THE * NEW
TREASURY
OF
SCRIPTURE
KNOWLEDGE

REVISED AND EXPANDED

Edited by

JEROME H. SMITH

THOMAS NELSON PUBLISHERS
Nashville, Tennessee

Published in Nashville, Tennessee, and
distributed in Canada by Lawson Falle, Ltd.,
Cambridge, Ontario.

Published in association with the literary agency of
Alive Communications, P.O. Box 49068, Colorado
Springs, Colorado 80949.

Printed in the United States of America.

Library of Congress Cataloging-in-Publication Data

The New treasury of scripture knowledge : the most complete listing of
    cross-references available anywhere—every verse, every theme, every
    important word / edited by Jerome H. Smith.
        p.   cm.
    Rev. ed. of: The treasury of scripture knowledge.
    Includes bibliographical references and indexes.
    ISBN 0-8407-7694-2
    1. Bible—Cross references.   I. Smith, Jerome H.   II. Treasury of
scripture knowledge.
BS430.N48   1992
220.5'2033—dc20   91-45487
                                                                CIP

2 3 4 5 6 7 8 9 — 97 96 95 94 93 92

CONTENTS

Order of the books of the Old and New Testaments

PREFACE

I first learned of *The Treasury of Scripture Knowledge* in a vacation Bible school class on "How to Study the Bible" taught to senior high school students at the Highland Park Baptist Church by Miss Ellen Groh. Miss Groh was a student at the Detroit Bible College at the time and later went to the mission field. The pastor of Highland Park Baptist Church then was Dr. Lehman Strauss. That was the summer of 1955.

That Christmas my Aunt Ethel Sherwin sent me a Christmas card with a five-dollar bill. On December 24, 1955, I rode my bicycle four miles to the Grand Bible and Book Store in Highland Park and had Mr. Bob Humphries, the proprietor, locate a copy of the book for me. To this day I believe this Bible study tool was the best investment I have ever made for Bible study.

I was convinced that I needed to buy the book for myself when in Miss Groh's class I looked up the encouraging references at 2 Timothy 1:7. During the years immediately after high school graduation, I used the volume as many as three hours a day in Bible study.

Over the years I have marked my copy of the *Treasury*, underlining particularly clear references, and noting printing errors as I found them. I added references to those already given in the *Treasury* in the wide margins of my study Bibles, as I prepared weekly Sunday school lessons over the years.

In the main reading room of the library at Bob Jones University I first saw *Scott's Commentary*, and found this to be the primary source of the references in the *Treasury*. The *Treasury* has many additional references not found in Scott, though in some passages, such as Exodus 20, the reverse is true. I have since obtained several used editions of *Scott's Commentary*. Many variations from Scott's original references (over 4,000) and printing errors (nearly 1,000) present in the original edition of the *Treasury* have been corrected in this new edition by consulting this source.

This is the only *new* edition of *The Treasury of Scripture Knowledge* ever prepared. All previous editions are merely reprints of the original edition which first appeared about 1836. In my preparation of this new edition I have incorporated the results of my thirty years of personal Bible study using the original *Treasury* into this revised and expanded edition. I almost did not live to finish my editorial work on the *New Treasury*, for I was shot in the head by an unknown assailant on March 13, 1986, when I had typed the text only as far as 1 Samuel 3. The Lord miraculously spared my life. During my recovery I kept working on the book, often without income. This time away from teaching permitted a more thorough revision and expansion than I originally planned.

The most significant feature of the *Treasury* is its nearly exhaustive collection of cross-references. These references are the source of its enduring usefulness to every Bible student. Therefore it has been to the cross-references themselves that the greatest effort has been given in this new edition to make this excellent reference tool even more usable to the modern reader and student of the Bible. I have added over 100,000 new cross-references and supplied many more key words to the Bible text, making this the most complete collection of biblical cross-references ever published.

I am thankful to Miss Ellen Groh, Dr. Lehman Strauss, my Aunt Ethel, the proprietors of many Christian and secular bookstores, and to the present publisher for their encouragement to me in making this new volume possible. Of course, I must not neglect to mention the many hours of assistance in looking up cross-references, preparing and checking indexes, and proofreading provided by my wife, Susanne. In a volume of this size and magnitude it is impossible to produce an entirely error-free manuscript, I am sure, but every effort has been made to provide an accurate reference tool for personal Bible study.

Jerome H. Smith

INTRODUCTION

The New Treasury of Scripture Knowledge has been designed for the ordinary Bible reader. As I have worked on the references and notes to this new edition, I have kept in mind several very ordinary Christian laymen and laywomen who helped me at the start of my Christian life. While this book is very simple to use, its contents are inexhaustible. It will provide the fullest help available on nearly every verse in the Bible. At several places I have provided notes of a more scholarly nature because the passage involved has been misunderstood by many interpreters or particular religious movements. It has been my purpose to help Bible students understand such verses at the verse where the difficulty arises. See, for example, the note on John 1:1.

The original *Treasury* was developed from the references in the Reverend Thomas Scott's *Commentary*, supplemented by the references in the center column of the English Polyglot Bible. The pages of the *Treasury* were designed to match the page content of editions of the Polyglot Bible in English published by Samuel Bagster and Sons of London. The effort to match the paging of this particular edition of the Bible led to what have been some unfortunate features in all former editions, most especially the tiny print in the Psalms and elsewhere, where the references are cramped into three columns on a page. In some portions of Scripture, where the number of cross-references to be adduced were few, the rest of the page was taken up with explanatory notes on the passages. Most of these notes have been retained. Additional notes have been provided where it was thought helpful, many from the *Comprehensive Bible*, the source of most of the original *Treasury* notes. Examples of these include notes at Genesis 38:21, Exodus 40:2, and Judges 9:54. I have modified a few of the original notes of the *Treasury* to reflect a more accurate understanding of Bible prophecy. Notes at Ezekiel 48:4, Daniel 2:44, and Micah 4:4 reflect such modification. I have written a number of new notes for this edition. These are identified under the Subject Index entry "Notes written for this edition." In this new edition, Roman numerals are no longer used, as they were in all former editions, to designate Bible chapter numbers.

The chapter headnotes have been expanded and given in greater detail. For the most part these were taken directly from *Scott's Commentary*, rarely supplemented by the headnotes in *Matthew Poole's Commentary*. I expanded the headnotes for Leviticus, chapter 19, and Deuteronomy, chapter 28. I modified the headnotes for several of the chapters of Zechariah to reflect a more accurate, consistent, literal view of prophetic interpretation. These headnotes are of much assistance in locating the subject matter of a chapter. Frequently I recall that a particular incident is mentioned in a book of the Bible, but I may not be able to think of a specific word used in the account, and therefore cannot use *Strong's Concordance* to locate the desired passage. The headnotes efficiently direct my attention to the passage sought.

Thomas Scott was the original compiler of the cross-references in *The Treasury of Scripture Knowledge*. I have adhered closely to Scott's original intent as expressed in the following quotes from his Preface Postscript:

"In numerous instances the references are entirely original, and in almost all many are so."

I have added many original references to those of the original *Treasury*, and still more from the *Commentary Wholly Biblical*, Robert Young's *Concise Critical Comments*, and *The New Testament with Fuller References*.

"In some of the original references, the Author's idea [i.e., Scott's] may not at once be perceived by the reader: but, if the several places referred to be consulted, it will generally appear."

I have remarked on this problem in the next section, "How to Use This Book."

"He has sometimes proceeded by way of *contrast*, that the reader, by comparing the opposite characters or conduct of the persons mentioned, may more clearly perceive the excellency or evil of the case in question."

I have extended this feature in some places (1 S 25:17; 2 K 5:13) with additional references, and have used a special symbol (◐) to indicate contrast.

"Or by comparing the different language of Scripture, used on the same subject, he may more readily see the true interpretation, especially on controverted subjects; or at least be better enabled to judge for himself."

I have attempted to advance the doctrine of private judgment (Ga 1:8n) and the perspicuity of Scripture (Is 8:20n) to this very purpose. Controversial subjects have not been shunned. Scripture evidence for valid alternative doctrinal or interpretative positions has been marshalled. The false doctrines held by those of Arian and Unitarian persuasion have been carefully addressed, particularly the doctrinal positions of the Jehovah's Witnesses.

"Some pains have likewise been taken, even on those parts of Scripture which chiefly consist of names, to point out other passages, in which the same persons or places are mentioned; and to mark the difference in spelling the same name, or the different names for the same person or place which occur in different parts, and the different places and persons called by the same name. Sometimes the unlearned reader is perplexed or misled by these variations; and this part of the references often contains all, which even the most learned know upon the subject, especially in the genealogies."

This feature of the original *Treasury* has been extended to the point that the *Treasury* is now exhaustively complete on these matters, with an accuracy surpassing, in some places, that of *Strong's Concordance* and other standard reference sources. The literal meaning of the original Hebrew and Greek names is given. The meanings were taken largely from Young's *Concise Critical Comments*, the tables of such names in volume three of *The Commentary Wholly Biblical*, supplemented by occasional reference to the definitions from several dictionaries of Bible names, particularly the dictionary revised and edited by Philip Schaff, "Comprehensive Bible Helps," in the Funk and Wagnalls edition of *Wilmore's New Analytical Reference Bible* (Copyright 1891, 1910, 1918). This information is readily accessed by means of the complete Index to the names in Scripture at the end of this volume.

"The meaning of scriptural phrases may also be often fixed, by comparing the several places where they are used. This is the intent of many sets of references; while others refer to the doctrine or promise inculcated in the passage, and tend to establish a scriptural interpretation."

Doctrinal topics have been carefully referenced, indexed, and expanded, utilizing the excellent material found in Charles Simmons' *A Scripture Manual* and other standard sources. Bible promises have been indexed and expanded, using Samuel Clark's *Precious Bible Promises*. Bible references to prayer have been expanded and indexed, using Philip Watters' work, *The Prayers of the Bible*. References to unfulfilled Bible prophecy have been made more complete by a thorough study of George N. H. Peters' *The Theocratic Kingdom of our Lord Jesus, the Christ*. The precise extent to which this is so may be determined by examining the subject index entries under this author's name. I have expanded the references which relate to prophetic subjects. Reference to Isaiah 55:3, Matthew 5:5, and Luke 21:36 will furnish a sampling of the extent to which this has been done.

On important themes of practical and contemporary interest, forward and backward referencing has been increased. Passages of practical (Hab 2:20, 1 C 15:55), prophetic (Am 9:14, 15, Lk 21:36), and doctrinal (Am 3:6, Mt 24:45, 28:19) significance have been so referenced. Thus, at Amos 3:6 will be found many references not supplied before to the other passages in Scripture which treat the same themes, which themselves (in the *Treasury*) contain a cross-reference to Amos 3:6.

Figures of speech are identified. I believe this edition of *The New Treasury of Scripture Knowledge* contains the most comprehensive listing and identification of the figures of speech in the Bible ever produced in English.

The "Preface to the Treasury Bible" supplies the following important explanation not found in any current printings of *The Treasury of Scripture Knowledge*:

> "To preserve the distinction between the *Various Readings* [from the A.V.] and the *editorial remarks* and *explanations* which occur, the word "or" in the one case is printed in italics, with a small *o*; in the other in Roman, with a capital O: thus, Ge 4:13, "*My punishment is greater than I can bear. or,* Mine iniquity is greater than that it may be forgiven." In Ge 19:1, it is said, "*And there came two angels.* Or rather, 'the two angels came.'"

I have adhered to this principle as far as possible. When adding alternative translations not provided by the A.V. translators, such as those I have adduced from Young's *Literal Translation* and its accompanying *Concise Critical Comments*, I have introduced the alternative rendering by an unitalicized "or."

> "When the references illustrate the whole verse, the italic words are not printed, because not required."

This feature has been eliminated. All sets of reference passages in this new edition of the *Treasury* are keyed to the appropriate words of the text of the Authorized Version, eliminating the ambiguity present in the original system.

Thomas Scott used the words "see on" to indicate a passage where a more complete set of references was collected. I have restored many instances of this feature which were inadvertently deleted or inconsistently retained in the original editions of the *Treasury*. I have expanded this most helpful feature by using the symbol "+" in many more places. Thomas Scott's system is thus left intact. It may be distinguished from mine by the two different markings for essentially the same feature.

Cross-references have an advantage over chain references in that all the references are presented at one location, and with the new system of symbols introduced to this edition of the *Treasury*, the relative clarity, significance, or relationships of the references is presented at a single glance to the reader.

Studying all the references given for a text, then the references which that text can lead to, and so forth, will enable the careful student of Scripture to consider all the material in the Bible which relates to the subject or passage being studied.

Frequently in Bible study the student will want to know, "But what does the rest of Scripture have to say on this matter?" The only resource which can provide an answer will often be found to be the *Treasury*. No combination of additional Bible study tools quite duplicates the content of *The New Treasury of Scripture Knowledge*. At many places in the Bible the *Treasury* will be found more complete. Almost always it will have far more cross-references than any other source or combination of sources.

Scott comments, "The degree of labor and attention, which has been used to render the printing of the references correct, cannot easily be conceived: yet probably some errors still remain." I have found five errors in Scott's London Edition that were corrected in the original *Treasury*; four errors in the London Edition that were corrected in the American edition; twenty-eight errors in the London edition, which I corrected in this new edition of the *Treasury* during my typing and proofreading of the manuscript. Something over 4,000 corrections involving unjustifiable changes and deletions from Scott's original references, and no less than 680 actual printing errors in the current edition of the original *Treasury*—459 from the Old Testament, 221 from the New Testament—have been found and corrected for this new edition of the *Treasury*. This new edition, therefore, is the most accurate collection of these extensive references available.

HOW TO USE THIS BOOK

The Bible is divided into separate books (such as Genesis, Exodus, or John). Each book is divided into chapters. Each chapter is divided into verses. This Bible study tool, *The New Treasury of Scripture Knowledge*, is arranged just like a Bible. It is divided into the same Bible books, chapters, and verses. To find information about any verse in the Bible, simply look up the book of the Bible where it is found, the chapter, and the verse. Whenever a Bible reference is given, the abbreviated name of the book is given first, followed by the chapter number, a colon, and the verse number. The reference John 3:16 means the book of John, chapter 3, verse 16.

This Bible study tool is designed to be used with any edition or translation of the Bible. This book provides for nearly every verse in the Bible a selection of other verses which shed light upon, clarify, or explain the verse you are consulting. Such verses are commonly known as "cross-references." Many study Bibles contain cross-references in their center column, and you may already be familiar with these. This book provides a far more complete selection of cross-references than can be found in any other source. The great advantage of having such a complete selection of references is that the Bible is allowed to comment upon and explain itself—something which it does very well. The Bible explains itself even better, and in far greater detail, than people who are otherwise quite familiar with its contents might suppose.

Why should you study the Bible in this way? Careful students of the Bible are aware that this is the way which the Savior Himself studied and discussed Scripture (Luke 24:27,44; John 1:45; 5:39). It is the way which the apostle Paul used to expound and explain the Bible (Acts 17:2,3). Reflections of this method of studying Scripture can be seen in the way the apostle Paul quotes a series of texts of Scripture in his epistles (see especially Romans 3:9-18). So while there are many other valuable methods of Bible study, the method of comparing Scripture with Scripture (made possible by the cross-references gathered in this volume) is certainly a valid, if not the best, method of Bible study. It is a Scriptural method, used by Christ in his teaching (Lk 4:18), reflected by the frequent use of composite quotations from the Old Testament in the New (Mt 27:9), and commended by Paul in Acts 17:11: "These were more noble than those in Thessalonica, in that they received the word with all readiness of mind, and searched the scriptures daily, whether those things were so."

The English text from the King James or Authorised Version of 1611 for 2 Timothy 1:7, a passage alluded to in the Preface, reads:

7. For God hath not given us the spirit of fear; but of power, and of love, and of a sound mind.

Here is an example of what *The New Treasury of Scripture Knowledge* provides at 2 Timothy 1:7.

7. **the spirit.** Ac *20:24. 21:13. Ro *8:15. He 2:15. 1 J *4:18. **but.** Mi *3:8. Zc *4:6. Lk 10:19. *24:49. Ac *1:8. 6:8. 9:22. *10:38. 1 C *2:4. **of love.** Ro *5:5. Ga *5:22. Col 1:8. 1 P *1:22. **a sound.** Ps *119:80. Pr *2:7. *8:14. Lk *8:35. *15:17. Ac *26:11, 25. 2 C 5:13, 14.

Rather than print out all the words of a verse, only the first words or the key words of a phrase or clause are printed in **bold** typeface. Following the key word will be found a set of cross-references to the other Bible passages which are helpful in understanding the verse you are reading. The key words are based on the King James or Authorized Version of 1611, but you will almost always find that the wording of any other version of the Bible is close enough that you can use the references with no difficulty. The asterisked verses represent especially clear passages that may be profitably consulted by even a new user of this volume.

Consider the references given above for the phrase "sound mind": Ps *119:80. Pr *2:7. *8:14.

Lk *8:35. *15:17. Ac *26:11, 25. 2 C 5:13, 14. So that the nature of the help to be derived from consulting such a series of Bible references may be immediately seen by the reader, the text of these several references is printed out in full below:

Psalms *119:80. "Let my heart be sound in thy statutes, that I be not ashamed."

Proverbs *2:7. "He layeth up sound wisdom for the righteous: he is a buckler to them that walk uprightly."

Proverbs *8:14. "Counsel is mine, and sound wisdom: I am understanding; I have strength."

Luke *8:35. "Then they went out to see what was done; and came to Jesus, and found the man, out of whom the devils were departed, sitting at the feet of Jesus, clothed, and in his right mind: and they were afraid."

Luke *15:17. "And when he came to himself, he said, How many hired servants of my father's have bread enough and to spare, and I perish with hunger!"

Acts *26:11, 25. (11) "And I punished them oft in every synagogue, and compelled them to blaspheme; and being exceedingly mad against them, I persecuted them even unto strange cities." (25) "But he said, I am not mad, most noble Festus; but speak forth the words of truth and soberness."

2 C 5:13, 14. (13) "For whether we be beside ourselves, it is to God: or whether we be sober, it is for your cause." (14) "For the love of Christ constraineth us; because we thus judge, that if one died for all, then were all dead."

Notice the common thread of thought through these several verses as represented by the words "sound heart," "sound wisdom," "right mind," "came to himself," "not mad," "sober." These comforting and reassuring words furnish a biblical answer to the attempts of others bent on discouraging new-found interest in the Bible and spiritual things.

The cross-references do not furnish the same information that a concordance does. A Bible concordance is an alphabetical index to the *words* of the Bible. The cross-references given in the *New Treasury* are not merely to the same word, although this is sometimes the case, but to the same or a related thought, theme, doctrine, subject, concept, or literary motif, even when expressed in entirely different words, as can be seen from even the short example above.

For example, if you consult the cross-references given to Genesis 3:15, regarded as the first biblical prophecy of a coming Redeemer or Messiah, you will find over one hundred cross-references to other related messianic prophecies and the New Testament passages which show their fulfillment. Such a collection of references could not be found by means of a concordance alone. If the student will turn in the *New Treasury* to the clearest references given at Genesis 3:15, such as Genesis 49:10, even more references to messianic prophecy will be found. Used in this manner, the *New Treasury* can be used in an exhaustive study of any Bible subject, and will lead to more explanatory verses than any other study tool available.

Some readers may benefit by some suggestions as to the actual mechanics of using the volume. I have found it helpful to study at a well-lighted table, with the *New Treasury* open to the passage I am studying. I find it easiest to use two Bibles with good print. I keep the largest one with the clearest print open to the verse being studied. I use a smaller Bible to turn to the various references cited for the passage I am studying.

Whenever possible, it is best to consult all the references given. Frequently the relevance of earlier references cited becomes abundantly clear when all the references have been consulted. My own experience has taught me that when I do not understand the bearing or relevance of a particular reference given, the trouble is with me. I usually discover that as I learn more about the Bible passage, or the theme involved, the relevance of the passage becomes clear. When the subject is an important one, and I encounter what seems to be an obscure reference—one that does not seem to pertain to the passage I am trying to understand—I find that turning to *that* passage and looking up its references generally makes the intended relationship clear. But when time and interest would make this procedure impractical to the reader, an effort has been made in this edition to assist the reader by identifying the clearest texts, or the most crucial ones, for understanding the text being studied through the use of special symbols.

The New Treasury of Scripture Knowledge probably has more cross-references than you could hope to consult in a lifetime of use. Yet that is the very heart of its advantage over other study tools—it is an inexhaustible study resource. Just how can a reader use this volume without becoming bogged down by the sheer quantity of cross-references?

In devotional reading, as I read a Bible chapter, I often come upon a verse that particularly strikes my interest, or meets a particular need. At that point, I open the *New Treasury* and consult the references for that verse. Sometimes discussing the Bible with others who have a totally different understanding of what it says will motivate me to look up the references on the verses pertaining to a disputed doctrine or interpretation. For Sunday school lesson preparation I will often study the lesson Scripture text, then select a particularly significant or relevant verse or two and consult the references to that passage. Then I share just the few clearest references with the class when that verse is discussed.

It is better to use the *New Treasury* in your personal study briefly and regularly, rather than to set up an overly ambitious program of extended study, only to give up for lack of time or discipline to put the program into effect. The book will do no good closed on the shelf, but it will prove to be a rich spiritual resource if used right along with your regular reading of the Bible.

Why should you study the Bible by consulting well-chosen cross-references? Those who are most familiar with the Bible know that the Bible is its own best commentary. It is most essential when arriving at an understanding of what the Bible teaches on any given theme that we first come to an understanding of what the Bible itself says. This can only be done when we consult all the Bible has to say on a subject. If we wish to arrive at the truth God has placed in His Word, we must make that Word our first authority, and it would be better if it were our only authority. We must not cite Bible texts in an arbitrary fashion with no regard to context, the culture which produced the text, and the statements elsewhere in the Bible which bear on the theme or doctrine being considered. Jesus said we are to "search the Scriptures" (Jn 5:39). Certainly *The New Treasury of Scripture Knowledge* is a most essential Bible study tool which will enable you to do just that.

This book is intended to be an essential companion to your Bible reading and study. No matter how much or how little prior knowledge of the Bible you bring to this study tool, it will provide the needed assistance to understand the Bible more accurately and deeply. If your experience is similar to mine, you will find this book the most helpful aid to in-depth Bible study you have ever used.

Features of *The New*

The New Treasury of Scripture Knowledge offers you truly inexhaustible resources for Bible study. At its heart is the most comprehensive listing available of cross-references from specific words of Scripture to other related Scripture portions. Many of these cross-references are marked with special symbols to indicate exactly what information they provide. This means that you can choose the specific references that will give you the information you want.

The many notes found through the book comment on the basic content of Bible chapters, on the meaning of words, on historical matters, and on practical and doctrinal teachings of Scripture. All of the notes in the original *Treasury* have been kept, and Jerome Smith has added many new ones.

Finally, much of the vast knowledge distributed throughout the whole book is made more

PAGE NUMBER

REFERENCE GUIDE HEADING. LEFT GUIDE TELLS WHICH NEW VERSE BEGINS THE PAGE. RIGHT GUIDE TELLS WHICH VERSE IS LAST ON THE PAGE. HELPS YOU FIND THE PAGE YOU NEED QUICKLY.

GENESIS 17:26

33

REFERENCES RELATED TO GENESIS 17:26 FOUND HERE.

are the descendants of Ishmael, retain the rite of circumcision to this day; and the latter perform it, as the other Mahometans also do, at the age of *thirteen*. ver. ◐12. Ge +14:4.

— 26. **In the.** Ge 12:4. 22:3, 4. Ps *119:60. **selfsame.** Ge +*7:13n.

27. **stranger.** ver. +12. **circumcised.** Ge *18:19. Ex 12:44.

BOLDFACE WORDS ARE THE SUBJECT FOR CROSS-REFERENCE AND COMMENTS THAT FOLLOW. ALL SUCH SUBJECT WORDS COME FROM THE KING JAMES VERSION.

GENESIS 18

HEADING FOR NEW CHAPTER

The Lord again appears to Abraham, who entertains angels, 1-9. A son is promised to Sarah, at which she laughs, and her misconduct is rebuked, 9-15. The Lord discovers to Abraham his purpose of destroying Sodom, 16-22; who earnestly intercedes for the inhabitants, 23-33.

CHAPTER HEADNOTE SUMMARIZES CONTENTS. HELPS YOU QUICKLY LOCATE THE SECTION YOU NEED.

1. **appeared.** T#1774. ver. 2, 13, 14, 17, 19, 22, 33. Ge 15:1. 16:7. 17:+1-3, 22. 26:2. 48:3. Ex 3:2, 4. 4:1, 5. Jg 13:21. 2 Ch 1:7. Pr 8:22-31. Ml 3:1, 2. Jn *8:56. Ac 7:2. **Mamre.** Ge +13:18. 14:13. **and he sat.** In these verses we have a delightful picture of genuine and primitive hospitality: a venerable father sits at the tent door, not only to enjoy the current of refreshing air, but that if he saw any weary and exhausted travelers, he might invite them to rest and refresh themselves during the heat of the day, and the same custom continues in the east. It was not the custom, nor was there any necessity, for strangers to knock at the door, or to speak first, but to stand till they were invited. **heat.** Ge ◐15:12. ◐19:1. 31:40. Mt 20:12. Lk 12:55. Ja 1:11.

EXCEPT FOR SPECIAL CASES, CROSS-REFERENCES ARE LISTED IN NORMAL BIBLICAL ORDER.

THIS NOTE COMMENTS ON THE SUBJECT WORDS "AND HE SAT." NOTES REFER TO BIBLICAL CUSTOMS, WORD MEANINGS, AND BIBLICAL TEACHINGS AND INTERPRETATION.

2. **And he.** Ge 22:4. Jg 13:3, 9. He 13:2. **lift.** ƒ144A12, Ge +22:13. **looked.** Ge +13:14. **lo.** ƒ40, Ge +3:22. **three.** ver. 22. Ge +1:26. 19:1. He 13:2. 1 P 4:9. **men.** Ge 32:24. Jn 1:14. **he ran.** Ge 24:29.

the end of that Abraha 1 S 25:41. **rest.** Mk 6 the *second* traveler.

5. **And I** the *third* order; as ea is very unv Heb. stay. Heb. ye ha

6. **hasten** hasten. **thro** 40. Ac 16:1 **measures.** Mt 13:33. 7:12. 24:5. Ho 7:8.

7. **ran.** (1:14. Mt 22

8. **he too** 30:33. Is 7: 17:8. Jn 12: Ge 19:3. E 30. *24:30,

9. **Wher** wife...and l tent." The "The Fiftee that "There mal appear are of the most ancier of the Soph

---

ISAIAH 12:3

DENOTES A CLEAR CROSS-REFERENCE.

3. **with joy.** Is 49:10. *55:1-3. Ps 36:9. 51:12. SS 2:3. Je *2:13. Jn 1:16. *4:10-14. *7:37-39. Re 7:17. 21:6. 22:1, 17. **wells.** Heb. *mayan*, Ge +7:11 (*S#4599h). **salvation.** Ge 49:18ℙ. Ex 14:13ℙ. 15:2ℙ. Dt 32:15ℙ.

TRANSLITERATION OF THE HEBREW WORD FOR THE SUBJECT WORD "WELLS."

MORE REFERENCES ARE FOUND AT THIS REFERENCE.

4. **in that day.** ver. 1. Ps 65:1. 106:47, 48. 113:1-3. ch. 117. **call upon his name.** *or,* proclaim his name. Ex 33:19. 34:5-7. 1 Ch 16:8. Ps 105:1. **declare.** Is 66:19. Ps 9:11. 22:31. 40:5. 71:16-18. 73:28. 96:3. 107:22. 145:4-6. Je 50:2. 51:9, 10. Jn 17:26. 2 Th 1:10. **his name.** Is 2:11, 17. 25:1. 33:5. Ex 15:2. 1 Ch 29:11. Ne 9:5. Ps +*9:10. 18:46. 21:13. 34:3. 46:10. 57:5. 97:9. 113:5. Ph 2:9-11.

INDICATES THAT ALL OCCURRENCES OF THIS HEBREW WORD, #4599 IN STRONG'S HEBREW LEXICON, ARE LISTED AT GENESIS 7:11 IN *THE NEW TREASURY*.

AN ITALICIZED *or* INTRODUCES AN ALTERNATE READING FOUND IN THE MARGIN OF THE KJV.

5. **Sing.** Ex 15:1, 21ℙ. Ps 68:32-35. 98:1. 105:2. Re *15:3. 19:1-3. **excellent things.** Mk 7:37. Lk 13:17. **this is known.** Is 40:9. Ps 72:19. Hab *2:14. Re 11:15-17.

THE SUBJECT WORD IS A QUOTE FROM THE PENTATEUCH—HERE, EXODUS.

6. **Cry out.** Is 40:9. 52:7-10. 54:1. Zp 3:14. Zc 9:9. Lk 19:37-40. **thou.** Is 10:24. 24:23. 30:19. 33:24. Zc 8:3-8. **inhabitant.** Heb. inhabitress. Je 10:17mg. Mi 1:11mg. **for great.** Is 8:18. 24:23. 25:9. 41:14, 16. Ps 9:11. 47:2. 68:16. 71:22. 89:18. 102:16. 132:14. Je 23:5, 6. Ezk 43:7. *48:35. Zp 2:5. 3:15-17. Zc 2:5, 10, 11. **in the midst.** Ps +*16:11. Jl *2:27. Zp 3:14, 15, 17. Zc *2:5, 10. 12:10. Jn 12:35, 36. Re 21:23.

THIS REFERENCE IS A PARTICULARLY CRITICAL CROSS-REFERENCE.

A MORE LITERAL TRANSLATION OF THE HEBREW.

THE MARGIN OF THE KJV CONTAINS THE PRECEDING ALTERNATE READING.

Treasury of Scripture Knowledge

quickly accessible through the seven comprehensive indexes at the end of the book. These present many additional benefits as you study the Bible with *The New Treasury of Scripture Knowledge*.

The following five samples are marked to help you quickly unlock the Bible study riches *The New Treasury* contains. The first sample illustrates basic elements of the page design, and the following four samples illustrate most of the symbols, abbreviations, and other features of *The New Treasury*. As an additional help, you are encouraged to remove the extended back jacket flap and use it as a quick-reference book mark with *The New Treasury* page you are using. It will provide on-the-spot translation of all the special symbols and abbreviations created for this revised and expanded edition.

MATTHEW 4:10

Da 3:5. Lk 4:7mg. **and worship.** 1 C 10:20, 21. 2 C 4:4. 1 T 3:6. 1 P 5:8, 9. Re +*19:10. +*22:8, 9.

10. **Then saith.** He =11:24, 25. **Get.** √34, Ps +50:16. Mt 16:23. Ja 4:7. 1 P 5:9. **Satan.** 1 Ch 21:1. Jb 1:6, 12. 2:1. Ps 109:6. Zc 3:1, 2. Gr. *Satanas*, i.e. *an adversary*, *S#4567g. Mt 4:10. 12:26. 16:23. Mk 1:13. 3:23, 26. 4:15. 8:33. Lk 4:8. 10:18. 11:18. 13:16. 22:3, 31. Jn 13:27. Ac 5:3. 26:18. Ro 16:20. 1 C 5:5. 7:5. 2 C *2:11. *11:14. 1 Th 2:18. 2 Th 2:9. 1 T 1:20. 5:15. Re 2:9, 13, 13, 24. 3:9. 12:9. 20:2, 7. See *S#4566g, 2 C 12:7. For *S#7854h, see Jb 1:6, Satan. **Thou shalt.** Dt √6:13, 14. 10:20. Jsh 24:14. 1 S 7:3. Lk 4:8. **worship.** T#744. Mt ◐+*14:33. Ex +*20:2, 3, *5. *34:14. Dt 11:16. Ps +22:28 (T#280). 96:4, 5, 8, 9. Ec +12:13 (T#295). Lk 4:8. Ac 14:15. Col +2:18 (T#80). Re +*19:10. +*22:8, 9. **and him only.** √92E. Gnome; or, Quotation B79L where the words are varied by omission, addition, or transposition. Here, the words are varied by addition, for the words "and him only shalt thou serve" are not quoted from Deuteronomy, but added by our Lord. For other instances of this figure see Mt 4:15, 16. 5:31. 12:18-21. 19:5. 22:24. Lk 4:8. Ro 11:3, 4. 1 C 2:9. 14:21. 1 P 1:24, 25. **shalt thou.** T#241. Mt 22:37, 38. Ex 20:2. Dt 10:20. 13:4. 1 S 7:3. 1 Ch 29:11. Ps +22:28 (T#280).

> **IDENTIFIES A TYPE OR ANTI-TYPE.**

> **A TRANSLITERATION OF THE GREEK WORD, FOLLOWED BY A TRANSLATION.**

> **THE CROSS-REFERENCE CONTRASTS WITH THE IDEA EXPRESSED IN THE SUBJECT WORD(S), OR, IF IT APPEARS TO CONTRADICT, AN EXPLANATION IS OFFERED.**

> **REFERS TO ITEM IN TOPIC INDEX, WHERE OTHER REFERENCES TO AND NOTES ON THE TOPIC ARE FOUND.**

> **PROVIDES RELEVANT PAGE NUMBER FOR BULLINGER'S *FIGURES OF SPEECH USED IN THE BIBLE.***

> **PARALLEL LINES INDICATE THAT A STRICT PARALLEL OCCURS BETWEEN THE SUBJECT REFERENCE AND CROSS-REFERENCE.**

> **THE "n" INDICATES THAT A RELEVANT NOTE OCCURS AT DANIEL 11:33.**

> **THE SOURCES OF NOTES QUOTING OR REFERRING TO NON-BIBLICAL AUTHORS ARE FOUND IN THE EXTENSIVE BIBLIOGRAPHY.**

> **ALL SIMILAR USES OF THE HEBREW WORD(S) WHICH CAN BE TRANSLATED "IN DUE SEASON" ARE LISTED AT GENESIS 17:21.**

42. **the Lord.** Lk 7:13. **Who then is.** Lk 19:15-19. Mt +√24:45, 46. *25:20-23. 1 C *4:1, 2. T 1:7. **faithful.** Ge +*18:19. Ps 101:2, *6. Is +*32:20. Je +*23:28n. Mt +√‖24:45. +*25:21. **wise.** Gr. *phronimos*, *S#5429g. Lk 12:42. 16:8. Mt 7:24. 10:16. *24:45. +25:2, 4, 8, 9. Ro 11:25. 12:16. 1 C 4:10. 10:15. 2 C 11:19. Thayer gives the meaning "prudent, denotes primarily one who has quick and correct perceptions, hence 'discreet,' 'circumspect'" (p. 582b), "mindful of one's interests" (p. 658b). Da +*11:33n. √12:3. **steward.** Lk 16:1-12. Mt 20:8. 1 C 4:1, 2. 1 P 4:10. **ruler.** 1 T 3:15. 5:17. He 3:5. 13:7, 17. **to give.** Je 23:4. Ezk 34:3. Mt +*13:52. Jn *21:15-17. Ac +*20:28. 1 P *5:1-4. **portion.** 2 Ch=31:14-16. Ne=13:13. Pr 31:15. **in due season.** Ge +17:21 (+S#4150h). Le 23:2n. Nu 28:2n. Pr 15:23. Ec 10:17. Is 50:4. Mt +√24:45. 2 T 4:2.

> **PROPHECY RECORDED IN CROSS-REFERENCE IS FULFILLED IN SUBJECT TEXT (MT 21:12).**

> **THIS OLD TESTAMENT VERSE IS QUOTED IN THE SUBJECT VERSE (MT 21:13).**

> **REFERS TO FIGURE OF SPEECH INDEX, WHERE EACH FIGURE IS DEFINED AND A REFERENCE WITH NOTE IS GIVEN. *THE NEW TREASURY* HAS THE MOST COMPREHENSIVE LISTING OF BIBLICAL FIGURES OF SPEECH AVAILABLE.**

12. **went.** Ml 3:1, 2. Mk 11:11. **and cast.** Mk 11:15. Lk *19:45, 46. Jn 2:14-17. **the temple.** Hg *2:7, 9. Ml *3:1. Lk 2:27, 32. **moneychangers.** Ex 30:13. Dt 14:24-26. **doves.** Le 1:14. 5:7, 11. 12:6, 8. 14:22, 30. 15:14, 29. Lk 2:24.

13. **It is.** Mt 2:5. Lk +*24:27. Jn 15:25. **My.** Ps 93:5. Is √56:7. **house of prayer.** 1 K 8:29, 30, 41-43. 2 Ch 6:40. **but ye.** √92G. Lk +4:18. **den of theives.** √102, Ge +2:24. Je √7:11. Ezk 7:22. Mk 11:17. Lk 19:46.

SYMBOLS AND ABBREVIATIONS

Below is an explanation of the symbols and abbreviations used in this edition of *The New Treasury of Scripture Knowledge*. (The extended back jacket flap lists all of these and, removed, may be used as a bookmark.)

*	placed before a cross-reference indicates an especially clear reference. These references should be looked up by the beginning user of this volume. As more experience is gained, all the references may be consulted.
√	placed before a cross-reference indicates a critically clear, pertinent, significant reference.
+	A fuller collection of references to this term are gathered at the verse so indicated.
+* or +√	Additional references to this topic, or a fuller collection for this topic is given at the verse so indicated.
◐	Contrast. Identifies groups of references gathered on another aspect of the topic, or identifies cross references which explain an apparent or alleged contradiction or alternate doctrinal position.
=	Identifies a type or antitype.
≐	Type or antitype identified on biblical authority.
▶	Identifies quotations in the New Testament from the Old Testament, and at Old Testament passages the fact that they are quoted in the New Testament.
▶𝒫	Identifies quotations from the Pentateuch in the prophets.
✦	Identifies references which are the fulfillment of prophecy.
‖	Indicates a strict parallel passage, as in the gospels, or the books of Samuel, Kings, and Chronicles. These have not been noted exhaustively, but only selectively.
✳S#	placed before a Strong's number (✳S#2313h) indicates that all the occurrences of the original Hebrew or Greek word so marked are given here.
✤S#	placed before a Strong's number (✤S#2313g) indicates that all the occurrences to the Hebrew or Greek word which are relevant or similar to the use there are given.
( )	When a cross-reference in a figure–of–speech listing is placed in parentheses, this indicates that the figure is not apparent in English versions (KJV, Young's *Literal Translation*, or Rotherham) and so is not cross-referenced back to the explanation of the figure at the passage so listed.
( )	In a series of references to a Hebrew or Greek word identified by its Strong's number, the English translation is given in parentheses when the word is rendered differently in a particular reference.
( )	An English word in parentheses after a verse reference lets the reader know which word in that verse translates the same underlying Hebrew or Greek word.
( )	A word placed in parentheses in connection with the figure of speech Ellipsis indicates the word is not present in the original language, but is to be supplied in accordance with the figure of speech as indicated.

CB   *Companion Bible*

F/L   In the book of Isaiah, sets of references to "first" (Is ch. 1-39) and "last" (Is ch. 40-66) portions of Isaiah are given to demonstrate the unity of the book. Words alleged by some authorities to occur in only the first portion of the book are seen to be used in the latter portion, demonstrating that the book is the work of a single author.

ſ   Figures of speech are identified with a reference number, such as *ſ*102, followed by the name of the figure of speech in the main entry, or a reference to where that figure is explained, and to where all the other instances of that particular figure, or a subset of that figure, can be found. This feature is an essential aid to Bible interpretation. This is the first time that such information has been made readily accessible to the ordinary Bible reader in one source. *The Companion Bible* identifies many of the figures of speech in its margins, and has a list with brief definitions in its Appendix 6. However, users of *The Companion Bible* who come across an important instance of the use of a figure of speech are not led in that volume to the other instances of its use. But to learn to identify a figure when it is used, one needs to see it in many contexts until one has developed a "feel" for the figure, and can learn its characteristics enough to be able to identify it wherever it occurs. Of course, one can consult E. W. Bullinger's *Figures of Speech Used in the Bible*, but there are many instances given in the margins of *The Companion Bible* which are not listed or discussed in that book, and many instances given in the book not given in *The Companion Bible*. This edition of the *Treasury* remedies that, and furnishes additional references to the figures not found in either of those two excellent sources.

            The names of the figures of speech have been alphabetized and given reference numbers from 1 to 180. Often the reference number is followed by additional letters and numbers to clearly identify the specific category of the figure of speech. The full alphabetical list of the figures with the subcategories is given in the Figure of Speech Index at the end of this volume.

B   B542 means a reference is made to page 542 of E. W. Bullinger's *Figures of Speech Used in the Bible*. All main figure of speech entries are so keyed to this volume.

g or h   Indicates verbal references to the same Hebrew or Greek words when used after a cross-reference. After a Strong's number, indicates whether the number refers to the Hebrew or Greek lexicon at the end of *Strong's Concordance*.

Gr.   Greek

Heb.   Hebrew

ISBE   *International Standard Bible Encyclopedia*

lit.   Literally

mg   A reference to the marginal reading found in the center column of many editions of the King James or Authorized Version of the Bible.

MM   James Hope Moulton and George Milligan, *The Vocabulary of the Greek Testament*.

n   Placed after a cross reference (Ge 2:7n) means that there is a pertinent note at that reference about the subject of the reference. This new feature makes the many notes throughout the *New Treasury* far more accessible than in previous editions and provides a unique internal cross-referencing system for the notes.

or,   Italicized "or," identifies a marginal reading supplied by the translators of the Authorized or King James Version.

or,	Unitalicized "or," identifies alternate renderings supplied by this editor from Robert Young's *Literal Translation* and its accompanying *Concise Critical Comments*, and other sources.
S#	There are selected references to the numbers of *Strong's Concordance* throughout this edition of the *Treasury*, so relating information in the *Treasury* with other published Bible study reference tools keyed to *Strong's Concordance*. Consult the Strong's Number Index at the end of this volume.
T#	Topic numbers are for the first time furnished in this edition of the *Treasury*, together with an index to these topics, to give the *New Treasury* all the advantages of a topical Bible or topical arrangement of the Scriptures. Sometimes the full set of references for more than one topic is located at the same verse. To help the user rapidly identify the appropriate set of references, the topic numbers are given at each major collection of indexed topical references.
TDNT	*Theological Dictionary of the New Testament*
w	"with." This symbol is used whenever cross-references are listed out of their normal biblical sequence in order to show important relationships between passages, relationships which would be lost if all the references were always cited only in the biblical order. Normally, however, references are cited in their biblical order, excepting that references are first given to verses within the same biblical book. All other references are cited in turn in biblical order. It is a sound rule of interpretation to seek first to understand the meaning of the language of an author by reference to the use of the same or similar language in the same book.
‡	placed after a topic number indicates the topic provides a set of proof texts used to support a false doctrine. The importance of including selected references of this category cannot be overestimated, for this furnishes the Bible-believing Christian with a defense against false doctrines promulgated by what are sometimes known as "false cults." Thus, by means of these symbols you can learn the commonly cited proof texts used to support a mistaken interpretation, and by reference to the cross-references not so marked, and especially by reference to cross-references marked with a ◐ symbol, the reader can learn the biblical answer to many of the false positions of the cults. Such helpful sets of cross-references are now marked out for the reader more fully in the *New Treasury* than in any other single reference source available.
? or x	placed before a cross-reference indicates doubtful validity of the reference, for it is a wrong identification of the source of a quotation, or it is a proof text underlying a mistaken doctrinal or prophetic interpretation, or it is a questionable identification of a figure of speech—questionable because it is misidentified, or arbitrarily supports a mistaken doctrinal viewpoint.

ABBREVIATIONS and order of the names of the Bible books:

Ge	Genesis	Mt	Matthew
Ex	Exodus	Mk	Mark
Le	Leviticus	Lk	Luke
Nu	Numbers	Jn	John
Dt	Deuteronomy	Ac	Acts
Jsh	Joshua	Ro	Romans
Jg	Judges	1 C	1 Corinthians
Ru	Ruth	2 C	2 Corinthians
1 S	1 Samuel	Ga	Galatians
2 S	2 Samuel	Ep	Ephesians
1 K	1 Kings	Ph	Philippians
2 K	2 Kings	Col	Colossians
1 Ch	1 Chronicles	1 Th	1 Thessalonians
2 Ch	2 Chronicles	2 Th	2 Thessalonians
Ezr	Ezra	1 T	1 Timothy
Ne	Nehemiah	2 T	2 Timothy
Est	Esther	T	Titus
Jb	Job	Phm	Philemon
Ps	Psalms	He	Hebrews
Pr	Proverbs	Ja	James
Ec	Ecclesiastes	1 P	1 Peter
SS	Song of Solomon	2 P	2 Peter
Is	Isaiah	1 J	1 John
Je	Jeremiah	2 J	2 John
La	Lamentations	3 J	3 John
Ezk	Ezekiel	Ju	Jude
Da	Daniel	Re	Revelation
Ho	Hosea		
Jl	Joel		
Am	Amos		
Ob	Obadiah		
Jon	Jonah		
Mi	Micah		
Na	Nahum		
Hab	Habakkuk		
Zp	Zephaniah		
Hg	Haggai		
Zc	Zechariah		
Ml	Malachi		

Note that Obadiah, Philemon, 2 John, 3 John, and Jude each contain only one chapter. Therefore, a reference to Ob 18 is to verse 18 of that book. But a reference to Nu ch. 7, 8, 10. would mean reference to the entire contents of chapters 7, 8, and 10 of the book of Numbers. A reference to Ge 3:15 means Genesis, the third chapter, verse fifteen. When the same verse numbers are repeated (Ge 3:15, 15, 16, 17, 17), this means that the word occurs as many times in the verse as the verse number is repeated. When references are to the first, second, or third occurrence of a word in the verse, this is indicated by placing an 'a,' 'b,' or 'c' after the verse reference (Jn 14:2b).

THE NEW TREASURY OF SCRIPTURE KNOWLEDGE

OLD TESTAMENT

GENESIS

GENESIS 1

God creates heaven and earth, 1; forms the light, and the firmament, 2-8; separates the dry land from the waters, and produces the vegetable tribes, 9-13; forms the sun, moon, and stars, 14-19; causes the waters to produce fishes and fowls, and the earth to bring forth cattle, wild beasts, and creeping things, 20-25; creates man in his own image; blesses him; gives him dominion; grants the fruits of the earth for food; and pronounces the whole "very good," 26-31.

1. **beginning.** Pr *8:22-24. 16:4. Mk 13:19. Jn *1:1-3. 15:27. Ac 1:1, 22. He *1:10. 1 J 1:1. Re 3:14. **God.** Heb. *Elohim.* S#430h. Ge 2:2. +19:29. Ex +2:24. Ps +45:6. 89:11, 12. Ep 3:9. Col *1:16, 17, 18. He *1:2. **created.** Ge 1:21, 27. 2:3. Dt 32:4. 2 S 22:31. Ne *9:6. Jb 38:4, 7. Ps *33:6, 9. 147:3-5. Pr 3:19. Ec 3:11-14. Is *40:22, 26. 42:5. 44:24. 45:7, 12, *18. Je *32:17. Ml +2:10 (✥S#1254h). Ac *17:24. Ro 1:19, 20. 11:36. 1 C 8:6. He 3:4. *11:3. Re 4:11. *10:6. **heaven.** Ge 2:4. 14:19, 22. Re *4:11. *10:6. 2 K 19:15. 1 Ch 16:26. *29:11. 2 Ch 2:12. Jb 9:8-10. 26:7-*13. 37:18. Ps 8:3. *19:1. 24:2. *89:11, 12. 96:5. *102:25. 104:2, 5, 24, *30. 115:15, 16. *121:2. 124:8. 134:3. 136:5, 6. 146:6. 147:8. 148:4, 5. Pr *8:22-30. Ec *12:1. Is 37:16. 40:21, *26, 28. 45:12. 48:13. 51:13, 16. *65:17. Je *10:12. 27:5. *32:17. *51:15. Zc *12:1. Mt 11:25. Ac 4:24. *14:15. 2 P 3:4, 5. Re 14:7. *21:1, 6. 22:13. **earth.** Ex 19:5. Ps 24:1, 2. 50:12. 74:16, 17. *90:2.

2. **And.** ſ148, Ge +8:22. **earth.** ſ16, Ge +1:27. **was.** or, became. Ge 2:7. 9:15. 19:26. Ex 32:1. Dt 27:9. 2 S 7:24. or, came to pass. Ge 4:3, 14. 22:1. 24:15. 27:1. Jsh 4:1. 5:1. 1 K 13:22. Is 14:24. **without form.** Heb. *tohu,* S#8414h, Is +45:18. ſ140, Ge +4:25. Jb 26:7. Is 24:1. 34:11h. *45:18. Je *4:23. Jl 2:31. Na 2:10. Mt 27:45. Ep 5:11, 13. Col 1:13. Re 6:12. 8:12. 9:2. 16:10. **and void.** Heb. *bohu.* ſ140, Ge +4:25. ✱S#922h. Ge 1:2. Is 34:11 (emptiness). Je 4:23. **and darkness.** Jb +*38:9. **was.** ſ63B, Ge +2:10. **deep.** or, sea. Ps 42:7. 104:24. Is 51:10. 63:13. Jon +*2:5. Hab 3:10. 2 C 11:25. **Spirit.** Heb. *ruach,* Is +48:16. Ge 6:17. Jb 26:13. Ps 33:6. *104:30. Is *40:12-14. 42:1. Mt ⬤+*12:32. Lk 24:49. Jn 3:6, 34. ⬤7:39. Ac 1:5. 2:17, 18. 4:8. 10:38, 44. 1 Th 5:19. Ja 1:18. **moved.** Dt 32:11. Is 31:5. Jn *3:3-8. Ro 8:5, 9, 14. 2 C 5:17, 18. Ga 4:29. **face.** ſ144A1, Ge +11:8. Ge 1:29. 2:6. 4:14. 6:1, 7. 7:3, 4, 18, 23. 8:8, 9, 13. 11:4. 41:56. Ex 10:5, 15. 32:12. 33:16. Nu 11:31. 12:3. 22:5, 11. Dt 6:15. 7:6. 1 S 20:15. 1 K 13:34. Jb 37:12. Is 14:21. 23:17. 27:6. Je 8:2. 28:16. Ezk 34:6. 38:20. Da 8:5. Am 5:8. 9:6. Lk 12:56. 21:35. **waters.** Ge 7:6. Ps *104:6.

3. **God.** Ps *33:6, 9. 148:3, 5. Mt 8:3. Jn 11:43, 44. **said.** ver. 6, 9, 11, 14, 20, 24, 26, 28, 29. **Let.** Ge 13:8. 18:4. 24:14-18. Jb +*42:2. Ec 8:4. Mt 7:4. *13:30. 27:22. Jn *14:1. Ph *2:5. **be.** or, become. ver. 2. **light.** Jb 36:30. 38:19. Ps 74:16. *97:11. 104:2. 118:27. *119:130. Is *45:7. 60:19. Jn *1:5, 9. 3:19. 9:5. Ac 9:3. 2 C *4:6. Ep 5:8, 14. Col 1:12. 1 T 6:16. 1 P

1:23-25. 1 J *1:5. 2:8. **was.** or, became. Ge ⬤1:14-19.

4. **saw.** ver. 10, 12, 18, 25, 31. Ec 2:13. *11:7. 1 P *2:9. **good.** or, beautiful. ver. 10, 12, 18, 21, 25, 31. ⬤2:18. Ps 145:9, 10. Ec 3:11. **divided.** ver. 7. Is *5:20. 45:7. 2 C *6:14. Ph 1:10. **light.** Ex 10:23. **darkness.** Jb 26:10.

5. **God.** Ps *74:16. **called.** ver. 5, 8, 10. Ge 5:2. Ps 92:2. Ec 3:11. 10:13. 11:6. Is 41:4. 44:6. 48:12. Re 1:8, 11, 17. 2:8. 21:6. 22:13. **Day, and.** Ge 8:22. Ps 19:2. Is *45:7. Je *33:20. Jn *8:12. 11:9. Ro 13:13. 1 C 3:13. 2 Cor *4:6. Ep 5:13. 1 Th *5:5. He 1:2, 3. **And the.** Heb. And the evening was, and the morning was. ſ171T5, Ge 1:31. ver. 8, 13, 19, 23, 31. Ge 19:27. Le 23:32. Ps 65:8. 74:16. *104:20. **day.** Ex *20:9, 10. Pr +*4:18. 1 J 2:8.

6. **Let there.** ver. 14, 20. Ge 7:11, 12. Jb *9:8. 26:7, 8, 10, 13. 37:11, 15, *18. 38:22-26. Ps *19:1. *33:6, 7, 9. 104:2. 136:*5, 6. *148:4. 150:1. Pr *8:27. Ec 11:3. Is 40:22. Je 10:10, *12, 13. *51:15. Zp 3:5. Zc 12:1. **firmament.** Heb. expansion. ver. 8. Jg ⬤5:4. Jb 26:8. 37:18. Ps 77:17. 104:5-9. ⬤147:8. Pr 8:28, 29. Is 14:12-14. 40:22. 44:24. Je 10:12. 51:15. Da ⬤7:13. 2 P 3:5-7.

7. **made.** ver. 16, 25, 31. Ge 2:2, 3. Ex 20:8-11. 31:17. **firmament.** or, expanse. ver. +6. Ge 7:11. Ps 19:1. **divided.** Pr 8:*28, 29. **were.** or, are. **above.** Jb 26:8. 37:16. 38:8-11. Ps 104:3, 10, 13. *148:4. Ec 11:3. **and it.** ver. 9, 11, 15, 24. Mt 8:27.

8. **God called.** ver. 5, 10. Ge 5:2. 32:28. **evening.** ver. 5, 13, 19, 23, 31.

9. **Let.** Jb 26:7, 10. Ps *33:7. 136:5, 6. Ec 1:7. Jl 2:3. Jon 1:9. Ro 6:14. Col 3:1. Re 10:6. **one.** Jb *38:8-11. Ps 104:3, 5-9. Pr 8:28, 29. Je *5:22. 2 P *3:5. **dry.** Ge ⬤+7:11. Jb 22:16. Ps 18:15. 24:1, 2. 83:5. 95:5. 102:25. *104:8. Pr 3:19. 8:29. Is 51:13-16. The exodus through the Red Sea is compared to the third day of creation in the following passages: Ps 66:5, 6. 77:15. Is 8:5-10. 17:13. **land.** lit. let the dry appear. ſ24G. Antimereia; or, Exchange of Parts of Speech B495. An adjective is used for a noun. Here, "dry" is put for "dry land." For other instances of this figure see Is 24:23. Ro 1:15, 19. 2:4. 1 C 1:27, 28. 2 C 8:8. Ep 6:12. Ph 2:6. 4:5. He 6:17.

10. **Earth.** Ge 2:5. Ps 24:2. Ec *1:4. **gathering.** Ps *33:7. 95:5. 146:6. **Seas.** Ge 9:2. Jb 38:8. Pr 8:29. **God saw.** ver. 4. Dt *32:4. Ps 104:31.

11. **Let the.** Ge 2:5. Jb 28:5. Ps 65:9-13. 104:14-17. *147:8. Is 42:5. Mt 6:30. He *6:7. **grass.** Heb. tender grass. Dt 32:2. Pr 27:25. Is 15:6. *40:8. Da 4:15, 23. Mk 6:39. **seed.** ſ147D, Ge +1:29. **fruit.** ver. 29. Ge 2:9, 16. Ps *1:3. Je *17:8. Mt 3:10. Mk 4:28. Ro 6:22. **after.** ver. 11, 12, 12, 21, 21, 24, 24, 25, 25, 25. Ge 7:14. 8:22. Je 13:23. 33:20. Ga *6:7-9. **kind.** Ge 6:20h. Dt +*14:13. Mt 7:16-20. Lk *6:43, 44. 1 C 15:36-38. Ja 3:12.

12. **earth.** Is 61:11. Mk 4:28. **herb.** Is *55:10, 11. Mt 13:24-26. Lk 6:44. 2 C 9:10. Ga *6:7. **good.** Ps 104:31. 1 T 4:4. Ja 1:17.

13. **evening.** Ps 65:8. *104:23. Ec 11:6. Zc 14:7. Lk 24:29. Jn 20:19. Ac 28:23. **morning.** Ge 19:15. Ex

16:21. 2 S 23:4. 1 K 18:26. Jb 7:21. 38:12. Ps *30:5. 59:16. 90:5, 6, 14. Mt 16:3. Mk 11:20. 16:2. Lk 21:38. Ac 5:21. **day.** Ge 1:5, 14. 2:4. 43:16. Ex 20:9. Le 23:32. Mt 27:64. Mk 9:31.

14. **Let there.** Dt *4:19. Jb 25:3, 5. 26:10. 38:12-14. Ps 8:3, 4. 19:1-6. *74:16, 17. 104:19-23. 119:91. *136:7-9. 148:3-6. Is *40:26. 45:7. Je *31:35. 33:20, 25. **lights.** or, light bearers. Or, rather, luminaries or light-bearers; being a different word from that rendered light, in ver. 3. ver. ◐3. Ex 25:6. 27:20. 35:8, 14, 28. 39:37. Le 24:2. Nu 4:9, 16. Ps 74:16. 90:8. Pr 15:30. **firmament.** Ge 1:+6, 7, 8, 20. Ps 19:1. 150:1. Ezk 1:22, 25. Da *12:3. **heaven.** Dt *26:15. Ps 19:1. 50:6. 97:6. Mt 24:29. Ac 2:19. **the day.** Heb. between the day and between the night. **and let.** Ge *8:22. 9:13. Jb 3:9. 38:31, 32. Ps 81:3. Ezk 32:7, 8. 46:1, 6. Jl 2:10, 30, 31. 3:15. Am 5:8. 8:9. Mt 2:2. Lk 21:25, 26. 23:45. Ac 2:19, 20. Re 6:12. 8:12. 9:2. **signs.** 2 K 20:9. Jb 37:14-17, 21, 22. Ps 72:5. 89:36, 37. Is 13:10. *47:12-14. Je +*10:2. Mt 12:38. 16:1-3. 24:29-31. Mk 8:11. 13:24-27. Lk 11:16. 12:54-56. 1 C 1:22. **seasons.** *Ge 8:22. +17:21 (✝S#4150h). 18:14. 21:2. Dt 11:14. Jb 38:22-32. 37:9. Ps 74:17. *104:19. Pr 26:1. SS 2:11-13. Je 31:36, 37. 33:25, 26. Jl 2:23. Ac 14:17.

15. **lights.** Ge 1:14-18. Dt 33:14. Jsh 10:12. Jb 31:26. Ps *8:3. 74:16. 121:6. 136:7-9. Ec 12:2. SS 6:10. Je *31:35. Hab 3:11. 1 C 15:51. Re 21:23. **firmament.** Ge 1:6-8, +14-17, 20. Ps *19:1. 150:1. Da *12:3. **light.** Is *45:7. 2 C *4:6. **earth.** Ge 1:1. Ex 20:11. 2 K 19:15. 2 Ch 2:12. Ne 9:6. Jb 38:4. Ps *90:2. 102:25. 115:15. 124:8. 146:6. Pr 8:22-26. Is 37:16. *45:18. Je 10:12. 27:5. 32:17. 33:25, 26. 51:15. Ezk 32:8. Jn 1:3. He 1:10. 2 P 3:5. Re 10:6. 14:7.

16. **made.** or, appointed. 1 S 12:6. Jb 14:5. Ps *104:19. **greater.** Ge 15:12, 17. Nu 2:3. Jsh *10:12, 13. 12:1. Is *38:8. Ml 4:2. Lk 4:40. Jn 9:5. **lesser.** Mt 5:14. Ro 10:18. Ph 2:15. **to rule.** Heb. for the rule, etc. Dt 4:19. Jsh 10:12-14. Jb 31:26-28. 38:7. Ps 8:3. *19:4-6. 74:16. 136:7-9. 148:3, 5. Is 13:10. 24:23. *40:26. 45:7. Je *31:35. Ezk 32:7, 8. Jl 2:10, 31. 3:15. Am 5:8. 8:9. Hab 3:11. Mt *24:29. 27:45. Ac 2:20. 1 C 15:41. Re 16:8, 9. *21:23. **he made the stars also.** Or, with the stars also. Ge 11:4. 37:9. Jg 5:20. 2 K 23:5. Jb 9:9. 38:31, 32. Ps 147:2. Is 13:10. Je +*10:2. Am 5:8.

17. **set them.** Ge 9:13. Jsh 10:12-14. Jb 38:12. Ps *8:1, 3. Je 4:23-26. 33:20, 25. Ac 13:47. 2 P 3:5-8.

18. **rule over.** Ps 19:6. Je 4:23-26. 31:35. 2 P 3:5-8. **darkness.** Jb +38:9.

19. **fourth.** Ge 15:16. Ex 20:5. Le 19:24. Da 2:40. 3:25. 7:23. Zc 8:19. Re 4:7. 6:7, 8. 8:12. 16:8.

20. **Let the waters.** ver. 22. Ge 2:19. 8:17. Jb 12:7-10. Ps 104:24, 25. 148:10. Ac 17:25. Ro 5:3, 4. Ph 1:12-18. **bring.** Ge 7:21. 8:17. 9:7. Ex 1:7. 8:3h. Le 11:29, 41-43. Ps 105:30. **moving.** or, creeping. Ge 7:21. Le 5:2. 11:20, 21, 23, 29, 41-44. 22:5. Dt +*14:19n. 1 K 4:33. **creature.** Ge +√2:19. 9:10, 12, 15, 16. **life.** Heb. a living soul. Heb. *nephesh*, soul, Ge +2:7. ver. 21, 24, 30. Ge +√2:7n, 19. 9:4, 5, 10, 12, 15, 16. Le 11:10, 46. 24:18. Nu 31:28. Jb 41:21. Ec ◐+*3:21. Ezk 47:9. Mt ◐+*10:28n. 1 C +*15:45n. √171Q3. Figure of speech Synecdoche of the Part, where a part is put for the whole, here 'soul,' a part, is used for the whole animal or living creature. For other instances of this figure see Ge 1:21, 24, 30. Re 16:3. **fowl that may fly.** Heb. let fowl fly. This marginal

reading is more conformable to the original, and reconciles this passage with Ge 2:19. The word fowl, from the Saxon *fleon*, to fly, exactly corresponds to the original, which denotes every thing that flies, whether bird or insect. **above.** √144C1, Ge +21:1. **open firmament.** Heb. face of the firmament. ver. 7, 14.

21. **great.** Ge 6:20. 7:14. 8:19. Jb 7:12. 26:5. Ps *104:24-26. Ezk 32:2. Jon 1:17. 2:10. Mt 12:40. **creature.** Heb. *nephesh*, soul, ver. +20. Ge +√2:7, 19. **brought.** Ge 8:17. 9:7. Ex 1:7. 8:3. **God saw.** ver. 18, 25, 31.

22. **blessed.** √43, Dt +28:3. ver. 28. **fruitful.** Ge 8:17. 9:1. 30:27, 30. 35:11. Le 26:9. Jb 40:15. 42:12. Ps *107:31, 38. 128:3. 144:13, 14. Pr 10:22. **fowl.** Le 11:9, 13. 1 K 4:33. Ps 148:10.

23. **evening.** Ex 12:6. 18:13. 1 S 17:16. Ps *65:8. 90:6. 104:23. Pr 7:8, 9. Ec 11:6. Zc *14:7. Lk 24:29. Jn 20:19. Ac *28:23. **morning.** Ge 1:5, 8, 13, 19, 31. 19:15. Ex *16:21. Nu 9:21. 2 S 23:4. 1 K 18:26. Jb 7:21. 38:12. Ps *30:5. *59:16. 90:5, 6, *14. Mt 16:3. 20:1. Mk *1:35. 11:20. 16:2. Lk 21:38. Ac 5:21.

24. **Let.** Ge 2:20. 6:20. 7:14. 8:19. Jb 38:39, 40. 39:1, 5, 9, 19. 40:15. Ps 50:9, 10. 104:18-23. 148:10. **creature.** Heb. *nephesh*, soul, ver. +20. Ge +√2:7, 19. **cattle.** Cattle, denotes domestic animals living on vegetables;—Beasts of the earth, wild animals; especially such as live on flesh; and—Creeping things, reptiles; or all the different genera of serpents, worms, and such animals as have no feet.

25. **God made.** Ge 2:19, 20. 7:21, 22. Jb 12:8-10. 26:13. Je *27:5.

26. **Let us.** Ge 3:22. *11:7. 18:1-3. *19:24. Ex ◐21:4, 6, 29. D+ ◐+√6:4. Jb 35:10n. Ps 97:7. 100:3. 149:2. Pr 8:12. Is *6:8. ◐40:25. 48:16. 64:8. Jn *5:17. *14:23. 17:5, 11, 21, 22. 1 J 5:7. **make.** Is 54:5. 62:5. Je 3:1, 6. 4:30. Ezk 16:32. Ho 1:2. 2:19. 3:1. **man.** In Hebrew, Adam; probably so called either from the red earth of which he was formed, or from the blush or flesh-tint of the human countenance: the name is intended to designate the species. **in our.** Ge 5:1, 3. 9:6. Ex 20:4. Le 26:1. Ps 73:20. 106:19. Ec 7:29. Is 40:19, 20. 44:9-17. 45:20. 48:5. Je *10:14. 51:17. Ac 17:26, 28, 29. Ro 1:20. 1 C *11:7. *15:49. 2 C *3:18. *4:4. Ep 4:24. Ph ◐2:7. Col *1:15. 3:10. He *1:3. Ja 3:9. 1 J 3:2. Re 3:14. 4:11. **image…likeness.** √93A. Figure of speech Hendiadys; or, Two for One B659: two words are used, but one thing is meant. One of the two words expresses the thing referred to, and the other (which may be of synonymous or even different signification, and is *not* a second thing or idea) intensifies and emphasizes it. The second word, if a noun, becomes in effect an adjective of the superlative degree, which is, by this means, made especially emphatic. The two words are always of the same part of speech, such as two nouns or two verbs. They are always joined by the conjunction "and." When the figure employs nouns, the two nouns are always in the same case. Just because two words are joined by "and" does not mean the presence of Hendiadys. It may be, instead, the figure Epitheton (√79, Ge +21:16). The very opposite of Hendiadys is Syntheton (√174, Ge +18:27). Sometimes, even in an undoubted Hendiadys, the two words may be equally true when taken separately and severally, as when joined together in one (as Ph 1:11 "the glory and praise of God" may equally mean either a reference to two things, to the glory of God, and to

the praise of God; or, by Hendiadys, it may mean just one, "unto the glorious praise of God"). Hendiadys is not present if the two words are opposed in any way in their signification, or when there is no real connection between them (as in Ph 1:25, "abide and continue" or "furtherance and joy"; likewise, there is no Hendiadys in Ro 15:4, "patience and comfort," for 'comforting' is not a proper qualification of patience). This figure of speech is one of the most important figures in the Bible, and is very frequently used in both the Old and New Testaments. About most of the examples cited there can be no doubt, but a few (such as Ge 2:9) may be open to question, and these are submitted for the judgment and consideration of the reader. Here, "image and likeness" by Hendiadys is "in the likeness of our image," thus one thing, not two. For Hendiadys of verbs, see Is +66:11. For additional instances of the figure Hendiadys of nouns see Ge 2:9. 3:16. 4:4. 5:29. 13:13. 19:24. Dt 30:15. 1 S 17:40. 28:3. 2 S 20:19. 1 K 20:33. 1 Ch 22:5. 2 Ch 2:9. 16:14. Jb 10:17, 21. ?34:14. Ps 74:16. 96:7. 116:1. 119:138. Is 1:13. 57:8. Je 22:3, 15. 29:11. 36:27. Da 8:10. Mi 2:11. Zp 1:16. Mt *3:11. 4:16. 24:30, 31. Lk 1:17. *21:15. Jn *1:17. √3:5. 4:23, 24. 11:25, 26. Ac 1:25. 3:14. 14:13. *23:6. Ro 1:5, 20. 2:27. 8:6. 11:17. ?15:4. 1 C 2:4. *11:7. 2 C 8:2. Ep *4:11. *5:5. 6:18. Col 1:26. 2:8, 18. 1 Th 2:12. 1 T ?1:4. 3:15. 2 T 1:10. 4:1, 2. T *2:13. Ja 3:9. 2 P 1:3, 16, 17. Re 5:10. 6:11. 13:5. **have dominion.** ver. 28. Ge *9:2-4. Jb 5:23. Ps *2:8. √8:4-8. 47:3. +*49:14. 104:20-24. *145:13. +*149:4-9. Is *11:6, 9. Je 27:6. Da *2:38. Zc +*14:9. Mt +*5:5. Lk +*1:32, 33. Ro 4:13. √8:19-23. 1 C +*15:24-28. Ep *1:18-21. He +*1:2. *2:6-9. 8:11. Ja *3:7. Re *11:15. +*20:4.

27. **created man.** Ge 5:1. Ps 100:3. Ec *7:29. Is 64:8. Ac *17:26. Ja 3:9. **own image.** 1 C 11:7. 2 C 3:18. Ep 4:24. Col *3:10. **in the image.** See ver. 26. Ps 139:14. Is 43:7. Ep *2:10. 4:24. Col *1:15. **image.** √16. Figure of speech Anadiplosis; or, Like Sentence Endings and Beginnings B251: the repetition of the same word or words at the end of one sentence and at the beginning of another. See Ge 1:1, 2, where Anadiplosis is the very first figure of speech employed in the Bible. For other instances of this figure see Ge 7:18, 19. 31:6, 7. 31:33, 34. Ex 7:16, 17. *12:4, 5. 32:16. Nu 33:3, 4. Dt 31:3, 4. 2 S *9:12, 13. 19:10, 11. Est 6:5, 6. *7:7, 8. Ps 98:4, 5. 113:8. 115:12. *121:1, 2. 122:2, 3. *126:2, 3. 127:1, 2. *145:18. Pr *13:21, 22. Is 24:4, 5. Ho 2:21, 22. Hab *3:2. Mt *10:40. Jn 14:11. 18:37. Ro 8:17. 9:30. *10:17. 2 C 5:17, 18. 2 C 9:6. Ga 4:31 and 5:1. Ph 2:8. Ja 1:3. **male.** Ge 2:21-25. 5:2. Ml 2:15. Mt *19:4. Mk 10:6. 1 C 11:8, 9. Ga ❍3:28.

28. **blessed.** √43, Dt +28:3. ver. 22. Ge 2:3. 8:17. 9:1, 7. 17:16, 20. *22:17, 18. *24:60. 26:3, 4, 24. 33:5. 49:25. Le 26:9. 1 Ch *4:10. 26:5. Jb *42:12. Ps 107:38. 127:1-5. 128:3, 4. Is *45:18. 1 T 4:3. **them.** Ge 2:20-23. √151. Figure of speech Prolepsis or Anticipation B914: anticipating what is going to be, and speaking of future things as present. Notice here the reference to "them" in anticipation of the creation of Eve which is not mentioned until Ge 2:20-23. Ge ❍2:18. For other instances of this figure see Ge 21:14. Ex 10:29. Jsh 4:19. 1 K 22:50. Is 37:22. 48:5-7. Lk 3:19-20. He 2:8. **fruitful.** Ge 1:22. ❍9:1. Ps +*127:3. 128:3, 4. Is 2:6. 23:2. Je 31:25. Ezk 26:2. 27:25. 1 T 4:1, 3. He

13:4. **replenish.** or, fill. ver. 22h. Ge 9:1. Ex 32:29mg. 1 K 18:33. Is *45:18. Je 51:11 (gather). **dominion.** ver. +*26. Ps 8:6. He 2:6-8. **moveth.** Heb. creepeth. Ps 69:34mg.

29. **I have.** Ps *24:1. *115:16. Ho 2:8. Ac *17:24, 25, 28. 1 T *6:17. **bearing.** Heb. seeding. √147D. Figure of speech Polyptoton; or, Many Inflections B275: the repetition of the same part of speech in different inflections; here, verb with cognate noun. For other instances of this figure see Ge 1:11. 8:21. +26:28. 27:3, 33, 34. *28:20. 30:8, 37. 35:14, 20. Nu 4:23. 11:4. 16:30. 1 S 4:5. 2 S 12:16. 13:36. 1 K 1:40. 2 K 4:13. 13:14. 19:7. Ps 14:5. 53:5. 64:6. 106:14. 144:6. Pr 30:24. Is 8:12. 22:17. Je 22:16. 48:5mg. 51:2. La 3:59. Ezk 13:5mg. 18:2. 38:12. Da 11:3. Ho 2:6mg. Jon 1:10. Mi 2:4. Na 1:15. Hab 3:2. Zc 1:2, 14, 15. 7:9. Mt 2:10. Mk 4:41. Lk 22:15. Jn 6:28. *7:24. Ac 23:12, 14. Ep *6:18. Col *2:19. 1 T *1:18. 2 T *4:7. Ja 5:17. Re 16:9. 17:6. **to you.** Ge 2:16. *9:3. Jb 36:31. Ps *104:14, 15, 27, 28. *111:15. 136:25. 145:15, 16. 146:7. 147:9. Is 33:16. Mt *6:11, 25, 26. Ac *14:17.

30. **to every beast.** Ge 9:3. Jb 38:39-41. 39:4, 8, 30. 40:15, 20. Ps 104:14. *145:15, 16. 147:9. **life.** Heb. a living soul. Heb. *nephesh*, ver. +*20. Ge 2:+*7, +√19.

31. **very good.** Ge ❍6:6. Dt 32:4. Jb 38:7. Ps *19:1, 2. 104:*24, 31. La 3:38. 1 T *4:4. **the evening.** √171T5. Synecdoche of the Part B656. Evening and morning are put for the full day; or, the whole of a day and night. ver. 5, 8, 13, 19, 23, 31. By this figure the beginning and end of anything is put for the whole of it. Compare Ps 92:2. Ec 3:11. 10:13. 11:6. Is 41:4. 44:6. 48:12. Re 1:8, 11, 17. 2:8. 21:6. 22:13. **and the.** ver. 5, 8, 13, 23. Ge 2:2. Ex *20:11. 31:17.

GENESIS 2

The sabbath is instituted, 1-3. Further particulars concerning the production of the vegetables, and the creation of man, 4-7. The garden of Eden, how planted, and where situated, 8-14; man is placed in it; and permitted to eat of the fruit, with a solemn interdiction of one tree, 15-17. The animals are named by Adam; and an account given of the creation of woman, and the institution of marriage, 18-25.

1. **Thus.** ver. 4. Ge 1:1, 10. Ex *20:11. 31:17. 2 K 19:15. 2 Ch 2:12. Ne 9:6. Jb 12:9. Ps 89:11-13. 104:2. 136:5-8. 146:6. Is 42:5. *45:18. 48:13. 55:9. *65:17. Je 10:12, 16. Zc 12:1. Ac 4:24. He 4:3. 2 P 3:5-8. **host.** Dt 4:19. 17:3. 2 K 21:3-5. Ps *33:6, 9. Is 24:21. 34:4. 40:26-28. 45:12. Je 8:2. Lk 2:13. Ac 7:42.

2. **And on.** Ge 1:31. Ex 16:23. 20:8, ❍*11. 23:12. 31:17. Dt 5:14. Is 58:13. Jn 5:17. Lk 23:56. ❍24:1. Col 2:16. He ▶4:4. **seventh day God.** The LXX, Syriac, and the Samaritan Text read the sixth day, which is probably the true reading; as the Hebrew letter *vau*, which stands for six, might easily be changed into the Hebrew letter *zain*, which denotes seven. **rested.** Or, rather, ceased, as the Hebrew word is not opposed to weariness, but to action; as the Divine Being can neither know fatigue, nor stand in need of rest. Is *40:28.

3. **blessed.** √43, Dt +28:3. Ex 16:22-30. *20:8-11. 23:12. 31:13-17. 34:21. 35:2, 3. Le 23:3. 25:2, 3. Dt 5:12-14. Ne 9:14. 13:15-22. Pr 10:22. Is 56:2-7. +√58:13n, 14. Je 17:21-27. Ezk 20:12. Mk 2:27. Lk

23:56. Jn ◐20:19, 26. Ac 16:13. ◐20:7. 1 C ◐16:2. He 4:4-10. **the seventh day**. Some would argue this account is given by *prolepsis* (♪151, Ge +1:28), and assert there is not even a single allusion to a sabbatical rest until the Mosaic law. However an allusion to the sabbath may be discerned at Ge 4:3mg and Ge 29:27. Furthermore, the sabbath is mentioned in Ex 16:26-30, *prior* to the giving of the law in Ex ch. 20. **created and made**. Heb. created to make.

4. **the generations**. Ge 1:4, ◐11-27. 5:1. 10:1. 11:10. 25:12, 19. 36:1, 9. Ex 6:16. Jb 38:4-11, 28. Ps 90:1, 2. **in**. Ge 1:3-31. **Lord**. i.e. *owner, master*. S#3068h, Jehovah. Ex 15:3. 1 K 18:39. 2 Ch 20:6. Ps +√9:10. 18:31. 86:10. Is 44:6. Re 1:4, 8. 11:17. 16:5. Jehovah-Elohim. First occurrence of this compound name. For other Jehovah compound names see Ge 15:2, 8. 22:8. Ex +√15:26n. 17:15. 20:2. 31:13. Jg 6:24. 1 S 1:3. Ps 7:17. 23:1. 95:6. 99:5. Je 23:6. Ezk 48:35. Zc 14:5. **earth**. Jb 38:4. Is 45:18.

5. **plant**. Ge 1:12. Ps *104:14. **had not**. Jb *5:10. 38:26-28. Ps 65:9-11. 135:7. Je 10:12, 13. 14:22. Mt *5:45. He 6:7. **to till**. Ge 3:23. 4:2, 12.

6. **there went up a mist**. *or*, a mist which went up. Ge ◐*2:5. ◐*7:4. Jb 26:27. Ps 135:7. 148:8. Je 10:12, 13. ♪63I1C1. Ellipsis of omitted negative particle from the preceding clause B93. Here, "mist" may be rendered "no mist" if three negative reasons why plants and herbs of the field did not grow are intended: (1) no rain; (2) no man; (3) no mist to water the ground. By the figure Ellipsis of repetition where an omitted negative particle is to be repeated from the preceding clause, the last of two or three negatives are not necessary and must be supplied, as in Dt 33:6. 1 S 2:3. 1 K +2:9n. Ps *9:18. 38:1. 75:5. Pr 24:12. 25:27. Is 38:18. **face**. Ge +1:2.

7. **Lord God**. ver. +4. **formed**. Ge 2:19. 2 K 19:25. Ps 94:9. 95:5. 100:3. 139:14, 15. Is 45:18. 64:8. Note that man's body was formed, but soul and spirit were created, Ge 1:26, 27, proving man is a compound being. **man**. ver. 8, 15. Note man is a compound being consisting of body and spirit, Jb +*14:22. Ec +*12:7. Mt +*10:28. Lk 8:55. 1 C 5:3. ▶15:45. 2 C 5:6, 8. 1 Th ◐5:23. He ◐4:12. 3 J 2. **of the**. Heb. dust of the ground. **dust**. Ge *3:19, 23. Jb *4:19. 33:6. Ps +*103:14. Ec 3:20. +*12:7. Is *64:8. Ro 9:20. 1 C *15:47. 2 C 4:7. 5:1. S#6083h, translated elsewhere "ashes," Nu 19:17. 2 K 23:4; "earth," Ge 26:15; "ground," Jb 14:8; "morter," Le 14:42, 45; "powder," 2 K 23:6, 15; "rubbish," Ne 4:2, 10. **and breathed**. Jb 27:3. 33:4. Ezk 37:9. Jn 20:22. Ac 17:25. **nostrils**. Ge 7:22. Ec +*3:21. Is 2:22. **breath**. Heb. *neshamah*. ✳S#5397h. Ge 7:22. Dt 20:16. Jsh 10:40: 11:11, 14. 2 S 22:16. 1 K 15:29. 17:17. Jb 4:9. 26:4. *27:3. 32:8. 33:4. +*34:14. 37:10. Ps 18:15. 150:6. Pr 20:27. Is 2:22. 30:33. 42:5. 57:16. Da 5:23. 10:17. Note that "spirit" or "soul" are not merely "breath." "Breath" constitutes function, "spirit" and "soul" often designate "being," or the immaterial part of man. "Breath" is distinct from "spirit" and "soul" as it cannot substitute for these terms in the following passages: Ge 34:3. 41:8. Le 20:27. Dt 2:30. 1 S 1:15. 28:7. 1 K 21:5. 22:21-24. Jb 34:14. Ps 16:10. 19:7. 34:18. 106:15. Pr 16:18, 19. 18:14. Ec 1:14. Is 29:24. 58:5. Mt +*10:28. Lk 12:19. Jn 4:23. Ac 23:8, 9. Ep 4:23. 1 Th 5:23. He 4:12. 1 J 4:1. Re 6:9-11. 20:4. Note also that the human soul or spirit is distinguished from the divine

Spirit from whom it proceeded, thus refuting pantheism, 1 C 2:11. Soul or spirit is distinguished from the body it inhabits, refuting materialism, Ge 35:18. 1 K *17:21. Jb +*14:22. Ec +*12:7. Zc +*12:1n. Ja 2:26. **of**. Genitive of Apposition, equivalent to "that is to say" or "consisting of," thus "breath, that is to say, life." For other instances of the Genitive of Apposition, see Is 14:14. Jn *2:21. Ro 4:11, 13, 18. 8:23. 2 C 1:22. 3:17, 18. 5:1, 5. Ep 4:3, *9. *6:14. He 6:1. 1 P 1:1. 2 P 2:6. **life**. Ge 6:17. 7:22. 17:15. Ac *17:25. 1 C *15:45. He *12:9. **became**. Ge +1:2. **living**. Ge 1:21, 24. 2:19. Jb 27:3. 32:8. 33:4. Note man's body is vitalized by a single principle, the living soul. **soul**. Heb. ✥S#5315h, *nephesh*. Ge +1:20. +√12:5. 35:18. Nu 16:22. 27:16. 1 K *17:21. 2 K 4:27. Jb +*14:22. 34:14. Ps 63:1. Pr 20:27. Ec +*12:7. Is *10:18. Da *7:15. Zc 12:1. Mt +*10:28n. Mk *12:26, 27. 1 C 15:45. 1 Th 5:23. He +*12:9. Ja 2:26. 1 P +*3:4. Note that Scripture uses the terms "soul" and "spirit" interchangeably in such passages as Ge 41:8 w Ps 42:6. Both depart the body at death: Ge 35:18 w Ps 146:4. 1 S 30:12 w La 1:11mg. Both are affirmed to be within man: Jb 14:22 w Zc 12:1. Mt 20:28 w 27:50. Jn 12:27 w 13:21. He 12:23 w Re 6:9. Both 'soul' (*nephesh*, Ge +23:8) and 'spirit' (*ruach*, Ge +26:35) are rendered *mind*: Ezk 23:18, 28 w Ezk 20:32. Both are used of the departed: 1 P 3:19 w Re 20:4. Both are used of sadness or sorrow: 1 K 21:5 w Ps 62:11. Mt 26:28 w Jn 13:21. Is 26:9a w Is 26:9b. Lk 1:46 w 1:47. Ph 1:27a w Ph 1:27b. An examination of its lexical uses shows immediately that "nephesh" is used with a broader range of meaning than the more theological English term "soul." The 754 occurrences of the Hebrew word *nephesh* (most often rendered "soul") may be classified as to its lexical uses as follows. (1) Ge +2:19, used of lower creatures; (2) Ge +9:15, used alike of lower creatures and man, rendered "creature," "life" (Le 17:11), "soul" (Nu 31:28); (3) Ge +12:5, used of man as an individual person; (4) Ge +12:13, used of mortal man, as though the soul could die or be destroyed; also rendered "life" (Ge +44:30), "ghost," etc. (Nu +23:10); (5) Ge +17:14, used of man as being "cut off" by God; (6) Ge +27:31, used of man, exercising certain powers, or performing certain acts, often rendered by emphatic pronouns; (7) Ge +34:3, used of man, exercising mental faculties, rendered "soul," "mind" (Ge +23:8), "heart" (Ex +23:9), "lust," etc. (Ex +15:9); (8) Le +19:28, used of man actually dead; (9) Nu +11:6, used of man as possessing animal appetites and desires; (10) Jsh +10:28, used of man being slain or killed by man. (11) Ps +30:3, used of man as going to a place described by the word "grave," etc. Compare the classification of the corresponding New Testament term *psyche* at Mt 2:20n. For "spirit," Heb. *ruach*, see Ge 6:3n.

8. ♪133. Ge 2:8-15 is a Parecbasis: a digression B906, a temporary turning aside from one subject to another; the original subject is resumed in verse 16, from verse 7. For other instances of the figure Parecbasis see Ge ch. 36, 38. Ro 1:2-6. **a garden**. Ge 13:10. SS 6:2. Is 51:3. Ezk 28:13. 31:8, 9. Jl 2:3. Jn ◐19:41. **eastward**. Ge 3:24. 4:16. 2 K 19:12. Ezk 27:23. 31:16, 18. **Eden**. LXX paradise. i.e. *delight*, ✳S#5731h. Ge 2:8, 10, 15. 3:23, 24. 4:16. 2 Ch 29:12. 31:15. Is *51:3. Ezk *28:13. 31:9, 16, 18. 36:35. Jl 2:3. **put the**. ver. 15. **formed**. Ro 9:20.

9. **every**. Ezk 31:8, 9, 16, 18. **tree of life**. Ge *3:22. Pr 3:18. *11:30. Ezk 47:12. Jn *6:48, 51, 53. Re *2:7. *22:2, 14. Genitive of cause, the tree supporting and continuing the life which had been imparted: Ge 3:22, +24. Jn 6:48, 51, 53. **midst**. Re *2:7. **tree of knowledge**. ver. 17. Ge 3:3, 22. Dt 6:25. Pr 1:7. Is 44:25. 47:10. Ro 3:20. 1 C 8:1. **good and evil**. ♪93A. Figure of speech Hendiadys, Ge +1:26. Thus here, tree of evil enjoyment.

10. **And a**. lit. And there was a. ♪63B. Figure of speech Ellipsis (Absolute, of verb substantive) B37. For other instances of this figure see Ge 1:2. 3:6. 4:13. 5:1. 14:9. 1 S 19:11. 2 K 6:33. 2 Ch 3:9. Ps 33:4. 99:9. 103:14. 119:89. Ec 7:12. Is *43:25. 44:6. Ezk 34:17. Lk 2:14. 22:21. Jn *4:24. Ac 2:9. 1 C 6:13. *15:29, 48. 2 C 11:22. Ep 3:1. Ph 4:16. 2 T +*3:16. Phm 11. **river**. Ps *36:8. 46:4. Ezk 47:1. Jl 3:18. Zc *14:8. Jn *7:38. Re *22:1. **thence it was parted**. or, thence it will part, or gets parted, or parts itself. ♪96C9. Figure of speech Heterosis; or, Exchange of Accidence B523, where there is an exchange of one voice, mood, tense, person, number, degree, or gender, for another; here it is heterosis of the tenses, the future for the present, in which what was then future at the time of speaking, remained, or remains, as a present fact. The present in this case is often in the subjunctive or reflexive mood. For instances of this figure see Nu 18:7. Jb 3:20. Ps 1:2. 3:5. 22:2. 25:1. 36:5. Ho 1:2. Mt 12:31. Lk 6:7. *23:46. Ro 3:30.

11. **Pison**. i.e. *overflowing*, ✳S#6376h, only here. The Phasis, a river of Colchis, emptying itself into the Euxine sea, where there is a city called Chabala. **Havilah**. Ge 10:7, 29. *25:18. 1 S *15:7. 1 Ch 1:9, 23.

12. **bdellium**. Bdellium is a transparent aromatic gum. Nu 11:7. **onyx**. The onyx is a precious stone, so called from a Greek word signifying a man's nail, to the color of which it nearly approaches. Ex 25:7. 28:9, 20. 35:9, 27. 39:13. Jb 28:16. Ezk 28:13.

13. **Gihon**. i.e. *the great breaking forth*, ✳S#1521h. 1 K 1:33, 38, 45. 2 Ch 32:30. 33:14. The Araxes, which runs into the Caspian sea. (1) The name of one of the rivers of Eden. (2) The name of a place near Jerusalem where there was a pool or watercourse, 1 K 1:33; 2 Ch 32:30. **Ethiopia**. Heb. Cush. The country of the ancient Cussaei. ✳S#3568h. Ge 10:6, 7, 8. 2 K 19:9. 1 Ch 1:8, 9, 10. Est 1:1. 8:9. Jb 28:19. Ps 68:31. 87:4. Is 11:11. 18:1. 20:3, 4, 5. 37:9. 43:3. 45:14. Je 46:9. Ezk 29:10. 30:4, 5, 9. 38:5. Na 3:9. Zp 3:10. For ✳S#3569h, see Nu +12:1. Ac *8:27.

14. **Hiddekel**. i.e. *sharp voice or sound*, ✳S#2313h. Da *10:4. The Tigris. **toward the east of**. or, eastward to. Ge 4:16. **Assyria**. i.e. *a step*, S#804h. Ge 10:11, 22. 25:18h. 2 K 15:19. 1 Ch 5:6, 26. 2 Ch 28:16, 20, 21. Ezr 6:22. Ne 9:32. Is 7:17, 18, 20. 8:4, 7. 10:12. 11:11, 16. 19:23, 24, 25. 20:1, 4, 6. 27:13. 36:1, 2, 4, 8, 13, 15, 16, 18. 37:4, 6, 8, 10, 11, 18, 21, 33, 37. 38:6. Je 2:18, 36. 50:17, 18. Ezk 23:7. Ho 7:11. 8:9. 9:3. 10:6. 11:11. Mi 5:6. 7:12. Na 3:18. Zp 2:13. Zc 10:10, 11. **Euphrates**. i.e. *fruitfulness*, ✳S#6578h. Ge 15:18. Dt 1:7. 11:24. Jsh 1:4. 2 S 8:3. 2 K 23:29. 24:7. 1 Ch 5:9. 18:3. 2 Ch 35:20. Je 13:4, 5, 6, 7. 46:2, 6, 10. 51:68. Re 9:14.

15. **the man**. or, Adam. Ge 5:2. Jb 31:33. **put**. ver. 8. Ps *128:2. Ep 4:28. 2 Th 3:10. 1 T 5:8. **dress**. Dt 28:39. **keep**. Heb. keep diligently, watch, guard, keep

safe, protect, preserve. Same Heb. word (S#8104h) used at Ge *3:24. Ex 16:28. 22:7, 10. 23:20. Nu 8:26. Dt 4:2. 5:12, 29. 6:2, 17. 7:8. Jsh *10:18. 22:5. 23:6. 1 S *7:1. 2 S 15:16. 16:21. 20:3. 1 K 2:3. 3:14. 8:58, 61. 11:38. 2 K 23:3. 1 Ch 22:12. 29:19. 2 Ch 34:31. Ps 19:11. *91:11. 119:*4, 5, 57, 60, 106. Pr 6:24. 7:5. Ec 3:6. Ezk 17:14. See also Ge 6:19, 20. 7:3. 17:9, 10. 18:19. 28:15, 20. Ps 17:8.

16. **God**. 1 S 15:22. **saying**. ♪22C10. Figure of speech Anthropopatheia or Anthropomorphism B888. Human actions are attributed to God: *speaking*, by way of discourse or command. For other instances of this figure see Ge 1:3. 3:9. 6:13. 12:1. 13:14. 15:18. Ex 3:4, 5. **thou mayest freely eat**. Heb. eating thou shalt eat. ver. 9. Ge 3:1, 2. 1 T *4:4. *6:17. ♪147B. Figure of speech Polyptoton B272: verb with infinitive or participle, involving the repetition of the same part of speech in different inflections for emphasis. May be used in strong and emphatic affirmation, or in strong negation. Here it is used in strong affirmation or exhortation. The conjugated verb is strengthened and emphasized by the infinitive preceding it. This infinitive Eve omitted in Ge 3:2, and thus "diminished" from the word of God. For other instances of this figure see Ge *2:17. 3:16. 28:22. 37:33. Ex 3:16. 19:12, 13. Jsh 24:10. 2 K 3:23. Ps 118:18. Is *6:9. Je 22:10. 23:17. 51:58. Da 11:13. Zc 8:21. Mt 13:13, 14. Mk 4:12. Lk 8:10. Jn 12:40. Ac 7:34. 28:26, 27. Ro 11:8. 12:15. He 6:14.

17. **of the tree**. ver. 9. Ge 3:1-3, 11, 17, 19. Ac 5:30. 10:39. 1 P 2:24. Re 2:7. 22:2. **good and evil**. Dt 6:4. Ro 3:20. **in the day**. Ezk *33:12. ♪171T2. Figure of speech Synecdoche; or, Transfer B652: the exchange of one idea for another associated idea. Here, Of the Part, when a part is put for the whole: "in the day" is put for an indefinite time. A noun with the preposition followed by the verb in the infinitive, as here, becomes an adverb of time, and means simply "when," or "after then," or "after that." For other instances of this figure see Ge 2:4. Le 13:14. 14:57. Dt 21:16. 2 S 21:12. 1 K *2:37. 2 K 20:1. Ps 18:18. Is 11:16. Je 11:3, 4. 31:32. 34:13. Ezk 20:5, 6. 36:33. 38:18. ♪12I12. Figure of speech Metonymy of the Subject B570, when the subject (the thing or action) is put for that which is connected with it. Here, of verb, where the action is put for the declaration concerning it. The meaning is not that he would die that very day, but that he would be sentenced to die "in that day." For other instances of this figure see Ge 27:37. 30:13. 34:12. 35:12. 41:13. Ex 13:2. 20:7. Le 13:3. Dt 9:1. 2 S 7:22. Is 6:10. 8:13. Je 1:5, 10. 4:10. 38:23. Ezk 13:19, 22. 20:25, 26. Ho 6:5. Mt 6:13. 13:14. 16:19. Mk 4:12. Lk 7:29, 35. 8:10. 10:29. 16:15. Jn 12:40. *20:23. Ac 10:15. 28:26, 27. Ro 7:9. 11:8. 2 C 3:6. Ga 3:23. Ja 2:21, 22, 24, 25. **thou shalt surely die**. Heb. dying thou shalt die. ♪147B. Figure of speech Polyptoton, Ge +2:16. Here again Eve in Ge 3:3 alters the Word of God by saying "Lest ye die"! Thus she changes a certainty into a contingency. Not only does she thus diminish from and alter the Word of God but she adds to it the words "neither shall ye touch it," which the Lord God had not spoken! **surely**. Ge 3:3, 4, 19. ●*5:5. 20:7. Nu 26:65. Dt 27:26. 30:15, 19, 20. Le 22:9. 1 S 14:39, 44. 20:31. 22:16. 1 K 2:37, 42. Je 15:1, 2. 26:8. Ezk *3:18-20. 18:*4, 13, 32. 33:8, 14. Ro 1:32. *3:23. 5:12-21. 6:16, *23. 7:10-13. 8:2. 13:4. 1 C *15:22, 56.

Ga 3:10. Ep 2:1-6. *4:18. 5:14. Col 2:13. 1 T 5:6. He +*9:27. Ja *1:15. 1 J +*5:16. Re 2:11. 20:6, 14. *21:8.

18. **It**. ⌐96G2,. Figure of speech Heterosis of Gender B533; here, the masculine for the neuter, as the Hebrew has no neuter gender. Heb. lit., "He is not good." For other instances of this figure, see Jn √16:13, 14. Ep 1:14. **good**. Ge 1:31. 3:12. 24:4. Ru 3:1. Pr *18:22. Ec 4:9-12. Mt 19:5. 1 C 7:◑1, 2, 36. 1 T *4:1, 3. He *13:4. **I will**. Ge 3:12. 1 C 11:7-12. 1 T +*2:11-13. 1 P 3:7. **meet for him**. Heb. as before him.

19. vv19-22. Ge ◑1:11-27. **And out**. Ge 1:20-25. **brought**. ver. 22, 23. Ge 1:26, 28. 6:20. *9:2. Ps *8:4-8. **Adam**. *or*, the man. ver. 15mg. i.e. *red earth*, S#120h. Ge 2:19, 19, 20, 20, 23. 3:8, 9, 20, 21. 4:1, 25. 5:1, 2. Dt 32:8. See S#121h: Ge 2:21. 3:17. 5:3, 4, 5. 1 Ch 1:1. Jb 31:33. Compare Jsh 3:16, the name of a town. **to see**. ⌐22C2. ⌐22C13. Figure of speech Anthropopatheia; or, Condescension (perhaps more commonly called anthropomorphism): the ascription of human passions, actions, or attributes to God. For instances of this figure in connection with "seeing" and "knowing," as if to acquire knowledge as though before ignorant, see Ge 1:4, 10, 12, 18, 21, 25. ◑+3:9. 6:5, 6. 7:1. 11:5. 16:13. +18:21. 22:12. 29:31. Ex 2:25. 3:4, 7, 9, 16. 32:9. Dt 8:2. 32:19. √1 S 16:7. 2 K 14:26. 2 Ch 12:7. Ps *1;6. 14:2. 31:7. 53:2. Is 59:15, 16. Jon 3:10. 2 T *2:19. **creature**. Mt +*2:20. ✚S#5315h. Heb. *nephesh*, soul, used of lower creatures in Ge 1:20, 21, 24, 30. 9:4, 10, 12, 15, 16. Le 11:10, 46. 17:11, 14. 24:18. Nu 31:28. Dt 12:23. Jb 12:10. 41:21. Pr 12:10. Is 19:10. Je 2:24. Ezk 47:9. For the other uses of *nephesh*, see ver. +√7n.

20. **gave names to**. Heb. called. **but**. ver. 18. 1 C 11:9.

21. **deep**. Ge 15:12. 1 S 26:12. Jb 4:13. 33:15. Pr 19:15. Da 8:18. Jn 12:24. 19:30. Ro 5:14.

22. **rib**. 1 C 11:8, 9. **made**. Heb. builded. 1 K 18:32. Ps 127:1. 1 T 2:13. ⌐22C28. Figure of speech Anthropopatheia or Anthropomorphism B889. Human actions are attributed to God: building. For other instances of this figure in connection with "building" see 2 S 7:27. Ps 28:5. Je 42:10. **brought**. ver. 19. Pr *18:22. *19:14. He +*13:4.

23. **bone**. Ge 29:14. Jg 9:2. 2 S 5:1. 19:13. Ep 5:28, 29, +*30. He 2:14. ⌐11. Figure of speech Ampliatio; or, Adjournment B689: an old name for a new thing, a retaining of an old name after the reason for it is passed away. Here, though the bone and flesh of Adam were changed and made into Eve, yet the name of the original source, "bone," is retained. For other instances of this figure, see Ex 7:12. 1 S 30:5. 2 S 3:3. Is 11:6. Am 6:8. Mt *10:3. 11:5. *26:6. Lk 2:11. Jn *9:17. 10:16. Ro 4:5. 1 C *15:5. 2 C 4:3. He 11:31. Ja 2:25. **flesh,** ver. 24. Mt *19:5, 6. **Woman**. Heb. Isha. 1 C 11:8, 9. **taken**. Pr 19:14. 1 C √11:8. **Man**. Heb. Ish.

24. **Therefore**. Ge 10:9. 26:33. 32:32. Mt ❭19:5. Mk ❭10:7. 1 C ❭6:16. Ep ❭5:31. **leave**. Ge 24:58, 59. 31:14, 15. Ps 45:10. **cleave**. Le 22:12, 13. Dt 4:4. 10:20. Jsh 23:8. Ps 45:10. Pr *12:4. 31:10. Ac *11:23. The word "leave" translates the Hebrew homonym "azav," which may mean "to leave or forsake," as here and at Ge 39:6. Ne 5:10. Ps 49:10. Ml 4:1, or it may mean "to restore, repair, or fortify," as at Ex 23:5. Dt 32:36. 1 K 14:10. 21:21. 2 K 9:8. 14:26. Ne 3:8. Je 49:25. ⌐102. Figure of speech Hyperbole; or, Exaggeration B423:

when more is said than is literally meant. This does not mean that he is to forsake and no longer to love or care for his parents. For other instances of this figure, see Ge +*7:19n. 41:47, 49. 42:28. Ex 8:17. Dt 1:28. 9:1. Jg 5:4, 5. √20:16. 1 S 5:12. 7:6. *25:37. 2 S 17:13. 1 K 1:40. 10:5. 2 K 19:24. 2 Ch 28:9. Ezr 9:6. Ne 8:4. Jb 20:17. 29:6. 39:19. 40:18. Ps 107:26. Pr 23:8. Is 5:25. 14:13, 14. 34:3, 4, 5, 7. 42:15. 57:9. Je 1:19. 4:29. 15:20. 51:9, 53. La 2:1, 11. Ezk 26:4. 27:28. 32:5, 6, 7, 8. Da 9:21. Am 9:13. Mi 6:7. Na 2:3. Mt 11:23. 19:5. 21:13. Lk √14:26. 18:5. Jn 3:26. *12:19. Ga 4:15. Ja 3:6. 4:1. **and they**. The LXX, Vulgate, Syriac, Arabic, and Samaritan read "they TWO;" as is also read in several of the Parallel Passages. Ml √2:14-16. Mt *19:3-9. Mk 10:6-12. Ro *7:2. 1 C 6:16, 17. 7:2-4, 10, 11. Ep *5:28-31. 1 T 5:14. 1 P *3:1-7. **one**. Ge 1:26, 27. Dt +*6:4n.

25. **naked**. Ge 3:7, 10, 11. ◑9:22. Ex ◑32:25n. Is +20:2. 2 C 5:3. He *4:13. Re 3:18. ◑7:9-14. **ashamed**. Ex 32:25. Ps 25:3. 31:17. Is 44:9. *47:3. 54:4. Je 6:15. *17:13. Ezk 16:61. Jl 2:26. Mk 8:38. Lk 9:26. Ro 9:33. 10:11. Ep 5:27. Col 1:22, 28. 2 P 3:11, 14. 1 J 2:28. Ju 24.

GENESIS 3

The woman, tempted by the serpent, eats the forbidden fruit, and induces Adam to do the same, 1-6. They are alarmed and ashamed, in vain attempt concealment, and are convicted by God, 7-13. Sentence is denounced against them, containing the gracious promise of a Redeemer, 14-19. They are clothed, but expelled from Eden, 20-24.

1. **Now**. ver. 13-15. Is 27:1. Mt 10:16. 2 C *11:3, 14. Re *12:9. 20:2. **serpent**. The Samaritan Copy, instead of nachash, 'a serpent,' reads cachash, 'a liar, or deceiver,' read Jn 8:44. Ezk 28:13, 14, 16, 17. 2 C 2:11. 11:3, 14. **subtil**. This word means wise, sometimes in a good sense, as in Ezk 28:12; rendered "prudent" in Pr 1:4. 8:12. 12:16, 23. 13:16. 14:8, 15, 18. 22:3. 27:12. For the evil sense see Ezk 28:17. Jb 5:12. 15:5. 1 S 23:22. Ps 83:3. **beast**. or, living being or creature. Re 4:6-9. 5:6, 8, 14. **And**. ⌐148. Figure of speech Polysyndeton or Many Ands B208: the repetition of the word "and" at the beginning of successive clauses, each independent, important, and emphatic, with no climax at the end. For other instances of this figure see Ge 1:2. +8:22. 22:9, 11. Jsh 7:24. Lk 14:21. **he said**. Nu 22:28, 29. Ec 4:10. 1 P 3:7. **Yea, hath**. Heb. Yea, because. ⌐85B, Ge ✚13:9. Figure of speech Erotesis or Interrogating: the asking of questions, not for information, or for an answer. Ps 35:10. **hath**. Jb 1:7, 9-11. 2:2, 4, 5. Mt 4:3, 6, 9.

2. **serpent**. Ps 58:4. **may eat**. Misquoted from Ge 2:16 by not repeating the emphatic figure of speech Polyptoton, and thus omitting the emphatic "freely." **fruit**. Ge 2:16, 17.

3. **But**. Ge 2:16, 17. Ja *2:19. **neither**. Pr 30:6. Lk 19:21. **touch**. Ge 20:6. Ex 19:12, 13. 1 Ch 16:22. Jb 1:11. 2:5. 19:21. 1 C 7:1. 2 C 6:17. Col 2:21. **lest**. Misquoted from 2:16, 17, by not repeating the emphatic figure of speech Polyptoton, thus changing the emphasis preserved in the word "surely." Thus Eve changed a certainty into a contingency.

4. **serpent**. Jn *8:44. **Ye**. ver. 13. Dt 29:19. 2 K 1:4, 6, 16. 8:10. Ps 10:11. Ezk +*13:22. 2 C 2:11.

11:3. 1 T *2:14. **not**. Ge ◐2:17. ✸60E. Figure of speech Deceptive Irony B815, where words are clearly false as well as hypocritical: false, for Satan knew the opposite, and Eve ought to have known the same, as they flatly contradicted the words of the Lord God. For another instance of this figure see Mt 2:8. **surely**. Ge 2:16. ✸147C. Figure of speech Polyptoton of verbs with their infinitives or participles B274, here used in strong negation. For other instances see Ex 5:23. 34:7. Ps 49:7.

5. **God**. Ex 20:7. 1 K 22:6. Je 14:13. 14. 28:2, 3. Ezk 13:2-6, 22. 2 C *11:3, 13-15. **your**. ver. 7, 10. Mt 6:23. Ac 26:18. 1 C ◐2:9. Ep ◐1:18. **ye**. Is 14:14. Ezk 28:2, 12-17. Pr ◐2:6. Ph ◐2:6. **as gods**. Ex 5:2. 2 Ch 32:15. Ps *12:4. 82:6n. Ezk 28:2, 9. 29:3. Da 4:30. 6:7. Ac 12:22, 23. 2 C 4:4. 2 Th 2:4. Re 13:4, 14. **knowing**. ver. 22. Ge 2:17.

6. **saw**. Jsh *7:21. Jg 16:1, 2. Ja *1:14, 15. **was**. ✸63B, Ge +2:10. **good**. Mt 4:3. 1 J *2:16. **pleasant**. Heb. a desire. Ezk 24:16, 21, 25. **to the eyes**. Ge 6:2. 39:7. Jsh 7:21. 2 S *11:2. Jb *31:1. Ps +*101:3. Mt 4:5. 5:28. 1 J *2:16. **make**. Mt 4:8. 1 J 2:16. **wise**. Ne 8:13mg. 9:20. Pr 21:11. Da 9:22mg. **and did**. 1 T *2:14. **and he did eat**. ver. 12, 17. Ho 6:7mg. Ro *5:12-19.

7. **And the**. ver. 5. Dt 28:34. 2 K 6:20. Lk 16:23. **opened**. Ge *21:19. Nu 22:31. 2 K 6:17-20. 1 Ch 21:16. Ps *119:18. Lk 4:18. *24:◐+16, +31, 45. Jn 9:39. 20:16. 21:7. Ac 9:17, 18. 26:18. 2 C 4:4, 6. Ep *1:18. **knew**. ver. 10, 11. Ge 2:25. +4:1. ✸121I1. Figure of speech Metonymy (of Subject) B567. They knew before, but their knowledge now received a new meaning. Adam becomes "naked" by losing something of Elohim's glorious likeness. Ro 8:3 may refer to this. Metonymy of the Subject occurs when the subject is put for the adjunct: for some circumstance pertaining to (or joined to) the subject: as when the place, or thing containing it, is put for that which is contained: the possessor for the thing possessed, etc. In this instance, the subject (the thing or action) for that which is connected with it (the adjunct). For other instances of this figure see 1 S 1:15. 1 Ch 12:38. Ps 7:9. 16:7. 26:2. 38:8. 62:8, 10. Pr 2:10. 6:32. 7:7. 8:5. 9:4, 16. 10:13, 21. 11:29. 15:14, 32. 16:21, 23. 22:17. 26:7. 28:26. Is 5:21. 29:13. 49:16. Je 11:20. 12:2. 17:10. 20:12. La 2:19. Ho 4:11. 7:11. Mt 6:21. 16:19. 18:18. 24:45. Jn 20:23. Ac 1:11, 24. Ro 6:6. 15:24, 32. 16:3, 7. 2 C 5:17. Ga 4:15. Ep 4:22. Ph 1:21. Re 2:23. **naked**. Ge +2:25. Is 47:3. La 1:8. **and they**. Ge 3:21. Jb 9:29-31. Ps 32:1. Pr 28:13. Is 28:20. 59:6. **sewed**. Jb 16:15. Ec 3:7. Ezk 13:8. **fig**. Mt 21:19. Ph 3:9. **aprons**. or, things to gird about.

8. **And they**. ver. 10. Dt 4:33. *5:25, 26. **voice**. Dt 18:16. 2 S 22:14. Jb 37:4. 38:1. Ps 18:13. 29:3-9. 46:6. 68:33. 81:11. 95:7. 106:25. Je 25:30. Jl 2:11. Mt 3:17. 17:5. Mk 1:11. 9:7. Lk 3:22. 9:35. Jn 10:27. 12:28. 2 P 1:17, 18. ✸144A9. Figure of speech Pleonasm, or Redundancy B413, when more words are used than the grammar requires. The figure involves certain idiomatic words, here the word "voice." For other instances of this figure involving this term see Ps 98:5. 102:5. Is 24:18 (noise). Je *16:9. 51:54. Zp 1:10. **walking**. Ge 18:33. Le *26:12. Dt 23:14. **cool of the day**. Heb. wind. Jb 34:21, 22. 38:1. **hid**. 2 Ch 16:9. Jb 22:14. *31:33. *34:21, 22. Ps ◐32:7. *94:9. *139:1-12. Pr +*15:3. Je *23:24. Ho 10:8. Am *9:2, 3. Jon 1:3, 9,

10. Ro *2:15. He *4:13. Re 6:15-17. **trees**. ✸96F1. Figure of speech Heterosis; or, Exchange of Accidence B528: the exchange of one voice, mood, tense, person, number, degree, or gender, for another. Here, heterosis of number, the singular for the plural. For other instances of this figure see Ge 49:6. Ex 14:17. 15:1, 21. Ex 23:28. Le 11:2. Nu 21:7, 31. Dt 17:9. 20:19. 21:10. (Jsh 2:4). 11:21n. (2 S 19:41). 2 K 3:3. Ne 13:4. (Ps 35:8). Pr 1:21. 17:22. (Ho 5:6). Jon 2:3. Jn 8:44. 1 C 6:5. 2 C 11:26. Ep 6:16. Ph 3:20. Re 21:21.

9. **the Lord**. Ge 4:9. 11:5. 16:8. 18:20, 21. Jsh 7:17-19. Re 20:12, 13. **called**. Ge 1:5, 8, 10. 2:19. 3:20. 4:17, 25. Jn 10:3. **Where**. Ge 18:9. 1 K 19:13. Mt ◐2:2. ✸22C2. Figure of speech Anthropopatheia; or, Condescension (more commonly known as "anthropomorphism") B884: the ascribing of human attributes to God. Here, not knowing, the opposite of knowing, is attributed to God. For other instances of this figure see Ge 4:9. Nu 22:9. 1 K 19:9, 13. 2 K 20:14, 15. Ps 7:9. Is 39:3, 4. Je 11:20. Ezk 20:8. Ho 11:8, 9. Mt 7:23. 22:20, 45. 25:12. Mk ◐+*13:32. Lk 8:45. 13:25. 27. 1 C 2:10. Re 2:23. ✸85K. Figure of speech Erotesis; or, Interrogating: the asking of questions without waiting for the answer, in expostulation B953. For other instances of this figure see Ge 12:18, 19. 23:15. 26:9, 10. 31:26, 27. 44:4,15,16. Ex 3:11. Ps 11:1. 50:16. Is 5:4. 58:3. Ezk 12:22. 18:2. Da 3:14. Ml 3:2, 8. Mt 17:17.

10. **voice**. Lk ◐24:15, 32. **I was afraid**. Ge 2:25. Ex 3:6. Dt *5:25. Jb *23:15. Ps *119:120. Is 33:14. 57:11. 1 J *3:20. **because**. ver. 7. Ge 2:25. Ex 32:25. Is 47:3. Re *3:17, 18. 16:15.

11. **Hast thou**. Ge 2:16, 17. 4:10. Ps 50:21. *90:8. Ro 3:20. 5:12-21.

12. **The woman**. ✸120, 1 K +18:18. Ge 2:18, 20, 22. Ex 32:21-24. 1 S 15:15, 20-24. Jb 31:33. Pr 19:3. √28:13. Lk 10:29. Ro 10:3. Ja *1:13-15.

13. **What**. Ge 4:10-12. 20:9. 31:26. 44:15. 1 S 13:11. 2 S 3:24. 12:9-12. Jn 18:35. Ga *6:7. ✸6. Figure of speech Aganactesis; or, Indignation B934. The figure is used when an exclamation proceeds from the deep feeling of indignation. For other instances of this figure see Ge 4:10. 20:9. 31:26. Ac 13:10. **The serpent**. ✸120, 1 K +18:18. ver. 1, 2, 4-6. 2 C *11:3, 14. 1 T *2:14. ✸103. Figure of speech Hypocatastasis; or, Implication B745: a declaration that implies the resemblance or representation; or comparison by implication. For other instances of this figure see Ge *49:17. 1 S 1:19. Ps 22:16. Je 4:7. ◐33:18n. Jl 2:25. Am 1:3. Mt 3:10, 12. *5:29, 30. 7:3-5, 6. 15:13, *26. 16:6. Mk 1:17. 8:15n. Lk *13:32. Jn √2:19. Ac 20:29. 2 T 4:17. For additional instances of Hypocatastasis, in the form of Extended or Continued Hypocatastasis, a form of Allegory, see ✸7, Ga +4:24.

14. **thou art**. ver. 1. Ge 9:6. Ex 21:28-32. Le 20:25. Dt 28:15-20. **upon**. Ps 44:25. **dust**. Ps 72:9. Is 29:4. 65:25. Mi 7:17.

15. **enmity**. Nu 21:6, 7. 35:21, 22. Ezk 25:15. 35:5. Am *9:3. Mk 16:18. Lk *10:19. Ac 28:3-6. Ro 3:13. Ja +*4:4. **thee**. Ho +11:1. Mt +16:23. **woman**. Is ◐?54:5. Ga ◐?4:26. **thy seed**. Ge 12:7. ◐17:7. *21:12. Mt *3:7. 12:34. *13:38. *23:33. Jn *8:44. Ac *13:10. Ro 9:7. Ga *3:16. He 11:18. 1 J *3:8, 10. Re 12:7, 9. **her seed**. T#1874. Ge 9:24-27. 12:1-3. +√49:10. Nu 24:15-19. Dt *18:15-19. 2 S 7:16. Ps ch. 2. 16:9, +10 (T#44-1), 11. ch. 22, 45, 72, 110. +*132:11. Is √7:14.

8:8-10. √9:6. 11:1-2, 10. 35:3-5, 10. Je 31:22, *31-34. Ezk 17:22-24. 34:23, 24. 37:22-25. Da 9:24-27. Ho 1-3. Am 9:11-15. Mi *5:1-3. Hg 2:7. Zc 3:8. 6:12. 9:9-10. Ml 1:10-11. 3:1. 4:2. Mt √1:18, 23, 25. Lk 1:31-35, 76. Ro 16:20. Ga +*♣4:4. 1 T 2:15. 1 J *3:8. Re 12:5. **it shall.** Ro *16:20. Ep 4:8. Col *2:15. He *2:14, 15. 1 J *3:8. 5:5. Re *12:7, 8, 17. √20:1-3, 10. **bruise.** Jb 9:17. Ps 139:11 (cover). **thou.** Ge 49:17. Is √53:3, 4, 12. Da *9:26. Mt *4:1-10. Lk 10:17-20. *22:39-44, √53. Jn √12:31-33. 14:30, 31. *16:11. Ac *3:15. 1 C *15:55. 2 T *1:10. He 2:18. 5:7. Re 2:10. *12:9-13. 13:7. 15:1-6. 20:7, 8.

16. **greatly.** ſ147B, Ge +2:16. **and.** ſ93A, Ge +1:26. **conception.** Ps 51:5. **in sorrow.** Ge 5:29. 35:16-18. 1 S 4:19-21. Ps 48:6. Is 13:8. 21:3. 26:17, 18. 42:14. 53:11. Je 4:31. 6:24. 13:21. 22:23. 49:24. Mi 4:9, 10. Jn 16:21. 1 Th 5:3. 1 T *2:15. **thy desire.** Ge 4:7. SS *7:10. **to.** *or,* subject to. **rule.** Nu 30:7, 8, 13. Est 1:20. 1 C 7:4. √11:3n. *14:34n. Ep √5:22-24. Col 3:18. 1 T √2:11, 12. T 2:5. 1 P 3:1-6.

17. **Adam.** Ho 6:7mg. **Because.** Ge *16:2. 1 S *15:23, 24. Mt 22:12. 25:26, 27, 45. Lk 19:22. Ro 3:19. **and hast.** ver. 6, 11. Ge 2:16, 17. Je 7:23, 24. **cursed.** Ge 5:29. Ps 127:2. Ec 1:2, 3, 13, 14. 2:11, 17. Is 24:5, 6. Ro *8:20-22. **in sorrow.** Jb *5:6, 7. *14:1. 21:17. Ps 90:7-9. 127:2. Ec *2:22, 23. 5:17. Jn *16:33.

18. **Thorns.** Nu 33:55. Jsh 23:13. Jg 8:7. Jb 5:5. Pr 22:5. 24:31. Is 5:6. 7:23, 24. 32:13. 34:13. 55:13. Je 4:3. 12:13. Ho 2:6. 9:6. Mt 13:7, 22. Jn 19:2. Ro 8:22. 2 C 12:7. He 6:8. **thistles.** Jb 31:40. 2 K 14:9. 2 Ch 25:18. Ho 10:8. Mt 7:16. **bring forth.** Heb. cause to bud. **herb.** Jb 1:21. Ps 90:3. 104:2, 14, 15. Ro 14:2.

19. **In.** Ec 1:3, 13. Lk 22:44. Ep *4:28. 1 Th 2:9. 2 Th *3:10. **face.** ſ171Q14. Figure of speech Synecdoche (of the part) B646, where a part is put for the whole, where one part or member is put for, and includes, every part or member. Here, "face" is put for the whole man, especially marking and emphasizing his presence. For other instances of this figure see Ge 19:21. 32:20. 2 S 17:11. 1 K 2:16, 17, 20. 10:24. Jb 11:19. Ps 42:5, 11. 43:5. 45:12. Pr 19:6. 28:21. Ec 8:1. Is 3:15. 36:9. La 5:12. Ac 20:25, 38. **bread.** ſ171I8. Figure of speech Synecdoche (of the species) B627. Synecdoche is the exchange of one idea for another associated idea. The difference between metonymy and synecdoche lies in this: that in metonymy, the exchange is between two related nouns, while in synecdoche, the exchange is made between two associated ideas. Synecdoche of the species occurs when the species (or subclass) is put for the genus (class), or particulars are put for universals. Here, bread is put for all kinds of food. For other instances of this figure see Ge 18:5. 39:6. 43:25, 31. 49:20. Le 3:11 (food). 21:6, 8, 17, 21, 22. Nu 28:2. Dt *8:3. Jg 13:16. 19:19. 1 S 14:24 (food). 20:24, 27 (meat). 28:20. Ne 5:15. Jb 6:7 (meat). 20:14 (meat). Ps 41:9. 102:4. 104:14. +107:18 (meat). 136:25. 146:7. Ec 9:11. 10:19 (feast). Is 3:1. 33:16. 58:7. Je 52:33. Da 5:1 (feast). Ho 9:4. Ml 1:7. Mt *4:4. √6:11. 15:2, 26. Lk 14:1. Jn 13:18. Ac 2:42, 46. **till.** Jb 1:21. Ps 90:3. 104:29. Ec 5:15. **return.** He 9:27. ſ132G. Parallelism (introverted) B356. Complex introversion occurs when the parallel lines are so placed that the first line corresponds in subject with the last, the second line corresponds in subject with the next to the last, and so on. If letters are assigned to the corresponding words, propositions, or subjects, they

would form the pattern ABCCBA, where the mention of subjects in the first half is reversed in order in the second half of the passage. This is done for emphasis, attention being called thereby particularly to the two central members of the series. In this passage the introversion is seen thus: A. End. "Till thou return unto the ground." B. Origin. "For out of it wast thou taken." B. Origin. "For dust thou art." A. End. "And unto dust shalt thou return." For other instances of this figure see Ex 9:31. Nu 15:35, 36. Dt 32:16. 1 S 1:2. 2 S 3:1. 1 K 16:22. 2 Ch 32:7, 8. Ps 76:1. 115:4-8. 135:15-18. Pr 1:26, 27. 3:16. Is 5:7. *6:10. 11:4. 50:1. *55:8, 9. 60:1-3. Da 5:19. Mt *6:24. 7:6. Ro 11:21-23. 1 C 1:24, 25. 2 C 1:3. 2 C 8:14. Ga 2:7-8. **thou taken.** Ge +*2:7. *18:27. **for dust.** Ge 2:7. 18:27. ſ121D10. Figure of speech Metonymy (of the cause) B560. Metonymy is the change of one noun for another related noun. Metonymy of the cause occurs when the cause is put for the effect, as here, the material is put for the thing made from or of it: dust is put for man who is made of dust. For other instances of this figure see Ge 18:27. Ps 103:14. Ec 12:7. **unto dust.** Ge 23:4. Jb 17:13-16. 19:26. *21:26. *34:15. Ps 22:15, 29. +*103:14. *104:29. Pr 21:16. Ec *3:20. +*12:7. Da *12:2. Ro *5:12-21. 1 C 15:21, 22. He +*9:27.

20. **Adam.** Ge 2:20, 23. 5:29. 16:11. 29:32-35. 35:18. Ex 2:10. 1 S 1:20. Mt 1:21, 23. **Eve.** Heb. Chavah; that is, living. i.e. *life giver,* *S#2332h. Ge 4:1. 2 C 11:3. 1 T 2:13. **of.** Ac 17:26. 1 C 15:21. **living.** Ro 4:17. ſ171E11. Figure of speech Synecdoche of the Genus B622: words of a wider meaning are used in a narrower sense; the universal for the particular, but of the same kind. Here, the living are put for men. For another instance of this figure see Ps 143:2.

21. **make.** ver. 7. Ps *32:1. Pr 28:13. Ro 3:22. 2 C 5:2, 3, 21. **coats.** Is *61:10. ◐64:6. Mt 22:11. Lk 15:22. Ro 10:3. 13:14. 1 C 1:30. Ph 3:9. **skins.** Ge 27:16. Jb 41:7.

22. **Behold.** ſ40. Figure of speech Asterismos; or, Indicating B926: employing some word which directs special attention to some particular point or subject. Ge 15:3, 12, 17. Ps *133:1. **as one.** ver. 5. Ge +1:26. 11:6, 7. Is 19:12, 13. 47:12, 13. Je 22:23. **become.** ſ27. Figure of speech Antiphrasis; or, Permutation: a new name for the old thing B691. A new and opposite name for a thing after the original meaning has ceased. Antiphrasis is a species of irony, with the difference that antiphrasis is used only of single words or phrases, while irony is used of connected sentences. Antiphrasis affects the meaning of words; irony affects the application of words. Antiphrasis is the use of a word or phrase in a sense opposite to its original signification. Here, Adam had become, not necessarily or really "a God," but what the tempter promised him; and now he will get the Tempter's doom and be cast out from God's presence. For other instances of this figure see Ps 60:9 (strong). Is 44:25. 57:12. Je 11:15. Zc *11:13 (goodly). Lk 11:13 (clean). **us.** Ge +√1:26. ſ60A. Figure of speech Eironeia; or, Irony B808: the expression of thought in a form that naturally conveys its opposite. Here, divine irony, for the speaker is divine. Man had not become "as one of us." He had become a wreck and a ruin, even as man. These words call our attention to verse 5, and show how false was the Serpent's promise. For other instances of this figure see Dt 32:37. Jg 10:14. Jb 38:4, 5. Ps 60:8, 9. Ec 11:9. Is

2:10. 8:9, 10. 17:3. 21:5. 29:1. 50:11. 57:12, 13. Je 7:21. 9:15. 22:20. 46:9, 11. 51:8. La 4:21. Ezk 3:24. *20:39. 28:3. Am 4:4, 5. Na 3:14. Zc 11:13. Ml 1:9. Mk 7:9. Lk 11:41. 13:33. Jn 3:10. 7:28. 1 C *6:4. 2 C 5:3. *13:5. **good.** Heb. *tov,* meaning general good. Ge 1:4, 10, 12, 18, 21, 25. 6:2. Dt 1:25. 3:25. Jg 8:2. Est 1:11. Pr 8:11. Ec 7:14. 11:7. **tree.** Ge 2:9. Pr 3:18. Re *2:7. 22:2. **eat.** Ps 22:26. Jn *6:48-58. **for ever.** Heb. *olam,* Ex +12:24. ✓37B. Figure of speech Aposiopesis; or, Sudden Silence B152. It is the sudden breaking off of what is being said (or written), so that the mind may be the more impressed by what is too wonderful, or solemn, or awful for words. Here, the figure is associated with anger and threatening, as it is also at Ge 20:3. Ja 3:1.

23. **sent.** Ge 21:14. 25:6. 28:5. 45:7. **to till.** ver. 19. Ge 2:5. *4:2, 12. *9:20. 2 S 9:10. Ec 5:9. Je 27:11.

24. **drove.** Ezk 31:11. **placed.** Ge 4:3, 7, 14, 16. 9:26, 27. **east.** Ge 2:8. **Cherubims.** Ex 25:2, 18, 20, 22. Nu 7:89. 1 S 4:4. 2 S 20:11. 1 K 6:25-35. 1 Ch 28:18. 2 Ch 3:7. Ps 18:10. 80:1. 99:1. 104:4. Ezk 9:3. 10:1, 2. 11:22. 28:14, 16. He 1:7. **a flaming.** Nu 22:23. Jsh 5:13. 1 Ch 21:16, 17. He 1:7. **turned.** Jb 37:12. 38:14. **keep.** Ge +2:15. **way.** Jn ✓14:6. He *10:18-22. **tree.** Ge 2:9. **of.** ✓181E. Genitive of relation and object B995. Here, "the way of the tree" signifies "the way pertaining (or leading) to the tree of life." For other instances of this use of the genitive see Ge 50:4. Jg 13:12. 2 S 7:19. Ps 4:1. 44:22. 102:20. 149:6. Pr 1:7. 30:24. Is 3:14. 34:5. 55:3. Je 50:28. Ezk 20:7. Jl 3:19. Zc 9:1. Mt 3:8. *4:23. 6:26, 28. 10:1. 14:1. *24:14. Mk 1:4. 6:7. 11:22. Lk 21:4. Jn 2:17. 5:29. 7:35. 17:2. Ac 4:9. 13:30, 34. *23:6. 24:15, 21. Ro 1:4. 3:22. 8:17, 36. 9:9. 10:2. 13:3. 16:2. 1 C 9:12. 15:13. 2 C *5:14. 10:5. Ep 4:16. Col 1:24. 2:18. T 2:14. He 3:12. 5:13. 9:21. 11:26. Ja 1:13. 1 P 2:19. 1 J 2:5. Re *3:10. 19:10.

GENESIS 4

Cain and Abel are born, 1,2. Abel's offering is accepted, and Cain's rejected, 3-7. Cain murders Abel; is convicted, condemned, and banished: his subsequent behavior, 8-17. His descendants to Lamech, the fifth in descent from him; with some particulars of Lamech and his children, 18-24. Seth is born, 25, 26.

1. **knew.** ✓88, Ge +15:15. ✓121C2A4, Ge +19:5. Ge 3:7. 4:+17, 25. 19:5. 38:26. Nu 31:17. Jg 11:39. 19:25. 1 S 1:19. 1 K 1:4. Mt *1:25. **Cain.** That is, gotten or acquired. i.e. *possession, acquisition,* ✻S#7014h. Ge 4:1, 2, 3, 5, 6, 8, 8, 9, 13, 15, 15, 16, 17, 24, 25. **I have.** ver. 25. Ge 3:15. 5:29. 1 J 3:12. **gotten.** ✓96C1. Figure of speech Heterosis of the Tenses B517: the past tense used for the present tense. Here, "have gotten"="have got" or "possess." For other instances of this figure see Ge 4:9. 23:11, 13. 32:10. 2 S 1:5. 2 K 3:11. Ps *1:1. 14:1. 25:2. 31:5. Is 9:2. Jn *1:4, 15. 3:16. 9:36. *20:17. Ac 12:14. Ro 5:2. 2 C 1:10. He 10:11. Ja 1:24. 1 J 3:6. **from the Lord.** Ge 33:5. Ps +*127:3.

2. **Abel.** Heb. Hebel. i.e. *vanity, transitory* ✻S#1893h. Ge 4:2, 2, 4, 4, 8, 8, 9, 25. **And Abel.** Ge 30:29-31. 37:13. Ex 3:1. Ps 78:70-72. Am 7:15. Lk 11:50, 51. **a keeper.** Heb. a feeder. ver. 25, 29. 46:32, 34. 47:3. Ps 127:3. **Cain.** Jn 8:44. 1 J 3:10, 12, 15. **tiller.** Ge 3:23. 9:20.

3. A.M. 129. B.C. 3875. **in the process of time.**

Heb. at the end of days. Either at the end of the year, or of the week, i.e. on the Sabbath. Daniel Wilson notes "as only one division of days had been mentioned, that of the days of the week, the Sabbath being the last or seventh of them—we may reasonably suppose that holy season to be termed 'the end of the days,' Ge 2:2 (*The Lord's Day,* p. 18). See related notes (Ge 2:3n. 29:27n. Ex 16:26n. Is 58:13n). Ge +*24:55mg. Le 25:29. Jg 11:40mg. 1 K 17:7mg, 15mg. Ne +13:6mg. **the fruit.** Ge *3:17. Le 2:1-11. Nu 18:12. Dt ❍26:2. Ro 3:28.

4. **the firstlings.** Ex 13:2, 12. 34:19. Le 27:26. Nu 18:12, 17. Dt 12:6. 14:23. Pr *3:9. He 9:22. 1 P 1:19, 20. Re 13:8. **flock.** Heb. sheep, or, goats. **and.** ✓93A. Figure of speech Hendiadys, Ge +1:26. By Hendiadys, "fattest firstlings," with the emphasis upon "fattest." Two words used, but one thing meant. **fat.** Ex 29:13. Le *3:4, 16, 17. **had.** Ge 15:17. Le *9:24. Nu 16:35. Jg 6:21. 1 S *15:22. 1 K *18:24, 38. 1 Ch 21:26. 2 Ch 7:1. Ps 20:3mg. He *11:4. 1 P *1:18, 19. Re *13:8. **respect.** ✓25. Figure of speech Antimetabole; or, Counterchange B301: a word or words repeated in reverse order, with the object of opposing them to one another, the form being that of introverted parallelism of lines. Here, note the words respect/his offering/his offering/had not respect. For other instances of this figure see 2 Ch *32:7, 8. Is *5:20. *55:8. Mk *2:27. Jn 8:47. 14:17. 15:16. 1 C *11:8, 9. Ga 5:17. 1 J 2:18. 2 J 6. 3 J 11.

5. **But.** Nu 16:15. 1 S *16:7. Pr *21:27. Ec 8:13. Ac *10:34. He 11:4. Ja 1:15. **wroth.** Ge 31:2, 5. Jb 5:2. Ps 20:3. Is 3:9-11. Mt *20:15. Lk 15:28-30. Ac 13:45. 1 J 3:12. Ju 11. **countenance.** Ge 31:2. Jb 29:24. Ps 4:6.

6. **Why.** ✓85K, Ge +3:9. 1 Ch 13:11-13. Jb 5:2. Is *1:18. Je 2:5, 31. Jon 4:1-4, 8-11. Mi 6:3-5. Mt 20:15. Lk 15:31, 32. **and why.** ✓85K, Ge +3:9.

7. **If.** Ex 19:5, 6. Le 26:3, 14, 15, 18, 21, 23, 24, 27, 28, 40-42. Dt 4:26-29. 8:19, 20. 11:22, 26-28. 15:5. 19:9. 30:9, 10, 17, 18. Jsh 24:20. 1 S 7:3. 12:14, 15. 1 K 6:12. 8:31, 32, 46-50. 9:2-9. 1 Ch 28:6-9. 2 Ch +*7:14. 15:1, 2. 30:9. Ne 1:8, 9. Is 1:19, 20. Je +7:5. **thou doest well.** Ge 19:21. 2 S 24:23. 2 K 8:28. Jb 42:8. Pr 18:5. Ec 8:12, 13. Is *3:10, 11. Je 3:12. 6:20. Mi ✓7:18. Ml 1:8, 10, 13. Ac 10:35. Ro 2:7-11. 12:1. 14:18. 15:16. Ep 1:6. 1 T 5:4. 1 P 2:5. **be accepted.** *or,* have the excellency. Ge 49:3. Jb 29:4. Pr 21:27. He 11:4. **and if.** Nu *32:23. **sin.** ver. 8-13. Ro 7:8, 9. Ep 5:2. Ja 1:15. ✓121L5. Figure of speech Metonymy of the Subject B584: the object is put for that which pertains or relates to it; here, sin is put for the offering for sin. For other instances of this figure see Ex 29:14. 30:10. Le 4:3. 6:25. 7:7. Nu 8:8. Ho ✓4:8. 2 C ✓5:21. **lieth.** ✓155F. Figure of speech Prosopopoeia; or, Personification B868: things represented as persons; human actions attributed to things. For other instances of this figure see Ge 18:20. 30:33. 44:34. Ex 18:8. Nu 20:14. Dt 31:17, 21, 29. Jb 16:8. 31:29. Ps ✓85:10. 116:3. 119:143. Ec 2:2. Is 59:12, 14. Je 14:7. 1 C 13:4, 5, 6, 7. Ja 1:15. Re 18:5. **unto thee.** *or,* subject unto thee. Ge 3:16mg. **rule.** Jb 11:14, 15. Ro 6:12, 16.

8. **talked.** 2 S 3:27. 13:26-28. 20:9, 10. Ne 6:2. Ps 36:3. 55:21. Pr *26:24-26. Mi 7:6. Lk 22:48. **Cain rose.** 2 S 14:6. Jb 11:15. Ps 24:3-6. 139:19. Mt 23:35. Lk 11:51. Jn 18:23. T 3:3. Ja *1:15. 1 J *3:12-15. Ju 11. **slew.** He 12:24.

9. **Where is.** *22C2, Ge +3:9. Ge 3:9-11. Nu +*32:23. Ps 9:12. **I know.** *96C1, Ge +4:1. Ge 37:32. Jb 22:13, 14. Ps *10:13, 14. Pr +*28:13. Jn *8:44. Ac 5:4-9.

10. **What.** *6, Ge +3:13. Ge 3:13. 20:9. 31:26. Jsh 7:19. 1 S 13:11. Ps 50:21. Jn 18:35. **voice.** Ge 18:20, 21. 19:13. 37:32. Ex 3:7, 9. Nu 35:33. Dt 21:1-9. Is *26:21. Hab 2:11. Mt *27:25. Re *6:10. **blood.** Heb. bloods. 2 K +*9:26mg. *96F2. Heterosis of Number B529: the plural for the singular, to express great excellence or magnitude. For other instances of this figure see Ge 19:11. Le 19:24. 2 S 3:28. 16:7, 8. 1 Ch 28:3. Jb 21:32. 40:10, 15. Ps 22:3. 28:8. 42:5, 11. 43:5. 45:15. 47:6. 49:3. 51:17. 53:6mg. 89:1. 90:10. 139:14. 144:7. Pr 1:20mg. 9:1. Ec 5:7. Is 26:2. 33:15. 58:11. Je 22:21. La 1:9. 3:22. Ezk 22:2. 25:17. 28:10. Da 2:18. Mt √26:65. Jn 1:13. Ac 1:7. Ro 12:1. 1 C 15:29? 2 C 1:3. 1 Th 5:1. 1 T 6:15. T 1:3. He 9:8, 12, √23. 10:28. Ja 1:17. 1 P 5:3. 2 P 3:11. Re 5:10. **crieth.** Ge 18:20. +27:34h. Ex 3:7. 2 K 9:26. Jb 16:18. 24:12. 31:38, 39. Ps 9:12. *72:14. 116:15. Is 5:7. Ac 5:3, 9. He 11:4. *12:24. Ja +*5:4. Re *6:10. *155D. Prosopopoeia; or, Personification B864: things represented as persons; the attribution of intelligence, by words or actions, to inanimate things. For other instances of this figure see Ge 4:11. 42:9, 12. 47:19. Ex 19:18. Le 18:25, 28. Dt 32:42. Jsh 24:27. Jg 5:20. 2 K 3:19. Jb 3:9. 7:10. 8:18. 28:22. 31:38. 38:7. 41:18. Ps *19:1. 77:16. 96:11, 12. 98:7, 8. 103:16. 104:19. 148:3. SS 1:6. Is 3:26. 5:14. 14:8, 10? 24:4, 7, 23. 33:9. 34:5, 6. 45:9. √55:12. Je 4:28. 12:4. 31:15. 46:10. 51:48. La 1:4. 2:8. Ezk ?32:21. Ho 2:22. 4:3. Jl 1:10. Am 1:2. Ro 8:19. 9:20. 10:6. Re ?6:10.

11. **cursed.** ver. 14. Ge 3:14. Dt 27:16-26. *28:15-20. 29:19-21. Ga 3:10. **opened.** Jb 16:18. 31:38-40. Is 26:21. Re 12:16. **mouth.** *155D, Ge +4:10. **hand.** Dt 28:20.

12. **it.** Ge 3:17, 18. Le 26:20. Dt 28:15-24. Jb 31:40. Jl 1:10-20. Ro *8:20. **strength.** *121C. Figure of speech Metonymy of the Cause, here, strength is put for that which it effects or produces. For another instance of this figure see Pr 5:10. **a fugitive.** ver. 14. Le 26:17, 36. Dt 28:65, 66. Ps 109:10. Je 20:3, 4. Ho 9:17.

13. **My punishment is greater than I can bear.** or, Mine iniquity is greater than that it may be forgiven. Ge +2:17. 19:15. 1 S 28:10. Jb 15:22. 21:19. Is 5:18. ●55:7. Mt 12:31, 32. Mk 3:28, 29. Lk 12:10. Jn ●*6:37. Ja +*5:19, 20. 1 J +*5:16. Re 16:9, 11, 21. **is.** *63B, Ge +2:10.

14. **driven.** Ge 3:24. Jb *15:20-24. Pr +*14:32. *28:1. Is 8:22. Je 52:3. Ho 13:3. **from thy.** ver. 16. 2 K 13:23. 24:20. Jb 21:14, 15. Ps *51:11-14. 143:7. Je 52:3. Mt 25:41, 46. 2 Th 1:9. **face.** Ge +1:2. **fugitive.** See ver. 12. Dt 28:64-67. Ps 109:10. **that.** ver. 15. Ge 9:5, 6. Le 26:17, 36. Nu 17:12, 13. 35:19, 21, 27. 2 S 14:7. Jb 15:20-24. Pr. 28:1.

15. **And.** Ro 2:4. **Therefore.** 1 K 16:7. Ps 59:11. Ho 1:4. Mt 26:52. **slayeth.** Ge *9:6. Nu 35:21. **sevenfold.** ver. 24. Le 26:18, 21, 24, 28. Ps 79:12. Pr. 6:31. **set a mark**, etc. Or, rather, 'gave a sign or token to Cain, that those who found him should not kill him.' **mark** (token). Ge 9:12, 13, 17. 17:11. Ex 3:12. 4:8, 9, 17, 28, 30. *12:13. 13:16. Nu 17:10. Dt 13:2. 22:15-21. Jsh 2:12. 1 S 2:34. 10:9. Jb 21:29. Ps 65:8. 86:17. 135:9. Is 44:25. Ezk *9:4, 6. 20:12, 20. (The same Hebrew word is translated "sign" and "signs" at Ge

1:14. Ex 4:8, 9, 17, 28, 30. 7:3. 8:23. 10:1, 2. 13:9. 31:13). Re 14:9, 11.

16. **went.** ver. 14. Ge 3:8. Ex 20:18. 2 K 13:23. 24:20. Jb 1:12. 2:7. 20:17. Ps 51:11. 68:2. Je 23:39. 52:3. Jon 1:3, 10. Mt 18:20. 27:5. Lk 13:26, 27. Jn 13:30. 2 C 7:10. 1 Th 1:9. **Nod.** i.e. *wandering*, *S#5113h. So called from *nad*, a vagabond, which Cain is termed in ver. 12. Ge +2:8. Is 51:3.

17. **knew.** Ge +4:1. 19:8. 24:16. Ex +34:15. **Enoch.** Heb. Chanoch. Ge 5:18, 22. **and he.** Ge 11:4. Ps 127:1. Ec 2:4-11. Da 4:30. Lk 12:16-21. 17:28, 29. **city.** He ●11:9, 10. **the name.** 2 S 18:18. Ps *49:11.

18. A.M. cir. 194. B.C. cir. 3810. **Irad.** i.e. *fugitive*, *S#5897h. **Mehujael.** i.e. *grief*, *S#4232h. **Methusael.** i.e. *man of God*, *S#4967h. **Lamech.** Heb. Lemech. i.e. *powerful, overthrower*, *S#3929h. Ge 4:18, 19, 23, 23, 24. 5:25, 26, 28, 30, 31. 1 Ch 1:3. Lk 3:36.

19. **two wives.** Ge 2:18, *24. 16:1-6. 25:1, 6. 26:34. 28:9. 29:25-30. 32:22. 36:2, 3. Le 18:18. Dt *17:17. 21:15-17. Jg 8:30, 31. Ru 4:11. 1 S 1:2. 27:3. 2 S 3:7. 5:13. 12:8. 1 K 11:1-3. 1 Ch 4:5. 14:3. 2 Ch 11:18, 21. 13:21. 24:3. SS 6:8. Is 4:1. Da 5:2. Ml 2:15. Mt *19:4, 5, 8. 1 T 3:2, 12. 5:9. T 1:6. **Adah.** i.e. *pleasure, ornament*, *S#5711h. Ge 4:19, 20, 23. 36:2, 4, 10, 12, 16. (1) One of the wives of Lamech, Ge 4:19. (2) One of the wives of Esau, Ge 36:2, etc. Called Bashemath in Ge 26:34. **Zillah.** i.e. *a shade*, *S#6741h. Ge 4:19, 22, 23.

20. **Jabal.** i.e. *flowing, leading, a river; nomad; a stream*, *S#2989h. **the.** ver. 21. 1 Ch 2:50-52. 4:4, 5. Jn 8:44. Ro 4:11, 12. **father.** The inventor or teacher. 1 S 10:12. **dwell.** ver. 2. Ge 9:21. 25:27. Je 35:7, 9, 10. He 11:9. **and of.** *180A. Figure of speech Zeugma; or, Unequal Yoke B131: when one verb is yoked on to two objects, while grammatically a second (and different) verb is required; here, "dwell" applies to "tents" but not "cattle." For other instances of this figure see Ex 3:16. Dt 4:12. 2 K 11:12. 2 Ch 23:11. Is 2:3. Lk *24:27. 1 C 3:2. 7:10. 14:34. 1 T 4:3. Re 11:1. **cattle.** Ge 26:14. 47:17. Ex 34:19. Ec 2:7.

21. A.M. cir. 500. B.C. cir. 3504. **Jubal.** i.e. *music*, *S#3106h. Ge 4:21. **father.** Ro 4:11, 12. **handle.** Je 2:8. 46:9. Ezk 27:29. 38:4. **the harp.** Ge 31:27. 1 S 10:5. Jb 21:12. Ps 137:2. 150:3. Is 5:12. 23:16. Am 6:5. **organ** (pipe). Jb 21:12. 30:31. Ps 150:4.

22. **Tubal-cain.** i.e. *possessor of the world*, *S#8423h. **instructor.** Heb. whetter, a sharpener. 1 S 13:20. Jb 16:9. Ps 7:12. 52:2. **artificer.** 1 Ch 29:5. 2 Ch 34:11. Is 3:3. **brass and.** Ge 27:40. Ex 25:3. Nu 31:22. 35:16. Dt 8:9. 27:5. 33:25. 2 S 12:31. 2 Ch 2:7. Jb 20:24. Is 2:4. **Naamah.** i.e. *pleasant, pleasing*, *S#5279h. (1) A daughter of Lamech and Zillah, Ge 4:22. (2) The mother of King Rehoboam, 1 K 14:21, 31. 2 Ch 12:13. (3) One of the cities of Judah, Jsh 15:41. Ru ●1:19, 20.

23. **wives.** ver. +19. **Hear.** Nu 23:18. Jg 9:7. *132A. Figure of speech Parallelism; or, Parallel Lines B349: the repetition of similar, synonymous, or opposite thoughts or words in parallel or successive lines; here, synonymous or gradational, where the lines are parallel in thought and use synonymous words: hear, hearken; voice, speech; man, young man; wounding, hurt; avenged, avenged (supply by ellipsis, *63B. Nu +24:19); seven fold, seventy and seven fold. For other instances of this figure see Jg 5:10. Ps √1:1. 7:14. 116:8.

Lk 1:46, 47. Ju 11. **I have slain a man to my wounding.** *or*, I would slay a man in my wound, etc. Ge 49:6. **to my hurt.** *or*, in my hurt. **slain.** Ex *20:13. 21:25. Le *19:18. Dt *32:35. Ps 94:1. He 10:30.

24. **If.** ver. 15. **avenged.** Ex 21:21mg. Dt +19:6. Ps 18:47. **sevenfold.** Le *26:21. 2 S 21:6. Ps 79:12. Pr. 6:31. **truly.** Ps 94:4. Pr 27:1. **seventy.** Mt 18:22.

25. A.M. 130. B.C. 3874. **Adam.** Ge *5:3. **knew.** Ge +4:1, 17. **and called.** Ge 5:3, 4. 1 Ch 1:1. Lk 3:38. **Seth.** Heb. Sheth; i.e. appointed, or put. i.e. *replacing*, ✱S#8352h. Ge 4:25, 26. 5:3, 4, 6, 7, 8. Nu 24:17. 1 Ch 1:1. ✐140. Figure of speech Paronomasia; or, Rhyming Words: the repetition of words similar in sound, but not necessarily in sense. Here, Seth (Sheth) and "appointed" Heb. shath) are similar in sound. At Ge 1:2, the Hebrew words underlying our "form" and "void" (*tohu, bohu*) are similar in sound. For other instances of this figure see Ge 9:27. *11:9. *18:27. 29:34, 35. 41:51, 52. 49:8, 16, 19. Ex 32:18. Nu 5:18. 18:2. 24:21. Dt 30:3. 1 S 1:27, 28. 13:7. 2 S 22:42. 1 K 2:36, 42. 2 K 5:25. 1 Ch 22:9. Jb 11:12. Ps 18:7. 25:16. 39:11. 40:3. *56:8. 64:4. 69:30, 31. 96:5. 119:13. *122:6. 137:5. Pr 6:23. 18:24. Ec 7:1, *6. Is 2:19, 21. 5:7. 7:9. 10:16. 13:4, 6. 15:9. 17:1, 2. 21:2. 22:18. 24:3, 4, 17, 18. 25:1, 6. 30:16. 32:6, 7, 19. 41:5. 54:8. 57:6. 61:3. Je 1:11, 12, 17. 6:1. 8:13. *10:11. 48:2, 9, 43, 44. La 2:5. 3:47. Ezk 7:6. 12:10. 24:21. 25:16. Da *5:26-28. Ho 8:7. 9:15. 12:11. Am 8:1, 2. Jon 4:6. Mi 1:10. Na 2:10. Hab 2:18. Zp 1:2. 2:4. Zc 9:3, 5. Mt 21:41. 22:3. *24:7. Lk 21:11. Ro 1:29, 31. 9:18. 1 C 9:17. 2 C 8:22. 9:8. Ph 3:2. 1 T 1:18. 4:3. 6:5, 6, 9. He 5:8. Ja 5:17. **For God.** ver. 1-3, 8, 10, 11. Ex 18:4. **seed.** ✐121D11. Figure of speech Metonymy of the Cause; here, "seed" is put for son or posterity, as also in Ge 15:13. For the same figure involving a different term, see Ge 3:19. Ge 21:12n. 1 S 1:11mg. 2 S 7:12. 1 Ch 17:11. **whom.** ver. 8.

26. A.M. 235. B.C. 3769. **Seth.** Lk 3:38. **to him.** Ge *5:6-8. **Enos.** Heb. Enosh. i.e. *mortal man*, ✱S#583h. Ge 4:26. 5:6, 7, 9, 10, 11. 1 Ch 1:1. **to call upon the name of the Lord.** *or*, call *themselves* by the name of the Lord. Ge 12:8. 13:4. 21:33. 26:25. Dt 26:17, 18. 1 K *18:24. Ps 79:6. *116:17. Is 12:4. 44:5. 48:1. 63:19. Je 33:16. Jl *2:32. Zp 3:9. Ac 2:21. 9:14. 11:26 *22:16. Ro √10:13. 1 C 1:2. Ep 3:14, 15. **call.** ✐171J6. Figure of speech Synecdoche of the Species; or, Transfer B631: the species (subclass) is put for the genus (class); here, a verb having a special meaning is used in a more general sense, where to 'call' upon the Lord is used of divine worship. For other instances of this figure see Is 43:22. Jn 4:23, 24. **name.** ✐144A4. Figure of speech Pleonasm; or, Redundancy B410: when more words are used than the grammar requires; here, call upon the 'name' of the Lord. For other instances of this figure see Is +30:27. Je 10:25. Mt 1:21, 23. *6:9. Lk 1:13. 2:21. *11:2. Jn *1:12. 2:23. *3:18. Ro *10:13.

GENESIS 5

A repeated account of Adam's creation, 1, 2. The birth of Seth, 3. The age and death of Adam, 4, 5; Seth, 6-8; Enos, 9-11; Cainan, 12-14; Mahalaleel, 15-17; and Jared, 18-20. Enoch walks with God, and is translated, 21-24. The age and death of Methuselah, 25-27; *and of Lamech, 28-31. An account of Noah, and his sons, 32.*

1. **book.** The original word rendered *book* signifies a register, account, history, or any kind of writing. Ge 2:4. 6:9. 10:1. Ex 17:14. 1 Ch 1:1. Ne 7:5. Mt 1:1. Lk 3:36-38. **in the likeness.** Ge 1:26, 27. ◗3:5, 22. Ec *7:29. 12:1. 1 C 11:7. 2 C 3:18. Ep *4:24. Col *3:10. He 1:3. 12:9.

2. **Male.** Ge 1:27. Ml 2:15. Mk ▶10:6. 1 C 12:12. Ga 3:28. **blessed.** Ge 1:28. **their.** Ge 2:15, 23mg. Ac 17:26.

3. A.M. 130. B.C. 3874. **in his.** Jb *14:4. 15:14-16. 25:4. Ps 14:2, 3. *51:5. Lk 1:35. Jn *3:6. Ro 5:12. 1 C 15:39. Ep 2:3. **called.** Ge 4:25.

4. **And the.** 1 Ch 1:1-3. Lk 3:36-38. **and he.** ver. 7, 10, 13, 19, 22, 26, 30. Ge 1:28. 9:1, 7. 11:12. Ps 127:3. 144:12. **begat sons and daughters.** This answers the frequently asked question, "Where did Cain get his wife?" Clearly, he married either a sister or other female descendent (i.e., sister's daughter) of Adam and Eve, who are said here to have begotten sons and daughters. Of necessity this must have been the case. See Le 18:6n. Some interpreters suppose that the genetic deterioration resulting from the curse placed on man for sin may have taken some generations to take effect, so marrying a sister would not have posed the problem then that it does now. Laws pertaining to incest are first mentioned in Le 18:10, 11. 20:17. Dt 27:22.

5. A.M. 930. B.C. 3074. **nine.** ver. 8, 11, 14, 17, etc. with Dt 30:20. Ps 90:10. **and he died.** ver. 8, 11, 14, etc. Ge ◗2:17. 3:19. 2 S 14:14. Jb 30:23. Ps 49:7-10. 89:48. Ec 9:5, 8. 12:5, 7. Ezk *18:4. Ro 5:12-14. 1 C 15:21, 22. He *9:27.

6. A.M. 235. B.C. 3769. **begat.** Ge 4:26.

7. **Seth.** Ge 4:25. **Enos.** 1 Ch 1:1.

8. A.M. 1042. B.C. 2962.

9. A.M. 325. B.C. 3679. **Cainan.** Heb. Kenan. i.e. *possession, acquisition; fixed*, ✱S#7018h. ver. 10, 12, 13, 14. 1 Ch 1:2. Lk 3:37.

10. **begat.** See ver. 4.

11. A.M. 1140. B.C. 2864. **died.** See ver. 5.

12. A.M. 395. B.C. 3609. **Mahalaleel.** Gr. Maleleel. i.e. *praise of God*, ✱S#4111h. ver. 13, 15, 16, 17. 1 Ch 1:2. Ne 11:4. Lk 3:37. (1) The son of Cainan, Ge 5:12; 1 Ch 1:2. He is called Maleleel in Lk 3:37. (2) An Israelite whose descendants lived in Jerusalem after the captivity, Ne 11:4.

13. **and begat.** See ver. 4.

14. A.M. 1235. B.C. 2769. **died.** See ver. 5.

15. A.M. 460. B.C. 3544. **Jared.** i.e. *descent*, ✱S#3382h. ver. 16, 18, 19, 20. 1 Ch 1:2. 4:18. Heb. Jered. 1 Ch 1:2.

16. **and begat.** See ver. 4.

17. A.M. 1290. B.C. 2714. **died.** See ver. 5.

18. A.M. 622. B.C. 3382. **Enoch.** Ge 4:17. 1 Ch 1:3. Henoch. Lk 3:37. Ju 14, 15.

19. **and begat.** See ver. 4.

20. **he died.** See ver. 5.

21. A.M. 687. B.C. 3317. **Enoch.** i.e. *dedicated; teacher*, ✱S#2585h. Ge 4:17, 17, 18. 5:18, 19, 21, 22, 23, 24. 25:4. 46:9. Ex 6:14. Nu 26:5. 1 Ch 1:3, 33. 5:3. (1) A son of Cain, Ge 4:17, 18. (2) The name given by Cain to a city which he built, Ge 4:17. (3) The son of Jared and father of Methuselah, Ge 5:18, 21. He is called in Ju 14 "the seventh from Adam" to

distinguish him from Enoch the son of Cain. He is said to have "walked with God," Ge 5:22, and was translated to heaven, for "God took him," Ge 5:24. **Methuselah.** i.e. *man of dart, or* he dies and it is sent—namely, the flood. ✱S#4968h. ver. 21, 22, 25, 26, 27. 1 Ch 1:3. The son of Enoch and grandfather of Noah, Ge 5:27; 1 Ch 1:3. He was the longest-lived man, and died at the age of nine hundred and sixty-nine years. Gr. Mathusala. Lk 3:37.

22. **walked.** Ex 2:5. 14:29. Jsh 5:6. 1 S 8:3. 12:2. ✓108B. Figure of speech Idioma; or, idiom B832: the peculiar usage of words and phrases; here, "walk" is used of one's continued course of action and life: i.e., the habitual habit and manner of life. For other instances of this idiom see Ge 5:24. Ro 8:1. 2 C 5:7. **with.** ver. 24. Ge 3:8. *6:9. *17:1. *24:40. 48:15. Ex 16:4. Le 26:12. Dt 5:33. *13:4. 28:9. 1 K *2:4. *3:6. 2 K +*20:3. *22:2. Ne *5:9. Ps *16:8. 26:11. 56:13. ✓86:11. ◐*89:30-32. *116:9. *128:1. SS 1:4. Ho 14:9. Am *3:3. Mi *4:5. +✓6:8. Ml *2:6. Lk *1:6. Ac *9:31. Ro 8:1. 1 C 7:17. 2 C ✓5:7. 6:16. Ga *5:16. Ep 5:1, 15. Col +*1:10. 4:5. 1 Th 2:12. 4:1. He *11:5, 6. 1 J *1:3, 6, 7. ✓2:6. **begat.** Jn 17:15. 1 T 4:3. Ju 14.

23. A.M. 987. B.C. 3017.

24. **walked.** See on ver. 22. **he was not.** The same expression occurs, Ge 37:30. *42:13, 32, 36. Jb 7:8. Je *31:15. Mt 2:18. **for.** 2 K 2:11. Lk 23:43. He *11:)5, 6. Ju *14, 15. **took.** 2 K 2:10. Ps 49:15. 73:24. Is *57:1. 1 C *15:51. 1 Th *4:17.

25. A.M. 874. B.C. 3130. **Lamech.** Heb. Lemech. Ge 4:18mg.

26. **begat sons and daughters.** See ver. 4.

27. A.M. 1656. B.C. 2348.· **he died.** See ver. 5. Ec 11:8. Is 65:20.

28. A.M. 1056. B.C. 2948.

29. **he called.** Ge 6:8, 9. 7:23. 9:24. Is +*54:9. Ezk *14:14, 20. Mt 24:37. Lk 3:36. 17:26, 27. He 11:7. 1 P 3:20. 2 P 2:5. **Noah.** Gr. Noe, i.e. rest *or* comfort. ✱S#5146h. Ge 5:29, 30, 32, 32. 6:8, 9, 9, 9, 10, 13, 22. 7:1, 5, 6, 7, 9, 9, 11, 13, 13, 13, 15, 23. 8:1, 6, 11, 13, 15, 18, 20. 9:1, 8, 17, 18, 19, 20, 24, 28, 29. 10:1, 32. 1 Ch 1:4. Is 54:9, 9. Ezk 14:14, 20. **comfort.** Ge 27:42. 37:35. Ps 23:4. 71:21. **work.** Ge 3:19. 6:3, 11, 12. Ex 23:24. Le 18:3. Jb 33:17. Ec 4:3. Mi 6:16. **and.** ✓93A, Ge +1:26. "Work and toil" by Hendiadys, toilsome work: two words used, one thing meant, the second word has the force of an adjective, and receives the emphasis. **because.** Ge 3:17-19. 4:11, 12. **which.** Ge 8:21. Ro 8:20-23.

30. **begat sons.** See ver. 4.

31. A.M. 1651. B.C. 2353. **he died.** See ver. 5.

32. A.M. 1556. B.C. 2448. **Noah.** Ge 7:6. **Shem.** i.e. *celebrated name,* ✱S#8035h. Ge 6:10. 7:13. 9:18, 19, 23, 26, 27. 10:1, 21, 22, 31. 11:10, 10, 11. 1 Ch 1:4, 17, 24. Lk 3:36. **Ham.** i.e. *raging,* ✱S#2526. Ge 6:10. 7:13. 9:18, 18, 22. 10:1, 6, 20. 1 Ch 1:4, 8. 4:40. Ps 78:51. 105:23, 27. 106:22. **Japheth.** i.e. *enlargement,* ✱S#3315h. Ge 6:10. 7:13. 9:18, 23, 27. 10:1, 2, 21. 1 Ch 1:4, 5.

GENESIS 6

The worshippers of God intermarry with the ungodly; wickedness rapidly increases; and the Lord in anger determines to destroy the earth, 1-7. Noah is accepted by God; warned of an approaching deluge;

and instructed to prepare an ark, 8-21. He implicitly obeys, 22.

1. A.M. 1556. B.C. 2448. **to multiply.** Ge 1:28. Ac 6:1. **face.** Ge +1:2.

2. **the sons.** Ge *4:26. Ex 4:22, 23. Dt *14:1. Jb 1:6. 2:1. 38:7. Ps 29:1. 82:6, 7. 89:6. Is 63:16. Ml 2:11. Jn 8:41, 42. Ro 9:7, 8. 2 C 6:18. 2 P 2:4. Ju 6. ✓108H11. Idioma; or, idiom B844. Here, "sons of God" is an idiomatic phrase meaning angels. For other instances of this idiom see Ge 6:4. Jb 1:6. 2:1. 38:7. Ps 29:1. 89:6. Da 3:25. **of God.** ✓24L. Antimereia; or, exchange of one part of speech for another B502; here, a divine name is used "in regimen" as an adjective, denoting wondrous, mighty, supernatural beings. "Sons of God" always used of angels in the O.T., as in the references given above for ✓108H11. For other instances of this figure of speech see Ge +*23:6mg. 30:8. Ex 9:28. 1 S *14:15. 26:12. 2 S 9:3n. 2 K 1:12. 1 Ch 12:22. +*16:42. 2 Ch 20:29. 28:13. Jb +*1:16mg. 4:9. Ps 36:6mg. 46:4. 65:9. 68:15. 80:10. 104:16. SS 8:6. Je 2:31. Ezk *28:13. 31:8, 9. Ac *7:20mg. **saw.** Jb +*31:1. 2 P *2:14. **that they.** Ge *3:6. 39:6, 7. 2 S *11:2. Jb *31:1. 1 J *2:16. **were fair.** 1 K *11:1, 3. Ne *13:25, 26. **and they.** Ge 24:3. *26:34, 35. 27:46. Ex *34:16. Dt *7:3, 4. Jsh 23:12, 13. Ezr 9:1, 2, 12. Ne 13:24-27. Ml *2:15. Mt ◐✓22:30. Lk ◐✓20:35, 36. 1 C +*7:39. 2 C *6:14-16.

3. A.M. 810. B.C. 3194. **My.** Nu 11:17. Ne *9:30. Is 1:5. *5:4. +*63:10. Je *11:7, 11. Lk 19:42. Jn 16:8. Ac 7:51. Ga ✓5:16, 17. 1 Th *5:19. 2 Th 2:6, 7. 1 P 3:18-20. 2 P 3:9. Ju 14, 15. **spirit.** Heb. *ruach.* Here *ruach* has reference to the invisible psychological part of man given to him by God at man's formation at birth, and returning to God at his death. ✚S#7307h. Nu 16:22. ✓27:16n. Jb 27:3. 34:14. Ps 31:5. 104:30. Ec *3:21, 21. 8:8, 8. 11:5. *12:7. Is 42:5. Ezk 37:9 (wind). Zc 12:1. The word *ruach,* spirit, is used of (1) God, Is 40:13. (2) The Holy Spirit, Is +48:16. (3) The operations of the Holy Spirit in (a) creation, Ge 1:2; (b) giving life, Ezk 37:14; (c) executing judgment, Ex +15:8. (4) Invisible power from on high in giving spiritual gifts, Ge +41:38. (5) Psychological uses. 1) The invisible part of man, rendered "breath," Ge +6:17; "spirit," Ge +6:3. See Ge 2:7n on the interchangeable uses of "soul," Heb. *nephesh,* and "spirit," Heb. *ruach.* 2) The invisible characteristics of man, rendered "mind," Ge +26:35; "breath," Is 33:11; "courage," Jsh 2:11; "anger," Jg 8:3; "blast," Is 25:4; "spirit," Ge +*41:8. (6) By Synecdoche, *spirit,* an integral part of man individually, is put for the whole person, Ps +106:33. (7) Invisible spirit beings, angels and cherubim, Ps +104:4. (8) Neutral spirit beings, Jb 4:15. Is 31:3. (9) Evil angels, Jg +9:23. For the corresponding Greek word, *pneuma,* see Mt 8:16n. **always.** Heb. *olam,* ✚S#5769h. 1 Ch 16:15. Jb 7:16. Ps 119:112. Je 20:17. **strive.** T#347-1, 349. Jb +*36:9. Ps 81:11-15. Is *55:6. Ho *5:6. 9:12. Ro 1:24-28. **flesh.** Jb 34:15. Ps 56:4. *78:37-39. Is 40:6-8. Je 17:5. Jn *3:6. Ro *8:1-13. 1 C 1:29. 15:39. Ga 5:16-24. 1 P 1:24. **yet.** 1 P 3:20. **his days.** Ge 47:9. Ps *39:5. Ja *4:14. **shall be.** Ge 15:13-16. Is 38:5. Je 25:12. Da 9:2, 23-27. Jn 21:18, 19, 21, 22, 23. Ac 1:6. 1 Th 5:1-4.

4. **giants.** Nu 13:33. Dt 2:11, 20, 21. 3:11, 13. Jsh 12:4. 13:12. 15:8. 17:15. 18:16. 1 S 17:4. 2 S 21:15-22. 1 Ch 20:4. **after.** ver. 3. **sons.** ✓108H11, Ge +6:2. **God.** ✓24L, Ge +6:2. **came in.** Ge 38:18. Dt +*22:13.

Ru +*4:13. Mt 1:18. **mighty.** Ge 10:8, 9. Is 2:17. 1 C 1:26. 2 C 10:5. **of old.** Heb. *olam*, ✛S#5769h. Dt 32:7. 1 S 27:8. Ps 25:6. 119:52. Is 46:9. 57:11. 63:9, 11. Je 28:8. La 3:6. Ezk 26:20. Am 9:11. Mi 7:14. Ml 3:4. **men of.** Ge 11:4. Nu 16:2.

5. **God.** Ge 13:13. 18:20, 21. Ps 14:1-4. 53:2. Ro 1:28-31. 3:9-19. **saw.** Ge 7:1. 11:5. 29:31. Ex 3:4. Dt 32:19. **of man.** ⌐121N1. Metonymy of the Adjunct, Abstract put for the concrete, Ge +31:54. The term *man* includes women and children. By this figure subjects are often spoken of as if they had an application only to men, when women are included; as only to adults, when children or infants are included; language used as applicable to an abstract question does not deny its applicability to a specific case. We are not to suppose that women and infants are excluded, merely because they are not specified. See related notes (Ac 8:12n. 1 P 3:21n). Jg 20:48n. **every.** Ep 4:17-19. 5:8. T 1:15. **imagination.** *or*, the whole imagination, *with* the purposes and desires of the heart. The Hebrew word signifies not only the imagination, but also the purposes and desires. Ge *8:21. Dt *29:19. 31:21. 1 K *8:46. 1 Ch +*28:9. 29:18. Jb 15:14, 16. Ps *14:2, 3. Pr *6:18. *20:9. Ec *7:20, 29. *9:3. Is *26:3. Je *17:9. Ezk 8:9, 12. Mt *15:19, 20. Mk *7:21-23. Ro *1:28. 3:10, 18. 8:7. Ep 2:1-3. T 3:3. **thoughts.** Is 66:4. Je 4:14. Ezk 14:3. **continually.** Heb. every day. 1 S 18:29. 2 K 13:3. Jb 1:5mg.

6. **repented.** Ge ◐1:31. Ex 32:14. Nu ◐*23:19. Dt 32:36. Jg 2:18. 1 S ◐*15:11, 29, 35. 2 S *24:16. 1 Ch 21:15. Ps 106:45. 110:4. Je 18:8-10. 26:19. Ho 11:8. Jon *3:10. Ml ◐+*3:6. Ro +*11:29. He 6:17, 18. Ja *1:17. ⌐22B. Anthropomorphism B882. Here, repentance is attributed to God. For other instances of this figure see Ex 32:12, 14. 2 S 24:16. Ps 106:45. Je *18:7-10. 26:3. Ho 11:8. Jl 2:13, 14. Am 7:3, 6. **grieved.** T#230. Nu 32:14. Dt 5:29. 25:16. 32:29. Ps 7:11-13. 10:3. 11:5. 78:40. 81:13. 95:8-10. 119:158. Pr 11:20. 15:9, 26. Is 48:18. +*63:10. Je 12:8. Ezk 33:11. Ho 7:2. 9:15. 12:2. 13:7, 8. Mi 6:2. Na 1:6. Mk *3:5. Lk 19:41, 42. Ep √4:30. He *3:10, 17, 18. Re +*6:16, 17. ⌐22B. Anthropomorphism B882. Here, sorrow and grief are attributed to God. For other instances of this figure see Jg √10:16n. Ps 78:40. Is 63:10. **heart.** ⌐22A17. Anthropomorphism B881. Here, a heart is attributed to God. For other instances of this figure see Ge 8:21. 1 S 13:14. Je 19:5 (mind). 32:41. Ac 13:22.

7. **I will.** Ps 24:1, 2. 37:20. Pr 10:27. 16:4. Is 48:18. Lk 19:41, 42. **destroy.** Dt 28:63. 29:20. Ph 3:19. 2 Th 1:9. **face.** Ge +1:2. **both man, and beast.** Heb. from man unto beast. Je 4:22-27. 12:3, 4. Ho 4:3. Zp 1:3. Ro 3:20-22. **repenteth.** Am 7:3, 6. He 3:11.

8. **found.** Ge 19:19. Ex 33:12-17. Ps *84:11. 145:20. Pr *3:4. 8:35. 12:2. Je 31:2. Lk *1:30. Ac 7:46. Ro 4:4. 11:6. 1 C 15:10. Ga 1:15. 2 T 1:18. T *2:11. 3:7. He *4:16. 2 P *2:5. ⌐171J4. Figure of speech Synecdoche of the Species B630, when the Species (subclass) is put for the Genus (class), particulars are put for universals. Here, a verb having a special meaning is used in a more general sense: to "find" is used for "receive" or "obtain." For other instances of this figure see Ge 26:12. Lk 1:30. Ro 4:1. He 9:12. **grace.** Ex 22:27. 33:19. 34:6. Nu 32:5. 2 Ch 30:9. Ne 9:17, 31. Ps 86:15. 103:8. 111:4. 112:4. 145:8. Pr 3:34.

9. **These.** Ge 2:4. 5:1. 10:1. **just.** Ge 7:1. Dt 32:4. Jb 12:4. Ps 37:39. Pr 4:18. Ec √7:20. Ezk *14:14, 20.

Mi +√6:8. Hab +*2:4. Mt 1:19. 27:19. Mk 6:20. Lk 2:25. ◐+*16:10. 23:50. Ac 10:22. 22:14. Ro 1:17. Ga 3:11. He 11:7. 2 P 2:5, 7. **perfect.** *or*, upright. Ge *17:1. Dt 18:13. 1 K +*20:3. 1 Ch 12:38n. 2 Ch 15:17. 25:2. Jb *1:1, 8. Ps 37:√18n, 37. Lk 1:6. Jn +*17:6. Ph 3:9-15. **and Noah.** See on Ge 5:22, 24. 17:1. 48:15. 1 K 3:6. Lk 1:6. 1 P 2:5.

10. A.M. 1556. B.C. 2448. **Shem.** Ge *5:32. 7:13. 9:18. 10:1. 1 Ch 1:4. **Ham.** Ge 9:22-24. **Japheth.** Ge 10:21. 1 Ch 1:5.

11. **earth.** ⌐121J17. Figure of speech Metonymy of the Subject B578: the place is put for the thing placed in it; here, the land or earth is put for its inhabitants. For other instances of this figure see Ge 11:1. 18:25. 41:30. 41:57. Jg 5:7. 1 S 14:29. 2 S 15:23. Ps 9:8. 22:27. 66:1, 4. 67:7. 82:8. 96:1. Pr 28:2. Ezk 14:13. Mt 5:13. **before.** Ge 7:1. 10:9. 13:13. 2 Ch 34:27. Lk 1:6. Ro 2:13. 3:19. **violence.** Ps 11:5. 55:9. 140:11. Is 60:18. Je 6:7. 20:8. 22:3. Ezk 7:23. 8:17. 9:9. 22:26. 28:16. *45:9. Ho 4:1, 2. Hab 1:2. 2:8, 17. Zp 3:4.

12. **God looked upon.** ver. 8. Ge 18:21. Jb 33:27. Ps 14:2. 33:13, 14. 53:2, 3. Pr 15:3. **corrupt.** Ex 32:7. Dt *31:29. 32:5. Jg *2:19. **for.** ver. 4, 5. Ge 7:1, 21. 9:12, 16, 17. Jb 22:15-17. Ps 14:1-3. Lk 3:6. 1 P 3:19, 20. 2 P 2:5. **all.** *⌐171M. Figure of speech Synecdoche of the Whole B636; the collective is put for the particular: what is said of the whole, collectively, is sometimes said (by Synecdoche) only of a part; and not all of the parts, precisely and singularly. Here, the "all" refers to all humanity, with the exception of Noah. For other instances of this figure see Ge 35:26 (except Benjamin: see ver. 16, 24). Mt 19:28 (except Judas Iscariot). 1 C 15:22 (except those who are "alive and remain" at Christ's coming: see ver. 51 and 1 Th 4:15, 17). He 11:13 (except Enoch: see ver. 5). See related note and figures given at Ge 24:10n, ⌐171B. **flesh.** ⌐171E1. Figure of speech Synecdoche of the Genus B620; a word of wider meaning is used in a narrower sense: the universal for the particular, but of the same kind. Here, "flesh" is put for man or mankind. For other instances of this figure see Ps 145:21. Is 40:5. 66:16, 23. Lk 3:6. Ro 3:20. ⌐171Q6. Synecdoche of the Part B642: the "flesh" is put for the whole person; here, "flesh" is the figure for "people." For other instances of this figure see Ps 56:4. 65:2. 145:21. Is 40:6. Mt 19:5. Jn √6:51. Ro 3:20. 1 C 1:29. 1 P 1:24. **earth.** 2 P 2:5. Re 11:18.

13. **The end.** Is 34:1-4. Je 51:13. Ezk 7:2-6. Am 8:2. Ro 3:19. 10:4. 1 P *4:7. **flesh.** ⌐171E1. Ge +6:12. ⌐171Q8. Figure of speech Synecdoche of the Part B643; "flesh" is put for all living beings. For other instances of this figure see Ge 6:17. Ps 136:25. **is come.** Is 60:1. Mt 12:28. He 12:22. **filled.** ver. 4, 11, 12. Ge 49:5. Ho 4:1, 2. **and, behold.** ver. 17. **destroy.** T#566. Ge 18:20, 21. 19:24, 25. Ex +*22:23, 24. Nu +*32:23 (T#733). Dt 15:9. Jg 9:24n. 2 S *3:39. 1 K +*8:32 (T#1751). Jb +*4:8. Ps *31:23. +37:9 (T#87). 54:5. +58:11 (T#630). 91:8. Pr *13:15. √22:22, 23. 24:17, *18. Is +*66:24. Ezk +39:23 (T#486). Ml +*3:5. Mt 18:6, 10. Lk +*18:7, 8. Ro +*1:27. √12:19. Col 3:25. 2 P 2:4-7. Re +*11:18. **with.** *or*, from. Ge 7:23. Ps 37:9, 10. **the earth.** Je 4:23-28. He 11:7. 2 P *3:6, 7, 10-12.

14. A.M. 1536. B.C. 2468. **Make.** Mt 24:38. Lk 17:27. 1 P 3:20. **ark.** Ex 2:3, 5. 1 Th 1:10. He 11:7. **wood.** Ga 6:14. **rooms.** Heb. nests. **shalt pitch.** Ex

2:3. 30:10. Le *17:11 (atonement). Dt +32:43h (merciful). **within.** Ex 25:2. 37:2.

15. **cubits.** Ge 7:20. Dt 3:11.

16. **window.** Ge 7:11. 8:6. 2 S 6:16. 2 K 9:30. **the door.** Ge 7:16. Lk 13:25. **with.** Ezk 41:16. 42:3. **lower.** ✻S#8482h, *tahti.* Dt +32:22.

17. **behold.** ver. 13. Ge 7:4, 21-23. 9:9. Ex 14:17. Le 26:28. Dt 32:39. Ps 29:10. Is 51:12. Ezk 5:8. 6:3. 34:11, 20. Ho 5:14. 2 P 2:5. **I.** *ſ*84. Figure of speech Epizeuxis; or, duplication B189: the repetition of the same word in the same sense, separated by one or more intervening words. Such repetition is for marked emphasis (see Ge 41:32). For other instances of this figure see Ge +7:19. +22:11. 25:30. 30:43. Ex +2:12. 4:16. 15:16. 23:30. 28:34. 34:6. Le 6:12. 24:8. Nu 8:16. 17:6mg, 12, 13. Dt 16:20. 28:43. 32:7. Jg 5:22. 1 S 2:3. 2 S 7:5. 18:33. 2 K 4:19. 2 Ch +4:3. Ps 22:1. 57:7. 67:6, 7. 77:16. 96:13. 118:11, 15, 16. 137:7. Pr 20:14. Ec 3:18. 7:24. Is 6:3. 21:9. +*24:16. *26:3. 28:10. 40:1. 51:9, 17. 52:1. 57:19. Je 4:19. *6:14. 22:29. Ezk 21:9, 27. 22:2. 33:11. 34:11, 17, 20. Da 5:11. 10:19. Zp 1:14. Mt 5:37. 23:37. Lk *23:21. Jn +1:51. Ep 3:9. He 10:37. **bring.** Ge 7:4, 17, 21-23. Jb 22:16. Ps 29:10. 93:3, 4. 107:34. Is 54:9. Am 9:6. Mt 24:39. Lk 17:27. He 11:7. 1 P 3:20. **is the.** Ge +*2:7. 7:15. Jb 27:3. Ps 31:5. Ec 3:19. *12:7. Mt 27:50. **breath.** Heb. *ruach.* Here *ruach* has reference to the invisible and psychological part of man given to him by God at man's formation at birth, and returning to God at death. ✚S#7307h. Ge 7:15, 22. Jb 9:18. 12:10. 17:1. Ps 104:29. 135:17. +√146:4. Ec 3:19. Je 10:14. 51:17. La 4:20. Ezk 37:5, 6, 8, 9, 10. Hab 2:19. For the other uses of *ruach* see ver. +*3n. **shall die.** ver. 7. Ps 104:29. 107:34. Ac 5:5. Ro 5:12-14, 21. √6:23. 8:20-22.

18. **establish.** Ge 9:9, 11. 17:4, 7, 21. **covenant.** Ge 15:18. He 13:20. **come.** Ge 7:1, 7, 13. Is 26:20. Ac +16:31. He 11:7. 1 P 3:20. 2 P *2:5, 9. Re 22:17.

19. **every.** Is 65:25. Ro 8:20, 21. **two.** Ge 7:2, 3, 8, 9, 15, 16. 8:17. Ps 36:6. Am 3:3.

20. **fowls.** Ge 1:20-24. Ac 10:11, 12. **two.** Ge 1:28. 2:19. 7:8-16. Jn 5:40. 6:37.

21. **all food.** Ge 1:29, 30. Jb 38:41. 40:20. Ps 36:6. 104:27, 28. 136:25. 145:16. 147:9. Mt 6:26.

22. **according to.** Ge 7:5, 9, 16. 17:23. Ex 40:16, 19, 21, 23, 25, 27, 32. Dt *12:32. Mt *7:24-27. Jn 2:5. 15:14. He 11:7, 8. 1 J 5:3, 4.

GENESIS 7

At God's command Noah enters the ark, with his family, and the living creatures; and the flood begins, 1-16. Its increase for forty days, 17-20. All flesh is destroyed by it, 21-23. Its duration, 24.

1. A.M. 1656. B.C. 2348. **Come.** ver. 7, 13. Jb 5:19-24. Ps *91:1-10. Pr *14:26. 18:10. Is 26:20, 21. Ezk 9:4-6. Zp +*2:3. Mt 11:28. 24:37-39. Lk 17:26. Ac 2:39. He 11:7. 1 P *3:20. 2 P 2:5. **house.** Jsh 2:18, 19. 24:15. Ac 16:31. *ſ*121J4. Figure of speech Metonymy; or, Change of Noun B573: the change of one noun for another related noun. Here, Metonymy of the Subject, where the subject is put for something pertaining to it: "house" is put for household, descendants, or family. For other instances of this figure see Ge 30:30. 43:16. Ex 1:21. 2:1. 2 S 7:11. 1 Ch 10:6. Ps 49:11. Is 36:3. Ezk 3:1. 27:14. Lk 19:9. Ac 10:2.

11:14. 16:+√15n, *31. 18:8. 1 ·C 1:16. 1 T 3:4. 2 T 1:16. 3:6. 2 T 4:19. T 1:11. He √11:7. **thee.** See on Ge 6:9. Ps *33:18, 19. Pr 10:6, 7, 9. 11:4-8. Is *3:10, 11. Ph 2:15, 16. 2 P 2:5-9. **seen righteous.** Ge *6:9. Jn +*17:6.

2. **every clean.** ver 8. Ge 6:19-21. 8:20. Le ch. 11. Dt 14:1-21. Ac 10:11-15. **sevens.** Heb. seven, seven. **not.** Le 10:10. Ezk 44:23.

3. **face.** ver 6 +1:2.

4. **For.** ver. 10. Ge 2:5. 6:3. 8:10, 12. 29:27, 28. Jb 28:25. 36:27-32. 37:11, 12. Am 4:7. **seven.** Jsh 6:3, 4. **forty days.** ver. 12, 17. Ge 5:3. Ex 24:18. 34:28. Nu 13:25. 14:34. Dt 9:18. 1 K 19:8. Ezk 4:6. Jon 3:4. Mt 4:2. Ac 1:3. **and every.** ver. 21-23. Ge 6:7, 13, 17. **destroy.** Heb. blot out. ver. 21, 23. Ge 6:7, 13, 17. Ex *32:32, 33. Jb 22:16. Ps *69:28. Re *3:5. **face.** Ge +1:2.

5. **all that.** Ge 6:22. Ex 39:32, 42, 43. 40:16. Ps 119:6. Mt 3:15. Lk 8:21. Jn 2:5. 8:28, 29. 13:17. Ph 2:8. He 5:8.

6. **six hundred.** Ge 5:32. 8:13.

7. **Noah went in.** ver. 1, 13-15. Ge 6:18. Pr +*22:3. Mt 24:38. Lk 17:27. He *6:18. 11:7. 1 P 3:20. 2 P 2:5.

8. **clean.** ver. 2, 3. Ge 6:19, 20.

9. **went in.** ver. 16. Ge 2:19. Is *11:6-9. 65:25. Je 8:7. Ac 10:11, 12. Ga 3:28. Col 3:11.

10. **after seven days.** *or*, on the seventh day. ver. 4. **waters.** ver. 4, 17-20. Ge 6:17. Jb 22:16. Mt *24:38, 39. Lk 17:27.

11. **second month.** The first month was Tisri, which answers to the latter end of September and first half of October; the second was Marchesvan, which answers to part of October and part of November. **same day.** Mt 24:27. Lk 17:26, 27. 1 Th *5:3. 2 P 2:5. 3:6. **all.** Ge 1:7. 6:17. 8:2. Jb 28:4. 38:8-11. Ps 33:7. 74:15. Pr 8:28, 29. Is 24:19. Je 5:22. 51:16. Ezk 26:19. Am 9:5, 6. Mt 24:38. 1 Th 5:3. **fountains.** Ge ◐+1:9. Ex 20:4. Le 11:36. Jsh 15:9. Jb 38:16, 25. Pr 24:2. *87:7. Jon 2:5, 6. Heb. *mayan*, a spring or fountain. ✻S#4599h. Ge 7:11. 8:2. Le 11:36. Jsh 15:9. 18:15 (well). 1 K 18:5. 2 K 3:19 (wells), 25 (wells). 2 Ch 32:4. Ps 74:15. 84:6 (well). *87:7 (springs). 104:10 (springs). 114:8. Pr 5:16. 8:24. 25:26. SS 4:12, 15. Is *12:3 (wells). 41:18. Ho 13:15. Jl 3:18. For ✻S#875h, *be-er*, a dug well, see Ge +16:14. For ✻S#953h, *bor*, a hewn cistern, well, etc., see Ge +37:20. For S#4726h, *maqor*, spring, dug well (even when naturally flowing), see Le +12:7. Pr 10:11. For ✚S#5869h, *ayin*, a fountain, see Ge +24:13. **deep.** Ge 1:2. 49:25. Dt 33:13. Ps 104:6. **windows.** *or*, flood-gates. Ge 1:7. 8:2. 2 K 7:2, 19. Ps 78:23, 24. Ec 12:3. Is *24:18. 60:8. Ho 13:3 (chimney). Ml *3:10.

12. **forty.** ver. 4, 17. Ex 24:18. Dt 9:9, 18. 10:10. 1 K 19:8. Mt 4:2.

13. **selfsame.** Heb. In the body, or essence, or strength of the day. ✚S#6106h. Ge 17:23, 26. Le 23:14, 21, 28 (same), 29, 30. Dt +32:48. Jsh 5:11. 10:27 (very). Jb 21:23h (strength). Ezk 2:3 (very). 24:2, 2 (same). 40:1. Not in the dark or twilight, like one ashamed of his action, or afraid of the people, but when it was a clear day, or about noon-tide, in the public view of the world (Matthew Poole). **day.** ver. 1, 7-9. Ge 6:18. He 11:7. 1 P 3:20. 2 P 2:5. **and Shem.** Ge 5:32. 6:10. 9:18, 19. 10:1, 2, 6, 21. 1 Ch 1:4-28.

14. **They.** ver. 2, 3, 8, 9. **kind.** Ge 1:21. 6:19. Le

11:14. Dt 14:13, 14. **sort**. Heb. wing. Ge 6:20. Ps 148:10mg. Is +24:16mg. Ezk 39:4mg.

15. **went**. Ge 6:20. Is 11:6. **two**. ver. 9. Ge 6:19. **breath**. Ge +*2:7. 6:17. Jb 27:3. Ps +*146:4.

16. **as**. ver. 2, 3. **and the**. Dt 33:27. 2 K 4:4, 5. Ps 36:6. *46:1-3. 91:1-10. Pr 3:23. Mt 25:10. Lk 13:25. Jn 10:27-30. 1 P *1:5. **shut**. Jg 9:51. Is 26:20. *55:6. Mt *25:10. Lk *13:25. Jn *10:28. Ro 8:1. Col 3:3. Re ◑*3:20.

17. **forty days**. ver. 4, 12. **bare up**. Ro 5:21.

18. **waters prevailed**. Ex 14:28. Jb 22:16. Ps 69:15. Jon 2:5. **ark**. Ps 104:26. **face**. Ge +1:2.

19. **waters**. Ps 69:1. **exceedingly**. ♪84, Epizeuxis. Ge +6:17. Ge 6:17. 17:2, 6, 20. 30:43. Ex 1:7. Nu 14:7. 1 K 7:47. 2 K 10:4. Ezk 9:9. 16:13. 37:10. **all**. ♪102. Figure of speech Hyperbole; or, Exaggeration B423: when more is said than is literally meant, also called overstatement. Here, if the flood of Noah was local, then this passage exhibits clear hyperbole. Sometimes "all" means every last one without exception (Ec 7:20. Ro √3:23. Col √1:16, 17. He 2:8); sometimes it means every one or kind without distinction, but not without exception (See √♪171B, Synecdoche of the Genus, Ge +√24:10n; ♪171.O.1, Synecdoche of the Whole, Jn +3:16; ♪121J8, Metonomy of the Subject, Jn +3:16; ♪142, Periphrasis, Jn +1:9. ◑♪171F, Synecdoche of the Species, where *many* is put for *all*, Is +53:12); sometimes it means "most" or the majority (Mk *1:33. Lk 3:12 w 7:30 w Mk 1:5); sometimes it means "all" in the purview of the author and his circumstances (Ge *41:56, 57. 1 K √18:10). Consideration of the context and related passages will usually clarify which sense is to be given to "all" and kindred expressions. For other instances of overstatement see Ge +2:24. 6:17, 19, 21. 7:21. +13:16. 19:4. *41:56, 57. Ex 8:17. 9:6, 25. 10:12. Dt *2:25. Jsh 6:21-25. Jg 7:21. 2 S 6:5, 15. 1 K 11:16. √18:10. 2 K *20:13. 24:14. 1 Ch *14:17. Ps *22:7, 17. *98:3. +139:8. Is 28:8. Je 13:13. 26:9. Da 2:37, *38. 7:23. Mt *2:3. *3:5, 6. 4:24. +√5:29, 30. *12:15. 14:35. Mk 1:5, 33. 9:23. 10:28. 12:44. Lk 1:65, 66. *2:1. *8:43. Jn 1:9. 3:26. *4:39. *10:8. 12:19, 32. Ac 2:*5, 44, 45, 47. 8:3. 10:12. Ro 1:8. *8:28. 10:18. 15:14. 16:26. 1 C 1:5. 6:12. 9:22. 10:24. *13:7. 2 C 8:3, 7. 11:8. Ph 4:13, 18. Col *1:6, 23. 1 T *2:4. 6:10. 2 T 1:15. 4:17. T 1:12, 15. *2:11. Re *13:8, 16. **the high hills**. Jb 12:15. Ps 46:2, 3. 104:6-9. Is 2:14. Je 3:23. 2 P 3:6.

20. **and the mountains**. Ge 8:4. Ps 104:6. Je 3:23.

21. **all flesh**. ver. 4. Ge 6:6, 7, 13, 17. Nu 23:19. Jb 22:15-17. Is 24:6, 19. Je 4:22-27. 12:3, 4. Ho 4:3. Jl 1:17-20. 2:3. Zp 1:3. Mt 24:39. Lk 17:27. Ro 8:20, 22. 2 P 2:5. 3:6.

22. **breath of life**. Heb. breath of the spirit of life. Ge +2:7. 6:17. Ps +*146:4.

23. **every living substance**. ver. 21, 22. Jb 22:15-17. Pr *11:21. Is 24:1-8. Mt 24:37-39. Lk 17:26, 27. 1 P 3:20. 2 P 2:5. **face**. Ge +1:2. **and Noah only**. Ex 14:28-30. Jb 5:19. Ps 91:1, 9, 10. Pr 11:4. Ezk *14:14-20. Ml 3:17, 18. Mt 24:38, 39. *25:46. Lk 17:26, 27. He 11:7. 1 P 3:20. 2 P 2:5, 9. 3:6.

24. **an hundred and**. ver. 11. Ge 8:3, 4. Jb 12:15.

GENESIS 8

God remembers Noah, and assuages the waters, 1-3. The ark rests on the mountains of Ararat, 4, 5. Noah sends forth a raven, and then a dove, to gain intelligence, 6-12. He leaves the ark, offers sacrifices, and is accepted and encouraged, 13-22.

1. **God remembered**. Ge *19:29. 30:22. Ex *2:24. 1 S 1:19. Ne 13:14, 22, 29, 31. Jb 14:13. Ps 94:14. 106:4. 132:1. 136:23. 137:7. Am 8:7. Hab *3:2. Re 16:19. 18:5. ♪22C3. Figure of speech Anthropomorphism B885: human actions are attributed to God; here, remembering. For other instances of this figure see Ge 9:15, 16. 19:29. 30:22. Ex 2:24. 6:5. 1 S 1:11, 19. Ps 25:6, 7. 78:39. 103:14. 105:8, 42. 106:45. 115:12. 119:49. 137:7. Is 43:25. Je 31:34. Re 18:5. **the cattle**. Ge 6:20. Nu 22:32. Ps *36:6. 145:9. Jon *4:11. Mt *10:29. Ro 8:20-22. **a wind**. Ex 14:21. Ps *104:7-9. Pr 25:23. **waters**. Jb 12:15. Ps 29:10. 33:7. Is 44:27. Na 1:4.

2. **fountains**. Ge +7:11 (S#4599h). Pr 8:28. Jon 2:3. **windows**. 2 K 7:2. **stopped**. Jb 38:8. **rain**. Ge 7:4, 12. Jb 37:11-13. 38:37. Mt 8:9, 26, 27.

3. **continually**. Heb. in going and returning. **hundred**. Ge 7:11, 24. **abated**. Jb 38:11. Ps *30:5. Is *30:18. Je 5:22.

4. **the ark**. Ge 7:17-19. **seventh month**. That is, of the year, not of the deluge. **rested**. Ro 6:9. Ep 2:6. **mountains**. ♪96F3. Figure of speech Heterosis of Number B532: the plural is put for an indefinite number, or for one of many. For other instances of this figure see Ge 19:29. Jg 12:7. 18:14. 1 S 18:21. Ne 3:8. Jb 21:32. Jon 1:5. Mt *2:20. 9:8. 21:5. **Ararat**. i.e. *mountain of descent; the curse reversed*, ✱S#780h. 2 K 19:37. Is 37:38. Je 51:27.

5. **decreased continually**. Heb. were in going and decreasing. ♪96B. Figure of speech Heterosis of Moods B515: here, infinitive for indicative. This figure is present in the Hebrew, but is not observable in the English translation, either here or in the other instances of this figure at Ex 8:15. 2 S 3:18. 1 K 22:30. 2 Ch 18:29. 31:10. Ps 8:1. *32:9 (where it is literally "not to understand," or "having no understanding": note the infinitive construction "to understand" for the indicative). 77:1. Pr 12:6. Is 5:5. 38:16. 49:7. Je 7:9. 14:5. Ezk 1:14. 11:7. Hab 2:15. **the tenth**. Ge 7:11.

6. **opened the window**. ver. +*13. Ge 6:16. 2 K 13:17. Da 6:10.

7. **a raven**. Ge 4:16. Le 11:15. 1 K 17:4, 6. Jb 38:41. Ps 147:9. Pr 30:17. SS 5:11. Is 34:11. Lk 12:24. Ep 4:20. **went forth to and fro**. Heb. in going forth and returning.

8. **a dove**. ver. 10-12. SS 1:15. 2:11, 12, 14. Mt 10:16. Lk 3:22. Jn 3:6. **face**. Ge +1:2.

9. **found**. Dt 28:65. Ps 55:6. Ezk 7:16. Mt *11:28. Jn 16:33. He 13:14. **and she**. Ps 116:7. Is 60:8. **face**. Ge +1:2. **pulled her**. Heb. caused her to come.

10. **stayed**. Ps *40:1. Is 8:17. 26:8. Ro 8:25. **seven**. ver. 12. Ge 7:4, 10.

11. **dove**. ver. +8. **evening**. Ge 15:12. Zc 14:7. **an olive**. Ne 8:15. SS 2:12. Zc 4:12-14. Ro 10:15. Ep 1:14. **abated**. ver. +3.

12. **And he**. Pr 27:14. 130:5, 6. Is 8:17. 25:9. 26:8. *30:18. Hab 2:3. Ja 5:7, 8. **seven**. ver. 10. Ge 2:2, 3. **dove**. ver. +8. Is 38:14. Je 48:28. **returned**. 2 P 3:13. Re 21:4.

13. A.M. 1657. B.C. 2347. **six**. Ge 7:6, 11. **first**. Ex 40:2. 2 Ch 29:17. Ezr 7:9. 10:17. Ezk 45:18. Lk 1:5. 2:1, 2. 2 P 1:16. 1 J 1:1. **covering**. Ex 26:14. 35:11. 36:19. 39:34. 40:19. Nu 3:25. 4:5, 10, 11, 12,

25. ✓171N. Figure of speech Synecdoche of the Whole B637: when the whole is put for a part. Here, the whole is put for one of its parts. When Noah removed the covering he did not remove the whole roof but the covering of the window. For other instances of this figure see Ex 22:13. 1 S 5:4. +19:24. Jb *22:6. 24:7, 10. Ps 102:5. Is 20:2, 3. Mi 1:8. Mt 25:36, 43. Jn 21:7. Ac 27:33. 1 C *4:11. He 10:5. Ja 2:15. **face.** Ge +1:2. **dry.** Ge 1:9.

14. **second month.** Ge 7:11, 13, 14. **dried.** Ex 14:21. Is 19:5. Je 23:10. 50:38. Jl 1:20.

15. **And God.** Ge 6:8, 13-21. 12:17. 20:3. 21:17, 19. 31:24, 29. 33:3-10. 35:3. 39:2, 21. **spake.** Ge 3:8. 11:7. 22:12. 35:12, 13. Ex 19:19.

16. **Go forth.** Ge 7:1, 7, 13. Jsh 3:17. 4:10, 16-18. Ps 91:11. 121:8. Da 3:25, 26. Zc 9:11. Ac 16:27, 28, 37-39. **with.** Ge 7:+1, 7. 1 P 3:20. 2 P 2:5.

17. **Bring.** Ge 7:14, 15. **flesh.** Ge 7:15. Ac ●17:26. 1 C 15:39. **fowl.** Ge 1:20. 2:19. 6:20. 9:2. Dt 14:11. Ps 8:8. Da 2:38. Mt 6:26. Ja 3:7. **cattle.** Ge 9:10. Ps 148:10. **creeping.** Le 11:21. Dt 14:19. Ac 10:12. Ja 3:7. **breed.** Ge 1:22, 28. 9:1, 7. Ps 107:38. 144:13, 14. Je *31:17, 28.

18. **went.** Ps 121:8. **sons.** Ge 5:32. 6:10. +7:1.

19. **Every.** Ge 7:14. **kinds.** Heb. families.

20. **builded.** Ge 4:4. 12:7, 8. 13:4, 18. 22:9. 26:25. 33:20. 35:1, 7. Ex *20:24, 25. 24:4-8. Jg 6:24. Ro 12:1. He *13:10, 15, 16. 1 P 2:5, 9. **altar.** Le 17:11. Dt 27:6. Jg 13:19. **clean beast.** Ge 7:2. Le ch. 11. 20:25. Dt 14:4. **fowl.** Dt 14:11, 20. **burnt offerings.** Ge 22:2. Ex 10:25. Le ch. 1. +*23:12.

21. **Lord.** Ps 91:4. He 12:29. **smelled.** Le 1:*9, 13, 17. 26:31. SS 4:10, 11. Is *65:5. Ezk *20:41. Am 5:21, 22. 2 C *2:15. Ep *5:2. Ph *4:18. ✓22C15. Figure of speech Anthropopatheia or Anthropomorphism B888. Human actions are attributed to God: smelling. For other instances of this figure see Ex 29:18, 25, 41. Le 1:9. 2:12. 3:16. 8:21. Nu 28:2. Ezk 20:28, 41. 2 C 2:15. Ep *5:2. Ph 4:18. **sweet savour.** Ex 29:18, 25. Le 4:31. Nu 15:3. Ezk 6:13. 16:19mg. 20:28, *41. Heb. savour of rest. ✓147D, Ge +1:29. Ge 5:29mg. Ex 29:18. Nu 15:7. Ezr 6:10. Jn 4:24. He 13:15, 16. **said.** Ge 24:45. 27:41. 1 S 27:1. Ho 7:2. **his heart.** ✓22A17, Ge +6:6. Ge 6:5, 6. Je 3:15. 7:31. **curse.** Ge 3:17. 4:12. 5:29. 6:7, 13, 17. Is *54:9. Col 3:13. **for.** or, though. **imagination.** Ge +6:5. Dt 31:21. 1 Ch +*28:9. Jb 14:4. 15:14-16. Ps *51:5. *58:3. Pr *20:9. Ec *7:20. Is 47:12, 15. 48:8. *53:6. Je 8:6. *17:9. 18:12. Mt *15:19. Jn 3:6. Ro 1:21. 3:10, *23. *8:7, 8. Ep *2:1-3. Ja *1:14, 15. 4:1, 2. 1 J 5:19. **youth.** Jb 14:4. Ps 51:5. Ec 7:20. 12:1. Ep 2:3. **neither.** Ge 9:11-15. Is +*54:9, 10. **as I.** 2 P *3:6, 7.

22. **While the earth remaineth.** Ge +9:12. Ps *72:+5, 7, 17. 78:69. 89:36, 37. 104:5. 119:90, 91. Ec +*1:4. Mt ●*24:35. Heb. as yet all the days of the earth. Is +*54:8. **seedtime.** Ge 45:6. Ex 34:21. Ps 74:16, 17. SS 2:11, 12. Is +*54:9. Je 5:24. Ja 5:7. **and.** ✓148. Figure of speech Polysyndeton; or, Many Ands B210: the repetition of the word "and" at the beginning of successive clauses. This figure asks us to unhurriedly stop and notice each point, weigh each matter, and consider each particular thus added and emphasized; there is never any climax at the end. This figure should be considered with its opposite, ✓41. Asyndeton or No Ands, Ge +10:1. For other instances of Polysyndeton see Ge 1:2, 26. 3:1. 6:18. 7:7, 8, 13,

21-23. 14:16. 19:12, 16, 19. 20:14. 22:9, 11. 24:35. 25:34. 43:8. Ex 1:7. Dt 16:11. Jsh 7:11, 24. 1 S 17:34-36. 2 K 2:12, 14. 5:26. 1 Ch 29:11-13. Ps 107:35-37. Is 2:11-19. 3:17. 37:37. Je 31:28. Hg 1:11. Zc *6:12, 13. Mt 7:25. 24:29-31. Mk 3:21-35. Lk 1:31, 32. 7:11-18, 38. 10:27. 12:45, 46. ✓14:21. 15:20, 22, 23. Jn *10:27-28. Ac *1:8. Ro 8:29, 30. 9:4. 1 C 1:30. Ep 4:31. 1 Th 2:11. 2 T 4:17, 18. He 13:8. Ja 1:24. 4:13. 2 P 1:5-7. Re 1:11. 3:17. 6:15. 12:2, 11. 13:1. 18:12, 13. **day.** Je ✓31:35, 36. 33:20-26.

GENESIS 9

The Lord blesses Noah and his family; grants them additionally flesh for food; prohibits them from eating blood; and requires that murderers should be punished with death, 1-7. His covenant with Noah and his posterity, of which the rainbow was constituted a pledge, 8-17. Noah's family and employment, 18-20. His drunkenness, and the different behavior of his sons; with his prophecy, age, and death, 21-29.

1. **blessed.** ver. 7. Ge 1:22, 28. 2:3. 8:17. 24:60. Ps 112:1. 128:3, 4. Is 11:6-8. 51:2. **Be.** ver. 7, 19. Ge 1:28. 8:17. 10:32. Jn 12:24. 15:2.

2. **the fear.** Ge 1:28. 2:19. 35:5. Le 26:6, 22. Jb 5:22, 23. Ps 8:4-8. 104:20-23. Ezk 34:25. Ho 2:18. Ja 3:7.

3. **Every.** Le ch. 11. 22:8. Dt 12:15. 14:3-21. Jn 6:53. Ac 10:12-15. 1 T 4:3-5. ✓66. Figure of speech Epanadiplosis; or, Encircling B245: the repetition of the same word or words at the beginning and end of a sentence; here, "Every" and "all things" are the same word in Hebrew. The words thus enclosed are given emphasis. For other instances of this figure see Ex 32:16. Le 7:19. 23:42. Nu 3:33. 8:12. 31:40. Nu 32:1, 41. Dt 31:3. Jsh 15:25. Jg 11:1. 1 S 26:23. 2 S 9:12. 19:7. 1 K 22:47. 2 K 23:25. 1 Ch 9:8. Ne 11:21. Est 7:7. Ps *27:14. 53:2. 122:7, 8. Ec 1:2. 7:2. Mk 7:14-16. *13:35-37. Lk *12:4, 5. *12:5. Jn ✓3:8. Ro 8:24. Ga 2:20. Ph *4:4. Ja 2:14-16. **even.** Ge *1:29, 30. Ps 104:14, 15. Ro 14:3, 14, 17, 20. 1 C 10:23, 25, 26, 31. Col 2:16, 21, 22. 1 T 4:3, 4. **green.** Ge 1:30. Ex 10:15. Nu 22:4. Ps 37:2. Is 15:6.

4. **the life.** Ge +*2:19. Le 3:17n. 7:26. *17:10-14. 19:26. Nu 31:28n. Dt 12:16, 23. 14:21. 15:23. 1 S 14:33, 34. Ac 15:20, 25, 29. 1 T *4:4. **blood.** Ro 6:23. He *9:22. **not eat.** Ezk 33:25. Ac 21:25.

5. **lives.** ✚S#5315h, *nephesh*, Ge +44:30. ✓121A7. Figure of speech Metonymy of the Cause B544. Metonymy, or change of noun, is a figure by which one name or noun is used instead of another, to which it stands in a certain relation. Here, by Metonymy of Cause, the word "soul" (Hebrew, *nephesh*; Greek, *psyche*) is used for "life," which is the effect of it. For instances of this usage see Ge *37:21. Ex 4:19. Le *17:11. Jg 9:17. 1 S 26:21. 1 K 2:23. Est 8:11. Ps 38:19. 38:12. 56:13. Je 40:14. 45:5. La 5:9. Jon 2:7. Mt +2:20. 6:25. 10:39. 16:25. *20:28. Mk 3:4. 8:35. 10:45. Lk 6:9. 9:24, 56. 12:22, 23. 14:26. 17:33. Jn 10:11, 15, 17. *12:25. 13:37, 38. 15:13. Ac 15:26. 20:10, 24. 27:10, 22. Ro 11:3. 16:4. Ph 2:30. 1 J 3:16. Re 12:11. **every beast.** Ex *21:28, 29. **require.** Ge 42:22. 2 Ch 24:22. Ps 9:12. Ezk *3:18. Ac *20:20, 26, 27. **hand of every.** Ex 20:13. **beast.** ✓155B. Figure of speech Prosopopoeia; or, Personification B863: things represented as persons; here, animals or beasts are

spoken of as intelligent and responsible. For other instances of this figure see Jb 12:7, 8. 41:29. Jl 1:4, 6. **at**. Ge 4:9, 10. Le 19:16. Nu 35:31-33. Dt 21:1-9. Ps 9:12. Mt 23:35. 1 J 3:15. Re 19:2. **hand**. *f*144A5. Figure of speech Pleonasm; or, Redundancy B410: when more words are used than the grammar requires. For other instances of this figure involving this idiom see Ex 4:13. 1 S 17:37. 1 K 8:53. 11:12. 2 K 17:13. 1 Ch 6:31. 25:2mg, 6mg. 2 Ch 23:18. 29:27. Ps 7:3. 22:20. 49:15. *107:2. Is *64:6. Mk 6:2. Lk 1:71. Ac 5:12. 7:25, 35. 15:23. Ga 3:19. Re 19:2. **man's**. *f*24.O. Figure of speech Antimereia of the Noun B505, the latter of two nouns used for an adjective. For other instances of this figure see Mt 3:17. Ro *3:23. 8:3. Col 1:11, 13. **brother**. Ac 17:26. **I require**. T#315. ver. 6. Ex *21:12-17. Nu 35:30-34. Dt *19:18, 19. 25:1-3. 32:35. Pr *17:15. *20:26. 28:17. Ac 25:10, 11. Ro 13:4. **life**. Ge +2:7. ✠S#5315h, *nephesh*, Ge +44:30.

6. **sheddeth**. Ex 21:25. Dt 32:43. Jn 19:11. **by man**. Ex *21:12-14. 22:2, 3. Le 17:4. *24:17. Nu 35:12, 25, 30, 33. Dt 19:6. Jsh 10:13. Jg 16:28. 2 S 4:8, 11. 1 K 2:5, 6, 28-34. Mt *26:52. Ro ❶12:19. 13:4. Re 13:10. 19:11. 21:8. **in the image**. Ge *1:26, 27. 5:1. Ps 51:4. 1 C 11:7. Ja 3:9.

7. **be ye fruitful**. ver. 1, 19. Ge 1:28. 8:17.

8. **God**. Heb. Elohim. Ge 1:1. **spake**. Ge 3:8. +8:15. **Noah**. Ge 5:28, 29, 32.

9. **establish my covenant**. ver. 11, +16, 17. Ge 6:18. +*17:7, 8. 22:17. Is +*54:9, 10. Je √31:35, 36. 33:20. Ro 1:3.

10. **with**. ver. 15, 16. Ge 8:1. Jb ch. 38, 41. Ps 36:5, 6. *145:9. Jon 4:11. **creature**. Heb. *nephesh*, soul. Ge +*2:19.

11. **And I**. Ge *8:21, 22. Is *54:9. **neither shall all**. Ge 7:21-23. 8:21, 22. Is +*54:9. 2 P +*3:7, 11.

12. **token**. ver. 13, 17. Ge *17:11. Ex 3:12. +*12:13. 13:16. Jsh 2:12. Ezk +9:4. Mt 26:26-28. 1 C 11:23-25. Ep 1:13. **creature**. ver. 10. Ge +*2:19. **perpetual**. Heb. *olam*, ✠S#5769h. Ex 29:9. 31:16. Le 3:17. 24:9. 25:34. Nu 19:21. Ps 78:66. Je 5:22. 18:16. 23:40. 25:9, 12. 49:13. 50:5. 51:39, 57. Ezk 35:5, 9. 46:14. Hab 3:6. Zp 2:9. **generations**. Ge +8:22. *13:15. 17:7, 19. Ex 3:15. Dt *5:29. *29:29. 2 S √7:24-26. 1 Ch 23:25. Ps 45:17. √72:5. 89:4. 102:*12, 24. 106:31. 145:13. 146:10. Ec +*1:4. Is √9:6, 7. 51:8. 59:21. Je √31:35-36. 32:38-40. Ezk 37:24-27. 43:7. Da 2:44, 45. 7:13, 14, 18, 27. Mt 8:11, 12. 19:28. Lk 1:32, 33, 55. 13:28-30. Re 11:15. 21:3, 24. 22:4, 5.

13. **bow**. Ge 27:3h. 48:22h. Ezk 1:28. Re 4:3. 10:1. **cloud**. Dt 4:11. Jg 5:4. 2 S 22:12. 23:4. 1 K 18:45. Jb 20:6. 22:14. 26:8. 37:16. 38:34, 37. Ps 18:11, 12. 77:17. 97:2. 104:3. 147:8. Ec 11:3, 4. 12:2. Is 5:6. 14:14. Je 4:13. Ezk 30:3. 34:12. Da 7:13. Jl 2:2. Na 1:3. Zp 1:15. Mt *24:30. 26:64. Mk *13:26. *14:62. 1 Th *4:17. Re *1:7. **token**. ver. +12.

14. **bow**. Ezk 1:28. Re 4:3. 10:1. **cloud**. Ge 2:5, 6. 1 K 18:43-45. Jb 37:21-22. Ec 11:4. Mt 16:2, 3. Lk 12:54-57.

15. **remember**. *f*22C3, Ge +8:1. Ge +*8:1. Ex 28:12. Le 26:42-45. Dt *7:9. 1 K 8:23. Ne 9:32. Ps 105:8, 9. *106:45. Je 14:21. Ezk 16:60. Lk 1:72. **creature**. Heb. *nephesh*. This is an instance where *nephesh* is used alike of lower creatures and man; rendered "creature" here and ver. 16; "the life," Le 17:11, 14, 14, 14; "soul," Nu 31:28. ver. 10. Ge +*2:7, 19. For

the other uses of *nephesh* see Ge +2:7. **the waters**. ver. 11. Ge 8:21. Is √54:8-10. 2 P 3:7.

16. **bow**. ver. 13, 14. **cloud**. ver. +13. **remember**. *f*22C3, Ge +8:1. ver. +15. **everlasting**. Heb. *olam*, Ge +17:7. **covenant**. ver. 9-11. Ge 8:21, +22. 13:15. 17:13, 19. Le 24:8. Nu 10:8. Dt 7:9. 1 S 1:22. 2 S 7:13. +*23:5. 1 Ch 16:17. Ps 89:3, 4. *105:8-10. 111:5. Is √9:7. 24:5. √54:8-10. +√55:3. 59:21. 61:8. Je *31:31-34. *32:40. √33:20, 21. Ezk 16:60. 37:26. He 6:18. 13:20. **creature**. Heb. *nephesh*, ver. +15n. ver. 10. Ge +*2:7. +*2:19.

17. **token**. ver. +12, 13. **covenant**. ver. +16.

18. **sons**. Ge 5:32. 7:7. Lk 3:36. **Shem**. Ge 5:32. 7:13. 10:1, 21. 1 Ch 1:4. **Ham**. Ge 7:13. 10:1, 6. **Japheth**. Ge 7:13. 10:1, 2. **Canaan**. Heb. Chenaan. Ge 10:6, 15.

19. **These**. Ge 5:32. 10:1. 1 Ch 1:4. **and of them**. Ge 8:17. 10:2-32. 1 Ch 1:4-28. 1 P 3:20. **whole**. Ge 11:4, 8. Ml 2:10. Ac 17:26.

20. **began**. Mt 26:47. Mk 10:41. 11:15. Lk *3:23. **to be**. *f*63BC. Figure of speech Ellipsis B36: where a gap is left in the sentence, which means that a word or words are left out or omitted. Here, absolute ellipsis when the verb infinitive is lacking after another verb, personal or impersonal. For other instances of this figure see 1 K 7:47. Pr 21:5. Mk 15:8. (Lk 13:33). (Ro 4:25). **an husbandman**. Ge 2:15. 3:18, 19, 23. 4:2. 5:29. 2 K 25:12. Pr 11:11. 12:11. Ec 5:9. Is 28:24-26. Am 5:16. Zc 13:5. Mt 21:33-41. Jn 15:1. 2 T 2:6. Ja 5:7. **planted**. Dt 20:6. 28:30. Pr 24:30. SS 1:6. 1 C 9:7.

21. **wine**. ver. +24. **drunken**. Ge 6:9. 19:32-36. Pr *20:1. *23:31, 32. 31:4. Ec *7:20. Lk *21:34. Ro 13:13. 1 C *10:12. Ga +√5:21. 1 T 4:4, 5. T 2:2. **uncovered**. Ge 3:7. Hab *2:15, 16. Lk 10:30. Re 3:17, 18.

22. **Ham**. ver. +18, 25. Ge 10:6, 15-19. 1 Ch 1:8, 13-16. **nakedness**. Le 18:7. Ezk 22:10. Hab *2:15. **told**. 2 S 1:19, 20. Ps 35:20, 21. 40:15. 70:3. Pr 12:13. *17:9. 25:9. *30:17. Ob 12, 13. Mt 18:15. 1 C *13:6. Ga 6:1. Ep 5:3, 4.

23. **garment**. Ge 37:34. Ex 22:27. **and went**. Ex *20:12. Le 19:32. Ro 13:7. Ga *6:1. 1 T 5:1, 17, 19. 1 P 2:17. *4:8. **nakedness**. Le 18:7. Is 58:7.

24. **awoke**. 1 S 25:37. Pr *23:35. Jl 1:5. Hab 2:7. 1 C 15:34. **wine**. 1 S 1:14. 25:37. Pr *20:1. 23:29-35. Hab *2:15. **younger**. Ge 27:15, 42. 42:13, 32. 44:2. 1 S 17:14.

25. **Cursed**. ver. 22. Ge 3:14. 4:11. 27:12. 49:7. Ex +20:5. Dt *27:16. 28:18. Pr *26:2. Mt 25:41. Jn 8:34. **Canaan**. Dt. 7:1. 20:17. Le 18:3. Jsh *17:13. Ro 1:27. **servant of**. Ge 10:15-20. 15:16. 25:23. 27:29. 37:10. 49:8. Jsh 9:23, 27. Jg *1:28-30. 1 K 9:20, 21. 2 Ch 8:7, 8. Pr 30:17. Jn 8:34. **servants**. *f*147H. Figure of speech Polyptoton; or, Many Inflections B283: the repetition of the same part of speech in different inflections; here, a noun is repeated in the genitive plural in order to express very emphatically the superlative degree which does not exist in Hebrew. Thus, "servant of servants" indicates the most degraded of servants, or the most abject slave. For other instances of this figure see Ex 26:33. Nu 3:32. Dt 10:17. 1 K 8:27. Ec 1:2. SS 1:1. Ezk 26:7. Da 2:37, 47. 8:25. Ho 10:15. Mi 2:4. Ph 3:5. 1 T 6:15. Re *1:6. 17:14. 19:16.

26. **Blessed**. Ge 14:20. 24:27. Ex 18:10. Dt 8:10. 33:26. 1 K 1:48. 1 Ch 29:20. Ps *144:15. Ezk 48:35. Lk 1:68. Ro +*9:5. 11:33. He *11:16. **the Lord**. Ge

11:10-26. *12:1-3. Lk 3:23-36. **Shem.** T#1875. He 11:16. **his servant.** *or,* servant to them. ver. +18, 27. Ge 27:37, 40. Jg 1:28. 1 K 9:21. 2 Ch 8:8.

27. **enlarge.** *or,* persuade. Ge 10:2-5. Dt 32:8. 1 Ch 1:5. Is 54:2. 60:3-9. 66:19. Ml *1:11. Ep *2:19. **Japheth.** ♪121A5. Figure of speech Metonymy; or, Change of Noun B544: the change of one noun for another related noun; parents and ancestors are frequently put for their posterity, and for children: and the name of the stock or race is put for the patronymic. Here, Metonymy of the Cause, where Japheth is put for his posterity. May also be considered as ♪121T3. Figure of Speech Metonymy of the Adjunct B608: some circumstances pertaining to the subject is put for the subject itself; here, the name of a man for his posterity. For other instances of this figure see Ge 12:3. 18:18. 26:4. 28:14. Ex 5:2. Nu 23:21. 24:5, *17. Dt 25:17. 33:28. 1 K 18:17, 18. Ps 14:7. 135:4. Ezk 34:23. Am 7:9, 16. Ml *1:2, 3. Ro √9:13. **dwell.** Is 11:10. Ho 2:14. Ml 1:11. Ac 17:14. Ro 11:12. 15:12. Ep 2:13, 14, 19. 3:6, 13. He 11:9, 10.

28. **lived.** Ge 17:18. 19:20. 25:7. **flood.** Ge 7:6.

29. A.M. 2006. B.C. 1998. **nine.** Ge 5:5, 20, 27, 32. 11:11-25. Ps 90:10. **died.** Ge +*2:17.

GENESIS 10

The posterity of Noah, by Japheth, 1-5; by Ham, with some particulars concerning Nimrod, and the descendants of Canaan, 6-20; by Shem, 21-32.

1. **are the.** Ge 2:4. 5:1. 6:9. Mt 1:1. **generations.** Ge 17:20. **Shem.** Ge 5:32. 6:10. 7:13. 9:18. 1 Ch 1:4. ♪41. Figure of speech Asyndeton; or, No-ands B137: without conjunctions. Contrast the Polysyndeton of Ge 7:13 (♪148, Ge +8:22). This figure asks us to hurry past the details listed and focus upon the climax to which they lead. For other instances of this figure see Ge 19:17. Ex 15:9, 10. Jg 5:27. 1 S 15:6. Is 21:11. 33:7-12. Ezk 33:15, 16. Mk 2:27, 28. *7:21-23. 16:6, 17, 18. Lk 1:17. 14:13, 14. 17:27-30. Ro 1:29-31. 2:19-23. 1 C 3:12, 13. 4:8. 12:28-31. 13:4-7. 13:13. 15:41-44. 2 C 7:2-4. 7:5, 6. Ga 5:19-21. 5:22. Ep *4:32. Ph 3:5-7. 1 Th 5:14-18. 1 T 1:17. *4:13-16. 2 T 3:1-5. 3:10, 11. √3:16, 17. 4:2, 3. He 11:32-38. Ja 1:19, 20. 5:6. Re 3:7, 8. **Ham.** ver. 6-20. Ge 9:24. **Japheth.** ver. 2-5, 21. 1 Ch 1:5. ♪68. Figure of speech Epanodos; or, Inversion B299: the repetition of the same words in an inverse order (but the same sense); after two, three, or more words have been mentioned, they are repeated, not in the same order again, but backward. Here, Shem is mentioned first, but elaborated last in ver. 21-31; Ham is mentioned second, but elaborated next to last, ver. 6-20; Japheth is mentioned last, but elaborated upon first in ver. 2-5. For other instances of this figure see Ex 9:31 (flax, barley, barley, flax). Ps 9:10 (note cause, effect, effect, cause: know, trust, not forsaken, seek). Is 6:10 (heart, ears, eyes, eyes, ears, heart). 24:4, 5. Ro 2:14g (not, law, law, not). 2 C 1:3 (God, Father, Father, God). 9:6 (sow, sparingly, sparingly, reap; sow, bountifully, bountifully, reap). 3 J 11 (evil, good, good, evil). **and unto.** Ge 9:1, 7, 19. **flood.** Ge 6:17. 8:13. 9:11, 15. 11:10. Jb 22:16. Ps 29:10. Is 54:9. Mt 24:38. Lk 17:27.

2. **sons.** ver. 21. 1 Ch 1:5-7. Is 66:19. Ezk 27:7, 12-14, 19. 38:2, 6, 15. 39:1. Re 20:8. **Gomer.** i.e. *complete, perfect,* ✱S#1586h. ver. 3. 1 Ch 1:5, 6. Ezk

38:6. Ho 1:3. (1) A son of Japheth, Ge 10:2, 3; 1 Ch 1:5, 6. (2) The people descended from him, who are supposed to have lived on the north side of the Black Sea, Ezk 38:6. (3) The wife of the prophet Hosea, Ho 1:3. **Magog.** i.e. *expansion, extension; region of Gog,* ✱S#4031h. 1 Ch 1:5. Ezk 38:2. 39:6. Re 20:8. (1) A son of Japheth, Ge 10:2; 1 Ch 1:5. (2) The word is used to denote the people descended from him, Ezk 38:2; 39:6. (3) It is used prophetically to denote one of the parties in the last assault on the camp of the saints and the beloved city, Re 20:8. **Madai.** i.e. *extended of the Lord,* ✱S#4074h. 2 K 17:6, Medes. 18:11. 1 Ch *1:5. Ezr +6:2, Medes. Est +1:3, Media. Da 11:2. **Javan.** i.e. *supple; clay; mired; effervescing,* ✱S#3120h. ver. 4. 1 Ch 1:5, 7. Is 66:19. Ezk 27:13, 19. Da 8:21h. 10:20h,mg. 11:2mg. Jl 3:6h. Zc 9:13h. **Tubal.** i.e. *flowing forth; carried or led,* ✱S#8422h. Ge ●4:22. 1 Ch 1:5. Is 66:19. Ezk 27:13. 32:26. 38:2, 3. 39:1. **Meshech.** i.e. *drawing out,* ✱S#4902h. 1 Ch 1:5, 17. Ps 120:5. Ezk 27:13. 32:26. 38:2, 3. 39:1. **Tiras.** i.e. *desire, longing; destroyer,* 1 Ch 1:5. Not mentioned elsewhere in Scripture. Tiras has been identified with Tarshish by some. See on ver. 4.

3. **Gomer.** ver. 2. 1 Ch 1:5. Ezk 38:6. **Ashkenaz.** i.e. *strong, fortified,* ✱S#813h. 1 Ch 1:6. Je 51:27. **Riphath.** i.e. *healing; bruising; a crusher, a terror,* ✱S#7384h. 1 Ch 1:6. **Togarmah.** i.e. *breaking or gnawing of bones,* ✱S#8425h. 1 Ch 1:6. Ezk 27:14. 38:6.

4. A.M. 1666. B.C. 2338. **Elishah.** i.e. *God of my salvation,* ✱S#473h. 1 Ch 1:7. Ezk 27:7. **Tarshish.** i.e. *breaking, subjection,* ✱S#8659h. 1 K 10:22, 22. 22:48. 1 Ch 1:7. 7:10, Tharshish. 2 Ch 9:21, 21. 20:36, 37. Est 1:14. Ps 48:7. 72:10. Is 2:16. 23:1, 6, 10, 14. 60:9. 66:19. Je 10:9. Ezk 27:12, 25. 38:13. Jon 1:3, 3, 3. 4:2. (1) One of the sons of Javan, the grandson of Noah, Ge 10:4; 1 Ch 1:7. (2) One of the seven princes of Persia who "saw the king's face," Est 1:13, 14. (3) Often mentioned place in the Old Testament, always as a distant place and situated on the sea-coast, but it has never been identified. Some consider it the same as Tarsis in Cilicia, and others as *Tartessus* in southern Spain, 1 K 10:22; 2 Ch 9:21. **Kittim.** i.e. *subduers, hidden; breaking, small,* ✱S#3794h. Nu 24:24. 1 Ch 1:7. Is 23:1, 12. Je 2:10. Ezk 27:6. Da 11:30, Chittim. **Dodanim.** *or,* Rodanim. i.e. *leaders,* ✱S#1721h. 1 Ch 1:7.

5. A.M. 1757. B.C. 2247. **isles.** ver. 25. Est 10:1. Ps 72:10. 97:1. Is 20:6. 24:15. 40:15. 41:5. 42:4, *10. 49:1. 51:5. 59:18. 60:9. 66:19. Je 2:10. 25:22. 31:10. 47:4mg. Ezk 26:15, 18. 27:3, 6. 39:6. Da 11:18. Zp 2:11. **Gentiles.** i.e. *foreigners,* ✢S#1471h. Ge 14:1, 9. Jsh 12:23. Jg 4:2, 13, 16. Is 9:1. 11:10. 42:1, 6. 49:6, 22. 60:3, 5, 11, 16. 61:6, 9. 62:2. 66:12, 19. Je 4:7. 14:22. 16:19. 46:1. Ezk 4:13. Ho 8:8. Jl 3:9. Mi 5:8. Zc 1:21. Ml 1:11. **divided.** Dt +32:8. ♪107. Figure of speech Hysterologia; or, the First, Last B705: the first of two things put last; here, the dispersion of the nations is mentioned before the cause of it. For other instances of this figure see Ge 12:1 w 11:31, 32. 30:22-24. 38:1. Jg 20, 21 w 18:1 & 19:1 (see Jg 18:30. 20:28. 1:8, 21 w ●19:10-12). 1 S 16-18. 2 S 23, 24. Is 38:21, 22. Am 6:2. Mt 27:52, 53. Lk *4:5 (mountain), 9 (temple) w Mt 4:5 (temple), 8 (mountain). Re 12. **in their lands.** ver. 20, 31. Re 5:9. 7:9. 10:11. 11:9. 13:7. 14:6. 17:15. **after his.** ver. 20. Ge 11:1-9.

6. A.M. 1676. B.C. 2228. **And the.** Ge 9:22. 1 Ch

1:8-16. 4:40. Ps 78:51. 105:23, 27. 106:22. **Ham.** ver. 1. **Cush.** i.e. *black; terror; blackness, burning; Ethiopian*, ✛S#3568h. ver. 7, 8. Ge 2:13mg. 1 Ch 1:8, 9. 2 Ch 12:3. 14:9, 12, 13. 16:8. Est 1:1. 8:9. Jb 28:19. Ps 68:31. 87:4. Is 18:1mg. 20:3-5. 37:9. 43:3. 45:14. Je 13:23. 46:9. Ezk 29:10. 30:4, 5, 9. 38:5. Na 3:9. Zp 3:10. (1) The oldest son of Ham, Ge 10:6, 7, 8; 1 Ch 1:8, 9, 10, brother of Mizraim, Phut, and Canaan, and, through his five sons, ancestor of the Cushites, who, moving in a southwestern direction from Chaldea through Arabia, crossed the Red Sea and formed an empire in the land south of Egypt, the present Nubia, but then called Ethiopia. (2) The name is applied in the original Hebrew to the people descended from Cush, but in the English Version it is translated Ethiopian. (3) It is frequently used to denote the land where the descendants of Cush lived; in which case it is generally translated *Ethiopia*, Is 11:11. (4) A man of the tribe of Benjamin, who appears to have been an enemy of David, Ps 7, title. **Mizraim.** i.e. *double distress*, S#4714h. ver. 13. Ge 50:11. 1 Ch 1:8, 11. Is 7:18. 19:6. 37:25. **Phut.** i.e. *extension; afflicted; a bow*, ✱S#6316h. 1 Ch 1:8. Is 66:19. Je 46:9mg. Ezk 27:10. 30:5. 38:5. Na 3:9, Put. (1) One of the sons of Ham, Ge 10:6. (2) The country which his descendants inhabited. (3) Phut was the ancestor of an African people usually known by the same name, and it is used in connection with Persia and with Lud, Ezk 27:10. **Canaan.** i.e. *humiliated; subjection; merchant, servant*, S#3667h. ver. 15. Ge 9:18, 22, 25, 26, 27. 1 Ch 1:8, 13.

7. **Cush.** ver. 6. **Seba.** i.e. *eminent; drink thou*, ✱S#5434h. 1 Ch 1:9. Ps 72:10. Is 43:3. (1) One of the sons of Cush, the son of Ham, Ge 10:7; 1 Ch 1:9. (2) The country occupied by his descendants. It is supposed to have been the southern part of Upper Egypt, Ps 72:10; Is 43:3. **Havilah.** i.e. *circular; trembling; childbirth; anguish*, ✱S#2341h. ver. 29. Ge 2:11. 25:18. 2 S 15:7. 1 Ch 1:9, 23. (1) A country supposed to lie on the east side of the river Indus—that is, in north-western India—or perhaps west of the Indus, along the shores toward the Persian Gulf, Ge 2:11. (2) A descendant of Ham, Ge 10:7; 1 Ch 1:9. (3) A descendant of Shem, Ge 10:29; 1 Ch 1:23. (4) A country or district apparently east of the Amalekites, Ge 25:18; 1 S 15:7. **Sabtah.** i.e. *terror; breaking through*, ✱S#5454h. 1 Ch 1:9. **Raamah.** i.e. *thunder; quivering in the wind; trembling; roaring*, ✱S#7484h. 1 Ch 1:9. Ezk 27:22. (1) One of the sons of Cush, the son of Ham. (2) A country which appears to have been named after Raamah, the son of Cush, and to have been settled by his descendants. It was probably on the southwest shore of the Persian Gulf, Ezk 27:22. **Sabtecha.** i.e. *beating, striking; terror*, ✱S#5455h. 1 Ch 1:9. **Sheba.** i.e. *oath*, ✛S#7614h. Ge 25:3. 1 K +10:1. 1 Ch *1:9. Ezk 27:22, 23. (1) A descendant of Ham, Ge 10:7; 1 Ch 1:9. (2) A descendant of Shem, Ge 10:28; 1 Ch 1:22. (3) A descendant of Abraham by Keturah, Ge 25:3; 1 Ch 1:32. (4) S#7652h. A man of Benjamin who raised a rebellion against David, 2 S +20:1. (5) S#7652h. One of the chiefs of Gad, 1 Ch 5:13. (6) S#7614h. A very fertile country in Arabia, adjoining the Red Sea, 1 K +10:1. (7) A town of Simeon, Jsh 19:2. **Dedan.** i.e. *leading forward; low*, ✱S#1719h. Ge 25:3, 3. 1 Ch 1:9, 32. Is 21:13, Dedanim, S#1720h. Je 25:23. 49:8. Ezk 25:13. 27:15, 20. 38:13. (1) A grand-

son of Cush, Ge 10:7; 1 Ch 1:9. (2) A son of Jokshan, Ge 25:3; 1 Ch 1:32. (3) A country in the Arabian peninsula, not far from the Edomites, Je 25:23; Ezk 25:13.

8. **Cush.** ver. 6. **Nimrod.** i.e. *rebel*, ✱S#5248h. ver. 9. 1 Ch 1:10. Mi 5:6. **mighty.** Ge 6:4h. Dt 10:17. Jsh 1:14. 6:2. 8:3. 10:2. Jg 5:13. **earth.** Jb 24:13. 34:37.

9. **a mighty.** Ge 6:4. 25:27. 27:40. Je 16:16. Ezk 13:18. Mi 7:2. 𝆑100. Figure of speech Hypallage; or, Interchange B535: interchange of construction. lit. a strong man of hunting. According to ordinary usage, the word "hunting" would be (by the figure Enallage B490: Is 32:12. La 1:7. Ro 7:24) the qualifying word: a hunting man of strength; but, by Hypallage, there is an Interchange, by which the noun becomes the adjective: a mighty hunter. For other instances of this figure see Ge 29:14. Le 12:4. Dt 12:3. Jsh 2:6. 2 S 12:27. 1 K *17:14. Ne 10:34. Jb 31:27mg. Ps 19:13. 139:23, 24mg. Pr 26:23. Is 30:30mg. Je 11:19. Ezk 21:29. Mt 8:3. Ac *5:20. Ro 5:17. *7:24. 9:31. 15:19. 2 C 3:7. Ga *6:1. Ep 1:9. He 9:15, 23. Ja 2:17. 3:4. Re 21:24. **before.** Ge 7:1. Nu 16:2. Jsh 7:12, 13. 1 S 26:12. 1 Ch 14:8. 2 Ch 14:10. Jb 23:4. **it is said.** 𝆑138A. Figure of speech Paroemia; or, Proverb B756: a wayside saying in common use, an adage. Here, a proverb quoted as already being in use as such. For other instances of this figure see Nu 21:27. 1 S 10:12. 24:13. 2 S 20:18. Je 31:29. Ezk 16:44. Lk 4:23. Jn 1:46. 4:37. 2 P 2:22. **Even as.** 2 Ch 28:22. **mighty.** ver. +8. 2 Ch 14:9. 16:8. Ps 52:1-3. 120:4. Is 5:22. 18:2. Je 9:23. **before the Lord.** Ge 6:11. 13:13. 2 Ch 28:22. Ps 52:7. 66:7. Mi 7:2.

10. A.M. 1745. B.C. 2259. **And the.** Je 50:21. Mi *5:6. **Babel.** Gr. Babylon. i.e. *confusion, mixture*, S#894h. Ge *11:9. 2 K 20:14. Ps 137:1, 8. Is *13:19. 14:4, 22. 22:9. 39:1. 43:14. Je 50:1. 51:8. Da 4:30. Mi 4:10. Ac 7:43. Re 14:8. 16:19. 17:5. 18:2. **Erech.** i.e. *length*, ✱S#751h. **Accad.** i.e. *strengthen; fortress; band, fortification, castle; a vessel, pitcher*, ✱S#390h. **Calneh.** i.e. *fortified dwellings; the wail is complete*, ✱S#3641h. Is 10:9. Am 6:2. **Shinar.** i.e. *casting out, scattering*, ✱S#8152h. Ge 11:2. 14:1, 9. Jsh 7:21mg. Is 11:11. Da 1:2. Zc 5:11. 𝆑146. Figure of speech Polyonymia; or, Many Names B776: an application of enigma to the names of persons or places, pointing to some important signification beyond what appears upon the surface. For other instances of this figure see Ge 11:2. Dt 1:2, 44. 2:8. 2 K 23:13mg. Ps 87:4. 89:10. Is 14:4. 29:1. 51:9. Je 25:26. Ezk *23:4. Ho 4:15. 10:5.

11. A.M. 1700. B.C. 2304. **went forth Asshur.** or, he went out *into* Assyria. Mi 5:6. **Asshur.** Ge 2:14. 25:18. Nu 24:22, 24. 2 K 15:19, 29. Ezr 4:2. Ps 83:8. Ezk 27:23. 32:22. Ho 14:3. **Nineveh.** i.e. *offspring of ease; offspring abiding*, ✱S#5210h. ver. 12. 2 K 19:36. Is 37:37. Jon 1:2. 3:2, 3, 4, 5, 6, 7. 4:11. Na 1:1. 2:8. 3:7. Zp 2:13. Mt 12:41. Lk 11:32. **the city of.** or, the streets of the city. **Rehoboth.** i.e. *broad places; wide places*, ✱S#7344h. Ge 26:22. 36:37. 1 Ch 1:48. Compare Am +*5:16n. (1) The name which Isaac gave to a well which he dug, Ge 26:22. (2) "Rehoboth by the river." The river referred to is supposed to be the Euphrates, Ge 36:37; 1 Ch 1:48. (3) One of the cities founded by Asshur, Ge 10:11. It is supposed to have been near the river Euphrates.

12. **Resen.** i.e. *bridle, curb*, ✱S#7449h. **Nineveh.** i.e. *agreeable*, ✱S#5210h. ver. +11. Na 1:14. **Calah.**

i.e. *full age, old age, completion,* ✳S#3625h. ver. 11. 2 K 15:19, 29. 1 Ch 5:26.

13. Mizraim. ver. 6. **Ludim.** i.e. *bending; travailings, generation,* ✳S#3866h. ver. 22. 1 Ch 1:11, 12, 17. Is 66:19. Je 46:9mg. Ezk 27:10. 30:5. **Anamim.** i.e. *answer of the waters; affliction of the waters; fountains of waters,* ✳S#6047h. 1 Ch 1:11. **Lehabim.** i.e. *flames; scorching heat,* ✳S#3853h. 1 Ch 1:11. 2 Ch 12:3. 16:8. Da 11:43. Na 3:9. **Naphtuhim.** i.e. *openings,* ✳S#5320h. 1 Ch 1:11.

14. Pathrusim. i.e. *southern region, Egypt,* ✳S#6625h. 1 Ch 1:12. Is 11:11. Je 44:1, 15. Ezk 29:14. 30:14. **Casluhim.** i.e. *protected boundary; pardoned,* ✳S#3695h. 1 Ch 1:12. **Philistim.** i.e. *wallowing,* ✳S#6625h. Ge 21:32, 34. 26:1, 8. Jsh 13:2. Jg 3:3. 1 Ch 1:12h. Is 14:31. Je 25:20. 47:1, 4. Ezk 25:16, 17. Am 1:8. 9:7. Ob 19. **Caphtorim.** i.e. *crowns, lintels,* ✳S#3732h. Dt 2:23. 1 Ch 1:12. Je 47:4. Am 9:7.

15. Canaan. ver. 6. 1 Ch 1:13. **Sidon.** Heb. Tzidon. Ge 49:13. Jsh 11:8. 19:28. Jg 1:31. 18:28. 2 S 24:6. 1 K 17:9. 1 Ch 1:13. Is 23:4, Zidon. **firstborn.** Ge 41:51, 52 w Je 31:9. Ex *4:22. Dt 21:15-17. Ps *89:20, 27. Col √1:15, 18. **Heth.** i.e. *terror; dread, fear, striking,* ✳S#2845h. Ge 15:18-21. 23:3, 5, 7, 10, 10, 16, 18, 20. 25:10. 27:46, 46. 28:3-20. 49:32. Ex 3:8. 34:11. Nu 34:2-15. Jsh 12:8-24. 2 S 11:3. 1 Ch 1:13.

16. Jebusite. i.e. *treading down,* ✳S#2983h. Ge 15:21. Ex 3:8, 17. 13:5. 23:23. 33:2. 34:11. Nu 13:29. Dt 7:1. 20:17. Jsh 3:10. 9:1. 11:3. 12:8. 15:8, 63, 63. 18:16, 28. 24:11. Jg 1:21, 21. 3:5. 19:11. 2 S 5:6, 8. 24:16, 18. 1 K 9:20. 1 Ch 1:14. 11:4, 6. 21:15, 18, 28. 2 Ch 3:1. 8:7. Ezr 9:1. Ne 9:8. Ezk 16:3, 45. Zc 9:7. **Amorite.** Ge 14:7, 13. 15:16, 21. 48:22. Ex 3:8, 17. 33:2. 34:11. Nu 13:29. 21:13, 21, 25, 26, 29, 31, 32, 34. 22:2. 32:33, 39. Dt 1:19, 44. 7:1. Jsh 2:10. 9:1. 11:3. 24:11. 1 K 21:26. 2 K 21:11. 1 Ch 1:14. Ezr 9:1. Ne 9:8. Ps 135:11. 136:19. Ezk 16:3, 45. Am 2:9, 10. **Girgasite.** i.e. *dweller in loamy soil,* ✳S#1622h. Ge 15:21. Dt 7:1. Jsh 3:10. 24:11. 1 Ch 1:14. Ne 9:8.

17. Hivite. Ge 34:2. 36:2. Ex 3:8, 17. 13:5. 23:23, 28. 33:2. 34:11. Dt 7:1. 20:17. Jsh 3:10. 9:1, 7. 11:3, 19. 12:8. 24:11. Jg 3:3, 5. 2 S 24:7. 1 K 9:20. 1 Ch 1:15. 2 Ch 8:7. **Arkite.** i.e. *fugitive; my gnawing,* ✳S#6208h. 1 Ch 1:15. **Sinite.** i.e. *dwellers in a marshy land,* ✳S#5513h. 1 Ch 1:15.

18. Arvadite. 1 Ch 1:16. Ezk 27:8, 11. **Zemarite.** Jsh 18:22. 1 Ch 1:16. **Hamathite.** Nu 13:21. 34:8. 2 S 8:9. 2 K 17:24, 30. 1 Ch 1:16. Is 10:9. Ezk 47:16, 17. Am 6:2. Zc 9:2. **Canaanites.** Ge 12:6. 13:7. 15:21. 24:3, 37. 34:30. 38:2. 46:10. 50:11. Ex 3:8, 17. 6:15. 13:5, 11. 23:23, 28. 33:2, 11. Nu 14:25. 21:3. 33:40. Dt 1:7. 11:30. Jsh 5:1. 7:9. 13:4. 16:10. 17:12. Jg 1:1. 3:5. 2 S 24:7. 1 K 9:16. 1 Ch 2:3. Ezr 9:1. Ne 9:8, 24. Ob 20. Zc 14:21. Mt 10:4. Mk 3:18.

19. And the border. Ge 13:12-17. 15:18-21. Nu 34:2-15. Dt 32:8. Jsh 12:7, 8. 14-21. **Sidon.** i.e. *hunting, fishery; plenty of fish,* ✳S#6721h. **as thou comest.** √178, Ge +25:18. Ge 13:10. **Gerar.** Ge 20:1, 2. 26:1, 6, 17, 20, 26. 2 Ch 14:13, 14. **Gaza.** Heb. Azzah. i.e. *strong, fortified,* ✳S#5804h. Dt 2:23. Jsh 10:41. 11:22. 15:47. Jg 1:18. 6:4. 16:1, 21. 1 S 6:17. 1 K 4:24. 2 K 18:8. 1 Ch 7:28. Je 25:20. 47:1mg, 5. Am 1:6, 7. Zp 2:4. Zc 9:5, 5. Ac 8:26. **Sodom.** i.e. *flaming, burning; mystery; dew, abundance; fettered,* ✳S#5467h. Ge 13:10-13. 14:2, 8, 10, 11, 12, 17, 21, 22. 18:16, 20, 22, 26. 19:1, 4, 24, 28. Dt 29:23. 32:32. Is 1:9, 10.

3:9. 13:19. Je 23:14. 49:18. 50:40. La 4:6. Ezk 16:46, 48, 49, 53, 55, 56. Am 4:11. Zp 2:9. Mt √10:15. Mk 6:11. Lk 10:12. Ro 9:29. 2 P 2:6. Ju 7. Re 11:8. **Gomorrah.** i.e. *people of fear; bondage; a ruined heap,* ✳S#6017h. Ge 13:10. 14:2, 8, 10, 11. 18:20. 19:24, 28. Dt 29:23. 32:32. Is 1:9, 10. 13:19. Je 23:14. 49:18. 50:40. Am 4:11. Zp 2:9. **Admah.** i.e. *earthy; red,* ✳S#126h. Ge 14:2, 8. Dt 29:23. Ho 11:8. **Zeboim.** i.e. *gazelles, gathering of troops; dyers, hyenas,* ✳S#6636h. Ge 14:2, 8. Dt 29:23. Also ✳S#6650h: 1 S 13:18. Ne 11:34. Also S#6636h: Ho 11:8. (1) One of the 'cities of the plain' near the Dead Sea, destroyed at the same time with Sodom. (2) A town of Benjamin, Ne 11:34. (3) 'valley of hyenas,' a ravine apparently east of Michmash in Benjamin, 1 S 13:18. **Lasha.** i.e. *fissure, pierced, to break through,* ✳S#3962h.

20. sons of Ham. ver. 6. Ge 11:1-9.

21. Shem. ver. 1. Ge *9:26. Lk 3:36. Ro *9:4, 5. **the father.** Ge 11:10-26. **Eber.** ver. +24, 25. Ge 11:15, 16. Nu 24:24. 1 Ch 1:19. **the brother.** ver. 2. **elder.** ver. +1. Ge 5:32.

22. children. Ge 9:26. 1 Ch 1:17-27. **Elam.** i.e. *eternal,* ✳S#5867h. Ge 14:1, 9. 2 K 15:19. 1 Ch 1:17. 8:24. 26:3. Ezr 2:7, 31. 4:9. 8:7. 10:2, 26. Ne 7:12, 34. 10:14. 12:42. Jb 1:17. Is 11:11. 21:2. 22:6. Je 25:25. 49:34-39. Ezk 32:24. Da 8:2. Ac 2:9. (1) A son of Shem. His descendants settled in that part of Persia afterward often called by this name, Ge 10:22; 1 Ch 1:17. (2) Name of a province in Persia; applied also to the whole country and to its inhabitants, Ge 14:1. (3) A son of Shashak, 1 Ch 8:24. (4) A son of Meshelemiah, 1 Ch 26:3. (5) The progenitor of a family who returned from Babylon, Ezr 2:7; Ne 7:12. (6) Another Israelite whose posterity returned from Babylon, Ezr 2:31; Ne 7:34. (7) An Israelite some of whose descendants returned from Babylon, Ezr 8:7. Perhaps same as either number 5 or 6. (8) An ancestor of Shechaniah, Ezr 10:2, 26. Perhaps the same as number 5 or 6. (9) A chief or family of the Jews who sealed the covenant of Nehemiah, Ne 10:14. (10) A priest who aided in the ceremony of purifying the rebuilt wall of Jerusalem, Ne 12:42. **Asshur.** i.e. *a step, going,* S#804h. 1 Ch 1:17. Ps 83:8. Ezk 27:23. 31:3. 32:22. **Arphaxad.** Heb. Arpachshad. i.e. *boundary of the Chaldeans; one that heals,* ✳S#775h. ver. 24. Ge 11:10, 11, 12, 13. 1 Ch 1:17, 18, 24. **Lud.** i.e. *bending, tortuous,* ✳S#3865h. 1 Ch 1:17. Is 66:19. Je 46:9mg. Ezk 27:10. 30:5h. **Aram.** Nu 23:7.

23. Uz. i.e. *counsel; impressible; fruitful in trees, fertile land,* ✳S#5780h. Ge 22:21. 36:28. 1 Ch 1:17, 42. Jb 1:1. 2:11. Je 25:20. La 4:21. (1) One of the sons of Aram, the son of Shem, Ge 10:23; 1 Ch 1:17. (2) One of the sons of Dishan, of the family of Seir, Ge 36:28; 1 Ch 1:42. (3) The country of Job, probably that part of Arabia which is east of Edom and south of Trachonitis, Jb 1:1. **Hul.** i.e. *circle; to have pain,* ✳S#2343h. 1 Ch 1:17. **Gether.** i.e. *fear, turning aside; spying a neighbor; a proud spy; seeing a wine press,* ✳S#1666h. 1 Ch 1:17. **Mash.** i.e. *drawn out, departed,* ✳S#4851h. ver. 2. 1 Ch 1:17.

24. Salah. Heb. Shelah. i.e. *sent, shooting forth; a missile,* ✳S#7974h. Ge 11:12-15. 1 Ch 1:18, 18, 24. Lk 3:35. **Eber.** i.e. *the region beyond; a shoot,* ✳S#5677h. ver. 21, 25. Ge 11:14, 15, 16, 17. 14:13. Nu 24:24. Jsh 24:2, 3, 14, 15. 1 Ch 1:18, 19, 25. 5:13. 8:12, 22. Ne 12:20. Lk 3:35. (1) The father of Peleg and the progenitor of the race of the Hebrews, Ge 10:21; 1 Ch 1:19. (2) The word is apparently used denoting, it may be, the Hebrews (descendants of Eber), but it may also be understood as referring to 'those beyond the river' (Euphrates), Nu 24:24. (3) A head of a family in Gad, 1 Ch 5:13. (4) A son of Elpaal, descendant of Benjamin, 1 Ch 8:12. (5) Apparently a son of Shashak, 1 Ch 8:22. (6) A priest of the family of Amok, Ne 12:20.

25. A.M. 1757. B.C. 2247. **Eber.** ver. 21, +24. 1 Ch 1:19. **the name.** Ge 11:16-19. Lk 3:35, 36. **Peleg.** i.e. Division. *S#6389h. i.e. *earthquake.* Ge 11:16, 17, 18, 19. 1 Ch 1:19, 25. Lk 3:35. **earth divided.** ver. 32. Dt *32:8. Ac 17:26. **Joktan.** i.e. *he will be small; small dispute,* *S#3355h. ver. 26, 29. 1 Ch 1:19, 20, 23.

26. **Joktan.** ver. +25. 1 Ch 1:20-23. **Almodad.** i.e. *immeasurable,* *S#486h. 1 Ch 1:20. **Sheleph.** i.e. *extract, drawn out, selected,* *S#8026h. 1 Ch 1:20. **Hazarmaveth.** i.e. *court of death,* *S#2700h. 1 Ch 1:20. **Jerah.** i.e. *moon, lunar,* *S#3392h. 1 Ch 1:20.

27. **And.** 1 Ch 1:20-23. **Hadoram.** i.e. *Hadar is high; exalted, power,* *S#1913h. 1 Ch 1:21. 18:10. 2 Ch 10:18. (1) A son of Joktan, of the family of Shem, Ge 10:27; 1 Ch 1:21. (2) A son of Tou, king of Hamath in the time of David, 1 Ch 18:10. (3) An Israelite over the tribute in the time of Rehoboam, 2 Ch 10:18. **Uzal.** i.e. *going to and fro; wandering; shall be flooded,* *S#187h. 1 Ch 1:21. Ezk 27:19mg. **Diklah.** i.e. *a palm tree,* *S#1853h. 1 Ch 1:21.

28. A.M. cir. 1797. B.C. cir. 2207. **Obal.** i.e. *bare; heaping confusion; bare district; stripped; bare of leaves,* *S#5745h. **Abimeal.** i.e. *a father sent from God,* *S#39h. 1 Ch 1:22. **Sheba.** Ge 25:3. 1 K 10:1. 1 Ch 1:9, 20-28. Jb 6:19. Ps 72:10. Is 60:6. Je 6:20. Ezk 27:22.

29. **Ophir.** i.e. *fruitful; abundance; reducing to ashes,* *S#211h. 1 K 9:28. 10:11, 11. 22:48. 1 Ch 1:23. 29:4. 2 Ch 8:18. 9:10. Jb 22:24. 28:16. Ps 45:9. Is 13:12. (1) A son of Joktan, a descendant of Shem, Ge 10:29; 1 Ch 1:23. (2) The gold region to which Solomon sent his fleet from a port on the Red Sea, has been variously located as being in Arabia, in eastern Africa, and in India. The Joktanite Ophir, on the coast of Arabia, is probably the place referred to, although the voyage may have been continued to India. **Havilah.** ver. +7. Ge *2:11. 25:18. 1 S 15:7. **Jobab.** i.e. *a desert; crying out,* *S#3103h. Ge 36:33, 34. Jsh 11:1. 1 Ch 1:23, 44, 45. 8:9, 18. (1) A son of Joktan, Ge 10:29; 1 Ch 1:23. (2) A king of Edom, Ge 36:33; 1 Ch 1:44. (3) A king of Madon who was overcome by Joshua, Jsh 11:1. (4, 5) Descendants of Benjamin, 1 Ch 8:9, 18.

30. **Mesha.** i.e. *retreat; bringing deliverance,* *S#4852h. **Sephar.** i.e. *numbering; census,* *S#5611h. **mount.** Ge 12:8. 14:10. 19:17, 30. 22:2. 31:21. Ex 3:1. **of the east.** Ge 25:6. 29:1. Nu *23:7. Jg 6:3, 33. 7:12. 8:10, 11. 1 K *4:30. Jb 1:3. Is 2:6. 11:14. Je 49:28. Ezk 25:4, 10.

31. **after their families.** ver. +5, 20. Ac 17:26.

32. **are the.** ver. 1, 20, 31. Ge 5:29-31. **and by.** Any man who can barely read his Bible, and has but heard of such people as the Assyrians, Elamites, Lydians, Medes, Ionians, and Thracians, will readily acknowledge that Asshur, Elam, Lud, Madai, Javan, and Tiras, grandsons of Noah, were their respective found-

ers. **nations.** ver. 25. Ge 9:1, 7, 19. Ac 17:26. **divided.** ver. +*25. Ge 11:8. Dt 32:8. Da 4:37. 5:28. Lk *1:51.

GENESIS 11

Only one language in the world, 1 The building of Babel interrupted by the confusion of tongues, and the builders dispersed, 2-9. A genealogy from Shem to Abram, 10-27. Some account of Abram and his family, and of his removal from his native country, 28-32.

1. A.M. 1757. B.C. 2247. **earth.** ſ121J17, Ge +6:11. **was of.** or, was. ſ119, Ge +49:9. Jb 12:20. Ps 81:5. Pr 17:7. Is *19:18. Zp 3:9. Ac ◑2:4-6. Re 7:9, 10. **language.** Heb. lip. ſ121BD. Figure of speech Metonymy of the Cause B546, where the organic cause or instrument is put for the thing effected by it; here, "lip" is put for the language. For other instances of this figure see Pr 12:19, 22. 14:7. 17:7mg. 18:6, 7. Is 19:18mg. 33:19. Zp 3:9mg. **speech.** Heb. words.

2. **from the east.** or, eastward. Ge 12:8. 13:11. 2 S 6:2. 1 Ch 13:6. **Shinar.** ſ146, Ge +10:10. See on ver. 9. Ge +10:10. 14:1. Is 11:11. Da 1:2. Zc 5:11.

3. **they said one to another.** Heb. a man said to his neighbor. **Go to.** The Hebrew word signifies *come,* or *make preparation,* as for a journey or the execution of a purpose. ver. 4, 7. Ps 64:5. Pr 1:11. Ec 2:1. Is 5:5. 41:6, 7. Ja 4:13. 5:1. **us.** ver. ◑√7. He ◑3:13. 10:24. **burn thoroughly.** Heb. burn to a burning. **brick.** Ex 1:14. 5:7-18. 2 S 12:31. Is 9:10. 65:3. Na 3:14. 1 P ◑2:5. **stone.** Ge 28:11. Is 9:10. **slime.** Ge 14:10. Ex 2:3. Re ◑21:19.

4. **Go to.** ver. 3, 7. Ge 38:16. Ex 1:10. **and let.** 2 S 8:13. Ps *49:11-13. Pr *10:7. Da *4:30. Jn 5:44. **city.** Ge 4:17. =13:12. Pr=25:28. Re=18:10, 13, 16. ◑=21:18, 21. **whose.** Ge 28:12. Ps 107:26. **top.** Dt 1:28. 9:1. Da 4:11, 22. Am 9:2. **name.** Ge 6:4. Ex 9:16. Dt 22:14. Ru 4:10. 2 S 7:9, 23. 8:13. Jb 18:17. Pr *10:7. Is 42:8. Da 4:30. Mk 6:14. Jn *5:44. Ro 9:17. Re 3:1. **lest.** ver. 8, 9. Dt *4:27. Ps 44:11. 92:9. Lk *1:51. **face.** Ge +1:2.

5. **came down.** Ge *18:21. Ex *3:8. 19:*11, 18, 20. 34:5. Nu 11:25. 12:5. Ps 11:4. 18:9. 33:13, 14. 144:5. Je 23:23, 24. Jn +√3:13. He *4:13. **see.** Ps 14:2. **children.** ſ144A3. Figure of speech Pleonasm; or, Redundancy B408, when more words are used than the grammar requires; here, "children," men viewed as the descendants of Adam, the human race. For other instances of this figure see Dt 9:2. 1 K 8:39. Ps 36:7. Ec 3:18. Jl 3:6. Mt 10:23. 16:13, 27, 28. Mk 2:28. 3:28. Lk 6:5. Jn 3:14. Ep 3:5.

6. **Behold.** Ge 3:22. Jg 10:14. 1 K 18:27. Ec 11:9. **the people.** ver. 1. Ge 9:19. Ac 17:26. **one.** Dt +*6:4. **imagined.** Ge 6:5. 8:21. Jb 5:12. Ps *2:1-4. Ec 7:29. Lk 1:51. 1 C 1:19.

7. **Go to.** ver. 4. **let us.** ver. 5. Ge +√1:26. 3:22. Pr 8:30. Is *6:8. Jn √1:1. **confound.** Ex 4:11. Jb 5:12, 13. 12:20. Ps *2:4. *33:10. 55:9. Ac *2:4-11. **language.** Is *28:11. Ac 2:4-6. 1 C 14:21, 22. **may.** Ge 10:5, 20, 32. 42:23. Dt 28:49. Ps 55:9. Je 5:15. 1 C 14:2-11, 23.

8. **scattered.** ver. 4, 9. Ge 49:7. Dt 32:8. Ps *92:9. Is *8:9. Lk *1:51. Ac 8:1. **upon.** Ge 10:25, 32. **face.** ſ144A1. Figure of speech Pleonasm; or, Redundancy B406: two nouns are used together, one of which appears to be redundant, but is used to emphasize and

enhance the force of the other noun; here, "face" emphasizes 'all over the earth.' Sometimes the word "face," though present in Hebrew, is omitted in translation. For other instances of this idiom see Ge 1:2. 16:8. 23:3. Ex 7:10. Le 23:40. Jg 11:3mg. 1 S 14:25. Is 14:21. 19:8. Ho 10:7. Am 5:8. Lk 21:35. Ac 3:19. 5:41. 17:26. Re 12:14. **left off.** ver. 4. Pr *10:24. **city.** ver. +4. Jb 12:14. Ps 127:1.

9. **name.** ♪144A4B. Figure of speech Pleonasm; or, Redundancy B409. The word "name" appears to be redundant when used with the verb "call," but it means emphatically to *name.* For other examples of this idiom see Ge 19:22. 27:36. 41:51. **Babel.** That is, Confusion. Ge 10:5, +10, 20, 31. Is ch. 13, 14. Je ch. 50, 51. 1 C 14:23. 1 P ◐5:13. Re 18:2. **scatter.** ver. +4. Ps 68:30. Lk *1:51. **the face.** Ge 10:25, 32. Ac 17:26.

10. A.M. 1658. B.C. 2346. **generations.** ver. 27. Ge 2:4. 5:1. 10:1, 21, 22. 1 Ch 1:17-27. Lk 3:34-36. **Shem.** Ge 6:10. +10:1, 21. 1 Ch 1:4. Lk 3:36. **Arphaxad.** Ge +10:22.

11. A.M. 2158. B.C. 1846. **Shem.** ver. 10. Ge 5:4, etc. **begat sons.** Ge 1:28. 5:4. 9:7. Ps 127:3, 4. 128:3, 4. 144:12.

12. A.M. 1693. B.C. 2311. **Arphaxad.** Ge 10:22. 1 Ch 1:17, 18. **begat.** Ge +10:24. Lk 3:36.

13. A.M. 2096. B.C. 1908.

14. A.M. 1723. B.C. 2281. **Eber.** Ge 10:+21, +24.

15. A.M. 2126. B.C. 1878.

16. A.M. 1757. B.C. 2247. **Eber.** Ge 10:21, 25. Nu 24:24. 1 Ch 1:19. **Peleg.** Ge +10:25. Lk 3:35, Phalec.

17. A.M. 2187. B.C. 1817.

18. A.M. 1787. B.C. 2217. **Reu.** i.e. *associate, friend,* *S#7466h. ver. 19, 20, 21. 1 Ch 1:25. Lk 3:35, Ragau.

19. A.M. 1996. B.C. 2008. **two.** Note the decreasing length of human life. Ge 5:27. 11:11. Dt 31:2. Ps *90:10.

20. A.M. 1819. B.C. 2185. **Serug.** i.e. *a branch, shoot, intertwined,* *S#8286h. ver. 21, 22, 23. 1 Ch 1:26. Lk 3:35, Saruch.

21. A.M. 2026. B.C. 1978.

22. A.M. 1849. B.C. 2155. **Nahor.** i.e. *snorer; snorting; burning or drying up; white, splendid,* *S#5152h. ver. 23, 24, 25, 26, 27, 29, 29. Ge 22:20, 23. 24:10, 15, 24, 47. 29:5. 31:53. Jsh 24:2, Nachor. 1 Ch 1:26. Lk 3:34. (1) The grandfather of Abraham, Ge 11:23; 1 Ch 1:26. (2) A brother of Abraham, Ge 11:26.

23. A.M. 2049. B.C. 1955.

24. A.M. 1878. B.C. 2126. **Terah.** Ge 11:32. Jsh 24:2. 1 Ch 1:26. Lk 3:34, Thara.

25. A.M. 1997. B.C. 2007.

26. A.M. 1948. B.C. 2056. **Terah.** i.e. *delay; breathing,* *S#8646h. ver. 24, 25, 27, 27, 28, 31, 32, 32. Jsh 24:2. 1 Ch 1:26. **Abram.** i.e. *exalted father; ambition,* *S#87h. ver. 27, 29, 29, 31, 31. Ge 12:1, 4, 4, 5, 6, 7, 9, 10, 14, 16, 17, 18. 13:1, 2, 4, 5, 7, 8, 12, 14, 18. 14:12, 13, 13, 14, 19, 21, 22, 23. 15:1, 1, 2, 3, 11, 12, 13, 18. 16:1, 2, 2, 3, 3, 3, 5, 6, 15, 15, 16. 17:1, 1, 3, *5. *18:19. 22:20-24. 29:4, 5. Ex 3:6. Jsh 24:2. 1 Ch 1:26, 27. Ne 9:7. Mt √22:31, 32. Mk √12:26, 27. Lk 20:37, 38. Jn 8:39, 52, 53, 56, +√58. Ro 4:11. Ga 3:16. He 11:17. Ja 2:23. **Haran.** i.e. *mountainous; parched,* *S#2039h. ver. 27, 27, 28, 29, 31, +32. 1 Ch 23:9. (1) i.e. *a mountaineer.* (2) A son of Shimei, of the tribe of Levi, 1 Ch 23:9. (3) i.e.

parched. A son of Caleb, the son of Jephunneh, 1 Ch 2:46. (4) i.e. *parched, dry.* The place to which Abram removed after leaving Ur, and before he went into Canaan, Ge 11:31; 2 K 19:12. The city was in Mesopotamia, and more definitely in Padan-aram, Ge 24:10; 25:20; Ac 7:2, 4, Charran.

27. A.M. 2008. B.C. 1996. Abram, though mentioned first, was born last. Ge 10:21. 17:15-21. 25:23. 27:15. 48:+18, 20. Ex 7:7. Jg 6:15. 1 S 16:10-12. 1 K 1:6. 2:22. Col +√1:15. **generations.** ver. +10. **Lot.** i.e. *a covering; myrrh,* *S#3876h. ver. 31. Ge 12:4, 5. 13:1, 5, 7, 8, 10, 11, 11, 12, 14. 14:12, 16. 19:1, 1, 5, 6, 9, 10, 12, 14, 15, 18, 23, 29, 29, 30, 36. Dt 2:9, 19. Ps 83:8. 2 P 2:7.

28. **Haran died before.** Thus, Lot was an orphan. Nu 3:4. 27:1-5. Dt +*10:18. 21:16. Jg 9:16-21. 2 S 9:3. 2 K 11:1-12. Est *2:7. La 5:3. Ur. ver. 31. Ge 15:7. Ne 9:7. Ac 7:2-4. **Ur.** i.e. *fire, light, flame,* *S#218h. ver. 31. Ge 15:7. 1 Ch 11:35. Ne 9:7. (1) The place where Abram lived before he was called to go into Canaan. (2) The father of Eliphal, one of David's valiant men, 1 Ch 11:35, called Ahasbai in 2 S 23:34. **Chaldees.** Ge 15:7. 2 K 24:2. 25:4. 2 Ch 36:17. Ne 9:7. Jb 1:17. Je 39:5. Ac 7:4.

29. **Nahor.** Ge 24:10, 15. 29:5. 31:53. Jsh 24:2. 1 Ch 1:26. **Sarai.** Ge 17:15. 20:12. 1 P 3:6. **Milcah.** i.e. *queen; counsel,* *S#4435h. Ge 22:20, 23. 24:15, 24, 47. Nu 26:33. 27:1. 36:11. Jsh 17:3. (1) A daughter of Haran. She was the wife of Nahor, a brother of Abraham. (2) A daughter of Zelophehad, Nu 26:33; Jsh 17:3. **Iscah.** i.e. *observant; she looks abroad,* *S#3252h. Iscah is called the *daughter-in-law* of Terah, (ver. 31,) as being Abram's wife; yet Abram afterwards said, "she is the daughter of my father, but not the daughter of my mother." (Ge 20:12.) Probably Haran was the eldest son of Terah, and Abram his youngest by another wife: and thus Sarai was the daughter, or *grand-daughter* of Terah, Abram's father, but not of his mother.

30. **barren.** Ge 15:2, 3. 16:1, 2. 18:11, 12. 21:1, 2. 25:21. 29:31. 30:1, 2. Dt 28:18. Jg 13:2. 1 S 1:2, 5. 2 S 6:23. Ps +*113:9. ◐+*127:3. Is +*54:1. Lk 1:7, 36. Ro 4:19. He 11:11.

31. A.M. 2078. B.C. 1926. **took.** ver. 26, 27. Ge 12:1. **Lot.** ver. 27. **Haran.** ver. 26. **daughter-in-law.** Ge 38:11. Le 18:15. 20:12. Ru 1:6, 22. 2:20. 4:15. 1 S 4:19. 1 Ch 2:4. Ezk 22:11. Mi *7:6. Mt *10:35. **they went.** ver. 28. Ge 12:1. Jsh 24:2, 3. He 11:8. **Ur.** ver. 28. Ge 15:7. Jsh 24:2. Ne 9:7. Ac 7:2-4. **the land.** Ge 10:19. 24:10. **Canaan.** Ge 10:18, 19. Nu 34:2. Ac 13:19. **Haran.** ver. 32. Ge 12:4, 5. 24:10, 15. 27:43. 28:10. 29:4, 5. 2 K 19:12. Ac 7:2-4, Charran. B.C. cir. 1923. A.M. cir. 2081. **and dwelt.** Nu *32:1-5. Mt *8:21. He √4:1.

32. A.M. 2083. B.C. 1921. **Terah.** ver. +24. **died.** Ru 1:3. Ac 7:4. **Haran.** ver. +31. Is 37:12. Ezk 27:23.

GENESIS 12

God calls Abram and blesses him, 1-3. He, with Lot, leaves Haran and comes to Canaan, 4, 5. The Lord appears to him, and Abram worships, 6-9. Abram in a famine goes down to Egypt, and feigns his wife to be his sister, 10-13. She is taken into Pharaoh's house, who by plagues is compelled to restore her, 14-17. He reproves Abram, and sends him away, 18-20.

1. **had.** Ge 11:31, 32. 15:7. Ne 9:7. Is 41:9. 51:2. Ezk 33:24. **said.** ♪107, Ge +10:5. **Get.** Jsh 24:2, 3. Ps 45:10, 11. Lk *14:26-33. Ac ⟩7:2-6. 2 C 5:16. 6:17. He 11:8. Re 18:4. **show.** 1 C *2:9, 10. Ep 2:6. 1 J 3:2. Re 21:9.

2. **And I.** Ge 13:16. 15:5. 17:5, 6. 18:18. *22:17, 18. 24:35. 26:4. 27:29. 28:3, 14. 35:11. 46:3. Ex 1:7. 32:10. Nu 14:12. 24:9, 10. Dt 26:5. 2 S 7:9. 1 K 3:8, 9. Mi *7:20. Ro *4:11. Ga 3:7. **will.** Ex 6:4-8. **great.** Is 51:2. Ezk 33:24. **bless.** Dt 9:5. Is 19:24, 25. Hg 2:19. Ep 1:3. **name.** Ge 2:19, 20. 11:4. *17:5. 32:28. Nu 6:27. 1 Ch 17:8, 21. Ps 52:9. Da 1:7. Mt *1:21. Ac *4:12. Ph *2:10. **thou shalt.** Ge 14:14-16. 18:18. 19:29. 28:4. 1 K 1:47. Je 4:2. Zc 8:13. Jn 7:38. Ga 3:14. He 6:14.

3. **And I.** Ge 27:29. Ex 23:22. Nu 24:9. Mt 25:40, 45. **bless them.** Ge +18:18. Ps +*122:6. **thee.** ♪121A5, Ge +9:27. **curse him.** Ex 23:22mg. Nu 23:8. Dt +*30:7. Je 30:16. Am 9:15. **in thee.** Ge 18:18. 22:18. 26:4. 28:14. 30:27, 30. 39:5. Ps 72:17. Zc 8:23. Mt 1:1. Lk 1:73. Ac *3:25, 26. Ro 4:11. 1 C 1:30. Ga *3:8, 16, 28. Ep 1:3. Col 3:11. Re 7:9.

4. **departed.** Ex 12:38. Ne 13:3. Is 51:2. Mt 10:37. **and Lot.** Ge 11:27. **departed out.** He 11:8.

5. **Lot.** Ge 13:1. **son.** Ac 12:25. Col 4:10. **substance.** Ge 13:6. Ec 5:19. **the souls.** ver. ◐+13. Ge 14:14, 21m 46:5-26. Ezk 27:13. Re 18:13. Heb. *nephesh,* ✚S♯ 15h, used of man as an individual person here and at Ge +*2:7. 46:15, 18, 22, 25, 26, 27. Ex 1:5. 12:4. Le 22:11. Ps 25:20. Pr 10:3. 11:25, *30. 14:25. 19:15. 22:23. 25:25. 27:7. Je 38:16. La 3:25. Ezk 13:18, 20. √18:4. *Nephesh* used in this same sense is rendered "person" at Ge 14:21. 36:6. Ex 16:16. Le 27:2. Nu 31:40, 46. Dt 10:22. Je 43:6. 52:29, 30. Ezk 16:5. 27:13. It is otherwise rendered "persons," Nu 31:35; "any," Dt 24:7; "man," 2 K 12:4; "men," 1 Ch 5:21; and left untranslated at Nu 31:35, where it is literally "and the soul of man...were 32,000 souls." For the other uses of *nephesh* see Ge +2:7. √√171Q1. Figure of speech Synecdoche of the part B640: when a part is put for the whole; here, an integral part of man individually, the *soul,* is put for the whole person. For other instances of this figure see Ge 14:21mg. 17:14. 46:15, 26, 27. Ex 12:19. 16:16mg. Le 5:2, 4. Jsh 20:3. Ezk √18:4, 20. Lk 6:9. Ac 2:41, 43. 7:14. Ro 13:1. 1 P 3:20. Re *6:9. 20:4. **gotten.** ♪121C. Metonymy of the Cause B556, where the thing or action is put for that which is the effect or product of it, in conjunction with certain verbs: here, a verb of operation, where the verb "to do" often denotes the effect rather than the act. "Gotten" (Heb. made) refers to the servants acquired in Haran. This figure may also be seen at Ge 30:30. Mt 25:16. **in Haran.** Ge 11:31. **and into.** Ge 10:19. Ac 7:4. He *11:8, 9. **land of Canaan.** Ge +11:31. 26:3.

6. **passed.** He 11:9. **place.** Ge 18:24. 19:12. 29:22. **Sichem.** i.e. *shoulder; early in the morning,* S♯7927h. Ge 33:18. 34:2. 35:4. Jsh 20:7. 24:32. Jg 9:1. 1 K 12:1, Shechem. Jn 4:5, Sychar. Ac 7:16, Sychem. **plain.** The word rendered *plain* should be rendered *oak,* or according to Celsius, the *turpentine tree.* Ge *13:18. 14:13. 18:1. Jg 4:11. 9:6, 37. 1 S 10:3. **Moreh.** i.e. *teacher; famous; dart flinger,* *S♯4176h. Dt 11:30. Jg 7:1. (1) The plain, plains, or oaks of Moreh, near Shechem. Abram stopped there after entering Canaan, Ge 12:6, and it is mentioned in Dt 11:30 as "the plains

of Moreh." (2) The name of a hill in the valley of Jezreel, where the Midianites and Amalekites were encamped before Gideon attacked them, Jg 7:1. It is the same as the "Little Hermon." **And.** Ge 13:7. Ps 23:5. Ep 6:12. 1 P 1:7. **Canaanite.** Ge 10:15, +18, 19. 13:7. 15:18-21.

7. **appeared.** Ge 13:14. 15. 17:1. 18:1. 21:12. 22:1, 15. 26:2. 32:30. 35:9. +46:29. Ex 3:16. 1 K 3:5. 9:2. 2 Ch 3:1. Ezk 40:3. Da 8:15. 10:18. Jn ◐1:18. 8:56, 58. **Unto thy.** Ge 13:15. *15:18. *17:3, 8. 21:12. *26:3. *28:13. Ex 33:1. Nu 32:11. Dt 1:8. 6:10. 30:20. Ps 105:9-12. Ac ⟩7:5. Ro 9:7, 8. Ga *3:16. **land.** Ge 15:7. Dt 34:4. **builded.** ver. 8. Ge 8:20. 13:4, 18. 22:9. 26:25. 33:20. He 11:13.

8. **removed.** 1 P 2:11. **Bethel.** i.e. *house of God,* *S♯1008h. Ge 13:3, 3. *28:19. 31:13. 35:1, 3, 6, 8, 15, 16. Jsh 7:2. 8:9, 12, 17. 12:9, 16. 16:1, 2. 18:13, 22. Jg 1:22, 23. 4:5. 20:18, 26, 31. 21:2, 19, 19. 1 S 7:16. 10:3. 13:2. 30:27. 1 K 12:29, 32, 32, 33. 13:1, 4, 10, 11, 11, 32. 2 K 2:2, 2, 3, 23. 10:29. 17:28. 23:4, 15, 17, 19. 1 Ch 7:28. 2 Ch 13:19. Ezr 2:28. Ne 7:32. 11:31. Je 48:13. Ho 10:15. 12:4. Am 3:14. 4:4. 5:5, 5, 6. 7:10, 13. **tent.** He 11:9. **Hai.** i.e. *heap of ruins,* S♯5857h. Ge 13:3. Jsh 7:2. 8:3, Ai. Ne 11:31, Aija. Is 10:28, Aiath. **altar.** Ge 8:20. Dt 27:2, 12. Jsh 8:9, 30. 1 P 2:5. **called.** Ge 4:26. 13:4. 21:33. 26:25. Ex 34:5. 1 Ch 4:10. Ps 99:6. 116:4. Pr 18:10. Jl *2:32. Ac 2:21. Ro *10:12-14. 1 C *1:2.

9. **going.** Ge 26:13. Ph 3:13. **on still.** Heb. in going and journeying. Ge 13:3. 24:62. Ps 105:13. He 11:13. 14. **south.** Ge 13:1, 3. 20:1. 24:62. Nu 13:17, 22, 29. Dt 1:7. Jsh 11:16. 15:21. Jg 1:9. 1 S 27:10. Ps 126:4. Is 21:1. Je 13:19. 17:26. 32:44. 33:13. Ezk 20:46, 47. 21:4. ♪171.O.8. Figure of speech Synecdoche of the Whole B639: a place is put for a part of it; here, the *south* is put for the Negev, or the hill country of Judea, with respect to Jerusalem. For other instances of this figure see the above references and Ge 13:1, 3. Ezk 20:46, 47.

10. A.M. 2084. B.C. 1920. **was a.** Ro 5:3. **famine.** Ge 26:1. 41:54. 42:5. 43:1. 47:13. Ru 1:1. 2 S 21:1. 24:13. 1 K ch. 17, 18. 2 K 4:38. 6:25. ch. 7. 8:1. 25:3. Ne 5:3. Ps 34:19. 105:16. 107:34. Is 51:19. Je 14:1, 15. 15:2. 24:10. 27:8. Ezk 5:12. 12:16. Am *8:11. Mt 24:7. Lk 15:14. 21:11. Jn 16:33. Ac 7:11. 11:28. 14:22. **went.** Ge 26:2, 3. 43:1. 46:3, 4. 1 S 27:1. 2 K 8:1, 2. Ps 105:13. Is 30:2. *31:1.

11. **he said.** Ge 20:2. 26:7. Lk 22:55-61. Ac 21:26. 23:6. Ga 2:12, 13. 6:12. **a fair.** ver. 14. Ge 26:7. 29:17. 39:6, 7. 2 S 11:2. 13:1. 14:27. 1 K 1:3, 4. Jb 42:15. Pr 11:22. 31:30. SS 1:14. 4:1, 7. 6:4, 10. Am 8:13.

12. **Egyptians.** i.e. *tribulation,* S♯4714h. ver. 14. Ge 41:55, 56. 43:32, 32, 32. 45:2. 46:34. 47:15. 47:20. 50:3, 11. Ex 1:13. 3:8, 9, 21, 22. Nu 14:13. Dt 26:6. Jsh 24:6, 7. 6:9. 10:11. 1 S 4:8. 6:6. 10:18. 2 K 7:6. Ezr 9:1. Is 19:2, 4, 21, 23. 20:4. 30:7. 31:3. Je 43:13. La 5:6. Ezk 16:26. 23:21. 29:12, 13. 30:23, 26. Ac 7:22. He 11:29. **will kill.** Ge 20:11. 26:7. 1 S 27:1. Pr 29:25. Mt *10:28. 1 J 1:8-10.

13. **Say.** Jn 8:44. Ro 3:6-8. 6:23. Col 3:6. **thou art.** Ge +11:29. 20:2, 5, *12, 13. *26:7. Is 57:11. Mt 26:69-75. Ga 2:12, 13. **that it.** Ge *20:11. Pr *29:25. Ec *7:20. Je *17:7. **and.** Ps +*146:3-5. Je 17:5-8. **soul.** Heb. *nephesh.* Used here and in the following passages of mortal man, as though the soul could die or be destroyed (Mt ◐+√10:28. Ac 2:37. 2 T ◐1:10): Ge

17:14. 19:20. Ex 30:12, 15, 16. Le 17:11. Nu 16:38. 31:50. Dt 19:6, 11. 22:26. 27:25. Jsh 2:13, 14. 10:28, 30, 32, 35, 37, 39. 11:11. 20:3, 9. Jg 5:18. 16:16, 30. 1 S 24:11. 25:29. 26:21. 1 K ●√17:21, 22. 19:4. 20:31. Jb 7:15. 11:20. 18:4mg. *33:22. *36:14mg. Ps 3:2. 6:4. 7:2, 5. 11:1. 17:13. 22:20, *29. 23:3. ●√49:8, 15. 66:9. 69:1. 78:50. 94:17. 106:15. 124:4. Pr 28:17. Is ●+*10:18. +*55:3. Je 2:34. *4:10. 18:20. 38:17. *40:14mg. Ezk *13:19. ●*14:14, 20. 17:17. √18:4. 22:25, 27. 33:6. Ho 9:4. Jon 2:5. Hab 2:10. Mt +2:20. +*12:18. For the other uses of *nephesh* see Ge +2:7. **live.** Je 38:17, 20.

14. **beheld.** Ge +*3:6. 6:2. 39:7. Jb +*31:1. Mt *5:28. He *13:4.

15. **princes.** Est 2:2-16. Pr 29:12. Ho 7:4, 5. **Pharaoh.** i.e. *sun king*, S#6547h. Pharaoh was a common name of the Egyptian kings, and signified a *ruler*, or *king*, or *father of his country.* Ge 40:2. 41:1. Ex 2:5, 15. 1 K 3:1. 2 K 18:21. Je 25:19. 46:17. Ezk 32:2. **taken.** Ge 20:2. Est 2:9. Ps 105:4. Pr 6:29. He 13:4. √63H. Figure of speech Ellipsis B62 (relative: of a combined word) where the omitted word is contained in another word, the one combining the two significations: here, "taken" translates Heb. *laqach*, which signifies to "catch" or "capture," in the sense of "lead." Thus, "The woman was taken and brought into Pharaoh's house." For other instances of this figure see Ge 43:33. Ex 23:18. 34:25. Le 17:3. Nu 25:1. Jsh 8:29. 10:27. 2 Ch 32:1. Ezr 2:62. Ps 21:12. 22:21. 55:18. 63:8. 66:14. *68:18. 73:27. 89:39. 104:22. 118:5. Pr 25:22. Mt 4:5. 5:23. Lk 4:1, 2, 38. 18:14. 19:44. *20:9. 21:38. Jn 1:23. 6:21. Ac 7:9. 20:30. 23:24. Ga *5:4. Ep *4:8. 2 T 1:10. 2:26. 4:18. He 5:3, *7. 9:16, 17. *10:22. 1 P 3:20. Re 13:3. 20:2.

16. **And he.** Ge 13:2. 20:14. **well.** Ge ●13:10. ●14:23. **he had.** Ge 24:35. 26:14. 32:5, 13-15. Jb 1:3. 42:12. Ps 14:13, 14. **maid-servants.** Ge 16:1. 20:14.

17. **plagued.** Ge 20:18. 1 Ch 16:21. 21:22. Jb 34:19. Ps *105:13-15. He *13:4. **plagues.** 1 S 5:11. **wife.** Ge +11:29. 17:15. 23:9. 1 Ch 16:21.

18. **What.** √85K, Ge +3:9. Ge 3:13. 4:10. 20:9, 10. 26:9-11. 31:26. 44:15. Ex 32:21. Jsh 7:19. 1 S 14:43. Pr 21:1. **why.** Le 19:17. Is 43:27. Ep 5:11. **wife.** Ro 7:3.

19. **Why.** √85K, Ge +3:9. Le *19:17. Ro 3:8. Ep *4:25. Col 3:9. **sister.** Ge 20:2, 12. 26:9.

20. **sent.** Ge 26:16. Ex 11:8. 18:27. 1 S 29:6-11. Ps *105:14, 15. Pr *21:1. Lk 21:24.

GENESIS 13

Abram and Lot return with great riches from Egypt, 1-5. Strife arises between Abram's herdsmen and those of Lot, 6, 7. Abram meekly refers it to Lot, to choose his part in the country, 8, 9; and Lot goes to Sodom, 10-13. God renews his promises to Abram, 14-17; who goes to Hebron and builds an altar, 18.

1. A.M. 2086. B.C. 1918. **up.** Ge ●12:10. **the south.** √171.O.8, Ge +12:9. The south of Canaan; as in leaving Egypt, it is said he 'came from the south,' (ver. 3,) and the southern part of the promised land lay northeast of Egypt. Ge +12:9. 20:1. 21:33. Jsh 10:40. 18:5. 1 S 27:10. 2 S 24:7. **Egypt.** i.e. *binds or oppresses*, S#4714h. ver. 10. Ge 12:10, 11, 14. 15:18. 21:21. 25:18. 26:2. 37:25, 28, 36. 39:1. 40:1, 1, 5. 41:8, 19, 29, 30, 33, etc.

2. **rich.** Ge *24:35. 26:12, 13. Dt *8:18. 1 S *2:7. Jb 1:3, 10. *22:21-25. Ps *112:1-3. Pr *3:9, 10. *10:22. Mt *6:33. Lk ●18:23. 1 T +*4:8.

3. **from.** Ge 12:6, 8, 9. **south.** √171.O.8, Ge +12:9. **beginning.** Ge 35:1. Re 2:4, 5. **Bethel and Hai.** i.e. The place which was afterwards called *Bethel* by Jacob, and so called when Moses wrote; for its first name was *Luz.* Ge +*28:19.

4. **Unto.** ver. 18. Ge 12:7, 8. 35:1-3. Ps *26:8. 42:1, 2. 84:1, 2, 10. **called.** Ge 4:26. 21:33. Ps 65:1, 2. 107:1, 8, 15. *116:2, 17. *145:18. Is 12:4. 58:9. Je *29:12. Zep 3:9. Ro *10:13. 1 C 1:2. Ep 6:18, 19.

5. **Lot.** Ge 11:27, 31. 12:5. **tents.** Ge 4:20. 25:27. Je 49:29. √121J16. Figure of speech Metonymy of the Subject B578. Metonymy is the change of noun for another related noun. The container is put for the contents, or the place for the thing placed in it. Here, "tents" are put for the dwellers therein. For other instances of this figure see Ps 78:67. 87:2. 91:10. Pr 14:11.

6. **bear.** Ge 36:6, 7. Ec 5:10, 11. Lk 12:17, 18. 1 T 6:9. **substance.** ver. 2. Ge 12:5, 16. **dwell together.** √76. Figure of speech Epistrophe; or, Like Sentence Endings B241, the repetition of the same word or words at the end of successive sentences. Epistrophe is thus the opposite of Anaphora (see Ps 115:12, 13, where there is Anaphora, and 115:9-11, where there is Epistrophe. Ps 115:12 also contains Anadiplosis, where the word or words at the end of one sentence are found at the beginning of the next sentence) where the same word is repeated at the beginning of successive sentences. Here, "dwell together" occurs at the end of successive sentences. For other instances of this figure Epistrophe see Dt 27:15-26 (amen). 32:10h (him), 12h (him). Ps 24:10 (King of Glory). 115:9-11 (he is their help and their shield). 118:8, 9, 10, 11. 120:2, 3. 121:3, 4. 123:3, 4. 125:1, 2. 131:2. 132:2, 5. *136. Is 65:14. Ezk 33:25, 26. Jl 2:26, 27. Ro 8:31 (us). Re 7:5-8. 18:21, 22, 23. 22:11, 17.

7. **a strife.** Ge 21:25. 26:20. Ex 2:17. 1 C 3:3. Ga 5:20. T 3:3. Ja 3:16. 4:1. **Canaanite.** Ge 10:+18, 19. 12:6. 15:18-21. 34:30. Ne *5:9. Ph 2:14, 15. Col *4:5. 1 Th 4:12. 1 P 2:12. **Perizzite.** i.e. *villagers*, *S#6522h. Ge 15:20. 34:30. Ex 3:8, 17. 23:23. 33:2. 34:11. Dt 7:1. 20:17. Jsh 3:10. 9:1. 11:3. 12:8. 17:15-18. 24:11. Jg 1:4, 5. 3:5. 1 K 9:20. 2 Ch 8:7. Ezr 9:1. Ne 9:8. **dwelled.** i.e. They were *there* when Abram and Lot came to pitch their tents in the land.

8. **said.** Pr *13:10. 15:18. 20:3. **Let.** Pr *15:1. Mt +*5:9. Ro *12:18. 1 C 6:6, 7. Ph 2:14. He *12:14. Ja 3:17, 18. **brethren.** Heb. men, brethren. Ge 11:27-31. 45:24. Ex 2:13. 2 Ch 2:17mg. Ps *133:1. Is +40:13mg. Ac 7:26. Ro *12:10. Ep *4:2, 3. 1 Th 4:9. He 13:1. 1 P *1:22. 2:17. *3:8. *4:8. 2 P 1:7. 1 J *2:9-11. *3:14-19. *4:7, 20, 21. √171G2. Figure of speech Synecdoche of the Species B624: when the species is put for the genus, particulars are put for universals, the subclass is put for the class; words of a limited and special sense are used with a wider and more universal meaning. Here, one relationship is put for and includes others: "brethren" is put for other relationships, put by Synecdoche of the Species for "relatives." For other instances of this figure see Ge 24:48. 29:5. 31:23. 35:15n, 16. Ex 1:7. Jsh 7:24. Jg 9:1. 2 S 9:7. 19:24n, 28. 1 K 15:10n, 13. 2 K 10:1n. 1 Ch 12:29. Ps 22:4. 106:6. Je 31:29. Da 5:2, 11, 18.

Am 6:10. Mt 1:1. 9:27. 12:23. 15:22. 20:30, 31. 21:9, 15. 22:42. Mk 12:35. Lk 1:32, 73. 13:16. 18:38, 39. 19:9. Jn 4:12. 8:39, 56. Ac 7:2. Ro 4:1.

9. **Is not**. Ge 20:15. 34:10. 47:6. ✓85B. Figure of speech Erotesis; or, Interrogating B947: the asking of questions without waiting for the answer; here, in negative affirmation, where the question is put in the negative form, and the answer must be in the affirmative, and very emphatically so, the truth being thus much more forcibly brought out by the question than by a mere cold and formal statement of the fact. For other instances of this figure see Ge 37:13. Ex 4:14. Dt 11:30. Ru 3:1. 2 S 15:27. 1 Ch 21:17. Jb 7:1. Ec *6:6. Is 50:2. Je 23:24. Jl 1:16. Am 2:11. 5:20. Ob 5, 8. Jon 4:11. Mt *7:22. Mk *12:24. Jn *4:35. 6:70. 11:9. 1 C 10:16. He 1:14. **if**. Ep 4:1-3. Ph 2:1-4. 4:5. **thou wilt take**. Ps 120:7. Ro *12:18. 1 C 6:7. He *12:14. Ja 3:13-18. 1 P 3:8-12. ✓63J1. Figure of speech Ellipsis of Repetition: Complex B110, where both clauses are involved, and where single words are involved. For other instances of this figure see Pr 10:1. 15:20. 17:25. 23:24. 30:17. Mt 23:29. Ro 5:16. *10:10. **left**. Ge 24:49. Nu 20:17. 22:26.

10. **lifted**. ✓144A12, Ge +22:13. Ge 3:6. 18:16. 2 T 4:10. 1 J *2:15. **and beheld**. Ge +*3:6. 6:2. Nu 32:1. 1 J *2:15, 16. **the plain**. Ge 19:17, 24, 25. Dt 34:3. 1 K 7:46. Ps *107:33, 34. 1 J *2:15. **the garden**. Ge 2:8-10. ◑19:28. Is 51:3. Ezk 28:13. 31:8. Jl 2:3. **land of**. Ge 47:6. **Zoar**. i.e. *little*, ✱S#6820h. Ge 14:2, 8. 19:22, 23, 30, 30. Dt 34:3. Is 15:5. Je 48:34. Instead of *Zoar*, which was situated at the extremity of the plain of Jordan, the Syriac reads *Zoan*, which was situated in the south of Egypt, and in a well-watered country. Nu 13:22. Ps 78:12, 43. Is 19:11, 13. 30:4. Ezk 30:14.

11. A.M. 2087. B.C. 1917. **chose**. Ge ◑15:1. 19:17. Jg 10:14. Pr 1:29. Is 65:12. 66:3. **they separated**. ver. 9, 14. Ps 16:3. ✓119:63. Pr *27:10. He *10:25. 1 P 2:17.

12. **Lot dwelled**. Ge 19:29. Jn 17:15, 16. Ep +*5:11, 12. **cities of**. Ge +=11:4. 14:2. 19:24, 25, 29. ✓171.O.12. Figure of speech Synecdoche of the Whole B639, when the whole is put for a part, a place is put for a part of it, as here, "cities" is put for one of them. **pitched**. Ge 14:12. 19:1. Ps *26:5. Is +*66:4. 1 C *15:33. 2 P 2:7, 8.

13. **But**. ✓137. Figure of speech Parenthesis B470: parenthetic addition by way of explanation, complete in itself. Parentheses are for the most part indicated; but there are others which are not marked. Here at Ge 13:13, the parenthetical statement shows the nature of Lot's choice. For other instances of this figure (unmarked) see Ge 14:18-20. Jsh 6:1 (see Jsh 5:15n). He 2:9 (for the suffering...glory and honor). 2 P 1:19 (as unto a light...daystar arise). **the men**. Ge 15:16. 18:20. 19:4, 5. 1 S 15:18. Is 1:9. 3:9. Ezk *16:46-50. Mt 9:10, 13. 11:23, 24. Jn 9:24, 31. Ro 1:27. 2 P *2:6-8, 10. Ju 7. **wicked**. S#7451h, *rah*, wicked, injurious. From its root, which indicates its nature as *breaking up* all that is good or desirable; injurious to all others. In Greek *poneros*, evil, or *kakos*, bad. Hence especially of moral depravity and corruption, and lewdness. For other occurrences of this word see Ge 38:7. Dt 17:5. 23:9. 1 S 30:22. 2 K 17:11. 2 Ch ✓7:14. Ne 9:35. Est 7:6. 9:25. Jb *21:30. Ps 101:4. Pr 2:14. *11:21. 12:13. *15:26. 26:23. Je 2:33. 5:28. 6:29. 15:21. Ezk 8:9. 11:2.

13:22. 20:44. 30:12. Rendered "evil" in such passages as Ge 2:9, 17. 3:5, 22. 6:5. 8:21. 44:4. Ex *23:2. Jb 1:1, 8. 2:3, *10. 5:19. *28:28. 42:11. Ps *5:4. 15:3. *23:4. 34:13, 14. 51:4. 97:10. 119:101. 121:7. 141:4. Pr 1:16, 33. 2:12, 14. 3:7. *13:21. **and**. ✓93A. Figure of speech Hendiadys, "very wicked sinners," Ge +1:26. **sinners**. Ge 39:9. Nu +*32:23. ✱S#2400h, *chatta*. This word signifies a habitual sinner who will reap the consequences of his sin. For other occurrences of this word see Nu 16:38. 32:14 (sinful). 1 S 15:18. 1 K 1:21 (offenders). Ps 1:*1, 5. 25:8. 26:9. *51:13. 104:35. Pr *1:10. 13:21. *23:17. Is 1:28. 13:9. 33:14. Am 9:10. **before**. Ge 6:11. 10:9. 38:7. 2 K 21:6. Is 3:8. Je 23:24. He *4:13.

14. **was**. ver. 11. **Lift**. ✓144A12, Ge +22:13. ver. 10. Is 49:18. 60:4. **look**. Ge 15:15. 18:2. *22:13. Dt 34:1-4. **northward**. Ge 28:14. Dt 3:27.

15. **For all**. Je 30:3. Ezk 28:25. Ro *11:29. **land**. Dt 11:12. Je *23:7, 8. Da 7:14. Mt *8:11. **to thee**. ver. 17. Ge 12:7. 15:7, 8, 18. *17:7, 8. 18:18. 24:7. 26:3, 4. 28:4, 13. 35:12. 48:4. Ex *3:6. Nu 34:2, 12. Dt 26:2-4. 34:4. 2 Ch 20:7. Ne 9:7, 8. Ps 37:*22, 29. 105:9-12. 112:1, 2. Is 63:18. Mt +*5:5. *8:11. ✓22:23-32. Lk 13:28. Ac 1:6. +*7:5n. Ro +*15:8. He +*11:13, 39. **thy seed**. Ga ▷3:16. **for ever**. Heb. *olam*, Ex +12:24. Ge +8:22. 9:+12, +16. *17:8. Is 11:11. Je 31:36. 33:26. Ezk 36:24. Am +9:14, 15. Lk 1:32, 33, *55. Ro +*11:1.

16. **I will**. Ge 12:2, 3. *15:5. 17:6, 16, 20. 18:18. 21:13. *22:17. *26:4. *28:3, 14. *32:12. 35:11. 36. 46:3. Ex 1:7. 32:13. Nu 23:10. Dt 1:10. Jg 6:3, 5. 1 K 3:8. 4:20. 1 Ch 21:5. 27:23. 2 Ch 17:14-18. Is *48:18, 19. Je *33:22. Ro 4:16-18. He *11:12. Re *7:9. **as the dust**. Ge 16:10. *28:14. Nu 23:10. ✓138B. Figure of speech Paroemia; or, Proverb B758, a wayside saying in common use: here, though not quoted as such, very probably already in use as a proverbial expression. For other instances of this figure see Ge 15:5. 22:17. 26:4. 28:14. 32:12. 41:49. Ex 32:13. Nu 23:10. Dt 1:10. 10:22. 28:62. Jsh 11:4. Jg 7:12. 1 S 2:6-8. 13:5. 14:45. 2 S 14:11. 17:11. 1 K 1:52. 4:20, 29. 1 Ch 27:23. 2 Ch 1:9. Ne 9:23. Jb 5:11. 22:24, 29. 27:16. 29:18. Ps 18:27. 78:27. 113:6. 139:18. Pr 29:23. Is 10:22. 48:19. Je 15:8. 33:22. Ho 1:10. Na 3:16. Hab 1:9. Zp 1:17. Zc 9:3. Mt 3:11. 7:2, 4, 12. 10:14, 25, 30. 12:25. 13:31, 32. 17:20. 19:24. 21:21. 23:12, 24. Mk 1:7. 3:24, 25. 6:11. 10:25. Lk 1:52, 53. 3:16. 6:31, 40. 9:5. 11:17. 14:11. 18:25. 21:18. 23:31. Jn 13:16. Ac 9:5. 13:51. 26:14. 27:34. Ro 9:27. 1 C 13:2. He 11:12. Re 20:8. ✓102B. Figure of speech Hyperbole; or, Exaggeration, involving comparisons B427: when more is said than is literally meant, where one thing is compared to another when there is nothing common between them. For other instances of this figure see Ge 22:17. 28:14. 32:12. Jsh 11:4. Jg 7:12. 1 S 13:5. 2 S 1:23. 1 K 4:20, 29. 10:27. 2 Ch 1:9, 15. 9:20. Jb 6:3. 29:18. 41:18. Je 4:13. La 4:7, 8, 19. Hab 2:5.

17. **walk**. Nu 13:17-24. Jsh 18:4. Ezk 43:7. Ep 1:18. 3:18. Col +*1:10. 1 Th *4:1. **give**. ver. +*15. Ge 12:7. 15:7. Dt 34:4.

18. **plain**. Heb. plains. Ge +12:6. Dt 11:30. Jsh 24:26. Jg 9:37. 1 S 10:3. **Mamre**. Ge 14:13, 24. 18:1. 23:17, 19. 25:9. +35:27. 49:30. 50:13. **Hebron**. Ge *23:2. 35:27. 37:14. Nu 13:22. Jsh 14:13. **altar**. ver. 4. Ge +8:20. 12:7, 8. Jsh 8:30. Jg 6:24, 26. 21:4. 1 S 7:17. 14:35. 2 S 24:25. 1 K ✓18:32. Ps 16:8. 1 T 2:8.

GENESIS 14

War is waged by four kings against the king of Sodom and his allies, who are conquered and plundered, 1-11. Lot is taken prisoner, but is rescued by Abram, 12-16. Abram returns, and is met by Melchizedek king of Salem, to whom Abram gives tithes; and by the king of Sodom, to whom he restores the spoil, except the portion of his own confederates, 17-24.

1. A.M. 2091. B.C. 1913. **came to pass.** Ru 1:1. 2 S 21:1. Is 7:1. Je 1:3. **Amraphel.** i.e. *speaker of hidden things; terrific giant,* ✳S#569h. ver. 9. **Shinar.** Ge +10:10. 11:2. Is 11:11. 39:6. Da 1:2. Zc 5:11. **Arioch.** i.e. *lion-like,* ✳S#746h. ver. 9. Da 2:14, 15, 15, 24, 25. (1) King of Ellasar. (2) Captain of Nebuchadnezzar's guard, Da 2:14. **Ellasar.** i.e. *God is chastener,* ✳S#495h. ver. 9. Is 37:12. **Chedorlaomer.** i.e. *handful of sheaves,* ✳S#3540h. ver. 4, 5, 9, 17. **Elam.** Ge +10:22. Is 21:2. 22:6. Je 25:25. 49:34-39. Ezk 32:24. **Tidal.** i.e. *fear, reverence; breaking the yoke,* ✳S#8413h. ver. 9.

2. **Bera.** i.e. *son of evil; excelling in science,* ✳S#1298h. **Sodom.** Ge +10:19. 13:10. 19:24. Is 1:9, 10. **Birsha.** i.e. *son of wickedness,* ✳S#1306h. **Shinab.** i.e. *tooth of father; change of father,* ✳S#8134h. **Admah.** Dt 29:23. Ho 11:8. **Shemeber.** i.e. *name of wing; flying wing; illustrious,* ✳S#8038h. **Zeboiim.** Dt *29:23. 1 S 13:18. Ne 11:34. **Bela.** i.e. *consumption; swallowing up; destroying,* ✳S#1106h. ver. 8. Also Ge 36:32, 33. 46:21. Nu 26:38, 40. 1 Ch 1:43, 44. 5:8. 7:6, 7. 8:1, 3. (1) A city, otherwise called Zoar, in the vale of Siddim, Ge 14:2, 8. (2) The first king of Edom mentioned in the Bible, Ge 36:32; 1 Ch 1:44. (3) The eldest son of Benjamin, Ge 46:21; Nu 26:38, 40; 1 Ch 7:6. (4) A son of Azaz, 1 Ch 5:8. **Zoar.** Ge +13:10. 19:20-30. Dt 34:3. Is 15:5. Je 48:34.

3. **joined.** ver. 13. Jg 20:11. **vale.** S#6010. ver. 8, 10. 37:14. Rendered *valley,* ver. 17. Nu 14:25. Jsh 7:24, 26. SS 2:1. **Siddim.** i.e. *furrows; open fields,* ✳S#7708h. ver. 8, 10. **salt sea.** Ge 19:24. Nu 34:12. Dt 3:17. Jsh 3:16. Ps 107:34mg.

4. **Twelve.** Ge 17:20. 35:22. 1 K=4:7. =10:20. Mt 26:53. Lk 2:42. 6:13. Re 21:21. 22:2. **they served.** Ge 9:25, 26. **thirteenth.** Ge=16:12 w 17:25. 1 K=7:1 w 11:6. Est 3:12, 13. Is 7:8. **they rebelled.** Ezk 17:15.

5. **Rephaims.** i.e. *the dead; giants.* Dt 3:20, 22. 2 S 21:18mg. ✳S#7497h: Ge 15:20. Dt 2:11, 20, 20 (giants). 3:11, 13. Jsh 12:4. 13:12. 15:8. 17:15mg. 18:16. 2 S 5:18, 22. 23:13. 1 Ch 11:15. 14:9. 20:4, 6, 8. Is 17:5. **Ashteroth.** The same as Ashteroth, a city of Bashan, where Og afterwards reigned. Dt 1:4. Jsh 9:10. 12:4. 13:12, 31. **Karnaim.** i.e. *two horned Astartes,* ✳S#6255h. **Zuzims.** i.e. *commotions, arousings,* ✳S#2104h. Dt 2:20-23. 1 Ch 4:40. Ps 78:51. 105:23, 27. 106:22. **Emims.** i.e. *terrors, horrors,* ✳S#368h. Dt 2:10, 11. **Shaveh Kiriathaim.** *or,* the plains of Kiriathaim; Kiriathaim was beyond Jordan, 10 miles westward from Medeba, and afterwards belonged to Sihon, king of Heshbon. i.e. *plain of the double city,* ✳S#7741h. Nu 32:37. Jsh 13:19. Je 48:1, 23.

6. **Horites.** i.e. *cave dwellers,* ✳S#2752h. Ge 36:8, 20-30. Dt 2:12, 22. 1 Ch 1:38-42. **Seir.** A region south of the Dead Sea, ✳S#8165. Ge 32:3. 33:14, 16. 36:8, 9, 21, 30. Nu 24:18. Dt 1:2, 44. 2:1, 4, 5, 8, 12, 22, 29. 33:2. Jsh 11:17. 12:7. 15:10. 24:4. Jg 5:4. 1 Ch 4:42. 2 Ch 20:10, 22, 23. 25:11, 14. Is 21:11. Ezk

25:8. 35:2, 3, 7, 15. **El-paran.** *or,* the plain of Paran. i.e. *the power of their adorning,* ✳S#364h. Ge 16:7. 21:21. Nu 10:12. 12:16. 13:3, 26. Dt 1:1. 33:2. 1 S 25:1. 1 K 11:18. Hab 3:3.

7. **Enmishpat.** i.e. *fount of judgment,* ✳S#5880h. **Kadesh.** i.e. *Sodomite; devoted to Venus; set apart; sacred,* ✳S#6946h. Ge 16:14. 20:1. Nu 13:26. 20:1, 14, 16, 22. 27:14. 33:36, 37. Dt 1:19, 46. 32:51. Jg 11:16, 17. Ps 29:8. Ezk 47:19. 48:28. **country.** Heb. field. ⌐171S7A. Figure of speech Synecdoche of the Part B650: a part of a thing is put for the whole of the thing. Here, "all the country" is Heb. "the whole field," "field" put by Synecdoche for country. For another example of this figure see 1 S 27:7. Other occurrences of this figure involving other terms include "gate" put for city, Ge 22:17. Ex 20:10. Dt 12:12. 14:27. 16:5. Ps 87:2. Je 15:7. "Gate" put for inhabitants or for the people who assemble at the city's gates, Ru 3:11. 4:10. Pr 31:23. "Stones" put for restored buildings, Ps 102:14. "Wall" put for whole city encompassed by it, Am 1:7, 10, 14. "Corner" put for "tower" which was usually placed at the corner, Zp 1:16. 3:6. "Gate" is put for place of business, 1 K 22:10. 2 K *7:1. Ezk 11:1; place of judgment or court, Dt +16:18n. 17:8. 21:19. 22:15. 25:7. 2 S 15:2. Jb 31:21. Is 29:21. Am *5:15. Zc 8:16; place of audience with the king, 2 S 19:8n. Est 2:19, 21. 3:2. Jb 29:7. La 5:14; place of legal transactions, Ge 23:10, 18; place of public assembly, 2 Ch 32:6. Ne *8:1, 3. Pr 1:21; place for public discourse, Je 17:19, 20. 26:10. *36:10. Am 5:10; place of honor, Ps 69:12. 127:5; symbol of power, Mt 16:18; symbol of entrance to life, death, or destruction, Jb 38:17. Ps 9:13. 107:18. Is 38:10. Mt √7:13, 14. **Amalekites.** Ge 36:12, 16. Ex 17:8-16. Nu 14:43, 45. 24:20. 1 S ch. 15, 27, 30. **Amorites.** ver. 13. Ge +10:16. **Hazezontamar.** i.e. *cutting off of the palm tree,* ✳S#2688h. 2 Ch 20:2. Called by the Chaldee, *Engaddi,* a town on the western shore of the Dead Sea. Jsh 15:62. 2 Ch 20:2.

8. **Zeboiim.** i.e. *gazelles,* ✳S#6636h. Ge +10:19. **same.** ver. 2. Ge +13:10. 19:20, 22. **joined.** ver. +3. **vale.** ver. +*3, 10.

9. **four kings with.** See on ver. 1.

10. **slime.** Places where asphalt or bitumen sprung out of the ground: this substance, which is properly denoted by the word *slime,* abounds in those parts. Ge +11:3. Ex 2:3. ✳S#2564. **pits.** Heb. *beer,* Ge +16:14. **fell.** Jsh 8:24. Ps 83:10. Is 24:18. Je 48:44. **the mountain.** Ge 19:17, 30.

11. **all the goods.** ver. 16, 21. Ge 12:5. Dt 28:31, 35, 51.

12. **took.** 2 Ch 28:31. 1 T 5:22. **Lot.** Ge 11:27. 12:5. **who dwelt.** Ge 13:12, 13. 19:1. Nu 16:26. Jb 9:23. Je 2:17-19. 1 T +*6:9-11. Ja *4:4. 2 P 2:6-9. 1 J *2:15-17. Re *3:19. √18:4.

13. **one.** 1 S 4:12. Jb 1:15. **the Hebrew.** i.e. *descendant of Eber,* ✳S#5680h. Ge 39:14, 17. 40:15. 41:12. 43:32. Ex 1:15, 16, 19. 2:6, 7, 11, 13. 3:18. 5:3. 7:16. 9:1, 13. 10:3. 21:2. Dt 15:12, 12. 1 S 4:6, 9. 13:3, 7, 19. 14:11, 21. 29:3. Je 34:9, 9, 14. Jon 1:9. Ac 6:1. 2 C 11:22. Ph *3:5. So called from "Eber," Ge 10:21, +24. 11:14. **dwelt.** Ge 13:18. **Mamre.** i.e. *bitter; causing fatness,* ✳S#4471h. ver. 24. Ge +13:18. 35:27. **Amorite.** ver. 7. Ge +10:16. Nu 21:21. **Eschol.** Nu 13:23. 32:9. Dt 1:24. **Aner.** i.e. *cast out, an exile; sprout; a lamp swept away,* ✳S#6063h. ver. 24. 1 Ch

6:70. (1) An Amorite ally of Abram in the pursuit of Chedorlaomer and rescue of Lot, Ge 14:13, 24. (2) A Levitical city in Manasseh, west of Jordan, 1 Ch 6:70. Some suppose it to be the same as Taanach, Jg 1:27, and Tanach, Jsh 21:25. **and these**. ver. 24. Ge 21:27, 32.

14. **his brother**. Ge 11:27-31. 13:8. Pr 17:17. 24:11, 12. Ga 6:1, 2. 1 P 3:9. 1 J 3:18. **armed**. *or,* led forth. Ps 45:3-5. 68:12. Is 41:2, 3. **trained**. *or,* instructed. Ge 12:5. 15:2. *18:19. 24:12-29. Pr *20:18. +*22:6. *24:6. Lk √14:31. **born**. Ge 12:5, 16. 15:3. 17:12, 27. +*18:19. 23:6. Ec 2:7. **Dan**. Dt 34:1. Jsh 19:47. Jg *18:29. 20:1. 1 S 3:20. 2 S 3:10. 17:11. 24:2, 15. 1 K 4:25. 12:29, 30. 15:20. 2 K 10:29. 1 Ch 21:2. 2 Ch 16:4. 30:5. Je 4:15. 8:16. Ezk 48:1, 2, 32. Am 8:14. For the tribe, see on Ex 31:6.

15. **And he**. Ps 112:5. **divided**. Ge 32:7. Jg 7:16. 9:34, 43. 1 S 11:11. **smote**. Is 41:2, 3. **Hobah**. i.e. *hiding place, lurking place,* *S#2327h. **Damascus**. i.e. *silent is the sackcloth weaver; city of Ham,* *S#1834h. Ge *15:2. 2 S 8:5, 6. 1 K 11:24, 24. *15:18. 19:15. 20:34. 2 K 5:12. 8:7, 9. 14:28. 16:9, 10, 11, 11, 12. 2 Ch 16:2. 24:23. 28:5. SS 7:4. Is 7:8, 8. 8:4. 10:9. 17:1, 1, 3. Je 49:23, 24, 27. Ezk 27:18. 47:16, 17, 18. 48:1. Am 1:3, 5. 5:27. Zc 9:1. Ac *9:2.

16. **And**. ♪148, Ge +8:22. **brought back**. ver. 11, 12. Ge 12:2. *19:16. 1 S 30:8, 18, 19. Is *41:2, 3. Ga 6:1. **people**. Ex 15:13.

17. **to**. Jg 11:34. 1 S 18:6. Pr 14:20. 19:4. **after**. He 7:1. **Shaveh**. i.e. *equalize,* *S#7740h. Compare ver. 5. **king's**. 2 S 18:18.

18. ver. 18-20. ♪137. Figure of speech Parenthesis, Ge +13:13. **Melchizedek**. i.e. *king of righteousness,* *S#4442h. Ps 110:4. He 5:6. 6:20. **king**. Ps 76:2. He ▶7:1, 2. **Salem**. i.e. *peace; complete, perfect,* *S#8004h. Ge 33:18. Ps *76:2. **bread**. Jg 19:19. Ps 104:15. Mt 26:26-29. Ga 6:10. **and wine**. ♪174, Ge +18:27. **the priest**. Ps *110:4. He 5:6, 10. *6:20. *7:1, 3, 10-22. **the most high**. Ru 3:10. 2 S 2:5. Ps 7:17. 50:14. 57:2. Mi 6:6. Ac 7:48. 16:17.

19. **he blessed**. Ge 27:4, 25-29. 47:7, 10. 48:9-16. 49:28. Nu *6:23-27. Mk 10:16. Ga *3:14. He *7:6, 7. **Blessed be**. Ru 3:10. 2 S 2:5. Ep 1:3, 6. **most high**. Dt 32:8. Nu 24:16. Ps 9:2. *83:18. Mi 6:6. Lk 1:76. Ac 16:17. **possessor**. ver. 22. Ps *24:1. 50:10. *115:15, 16. Mt *11:25. Lk 10:21. Re 10:6.

20. **blessed**. Ge 9:26. 24:27. 1 Ch 29:10-12. Ps 68:19. 72:17-19. *144:1. Ep *1:3. 1 P 1:3, 4. **which**. Jsh 10:42. Ps 44:3. **he**. ♪63A1. Figure of speech Ellipsis (Absolute: of the Nominative) B4: Absolute ellipsis requires us to supply the omitted word or words from the nature of the subject alone; here it is clear from the context and He 7:4 that it was Abram who gave tithes to Melchizedek, and not Melchizedek to Abram. For other instances of this figure see Ge 39:6. 2 S 3:7. 23:20. 24:1. 1 Ch 6:28. 11:19. Ps 34:17. 105:40. Pr 22:27. Is 26:1. Je 51:19. Ezk 46:12. Zc 7:2. Mt 5:11. *16:22. Ac 13:29. 1 C 15:√24n, 25, 53, 54. Ep 1:8. 2 Th 2:7n. T *1:15. He 9:1. 2 P 3:1. 1 J *5:16. **tithes**. This reference to tithing shows that tithing originated before the law of Moses, and thus can be considered a pre-Mosaic institution. Later, under Mosaic law, the obligation of the Jew in Israel involved the payment of several tithes amounting to about one quarter of his income. It appears that the first tithe was paid for the support of the Levites (Le 27:30-33. Nu 18:21-32). The second

tithe was to be applied to festival purposes (Dt 12:5-7, 17. 14:22-29). The third tithe was established for the support of the poor (Dt 26:12-15). Scholars differ in their opinion as to whether the third tithe was a substitute for the second tithe every third year, or whether it constituted a tithe in addition to the first two. Also, it is not clear whether the second and third tithe was based on one tenth of the whole, or on one tenth of what remained after the payment of the first tithe. See related notes (Ml 3:10n. Mt 6:2n. √23:23n. Lk ❍11:41n, 42n. 2 C 8:12n). Ge *28:22. Le 27:17, 18, 30-33. Nu 18:21, 24. 28:26. Dt 12:17. 14:23, 28, 29. 26:12-14. 2 Ch 31:5, 6, 12. Ne 10:37. 13:10, 12, 13. Am 4:4. Ml *3:8, 10. Mt 5:19. *23:23. Mk 7:11, 13. Lk 11:42. 18:12. Ac +*20:35. Ro 12:8. 1 C 9:14. √16:2. 2 C *9:6-12. Ga 6:6, 7. 1 T 5:17, 18. He 7:4-9. 13:15, 16.

21. **persons**. Heb. *nephesh,* souls. √♪171Q1, Ge +12:5. Ge +*12:5. 46:15. Je 39:18.

22. **lifted**. Ex 6:8. Nu 14:30mg. Dt 32:40. Ps 106:26. Is 3:7mg. Da *12:7. Re *10:5, 6. ♪22A14.8K, Ex +6:8. ♪121S3. Figure of speech Metonymy (of the Adjunct); or, Change of Noun B607, involving connected words and phrases, where the sign is put for the thing signified. Here, to *lift up* the hand, or hands, is put for swearing an oath, or making a promise. For other instances of this figure see Ex 6:8. Ps 106:26. Is 3:7mg. Put also for praying: Ps 28:2. 68:31. 1 T 2:8. **unto**. Ge 21:23-31. Jg *11:35. **the most high God**. ver 20. Ge 17:1. Ps *83:18. Is +*57:15. Da 4:34. Hag 2:8. Heb. El Elyon. ♪171E12. Figure of speech Synecdoche (of the Genus); or, Transfer B622: the exchange of one idea for another associated idea; of the Genus, where words of a wider meaning are used in a narrower sense: the universal for the particular, but of the same kind. Here, a common name is put for a proper one, a name common to many is used of one par excellence. For other instances of this figure see Ge 21:33. Ps 5:4. 22:1. Moses is called *the prophet,* Dt 18:15, 18. 34:10. Ho 12:13. Euphrates is called *the river* because of its magnitude, Ge 31:21. Ex 23:31. Jsh 24:2. Ps 72:8. 80:11. Mi 7:12. Christ is called Lord, etc., Mt 21:3. 22:24. Jn 11:3. The emperor Nero is called *lord,* Ac 25:26. **possessor**. ver. 19. Ge 21:23. Ps *24:1.

23. **That I**. Ge 21:23. 26:29. 42:15. Ps 95:11. He 4:5. **will not**. Ge 23:13. 2 S 24:24. 1 K 13:8. 2 K *5:16, 20. 1 Ch *21:24. Est 9:15, 16. Da 5:17. Ac 20:33. 1 C 9:18, 19. 2 C 11:7, 9-11. 12:14. 3 J 7. **lest**. 2 C 11:12. He *13:5.

24. **Save**. Pr *3:27. Mt *7:12. Ro *13:7, 8. **Aner**. ver. 13. **let**. 1 C *9:14, 15. 1 T *5:18.

GENESIS 15

The Lord encourages Abram; who complains that he continues childless, but is assured of a numerous posterity, 1-5. He is justified by faith, 6. He requests a pledge to confirm his faith; and being directed to prepare a sacrifice, obeys, 7-11. He is favored with a vision, prophetic of the condition of his posterity till brought out of Egypt: and Canaan is ensured by a covenant to them, 12-21.

1. A.M. 2093. B.C. 1911. **word**. 1 S 15:10. Ps 33:4-6. 147:15. Is *55:10, 11. Ezk 1:3. 9:3. **in a**. Ge 46:2. Nu 12:6. 1 S 9:9. Ezk 1:1. 8:4. 11:24. Da 10:1-16. Ac 10:10-17, 22. He 1:1. **vision**. Nu 24:4, 16. Ezk 13:7.

Fear not. ver. 14-16. Ge 21:17. 26:24. 46:3. Ex 14:13. Dt 31:6. 1 Ch 28:10. Ps *27:1. Is 35:4. *41:10, 14. 43:1, 5. 44:2, 8. 51:12. Da *10:12. Mt 8:26. *10:28-31. 28:5. Lk *1:13, 30. 12:32. Re *1:17. **thy shield.** Dt 33:29. 2 S *22:3, 31. Ps 3:3. *5:12. 18:2. *84:9, 11. *91:4. *119:114. Pr *30:5. Jn 8:56. Ep 6:16. ♪22D5F. Figure of speech Anthropomorphism B893: ascribing human attributes, etc., to God. Here, circumstances are attributed to God as to a person, namely, being a shield or buckler. For other instances of this figure see Dt 33:29. Ps 3:3. 18:2. 28:7. 84:11. **reward.** Ge 17:6. Nu 18:20. Dt 33:26-29. Ru 2:12. Ps 16:5, 6. 58:11. 73:25. *142:5. Pr 11:18. La *3:24. 1 C 3:22. He 11:9, 13, 16, 39. +*13:5, 6. Re 21:3, 4.

2. **what.** Ge 12:1-3. **go.** 2 Ch 21:20. Ps 39:13. **childless.** Ge 3:15. +*11:30. 25:21. 30:1, 2. Le 20:20. 1 S 1:11. Ps +*127:3. Pr 13:12. Is 56:5. Je 22:30. Ac +*7:5n. **the steward.** Ge 24:2, 10. 39:4-6, 9. 43:19. 44:1. Pr 17:2. **Eliezer.** i.e. *God of help,* ✱S#461h. Ex 18:4. 1 Ch 7:8. 15:24. 23:15, 17, 17. 26:25. 27:16. 2 Ch 20:37. Ezr 8:16. 10:18, 23, 31. (1) A man of Damascus who was steward of Abram's house, Ge 15:2. (2) A son of Moses, Ex 18:4; 1 Ch 23:15. (3) A son of Becher, 1 Ch 7:8. (4) A priest who assisted in bringing up the ark out of the house of Obed-edom, 1 Ch 15:24. (5) Ruler of the tribe of Reuben in the time of David, 1 Ch 27:16. (6) A prophet who prophesied against Jehoshaphat, 2 Ch 20:37. (7) A chief man who went with Ezra from Babylon to Jerusalem, Ezr 8:16. (8) A priest who took a foreign wife, Ezr 10:18. (9) A Levite who took a foreign wife, Ezr 10:23. (10) A Jew of the sons of Harim who took a foreign wife, Ezr 10:31. (11) An ancestor of Joseph, the husband of Mary, Lk 3:29.

3. **Behold.** ♪40, Ge +3:22. Ge 12:2. 13:16. Pr 13:12. Je 12:1. He 10:35, 36. **born.** Ge 14:14. Pr 29:21. 30:23. Ec 2:7. **heir.** Heb., inherits me. ♪121K2. Figure of speech Metonymy of the Subject B583: the possessor is put for the thing possessed; here, a person is put for possessions. For another instance of this figure see 2 C 11:20.

4. **shall come.** Ge 17:16. 21:12. 2 S 7:12. 16:11. 2 Ch 32:21. Ga 4:28. Phm 12.

5. **Look.** Ge +13:14. **tell.** ♪138B, Ge +13:16. Ge *22:17. 26:4. Dt 1:10. Ps 147:4. Je 33:22. Ro 9:7, 8. **So.** Ge 12:2. 13:16. 16:10. 22:17. 28:14. Ex 32:13. Dt 1:10. *10:22. 1 Ch 27:23. Ro ▶4:18. He *11:12.

6. **believed.** Ro ▶4:3, 6, 22. Ga ▶3:6. Ja ▶2:23. Ge ◖28:20. Ro *4:3-6, 9, 20-25. *10:17. Ga *3:6-14. He *11:8. Ja *▶2:23. **he counted.** Ps 106:31. Ro 4:▶9, 11, *22. 2 C *5:19. Ga *▶3:6. S#2803h: Ge 31:15 (counted). Le 7:18 (imputed). Nu 18:27 (reckoned). Ps *32:2 (imputeth). 40:17 (thinketh). Je 26:3 (purpose). La 4:2 (esteemed). Ml 3:16 (thought upon). **righteousness.** Ge 6:9 (just). 7:1. Ro *10:3, 4. S#6666. Ge 18:19 (justice). 30:33. Dt 6:25. 9:4, 5. Ps 5:8. 11:7. 51:14. Pr 8:18, 20. 11:4, 18. 12:28. 15:9. 16:8. Is √64:6. Ezk 33:12, 13. Ml 4:2.

7. **brought.** Ge *11:28-31. *12:1. Ne *9:7. Ac 7:2-4. **to give.** Ge 12:7. 13:15-17. Ne 9:8. Ps 105:11, 42, 44. Ro 4:13.

8. **whereby.** Ge 24:2-4, 13, 14. Jg *6:17-24, 36-40. 1 S 14:9, 10. 2 K 20:8. Ps 86:17. Is 7:11. Lk *1:18, 34. **know.** Ml 3:10. 1 J *5:13.

9. **Take.** Je 34:18, 19. He 6:17, 18. **heifer.** Ge 22:13. Le 1:3, 10, 14. 3:1, 6. 9:2, 4. 12:8. 14:22, 30. Ps 50:5. Lk 2:24. **three.** Is 15:5.

10. **divided them.** ver. 17. Je 34:+*18n, 19. 2 T 2:15. **the birds.** Le 1:17.

11. **fowls.** Ezk 17:3, 7. Mt 13:4. **Abram.** Ps 119:13. **drove.** 2 S 21:10.

12. **sun.** Ge 19:1. 28:11. **deep.** Ge *2:21. 28:11. 1 S 26:12. Jb 4:13, 14. 33:15. Da 10:8, 9. Ac 20:9. 2 C 1:9. **lo.** ♪40, Ge +3:22. **horror.** Ps 4:3-5. Ac 9:8, 9. **darkness.** Jb +38:9.

13. **Know.** ♪147B, Ge +2:16; +26:28. 2 P 1:19. **thy.** Ge 17:8. *21:12. Ex ch. 1, 2, 5. 22:21. 23:9. Le 19:34. Dt 10:19. Ps *105:11, 12, 23-25. Ac ▶7:6, 7. He 11:8-13. **land.** Ge 46:3. Ac 7:17. **shall serve.** Dt 5:15. Ps 105:25. ♪81. Figure of speech Epitrechon; or, Running Along B472: parenthetic addition by way of a statement thrown in which is not complete in itself. Here, "and shall serve them and they shall afflict them" pertains to the servitude in Egypt. The outer or first and last members of this structure (introversion) pertain to the whole sojourning and duration and can be read together: "Thy seed shall be a stranger four hundred years." For other instances of this figure see Ge 19:20. 46:26. Ex 12:40. 1 K 8:39, 42. Ps 68:18. Mt 9:6. Jn 2:9. 4:8. Ac 1:15. Ro 3:8. 8:20. Ro 9:3. 10:6, 7. Ep *2:5. Col 2:21, 22. He 12:20, 21. **four hundred.** Ex *12:40, 41. Ga 3:17. The four hundred years date from Isaac's birth (Ac 7:6). The 430 from the "promise" or Covenant here made (Ga 3:17), and include the whole "sojourning" (Ex 12:40), *Companion Bible.* See further notes on Ge 17:7. 21:12. Ex 12:40.

14. **that.** Ge ch. 46. Ex 6:5, 6. ch. 7-14. Dt 4:20. *6:22. 7:18, 19. 11:2-4. Jsh 24:4-7, 17. 1 S 12:8. Ne 9:9-11. Ps 51:4. 78:43-51. 105:27-37. 135:9, 14. **judge.** Ex 7:4. *12:12. Nu 33:4. ♪121C2D2. Figure of speech Metonymy (of the cause) B557: the thing or action is put for that which is the effect or product of it, involving a verb of action, where to judge is put for punish or condemn, not simply rule. For other instances of this figure see 2 Ch 20:12. Ps 9:19. Jn 3:18. Ro 14:3. He 13:4. Similarly, *to judge* is also used in the sense of *acquit,* which is also an effect of judging, as in Ps 35:24. **with great.** Ex 3:21, 22. *12:35, 36, 38. Ps *105:37.

15. **And thou.** Ge 25:8. +*35:29. 47:30. Nu 20:24. 27:13. Jg 2:10. 2 S 12:23. Ec +12:7. Lk *20:37, 38. Ac 13:36. **go to.** ♪88. Figure of speech Euphemism B685: where a pleasing expression is used for one that is unpleasant. Here, "thou shalt go to thy fathers" means thou shalt die and be buried. Abram's fathers were idolaters, Jsh 24:2. For other instances of euphemism in various forms see Ge +4:1, knew. 24:2. 25:8. 42:38. Dt 23:13. Jg 3:24. Ru 3:9. 1 S 24:3. 2 S 18:32. 2 K 22:20. Ne 4:23mg. Jb 10:21, 22. 16:22. 18:13, *14. Ps 94:17. Ec 3:21. 12:5. Is 38:10. Mt 8:11. 11:19. Lk 7:35. Jn 2:25. 11:11. Ac 2:39. Ph 1:23. 2 P 1:13, 14. **in peace.** 2 Ch 34:28. Ps *37:37. Is *57:1, 2. Da 12:13. Mt 22:32. He 6:13-19. 11:13-16. **buried.** Ge 23:4, 19. 25:8-10. 35:29. 49:29, 31. 50:13. Ec 6:3. Je 8:1, 2. **good.** Ge 25:7, 8. 1 Ch 23:1. 29:28. Jb *5:26. 42:17.

16. **in the.** Ex 12:40, 41. **come hither.** Jsh 14:1. Ac 7:7. **Amorites.** Ge +10:16. 1 K 21:26. 2 P 3:8, 9. **not yet full.** Le 18:24-28. 1 K 21:26. 2 K 21:11. Da 8:23. Zc 5:5-11. Mt *23:32-35. Lk 6:35. 1 Th 2:16. 2 P *3:8, 9. Re 6:11. 14:17-19.

17. **dark.** Jb +38:9. **behold.** ♪40, Ge +3:22. **smok-**

ing. Ge 19:28. Ex 3:2, 3. *19:18. Dt 4:20. Jg 6:21. 13:20. 1 Ch 21:26. Is *48:10. 62:1. Je 11:4. He *12:29. **furnace**. Dt=4:20. 1 K 8:51. Is 31:9. Ezk 22:18-22. Je 11:4. **a burning lamp**. Heb. a lamp of fire. 2 S 21:17. 22:9, 29. 1 K=11:36. 15:4. Ps 27:1. 132:17. Is 62:1. **passed**. Dt 29:12n. Jsh 9:6mg. Je 34:18, 19.

18. **made**. Ge 9:8-17. ch. 17. 24:7. 2 S +*23:5. Is +√55:3. Je *31:31-34. *32:40. +√33:20-26. Ga 3:15-17. He 13:20. **covenant**. Ge 6:18. +*9:16. **Unto thy.** Ge 12:7. +*13:15. 17:8. 26:4. 28:4, 13, 14. 35:12. 50:24. Ex 3:8. 6:4. *23:23, 27-31. 34:11. Nu 34:3. Dt 1:7, 8. 7:1. 11:24. *34:4. Jsh 1:3, 4. ch. 12, 19. 1 K *4:21n. 2 Ch 9:26. Ne 9:8. Ps 105:11. **this land**. Ge +*13:15. **river of Egypt.** Ex 23:31. Nu 34:5. Jsh 15:4. Is +*27:12. **river Euphrates.** Ge 2:14. 2 S 8:3. 1 K 4:21. 1 Ch 5:9. Is +*27:12.

19. **Kenites**. Nu 24:21, 22. Jg 1:16. 4:11, 17. 5:24. 1 S 15:6. 27:10. 30:29. 1 Ch 2:55. **Kenizzites.** i.e. *hunter*, ✳S#7074h. Ge 36:11. Nu 32:12. Jsh 14:6, 14. **Kadmonites.** i.e. *ancients, easterners,* ✳S#6935h.

20. **Hittites**. Ex 3:8, 17. 13:5. Jsh 1:4. 3:10. 12:8. 24:11. Jg 1:26. 3:5. 1 K 9:20. 10:29. 11:1. 2 K *7:6. 2 Ch 1:17. 8:7. Ezr 9:1. Ne 9:8. **Perizzites**. Ge +13:7. **Rephaims**. Ge +14:5. Is 17:5.

21. **Amorites**. Ge +10:16. Ex 23:23-28. 33:2. 34:11. Dt 7:1. **Canaanites**. Ge +10:18. **Girgashites.** i.e. *dwellers on clay soil; a stranger drawing near,* ✳S#1622h. Ge +10:16. Dt 7:1. Jsh 3:10. 24:11. 1 Ch 1:14. Ne 9:8. Mt 8:28. **Jebusites**. Ge +10:16.

GENESIS 16

Sarai being barren gives Hagar to Abram, 1-3. Hagar despises Sarai, who complains to Abram; he gives up Hagar to her, and Hagar, being harshly treated, flees from her, 4-6. An Angel commands her to return and submit, promises her a son and a numerous posterity, and shows their character and condition, 7-12. Hagar gives a name to the place, and returns to Sarai, 13, 14. The birth of Ishmael, and the age of Abram, 15, 16.

1. A.M. 2092. B.C. 1912. **bare**. Ge +*11:30. 15:2, 3. 21:10, 12. 25:21. Jg 13:2. Lk 1:7, 36. **handmaid**. 1 S 25:41. **Egyptian**. Ge 12:16. 21:9, 21. **name**. Ga 4:24, Agar. **Hagar**. i.e. *the sojourner, stranger; southern, flight,* ✳S#1904h. Ge 16:1, 3, 4, 8, 15, 15, 16. 21:9, 14, 17. 25:12.

2. **the Lord**. Ge 17:16. 18:10. 20:18. 25:21. 30:2, 3, 9, 22. Ru ◐+*1:13. 1 S 1:5. Ps +*127:3. **go in**. Ge ◐21:10. 27:8. **obtain children**. Heb. be builded. Ge 30:3, 6. Ex 21:4. Ru 4:11. **hearkened**. Ge 3:1-6, 12, *17. Ep *5:21. 1 P ◐3:6.

3. A.M. 2093. B.C. 1911. **after**. Ga 3:3. **had**. Ge 12:4, 5. **gave**. ver. 5. Ge 30:4, 9. **his**. Ge 25:6. 28:9. 32:22. 35:22. Jg 19:1-4. 2 S 5:13. 1 K 11:3. Ga 4:25. **wife**. Ge +4:19.

4. **her mistress**. 1 S 1:6-8. 2 S 6:16. Pr *30:20, 21, 23. 1 C 4:6. 13:4, 5. ✸63A1, Ellipsis (absolute, of the nominative), Ge +14:20. Supply "Sarai." **despised**. Ge 21:9. Ro 3:27. **despised**. ver. 5. S#7043h. Other renderings of this Hebrew word in its various grammatical forms include *shall be lightly esteemed,* 1 S 2:30. *light thing,* 1 S 18:23. 2 K 3:18. Is 49:6. *easy,* Pr 14:6. *curse,* Ge 8:21. 12:3. Jsh 24:9. Pr 20:20. Ec *7:21. *despise,* 2 S 19:43. *contempt,* Is 23:9.

5. **My wrong**. Lk 10:40, 41. **despised**. ver. +4. Ge

+21:9. **the Lord**. Ge 31:53. Ex 5:21. 1 S 24:12-15. 2 Ch 24:22. Ps 7:8. 35:23. 43:1.

6. **Abram**. Ge 13:8, 9. Pr 14:29. 15:1, 17, 18. 1 P *3:7. **Sarai**. i.e. *my princesses; contentious,* ✳S#8297h. Ge 11:29, 30, 31. 12:5, 11, 17. 16:1, 2, 2, 3, 5, 6, 6, 8, 8. 17:15, 15. **in**. Ge 24:10. Jb 2:6. Ps 106:41, 42. Je 38:5. **as it pleaseth thee**. Heb. that which is good in thine eyes. Jsh +22:30mg. 1 K 21:2mg. 2 Ch 30:4mg. Zc 11:12mg. **dealt hardly with her**. Heb. afflicted her. Pr 29:19. **fled**. Ex 2:15. Pr *15:12. 27:8. Ec 10:4. 1 C *7:10-16. 1 P 2:20.

7. **angel of**. ver. 13. 18:1. 22:11. Ex *23:20, 21. Is *63:9. Ml *3:1. **found**. Ge 2:17-19. Pr 15:3. **the fountain**. Ge 25:18. Ex 15:22. 1 S 15:7. **Shur**. i.e. *a wall, rampart, fort,* ✳S#7793h. Ge 16:7. 20:1. *25:18. Ex 15:22. 1 S 15:7. 27:8. The desert of Shur being between the south of Canaan, where Hebron was situated, and Egypt, it is likely that Hagar was returning to her own country.

8. **Sarai's maid**. ver. 1, 4. Ep 6:5-8. 1 T 6:1, 2. **whence**. Ge 3:9. 4:10. Ec 10:4. Je 2:17, 18. **I flee**. 1 S 26:19. **face**. ✸144A1, Ge +11:8.

9. **Return**. Ps 74:21. Pr *24:10. Je 12:5. Mt 25:21. Mk 5:19. Lk *16:10. 1 C 7:13. T +*2:4. Phm 12. **submit**. Ec 10:4. Mt 20:27. Ro 12:10. 1 C 11:3. +*14:34. Ep 5:21, 22. 6:5, 6. Ph +*2:3. Col 2:11n. +*3:18. T 2:9. Phm 21. He 13:17. 1 P *2:18-25. *5:5, 6. S#6031h. This is the only place where this Hebrew word is translated *submit*. Other renderings of this Hebrew word in its various grammatical forms include *afflict,* Ex 22:22, 23. Ezr 8:21. Ps 116:10. 119:67, 71. Is 53:4, 7. 58:10. Na 1:12. *chasten,* Da 10:12. *dealt hardly,* Ge 16:6. *force,* Jg 10:25. 2 S 13:12, 14, 22. See also Ezk 22:10, 11 (humbled). *humble,* Ex 10:3. Dt 8:2, 16.

10. **the angel**. Ge 22:15-18. 31:11-13. 32:24-30. 48:15, 16. Ex 3:2-6. Jg 2:1-3. 6:11, 16, 21-24. 13:16-22. Is 63:9. Ho 12:3-5. Zc 2:8, 9. Ml 3:1. Jn 1:18. Ac 7:30-38. 1 T 6:16. **I will**. Ge 17:20. 21:13, 16. 25:12-18. 1 Ch 1:29. Ps 83:6, 7. Ep 6:8.

11. **shalt**. Ge 17:19. 29:32-35. Is 7:14. Mt 1:21-23. Lk 1:13, 31, 63. **Ishmael**. i.e. God shall hear. ✳S#3458h. Ge 16:11, 15, 16. 17:18, 20, 23, 25, 26. 25:9, 12, 13, 13, 16, 17. 28:9, 9. 36:3. 2 K 25:23, 25. 1 Ch 1:28, 29, 31. 8:38. 9:44. 2 Ch 19:11. 23:1. Ezr 10:22. Je 40:8, 14, 15, 16. 41:1, 2, 3, 6, 7, 8, 9, 9, 10, 10, 11, 12, 13, 14, 15, 16, 18. (1) The son of Abraham by Hagar. (2) A descendant of the royal family of Judah, who murdered Gedaliah, the governor appointed by Nebuchadnezzar, in the basest manner and then was compelled by Johanan to flee to the Ammonites, Je ch. 41; 2 K 25:23, 25. (3) A son of Azel, a descendant of Benjamin, 1 Ch 8:38; 9:44. (4) Father of Zebadiah, a ruler of the house of Judah, 2 Ch 19:11. (5) One of the captains by whose aid Jehoiada the priest set Joash on the throne of Judah, 2 Ch 23:1. (6) A priest who had a foreign wife, Ezr 10:22. **because**. Ge 41:51, 52. 1 S 1:20. **hath**. Ge 29:32, 33. Ex 2:23, 24. 3:7. Jb 38:41. Ps 22:24. **heard**. ✸22C14. Figure of speech Anthropomorphism B888: human actions are attributed to God. Here, hearing. For other instances of this figure see Ge 21:17. Ex 2:24. Ps 4:3. 5:1, 2, 3. 10:17. *66:18. 130:2. Is *65:24. 1 J *5:14.

12. **be a**. Ge 21:20. Jb 11:12. 39:5-8. **wild**. The word rendered *wild* also denotes the *wild ass*; the description of which animal in Job 39:5-8, affords the very best representation of the wandering, lawless, freebooting

life of the Bedouin and other Arabs, the descendants of Ishmael. ✻S#6501. Jb 6:5. 11:12. 24:5. *39:5. Ps 104:11. Is 32:14. Je 2:24. 14:6. Ho 8:9. **his hand.** Ge 27:40. **against every.** Ge 21:20. Ezr 8:31. Ps 10:8, 9. Is 21:13. Je 3:2. **he shall.** Ge ✻25:18. **brethren.** Ge 37:28. Jg 8:22, 24.

13. **called.** ver. 7, 9, 10. Ge 22:14. 28:17, 19. 32:30. Jg 6:24. **Lord that.** Ge +12:7. 17:1. 18:1. **Thou God.** Ex 33:18-23. *34:5-7. Ps *139:1-12. Pr *15:3. **seest.** 2 Ch 16:9. Jb 31:4. Ps *139:7. Pr *5:21. Je 16:17. Zc 4:10. He 4:13. ♪22C13. Figure of speech Anthropomorphism B888. Human actions are attributed to God: seeing. For other instances of this figure see Ge 1:4, 10, 12, 18, 21, 25. Ex 2:25. 32:9. 1 S 16:8. Ps 11:4. **looked.** Ge 32:30. Ex 24:10. ◖33:20. 23. Dt 5:24. Jg 6:22. 13:22. Is 6:5. Jn ◖1:18. 1 T ◖6:16. 1 J ◖4:12. ♪121S3. Figure of speech Metonymy (of the adjunct) B607: the sign is put for the thing signified, involving connected words or phrases. Here, "looking" is put for living or being alive because Hagar had seen God and yet lived. **him that.** Ge 31:42.

14. **well.** Ge *21:19. ✻S#875h, *be-er,* a dug well. Ge 14:10. 16:14. 21:19, 25, 30. 24:11, 20. 26:15, 18, 19, 20, 21, 22, 25, 32. 29:2, 2, 3, 3, 8, 10. Ex 2:15. Nu 20:17. 21:16, 17, 18, 22. 2 S 17:18, 19, 21. Ps 55:23. 69:15. Pr 5:15. 23:27. SS 4:15. For ✻S#953h, *bor* or *bore,* a hewn cistern, well, etc., see Ge +37:20. For ✛S#5869h, *ayin,* a fountain, see Ge +24:13. For ✻S#4599h, *mayan,* a spring or fountain, see Ge +7:11. For S#4726h, *maqor,* spring, dug well (even when naturally flowing), see Le +12:7. Pr 10:11. **Beer-lahai-roi.** That is, The well of him that liveth and seeth me. ✻S#883h. Ge 21:31. *24:62h. *25:11h. **Kadesh.** Nu 13:26. **Bered.** i.e. *hail; seed place,* ✻S#1260h. (1) A place in the south of Canaan, Ge 16:14. (2) A grandson of Ephraim, 1 Ch 7:20. Same as Becher, Nu 26:35.

15. A.M. 2094. B.C. 1910. **Hagar.** ver. 11. Ge 25:12. 1 Ch 1:28. Ga 4:22, 23. **Ishmael.** Ge 17:18, 20, 25, 26. 21:9-21. 25:9, 12. 28:9. 37:27, 28. 39:1.

16. **years old.** Ge 12:4. 17:1, 17, 24. 21:5. **Hagar.** ver. 1. Ge 21:14. 25:12. **Ishmael.** Ge 17:18, 20. *21:10, 20. 25:12.

GENESIS 17

The Lord again ratifies the covenant with Abram; changes his name to Abraham, and Sarai's to Sarah, and institutes circumcision, 1-15; he promises him a son by Sarah; accepts his prayer for Ishmael; and fixes the time for the birth of Isaac, 16-22. Abraham circumcises himself and the males of his family, 23-27.

1. A.M. 2107. B.C. 1897. **was.** Ge 16:16. **the Lord.** Ge 12:1. **appeared.** Ge +12:7. +16:13. 26:2. 35:9. Ex 3:16. 1 K 3:5. 9:2. 2 Ch 3:1. Jn ◖1:18. **I am.** Ex 6:3. Jn 1:3. 8:56. Ac 7:38. Re 1:8. 15:3. 16:7. **Almighty God.** Heb. El Shaddai. S#7706h. Ge 18:14. 28:3. 35:11. 43:14. 48:3. 49:25. Ex *6:3. Nu 11:23. 24:4, 16. Dt 10:17. Ru 1:20, 21. Jb +5:17. Ps 68:14. 91:1. 115:3. Is 13:6. Je 32:17. Ezk 1:24. 10:5. Da 4:35. Jl 1:15. Mt 19:26. 2 C *6:18. Ep 3:20. Ph 4:13. He 7:25. Re +*1:8. **walk.** Ge *5:22, 24. *6:9. 24:40. 48:15. 1 K *2:4. 3:6. 8:25. 2 K +*20:3. Ps 15:2. 116:9. Is 38:3. Mi +*6:8. Lk 1:6. Ac 23:1. 24:16. Col +√1:10. He 12:28. 1 J *2:6. **perfect.** *or,* upright, *or* sincere. Ge 6:9. Dt 18:13. 2 S *22:33. Jb *1:1. Ps 18:23. *37:18n. Mt *5:48. Ep 1:4. *3:20. 5:27. Ph 2:15. 3:6, ◖√12.

Col 3:22. 1 Th 2:10. 3:13. *5:23. He 8:7. 9:14. *12:14. Ja ◖√3:2, 8. 1 P 1:19. 2 P *3:14. Ju *24. Re 14:5.

2. **And I.** ver. 4-6. Ge 9:9. 15:18. Ps 105:8-11. Ga 3:17, 18. **multiply.** Ge *12:2. *13:16. *22:17. Dt 1:10. He 11:12. **exceedingly.** ♪84, Ge +6:17. Ge +7:19.

3. **fell.** ver. +17. Ge 18:2. 19:1. 33:3. Ex 3:6. 18:7. Le 9:23, 24. Nu 14:5. 16:4, 22, 45. 20:6. *22:31. Dt 9:18, 25. Jsh *5:14. 7:6. Jg 13:20. 1 K 18:39. Ezk +1:28. 3:23. 9:8. Da 8:17, 18. 10:9. Mt +*14:33. 17:6. Lk 17:16. Re 1:17. 5:8, +*12, 14. *7:11. 11:16.

4. **a father.** Ge 12:2. 13:16. 16:10. 22:17. 25:1-18. 32:12. 35:11. ch. 36. Nu ch. 1, 26. Ro *4:11-18. Ga *3:28, 29. **many nations.** Heb. multitude of nations. Ge 48:19.

5. **but thy name.** ver. 15. Ge 25:26. 27:36. 32:28. Nu 13:16. Ru 1:20. 2 S 12:25. Ne 9:7. Is 62:2-4. 65:15. Je 20:3. 23:6. 33:16. Ezk 48:35. Mt 1:21-23. 16:18. Jn 1:42. Re 2:17. **Abraham.** i.e. *father of a great multitude.* ✻S#85h. Ge 17:5, 9, 15, 17, 18, 22, 23, 23, 24, 26. 18:6, 7, 11, 13, 16, 17, 18, 19, 22, 23, 27, 33, 33. 19:27, 29. 20:1, 2, 9, 10, 11, 14, 17, 18. 21:2, 3, 4, 5, 7, 8, 9, 10, 11, 12, 14, 22, 24, 25, 27, 28, 29, 34. 22:1, 1, 3, 4, 5, 6, 7, 8, 9, 10, 11, 11, 13, 13, 14, 15, 19, 19, 20, 23. 23:2, 3, 5, 7, 10, 12, 14, 16, 16, 18, 19, 20. 24:1, 1, 2, 6, 9, 12, 12, 15, 27, 34, 42, 48, 52, 59. 25:1, 5, 6, 6, 7, 8, 10, 10, 11, 12, 12, 19, 19. 26:1, 3, 5, 15, 18, 18, 24, 24. 28:4, 4, 9, 13. 31:42, 53. 32:9. 35:12, 27. 48:15, 16. 49:30, 31. 50:13, 24. Ex 2:24. 3:6, 15, 16. 4:5. 6:3, 8. 32:13. 33:1. Le 26:42. Nu 32:11. Dt 1:8. 6:10. 9:5, 27. 29:13. 30:20. 34:4. Jsh 24:2, 3. 1 K 18:36. 2 K 13:23. 1 Ch 1:27, 28, 32, 34. 16:16. 29:18. 2 Ch 20:7. 30:6. Ne 9:7. Ps 47:9. 105:6, 9, 42. Is 29:22. 41:8. 51:2. 63:16. Je 33:26. Ezk 33:24. Mi 7:20. **for.** Ro 14:17. **many.** ♪24N. Figure of speech Antimereia; or, Exchange of Parts of Speech B505. Here, of the noun, the first of two nouns used as an adjective. For other instances of this figure see Ge 45:22. Ac 7:30. Ro 5:2. *8:2. 2 C 4:4, 6. Ep 1:6. 1 T 1:11. T 2:13. Re 18:3.

6. **exceedingly.** ♪84, Ge +6:17. **nations.** ver. 4, 20. Ge 35:11. **kings.** ver. 16, 19. Ge 35:11. 36:31. Ex 19:6. Ezr 4:20. Mt *1:6-11. Ro +*4:13. Re 1:5, 6. √5:9, 10. √20:6.

7. **And I.** Ge 15:18. 26:24. Ex 6:4. Ps 105:8-11. Mi 7:20. Lk 1:54, 55, 72-75. Ro 9:4, 8. Ga 3:17. Ep 2:2. **thy seed.** Here, the collective noun *zer'a* is shown to be plural by the words "after thee" (compare verses 8, 9), and by the plural pronoun "their generations" (verses 7, 9). This is not the verse referred to in Galatians 3:16, but Ge 21:12. See note on 21:12, where "seed" must be in the singular because of the verb. See note on Ge 15:13 (*Companion Bible*). **generations.** Ge +9:12. **everlasting.** ver. 13, 19. Ge +9:16. Jg 2:1. Ps 105:9, 10. 111:5. Is 44:7mg. He *13:20. 1 P *1:20. Heb. *olam,* ✛S#5769h: Ge 9:16. 17:7, 8, 13, 19. *21:33. 48:4. 49:26. Ex 40:15. Le 16:34. 24:8. Nu 25:13. Dt 33:27. 2 S 23:5. 1 Ch 16:17. Ps 24:7, 9n. 93:2. 100:5. 105:10. 112:6. 119:142, 144. 139:24. Pr 8:23. 10:25. Is 24:5. *33:14. 35:10. *40:28. 51:11. 54:8. 55:3, 13. 56:5. 60:19, 20. 61:7, 8. 63:12, 16. Je 10:10. 20:11. 23:40. 31:3. 32:40. Ezk 16:60. 37:26. Da 4:3, 34. 7:14, 27. 12:2, 2. Mi *5:2. Hab 3:6. For passages where *olam* is rendered *for ever,* see Ex +12:24. See related note (Jn +*6:54n). **to be a God.** Ge 24:12. *26:24. *28:13. 31:42. 32:9. Ex 3:6, 15. 20:2. 29:45. Le 11:45. 26:12, 45. Ps 47:9. 81:10. Je *24:7. 30:22.

*31:33. Ezk 11:20. 28:26. Zc +*13:9. Mt 22:32. Jn +20:17. 2 C *6:16. He 8:10. *11:16. Re 21:3, 7. **and to.** Ex 19:5, 6. Dt +*29:11n. Ne +*12:43. Mt *19:14. Mk 10:14. Lk *1:54, 55. Ac +*2:39. Ro *9:7-9. 1 C √7:14n. Ga ?♭3:16.

8. **And I.** Ge 12:7. 13:15, 17. 15:7-21. Ps 105:9, 11. Ac +*♭7:5. **thy seed.** ver. +*7. **the land.** Is +*60:21. *63:18. **wherein thou art a stranger.** Heb. of thy sojournings. Ge 23:4. 28:4. **everlasting.** Heb. olam, ver. +*7. Ge +*8:22. +*13:15. 48:4. Ex 21:6. 31:16, 17. 40:15. Le 16:34. Nu 25:13. Dt 32:8. 2 S +*23:5. Ps 103:17. He 9:15. 1 P *1:4. 2 P *1:11. **their God.** ver. +*7. Ex 6:7. Le 26:12. Dt 4:37. *14:2. *26:18. *29:13.

9. **keep.** Ge +4:7. Ps 25:10. *103:17, 18. Is 56:4, 5.

10. **Every.** ver. 11. Ge 34:15. Ex 4:25. 12:48. Dt 10:16. 30:6. Jsh 5:2, 4. Je 4:4. 9:25, 26. Ac 7:8. Ro 2:25, 28, 29. 3:1, 25, 28, 30. 4:9-11. 1 C 7:18, 19. Ga 3:28. 5:3-6. 6:12. Ep 2:11. Ph 3:3. Col *2:11, 12.

11. **circumcise.** Ro *2:28, 29. 1 C 7:19. Ga 5:6. Ph 3:3. Col *2:11. **the flesh.** Ex 4:25. Jsh 5:3. 1 S 18:25-27. 2 S 3:14. ♪88. Euphemism B684. "Flesh" put for male organ of generation (BDBG, p. 142, S#3). Compare Ge 24:2, thigh; Dt 23:1; Ho ◐2:10, S#5040h, lewdness, lit. pudenda. For other instances of this figure see Ge 17:14, 23, 24, 25. Ex +*19:15. 28:42mg. Le 15:2, 3, 7, 13, 16, ◐19. Ezk *16:26. *23:20. 44:7, 9. **a token.** Ex *12:13. Jsh *2:12. Ac 7:8. Ro *4:11. 2 T *2:19. He 11:28.

12. **he that is eight days old.** Heb. a son of eight days. ver. ◐25. Ge 21:4. Le *12:3. Jon 4:10mg. Lk 1:59. *2:21. Jn 7:22, 23. Ac 7:8. Ro 2:28. Ph *3:5. **is born.** ver. 23. Ex 12:48, 49. **stranger.** ver. 27. Ge 35:2, 4. Ex +12:43 (✻S#5236h).

13. **born.** Ge 14:14. 15:3. Ex 12:44. 21:4. **bought.** Ge 37:27, 36. 39:1. Ex 21:2, 16. Ne 5:5, 8. Mt 18:25. **flesh.** ♪171Q5. Figure of speech Synecdoche (of the part) B642, where "flesh," an integral part of man, is put for the whole body. For other instances of this figure see Ps 16:9. Pr 14:30. Ac 2:26. 2 C 7:1. **everlasting.** Heb. olam, ver. +7. Ge +9:16.

14. **soul.** Heb. nephesh, used here as being "cut off" by God. √√171Q1, Ge +12:5. Ex 12:15, 19. 31:14. Le 7:20, 21, 25, 27. 17:10. 18:29. 19:8. 20:6. 22:3. 23:29, 30. Nu 9:13. 15:30, 31. 19:13, 20. Ezk 18:4, 20. For the other uses of nephesh see Ge +2:7. **cut off.** Ge 9:11. Ex *4:24-26. 12:15, 19. 30:33, 38. 31:14. Le 7:20, 21, 25, 27. 18:29. 19:8. Nu 15:30, 31. Jsh 5:2. Ps 101:5. Is 53:8. Da 9:26. Ml 2:12. **broken.** Ps 55:20. Is 24:5. 33:8. Je 11:10. 31:32. 1 C 11:27, 29.

15. **As.** ver. 5. Ge 32:28. 2 S 12:25. **Sarah.** i.e. princess. ✻S#8283h. Ge 17:15, 17, 19, 21. 18:6, 9, 10, 10, 11, 11, 12, 13, 14, 15. 20:2, 2, 14, 16, 18. 21:1, 1, 2, 3, 6, 7, 9, 12. 23:1, 1, 2, 2, 19. 24:36, 67. 25:10, 12. 49:31. Is 51:2.

16. **And I.** Ge 1:28. 12:2. 24:60. Ro 9:9. **give.** Ge 18:10-14. **be a mother of nations.** Heb. become nations. Ge 35:11. Ga 4:26-31. 1 P 3:6. **kings.** See on ver. 6. Is 49:23.

17. **fell.** ver. +3. Le 9:24. Nu 14:5. 16:22, 45. Dt 9:18, 25. Jsh 5:14. 7:6, +10mg. Jg 13:20. 1 Ch 21:16. Jb 1:20. Ezk +1:28. Da 8:17. Mt 2:11. Re 5:8. 11:16. **laughed.** Ge 18:12. 21:6. Ps *4:7. Jn *8:56. Ro 4:19, 20. **Shall.** ♪85E. Figure of speech Erotesis; or, Interrogating B951: the asking of questions without waiting

for the answer, in wonder and admiration. For other instances of this figure see Ge 27:20. 42:28. 1 S 9:21. (Ps 133:1). Is 63:1, 2. (Ezk 16:30). Hab 3:8. Mt 21:20. Mk 6:37.

18. **O that.** Ge 21:11. Je 32:39. Ac 2:39. **might live.** Dt 33:6. **before.** Ge 4:12, 14. Ps 4:6. 41:12. Is 59:2.

19. **Sarah.** ver. 21. Ge 18:10-14. 21:2, 3, 6. 2 K 4:16, 17. Lk 1:13-20. Ro *9:6-9. Ga 4:28-31. **Isaac.** ✻S#3327h. Ge 17:19, 21. 21:3, 4, 5, 8, 10, 12. 22:2, 3, 6, 7, 9. 24:4, 14, 62, 63, 64, 66, 67, 67. 25:5, 6, 9, 11, 11, 19, 19, 20, 21, 26, 28. 26:1, 6, 8, 9, 9, 12, 16, 17, 18, 19, 20, 25, 27, 31, 32, 35. 27:1, 5, 20, 21, 22, 26, 30, 30, 32, 33, 37, 39, 46. 28:1, 5, 6, 8, 13. 31:18, 42, 53. 32:9. 35:12, 27, 27, 28, 29. 46:1. 48:15, 16. 49:31. 50:24. Ex 2:24. 3:6, 15, 16. 4:5. 6:3, 8. 32:13. 33:1. Le 26:42. Nu 32:11. Dt 1:8. 6:10. 9:5, 27. 29:13. 30:20. 34:4. Jsh 24:3, 4. 1 K 18:36. 2 K 13:23. 1 Ch 1:28, 34, 34. 16:16. 29:18. 2 Ch 30:6. Yitzchak, which we change into Isaac, signifies laughter; in allusion to Abraham's laughing, ver. 17. By this Abraham did not express his unbelief or weakness of faith, but his joy at the prospect of the fulfillment of so glorious a promise; and to this our Lord evidently alludes, Jn 8:56. **everlasting.** Heb. olam, ver. +7. Ge 9:+12, +16. **his seed.** T#1877. Ge *21:12. 26:2-5. Mt 1:2. Lk +*3:23, 24. Ro 9:6-8. He *11:17-19.

20. **heard thee.** Ge +*18:32. Ps +*27:7. +*99:6. Examples of intercessory prayer answered: Abraham, Ge 17:18, 20. 18:23-32. 20:7, 17, 18. Moses for Pharaoh, Ex 8:12, 13, 30, 31. 9:33. 10:18, 19; for Israelites, Ex 17:11, 13. 32:11-14, 31-34. 33:15-17. Nu 11:2. 14:13-20. 21:7, 8. Dt 9:18, 19, 25. 10:10. Ps 106:23; for Miriam, Nu 12:13; and for Aaron, Dt 9:20. Samuel, 1 S 7:5-12. Solomon, 1 K ch. 8. 2 Ch ch. 6. 7:12-16. A prophet, 1 K 13:6. Elijah, 1 K 17:20-23. Elisha, 2 K 4:33-36. Isaiah, 2 K ch. 19. Jeremiah, Je 42:2-10. Shadrach, Da 2:17-23. Peter, Ac 9:40. The church, Ac 12:5-12. Paul, Ac 28:8. **blessed him.** Ge 16:10-12. **exceedingly.** ♪84, Ge +6:17. **twelve.** Ge *25:12-18. **and I.** Ge 21:13, 18.

21. **my.** Ge 21:10-12. 26:2-5. 46:1. 48:15. Ex 2:24. 3:6. Lk 1:55, 72. Ro 9:5, 6, 9. Ga 3:29. He 11:9. **at.** Ge 18:10. *21:2, 3. Jb 14:13. Ac +*1:7. Ga 4:4. **set time.** ✤S#4150h. Ge 1:14. 18:14. 21:2. Ex 9:5. 13:10. 23:15. 34:18. Le *23:2n (feasts), 4, 37, 44. Nu 9:2, 3, 7, 13. 10:10 (solemn days). 15:3. *28:2 (due season). 29:39. Dt 16:6 (season). 31:10. Jsh 8:14. Jg 20:38mg. 1 S 9:24 (time). 13:8, 11 (appointed). 20:35. 2 S 20:5. 24:15. 2 K 4:16mg, 17. 1 Ch 23:31. 2 Ch 2:4. 30:22. *31:3. Ezr 3:5. Ne 10:33. Jb *30:23 (appointed). Ps *102:13. 104:19 (seasons). Is 1:14. 33:20. Je 8:7. 46:17. La 1:4. 2:6, 7, 22. Ezk 36:38. 45:17. 46:9, 11. Da *8:19. *11:27, 29, 35. *12:7. Ho 2:9, 11. 9:5. 12:9. Hab *2:3. Zp 3:18. Zc 8:19mg. For S#4150h rendered tabernacle of the congregation, etc., see Ex 27:21n. Mt +*24:45.

22. **talking.** ver. 3. Ge *18:33. 35:9-15. Ex 20:22. Nu 12:6-8. Dt *5:4. Jg 6:21. *13:20. Jn +*1:18. *10:30. **went.** +1.

23. **circumcised.** ver. 10-14, 26, 27. Ge +*18:19. 34:24. Jsh 5:2-9. Ps *119:60. Pr 27:1. Ec 9:10. Ac 16:3. Ro 2:25-29. 4:9-12. 1 C *7:18, 19. Ga 5:6. 6:15. **self-same.** Ge +*7:13n.

24. **Abraham was.** ver. 1, 17. Ge 12:4. Ro *4:11, 19, 20.

25. **thirteen.** Not only the Jews, but the Arabs, who

are the descendants of Ishmael, retain the rite of circumcision to this day; and the latter perform it, as the other Mahometans also do, at the age of *thirteen*. ver. ◑12. Ge +14:4.

26. **In the**. Ge 12:4. 22:3, 4. Ps *119:60. **selfsame**. Ge +*7:13n.

27. **stranger**. ver. +12. **circumcised**. Ge *18:19. Ex 12:44.

GENESIS 18

The Lord again appears to Abraham, who entertains angels, 1-9. A son is promised to Sarah, at which she laughs, and her misconduct is rebuked, 9-15. The Lord discovers to Abraham his purpose of destroying Sodom, 16-22; who earnestly intercedes for the inhabitants, 23-33.

1. **appeared**. T#1774. ver. 2, 13, 14, 17, 19, 22, 33. Ge 15:1. 16:7. 17:+1-3, 22. 26:2. 48:3. Ex 3:2, 4. 4:1, 5. Jg 13:21. 2 Ch 1:7. Pr 8:22-31. Ml 3:1, 2. Jn *8:56. Ac 7:2. **Mamre**. Ge +13:18. 14:13. **and he sat**. In these verses we have a delightful picture of genuine and primitive hospitality: a venerable father sits at the tent door, not only to enjoy the current of refreshing air, but that if he saw any weary and exhausted travelers, he might invite them to rest and refresh themselves during the heat of the day, and the same custom continues in the east. It was not the custom, nor was there any necessity, for strangers to knock at the door, or to speak first, but to stand till they were invited. **heat**. Ge ◑15:12. ◑19:1. 31:40. Mt 20:12. Lk 12:55. Ja 1:11.

2. **And he**. Ge 22:4. Jg 13:3, 9. He 13:2. **lift**. ♪144A12, Ge +22:13. **looked**. Ge +13:14. **lo**. ♪40, Ge +3:22. **three**. ver. 22. Ge +1:26. 19:1. He 13:2. 1 P 4:9. **men**. Ge 32:24. Jn 1:14. **he ran**. Ge 24:29. 29:13. Ro 12:13. **bowed**. Ge 23:7. 33:3-7. 43:26, 28. 44:14. Ru 2:10. 2 K 2:15.

3. **Lord**. Heb. Adonai, S#136h. This is the first of 134 places where the ancient Sopherim altered "Jehovah" to "Adonai" out of extreme (but mistaken) reverence for the Ineffable Name "Jehovah." The other passages where this change was made are: Ge 18:27, 30, 32. 19:18. 20:4. Ex 4:10, 13. 5:22. 15:17. 34:9, 9. Nu 14:17. Jsh 7:8. Jg 6:15. 13:8. 1 K 3:10, 15. 22:6. 2 K 7:6. 19:23. Ezr 10:3. Ne 1:11. 4:14. Jb 28:28. Ps 2:4. 16:2. 22:19, 30. 30:8. 35:3, 17, 22. 37:12. 38:9, 15, 22. 39:7. 40:17. 44:23. 51:15. 54:4. 55:9. 57:9. 59:11. 62:12. 66:18. 68:11, 17, 19, 22, 26, 32. 73:20. 77:2, 7. 78:65. 79:12. 86:3, 4, 5, 8, 9, 12, 15. 89:49, 50. 90:1, 17. 110:5. 130:2, 3, 6. Is 3:17, 18. 4:4. 6:1, 8, 11. 7:14, 20. 8:7. 9:8, 17. 10:12. 11:11. 21:6, 8, 16. 28:2. 29:13. 30:20. 37:24. 38:14, 16. 49:14. La 1:14, 15, 15. 2:1, 2, 5, 7, 18, 19, 20. 3:31, 36, 37, 58. Ezk 18:25, 29. 21:13. 33:17, 29. Da 1:2. 9:3, 4, 7, 9, 15, 16, 17, 19, 19, 19. Am 5:16. 7:7, 8. 9:1. Zc 9:4. Mi 1:2. Ml 1:12, 14. In the following passages "Elohim" was altered to "Adonai": 2 S 5:19-25. 6:9-17. 1 Ch 13:12. 14:10, 11, 14, 16. Ps 14:1, 2, 5. 53:1, 2, 4, 5. **favor**. Ge 19:19. 32:5. 39:4. Ru 2:2, 10, 13. **pass not**. Ac 16:15. He *13:2. 1 P *4:9. **servant**. Ge 33:5.

4. **wash your feet**. In those ancient times, shoes such as ours, were not in use; and the foot was protected only with sandals or soles, fastened round the foot with straps. It was, therefore, not only necessary from motives of cleanliness, but also a very great refreshment, in so hot a country, to get the feet washed at the end of a day's journey; and this is the *first* thing that Abraham proposes. Ge 19:2. 24:32. 43:24. Jg 19:21. 1 S 25:41. 2 S 11:8. Lk 7:44. Jn 13:5-15. 1 T 5:10. **rest**. Mk 6:31. Jn 6:10. **tree**. Rest in the shade was the *second* requisite for the refreshment of a weary traveler.

5. **And I**. Jg 6:18. 13:15. Mt 6:11. **bread**. This was the *third* requisite, and is introduced in its proper order; as eating immediately after exertion or fatigue is very unwholesome. ♪171.I.8, Ge +3:19. **comfort**. Heb. stay. Jg 19:5. Ps 104:15. Is 3:1. **are ye come**. Heb. ye have passed. Ge 19:8. 33:10.

6. **hastened**. Ge 22:3. **Make ready quickly**. Heb. hasten. **three**. Nu 15:9. Is 32:8. Mt +*13:33. Lk 10:38-40. Ac 16:15. Ro 12:13. Ga 5:13. He 13:2. 1 P 4:9. **measures**. 1 S 25:18. 2 K *7:1, 16. Ps 80:5. Is 40:12. Mt 13:33. Lk 13:21. **cakes**. Ge 19:3. Ex 12:39. Le 7:12. 24:5. Nu 11:8. 1 K *17:13. Je 7:18. Ezk 4:12. Ho 7:8.

7. **ran**. Ge 19:3. 22:3. Jg 13:15, 16. Am 6:4. Ml 1:14. Mt 22:4. Lk 15:23, 27, 30. **calf**. Le 3:1.

8. **he took**. Ge 19:3. Dt 32:14. Jg 5:25. **butter**. Pr 30:33. Is 7:15. **stood**. 1 K 10:8. Ne 12:44. Lk 12:37. 17:8. Jn 12:2. Ro *12:13. Ga 5:13. Re *3:20. **and they**. Ge 19:3. Ex 24:11. Jg 13:15. Ps 78:25. Lk 22:16, 18, 30. *24:30, 43. Ac 10:41.

9. **Where**. Ge 4:9. Translate "And as to Sarah thy wife...and he (interrupting) said, Lo! (she is) in the tent." The *Companion Bible* states in Appendix 31, "The Fifteen Extraordinary Points of the Sopherim," that "There are fifteen words which present an abnormal appearance in the printed Hebrew Bibles. These are of the utmost importance, as they represent the most ancient result of Textual Criticism on the part of the *Sopherim*. Some are without effect as to translation or interpretation; others are more important, and will be noted in the passages where they occur. The following is the list": Ge 16:5. 18:9. 19:33, 35. 33:4. 37:12. Nu 3:39. 9:10. 21:30. 29:15. Dt 29:29. 2 S 19:29. Ps 27:13. Is 44:9. Ezk 41:20. 46:22. **in**. Ge 24:67. 31:33. T 2:5.

10. **he said**. ver. 13, 14. Ge 16:10. 22:15, 16. **certainly**. ♪147B, Ge +2:16. +26:28. **according**. Ge 17:21. 21:2. 2 K 4:16, 17. **lo**. ♪40, Ge +3:22. **Sarah thy**. Ge 17:16, 19, 21. 21:2. Jg 13:3-5. Mt 3:9. Lk 1:13. Ro 9:8, ♭9. Ga 4:23, 28. **heard**. Ge 27:5, 6. 37:17, 21. 42:23. Jg 7:11. Mt 10:27. Lk 12:2, 3. Jn 7:12, 13. Ac 23:16. Ep 5:11, 12. S#8085h.

11. **old**. Ge *17:17, 24. Lk 1:7, 18, 36. Ro *4:18-21. He *11:11, 12, 19. **ceased**. Ge +11:30. **the manner**. Ge 31:35. Le 15:19. Ro 4:19. ✢S#734h. Frequently translated *path* or *way*. Ge 49:17. Jg 5:6. Jb 6:18. 8:13. *16:22. 19:8. 22:15. 30:12. 31:32mg. 33:11. 34:11. Ps *16:11. *25:4, 10. 27:11. 44:18. 119:*9, 15, 101, 104, 128. Pr 1:19. 2:8, 13, 15, 19, 20. √3:6. 4:14, 18. 5:6. 8:20. 9:15. 10:17. *12:28. 15:10, 19, *24. 17:23. 22:25. Is 2:3. 3:12. 26:7, 8. 30:11. 33:8. 40:14. 41:3. Jl 2:7 (ranks). Mi 4:2.

12. **laughed**. ver. 13. Ge 17:17. 21:6, 7. Ps 126:2. Lk 1:18-20, 34, 35. He 11:11, 12. **After**. ♪85I. Figure of speech Erotesis; or, Interrogating B953: the asking of questions without waiting for the answer, here, in doubts. For other instances of this figure see Ho 6:4. 11:8. Mi 6:6. Ro 10:6, 7. **old**. Jb 13:28. Ps 32:3. **pleasure**. ✢S#5730h. 2 S 1:24 (delights). Ps 36:8. Je 51:34 (delicates). **my**. Ep 5:33. 1 P 3:6.

13. **Wherefore**. Jn 2:25. *85K. Figure of speech Erotesis, in expostulation, Ge +3:9. **Shall**. *85I. Erotesis, in doubts, ver. +12. **old**. Ge 17:17.

14. **Is**. Nu 11:23. Dt 7:21. 17:8. 1 S 14:6. 2 K 7:1, 2. Jb 36:5. 42:2. Ps 93:1. 95:3. Je *32:17. Mi *7:18. Zc 8:6. Mt *3:9. 14:31. *19:26. Mk *10:27. Lk 1:13, 37. 8:50. *18:27. Ro 4:17. 1 C 1:28. Ep 3:20. Ph 3:21. √4:13. He 11:19. *85C. Figure of speech Erotesis; or, Interrogating B949: the asking of questions without waiting for the answer; here, in affirmative negation, where the question is put in the affirmative, and the answer to be supplied by the mind is a very emphatic negative. For other instances of this figure see Ge 18:17. 50:19. Ex 15:11. Dt 7:17. 1 S 2:25. Jb 40:2, 4. 41:11. Ps 35:10. 106:2. Ec 3:21. Is 40:13, 14. Je 23:24. Jl 1:2. Zc 8:6. Mt 7:16. 12:26. Mk 4:21. Jn √8:46. Ac 10:47n. Ro 3:3. 8:31, 33, 34, 35. 11:34, 35. 1 C 9:7. 12:30. He *1:5, 13. **I will**. ver. 10. Ge 17:21. Dt 30:3. 2 K 4:16. **see**. Ps 90:13. Mi 7:18. Lk 1:13, 18. Ro ❿9:9.

15. **denied**. Ge 4:9. 12:13. 27:20. 31:35. Jb 2:10. Pr *28:13. Jn 18:17, 25-27. Ep 4:23. Col 3:9. 1 J 1:8. **Nay**. Ps 44:21. Pr 12:19. Mk 2:8. Jn +*2:25. Ro 3:19. He *4:13.

16. **looked**. Ge ❿13:10. **to bring**. 2 S 19:31. Ac 15:3. 20:38. *21:5. Ro 15:24. 3 J 6.

17. **Shall**. *85C, Ge +18:14. 2 K 4:27. 2 Ch 20:7. Ps *25:14. Am +*3:7. Jn *15:15. Ja 2:23.

18. **Abraham**. *121A5, Ge +9:27. **become**. See on Ge 12:2, 3. 22:17, 18. 26:4. Ps 72:17. Ac *3:25, 26. Ga *3:❭8, 14. Ep 1:3. **blessed**. Ge 12:3. Ps 51:18, 19. *122:6. Zc 8:23.

19. **For I**. 2 S 7:20. Ps *1:6. 11:4. *34:15. *40:17. Jn *10:14. 21:17. 2 T *2:19. **command**. Ge 17:23-27. 26:5. 35:2. Ex +*13:8. Dt *4:9, 10. *6:6, 7, +*20. *11:19-21. 32:46. Jsh √24:15. 1 S ❿3:13. 1 Ch +*28:9. Est 1:22n. Jb +*1:5. 4:3, 4. Ps √78:2-8. 101:2. *119:9. Pr *6:20-22. +*22:6. Is 38:19. Ml +*4:6. Ep +*6:4. 1 T *3:4, 5, 12. 2 T 1:5. +*3:15. **justice and**. 2 S 22:25. Ps 15:2. Pr 2:9. 21:3. Ezk *18:5. Mi +*6:8. **that the**. Ge +*22:18. 1 S *2:30, 31. Ac *27:23, 24, 31.

20. **the cry**. *155F, Ge +4:7. Ge 4:10. 19:13. Pr 21:13. Is 3:9. 5:7. Je 14:7. Ja +*5:4. 2 P 2:8. **Sodom and**. Dt 32:32. Is 1:10. Je 23:14. Ezk 16:46. Mt 11:23. Re 11:8. **sin**. Ge 13:13. **grievous**. Ge 13:13. Is 3:9. Ju 7.

21. **I will go down**. This is spoken figuratively; and as the Jewish writers speak, according to the language of men. So eyes, ears, hands, and other members of the body are attributed to God, for effecting those things which men cannot accomplish without these members. Ge 11:5, 7. Ex 3:8. 33:5. Mi 1:3. Jn 6:38. 1 Th 4:16. **see**. Jb 34:22. Ps 14:2. 90:8. Je 17:1, *10. Zp 1:12. He *4:13. **cry**. Ge 19:13. La 4:6. Ezk *16:49, 50. **I will know**. Ex 33:5. Dt 8:2. 13:3. Jsh 22:22. Ps 139. Lk 16:15. 2 C 11:11. *22C1. Figure of speech Anthropomorphism B883: human actions are attributed to God; here, "knowing." Not actual knowledge as such, but the acquiring of knowledge as though before ignorant. For other instances of this figure see Ge 22:12. Dt 8:2. Ps 14:2. 53:2.

22. **the men**. ver. 2. Ge 19:1. **stood**. The two, whom we suppose to have been created angels, departed at this time; and accordingly *two* entered Sodom at evening: while the one, called Jehovah throughout the chapter, continued with Abraham, who "stood yet before the Lord."—Scott. ver. 1. Ge 19:27. Ex 32:31.

Ps 106:23. Je 15:1. 18:20. Ezk 22:30. Ac 7:55. 1 T 2:1. Ja 5:16. *22C11. Figure of speech Anthropomorphism B888: human actions are attributed to God; here, "standing." *182. Emendations of the Sopherim. The primitive text read "But the Lord stood yet before Abraham." This is one of the eighteen passages altered by the Sopherim to remove the harshness of the Anthropomorphism. It was felt to be derogatory for the Lord to stand and wait Abraham's pleasure; and so the text was altered, as we have it in the present Hebrew Bible and all its versions. Other passages altered by the Sopherim are: Nu 11:15. 12:12. 1 S 3:13. 2 S 20:1. 1 K 12:16. +21:10n. 2 Ch 10:16. Jb 7:20. 32:3. Ps 106:20. Je 2:11. La 3:20. Ezk 8:17. Ho 4:7. Hab 1:12. Zc 2:8. Ml 1:13. Three other passages that have been altered, noted by the Massorah, but not included in any of the special lists, are: 2 S 12:14. Jb +2:9n. Ps 10:3. Ec 3:21. **Lord**. Ge +17:1. 31:11. 32:30. Jg 6:11.

23. **drew**. Ps 73:28. Je 30:21. He *10:22. Ja 5:17. **Wilt**. ver. 25. Ge 20:4. Ex *23:7. Nu 16:22. 2 S 24:17. Jb 8:3. 34:17. Ps 11:4-7. Je *12:1. 15:1. Mt 13:49. Ro 3:5, 6. **destroy**. S#5595h. Ge 19:15. Dt 32:23. 1 S 12:25. 26:10. 27:1. 1 Ch 21:12, 13. Ps 40:15. Is 7:20. Je 12:4. **the righteous**. T#1680. Ge 20:3, 4. Nu *16:22. 2 S *24:17. S#6662h. Ge 6:9. 2 S 23:3. Jb 12:4. Ps 5:13. 145:17. Pr 29:7. Ec 7:16, 20. **with**. Ezk 21:3. Mt 5:45. **wicked**. S#7563h. Ex 23:7. Jb 3:17. 9:22. Ps 1:6. 119:155. Pr 4:19. 5:22. 10:16, 20, 24, 25, 27, *28, 30, 32. Is 53:9. *57:20, 21. Mi 6:10.

24. **there**. ver. 32. Is 1:9. Je *5:1. Ezk❿14:14. 22:30. Mt √7:13, 14. 2 P 2:8. **spare**. Ac 27:24.

25. **be far**. Je *12:1. **with the wicked**. Ps *37:10. Pr 29:16. **righteous should**. Jb *8:20. 9:22, 23. Ec 7:15. *8:12, 13. Is *3:10, 11. *57:1, 2. Ml 3:18. **as the wicked**. Ex *23:7. Dt 1:16, 17. **Shall**. Dt +*32:4. Jb *8:3. 34:*12, 17-19. Ps 11:5-7. 50:6. *58:11. 98:9. *145:9. Is +*30:18. 33:22. Ezk +*18:25. Zc +*7:9. Lk +*6:35. Ac *17:31. Ro *2:2. *3:6. **Judge**. Ps *50:6. 67:4. Jn 5:22-27. 2 C 5:10. **earth**. *121J17, Ge +6:11. Ps +√94:2. **do right**. Ps 9:4mg, 8. +33:5 (T#232). +*145:17. Is 11:4. 2 T +*4:8.

26. **If**. ver. 24. Is 6:13. 10:22. 19:24. 65:8. Je *5:1. Ezk *22:30. Mt 24:22.

27. **I have**. ver. 30-32. Ezr 9:6. Jb 42:6-8. Is 6:5. Lk *18:1. **dust**. Ge 2:7. *3:19. Jb *4:19. 30:19. Ps *8:4. 113:7. 144:3. Ec 12:7. Is *6:5. *64:8. Lk *5:8. 1 C 15:47, 48. 2 C 5:1, 2. *111. Figure of speech Meiosis; or, A Belittling B155: a belittling of one thing to magnify another. This figure is also known by the name *litotes*. By this figure one thing is diminished in order to increase another thing. It thus differs from *175, Tapeinosis (Ge +27:44), in which a thing is lessened in order to emphasize its own greatness and importance. For other instances of this figure see Nu 13:33. 1 K 16:2. 1 S 24:14. Ezr 9:8. Jb 25:6. Ps 22:6. Is 40:15, 17. 41:14. Am 6:13. Mt 6:13. 15:26. 18:14. *22:3. Lk +*11:4n. 17:9. Jn 15:20. Ro 10:19. 1 C 9:17. 15:9. Ep 3:8. Phm 11. He 9:12, 13. 13:17. 1 P 2:10. 1 J 3:17. **and ashes**. *174. Figure of speech Syntheton; or, Combination B442: a placing together of two words by usage. The opposite of this figure is Hendiadys (*93A, Ge +1:26. *93B, Is +66:11), by which, though two words are used, only one thing is meant. Here, in *Syntheton*, much more is meant than is expressed and embraced by the conjunction of the two words. For other instances of this figure see Ps 115:13, "small

and great." Ac 7:22, "words and deeds." Other words similarly paired in Scripture include (note that parenthetical references indicate paired words in context not joined by "and" as required in the figure): babes and sucklings: Ps 8:2. Mt 21:16. bread and flesh: 1 K 17:6. bread and vineyards: 2 K 18:32. Is 36:17. bread and water: 1 K 18:4, 13. 2 K 6:22. Ezk 4:17. Ho 2:5. bread and wine: Ge 14:18. Jg 19:19. Ne 5:15. child and suckling: Je 44:7. corn and wine: Ge 27:28, 37. Dt 33:28. 2 K 18:32. Ps 4:7. Is 36:17. La 2:12. Ho 7:14. eat and drink: 2 K 6:22. faith and love: (1 C 13:13). Ga 5:6. Ep 6:23. 1 Th 1:3. 3:6. *5:8. 1 T 1:14. 2:15. (6:10). 2 T 1:13. (2:22). T (2:2). (3:15). Phm 5. (Re 2:19). faith and patience: (1 T 6:11). (2 T 3:10). He 6:12. (Ja 1:3). Re 13:10. (faith and works): (He 6:1). (Ja 2:14, 17, 18, 20, 22, 24, 26). fear and dread: (Ge 9:2). Ex 15:16. Dt (2:25). 11:25. flesh and blood: Mt +16:17. 1 C 15:50. Ga 1:16. Ep 6:12. flesh and bone: Ge ◖+29:14. Jg 9:2. 2 S 5:1. 19:12, 13. Lk +√24:39. Ep 5:30. God and man: Lk 2:52. 1 T 2:5. goodness and mercy: Ps 23:6. grace and truth: Jn 1:14, 17. iniquities and sins: Jb 13:23. (Je 14:10). Ho (8:13). (9:9). justice and judgment: Ge 18:19. man and woman: Je 44:7. meat and drink: (Ezr 3:7). Jl (1:9, 13). (2:14). Ro 14:17. mercy and peace: 1 T 1:2. 2 T 1:2. T 1:4. 2 J 3. Ju 2. mercy and truth: Ge 24:27, 49mg. 2 S 15:20. Ps 25:10. 61:7. *85:10. 86:15. 89:14. 98:3. (115:1). Pr 3:3. 14:22. 16:6. 20:28. (Ho 4:1). milk and honey: Ex 3:8, 17. 13:5. 33:3. Le 20:24. Nu 13:27. 14:8. 16:13, 14. Dt 6:3. 11:9. 26:9, 15. 27:3. 31:20. Jsh 5:6. SS 4:11. Je 11:5. 32:33. Ezk 20:6, 15. new and old: Mt 13:52. old and young: Ge 19:4. (Ex 10:9). Je 51:22. Ezk 9:6. rich and poor: Ps 49:2. Pr 22:2. Re 13:16. sackcloth and ashes: Est 4:1, 3. Is 58:5. Da 9:3. Jon 3:6. Mt 11:21. Lk 10:13. silver and gold: Ps 115:4. Ac *3:6. sins and iniquities: He 8:12. 10:17. sword and bow: Ge 48:22. 2 K 6:22. thoughts and deeds: (Jb 21:27). (Is 66:18). young and old: Jsh 6:21. Est 3:13. Is 20:4. 30:6. Je 31:13. La 2:21.

28. **wilt.** Nu 14:17-19. 1 K 20:32, 33. Jb 23:3, 4. **If I.** ver. 26, 29. Ps 78:38. Is *65:8.

29. **yet again.** Ge 22:15. 1 S +*23:4. Lk 18:1, 5, 7. Ep 6:18. He *4:16.

30. **Oh.** Ge 44:18. Jg 6:39. Es 4:11-16. Jb 40:4. Ps 9:12. 10:17. 89:7. Is 6:5. *55:8, 9. He 12:28, 29. **I will.** Ex 34:6. Ezr ◖5:12. Ps 86:15.

31. **Behold.** ver. 27. Mt 7:7, 11. Lk *11:8. *18:1. Ep 6:18. He *4:16. 10:20-22. **speak.** Jb 40:4. Ps 9:12.

32. **Oh.** ver. 30. Ge +*17:20. 20:7, 17. 47:7. ch. 49. Ex 32:10-14, 31, 32. 34:9. Nu +*12:13. 14:11-21. 16:20-22. Dt 1:11. 9:18-20. 33:6-17. Jg 6:39. Ru 1:8, 9. 1 S √12:23. 2 S *12:16. 24:3. 1 K 1:37. 2 Ch 30:18-20. Ezr 9:3-15. Ne 1:4-9. Jb 1:5. *42:7-10. Ps 106:23. Pr 15:8. Is *62:6, 7. Ezk 22:30. Am 7:1-3. Ja +*5:14-17. 1 J +*5:15, 16. **speak.** Jg *6:39. Ps 86:6. **I will not.** Ex 32:9, 10, 14. 33:13, 14. +*34:6, 7, 9, 10. Nu 14:11-20. Jb 33:23. Ps *86:5. Is 1:9. *65:8. Ezk ◖14:16. Mi *7:18. Mt *7:7. Ac 27:24. Ep 3:20. He *7:25. Ja *5:16.

33. **And the.** ver. 16, 22. Ge 17:22. 32:26. **communing.** Ex 31:18. **and Abraham.** Ge 31:55.

GENESIS 19

Lot entertains two angels, 1-3. The abandoned Sodomites are smitten with blindness, 4-11. Lot is warned, *and in vain warns his sons-in-law, 12-14. He is directed to flee with his family to the mountain, but obtains leave to retire to Zoar, 15-23. Sodom and Gomorrah are destroyed; and Lot's wife, looking back, becomes a pillar of salt, 24-26. Abraham beholds the destruction of Sodom, 27-29. Lot retires from Zoar; and is betrayed into drunkenness and incest, 30-35. The birth of Moab and Ammon, 36-38.*

1. **And there came two angels.** Or, rather, 'the two angels came,' referring to those mentioned in the preceding chapter, and there called 'men.' It seems (from Ge 18:22) that these two angels were sent to Sodom, while the third, who was the Lord or Jehovah, remained with Abraham. Ge 18:1-3, 16, 22. **sat.** Ps 1:1. Pr 1:14. Jn 18:18. **gate.** Ge +14:7. Est 2:19. Pr 31:23. **rose.** Ge 18:1-5. Jb 31:32. He 13:2. **bowed.** Ge 18:2. 1 S 24:8.

2. **turn.** Jb 31:32. Lk 24:29. He +*13:2. **tarry.** or, lodge. Ru 3:13. **wash.** Ge +18:4. **rise.** Jg 19:9. 1 S 29:10. **Nay.** Jg 19:17-21. Je 14:8. Lk 19:5. 24:28, 29. Ac 16:15. Ep 5:11. *60C. Figure of speech Peirastic Irony B814: irony used to test the character or resolve of the person or persons so addressed. Here, the angels had no intention to abide in the street of Sodom all night, but said what they did to see what response Lot would make. For other instances of this figure see Ge *22:2. Mt 15:24, 26. **street.** or, broad place. Where travellers could pitch their tents, and pass the night under the mild influence of Eastern moonlight (Young). Jg 19:15. *143. Figure of speech Peristasis; or, Description of Circumstances B456. For other instances of this figure see 2 S 18:24. Mk 11:4. 12:41. Lk 21:5. Jn 4:6. 5:2. 18:18. 21:8, 9.

3. **pressed.** Jg 19:20. 2 K 4:8. Lk 11:8. 14:23. *24:28, 29. Ac 16:15. 2 C 5:14. **a feast.** Ge 18:6-8. 21:8. 26:30. 29:22. Jg 14:12. 2 K 6:23. Lk 5:29. Jn 12:2. He 13:2. **unleavened.** Ge 18:6. Ex 12:15, 33, 34, 39. Jg 6:19. 1 S 28:24. 1 C 5:8, 11.

4. **But.** Pr 4:16. 6:18. Mi 7:3. Ro 3:15. **men of.** Jg 19:22. Ep 4:19. **and young.** *174, Ge +18:27. **all.** *102, Ge +7:19. Ge 13:13. 18:20. Ex 16:2. 23:2. Je 5:1-6, 31. Mt 27:20-25. Mk 1:33.

5. **Where.** Le 18:22. 20:13. Jg *19:22. Is 1:9. *3:9. Je 3:3. 6:15. Ezk +*16:49, 51. Mt 11:23, 24. Ro *1:23, 24, 26, 27. 1 C +*6:9. 1 T 1:10. 2 T 3:13. Ju *7. **know.** *88. Ge +15:15. Ge +4:1. *121C2A4. Metonymy of the Cause with verbs of "knowing": Ge 4:+1, +17, 25. 24:16. 38:26. Ex +34:15. Nu 31:17. Jg 11:39. 19:25. 1 S 1:19. 1 K 1:4. Mt *1:25.

6. **Lot.** Jg 19:23. **door.** Two words are here used for door: the first *pethach* (S#6607, as in Ge 4:7. 6:16. 18:1, 2, 10. 19:11. 38:14. 43:19. Ex *12:22, 23. 26:36. 29:4. Le 1:3. Dt 22:21. 1 K 19:13. 22:10. Ps 24:7, 9. Pr 1:21. 5:8. 8:3, 34. 9:14. 17:19), which is the *doorway*, at which Lot went out; the latter, *deleth* (S#1817, as in Ge 19:9, 10. Ex 21:6. Dt 3:5. 15:17. Jg 19:22, 27. Jb 3:10. 31:32. 38:8, 10. 41:14. Ps 78:23. 107:16. *141:3. Pr 8:34. 26:14. Ec 12:4. SS 8:9. Is 45:1, 2), the *leaf* of the door, which he shut after him when out.

7. **I pray.** Ge 37:21. 42:22. Ex *23:2. Jg 19:23. 1 S 30:23, 24. Pr *1:10. Ac 17:26. **do not.** Ex 32:22. Dt 23:17. Ro *1:24. 1 C +*6:9-11. Ju *7.

8. **I have.** Ex 23:32. 32:22. 34:12, 16. Dt 7:3. Jsh 23:12, 13. Ezr 9:2, 12. Ne 10:30. 13:25. 1 C 6:13, 16-20. 2 C 6:14-18. **known.** Ge +4:1, 17. Ge 24:16. Ex

+34:15. ✍121C2A4, Ge +19:5. **let**. ver. 31-38. Ge 42:37. Jg *19:24. Mk *9:6. Ro *3:8. **therefore**. Ge 18:5. Jg 9:15. Is 58:7. **roof**. ✍117. Figure of speech Metalepsis; or, Double Metonymy B609. Metalepsis occurs when there are two metonymies, one contained in the other, but only one is expressed. Here, "roof" is first put (by Synecdoche) for the whole house, of which it is a part: and then the house is put for the protection it afforded. For other instances of this figure see Ge 31:1. Le *20:9. Pr 1:11. Ec 12:5. Is 10:3. 33:15. 66:12. Ho 14:2. Ac 20:28. Ro 3:25. 5:9. 1 C 1:17, 18. Ep 1:7. 2:13. Col 1:14, 20. He 9:12, 14. 10:19. 12:24. 13:12. 1 P 1:2, 19. 1 J 1:7. Re *1:5. 7:14. 12:11.

9. **Stand**. 1 S 17:44. 25:17. Pr 9:7, 8. Is +*65:5n. Je 3:3. 6:15. 8:12. Mt +*7:6. **This**. Ge 13:12. Ex *2:14. Ac 7:26-28. 2 P 2:7, 8. **pressed**. Ge 11:6. 1 S 2:16. Ps 118:13. Pr 14:16. 17:12. 27:3. Ec 9:3. 10:13. Da 3:19-22.

10. **men**. ver. 1. **pulled**. Dt 33:12. 1 S 2:9. Ps 4:8. 34:7. Is 63:9. Mt 18:10. Lk 21:18.

11. **with blindness**. The word _sanverim_ rendered "blindness," and which occurs only here, and in 2 K 6:18, is supposed to denote _dazzlings_, _deceptions_, or _confusions_ of sight from excessive light. The Targums, in both places where it occurs, render it by _eruptions_, or _flashes_ of light, or as Mercer, in Robertson, explains the Chaldee word, _irradiations_. ✍96F2, Ge +4:10. Ge 27:1. 48:10. Dt 28:28, 29. Jg 16:21. 1 S 4:15. 1 K 14:4. 2 K *6:18-20. 25:7. Is *44:18. Mk 14:44. *16:12. Lk +*4:30. *24:16. ●+*24:31. Jn 20:14. 21:4. Ac *13:11. **small and**. ✍174, Ge +18:27. Je 8:10. **wearied**. Ec 10:15. Is 57:10. Je 2:36. Mt 15:14.

12. **Hast**. Ge *7:1. Nu 16:26. Jsh +2:13. 6:22, 23. 1 S 15:6. Je 32:39. 51:6. 2 P *2:7, 9. **son**. ver. 14, 17, 22. Re 18:4. **and**. ✍148, Ge +8:22.

13. **cry**. Ge 13:13. 18:20. Ja +*5:4. **face of**. ✍22A4. Anthropomorphism; or, Condescension B873: the ascribing of human attributes to God; here, a "face," signifying "presence." For other instances of this figure see Ex 23:15, 20. 25:30. 33:14, 15, 20, 23. Le 17:10. 20:5. Nu 6:25, 26. Dt 5:4. 34:10. 2 S 21:1mg. 2 K 25:19mg. 1 Ch 29:12. 2 Ch *7:14. Est 1:14. Jb 23:15 (presence). Ps 4:6. 9:3. 13:1. *16:11. 17:15. 21:9 (anger). 27:8, 9. 30:7. 31:16. 34:16. 51:11. 80:3, 7, 19. 100:2. 105:4. 139:7. Is 63:9. Je 21:10. La 4:16. Ezk 39:24. Da 9:17. Jon 1:3. Mt 18:10. 1 P 3:12. **Lord hath**. 1 Ch 21:15, 16. Ps 11:5, 6. Is 3:11. 36:10. 37:36. Ezk 9:5, 6. Mt *13:41, 42, 49, 50. Ac 12:23. Ro 3:8, 9. Ju 7. Re 16:1-12. **destroy**. Le 26:30-33. Dt 4:26. 28:45.

14. **which**. Mt 1:18. **Up**. ver. 17, 22. Nu *16:21, 26, 45. Je 51:6. Lk 9:42. Re 18:4-8. **as one**. Ex *9:21. 12:31. 2 Ch 30:10. 36:16. Pr 29:1. Is 28:22. Je 5:12-14. 20:7. 43:1, 2. Ezk 20:49. Mt 9:24. Lk *17:28-30. *24:11. Ac 17:32. 1 Th *5:3. 2 P 3:3, 4.

15. **morning**. Ge 32:24, 26. Jsh 6:15. Jg 19:25. **hastened**. ver. 17, 22. Ex 12:11. Nu *16:24-27. Pr 6:4, 5. Lk 13:24, 25. 2 C +*6:2. He 3:7, 8. Re *18:4. **are here**. Heb. are found. Jg 20:48mg. 2 Ch +29:29mg. Est +*1:5mg. 4:16mg. **lest**. Lk 17:31. **iniquity**. or, punishment. ✍121C1E. Figure of speech Metonymy (of the Cause); or, Change of Noun B550: sin and its synonyms are put for the effects or punishment of sin. Here, "iniquity" is put for "punishment," as in the AV margin. For other instances of this figure see Ex 28:43. Le 5:1. 7:18. 10:17. 20:20. 22:9. Nu 5:31. 9:13.

Is *53:4. Je 14:16. Ezk 23:35, 49. 16:58. 18:20. Zc 14:19. Mt 8:17. He *9:28. 1 P *2:24.

16. **lingered**. Ge ●22:3. 24:55. Ps *119:60. Jn 6:44. Ro +*12:11. **the men**. He 1:14. **laid**. ver. 10. Dt 5:15. 6:21. 7:8. **and**. ✍148, Ge +8:22. **the Lord**. Ex 33:19. +*34:6. Nu 14:18. Dt 4:31. 1 Ch 16:34. Ps 34:12. 86:5, 15. 103:8-10, 13. 106:1, 8. 107:1. 111:4. 118:1. 136:1. Is *63:9. La *3:22. Jl 2:18. Mi *7:18, 19. Lk +*6:35, 36. 18:13. Ro *9:15, 16, 18. 2 C 1:3. Ep 2:4, 5. T 3:5. **brought**. Jsh 6:22. Ps *34:22. Am 4:11. Zc 3:2. 2 P 2:9.

17. **he said**. Ge 18:22. **Escape**. ver. 14, 15, 22. Nu 16:26. 1 S 19:11. 1 K 19:3. Ps 121:1. Je 48:6. Mt 3:7. *24:16-18. He 2:3. **life**. Ge +44:30. **look**. ✍41, Ge +10:1. ver. 26. Lk √9:62. 17:31, 32. Ac 7:39. Ph *3:13, 14. He 10:38, 39. **lest**. Re *18:14, 15.

18. **Oh**. Ge 32:26. 2 K 5:11, 12. Is 45:11. Mt *16:22. Jn 13:6-8. Ac 9:13. 10:14.

19. **and thou**. Ps 18:40. 103. 106. 107. 116. 1 T 1:14-16. **saving**. Ps 41:2. 143:11. **life**. Ge +44:30. **and**. ✍148, Ge +8:22. **lest some**. Ge 4:14. 12:12, 13. Ex 14:11. Nu 14:3. Dt 31:17. 1 S *27:1. 1 K 9:9. Ps 6:4. 77:7-11. 116:11. Mt 8:25, 26. Mk 9:19. Ro *8:31. Ga 1:4. He +*13:6.

20. **this**. ver. 30. Pr √3:5-7. Am *3:6. **it is,**. ✍81, Ge +15:13. **little**. 1 S *15:13-23. 2 K 3:18. SS 2:15. 1 C 5:6. Ga 5:9. **let me**. Ps *106:15. Is +*66:4. **and my**. Ge 12:13. Ps 68:20. 119:175. Is 55:3. **soul**. Heb. _nephesh_, Ge +12:13.

21. **See, I**. Ge 4:7. Jb 42:8, 9. Ps 34:15. 102:17. *145:19. Je 14:10. Mt 12:20. Lk 11:8. He 2:17. *4:15, 16. **accepted**. Mt 19:8. Ac 17:30. **thee**. Heb. thy face. ✍171Q14, Ge +3:19. **that**. Ge 12:2. 18:24.

22. **Haste**. 2 K 10:23. Ezk 9:6. Am 9:9. Re 7:3. **for**. Ge 32:25-28. Ex 32:10. Dt 9:14. Ps 91:1-10. Is 65:8. Mk 6:5. 1 Th *5:9. 2 T 2:13. T 1:2. He 11:40. 2 P 3:9. **name**. ✍144A4B, Ge +10:9. **called**. Ge 13:10. 14:2. Is 15:5. Je 48:34. **Zoar**. i.e. little. ver. 20. Ge +13:10.

23. **risen**. Heb. gone forth. 1 Th 5:3. 2 P 2:21, 22.

24. **the Lord**. Ge 20:13. Dt 29:23. Jsh 22:22. Jb 18:15. Ps *11:6. Is *1:9. 13:19. 50:1-9. Je *20:16. *49:18. 50:40. La 4:6. Ezk +*16:49, 50. Ho *11:8. Am *4:11. Zp 2:9. Zc 2:8, 9. Mt 11:23, 24. Lk *17:28, 29. 2 P *2:6. Ju *7. **Sodom and**. Mt 10:15. **brimstone**. The word rendered _brimstone_ is always rendered by the LXX _sulphur_, and seems to denote a meteorous inflammable matter. Re 21:8. **and**. ✍93A, Ge +1:26. **Lord**. Note the mention here of two Jehovahs, one in heaven who sends judgment upon Sodom and Gomorrah at the bidding of the Jehovah on earth. This gives significant evidence for more than one person in the Godhead. The Jehovah upon earth was one of the three persons to visit Abraham, one of whom stays behind to speak further to Abraham and is called Jehovah, Ge 18:13, 14, 17, 19, 20, *22, 26, 33. Jn 3:13, 31. 6:38, 42. 8:*56, 58. 1 C 2:8. +12:3. Ja 2:1. See also on Ge +12:7. +16:13. +17:1. Da +*3:28.

25. **overthrew**. Dt 29:23. Is 13:19. La 4:6. 2 P 2:6. **plain**. Ge 13:10. 14:3. Ps 107:34. **cities**. ✍132D. Figure of speech Parallelism; or, Parallel Lines B352: the repetition of similar, synonymous, or opposite thoughts in parallel or successive lines. Here, Complex Alternate, two lines repeated only once (four lines in all): cities, plain, cities, plain (A.V., ground). The lines are placed alternately, so the first and third lines, and

the second and fourth lines, may, as a rule, be read continuously, while the intervening line is thus placed in a parenthesis. These alternate lines may be either synonymous or antithetic. For other instances of this figure see Dt 32:21, 42. 1 Ch 21:22. Est 8:5. Pr *18:24. 24:19, 20. Is 1:29, 30. 9:10. 14:26, 27. 17:7, 8. 18:6. 31:3. Is 34:6. 51:20. 59:5, 6. 61:4.

26. **looked back.** ver. 17. Pr 14:14. Lk √9:62. He +*10:38. **and.** Nu 16:33. Lk *17:31, ▶32. The Reverend Thomas Scott states "This unhappy woman, contrary to God's express command, in unbelief and love to Sodom and its riches, regretting what was left behind, and probably purposing to return, *looked back*, and as some think, actually attempted to return; and our Lord's words, 'Let him not *return back*; remember Lot's wife' favor this supposition. She was therefore struck dead and petrified, and thus remained to after-ages a visible monument of the divine displeasure; being punished as a warning to others through successive generations. Perhaps she was a native of Sodom, as nothing is said of Lot having a wife, when with Abraham. Above twenty years had passed, from the time that Lot went to Sodom."

27. **early.** Ge +21:14. 22:3. Ps 5:3. 63:1. Ec 9:10. **to the.** Ge 18:22-33. Ezk 16:49, 50. Hab 2:1. He 2:1.

28. **looked.** Ps 91:8. Is 66:24. Re 3:10. **lo.** √40, Ge +3:22. **smoke.** Ge 13:10. Dt 29:23. Ps 107:34. Is 3:9. 2 P 2:7. Ju 7. Re 14:10, 11. *18:9, 18. 19:3. 21:8. **furnace.** Ex 9:8, 10. 19:18.

29. **that God.** Ge *8:1. 12:2. 18:23-33. 30:22. Dt 9:5. Ne 13:14, 22. Ps 25:7. 105:8, 42. 106:4. 136:23. *145:20. Ezk 36:31, 32. Ho 11:8. **remembered.** √22C3, Ge +8:1. Ge 30:22. Ex +*2:24. **sent.** Lk +*21:36. 2 P *2:6-10. **cities.** √96F3, Ge +8:4.

30. **Lot.** ver. 17-23. **for he.** Ge 49:4. Je 2:36, 37. Ja *1:8. **feared.** Ge ●15:1. Dt ●33:12. Jb ●4:7. ●11:18. Ps ●4:8. ●16:8. ●27:1. ●118:6, 7. Pr ●*1:33. ●3:24. Je 41:17n, 18. Mt 14:30, 31. 17:6, 7. 25:24, *25. Mk 4:38-41. 5:33. 16:5, 6. Lk 1:12, 13. Ro ●*8:15. 2 T ●*1:7. He ●13:5, 6. **Zoar.** Ge +13:10. 14:22. Dt 34:3. Is 15:5. Je 48:34. **cave.** Ge 23:9, 11, 17, 19, 20. 25:9. 49:29, 30, 32. 50:13. Jsh 10:16, 17, 18, 22, 23, 27. Jg 6:2. 1 S 13:6. 22:1. 24:3, 7, 8, 10. 2 S 23:13. 1 K 18:4, 13. 19:9. 1 Ch 11:15. Ps 57, title. 142, title. Is 2:19. Ezk 33:27. Jn 11:38. He 11:38.

31. **not.** ver. 28. Mk 9:6. **to come.** Ge +4:1. 6:4. 16:2, 4. 38:8, 9, 14-30. Dt 25:5. Is 4:1. **manner.** Ge 38:8. Ep 5:7. Col 3:1. Ja 4:4.

32. **Come.** Ge 11:3. **drink.** Ge +9:21. Pr *20:1. *23:31-33. Hab 2:15, 16. Ga 5:21. Ep 5:18. **lie.** Le 18:6, 7. 20:12. Ga 5:19. **seed.** Ge 38:8. Dt 25:5-10. Mk 12:19.

33. **drink.** Pr 20:1. 23:29-35. Hab 2:15, 16. **night.** 1 Th 5:7.

34. **I lay.** Is 3:9. Je 3:3. 5:3. 6:15. 8:12.

35. **that night also.** Ps 8:4. Pr *24:16. Ec *7:26. Lk 21:34. Jn ●+√17:6. 1 C *10:11, 12. 1 P 4:7. 2 P ●*2:7, 8.

36. **were.** ver. 8. Le 18:6, 7. Jg 1:7. 1 S 15:33. Hab 2:15. Mt 7:2. **father.** Ezk 22:10.

37. A.M. 2108. B.C. 1896. **Moab.** This name is generally interpreted "of the father"; from *mo*, of, and *av*, a father. i.e. *water (seed) of a father*, ⁕S#4124h. Ge 36:35. Ex 15:15. Nu 21:11, 13, 13, 15, 20, 26, 28, 29. 22:1, 3, 3, 4, 4, 7, 8, 10, 14, 21, 36. 23:6, 7, 17. 24:17. 25:1. 26:3, 63. 31:12. 33:44, 48, 49, 50.

35:1. 36:13. Dt 1:5. 2:8, 9, 18. 29:1. 32:49. 34:1, 5, 6, 8. Jsh 13:32. 24:9. Jg 3:12, 14, 15, 17, 28, 28, 29, 30. 10:6. 11:15, 17, 18, 18, 18, 25. Ru 1:1, 2, 6, 6, 22. 2:6. 4:3. 1 S 12:9. 14:47. 22:3, 4. 2 S 8:2, 2, 12. 23:20. 1 K 11:7, 33. 2 K 1:1. 3:4, 5, 7, 7, 10, 13, 18, 21, 22, 23, 24, 24, 26. 13:20. 23:13. 24:2. 1 Ch 1:46. 4:22. 8:8. 11:22. 18:2, 2, 11. 2 Ch 20:1, 10, 22, 23. Ps 60:8. 83:6. 108:9. Is 11:14. 15:1, 1, 1, 2, 4, 5, 8, 9. 16:2, 4, 6, 7, 7, 11, 12, 13, 14. 25:10. Je 9:26. 25:21. 27:3. 40:11. 48:1, 2, 4, 9, 11, 13, 15, 16, 18, 20, 20, 24, 25, 26, 28, 29, 31, 31, 33, 35, 36, 38, 38, 39, 39, 40, 41, 42, 43, 44, 45, 46, 47, 47. Ezk 25:8, 9, 11. Da 11:41. Am 2:1, 2, 2. Mi 6:5. Zp 2:8, 9. **Moabites.** Ex 15:15. Nu *21:29. ch. 22-24. *25:1-3. Dt *2:9, 19. 23:3. Jg ch. 3. Ru 2:6. 4:5, 10. 1 S 14:47. 2 S ch. 8. 1 K 11:7. 2 K ch. 3. 24:2. 1 Ch 18:2. Is 15:1. 16:6, 7. Je 27:3. 48:1, 4, 11-18. **unto.** ver. +38.

38. **Ben-Ammi.** i.e. *Son of my people*, from *ben*, a son, and *ammi*, my people. ⁕S#1151h. **children of Ammon.** i.e. *unique, or great people*, ⁕S#5983h. Nu 21:24, 24. Dt 2:9, *19, 37. 3:11, 16. *23:3. Jsh 12:2. 13:10, 25. Jg 1:6-18. 3:13. 10:6, 7, 9, 11, 17, 18. 11:4, 5, 6, 8, 9, 12, 13, 14, 15, 27, 28, 29, 30, 31, 32, 33, 36. 12:1, 2, 3. 1 S 11:11. 12:12. 14:47. 2 S 8:12. 10:1, 2, 3, 6, 6, 8, 10, 11, 14, 14, 19. 11:1. 12:9, 26, 31. 17:27. 1 K 11:1-5, 7, 33. 2 K 23:13. 24:2. 1 Ch 18:11. 19:1, 2, 3, 6, 6, 7, 9, 11, 12, 15, 19. 20:1, 3. 2 Ch 20:1, 10, 22, 23. 27:5, 5, 5. Ne 13:1-3, 23-28. Ps 83:4-8. Is 11:14. Je 9:26. 25:21. 27:3. 40:11, 14. 41:10, 15. 49:1, 2, 6. Ezk 21:20, 28. 25:2, 3, 5, 10, 10. Da 11:41. Am 1:13. Zp 2:8, 9. **unto this day.** ver. 37. Ge 26:33. 32:32. 35:20. 47:26. 48:15. 50:20. Ex 10:6. Dt +*29:4, 28. Jsh +*4:9. Jg 18:12.

GENESIS 20

Abraham sojourns in Gerar, and denies his wife; whom Abimelech takes, but is warned in a dream to restore, 1-7. Abimelech expostulates with Abraham, and restores Sarah with presents and a gentle reproof, 8-16. Abimelech and his family are healed, in answer to Abraham's prayer, 17, 18.

1. A.M. cir. 2107. B.C. cir. 1897. **from.** Ge 13:1. 18:1. 24:62. **Kadesh.** Ge 14:7. 16:1, 7, 14. Nu 13:26. 20:16. Dt 1:19. 32:51. 1 S 15:7. Ps 29:8. **Gerar.** i.e. *sojourning, journeying, lodging*, ⁕S#1642h. Gerar was a city of Arabia Petraea, under a king of the Philistines, 25 miles from Eleutheropolis beyond Daroma, in the south of Judah. From Ge 10:19, it appears to have been situated in the angle where the south and west sides of Canaan met, and to have been not far from Gaza. Jerome, in his Hebrew Traditions on Genesis, says, from Gerar to Jerusalem was three days' journey. There was a wood near Gerar, on which was a monastery, noticed by Sozomen. ver. 2. Ge 10:19. 26:1, 6, 17, 20, 26. 2 Ch 14:13, 14.

2. **said.** Ge 12:11-13. *13:15. *26:7. 2 Ch 19:2. 20:37. *32:31. Pr 24:16. *29:25. Ec *7:20. Ga *2:11, 12. Ep *4:25. Col 3:9. **Abimelech.** i.e. *father of the king; my father is king*, ⁕S#40h. ver. 3, 4, 8, 9, 10, 14, 15, 17, 18. Ge 21:22, 25, 25, 26, 27, 29, 32. 26:1, 8, 9, 10, 11, 16, 26. Jg 8:31. 9:1, 3, 4, 6, 16, 18, 19, 20, 20, 21, 22, 23, 23, 24, 25, 27, 28, 29, 29, 31, 34, 35, 38, 39, 40, 41, 42, 44, 45, 47, 48, 48, 49, 50, 52, 53, 55, 56. 10:1. 2 S 11:21. 1 Ch 18:16. Ps 34, title. Ge ●12:15. (1) A king of Gerar of the Philistines who

made a league with Abraham. (2) Another king of Gerar contemporary with Isaac. He made a league with Isaac at Beersheba, Ge ch. 26. (3) A son of Gideon by a concubine in Shechem. He made himself king after the death of his father and slew his father's seventy sons, leaving only Jotham, the youngest. Abimelech was disgracefully killed in attacking Thebez. (4) Abimelech, the son of Abiathar, who was high-priest in David's time, 1 Ch 18:16. (5) The name given in one place apparently to Achish, the king of Gath, to whom David fled (1 S 21:10), Ps 34, title.

3. **a dream**. Ge 28:12. 31:24. 37:5, 9. 40:8. 41:1. Jg 7:13. 1 K 3:5. Jb 4:12, 13. 33:15. Da 2:3. 4:5. 7:1. Mt 1:20. 2:12, 13. 27:19. **Behold**. ⌐40, Ge +3:22. **a dead**. ver. 7. Ps *105:14. Ezk *33:14, 15. Jon 3:4. **man**. ⌐37B. Aposiopesis, or Sudden Silence, Ge +3:22. Here we must supply "If thou dost not restore her" or "I will slay thee," as implied by Abimelech's response in ver. 4 and 7. **a man's wife**. Heb. married to an husband. Dt 21:13. 22:22. 24:1. Is 62:+4mg, 5. Ml 2:11. 2 C 11:2.

4. **had**. ver. 6, 18. **near**. Le 18:19. **wilt**. ver. 17, 18. Ge *18:23-25. 19:24. 2 S 4:11. 1 Ch 21:17. **nation**. T#1622. Ex 5:22, 23. 8:8, 28-30. 14:10. 35:15, 16. Nu 6:22-26. 20:3-6. 27:15-17. Dt *4:17. 26:15. Jsh 7:7-9. Ps 25:22. 60:1-3, 9-11. Ro 10:1.

5. **in the integrity**. or, simplicity, or sincerity. Ge 17:1. Jsh 22:22. 2 S 15:11. 1 K 9:4. 2 K +*20:3. 1 Ch 29:17. Ps 7:8. 25:21. 26:6. *37:14n. 78:72. Pr 11:3. 20:7. 2 C *1:12. 1 Th 2:10. 1 T 1:13. *S#8537h: ver. 6. Ex 28:30 (Thummim). Le 8:8. 2 S 15:11 (simplicity). 1 K 9:4. 22:34mg. 2 Ch 18:33mg. Ezr 2:63. Ne 7:65. Jb 4:6 (uprightness). 21:23 (full. mg, perfection). Ps 7:8. 25:21. 26:1, 11. 41:12. 78:72. 101:2 (perfect). Pr 2:7 (uprightly). 10:9, 29. 13:6. 19:1. 20:7. 28:6. Is 47:9 (perfection). **and innocency**. Jb 33:9. Ps 24:4. 26:6. 73:13. Da 6:22.

6. **dream**. ver. +3. Dt ☽*13:1-5. Jb ☽20:8. Ps 126:1. Ec ☽*5:3. Ju 8. **know**. 1 S 16:7. Pr 21:1. Je 17:10. **thou didst**. Lk *12:48. **withheld**. ver. 18. Ge *31:7. 35:5. Ex 34:24. 1 S 25:26, 34. Ps *84:11. Pr *21:1. Ho 2:6, 7. 2 Th 3:3. **sinning**. Ge *39:9. Le 6:2. Ps *51:4. 81:12. 2 Th 2:7, 11. **to touch**. Ge *3:3. 26:11. 1 C *7:1. 2 C *6:17. ⌐108B. Figure of speech Idiom B827. To touch is used for cohabitation. For other instances of this idiom see Pr 6:29. 1 C 7:1.

7. **a prophet**. The word navi, rendered "a prophet," not only signifies one who foretells future events, but also an intercessor, instructor. See 1 S ch. 10. 1 K ch. 18. 1 C 14:4. The title was also given to men eminent for eloquence and literary abilities; hence Aaron, because he was the spokesman of Moses to the Egyptian king, is called a prophet, as in Ex 4:16 and *7:1. Ge 12:1-3. 18:17. 1 Ch 16:22. Ps 25:14. 105:9-15. He 1:1. **shall**. ⌐96B. Figure of speech Heterosis (of Mood): or, Exchange of Accidence B513; here, of the verb, Imperative for Indicative. "Let him pray" is rendered "he shall pray." For other instances of this figure see Ge 42:18. 45:18. Dt 32:50. Ps *22:8mg. *37:27. Pr 3:4. 4:4. Is 8:10. 29:9. 37:30. 54:1. Jn 2:19. 1 C *16:22. **pray for**. Le 6:4, 7. Dt 9:20. 1 S *7:5, 8. 12:19, √23. 2 S 24:17. 1 K 13:6. 2 K 5:11. 19:2-4. Jb +*42:8. Je 14:11. 15:1. 27:18. Ja *5:14-16. 1 J *5:16. Re 11:5, 6. **surely**. ⌐147B, Ge +2:16. ver. 18. Ge +2:17. 12:17. Jb 34:19. Ps 105:14. Ezk *3:18. 33:8, 14-16. He 13:4. **all**. Ge 12:15. Nu 16:32, 33. 2 S 24:17.

8. **morning**. Ge +21:14. 22:3. **servants**. Ge 9:25, 26. 14:14. 16:6. 24:34. 43:18. Le 25:46. **afraid**. Ge ☽+19:30. 22:12. Dt 4:10. 10:12. Jb 28:28. Ps 111:10. Pr 1:7. 9:10. 15:33. 2 C 5:11. He 10:31. Ju 23. Re 19:5.

9. **What hast**. ⌐6, Ge +3:13. Ge 3:13. 4:10. 12:18. ☽21:25. *26:10. 31:26. Ex *32:21, 35. Jsh 7:25. 1 S 13:11. 26:18, 19. Pr 28:10. Jn 18:35. **a great**. Ge 38:24. 39:9. Le 20:10. 2 S 12:5, 10, 11. Ro 2:11. He 13:4. **ought not**. Ge 29:26. 34:7. 1 S 26:16. 2 S 13:12. Pr *28:10. T 1:11.

10. **What**. Ge 12:18. 26:10. Ps 15:2, 4. 1 P 3:15.

11. **Surely**. Ge *22:12. 42:18. Ne 5:15. Jb *1:1. *28:28. Ps 14:4. *36:1-4. Pr *1:7. 2:5. *8:13. *16:6. Ro 3:18. **slay**. Ge *12:12. *26:7.

12. **And yet**. Ge *11:29. 12:13. 1 Th *5:22. **is the**. Ebn Batrik, in his annals, among other ancient traditions, has preserved the following: "Terah first married Yona, by whom he had Abraham; afterwards he married Tehevita, by whom he had Sarah." Ge 11:25-29.

13. **God**. Heb. Elohim. Ge *12:1, 9, 11. 35:7. 2 Ch 18:31. Is 63:7-14. Ac +*7:3-5. He *11:8. **caused**. This verb is plural, as is Elohim, in harmony with the teaching of three persons in the Godhead. Ge +√15. **This**. 1 S 23:21. Ps 64:5. Ac 5:9. **kindness**. Ge 47:29. Ru 3:10. 2 S 9:7. Col 3:10. ⌐121C1B. Figure of speech Metonymy (of the Cause); or, Change of Noun B549: the thing or action is put for that which is the effect or product of it. In certain nouns, the feeling or affection is put for the effects resulting or proceeding from the feeling, as "mercy" is put for the offices and benefits which are the outcome of it. Here, "kindness" is put for the kind deeds caused by it. For other instances of this figure see Ge 21:23. *24:27. 32:10. 2 Ch 32:32. 35:26. Ne 13:14mg. Ps 98:3. Mt 6:1. Lk 11:41. Ac 10:2, 4. **say**. Ge 12:13. Ep *5:22. 1 P 3:1-6.

14. **And**. ⌐148, Ge +8:22. **took**. ver. 11. Ge *12:16. **restored**. ver. 2, 7. Ge 12:19, 20.

15. **Behold**. ⌐40, Ge +3:22. **my land**. Ge 13:9. 34:10. 47:6. **where it pleaseth thee**. Heb. as is good in thine eyes. Ge 16:6. 41:37. Pr 16:7.

16. **thy**. ver. 5. Pr 27:5. **brother**. ⌐60B. Figure of speech Human Irony B813: where the speaker is a human being. Abimelech now knew Abraham was not Sarah's brother, but husband, as the context shows, but in irony and reproof he calls Abraham Sarah's "brother" here. For other instances of human irony see 1 S 26:15. 1 K *18:27. 22:15. 2 K 8:10. Jb 12:2. 26:2, 3. 32:11n. Mt 11:19. Lk 15:2. Jn 18:38. 19:14. 1 C 4:8. 2 C 10:12. 11:19. 12:13. **thousand**. What these pieces were is not certain; but it is probable they were shekels, as it is so understood by the Targum; and the LXX renders it didrachma, by which the Hebrew shekel is rendered in Ge 23:15, 16. **behold**. Or, 'behold it (the 1000 shekels) is to thee.' Ge 26:11. **a covering**. Ge 24:65. Ru 3:9. Pr 12:16. 1 C 11:5. ⌐142. Figure of speech Periphrasis; or, Circumlocution B419: when a description is used instead of the name. Here, "a covering of the eyes" is a periphrasis for a husband. For other instances of this figure see Ge 46:26. Jg *5:10. 2 S 3:29. 2 Ch 26:5. 32:21. Jb 14:1. 15:14. 25:4. Ps 4:7. 105:18. 132:3, 4. Pr 30:31mg. Ec 12:3, 6. Is ?*14:15. Je 21:13. Ezk 1:22. Ezk 24:16, 21, 25. 24:25. 26:9. 31:14. Mi 7:5. Zc 9:1. Zp 1:9. Mt 11:11. 26:29. 27:62. Lk 2:11, 23. 7:28. 21:35. Jn *1:9. 2 C 5:1.

1 Th 4:5, 12, 13. He 1:14. 2 P 1:13, 14. **thus**. Ge 21:25. 1 Ch 21:3-6. Pr *9:8, 9. *12:1. 25:12. 27:5. Jon 1:6. Re 3:19.

17. **prayed**. See on ver. 7. Ge 29:31. Nu 12:13. 21:7. 1 S 5:11, 12. Ezr 6:10. Jb *42:9, 10. Pr 15:8, 29. Is 45:11. Mt 7:7. 21:22. Ac 3:24. Ph 4:6. 1 Th 5:25. Ja *5:16.

18. **closed**. ver. 7. Ge *12:17. 16:2. 30:2. 1 S 1:6. 5:10. **because**. Jsh ch. 7. 22:20. Jon 1:12. Mt ◐5:13. Ac ◑27:20-25.

GENESIS 21

Isaac is born and circumcised, and Abraham and Sarah rejoice, 1-7. Isaac is weaned, 8. Ishmael mocks, and, at Sarah's insistence and by God's direction, is sent away with Hagar, 9-14. They are distressed, but delivered; and Ishmael prospers and marries an Egyptian, 15-21. Abraham covenants with Abimelech, and worships God at Beersheba, 22-34.

1. **visited**. Ge 50:24. Ex 3:16. 4:31. 13:19. +*20:5. Ru 1:6. 1 S 2:21. Ps 106:4. Lk 1:68. 19:44. Ro 4:17-20. **Sarah as**. Ge *17:19. 18:10, 14. Ps 12:6. Mt 24:35. Ga *4:23, 28. T 1:2. **spoken**. ∫144C1. Figure of speech Pleonasm; or, Redundancy B415: when more words are used than the grammar requires. Here, involving sentences repeated in another form, affirmatively. This figure is nearly identical with ∫173, Synonymia, Ge +27:44. In this passage note and compare "as he had *said*" with "as he had *spoken*." For other instances of this figure see Ge 1:20. Nu 19:2. Dt 32:6. Jn 1:22. 5:24. Ac 13:45. Ph 1:23.

2. **conceived**. 2 K 4:16, 17. Lk 1:24, 25, 36. Ac 7:8. Ga 4:22. He *11:11. **at the set**. Ge *17:19, 21. 18:10, 14. Ro 9:9.

3. **called**. ver. 6, 12. Ge *17:19. 22:2. Jsh *24:3. Is *54:1. Mt 1:2. Ac 7:8. Ro 9:7. He 11:18.

4. **eight days**. Ge *17:10-12. Ex 12:48. Le 12:3. Dt 12:32. Lk 1:6, 59. 2:21. Jn 7:22, 23. Ac *7:8.

5. **an hundred**. Ge *17:1, 17. Ro 4:19. He 6:15.

6. **God**. Ge 17:17. 18:12-15. 1 S 1:26-28. 2:1-10. Ps +*113:9. *126:2. Is 49:15, 21. +*54:1. Lk 1:46-55. Jn 16:21, 22. Ga 4:27, 28. He 11:11. **to laugh**. Sarah most likely remembered the circumstance mentioned in Ge 18:12; and also the name *Isaac*, which implies *laughter*. **will laugh**. Lk *1:14, 58. Ro 12:15. ∫121S2. Figure of speech Metonymy (of the Adjunct, Verbs) B604: the sign is put for the thing signified. Here, "laughter" is put for the "rejoicing" it signifies. For other instances of this figure see Ge 31:49. 41:40mg. Dt 10:8. 22:1. 1 K *19:18. Jb 5:22. 8:21. 31:27. Ps *2:12. 3:5. 4:8. 10:5. 12:5. 27:5. 31:20. 64:2. 126:2. Ezk 8:11. Zc 3:1. Mt 5:47. Lk 6:21, 25. He 11:13.

7. **Who**. Nu 23:23. Dt 4:32-34. Ps 86:8, 10. Is 49:21. 66:8. Ep 3:10. 2 Th 1:10. **children**. ∫171E13, Ge +46:7. **for I**. Ge 18:11, 12.

8. A.M. 2111. B.C. 1893. **and was weaned**. 1 S 1:22. 1 K 11:20. Ps 131:2. Is 11:8. *28:9. Ho 1:8. **feast**. Ge 19:3. 26:30. 29:22. 40:20. Jg 14:10, 12. 1 S 25:36. 2 S 3:20. 1 K 3:15. Est 1:3.

9. **Sarah**. Ge *16:3-6, 15. 17:20. **Egyptian**. Ge 16:1, 15. **mocking**. or, playing. Ge 16:4, 5. 19:14. 26:8h. 39:14, 17. Ex 32:6h. 2 K 2:23, 24. 2 Ch 30:10. 36:16. Ne 4:1-5. Jb 30:1. Ps 22:6. 42:10. 44:13, 14. Pr 17:5. 20:11. 30:17. La 1:7. Ga *4:22, 29. He 11:36. Ju 18.

✳S#6711h. Ge 17:17 (laugh). 18:12, 13 (laugh), 15. 19:14 (mocked). 21:6 (laugh), 9 (mocking). 26:8 (sporting). 39:14, 17 (mock). Ex 32:6 (play). Jg 16:25 (sport).

10. **Cast out**. The word rendered *cast out*, signifies also to *divorce*. See Le 21:7. In this latter sense, it may be understood here. Ge 25:6, 19. 17:19, 21. 20:11. 22:10. 36:6, 7. Pr 22:10. Mt 8:11, 12. 22:13. Jn 8:35. Ga *4:22-31. 1 J 2:19. **heir**. Jn 8:35. Ga 3:18. 4:7, ▸30. 1 P 1:4. 1 J 2:19.

11. **because**. Ge 17:18. 22:1, 2. 2 S 18:33. Mt 10:37. He 12:11.

12. **hearken**. 1 S 8:7, 9. Is 46:10. **in Isaac**. Ge 17:+*19, 21. Ro ▸9:7, 8. He ▸11:18. **thy seed**. Here "seed" (zera) is in the singular sense, because of the word "Isaac," and because of the singular verb "it shall be called." *Zera* is a collective noun (like English *sheep*), but the context must determine whether it is singular or plural. It is to this verse Ga 3:16 refers; not to Ge 12:7, where it is indefinite; or Ge 17:7 where the verb and pronouns show it is plural. "Thy seed" is therefore "Christ." The difference of the 30 years comes in here: 430 to the Exodus (Ex 12:40) from Ge 12:4, when Abraham was 75: 25 thence to Isaac's birth: and now, 5 to his recognition as the seed= 30 years (Adapted from *Companion Bible* note, p. 29, at this place).

13. **the son**. ver. 18. Ge +13:16. 16:10. 17:20. 25:12-18.

14. A.M. 2112. B.C. 1892. **rose up**. Ge +18:2. +19:27. 22:3. 24:54. 26:31. Ps 119:60. Pr 27:14. Ec 9:10. **took**. Ge 25:6. 36:6, 7. **child**. Or, *youth*, (see ver. 12, 20) as Ishmael was now 16 or 17 years of age. S#3206h, Da +*1:4n. 2 K 2:23n, 24h. **sent**. Jn *8:35. **wandered**. Ge 16:7. 37:15. Ps 107:4. Is 16:8. Ga 4:23-25. **Beersheba**. So called when Moses wrote; but not before Abraham's covenant with Abimelech, ver. 31. Such instances of the figure of speech Prolepsis (∫151, Ge +1:28) are not unfrequent in the Pentateuch. ver. 33. Ge 22:19. 26:33. 46:1. 1 K 19:3.

15. **the water**. ver. 14. Ex 15:22-25. 17:1-3. 2 K 3:9. Ps 63:1. Is 44:12. Je 14:3. **and she cast the child**. Or, 'and she sent the lad,' to screen him from the intensity of the heat.

16. **bowshot**. ∫79. Figure of speech Epitheton; or, Epithet B440: a naming of a thing by describing it. Here, "bowshot" is an epithet for a certain distance. For other instances of this figure see Ex 25:25. 37:12. Nu 24:20. Jg *20:16. 1 K 7:26. 2 Ch 4:5. Ps 39:5. Ezk 40:5. Lk 22:41. Jn 17:3. 1 Th 1:9. 1 P 4:3. 1 J 5:20. **Let**. Ge 44:34. 1 K 3:26. Est 8:6. Is 49:15. Zc 12:10. Lk 15:20. **not**. ∫175B. Figure of speech Tapeinosis; or, Demeaning B159: a lessening of a thing in order to increase it. This differs from Meiosis (∫111, Ge +18:27) in that in Meiosis one thing is diminished in order, by contrast, to increase the greatness of *another*, or something else. In Tapeinosis the thing that is lessened is the same thing which is increased and intensified. Here, Hagar prayed to not see the death of her child, but let him live and prosper. For other instances of this figure see Ge 26:29. Ex 20:7. Le 10:1. Nu 21:23. Ps 43:1mg. 51:17. 78:50. 83:1. *84:11. 107:38. Pr 12:3. 17:21. 18:5. 30:25. Is 14:6. 42:3. Je 2:8, 11. Zc 8:17. Mt 2:6. *12:32. Jn *6:37. *14:18. Ac 20:12. 21:39. 22:18. 26:19. Ro 1:13, *16. 4:19. 5:5. 9:25. 10:2. 13:10. 1 C *2:14. 10:1, 5. 12:1. 2 C 1:8. 2:11. Ga √5:21. 1 Th *4:13. He 11:16. 13:2. Re 12:11.

18:7. **see**. ✸108B. Figure of speech Idiom B828, 829: here, involving special idiomatic use of the verb "to see," implying sorrow and grief. For other instances of this use see Ge 44:34. Zc 12:10. Jn 19:37. Re 1:7.

lift. ✸144A12, Ge +22:13. Ge 27:38. 29:11. Jg 2:4. Ru 1:9. 1 S 24:16. 30:4. 2 S 13:36.

17. **heard**. ✸22C14, Ge +16:11. Ge 16:11. Ex 3:7. 22:23, 27. 2 K 13:4, 23. Ps 50:15. 65:2. 91:15. Mt 15:32. **the angel**. See on Ge 16:9, 11. **What**. ✸85K, Ge +3:9. Jg 18:23. 1 S 11:5. Is 22:1. **fear**. Ge 15:1. 46:3. Ex 14:13. Ps 107:4-6. Is 41:10, 13, 14. 43:1, 2. Mk 5:36.

18. **I will**. ver. 13. Ge 16:10. 17:20. 25:12-18. 1 Ch 1:29-31.

19. **opened**. Ge +*3:7. Nu *22:31. 2 K 6:17-20. Ps 119:18. Is 35:5, 6. Lk 24:◉16, +31. **well**. Heb. *beer*, Ge +16:14.

20. **God**. Ge 17:20. 28:15. 39:2, 3, 21. Jg 6:12. 13:24, 25. Lk 1:80. 2:40. **an archer**. Ge 10:9. 16:12. 25:27. 27:3. 49:23, 24.

21. **Paran**. i.e. *place of caverns; abounding in foliage; their beautifying*, ✸S#6290h. Nu 10:12. 12:16. 13:3, 26. Dt 1:1. +*33:2. 1 S 25:1. 1 K 11:18, 18. Hab *3:3. Paran is an extensive wilderness region on the south and southwest of Palestine, often called the wilderness of Paran, sometimes Mount Paran, and, in Ge 14:6, El-paran. Hagar and Ishmael went into the wilderness of Paran, Ge 21:21. It was entered by the Israelites soon after they left Sinai, Nu 10:12, and they encamped there many times during their wanderings, Nu 12:16; 13:3, 26. David fled to it from Saul, 1 S 25:1, after the death of Samuel, and Hadad escaped through it to Egypt, 1 K 11:18. Mount Paran, probably in the northeast part of the wilderness of Paran, is the place where the "Lord shined forth," Dt 33:2. It is also mentioned in Hab 3:3. **a wife**. Ge 24:3, 4, +*57. 26:34, 35. 27:46. 28:1, 2. 34:4. 36:2. Ex 2:21. Nu +*12:1. 36:6. Jg 14:2. 1 C 7:38.

22. A.M. 2118. B.C. 1886. **Abimelech**. Ge 20:2. 26:26. **Phicol**. i.e. *mouth of all*, ✸S#6369h. ver. 32. Ge 26:26. **God**. Ge 20:17. *26:28. 28:15. 30:27. 39:2, 3. Jsh 3:7. 2 Ch 1:1. Is 8:10. 45:14. Zc *8:23. Mt 1:23. Ro 8:31. 1 C 14:25. He 13:5. Re 3:9.

23. **swear**. Ge 14:22, 23. 24:3. 26:28. 31:44, 53. Dt 6:13. Jsh *2:12. 1 S 20:13, 17, 42. *24:21, 22. 30:15. Je 4:2. 2 C 1:23. He 6:16. **that thou wilt not deal falsely with me**. Heb. if thou shalt lie unto me. **kindness**. ✸121C1B, Ge +20:13. I have. Ge 20:14.

24. **will swear**. Ge 14:13. Ro 12:18. He 6:16.

25. **reproved**. Le +*19:17. Pr *17:10. 25:9. 27:5. Mt *18:15-18. Ga *6:1. **because**. Wells of water were of great consequence in those hot countries, especially where the flocks were numerous; because water was scarce, and digging to find it was attended with the expense of much time and labor. Ge *26:15-22. 29:8. Ex 2:15-17. Jg 1:15. **well**. Heb. *beer*, Ge +16:14. **servants**. Ge 13:7. 26:15-22. Ex 2:16, 17.

26. **I wot**. *Wot*, though used for the present tense, is the past tense of the almost obsolete word *to wit*, from the Saxon *witan*, to know. Ge 13:7. 2 K 5:20-24.

27. **took**. Ge 14:22, 23. Pr 17:8. 18:16, 24. 21:14. Is 32:8. **made**. Ge 26:28-31. 31:44. 1 S 18:3. Ezk 17:13. Ro 1:31. Ga 3:15.

28. **Abraham**. Ge 17:5. **seven**. Ge 7:2. 41:26, 27. Le 4:6. 14:7, 16. 23:15, 18. 25:8. 26:18-21. Nu 23:1.

29:32. Jsh 6:4. Ru 4:15. 1 S 2:5. 1 K 18:43. 2 K 5:10. 1 Ch 15:26. 2 Ch 29:21. Jb 42:8. Ps 12:6. 119:164. Pr 26:16. Is 4:1. 30:26. Je 15:9. Ezk 45:23. Da 3:19. 4:32. 9:24, 25. Am 5:8. Mi 5:5, 6. Zc 3:9. 4:2, 10. Ac 6:3. Re 1:4, 12, 20. 3:1. 4:5. 5:1, 6. 8:2. 10:3. 12:3. 13:1. 15:1, 6, 7. 17:3, 7, 9, 10. The foregoing references show the frequency of and prominence given to the number seven in Scripture, a prominence present also in this very passage. While the number is to be understood literally, it also clearly possesses additional symbolic and spiritual significance. Generally, it is the symbol of spiritual completeness or perfection, and may well be contrasted with the symbolism of the numbers six, eight, and thirteen. **lambs**. Ge 22:7, 8. Ex 12:3, 4, 5, 21. 29:39, 41. Le 3:7. 4:32, 35. Is 34:6. *53:7. 66:3. Jn 1:29, 36. Ac 8:32. 1 P 1:19. Re 5:6, 8, 12, 13.

29. **What mean**. Ge 33:8. Ex 12:26. 1 S 15:14.

30. **a witness**. Ge 31:44-48, 52. Jsh 22:27, 28. 24:27. **well**. Heb. *beer*, Ge +16:14.

31. **called**. Ge 26:33. **Beer-sheba**. i.e. the well of the oath, or the well of the seven: alluding to the seven ewe lambs. ✸S#884h. ver. 14, 32, 33. Ge 22:19, 19. 26:23, 33. 28:10. 46:1, 5. Jsh 15:28. 19:2. Jg 20:1. 1 S 3:20. 8:2. 2 S 3:10. 17:11. 24:2, 7, 15. 1 K 4:25. 19:3. 2 K 12:1. 23:8. 1 Ch 4:28. 21:2. 2 Ch 19:4. 24:1. 30:5. Ne 11:27, 30. Am 5:5. 8:14. **sware**. The verb rendered *to swear* (S#7650h) is derived from the word translated *seven* (S#7651h). Abraham used seven lambs (ver. 28) to seal the covenant with Abimelech. When God sware unto Abraham (Ge 22:16, 17), he *sevened* or confirmed the blessing with the seal of the seven. See also Ge 26:31-33. The Hebrew stem for *seven* also signifies fullness or completeness, as in Ge 4:15. Le *26:18. Dt 33:23. 28:7. Pr 6:30, 31.

32. **made a covenant**. ver. 27. Ge 14:13. 31:53. 1 S 18:3. **the Philistines**. Ge 10:14. 26:8, 14. Ex 13:17. Jg 13:1.

33. **grove**. *or*, tree. T#1192. Am 8:14. The original word *eshel*, has been variously translated a *grove*, a *plantation*, an *orchard*, a *cultivated field*, and an *oak*; but it may denote a kind of *tamarisk*, as it is rendered by Gesenius, the same with the Arabic *athl*. 1 S 22:6. 31:13. **Beersheba**. ver. 14. Dt *16:21. Jg *3:7. **called**. Ge +*4:26. *12:8. *26:23, 25, 33. **on the name**. Dr. Shuckford justly contends, that the expression rendered, 'he called on the name,' signifies 'he invoked in the name.' **Lord**. or, Jehovah. **everlasting**. Heb. *olam*, Ge +17:7. ✸171E12, Ge +14:22. Dt *33:27. Ps *90:2. Is *40:28. +*57:15. 63:16. Je *10:10. Da 12:7. Mi 5:2. Jn 8:56-58. Ro *1:20. *16:26. 1 T *1:17. Notice here the divine definition of Jehovah as the everlasting God.

34. **sojourned**. Ge 20:1. 1 Ch 29:15. Ps 39:12. He 11:9, 13. 1 P 2:11.

GENESIS 22

Abraham, tested by the command to sacrifice Isaac, shows his faith by obeying, 1-10. He is prevented from slaying his son, and offers a ram in his stead, 11-13. A name is given to the place; and the covenant renewed with Abraham, 14-19. The generations of Nahor unto Rebekah, 20-24.

1. A.M. 2132. B.C. 1872. **God**. Ex *15:25, 26. 16:4. Dt 8:2. *13:3. Jg 2:22. 2 S *24:1. 2 Ch 32:31. Pr 17:3.

1 C +*10:13. He *11:17. Ja √1:12-14. 2:21. 1 P *1:7.
tempt. Or, *prove*, or *try*, as *tempt* originally signified.
Ex 20:20. Dt 8:16. 1 S 17:39. 1 K 10:1. 2 Ch 9:1. Jb
1:12. Mt 13:21. Lk +*8:13. Ac 20:19. He *2:18. √4:15.
1 P 1:6. **Behold, here I am.** Heb. Behold me. ver.
7, 11. Ex 3:4. Jb 38:35mg. Is *6:8mg.

2. **Take.** ♪60C, Ge +19:2. Ge 17:19. 21:12. Jn *3:16.
Ro *5:8. *8:32. He 11:17. 1 J *4:9, 10. **only.** Heb.
yachid, ❋S#3173h, Ps +22:20mg. ver. 12, 16. Dt
◑6:4n. Jg 11:34. Lk +7:12. Jn 3:16n. He *11:17. 1 J
4:9. **whom.** Pr 4:3. 8:30. Mk 12:6. Jn=3:16. Ro=*8:32.
Col 1:13. 1 J 4:9, 10. **Moriah.** i.e. *chosen of the Lord;
my teacher is Jehovah*, ❋S#4179h. 1 Ch 21:22. 22:1.
2 Ch *3:1h. Mt 27:33. (1) The land to which Abraham
was commanded to go to offer up Isaac for a burnt
offering, Ge 22:2. (2) The mount on which Solomon
built the Temple in Jerusalem, 2 Ch 3:1. **and offer.**
Jg 11:31, 39. 2 K 3:27. Mi *6:7. Jn *3:16. **burnt offering.**
Le 1:3. +*23:12. Ep 5:2.

3. **And.** ♪148. Polysyndeton, Ge +8:22. The use
of Polysyndeton here emphasizes the deliberateness
of each step of Abraham's action and the calmness of
his faith. **rose.** Ge 17:23. Ps *119:60. Ec 9:10. Is *26:3,
4. Mt *10:37. Mk 10:28-31. Lk *14:26. Ga 1:16. He
11:8, *17-19. **early.** Ge 18:6. +21:14. Jsh 3:1. Je 7:13.
place. Dt 12:14.

4. **third.** Ge 31:22. 34:25. +40:20. Ex 5:3. +10:22.
15:22. 19:11, 15. Le 7:17. +19:6. Nu 10:33. 19:12,
19. 31:19. Jsh 1:11. 2 K 20:5. Est 5:1. Ho *6:2.
Mt=*16:21. *17:23. 27:64. Lk *13:32. 24:21. 1 C
+=*15:4. **lifted.** ♪144A12, Ge +22:13. **saw.** 1 S 26:13.

5. **Abide.** Ge 45:1. Jn 16:32. He 12:1. **come.** He
11:19. First person plural, "We will come again," evidence of Abraham's faith.

6. **laid it.** Is=*53:6. Mt 8:17. Lk *24:26, 27. Jn
*19:17. 1 P=*2:24. =3:18. **fire.** 1 K 18:38. He 12:29.
knife. Zc 13:7. **both.** Jn=10:30. =14:10, 11. =*16:32.

7. **My father.** Mt *26:39, 42. Jn 18:11. Ro 8:15.
Here am I. Heb. Behold me. ver. 1. Is 58:9. Jn 8:29.
but. Ge 4:2-4. 8:20. **lamb.** *or*, kid. Ex *12:3mg. 29:38-
42. Is 43:23. 53:7. Jn *1:29. 1 P 1:19. Re 5:6. 13:8.

8. **God will.** Ge 18:14. 2 Ch 25:9. Mt *19:26. Jn
*1:29, 36. 1 P *1:19, 20. Re *5:6, 12. 7:14. 13:8. **provide.** 1 S 16:1. Ro *8:32. **burnt.** Ep 5:2. He 10:5.

9. **And.** ♪148, Ge +8:22. **place.** ver. 2-4. Mt ch.
21, 26, 27. **built.** Ge 8:20. **altar.** Ge 12:7. Ex 20:25.
He 13:10. **bound.** Ps 118:27. Is *53:4-10. Mt *27:2.
Mk 15:1. Jn *10:17, 18. Ac 8:32. Ga 3:13. Ep 5:2. Ph
*2:7, 8. He +*9:28. 1 P 2:24.

10. **And.** ♪148, Ge +8:22. **stretched.** Is *53:6-12.
He 11:17-19. Ja 2:21-23.

11. **angel.** ver. *12, 16. See on Ge *16:7, 9, 10.
21:17. Ps 34:7. 91:11. Mt 17:5. **Abraham.** ver. 1. Ex
*3:4. 1 S *3:10. Ac *9:4. 26:14. **Abraham.** ♪84, Ge
+6:17. Ge 46:2. Ex 3:4. 1 S 3:10. Ps 22:1. Mt 7:21,
22. 23:37. 27:46. Mk 15:34. Lk 6:46. 10:41. 13:25,
34. 22:31. Ac 9:4. **and.** ♪148, Ge +8:22. **Here.** 1 K
◑19:13.

12. **Lay.** Ge +37:22. 1 S *15:22. Jb 5:19. Je *19:5.
Mi +*6:6-8. 1 C +*10:13. 2 C 8:12. He *11:19. **neither.**
Ex 12:46. Nu 9:12. Ps 22:14. =34:20. 35:10. Jn=19:36.
1 C 5:7. **now.** Ge 20:11. 26:5. 42:18. Ex 20:20. 1 S
12:24, 25. 15:22. Ne 5:15. Jb 28:28. Ps *1:6. 2:11.
*25:12, 14. *111:10. 112:1. *147:11. Pr 1:7. Ec 8:12,
13. *12:13. Je *32:40. Mal *4:2. Mt 5:16. *10:37, 38.
16:24. 19:29. Ac 9:31. Ep *2:10. He *11:17. 12:28. Ja

*2:18, 21, 22. 1 J 4:10. 5:3. Re 19:5. **know.** ♪22C1,
Ge +18:21. **seeing.** Jn *3:16. Ro *5:8. √8:32. 1 J *4:9,
10. **only.** ver. 2. Mk ◑+6:3. Lk ◑+7:12. Jn=1:14,
18. +=3:16n, 18. 1 J 4:9.

13. **lifted.** ♪144A12. Figure of speech Pleonasm; or,
Redundancy B413: when more words are used than
the grammar requires, for the sake of emphasis. For
other instances of this figure involving this term see
Ge 13:10, 14. 18:2. 21:16. 22:4. 24:63. 27:38. 29:11.
31:10, 12. 33:1, 5. 37:25. 39:15, 18. 43:29. Nu 24:2.
Dt 3:27. 4:19. Jg 9:7. 19:17. 21:2. Ru 1:9, 14. 1 S
6:13. 11:4. 24:16. 30:4. 2 S 3:32. 13:34, 36. 18:24.
1 Ch 21:16. 2 Ch 5:13. Jb 2:12. Ps 93:3. 121:1. 123:1.
Is 40:9, 26. 42:11. 49:18. 51:6. 52:8. 60:4. Je 13:20.
22:20. Ezk 8:5. 18:6, 12, 15. Da 4:34. 8:3. 10:5. Zc
1:18. 2:1. 5:1, 5, 9. 6:1. Mt 17:8. Lk 6:20. 11:27. 17:13.
Jn *4:35. 6:5. 11:41. 17:1. Ac 2:14. 4:24. 14:11. 22:22.
looked. Ge +13:14. **behold.** ♪40, Ge +3:22. **behind.**
ver. *8. Ps 40:6-8. 89:19, 20. Is 30:21. 1 C +*10:13.
2 C 1:9, 10. **burnt.** ver. 2, 8. Le 16:3. +*23:12. **in
the.** 1 C *5:7, 8. 1 P 1:19, 20. **stead.** Is 53:10, 11.
Mt 20:28. Jn 6:51. Ro 4:25. 5:6, 8. 2 C=5:14, 15, 21.
Ga 3:13. He 9:28. 10:10.

14. **called.** Ge *16:13, 14. *28:19. *32:30. Ex *17:15.
Jg *6:24. 1 S *7:12. Ezk *48:35. **Jehovah-jireh.** i.e.
The Lord will see, *or* provide. ❋S#3070h, only here.
ver. *8, *13. Ex *17:15. **said.** ♪138C. Figure of speech
Paroemia; or, Proverb B761: a saying which appears
first in Scripture, but has since passed into general
use as a proverbial saying. For other instances of this
figure see Dt 25:4. 1 K 8:46. 20:11. 2 Ch 6:36. Jb
6:5. 14:19. 28:18, 28. Ps 62:9. 111:10. Pr 1:7, 17, 32.
3:12. 6:6, 27. 9:10. 10:5, 13, 19. 11:15. *22:6. 26:11.
27:6, 7, 17. 28:21. Ec 1:15, 18. 9:4. 10:1. 11:6. *12:12.
Je *13:23. *23:28. Mi *7:5, 6. Hab 2:6. Ml 2:10. Mt
5:13, 14, 15. *6:3, 21, 24, 34. 7:*2, *5, 16. 9:12, 16.
10:10, 22, 24, *26. 12:34. 13:*12, 57. *15:14. Mk 9:50.
Lk *9:62. *12:48. 17:37. 20:35. 1 C 5:6. *10:12. 15:33.
2 C 9:6, 7. 2 Th *3:10. T *1:15. **day.** Ge +19:38. **In.**
Dt 32:36. Ps 22:4, 5. Da 3:17. Mi 4:10. Jn *1:14. 2 C
1:8-10. 1 T *3:16. **it shall be seen.** 2 S 24:25. 1 Ch
21:26. 2 Ch 7:1-3. Is 25:6. 'In the mount of the Lord
it shall be provided.' The meaning is, that God, in
the greatest difficulties, when all human assistance is
vain, will make a suitable provision for the deliverance
of those who trust in Him. Jb 11:16. Ps 16:8. 30:5.
112:4. 146:8. Is √30:18. 43:2, 3.

15. **angel.** ver. 11. Ge +19:24. 21:17. **second time.**
Ge 24:44. 41:5, *32. Dt 17:6. Jg 6:39, 40. 1 S 10:22.
+*23:4. Je 1:13. Jon 3:1. 1 C *2:9.

16. **By myself.** Ge *12:2. Ps 89:35. 105:9. 110:4.
132:11. Is *45:23. Je 22:5. 49:13. 51:14. Am 6:8. Lk
1:73. Ac 2:30. Ro 4:13, 14. He *▶6:13, 14. **sworn.** Ge
26:3. Ps 89:35. 110:4. 132:11. Is *45:23. Je 22:5. Ac
2:30.

17. **in blessing.** ♪147B, Ge +2:16. Ge *12:2. 27:28,
29. 28:3, 14. 49:25, 26. Dt 28:2-13. Ep *1:3. **I will
multiply.** See on Ge *13:16. 15:5. 17:6. 26:4. Dt *1:10.
Is +*54:1. Je 33:22. **as the stars.** ♪102B, Ge +13:16.
♪138B, Ge +13:16. **as the sand.** ♪102B, ♪138B, Ge
+13:16. Ge 13:16. 32:12. 41:49. Jsh 11:4. 2 S 17:11.
1 K 4:20. Is 48:19. **shore.** Heb. lip. 1 K 9:26mg. **thy
seed.** Ge *24:60. Nu *24:17-19. Dt *21:19. Jsh ch. 1-
10. 2 S ch. 8, 10. Ps *2:8, 9. *72:8, 9. Je *32:22. Da
*2:44. 45. Mi *1:9. Lk *1:68-75. 1 C *15:57. Re
+*11:15. **gate.** Ps 87:2. Is 14:31. 24:12. ♪171S6. Figure

of speech Synecdoche (of the Part) B650: when a part is put for the whole; here, "gate" is put for the whole city. For other instances of this figure (compare Ge +14:7) see Ex +20:10. Dt 12:12. 14:27. 16:5. Ps 87:2. Je 15:7. **of his enemies.** Dt +*28:13. Ps +*18:43. 127:5. Ro +*11:25n.

18. **thy seed.** T#1876. See on Ge *12:3. *18:18. *26:4. 28:14. Ps *72:17. Zc 8:23. Mt *1:1. Lk *1:54, 55, 72-75. +*❋3:34. Jn *11:51, 52. Ac ▶3:25. Ro 1:3. +*4:13. Ga 3:❳8, 9, *16, 18, 28, 29. Ep *1:3. **because.** ver. 16. Ps +*9:10. Is 50:10. Zc 6:15. Mt 7:*21, 24-27. Lk 6:46. Jn 3:36. Ac 5:32. Ro 1:5. 2:8. 6:17. 10:16. 15:18. 2 C 10:5. 2 Th 1:8. He *5:9. 1 P 1:22. **obeyed.** ver. 3, 10. Ge 26:5. Dt +*28:1, 2, 15. 1 S 2:30. Je *7:23. He ch. 11.

19. **So Abraham.** ver. 5. **to Beer-sheba.** Ge 21:31. Jsh 15:28. Jg 20:1.

20. A.M. 2142. B.C. 1862. **told.** Pr 25:25. **Milcah.** Ge 11:29. 24:15, 24. **Nahor.** Ge 11:26. 24:10, 24. 31:53.

21. **Huz.** i.e. *the strong; counsellor,* *S#5780h. Ge +10:23. 36:28. 1 Ch 1:17, 42. Jb 1:1, Uz. Je 25:20. La 4:21. **Buz.** i.e. *contempt,* *S#938h. 1 Ch 5:14. Jb ◑32:2, 6. Je 25:23. (1) Son of Nahor, Ge 22:21. (2) An Israelite of Gad, 1 Ch 5:14. (3) A people and region whose situation is uncertain, but who are supposed to have occupied part of Arabia Petraea, Je 25:23. **Kemuel.** Kemuel might have given name to the Kamilites, a people of Syria, mentioned by Strabo, to the west of the Euphrates. **Aram.** i.e. *high, exalted,* *S#758h. (1) A son of Shem, Ge 10:22, 23; 1 Ch 1:17. (2) A descendant of Nahor, the brother of Abraham, Ge 22:21. (3) Son of Shamer of Asher, 1 Ch 7:34. (4) The son of Esrom, Mt 1:3, 4; Lk 3:33, elsewhere called Ram. (5) The elevated country northeast of Palestine, toward the river Euphrates, Nu 23:7; 1 Ch 2:23. It was nearly the same as Syria. Ge 24:10. Nu 23:7. Ps 60, title.

22. **Chesed.** i.e. *increase,* *S#3777h. **Hazo.** i.e. *vision,* *S#2375h. **Pildash.** i.e. *lamp of fire,* *S#6394h. **Jidlaph.** i.e. *shedding tears,* *S#3044h. **Bethuel.** i.e. *man of God; abode of God,* *S#1328h. ver. 23. Ge 24:15, 24, 47, 50. 25:20. 28:2, 5. 1 Ch 4:30.

23. **Bethuel.** Ge 24:15, 24, 47. 25:20. 28:2, 5. **Rebekah.** i.e. *a rope with a noose,* *S#7259h. Ge 24:15, 29, 30, 45, 51, 53, 58, 59, 60, 61, 64, 67. 25:20, 21, 28. 26:7, 8, 35. 27:5, 6, 11, 15, 42, 46. 28:5. 29:12. 35:8. 49:31. Ro 9:10, Rebecca. **these.** Ge 25:13-16. 35:22-26.

24. **concubine.** Ge 16:3. 25:6. 30:4. 36:12. Jg 8:31. 2 S 3:7. 5:13. 15:16. 21:11. 1 K 11:3. 1 Ch 1:32. 2:46-48. 7:14. 2 Ch 11:21. 13:21. Pr 15:25. Da 5:2. **Reumah.** i.e. *exalted, high, lofty,* *S#7208h. **Tebah.** i.e. *confidence; slaughter,* *S#2875h. **Gaham.** i.e. *having large flaming eyes; sunburnt or swarthy,* *S#1514h. **Thahash.** i.e. *badger, seal,* *S#8477h. **Maachah.** Dt 3:14. Jsh 12:5. 2 S 10:6. 1 K +2:39.

GENESIS 23

The age and death of Sarah, 1, 2. Abraham communes with the sons of Heth, and purchases the field and cave of Machpelah of Ephron, 3-18; where Sarah is buried, 19, 20.

1. A.M. 2144. B.C. 1860. **Sarah.** It is worthy of remark that Sarah is the only woman whose age, death,

and burial are distinctly noted in the Sacred Writings. **an.** Ge 17:17.

2. **Kirjath-arba.** ver. 19. Ge 13:18. Nu 13:22. Jsh 10:39. 14:14, 15. 20:7. Jg 1:10. 1 S 20:31. 2 S 2:11. 5:3, 5. 1 Ch 6:57. **mourn.** Ge 24:67. 27:41. 50:10. Nu 20:29. Dt 34:8. 1 S 28:3. 2 S 1:12, 17. 2 Ch 35:25. Je 22:10, 18. Ezk 24:16-18. Jn 11:31, 33, 35. Ac 8:2.

3. **before.** ℐ144A1, Ge +11:8. **Heth.** ver. 5, 7. Ge 10:15. 25:10. 27:46. 49:30. 1 S 26:6. 2 S 23:39.

4. **stranger.** Ge 17:8. 47:9. Le 25:23. 1 Ch *29:15. Ps 39:12. *105:12, 13. 119:19. Mt 25:35. Ac +*7:5n. He *11:9, 13-16. 1 P 2:11. ✛S#1616h: Ge 15:13. 23:4. Ex 2:22. 12:19, *48, 49. 18:3 (alien). 20:10. 22:21. 23:9, 12. Le 16:29. 17:8, 10, 12, 13, 15. 18:26. 19:10, 33, 34. 20:2. 22:18. 23:22. 24:16, 22. 25:23, 35, 47. Nu 9:14. 15:14, 15, 16, 26, 29, 30. 19:10. 35:15. Dt 1:16. 5:14. 10:18, 19. 14:21, 29. 16:11, 14. 23:7. 24:14, 17, 19, 20, 21. 26:11, 12, 13. 27:19. 28:43. 29:11. 31:12. Jsh 8:33, 35. +20:9. 2 S 1:13. 1 Ch 22:2. 29:15. 2 Ch 30:25. Jb 31:32. Ps 39:12. 94:6. 119:19. 146:9. Is 14:1. Je 7:6. 14:8. 22:3. Ezk 14:7. 22:7, 29. 47:22, 23. Zc 7:10. Ml *3:5. For *S#5236h, see Ex +12:43 (stranger). For *S#5237h, see Ge +31:15 (strangers). **sojourner.** ✛S#8453h: Ge 23:4. Ex 12:45 (foreigner). Le 22:10. 25:6 (stranger), 23, 35, 40, 45 (strangers), 47 (stranger). Nu 35:15. 1 K 17:1 (inhabitants). 1 Ch 29:15. Ps 39:12. **burying place.** Ge *3:19. 49:30. 50:13. Jb 30:23. Ec 6:3. 12:5, 7. Ac +*7:5. *S#6913h, *qeber.* Ge 23:4, 6, 6, 9, 20. 49:30. 50:5, 13. Ex 14:11. Nu 11:34, 35. 19:16, 18. 33:16, 17. Dt 9:22. Jg 8:32. 16:31. 2 S 2:32. 3:32. 4:12. 17:23. 19:37. 21:14. 1 K 13:22, 30, 31. 14:13. 2 K 13:21. 22:20. 23:6, 16, 16, 17. 2 Ch 16:14. 21:20. 24:25. 28:27. 32:33. 34:4, 28. 35:24. Ne 2:3, 5. 3:16. Jb 3:22. 5:26. 10:19. 17:1. 21:32. Ps 5:9. 88:5, 11. Is 14:19. *22:16, 16. 53:9. 65:4. Je 5:16. 8:1. 20:17. *26:23. Ezk 32:22, 23, 25, 26. 37:12, 12, 13, 13. 39:11. Na 1:14. For *S#6900h, *qeburah,* grave, see Ge +35:20. For *S#7845h, *shachath,* pit, ditch, destruction, corruption, see Jb +9:31. For *S#7585h, *sheol,* grave, hell, pit, see Ge +37:35. **bury.** ver. 19.

5. **answered.** ver. 14.

6. **my lord.** Ge 18:12. 24:18, 35. 31:35. 32:4, 5, 18. 42:10. 44:5, 8. Ex 32:22. Ru 2:13. **a mighty prince.** Heb. a prince of God. ℐ24L, Ge +6:2. Ge ◑10:9. 21:22. 30:8. Ex 9:28. 1 S 14:15. 26:12. 2 S 9:3n. 2 K 1:12. 1 Ch 12:22. Jb +1:16. Ps 36:6. 80:10. SS 8:6. Is 45:14. Ezk 28:13. Ho 13:15. Jon 3:3mg. Ac *7:20mg. 1 J 3:1, 2. **prince.** Ge *13:2. *14:14. 24:35. **choice.** Ex 15:4. Dt 12:11. Is 22:7. Ezk 24:5. **sepulchres, sepulchre.** Heb. *qeber.* ver. +*4.

7. **bowed.** Ge 18:2. 19:1. Pr 18:24. Ro 12:17, 18. He 12:14. 1 P 3:8.

8. **mind.** Heb. *nephesh,* soul. Dt 18:6. 28:65. 1 S 2:35. 2 S 17:8. 2 K 9:15. 1 Ch 28:9. Je 15:1. Ezk 23:17, 18, 22, 28. 24:25. 36:5. ℐ121A9. Figure of speech Metonymy (of the Cause) B545: the *soul* is put for the will, affection, or desire, which are its operations and effects. For other instances of this figure see Ex 23:9mg. Dt 23:24. 1 K 19:3. Pr 23:2. Je 34:16. Jn 10:24. Compare Ge +34:3; Ex +15:9; +23:9. For the other uses of *nephesh* see Ge +2:7. **intreat.** 1 K 2:17. Lk 7:3, 4. He 7:26. 1 J 2:1, 2. **Ephron.** i.e. *fawnlike; strong.* S#6085h. Ge 23:10, 10, 13, 14, 16, 16, 17. 25:9. 49:29, 30. 50:13. (1) A son of Zohar the Hittite,

from whom Abraham purchased the field and cave of Machpelah, Ge 23:8; 49:30; 50:13. (2) A mountain between Judah and Benjamin, Jsh 15:9.

9. **Machpelah.** i.e. *double, folded together,* **✱**S#4375h. ver. 17, 19. Ge 25:9. 49:30. 50:13. **much money.** Heb. full money. Ro 12:17. 13:8. ✐121D5. Figure of speech Metonymy (of the Cause): or, Change of Noun B558: the material is put for the thing made of or from it. Here, "silver" is put for "money." For other instances of this figure see Ge 24:22. 2 K 5:5. 12:4. 1 Ch 21:22, ✱24. 29:2. Ps 115:4. Mt 10:9. Ac 3:6. **buryingplace.** Heb. *qeber,* ver. +✱4.

10. **dwelt.** Or, *sitting* (as the word frequently denotes) among the children of Heth (Hittites), at the gate of the city, where all public business was transacted. Ephron, though a chief man, might have been personally unknown to Abraham; but now he answers for himself, making a free tender of the field and cave to Abraham, in the presence of all the people, which amounted to a legal conveyance to the Patriarch. **audience.** Heb. ears. **all that.** ver. 18. Ge 34:20, 24. Ru 4:1-4. Jb 29:7. Is 28:6. **his.** Ge 24:10. Mt 9:1. Lk 2:3, 4. **gate.** ✐171S7B. Synecdoche of the Part, "gate" put for place of legal transactions, Ge +14:7. **his.** Ge 24:10. Mt 9:1. Lk 2:3, 4.

11. **my lord.** ver. 6. 2 S 24:20-24. 1 Ch 21:22-24. Is 32:8. **give.** ✐96C1. Heterosis, Ge +4:1. **in the.** ver. 18. Nu 35:30. Dt 17:6. 19:15. Ru 4:1, 4, 9, 11. Je 32:7-12. Lk 19:24.

12. **bowed.** See ver. 7. Ge 18:2. 19:1.

13. **I will.** Ge 14:22, 23. 2 S 24:24. Ac 20:35. Ro 13:8. Ph 4:5-8. Col 4:5. He 13:5.

14. **answered.** ver. 5.

15. **shekels.** Ge 17:12, 13. 20:16. Ex 21:32. 30:13, ✱15. Jsh 7:21. Ezk 45:12.

16. **weighed.** Ge 43:21. 2 S ✱24:24. 1 Ch 21:25. Ezr 8:25-30. Jb 28:15. Je ✱32:9. Zc 11:12. Mt 7:12. 26:15g. Ro 13:8. Ph 4:8. 1 Th 4:6. **four.** ver. 15. Ex 30:13. Ezk 45:12. **current.** 2 K 12:4. ✐24B. Figure of speech Antimereia; or, Exchange of Parts of Speech B493: the exchange of one part of speech for another. Here, the active participle for a noun, "current money of purchasing" for "silver which passes with the merchant." For other instances of this figure see Jb 13:4. Ps 17:14. Pr 14:20mg. Jl 1:17. Mt 4:3. 11:3. Mk 6:14. 15:29. 1 C 9:25. 1 Th 3:5. He 1:6. 9:17. 12:18. Re ✱9:11mg. **merchant.** Ge 37:28. 2 S 14:26. 1 K 10:15, 28.

17. **the field.** ver. 20. Ge 25:9. 49:30-32. 50:13. Ac 7:16. **made sure.** ver. 20. Ru 4:7-10. Ps 112:5. Je 32:7-14. Mt 10:16. Ep 5:15. Col 4:5.

18. **all.** Ge 34:20. Ru 4:1. Je 32:12. **gate.** ✐171S7B, Ge +14:7. ver. 10.

19. **buried.** Ge 3:19. 25:9, 10. 35:27-29. 47:30. 49:29-32. 50:13, 25. Jb 30:23. Ec 6:3. 12:5, 7. **Mamre.** Ge +13:18.

20. **were.** Ru ✱4:7-10. 2 S ✱24:24. Je ✱32:10, 11. **for a.** Ge 25:9. 49:31, 32. 50:5, ✱13, 24, 25. 2 K 21:18. **buryingplace.** Heb. *qeber,* ver. +✱4.

GENESIS 24

Abraham commissions his servant to go to Mesopotamia in order to take a wife for Isaac, 1-9. The servant's journey, 10, 11. His prayer, 12, 13. His sign, 14. Rebekah meets him, 15-17; fulfils his sign, 18-21; receives jewels, 22; shows her kindred, 23, 24; and invites him home, 25. The servant blesses God, 26, 27. Laban entertains him, 29-33. The servant proposes a marriage between Isaac and Rebekah, 34-49. Laban and Bethuel approve it, 50-57. Rebekah consents to go, and departs, 58-61. Isaac meets and marries her, 62-67.

1. ✐133. Parecbasis; or, Digression, vv. 1-62, Ge +2:8. **was old.** Ge 18:11. ✱21:5. 25:20. 1 K 1:1. Lk 1:7. **well stricken in age.** Heb. gone into days. **blessed.** ver. 35. Ge 12:2. ✱13:2. 49:25. Ps ✱112:1-3. Pr ✱10:22. Is 51:2. Mt 6:33. Ga ✱3:9. Ep ✱1:3. 1 T +✱4:8.

2. **eldest.** Ge 15:2. 1 T 5:17. **ruled.** ver. 10. Ge 39:4-6, 8, 9. 44:1. **Put.** ver. 9. Ge 47:29. 1 Ch +✱29:24mg. **thigh.** ✚S#3409h. ✐88. Figure of speech Euphemism B684: the change of what is unpleasant or immodest to what is pleasant or modest. Here, "thigh" is put for the organs of generation (compare Ge +17:11, "flesh"). For other instances of this figure involving this term see Ge 24:9. 32:25, 31, 32. 46:26mg. ✱47:29. Ex 1:5mg. 28:42. Nu ❶5:21, 22, 27. Jg 8:30mg. 1 Ch +✱29:24mg.

3. **swear.** Ge 21:23. 26:28-31. 31:44-53. 50:25. Ex 20:7. 22:11. 23:13. Le 19:12. Nu 5:21. Dt ✱6:13. 10:20. Jsh 2:12. 1 S 20:17. Ne 13:25. Is 45:23. 48:1. 65:16. Je 4:2. 12:16. Zp 1:5. He 6:16. **the God.** Ge 14:22. 2 K 19:15. 2 Ch 2:12. Ne 9:6. Ps 115:15. Je 10:11. **that.** Ge 6:2, 4. 26:34, 35. ✱27:46. 28:1, 2, 8. Ex 34:16. Dt 7:3, 4. 1 C ✓7:39. 2 C ✓6:14-17. **Canaanites.** S#3669h. ver. 37. Ge 10:+18, 19. 15:21. Nu 13:29. 14:43, 45. Dt 7:1. 20:17. Jsh 3:10. 12:8. 17:13, 16, 18. 24:11. Jg 1:3, 4, 5, 9, 10, 17, 27, 28, 29, 30, 32, 33. 3:3.

4. **to my kindred.** Ge 11:25. 12:1, 7. 22:20-23. 28:2. Nu 36:6.

5. **Peradventure.** ver. 39, 58. Ex 9:2. 20:7. Pr 13:16. Ec 5:2. Je 4:2.

6. **Beware.** Ga 5:1. He 10:39. 11:9, 13-16. 2 P 2:20-22.

7. **Lord.** Ezr 1:2. Da 2:44. Jon 1:9. Re 11:13. **took.** Ge 12:1-7. **which spake.** Ge 13:15. 15:18. 17:8. 22:16-18. 26:3, 4, 24. Ex 13:5. ✱32:13. Nu 14:16, 30. 32:11. Dt 1:8. 34:4. Jsh 1:6. Jg 2:1. Ac +✱7:5. Ga ▶3:16. He 11:9. **send.** Ex 32:34. 33:2. Nu 20:16. **angel.** Ex ✱23:20-23. 33:2. Ps ✱32:8. ✱34:7. 73:24. 103:20. Pr ✓3:5, 6. Is ✱63:9. He ✱1:14.

8. **clear.** Nu 30:5, 8. Jsh 2:17-20. 9:20. Jn 8:32. **only.** ver. 4, 5, 6. Ac 7:2.

9. **thigh.** ✐88, ver. +2. ver. +2.

10. **camels.** Ge 12:16. **for.** *or,* and. **all.** ver. 2. Ge 39:4-6, 8, 9, 22, 23. ✓✐171B. Figure of speech Synecdoche (of the Genus); or, Transfer B616: where genus is put for the species, or universals for particulars, when a universal affirmative does not affirm particularly, as when "all" and "every," as universal affirmations, extend not to all the individuals, but to all kinds, or all that are specified or implied. Here, "all the goods of his master were in his hand" refers only to all that his master had given him, ver. 53. For other instances of this very significant figure (some highly debatable instances are marked by this editor with a preceding "?"), see Ge +✱7:19. Nu 1:45. 8:9. Jsh 11:10n. 2 K 8:9. 24:14. Jl 2:28. Zp 2:14. Mt 4:23. Lk ✱11:42, herb of every (tithable) kind. Jn ✱1:9, *every* man without distinction, not without exception. Jn ✓12:32, *all* without distinction, not all without exception. Ac 10:12. 1 T ?✓2:4, 6. **all** kinds of men without distinction (Jn ❶4:22), not all or every man without exception. He

?√2:9, *every*, meaning all manner of men, without distinction, not all men without exception. He 13:4. 2 P ?√3:9, *any* kind of person, without distinction, not all kinds without exception. See further on √*J*171O1, Jn +3:16. ◑*J*171F, Synecdoche (of the Species), where *many* is put for *all*, Is +53:12. *J*121J9A, Jn 1:10, Metonymy of the Subject, where the *world* is put for a portion of its inhabitants. *J*108B, 1 C 8:1, Idiom, where *all* signifies the greater part. *J*108B, 1 C 13:2, Idiom, where *all* signifies the greatest degree or quality of that to which it is applied. *J*108B, Mt 4:23, Idiom, where *all* signifies some of every kind. *J*171M, Synecdoche of the Whole, where what is said of the whole, collectively, is sometimes said of only a part, and not all of the parts, precisely and singularly, Ge 6:12. √*J*171A, Ex 9:6, Synecdoche of the Genus, where *all* is put for the greater part. *J*171D, Mk 16:20, Synecdoche of the Genus, when words denoting universality do not always affirm it of particulars. *J*121N1, Metonymy of the Adjunct, abstract put for the concrete, Ge 6:5n. √*J*102, Hyperbole, Ge √7:19n. Caution is required when assigning such figure of speech categories lest our presuppositions or theology dictate our categories (see Ps 16:10n); otherwise, if Christ really died for all men (2 C 5:15), how could God by the Holy Spirit inspire the Scripture writers to say so, if we by our arbitrary categories have removed every possible way of Him saying so? **hand**. Ge +43:26. **Mesopotamia**. i.e. *exalted*, ✳S#763h. Dt 23:4. Jg 3:8-10. 1 Ch 19:6. Ps 60, title. Ac 2:9. **city**. Ge 11:31. 27:43. 29:1, 4, 5.

11. **kneel**. Ge 33:13, 14. Pr 12:10. **well**. Heb. *beer*, Ge +16:14. **women go out to draw water**. Heb. women which draw water go forth. ver. 13-20. Ex 2:16. 1 S 9:11. Jn *4:7.

12. **O Lord**. ver. 27. Ge 15:1. 17:7, 8. 26:24. 28:13. 31:42. 32:9. Ex *3:6, 15. 1 K 18:36. 2 K 2:14. Mt 22:32. **I pray**. T#1616. Ge 27:10. 43:14. Ne *1:11. 2:4. Ps *37:5. 90:16, 17. 118:25. 122:6. 127:1. Pr *3:6. Ph *4:6. 1 Th 3:10, 11.

13. **Behold**. *J*40, Ge +3:22. **I stand**. ver. 43. Ps *37:5. Pr *3:6. **well**. ✛S#5869h, *ayin*, a fountain. Ge 24:13, 16, 29, 30, 42, 43, 45. 49:22. Ex 15:27. Ne 2:13. For ✳S#875h, *be-er*, a dug well, see Ge +16:14. For ✳S#4599h, *mayan*, a spring or fountain, see Ge +7:11. For S#4726h, *maqor*, spring, dug well (even when naturally flowing) see Le +12:7, issue. Pr 10:11. For ✳S#953h, *bor* or *bore*, a hewn cistern, well, dungeon, pit, see Ge +37:20. **daughters**. ver. 11. Ge 29:9, 10. Ex 2:16. Jg 5:11. 1 S 9:11. Jn 4:7.

14. **And let**. Jg 6:17, 37. 1 S 14:9. **damsel**. Heb. *naarah*, ✳S#5291h. ver. 16, 28, 55, 57, 61. Ge 34:3, 12. Ex 2:5 (maidens). Dt 22:15 (damsel), 15, 16, 19, 20, 21, 23, 24, 25, 26, 27, 28, 29. Jg 19:3, 4, 5, 6, 8, 9. 21:12. Ru 2:5, 6, 8 (maidens), 22, 23. 3:2 (maidens). 4:12 (young woman). 1 S 9:11. 25:42. 1 K 1:2 (young), 3 (damsel), 4. 2 K 5:2 (maid), 4. Est 2:2 (young), 3 (young), 4 (maiden), 7, 8, 9, 9, 9, 12, 13. 4:4, 16. Jb 41:5. Pr 9:3. 27:27. 31:15. Am 2:7. **pitcher**. Jn 4:28. **give**. Ge ◑29:10. Jn 4:9. **she that**. ver. 44. Pr *19:14. **thereby**. ver. +50. Ge 15:8. Ex 4:1-9. Jg *6:17, 37. 7:13-15. 18:5. 1 S 6:7-9. 10:2-10. 14:8, 10. 20:7. 2 S 5:24. 20:9. 2 K 20:8-11. Is 7:11. Ro 1:10.

15. **before**. ver. 45. Jg 6:36-40. Ps *34:15. 65:2. 145:18, 19. Is 58:9. +*65:24. Da *9:20-23. **Rebekah**. ver. 24. Ge 22:20-23. **Milcah**. Ge 11:27, 29. 22:23.

pitcher. Ge 21:14. 29:9. Ex 2:16. Ru 2:2, 17. Pr *31:27.

16. **fair to look upon**. Heb. good of countenance. Ge 26:7. 29:17. 39:6. Est 1:11mg. **virgin**. Heb. *bethulah*. ver. ◑+43. Le +21:13. S#1330h. Dt 22:19, 23, 28. 32:25. 2 Ch 36:17. Ps 148:12. Is 62:5. Je 51:22. La 1:18. 2:21. Jl √1:8. **known**. Ge +4:1, +17. Ex +34:15. Nu 31:17, 18. SS 5:2. **well**. Heb. *ayin*, ver. +13.

17. **Let**. 1 K 17:10. Jn 4:7, 9. **water of**. Ge ch. 26. Is 21:14. 30:25. 35:6, 7. 41:17, 18. 49:10.

18. **Drink**. Pr *31:26. 1 P *3:8. 4:8, 9.

19. **she said**. ver. 14, 45, 46. 1 P 4:9.

20. **hasted**. Ge 18:2. 19:27. 21:14. **well**. Heb. *beer*, Ge +16:14.

21. **wondering at**. 2 S 7:18-20. Ps 34:1-6. 107:1, 8, 15, 43. 116:1-7. Lk 2:19, 51. **to wit**. i.e. *to know*, or *to learn*. **the Lord**. ver. 12, 56.

22. **took**. ver. 30. Ex 32:2, 3. Est 5:1. Je 2:32. 1 T 2:9, 10. 1 P 3:8. **earring**. *or*, jewel for the forehead. ver. 30, 47. Ge ◑35:4. Ex 32:2, 3. 35:22. Jg 8:24-26. Jb 42:11. Pr◑11:22. 25:12. Is 3:19-23. Ezk 16:11, 12mg. Ho 2:13. **of half**. Ge 23:15, 16. **gold**. *J*121D5, Ge +23:9.

23. **Whose**. ver. 47. **room**. Jg 19:15. 20:4. Lk ◑2:7. He 13:2.

24. **I am**. ver. 15. Ge 11:29. 22:20, 23.

25. **We have**. Ge 18:4-8. Jg 19:19-21. Is 32:8. 1 P 4:9.

26. **bowed**. ver. 48, 52. Ge 22:5. Ex 4:31. 12:27. 34:8. 1 Ch 29:20. 2 Ch 20:18. 29:30. Ne 8:6. Ps 22:29. 66:4. 72:9. 95:6. Mi 6:6. Ph 2:10.

27. **Blessed**. ver. 12. Ge 9:26. 14:20. Ex 18:10. Ru 4:14. 1 S 25:32, 39. 2 S 18:28. 1 Ch 29:10-13. Ps 68:19. 72:18, 19. Lk 1:68. Ep 1:3. 1 T 1:17. **of his**. Ge *32:10. Ps *98:3. 100:5. Mi 7:20. Jn 1:17. **mercy**. *J*121C1B, Ge +20:13. **and**. *J*174. Syntheton, Ge +18:27. **I being in the way**. Am +√7:15. Mt 4:18. 9:9. **the Lord**. ver. 48. Pr 3:6. 4:11-13. 8:20. **of my**. ver. 4. Ge 13:8. Ex 2:11, 13.

28. **of**. ver. 48, 55, 67. Ge 29:12. 31:33.

29. **a brother**. ver. 55, 60. Ge 25:20. 27:43. 28:2, 5. 29:5, 12. **Laban**. i.e. *white, clean*, ✳S#3837h. ver. 50. Ge 25:20. 27:43. 28:2, 5. 29:5, 10, 10, 13, 13, 14, 15, 16, 19, 21, 22, 24, 25, 26, 29. 30:25, 27, 34, 36, 40, 40, 42. 31:1, 2, 12, 19, 20, 22, 24, 25, 25, 26, 31, 33, 34, 36, 36, 43, 47, 48, 51, 55, 55. 32:4. 46:18, 25. Dt 1:1. (1) The son of Bethuel and brother of Rebekah. (2) The name of a place, perhaps Libnah, near the Arabah desert, Dt 1:1. **ran**. Ge 18:2. 29:13. **well**. Heb. *ayin*, ver. +13.

30. **earring**. ver. +22. Ezk 16:11, 12. **well**. Heb. *ayin*, ver. +13.

31. **thou**. Ge 26:29. Jg 17:2. Ru 3:10. Ps 115:15. Pr 17:8. 18:16. *19:6. **for I**. ver. 25.

32. **he ungirded**. i.e. Laban ungirded. **straw**. Straw, by the eastern mode of threshing, was cut or shattered and reduced to a kind of chaff. With this, sometimes mixed with a little barley, the eastern people still feed their laboring beasts, as they anciently did. ver. 25. Jg 19:19n. **wash**. Ge +18:4. 19:2. 43:24. Jg 19:21. 1 S 25:41. Lk *7:44. Jn 13:4-14. 1 T 5:10.

33. **not eat**. Jb *23:12. Jn *4:14, 31-34. **until**. Ps 132:3-5. Pr 22:29. Ec 9:10. Mt *6:33. Ep *6:5-8. 1 T 6:2.

34. **servant**. ver. 2. Ge 15:3.

35. **And**. *J*148, Ge +8:22. **the Lord**. ver. 1. Ge

+*12:2. 13:2. 25:11. 26:12. 49:25. Ps 18:35. 112:3. Pr +*10:22. *22:4. 1 T +*4:8. **flocks.** Ge 12:16. 13:2. 26:13, 14. Jb 1:3. 42:10-12. Ps 107:38. Mt *6:33.

36. **Sarah.** Ge 11:29, 30. 17:15-19. 18:10-14. 21:1-7. Ro 4:19. **unto.** Ge 21:10. 25:5.

37. **And my.** ver. 2-9. Ge 6:2. 27:46. Ezr 9:1-3. **Thou shalt not.** Ge 28:1. Ex 34:12-16. Dt 7:3, 4. Jsh 23:12, 13. Ezr 9:2, *12. Ne 10:30. 13:25. 2 C +*6:14. **Canaanites.** Ge +10:18.

38. **But.** ver. 4. Ge 12:1. +21:21.

39. **Peradventure.** ver. 5. Jsh 9:18, 19. Ps 15:4. Je 34:8-21. Ezk 17:14-18. Ga *3:15.

40. **And he.** ver. 7. **before.** Ge 5:22, 24. 6:9. +*17:1. 48:15. 1 K 2:3. *8:23. 2 K +*20:3. Ps 16:8. **will.** ver. 7. Ex 23:20. 33:2. Ps *1:3. 91:11. Da 3:28. He 1:14. Re 22:8, 16.

41. **clear from.** ver. 8. Dt 29:12. 1 C 7:*15, 39.

42. **well.** Heb. *ayin*, ver. +13. **O Lord.** ver. 12-14. Ac 10:7, 8, 22. **prosper.** ver. 12, 31. Ge 39:3. Ezr 8:21. Ne 1:11. Ps 37:5. 90:17. Ro 1:10.

43. **I stand.** ver. 13, 14. **well.** Heb. *ayin*, ver. +13. **virgin.** Heb. *almah*. *S#5959h. Ex 2:8. Ps 68:25. Pr 30:19. SS 1:3. 6:8. Is √7:14.

44. **Both.** Ge +*22:15. Is 32:8. 1 T 2:10. He 13:2. 1 P 3:8. **the woman.** ver. 14. Ge 2:22. Pr 16:33. 18:22. 19:14. **appointed.** Ge 20:16. 45:8. S#3198h, used in this sense only here and ver. 14. Other renderings of this word include "correcteth," Jb 5:17; "chastened," Jb 33:19; "reason," Is *1:18; "plead," Mi 6:2. Those events which appear to us the effect of choice, contrivance, or chance, are matters of appointment with God (Pr √16:33. 21:1); and the persuasion of this does not prevent, but rather encourage, the use of all proper means; at the same time that it confines us to proper means, and delivers the mind from useless anxiety about consequences. Ps *37:23. 48:14. 73:24. Pr 3:5, 6. 11:5. *16:9. Is 28:26. *30:18. 42:16. ◑√65:11h,mg. Arthur Carr, in the opening sentence of an intriguing essay titled "The Exclusion of Chance from the Bible," states that "There is, perhaps, no point more impressively dwelt upon by the Hebrew Prophets in their interpretation of history or of human life than the exclusion of chance as an element to be taken into account" (*Horae Biblicae*, p. 33. See related note, Is 65:11n). Carr states further that "The pervading prophetical interpretation of history and of men's lives is that events are ordered and determined by the divine will, and not by luck or chance or happy accident" (p. 34). "It is remarkable that neither *tukee* nor any other word signifying luck or chance or accident occurs in the New Testament....We meet with the same phenomenon in the Old Testament" (pp. 36, 37). Thus the Biblical worldview or philosophy of sacred history identifies purpose and result in the Hebrew mind, and leaves no place for chance or fortune in any theory of life or in religious terms. Ge ◑30:11. Jsh ◑14:2n. Jg 20:22n. Ru ◑+2:3. 1 S +6:9. 2 S +1:6. 1 K ◑22:34. Est 3:7n. ◑9:24n. Ec +9:11. Is *65:11n. Am +*3:6. Lk ◑10:31.

45. **before.** ver. 15-20. Is 58:9. +*65:24. Da 9:19, 23. Mt 6:8. 7:7. Ac 4:24-33. 10:30. 12:12-17. **speaking.** 1 S 1:13-15. 2 S 7:27. Ne 2:4. Ro 8:26. **well.** Heb. *ayin*, ver. +13.

46. **Drink.** ver. +18-20.

47. **I put.** ver. 22, 53. Ps 45:9, 13, 14. Is 62:3-5. Ezk 16:10-13. Ep 5:26, 27.

48. **bowed.** ver. 26, 27, 52. **led me.** ver. 27, +44.

Ge 22:23. Ex 18:20. Ezr 8:21. Ps +*32:8. *48:14. 107:7. Pr √3:5, 6. 4:11. Is √48:17. **daughter.** ƒ171G. Synecdoche of the Species, Ge +13:8. Here, "daughter" is put for "granddaughter."

49. **now if.** Ge 47:29. Jsh 2:14. **deal kindly and truly.** Heb. do mercy and truth. ƒ174, Ge +18:27. Ge 32:10. Pr 3:3. Mi +*6:8. Mt 23:23. **that I.** Nu 20:17. Dt 2:27.

50. **Laban.** These seem both to be brothers, of whom Laban was the eldest and chief: the opinion of Josephus appears to be very correct, that Bethuel, the father, had been dead some time. See ver. 15, 28, 53, 55, 60. **The thing.** ver. +14, 27. 1 S +*23:4. 1 K +√13:9n. Ps *118:23. 126:3. Is 28:21. 29:14. Mt 21:42. Mk 12:11. Ac 16:10. 15:25, 28. **we.** Ge 31:24, 29. 2 S 13:22. Ac 11:17.

51. **Rebekah.** Ge 20:15. **hath.** ver. 15, +44. 2 S 16:10.

52. **worshipped.** ver. 26, 48. 1 Ch 29:20. 2 Ch 20:18. Ps 34:1, 2. 95:6. 107:21, 22. *116:1, 2. Mt 2:11. Ac 10:25, 26.

53. **jewels.** Heb. vessels. The original word denotes vessels, utensils, instruments, furniture, or dress; and these presented by Abraham's servant might have been of various kinds. Ex 3:22. 11:2. 12:35. **brother.** Pr 18:24. No mention is made of her father. Ex 22:22. Dt +*10:18. Ps 10:14. Ho 14:3. Ja *1:27. **precious.** Dt 33:13-16. 2 Ch 21:3. Ezr 1:6. SS 4:13. Is 39:2.

54. **Send me.** ver. 56, 59. Ge 28:5, 6. 30:25. 45:24. 2 S 18:19, 27, 28. Pr 22:29. Ec 7:10. Lk 8:38, 39.

55. **a few days.** or, a full year, or ten *months*. Ge +4:3mg. Le 25:29. Jg 14:8. ƒ171T2C. Figure of speech Synecdoche (of the Part); or, Transfer B654: the exchange of one idea for another associated idea; of the part, where a part of the time is put for the whole time, as here, the plural "days" is put for a whole year. For other instances of this figure see Ge 40:4. Ex 13:10. Le 25:29. Jg 11:40. 17:10. 21:19. 1 S 1:3. 27:7. 1 K 17:7mg, 15mg. 18:1. Am 4:4mg.

56. **Hinder.** Ge 45:9-13. Pr 25:25. **prospered.** Jsh *1:8. Is 48:15.

57. **call the damsel.** Jg 19:3. 1 S 18:20, 21. 25:40, 41. Jn 9:21, 23. **enquire at.** Ex ◑+*2:21. Nu ◑+*12:1.

58. **Wilt thou.** Ge 2:24. Ps 45:10, 11. Ru 1:16. Lk 1:38. **I will go.** Nu ◑10:30. 1 C 7:39.

59. **their.** ver. 50, 53, 60. **nurse.** Ge 35:8. Nu 11:12. 1 Th 2:5.

60. **they.** Ge 1:28. 9:1. 14:19. 17:16. 28:3. 48:15, 16, 20. Ru 4:11, 12. **be thou the mother.** or, 'be thou for thousands of myriads'; a large family being always considered in ancient times as a proof of the peculiar blessing and favor of God, Dt 7:13. Ps 113:9. *127:3-5. **thousands.** Ge 17:16. 25:23. Da 7:10. **thy seed.** See on Ge *22:17. Le 25:46. Ps 127:5. **gate.** ƒ171S7B, Ge +14:7. Dt 21:19.

61. **they rode.** Ge 31:34. 1 S 30:17. Est 8:10, 14. **followed.** Ge 2:24. Ps 45:10.

62. **Lahai-roi.** i.e. *the living God looking on me*, *S#883h. Ge *16:14. 25:11. **south.** Ge 12:9.

63. **to meditate.** or, to pray. Jsh √1:8. Ps *1:2. 55:17. *77:11, 12. 104:34. 119:*15, 27, 48, 97, 148. 139:17, 18. *143:5, 6. The meaning of this Hebrew word is uncertain; consideration of the context of this passage (especially Ge 23:19 and *24:67) may suggest *mourn*, and that this verse marks the return to the narrative (broken off after Ge 23:20 to introduce the account of

taking a wife for Isaac), as the figure of speech Parecbasis, noted in Ge 24:1, shows. **lifted**. *∫*144A12, Ge +22:13. **behold**. *∫*40, Ge +3:22.

64. **lifted**. *∫*144A12, Ge +22:13. **lighted**. Jsh 15:18. Jg 1:14.

65. **a vail**. Ge 20:16. 38:14. SS 1:7mg. 4:1, 3. 6:7. 1 C 11:5, 6, 10. 1 T 2:9.

66. **the servant**. Mk 6:30.

67. **his mother**. Ge 18:6, 9, 10. SS 8:2. Is 54:1-5. **Sarah's tent**. Sarah being dead, her tent, which according to the custom of the east, was distinct from that of Abraham (see Ge 31:33), became now appropriated to the use of Rebekah. **and took**. Ge 2:22-24. 25:20. 49:31. 2 C 11:1, 2. Ep 5:22-33. **loved her**. Ge 26:8. 29:18, 20. 34:3. Jg 16:4. Ep *5:25, 28. **comforted**. ver. 63. Ge 23:2, 19. 37:35. 38:12. 2 S 13:39. 1 Th 4:13, 15.

GENESIS 25

Abraham marries Keturah, 1; his sons by her, 2-4. He gives his substance to Isaac; and sends them away with gifts, 5, 6. His age, death, and burial, 7-10. God blesses Isaac, 11. The posterity, age, and death of Ishmael, 12-13. Isaac prays for Rebekah, who was barren; and is heard, 19-21. Circumstances preceding and attending the birth of Esau and Jacob, 22-26. Their different characters and pursuits, 27, 28. Esau sells his birthright to Jacob, 29-34.

1. A.M. cir. 2151. B.C. cir. 1853. **again**. Ge +4:19. 23:1, 2. 28:1. 1 Ch 1:32, 33. **Keturah**. i.e. *incense, perfume,* ✱S#6989h. ver. 4. 1 Ch 1:32, 33.

2. A.M. cir. 2152. B.C. cir. 1852. **she bare him Zimran**. i.e. *musical, psalmody; fine chamois,* ✱S#2175h. 1 Ch 1:32h, 33. Je 25:25, Zimri. **Jokshan**. i.e. *sportsman; a fowler; difficult, their snare,* ✱S#3370h. ver. 3. 1 Ch 1:32, 32. **Medan**. i.e. *strife, discernment,* ✱S#4091h. 1 Ch 1:32. **Midian**. i.e. *contention, strife,* ✱S#4080h. (1) A son of Abraham by Keturah. Ge 25:2, 4. 1 Ch 1:32, 33. (2) The country which the descendants of Midian occupied. Ge 36:35. 37:28, 36. Ex 2:15, 16. 3:1. 4:19. 18:1. Nu 22:4, 7. 25:15, 18. 31:3, 8, 8, 9. Jsh 13:21. Jg 6:1, 2. 7:8, 13, 14, 15, 25. 8:3, 5, 12, 22, 26, 28. Jg 9:17. 1 K 11:18. 1 Ch 1:46. Is 9:4. 10:26. 60:6. Hab 3:7. **Ishbak**. i.e. *he will remain,* ✱S#3435h. 1 Ch 1:32. **Shuah**. i.e. *prostration, depression,* ✱S#7744h. 1 Ch 1:32h. Jb 2:11. 8:1.

3. A.M. cir. 2180. B.C. cir. 1824. **Sheba**. 1 K 10:1. Jb 6:19. Ps 72:10. **Dedan**. Is 21:13. Je 25:23. 49:7, 8. Ezk 25:13. 27:20. **Asshurim**. i.e. *steps; going forward,* ✱S#805h. 2 S 2:9h. Ezk 27:6, 23. **Letushim**. i.e. *oppressed; sharpened,* ✱S#3912h. **Leummim**. i.e. *nations, gatherings,* ✱S#3817h.

4. A.M. cir. 2200. B.C. cir. 1804. **Ephah**. i.e. *darkness, obscurity,* ✱S#5891h. 1 Ch 1:33. 2:46, 47. Is 60:6. (1) A son of Midian and grandson of Abraham. The name is apparently also applied to the district where he settled or to his posterity, Ge 25:4; Is 60:6. (2) The concubine of Caleb the son of Hezron, 1 Ch 2:46. (3) A son of Jahdai, 1 Ch 2:47. **Epher**. i.e. *young deer or calf,* ✱S#6081h. (1) A son of Midian, Ge 25:4; 1 Ch 1:33. (2) An Israelite of the tribe of Judah, 1 Ch 4:17. (3) A head of the house of their fathers, in Manasseh, 1 Ch 5:24. **Hanoch**. i.e. *dedicated,* ✥S#2585h. (1) A son of Midian, Ge 25:4, called Henoch

in 1 Ch 1:33. (2) A son of Reuben, Ge 46:9; Ex 6:14. **Abidah**. i.e. *father of knowledge,* ✱S#28h. 1 Ch 1:33. **Eldaah**. i.e. *whom God called,* ✱S#420h. 1 Ch 1:33.

5. A.M. cir. 2175. B.C. cir. 1829. **gave**. Ge ◐21:10-12. 24:36. Jg ◐11:2. Ps 68:18. Mt 11:27. 28:18. Jn 3:35. 17:2. Ro *8:17, 32. 9:7-9. 1 C 3:21-23. Ga *3:29. 4:28, ◐30. Col 1:19. He *1:2. Isaac typified the Son of God, 'whom He hath appointed Heir of all things.'

6. **concubines**. ver. 1. Ge 16:3. 30:4, 9. 32:22. 35:22. Jg 19:1, 2, 4. 1 Ch +2:48. **had**. Ge +4:19. **gifts**. Ps 17:14, 15. Mt 5:45. Lk 11:11-13. Ac 14:17. **sent**. Ge 21:14. **east country**. Arabia Deserta, which was eastward of Beer-sheba, where Abraham dwelt. Ge +29:1. Jg 6:3. Jb 1:1, 3.

7. A.M. 2183. B.C. 1821. **years**. Ge 12:4.

8. **gave**. ver. 17. Ge 35:18. 49:33. Ac 5:5, 10. 7:59. 12:23. **good**. Ge *15:15. 35:28, 29. 47:8, 9. 49:29. Jg 8:32. 1 Ch 29:28. Jb 5:26. 42:17. Pr 9:11. 20:29. Je 6:11. He *12:23. **old man**. Ge 43:27. 44:20. Jg 19:16, 17, 20, 22. 1 S 4:18. Lk 1:18. **and full**. Ge 35:29. Ex +23:26. **gathered**. *∫*88. Euphemism, Ge +15:15. ver. 7. Ge +35:29. 49:33. 50:13. Nu 20:24. 27:13. 31:2. Dt 32:49, 50. Jg 2:10. 1 K 2:10. 11:43. Ac 13:36. The expression 'was gathered to his people' does not relate to burial, for this was not so: Abraham's "people" dwelt at this time in Haran, and he was buried at Hebron. Besides which, the fact of burial is here, and in many other places, specified over and above (see Ge 15:15. 35:29. 1 K 2:10. 11:43, etc.). Nor is it a mere synonym for dying: for in many places, as here, it is specified over and above the fact, here repeatedly expressed, of death (see ver. 17. Ge 35:29. 49:33. Nu 20:26. Dt 32:50). The only assignable sense, therefore, is that of reference to a state of further personal existence beyond death: and the expression thus forms a remarkable testimony to the O.T. belief in a future state (Henry Alford, *The Book of Genesis and Part of the Book of Exodus,* p. 111-112).

9. **Isaac**. Ge 21:9, 10. 35:29. **in the cave**. Ge 23:9-20. 49:29, 30. *50:13.

10. **The field**. Ge 23:16. **there**. ver. 8. Ge *49:31. 1 K 2:10. 16:28. 2 K 21:18.

11. **after**. Ge 12:2. 17:19. 22:17. 50:24. **La-hai-roi**. Ge 16:14. 24:62.

12. **Now these**. Ge *16:10-15. *17:20. 21:13. Ps 83:6.

13. **the names**. 1 Ch 1:29-31. 5:19, 20. **Nebajoth**. i.e. *heights,* ✱S#5032h. Ge 28:9. 36:3. 1 Ch 1:29. Is 60:7. **Kedar**. i.e. *darkness; dark skinned,* 1 Ch 1:29. Ps 120:5. SS 1:5. Is 21:16, 17. 42:11. 60:7. Je 2:10. 49:28, 28. Ezk 27:21. **Adbeel**. i.e. *disciplined of God,* ✱S#110h. 1 Ch 1:29. **Mibsam**. i.e. *fragrant, sweet odor,* ✱S#4017h. 1 Ch 1:29. 4:25. (1) A son of Ishmael, Ge 25:13; 1 Ch 1:29. (2) One of the sons of Simeon, 1 Ch 4:25.

14. **Mishma**. i.e. *a report, a hearing,* ✱S#4927h. (1) One of the sons of Ishmael, Ge 25:14; 1 Ch 1:30. (2) A son of Simeon, 1 Ch 4:25. **Dumah**. i.e. *silence,* ✱S#1746h. Jsh 15:52. 1 Ch 1:30. Is 21:11. (1) A son of Ishmael, Ge 25:14; 1 Ch 1:30. (2) A town of Judah ten miles southwest of Hebron, Jsh 15:52. (3) A city or tribe, Is 21:11. **Massa**. i.e. *gift; burden, a prophecy; enduring,* ✱S#4854h. 1 Ch 1:30.

15. **Hadar**. *or,* Hadad. More than 300 MSS. and printed editions read *Hadad,* as in 1 Ch 1:30. **Tema**. i.e. *south desert; southerner,* ✱S#8485h. 1 Ch 5:19. Jb ◐2:11. 6:19. Is 21:14. Je 25:23. (1) One of the sons

of Ishmael, Ge 25:15; 1 Ch 1:30. (2) An Ishmaelite tribe in northern Arabia descended from Tema, son of Ishmael. (3) The name Tema is also applied to the country occupied by that tribe, Jb 6:19; Is 21:14; Je 25:23. **Jetur.** i.e. *an enclosure; defence,* *S#3195h. 1 Ch 1:31. 5:19. Compare Lk 3:1, Ituraea. **Naphish.** i.e. *refreshed; recreation; taking breath,* *S#5305h. 1 Ch 1:31. 5:19. **Kedemah.** i.e. *eastward,* *S#6929h. 1 Ch 1:31.

16. **towns.** or, villages. Is 42:11. **castles.** or, encampments. Nu 31:10. Ps 83:6. The word *tiroth,* rendered *castles,* is supposed by some to denote here towers, fortified rocks, or mountain tops, and fastnesses of various kinds in woods and hilly countries; but it rather means, *shepherds' cots,* surrounded by sufficient enclosures to prevent the cattle from straying, as the cognate Syriac word *teyaro,* and Arabic *tawar,* signify *a sheep fold.* 1 Ch 6:54. Ne 8:16. **twelve.** Ge 17:20, 23. **nations.** Nu 25:15. Ps 117:1.

17. A.M. 2231. B.C. 1773. **these are.** ver. 7, 8. **gave up.** ver. 8. Ge 35:29. 49:33. Ac 7:59. **gathered.** ♪88, Ge +15:15. ver. 8. Ge 15:15. 49:*29, 33. Dt 32:49, 50.

18. **Havilah.** Ge 2:11. 10:7, 29. 20:1. 21:14, 21. 1 S *15:7. **before.** ♪178. Topographia; or, Description of Place B453. This figure adds something to what is said by describing a place; or any peculiarity which marks the place, and throws light on what is being treated of. *Topographia* is such a description of a place as exhibits it to our view; as the description of *Sheol,* Is 14:9-12; 30:33. The New Heaven and Earth, Is 65:17, etc. Re 21:1, etc. The future glory of Jerusalem and the Land, Ps 46:5, 6. 60:6-9. Is 33:20, 21. 35:6-10. In Ps 89:12, the description shows that the points of the compass are always (excepting perhaps parts of Ezekiel written in Babylon) reckoned with reference to Jerusalem, "The north and the south thou hast created them: Tabor (in the west) and Hermon (in the east) shall rejoice in thy name." The "Sea" is frequently mentioned by way of description to show that the *West* is intended: the Mediterranean being on the West of the Land. See Nu 2:18h. Jsh 16:5, 6. Ezk 42:19h. In Ps 107:3, however, the Sea evidently denotes the Red Sea, and though the word "sea" is in the Hebrew, it is rendered "South." The emphasis put upon the wonderful Exodus is thus quietly but very powerfully introduced: "And gathered them out of the lands, from the east, and from the west, from the north, and from the sea!" because the deliverance from Egypt was through the sea. In Ps 72:8, "from sea to sea" means from the Mediterranean to the Red Sea and the Persian Gulf. Compare Ex 23:31. Sometimes a description of place is added and thrown in to convey a lesson, *e.g.,* Jn 4:10, "Now there was much grass in the place." Ac 8:26, "Which is desert," to show that it mattered not to the true servant whether he ministered in a city (ver. 5), and gave joy to crowds of people (ver. 8), or whether he ministered to one soul in the desert. See also Is 65:17-25. Jl 2:3. Lk 16:24-26. Jn 11:18. For other instances of this figure see Ge 10:19. Jg 21:19. **as thou.** Ge 13:10. **toward.** 2 K 23:29. Is 19:23, 24. **died.** Heb. fell. Ge 14:10. ♣16:12. Jsh 23:4. Jg 18:1. 1 Ch 12:20. 26:14. 2 Ch 15:9. Ps 16:6. 78:64. Pr 1:14. **in the.** Ge ♣16:12.

19. A.M. 2108. B.C. 1896. **Abraham.** 1 Ch 1:32, 34. Mt 1:2. Lk 3:34. Ac 7:8.

20. A.M. 2148. B.C. 1856. **when he.** Ge 22:23. 24:67. **the Syrian.** i.e. *sublime, deceiving,* *S#761h. Ge 24:29. 28:5. 31:20, 24. Dt 26:5. 2 K 5:20. 8:28, 29. 9:15. 1 Ch 7:14. Lk 4:27. **Padan-aram.** i.e. *table land of Aram,* *S#6307h. Ge 28:2, 5, 6, 7. 31:18. 33:18. 35:9, 26. 46:15. ◖48:7.

21. A.M. 2167. B.C. 1837. **intreated.** Ex 8:30. 10:18. Jg 13:8. 1 S 1:11, 27. Ps +*50:15. 65:2. 91:15. Is 45:11. 58:9. +*65:24. Lk 1:13. **because.** Ge +11:30. 15:2, 3. 16:2. 17:16-19. 1 S 1:2. Lk 1:7. **and the.** 1 Ch *5:20. 2 Ch *33:13. Ezr *8:23. Ps *145:19. Pr *10:24. Mt *7:7. **and Rebekah.** Ro 9:10-12.

22. A.M. 2168. B.C. 1836. **struggled.** Nu 20:20, 21. 2 S 8:13, 14. Ps 137:7. Jl 3:19. Ml 1:4. **If.** ♪37C. Figure of speech Aposiopesis; or, Sudden Silence B153: the speaker's words are suddenly broken off to emphasize the importance of what is being said. Here, in grief and complaint, for Rebekah does not understand why her new condition entails suffering as hard to be borne as her former condition. For other instances of this figure see Ge 27:46. Jg 5:29, 30. Ps 6:3. Lk 15:21. 19:42. **why am I.** T#1481. Hab 1:12, 13. **she went.** 1 S *1:15. 2 K 4:22, 23. 22:14. Est 4:16. Lk 1:25, 38, 46. 2:36. 10:42. Ac 16:14. Ro 16:1, 12. **inquire.** T#1567. Ex 3:7. 5:22, 23. 18:15. 28:30. Le 24:12. Nu 9:6-8. 11:10-15, 21, 22. 15:34. 27:5, 21. Dt 17:9. Jg 1:1, 2. 6:15, 16. 13:8, 9. 18:5. 20:18, 27. 1 S 8:6. *9:9. 10:22. 14:36, 37. 16:1, 2. 22:10, 13, 15. 23:1-4, 10-12. 28:6. 30:6-8. 2 S 2:1. 5:19, 22-24. 21:1. 1 K 14:5. 20:13, 14. 22:5, 7, *8. 2 K 3:11. 8:7, 8. *22:12, 13. 1 Ch 14:14. 2 Ch 18:4, 6. 25:7, 8. 34:21. Ps +25:4 (T#1469). 78:34. Is *30:2. Je 21:1, 2. 37:7, 17. Ezk 14:3, 7, 8. 20:1, 3, 31. 36:37. Zc 7:1-3. Ac *1:6.

23. **Two nations.** Ge 17:16. 24:60. ♪121E1. Figure of speech Metonymy of the Effect; or, Change of Noun B560: the change of one noun for another related noun; here, of the Effect, when the effect is put for the person producing the effect, or for the author of it. Here, "nations" in the womb refer to the two infants whose progeny should become two different nations. For other instances of this figure see Ge 26:35mg. 49:18. Ne 12:31, 38, 40. Ps 18:1. 22:19. 27:1. 106:20. Is 49:6. Je 16:19. 23:6. Mt 9:33. Mk 9:17, 25. Lk 2:30. 3:6. *11:14. 13:11. Jn 1:23. *11:25. Ro 13:3. 2 C 1:14. 1 Th 2:19, 20. Re 1:12. **two manner.** ver. +22, 27. Ge 32:6. 33:3. 36:31. Nu 20:14. **the elder.** Ge 27:29, 40. +*48:14, 18. 2 S *8:14. 1 K 22:47. 1 Ch 18:13. 2 Ch 25:11, 12. Ps 60:8, 9. 83:5-15. Is ch. 34. 63:1-6. Je 49:7-22. Ezk 25:12-14. ch. 35. Am 1:11, 12. Ob 1-16. Ml 1:2-5. Ro ♪9:10-13. Col +√1:15.

24. **delivered.** Lk 1:57. 2:6. **twins.** Ge 38:27. SS 4:2, 5. 6:6. 7:3. Jn 11:16. 20:24. 21:2. Ac 28:11. **womb.** Ps 139:15. Ec 11:5.

25. **all over.** Ge 27:11, 16, 23. **Esau.** i.e. *hairy, rough,* *S#6215h. ver. 26, 27, 28, 29, 30, 32, 34, 34. Ge 26:34. 27:1, 5, 5, 6, 11, 15, 19, 21, 22, 23, 24, 30, 32, 34, 37, 38, 38, 41, 41, 42, 42. 28:5, 6, 8, 9. 32:3, 4, 6, 8, 11, 13, 17, 18, 19. 33:1, 4, 9, 15, 16. 35:1, 29. 36:1, 2, 4, 5, 6, 8, 8, 9, 10, 10, 10, 12, 12, 13, 14, 14, 15, 15, 17, 17, 18, 18, 19, 40, 43. Dt 2:4, 5, 8, 12, 22, 29. Jsh 24:4, 4. 1 Ch 1:34, 35. Je 49:8, 10. Ob 6, 9, 18, 18, 19, 21. Ml 1:2, 3.

26. **And after.** Ge 38:28-30. **took.** Ge *27:36. Ho *12:3. **Jacob.** i.e. *supplanter,* S#3290h. ver. 29-34. Ge 27:6, 18-30, 36, 41-43. 28:1, 10, 12-22. 29:1, 15-30. 30:25. 31:3, 40, 45-54. 32:1-12, 24-32. 33:10, 17,

19. 35:1, 29. 37:3, 28. 42:1, 36. 43:11. 45:26. 46:5. 47:9. 48:2. 49:33. 50:13. Ex 1:1, 5. 2:24. 3:6, 15, 16. 4:5. 6:3, 8. 19:3. 33:1. Le 26:42. Nu 23:7, 10, 21, 23, 23. 24:5, 17, 19. 32:11. Dt 1:8. 6:10. 9:5, 27. 29:13. 30:20. 32:9. 33:4, 10, 28. 34:4. Jsh 24:4, 4, 32. 1 S 12:8. 2 S 23:1. 1 K 18:31. 2 K 13:23. 17:34. 1 Ch 16:13, 17. Ps 14:7. 20:1. 22:23. 24:6. 44:4. 46:7, 11. 47:4. 53:6. 59:13. 75:9. 76:6. 77:15. 78:5, 21, 71. 79:7. 81:1, 4. 84:8. 85:1. 87:2. 94:7. 99:4. 105:6, 10, 23. 114:1, 7. 132:2, 5. 135:4. 146:5. 147:19. Is 2:3, 5, 6. 8:17. 9:8. 10:20, 21. 14:1, 1. 17:4. 27:6, 9. 29:22, 22, 23. 40:27. 41:8, 14, 21, 23. 45:4, 19. 46:3. 48:1, 12, 20. 49:5, 6, 26. 58:1, 14. 59:20. 60:16. 65:9. Je 2:4. 5:20. 10:16, 25. 30:7, 10, 10, 18. 31:7, 11. 33:26, 26. 46:27, 27, 28. 51:19. La 1:17. 2:2, 3. Ezk 20:5. 28:25. 37:25. 39:25. Ho 10:11. 12:2, 12. Am 3:13. 6:8. 7:2, 5. 8:7. 9:8. Ob 10, 17, 18. Mi 1:5, 5. 2:7, 12. 3:1, 8, 9. 4:2. 5:7, 8. 7:20. Na 2:2. Ml 1:2, 2. 2:12. 3:6. He 11:21. **Isaac was.** ver. 20.

27. **a cunning.** Ge 10:9. 21:20. 27:3-5, 40. **a plain man.** Ge 6:9. 28:10, 11. 31:39-41. 46:34. Jb 1:1, 8. 2:3. 8:20. Ps 37:37. 64:4. Pr 29:10. **dwelling.** He 11:9.

28. **loved.** Ge +*44:30. **he did eat of his venison.** Heb. venison *was* in his mouth. Ge 27:4, 19, 25, 31. ♪121C1J. Figure of speech Metonymy of the Cause B552: in certain nouns; here, "hunting" is put for the flesh of the animal that is caught, so that the verse reads "And Isaac loved Esau because hunting was in his mouth," where *mouth* is put for the eating it performs, and *hunting* for the venison which it caught. For another instance of this figure see Ge 27:3. ♪63B. Figure of speech Ellipsis (Absolute, of the Finite Verb); or, Omission B26: the verb is omitted, thus emphasizing what is done, not the doing of it. Here, *venison* is Heb. *hunting*, thus Isaac loved what Esau *obtained* (the omitted verb) by hunting. For other instances of this figure see Nu 16:28. 1 S 19:3. 2 S 4:10. 18:12. 23:17. 1 K 11:25. 14:6. 22:36. 2 K 25:4. Ezr 10:14mg. 10:19. Jb 3:21. 4:6. 39:13. Ps 4:2. ?22:16. 25:15. 120:7. Ec 8:2. Is 61:7. 66:6. Je 18:14. 19:1. Ho 8:1. Am 3:11. Mt 26:5. Mk 14:2. Ac 15:24. Ro 2:7-10. 4:9. 6:19. 11:18. 13:11. 1 C 2:12. 4:20. 14:33. 2 C 9:14. 12:18. Ga 5:13. Ep 4:9. 5:9. Ph 3:15. 1 T 2:6mg. Phm 6. 1 P 4:11. 2 P 2:3. 1 J 3:20. **Rebekah.** Ge 27:6. **loved.** Ge +*44:30.

29. A.M. 2199. B.C. 1805. **and he.** Jg 8:4, 5. 1 S 14:28, 31. Pr 13:25. Is 40:30, 31.

30. **with that same red pottage.** Heb. with that red, *with that* red *pottage.* This, we are informed (ver. 34), was of lentiles, a sort of pulse. ♪84, Ge +6:17. **Edom.** i.e. *red.* ✛S#123h. Ge 32:3. 36:1, 8, ●9, 16, 17, 19, ●+*21, ●43. Ex 15:15. Nu 20:14-21. 24:18. Dt 23:7. 2 K 8:20.

31. **this day.** ♪160B. Figure of speech Simile; or, Resemblance B728: a declaration that one thing resembles another; or, comparison by resemblance. Sometimes a Simile is really used as a figure, implying not merely a resemblance but the actual thing itself. Here, "Sell me *as* on this day," means 'on this very day' (Dt +4:26). For other instances of this type of Simile see (Ge 25:33). Nu 11:1mg. Ne 7:2. Ps *122:3. Is 1:7, 9. 24:2. 55:10, 11. Ho 5:10. Mt 14:5. Lk 22:44. Jn 1:14. Ro 9:32. 2 C 2:17. *3:18. **birthright.** Ge 27:36. 43:33. Dt *21:16, 17. 2 Ch 21:3.

32. **at the point to die.** Heb. going to die. Ge 26:1. **and what.** Jb 21:15. 22:17. 34:9. Ml 3:14. **birthright.**

Ex 22:9. **me.** ♪63C. Figure of speech Ellipsis (Absolute: Brachyology) B47: when certain connected words are omitted in the same member of a passage. Here, to Esau's statement the words to be supplied are "I will sell it." For other instances of brachyology see Ge 45:12. (Jg 6:17). 2 K (19:9). 22:18. 1 Ch 18:10. Ezk 47:13. Mt (*21:22). *25:9. Mk 14:49. Lk 7:43. Jn (2:18). (*7:38). (13:18). 15:25, (27). Ro 9:16. (1 C 9:4). (2 C 5:3). Ga 2:9. (Ep 4:29). Ph 4:11. (1 J 3:8).

33. **Swear.** Ge 14:22. 24:3. Mk 6:23. He 6:16. **this day.** ♪160B, Ge +25:31. Dt +4:26. **and he sold.** Ge 27:36. 36:6, 7. He 12:16.

34. **eat.** Ec 8:15. Is *22:13. 1 C *15:32. **thus Esau.** Ps 106:24. Zc 11:13. Mt 22:5. 26:15. Lk 14:18-20. Ac 13:41. Ph +*3:18, 19. He *12:16, 17.

GENESIS 26

Isaac, because of a famine, sojourns in Gerar, and the Lord instructs and blesses him, 1-5. He denies his wife, and is detected and reproved, 6-11. The Philistines envy his prosperity; he removes from them, and they fill up, or take from him, the wells which his father and he had dug, 12-17. He digs several other wells, 18-22. The Lord blesses him at Beer-sheba, 23-25. Abimelech covenants with him, 26-33. Esau marries two Canaanitish wives, to the grief of his parents, 34, 35.

1. A.M. 2200. B.C. 1804. **the first.** Ge *12:10. **And Isaac.** Ge 25:11. **Abimelech.** Ge 20:2. 21:22-32.

2. **appeared.** Ge 12:7. 17:1. 18:1, 10-20. **dwell.** Ge 12:1. Ps 37:3.

3. **Sojourn.** ver. 12, 14. Ge 20:1. Ps 32:8. 37:1-6. *39:12. He *11:9, 13-16. **I will be.** Ge *28:15. 39:2, 21. Is 43:2, 5. Ph 4:9. **unto thee.** Ge 12:1, 7. 13:15, 17. *15:18. 17:8. **oath.** Ge *22:16, 18. Ps *105:9. Mi *7:20. He *6:17.

4. **multiply.** Ge 13:16. 15:5, 18. 17:4-8. 18:18. *22:17. He 11:12. **as the stars.** ♪138B, Ge +13:16. **seed shall.** ♪121A5, Ge +9:27. Ge 12:2, 3. *22:18. Ps 72:17. Ac ❭3:25. Ga *3:8, 16.

5. **obeyed.** Ge 12:4. 17:23. +*18:19. 22:16, 18. Ps *112:1, 2. ch. 128. Mt 5:19. *7:24. 1 C *7:19. +*15:58. Ga 5:6. He 11:8. Ja 2:21, 22.

6. **Gerar.** ver. 17. Ge +10:19. 20:1.

7. **She is my sister.** Ge 12:13. 20:2, 5, 12, 13. Pr 29:25. Mt 10:28. Ep 5:25. Col 3:9. **said he.** ♪63BA. Figure of speech Ellipsis (Absolute: the Verb "to say"); or, Omission B32. The verb "to say" is frequently omitted in the original, but is often supplied in italics in the A.V. This omission places the emphasis on what is said rather than on the act of saying it. For other examples of this figure see Ge 4:25. Ex 18:4. 2 S 9:11. 1 K 20:34. Jb 8:18. 32:17. Ps 2:2. (109:5). (144:12). Is 5:9. 14:8. 18:2. (22:13). (24:14, 15). (28:9). Je 4:31. (9:19). 11:19. 50:5. (La 3:41). Ho 14:8. Ac 1:4. 9:6. 10:15. (14:22). 17:3mg. 23:22mg. (2 C 12:16). **he feared.** Pr *29:25. Ec *7:20. **fair.** Ge 24:16.

8. **long time.** Nu +9:22. **a window.** Jg 5:28. Pr 7:6. SS 2:9. **sporting.** Ge +21:9, *S#6711h. Ex 32:6. Jg 16:25. Pr 5:18, 19. Ec 9:9. Is 62:5.

9. **Behold.** ♪40, Ge +3:22. **how.** ♪85K, Ge +3:9. Ge 12:19.

10. **What.** ♪85K, Ge +3:9. Ge 12:18, 19. 20:9, 10.

11. **toucheth.** Ge 20:6. 1 Ch *16:21, 22. Ps *105:15. Pr 6:29. Zc 2:8. **surely.** ♪147B, Ge +2:16.

12. **sowed**. Ge 8:22. 47:23. Ex 23:10, 16. Is 55:10. 2 C 9:10. **received**. Heb. found. ⨍171J4, Ge +6:8. **an hundredfold**. Ps 67:6. 72:16. 126:5, 6. Ec 11:6. Zc 8:12. Mt +*13:8, 23. *19:29. Mk 4:8. +*10:30. Lk *18:30. 1 C 3:6. 2 C 9:10, 11. Ga 6:7, 8. **blessed**. ver. 3, 29. Ge 24:1, 35. *26:3. 30:30. Jb 42:12. Pr *10:22. 1 T +*4:8.

13. **waxed great**. Ge 24:35. Ps 112:3. **went forward**. Heb. went going. Ge 12:9. Ph 3:13.

14. **had possession**. Ge 12:16. 13:2. Jb 1:3. 42:12. Ps 112:3. 144:13, 14. Pr 10:22. **servants**. *or*, husbandry. **envied**. Ge 37:11. 1 S 18:9. Jb 5:2. Ps 112:10. Pr 27:4. Ec *4:4.

15. **wells**. Heb. *beer*, Ge +16:14. ver. 18, 19, 20, 21, 22, 25, 32. **his father's**. Ge *21:30. **had stopped**. 2 Ch 32:3.

16. **Go**. ver. 27. Jg 11:7. Mk 5:17. Ac 16:39. **mightier**. Ex *1:9. Ps 105:24.

17. **Gerar**. ver. 6. Ge +10:19. 20:1.

18. **wells**. ver. +15. **stopped**. 2 Ch 32:3. **and he**. Ge 21:31. Nu 32:38. Ps 16:4. Ho 2:17. Zc 13:2.

19. **well**. Heb. *beer*, Ge +16:14. ver. +15. **springing water**. Heb. living. Le 14:5. Nu 19:17n. SS +*4:15. Je *2:17. 51:13, 36. Zc 14:8. Jn 3:23. 4:10, 11. 7:38. Ac 8:36.

20. **did strive**. Ge 21:25. **well**. ver. +15. **Esek**. i.e. Contention. or, strife. ✱S#6230h, only here.

21. **well**. ver. +15. **Sitnah**. i.e. Hatred. or, accusation. ✱S#7856h, only here. Ezr 4:6.

22. **removed**. Mt *5:39. Ro *12:18. 14:19. He 12:14. **digged**. The wells in Arabia are generally dug in the rock: their mouths are about six feet in diameter, and they are from nineteen to twenty feet in depth. But Niebuhr informs us, that many wells are from 160 to 170 feet deep. **well**. Heb. *beer*, Ge +16:14. ver. +15. **Rehoboth**. i.e. Room. **the Lord**. Ps 4:1. 18:19. 118:5. **made room**. ⨍22C36. Figure of speech Anthropomorphism B890: human actions are attributed to God; here, *enlarging*. For another instance of this figure see Ps 4:1. **be fruitful**. Ge 17:6. 28:3. 41:52. Ex 1:7.

23. **Beer-sheba**. Ge 21:31. 46:1. Jg 20:1.

24. **appeared**. Ge 12:7. 16:13. +17:1. **I am the**. Ge 15:1. 17:7. 24:12. 28:13. 31:5. Ex 3:6. Mt √22:32. Ac 7:32. **fear not**. ver. 3, 4. Ge 13:16. 22:19. Ps *27:1-3. +*34:4. 46:1, 2. Is 12:2. *41:10, 13-15. 43:1, 2. 44:2. 51:7, 12. Lk 12:32. He +*13:5, 6. Re 1:17.

25. **builded**. Ge 8:20. *12:7. 13:18. 22:9. 33:20. 35:1. Ex 17:15. **called**. Ps *116:17. **well**. ver. +15.

26. **Abimelech**. Ge 20:3. 21:22-32. **Ahuzzath**. i.e. *possession*, ✱S#276h. **Phichol**. Phichol, as well as Abimelech, *father king*, seems to have been a name of office or dignity among the Philistines; for it is not probable that they were the same as are mentioned in the days of Abraham, Ge 21:22, 32. Ps 34, title, note.

27. **seeing**. ver. 14, 16. Jg 11:7. Ac 7:9, 14, 27, 35. Re 3:9. **sent me**. ver. 16.

28. **We saw certainly**. Heb. Seeing we saw. ⨍147B. Figure of speech Polyptoton; or, Many Inflections B272: the repetition of the same part of speech in different inflections. Here, verbs with their infinitives or participles. For other instances of this figure see Ge +1:29. +2:16. 27:30. 43:3, 7, 20. +50:24, 25. Ex 3:16. 5:23. 13:19. 18:18. 21:5. Nu 22:17, 37. 23:11. 24:10. 26:65. 30:12. 1 S 20:6. Jb 37:2. **was with**. Ge 21:22, 23. 39:5. Jsh 3:7. 2 Ch 1:1. 15:14. 60:14.

61:6, 9. Zc *8:23. Ro 8:31. 1 C 14:25. He 13:5. **Let there**. Ge *21:31, 32. 24:3, 41. 31:49-53. Ps *115:13. He 6:16.

29. **That thou wilt**. Heb. If thou shalt. Ge 21:23. 31:29, 52. **not touched**. ver. 11, 14, 15. Ge 20:6. ⨍175B, Ge +21:16. ⨍108B. Figure of speech Idiom B827. *To touch* is an idiom which means to hurt or to do any harm to. For other instances of this idiom, see Ru 2:9. Jb 1:11. 2:5. 19:21. Ps 105:15. Je 12:14. Ezk 17:10. He 11:28. 1 J 5:18. **the blessed**. ver. 12. Ge 12:2. 21:22. 22:17. 24:31. Ps 115:15.

30. **made them a feast**. Ge 19:3. 21:8. 31:54. Ro 12:18. He 12:14. 1 P 4:9.

31. **betimes**. Ge 19:2. 21:14. 22:3. 31:55. **sware**. Ge 14:22. 21:23, 31, 32. 25:33. *31:44, 53, 54. 1 S 14:24. 20:3, 16, 17. 30:15. He 6:16. **peace**. Ro *12:18.

32. **well**. ver. +15. **We have**. ver. 25. Pr 2:4, 5. 10:4. 13:4. Mt 7:7.

33. **Sheba**. i.e. an oath. **therefore**. Ge 21:31. **Beersheba**. i.e. the well of the oath. ✱S#7656h. ver. 28. This may have been the same city which was called Beer-sheba a hundred years before this, in the time of Abraham; but as the well, from which it had its name originally, was closed up by the Philistines, the name of the place might have been abolished with the well; when, therefore, Isaac reopened it, he restored the ancient name of the place. **unto this day**. Ge +19:38. Dt +29:4.

34. A.M. 2208. B.C. 1796. **And Esau**. Ge 36:2, 5, 13. **wife**. Ge +4:19. **Judith**. i.e. *praised; Jewess*, ✱S#3067h, only here. ⨍146, Ge +10:10. Ge 28:9. 36:+2, 3, 5, 14, 25. **the daughter**. Ge 24:3. *27:46. *28:1. Ex 34:16. Dt *7:1-4. 1 C 7:2. He 12:16. **Beeri**. i.e. *spring man; fountained; illustrious; expounder*, ✱S#882h. Ge 36:24. Ho 1:1. (1) Father of Judith, Ge 26:34. (2) Father of Hosea the prophet, Ho 1:1. **Bashemath**. ⨍146. Polyonymia, Ge +10:10. Ge 36:2. **Elon**. i.e. *mighty oak*, ✱S#356h. Ge 36:2. Jsh 19:43. Jg 12:11, 12. (1) Father of Bashemath, a wife of Esau, Ge 26:34; 36:2. (2) A son of Zebulun, Ge 46:14; Nu 26:26. (3) A town in Dan, Jsh 19:43. (4) A Zebulonite judge in Israel, Jg 12:11, 12.

35. **Which**. Ge 6:2. *27:46. *28:1, 2, 8. **grief of**. Heb. bitterness of spirit. ⨍121E1. Metonymy of the Effect, Ge +25:23. Put for *source of much sorrow*. **mind**. Mk +*2:8. Heb. *ruach*, spirit. S#7307. Pr 29:11. Ezk 11:5. 20:32. Da 5:20. Hab 1:11. ⨍121A10. Figure of speech Metonymy (of the Cause) B545; the word "spirit" is put for the soul or life in its manifestations. For other instances of this figure see Ge 45:27. Nu 14:24. Jg 8:3. 1 Ch 5:26. 2 Ch 21:16. 36:22. Ezr 1:1. Ps 76:12. 77:3, 6. Pr 1:23. 18:14. 29:11. Ec 7:9. Is 29:10. Je 51:11. Ezk 13:3. Da 2:1, 3. Hg 1:14. Ro 11:8. 1 C 2:12. For the other uses of *ruach*, see Ge 6:3n.

GENESIS 27

Isaac when old sends Esau to take venison, intending to bless him, 1-4. Rebekah instructs Jacob how to secure the blessing, and over-rules his objections, 5-13. The strategem succeeds, and Isaac blesses Jacob, supposing him to be Esau, 14-29. Esau afterwards arrives, complains bitterly, and by importunity obtains a blessing, 30-40. Esau purposes to murder Jacob, who is sent away to Mesopotamia, 41-46.

1. **A.M.** 2244. **B.C.** 1760. **dim**. Ge 48:10. 1 S 3:2. 4:15. Ec 12:3. Jn 9:3. **eldest son**. Ge 25:23-25.

2. **Behold**. ꭲ40, Ge +3:22. **I know not**. Ge 48:21. 1 S 20:3. Pr *27:1. Ec *9:10. Is *38:1, 3. Mk 13:35. Lk *12:40. Ja *4:14.

3. **take, I**. Ge 10:9. 25:27, 28. **take me**. Heb. hunt. ꭲ147D, Ge +1:29. ver. 33. Ge 25:27, 28. 1 C 6:12. **venison**. ꭲ121C1J, Ge +25:28.

4. **thatmy**. ver. 7, 23, 25, 27. Ge 14:19. 24:60. 28:3. 48:9, 15-20. 49:28. Le 9:22, 23. Dt 33:1. Jsh 14:13. 22:6. Lk 2:34. 24:51. He 11:20. **soul**. Heb. *nephesh, myself*. ver. 19, 25, +31.

5. **Rebekah**. Ge 26:7. 28:5. 29:12. 35:8. 49:31. Ro 9:10. **heard**. Ge +18:10. **Esau went**. ver. 30. **field**. Ge 25:27, 29.

6. **Jacob**. Ge 25:28. **heard**. ver. 5. Ge +18:10.

7. **Bring me**. ver. 4. **before the**. Dt 33:1. Jsh 6:26. Jg 11:11. 1 S 11:15. 12:7. 23:18. 24:19. 26:19. 1 T 5:21. 6:13. 2 T 2:14. 4:1.

8. **obey**. ver. 13. Ge 25:23. Lk *16:1-12. Ac 4:19. *5:29. Ep *6:1.

9. **two**. Jg 13:15. 1 S 16:20. **savoury**. ver. 4.

10. **thou shalt**. Ro *3:8. **may bless thee**. ver. +4, 10, 25, 31.

11. **hairy man**. ver. 23. Ge 25:25.

12. **feel**. ver. 22. Jb 12:16. 2 C 6:8. **a deceiver**. ver. 36. Ge 25:27. Je +*48:10. 1 Th *5:22. **and I shall**. Ge 9:25. Dt *27:18. Ps 5:6. *24:5, 6. Je +*48:10. Ml 1:14.

13. **Upon**. Ge 25:23, 33. 43:9. 1 S 14:24-28, 36-45. 25:24. 2 S 14:9. Mt 27:25.

14. **mother**. ver. 4, 7, 9, 17, 31. Ge 25:28. Ps 141:4. Pr 23:2, 3. Lk 21:34.

15. **goodly**. Heb. desirable. ver. 27. ꭲ121R5. Figure of speech Metonymy (of the Adjunct); or, Change of Noun B601: of the adjunct, for some circumstance pertaining to the subject is put for the subject itself; as when the affection relating to the object is put for the object itself; as here, "desire" is put for the person or thing desired. For other instances of this figure see 1 S 9:20. 2 Ch 36:10mg. Is 32:12mg. 44:9mg. Je 3:19mg. La 1:7mg, 10mg. 2:4mg. Ezk 24:16. Da 9:23mg. 10:11mg, 19mg. 11:37. Ho 9:16mg. Am 5:11. Hag *2:7. 1 J 2:16. **raiment**. The Septuagint translates it *a goodly robe*, which was a long garment that great men used to wear (Lk 15:22. 20:46). The priest afterwards in the law had *holy garments* to minister in (Ex 28:2-4). Whether the firstborn before the law had such to minister in is not certain; for, had they been common garments, why did not Esau himself or his wives keep them? But being, in likelihood, holy robes, received from their ancestors, the mother of the family kept them in sweet chests, from moths and the like; whereupon it is said (ver. 27), 'Isaac smelled the smell of his garments.' "Goodly" (Heb. *desirable*) is put for things desired or coveted. Raiment marked the social rank and position of the wearer, which accounts for Jacob's desire here, and his act with Joseph (Ge 37:3). Being the garment of the firstborn it doubtless denoted also his official and priestly position. Here, Heb. *beged* (see Ex 28:2, 4. 35:19. Le 10:6. 21:10) used of sacred things. Not the word rendered "clothes" in Dt 29:5. Perhaps this adds meaning to He 12:16, where Esau is called "profane" for having sold this his birthright (some of this material adapted from CB margin at this place).

16. **skins**. ver. 22, 23. Ge 38:14. 42:7. Jsh 9:3-21. 1 S 19:13. +21:14. 28:8. 1 K 14:2. 20:38. 22:30, 34. 2 Ch 18:29. 35:22. Ezk 12:6. Mk ◐14:44. ◐16:12. Lk ◐+4:30. +24:16. **smooth**. ver. 11, 23. Ge 25:25. 2 K ◐1:8. Zc ◐*13:4.

17. **savoury**. ver. 4, 9. Ex 12:8. Nu 11:5. Lk 11:42.

18. **who art**. ver. 32.

19. **I am**. ver. 21, 24, 25. Ge 3:4. 4:9. 18:15. 29:23-25. 37:32. Le +*19:11. 1 K *13:18. 14:2. 2 K 5:25-27. Ps 58:3. 63:11. 101:7. 119:29, 163. 120:2-4. Pr *6:16, 17. *12:19, 22. *13:5. *19:5, 9. 21:6. 30:8. Is *28:15. 63:8. Zc *13:3, 4. Mt *26:70-74. Jn 8:44. Ac 5:4, 5, 8, 10. Ep *4:25. Col *3:9. Re *21:8, 27. *22:15. **Esau**. Ge 25:25. **that thy**. ver. 4. **soul**. Heb. *nephesh, thou*. ver. 4, 25, +31.

20. **How**. ꭲ85E, Ge +17:17. **Because**. Ex *20:7. Jb *13:7. **to me**. Heb. before me.

21. **Come**. Ps 73:28. Is 57:19. Ja 4:8. **may feel**. ver. 12.

22. **near**. Ge 45:4. **felt**. ver. +12. **voice**. Jn 10:4, 5, 8, 16, 27. Ro 10:17. 2 C 5:7.

23. **his hands**. ver. 16. **he blessed**. Dt 21:16, 17. Ro 9:11, 12. He 11:20.

24. **I am**. 1 S 21:2, 13. 27:10. 2 S 14:5. Jb 13:7, 8. 15:5. Pr 12:19, 22. 30:8. Zc 8:16. Ro 3:7, 8. Ep 4:25. Col 3:9.

25. **my soul**. Heb. *nephesh*. ver. 4, 19, +31.

26. **Come near**. ver. 22. Ge 45:4. **kiss**. Ge 48:10.

27. **kissed**. Ge 29:11, 13. 31:35. *33:4. 45:15. 48:10. 50:1. Ex 4:27. 18:7. Ru 1:9, 14. 1 S 10:1. **blessed**. ver. ◐39. Ge 14:19. 24:60. 28:1-4. 31:55. 47:7, 10. 48:15, 20. 49:28. Ex 39:43. Dt 33:1. He 11:20. **smell**. Ex 30:38. **the smell of a field**. A field where aromatic plants, flowers, fruits, and spices grew in abundance, with which these garments (see ver. 15) of Esau might probably have been perfumed by being laid up with them. SS 2:13. 4:11-14. 7:12, 13. Ho 14:6, 7. **which**. Ge 26:12. He *6:7.

28. **of the dew**. Dt 11:11, 12. 32:2. *33:13, 28. 2 S 1:21. 1 K 17:1. Ps 65:9-13. 133:3. Is 45:8. Je 14:22. Ho 14:5-7. Mi *5:7. Zc *8:12. He 11:20. **the fatness**. ver. 39. Ge 45:18. 49:20. Nu 13:20. Ps 36:8. Ro 11:17. Or, fat places. ver. 39. Da 11:24. **plenty**. Dt 7:13. 8:7-9. 33:28. Jsh 5:6. 1 K 5:11. 2 Ch 2:10. Ps *65:9, 13. 104:15. Jl 2:19. Zc 9:17. **corn**. ꭲ121D4. Figure of speech Metonymy (of the Cause); or, Change of Noun B558: the change of one noun for another related noun; here, "corn" is put for bread or food generally. For other instances of this figure see Ge 27:37. 42:1, 2. Dt 33:28. 2 K 18:32. Ps 4:7. Is 36:17. La 2:12. Ho 7:14. Ac 7:12. **and**. ꭲ174, Ge +18:27. **wine**. ꭲ121D13. Figure of speech Metonymy (of the Cause); or, Change of Noun B560: Here, "wine" is put for liquid beverage generally. For other instances of this figure see Ge 27:37. Dt 33:28. Jg 19:19. 2 K 18:32. Ne 5:15. Ps 4:7. Is 36:17. La 2:12. Ho 7:14.

29. **Let people**. Ge 9:25, 26. 22:17, 18. 49:8-10. 2 S 8:10. 1 K +*4:21n. Ps 2:6-9. 72:8. Is *9:7. Da 2:44, 45. Re 19:16. **be lord**. ver. 37. Ge *25:22, 23, 33. 2 S *8:14. 1 K 11:15, 16. 22:47. 1 Ch 5:2. 2 Ch 25:11-14. Ps 60, title. Is 63:1-6. Ml 1:2-5. Ro 9:12. **cursed**. Ge +*12:3. Nu 22:11, 12. 23:8. 24:9. Zp 2:8, 9. Mt 25:40, 45.

30. **scarce**. ꭲ147B, Ge +2:16. **came**. Ge 32:6. Nu 20:18. **hunting**. ver. 3-5. Ge +10:9. 21:20. 25:27. Le 17:13. 1 S 26:20. Jb 10:16. 38:39. Ps 140:11. 141:9,

10. Pr 1:17. 6:5. 12:27. Ec 9:12. Je 16:16. 50:17. La 3:52. Ezk 13:18. Am 3:5.

31. **eat.** ver. 4. **savoury.** ver. 9, +17. **thy soul.** Heb. *nephesh*, thou. Used of man as exercising certain powers, or performing certain acts, often rendered by emphatic pronouns. ✛S#5315h. ver. 4, 19, 25. Ex 12:16 (man). Le 2:1 (any). 4:2, 27 (one). 5:1, 2, 4, 15, 17. 6:2. 7:18, 20, 21, 27. 11:43, 44 (yourselves). 16:29, 31. 17:12, 15. 20:6, 25. 22:6. 23:27, 30, 32. Nu 5:6 (person). 15:27, 28, 30. 19:22. 29:7. 30:2, 4, 4, 5, 6, 7, 8, 9, 10, 11, 12, 13. Dt 13:6. Jg 5:21. 1 S 1:26. 17:55. 18:1, 3. 20:3, 17. 25:26. 2 S 11:11. 14:19. 2 K 2:2, 4, 6. 4:30. Est 9:31 (themselves). Jb 16:4, 4. 18:4 (himself). 31:30. 32:2 (himself). Ps 35:13. 105:18 (he). 120:6. Pr 6:32. 8:36. 11:17. 13:2. 15:32. 16:17. 19:8, 16. 20:2. 21:23. 22:5. 29:24. Ec 4:8. 6:2. Is 46:2 (themselves). 51:23. 58:3, 5. Je 3:11 (herself). 4:19. 17:21 (yourselves). 51:14 (himself). Ezk 4:14. Am 6:8 (himself). Mi 6:7. For the other uses of *nephesh*, see Ge +2:7. For the equivalent New Testament use of *psyche* to emphasize the personal pronoun in the third person, see 1 P +4:19. **bless.** He 7:7.

32. **Who.** ver. 18. **I am.** ver. 19. **firstborn.** Ge 4:4, 5, 9-16. 17:19-21. ◖*25:31. 48:15-20. 49:3, 4. Dt ◖*21:17. 1 S 16:2-12. 1 K 2:15. 1 Ch 5:1, 2. 26:10. **Esau.** Ge 25:25.

33. **trembled very exceedingly.** Heb. trembled with a great trembling greatly. ⌐147D, Ge +1:29. Ru 3:8. Jb 21:6. 37:1. Ps 55:5. **taken.** Heb. hunted. **thou camest.** ver. 25. **yea.** Ge 28:3, 4. Jn 10:10, 28, 29. Ro 5:20, 21. +*11:29. Ep 1:3. He 11:20.

34. **he cried.** 1 S 30:4. Pr 1:24-28, 31. 19:3. Lk 13:24-28. He *12:17. **great and.** ⌐147D, Ge +1:29. **cry.** Ge 4:10. 41:55. Ex 5:15. 8:12. 14:10, 15. 15:25. 17:4. 22:27. Ps 107:6. He 5:7.

35. **Thy brother.** ver. 19-23. 2 K 10:19. Jb 13:7. Ml 2:10. Ro 3:7, 8. 2 C 4:7. 1 Th 4:6. **subtilly.** 1 S 23:22. 2 S 13:3. 2 K 10:19. Je 9:4. Mt 26:4. Ac 13:10. 2 C 11:3.

36. **Jacob.** i.e. a supplanter. Ge 25:26, 31-34. 32:28. Jn 1:47. **named.** ⌐144A4B, Ge +11:9. **he took.** Ge 25:26, 33, 34.

37. **Behold.** ⌐40, Ge +3:22. **I have.** ver. 29. Ge 25:23. 2 S 8:14. Ro 9:10-12. **him thy.** ⌐121I2, Ge +2:17. **with.** ver. 28. **corn.** ⌐121D4, Ge +27:28. **and.** ⌐174, Ge +18:27. **wine.** ⌐121D13, Ge +27:28. **sustained.** *or*, supported. ver. 28. S#5564. Le 1:4 (And he shall put). 4:4 (and shall lay). Dt 34:9 (had laid). Ps 3:5. 51:12 (uphold). 111:8 (stand fast). 119:16 (uphold). Is √26:3 (stayed). 59:16. 63:5 (upheld).

38. **Hast thou.** ver. 34, 36. Ge 49:28. Pr 1:24-26. Is 32:10-12. 65:14. He 12:17. **lifted.** ⌐144A12, Ge +22:13. Ge 21:16.

39. **Behold.** ⌐40, Ge +3:22. Ge 36:6-8. Jsh 24:4. He *11:20. **the fatness.** *or*, of the fatness. ver. 28. Nu ◖*20:17. A better rendering would be *far from the fatness* and *far from the dew*, for Esau dwelt in the desert. Jsh 24:4.

40. **thy sword.** Ge 32:6. Mt 10:34. **serve.** Ge 25:23. 1 S 14:47. 2 S 8:14. 1 K 11:15-17. 2 K 14:7, 10. 1 Ch 18:11-13. 2 Ch 25:11, 12. Ps 60:8. Ob 17-21. **that thou.** Nu *20:14, 17. 2 K *8:20-22. 2 Ch 21:8, 10. 28:17.

41. **hated.** Ge 4:2-8. 37:4, 8. Ezk 25:12-15. 35:5. Am 1:11, 12. Ob *10-14. 1 J *3:12-15. **The days.** Ge 35:29. 50:3, 4, 10, 11. Dt 34:8. 2 Ch 35:24. Ps 35:14. **then.** Ge 32:6. 2 S 13:28, 29. Ps 37:12, 13, 16. 140:4,

5. 142:3. Pr 1:12, 13, 16. 6:14. Ec 7:9. Ob 10. Ep 4:26, 27. T 1:15, 16. 3:3. 1 J *3:12-15.

42. **Behold.** ⌐40, Ge +3:22. **comfort himself.** Ge 37:18-20. 42:21, 22. 1 S 30:5. Jb 20:12-14. Ps *64:5. Pr 2:14. 4:16, 17.

43. **obey.** ver. 8, 13. Ge 28:7. Pr 30:17. Je 35:14. Ac 5:29. **Haran.** Ge 11:31. 12:4, 5. 24:4. 28:10. 29:4.

44. **a few days.** Ge ◖31:38, 41. ⌐175A. Figure of speech Tapeinosis; or, Demeaning B159: a lessening of a thing in order to increase it. Here, "one" in the plural (in Hebrew) is used for a few. For other instances of this figure see Ac 5:36. Ro 3:3 (*some* used for by far the greater number). 5:6. 2 C 2:6mg. Ga 2:6. 1 T *4:1 (*some* used for a great many, if not majority). **until.** Pr 18:19. 20:3. 22:24. 29:22. **fury.** ⌐173. Figure of speech Synonymia; or, Synonymous Words B324: the repetition of words similar in sense, but different in sound and origin. Here, "fury" in one clause is a near-synonym for "anger" in v. 45. For further instances of this figure see Ex 1:7. 2:23, 24, 25. 12:2. 15:16. 34:6, 7. Dt 13:4. 20:3. Ps 5:1, 2. 6:8, 9. 7:14, 15. 8:4. 10:17. 29:1, 2. *32:1, 2. 89:30, 31. Pr 4:14, 15. Is 1:4. 2:11-17. 52:13. Je 13:17. 48:29. Na 2:11, 12. Zp *1:15. 2:9. Mk *12:30. Lk 10:27. Ac 2:23. Ro 2:4, 7, 8, 9, 10, 18, 19, 20. 6:6. 9:33. 10:15. 1 C 14:21. Ga 1:12. Ga 5:19-21. Ep 1:21. *5:19. Ph 4:9. Col 1:16. 3:16. 1 T 1:2. 3:15. 2 T 1:2. 3:14, 15. T 1:4.

45. **then I.** Pr *19:21. La 3:37. Ja 4:13-15. **why.** Ge 4:8-16. *9:5, 6. 2 S 14:6, 7. Ac 28:4. ⌐85L. Figure of speech Erotesis; or, Interrogating B954: the asking of questions without waiting for the answer, in prohibitions. For other instances of this figure see 1 S 19:17. 2 S 2:22. 2 Ch 25:16. Ps 79:10. Ec 5:6. 7:17. Je 27:13, 17. Ezk 18:31. 33:11. Da 1:10. **both.** Jacob by Esau's hand, and Esau by the avenger of blood, Ge +9:6 (CB margin).

46. **I am.** Nu 11:15. 1 K 19:4. Jb 3:20-22. 7:16. 14:13. Jon 4:3, 9. **because.** Ge 26:34, 35. *28:8. 34:1, 2. **if Jacob.** Ge *24:3. **what.** Jb 6:8-11. 7:6, 7. Ps ◖118:24. 1 C◖15:58. ⌐37C. Aposiopesis; or, Sudden Silence, in grief and complaint, Ge +25:22. ⌐85P. Figure of speech Erotesis; or, Interrogating B955: the asking of questions without waiting for the answer, in lamentation. For other instances of this figure see Ps 3:1. 22:1. 77:7-9. 73:11. Is 1:21. La 2:20.

GENESIS 28

Isaac blesses Jacob, and sends him to Padan-aram to take a wife from thence, 1-5. Esau marries Mahalath the daughter of Ishmael, 6-9. Jacob journeys, has a vision of a ladder, sets up a stone as a pillar, calls the place Beth-el, and makes a solemn vow, 10-22.

1. **blessed.** ver. 3, 4. Ge 27:4, 27-33. 48:15. 49:28. Dt 33:1. Jsh 22:7. **Thou shalt.** Ge 6:2. 24:3, 37. 26:34, 35. 27:46. 34:9, 16. Ex 34:15, 16. 1 C *7:39. 2 C *6:14-16.

2. **Arise.** Ho 12:12. **Padan-aram.** ver. 5. Ge 22:20-23. 24:10, 15-24. 25:20. 29:1. 31:18. 32:10. 35:9. 46:15. **Laban.** Ge 24:29, 50.

3. **And.** ⌐148, Ge +8:22. **God.** Ge 17:1-6. 22:17, 18. 35:11. 43:14. 48:3. Ex 6:3. Ps 127:1. 2 C 6:18. Re 21:22. **and make.** Ge 1:28. 9:1. 13:16. 24:60. 41:52. Ps *127:3-5. 128. **a multitude.** Heb. an assembly. Ge 49:6. Ps 22:22, 25.

4. **the blessing.** Ge *12:1-3, 7. 15:5-7. *17:6-8.

22:17, 18. Ps 72:17. Ro 4:7, 8. Ga 3:8, 14. Ep 1:3. **wherein thou art a stranger**. Heb. of thy sojournings. Ge 17:8. **which**. Ge 12:7. 13:14-17. 15:18-21. 2 Ch +*20:7. Ps 39:12. 105:6-12. Ac +*7:5. He *11:9-13.

5. **sent**. Ge 11:31. **he went**. Ho 12:12. **Padan-aram**. ver. 2. **Bethuel the**. Ge 25:20. Dt 26:5. **Rebekah**. Ge 24:15.

6. **Esau**. Ge 27:33. **and**. ∫148, Ge +8:22. **Thou**. See ver. 1.

7. **obeyed**. Ge 27:43. Ex 20:12. Le 19:3. Pr 1:8. 30:17. Ep +*6:1-3. Col 3:20.

8. **the daughters**. ver. 1. Ge 24:3. *26:34, 35. **pleased not**. Heb. were evil in the eyes. Ge 38:10mg. Ex 21:8mg. Nu +22:34mg. Jg ◐+14:3mg. 1 S +8:6mg.

9. **Then went**. 1 S √15:23. **unto Ishmael**. Ge 25:13-17. 36:3, 13, 18. **wives**. Ge +4:19. **Mahalath**. called also, Bashemath, Ge 36:3. **the sister**. Ge 25:13.

10. **And**. ∫148, Ge +8:22. **went toward**. Ge 11:31. 32:10. Ho *12:12. **Beer-sheba**. Ge 21:14. 26:23, 33. **Haran**. Ge +11:31. Ac 7:2, Charran.

11. **took**. ver. 18. Ge 31:46. Mt 8:20. 2 C 1:5. **put them**. ver. ◐18.

12. **he dreamed**. Ge 15:1, 12. 20:3, 6, 7. 37:5-11. ch. 40, 41. Nu 12:6. Jb 4:12-21. 33:15, 16. Da ch. 2, 4. 7:1. Mt 1:20. 2:12, 13, 19. He 1:1. **behold**. ∫40, Ge +3:2. **ladder**. Ge 32:1, 2. 2 Ch 16:9. Is 41:10. Jn *1:51. 2 T 4:16, 17. He *1:14. **to heaven**. Ge 11:4.

13. **the Lord stood**. Ge 35:1, 6, 7. *48:3. **I am**. Ge 15:1. 17:6, 7. 26:24. 31:42. 32:9. 46:3. Ex 3:6, 15, 16. Mt √22:32. He 11:16. **the land**. See on ver. 4. Ge 12:7. 13:15. 35:12, 15, 17. Ps 105:11. Ezk 37:24, 25. Ac +*7:5.

14. **thy seed**. Ge *13:16. *32:12. 35:11, 12. Nu *23:10. Ac 3:25. Re 7:4, 9. **as**. ∫102B, Ge +13:16. **dust**. ∫138B, Ge +13:16. **spread abroad**. Heb. break forth. Ge 30:30mg, 43. Ex 1:12. 1 Ch 4:38mg. 13:2mg. 2 Ch 31:5mg. Pr 3:10. **to the west**. Ge 13:14. Dt 12:20. Mt *8:11. **and in thee**. Ge *12:3. 18:18. *22:18. 26:4. Ps 72:17. Ac *3:25. Ga *3:8, 16. Ep 1:3.

15. **I am**. ver. 20, 21. Ge 26:24. 31:3. 32:9. 39:2, 21. 46:4. Ex 3:12. Jg *6:16. Ps 46:7, 11. Is *7:14. 8:10. 41:10. *43:2. Je *1:19. Mt 18:20. 28:20. Ro 8:31, 32. 1 T 4:8. **keep**. Ge 48:16. Ps *121:5-8. **bring**. Ge 35:6, 7. **for I**. Dt 31:6. Jsh *1:5. 1 K *8:57. Jn *10:28, 29. He +*13:5, 6. Ju 1. **until**. Nu *23:19. Jsh *23:14-16. Mt 24:35.

16. **awaked**. 1 K 3:15. Je 31:26. **Surely**. ∫59. Figure of speech Ecphonesis; or, Exclamation B927: an expression of feeling by way of exclamation. For other instances of this figure see Jsh 7:7. 1 Ch 11:17. Ps 22:1. 57:7. 84:1. Is 1:4. 6:5. Ezk 4:14. 9:8. 11:13. Mt 15:28. 17:17. 27:46. Mk 15:34. Jn ◐X20:28. Ac 7:51. Ro 7:24. **and I**. Ex *3:5. 15:11. Jsh *5:15. 1 S 3:4-7. Jb *9:11. 33:14. Ps 68:35. Is 8:13.

17. **he was**. Ex 3:6. Jg 13:22. Ps *5:7. Mt 17:6. Lk 2:9. 8:35. Re 1:17. **the house**. ver. 22. Ge 35:1-13. 2 Ch 5:14. Ec *5:1. 1 T 3:15. He 10:21. 1 P 4:17.

18. **rose up**. Ge 22:3. Ps 119:60. Ec 9:10. **set it**. Ge 31:13, 45. 35:14, 20. Jsh 4:9, 20. 24:26, 27. 1 S 7:12. 2 S 18:18. Is 19:19. **poured**. Le 8:10-12. Nu 7:1. **oil**. S#8081h. Ge 35:14. Ex 25:6. 27:20. Le 23:13. 24:2. Dt *32:13. 33:24. Mt 26:26. Ja 5:14.

19. **the name**. Ge 12:8. 35:1. 48:3. Jg 1:22-26. 1 K 12:29. Ho 4:15. 12:4, 5. **Beth-el**. i.e. the house of God. Ge 12:8. 13:3. *31:13. 35:1, *15. Jsh 7:2. 12:9. 16:2. 18:13. Jg 1:22, *23. **Luz**. i.e. *almond tree; per-*

verse, bending, going back, *S#3870h. Ge 35:6. 48:3. Jsh 16:2. 18:13, 13. Jg 1:*23, 26. (1) A city of the Canaanites which was afterward called Bethel, Ge 28:19; Jsh 16:2. (2) A city of the Hittites, Jg 1:26.

20. **vowed**. Ge 31:13. Le ch. 27. Nu 6:1-20. 21:2, 3. Jg 11:30, 31. 1 S 1:11, 28. 14:24. 2 S 15:8. Ne ch. 9, 10. Ps 22:25. 56:12. 61:5, 8. 66:13. 76:11. 116:14, 18. 119:106. 132:2. Ec *5:1-7. Is 19:21. Jn 1:16. Ac 18:18. 23:12-15. **vow**. ∫147D, Ge +1:29. Le 27:29n. +*23:38. **If God**. See on ver. 15. Da ◐*3:18. **will keep**. T#1659. Dt 33:7, 12, 24, 25. Ps 17:5-9. 72:12-14. 84:9-12. Jn 17:15. **will give**. Ge 48:15. Dt 2:7. 8:3, 4. Pr 27:23-27. 30:8, 9. Ec 2:24-26. 3:12, 13. Mt *6:11, 25-33. 1 T *6:8. He 13:5, 6. **raiment**. T#1664. Mt *6:28-33. 1 T *6:8. He 13:5.

21. **I come**. Jg 11:31. 2 S 19:24, 30. **then**. Ex 15:2. Dt *26:17. 2 S 15:8. 2 K 5:17.

22. **stone**. ∫121.O. Metonymy (of the Adjunct); or, Change of Noun B591: the change of one noun for another related noun; here, what is placed (a "stone") for the place where it is located, of which the stone formed a part. For other instances of this figure see Jsh 15:19. 1 Ch 9:24. Jb 38:22. Ps 135:7. Is 23:3. 37:25. Je 12:7. 49:32. Ezk 5:12. 26:5. Ho 8:1. *9:6, 15. Am 8:5. Zc +9:8. Mt 2:11. 12:35. 13:52. 24:31. 25:10, *21, *23. Lk 21:4. Ac 16:13. 1 C 9:24. Ga 2:12. He 12:1. Re 8:3. **pillar**. ver. 18. Le ◐26:1mg. Dt ◐16:22mg. **God's**. ver. 17. Ge 12:8. 21:33. 33:20. 35:1-15. **I will**. Ge 14:20. Le 27:30-33. Dt 14:22, 23.

GENESIS 29

Jacob comes to the well of Haran and confers with some shepherds, 1-8. He becomes acquainted with Rachel, 9-12. Jacob is entertained by Laban, and serves seven years for Rachel, 13-20. He is deceived by Laban with Leah; he remonstrates, and Laban excuses himself; Jacob also marries Rachel, and serves other seven years for her, 21-30. Rachel is barren; but Leah bears Reuben, Simeon, Levi, and Judah, 31-35.

1. **Jacob**. Ps 119:32, 60. Ec 9:7. **went on his journey**. Heb. lifted up his feet. **came**. Ge 22:20-23. 24:10. 25:20. 28:5-7. Nu 23:7. Jg 6:3, 33. 7:12. 8:10. 1 K *4:30. Ho *12:12. **people**. Heb. children. 1 K *4:30. Jb 1:3. Je 49:28. Ezk 25:4, 10. **east**. the district of Mesopotamia, and the whole country beyond the Euphrates, are called *Kedem*, or the East, in the Sacred Writings. Ge +25:6.

2. **a well**. Heb. *beer*, Ge +16:14. Ge 24:11, 13. Ex 2:15, 16. Jn 4:6, 14. **there**. Ps 23:2. SS 1:6, 7. Is 49:10. Re 7:17. **a great stone**. ver. 3, 8, 10. Jsh ◐10:27. Mt ◐27:60, 66. ◐28:2. Mk ◐15:46. ◐16:3. A stone was used as a cover to keep the blowing sands of the desert from clogging the well. Compare Dt 28:24n.

3. **all**. Ps ◐23:2. Ps +*149:9. Jn +*10:16. 1 C *12:13. The shepherds by agreement waited until all the flocks were present before opening the well, perhaps to share equally in the water, as well as to keep the well open the briefest length of time to keep out the blowing desert sand. **well's**. ver. +2.

4. **of Haran**. Ge 11:31. *24:10. 27:43. 28:10. Ac 7:2, 4, Charran.

5. **son of**. Ge *24:24, 29. 31:53. ∫171G. Synecdoche of the Species, Ge +13:8. Here, "son" is put for "grandson."

6. **Is he well**. Heb. *Is* there peace to him? Ge

37:14mg. 43:27mg. Ex 18:7mg. Jg 18:15mg. 1 S 17:18, 22mg. 25:5. 2 S 8:10mg. 11:7mg. 20:9. 2 K 4:23mg. 9:11.

7. **Lo.** ƒ40, Ge +3:22. Ga 6:9, 10. Ep 5:16. **it is yet high day.** Heb. yet the day *is* great.

8. **until.** ver. 3. Ge 34:14. 43:32. **roll.** Mk 16:3. Lk 24:2. **well's.** ver. +2.

9. **Rachel.** Ge 24:15. Ex *2:15, 16, 21. SS 1:7, 8. **for she kept them.** Ge 24:19. ◐37:14 w 34:25-30. 1 S 17:14, 15. Pr 31:13. Lk 16:10-12.

10. **Jacob.** Ge ◐24:19, 20. **rolled.** Ex 2:17. Mt 28:2. Mk 16:4. **well's.** ver. +2.

11. **kissed.** ver. 13. Ge 27:26. 33:4. 43:30. 45:2, 14, 15. Ex 4:27. 18:7. Ro 16:16. **lifted.** ƒ144A12, Ge +22:13. **and wept.** Ge 33:4. +42:24. 43:30. 45:2, 14, 15.

12. **brother.** ver. 5. Ge 13:8. 14:14-16. ƒ171G. Synecdoche of the Species, Ge +13:8. Here, "brother" put for nephew, see ver. 13. **and she.** Ge 24:28.

13. **tidings.** Heb. hearing. ƒ147A, Ge +50:24. **he ran.** Ge +18:2. 24:29. **and.** ƒ148, Ge +8:22. **kissed.** ver. 11. Ge 45:15. Ex 4:27. 18:7. 2 S 19:39. Lk 7:45. 15:20. Ac 20:37. Ro +*16:16n. **all these.** Col 4:5.

14. **art my.** ver. 12, 15. Ge *2:23. 13:8. Jg 9:2. 2 S 5:1. 19:12, 13. Mi 7:5. Ep +*5:30. **and.** ƒ174, Ge +18:27. **the space of a month.** Heb. a month of days. ƒ100, Ge +10:9. ƒ144A10. Figure of speech Pleonasm; or, Redundancy B413: when more words are used than the grammar requires. Here, *a month of days*, or a full month. For other instances of this figure see Ge 47:8mg. Ex 13:10. Nu 11:20mg, 21. Jg 19:2mg. 2 S 19:34mg. Ps *90:10.

15. **brother.** ver. 12. **for nought.** Dt 25:4. 1 Ch +*21:24. Mt 10:10. Lk *10:7. 1 C 9:4-9. Ja ◐+*5:4. **tell me.** Ge 30:28. 31:7. **wages.** Le √19:13. Dt +*24:14. Pr +22:23. +23:11. Mal +*3:5. Mt 20:1-15. Lk 3:14. 1 T 5:18.

16. **was Leah.** i.e. *weary*, ＊S#3812h. ver. 17, 23, 25, 30, 31, 32. Ge 30:9, 10, 11, 12, 13, 14, 14, 16, 17, 18, 19, 20. 31:4, 14, 33, 33. 33:1, 2, 7. 34:1. 35:23, 26. 46:15, 18. 49:31. Ru 4:11.

17. **Rachel.** ver. 6-12, 18. Ge 30:1, 2, 22. 35:19, 20, 24. 46:19-22. 48:7. 1 S 10:2. Je 31:15. Mt 2:18. **beautiful.** Ge 12:11, 14. 24:16. 26:7. 39:6. 1 S 25:3. 2 S 11:3. 13:1. 14:27. 1 K 1:4. Est 1:11. 2:7. Jb 42:15. Ps 144:12. Pr *31:30.

18. **loved.** ver. 20, 30. **I will serve.** In ancient times, it was a custom among many nations to give dowries for their wives; but Jacob, being poor, offered for Rachel seven years' service. Ge 31:41. 34:12. Ex 22:16, 17. 2 S 3:14. Ho 3:2. 12:12.

19. **better.** Ps 12:2. Is 6:5, 11.

20. A.M. 2251. B.C. 1753. **served.** Ge 30:26. Ho 12:12. **seemed.** He 12:2. **for the love.** Ge 24:67. SS 8:6, 7. 1 C 13:7. 2 C 5:14. Ep *5:2, 25.

21. **Give me.** Mt 1:18. **my days.** ver. 18, 20. Ge 31:41. go in. Ge +4:1. 38:16. Jg 15:1.

22. **and made.** Jg 14:10-18. Ru 4:10-13. Mt 22:2-10. 25:1-10. Jn 2:1-10. Re 19:9.

23. **brought her.** ver. +15. Ge *24:65. 38:14, 15. Mi 7:5. **went in.** ver. +21.

24. **Zilpah.** i.e. *flippant mouth; to drop, trickle; contempt of the mouth*, ＊S#2153h. Ge 30:9, 10, 12. 35:26. 37:2. 46:18. **handmaid.** Ge 16:1. 24:59.

25. **in the morning.** 1 C 3:13. **wherefore.** Ge *27:35, 36. Jg 1:7. Nu 32:23. Pr *5:22. 11:31. 13:15, *21. 26:27. Mt *7:2, 12. Lk ◐6:38. Jn 21:17. Ga 6:7. Re *3:19.

26. **must not.** Ge 20:9. 34:7. **country.** Heb. place. Mk 7:1-13. **younger before.** Jg 15:2. 1 S 18:17. **first-born.** 1 S 14:49.

27. **week.** Thomas Scott notes that the *week*, here mentioned, was that of the marriage feast; and did not relate to the years Jacob afterwards served. The division of time by *weeks* intimates that some regard was paid to the sabbath (See related notes, Ge 2:3n. 4:3n. Ex 16:26n. Is 58:13n). Ge 2:2, 3. 8:10-12. Le 18:18. Jg 14:10, 12. Ml 2:15. Mt 19:5. 1 T 6:10. **we will.** ver. 20. ƒ96D4. Figure of speech Heterosis (of Person and Number); or, Exchange of Accidence B525: the plural is put for the singular; as here, "we" is put for "I." For other instances of this figure see Nu 22:6. 2 S 16:20. Jb 18:2. Da 2:36. Mk 4:30. Jn 3:11. 21:24. Ro 1:5. 1 T 2:15.

28. **fulfilled her week.** The public marriage feast made on this occasion (ver. 22), seems to have formed the regular method of recognizing the marriage, and lasted seven days: it would therefore have been improper to have broken off the solemnities to which all the men of the place had been invited (ver. 22) and probably Laban wished to keep the fraud from the public eye. It is perfectly plain that Jacob did not serve seven years more before he got Rachel to wife. Jg *14:12. **Rachel.** i.e. *an ewe*, ＊S#7354h. ver. 6, 9, 10, 11, 12, 16, 17, 18, 18, 20, 25, 29, 30, 30, 31. Ge 30:1, 1, 2, 6, 7, 8, 14, 15, 22, 25. 31:4, 14, 19, 32, 33, 34. 33:1, 2, 7. 35:16, 19, 20, 24, 25. 46:19, 22, 25. 48:7. Ru 4:11. 1 S 10:2. Je 31:15. **wife.** Ge +4:19.

29. **Bilhah.** i.e. *tender; alarm; timid*, ＊S#1090h. See on ver. 24. Ge 30:3, 4, 5, 7. 35:22, 25. 37:2. 46:25. 1 Ch 4:29. 7:13. (1) The handmaid of Rachel, Ge 29:29; 1 Ch 7:13. (2) A town of Simeon, 1 Ch 4:29. Probably same as Balah in Jsh 19:3.

30. **went in.** ƒ88, Ge +15:15. ver. 23. Ge +4:1. **he loved.** ver. 20, 31. 44:20, 27. Dt *21:15. Pr +13:24. Ml 1:2. Mt 6:24. 10:37. Lk 14:26. 16:13. Jn 12:25. Ro 9:13. **served.** ver. 18. Ge 30:25, 26. 31:15, 41. 1 S 18:17-27. Ho 12:12.

31. **saw.** ver. 33. Ge 31:42. Ex 2:23-25. *3:7. Ne 9:9. Ps 106:44. Ac 7:34. **was hated.** ver. 30. Ge 27:41. Dt *21:15. Ml 1:3. Mt 6:24. 10:37. Lk 14:26. Jn 12:25. ƒ121C2C2. Figure of speech Metonymy (of the Cause) B566, with verbs of loving and hating, where "love" and "hate" are put for the esteem or neglect caused by love or hate; "hate" indicates *less loved*. For other instances of this figure see Dt 21:15. Mt *6:24. 16:25. Lk √14:26. Jn 12:25. **he opened.** Ge ◐+11:30. 16:1. ◐20:18. 21:1, 2. 25:21. 30:1, 2, 22. Dt 28:4. Jg 13:2, 3. Ru +4:13. 1 S 1:5, 20, 27. 2:21. Ps +*127:3. Lk 1:7. 1 T 2:15. 4:8. **barren.** Ge +11:30.

32. A.M. 2252. B.C. 1752. **his name.** Ge 35:22. 37:21, 22, 29. 42:22, 27. 46:8, 9. 49:3, 4. 1 Ch 5:1. **Reuben.** that is, See a son. ✚S#7205h. Ge 30:14. 35:22, 23. 37:21, 22, 29. 42:22, 37. 46:8, 9. 48:5. 49:3. Ex 1:2. 6:14, 14. Nu 1:20. 16:1. 26:5, 5. Dt 11:6. Jsh 15:6. 18:17. 1 Ch 2:1. 5:1, 3. For the tribe of Reuben, see on Nu 1:5. **looked.** ver. +31. Ex 3:7. 4:31. Dt 26:7. 1 S 1:11, 20. 2 S 16:12. Ps 25:18. 106:44. Lk 1:25.

33. A.M. 2253. B.C. 1751. **Because.** Ge 30:6, 8, 18, 20. **heard.** ƒ140, Ge +4:25. **called.** Ge 34:25, 30. 35:23. 42:24. 49:5, 6. **Simeon.** that is, hearing. ✚S#8095h. Ge 34:25, 30. 35:23. 42:24, 36. 43:23. 46:10. 48:5. 49:5. Ex 1:2. 6:15, 15. For the tribe of Simeon,

see on Nu 1:6. (1) The second son of Jacob and Leah, Ge 29:33; Ex 1:2. He was one of "the twelve patriarchs," and was the ancestor of the tribe of Simeon. (2) A just and devout man of Jerusalem, who waited for the consolation of Israel and was permitted to see the infant Savior, Lk 2:25, 34. (3) A disciple and prophet who was at Antioch when Barnabas and Saul returned from Jerusalem, Ac 13:1. (4) Simeon, in Ac 15:14, is applied to the apostle Peter, who was more frequently called Simon. (5) An ancestor of Joseph, the husband of Mary, Lk 3:30.

34. A.M. 2254. B.C. 1750. **joined.** ⌐140, Ge +4:25. Nu 18:2, 4. Je 50:5. **because.** Ge 30:20. **was.** Ge 34:25. 35:23. 46:11. 49:5-7. Ex 2:1. 32:26-29. Dt 33:8-10. **Levi.** that is, joined. ✦S#3878h. Ge 34:25, 30. 35:23. 49:5. Ex 1:2. 6:16, 16. Nu 3:17. 16:1. 26:59, 59. 1 Ch 6:38, 43, 47. Ezr 8:18. (1) The third son of Jacob by Leah, Ge 29:34; 34:25-31. (2) The tribe descended from Levi, Number 1, Ex +2:1; Nu 1:49. (3) Two ancestors of Joseph, the husband of Mary, Lk 3:24, 29. (5) The original name of Matthew the publican and apostle, Mt 9:9; Mk 2:14; Lk 5:27, 29.

35. A.M. 2255. B.C. 1749. **called.** Ge 35:26. 38. 43:8, 9. 44:18-34. 46:12. 49:8-12. Dt 33:7. 1 Ch 5:2. Mt *1:2. **Judah.** that is, praise. **left bearing.** Heb. stood from bearing. Ge 49:8. That is, for a time; for she had several children afterwards, Ge 30:17.

GENESIS 30

Rachel envies Leah, and complains impatiently to Jacob, who sharply rebukes her; yet at her instance takes Bilhah to wife, who bears Dan and Naphtali, 1-8. Leah gives Zilpah to Jacob, and she bears Gad and Asher, 9-13. Leah purchases Jacob's company, of Rachel, by her son's mandrakes; and bears Issachar, Zebulun, and Dinah, 14-21. Rachel bears Joseph, 22-24. Jacob desires to leave Laban, who agrees with him for his future services, 25-36. Jacob's policy, whereby he becomes rich, 37-43.

1. **when Rachel.** Ge 29:31. **Rachel envied.** Ge 26:14. 37:11. 1 S 1:4-8. Ps 106:16. Pr 14:30. 27:4. Ec 4:4. 1 C 3:3. Ga 5:21. T 3:3. Ja 3:14. 4:5. **or else I die.** Ge *35:16-19. 37:11. Nu 11:15, 29. 1 K 19:4. Jb 3:1-3, 11, 20-22. *5:2. 13:19. Je 20:14-18. Jn 4:3, 8. 2 C 7:10.

2. **anger.** Ge 31:36. Ex 32:19. Mt 5:22. Mk 3:5. Ep *4:26. **Am I.** Ge 16:2. 25:21. 50:19. 1 S *1:5. 2:5, 6. 2 K 5:7. **withheld.** Ge +*11:30. Dt 7:13, 14. Ps +*113:9. +*127:3. Lk 1:42.

3. **Behold.** ver. 9. Ge 16:2, 3. **Bilhah.** Ge 29:29. **she shall.** Ge 50:23. Jb 3:12. **have children by her.** Heb. be built up by her. Ge 16:2mg. Ru 4:11.

4. **to wife.** Ge 16:3. 21:10. 22:24. 25:1, 6. 33:2. 35:22. 2 S 12:11.

6. A.M. 2256. B.C. 1748. **God.** Ge 29:32-35. Ps 35:24. 43:1. La 3:59. **Dan.** that is, judging. ⌐140, Ge +4:25. ✦S#1835h. Ge 35:25. 46:23. 49:16, 17. Ex 1:4. Dt 33:22. Jsh 19:47, 47. Jg 13:2, 24. 15:14-20. 18:29. 1 Ch 2:2. Ezk 27:19. (1) The name (afterward given) of a place to which Abram pursued the kings who had ravaged Sodom and carried away Lot, Ge 14:14; Jg 18:29; 1 Ch 21:2. It is stated in Jg 18:29 that a colony of the tribe of Dan settled there and changed the name of the city of which they took possession from Laish to Dan, which was the principal city of

the northern part of the territory of the tribe of Dan, Jg 20:1. (2) The fifth son of Jacob, and the first of Bilhah, Rachel's maid, Ge 30:6; 49:16; 1 Ch 2:2. (3) The name of the tribe descended from Dan, or the territory they occupied in the land of Canaan, Nu +1:12. (4) Dan, Ezk 27:19, may be the same as Number 1, but is identified with *Dedar* by some, and by others with Aden in Arabia.

7. A.M. 2257. B.C. 1747. **Bilhah.** ver. 3, 5.

8. **And.** ⌐148, Ge +8:22. **great wrestlings.** Heb. wrestlings of God. ⌐147D, Ge +1:29. ⌐24L, Ge +6:2. Ge +23:6mg. 32:24. Ex 9:28. 1 S 14:15mg. Jon 3:3mg. **wrestled.** ⌐140, Ge +4:25. **and she.** Ge 35:25. 46:24. 49:21. Dt 33:23. **Naphtali.** that is, my wrestling. ⌐140, Ge +4:25. ✦S#5321h. Ge 32:24, 25. 35:25. 46:24. 49:21. Ex 1:4. 1 Ch 2:2. 7:13. Ezk 48:34. Mt 4:13, Nephthalim. For the tribe and land, see Nu +1:15.

9. A.M. 2256. B.C. 1748. **left.** ver. 17. Ge 29:35. **gave her.** ver. 4. Ge 16:3.

11. **she.** Ge 35:26. 46:16. 49:19. Dt 33:20, 21. **a troop.** Carr remarks "Whether Leah's exclamation refers to the Syrian God of Fortune, as has been conjectured, or whether *Gad* is an abstract term for prosperity or happiness, there is certainly nothing in the expression to imply a formal recognition of good luck or fortune as a force determining events" (*Horae Biblicae*, p. 38). Ge +*24:44n. **Gad.** that is, a troup, or company. *i.e. the seer; fortune.* Jsh 11:17. 12:7. Is 65:11mg. ✦S#1410h: Ge 35:26. 46:16. 49:19. Ex 1:4. 1 Ch 5:11. (1) The seventh son of Jacob, Ge 30:11; Ex 1:4. (2) The name is also used to denote the tribe which sprang from Gad and the land which they inhabited, which was east of the Jordan and between Reuben and Manasseh, Nu +1:14. (3) A prophet who lived in the time of David, and was his friend, 1 S +22:5; 2 S 24:13, 14.

13. A.M. 2257. B.C. 1747. **Happy am I.** Heb. In my happiness. **will call.** ⌐121I2, Ge +2:17. Pr 31:28. SS 6:9. Lk 1:48. **and she.** Ge 35:26. 46:17. 49:20. Dt 33:24, 25. **Asher.** that is, happy. ⌐140, Ge +4:25. ✦S#836h. Ge 35:26. 46:17. 49:20. Ex 1:4. Nu 26:46. 1 Ch 2:2. 7:30, 40. For the tribe of Asher, see on Nu 1:13. (1) The eighth son of Jacob. (2) One of the twelve tribes, Nu 1:13. (3) A territory about sixty miles long, extending from Carmel to Lebanon, and from ten to twelve miles wide. The Phoenicians retained the plain by the sea, and Asher occupied the mountains, Jsh 19:24-31; Jg 1:31, 32. (4) A town on the border of Ephraim and Manasseh, Jsh 17:7.

14. A.M. 2256. B.C. 1748. **wheat harvest.** Ex 34:22. Jg 15:1. Ru 2:23. 1 S 6:13. 12:17. 1 Ch 21:20. Jl 1:11. **mandrakes.** SS 7:13. **Give me.** Ge 25:30.

15. **Is it.** Nu 16:9, 10, 13. Is 7:13. Ezk 16:47. 34:18. 1 C 4:3. **Therefore.** Ge 19:31-36. 38:16. Ezk 16:33. Ho 2:5. 8:9. 9:1.

16. **come in.** ⌐88, Ge +15:15. Ge 29:21, 30. **mandrakes.** ver. 14. **And he.** 1 C 7:3-5. 1 P 3:7. **lay.** Ge 19:33, 34, 35. 34:2. 35:22. He 13:4.

17. A.M. 2257. B.C. 1747. **God hearkened.** ver. 6, 22. Ge +29:31. Ex 3:7. 1 S 1:20, 26, 27. Lk *1:13.

18. **and she.** Ge 35:23. 46:13. 49:14, 15. Dt 33:18. 1 Ch 12:32. **Issachar.** that is, a hire. ⌐140, Ge +4:25. *i.e. he brings reward or wages,* ✦S#3485h. Ge 35:23. 46:13. 49:14. Ex 1:3. 1 Ch 2:1. 7:1. (1) The fifth son of Jacob and Leah, Ge 30:18; Ex 1:3. (2) The tribe

and territory inhabited by the descendants of Issachar, comprised the great plain called Esdraelon or Jezreel, and extended from Mount Carmel to the Jordan and from En-gannim to Mount Tabor. It was one of the most fertile districts in Palestine and contained sixteen famous cities. Its boundaries are given in Jsh 19:17-23. For the tribe, see on Nu +1:29. (3) A porter for the Tabernacle in the time of David, 1 Ch 26:5.

20. A.M. cir. 2258. B.C. cir. 1746. **good dowry.** ⌐147D, Ge +1:29. Ge 34:12. Ex 22:16-17. 1 S 18:25. Ru 4:3-9. **now will.** ver. 15. Ge 29:34. **and she.** Ge 35:23. 46:14. 49:13. Jg 4:10. 5:14. Ps 68:27. **Zebulun.** that is, dwelling. ⌐140, Ge +4:25. *S#2074h. Ge 35:23. 46:14. 49:13. Ex 1:3. 1 Ch 2:1. Mt 4:13, Zabulon. For the tribe and descendants, see Nu 1:9.

21. A.M. cir. 2259. B.C. 1745. **and called.** Ge 34:1-3, 26. 46:15. **Dinah.** that is, judgment. i.e. *avenged*, *S#1783h. Ge 34:1, 3, 5, 13, 25, 26. 46:15.

22. **And.** ⌐107, Ge +10:5. Hysterologia, for Joseph was born after Naphtali, not after Dinah. This figure is used here to keep Leah's children together. **remembered.** ⌐22C3, Ge +8:1. Ge 8:1. 21:1. 29:31. 1 S *1:19, 20. Ps 105:42. **opened.** ver. 2. Ge 21:1, 2. 25:21. +29:31. Ps +*113:9. +*127:3.

23. **taken away.** 'Be fruitful and multiply' was the blessing of God: barrenness therefore was reckoned a reproach. The intense desire of having children, observable among the Jewish women, arose not only from this reproach of barrenness, but from the hope of being the mother of the promised seed, and Him in whom all the nations of the earth were to be blessed. Ge +*3:15. ◑+*11:30. *12:3. +*29:31. Ru +4:13. 1 S 1:5, 6. Ps +*127:3. Is 4:1. Lk 1:21, 25, 27.

24. **And she.** Ge 35:24. 37:2, 4. ch. 39. 42:6. 48:1. 49:22-26. Dt 33:13-17. Ezk 37:16. Ac 7:9-15. He 11:21, 22. Re 7:8. **Joseph.** that is, adding. ⌐140, Ge +4:25. ✛S#3130h. ver. 25. Ge 33:2, 7. 35:24. 37:2, 2, 3, 5, 13, 17, 23, 23, 28, 28, 28, 29, 33. 39:1, 2, 4, 6, 7, 10, 11, 21. 40:3, 4, 6, 8, 9, 12, 16, 18, 22, 23. 41:14, 15, 16, 17, 25, 39, 41, 44, 45, 46, 46, 49, 50, 51, 54, 55, 56, 57. 42:6, 7, 8, 9, 14, 18, 23, 25, 36. 43:15, 16, 17, 25, 26, 30. 44:2, 4, 15. 45:1, 1, 3, 3, 4, 4, 9, 17, 21, 26, 27, 27, 28. 46:4, 19, 20, 27, 28, 29, 30, 31. 47:1, 5, 7, 11, 12, 14, 14, 15, 16, 17, 17, 20, 23, 26, 29. 48:1, 2, 3, 9, 11, 12, 13, 15, 17, 18, 21, 22, 26. 50:1, 2, 4, 7, 8, 14, 15, 16, 17, 17, 19, 22, 22, 23, 24, 25, 26. Ex 1:5, 6, 8. 13:19. 27:1. 32:33. 34:23. 36:12. Dt 27:12. Jsh 14:4. 16:1, 4. 17:1, 2, 14, 16. 24:32. 1 Ch 2:2. Ps 105:17. Jn 4:5. Ac 7:9, 13, 14, 18. He 11:21, 22. For the descendants and tribe of Joseph, see on Nu 1:10. (1) The eleventh son of Jacob, the first whom he had by Rachel, Ge 30:24. (2) The father of Igal the spy, Nu 13:7. (3) A Jew who married a foreign wife, Ezr 10:42. (4) A priest in the time of Joikim, Ne 12:14. (5) A son of Asaph, 1 Ch 25:2, 9. (6, 7, 8) Three ancestors of Christ, Lk 3:24, 26, 30. (9) The husband of Mary, the mother of Jesus, Mt 1:19; 13:55. (10) Joseph of Arimathaea, Mt 27:57-60. (11) A disciple called also Barsabas, who was a candidate with Matthias to take the place of Judas among the apostles, Ac 1:23. **another son.** Ge 35:17, 18.

25. **Send me away.** Ge 24:54, 56. **mine.** Ge 18:33. 31:55. **and to.** Ge 24:6, 7. 26:3. 27:44, 45. 28:13, 15. 31:13. Ac 7:4, 5. He 11:9, 15, 16.

26. **my wives.** Ge +4:19. 29:19, 20, 30. 31:26, 31,

41. Ho 12:12. **for thou.** ver. 29, 30. Ge 31:6, 38-40.

27. **favor.** Ge 18:3. 33:15. 34:11. 39:3-5, 21. 47:25. Ex 3:21. Nu 11:11, 15. Ru 2:13. 1 S 16:22. 1 K 11:19. Ne 1:11. 2:5. Da 1:9. Ac 7:10. **tarry.** ⌐63D2. Figure of speech Ellipsis (Absolute: of Anantapodoton) B53: Ellipsis of a latter clause, a hypothetical proposition without the consequent clause. Here, "if..., *tarry*." For other instances of this figure see 2 S 2:27. 5:6-8. 2 Ch 2:3. Da 3:15. Mt (6:25). (8:9). Mk (11:32). Lk (2:21). 13:9. Jn (3:2). (6:62). Ro (9:22-24). Ja (2:13). 2 P (2:4). **learned.** Ge 44:15. Nu 23:23. 24:1. 1 K 20:33. Da 4:34, 36, 37. 2 C 5:7. **experience.** or, divination. Ge 3:1. Nu 22:7. Jsh 13:22mg. Je 27:9. *S#5172h, *nachash.* Ge 44:5, 15. Le 19:26 (enchantment). Dt *18:10 (enchanter). 1 K 20:33 (diligently observe). 2 K 17:17 (enchantments). 21:6 (enchantments). 2 Ch 33:6 (enchantments). **the Lord.** ver. 30. Ge *12:3. *39:2-5, 21-23. Ps *1:3. Is 61:9. **for thy.** ver. 30. Ge 26:24, 28. *39:3, 23. 41:38, 39. 1 S 18:28. 1 K 3:28. Zc 8:23. Mt *5:16.

28. **wages.** ver. 32. Ge 29:+*15, 19. 31:7, 41.

29. **Thou knowest.** See on ver. 5. Ge *31:6, 38-40. Mt 24:45. Ep *6:5-8. Col *3:22-25. T *2:9, 10. 1 P *2:15, 18.

30. **increased.** Heb. broken forth. ver. 43. **and the Lord.** ver. +27. **since my coming.** Heb. at my foot. Ex 11:8mg. Dt 11:+6mg, 10. 2 K 3:9mg. **when.** 2 C 12:14. 1 T √5:8. **provide.** ⌐121C, Ge +12:5. **house.** ⌐121J4, Ge +7:1.

31. **Thou shalt.** 2 S 21:4-6. Ps 118:8. He *13:5. **not give.** 2 S 24:24.

32. **of such.** ver. 35. Ge 31:8, 10, 12.

33. **righteousness.** Ge 31:37. 1 S 26:23. 2 S 22:21. Jb 6:29. Ps *37:6. **answer.** ⌐155F, Ge +4:7. Is 59:12. **in time to come.** Heb. tomorrow. Ex 13:14. Jsh +4:6. +22:24. Dt +6:20. ⌐24E. Figure of speech Antimeria (of the Adverb); or, Exchange of Parts of Speech B494: adverb for adjective. Here, "tomorrow" is put for some future day. For other instances of this figure see Ex 13:14mg. 1 S 25:31. Ne 2:12. Pr 3:25. 15:24. 24:28. *27:1mg. Mt *6:34. Jn 1:3. 15:5mg. 20:7. 2 C 4:16, 17. **that shall be.** Supply the ellipsis (⌐63C, Ge +25:32) by inserting *if found* after *stolen*, and the sense will be clear.

34. **I would.** Nu 22:29. 1 C 7:7. 14:5. Ga 5:12. Re 3:15.

35. **the hand.** Ge 31:9.

36. **three days.'** Ge +22:4. 31:22. 40:13. Ex 3:18. 8:27. 13:17, 18. 1 C +*15:4. **betwixt.** Pr 14:7. Mt +*15:14.

37. **Jacob.** Ge 31:9-13. **green poplar.** Ho 4:13. **hazel.** or, almond. Nu 17:8. Ec 12:5. Je 1:11. **chestnut.** Ezk 31:8. **pilled.** Heb. peeled a peeling. ⌐147D, Ge +1:29. **rods.** ver. 41. Nu 21:18. Zc 11:7.

38. **gutters.** ver. 41. **watering troughs.** Ge 24:20. Ex 2:16. **conceive.** ver. 41. Je 2:24.

39. **brought forth.** Ge 31:9-12, 38, 40, 42. Ex 12:35, 36. Je 27:5, 6.

40. **brown.** ver. 32.

41. **stronger.** Jb 39:4. **conceive.** ver. +38. **gutters.** ver. 38. Ex 2:16. **rods.** ver. +37.

42. **stronger.** Ge 31:1, 9, 16, 43. 32:5.

43. **increased.** ver. 30. Ge 13:2. 24:35. 26:13, 14. 28:15. 31:7, 8, 42. 32:10. 33:11. 36:7. Ec 2:7. Ezk 39:10. **exceedingly.** Heb. greatly, greatly. ⌐84, Ge +6:17. **camels.** Ge 12:16. 24:10. The Lord will, in

one way or other, honor those who simply trust his providence (Ge 24:44n).

GENESIS 31

Jacob is envied by Laban and his sons, 1, 2. Being commanded by God to return to his kindred, he proposes it to his wives; explains the Lord's dealings with him; and, with their consent, privately departs, taking his family and substance, 3-21. Laban pursues him, but is warned in a dream not to injure him; he overtakes Jacob and expostulates with him, 22-32. Laban searches in vain for his images, which Rachel had stolen and concealed, 33-35. Jacob vindicates himself, and complains of Laban, 36-42; they enter into a covenant, and Laban returns home, 43-55.

1. **Jacob.** ver. 8, 9. Jb 31:31. Ps 57:4. 64:3, 4. 120:3-5. Pr 14:30. 27:4. Ec 4:4. Ezk 16:44. T 3:3. **glory.** ✓121G1. Figure of speech Metonymy of the Effect B564. *Glory* is here used for *wealth*, riches, or property; since those who possess riches, generally make them the subject of glory. The original word *cavod*, signifies both *glory* and *weight*. Ge 45:13. Est 5:11. Jb 31:24, 25. Ps 17:14. 49:16, 17. Ec 4:4. Is 5:14. 10:3. 66:12. Je 9:23. Mt 4:8. 1 T 6:4. 1 P 1:24. For other instances of this figure, see Ex 10:17. Dt 30:15. 2 K 4:40. Pr 10:2. 19:13. 20:1. Ec 11:1. Is 10:3. 28:12. 58:9. √60:5mg. +*63:15n, ✓22A18. Je 3:24. La 2:14. Ezk 44:18. Ho 4:18. Mi 1:5. Hab 2:5. Jn 3:19. 12:50. 17:3. Ro 6:6. 7:7, 24. 8:6. 1 C 12:6. 14:3. 2 C 1:10. 11:23. Ph 1:13. He 6:1. Re 6:8.

2. **countenance.** Ge 4:5. Dt 28:54. 1 S 18:9-11. Da 3:19. **it was.** Ge 30:27. **as before.** Heb. as yesterday and the day before. ver. 5. Ex +4:10mg. 5:7, 8, 14. 21:29, 36. Dt 19:4mg. Jsh 4:18. 1 S 19:7mg. 2 S 3:17mg. 5:2h.

3. **Return.** Ge 28:15, 20, 21, etc. 32:9. 35:1. 46:2, 3. 50:24. Ps 46:1. 50:15. 90:15. **land.** ver. 13, 18. Ge 13:15. 26:3-5. 28:4, 13, 15. 30:25. **with thee.** Ge 21:22. 26:24. +*28:15. *32:9. Is √41:10. He +*13:5.

5. **I see.** ver. 2, 3. **the God.** ver. 3, 13, 42, 53. Ge 32:9. 48:15. 50:17.

6. **with all.** ver. 38-42. Ge 30:29. Ep 6:5-8. Col 3:22-25. T 2:9, 10. 1 P 2:18.

7. **your father.** ✓16, Ge +1:27. **deceived.** Or, mocked. Ge 29:25. 34:13. Ex 8:29. Le 6:2. 19:*15, 35, 36. Ezk 45:10. Am 8:5. **changed.** ver. 41. Ge +*29:15. Le +*19:13. Pr +22:23. +23:11. Mt ●20:1-15. Ja +*5:4. ✓106. Hysteresis; or, Subsequent Narration B709. A subsequent narration of prior events. Here, Jacob mentions facts in his history which had taken place before, but were not previously mentioned in the narrative. For other instances of this figure see 1 S 12:12. 22:9-16. Ps 105:18. Ho 12:3-5. Am 1:1. 2:1. 5:25, 26. Zc 14:5. Mt 2:23. 23:35, 36. 27:9, 10. Ac ch. 8, 22, 26. 2 T 3:8. He 9:19. 11:21. 12:21. Ja 5:17. Ju 9. **ten times.** The Hebrew, *asereth monim*, is literally, as Aquila renders, ten numbers; and Symmachus, ten times in number; which probably implies an indefinite number: see ver. 41. Le 26:26. Nu *14:22. Ne 4:12. Jb *19:3. Is 4:1. Zc 8:23. Mt ●18:21. **God.** ver. 29, 52. Ge +*20:6. Jb 1:10. Ps 37:28. *84:11. 105:14, 15. Ec 8:12. Is 54:17. 1 P 3:13. **suffered.** √✓108A4. Figure of speech Idiom B823: Active verbs were used by the Hebrews to express, not the doing of the thing, but the *permission* of the thing which

the agent is said to do. See related notes and references, Am +√3:6. For other instances of this figure see Ex 4:21. 5:22. Ps 16:10. Je 4:10. Ezk 14:9. 20:25. Am +*3:6. Mt 6:13. 11:25. 13:11. Ac 13:29. Ro 9:18. 11:7, 8. 2 Th *2:11.

8. **The speckled.** Ge 30:32.

9. **God hath.** ver. 1, 16. Est 8:1, 2. Ps 50:10. Pr 13:22. Mt 20:15.

10. **lifted.** ✓144A12, Ge +22:13. **a dream.** ver. 24. Ge 20:6. 28:12. Nu 12:6. Dt 13:1. 1 K 3:5. **rams.** *or*, he-goats. **ringstraked.** Ge 30:39. **grisled.** The original word, *beroodim*, means marked with white spots like hail, hence, spotted with white on a dark ground.

11. **the angel.** ver. 5, 13. See on Ge 16:7-13. 18:1, 17. *48:15, 16. **Here am I.** Ge 22:1. Ex 3:4. 1 S 3:4, 6, 8, 16. Is 58:9.

12. **Lift up.** ✓144A12, Ge +22:13. Ge 30:37-43. **I have seen.** ver. 42. Ex 3:7, 9. Le *19:13. Dt *24:15. Ps 12:5. 139:3. Ec 5:8. Ac 7:34. Ep 6:9.

13. **the God.** Ge *28:12-22. 35:7mg. **vow.** Le +*23:38. 27:29n. **return.** ver. 3. Ge 32:9.

14. **Rachel.** Ru 4:11. **yet any.** Ge 2:24. 29:24, 29.

15. **strangers.** Heb. *nokri*, *S#5237h. A permanent resident alien, a term never applied to Israel. Ex 2:22 (strange). 18:3. 21:8. Dt 14:21 (alien). 15:3 (foreigner). 17:15. *23:20. 29:22. Jg 19:12. Ru 2:10. 2 S 15:19. 1 K 8:41, 43. 11:1, 8. 2 Ch 6:32, 33. Ezr 10:2, 10, 11, 14, 17, 18, 44. Ne 13:26 (outlandish), 27. Jb 19:15 (alien). Ps *69:8. Pr 2:16 (stranger). 5:10, 20. 6:24 (strange woman). 7:5. 20:16. 23:27. 27:2, 13. Ec 6:2. Is 2:6. *28:21. Je 2:21. La 5:2 (aliens). Ob 11 (foreigners). Zp 1:8 (strange). Compare *S#5236h, Ex +12:43. Contrast with *ger* (*S#1616h, Ge +23:4), a term which is applied to Israelites. S. C. Mooney observes that "The *Ger* were favored aliens, who were to enter into the life of Israel. The *Nokri* were the wicked people whom God had promised to drive out of the land" (*Usury: Destroyer of Nations*, p. 148). **sold us.** ver. 41. Ge 29:15-20, 27-30. 30:26. Ex 21:7-11. Ne 5:8.

16. **which God.** See on ver. 1, 9. Ge 30:35-43. **whatsoever.** Ps 45:10.

17. **upon camels.** Ge 24:10, 61. 1 S 30:17.

18. **for to go.** Ge 27:1, 2, 41. 28:21. 35:27-29.

19. **images.** Heb. *teraphim.* ver. 30, 32. Ge ●+30:27. *35:2. Jsh 24:2. Jg 17:4, 5. 18:14-24, 31. 1 S √15:23. 19:13, 16. 2 K 23:24mg. Ezk +21:21mg. Ho 3:4. Zc 10:2. These might have been **images** devoted to superstitious or idolatrous purposes, as they are termed **gods** by Laban in ver. 30. *S#8655h. ver. 34, 35. Jg 17:5. 18:14, 17, 18, 20. 1 S 15:23. 19:13, 16. 2 K 23:24. Ezk 21:21. Ho 3:4. Zc 10:2mg.

20. **unawares to Laban.** Heb. the heart of Laban. See references on ver. 27. ✓171Q20. Figure of speech Synecdoche of the Part B648. The *heart* is put for the whole man, in respect to his knowledge or affection. Here, Jacob baffled Laban's knowledge by hiding his intentions. For other instances of this figure see ver. 26mg, 27. 2 S 15:6. Lk 21:34.

21. **passed.** Ge 2:14. *15:18. Jsh 24:2, 3. **river.** ✓32. Figure of speech Antonomasia; or, Name Change B682. The change of a proper name for a common or appellative noun, or *vice versa*. Here, the Euphrates is called *the river* on account of its greatness. For other instances of this figure, see Jsh 24:2. 1 S 4:21. Ps 72:8. 80:11. Is 62:4. Ho 1:6. 12:13, 14. Mi 7:12. Mt 11:14n. Mk 8:20. Ac 3:14. 22:14. 25:26. **set his.** Ge 46:28. Nu 24:1.

2 K 12:17. Je 50:5. Lk 9:51-53. **Gilead**. ver. 23. Nu 32:1. Dt 3:12. Jsh 13:8, 9. Jg 10:18. 1 K 17:1.

22. third day. Ge 30:36. Ex 14:5, etc. Jb 5:12, 13.

23. brethren. ♪171G, Ge +13:8. Ge 13:8. 24:27. Ex 2:11, 13. **Gilead**. i.e. *perpetual fountain; heap of witness; rolling forever*, ✚S#1568h. ver. 21, 25. Dt 3:12. Jg 7:3. SS 4:1. (1) An extensive and mountainous district which formed the chief part of Manasseh east of Jordan and of Gad, Ge +37:25. (2) A grandson of Manasseh, Nu +26:29; Jsh 17:1. (3) The father of Jephthah, one of the judges of Israel, Jg 11:1, 2. (4) One of the chiefs of the families of Gad, 1 Ch 5:14.

24. the Syrian. Ge 28:5. Dt 26:5. Ho 12:12. **dream**. ver. 10, 29. Ge *20:3. 40:5. 41:1. Nu 12:6. 22:20, 26. 1 K 3:5. Jb *33:15-17, 25. Mt 1:20. 2:12. 27:19. **Take heed**. ver. 42. Ge 24:50. Nu 24:13. 2 S 13:22. Ps 105:14, 15. Is 37:29. **either good or bad**. Heb. from good to bad.

25. pitched. Ge 12:8. 33:18. He 11:9.

26. What. ♪85, Ge +3:9. ♪6, Ge +3:13. ver. 36. Ge 3:13. 4:10. 12:18. 20:9, 10. 26:10. Jsh 7:19. 1 S 13:11. 14:43. 17:29. Jn 18:35. **unawares**. ♪171Q20, Ge +31:20. **carried**. ver. 16. Ge 2:24. 34:29. 1 S 30:2.

27. Wherefore. ♪85K, Ge +3:9. ver. 3-5, 20, 21, 31. Jg 6:27. **secretly**. ♪171Q20, Ge +31:20. **steal away from me**. Heb. hast stolen me. ver. 20mg. **that I**. Pr *26:23-26. **with mirth**. Ge 24:59, 60. Jb 21:11-14. **tabret**. Ex 15:20.

28. kiss. ver. 55. Ge 29:13. Ex 4:27. Ru 1:9, 14. 1 K 19:20. Ac 20:37. **foolishly**. ver. 3, 13, 24. 1 S 13:13. 2 Ch 16:9. 1 C 2:14.

29. the power. Dt 28:32. Ne 5:5. Jb 12:6. Ps 52:1. Pr *3:27. Mi 2:1. Jn 19:10, 11. **the God**. ver. 42, 53. Ge 28:13. Jsh 24:2, 3. 2 K 19:10. Da 2:47. 3:28. 6:20, 26. S#430h. ver. ◑30. Ge 1:1. **yesternight**. ver. 24. Take. Ac 5:38, 39. 9:5.

30. my gods. ver. +*19. Ex 12:12. Nu 33:4. Jg 6:31. *18:24. 1 S 5:2-6. 2 S 5:21. Ps +*82:1. +*138:1. Is 37:19. 46:1, 2. Je 10:11. 43:12. Jn +*10:35. S#430. ver. ◑29. Ex 18:11. 1 S 5:7. 1 K 18:24. 2 K 18:34. Ps 86:8.

31. Because. ver. 26, 27. Ge 20:11. Pr 29:25.

32. whomsoever. This was rash, and might have produced fatal effects; but Jacob was partial to Rachel, and did not suspect her; and he was indignant at being accused of a crime which he deeply abhorred (Scott). ver. 19, 30. Ge 44:9-12. Jg ◑11:29-40. **before**. ver. 23. Ge 13:8. 19:7. 30:33. 1 S 12:3-5. 2 C 8:20, 21. 12:17-19. **For Jacob**. 1 S 14:24-29. 1 C 13:5.

33. Leah's. Ge 24:28, 67.

34. had taken. ver. 17, 19. **furniture**. The word *car* rendered *furniture*, from the Arabic root *to be round*, properly denotes *a large round pannier*, placed one on each side of a camel, for women to ride in. It is a hamper, like a cradle, having a back, head, and sides, like a great chair. Moryson describes them as 'two long chairs like cradles, covered with red cloth, to hang on the two sides of the camel' (*Journey from Aleppo to Jerusalem*, 1596, p. 247). Hanway (*Travels*, Vol. i. p. 190) calls them *kedgavays*, which 'are a kind of covered chairs, which the Persians hang over their camels in the manner of panniers, and are big enough for one person to sit in.' Thevenot (vol. i. p. 177) who calls them *counes*, says that they lay over them a cover which keeps them both from the rain and sun; and Mailet (Lett. p. 230) describes them as covered cages,

hanging on each side of a camel. (See Harmer, Obser. vol. i. p. 445.) The late Editor of Calmet has furnished a correct delineation of these *cars*, as seen on one side of a camel, copied from Mr. Dalton's *Prints of Egyptian Figures*. Is 66:20n. **searched**. Heb. felt.

35. my lord. Ge 18:12. Ex +*20:12. Le 19:3. Ep +*6:1. 1 P 2:18. 3:6. Heb. the eyes of my lord. ♪155A. Figure of speech Prosopopoeia; or, Personification: things represented as persons B861: the members of the human body. Here, eyes. For other instances of this figure, see Ge 45:5mg. 48:14. Dt 13:8. 1 K 20:6. Jb 29:11. 31:7. Ps 35:10. 68:31. 73:9. 103:1. 119:82. 137:5. 145:15. Pr 10:32. Is 13:18. Ezk 20:7. Mt 6:3. 1 C 12:15, 16. 2 P 2:14. **rise up**. Le *19:32. 1 K 2:19. **custom**. Ge 18:11. Le 15:19.

36. was wroth. Ge 30:2. 34:7. 49:7. Nu 16:15. 2 K 5:11. 13:19. Pr 28:1. Mk 3:5. Ep 4:26. Ja 1:19, 20. **pursued**. 1 S 17:53.

37. set it here. See on ver. 32. Jsh 7:23. 1 S 12:3, 4. Mt 18:16. 1 C 6:4, 5. 1 Th 2:10. He 13:18. 1 P 2:12. 3:16.

38. twenty. ver. 41. **ewes**. Ge 30:27, 30. Ex 23:26. Dt 28:4. **the rams**. Ezk 34:2-4.

39. torn of. Ex 22:10, 31. Le 22:8. 1 S 17:34, 35. Jn 10:12, 13. **I bare**. Ex 22:10-13. **or stolen**. Ex 22:12. Lk 2:8.

40. in the day. Ex 2:19-22. 3:1. Ps 78:70, 71. Ho 12:12. Lk 2:8. Jn 21:15-17. He 13:7. 1 P 5:2-4. **frost by night**. Je *36:30n.

41. fourteen. ver. 38. Ge 29:18-30. 30:33-40. 1 C 15:10. 2 C 11:26. **ten times**. See on ver. +*7.

42. Except. ver. 24, 29. Ps *124:1-3. **the fear**. ver. 53. Ge 27:33. Ps 76:11, 12. 124:1. Is *8:13. ♪121R6. Figure of speech Metonymy of the Adjunct B601. Fear is put for God who is feared, or for any object of fear. For other instances of this figure see ver. 53. Ps 53:5. Pr 1:26, 27. 3:25. Is 8:13. 2 C 5:11. **hath seen**. See on ver. 12. Ge 11:5. 16:11, 13. 29:32. Ex *3:7. 1 Ch 12:17. Ps 31:7. **rebuked**. Ju *9.

43. cattle. ver. 1. Ge 30:32, 42. **do**. Ge 22:12. 27:45. Ex 14:11.

44. let us. Ge 15:18. 21:22-32. 26:28-31. 1 S 20:14-17. **a witness**. ver. 48, 52. Ge 21:30. Dt 31:19, 21, 26. Jsh 22:27. 24:25-27.

45. stone. Ge 28:18-22.

46. brethren. ver. 23, 32, 37, 54. **Gather**. Jsh 4:5-9, 20-24. 7:26. 2 S 18:17. Ec 3:5. **an heap**. The word *gal* rendered *heap* properly signifies a round heap or circle. Jsh 4:5. Jg 2:1. 3:19. 20. 1 S 7:16. 10:8, 17. 11:15. 13:7. 15:33. 2 S 19:15, 40. 2 K 2:1.

47. Jegar-sahadutha. *Chald.* that is, the heap of witness. ✱S#3026h. **Galeed**. Heb. that is, the heap of witness. ✱S#1567h. ver. 48. Ps 108:8. He 12:1.

48. This heap. Jsh 24:27. **Galeed**. *or*, Gilead. ver. 23. Dt 2:36. 3:16. Jsh 13:8, 9.

49. Mizpah. ♪Gal i.e. a beacon, or watch-tower. Jsh 11:3n. 13:26. Jg 10:17. 11:11, *29, 34, Mizpeh. 1 S 7:5. 1 K 15:22. Ho 5:1. ✱S#4708h; Jsh 11:8. 15:38. 18:26. Jg 11:29, 29. 1 S 7:5, *6, 7. 22:3. 2 Ch 20:24. Je 40:6, 8, 12, 13. 41:1. (1) The place on Mount Gilead where Jacob made a covenant with Laban and put up a heap of stones as a witness, Ge 31:43-49. It is called Mizpeh of Gilead in Jg 11:29. Jephthah met his daughter there, Jg 11:34. (2) A city of Moab, 1 S 22:3. (3) The land of Mizpeh, in northern Palestine, occupied by the Hivites, Jsh 11:3. It may be the same as Number 4. (4) The valley of Mizpeh, Jsh 11:3, 8. (5) A city of Judah, Jsh 15:38. (6) A city of Benjamin, Jsh 18:26. Saul was elected king there, 1 S 10:17-21. **watch between**. 1 S 12:22-24. *20:42. 2 Ch 16:9. Jb 31:4. 34:21. Pr 5:21. 15:3. Je 16:17. 32:19. Ho 7:2. **when we**. Nu ●6:24-26. Ac 20:32-38. 2 C 13:11. Ph 1:4, 5. 2 T 1:3, 4. He 13:18-21. **absent**. ʃ121S2, Ge +21:6.

50. **afflict**. Le 18:18. Mt 19:5, 6. **God is witness**. Jg 11:10. 1 S 12:5. Je 29:23. +*42:5. Mi 1:2. Ml 2:14. 3:5. 1 Th 2:5.

51. **I have cast**. For *yarithi*, I have set up, we may read, Thou hast set up, with one Heb. and one Sam. MS.: see ver. 45.

52. **heap**. See on ver. 44, 45, 48.

53. **God of Abraham**. Ge 11:24-29, 31. 17:7. 22:20-24. 24:3, 4. Ex 3:6. Jsh 24:2. **their father**. For *avihem*, Their father, several MSS. read *avichem*, Your father, for Terah was an idolater: see Jsh 24:2. **judge**. Ge 16:5. **sware**. Ge 14:22. 21:23, 24. 24:3. 26:28-31. **fear**. ʃ121R6, Ge +31:42. See on ver. 42. Dt 6:13.

54. **offered sacrifice**. *or*, killed beasts. ʃ121N1. Figure of speech Metonymy of the Adjunct B587. The adjunct or accident is put for the subject. The abstract is put for the concrete; or the attribute is put for that to which anything is attributed. Here, killing of beasts is put for offering sacrifice, see marginal rendering. For other instances of this figure, see Ge +*6:5n. 42:38. 46:34. Jg *20:42n. 1 S 15:29. 2 S 23:23. Ne 5:9. Jb 5:16. 31:21. 32:7. Ps 12:1. 65:8. 68:18. 110:3. Pr 23:21. Is 57:13. Je 2:5. Ezk 44:6. Am 8:3. Lk 1:78. Jn 11:40. Ro 3:30. 8:19. 11:7. Ep 1:21. Ph 1:16. 1 P 2:17. Re 9:11. **did eat**. Ge 21:8. 26:30. 37:25. Ex 18:12. 2 S 3:20, 21.

55. **and kissed**. ver. 28. Ge 33:4. Ru 1:14. **blessed**. Ge 24:60. 28:1. Nu 23:5, 8, 11. Dt 23:5. Pr *16:7. **returned**. Ge 18:33. 30:25. Nu 24:25. Dt 32:36. Ps 76:10. Ac 28:4, 5.

GENESIS 32

Jacob has a vision of angels, 1, 2. He sends a message to Esau; and, alarmed by the report of his coming with four hundred men, prays for deliverance, 3-12. He prepares a present for Esau; instructs his servants, and passes the brook Jabbok, 13-23. He wrestles at Peniel; prevails, is blessed, and called Israel; yet goes away halting, 24-32.

1. **angels**. Ps *91:11. 1 C 3:22. Ep 3:10. He *1:14.

2. **God's**. Jsh 5:14. 2 K 6:17. Ps 34:7. *103:21. 148:2. Da 10:20. Lk *2:13. **the name**. Jsh 21:38. 2 S 2:8, 12. 17:24, 26, 27. 1 K 2:8. 4:14. **Mahanaim**. i.e. two hosts, or camps. ✱S#4266h. Jsh 13:26, 30. *21:38. 2 S 2:8, 12, 29. 17:24, 27. 19:32. 1 K 2:8. +4:14. 1 Ch 6:80. SS ●6:13.

3. **sent**. Ml 3:1. Lk 9:52. 14:31, 32. **Seir**. Ge 14:6. 33:14, 16. 36:6-8. Nu 24:18. Dt *2:5, 22. *33:2. Jsh 24:4. **country**. Heb. field. **Edom**. See on Ge 25:30.

4. **my lord**. ver. 5, 18. Ge 4:7. 23:6. 27:29, 37. 33:8. Ex 32:22. 1 S 26:17. Pr 6:3. *15:1. Lk 14:11. 1 P 3:6. **servant**. 1 K 20:32. Ec 10:4.

5. **have oxen**. Ge 30:43. 31:1, 16. 33:11. Jb 6:22. **may find**. Ge 33:8, 15. 47:25. Ru 2:2. 1 S 1:18. 2 S 16:4.

6. **and four**. ver. 8, 11. Ge 27:40, 41. 33:1. Am 5:19.

7. **greatly**. Ex 14:10. Ps 18:4, 5. 31:13. 55:4, 5. 61:2. 142:4. Mt 8:26. Jn 16:33. Ac 14:22. 2 C 1:4, 8-10. 2 T 3:12. **distressed**. Ge 35:3. Ps 107:6. **and he**. Ps 112:5. Pr 2:11. Is 28:26. Mt 10:16.

8. **If Esau come**. Ge 33:1-3. Pr +*22:3. Mt 10:16.

9. **Jacob**. 1 S *30:6. 2 Ch *20:6, 12. 32:20. Ps 34:4-6. +*50:15. *91:15. Ph *4:6, 7. **O God**. Ge 17:7. *28:13. 31:29, 42, 53. Ex 3:6. **the Lord**. Ge *31:3, 13.

10. **am**. ʃ96C1, Ge +4:1. **not worthy of the least of all**. Heb. less than all. Ge 18:27. 2 S *7:18. Jb 42:5, 6. Ps 16:2. Is 6:5. *63:7. Da 9:8, 9. Lk 5:8. 17:10. 2 C 12:11. 1 T 1:12-15. 1 P 5:5. 1 J 1:8-10. **mercies**. ʃ121C1B, Ge +20:13. Ge *24:27. Ps 8:5. **truth**. Ge 24:27. 28:15. Ps 61:7. 85:10. Mi 7:20. **my staff**. Ge 28:10, 11. Jb *8:7. Ps 18:35. **two bands**. ver. 5, 7. Ge 30:43. Dt 8:18. Jb 17:9. Ps 18:35. 84:7. Pr *4:18.

11. **Deliverer**. 1 S 12:10. 24:15. Ps 16:1. 25:20. 31:2. 43:1. 59:1, 2. 119:134. 142:6. Pr 18:19. Da 3:17. Mt 6:13. **the mother**. Dt 22:6. Ho 10:14. **with**. Heb. upon.

12. **thou**. Ge 32:6. Ex 32:13. Nu 23:19. 1 S 15:29. 2 S 7:25. 1 K 8:25. Ps 119:58. Is *43:26. Mt *24:35. 2 T 2:13. T 1:2. He 6:17. *10:23. **I will**. Ge 28:13-15. 46:3, 4. **as the sand**. ʃ102B, Ge +13:16. ʃ138B, Ge +13:16.

13. **which**. 1 S 25:8. **to his hand**. Or, *under his hand* or power; i.e. what Providence had put in his power or possession. 1 K 10:14. Ps 90:12. **a present**. ver. 20, 21. Ge 18:2. 33:10. 42:6. 43:11, 26. 1 S 25:27. Pr 17:8. *18:16. 19:6. 21:14.

14. **hundred**. Ge 30:43. 31:9, 16. Dt 8:18. 1 S 25:2. Jb 1:3. 42:12.

16. **space**. ver. 20. Ge 33:8, 9. Ps 112:5. Pr 2:11. Is 28:26. Mt 10:16.

17. **Whose art**. Ge 33:3.

18. **thy servant**. See on ver. 4, 5.

20. **I will appease**. Ge 43:11. 1 S 25:17-35. Jb 42:8, 9. Pr 15:18. 16:14. *21:14. **peradventure**. 1 S 6:5. 1 K 20:31. Jon 3:9. 2 T 2:25. **of me**. Heb. my face. ʃ171Q, Ge +3:19. Jb 42:8mg, 9mg. Pr 6:35mg.

22. **his two wives**. ver +4:19. 29:21-35. 30:1-24. 35:18, 22-26. 1 T 5:8. **the ford Jabbok**. i.e. *emptying, pouring out, flowing*, ✱S#2999h. Nu 21:24. Dt 2:37. 3:16. Jsh *12:2. Jg 11:13, 22.

23. **sent them**. Heb. caused to pass.

24. **left alone**. Ps 127:2. Ac 12:6. **wrestled**. T#1300. Ge 30:8. Lk 13:24. 22:44. Ro 8:26, 27. *15:30. Ep 6:12, 18. Col 2:1. *4:12. He 5:7. **man**. ver. 28, 30. Ge 48:16. Is 32:2. Ho 12:3-5. 1 C *15:47. **breaking of the day**. Heb. ascending of the morning. ver. 26. Ge 19:15. Ex 14:27. Jg 19:25. Ps +*30:5. +*46:5mg. SS 2:17. ʃ24A. Anitimereia of the Verb B492: Infinitive for a Noun. For other instances of this figure see 1 K 8:52. 1 Ch 16:36. 2 Ch 3:3. Ps 101:3. 132:1. Is 4:4. Da 10:1. Lk 7:21. Ph x?1:23. He 2:15. 4:1.

25. **that he**. Ge 19:22. Nu 14:13, 14. Is 41:14. 45:11. Ho 12:3, 4. Mt 15:22-28. Lk 11:5-8. **touched**. ver. 32. Ps 30:6, 7. Mt 26:41, 44. 2 C *12:7-9. **thigh**. ʃ88, Ge +24:2.

26. **Let me go**. Ex 32:10. Dt 9:14. SS 7:5. Is 45:11. *64:7. Lk *24:28, 29. **I will not**. SS 3:4. Ho 12:4. Mt 15:28. Lk *18:1-7. Ro 8:37. 1 C 15:58. 2 C 12:8, 9. He 5:7. **thou bless**. 1 Ch 4:10. Ps 67:1, 6, 7. 115:12, 13.

27. **what**. ver. 29. Ge ●27:8.

28. **Thy name.** Ge 17:5, 15. 33:20. 35:10. Nu 13:16. 2 S 12:25. 2 K 17:34. Is 62:2-4. 65:15. Jn 1:42. Re 2:17. **Israel.** i.e. *a prince of God; prevailing with God,* ✣S#3478h. Ge 35:10, 10, 21, 22, 22. 37:3, 13. 42:5. 43:6, 8, 11. 45:21, 28. 46:1, 2, 5, 8, 29, 30. 47:27, 29, 31. 48:2, 8, 10, 11, 14, 20, 21. 49:2. 50:2. Ex 1:1, 7. 6:14. 32:13. Nu 26:5. Jg 18:29. 1 K 18:31, 36. 2 K 17:34. 1 Ch 1:34. 2:1. 5:1, 1, 3. 6:38. 7:29. 29:10, 18. 2 Ch 30:6. Ezr 8:18. **as a prince.** Or, according to the LXX., Vulgate, Houbigant, Dathe, and Rosenmuller, 'because thou hast had power with God, thou shalt also prevail with men.' There is a beautiful antithesis between the two terms, with *Elohim,* God, the Almighty, with *anashim,* weak, feeble men, as the word imports; seeing thou hast had power with the Almighty, surely thou shalt prevail over perishing mortals. **power.** ver. 24. Ho *12:3-5. **with men.** Ge *25:31. *27:33-36. 31:24, 36-57. *33:4. 1 S 26:25. Pr *16:7. **prevailed.** ſ22D1. Anthropopatheia or Anthropomorphism B891: Circumstances are attributed to God: Negative, when He is represented as not being able to do something. For other instances of this figure see Ex 32:10. Ps 106:23. Is 1:13. Ezk 23:18.

29. **thy name.** T#1534. Ex 3:13, 14. **Wherefore.** ver. 27. Dt 29:29. Jg *13:16-18. Jb 11:7. Pr 30:4. Is 9:6. Lk 1:19. **blessed.** ver. 26. Ge 27:28, 29. 28:3, 4, 13, 14. Ho 6:1.

30. **Jacob.** ver. 31, Penuel. Ge 28:19. Jg 8:8, 17. 1 K 12:25. **Peniel.** i.e. *the face of God; divine presence,* ✳S#6439h. ver. 31. Jg 8:8, 8, 9, 17. 1 K 12:25. 1 Ch 4:4. 8:25. Peniel, or Penuel, was evidently situated near the ford of Jabbok, on the north of that stream, about forty miles from Jerusalem. **I have seen.** T#1772. Ge 16:13. Ex *24:10, 11. 33:14, 19-23. Nu 12:8. Dt *5:24. *34:10. Jg *6:22, 23. *13:21, 22. Is *6:5. Jn √1:18. 1 C *13:12. 2 C 3:18. 4:6. Ga 1:6. Ep 1:17. Col *1:15. 2 T 1:10. He 11:27. **life.** Heb. *nephesh,* soul. Ge +44:30. **preserved.** or, delivered. The common opinion very naturally was, that the sight of God would cause death (Young); see Ge 16:13. 32:30. Ex *20:19. 33:18, √20. Dt 5:25. Jg 6:22. 13:22.

31. **rose upon.** Ge 19:15, 23. Ml 4:2. **he halted.** ver. 25. Ps 38:17. 2 C 12:7, 9. **thigh.** ſ88, Ge +24:2.

32. **eat not.** 1 S 5:5. **unto this day.** Ge +19:38.

GENESIS 33

Esau and Jacob meet, and after an amicable conference, Esau departs, 1-16. Jacob abides at Succoth; and buys a field, and builds an altar at Shechem, 17-20.

1. **lifted.** ſ144A12, Ge +22:13. **Esau came.** Ge 27:41, 42. 32:6. **And he.** Ge 32:7, 16.

2. **Rachel.** Ge 29:30. 30:22-24. 37:3. Ml 3:17. **hindermost.** Ge +*44:30.

3. **passed.** Jn 10:4, 11, 12, 15. **bowed.** Ge 18:2. 42:6. 43:26. Pr 6:3. Ec 10:4. Lk 14:11. **seven times.** 1 S 2:5.

4. **embraced.** Ge *32:28. 43:30, 34. 45:2, 15. Ezr 7:27, 28. Ne 1:11. Jb 2:12. Ps +*34:4. Pr +*16:7. *21:1. **fell on.** Ge 45:14, 15. 46:29. Lk 15:20. Ac 20:37.

5. **lifted.** ſ144A12, Ge +22:13. **with.** Heb. to. **children.** Ge 30:2. *41:52. 48:9. Ru 4:13. 1 S 1:27. 1 Ch *28:5. Ps +*127:3. Is 8:18. He 2:13.

8. **What meanest thou by all this drove?** Heb. What is all this band to thee? Ge 32:13-20. **to find.** Ge 32:5. 39:5. Est 2:17.

9. **have enough.** Ge 27:39. Pr 30:15. Ec 4:8. **my brother.** Ge 4:9. 27:41. Jg 20:23. Pr 16:7. Ac 9:17. 21:20. Phm 7, 16. **keep that thou hast unto thyself.** Heb. be that to thee that *is* thine.

10. **said.** ſ63F. Ellipsis B58: Where the omitted word is to be supplied from a *contrary* word. Here, supply "Jacob *refused and* said." This is latent in the contrary words which follow. Other instances (proposed by EWB in B) of this figure are: Ge 33:15. 49:4. Jg 5:6. Ps 7:11. 65:8. 66:20. 84:10. Pr 19:1. 24:17, 18. 28:16. Je 18:15. Da 3:15. Lk 13:9. Ro 6:17. 1 C 7:19. 2 C 8:14. 1 T 4:3. **if now.** Ge 19:19. 47:29. 50:4. Ex 33:12, 13. Ru 2:10. 1 S 20:3. Je 31:2. **receive.** To accept a present from an inferior was a customary pledge of friendship; but returning it implied disaffection. It was on this ground that Jacob was so urgent with Esau to receive his present. **present.** Ge +32:13. **I have seen.** Ge 32:30. 43:3. 2 S 3:13. 14:24, 28, 32. Jb 33:26. Ps 41:11. Mt 18:10. Re 22:4.

11. **my blessing.** Ge 32:13-20. Jsh 15:19. Jg 1:15. 1 S 25:27. 30:26. 2 K *5:15. 2 C 9:5, 6. ſ108B. Idiom B825: *blessing* signifies a gift. For other instances of this idiom, see 1 S 25:27. Ro 15:29. 2 C 9:5. **and because.** ver. 9. Ph 4:11, 12, 18. **enough.** Heb. all things. Ro 8:31, 32. 1 C 3:21. 2 C 6:10. Ph 4:12, 18. 1 T 4:8. **urged him.** 2 K 2:17. 5:16, 23. Lk 14:23.

13. **the children.** 1 Ch 22:5. Pr 12:10. Is 40:11. Ezk 34:15, 16, 23-25. Jn 21:15-17.

14. **according as,** etc. Heb. according to the foot of the work, etc.; and according to the foot of the children. Dt +11:6mg. **be able.** Is 40:11. Mk 4:33. Ro 15:1. 1 C 3:2. 9:19-22. **unto Seir.** See on Ge *32:3. Dt 2:1. Jg 5:4. 2 Ch 20:10. Ezk 25:8. 35:2, 3.

15. **leave.** Heb. set, *or* place. **some.** ſ63F, ver. +10. **What needeth it?** Heb. Wherefore *is* this? **find grace.** Ge 34:11. 47:25. Ru 2:13. 1 S 25:8. 2 S 16:4.

17. **Succoth.** Jsh 13:27. Jg 8:5, 8, 16. 1 K 7:46. Ps 60:6. **Succoth.** i.e. Booths. ✳S#5523h. Ex 12:37. 13:20. Nu 33:5, 6. Jsh 13:27. Jg 8:5, 6, 8, 14, 14, 15, 16. 1 K 7:46. 2 Ch 4:17. Ps *60:6. *108:7. (1) The place to which Jacob went after leaving Esau, and built a house and made booths for his cattle, Ge 33:17. (2) It was given to Gad, Jsh 13:27. Jg 8:5, 6, 8, 14, 14, 15, 16. (3) The Israelite's first encampment in the desert after leaving Egypt, Ex 12:37. 13:20. Nu 33:5, 6. (4) A city in Ephraim, 1 K 7:46. 2 Ch 4:17. Ps 60:6. 108:7.

18. **Shalem.** i.e. *complete, perfect,* ✳S#8003h. Strong's Hebrew Lexicon notes 'by mistake for a name.' The name is given as ✳S#8004h. The word *Shalem,* in the Samaritan *Shalom,* should probably be rendered *in peace,* or *in safety,* as it is translated by the Chaldee, Arabic, Coverdale, and Matthewes. Ge 14:18. 18:21. *34:2. Ps 76:2. Jn *3:23. 4:5. Ac *7:16. **a city of Shechem.** Or, rather, the city of Shechem. i.e. *shoulder, back, ridge; diligence; early rising, early in the morning,* ✣S#7927h. Ge 35:4. 37:12, 13, 14. Jsh 17:7. 20:7. 21:21. 24:1, 25. Jg 8:31. 9:1, 2, 3, 6, 6, 7, 18, 20, 20, 23, 23, 24, 25, 26, 26, 31, 34, 39, 41, 46, 47, 49, 57. 21:19. 1 K 12:1, 1. 12:25. 1 Ch 6:67. 7:28. 2 Ch 10:1, 1. Ps 60:6. 108:7. Je 41:5. Jn 4:5, Sychar. Ac 7:16, Sychem. (1) The son of Hamor, Ge +*33:19. (2) A son of Gilead, the son of Manasseh,

✳S#7928h: Nu 26:31; Jsh 17:2. (3) An Israelite, the son of Shemidah, 1 Ch 7:19. (4) A city of Samaria, thirty-four miles north of Jerusalem, also called Sichem, Ge 12:6; Sychem, Ac 7:16; and is generally supposed to be the same as Sychar, Jn 4:5. **Padan-aram**. Ge 25:20. 28:6, 7. 35:9. 46:15.

19. **bought**. Ge 23:17-20. 49:30-32. Jsh *24:32. Jn *4:5. Ac 7:16. **Hamor**. i.e. *an ass*, ✳S#2544h. Ge 34:2, 4, 6, 8, 13, 18, 18, 20, 24, 26. Jsh 24:32. Jg 9:28. Ac 7:16, Emmor. **Shechem**'s. ✛S#7928h. Ge 34:2, 4, 6, 8, 11, 13, 18, 20, 24, 26, 26. Jsh 24:32, 32. Jg 9:28, 28. **pieces of money**. Jb 42:11. *or*, lambs.

20. **altar**. Ge 8:20. 12:7, 8. 13:18. 21:33. **El-elohe-Israel**. i.e. God, the God of Israel. ✳S#415h, only here. Ge *32:28. 35:7.

GENESIS 34

Dinah visits the daughters of the land, and is defiled by Shechem, who loves her and proposes to marry her, 1-12. Jacob's sons insidiously consent, on condition that all the Shechemites be circumcised; to which at Shechem's instance they submit, 13-24. Simeon and Levi murder all the men of Shechem, plunder the city, make captives of the women and children, and recover Dinah, 25-29. Jacob bitterly complains, and his sons excuse their conduct, 30, 31.

1. A.M. 2272. B.C. 1732. **Dinah**. Ge 30:21. 46:15. **the daughters**. Ge 26:34. *27:46. 28:6. 30:13. Je 2:36. 1 T *5:13. T *2:4, 5.

2. **Shechem**. Ge 10:17. 33:19. **Hivite**. Ge +10:17. **saw her**. Ge 6:2. 39:6, 7. Jg 14:1. 2 S 11:2. Jb +*31:1, 9. Pr 13:20. Mt *5:28. **took her**. Ge 20:2. **defiled her**. Heb. humbled her. Dt 21:14. 22:24, 29. Jg 19:24, 25. 20:5. 2 S 13:22. La 5:11. Ezk 22:10, 11.

3. **soul**. Ru 1:14. 1 S 18:1. Ps +*84:2. Mt +*11:29. +*22:37. Re +*18:14. Heb. *nephesh*. ✛S#5315h. "Nephesh" is sometimes used of man manifesting feelings, affections, passions, and exercising mental faculties. In this sense also rendered "soul" in the following passages: Ge 34:8. 42:21. 49:6. Le 26:11, 15, 30, 43. Nu 21:4. Dt 4:9, 29. 6:5. 10:12. 11:13, 18. 13:3. 26:16. 30:2, 6, 10. Jsh 22:5. 23:14. Jg 10:16. 16:16. 1 S 1:10, 15. 18:1, 1. 20:4. 23:20. 30:6. 2 S 5:8. 1 K 2:4. 8:48. 11:37. 2 K 4:27. 23:3, 25. 1 Ch 22:19. 2 Ch 6:38. 15:12. 34:31. Jb 3:20. 7:11. 9:21. 10:1, 1. +√14:22. 19:2. 21:25. 23:13. 24:12. 27:2. 30:16, 25. Ps 6:3. 11:5. 13:2. *19:7. 24:4. 25:1, 13. 31:7, 9. 33:20. 34:2. 35:9. 42:1, 2, 4, 5, 6, 11. 43:5. 44:25. 49:18. 57:1, 6. 62:1, 5. 63:1, 5, 8. 69:10. 77:2. 84:2. 86:4, 4. 88:3. 94:10. 103:1, 2, 22. 104:1, 35. 107:5, 9, 9, 26. 116:7. 119:20, 25, 28, 81, 129, 167. 123:4. 130:5, 6. 131:2. 138:3. 139:14. 143:6, 8, 11, 12. 146:1. Pr 2:10. 3:22. 13:4, 4, 19. 16:24. 19:2, 18. 21:10. 22:25. 24:14. 25:13. 29:17. Ec 2:24. 6:3. 7:28. SS 1:7. 3:1, 2, 3, 4. 5:6. 6:12. Is 1:14. 26:8, 9. 32:6. 38:15. 42:1. 55:2. 58:10, 10, 11. 61:10. 66:3. Je 4:31. 5:9, 29. 6:8, 16. 9:9. 12:7. 13:17. 14:19. 31:12, 14, 25, 25. 32:41. 50:19. La 3:17, 20, 24. Ezk 7:19. 24:21. Jon 2:7. Hab 2:4. Zc 11:8, 8. For the other uses of *nephesh* see Ge +2:7. **kindly unto the damsel**. Heb. to the heart of the damsel. Ge 50:21mg. Jg 19:3mg. 2 S 19:7mg. 2 Ch 30:22mg. 32:6mg. Is 40:2mg. Ho 2:14mg.

4. **Get me**. Ge 21:21. Jg 14:2. 2 S 13:13.

5. **defiled**. ver. 13, 17. Nu 19:13. 2 K 23:10. Ps 79:1. Ezk 18:6. 22:11. 23:17. **now his**. Ge 30:35. 37:13,

14. 1 S 10:27. 16:11. 17:15. 2 S 13:22. Lk 15:25, 29. **held**. Le 10:3. Ps 39:9.

7. **were**. Ge 46:7. 2 S 13:21. **wrought folly**. Ex 19:5, 6. Dt 22:21. Jsh +*7:15. Jg 19:22-25. 20:6. 2 S 13:12, 13. Ps 93:5. Pr 7:7. Is 9:16 (✳S#5039h). Ho 2:10. 1 P 2:9. **in Israel**. Jg 20:6, 10. **which thing**. Ge 20:9. Le 4:2, 13, 27. Dt 23:17. 1 C 6:18. 10:8. Ep 5:3. Col 3:5. 1 T 5:13. He 13:4. Ja 3:10.

8. **The soul**. ver. +3. 1 K 11:2. Ps 63:1. 84:2. 119:20.

9. **make ye marriages**. Ge 6:2. 19:14. 24:3. 26:34, 35. 27:46. Dt 7:3.

10. **and the land**. ver. 21-23. Ge 13:9. 20:15. 42:34. 47:27.

11. **Let me find**. Ge 18:3. 33:15.

12. **dowry**. Ge 24:53. 29:18. 31:41. Ex 22:16, 17. Dt 22:28, 29. 1 S 18:25-27. 2 S 3:14. Ho 3:2. Mt 14:17. **gift**. √121I2, Ge +2:17.

13. **deceitfully**. Ge 25:27-34. +*27:19. Jg 15:3. 2 S 13:23-29. Jb 13:4, 7. Ps 12:2. Pr 12:13, 18-20. 24:28, 29. 26:24-26. Is 59:13. Mi 7:2. Mt 28:13. Ro 12:19. Ep *4:25. 1 Th 5:15. **said**. 2 Ch 22:10. Ps 137:5-9.

14. **uncircumcised**. Ge 17:11. Jsh 5:2-9. 1 S 14:6. 17:26, 36. 2 S 1:20. 15:7. 1 K 21:9. Mt 2:8, 13. 23. Ro 4:11.

15. **If ye**. Ga 4:12.

19. **because**. Ge 29:20. SS 8:6. Is 62:4. **honorable**. Ge 41:20. Nu 22:15. 1 S 22:14. 2 K 5:1. 1 Ch 4:9. Is 3:3-5. 5:13. 23:8, 9. Ac 13:50. 17:12.

20. **the gate**. Ge +14:7. 22:17. 23:10. Dt 17:5. Ru 4:1. Jb 29:7. Pr 31:23. Am 5:10, 12, 15. Zc 8:16.

22. **consent**. ver. 15-17.

23. **not their**. Pr 1:12, 13. 23:4, 5. 28:20. Jn 2:16. 6:26, 27. Ac 19:24-26. 1 T 6:6-10.

24. **went out**. Ge 23:10, 18. **every male**. Ge 17:23. Is 1:10-16. Mt 7:6. Ro 2:28, 29. 1 C 7:19.

25. **sore**. Jsh 5:6, 8. **Simeon**. Ge 29:33, 34. 49:5-7. Nu 31:7, 17. Pr 4:16. 6:34, 35. **took**. Ro *12:19. 1 *Th 5:15. **slew**. Ge 49:6. 2 Ch 32:25.

26. **edge**. Heb. mouth. Ex 17:13. Nu 21:24. Dt 13:15. 32:42. Jsh 6:21. 2 S 2:26. 2 K 10:25mg. Is 31:8. √144A2. Pleonasm B407: "mouth" seems redundant when used with the word *sword*. The figure emphasizes the fact that it is not a mere sword, but a sword with its sharp devouring edge, which is thus compared to a mouth. For other instances of this figure see Ge 43:7mg. Ex 17:13. Nu 26:56. Dt 13:15. Pr 22:6. Ezk 6:11. Am 7:11. Lk 21:24. He 11:34.

27. **spoiled**. Est 9:10, 16. 1 T 6:10. **they**. ver. 2, 31. Ex 2:14. Jsh 7:1, 21. See on ver. 13.

28. **They took**. Nu 31:17. Dt 8:17, 18. Jb 1:15, 16. 20:5.

29. **wealth**. Heb. strength. √121N2. Figure of speech Metonymy of the Adjunct B589, here *strength* put for wealth. For other instances of this figure see Ex 14:4. Le 13:4, 13, 31, 50. Dt 8:17. 1 S 14:48. 1 K 7:9. Jb 6:22. 31:26mg. 37:21. Ps 22:3. Pr 5:10. 15:6. 27:24mg. Is 1:18. 10:14, 27. 30:6, 7. Is √60:5mg. Je 20:5. 40:7. Ezk 38:4. Ob 11mg. Hab 3:4. Mt 8:3. Mk 14:54. Ac 14:15. Ro √11:25. Ga 3:13. Ep 5:8. **and spoiled**. Ge *35:5.

30. **Ye have**. Ge 49:5-7. Jsh 7:25. 1 K 18:18. 1 Ch 2:7. Pr 11:17, 29. 15:27. **to stink**. Ex 5:21. 1 S 13:4. 27:12. 2 S 10:6. 1 Ch 19:6. **Canaanites**. Ge +10:18. **Perizzites**. Ge +13:7. 15:20, 21. **and I being**. Dt 4:27. 7:7. 26:5. 33:6. 1 Ch 16:12, *19. Ps 105:12. **and I**

shall. Ge 12:2, 12. 28:13, 14. *42:36. 1 S 16:2. 27:1. Ro 4:18-20.

31. **Should he.** See on ver. 13. Ge 49:7. Pr 6:34.

GENESIS 35

God commands Jacob to go to Bethel, 1. He purges his house of idols, 2-5. He builds an altar at Bethel, 6, 7. The death of Deborah, Rebekah's nurse, 8. The Lord appears to Jacob, and encourages him, and Jacob worships, 9-15. Benjamin is born and Rachel dies, 16-20. Reuben commits incest with Bilhah, 22. The names of Jacob's sons, 23-26. Jacob visits Isaac; Isaac's age, death, and burial, 27-29.

1. **God said.** Ge 22:14. Dt 32:36. Ps 46:1. 91:15. **Bethel.** ver. 7. Ge 12:8. 13:3, 4. *28:10-22. 31:3, 13. Ps 47:4. Ec 5:4-6. Ho 12:4. Na 1:15. **when thou.** Ge 16:8. 27:41-45. Ex 2:15.

2. **unto his.** Ge +*18:19. Jsh *24:15. Ps 101:2-7. **Put away.** Ezk 20:7, 18. 37:23. Ps *101:2-7. **strange.** ver. 4. Ge 17:12, 27. 31:*19, 34. Ex 12:43 (*S#5236h). 20:3, 4. 23:13. Dt 5:7. 6:14. 7:25. 11:28. 32:16. Jsh 23:7. 24:2, 20, 23. Jg 10:16. Ru 1:15. 1 S 7:3. 2 S 7:23. 2 K 17:29. 1 Ch 16:26. Je 5:7. 16:20. Da 5:4. Ac 19:26. 1 C 10:7. 2 C *6:15-17. Ga 4:8. **clean.** ver. 22. Ge 34:2, 24, 25. Ex *19:10, 14. 29:4. 40:12. Le 8:6. 15:5. 17:16. Nu 31:24. 2 K 5:10, 12, 13. Jb 1:5. Ps 51:2, 7. 119:9-11. Ec 5:1. Is 1:16. 52:11. Je 13:27. Ezk *18:31. 20:7. *36:25. Jn 13:10, 11. 2 C 7:1. Ep 5:26. He *10:22. Ja 4:8. 1 P 2:1, 2. Ju 23. **change.** Le 14:9. Nu 8:7, 21. 19:19. Zc 3:3-5. Mt ◑22:11, 12. Ju 23.

3. **who answered.** Ge 28:12, 13. *32:7, 24. Ps 46:1. +*50:15. *66:13, 14. 91:15. *103:1-5. 107:6, 8, 15. *116:1, 2, 16-18. 118:19-22. Is 30:19. **was with.** Ge *28:20. 31:3, 42. Pr *3:6. Is √43:2. ♪15G. Anacoluthon; or, Non-sequence B724: A breaking off of the sequence of thought. Sometimes two equivalent constructions are united in the same proposition. For other instances of this figure see Jsh 23:16. Jg 16:24. Ne 10:30. Mk 6:7. 12:38. Ro 12:4. 1 C 14:5. Ep 5:27, 33.

4. **gave.** Ac 19:18-20. **strange.** ver. +2. Dt 18:10. **earrings.** These rings were not worn as mere ornaments, but for superstitious purposes; perhaps as amulets or charms, first consecrated to some false god, or formed under some constellation, and stamped with magical characters. Maimonides mentions rings and jewels of this kind, with the image of the sun, moon, etc., impressed upon them; and Augustine describes them (Epist. 73) as used for this execrable purpose. Ex 32:2-4. Jg 8:24-27. Is 3:20. Ho 2:12, 13. **hid them.** Ex 32:20. Dt 7:5, 25. 1s 2:20. 30:22. **the oak.** Ge 12:6, 7. Jsh *24:25, 26. Jg 9:6.

5. **terror.** Ge 34:30. Ex *15:15, 16. 23:27. 34:24. Dt *11:25. Jsh *2:9-11. *5:1. 1 S *11:7. 14:15. 2 Ch 14:14. 17:10. Ps 14:5. Ezk 26:17. 32:23.

6. **Luz.** Ge 12:8. 28:19, 22. Jg 1:22-26.

7. **built.** ver. 1, 3. Ec 5:4, 5. **El-bethel.** i.e. the God of Bethel. *S#416h, only here. Ge 28:12, 13, 19, 22. Ex 17:15. Jg 6:24. Ezk 48:35.

8. **Deborah.** i.e. *bee, eloquent,* *S#1683h. (1) The name of the nurse of Rebekah, Ge 35:8. (2) A prophetess and judge of the people of Israel, whose history is told in the most charming manner in Judges. Jg 4:4, 5, 9, 10, 14. 5:1, 7, 12, 15. **Rebekah's.** Ge 24:59.

under an oak. 1 S 31:13. **Allon-bachuth.** i.e. the oak of weeping. *S#439h, only here. Jg 2:1, 5.

9. **God appeared.** Ge 12:7. 17:1. 18:1. 26:2. 28:13. *31:3, 11-13. *32:1, 24-30. *35:1. 46:2, 3. 48:3, 4. Je 31:3. Ho 12:4. Ac 7:2.

10. **thy name shall not.** Ge 17:5, 15. 32:27, 28. 1 K 18:31. 2 K 17:34.

11. **God Almighty.** Ge 17:1. 18:14. 43:14. *48:3, 4. Ex *6:3. 2 C 6:18. **a nation.** Ge 12:2. 13:16. 15:5. 17:5-7, 16. 18:18. 22:17. 28:3, 4, 14. 32:12. 46:3. 48:4. Ex 1:7. Nu ch. 1—26. 1 S to 2 Ch. **and a company of.** Is +*54:1. **and kings.** Ge +*17:6.

12. **the land.** Ge *12:7. 13:14-17. 15:18. *26:3, 4. 28:3, 4, 13. 48:4. Ex 3:8. Jsh ch. 6-21 to Ne ch. 13. **gave.** ♪121I2, Ge +2:17. **thy seed.** Nu +*24:17.

13. **God went.** Ge 11:5. *17:22. 18:33. Jg 6:21. 13:20. Lk 24:31.

14. **set up.** ver. 20. Ge 28:18, 19. Ex 17:15. 1 S 7:12. **pillar.** ♪147D, Ge +1:29. **drink offering.** Le +*23:13.

15. **Bethel.** Ge +12:8. +*28:19.

16. **a little way to come.** Heb. a little piece of ground. Ge 48:7. 2 K 5:19mg. **Ephrath.** Ge 48:7. Ru 1:2. 1 Ch 2:19. Ps 132:6. Mi 5:2. Mt 2:1, 16, 18. **hard labor.** Ge 3:16. Ps 48:6. Is 13:8. 26:17. 42:14. *66:7. Je *30:6. Ho 13:13. Mi 4:9, 10. Mt 24:8. Jn 16:21. 1 Th 5:3. 1 T *2:15.

17. **midwife.** Ge 35:28. Ex 1:15-21. Ezk 16:4. **Fear not.** Ge *30:24. 1 S 4:19-21.

18. A.M. cir. 2275. B.C. cir. 1729. **her soul.** Heb. *nephesh,* Ge +44:30. Ge +*25:8n, 9, 17. 30:1. 1 S 4:20, 21. 1 K √17:22. 2 K 4:32-37. Jb 14:22. 33:18, 22. Ps +*16:10n. ◑+31:5. 88:3. Ec 12:7. La 2:12. Mt +√10:28. Lk 12:20. 23:46. Ac 7:59. 15:26. **Benoni.** i.e. the son of my sorrow. *S#1126h, only here. 1 Ch 4:9. **Benjamin.** i.e. the son of my right hand. Ge 42:38. 44:27-31. Ps 80:17. ✛S#1144h. ver. 24. Ge 42:4, 36. 43:14, 15, 16, 29. 45:12, 14, 22. 46:19, 21. Ex 1:3. 1 Ch 2:2. 7:6. 8:1. The Samaritan has *ben yamim,* the son of days, i.e. of his old age, Ge 44:20. (1) The twelfth and youngest son of Jacob and the second son of Rachel, Ge 35:18. (2) The tribe of Benjamin had their part of the Promised Land adjoining Judah, and when the ten tribes revolted it became part of the kingdom of Judah, Ge +49:27. (3) A grandson of Jediael, 1 Ch 7:10. (4) A descendant of Harim who took a foreign wife, Ezr 10:32. (5) A Jew who repaired part of the wall of Jerusalem, Ne 3:23. (6) A Jew who took part in the ceremonial of purifying the wall of Jerusalem, Ne 12:34. (7) A gate of Jerusalem, Je 20:2; Zc 14:10.

19. **Rachel died.** Ge 48:7. **Ephrath.** Jsh 19:15. Ru 1:2. 4:11. Mi *5:2, 16. Mt *2:1, 6, 18.

20. **a pillar.** ♪147D, Ge +1:29. **the pillar.** ver. 9, 14. 1 S *10:2. 2 S 18:17, 18. **grave.** Heb. *qeburah.* *S#6900h. Ge 35:20, 20. 47:30. Dt 34:6. 1 S 10:2. 2 K 9:28. 21:26. 23:30. 2 Ch 26:23. Ec 6:3. Is 14:20. Je 22:19. Ezk 32:23, 24. For *S#6913h, *qeber,* grave, buryingplace, sepulchre, see Ge +23:4. For *S#7585h, *sheol,* see Ge +37:35. **unto this day.** Ge +19:38.

21. **tower.** Mi 4:8. Lk 2:8. **Edar.** i.e. *flock,* *S#5740h. *S#4029h: Ge 35:21. Mi 4:8. ✛S#5740h: here rendered *Edar,* rendered *Eder,* 1 Ch +23:23. (1) A place near which Jacob pitched his tent after leaving Ephrath, where Rachel was buried, Ge 35:21.

(2) A border city on the south side of Judah, Jsh 15:21. It may be the same as Number 1. (3) A grandson of Merari, 1 Ch 23:23; 24:30.

22. **Israel.** Ge 37:3. 45:28. 46:30. 50:2. **lay with.** Ge 49:4. Le 18:8. Dt 22:30. 2 S 16:21, 22. 20:3. 1 Ch *5:1. 1 C *5:1. **Now the sons.** In the Hebrew text, a break is here left in the verse, opposite to which there is a Masoretic note, which states that 'there is a hiatus in the verse.' This hiatus the LXX. thus supplies: 'and it appeared evil in his sight.' ver. 18. Ge 29:31-35. 30:5-24. 46:8-27. 49:1-28. Ex 1:1-5. 6:14-16. Nu 1:5-15, 20, etc. 2:3-33. 7:12, etc. 26:5-51, 57-62. 34:14-28. Dt ch. 33. Jsh ch. 13-21. 1 Ch 2:1, 2. 12:23-40. 27:16-22. Ezk ch. 48. Ac 7:8. Re 7:4-8. 21:14.

23. **sons of Leah.** Ge 29:32-35. 30:18-20. 33:2. 46:8-15. **Judah.** i.e. *praise, celebrated,* ✤S#3063h. Ge 29:35. 37:26. 38:1, 2, 6, 8, 11, 12, 15, 20, 22, 23, 24, 24, 26. 43:3, 8, 14, 16, 18. 46:12, 28. 49:8, 9. Ex 1:2. Nu 26:19. Ru 4:12. 1 Ch 2:1, 3, 3, 4, 10. 4:1, 21, 27. 5:2. 9:4. Ne 11:24. (1) The fourth son of Jacob and Leah, Ge 29:35, one of the patriarchs, Ge +35:23. (2) The tribe of Judah was the largest which came out of Egypt, Nu 1:27. It was composed of the descendants of the patriarch Judah, Ge +*49:10; Nu 1:27. (3) The territory of Judah, occupied by the tribe of Judah in Canaan, comprised western Palestine from the Dead Sea to the Mediterranean. Its northern boundary extended from Beth-hogla, a little southeast of Jericho, to Jabneel, about four miles below Joppa, on the Mediterranean. Its southern boundary extended from the south end of the Dead Sea westward to the river of Egypt, now called Wady el Arish. Part of this territory was afterward cut off for Simeon. The northwestern part was given to Dan. (4) The Kingdom of Judah embraced the territory of the tribe of Judah and also the greater part of that of Benjamin on the northeast, Dan on the northwest, and Simeon on the South. Edom, which was conquered by David, was faithful to Judah for a time. After the kingdom of Israel was divided, B.C. 975, Judah existed as a separate kingdom until B.C. 588. Jerusalem, its capital, was taken at that time by Nebuchadnezzar. 1 K 12:17. (5) The city of Judah is mentioned in 2 Ch 25:28, and is probably the city of David, a name of Mount Zion at Jerusalem. (6) Father of two Levites who were overseers of the rebuilding of the Temple, Ezr 3:9. (7) A Levite who took a foreign wife, Ezr 10:23. (8) A Benjamite, Ne 11:9. (9) A Levite with Zerubbabel, Ne 12:8. (10) An exile, Ne 12:34. (11) A musician in exile, Ne 12:36.

24. **sons of Rachel.** ver. 16-18. Ge 30:22-24. 46:19-22.

25. **sons of Bilhah.** Ge 30:4-8. 37:2. 46:23-25.

26. **And the sons.** Ge 30:9-13. 46:16-18. **sons of Jacob.** ∫171M, Ge +6:12. **in Padan-aram.** Except Benjamin, ver. 18. Ge 25:20. 28:2. 31:18.

27. **Jacob.** Ge 27:43-45. 28:5. **Mamre.** Ge +13:18. 14:13. 18:1. *23:2, 19. Jsh *14:12-15. *15:13. 21:11. 2 S 2:1, 3, 11. 5:1, 3, 5. **Arbah.** i.e. *four sided, square,* ✤S#704h. Rendered Arba: Jsh 15:13. 21:11. Compare Kirjath-arbah (Jsh +15:54) and Hebron (Ex +6:18).

28. **hundred and fourscore.** Ge 25:7. 47:28. 50:26.

29. A.M. 2288. B.C. 1716. **Isaac.** Ge 3:19. 15:15. *25:7, 8, 17. 27:1, 2. 49:33. Jb 5:26. Ec 12:5-7. He *11:13. **gathered.** Ge 15:15. +*25:8. +√49:33 w 50:13.

full of days. Ge +*25:8. Ex +*23:26. **his sons.** Ge 23:19, 20. 25:9. 27:41. 49:31.

GENESIS 36

Esau's three wives, 1-5. His removal to mount Seir, 6-8. His sons, 15-19. The sons and dukes of Seir the Horite, 20-30. Anah finds mules, 24. The kings of Edom, 31-39. The dukes that descended of Esau, 40-43.

1. A.M. 2208. B.C. 1796. ∫133. Digression, Ge +2:8. **the generations.** Ge 22:17. *25:24-34. 27:35-41. 32:3-7. Nu 20:14-21. Dt 23:7. 1 Ch *1:35. Is 63:1. Ezk 25:12.

2. **Esau.** Ge 9:25. *26:34, 35. 27:46. **wives.** Ge +4:19. **Adah.** *or,* Bashemath, Ge 26:34. **Aholibama.** ver. 25. Ge 26:34, Judith. ∫146. Polyonymia; or, Many Names B775: An application of Enigma to the names of persons or places. Here, Aholibama, elsewhere called the daughter of Anah the daughter of Zibeon the Hivite, is not the Aholibama of verse 25, who was her aunt (compare ver. 2 and 25). She was also called Judith, and in Ge 26:34 this Judith is said to be the daughter of Berri the Hittite. But there is no contradiction in this, for Anah appears to have been called Beeri, or *the spring-man,* because he discovered the *hot springs* (Ge 36:24), not mules, as in the A.V. For other instances of Polyonymia, see Ge 10:10. 11:2. Dt 1:2, 44. 2:8. 2 K 23:13. Ps 87:4. 89:10. Is 14:4. 29:1. 51:9. Je 25:26. Ezk 23:4. Ho 4:15. 10:5. **the daughter.** We ought, most probably, to read here and in ver. 14, as in ver. 20, "the *son* of Zibeon"; which is the reading of the Samaritan, Septuagint, (and Syriac, in ver. 2) and which Houbigant and Kennicott contend to be genuine. **Hittite.** Ge +15:20. **Zibeon.** i.e. *many colors, variegated,* ✤S#6649h. ver. 14, 20, 24, 24, 29. 1 Ch 1:38, 40. **Hivite.** Ge +10:17.

3. **Bashemath.** i.e. *fragrant,* ✤S#1315h. ver. 3, 4, 10, 13, 17. Ge 26:34. 1 K 4:15. **Nebajoth.** Ge 25:13. *28:9, Mahalath.

4. **Adah.** 1 Ch 1:35. **Eliphaz.** i.e. *God of fine gold; God his strength; my God has refined,* ✤S#464h. ver. 10, 11, 12, 12, 15, 16. 1 Ch 1:35, 36. Jb 2:11. 4:1. 15:1. 22:1. 42:7, 9. (1) A son of Esau, Ge 36:4; 1 Ch 1:35. (2) One of Job's friends, Jb 2:11; 42:9. **Reuel.** i.e. *friend of God,* ✤S#7467h. ver. 10, 13, 17, 17. Ex 2:18. Nu 2:14. 10:29. 1 Ch 1:35, 37. 9:8. (1) A son of Esau, Ge 36:4; 1 Ch 1:35. (2) The father-in-law of Moses, Ex 2:18. He is elsewhere called Jethro, and in Nu 10:29, Raguel. (3) The father of the captain of the tribe of Gad, Nu 2:14. He is called Duel in Nu 1:14. (4) A descendant of Benjamin, 1 Ch 9:8.

5. **Jeush.** i.e. *to whom God hastens; devoured; he will gather together; he will succor,* ✤S#3266h. ver. 14, 18. 1 Ch 1:35. 7:10. 8:39. 23:10, 11. 2 Ch 11:19. (1) A son of Esau, Ge 36:5; 1 Ch *1:35. (2) A descendant of Benjamin, 1 Ch 7:10. (3) A descendant of Shimei, 1 Ch 23:10, 11. (4) A son of Rehoboam, 2 Ch 11:19. (5) Jehush. i.e. *a collector,* a descendant of Saul, 1 Ch 8:39. **Jaalam.** i.e. *hidden,* ✤S#3281h. ver. 14, 18. 1 Ch 1:35. **Korah.** i.e. *icy, ice, hail; baldness,* ✤S#7141h. (1) A son of Esau and Aholibamah, Ge 36:5; 1 Ch 1:35, named as a son of Eliphaz in Ge 36:16. (2) A son of Izhar, the grandson of Levi. He was leader in the rebellion against Moses and Aaron, and was destroyed, with many of his companions, by the Lord. Ex 6:18, 21, 24; Nu 16:1, 5, 6, 8, 16, 19,

24, 27, 32, 40, 49. 26:9, 10, 11. 27:3. 1 Ch 6:37. 9:19. (3) A son of Hebron, 1 Ch 2:43. (4) A grandson of Kohath: 1 Ch 6:22. Ps ch. 42, 44, 45, 46, 47, 48, 49, 84, 85, 87, 88, titles. **in the land.** ver. 6. Ge 35:29.

6. A.M. cir. 2264. B.C. cir. 1740. **persons.** Heb. souls. *nephesh,* Ge +12:5. Ezk 27:13. Re 18:13. **went.** Ge 13:6, 11. 17:8. 25:23. 28:4. 32:3.

7. **their riches.** Ge 13:6, 11. **the land.** Ge 17:8. 28:4.

8. **mount Seir.** ver. 20. Ge 14:6. 32:3. Dt 2:5. Jsh 24:4. 1 Ch 4:42. 2 Ch 20:10, 23. Ezk 35:2-7. Ml 1:3. **Esau.** ver. 1.

9. **the Edomites.** Heb. Edom. ✛S#130h. ver. 43. Dt ◐+23:7. 1 K 11:1, 17. 2 K 8:21. 1 Ch 18:12, 13. 2 Ch 21:8, 9, 10. 25:14, 19. 28:17. **the father of.** Ge 19:37.

10. A.M. cir. 2230. B.C. cir. 1774. **Eliphaz.** ver. 3, 4. 1 Ch 1:35, etc.

11. A.M. cir. 2270. B.C. cir. 1734. **Teman.** i.e. *southward, the southern country, south desert,* ✳S#8487h. ver. 15, 42. Jsh 12:3. 13:4. 15:1. 1 Ch 1:36, 53. Je 49:7, 20. Ezk 25:13. Am 1:12. Ob 9. Hab 3:3. (1) One of the sons of Eliphaz, son of Esau, Ge 36:11, 15; 1 Ch 1:36. (2) An Edomite chief, apparently of a later period, Ge 36:42; 1 Ch 1:53. (3) A district east of Edom, Je 49:7, 20; Am 1:12. **Zepho.** i.e. *watchtower,* ✳S#6825h. ver. 15, 16. 1 Ch 1:35, 36, Zephi. **Gatam.** i.e. *great fatigue; their touch; moving to laughter,* ✳S#1609h. ver. 16. 1 Ch 1:36. **Kenaz.** i.e. *a hunt, hunting; to chase,* ✳S#7073h. ver. 15, 42. Ge ◐15:19. Nu ◐32:12. Jsh 15:17. Jg 1:13. 3:9, 11. 1 Ch 1:36, 53. 4:13, 15. (1) A son of Eliphaz, the son of Esau, Ge 36:11, 42; 1 Ch 1:36. (2) Father of Othniel, who was a judge of Israel, Jsh 15:17; 1 Ch 4:13. (3) A grandson of Caleb, the son of Jephunneh, 1 Ch 4:15, but the marginal note for this verse reads 'or, Uknaz,' which is the same as Kenaz with a prefix.

12. **Timna.** i.e. *inaccessible; restraint,* ✳S#8555h. ver. 22, 40. 1 Ch 1:36, 39, 51. (1) The concubine of Eliphaz, the son of Esau, Ge 36:12, 22; 1 Ch 1:39. (2) One of the chiefs of Edom descended from Esau, Ge 36:40; 1 Ch 1:51. (3) A son of Eliphaz, the son of Esau, 1 Ch 1:36. **Amalek.** ver. 16. Ge 14:7. Ex *17:8-16. Nu *24:18-20. Dt 23:7. *25:17-19. 1 S 15:2, 3, etc.

13. **these are.** ver. 17. 1 Ch 1:37. **Nahath.** i.e. *rest,* ✳S#5184h. ver. 17. 1 Ch 1:37. 6:26. 2 Ch 31:13. (1) A grandson of Esau. He was a duke (chief) in Edom, Ge 36:13; 1 Ch 1:37. (2) One of the Levites, a descendant of Kohath, 1 Ch 6:26. (3) A Levite who lived in Hezekiah's reign, 2 Ch 31:13. **Zerah.** i.e. *rising of light,* ✳S#2226h. ver. 17, 33. Ge 38:30. 46:12. Nu 26:13, 20. Jsh 7:1, 18, 24. 22:20. 1 Ch 1:37, 44. 2:4, 6. 4:24. 6:21, 41. 9:6. 2 Ch 14:9. Ne 11:24. (1) A king of Ethiopia who made war against Asa, king of Judah, 2 Ch 14:9. (2) One of the sons of Reuel, the son of Esau, Ge 36:13, 17. 1 Ch 1:37. (3) One of the sons of Simeon, Nu 26:13; 1 Ch 4:24, called Zohar in Ge 46:10. (4) A Levite of the family of Gershom (Gershon), 1 Ch 6:21, 41. (5) A son of Judah and Tamar, Nu 26:20; Jsh 7:1, 18, etc. He is called Zarah in Ge 38:30; 46:12. (6) The father of Jobab, king of Edom, Ge 36:33; 1 Ch 1:44. **Mizzah.** i.e. *dropping; from sprinkling,* ✳S#4199h. ver. 17. 1 Ch 1:37.

14. A.M. cir. 2292. B.C. cir. 1712. **Aholibamah.** ver. 2, 5, 18. 1 Ch 1:35.

15. First aristocracy of dukes, from A.M. cir. 2429, to A.M. cir. 2471; from B.C. cir. 1575, to B.C. cir. 1533. **dukes.** ver. 18. 1 Ch 1:35. Pr 16:28. Je 13:21. **sons of Eliphaz.** "Korah is not mentioned before among the sons of Eliphaz: probably he was one of his grandsons" (Scott). ✠171G2, Ge +13:8. By Synecdoche of the Species, "son" is put for "grandson." **duke Teman.** ver. 4, 11, 12. 1 Ch 1:36, 45, 51-54. Jb 2:11. 4:1. Je 49:7, 20. Ezk 25:13. Am 1:12. Ob 9. Hab +*3:3.

16. **Duke Korah.** As it is certain from ver. 4, that Eliphaz was Esau's son by Adah, and from ver. 11, 12, that Eliphaz had but *six* sons, 'Teman, Omar, Zepho, Gatam, Kenaz, and Amalek;' as it is also certain, from ver. 5, 14, that *Korah* was the son of *Esau* (not Eliphaz) by *Aholibamah*; and as the words *duke Korah* are omitted by both the Samaritan Text and Version, Dr. Kennicott pronounces them to be an interpolation. **dukes.** Ex 15:15.

17. **Reuel.** ver. 4, 13. 1 Ch 1:37.

18. **Aholibamah.** ver. 5, 14. 1 Ch 1:35.

19. **who is Edom.** See on ver. 1.

20. A.M. cir. 2198. B.C. cir. 1806. **Seir.** i.e. *shaggy; goat-like; hairy,* ✳S#8165h. ver. 2, 22-30. Ge 14:6. Dt 2:12, 22. 1 Ch 1:*38-42. (1) The grandfather of Hori, Ge 36:20. His name was probably given to the mountainous district in which he lived. (2) A mountainous district extending from the Dead Sea to the eastern gulf of the Red Sea. It was occupied by the Horites, and afterward by the descendants of Esau: Ge 14:6. 32:3. 33:14, 16. 36:8, 9, 21, 30. Nu 24:18. Dt 1:2, 44. 2:1, 4, 5, 8, *12, 22, 29. √33:2. Jsh 11:17. 12:7. 24:24. Jg 5:4. 1 Ch 4:42. 2 Ch 20:10, 22, 23, 23. 25:11, 14. Is 21:11. Ezk 25:8. 35:2, 3, 7, 15. Seir sometimes means Edom. (3) Mount Seir, a landmark of Judah, Jsh 15:10. **inhabited.** Ex 23:31. Nu 32:17. Jg 1:33. **Lotan.** i.e. *covering up,* ✳S#3877h. ver. 22, 22, 29. 1 Ch 1:38, 39, 39. **Shobal.** i.e. *flowing; increasing; waving,* ✳S#7732h. ver. 23, 29. 1 Ch 1:38, 40. 2:50, 52. 4:1, 2. (1) A son of Seir, Ge 36:20; 1 Ch 1:38. (2) A son of Caleb, the son of Hur, 1 Ch 2:50, 52. (3) Shobal, in 1 Ch 4:1, 2, is probably the same as Shobal, number 2. **Anah.** i.e. *afflicted; answered,* ✳S#6034h. ver. 2, 14, 18, 24, 24, 25, 25, 29. 1 Ch 1:38, 40, 41. The father of Aholibamah, a wife of Esau, Ge 36:2, 14, 24. He is said to have discovered some *warm springs,* translated *mules* in the Authorized Version, Ge 36:24.

21. A.M. cir. 2204. B.C. cir. 1800. **Dishon.** i.e. *gazelle, wild goat; a thresher,* ✳S#1787h. ver. 25, 30. 1 Ch 1:38, 41. (1) Another son of Seir the Horite, Ge 36:21; 1 Ch 1:38. (2) A son of Anah, Ge 36:25; 1 Ch 1:41. **Ezer.** i.e. *union; treasure,* ✳S#687h. ver. 27, 30. 1 Ch 1:38, 42. A son of Seir. **Dishan.** i.e. *antelope; a threshing,* ✳S#1789h. ver. 26, 28, 30. 1 Ch 1:38, 42. **Edom.** ✛S#123h. ver. 31, 32, 43. Ex 15:15. Nu 20:14, 18, 20, 21, 23. 21:4. 24:18. 33:37. 34:3. Jsh 15:1, 21. Jg 5:4. 11:17, 17, 18. 1 S 14:47. 2 S 8:14, 14, 14. 1 K 9:26. 11:14, 15, 15, 16. 22:47. 2 K 3:8, 9, 12, 20, 26. 8:20, 22. 14:7, 10. 1 Ch 1:43, 51, 54. 18:11, 13. 2 Ch 8:17. 25:20. Ps 60:8, 9. 83:6. 108:9, 10. 137:7. Is 11:14. 63:1. Je 9:26. 25:21. 27:3. 40:11. 49:7, 17, 20, 22. La 4:21, 22. Ezk 25:12, 13, 14, 14. 32:29. Da 11:41. Jl 3:19. Am 1:6, 9, 11. 2:1. 9:12. Ob 1, 8. Ml 1:4.

22. A.M. cir. 2248. B.C. cir. 1756. **Hori.** i.e. *cave dweller,* ✳S#2753h. ver. 20, 21, 29, 30. Ge 14:6. Nu

13:5. Dt 2:12, 22. 1 Ch 1:39. (1) A son of Lotan and grandson of Seir, Ge 36:22; 1 Ch 1:39. (2) A man of Simeon, Nu 13:5. (3) Horims, Horites: a people who dwelt on the south and southeast of the Dead Sea, in the mountainous country about Petra, and who were, as is supposed, descended from Hori, the grandson of Seir, Ge 14:6; Dt 2:12. **Hemam.** i.e. *exterminating; raging,* *S#1967h, only here. 1 Ch 1:39, Homan. **Timna.** ver. 12.

23. **Alvan.** i.e. *unrighteous; iniquitous one; their ascent; sublime,* *S#5935h. 1 Ch 1:40, Alian. **Manahath.** i.e. *rest,* *S#4506h. 1 Ch 1:40. 8:6. (1) A descendant of Seir, Ge 36:23; 1 Ch 1:40. (2) A place in the territory of Benjamin, 1 Ch 8:6. **Ebal.** i.e. *heap of barrenness; stone,* *S#5858h. Dt 11:29. 27:4, 13. Jsh 8:30, 33. 1 Ch 1:22, 40. (1) A son of Shobal, Ge 36:23; 1 Ch 1:40. (2) A son of Joktan, 1 Ch 1:22, called Obal in Ge 10:28. (3) One of two mountains (the other being Gerizim) of Samaria from which the cursings and blessings were pronounced, Dt 11:29; Jsh 8:30-35. **Shepho.** or, Shephi. i.e. *smoothness; barrenness; a naked hill,* *S#8195h. 1 Ch 1:40. **Onam.** i.e. *iniquity; strong,* *S#208h. 1 Ch 1:40. 2:26, 28. (1) A son of Shobal, Ge 36:23; 1 Ch 1:40. (2) One of the sons of Jerahmeel, 1 Ch 2:26, 28.

24. **Ajah.** i.e. *the screamer; a vulture,* *S#345h. 2 S 3:7. 21:8, 10, 11. 1 Ch 1:40. (1) A son of Zibeon, Ge 36:24; 1 Ch 1:40. (2) Father of Saul's concubine, Rizpah, 2 S 3:7; 21:8, 10. **found.** Le 19:19. Dt 2:10. 2 S 13:29. 18:9. 1 K 1:38, 44. 4:28. Zc 14:15. **mules.** or, hot springs. Jsh 15:19.

25. **Dishon.** ver. 21. **Anah.** ver. 2, 5, 14, 18. 1 Ch 1:41.

26. **Hemdan.** i.e. *pleasant,* *S#2533h. 1 Ch 1:41, Amram. **Eshban.** i.e. *very red; vigorous,* *S#790h. 1 Ch 1:41. **Ithran.** i.e. *exalted, very iminent; abundance,* *S#3506h. 1 Ch 1:41. 7:37. (1) One of the Horites, Ge 36:26; 1 Ch 1:41. (2) A son of Zophah, an Asherite, 1 Ch 7:37. **Cheran.** i.e. *lyre; lamb,* *S#3763h. 1 Ch 1:41.

27. **Ezer.** ver. 21. 1 Ch 1:38. **Bilhan.** i.e. *tender; timid, fearful,* *S#1092h. 1 Ch 1:42. 7:10, 10. (1) A son of Ezer, Ge 36:27; 1 Ch 1:42. (2) A son of Jediael, 1 Ch 7:10. **Zaavan.** i.e. *disquieted,* *S#2190h. 1 Ch 1:42, Zavan. **Akan.** i.e. *acute; tortuous,* *S#6130h. 1 Ch 1:42, Jakan.

28. **Uz.** Jb 1:1. Je 25:20. La 4:21. **Aran.** i.e. *wild goat,* *S#765h. 1 Ch 1:42.

29. **Horites.** ver. 20, 28. 1 Ch 1:41, 42. **duke Lotan.** ver. 20. 1 Ch 1:38.

30. From A.M. cir. 2093, to A.M. cir. 2429; from B.C. cir. 1911, to B.C. cir. 1575. **dukes in the.** 2 K 11:19. Is 23:15. Da 7:17, 23.

31. **the kings.** Ge 17:6, 16. 25:23. Nu 20:14. 24:17, 18. Dt 17:14-20. 33:5, 29. 1 Ch 1:43-50. **before there.** Moses may here allude to the promise which God made to Jacob (Ge 35:11) that kings should proceed from him; and here states that these kings reigned before that prophecy began to be fulfilled.

32. **Dinhabah.** i.e. *judgment, concealment,* *S#1838h. 1 Ch 1:43.

33. A.M. cir. 2135. B.C. cir. 1869. **Bozrah.** i.e. *stronghold; sheepfold,* *S#1224h. 1 Ch 1:44. Is 34:6. 63:1. Je 48:24. 49:13, 22. Am 1:12. Mi 2:12. (1) A city of the Edomites, Ge 36:33; Je 49:13. (2) A city of Moab, Je 48:24.

34. A.M. cir. 2177. B.C. cir. 1827. **Husham.** i.e. *great haste,* *S#2367h. 1 Ch 1:45, 46. **Temani.** i.e. *southward,* *S#8489h. See on ver. 11, 15. 1 Ch 1:45. Jb 2:11. 4:1. 15:1. 22:1. 42:7, 9. Je 49:7.

35. A.M. cir. 2219. B.C. cir. 1785. **Hadad.** i.e. *brave, mighty,* *S#1908h. ver. 36. 1 K 11:14, 17, 19, 21, 21, 25. 1 Ch 1:46, 47, 50, 51. (1) An early king of the Edomites, Ge 36:35; 1 Ch 1:46. (2) Another king of Edom, 1 Ch 1:50, 51, called Hadar in Ge 36:39. (3) One of the royal house of Edom, 1 K 11:14, 25. (4) Compare Hadad, i.e. *fierce; sharpness,* *S#2301h, 1 Ch 1:30, called Hadar in Ge 25:15. (5) Hadad, *S#111h, 1 K 11:17. (6) A deity worshiped by the Aramaeans. It occurs in proper names, as in Benhadad, Hadadezer. The Assyrian scribes identified Hadad with their own weather-god Ramman, i.e. Rimmon (J. D. Davis, *Dictionary of the Bible,* p. 281). **Bedad.** i.e. *solitary,* *S#911h. 1 Ch 1:46. **Midian.** Ge +25:2. **Moab.** Ge +19:37. Nu 21:11, 13. Dt 2:9. **Avith.** i.e. *ruins; subverted; overturning; iniquity,* *S#5762h. 1 Ch 1:46.

36. A.M. cir. 2261. B.C. cir. 1743. **Samlah.** i.e. *peaceable; enwrapping,* *S#8072h. ver. 37. 1 Ch 1:47, 48. **Masrekah.** i.e. *vineyard,* *S#4957h. 1 Ch 1:47.

37. A.M. cir. 2303. B.C. cir. 1701. **Rehoboth.** Ge 10:11. 1 Ch 1:48.

38. A.M. cir. 2315. B.C. cir. 1659. **Baalhanan.** i.e. *lord of grace; the lord is gracious,* *S#1177h. ver. 39. 1 Ch 1:49, 50. 27:28. (1) The seventh of the ancient kings of Edom, Ge 36:38; 1 Ch 1:50. (2) Superintendent of olive and sycamore tres under David, 1 Ch 27:28. **Achbor.** i.e. *a mouse; agility,* *S#5907h. ver. 39. 2 K 22:12, 14. 1 Ch 1:49. Je 26:22. 36:12. (1) The father of the seventh Edomite king, Ge 36:38, 39; 1 Ch 1:49. (2) A messenger of Josiah sent to inquire concerning the denuciation of wrath against the national sins as recorded in the book of the law found by Hilkiah in the temple, 2 K 22:12, 14. In 2 Ch 34:20 Abdon is used in place of Achbor. (3) A Jew whose son was sent by Jehoiakim to bring back Urijah the prophet, Je 26:22; 36:12.

39. A.M. cir. 2387. B.C. cir. 1617. **Hadar.** i.e. *honor,* *S#1924h. 1 Ch 1:50, Hadad. After his death was an aristocracy. Ex 15:15. **Pau.** i.e. *sighing,* *S#6464h. 1 Ch 1:50, Pai. **Mehetabel.** i.e. *benefited of God,* *S#4105h. 1 Ch 1:50. Ne 6:10. (1) Wife of Hadar, a king of Edom, Ge 36:39; 1 Ch 1:50. (2) The father of Delaiah, Ne 6:10. **Matred.** i.e. *wand of government; causing pursuit; thrusting forward; propelling,* *S#4308h. 1 Ch 1:50. **Mezahab.** i.e. *waters of gold,* *S#4314h. 1 Ch 1:50.

40. Second aristocracy of dukes, from A.M. cir. 2471, B.C. cir. 1533; to A.M. cir. 2513, B.C. cir. 1491. **And these.** ver. 31. 1 Ch 1:51-54. **dukes.** See on ver. 15, 16. Ex 15:15. 1 Ch 1:51-54. **Timnah.** i.e. *portion assigned,* *S#8555h. ver. 12, 22. 1 Ch 1:36, 39, 51. (1) The concubine of Eliphaz, the son of Esau, Ge 36:12, 22; 1 Ch 1:39. (2) One of the chiefs of Edom descended from Esau, Ge 36:40; 1 Ch 1:51. (3) A son of Eliphaz, the son of Esau, 1 Ch 1:36. (4) Timnah, i.e. *portion assigned,* *S#8553h, A town in the north border of Judah, Jsh 15:10; 2 Ch 28:18. It is probably the same as Timnath, number 1. (5) A town in the mountains of Judah, Jsh 15:57. **Alvah.** or, Aliah. i.e. *iniquity,* *S#5933h. 1 Ch 1:51. **Jetheth.** i.e. *nail; subjugation,* *S#3509h. 1 Ch 1:51.

41. **Aholibamah**. i.e. *tent of the high place*, ✳S#173h. ver. 2, 5, 14, 18, 25. 1 Ch 1:52. (1) A Hittite woman of Mount Hor. She was one of the three wives of Esau, and in Ge 26:34 is called Judith. Ge 36:2, 5, 14, 18, 25. (2) A chief that sprang from Esau, Ge 36:41; 1 Ch 1:52. **Elah**. i.e. *an oak*, ✳S#425h. 1 S 17:2, 19. 21:10. 1 K 16:6, 8, 13, 14. 2 K 15:30. 17:1. 18:1, 9. 1 Ch 1:52. 4:15, 15. 9:8. (1) A duke (or chief) of Edom, Ge 36:41; 1 Ch 1:52. (2) A valley in Judah where Saul's army encamped when David slew Goliath, 1 S 17:2; 21:9. (3) Father of one of Solomon's officers, 1 K 4:18. (4) Son of Baasha, king of Israel, 1 K 16:6, 8. (5) Father of Hoshea, 2 K 15:30; 18:1. (6) A son of Caleb, 1 Ch 4:15. (7) An Israelite whose family dwelt in Jerusalem, 1 Ch 9:8. Perhaps the same as number 3. **Pinon**. i.e. *perplexity, distraction*, ✳S#6373h. 1 Ch 1:52.

42. **Mibzar**. i.e. *fortress, defence*, ✳S#4014h. 1 Ch 1:53.

43. **Magdiel**. i.e. *prince of God, declaring of God, praise*, ✳S#4025h. 1 Ch 1:54. **Iram**. i.e. *belonging to a city; watchful*, ✳S#5902h. 1 Ch 1:54. **the dukes**. ver. 15, 18, 19, 30, 31. Ex 15:15. Nu 20:14. **their**. ver. 7, 8. Ge 25:12. Dt 2:5. **father**. Ge 25:30. 45:8. 1 Ch 4:14. **the Edomites**. Heb. Edom. ver. 9.

GENESIS 37

Joseph is loved by Jacob, but hated by his brethren, 1-4. His dreams and the interpretation, 5-11. Jacob sends him to his brethren, who counsel to slay him, 12-20. At Reuben's desire they cast him into a pit, 21-24; and afterwards sell him to the Ishmaelites; while Reuben grieves at not finding him, 25-30. His coat, covered with blood, is sent to Jacob, who mourns inordinately, 31-35. Joseph is brought to Egypt and sold to Potiphar, 36.

1. A.M. 2276. B.C. 1728. **wherein his father was a stranger**. Heb. of his father's sojournings. Ge *17:8. 23:4. 28:4mg. 36:7. He *11:9-16.

2. **the generations**. *Toledoth*, the history, narrative, or account of the lives and actions of Jacob and his sons; for in this general sense the original must be taken, as in the whole ensuing history there is no genealogy of Jacob's family. Ge 2:4. 5:1. 6:9. 10:1. 11:10, 27. 25:12, 19. 36:1, 9. **feeding**. Jn=10:11, 14. **wives**. Ge 30:4, 9. 35:22, 25, 26. **evil report**. 1 S 2:22-24. Jn=3:19, 20. 7:7. 1 C 1:11. 5:1. 11:18.

3. **loved**. Jn 3:35. 13:22, 23. **more**. Ge +*44:30. **son**. Ge *44:20-30. **a coat**. ver. 23, 32. Ge ◐27:15. Jg 5:30. 2 S 13:18. Ps 45:13, 14. Ezk 16:16. **colors**. or, pieces. *Kethoneth passim*, a coat made of stripes of different colored cloth.

4. **more**. Ge +*44:30. Ep *6:4. **hated him**. ver. 5, 11, 18-24. Ge 4:5. 27:41. 49:23. 1 S 16:12, 13. 17:28. Ps 38:19. 69:4. Jn 7:3-5. 15:18, 19,=24,=25. T 3:3. 1 J 2:11. 3:10, 12. 4:20.

5. **dreamed**. ver. 9. Ge 28:12. 40:5. 41:1. *42:9. Nu 12:6. Jg 7:13, 14. 1 K 3:5. Ps 25:14. Da 2:1. 4:5. Jl 2:28. Am 3:7. **brethren**. Jn=7:5. **and they**. ver. 4, 8. Ge 49:23. Jn=15:24, 25. 17:14.

6. **Hear**. Ge 44:18. Jg 9:7.

7. **your sheaves**. Ge *42:6, 9. *43:26. *44:14, 19. **obeisance**. Ph=2:10. Col=1:18.

8. **reign over us**. ver. 4. Ex 2:14. 1 S 10:27. 17:28. Ps 2:3-6. 118:22. Lk=19:14. 20:17. Ac *4:27, 28. 7:35. He 10:29.

9. **another dream**. ver. 7. Ge 41:25, 32. **the sun**. ver. 10. Ge 43:28. 44:14, 19. 45:9. 46:29. 47:12. 50:15-21. Ac 7:9-14. Re 12:1. **eleven**. 2 K 23:5. Jb 38:22. **stars**. Da 8:10. Ph 2:15. **obeisance**. Ph=2:10. Col=1:18.

10. **Shall I**. Ge 27:29. Is 60:14. Ph 2:10, 11.

11. **envied**. Ge 26:14-16. Ps 106:16. Ec 4:4. Is 11:13. 26:11. Mt=27:18. Mk=15:10. Ac 7:9. 13:45. Ga 5:21. T 3:3. Ja 3:14-16. 4:5. **observed**. Ge 24:31. Da 7:28. Lk=2:19, 51.

12. **in Shechem**. ver. 1. Ge 33:18. 34:25-31.

13. **Do**. ♪85B, Ge +13:9. **the flock**. ♪63K. False Ellipsis B114. EWB notes that the words rendered *their father's flock* are one of the fifteen dotted words given in the Massorah, words which ought to be cancelled in reading, though they have not been removed from the Text. If these words are removed, then the inference is that they had gone to feed themselves and make merry, and the words *the flock* in this verse need not be inserted in italics. Other instances given by EWB in Bof false ellipsis are: Nu 16:1. Dt 29:29. 32:35. Jsh 24:17. 1 S 24:9, 10. 2 S 1:18, 21. 1 K 20:33. Ne 4:12. Ps 1:4. 2:12. 10:3. 19:3. 27:13. 68:16. 69:4, 20. 75:5. 118:5. 126:3. 127:2. SS 8:6. Ezk 22:20. Ho 4:7. Jon 3:9. Ml 3:9. Mt 20:23. Mk 11:13. Jn 8:6. Ro 1:1, 7. 12:3. 1 C 1:1, 2. 2 C 6:1. Ga 3:20, 24. He 2:16. 4:15. 12:2. 2 P 1:21. 1 J 3:16. **come**. 1 S 17:17-20. Mt 10:16. Lk 20:13. **send**. Lk=20:13. **Here am I**. Ge 22:1. 27:1, 18. 1 S 3:4-6, 8, 16. Ps=40:7, 8. Ep 6:1-3.

14. **see whether it be well with**. Heb. see the peace of thy brethren, etc. Ge 29:6. 41:16. 1 S 17:17, 18, 22mg. 2 S 18:32. 1 K 2:33. Est 2:11mg. Ps 125:5. Je 29:7. Lk 19:42. **bring**. Jn=17:3. **out of**. Jn=17:5, 24. **vale of Hebron**. Ge 23:2. 35:27. Nu 13:22. Jsh 14:13, 15. **came to**. Jn=4:4, 5.

15. **he was**. Ge 21:14. **wandering**. Mt=13:38. Lk=9:58. **What**. Jg 4:22. 2 K 6:19. Jn 1:38. 4:27. 18:4, 7. 20:15.

16. **seek**. Lk=19:10. **tell me**. SS 1:7.

17. **went after**. Lk =15:4. **Dothan**. i.e. *double fountain; two cisterns*, ✳S#1886h. 2 K 6:13.

18. **came**. Jn=1:11. **conspired**. 1 S 19:1. Ps 31:13. 37:12, *32. 94:21. 105:25. 109:4. Mt 21:38. =27:1. Mk 12:7. 14:1. Lk 20:14, 15. Jn=11:53. Ac 23:12.

19. **Behold**. ♪60D. Simulated Irony B815: Where the words in question are used by man either in dissimulation or hypocrisy. For other instances of this figure see 2 S 6:20. Ps 22:8. Is 5:19. Mt 22:16. 27:29. 27:40, 42, 43. Mk 15:29. **dreamer**. Heb. master of dreams. ver. 5, 11. Ge +28:12. 49:23mg.

20. **let us**. Ps 64:5. Pr 1:11, 12, 16. 6:17. *27:4. Mk=15:14. T 3:3. **pit**. Heb. *bor* or *bore*, a hewn cistern, well, dungeon, pit. ✳S#953h. Ge 37:20, 22, 24, 28, 29, 29. 40:15. 41:14. Ex 12:29. 21:33, 34. Le 11:36. Dt 6:11. 1 S 13:6. 19:22. 2 S 3:26. 23:15, 16, 20. 2 K 10:14. 18:31. 1 Ch 11:17, 18, 22. 2 Ch 26:10. Ne 9:25. Ps 7:15. 28:1. +√30:3. 40:2. 88:4, 6. 143:7. Pr 1:12. 5:15. 28:17. Ec 12:6. Is 14:15, 19. 24:22. 36:16. 38:18. 51:1. Je 6:7. 37:16. 38:6, 6, 7, 9, 10, 11, 13. 41:7, 9. La 3:53, 55. Ezk 26:20, 20. 31:14, 16. 32:18, 23, 23, 25, 29, 30. Zc 9:11. Contrast ✳S#875h, *be-er*, a dug well, Ge +16:14. ✥S#5869h, *ayin*, a fountain, Ge +24:13. ✳S#4599h, *mayan*, a spring or fountain, Ge +7:11. S#4726h, *maqor*, spring, dug well (even when naturally flowing), Le +12:7, issue. Pr 10:11. **Some**.

1 K 13:24. 2 K 2:24. Pr 10:18. 28:13. **and we.** 1 S 24:20. 26:2. Mt 2:2-16. *27:40-42. Mk 15:=14, 29-32. Jn 3:12. 12:10, 11. Ac 4:16-18.

21. **Reuben heard.** Ge 35:22. 42:22. **not kill him.** Heb. *nephesh*, Jsh +10:28. ✓121A7, Ge +9:5. Mt ◐+*10:28.

22. **Reuben said.** Ge *42:22. **Shed.** Mt=27:24. **lay.** Ge 22:12. Ex 24:11. Dt ◐13:9. Ac 12:1.

23. **stript.** ver. 3, 31-33. Ge *42:21. Ps 22:18. Mt=27:28. **colors.** *or*, pieces. ver. 3mg.

24. **and cast.** Ps 35:7. Is=38:17mg. La 4:20. **the pit.** Ps 40:1, 2. =69:2, 14, 15. 88:6, 8. 130:1, 2. Je 38:6. La 3:52-55. Zc 9:11.

25. **they sat.** Est 3:15. Ps 14:14. Pr *30:20. Am *6:6. Mt=27:36. **lifted.** 144A12, Ge +22:13. **Ishmeel-ites.** ver. 28, 36. Ge 16:11, 12. 25:1-4, 16-18. 31:23. Ps 83:6. **Gilead.** Ge 31:21. 43:11. Je 8:22. ✤S#1568h: Nu 32:1, 26, 29, 39, 40. Dt 2:36. 3:10, 13, 15, 16. 4:43. 34:1. Jsh 12:2, 5. 13:11, 25, 31. Jsh 17:1, 5, 6. 20:8. 21:38. 22:9, 13, 15, 32. Jg 5:17. 10:4, 8, 17, 18. 11:5, 7, 8, 8, 9, 10, 11, 29, 29, 29. 12:4, 4, 5, 7. 20:1. 1 S 13:7. 2 S 2:9. 17:26. 24:6. 1 K 4:13, 19. 17:1. 22:3. 2 K 10:33, 33. 15:29. 1 Ch 2:22. 5:9, 10, 16. 6:80. 26:31. 27:21. Ps 60:7. 108:8. SS 6:5. Je 8:22. 22:6. 46:11. 50:19. Ezk 47:18. Ho 6:8. 12:11. Am 1:3, 13. Ob 19. Mi 7:14. Zc 10:10. **spicery.** or, gum traga-canth or storax. Ge 43:11. **balm.** Je 8:22. 46:11. 51:8. **myrrh.** Ge 43:11.

26. **What profit.** Ge 25:32. Ps 30:9. Je 41:8. Mt 16:26. Ro 6:21. **conceal.** ver. 20. Ge *4:10. Dt 17:8. 2 S 1:16. Jb 16:18. Ezk 24:7.

27. **sell him.** ver. 22. Ex 21:16, 21. Ne 5:8. Mt 16:26. 26:15. 1 T 1:10. Re 18:13. **let not.** 1 S 18:17. 2 S 11:14-17. 12:9. **he is our.** Ge 29:14. 42:21. Jg 9:2. **were content.** Heb. hearkened.

28. **Midianites.** ver. 25. Ge *25:2. Ex 2:16. Nu 25:15, 17. 31:2, 3, 8, 9. Jg *6:1-3. Ps 83:9. Is 60:6. **sold.** Ge 45:4, 5. Ps 105:17. Zc 11:12, 13. Mt=26:15. =27:9. Ac *7:9. **twenty pieces.** Ge 20:16. 33:19. 45:22. Ex=21:32. Jg 9:4. 16:5. 2 K 5:5. **brought.** Mt=2:14.

29. **he rent.** ver. 34. Ge 44:13. Nu 14:6. Jg 11:35. 2 K 19:1. Jb 1:20. Jl 2:13. Ac 14:14.

30. **The child is not.** ver. 20. Ge 42:13, 32, 36. Je +*31:15.

31. **Joseph's coat.** ver. 3, 23. Pr 28:13.

32. **thy son's.** ver. 3. Ge 44:20-23. Lk 15:30.

33. **evil beast.** ver. 20. Ge 44:28. 1 K 13:24. 2 K 2:24. Pr 14:15. Jn 13:7. **rent.** ✓147B, Ge +2:16.

34. **Jacob rent.** ver. 29. Jsh 7:6. 2 S 1:11. 3:31. 1 K 20:31. 21:27. 2 K 19:1. 1 Ch 21:16. Ezr 9:3-5. Ne 9:1. Est 4:1-3. Jb 1:20. 2:12. Ps 69:11. Is 22:12, 13. 32:11. 36:22. 37:1, 2. Je 36:24. Jl 2:13. Jon 3:5-8. Mt 11:21. 26:65. Ac 14:14. Re 11:3. **sackcloth.** ✤S#8242h. Ge 42:25 (sack), 27, 35, 35. Le 11:32. Jsh 9:4. 2 S *3:31. *21:10. 1 K *20:31, 32. *21:27, 27. 2 K *6:30. *19:1, 2. 1 Ch *21:16. Ne *9:1. Est *4:1, 2, 3, 4. Jb *16:15. Ps *30:11. *35:13. *69:11. Is *3:24. *15:3. 20:2. 22:12. 37:1, 2. 50:3. 58:5. Je 4:8. 6:26. 48:37. 49:3. La 2:10. Ezk 7:18. 27:31. Da 9:3. Jl 1:8, 13. Am 8:10. Jon 3:5, 6, 8.

35. **his daughters.** Ge 31:43. 35:22-26. **rose up.** 2 S 12:17. Jb 2:11. Ps 77:2. Je 31:15. **For I.** Ge *42:38. 44:29-31. 45:28. **grave.** Nu 16:30. Dt *32:22. Jb 11:8. 14:3. Pr 30:15, 16. Is 5:14. Hab 2:5. T#1003‡: Jb 14:13. Ps *9:17. 16:10. Heb. *sheol*. First mention. ✤S#7585h. Rendered *grave* in the following passages: Ge 37:35.

42:38. 44:29, 31. 1 S 2:6. 1 K 2:6, 9. Jb 7:9. 14:13. 17:13. 21:13. 24:19. Ps 6:5. 30:3. 31:17. 49:14, 14, 15. 88:3. 89:48. 141:7. Pr 1:12. 30:16. Ec 9:10. SS 8:6. Is 14:11. 38:10, √18. Ezk 31:15. Ho 13:14, 14. Rendered *hell* in the following passages: Dt 32:22. 2 S 22:6. Jb 11:8. 26:6. Ps 9:17. 16:10. 18:5. 55:15. 86:13. 116:3. 139:8. Pr 5:5. 7:27. 9:18. 15:11, 24. 23:14. 27:20. Is 5:14. 14:9. 14:15. 28:15, 18. 57:9. Ezk 31:16, 17. 32:21, ◐√27. Am ◐√9:2. Jon 2:2. Hab 2:5. Rendered *pit* in the following passages: Nu 16:30, ◐√33. Jb 17:16. For ✱S#6900h, *qeburah*, grave, see Ge +35:20. For ✱S#6913h, *qeber*, grave, buryingplace, sepulchre, see Ge +23:4. For ✱S#7845h, shachath, pit, ditch, de-struction, corruption, see Jb +9:31. R.B. Girdlestone suggests (*Synonyms of the Old Testament*, Chapter 24, "Destruction, Death, Hell") that the state which we call death, i.e., the condition consequent upon the act of dying, is to be viewed in three aspects. First, there is the tomb, or sepulchre, the local habita-tion of the physical frame, which is called *qeber*, Ge 50:5 (Ge +23:4). Secondly, there is the corruption whereby the body itself is dissolved, which is repre-sented by the word *shachath*, Ge 6:13, 17. 9:11, 15, with reference both to the moral corruption and also to the physical destruction of all that was living on the earth; and of the earth itself, which, as Peter said, *perished* (2 P 3:6). In the N.T. the verb used here (2 P 3:6, *apollumi*) is applied to the waste of ointment (Mt 26:8), to the destruction of physical objects, e.g., wine-skins (Mt 9:17), gold (1 P 1:7), food (Jn 6:27), and the hair of the head (Lk 21:18). In these cases it is not annihilation that is spoken of, but such injury as makes the object practically useless for its original purpose. It is applied to the destruction of the world in 2 P 3:6 in exactly the same sense; for as the world was destroyed at the Deluge, so shall it be hereafter; it will be rendered useless as a habitation for man. Nevertheless, as after the first destruction it was re-stored, so it may be after the second. Again, the word is applied to the perishing or being destroyed from off the face of the earth in death, when the physical frame which is the temple of life becomes untenanted; and a contrast is drawn between the power of those who can bring about the death of the body, and of Him who can destroy both body and soul in gehenna. Death is spoken of in this sense in Matthew 2:13. 8:25. 12:14. 21:41. 22:7. 26:52. 27:20. and probably in Mt 18:14. Ro 2:12. 14:15. and 1 C 8:11. The destruc-tion of the body is compared to the disintegration of the seed which falls into the ground and dies. It is dismemberment and dissolution, and renders the body useless for the time being, so far as its original purpose is concerned, but it is not annihilation. The use of the word in the argument in 1 C 15:18 is worthy of note; it here implies, that, physically speaking, the Christian has perished, if Christ be not risen. There is not a word here about annihilation of the person (which would continue in hades), but simply of the blotting out of existence in death. See also, for the moral sense, such passages as Mt 18:11. Lk 15:32. Is 53:6. Jn 3:15, 16. 2 P 3:9. Thirdly, there is sheol, which represents the locality or condition of the de-parted. There is no reason to doubt that what the grave or pit is to the body, that sheol is to the soul. **unto my son.** As far as Jacob knew, Joseph had been devoured by a wild beast (ver. 33), and was not buried in a grave at all; even had he supposed Joseph perished in some *pit*, Jacob certainly did not expect his own *body* to be deposited in the same place: therefore, the use of *sheol* in the preceding clause, considering these factors in the case, shows that Jacob expected to meet Joseph in a conscious existence after the death of his own body. 2 S +*12:23. Je 31:15-17. Am +*9:2.

36. **the Midianites.** ver. 28. Ge 25:1, 2. 39:1. **into Egypt.** Mt=2:14, 15. **officer.** Heb. eunuch. But the word signifies not only eunuchs, but also chamberlains, courtiers, and officers. *S#5631h. Ge 39:1 (officer). 40:2, 7. 1 S 8:15mg. 1 K 22:9mg. 2 K +8:6mg. 9:32. 18:17, Rabsaris. 20:18. +23:11mg. 24:12mg, 15mg. 25:19mg. 1 Ch 28:1mg. 2 Ch 18:8mg. Est 1:10mg, 12mg, 15 (chamberlains). 2:3, 14, 15, 21. 4:4mg, 5. 6:2, 14. 7:9. Is 39:7. 56:3, 4. Je 29:2. 34:19. 38:7. 39:3, 13. 41:16. 52:25. Da 1:3, 7, 8, 10, 11, 18. **captain.** *Or*, chief marshal. Heb. chief of the slaughtermen, *or* executioners. Ge ch. 39. 40:4. 1 S 9:23. 2 K 25:8mg. Je 39:9mg.

GENESIS 38

Judah's marriage and children, 1-5. His son Er's marriage and death, 6, 7. Onan marries his brother's widow; is cut off for his sin; and Tamar his widow is reserved for Shelah, 8-11. Judah's wife dies; he is deceived by Tamar and commits incest with her; his crime is detected, and Tamar bears to him Pharez and Zarah, 12-30.

1. A.M. 2265. B.C. 1739. **And.** ♪107, Ge +10:5. **it came to pass.** ♪144A11. Pleonasm; or, Redundancy B413. Sometimes this phrase appears to be redundant, as the sense is complete without it. It is added for the sake of emphasis. For other instances of Pleonasm involving this phrase see ver. 9, 24, 38. Dt 18:19. Jsh 2:14. Is 7:23. Mt 7:28. 9:10. 11:1. 13:53. 19:1. 26:1. Mk 1:9.」2:15. Lk 1:23, 41. 2:1, 6. 5:1. Ac 2:6. 3:23. Ro 9:26. **at that time.** As there cannot be above 23 years from the selling of Joseph, unto Israel's going down into Egypt; and as it is impossible that Judah should take a wife, and by her have three sons successively, and Shelah, the youngest, marriageable when Judah begat Pharez of Tamar, and Pharez be grown up, married, and have two sons, all within so short a period; Mr. Ainsworth conceives that the *time* here spoken of is soon after Jacob's coming to Shechem (Ge 33). We have accordingly adapted the chronology to correspond with that time. **turned.** Ge 19:2, 3. Jg 4:18. 2 K 4:8. Pr 9:6. 13:20. **Adullamite.** i.e. *a native of Adullam* (i.e. *hiding place, retreat; justice of the people*, Jsh +12:15), *S#5726h. ver. 12, 20h. Jsh 12:15. 15:35. 1 S 22:1. 2 S 23:13. Mi 1:15. **Hirah.** i.e. *liberty; nobility, noble race*, *S#2437h. ver. 12.

2. **saw.** Ge 3:6. 6:2. 24:3. 34:2. Jg 14:2. 16:1. 2 S 11:2. 2 C 6:14. 1 J 2:16. **Canaanite.** Ge +10:18. **Shuah.** Ge 46:12. 1 Ch 2:3, Shua. **took.** Ge 6:4. ◐*24:3. 36:2. 46:10. Jg 14:2. **went in.** Ge +29:30.

3. A.M. 2266. B.C. 1738. **Er.** i.e. *watchful*, *S#6147h. ver. 6, 7. Ge 46:12, 12. Nu 26:19, 19. 1 Ch 2:3, 3. 4:21. (1) The eldest son of Judah by the daughter of Shua the Canaanite, Ge 38:3; Nu 26:19. (2) A son of Shelah, the youngest son of Judah by the daughter of Shua the Canaanite, 1 Ch 4:21. (3) An ancestor of Joseph, the husband of Mary, Lk 3:28.

4. A.M. 2267. B.C. 1737. **Onan.** i.e. *strong; weari-*

ness, vanity, iniquity, *S#209h. ver. 8, 9. Ge 46:12, 12. Nu 26:19, 19. 1 Ch 2:3. The second son of Judah by the daughter of Shuah the Canaanite. He refused to obey the law concerning raising up children by the wife of his deceased elder brother.

5. A.M. 2268. B.C. 1736. **Shelah.** i.e. *petition, a request*, *S#7956h. ver. 11, 14, 26. Ge 46:12. Nu 26:20. 1 Ch 2:3. 4:21. Contrast *S#7974h, also rendered Shelah, 1 Ch 1:18, more usually rendered Salah, Ge +10:24. i.e. *sprout*, the son of Arphaxad, 1 Ch 1:18, 24. He is called Salah in Ge 10:24; 11:12. **Chezib.** i.e. *lying, deceptive*, *S#3580h. Jsh 15:44, Achzib.

6. **took.** Ge 21:21. 24:3. **Tamar.** i.e. *palm tree*, *S#8559h. Ge 38:6, 11, 11, 13, 24. Ru 4:12. 2 S 13:1, 2, 4, 5, 6, 7, 8, 10, 10, 19, 20, 22, 32. 14:27. 1 Ch 2:4. 3:9. Mt 1:3. (1) The wife of Er, the son of Judah, and afterward of his brother Onan, Ge 38:6-30. (2) A daughter of David, 2 S ch. 13; 1 Ch 3:9. (3) One of the daughters of Absalom, 2 S 14:27. (4) A place on the southeast of Palestine, 1 K 9:18; Ezk 47:19; 48:28.

7. **Er.** Ge 46:12. Nu 26:19. **wicked.** Ge 6:8. 13:13. 19:13. 2 Ch 33:6. Jb *34:22. Pr *15:3. **and the.** ver. 10. Le 10:2. Nu 26:19. +*32:23. 1 Ch 2:3. Jb 15:32. 22:16. Ps 37:22, 38. 55:23. ◐102:24. Pr 10:27. Ec 7:17. *12:14. Is 40:24.

8. A.M. 2282. B.C. 1722. **Go in.** Le ◐18:16. Nu 36:8, 9. Dt *25:5-10. Ru 1:11. 4:5-11. Mt *22:23-27. Mk 12:19-23. Lk ▶20:28-33.

9. **be his.** Dt *25:6. Ru 1:11. 4:10. Jb ◐5:2. 1 T ◐1:10. T ◐3:3. **came to pass.** ♪144A11, Ge +38:1. **spilled.** Onan's sin was not masturbation, but failing to fulfill the duty required by the Levirate law, whereby he was obliged to raise up seed by the widow of his deceased brother, to continue her family's name and inheritance, since his brother died without leaving any male heirs (ver. 8. Dt 25:5-10. Ru 3:6-9. 4:5-11. Mt 22:24-28). Le *15:16-18. *22:4. Dt *23:10. Pr 25:26 (corrupt). Je 11:19 (destroy). Ezk 16:26. 23:11 (corrupt), 20. **lest that.** Jb 5:2. Pr 27:4. 1 T 1:10. T 3:3. Ja 3:14, 16. 4:5. **give seed.** Le +*15:16.

10. **displeased.** Heb. was evil in the eyes of. Ge 28:8mg. 48:17mg. Nu 11:1mg. 22:34. 1 S 8:6mg. 2 S 11:27. 1 Ch 21:7. Pr 14:32. 24:18. Is 59:15mg. Je 44:4. Jon 4:1. Hab 1:13. **him also.** ver. +7. Ge *46:12. Nu 26:19.

11. **till Shelah.** Ru *1:11, 13. **in her.** Le *22:13.

12. **in process of time.** Heb. the days were multiplied. Nu +9:22. **comforted.** Ge 24:67. 37:35. 2 S 13:39. **sheep shearers.** Ge 31:19. 1 S 25:4-8, 36. 2 S 13:23-29. **Timnath.** i.e. *portion assigned*, *S#8553h. ver. 13, 14. Jsh 15:10, 35, 57, Timnah. 19:43, Thimnathah. Jg 14:1, 1, 2, 5, 5. (1) The place mentioned in Ge 38:13. It is perhaps the same as Timnah, Jsh 15:10. (2) A city of the Philistines and the home of Samson's wife, Jg 14:1, 2, 5. Probably the same as Thimnathah.

13. **Timnath.** Jg *14:1. **shear.** Ge 31:19. 1 S 25:2, 11.

14. **widow's garments off.** Dt 24:17 1 T ◐5:3-16. **covered.** Ge +27:16. Pr 7:10. **vail.** Ge 21:16. +24:65. **and sat.** Pr *7:12. *9:14, 15. Je 3:2. Ezk 16:25. **an open place.** Heb. the door of eyes, *or* of Enajim. Some think *ainayim* means *the two fountains*, or *double fountain*; while others regard it as a proper name, and the same as *Enaim*, a city of Judah (Jsh 15:34). So the LXX. render it *Enan*. Jn +3:23. **Timnath.** See

ver. 12, 13. **that Shelah**. ver. 11, 26. ·Dt 25:5. Ru 1:11. Mt 22:24.

15. **harlot**. Ge 34:31. Le 19:29. 21:14. Nu 25:1, 6. Dt 23:18. Jg 11:1. 16:1. 19:2, 25. 1 K 3:16. Pr ❶*2:18, 19. Am 2:7. **because**. 1 Th *5:22. 1 P ❶*3:3-6. **covered**. ver. +14.

16. **Go to**. 2 S 13:11. **What wilt**. Dt 23:18. Ezk 16:33. Mt 26:15. 1 T 6:10.

17. **I will**. Ezk 16:33. **a kid**. Heb. a kid of the goats. **Wilt thou**. ver. 20, 24, 25. Pr 20:16. 27:13. Lk 16:8.

18. **Thy signet**. ver. 25. A *ring seal*, with which impressions were made to ascertain property, etc. ver. 25, 26. Ge 41:42. Je 22:24. Lk 15:22. **gave it her**. ver. 25, 26. Ge ❶39:12-20. Ho 4:11.

19. **laid by her vail**. ver. 14. 2 S 14:2, 5.

20. **his friend**. Ge 20:9. Le 19:17. Jg 14:20. 2 S 13:3. Lk 23:12. **pledge**. Dt 24:10-13, 17.

21. **the harlot**. Tamar is not here called a *harlot*, as in our version, but *kedaishah*, which from *kadash*, to consecrate to religious purposes, must mean a person consecrated by prostitution to the worship of some impure goddess. So Strabo (l. viii) calls the public prostitutes, who, it is well known, were dedicated to Venus, among the Greeks, *ierodoulai*, or *consecrated servants* or *votaries*. Le 19:29. Dt *22:21. 23:17. 1 K 14:24. 15:12. 22:46. 2 K 23:7. Jb 36:14mg. Pr 2:16. Ho 4:14. **openly by the wayside**. *or*, in Enajim. ver. 14.

23. **lest we**. 2 S 12:9. Pr 6:33. Ro 6:21. 2 C 4:2. Ep 5:12. Re 16:15. **be ashamed**. Heb. become a contempt.

24. **came to pass**. ℐ144A11, Ge +38:1. **played the harlot**. Ge 34:31. Jg 19:2. Ec 7:26. Je 2:20. 3:1, 6, 8. Ezk 16:15, 28, 41. 23:5, 19, 44. Ho 2:5. 3:3. 4:15. **with child**. Ge 16:11. 19:30-38. Ex 21:22. Is ❶7:14. **let her**. Ge 20:3, 7, 9. Le 20:10, 14. *21:9. Dt *22:21-27. 24:16. Jsh 7:25. 2 S *12:5, 7. Je 29:22, 23. Ezk 16:40. 23:47, 48. Mt *7:1-5. Jn ❶8:3-11. Ro *2:1, 2. 14:22.

25. **Discern**. ver. 18. Ge 37:32. Ps 50:21. Je 2:26. Ro 2:16. 1 C 4:5. Re 20:12.

26. **acknowledged**. Ge 37:33. Nu +*32:23. **She hath**. 1 S *24:17. 2 S 24:17. Ezk 16:52. Hab *1:13. Jn 8:9. Ro 3:19. **more righteous**. Not less to blame, but more righteous. Jb 33:26, 27. Pr 11:6. **because**. ver. 14. Dt 25:5. Ru 3:9-12. **And he knew**. Ge +4:1. 2 S 16:22. 20:3. Jb 4:5. *34:31, 32. 40:5. Mt 3:8. Jn *8:11. Ro 13:12. T 2:11, 12. 1 P 4:2, 3.

27. **twins**. Ge +25:24.

28. **came to pass**. ℐ144A11, Ge +38:1. **travailed**. Ge +35:16. **midwife**. Ge +35:17. **scarlet thread**. Jsh 2:18.

29. A.M. 2283. B.C. 1721. **his brother**. Ge 25:26. **How hast**, etc. *or*, Wherefore hast thou made *this* breach against thee? **his name**. Ge 46:12. Nu 26:20. 1 Ch 2:4. 9:4. Ne 11:4, 6, Perez. Mt 1:3. Lk 3:33, Phares. **Pharez**. i.e. a breach.

30. **Zarah**. i.e. *clearness; rising of light*, ✢S#2226h. Ge 46:12. 1 Ch 9:6, Zerah. Mt 1:3, Zara.

GENESIS 39

Joseph is bought by Potiphar, and preferred in the family, 1-6. tempted by his mistress, but overcomes the temptation, 7-12; accused by her, and imprisoned by Potiphar, 13-20; favored by the Lord's presence, and advanced by the keeper of the prison, 21-23.

1. A.M. 2276. B.C. 1728. **Joseph**. Ge 37:36. 45:4. Ps 105:17. Ac 7:9. **Potiphar**. i.e. *priest of the bull; my affliction was broken*, ✳S#6318h. Ge 37:36. **officer**. Is=49:7. **bought**. Ph=2:7. **the Ishmeelites**. Ge 37:25, 28.

2. **the Lord**. ver. 21, 22. Ge 21:22. 26:24, 28. 28:15. 1 S 3:19. 16:18. *18:14, 28. Ps 1:3. 46:7, 11. 91:15. Is 8:9, 10. 41:10. 43:2. Je 15:20. Mt 1:23. Ac *7:9, 10. Ro 8:31. **with**. Jn=16:32. **house**. 1 C 7:20-24. 1 T 6:1. T 2:9, 10.

3. **saw that**. ver. 23. Ge 21:22. 26:24, 28. 30:+27, 30. 1 S 18:14, 28. Zc 8:23. Mt *5:16. Ac=10:38. Ph 2:15, 16. Re 3:9. **prosper**. ver. 23. Ge 30:27. Dt +29:9. Jsh *1:7, 8. 1 Ch 22:13. 2 Ch 26:5. Ne 2:20. Ps *1:3. Is 44:4. 53:10. 1 C 16:2. Col 1:6.

4. **Joseph**. ver. 21. Ge 18:3. 19:19. 32:5. 33:8, 10. 1 S 16:22. Ne 2:4, 5. Pr 16:7. Lk=2:52. **overseer**. ver. 22. Ge 15:2. 24:2. 41:40, 41. Pr 14:35. 17:2. 22:29. 27:18. Ac 20:28. **all**. Jn=3:35.

5. **blessed**. Ep=1:3. =4:32. **for Joseph's**. Ge 12:2. 19:29. *30:27. Dt 28:3-6. 2 S 6:11, 12. Ps 21:6. 72:17. Mt 24:22. Ac 27:24. Ep 1:3. 2 Th 2:6, 7.

6. **he left**. ver. 4, 8, 23. Lk 16:10. 19:17. 2 T=1:12. **he**. ℐ63A1, Ge +14:20. **knew**. ℐ121C2A2. Metonymy of the Cause B553. Verbs of knowing are sometimes put for *caring for* or manifesting affection to. For other instances of this figure see Ex 2:25. Dt 33:9. Jg 2:10. 1 Ch 17:18. Ps 37:18. 142:4. Pr 12:10. 29:7. Je 1:5. 24:5. Ho 5:3. Am 3:2. 1 Th 5:12. 2 T 2:19. **save**. Ge 43:32. Pr 31:11. **bread**. ℐ171I8, Ge +3:19. **a goodly person**. *Yephaih toar, weephaih maraih*, ' beautiful in person and beautiful in countenance.' Joseph's beauty is so celebrated in the East, that a handsome man is frequently compared to him; and the Persian poets vie with each other in descriptions of his comeliness. Ge 12:14, 15. 29:17. 1 S 16:12. 17:42. SS=5:16. Ac 7:20. **well favored**. Lk=2:52.

7. A.M. 2285. B.C. 1719. **cast**. Ge 6:2. Jb +*31:1. Ps 119:37. Ezk 23:5, 6, 12-16. Mt ❶*5:28. 2 P 2:14. 1 J 2:16. **Lie**. 2 S 13:11. Pr 2:16. 5:9. 7:13. Je 3:3. Ezk 16:25, 32, 34.

8. **refused**. Est +*1:12. Pr √1:10. *2:10, 16-19. 5:3-8. 6:20-25, 29, 32, 33. *7:5, 25-27. 9:13-18. 22:14. 23:26-28. Is=7:15. Jn=8:46. **my master**. Pr 18:24. **all**. Jn=3:35.

9. **none**. Ge 24:2. Ne 6:11. Lk *12:48. 1 C 4:2. T 2:10. **how then**. Ge *20:3, 6. Le *20:10. 2 S 11:27. Jb 31:9-12, 23. Pr *6:29, 32. Je 5:8, 9. 1 C +√6:9, 10. Ga +√5:19-21. He 13:4. Re +√21:8. 22:15. **sin**. Ge 42:18. Le 6:2. Nu +*32:23. 2 S *12:13. Ne *5:15. Ps *51:4. Je 28:16. 50:7. He=4:15. 1 J 3:9.

10. **came to pass**. ℐ144A11, Ge +38:1. **as she spake**. ver. 8. Pr 2:16. 5:3. 6:25, 26. 7:5, 13. 9:14, 16. 22:14. 23:27. **or to be**. Ps *1:1. Pr *1:15. *4:15. *5:8. Mt *6:13. 1 C 6:18. *10:13. 15:33. 1 Th *5:22. 2 Th *3:14. 1 T 5:14. 2 T *2:22. 1 P 2:11.

11. **none of the men**. Jb 24:15. Pr 9:17. Je *23:24. Ml 3:5. Ep 5:3, 12.

12. **caught**. ver. 8, 10, 15. Pr 7:13, etc. Ec *7:26. Ezk 16:30, 31. **and he left**. 1 S 15:27. Pr 1:15. 5:8. *6:5. Ec *7:26. Mk 14:51, 52. 1 C 15:33. 2 T 2:22. 1 P 2:11.

13. **came to pass**. ℐ144A11, Ge +38:1. **garment in her hand**. Ge ❶38:25.

14. **he hath**. The base affection of this woman being disappointed, was changed into rancorous hatred, and

she exults in the opportunity of being revenged on Joseph. She begins her accusation in the affected language of offended modesty, rage, and disdain, by charging her husband, whom we may reasonably suppose she did not greatly love, with being an accessary to the indignity she pretended to have received: 'He hath brought in a Hebrew,' a very abomination to an Egyptian, 'to mock us,' insult and treat me in a base, unworthy manner. **an Hebrew.** ver. 17. Ge 10:21. 14:13. 40:15. Ps 120:3. Ezk 22:5. **mock.** Ge +21:9. +26:8. **he came.** ver. 7. Ps 35:11. 55:3. Pr 10:18. Is 51:7. 54:17. Mt 5:11. 26:59. Lk 23:2. 2 C 6:8. 1 P 2:20. 3:14-18. 4:14-19. **loud.** Heb. great. Dt 22:24, 27.

15. **came to pass.** ∫144A11, Ge +38:1. **lifted.** ∫144A12, Ge +22:13. **his garment.** ver. 12, 13.

16. **laid up.** Je 4:22. 9:3-5. 20:10.

17. **she spake.** Ge +*27:19. Ex +*20:16. *23:1. Dt 5:20. Ps 120:3. Pr *19:9. Is √54:17. Mt *5:11, 12. Ja 3:8. 1 P *3:14-17. **Hebrew servant.** ver. 14. Ex 20:16. 23:1. 1 K 18:17. 21:9-13. Ps 37:14. 55:3. 120:2-4. Pr 12:19. 19:5, 9. Mt 26:65.

18. **came to pass.** ver. 14. Ex 20:16. *23:1. Le 19:16. Pr 6:19. 12:22. 19:5. **lifted.** ∫144A12, Ge +22:13.

19. **heard.** Jb 29:16. Pr 18:17. +*29:12. Ac 25:16. 2 Th 2:11. 1 T +*5:19n. **his wrath.** Ge 4:5, 6. 34:7. Ps *76:10. Pr *6:34, 35. SS 8:16.

20. **into the prison.** or, roundhouse. So called from the form of the building, according to some; or, 'the watch or guard house,' according to others. Ge 40:3, 5, 15. 41:14. Ps *105:18, 19. Is 53:8. Da 3:21, 22. 2 T 2:9. 1 P *2:19. **into the prison.** 1 P=3:19. **the king's.** Ge 40:1-3, 15. 41:9-14. Ps 76:10. **bound.** Ps=22:16. =105:18, 19. Mt=27:2.

21. **the Lord.** See on ver. 2. Ge 21:22. 49:23, 24. Ps 91:15. Is 41:10. 43:2. Da 6:22. Ro 8:31, 32, 37. 1 P 3:13, 14, 17. 4:4-16. **with.** Jn=16:32. **showed him mercy.** Heb. extended kindness to him. **gave him.** Ge 40:3. Ex 3:21. 11:3. 12:36. Ps *37:5, 6. 105:19, 22. *106:46. *112:4. Pr +*16:7. Da *1:9. Ac 7:9, 10.

22. **committed.** ver. 4, 6, 7, 9. Ge 40:3, 4. 1 S 2:30. Ps 37:3, 11. Mt 25:14-30. Lk 12:48. 16:10. 19:17.

23. **keeper.** Ge 40:3, 4. **because.** See on ver. 2, 3. Ge 49:23, 24. 1 S 2:30. Ps 1:3. 37:3-11. Is 43:2. Da 6:22. **with him.** ver. +3. Ge +*30:27. Ps 91:5. Jn=16:32. **prosper.** Ps *1:1-3.

GENESIS 40

Pharaoh's chief butler and chief baker being imprisoned, Joseph is charged with them, 1-4. He interprets their dreams, and offers a petition to the chief butler, 5-19. The dreams are accomplished, and the chief butler forgets Joseph, 20-23.

1. **it came.** Ge 39:20-23. Est 6:1. **the butler.** or, cup-bearer. ver. 13. Ne 1:11. 2:1, 2.

2. **wroth.** Ps *76:10. Pr *16:14. 19:12, 19. 27:4. Ac 12:20. **two.** Lk=23:32. **the chief of the butlers.** 1 Ch 27:27.

3. **the place.** Ge 39:20, 23. 2 S 20:3mg. Lk=23:32. **where Joseph was bound.** Or, 'where Joseph was confined,' for he doubtless had his personal liberty.

4. **the captain.** Ge 37:36. 39:1, 21-23. Ps 37:5. **served.** Lk=22:27. **a season.** Heb. *Yamim,* literally *days;* how long is uncertain, though the word may signify, as many suppose, a complete year (see Ge 4:3. 24:55); and as Pharaoh called them to an account

on his birthday (ver. 20), Calmet supposes they had offended on the preceding birthday, and thus had been one whole year in prison. ∫171T2C, Ge +24:55.

5. **A.M. 2287. B.C. 1717. dreamed a dream.** ver. 8. Ge 12:1-7. 20:3. 37:5-10. 41:1-7, 11. Nu 12:6. Jg 7:13, 14. Est 6:1. Jb 33:15-17. Da 2:1-3. 4:5, 9, 19. ch. 7, 8.

6. **and, behold.** ver. 8. Ge 41:8. Da 2:1-3. 4:5. 5:6. 7:28. 8:27.

7. **Wherefore.** Jg 18:24. 1 S 1:8. 2 S 13:4. Ne 2:2. Lk 24:17. **look ye so sadly today.** Heb. *are* your faces evil. Lk=24:17.

8. **Do not,** etc. Ge *41:15, 16. Jb 33:15, 16. Ps 25:14. Is 8:19. Da *2:11, 28, 47. 4:8. 5:11-15. Am 3:7. 1 C 12:10, 11.

9. **a vine.** Ge 37:5-10. Jg 7:13-15. Da 2:31. 4:8, 10, etc.

10. **budded.** Nu 13:23. Dt 1:24. **blossoms.** SS 6:11. Is 27:6. 35:1, 2. 37:31. Ho 14:7. Jl 2:22. Zc 8:12.

11. **and I took,** etc. From this we find that *wine* anciently was the mere expressed juice of the grape, without fermentation. The *saky,* or cupbearer, took the bunch, pressed the juice into the cup, and instantly delivered it to his master. **pressed.** Ge 49:11. Le 10:9. Pr 3:10. **hand.** ver. 21. 1 K 10:5. 2 Ch 9:4. Ne 1:11. 2:1.

12. **This.** ver. 18. Ge 41:12, 25, 26. Jg 7:14. Da 2:36, etc. 4:19, etc. **The three.** Ge 41:26. Jg 7:14. Mt 26:26. 1 C 10:4. Ga 4:25.

13. **Yet.** Lk=23:43. **within.** Ge 7:4. **three.** 1 C +=15:4. **shall.** ver. 20-22. 2 K 25:27. Ps 3:3. Je 52:31. **lift up thine head.** or, reckon. ver. 19mg, 20mg. 2 K 25:27.

14. **think on me.** Heb. remember me with thee. 1 C=11:24. **on me.** 1 S 25:31. Lk 23:42. 1 C 7:21. **show kindness.** Jsh *2:12. 1 S 20:14, 15. 2 S 9:1. 1 K 2:7. Mt=25:40. **make mention.** Mt=10:32. **bring.** 1 C *7:21.

15. **stolen.** Ge 37:28. Ex 21:16. Dt 24:7. 1 T 1:10. **the Hebrews.** i.e. *descendants of Eber,* ✢S#5680h. Ge +14:13. 41:12. 43:32. Ex 2:13. 3:18. 5:3. 7:16. 9:1, 13. 10:3. 1 S 4:6, 9. 13:3, 7, 19. 14:11, 21. 29:3. **done nothing that.** Ge 39:8-12, 20. 1 S 24:11. Ps 59:3, 4. Da 6:22. Lk=23:41. Jn=8:46. 10:32. 15:25. Ac 24:12-21. 25:10, 11. 1 P *3:17, 18.

16. **the chief.** ver. 1, 2. **white baskets.** or, baskets full of holes. Am ◖8:1, 2. Hg ◖1:6.

17. **bake-meats.** Heb. meat of Pharaoh, the work of a baker, *or* cook. Ge 49:20. 1 Ch 12:20.

18. **This is.** See on ver. 12. Ge 41:26. 1 C 10:4. 11:24.

19. **within.** ver. 13. **lift up thy head from off thee.** *or,* reckon thee *and take thy office* from thee. **hang thee.** ver. 22. Ge 41:13. Dt 21:22, 23. Jsh 8:29. 10:26. 2 S 21:6. Pr 30:17. Ga 3:13. **tree.** ∫121D8. Metonymy of the Cause B559. Wood is put for things made of wood. Here, *tree* is put for gallows. For other instances of this figure see Dt 21:22, 23. Jsh 8:29. 2 S 21:19. Est 7:9mg, 10. Ezk 37:16. Ac 16:24. Ga 3:13. 1 P 2:24. **and the birds.** ver. 17. Dt 28:26. 1 S 17:44, 46. 2 S 21:10. 1 K 14:11. 16:4. 21:24. Ps 79:2. Je 7:33. 12:9mg. 16:4. 34:20. Ezk 39:4. Mt 13:4, 19, 32. Ac 20:27.

20. **third day.** ver. 13, 19. Ge +=22:4. Ex +10:22. Jon=1:17. Mt=12:40. 1 C +=15:4. **birthday.** Ge 21:8. Est 1:3. Jb 3:1. Mt 14:6. Mk 6:21. **lifted up.** *or,* reck-

oned. ver. 13mg, 19mg. 2 K 25:27. Mt 18:23-25. 25:19. Lk 16:1, 2.

21. **restored**. Je 52:31, 32. **gave the cup**. ver. 13. Ne 2:1.

22. **he hanged**. ver. 8, 19. Ge 41:11-13, 16. Je 23:28. Da 2:19-23, 30. 5:12. Mt *25:19. Ac 5:30.

23. **but forgat him**. Ge 42:21. Jg 8:33. Jb *19:14. Ps *31:12. 105:19. Ec 9:=15, 16. Am *6:6. Lk=23:39-43. ∫144D. Pleonasm B416. When the sense is first put positively, and then negatively (or *vice versa*), this greatly emphasizes the original statement, and calls very special attention to it. For other instances of this figure see Ge 42:2. Ex 9:19. 12:20. Dt 28:13. 32:6. 33:6. 1 S 1:11. 1 K 6:18. 2 K 20:1. Is 3:9. 31:3. 38:1. 45:22. Je 20:14. Ezk 18:13. 28:2. 33:15. Ho 5:3. 11:9. Am 5:20. Hab 2:3. Lk 18:34. Jn 1:3, 20. 3:15. Ac 18:9. Ro 4:20. 12:11. 12:14. 1 C 1:10. Ga 5:1. 1 J 1:5, 8. 2:4.

GENESIS 41

Pharaoh has two dreams, which the magicians cannot interpret, 1-8. The chief butler recommends Joseph, who is sent for, and interprets the dreams to foretell seven years of great plenty and seven of as great scarcity, 9-32. He gives counsel to Pharaoh; and is highly preferred, 33-44; and married, 45. The seven years of plenty, and Joseph's wise management, 46-49. The names of his two sons, 50-52. The seven years of scarcity begin, and the Egyptians are relieved by Joseph, 53-57.

1. A.M. 2289. B.C. 1715. **two full years**. Heb. *She-nathayim yamim*, two years of days, two complete solar revolutions; as a *month of days* is a full month, Ge 29:14. **that Pharaoh**. Ge 20:3. 37:5-10. 40:5. Jg 7:13, 14. Est 6:1. Jb 33:15, 16. Da 2:1-3. 4:5, etc. 7:8. Mt 27:19. **the river**. Ge 31:21. Ex 1:22. 4:9. Dt 11:10. Is 19:5. Ezk 29:3, 9.

2. **there came**. ver. 17-27. **a meadow**. Or, rather, "on, or among the reeds or sedges"; for so *achoo* is generally supposed to denote (see Jb 8:11).

3. **ill favored**. ver. 4, 20, 21.

4. **So Pharaoh awoke**. 1 K 3:15.

5. **seven ears**. A species of wheat, which grows in Egypt, bears, when perfect, seven ears on one stalk, as its natural conformation. It differs from ours in having a solid stem, or at least a stem full of pith, in order to yield sufficient nourishment and support to so great a weight as the ears which it bears. **rank**. Heb. fat. Dt 32:14.

6. **blasted**. Ezk 17:10. 19:12. Ho 13:15. **east wind**. Ge 8:1. *S#6921h. ver. 23, 27. Ex 10:13. 14:21. Jb 15:2. 27:21. 38:24. Ps 48:7. 78:26. Is 27:8. Je 18:17. Ezk ◐+11:1. 17:10. 19:12. 27:26. Ho 12:1. 13:15. Jon 4:8. Hab 1:9.

7. **a dream**. Ge 20:3. 37:5.

8. **his spirit**. Ge 40:6. Da 2:1-3. 4:5, 19. 5:6. 7:28. 8:27. Hab 3:16. The use of *spirit* and *soul* are sometimes interchangeable: Ps ◐42:6. Mt ◐20:28. ◐27:50. Jn 12:27. ◐13:21. He 12:23. Re ◐6:9. In Hebrew thought man is technically neither dichotomous or trichotomous, but a being possessing an inner and outer aspect (see especially 1 S √16:7). Nevertheless, in the light of New Testament teaching we can look back at Old Testament statements and find passages which are not out of harmony with its teachings; see the references

gathered at such passages as Ge +√2:7. Mt +√10:28. Here, "spirit" is Heb. *ruach*. ✛S#7307h. This term is used to represent the invisible characteristics of man manifesting themselves in states of mind (Ge +26:35) or feeling by the figure of speech ∫121A10, Metonymy (of the Cause); the word "spirit" is put for the soul or life in its manifestations, Ge +26:35. Ge 45:27. Ex 6:9. 35:21. Nu 5:14, 14, 30. 14:24. Jsh 5:1. Jg 15:19. 1 S 1:15. 30:12. 1 K 10:5. 21:5. 1 Ch 5:26, 26. 2 Ch 9:4. 21:16. 36:22. Ezr 1:1, 5. Jb 6:4. 7:11. 10:12. 15:13. 20:3. 21:4. 32:8, 18. Ps 32:2. 34:18. 51:10, 11, 12, 17. 76:12. 78:8. 142:3. 143:4, 7. Pr 11:13. 14:29. 15:4, 13. 16:2, 18, 19, 32. 17:22, 27. 18:14, 14. 25:28. 29:23. Ec 1:14, 17. 2:11, 17, 26. 4:4, 6, 16. 6:9. 7:8, 8, 9. 10:4. Is 19:3, 14. 26:9. 29:10, 24. 33:11. 38:16. 54:6. 57:15, 15, 16. 61:3. 65:14. 66:2. Je 51:11. Ezk 13:3, 14b. Da 7:15. Ho 4:12. 5:4. Mi 2:11 (where by the figure of speech ∫93A, Hendiadys, Ge +1:26, *ruach* is put for a false or lying spirit), CB, Ap. 9, VI. Hg 1:14. Mk +*2:8. For the other uses of *ruach*, see Ge 6:3n. **troubled**. Jb *7:13, 14. **the magicians of Egypt**. The word here used (*chartummim*) may mean no more than 'interpreters of abstruse or difficult subjects'; especially of dreams and visions, which formed a considerable part of the ancient Pagan religion; and the Egyptian priests were the first who professed this art. The word may be of affinity with, or derived from, the Persian *chiradmand*, wise, learned, judicious, intelligent, from *chirad*, understanding, judgment, and *mand*, endowed with. They seem to have been such persons as Josephus calls 'sacred scribes'; or professors of sacred learning. Ex 7:11, 22. 8:7, 18, 19. 9:11. 15:9, 11. Le 19:31. 20:6. Dt 18:9-14. Is 8:19. 19:3. 29:14. 47:12, 13. Da 1:20. 2:2, 10, 27. 4:7, 9. 5:7, 11. Ac 17:18. **the wise men**. Mt 2:1. Ac 7:22. **but there**. Ge 40:8. Jb 5:12, 13. Ps 25:14. Is 19:11-13. *29:14. Da 2:4-11, 27, 28. 5:8. 1 C 1:19. 3:18-20.

9. **I do remember**. Ge 40:1-3, 14, 23. Lk=23:41.

10. **Pharaoh**. Ge 39:20. 40:2, 3. **captain**. Ge 37:36.

11. **dreamed**. Ge 40:5-8.

12. **with us**. Lk=23:41. **Hebrew**. Ge +14:13. **servant**. Ge 37:36. 39:1, 20. **interpreted**. Ge 40:12-19.

13. **me he restored**. ∫121I2, Ge +2:17. Ge 40:12, 20-22. Je 1:10. Ezk 43:3. **hanged**. ∫121I2, Ge +2:17.

14. **sent**. 1 S 2:7, 8. Ps 105:19-22. *113:7, 8. **and they brought him hastily**. Heb. made him run. Ex 10:16. 1 S *2:8. Ps 113:7, 8. Da 2:25. **out**. Ec=4:14. **he shaved**. 2 S 19:24. 2 K 25:29. Est 4:1-4. 5:1. Is 61:3, 10. Je 52:32, 33.

15. **I have heard**. ver. 9-13. Ps *25:14. Da 5:12, 16. **that thou canst understand a dream to interpret it**. *or*, when thou hearest a dream, thou canst interpret it. ver. 12, 25. Ge 40:12. Jg 7:13, 14. Da 2:36. 4:19.

16. **It is not**. Ge 40:8. Nu 12:6. 2 K 6:27. Da *2:18-23, 28-30, 47. *4:2. Jn=5:19. Ac *3:7, 12. 14:14, 15. 1 C 15:10. 2 C *3:5. **peace**. Ge 37:14. Lk 19:42.

17. **In my dream**. ver. 1-7.

18. **fat fleshed**. Je 24:1-3, 5, 8.

19. **poor**. Ru +3:10.

21. **eaten them up**. Heb. come to the inward parts of them. Je 9:8mg. Ezk 3:3. Re 10:9, 10. **still**. Ps 37:19. Is 9:20.

23. **withered**. *or*, small. **thin**. ver. 6. 2 K 19:26. Ps 129:6, 7. Ho 8:7. 9:16. 13:15. **east wind**. ver. +6.

24. **I told this**. ver. 8. Ex 8:19. Da 4:7.

25. **God hath showed**. See on ver. 16. Ex 9:14.

Jsh 11:6. Ps 98:2. Is 41:22, 23. 43:9. Da 2:28, 29, 45, 47. Am 3:7. Mt 24:40. Mk 13:23. Jn=5:19. Ep 1:17. Re *4:1.

26. **are.** or, signify. ver. 2, 5, 29, 47, 53. Ge 40:18. Ex 12:11. 1 C 10:4. **good ears are seven.** See on Ge 40:12. **the dream is one.** Ge 2:24. Ex 26:6. 1 J 5:7.

27. **seven years of famine.** 2 S 24:13. 2 K 8:1.

28. **What God.** See on ver. 16, 25. Ge 40:8.

29. **seven years.** ver. 26, 46, 47, 49.

30. **seven years.** ver. 27, 54. 2 S 24:13. 1 K 17:1. 2 K 8:1. Lk 4:25. Ja 5:17. **shall be.** ver. 21, 51. Pr 31:7. Is 65:16. **consume.** Ge 47:13. Ps 105:16. **land.** 121J17, Ge +6:11.

31. **grievous.** Heb. heavy. 1 S 5:6. Is 24:20.

32. **dream.** Jl 2:28-32. Ac 2:16-21, 38, 39. **doubled.** Ge 37:7, 9. Jb *33:14, 15. 2 C *13:1. **twice.** Ge +22:15. Pr 14:12. 16:25. Je 1:13. **it is because.** Nu *23:19. Is 14:24-27. *46:10, 11. Mt *24:35. **established by.** or, prepared of. Ps 51:10mg. 57:7mg. Is 2:2mg. 30:33. Ho +*6:3. Mt *25:34, 41. Mk 10:40. 1 C *2:9. Re 9:15.

33. **therefore.** Da 4:27. **look out.** Ex 18:19-22. Dt 1:13. Ac 6:3.

34. **officers.** or, overseers. Nu 31:14. 2 K 11:11, 12. 2 Ch 34:12. Ne 11:9. 12:42. *S#6496h. Jg 9:28. 2 K 25:19 (was set). 2 Ch 24:11. 31:13 (overseer). Ne 11:9, 14, 22. 12:42 (overseer). Est 2:3. Je 20:1 (governor). 29:26. 52:25 (had the charge). **and take.** Jb 5:20. Ps 33:19. Pr 6:6-8. +*22:3. 27:12. Lk 16:5.

35. **gather.** ver. 48, 49, 56. Ge 45:6, 7. **under.** 2 K 13:5. Is 3:6. **hand.** Ex 4:13.

36. **that the.** Ge 47:13-25. **perish not.** Heb. be not cut off. ver. 30.

37. **the thing.** Ps 105:19. Pr 10:20. 25:11. Ac 7:10. **good.** Jsh 22:30mg. 2 S 3:36mg. 1 K 21:2mg.

38. **we.** Ge +30:27. **in whom.** Nu *27:18. Jb *32:8. Ps *84:11. Pr *2:6. Da *4:6, 8, 18. *5:11, 14. *6:3. Ac=10:38. **spirit.** Heb. ruach. ✣S#7307. Here this word represents invisible 'power from on high' (Lk 24:49) manifesting itself as divine power in giving spiritual gifts (Ep 5:18), spoken of as coming upon, clothing, falling on, and being poured out. Rendered "Spirit," but should be "spirit." Ex 28:3. 31:3. 35:31. Nu 11:17, 25, 25, 26, 29. 24:2. 27:18. Dt 34:9. Jg 3:10. 6:34. 11:29. 13:25. 14:6, 19. 15:14. 1 S 10:6, 10. 11:6. 16:13, 14. 19:20, 23. 2 K 2:9, 15. 1 Ch 12:18. 28:12. 2 Ch 15:1. 20:14. 24:20. Ps 51:11, 12. 143:10. Pr 1:23. Is 11:2, 2, 2. 30:1. 32:15. 42:1, 5. 44:3. 59:21. 61:1. 63:11. Ezk 2:2. 3:24. 11:5, 19. 36:27. 39:29. Da 4:8, 9, 18. 5:11, 12, 14. Jl 2:28, 29. Hg 2:5. Zc 12:10. For the other uses of ruach, see Ge 6:3n.

39. **said.** Ge 30:27. **God hath.** See on ver. 16, 25, 28, 33. Jn=5:20. **Forasmuch.** ver. 32. 1 S 10:6-10. Ac 5:32. 8:15. Ro 5:5. 1 C 13:4-10. Ep *5:18. Col 1:9, 10. Ju 20. **discreet.** Is 28:26. Lk=2:47.

40. **Thou shalt.** Ge 39:4-6. 45:8, 9, 26. Ps 105:21, 22. Pr 22:29. Da 2:46-48. 5:29. 6:3. Mt=24:47. He =3:6. **according.** Is=9:6, 7. **be ruled.** Heb. be armed, or kiss. ʃ121S2, Ge +21:6. 1 S 10:1. 1 K *19:18. Jb 31:27. Ps 2:12. Ho 13:2. **only.** Ge 44:18 w Jn √14:28. **greater than.** Ge ◗*44:18 w Jn 14:28.

41. **See, I have set.** ver. 44. Ge 39:5, 22. Est 10:3. Ps *105:21, 22. Pr 17:2. 22:29. Da 2:7, 8. 4:2, 3. 6:3. Mt 28:18. Ph 2:9-11.

42. **his ring.** Est *3:10, 12. 6:7-12. 8:2, 8, 10, 15. 10:3. Da 2:46, 47. *5:7, 29. Lk 15:22. **fine linen.** or,

silk. Ezk 27:7. **a gold chain.** Pr 1:9. 31:22, 24. SS 1:10. Ezk 16:10, 11. Da *5:7, 16, 29. Lk 19:16-19. Re=1:13.

43. **and they.** Est 6:8, 9. **Bow the knee.** or, Tender father. Ge 45:8. Heb. Abrech. Ph=2:10. **ruler.** Ge 42:6, 30, 33. 45:8, 26. Ac *7:10.

44. **without thee.** Jn=15:5. **lift up his hand.** Ex 11:7.

45. **Zaphnath-paaneah.** or, prince. i.e. discovering hidden things, *S#6847h, only here. Ex 2:16. 2 S 8:18. Which in the Coptic signifies 'A revealer of secrets,' or, 'The man to whom secrets are revealed.' Jerome says this name signified in Egyptian, Salvatorem mundi, the Saviour of the world. If this interpretation be correct, Pharaoh must have meant Egypt by the world, of which Joseph might justly be termed the Saviour. See the same phraseology applied to Syria, Palestine, etc. Lk 2:1. Ac 11:28. **Asenath.** i.e. fairness; beautiful; devoted to Neith (the titular goddess of Sais), *S#621h. ver. 50. Ge 46:20. **Potipherah.** i.e. priest of the sun; affliction of the locks (of hair), *S#6319h. ver. 50. Ge 46:20. **priest of.** or, prince. Ge 14:18. Ex 2:16mg. 2 S 8:18. 20:26h. Is +24:2mg. **On.** ver. 50. Ge 46:40. Ezk 30:17, Aven.

46. **thirty years.** Ge 37:2. Nu=4:3. 2 S=5:4. Lk=3:23. **he stood.** 1 S 16:21. 1 K 12:6, 8. Pr 22:29. Da 1:19. Lk +*21:36. Ju 24.

47. From A.M. 2289, B.C. 1715, to A.M. 2296, B.C. 1708. **handfuls.** ʃ102, Ge +2:24. Ge 26:12. Ps 72:16.

48. **he gathered.** ver. 34-36. Ge 47:21.

49. **as.** ʃ102, Ge +2:24. **the sand.** ʃ138B, Ge +13:16. Ge 22:17. Jg 6:5. 7:12. 1 S 13:5. Jb 1:33. Ps 78:27. Je 33:22. **without.** Ep=3:8.

50. **unto Joseph.** Ge 46:20. 48:5. **Asenath.** ver. 45. Ge 46:20. **priest.** or, prince. 2 S 8:18. Is +24:2mg.

51. A.M. 2292. B.C. 1712. **called.** Ge 48:5, 13, 14, 18-20. Dt 33:17. **the name.** ʃ144A4B, Ge +11:9. **firstborn.** Ge √48:18. 1 Ch 26:10. Ps 89:27. Je ◗+√31:9. Col +√1:15. **Manasseh.** i.e. Forgetting. causing to forget, *S#4519h. see on ver. ◗30. Ge 46:20. 48:1, 5, 13, 14, 20, 20. 50:23. Nu ◗1:34. 26:28, 29. 27:1, 1. 32:39, 40, 41. 36:1. Dt 3:14. ◗33:17. Jsh ◗4:12. 17:1, 2, 3. 1 K 4:13. 1 Ch 7:14, 17. (1) Joseph's firstborn son, Ge 41:51; 46:20. (2) The tribe descended from Manasseh, the son of Joseph, Nu +1:10. Their territory was divided into two portions, one lying east of the river Jordan and the other west of it. The latter is frequently joined with the territory of Ephraim in Biblical references. (3) A king of Judah, 2 K 20:21; 1 Ch 3:13; 2 Ch 32:33. He was the son and successor of King Hezekiah, and became king B.C. 696, when twelve years old. He was taken captive by an Assyrian king and carried to Babylon, but was allowed to return to Jerusalem. He died B.C. 641. He is called Manasses in Mt 1:10. Is 38:19n. (4) A Levite whose grandson Jonathan became an idolatrous priest of the tribe of Dan, Jg 18:30. (5) A Jew who married a foreign wife, Ezr 10:30. (6) Another Jew who married a foreign wife, Ezr 10:33. **forget.** Jb *11:16. Ps 30:5, 11. 45:10. Pr 31:7. Is 57:16. 65:16.

52. A.M. 2293. B.C. 1711. **called he.** Ge 29:32-35. 30:6-13. 50:23. **Ephraim.** i.e. Fruitful, in Hebrew sounding like the word for twice fruitful. Ge 48:16, 19. 49:22. ✣S#669h: Ge 46:20. 48:1, 5, 13, 17, 20, 20. 49:22. Nu 1:10, 32, 33. 2:18, 24. 7:48. *26:28. Dt 33:17. 34:2. Jsh 14:4. 16:4, etc. 17:8-18. Jg 1:29. 5:14.

8:1. 1 Ch *7:20, 22. 2 Ch 30:1. Ps 60:7. 78:9, 10, 67. 80:2. 108:8. Is 7:2, etc. 9:9, 21. *11:13. 17:3. 28:1, 3. *40:1, 2. Je 7:15. 31:6, +√9, 18, *20. Ezk 37:16, 19. 48:5, 6. Ho *4:17. 5:3, etc. 6:4, 10. 7:1, *8, 11. 8:9, 11. 9:3, 8, 11, 13, 16, 17. 10:6. 11:3, etc. 12:1, 8, 14. 13:1, 12. *14:8. Ob 1:19. Zc 9:10, 13. 10:7. (1) Joseph's second son by his wife Asenath, Ge 41:52. (2) The tribe which sprang from Ephraim or the territory which they occupied, Nu 1:33. (3) Mountains in Samaria, Jsh 17:15. (4) A city belonging to Benjamin, 2 S 13:23; Jn 11:54. Supposed to be the same as Ephrain. (5) The name of one of the gates of Jerusalem, 2 K 14:13; 2 Ch 25:23. Ne 8:16. 12:39. (6) The wood of Ephraim, a woody and rugged district in Gad, so named from the slaughter of the Ephraimites recorded in Jg ch. 12, which took place near it, 2 S 18:6. **fruitful.** Jn=12:24. **the land.** Ps 105:17, 18. Am 6:6. Ac 7:10.

53. A.M. 2296. B.C. 1708. **years of plenteousness.** ver. 29-31. Ps 73:20. Lk 16:25.

54. **the seven.** ver. 3, 4, 6, 7, 27. Ge 45:11. Ps 105:16. Ac 7:11. **according.** ver. 30. **as.** Jn=2:22. **and the dearth.** Ge 42:2, 5, 6. 43:1. 45:11. 47:13. **all.** ver. 56, 57. Ge +*7:19. ʃ102. Hyperbole, Ge +2:24. Ge +7:19. **but in.** Ex 10:23. Ps *37:25. Jn 6:22-59.

55. **famished.** 2 K 6:25-29. Je 14:1-6. La 4:3-10. **Go unto.** ver. 40, 41. Ps 105:20-22. Mt 3:17. 17:5. Jn 1:14-16. =2:5. =6:68. Ph 4:19. Col 1:19. **what he.** Jn=2:5.

56. **famine.** Am=8:11. Lk=15:14. **the face.** Ge +1:2. Is 23:17. Zc 5:3. Lk 21:35. Ac 17:26. **opened.** Ml=3:10. Lk=24:27, 32. **all the storehouses.** Heb. all wherein *was.* **sold.** Ge 42:6. 47:14-24.

57. **all.** ʃ171.O.3. Synecdoche of the Whole B638. "All" is put for the greater part, or for all in the purview of the writer, in the phrase "all the earth." See related note and figures listed at Ge 24:10n. For other instances of this figure see Jg 6:37. 2 S 15:23. Is 13:5. **countries.** ʃ121J17, Ge +6:11. Ge 42:1, 5. 50:20. Dt 9:28. Ps 105:16, 17. Is=49:6. **famine.** Am=8:11. **in all lands.** ver. 54, 56.

GENESIS 42

Jacob sends ten of his sons to Egypt to buy corn, 1-5. Joseph, who knows them but is unknown to them, imprisons them as spies, 6-17. They betray before Joseph remorse for their cruelty to him: he conceals his sympathy; retains Simeon, and sends the rest home, with provisions, requiring them to bring their younger brother, 18-25. They find their money in their sacks' mouths, and are alarmed: they report the matter to Jacob, who complains, laments, is affrighted, and refuses to send Benjamin, 26-38.

1. **when Jacob.** Ge 41:54, 57. Ac *7:12. **saw.** i.e. heard, from the report of others, that there was plenty in Egypt. The operations of one sense are frequently put for those of another in Hebrew; (see the parallel passages). ver. 2. Ex 5:19. 20:18. 1 K 19:3. Ho 5:13. Ga 2:7. ʃ171J15. Synecdoche of the Species B629. Verbs expressing the operation of one sense are in Hebrew often put for those of another. Here, seeing is put for hearing. Re 1:12. Seeing is put for smelling, Ex 5:21; for tasting, Ps 34:8; for touching, Jn 20:29. Compare the figure Idiom, ʃ108B, Ge +21:16. **corn.** ʃ121D4, Ge +27:28, **Why do ye.** Jsh 7:10. 2 K 7:3, 4. Ezr 10:4. Je 8:14.

2. **corn.** ʃ121D4, Ge +27:8. **get you.** Ge 43:2, 4. 45:9. **that we.** Ge 43:8. Ps 118:17. Is 38:1. Mt 4:4. **not die.** ʃ144D, Ge +40:23.

3. **ten brethren.** ver. 5, 13. Ge 43:20.

4. **Benjamin.** Ge 35:16-19. **Lest.** ver. 38. Ge 3:22. 11:4. 33:1, 2. 43:14, 29. 44:20-22, 27-29, +*30, 31-34.

5. **for.** Ge 12:10. 26:1. 41:57. Ac 7:11. 11:28.

6. **governor.** Ge 41:40, 41. 45:8, 26. Ps 105:16-21. Ec 7:19. 8:8. 10:5. Ezk 7:24. Da 2:10, 15. 4:*17, 25, 26, 32. 5:21, 29. Ac 7:10. **he it was.** Ge 41:55, 56. Pr=11:26. Ac=4:12. **bowed.** Ge 18:2. 19:1. *37:7, 9. 43:26, 28. 44:14. 50:18. Re 3:9.

7. **knew.** Jn=2:24, 25. **made.** Ge +27:16. Lk= 24:16. **spake.** Jb 36:8-10. **roughly unto them.** Heb. hard things with them. ver. 9-12, 14-17, 19, 20. Pr *18:19. Mt 15:23-26.

8. **Joseph knew.** Jn=2:24, 25. He +4:13. **they knew not.** Lk=24:16. Jn=1:10, 11. 20:14. 21:4.

9. **remembered.** Ge 37:5-9. **Ye are spies.** ver. 9, 16, 30, 31, 34. Nu 13:2, 16-20. Jsh 2:1. 6:23. Jg 1:24. 1 S 26:4. Lk 20:20. He 11:31. **nakedness.** ʃ155D, Ge +4:10. Ex 32:25.

10. **my lord.** Ge 27:29, 37. 37:8. 44:9. 1 S 26:17. 1 K 18:7.

11. **We are.** ver. 31. **true men.** ver. 19, 33, 34. Jn 7:18. 2 C 6:8. **thy servants.** ver. 13. Ge 44:7. 46:34. 47:3.

12. **nakedness.** ʃ155D, Ge +4:10. ver. 9.

13. **Thy servants.** ver. +11, 32. Ge 29:32-35. 30:6-24. 35:16-26. 43:7. 46:8-27. Ex 1:2-5. Nu ch. 1, 10, 26, 34. 1 Ch ch. 2-8. **youngest.** Ge 9:24. **one is not.** ver. 36, 38. Ge 5:24. 37:30. 44:20, 28. 45:26. Je 31:15. La 5:7. Mt 2:16, 18.

14. **That.** ver. 9-11. Jb 13:24. 19:11. Mt 15:21-28.

15. **By the life.** ver. 7, 12, 16, 30. Dt 6:13. 1 S 1:26. 17:55. 20:3. Je 5:2, 7. Mt 5:33-37. 23:16-22. Ja *5:12. **except.** ver. 20, 34. Ge 43:3. 44:20-34.

16. **brother.** ver. 15. **kept in prison.** Heb. bound. ver. 19. **that your.** ver. 7, 12, 30. **truth.** ver. 11. **spies.** ver. 9, 11.

17. **put.** Heb. gathered. Ps +27:10mg. Is 24:22. +58:8mg. Ac 5:18. **ward.** Ge 40:4, 7. 41:10. Le 24:12. Jb 36:8-10. Ps 119:65. Ac 4:3. He 12:10.

18. **live.** ʃ96B, Ge +20:7. **I fear God.** Ge 20:11. Le *25:43. Ne *5:9, 15. Lk 18:2, 4.

19. **house.** Ge 40:3. Is 42:7, 22. Je 37:15. **carry corn.** ver. 1, 2, 26. Ge 41:56. 43:1, 2. 45:23.

20. **bring.** ver. 15, 34. Ge 43:5, 19. 44:23. **And they.** ver. 26. Ge 6:22. Jn 2:5.

21. **they said.** Ge 41:9. Nu +*32:23. 2 S *12:13. 1 K 17:18. Jb 33:27, 28. 34:31, 32. *36:8, 9. Pr *28:13. Ho *5:15. Mt 27:3, 4. Mk 9:44, 46, 48. Lk 16:28. Ac 19:18. **we saw.** Ge 37:23-28. Jg 1:7. Pr *21:13. 24:11, 12. 28:17. Je 2:17, 19. 4:18. 34:17. Mt *7:2. Ja *2:13. 1 J 1:9. **soul.** Heb. *nephesh,* S#5315h, Ge +34:3. **therefore.** Ge +*6:13 (T#566). Ps +*9:10. **this distress.** Pr 1:27, 28.

22. **Spake I.** Ge 37:21, 22, 29, 30. Lk 23:51. Ro 2:15. **his blood.** Ge 4:10. *9:5, 6. 1 K 2:32. 2 Ch 24:22. Ps *9:12. Ezk 3:18. Mt=27:25. Lk 11:50, 51. Ac 28:4. Re 13:10. 16:9.

23. **understood.** Ge +18:10. Is=11:3. **he spake unto them by an interpreter.** Heb. an interpreter *was* between them. The *mailitz* does not seem to have been an interpreter in our sense of the term; as we have

many evidences in this book that the Egyptians, Hebrews, Canaanites, and Syrians could understand each other in a general way; and it appears from several passages in this very chapter (particularly ver. 24) that Joseph and his brethren understood each others' language, as his brethren and Joseph's steward also did (Ge 43:19, etc.; compare Ge ch. 39, 49). It seems to denote an officer who is called in Abyssinia, according to Mr. Bruce, *Kal Hatze,* 'the voice or word of the king,' who always stands at the side of a lattice window of a balcony, within which the king sits; who is never seen, but who speaks through a hole in the side of it, covered in the inside with a curtain, to this officer, by whom he speaks to the persons present. Jn=16:13, 14. 2 C=5:20.

24. **wept.** Ge 43:30. Is 63:9. Lk=19:41. Ro 12:15. 1 C 12:26. He 4:15. Note the seven times Joseph wept: Ge 43:30. 45:2, 14. 46:29. 50:1, 17. **Simeon.** Ge 34:25. 49:5-7. Ju 22, 23.

25. **commanded.** Ge 44:1, 2. Is 55:1. **fill.** Jn=1:16. **restore.** Is =55:1. **to give them.** Ge 45:21. Mt 6:33. **provision.** Ph=4:19. **and thus.** Jsh=21:45. =23:14. Mt *5:44. Ro *12:17-21. 1 P 3:9.

26. **laded their asses.** Ge 12:16. 24:35. 30:43. 32:5, 15. 34:28. 44:3, 13. 45:17, 23. 1 S 25:18. 2 S 16:2. 1 Ch 12:40. 2 Ch 28:15. Ne 13:15. Jb 1:3. Is 30:6.

27. **the inn.** Ge *43:21. 44:11. Ex 4:24. Lk 2:7. 10:34.

28. **their heart.** ver. 36. Ge 27:33. Le 26:36. Dt 21:26. 28:65. 1 K 10:5. SS 5:6. Lk *21:26. **failed them.** Heb. went forth. ℐ102, Ge +2:24. Ex 15:15. Jsh 2:9, 11. 5:1. 7:5. Ps 22:14. Is 13:7. Mk 5:33. **What is.** ℐ85E, Ge +17:17. Is +*45:7. La 2:17. 3:37. Am +*3:6.

29. **Canaan.** ver. 5, 13. Ge 37:1. 45:17. **told.** Ge 44:24.

30. **roughly to us.** Heb. with us hard things. ver. 7-20. Pr *13:15. *22:5.

31. **true.** ver. 11.

32. **twelve brethren.** ver. 13.

33. **Hereby.** ver. 15, 19, 20.

34. **traffick.** Ge 34:10, 21. 1 K 10:15. Ezk 17:4.

35. **every man's.** ver. 27, 28. Ge *43:21.

36. **Me have ye.** Ge 37:20-35. 43:14. **all these.** Ge 45:28. 47:12. 1 S *27:1. Jb 7:7. ◖42:10. Ps *34:19. Ec 7:8. Is 27:9. 38:10. 41:10, 13, 14. Mt 14:31. Ro √8:28, 31. 1 C +*10:13. 2 C *4:17. Ja 5:7-11. **against me.** Ru +√1:13. Je ◖+*29:11.

37. **Slay my.** Ge 43:9. 44:32-34. 46:9. Mi 6:7.

38. **his brother.** ver. 13. Ge 30:22-24. 35:16-18. 37:33, 35. 44:20, 27-34. **if mischief.** ver. 4. Ge 44:29. **then.** ℐ88, Ge +15:15. **bring down.** Ge 37:35. 44:29, 31. Nu 16:30. 1 K 2:6. Ps 49:14. 71:18. 89:48. 90:10. Ec 1:14. 2:26. 9:10. Is 38:10. *46:4. Ho 13:14. Ac 2:27. Re 20:13. ℐ121E2. Metonymy of the Effect B562. The effect is put for the cause producing it: the verb expressing the effect is put for the cause, author, or occasion of it. Here, this would be the cause of my death. For other instances of this figure see Ge 43:6. Ex 23:8. 1 K 18:9. Ps 76:10. Is 43:24. Je 38:23mg. Ezk 19:7. Ac 1:18. Ro 14:15. 1 C 7:16. ℐ108A5. Idiom B824: Active verbs are used to express, not the doing of a thing, but the occasion of a thing's being done. For other instances of this figure see 1 K 14:16. Ac 1:18. **my.** ℐ121N1, Ge +31:54. **the grave.** Heb. *sheol,* Ge +37:35.

GENESIS 43

Jacob at length is persuaded to send Benjamin, who goes with his brethren into Egypt, 1-15. They are brought into Joseph's house, and are greatly alarmed, but are encouraged by Joseph's steward, 16-25. Joseph is kind to them, inquires about their father, is affected at seeing Benjamin; and they do obeisance to him, 26-29. Joseph retires to weep, and then hospitably entertains them, 30-34.

1. **the famine.** Ge 18:13. 41:54-57. 42:5. Ec 9:1, 2. La 5:10. Ac 7:11-13.

2. **Go again.** ver. 4, 20. Ge 42:1, 2. Pr 15:16. 16:18. 31:16. 1 T 5:8. 6:6-8.

3. **The man.** Ge 42:15-20, 33, 34. 44:23. ℐ52B. Chiasmus; or, Introverted Correspondence B374. Here, Chiasmus is displayed thusly: (A) Judah's words, "The man did solemnly protest," etc. (B) Jacob's act: "If thou wilt send." (B) Jacob's act: "But if thou wilt not send him." (A) Joseph's words: "For the man said unto us," etc. The figure consists of a series of words or topics, which are repeated in reverse order, which, if assigned letters for each member or topic, would appear as A, B, C, D, E, E, D, C, B, A. Generally there is intended great emphasis upon the central members of the Chiasmus. This figure has been noted by various authorities in the following passages: Le 14:51, 52. Nu 15:35, 36. Dt 32:1-43. Ps 3:7, etc. 6:3. 7:16. ch. 23. 58:6. 89:30-34. ch. 103. Is 55:8, 9. 60:1-3. Mt 3:10-12. 7:6. 9:17. 12:22. Mk 5:2-6. Jn 5:8-11. 5:21-29. 6:36-40. 10:14, 15. 12:23-32. Ro 1:22. 2:6-11. 10:9, 10. 14:7, etc. 1 C 4:10? 5:2-6. 7:3. 7:1-7. 9:19-22. 11:8-12. Ga 1:1. 2:16. 3:2. 4:4n, 5, 6. Ep 2:11-22 (11-13, 13-17, 18-22). Ph 1:15, etc. 3:10, etc. 4:11-13. Col 1:13-20. 3:3, etc. 3:11. 1 Th 1:2-5. 5:5. 5:6. Phm 5. 3 J 11. Re 2:13. Even whole books of Scripture are based upon this structure. Scholars have noticed this is true for Galatians. The book of James, as outlined in the Companion Bible, is a striking example. Many more instances of Chiasmus are given in N. W. Lund, *Chiasmus in the New Testament. A Study in Formgeshichte,* N. Carolina, 1942. Lund wrote numerous journal articles which furnish yet more examples. Lund's work needs to be reprinted to make his research available today, for it has great significance for the study of the style of the writers of the New Testament, elucidates many obscure passages, and provides valuable assistance for textual criticism, for both the Hebrew and Greek text of Scripture. Only 500 copies of his book were ever printed, and they are exceedingly scarce today. Though his work is scholarly, it would certainly be understandable to most serious adult students of the Bible. **did solemnly protest.** Heb. protesting, protested. ℐ147B, Ge +2:16. Ac 7:34. **see my face.** ver. 5. 2 S 3:13. 14:24, 28, 32. Est 1:14. Ps 11:7. *16:11. 17:15. Ac 20:25, 38.

5. **will not.** Ge 42:38. 44:26. Ex 20:12.

6. **dealt.** ℐ121E2, Ge +42:38.

7. **asked us straitly.** Heb. asking asked us. ver. 3mg. ℐ147B, Ge +2:16. **tenor.** Heb. mouth. **could we certainly know.** knowing could we know. ver. 3mg. ℐ147B, Ge +2:16.

8. **lad with me.** Ge 42:38. 44:26. Ex 20:12. **and.** ℐ148, Ge +8:22. **that we.** Ge 42:2. Dt 33:6. 2 K 7:4, 13. Ps 118:17. **also our.** Ge 45:19. 50:8, 21. Nu 14:31. Ezr 8:21.

9. **will be**. Ge 42:37. 44:32, 33. 1 K 1:21. Jb 17:3. Ps 119:122. Phm *18, 19. He 7:22. **of my hand**. Ge 9:5. 31:39. Ezk 3:18, 20. 33:6, 8. Lk 11:50.

10. **lingered**. Ge 19:16. 45:9. **this second time**. or, twice by this.

11. **Israel**. Ge 35:22. 37:3. 45:28. 46:30. 50:2. **If it must be**. ver. 14. Est 4:16. Ac 21:14. **take**. Ge 32:14. 1 K 10:25. Mt 2:11. **fruits**. lit. praise. ℐ121R7. Metonymy of the Adjunct B602. Actions are put for the object connected with, or related to them, the object is shown by the context. Here, *praise* is put for the choice fruits which called forth the praise. For other instances of this figure see Ex 15:2. Dt 12:7. 28:8. 1 S 1:27. Ne 8:8. Jb 6:8. Ps 118:14. Is 60:1. Lk 16:15. Ac 1:4. Ga 3:2, 5. 2 Th 1:11. He 11:13. **land**. Je 51:41. **carry down**. Ge *32:13-21. 33:10. *37:25. Dt 33:14. 1 S 9:7. 25:27. 1 K 4:21. 10:25. 15:19. 2 K 8:8. 16:8. 20:12. Ps 68:29. 72:10. 76:11. Pr 17:18. *18:16. 19:6. 21:14. Ezk 27:15. **a little balm**. Ge 37:25. Je 8:22. Ezk 27:17. **balm**. For an explanation of the Hebrew words *tzori*, *nechoth*, and *lot*, here rendered respectively **balm**, **spices**, and **myrrh**, see on Ge 37:25. Ge 37:25. **honey**. Heb. *davash*. *Davash* is supposed by some (as Bochart and Celsius) not to have been that produced by bees, but a sweet syrup produced from dates when in maturity. The Jewish doctors (Talm. tract. Nedarim. c. 6. sec. 10. Terumoth, c. 11. sec. 2. Maimon. Comment. in Tr. Biccurim. c. 1) observe, that the word in 2 Ch 31:5, properly signifies dates; and the Arabians, at this day, call the choicest dates preserved with butter, *dabous*, and the honey obtained from them *dibs* or *dabs*. Le 20:24. 2 Ch 31:5. Ezk 27:17. **spices**. 1 K 10:15. 2 Ch 32:27. SS 4:10, 14-16. 5:1. 8:14. **nuts**. Heb. *betanim. Betanim, nuts*, signifies, according to Bochart, Celsius, Dr. Shaw, and Parkhurst, *pistachio nuts*, the finest in the world being found in Syria; but, according to others, a small nut, the produce of a species of the turpentine tree, which some refer to the pistachio, and others think superior to the almond. See related notes (Ge 37:25n. 2 Ch 31:5n). **almonds**. Je 1:11, 12.

12. **double**. ver. 15. Ro 12:17. 13:8. 2 C 8:21. Ph 4:8. 1 Th 4:6. 5:21. He 13:8. ℐ121L9. Metonymy of the Subject B585. "Double" is used for that which is complete, thorough, or ample; and of full compensation, whether of judgment or blessing. For other instances of this figure see Ex 16:5. 22:7, 9. Dt 15:18. Jb 11:6. 41:13. Is 40:2. 61:7. Je 16:18. 17:18. Zc 9:12. 1 T 5:17. **mouth**. Ge 42:25, 35.

13. **Take also**. Ge 42:38.

14. **And God**. Ge 17:1. 22:14. 32:11-28. 39:21. Ezr 7:27. Ne *1:11. Est 4:16. Ps *37:5-7. 85:7. 100:5. 119:41. Pr 1:1. +*16:7. 21:1. Is 49:13. Lk 1:50. Ac 7:10. 21:14. 1 T 1:2, 16. T 1:4. 2 J 3. **If I be**, etc. or, and I as I have been, etc. Est 4:16. See on ver. 11.

15. **double money**. ver. 12. Ex 22:4, 7. Pr ◐6:31. **went down**. Ge 39:1. 46:3, 6. **stood before**. Ge 37:7. 47:2, 7. Mt 2:11. Ac 7:13.

16. **the ruler**. ver. 19. Ge 15:2. 24:2-10. 39:4, 5. 44:1. **house**. ℐ121J4, Ge +7:1. Metonymy of the Subject. House is put for the servants of it. **Bring**. Lk=14:23. **slay**. Heb. kill a killing. Ge 21:8. 26:30. 31:54. 1 S 25:11mg. *Tevoch taivach*, slay a slaying, or make a great slaughter: let preparations be made for a great feast or entertainment. See a similar form of speech in Ge 31:54. 1 S 25:11. Pr 9:2. ℐ147B, Ge +26:28. **make**. Mt=22:4. **dine with**. Heb. eat.

18. **the men**. Ge 42:21, 28, 35. Jg 13:22. Jb 15:21. Ps 53:5. 73:16. Is 7:2. Mt 14:26, 27. Mk 6:16. **afraid**. 1 J=4:18. **seek occasion against us**. Heb. Roll himself upon us. Dt 22:14, 17. Jg 14:4. Jb 30:14. Ro 7:8. ℐ108J, Idiom B854. Compare Ge 26:20. Le 6:2. Dt 24:14. Jb 10:3. 35:9. Ps 72:4. 119:122, 134. Pr 14:31. 22:16. 28:3, 16. Ec 4:1. 5:8. 7:7. Je 6:6. Ezk 22:12, 29. Lk *3:14. *19:8. **bondmen**. Ge 44:9, 33. Ex 22:3. 2 K 4:1-7.

19. **steward**. ver. 16, 24. 2 S 19:17. Is 22:15. **communed**. Jn=14:26.

20. **we came indeed down**. Heb. coming down we came down. ℐ147B, Ge +2:16. ver. 3, 7. Ge 42:3, 10, 27, 35.

21. **we came**. Ge 42:27-35. **we have**. See on ver. 12. Ro 12:17. 13:8. He 13:5, 18. 1 P 2:12. 3:16.

22. **other money**. Ro=10:3.

23. **Peace**. Jg 6:23. 19:20. 1 S 25:6. 1 Ch 12:18. Ezr 4:17. Lk 10:5. 24:36. Jn 14:27. 20:19, 21, 26. Ro=15:13. ℐ17I9A. Synecdoche of the Species B627. Peace is used for plenty, happiness, and all kinds of earthly good and blessing. For other instances of this figure see Nu 6:26. Ps 119:165. Ro 2:10. **I had your money**. Heb. Your money came to me. *Caspechem ba ailai*, "your money comes to me": as I am the steward, the cash for the corn belongs to me. Ye have no occasion to be apprehensive of any evil; the whole transaction is between myself and you; receive therefore the money as a present from "the God of your father," no matter whose hands he employs to convey it. **Simeon**. ver. 14. Ge 42:24, 36.

24. **gave them water**. Ge 18:4. 19:2. 24:32. Lk 7:44. Jn 13:4-17.

25. **made ready**. ver. 11, 16. Ge 33:10. 1 S 16:20. Pr 17:8. **bread**. ℐ17I18, Ge +3:19.

26. **hand**. Ge *24:10. 35:4. Nu 22:7. **bowed**. ver. 28. Ge 27:29. 37:7-10, 19, 20. 42:6. Ps 72:9. Ro 14:11. Ph 2:10, 11. Re=1:17.

27. **welfare**. Heb. peace. Ge 37:14mg. 41:16. Ex 18:7. Jg 18:15. 1 S 17:22. 25:5. 1 Ch 18:10. Je 38:4mg. **Is your father well**. Heb. *Is there* peace to your father. Ge 29:6mg. 37:14. Jg 18:15mg. 1 S 10:4. 17:22mg. 2 S 11:7. 2 K 4:26. **the old**. Ge 37:3. 42:11, 13. 44:20. Le +*19:32. Jb 32:6. Pr 23:22. 1 T 5:1, 2.

28. **bowed**. ver. 26. Ge 37:7, 9, 10. **made obeisance**. Ex 18:7. 2 S 1:2. 14:4. 1 K 1:16. 2 Ch 24:17.

29. **lifted**. ℐ144A12, Ge +22:13. **mother's son**. Ge 30:22-24. 35:17, 18. **of whom**. Ge 42:11, 13. **God**. Ge 45:8. Jsh 7:19. 2 Ch 29:11. Ps 133:1, 2. Mt 9:2, 22. Mk 10:24. 1 T 1:2. He 13:1. **my son**. Nu 6:25. Ps 111:4. 112:4. Is 30:19. 33:2. Ml 1:9.

30. **his bowels**. ℐ121G1, Is +63:15. 1 K *3:26. Is 47:6. Je *31:20. Ho 11:8. Am 1:11. Zc 7:9. Ph 1:8. 2:1. Col 3:12. Phm 7, 12. 1 J 3:17. **chamber**. or, inner chamber. Ex 8:3. Dt 32:25. Jg 3:24. 15:1. 16:9, 12. 2 S 4:7. 13:10. 1 K 20:30. **wept there**. Ge +42:24. Jn 11:33-38. Ac 20:19, 31, 37. 2 T 1:4.

31. **refrained**. Ge 45:1. Is 42:14. Je 31:16. 1 P 3:10. **Set**. Jn=21:12. **bread**. ℐ17I18, Ge +3:19. ver. 25.

32. **eat bread**. ver. 16. Ge 31:54. **for that is an abomination**. The Chaldee Paraphrast renders this clause, "Because the Hebrews eat the cattle which the Egyptians worship." But, as we learn from ver. 16, compared with this verse, that the provision for the entertainment of the Egyptians themselves was animal food, this reason cannot be just. The true reason

seems to be that assigned by the LXX., "For every shepherd is an abomination to the Egyptians." Ge 46:34. Ex *8:26.

33. **sat.** Ge 42:7. 44:12. **firstborn.** Ge 35:23. 46:8. 49:3. **according.** Ge 44:5, 12, 15. **birthright.** Ge 25:31. **marvelled.** ♪63H, Ge +12:15.

34. **messes.** 2 S 11:8. **was five.** Alford states that "The number five seems to have been in especial regard in Egypt: see Ge 41:34. 45:22. 47:2, 24. Is 29:18. The reason is stated to have been, that the Egyptians recognized only five planets." 2 K +7:13. **times.** 1 S 1:5. 9:22-24. Is 19:18. Sir John Chardin observes that "in Persia, Arabia, and in the Indies, there are some houses where they place several plates in large salvers, and set one of these before each person, or before two or three, according to the magnificence of each house. The great men of the state are always served by themselves, in the feasts that are made for them; and with great profusion, their part of each kind of provision being always double, treble, or a larger proportion of each kind of meat." **were merry.** Heb. drank largely. Ge 9:21. 1 S 1:14. 2 S 11:13. Pr 31:6. Ec 9:7. 10:19. SS 5:1. Is 29:9. Je 25:27. Hg 1:6. Mt 11:19. Lk=15:24. Jn 2:10.

GENESIS 44

Joseph directs his steward to put the money into the mouths of his brethren's sacks, and his silver cup into that of Benjamin, 1, 2; and afterwards to pursue them and accuse them of theft, 3-6. Their sacks are searched; the cup is found; and in deep distress they return to Joseph, 7-13. They humble themselves before him, 14-17; and Judah makes a most pathetic speech, concluding with a most generous request, 18-34.

1. **the steward.** Heb. *him* that *was* over his house. Ge 24:2. 43:16, 19. **Fill the.** Ge 42:25. 43:2. Is 3:1. **as much.** Jn=6:11.

2. **cup.** Ge 42:15, 16, 20. 43:32. Dt 8:2, 16. 13:3. Mt 10:16. 2 C 8:8.

4. **Up.** Dt 2:16. **Wherefore.** ♪85, Ge +3:9. 1 S 24:17. 2 Ch 20:11. Ps 35:12. 109:5. Pr 17:13. Jn 10:32.

5. **divineth.** *or*, maketh trial. lit. divining he divineth. ♪147B, Ge +2:16. ver. 15mg. Ge +30:27. Le 19:26. 1 K 20:33. 2 K 21:6.

7. **Wherefore.** Ge 34:25-31. 35:22. 37:18-32. 38:16-18. Jsh 22:22-29. 2 S 20:20. 2 K 8:13. Pr 22:1. Ec 7:1. He 13:18. **forbid.** ver. 17. Ge 18:25.

8. **the money.** Ge 42:21, 27, 35. 43:12, 21, 22. **how then.** See on ver. 7. Ex 20:15. Dt 5:19. Mt 19:18. Ro 13:9. Ja 2:10, 11.

9. **both.** Ge *31:32. Jb 31:38-40. Ps 7:3-5. Ac 25:11. **and we.** Ge 43:18.

10. **he with whom.** ver. 17, 33. Ex 22:3. Mt 18:24, 25.

12. **began.** Ge 43:33. **and the cup.** ver. 26-32. Ge 42:36-38. 43:14.

13. **rent their clothes.** Ge 37:29-34. Nu 14:6. 2 S 1:2, 11. 13:19.

14. **he was yet.** Ge 43:16, 25. **fell.** Ge 37:7-9. 50:18. Ph 2:10, 11.

15. **What.** ♪85, Ge +3:9. ver. 4, 5. Ge 3:13. 4:10. **wot ye not.** Ge 21:26. 39:8. Ex 32:1. **divine.** *or*, make trial. ♪147B, Ge +2:16. ver. 5. Ge +30:27.

16. **Judah.** ver. 32. Ge 43:8, 9. **What shall we say.**

♪85, Ge +3:9. Dt 25:1. Ezr 9:10, 15. Jb 40:4. Pr 17:15. Is 5:3. Da 9:7. Ac 2:37. **God hath.** Ge *37:18-28. 42:21, 22. Nu +√32:23. Jsh 7:1, 18. Jg 1:7. Pr 28:17. Mt 7:2. Lk 12:2. **found out.** Jn=16:8, 9. **iniquity.** Ge 43:9. Is 27:9. Da 9:7. **behold.** ver. 9. Ge 37:7, 9.

17. **God forbid.** Ge +*18:25. 42:18. 2 S 23:3. Ps 75:2. Pr 17:15. **he shall.** ver. 10. **in peace.** Ge 26:29. 37:32, 33.

18. **Oh my Lord.** ver. 22, 24. Ge 37:8. 43:20. **let thy.** Ge 18:30, 32. 2 S 14:12. Jb 33:31. Ac 2:29. **ears.** Ge 50:4. 1 S 18:23. **anger.** Ex 32:22. Est 1:12. Ps 79:5. **even as.** or, as great as (NEB), or, equal to (NASB, NIV). Ge 41:40 w Jn +√14:28. Jn ◖/5:18. Just as Jesus said "my father is greater than I" (Jn 14:28), yet the Evangelist records that the Jews rightly understood him to be "making himself equal to God" (Jn 5:18), so in the history of Joseph, which demonstrates so many parallels with the life of our Lord, Joseph is said to be "equal to Pharaoh," and yet of him Pharaoh said, "only in the throne will I be greater than thou." Here then is demonstrated the possibility of being equal to, yet in some respect not as great as another, even on a human scale. **Pharaoh.** Ge 41:40, 44. Pr 19:12. Da 3:15, 19-23. 5:19. Jn 5:22.

19. **asked his servants.** Ge 42:7-10. 43:7, 29.

20. **we said.** Every word in this verse is simplicity and pathos itself. No man of the least sensibility can read it without great emotion. Indeed the whole speech is exquisitely beautiful, and perhaps the most complete pattern of genuine natural eloquence extant in any language. When we read this generous speech, we forgive Judah all the past, and cannot refuse to say, "Thou art he whom thy brethren shall praise." Ge 49:8. **a child.** Ge 35:18. *37:3, 19. 43:7, 8. 46:21. **little.** Ge 43:29. 43:8. 44:30-34. 46:21. **and his brother.** Ge 37:33-35. 42:36, 38. **he alone.** ver. 27-29. Lk 7:12.

21. **Bring.** Ge 42:15, 20. 43:29. **that I may.** Je 24:6. 40:4. Am 9:4.

22. **his father would die.** ver. 30. Ge 42:38.

23. **Except.** Ge 42:15-20. 43:3, 5.

24. **we told him.** Ge 42:29-34.

25. **Go again.** Ge 43:2, 5.

26. **We cannot.** Ge 43:4, 5. Lk 11:7.

27. **my wife.** Ge 29:18-21, 28. 30:22-25. 35:16-18. 46:19.

28. **the one.** Ge 37:13, 14. **Surely.** Ge 37:33. 42:36, 38.

29. **And if.** Ge 42:36, 38. 43:14. Ps 88:3, 4. **sorrow.** ver. 31. Ge 42:38. Dt 31:17. Ps 88:4. **grave.** Heb. *sheol*, *S#7585h, Ge +√37:35. ver. 31. Ge +√37:35. 42:38. Ps *16:10. *88:3. Ec 9:10. Ho 13:14. Mt 11:23. Ac *2:31. Re 20:13.

30. **when I.** ver. 17, 31, 34. **his life.** Heb. his soul is knit with the lad's soul. 1 S 18:1. 25:29. 2 S 18:33. Mt +√2:20. Lk 12:22. ✛S#5315h, *nephesh. Nephesh* is sometimes used of man as being mortal, subject to death, as here and at Ge 9:5, 5. +12:13. 19:17, 19. 32:30. +√35:18. 44:30, 30. Ex 4:19. 21:23, 23, 30. Nu 35:31. Dt 19:21, 21. 24:6. Jsh 2:13, 14. 9:24. Jg 5:18. 9:17. 12:3. 18:25, 25. Ru 4:15. 1 S 19:5, 11. 20:1. 22:23, 23. 23:15. 26:24, 24. 28:9, 21. 2 S 1:9. 4:8. 16:11. 18:13. 19:5, 5, 5. 23:17. 1 K 1:12, 12. 2:23. 3:11. 19:2, 2, 3, 4, 10, 14. 20:31, 39, 39, 42, 42. 2 K 1:13, 13, 14. 7:7. 10:24, 24. 1 Ch 11:19, 19. 2 Ch 1:11. Est 7:3, 7. 8:11. 9:16. Jb 2:4, 6. 6:11. 13:14. 31:39. Ps 31:13. 38:12. Pr 1:18, 19. 6:26. 7:23. 13:3,

8. Is 15:4. 43:4. Je 4:30. 11:21. 19:7, 9. 21:7, 9. 22:25. 34:20, 21. 38:2, 16. 39:18. 44:30, 30. 45:5. 46:26. 48:6. 49:37. La 2:19. 5:9. Ezk 32:10. Jon 1:14. 4:3. **bound.** Ge *25:28. 33:2. 37:3, 4. 42:4. 48:22. 2 S 13:21n. 1 Ch 26:10. 1 T 5:21. Ja 2:9. 3:17.

31. **when he.** 1 S 4:17, 18. 2 C 7:10. 1 Th 4:13. **is not.** Ge 37:30. 42:13. **servants shall.** ver. 29. Ge 37:26, 27, 35. 1 S 22:22. **grave.** ver. +29. Ge +√37:35.

32. **surety for.** See on Ge 43:8, 9, 16.

33. **therefore.** What must Benjamin have felt when he heard his brother conclude his speech by a proposal which could never have been thought of if it had not been made! Perhaps the annals of the whole world do not produce an instance of so heroic and disinterested affection in any mere man. **I pray thee.** Ex *32:32. Ro 5:7-10. 9:3. **instead.** He 7:22. 1 J 3:16.

34. **lest.** 1 S 2:33, 34. 2 Ch 34:28. Est 8:6. Je 52:10, 11. **see.** ✓108B, Ge +21:16. **come on.** Heb. find. ✓155F, Ge +4:7. Ex 18:8mg. Nu 20:14mg. 2 K +9:21mg. Ne 9:32mg. Jb 31:29. Ps 116:3mg. 119:143mg.

GENESIS 45

Joseph makes himself known to his brethren, 1-3; encourages them by showing them the Lord's merciful purposes in these transactions, 4-8; orders them to fetch his father and family into Egypt; and cordially embraces them, 9-15. Pharaoh confirms the invitation, 16-20. Joseph furnishes his brethren for their journeys, and exhorts them to concord, 21-24. They report the whole to Jacob, who hardly believes the tidings, but is at length revived by them, 25-28.

1. **could not.** Ge 43:30, 31. Is 42:14. Je 20:9. **Cause.** 2 S 1:20. Mt 18:15. Ac 10:41. 1 C 13:5. **no man.** Mt=17:8. **known.** Lk=24:31, 35. Ac *7:13.

2. **wept.** Heb. gave forth his voice in weeping. Ge +42:24. Nu 14:1. Ru 1:9. 2 K 20:3. Ac 20:37.

3. **I am Joseph.** Mt 14:27. Ac 7:13. 9:5. **doth.** ver. 9. Ge 46:29. 48:1, 21. 50:1. Ru 1:8-11, 16-18. 2 K 13:4. **for they.** Jb 4:5. 23:15. Zc 12:10. Mt 14:26. Mk 6:50. Lk 5:8. 24:37, 38. Re 1:7. **troubled.** *or*, terrified. Ex 15:15. Jg 20:41. Jb 4:5. 21:6. 22:10. 23:15, 16. Zc=12:10. Mt 14:26. Mk 6:50.

4. **near.** Ps 73:28. Is 48:16. Ep=2:13. Ja *4:8. **I am Joseph.** Ge 37:28. 50:18. Mt 14:27. Ac=9:5.

5. **be not grieved.** Is *40:1, 2. Lk 23:34. 2 C *2:7, 11. **nor angry with yourselves.** Heb. neither let there be anger in your eyes. ✓155A, Ge +31:35. **for God.** T#268. ver. 7, 8. Ge 47:25. *50:20. Ex 9:16. 10:1, 2. 1 S 1:19. 2 S 12:12. 16:10-12. 17:14. Jb 1:21. Ps +46:10 (T#277). 76:10. *105:16, 17. Mt *18:7. Ac 2:23, 24. 4:24-28. 7:9-15. Ro 3:5-8. 5:20. 6:17. *8:28. 1 C +11:19. **send.** 1 J=4:9.

6. **two years.** Ge 41:29-31, 54-56. 47:18. **in.** lit. in the midst. ✓144A6. Pleonasm; or, Redundancy B411. The phrase "in the midst" is used pleonastically when it is not to be taken literally as being equidistant from the extremes, or when it only adds emphasis to the sense. For other instances of this figure see Nu 14:13. Jsh 3:17. 1 K 3:28mg. 2 K 4:13. Ps 22:14, 22. 40:8, 10. 48:9. Is 10:23. Hab 3:2. Zc 2:5, 10, 11. Mt 13:25, 49. Lk 17:11. Ac 17:33. 2 C 6:17. He 2:12. **earing.** Earing means plowing or seed-time. Ge 47:23. Ex 34:21. Dt 21:4. 1 S 8:12. Is 30:24.

7. **sent.** 1 J=4:9. **to preserve you a posterity.** Heb. to put for you a remnant. 2 S 14:7. Je 44:7. **to save.**

Jg 15:18. 1 Ch 11:14. Ps 18:50. 44:4. Ac 7:35. **great.** 2 C=1:10.

8. **it was not.** ver. 5. Ge +√24:44. Jn 15:16. 19:11. Ac=2:23. Ro 9:16. **father.** Ge 41:39-48. Jg 17:10. Jb 29:16. Ps 105:21, 22. **lord.** He=3:6. 1 P=3:22.

9. **and say.** ✓96C2. Heterosis of Tenses B519: Past Tense for the Future. Here it is literally "have said," which is put for "will say." For other instances of this figure see Ge 45:10. Ex 17:4. 1 S 2:31. 6:7. 10:2. Jb *19:27. Ps 23:5. 107:42. Pr *1:22. 11:7, 21. 12:21. Is 11:1. Je 21:9. Jn 3:13. 4:38. Ro *8:30. 1 C 15:27. Ep 2:6. He 2:7. 3:14. 12:22. **Thus saith.** ver. 26-28. **come.** ver. 13, 19, 20. Mt=11:30. **tarry not.** 2 C=6:2.

10. **shalt dwell.** lit. hast dwelt. ✓96C2, Ge +45:9. **in the land.** Ge 46:29, 34. 47:1-6. Ex 8:22. 9:26. **Goshen.** Ge 46:28, 34. 47:11. 50:8. Ex 8:22. 9:26. Jsh 10:41. 11:16. 15:51. **be near.** Jn 14:2, 3. 17:24.

11. **nourish.** Ge 47:6, 12. Ps 36:7-9. Mt 15:5, 6. Mk 7:9-12. Jn=6:35. 1 T 5:4.

12. **your eyes.** Ge 42:23. Lk=24:39. Jn 20:27. **it is.** ✓63C, Ge +25:32. **my mouth.** Not as Ge 42:23.

13. **my glory.** Jn=17:22, 24. 2 C=4:4. 1 P 1:10-12. Re 21:23. **bring.** Ac *7:14.

14. **fell.** Ge 29:11. 33:4. 46:29. Ro 1:31. **wept.** Ge +42:24. Ps *30:5.

15. **Moreover.** ver. 2. Ge 29:11, 13. 33:4. Ex 4:27. Ru 1:9, 14. 1 S 10:1. 20:41. 2 S 14:33. Lk 15:20. Ac 20:37. **talked.** Ps 77:4. Lk=24:15.

16. **it pleased Pharaoh well.** Heb. was good in the eyes of Pharaoh. Ge 16:6mg. 20:15mg. 34:18. 41:37. Dt 1:33. Jsh +22:30mg. 2 S 3:36. 2 Ch 30:4. Est 1:21. 2:4. 5:14. Ac 6:5.

17. **lade your.** Ge 42:25, 26. 44:1, 2.

18. **come.** Mt=11:28. **shall.** ✓96B, Ge +20:7. **the fat.** Ge 27:28. 47:6. Nu *18:12, 29. Dt 32:14. Ps 81:16. 147:14. Is 28:1, 4.

19. **commanded.** Is 49:1, 23. 1 J=3:23, 24. **this do.** Mt=7:21. Lk=6:46. Jn=13:17. Ja=1:22. 1 J=2:3, 4. **wagons.** ver. 27. Ge 46:5. **for your.** Ge 31:17, 18. **come.** Mt=11:28. Jn=6:37. =7:37, 38. Re=22:17.

20. **regard not.** Heb. let not your eye spare, etc. Dt 7:16. 19:13, 21. 2 Ch 25:9. Is 13:18. Ezk 7:4, 9. 9:5. 20:17. Mt *6:19, 20. Ph 3:8, =13, =14. Col 3:1-3. He 10:34. **stuff.** Ex 22:7. Jsh 7:11. 1 S 10:22. 25:13. 30:24. Ezk 12:3, 4. Mt 24:17. Lk 17:31. **the good.** ver. 18. Ge 20:15. Ezr 9:12. Is 1:19.

21. **wagons.** ver. 19, 27. Ge 41:43. 46:5, 29. 50:9. Ex 14:6. 15:1, 4, 19. Nu 7:3-9. 1 K 10:28. Is 31:1. 36:9. Ezk 23:24. **commandment.** Heb. mouth. ver. 19. Ex 17:1. 38:21. Nu 3:16mg. 2 Ch 8:13. 35:16. Jb 39:27. Ec 8:2. La 1:18mg. ✓121BA. Metonymy of the Cause B545. The organs of speech are put for the testimony borne: the mouth is put for the *witness* or testimony borne by it. For other instances of this figure see Ex 17:1. Nu 3:16mg, 39. 20:24mg. Dt 1:26, 43. 34:5.

22. **To all.** Ge 24:53. Ex 3:22. 12:35. 2 K *5:5, 22, 23, 26. Zc *3:4. **each.** Jg 14:12, 19. 2 K 5:5, 22, 23. Re 6:11. **changes.** ✓24N, Ge +17:5. **to Benjamin.** Ge 43:34. **five.** Ge +43:34n.

23. **laden with.** Heb. carrying. ver. 17. **good things.** Ge 24:10. 43:11. Ex 16:3.

24. **See that.** Ge 37:22. 42:21, 22. Ps ch. 133. Jn 13:34, 35. Ep *4:31, 32. Ph 2:2-5. Col 3:12, 13. 1 Th 5:13. **fall.** Pr 29:9. Is 28:21.

26. **Joseph.** Lk=24:34. Re=1:18, 19. **alive.**

Ac=25:19. **and he is.** ver. 8, 9. Ps 105:21. **And Jacob's.** Heb. And his. Ge 37:35. 42:36, 38. 44:28. Jon 2:7. **he believed.** Jb 9:16. 29:24. Ps *126:1. Lk=24:11, 41.

27. **the spirit.** Jg 15:19. 1 S 30:12. Ps 85:6. Is 57:15. Ho 6:2. Heb. *ruach*, S#7307. Ge +41:8. ʄ121A10, Ge +26:35. Metonymy of the Cause B545. "Spirit" is put for soul or life in its its manifestations. Ge +*26:35. 1 Ch 5:26. Is 37:7. Da 5:20. Hab 1:11.

28. **It is enough.** Ge *46:30. Ex 9:28. Nu 16:3, 7. 2 S 24:16. 1 K 19:4. Lk 2:28-30. Jn 16:21, 22. **alive.** Ac=25:19.

GENESIS 46

Jacob offers sacrifices, and has an encouraging vision, 1-4. He goes with his family into Egypt, 5-7. The names and the number of his descendants, 8-27. He meets and confers with Joseph, who instructs his brethren how to answer Pharaoh, 28-34.

1. A.M. 2298. B.C. 1706. **Beer-sheba.** Ge 21:14, 31, 33. *26:22, 23. *28:10. 1 S 3:20. **and offered.** Ge 4:4. 8:20. 12:8. 22:13. 33:20. 35:3, 7. Jb 1:5. 42:8. **unto.** Ge 21:33. 26:23-25. *28:13. *31:42, 53.

2. **in the visions.** Ge 15:1, 13. 22:11. Nu 12:6. 24:4. 2 Ch 26:5. Jb 4:13. 33:14, 15. Da 2:19. Ac 9:10. 10:3. 16:9. **Jacob.** Ge 22:1. Ex 3:3, 4. 1 S 3:4, 10. Ac 9:4. 10:13.

3. **the God.** Ge 28:13. **fear not.** Ge 15:1, 13. 26:2, 3. Is 41:10. 43:1, 2. Je 40:9. Ac 27:24. **I will.** Ge 12:2. 13:15, 16. 18:18. 22:17. 28:14. 35:11. 47:27. Ex *1:7-10. 12:17, 37. Dt 1:10. *10:22. *26:5. Ac 7:17.

4. **will go.** Ge *28:15. 48:21. Is 43:1, 2. **and I will.** Ge 15:14-16. 50:5, 13, 24, 25. Ex *3:8. **and Joseph.** Ge 50:1. This last and most solemn office, as Mr. Hewlett observes, that could be paid to a parent, was generally performed by the nearest relation of the deceased. This promise must have given great consolation to the venerable patriarch's mind.

5. **Jacob.** Ac *7:15. **in the wagons.** Ge 31:17, 18. 45:19, 21, 27. Ex 10:24, 26.

6. **into Egypt.** Ge 15:13. Nu 20:15. Dt 10:22. 26:5. Jsh 24:4. 1 S 12:8. Ps 105:23. Is 52:4. Ac 7:15.

7. **his daughters.** Ge 37:35. Jsh 24:4. Ps 105:23. Is 52:4. ʄ171E13. Synecdoche of the Species B623. Plural put for the singular, in reference to his one daughter, Dinah. See verses 15, 17. For other instances of this figure see ver. 23. Ge 21:7. 1 Ch 1:41. 2:7. 7:12. 2 Ch 24:25. Mk 1:2. Jn 6:45. Ac 7:42.

8. **the names.** Ge ch. 29, 30. 35:23. ch. 49. Ex 1:1-5. 6:14-18. 1 Ch 2:1, 2. ch. 8. 2 Ch ch. 1, 26. **Reuben.** Ge 29:32. 35:22, 23. 49:3, 4. Ex 6:14. Nu 1:5, 20, 21. 2:10-13. 26:5-11. Dt 33:6. 1 Ch 2:1-10. 5:1, 3.

9. **Phallu.** i.e. *wonderful, distinguished,* *S#6396h. Ex 6:14, Pallu. Nu 26:5, 8. 1 Ch 5:3. **Hezron.** i.e. *blooming; courtyard,* *S#2696h. ver. 12. Ex 6:14. Nu 26:6, 21. Ru 4:18, 19. 1 Ch 2:5, 9, 18, 21, 24, 24, 25. 4:1. 5:3. (1) A son of Reuben, Ge 46:9; Ex 6:14. (2) A son of Pharez, Ge 46:12; Ru 4:18. (3) A town of Judah, Jsh 15:25. See Hazor, number 4, Jsh +15:23.

10. **Simeon.** Ge 29:33. 34:25, 30. 49:5-7. Ex 6:15. Nu 1:6, 22, 23. 2:12, 13. 26:12, 13. 1 Ch 2:1. 4:24-43. **Jemuel.** *or,* Nemuel. i.e. *day of God,* *S#3223h. Ex 6:15. **Jamin.** i.e. *prosperity, right hand; dextrous,* *S#3226h. Ex 6:15. Nu 26:12. 1 Ch 2:27. 4:24. Ne 8:7. (1) Second son of Simeon and founder of the Jamin-

ites, Ge 46:10; Ex 6:15. (2) An Israelite of the tribe of Judah, 1 Ch 2:27. (3) One of the priests who expounded the law with Ezra, Ne 8:7. **Ohad.** i.e. *union, power,* *S#161h. Ex 6:15. **Jachin.** *or,* Jarib. i.e. *he shall establish,* *S#3199h. Ex 6:15. Nu 26:12. 1 K 7:21. 1 Ch 9:10. 24:17. 2 Ch 3:17. Ne 11:10. (1) A son of Simeon, Ge 46:10; Ex 6:15. (2) Head of the twenty-first course of priests, 1 Ch 9:10; 24:17; Ne 11:10. (3) The name given by Solomon to the pillar which he set up on the right side of the porch of the Temple, 1 K 7:21; 2 Ch 3:17. See Boaz, number 2. **Zohar.** *or,* Zerah. i.e. *whiteness, dryness,* *S#6714h. Ge 23:8. 25:9. Ex 6:15. 1 Ch 4:7, 24, Zerah. (1) The father of Ephron, from whom Abraham purchased the cave of Machpelah, Ge 23:8; 25:9. (2) A son of Simeon, Ge 46:10; Ex 6:15. See Zerah, number 3, Ge +36:13. **Shaul.** i.e. *desired; eagerness,* ✛S#7586h. (1) A son of Simeon: Ge 46:10. Ex 6:15. Nu 26:13. 1 Ch 4:24. (2) An ancient king of Edom: 1 Ch 1:48, 49. Called Saul in Ge 36:37, 38. (3) A descendant of Kohath, the son of Levi: 1 Ch 6:24. **Canaanitish.** Ge +10:18. 28:1.

11. **Levi.** Ge 29:34. 49:5-7. Ex 6:16. Nu 3:17-22. ch. 4, 8. 26:57, 58. Dt 33:8-11. 1 Ch 2:1, 11, 16. 6:1-3. ch. 22-26. **Gershon.** *or,* Gershom. i.e. *expulsion; exile,* *S#1648h. Ge 46:11. Ex 6:16, 17. Nu 3:17, 18, 21, 25. 4:22, 38, 41. 7:7. 10:17. 26:57. Jsh 21:6, 27. 1 Ch 6:1, ◐16 (Gershom). ◐15:7 (Gershom). 23:6. **Kohath.** i.e. *assembly; obedience,* *S#6955h. Ex 6:16, 18, 18. Nu 3:17, 27. 26:57, 58. Jsh 21:5, 20, 20, 26. 1 Ch 6:1, 2, 16, 18, 22, 38, 61, 66, 70. 15:5. 23:6, 12. Also *S#6955h: Nu 3:19, 29. 4:2, 4, 15, 15. 7:9. 16:1. **Merari.** i.e. *bitterness,* *S#4847h. Ex 6:16, 19. Nu 3:17, 20, 33, 35, 36. 4:29, 33, 42, 45. 7:8. 10:17. 26:57. Jsh 21:7, 34, 40. 1 Ch 6:1, 16, 19, 29, 44, 47, 63, 77. 9:14. 15:6, 17. 23:6, 21. 24:26, 27. 26:10, 19. 2 Ch 29:12. 34:12. Ezr 8:19.

12. **Judah.** Ge 29:35. 38:1-3, 7, 10, 24-30. 49:8-12. Nu 1:7, 26, 27. 26:19-21. Dt 33:7. Jg 1:2. 1 Ch 2:1, 3-5. ch. 3. 4:1, 21. 5:2. Ps 78:68. Mt 1:1-3. He 7:14. Re 5:5. **died in.** Ge 38:7-10. **Pharez.** i.e. *a breach,* *S#6557h. Ge 38:29. Nu 26:20, 21. Ru 4:12, 18, 18. 1 Ch 2:4, 5. 4:1. 9:4. 27:3. Ne 11:4, 6, Perez. Mt 1:3, Phares. Lk 3:33. **Hamul.** i.e. *pitied,* *S#2538h. Nu 26:21. 1 Ch 2:5.

13. **Issachar.** Ge 30:14-18. 35:23. 49:14, 15. Nu 1:8, 28-30. 26:23-25. Dt 33:18. 1 Ch 2:1. 7:1-5. 12:32. **Tola.** i.e. *worm; scarlet,* *S#8439h. Nu 26:23. Jg 10:1. 1 Ch 7:1, 2, 2. (1) A son of Issachar, Ge 46:13; Nu 26:23. (2) One of the judges of Israel, Jg 10:1, 2. **Phuvah.** *or,* Puah. i.e. *mouth; puff, blast,* *S#6312h. Nu 26:23. Jg 10:1, Pua. 1 Ch 7:1, Puah. **Job.** *or,* Jashub. i.e. *desire,* *S#3102h, only here. 1 Ch 7:1, Jashub. **Shimron.** i.e. *watch post; a guardian,* *S#8110h. (1) One of the sons of Issachar, Ge 46:13; Nu 26:24; 1 Ch 7:1, Shimrom. (2) One of the ancient cities of Canaan, Jsh 11:1; 19:15, is probably the same as Shimron-meron in Jsh 12:20.

14. **Zebulun.** Ge 30:19, 20. 49:13. Nu 1:9, 30, 31. 26:26, 27. Dt 33:18, 19. 1 Ch 2:1. **Jahleel.** i.e. *hoping in God,* *S#3177h. Nu 26:26.

15. **Leah.** Ge 29:32-35. 30:17-21. 35:23. 49:3-15. Ex 1:2, 3. Nu 1. 10. 26. 1 Ch 2:1. **Padan-aram.** Ge 25:20. **with his.** Ge 30:21. 34:1, etc. **souls.** Heb. *nephesh,* Ge +12:5. ʄ171Q1, Ge +12:5. ver. 18, 22, 25, 26, 27.

16. **sons of**. Ge 30:11. 35:26. 49:19. Nu 1:11, 24, 25. 26:15-17. Dt 33:20, 21. 1 Ch 2:2. 5:11-16. **Ziphion**. or, Zephon. i.e. *watchtower*, *S#6837h. **Haggi**. i.e. *festive*, *S#2291h. Nu 26:15. **Shuni**. i.e. *my rest*, *S#7764h. Nu 26:15. **Ezbon**. or, Ozni. i.e. *splendor of God*, *S#675h. 1 Ch 7:7. (1) A son of Gad, Ge 46:16. (2) A son of Bela, 1 Ch 7:7. **Eri**. i.e. *watcher of the Lord*, *S#6179h. Nu 26:16. **Arodi**. or, Arod. i.e. *my posterity; untamed*, *S#722h. Nu 26:17. **Areli**. i.e. *heroic; lion of my God*, *S#692h. Nu 26:17.

17. **Asher**. Ge 30:13. 35:26. 49:20. Ex 1:4. Nu 1:13, 40, 41. 26:44-46. Dt *33:24. 1 Ch 2:2. 7:30-40. **Jimnah**. i.e. *prosperity; good fortune*, *S#3232h. Nu 26:44, 44. 1 Ch 7:30, Imnah. 2 Ch 31:14. **Ishuah**. i.e. *quiet; he will be even or equal*, *S#3438h. 1 Ch 7:30, Isuah. **Isui**. i.e. *quiet; level*, *S#3438h. 1 Ch 7:30, Ishuai. See Nu 26:44, Jesui. **Serah**. i.e. *princess*, *S#8294h. Nu 26:46, Sarah. 1 Ch 7:30. **Heber**. i.e. *alliance; community*, *S#2268h. Nu 26:45. Jg 4:11, 17, 17, 21. 5:24. 1 Ch 4:18. 7:31, 32. 8:17. (1) The grandson of Asher, Ge 46:17; 1 Ch 7:31. (2) A Judite, a son of Ezra, 1 Ch 4:18. (3) The head of a family in Gad, 1 Ch 5:13. (4) A son of Elpaal, a Benjamite, 1 Ch 8:17. (5) A son of Shashak, a Benjamite, 1 Ch 8:22. (6) A Kenite, the husband of Jael, who killed Sisera, the captain of Jabin's army, Jg 4:11, 17, 21, 22. (7) Heber, the father of Phalec, Lk 3:35. See Eber, Ge +10:24. **Malchiel**. i.e. *my king is God*, *S#4439h. Nu 26:45. 1 Ch 7:31.

18. **Zilpah**. Ge 29:24. 30:9-13. 35:26. Ex 1:4. **souls**. Heb. *nephesh*, Ge +12:5. ver. 15, 22, 25, 26, 27.

19. **Rachel**. Ge 29:18. 30:24. 35:16-18, 24. 44:27. Ex 1:3, 5. 1 Ch 2:2. **Joseph**. Ge ch. 37, 39, 40-45, 47. 49:22-27. 50:1, etc. Nu 1:36, 37. 26:38-41. Dt 33:12-17.

20. **Manasseh**. Ge 41:50-52. 48:4, 5, 13, 14, 20. Nu 1:32-35. 26:28-37. Dt 33:13-17. 1 Ch 5:23-26. 7:14-29. **priest**. or, prince. Ge 41:45, 50mg.

21. **sons of Benjamin**. Ge 49:27. Nu 1:11, 36, 37. Dt 33:12. 1 Ch 7:6-12. 8:1-7. **Belah**. i.e. *consumption; destroying*, *S#1106h. Ge 14:2, 8. 36:32, 33. Nu 26:38, 40. 1 Ch 1:43, 44. 5:8. 7:6, 7. 8:1, 3. (1) A city, otherwise called Zoar, in the vale of Siddim, Ge 14:2, 8. See Zoar, Ge +13:10. (2) The first king of Edom mentioned in the Bible, Ge 36:32; 1 Ch 1:44. (3) The eldest son of Benjamin, Ge 46:21; Nu 26:38, 40; 1 Ch 7:6. (4) A son of Azaz, 1 Ch 5:8. **Becher**. i.e. *youth; firstborn; firstfruits*, *S#1071h. Nu 26:35. 1 Ch 7:6, 8, 8. (1) A son of Benjamin, Ge 46:21; 1 Ch 7:6. (2) A son of Ephraim, Nu 26:35. He is called Bered in 1 Ch 7:20. **Ashbel**. i.e. *man of Baal; vain or decaying fire; fire of Bel*, *S#788h. Nu 26:38. 1 Ch 8:1. **Gera**. i.e. *enmity; a grain; sojourning*, *S#1617h. Jg 3:15. 2 S 16:5. 19:16, 18. 1 K 2:8. 1 Ch 8:3, 5, 7. (1) A son or grandson of Benjamin, Ge 46:21; 1 Ch 8:3, 5, 7. (2) A Benjamite, the father of Ehud, Jg 3:15. (3) A Benjamite, the father of Shimei, 2 S 16:5; 1 K 2:8. **Naaman**. i.e. *pleasantness*, *S#5283h. Nu 26:40, 40. 2 K 5:1, 2, 6, 9, 11, 17, 20, 21, 21, 23, 27. 1 Ch 8:4, 7. (1) One of the sons of Benjamin, Ge 46:21. (2) A son of Bela, the son of Benjamin, Nu 26:40; 1 Ch 8:4. (3) The name apparently of a son of Ehud (or Abihud?), 1 Ch 8:7. (4) The "captain of the host" of the king of Syria, a leper, who was miraculously cured of his leprosy after washing seven times in the river Jordan, according to the direction

of the prophet Elisha, 2 K 5:1, etc. **Ehi**. i.e. *unity; my brother*, *S#278h. Nu 26:38, Ahiram. Supposed by some to be the same with Ehud, 1 Ch 8:6. See Aharah, 1 Ch +8:1. **Rosh**. i.e. *head, chief*, *S#7220h. Also Ezk 38:2, 3. 39:1, chief. (1) One of the sons of Benjamin, Ge 46:21. (2) A northern people mentioned with Meshech and Tubal (Ezk 38:2, 3; 39:1, both RV text). Gesenius believes Rosh to be the Russians, though they are nowhere else mentioned by this or any similar name for centuries afterwards. The text of the AV and the margin of the RV render Rosh "chief prince," in which case Rosh as a proper name disappears (J. D. Davis, *Dictionary of the Bible*, p. 661). **Muppim**. i.e. *anxieties, serpent*, *S#4649h. Nu 26:39, Shupham. 1 Ch 7:12, Shuppim. **Huppim**. i.e. *protection; coverings*, *S#2650h. Nu 26:39, Hupham. 1 Ch 7:12, 15. **Ard**. i.e. *fugitive*, *S#714h. Nu 26:40. 1 Ch 8:3, Addar.

22. **souls**. Heb. *nephesh*, Ge +12:5. ver. 15, 18, 25, 26, 27.

23. **sons**. ƒ171E13, Ge 46:7. **Dan**. Ge 30:6. 35:25. 49:16, 17. Nu 1:12, 38, 39. 10:25. Dt 33:22. 1 Ch 2:2. 7:12. 12:35. **Hushim**. i.e. *hasters; who hasten their birth*, *S#2366h. Nu 26:42, 43, Shuham. 1 Ch 7:12. 8:8, 11. (1) A son of Dan, Ge 46:23. (2) A descendant of Benjamin, 1 Ch 7:12. (3) A wife of Shaharaim, a descendant of Benjamin, 1 Ch 8:8, 11.

24. **Naphtali**. Ge 30:7, 8. 35:25. 49:21. Nu 1:15, 42, 43. 26:48-50. Dt 33:23. 2 K 15:29. 1 Ch 2:2. 12:34. **Jahzeel**. i.e. *whom God allots*, *S#3183h. Nu 26:48. 1 Ch 7:13, Jahziel. **Guni**. i.e. *protected*, *S#1476h. Nu 26:48. 1 Ch 5:15. 7:13. (1) A son of Naphtali, Ge 46:24; Nu 26:48. (2) An Israelite of Gad, 1 Ch 5:15. **Jezer**. i.e. *frame, form; imagination, purpose*, *S#3337h. Nu 26:49. 1 Ch 7:13. **Shillem**. i.e. *requital; recompense*, *S#8006h. Nu 26:49. Called Shallum, 1 Ch 7:13.

25. **Bilhah**. Ge 29:29. 30:3-8. 35:22, 25. Ex 1:2. **souls**. Heb. *nephesh*, Ge +12:5. ver. +15.

26. **souls**. √ƒ171Q1, Ge +12:5. **which**. ƒ81, Ge +15:13. **loins**. Pr 17:21. 23:24. Is 45:10. He +7:10. Heb. *thigh*. ƒ88, Ge +24:2. ƒ142, Ge +20:16. Ge +24:2n. 35:11. Ex 1:5mg. Jg 8:30. S#3409. **souls**. Heb. *nephesh*, Ge +12:5. ver. +15. **threescore and**. Ex ◖1:5.

27. **souls**. Heb. *nephesh*, Ge +12:5. √ƒ171Q1, Ge +12:5. ver. +15. **threescore and ten**. Nu 11:16. Threescore and six were before mentioned (ver. 26), so that Joseph and his two sons, together with Jacob himself, complete the seventy persons here enumerated; and the number in ver. 15, 18, 22, 25, amount to that number. The addition of five persons in the LXX. in ver. 20, was either the cause or the consequence of another difference here; for in that version the number is seventy-five. ver. 15, 18, 22, 25. Ex 1:5. 24:1. Dt 10:22. Ac *7:14.

28. **Judah**. Ge 43:8. 44:16-34. *49:8-10. **to direct**. Ge 31:21. **Goshen**. ver. 34. See on Ge 45:10. 47:1.

29. **his chariot**. Ge 41:43. 45:19, 21. **presented**. Ge 12:7. 17:1. 18:1. 26:2, 24. 35:1, 9. 48:3. Alford notes that "*presented himself* is literally *appeared*, a word almost reserved for divine appearances (see references): and Knobel thinks it is used here as according with the royal pomp with which Joseph was invested" (*Genesis and Part of Exodus*, p. 197). **fell on**. Ge 33:4. 45:14. Lk 15:20. Ac 20:37. **wept**. Ge +42:24n.

30. **Now let.** Ge 45:28. Lk=2:29, 30.

31. **I will.** Ge 45:16-20. 47:1-3. Ac 18:3. He 2:11. **My brethren.** He=*2:11.

32. **shepherds.** Ge 4:2. 31:18. 37:2. 47:3. Ex 3:1. 1 S 16:11. 17:15. Ps 78:70-72. Is 40:11. Zc 13:5. **their trade hath been to feed cattle.** Heb. they are men of cattle. ver. 34. Ge 9:20. 1 K 9:27. 18:5, 6. **and they.** Ge 45:10.

33. **What is.** ver. 32. Ge 47:2-4. Jon 1:8.

34. **Thy servants.** ver. 32. Ge 30:35. 32:13-15. 34:5. 37:12. **for every.** Ge 43:32. Ex 8:26. **abomination.** ʃ121N1, Ge +31:54.

GENESIS 47

Joseph presents, first his brethren, and then his father, to Pharaoh; with the conference between them, 1-12. The terms on which Joseph dealt out corn to the Egyptians: and the compact which he finally settled between Pharaoh and his subjects; with their grateful acknowledgements, 13-26. Jacob on the approach of death calls Joseph, and gives orders concerning his burial, 27-31.

1. **Joseph.** Ge 45:16. 46:31. **my brethren.** He=2:11. **in the land.** Ge 45:10. 46:28, 34. Ex 8:22. 9:26.

2. **five.** Ge +43:34n. **presented.** Ac 7:13. 2 C 4:14. Col 1:28. Ju *24.

3. **What is.** Ge 46:33, 34. Am 7:14, 15. Jon 1:8. 2 Th 3:10. **shepherds.** Ge 4:2. 46:33, 34.

4. **For to.** Ge 12:10. 15:13. Dt 26:5. Ps 105:23. Is 52:4. Ac 7:6. **for the famine.** Ge 43:1. Ac 7:11. **let thy.** Ge 46:34.

6. **is.** ver. 11. Ge 13:9. 20:15. 34:10. 45:18-20. Pr 21:1. Jn 17:2. **Goshen.** ver. 4, 11. **men of activity.** *Anshey chayil*, men of strength, power, ability, or prowess. It implies both fitness of mind and body; and so valor, prudence, diligence, and virtue. Pr +*22:3, *29. **rulers.** Ex +*18:21. 1 S 21:7. 1 Ch 27:29-31. 2 Ch 26:10. Pr 22:29. **cattle.** The word signifies property or possession of any kind, though it frequently is used for *cattle*, because in ancient times they constituted the principal part of a man's possessions. See ver. 16. Ex 9:3-6, 10-21.

7. **And Jacob.** See on ver. 10. Ge 14:29. Ex 12:32. Nu 6:23, 24. Jsh 14:13. 1 S 2:20. 2 S 8:10. 16:16. 19:39. 1 K 1:47. 2 K 4:29. Da 2:4. 5:10. Mt 26:26. Lk 22:19. 1 P 2:17.

8. **How old art thou.** Heb. How many *are* the days of the years of thy life? ver. 9. 2 S 19:34. ʃ144A10, Ge +29:14.

9. **The days.** Ge 25:7. 35:28. 1 Ch *29:15. Ps *39:12. 119:19, 54. 2 C 5:6. He *11:9-16. *13:14. 1 P *2:11. **an hundred.** Jb *14:1. Ps *39:5. 89:47, 48. *90:3-12. Ja *4:14. **few and evil.** Ge *27:42. *31:41. *32:6, 7. 34:2. 35:19, 20, 22. *37:33, 34. *42:36. **have not.** ver. 28. Ge 5:27. 11:11, 24, 25. 25:7, 8. 35:28. 50:26. Ex 6:4. 7:7. Dt 34:7. Jsh 24:29. 2 S 19:32-35. Jb 8:8, 9. 42:16, 17. He *11:13. *13:14.

10. **blessed.** ver. 7. Ge 14:19. Nu 6:23-27. Dt 33:1. Ru 2:4. 2 S 8:10. 19:39. Ps 119:46. 129:8. He 7:7.

11. **Rameses.** i.e. *son of the sun*, *S#7486h. ver. 6. Ex 1:11. 12:37. Nu 33:3, 5. Jn 10:10, 28. 14:2, 23. 17:2, 24.

12. **nourished.** Ru 4:15. **his father.** Ex 20:12. Mt 15:4-6. Mk 7:10-13. 1 T 4:8. √5:4, 8. **according to their**

families. *or*, as a little child is nourished. Heb. according to the little ones. ver. 1, 21, 24. Ge 50:24. Ps=23:1. 1 Th 2:7.

13. A.M. 2300. B.C. 1704. **so that.** Ge 41:30, 31. 1 K 18:5. Je 14:1-6. La 2:19, 20. 4:9. Ac *7:11. **fainted.** Je 9:12. Jl 1:10-12.

14. **the money.** Ge 41:56. **Joseph brought.** Lk 16:1, 2, 10-12. 1 C 4:2. 1 P 4:10.

15. A.M. 2301. B.C. 1703. **the Egyptians.** lit. Egypt. ʃ121J14. Metonymy of the Subject B577: A region is put for its inhabitants. For other instances of this figure see Jb 1:15. 6:19. Jb 68:31. 105:38. Is 43:3. Je 47:5. Mt 3:5. Ro 15:26. **Give us bread.** ver. 18, 19, 24. Jg 8:5, 8. 1 S 21:3. 25:8. Ps 37:3. Is 33:16. Mt 6:11. **why.** Jn=11:25.

16. **Give your cattle.** Pr 12:17. Da 6:5-7. 1 C 10:32. Ph 4:8. Col 4:5.

17. **for horses.** Ex 9:3. 1 K 10:28. Jb 2:4. Is 31:1. Mt 6:24. **fed them.** Heb. led them. Ex 15:13. 2 Ch 28:15. 32:22. Ps *23:2. 31:3. Is *40:11. *49:10. 51:8. Jn 21:16.

18. A.M. 2302. B.C. 1702. **We will.** 2 K 6:26. Je 38:9. **spent.** Mk=5:26. Lk=7:42. =15:14. **bodies.** Ro=12:1.

19. **die.** Jn=11:25. **land.** ʃ155D, Ge +4:10. **buy us.** Ne 5:2, 3. Jb 2:4. La 1:11. 5:6, 9. Mt 16:26. Ph 3:8, 9. **and give.** See on ver. 23.

21. A.M. 2303. B.C. 1701. **And as.** Ge 41:48. **removed them.** Jb 5:20. Ps 33:19. 37:19. *107:36. **to cities.** Ge *41:48.

22. **of the priests.** *or*, princes. Ge 14:18. 41:45, 50mg. 2 S 8:18. **for the priests.** Dt 12:19. Jsh 21. Ezr *7:24. Ne 13:10, 13. Mt 10:10. 1 C *9:13. Ga 6:6. 2 Th 3:10. 1 T 5:17. **portion.** lit. statute. ʃ171E9. Synecdoche of the Genus B621. *Statute* is put for *allowance*, or *necessary food*. For other instances of this figure see Jb 23:12mg. Pr 30:8mg. Ezk 16:27.

23. **bought.** ver. 19. 1 C=6:20. **here is seed.** Ge 41:27. 45:6. Ps 41:1. 107:36, 37. 112:5. Pr 11:26. 12:11. 13:23. Ec 11:6. Is 28:24, 25. =55:10, 11. Mt 24:45. 2 C=9:10.

24. **the fifth part.** ver. 25. Ge 41:34. Le 27:32. 1 S 8:15-17. Ps 41:1. 112:5.

25. **Thou hast.** Ge 6:19. 41:45mg. 45:6-8. 50:20. Pr 11:26, 27. **let us.** Ge 18:3. 33:15. Ru 2:13.

26. **made it a law.** From this history, and from Diodorus Siculus (lib. i.), we learn that the land of Egypt was divided into three parts: one belonged to the priests (ver. 22, 26); a second was the king's (which appears to have been the land of Rameses, or Goshen, ver. 11); the remainder was the subjects'. Now Joseph, having purchased the land of the people (ver. 19, 20), restored it, on the condition of their paying a fifth part of the produce to the king, beyond which he appears to have made no demand. **unto this day.** Ge +19:38. **except.** ver. 22. Ezk 7:24. **priests.** *or*, princes. See on ver. 22.

27. **dwelt.** ver. 11. **grew.** Ge 8:7, 9. 13:16. 26:4. 28:14. 46:3. Ex 1:7, 12. Dt 10:22. 26:5. Ne 9:23. Ps 105:24. 107:38. Zc 10:8. Ac 7:17.

28. A.M. 2315. B.C. 1689. **seventeen.** Ge 37:2. **the whole age.** Heb. the days of the years of his life. ver. 8mg, 9. Ps 90:10mg, 12. 119:84. Je +28:3mg.

29. **must die.** ver. 9. Ge 3:19. 50:24. Dt *31:14. 2 S 7:12. 14:14. 1 K *2:1. Jb 7:1. *14:14. 30:23. Ps 6:5. 23:4. 49:7, 9. 89:48. He +*9:27. **put.** See on Ge *24:2.

thigh. ⨍88, Ge +24:2. **deal kindly.** Ge 24:49. **bury me not.** Ge *50:24, 25. Ac 7:15, 16. He 11:22.

30. **lie.** Ge 23:19. 25:9. 49:29-32. *50:5-14, 25. 2 S *19:37. 1 K 13:22. Ne 2:3, 5. **burying place.** Heb. *qeburah*, S#6900h, Ge +35:20.

31. **Swear.** Ge 24:3. **And Israel bowed.** ver. 29. Ge 24:26. 48:1, 2. 1 K 1:47. He ❭11:21.

GENESIS 48

Jacob being sick is visited by Joseph with his two sons, 1, 2. He adopts Joseph's sons as his own children; with an affectionate mention of Rachel's death, 3-8. He blesses Joseph and them, prophetically preferring the younger to the elder, 9-20. He predicts the return of his family to Canaan, and assigns a portion there to Joseph, 21, 22.

1. **thy father.** Jn 11:3. **his two sons.** Ge 41:50-52. 46:20. 50:23. Jb 42:16. Ps 128:6.

2. **strengthened.** Dt 3:28. 1 S 23:16. Ne 2:18. Ps 41:3. Pr 23:15. Ep 6:10.

3. **God.** Ge 17:1. 28:3. 35:11. Ex 6:3. Re 21:22. **appeared.** Ge *28:12-19. 35:6, 7, 9, 11, 12. Ho 12:4. **Luz.** Ge *28:13, +19. *35:6. Jsh 16:2. Jg 1:23. **land of.** Ge 11:31. 12:5. 13:12. 16:3. 17:8. 31:18. 33:18. 35:6. 36:5. 37:1. 42:5. 45:17. 46:6. 47:1. 49:30.

4. **Behold, I.** Ge 12:2. 13:15, 16. 22:17. 26:4. 28:3, 13-15. 32:12. 35:11. 46:3. 47:27. Ex 1:7, 11. **will give.** Dt 32:8. 2 Ch +*20:7. Am +*9:14, 15. **everlasting.** Heb. *olam*, Ge +17:7. Ge +*8:22. +√9:16. +*13:15. 17:+8, 13.

5. **two sons.** Ge 41:50-52. 46:20. Jsh *13:7. *14:4. ch. 16, 17. **are mine.** Le 20:26. Nu 1:10, 32-35. 26:28-37. Is 43:1. Ezk 16:8. Ml *3:17. 2 C 6:18. Ep 1:5. **Reuben.** 1 Ch 5:1, 2. Re 7:6, 7.

6. **and shall be called.** Jsh 13:29. 14:4. 16:5. 1 Ch 5:1, 2. Ps 77:15.

7. **Padan.** i.e. *plain*, ✲S#6307h. Ge ◖+25:20. **Rachel.** Ge 35:9, 16-19. 1 S 10:2. Mt 2:18. **to Ephrath.** i.e. *fruitfulness*, ✲S#672h. Ru 1:2. 1 S 1:1. 17:12. Mi 2:4.

9. **my sons.** Ge 30:2. *33:5. Ru 4:11-14. 1 S 1:20, 27. 2:20, 21. 1 Ch 25:5. 26:45. Ps +*127:3. Is 8:18. 56:3-5. **bless them.** Ge 27:4, 28, 29, 34-40. 28:3, 4. 49:28. Dt 33:1. He 11:21.

10. **the eyes.** Ge 27:1. 1 S 3:2. 4:15. **dim.** Heb. heavy. Is 6:10. 59:1. **kissed.** Ge 27:27. 31:55. 45:15. 1 K 19:20.

11. **I had not.** Ge 37:33, 35. 42:36. 45:26. **God.** Ep 3:20.

12. **he bowed himself.** Ge 18:2. 19:1. 23:7. 33:3. 42:6. Ex +*20:12. 34:8. Le 19:3, 32. 1 K 2:19. 2 K 4:37. Pr 31:28. 1 C=15:28. Ph=2:5-8. Ep 6:1.

13. **Israel's left.** Ge 41:52. Jg 3:15n. +20:16n. Ec 10:2. Mt ◖25:41. **Israel's right.** Ge 41:51. 1 K 2:19. Ps 16:8. 45:9. 73:23. 89:13. 110:1. Mt 20:23. 25:33. 26:64. Mk 16:19. Lk 22:69. Ac 2:34. 7:55. Ep 1:20. Col 3:1. He 1:3. 8:1. 10:12. 1 P 3:22.

14. **right hand.** ver. +13. Ex 15:6. Ps 110:1. 118:16. **and laid.** Nu 8:10, 18. 27:18-23. Dt 34:9. Mt 19:13, 15. Mk 6:5. 16:18. Lk 4:40. 13:13. Ac 6:6. 8:17-19. 13:3. 1 T 4:14. 5:22. **guiding.** *or*, making his hands wise. ver. 19. **wittingly.** ⨍155A, Ge +31:35. **firstborn.** ver. 18. Ge 41:51. 46:20. 1 Ch +*26:10. Col +√1:15.

15. **blessed.** ver. 16. Ge 27:4. 28:3. 49:28. Dt 33:1. He *11:21. **Joseph.** i.e. Ephraim and Manasseh, his

representatives. We have the same form of comprehension of the two in the dying blessing of Jacob, Ge 49:22; of Moses, Dt 33:13 (Alford, p. 204). **did walk.** Ge 5:22-24. 6:9. 17:1. 24:40. 1 K 3:6. Ps 16:8. Is 30:21. Je 8:2. Lk 1:6. 1 C 10:31. 2 C 1:12. Col *2:6. 1 Th 2:12. **fed me.** Ge 28:20, 22. +47:17. Ps 23:1. 28:9. *37:3. 103:4, 5. Ec 2:24, 25. 5:12, 18. 6:7. Is 33:16. Mt *6:25-34. 1 T *6:6-10. Ge +19:38.

16. **The Angel.** Ge 16:7-13. 28:15. 31:11-13, 24. Ex 3:2-6. *23:20, 21. Jg 2:1-4. 6:21-24. 13:21, 22. Ps *34:7, 22. 121:7. Is *47:4. *63:9. Ho 12:4, 5. Ml *3:1. Ac *7:30-35. 1 C 10:4, 9. ⨍171E12. Synecdoche of the Species B622. A common name is put for a proper one. A name common to many is used of one *par excellence*. For other instances of this figure see Ex 3:2. 23:20. Jg 6:11. Mt 21:3. 22:24. Jn 11:3, 12, 28. **redeemed.** Ps 34:2. Mt *6:13. Jn *17:15. Ro 8:23. 2 T 4:18. T 2:14. **my name.** ver. 5. Ge *32:28. Nu +*6:27. Dt *28:10. 2 Ch +*7:14. Je 14:9. Am 9:12. Ac *15:17. **grow into.** Heb. as fishes do increase. Ge 1:21, 22. Nu 1:46. 26:34, 37. **a multitude.** Ge 49:22. Ex *1:7. Nu 26:28-37. Dt 33:17. Jsh *17:17.

17. **laid his.** ver. 14. **displeased him.** Heb. was evil in his eyes. Ge 28:8mg. +38:10mg. Nu 11:1mg. 22:34mg. 1 S 8:6mg. 16:7. 1 K 16:25. 1 Ch 21:7mg. Pr 24:18mg. Ro 9:7, 8, 11.

18. **Not so.** Ge 19:18. Ex 10:11. Mt 25:9. Ac 10:14. 11:8. **for this.** Ge 27:15. 29:26. 43:33. 49:3. **firstborn.** Ge ◖*41:51. 1 Ch +26:10. Je √31:9. Col +√1:15. **right hand.** ver. +13.

19. **said, I know it.** ver. 14. Ge 17:20, 21. 25:23. Nu *1:33-35. 2:19-21. Dt *33:17. Is 7:17. Ezk 37:10. Re 7:6, 8. **become.** Dt 1:10. Ru 4:11, 12. **multitude.** Heb. fulness.

20. **Israel bless.** Ge 24:60. 28:3. Ru *4:11, 12. **and he set.** Nu 2:18-21. 7:48, 54. 10:22, 23. 13:8, 11, 16.

21. **Behold.** Ge *50:24. 1 K 2:2-4. Ps 146:3, 4. Zc 1:5, 6. Lk 2:29. Ac 13:36. 2 T 4:6. He 7:3, 8, 23-25. 2 P 1:14. **God.** Ge 15:14. *28:15. *46:4. Dt ch. 1. *23:14. *31:8. Jsh 1:5, 9. 3:7. *23:14. ch. 24. Ps 18:46. **land.** Ge 12:5. 26:3. 37:1.

22. **given.** Ge 33:19. Dt 21:17. Jsh 24:32. 1 Ch *5:2. Ezk *47:13. Jn 4:5. **above.** Ge +44:30. **Amorite.** Ge +10:16. *15:16. 34:28. Jsh *17:14-18. Jg *11:23. Am *2:9. **sword and.** ⨍174, Ge +18:27.

GENESIS 49

Jacob calls his sons together to receive his prophetical benediction, 1, 2. He addresses each of them by name, and utters predictions concerning their posterity, 3-28. He gives them a charge respecting his burial, and dies, 29-33.

1. **Gather.** Dt 31:12, 28, 29. 33:1, etc. Ps 25:14. 105:15. Is 22:14. 53:1. Da 2:47. 10:1. Am *3:7. Lk 2:26. Ro 1:17, 18. He 10:24, 25. 13:1. Re 4:1. **last days.** This expression always denotes the period of the ultimate completion of the Kingdom of God, in other words, the Messianic age (Kurtz, *History of the Old Covenant*, vol. 3, p. 440, cited by Peters, *Theocratic Kingdom*, vol. 2, p. 423, note 1). Nu *24:14. Dt *4:30. 31:29. Ps +*118:24. Is *2:2. +*13:6. 39:6. Je 23:20. 30:24. 48:47. 49:39. Ezk 38:16. Da 2:28, 29. 8:17. 10:14. *12:13. Ho 3:5. Jl *2:28. Mi *4:1. Mt 24:6, 14. Jn *6:39, 40, +√54n. Ac *2:17. 1 C +√3:13. 1 T *4:1. 2 T *3:1. He *1:2. Ja 5:3. 1 P 1:5. 2 P 3:3.

2. **hearken.** ver. 29, 33. Ex *18:24-27. 1 S 3:16-18. Ps *34:11. Pr *1:8, 9. 2:1-6. 4:1-4. 5:1. 6:20. 7:1, 24. 8:32. 23:19-22, 26.

3. **my firstborn.** Ge *29:32. 46:8. 48:18. Nu *1:20. 26:5. 1 Ch 2:1. 5:1, 3. **my might.** Dt *21:17, 27. Ps 78:51. 105:36.

4. **Unstable.** Jg *5:15, 16. Ja 1:6-8. 2 P 2:14. 3:16. **water.** ℐ63F, Ge +33:10. **thou shalt not excel.** Heb. do not thou excel. Ge 46:8. Nu ch. 32. Dt 33:6. **because.** Ge *35:22. Dt 5:21. *27:20. 1 Ch *5:1. 1 C *5:1. **he went up to my couch.** or, my couch is gone. 2 K 1:16n. Ps 132:3. ℐ96D3. Heterosis of Person B524: The Third person for the First or Second. For other instances of this figure see Is 54:1. La 3:1. Mi 7:18.

5. **Simeon.** Ge *29:33, 34. *34:25-31. 46:10, 11. Pr 18:9. **instruments,** etc. or, their swords *are* weapons of violence. Ge 34:25-29, 35.

6. **O my soul.** Heb. *nephesh,* S#5315h, Ge +34:3. Jg 5:21. Ps 42:5, 11. 43:5. 103:1. Je 4:19. Lk 12:19. **come.** Ge 34:30. Ps 5:10. 26:4, 5. 28:3. 64:2. 94:20, 21. 139:19. Pr *1:11, 15, 16. 12:5. **secret.** Dt 27:24. Ps *26:9. 64:2. Pr 11:13. Je 15:17. Ep *5:11. **unto their.** Ps 1:1. 26:9. 94:20. 2 C 6:14. **honor.** Ps 7:6. +*16:9 (glory). +*30:12mg,n. 57:8. ℐ121F. Metonymy of the Effect B563. The thing effected by an instrument is put for the instrument or organic cause of it. Here, *honor* is put for the tongue which gives it. He would not honor them by speaking or taking part in their assembly. For other instances of this figure see Dt 24:6. Ps 7:5. 16:9. *30:12mg,n. 57:8. Pr 27:27. Mk 12:44. Lk 15:12. Ac 17:31. Ro 1:16. 1 J 5:4. **a man.** Ge 34:7, 25, 26, 36. Le 19:18. Dt 32:35. 2 S 13:22-39. Ps 94:1. Pr 20:22. Na 1:2. Ro 12:17, 19. He 10:30. ℐ96F1, Ge +3:8. **selfwill.** Ne 9:24, 37. Is 28:12. 30:15. Da 11:3, 16. Lk *19:14. 2 P 2:10. **digged down a wall.** or, houghed oxen. Jsh 11:6, 9.

7. **Cursed.** Nu 18:23. Jsh 21:3. 2 S 13:15, 22-28. Pr 26:24, 25. 27:3. **I will divide.** Jsh 19:1-9. ch. 21. 1 Ch 4:24-31, 39, 40. 6:65.

8. **shall praise.** Ge 29:35. 44:18-34. 46:12. Dt *33:7. 1 Ch *5:2. Ps 76:1. Ho *11:12. He 7:14. **thy hand.** Nu 1:27. *10:14. 26:22. Jg *1:1, 2. 20:18. 2 S 24:9. 1 K ch. 4. 1 Ch ch. 12. 2 Ch 11:12-17. 14:8. 15:9. 17:2, 14-16. 30:11. Ps *18:40-43. 78:68-71. Is 9:7. Ph *2:10, 11. He 7:14. *10:13. Re 5:5. 11:15. **the neck.** Jsh 10:24. 2 S 22:41. Ezk 21:29. **thy father's.** Ge 27:29. 37:7-10. 42:6. 2 S 5:3.

9. **is.** ℐ119. Metaphor; or, Representation B737. A declaration that one thing is (or represents) another; or, comparison by representation. The rest of the verse is Allegory, in the form of extended or continued metaphor. For other instances of the figure Metaphor see Ge 11:1. Ezr 10:13. Jb 8:9. Ps 23:1. 45:8. 84:11. *109:4. 120:7. SS 2:13. Is 5:12. Ezk 2:7mg. Mt 5:13. 13:38. √26:26. Mk +*14:22n, 24. Lk 8:14. Jn 6:35. 8:12. *10:9. 15:5. 1 C 10:16. Ga 4:24. **a lion's.** Nu 23:24. 24:9. Dt 33:22. Ps 7:2. 10:9. Is *31:4. Ezk 19:2, 5. Ho 5:4, 14. Mi *5:8. 1 C 15:24. Re *5:5. **from the.** As this continues and expands upon the Metaphor, it constitutes the figure Allegory. ℐ7, Ga +4:24. **prey.** ver. 27. Jb 38:39. Ps 17:12. 22:13. 104:21. **gone up.** SS 4:8. **he stooped.** Nu *23:24. *24:9. Ps 10:10. **rouse.** 1 K *4:25.

10. ℐ3. Enigma; or, Dark Saying B772. A truth expressed in obscure language. Compare ℐ146, Polyonymia, an application of Enigma to the names of persons or places, Ge +36:2. For other instances of the figure Enigma, see Jg *14:14. Is 11:1. 21:11, 12. Ezk 17:2-10. Da 5:25-28. **scepter.** Nu *24:17, 19. 2 S 7:14. 1 Ch *5:2. 28:4. Jb 9:34. Ps 2:9. *45:6. *60:7. 89:32. 110:2. Pr 10:13. Is 2:4. 14:5. Je 30:21. Ezk 19:11, 14. Ho 11:12. Am 1:5. Zc 10:11. Re 2:7. 12:5. +*19:15. ℐ121S1. Metonymy of the Adjunct B603. The sign put for the thing signified: nouns. Here the scepter, which is the Rod of tribal supremacy, is put for Him who is entitled to hold it. For other instances of this figure see Ex 18:10. Nu 18:8. 2 S 12:10. 1 K 19:10. 2 Ch 6:11n. Jb 5:21. Ps 23:4. 44:6. 89:4, 39. Pr 25:22. Is 2:4. Je *47:5. La 5:9. Ezk 7:15. 21:26. Mt *23:2. Lk √11:52. Ac 15:10. Ro 13:4. Re 3:7. **not depart.** Ps 89:39. Ezk 21:26, 27. **from Judah.** T#1879. 2 S 2:4. 1 Ch +5:2. Ps +60:7. Mi +*5:2. Mt 1:2. 2:6. He +*7:14. Re *5:5. **lawgiver.** or, ruler's staff. Nu 21:18. Ezr 1:5, 8. Ps 60:7. 108:8. Is 33:22. **between.** Dt +17:15. *28:57. Je 30:21. **feet.** Dt +11:6mg. Jg 5:27mg. **until.** Peters cites Isaac Leeser, who translates "The scepter shall not depart from Judah nor the lawgiver from his descendants *forever*; because Shiloh shall come; and to him shall be the gathering of the nations." Peters notes, "He appends this significant sentence, expressive of his own opinion: 'The scepter will *return*, when the Shiloh, the King Messiah, shall come, and to Him shall be both the obedience and the assembling of people or nations.' This is *precisely* what the general analogy of Scripture teaches, and this sublime prediction is in full accord with the same" (George N. H. Peters, *The Theocratic Kingdom,* vol. 3, p. 401). LXX., until that which is his shall come. Ge +*3:15. Ps +16:10 (T#44-1). Is +*9:6. 11:1-5. *62:11. Je *23:5, 6. Ezk +*21:26, 27. Da √9:25, 26. Hg √2:7-9. Mt 1:21. 17:5. *21:9. Lk 1:32, 33. +23:44n. Jn 9:7. ◐√18:31. *19:12, 15. 1 C ?11:26. ?13:10. +√15:4. **Shiloh.** i.e. *a Savior; peace bringer,* ✻S#7886h, only here. For ✻S#7887h, Shiloh, see Jg +21:19. **unto him.** Jn 12:32. 2 C 5:15. Ep 3:21. 2 Th 2:1. He 13:13. **the gathering.** or, obedience. Dt *18:15, 18, 19. Ps 2:8. 72:8-11. 98:3. +*102:18. Is *2:2. *11:10, 12, 13. ◐26:18. *42:1, 3, 4. 45:22. *49:6, 7, 22, 23. 51:5. *55:4, 5. *60:1, 3-5. Ezk +*17:23. 21:27. Mi *4:1. +*5:2. Hg 2:7. Zc 2:11. *8:20-23. +*14:9, 16. Mt 2:6. 25:32. Mk 16:15. Lk *1:32, 33. *2:30-32. Jn 3:17. 11:52. *12:32. Ro +*11:25. 15:12. 2 C 5:10. He 7:14. Re +*11:15.

11. **his foal.** Is 63:1-3. **he washed.** Dt *33:28. 1 K 4:20, 25. 2 K *18:31, 32. Jl 3:18. Mi 4:4. Re 7:14. 19:18.

12. **red with wine.** Pr 23:29. **with milk.** Ex *3:8. SS 5:12.

13. **Zebulun.** Ge 30:20. Dt *33:18, 19. Jsh *19:10-16. **Zidon.** i.e. *fishery; plenty of fish, hunting,* ✻S#6721h. (1) A city in Asher. Jsh 11:8. 19:28. Jg 1:31. 10:6. 18:28. 2 S 24:6. 1 K 17:19. Ezr 3:7. Is 23:2, 4, 12. Je 25:22. 27:3. 47:4. Ezk 27:8. 28:21, 22. Jl 3:4. Zc 9:2. (2) A son of Canaan, 1 Ch 1:13. Also rendered Sidon, Ge 10:15. For ✻S#6721h, rendered Sidon, see on Ge +10:19. For ✻S#4605g, see on Mt +11:21.

14. **Issachar.** Ge 30:18. Dt 33:18. Jsh *19:17-23. Jg 5:15. 10:1. 1 Ch 12:32.

15. **rest.** Jsh 14:15. Jg 3:11. 2 S 7:1. **bowed.** Ps 81:6. Ezk 29:18. Mt 23:4.

16. **shall judge.** Ge 30:6. Nu 10:25. Dt 33:22. Jg *13:2, 24, 25. *15:20. 16:21, 30. 18:1, 2.

17. **shall be.** Jg ch. 14, 15. 16:22-30. *18:22-31. 1 Ch 12:35. **serpent.** ♪103, Ge +3:13. **an adder.** Heb. an arrow snake. or, horned snake. S#8207h, only here. Ps 58:4. 91:13. 140:3. Pr 23:32. Je 8:17.

18. **waited for.** Jb *14:14. Ps 14:7. *25:5, 6. 40:1. 62:1, 5. 85:7. *119:41, 166, 174. 123:2. *130:5. Is 8:17. *25:9. *26:8. *30:18. 33:2. 36:8. La 3:25. Mi 7:7. Mt 1:21. Mk 15:43. Lk *1:29, 30. *2:25, 30, 38. *12:35, 36. 23:51. Ro *8:19, 23, 25. 1 C *1:7. Ga *5:5. Ph *1:23. 1 Th 1:10. 2 Th *3:5. He *10:36. **salvation.** ♪121E1, Ge +25:23. La *3:26. 2 T *2:10.

19. **Gad.** Ge *30:11. 46:16. Nu ch. 32. Dt *33:20, 21. Jsh 13:8. Jg ch. 10, 11. 1 Ch 3:18-22. 5:11-22, 26.

20. **Asher.** Ge 30:13. 46:17. Dt +*33:24n, 25. Jsh 19:24-31. **bread.** ♪17I18, Ge +3:19. **fat.** ❋S#8082h. Nu 13:20. Jg 3:29. 1 Ch 4:40. Ne 9:25, 35. Is 30:23. *35:2. Ezk 34:14, 16. Hab 1:16.

21. **Naphtali.** Ge 30:8. 46:24. Dt *33:23. Jsh 19:32-39. Jg 4:6, 10. 5:18. Ps 18:33, 34. Mt 4:15, 16, Nepthalim.

22. **a fruitful.** Ge 30:22-24. 41:52. 46:27. 48:1, 5, 16, 19, 20. Nu ch. 32. Dt *33:17. Jsh ch. 16. 17:14-17. Ps *1:1-3. 128:1, 3. Ezk 19:11. Jn=15:1. **well.** Heb. ayin, a fountain. Ge +24:13. Jn=4:14. **branches.** Heb. daughters.

23. **archers.** Ge *37:4, 18, 24, 28. 39:7-20. *42:21. Ps 64:3. *118:13. Jn 16:33. Ac 14:22. **grieved.** Is=53:3.

24. **his bow.** Ne 6:9. Jb *29:20. Ps *18:32, 34. *27:14. 28:8. 89:1. Col *1:11. 2 T 4:17. **arms.** Jb 22:8mg. Ps 77:15. **were made.** Jb 29:20. Ps 18:32-35. 37:14, 15. 44:7. Zc 10:12. Ro 14:4. **strong.** Ps=89:19. **the mighty.** Ge 35:10, 11. Ex 3:6. Ps 18:1, 30, 32, 34. 132:2, 5. Is 29:26. 60:16. **the shepherd.** Ge 45:5, 7, 11. *47:12. 48:15. 50:21. Nu 27:16-18. Dt 34:9. Jsh 1:1-9. ch. 24. Ps *80:1. He=13:20. **the stone.** Dt 32:4. Ps 2:12. *118:22, 23. Is 17:10. *28:16. 30:29. 63:1-6. Da *2:45. Zc 3:9. Mt=21:42, 44. Mk 12:10. Lk 20:17. Ac 4:11. Ro 9:33. 1 C 15:24. Ep 2:20. 1 P 2:4-8.

25. **the God.** Ge *28:13, 21. 35:3. 43:23. *48:15, 16. Dt 8:17. 28:12. 33:1, 13-17. He=1:9. **the Almighty.** Ge 17:1. 35:11. **bless.** Ps=45:7. **with blessings.** Dt 28:2-12. 33:13. Ps 84:11. 85:12. Mt *6:33. 1 C 3:21, 22. Ep 1:3. Ph 4:19. 1 T +*4:8. **of heaven.** Ge 27:28, 39. Le 26:4. Dt 28:12. √33:13, 14. Is +*26:19n. Je *5:24. **of the deep.** That is, of that great sea of waters both about the earth, and in the earth, whence come those springs and rivers by which the earth is moistened and made fruitful (Matthew Poole). Ge 1:2. 7:11. Dt *8:7. +*33:13. Jon +*2:5. **lieth under.** Dt +33:13 (✢S#8478h). **womb.** Ge +29:31. Ps *128:3.

26. **The blessings.** Dt *33:16. **have prevailed.** Ge 27:27-29, 39, 40. 28:3, 4. *37:4. Ep 1:3. **everlasting.** Heb. olam, Ge +17:7. **hills.** Dt 33:15. Ps 89:36. Is 54:10. Ezk 37:25, 26. Jon 2:6. Hab 3:6. **they shall.** Dt 33:16. Ps 132:18. **was separate.** Ge 37:28. Nu 6:2. Ps 105:17-22. Is 66:5. Ac 7:9. He=7:26.

27. **Benjamin.** Nu +*1:37. 2 S 2:15. 1 Ch 8:40. 12:2. 2 Ch 14:8. 17:17. **ravin.** Ge 35:18. 46:21. Dt 33:12. **a wolf.** Nu 23:24. Jg 3:15-29. *20:21, 25. 1 S 11:4-11. ch. 14, 15, 17. Ac 8:3. 9:1. Ph 3:5. **morning.** Ps 49:14. 55:17. *92:2. Ec 11:6. **the prey.** Zp +*3:8. **at night.** Je 5:6. Ezk 22:25, 27. Ho 13:7, 8. Zp 3:3. Mt 7:15. 10:16. Ac 20:29.

28. **the twelve.** Nu 23:24. Est 8:7, 9, 11. ch. 9, 10. Ezk 39:8-10. Zc 14:1-7. He 12:23. **every one.** Ge

35:22. Ex 28:21. 1 K 18:31. Ac 26:7. Ro 12:6. 1 C 12:4, 7, 13. Ja 1:1. 1 P 4:10. Re 7:4.

29. **charged.** Ge 50:16. **gathered.** ver. 33. Ge 25:8, 17. 35:29. Nu 20:24, 26. 27:13. 31:2. Dt 32:50. He 12:23. **bury me.** Ge *15:15. 25:8-17. 35:29. 47:30. 2 S 2:32. 19:37. He 12:23. **in the cave.** Ge 23:17. 25:9. 47:30. *50:13. 2 S 19:37. **Ephron.** Ge 50:13.

30. **Abraham bought.** Ge 23:8. **buryingplace.** Heb. qeber, S#6913h, Ge +23:4.

31. **they buried.** Ge 23:3, 16-20. 25:9. 35:29. 47:30. 50:13. Ac 7:16. He *11:13.

32. **The purchase.** Ge 23:17-20.

33. **had made.** ver. 1, 24-26. Jsh 24:27-29. He 11:22. **and yielded.** ver. 29. Ge 15:5. 25:8, 17. 35:29. Jb 3:11. 10:18. ◐11:20. 13:19. 14:10. Ps 37:37. Je ◐15:9. La 1:19. Mt ◐27:50. Mk 15:37, 39. Lk 23:46. Jn 19:30. Ac 5:5, 10. +*7:59. 12:23. **ghost.** Ac +*7:59. Heb. gava, ❋S#1478h. Ge 6:17 (die). 7:21 (died). 25:8, 17. 35:29. 49:33. Nu 17:12 (die), 13 (dying). 20:3 (died), 3, 29 (dead). Jsh 22:20 (perished). Jb 3:11. 10:18. 13:19. 14:10. 27:5 (die). 29:18 (die). 34:15 (perish). 36:12 (die). Ps 88:15 (die). 104:29 (die). La 1:19. Zc 13:8. **gathered.** ver. 29. Ge 25:8, 17. 35:29. Dt 32:49, 50. **unto.** Jb 5:26. 30:23. Ec 12:7. Is 57:1, 2. Lk 2:29. He 11:13-16. 12:23.

GENESIS 50

Jacob mourned for, and embalmed, 1-3. Joseph requests Pharaoh that he may go and bury his father, and obtains leave, 4-6. Jacob is buried in Machpelah, 7-13. Joseph and his brethren return to Egypt; their suspicious fears of him; and his kindness to them, 14-21. Joseph's age, posterity, prophecy, and charge concerning his bones; his death, and interment, 22-26.

1. **fell.** Ge *46:4. Dt 6:7, 8. Ep 6:4. **wept.** Ge 23:2. +42:24n. 2 K 13:14. Mk 5:38, 39. Jn 11:35-36. Ac 8:2. 1 Th 4:13.

2. **the physicians.** 2 Ch ◐*16:12. Jb 13:4. Je 8:22. Mt 9:12. Mk 2:17. 5:26. Lk 4:23. 5:31. 8:43. Col 4:14. **embalmed.** ver. 26. 2 Ch *16:14, 18. Mt 26:12. Mk 14:8. 16:1. Lk 24:1. Jn 12:7. 19:39, 40.

3. **forty days.** Ge +7:12. 8:6. Ex 24:18. 34:28. Nu 13:25. Dt 9:25. We learn from the Greek historians, that the time of mourning was while the body was with the embalmers, which Herodotus says was *seventy* days. During this time the body lay in nitre, the use of which was to dry up all its superfluous and noxious moisture: and when, in the space of 30 days, this was sufficiently effected, the remaining *forty*, the time mentioned by Diodorus, were employed in anointing it with gums and spices to preserve it, which was properly the embalming. This sufficiently explains the phraseology of the text. **mourned.** Heb. wept. **threescore.** Nu *20:29. Dt 21:13. *34:8.

4. **the days.** ver. 10. **of.** ♪181E, Ge +3:24. **Joseph.** Est 4:2. **found grace.** Ge 18:3.

5. **made me.** Ge 47:29-31. **Lo, I die.** ver. 24. Ge 48:21. 49:29, 30. Dt 4:22. 1 S 14:43. **I have.** 2 Ch 16:14. Is 22:16. Mt 27:60. **bury me.** Ge 3:19. Jb 30:23. Ps 79:3. Ec 6:3. 12:5, 7. **let me go.** Mt 8:21, 22. Lk 9:59, 60.

6. **as he made.** Ge 48:21.

7. **and with him.** Ge 14:16.

8. **only their.** Ex 10:8, 9, 26. Nu 32:24-27.

9. **chariots**. Ge 41:43. 46:29. Ex 14:7, 17, 28. 2 K 18:24. SS 1:9. Ac 8:2.

10. **the threshingfloor**. Nu 15:20. 18:27. Dt +16:13mg. Jg *6:37. Ru 3:2. 2 S 6:6. *24:18-21. 1 Ch 13:9. 2 Ch 3:1. Da 2:35. Mt 3:12. Lk 3:17. This place was situated, according to Jerome, between the Jordan and the city of Jericho, two miles from the former, and three from the latter, where Bethagla was afterwards built. **beyond Jordan**. As Moses wrote or revised his history on the east side of Jordan, the term "beyond Jordan" in his five books, means *westward* of Jordan; but in other parts of Scripture it generally means *eastward*. ver. 11. Dt 1:1. **Atad**. i.e. *bramble*, *S#329h. ver. 11. Jg 9:14mg. **seven days**. ver. 4. Nu 19:11. Dt 34:8. 1 S *31:13. 2 S 1:17. Jb *2:13. Ac *8:2.

11. **the Canaanites**. Ge 10:15-17, +18, 19. 13:7. 24:3. 34:30. **Abel-mizraim**. i.e. The mourning of the Egyptians. *S#67h. 1 S 6:18. **beyond Jordan**. ver. 10n. Dt 3:25, 27. 11:30.

12. **according**. Ge 47:29-31. 49:29-32. Ex 20:12. Ac 7:16. Ep 6:1.

13. **his sons**. Ge 49:29, 30. Ac 7:16. **buried**. Ge +15:15. 25:9. +35:29. ◑*49:33. **the cave**. Ge 23:16-18. 25:9. 35:27, 29. 49:29-31. 2 K 21:18. **buryingplace**. Heb. *qeber*, Ge +23:4.

15. **their father**. Ge 27:41, 42. **Joseph**. Ge 42:17. Le 26:36. Jb 15:21, 22. Ps 14:5. 58:5. Pr 28:1. Ro 2:15.

16. **sent**. Heb. charged. Pr 29:25.

17. **Forgive**. Mt 6:12, 14, 15. 18:35. Lk 17:3, 4. Jn=14:9. Ep *4:32. Col 3:12, 13. **they did**. ver. 20. Jb 33:27, 28. Ps 21:11. Pr *28:13. Ja *5:16. **servants**. Ge 31:42. 49:25. Mt 10:42. 25:40. Mk 10:41. Ga 6:10, 16. Phm 8-20. **wept**. Ge 42:21-+24n. 45:4, 5, 8.

18. **fell**. Ge 23:28. *37:7-11. 42:6. 44:14. 45:3.

19. **Fear not**. Ge 45:5. Mt 14:27. Lk 24:37, 38. **for am I**. ⌐85C, Ge +18:14. It belongs to God to execute vengeance (Ge +49:6), and Joseph did not intend to usurp his prerogative. Thus he instructed his brethren not to fear him, but to fear God; to humble themselves before God, and to seek *his* forgiveness. Ge 30:2. Dt *32:35. 2 K 5:7. Jb *34:19-29. Ro +*12:19. He 10:30.

20. **ye thought**. Ge 37:4, 18-20. Ps 56:5. **evil**. ⌐96G3. Heterosis of Gender B533: The Feminine for the Neuter. "Evil" is feminine; "meant" is masculine. The feminine form of *evil* is used to express the consequence of moral evil, which is physical evil, mischief or hurt. Jb 5:9. Ps 12:3. 27:4. This figure occurs in the use of pronouns, but as this is not observable in English translation, the figure is not marked at the following passages: Ge 15:6. 43:32. Ex 10:11. Nu 23:23. Ps 118:23.

Mt 21:42. Mk 12:11. **God meant**. T#270. Ge 45:+*5-8. Ps *76:10. 105:16, 17. 119:71, *91. Pr 19:21. Is *10:5-7, 12. Je +*29:11. Mk 15:9, 10. Jn 3:16. Ac *2:23, 24. *3:13-15, 26. Ro *8:28. He =2:10. lit. thought. ⌐22C5. Anthropopatheia or Anthropomorphism B886. Human actions are attributed to God: thinking. For other instances of this figure see Ps 40:5, √17. 92:5. 139:17. Is √55:8. Je √29:11. **this day**. Ge +19:38.

21. **fear**. Jn =14:1. **I will nourish**. Ge 45:10, 11. 47:12. Mt *5:44. 6:14. Ro *12:20, 21. 1 Th 5:15. 1 P 3:9. **kindly to them**. Heb. to their hearts. Ge +34:3mg. Is 40:2mg.

22. **an hundred**. Joseph's life was the shortest of all the patriarchs; for which Bp Patrick gives this reason, he was the son of his father's old age.

23. **the children**. Ge 48:19. 49:12. Nu 32:33, 39. Jsh 17:1. Jb 42:16. Ps *128:4, 6. **Machir**. i.e. *sold; salesman*, *S#4353h. (1) A son of Manasseh and the father of Gilead: Ge *50:23. Nu 26:29, 29. 27:1. 32:39, 40. 36:1. Dt 3:15. Jsh 13:31, 31. 17:1, 3. Jg 5:14. 1 Ch 2:21, 23. *7:14, 15, 16, 17. (2) A son of Ammiel, 2 S 9:4, 5; 17:27. **brought up**. Heb. born. ⌐63G. Ellipsis: Relative, of related or analogous words B61. Here, the Ellipsis of relation is: "(*and educated*) at Joseph's knees." Other instances of this form of Ellipsis are noted by EWB in B for the following passages: Ex 13:15. Le 21:4. Dt *15:12. Ps 142:4. Is 30:17. 38:12. Mt 3:4. Jn 7:39. Ro 14:21. 16:16. **Joseph's**. Ge 30:3.

24. **I die**. ver. 5. Ge 3:19. Jb 30:23. Ec 12:5, 7. Ro 5:12. He +*9:27. **surely**. ⌐147A. Polyptoton B268. Verbs repeated in different moods and tenses. Here, the figure is used to emphasize the certainty of Joseph's belief in the promise of God, as is stated in He 11:22. It might be rendered, "God will most certainly visit you," with great emphasis on the words "most certainly." For other instances of this figure see Ex 23:5. 2 K 21:13. Je 8:4. Mt 11:15. 13:9, 43. 19:12. Mk 4:12, 23. 7:16. Lk 8:8. 14:35. Jn 12:40. 13:7, 10. 17:25, 26. Ro 2:21-23. 1 C 6:2. 2 C 1:10. Ga 1:8, 9. 2 T 3:13. 4:17, 18. He 10:37. 1 J 3:7. Re 2:7, 11, 17, 29. 3:6, 13, 22. 13:9. **visit you**. Ge 21:1. Ex 4:31. Ezk 25:12mg. **you out**. Ge *15:13-16. 26:3. 35:12. 46:4. *48:21. Ex *3:16, 17. He *11:22. **sware**. Ge 12:7. 13:15, 17. 15:7, 18. *17:8. 26:3. 28:13. 35:12. 46:4. Ex 33:1. Nu 32:11. Dt 1:8. 6:10. +30:20. He *11:13. **to Abraham**. Je +*33:26.

25. **took an**. ver. 5. Ge 47:29-31. **and ye**. Ex *13:19. Jsh *24:32. Ac *7:15, 16. He *11:22.

26. **being an hundred and ten years old**. *Ben meah weaiser shanim*, "the son of an hundred and ten years"; the period he lived being personified. ver. 22. Ge 47:9, 28. Jsh 24:29. **they embalmed**. ver. 2, 3.

EXODUS

EXODUS 1

The names of Jacob's sons, 1-5. The death of that generation, and the vast increase of their posterity, 6, 7. The politic, but vain attempts of the king of Egypt to check their increase, 8-14. His cruel orders to the midwives, and their pious disobedience accepted by the Lord, 15-21. Pharaoh commands his subjects to destroy the male infants, 22.

1. A.M. 2299. B.C. 1705. **these are.** Ex 6:14-16. Ge 29:31-35. 30:1-21. 35:18, 23-26. 46:8-26. 49:3-27. 1 Ch 2:1, 2. 12:23-40. 27:16-22. Re 7:4-8.

2. **Reuben.** Ge 35:22.

3. **Issachar.** Ge 35:23. **Benjamin.** Ex 28:20.

4. **Dan.** Ge 35:25. 1 Ch *2:2. **Asher.** Ge 35:26. +46:17. 1 Ch 2:2.

5. **loins.** Heb. thigh. ♪88, Ge +24:2. Ge +24:2n. 35:11. 46:26. Jg 8:30mg. S#3409. **seventy.** ver. 20. Ge 46:26, 27. Dt *10:22. **souls.** Heb. *nephesh*, Ge +12:5.

6. A.M. 2369. B.C. 1635. **Joseph died.** Ge *50:24, 26. Ac *7:14-16. **and all.** Ec *1:4. He +*9:27.

7. **And.** ♪148, Ge +8:22. **children.** ♪171G, Ge +13:8. **fruitful.** ♪173, Ge +27:44. Ex *12:37, 38. Ge 1:20, 28. 9:1. 12:2. 13:16. 15:5. 17:4-6, 16. 22:17. 26:4. 28:3, 4, 14. 35:11. *46:3. 47:27. 48:4, 16. Dt 10:22. *26:5. Ne *9:23. Ps 105:24. Ac *7:17, 18.

8. **a new king.** Dt 32:17. Jg 5:8. Ec 1:9. Is 42:9. Ezk 11:19. Probably Rameses Miamum, or his son Amenophis, who succeeded him about this period; and by his not *knowing* Joseph is meant his not *acknowledging* his obligation to him. Ec 2:18, 19. *9:15. Ac ⟩7:18. **knew not.** Jn ❰=10:4, 5. 1 C=2:8. He *6:10.

9. **the people.** Nu 22:4, 5. Jb 5:2. Ps 105:24, 25. Pr 14:28. 27:4.⟨Ec 4:4. T 3:3. Ja 3:14-16. 4:5.

10. **Come on.** Ps 2:1-4. *10:2. +*83:3, 4. Pr 1:11. **wisely.** Nu 22:6. Jb *5:13. Ps 105:25. Pr *16:25. +*21:30. Ac 7:19. 23:12. 1 C 3:18-20. Ja 3:15-18.

11. **to afflict.** Ex 3:7. 5:15. Ge *15:13. Nu 20:15. Dt *26:6. **burdens.** Ex 2:11. 5:4, 5. Ps 68:13. *81:6. 105:13. **treasure cities.** 1 K 9:19. 2 Ch 8:4, 6. 16:4. 17:12. 32:28. **Pithom.** i.e. *a dilation of the mouth; mouth of integrity,* *S#6619h. **Raamses.** i.e. *thunder of the standard,* *S#7486h. Ge *47:11. Pr 27:4.

12. **But the more,** etc. Heb. and as they afflicted them, so they multiplied, etc. **multiplied.** Ps *105:24. Pr 21:30. Ro 8:28. He 12:6-11. **grieved.** ver. 9. Ge 27:46. Le 20:23. Nu 21:5. 22:3. 1 K 11:25. Jb 5:2. Pr 3:11. 27:4. Is 7:6, 16. Jn 12:19. Ac 4:2-4. 5:28-33.

14. **their lives.** Ex *2:23. *6:9. Ge 15:13. Nu 20:15. Dt 4:20. 26:6. Ru 1:20. Ac *7:19, 34. **in mortar.** Ps 68:13. 81:6. Na 3:14. **was with rigour.** ver. 13. Ex 5:7-21. 20:2. Le 25:43, 46, 53. Is 14:6. 51:23. 52:5. 58:6. Je 50:33, 34. Mi 3:3.

15. **midwives.** Ge +35:17. 38:28. **Shiphrah.** i.e. *beauty, brightness, fairness,* *S#8236h. **Puah.** i.e. *splendor, splendid; light; displayed; pained in travail,* *S#6326h.

16. **and see them.** Jb 10:9. 33:6. Pr 25:11. Is 29:16. 45:9. 64:8. Je ⟨18:6: Or, possibly, "and ye see them by the *stone troughs,*" for so *ovnayim*, from *aven,* a stone, seems to signify (compare Ex 7:19), in which they washed the new-born infants. Alford states "The word literally signifies *two stones,* but is applied in Je 18:3 to the wheels of a potter, which, though of wood, are similar to two mill-stones in form and motion. The similitude of creation, or birth, to the making of a potter's vessel is often found in Scripture (see above references). Hence it has been inferred by some Hebraists that the word here signifies the place of birth, the mouth of the womb, whence the babe issues, as the vessel from the wheels of the potter." **then ye shall.** ver. 22. Mt 21:38. Re 12:4.

17. **feared God.** Ge 20:11. 42:18. Ne *5:15. Ps 31:19. Pr 8:13. *16:6. 24:11, 12. Ec 8:12. 12:13. Da *3:16-18. *6:13. Ho 5:11. Mi 6:16. Mt 10:28. Lk 12:5. Ac 4:19. 5:29. 1 P *2:17. **did not.** Da *6:10. Mt 2:*12, 13, 14, 16. Ac +*4:19. *5:29.

18. **Why have.** 2 S 13:28. Ec 8:4.

19. **midwives said.** Jsh 2:4, etc. 1 S 21:2. 2 S 17:19, 20.

20. **God.** Ps 41:1, 2. 61:5. 85:9. 103:11. 111:5. 145:19. Pr *11:18. 19:17. Ec *8:12. Is *3:10. Mt 10:42. 25:40. Lk 1:50. He +*6:10. **the people.** See ver. 7, 12.

21. **made them.** 1 S *2:35. 25:28. 2 S *7:11-13, 27-29. 1 K 2:24. 11:38. Ps 37:3. *127:1, 3. Pr 24:3. Ec 8:12. Je 35:2. **houses.** ♪121J4, Ge +7:1. Ge 24:60. 30:11, 13. Dt 7:14. Ps 128:3.

22. A.M. 2431. B.C. 1573. **Every son.** ver. 16. Ex 7:19-21. Ps 105:25. Pr 1:16. 4:16. 27:4. Ac *7:19. Re 16:4-6. **cast.** Mt=2:13-16. Ac *7:19.

EXODUS 2

Moses is born, and exposed in an ark among the flags, 1-4. He is found by Pharaoh's daughter, 5, 6; who employs his own mother to nurse him, and brings him up as her son, 7-10. He visits his brethren, slays an Egyptian who had injured one of them, and flees into Midian, 11-15. The priest of Midian entertains him, and gives him his daughter, of whom Gershom is born, 16-22. The king of Egypt dies, and the Lord regards the cry of the Israelites, 23-25.

1. A.M. 2432. B.C. 1572. **house.** ♪121J4, Ge +7:1. **of Levi.** Ex *6:16-20. Nu +*1:49. *26:59. 32:26, 28. 1 Ch 6:1-3. 23:12-14.

2. A.M. 2433. B.C. 1571. **she saw.** Ps 112:5. Ac *7:20. He *11:23. **goodly.** Lk=2:40, 52. Ac 7:20. **three.** He 11:23.

3. **could not.** Ex 1:22. Mt *2:13, 16. Ac 7:19. **an ark.** Is 18:2. **bulrushes.** Jb 8:11. Is 18:2. 35:7. **with slime.** Ge 6:14. 11:3. 14:10. **pitch.** Is 34:9.

4. **his sister.** Ex *15:20. Nu 12:1-15. 20:1. 26:59. Mi 6:4.

5. **daughter.** Ac *7:21. **wash herself.** Heb. *rahats,* S#7364h, Ex +29:4. Ex 7:15. 8:20. **when she.** 1 K 17:6. Ps 9:9. 12:5. 46:1. 76:10. Pr 21:1. Jon 1:17. 2:10.

6. **she had compassion.** 1 K 8:50. Ne 1:11. Ps 106:46. Pr 21:1. Ac 7:21. 1 P 3:8.

7. **his sister.** ver. 4. Ex 15:20. Nu 12:1. 26:59.

8. **Go.** Ps 27:10. Is 46:3, 4. Ezk 16:8. **mother.** Ex 6:20.

9. **Take.** Jg 13:8.

10. **and he.** Ge 48:5. Ps *113:7, 8. Ac 7:21, 22. Ga 4:5. He *11:24. 1 J 3:1. **Moses.** i.e. Drawn out. S#4872h. Ex 3:3, 11. 12:21. 14:21. 19:20. 33:11. 34:29. Nu 10:29. 12:3. 20:10. 31:3. Dt 33:1. 34:5. Mt 17:3. Ac 7:22. He 11:24. **Because.** Ge 4:25. 16:11. 1 S 1:20. Mt 1:21.

11. A.M. 2473. B.C. 1531. **in.** Jg 19:1. Ac 7:23, 25. **Moses.** Ac *7:22-24. He *11:24-26. **grown.** Ge 21:20. **looked.** Mt=11:28. **burdens.** Ex 1:11. 3:7. 5:9, 14. Is 58:6. Mt 11:28. Lk 4:18.

12. **looked.** Pr 4:25. Lk 9:62. Ac 7:24-26. **this.** ♪84, Ge +6:17. **slew.** If the Egyptian killed the Hebrew, Moses only acted agreeably to the divine law (Ge 9:6) in thus slaying the Egyptian; nor did he violate the law of Egypt; for, according to Diodorus Siculus (l.1.17), "he who saw a man killed, or violently assaulted on the highway, and did not rescue him if he could, was punished with death." Moses, therefore, in this transaction, acted as a brave and good man; especially as at this time there was little probability of obtaining justice on an Egyptian murderer. Ge *9:6. Mk ☾=1:25, 26.

13. **strove.** Mt *5:9. Mk *9:33. **and he said.** Ac 7:26. 1 C 6:7, 8. **him.** Ex 23:1. Dt 25:1.

14. **Who.** Ge 19:9. 37:8-11, 19, 20. Nu 16:3, 13. Ps 2:2-6. Ml *2:10. Mt 21:23. Lk 12:14. 19:14, 27. Ac ⟩7:26-28, 35. **a prince.** Heb. a man, a prince. Ge 13:8mg. Is +40:13mg. **intendest.** 1 S 20:4. 1 K 5:5. **Moses.** Pr 19:12. 29:25. **feared.** He ☾11:27.

15. **fled.** Ex 4:19. Ge 28:6, 7. 1 K 19:1-3, 13, 14. Pr +*22:3. Je 26:21-23. Mt 10:23. Ac 7:29. He *11:27. **Midian.** Ge *25:2, 4. **sat down.** Ge 24:11. 29:2. Jn=4:6. **well.** Heb. be-er, Ge +16:14.

16. **the priest.** or, prince. Ex 3:1. Ge 14:18. 41:45mg. Nu *10:29. Jg *4:11. Is +24:2mg. **they came.** Ge 24:11, 14-20. *29:6-10. 1 S *9:11.

17. **shepherds.** Ge 21:25. 26:15-22. **watered.** ver. 12. Ge 29:10.

18. **Reul.** Ex 3:1. 4:18. 18:1-12. Jethro, or Jether. Nu 10:29, Raguel.

19. **An Egyptian.** Ge 50:11. **and also.** Ge 29:10.

20. **call him.** Ge 18:5. 19:2, 3. 24:31-33. 29:13. 31:54. 43:25. Jb 31:32. 42:11. 1 T 5:10. He 13:2.

21. **content.** ver. 10. Ge 31:38-40. Ph 4:11, 12. 1 T 6:6. He 11:25. 13:5. Ja 1:10. **he gave.** Ge ☾21:21. ☾+*24:57, 58. Nu *12:1. Jsh 15:16, 17. Jg ☾14:2. 1 S 18:27. **Zipporah.** i.e. little bird; a sparrow, ✳S#6855h. Ex 4:20-25. 18:2-6. Nu 12:1.

22. **Gershom.** i.e. a stranger here; expulsion, ✳S#1647h. Ex 18:3. Jg 18:30. 1 Ch 6:16, 17, 20, 43, 62, 71. 15:7. 23:15, 16. 26:24. Ezr 8:2. (1) The eldest son of Moses and Zipporah, Ex 2:22; 18:3. (2) A corruption of Gershon, 1 Ch 6:16, 17; 15:7. (3) A Levite who went up with Ezra from Babylon, Ezr 8:2. (4) Father of Jonathan, a Levite who became priest to a colony of Dan at Laish, Jg 18:30. **for he said.** ver. 10. Ex 18:3. 22:21. 1 Ch 16:20. 29:15. Ps 39:12. 119:19. Ac *7:29. He *11:13, 14.

23. A.M. cir. 2504. B.C. cir. 1500. **in process.** Ex 7:7. Ac *7:30. **the king.** Ex 4:19. Mt 2:19, 20. Ac 12:23, 24. **sighed.** ♪173, Ge +27:44. Ge 16:11. Nu *20:16. Dt *26:6, 7. Ps *12:5. **by reason.** T#1228. Dt 4:27-29. Jg 3:9, 14, 15. 4:2, 3. 6:2, 6. 10:7, 10. 2 Ch +6:37 (T#1232). Ezr 9:8, 9. Ne 9:36, 37. Ps 116:16. +119:134 (T#1268). **cry.** Ex 3:7-9. +*22:22-27. Ge 4:10. 18:20,

21. Dt +*24:15. 33:36. Jg 10:11, 12. Ne 9:9. Ps 18:6. 81:6, 7. 107:19, 20. Is 5:7. 19:20. Ja +√5:4.

24. **God heard.** ♪22C14, Ge +16:11. ♪173, Ge +27:44. Ex *6:5. +*22:23. Jg 2:18. Ne 9:27, 28. Ps 22:5, 24. 79:11. *81:7. 102:20. *106:44. 138:3. **remembered.** ♪22C3, Ge +8:1. Ge *15:14-18. *17:7. 18:18. +19:29. *26:3, 24. 28:12-14. 32:28. *46:2-4. Ne *9:8, 9. Ps *105:6-13, 42. *106:45. Lk 1:72, 73.

25. **looked.** ♪173, Ge +27:44. Ex *4:31. 1 S 1:11. 2 S 16:12. Jb 33:27. Lk 1:25. **God.** For elohim, God, Houbigant reads alehem, unto them, which is countenanced by the LXX., Vulgate, Chaldee, Coptic, and Arabic, and appears to have been the original reading. **had respect.** Heb. knew. ♪121C2A2, Ge +39:6. Ex 1:8. 3:7, 8. Ge 39:6. Jb 34:4. Ps *1:6. 55:22. 144:3. Mt *7:23.

EXODUS 3

Moses feeds the flock of Jethro, 1. God appears to him in a flame of fire in a bush, and sends him to deliver Israel, 2-12. Moses inquires, and is told, the name of God, 13, 14. He is instructed what to speak to Israel, and to Pharaoh, whose decided opposition is foretold, 15-19; and is assured that at last the people shall leave Egypt greatly enriched, 20-22.

1. A.M. 2513. B.C. 1491. **kept.** Ps 78:70-72. Am 1:1. 7:14, 15. Mt 4:18, 19. Lk 2:8. 1 C *1:27-29. *7:20. Ph *4:11. **flock.** Ge ☾46:34. Is 63:11. Jn=10:11, 14. **Jethro.** i.e. his excellence. ✳S#3503h. Ex 3:1. 4:18. 18:1, 2, 5, 6, 9, 10, 12. **his father.** Ex 2:16, 21. 18:1-6. Nu 10:29. Jg 4:11. **backside.** Jsh 8:2. Jg 18:12. 1 K 17:3. Ezk 1:1. Mk +*6:31, 32. Ga 1:15-17. He 11:37-40. Re 1:9. **the mountain.** ver. 5. Ex 4:27. 18:5. 19:3, 11. 24:15-17. Nu 10:33. 1 K 19:8. **Horeb.** i.e. desolate. ✳S#2722h. Ex 17:6. 33:6. Dt 1:2, *6, 19. 4:10, 15. 5:2. 9:8. 18:16. 29:1. 1 K 8:9. 19:8. 2 Ch 5:10. Ps 106:19. Ml 4:4.

2. **angel.** ver. 4, 6. Ge *16:7-13. 21:17, 18. 22:11, 12, 15, 16. 31:11, 13. *48:15, 16. Dt *33:16. Jg 6:11-16. *13:20-23. Is *63:9. Ho 12:4, 5. Ml 3:1. Mk 12:26. Lk 20:37. Ac ⟩7:30-35. **flame.** Is *10:17. **bush burned.** Ge 15:13-17. Dt 4:11, 20. 5:23. Ps 66:12. Is 43:2. 53:10, 11. Da 3:27. Zc 13:7. Jn 1:14. Ro 8:3. 2 C 1:8-10. **with fire.** Ge 15:17. Ex 13:21. 19:18. 24:17. 1 K 19:12. Is 4:5. Ezk 1:27, 28. 8:2. He 10:27. 12:29. **not consumed.** Nu 21:28. 26:10. Jb 15:34. Ps 129:2. Is *43:2.

3. **turn aside.** Jg 14:8. Ru 4:1. Ja 4:8. **and see.** Jb 37:14. Ps 107:8. *111:2-4. Da *3:26, 27. Ac 7:31.

4. **unto him.** Dt 33:16. **Moses.** Ge 22:1, 11. *46:2. 1 S 3:4, 6, 8, 10. Ps 62:11. Ac 9:4. 10:3, 13.

5. **Draw not.** Ex *19:12, 21. Le 10:3. He ☾10:22. 12:20. **put off.** Ge 28:16, 17. Jsh *5:15. Ec *5:1. Ac 7:33. **holy.** Heb. kodesh, the quality of holiness. First occurrence. Jn 13:10. Ep 2:18. 3:12. S#6944h. Ex 3:5. 12:16, 16. 15:11, 13. 16:23. 22:31. 26:33, 34. 28:2, 4, 29, 35, 36, 38, 38, 43. 29:6, 29, 30, 33, 34, 37. 30:10, 13, 24, 25, 25, 29, 31, 32, 35, 36, 37. 31:10, 11, 14, 15. 35:2, 19, 21. 36:1 (sanctuary), 3, 4, 6. 37:29. 38:24, 24, 25, 26, 27. 39:1, 30, 30 (Holiness), 41, 41. 40:9, 10, 13.

6. **I am.** ver. 14, 15. Ex 4:5. 29:45. Ge 12:1, 7. 17:7, 8. 26:24. 28:13. 31:42. 32:9. 1 K 18:36. Est 14:14. Ps 132:2. Je 24:7. 31:33. 32:38. Ezk 11:20. Zc 8:8. Mt +*22:32. Mk ⟩12:26. Lk ⟩20:37. Ac ⟩3:13. ⟩7:31, 32. He *11:16. **thy father.** Ex 15:2. 18:4. 2 K 20:5.

2 Ch 21:12. Though the word *avicha*, thy father, is here used in the singular, yet Stephen, quoting this passage (Ac ▶7:32), uses the plural, "the God of thy fathers"; and that this is the meaning, the following words prove. This reading is confirmed by the Samaritan and Coptic. **hid.** Ge 17:3. Dt 18:16. Jg 13:22. 1 K *19:13. Ne 9:9. Jb 42:5, 6. Ps 106:44, 45. Is *6:1-5. Da 10:7, 8. Mt 17:6. Lk 5:8. Ac *7:34. 22:11. He 12:21. Re 1:17.

7. **I have.** Ex *2:23-25. 22:23. Ge 29:32. 1 S 9:16. Ne 9:9. Ps 22:24. 34:4, 6. 102:20. 106:44. 145:19. Is *63:9. He 4:15. **by reason.** Ex 1:11. **I know.** Ge 18:21. Jb *23:10. Ps *142:3.

8. **I am.** Ge 11:5, 7. 18:21. *50:24. Ps 12:5. 18:9-19. 22:4, 5. 34:8. 91:15. Is 64:1. Jn 3:13. *6:38. Ph *1:6. **come.** Mt=5:17. Lk +=*19:10. **deliver.** Ex *6:6-8. 12:51. Ge 15:14. 50:24. **unto a good.** ver. 17. Ex 13:5. 33:2, 3. Ge 13:14, 15. *15:18. Le 20:24. Nu *13:19, 27. 14:7, 8. 16:14. Dt *1:7, 25. 6:3. *8:7-9. 11:9-24. *26:9-15. 27:3. 28:11. 31:20. Jsh 5:6. Ne 9:22-25. Je 2:7. *11:5. 32:22. Ezk 20:6, 15. **milk and.** ⟋174, Ge +18:27. **honey.** ⟋117I7. Synecdoche of the Species B626. Honey is put for whatever is sweet and delicious. For other instances of this figure see ver. 17. Ex 13:5. 33:3. Le 20:24. Nu 13:27. 14:8. 16:13. Dt 6:3. 8:8. 11:9. 26:9, 15. 27:3. 31:20. *32:13. Jsh 5:6. 2 K 18:32. Jb 20:17. Je 11:5. 32:22. Ezk 16:13, 19. 20:6, 15. **unto the place.** Ezk *20:5-10. **Canaanites.** Ex 22:23-31. 34:11. Ge +10:18. 15:18-21. Dt 7:1. Jsh 9:1. Ne 9:8. **Hittites.** Ge +15:20. **Amorites.** Ge +10:16. **Perizzites.** Ge +13:7. **Hivites.** i.e. *villager, serpent*, ✱S#2340h. ver. 17. Ex 13:5. 23:23, 28. 33:2. 34:11. Ge +10:17. 34:2. 36:2. Dt 7:1. 20:17. Jsh 3:10. 9:1, 7. 11:3, 19. 12:8. 24:11. Jg 3:3, 5. 2 S 24:7. 1 K 9:20. 1 Ch 1:15. 2 Ch 8:7. **Jebusites.** Ge 10:16.

9. **the cry.** ver. 7. Ex *2:23. Ge 4:10. 19:13. Nu *20:16. **and I have.** ver. 7. Ex 1:11, 13, 14, 22. Ps +*12:5. Pr 22:22, 23. Ec 4:1. 5:8. Je 50:33, 34. Am 4:1. Mi 2:1-3.

10. **Come now.** Is 1:18. Mt=11:29. Jn 6:37. He=7:25. 11:26. **and I.** 1 S 12:6. Ps 77:20. 103:6, 7. *105:26. Is 63:11, 12. Ho 12:13. Mi *6:4. Ac 7:34, 36.

11. **Who am I.** ⟋85, Ge +3:9. Ex 4:10-13. 6:12. 1 S 18:18. 2 S 7:18. 1 K 3:7, 9. Pr *29:25. Is *6:5-8. Je *1:6. Lk *14:18. Ac 7:23-25. 2 C 2:16. 3:5, 6, 12. Ep *6:10.

12. **Certainly.** Ex 4:12, 15. Ge 15:1. 31:3. Dt 31:8, 23. Jsh *1:5. Jg 6:16. Is 41:10. 43:2. Mt *28:20. Mk 16:20. Jn=8:29. Ac 11:21. Ro *8:31. 2 C *12:9. He +*13:5. **token.** Ex 4:1-9. Ge 15:8. Jg 6:17, 21, 36-40. 7:11, 13, 14. Ps 86:17. Is 7:14. 37:30. Je 43:9, 10. 51:63, 64. **ye shall.** Ex ch. 19-40. Le ch. 1-27. Nu ch. 1-10.

13. **Moses said.** Ex 4:11. Ps 32:3, 8. Is 58:1. 59:1. Ezk 3:14, 17. *Jn 8:24. **What is his.** ver. 14. Ex 15:3. Ge 32:29. Jg 13:6, 17. Pr 30:4. Is +*7:14. +√9:6. Je 23:6. Mt 1:21, 23. **name.** See for Jehovah, Ex +*6:3n. Ps +*83:18. Is 12:2. 26:4. 42:8. Je ◐10:16.

14. **I AM hath.** Ex 6:3. Jb 11:7. Ps +*68:4. 90:2. Is 44:6. Mt 18:20. 28:20. Jn 8:58. 2 C 1:20. He *13:8. Re *1:4, 8, 17. 4:8. 16:5.

15. **The Lord.** ver. 6. Ex 4:5. Ge +*17:7, 8. Dt 1:11, 35. 4:1. 2 Ch 28:9. Mt ▶22:32. Mk ▶12:26. Ac ▶3:13. 7:32. **this is my name.** The name here referred to is that which immediately precedes, Jehovah, which we translate *Lord*, the name by which God had been

known from the creation of the world (Ge 2:2), and by which he is known to the present day. *Jehovah*, from *hawah*, to be, subsist, signifies He who is, or subsists, i.e. eminently and in a manner superior to all other beings; and is essentially the same with *eheyeh*, "I, AM," in the preceding verse. Ps 72:17, 19. *111:5. *135:13. 145:1, 2. Is 9:6. 63:12. **for ever.** Heb. *olam*, Ex +12:24. **my memorial.** Ps 102:12. Ho *12:5. Mi 4:5. Ml 3:6. He *13:8. **generations.** Ge +9:12.

16. **elders.** Ex 4:29. 12:21. 18:12, +21. 19:7. 24:11. Ge 50:7. Nu *11:16. Jsh +20:4. Mt 26:3. Ac 11:30. 20:17. 1 P 5:1. **surely visited.** ⟋147B, Ge +2:16. Ex 2:25. 4:31. 13:19. 15:14. Ge 21:1. *50:24. Ru 1:6. Ps 8:4. Lk *1:68. 19:44. Ac 15:14. He 2:6, 7. 1 P 2:12. **seen.** ⟋180A, Ge +4:20.

17. **I will bring.** ver. 9. Ex 2:23-25. Ge *15:13-21. 46:4. 50:24. **unto the land.** See on ver. +8. Ge 15:14, 18-21. **milk and.** ⟋174, Ge +18:27. **honey.** ⟋117I7, Ex +3:8.

18. **And they.** ver. 16. Ex *4:31. Jsh 1:17. 2 Ch 30:12. Ps 110:3. Je 26:5. **and thou.** Ex 5:1-3. **The Lord.** Ex 7:16. 9:1, 13. 10:3. **met.** Ex 4:24. *5:3. 25:22. 29:42, 43. 30:6, 36. Ge 12:1. 15:1. 17:1. 48:3. Nu 17:4. 23:3, 4, 15, 16. Is 64:5. **three days.'** Ex 8:27. 13:17, 18. **that we may.** ver. 12. Ex 7:16. 8:25-28. 9:1. 10:24-26. 19:1. Je 2:2, 6.

19. **will not.** Ex *5:2. *7:4. **no, not by a mighty hand.** *or*, but by a strong hand. Ex 6:1. ch. 7-14. Dt +34:12. Ps 136:11, 12. Is 63:12, 13. ⟋77. Epitasis B462. The addition of conclusion by way of emphasis. The figure is used when a concluding sentence is added by way of increasing the emphasis. It is not independent of what has gone before, but it is some emphatic increase added to it by way of conclusion. It differs from the figure Amplification (⟋144, Pleonasm) in that it comes by way of *conclusion*. For other instances of this figure see Mt 6:30. 10:18. 18:19. 22:37. Mk 10:43, *44. Jn 1:1. 13:34. 18:20. Ac 4:12. 7:5. 10:39. 13:33. Ro 1:4. 8:3. 9:7. 13:1. 1 C 7:30. 11:5. 13:13. 2 C 3:5, *6. 5:8. 8:3. Ga 1:9. 5:3. Ph 4:4. He 1:13.

20. **stretch.** Ex 6:6. *7:5. 9:15. Ezk 20:33. **smite.** Ex 7:3. 11:9. Dt 4:34. *6:22. Ne *9:10. Ps 105:27. 106:22. *135:8, 9. *136:11, 12. Is 19:22. Je 32:20, 21. Ac *7:36. See Ex ch. 7-13. **after that.** Ex 11:8. *12:31, 39. Ge 15:14. Jg 6:8. 8:16. Ps *105:38. Is 26:11.

21. **will give.** Ex *11:3. 12:36. Ge 39:21. Ne 1:11. Ps 106:46. Pr +*16:7. Da *1:9. Ac 7:10.

22. **But.** Ex 11:2. *12:35, 36. Ge *15:14. Ps 105:37. **borrow.** Ex 22:14. 2 K 4:3. 6:5. *or*, ask. Ex 13:14. 18:7. Jsh 19:50. Jg 5:25. 1 S 1:17, 20. 12:13. **spoil.** Jb *27:16, 17. Pr +*13:13. Is 33:1. Ezk *39:10. **the Egyptians.** *or*, Egypt.

EXODUS 4

The Lord assures Moses of his effectual assistance, by miraculous signs and gracious promises, 1-12; and is angry at his backwardness to the service; yet appoints Aaron to assist him, 13-17. Moses leaves Jethro, and sets out on his journey; and is charged with a message to Pharaoh, 18-23. He is rebuked by the way; Zipporah circumcises her son: Aaron meets Moses, and they are welcomed by the Israelites, 24-31.

1. **will not.** ver. 31. Ex 2:14. 3:18. 1 S 16:2. 1 K 18:14. Je 1:6. Ezk 3:14. Jn *8:47. Ac 7:25. Ro 1:16. 2 C 4:4.

2. **hand**. Ac 28:5, 6. **rod**. ver. 17, 20. Ge 30:37. Le 27:32. 1 S 14:27, 43. Ps 110:2. Is 11:4. 28:27. Mi 6:9. 7:14.

3. **it became**. ver. 17. Ex 7:10-15. Am 5:19.

4. **Put forth**. Ge 22:1, 2. Ps 91:13. Mk 16:18. Lk 10:19. Ac 28:3-6. **And he put**. Jn 2:5.

5. **That they**. ver. 1. Ex 3:18. 4:31. 19:9. 2 Ch 20:20. Is 7:9. Jn *3:2. 5:36. 11:15, 42. *20:27, 31. Ac 28:5, 6. **the Lord**. Ex 3:15. Ge 12:7. 17:1. 18:1. 26:2. 48:3. Je 31:3. Ac 7:2.

6. **leprous as snow**. Nu *12:10. 2 K *5:27.

7. **it was turned**. Nu 12:13, 14. Dt *32:39. 2 K 5:14. Mt *8:3.

8. **if they**. ver. 30, 31. Is 28:10. Jn 12:37. **voice**. Jb 12:7. Ps 19:2. **that they**. Dt 32:39. 2 K 5:7. Jb 5:18.

9. **the water**. Ex 7:19. **pour**. Heb. *shaphak,* *S#8210h. Kal, Preterite: Le 14:41. 17:4, 13. Dt 21:7. 1 K 2:31. 2 K 21:16. 24:4. 1 Ch 22:8, 8. 28:3. Ps 79:3. Is 57:6 (poured). Je 14:16. La 2:4. 4:11. Ezk 4:2 (cast). 14:19 (pour). 21:31. 22:4 (shed), 22 (poured out). 24:7. 26:8 (cast. mg, pour out). 30:15. 36:18. 39:29. Jl 3:19. Zc 12:10. Kal, Infinitive: 1 S 25:31 (shed). 1 K 18:28 (gushed. mg, poured). Pr 1:16. Is 59:7. Je 6:11. 22:17. Ezk 9:8. 17:17. 20:8, 13, 21. 21:22. 22:6, 9, 12, 27. Zp 3:8. Kal, Imperative: Jg 6:20. Ps 62:8. 69:24. 79:6. Je 6:6. 10:25. La 2:19. Kal, Future: Ge 37:22. Ex 29:12. Le 4:7, 18, 25, 30, 34. Dt 12:16, 24. 15:23. 1 S 1:15. 7:6. 2 S 20:10, 15. 2 K 19:32. Jb 16:13. Ps 42:4. 106:38. 142:2. Is 37:33 (cast). 42:25. Je 7:6. 22:3. Ezk 7:8. 16:15. 22:31. 23:8. 33:25. 36:18. Da 11:15. Ho 5:10. Jl 2:28, 29. Am 5:8. 9:6. Kal, Participle, Poel: Ge 9:6 (sheddeth). Nu 35:33. Jb 12:21. Ps 107:40. Pr 6:17. La 4:13. Ezk 16:38. 18:10. 22:3. 23:45. Kal, Participle, Paul: Ps 79:10. Ezk 20:33, 34. Niphal, Preterite: 1 K 13:3. Ps 22:14. La 2:11. Niphal, Infinitive: Ezk 16:36. Niphal, Future: Ge 9:6. Dt 12:27. 19:10. 1 K 13:5. Pual, Preterite: Nu 35:33. Ps 73:2 (slipped). Zp 1:17. Hithpael, Infinitive: La 2:12. Hithpael, Future: Jb 30:16. La 4:1. **shall become**. Heb. shall be, and shall be. **blood**. Ex 1:22. 7:19-25. Mt 7:2. Jn 2:8-11. Re 16:3-6.

10. **am not**. 1 K 3:7. **eloquent**. Heb. a man of words. ver. 1. Jb 12:2. 1 C 2:1-4. 2 C 10:10. 11:6. **heretofore**. Heb. since yesterday, nor since the third day. Ex 21:29. Ge +31:2. Dt 19:4, 6. Jsh +3:4mg. +*4:18mg. 1 S 4:7. **slow of speech**. Ex 6:12. Je *1:6. Ac 4:13. 7:22.

11. **Who hath**. Ge 18:14. Ps 51:15. 94:9. 146:8. Is 6:7. 35:5, 6. 42:7. 49:2. 50:4. Je 1:6, 9. Ezk 3:26, 27. 33:22. Am +√3:6. Mt 10:19, 20. Lk 2:14, 15. Lk ◑13:1-5. Jn ◑9:2, 3. Ja 3:8, 9.

12. **I will**. Ps 25:4, 5. 32:9. 143:10. Is 49:2. *50:4. Je 1:9. Mt 10:19, 20. Mk 13:11. Lk 11:1. *12:11, 12. 21:14, 15. Jn 14:26. Ac *7:22. Ep 6:19.

13. **send**. ver. 1. Ex 23:20. Ge 24:7. 48:16. Jg 2:1. 1 K 19:4. Is 6:8. Je 1:6. 20:9. Ezk 3:14, 15. Jon *1:3, 6. Mt 13:41. Jn 6:29. Ro 12:1. **hand**. √144A5, Ge +9:5. **wilt send**. *or,* shouldest.

14. **anger**. 2 S 6:7. 1 K 11:9. 1 Ch 21:7. Lk 9:59, 60. Ac 15:38. Ph 2:21. **Is not**. √85B, Ge +13:9. **Aaron**. i.e. *teaching,* S#175h. Ex 5:20. 6:20. 7:1, 7, 12. 12:1. 16:34. 17:12. 19:24. 24:14. 28:1, 12. 30:10. 32:2-4. Le 10:6. Nu 12:1. 16:11. 17:3. 20:12, 25, 28. **cometh**. ver. 27. 1 S 10:1-7. Mk 14:13-15. 2 C 2:13. 7:6, 7. 1 Th 3:6, 7.

15. **and put**. Ex 7:1, 2. 2 S 14:3. Is 51:16. 59:21. **and I**. Nu *22:38. 23:5, 12, 16. Dt *18:18. Is 51:16.

Je 1:9. Mt 28:20. Lk 21:15. Jn *17:8. 1 C 11:23. 15:1. **will teach**. Dt 5:31. 1 S 16:3. Is 50:4.

16. **shall**. √84, Ge +6:17. **be to thee**. Ex *7:1, 2. 18:19. Ps +*82:6. Jn +*10:34, 35.

17. **this rod**. ver. 2. Ex 7:9, 19. 1 C 1:27.

18. **Jethro**. Heb. Jether. See on Ex 3:1. **Let me go**. 1 T 6:1. **and see**. Ge 45:3. Ac 15:36. **Go in peace**. 1 S 1:17. Lk 7:50. Ac 16:36.

19. **Midian**. Ex *2:15, 23. 3:1. 18:1. Ge 37:28. Nu 10:29. **for all**. Ex 2:15, 23. Mt=2:20. **life**. Heb. *nephesh,* soul. Ge +44:30. √121A7, Ge +9:5.

20. **his wife**. Ex *2:21, 22. *18:2-4. **an ass**. Jsh 15:18. 1 S 25:20. 2 S 17:23. 1 K 13:13. **the rod of God**. ver. 2, 17. Ex 17:9. Nu 20:8, 9.

21. **wonders**. Ex 3:20. **I will harden**. √√108A4, Ge +31:7. Ex 7:3, ◑+13. ◑*8:15. 9:12, 35. 10:1, 20, 27. 11:10. 14:8. Ge 6:3. Dt *2:30-33, 36. ◑15:7. Jsh *11:20. 1 S ◑*6:6. 1 K 22:22. 2 Ch ◑*36:13. Jb ◑*9:4. Ps 105:25. Pr ◑*29:1. Is 6:10. *63:17. Je *5:3. Ezk◑33:11. *36:26. Da ◑*5:20. Am +√3:6. Zc ◑*7:11, 12. Jn *12:40. Ac ◑*28:26, 27. Ro √1:28. *2:5. *9:18, 22. 11:8-10. 2 C 2:16. 2 Th √2:10-12. He ◑*3:8, 13. Ja ◑√1:13, 14. 1 P 2:8.

22. **Israel**. Ex 19:5, 6. Dt *14:1, 2. Je *31:9. Ho *11:1. Mt *2:15. Ro *9:4. 2 C *6:18. He 12:23. Ja *1:18. **firstborn**. Ps √89:27. Je √31:9. Col +√1:15.

23. **I will slay**. Ex 11:5. *12:29. Ps 78:51. 105:36. 135:8.

24. **the inn**. See on Ge 42:27. **the Lord**. Ex 3:18. Nu 22:22, 23. 1 Ch 21:16. Ho 13:8. **sought**. Ge *17:14. Le 10:3. 1 K 13:24. 1 T 3:4, 5.

25. **a sharp stone**. *or,* knife. Jsh *5:2n, 3. Is 5:28. Ezk 3:9. **cast it**. Heb. made it touch. **a bloody**. 2 S 16:7.

27. **Go into**. ver. 14-16. Ec 4:9. Ac 10:5, 6, 20. **the mount**. Ex 3:1. 19:3. 20:18. 24:15-17. 1 K 19:8. **kissed him**. Ex 18:7. Ge 29:11. 33:4. 2 S 19:39. 20:9.

28. **told Aaron**. ver. 8, 9, 15, 16. Jon 3:2. Mt 21:29. **and all**. ver. 11-13.

29. **gathered**. Ex 3:16. 24:1, 11.

30. **And Aaron**. ver. 16. **did the**. ver. 2-9.

31. **believed**. ver. 8, 9. Ex *3:18. Ps 106:12, 13. Lk 8:13. **visited**. See on Ex 3:16. Lk 1:68. **looked**. Ex 2:25. 3:7. **bowed**. Ex 12:27. Ge 17:3. 24:26. 1 Ch 29:20. 2 Ch 20:18.

EXODUS 5

Moses and Aaron deliver their message to Pharaoh, who disdainfully rejects it, 1-5. He increases the task of the Israelites, allows them no straw, and silences their complaints, 6-19. They despond and murmur, and Moses complains to the Lord, 20-23.

1. **and told**. 1 K 21:20. Ps 119:46. Ezk 2:6. Jon 3:3, 4. Mt 10:18, 28. Ac 4:29. **a feast**. Ex *10:9. Is 25:6. 1 C 5:8.

2. **Who**. Ex *3:19. 2 K 18:35. 2 Ch 32:15, 19. Jb *21:15. Ps 10:4. 12:4. 14:1. **Israel**. √121T3, Ge +9:27. **I know not**. 1 S 2:12. Jn 16:3. Ro 1:28. 2 Th 1:8. **neither**. Ex 3:19. Je 44:16, 17.

3. **The God**. Ex 3:18. **lest he**. Dt 28:21. 2 K 17:25. 2 Ch 30:8. Ezr 7:23. Ezk 6:11. Zc 14:16-19. **with pestilence**. Ezk +*38:22. **the sword**. √121B. Metonymy of the Cause B548. The sword is put for slaughter. For other instances of this figure see Le 26:16. Is 1:20. Je 14:12, 13, 15, 16. Ezk 14:17. Mt 10:34.

4. **Wherefore**. Je 38:4. Am 7:10. Lk 23:2. Ac 16:20, 21. 24:5. **let**. *or*, loose. Ex 32:25h. Ye hinder the people from their work: "Get you unto your burdens." "Let religion alone and mind your work." The language not only of tyranny, but of thoughtless irreligion. **burdens**. Ex 1:11. 2:11. 6:6.

5. **many**. Ex *1:7-11. Pr 14:28. **rest**. Mt=11:28.

6. **taskmasters**. or, exactors, oppressors. Jb 3:18. Is 3:12. 60:17. Zc 10:4. These taskmasters were Egyptians (Ex 1:11), but the *officers* were Hebrews. See ver. 14. ver. 10, 13, 15, 19. Ex 1:11. Pr 12:10. **officers**. Compare Ex 2:14. Nu 11:16. Dt 1:15. 16:18. Jsh 8:33. 24:1, 4. 2 Ch 26:11. They may have been somewhat like the chiefs of trade, where every trade has a head, who is entrusted with authority, and in some measure answerable to the Government. "Officers" (see references) may be evidence of political or governmental organization among the Israelites themselves.

7. **straw**. Ge 24:25. Jg 19:19.

8. **tale**. Ex 30:32, 37h. 2 Ch 24:13h. Ezk 45:11h. **heretofore**. ver. 7, 14. Ex 4:10mg. Ge 31:2. 1 S 19:7. **ye shall lay**. Ps 106:41. **idle**. ver. 17. **therefore**. Ex 10:11, 25.

9. **Let there more work be laid upon the men**. Heb. Let the work be heavy upon the men. 2 T=3:12. **vain words**. *or*, lying words. 2 K 18:20. Jb 16:3. Je 7:4. 43:2. Zc 1:6. Ml 3:14. Ep 5:6.

10. **taskmasters**. Ex 1:11. Pr 29:12.

11. **not ought**. ver. 13, 14.

12. **stubble**. Ex 15:7. Is 5:24. 47:14. Jl 2:5. Na 1:10. Ob 18. 1 C 3:12.

13. **hasted**. Jsh 10:15. 17:15. Pr 19:2. **daily tasks**. Heb. a matter of a day in his day. ver. 19. Ex 16:4mg. Le 23:37. 1 K 8:59mg. 2 K 25:30. 1 Ch 16:37. 2 Ch 8:14. 31:16. Ezr 3:4mg. Ne 11:23. Je 52:34mg.

17. **Ye are idle**. Mt 26:8. Jn 6:27. 2 Th 3:10, 11.

18. **yet shall ye deliver**. Ezk 18:18. Da 2:9-13.

19. **evil case**. Dt 32:36. Ec 4:1. 5:8.

21. **The Lord**. Ex 4:31. 6:9. Ge 16:5. **our savor**. Ec 10:1. Jl 2:20. 2 C 2:15, 16. **to be abhorred**. Heb. to stink. Ge 34:30. 1 S 13:4. 27:12. 2 S 10:6. 1 Ch 19:6. **in the eyes**. ſ171J15, Ge +42:1. ſ46B. Catachresis; or, Incongruity B677. Of two words, where the meanings are different. Here "stink" and "eyes" are incongruously conjoined to call our attention to the highest degree of abhorrence. For other instances of this figure see Ex 20:18. Mk 7:21, *22. 1 T 6:19. Re *1:12.

22. **returned**. Ex 17:4. 1 S 30:6. 2 K *19:14. Ps 73:25. Je 12:1. **evil intreated**. √ſ108A4, Ge +31:7. **why is it**. Nu 11:14, 15. 1 K 19:4, 10. Je *20:7. Hab 2:3.

23. **in thy name**. Ps 118:26. Je 11:21. Jn 5:43. **neither hast thou delivered**. Heb. delivering, thou hast not delivered. ſ147C, Ge +3:4. Is 26:17, 18. 28:16. He 10:36, 37. **at all**. ſ147B, Ge +26:28.

EXODUS 6

God encourages Moses, by his name JEHOVAH, and by promises, 1-8. Moses in vain attempts to encourage the Israelites, 9. He and Aaron are charged to go again unto Pharaoh, 10-13. The geneology of Reuben and of Simeon; and of Levi the ancestor of Moses and Aaron, 14-25. The history is resumed, 26-30.

1. **Now shalt**. Ex 14:13. Nu 23:23. Dt 32:39. 2 K 7:2, 19. 2 Ch 20:17. Ps 12:5. **with a strong**. Ex *3:19, 20. Dt 4:34. Ps 89:13. 136:12. Is 63:12. Ezk 20:33, 34. **drive them**. Ex 11:1. *12:31, 33, 39.

2. **I am the Lord**. *or*, Jehovah. ver. 6, 8. Ex 14:18. 17:1. 20:2. Ge 15:7. Is 42:8. 43:11, 15. 44:6. Je 9:24. Ml 3:6. Ac 17:24, 25.

3. **name of**. Ex *3:13, 14. Ps +*83:18. Is 12:2. 26:4. Jn 1:3. 8:56. Ac 7:38. Re +*1:8. 15:3. **God Almighty**. *El shadday*, God Almighty; for *shadday* means *strong, mighty*. Ge *17:1. 28:3. 35:11. 43:14. 48:3. 49:25. Nu 24:4, 16. Ru 1:20, 21. Ps 68:14. 91:1. Is 13:6. Ezk 1:24. 10:5. Jl 1:15. S#7706h, Jb +5:17. **but by my name**. If Abraham, Isaac, and Jacob, did not know the name Jehovah, then Moses must have used it in Genesis by *prolepsis*, or anticipation (ſ151, Ge +1:28). This, however, is most unlikely, for Abraham called the place where Isaac was about to be sacrificed "Jehovah-jireh"; and God, speaking to Jacob in Bethel, said "I am Jehovah, the God of Abraham" (Ge 22:14. 28:13). Mr. Locke and others read it *interrogatively*, for the negative particle, *lo*, not, has frequently this power in Hebrew: "I appeared unto Abraham, Isaac, and Jacob, by the name of God Almighty, and by my name Jehovah was I not also made known unto them?" **name**. Note that God has more than one name, explicitly stated here and in Ex 3:13, 14. Ps +*68:4. +*83:18. Is 42:8. Je ●10:16. In Scripture his several names are not merely titles, but are divine names given to reveal his many-sided character. Ps +√9:10. **JEHOVAH**. i.e. *he will be; self-existent*, S#3068h. Ex ●3:14. ●15:2mg. 17:15. Ge 2:4. 4:1, 3. +*12:7, 8. 13:18. +*17:1. √19:24. *21:33. 22:14. Jg 6:24. 2 Ch 18:31. Ps *68:4, JAH. Ps +*83:18. Is 12:2. 26:4. 42:8. 44:6. 52:5, 6. Jn *8:58. 1 P +*2:3n. Re *1:4, 8.

4. **established**. Ge 6:18. *15:18. 17:7, 8, 13. 28:4. 2 S 23:5. Is +*55:3. **covenant**. Ge *26:3. *35:12. **the land of their**. Ge 15:13. 17:8. 23:4. *26:3. Ps 105:12. Ac 7:5.

5. **the groaning**. Ex 2:24. 3:7. Ps 106:44. Is 63:9. **I have remembered**. ſ22C3, Ge +8:1. Ex 2:24. Ge 8:1. 9:15. Ps *105:8. *106:45. Lk *1:54, 72.

6. **I am the Lord**. See on ver. 2, 8, 29. Ezk 20:7-9. **I will bring**. Ex 3:17. 7:4. Dt *26:8. Ps 81:6. *136:11, 12. **redeem**. Ex 15:13. Dt 4:34. *7:8. 15:15. 2 K 17:36. 1 Ch 17:21. Ne 1:10. Is 9:12, 17, 21. **stretched**. Ex *15:12. Dt 5:14. 7:19. 1 K 8:42. Ps 136:12. Je 27:5. **judgments**. lit. justice. ſ121C1D. Metonymy of the Cause B550. Justice is put for the judgment or punishment which manifests it. For other instances of this figure see Je 26:11. Jn 3:19.

7. **will take**. Ex 19:5, 6. Ge 17:7, 8. Dt *4:20. *7:6. 14:2. *26:18. 2 S *7:23, 24. Je *31:33. Ho *1:10. 3:3. 1 P 2:9, 10. **I will be**. Ex 29:45, 46. Ge +*17:7, 8. Dt 29:13. Zc 13:9. Mt 22:32. Ro 8:31. He 11:16. Re 21:3, 7. **from under**. Ex 5:4, 5. Ps 81:6.

8. **swear**. Heb. lift up my hand. The ancient mode of appealing to God was by lifting up the *right hand*, and was considered as a form of swearing. Hence *yamin*, in Hebrew the *right hand*, is in Arabic an *oath*, and as a verb, *to take an oath*. A similar custom prevailed among the heathens. See Virgil, *Aeneid*. l. xii. v. 196. ſ121S3, Ge +14:22. Ge 14:22. Dt 32:40. Nu 14:30. Ezk 20:5, 6, 15, 23, 28, 42. 36:7. 47:14. Da 12:7. Re 10:5, 6. ſ22A14.8K. Anthropomorphism B880. A hand is attributed to God in the idiomatic expression "to lift up the hand," meaning to swear solemnly. For

other instances of this figure see Ge 14:22. Dt 32:40. Ezk 20:5, 6. 36:7. **to give.** Ex 32:13. Ge 15:18. 22:16, 17. 26:3. 28:13. 35:12. **will give.** Mt +8:11. Ph 1:6. T 1:2. He √11:39. **I am.** See on ver. 2. Nu *23:19. 1 S *15:29.

9. **hearkened not.** Ex 5:21. 14:12. Jb 21:4. Pr 14:19. **anguish.** *or,* impatience. Heb. shortness, *or,* straitness. Nu 21:4. Jb +21:4mg. **spirit.** Heb. *ruach,* Ge +41:8.

11. **speak unto.** ver. 29. Ex 3:10. 5:1, 23. 7:1.

12. **children.** ver. 9. Ex 3:13. 4:29-31. 5:19-21. Ac *7:25. **am.** The italics show that this word has been supplied by our translators; hence it may be inferred by some that Moses was uncircumcised. The difficulty is in some measure cleared away, by using the word *uncircumcised* in the sense of *unsuitable* or *incapacitated,* see ver. 30, which agrees with Ex 4:10, where Moses complains of want of eloquence: but by substituting *is* for *am* in this place, the connection with the former part of the verse is preserved: "For if the chosen seed, the circumcised sons of Jacob, refuse to hear me," as though Moses had said, "how can I expect to make uncircumcised Pharaoh pay attention to me?" **uncircumcised.** ver. 30. Ex 4:10. Le 26:41. Dt 30:6. Is 6:5. Je 1:6. 6:10. 9:26. Ac 7:51.

13. **gave them.** Nu 27:19, 23. Dt 31:14. Ps 91:11. Mt 4:6. 1 T 1:18. 5:21. 6:13, 17. 2 T 2:4. 4:1.

14. **the heads.** ver. 25. Jsh 14:1. 19:51. 1 Ch 5:24. 7:2, 7. 8:6. **The sons.** Ge *46:9. 49:3, 4. Nu 26:5, 6. 1 Ch *5:3. **these be.** Nu 26:7. Jsh 13:15, 23.

15. **sons.** Ge 46:10. Nu 26:12, 13. 1 Ch *4:24, Nemuel, Jarib, Zerah. **Canaanitish.** Ge +10:18.

16. **sons.** Ge 46:11. Nu *3:17. 1 Ch *6:1, 16. **according.** Ge 10:32. 25:13. **Kohath.** Nu 26:57. 1 Ch 23:6. **an hundred.** ver. 18, 20. Ge 35:28. 47:28. 50:26.

17. **sons of Gershon.** Ge 46:11. Nu 3:18, Shimei. 1 Ch 6:17. 23:7, Laadan, Shimei. **Shimi.** i.e. *a hearkener,* *S#8096h, so rendered only here. For Shimei, see 2 S +16:5; for Shimhi, see 1 Ch +8:21.

18. **sons of Kohath.** Nu 3:19, Izehar. *26:57. 1 Ch *6:2, 18. **Amram.** i.e. *exalted people,* *S#6019h. ver. 20, 20. Nu 3:19. 26:58, 59, 59. 1 Ch 6:2, 3, 18. 23:12, 13. 24:20. Ezr 10:34. (1) A son of Kohath and father of Aaron, Miriam, and Moses. The faith of Amram and his wife Jochebed is commended in He 11:23. (2) A son of Bani who had taken a foreign wife during the exile, Ezr 10:34. (3) S#2566h, A descendant of Seir, 1 Ch 1:41. **Izhar.** i.e. *anointed; oil,* *S#3324h. ver. 21. Nu 3:19, Izehar. 16:1. 1 Ch 6:2, 18, 38. 23:12, 18. **Hebron.** i.e. *friendship; confederation, conjunction,* +S#2275h. Nu 3:19. 1 Ch 2:42, 43. 6:2, 18. 15:9. 23:12, 19. (1) A city of Palestine, Ge +13:18. Also called Kirjath-arba, Jsh 15:13, 14; 21:11. (2) A city of Asher, Jsh 19:28. (3) One of the sons of Kohath, the son of Levi, Ex 6:18; 1 Ch 6:2. (4) The name of the son of Mareshah, 1 Ch 2:42; 15:9. **Uzziel.** i.e. *strength of God,* *S#5816h. ver. 22. Le 10:4. Nu 3:19, 30. 1 Ch 4:42. 6:2, 18. 7:7. 15:10. 23:12, 20. 24:24. 25:4. 2 Ch 29:14. Ne 3:8. (1) A son of Kohath, the son of Levi, Ex 6:18; Le 10:4. (2) A captain of the Simeonites who destroyed the remnant of the Amalekites, 1 Ch 4:42, 43. (3) A son of Bela, the son of Benjamin, 1 Ch 7:7. (4) One of the sons of Heman. He was a Levite musician, 1 Ch 25:4; is called Azareel in 1 Ch 25:18. (5) One of the Levites who cleansed the house of the Lord in the time of Hezekiah, 2 Ch 29:14-19.

(6) A Jew who aided in repairing the walls of Jerusalem, Ne 3:8. **and the years.** See on ver. 16.

19. **sons of Merari.** Nu 3:20. 1 Ch 6:19. *23:21. **Mahali.** i.e. *infirmity, disease; instability,* *S#4249h, elsewhere rendered Mahli. Nu +3:20. 1 Ch 6:19, 29, 47. 23:21, 21, 23. 24:26, 28, 30. Ezr 8:18. **Mushi.** i.e. *forsaking; proved of the Lord; sensitive,* *S#4187h. Nu 3:20. 1 Ch 6:19, 47. 23:21, 23. 24:26, 30.

20. **Amram.** Ex 2:1, 2. Nu *26:59. **Jochebed.** i.e. *whose glory is Jehovah,* *S#3115h. Nu 26:59. **his father's sister.** Heb. *dodatho,* has been supposed to mean his *cousin* and not his *aunt,* on the authority of the LXX. and Vulgate, who render it *his paternal cousin.* But this construction was probably put on the original word to save the credit of Moses and Aaron, because the marriage of an aunt is afterwards forbidden (Le 18:12, 14); for the meaning of the word is fixed by another passage, where it is said, "The name of Amram's wife was Jochebed, the daughter of Levi, whom her mother bare to Levi, in Egypt" (Nu 26:59). Moses, then, is more impartial than his commentators. **and the years.** The Samaritan, LXX., Syriac, and one Hebrew MS. add, "And Miriam their sister;" which some of the best critics suppose to have been originally in the text. See on ver. 16, 18.

21. **Korah.** ver. 24. Nu 16:1, 32. 26:10, 11. 1 Ch 6:37, 38.

22. **sons of Uzziel.** Le *10:4. Ne 3:30. **Mishael.** i.e. *who is what God is?,* *S#4332h. Le 10:4. Ne 8:4. Da 1:6, 7, 11, 19. (1) One of the sons of Uzziel, Ex 6:22; Le 10:4. (2) One of those who stood at Ezra's left hand when he read the law to the people, Ne 8:4. (3) The Babylonian name given to Meshach, one of the three companions of Daniel who were thrown into a fiery furnace and miraculously delivered, Da 1:6, 7; 3:20-30. **Elzaphan.** i.e. *whom God protects; God of treasure,* *S#469h. Le 10:4. Nu 3:30. 34:25. 1 Ch 15:8. 2 Ch 29:13. (1) A son of Uzziel, Ex 6:22; Le 10:4. (2) Elizaphan, a Levite of the sons of Kohath, Nu 3:30; 1 Ch 15:8. (3) Prince of Zebulun in the time of Moses, Nu 34:25. **Zithri.** i.e. *protection of the Lord,* *S#5644h.

23. **Elisheba.** i.e. *God of the oath,* *S#472h. Lk 1:5. **Amminadab.** Nu 1:7. 2:3. Ru 4:19, 20. 1 Ch 2:10. Mt *1:4. **Naashon.** i.e. *enchanter,* +S#5177h, so rendered only here. See 1 Ch +2:10, Nahshon. **Nadab.** i.e. *liberal; volunteer, self-impelled,* *S#5070h. Ex 24:1, 9. Le 10:1, 2. Nu 3:2-4. 20:25. 26:60, 61. 1 K 14:20. 15:25, 27, 31. 1 Ch 2:28, 30. 6:3. 8:30. 9:36. 24:1, 2. (1) One of the sons of Aaron. He and his brother Abihu were miraculously destroyed for offering strange fire to the Lord, Le 10:1-3. (2) A son of Jeroboam I., whom he succeeded as king of Israel, 1 K 14:20; 15:25-31. (3) A son of Shammai, 1 Ch 2:28. (4) A son of Gibeon. He was the uncle of King Saul, 1 Ch 8:30. **Abihu.** i.e. *father of him,* *S#30h. Ex 24:1, 9. 28:1. Le 10:1. Nu 3:2, 4. 26:60, 61. 1 Ch 6:3. 24:1, 2. **Eleazar.** i.e. *God has helped,* *S#499h. (1) The third son of Aaron, Ex 6:23, and his successor in the office of high-priest. Ex 6:25. 28:1. Le 10:6, 12, 16. Nu 3:2, 4, 32. 4:16. 16:37, 39. 19:3, 4. 20:25, 26, 28, 28. 25:7, 11. 26:1, 3, 60, 63. 27:2, 19, 21, 22. 31:6, 12, 13, 21, 26, 29, 31, 41, 51, 54. 32:2, 28. 34:17. Dt 10:6. Jsh 14:1. 17:4. 19:51. 21:1. 22:13, 31, 32. 24:33. Jg 20:28. 1 Ch 6:3, 4, 50. 9:20. 24:1, 2, 3, 4, 4, 5, 6. Ezr 7:5. (2) The son of Abinadab, 1 S 7:1. (3) One of the three

mighty men who aided David in smiting the Philistines, 2 S 23:9; 1 Ch 11:12. (4) A son of Mahli, 1 Ch 23:21, 22; 24:28. (5) A priest who went up with Ezra to Jerusalem, Ezr 8:33. (6) A priest in the time of Nehemiah, Ne 12:42. Perhaps the same as number 5. (7) A Jew who had taken a foreign wife, Ezr 10:25. (8) An ancestor of Joseph, the husband of Mary, Mt 1:15. **Ithamar**. i.e. *land of palms; he is bitter*, *S#385h. Ex 28:1. 38:21. Le 10:6, 12, 16. Nu 3:2, 4. 4:28, 33. 7:8. 26:60. 1 Ch 6:3. 24:1, 2, 3, 4, 4, 5, 6. Ezr 8:2.

24. **sons of Korah**. ver. 21. Nu 16:1, 32. 26:9-11. 1 Ch 6:22, 33, 37, 38. Ps 84, 85 titles. **Assir**. i.e. *prisoner*, *S#617h. 1 Ch 3:17. 6:22, 23, 37. (1) A Levite, the son of Korah, Ex 6:24; 1 Ch 6:22. (2) A son of Ebiasaph, 1 Ch 6:23, 37. (3) A son of Jeconiah, 1 Ch 3:17. **Elkanah**. i.e. *whom God has redeemed*, *S#511h. (1) A son or grandson of Korah, Ex 6:24; 1 Ch 6:23. (2) A descendant, as it appears, of number 1, 1 S 1:1; 1 Ch 6:27. He was the husband of Hannah and father of Samuel. 1 S 1:1, 4, 8, 19, 21, 23. 2:11, 20. 1 Ch 6:27, 34. (3) A descendant of Kohath, 1 Ch 6:25, 36. (4) Apparently a descendant of Kohath, 1 Ch 6:26, 35. Perhaps same as number 3. (5) A Levite whose descendants dwelt in the villages of the Netophathites, 1 Ch 9:16. (6) An Israelite who joined David at Ziklag, 1 Ch 12:6. (7) A Levite, one of the porters for the ark, 1 Ch 15:23. (8) A chief officer of Judah in the time of Ahaz, 2 Ch 28:7. **Abiasaph**. i.e. *gatherer*, *S#23h. **Korhites**. i.e. *descendants of Korah*, *S#7145h. Nu 26:58, Korathites. 1 Ch 9:19 (Korahites), 31 (Korahite). 12:6. 26:1, 19. 2 Ch 20:19.

25. **Putiel**. i.e. *afflicted of God*, *S#6317h. **Phinehas**. i.e. *brazen mouth; mouth of brass; mouth of pity*, *S#6372h. Nu 25:7, 11. 31:6. Jsh 22:13, 30, 31, 32. 24:33. Jg 20:28. 1 S 1:3. 2:34. 4:4, 11, 17, 19. 14:3. 1 Ch 6:4, 4, 50. 9:20. Ezr 7:5. 8:2, 33. Ps 106:30, 31. (1) A son of Eleazar, one of the sons of Aaron, Ex 6:25; Nu 25:7. He was high-priest for many years. (2) One of the sons of Eli the priest. He was notoriously wicked, 1 S 1:3; 2:34; 4:4, 17, 19; 14:3. (3) A Levite in the time of Ezra, Ezr 8:33. **the heads**. ver. 14.

26. **that Aaron**. ver. 13, 20. Jsh 24:5. 1 S 12:6, 8. 1 Ch 6:3. Ps 77:20. 99:6. Mi 6:4. **Bring**. ver. 7. Ex 3:10, 11. 20:2. 32:1, 7, 11. Ac 7:35, 36. **armies**. Ex 7:4. 12:17, 51. *13:18. Ge 2:1. Nu 1:3, 52. 2:3, 9. 10:14, 18, 22, 28. *33:1.

27. **spake**. Ex 5:1-3. 7:10. **to bring**. ver. 13, 26. Ex 32:7. 33:1. Ps *77:20. Mi 6:4.

29. **I am the**. See on ver. 2, 6, 8. **speak**. ver. 11. Ex 7:2. 1 S 3:18. Je 1:7, 8, 17-19. √23:28. 26:2. Ezk 2:6, 7. 3:11, 17. Mt *28:20. Jn=12:49, 50. Ac 20:27.

30. **uncircumcised**. See on ver. 12. Ex *4:10. 1 C 9:16, 17.

EXODUS 7

The Lord encourages Moses and Aaron to go unto Pharaoh, 1-6. Their ages are noted, 7. Aaron casts down his rod, which becomes a serpent, and the magicians do the same; but their rods are swallowed up by Aaron's rod: yet Pharaoh's heart is hardened, 8-13. Another message is sent to Pharaoh, and the river is turned into blood, 14-23. The distress of the Egyptians, 24, 25.

1. **See**. Ex 16:29. Ge 19:21. 1 K 17:23. 2 K 6:32. Ec 1:10. **a god**. Ex *4:15, 16. 22:9h. Ps +√82:6. Je

*1:10. Lk *21:15. Jn 10:+√35, 36. Ac ❰14:11. **thy prophet**. Ex 4:15, 30. Ac 14:12.

2. **speak all**. Ex 4:15. 6:29. Dt 4:2. 1 K 22:14. Je *1:7, 17. Ezk 3:10, 17. Mt 28:20. Ac 20:27.

3. **And I**. See on Ex 4:21, 29. **multiply**. Ex 4:7. 9:16. 11:9. Dt 4:34. 7:19. Ne 9:10. Ps 78:43-51. 105:27-36. 135:9. Is 51:9. Je 32:20, 21. Mi 7:15. Jn 4:48. Ac 2:22. 7:36. Ro 15:19.

4. **that I**. Ex 9:3. 10:1. 11:9. Jg 2:15. La 3:3. **armies**. Ex 6:26. 12:41, 51. Nu 1:3. 2:32. **by great**. Ex 6:6. Pr 19:29. Is 26:9. Ezk 14:21. 25:11. 30:14, 19. Re 15:4. 16:7. 19:2.

5. **Egyptians**. ver. 17. Ex 8:10, 22. 14:4, 18. Ps *9:16. Ezk 25:17. 28:22. 36:23. 39:7, 22. **I stretch**. See on Ex 3:20. ♪22A14.8A. Anthropomorphism B879. A hand is attributed to God in the idiomatic expression, to "stretch forth the hand" in sending judgments. For other instances of this idiom see Ps 138:7. Is 5:25. 9:12, 17, 21. 10:4. 14:27. 31:3. Je 6:12. Ezk 16:27. 25:7. Zp 1:4. 2:13.

6. **did as**. ver. 2, 10. Ex 12:28. 39:43. 40:16. Ge 6:22. 22:18. Ps 119:4. Jn 15:10, 14.

7. **fourscore**. Ex 2:23. Ge 41:46. Dt *29:5. *31:2. *34:7. Ps 90:10. Ac *7:23, 30.

9. **Show**. Is 7:11. Mt 12:39. Jn *2:18. *6:30. 10:38. **Take**. ver. 10-12. Ex 4:2, 17, 20. 9:23. 10:13. **a serpent**. Ps 74:12, 13. Ezk 29:3.

10. **as the Lord**. ver. 9. **before**. ♪144A1, Ge +11:8. **it became**. Ex *4:3. Am 9:3. Mk 16:18. Lk 10:19. **serpent**. S#8577h. Ge 1:21, Heb. sea monster.

11. **wise men**. Ge *41:8, 38, 39. Is 19:11, 12. 47:12, 13. Da *2:2, 27. 4:7-9. 5:7, 11. 2 T *3:8. Re 19:20. **sorcerers**. *mechashshaphim*, probably from the Arabic *kashaph*, to discover, reveal, signifies *diviners*, or those who pretended to reveal futurity, to discover things lost, or to find hidden treasures. *S#3784h. Ex 7:11. 22:18 (witch). Dt 18:10 (witch). 2 Ch 33:6 (witchcraft). Da 2:2. Ml 3:5. **magicians**. *S#2748h. Ge 41:8, 24. Ex 7:11, 22. *8:7, 18, 19. 9:11, 11. Da 1:20. 2:2. **they also**. ver. 22. Ex *8:7, 18. Dt 13:1-3. Mt 24:24. Ga 3:1. Ep 4:14. 2 Th 2:9. Re 13:11-15. **enchantments**. By the word *lahatim*, from *lahat*, to burn, may be meant such incantations as required lustral fires, fumigations, etc. S#3858h, only here.

12. **but Aaron's**. Ex 8:18, 19. 9:11. Ac 8:9-13. 13:8-11. 19:19, 20. 1 J 4:4. **rod**. ♪11, Ge +2:23.

13. **hardened**. ver. 4. Ex 4:21. 8:15. 10:1, 20, 27. 14:17. Dt +*2:30. Zc 7:11, 12. Ro 1:28. 2:5. He 3:7, 8, 13.

14. **Pharaoh's**. Ex *10:1, 20, 27. Zc 7:12. **heart**. ver. 22. Ex ❰+4:21. 8:15, 19, 32. 9:7, 34, 35. **hardened**. Heb. heavy. *S#3515h. Ge 12:10 (grievous). 41:31 (grievous, mg. heavy). 43:1 (sore). 47:4 (sore), 13. 50:9 (great), 10 (sore), 11 (grievous). Ex 4:10 (slow). 7:14 (hardened). 8:24 (grievous). 9:3, 18, 24. 10:14. 12:38 (much). 17:12 (heavy). 18:18. 19:16 (thick). Nu 11:14. 20:20. 1 K 3:9. 10:2. 12:4, 11. 2 K 6:14mg. 18:17mg. 2 Ch 9:1. 10:4, 11. Ps 38:4. Pr 27:3. Is 1:4 (laden). 32:2mg. 36:2. Ezk 3:5mg, 6mg. **he refuseth**. Ex 4:23. 8:2. 9:2. 10:4. Is 1:20. Je 8:5. 9:6. He 12:25.

15. **he goeth**. Ex 2:5. 8:20. Ezk 29:3. **the rod**. ver. 10. Ex 4:2-4.

16. **The Lord**. Ex 3:18. 5:3. 9:1, 13. 10:3. 1 S 4:6-9. **Let my**. Ex 8:1, 20. 13:15. 14:5. Is 45:13. Je 50:33. Ac 4:21-23. **serve**. Ex 3:12, 18. *5:1-3. 9:1.

17. **this**. ♪16, Ge +1:27. **thou shalt**. ver. 5. Ex 5:2.

6:7. 1 S 17:46, 47. 1 K 20:28. 2 K 19:19. Ps 9:16. 83:18. Ezk 29:9. 30:8, 19. 32:15. 38:23. 39:28. Da 4:17, 32, 37. 5:21, 23. **and they**. Ex 1:22. 4:9. Ps 78:44. 105:29. Re 8:8. *16:3-6.

18. **the fish**. ver. 21. **shall loathe**. Heb. weary themselves. ver. 24. Ge 19:11. Nu 11:20. 21:5. Is 1:14. Je 6:11.

19. **stretch**. Ex 8:5, 6, 16. 9:22, 23, 33. 10:12, 21. 14:21, 26. **their pools**. Heb. gathering of their waters. Ge 1:10. Le 11:36. **stone**. ♪121D7. Metonymy of the Cause B559. Stones are put for things made of them. For other instances of this figure see Dt 25:13. Pr 11:1. Is 34:11. Je 2:27. Zc 4:10.

20. **he lifted**. Ex 17:5, 6, 9-12. Nu 20:8-12. **all the waters**. ver. 17, 18. Ps *78:44. *105:29. Jn *2:9-11. Re 8:8.

21. **the fish**. ver. 18. Re 8:9. The first miracle of Christ turned water into wine, the first plague upon Egypt turned all their water into blood. Jn ◑=2:1-10.

22. **magicians**. ver. 11. Ex 8:7, 8. Je 27:18. 2 T 3:8. **and Pharaoh's**. See on ver. 13. **as the**. ver. 3.

23. **neither**. Ex 9:21. Dt 32:46. 1 S 4:20mg. 2 S 13:20. Jb 7:17. Ps 62:10. Pr 22:17. 24:32mg. 29:1. Is *26:11. Je 5:3. 36:24. Ezk 40:4. Am 4:7-12. Hab 1:5. Ml 2:2.

24. **for they**. ver. 18-21.

25. **seven days**. Ex 8:9, 10. 10:23. 2 S 24:13.

EXODUS 8

The plague of frogs is threatened and sent, 1-6; is imitated by the magicians, 7; and removed in answer to the prayer of Moses, made at Pharaoh's request, who yet hardened his heart, 8-15. The plague of lice, which the magicians could not imitate, 16-19. The plague of flies, 20-24; Pharaoh relents, the plague is removed, and his heart is hardened, 25-32.

1. **Go**. Je 1:17-19. 15:19-21. Ezk 2:6, 7. **Let my**. See on Ex *3:12, 18. 5:1. 7:16.

2. **refuse**. See on Ex 7:14. 9:2. **frogs**. Ps *78:45. *105:30. Re *16:13, 14.

3. **bedchamber**. 2 K 1:16n. Ec +10:20. **ovens**. Le 2:4. 7:9. 26:26. **kneading troughs**. *or*, dough. Ex 12:34. Ge 40:17.

4. **on thee**. ver. 9, 11, 21. Ex 9:14. 10:6. Ps 107:40. Is 19:11, 22. 23:9. Da 4:37. Ac 12:22, 23.

5. **Stretch forth**. Ex 7:19.

6. **and the frogs**. Le 11:12. Ps 78:45. 105:30. Re 16:13.

7. **magicians did so**. Ex 7:11, 22. ◑*8:18. Dt 13:1-3. Mt √24:24. 2 Th √2:9-11. 2 T *3:8. Re 13:14.

8. **Intreat**. Ex 5:2. *9:28. *10:17. Nu 21:7. 1 S 12:19. 1 K *13:6. Ac +*8:24. **and I will**. ver. 25-28. Ex 10:8-11, 24-27. 12:31, 32. 14:5. Ps 66:3mg. 78:34-36. Je 34:8-16.

9. **Glory over me**. *or*, Have *this* honor over me. Jg 7:2. 1 K 18:25. Ps 60:8mg,n. Is 10:15. **when**. *or*, against when. **to destroy**. Heb. to cut off. ver. 13.

10. **Tomorrow**. *or*, against tomorrow. Pr 27:1. Ja 4:14. **there is none**. Ex 9:14, 29. 15:11. Dt *32:31. *33:26. 2 S *7:22. 1 Ch 17:20. Ps 9:16. 83:18. *86:8. 89:6-8. Is 40:25. *46:9. Je *10:6, 7.

11. **the frogs**. ver. 3, 9.

12. **cried unto**. See on ver. 8, 30. Ex 9:33. 10:18. 32:11. 1 S √12:23. Ezk 36:37. Mt *5:44. Ja 5:16-18.

13. **according**. Jn=18:9. Ja +*5:16. **word of**. Dt 34:10-12.

14. **and the**. ver. 24. Ex 7:21. Is 34:3. Ezk 39:11. Jl 2:20.

15. **saw**. Ex 14:5. Ec √8:11. Is √26:10. Je 34:7-11. Ho 6:4. **respite**. Est 4:14. **he hardened**. ♪96B, Ge +8:5. See on Ex +*4:21. *7:4, 13, 14. Pr 29:1. Zc 7:11, 12. He 3:8, 15. Re 16:9. S#3515h. Ex +7:14. or, S#3513h. Ex 8:32. 9:34. 10:1. 1 K 10:1 (made heavy), 14. 2 Ch 10:10, 14. 25:19 (boast). La 3:7. Zc 7:11mg.

16. **Stretch**. ver. 5, 17.

17. **lice in man**. Ps 105:31. Is 23:9. Ac 12:23. **all**. Ex 9:6, 25. 10:12. ♪102. Hyperbole or Overstatement, Ge +7:19.

18. **the magicians**. Ex 7:11. **did so**. ♪108A1. Idiom B821. Idiomatic usage of verbs. Active verbs used to express the agent's design or attempt to do anything, even though the thing was not actually done. For other instances of this figure see Dt 28:68. Ezk 24:13. Mt 17:11. Ga 5:4. Ph 3:15. 1 J 1:10. 2:26. 5:10. **they could not**. Ex 9:11. Ge 41:8. Is 19:12. 47:12, 13. Da 2:10, 11. 4:7. 5:8. Lk 10:18. 2 T *3:8, 9.

19. **This is**. 1 S *6:3, 9. Ps 8:3. Da 2:10, 11, 19. Mt *12:28. Lk √11:20. Jn 11:47. Ac 4:16. **the finger**. Ex 10:7. Lk =11:20. ♪22A16. Anthropomorphism B881: A finger is attributed to God. For other instances of this figure see Ex 31:18. Ps 8:3. Is 40:12. 48:13. Lk 11:20. **and Pharaoh's**. See on ver. 15.

20. **lo**. Ex 7:15. **Let my**. ver. 1.

21. **swarms**. Ex 12:38. Ne 13:3. Ps 78:45. 105:31. Is *7:18.

22. **sever**. Ex *9:4, 6, 26. *10:23. *11:6, 7. *12:13. Ml 3:18. **know**. See on ver. 10. Ex 7:17. Ezk 30:19. **midst**. Ps 74:12. 110:2.

23. **put**. Ex 11:7. Ps 50:5. **a division**. Heb. a redemption. Ex 33:16. Le 20:24. Nu 23:9. Dt 33:28. Ps 111:9. 130:7. Is 50:2. ♪121M. Metonymy of the Adjunct B586. The thing signified is put for the sign. Here, redemption is put for the judgment, which would be the sign of the redemption. For other instances of this figure see Nu 6:7mg. Dt 16:3. 22:15, 17. 2 K 13:17. 1 Ch 16:11. Ps 78:61. Is 49:6mg, +8n. Ezk 7:27. **tomorrow**. *or*, by tomorrow. ver. 10. **sign**. Ex 4:8. +12:13. Jg 6:17, 37.

24. **there**. ver. 21. Ps 78:45. 105:31. **the land**. How intolerable a plague of flies can prove, is evident from the fact that whole districts have been laid waste by them. Such was the fate of Myuns in Ionia (Pausan. l. vii) and of Alarnae. The inhabitants were forced to quit these cities, not being able to stand against the flies and gnats with which they were pestered. Trajan was obliged to raise the siege of a city in Arabia, before which he had sat down, being driven away by the swarms of these insects (Dion Cassius, l. lxviii. Aelian de Animal. l. xi. c. 28). Hence different people had deities whose office it was to defend them against flies. Among these may be reckoned Baalzebub, the fly-god of Ekron (2 K 1:16n); Hercules, muscarum abactor, Hercules the expeller of flies; and hence Jupiter had the titles of *apomuios, muiagros, muiokoros*, because he was supposed to expel flies, and especially clear his temples of these insects (See Bryant, pp. 54-56). ver. 14. **corrupted**. *or*, destroyed. Ge 6:11, 12.

25. **called for**. See on ver. 8. Ex 9:27. 10:16. 12:31. Re 3:9. **in the land**. Ex 8:11. 10:11, 24.

26. **It is not**. Ex 3:18. 2 C 6:14-17. **we shall**. Ge 43:22. 46:34. Dt *7:25, 26. *12:30, 31. Ezr 9:1. Is 44:19. **the abomination**. i.e. The animals which the Egyptians worshipped, when sacrificed by the Israelites in their worship, would cause the Egyptians great offense, as did all these plagues, for they struck at the very objects and creatures most worshipped by the Egyptians. Ex 9:3. 1 K 11:5-7. 2 K 23:13.

27. **three days'**. Ex 3:18. 5:1. 2 C *6:17. **as he shall**. Ex 3:12. 10:26. 34:11. Le 10:1. Mt 28:20.

28. **I will**. Ho 10:2. **only**. Ex 8:25. 10:11, 24. **intreat**. See on ver. 8, 29. Ex 9:28. 10:17. 1 K 13:6. Ezr 6:10. Ec 6:10. Ac 8:24.

29. **tomorrow**. ver. 10. **deal**. ver. 8, 15. Ps 66:3mg. 78:34-37. Je 42:20, 21. Ac *5:3, 4. Ga *6:7.

30. **entreated**. ver. 12. Ex 9:33. Ja *5:16.

31. **according**. Ps 65:2. **removed**. 1 K 13:6.

32. **hardened**. See on ver. 15. Ex 4:21. 7:13, 14. Pr 28:14. Is 63:17. Ac 28:26, 27. Ro +*2:5. +*9:18. Ja *1:13, 14.

EXODUS 9

The plague of murrain predicted, and sent on the cattle of the Egyptians, while the cattle of Israel are exempted, 1-7. The plague of boils, 8-12. Moses expostulates with Pharaoh, and predicts the plague of hail, which is sent, and causes immense devastation, 13-26. Pharaoh confesses his wickedness, deprecates further judgments, and promises to let Israel go, 27, 28. Moses intercedes, the hail ceases, and Pharaoh continues hardened, 29-35.

1. **Go in**. ver. 13. Ex 3:18. 4:22, 23. 5:1. 8:1, 20. 10:3. **the Lord**. Ex 3:18. 5:3. 7:16.

2. **if thou refuse**. Ex 4:23. 8:2. 10:4. Le 26:14-16, *21, 23, 24, 27, 28. Ps 7:11, 12. *68:21. Is 1:20. Ro 2:8. Re 2:21, 22. *16:9.

3. **the hand**. Ex 7:4. 8:19. 1 S 5:6-11. 6:9. Jb 13:21. 33:7. Ps 32:4. 38:2. 39:10. Ac 13:11. ʃ22A14.7. Anthropomorphism B879. A *hand* is attributed to God, in the action of punishment. For other instances of this figure see Jb 19:21. Ps 17:14. 21:8. 38:2. Ezk 39:21. Ac 13:11. **murrain**. *or*, pestilence. ver. 15. Ex 5:3. Le 26:25. Ezk 38:22.

4. **sever**. Ex *8:22. 10:23. 12:13. Is 65:13, 14. Ml *3:18.

5. **a set time**. ver. 18. Ex 8:23. 10:4. Nu 16:5. Jb 24:1. Ec 3:1-11. Je 28:16, 17. Mt 27:63, 64.

6. **all**. Ex 9:25. 10:12. ʃ102, Hyperbole or Overstatement, Ge +√7:19. ʃ171A. Synecdoche of the Genus B614: "All" is put for the greater part. What is meant is all kinds of cattle, not all the individual animals of all species. The kinds of cattle are particularized in verse 3. This must be so, for no sane writer could stultify himself by meaning "all" in any other sense, when he goes on to speak of other beasts immediately after, in verse 10. See listing of related figures at Ge 24:10n. For other instances of this figure see Ex 9:25. 32:3, 26. Ge 6:17. Nu √16:32n. Dt 28:64. Jsh 6:21. 11:23n. √21:43n. 2 S 6:5, 15. 16:22. 17:24. 2 K 11:16. 1 Ch 10:6. √14:17. Ps 22:7. *118:10. Is 2:2. Je 26:9. Ho 7:4. Hg 2:7. Mt 3:5. 8:34. 10:22. 16:19. 18:18. 21:26. 24:9. Mk 1:33. 9:23. Lk 2:1, 3. 15:1. Jn 1:16. 10:8. Ro 1:8. 10:18. 1 C 6:2. 9:19, 22. 13:7. Ph 2:21. 4:13. Col 1:23, 28. He 6:16. Re *13:7, 8, 16. **the cattle**. ver. 19, 25. Ps 78:48, 50. Mt 10:29. 1 C 9:9, 10.

7. **the heart**. ver. 12. Ex 7:14. 8:32. Jb 9:4. Pr 29:1. Is 48:4. Da 5:20. Ro 9:18.

8. **Take to**. Ex 8:16. **furnace**. Ex 19:18. Ge 11:3. 19:28. **toward the heaven**. ver. 10.

9. **a boil**. Le 13:18-20. Dt 28:27, 35. 2 K 20:7. Jb 2:7. Is 38:21. Re *16:2.

10. **up toward**. ver. 8. **a boil**. ver. +9. Dt *28:27.

11. **magicians**. Ex 8:7, 18, 19. Da 1:20. 2:2. 4:7, 9. 5:11. **could not**. Ex 7:11, 12. 8:18, 19. Is 47:12-14. 2 T *3:8, 9. Re 16:2. **stand**. Ps 147:14. Pr 27:7. Da 8:7.

12. **the Lord hardened**. Hardness of heart is a figurative expression, denoting that insensibility of mind upon which neither judgments nor mercies make any abiding impressions; but the conscience being stupified, the obdurate rebel persists in determined disobedience. ver. 35. See on Ex +*4:21. 7:3, 13, +14. 8:15. 10:1, 20, 27. 11:10. 14:4, 8. Dt 2:30. Jsh 11:20. Jg 9:23. 14:4. 1 S 2:25. 6:6. *16:14. 1 K 12:15. 22:23. 2 Ch 10:15. 22:7. 25:20. Jb 12:16. Ps 81:11, 12. 105:25. Pr 21:1. Is 6:9, 10. 19:2, *14. 29:10. *63:17. Je 4:10. Ezk 12:2. 14:9. Am +√3:6n. Mt 13:11, 14. Mk 4:11, 12. Lk 8:10. Jn 12:39, 40. Ac 28:26, 27. Ro √9:18. 11:8. 2 C 3:14, 15. 2 Th *2:10-12. Re 16:10, 11.

13. **Rise up early**. ver. 1. Ex 7:15. 8:20. Ge ◐+*21:14. **the Lord God**. Ex 7:16. Let. Is=61:1.

14. **send all**. Le 26:18, 21, 28. Dt 28:15-17, 59-61. 29:20-22. 32:39-42. 1 S 4:8. 1 K 8:38. Je 19:8. Mi *6:13. Re 18:8. 22:18. **that thou**. See on Ex 8:10.

15. **stretch**. ver. 3, 6, 16. 3:20. Ex 11:4-6. 12:29, 30. **cut off**. Ex 14:28. 1 K 13:34. Pr 2:22.

16. **deed**. Ex 14:17. Ps 83:17, 18. Pr *16:4. Ro *9:♦17, 22. 1 P 2:8, 9. Ju 4. **raised thee up**. Heb. made thee stand. **for to**. Ex 14:4. 15:11-16. 18:11. Jsh 2:10, 11. 1 S 4:8. Ps *76:10. 136:10-15. **that my**. 1 Ch 16:24. Ne *9:10. Ps 64:9. 83:17, 18. Is 63:12-14. Ml 1:11, 14. Ro 9:17.

17. **exaltest**. Jb 9:4. 15:25, 26. 40:9. Is 10:15. 26:11. 37:23, 24, 29. 45:9. Ac 12:23. 1 C 10:22.

18. **tomorrow**. 1 K 19:2. 20:6. 2 K 7:1, 18. **I will cause**. ver. +12, 22-25. Jb 9:17. Ps 83:15. **rain**. ver. 34. Ge 7:4. 1 S 12:17, 18. Ps 77:17. **hail**. Jsh 10:11. Jb 38:22. Ps 18:13, 14. 78:47-48. 105:32. 148:8. Is 28:2. 30:30. Ezk 13:11. 38:22. Hag 2:17. Re 8:7. 11:19. 16:21. **such as**. ver. 24. Ex 10:6, 14.

19. **and gather**. Hab 3:2. **shall not**. ʃ144D, Ge 40:23. **the hail**. ver. +18, 25.

20. **feared the word**. Pr 16:16. +*22:3, 23. Jon *3:5, 6. Mk 13:14-16. He 11:7.

21. **regarded not**. Heb. set not his heart unto. Ex 7:23. 1 S 4:20mg. 2 S 13:26. 1 Ch 22:19. Jb 1:8mg. 7:17. 34:14. Ps +78:43mg. Pr 24:32mg. Ezk 40:4. 44:5mg. Da 10:12.

22. **Stretch forth**. Ex 7:19. 8:5, 16. 10:12, 21. Re 16:21. **toward heaven**. Mt 14:19. Lk 15:18.

23. **the Lord sent**. Ex 19:16. 20:18. 1 S 12:17, 18. Jb 37:1-5. Ps 29:3. 77:18. Re 16:18, 21. **thunder**. Heb. voices. Ex 19:16. 20:18. Ps 29:3, 9. **and hail**. ver. +18. Jsh *10:11. Jb 38:22, 23. Ps 18:13. *78:47, 48. *105:32, 33. *148:8. Is *30:30. Ezk *38:22. Re *8:7.

24. **mingled**. Ezk 1:4. **none like**. ver. 18, 23. 10:6. Mt 24:21.

25. **smote**. Ps *105:33. **all**. √ʃ171A, Ex +9:6. **every**. ʃ102, Hyperbole or Overstatement, Ge +7:19. ver. 6. Ex 8:17. ◐*10:12.

26. **Only in the land**. Ex *8:22, etc. *9:4, 6. *10:23.

11:7. 12:13. Ps 91:7. Is *32:18, 19. **Goshen.** Ge +45:10.
where. Ex 10:23. *11:7. *12:13. 14:29. 15:19. Ps 78:53.
Am 4:7.

27. **I have.** Ex 10:16. Nu *22:34. 1 S *15:24, 30.
*26:21. Jb *34:31, 32. Pr *28:13. Mt 27:4. **the Lord.**
2 Ch *12:6. Ps 9:16. 129:4. *145:17. La *1:18. Da
*9:14. Ro 2:5. 3:19.

28. **Intreat.** T#1724. Ex 8:8, 28. 10:17. Ac 8:24.
enough. Ge 45:28. Nu 16:3. **mighty thunderings.** Heb.
voices of God. Ge +*23:6. Ps 29:3, 4. √24L, Ge +6:2.
ye shall. Ex 11:1.

29. **spread.** ver. 33. 1 K 8:22, 38. 2 Ch 6:12, 13.
Ezr 9:5. Jb 11:13. Ps 143:6. Is 1:15. **that the earth.**
Dt 10:14. Ps *24:1, 2. 50:12. 95:4, 5. 135:6. 1 C *10:26,
28.

30. **as for.** Pr 16:6. Ec 8:12. Is √26:10. 63:17. Ro
2:4. **I know.** Lk ◑+*6:35. **not yet fear.** Dt 25:18.
2 K 17:25. Jb *6:14mg. Ps 36:1. 55:19. Pr 1:29. Ec 8:13.
Is 57:11. Je *2:19. 5:22, 24. 44:10. Ho 10:3. Ml 3:5.
Lk √16:31. 18:4.

31. **flax.** √68, Ge +10:1. √132G, Ge +3:19. Ru 1:22.
2:23. Am 4:9. Hab 3:17. **barley.** Le 27:16. **in the ear.**
Le 2:14. **bolled.** or, in bud.

32. **rie.** or, spelt. Is 28:25. Ezk 4:9. **not grown up.**
Heb. hidden, or dark. Ex 10:22.

33. **spread.** ver. 29. Ex 8:12. **and the thunders.**
Ex 10:18, 19. Ja 5:17, 18. **poured.** Heb. nathak,
❊S#5413h. Kal, Future: 2 Ch 12:7. 34:25. Jb 3:24.
Je 42:18. 44:6. Da 9:11, 27. Niphal, Preterite: Ex 9:33.
2 S 21:10 (dropped). 2 Ch 34:21. Je 42:18. Ezk 22:21
(melted). 24:11 (molten). Na 1:6. Niphal, Participle:
Je 7:20. Hiphil, Preterite: 2 K 22:9 (gathered. mg,
melted). Ezk 22:20 (melt). Hiphil, Infinitive: Ezk 22:20
(melt). Hiphil, Future: 2 Ch 34:17 (gathered together.
mg, poured out, or, melted). Jb 10:10. Hophal, Future:
Ezk 22:22 (melted).

34. **saw.** Ex 8:15. Ec √8:11. **and hardened.** Ex
+4:21. +7:14. 1 S 6:6. 2 Ch 28:22. *33:23. 36:13. Ro
2:4, 5.

35. **was hardened.** Ex +7:13. **as the Lord.** Ex
+*4:21. 7:3, 4. 11:9, 10. **by Moses.** Heb. by the hand
of Moses. Ex 4:13.

EXODUS 10

*Moses is sent to denounce the plague of locusts, 1-
6. The servants of Pharaoh persuade him to let Israel
go, 7; he sends for Moses, treats with him, but drives
him away, 8-11. The plague of locusts, 12-15. Moses
is sent for, and entreats the Lord; the locusts are removed, and Pharaoh is hardened, 16-20. The plague
of darkness; Pharaoh again treats with Moses, but is
again hardened, and drives him away with menaces,
21-29.*

1. **I have hardened.** See on Ex +*4:21. 7:13, +14.
8:15. 9:27, 34, 35. Ps 7:11. **that I.** Ex 3:20. 7:4. 9:16.
14:17, 18. 15:14, 15. Jsh 2:9, 10. 4:23, 24. 1 S 4:8.
Ro 9:17.

2. **And that.** Ex 13:8, 9, 14. Dt *4:9. 6:20-22. Ps
*44:1. 71:18. 78:5, 6. Jl *1:3. Ep *6:4. **wrought.** Nu
22:29. 1 S 6:6. 31:4. **that ye.** √96F4. Heterosis of Number or Person B532. Transition or change from the
singular to the plural. Here, a sudden transition from
"thou" to "ye." For other instances of this figure see
Ps 14:1. Is 2:20. Ga 4:6-8. 6:1. **may know.** See on Ex
7:17. Ps 58:11. Ezk 20:26, 28.

3. **How long.** Ex 9:17. 16:28. Nu 14:27. 1 K 18:21.
Pr 1:22, 24. Je 13:10. Ezk 5:6. He 12:25. **humble.**
1 K *21:29. 2 Ch +√7:14. 33:12, 19. 34:27. Jb *42:6.
Pr *18:12. Is 1:5. 2:11. Je 13:18. Ro 2:4. Ja *4:10.
1 P *5:6.

4. **tomorrow.** Ex 8:10, 23. 9:5, 18. 11:4, 5. **locusts.**
Pr 30:27. Jl 1:4-7. 2:2-11, 25. Re 9:3.

5. **face.** Heb. eye. ver. 15. Ge +1:2. Nu 11:7. 22:5,
11. **the residue.** Ex 9:32. Jl 1:4. 2:25.

6. **fill.** Ex 8:3, 21. **which.** ver. 14, 15. Ex 9:24. 11:6.
Jl 2:2. **unto this day.** Ge +19:38. **And he.** ver. 11.
Ex 11:8. He 11:27. **went out.** Mt *10:14.

7. **servants said.** Ex 8:19. **How long.** ver. 3. **snare.**
Ex 23:33. 34:12. Dt 7:16. Jsh 23:13. 1 S 18:21. Jb
40:24. Pr 29:6. Ec 7:26. Is 8:14. 1 C 7:35. 1 P=2:8.
that Egypt. Ps 107:34. Is 14:20. 51:9. Je 48:4. 51:8.
Zp 1:18.

8. **brought.** ver. 16, 24. Ex 12:31. **who.** Heb. who,
and who, etc.

9. **We will go.** Ge 50:8. Dt 31:12, 13. Jsh 24:15.
Ps 148:12, 13. Ec 12:1. Ep 6:4. **our flocks.** Pr 3:9. **a
feast.** The original word, though generally rendered
feast, is an entirely different word from that which
occurs in Ge 19:3; the latter is properly a *drinking*,
and is used of ordinary entertainments; the former is
used only of religious rejoicings, accompanied with
eating and *dancing*, the literal meaning of the word
being *to move in a circle* (compare Ps 107:27), so ver.
12, 14; 13:6; 23:15, 16, 18; 32:5; 34:18, 22, 25, etc.;
according to Dt 16:10, 11, all the people, without exception, were required to observe these *festivals* (Young,
Concise Critical Comments, p. 52). Ex 3:18. 5:1, 3.
8:25-28. ❊S#2282h: Ex 12:14. 13:6. 23:15, 16, 16, 18.
32:5. 34:18, 22, 22, 25. Le 23:6, 34, 39, 41. Nu 28:17.
*29:12. Dt 16:10, 13, 14, 16, 16, 16. 31:10. Jg 21:19.
1 K 8:2, 65. 12:32, 32, 33. 2 Ch 5:3. 7:8, 9. 8:13, 13,
13. 30:13, 21. 35:17. Ezr 3:4. 6:22. Ne 8:14, 18. Ps
81:3 (solemn feast). 118:27 (sacrifice). Is 29:1 (sacrifices).
30:29 (solemnity). Ezk 45:17, 21, 23, 25. 46:11. Ho
2:11. 9:5. Am 5:21. 8:10. Na 1:15. Zc 14:16, 18, 19.
Ml 2:3. 1 C *5:7, 8.

10. **Let.** ver. 24. Ex 8:25. **be so.** Ex 12:30, 31. 13:21.
look to it. 2 Ch 32:15. La 3:37.

11. **Not so.** Ex ◑8:25, 26. 10:24. **for that.** Ps 52:3,
4. 119:69. **And they.** ver. 28. Ex 5:4.

12. **Stretch.** Ex 7:19. **eat every.** ver. 4, 5. **all that.**
Ex ◑9:25. √102. Hyperbole or Overstatement, Ge
+7:19.

13. **east wind.** Ex 14:21. Ge +√41:6. Ps 78:26.
107:25-28. 148:8. Jon 1:4. 4:8. Mt 8:27.

14. **the locusts.** Dt 28:42. 1 K 8:37. Ps 78:46. 105:34,
35. Re 9:3-7. **very grievous.** ver. 5. Jl 1:2-4. **before.**
ver. 6. Ex 11:6. Jl 2:2. **no such.** Ex 9:18.

15. **For they.** ver. 5. Jl 1:6, 7. 2:1-11, 25. **face.**
Ge +1:2. **eat.** Ps 78:46. 105:35.

16. **called for.** Heb. hastened to call. **I have.** Ex
*9:27. Nu 21:7. 22:34. 1 S 15:24, 30. 26:21. 2 S 19:20.
Jb 34:31, 32. Pr *28:13. Mt 27:4.

17. **forgive.** 1 S 15:25. Pr 28:13. **and intreat.** See
on Ex *8:8. 9:28. 1 K 13:6. Is 26:16. Ro 15:30. Ac
8:24. **this death.** √121G, Ge +31:1. 2 K 4:40. 2 C
1:10.

18. **went.** Ex 8:30. **and intreated.** See on Ex 8:9,
28, 29. Mt 5:44. Lk 6:28.

19. **a mighty.** ver. 13. **cast.** Heb. fastened. **the Red
sea.** Ex 13:18. 15:4. Jl 2:20. He 11:29.

20. **the Lord hardened**. See on Ex +*4:21. 7:13, +14. 9:12. 11:10. 14:4, 8. Dt +*2:30. Is 6:9, 10. Jn 12:39, 40. Ro *9:18. 2 Th 2:11, 12.

21. **Stretch**. Ex 9:22. **darkness**. Ps 35:6. 78:49. 105:28. Pr 4:19. Ec 2:14. 6:4. Is 8:21, 22. Mt 27:45. Mk 15:33. Lk 23:44. 2 P 2:4, 17. Ju 6, *13. Re 16:10, 11. **even darkness which may be felt**. Heb. that *one* may feel darkness. Dt 28:29.

22. **thick darkness**. Ex 20:21. Ge 15:12. Dt +*4:11. 5:22. Ps *105:28. Pr +*20:20. Jl 2:2, 31. Am 4:13. Zp *2:15. Re 16:10. **three days**. Ex 3:18. 5:3. Ge +22:4. 30:36. +40:20. Le +19:6. Jsh 3:11.

23. **but all**. Ex *8:22. 9:4, 26. 14:20. Jsh 24:7. Is 42:16. 60:1-3. 65:13, 14. Ml *3:18. Ep *5:8. Col 1:13. 1 P *2:9.

24. **Go ye**. ver. 8, 9. Ex 8:28. 9:28. **only**. Ex 8:25, 28. 10:11. **flocks**. Ge 34:23. **little ones**. ver. 10.

25. **us**. Heb. into our hands. **sacrifices**. Ex 29:36-41. Le 9:22. 16:9.

26. **cattle**. Ex 12:32. Is 23:18. 60:5-10. Ho 5:6. Zc 14:20. Ac 2:44, 45. 2 C 8:5. **shall go**. Jsh 4:11. 1 C 10:1. **and we**. Pr 3:9. He 11:8.

27. **the Lord hardened**. See on ver. 1, 20. Ex +4:21. ◑+7:14. 14:4, 8. Re 9:20. 16:10, 11.

28. **Get thee**. ver. 11. **for in that**. 2 Ch 16:10. 25:16. Am 7:13.

29. **I will see**. Ex 11:4-8. 12:30, 31. He *11:27. **no**. ∫151, Ge +1:28.

EXODUS 11

The Lord shows Moses that one more plague is coming on Egypt, and directs that the Israelites should ask jewels of the Egyptians, 1, 2. Moses is honored by the Egyptians, 3. He denounces the death of the firstborn, and goes out from Pharaoh, 4-8. The Lord hardens Pharaoh's heart, 9, 10.

1. **Yet will**. Ex 9:14. Le *26:21. Dt 4:34. 1 S 6:4. Jb 10:17. Re 16:9. 22:18. **afterwards**. Ex 3:20. Ge 15:14. **thrust you**. Ex 12:31-39.

2. **borrow**. Ex +*3:22. *12:1, 2, 35, 36. Ge 31:9. Jb 27:16, 17. Ps 24:1. 105:37. Pr 13:22. Hg 2:8. Mt 20:15. **jewels**. Ex 32:2-4, 24. 35:22. Ezk 16:10-13. Ho 2:8.

3. **the Lord**. Ex 3:21. 12:36. Ge 39:21. Ps 106:46. Ac 7:10. **Moses**. Ge 12:2. 2 S 7:9. Est 9:4. Is 60:14. Ac 7:22. Re 3:9.

4. **About**. Ex 12:12, 23, 29. 2 K *19:35. Jb 34:20. Am *4:10. 5:17. Mt 25:6. **midnight**. Mt=25:6. **will I go**. 2 S 5:24. Ps 60:10. Is 42:13. Mi 2:13. Zc 14:3.

5. **the firstborn**. Ex 4:23. 12:12, 29. 13:15. Ps 78:51. 105:36. 135:8. 136:10. He 11:28. **behind**. Jg 16:21. Is 47:2. La 5:13. Mt 24:41.

6. **a great**. Ex 3:7. *12:30. Pr 21:13. Is 15:4, 5, 8. Je 31:15. La 3:8. Am 5:17. Zp 1:10. Lk 13:28. Re 6:16, 17. 18:18, 19. **cry**. Mt=25:6. **such as**. Ex ◑8:10. +9:24. 10:6.

7. **dog**. Jsh 10:21. Jb 5:16. **a difference**. See on Ex 7:22. +8:23. 10:23. Le 10:10. Ml 3:18. 1 C 4:7.

8. **And all**. Ex *12:31-33. Is 49:23, 26. Re 3:9. **bow**. Ph=2:10. **follow thee**. Heb. is at thy feet. Ge 30:30mg. Dt +11:6mg. Jg 4:10. 8:5. 1 K 20:10mg. 2 K +3:9mg. Da 11:43. **a great anger**. Heb. heat of anger. Ex *32:19. Nu *12:3. Dt 29:24. 32:24. Ps 6:1. Ezk 3:14. Da 3:19. Mk=3:5. Ep *4:26, 27.

9. **Pharaoh**. Ex 3:19. 7:4. 10:1. Ro *9:16-18. **wonders**. See on Ex 7:3.

10. **the Lord**. See on Ex +*4:21. 7:13, +14. 10:20, 27. Dt 2:30. 1 S 6:6. Jb 9:4. Ro *2:4, 5. 9:22.

EXODUS 12

The month of Israel's deliverance is appointed to be the first of their year, 1, 2. The institution of the passover, and the feast of unleavened bread, 3-28. The firstborn throughout Egypt are cut off at once, 29, 30; the Israelites are sent away in haste, 31-33; they spoil the Egyptians and march out, attended by a mixed multitude, 34-39. The term of their sojourning, and the fulfilment of God's promise to Abraham, 40-42. Further rules respecting the passover, 43-51.

1. A.M. 2513. B.C. 1491. **in**. Lk 10:33.

2. **month**. ∫173, Ge +27:44. **beginning**. 2 C=5:17. **first month**. Abib or Nisan. Ex *13:4. 23:15. 34:18. Le 23:5. Nu 28:16. Dt *16:1. Est *3:7.

3. **Speak ye**. Ex 4:30. 6:6. 14:15. 20:19. Le 1:2. **congregation**. The first instance of the occurrence of this word, which literally means *an appointed meeting*; it is rendered in the Common Version (AV) 121 times congregation, 13 times company, 9 times assembly, once multitude, once swarm, once people. It is applied to all Israel, to the followers of Korah, to a band of wicked men (Ps 22:17), and to a swarm of bees (Jg 14:8), Young. Newberry states it denotes *to appoint*, describes a general congregation, inclusive of all. Darby renders it *assembly* at this place, noting it means the congregation looked at as a moral whole, a corporate person before God: see Le 4:13; 8:3. *S#5712h. Ex 12:3, 6, 19, 47. 16:1, 2, 9, 10, 22. 17:1. 34:31. 35:1, 4, 20. Le 4:13, 15. 8:3, 4 (assembly), 5. 9:5. 10:6 (people), 17. 16:5. 19:2. 24:14, 16. Nu 1:2, 16, 18, 53. 3:7. 4:34. 8:9, 20. 10:2, 3. 13:26, 26. 14:1, 2, 5, 7, 10, 27, 35, 36. 15:24, 25, 26, 33, 35, 36. 16:2, 3, 5, 6, 9, 9, 11, 16, 19, 21, 22, 24, 26, 40, 41, 42, 45, 46. 19:9. 20:1, 2, 8, 8, 11, 22, 29. 25:6, 7. 26:2, 9, 9, 10. 27:2, 3, 3, 14, 16, 17, 19, 20, 21, 22. 31:12, 13, 16, 26, 27, 43. 32:2, 4. 35:12, 24, 25, 25. Jsh 9:15, 18, 18, 19, 21, 27. 18:1. 20:6, 9. 22:12, 16, 17, 18, 20, 30. Jg 14:8. 20:1. 21:10, 13, 16. 1 K 8:5. 12:20. 2 Ch 5:6. Jb 15:34. 16:7. Ps *1:5. 7:7. 22:16. 68:30 (multitude). 74:2. 82:1. 86:14. 106:17, 18. 111:1. Pr 5:14. Je 6:18. 30:20. Ho 7:12. **tenth**. ver. 6. Ps 40:8. Mt 3:17. Jn 12:1, 12. Ga=4:4. **take to**. Ge 4:4. 22:8. 1 S 7:9. Jn 1:29, 36. 1 C 5:7. Re 5:6-13. 7:9-14. 13:8. **lamb**. *or*, kid. The word *seh* means the young of both sheep and goats, and may be indifferently rendered either *lamb* or *kid*. It is evident from ver. 5 that the Hebrews might take either; but they generally preferred a lamb, from being of a more gentle nature. Ex 13:13. 22:1, 9, 10. 34:20. Ge 22:7, 8. Le 5:6. 22:23. Nu 15:11. Dt 17:1. 1 S 14:34. 17:34. 2 Ch 35:7. Is 53:7. 1 C 5:7. 1 P 1:19. Re 5:6. 7:10. **according**. Ex 6:11. 2 Ch 25:5. 35:12. **for an**. Ge 7:1. 30:30. Pr 31:15. Ac +16:31. **house**. The Israelites were divided into twelve tribes, these tribes into families, the families into houses, and the houses into particular persons. Nu ch. 1. Jsh 7:14.

4. **too little**. Jsh 19:9. **it**. ∫63I1A. Ellipsis of Repetition B71: Noun from preceding clause. Where the ellipsis is to be supplied by repeating a word or words out of the preceding clause, involving nouns and pro-

nouns. Here, "it" may be replaced by "lamb" from verse 3. Other passages cited by EWB in B exhibiting this figure are: 1 K 1:6. 2 K 3:25. Ps 12:6. 68:18. Ec 12:11. Is 40:13. Am 3:12. Ml 2:14. Ac 7:15, 16. Ro 6:5. 12:11. 1 C 2:11. 2:13. 4:4. 2 C 3:16. 6:16. 11:14, 15. Ep 3:17-19. 1 T 1:16. T 3:8. He 2:11. 7:4. 1 J 2:2. souls. Heb. *nephesh*, Ge +12:5. according to his eating. Ex 16:16.

5. lamb. Jn=1:29. *J*16, Ge +1:27. be without. Le *1:3, 10. *22:19-24. Dt *17:1. Ml 1:7, 8, 14. Jn=8:46. He 7:26. *9:13, 14. 1 P=1:18, 19. =2:22. a male. Le ●4:28. of the first year. Heb. son of a year. Le 23:12. 1 S 13:1mg. Ps 102:23, 24. 110:3.

6. fourteenth. Le 23:5. Nu 9:3. 28:16, 18. Dt *16:1-6. Jsh 5:10. 2 Ch *30:15. Ezr 6:19. Ezk 45:21. the whole. 2 Ch 30:15-18. Is *53:6. Mt *27:20, 25. Mk 15:1, 8, 11, 25, 33, 34, 37. Lk 23:1, 18. Jn 11:50. Ac 2:23. 3:14. 4:27. 2 C 5:14. assembly. Newberry states *kahalh* means *to call together; an assembly, local and partial.* ✳S#6951h. Ge 28:3mg. 35:11. 48:4. 49:6. Ex 12:6. 16:3. Le 4:13, 14, 21. 16:17, 33. Nu 10:7. 14:5. 15:15. 16:3, 33, 47. 19:20. 20:4, 6, 10, 12. 22:4. Dt 5:22. 9:10. 10:4. 18:16. 23:1, *2, 2, 3, 3, 8. 31:30. Jsh 8:35. Jg 20:2. 21:5, 8. 1 S 17:47. 1 K 8:14, 22, 55, 65. 12:3. 1 Ch 13:2, 4. 28:8. 29:1, 10, 20, 20. 2 Ch 1:3, 5. 6:3, 12, 13. 7:8. 20:5, 14. 23:3. 24:6. 28:14. 29:23, 28, 31, 32. 30:2, 4, 13, 17, 23, 24, 24, 25, 25. 31:18. Ezr 2:64. 10:1, 8, 12, 14. Ne 5:13. 7:66. 8:2, 17. 13:1. Jb 30:28. Ps 22:22, 25. 26:5. 35:18. 40:9, 10. 89:5. 107:32. 149:1. Pr 5:14. 21:16. 26:26. Je 26:17. 31:8. 44:15. 50:9. La 1:10. Ezk 16:40. 17:17. 23:24, 46, 47. 26:7. 27:27, 34. 32:3, 22, 23. 38:4, 7, 13, 15. Jl 2:16. Mi 2:5. in the evening. Heb. between the two evenings. The Jews divided the day into morning and evening: till the sun passed the meridian, all was morning or forenoon; after that, all was evening or afternoon. Their first evening began just after twelve o'clock, and continued till sunset; their second evening began at sunset, and continued till night, i.e. during the whole time of twilight; between twelve o'clock, therefore, and the termination of twilight, the passover was to be offered. See Parallel Passages. ver. 18. Ex 16:12. Le *23:5. Nu 9:3. Dt 16:6. Pr 7:9mg. Mt *27:46-50. Mk 15:33. Jn 13:30.

7. blood. ver. *13, 22, 23. Le 17:11. Mt=20:28. Ro 5:9. Ep *1:7. He 9:13, 14, +*22. 10:14, 29. 11:28. *12:24. 1 P *1:2. 1 J 1:7. Re *13:8. strike. Ro 4:24, 25. 5:1.

8. eat the. Mt 26:26. Jn 6:52-57. 1 J=1:3. that night. ver. 12, 14, 17. Mt 26:17. Lk 17:34. roast. Ex ●29:31. Dt 16:7. Ps 22:14. Is 53:10. He 12:29. unleavened. Ex 13:3, 7. 34:25. Nu 9:11. Dt *16:3. 2 Ch 30:2, 5. Ps 32:2, 5. Am 4:5. Mt 16:12. Ac 24:16. 1 C *5:6-8. Ga 5:9. with bitter. Ex 1:14. Nu 9:11. La 3:15, 19, 20. Zc 12:10. Ep 2:11, 12. 1 Th 1:6. 1 T 1:12-15.

9. sodden. Nu 6:19. Dt 16:7. but roast with fire. ver. 8. Dt 16:7. La 1:13. head. Col=2:3. legs. Jn =8:29. purtenance. Ex 29:13. Le 1:13. Ps=40:8.

10. let nothing. Ex 23:18. 29:34. 34:25. Le *7:15-17. 22:30. Dt *16:4, 5. remain. Ex 16:19. Le 7:15.

11. loins girded. 1 K 18:46. 2 K 4:29. Mt 26:19, 20. Lk *12:35, 36. Ep 6:14. 1 P 1:13. *2:11. shoes. Jsh 9:5, 13. SS 7:1. Lk 7:38. 15:22. Ac 12:8. Ep 6:15. staff. Ge 32:10. 2 K 4:29. Mk 6:8. haste. Ge 19:15. Dt 20:3. 2 K 7:15. Ps 31:22. it is the. ver. 27. Le

23:5. Nu 28:16. Dt 16:2-6. 1 C 5:7. passover. 1 C 11:26.

12. pass through. ver. 23. Ex 11:4, 5. Am 5:17. *J*22C22. Anthropomorphism B889. Human actions are attributed to God: passing through. For other instances of this figure see ver. 23. Am 5:17. this night. ver. +8. will smite. See on ver. 29, 30. Ex 11:4-6. against. Nu *33:4. 1 S 5:3. 6:5. 1 Ch 14:12. Is *19:1. Je 43:13. Zp 2:11. gods. *or*, princes. Ex 15:11. 18:11. 21:6. 22:8, 9, *28mg. Nu *33:4. 2 Ch 2:5. Ps √82:1, +*6. 95:3. 96:4, 5. 97:9. 135:5. +*138:1. Je 43:12. 44:8. 46:25. Jn 10:+√34, 35. Re 12:8. execute. Ge 15:14. Ac 17:31. I am the Lord. Ex 6:2. Is 43:11-15. Ezk 12:16. 1 C +*8:6.

13. the blood. ver. 7, 23. He 11:28. token. Ge 9:13. +17:11. Jsh 2:+12, 21. and when. 1 Th 1:10. 1 J 1:7. I see the. Ge ●6:5. Ro 3:26. 8:33. blood. ver. 7. Mt 20:28. Mk 10:45. Col 1:14. He 9:11-14, +*22. 1 J *1:7. Re +*1:5. pass over. Le +*23:5. Jsh 4:7. Lk 21:36. 1 C 5:7. 1 Th 5:9. Re 3:10. shall not. Ex 8:22. 9:4, 6. 10:23. 11:6, 7. 14:28, 29. 15:19. Ps 78:53. Ro +*5:9. 1 Th +*5:9. Re +*3:10. to destroy you. Heb. for a destruction.

14. this day. ver. +8. memorial. Ex 13:9. Nu 16:40. Jsh 4:7. Ps 107:1, 2. 111:4. 126:2. 135:13. Zc 6:14. Mt 26:13. Lk *22:19. 1 C *11:23-26. a feast. Ex 5:1. Dt 16:11. Ne 8:9-12. by an ordinance. ver. 17, 24, 43. Ex 13:10. Le 23:4, 5. Nu 10:8. 18:8. Dt 16:1. 1 S 30:25. 2 K *23:21. Ezk 46:14. 1 C *5:7, 8. for ever. Heb. *olam*, ver. +24.

15. Seven. See on ver. 8. Ex 13:6, 7, etc. 23:15. 34:18, 25. Le 23:5-8. Nu 28:17. Dt 16:3, 5, 8. Mt 16:12. Lk 12:1. Ac 12:3. 1 P=4:2. unleavened. Le +*23:6. that soul. ver. 19, 20. Ex 31:14. Ge 17:14. Le 17:10, 14. Nu 9:13. Ml 2:12. Ga 5:12. soul. Heb. *nephesh*, Ge +17:14. cut off. 1 C 11:30-32.

16. first day. Le 23:2, 3, 7, 8. 8, 21, 24, 25, 27, 35. Nu 28:18, 25. 29:1, 12. no manner. Ex 16:5, 23, 29. 20:10. 35:2, 3. Je 17:21, 22. Ro=4:4, 5. man. Heb. *nephesh*, soul. Ge +27:31.

17. unleavened. Le +*23:6. in this selfsame. Ex 7:5. *13:3, 8. Nu 20:16. this day. ver. +8. an ordinance. See on ver. 14. for ever. Heb. *olam*, ver. +24.

18. In the first. See on ver. 1, 15. Le 23:5, 6. Nu 28:16.

19. Seven. Ex 23:15. 34:18. Dt 16:3. 1 C 5:7, 8. even that. See on ver. 15. Nu 9:13. soul. Heb. *nephesh*, Ge +17:14. √*J*171Q1, Ge +12:5. whether. ver. 43, 48. born in. ver. +48.

20. all your habitations. ✳S#4186h. Ex 10:23 (dwellings). 12:20, 40 (sojourning). 35:3. Ge 10:30 (dwelling). 27:39. 36:43. Le 3:17. 7:26. 13:46. 23:3, 14, 17, 21, 31. 25:29. Nu 15:2. 24:21. 35:29. 1 S 20:18 (seat), 25. 2 S 9:12. 1 K 10:5 (sitting). 2 K 2:19 (situation). 1 Ch 4:33. 6:54. 7:28. 2 Ch 9:4 (sitting). Jb 29:1 (seat). Ps *1:1. 107:4, 7, 32 (assembly), 36. 132:13. Ezk 6:6, 14. 8:3. 28:2. 34:13. 48:15 (dwelling). unleavened bread. ver. 15. Le 13:3, 4, 6, 7. 23:18. 23:17. Nu 9:11. *J*144D, Ge +40:23.

21. elders. Ex 3:16. 17:5. 19:7. Nu 11:16. Draw out. Jg 4:6. 5:14. 20:37. Jb 21:33. and take. ver. 3. Nu 9:2-5. Jsh *5:10. 2 K 23:21. 2 Ch 30:15-17. 35:5, 6. Ezr 6:20. Mt *26:17-19. Mk *14:12-16. Lk *22:7-13. 1 C 10:4. lamb. *or*, kid. ver. 3n. Ge 4:4. Le 22:21. the passover. That is, the *lamb* which was called the *paschal*, or *passover* lamb; the *animal* sacrificed obtain-

ing the name of the *institution*. Paul copies the expression in 1 C 5:7. Ezr *6:19. Ezk 45:21. Lk 22:15. ſ121P8. Metonymy of the Adjunct B596. Passover is put for the lamb slain at the passover. For other instances of this figure see 2 Ch 30:17. Mt 26:17. Mk 14:12, 14. Lk 22:8, 11, 15.

22. **a bunch**. Le 14:6, 7. Nu 19:18. Ps 51:7. He 9:1, 14, 19. *11:28. 12:24. 1 P 1:2. **hyssop**. 1 K 4:33. Lk=18:14. Jn 19:29. Ac 20:21. **dip**. Heb. *tabal*, ✳S#2881h, 2 K +5:14. Here it is to be observed, the quantity of blood was, probably, insufficient for an immersion of the hyssop; a partial dipping, a smearing, or moistening, was all that was required by the circumstances of the case; and here, also, the occurrence of *apo* with the genitive after the verb constitutes a form of speech unadapted to convey the idea of dipping (Hibbard, *Christian Baptism*, Part 2, p. 45). He 11:28. **strike**. ver. 7. **and none**. Jsh 2:18, 19. Is *26:20. Mt 26:30. Jn 15:6. He 6:6.

23. **will pass through**. ſ22C22, Ex +12:12. See on ver. 12, 13. **pass over**. Is 31:5. Mt 26:39. **and will not**. 2 S *24:16. Is 37:36. Ezk *9:4, 6. Ro 8:33. 1 C 10:10. 1 Th 1:10. He 11:28. 12:24. Re *7:3. *9:4.

24. **for an**. See on ver. 14. Ge 17:8-10. **for ever**. Ezk 45:17. 46:14. Ep ●2:15. Col ●2:14. He ●8:13. ✛S#5769h, *olam*. Rendered "forever" in the following passages: Ge 3:22. 13:15. Ex 3:15. 12:14, 17, 24. 14:13. 19:9. 21:6. 27:21. 28:43. 29:28. 30:21. 31:17. 32:13. Le 6:18, 22. 7:34, 36. 10:9, 15. 16:29, 31. 17:7. 23:14, 21, 31, 41. 24:3. 25:46. Nu 10:8. 15:15. 18:8, 11, 19, 19, 23. 19:10. Dt 5:29. 12:28. 13:16. 15:17. 23:3, 6. 28:46. 29:29. 32:40. Jsh 4:7. 8:28. 14:9. 1 S 1:22. 2:30. 3:13, 14. 13:13. 20:15, 23, 42. 27:12. 2 S 3:28. 7:13, 16, 16, 24, 25, 26, 29, 29. 1 K 1:31. 2:33, 33, 45. 9:3, 5. 10:9. 2 K 5:27. 21:7. 1 Ch 15:2. 16:34, 41. 17:12, 14, 22, 23, 24, 27, 27. 22:10. 23:13, 13, 25. 28:4, 7, 8. 29:18. 2 Ch 2:4. 5:13. 7:3, 6, 16. 9:8. 13:5. 20:7, 21. 30:8. 33:4, 7. Ezr 3:11. 9:12, 12. Ne 2:3. 13:1. Jb 41:4. Ps 9:7. 12:7. 28:9. 29:10. 30:12. 33:11. 37:18, 28. 41:12. 44:8. 45:2. 48:8. 49:8, 11. 52:9. 61:7. 66:7. 72:17, 19. 73:26. 75:9. 78:69. 79:13. 81:15. 85:5. 89:1, 2, 4, 36, 37. 102:12. 103:9. 104:31. 105:8. 106:1. 107:1. 110:4. 111:9. 112:6. 117:2. 118:1, 2, 3, 4, 29. 119:89, 111, 152, 160. 125:1, 2. 131:3. 135:13. 136:1-26. 138:8. 146:6, 10. Pr 27:24. Ec 1:4. 2:16. 3:14. 9:6. Is 9:7. 32:14, 17. 34:10, 17. 40:8. 47:7. 51:6, 8. 57:16. 59:21. 60:21. Je 3:5, 12. 17:4, 25. 31:40. 33:11. 35:6. 49:33. 51:26, 62. La 3:31. 5:19. Ezk 37:25, 25. 43:7, 9. Da 2:4, 44. 3:9. 4:34. 5:10. 6:6, 21, 26. 7:18. 12:7. Ho 2:19. Jl 3:20. Ob 10. Jon 2:6. Mi 2:9. 4:7. Zc 1:5. Ml 1:4. For passages where this term is rendered "everlasting," see Ge +17:7. For "perpetual," see Ge +9:12. For "for evermore," see Ps +18:50. For "of old" and "ever of old," see Ge +6:4. For "old" or "ancient," see Jb +22:15. For "of" or "in old time," see Jsh +24:2. For "alway" or "always," see Ge +6:3. For "ever," see Ps +5:11. For miscellaneous renderings see Le +25:32. For passages where *olam* is doubled, rendered "for ever and ever," see Da +2:20; rendered "from everlasting to everlasting," see Ps +41:13. For the use of *olam* in the plural see Ps +61:4. For its use in conjunction with *ad*, see Ex +15:18. For the Hebrew word *ad*, see Nu +24:20. See also for *nezach*, 2 S +2:26; *kedem*, Mi +5:2; *zmithuth*, Le 25:23; *tamid*, Le +6:13; *dor*, Ps 77:8; *yom*, Ge +43:9. Ps 23:6. For

an explanation of the limited sense contrasted with the infinite sense of *olam*, see Jn +*6:54n.

25. **when**. Dt 4:5. 12:8, 9. 16:5-9. Jsh 5:10-12. Ps 105:44, 45. **according**. Ex *3:8, 17.

26. **when**. Dt 6:20. **your children**. Ex 13:8, 9, 14, 15, 48. Dt 6:7. 11:19. 32:7. Jsh 4:6, 7, 21-24. Ps 78:3-6. 145:4. Is 38:19. Ep 6:4.

27. **It is the sacrifice**. See on ver. 11, 23. Ex 34:25. Dt 16:2, 5. 1 C 5:7. 11:26. **bowed**. Ex *4:31. 34:8. 1 Ch 29:20. 2 Ch 20:18. 29:30. Ne 8:6.

28. **and did**. ver. 50. Ex 40:16. Ge +6:22. 7:5. He 11:28.

29. **at midnight**. See on ver. 12. Ex 11:4. 13:15. Jb *34:19, 20. 1 Th *5:2, 3. **the Lord smote**. Ge 15:14. Nu 3:13. 8:17. 33:4. 2 Ch 32:21. Ps 78:51. 105:36. 135:8. 136:10. Zc=12:10. Lk 12:20. Ro 6:23. He 11:28. 12:23. **the firstborn of Pharaoh**. Ex 4:23. 11:5. **dungeon**. Heb. *bor*, Ge +37:20. house of the pit. Ge 40:15. Is 24:22. 51:14. Je 38:6, 13. Zc 9:11. **of cattle**. Ex 11:5. Nu 3:13. Ps 135:8.

30. **and there was a great cry**. See on Ex 11:6. Pr *21:13. Am 5:17. Zc=12:10. Mt 25:6. Ja *2:13.

31. **called**. Ex 10:29. **Rise up**. Ex 3:19, '20. 6:1. *11:1, 8. Ps *105:38. **the children**. See on Ex *10:9, 11.

32. **your flocks**. See on Ex 10:26. **bless me**. Ex 8:28. 9:28. Ge 27:34, 38.

33. **urgent**. Ex 10:7. 11:1, 8. Ps 105:38. **We be all**. Ge 20:3. Nu 17:12, 13.

34. **before**. Ge 19:3. Ac 12:3. **kneading troughs**. or, dough. Ex 8:3.

35. **did**. ver. 28. **borrowed**. Ex 3:21, +*22. *11:2, 3. Ge 15:14. Ps *105:37.

36. **the Lord**. Ex 3:21. 11:3. Ge 39:21. Pr *16:7. Da 1:9. Ac 2:47. 7:10. **lent**. 1 S 1:28. **they spoiled**. Ex 3:22. Ge *15:14. 31:9, 16. 1 S 30:22. Ps 105:37. 119:43. Is 14:2. Ezk 39:10.

37. **the children**. Nu *33:3, 5. **Rameses**. Ex 1:11. Ge *47:11. **six hundred thousand**. Ex 38:26. Ge 12:2. 15:5. 46:3. Nu 1:46. 2:32. 11:21. 26:51.

38. **mixed**. Ge 12:4. Ne 13:3. Is 51:2. Mt 10:37. **multitude**. Ge 17:6. 22:17. 26:4. 28:3, 14. 32:12. 35:11. *46:3 w 47:27. Heb. a great mixture. Nu *11:4. Zc 8:23. Lk 14:25-27. **very much**. Ex 17:3. Nu 20:19. 32:1. Dt 3:19.

39. **thrust**. ver. 33. Ex 3:20. 6:1. 11:1.

40. The Samaritan Pentateuch reads, "Now the sojourning of the children of Israel, *and of their fathers in the land of Canaan and* in the land of Egypt, was 430 years." The Alexandrine copy of the LXX. has the same reading; and the same statement is made by the apostle Paul in Ga 3:17, who reckons from the promise made to Abraham to the giving of the law. That these three witnesses have the truth, the chronology itself proves; for it is evident that the descendants of Israel did not dwell 430 years in *Egypt*; while it is equally evident, that the period from Abraham's entry into Canaan to the Exodus, is exactly that number. Thus, from Abraham's entrance into the promised land to the birth of Isaac, was 25 years; Isaac was 60 at the birth of Jacob; Jacob was 130 at his going into Egypt; where he and his children continued 215 years more; making in the whole 430 years. Ge 15:13n. 17:7n. 21:12n. **sojourning**. Ac 13:17. He 11:9. **Israel**. ſ171R. Synecdoche of the Part B648. An integral part of men (collectively) is put for the whole, or others associated

with them. Here, in *Israel* is comprehended his father Isaac and his grandfather Abraham. For other instances of this figure see Ex 17:8, 13. Dt 33:7. Jsh 10:28, 40. 1 S 18:7. 1 K 8:66. 10:11. 11:32. 2 K 17:18. Jb 32:4. Ps 78:9n. 80:1, 2. Is 7:2, 5, 8, 9. Je 6:1. Am 5:15. 6:6. **who.** ♪81, Ge +15:13. **four hundred and thirty.** Ge 12:1-3. *15:13. Ac 7:6. Ga *3:16, 17.

41. **four hundred and.** ver. 40. Ge 15:16. **selfsame.** ver. 51. Ps 102:13. Da 9:24. Hab *2:3. Jn 7:8. Ac 1:7. **hosts.** ver. 51. Ex 7:4. Jsh 5:14. 1 S 17:26.

42. **a night to be much observed.** Heb. a night of observations. **observed.** ver. 14. Dt *16:1-6. **in their.** Ex 13:10. Le 3:17. Nu 9:3.

43. **passover.** Le +23:5. Jsh 5:10. Mk 14:1. 1 C 5:7. **There shall.** ver. 48. Ge 17:12, 27. Le 22:10, 25. Nu 9:14. Ac 2:46. 5:13. 2 C 6:14. Ep 2:12, 19. **stranger.** Heb. foreigner. Dt +*17:15. ✢S#5236h. Ge 17:12, 27. 35:2, 4. Ex 12:43. Le 22:25. Dt 31:16. 32:12. Jsh 24:20, 23. Jg 10:16mg. 1 S 7:3. 2 S 22:45, 46. 2 Ch 14:3. 33:15. Ne 9:2. 13:30. Ps 18:44, 45. 81:9. 137:4. 144:7, 11. Is 56:3, 6. 60:10. 61:5. 62:8. Je 5:19. 8:19. Ezk 44:7, 9. Da 11:39. Ml 2:11. For S#1616h, see Ge ◑+*23:4. ver. ◑+48. For ✢S#8453h, see Ge +23:4.

44. **bought.** Ge 17:27. Le 22:11. Ep 2:13. **circumcised.** Ge *17:12, 13, 23. Ep 2:19. Col 2:11.

45. **A foreigner.** Ge 23:4. Le *22:10. 25:6. Ps 39:12. Ep *2:12. **hired.** Lk 15:19, 29. Ro 4:4, 5.

46. **one house.** 1 C 12:12, 13. Ep *2:19-22. 4:4. **neither.** Nu *9:12. Ps 34:20. ◑51:8. Jn *19:33, ♪36.

47. **All the.** ver. 3, 6. Nu *9:13. Mt=26:27. **keep it.** Heb. do it. ver. 48. Ex 29:36, 38, 39, 41. Is *53:6. Mt 7:21. Lk 11:28.

48. **a stranger.** Heb. sojourner. ver. ◑+43. Ge +23:4 (✸S#1616h). Nu *9:14. 15:15, 16. Dt ◑+17:15. +26:11. Jsh +20:9. Is *56:6, 7. **let all.** Ex 17:12. Ezk 44:9. 47:22. **circumcised.** Ph 3:3. **near.** He 10:22. **shall be.** Ga *3:28. Col 3:11. **born in.** ver. 19. Le 16:29. 23:42. 24:22. Ps 37:4. Jn=3:3.

49. **One law.** Le 24:22. Nu *9:14. 15:15. 16, 29. Ga *3:28. Ep *4:4-6. Col *3:11.

50. **as the Lord.** Dt 4:1, 2. 12:32. Mt 7:24, 25. 28:20. Jn 2:5. 13:17. 15:14. Re 22:14. **so did they.** ver. 28, 35. Ex 7:6. 39:32. Nu 9:5. Dt *12:32.

51. **selfsame.** ver. +41. **by their armies.** ver. 41. Ex 6:26. 7:4. 13:18.

EXODUS 13

The firstborn of man, and firstlings of cattle, are sanctified to God, 1, 2. The feast of unleavened bread is appointed to be kept annually as a memorial of Israel's deliverance from Egypt, 3-10. Their children must be instructed in the meaning of these observances, 11-16. The Lord guides forth the people, 17, 18; who take with them the bones of Joseph, 19; and, under the guidance of a pillar of cloud and of fire, arrive at Etham, 20-22.

2. **Sanctify.** ♪121I2, Ge +2:17. The word *kadash* (S#6942h) is to *consecrate, separate,* and *set apart* a person or thing from all common or secular purposes to some religious use; and exactly answers to the Greek *hagiazo* (S#37g), from *a*, privative, and *ge*, the earth; because everything offered or consecrated to God was separated from all earthly uses. ver. 12-15. Ex 4:22.

*22:29, 30. 23:19. 34:19, 20. Le *27:26. Nu *3:13. 8:16, 17. 18:15. Dt *15:19. Lk ♪2:23. 1 C *15:20. Col *1:15. He *12:23. **openeth.** ver. 12. Mt 1:25. Lk 2:21. **womb.** Nu 3:12. 12:12. Jb 10:18. Ho 9:14.

3. **Remember.** Ex *12:42. 20:8. 23:15. Dt 5:15. 15:15. *16:3, 12. 24:18, 22. 1 Ch 16:12. Ps 105:5. Lk 22:19. 1 C 11:24. **out of the.** ver. 14. Ex 20:2. Dt 5:6. 6:12. 8:14. 13:5, 10. Jsh 24:17. Jg 6:8. **house of bondage.** Heb. servants. Dt 7:8. **strength.** Ex 6:1. Dt 4:34. 11:2, 3. Ne 9:10. Ep 1:19. **there.** See on Ex 12:8, 15. Mt 10:12. 1 C 5:8.

4. **Abib.** i.e. *green ear of corn,* ✸S#24h. Ex 9:31 (in the ear). 23:15. 34:18. Le 2:14 (green ears of corn). Dt *16:1-3. Ezk 3:15.

5. **shall bring.** Ex *3:8, 17. 23:23. 33:2. 34:11. Ge 15:18-21. Dt 7:1. 12:29. 19:1. 20:17. 26:1. Jsh 3:10. 12:8. 24:11. Jg 3:5. **Canaanites.** Ge +10:18. **Hittites.** Ge +15:20. **Amorites.** Ge 10:16. **Hivites.** Ge +10:17. **Jebusites.** Ge +10:16. **which he sware.** Ex *6:8. 33:1. Ge 17:7, 8. 22:16-18. 26:3. 50:24. Nu 14:16, 30. 32:11. **a land.** See on Ex 3:17. **flowing.** Ex +3:8. **milk and.** ♪174, Ge +18:27. **honey.** ♪171I7, Ex +3:8. **thou shalt keep.** See on Ex *12:25, 26.

6. **Seven days.** See on Ex *12:15-20. 34:18. Le 23:8.

7. **no leavened bread.** Ex 12:19. Mt 16:6, 12. 1 C *5:7. *11:28.

8. **show thy son.** See on ver. 14. Ex *12:26, 27. Ge +*18:19. Dt 4:9, 10. +*6:7, 20. 11:19. Jsh 8:35. √24:15. 1 K 2:1-3. 1 Ch 22:11-13. +*28:9. Ps 34:11. 44:1. √78:3-8. Pr +*19:18. +*22:6, 15. 23:13, 14. 29:15, 17. Is *38:19. Ml +*4:6. Ep +*6:4. Col 3:21. 2 T 1:5. +√3:15. He 12:7-10.

9. **a sign.** ver. 16. Ex 12:14. Nu 15:39. Dt 6:6, 8. *11:18, 19. Pr 1:9. 3:21. *6:20-23. 7:23. SS 8:6. Is 49:16. Je 22:24. Mt 23:5. **may be.** Dt *30:14. Jsh √1:8. Is 59:21. Ro 10:8. **strong hand.** ver. 3. Ex 6. Jsh 1:9. Ne 1:10. Ps 89:13. Is 27:1. 40:10. 51:9. Jl 2:11. 1 C 11:26. Re 18:8.

10. **keep.** Ex 12:14, 24. 23:15. Le 23:6. Dt 16:3, 4. **year to.** Jg 11:40. 21:19. 1 S 1:3. 2:19. **year.** Heb. days. ♪171T2C, Ge +24:55. ♪144A10, Ge +29:14.

11. **Canaanites.** Ge +10:18. **as he sware.** See on ver. 5.

12. **thou shalt.** ver. 2. Ex 22:29. 34:19. Le 27:26. Nu *8:17. 18:15. Dt *15:19. Ezk *44:30. **set apart.** Heb. cause to pass over. **openeth.** ver. +2. Ex 34:19. Nu 3:12. 18:15.

13. **every firstling of.** Ex 34:20. Nu 18:15-17. **an ass.** ♪171I2. Synecdoche of the Species B626. The *ass* is put for all kinds of animals not sacrificed. For another instance of this figure see Ex 34:20. **lamb.** *or,* kid. Ex 12:3n, 21. **shalt thou.** Nu *3:46-51. *18:15, 16. Re *5:9, 12. 14:4.

14. **thy son.** ver. +8. Ex 12:26. Dt *6:20-25. Jsh 4:6, 21-24. Ps 145:4. **in time to come.** Heb. tomorrow. ♪24E, Ge +30:33. Ex 12:26. Ge +*30:33mg. Dt +6:20mg. Jsh +4:6mg. +22:24mg. **By strength.** ver. 3.

15. **the Lord slew.** See on Ex *12:29. **therefore I.** See on ver. 12. **all that.** ♪63G, Ge +50:23. Supply by Ellipsis, "I sacrifice to the Lord all (*beasts*), etc.

16. **a token upon.** ver. 9. Ex +*12:13. Pr 3:3. 6:21. 7:3. SS 8:6. Is 49:18. Je 22:24. Hg 2:23. **frontlets.** Dt 6:7-9. 11:18. Mt 23:5. **for by.** ver. 9, 14. Dt 26:8. Ps *46:1. Is *49:24, 25.

17. **God led**. Ps *107:7. Pr *16:9. Je *10:23. **the people repent**. Ex *14:11, 12. Nu *14:1-4. Dt 20:8. Jg 7:3. 1 K 8:47. Lk 14:27-32. Ac 15:38. 1 C *10:13. **return**. Ex 16:2, 3. Dt 17:16. Ne 9:17. Ac 7:39.

18. **led the**. Ex 14:2. Nu *33:6-8. Dt *32:10. Ps 107:7. **harnessed**. *or*, by five in a rank. Ex 12:51. Jsh 1:14. 4:12. Jg 7:11.

19. **for he had**. Ge *50:24, 25. Jsh *24:32. Ac *7:16. **God**. Ex 4:31. Ge 48:21. Lk 1:68. 7:16. **surely**. ✓147B, Ge +26:28.

20. **they took**. Ex 12:37. Nu 33:5, 6. **Etham**. i.e. *desolate; limit of habitation*, ❋S#864h. Nu 33:6, 7, 8.

21. **the Lord went**. Ex *14:19-24. 40:34-38. Nu *9:15-23. 10:34. 14:14. Dt 1:33. Ne *9:12, 19. Ps *78:14. *99:7. 105:39. Is *4:5, 6. Ac *7:38. 1 C *10:1, 2. **before**. Dt 31:3, *8. 32:10. Jn 10:3. **in a**. ✓22D3J5. Anthropopatheia or Anthropomorphism B893. God is spoken of as being in circumstances which have to do with place and time as men are. Here, in the Shekinah. For other instances of this figure see Ex 16:10. Le 16:2. Nu 9:15. Is 6:4. Mt 17:5. **cloud**. Ex 14:19. 16:10. 33:9. 40:36. Nu 9:17. 10:11. 12:5. 16:42. Dt 1:33. 31:15. 2 Ch +*5:13. Ne 9:12. Ps 78:14. 105:39. Is 4:5. Zc +*2:5. Mt +*24:30. +*25:31. **light**. Ps *119:105.

22. **He took**. Ne *9:19. Ps *121:4-8. **pillar of fire**. Ex 40:38. Re 10:1.

EXODUS 14

The way taken by Israel proves the occasion of hardening Pharaoh's heart, 1-4. He pursues them, 5-9. Being affrighted, they murmur; but are encouraged by Moses, 10-14. God instructs Moses, 15-18. The cloud removes behind the camp; the Red Sea is divided; the Israelites pass through it; but the Egyptians following them are drowned, 19-30. The Israelites are suitably affected, 31.

1. **the Lord spake**. Ex 12:1. 13:1.

2. **that they**. ver. 9. Ex 13:17, 18. Nu 33:7, 8. **Pihahiroth**. i.e. *mouth of caves*, ❋S#6367h. Nu 33:7. Pihachiroth, *the mouth of Chiroth*, as it is rendered by the LXX. *Chiroth* denotes the valley which extends from the wilderness of Etham to the Red Sea. **Migdol**. i.e. *a tower*. Ge 11:4. Jsh 15:37. Jg 8:17. Is 5:2. Je 44:1. 46:14. Ezk 29:10. 30:6. ❋S#4024h: Nu 33:7. Je 44:1. 46:14. **Baal-zephon**. i.e. *lord of the unknown*, ❋S#1189h. ver. 9. Nu 33:7. This may have been the name of a town or city in which Baal was worshipped; and probably called *zephon*, from being situated on the *north* point of the Red Sea, near the present Suez. Nu 33:7.

3. **Pharaoh**. Ex 7:3, 4. Dt 31:21. Ps 139:2, 4. Ezk 38:10, 11, 17. Ac 4:28. **They are entangled**. Jg 16:2. 1 S 23:7, 23. Ps 3:2. *71:11. Je 20:10, 11.

4. **harden**. ver. 8, 17. Ex +4:21, etc. 7:3, 13, +14. Ro 11:8. **I will be**. ver. 18. Ex *9:16. 15:10, 11, 14-16. 18:11. Ne 9:10. Is 2:11, 12. Ezk 20:9. 28:22. 39:13. Da 4:30-37. Ro *9:17, 22, 23. Re 19:1-6. **host**. ✓121N2, Ge +34:29. **that the Egyptians**. See on Ex 7:5, 17. Jsh 10:14.

5. **and the heart**. Ex 12:33. Ps *105:25. **Why have we**. Je 34:10-17. Lk 11:24-26. 2 P 2:20-22.

6. **people**. ver. 23. Nu 21:23. Dt 2:32. 3:1.

7. **six hundred chosen**. ver. 23. Ex *15:4. Jsh 17:16-

18. Jg 4:3, 15. Ps *20:7. 68:17. Is 37:24. **captains**. Ex 15:4.

8. **the Lord**. See on ver. 4. **with an high hand**. Ex 6:1. 13:9, 16, 18. Nu 33:3. Dt *26:8. 32:27. Jb ◖38:15. Ps 89:13. Is 26:11. Ac 13:17.

9. **the Egyptians**. Ex 15:9. Jsh 24:6. **encamping**. See on ver. 2.

10. **sore afraid**. Ex 14:30. 15:1. Ps *53:5. Is 7:2. *8:12, 13. *51:12, 13. Mt *8:26. 14:30, 31. 1 J 4:18. **cried out**. Jsh 24:7. 2 Ch *18:31. Ne *9:9. Ps *34:17. 106:44. *107:6, 13, 19, 28. Is *26:16. Je 22:23. Mt 8:25.

11. **Because**. Ex 15:23, 24. 16:2, 3. 17:2, 3. Nu 11:1. 14:1-4. 16:41. Ps *106:7, 8. **graves**. Heb. *qeber*, Ge +23:4. **wherefore**. Ex 5:22. Ge 43:6. Nu 11:15.

12. **Is not this**. Ex *5:21. *6:9. **Let us alone**. Ho 4:17. Mk 1:24. 5:7, 17, 18. **For it had**. Jon 4:3, 8.

13. **Fear ye not**. Nu 14:9. Dt 20:3. 2 K *6:16. 2 Ch *20:15, 17. Ps *27:1, 2. *46:1-3. Is 26:3. 30:15. 35:4. *41:10-14. Mt 28:5. **stand still**. Nu 9:8. 1 S *9:27. 12:7. 2 Ch 20:17. Jb 37:14. Ps 46:10. Is *30:7, 15, 18. Mt 8:25, 26. **see the**. ver. 30. Ex 15. Ge 49:18. 1 S 12:16. 1 Ch 11:14. Ps 3:8. Is 43:11. Je *3:23. La *3:26. Ho 13:4, 9. Hab 3:8, 13. **for the Egyptians whom ye have seen today**. *or*, for whereas ye have seen the Egyptians today, etc. **ye shall see**. ver. 30. Ex 15:4, 5, 10, 19, 21. Ne 9:9. **for ever**. Heb. *olam*, Ex +12:24.

14. **The Lord**. ver. 25. Ex 15:3. Dt 1:30. 3:22. 20:4. Jsh 10:10, 14, 42. 23:3, 10. Jg 5:20. 2 Ch *20:17, 29. Ne 4:20. Ps *46:10. Is *7:4. 31:4, 5. **hold**. Ge 34:5. Ps 50:3. 83:1. Is *30:15.

15. **Wherefore**. Ex 17:4. Jsh 7:10. Ezr 10:4, 5. Ne 9:9. Is *65:24. Ro *8:26.

16. **lift**. ver. 21, 26. Ex 4:2, 17, 20. 7:9, 19. **stretch out**. Ex 10:12, 21. **and the**. See on ver. 21, 22.

17. **I, behold**. Ge 6:17. 9:9. Le 26:28. Dt 32:39. Is 48:15. 51:12. Je 23:39. Ezk 5:8. 6:3. 34:11, 20. Ho 5:14. **I will**. See on ver. 8. Ex 4:23. 7:3, 13, 14. **and I will**. ver. 18. See on ver. 4. **chariots**. ✓96, Ge +3:8.

18. **shall know**. ver. 4. Ex 7:5, 17.

19. **the angel**. ver. 24. Ex 13:21. *23:20, 21. 32:34. Nu *20:16. Is *63:9. Ac 7:38. **and the pillar**. See on Ex 13:21, 22.

20. **it was a**. Jsh 5:13, 14. 1 S 5:11. 1 Ch 21:16. Ho 14:9. Mt 21:44. 1 P 2:6, 7. **cloud and darkness**. Ps 18:11. Pr 4:18, 19. Is 8:14. 2 C 2:15, 16. *4:3. Col *1:12. Ju *13.

21. **stretched**. ver. 16, 26, 27. Ex 7:19. 8:5, 6, 16. 9:22. 10:12, 21. 2 K 5:11. Mt=8:27. **the Lord caused**. Ex 15:8. Jsh 3:13-16. 4:23. Ne *9:11. Jb 26:12. Ps *66:6. *74:13. 78:13. *106:7-10. 114:3-5. 136:13. Is 14:27. 23:11. 51:10, 15. 63:12. Je 31:35. Ac 7:36. **go back**. *or*, part. Jb 12:17, 19. Ps 125:5. Ezk 32:14. **east wind**. T#1782. Ex 15:8. Ge 8:1. +✓41:6. 2 S 22:16. 1 K 19:11. Jb 4:9mg. 38:1. 40:6. Ps 18:10, 11. *104:3. Je 23:19. 25:32. Ezk 1:4. Na 1:3. **dry land**. Ge 7:22. Jsh 3:17. 4:18. 2 K 2:8. Hg 2:6. **divided**. ver. 22, 27, 28. Jsh *3:15, 16. 4:23. Ne 9:11. Ps 74:13. 77:16. 78:13. 106:9. 114:3, 5. 136:13. Is 63:12. Hab 3:8.

22. **the children**. ver. 29. Ex 15:19. Nu 33:8. Ps 66:6. 78:13. Is 63:13. 1 C *10:1. He 11:29. **and the waters**. This verse demonstrates that this event was wholly miraculous, and cannot be ascribed, as some have supposed, to an extraordinary *ebb*, which *happened* just then to be produced by a strong east wind:

for this would not have caused the waters, contrary to every law of fluids, to stand as *a wall on the right hand and the left.* **a wall.** ver. 29. Ex 15:8. Jsh 3:13. Ps 78:13. Hab *3:8-10. Zc 2:5.

23. **Egyptians pursued.** ver. 17. Ex 15:9, 19. 1 K 22:20. Ec 9:3. Is 14:24-27.

24. **that in the.** 1 S 11:11. **looked unto.** Jb 40:12. Ps 18:13, 14. 77:16-19. 104:32. **through.** ver. 19, 20. **and troubled.** ver. 25. Jb 22:13. 23:15, 16. 34:20, 29. Ps 48:5. **host.** Ge 32:8. 33:8. 50:9.

25. **took off.** Jg 4:15. Ps 46:9. 76:6. Je 51:21. **that they drave them heavily.** *or,* and made them go heavily. **Let us flee.** Jb 11:20. 20:24. 27:22. Ps 68:12. Am 1:14. 5:19. 9:1. **for the Lord.** See on ver. 14. Dt 3:22. 1 S 4:7, 8.

26. **Stretch out.** ver. 16. Ex 7:19. 8:5. Mt 8:27. **the waters.** Ex *1:22. Jg 1:6, 7. Ps *77:16-19. Mt 7:2. Ja 2:13. Re 16:6.

27. **and the sea.** ver. 21, 22. Ex 15:1-21. Jsh 4:18. **Lord.** Dt *11:4. Jg 5:20, 21. Ps 78:53. **overthrew.** Heb. shook off. Dt 11:4. Ne 5:13. 9:11. Ps *136:15. He *11:29.

28. **the waters.** Ex 15:10. Dt 11:4. Ne 9:11. Ps 78:53. Hab *3:8-10, 13. He *11:29. **remained.** ver. 13. Jg 3:29. 2 Ch 20:24. Ps *106:9-11. 136:15. Am *4:6-12.

29. **walked.** ver. 22. Jb 38:8-11. Ps 66:6, 7. 77:19, 20. 78:52, 53. Is 43:2. 51:10, 13. 63:12, 13. **a wall.** ver. +22n. Jsh 3:16.

30. **the Lord.** ver. 13. 1 S 14:23. 2 Ch 32:22. Ps 44:6, 7. *106:8, 10. Pr 11:8. 21:18. Is 43:3. 63:9. Ho 1:7. Ju 5. **saved.** Ex 14:10. 15:1. Re 5:9. 14:3. **saw.** Ps 58:10. 59:10. 91:8. 92:9-11. Is 66:10.

31. **work.** Heb. hand. Jb 27:11. Ps 78:42. **feared.** 1 S 12:18. Ps 119:120. **believed.** Ex 4:31. 19:9. Ge √15:6. Nu *14:11. 2 Ch +*20:20. Ps 95:8. *106:12, 13. Lk +√8:13. Jn 2:11, 23-25. *8:30-32. 11:45. Ac *8:13, ●18-24. 1 C +*15:2. He 2:1. *3:7-12, +√14, 15, 18, 19. 4:1, 2, 6. 10:35-39.

EXODUS 15

The song of Moses, Miriam, and Israel on their deliverance, 1-21. In the wilderness they want water, 22; the waters of Marah are bitter, they murmur, Moses prays, and the waters are made sweet by means which God appointed, who also gives them his charge and promise, 23-26. They encamp at Elim, 27.

1. **Then.** Ex ●2:23, 24. 14:10, 30. Jg 5:1, etc. 2 S 22:1, etc. Ps 106:12. 107:8, 15, 21, 22. Is 12:1, etc. 51:10, 11. Re 1:5. 5:9. 14:3. =15:3. **hath triumphed.** ver. 21. Ex 14:17, 18, 27. 18:11. Col 2:15. **horse.** √96, Ge +3:8.

2. **The Lord.** Heb. *Jah.* Ex 17:16. Ps 68:√4, 18. 77:11. 89:8. 94:7, 12. 102:18. 104:35. 105:45. 106:1, 48. 111:1. 112:1. 113:1, 9. 115:17, 18, 18. 116:19. 117:2. 118:5, 5, 14, 17, 18, 19. 122:4. 130:3. 135:1, 3, 4, 21. 146:1, 10. 147:1, 20. 148:1, 14. 149:1, 9. 150:1, 6; 6. SS 8:6. Is 12:2. 26:4. 38:11, 11. Re 19:1, 3, 4, 6. Note that "Jah" is explicitly declared to be a *name* of God at Ps 68:4, thus demonstrating that God has more than one name. See on Ex +6:3n. **strength.** Ps 8:3. 18:1, 2. 27:1. 28:7, 8. 29:1. 59:17. *62:6, 7. 68:35. 99:4. 118:14. Hab 3:17-19. Ph 4:13. **song.** 121R7, Ge +43:11. Dt 10:21. Ps 22:3. *59:17. 109:1. 140:7. Is *25:1. Re *15:3. **my salvation.** Ex 14:13. 2 S 22:51. Ps 68:20. Is *12:2. *45:17. 49:6. Je 3:23. Lk 1:77. 2:30.

Jn 4:22. Ac √4:12. Re 19:1. **my.** Ex 4:22. Ge 17:7. Ps 22:10. Je 31:33. 32:28. Zc 13:9. **God.** Heb. *El.* ver. ●+11n. Ge 14:18, 19, 20, 22. 16:13. 21:33. 31:13. 35:1, 11. 49:25. Ex 6:3. 15:2. 20:5. 34:6. Nu 12:13. +*16:22. Dt *3:24. 4:24, *31. 7:9, 21. 10:17. *32:4. Jsh 3:10. 22:22. 24:19. 1 S 2:3. 2 S 22:31, 32, 33, 48. 23:5. Jb 9:2. 13:3. Ps *5:4. 7:11. 16:1. 17:6. 18:2, 30, 32, 47. *19:1. *22:1. 29:3. 31:5. 42:2, +8. 52:1. 68:35. 73:11, 17. 78:7, 8, 18, 19, 34, 35, 41. 85:8. *86:15. 89:7, 26. *90:2. 94:1. 106:14, 21. 107:11. 118:27, 28. 136:26. 139:17, *23. 149:6. 150:1. Is 5:16. 8:10. 9:6. 12:2. 14:13. 31:3. 43:10. 45:20, 21, 22. Je +32:18. 51:56. La 3:41. Jon 4:2. Mi 7:18. Ml 1:9. 2:10, 11. Note the frequency with which the divine attributes are associated and specified with this name. **an habitation.** Ex 40:34. Ge 28:21, 22. 2 S 7:5. 1 K *8:13, 27. Ps *132:4, 5. Is *57:15. 66:1. Jn *14:23. 2 C 5:19. Ep *2:22. Col 2:9. **my father's.** See on Ex *3:15, 16. **God.** Heb. *Elohim.* Ge 1:1. 6:13, *18. 17:3, +*7, 8. 19:29. 30:22. 50:24. Ex 2:24. Nu 23:19. 2 S 23:1, 3. 2 Ch √18:31. Is 45:22, 23. Note that the divine name *Elohim* frequently speaks of God as creator or in covenant relations ratified by an oath. **exalt him.** 2 S 22:47. Ps 18:46. 30:1. 34:3. 99:5, 9. 118:28. 145:1. Is *25:1. Jn 5:23. Ph 2:11. Re 5:9-14. *19:1, 2.

3. **man of war.** Jsh 17:1. 2 S 17:8. Ps *24:8. 45:3. Re *19:11-21. ♪22D2C. Anthropopathia or Anthropomorphism B891. Circumstances are attributed to God; here, God is spoken of as a warrior. For other instances of this figure see Ps 45:3-5. 46:8, 9. 76:3. **name.** See on Ex 3:13, 15. 6:3, 6. Ps *83:18. Is 42:8.

4. **chariots.** Ex 14:13-28. **chosen.** Ex 14:7. Ge +23:6. **captains.** Ex 14:7.

5. **depths.** Ex 14:28. Ezk 27:34. Jon 2:2. Mi 7:19. Mt 18:6. **have covered.** lit. will cover. ♪96C8. Heterosis of Tenses B522: the future for the past. The future is used for the past when it is understood that the thing or matter was future at the time of writing or speaking. For other instances of this figure see Jg 2:1. 5:8. 21:25. 2 S 3:33. 12:3. Is *63:3. **they.** Ne 9:11. Je 51:63, 64. Re *18:21.

6. **right hand.** ver. 11. 1 Ch 29:11, 12. Ps 17:7. 44:3. 60:5. 74:11. 77:10. 89:8-13. 98:1. *118:15, 16. Is 51:9. 52:10. Mt 6:13. ♪22A15A. Anthropomorphism B880. A *right hand* is attributed to God to denote the highest power, and most divine authority. For other instances of this figure see ver. 12. Ps 77:10. 118:15, 16. 139:10. Is 48:13. **dashed.** Jg 10:8h. Ps 2:9. Is 30:14. Je 13:14. Re 2:27.

7. **the greatness.** Ex 9:16. Dt *33:26. Ps 68:33. 148:13. Is 5:16. Je 10:6. **overthrown.** Jg 6:28. 1 K 19:10. 1 Ch 20:1. Ps 28:5. Is 14:17. **them that.** Is 37:17, 23, 29, 36, 38. Mi 4:11. Na 1:9-12. Zc 2:8. 14:3, 8. Ac 9:4. **rose up.** Ex 32:25. Dt 33:11. Ps 18:40. **sentest forth.** Ex 14:24. Nu 16:35. Is 5:24. 9:18. 10:17. Ezk 7:3. **thy wrath.** ♪22B. Anthropomorphism B882. Anger, vengeance, and hatred are attributed to God. For other instances of this figure see Ps 5:5. Is 1:14, 24. Je 9:9. Na *1:2. **consumed.** Ps 59:13. 83:13. Is 5:24. *47:14. Na 1:10. Ml *4:1. Mt *3:12. ♪22C35. Anthropomorphism B890. Human actions are attributed to God: eating, swallowing. For other instances of this figure see Is 25:7mg, 8. 1 C 15:54.

8. **blast.** Ex +14:21. 2 S 22:16. Jb *4:9. Ps 18:15. Is 11:4. 37:7. 2 Th *2:8. Heb. *ruach*, S#7307h, used in reference to invisible divine power manifesting itself

in executing judgment. 2 K 19:7. Is 37:7. Rendered *breath*: 2 S 22:16. Jb 4:9. 15:30. Ps 18:15. 33:6. Is 11:4. 30:28. Rendered *spirit*: Is 4:4. 28:6. 34:16. 40:7. For the other uses of *ruach*, see Ge 6:3n. **thy nostrils.** ſ22A9. Anthropomorphism B876. Nostrils are attributed to God. For other instances of this figure see Dt 33:10mg. Jb 4:9. Ps 18:15. Ezk 8:17. **waters.** Ps 78:13, 16. Is 44:3. **the floods.** See on Ex +14:22. Ps 78:13. Hab *3:10. **heap.** Jsh *3:13, 16. Ps 33:7. 78:13. **heart.** ſ144A7. Pleonasm B412. "Heart" is sometimes used pleonastically by Metonymy for *the midst*, when it does not mean literally the precise middle point. For other instances of this figure see Ps 46:2mg. Pr 23:34mg. 30:19mg. Ezk 27:4mg. Mt 12:40.

9. **said.** ſ122. Mimesis; or, Description of Sayings B451. This figure is used when the sayings (and sometimes motions and thoughts) of another are described or imitated by way of emphasis. Sometimes the figure is used when only a single word typically used by another is delicately repeated to direct him aright. For other instances of this figure see Ps 137:7. 144:12-15. Is 14:13, 14. 28:15. Ezk 36:2. Ho 14:2, 3. Mi 2:11. 3:11. 1 C 15:35. 2 C 10:1, 10. Ph 3:4, 5. Ga (6:2). **I will pursue.** Ge 49:27. Jg 5:30. 1 K 19:2. 20:10. Is 10:8-13. *17:13, 14. 36:20. 53:12. Hab 3:14. Lk 11:22. **I will overtake.** ſ41. Ge 10:1. ſ82. Epitrochasmos; or, Summarizing B438. A running lightly over by way of summary. Here it is a figure of omission, in that the conjunction "and" is omitted for the sake of running quickly through the enumeration, as in the figure Asyndeton (ſ41, Ge 10:1). It is an omission of sense also, in that it abbreviates and summarizes. Another example of this figure is He 11:32, where a number of persons are named or alluded to, but not dwelt upon. **lust.** Heb. *nephesh*, soul. Ge 23:8. Dt 12:20. Ec 6:7. Here, *nephesh* is used of man manifesting certain feelings and passions, here strong desire. For other instances of *nephesh* used similarly to express man's exercising various mental faculties and expressing or exercising various feelings, affections, or passions, see Dt 21:14 (she will). Jg 18:25 (angry). 1 S 22:2 (discontented). Est 4:13 (thyself). Ps 27:12 (will). 35:25 (so would we have it). 41:2 (will). 105:22 (pleasure). 131:2 (myself). Pr 6:16 (Him), used of God. 14:10 (his own). 16:26 (he). 27:9 (hearty). Ec 6:9 (desire). Is 5:14 (herself). 49:7 (man). Je 22:27 (desire). 34:16 (pleasure). 37:9 (yourselves). 44:14 (desire). Ezk 16:27 (will). Jon 4:8 (himself). Mi 7:3 (desire). Hab 2:5 (desire). Compare Ex +23:9; Ge +34:3. For the other uses of *nephesh* see Ge +2:7. ſ108K40B. Idiom B859. There is an instance of Idiom here involving changes in the usage of words in the English language. In the time of the translators, "lust" meant simply pleasure or desire generally, whereas now we use the word of a particular kind of desire. Passages affected by this idiom include Dt 12:15. Jn 8:44. 2 T 4:3. 1 J 2:16. **destroy.** *or*, repossess. Ex 14:5, 9. Nu 14:12. 32:21. Dt 4:38. 1 S 2:7.

10. **blow.** Ex +14:21. Ge 8:1. Ps 74:13, 14. 135:7. 147:18. Is 11:15. Je 10:13. Am 4:13. Mt 8:27. **the sea.** Ex 14:28. Dt 11:4. **they sank.** See on ver. 5. **mighty.** Heb. lordly, S#117h. Jg *5:25. 1 S 4:8. 2 Ch 23:20. Ne 3:5. Ps 8:1 (excellent). Is 33:21 (glorious). Ezk 17:23 (goodly). Na 2:5. 3:18.

11. **Who.** ſ85C, Ge +18:14. **like unto thee.** Dt 3:24. 33:26. 1 S 2:2. 2 S *7:22. 1 K *8:23. Ps 35:10. 77:19. *86:8. *89:6-8. Is 40:18, 25. Je *10:6, 16. *49:19. **gods.**

or, mighty ones. S#410, *El*. This Hebrew noun emphasizes might. It is used as a name of God himself, ver. +2. It is also used of men, Jb 41:17; Ezk 32:21. It is used in reference to pagan gods or idols, Is 43:10. It is used of angels, Ps 29:1. It is even used of great natural objects, Ps 36:6 (great) mountains; Ps 80:10 (goodly) cedars. Ps *82:1, 2. **glorious.** Le *19:2. Ps *2:11. 89:18. *145:17. Is *6:3. 30:11. +*57:15. Hab *1:13. 1 P 1:15, 16. Re 4:8. **fearful.** Ps 66:5. *77:14. 89:5, 7. 90:11. 119:120. *130:4. Is 64:2, 3. Je 10:7. Lk 12:5. He 12:28, 29. Re *15:4. 19:1-6.

12. **stretchedst.** See on ver. 6. **right hand.** ſ22A15A, Ex +15:6.

13. **Thou.** Ge 19:16. Ep 2:4. **led.** Ps *73:24. 77:14, 15, 20. 78:52, 53. 80:1. 106:9. Is 63:12, 13. Je 2:6. **guided.** 1 P 1:5. **holy.** Ps *78:54. *135:21.

14. **hear.** Nu 14:14. 22:5. Dt 2:4, 5. Jsh *2:9, 10. 9:24. Ps *48:6. **of Palestina.** i.e. *wallowing*, *S#6429h. Ex 15:14. Ps 60:8. 83:7. 87:4. 108:9. Is 14:29, 31. Jl 3:4.

15. **dukes.** Ge 36:40. Nu 20:14-21. Dt 2:4. 1 Ch 1:51-54. **Moab.** Nu *22:3-5. Hab *3:7. **all the.** Jsh 2:11. *5:1. **melt.** Dt 20:8. Jsh 2:9mg. 14:8. 1 S 14:16. 2 S 17:10. Ps 68:2. Is 13:7. 19:1. Ezk 21:7. Na 2:10.

16. **Fear.** ſ173, Ge +27:44. **and.** ſ174, Ge +18:27. **dread.** Dt 2:25. 11:25. Jsh 2:9. **greatness.** ſ22I2. Anthropomorphism B895. Magnitude or greatness is attributed to God. For other instances of this figure see Ex 18:11. Nu 14:19. Dt 3:24. Ezr 5:8. Ps 47:2. 48:1. Je 32:17, 18, 19. Da 2:45. Ml 1:14. **thine arm.** ſ22A12. Anthropomorphism B877. Arms are attributed to God, to indicate His strength and power. For other instances of this figure see Jb 40:9. Ps 77:15. 79:11mg. 89:10mg, 13. Is 30:30. 51:9. 59:16. 62:8. Lk 1:51. **still.** Ex 11:7. 1 S 2:9. 25:37. **thy people.** Ex 19:6. Dt 7:6. 14:2. 26:18. 1 C 6:19, 20. T 2:14. 1 P 1:18, 19. **people.** ſ84, Ge +6:17. **which thou.** Ex 19:5, 6. Dt 32:6, 9. 2 S 7:23. Ps 74:2. Is *43:1-3. 51:10. Je 31:11. Ac *20:28. 1 C *6:19, 20. T *2:14. 1 P *2:9. 2 P 2:1.

17. **plant.** Ps *44:2. 78:54, 55. *80:8. Is 5:1-4. Je 2:21. 32:41. **mountain.** Ex 3:1, 2. Ge 22:2. Nu 22:41. 33:52. Ps 15:1. 78:54, 68, 69. *87:1, 2. Is *57:13. Je 31:23. Mi 4:1, 2. Re 14:1. **place.** 1 K 8:13. Is 4:5. **Sanctuary.** i.e. *a holy* or separate place. Heb. *mikdash*, holy as to place; hallowed (Darby). Ps 107:36. 114:2. Ha 2:12. *S#4720: Ex 15:17. *25:8. Le 12:4. 16:33. 19:30. 20:3. 21:12, 23. 26:2, 31. Nu 3:38. 10:21. 18:1, 29. 19:20. Jsh 24:26. 1 Ch 22:19. 28:10. 2 Ch 20:8. 26:18. 29:21. 30:8. 36:17. Ne 10:39. Ps 68:35. *73:17. 74:7. *78:69. 96:6. Is 8:14. 16:12. 60:13. 63:18. Je 17:12. 51:51. La 1:10. 2:7, 20. Ezk 5:11. 8:6. 9:6. 11:16. 21:2. 23:38, 39. 24:21. 25:3. 28:18. 37:26, 28. 43:21. 44:1, 5, 7, 8, 9, 11, 15, 16. 45:3, 4, 4, *18. 47:12. 48:8, 10, 21. Da 8:11. 9:17. 11:31. Am 7:9, 13 (chapel). For *S#6944h, *kodesh*, see Ex +*3:5. 28:29.

18. **shall reign.** Ps 10:16. 29:10. *146:10. Is *57:15. Da *2:44. 4:3. +*7:14, 27. Mt *6:13. Re +*11:15-17.

19. **horse.** Ex 14:23. Pr *21:31. **brought.** Ex 14:28, 29. He 11:29. **sea.** Re=15:2.

20. **Miriam.** i.e. their rebellion, *S#4813h. Ex 15:20, 21. Nu 12:1, 4, 5, 10, 10, 15, 15. 20:1. 26:59. Dt 24:9. 1 Ch 4:17. 6:3. Mi *6:4. (1) A daughter of Amram and the sister of Moses and Aaron, 1 Ch 6:3. She was watching the ark of bulrushes in which the

infant Moses was laid, and when the daughter of Pharaoh discovered it Miriam called her mother as a nurse for Moses, Ex 2:4-10. She led the women of Israel in a triumphant song after the passage of the Red Sea, Ex 15:20. She was smitten with leprosy for murmuring against Moses, but was restored to health in answer to Moses' prayer, Nu 12:1-15. She died at Kadesh and was buried there, Nu 20:1. (2) A descendant of Judah, 1 Ch 4:17. **prophetess.** Young renders, inspired one. Prophet of the Common Version (Ge 20:7) does not at all give the meaning of the Hebrew word *Nabi;* the one is now used in English invariably to express the individual who foretells future events; the Hebrew word rarely, if ever, expresses this, but simply the recipient of a divine influence, which may or may not concern future circumstances. At Ex 7:1, Young notes thy prophet. i. e. thy mouth-piece; as already remarked, the Hebrew idea of a prophet is not that of one who foretells future events, but one who receives a revelation of God's will, and proclaims it to others. Miriam (Nu 12:2), Deborah (Jg 4:4), Huldah (2 K 22:14; 2 Ch 34:22), Noadiah (Ne 6:14), are the only females thus denominated in Scripture; Isaiah's wife is called by the same name (Is 8:3), but whether it was simply because she was the wife of the prophet, or because she really received Divine revelations, it is impossible to say positively (Young). Jg 4:4. 1 S 10:5. 2 K 22:14. Lk 2:36. Ac 21:9. 1 C 11:5. 14:34. **sister.** Ex 2:4. Nu 12:1. 20:1. 26:59. Mi 6:4. **a timbrel.** Ge 31:27. Jg 11:34. 1 S 18:6. Ps 68:25. 81:2. 149:3. 150:4. Is 30:32. Re ◐=15:2. A kind of hand-drum, very common in the East, used principally by females, accompanied by dancing, or slow movements of the feet; in all Eastern festivals and entertainments, civil and sacred, the sexes are kept separate from each other (Jg 21:21n): in every instance of singing recorded in Scripture, where the posture is mentioned, it is always standing; it was reserved for some modern churches to sanction the unnatural and unseemly—not to say un-Scriptural—practice of sitting during praise in the worship of God (Young). But contrast Jg +*20:26n. **all the women.** Jg 11:34. +*21:21n. 1 S 18:6. 2 S 6:5, 14, 16. 2 K *4:23. 1 Ch 15:20n. Ps 68:11, 25. 81:2. *149:3. *150:4. **with dances.** 1 Ch +15:29. Ps +*30:11. SS 6:13mg. Je 31:4, 13.

21. **answered.** 1 S *18:7. 2 Ch 5:13. Ps 24:7-10. ch. 134. **Sing ye.** See on ver. 1. Jg 5:3. Ezr *3:11. Is ch. 5. Re 7:10-12. 5:9. 14:3. 15:3. 19:1-6. **horse.** ♪96, Ge +3:8.

22. **wilderness of Shur.** Ge *16:7. *25:18. 1 S 15:7. **three days.** Ex 3:18. +10:22.

23. **Marah.** Nu 33:8. **Marah.** i.e. bitterness; calamity, ✱S#4785h. Ex 15:23, 23, 23. Nu 33:8, 9. Ru 1:20.

24. **murmured.** Ex 14:11. 16:2, 8, 9. *17:3, 4. Nu +*11:1-6. 14:1-4. 16:11, 41. 17:10. 20:2-5. 21:5. 1 C 10:10. Ph *2:14. Ju *16. **What.** Ex 17:3. Ps 78:19, 20. Mt 6:25.

25. **cried.** Ex 14:10. 17:4. Ps +*50:15. 91:15. 99:6. Je 15:1. **a tree.** 2 K 2:21. 4:41. 1 C 1:18. **a statute.** Jsh 24:21-25. **proved.** Ex *16:4. 20:20. Dt 8:2, 16. 13:3. 33:8. Jg *2:22. 3:1, 4. Ps *66:10. *81:7. Pr 17:3. Je 9:7. 1 P 1:6, 7.

26. **diligently.** Dt 4:9. 6:7, 17. 11:13, 22. 13:14. 24:8. Jsh 22:5. Ps 77:6. 119:4. Pr 11:27. Is 55:2. Je 12:16. 17:24. Zc 6:15. Ro *12:7, 8. Ep 4:3. 1 T 4:15. 5:10. 2 T 2:15. 4:2. T 3:13. He 4:11. 6:11. 1 P 1:10. 3:13. 2 P 1:5, 10. 3:14. Ju +*3. **hearken.** Le 26:14, 18. Dt

7:12, 13, 15. *28:1-15. **and wilt.** Dt 12:28. 13:18. 1 K 11:33, 38. 2 K 22:2. Ezk 18:5. **put none.** Ex +23:25. Ezk ◐7:9. Ho 6:1. **diseases.** Ex 9:10, 11. 12:29. Dt *7:15. 28:27, 60. **for I am.** Ex 23:25. 2 K 20:5. 2 Ch *30:20. Jb 5:18. Ps 6:2. *41:3, 4. +*103:3. *147:3. Pr *4:22. Is 57:18. Je 8:22. 33:6. Ho 6:1. 1 T +*4:8. Ja 5:11-16. **the Lord that healeth thee.** or, *Jehovah-ropheka,* one of the compound names of Jehovah. For other compound names of Jehovah, see (2) *Jehovah-jireh,* the Lord will provide, Ge 22:14. (3) *Jehovah-nissi,* the Lord our banner, Ex 17:15. (4) *Jehovah-me-kaddishkem,* the Lord that doth sanctify you, Ex 31:13; Le 20:8; 21:8; 22:9, 16, 32; Ezk 20:12. (5) *Jehovah-shalom,* the Lord our peace, or the Lord send peace, Jg 6:24. (6) *Jehovah-tsebahoth (sabaoth),* Ro 9:29. Ja 5:4), the Lord of hosts, 1 S 1:3. (7) *Jehovah-roi,* the Lord my shepherd, Ps 23:1. (8) *Jehovah-elyon,* the Lord most high, Ps 7:17; 47:2; 97:9. (9) *Jehovah-tsid-kenu,* the Lord our righteousness, Je 23:6; 33:16. (10) *Jehovah-shammah,* the Lord is present, or the Lord is there, Ezk 48:35. (11) *Jehovah-hoseenu,* the Lord our maker, Ps 95:6. (12) *Jehovah-elohim,* the eternal creator, Ge 2:4. (13) *Adonai-Jehovah,* the Lord our sovereign, or Master Jehovah, Ge 15:2, 8. (14) *Jehovah-eloheenu,* the Lord our God, Ps 99:5, 8, 9. (15) *Jehovah-eloheka,* the Lord thy God, Ex 20:2, 5, 7. (16) *Jehovah-elohay,* the Lord my God, Zc 14:5. **healeth.** ♪22D2E. Anthropopatheia or Anthropomorphism B891. God is spoken of as a physician. For another instance of this figure, see Ps 147:3.

27. **Elim.** i.e. strong ones, ✱S#362h. Ex 15:27h. 16:1, 1h. Nu 33:9, 9, 10h. Is 12:3. Ezk 47:12. Re 7:17. 22:2. **twelve.** Ex 24:4. 28:21. Ge 35:22. Le 24:5. Nu 17:2. 29:17. Dt 1:23. Jsh 4:3. 1 K 4:7. 7:25. 10:20. 18:31. 19:19. **wells.** Ex 2:15. Ge 16:14. 21:30. 24:11. 26:18. 29:2. 1 S 19:22. Here, S#5869, ayin, a fountain, Ge +24:13. **palm trees.** Le 23:40. Nu 33:9. Dt 34:3. Jg 1:16. 3:13. 2 Ch 28:15.

EXODUS 16

The Israelites come to the wilderness of Sin, and murmur for want of bread, 1-4. Manna and flesh is promised, and the people are rebuked, 5-12. Quail and manna are sent, 13-15. Manna is described, and rules are given for gathering it; the people disobey in hoarding it, and in seeking it on the sabbath day, 16-31. God commands that an omer of it should be preserved, 32-36.

1. A.M. 2513. B.C. 1491. **took.** Ex 15:27. Nu *33:10-12. **Sin.** Ex 17:1. Nu 33:12. Ezk 30:15, 16. **Sinai.** i.e. *bush of the Lord;* jagged; my thorns, ✱S#5514h. Ex 16:1. 19:1, 2, 11, 18, 20, 23. 24:16. 31:18. 34:2, 4, 29, 32. Le 7:38, 38. 25:1. 26:46. 27:34. Nu 1:1, 19. 3:1, 4, 14. 9:1, 5. 10:12. 26:64. 28:6. 33:15, 16. Dt 33:2. Jg 5:5. Ne 9:13. Ps 68:8, 17.

2. **murmured against.** Ex 15:24. Ge 19:4. Ps 106:7, 13, *25. 1 C *10:10.

3. **Would.** Nu 20:3-5. Dt 28:67. Jsh 7:7. 2 S 18:33. La *4:9. Ac 26:29. 1 C 4:8. 2 C 11:1. **we had.** Nu 11:15. 14:2. Jb 3:1, 10, 20. Je 20:14-18. Jon 4:8, 9. **flesh.** Ex 2:23. Nu *11:4, 5. **to kill.** Ex 5:21. 17:3. Nu 16:13, 41. **hunger.** Dt 8:3. Je 2:6. La 4:9.

4. **I will rain.** Nu *11:7, 8. Ps *78:24, 25. 105:40. Jn *6:31, 32. 1 C *10:3. **a certain rate every day.** Heb. the portion of a day in his day. Ex +*5:13mg,

19. Le 23:37. 1 K 8:59mg. 2 Ch 31:16. Ezr 3:4mg. Ne 11:23. Pr 30:8. Je 52:34mg. Mt 6:*11, 32, 33. Lk 11:3. Jn=6:31. **prove them.** See on Ex +15:25. 20:20. Dt *8:2, 16. 13:3. Jsh 24:15. Jg 3:1.

5. **prepare.** ver. 23. Ex 35:2, 3. Le 25:21, 22. **twice.** ſ121L9, Ge +43:12.

6. **even.** ver. 8, 12, 13. **the Lord.** ver. 3. Ex 6:7. 12:51. 32:1, 7, 11. Nu 16:28, 30. Ps 77:20. Is 63:11, 12.

7. **the morning.** ver. 13. **ye shall.** ver. 10. Ex 24:10, 16. 40:34. Le 9:6. Nu 14:10. 16:42. Is 35:2. 40:5. Jn 11:4, 40. **the glory of.** Is 6:8-10 w Ac 28:25-27. Ac +5:3, 4. He 3:7-9. **what are we.** ver. 2, 3, 8. Nu 16:11.

8. **the Lord heareth.** ver. 9, 12. Nu 14:27. Mt 9:4. Jn 6:41-43. 1 C 10:10. **but against.** Nu 21:7. 1 S *8:7. Ps 51:4. Is 32:6. 37:29. Mt 10:40. Lk *10:16. Jn 13:20. Ac 5:4. Ro *13:2. 1 Th 4:8.

9. **Come near.** Nu 16:16. **heard.** See on ver. 2, 8.

10. **that they.** ver. 7. Nu 14:10. 16:19, 42. **appeared.** ver. 7. Ex 3:2. 13:21, 22. 14:24. 40:34-38. Le 9:6, 23, 24. Nu 14:10. 16:19, 42. 1 K *8:10, 11. Mt 17:5. **in the cloud.** ſ22D3J5, Ex +13:21.

12. **I have.** ver. 8. **At even.** ver. 6. **in the morning.** ver. 7. **ye shall know.** Ex 4:5. 6:7. 7:17. Je 31:34. Ezk 34:30. 39:22. Jl 3:17. Zc 13:9.

13. **the quails.** Nu *11:31-33. Ps *78:27, 28. *105:40. **the dew.** Nu *11:9.

14. **the dew.** Nu 11:7-9. Dt *8:3. Ne 9:15. Ps *78:24. 105:40. **the hoar frost.** Jb 38:29. Ps 147:16.

15. **It is manna.** *or,* What is this? *or,* It is a portion. ver. 31, 33, 35. Nu 11:6, 7, 9. Dt 8:3, 16. Jsh 5:12. Ne 9:15, 20. Ps 78:24. Jn *6:31, 32, 49, 58. 1 C 10:3. He 9:4. Re *2:17. **This is.** ver. 4. Nu 21:5. Ps *136:5. Pr 9:5. Lk 12:30. 1 P=2:2.

16. **according.** Ex 12:4. **omer.** ver. 18, 33, 36. Le 23:10, 11, 12, 15. **for every man.** Heb. by the poll, or head. Ex 38:36. Nu 1:2, 18, 20, 22. 3:47. Jg 9:53. 2 K 9:35. 1 Ch 10:10. 23:3, 24. **persons.** Heb. *nephesh,* souls, Ge +12:5. √ſ171Q1, Ge +12:5. **tents.** Ex 27:21n. 33:7n. Heb. *ohel.* a2168h. Ge 4:20. 9:21, 27. 12:8. 13:3, 5. 18:1, 2, 6, 9, 10. 24:67. 25:27. 26:25. 31:25, 33, 34. 33:19. 35:21. Ex 16:16. 18:7. 26:7 (covering), 9 (tabernacle), 11, 12, 13, 14, 36. +27:21n.

17. **more.** Heb. multiplying. ver. 18. Ex 36:5. Le 11:42. 1 Ch 8:40. Ne 6:17. 9:37. Pr 28:8. Ec 6:11. Hab 2:6. **less.** Heb. lessening. ver. 18. Nu 11:32.

18. **gathered much.** 2 C *8:14, 15.

19. **leave.** Ex 12:10. 23:18. Mt 6:34.

20. **bred worms.** Mt 6:19. Lk 12:15, 33. He 13:5. Ja *5:2, 3. **and Moses.** Nu 12:3. 16:15. Mk 3:5. 10:14. Ep 4:26.

21. **every morning.** Pr 6:6-11. Ec 9:10. 12:1. Mt *6:33. Jn 12:35. 2 C 6:2.

22. **on the sixth.** What the substance called *manna* was, is utterly unknown; but, from the circumstances in the text, it is evident that it was not a *natural* production, but was miraculously sent by Jehovah. These circumstances the learned Abarbinel, a most judicious Jewish interpreter, has thus enumerated: The natural manna was never found in the desert where this fell; where the common manna does fall, it is only in the spring time, in March and April, whereas this fell throughout all the months in the year; the ordinary manna does not melt in the sun, as this did (ver. 21);

it does not stink and breed worms, as this did, when kept till the morning (ver. 20); it cannot be ground, or beaten in a mortar, so as to make cakes, as this was; the common manna is medicinal and purgative, and cannot be used for food and nutriment, as this was; this fell in a double proportion on the sixth day, and not on the sabbath, as it certainly would have done had it fallen naturally; it followed them in all their journeys, wherever they pitched their tents; and it ceased at the very time of the year when the other falls, namely in March, when the Israelites were come to Gilgal. Whatever this substance was, it does not appear to have been common to the wilderness. From Dt 8:3, 16, it is evident that the Israelites never saw it before; and from a pot of it being preserved, it is certain that nothing of the kind ever appeared again. ver. 5, 16. Le 25:12, 22. **rulers.** or, princes, elders. Heb. lifted up ones. Ex 12:21. 17:5. 22:28. 34:31. 35:27. Ge 17:20.

23. **Tomorrow.** Le 10:3. **rest.** Ex +*20:8-11. *31:15. *35:3. Ge *2:2, 3. Le 23:3. Mk 2:27, 28. Lk 23:56. Re 1:10. **bake.** Nu 11:8.

24. **did not stink.** ver. 20, 33.

25. **a sabbath.** ver. 23, 29. Ne 9:14.

26. **Six days.** Ex *20:9-11. Dt 5:13. Ezk 46:1. Lk 13:14. **the sabbath.** "The language is not that of delivering a new precept, but restoring an old and well known, though neglected one" (Daniel Wilson, *The Lord's Day,* p. 22). "It is remarkable, that three miracles were wrought, every week, in honor of the sabbath, even before the promulgation of the Mosaic law. Double the quantity fell the day before; none fell on the sabbath day; nor did that stink, which they kept for that day. This confirms the opinion, that the institution of the sabbath was from the beginning. Indeed the whole narrative implies, that reference was made to an institution before known, but not properly remembered or regarded; and not to any new law given on the occasion. Neither the inquiry of the elders, nor the language of Moses, can be consistently interpreted of an entirely new institution" (Thomas Scott). See related notes (Ge 4:3n. 29:27n. Is +*58:13n).

27. **and they found none.** Pr 20:4.

28. **How long.** Ex 10:3. Nu 14:11. 20:12. 2 K *17:14. Ps *78:10, 22. 81:13, 14. *106:13. Is 7:9, 13. Je 4:14. 9:6. Ezk 5:6. 20:13, 16. Mk 9:19.

29. **hath given.** Ex 31:13. Ne 9:14. Is 58:13, 14. Ezk 20:12. **abide ye.** Lk 23:56.

30. **rested.** Le 23:3. Dt 5:12-14. He 4:9.

31. **called the name.** See on ver. 15. In consequence of the term *manna* having been given to a drug which is now much used in England, many persons have ignorantly supposed it to be the same sort of thing as that miraculously sent for the sustenance of the children of Israel in the wilderness. The manna of commerce comes from Calabria and Sicily, where it oozes out of a kind of ash tree, from the end of June to the end of July, and is a thick, clammy, sweet juice, partly drawn from the tree by the rays of the sun, partly by the puncture of insects, and partly by artificial means. The European manna is not so good as the Oriental, which is gathered in Syria, Arabia, and Persia, from the Oriental oak, and from a shrub which is called in Persia *teranjabin.* **and it was.** Nu *11:6, 7. SS 2:3. **wafers.** only here; another word from the same root (per Young) is generally rendered cruse, i.e. *of oil,*

water, etc.; see 1 S 28:11, 12, 16. 1 K 17:12, 14, 16. 19:6. **honey.** Ge 43:11. Ex 3:8, 17. 13:5. Le 2:11.

32. **Fill.** Ps 103:1, 2. 105:5. 111:4, 5. Lk 22:19. He 2:1.

33. **Take a pot.** He *9:4.

34. **testimony.** Ex *25:16, 21. 26:33, 34. 27:21. 30:6, 26, 36. 31:18. 38:21. 40:20. Nu 1:50, 53. *17:10. Dt *10:5. 1 K 8:9.

35. **forty years.** Nu 33:38. Dt 8:2, 3. Ne 9:15, 20, 21. Ps 78:24, 25. Mt *5:45. Jn 6:30-58. Re *7:16. **did eat.** ✓70. Epibole; or, Overlaid Repetition B346. The repetition of the same phrase at irregular intervals. For other instances of this figure see Nu 9:18. Jg 5:27. Ps 29:3, 4, 5, 7, 8, 9. Is 2:7, 8. 5:8, 11, 18, 20, 21, 22. Mt 6:19, 20. Ac 20:22, 25. **until they came to.** Jsh *5:12. **the borders.** Nu 33:48-50. Dt 1:8. 34:1-4.

36. **an omer is.** ver. 16, 32, 33. **the tenth part.** Le 5:11. 6:20.

EXODUS 17

The people want water, chide with Moses, and tempt the Lord, 1, 2. Moses expostulates with them, and complains to God; and, at his command, smites the rock in Horeb, which pours out water, 3-6; the place is named Massah, and Meribah, 7. Amalek assaults Israel, and is overcome by Joshua, while Moses holds up his hands with the rod of God, 8-13. Amalek is doomed to destruction, and Moses builds an altar, called Jehovah-nissi, 14-16.

1. **Sin.** Ex 16:1. Nu 33:12-14. **commandment.** lit. mouth. ✓121BA, Ge +45:21. Nu *9:18. **Rephidim.** i.e. *supports, props; shrinking of hands,* ✱S#7508h. ver. 8. Ex 19:2. Nu 33:14, 15.

2. **the people.** Ex 5:21. 14:11, 12. 15:24. 16:2, 3. Nu 11:4-6. 14:2. *20:3-5. 21:5. **Give us.** Ge 30:1, 2. 1 S 8:6. Lk 15:12. **wherefore.** ver. 7. Ex 16:2. Nu 14:22. Dt 6:16. Ps *78:18, 41, 56. *95:9. 106:14. Is 7:12. Ml 3:15. Mt 4:7. 16:1-3. Lk 4:12. Ac 5:9. 15:10. 1 C *10:9. He *3:9.

3. **thirsted.** Jn=7:37. **murmured.** Ex *14:11, 12. *15:24. 16:2, 7, 8. Nu *14:2, 27, 29, 36. 16:11, 41. 17:5. *21:5. **thou hast.** See on *16:3.

4. **cried.** Ex 14:15. 15:25. Nu 11:11. **almost.** Nu 14:10. 16:19. 1 S *30:6. Jn=8:59. 10:31. Ac +*7:59. 14:19. **stone.** ✓96C2, Ge +45:9. Ex 19:13. 21:28, 29, 32. Le 24:14, 16. Dt 13:10. 17:5. 22:21, 24. Jsh 7:25.

5. **Go on.** Ezk 2:6. Ac 20:23, 24. **thy rod.** Ex *7:19, 20. Nu 20:8-11.

6. **I will.** Ex 16:10. **the rock in.** Ex 33:22. Is 32:2. **Horeb.** Ex 3:1-5. **and thou.** Nu *20:9-11. Dt 8:15. Ne 9:15. Ps 78:15, 16, 20. *105:41. *114:8. Is 48:21. 1 C *10:4. **come water.** Jn =19:34. **out of.** Jg 6:21. Ps 81:16. **that the people.** Ps 46:4. Is *41:17, 18. *43:19, 20. *55:1. Jn *4:10, 14. *7:37, 38. Re *22:17.

7. **Massah.** i.e. *Temptation.* ✱S#4532h. Nu *20:13. Dt 6:16. 9:22. 33:8. **Meribah.** that is, *Chiding,* or *Strife.* ✱S#4809h. ver. 2. Nu 20:13, 24. 27:14. Dt 32:51. Ps *81:7. **chiding.** See on ver. 2. **tempted.** Ps *95:8. He *3:8, 9. **Is the Lord.** Ex 34:9. Dt 31:17. Jsh 22:31. Is 12:6. Mi 3:11. Jn 1:14. Ac 7:37-39. **among us.** Nu 14:42. Dt +23:14.

8. **Amalek.** ✓171R, Ex +12:40. i.e. *a people that*

licks up; people lapping, ✱S#6002h. ver. 9, 10, 11, 13, 14, 16. Ge *36:12, 16. Nu 13:29. 14:43. *24:20, 20. Dt *25:17, 19. Jg 3:13. 5:14. 6:3, 33. 7:12. 10:12. 1 S 14:48. *15:2, 3, 5, 6, 7, 8, 18, 20, 20, 32. 27:48. 28:18. 30:18. 2 S 1:1. 8:12. 1 Ch 1:36. 4:43. 18:11. Ps 83:7.

9. **unto Joshua.** i.e. *Lord of salvation, the Lord is his salvation,* S#3091h. ver. 10, 13, 14. Ex 24:13. 32:17. 33:11. Nu 11:28. 13:16, Oshea, Jehoshua. 14:6, 30, 38. 26:65. 27:18, 22. 32:12, 28. 34:17. Dt 1:38. 3:21, 28. 31:3, 7, 14, 14, 23. 32:44, Hoshea. 34:9. Jsh 1:1, 10, 12, 16. Jg 1:1. 2:6, 7, 7, 8, 21, 23. 1 S 6:14, 18. 1 K 16:34. 2 K 23:8. 1 Ch 7:27. Hg 1:1, 12, 14. 2:2, 4. Zc 3:1, 3, 6, 8, 9. 6:11. Ac 7:45, called Jesus. He 4:8, Jesus. **Choose.** Nu 31:3, 4. **will stand.** He *2:10. *7:25. **the rod.** Ex 4:2, 20.

10. **Joshua.** Jsh 11:15. Mt 28:20. Jn 2:5. 15:14. **and Moses.** ver. 9. **Hur.** i.e. *a hole or cavern,* ✱S#2354h. ver. 12. Ex 24:14. 31:2. 35:30. 38:22. Nu 31:8. Jsh 13:21. 1 K 4:8. 1 Ch 2:19, 20, 50. 4:1, 4. 2 Ch 1:5. Ne 3:9. (1) One of the chief men of the Israelites, who with Aaron held up the hands of Moses on the mountain at the battle with Amalek, Ex 17:10; 24:14. (2) A son of Caleb, the son of Hezron, Ex 31:2; 35:30. (3) A king of Midian, Nu 31:8; Jsh 13:21. (4) Father of one of Solomon's officers, 1 K 4:8. (5) A man of Judah, 1 Ch 2:50; 4:4. May be same as Number 2. (6) A son of Judah, 1 Ch 4:1. (7) Father of one who helped to repair the wall of Jerusalem, Ne 3:9.

11. **Moses held.** 1 S 7:8, 9. Ps *56:9. Lk 18:1. 1 T 2:8. Ja *5:16. **prevailed.** Ro=8:37. **let down.** Mt *26:41.

12. **Moses' hands.** Mt 26:40-45. Mk 14:37-40. Ep 6:18. Col 4:2. **stayed up his hands.** Ps 35:3. Is 35:3. 2 C 1:11. Ph 1:19. 1 Th 5:25. He 12:12. Ja 1:6. **were steady.** He=7:25.

13. **Joshua.** Jsh 10:28, 32, 37, 42. 11:12. **discomfited.** Heb. weakened. Jsh 14:10mg. Is 14:12. Jl 3:10. **Amalek.** ✓171R, Ex +12:40. **edge.** ✓144A2, Ge +34:26.

14. **Write.** This is the first mention of writing in the Bible. Ex 24:4, 7. Nu 33:2. 36:13. Dt 28:61. Jsh 1:7, 8. **memorial.** Ex 12:14. 13:9. 34:27. Dt 31:9. Jsh 4:7. Jb 19:23. Hab 2:2, 3. **for I will.** Nu 24:20. Dt 25:17-19. 1 S *15:2, 3, 7, 8, 18. 27:8, 9. *30:1, 17. 2 S 1:1, 8-16. 8:12. 1 Ch 4:43. Ezr 9:14. **put out.** S#4229h. Ge 6:7 (destroy). 7:4, 23. Ex 32:32 (blot), 33. Nu 5:23 (blot out). Dt 9:14. 25:6, 19. 29:20. Ps *51:1, 9. Pr 6:33. Is *43:25. **the remembrance.** Ex 3:15 (memorial). Dt 25:19. Jb 18:17. Ps 9:6. ◑*83:4, 7. Pr *10:7. Re *17:14.

15. **altar.** Ge +8:20. 12:7. 26:25. 35:7. **Jehovah-nissi.** i.e. *the Lord my banner,* ✱S#3071h, only here. Ex +15:26. Ge 22:14. 33:20. Jg 6:24. Ps *20:5. *60:4. Is 11:10. **nissi,** ✱S#5251h. Ex 17:15. Nu 21:8 (pole), 9 (pole). 26:10 (sign). Ps 60:4 (banner). Is 5:26 (ensign). 11:10, 12. 13:2. 18:3. 30:17. 31:9. 33:23 (sail). 49:22 (standard). 62:10. Je 4:6, 21. 50:2. 51:12, 27. Ezk 27:7 (sail). **banner.** ✓22D5Q. Anthropomorphism B894. A banner or flag is attributed to God. For other instances of this figure see Ps 60:4. SS 2:4. Is 5:26. 11:10. 59:19.

16. **Because,** etc. or, Because the hand of Amalek is against the throne of the Lord, therefore, etc. **the Lord,** etc. Heb. the hand upon the throne of the Lord (Heb. *Jah,* Ex +15:2. Ps *68:4. 89:8. Is 26:4), Is 66:1. Ac 7:49. **sworn.** Ge 22:16. Nu 32:10. Dt 4:21. **will have war.** Nu *24:20. Dt *25:19. 1 S 15:3, 7. *28:18. Ps 21:8-11. **Amalek.** Ge +14:7. 36:12.

EXODUS 18

Jethro brings to Moses his wife and sons, 1-6. Moses entertains him; and relates the Lord's goodness to Israel, 7, 8. Jethro rejoices, blesses God, and offers sacrifices, 9-12. He gives good counsel to Moses, and Moses acts according to it, 13-26. He departs from Moses, 27.

1. **Jethro.** Ex 2:16, 21. 3:1. 4:18. Nu 10:29. Jg 4:11. **heard.** Ps 34:2. 44:1. 77:14, 15. 78:4. 105:5, 43. 106:2, 8. Je 33:9. Zc 8:23. Ga 1:23, 24. **God.** Ac 7:35, 36. 14:27. 15:12. 21:19, 20. Ro 15:18. **done.** Ex chs. 7-15. Jsh 2:10. 9:9. Ne 9:10, 11. Ps 77:14, 15. 78:50-53. 105:36-41. 106:8-11. 136:10-16. Is 63:11-13.

2. **Zipporah.** Ex 2:21. 4:25, 26.

3. **two sons.** Ac *7:29. **Gershom.** i.e. *A stranger there.* Ex 2:22. Ps 39:12. He 11:13. 1 P 2:11.

4. **Eliezer.** i.e. *My God is an help.* Ps 46:1. Is 50:7-9. He 13:6. **said he.** ♪63BA, Ge +26:7. **delivered.** Ex 2:15. Ps 18, title, 48. 34:4. Da 6:22. Ac 12:11. 2 C 1:8-10. 2 T 4:17.

5. **came with.** Ex *3:1, 12. 19:11, 20. 24:16, 17. 1 K 19:8.

6. **said.** i.e. *by means of messengers sent before-hand.* Mt=12:47.

7. **went.** Ge 14:17. 46:29. Nu 22:36. Jg 11:34. 1 K 2:19. Ac 28:15. **did obeisance.** Ge 18:2. 19:1. 33:3-7. **kissed.** Ge 29:13. 31:28. 33:4. 45:15. Ps 2:12. Lk 7:45. Ac 20:37. **welfare.** Heb. peace. Ge 37:14. 43:27. 2 S 11:7. Je 15:5mg.

8. **told.** ver. 1. Ne 9:9-15. Ps 66:16. 71:17-20. *105:1, 2. *145:4-12. **and all the.** Ex 15:22-24. 16:3. **come upon them.** Heb. found them. ♪155F, Ge +4:7. Ge +44:34mg. Nu 20:14mg. 2 K 9:21mg. Ne 9:32mg. **how the Lord.** Ps 78:42, 43. 81:7. 106:10. 107:2.

9. **rejoiced.** Is 44:23. 66:10. Ro 12:10, 15. 1 C 12:26. **goodness.** Ho +*3:5.

10. **Blessed be.** Ge *14:20. 2 S *18:28. 1 K 8:15. Ps 41:13. 106:47, 48. Lk *1:68. Ro *12:15. Ep 1:3. 1 Th 3:9. 1 P 1:3. Re 5:11-13. 19:1-6. **hand.** ♪121S1, Ge +49:10. Metonymy of the Adjunct, the sign is put for the thing signified B603. Here, the "hand" is put for power, of which it is the sign; and it is repeated three times in order to emphasize the greatness of the power and the wonderful deliverance from it.

11. **Now I know.** Ex 9:16. 1 K 17:24. 2 K 5:15. Pr +*19:25. **the Lord.** Ex 15:11. 1 Ch 16:25. 2 Ch 2:5. Ps *95:3. 97:9. 135:5. **greater.** ♪22I2, Ex +15:16. **in the thing.** Ex 1:10, 16, 22. *5:2, 7. *14:8, 18. **proudly.** Ex 9:17. 10:3. 1 S 2:3. Ne 9:10, 16, 29. Jb 40:11, 12. Ps 31:23. 119:21. Da *4:37. Lk 1:51. Ja 4:6. 1 P 5:5.

12. **took.** Ex 24:5. Ge 4:4. 8:20. 12:7. 26:25. 31:54. Jb 1:5. 42:8. **burnt offering.** Le +*23:12. **Aaron.** Ex 24:11. Le 7:11-17. Dt 12:7. 27:7. 1 Ch 29:21, 22. 2 Ch 30:22. 1 C *10:18, 21, 31. **eat bread.** Ex 2:20. Ge 43:25. 2 S 9:7. Jb 42:11. Da 10:3. Lk 14:1, 15.

13. **sat to.** Jg 5:10. Jb 29:7. Is 16:5. Jl 3:12. Mt 23:2. Ro 12:8. 13:6. **judge.** Jn=5:27. Ac=17:31.

14. **he said.** Pr *1:5. 9:9. 11:14. 12:15. *19:20. 20:18. 24:6. **What is this.** Young (*Concise Critical Comments*) notes "The question does not imply ignorance of what was going on, but is simply a graceful way of opening up a conversation, in which he might find an opportunity of giving utterance to his sentiments." This is a much needed grace, whether in family, business, or spiritual affairs, and this is a fine example of its practice.

Further insight on this grace is given in notes at Ps 9:10 and Ro 12:8, where we see that correction given regarding the root cause of a problem, rather than to the sensitive problem itself, may win a receptive audience. Here, Jethro and Moses both demonstrate valuable qualities: the ability to give advice, and the ability to receive and profit therefrom (2 K +*5:13. Pr *9:8, 9). Moses needed to learn the valuable skill of delegating authority, a skill valuable in application to both business and worship. There is the need to set priorities, and as often as possible, to limit ourselves to do the things which we can do (by training, gift, or position) that others cannot, lest, like Moses, we assume for ourselves too much of the burden. Nu 11:16, 17, 24, 25. Dt 1:9-17. 16:18. 2 Ch 19:5, 8. Ezr 7:10, √25. Mt 17:27. 21:1-3. Mk *6:31. Lk 10:38-42. Ac *6:2-4. 1 T 4:16. 2 T √2:2.

15. **to enquire.** ver. 19, 20. Ge 25:22. Dt *4:29. Le 24:12-14. Nu 15:34. *27:5. 2 K 8:8. 1 Ch 10:14. 2 Ch 14:7. 17:4. 22:9. Ps 34:5. 77:2. 78:34. Is *26:9, 16.

16. **a matter.** Ex 23:7. 24:14. Dt *17:8-12. 2 S 15:3. Jb 31:13. Ac 18:14, 15. 1 C *6:1. **one and another.** Heb. a man and his fellow. ver. 7. Ex 2:13. 21:18. **make.** Le 24:15. Nu 15:35. 27:6, etc. 36:6-9. Dt 4:5. 5:1. 6:1. 1 S 12:23. Mt 28:20. 1 Th 4:1, 2.

17. **not good.** ver. +*14n. Dt 1:12. 1 K 3:8, 9. ●*13:18. 2 Ch 19:6. Mt ●17:4. Jn ●13:6-10.

18. **Thou wilt surely wear away.** Heb. fading thou wilt fade. ♪147B, Ge +2:16. Jb 14:18mg. Ps ●1:3mg. 18:45. 37:2. 90:5, 6. 103:15. Is 40:6, 7, *8. 2 C 12:15. Ph 2:30. 1 Th 2:8, 9. **thou art.** Nu *11:14-17. Dt *1:9-12. Ac 6:1-4.

19. **Hearken.** ver. 24. Pr 9:9. **God shall.** Ex 3:12. 4:12. Ge 39:2. Dt 20:1. Jsh 1:9. 2 S 14:17. Mt 28:20. **Be thou.** See on ver. 15. Ex *4:16. *20:19. Dt *5:5. **bring.** Nu 27:5.

20. **teach.** ver. 16. Dt *4:1, 5. 5:1. 6:1, 2. 7:11. 2 Ch 17:7. Ezr *7:25. Ne 9:13, 14. Ml 2:7. 1 T 3:2. 2 T *2:2. T 1:9mg. **the way.** 1 S 12:23. Ps 32:8. *143:8. Is 30:21. Je 6:16. 42:3. Mi 4:2. 1 Th 4:1. **work.** Dt 1:18. Ezk 3:17. Mt 28:20. Mk 13:34. 2 Th 3:6-12.

21. **Moreover.** Dt 1:13-17. Ac 6:3. **provide.** or, see. i.e. look out for. Ex 24:11. Ge 22:8. Jb 19:26, 27. Ps 11:4, 7. 17:2. Pr 24:32. SS 6:13. Is 30:10 (prophesy). La 2:14. (S#2372h). **able men.** T#312. ver. 25. Dt 1:13, 15. 16:18. 1 K 3:9-12. 1 Ch 26:8. Pr 28:2. 2 T *2:2. T 1:5-9. **such as fear God.** Ex 9:20. 23:2-9. Ge 22:12. *42:18. 2 S *23:3. 1 K 18:3, 12. 2 Ch *19:5-10. Ne 5:9, *15. 7:2. Jb 1:1, 8. 2:3. Pr 1:7. Ec 12:13. Mt *10:28. Lk 18:2, 4. **men of truth.** Jb 29:16. 31:13. Is 16:5. 59:4, 14, 15. Je 5:1. Ezk 18:8. Zc 7:9. 8:16. Ac +*6:3. **hating covetousness.** Ex 23:8. Dt *16:18, 19. 1 S 8:3. 12:3, 4. 2 K +*12:15. Ps 26:9, 10. 119:36. Pr *28:16. Is *33:15. Ezk 22:12. *33:31. Mt 13:22. Mk *7:21, 22. Lk *12:15. Ac +*6:3. 20:33. 1 C +*4:2. 2 C +*7:2. √8:20. 1 T 3:3. 6:5, 9-11. 2 P 2:14, 15. **rulers of thousands.** Ex 24:1, 9. Jsh +*22:21. Jg 6:15. Ps *84:10n. Mi +*5:2. Lk 10:1, 17. Ac 4:32-37. Whatever matter the *decarch*, or ruler over ten, could not decide, went to the *pentecontarch*, or ruler over fifty, and thence by degrees to the *hecatontarch*, or ruler over a hundred, to the *chiliarch*, or ruler over a thousand, to Moses, and at length to God himself. Each magistrate had the care or inspection of only ten men; the decarch superintended ten private individuals; the hecatontarch, ten decarchs; and the chiliarch, ten

hecatontarchs. Nu 10:4. Dt 1:15. Jsh 22:14. 1 S 8:12. But contrast Young's comment here (*Concise Critical Comments*), "This advice, though excellent as a whole, was carrying the divisions too far; for 600,000 men there must have been, according to this plan, 60,000 heads of tens, 6000 heads of hundreds, 600 heads of thousands, in all 78,600 judges! It was apparently found unworkable, for at a later period seventy elders were chosen, and fitted to assist him." Yet reference to thousands throughout the rest of the Old Testament may suggest some form of this organization remained in place (Mi +*5:2). **rulers of hundreds.** Jg 7:16. 1 S 25:13. Ac 1:15. **rulers of fifties.** Ge 18:24, 26. Mk 6:40. Lk ◑10:1, 17. **rulers of tens.** As noted, by this system each magistrate, ruler, or leader would have the care of only ten men. Studies of small-group dynamics suggest that 10 or 12 is the maximum size for a group where effective listening to one another (Ro +12:5. 1 C 14:26. Ep 5:19-21. Ja 5:16) can occur, essential for effective nurturing (Ep 6:4), comfort (2 C 1:4), caring (1 T +*3:5), exhortation (He +*3:13), and fellowship (Ml 3:16) for spiritual growth and the discipling of new leadership (1 T 4:16. 2 T 2:2). It was prescribed in Jewish practice that ten men as heads of families were required to establish a local synagogue, or to conduct a service. Where a building for the purpose was not available, Edersheim notes "they might meet for worship in a private dwelling, a sort of 'Synagogue in the house' (Phm 2)" (*The Life and Times of Jesus the Messiah*, vol. 1, p. 433). Ge *18:32. 1 S 25:5. Mt 10:1. Ac 19:7.

22. **at all seasons.** ver. 26. Ro 13:6. **great.** Le 24:11. Nu 15:33. 27:2. 36:1. Dt 1:17. 17:8, 9. **they shall.** ver. 18. Nu *11:16, 17. Dt 1:9.

23. **do.** 2 Ch 19:6. **and God command thee so.** Young notes, "This language shows Jethro to have been a man of a truly godly spirit, proposing that his plans should only be adopted after receiving the Divine sanction." Ge 21:10-12. 1 S 8:6. Ac 15:2. Ga 2:2. **able to endure.** ver. 14n, 18. Ex 21:21h. **and all this.** Ex 16:29. Ge 18:33. 30:25. 2 S 18:3. 19:39. 21:17. Ph 1:24, 25.

24. **Moses hearkened.** ver. 2-5, 19. Ezr 10:2, 5. Pr +*1:5. 1 C 12:21.

25. **chose able.** ver. 21. Dt *1:13-15. Ac 6:5.

26. **at all.** ver. 14, 22. **the hard causes.** ver. 15, 22. Dt 17:8. 1 K 3:16-28. 10:1. Jb 29:16.

27. **let his.** Ge 24:59. 31:55. Nu *10:29, 30. Jg 19:9. **his own land.** i.e. Midian. Ex 2:15, 16. 3:1. Nu 24:21. Jg *1:16. 4:11. 1 S 15:6. 2 K 10:15. 1 Ch 2:55. Je 35:2.

EXODUS 19

Israel arrives at mount Sinai, and encamps there, 1, 2. Moses hears the message of God, and delivers it to the people; they engage to obey, and he reports it to the Lord, 3-8. Preparations are made, regulations prescribed, and the time set, for the giving of the law, 9-15. The tremendous introduction to that solemn transaction, 16-25.

1. A.M. 2513. B.C. 1491. **the third.** Ex 12:2, 6. Le 23:16-18. **came.** Ex 16:1. Nu 33:15.

2. **Rephidim.** Ex *17:1, 8. **camped.** Ex *3:1, 12. 18:5. Ac 7:30, 38. Ga 4:24.

3. **went up.** Ex 20:21. 24:15-18. 34:2. Dt 5:5-31. Ac 7:38. **called.** Ex 3:4.

4. **seen.** Ex 7-14. Dt 4:9, 33-36. 29:2. Is *63:9. **I bare you.** Dt *32:11, 12. Is 40:31. *63:9. Mt *23:37. Re 12:14. **eagles'.** Dt 28:49. 2 S 1:23. Jb 9:26. Ps 103:5.

5. **if ye.** Ex 23:22. 24:7. Ge +4:7. Dt 11:27. 28:1. Jsh 24:24. 1 S 15:22. Is 1:19. Je 7:23. 11:4-7. He 11:8. **keep.** Dt 5:2. Ps 25:10. 103:17, 18. Is 56:4. Je 31:31-33. **covenant.** Ge *12:1-3. *17:1-14. Dt *29:9. Mt ◑26:28. Ga 4:24. He 8:9. **a peculiar.** Le 20:26. *26:12. Dt 4:20. *7:6. *14:2, 21. *26:18. 32:8, 9, +*43. 1 K 8:53. Ps *135:4. Ec 2:8. SS 8:12. Is 41:8. 43:1. Je 10:16. Ml *3:17. Ac 20:28. 1 C 6:20. 7:23. Ep 1:14. T *2:14. 1 P *2:9. **treasure.** 1 Ch 29:3. Ml 3:17. **above all people.** Dt *10:15. Ro 11:28, 29. **all the earth.** Ex 9:29. Dt 10:14. Jb 41:11. Ps *24:1. *50:12. Da 4:34, 35. 1 C 10:26, 28.

6. **a kingdom of.** Ex 15:16. Dt 7:6. 14:2. 26:18. *33:2-4. Ps 122:5. *148:14. Pr 25:5. Is 61:6. *66:21. Ro 12:1. T 2:14. 1 P *2:5, ▶9. Re +*1:5, 6. +*5:9, 10. +*20:6. ʃ29. Antiptosis; or, Exchange of Cases B507. The governing noun becomes the adjective instead of the noun in regimen. Here, "a kingdom of priests" denotes "a royal priesthood." For other instances of this figure see Ps 1:1. Mt 13:5. Lk 1:48, 55. 5:9. Ro 2:4. 5:17. 1 C 1:17, 21. 14:12mg. 2 C 8:8. Ga 3:14. 4:4. Ep 1:7, 18. 4:29. Col 1:27. 1 Th 1:3. He 6:17. 9:15. 10:5. 1 P 3:20. Re 1:5, 6. **and an holy nation.** Le *10:3. 11:44, 45. 19:2. *20:24, 26. 21:7, 8, 23. Dt 7:6. 14:2, 21. 26:19. 28:9. Ps *93:5. Is +*60:21. *62:12. 1 C *3:17. 1 Th 5:27. 1 P 1:15, 16. 2:5, 9.

7. **the elders.** See on Ex 3:16. **and laid.** Ex 4:29, 30. 1 C 15:1.

8. **answered.** Ex 20:19. 24:3, 7. Dt *5:27-29. *26:17-19. Jsh 24:24. Ne 10:29. **returned.** Ge 37:14. Dt 1:32, 35. Jsh 22:32. Jg 11:11n. 1 S 8:21.

9. **Lo.** ver. 16. Ex 20:21. *24:15, 16. Dt 4:11. 1 K 8:12. 2 Ch 6:1. Ps *18:11, 12. 97:2. Is 19:1. Mt 17:5. Mk 9:7. Lk 9:34, 35. Re 1:7. **thick cloud.** Ex 40:34. Le 16:2. Nu 9:15. 1 K 8:10, 11. 2 Ch 5:13, 14. 7:2. Ps 18:11. 104:3. Is 6:4. 19:1. 29:6. Hg 2:7, 9. Mt *17:5. Re 10:1. 15:8. **that the.** Dt 4:12, 36. Jn 12:29, 30. **believe.** Ex 14:31. 2 Ch +*20:20. Is 7:9. Lk 10:16. **for ever.** Heb. *olam*, Ex +12:24.

10. **sanctify.** ver. 15. Le 11:44, 45. *19:2. Jsh *3:5. *7:13. 1 S 16:5. 2 Ch 29:5, 34. 30:17-19. Jb 1:5. 1 C 6:11. **wash.** ver. 14. Ge *35:2. Le 11:25. 15:5. Nu 8:7, 21. 31:24. Zc 3:3, 4. He *10:22. *12:28, 29. Re 7:14.

11. **the Lord.** ver. 16, 18, 20. Ex 3:8. 34:5. Nu 11:17. Dt +*33:2. Ps 18:9. 144:5. Is 64:1, 2. Hab *3:3-6. Jn *3:13. 6:38.

12. **set bounds.** ver. 21, 23. Jsh 3:4. **Take.** Ex 10:28. 34:12. Dt 2:4. 4:9. **or touch.** He ▶12:20, 21. **surely.** ʃ147B, Ge +2:16. Ro *3:20.

13. **shall not.** He *12:18, 19. **surely.** ʃ147B, Ge +2:16. **shot.** 1 S 20:36, 37. Ps 11:2. **whether.** Ex 21:28, 29. Le 20:15, 16. **when the trumpet.** *or*, cornet. ver. 16, 19. 1 C 15:52. 1 Th *4:16.

14. **and sanctified.** See on ver. 10.

15. **be ready.** Am *4:12. Ml 3:2. Mt 3:10-12. 24:44. 2 P 3:11, 12. **the third.** ver. 11, 16. Ex +10:22. Zc 6:3. **come not.** 1 S 21:4, 5. Jl *2:16. Zc 7:3. 12:12-14. 1 C *7:5. ʃ88. Euphemism, Ge +17:11. Ge 20:6. 26:29. Ru 2:9. Pr 6:29.

16. **thunders.** Ex 9:23, 28, 29. 20:18. 1 S 12:17, 18. Jb 37:1-5. 38:25. Ps 18:11-14. 29:3-11. 50:3. 77:18. 97:4. He 12:18, 19. Re *4:5. *8:5. *11:19. **thick.** See

on ver. 9, 40:34. 2 Ch 5:14. **voice**. Re 1:10. 4:1. **trumpet**. Mt 16:27. 25:31. 1 Th *3:13. *4:16. **all the people**. Je 5:22. He *12:21.

17. **Moses brought**. Dt 4:10. 5:5. **nether**. Dt +32:22. **meet with**. Dt 4:7. Ps 73:28. 145:18. Is 55:6. Jn 14:6. Ep 3:12. He 4:16. 7:19, 25. 10:19, 22. 11:6. Ja 4:8.

18. **mount Sinai**. See on ver. 13. Ex 20:18. Dt *4:11, 12. 5:22. *33:2. Jg *5:5. Ps *68:7, 8. 104:32. 144:5. Is *6:4. Hab *3:3. Re *15:8. **in fire**. Ex 3:2. *24:17. 2 Ch *7:1-3. Je *23:29. 2 Th *1:8. He 12:18-20. 2 P 3:10. **as the smoke**. Ge *15:17. 19:28. Ps *144:5. Re 15:8. **whole mount**. 1 K 19:11, 12. Ps 18:7-13. 68:8. 77:18. 114:7. Je 4:24. Na 1:5, 6. Hab 3:10. Zc 14:5. Mt 24:7. He *12:26. **quaked**. ♪155D, Ge +4:10.

19. **And when**. ver. 13, 16. **Moses**. He 12:21. **God**. Ps 81:7.

20. **the Lord came**. See on ver. 11. Ne 9:13. Ps 81:7. **Moses went up**. ver. 3. Ex 24:12, 13, 18. 34:2, 4. Dt 9:9.

21. **charge**. Heb. contest or, protest. ver. 12, 13, 23. Ex 21:29. Ge 43:3. Dt 4:26. 8:19. 30:19. 31:28. 32:46. Je 32:25. Am 3:13. **break**. Ex 3:3, 5. 33:20. 1 S *6:19. Ec 5:1. He 12:28, 29.

22. **the priests**. Ex 24:5. Le 10:1-3. Is 52:11. **sanctify**. See on ver. 5, 14, 15. **break**. 2 S *6:6-8. 1 Ch 13:9-11. 15:13. 2 Ch 30:3, 15, 18, 19. Ac 5:5, 10. 1 C 11:30-32.

23. **Set bounds**. ver. 12. Jsh *3:4, 5.

24. **and thou**. See on ver. 20. **but let**. See on ver. 12, 21. Mt 11:12. Lk 13:24. 16:16. Jn 1:17. He 4:16. 10:19-22. 12:18-25, 29. **lest**. See on ver. 22. Ro 4:15. 2 C 3:7-9. Ga 3:10, 11, 19-22.

25. **went down**. ver. 24. Je 26:2. Ac 20:20, 27.

EXODUS 20

The ten commandments are spoken in an audible voice, by Jehovah, to the whole congregation of Israel, 1-17. The people are alarmed, and confer with Moses, 18-20. Moses receives from God an additional prohibition of idolatry, and rules for erecting an altar, 21-26.

1. **God spake**. Dt 4:33, 36. 5:4, *22. Ac 7:38, 53.

2. **I am**. Ex ◐32:7. ◐33:1. Dt *5:6. Ps *81:10. **the Lord**. Ex +15:26. Ge 17:7, 8. Le 26:1, 13. Dt 5:6. 6:4, 5. 2 Ch 28:5. Ps 50:7. 81:10. Je 31:1, 33. Ho *13:4. Ro 3:29. 10:12. **brought**. Ex ch. 10-15. Le 19:36. 23:43. **out of the**. Ex 13:3. Dt 5:15. 7:8. 13:10. 15:15. 26:6-8. **bondage**. Heb. servants. Ex 13:3mg, 14mg.

3. **The First Commandment. Thou shalt have no other gods before me**. **shalt**. lit. wilt. ♪96C10, Jg +5:21. Heterosis of Tenses: The future for the imperative B523. The future of the Indicative is by Hebrew idiom frequently used for the Imperative. When this is the case, the Imperative is very forcible and emphatic; not being so much a mere command as the assertion of a fact which could hardly be otherwise. All the ten commandments are in this form. **have no other**. ver. 23. Ex 15:11. 34:14. Dt *5:7. 6:5, *14. +*18:10. Jsh 24:18-24. 2 K *17:29-35. *19:17, 18. Ps 29:2. 73:25. 81:9. Is 26:4. 43:10. 44:8. 45:21, 22. 46:9. Je *25:6. *35:15. Ho 13:4. Hab 1:11. Mt *4:10. 6:24. Lk 16:13. 1 C 8:4, 6. Ep 5:5. Ph 3:19. Col 2:18. *3:5. 1 J 5:20, 21. Re 19:10. 22:9. **before**. or, beside. Heb. against my face, or presence. ver. 20, with me. Ge

31:50. Dt 19:19. 1 C *8:5. Ep *4:6. He 3:12. Ja *4:4.

4. **The Second Commandment. Thou shalt not make unto thee any graven image**. ver. 23. Ex 23:24. 32:1, 8, 23. 34:13, 17. Le 19:4. 26:1. Nu *33:52. Dt 4:15-19, 23-25, +28. *5:8. 7:5, 25. 12:2, 31. *17:2-6. *27:15. 1 K 12:28. 21:26. 2 Ch 15:8. 33:7. Ps *97:7. 115:4-8. 135:15-18. Is 30:22. 40:18-20. 41:24. 42:8, 17. 44:9-20. 45:16. 46:5-8. Je 10:3-5, 8, 9, 14-16. 44:4. Ezk 8:10. +*14:3. Jn 4:24. Ac 14:15. 15:20. *17:29. 19:26-35. Ro 1:23, 25. 2:22. 1 C 5:11. 6:9, 10. 10:7, *14. 2 C *6:16. Ga 5:20. Ep *5:5. 1 P 4:3. 1 J *5:21. Re 9:20. 13:14, 15. 14:9-11. 16:2. +*21:8. *22:15. **graven**. Jg 17:3. 2 K 21:7. Ps 97:7. Is 40:19. 1 C 8:4. **image**. Le 26:1. Dt 4:16, 23, 25. 5:8. *27:15. Jg 17:3. Compare the use of the verb to grave in Ex 34:1, 4. Dt 10:1, 3. 1 K 5:18. Hab *2:18. **likeness**. Nu 12:8 (similitude). Dt 4:12, 15, 16, 23. *5:8. Jb 4:16. Ps *17:15. Young (*Concise Critical Comments*) states "The prohibition is not against making statues or pictures of any object for ornament, (witness the *cherub* work in the tabernacle, Ex 25:18-20; compare Ex 25:34; 26:32; Nu 41:8, 9; the *twelve oxen*, 1 K 7:25; the *fourteen lions*, 1 K 10:20; the *brazen serpent*, Nu 21:9, etc.); but for *religious adoration*, as the next verse explicitly shows." **earth**. Ph 2:9, 10. Col 3:5.

5. **not bow down**. Ex *23:24. *34:14. Le 26:1. Jsh 23:7, 16. Jg 2:19. 2 K 17:35, 41. 2 Ch 25:14. Is 44:15, 19. Mt 4:9. **nor serve**. Ex 3:12. Ge 35:2. 2 K 10:18. Is 19:21. Je 44:3. 1 C 10:20. 1 J 5:21. **for I**. Ex 34:14. Dt *4:24. 6:15. 32:21. Jsh *24:19. Ps 78:58. Pr 6:34, 35. Is *48:11. Ezk 8:3. Da 1:2. Na 1:2. 1 C 10:22. **Lord thy God**. Ex +15:26. **jealous**. Nu 25:11. Mt 4:10. ♪22B. Anthropomorphism B883. Jealousy is attributed to God. For other instances of this figure see Nu 25:11. Dt 32:16, 21. 1 K 14:22. Ezk 8:3. Jl 2:18. Zc 1:14. **God**. Heb. *El*, Ex +15:2. **visiting**. T#246. Ex 34:7. Ge 9:25. Le *20:5. *26:29, 39, 40. Nu *14:18, 33. 1 S +3:13 (T#497), +*14. 15:2, 3. 2 S 21:1, 6. 1 K *21:29. 2 K 23:26. Jb 5:4. *21:19. Ps *79:8. 109:14. Pr *13:21. +*17:13. Is *14:20, 21. ◐+*24:21mg, 22. *65:6, 7. Je *2:9. +11:22mg. 31:29. 32:18. Ezk 18:1-4. Da 9:6. Ml 4:5, 6. Mt 23:34-36. Young argues a better rendering would be "charging," and states "the original word *never* means *to visit*, i.e. *come to see*, though it is so translated several hundreds of times in the A.V.; it always has the idea of *looking over*, *looking after*, *inspecting*, *examining*; and is sometimes used causitively, *to set, appoint, lay a charge* upon anyone. 'Those hating me,' refer to the *children*, not to the *parents*. The vulgar interpretation is directly opposed to Dt 24:16. 2 K 14:5, 6. (Ex 32:33); compare Ge 18:25; Le 26:39, 40; Je 31:29, 30; Ezk 18:20-24." **of them**. Dt 5:9. 7:10. 32:41. Ps 81:15. Pr 8:36. Jn 7:7. 15:18, 23, 24. Ro 1:30. 8:7. Ja *4:4.

6. **showing mercy**. or, doing kindness. Dt 4:37. 5:10, 29. *7:9. Ps *89:34. Je 32:39, 40. Mi *7:18. Jn *14:21. Ac 2:39. Ro *11:28, 29. **love me**. Jn 14:15, 21. 1 C +*2:9. 1 J 4:19. 5:3. 2 J 6. **keep**. Ec 12:13.

7. **The Third Commandment. Thou shalt not take the name of the Lord thy God in vain**. **take**. T#718. Ex ◐+*22:11. *23:1h. Ge ◐+22:16. Le 18:21. 19:+8, 11, *12. 20:3. +*21:6. *24:11-16. Nu 23:7h. Dt *5:11. ◐+*6:13. 23:21-23. Jg 11:35. 2 S √12:14. 1 K ◐17:1. ◐22:14. Jb 27:1h. Ps +*15:4. 50:14-16. 74:10. 81:3h. *139:20. Pr 30:8, 9. Ec 5:4-6. Is 29:13. 48:11. Je 4:2. 23:10. 34:16. Ezk 20:9. 36:21. Ho 4:2. Zc 5:3. Mt *5:33-

37. 23:16-22. 26:63, 64. Ro +*2:24. 2 C 1:23. 11:31. Col +√4:5. 1 Th ◑+2:5. 1 T *6:1. He 6:16, 17. Ja 2:7. 5:12. Re ◑10:5. 13:6. 16:9. **the name.** Ps +√9:10. Lk 1:49. **Lord.** Ex +15:26. **vain.** or, for vanity or falsehood. Ps 12:2h. 41:6h. 139:20. Is 59:4. **not hold.** lit. make. ∫121I2, Ge +2:17. Metonymy of the Subject B570: verbs. Where the action is put for the declaration concerning it. Here, *make* is put for declare or pronounce, or "hold," as rendered in the A.V. ∫175B, Ge +21:16. **guiltless.** Ex 34:7. Le 24:16, 23. Dt 23:21-23. Jsh 2:12, 17. 9:20. 2 S 21:1, 2. 1 K 2:9. Jb 9:28. *10:14. Ps 19:13. Je 30:11. Ezk 17:13-19. Zc 5:3, 4. or, declare innocent. Nu 14:18. Dt 5:11. Je 46:28. 49:12. Na 1:3.

8. The Fourth Commandment. **Remember the sabbath day, to keep it holy.** The Fourth Commandment is an example of ∫52C. Complex Correspondence B380, a literary structure combining alternation and introversion. (A) 8. The Sabbath day to be kept in remembrance by man. (B. a.) 9. The six days for man's work. (b) 10. The seventh day for man's rest. (B. a.) 11. The six days for Jehovah's work. (b) 11. The seventh day for Jehovah's rest. (A) 11. The Sabbath day blessed and hallowed by Jehovah. As this figure represents greater complexity than the format of the *Treasury* permits to be displayed in a note, see either the *Companion Bible* margins or *Figures of Speech Used in the Bible* (B380) for illustrations of this figure. Other instances of this figure noted by EWB in B are Ps ch. 39, 84, 105, 144, 148. Mk 3:21-25. **Remember.** Ex 13:3. 16:23-30. *31:13, 14. Ge *2:2, 3. Le *19:3, 30. *23:3. 26:2. Dt *5:12, 13. 2 K 4:22, 23 w He 10:25. Ne *8:9, 10. Is 1:13. 56:2, 4-6. +*58:13n. Je *17:27. La 2:6. Ezk 20:12, 13, 16, 21. 22:8, 26. 23:38. 44:24. 46:3. Ho 2:11. Mk ◑2:27, 28. Lk 4:16. ◑6:5. *13:14n. 14:1. Jn ◑20:1. Ac ◑20:7. Col ◑2:16n. lit. To remember. ∫96B. Heterosis of Moods B516: Infinitive for Imperative. For other instances of this figure see Jsh 1:13. Jb 32:10. Ps 17:5. 22:8. Is 32:11. Je 2:2. Lk 9:3. Ro 12:15. Ph 3:16. **the sabbath.** T#638. Dt 5:14. Ne 13:15-18. Ezk 44:24.

9. **Six days.** Ex *23:12. Le 23:3. Dt 5:13. Lk *13:14-16. **labor.** Ge *3:19. Ro *12:11. Ep *4:28. 2 Th *3:8-10.

10. **the seventh.** Ex *31:13. *34:21. Le *23:3. **sabbath.** Ex *16:26. Ezk *20:12. Jn 7:23. **thou shalt.** Ex 16:23, 27-29. *34:21. *35:2, 3. Le *23:7. Nu *15:32-36. Ne 10:31. *13:15-17, 19. Je *17:21. Am +*8:5. Mt 24:20. Lk 23:56. **any work.** ∫171C. Synecdoche of the Genus B618. Where the genus is put for the species; or universals for particulars. A universal negative does not deny particularly. Here, not do work that is specifically forbidden, such as servile or mechanical work (Le 23:7, 8. Nu 28:18). For a listing of related figures, see Ge 24:10n. For other instances of this figure see 1 S 20:26. Je 8:6. Mt 5:34. 10:26. Jn 3:32. 15:5. 18:20. Ac 27:33. 2 Th 3:11. 1 T 6:3, *4. **thy manservant.** Le 25:6, 7. Dt 5:14, 15. **thy stranger.** Ex 12:48, 49. 22:21. 23:9-12. Ge 17:12, 13, 23. Le 19:33, 34. 22:25. Nu 15:14-16, 26, 29, 30. Dt 16:11, 12. 24:14-22. Ne 10:31. 13:15-21. **within.** Ex 16:29. Dt 5:14. **thy gates.** i.e. cities, or even the gates of a private dwelling (Dt 6:9). ∫171S6, Ge +14:7. Ge +14:7. Dt 12:12. 14:27. 17:2. 1 K 8:37h. 2 Ch 6:28mg.

11. **six days.** T#140. Ex *31:17. Ge 2:1-4. Ps 95:4-7. Mk 2:27, 28. Jn 20:19, 26. Ac 20:7. 1 C 16:2. He

4:2-5, 9-11. Re 1:10. **made.** Ge ◑2:2. Ac 4:24. 14:15. Re 10:6. 14:7. **seventh.** Ex 12:15 w Dt 16:8. Le 16:29. 23:32. He 4:4. **sabbath.** T#637. ver. +8. Ge 2:2, 3. **hallowed it.** Le 22:32. Dt 5:12. Je 17:20-27. Ezk 20:20. 44:24. Mt 6:9. Lk 11:2.

12. The Fifth Commandment. **Honor thy father and thy mother. Honor.** Ex 21:15, 17. 22:28. Ge 9:22, 23. Le 19:3, 32. *20:9n. Dt *5:16. 21:18-21. 27:16. 1 K 2:19. 2 K 2:12. 5:13. 13:14. Pr 1:8, 9. 6:20. 15:5. 19:26. 20:20. 23:22-25. 28:24. 30:11, 17. Is 3:5. Je 35:18, 19. Ezk 22:7. Ml 1:6. Mt 15:♪4-6. 19:♪19. Mk 7:♪10-12. ♪10:19. 12:17. Lk 2:51. ♪18:20. Jn 19:26. Ro 1:30. 13:7. Ep 5:21. +√6:1, ♪2, 3. Col +*3:20, 21. 1 T 5:1, 2, 4, 17. 6:1, 2. 2 T 3:2. T 1:6. He 13:7. 1 P 2:17. 3:1-7. 5:5, 6. Ju 8. Heb. make heavy, but always in a figurative sense. 1 S 15:30. Ps 22:23 (glorify). Pr 3:9. Is 24:15 (glorify). S#3513h, 1 S +2:30. Young suggests such honor includes reverence, love, obedience, and support. ∫171K2, Ex +23:2. By this figure, the command applies also to all who stand in the place of parents, thus all who legitimately have the rule over us. **father and mother.** Ex 21:15, 17. Le *19:3. 20:9. Dt *21:18-21. Pr 10:1. 15:20. 17:25. 19:26. 20:20. 23:22, 24, 25. 28:24. 30:11, *17. Ml 1:6. Ep 6:2. He 12:9. **that thy days.** Dt 4:26, 40. 5:16, 33. 6:2. 11:9. 17:20. 25:15. 32:47. Pr 3:16. Je *35:18, 19. Ep ♪6:3. **long.** ✱S#748h. Ge 26:8. Ex 20:12. Nu 9:19 (tarried long; mg, prolonged), 22. Dt 4:26 (prolong), 40. 5:16, 62. 11:9. 17:20. 25:15 (lengthened). 30:18. 32:47. Jsh 24:31 (overlived; mg, prolonged). Jg 2:7 (outlived; mg, prolonged). 1 K 3:14 (lengthen). 8:8 (drew out). 2 Ch 5:9 (drew out). Jb 6:11. Ps 129:3 (made long). Pr 19:11 (deferreth). 28:2, 16. Ec 7:15. 8: 12, 13. Is 48:9 (defer). 53:10. 54:2 (lengthen). 57:4 (draw out). Ezk 12:22. 31:5 (became long). **land.** Ps 115:16.

13. The Sixth Commandment. **Thou shalt not kill.** or, murder. Ex 21:12, 14, 20, 29. 22:2, 3. Ge *4:8-15, 23. ◑*9:5, 6. 27:41, 45. 49:6. Le 24:17, 21. Nu 35:16-21, 31-34. ◑35:6, 11, 12, 15-31. Dt 4:42. *5:17. 19:11-13. 21:1-9. ◑22:26. 2 S *12:9, 10. 1 K 2:5, 6. 2 K 21:16. 2 Ch 24:22. Ps 10:8-11. *51:14. Pr 1:11, 18. 28:17. Is 1:15. 26:21. Je 26:15. Mt 5:♪21, 22. *15:19. ♪19:18. Mk ♪10:19. Lk ♪18:20. Jn *8:44. Ac 3:15. 28:4. Ro ♪13:9. Ga 5:21. 1 T 1:9. Ja 2:♪11, 13. 4:1, 2. 1 P *4:15. 1 J *3:12-15. Re 16:6. 17:6. *21:8. *22:15.

14. The Seventh Commandment. **Thou shalt not commit adultery.** Ge 39:9. Le 18:20. 19:29. 20:10. Dt *5:18. 22:21-24. 2 S 11:4, 5, 27. *12:9-11. Jb 24:15. 31:1, 9, 10. Ps 50:18. Pr 2:15-18. 5:15-20. 6:24-35. 7:18-27. *22:14. *31:3. Je *5:8, 9. 7:9. 13:27. 23:14. 29:22, 23. Ezk 18:6, 11, 15. 22:9-11. Ho *4:11. Ml +*3:5. Mt *5:♪27, 28. *19:9, ♪18. Mk 10:11, 12, ♪19. Lk ♪18:20. Jn 8:3-11. Ro 1:24-29. 7:2, 3. 13:♪9. 1 C 6:9-11, 18. 7:4. 2 C 11:2. Ga *5:19, 20. Ep *5:3-5. Col 3:5. 1 Th *4:3-7. He *13:4. Ja ♪2:11. 4:4. 2 P *2:14, 18. Ju 7, 10. Re 2:20-22. 17:1-5. +*21:8. 22:15.

15. The Eighth Commandment. **Thou shalt not steal.** Ex 21:16. *22:1-5, 7-13. Le 6:1-7. +*19:11, 13, 35-37. 25:17. Dt *5:19. 19:14. 23:24, 25. 24:7. 25:13-16. 27:17. Jsh *7:24, 25. Jb 20:19-22. 24:2. Ps 37:21. 50:18. *62:10. Pr 1:13-15. *3:27. 6:30, 31. 11:1. 16:11. 20:10, 23. *22:22, 28. 23:10. *28:24. *29:24. *30:8, 9. Is 1:23. 61:8. Je 5:26-29. 7:8-11. 22:13. Ezk *33:15. 45:10. Ho 4:2. 12:7. Am 3:10. 5:11, 12. 8:4-6. Mi 6:10, 11. 7:3. Zc +*5:3, 4. Ml 3:5, 8. Mt 15:19. ♪19:18. 21:13. 22:21. 23:14, 25. Mk 7:22. ♪10:19. 11:17. 12:17,

*40. Lk 3:13, 14. 18:11, ▶20. 19:+*8, 46. 20:25, *47. Jn 12:6. Ro 2:21. 13:7, ▶9. 1 C 5:11. √6:10. Ep *4:28. Col +*4:1. 1 Th 4:6. 1 T 1:10. T *2:10. Ja +*5:4. 1 P 4:15. Re 9:21. Under this commandment A. C. Price observes "In one sense this Commandment would cover also breaches of all the other Commandments, for every violation of duty to God or man is really robbing them of what is their due, but the reference here is clearly to what we know as theft, i.e. the wrongful acquisition of the property of some other person. It is not however always recognized how much even in this narrower sense it involves. We are apt...to neglect...the perversion of character and moral blindness from which it springs, for thefts are included by Christ among the evil things which 'proceed from the heart' (Mk 7:21, 22)." "We forget also that law is only an imperfect embodiment of morality, and tend to regard all that is not punishable by law as morally justifiable. For the Christian at any rate the Commandment must be interpreted by the Law of Love (Mt 7:12), and the gist of it seems to be that he should himself be thoroughly honest in heart, that honesty should characterize all his dealings with others, and that to enrich himself by taking advantage of the weakness or necessities or ignorance of others is a sin in the sight of God." "...it is hard to see how the teaching of Christ can be made to square with such things as the confiscations that have been the scandal of most revolutions, ...the 'bearing' and 'bulling' on the Stock Exchange, ...the extortion of enormous rents when there is dearth of accommodation; nor how any nation is entitled to be called Christian in which inferior goods are foisted on poor or ignorant purchasers and *caveat emptor* is regarded as a legitimate basis for business transactions, or employees are 'sweated' by their employers, or workmen cannot be trusted to do their best unless under the eye of a master. As to the last point it may be noticed how stress is constantly laid in the Bible on diligence, both in religious matters (Ex +*15:26), and also generally (Pr +*10:4); and as to idleness (Pr +*18:9), to which we may add the parables of the Talents (Mt 25:14, etc.) and the Pounds (Lk 19:12, etc.), and the references to the continual work of God and Christ (Jn 5:17; 9:4) and to Paul's labor both religious and manual (Ac +*18:3)" (*Biblical Studies*, pp. 147, 148). **steal.** Young notes "The primary idea of the original word is, to do a thing secretly, as in Ge 31:27; 40:15; 2 S 15:6; 19:3, 41; Jb 4:12; 21:18; 27:20." ❋S#1589h: Ge 30:33. 31:19, 20, 26, 27, 30, 32, 39. 40:15. 44:8. Ex 20:15. 21:16. 22:1, 7, 12. Le 19:11. Dt 5:19. Jsh 7:11. 2 S 15:6. 19:3, 3, 41. 21:12. 2 K 11:2. 2 Ch 22:11. Jb 4:12 (secretly brought; mg, by stealth). 21:18 (carried away; mg, stealeth away). 27:20. Pr 6:30. 9:17. +30:9 (T#1712). Je 7:9. Ho 4:2. Ob 5. Zc *5:3.

16. The Ninth Commandment. **Thou shalt not bear false witness. false.** Ex 23:1, 6, 7. Le 19:11, 16. Dt *5:20. √19:15-21. 1 S 22:8-19. 1 K 21:10-13. Ps *15:3. 27:12. 50:20. 52:2-4. *101:5-7. Pr 6:19. 10:18. 11:13. 12:17. 14:5. 18:8. 19:5, 9. 20:19. 25:18, 23. 26:20-22. Is 59:3, 4. Je 9:4. Ezk 22:9. Mt 5:11. ▶19:18. 26:59, 60. Mk ▶10:19. Lk 3:14. ▶18:20. Ac 6:13. Ro 1:30. ▶13:9. 1 C 6:10. Ep 4:31. Col 3:9. 1 T 1:10. 3:11. 2 T 3:3. T 2:3. Ja 4:11. 1 P 2:1. 4:14. 2 P 2:10, 11. Re 12:10. 22:15. **witness.** Dt 17:6. 19:15. Ru 4:9-11. Is 8:2. Mk 14:55, 56. **neighbor.** Le 19:18. Dt 5:20. Ep 4:25.

17. The Tenth Commandment. **Thou shalt not covet.** Ge 3:6. 14:23. 34:23. Dt *5:21. Jsh 7:21. 1 S 15:19. 1 K 21:6-16. 2 K 5:20. Jb 31:24, 28. Ps +*10:3. 119:36. Pr 21:25, 26. 23:4, 5. Ec 4:8. 5:10, 11. Is 5:8. 33:15. 56:11. 57:17. Je 22:17. Ezk +*33:31. Am 2:6, 7. Mi 2:2. Hab *2:9. Mt 6:19-24. 13:22. 16:26. Mk 7:21-23. Lk +*12:15. 16:14. Jn 12:6. Ac *20:33. Ro ▶7:7. ▶13:9. 1 C 5:10, 11. 6:10. Ep *5:3, 5. Ph 3:19. Col +*3:5. 1 T +*6:6-10. 2 T 3:2. He *13:5. Ja *4:1, 2. 1 P 5:2. 2 P 2:14, 15. 1 J *2:16. or, desire. ❋S#2530h. Ge 2:9 (pleasant). 3:6. Ex 20:17, 17. 34:24. Dt 5:21. 7:25. Jsh 7:21. Jb 20:20. Ps 19:10. 39:11mg. 68:16. Pr 1:22 (delight). 6:25 (lust). 12:12. 21:20. SS 2:3. Is 1:29. 44:9 (delectable; mg, desirable). 53:2. Mi 2:2. **neighbor's wife.** 2 S 11:2-4. Jb 31:1, 9. Pr 4:23. *6:24, 25, 27-29. Je 5:8. Mt *5:28. Ja 1:14, 15. 2 P 2:14. **nor anything that is thy neighbor's.** Mt 20:15. Ac 5:4. 2 Th 3:12. There is difference of opinion and practice in counting and dividing the ten commandments. That there are expressly ten commandments (Heb. words) is stated at Ex 34:28; Dt 4:13; 10:4. This tenth commandment is sometimes made into two, the clause regarding coveting thy neighbor's wife being made the tenth. Some who arbitrarily choose to make the division here eliminate commandment number two, "Thou shalt not make unto thee any graven image," for the second commandment is an embarrassment to their own unscriptural practice of 'venerating' images in religious worship. Clearly, the first commandment forbids polytheism; the second forbids idolatry. This tenth commandment is never cited in the New Testament as two separate commandments. If one counts the separate prohibitions it contains, there are eight separate prohibitions, prohibitions against inordinate, unrestrained, desire for a neighbor's (1) house, (2) wife, (3) manservant, (4) maidservant, (5) ox, (6) ass, (7) anything else of his, (8) or (see Dt 5:21) his field. Why should a division be made for a separately enumerated commandment at the clause regarding coveting thy neighbor's wife? The first and second commandments are not cited as such in the New Testament. Their subject matter is not always considered separately, for the subject of polytheism is found at Mt 4:10 and Ac 17:23, 24, 25; 1 C 8:5, 6; the subject of idolatry is found at Ac 17:29; 1 C 8:4; 10:7, 14, 19, 20; 1 J 5:21. There does not appear in this listing any reason why the tenth commandment should be enumerated as two, and the second commandment combined with the first, as some have done, particularly when the probable motive for doing so is considered.

18. **And all.** Ex 19:16-18. See on Dt 4:10, 11, 36. 5:22, 23. **saw.** Ge 42:1. Is 44:16. Je 33:24. He *12:18. ƒ171J15, Ge +42:1. ƒ180D. Synezeugmenon; or, Joint Yoke B135: when the verb is joined to more than two clauses, each of which would require its own proper verb in order to complete the sense. Here, the verb "saw" is appropriate to the "lightnings" and "mountain." By the omission of the second verb "heard" we are informed that the people were impressed by what they saw, rather than by what they heard. For other instances of this figure see Ps ch. 15. Ep 4:31. Ph 3:10. **smoking.** Ge 15:17. **they removed.** Ps 139:7, 8. Je 23:23, 24. or, were moved (with fear). Is 7:2. 19:1. Ro 4:15. **afar.** Ep ◐2:13.

19. **Speak thou.** T#1619. Dt *5:5, 23-28. *18:15, 16. Ac 7:38. Ga *3:19, 20. 1 T *2:5. He =1:2. 12:18,

19. **let not God**. Ex 33:20. Ge 32:30. Dt 5:24, 25, 26. He 12:19.

20. **Fear not**. Ex 14:13. 1 S 12:20, 24. Is *41:10, 13. **prove**. Ex 15:25, 26. 16:4. Ge 22:1, 12. Dt *8:2, 16. *13:3. Jg 3:1. **his fear**. Ge 20:11. 42:18. Dt 4:10. 6:2, 24. 10:12. 17:13, 19. *28:58. Jsh 24:14. Ne *5:15. Jb 28:28. Pr 1:7. *3:7. *16:6. Is *8:13. Je 32:39, 40. Mt +*10:28. He 12:28.

21. **the people**. Ex *19:16, 17. Dt *5:5. **thick**. Ex 19:16. Dt 5:22. 2 S 22:10, 12. 1 K 8:12. 2 Ch 6:1. Ps 18:9, 11. 97:2. 104:2. 1 T 6:16. **darkness**. Jb +38:9.

22. **said**. Ex 33:1. **I have talked**. Dt 4:36. 5:24, 26. Nu 12:8. Ne *9:13. He *12:25, 26.

23. **shall not make**. ver. 3-5. See on Ex *32:1-4. 1 S 5:4, 5. 2 K *17:33, 41. Je *7:9, 10. Ezk *20:39. 43:8. Da *5:4, 23. Zp 1:5. 1 C 10:21, 22. 2 C *6:14-16. Col 2:18, 19. 1 J 5:20, 21. Re 22:15. **silver**. Dt 29:17. Ac 17:29.

24. **altar**. Ex 27:1-8. 2 K 5:17. Jn 4:24. Ro 10:6-9. **burnt offerings**. Ex 10:25. 18:12. Le ch. 1, 3. 6:9. +*23:12. Jb 1:5. **peace offerings**. Ex 24:5. Le +*23:19. **in all places**. Dt *12:5, 11, 21. 14:23. 16:5, 6, 11. 26:2. 1 K *8:29, 43. *9:3. 2 Ch *6:6. *7:16. 12:13. Ezr 6:12. Ne 1:9. Ps *74:7. 76:2. 78:68. 132:13, 14. Je 7:10-12. Ml 1:11. Mt *18:20. 28:20. Jn *4:20-23. 1 T 2:8. **will bless thee**. Ge 12:2. Nu 6:24:27. Dt *7:13. 2 S 6:12. Ps 128:5. 134:3.

25. **And**. Dt *27:5, 6. Jsh *8:30, 31. **building it of hewn stone**. Heb. build them with hewing. 1 K 5:17. Ro=4:4, 5. 1 C=1:17. **lift up**. 2 K 5:11mg.

26. **by steps**. Ph=3:3. **thy nakedness**. Ex 28:42, 43. Le 10:3. Ps 89:7. Ec 5:1. He 12:28, 29. 1 P 1:16.

EXODUS 21

Laws concerning the release or detention of Hebrew slaves, 1-6; the treatment of female slaves, 7-11; murder, manslaughter, smiting or cursing parents, manstealing, maiming any person, killing or wounding a slave, hurting women with child, and other injuries, 12-27; mischiefs by cattle, and by pits, 28-36.

1. **the judgments**. Le 18:5, 26. 19:37. 20:22. Nu 35:24. 36:13. Dt 5:1, 31. *6:20. 1 K 6:12. 2 Ch 19:10. Ne 9:13, 14. 10:29. Ps 147:19. Ezk 20:11, 25. Ml 4:4. **which**. Ex 19:7. *24:3, 4. Dt 4:5, 8, *14, 45. 6:20. Mt 28:20. 1 Th 4:1, 2.

2. **buy**. T#677-2. Le *25:39-43. Dt *15:12-18. 2 K 4:1. Ne 5:2, 5. **an Hebrew**. Ex 12:44. 22:3. Ge 37:28, 36. Le 25:39-41, 44. 2 K 4:1. Ne 5:1-5, 8. Mt 18:25. Ro *6:17, 18. 1 C *6:20. **and in the**. Le 25:40-43, 45. Dt 15:1, 12-15, 18. 31:10. Je *34:8-17. Ga *5:1.

3. **by himself**. Heb. with his body. Dt 15:12-14. ƒ171Q4. Synecdoche of the Part B641. The body is put for the person himself. For other instances of this figure see Ro 12:1. 1 C 6:15. Ja 3:6.

4. **shall be her**. Ex 4:22. Ge 14:14. 15:3. 17:13, 27. 18:19. Ec 2:7. Je 2:14.

5. **And if**. Dt *15:16, 17. Is 26:13. 2 C 5:14, 15. **shall plainly say**. Heb. saying shall say. ƒ147B, Ge +2:16. **master**. 1 S 25:10. **will not**. T#677-1. Le 25:47-54. Dt *15:16, 17.

6. **master**. Ge 24:9. Re 22:3. **the judges**. ver. 22. Ex 12:12. 18:21-26. 22:8, 9, 28. Nu 25:5-8. Dt 1:16. *16:18. 19:17, 18. 1 S 8:1, 2. Js 1:26. Zp 3:3. **bore his ear**. Jb ◐33:16. Ps ◑=40:6-8. Is 48:8. 50:4, 5. **for ever**. Heb. *olam*, Ex +12:24. Le 25:23, 40, 41.

Dt 15:17. 1 S 1:11, 22, 28. 27:12. 28:2. 1 K 12:7. Ps 15:4.

7. **sell**. Ne *5:5. **maidservant**. Ge 20:17. 21:10. Jg 9:18. **go out**. ver. 2, 3.

8. **please not**. Heb. be evil in the eyes of, etc. Ge 28:8mg. Jg 14:3. 1 S 8:6. 18:8mg. **who hath**. Dt 20:7. *21:11-14. **seeing**. Ex 8:29. Jg 9:19. Jb 6:15. Ml 2:11-15. **dealt**. Ge 38:14, 26. Je 3:20. Ml *2:14.

9. **betrothed her unto**. Ex *22:17. Ge 38:11. Le 22:13.

10. **her food**. Heb. her flesh. He shall not only afford her a sufficient quantity of food, as before, but of the same quality. She is not to be fed, like a common slave, with a sufficiency of bread, vegetables, milk, etc., but with her customary supply of flesh, and other agreeable articles of food. 1 C *7:1-6. **diminish**. or, withdraw. Ex 5:8, 19. Dt *4:2. 12:32. Jb 36:7.

11. **then shall**. See on ver. 2. Mt 19:8.

12. **smiteth a man**. Ex 20:13. Ge *9:6. Le *24:17. Nu *35:16-24, 30, 31. Dt 19:11-13. 2 S 12:13. Mt *26:52. **surely**. ƒ147B, Ge +2:16.

13. **lie not**. Nu *35:11, 22-25. Dt *19:4-6, 11. Mi 7:2. **God**. 1 S *24:4, 9, 10, 17, 18. 2 S 16:10. Is 10:7. Mt *10:29, 30. **I will appoint**. Nu *35:11. Dt 4:41-43. 19:1-3, 9. Jsh 20:2-9.

14. **presumptuously**. Ex 18:11. Nu 15:30, 31. Dt 1:43. 17:12, 13. 18:20, 22. *19:11-13. 1 K 2:28-34. Ps 19:13. He +*10:26. 2 P 2:10. **slay**. Nu *35:20, 21. Dt 27:24. 2 S 3:27. 20:9, 10. **take him**. 1 K 1:50, 51. 2:28-34. 2 K 11:15.

15. **father, or his mother**. Ex +20:12. Dt 21:18-21. 27:24. Pr 30:11, 17. 1 T *1:9. **put to death**. T#316. Capital crimes under the Mosaic code included: (1) Murder: Nu 35:16. (2) Blasphemy: Le 24:16. Jn 10:32n. (3) Manstealing: Ex 21:16. 1 T 1:9. (4) Idolatry: Ex 22:20. Dt 17:2. (5) Enticement to Idolatry: Dt 13:6, 9. (6) Adultery: Le 20:10. (7) Sodomy and Uncleanness: Le 20:13, 17-20. (8) Incest: Le 20:14, 21. (9) Bestiality: Le 20:15, 16. (10) Witchcraft: Ex 22:18. (11) Smiting Parents: Ex 21:15. Dt +27:16 (T#54). (12) Cursing Parents: Ex 21:17. Le 20:9. (13) Disobeying Parents: Dt 21:20, 21. (14) Sabbath Profanation. Ex 35:2. Nu 15:32. (15) Endangering Human Life: Ex 21:29.

16. **stealeth**. Ge 40:15. Dt *24:7. 1 T 1:10. Re 18:12. **selleth him**. Ge *37:28. Re 18:12, 13. **found in**. Ex 22:4.

17. **curseth**. or, revileth. Ex 22:28. Le 19:14. 24:11. Ec 7:21, 22. Is 8:21. Ac 23:4, 5. **father, or his mother**. ver. 15. Ex +*20:12. Le *20:9. Dt 27:16. Pr *20:20. 30:11, 17. Mt ▶15:3-6. Mk ▶7:10, 11. **surely**. ƒ147B, Ge +2:16.

18. **men**. ver. 22. Ex 2:13. Dt 25:11. 2 S 14:6. **another**. or, his neighbor. ver. 35. Ex 18:16. **a stone**. ver. 20. Nu 35:16-24.

19. **upon his staff**. 2 S 3:29. Zc 8:4. **shall pay**. ver. 28-34. Le 6:1-5. Nu 5:5-8. Dt 22:13-19, 28, 29. **the loss**. Heb. his ceasing.

20. **smite**. ver. 26, 27. Le 25:45, 46. Dt 19:21. Pr 29:19. Is 58:3, 4. Ep *6:9. **he shall**. Ge 9:6. Nu 35:30-33. **punished**. Heb. avenged. Ge 4:15, 24. Nu 35:19. Ro 13:4.

21. **punished**. or, avenged. **for**. Le 25:45, 46. **his money**. lit. silver. ƒ121B. Metonymy of the Cause B548. Silver is put for the thing procured by it.

22. **strive**. ver. 18. **hurt**. S#5062h. Ex 8:2 (smite). 12:23, 27. 21:35. 32:35 (plagued). 2 S 12:15 (struck).

2 K 14:12 (put to the worse). Ps 91:12 (dash). Pr 3:23 (stumble). **fruit depart.** Lk +*1:44n. **as the judges.** ver. *30. Dt 16:18. 22:18, 19.

23. **life.** Heb. *nephesh*, soul, Ge +44:30. **for life.** Le *24:20. Nu 35:31. Dt *19:21. Mt *5:38.

24. **Eye for eye.** ver. 26, 27. Le 24:19, 20. Dt 19:21. Jg 1:6, 7. 1 S 15:33. Mt 5:ʒ38, 39-40. 7:2. Lk 6:38. Re 16:6.

25. **burning.** only here. Pr 6:28. Is 43:2. **wound for.** Ge 4:23. 9:6. Jn 19:11. Ro 13:4.

26. **smite the eye.** ver. 20. Dt 16:19. Ne 5:5. Jb 31:13-15. Ps 9:12. 10:14, 18. 72:12-14. Pr 22:22, 23. Ep 6:9. Col 4:1.

27. **smite.** ver. +19.

28. **the ox.** ver. 32. Ge *9:5, 6. Le 20:15, 16.

29. **his owner also.** Dt 21:1-9.

30. **sum of money.** or, ransom. Ex 30:12. **for the ransom.** or, redemption. ver. 22. Ex 30:12. Nu 3:49. *35:31-33. Pr 13:8. **life.** Heb. *nephesh*, soul, Ge +44:30.

31. **judgment.** or, sentence.

32. **thirty shekels.** Ge=37:28. Zc *11:12, 13. Mt= 26:15. =27:3-9. Ph *2:7. **and the ox.** ver. 28, 29.

33. **shall open a.** Ps 9:15. 119:85. Pr 28:10. Ec 10:8. Je 18:20, 22. **pit.** Heb. *bor*, Ge +37:20.

34. **owner.** ver. 29, 30. Ex 22:6, 14. **pit.** ver. 33. Ge +37:20.

36. **if it be.** ver. 29. **owner hath not kept.** Pr +*22:3. **surely pay.** Le 24:21.

EXODUS 22

Laws concerning theft, 1-4; and fraud, 5; kindling fires which occasioned damage, 6; breach of trust, 7-13; and things borrowed and hired, 14, 15. Concerning seducers, 16; witchcraft, 18; beastiality, 19; idolatry, 20; and the treatment of strangers, 21; widows, and orphans, 22-24. Against usury and reviling rulers; concerning the first-fruits and firstlings, and against eating the flesh of torn animals, 25-31.

1. **sheep.** *or*, goat. ver. 4, 9, 10. Ex 12:3, 5. **he shall restore.** Le 6:1-6. Nu 5:7. 2 S *12:6. Pr 6:31. Lk +*19:8. **five oxen.** Pr 14:4.

2. **breaking.** Jb 24:14, 16. 30:5. Ho 7:1. Jl 2:9. Mt 6:19, 20. 24:43. 1 Th 5:2. **no blood.** Nu 35:27.

3. **full restitution.** Lk +*19:8. **sold for his theft.** See on Ex 21:2. Ge 44:9. Jg 2:14. 10:7. 2 K 4:1-7. Is 50:1. Mt 18:25.

4. **found.** Ex 21:16. **he shall restore double.** ver. 1, 7, 9. Ge 43:12. Pr *6:30, 31. Is 40:2. Je 16:18. Re 18:6.

5. **be eaten.** lit. burned or consumed. ver. 6. Jg 15:5. 2 Ch 28:3. Ezk 5:2. Na 2:13. **beast.** Ge 45:17. Nu 20:4, 8, 11. Ps 78:48. **feed.** lit. burn or consume. Le 6:12. Nu 24:22. **shall he make restitution.** ver. 3, 12. Ex 21:34. Jb 20:18.

6. **and catch in.** S#4672h. Ge 2:20 (found). 44:34mg. Ex 18:8. Nu 20:14mg. *32:23 (find). Jsh 2:23. Jg 6:13. Ps 116:3. 119:143mg. **so that the stacks of corn.** Jg 15:4, 5. 2 S 14:30, 31. **he that kindled the fire.** ver. 9, 12. Ex 21:33, 34.

7. **if the thief be found.** Pr 6:30, 31. Je 2:26. Jn 12:6. 1 C 6:10. **let him pay double.** ʃ121L9, Ge +43:12. See on ver. 4.

8. **the judges.** ver. 28mg. Ex 21:6. Ge ●1:26. Dt

16:18. 19:17, 18. 1 Ch 23:4. Ps 82:1, +*6n. 86:8. 97:7. Jn +*10:34.

9. **for all manner of trespass.** Nu 5:6, 7. 1 K 8:31. Mt 6:14, 15. 18:15, 35. Lk 17:3, 4. **the cause of both parties.** Ex 18:21, 22. 23:6-8. Dt 16:18, 19. *25:1. 2 Ch *19:10. **pay double.** ʃ121L9, Ge +43:12. **unto his.** ver. 4, 7.

10. **deliver.** Ge 39:8. Lk 12:48. 16:11. 2 T 1:12. **driven.** 1 Ch 5:21. 2 Ch 14:15. Jb 1:15, 17. Je 13:17.

11. **an oath of the Lord.** Le 5:1. 6:3. 1 K *2:42, 43. 8:31. Pr 29:24. 30:9. Mt *26:63. He *6:16. **that he hath not.** ver. 8. Ex 23:1.

12. **stolen from.** ver. 7. Ge *31:39. **him.** i.e. his premises or custody. Ge 30:33. 31:39.

13. **torn in pieces.** Ezk 4:14. Am 3:12. Mi 5:8. Na 2:12. **let him bring it for witness.** Or, rather, "Let him bring" an evidence of the thing torn, such as the horns, hoofs, etc. **it.** ʃ171N, Ge +8:13.

14. **borrow.** Dt 15:2. 23:19, 20. Ne 5:4. Ps 37:21. Mt 5:42. Lk 6:35. **make it good.** ver. 11. Ex 21:34. Le 24:18.

15. **it came for his hire.** Zc 8:10.

16. **a man entice.** Ge 34:2-4. Dt *22:28, 29.

17. **utterly.** Dt 7:3, 4. **pay.** Heb. weigh. Ge 23:16. **dowry of virgins.** Ge *34:12. Dt 22:29. 1 S 18:25.

18. **not suffer.** Le *19:26, 31. *20:6, 27. Dt +*18:10, 11. 1 S *28:3, 9. Is 19:3. Ac 8:9-11. 16:16-19. 19:19. Ga *5:20. Re *22:15. **witch.** Dt 18:10. Ml +*3:5 (sorcerers).

19. **lieth with a beast.** Le *18:23, 25. *20:15, 16. Dt 27:21.

20. **sacrificeth.** Nu 25:2-4, 7, 8. Dt *13:1-15. 17:2-5. 18:20. **unto any god.** T#362. Dt 8:19. 27:15. 30:17, 18. Jg 2:11-14. 10:6, 7. 1 K 9:6, 7. 2 K 17:9-11, 16, 18-20. 22:17. Ps 78:58, 59. Je 44:2-4. Ezk 36:18, 19. **utterly.** Nu 21:3. Jsh 23:15, 16. **destroyed.** Heb. devoted. S#2763h. Young notes, "to the Lord (either for destruction or preservation), as the word always signifies." Le 27:+21n, 28, 29. Nu 21:2, 3. Dt 3:6. 7:2. 20:17. 1 S 15:3. Ezr 10:8mg. 1 C *16:22.

21. **neither vex.** Ex 12:40. *23:9. Le *19:33, 34. *25:35. Dt *10:19. 24:18, 22. Je *7:6, 7. 22:3. Zc *7:10. Ml +*3:5. **a stranger.** Ge +23:4 (⊛S#1616h). Ex12:48. Dt +26:11. Jsh +20:9. Mt +25:35. **for ye were strangers.** Ex 20:2. 23:9. Dt 10:19. 15:15. 23:7.

22. **not afflict.** Dt *10:18. *24:17. *27:19. 2 K 4:1. Jb 24:3, 9. Ps *94:6, 7. Is *1:17, 23. *10:2. Je 5:28. Ezk *22:7. Mi 2:9. Zc 7:10. Ja *1:27. **widow.** ʃ171I14. Synecdoche of the Species B629. Widows and fatherless are put for all kinds of afflicted. For other instances of this figure see Dt 10:18. 27:19. Ps 146:9. Pr 23:10. Is 1:17, 23. Je 7:6. 22:3. Ezk 22:7. Ja 1:27.

23. **they cry at all.** ver. +*27. Ex 3:9. Ge *4:10. 18:20, 21. Dt 15:9. √24:14, 15. 1 S 25:17, 31. Jb 31:16, 21-23, 38, 39. *34:28. 35:9. Ps +*12:5. 34:6, *17. 35:10. 43:1. 68:5. *140:12. Pr 22:23. 23:11. 30:10. Is 33:10. Je *22:13, 16. Hab 2:9-11. Lk *18:7. Ja +√5:4. **I will surely.** Ge +*6:13 (T#566). Jb 34:28. Ps 10:17, 18. *18:6. 140:12. *145:19. 146:7-9. Pr 22:22, 23. 23:10, 11. Ja +√5:4.

24. **my wrath.** Jb *20:23. 31:23. Ps *69:24. 76:7. 90:11. Na 1:6. Ro 2:5-9. He 10:31. **your wives.** Jb 27:13-15. Ps 78:63, 64. *109:9. Is 9:17. Je 15:8. 18:21. La *5:3. Lk 6:38.

25. **lend money.** Le *25:35-37. Dt *23:19, 20. 2 K 4:1, 7. Ne *5:2-5, 7, 10, 11. Ps *15:5. Pr 28:8. Je

15:10. Ezk *18:8, 17. Mt 25:27. Lk 19:23. **userer**. Ps 109:11. **usury**. Is +*24:2.

26. **to pledge**. Dt *24:6, 10-13, 17. Jb 22:6. 24:3, 9. Pr 20:16. 22:27. Ezk 18:7, 16. 33:15. Am 2:8.

27. **when he crieth**. ver. +√23. Ex 2:23, 24. Ex 34:6. 72:12. Is 19:20. **for I am gracious**. Ex +*34:6. 2 Ch *30:9. Ps *86:15. 136:10, 11.

28. **the gods**. or, judges. ver. +8, 9. Ps 32:6. *82:6n. 86:8. 138:1. Jn 10:+√34, 35. **nor curse**. Ex 21:17. 1 S 24:6, 10. 26:9. Ec √10:20. Ac ▶23:3, 5. Ro *13:2-7. T *3:1, 2. 1 P 2:17. 2 P 2:10. Ju *8.

29. **shalt not delay**. Ex *23:16, 19. Ge 24:56h. 34:19. Dt 7:10. *23:21. 26:2-10. 2 K 4:42. 2 Ch 31:5. Pr *3:9, 10. Ezk 20:40. Mi 7:1. Ml *3:10. Mt √6:33. Ro 8:23. Ja *1:18. **the first of thy ripe fruits**. Heb. thy fulness. i.e. the abundance of thy corn which was to be offered to the Lord as first-fruits. Le +*23:10. Nu 18:29. Dt 22:9. **liquors**. Heb. tear. only here; used metaphorically of olives and grapes. **the firstborn**. Ex *13:2, 12. *34:19.

30. **Likewise**. Dt *15:19. **seven days**. Le *22:27.

31. **holy**. Ex *19:5, 6. Le 11:45. *19:2. Dt *14:21. Ps *93:5. 1 P *1:15, 16. *2:9. **neither**. Le 17:15, 16. 20:25. *22:8. Dt 14:21. Ezk *4:14. *44:31. Ac 10:14. 15:20.

EXODUS 23

Laws forbidding slander, false witness, wresting judgment, bribery, and oppression; and requiring kindness to enemies, 1-9. The law of the sabbatical year and the weekly sabbath, with a caution against idolatry, 10-13. The three great annual feasts appointed, 14-19. The Lord promises to conduct Israel safe to Canaan, to put them in possession of it, to enlarge their borders, and destroy their enemies; an angel is promised, with a blessing, if they obey him, 20-33.

1. **shalt not**. ver. 7. Ex +*20:16. *23:7. Le *19:16. 2 S 16:3. 19:27. Ps *15:3. *101:5. 120:3. Pr *10:18. 17:4. 25:23. Je 20:10. Mt 28:14, 15. Ro 3:8. **raise**. or, receive. Ps 15:3mg. 1 T +*5:19n. **an unrighteous witness**. Dt 5:20. *19:16-21. 1 K *21:10-13. Ps 27:12. *35:11. Pr 6:19. 12:17. 19:5, 9, 28. *24:28. 25:18. Mt 19:18. *26:59-61. Lk 3:14. 19:8. Ac *6:11-13. Ep √4:25. 2 T 3:3. 1 P 3:16. Re 12:10.

2. **follow**. Ex *32:1-5. Ge 6:12. *7:1. 19:4, 7-9. Nu 14:1-10. Jsh √24:15. 1 S *15:9, 24. 1 K *19:10. Jb *31:34. Pr √1:10, 11, 15. *4:14. Mt +*7:13. *27:24-26. Mk *15:15. Lk 23:23, 24, 51. Jn 7:50, 51. Ac *24:27. 25:9. Ro 1:32. Ga 2:11-13. **speak**. or, answer. **to decline**. ver. 6, 7. Le 19:15. Dt *1:17. Ps 72:2. Je 37:15, 21. 38:5, 6, 9. Ezk 9:9. Hab +*1:4. **to wrest**. or, incline. Dt 16:19. or, stretch out. Ps 56:5.

3. **countenance**. Le +*19:15. Dt 1:17. Jb *34:19. Ps *72:2. 82:2, 3. Ac +*10:34. Ja 3:17. Ju *16. **poor**. Ex 30:15. Le 14:21. 19:15. Dt ◑*15:11. Jg 6:15. Ru 3:10. Pr 22:2. Mt 26:11. Mk +14:7. Jn 12:8. 1 J ◑*3:17.

4. **meet thine**. Dt 22:1-4. Jb 31:29, 30. Pr *24:17, 18. *25:21. Mt *5:44. Lk 6:27, 28. Ro *12:17-21. 1 Th *5:15. **ox or**. √171K2. Synecdoche of the Species B635. One example or specimen is put for all kinds of similar things in divine precepts, etc. For other instances of this figure see Ex 20:12. 1 S 25:41. Pr 25:21. Lk 3:11. Jn 13:14. Ro 12:20. 1 T 5:10. 6:8. See Paul's implicit application of this principle in 1 C 9:9.

5. **If thou see**. Dt 22:4. **and wouldest forbear to help him**. or, Wilt thou cease to help him? or, wouldest cease to leave *thy business* for him; thou shalt surely leave it to join with him. **surely**. √147A, Ge +50:24.

6. **not wrest**. ver. 2, 3. Dt 16:19. *27:19. 2 Ch 19:7. Jb 31:13, 21, 22. Ps 82:3, 4. Ec +*5:8. Is *10:1, 2. Je 5:28. 6:28. 7:6. Am *5:11, 12. Mi 3:1-4. Zp 3:1-4. Ml +*3:5. Ja 2:5, 6.

7. **far from**. ver. 1. Le *19:11. Dt 19:16-21. Jb 22:23. Pr 4:14, 15. Is 33:15. Lk 3:14. Ep *4:25. 1 Th 5:22. **the innocent**. Dt *27:25. Ps *94:21-23. Mt *27:4. **for I will not**. Ex 34:7. Pr *17:15. Na 1:3. Ro *1:18. 2:5, 6.

8. **thou shalt take**. Dt 10:17. *16:19. 27:25. 1 S ◑*8:3. *12:3. Ps 26:10. Pr *15:27. 17:8, 23. 19:4. *29:4. Ec 7:7. Is 1:23. 5:23. Ezk *22:12. Ho 4:18. Am *5:12. Mi 7:3. Ac *24:26. **no gift**. 2 Ch *19:7. Da 5:17. **blindeth**. √121E2, Ge +42:38. **the wise**. Heb. the seeing. Ex 4:11. Ge +21:19. **perverteth**. Pr *27:8, 23. **words**. or, cause.

9. **not oppress**. Ex 22:21. Dt *10:19. +*24:14-18. *27:19. Ps +*12:5. 94:6. Ezk +*16:49. 22:7. Ml +*3:5. **a stranger**. Ex +12:48. Ge +23:4 (S#1616h). Dt +26:11. Jsh +20:9. Mt +25:35. **ye know**. Mt 18:33. He 2:17, 18. **heart**. Heb. *nephesh*, soul, Ge +34:3. √121A9, Ge +23:8. Ex +15:9. Le 26:16. Dt 24:15. 1 S 2:33. 2 S 3:21. Ps 10:3. Pr 23:7. 28:25. 31:6. Je 42:20. La 3:51. Ezk 25:6, 15. 27:31. Ho 4:8.

10. **six years**. Le *25:3, 4. Ne 10:31.

11. **the seventh**. See on Le 25:2-7, 11, 12, 20, 22. 26:34, 35. **let it rest**. or, release it. Dt *15:1, 2, 9. **olive-yard**. or, olive-trees. Ge 8:11. Dt 6:11.

12. **Six days**. See on Ex *20:8-11. 31:15, 16. Lk *13:14. **and the son**. Dt 5:13-15. Is 58:3. **refreshed**. Ex 31:17. 2 S 16:14.

13. **be circumspect**. Dt *4:9, 15. Jsh *22:5. 23:11. 1 Ch 28:7-9. Ps √39:1. Ep *5:15. 1 T *4:16. He *12:15. **make no mention**. Nu 32:38. Dt *12:3. Jsh 23:7. Ps *16:4. Je 10:+*2, 11. Ho *2:17. Zc *13:2. Ep 5:12.

14. **Three**. Ex *34:22, 23. Le *23:4, 5, 16, 34. Dt *16:16. **times**. lit. feet. Nu 22:28.

15. **the feast**. Ex *12:14-28, 43-49. 13:6, 7. 34:18. Le *23:5-8. Nu 9:2-14. 28:16-25. Dt *16:1-8. Jsh 5:10, 11. 2 K 23:21-23. Mk 14:12. Lk 22:7. 1 C 5:7, 8. **and none**. Ex 34:20. Le 23:10. Dt *16:16. 1 S 9:7, 8. 2 S *24:24. 1 Ch +*21:24. Pr 3:9, 10. Lk 21:4. Ph 3:8. 1 C +*16:2. **me**. √22A4, Ge +19:13.

16. **feast of harvest**. Ex 22:29. *34:22. Le *23:9-21. Nu 28:26-31. Dt 16:9-12. Ac 2:1. **firstfruits**. The Hebrew word is from the same root as the word *firstborn* (Le +27:26, *S#1060h). Note the accuracy of the type at Col 1:15, 18: Christ is firstborn not because he was born first, but because he was, in answer to the type of the firstfruits, the firstborn from the dead by resurrection, in full harmony with the typical significance of the feast of firstfruits at Le +*23:10. *S#1061h: Ex 23:19. 34:22, 26. Le 2:14, 14. *23:17, 20. Nu 13:20 (firstripe). 18:13. 28:26. 2 K 4:42. Ne 10:35, 35. 13:31. Is 28:4. Ezk 44:30. Na 3:12. **in-gathering**. Ex 34:22. Le 23:+34-44. Nu 29:12-39. Dt 16:13-15. Ne 8:14-18. Zc 14:16-19. Jn 7:2, 37. **end of**. Le 23:36. Dt *16:13.

17. **males shall appear**. Ex 34:23. Dt 12:5. *16:16. 31:11. Ps 84:7. Lk 2:42.

18. **offer**. √63H, Ge +12:15. **blood**. Ex *12:8, 15. *34:25. Le *2:11. 7:12. Dt *16:4. **sacrifice**. or, feast. √121P7. Metonymy of the Adjunct B596. Feast or feast

day is put for the sacifices offered at the festival. For other instances of this figure see Ps 118:27. Is 29:1. Ml 2:3. **remain**. Ex 12:10. Le 7:15.

19. **first of the**. Ex *22:29. 34:26. Le *23:10-17. Nu *18:12, 13. Dt 12:5-7. *14:22. *26:10. Ne *10:35. 1 C 15:20. Re 14:4. **firstfruits**. Le +*23:10. **Thou shalt not seethe a kid**. The true sense of this passage seems to be that assigned by Dr. Cudworth, from a MS. comment of a Karaite Jew. "It was a custom with the ancient heathens, when they had gathered in all their fruits, to take a kid, and boil it in the dam's milk; and then in a magical way, to go about and sprinkle all their trees, and fields, and gardens, and orchards with it, thinking by these means, that they should make them fruitful, and bring forth more abundantly in the following year. Wherefore, God forbad his people, the Jews, at the time of their in-gathering, to use any such superstitious or idolatrous rite." Ex 34:26. Dt 14:21. Pr 12:10. Je 10:3.

20. **Angel**. ♪171E12, Ge +48:16. Ex 3:2-6. *14:19. 32:34. *33:2, 14. Ge *48:16. Nu 20:16. Jsh 5:13. 6:2. Ps 91:11. Is +*63:9. Ml ▶3:1. Mt ▶11:10. Mk ▶1:2. Lk ▶7:27. Jn *1:18. Ac *7:38. 1 C *10:9, 10. **place**. Ex +29:24. 32:34. Dt *16:16. **prepared**. Ge 15:18. Mt 25:34. Jn *14:3.

21. **Beware of him**. Ps 2:12. Mt 17:5. He 12:25. **provoke him not**. Nu *14:11. Ps *78:40, 56. Ep *4:30. He *3:10, 16. **he will not**. Ex 32:34. Nu *14:35. Dt *18:19. Jsh 24:19. Je 5:7. He 3:11. 10:26-29. 12:25. 1 J +*5:16. **my name**. Ex 3:14. 34:5-7. Ps +√9:10. 72:19. 83:18. 91:14. Is 7:14. *9:6. 42:8. 45:6. 57:15. Je √23:6. Mt 1:23. Jn 5:23. *10:30, 38. *14:9, 10. *17:21. Col 2:9. Re √1:8. 2:8, 23. 3:7.

22. **an enemy**. Ge 12:3. Nu 24:9. Dt 30:7. Je 30:20. Zc 2:8. Ac 9:4, 5. **an adversary unto thine adversaries**. *or*, I will afflict them that afflict thee. Ex +*22:22, 23. Ge +6:13 (T#566). +*12:3. 2 Ch 16:9. Ps 34:7. 91:4. 125:2. Is *41:11. Zc 2:5. Lk 21:18.

23. **mine Angel**. ver. 20. Ex 32:2. Is 5:13. **thee in**. Ex 3:17. Ge 15:19-21. 34:2. Jsh *24:8-11. **Amorites**. Ge +10:16. **Hittites**. Ge +15:20. **Perizzites**. Ge +13:7. **Canaanites**. Ge +10:18. **Hivites**. Ge 10:17. **Jebusites**. Ge 10:16. The LXX, Samaritan, Coptic, and one Hebrew MS. add, "and the Girgashite;" thus making the seven nations.

24. **shalt not**. See on Ex +*20:5. **do after**. Le *18:3, 26-30. Dt *12:30, 31. 2 Ch 33:2, 9. Ps 101:3. 106:35-38. Ezk 16:47. **overthrow**. Ex *32:20. *34:13, 14. Nu *33:52. Dt *7:5, 25, 26. 12:3. 2 Ch *34:3-7.

25. **And ye**. Dt 6:13. *10:12, 20. *11:13, 14. 13:4. 28:1-6. Jsh *22:5. *24:14, 15, 21, 24. 1 S 7:3. *12:20, 24. Je 8:2. Mt *4:10. **he shall**. Dt *7:13. *28:5-8. Is 33:16. Ml 3:10. Mt *6:33. 1 T +*4:8. **bread**. Is 3:1. 30:20. **take sickness**. T#770. Ex +*15:26. Le ◑26:16. Nu +12:13. Dt *7:15. ◑28:21. Jb 33:24-26, 28. Ps +*30:2. +*103:3. Is 33:24. Je +*17:14. *33:6. Mt *8:17. Ac *10:38.

26. **shall nothing**. Dt 7:14. *28:4. Jb 21:10. Ps 107:38. 144:13. Ml *3:10, 11. **nor be**. Ge +11:30. Le 26:9. Dt 28:11. 30:9. **the number**. Ge +*25:8. *35:29. 1 Ch *23:1. Jb *5:26. *14:5. 15:20. 21:21. 36:26. *42:17. Ps ◑55:23. *90:10. Ec 2:3mg. 5:18mg. Is 65:20. Ac ◑1:18.

27. **my fear**. Ex 15:14-16. Ge *35:5. Dt *2:25. *11:23, 25. Jsh *2:9-11. 1 S 14:15. 2 K 7:6. 2 Ch 14:14. **destroy**. or, trouble. Ex 14:24. Dt 7:23. **backs**. Heb.

neck. Ge 49:8. Jsh 7:8mg, 12. 2 S 22:41. 2 Ch 29:6mg. Ps 18:40.

28. **hornets**. lit. hornet. ♪96, Ge +3:8. Dt 7:20. Jsh *24:11, 12. **Hivite**. Ge +10:17. **Canaanite**. Ge +10:18. **Hittite**. Ge +15:20.

29. **in one year**. Dt 7:22. Jsh 15:63. 16:10. 17:12, 13. Jg 3:1-4. **lest**. Dt 7:22. Jn=15:19. 2 C=12:7-10. Ph=1:24. 1 P=5:10.

30. **By little and little**. ♪84, Ge +6:17. Dt 7:22. Ph=3:12-14. 2 P=3:18. **drive them out**. Ex 33:2. 34:11. Dt 7:22. Jsh 23:5. 24:11, 12.

31. **I will set**. Ge *15:18. Nu *34:3-15. Dt *11:24. Jsh *1:4. 1 K *4:21n, 24. Ps *72:8. **the river**. ♪171E12, Ge +14:22. **deliver the**. Nu 21:34. Dt 3:2. Jsh 8:7, 18. 10:8, 19. *21:44. 23:14. 24:8. Jg *1:4. *11:21. 1 S 23:4. 2 S *8:3. 1 K 20:13.

32. **shalt make**. Ex *34:12, 15. Dt 7:2. Jsh 9:6, 14-23. 1 S 11:1. 2 S 21:1, 2. Ps *106:35. 2 C *6:15. **nor with**. Nu 25:1, 2. Dt 7:16.

33. **they make**. 1 K 14:16. 2 Ch 33:9. **it will surely**. Ex 34:12. Dt 7:16. 12:30. Jsh *23:13. Jg *2:3. 1 S 18:21. Ps 106:36. 2 T 2:26.

EXODUS 24

Moses, being called to go up to the mount, delivers the laws to Israel, and they consent to covenant with God, 1-3. An altar and twelve pillars are prepared, and the covenant is ratified, with sacrifices, and the sprinkling of blood, 4-8. Moses, Aaron, and his sons, and the elders of Israel, are favored with a vision of God, and feast before him, 9-11. Moses ascends the mount, Joshua at first accompanying him; he leaves Aaron and Hur to rule the people; and abides in the mount forty days and nights, 12-18.

1. **Come up**. ver. 15. Ex 3:5. 19:9, 20, 24. 20:21. 34:2. **Nadab**. Ex 6:23. *28:1. Le *10:1, 2. 1 Ch 6:3. 24:1, 2. **seventy**. ver. 9. Ex 1:5. ◑+18:21n. Nu *11:16, 24, 25. Ezk 8:11. Lk 10:1, 17.

2. **alone**. ver. 13, 15, 18. Ex 20:21. Nu 16:5. Je 30:21. 49:19. He 9:24. 10:21, 22. **neither shall**. Ex *19:12.

3. **all the judgments**. Ex ch. 21-23. Dt 4:1, 5, 45. 5:1, 31. 6:1. 11:1. **All the words**. ver. 7. Ex 19:8. Dt 5:27, 28. Jsh 24:22. Ga *3:19, 20.

4. **Moses wrote**. Ex 34:27, 28. Nu 21:14. 33:2. Dt 17:18, 19. 27:3, 8. 28:58, 61. 29:20, 21, 27. *31:9, 19, 22, 24, 26. Jsh 1:8. 8:31, 34. 23:6. 24:26. 1 S 10:25. 1 K 2:3. 2 K +14:6n. *22:8n. 23:3, 21, 24. 1 Ch 16:40. 2 Ch *17:9. 25:4. 31:3. +*34:14n. 35:12. Ezr 3:2. Ne 8:1. 9:3. 13:1. Da 9:11, 13. Mk 12:26. Lk 4:17. *16:31. 20:42. Jn 1:45. 5:45, √46, 47. Ac 1:20. Ga 3:10. He 9:19. **and builded**. Ex 20:24-26. **twelve pillars**. Ge 28:18, 22. 31:45. Jsh 24:27. Ga 2:9. **according**. Ex 28:21. Le 24:5. Nu 17:2. Jsh 4:2, 3, 8, 9, 20. 1 K 11:30. Ezr 6:17. Lk 22:30. Re 21:14.

5. **young men**. Ex *19:22. 33:11. 2 S 18:15. 1 K 20:14. Ac 5:6, 10. **burnt offerings**. Ex 18:12. Le ch. 1. +*23:12. **peace offerings**. Le ch. 3. 7:11-21. +*23:19.

6. **the blood he**. ver. 8. Ex *12:7, 22. Col 1:20. He 9:18. 12:24. 1 P 1:2, 19. **on the altar**. Ex 29:16, 20. Le 1:5, 11. 3:2, 8. 4:6.

7. **the book**. ver. 4. He 9:18-23. **read**. Dt 31:11-13. Jsh 8:34, 35. 2 K 23:2. Ne 8:3, √8, 18. 13:1. Je *23:22. 36:6, 8. Mt ◑22:29. Mk 12:24. Lk 4:16. Jn

+5:39. Ac 8:30-32. 13:15. Col 4:16. 1 Th 5:27. 1 T
*4:13. Re 1:3. **All that**. ver. 3. Jsh *24:24. Je 7:23,
24.

8. **blood**. Mt 26:28. Mk 14:24. Lk=22:30. 1 C 11:25.
Ep *1:7. Col 1:20. He *9:18. **sprinkled**. See on ver.
6. Le 8:30. Is 52:15. Ezk 36:25. He *9:18-21. 12:24.
1 P 1:2, 19. **Behold**. Zc 9:11. Mt 26:28. Mk 14:24.
Lk 22:20. 1 C 11:25. Ep 1:7. He ♭9:20. 10:4, 5. *13:20.
1 P *1:2.

9. **went up**. See on ver. 1.

10. **saw**. Ex *3:6. *33:20, 23. Ge *32:30. Jg 6:22.
*13:21, 22. 1 K *22:19. Is *6:1-5. Ezk *1:28. Jn √1:18.
14:9. 1 T *6:16. 1 J 4:12. **of a sapphire stone**. Ezk
*1:26, 27. *10:1. Re *4:3. 21:19-23. **in his clearness**.
SS 6:10. Mt *17:2. Re 1:16. 21:11, 18.

11. **nobles**. ver. 1, 9. Nu 21:18. Jg 5:13. 1 K 21:8.
2 Ch 23:20. Ne 2:16. Je 14:3. **laid not**. Ex 19:21. 33:20-
23. Ge 32:24-32. Dt *4:33. Jg 13:22. **they saw**. ver.
10. Ge *16:13. **and did**. Ex 18:12. Ge 18:18. 31:54.
Dt 12:7. Ec 9:7. Lk 15:23, 24. 1 C 10:16-18. **eat and
drink**. √121S3R. Metonymy of the Adjunct B607. Eating and drinking is put for living or being alive.

12. **Come up**. ver. 2, 15, 18. Ex ◐3:5. **tables**. Ex
*31:18. 32:15, 16. Dt *5:22. Ne 9:13. Je 31:33. 2 C
3:3, 7. He 9:4. **that thou**. Dt 4:14. Ezr *7:10. Mt
5:19.

13. **his minister**. Ex 17:9-14. 32:17. 33:11. Nu 11:28.
went up. ver. 2.

14. **Tarry ye**. Ex *24:2. 32:1. Ge 22:5. 1 S 10:8.
13:8-13. **Hur**. Ex *17:10, 12. **if any man**. Ex *18:25,
26.

15. **a cloud**. Ex *19:9, 16. 2 Ch 6:1. Mt *17:5.

16. **the glory**. ver. 17. Ex 16:10. Le 9:23. Nu 14:10.
16:42. Ezk 1:28. 2 C 4:6. **seventh day**. Ex 19:11. 20:10.
Re 1:10.

17. **like a devouring fire**. Ex *3:2. *19:18. Dt 4:24,
36. Ezk 1:27. Na 1:6. Hab 3:4, 5. He *12:18, 29.

18. **went into**. ver. 17. Ex 9:29, 33. 19:20. Pr 28:1.
forty days. Ex *34:28. Dt 9:9, 18, 25. 10:10. 1 K 19:8.
Mt 4:2. Mk 1:13. Lk 4:2.

EXODUS 25

*The Lord directs Moses concerning an offering from
the people, in order to erect a tabernacle, 1-9. The
form of the ark of the covenant, and the mercy-seat,
10-22. The table of showbread, 23-30. The golden
candlestick, with the tongs and snuff-dishes, 31-40.*

1. **the Lord spake**. Ex 6:1. 7:1. 8:1. 9:1. 10:1. 11:1.
12:1. 13:1. 14:1. 20:1.

2. **they**. Ex 35:5-29. Nu 7:3-88. Dt 16:16, 17.
1 Ch 29. **bring me**. Heb. take for me. **offering**. or, heave
offering. Nu 18:24. **willingly**. Ex 35:5, 21. Le +*23:38.
Jg 5:9. 1 Ch *29:3, 5, 9, 14, 17. Ezr 1:6. 2:68. 3:5.
7:16. Ne 11:2. Ps 110:3. Pr *11:25. Ro *12:8. 2 C
*8:12. *9:7.

3. **brass**. rather, copper. Dt 8:9. Jb 28:2.

4. **blue**. Ex 26:1. 2 Ch 3:14. Lk +=1:35. Jn=3:13.
1 P=2:22. **purple**. Jg 8:26. Est 1:6. 8:15. Je 10:9. Ezk
27:7, 16. Da 5:7, 16, 29mg. Ac 16:14. **scarlet**.
✳S#8144h: Ge 38:28, 30. Ex 25:4. 26:1, 31, 36. 27:16.
28:5, 6, 8, 15, 33. 35:6, 23, 25, 35. 36:8, 35, 37. 38:18,
23. 39:1, 2, 3, 5, 8, 24, 29. Le 14:4, 6, 49, 51, 52.
Nu 4:8. 19:6. Jsh 2:18, 21. 2 S 1:24. Pr 31:21. SS
4:3. Is *1:18. Je 4:30. ✳S#8438h: Ex 25:4. 26:1, 31,
36. 27:16. 28:5, 6, 8, 15, 33. 35:6, 23, 25, 35. 36:8,

35, 37. 38:18, 23. 39:1, 2, 3, 5, 8, 24, 29. Le 14:4, 6,
49, 51, 52. Nu 4:8. 19:6. Dt 28:39 (worms). Jb 25:6
(worm). Ps *22:6 (worm). Is 14:11. 41:14. *66:24. Jon
4:7. Ada Habershon suggests scarlet typifies Christ's
earthly glory, noting the same word means worm at
Jb 25:6; Ps 22:6. Specially connected with Israel or
Judah—the national color (*Outline Studies of the Tabernacle*, p. 32). **fine linen**. *or*, silk. Ex 26:1, 31. Ge
41:42. Pr 31:22. Ezk 16:10. Re=19:8. **goats' hair**. Nu
31:20. 1 S 19:13, 16.

5. **rams' skins**. Ex 26:14. 39:24. He +=2:10. **badgers' skins**. Ex 26:14. 39:34. Ps=22:6. Is=53:2, 3. Ezk
16:10. Mk=6:3. Jn=*1:10. Ph=2:6, 7. He=7:26. The
original word thus translated occurs out of the Pentateuch only in Ezk 16:10, so that the context throws
no light on the subject. Many ancient interpreters understand it to denote a color, though they differ in
determining it; jackal, weasel, seal, boar, pardale,
fitchet, dolphin, mermaid, dudong, hyaena, walrus,
antelope, etc. have all been suggested in addition to
badger, which has been objected to as an unclean animal, whose skin would have been unlawful for the
tabernacle (Young). **shittim wood**. Ex 26:15, 26, 37.
27:1. 36:20. Is *41:19. or, acacia wood, which is the
largest and most common tree in Arabia, especially
near Sinai; whence the name of a place, Nu 25:1; 33:49;
Jl 3:18 (Young).

6. **Oil for**. ver. 37. Ex *27:20. 40:24, 25. **spices**.
Ex *30:23-38.

7. **Onyx stones**. Ex 28:9-21. Ge 2:12n. **ephod**. Ex
*28:4, 6, 15.

8. **a sanctuary**. Ex 15:2. 36:1-4. Le 4:6. 10:4. 21:12.
He 8:2. *9:1, 2. S#4720h, Ex +*15:17n. **I may dwell**.
Ex *29:45. Nu 5:3. 16:9. 1 K 6:13. Is 12:6. Zc 2:10.
8:3. Mt=1:23. Jn=14:23. 2 C *6:16. He *3:6. Re
*21:3.

9. **the pattern of the**. ver. 40. Dt 4:17h. 2 K 16:10.
1 Ch *28:11-19. Ps 144:12. He 8:5. 9:9. **tabernacle**.
Ex 26:1n. *27:21n. 33:7n. Heb. *mishkan*, habitation,
dwelling place. Newberry notes that, according to ver.
8, this term is suggestive of the presence of God. It
is to be distinguished from the tent of meeting (see
Ex 27:21n), for it refers to the place where God is
pleased to dwell, not a meeting place for man.
✳S#4908h: Ex 25:9. 26:1, 6, 7, 12, 15, 17, 18, 20,
22, 23, 26, 27, 27, 30, 35. 27:9, 19. 35:11, 15, 18.
36:8, 13, 14, 20, 22, 23, 25, 27, 28, 31, 32. 38:20,
21, 31. 39:32, 33, 40. 40:2, 5, 6, 9, 17, 18, 19, 21,
22, 24, 28, 29, 33, 34, 35, 36, 38. Le 8:10. 15:31.
17:4. 26:11. Nu 1:50, 50, 50, 51, 51, 53, 53. 3:7, 8,
23, 25, 26, 29, 35, 36, 38. 4:16, 25, 26, 31. 5:17. 7:1,
3. 9:15, 15, 18, 19, 20, 22. 10:11, 17, 17, 21. 16:9,
24, 27. 17:13. 19:13. 24:5. 31:30, 47. Jsh 22:19, 29.
2 S 7:6. 1 Ch 6:32, 48. 16:39. 17:5. 21:29. 23:26. 2 Ch
1:5. 29:6. Jb 18:21. 21:28mg. 39:6. Ps 26:8mg. 43:3.
46:4. 49:11. 74:7. 78:28, 60. 84:1. 87:2. 132:5, 7. SS
1:8. Is 22:16. 32:18. 54:2. Je 9:19. 30:18. 51:30. Ezk
25:4. 37:27. Hab 1:6. Note that in passages after the
Pentateuch, particularly in Job and Song of Solomon,
etc., that the idea of God's presence discussed above
does not hold, where its meaning is simply dwelling
place.

10. **an ark**. or, chest. or, coffer. Ex *37:1-3. Dt
10:1-3. 2 Ch 8:11. He 9:4. Re 11:19. **shittim wood**.
Ex 37:1. He=2:14.

11. **overlay**. ver. 24. Ex 30:3. 1 K 6:20. 2 Ch 3:4.

pure gold. Jn=1:1, 14. +*20:28. **crown.** ver. 24. Ex 30:3. 38:2, 11, 26.

12. **four rings.** ver. 15, 26. Ex 26:29. 27:7. 37:5. 38:7.

13. **staves.** ver. 28. Ex 12:11. 27:6. 30:5. 37:4. 40:20. Ge 32:10. Nu 4:6, 8, 11, 14. 21:18. 1 Ch 15:15. 2 Ch 5:9. Mk 6:8.

14. **staves.** lit. parts, separated things. S#905h. Jb 17:16 (bars). 18:13 (strength; mg, bars), 13. Ezk 17:6 (branches). 19:14. Ho 11:6.

15. **staves.** 1 K *8:8. 2 Ch 5:9.

16. **into.** 2 Ch 6:11. Ps=40:8. He ◑9:15. **the testimony.** Ex 16:34. 27:21. 30:6, 36. 31:18. 32:15. 34:29. 38:21. Nu 17:4. Dt *10:2-5. *31:26. 1 K *8:9. 2 K 11:12. 2 Ch *5:10. 34:14, 15. Ac 7:44. Ro 3:2. He 9:4.

17. **mercy seat.** Ex 26:34. *37:6. 40:20. Le 16:12-15. 1 Ch 28:11. Lk 18:13. Ro=3:25. He 4:16. 9:5. 1 J *2:2.

18. **two cherubims of gold.** Ex 37:7-9. Ge 3:24. 1 S 4:4. 1 K 6:23-28. 8:6, 7. 1 Ch 28:18. Ezk 10:2, 20. 41:18, 19. He 9:5.

19. **of the.** or, of the matter of the. The cherubim were thus looking toward each other, and toward the Mercy-seat, and therefore gazing on the blood. Habershon suggests "These last facts seem to show that the cherubim typify the redeemed; rent in the vail—crucified with Christ, Ga 2:20; one with Him, Jn 17:21, 23; fellowship with one another and with Himself, 1 J 1:3, 7; owing all to the blood, 1 J 1:7" (*Outline Studies*, p. 57).

20. **cherubims shall.** ver. 18. 1 K 8:7. 1 Ch 28:18. 2 Ch 3:10. He *9:5. **covering.** Ezk 28:14. **toward.** Ge 28:12. Is 6:1-5. Ezk 1:20. Mt 24:31. Jn 1:51. 1 C 4:9. 11:10. Ep 3:10. Col 2:10. He 1:14. 1 P 1:12. 3:22. Re 5:11, 12.

21. **mercy seat.** ver. 17. Ex 26:34. Ro 10:4. **in.** See on ver. 16. **testimony.** ver. 16. Pr=3:3. =7:3. Je=17:1. =31:33. 2 C=3:3, 7. He=8:10. =10:16.

22. **there.** Jg 20:26, 27. **meet.** Ex *29:42, 43. 2 C=5:19. He *4:16. **and I will.** Ex 20:24. 30:6, 36. 31:18. Ge 18:33. Le 1:1. 16:2. Nu *7:89. 17:4. Dt 5:26-31. Jg 20:27. **from above.** T#1199. Nu 7:89. **between.** Ex 29:42, 43. 31:6. 1 S 4:4. 2 S 6:2. 2 K *19:15. Ps *80:1. 90:1. 99:1. Is 37:16. 1 P *1:12.

23. **a table.** Ex *37:10-16. 40:22, 23. Le 24:6. Nu 3:31. 1 K *7:48. 1 Ch 28:16. 2 Ch 4:8, 19. Ezk 40:41, 42. He *9:2. **shittim wood.** ver. +5n, 10.

24. **overlay.** See on ver. 11. 1 K 6:20-22. **crown.** ver. +11.

25. **hand breadth.** ⨍79, Ge +21:16. **a golden crown to the border.** Ex 30:3. 37:2.

26. **four rings of gold.** See on ver. 12.

27. **for places of the staves.** ver. 14, 18.

28. **the table.** ver. 14, 27. Nu 10:17. Ac 9:15.

29. **the dishes.** Ex 37:16. Nu *4:7. 7:13, 19, 31, etc. 1 K 7:50. 2 Ch 4:22. Ezr 1:9-11. Je 52:18, 19. **covers.** Ex 37:16. Nu 4:7. 1 Ch 28:17. **bowls.** Ex 37:16. Nu 4:7. Je 52:19. **to cover.** or, to pour out. Le 24:5-9. SS 5:1. Re 3:20.

30. **showbread.** Ex 35:13. 39:36. Le *24:5, 6. Nu *4:7. 1 S 21:6. 1 Ch 9:32. 23:29. 2 Ch 13:11. Ml 1:7, 12. Mt 12:4. bread of faces, Ex 35:13. 39:36. Nu 4:7. 1 Ch ◑+9:32. **me.** ⨍22A4, Ge +19:13. Ps *23:5. 1 C *10:31.

31. **a candlestick.** Ex 35:14n. 37:17-24. 40:24, 25.

1 K *7:49. 2 Ch 13:11. Pr *6:23. Zc *4:2. He *9:2. 2 P 1:19. Re *1:12, 20. 2:1, 5. *4:5. **pure gold.** Ex 31:8. 39:37. Le 24:4. **beaten.** Ex +27:20. Is=53:5. He +=2:10. **shaft.** or, base. Heb. thigh. Ge ◑+24:2. 41:5. Ex 1:5. 28:42. Nu 5:27. 1 K 14:15. **branches.** Ge 41:5 (stalk), 22. **bowls.** Ge 44:2. Je 35:5. **his knops.** 1 K 6:18. 7:24. Am 9:1. Zp 2:14. **flowers.** Nu 17:8. Is 5:24. 18:5. Na 1:4.

33. **like unto.** Nu 17:4-8. Je 1:11, 12. **and three.** Ex 37:19, 20. Zc 4:3.

36. **beaten.** ver. 18, +31. Nu 8:4. 1 K 10:16, 17. 2 Ch 9:15.

37. **seven.** Ex 37:23. Zc 4:2. Re 1:4, 12, 20. 2:1. 4:5. **they shall.** Ex *27:21. 30:8. Le 24:2-4. 2 Ch *13:11. **light.** or, cause to ascend. Ex 27:20. 30:8. 40:4, 25. Le 24:2. Nu *8:2, 3. 1 S *3:3. **give.** Ex 40:24. Nu 8:2. Ps *119:105. Pr 6:23. Is +√8:20. Mt 5:14. Lk 1:79. Jn 1:9. *8:12. 12:35. Ac 26:18. Re 21:23-25. 22:5. **it.** Heb. the face of it. Nu 8:2.

38. **the tongs.** Ex 37:23. Nu 4:3. 1 K *7:49. 2 Ch 4:21. Is *6:6. **snuff dishes.** Ex 27:3. 37:23. Le 16:12. Nu 4:9. 16:37. 1 K 7:50. 2 K 12:13. 25:14. Je 52:18, 19.

39. **talent.** Ex 37:24. Zc ◑5:7.

40. **that thou make.** Ex 26:30. 39:42, 43. Nu *8:4. 1 Ch 28:11, 19. Ezk 43:11, 12. Ac *7:44. He ⟩8:5. **pattern.** 1 Ch 28:19. **was showed thee in the mount.** Heb. thou wast caused to see in the mount.

EXODUS 26

Directions for making the ten curtains of the sanctuary, 1-6. The eleven curtains of goats' hair; and the coverings of rams' skins and badgers' skins, 7-14. The boards, sockets, and bars, 15-30. The veil and pillars to separate the most holy place, 31-33. The arrangement of the furniture in the sanctuary; and the hanging for the door, 34-37.

1. **the tabernacle with ten curtains.** The word *mishcan*, here rendered tabernacle, from *shachan*, to dwell, means simply a dwelling-place *or* habitation (✻S#4908h, Ex +25:9n). "When God had brought the children of Israel out of Egypt," says the very learned Dr. Cudworth, "resolving to manifest himself in a peculiar manner present among them, he thought good to dwell amongst them in a visible and external manner; and therefore, while they were in the wilderness, and sojourned in tents, he would have a tent or tabernacle built, to sojourn with them also. Now, the tabernacle being thus a house for God to dwell in visibly, to make up the notion of dwelling or habitation complete, there must be all things suitable to a house belonging to it. Hence, in the holy place, there must be a table and a candlestick, because these were the ordinary furniture of a room. The table must have its dishes, and spoons, and bowls, and covers, belonging to it, though they were never used; and always be furnished with bread upon it. The candlestick must have its lamps continually burning," etc. Ex 16:16 (◑S#168h). 25:8, 9n. 27:21n. ◑33:7n. *36:8-19. 40:◑2n, 17-19, 33n. 1 Ch 17:1. 21:29. Jn=1:14. 2:21. He 8:2. 9:9, 23, 24. Re 21:3. **fine twined linen.** ver. 36. Ex 25:4. 35:6, 35. Re 19:8. **cherubims.** See on Ex 25:18. **cunning work.** Heb. the work of a cunning workman, *or*, embroiderer. ver. 31. Ex 28:6, 15. *36:8, 35. 39:3, 8.

2. **curtain.** ver. 7, 8. Nu 4:25. 2 S 7:2. 1 Ch 17:1.

3. **coupled together**. ver. 9. Ex 36:10. Jn 17:21.
1 C 12:4, 12-27. Ep 2:21, 22. 4:3-6, 16. Col 2:2, 19.
4. **loops of blue**. ver. 5, 10, 11. Ex 36:11, 12, 17.
6. **taches of gold**. ver. 11, 33. Ex 35:11. 36:13, 18.
39:33. **one tabernacle**. Ep 1:22, 23. 4:16. 1 P 2:4, 5.
7. **curtains**. Ex 35:26. *36:14-18. Nu 4:25. Ps 45:13.
1 P 3:4. 5:5. **goats' hair**. *Izzim*, goats, but used here
elliptically for goats' hair. In different parts of Asia
Minor, Syria, Cilicia, and Phrygia, the goats have long,
fine, and beautiful hair; in some cases, almost as fine
as silk, which is shorn at proper times, and manufactured into garments. Ex 25:4. 35:6, 23. Nu 31:20. **a
covering**. ver. 14. Is 4:5mg. **eleven**. ver. 1, 9, 12.
8. **length of one curtain**. ver. 2, 13.
9. **five curtains by themselves**. ver. 3.
10. **fifty loops**. ver. 4-6.
11. **tent**. *or*, covering. See on ver. 3, 6.
12. **shall hang over**. ver. 9.
13. **a cubit**. ver. 2, 8. **of that which remaineth**.
Heb. in the remainder, or surplusage.
14. **a covering**. Ex *36:19. Nu 4:5. Ps 27:5. 121:4,
5. Is 4:6. 25:4. 1 C *12:13. **rams' skins dyed red**. Ex
25:5. 35:7, 23. 39:34. Nu 4:10. Ezk 16:10. **badgers'
skins**. Ex 25:5.
15. **boards**. ver. 18, 22-29. Ex 35:11. 36:20-33.
39:33. 40:17, 18. Nu 3:36. 4:31, 32. Ezk 27:5, 6. Ep
2:20, 21. **of shittim**. Ex 25:5.
17. **tenons**. or, handles. Heb. hands. ver. 19. Ex
36:22, 24.
19. **forty sockets of silver**. ver. 25, 37. Ex 27:10,
12-18. 36:24-26. 38:27, 30, 31. 40:18. Nu 3:36. 4:31,
32. Jb 38:6mg. SS 5:15.
21. **two sockets under one board**. ver. 19.
23. **corners**. *S#4742h. Ex 36:28.
24. **be coupled**. Heb. double; twined. or, twinned.
or, paired. Ex 36:29. SS 4:2. 6:6. **and they shall be
coupled together above**. Ex 36:29, 30. Ps 133:1-3.
1 C 1:10. 3:16. Ep *4:15, 16. 1 P 2:5. **corners**. *S#4740h.
Ex 36:29. 2 Ch 26:9. Ne 3:19, 20, 24, 25. Ezk 41:22.
46:21, 22.
26. **bars**. ver. 27, 28, 29, etc. Dt 3:5. Jg 16:3. **of
shittim wood**. Ex 36:31-38. Nu 3:36. 4:31. Ro 15:1.
1 C 9:19, 20. Ga 6:1, 2. Ep *4:16. Col 2:19.
28. **reach**. lit. flee. 1 Ch 12:15. Ne 13:28. Jb 41:28.
Pr 19:26.
29. **overlay the boards with gold**. See on Ex 25:11,
12. **places**. lit. houses. Ex 23:19. 25:27. 36:34. 37:14,
27. 38:5.
30. **rear up the tabernacle**. Ex 40:2, 17, 18. Nu
10:21. Dt 27:2. Jsh 18:1. Ep *2:19-22. He 8:2. **according
to the**. Ex 25:9, 40. 27:8. Ac *7:44. He *8:5. 9:23.
fashion. lit. judgment. Ex 28:15, 29, 30. **showed thee**.
lit. was caused to see. Ex 25:40mg. Le 13:49. Dt 4:35.
31. **a vail of**. ver. +33, 35. Ex 36:35. 40:3, 21. Le
16:2, 15. 2 Ch *3:14. Mt *27:51. Mk 15:38. Lk 23:45.
Jn=1:14. 2 C 3:18. Ep 2:14. 1 T=3:16. 2 T *1:10.
He 6:19. *9:3-8. *10:20, 21. 1 J=4:2, 3. 2 J=7. **blue**.
Ex 25:4. 35:6, 25, 35. 36:8. **purple**. *Argaman*, a very
precious color, extracted from the *purpura*, or *murex*,
a species of shell-fish; and supposed to be the same
with the costly and much celebrated Tyrian purple.
scarlet. *Tolaath*; properly the worm whence the scarlet
color was produced. Ex +25:4. 2 Ch 3:14. **cunning
work**. ver. 1. Ex 28:15. 38:23. 2 Ch 2:7-13. Ps 137:5.
SS 7:1. **cherubims shall it be made**. See on Ex
25:18.

32. **pillars**. Ex 13:21. 26:37. 27:10-17. Jg 16:25, 26,
29, etc. **of shittim**. ver. 37. Ex 36:38. Est 1:6. **their
hooks shall be of gold**. or, pegs. ver. 37. Ex 27:10,
11, 17. 36:36, 38. 38:10, 11, 12, 17, 19, 28. The Hebrew
waveyhem, which we translate their hooks, is rendered
by the LXX. *kephalides*, and by the Vulgate, *capita*,
capitals. But as the root *wavah* seems to signify to
connect, and as the letter *wav*, if it has not its name
from its hook-like form, is yet used as a connective
particle, it would rather appear to denote hooks, which
connected the curtains or vails to the pillars. The LXX.
also render it *agkulai*, handles, and *krikoi*, rings or
clasps.
33. **vail**. Mt *27:51. Mk *15:38. Lk=4:22. 23:45.
Jn=7:46. He +=2:10. =10:20. **the taches**. Ex 27:10.
36:36. **within the vail**. He 9:4, 5. **the ark of the testimony**. Ex 25:16. *40:21. **divide**. Ro=8:3. 2 C=5:15,
16. He 2:9,=14. =9:8. **the holy place**. Le *16:2.
1 K 8:6, 10. 2 Ch 5:7-10. He 9:2, 3. **most holy**. ♪147H,
Ge +9:25.
34. **put the mercy seat**. See on Ex 25:21. 40:20.
He *9:5.
35. **the table**. See on Ex 40:22. He 9:2, 8, 9. **the
candlestick**. See on Ex 25:31-37. 40:24. **side**. Heb.
rib. ver. 20, 26, 27, 35, etc. Ex 25:12, 14. Ge 2:21,
22.
36. **hanging**. or, covering. Jg 3:24. Ezk 28:13. This
may be termed the first vail, as it occupied the door
or entrance to the tabernacle: the vail that separated
the Holy of Holies is called the second vail, He 9:3,
Ex 36:37. 40:28. Jn 10:9. 14:6. **door**. or, opening. i.e.
the open space of the door, as distinguished from the
leaf of the door itself. **the tent**. Ex 35:11. 39:33. 40:29.
Nu 3:25. 9:15. 2 S 7:6. Ps 78:60. **of blue**. See on ver.
31. **wrought with**. Ex 27:16. 28:39. 35:35. 36:37. 38:18,
23. 39:29. Jg 5:30.
37. **overlay them with gold**. Ex 36:38. **cast**. lit. pour
out. Ex 25:12. Ge 28:18. 35:14.

EXODUS 27

*The brazen altar for burnt sacrifice, and its vessels,
1-8. The court of the tabernacle, its hangings, pillars,
and dimensions, 9-19. The oil for the candlestick, and
the ordering of it, 20, 21.*

1. **altar of shittim wood**. ver. 2. Ex 20:24-26. 24:4.
*38:1-7, 30. 40:10, 29. 2 S 24:18. 2 Ch 4:1. Ezk *43:13-
17. He *13:10.
2. **horns of it upon the four corners thereof**. The
horns might have been designed not only for ornament,
but to prevent the sacrifices from falling off, and to
tie the victim to, previous to its being sacrificed. Ex
29:12. Le *4:7, 18, 25. 8:15. *16:18. 1 K *1:50, 51.
2:28. Ps *118:27. He *6:18. **overlay it with brass**. Nu
*16:38, 39. 1 K 8:64.
3. **pans**. or, pots. Ex 16:3. 38:3. 1 K 7:45. **ashes**.
Le +=1:16. Nu 4:13. Ps 20:3mg. **his shovels**. Ex 38:3.
Le 16:12. Nu 4:14. 1 K 7:40, 45. 2 K 25:14. 2 Ch
4:11, 16. Je 52:18. **basons**. or, bowls. Ex 24:6. 38:3.
Nu 4:14mg. 7:13. Am 6:6. Zc 9:15. 14:20. **flesh-hooks**.
or, forks. Ex 38:3. Nu 4:14. 1 S 2:13, 14. 1 Ch 28:17.
2 Ch 4:16. **firepans**. Ex 38:3. 1 K 7:45. 2 K 25:15. Je
52:19, 20.
4. **a grate of network**. Ex 35:16. 38:4, 5. **rings in
the four corners thereof**. See on Ex 25:12.
5. **compass of the altar**. Ex 38:4.

6. **staves for the altar**. See on Ex 25:13-15. 30:4. Nu 4:14.

7. **bear it**. Ex 25:28. 30:4. Nu 4:13, 14.

8. **as it was showed**. Heb. he showed. Ex 25:9, 40. *26:30, etc. 1 Ch 28:11, 19. Mt 15:9. Col 2:20-23. He 8:5.

9. **the court**. Ex *38:9-20. 40:8. 1 K 6:36. 8:64. 2 Ch 33:5. Ps 84:10. 92:13. 100:4. 116:19. Ezk 40:14, 20, 23, 28, 32, 44. 42:3, 19, 20. 46:20-24. **hangings for**. Ex 26:31, 37. 35:17. 39:40.

10. **sockets shall be of brass**. See on Ex 26:19-21. **fillets shall be of silver**. Ex 36:38. Je 52:21.

14. **hangings of one side**. ver. 9. Ex 26:36.

16. **gate**. This word which generally expresses the large outer gate of a court, city, etc., here denotes the open space, not the gate itself (Young). Ge +14:7. **of blue**. See on Ex 26:31, 36. **needlework**. Ex 28:39. 36:37. 39:29. Jg 5:30. Ps 45:14.

18. **length of the court**. ver. 9-12. **fifty every where**. Heb. fifty by fifty.

19. **all the pins thereof**. ver. 3. Ex 35:18. 38:20, 31. 39:40. Nu 3:37. 4:32. Dt +23:13mg. Ezr 9:8. Ec 12:11. Is 22:23-25. 33:20. Zc 10:4.

20. **pure oil olive**. That is, such oil as could be easily expressed from the olives, after they had been bruised in a mortar; and which is much purer than that obtained after the olives are put under the press. Ex 39:27. Le 24:2-4. Jg 9:9. Ps 23:5. Zc 4:11-14. Re 11:4. **beaten**. Ex 25:31, 36. 29:40. 30:36. 37:7. Le=2:1, 14. 24:5. Nu 8:4. 11:8. Is 28:28. Things bruised, crushed, or beaten symbolize the Lord's sufferings. Is=53:5. He +=2:10. **for the light**. See on Ex 25:31-37. **to cause the lamp**. Josephus says, that the whole of the seven lamps burned all night; and that in the morning four were extinguished, and three burned the whole of the day. Such might have been the practice in his time; but it appears sufficiently evident from Ex 30:8, and 1 S 3:3, that they were extinguished in the morning. **to burn**. Heb. to ascend up. Ex 25:37. Ps *119:105. Mt *5:16. 1 J *2:20.

21. **the tabernacle of the congregation**. Rather, tent of meeting. The Holy Spirit never speaks of the "tabernacle of the congregation," as the Hebrew *ohel moheed* is frequently but erroneously rendered. The tabernacle, Heb. *mishkan* (✳S#4908h, Ex +25:9), is properly the dwelling place of God, containing the presence of Jehovah evidenced in the light of the Shekinah Glory, or cloud, in the Holy of Holies. Such was certainly not the place where the people gathered for worship! Thus the tent of meeting, or tent of meeting by appointment, or at appointed seasons, Heb. *ohel moheed*, is connected with the assembly of the people. For S#168h, *ohel*, tent, Ex +16:16. Ex 26:1n. 29:10, 44. 33:7n. Le 3:8. Nu 8:9. ✳S#4150h, *moheed*, assembly, meeting, congregation in the expression "tabernacle (or tent) of the congregation": Ex 27:21. 28:43. 29:4, 10, 11, 30, 32, 42, 44. 30:16, 18, 20, 26, 36. 31:7. 33:7, 7. 35:21. 38:8, 30. 39:32, 40. 40:2, 6, 7, 12, 22, 24, 26, 29, 30, 32, 34, 35. Le 1:1, 3, 5. 3:2, 8, 13. 4:4, 5, 7, 7, 14, 16, 18, 18. 6:16, 26, 30. 8:3, 4, 31, 33, 35. 9:5, 23. 10:7, 9. 12:6. 14:11, 23. 15:14, 29. 16:7, 16, 17, 20, 23, 33. 17:4, 5, 6, 9. 19:21. 24:3. Nu 1:1. 2:2, 17. 3:7, 8, 25, 25, 38. 4:3, 4, 15, 23, 25, 25, 28, 30, 31, 33, 35, 37, 39, 41, 43, 47. 6:10, 13, 18. 7:5, 89. 8:9, 15, 19, 22, 24, 26. 10:3. 11:16. 12:4. 14:10. 16:18, 19, 42, 43, 50. 17:4. 18:4, 6, 21, 22,

23, 31. 19:4. 20:6. 25:6. 27:2. 31:54. Dt 31:14, 14. Jsh 18:1. 19:51. 1 S 2:22. 1 K 8:4. 1 Ch 6:32. 9:21. 23:32. 2 Ch 1:3, 6, 13. 5:5. For ✚S#4150h, rendered set time, due season, etc., see Ge +17:21. **without the vail**. Ex *26:31-33. 40:3. **testimony**. See on Ex 16:34. 25:16, 21. **Aaron**. Ex 30:8. 1 S 3:3. 2 Ch 13:11. Ml 2:7. Mt 4:16. Lk 12:35. Jn 5:35. 2 C 4:6. Ac 20:27, 28. 2 P 1:19. Re 2:1. **evening to**. Ex +30:8. Ge 1:5, 8. Le 24:3. Ps 134:1. **a statute**. Ex 28:43. 29:9, 28. Le 3:17. 16:34. 24:9. Nu 18:23. 19:21. 1 S 20:35. **for ever**. Heb. *olam*, Ex +12:24.

EXODUS 28

Aaron and his sons are appointed to the priesthood, 1. The holy garments prescribed for the high priest, 2-5; consisting of the ephod and girdle, 6-14; the breastplate of judgment with Urim and Thummim, 15-30; the robe of the ephod, the mitre, and the coat of fine linen, 31-39. The garments of the other priests, 40-43.

1. **take**. Le 8:2. Nu 16:9-11. 17:2-9. 2 Ch 26:18-21. He *5:1-5. **with him**. Col=2:20. =3:1, 3, 4. **among**. ver. 41. Ex 29:1, 9, 44. 30:30. 31:10. 35:19. Nu *18:7. Dt 10:6. 1 Ch 6:10. 2 Ch 11:14. Lk 1:8. **unto me**. Jn =14:12. =15:15. **Nadab**. Ex 6:23. 24:1, 9. Le 10:1, 12. Nu 2:4. 26:61. 1 Ch 24:1-4.

2. **holy garments**. Ex *29:5-9, 29, 30. 31:10. 39:1, 2. 40:13. Le 8:7-9, *30. Nu 20:26-28. Ps *132:9, 16. Is *61:3, 10. *64:6. Zc 3:3, 4. Ro 3:22. *13:14. Ga *3:27. He *7:26. Re 19:8. **glory**. ver. 40. Ex 19:5, 6. Nu 27:20, 21. Jb 40:10. Ps 90:16, 17. 96:6. 149:4. Is 4:2. Je 9:23, 24. Jn *1:14. 1 C *1:30, 31. He=2:9. 2 P=1:17. 1 J=3:2. Re 5:10. 19:8. **and**. J93A, Ge +1:26.

3. **wise hearted**. Ex *31:3-6. 35:30, 35. *36:1, 2. Pr 2:6. Is 28:24-26. **filled**. Dt 34:9. Is 11:2. 1 C *12:7-11. Ep 1:17. Ja *1:17. **spirit**. Heb. *ruach*, Ge +41:38.

4. **a breastplate**. *Choshen*, in Hebrew is used for the square breastplate of the high priest, in which were set twelve precious stones, each being engraved with the name of one of the sons of Jacob. ver. 15. Ex 39:8-21. Is 59:17. Ep 6:14. 1 Th 5:8. Re 9:17. **ephod**. The ephod seems to have been a short cloak, without sleeves. ver. 6-14. Ex 39:2-5, 21, 22. Le *8:7, 8. 1 S 2:18. 22:18. *23:6. 30:7. 2 S 6:14. **a robe**. The word *meil*, from *alah*, to ascend, go up on, may be considered as an upper garment that goes up or over the rest, a surtout. ver. 31-34. Ex 39:25, 26. **broidered**. ver. 39, 40. Le 8:7. **a mitre**. Ex 39:28. Le 8:9. Zc 3:5. **a girdle**. Is 11:5.

5. **gold**. Ex 25:3, 4. 39:2, 3.

6. **linen**. See on Ex 26:1. 1 S *2:18. *22:18. 2 S *6:14, 15.

7. **shoulderpieces**. Ex 39:4. Ps 55:2. Is 40:11. 63:9. 1 P 5:7.

8. **curious**. *or*, embroidered. ver. 27, 28. Ex 29:5. 39:20, 21. Le 8:7. Is *11:5. Ep *6:14. 1 P 1:13. Re *1:13.

9. **onyx**. ver. 20. Ex 39:13. Ge 2:12. Jb 28:16. Ezk 28:13. **grave**. ver. 36. Ex 39:6. 2 Ch 2:7. SS 8:6. Is 49:16.

10. **according to their birth**. Ex 1:1-4. Ge 43:33.

11. **engraver**. Ex 35:35. 38:23. Dt 27:15. 1 S 13:19. 2 S 5:11. 2 K 12:11. 22:6. 24:14, 16. **engravings of a**. ver. 21, 36. Je 22:24. Zc 3:9. Ep 1:13. 4:30. 2 T 2:19. Re 7:2. **signet**. ver. 21, 36. Ex 39:6, 14, 30. Ge 38:18.

1 K 21:8. Jb 38:14. 41:15. SS *8:6. Je 22:24. Hg *2:23. **ouches of gold.** ver. 13, 14, 25. Ex 39:6, 13, 18.

12. **the shoulders.** ver. 7. Ps 89:19. Is *9:6. 12:2. Zc 6:13, 14. He 7:25-28. **Aaron shall bear.** ver. 29. Ex 39:6, 7. Ep *5:27. He *7:25. **for a memorial.** Ex 12:14. 13:9. 39:7. Ge 9:12-17. Le 24:7. Nu 16:40. 31:54. Jsh 4:7. Is 62:6. Zc 6:14. Lk 1:54, 72. Ac *10:4. 2 T *2:19.

14. **chains of.** ver. 24. Ex 39:15. **of wreathen.** ver. 22-25. Ex 39:17, 18. 1 K 7:17. 2 K 25:17. 2 Ch 4:12, 13.

15. **the breastplate.** See on ver. 4, 30. Ex 39:8. Le 8:8. **after.** See on ver. 6. Ex 26:1.

17. **thou shalt.** See on ver. 9, 11. Ex 39:10, etc. Ml 3:17. **set it in settings of stones.** Heb. fill in it fillings of stone. Ex 25:7. 31:5. 35:9, 27, 33. 39:10. **the first row.** Ezk 28:13. Re 21:19-21. **a sardius,** or, ruby. Ex 39:10. The Hebrew *odem,* from *adam,* to be red, ruddy, seems to denote the ruby; as *adam* does in Persian a beautiful gem, of a fine deep red color, with a mixture of purple. Jb 28:18. Pr 3:15. 8:11. 20:15. 31:10. La 4:7. **a topaz.** *Pitdah* is constantly rendered by the LXX. *topadzion,* and Vulgate, *topazius,* with which agrees Josephus. The topaz is a precious stone, of a pale, dead green, with a mixture of yellow, sometimes of a fine yellow; and hence called chrysolyte by the moderns, from its gold color. Jb 28:19. Re 21:20. **a carbuncle.** *Bareketh,* from *barak,* to lighten, glitter, a very elegant gem, of a deep red color, with a mixture of scarlet. Is 54:11, 12.

18. **emerald.** *Nopech,* an emerald, the same with the ancient *smaragdus;* one of the most beautiful of all the gems, and of a bright green color, without any mixture. Ex 39:11. Ezk 27:16. **sapphire.** Ex 24:10. Jb 28:6, 16. SS 5:14. Ezk 1:26. 10:1. Re 4:3. **diamond.** Je 17:1. Ezk 28:13.

19. **a ligure.** Ex 39:12. **an agate.** Is 54:12.

20. **a beryl.** Ezk 1:16. 10:9. Da 10:6. Re 21:20. **an onyx.** See on ver. 9. **a jasper.** Re 4:3. 21:11, 18-20. **inclosings.** Heb. fillings. ver. 13.

21. **twelve.** ver. 9-11. **every one.** Is *43:4. Ml *3:17. Ep 4:7. **according to the twelve.** 1 K 18:31. Lk 22:30. Ja 1:1. Re 7:4-8. 21:12.

22. **upon the breastplate.** ver. 14.

23. **two rings.** Ex 25:11-15.

25. **wreathen chains.** ver. 14. Ex 39:15. **on the shoulder pieces.** ver. 7. **of the ephod.** Ex 39:4.

27. **the curious girdle.** See on ver. 8.

28. **a lace.** ver. 31, 37. Ex 39:30, 31. Nu 15:38.

29. **in the.** See on ver. 15, 30. **upon.** See on ver. 12. Je 30:21. Ro 10:1. **a memorial.** SS *8:6. Is *49:15, 16.

30. **the Urim.** i.e. enlightening, *S#224h. Le 8:8. Nu *27:21. Dt 33:8. 1 S *28:6. Ezr *2:63. Ne 7:65. Is 24:15 (fires. mg, valleys). 31:9 (fire). 44:16. 47:14. 50:11. Ezk 5:2. **and Thummim.** i.e. perfections, *S#8550h, plural of *S#8537h. Strong states "one of the epithets of the objects in the high-priest's breastplate as an emblem of complete Truth." Le 8:8. Dt 33:8. Ezr 2:63. Ne 7:65. For *S#8537h, see Ge 20:5 (integrity). The lights and perfections; rendered by the LXX. manifestation and truth; and, by the Vulgate, *doctrina et veritas,* doctrine and truth. Among the various and contradictory opinions respecting the form and substance of these mysterious appendages, the most probable seems to be that of Josephus, Philo,

Bp. Patrick, Parkhurst, and the Jewish writers generally; who state, that they were no other than the twelve precious stones of the high priest's breastplate. In support of this statement, it is observed, (1) That in the description of the high priest's breastplate, Ex 39:8, et seq., the Urim and Thummim are not mentioned, but only the rows of stones; and on the contrary, in Le 8:8, the Urim and Thummim are expressly mentioned, but not a word is said of the four rows of stones. (2) As Moses has given such a particular description of every thing relative to the high priest's dress, these would certainly have been described had they been different from what was previously mentioned. Le 8:8. Nu 27:21. Dt 33:8. Jg 1:1. 20:18, 23, 27, 28. 1 S 23:9-12. 28:6. 30:7, 8. Ezr 2:63. Ne 7:65. Jn *1:9, 18. *16:13, 14. Ro *12:1, 2. He *1:1, 2. **Aaron's heart.** SS 8:6. Re ○22:4. **bear the judgment.** Zc 6:13. He *9:24. **upon his heart.** 2 C 6:11, 12. 7:3. 12:15. Ph 1:7, 8. He 2:17. +*4:15. *9:12, 24.

31. **the robe.** ver. 4, 28. Ex 39:22. Le 8:7. Is 61:10. Ro 3:22.

32. **as it were.** Ex 39:28. 2 Ch 26:14. Ne 4:16. Jb 41:26. **that it be not rent.** Jn 19:23, 24. Ep 4:3-16.

33. **And.** Ex 39:24-26. **hem,** or, skirts. ver. 34. Ex 39:24, 25, 26. **pomegranates.** 1 K 7:18. 2 K 25:17. **bells.** Zc 14:20. Lk=4:22. 11:54. Jn 7:46. He 7:25. 9:24.

34. **golden bell.** Ps 89:15. SS 2:3. 4:3, 13. 6:7, 11. 8:2. Jn 15:4-8, 16. Col 1:5, 6, 10. **golden.** ♪84, Ge +6:17.

35. **goeth in.** Le 16:2. He 9:12. **die not.** Ps *2:11.

36. **grave upon it.** See on ver. 9, 11. **HOLINESS.** Ex 39:30. Le 8:9. *10:3, 4. 19:2. *21:1, 7, 8. Ps 93:5. Ezk 43:12. Zc 14:20. 1 C *1:30. He *7:26. √12:14. 1 P 1:15, 16. 2:9. Re 21:27.

37. **blue.** See on ver. 28, 31. **the mitre it.** ver. 4. Ex 29:6. 39:30, 31. Le 8:9. Zc 3:5.

38. **forehead.** Re 19:12. **bear the iniquity.** ver. 43. Le *10:17. 22:9. Nu *18:1. Is *53:6, 11, 12. Ezk 4:4-6. Jn *1:29. 2 C *5:21. He *9:28. 1 P *2:24. *3:18. **shall hallow.** Jn *17:19. He *4:14-16. **gifts.** He=13:15. **accepted.** Le *1:4. 22:27. 23:11. Is 56:7. 60:7. Ep 1:6. 1 P *2:5.

39. **embroider.** See on ver. 4. **the girdle.** See on ver. 8. Is 22:21. Mk 10:45. Lk 17:8. Jn 13:2-17. Re 1:13. **needlework.** Ps 45:14.

40. **Aaron's.** ver. 4. Ex *39:27, 29, 41. Le 8:13. Ezk *44:17, 18. Mt *22:12, 13. Ep *6:13. **bonnets.** Ex 29:9. **glory.** See on ver. 2. 1 T 2:9, 10. 6:9-11. T 2:7, 10. 1 P 3:3, 4. 5:5.

41. **with him.** 1 J=3:2. **anoint them.** Ex 29:7. 30:23-30. 40:15. Le 7:35. *8:12. 10:7. 1 S 9:16. 10:1, 7. 16:1-3, 12, 13. 2 S 2:4. 1 K 1:34. 19:15, 16. 2 K 11:12. Ps 45:2, 7. Is 10:27. 11:2. 61:1. Lk 1:15. 2:11. Jn 3:34. 2 C=1:21, 22. 1 J=2:20, 27. **and consecrate them.** Heb. fill their hand. Ex 29:9, 24, 35. Le ch. 8. Nu 3:3. Ezk 43:26. He 5:4. 7:28. √121S3P. Metonymy of the Adjunct B607. To fill the hand or hands is put for consecrating anyone to a sacred office, because the person so appointed received the sign or symbol of the office in his hands. For other instances of this figure see Ex 29:9mg, *27n, 33, 35. 32:29mg. Le 8:33. 16:32mg. Nu 3:3mg. Jg 17:5mg, 12. 1 K 13:33mg. **sanctify.** 1 Th=5:23. **minister.** See on ver. 1, 4.

42. **breeches.** Ex 20:26. 39:28. Le 6:10. 16:4. Ezk

44:18. Re 3:18. 16:15. **their nakedness.** Heb. flesh of their nakedness. ♪88, Ge +17:11. **thighs.** ♪88, Ge +24:2. **reach.** Heb. be.

43. **unto the altar.** Ex 20:26. **bear not iniquity.** ♪121C1E, Ge +19:15. Le *5:1, 17. 20:19, 20. *22:9. Nu 9:13. 18:22. Mt 22:12, 13. **a statute.** Ex 27:21. Le 17:7. **for ever.** Heb. *olam,* Ex +12:24.

EXODUS 29

The ceremonies and sacrifices to be used in consecrating the priests, and the altar, 1-37. The daily oblation, 38-41. God's gracious promises to meet with and dwell among the children of Israel, 42-46.

1. **hallow them.** ver. 21. Ex 20:11. 28:41. Le 8:2, etc. Mt 6:9. **to minister.** See on Ex 28:3. **Take.** Le 8:2. 9:2. 16:3. 2 Ch 13:9. **without.** Ex 12:5. Le 4:3. 5:15, 16. 6:6. 22:20. Ml *1:13, 14. He 7:26. 1 P 1:19.

2. **bread.** See on Ex 12:8. Le 2:4. *6:20-22. 8:2. 1 C 5:7. **tempered.** ver. 23. Le 2:4, 5, 15. 7:10. Nu 6:15. **wafers.** Le 7:12. 8:26. Nu 6:15, 19.

3. **in the basket.** Le 8:2, 26, 31. Nu 6:17.

4. **unto the door.** Ex 26:36. 40:28. Le *8:3-6. **wash.** Heb. *rahats,* S#7364h. Kal, Preterite: Ex 29:4, 17. 30:19, 21. 40:12, 31. Le 8:21. 14:8, 9. 15:5 (bathe), 6, 7, 8, 10, 13, 16, 18, 21, 22, 27. 16:4, 24, 26, 28. 17:15. 22:6. Nu 19:7, 8, 19. Ru 3:3. 1 K 22:38. 2 K 5:10. SS 5:3. Is 4:4. Ezk 23:40. Kal, Infinitive: Ge 24:32. Ex 2:5. 30:18. 40:30. 1 S 25:41. 2 Ch 4:6, 6. Jb 29:6. Kal, Imperative: Ge 18:4. 19:2. 2 S 11:8. 2 K *5:13. Is 1:16. Kal, Future: Ge 43:24, 31. Ex 30:20. 40:32. Le 1:9, 13. 8:6. 9:14. 17:16 (bathe). Dt 21:6. 23:11. Jg 19:21. 2 S 12:20. 2 K *5:12. Ps 26:6. 58:10. 73:13. Ezk 16:9. Kal, Participle: 2 S 11:2. SS 5:12. Pual, Preterite: Pr 30:12. Ezk 16:4. Hithpael, Preterite: Jb 9:30. See related notes (2 K 5:10n. He 9:10n). **them with water.** Ex 30:18-21. 40:12. Le 8:6. 14:8. Dt 23:11. Ezk 36:25. Jn 13:8-10. 1 C=6:11. Ep=5:26, 27. T 3:5. He +*10:22. 1 P *3:21. Re *1:5, 6.

5. **garments.** Ex 28:2-8. Le 8:7, 8. **put upon.** Ro=3:22. **curious.** The word *cheshev,* translated curious girdle, simply signifies a kind of embroidered work, of the same texture as the ephod itself. Ex 28:8.

6. **mitre.** *Mitznepheth,* from *tzanaph,* to wrap around, evidently means that covering of the head so universal in eastern countries, which we call turban, which consists of a cap, and a sash of fine linen or silk wound round its bottom. See on Ex 28:36-39. Le 8:9.

7. **anointing oil.** Ex 28:41. 30:23-31. Le 8:10-12. 10:7. 21:10. Nu 35:25. Ps 89:20. 133:2. Is 61:1. Jn 3:34. He *1:9. 1 J *2:27.

8. **his sons.** Ex 28:40. Le 8:13. **coats.** Ro=13:14.

9. **put.** Heb. bind. Le 8:13. **on them.** Jn=14:6. Ep=1:6. =6:14. Col=3:12, 14. 1 Th=5:8. **the priest's.** Ex 28:1. Nu 16:10, 35, 40. 18:7. He 5:4, 5, 10. 7:11-14. **theirs.** Re=1:6. **perpetual.** Heb. *olam,* Ge +9:12. **consecrate.** Heb. fill the hand of. Ex 28:41. 32:29mg. Le 8:22-28. 1 Ch 29:5mg. Col=2:9, 10. He *7:23-28.

10. **cause.** ver. 1. **put.** ver. 15, 19. Le 1:4. 3:2. 8:14, 18. 16:21. Is *53:6. 2 C *5:21.

11. **And.** Le *1:4, 5. 8:15. 9:8, 12. **door.** ver. 4. Le 1:3.

12. **the blood.** Le *8:15. 9:9. 16:14, 18, 19. He 9:13, 14, 22. 10:4. **the horns.** Ex 27:2. 30:2. 38:2. **thy finger.**

Mt 12:28. Lk=11:20. **pour all.** Le 4:7, 18, 25, 30, 34. 5:9. 9:9.

13. **all the fat.** ver. 22. Le 3:3, 4, 9, 10, 14-16. 4:8, 9, 26, 31, 35. 6:12. 7:3, 31. Ps 22:14. Is 1:11. 34:6. 43:24. **and the caul.** It seemeth by anatomy, and the Hebrew doctors, to be the midriff. Le 8:16, 25. 9:10, 19. **burn them.** ver. 18, 25. Le 1:9, 15. 16:25. 17:6. Nu 18:17. 1 S 2:16.

14. **flesh.** Le 4:11, 12, 21. 8:17. 16:27. He *13:11-13. **it is a.** Ex 30:10. Le 4:3, 25, 29, 32. 5:6, 8. 6:25. 9:2. 16:3, 11. Nu 7:16. 2 Ch 29:24. Ezr 8:35. **sin.** ♪121L5, Ge +4:7.

15. **one.** ver. 3, 19. Le 8:18-21. **put.** ver. 10. Le 1:4-9.

16. **slay the ram.** See on ver. 11, 12. **sprinkle.** 1 P *1:2.

17. **wash the.** Le 1:9, 13. 8:21. 9:14. Je 4:14. Mt 23:26. **unto.** or, upon. Le 8:20.

18. **a burnt offering.** Ge 22:2, 7, 13. Le 9:24. +*23:12. 1 S 7:9. 1 K 3:4. 18:38. Ps 50:8. Is 1:11. Je 6:20. 7:21, 22. Mk 12:33. He 10:6-10. **sweet savor.** ♪22C15, Ge +8:21. Ge *8:21. Le 1:17. Ep *5:2. Ph 4:18.

19. **other.** ver. 3. Le *8:22-29. **Aaron.** See on ver. 10.

20. **and put.** Le 8:24. 14:14. Is 50:5. Mk 7:33. **tip.** Ro=12:1. 1 C=6:19, 20. **sprinkle.** Le 14:7, 16. 16:14, 15, 19. Is 52:15. He 9:19-23. +*10:22. 12:24. 1 P 1:2.

21. **blood.** He *9:12. 1 P 2:5. Re 1:5, 6. **the anointing oil.** ver. 7. Ex *30:25-31. Le 8:30. 14:15-18, 29. 133:2. Is 11:2-5. 61:1-3. **shall be.** ver. 1. Jn 17:19. He *9:22. 10:29.

22. **Also thou.** ver. 13. Le 8:25-27. **the rump.** Le 3:9. 7:3. 9:19. **right shoulder.** Le 7:32, 33. 9:21. 10:14. Nu 18:18.

23. **one loaf.** ver. 2, 3.

24. **put.** Le 8:27. **wave them.** Heb. shake to and fro. ver. 26, 27. Le 7:30. 8:27, 29. 9:21. 14:12. 23:11. Nu 5:25. 6:20. 2 K +5:11mg. **a wave offering.** ver. 26, 27. Le 7:30. 9:21. 10:14. +*23:15. **before.** Ex 23:20. Le 16:12. Dt *16:16. 26:2.

25. **thou.** Le 7:29-31. 8:28. Ps 99:6. **for a sweet.** See on ver. 18. **savor.** ♪22C15, Ge +8:21. **offering.** ver. 41. Le 1:9, 13. 2:2, 9, 16. 3:3, 5, 9, 11, 14, 16. 7:5, 25. 10:13. 1 S 2:28.

26. **the breast.** Le 8:29. **it shall be thy.** Ps 99:6.

27. **the breast.** Le 7:31-34. 8:29. 9:21. 10:15. Nu 6:20. 18:11, 18, 19. Dt *18:3. **the wave offering.** The wave offering and the heave offering are thus distinguished by the Jewish writers: the former was waved horizontally towards the four cardinal points, to signify that He to whom it was consecrated was the Lord of the whole earth; the latter was lifted perpendicularly upward and downward, in token of its being devoted to the God of heaven. For heave offering, see on Ezr +8:25. Le +*23:15. **heave offering.** Nu 18:11, 18. Ezr +8:25. **the ram of the consecration.** ♪121S3P, Ex 28:41. ver. 22, 34. Le 7:37. 8:28-31. Literally, the ram of filling; so called, according to some, because at the consecration of the priests, certain pieces of the sacrifice were put into their hands (ver. 24); on which account their consecration itself is called filling their hands (Ex 28:41). Rabbi Solomon gives a different reason for the ram being so called; because the sacrifice completed the consecration, and thereupon the priests

were fully invested in their office. Accordingly, the LXX. render it by *teleiosis*, consummation. See He 7:28.

28. **Aaron**'s. Le 7:32-34. 10:14, 15. Dt 18:3. **for ever**. Heb. *olam*, Ex +12:24. **is an heave**. ver. 27. Le 7:14, 34. Nu 15:19, 20. 18:24, 29. 31:29, 41. **sacrifice**. Le 3. 7:11, etc. **peace offering**. Le +*23:19.

29. **holy**. Ex 28:3, 4. **his**. Nu *20:26-28. **anointed**. ver. 5-7. Ex 30:30. 40:15. Le 8:7-12. Nu 18:8. 35:25.

30. **that son**. Heb. he of his sons. Nu 20:28. He 7:26. **seven days**. ver. 35. Ex 12:15. Ge 8:10, 11. Le 8:33-35. 9:1, 8. 12:2, 3. 13:5. Jsh 6:14, 15. Ezk 43:26. Ac 20:6, 7.

31. **the ram**. See on ver. 27. **seethe his flesh**. Le 8:31. 1 S 2:13, 15. Ezk 46:20-24.

32. **Aaron**. Ex 24:9-11. Le 10:12-14. **and the bread**. ver. 2, 3, 23. Mt 12:4.

33. **eat those**. Le *10:13-18. Ps 22:26. Jn 6:53-55. 1 C 11:24, 26. **atonement**. Jn=6:54-57. **consecrate**. ſ121S3P, Ex +28:41. **a stranger**. Le 22:10-13. Nu 1:51. 3:10, 38. 16:40. 18:4, 7. **they are holy**. Nu 16:5.

34. **flesh**. ver. 22, 26, 28. **burn**. Ex 12:10. 16:19. Le 7:18, 19. 8:32. 10:16.

35. **thus shalt thou do**. Ex 40:12-15. Le 8:4, etc. **according**. Ex 39:42, 43. 40:16. Jn 15:14. **seven days**. ver. 30, 37. Ex 40:12, 13. Le *8:33-35. 14:8-11. **consecrate**. ſ121S3P, Ex +28:41.

36. **every day**. See on ver. 10-14. Ezk 43:25, 27. 48:18-20. He *10:11. **cleanse**. Le 16:16-19, 27. He 9:22, 23. **anoint it**. Ex *30:26, 28, 29. 40:9-11. Le 8:10, 11. Nu 7:1.

37. **and sanctify it**. Ex 40:10. Da 9:24. **it shall be an**. Ex 30:29. Mt 23:17, 19.

38. **two lambs**. Nu *28:3-8. 1 Ch 16:40. 2 Ch 2:4. *13:11. 31:3. Ezr 3:3. Da 9:21, 27. 12:11. Jn *1:29. He *7:27. 1 P *1:19. Re 5:9-12.

39. **in the morning**. 2 K 16:15. 2 Ch 13:11. Ps 5:3. *55:16, 17. Ezk 46:13-15. Lk 1:10. Ac 26:7. **at even**. See on ver. 41.

40. **a tenth**. Ex 16:36. Nu 15:4, 9. 28:5, 13. **hin**. Ex 30:24. Le 23:13. Nu 15:4. 28:14. Ezk 4:11. 45:24. 46:5, 7, 11, 14. **beaten**. Ex +27:20. Is=53:5. He +=2:10. **oil**. Mt=26:36n. **a drink offering**. Ge 35:14. Le +*23:13. Nu 6:15-17. 15:5, 7, 10, 24. 28:10, 14, 15, 24. 29:16. Dt 32:38. Is 57:6. Ezk 20:28. 45:17. Jl 1:9, 13. 2:14. Ph 2:17g.

41. **offer at even**. 1 K 18:29, 36. 2 K *16:15. Ezr 9:4, 5. Ps 141:2. Ezk 46:13-15. Da *9:21. **meat offering**. Le +*23:13. **drink offering**. Le +*23:13. **for a sweet**. ver. 18, 25. **savor**. ſ22C15, Ge +8:21.

42. **a continual**. ver. 38. Ex 30:8. Nu *28:6. Da 8:11-13. 12:11. **where**. Ex 25:22. 30:6, 36. Le 1:1. Nu 17:4. **meet**. Ex *25:22. Le *16:2. 2 C=5:19. **speak**. Jn =1:1. =8:26, 43, 47. He=1:2.

43. **the tabernacle**. or, **Israel. sanctified**. Ex *40:34. 1 K 8:11. 2 Ch *5:14. *7:1-3. Is 6:1-3. 60:1. Ezk 43:5. Hg *2:7-9. Ml *3:1. 2 C 3:18. 4:6. 1 J 3:2. Re 21:22, 23.

44. **sanctify also**. Le 21:15. 22:9, 16. Jn 10:36. =17:19. Re 1:5, 6.

45. **dwell**. Ex 15:17. 25:8. Le 26:12. Ps 68:18. Zc *2:10. Mt=1:23. Jn *14:17, 20,=23. 2 C *6:16. Ep 2:22. Re *21:3.

46. **know**. Jn=14:7-9. **that I am**. See on Ex 20:2.

Je 31:33. **dwell among**. Jn *1:14. **them: I am**. Le 11:44. 18:30. 19:2. Ezk 20:5.

EXODUS 30

Directions concerning the altar of incense, 1-10; the half shekel of ransom money, 11-16; the brazen laver, 17-21; the holy anointing oil, 22-33; and the incense, 34-38.

1. The Samaritan inserts the first ten verses of this chapter after ver. 32 of chapter 26. **an altar**. ver. 7, 8, 10. Ex 37:25-28. 40:5. Le 4:7, 18. 1 K 6:20. 2 Ch 26:16. Re 8:3. **to burn incense**. Where so many sacrifices were offered, it was essentially necessary to have some pleasing perfume to counteract the disagreeable smells that must have arisen from the slaughter of so many animals, the burning of so much flesh, the sprinkling of blood, etc. No blood was ever sprinkled on this altar, except once a year, on the grand day of expiation. It was called also the golden altar (Nu 4:11); and the incense was as constantly burnt on it every day, as the morning and evening sacrifice of a lamb was burnt on the brazen altar. **incense**. Ps=*141:2. Pr=27:9. SS=1:3, +=12. Lk=23:44n. Jn=16:23, 26. 2 C=2:14, 15. Ph=4:18. He=7:25. =9:24. Re=⅃5:8. =⅃8:3.

2. **the horns**. See on Ex 27:2.

3. **overlay it**. Ex 25:11, 24. **top**. Heb. roof. **sides**. Heb. walls. Ex 37:26.

4. **rings**. Ex 25:12, 14, 27. 26:29. 27:4, 7. **two corners**. Heb. ribs. Ex 25:14. 26:26, 27, +*35. 37:27.

5. **staves**. Ex 25:13, 27.

6. **vail**. Ex 26:31-35. 40:3, 5, 26. Mt 27:51. He 9:3, 4. **mercy seat**. Ex 25:21, 22. Le 16:13. 1 Ch 28:11. He 4:16. 9:5. **I will**. ver. 36. Ex 29:42, 43. Nu 17:4. He *9:24.

7. **sweet incense**. Heb. incense of spices. ver. 34-38. **dresseth**. Ex 27:20, 21. 1 S 2:28. 3:3. 1 Ch 23:13. Lk *1:9. Ac 6:4.

8. **lighteth**. *or*, setteth up. Ex 27:20, 21. Le 24:2, 3. 1 S 3:3. 2 Ch 13:11. Heb. causeth to ascend. Ex 25:37. *27:20. **at even**. Heb. between the two evens. Ex 12:6mg. **a perpetual**. Ro 8:34. 1 Th 5:17. He 7:25. 9:24. **incense**. ver. +1. Ex 30:34. SS 2:13. 4:13, 14.

9. **strange incense**. Le *10:1. **meat offering**. Le +*23:13. **drink offering**. Le +*23:13.

10. **Aaron**. Ex 29:36, 37. Le *16:18, 29, 30. 23:27. He 1:3. 9:7, 22, 23, 25. **it once**. Le 16:14, 18, 19. Nu 29:7. He +=2:10. **sin offering**. Le 16:5, 6. **of atonements**. Le +*23:27.

12. **takest**. Ex *38:25, 26. Nu 1:2-5. 26:2-4. 2 S 24:2. **their number**. Heb. them that are to be numbered. **a ransom**. Nu 31:50. 2 Ch 24:6. Jb 33:24. 36:18. Ps 49:7. Mt 20:28. Mk 10:45. 1 T *2:6. 1 P *1:18, 19. **soul**. Heb. *nephesh*, Ge +12:13. Jb 32:2mg. 1 P +*4:19. **no plague**. 2 S 24:2-15. 1 Ch 21:12, 14. 27:24.

13. **a shekel is**. Le 27:25. Nu 3:47. Ezk 45:12. **an half shekel**. Ex *38:26. Ne 10:32. Mt 17:24g.

14. **from twenty**. Nu 1:3, 18, 20. 14:29. 26:2. 32:11.

15. **rich**. Jb *34:19. Pr *22:2. Ep *6:9. Col 3:25. Ja *2:1. **give more**. Heb. multiply. **give less than**. Heb. diminish. Je +10:24mg. **an atonement**. ver. 12. Le 17:11. Nu 31:50. 2 S 21:3. **souls**. Heb. *nephesh*, Ge +12:13.

16. **atonement money**. Ex *38:25-28. 1 P =1:18,

19. **appoint.** Ex 38:25-31. Ne 10:32, 33. **a memorial.** See on Ex 12:14. Nu 16:40. Lk 22:19. **souls.** Heb. *nephesh,* +Ge 12:13.

18. **a laver.** Ex 31:9. *38:8. Le 8:11. 1 K 7:23, 38. 2 Ch 4:2, 6, 14, 15. Zc 13:1. Ep=5:26. T 3:5g. 1 J 1:7. *S#3595h: ver. 28. Ex 31:9. 35:16. 38:8. 39:39. 40:7, 11, 30. Le 8:11. 1 S 2:14 (pan). 1 K 7:30, 38, 38, 38, 38, 40, 43. 2 K 16:17. 2 Ch 4:6, 14 (mg. caldrons). 6:13 (scaffold). Zc 12:6 (hearth). **brass.** Ex 38:8. **wash.** Heb. *rahats,* Ex +29:4. 2 S 22:21, 25. Jb 17:9. Ps 24:3, 4. 26:6. Jn=13:10. Ja 4:8. **put it.** Ex 40:7, 30-32.

19. **wash.** Heb. *rahats,* Ex +29:4. Ex 40:31, 32. Ps *26:6. Is *52:11. Jn *13:8-10. 1 C 6:9-11. T *3:5. He +*9:10n. +*10:22. Ja 3:2. *4:8. Re +*1:5, 6. **thereat.** or, at it. lit. out of it. Orientals never put their hands or feet in water to cleanse them, but pour water upon them (Young). Samuel J. Baird notes that "In fact, the laver was not a bath tub, nor ever used as such, but a containing vessel from which was drawn water for all the uses of the sanctuary" (*The Great Baptizer: A Bible History of Baptism,* p. 130).

20. **wash.** Heb. *rahats,* Ex +29:4. **with water.** ver. 19n. Ac +*1:5n. **die not.** Ex 12:15. Le 10:1-3. 16:1, 2. 1 S 6:19. 1 Ch 13:10. Ps 89:7. Ac 5:5, 10. He 12:28, 29.

21. **wash.** Heb. *rahats,* Ex +29:4. **their hands.** Baird pointedly asks, "will it be insisted that the priests as they came into the sanctuary at the appointed times of service, successively, climbed to the top of the laver and, balancing on its brim, immersed their hands and feet; and, then, in fulfillment of their official duties, immersed in the water thus fouled, the inwards, or bowels and intestines, and the pieces of the sacrifices, about to be offered to God? The supposition would be indecent and profane. And yet, this is the unavoidable result of demanding immersion, in this case. For, the same language is used in requiring the washing of the priests and of the sacrifices, and there was but one laver, to supply all demands for water at the sanctuary" (p. 132). See related notes (ver. 19n. Ex 40:12n. Le 16:24n. 1 K 7:23n). **a statute.** Ex 28:43. **for ever.** Heb. *olam,* Ex +12:24.

23. **principal spices.** Ex 25:6. 37:29. Ps 45:8. Pr 7:17. SS 1:3, 13. 4:14. Je 6:20. Ezk 27:19, 22. There is a nine-fold enumeration here; so also at SS 4:13, 14; 1 C=12:8-10; 2 C=6:4, 5; Ga=5:22, 23; 2 P=1:5-7. **pure myrrh.** Young renders *wild* or *free honey.* On *free,* see Le 25:10. Is 61:1. Je 34:8, 15, 17. Ezk 46:17. **cinnamon.** Pr 7:17. SS 4:14, only. **sweet calamus.** Young renders spice-cane. On *cane,* see Ge 41:5. SS 4:14. Is 43:24. Je 6:20. Ezk 27:19.

24. **cassia.** Ps 45:8. **the shekel.** Nu 3:47. Ezk 45:12. **hin.** Ex 29:40. Le 19:36. Nu 15:5.

25. **ointment.** SS 1:3. **apothecary.** or, perfumer. 1 Ch 9:30. **an holy.** Ex 37:29. Nu 35:25. Ps 89:20. 133:2. He *1:9.

26. **anoint.** Ex 40:9-15. Le *8:10-12. Nu 7:1, 10. Is *61:1. Ac 10:38. 2 C *1:21, 22. 1 J *2:20, 27.

29. **whatsoever.** Ex 29:37. Le 6:18. Mt 23:17, 19.

30. **anoint.** Ex 29:7, etc. 40:15. Le *8:12, 30. Nu 3:3. **consecrate.** See on Ex 28:3. 29:9, 35. **priest's.** 1 P=2:5, 9.

31. **an holy.** Ex 37:29. Le 8:12. 21:10. Ps 89:20. **oil.** Ro 8:9. 1 C 12:3.

32. **man's.** Le 21:10. Mt 7:6. **flesh.** 1 C 2:14. **poured.** Heb. *yasak,* *S#3251h, only here. **composition.** ver. 37. Ex +5:8. **it is.** ver. 25, 37, 38.

33. **compoundeth.** ver. 38. Lk 12:1, 2. He 10:26-29. **a stranger.** Ex 29:33. **cut off.** Ex 12:15, 19. Ge 17:14. Le 7:20, 21. 17:4, 9. 19:8. 23:29. Nu 9:13.

34. **unto thee.** ver. +8, 23. Ex 25:6. 37:29. **stacte.** Heb. *nataph.* The Jews and others suppose it to be what was afterwards called the balm of Jericho, or Gilead. The word only occurs elsewhere at Jb 36:27, rendered there as "drops." **onycha.** only here. The word *shechaileth* is generally allowed to denote *onycha,* (nail-fish, from its form), as it is rendered by the LXX. and Vulgate. It is the shell of the *purpura,* and of the whole class of murex; and serves as the basis of the principal perfumes in India. **galbanum.** only here. *Chelbenah,* (probably from chalay, milk or gum, and lavan, white), is the gummy, resinous juice of an umbeliferous plant, the *bubon gumniferum* of Linnaeus, growing in Syria, Persia, and Africa. When any part of the plant is broken, there issues out a little thin juice, of a cream color, of a fat, tough substance, like gum ammoniac, composed of many small, shining grains, of a strong, piercing smell and a sharp, warm taste. **frankincense.** Le 2:1, 15. 5:11. 24:7. 1 Ch 9:29, 30. Ne 13:5. SS 3:6. Mt 2:11.

35. **perfume.** Pr 27:9. SS 1:3. 3:6. Jn 12:3. **after the.** ver. 25. **tempered.** Heb. salted. Le 2:13. Ezk 16:4.

36. **beat.** Ex +*27:20n. Is =53:5. He +=2:10. **the testimony.** See on Ex 16:34. **where I will.** ver. 6. Ex 25:22. 29:42, 43. Le *16:2.

37. **ye shall.** ver. 32, 33. **composition.** ver. 32. Ex +5:8. 2 Ch 24:13h. **it shall.** Ex 29:37. Le 2:3.

38. **to smell.** Ge 8:21. 1 S 16:23h. **be cut off.** See on ver. 33.

EXODUS 31

Bezaleel and Aholiab are appointed and qualified to erect the tabernacle, and make the sacred furniture, 1-11. The observance of the sabbath is enforced, 12-17. The tables of the law are delivered to Moses, 18.

2. **I have.** Ex 33:12, 17. 35:30. 36:1. Is *45:3, 4. Mk 3:16-19. Jn 3:27. **Bezaleel.** i.e. God is protection; in the shadow of God, in God's shade, *S#1212h. Ex 35:30. 36:1, 2. 37:1. 38:22. 1 Ch 2:20. 2 Ch 1:5. Ezr 10:30. (1) A man of Judah fitted by God for work on the ark of the testimony and the Tabernacle, Ex 31:2; 2 Ch 1:5. (2) A Jew who returned from Babylon and had taken a foreign wife, Ezr 10:30. **Uri.** i.e. my light; fiery, *S#221h. Ex 31:2. 35:30. 38:22. 1 K 4:19. 1 Ch 2:20, 20. 2 Ch 1:5. Ezr 10:24. (1) The father of Bezaleel, Ex 31:2; 35:30; 38:22; 1 Ch 2:20; 2 Ch 1:5. (2) The father of Geber, 1 K 4:19. (3) A porter who took a foreign wife, Ezr 10:24.

3. **filled.** Ex 35:31. *36:1. 1 K 3:9. 7:14. Is 28:6, 26. *54:16. Ac *2:4. 1 C *12:4-11. Ja *1:17. **the spirit of God.** Heb. *ruach,* Ge +41:38. *Ruach Elohim,* rather, "a spirit of God;" which is a usual Hebraism, signifying "an excellent spirit;" or, as we should now say, "a distinguished genius for the work he had to perform." No man, by course of reading or study, ever acquired a genius of any kind: we call it natural, and say it was "born with the man:" Moses teaches us to consider it divine. The prophet Isaiah (Is 28:24-29) pointedly

refers to this sort of teaching as coming from God, even in the most common and less difficult arts of life. Dark as the heathens were, yet they acknowledged that all talents and the seeds of all arts came from God. **workmanship**. 1 C=3:10.

4. **devise cunning works**. Ex 25:32-35. 26:1. 28:15. 1 K 7:14. 2 Ch 2:7, 13, 14.

5. **in cutting**. Ex 28:9-21.

6. **I have given**. Ex 4:14, 15. 6:26. Ezr 5:1, 2. Ec 4:9-12. Mt 10:2-4. Lk 10:1. Ac 13:2. 15:39, 40. **Aholiab**. i.e. tent of my father, *S#171h. Ex 35:34. 36:1, 2. 38:23. **Ahisamach**. i.e. brother of support, *S#294h. Ex 35:34. 38:23. **tribe of Dan**. Ex 35:34. 38:23. Le 24:11. Nu 1:12, 38, 39. 2:25, 25, 31. 7:66. 10:25. 13:12. 26:42, 42. 34:22. Dt 27:13. 33:22. Jsh 19:40, 47, 47, 48. 21:5, 23. Jg 1:34. 5:17. 13:25. 18:2, 16, 22, 23, 25, 26, 30, 30. 1 Ch 27:22. 2 Ch 2:14. **wise hearted**. Ex 28:3. 35:10, 25, 26, 35. 36:1, 8. 1 K 3:12. Pr 2:6, 7. Ja 1:*5, 16, 17. **that they**. Ex chs. 37. 38. Nu ch. 4. 1 K chs. 6. 7. 8. 2 Ch chs. 3. 4. Ezk chs. 43, etc.

7. **tabernacle**. Ex ch. 26. 27:9-19. 36:8-38. **ark**. Ex 25:10-22. 37:1-9. **furniture**. Heb. vessels. Ex 30:27, 28. 39:33.

8. **the table**. Ex 25:23-30. 37:10-16. **pure candle-stick**. Ex 25:31-40. 37:17-24. **the altar**. Ex 30:1-10. 37:25-28.

9. **the altar**. Ex 27:1-8. 38:1-7. **the laver**. Ex 30:18-21. 38:8. 40:11.

10. **the cloths**. Ex chs. 28. 39. Le 8:7, 8, 13. Nu 4:5-14.

11. **the anointing**. Ex 30:23-33. 37:29. **sweet incense**. Ex 30:34-38.

13. **Verily**. See on Ex +*20:8-11. Le *19:3, 30. 23:3. 25:2. 26:2. **a sign**. ver. 17. Ne 9:14. Ezk 20:12, 20. 44:24. **that ye may**. Le 20:8. 21:8. Ezk *37:28. Jn 17:17, 19. 1 Th 5:23. Ju 1. **Lord**. Ex +15:26. **that doth sanctify**. lit. *Jehovah-Mekaddishkem*. Le 20:8. 21:8. 22:32. Ps=23:5. Ezk 20:12.

14. **keep**. Ex +*20:8. Dt *5:12-15. Ne 9:14. Is 56:2-6. +*58:13, 14. Je √17:21, 22, 27. Ezk 20:12. 44:24. **every one**. Is 56:2-6. Ezk 20:13, 16, 21, 24. **surely**. √147B, Ge +2:16. **doeth**. Ex *35:2, 3. Nu *15:35. **soul**. Heb. *nephesh*, Ge +17:14.

15. **Six days**. ver. 17. Ex 16:26. *20:9. 34:21. Le 23:3. Ezk 46:1. Lk 13:14. **the sabbath**. Ex 16:23. 20:10. Ge *2:2. Le 23:3, 32. Lk 23:56. He 4:9g. **holy**. Heb. holiness. ver. 10, 14. Ex 16:23. 30:25, 32, 35, 37, etc. **whosoever**. Nu 15:32-36. Je 17:24-27. **surely**. √147B, Ge +2:16.

16. **a perpetual**. Heb. *olam*, Ge +9:12. **covenant**. Ge 9:13. 17:11. Je 50:5.

17. **a sign**. ver. 13. Ezk 20:12, 20. **six days**. Ge 1:31. 2:2, 3. He 4:3, 4, 10. **for ever**. Heb. *olam*, Ex +12:24. **and was refreshed**. God, in condescension to human weakness, applies to himself here what belongs to man; though it may refer to the delight and satisfaction with which he contemplated the completion of all his works, and pronounced them very good. Ge 1:31. Jb 38:7. Ps 104:31. Je 32:41.

18. **gave**. Ex *24:12, 18. 32:15, 16. 34:1-4, 28, 29. Dt 4:13. 5:22. 9:9-11. Jn *1:17. 2 C *3:3. **written**. √22C43. Anthropopatheia or Anthropomorphism B890. Human actions are attributed to God: writing. For other instances of this figure see Ex 32:16. Dt 9:10. Is 4:3. Je *31:33. Da 12:1. He 8:10. **the finger**. √22A16,

Ex +8:19. Ex 8:19. 32:16. Je 31:33. Mt 12:28. Lk *11:20. 2 C 3:7, 8.

EXODUS 32

Aaron, at the people's instigation, makes a golden calf, and they worship it, 1-6. God informs Moses, who intercedes for Israel, and prevails, 7-14. He comes down from the mount, breaks the tables of the law, destroys the idol, and expostulates with Aaron, 15-24. He commissions the Levites, who slay three thousand of the criminals, 25-29. He again intercedes for the nation, 30-35.

1. A.M. 2513. B.C. 1491. **saw**. 1 S 8:5. **delayed**. Ex *24:18. Dt 9:9. Mt=24:48, 50, 51. Lk 12:45. 2 P=3:3, 4. **Up**. Ge 19:14. 44:4. Jsh 7:13. **make**. Ex 20:3-5. Dt 4:15-18. Ac 7:40. 17:29. 19:26. **which shall**. Ex 13:21. 33:3, 14, 15. **the man**. ver. 7, 11. Ex 14:11. 16:3. Ho 12:13. Mi 6:4. **we wot**. Ge 21:26. 39:8. 44:15. Mt=24:48. Ac ▶7:40. 2 P=3:4.

2. **golden earrings**. Ex *12:35, 36. Ge 24:22, 47. Jg 8:24-27. Ezk 16:11, 12, 17. Ho 2:8. **bring**. Ex 35:22.

3. **all**. √171A, Ex +9:6. **brake off**. Jg 17:3, 4. Is 40:19, 20. 46:6. Je 10:9.

4. **fashioned**. Ex *20:23. Dt 9:16. Ps *106:19-21. Is 44:9, 10. 46:6. Ac 7:41. 17:29. **a graving**. Ex 28:9, 11. **calf**. 1 K 12:28, 32. 2 K 10:29. 2 Ch 11:15. 13:8. Ho 8:4, 5. 10:5. 13:2. **These**. ver. 8. Jg 17:3, 4. Ne 9:18. Is 40:18, 19. Ro 1:21-23. **which brought**. ver. 1, 8. Ex 20:2.

5. **Aaron**. 1 S 14:35. 2 K 16:11. Ho 8:11, 14. **made proclamation**. Le 23:2, 4, 21, 37. 1 K 21:9. 2 K 10:20. 2 Ch 30:5. **a feast**. ver. 4. Ex 10:9. 12:14. 1 K 12:32, 33. 1 C 5:8.

6. **offered**. Ex 24:4, 5. **sat down**. No doubt at this feast they sacrificed after the manner of the Egyptians. Nu 25:2. Jg 16:23-25. Am 2:8. 8:10. Ac 7:41, 42. 1 C ▶10:7. Re 11:10.

7. **Go**. Ex 19:24. 33:1. Dt 9:12. Da 9:24. **thy people**. ver. 1, 11. **thou broughtest**. Ex ◐20:2. *33:1. Dt ◐5:6. **corrupted**. Ge 6:11, 12. Dt 4:16. 32:5. Jg 2:19. Ho 9:9.

8. **have turned**. Ex ◐19:8. Dt 9:16. Jg 2:17. **which I**. Ex *20:3, 4, 23. **These be**. ver. 4. 1 K 12:28.

9. **I have seen**. √22C13, Ge +16:13. Dt 9:13. Je 13:27. Ho 6:10. **a stiffnecked**. Ex 33:3, 5. 34:9. Dt 9:6, 13. 10:16. 31:27. 2 Ch 30:8. Ne *9:17. Ps 78:8. Pr *29:1. Is *48:4. Zc 7:11, 12. Ac *7:51.

10. **let me alone**. Ge 18:32, 33. 32:26-28. Nu 14:19, 20. 16:22, 45-48. Dt 9:14, 19. Je +*14:11. *15:1. Ja +*5:16. **that**. √22D1, Ge +32:28. **my wrath**. ver. 11, 19. Ex 22:24. **and I will**. Nu 14:12. Dt 9:14, 19. Mt *3:9.

11. **besought**. Dt *9:18-20, 26-29. Ps *106:23. **the Lord his God**. Heb. the face of the Lord. 1 S +13:12mg. Jb +11:19mg. Je +26:19mg. Zc 7:2mg. Ml 1:9mg. **why doth**. Nu 11:11. 16:22. Dt 9:18-29. Ps 74:1, 2. Is 63:17. Je 12:1, 2. **which thou**. ver. 7.

12. **Wherefore**. Jsh 7:6, 9. 2 Ch 20:9, 11. Je 14:21. **should**. Nu 14:13-16. Dt 9:28. *32:26, 27. Jsh 7:9. Ps 74:18. *79:9, 10. Ezk 20:9, 14, 22. **Turn from**. Dt 13:17. Jsh 7:26. Ezr 10:14. Ps 78:38. 85:3. **repent**. √22B, Ge +6:6. ver. 14. Ge 6:6. Dt 32:36. Ps 90:13. 106:45. Am 7:3, 6. Jon 3:9. Zc 8:14.

13. **Remember**. Ge 32:12. Le 26:42. Dt 7:8. *9:27. 2 S 7:25. 1 K 8:25. Ps 119:58. Lk 1:54, 55. **to whom**.

Ge *22:16. 26:3, 4. He *6:13, 14. **I will multiply.** Ge 12:2, 7. 13:15, 16. 15:5, 7, 18. 26:4. +*28:13, 14. 35:11, 12. 48:16. **as.** ♪138B, Ge +13:16. **for ever.** Heb. *olam,* Ex +12:24.

14. **repented.** ♪22B, Ge +6:6. Dt 32:26. 2 S 24:16. 1 Ch 21:15. Ps *106:45. Je *18:8. *26:13, 19. Jl *2:13. Jon 3:10. *4:2.

15. **turned.** Ex 24:18. Dt *9:15. **the testimony.** Ex 16:34. 40:20. Dt 5:22. Ps 19:7. **written.** Re 5:1.

16. **the tables.** ♪66, Ge +9:3. Ex 31:18. 34:1, 4. Dt 9:9-11, 15. 10:1. 2 C 3:3, 7. He 8:10. **writing.** ♪22C43, Ex +31:18. **writing.** ♪16, Ge +1:27. **the tables.** ♪72. Epidiplosis; or, Double Encircling B250. Repeated Epanadiplosis, words repeated at the beginning and end of successive sentences. For other instances of this figure see Ps 47:6. Ro 14:8.

17. Joshua had waited patiently during all the forty days, in the place where Moses had left him—below the summit of the mount, at a distance from the people, and out of the way of temptation. **Joshua.** Ex 17:9. 24:13. **they shouted.** ver. 18. Ezr 3:11-13. Ps 47:1. **There is a noise.** Jsh 6:5, 10, 16, 20. Jg 15:14. 1 S 4:5, 6. 17:20, 52. Jb 39:25. Je 51:14. Am 1:14. 2:2.

18. **being overcome.** Heb. weakness. Jl 3:10. **but the.** Ex 15:1, etc. Da 5:4, 23.

19. **he saw.** ver. 4-6. Dt 9:16, 17. **the dancing.** Ex 15:20. 2 S 6:14. La 5:15. **anger.** ver. 11. Nu 12:3. Mt 5:22. Mk *3:5. 10:14. Ep 4:26. **brake them.** Dt 9:17. 27:26. Ps ◐=40:8. Je *31:32. Zc 11:10, 11, 14.

20. **took the calf.** Dt 7:5, 25. *9:21. 2 K 23:6, 15. **made the.** Ps *109:18. Pr 1:31. *14:14.

21. **What did.** Ge 20:9. 26:10. Dt 13:6-8. Jsh 7:19-26. 1 S 26:19. 1 K 14:16. 21:22. 2 K 21:9-11.

22. **anger.** Dt *9:20. **knowest.** Ex 14:11. 15:24. 16:2-4, 20, 28. *17:2-4. Dt 9:7, 24. **that they are.** Dt 31:27. 1 S 15:24. Ps 36:4. Pr 4:16. Ro *3:10.

23. **they said.** See on ver. 1-4, 8. **we wot.** Ac ⸗7:40.

24. **So they.** ver. 4. Ge 3:12, 13. Lk 10:29. Ro 3:10.

25. **naked.** The term naked may mean either that they were unarmed and defenseless, or ashamed from the consciousness of guilt. Ex 33:4-6. Ge *3:10. 2 S 6:20n. 2 Ch *28:19. Is 47:3. Ho 2:3. Mi 1:11. Jn 21:7n. Re 3:17, 18. 16:15. **Aaron.** Dt 9:20. 2 Ch 28:19. **shame.** Ezk 16:63. Da 12:2. Ro 6:21. **their enemies.** Heb. those that rose up against them.

26. **camp.** He=13:13. **Who is on.** Jsh 5:13. 2 S 20:11. 2 K 9:32. Mt=12:30. Lk=11:23. **come unto.** Jsh *24:15. **all.** ♪171A, Ex +9:6.

27. **sword.** Ep=6:17. **slay every man.** ver. 26, 29. Nu *25:5, 7-12. Dt 33:8, 9. Lk 14:26. 2 C 5:16.

28. **children.** Dt 33:9. Ml 2:4-6. **there fell.** Nu 16:32-35, 41. 1 C 10:8. He *2:2, 3.

29. **For.** *or,* another reading of this verse is: And Moses said, Consecrate yourselves today to the Lord; because every man hath been against his son and against his brother, etc. **Moses.** Nu *25:11-13. Dt *13:6-11. 33:9, 10. 1 S 15:18-22. Pr 21:3. Jl 2:12-14. Zc 13:3. Mt *10:37. **Consecrate.** Heb. fill your hands. ♪121S3P, Ex +28:41.

30. **Ye have.** ver. 31. 1 S 2:17. *12:20, 23. 2 S 12:9. 2 K 17:21. Ps *25:11. Lk 7:47. 15:18. **peradventure.** 2 S 16:12. Am 5:15. Jon 3:9. 2 T 2:25. **an atonement.** T#1224. ver. 32. Nu 16:44-47. 25:13. Jb 42:7, 8. Ro 9:3. Ga *3:13. Ja +*5:16.

31. **returned.** Ex 34:28. Dt *9:18, 19. **sinned.** ver.

30. Ezr 9:6, 7, 15. Ne 9:33. Da 9:5, 8, 11. **made.** Ex *20:4, 23.

32. **if thou.** Nu 14:19. Da 9:18, 19. Is 1:18. Am 7:2. Lk 23:34. **their sin.** Ge 30:27. ♪37A. Aposiopesis; or, Sudden Silence B151: In Promise, where some great thing is promised, too great to be conveyed in words. For other instances of this figure see 2 S 5:8. 1 Ch 4:10. Da 3:15. Lk 13:9. **blot.** ver. 10. Dt *9:14. 25:19. 29:20. Ps 56:8. 69:28. 139:16. Is 4:2. Ezk 13:9. Da 7:10. *12:1. Ml ◐*3:16. Lk ◐*10:20. Jn ◐10:27, 28. Ro √9:3. Ph *4:3. He ◐*12:23. Re *3:5. *13:8. 17:8. *20:12, 15. 21:27. *22:19. ♪55. Deprecatio; or, Deprecation B936. An expression of feeling by way of deprecation. A related figure, though not here classed as such, is Imprecatory Prayer, Je +*10:25. **me.** Is ◐=53:4-6. 1 P ◐=2:24. **thy book.** ♪22D5K1A. Anthropopatheia or Anthropomorphism B893. Circumstances connected with a person are attributed to God: a book of life. For other instances of this figure see Ps 56:8. 69:28. Da 12:1. Ml 3:16. Ph 4:3. Re 3:5. 13:8.

33. **Whosoever.** Ps 49:7, 8. Je ◐15:1. **sinned.** Le 23:30. Ps 69:28. Ezk *18:4. **blot out.** ♪22C34. Anthropomorphism B890. Human actions are attributed to God: blotting out. For other instances of this figure see Ex 32:33. Ps 51:1. Is 43:25. 44:22. **my book.** Ps 109:13, 14. Ph 4:3. Re 13:8. 20:12.

34. **mine Angel.** Ex *14:19. *23:20. *33:2, 14, 15. Nu *20:16. Is 63:9. **the day.** Ex 20:5. Nu 14:27-30. Dt 32:35. 2 S *7:14. Ps 89:32. 94:23. 99:8. Je *5:9, 29. 9:9. 11:22mg. *23:2. 43:11. Ho 12:2mg. Am 3:14. Ml +*3:5. Mt 23:35. Ro *2:4-6.

35. **they made.** ver. 25. 2 S 12:9, 10. Je *2:19. Mt 27:3-7. Ac 1:18. 7:41.

EXODUS 33

The Lord orders Moses to Lead the people to Canaan, under the conduct of an angel, refusing himself to go with them, 1-3. The people express sorrow and humiliation, 4-6. Moses removes the tabernacle out of the camp; and the Lord there displays his glory, and communes with Moses, while the people worship at their tent doors, 7-11. Moses prevails with the Lord to accompany them, and desires to behold his glory, 12-23.

1. **Depart.** Ex 32:24. **thou hast.** Ex 17:3. ◐20:2. 32:1, 7. Dt ◐5:6. **the land.** Ex 32:13. Ge 22:16-18. 26:3. 28:13-15. **Unto.** Ge 12:7. 13:14-17. 15:18.

2. **an angel.** Ex 23:20. 32:34. 34:11. **the Canaanite.** See on Ex 3:8. 17. Ge +10:18. Dt 7:22. Jsh *24:11. **Amorite.** Ge +10:16. **Hittite.** Ge +15:20. **Perizzite.** Ge +13:7. **Hivite.** Ge +10:17. **Jebusite.** Ge +10:16.

3. **a land.** Ex 3:8. 13:5. Le 20:24. Nu 13:27. 14:8. 16:13. Jsh 5:6. Je 11:5. **milk and.** ♪174, Ge +18:27. **honey.** ♪17117, Ex +3:8. **for I.** ver. 15-17. Ex 32:10, 14. Nu 14:12. Dt 32:26, 27. 1 S 2:30. Je 18:7-10. Ezk 3:18, 19. 33:13-16. Jon 3:4, 10. **stiffnecked.** Ex 32:9. *34:9. Dt 9:6-13. Ps 78:8. Ac 7:51. **lest I.** Ex *23:21. 32:10. Nu 16:21, 45. Am 3:13, 14. Hab *1:13.

4. **they mourned.** Nu 14:1, 39. Ho 7:14. Zc 7:3, 5. **and no.** Le 10:6. 2 S 19:24. 1 K 21:27. 2 K 19:1. Ezr 9:3. Est 4:1-4. Jb 1:20. 2:12. Is 32:11. Ezk 24:17, 23. 26:16. Jon 3:6.

5. **Ye are.** ver. 3. Nu 16:45, 46. **in a moment.** Nu 16:21, 45. Jb 34:20. Ps 73:19. La 4:6. **put off.** Is 22:12. **I may.** Ge 18:21. 22:12. Dt 8:2. Ps 139:23.

6. **stripped**. ver. 4. Ex 32:3. Je 2:19.

7. **the tabernacle**. *Eth haohel*, the tent (S#168h, Ex +16:16), not *eth hammishcan* (*S#4908h, Ex +25:9n), the tabernacle, for this was not erected; but probably the tent of Moses, which was before in the midst of the camp, and to which the people came for judgment; and where, no doubt, God frequently met his servant. The situation, as well as the superior elegance, of a chief's tent, was one mode by which he was honored. Ex ◐26:1n. Nu ◐16:24n. **afar off**. Jsh 3:4. Ps 10:1. 35:22. Pr 15:29. Is 59:2. Ho 9:12. **the Tabernacle of the congregation**. Ex +*27:21n. See on *29:42, 43. **sought**. Dt 4:29. 2 S 21:1. Ps 27:8. Is 55:6, 7. Mt 7:7, 8. **went out**. He 13:11-13. **unto the**. T#1209. Nu 11:16, 17. 16:19-22. 20:6.

8. **and stood**. Nu 16:27. **until**. 1 T=2:5.

9. **cloudy**. Ex 13:21, 22. Ps *99:7. **talked**. ver. 11. Ex *25:22. 31:18. 34:3, 9. Ge 17:22. 18:33. Nu 11:17. Ezk 3:22.

10. **worshipped**. Ex 4:31. 1 K 8:14, 22. Lk 18:13.

11. **spake**. ver. 9. Ge 32:30. Nu *12:8. Dt 5:4. *34:10. **his friend**. 2 Ch +*20:7. Jb 16:21. Is *42:8. Jn 3:29. 11:11. 15:14, 15. Ja *2:23. **his servant**. Ex 17:9. 24:13. 32:17. **Nun**. i.e. noon, fish; eternal. *S#5126h. Ex 33:11. Nu 11:28. 13:8, 16. 14:6, 30, 38. 26:65. 27:18. 32:12, 28. 34:17. Dt 1:38. 31:23. 32:44. 34:9. Jsh 1:1. 2:1, 23. 6:6. 14:1. 17:4. 19:49, 51. 21:1. 24:29. Jg 2:8. 1 K 16:34. Ne 8:17. **departed not**. Pr 8:34. Lk 2:37.

12. **See**. ver. 1. Ex *32:34. **I know**. ver. 17. Ge +*18:19. Ps *1:6. +*40:17. Is 43:1. Je 1:5. Am 3:2. Jn *10:+3, 14, 15. 2 T *2:19.

13. **if**. ver. 15, 17, 18. Ex 34:9. Ps *16:11. *103:7. **show**. Ps 25:4. 27:11. *86:11. 119:33. SS 1:7, 8. Is *30:21. **thy way**. Nu *12:7, 8. Dt *29:29. Ps √103:7. **know thee**. ver. 18. Ps +*9:10. Jn √17:3. Ep *1:17. Col +√1:10. 2 P +*3:18. **consider**. Ex ◐32:7. Dt *9:26, 29. +*32:43. Is 63:17, 19. Jl *2:17. Ro 11:28.

14. **My presence**. ♪22A4, Ge +19:13. Ex *13:21. *40:34-38. Jsh 1:5. Ps *32:8. Is *63:9. Mt *28:20. **rest**. Dt 3:20. Jsh *21:44. 22:4. 23:1. Ps 95:11. Je 6:16. Mt *11:28. He 4:8, 9.

15. **thy presence**. ♪22A4, Ge +19:13. ver. 3. Ex 34:9. Ps 4:6.

16. **wherein**. Ps 73:24. **in that**. Nu *14:14. Mt 1:23. **separated**. Ex 8:22. 19:5, 6. 34:10. Nu 23:9. Dt *4:7, 34. 2 S *7:23. 1 K *8:53. Ps 147:20. 2 C 6:16, 17. **face**. Ge +1:2.

17. **I will do**. Ge 18:32. *19:21. Is +*65:24. Jn 16:23. Ja +*5:16. 1 J *5:14, 15. **thou hast**. ver. 12. Ge 6:8. 19:19, 21. Mt=17:5. **know thee**. ver. +*12. Est 2:14. Ps +*40:17.

18. **show me**. ver. 20. Ps 4:6. Jn 1:18. 2 C 3:18. *4:6. 1 T *6:16. T *2:13. 1 J *3:2. Re 21:23. **glory**. Ex *24:16, 17. Ps *84:11. Lk *9:32.

19. **all my goodness**. Ne 9:25. Ps 25:13mg. 65:4. Je 31:12, 14. Zc 9:17. Ro 2:4. Ep 1:6-8. **proclaim**. Ex 3:13-15. 34:5-7. Is *7:14. *9:6. 12:4. **I will be gracious**. Ex +*34:6, 7. Ro 9:◑15, 16-18, 23. **to whom**. Dt 7:6, Mt 20:15. Ro 9:10-24. 11:4-6, 23-36. Ep 1:5.

20. **Thou canst not**. Ex 24:10. Ge *32:30. Dt *5:24. Jg 6:22. 13:22. Is *6:5. Jn √1:18. 13:22. 1 C *13:12. 1 T √6:16. He *1:3. 1 J *3:2. Re 1:16, 17. **face**. ♪22A4, Ge +19:13.

21. **place by**. Dt *5:31. Jsh 20:4. Is *56:5. Zc *3:7. Lk 15:1.

22. **in a clift**. Ge 49:24. Ps 18:2. *27:5. SS 2:3. Is *2:21. 32:2. 1 C 10:4. 2 C 5:19. **rock**. Ex 17:6. 1 K 19:9. Is *32:2. Jn 19:34. **cover thee**. Dt 33:12. Ps *91:1, 4. Is 49:2. *51:16.

23. **thou shalt**. ver. 20. Jb 11:7. 26:14. Jn *1:18. 1 C 13:12. 1 T *6:16. 1 J 4:12. **back parts**. EWB notes, i.e. *shadow*. ♪22L8, Ps +121:5. **face**. ♪22A4, Ge +19:13. Re ◐22:4.

EXODUS 34

Moses is commanded to hew two tables of stone, and to ascend mount Sinai alone, 1-4. The Lord proclaims his name, and Moses worships, 5-9. The Lord renews his covenant with Israel, and repeats many laws before given, 10-27. Moses, after forty days' fasting, returns with the tables of the law: his face shines, and he covers it with a veil, 28-35.

1. **Hew**. See on Ex 31:18. *32:16, 19. Dt *10:1, 2. 2 C *3:3. **I will**. ver. 28. Dt 10:1-4. **the words**. Ps 119:89. **which**. Ex 32:19. Dt 9:15-17.

2. **in the morning**. Ge +*21:14. 22:3. **in the top**. Ex 19:20, 24. 24:12. Dt 9:25.

3. **come**. Ex *19:12, 13, 21. Le 16:17. Mk ◐=9:15. 1 T 2:5. He 12:20.

5. **descended**. Ex 19:18. *33:9. Nu 11:17, 25. 1 K 8:10-12. Lk *9:34, 35. **the name**. Ex 33:19. Nu 14:17. Dt *32:3. Ps +*9:10. *102:21. Pr 18:10. Is *50:10. Jn *17:26.

6. **passed**. Ex 33:20-23. 1 K 19:11. **proclaimed**. Nu 14:17-19. Is 12:4. **The Lord**. Ex 3:13-16. **The Lord**. ♪84, Ge +6:17. **God**. Heb. *El*. Ex +15:2. **merciful**. ♪173, Ge +27:44. Ex +*20:6. 33:19. Nu 14:18. Dt *4:31. 5:10. 2 S +*7:15. *24:14. 2 K √8:23. 1 Ch 16:34. 2 Ch *5:13. 7:3, 6. *30:9. Ezr 3:11. Ne 1:5. *9:17, 32. Ps +*25:6. 57:10. 62:12. 86:5, 15. *89:1. 100:5. *103:8-14, 17. 106:1. 107:1, 43. 111:4. 112:4. 116:5. 118:1. 136:1. *145:8. Is *54:7. √55:7. Je +*29:11. 33:11. La *3:22, 32. Da *9:9. Jl *2:13. Jon +*4:2. Mi √7:18. Mk 5:19. Lk 1:50, 54, 58, 72. *6:36. 8:39. *18:13. Ro +*2:4. +*12:1. 15:9. 2 C √1:3. Ga 6:16. Ep +*2:4. Ph *2:27. T *3:5. He √4:16. 1 P 1:3. 2:10. **and gracious**. Nu +*6:25. 2 S 12:22. 2 K 13:23. Jb 33:24. Ps 77:9. Is +*30:18. 33:2. Am *5:15. Ml 1:9. **longsuffering**. Nu +*14:18. Is 48:9. Ezk 20:17. Ro *9:22. 1 P *3:20. 2 P *3:9. **abundant**. Ps 31:19. Is 55:7. Mi 7:18. Ro 2:4. 5:20, 21. Ep 1:7, 8. **goodness**. Ex 18:9. 33:19. Ge 1:31. 1 K 8:66. 2 Ch 5:13. 7:3. 30:18. Ezr 3:11. 7:9. 8:18. Ne 9:13, *20, 25. Ps 23:6. 25:7. *31:19. *34:8. 65:11. *68:10. 73:1. *86:5. *100:5. 106:1. 107:1. 118:1. 119:39. 135:3. 136:1. +*143:10. *145:7, +*9. Is 63:7. Je *31:12. 33:11. La *3:25. Ho *3:5. Na √1:7. Mt 7:11. 19:17. 20:15. +*28:19n. Mk +*10:18n. Lk ◐+*6:35. 11:13. 18:19. Ac 14:17. Ro 2:4. *7:12. √11:22. Ga 5:22. Ja √1:17. **truth**. T#235. Nu 23:19. Dt 32:4. 1 S 15:29. Ps 19:9. 57:3, 10. 89:14. 91:4. 108:4. 111:8. 117:2. 119:142. 138:2. 146:6. Is 25:1. La 3:23. Da 4:37. Mi *7:20. Mt +*28:19n. Jn *1:17. 7:28. Ro 3:3, 4. T +*1:2n. 1 P +4:19 (T#226). Re 15:3.

7. **Keeping**. Ex 20:6. Dt 5:10. Ne 1:5. 9:32. Ps 86:15. Je 32:18. Da 9:4. **forgiving**. Ex 32:32. Ps 32:1, 5. 85:3. *103:3. *130:4. Is 33:24. Da 9:9. Mi *7:18. Mt 6:14, 15. 12:31. 18:32-35. Lk 7:42, 48. Ac 5:31. 13:38. Ro 4:7, 8. Ep 1:7. √4:32. 1 J √1:9. **iniquity**. ♪173, Ge +27:44. **that will by no means clear the guilty**. ♪147C, Ge +3:4. The Hebrew *nakkeh lo yenakkeh*, has been

rendered "Acquitting him who is not innocent." Nothing can more strongly express the goodness of God to frail mortals than this declaration, "which has been misunderstood and misinterpreted by all our translators." Ex *23:7, 21. Nu 14:18-23. Dt 32:35. Jsh 24:19. Jb 10:14. Ps 9:16, 17. 11:5, 6. 58:10, 11. 136:10, 15. Is 45:21. Je 49:12. Mi 6:11. Na *1:2, 3, 6. Ro 2:4-9. 3:19-26. 9:22, 23. He 12:29. Re 20:15. *21:8. visiting. See on Ex 20:5, 6.

8. **bowed his head.** Ex 4:31. Ge 17:3. 2 Ch 20:18.

9. **If now.** Ex 33:13, 17. **let my Lord.** See on Ex 33:14-16. Mt 28:20. **stiffnecked.** See on Ex 32:9. 33:3-5. Is 48:4. **pardon.** Nu 14:19. Ps 25:11. **take us.** Ex 19:5. Dt *32:9. Ps 28:9. *33:12. 78:62. +√94:14. 135:4. Je *10:16. Zc √2:12.

10. **I make.** Ex 24:7, 8. Dt 4:13. 5:2, 3. 29:12-14. Jsh 24:25. **I will do marvels.** Dt 4:32-37. 32:20. Jsh 6:20. 10:12, 13. 2 S *7:23. Ps 77:14. 78:12. *147:20. **a terrible.** Dt *10:21. Ps *65:5. 66:3, 5. 68:35. 76:12. 106:22. 145:6. Is 64:3. Je 32:21.

11. **Observe.** Dt 4:1, 2, 40. *5:32. 6:3, 25. *12:28, 32. *28:1. Mt 28:20. **I drive.** See on Ex 3:8, 17. 33:2. Ge 15:18-21. Dt 7:1, 19. 9:4, 5. **Amorite.** Ge +10:16. **Canaanite.** Ge +10:18. **Hittite.** Ge +15:20. **Perizzite.** Ge +13:7. **Hivite.** Ge +10:17. **Jebusite.** Ge +10:16.

12. **Take heed.** Ex 23:32, 33. Dt 7:2. Jg 2:2. **lest.** Dt 7:16. Jsh *23:12, 13. Jg 2:3. 8:27. Ps *106:36.

13. **ye shall.** Ex 23:24. Dt 7:5, 25, 26. *12:2, 3. Jg 2:2. 6:25. 2 K 18:4. 23:14. 2 Ch 31:1. 34:3, 4. **images.** Heb. statues. *S#4676h. Ex 23:24. 24:4 (pillars). Ge 28:18 (pillar), 22. 31:13, 45, 51, 52, 52. 35:14, 20. Le 26:1. Dt 7:5. 12:3. 16:22. 1 K 14:23mg. 2 K 3:2. 10:26, 27. 17:10. 18:4. 23:14. 2 Ch 14:3mg. 31:1. Is *19:19. Je 43:13. Ezk 26:11 (garrisons). Ho 3:4. 10:1, 2. Mi 5:13mg.

14. **worship.** Ex +*20:3-5. Dt 4:24. 5:7, 9. 6:13. 10:20. 11:16. Jsh 24:14, 19. Ps 29:2. Da 3:5. Na 1:2. Mt *4:9, 10. 6:24. Lk 4:7. Jn ❂*20:28. Re 19:10. 22:9. **whose.** ver. 5-7. Ex 33:19. Is *9:6. 57:15. **jealous God.** Ex 20:5. Dt 4:24. 6:15. 29:20. 32:16, 21. Jsh 24:19. Na 1:2. 1 C 10:22. Ja *4:4.

15. **make.** ver. 10, 12. Ex 23:32. Dt 7:2. **whoring.** Ge 4:+1, +17. 19:8. 24:16. Le 17:7. 20:5, 6. Nu 15:39. 31:17, 18. Dt 31:16. Jg *2:17. Ps *73:27. 106:39. Je *3:2, 6, 9. Ezk 6:9. 23:3. Ho 2:2. 4:12. 9:1. Ml 2:11. Jn 8:41. 1 C 10:20. Ja *4:4. 2 P 2:14mg. Re 2:14, 20-22. 17:1-5. 18:3, 9. 19:2. **call thee.** Nu 25:2. 1 C 10:27. **eat.** Ps 106:28. 1 C 8:4, 7, 10. *10:20, 21. Re 2:20.

16. **thou take.** Nu *25:1, 2. Dt 7:3, 4. 1 K 11:2-4. Ezr *9:2. Ne 13:23, 25. 2 C *6:14-17.

17. **no molten gods.** Ex 32:8. Le 19:4. Is 46:6, 7. Je 10:14. Ac 17:29. 19:26.

18. **feast of unleavened.** Ex *12:15-20. 13:4, 6, 7. 23:15. Le +*23:6. Dt 16:1-4. Mk 14:1. Lk 22:1. Ac 12:3.

19. **openeth.** Ex 13:2, 12. 22:29. Nu 18:15-17. Ezk 44:30. Lk *2:23. **matrix.** *S#7358h. Ex 13:2 (womb), 12, 15. 34:19. Ge 20:18. 29:31. 30:22. Nu 3:12. 8:16. 12:12. 18:15. 1 S 1:5, 6. Jb 3:11. 10:18. 24:20. 31:15. 38:8. Ps 22:10. *58:3. 110:3. Je *1:5. 20:17, 17, 18. Ho 9:14.

20. **firstling.** Ex 13:10. Nu 18:15. **ass.** √17I12, Ex +13:13. **lamb.** or, kid. Ex 12:3n. **All the.** Ex 13:15. Nu 3:45-51. **none.** Ex 23:15. Dt 16:16. 1 S 9:7, 8. 2 S 24:24. 1 Ch +*21:24. Lk 21:4. 1 C +*16:2. Ph 3:8.

21. **Six.** Ex +*20:9-11. 23:12. 35:2. Ge 2:3. Dt *5:12-15. Lk +*13:14. 23:56. **earing time.** Ge 45:6n. Dt 21:4. 1 S 8:12. Is 30:24.

22. **feast of weeks.** Ex 23:16. Nu 28:16-31. 29:12-39. Le +*23:15. Dt *16:10-15. Jn 7:2. Ac 2:1. **firstfruits.** Le +*23:10. **year's end.** Heb. revolution of the year. 1 S 1:20h. 2 Ch 24:23h. Ps 19:6h.

23. **Thrice.** Ex 23:14, 17. Dt *16:16. Ps 84:7. **the God.** Ge 32:28. 33:20.

24. **I will.** ver. 11. Ex 23:27-30. 33:2. Le 18:24. Dt 7:1. Ps *78:55. *80:8. **enlarge.** Ex 23:31. Dt 12:20. 19:8. 1 Ch 4:10. **desire.** Ge 35:5. 2 Ch 17:10. Jb 1:10. Pr +*16:7. Ac 18:10. **when.** 1 S 2:30. Mt 6:33. He 10:25.

25. **offer.** ♪63H, Ge +12:15. **leaven.** Ex 12:20. 23:18. Dt 16:3. 1 C 5:7, 8. **be left.** Ex *12:10. 23:18. 29:34. Le 7:15. Nu 9:12.

26. **first.** Ex 23:19. Dt *26:2, 10. Pr *3:9, 10. Mt *6:33. 1 C *15:20. Ja *1:18. **firstfruits.** Le +*23:10. **seeth.** Ex 23:19. Dt 14:21.

27. **Write.** Ex 17:14. 24:4, 7. Dt 31:9. **I have.** See on ver. 10. Dt 4:13. *31:9.

28. **forty days.** See on Ex 24:18. Dt 9:9, 18, 25. Mt ❂=4:2. **he wrote.** ver. 1. Ex *31:18. *32:16. Dt 4:13. 10:2-4. Is *49:8. 2 C 3:7. **commandments.** Heb. words. ♪108B, Lk +1:2. Dt 4:13.

29. A.M. 2513. B.C. 1491. **two tables.** See on Ex 32:15. **wist.** Ex 16:15. Jsh 2:4. 8:14. Jg 16:20. Mk 9:6. 14:40. Lk 2:49. Jn 5:13. Ac 12:9. 23:5. Ro *10:4. **the skin.** Mt 17:2. Lk 9:29. Ac 6:15. 2 C *3:7-9, 13. Re 1:16. 10:1. **face shone.** ver. 30, 35. Ps 67:1. Mt=17:2. Ac 6:15. 2 C 3:7.

30. **face.** Mt=17:2. **afraid.** Nu 12:8. Mk 9:3, 15. Lk 5:8.

31. **called.** Ex 3:16. 24:1-3. **and Moses talked.** Ge 45:3, 15.

32. **he gave.** Ex 21:1. Nu 15:40. 1 K 22:14. Mt 28:20. 1 C 11:23. 15:3.

33. **a vail.** Nu 12:3. Mk 4:33. Ro *10:4. 1 C 2:1-3. 9:22. 2 C *3:13-18. 4:4-6.

34. **he took.** 2 C 3:16. He *4:16. 10:19-22.

35. **saw the face.** ver. 29, 30. Ec 8:1. Da 12:3. Mt 5:16. 13:43. Jn 5:35. Ph 2:15.

EXODUS 35

Moses shows the will of God, concerning the sabbath, 1-3; the voluntary offering, 4-9; and the tabernacle and its furniture, 10-19. The people readily contribute and assist, 20-29. Bezaleel and Aholiab are called to the work, 30-35.

1. **These.** Ex ch. 25. 31:1-11. 34:32. **do them.** Mt *7:21-27. Ro 2:13. Ja *1:22.

2. **Six days.** Ex +*20:9, 10. 23:12. 31:13-16. 34:21. Ge 2:3. Le *23:3. Dt *5:12-15. Lk +*13:14n. **an holy day.** Heb. holiness. ver. 19, 21. Ex 26:33. 39:1. +31:15. 40:13. Le 21:6. 22:2, etc. **whosoever doeth work.** T#643. Nu *15:32-36. Dt 5:12-14. Je *17:27. Ezk 20:15, 16, 20, 21. 22:26, 31. Lk 13:14, 15. Jn 5:16. He *2:2, 3. 10:28, 29.

3. **kindle no fire.** Ex 12:16. *16:23. Nu 15:32, etc. Is +*58:13n.

4. **This is.** Ex *25:1, 2.

5. **whosoever.** See on Ex *25:2-7. Jg 5:9. Ps *110:3. Mk 12:41-44. 2 C *8:11, 12. *9:7. **willing.** Le +*23:38. **gold.** 1 Ch 22:14, 16. 28:14-18. 2 Ch 4:19-22. Jb

22:25mg. Jn=1:1. 1 C 3:12. 2 P=1:4. Re 3:18. 21:18, 21.

6. **blue.** See on Ex 25:4n. 26:1, 31, 36. 28:5, 6, 15, 33. **goats' hair.** See on Ex 26:7n, 8-14.

8. **And oil.** See on Ex 27:20. **spices.** Ex 25:6. 30:23n, 28.

9. **onyx stones.** Ex 25:5. See on 28:9, 17-21. 39:6-14. Ge 2:12n.

10. **wise hearted.** Ex *31:1-6. *36:1-4. 1 P *4:10.

11. **tabernacle.** See on Ex 26:1n, 2, etc. 31:7-9. 33:7n. 36:8-34. **taches.** *Keraism,* from *karas,* to bend, so called from their curved form; hooks, clasps, or any thing used for the purpose of fastening: the word *taches* is formed by aphaeresis from the French *attacher,* to fasten. They were equivalent, perhaps, to our hooks-and-eyes.

12. **ark.** See on Ex *25:10-22. 37:1-9. **the vail.** See on Ex 26:7, 31-33. 36:35, 36.

13. **The table.** Ex *25:23-30. 37:10-16. Le *24:5, 6. **showbread.** Ex +25:30. 1 Ch ●+9:32.

14. **candlestick.** *Menorah,* rather, a chandelier, or lampstand, candles not used in Scripture in connection with worship. The lampstand was of pure gold, and is described as having one shaft, with six branches proceeding from it, adorned at equal distances with six flowers, like lilies, with as many bowls and knops placed alternately. See on Ex *25:31-39. 37:17-24. Ps 148:3. Mt 5:14, 15.

15. **the incense.** Ex *30:1-10, 22-38. 37:25-28. Ps 141:2. **the hanging.** Ex 26:36, 37. 36:37, 38.

16. **the altar.** Ex *27:1-8. 38:1-7. **the laver.** Ex 30:18-21. 38:8.

17. **The hangings.** See on Ex *27:9-19. 38:9-20. 2 S 7:2.

18. **The pins.** These, as Dr. Wall observes, were not particularly mentioned. Josephus says, that to every board of the tabernacle, and to every pillar of the hangings of the court, there were ropes or cords, fastened at the top of the board or pillar, and that the other end of the rope was fastened to a *passalaos,* a nail, or pin, which at a good distance off, was driven into the ground up to the head, a cubit deep. This was to keep the tabernacle from being blown down by the wind. Dr. Shaw, describing the tents of the Bedouins, says, "These tents are kept firm and steady by bracing or stretching down their eaves with cords tied to wooden hooked pins, well pointed, which they drive into the ground with a mallet; one of these pins answering to the nail, as the mallet does to the hammer, which Jael used in fastening to the ground the temples of Sisera" (Jg 4:21). Ex 27:19.

19. **The cloths.** See on Ex 31:10. 39:1, 41. Nu *4:5-15. **the holy.** See on Ex 28. 39:1-31.

21. **whose heart.** ver. 5, 22, 26, 29. Ex 25:2. 36:2. Jg 5:3, 9, 12. 2 S 7:27. 1 Ch 28:2, 9. 29:3, 5, 6, 9, 14, 17, 18. Ezr 1:5, 6. 7:27. Ps 110:3. Pr 4:23. Je 30:21. Mt 12:34. 2 C 8:12. 9:7. **spirit.** Heb. *ruach,* Ge +41:38. **offering.** Le +*23:38.

22. **brought.** Ex ●32:2, 3. **bracelets.** *Chach,* either a hook or clasp, to join garments together. Ex 32:3. ●35:11n. 2 K 19:28. Is 3:19. 37:29. Ezk 16:11. 19:4, 9. 29:4. **earrings.** Ge 24:22. **tablets.** *Kumoz,* as Bochart thinks, a kind of girdle, swathe, or zone. Nu 31:50. **every man.** 1 Ch 29:6, 7. 2 Ch 24:9-14. Ezr 2:68, 69. Ne 7:70-72. Is 60:9, 13. Mt 2:11. Mk 12:41-44.

23. **blue.** See on ver. 6-10. Ex 25:2-7. 1 Ch 29:8.

24. **whom.** 2 C 8:12.

25. **wise hearted.** Ex 28:3. 31:6. 36:1. 2 K 23:7. Pr 14:1. 31:19-24. Lk 8:2, 3. Ac 9:39. Ro 16:1-4, 6, 12. Ga 3:28. Ph 4:3.

26. **whose heart.** ver. 21, 29. Ex 36:8.

27. **onyx.** ver. 9. 1 Ch 29:6. Ezr 2:68.

28. **spice.** ver. 8. Ex 30:23-38.

29. **willing offering.** Le +*23:38. **whose heart.** ver. 21, 22. Jg 5:2, 9. 1 Ch *29:3, 6, 9, 10, 14, 17. 1 C 9:17. 2 C √9:7. **the Lord.** ver. 4. Dt 4:2. 11:32. 12:32. Is +√8:20n. Mt 28:20. 1 C 3:5. Ga 6:16. 2 T 3:15-17. 2 P 1:19.

30. **See.** Ex 31:2-6. 1 K 7:13, 14. Is 28:26. 1 C 3:10. 12:4, 11. Ja 1:17.

31. **And he.** Ex +*31:3n. Nu ●11:25, 26. 27:18. Is 11:2-5. 28:26. 61:1-3. 1 C 12:4-10. Col 2:3. Ja 1:17. **spirit.** Heb. *ruach,* Ge +41:38. **workmanship.** 2 Ch 2:7, 14.

34. **he hath.** Ex +18:20, 21. Ezr *7:10, 27. Ne 2:12. Ja 1:16, 17. **teach.** Ps 94:10. **Aholiab.** Ex *31:6. 2 Ch 2:14. Is 28:24-29. 1 C 1:5-7. 12:7.

35. **he filled.** ver. 31. Ex *31:3, 6. 1 K 3:12. 7:14. 2 Ch 2:14. Is 28:26. **the cunning.** Ex 26:1. Ac 19:6, 8. 1 C 1:5, 7. 12:4, 8, 12. Ga 3:2, 5. 1 T *3:15. 4:16. 2 T *2:15. **of the weaver.** Jb 7:6. Is 38:12.

EXODUS 36

Bezaleel and Aholiab receive the oblations and begin to work, 1-3. The liberality of the people is restrained, 4-7. The several parts of the sanctuary are made: The curtains with cherubims, 8-13. The curtains of goat's hair, 14-18. The covering of skins, 19. The boards with their sockets, 20-30. The bars, 31-34. The vail, 35, 36. The hanging for the door, 37, 38.

1. **Bezaleel.** See on Ex 31:1-6. 35:30-35. **wise hearted man.** Ex 28:3. 31:6. **for the service.** ver. 3, 4. Ex 25:8. Nu 7:9. He 8:2. **according.** Ex 23:21, 22. 39:1-43. ch. 40. Ps 119:6. Mt 28:20. Lk 1:6.

2. **in whose.** Ex 28:3. 31:6. 35:10, 21-35. Ac 6:3, 4. 14:23. Col 4:17. He 5:4. **one whose.** Ex 35:2, 21, 25, 26. 1 Ch 29:5.

3. **the offering.** Ex 35:5-21, 27, 29. **free offerings.** Le +*23:38. **every morning.** Ps 5:3. 101:8. Pr 8:15. Is 50:4. Je 21:12.

4. **wise men.** 2 Ch 24:13. Mt 24:45. Lk 12:42. 1 C *3:10.

5. **much more.** Ex 32:3. 2 Ch 24:14. 31:6-10. 2 C 8:2, 3. Ph 2:21. +*4:17, 18.

6. **gave commandment.** Ex 35:21-29. 38:8. Ge 14:21. 28:22. 45:18-20. Le 26:10. Nu 7:1-88. 31:48-54. 2 S 8:10, 11. 2 Ch *31:10. Pr *11:25. Ml *3:10. Lk *5:6, 7. *6:38. 12:16, 17. Jn 21:6-11. **proclaimed.** 2 Ch 30:5h. 36:22. Ezr 1:1mg. 10:7. Ne 8:15. **restrained.** Ge 8:2h. Ezk 31:15h.

7. **and too much.** ver. +6. 2 Ch 31:10. Ml *3:10.

8. **wise.** Ex 31:6. 35:10. **made.** See on Ex 26:1-37. 1 Ch 15:1. **cherubims.** *Keroovim,* cherubim, not cherubims, for the word is already plural. See on Ex 25:18, 22. Ge 3:24. 1 K 6:23. 2 Ch 3:10. Ezk 1:5, etc. 10:1-19.

10. **coupled.** Ex 26:3. Ps 122:3. 133:1. Zp 3:9. Ac 2:1. 1 C *1:10. 12:20, 27. Ep 1:23. 2:21, 22. 4:2-6. Ph 2:2. 3:15.

11. **loops.** Ex 26:4.

12. **Fifty loops.** Ex 26:5, 10.

13. **so it became**. 1 C 12:20. Ep *2:20-22. 1 P *2:4, 5.

14. **curtains**. See on Ex 26:7-13.

19. **covering**. See on Ex 26:14n. **rams' skins dyed red**. This was the third covering of the tabernacle. The first and lowermost was made of fine linen, richly embroidered with figures of cherubim, in shades of blue, purple, and scarlet (ver. 8-13). It is reasonable to suppose, that the right side of this curtain was undermost, and so it formed a beautiful ceiling on the inside of the tabernacle. The second covering, which lay over the embroidered one, was made of a sort of mohair (ver. 14-17), and the fourth, or uppermost one, which was to keep the others from the weather, was made of *tachash*, or badgers' skins. Ex ❶25:5n.

20. **boards**. See on Ex 26:15-25. 40:18, 19. **shittim wood**. Ex 25:5, 10. Nu 25:1. Dt 10:3.

21. **The length**. Each of these boards, taking the cubit at nearly twenty-two inches, was about eighteen feet long, and two feet nine inches broad. As these boards are said to be standing up (ver. 20), their length was consequently the height of the tabernacle; and as the two sides were composed of twenty of these, standing up (ver. 23, 25), and the west end of six, with two boards to project at the corners (ver. 27, 28), the tabernacle must therefore have been thirty cubits, or fifty-five feet long, and about ten cubits, or eighteen feet broad. These boards were fastened at the bottom by two tenons in each board (Ex 26:17), which fitted into two mortices in the foundation, at the top by links or hasps, and on the sides by the wooden bars, which ran through rings or staples in each of the boards. The boards and bars were all overlaid with gold; and their rings for the staves, and their hasps at top, were of the same metal. The foundation on which they stood consisted of about ninety-six solid blocks of silver, two under each board, about eighteen inches long, and of a suitable thickness; and each weighing about a talent, or about a hundredweight. Four blocks of silver formed the bases of the columns which supported the curtain that divided the inside of the tabernacle into two rooms.

27. **westward**. Ex 26:22, 27.

29. **coupled**. Heb. twined. Ex 26:24mg. Ps 122:3. 133:1. Ac 2:46. 4:32. 1 C=1:10. =*12:13. 2 C 1:10x. Ep 2:15, 19, 21. 3:18, 19. 4:2-6, 15, 16.

30. **under every board two sockets**. Heb. two sockets under one board. Ex 26:25.

31. **bars**. See on Ex 25:28. 26:26-29. 30:5.

32. **the tabernacle**. Ex 26:26.

35. **a vail of blue**. *Parachoth*, from *parach*, to separate, divide, make a distinction between somewhat, the inner vail, which divided the tabernacle into two, and separated, and made a distinction, between the Holy place and the Holy of Holies. This vail was made of the same rich materials as the inner covering of the tabernacle, and curiously embroidered with the cherubim and other ornaments. Though it does not appear from Scripture at what distance from either end of the tabernacle this vail was hung, yet it is reasonably conjectured, that it divided it in the same proportion in which the temple, built after this model, was divided; that is, two thirds of the whole length were allotted to the first room, and one third to the second; so that the room beyond the vail, the Holy of Holies, was exactly square, being ten cubits each way, and

the first room, the sanctuary, was twice as long as it was broad. See on Ex 26:31-35. 30:6. 40:21. Mt 27:51. He 10:20.

36. **pillars**. Je 1:18.

37. **an hanging**. This vail was a fine embroidered curtain, of the same materials and of the same workmanship as the inner vail and inner covering of the tabernacle. The text does not say how low it hung. Philo makes it touch the ground; but Josephus will have it to come down but half way, so that the people might have a view of the inside of the tabernacle; but then he says there was another curtain over that, which came to the ground, to keep it from the weather, and was drawn aside on the sabbath and other festivals. Ex 26:36, 37. 40:28. **of needlework**. Heb. the work of a needle worker, or embroiderer. Ex 26:36.

38. **fillets with gold**. Ex 27:10, 11, 17. 38:10, 17, 19, 28.

EXODUS 37

The ark and mercy seat made, 1-9. The table of showbread, 10-16. And the candlestick, 17-24. The altar of incense, 25-28; and the holy oil and incense, 29.

1. **the ark**. Ex 25:10-16. 26:33. 31:7. 40:3, 20, 21. Nu 10:33-36.

2. **he overlaid**. Ex 30:3.

4. **staves**. Nu 4:14, 15. Ac 9:15. **with gold**. 1 P 1:7, 18, 19.

5. **the staves**. Nu 1:50. 4:15. 2 S 6:3-7.

6. **mercy seat**. See on Ex 25:17-22. Le 16:12-15. 1 Ch 28:11. Ro=3:25. Ga 4:4. T 2:14. He 9:5. 1 J 2:2. **pure gold**. Jn=1:1, 14. =20:28.

7. **cherubims**. Ex 36:8n. 1 K 6:23-29. Ps 80:1. 104:4. Ezk 10:2. **beaten**. ver. 22. Ex +27:20n. Is=53:5. He +=2:10.

8. **on the end**. *or*, out of, etc. **on the other end**. *or*, out of, etc.

9. **cherubims spread**. Ex 36:8n. Ge 3:24. 28:12. Is 6:2. Ezk 10. Jn 1:51. 2 C 3:18. Ph 3:8. 1 T 3:16. He 1:14. **to the mercy seatward**. Ex 25:20. Ep 3:10. 1 P *1:12.

10. **the table**. See on Ex *25:23-30. 35:13. 40:4, 22, 23. Ezk 40:39-42. Ml 1:12. Jn 1:14, 16. Col 1:27.

12. **handbreadth**. *f*79, Ge +21:16.

16. **dishes**. See on Ex 25:29. 1 K 7:50. 2 K 12:13. Je 52:18, 19. 2 T 2:20. **cover withal**. *or*, pour out withal.

17. **the candlestick of**. See on Ex 25:31-39. 40:24, 25. 1 Ch 28:15. 2 Ch 13:11. Zc 4:2, 11. Mt 5:15. Jn *1:4-9. 14:26. Ph 2:15. He 9:2. Re *1:12-20. 2:1-5.

20. **almonds**. Ex 25:33. Nu 17:8. Ec 12:5. Je 1:11.

21. **a knop**. Ex 25:35.

22. **were**. Ex 25:31. 1 C 9:27. Col 3:5. **beaten work**. ver. +7. Ex +27:20. Ps 51:17. Is 5:4, 5, 10. =53:5. He +=2:10.

23. **seven lamps**. Ex 25:37. Nu 8:2. Zc 4:2. Re 1:12, 20. 2:1. 4:5. 5:5.

25. **incense altar**. See on Ex 30:1-5. 40:5, 26, 27. 2 Ch 26:16. Mt 23:19. Lk 1:9, 10. He 7:25. 13:10. 1 P 2:5. Re *8:3, 4.

29. **he made**. See on Ex *30:23-38. Ps 23:5. 92:10. Is 11:2. 61:1, 3. Jn 3:34. 2 C 1:21, 22. 1 J 2:20, 27. **incense**. Ex 30:1n, 7, 34. Ps 14:1, 2. 141:2. He 5:7.

*7:25. Re 8:3, 4. **sweet spices.** 2 C *2:15. **the apothecary.** Ex 30:25, 35. Ec 10:1.

EXODUS 38

The altar of burnt offering, 1-7. The laver of brass, 8. The court, the pillars, and the hangings for the court, 9-20. The sum of what the people offered, and the use to which it was applied, 21-31.

1. **the altar.** Ex 27:1-8. 40:6, 29. 2 Ch 4:1. Ezk 43:13-17. Ro 8:3, 4. 12:1. He 3:1. 9:14. 13:10. 1 P 2:5. **foursquare; and three cubits the height thereof.** Ezk 43:16. Jn 6:37. He 13:8. Re 21:16.

2. **he made.** Ex 27:2. **brass.** Jb 6:12.

3. **he made.** Ex 27:3. **flesh hooks.** 1 S 2:13.

5. **the grate.** Ex 27:4.

6. **shittim wood.** Ex 25:6. Dt 10:3.

7. **to bear it withal.** Ac 9:15. 1 C 1:24. 2:2.

8. **the laver.** See on Ex 30:18-21. 40:7, 30-32. 1 K 7:23-26, 38. Ps 26:6. Zc 13:1. Jn 13:10. T 3:5, 6. He *9:10. 1 J 3:7. Re 1:5. **looking glasses.** *or,* brazen glasses. Jb 37:18. Is 3:23mg. 1 C =13:12. Ja 1:23-25. **assembling.** Heb. assembling by troops. Nu 4:23. 8:24. 1 S 2:22mg. It is supposed that these women kept watch during the night. Among the ancients, women were generally employed as door-keepers. See 1 S 2:22. Ps 84:10. Pr 8:34. Mt 26:69. Lk *2:37. Jn 18:16. Ac 12:13. 1 T 5:5.

9. **the court.** See on Ex *27:9-19. 40:8, 33. 1 K 6:36. Ps 84:2, 10. 89:7. 92:13. 100:4. Is *54:2, 3.

14. **hangings.** Ex 27:14.

18. **needlework.** 2 Ch 3:14.

20. **the pins.** Ex 27:19. 2 Ch 3:9. Ezr 9:8. Ec 12:11. Is 22:23. 33:20. Ep 2:21, 22. Col 2:19.

21. **sum.** He=8:1, 2. **tabernacle of testimony.** Ex 25:16. 26:33. 40:3. Nu *1:50, 53. 9:15. 10:11. 17:7, 8. 18:2. 2 Ch 24:6. Ac 7:44. Re 11:19. The word tabernacle is used in many different senses, and signifies (1) A tent or pavilion, Nu 24:5; Mt 17:4. (2) A house or dwelling, Jb 11:4; 22:23. (3) A kind of tent, which is designated, to speak after the manner of men, the palace of the Most High, the dwelling of the God of Israel, Ex 26:1; He 9:2, 3. (4) Christ's human nature, of which the Jewish tabernacle was a type, wherein God dwells really, substantially, and personally, He 8:2; 9:11. (5) The true church militant, Ps 15:1. (6) Our natural body, in which the soul lodges as in a tabernacle, 2 C 5:1; 2 P 1:13. (7) The token of God's gracious presence, Re 21:3. **by the hand.** Nu 4:28-33. Ezr 8:26-30. **Ithamar.** Ex 6:23. 1 Ch 6:3. 24:4.

22. **Bezaleel.** Ex 31:1-5. 35:30-35. 36:1-3. **all that the Lord.** Ps 119:6. Je 1:7. Mt 28:20.

23. **Aholiab.** Ex 35:34. **a cunning.** Ex 35:34.

24. **All the gold.** 1 K 6:21, 22, 28, 30. 1 Ch 22:14-16. 29:2-7. Hg 2:8. If we follow the estimation of the learned Dean Prideaux, the gold weighed 4245 pounds, the silver, 14,603 pounds, and the brass, 10,277 pounds, troy weight. The total weight of these three metals will amount to 29,124 pounds troy, which, reduced to avoirdupois weight, is equal to fourteen tons, 266 pounds! See notes on Nu 3:25n. 4:44n. **offering.** Ex 25:2. 29:24. 35:22. **the shekel.** Ex 30:13, 14, 24. Le 5:15. 27:3, 25. Nu 3:47. 18:16.

26. **bekah.** Ex *30:13. 15, 16. Ge 24:22. **every man.** Heb. a poll. Ex +16:16mg. Nu *1:46. **every one.** Ex

30:11-16. 1 P=1:18, 19. **six hundred.** Ex *12:37. Nu 1:46. 26:51.

27. **and the sockets.** Ex 26:19, 21, 25, 32.

28. **and filleted them.** Ex 27:17.

30. **the sockets.** Ex 26:37. 27:10, 17. **the brasen altar.** Ex 27:2-4.

31. **And the sockets.** Ex 27:10-12. **and the sockets.** Ex 27:16, 17. **the pins.** Ex 27:19. 35:18n.

EXODUS 39

The cloths of service and holy garments, 1. The ephod, 2-7. The breast-plate, 8-21. The robe of the ephod, 22-26. The coats, mitre, and girdle of fine linen, 27-29. The plate of the holy crown, 30, 31. All is finished, reviewed, and approved by Moses, 32-43.

1. **the blue.** Ex 25:4. 26:1. *35:23. **cloths.** Ex 31:10. 35:19. **holy place.** Ps 93:5. Ezk 43:12. He 9:12, 25. **the holy.** Ex 28:2-4. 31:10. Ezk 42:14.

2. **the ephod.** See on Ex 25:7. 28:6-12. Le 8:7.

3. **cunning work.** Ex 26:1. 36:8.

5. **curious.** See on Ex 28:8. 29:5. Le *8:7. 1 S *2:18. Is 11:5. Re 1:13. **as the Lord.** Mt 28:20. 1 C 11:23.

6. **onyx stones.** See on Ex 25:7. *28:9. 35:9. Jb 28:16. Ezk 28:13. **ouches.** *mishbetzoth,* strait places, sockets, to insert the stones in, from *shavatz,* to straiten, enclose. ver. 13, 16, 18. Ex 28:+11, 13, 14, 25.

7. **a memorial.** Ex *28:12, 29. Jsh 4:7. Ne 2:20. Mk 14:9, 22-25.

8. **breastplate.** See on Ex 25:7. *28:4, 13-29. Le 8:8, 9. Ps 89:28. Is *59:17. Ep *6:14. 1 Th *5:8. He *7:24, 25.

10. **the first row.** See on Ex 28:16, 17, 21. Re 21:19-21. **sardius.** or, ruby. Ex 28:17. Ezk 28:13. **topaz.** Jb 28:19. **carbuncle.** Ezk 28:13.

11. **emerald.** Ex 28:18. Ezk 27:16. **sapphire.** Jb 28:6, 16. **diamond.** or, sardonyx. Ex 28:18. Ezk 28:13.

12. **ligure.** or, jacinth. Ex 28:19. *Leshem,* the ligure, the same as the jacinth, or hyacinth, a precious stone of a deep red, with a considerable tinge of yellow. **agate.** Ex 28:19. **amethyst.** Ex 28:19. Re 21:20.

13. **beryl.** or, chalcedony. Ex 28:20. SS 5:14. **onyx.** ver. 6. **jasper.** Ex 28:20. Ezk 28:13. Re 4:3. 21:11, 18, 19.

14. **the names.** Re 21:12.

15. **chains at the ends.** Ex 28:14. 2 Ch 3:5. SS 1:10. Jn 10:28. 17:12. 1 P 1:5. Ju 1.

16. **gold rings.** Ex 25:12.

18. **two wreathen.** Ex 28:14. SS 1:10. **ephod.** ver. 2.

20. **coupling.** Ex 26:3.

21. **as the Lord.** Mt 16:24. 1 C 1:25, 27. 1 P 3:16.

22. **the robe.** See on Ex 28:31-35.

24. **they made.** Ex 28:33. **pomegranates.** Ga 5:22.

25. **bells.** Ex 28:33, 34. Ps 89:15. **the pomegranates.** SS 4:13.

26. **pomegranate.** Ex 28:34. SS 4:3, 13. 6:7. **hem.** Dt 22:12. Mt 9:20.

27. **coats.** See on Ex *28:39-42. Le 8:13. Is *61:10. Ezk 44:18. Ro 3:22. 13:14. Ga 3:27. Ph 2:6-8. 1 P 1:13. **fine.** The word *shesh* seems rather to mean cotton, than either fine linen or silk. Pr 31:22n. Re *19:8.

28. **a mitre.** Ex 28:4, 39. 29:6n. Ezk *44:18. **linen.** Ex 28:42. **bonnets.** Ex 29:9. Le 8:13. **breeches.** *Michnasim,* from *kanas,* to wrap around. Ex 28:42. Le 6:10. 16:4. Ezk 44:18.

29. **a girdle**. Ex 28:39. 29:9. Le 8:7, 13. Is *11:5. **needlework**. Ex 38:18, 23.

30. **the plate**. See on Ex 26:36. 28:36-39. 1 C *1:30. 2 C 5:21. He 1:3. 7:26. **Holiness**. Ex 28:36. Zc *14:20. T *2:14. Re 5:10.

32. **all the**. ver. 33, 42. Ex ch. 25-31. ch. 35-40. Le ch. 8, 9. Nu 3:25, 26, 31, 36, 37. 4:4-32. Jn *1:14. Col *2:9. 1 J *3:24. Re *21:3. **according**. ver. 42, 43. Ex 25:40. 40:32. Dt 12:32. 1 S 15:22. 1 Ch 28:19. Mt 28:20. He 3:2. 8:5.

33. **the tent**. Ex ch. 25-30. 31:7-11. 35:11-19. ch. 36-40.

35. **the mercy seat**. Ex 25:17. He 9:5, 8.

36. **the showbread**. Ex +25:30. 1 K 7:48. 1 Ch ◑+9:32.

37. **even with**. Ex 27:21. Mt 5:14-16. Ph 2:15.

38. **golden altar**. Ex 37:25-28. **anointing oil**. Ex 37:29. **sweet incense**. Heb. the incense of sweet spices. Ex 25:6. 30:7. 31:11. 35:8. 37:29. 2 Ch 2:4.

39. **brasen altar**. Ex 27:1, 2. 30:28. 31:9. 35:16. 38:1, 30. 40:6. 1 K 8:64. **laver**. Ex 30:18. 31:9. 35:16. 38:8. 40:7. 1 K ◑7:23.

40. **court**. Ex 27:9. 35:17. 38:9. 40:7. **cords**. Ex 35:18. Nu 3:26, 37. **pins**. Ex 27:19. 35:18n. 38:20, 21. Nu 3:37.

41. **cloths**. ver. 1. Ex 31:10. **the holy**. Ex 28:2.

42. **According**. ver. 32. Ex 23:21, 22, 25-31. Dt 12:32. Mt 28:20. 2 T 2:15. 4:7. **made**. Ex 35:10.

43. **did look**. Ex 40:25. Ge 1:31. Ps 104:31. **blessed them**. Ge 14:19. 49:28. Le 9:22, 23. Nu *6:23-27. Jsh 22:6. 2 S 6:18. 1 K 8:14. 1 Ch 16:2. 2 Ch 6:3. 30:27. Ne 11:2. Ps 19:11.

EXODUS 40

The tabernacle is commanded to be reared, anointed, and consecrated, 1-12. Aaron and his sons to be sanctified, 13-15. Moses performs all things accordingly, 16-33. A cloud covers the tabernacle, 34-38.

2. **the first month**. ver. 17. Ex 12:1, 2. 13:4. Nu 7:1. **tabernacle**. ver. 6, 18, 19. Ex 26:1, 7, 30. 27:21. 30:36. 35:11. 36:18. The heathen temples were evident imitations of the tabernacle and temple. They consisted of, (1) the area, or porch; (2) the *naos*, or temple; (3) the *adytum*, or holy place, also called *penetrale* and *sacrarium*; (4) the *apisthodomos*, or inner temple, where they had their mysteria, and which answered to the Holy of Holies. One of the most complete imitations of the tabernacle and its whole service is found in the ancient temple of Hercules at Gades, now Cadiz, in Spain; in which the beams were so ancient that they were supposed to be incorruptible. Women were not permitted to enter, nor swine to come near it; the priests wore no parti-colored vests, but were clothed in fine linen, with bonnets of the same; they offered incense with their clothes ungirded (ch. 20:26); they wore a stud of purple on their vest; they ministered bare footed, kept the strictest continency, kept a perpetual fire on their altars; and had no image in their sacred place (See Silius Italicus, *Punicor*. l. iii. v. 77-31).

3. **the ark**. ver. 20, 21. Ex 25:10, 22. 26:31, 33, 34. 35:12. 36:35, 36. 37:1-9. Le 16:14. Nu 4:5. Re 11:19. 15:5.

4. **the table**. ver. 22, 25. Ex 25:23-30. 26:35, 36. 37:10-24. **the things that**, etc. Heb. the order thereof.

ver. 23. Ex 39:37. Le 24:5, 6, 8. 2 Ch 2:4. 29:18. Ne 10:33. **the candlestick**. ver. 24, 25. See on Ex 25:31-39. 35:14n.

5. **the altar**. ver. 26, 27. Ex 30:1-5. 35:25-28. 37:25-28. Jn *14:6. He 9:24. 10:19-22. 1 J 2:1, 2. **put**. ver. 28. Ex 26:36, 37. 36:37, 38. **tabernacle**. He *9:11-14.

6. **altar of the burnt offering**. ver. 29. See on Ex 27:1-8. 38:1-7. Ep 1:6, 7. He *13:10. 1 J 2:2. 4:9, 10.

7. **the laver**. ver. 30-32. See on Ex 30:18-21. 38:8. Ps 26:6. Zc 13:1. T 3:5. He 10:22. 1 J 1:7. Re 1:5, 6.

8. **the court**. ver. 33. See on Ex 27:9-19. 38:9-20. 39:40. Mt 16:18. 1 C 12:28. Ep 4:11, 12.

9. **the anointing oil**. Ex 30:23-33. 37:29. 39:39. Le 8:10. Nu 7:1. Ps 45:7. Is 11:2. 61:1. Mt 3:16. Jn 3:34. 2 C 1:4, 22. 1 J 2:20, 27.

10. **sanctify**. Ex 29:36, 37. Le 8:11. Is 11:2. 61:1. Jn 3:34. 17:19. **most holy**. Heb. holiness of holinesses. Ex 29:37. 30:10, 29, 36. Le 2:3, 10. 6:17, 25, 29. 7:1, 6. 10:12, 17. 14:13. 21:22. 24:9. 27:28. Nu 18:9. Lk=1:35. 1 C 1:30. 2 C 5:21. He 7:26.

12. **bring Aaron**. See on Ex 29:1-35. Le 8:1-13. ch. 9. Is 11:1-5. 61:1-3. Mt 3:16. Lk 1:35. Jn 3:34. Ro 8:3. Ga 4:4. **unto the door**. Moses washed Aaron and his sons at the door of the tabernacle, not in the laver, as immersion would require. See related notes (Ex 30:19n, 21n. Le *16:24n. 1 K 7:23n). Le 8:4-6. **wash**. Heb. *rahats*, Ex +29:4. **with water**. Ac +*1:5n.

13. **anoint him**. See on Ex 28:41. Is 61:1. Jn 3:34. 17:19. Ac *10:38. He 10:10, 29. 1 J 2:20, 27.

14. **bring his sons**. Is 44:3-5. 61:10. Jn 1:16. Ro 8:30. 13:14. 1 C 1:9, 30.

15. **as**. Jn=3:34. 1 J=2:20. **everlasting**. Heb. *olam*, Ex +12:24. Ex 12:14. 30:31, 33. Nu *25:13. Ps *110:4. He ch. 5. 7:3, 7, 17-24. ch. 8-10.

16. **according**. ver. 17-32. Ex 23:21, 22. 39:42, 43. Dt 4:2. 12:32. Is +√8:20n. Mt 28:20. Jn=15:10. 1 C 4:2.

17. **the first month**. ver. 1, 2. Nu 7:1. 9:1.

18. **reared**. ver. 2. Ex 26:15-30. 36:20-34. Le 26:11. Ezk 37:27, 28. Jn 1:14. Ga 4:4. 1 P 1:5. Re 21:3. **and fastened**. Is 33:26. Mt 16:18. 1 T 3:15.

19. **the tent**. Ex 26:1-14. 36:8-19.

20. **the testimony**. Ex 16:34. 25:16-21. 31:18. Ps 40:8. Mt 3:15. **mercy**. ver. 3. Ex 37:6-9. Ro 3:25. 10:4. He 4:16. 10:19-21. 1 J 2:2.

21. **he brought**. ver. 3. Ex 26:33. 35:12. **and covered**. He 10:19, 20.

22. **he put**. Jn *6:53-57. Ep 3:8. **northward**. ver. 24. Ex 26:35.

23. **set**. ver. 4. Ex *25:30. Mt 12:4. He 9:2. **bread**. Re=2:17.

24. **the candlestick**. Ex 25:31-35. 37:17-24. Ps *119:105. Jn *1:1, 5, 9. *8:12. Re 1:20. 2:5.

25. **he lighted**. ver. 4. Ex 25:37. Re 4:5.

26. **golden altar**. ver. 5. Ex 30:1-10. Mt 23:19. Jn 11:42. ch. 17. He *7:25. 10:1. 1 J *2:1. Re 8:3, 4.

27. **he burnt**. Ex 30:7.

28. **set up**. ver. 5. Ex 26:36, 37. 38:9-19. Jn *10:9. *14:6. Ep 2:18. He 10:19, 20.

29. **the altar**. ver. 6. Ex 27:1-8. 38:1-7. Mt 23:19. Ro 3:24-26. He 9:12. 13:5, 6, 10. **offered**. Ex 29:38, etc. **burnt offering**. Le +*23:12. **meat offering**. Le +*23:13.

30. **laver**. ver. 7. Ex 30:+18, 19-21. 38:8. Ezk 36:25. He 10:22.

31. **washed**. Ps 26:6. 51:6, 7. Jn 13:10. 1 J 1:7, 9. **feet**. Jn=13:10.

32. **washed**. Jn=13:10. **as the Lord**. ver. 19. Ex 30:19, 20. Ps 73:19.

33. **up the court**. ver. 8. Ex 27:9-16. Nu 1:50. Mt 16:8. 1 C 12:12, 28. Ep 4:11-13. He 9:6, 7. **tabernacle**. *S#4908h. Ex +*25:9n. The tabernacle might either be called a house or a tent, because it had wooden walls and partitions like a house, and curtains and hangings like a tent; but as it externally resembled a common oblong tent, and the wooden walls were without a roof, and properly only supports for the many curtains and hangings spread over them, it is more properly called a tent. Even ordinary tents of the Arabs have at least two main divisions; the innermost for the women, and hence called *sacred*, i.e. *cut off*, inaccessible. In the tent of an emir the innermost space is accessible to himself only, or those whom he particularly honors; into the outer tent others may come. The furniture is costly, the floor covered with a rich carpet, and has a stand with a censer and coals, on

which incense is strewed. Hence we have the simple idea after which this magnificent royal tent of the Hebrews, was made. **hanging**. Jn 10:9. 14:6. Ep 2:18. He 4:14-16. **So Moses**. Ex 39:32. 1 K 6:9. Zc 4:9. Jn 4:34. =17:4. 2 T 4:7. He *3:2-5.

34. **a cloud**. Ex 13:21, 22. 14:19, 20, 24. 25:8, 21, 22. 29:43. 33:9. Le *16:2. Nu *9:15-23, 35. 1 K *8:10, 11. 2 Ch 5:13. 7:2. Ps 18:10-12. Is 4:5, 6. 6:4. Ezk 43:4-7. Hg *2:7, 9. Zc *2:5. Re *15:8. 21:3, 23, 24.

35. **not able**. Le 16:2. 1 K 8:11. 2 Ch *5:14. 7:2. Is *2:10. 6:4. Re 15:8. **cloud**. Ex +*13:21. Le 16:2. 2 S 6:2. 1 K 8:10. 2 Ch +*5:13. Ps 80:1. Is 37:16. Ezk 9:3. **glory**. Zc +*2:5. Jn *1:14. Ep *2:21, 22. Col *2:9. He *9:24.

36. **when**. Ex 13:21, 22. Nu *10:11-13, 33-36. 19:17-23. Ne *9:19. Ps *78:14. 105:39. 1 C 10:1. 2 C 5:19, 20. **went onward**. Heb. journeyed. ver. 37.

37. **if the cloud**. Nu *9:19-22. Ps *31:15. Pr *3:5, 6.

38. **the cloud**. Ex +*13:21. Nu 9:15. **fire**. Ps *78:14. 105:39. Is 4:5, 6. He *12:29. 1 J *1:5. **throughout**. Ne *9:19.

LEVITICUS

LEVITICUS 1

The law of the burnt offering, of a bullock, 1-9; of a sheep, or goat, 10-13; of fowls, 14-17.

1. A.M. 2514. B.C. 1490. **called**. Ex 19:3. 24:1, 2, 12. 29:42. Jn 1:17. 2 P 1:17. **unto Moses**. Nu 12:7, 8. He 3:5. **spake**. Ex 29:42. Jn=8:26. He=1:2. **out of**. Ex 25:22. 33:7. 39:32. 40:34, 35. Nu 12:4, 5. He 9:11.

2. **If any**. Le 22:18, 19. Ge 4:3-5. 1 Ch 16:29. Ro 12:1, 6. Ep 5:2. **an offering**. *Korban*, from *karav*, to approach, an introductory offering, or offering of access, in allusion to the present which is always required in the East, on being introduced to a superior.

3. **a burnt**. Le 6:9-13. 8:18, 21. +*23:12. Ge 8:20. 22:2, 8, 13. Ex 24:5. 29:18, 42. 32:6. 38:1. Nu 28:3, 10, 11, 19, 23, 24, 27, 31. 29:8-11, 13. Is 1:11. He 10:8-10. **a male**. Le 3:1. 4:23. 22:19-25. Ex 12:5. Dt 15:21. Zc 13:7. Ml 1:14. Lk +*1:35. Jn 1:36. *8:46. *14:30. Ep 5:27. He +*4:15. 7:26. 9:14. 1 P *1:18, 19. *2:22-24. **own voluntary will**. Le 7:16. 22:19, 21. Ex 35:5, 21, 29. 36:3. Ps *40:8. *110:3. Is=50:6. Ezk 46:12. Jn=10:11, 15, 17, +√18. 15:13. Ro *8:32. 2 C 8:12. √9:7. Ga 2:20. He=*9:14. 10:10. **at the**. Le 16:7. 17:4. Ex 29:4. Dt 12:5, 6, 13, 14, 27. Ezk 20:40. Jn 10:7, 9. Ep 2:18.

4. **put**. 3:2, 8, 13. 4:4, 15, 24, 29. 8:14, 22. 16:21. Ex 29:10, 15, 19. Nu 8:12. Is 53:4-6. 2 C 5:20, 21. **hand upon**. 1 J=1:1. **burnt offering**. Le 6:8-13. Ge 8:20. Ezr 3:2. Ps 51:19. Ac 13:39. 2 C 5:19. Ep 2:1-6. **be accepted**. Le 22:21, 27. Ps *51:17. Is 56:7. Ro *12:1. Ep=1:6. Ph 4:18. 1 P 2:5. **atonement**. Le 4:20, 26, 31, 35. 5:6. 6:7. 9:7. 16:24. Nu 15:25, 28. 25:13. 2 Ch 29:23, 24. Da 9:24. Ro 3:25. 5:11. He 10:4. 1 J 2:2.

5. **kill**. ver. 11. Le 3:2, 8, 13. 16:15. 2 Ch 29:22-24. Mi 6:6. Col 1:22. **bullock**. Pr=14:4. **the priests**. ver. 11, 15. 2 Ch 35:11. He 10:11. **sprinkle**. ver. 11. Le 3:2, 8, 13. Ex 24:6-8. 29:16. Nu 18:17. 2 Ch 35:11. Is 52:15. Ezk 36:25. He 10:11. *12:24. 1 P *1:2.

6. **flay**. Le 7:8. Ge 3:21. 2 Ch 29:34. Ps 2:2. Ac 4:27, 28.

7. **fire**. Le 6:12, 13. 9:24. 10:1. 1 Ch 21:26. 2 Ch 7:1. Ml 1:10. **lay**. Ge *22:9. Ne 13:31.

8. **lay the parts**. Le 8:18-21. 9:13, 14. Ex 29:17, 18. 1 K 18:23, 33.

9. **inwards**. ver. 13. Le 8:21. 9:14. Ps 51:6. Je 4:14. Mt 23:25-28. **wash**. 1 J 5:8. **burn all**. ver. 13, 17. Le 3:11. Ps 66:15. Zc 13:7. He 9:14. **a sweet**. Ge *8:21. Ezk 20:28, 41. 2 C 2:15. Ep *5:2. Ph *4:18. **savor**. ƒ22C15, Ge +8:21.

10. **of the flocks**. ver. 2. Ge 4:4. 8:20. Is *53:6, 7. Jn 1:29. Ac 8:32. **sheep**. Ge *22:8. Ex 29:38, 39, 42. Is=53:7. **a male**. See on ver. 3. Le 4:23. 22:19. Ml *1:14. Jn *6:37. **without blemish**. He *9:14.

11. **he shall**. See on ver. 5. Ex 40:22. Ezk 8:5. Zc 13:7. Lk 24:46. **northward**. Le 6:25. 7:2. **and the**. ver. 7-9. Le 9:12-14.

12. **shall cut**. ver. 6-8.

13. **shall wash**. See ver. 9. Ezk 36:25. Jn 13:10. **the inwards**. Mt 23:26. Mk *7:21. Ja 4:8.

14. **of fowls**. Le 5:7. 12:8. Mt 11:29. Lk *2:24. Jn 2:14. 2 C 8:12. He 7:26. **turtledoves**. Is=38:14. =59:11. Mt=10:16.

15. **wring off his head**. *or*, pinch off the head with the nail. Le 5:8. Ps 22:1, 21. 69:1-21. Is 53:4, 5, 10. Mt ch. 26, 27. Jn 12:27.

16. **his feathers**. *or*, the filth thereof. Lk 1:35. 1 P 1:2. **east**. 2 Ch 5:12. Ps=103:12. Je 31:40. Ezk 43:1, 2, 4. Jn=14:6. **by the place**. Le 4:12. 6:10, 11. 16:27. He 13:11-14. **ashes**. 2 Ch=5:12. Ps 20:3mg. Pr ◑30:16. Je 31:40. Ep=1:6.

17. **shall not**. Le *15:10. Ps 16:10. 22:14. Mt 27:50. Jn 19:30. Ro 4:25. 1 P 1:19-21. 3:18. **it is**. ver. 9, 10, 13. Ge 8:21. Ro 12:1. He 10:6-12. 13:15, 16.

LEVITICUS 2

The law of the meat offerings of flour, with oil and incense, raw or baken, 1-10. No leaven or honey to be used in them, 11. The firstfruits not to be burnt on the altar, 12. Salt to be used with every offering, 13. The meat offering of firstfruits in the ear, 14-15.

1. **any.** Heb. *nephesh*, soul, Ge +27:31. **meat offering.** *Minchah*, from the Arabic *manacha*, to give, especially as a reciprocal gift, gift, oblation, or eucharistical or gratitude offering, for the bounties of providence displayed in the fruits of the earth. It is termed a *meat offering* by our translators, because the term *meat* in their time was the general name for food. Le 6:14-18, 20-23. 9:17. +*23:13. Nu 15:4-21. Is 66:20. Jn 6:35. **fine flour.** Ex +27:20. 29:2. Nu 7:13, 19. Is=53:10. Jl 1:9. 2:14. He +=2:10. **pour oil.** ver. 4-8, 15, 16. Le 7:10-12. Ps 45:7, 8. Is 61:1. 1 J 2:20, 27. Ju 20. **frankincense.** Ml 1:11. Mt 2:11. Lk 1:9, 10. Re 8:3.

2. **sons.** 1 C 9:13, 14. **the memorial.** ver. 9. Le 5:12. 6:15. 24:7. Ex 30:16. Nu 5:18. Ne 13:14, 22. Is 66:3. Ac *10:4. Ep *2:18.

3. **the remnant.** Le 6:16, 17, 26. 7:9. *10:12, 13. 21:22. Nu 18:9. 1 S 2:28. Ps 78:24, 25. Jn 6:51. Re 2:17. **meat offerings.** 1 J=1:3. **most holy.** Le 6:17. 10:12. 21:22. Ex 29:37. Nu 18:9.

4. **meat offering.** 1 Ch 23:28, 29. Ps 22:14. Ezk 46:20. Mt 26:38. Jn 12:27. **unleavened cakes.** ver. 1, 11. Le 6:17. 7:12. 10:12. Ex 12:8. 29:2. 1 C 5:7, 8. He 7:26. 1 P 2:1, 22. *or*, pierced cakes. Heb. *chaloth*, from *chalhal*, to be pierced, or wounded. Ps=22:16. Jn=19:34, 37. 1 C=11:24. He +=2:10. **wafers.** Ex 16:31. 29:2. Is 42:1. 44:3-5. 61:1. Jn 3:34.

5. **in a pan.** *or*, on a flat plate, *or* slice. Le 6:21. 7:9. 1 Ch 23:29. Ezk 4:3.

6. **part.** Le 1:6. Ps 22:1-21. Mk chs. 14. 15. Jn chs. 18. 19. 1 C=11:26. He +=2:10.

7. **the fryingpan.** *Marchesheth*, a shallow earthen vessel, like a fryingpan. Le 7:9. **of fine.** See on ver. 1, 2.

9. **a memorial.** ver. 2. Le 6:15. **an offering.** ver. 2. Ex *29:18. Ps 22:13, 14. Is 53:10. Zc 13:7, 9. Ro 12:1. 15:16. Ep 5:2. Ph 2:17. 4:18.

10. **is left.** See on ver. 3. 1 C 9:13, 14. **meat offering.** Jn=6:50, 51.

11. **no leaven.** Le 6:17. Ex 12:19, 20. Am 4:5. Mt 16:6, 11, 12. Mk *8:15. Lk *12:1. 1 C *5:6-8. Ga *5:9. **honey.** Pr 24:13. 25:16, 27. Lk 21:34. Ac 14:22. 1 P 4:2.

12. **the oblation.** Le 23:10, 11, 17. Ex *22:29. 23:10, 11, 19. Nu 15:20. Dt 26:10. 2 Ch 31:5. 1 C 15:20. Re 14:4. **firstfruits.** Le +*23:10. Pr *3:9, 10. Mt *6:33. **be burnt.** Heb. ascend. S#5927h. Le 19:19 (come). Ge 2:6 (went up). 13:1. 17:22. 19:30. Ex 2:23 (came up). savor. ⌐22C15, Ge +8:21.

13. **with salt.** Ezr 7:22. Ezk 43:24. Mt 5:13. Mk *9:49, 50. Ac *2:27. 3:15. Col *4:6. **the salt.** Nu 18:19. 2 Ch 13:5. **with all thine.** Ezk 43:24.

14. **a meat offering.** These first fruits seem to have been the voluntary oblation brought by individuals, of the finest ears of corn out of the field, before the harvest was ripe. Le 22:29. 23:10, +*13, 14-17, 20. Ge 4:3. Nu 28:2. Dt 26:2. Pr *3:9, 10. Is 53:2-10. Ml 1:11. Ro 11:16. 1 C *15:20. Re 14:4. **firstfruits.** Le 23:10, 11, 14. 1 C=⌐15:23. **corn beaten.** Ex +27:20. 2 K 4:42. Is=53:5. He +=2:10.

15. **put oil.** See on ver. 1.

16. **the memorial.** See on ver. 1, 2, 4-7, 9, 12. Ps 141:2. Is 11:2-4. 61:1. Jn 1:45. 7:41. Ro 8:26, 27. He 5:7.

LEVITICUS 3

The law of the peace offerings, of the herd, 1-5; of the flock, 6-11; of a goat, 12-16. A prohibition to eat the fat, or the blood, 17.

1. **a sacrifice.** Le 7:11-21, 29-34. 22:19-21. Ex 20:24. 24:5. 29:28. Nu 6:14. 7:17. Jg 20:26. 21:4. 1 Ch 21:26. Pr 7:14. Is *9:6. Je +*29:11. Ezk 45:15. Am 5:22. Mi *5:5. Lk *2:24. *19:38. Ro *5:1, 2. Col 1:20. 1 J 1:3. **peace offering.** Le +*23:19. Dt 33:27, 28. Jg +6:24. Is 40:11. Ro 5:1. Col 1:20. **without.** See on Le 1:3. Nu 6:14. Ml 1:8, 14. He +*10:22.

2. **lay.** Le 1:4, 5. 8:22. 16:21, 22. Ex 29:10, 15. *53:5, 6. 2 C 5:21. 1 J 1:9, 10. **kill it.** Le 1:11. Zc 12:10. Ac 2:36-38. 3:15, 26. 4:10-12, 26-28.

3. **the fat.** *or*, suet. ver. 16. Le 4:8, 9. 7:3, 4. Ex 29:13, 22. Dt 30:6. Ps 7:9. 119:70. Pr 23:26. Is 6:10. Ezk 36:26. Mt 13:15. 15:8. Ro 5:5. 6:6. Ep 2:14, 15.

4. **caul above the liver, with the kidneys.** *or*, midriff over the liver, and over the kidneys. ver. 10, 15. Le 4:9. 7:4. 8:16, 25. 9:10, 19. Ex 29:13mg, 22.

5. **Aaron's.** Le 1:9. 4:31, 35. 6:12. 9:9, 10. Ex 29:13. 1 S 2:15, 16. 1 K 8:64. 2 Ch 35:14. Ezk 44:7, 15. He 13:15. **upon the burnt.** Le 6:12. 1 P 2:5.

6. **a sacrifice.** Is 32:17. 42:1. Ga 4:4. Ep 1:10. 2:13-22. He 7:2. **be of.** ver. 1. Le 1:2, 10. Is 60:7. **male.** Ga 3:28. **he shall.** ver. 1, etc. Ac 4:27. Ro 12:1, 2. T 2:11, 12.

7. **offer it.** ver. 1. 1 K 8:62. Ep 5:2, 12. He 9:14.

8. **he shall.** See on ver. 2-5, 13. Le 4:4, 15, 24. Is 53:6, 11, 12. 2 C 5:21. 1 P 2:24. **kill it.** Ep 2:18. 3:12. He *10:19-22. Re 5:6. **sprinkle.** Le 1:5, 11. Mt 3:17. 2 C 5:19. 1 P 1:19.

9. **the fat.** ver. 3, 4. Pr 23:26. Is 53:10. **the whole rump.** Le 7:3. 8:25. 9:19. Ex 29:22.

10. **the caul.** ver. +4.

11. **burn.** ver. 5. Ps 22:14. Is 53:4-10. Ro 8:32. **the food.** ⌐17118, Ge +3:19. ver. 16. Le 21:6, 8, 17, 21, 22. 22:25. Nu 28:2. Ezk 44:7. Ml 1:7, 12. 1 C 10:21. 1 J=1:4. Re *3:20.

12. **a goat.** ver. 1, 7, etc. Le 1:2, 6, 10. 9:3, 15. 10:16. 22:19-27. Is 53:2, 6. Mt 25:32, 33. Ro 8:3. 2 C 5:21.

13. **lay his hand.** See on ver. 1-5, 8. Is 53:6, 11, 12. 2 C 5:21. 1 P 2:24. 3:18. **sprinkle.** ver. 2, 8. Is 52:15. Ro 5:6-11, 15-21. He 12:24. 1 P 1:2.

14. **the fat that covereth.** ver. 3-5, 9-11. Ps 22:14, 15. Pr 23:26. Je 20:21. Mt 22:37. 26:38. Ro 12:1, 2.

15. **caul above.** See on ver. +4.

16. **it is the food.** See on ver. 11. **all the fat.** ver. 3-5, 9-11, 14, 15. Le 4:8-19, 26, 31. *7:23-25. 8:25. 9:24. 17:6. Ex 29:13, 22. 1 S 2:15, 16. 2 Ch 7:7. Is 53:10. Mt 22:37. **savor.** ⌐22C15, Ge +8:21.

17. **a perpetual.** Heb. *olam*, ever +9:12. Le 6:18. 7:36. 16:34. 17:7. 23:14. Nu 19:21. **eat neither.** ver. 16. Dt 32:14. Ne 8:10. Ezk 34:3. **blood.** Le 7:23, 25-27. 17:10-14. Ge *9:4. Dt *12:16, 23. 15:23. 1 S *14:32-34. Ezk 33:25. 44:7, 15. Mt 16:24. 26:28. Ac √15:9, 10, 19, 20, 21, 24, 29. Ep 1:7. 5:26. Col √2:16, 20-23. 1 T √4:4. The law against eating the fat or eating the blood pertained to the blood contained in the larger veins and arteries, and the fat or suet within the animal, which exists in a separate or unmixed state (as the caul, mesentery, kidneys, and whatever else of the internal fat which was easily separable, together with the whole of the tail); for the blood which assumes

the form of gravy, and the fat which is intermixed with the other flesh, might be eaten. The provision against *eating* blood has no bearing upon the modern day medical practice of blood transfusion, which was not in view; and, as it does not have anything to do with eating or digesting of the blood, has no possible legitimate connection with this law.

LEVITICUS 4

The law of the sin offering for a priest, 1-12; for the congregation, 13-21; for a ruler, 22-26; for a private person, 27-35.

2. **soul**. Heb. *nephesh*, Ge +27:31. ver. 27. Le 5:15, 18. Ex 29:14. Nu 15:22, 27. Ps *19:12. **sin through ignorance**. Le 5:15, 17. Nu 15:22-29. Dt 19:4. 1 S 14:27. Jb 10:6. *13:23. *15:15. Ps *19:12. *32:5. Ro *14:23. 1 T 1:13. He 5:2. 9:7. Ja +*4:17. **things**. or, sins. ƒ63E1. Ellipsis (Relative: of cognate words) B56. Where the omitted word is supplied from a cognate word in the immediate context: where the noun is suggested by the verb. Here the verb "shall sin" supplies the noun "sins," i.e., "concerning sins" which ought not to be done." For other instances of this figure given by EWB see Nu 11:14. 2 K 17:14. Ps 13:3. 76:11. 107:41. Ho 9:4. Ga 4:24. **which ought**. ver. 27. Ge 20:9. Ja 3:10.

3. **the priest**. Le 8:12. 21:10-12. Ex 29:7, 21. **a young bullock**. ver. 14. Le 9:2. 16:6, 11. Ezk 43:19. **for a sin offering**. ƒ121L5, Ge +4:7. Le 5:6. 6:1-7. Ex 29:14. 30:10. Nu 8:8. Ezr 8:35. Ro 8:3. 1 C *3:17. 2 C 5:19, 21. Ga=2:20. Col=2:13, 14. He *1:2, 3. 5:3. *7:27, 28. =9:13, 14. 13:11. 1 P 2:24. 1 J=1:7. *2:2. Re 1:5, 6.

4. **bring**. Le 1:3. Ex 29:10, 11. **lay his hand**. See on Le 1:4. 16:21. Is 53:6. Da 9:26. 1 P 3:18.

5. **shall take**. ver. 16, 17. Le 16:14, 19. Nu 19:4. 1 J 1:7.

6. **dip**. ver. 17, 25, 30, 34. Le 8:15. 9:9. 16:14, 19. Nu 19:4. **seven times**. The number seven is what is called a number of perfection among the Hebrews; and is often used to denote the completion, fullness, or perfection of a thing. Le 14:16, 18, 27. 25:8. 26:18, 24, 28. Jsh 6:4, 8. **vail**. He 10:20.

7. **the horns**. Le 8:15. 9:9. 16:18. Ex 30:1-10. Ps 118:27. He 9:21-25. **all the blood**. ver. 18, 34. Le 5:9. 8:15. Ep 2:13.

8. **all the fat**. See on ver. 19, 26, 31, 35. Le 3:3-5, 9-11, 14-16. 7:3-5. 16:25. Is 53:10. Jn 12:27.

10. **peace offering**. Le +*23:19. Ps 32:1. 1 T *2:5, 6.

11. **the skin**. ver. 21. Le 6:30. 8:14-17. 9:8-11. 16:27. Ex 29:14. Nu 19:5. Ps 103:12. He *13:11-13.

12. **without the camp**. Heb. to without the camp. ver. 21. Le 6:11. 10:4, 5. 13:46. 14:3, 40, 41, 45, 53. 16:27. 24:14, 23. Ex 29:14. 33:7. Nu 5:3, 4. 15:35. 19:3. This was intended, figuratively, to express the enormity of this sin, and the availableness of the atonement. The sacrifice, as having the sin of the priest transferred from himself to it, by his confession and imposition of hands, was become unclean and abominable, and was carried, as it were, out of God's sight; and thus its own offensiveness was removed, with the sin of the person in whose behalf it was offered. **the ashes**. Le 6:10, 11. **burn him**. Ex 29:14. Nu 19:5. He *13:11. **where the ashes are poured out**. Heb. at

the pouring out of the ashes. **poured**. Heb. *shephek*, *S#8211h, only here.

13. **the whole congregation**. 1 S 14:32, etc. **through ignorance**. See on ver. 1, 2. Le 5:2-5, 17. 22:14. Nu 15:24-29. Jsh 7:11, 24-26. 1 S 14:33. Ro 3:9-12. 1 T 1:13. He 2:1. 10:26-29. **and are guilty**. Le 5:2-5, 17. 6:4. Ezr 10:19. Ho 5:15mg. 1 C 11:27.

14. **young bullock**. See on ver. 3. Mk 10:45. 1 P 3:18.

15. **the elders**. Ex 24:1, 9. Nu 11:16, 25. Dt 21:3-9. **lay**. See on ver. 4. Le 1:4. 16:21. Is *53:6. 1 C 15:56, 57.

16. **the priest**. See on ver. 5-12. He *9:12-14.

17. **the priest**. See ver. 6, 7. Da 9:24. He 10:10-12. 1 J 1:7. 2:2.

18. **upon the**. ver. 7.

19. **fat**. ver. 8-10, 26, 31, 35. Le 5:6. 6:7. 12:8. 14:18. Nu 15:25. Ps 22:14. He 1:3. 9:14. **burn**. Le 10:2. Ge 19:24. Ex 9:23, 24. Nu 11:1. 16:35. 26:10. 2 K 1:10-14.

20. **with the**. ver. 3. **an atonement**. ver. 26. Le 1:4. 5:6. 6:7. 12:8. 14:18. Ex 32:30. Nu 15:25. Da 9:24. Ro 5:11. Ga 3:13. He 1:3. 2:17. 9:14. 10:10-12. 1 J 1:7. 2:2. Re 1:5. **forgiven**. ver. 26, 31, 35. Le 5:10, 16, 18. 6:7. Ep=1:7.

21. **burn him**. Ge 22:8. **as he**. ver. 11, 12. **a sin offering**. Le 16:15, 21. 2 Ch 29:21-24. Ezr 8:35. Mt 20:28. 2 C 5:21. 1 T 2:5, 6.

22. **a ruler**. Nu 1:4, 16. 7:2. **hath sinned**. Ex 18:21. Nu 16:2. 2 S 21:1-3. 24:10-17. **and done**. See on ver. 2, 13.

23. **if his sin**. ver. 14. Le 5:4. 2 K 22:10-13. **a kid**. Le 9:3. 23:19. Nu 7:16, 22, 28, 34. 15:24. 28:15, 30. 29:5, 11, 16, 19. Ro 8:3.

24. **And he**. ver. 4, etc. Is 53:6. **in the place**. Le 1:5, 11. 3:2, 8, 13. 4:4, 15, 29, 33. 6:25. 7:2. 16:15. Ex 29:38. **burnt offering**. Le +*23:12. **it is a sin**. See on ver. 3, 21, 31, 35.

25. **put**. ver. 7, 18, 30, 34. Le 8:10, 15. 9:9. 16:18. Is 40:21. Ro 3:24-26. 8:3, 4. 10:4. He 2:10. 9:22.

26. **the fat**. ver. 8-10, 35. See on Le 3:5. 6:20-30. **an atonement**. See on ver. 20. Nu 15:28. **forgiven**. Ro *4:7, 8. 2 C *5:21.

27. **any one**. Heb. *nephesh*, any soul, Ge +27:31. ver. 2. Nu 15:27. **common people**. Heb. people of the land. *Am haaretz*; that is, any individual who was not a priest, king, or ruler among the people; an ordinary person. Any of these having transgressed, was obliged to bring a lamb or kid, the ceremonies being nearly the same as in the preceding cases. See on ver. 2, 13. Ex 12:49. Nu 5:6. 15:16, 29. **through ignorance**. Pr *20:9. 1 J *1:8-10. *3:4.

28. **a kid**. ver. 23, 32. Le 5:6. Ge 3:15. Is 7:14. Je 31:22. Ro 8:3. Ga 4:4, 5. **a female**. ver. 23. Ga 3:28.

29. **lay his hand**. See on ver. 4, 15, 24, 33. He 10:4-14.

30. **upon the horns**. ver. 25, 34. Is 42:21. Ro 8:3, 4. 10:4. He 2:10. **pour out**. There may have been some place at the bottom of the altar to receive and carry off the blood. Is=53:12. He *9:22.

31. **all the fat**. ver. 8-10, 19, 26, 35. Le 3:3-5, 9-11, 14-16. **a sweet**. Le 1:9, 13, 17. 3:3, 5. 8:21. Ex 29:18. Ezr 6:10. Jb 42:8. Ps 40:6, 7. 51:16, 17. 69:30, 31. Is 42:21. 53:10. Mt 3:17. Ep 5:2. He 1:3. 9:12, 14, 15. 10:12, 14. 1 P 2:4, 5. 1 J 1:7. 4:9, 10. Re 5:9. **and the priest**. ver. 26, 35.

32. **a lamb**. ver. 28. Le 3:6, 7. 5:6. Ex 12:3, 5. Is 53:7. Lk +*1:35. Jn *1:29, 36. He 7:26. 1 P 1:18-20. 2:22, 24. 3:18. Re 5:6, 8, 9. **without blemish**. ver. 28. Ep 5:27. He 9:14. 1 P 2:22. 3:18.

33. **lay his hand**. See on ver. 4, 29-31.

34. **the horns of the altar**. ver. 25, 30. Is 42:21. Jn 17:19. Ro 8:1, 3. 10:4. 2 C 5:21. He 2:10. 10:29. 1 P 1:18-20. 2:24. 3:18.

35. **And he**. See ver. 31. **according**. Le ch. 1-6. **and the priest shall make**. ver. 20, 26, 30, 31. Le 1:4. 5:6, 10, 13. 6:7. 9:7. 12:8. 14:18, 53. ch. 16. Nu 15:25. Ro 3:24-26. 4:25. 5:6-11, 15-21. 8:1, 3, 4. 10:4. 2 C *5:21. Ga *1:4. Ep 1:6, 7. 5:2. Col 1:14. He 1:3. 4:14. 7:26. 9:14, 26-28. 1 P 1:18, 19. 2:22, 24. 3:18. 1 J 1:7. 2:2. 4:9, 10. Re 1:5, 6.

LEVITICUS 5

He that sinneth in concealing his knowledge, 1; in touching an unclean thing, 2, 3; or in making an oath, 4, 5. His trespass offering, of the flock, 6; of fowls, 7-10; or of flour, 11-13. The trespass offering in sacrilege, 14-16; and in sins of ignorance, 17-19.

1. **a soul**. Heb. *nephesh*, Ge +27:31. ver. 15, 17. Le 4:2. Ezk +*18:4, 20. **hear**. Ex 22:11. Jg 17:2. 1 K *8:31. 22:16. 2 Ch 18:15. Pr *29:24. 30:9. Mi +*6:8. Mt *26:63. **the voice of swearing**. *Kol alah*, rather, "the voice of *adjuration*," *phoneen orkismou*, as the LXX. render; for this does not relate to the duty of informing against a common swearer, but to the case of a person who, being adjured by the civil magistrate to answer upon oath, refuses to declare what he knows upon the subject—such an one shall bear his iniquity— shall be considered as guilty in the sight of God of the transgression which he has endeavored to conceal, and must expect to be punished for hiding the iniquity with which he was acquainted. **if he do not**. Le ❶*19:17. Ep ❶*5:11. **bear**. ver. 17. Le 7:18. 17:16. 19:8. ❶*17mg. 20:17. Nu 9:13. Ps 38:4. 90:8. Is=53:11. 1 T ❶*5:22. 1 P=2:24. **iniquity**. ✔121C1E, Ge +19:15.

2. **soul**. Heb. *nephesh*, Ge +27:31. ✔171Q1, Ge +12:5. **touch**. Le 7:21. 11:24, 28, 31, 39. Nu *19:11-16. Dt 14:8. Is 52:11. Da *1:8. Hg 2:13. 2 C *6:17. **hidden**. ver. 4, 17. Ps *19:12. Lk 11:44. **and guilty**. ver. 17. Le 4:13. 1 J *3:4.

3. **the uncleanness**. Le ch. 12, 13, 15. 22:4-6. Nu *19:11-16. **when**. ver. 4. He 3:13.

4. **if a soul**. Heb. *nephesh*, Ge +27:31. ✔171Q1, Ge +12:5. This relates to rash oaths or vows, which a man was afterwards unable, or which it would have been sinful, to perform. Nu +*30:2n. Jg +*11:30, 31n. Pr *10:19. **to do evil**. Le 27:2, etc. Jsh 2:14. 9:15. Jg 9:19. ✔11:31, 34, 35. 21:7, 18. 1 S 1:11. 14:24-28. 24:21, 22. 25:22. 2 S 21:7. 2 K 6:31. Ps *39:1. 132:2-5. Pr *14:9. Ec 5:2-6. Ezk 17:18, 19. Mt *14:7, 9. Mk 6:23. Ac *23:12.

5. **confess**. Le 16:21. 26:40. Nu 5:7. Jsh *7:19. Ezr 10:11, 12. Jb 33:27. Ps *32:5. *51:4. Pr *28:13. Je 3:13. Da 9:4. Ro *10:10. 1 J ✔1:8-10.

6. **trespass offering**. It is remarkable, that in this and the following verse, the sacrifice offered is indifferently called *asham*, a trespass offering, and *chattath*, a sin offering; yet the Marginal References show that these differ in several respects. Sin offerings were sometimes offered for the whole congregation; trespass offerings never, but only for particular persons. Bullocks were sometimes used for sin offerings, never for trespass offerings. The blood of the sin offerings was put on the horns of the altar, that of the trespass offerings was only sprinkled round the bottom of the altar. The sin offering seems to have been for the expiation of offences committed in matters of religion, from a mistake or inadvertency respecting the law; but the trespass offering was required for the casual deviations from the ritual law, when well known, or for crimes against moral precepts, implying injustice to man. Le 4:28, 32. 6:6, 17. 7:1-7. 14:12, 13. 19:21, 22. Nu 6:12. 18:9. 1 S 6:3. 2 K 12:16. Ezr 10:19. Ps=40:12. Is 53:10. Ezk 40:39. 42:13. 44:29. 46:20. Mt=1:21. =26:28. 1 C=15:3. 2 C=5:19. Ga=1:4. Ep=1:7. Col=1:14. =2:13. He=*10:12. 1 P=*2:24. =3:18. 1 J=1:9. **a female**. Le 4:28, 32. **the priest**. See on Le 4:20.

7. **he be not able to bring a lamb**. Heb. his hand cannot reach to the sufficiency of a lamb. ver. 11. Le 12:8. 14:21, 30. 25:26mg. Lk +*11:41n. 2 C 8:12. Ja 2:5, 6. **two turtle doves**. Le 1:14, 15. Mt 3:16. 10:16. Lk 2:24. **one**. ver. 8, 9. Le 9:3. 14:22, 31. 15:14, 15, 30. 16:5. He 10:6-10.

8. **wring off**. Le 1:15. Ro 4:25. 1 P 3:18.

9. **sprinkle**. See on Le 1:5. 4:25, 30, 34. 7:2. Ex 12:22, 23. Is 42:21. He *2:10. 12:24. **the rest**. Le 4:7, 18, 25, 30, 34.

10. **offer**. Le 1:14-17. Ep 5:2. **manner**. *or*, ordinance. See on Le 1:14-17. 9:16. Ge 40:13. **make**. ver. 6, 13, 16. Le 4:20, 26, 31, 35. Ro 5:11. He *10:12. 1 J 2:2. **it**. Ja 5:15.

11. **But if**. See on ver. 7. 2 C *8:9. **the tenth part**. Ex 16:18, 36. **fine flour**. Le 2:1. Nu 7:13, 19, etc. 15:4-9. He *9:22. **no oil**. Le 2:1, 2, 4, 5, 15, 16. Nu 5:15. Ps 22:1-21. 69:1-21. Is 53:2-10. **for it is**. ver. 6, 9, 12. 2 C 5:21.

12. **a memorial**. Le 2:2, 9, 16. 6:15. Nu 5:26. Ac +*10:4. Ep *5:2. **according**. Le 1:9, 13, 17. 2:9. 3:4, 11. 4:35.

13. **the priest**. ver. 6. Le 4:20, 26, 31. **shall be**. Le 2:3, 10. 7:6. 1 S 2:28. Ho 4:8. 1 C 9:13. **meat offering**. Le +*23:13.

15. **a soul**. Heb. *nephesh*, Ge +27:31. ver. 1, 2. **trespass**. Ec 5:6. **sin through ignorance**. Le +*4:2. Pr *24:9. **in the holy**. ver. 16. Le 7:1, 6. 10:17, 18. 22:1-16. 24:5-9. 27:9-33. Nu 18:9-32. Dt 12:5-12, 26. 15:19, 20. 26:1-15. **then**. Le ❶6:5, 6. **ram**. ver. 18. Le 6:6. Ezr *10:19. **thy estimation**. Le 27:2-8, 12, 13, 17, 18, 23-27. **the shekel**. Le *27:25. Ex 30:13. Ps 89:19.

16. **make**. Le 22:14. Ex 22:1, 3, 4. Ps 69:4. Lk 19:8. Ac 26:20. **the fifth**. Le 6:4, 5. 27:13, 15, 27, 31. Nu 5:7. **and the priest**. ver. 6, 10, 13. Le 4:26. He *9:13, 14. 1 J *2:1, 2.

17. **soul**. Heb. *nephesh*, Ge +27:31. **sin**. This case is supposed to differ from the preceding, merely in that the person concerned was not certain whether he had or had not committed the trespass. It is therefore called by the Hebrews a doubtful trespass offering. ver. 1. Le 4:2-4, 13, 22, 27. **though**. ver. 15. Le +*4:2. Ps *19:12. Lk *12:48. Ro 14:23. 1 T *1:13. **yet is he**. ver. 1, 2. Le 4:2, 13, 27.

18. **And he**. See on ver. 15, 16. **for a trespass**. Le 6:6. 1 T 2:5, 6. **and the priest**. ver. 16. Le 1:4. 4:20. 6:7.

19. **trespassed**. Ezr *10:2. Ps 51:4. Ml 3:8. Ro *7:7-12. 2 C 5:19-21.

LEVITICUS 6

The trespass offering for sins done wittingly, 1-7. The law for the priest respecting the burnt offering, 8-13; and the meat offering, 14-18. The offering at the consecration of a priest, 19-23. The law of the sin offering, 24-30.

2. **soul.** Heb. *nephesh*, Ge +27:31. **commit.** Le 5:15, 19. Nu 5:6-8. Ps 51:4. **against.** Mt 25:40, 45. Ac 9:5. **lie.** Le 19:11. Ge 26:7. Jn *8:44. Ac 5:4. Ep *4:25. Col 3:9. Re *22:15. **lie.** ſ108J, Ge +43:18. **in that.** Ex 22:7-10. **in fellowship.** *or*, in dealing. Heb. in putting of the hand. Is 21:2. 24:16. 33:1. Hab 1:13. ſ121S3J. Metonymy of the Adjunct B607. The sign put for the thing signified in connected words and phrases; "to place the hand on" is put for association. **deceived.** Pr 24:28. 26:19. Is 59:13-15. Je 9:5. Am +*8:5. Mi 6:10-12.

3. **have found.** Ex 23:4. Dt 22:1-3. **sweareth.** Le *19:12. Ex 22:9-11. Pr 30:9. Je 5:2. 7:9. Zc 5:4. Ml +*3:5. Ac *5:3, 4. Col *3:9. 1 J *4:20.

4. **because.** Le 4:13-15. 5:3, 4. **which he.** Ge 21:25. Jb 20:19. 24:2. Is 59:6. Ezk 18:7, 12, 18. Am 3:10. Mi 2:2. Zep 1:9. **to keep.** Ex *22:7-9.

5. **restore.** Le 5:16. Ex 22:1, 4, 7, 9. Nu *5:7, 8. 1 S 12:3. 2 S 12:6. Ps ●69:4. Pr 6:30, 31. Is 58:6, 9. Lk 19:8. **of his trespass offering.** *or*, of his being found guilty. Heb. of his trespass. Mt 5:23, 24.

6. **And he shall.** Le ●5:15, 16. Mt *5:23, 24. **a ram.** Le 5:15, 18. Is 53:10, 11. 2 C 9:15.

7. **make.** Le 4:20, 26, 31. 5:10, 13, 15, 16, 18. Ex 34:7. Ezk 18:21-23, 26, 27. 33:14-16, 19. Mi 7:18. 1 J 1:7, 9. 2:1, 2. **it shall be.** Is 1:18. Mt 12:31. 1 C 6:9-11.

9. **of the burnt.** See on Le 1. Ex 29:38-42. Nu 28:3. **because of the burning.** *or*, for the burning. ver. 12, 13. Ps *66:13-15.

10. **linen garment.** Le 16:4. Ex *28:39-43. 39:27-29. Ps *132:16. Ezk 44:17, 18. Re 7:13. 19:8, 14. **consumed.** Le 1:9, 13, 17. Nu 16:21, 35. Ps 20:3mg. 37:20. **beside.** Le 1:16.

11. **put off.** Ex 16:23, 24. Ezk 44:19. Is 53:9. Jn 19:30. **without.** Le 4:12, 21. 14:40, 41. 16:27. Jn *19:41, 42. He 13:11-13.

12. **the fire.** Le 9:24. Nu 4:13, 14. Mk 9:48, 49. He 10:27. *12:29. **burn wood.** Le 1:7-9. 3:3-5, 9-11, 14-16. Ex 29:38-42. Ne 13:31. The efficacy of the priesthood and mediation of Christ is perpetual, and we can never approach to God in his name, by day or night, unseasonably. The ministers of Christ should have the fire of their zeal constantly burning. **morning.** ſ84, Ge +6:17. **peace offerings.** Le +*23:19. 2 Th *3:16.

13. **fire.** Is *6:6, 7. Re *8:5. **ever be burning.** Re *4:8.

14. **the meat offering.** See on Le 2:1, 2. +*23:13. Nu 15:4, 6, 9. Jn 6:32.

15. **the memorial.** See on Le 2:2, 9.

16. **the remainder.** Le 2:3, 10. 5:13. Ezk 44:29. 1 C 9:13-15. **his sons.** Le 24:9. 1 C 11:24. **unleavened.** Ex 12:8. 1 C 5:8. **shall it.** ver. 26. Le 10:12, 13. Nu 18:9, 10.

17. **baken.** Le *2:11. 1 C *5:6-8. 1 P 2:22. **I have.** Nu 18:9, 10. **it is most holy.** ver. 25. Le 2:3. 7:1, 6. Ex 29:33, 34, 37.

18. **the males.** ver. 29. Le 21:21, 22. Nu 18:10. **It**

shall. See on Le 3:17. **for ever.** Heb. *olam*, Ex +12:24. **every one.** Le 22:3-7. Ex 29:37. Ps *89:7. Hg 2:12-14. Zc 14:20, 21. 1 P 1:16. 2:9.

20. **the offering.** Ex 29:2. Nu 18:26-32. He 5:1. 7:27. 8:3, 4. **in the day.** The word *beyom*, signifies not only in the day, but from that day forward; for it was a daily oblation, and for them and their successors, a statute forever. ver. 22. He *7:19. **the tenth.** Le 5:1. Ex *16:36. **a meat offering.** Le 2:1, etc. Ex 29:35-42. Nu 28:3, 10.

21. **a pan.** Le 2:5. 7:9. 1 Ch 9:31.

22. **is anointed.** Le 4:3. Dt 10:6. He 7:23. **for ever.** Heb. *olam*, Ex +12:24. **wholly.** Le 8:21. Ex 29:22-25. Is 53:10.

23. **shall be.** The meat offering of the people was eaten by the priests, who typically bore and expiated their sins; but as no priest, being a sinner, could make atonement for himself, his meat offering must not be eaten, but wholly burnt on the altar, which was a typical transfer of his guilt to the great antitype who actually bore and expiated it. Ex 29:25. He 7:23. **it shall not be.** ver. 16, 17. Le 2:10.

25. **the law.** See on Le 4:2, 3, etc., 21, 24, 33, 34. **offering.** ſ121L5, Ge +4:17. **In the place.** Le 1:3, 5, 11. 4:24, 29, 33. **offering.** ſ121L5, Ge +4:7. **it is.** ver. 17. Le 21:22.

26. **priest.** Le 10:17, 18. Nu 18:9, 10. Ezk 44:28, 29. 46:20. Ho 4:8. Jn 6:52-57. Ep 5:32. **in the holy.** ver. 16. **in the court.** Ex 27:9-18. 38:9-19. 40:33. Ezk 42:13.

27. **touch.** ver. 18. Ex 29:37. 30:29. Hg 2:12. Mt 9:21. 14:36. **wash.** Heb. *kabas*, Nu +19:21. Le 11:32. 2 C 7:1, 11.

28. **the earthen.** Such vessels are very common in the East, and are very cheap, sometimes even as low as a farthing, hence they are commanded to be broken (Young). Le 11:33. 15:12. He 9:9, 10. **vessel.** Pr 25:4. 2 C 4:10, 11. **brazen pot.** Brass is a very common material of which cooking pots and washing vessels are made, in the East, even to this present day, and the accuracy of the Scriptures in such little and incidental details is a most satisfactory proof of their authenticity (Young). **and rinsed.** Heb. *shatap*, Le +15:11. Le 11:32n. T 2:13, 14.

29. **the males.** See on ver. 18. Nu 18:10. **it is.** ver. 25. Ps 99:1.

30. **no sin offering.** Le 4:3-21. 10:18. 16:27, 28. He 9:11, 12. *13:11. **holy place.** He 9:12. 10:3, 12-14. Re 7:13-15. **burnt.** Le *4:12.

LEVITICUS 7

The law of the trespass offering, 1-10; and of the peace offering, 11; whether it be for a thanksgiving, 12-15; or a vow, or a free will offering, 16-21. The fat and the blood are forbidden, 22-27. The priests' portion in the peace offerings, 28-34. The whole summed up, 35-38.

1. **the law.** Le ch. 5. 6:1-7. 14:12, 13. 19:21, 22. Nu 6:12. Ezk 40:39. 44:29. 46:20. **it is.** Le 6:17, 25. 21:22.

2. **in the place.** Le 1:3, 5, 11. 4:24, 29, 33. 6:25. Nu 6:12. Ezk 40:39. **and the.** Le 1:5. 3:2, 8. 5:9. Is 52:15. Ezk 36:25. He 9:19-22. 11:28. 12:24. 1 P 1:2.

3. **all the fat.** See on Le 3:3-5, 9-11, 15, 16. 4:8-10. Ex *29:13. Ps 51:6, 17.

5. **burn them.** Le 1:9, 13. 2:2, 9, 16. 3:16. Ga 2:20. 5:24. 1 P 4:1, 2.

6. **male.** Le 6:16-18, 29. Nu *18:9, 10. **it is most holy.** Le 2:3.

7. **sin offering.** ſ121L5, Ge +4:7. **the trespass.** Le 6:25, 26. 14:13. **have it.** Lk 10:7.

8. **have to himself.** Ezk *44:29. 1 T *5:17, 18. **skin.** Le 1:6. 4:11. 15:17. Ge=3:21. Ex 29:14. Nu 19:5. Ro 13:14. Ep=1:6. Ph 3:9. Col=3:12, 14.

9. **the meat offering.** Le 2:4-7. +*23:13. Nu 18:9. Ezk 44:29. **in the pan.** or, on the flat plate, or slice. Le 2:5mg. 6:21. **shall be.** Le 2:3, 10. 5:13. 6:16-18. Is *33:16. Lk *22:35. 1 C 9:7, 13. Ga 6:6.

10. **all.** Jn=1:16. **one as much.** Ex 16:18. 2 Ch +31:10. 2 C 8:14. Ph=4:18.

11. **the sacrifice.** Le ch. 3. 22:18-21. Nu 10:10. 1 S 10:8. 11:15. 1 K 8:63. Ezk 45:15. Ep=5:2. He=10:5. **peace offerings.** Le +*23:16. Jg +6:24. Ps 116:17. *119:108. Jn *4:27. Col 1:2. He *13:15.

12. **a thanksgiving.** Le 22:29. 2 Ch *29:31. 33:16. Ne 12:43. Ps *50:13, 14, 23. 103:1, 2. *107:8, 21, 22. *116:17. Je 33:11. Ho 14:2. Lk 17:16, 18. Ro 1:21. 2 C 9:11-15. Ep 5:20. He 13:15. 1 P 2:5. **unleavened wafers.** Le 2:4. 6:16. Nu 6:15.

13. **leavened.** Le √23:17n. Am *4:5n. Mt +*13:33n. **thanksgiving.** 1 T 4:4. He *13:15. Ja √3:2, 8, 9.

14. **an heave offering.** Le 7:32, 34. 10:14, 15. See on Ex 29:27, 28. Nu 5:9mg. 6:20. 15:19-21. *18:8, 11, 19, 24-30, 32. 31:29, 41, 52mg. Dt 12:6, 11, 17. **the priest's.** Le 6:26. Nu 18:8-11, 19, 26-32.

15. **for thanksgiving.** Col *3:15. **be eaten.** Le 22:29, 30. See on Ex 12:10. 16:19. Ec 9:10. Jn 9:4. 1 C 10:3. 2 C +*6:2. He *3:13-15. **he shall not.** Le 22:30. Ex 12:10. 23:18. 29:34. 34:25.

16. **be a vow.** Le 22:18-21. +*23:38. Nu 15:3. Dt 12:6, 11, 17, 26. Ps 66:13. 116:14, 18. Na 1:15. **a voluntary offering.** Le 22:23, 29. +*23:38. Dt 12:6. Ezk 46:12. **also the.** Le 19:5-8.

17. **the remainder.** Ps 16:10, 11. **on the third.** Le 19:7. Ge +22:4. Ex 19:11. Ho 6:2. 1 C +*15:4. **burnt.** Le 6:22, 23. 10:16. Ex 12:10. 29:14.

18. **it shall.** Le 10:19. 19:7, 8. 22:23, 25. Je 14:10, 12. Ho 8:13. Am 5:22. Ml 1:10, 13. **be imputed.** Nu 18:27. Ro 4:11. **an abomination.** Le 11:10, 11, 41. Is 1:11-14. 65:4. 66:3. Lk 16:15. **soul.** Heb. *nephesh*, Ge +27:31. **bear.** Le 5:17. 10:17. 17:16. 19:7, 8. 20:17, 19. 22:16. Is *53:11, 12. Ezk *18:20. He +*9:28. 1 P *2:24. **iniquity.** ſ121C1E, Ge +19:15.

19. **flesh.** ſ66, Ge +9:3. **toucheth.** Le 11:24-39. Nu 19:11-16. Hg *2:13. Lk 11:41. Jn *18:28. Ac 10:15, 16, 28. Ro 14:14, 20. 2 C *6:17. T 1:15. **clean shall eat.** SS 5:1.

20. **soul.** Heb. *nephesh*, Ge +27:31. **having.** Le 15:2, 3, etc. 1 C 11:28. **soul.** Heb. *nephesh*, Ge +17:14. **shall be.** ver. 21, 25, 27. Ge 17:14. Ex 30:33.

21. **soul.** Heb. *nephesh*, Ge +27:31. **the uncleanness.** Le 5:2, 3. ch. 12, 13, 15. 22:4. Nu 19:11-16. **any unclean.** Le 11:24-42. Dt 14:7, 8, 10, 12-20. **uncleanness of man.** Le 15:3. 22:4-9. Ep 1:4. He 12:10. **abominable.** Le 11:10-13, 20, 41, 42. Dt 14:3. Ezk 4:14. **soul.** Heb. *nephesh*, Ge +17:14. **cut off.** ver. 20, 25, 27. Le 17:10, 14. 18:29. Ge 17:14. Ex 12:15, 19. 30:33-38.

23. **fat.** Le 3:16, *17n. 4:8-10. 17:6, 10. Dt 32:◉12-14, 38. 1 S 2:15-17, 29. Ac 28:27. Ro 8:13. 13:13.

24. **beast.** Heb. carcase. Le 11:8. 17:15. 22:8. Ex 22:31. Dt 14:21. Ezk 4:14. 44:31.

25. **soul.** Heb. *nephesh*, Ge +17:14. **shall be cut off.** ver. +21.

26. **ye shall eat no.** The prohibition of the fat or suet, which was restricted to animals offered in sacrifice, taught reverence to the altar and ordinances of God; but that of blood, which was extended to all land animals, had special respect to the atoning blood of the sacrifice, and of the great antitype which the sacrifice prefigured. Le 3:17n. 17:10-14. Ge 9:4. Nu 33:25. 1 S 14:33, 34. Ezk 33:25. Jn 6:53. Ac 15:20, 29. 21:25. Ep 1:7. 1 T 4:4.

27. **soul.** Heb. *nephesh*, Ge +27:31. **that eateth.** Le +*3:17n. Ge *9:4. Mt 22:21. Lk 22:17-20. Jn *6:53, 54. **that soul.** Heb. *nephesh*, Ge +17:14. ver. 20, 21, 25. He 10:29. **shall be.** Shall be excommunicated or cut off from the people of God, and so deprived of any part of their inheritance or of their blessings.

29. **He that.** Le 3:1. Col 1:20. 1 J 1:7.

30. **own hands.** Le 3:3, 4, 9, 14. Ps 110:3. Jn 10:18. 2 C *8:12. **with the breast.** Le 8:27. 9:21. See on Ex *29:24-28. Nu *6:20. **wave offering.** Le +*23:15.

31. **the priest.** Le 3:5, 11, 16. **the breast.** ver. 34. Le 5:13. 6:16, 26. 8:29. Nu 18:18.

32. **right shoulder.** ver. 34. Le 8:25, 26. 9:21. 10:14. Nu 6:20. 18:18, 19. Dt 18:3. 1 C 9:13, 14. **heave offering.** ver. +*14.

33. **that offereth.** ver. 3. Le 6:26. **his part.** Ep 1:6.

34. **the wave.** See on ver. 30-32. Le 10:14, 15. Ex *29:28. Nu 18:18, 19. Dt *18:3. **breast.** Jb=36:5mg. Pr=8:17. Ep=3:17-19. **shoulder.** Dt=33:12. Pr=8:14. Is 40:11. Ep=1:19. **by a statute.** See on Le 3:17. Ex 29:9. **for ever.** Heb. *olam*, Ex +12:24.

35. **portion.** Le 8:10-12, 30. Ex 29:7, 21. 40:13-15. Is 10:27. 61:1. Jn 3:34. 2 C 1:21. 1 J 2:20, 27. **he presented.** Ex 28:1. 29:1. Nu 18:7-19.

36. **in the day.** Le 8:12, 30. Ex 40:13, 15. **for ever.** Heb. *olam*, Ex +12:24.

37. **the law.** Le ch. 1. 6:9-13. Ex 29:38-42. Mt 20:28. Ro 5:10, 11. 2 C 5:18, 19. 1 J 2:1, 2. **meat.** Le ch. 2. 6:14-18. **sin.** Le ch. 4. 6:24-30. **trespass.** ver. 1-7. Le ch. 5. 6:1-7. **consecrations.** Le 6:20-23. Ex 29:1. **sacrifice.** ver. 11-21. Le ch. 3.

38. **commanded.** See on Le 1:1, 2. Ml 3:3.

LEVITICUS 8

The Lord commands Moses to consecrate Aaron and his sons, 1-5. He washes and clothes them; and anoints Aaron; and also the tabernacle and its furniture, the altar and the laver, 6-13. The sin offering, burnt offering, and ram of consecration sacrificed for Aaron and his sons, with the appointed rites, 14-32. The place and time of their consecration, 33-36.

2. **Aaron.** Ex 29:1-4. Ep 2:18. He 10:5-7. **garments.** Ex *28:2-4, 40-43. 39:1-31, 41. **anointing.** Ex 30:23-37. 40:12-15. **bullock.** Ex *29:1, 2. He *7:27, 28.

3. **gather.** Nu 20:8. 21:16. 1 Ch 13:5. 15:3. 2 Ch 5:2-6. 30:2, 13, 25. Ne 8:1. Ps 22:25. Ac 2:1.

4. **did as.** ver. 9, 13, 17, 29, 35. Ex 39:1, 5, 7, 21, 26, 29, 31, 32, 42, 43. Dt 12:32. Mt 28:20. 1 C 11:23. 15:3. **unto the door.** Ex *29:4.

5. **Lord commanded to be done.** Ex 29:4, etc.

6. **washed.** Ex 29:4. 40:12. Ps 51:2, 7. Is 1:16. Ezk

36:25. Zc 13:1. Jn *13:8-10. 1 C 6:11. Ep 5:26. He 9:10. 10:22. Re 1:5, 6. 7:14.

7. **he put.** See on Ex 28:4. *29:5. 39:1, etc. 1 S 2:28. Ps 132:9, 16. Is 61:3, 10. Ro 3:22. 13:14. Ga 3:27. **the ephod.** Ex 28:6, etc. 2 S 6:4.

8. **the breastplate.** Ex 28:15-29. 39:8-21. Ps 40:8. SS 8:6. Is 59:17. Ep 6:14. 1 Th 5:8. **the Urim.** Ex *28:30. Ezr 2:63.

9. **the mitre.** Ex *28:4, 36-38. 29:6. 39:28-30. Zc 3:5. 6:11-14. Ph 2:9-11. **holy crown.** Ps *93:5. Col *3:12. Re *4:8.

10. **anointing oil.** Ex 30:23-29. 40:9-11.

11. **he sprinkled.** Le 4:6, 17. 16:14, 19. Is 52:15. Ezk 36:25. T 3:6. **anointed.** Le 21:10, 12. Ex 29:7. **laver.** Ex 30:18-21. 38:8. Pr 27:19. 1 C=6:11. Ep=5:26. He=10:22. Ja=1:22-24. **sanctify them.** Ex 30:29. Ps 45:8.

12. **he poured.** Le 4:3. 21:10, 11, 12. Ex 28:41. 29:7. *30:30. Ps *133:2. **anointing oil.** ver. 30. Ps 133:2. 1 J 2:20.

13. **Moses.** Ex *28:40, 41. 29:8, 9. 40:14, 15. 1 Ch *16:29. Ps 30:4. 132:9. Is 61:6, 10. 63:1. 1 P 2:5, 9. Re 1:6. 5:10. **coats.** Ex 28:4. Re 1:13. **girded them.** Is 11:5. **put.** Heb. bound. **bonnets.** Ex 39:28, 29.

14. **he brought.** ver. 2. Le 4:3-12. 16:6. Ex *29:10-14. Is 53:10. Ezk *43:19. Ro 8:3. 2 C 5:21. He *7:26-28. 1 P 3:18. **laid.** Le 1:4. 4:4. 16:21.

15. **he slew it.** Le 1:5, 11. 3:2, 8. Ex 29:10, 11. **Moses.** Le 4:7, 17, 18, 30. Ex *29:12, 36, 37. Ezk *43:19-27. He 9:18-23. **to make.** Le 6:30. 16:20. 2 Ch 29:24. Ezk 45:20. Da 9:24. Ro 5:10. 2 C 5:18-21. Ep 2:16. Col 1:21, 22. He 2:17. The beginning of this verse may be rendered, "And Moses slew it, and took the blood," etc. We find it expressly said in Exodus, that Moses slew sacrifices, Ex 29:11. Yet, in general, the offerer seems to have killed his own sacrifice.

16. **all the fat.** Le 3:3-5. 4:8, 9. Ex 29:13.

17. **the bullock.** Le 4:11, 12, 21. 6:30. 16:27. Ex *29:14. Ga 3:13. He 13:11-13. **without the camp.** Ps 38:4. 40:12. 69:5.

18. **the ram.** See on Le 1:4-13. Ex *29:15-18.

21. **a sweet savor.** f22C15, Ge +8:21. Le 1:17. 2:9. Ge 8:21. Ex 29:18. Ep 5:2. **by fire.** Le 1:6-8. Ex 29:18.

22. **the ram of consecration.** ver. 2, 29. Le 7:37. Ex *29:19-31. Jn 17:19. 1 C 1:30. 2 C 5:21. Ep 5:25, 27. Re 1:5, 6.

23. **Moses took.** Le 14:14, 17, 28. Ex *29:20. Ro 6:13, 19. 12:1. 1 C 1:2, 30. 6:20. 1 Th 5:22. Ph 1:20. 2:17. He 2:10. 5:8. 9:11, 12. 13:12. Re 7:14, 15.

24. **Moses sprinkled.** He 9:22.

25. **the fat.** See on Le 3:3-5, 9. Ex *29:22-25. Pr 23:26. Is 53:10.

26. **out of.** Ex *29:23. Jn 1:14. Ac 5:12. 1 T 2:5.

27. **upon Aaron's.** Ex *29:24-28. Je 30:21. He 9:14. **and waved.** See on Le 7:30, 31. 1 P 2:5. **wave offering.** Le +*23:15.

28. **Moses.** Ex *29:25. Ps 22:13, 14. Zc 13:7. He 3:5. 10:14-22. **they were.** See on ver. 22.

29. **the breast.** Le 7:30-34. Ex 29:26, 27. Is 66:20. 1 C 10:31. 1 P 4:11. **before the Lord.** He 13:15. **wave offering.** Le +*23:15.

30. **the anointing.** See on Ex *29:21. *30:30. Is 61:1, 3. Ga 5:22-25. He 2:11. 1 P 1:2. 1 J 2:27. Re 7:14. **sprinkled.** He=12:24. 1 P=1:2. **his garments.** Re 3:4. 6:11. 16:15. 19:8. **and sanctified.** Le 10:3. Nu 3:3.

31. **Boil.** Le 6:28. 7:15. Ex *29:31, 32. Dt 12:6, 7. 1 S 2:13-17. Ezk 46:20-24. **eat it.** Le 10:17. Jn 6:33, 35, 51, 53-56. Ga 2:20.

32. **remaineth.** Le 7:17. Ex 12:10. *29:34. Pr 27:1. Ec 9:10. 2 C +*6:2. He 3:13, 14.

33. **seven days.** Le 14:8. Ex *29:30, 35. Nu 19:12. Ezk *43:25-27. **consecrate.** f121S3P, Ex +28:41.

34. **hath done.** He *7:16, 27. 10:11, 12.

35. **abide.** Ps *84:4. Pr *8:34. **the tabernacle.** Le 14:8. Ex *29:35. Nu 19:12. Ezk 43:25. 2 C 7:1. Col 2:9, 10. He 7:28. 9:23, 24. **keep.** Le 10:1. Ge 26:5. Nu 1:53. *3:7. *9:19. Dt *11:1. 1 K *2:3. Zc 3:7. 1 T 1:3, 4, 18. 5:21. 6:13, 17, 20. 2 T *4:1.

36. **Aaron.** Ex 39:43. 40:16. Dt 4:2. *12:32. 1 S *15:22. **did all.** Ge 6:22. Mt 5:48. *7:21. Jn=15:10. He 10:14. 12:23. Ja *1:22. 1 J *4:17.

LEVITICUS 9

The newly consecrated priests, directed by Moses, enter on their office with the first offerings of Aaron for himself and the people, 1-7. The sin offering, 8-11, and the burnt offering for himself, 12-14. The offerings for the people, 15-22. Moses and Aaron bless the people; and the glory of the Lord appears, 22, 23. Fire from before the Lord consumes the sacrifices, and the people worship, 24.

1. **the eighth day.** Not on the eighth day of the month, but on the first day after their consecration, which occupied seven days, and before which they were deemed unfit to minister in holy things, being considered in a state of imperfection. All creatures, for the most part, were considered as in a state of uncleannesss and imperfection, *seven* days, and perfected on the *eighth* (see Le 12:2, 3. 14:8-10. 15:13, 14. 22:27. Nu 6:9, 10). Le 8:33. 14:10, 23. 15:14, 29. Nu 6:10. Ezk 43:26, 27. Mt 28:1. Col=3:4.

2. **a young.** ver. 7, 8. Le 4:3. 8:14. Ex 29:1. 2 C 5:21. He 5:3. 7:27. 10:10-14. **and a ram.** Ex 8:18.

3. **Take ye.** Le 4:23. 16:5, 15. Ezr 6:17. 10:19. Is 53:10. Ro 8:3. 2 C 5:21. T 2:14. He 9:26-28. 1 P 2:24. 3:18. Re 5:9. **a kid.** As the offering here is a kid, which was the sacrifice for the sin of the ruler, some think that the reading of the Samaritan and LXX. is to be preferred: "Speak unto the *elders* of Israel." **a calf.** See on ver. 2. **both.** Le 12:6. 14:10. 23:12. Ex 12:5.

4. **a bullock.** See on Le ch. 3. **peace offerings.** Le +*23:19. **and a meat offering.** Le ch. 2. 6:14-23. +*23:13. Nu 15:3-9. **today.** ver. 6, 23. Ex 16:10. 19:11. 24:16. 29:43. 40:34, 35. Nu 14:10. 16:19. 1 K 8:10-12. Ezk 43:2.

5. **and all the congregation.** Ex 19:17. Dt 31:12. 1 Ch 15:3. 2 Ch 5:2, 3. Ne 8:1.

6. **and the glory.** ver. 23. Ex 16:10. 24:16. 40:34, 35. 1 K 8:10-12. 2 Ch 5:13, 14. Ezk 43:2.

7. **offer thy.** ver. 2. Le 4:3, 20. 8:34. 1 S 3:14. He 5:3. 7:27, 28. 9:7. **offer the.** Le 4:16-20. He 5:1.

8. **slew the calf.** Le 1:4, 5. 4:4, 29.

9. **blood.** He=10:19-22. **he dipped.** Le 4:6, 7, 17, 18, 25, 30. 8:15. 16:18. He 2:10. 9:22, 23. 10:4-19.

10. **the fat.** See on Le 3:3-5, 9-11. 4:8-12, 34, 35. 8:16, 17. Ps 51:17. Pr 23:26. Is 53:10. 57:15. 66:2. **as the Lord.** Le 4:8.

11. **the flesh.** Le 4:11, 12, 21. 8:17. 16:27, 28. He 13:11, 12.

12. **the burnt offering**. See on Le 1. 8:18-21. Ep 5:2, 25-27. **sprinkled**. He=10:22.

14. **did wash**. Le 8:21.

15. **the goat**. ver. 3. Le 4:27-31. 9:15. Nu ch. 28, 29. Is 53:10. 2 C *5:21. T 2:14. He 2:17. 5:3.

16. **manner**. *or*, ordinance. ver. 12-14. Le 1:3-10. 5:10. 8:18-21. He 10:1-22.

17. **the meat**. ver. 1. Le 2:1, 2. Ex 29:38, 41. Jn 6:53. Ga 2:20. **took an handful thereof**. Heb. filled his hand out of it. Le 2:2. **beside**. Ex 29:38-42.

18. **a sacrifice**. Le ch. 3. 7:11-18. Ro 5:1, 10. Ep 2:14-17. Col 1:20.

19. **the fat**. ver. 10. Le 3:5, 16.

20. **they put**. Le 7:29-34. **burnt**. Le 3:14-17.

21. **the breasts**. Le 7:24, 26, 30-34. Ex 29:27, 28. Is 49:3. Lk 2:14. 1 P 4:11. **wave offering**. Le +*23:15. **as Moses commanded**. The Samaritan text, and thirty MSS. have, *kaasher tzivvah yehowah eth Moshe*, "as Jehovah commanded Moses;" which is also the reading of the LXX., Arabic, and Targum of Onkelos, and seems to be the true reading, being supported, not only by these authorities, but by the whole chapter itself.

22. **his hand**. *or*, as the Greek has it, his hands. Menachem gives the reason why it is written hand, to signify the right hand, because that was lifted up higher than the left. The lifting up of the hand was a gesture used in speaking, and signifying any weighty thing, Is 49:22; and particularly in swearing, Ge 14:22; praying, Ps 28:2; and blessing, either of God, Ps 134:2, or of men, as in this place. Paul, speaking of prayer, uses the phrase, "lifting up holy hands," 1 T 2:8; as also David: "Let the lifting up of my hands be as the evening sacrifice," Ps 141:2. Ge 14:18-20. Nu 6:23-27. Dt 10:8. 21:5. 1 K 8:55. 1 Ch 23:13. 2 Ch 6:3. Ps 72:17. Mk 10:16. Lk 24:50. Ac 3:26. 2 C 13:14. He 7:6, 7. 1 P 3:9.

23. **came out**. Lk 1:21, 22. He 9:24-28. **the glory**. ver. 6. Nu 14:10, 21. 16:19, 42. 1 K 8:11. Ps 72:19. Is 40:5. Ezk 1:28. 3:23. 10:18. 43:2-5. 44:4. Mt 17:2. Jn 1:14. 2:11. 2 C 3:18. 4:4, 6. Re 21:10, 11. 22:5.

24. **there came a fire**. These victims were consumed by a fire of no human kindling. Josephus says that "a fire proceeded from the victims themselves, of its own accord, which had the appearance of a flash of lightning, and consumed all that was upon the altar." Le 6:13. Ge 4:3, 4. 15:17. Ex 3:2. Jg 6:21. 13:19, 20, 23. 2 S=22:9, 13. 1 K *18:24, 38. 2 K 19:15. 1 Ch 21:26. 2 Ch 6:2. 7:1-3. Ps 20:3mg, 4. 80:1mg. **the fat**. ſ108H10, Ps +20:3mg. **they shouted**. Ge 17:3. Nu 14:5. 16:22. 1 K 18:39. 2 Ch 7:3. Ezr 3:11. Mt 26:39. He 11:4. Re 4:9. 5:8. 7:11.

LEVITICUS 10

Nadab and Abihu, burning incense with strange fire, are consumed by fire from the Lord, 1, 2. Moses shows the reason of this judgment, and orders their burial; while Aaron holds his peace, 3-5. Aaron and his other sons are forbidden to mourn for them, 6, 7. The priests are forbidden to use wine, or strong drink, when going into the sanctuary, 8-11. Moses gives directions about eating the holy things, 12-15. A mistake is discovered about the people's sin offering; Moses reproves the priests, and Aaron excuses it, 16-20.

1. **Nadab**. Le 16:1. 22:9. Ex 6:23. 24:1, 9. 28:1.

Nu 3:3, 4. 26:61. **censer**. Le 16:12. Ex 27:3. 38:3. Nu 16:6, 7, 16, 17, 46. He 9:4. **put incense**. Ex 30:1-9, 34-36. 31:11. 37:29. 40:27. 1 K 13:1, 2. 2 Ch 26:16-20. Ps 141:2. Je 44:8, 15, 19-21. Lk 1:9-11. Re 8:3-5. **strange**. Le 9:24. 16:12. Nu 16:18, 46. 2 K 15:1-7. 2 Ch 26:16-23. Ps 50:16. Mk 1:24, 25. Ep 5:18. Ph 3:3. **which**. Ex 30:9. Dt 4:2. 12:32. 17:3. Je 7:31. 19:5. 32:35. Bishop Hall says, "It is a dangerous thing, in the service of God, to decline from his own institutions; we have to do with a God, who is wise to prescribe his own worship—just to require what he has prescribed—and powerful to avenge what he has not prescribed." **not**. ſ175B, Ge +21:6.

2. **fire**. Le 9:24n. 16:1. Nu 3:3, 4. 16:35. 26:61. 2 S 6:7. 2 K 1:10, 12. 1 Ch 24:2. **they died**. Nu 3:3, 4. 16:32, *33, 49. 26:61. 1 S 6:19. 1 Ch 13:10. 15:13. Is 30:33. Ac 5:5, 10. 1 C 10:11.

3. **said**. ver. 6. 1 S 3:18. **I will be**. Le 8:35. 21:6, 8, 15, 17, 21. 22:9. Ex 14:4. 19:22. 29:43, 44. Nu 20:12. Dt 32:51. 1 S 6:20. 1 Ch 15:12, 13. 2 Ch 26:16-21. Ps 89:7. 119:120. Is 52:11. Ezk 20:41. 42:13. He 12:28, 29. **before**. 1 S 2:30. Is 49:3. Ezk 28:22. Jn 12:28. 13:31, 32. 14:13. Ac 5:11-13. 1 Th *1:10. 1 P *4:17. **Aaron**. Ge +*18:25. Dt 26:14. 1 S 3:18. Jb 1:20, 21. 2:10. Ps *39:9. 46:10. Is 39:8. Mt 10:37. Ac +*21:14.

4. **Uzziel**. Ex 6:18, 22. Nu 3:19, 30. 1 Ch 6:2. **carry**. Lk 7:12. Ac 5:6, 9, 10. 8:2.

6. **Uncover**. Le 13:45. 21:1-15. Ex 33:5. Nu 5:18. 6:6, 7. 14:6. Dt 33:9. 1 S 16:1. Je 7:29. Ezk 24:16, 17. Mi 1:16. **lest wrath**. Nu 16:22, 41-47. Jsh 7:1, 11. 22:18, 20. 2 S 24:1, 15-17.

7. **ye shall**. Le 21:12. Mt 8:21, 22. Lk 9:60. **the anointing**. Le 8:12, 30. Ex 28:41. 30:30. 40:13-15. Ac 10:38. 2 C 1:21.

9. **Do not**. Nu 6:3, 20. 1 S ❶1:13-16. Pr 31:4, 5. Ec 5:1. Is 28:7. Je 35:5, 6. Ezk 44:21. Lk ❱15:15. Ac ❷2:13, 15. 1 C 11:21, 22. Ep=5:18. 1 T 3:3, 8. 5:23. T 1:7. 1 J=2:15-17. **strong drink**. The Hebrew *shecher*, Greek *sikera*, from *shachar*, to inebriate, signifies any kind of fermented and inebriating liquor beside wine. Ge +9:21. 1 C 10:12. **it shall be**. See on Le 3:17. **for ever**. Heb. *olam*, Ex +12:24.

10. **put difference**. Le 11:47. 20:25, 26. Ex +11:7. Je 15:19. Ezk 22:26. 44:23. Ph *1:10mg. T 1:15. 1 P 1:14-16.

11. **teach**. Dt 24:8. 33:10. 2 Ch 17:9. 30:22. Ne 8:2, 8. 9:13, 14. Je 2:8. 18:18. Ml 2:7. Mt 28:20. Ac 20:27. 1 Th 4:2.

12. **Take**. Le ch. 2. 6:15-18. 7:9. 21:22. Ex 29:2. Nu 18:9, 10. Ezk 44:29. **beside the altar**. He=13:10. **for it is most**. Le 21:22.

13. **ye shall**. Nu 18:10. **thy due**. 1 C=9:13, 14. **for so I**. Le 2:3. 6:16.

14. **wave breast**. Le 7:29-34. 9:21. Ex 29:24-28. Nu 18:11. Jn 4:34. **peace offerings**. Le +*23:19.

15. **heave shoulder**. Ex 7:29, 30, 34. **wave offering**. Le +*23:15. **for ever**. Heb. *olam*, Ex +12:24. Le 7:34. Ge 13:15. 17:8, 13, 17. 1 C 9:13, 14.

16. **the goat**. Le 6:26, 30. 9:3, 15. Ezk 44:29. **angry**. Ex 32:19-22. Nu 12:3. Mt 5:22. Mk 3:5. 10:14. Ep 4:26.

17. **Wherefore**. Le 6:26, 29. 7:6, 7. **to bear**. Le 16:22. 22:16. Ex 28:38, 43. Nu 18:1. Is 53:6-11. Ezk 4:4-6. 18:19, 20. Jn *1:29. 2 C *5:21. He *9:28. 1 P *2:24. **iniquity**. ſ121C1E, Ge +19:15.

18. **the blood.** Le 6:30. **as I commanded.** Le 6:26, 30.

19. **this day.** Le 9:8, 12. He 7:27. 9:8. **should.** Dt 12:7. 26:14. 1 S 1:7, 8. Is 1:11, 15. Je 6:20. 14:12. Ho 9:4. Ml 1:10, 13. 2:13. Ph *4:4.

20. **he was content.** 2 Ch 30:18-20. Zc 7:8, 9. Mt 12:3-7, 20.

LEVITICUS 11

What beasts may, 1-3; and what may not be eaten, 4-8. What fishes, 9-12. What fowls, 13-23. How ritual uncleanness would be contracted, by touching the carcasses of unclean animals; and how it must be cleansed, 24-40. Reptiles not to be eaten, 41-43. The reason of these laws, 44-47.

2. **the beasts.** ✗96, Ge +3:8. Dt 14:3-8. Ezk 4:14. Da 1:8. Mt 15:11. Mk 7:15-19. Ac 10:12, 14. 15:29. Ro 14:2, 3, 14, 15. Ph 4:8. 1 T 4:4-6. He 9:10. 13:9.

3. **parteth.** Ps *1:1. Pr 9:6. 2 C 6:17. **cheweth.** Dt 6:6, 7. 16:3, etc. Ps *1:2. Pr 2:1, 2, 5, 9, 10. *4:20-22. Ac *17:11. 1 T 4:15. 3 J 2.

4. **unclean unto you.** Ge 7:1, 2. Dt 14. Is 52:11. 1 C 8:13. 1 Th *5:22. 1 J 3:4.

5. **the coney.** Ps 104:18. Pr 30:26. **but divideth.** Jb 36:14. Mt 7:26. Ro 2:18-24. Ph 3:18, 19. 2 T 3:5. T 1:16.

6. **the hare.** Dt 14:7.

7. **swine.** Dt 14:8. Is 65:4. 66:3, 17. Mt 7:6. Lk 8:33. 15:15. Ro *14:14, 17. 1 C 8:8. Col 2:16, 17. 1 T ✓4:3, 4. He 9:9, 10. 2 P 2:18-22.

8. **they are unclean.** Le 5:2. Is 52:11. Ho 9:3. Mt 15:11, 20. Mk 7:2, 15, 18. Ac 10:10-15, 28. 15:29. Ro 14:14-17, 21. 1 C 8:8. 2 C 6:17. Ep 5:7, 11. Col 2:16, 21-23. He 9:10.

9. **fins and scales.** Dt 14:9, 10. Ac 20:21. Ga 5:6. Ja 2:18. 1 J 5:2-5.

10. **thing.** Heb. *nephesh*, soul. Ge +✓2:19. Ezk 47:9. **they shall be.** Le 7:18. Dt 14:3. Ps 139:21, 22. Pr 13:20. 29:27. Re *21:8.

13. **the eagle.** Dt 14:12-20. Jb 28:7. 38:41. 39:27-30. Je 4:13, 22. 48:40. La 4:19. Ho 8:1. Hab 1:8. Mt 24:28. Ro 1:28-32. 3:13-17. T 3:3.

15. **raven.** Ge 8:7. 1 K 17:4, 6. Pr 30:17. Lk 12:24.

16. **the owl.** Dt 14:15-18. Ps 102:6. Is 13:21, 22. 34:11-15. Jn 3:19-21. Ep 2:2, 3. 4:18, 19. 5:7-11. Ph 3:18, 19. 1 Th 5:5-7. Re 18:2.

19. **bat.** Is 2:20. 66:17.

20. **fowls that creep.** ver. 23, 27. Dt 14:19. 2 K 17:28-41. Ps 17:14. Mt 6:24. Ph 3:18, 19. 2 T 4:10. 1 J 2:15-17. Ju 10, 19.

22. **the locust.** Ex 10:4, 5. Is 35:3. Mt 3:4. Mk 1:6. Ro 14:1. 15:1. He 5:11. 12:12, 13.

24. **toucheth the carcass.** ver. 8, 27, 28, 31, 38-40. Le 17:15, 16. Is 22:14. 1 C 15:33. 2 C 6:17. Ep 2:1-3. *5:11. Col 2:16, 17, 20. He 9:26. 1 J 1:7.

25. **wash his clothes, and be unclean.** ver. 28, 40. Le 14:8. 15:5, 7-11, 13. 16:28. Ex 19:10, 14. Nu 19:8, 10, 19, 21, 22. 31:24. Ps 51:2, 7. Zc 13:1. Jn 13:8. Ac 22:16. He 9:10. 10:22. 1 P 3:21. 1 J 1:7. Re 7:14.

27. **whatsoever goeth.** See ver. 20, 23.

28. **beareth.** ver. 24, 25. **shall wash.** ver. 14. **until the even.** Ro 13:12.

29. **creeping things that creep.** ver. 20, 21, 41, 42. Ps 10:3. 17:13, 14. Hab 2:6. Lk 12:15. 16:14. Jn 6:26,

66. Ep 4:14. Ph 3:19. Col 3:5. 2 T 3:2-5. He 13:5. **the mouse.** Is 66:17.

31. **doth touch.** ver. 8, 24, 25.

32. **vessel.** Dt +*23:24. **it must be put into water.** Note that "put into water" means to be rinsed and scoured, Le 6:28n; Dt ◑+23:11. Although Samuel J. Baird identifies this as the single instance of an immersion mentioned in connection with any of the Mosaic ritual (*A Bible History of Baptism*, p. 136), closer examination of this text and the related passages would point rather to a rinsing, than an immersion. Even if this were conceded to be an instance of immersion, it would be of an object, not a person. See related notes (He ✓9:10n). Le 6:28n. 15:12. T 2:14. 3:5.

33. **ye shall break it.** Earthen vessels being, as before noted (Le 6:28n), of little value, but those of more valuable materials were rinsed and scoured (Young). ver. 35. Le 6:28n. 14:45. 15:12. Je 48:38. 2 C 5:1-8. Ph 3:21.

34. **all meat.** Pr 15:8. 21:4, 27. 28:8. T 1:15.

35. **they shall be.** ver. 33. Le 6:28. 15:12. 2 C 5:1-7. **broken down.** Ps 2:9. Je 48:11.

36. **a fountain.** Zc 13:1. Jn 4:14. S#4599h, *mayan*, Ge +7:11. **pit.** Heb. *bor*, Ge +37:20. **wherein there is plenty of water.** Heb. a gathering together of waters. Ge 1:10. Ex 7:19.

37. **sowing seed.** Is 61:11. 1 C 15:37. Ph 1:15-18. 1 P=*1:23. 1 J=*3:9. 5:18.

39. **that toucheth.** ver. 24, 28, 31, 40. Le 7:24. 15:5, 7. Nu 19:11, 16.

40. **eateth.** See on ver. 25. Le 17:15, 16. 22:8. Ex 22:31. Nu 15:30. Dt 14:21. Is 1:16. Ezk 4:14. 36:25. 44:31. Zc 13:1. 1 C 6:11. 10:21. 1 J 1:7. **shall wash.** ver. 28. Le 14:8, 9. 15:5-10, 27. 16:26, 28. Nu 19:7, 8, 19.

41. **creeping thing.** See ver. 20, 23, 29.

42. **goeth upon the belly.** Ge 3:14, 15. Is 65:25. Mi 7:17. Mt 3:7. 23:23. Jn 8:44. 2 C 11:3, 13. T 1:12. **hath more feet.** Heb. doth multiply feet.

43. **Ye shall.** ver. 41, 42. Le 20:25. **yourselves.** Heb. *nephesh*, Ge +27:31, your souls. ver. 44. Le 20:25.

44. **I am the.** See on Ex 20:2. **ye shall.** Le 10:3. 19:2. 20:7, 26. Ex 19:6. Dt 14:2. 1 S 6:20. Ps 99:5, 9. Is 6:3-5. Ezk 4:14. Am 3:3. Mt 5:48. 1 Th 4:7. 1 P 1:15, 16. 2:9. Re 22:11. **yourselves.** Heb. *nephesh*, Ge +27:31, your souls. ver. 43.

45. **that bringeth.** Ex 6:7. Ps 105:43-45. **be holy.** See on ver. 44. Ex 6:7. 20:2. Ps 105:43-45. Ho 11:1. 1 Th 4:7.

46. **This.** Le 7:37. 14:54. 15:32. Ezk 43:12. **creature.** Heb. *nephesh*, soul, Ge +✓2:19. Ge 1:21, 24. 9:10, 12.

47. **make a difference.** Le 10:10. Ezk 44:23. Ml *3:18. Mt 15:17, 18. 23:23-26. Ac 15:10, 18-20. Ro 14:2, 3, 13-23. 1 C 10:25, 26, 31. Col 2:16, 17. 1 T ✓4:3-5.

LEVITICUS 12

The purification of a woman after childbirth, 1-5. Her offerings for her purifying, 6-8.

2. **If a woman.** Ge 1:28. 3:16. Jb 14:4. 15:14. 25:4. Ps 51:5. Is 43:27. Lk 2:22. Ro 5:12-19. **according.** Le 15:19.

3. **eighth day.** Ge 17:11, 12. Dt 30:6. Lk 1:59. 2:21. Jn 7:22, 23. Ro 3:19. 4:11, 12. 1 C 7:19. Ga 3:17.

5:3, 5, 6. 6:15, 16. Ph 3:3, 5, 7-11. Col 2:11.

4. **in the blood.** Le 15:25-28. Hag 2:13. Lk 2:22, 23. **purifying.** ✶100, Ge +10:9. **nor come.** Le 15:31n. Ne 12:45.

5. **maid child.** ver. 2, 4. Ge 3:13, 28. 1 T 2:14, 15.

6. **a lamb.** Le 1:10-13. 5:6-10. 14:22. 15:14, 29. Nu 6:10. Lk 2:22. Jn 1:29. 2 C 5:21. He 7:26. 1 P 1:18, 19. **of the first year.** Heb. a son of his year. Le 14:10. 23:12. Ezk 46:13mg.

7. **make.** See on Le 1:4. 4:20, 26, 31, 35. Jb 1:5. 14:4. Ro 3:23, 26. 1 C 7:14. He 9:12-14. **be cleansed.** Le 15:28-30. **issue.** Le 20:18. ✶S#4726h, *maqor*, a spring, dug well, even when naturally flowing. Here used of the flow of blood after childbirth; in Le 20:18, used of the source of menstruous blood. Ps ✶36:9 (fountain). 68:26. Pr 5:18. ✶10:11 (well). 13:14. 14:27. 16:22 (wellspring). 18:4. 25:26 (spring). Je ✶2:13. 9:1. ✶17:13. 51:36 (springs). Ho 13:15. Zc ✶13:1. For ✶S#953h, *bor*, a hewn cistern, well, etc., see Ge +37:20. For ✤S#5869h, *ayin*, a fountain, see Ge +24:13. For ✶S#4599h, *mayan*, a spring or fountain, see Ge +7:11. **a male.** Ga 3:28.

8. **she be not able to bring a lamb.** Heb. her hand find not sufficiency of a lamb. Le 1:14. 5:7. 14:22. 15:14, 29. 25:26, 28. Lk 2:22, ▶24. 2 C 8:9. **make atonement.** Le 4:26. When burnt offerings and sin offerings were brought together the sin offerings were first offered.

LEVITICUS 13

Rules for distinguishing the plague of leprosy, 1-44. The conduct prescribed to lepers, 45, 46. The leprosy in garments, 47-59.

2. **skin of.** Le ◐7:8. Is=3:9. **rising.** *or*, swelling. ver. 10, 19, 43, etc. **a scab.** Le 14:56. Dt ✶28:27. Is ✶3:17. **the plague of leprosy.** Le 14:3, 35. Ex 4:6, 7. Nu 12:10, 12. Dt 24:8. 28:27. 2 S 3:29. 2 K 5:1, 27. 2 Ch 26:19-21. Ps ✶38:5-7. Is ✶1:5, 6. Mt 10:6-8. 11:4, 5. 1 C=6:11. **he shall.** Dt 17:8, 9. ✶24:8. Ml 2:7. Mt 8:4. Mk 1:44. Lk 5:14. ✶17:14. **the priest.** Ps=19:12. Jn=2:25. He 4:13. Re=1:14.

3. **shall look.** ver. 2. Le 10:10. Ezk 44:23. Hg 2:11. Ml 2:7. Ac 20:28. Ro 3:19, 20. 7:7. He 13:7. Re 2:23. **turned.** ver. 4, 10. Nu ◐6:5. Ezk 16:30. Ho 7:9. **white.** Ex 4:6. Nu 12:10, 12. 2 K ✶5:27. 2 Ch ✶26:20. **deeper.** Ge 13:3. Je =17:9. Mt 15:19, 20. 2 T 2:16, 17. 3:13. **pronounce.** ✶121I2, Ge +2:17. 2 K 5:27. 2 Ch 26:20. Mt 16:19. 18:17, 18. Jn=20:23. Ro 3:19, 20. 1 C 5:4-6. =6:11. 2 Th 3:14, 15. 1 T 1:20.

4. **shut up.** Le 24:12. Nu 12:15. Dt 13:14. Ezk 44:10. 1 C 4:5. 2 Th=3:14, 15. 1 T 5:24. Ju 22. **plague.** ✶121N2, Ge +34:29.

6. **look.** Is=1:16-18. Jn=15:6. 2 C 2:6, 7. Ga=6:1. Ja=✶5:19, 20. **pronounce.** Is 11:3, 4. 42:3. Ro 14:1. 2 C ✶2:6, 7. Ju 22, 23. **a scab.** ver. 2. Dt 32:5. Ja 3:2. **wash.** Le 11:25, 28, 40. 14:8. Ge 35:2. 1 K 8:38, 45. Ps ✶19:12. Pr ✶20:9. Ec √7:20. Is ✶1:16-18. Jn 13:8-10. =15:3. 2 C 7:1. Ga ✶6:1. He 9:10. 10:22. Ja ✶5:19, 20. 1 J 1:7-9.

7. **the scab.** ver. 27, 35, 36. Le 14:4, 10, 21, 22. Ps 38:3. Is 1:5, 6. Lk 5:14. 17:14. Ro 6:12-14. 2 T 2:16, 17.

8. **pronounce him.** See on ver. 3. Mt 15:7, 8. Ac 8:21. Ph 3:18, 19. 2 P 2:19.

10. **white.** ver. 3. **shall see him.** ver. 3, 4. Nu ✶12:10-

12. 2 K 5:27. 2 Ch 26:19, 20. **quick raw flesh.** Heb. the quickening of living flesh. ver. 14, 15, 24. Pr 12:1. Am 5:10. Jn 3:19, 20. 7:7. T 3:11.

11. **old leprosy.** Mt 8:2-4. Lk 5:14.

12. **cover all.** 1 K 8:33. Jb 40:4. 42:6. Is ✶64:6. Jn 16:8, 9. Ro 7:14. 1 T 1:15. 1 J 1:8-10.

13. **covered all.** 2 S + =12:13. Jb=33:27, 28. =40:4. 42:6. Is=6:5. Lk=5:8, 12. 15:21. 18:13. 23:41. Ro=7:18. **turned white.** Nu 12:10. **plague.** ✶121N2, Ge +34:29. **he is clean.** Is ✶64:6. Jn 9:41.

14. **when.** ✶171, Ge +2:17. **raw flesh.** ver. 10.

15. **raw flesh.** Nu + =22:34.

16. **turn again.** Ro 7:14-24. Ga 1:14-16. Ph 3:6-8. 1 T 1:13-15.

18. **a boil.** Ex 9:9. +15:26. 2 K 20:7. 2 Ch 16:12. Jb 2:7. Ps 38:3-7. Is 38:21.

20. **in sight.** See on ver. 3. Mt 12:45. Jn 5:14. 2 P 2:20.

21. **shut him.** 1 C 5:5.

22. **a plague.** i.e. "The plague of the leprosy."

23. **stay.** Ge 38:26. 2 S 12:13. 2 Ch 19:2, 3. Jb 34:31, 32. 40:4, 5. Pr ✶28:13. Mt 26:75. 2 C 2:7. Ga ✶6:1. 1 P 4:2, 3.

24. **a hot burning.** Heb. a burning of fire. Is 3:24. He 12:5, 11. 1 P=4:12. This is supposed to state the case of such as had been hurt by fire; which would leave a scar, in which the leprosy might appear, and which was to be distinguished by the rules here given.

25. **turned white.** ver. 4, 18-20.

26. **then the priest.** ver. 4, 5, 23.

27. **it is the plague of leprosy.** See on ver. 2.

28. **And if.** Ps ✶38:3-7, 11. Je ✶3:12-14. ✶8:4-6. Re ✶2:5.

29. **upon the head or.** 1 K 8:38. 12:28. 2 Ch 6:29. Ps 53:4. Is 1:5. 5:20. 9:15. Mi 3:11. Mt 6:23. 13:14, 15. Jn 16:2, 3. Ac 22:3, 4. 26:9, 10. 2 C 4:3, 4. =11:3. Col=2:18. 2 Th 2:11, 12. T=1:15.

30. **scall.** ver. 34-37. Le 14:54. **leprosy.** Je ✶14:7-9. Ho ✶11:7, 8. ✶14:4.

31. **plague.** ✶121N2, Ge +34:29. **seven days.** ver. 4-6.

32. **yellow hair.** ver. 30. Mt 23:5. Lk 18:9-12. Ro 2:23.

33. **be shaven.** 1 P=5:6.

34. **the seventh.** 1 J 4:1. Ju 22. Re 2:2. **be not.** ver. 23. **and he shall.** See on ver. 6.

35. **spread much.** ver. 7, 27. 2 T 2:16, 17. 3:13.

37. **the priest.** Jn ✶5:22.

39. **if the bright.** Ec 7:20. Ro 7:22-25. Ja 3:2.

40. **hair is fallen off his head.** Heb. head is pilled. ver. 41. SS ◐5:11. Ro 6:12, 19. 8:10. Ga 4:13. **bald.** Le ◐✶21:5. 2 K 2:23. Ezr 9:3. Jb 1:20. Is 3:24. 15:2. 22:12. Je 7:29. 16:6. 47:5. Ezk 7:18. 27:31. 29:18. Am 8:10. Mi 1:16.

42. **forehead.** 2 Ch 26:16-20.

44. **utterly unclean.** Jb 36:14. Mt 6:23. 2 P 2:1, 2. 2 J 8-10. **his plague.** Is 1:5. **head.** 2 C=10:5.

45. **his clothes.** Ge 37:29. Jsh 7:6. 2 S 13:19. Jb 1:20. Is 6:5. Je 3:25. 36:24. Jl 2:13. **and his head.** Le 10:6. 21:10. **bare.** Nu 5:18. Ps 140:7. Pr 28:13. Jn 3:36. He=4:13. **put.** Jb 40:4. Ezk ✶24:17, 22. Mi ✶3:7. **Unclean.** Jb 42:6. Ps 51:3, 5. Is 6:5. ✶52:11. ✶64:6. La ✶4:15. Lk 5:8. 7:6, 7. 17:12. Ep=✶5:5.

46. **the days.** Pr 30:12. **alone.** Is=59:2. Jn ◐8:16, 29. **without.** Le ◐16:27. Nu ✶5:2. ✶12:12, 14, 15. 2 K ✶5:1. ✶7:3. ✶15:5. 2 Ch ✶26:21. La 1:1, 8. 4:15. Is

52:11. Ezk *24:17, 22. Lk *17:12. 1 C 5:5, 9-13. 2 Th 3:6, 14. 1 T 6:5. He 12:15, 16. Re 21:27. 22:15.

47. **The garment.** Ps 109:18. Is 3:16-24. 59:6. *64:6. Ezk 16:16. Ro 13:12. Ep 4:22. Col 3:3. Ju *23. Re ◐19:8.

48. **thing made of.** Heb. work of. ver. 51. Dt 8:11. Ju 23. Re *3:4.

49. **thing of skin.** Heb. vessel, *or* instrument. ver. 52, 53, 57-59. Le 15:4. **it is.** See on ver. 2. **showed unto.** Mk 1:44.

50. **look upon.** Ezk 44:23. **plague.** ʃ121N2, Ge +34:29.

51. **fretting leprosy.** Le 14:44.

52. **burn.** Le 11:33, 35. Dt 7:25, 26. Is 30:22. Ac 19:19, 20. Col=3:5. **fretting leprosy.** Le 14:44, 45.

54. **wash.** Hg 1:6.

55. **after.** Ezk 24:13. He 6:4-8. 2 P 1:9. 2:20-22. **not changed.** Je=13:23. Lk=13:6-9. 1 C 7:20, 24. T 3:5. **color.** lit. eye. ʃ121R1. Metonymy of the Adjunct B598. The action or affection relating to an object is put for the object itself. The senses are put for the object of them, or for the things which are perceived by the senses. Here, "eye" is put for color perceived by the eye. For other instances of this figure see Nu 11:7mg. Ps 112:7. Pr 23:31. Is 28:9mg, 19. 53:1mg. Ezk 1:4. 7:26. Ob 1. Hab 3:2mg. Mt 4:24. 24:6. Jn 12:38. Mk 13:7. Ro 10:16mg. Ga 3:2, 5. **it be bare within or without.** Heb. it *be* bald in the head thereof, or in the forehead thereof. ver. 43.

56. **rend it out.** Ep 4:25.

57. **shalt burn.** Is 33:14. Mt 3:12. 22:7. 25:41. Re 21:*8, 27.

58. **be washed.** 2 K 5:10, 14. Ps 51:2. 2 C 7:1. 12:8. He 9:10. Re 1:5. 7:14. **the second time.** Ac 19:1-5.

59. **pronounce.** 1 C *5:3-5. Re *19:8.

LEVITICUS 14

The ceremonies and sacrifices appointed, when a leper had been healed, 1-32. The signs of leprosy in a house, 33-47. The cleansing of that house, 48-53. The subject closed, 54-57.

2. **the law.** ver. 54-57. Le 13:59. **leper.** Lk 4:27. **in the day.** Nu 6:9. **He shall.** Mt *8:2-4. Mk 1:40-44. Lk 5:12-14. *17:14.

3. **go forth.** Mt 9:10, 11. *11:19. 21:31, 32. Lk 7:34. =19:10. **out of.** Le 13:46. Lk=10:33. He=13:13. **be healed.** Ex +15:26. 2 K 5:3, 7, 8, 14. Jb 5:18. Mt 10:8. 11:5. Lk 4:27. 7:22. 17:15-19. 1 C 6:9-11.

4. **two.** Le 4:21. Ge 22:8. Mt 10:29. **birds.** *or,* sparrows. ver. 49. Le 1:14. 5:7. 12:8. Mt 10:29, 31. Lk 12:6, *7. Jn=6:38. **cedar.** ver. 6, 49-52. Nu *19:6. 1 K 6:9. Is 2:13. **scarlet.** 2 S 1:24. Is *1:18. He *9:19. **hyssop.** Ex 12:22. Nu 19:18. 1 K 4:33. Ps *51:7. Jn *19:29, 30. He 9:19.

5. **kill one.** Jn 11:49-52. Ac 2:23. Ro 5:6. 2 C *5:21. **earthen vessel.** ver. 50. Nu 5:17. 2 C *4:7. 5:1. 13:4. Ph 2:7, 8. He 2:14. **running.** Ge +*26:19. Nu *19:17n. SS +*4:15. Ezk ◐*34:18, 19. Zc 13:1. Ac *1:5n. He=9:14. **water.** 2 K 5:10, 14. Ezk ◐*34:18, 19. Ro 6:3, 4. 8:1, 2, 21. 1 J *5:6, 8.

6. **the living bird.** Jn 14:19. Ro 4:25. 5:10. Ph 2:9-11. He 1:3. Re 1:18. **dip them.** ver. 51-53. Zc *13:1. Ga 6:14. Re 1:5. **blood.** Jn *19:34. He *9:13, 14, 19. 1 J *5:6, 8. **over.** Zp *3:17.

7. **sprinkle.** Nu 19:18, 19. Is 52:15. Ezk 36:25. Jn 19:34. He 9:13, 19, 21. 10:22. 12:24. 1 P 1:2. 1 J 5:6. **seven times.** ver. 51. Le 4:6, 17. 8:11. 16:14, 19. 2 K *5:10, 14. Ps 51:2, 7. Ep 5:26, 27. **pronounce.** Le 13:13, 17. 2 C 5:21. **let.** Le 16:22. Ge 49:21. Da 9:24. Mi 7:19. Ro=4:25. Col 3:1. He 9:26. **into the open field.** Heb. upon the face of the field. ver. 53. Le 17:5. Is 1:18. Zp 3:17. Jn *8:36. 1 C *15:42-44, 54, 55. Ga *5:1, 13.

8. **wash his.** Le 11:25. 13:6, 34. 15:5-8. Ex 19:10, 14. *33:5, 6. Nu 8:7. Jb *19:9. Is *32:11. Re 7:14. **and shave.** Nu *6:9. Jb *1:20. Ps *89:38, 39. Je *48:37. **wash himself.** Le 8:6. 1 P 3:21. Re 1:5, 6. **come into.** Jn=21:15-19. 2 C=2:6, 7. Ep 2:13. **and shall.** Nu 12:15. **tarry.** Mk=5:19. 2 C=5:6. **seven days.** Le 8:33-35. 13:5.

9. **on the seventh.** Nu 19:19. **shave all his hair.** Le ◐19:27. 21:5. Nu 6:9. 8:7. 2 S 10:4, 5. Ps=69:19, 20. Is 15:2. *50:6. *52:14. Je 41:5. 48:37. He=10:33. =13:13. **wash his flesh.** Nu 19:19. 2 C=7:1. **clean.** Is=44:22.

10. **eighth day.** ver. 23. Le 9:1. 15:13, 14. Mk=16:2-6. Jn=11:25-27. Ac=4:2. Ep 2:4-7. Col=1:21, 22. Re=21:5. **take.** Mt 8:4. Mk 1:44. Lk 5:14. **he lambs.** Le 1:10. Jn 1:29. 1 P 1:19. **ewe lamb.** Le 4:32. Nu 6:14. **of the first year.** Heb. the daughter of her year. Le ◐12:6mg. **three tenth.** Le 23:13. Ex 29:40. Nu 15:9. 28:20. **a meat offering.** Le 2:1n. +*23:13. Nu 15:4-15. Jn 6:33, 51. **log of oil.** ver. 12, 15, 21, 24.

11. **shall present.** Le 8:3. ◐13:3. Ex 29:1-4. Nu 8:6-11, 21. Mt *8:4. Mk 1:44. Lk 5:14. Ep 5:26, 27. Ju 24.

12. **trespass.** Le 5:2, 3, 6, 7, 18, 19. 6:6, 7. Ps 51:4. Is 53:10. **wave them.** Le 7:30. 8:27-29. Ex *29:24, 27n. **wave offering.** Le +*23:15.

13. **in the place.** Le 1:5, 11. 4:4, 24. Ex 29:11. **as the sin.** Le 7:7. 10:17. **it is most holy.** Le 2:3. *7:6. *21:22.

14. **upon the tip.** Le 8:23, 24. Ex *29:20. Is 50:5. Ro 6:13, 19. 12:1. 1 C 6:20. 2 C 7:1. Ph 1:20. 1 P 1:14, 15. 2:5, 9, 10. Re 1:5, 6.

15. **oil.** Ps 45:7. Jn 3:34. 1 J 2:20.

16. **sprinkle.** Le 8:11, 12. **before the Lord.** Le 4:6, 17. Lk 17:18. 1 C 10:31.

17. **the tip.** ver. 14. Le 8:30. Ex 29:20, 21. Ezk 36:27. Jn 1:16. T 3:3-6. 1 P 1:2.

18. **the remnant.** Le 8:12. Ex 29:7. 2 C 1:21, 22. Ep 1:17, 18. **make an atonement.** Le 4:26, 31. 5:16.

19. **sin offering.** ver. 12. Le 5:1, 6. 12:6-8. +*23:19. Ro 8:3. 2 C 5:21.

20. **shall offer.** ver. 10. Ep 5:2. **burnt offering.** Le +*23:12.

21. **poor.** Le 1:14. 5:7. 12:8. 1 S 2:8. Jb 34:19. Pr 17:5. 22:2. Lk 6:20. 21:2-4. 2 C *8:9, 12-15. Ja 2:5, 6. **cannot.** Heb. his hand reach not. ver. 22, 30-32. **one lamb.** See on ver. 10. **to be waved.** Heb. for a waving. ver. 12, 24. Ex 29:24.

22. **two turtle doves.** Ps 68:13. SS 2:14. Is 38:14. 59:11. Je 48:28. Ezk 7:16.

23. **he shall bring.** ver. 11.

24. **the priest.** See on ver. 10-13. **wave offering.** Le +*23:15.

25. **trespass offering.** See on ver. 14-20. Le +*5:6. Ps 40:6. Ec 5:1.

29. **make an atonement.** ver. 18, 20. Ex 30:15, 16. Jn 17:19. 1 J 2:1, 2. 5:6.

30. **turtledoves.** ver. 22. Le 12:8. 15:14, 15. Lk 2:24. Ro 8:3. **such as he can.** Le 5:7. Lk +*11:41n.

32. **the law.** ver. 2, 54-57. Le 13:59. **whose hand.** See on ver. 10, 21. Ps 72:12-14. 136:23. Mt 11:5. 1 C 1:27, 28.

34. **When.** Le 23:10. 25:2. Nu 35:10. Dt 7:2. 12:1, 8. 17:14. 19:1. 26:1. 27:3. Ep=5:3-11. **which I.** Ge 12:7. 13:17. 17:8. Nu 32:32. Dt 12:9, 10. 32:49. Jsh 13:1. **I put the plague of leprosy.** It was probably from this text, that the leprosy has been in general considered to be a supernatural disease, inflicted immediately by God himself; but it cannot be inferred from this expression, as it is well known, that in Scripture, God is frequently represented as *doing* what, in the course of his providence, he only *permits* to be done. Ge +*24:44n. Ex +15:26. Dt 7:15. 1 S 2:6. Pr 3:33. Is *45:7. Am +√3:6. 6:11. Mi 6:9. **house.** Pr 3:33. 1 C 3:16. 2 T 2:20, 21.

35. **come and tell.** Ps *32:5. **a plague.** Dt 7:26. Jsh 7:21. 1 S 3:12-14. 1 K 13:34. Ps 91:10. Pr 3:33. Zc 5:4.

36. **empty.** *or*, prepare. ✛S#6437h. Ge 24:31. Ps 80:9. Zp 3:15 (cast out). Ml 3:1. **be not made.** 1 C 15:33. 2 T 2:17, 18. He 12:15. Re 18:4. **house.** Pr *3:33. Zc *5:3, 4.

37. **with hollow streaks.** Le 13:3, 19, 20, 42, 49.

38. **shut.** Le 13:50. 1 C 5:2. 2 C 12:20, 21. 2 P=3:9-11.

39. **come again.** Lk 13:6-9. **spread in.** Le 13:7, 8, 22, 27, 36, 51. **house.** Jb 19:25-27. Jn ◖14:2. 1 C 5:5. 15:53. 2 C 5:1-4.

40. **take away.** Ezr 9:2. 10:17. Ps 101:5, 7, 8. Pr 22:10. 25:4, 5. Is 1:25, 26. Mt 18:17. Jn 15:2. 1 C 5:5, 6, 13. T 3:10. 2 J 10, 11. Re 2:2, 6, 14-16, 20. **without the city.** Re 22:15.

41. **scraped.** Ne 13:4-10. Ezk 26:4. 2 C 7:11. **into an unclean place.** ver. 45. Jb 36:13, 14. Is 65:4. Mt 8:28. 24:51. 1 T 1:20. Re 22:15.

42. **take other stones.** Ge 18:19. Jsh 24:15. 2 Ch 17:7-9. 19:5-7. 29:4, 5. Ps 101:6. Lk 13:6-9. Ac 1:20-26. 1 T 5:9, 10, 21, 22. 2 T 2:2. T 1:5-9.

43. **the plague.** Je 6:28-30. Ezk 24:13. He 6:4-8. 2 P 2:20, 22. Ju 12.

44. **fretting leprosy.** Le *13:51, 52. Pr *4:14, 15. Zc *5:4. 1 C *15:33.

45. **break down.** Le 11:35. 1 K 9:6-9. 2 K 10:27. 17:20-23. 18:4. 25:4-12, 25, 26. Ezr 6:11. Jb 19:25-27. Je 52:13. Ezk 5:4. Mt 22:7. 24:2. Jn 14:2. Ro 11:7-11. 1 C 5:5. *15:53. 2 C *5:1-4. Re 2:5. 11:2. **and the timber.** Zc 5:1-4. **into an unclean place.** See on ver. 41.

46. **goeth into.** 2 J 10, 11. **shall be unclean.** Le 11:24, 25, 28. 15:5-8, 10. 17:15. 22:6. Nu 19:7-10, 21, 22.

47. **wash his clothes.** See on ver. 8, 9.

48. **shall come in.** Heb. in coming shall come in, etc. **because.** ver. 3. Jb 5:18. Ho 6:1. Mk 5:29, 34. Lk 7:21. 1 C 6:11.

49. **to cleanse.** See on ver. 4-7.

51. **cedar.** √52B, Ge +43:3. **scarlet.** Jsh *2:18-21. **blood of the.** He *9:19. **slain bird.** Mk *15:12-20. He 2:14.

53. **let go.** Ps *55:6. *124:7. Is *35:10. Lk *4:18. Jn *18:8. Ro *6:18. 2 C *3:17. **and make.** ver. 20. **it shall be clean.** Ps=118:15.

54. **the law.** ver. 2, 32. Le 6:9, 14, 25. 7:1, 37.

11:46. 15:32. Nu 5:29. 6:13. 19:14. Dt *24:8. **scall.** Le 13:30, 31.

55. **the leprosy.** Le 13:47-59. **of a house.** ver. 34.

56. **a rising.** Le 13:2.

57. **teach.** Le 10:10. Je 15:19. Ezk *44:23. **when it is unclean, and when it is clean.** Heb. in the day of the unclean, and in the day of the clean. √171, Ge +2:17. Jn=17:15. **this is.** Dt *24:8.

LEVITICUS 15

The uncleanness of men in their issues, 1-12. The cleansing of them, 13-18. The uncleanness of women in their issues, 19-27. Their cleansing, 28-33.

1. **Aaron.** Le 11:1. 13:1. Ps 25:14. Am 3:7. He 1:1.

2. **unto the.** Dt 4:7, 8. Ne 9:13, 14. Ps 78:5. 147:19, 20. Ro 3:2. **when any man.** It may be observed, that from the pains which persons rendered unclean were obliged to take, the ablutions and separations which they must observe, and the privations to which they must in consequence be exposed, in the way of commerce, traffic, etc., these laws were admirably adapted to prevent contagion of every kind, by keeping the whole from the diseased, and to hinder licentious indulgences and excesses of every description. Le *22:4. Nu *5:2. 2 S 3:29. Mt *9:20. Mk *5:25. 7:20-23. Lk 8:43. **running issue.** *or*, running of the reins. Le 22:4mg. **flesh.** √88, Ge +17:11.

3. **issue.** Le 22:4. Nu 5:2. Mt 9:20. Mk *5:29. Lk 8:43. **flesh run.** Le 12:3. Ezk 16:26. 23:20.

4. **thing.** Heb. vessel. ver. 6, 22, 23, 26. Le 13:49. **be unclean.** 1 C 15:33. Ep 5:11. T 1:15.

5. **wash his clothes.** Le 11:25, 28, 32. 13:6, 34. 14:8, 9, 27, 46, 47. 16:26, 28. 17:15. Nu 19:10, 22. Ps 26:6. 51:2, 7. Is 1:16. 22:14. Ezk 36:25, 29. He 9:14, 26. 10:22. Ja 4:8. Re 7:14. **and bathe himself.** Heb. *rahats*, S#7364h, Ex +29:4. Rendered *bathe*: Le 15:5, 6, 7, 8, 10, 11, 13, 18, 21, 22, 27. 16:26, 28. 17:15, 16. Nu 19:7, 8, 19. See related notes (Nu 19:17n. 2 K +*5:10n. He 9:10n) which demonstrate that the English word *bathe* is not synonymous with Hebrew and Greek terms which are synonymous with the English word *wash*.

6. **and bathe.** Heb. *rahats*, S#7364h, Ex +29:4. ver. +5n. Is 1:16. Ja 4:8.

8. **wash his clothes.** Is *1:16. Ga *1:8, 9. 1 T 4:1-3. T 1:9, 10. Ja *4:8. 2 P 2:1-3. Ju 4.

9. **saddle.** Ge 31:34.

10. **wash his clothes.** See on ver. 5, 8. Ps 26:6. Ja *4:8.

11. **whomsoever.** It is rather doubtful whether the words "hath not rinsed his hands in water," refer to him who was diseased, or to him who had his hands touched. Most understand it of the former, that if the person who had the issue rinsed his hands in water, just before he touched any one, he did not communicate any pollution; otherwise, he did. But the Syriac refers it to the person touched by him, though it seems strange that he should be cleansed by washing his hands, when perhaps some other part was touched. See related note (Nu 19:19n). **rinsed.** Heb. *shataph*, *S#7857h. Kal, Preterite: Le 15:11. Ps 69:2 (overflow). 124:4 (overwhelmed). Is 8:8. Da 11:10, 40. Kal, Future: 1 K 22:38 (washed). Jb 14:19 (washest away. mg. overflowest). Ps 69:15. 78:20. SS 8:7 (drown). Is 28:17. 43:2. Je 47:2. Ezk 16:9 (throughly washed away). Da 11:26.

Kal, Participle, Poel: 2 Ch 32:4 (ran. mg, overflowed).
Is 10:22. 28:2, 15, 18. 30:28. 66:12. Je 8:6. 47:2. Ezk
13:11, 13. 38:22. Niphal, Future: Le 15:12 (rinsed).
Da 11:22 (overflown). Pual, Preterite: Le 6:28 (rinsed).
See related note (He 9:10n).

12. **vessel.** Le 6:28. 11:32, 33. Pr 1:21, 23. 3:21.
2 C 5:1. Ph 3:21. **shall be broken.** Ps 2:9. 2 P=3:11.

13. **seven days.** ver. 28. Le 8:33. 9:1. 14:8, 10. Ex
29:35, 37. Nu 12:14. 19:11, 12. **wash.** ver. 5, 10, 11.
Je 33:8. Ezk 36:25-29. 2 C 7:1. Ja 4:8. Re 1:5. **clean.**
Ps 51:6.

14. **two turtledoves.** ver. 29, 30. Le 1:14. 12:6, 8.
14:22-31. Nu 6:10. 2 C 5:21. He 7:26. 10:10, 12, 14.

15. **the one.** Le 5:7-10. 14:19, 20, 30, 31. **sin offering.** Le +*23:19. **burnt offering.** Le +*23:12. **an atonement.** Le 4:20, 26, 31, 35. 12:7. 14:18. Nu 15:25. 25:13.
Mt 3:17. Ep 1:6. He 1:3.

16. **man's seed.** ver. 5. Le *22:4. Ge +*38:9. Dt
*23:10, 11. 2 C 7:1. 1 P 2:11. 1 J 1:7. **of copulation.**
Le 18:6-16, 19, 23. 20:15, 16. Ge +*38:9. Ex 22:19.
*S#7902h. Ex 16:13 (lay), 14. Le 15:16 (lit. lying),
17, 18, 32. 19:20 (carnally; lit. the lying of seed). 22:4.
Nu 5:13.

18. **The woman.** ver. 5. Ep 4:17-19. 5:3-11. 2 T
2:22. 1 P 2:11. **unclean.** Ex 19:15. 1 S *21:4, 5. Ps
*51:5, 6. 1 C 6:12, 18. 2 C *7:1. 1 Th 4:3-5. He +*13:4.

19. **and her issue.** Le *12:2, 4. 20:18. La 1:8, 9,
17. Ezk 36:17. Mt 15:19. Mk 5:25. **put apart.** Heb.
in her separation. ver. 20. Le 12:2, 5.

20. **every thing.** See on ver. 4-9. Pr 2:16-19. 5:3-
13. 6:24, 35. 7:10-27. 9:13-18. 22:27. Ec 7:26. 1 C
15:33.

21. **shall wash.** See on ver. 5, 6. Is 22:14. 2 C 7:1.
He 9:26. Re 7:14.

24. **any man.** ver. 33. Le 20:18. Ezk 18:6. 22:10.
1 Th 5:22. He 13:4. 1 P 2:11. **flowers.** or, monthly
flow. *S#5079h. Le 12:2 (separation), 5. 15:19 (put
apart; mg, in her separation), 20, 24 (flowers), 25, 25,
25, 26, 26, 33 (flowers). 18:19 (put apart). 20:21 (unclean
thing; mg, a separation). Nu 19:9, 13, 20, 21, 21. 31:23.
2 Ch 29:5 (the filthiness). Ezr 9:11 (unclean with the
filthiness). La 1:17 (menstruous woman). Ezk 7:19 (removed; mg, for a separation, or, uncleanness), 20 (far;
mg, unclean thing). 18:6 (menstruous). 22:10. 36:17
(removed woman). Zc 13:1 (uncleanness; mg, separation for uncleanness). OS#2931h, ver. +25.

25. **an issue.** Nu 5:2. **many days.** ver. 19-24. Mt
*9:20. Mk 5:25. 7:20-23. Lk *8:43. **unclean.** S#2931h.
Le 5:2. 15:2, 25, 26, 33. Jb 14:4. Is 6:5. 35:8. Is 52:1,
11. √64:6. Je *19:13 (defiled). La 4:15. Ezk 4:13. 22:5
(infamous; mg, polluted of name), *10 (pollution), 26.
44:23. Ho 9:3. Am 7:17. Hg 2:13, 14. O*S#5079h,
ver. +24.

27. **shall wash.** ver. 5-8, 13, 21. Le 17:15, 16. Ezk
36:25, 29. Zc 13:1. He *9:14. +*10:22. 1 P 1:18, 19.
1 J *1:7.

28. **number.** See on ver. 13-15. Mt 1:21. 1 C 1:30.
6:11. Ga 3:13. 4:4. Ep 1:6, 7.

29. **eighth day.** See on ver. 14.

30. **sin offering.** Le +*23:19. **burnt offering.** Le
+*23:12. **for the issue.** Ps *103:3. Ezk *44:23.

31. **Thus shall.** Le 11:47. 13:59. Nu 5:3. Dt 24:8.
Ps 66:18. Ezk 44:23. He 10:29. 12:*14, 15. Ju 4. **that
they.** Le 19:30. 21:23. Nu 5:3. 19:13, 20. Ezk 5:11.
23:38. 44:5-7. Da 9:27. 1 C 3:17. These laws were
principally intended to impress the minds of the Israelites with reverence for the sanctuary; and, on the one
hand, to show them what need they had for circumspection, and purity of heart and life, in order to worship
the holy God with acceptance; and, on the other hand,
that being sinners in a world full of temptations and
defilements, they would continually need forgiveness,
through the great atonement typified by all the sacrifices, and the sanctification of the Spirit, shadowed
forth by all the purifications. While they were encamped in the desert, it would not be very burdensome
to bring the prescribed oblations; but after they were
settled in Canaan, many of them at a great distance
from the tabernacle, this would become much more
difficult. We may, however, observe, continues Mr.
Scott, that many of these cases stated only required
such washings as might any where be performed; and
that those, respecting which sacrifices were appointed,
would more rarely occur. We may also suppose, that
provided these were brought, when the person who
had been unclean first came to the sanctuary, it would
suffice: though distance or other hindrances prevented
its being done immediately, at the expiration of the
seven days.

32. **law of him.** ver. 1-18. Le 11:46. 13:59. 14:2,
32, 54-57. Nu 5:29. 6:13. 19:14. Ps *119:1, 2, 18, 73,
128, 140. Is *4:4. Ezk 43:12. Zc 13:1. Mt *5:8. Ep
*5:25-27. T *1:15. He *9:8-14. *12:28. Re 14:1-5.

33. **of her.** ver. 19-30. **flowers.** ver. +24. **and of
him.** ver. 24. Le 20:18.

LEVITICUS 16

*The high priest must not enter the most holy place
at all times, but on a day of atonement yearly observed,
1-10; having slain a sin offering for himself, 11-14;
and another for the people, 15; he must enter with
the sprinkling of blood, and burning of incense, 16,
17. The altar of incense, purified with blood, 18, 19.
The scape goat sent away, 20-22. Aaron the high priest
to enter the holy place and wash himself, then go forth.
The burnt offerings sacrificed, and the sin offerings
burnt without the camp, 23-28. The yearly feast of
the expiation instituted, 29-34.*

1. **after the death.** Le 10:1, 2. 2 C *1:4.

2. **he come not.** ver. 34. Le 23:27. Ex 26:33, 34.
30:10. 40:20, 21. 1 K 8:6. Ep O=2:18. He 9:3, 7, 8.
10:19, 20. **that he die not.** ver. 13. Le 8:35. Nu 4:19.
17:10. Mt 27:51. He 4:14-16. 10:19. **in the cloud.**
J22D3J5, Ex +13:21. ver. O13. Ex 40:34, 35. 1 K
8:10-12. 2 Ch +*5:13, 14. **the mercy seat.** Ex 25:17-
22.

3. **Aaron.** He 9:7, 12, 24, 25. **a young.** Le 4:3. 8:14.
Nu 29:7-11. **a ram for a burnt offering.** Le 1:3, 10.
8:18. 9:3. +*23:12.

4. **holy linen coat.** Heb. of holiness. Le 6:10. Ex
28:2, 39-43. 39:27-29. Is 53:2. Ezk 44:17, 18. Lk 1:35.
2 C=8:9. Ph *2:7. He 2:14. 7:26. Re 19:8. **therefore.**
Le 8:6, 7. Ex 29:4. 30:20. 40:12, 31, 32. He 10:22.
Re 1:5, 6.

5. **two kids.** Le 4:14. 8:2, 14. 9:8-16. Nu 29:11.
2 Ch 29:21. Ezr 6:17. Ezk 45:22, 23. Ro 8:3. He 7:27,
28. 10:5-14.

6. **which.** Le 8:14-17. He 9:7. **an atonement for
himself.** Le 9:7. Ezr 10:18, 19. Jb 1:5. Ezk 43:19-27.
He 5:2. 7:27, 28. 9:7. **house.** Ps 115:12. He=3:6.
1 P=2:5.

7. **present them**. Le 1:3. 4:4. 12:6, 7. Mt 16:21. Ro 12:1.

8. **cast lots**. Nu 26:55. 33:54. Jsh +*14:2n. 18:10, 11. 1 S 14:41, 42. Pr 16:33. Ezk 48:29. Jon 1:7. Ac 1:23-26. **scape goat**. Heb. *Azazel*, that is, the goat gone away. ver. 10, 26. Dt 32:26.

9. **upon which**. Ac 2:23. 4:27, 28. **fell**. Heb. went up. ver. 10.

10. **the scape goat**. ver. 21, 22. **to make**. Is 53:5, 6, 10, 11. Ro 4:25. 2 C 5:21. He 7:26, 27. 9:23, 24. 1 J 2:2. 3:16. **let him**. Le 14:7. **into**. Jn 1:29. 1 J 2:2.

11. **the bullock**. See on ver. 3, 6.

12. **censer**. Nu 16:46. Is 6:6, 7. Re 8:3, 5. **from off**. Le 10:1. Nu 16:18, 46. Is 6:6, 7. He 9:14. 1 J 1:7. **hands full**. Ex 29:24. Dt 16:16. 26:2. **sweet incense**. Ex 30:34-38. 31:11. 37:29. Ps 141:2. Re 8:3, 4. **beaten**. Ex +27:20n. Is=53:5. He +=2:10.

13. **And he**. Ex 30:1, 7, 8. Nu 16:7, 18, 46. Re 8:3, 4. **the cloud**. Ex 25:21. He 4:14-16. 7:25. 9:24. 1 J 2:1, 2. **cover**. Ps=84:11.

14. **the blood of**. Le 4:5, 6, 17. 8:11. Ro 3:24-26. He 9:7, 13, 25. 10:4, 10-12, 19. 12:24. **eastward**. Le +1:16. **blood with**. Le 4:6. 17:11. He 9:22, 25. 10:4. 12:24. 13:20. **seven**. ver. 19. Nu 19:4. 1 K 18:43, 44.

15. **Then shall**. ver. 5-9. He 2:17. 5:3. 9:7, 25, 26. **bring**. ver. 2. He 6:19. 9:3, 7, 12. **mercy seat**. He 2:17. 5:2. 6:19, 20. 9:28.

16. **an atonement**. ver. 18. Le 8:15. Ex 29:36, 37. Ezk 45:18, 19. Jn 14:3. He 9:22, 23. **all their sins**. Ps 69:5. Is 53:4, 6. **remaineth**. Heb. dwelleth. Le 15:31.

17. **no man**. Ex 34:3. Ps 22:1. 69:20. Is 43:11. 45:21. 53:6. 63:3, 5. Da 9:24. Mt=26:56. 27:46. Lk 1:10. Jn=16:32. Ac √4:12. 1 T *2:5. He 1:3. 9:7. 1 P 2:24. 3:18. **and have made**. ver. 10, 11. Lk 1:10.

18. **go out**. ver. 16. Le 4:7, 18. Ex 30:10. Ezk 43:20. Jn 17:19. He 2:11. 5:7, 8. 9:12-14, 22, 23.

19. **hallow it**. Ezk 43:18-22. Zc 13:1.

20. **reconciling**. ver. 16. Le 6:30. 8:15. Ezk 45:20. 2 C 5:19. Col=1:20. **live goat**. Ro 4:25. 8:34. He 7:25. Re 1:18.

21. **lay**. See on Le 1:4. Ex 29:10. **confess over**. Le 26:40. Ezr 10:1. Ne 1:6, 7. 9:3, etc. Ps 32:5. 51:3. Pr 28:13. Da 9:3-20. Ro 10:10. **putting**. Is 53:6. 2 C 5:21. **a fit man**. Heb. a man of opportunity. ✳S#6261h, only here. The man that took the scape goat into the wilderness, and they that burned the sin offering, were to be looked upon as ceremonially unclean, and must not come into the camp till they had washed their clothes and bathed their flesh in water, which signified the defiling nature of sin; even the sacrifice which was made sin, was defiling: also the imperfection of the legal sacrifices, they were so far from taking away sin, that they left some stain even upon those that touched them.

22. **bear upon**. Is 53:11, 12. Jn 1:29. Ga 3:13. He 9:28. 1 P 2:24. **not inhabited**. Heb. of separation. Ps 103:10, 12. Ezk 18:22. Mi 7:19. **let go**. Le 14:7. **in the wilderness**. Ps=103:12. Is 38:17. 44:22. Je 31:34. 50:20. Jn=1:29. 1 J 1:7.

23. **shall put off**. ver. 4. Ezk 42:14. 44:19. Ro 8:3. Ph 2:6-11. He 9:28.

24. **wash**. Heb. *rahats*, Ex +29:4. ver. 4. Le 8:6. 14:9. 22:6. Ex 29:4. He +*9:10n. +*10:19-22. Re 1:5, 6. **his flesh**. He +√9:10n. **with water**. Ex *30:19n. Ac +*1:5n. **in the holy place**. This phrase specifies where the washing took place. Samuel J. Baird notes

"On the day of atonement, the high priest was required, at a certain time in the order of the observance for the day, being alone in the sanctuary, to 'wash his flesh with water in the holy place.' Here, at least, there is no room for controversy. The laver was outside the door of the tabernacle. The priest was within, 'in the holy place.' In it, there was no vessel in which an immersion could take place. Immersion was not only improbable.—It was impossible. The circumstances require us to accept the language of the place, just as it stands; and to believe that the high priest, on this occasion *washed* himself, and that he did so, as all washings of the person are performed, '*with* water,' as an instrumental means; and that it was applied with his own hands to his own person" (*A History of Bible Baptism*, p. 132). See related notes (Ex 30:19n, 21n. Lk 7:44n. He +*9:10n). **his garments**. Le 8:7-9. Ex 28:4, etc. 29:5. **his burnt**. ver. 3, 5. **and make**. ver. 17.

25. **the fat**. ver. 6. Le 4:8-10, 19. Ex 29:13.

26. **he that**. ver. 10, 21, 22. **wash**. ver. 28. Le 14:8. 15:5-11, 27. Nu 19:7, 8, 21. He 7:19. 13:11.

27. **bullock**. Le 4:11, 12, 21. 6:30. 8:17. **without**. Mt 27:31-33. He 13:11-14.

28. **wash his clothes**. See on ver. 26.

29. **for ever**. Heb. *olam*, Ex +12:24. **in the seventh**. Le 23:27-32. Ex 30:10. Nu 29:7. 1 K 8:2. Ezr 3:1. Ga=4:4. **shall afflict**. Le 23:27, 29, 32. Ps *35:13mg. 69:10. Is *58:3, 5. Da 10:3, 12. Mt 26:36-39. Lk 12:50. 1 C 11:31. 2 C 7:10, 11. Ph 2:5-8. He 5:7, 8. **souls**. Heb. *nephesh*, Ge +27:31. **do no**. Le 23:3, 7, 8, 21, 28, 36. Ex 12:16. 20:10. Is 58:13. He 4:10.

30. **atonement**. Le +23:27. He 9:14. **to cleanse**. Ps 51:2, 7, 10. Je 33:8. Ezk 36:25-27. Ep 5:26. T 2:14. He 9:13, 14. 10:1, 2. 1 J 1:7-9. **your sins**. Mt 26:27, 28. Lk 7:47, 50. 1 C 15:3. 1 P 2:24. 3:18.

31. **a sabbath**. Le 23:32. 25:4. Ex 31:15. 35:2. **of rest**. He 4:10, 11. **souls**. Heb. *nephesh*, Ge +27:31. **for ever**. Heb. *olam*, Ex +12:24.

32. **the priest**. Le 4:3, 5, 16. **consecrate**. Heb. fill his hand. ✍121S3P, Ex +28:41. Ex 29:9mg. **father's stead**. He 5:4, 6. 7:23. **to minister**. Ex 29:29, 30. Nu 20:26-28. **put on the linen**. See on ver. 4. **holy garments**. Ex 29:29, 30.

33. **an atonement**. See on ver. 6, 16, 18, 19, 24. Ex 20:29, 30. He 5:3. 9:14. 1 P 1:19. **for all**. Mk 16:15. Lk 2:10. 2 C=5:15. 1 T=2:6. He=2:9. 1 J 2:2.

34. **an everlasting**. Heb. *olam*, Ge +17:7. Le 23:31. Ex 12:14. Nu 29:7. 2 S 23:5. **atonement**. Le +23:27. **once a year**. Ex 30:10. He 9:7, 25. 10:3, 14.

LEVITICUS 17

The blood of all slain beasts must be offered to the Lord at the door of the tabernacle, 1-6. No sacrifices may be offered to devils, 7-9. All eating of blood is forbidden, 10-14; and of all that dieth by itself, or is torn, 15, 16.

3. **be of**. ver. 8, 12, 13, 15. **that killeth an**. ✍63H, Ge +12:15. Dt 12:5-7, 11-15, 20-22, 26, 27.

4. **bringeth**. Le 1:3. Dt *12:5, 6, 13, 14. Ezk 20:40. Jn 10:7, 9. 14:6. Ro *5:13. He *3:12. Ja +*4:17. **blood shall**. Le 7:18. Ps 32:2. Ro 4:6. 5:13, 20. Phm 18, 19. **he hath**. Is *66:3. **be cut off**. ver. 10, 14. Le 18:29. 20:3, 16, 18. Ge 17:14. Ex 12:15, 19. Nu 15:30, 31.

5. **in the open.** Ge *21:33. *22:2, 13. 31:54. Dt *12:2. 1 K 14:23. 2 K 16:4. 17:10. 2 Ch 28:4. Ps *16:4. Ezk 20:28. 22:9. **and offer them.** Le ch. 3. 7:11-21. Ex 24:5. **peace offerings.** Le +23:19.

6. **sprinkle.** Le 3:2, 8, 13. **burn the fat.** Le 3:5, 11, 16. *4:31. Ex 29:13, 18. Nu *18:17. **sweet savor.** Ex 29:18.

7. **unto devils.** Dt *32:17. 2 Ch *11:15. Ps *106:37, 39. Jn 12:31. 14:30. 1 C *10:20. 2 C 4:4. Ep 2:2. Re 9:20. **devils,** *Seirim,* properly signifies *hairy,* or *hairy ones;* and hence is used not only for *he-goats,* but also for some fabulous beings or sylvan gods, to whom was ascribed the form of goats. Maimonides says that the Zabian idolaters worshipped demons under the form of goats; and that this custom being spread among other nations, gave occasion to this precept. He-goats, however, are probably intended here, which were objects of divine honor among the Egyptians under the name of Mendes. Herodotus says that all goats were worshipped in Egypt; but particularly *he-goats.* From these seem to have sprung Pan, Silenus, and the innumerable herd of those imaginary beings, fauns, satyrs, dryads, etc., all woodland gods, and held in veneration by the Greeks and Romans. **gone a whoring.** Though this phrase is equivalent, in Scripture, to that of committing idolatry, yet it is to be taken sometimes in a literal sense. Baalpeor and Ashtaroth were worshipped with obscene rites; and public prostitution formed a great part of the worship among the Egyptians, Moabites, Canaanites, Greeks, and Romans. Le 20:5. Ex 34:15. Dt 31:16. Je 3:1. Ezk 23:8. Re 17:1-5. **for ever.** Heb. *olam,* Ex +12:24.

8. **that offereth.** ver. 4, 10. Le *1:2, 3. Jg 6:26. 1 S 7:9. 10:8. 16:2. 2 S 24:25. 1 K 18:30-38. Ml 1:11. **burnt offering.** Le +23:12.

9. **bringeth.** ver. 4.

10. **soul.** Heb. *nephesh,* Ge +17:14. **that eateth.** ver. 11. Le *3:17n. 7:26, 27. 19:26. Ge *9:4. Dt 12:16, 23. 15:23. 1 S *14:33. Ezk 33:35. 44:7. Ac *15:20, 29. +*21:25. He 10:29. **I will.** Le 20:3-6. 26:17. Ps 34:16. Je 21:10. 44:11. Ezk 14:8. 15:7. **face.** ✕22A4, Ge +19:13.

11. **the life.** Heb. *nephesh,* soul, Ge +√2:19. ✕121A7, Ge +9:5. ver. 14. Ge 9:4, +15. Dt 12:23. 2 S 14:7. 1 Ch 11:19. Est 8:11. Mt +*2:20. 27:4, 24. Lk 12:22. **flesh.** Nu 16:22. **I have given.** Le 8:15. 16:11, 14-19. Mt 20:28. *26:28. Mk 14:24. Jn *6:53. *19:34. Ro *3:25. *5:9. Ep *1:7. Col *1:14, 20. He +=2:10. =9:22. 13:12. 1 P 1:2. 1 J √1:7. 2:2. Re *1:5. **souls.** Heb. *nephesh,* Ge +12:13. Le 26:15. 1 S 1:26. 2 C +*12:15mg.

12. **soul.** Heb. *nephesh,* Ge +27:31. **eat blood.** Le 3:17n. 7:26, 27. 19:26. Dt 12:16, 23. 15:23. 1 S 14:33, 34. 1 Ch *11:19. Ezk 33:25. Ac 15:20, 29. 21:25. **neither.** Ex 12:49.

13. **which hunteth.** Le 7:26. **hunteth.** Heb. hunteth any hunting. **pour out.** Dt 12:16, 24. 15:23. 1 S 14:32-34. Jb 16:18. **cover.** Ezk *24:7, 8.

14. **life.** Heb. *nephesh,* soul, Ge +√2:19. ver. +11, +12. Ge *9:4, +15. Dt 12:23.

15. **every.** Le 22:8. Ex 22:31. Dt 14:21. Ezk 4:14. 44:31. **soul.** Heb. *nephesh,* Ge +27:31. **that which died of itself.** Heb. a carcass. S#5038h, Le 5:2. 7:24mg. 11:8, 11, 24, 25, 27, 28, 35, 36, 37, 38, 39, 40, 40. 22:8. **both wash.** S#3526h, Nu +19:21. Le 11:25. 15:5, 10, 21. Nu 19:8, 19, 21. Re 7:14. **bathe.** S#7364h,

Ex +29:4. 2 K 5:10n. **in water.** Le 11:32n. ❶16:24n. Ex 30:19n.

16. **shall bear.** Le 5:1. 7:18. 19:8. 20:17, 19, 20. Nu 19:19, 20. Is *53:11. Jn *13:8. Ac *15:20. He *9:28. 1 P *2:24. Re *2:18. *3:4.

LEVITICUS 18

The customs of Canaan and Egypt to be avoided, and God's commands obeyed, 1-5. Laws restricting marriage among relations, 6-18; and against base lusts and idolatries, enforced by the judgments about to be executed on the Canaanites, 19-30.

2. **I am the.** ver. 4. Le 11:44. 19:3, 4, 10, 34. 20:7. Ge 17:7. Ex 6:7. 20:2. Ps 33:12. Ezk 20:5, 7, 19, 20.

3. **the doings.** Ps 106:35. Ezk 20:7, 8. 23:8. Ep 5:7-11. 1 P 4:2-4. **not do.** Dt 12:30, 31. 2 C 6:17, 18. **and after.** Le 20:23. Ex 23:24. Dt 12:4, 30, 31. Je 10:2, 3. Ro 12:2.

4. **do my.** ver. 26. Le 19:37. 20:22. Dt 4:1, 2. 6:1. Ps 105:45. 119:4. Ezk 20:19. 36:27. 37:24. Lk 1:6. Jn 15:14.

5. **which if a man do.** Ge 4:7. Dt 4:1, 2. 6:25. Ne 9:29. Ec *7:20. Ezk 20:11, 13, 21. Lk 10:28, 29. Ro *3:10. 10:3,)5, 6. Ga *)3:12. Ja 2:10. 2 P 1:4. **I am the Lord.** Ex 6:2, 6, 29. Ml 3:6.

6. **near to kin.** Heb. remainder of his flesh. Le 20:19. Notwithstanding the prohibitions here, it must be evident, that in the infancy of the world, persons very near of kin, and even brothers and sisters, must have joined in matrimonial alliances; and therefore we cannot pronounce them immoral in themselves. But, in these first instances, necessity required it; but when this necessity no longer existed, the practice became inexpedient and improper. These prohibitions are, therefore, to be considered so eminently moral obligations as to be observed by all mankind. Ge 5:4n. Je 51:35mg. **to uncover.** ver. 7-19. Le 20:11, 12, 17-21. Mk 7:21, 22. 1 C 5:1. 6:9, 10, 13. Ga 5:19-21. Ep 5:3-7.

7. **not uncover.** Le 20:11. Ge 19:32. Ezk 22:10.

8. **nakedness of.** Le 20:11. Ge 35:22. 49:4. Dt 22:30. 27:20. 2 S 16:21, 22. Ezk 22:10. Am 2:7. 1 C 5:1. 7:2.

9. **thy sister.** Le 20:17. Dt 27:22. 2 S 13:11-14. Ezk 22:11.

11. **thy sister.** 2 S 13:12. Ezk 22:11.

12. **father's sister.** Le 20:19. Ex 6:20.

14. **father's brother.** Le 20:20.

15. **daughter-in-law.** Le 20:12. Ge 38:18, 19, 26. Ps 19:12, 13. Ezk 22:11.

16. **brother's wife.** Le 20:21. Dt 25:5. Mt 14:3, 4. 22:24. Mk 6:17. 12:19. Lk 3:19.

17. **a woman.** Le 20:14. Dt 27:23. Am 2:7. **it is wickedness.** Le 20:14.

18. **wife.** *or,* one wife to another. Ge +4:19. 29:28. Ex 26:3. **to vex her.** Ge 29:21-30. 30:15. 1 S 1:6-8. Ml 2:15.

19. **as long.** Le 15:19, 24. 20:18. Ezk 18:6. 22:10.

20. **shalt not lie.** Le 20:10. Ge ❶38:9. Ex 20:14. Dt 5:18. 22:22, 25. 2 S 11:3, 4, 27. Pr 6:25, 29-33. Ml 3:5. Mt 5:27, 28. Ro 2:22. 1 C 6:9. Ga 5:19. 1 Th 4:3-8. He 13:4. **with.** Le 20:13 (both), w Jn 8:5, 6.

21. **pass through.** Le 20:2. Ex 13:12mg. Dt 12:31. 18:10. 2 K 16:3. 17:17. 21:6. +23:10. 2 Ch 28:3. 33:6. Ps 106:37, 38. Je 7:31. 19:5. 32:35. Ezk 20:31. 23:37,

39. **to Molech**. i.e. *king*, *S#4432h. Le 18:21. 20:2, 3, 4, 5. 1 K 11:7h, 33. 2 K 23:10h. Je 32:35h. Am 5:26. Ac 7:43, Moloch. **profane**. Le 19:12. 20:2-5. 21:6. 22:2, 32. Ezk 36:20-23. Ml 1:12. Ro 1:23. 2:24.

22. **lie with mankind**. Homosexuality is not a legitimate alternative life style, it is a sin which in Israel merited the death penalty. In the New Testament it is a sin the practice of which disqualifies the individual from inheriting the kingdom of God (1 C √6:9, 10. Ga 5:21. Ep 5:5). No saved individuals practice this sin. Believers are to hate the sin, but love the sinner, and exercise compassion toward such lost individuals, seeking to win them to a saving knowledge of Christ (1 C 6:11. Ja 5:20. Ju 22, 23). The passage of human laws in an attempt to legitimatize the practice as a life style are directly contrary to the word of God, and will subject the offending nation to the wrath of God (ver. 24. Ps 9:17). Under no circumstances are Bible believing Christians to support financially or otherwise the activities of groups which support the practice of homosexuality or lesbianism, or which otherwise advocate the "rights" of those who practice these sins (2 Ch +*19:2. Ps +*119:63. 2 C *6:17. Ep 5:7). Le *20:13. Ge *19:5, 24. Jg *19:22. 1 K *14:24. Ro +*1:26, 27. 1 C +√6:9. 1 T *1:10. He ❍*13:4. 2 P +*2:6. Ju *7.

23. **any beast**. Le 20:15, 16. Ex 22:19. **confusion**. Le 20:12.

24. **Defile**. ver. 6-23, 30. Je 44:4. Mt 15:18-20. Mk 7:10-23. 1 C *3:17. +*6:9-11. 2 C *6:17. **for**. Le 20:22, 23. Dt 12:31. 18:12.

25. **the land**. Nu 35:33, 34. Ps 106:38. Is 24:5. Je 2:7. 16:18. Ezk 36:17, 18. Ro 8:22. **therefore**. Ps 89:32. Is 26:21. Je 5:9, 29. 9:9. 14:10. 23:2. Ho 2:13. 8:13. 9:9. Col 3:5-11. Ju 7, 8. **vomiteth**. ✓155D, Ge +4:10. ver. 28. Le 20:22.

26. **keep**. ver. 5, 30. Dt 4:1, 2, 40. *12:32. Ps 105:44, 45. Lk +*8:15. +*11:28. Jn 14:15, 21-23. +*15:14. **nor any stranger**. Le 17:8, 10. Je +*10:2.

27. **abominations**. ver. 24. Dt 20:18. 23:18. 25:16. 27:15. 1 K 14:24. 2 K 16:3. 21:2. 2 Ch 36:14. Ezk *16:50. 22:11. Ho 9:10.

28. **spew**. ✓155D. Ge +4:10. ver. 25. Le 20:22. Je 9:19. Ezk 36:13, 17. Ro *8:22. Re 2:20, 21. *3:16.

29. **souls**. Heb. *nephesh*, Ge +17:14. **cut off**. Le 17:10. 20:6. See on Ex 12:15.

30. **abominable**. ver. 3, 26, 27. Le 20:23. Dt 18:9-12. **that ye defile**. ver. 24. Ps 69:5. 106:29-31. Ezk +*16:49. **I am**. See on ver. 2, 4. Le 19:4.

LEVITICUS 19

Miscellaneous laws, moral and ceremonial, being in general repetitions or explanations of precepts before given, regarding honor to parents and sabbath observance, 1-4; against idolatry, 5; free will peace offerings, 5-8; the law of gleanings and benevolence to the poor, 9, 10; theft, falsehood, forbidden, 11, 12; wage fraud and oppression of employees forbidden, prompt payment of wages commanded, 13; cruelty to the handicapped forbidden, 14; all unjust legal decisions forbidden, 15; talebearing forbidden, 16; love to brother, neighbor, and reproof enjoined, 17; law against revenge and retaliation, command to love neighbor as thyself, 18; additional laws regarding agricultural practice, etc., 19; against adultery and its atonement,

20-22; horticultural laws, 21-25; laws against eating blood, the use of enchantment, and the practice of augury and astrology, 26; prostitution forbidden, 29; occult practices and witchcraft forbidden, 31; honor and respect for the aged enjoined, 32; justice and love for foreigners commanded, 33, 34; honest dealings in business required, 35-37.

2. **Ye shall**. Le 11:44, 45. 20:7, 26. 21:8. Ge *5:24. +*17:1. Ex 19:6. Jb *1:1. Ps *37:31, 37. Is 6:3, 4. Am *3:3. Mt *5:48. Jn +*17:6. 2 C 6:14-16. 7:1. Ph *3:20, 21. Col √1:28. 1 P *1:15, ▸16. Ju *24, 25.

3. **fear**. Ex +*20:12. 21:15, 17. Dt 21:18-21. 27:16. Pr 1:8. 6:20, 21. 23:22. 30:11, 17. Ezk 22:7. Ml 1:6. Mt 15:4-6. Lk *2:51. Ep √6:1-3. He 12:9. **keep**. ver. 30. Le 26:2. Ex 16:29. +*20:8. *31:13-17. Is 56:4-6. +*58:13n. Ezk 20:12, 20. 22:8. Mk ❍2:27, 28. Col ❍*2:16.

4. **not unto**. Le *26:1. See on Ex +*20:3-5. 1 C *10:14. 1 J *5:21. **molten gods**. Ex 20:23. 32:4. 34:17. Dt 27:15. Hab 2:18.

5. **peace offerings**. Le ch. 3. 7:16. 22:21. Ex 24:5. Le +*23:19. 2 Ch 31:2. Ezk 45:15-17. 46:2, 12. Ep 2:13, 14. **ye shall**. Le 1:3. 22:19, 23, 29. **your own will**. The Hebrews had several kinds of offerings, which they called *corban* (Le 1:2n. Mk 7:11n) Some were free-will offerings, and others were of obligation. The firstfruits, the tenths, and the sin offerings were of obligation; the peace offerings, vows, offerings of oil, wine, bread, and other things which were made to the temple, or to the ministers of the Lord, were offerings of devotion: these constituted the greater part. They indeed were a shadow of good things to come, which we enjoy in full fruition through the one great sacrifice, even Jesus Christ.

6. **shall be eaten**. Le 7:11-17. **third**. Le=23:11. Ge +22:4. 40:20. Ex 10:22. Lk=24:46. Ro 5:1. 1 C 11:26-28. +=15:4. Ep 2:14.

7. **abominable**. Is 1:13. 65:4. 66:3. Je 16:18. **third day**. Lk *24:46. Ro 5:1. Ep 2:14. **it shall**. See on Le 7:18-21. 22:23, 25. 1 C 11:26-28.

8. **shall bear**. Le 5:1. **profaned**. Le 22:2, 32. Ex +*20:7. Nu 30:2mg. Ne 13:17. Ps 55:20mg. Je 23:11. Ezk 22:8, 26. 23:38. Am +2:7. Mt 12:5. 1 T 1:9. 4:7. 6:20. 2 T 2:16. He 12:16. **soul**. Heb. *nephesh*, Ge +17:14. **cut off**. Ex 30:33.

9. **ye reap the harvest**. In what code of laws merely human, is a requisition to be found so counteracting to selfishness, so encouraging to liberality, and so beneficently considering to the poor and needy? But the Mosaic dispensation, like the Christian, breathed with love to God, and benevolence to man. Le 23:22. Dt *24:19-21. Ru *2:2, 15, 16. Ps 10:2, 11, 12. Mt 26:11. Ga 2:10.

10. **glean**. Jg 8:2. Is 17:6. 24:13. Je 49:9. Ob 5. Mi 7:1. **thou shalt leave**. Le 25:6. **for the poor**. Ps 10:2, 11, 12. Pr 29:8. Ezk +*16:49. Mt *26:11. Lk +*14:13. Ga *2:10. **stranger**. Ge +*23:4 (S#1616h). Ex 12:48. Dt +26:11. Jsh +20:9. Mt +25:35.

11. **not steal**. Le 6:2. Ex +√20:15, 17. 22:1, 7, 10-12. Dt 5:19. Ps √37:21. Je 6:13. 7:9-11. Zc *5:3, 4. 8:16, 17. 1 C +*6:8-10. Ep *4:28. **deal falsely**. Am +*8:5. Mt ❍7:15. Ac +*6:3. **lie one**. Ge +*27:19. 1 K *13:18. Ps +*15:2. 101:7. 116:11. Pr 6:17, 19. 12:19, 22. 13:5. 21:6. 26:28. Is 32:7. Je 9:3-5. Jn *8:44. Ac 5:3, 4. Ro 3:4. Ep *4:25. Col *3:9. 2 Th 2:9. 1 T 1:10. 4:2. Ja 3:14. 1 J 2:21, 22. Re +*21:8. 22:15.

12. **ye shall.** Le 6:3. Ex +*20:7. Dt 5:11. Ps=15:4. Je 4:2. 7:9. Zc *5:4. Ml +*3:5. Mt *5:)33, 34. Ja *5:12. **profane.** Le 18:21. 24:11, 15, 16. Ezk 36:20-23.

13. **not defraud.** Pr 20:10. 22:22. Je 22:3. Ezk 22:29. Mk)10:19. Lk 3:13. 1 Th *4:6. **the wages.** T#1852. Dt √24:14, 15. Jb 31:39. Je +*22:13. Ml +*3:5. 1 T +√5:19n, 18. +*Ja 5:4. lit. **work.** ƒ121C1F. Metonymy of the Cause B551. Work is put for the wages paid for it. For other instances of this figure see Je 22:13. Ro 11:6. Re 14:13.

14. **not curse.** Dt *27:18. Ps 37:28. Ro 12:14. *14:13. 1 C 8:8-13. 10:32. Ja 2:1, 9, 10. Re 2:14. **fear.** ver. 32. Le 25:17. Ge 42:18. Ne 5:15. 1 P 1:17. *2:17.

15. **no unrighteousness in.** ver. 35. Ex 18:21. 23:2, 3, 7, 8. Dt 1:17. 16:19. 25:13-16. 27:19. 2 Ch 19:6, 7. Ps *37:28. 82:1-4. Pr 18:5. 24:23. 29:27. 31:4, 5. Ec 3:16. Hab +*1:4. Lk +*16:10. Jn +*7:24. Ja *2:6-9. **respect the person of the poor.** Ex +*23:3, 6. Dt 10:17. 16:19. Jb 13:10. Ps *82:1-4. Je 22:3. La 3:36. **nor honor.** Dt 1:17. Jb *32:21. *34:19. 36:19. Ml 2:9. 1 T *5:21. +*6:5. Ja *2:9. Ju *16. **in righteousness.** Dt 16:20. Ps 82:3. Pr +*18:13. 21:3. Is 56:1. Mi +*6:8. Jn +*7:24, 51. 1 T +√5:19n.

16. **talebearer.** Ex 23:1. Ps *15:3. 50:20. Pr *11:13. 20:19. Je 6:28. 9:4. Ezk *22:9. 1 T 3:11. *5:13. 2 T 3:3. T 2:3. Ja *3:6. 1 P 2:1. **stand.** Ex 20:16. *23:1, 7. 1 K 21:10-13. Mt *26:60, 61. *27:4. Ac 6:11-13. 24:4-9.

17. **hate.** Ge 27:41. Pr 26:24-26. 1 J 2:9, 11. 3:12-15. **rebuke.** Ps 141:5. Pr *3:12. 9:8. 27:5, 6. Mt √18:15-17. Lk *17:3. 1 C 13:6. Ga 2:11-14. *4:16. √6:1. Ep √5:11. 1 T *5:20. 2 T *4:2. T 1:13. 2:15. He *3:12, 13. *10:24, 25. **and not suffer sin upon him.** or, that thou bear not sin for him. Le 22:9n. Ezk 3:17, 18. Ac 20:26, 27. Ro 1:32. 1 C 5:2. 1 T 5:22. Ja *5:19, 20. 1 J 5:16. 2 J 10, 11. Ju 23.

18. **not avenge.** Ex 23:4, 5. Dt 32:35. 2 S 13:22, 28. Pr *20:22. *24:29. Mt 5:43, 44. Ro √12:17, 19. 13:4. He *10:30. **grudge.** Ga 5:20. Ep *4:31. Col 3:8. Ja *5:9. 1 P *2:1. **thou shalt love.** Mi +*6:8. Mt)5:43. 18:15.)19:19. 22:)39, 40. Mk 12:)31-34. Lk 10:)27-37. 17:3. Ro)13:9. Ga)5:14. 6:1. 1 Th *4:9. Ja)2:8. 1 P *1:22. *3:8-12. *4:15. 1 J *2:9, 11. *3:10-18. **thy neighbor.** Ex 20:16. Pr 3:28, 29. 14:21. 16:28, 29. Hab 2:15. Mk 12:31. Lk √10:29-36. Ro +12:5. 13:10. 15:2. Ga +*6:10. Ja 2:8, 9. **as thyself.** Ps +*40:17. Mt 10:31. 16:26. Ro 8:17, 18. Ga *6:4. Ep 5:29. Ph ◐+*2:3.

19. **thy cattle gender.** Ge 36:24. 2 S 13:29. 18:9. 1 K 1:33. Ezr 2:66. **diverse.** Mt *6:22, 24. Ga *2:11-18. *4:21-23. **mingled.** Dt 22:9-11. Mt 9:16, 17. Ro 11:6. 2 C 6:14-17. Ga 3:9-11. **neither.** 1 P 3:3-5.

20. **bondmaid.** Ge 12:16. 16:1, 2, 3, 5, 6, 8. **betrothed to an husband.** or, abused by any. Young states (*Concise Critical Comments*) "The original word occurs nowhere else, and has been variously rendered, e.g. gathered, plucked, reproached, by to or for a man." **she shall be scourged.** or, they. Le 20:10. Jn ◐8:5, 6. Heb. there shall be a scourging. or, there shall be an investigation. Young states "There is not the slightest ground for the monstrously unjust rendering of the Common (A.V.) Version; the noun occurring here is not found elsewhere, but the verbal form of the root occurs after. It never signifies "to scourge," nor "to animadvert or punish anyone," as Gesenius pretends. The simple meaning is "to search, seek, open up by examination;" compare all the passages where the verb

occurs, *viz.*, Le 13:36; 27:33; 2 K 16:15; Ps 27:4; Pr 20:25; Ezk 34:11, 12; compare also Ezr 5:15, 19; 5:17; 6:1; 7:14." **they shall.** Ex 21:20, 21. Dt 22:23, 24. He 7:19.

21. **trespass offering.** Le +*5:6. 6:1-7.

22. **and the sin.** See on Le 4:20, 26. 1 T *1:8-11.

23. **And when.** See on Le 14:34. **fruit.** ƒ155C. Prosopopoeia; or, Personification: the products of the earth B864. For other instances of this figure see Is 16:8. Ho 9:2. Jl 1:10. Na 1:4. Hab 3:17. **uncircumcised.** Le 12:3. 22:27. Ex 6:12, 30. 22:29, 30. Je 6:10. 9:25, 26. Ac 7:51.

24. **all the.** Nu 18:12, 13. Dt 12:17, 18. *14:28, 29. 18:4. Pr 3:9. **holy to praise the Lord withal.** Heb. holiness of praises to the Lord. Ps √50:23. *65:1. Je *17:26. **holiness.** ƒ24J, Dt +32:42. **praises.** ƒ96F2, Ge +4:10.

25. **that it may.** Le 26:3, 4. Pr 3:9, 10. Ec 11:1, 2. Hag 1:4-6, 9-11. 2:18, 19. Ml 3:8-10.

26. **with the blood.** See on Le 3:17n. 7:26. *17:10-14. Dt 12:23. 1 S *14:33. **use.** Ex 7:11. 8:7. 1 S +*15:23. Je 10:2. Da 2:10. Ml 3:5. **enchantment.** Ge +30:27. 44:5, 15. 1 K 20:33. 2 K 17:17. +*21:6. 2 Ch 33:6. **nor.** Ge ◐9:14h. Dt +*18:10-14. Jg 9:37mg. 2 K 17:17. 21:6. 2 Ch 33:6. Is 2:6. 57:3. Je *27:9. Mi 5:12.

27. **round the corners.** Le 21:5. Dt *14:1. Is *15:2. Je *9:26mg. 16:6. *48:37. Ezk 7:18. 44:20. 1 C *11:3, 4. Ep *1:22, 23. Col *1:18, 19.

28. **cuttings.** Le *21:5. Dt 14:1. 1 K *18:28. Je 16:6. 48:37. Mk 5:5. **for the.** Dt 14:1. 1 C ◐15:29. **dead.** Heb. *nephesh*, soul. Here, *nephesh* is used of man as actually dead. *Nephesh* is similarly used elsewhere, rendered *the dead* at Le 21:1. 22:4. Nu 5:2. 6:11. Rendered *dead body* at Nu 9:6, 7, 10. Rendered *body* at Le 21:11. Nu 6:6. 19:11, 13. Hag 2:13. For the other uses of *nephesh* see Ge +2:7. However, Young states here, "There is not the slightest authority for abandoning the usual meaning of the word *nephesh*, or to suppose it denotes here a corpse or dead person." Rather, it should be observed that such texts do not justify the mistaken notion that the body is the soul. While "soul" is sometimes used with reference to a body, it does not always, or usually, have this significance. Mt +√10:28n. **print.** Re 13:16, 17. 14:9, 11. 15:2. 16:2. 19:20. 20:4.

29. **prostitute.** Heb. profane. Le 18:21. 20:3. *21:9. Is 53:5 (wounded). Ezk 9:6 (begin, began). S#2490h. **to cause.** Le 21:7. Ge 18:20, 21. *19:6-8. Dt *23:17. Ho 4:12-14. Mt √18:6, 10, 14. 23:15. Mk 9:42. Lk 17:2. 1 C 6:15. **fall.** lit. go a whoring. The practice condemned is that of dedicating them to heathen temples, but the form in the original is sometimes only permissive, not causative (Young). ✚S#2181h, Kal, Future: Jg 8:27, 33. 19:2. 1 Ch 5:25. Ps 106:39. Is 57:3. Je 3:6, 8. Ezk 16:15, 16, 17, 26, 28, 28. 23:3, 5, 43. Ho 1:2. 3:3. 4:12, 13, 14. Am 7:17.

30. **keep.** See on ver. *3. Le 26:2. Ge *2:2, 3. He *4:3, 10, 11. **reverence.** Le 10:3. 15:31. 16:2. Ge *28:16, 17. 2 Ch 33:7. 36:14. Ps *89:7. Ec *5:1. Ezk 9:6. Hab *2:20. Mt 21:13. Jn 2:15, 16. 2 C 6:16. 1 T *3:15. 1 P 4:17.

31. **Regard not.** lit., turn or look, i.e. *turn the face to look*. S#6437h, Le +14:36. 19:4, 31. 20:6. Jb 36:21. **familiar spirits.** or, necromancers. ✱S#178h. ver. 26. Le 20:6, 27. Ex *22:18. Dt *18:10-14. 1 S *28:3, 7-9. 2 K 17:17. +21:6. 23:24. 1 Ch *10:13.

2 Ch 33:6. Jb 32:19h. Is *8:19. 19:3. 29:4. 47:13. Ac 8:11. 13:6-8. *16:16-18. *19:19, 20. Ga 5:20. Re +*21:8. **wizards**. lit. knowing ones. ✸S#3049h. Le 20:6, 7. Dt 18:11. 1 S 28:3, 9. 2 K +21:6. 23:24. 2 Ch 33:6. Is 8:19. 19:3.

32. **rise up**. ver. 14. Ge *31:35. +*43:27. 1 K 2:19. Jb 32:4, 6. Pr 16:31. *20:29. *23:22. *31:28. Is 3:5. La 5:12. Ro 13:7. Ep *6:1-3. 1 T *5:1. 1 P 2:17.

33. **And if**. Ex *12:48, 49. *22:21. *23:9. Dt *10:18, 19. +*24:14. Ml +*3:5. Lk √10:29, 30, 36, 37. Jn *4:6, 7, 9. **stranger**. ver. 10. Ge +23:4. **vex him**. *or*, oppress him. Le 25:14. Ex 22:21. Ps +*12:5. Je 7:6. Ezk 22:7, 29.

34. **the stranger**. ver. +10. Ge +23:4. **love him as**. See on ver. 18. Ex 12:48, 49. Dt 10:19. Mt 5:43.

35. **no unrighteousness**. See on ver. 15. **in mete-yard**. Dt *25:13, 15. Pr *11:1. *16:11. *20:10. Ezk 22:12, 13. Am *8:5, 6. Mi *6:10, 11. Mt 7:2.

36. **Just balances**. Pr *11:1. **weights**. Heb. stones. Pr 11:1mg. +16:11mg. **I am**. See on Ex 20:2.

37. **observe all**. See on Le 18:4, 5. Dt 4:1, 2, 5, 6. *5:1. 6:1, 2, 25. 8:1. Ps 119:4, 34. Mt *3:16, 17. *5:17-19. *7:21. Lk 9:35. 1 J *3:22, 23. **do them**. Ro *13:10. 1 C *13:4, 7. 1 J √2:3.

LEVITICUS 20

The man who gave of his seed to Molech must be stoned; or the Lord would cut him off, with those who connived at him, and those who consulted wizards, 1-6. Holiness required, 7, 8. Capital punishments appointed for him who cursed his parents, 9; or committed adultery, 10; or some kinds of incest, 11, 12; or sodomy, 13, 14; or bestiality, 15-17. Of uncleanness, 18-21. Obedience is required with holiness, 22-26. Witches and wizards to be stoned, 27.

2. **Again**. Is 28:10, 13. **Whosoever**. Le 17:8, 13, 15. **giveth**. Le 18:21. Dt 12:31. 18:10. 2 K 17:17. 23:10. 2 Ch 28:3. 33:6. Ps 106:38. Is 57:5, 6. Je 7:31. 32:35. Ezk 16:20, 21. 20:26, 31. 23:37, 39. Ac 7:43, Moloch. **surely**. ℐ147B, Ge +2:16. **the people**. ver. 27. Le 24:14, 23. Nu 15:35, 36. Dt 13:10, 11. 17:5-7. 21:21. Ac 7:58, 59.

3. **I will set**. Le 17:10. Pr 29:1. 1 P 3:12. **hath given**. ver. 2. 1 K 11:6-13. Is 1:2-4. Nu 19:20. Ezk 5:11. 23:38, 39. **profane**. Le 18:21. Ezk 20:39. 2 C 6:16.

4. **hide**. 1 S 3:11-13. Ps 50:18. Pr 10:10. 24:24. 28:4. Ho 7:3. Mk 14:11. Lk 11:48. Ac ◉17:30. 22:20. Ro 1:32mg. Ep 5:11. **and kill**. Dt 13:8. 17:2-5. Jsh 7:12. 1 S 3:13, 14. 1 K 20:42. Ho 9:17. Ml 2:11. Re 2:14.

5. **I will**. Le 17:10. **face**. ℐ22A4, Ge +19:13. **against his**. Ex 20:5. Je 32:28-35, 39. **whoring**. Le 17:7. Ps 106:39. Je 3:2. Ho 2:5, 13.

6. **soul**. Heb. *nephesh*, Ge +27:31. **familiar**. ver. 27. Le 19:+26, +31. Dt 18:10-14. Is 8:19. Ezk 21:21-24. **go**. Ex 34:15, 16. Nu 15:39. Ps 73:27. Ezk 6:9. Ho 4:12. **I will**. Nu 23:19. **soul**. Heb. *nephesh*, Ge +17:14. **cut him**. 1 Ch 10:13, 14.

7. **Sanctify yourselves**. Le 11:44. 19:2. Ezk 37:28. Jn 17:17, 19. Ep 1:4. 5:25-27. Ph 2:12, 13. Col 3:12. 1 Th 4:3, *6n, 7. *5:23. He *12:14. 13:12. 1 P 1:15, 16.

8. **And ye**. See on Le 18:4, 5. 19:37. Mt 5:19. 7:24. 12:50. 28:20. Jn 13:17. Ja 1:22. Re 22:14. **Lord**. Ex

+15:26. **sanctify**. Le 21:8. 22:32. Ex +15:26. 28:36. 31:13. Ezk 20:12. 37:28. 1 C 1:30. Ep 4:24. 1 Th 5:23. 2 Th 2:13. 2 T 1:9. He 3:1. *12:14.

9. **curseth**. The term *yekallel* signifies not only to *curse*, but to speak contemptuously, disrespectfully, or to make light of a person: so that all speeches which have a tendency to lessen our parents in the eyes of others, or to render their judgment, piety, etc., suspected or contemptible, is here included; though the act of cursing, or of treating the parent with injurious or opprobrious language, is what is particularly intended. He who conscientiously keeps the *fifth* commandment, can be in no danger of the judgment here denounced. Ex 21:17. Dt 27:16. Pr 20:20. 30:11, 17. Mt 15:4. Mk 7:10. Col 3:20. **surely**. ℐ147B, Ge +2:16. **his blood**. ver. 11-13, 16, 27. Jsh 2:19. Jg 9:24. 2 S 1:16. 1 K 2:32. Mt 27:25. Ac 5:28. 18:6. ℐ171I12. Synecdoche of the Species B628. *Blood* is put for *guilt* or punishment. For other instances of this figure see Dt 19:10. 21:8. 2 K 24:4. Ps 51:14. Is 1:15. ℐ117. Metalepsis; or, Double Metonymy B609. "Blood" is put by the figure Metonymy of Adjunct (ℐ121P12, B597) for guilt, and "guilt" is put by the figure Metonymy of Cause (ℐ121C1K, B552) for the penalty. For other examples of the figure Metalepsis see Ge +19:8.

10. **the adulterer**. Le 18:20. Dt 22:22-24. 2 S 12:13. Ezk 23:45-47. Jn 8:4, 5. **and the adulteress**. Le 19:20mg. Jn 8:5, 6. **surely**. ℐ147B, Ge +2:16.

11. **lieth with**. Le 18:8. Dt 27:20, 23. Am 2:7. 1 C 5:1. **surely**. ℐ147B, Ge +2:16. **their**. See on ver. 9.

12. **lie**. Le 18:15. Ge 38:16, 18, 24-26. Dt 27:23. **surely**. ℐ147B, Ge +2:16. **confusion**. Le 18:23.

13. **lie with mankind**. Le +*18:22n. Ge *19:5. Dt *23:17. Jg *19:22. Ro +*1:26, 27. 1 C +*6:9. 1 T *1:10. 2 P +*2:6. Ju *7. **surely**. ℐ147B, Ge +2:16.

14. **a wife**. Le 18:17. Dt 27:23. Am 2:7. **burnt**. Le 21:9. Jsh 7:15, 25.

15. **lie with a beast**. Le 18:23. Ex 22:19. Dt 27:21. **surely**. ℐ147B, Ge +2:16.

16. **And if a woman**. Ju 17-19. We are assured by Herodotus (in *Euterp.*) that the abominations here referred to existed among the Egyptians, and even formed a part of their superstitious religious system, and we have reason to believe that they were not uncommon among the Canaanites (See Le 18:24, 25). Need we wonder then, that God should have made laws of this nature, and appointed the punishment of death for these crimes? This one observation will account for many of those strange prohibitions which we find in the Mosaic law. **and the beast**. Ex 19:13. 21:28, 32. He 12:20. **surely**. ℐ147B, Ge +2:16.

17. **sister**. Le 18:9. Ge 20:2, 10-12. Dt 27:22. 2 S 13:12. Ezk 22:11. Ro 5:13. **wicked thing**. or, a shame. The original word (S#2617h) occurs very often in the Old Testament, and with only two other exceptions is uniformly rendered kindness, loving kindness, (goodness, mercy, in the A.V.), etc. In Job 6:14 (pity), and in Pr 14:34 (reproach), besides the present passage (in Young's *Literal Translation*), it is rendered (by way of antiphrasis) shame. ℐ27B. Figure of speech Antiphrasis; or, Permutation B691, 807: this name is given to Irony (ℐ60, Ge +3:4. +3:22; +19:2; +20:16) when it consists of one word or a single expression, as when "a court of justice" is called "a court of vengeance." For other instances of this figure see Jb 6:14. Pr 14:34.

18. **having**. Le 15:24. 18:19. Ezk 18:6. 22:10. **discovered**. Heb. made naked. ❋S#6168h. ver. 19. Ge 24:20 (emptied). Le 20:18 (discovered; mg, made naked), 19 (uncovereth). 2 Ch 24:11 (emptied). Ps 37:35 (spreading himself). 137:7 (Rase; mg, Make bare). 141:8 (destitute; mg, bare). Is 3:17 (discover; mg, make naked). 22:6 (uncovered; mg, made naked). 32:15 (be poured). ❋53:12 (hath poured out). La 4:21 (make thyself naked). Hab 3:13 (by discovering; mg, making naked). Zp 2:14 (uncover). **fountain**. ❋S#4726h, Le 12:7 (issue). Ps ❋36:9 (fountain). 68:26. Pr ❋10:11 (well).

19. **mother's**. Le 18:12, 13, etc. Ex 6:20. **uncovereth**. Le 18:6.

20. **uncle's wife**. Le 18:14. **sin**. ℐ121C1E, Ge +19:15. **childless**. Jb 18:19. Ps 109:13. Je 22:30. Lk 1:7, 25. 23:29.

21. **his brother's**. Le 18:16. Mt 14:3, 4. **an unclean thing**. Heb. a separation. Le 12:2, 5, etc.

22. **statutes**. Le 18:4, 5, 26. 19:37. Ps 19:8-11. 105:45. 119:80, 145, 171. Ezk 36:27. **judgments**. Ex 21:1. Dt 4:45. 5:1. Ps 119:20, 106, 160, 164, 175. Is 26:8, 9. **spue you**. Le 18:25-28. 26:33. Dt 28:25, 26.

23. **in the manners**. Le 18:3, 24, 30. Dt 12:30, 31. Je 10:1, 2. 1 Th 4:3-7. T 3:3-6. **therefore**. Le 18:27. Dt 9:5. Ps 78:59. Zc 11:8.

24. **But I**. See on Ex 3:8, 17. 6:8. He ◐11:16. **a land**. Ex 3:17. Dt 32:13, 14. Jg 14:8. 1 S 14:25, 26. Ps 16:11. 81:11-16. Jn=14:2. 1 C 2:9. Re 22:2. Milk and honey were the chief dainties of the ancients. Hence not only the Hebrews, but also the Greeks and Romans, painted the highest pleasantness and fertility by an abundance of milk and honey. The image used in the text, and frequently by ancient authors on similar subjects, is a metaphor, derived from a breast, producing copious streams of milk. **milk and**. ℐ174, Ge +18:27. **honey**. ℐ171I7, Ex +3:8. **which**. ver. 26. Ex 19:5, 6. 33:16. Nu 23:9. Dt 7:6. 14:2. 1 K 8:53. Ho 11:1-3. Jn 15:19. 2 C 6:17. 1 P 2:9.

25. **put a difference**. Le ch. 11. Dt 14:3-21. Ac 10:11-15, 28. Ep 5:7-11. **souls**. Heb. *nephesh*, Ge +27:31. **abominable**. Le 11:43. **creepeth**. or, moveth. Le 11:44, 46. Ge 1:21. 7:8. Ps 69:34. 104:20.

26. **the Lord**. ver. 7. Le 19:2. Ps 99:5, 9. Is 6:3. 30:11. 1 P 1:15, 16. Re 3:7. 4:8. **severed**. ver. 24. Dt 7:6. 14:2. 26:18, 19. T 2:14.

27. **a familiar**. ver. 6. Le +❋19:31. Ex 22:18. Dt +❋18:10-12. 1 S 28:7-9. 1 Ch 10:13, 14. **surely**. ℐ147B, Ge +2:16. **they shall stone**. ver. 2. **their blood**. See on ver. 9.

LEVITICUS 21

Laws for the mourning of the priests, 1-5; for their holiness, 6; for their marriages, 7; of their estimation, 8; the punishment of a priest's daughter convicted of fornication, 9; of the high priest's holiness, 10-12; of his marriage, 13-15. The bodily blemishes which excluded from the work of the priesthood in the sanctuary, 16-24.

1. **Speak**. Ho 5:1. Ml 2:1, 4. **There**. ver. 11. Le 10:6, 7. Nu 19:14, 16. Ezk 44:25. **the dead**. Heb. *nephesh*, soul, Le +19:28.

2. **kin**. Le 18:6. Ezk 24:16-18. 1 Th 4:13.

4. **he shall**. or, the verse may be read, *being an husband among his people, he shall not defile himself for his wife*, etc. Ezk 24:16, 17. **chief man**. ℐ63G,

Ge +50:23. Supply by ellipsis "a chief man (*a priest*) among his people, shall not defile himself (*for his wife*) to profane himself" B61. ver. 14.

5. **not make baldness**. This custom is also called 'rounding the corners of the head' (Le 19:27), and seems to have been performed in honor of some idol. Herodotus observes (l. iii. c. 8) that the Arabs shave, or cut their hair round, in honor of Bacchus, who, they say, had his hair cut in this way. He also says (l. iv. c. 175) that the Macians, a people of Lybia, cut their hair round, so as to leave a tuft on the top of the head. In this way the Chinese still cut their hair. The hair was much used in divination among the ancients: and for purposes of religious superstition among the Greeks (See Homer, *Iliad*, xxiii. v. 142. and Virgil, *Aenead*, iv. 698). Le 10:6. 19:27, 28. Dt 14:1. Is 15:2. 22:12. Je 9:26n. 16:6. 41:5. 48:37. Ezk 44:20. Am 8:10. Mi 1:16.

6. **holy**. ver. 8. Le 10:3. Ex 28:36. 29:44. Ezr 8:28. Ps 132:9, 16. 1 P 2:5, 9. Re 1:6. 20:6. **profane**. Le 18:21. 19:+❋8, 12. 22:2, 22. Je 23:11. Ezk 22:26. Ml 1:6, 11, 12. **bread**. ℐ171I8, Ge +3:19. Le 3:11. Ezk 44:7. Ml 1:7. **therefore**. Is 52:11.

7. **that is a whore**. ver. 8. Ezk 44:22. 1 T 3:11. **put away**. Dt 24:1-4. Is 50:1. **for he**. 1 T 3:2, 8, 9, 11, 12.

8. **sanctify**. ver. 6. Ex 19:10, 14. 28:41. 29:1, 43, 44. Jn 17:17, 19. **bread**. ℐ171I8, Ge +3:19. **for I**. Le 11:44, 45. 19:2. 20:7, 8. Jn 10:36. 17:19. He 7:26. 10:29. **Lord**. Ex +15:26.

9. **the daughter**. 1 S 2:17, 34. 3:13, 14. Ezk 9:6. Ml 2:3. Mt 11:20-24. 1 T 3:4, 5. T 1:6. **she shall be burnt**. Le 20:14. Ge 38:24. Jsh 7:15, 25. Is 33:14. Re 21:8.

10. **high priest among**. He 2:17. 3:1. 4:14, ❋15. 7:26. **upon**. Le 8:12. 10:7. 16:32. Ex 29:29, 30. Nu 35:25. Ps 133:2. **consecrated**. Le 8:7-9. Ex 28:2-4. **uncover**. Le 10:6, 7. 13:45. 2 S 15:30. Est 6:12. **nor rend**. Ge 37:34. Jb 1:20. Mt 26:65.

11. **body**. Heb. *nephesh*, soul, Le +19:28. **his father**. ver. 1, 2. Nu 6:7. 19:14. Dt 33:9. Mt 8:21, 22. 12:46-50. Lk 9:59, 60. 14:26. 2 C 5:16.

12. **go out**. Le 10:7. **for the crown**. Le 8:9-12, 30. Ex 28:36. 29:6, 7. Is 61:1. Ac 10:38.

13. **take a wife**. ver. 7. Ezk 44:22. 2 C 11:2. Re 14:4. **virginity**. ❋S#1331h. Dt 22:14, 15, 17, 20. Jg 11:37, 38. Ezk 23:❋3, 8. For ❋S#1330h, see Ge 24:16. For ❋S#5959h, *almah*, see Ge +24:43.

14. **take a virgin**. SS 6:9. 2 C 11:2. Ep 5:27. ❋S#1330h, Ge +24:16.

15. **profane**. Ge 18:19. Ezr 2:62. 9:2. Ne 13:23-29. Ml 2:11, 15. Ro 11:16. 1 C 7:14. 2 C 6:14-18. **for I the**. ver. 8.

17. **blemish**. Le 22:20-25. 1 Th 2:10. 1 T 3:2. He 7:26. **let him**. ver. 21. Le 10:3. Nu 16:5. Ps 65:4. 1 T 4:12. 1 P 5:3. **bread**. or, food. ℐ171I8, Ge +3:19. Le 3:11, 16.

18. **a blind man**. Is 56:10. Mt 23:16, 17, 19. 1 T 3:2, 3, 7. T 1:7, 10. **superfluous**. Ge 22:23.

20. **a dwarf**. or, too slender. ❋S#1851h. Ge 41:3 (lean), 4, 6 (thin), 23, 24. Ex 16:14 (small). Le 13:30 (thin). ❋16:12 (small). 21:20 (dwarf; mg, too slender). 1 K ❋19:12 (small). Is 29:5. 40:15 (very little thing). **or hath**. Dt 23:1n. **stones**. ❋S#810h, only here. **broken**. ver. 24. Is 56:3. Mt 19:12.

21. **a blemish**. In the above list of blemishes, we

meet with some that might render the priest contemptible in the eyes of men; and others that would be very great impediments in the discharge of his ministerial duties. Mt 5:48. Lk 6:40. 2 C 13:9. Col 1:28. 2 T 3:17. Ja 1:4. 3:2. 1 P 5:10. **to offer.** ver. 6, 8, 17. Jn 6:51. He 7:27. **bread.** ♪171I8, Ge +3:19.

22. **bread.** ♪171I8, Ge +3:19. **both.** Le 2:3, 10. 6:16, 17, 29. 7:1. 24:8, 9. Nu 18:9, 10. **and of the holy.** Le 22:10-13. Nu 18:10, 19.

23. **go in.** Ex 30:6-8. 40:26, 27. Ezk 44:9-14. **profane.** ver. 12. Le 15:31. **for I the Lord.** ver. 8. 1 P 1:15, 16.

24. **Moses told.** He 3:2. **Aaron.** Ml 2:1-7. Col 4:17. 1 T 1:18. 2 T 2:2.

LEVITICUS 22

The priests must not eat of the holy things when unclean, 1-5; how they shall be cleansed, 6-9; Who of the priest's house may eat of the holy things, 10-13. The restitution to be made by him who had unwittingly eaten of them, 14-16. The sacrifices must be without blemish, and above seven days old, 17-28. The law of eating the sacrifices of thanksgiving, 29, 30. Calls to obedience, 31-33.

2. **separate themselves.** ver. 3-6. Le 15:31. Nu 6:3-8. **that they profane not.** ver. 32. Le 18:21. 19:12. 20:3. 21:6. Nu 18:32. 1 S 2:12-17. Ezk 44:21. **hallow.** Ex 13:12. 28:38. Nu 18:32. Dt 15:19.

3. **having his uncleanness upon him.** Le 7:20, 21. Ps 89:7. **that soul.** Heb. *nephesh*, Ge +17:14. **cut off.** Le 10:1, 2. Ex 30:33. **from my.** Ex 33:14, 15. Ps 16:11. 51:11. Mt 25:41. 2 Th 1:9.

4. **the seed.** These words include the daughters as well as the sons of Aaron. **a leper.** Le 13:2, 3, 44-46. **running issue.** Heb. running of the reins. Le 15:2, 3. **shall not eat.** Lk=15:17. **holy things.** Le 2:3, 10. 6:25-29. 21:22. Nu 18:9, 19. **until.** Le 14:2, etc. 15:13-15. **unclean.** Le 21:1. Nu 19:11-16. 1 Th 4:3, 4, 7. Ju 23. **the dead.** Heb. *nephesh*, soul, Le +19:28. **whose.** Le 15:16. **seed goeth.** S#7902h, Le +15:16. Ge +*38:9.

5. **whosoever.** Le 11:23, 24, 43, 44. **or a man.** Le 15:7, 19.

6. **soul.** Heb. *nephesh*, Ge +27:31. **which hath.** Le 11:24, 25. 15:5. 16:24-28. Nu 19:7-10. Hg 2:13. 1 C 6:11. He 7:26. *10:22.

7. **sun is down.** 1 J=1:6, 7. **because it.** Le 21:22. Nu 18:11-19. Dt 18:3, 4. 1 C 9:4, 13, 14.

8. **dieth of itself.** Le 17:15. Ex 22:31. Dt 14:21. Ezk 44:31.

9. **bear sin for it.** ♪121C1E, Ge +19:15. That is, be punished if he break it. Le 10:1, 2. 16:2. *19:17mg. Ex 28:43. Nu 18:22, 32. **profane.** La 4:13, 14. Ezk 22:26. Mi 3:11, 12. Zp 3:4. **Lord.** Ex +15:26.

10. **shall no.** 1 S 21:6. Mt 12:4. **stranger.** The word *zar*, a stranger, does not mean one of another nation, a *foreigner*, which is expressed by *hechar*, but one who is not of the seed of Aaron, or does not belong to his family. Ep=2:12, 19. **sojourner.** 1 J=2:19. **hired servant.** Lk=15:18, 19. Jn 10:12, 13. =15:15.

11. **buy.** Ac=20:28. 1 C=6:20. 1 P=1:18, 19. **soul.** Heb. *nephesh*, Ge +12:5. **his money.** Heb. the purchase of his money. Ge 17:13. Nu 18:11-13. 1 C 6:19, 20. **born.** 2 C 6:18. Ga 6:10. Ep 3:14, 15. 1 P=1:23. 2:2. **eat of.** 1 C 9:13, 14.

12. **a stranger.** Heb. a man, a stranger. Le 21:3. Is +40:13mg.

13. **returned unto her father's house.** Ge 38:11. **as in her.** Le 10:14. Nu 18:11-19.

14. **eat of.** Le 5:15-19. 27:13, 15. **unwittingly.** Nu 15:24-29. **fifth part.** Le 6:5. 27:13. Ps 19:12. 139:23, 24.

15. **not profane.** ver. 9. Le 19:8. Nu 18:32. Ezk 22:26.

16. **suffer them to bear the iniquity of trespass.** *or*, lade themselves with the iniquity of trespass in their eating. Le 19:17. **bear.** Le 7:18. 1 S 2:12-17. Ps 38:4. Is 53:11, 12. 1 P 2:24. **for I.** ver. 9. Le 20:8. **Lord.** Ex +15:26.

18. **Whatsoever.** Le 1:2, 10. 17:10, 13. **of the strangers.** Nu 15:14-16. **vows.** Le 7:16. +*23:38. Nu 15:3. Dt 12:6. Ps 22:25. 56:12. 61:5, 8. 65:1. 66:13. 116:14, 18. Ec 5:4. Jon 1:16. 2:9. Na 1:15. Ac 18:18. **freewill offerings.** Le +*23:38. Nu 15:3. Dt 12:6, 17. 16:10. **burnt offering.** Le +*23:12.

19. **a male.** Le 1:3, 10. 4:32. Ex 12:5. Mt 27:4, 19, 24, 54. Lk 23:14, 41, 47. Jn 19:4. 2 C 5:21. Ep 5:27. He 9:14. 1 P 1:19. 2:22-24. 3:18.

20. **hath a blemish.** ver. 25. Dt 15:21. 17:1. Ml *1:8, 13, 14. Ro 12:1, 2. Ep 5:27. He 9:14. 1 P 1:18, 19.

21. **peace offerings.** Le 3:1, 6. 7:11, etc. +*23:19. **to accomplish.** Ge 28:20. 35:1-3. Nu 15:3, 8. Dt 23:21-23. Ps 50:14. Pr 7:14. Ec 5:4, 5. **sheep.** *or*, goats. Ge 4:4. Ex 12:3n, 21. **it shall be perfect.** Le 1:3, 10. Ex 12:5. 29:1. Dt 15:21. 17:1. Ezk 43:23. Ml 1:8, 14. He 9:14. 1 P 1:19.

22. **Blind.** ver. 20. Le 21:18-21. Ml 1:8. **an offering.** Le 1:9, 13. 3:3, 5.

23. **lamb.** *or*, kid. Ex 12:3n. **superfluous.** Le 21:18. **vow.** Le +*23:38.

24. **broken, or cut.** ver. 20. Dt 23:1.

25. **a stranger's.** lit. son of a stranger. (*S#5236h). Ex 12:43 Nu 15:14-16. 16:40. Dt 31:16. Ezr 6:8-10. **the bread.** Le 21:6, 8, 21, 22. Ml 1:7, 8, 12-14. **because.** Ep 2:12. 1 J 5:18.

27. **seven days.** Le 12:2, 3. 19:23, 24. Ex 22:30.

28. **ewe.** *or*, she goat. Ex 12:3n. **ye shall not kill it.** This law was certainly intended to inculcate mercy and tenderness of heart; and so the Jews have understood it. Ex 23:19. 34:26. Dt 14:21. 22:6, 7. Ps 119:156. 145:8, 9. Is 49:15. 66:13. Mt 23:37. Ja 5:11. 1 J 4:16.

29. **sacrifice of thanksgiving.** Le 7:12-15. Ps 22:25. 107:22. 116:17. Ho 14:2. Am 4:5. He +*13:15. 1 P 2:5.

30. **leave none.** Le 7:15-18. 19:6. Ex 16:19, 20. Ac=2:27-32.

31. **keep my commandments.** See on Le 18:4, 5. 19:37. Nu 15:40. Dt +*4:40. Ps 19:7-11. 119:1-4, 9, 14-16. 1 Th 4:1, 2.

32. **profane.** See on ver. 2. Le 18:21. **holy name.** Ps 8:9. √9:10. 25:11. 115:1. SS 1:3. Is *26:8. Mt *6:9. Lk 11:2. Jn 17:11. Re 15:3, 4. **I will.** Le 10:3. Is 5:16. Mt 6:9. Lk 11:2. **Lord.** Ex +15:26. **hallow you.** ver. 16. Le 20:8. 21:8, 15. Ex 19:5, 6. Jn 17:17. 1 C 1:2.

33. **That brought.** Le 11:45. 19:36. 25:38. Ex 6:7. 20:2. Nu 15:41. 24:8, 9. Ps 80:8-11. 81:10. Je 10:7.

LEVITICUS 23

The feasts of the Lord, 1, 2. The sabbath, 3. The passover and feast of unleavened bread, 4-8. The sheaf of firstfruits, 9-14. The feast of Pentecost, 15-21. Gleanings to be left for the poor, 22. The feast of trumpets, 23-25. The day of atonement, 26-32. The feast of tabernacles, 33-44.

2. the feasts of the Lord. ver. 4, 37. Ex 23:14-17. 32:5. 1 S 15:22. Is 1:14. 33:20. La 1:4. Ho 2:11. Na 1:15. Jn ❍2:13. 5:1. 7:2. Col 2:16. or, appointed seasons, as Ge 1:14. Ge +17:21 (✚S#4150h). God appointed several festivals among the Jews. The *Passover* was celebrated on the 14th, or rather 15th day of the first month in the ecclesiastical year, which was the seventh of the civil year, and lasted seven days. The *Pentecost* was celebrated on the fiftieth day after the passover, in memory of the law's being given to Moses on Mount Sinai, fifty days, or seven weeks after the departure out of Egypt. The word is derived from the Greek word *Pentakosta*, which signifies the fiftieth. The Hebrews call it the feast of weeks, Ex 34:22. The feast of *trumpets*, celebrated on the first day of the civil year, when a trumpet was sounded, to proclaim its commencement, which was in the month *Tisri*, answering to our September, Le 23:24, 25. The *new moons*, or first days of every month, were, in some sort, a consequence of the feast of trumpets. God ordained that, by giving him the firstfruits of every month they should acknowledge him as the Lord of all their time, and own his providence, by which all times and seasons are ordered. The feast of *expiation* or *atonement* was kept on the tenth day of *Tisri* or September: the Hebrews call it *Kippur*, i.e. *pardon*, or *expiation*, because it was instituted for the *expiation* of all their sins. The feast of *tents* or *tabernacles* was so called, because the Israelites kept it under green tents or arbors, in memory of their dwelling in tents in their passage through the wilderness. It was celebrated on the 15th day of Tisri, and continued eight days: the first and last days were most solemn. Besides the feasts mentioned by Moses, we find the feast of lots, or *Purim*, which was celebrated among the Jews of Shushan on the 14th of *Adar*, which answers to our February. The feast of the *dedication of the temple*, or rather, of the restoration of the temple, which had been profaned by Antiochus Epiphanes, which is thought to be the feast mentioned in the gospel, Jn 10:22, was celebrated in the winter. **feasts.** *Moadim*, properly means assemblies, convened at an appointed time and place. ver. 4, 37. Ex 23:14-17. Is 1:13, 14. 33:20. La 1:4. Ho 2:11. Na 1:15. Jn 5:1. Col 2:1. **proclaim.** Ex 32:5. Nu 10:2, 3, 10. 2 K 10:20. 2 Ch 30:5. Ps 81:3. Jl 1:14. 2:15. Jon 3:5-9. **convocations.** Ge *49:10. Ex 12:16. He 12:23. Re *7:9. Young notes "lit. (1) a calling together, (2) those called together, (3) the place where they are called together. 'my appointed seasons,' and therefore not of human origin" (*Concise Critical Comments*).

3. Six days. Le *19:3. Ex 16:23, 29. +*20:8-11. 23:12. 31:15. *34:21. 35:2, 3. Dt 5:13. Ne *13:15-22. Is *56:2, 6. +*58:13n, 14. Lk +*13:14. 23:56. Ac 15:21. Col 2:16. Re 1:10. **sabbath of rest.** Ex 31:13. Ezk 20:12. 46:1. Ac 15:21. He *4:3-5, 9. Young states "This is the first of the 'appointed seasons of Jehovah.' It is here said to be a 'holy convocation,' which shows or implies that it was the design of God that they should have stated meetings on that day; and it need not be doubted but that these were for the reading of the Law, and the worship of God, by the priests, and

especially the Levites, who are everywhere regarded as the instructors of Israel (see on 2 Ch 35:3n); compare 2 K 4:23, etc."

4. are the feasts. or, set feasts. ver. 2, 37. Ex 23:14. Dt 12:14. 16:6. Ps 102:13. Na 1:15. Ro 15:4. Col 2:17.

5. the fourteenth. Ex 12:2-14, 18. 13:3-10. 23:15. Nu 9:2-7. 28:16. Dt 16:1-8. Jsh 5:10. 2 Ch 35:18, 19. Mt 26:17. Mk 14:12. Lk 22:7. 1 C *5:7, 8. **at even.** Heb. between the two evenings. Ex +12:6n. 30:8. Nu 9:3. **passover.** Ge 40:20. Ex *12:13, 27, 43-49. *13:10. 34:25. Nu 9:2, 10. 28:16. 33:3. Dt 16:1, 2, *6. 2 K *23:21, 22. 2 Ch 30:1, 13-17. 35:17. Ezr 6:19. Is 31:5. Ezk 45:21. Mt *26:2, 17, 19, 26-29. Mk 14:1, 12. Lk 22:1, 7. Jn 13:1. 19:14. 1 C=❘5:7. Col 1:14.

6. the feast of unleavened bread. Ex 12:15, 16, 17. 13:6, 7. 23:15. *34:18. Nu 28:17, 18. Dt 16:3, 8, 16. 2 Ch *8:13. 30:13. 35:17. Ezr 6:22. Ezk 45:21. Mt 26:17. Mk 14:1, 2. Lk 22:1, 7. Ac 12:3, 4. 20:6. 1 C=❘5:7, 8. **seven.** Lk 1:74, 75. **eat.** Jn=6:50, 51.

7. ye shall have. Nu 28:18-25.

8. by fire. Le 1:9. Young renders, "fire offering." Nu 28:19-24. **seven days.** i.e. daily for that period (Young). **seventh day.** in which the Egyptians were drowned, Ex 12:16. 14:23-28.

10. When. See on Le 14:34. **and shall.** Le 2:12-16. Ex 22:29. 23:16, 19. 34:22, 26. Nu 15:2, 18-21. 28:26. Dt 16:9. Jsh 3:15. **harvest.** i.e. of barley; see Ex 9:31; the wheat harvest was seven weeks later (Young). **sheaf.** "as in ver. 11, 12, 15; Dt 24:19; Ru 2:7, 15; Jb 24:10; it is elsewhere (Ex 16:16, 18, 22, 32, 33, 36) considered as a measure called an *omer*, hence it is a question whether the barley was to be waved before Jehovah before or after it was thrashed out" (Young). **or,** handful. Je 9:22. Heb. *omer.* ver. 11, 12, 15. Dt 24:19. Ru 2:7, 15. Jb 24:10. Ps 129:7. Am 2:13. Mi 4:12. Zc 12:6. **the firstfruits.** Le 2:12-16. Ex 22:29. 23:16, 19. *34:22, 26. Nu 15:20, 21. 28:26. Dt 16:10. 26:2, 11. Ne 12:44. Pr *3:9. Je 2:3. Ezk 20:40. This offering was a public acknowledgment of the bounty and goodness of God for the kindly fruits of the earth. From the practice of the people of God, the heathen borrowed a similar one, founded on the same reason. 2 Ch 31:4-12. Ne 10:35-37. Pr 3:9, 10. Is 4:2. Ezk 20:40. 44:30. Mt *28:5, 6. Jn 12:24. *20:17. Ro *11:16. 1 C=15:20-23. Col *1:15, 18. *3:3, 4. Ja 1:18. Re *14:4.

11. wave the. Le 9:21. 10:14. Ex 29:24. **sheaf.** Ps=22:22. Jn=20:17. He=2:11. **accepted.** Ro=4:25. =8:34. **on the morrow after.** Ge +22:4. +49:10. Mt 28:1-10. Lk *23:44n. 1 C +*15:4, 20, 23. Ada Habershon writes "The sheaf of the firstfruits, which they waved on the first day of the week on the morrow after the Sabbath, plainly prophesied His resurrection" (*The Study of the Types*, p. 32). **the sabbath.** Jn 19:31.

12. an he lamb. Le 1:10. Nu 28:4, 5. Jn *1:29. Ro *6:9, 10. He *9:11, 12, 14, 24. 10:10-12. 1 P 1:19. Re *5:6. **burnt offering.** Le +1:3. 3:5. 4:24. 5:7-10. 6:9-13. 7:2. 12:6, 8. 14:13, 20. 15:15, 30. 16:3. 17:8, 9. 22:18. Ge 8:20. 22:2. Ex 18:12. 20:24. 24:5. 29:15-18. 40:29. Nu 6:11, 14. 7:15, 16. 8:12. 10:10. 15:3, 5, 8, 24. 28:10, 15. 29:6, 11, 39. Dt 12:6. 27:6. Jsh 8:31. 22:23, 29. Jg 13:23. 20:26. 21:4. 1 S 6:14. 7:9. 10:8. 13:9. 2 S 6:17, 18. 1 K 3:15. 8:64. 9:25. 2 K 16:13, 15. 1 Ch 16:1, 2. 21:23, 26. 29:35. 2 Ch 7:7. 29:35. 33:16. Ezr 3:5, 6. 8:35. Ps 40:6. 51:16. 66:13. Is 1:11-15. =50:6. =53:11. Je 6:20. 7:21, 22. 14:12.

17:26. Ezk 40:39. *43:27. 45:15, 17, 25. 46:2, 12. Ho *6:6. Am 4:4. *5:2. Mt=26:39. Jn=4:34. =√10:18. Ac=13:39. Ro=5:19. Ep=*1:6. Ph=2:5-8. He=*9:14. 10:6,=7. 1 P=2:5.

13. **the meat offering.** Le *2:1n, 14-16. 5:13. 6:14. 7:9. 9:4. 14:10. Ex 29:41. 30:9. 40:29. Nu 4:16. 6:15, 17. 8:8. 15:3-12, 24. 18:9. 28:5. 29:3, 6, 11, 39. Jsh 22:23, 29. Jg 6:18mg. 13:23. 1 K 8:64. 2 K 3:20. 16:13, 15. 1 Ch 21:23. 23:29. 2 Ch 7:7. Ezr 7:17. Ne 13:5, 9. Is=53:5, 10. 57:6. 66:20. Je 17:26. Ezk 42:13. 44:29. 45:15, 17, 25. 46:20. Jl 1:9, 13. 2:14. Am 5:22. Jn *4:34. *6:51. 15:1. He=7:26. **two tenth.** Nu ◖28:5. "From Ex 29:40, it appears that only one-tenth deal was commonly required for a present, here it is doubled, probably to express thankfulness" (Young). **the drink offering.** Ge 35:14. Ex 29:40, 41. 30:9. Nu 6:15, 17. 15:5, 24. 28:7, 10, 15. 29:6, 11, 39. 2 K 16:13, 15. 1 Ch 29:21. 2 Ch 29:35. Ezr 7:17. Ps 16:4. *104:15. Is 57:6. Je ◖7:18. ◖19:13. ◖32:29. ◖*44:17. Ezk ◖20:28. 45:17. Jl 1:9, 13. 2:14. Ph=2:17mg. **wine.** Le ◖10:9. **the fourth.** Ex 29:40. 30:24. Nu 28:7. Ezk 4:11. 45:24. 46:14.

14. **eat.** Le 19:23-25. 25:2, 3. Ge 4:4, 5. Ex *22:29. *23:19. Dt *26:2. Jsh 5:11, 12. Mi *7:1. **green ears.** rather, full ears; see Le 2:14, etc. (Young). **selfsame.** ver. 21. Ge +*7:13n. Dt +*32:48. **it shall be.** Le 3:17. 10:11. Nu 10:8. Dt 16:12. Ne 9:14. Ps 19:8. **for-ever.** Heb. *olam*, Ex +*12:24. Ml *3:6.

15. **from the morrow.** ver. 10, 11. Le 25:8. Ex *34:22. Dt 16:9, 10. **wave offering.** Ex ◖+29:27n. Le 7:30, 34. 8:27, 29. 9:21. 10:14, 15. 14:12, 24. Ex 29:24, 26, 27n. 35:22h. 38:24h, 29h. Nu 5:25. 6:20. 8:11mg. 18:11, 18. Ro=▶12:1.

16. **fifty days.** Ex 34:22, 26. Nu 15:19-21. 28:26, 27. Dt *16:9. Mt 9:37, 38. Jn 4:35, 36. Ac *2:1-4, 41. 20:16. 1 C 12:13. Re 14:1-4.

17. **two wave loaves.** The Feast of Weeks foreshadowed Pentecost in Ac ch. 2. The *two* loaves prefigured saved Jews *and* Gentiles. As the old nature remains in those who are born again, the "leaven" was needed in the loaves which represented these believers. Whenever the typical bread represented Christ it must be unleavened; whenever it typified his people it must be leavened (A. W. Pink, *The Prophetic Parables of Matthew Thirteen*, p. 48). Two loaves may typify the fellowship of God's people (F.W. Grant, *Numerical Bible*, vol. 1, p. 360). ver. +*15. Nu 28:26, 28. Am=3:3. Mt=18:20. Jn=10:16. Ep=2:14, 15. 1 J=1:3. **fine flour.** Le +*2:1. Ex +27:20n. 29:2. Jn +=17:6. He +=2:10. **with.** Ho ◖7:4. Am ◖*4:5. Ac 5:1-11. Ro =5:12. =7:18, 23. **leaven.** See preceding note for the significance of leaven here. Le 7:13. Mt +*13:33n. *or* yeast; none of these loaves were burnt; they became the priest's property (Young). **the firstfruits.** ver. 10. Ex 22:29. 23:16, 19. *34:22, 26. Nu *15:17, 19-21. *28:26. Dt 26:1, 2. Pr *3:9, 10. Ro 8:23. 1 C 15:20. Ja 1:18. Re *14:4. "as in Ex 23:16, etc., hence in Ex 34:22, it is called the 'feast of the first fruits,' of wheat harvest" (Young).

18. **seven.** Ge *4:15. Ps *79:12. Pr *6:31. **lambs.** ver. 12, 13. Nu 28:27-31. Ml 1:13, 14. He 10:14. **without blemish.** Le 3:1. 2 C *5:21. **burnt offering.** Ge *8:20, 21. **with their.** ver. +13. Nu 15:4-12. **sweet savor.** Ep *5:2.

19. **one kid.** Le 4:23-28. 16:15. Nu 15:24. *28:30. Ro 8:3. 2 C *5:19, 21. **sin offering.** Le 4:3. 6:17. 7:7,

37. 8:2, 14. 9:2. 10:16. 12:6, 8. 14:13, 19. 15:15, 30. 16:3. Ex 29:14. 30:10. Nu 6:11, 14, 16. 7:16. 8:8, 12. 15:24. 18:9. 19:9mg, 17mg. 28:15, 22. 29:5, 11. 2 Ch 29:21. Ezr 6:17. 8:35. Ne 10:33. Ps ch.=22. 40:6. Is=53:*6, 10, 12. La=1:12. =3:1-19. Ezk 40:39. 42:13. 43:19. 44:29. 45:17, 22, 25. 46:20. Jn=1:29. Ac=13:38. Ro=5:8. =8:3. 2 C=*5:21. Ga =3:13. 1 T=1:15. He=10:18. 1 J=*1:7. **two lambs.** Le ch. 3. 7:11-18. **peace offerings.** Le *3:1, +11. 4:10. 6:12. +*7:11. 9:4. 10:14. 17:5. 19:5. 22:21. Ex 20:24. 24:5. 29:28. Nu 6:14, 17. 7:17. 10:10. 15:8. 29:39. Dt 12:6. 27:7. Jsh 8:31. 22:23. Jg 20:26. 21:4. 1 S 10:8. 11:15. 13:9. 2 S 6:17, 18. 24:25. 1 K 3:15. 8:63, 64. *9:25. 2 K 16:13. 1 Ch 16:1, 2. 21:26. 2 Ch 7:7. 29:35. 30:22. 31:2. 33:16. Ps 50:14. 76:11. Pr 7:14. Is=53:5. Ezk 43:27. 45:15, 17. 46:2, 12. Am 5:22. Jon 2:9. Jn=6:51-57. 1 C=10:16. 2 C=9:15. Ep=2:13, *14, 17, 18. Col=1:20. He=13:15.

20. **wave them.** ver. 17. Le 7:29, 30. Ex *29:24. Lk 2:14. Ep 2:14. **holy to.** Le 7:31-34. 8:29. 10:14, 15. Nu *18:8-12. Dt *18:4. Jn *6:57. 1 C 9:11.

21. **proclaim.** ver. 2, 4. Ex 12:16. Dt 16:11. Is 11:10. **selfsame.** ver. 14. Dt +*32:48. **convocation.** He *10:25. **a statute.** ver. 14. Ge 17:7. Ex 12:17. Nu 18:23. **for ever.** Heb. *olam*, Ex +*12:24.

22. **thou shalt not make clean riddance.** Le 19:9, 10. Dt 16:11-14. *24:19-21. Ru 2:3-7, 15, 16, etc. Jb 31:16-21. Ps 41:1-3. 112:9. Pr 11:24, 25. Is 58:7, 8, 10. Lk 11:41. Jn ◖=6:12. *12:8. 2 C *8:9. 9:5-12. Ja *1:27. **corners.** Mt=24:14. Ac=1:8. Ro 10:12-15. **field.** Ps=22:27. 72:11. Mt=13:38. **gather.** Is=2:2-4. 25:7. Je=3:17. Zc=2:11. =8:22. Mt =25:32. **gleaning.** Is 27:12mg. Re =7:14-17. 20:4. **stranger.** Mt 25:31-46. Re=7:9. To the institution of the feast of pentecost is annexed a repetition of that law, by which they were required to leave the gleanings of their fields, and the corn that grew on the ends of the butts, for the poor. It may come in *here* as a thing which the priests must take occasion to remind the people of, when they brought their firstfruits, intimating to them, that to obey even in this small matter was better than sacrifice; and that unless they were obedient, their offerings should not be accepted. It also taught them that the joy of harvest should express itself in charity to the poor, who must have their due out of what we have, as well as God his. They that are truly sensible of the mercy they receive from God, will without grudging show mercy to the poor.

24. **Speak.** He 12:25. **In the seventh.** Nu *10:10. 29:1-6. 1 Ch 15:28. 2 Ch 5:13. Ezr 3:6. Ne 8:2, 3, 8. Ps *81:1-4. *89:15. 98:6. Is *27:13. 1 C *15:52. 1 Th *4:16. He 12:25. **month.** Jn 4:35. **a memorial.** *Zichron terooah,* here rendered "a memorial of blowing the trumpets," properly signifies *a memorial of triumph,* or *shouting for joy.* This festival is generally called the *feast of trumpets*; and, though the Scriptures have not expressly declared the reason of its celebration, yet, as it fell in the seventh month of the sacred year, which was the first of the civil year, that is, the month *Tisri,* answering to our September, the opinion very generally embraced by both Jews and Christians is, that it was a memorial of the creation of the world, at which "the sons of God shouted for joy" (Jb 38:7); and which is supposed, not altogether without reason, to have been at this season of the year. The month *Tisri* was not only anciently, but still is, reckoned by

the Jews the first month of the year; and the feast of tabernacles, kept in this month, was said to be, as it is correctly rendered in the margin, "at the revolution of the year" (Ex 34:22); importing, that at this season the year had revolved, and was beginning anew. So that this feast was the new year's day, on which the people rejoiced in a grateful remembrance of God's benefits, and implored his blessing for the future year. Le 25:9. Nu 29:1-6. Ne 8:2, 9-12. **memorial.** Nu 10:9. Is 49:14-16. Ezk 16:60. Ro 11:1, 2. **trumpets.** Le 25:9. Nu 10:2, 9. 31:6. 1 K 1:34. 2 K 11:14. 2 Ch 13:12. Ps 72:8. 81:1-3. 89:15 (joyful sound; RV mg, trumpet sound). 98:6. Is 18:3-7. 27:13. 58:1. Je 50:4. Jl 2:*1, 12. Zc 10:8. 14:9. Mt=24:31. 1 C =15:51, 52. 1 Th =4:16, 17. or, shouting (*S#8643h); as in Le 25:9. Nu 10:5, 6. *23:21. 29:1. 31:6. Jsh *6:5, 20. 1 S *4:5, 6. 2 S *6:15. 1 Ch 13:12. 15:14, 28. Ezr *3:11, 12, 13. Jb 8:21mg. 33:26 (with joy). *39:25. Ps 27:6mg. 33:3 (loud noise). *47:6. 89:15 (joyful sound). 150:5 (high sounding). Je 4:19 (alarm). *20:16. 49:2 (alarm). Ezk 21:22. Am 1:14. 2:2. Zp 1:16 (alarm).

25. **offering made by fire.** Young renders, "fire offering." ver. 8. Nu 29:1-6.

27. **the tenth.** Le 16:29, 30. 25:9. Nu 29:7-11. **day of atonement.** Le 16:30, 34. 25:9. Ex 30:10. Nu *29:7. Zc 12:10. 13:1. Jn 11:50. He=9:7, 28. Young notes *atonement* here is plural, *atonements*, as in Ex 29:36. 30:10, 16. Le 23:27, 28. 25:9. Nu 5:8. 29:11. **convocation.** 2 C=5:10. Re 22:12. **afflict.** Le 16:31. Nu 29:7. Ezr 8:21. Ps 35:13. ch. 51. Is ch. 53. 58:5. Je 31:9, 15-20. La ch. 1-5. Ezk 20:35-38, 43. 36:31. Da 10:2, 3. Ho *6:1-3. 14:8. Jon ch. 2. Mi 7:9. Zc 12:10. Ac 2:37, 38. 2 C 7:10, 11. Ga *2:20. *5:24. Ph *3:10. Ja 4:9. 1 P *4:13. **souls.** Heb. *nephesh*, Ge +27:31. **offer.** Le 16:11, 15, 24. **offering made by fire.** Young renders, "fire offering." Nu 29:8-11.

28. **a day of atonement.** Le 16:34. Is 53:10. Da 9:24. Zc 3:9. Ro 5:10, 11. He 9:12, 26. 10:10, 14. 1 J 2:2. 4:10. 5:6.

29. **soul.** Heb. *nephesh*, Ge +17:14. **that shall.** See on ver. 27, 32. Is 22:12. Je 31:9. Ezk 7:16. **he shall be.** Ge 17:14. Ac ▸3:23.

30. **soul.** Heb. *nephesh*, Ge +27:31. **the same.** Le 20:3, 5, 6. Ge 17:14. Je 15:7. Ezk 14:9. Zp 2:5. 1 C 3:17. **soul.** Heb. *nephesh*, Ge +17:14. **from among.** Ac 3:23.

31. **no manner of work.** ver. 28. Mt ◑12:12. Mk 3:4. Ro=4:4, 5. *11:6. Ep √2:7-10. He *4:8-11. **for ever.** Heb. *olam*, Ex +*12:24.

32. **a sabbath.** See on Le 16:31. Mt 11:28-30. He 4:3, 11. **afflict.** See on ver. 27. Ps 35:13. 51:17. 69:10, 11. 126:5, 6. Is 57:15, 18, 19. 58:3-7. 61:3. Je=8:20. Zc 12:10-14. Mt +*5:4. 1 C 11:31. Re +*1:7. **souls.** Heb. *nephesh*, Ge +27:31. **celebrate your sabbath.** Heb. rest. Le 25:2.

34. **The fifteenth.** Ex 23:16. 34:22. Nu 29:12. Dt 16:13-15. Ezr 3:4. Ne 8:14. Ezk 45:25. Zc 14:16-19. Jn 1:14. 7:2. He 11:9, 13. **seventh month.** 1 K 8:2. Hg 2:1. i.e. *Tisri*, part of September (Young). **the feast.** See on Ex 10:9n, *S#2282h. **of tabernacles.** Ge 30:14. 33:17. Ex 23:16. 34:22. Nu 29:12, 40. 31:10. Dt 16:13. 26:11. 31:10. 2 S *7:6. 1 K 8:2. 2 Ch 8:13. Ezr *3:4. Ne 8:17. Ezk 45:25. Ho *12:9. Zc 8:19, 23. =*14:16. Jn 7:*2, 3, 6, *14, *37-39. This feast was celebrated in commemoration of the Israelites' dwelling in tents in the wilderness for forty years; and was kept with

greater jollity than any of the other festivals. Hence, in the Talmud, it is often called *chag, the* feast, by way of excellence; and by Philo, *eorton megistan,* the greatest of the feasts; it was therefore more noticed by the heathen than any other. It is probable that *Cecrops* borrowed from it the law which he made in Athens, "that the master of every family should after harvest make a feast for his servants, and eat together with them who had taken pains with him in tilling his grounds." **seven days.** Ga=4:4. 1 T 3:16. Re 13:8.

35. **an holy convocation.** ver. 7, 8, 24, 25.

36. **Seven.** Nu 29:12-38. **the eighth.** Nu 29:35, 36. 2 Ch 7:8-11. Ne 8:18. Is=65:17. Jn 7:37. 2 P=3:13. Re=21:1-8. **solemn.** Heb. day of restraint. Nu 29:35. Dt 16:8. 1 K 8:2. 2 K 10:20. 2 Ch 7:9. Ne 8:18. Is 1:13. Je 9:2. Jl 1:14. 2:15mg. Am 5:21.

37. **the feasts.** See on ver. 2, 4. Dt 16:16, 17. **drink offerings.** ver. +13. Ex 29:40. Nu 15:5. 28:7. Ph 2:17mg. **every thing.** Ec *3:1. Ga 4:4. 1 T 3:16. Re 13:8.

38. **the sabbaths.** See on ver. 3. Le 19:3. Ge 2:2, 3. Ex 20:8-11. **and beside.** Nu 29:39. Dt 12:6. 1 Ch 29:3-8. 2 Ch 35:7, 8. Ezr 2:68, 69. **vows.** Le 7:16. 22:18, 23. 27:29n. Ge 28:20. 31:13. Nu 15:3, 8. 29:39. Dt 12:6, 11. *23:18, 21. Jg *11:30. 1 S 1:11. 2 S 15:7, 8. Jb 22:27. Ps 22:25. 50:14. 56:12. 61:5, 8. 65:1. 66:13. 76:11. 116:14, 18. 132:2. Pr 7:14. Ec 5:4, 5. Is 19:21. Je ◐44:25. Jon 1:16. 2:9. Na 1:15. Ac 18:18. 21:23. ch. 24. **freewill offerings.** Le 7:16. 22:18. Ex 25:2. 35:5, 21, 29. 36:3. Nu 15:3. 29:39. Dt 12:6, 17. 16:10. 23:23. Jg 5:2, 9. 1 Ch 29:9. 2 Ch 31:14. 35:8. Ezr 1:4. 2:68. 3:5. 8:28. Ne 7:70. Ps 54:6mg. +*119:108. Ezk 46:12. Am 4:5. 2 C 9:7.

39. **fifteenth day.** i.e. as in ver. 34 above, where the festival of booths is appointed (probably) to commemorate the dwelling of Israel in booths in the wilderness 40 years; in this 39th verse, the same festival is apparently to give thanks for the ingathering of the fruits of the land in autumn, hence in Ex 23:16, and in 34:22, it is called the feast of ingathering (Young). **when.** See on ver. 34. Ex *23:16. Dt 16:13. **feast.** Dt 16:13. Zc 14:16. Mt=6:10. 13:39. **gathered in the fruit.** Zc √14:5. Mt *1:23. *13:24-30, 34-39. 24:31. *25:10. Mk *13:26, 27. 1 C *2:9, 10. *15:23. 1 Th √4:16-18. Re 7:9-17. *21:3, 4. **on the first.** See on ver. 24, 36. **eighth.** Lk 9:28.

40. **the boughs.** Heb. fruit. Ge 1:11. Ne 8:15. Mt 21:8. **goodly.** or, beautiful. *S#1926h. Le 23:40 (goodly). Dt 33:17 (glory). 1 Ch 16:27 (honor). Jb 40:10 (beauty). Ps 8:5 (honor). 21:5 (majesty). 29:4. 45:3, 4. 90:16 (glory). 96:6 (majesty). 104:1 (majesty). 110:3 (beauties). 111:3 (glorious). 145:5 (honor), 12 (majesty). *149:9 (honor). Pr 20:29 (beauty). 31:25 (honor). Is 2:10 (glory), 19, 21. 5:14. 35:2 (excellency), 2. *53:2 (comeliness). La 1:6 (beauty). Ezk 16:14 (comeliness). 27:10. Mi 2:9 (glory). See also *S#1925h, Da 11:20. *S#1923h, Da 4:30 (majesty), 36 (honor). 5:18. **branches.** lit. bendings, or hands, the word being used of the *sole* of the foot (Ge 8:9), the *palm* of the hands (Le 14:15); compare also Jb 36:32 (clouds); Hab 2:9 (power; mg, palm of the hand). Compare also Jb 15:32. Is 9:14. 19:15. **of palm trees.** Ex 15:27. 1 K 6:29. Ps 92:12. Is 35. 52:1, 2. Ezk 40:16. Jn=12:13. Re=7:9. **boughs.** Ps 80:10. Ezk 17:23. 31:3, 10, 14. 36:8. Da 4:12, 14, 21. Ml 4:1. **thick.** Ne 8:15. Jb 15:26. Ezk 6:13. 20:28. **willows.** Jb 40:22. Ps 137:1, 2. Is 15:7.

40:1, 2. 44:4. **brook**. Ge 32:23. Ne 2:15. Jb 6:15. 40:22. Ps 83:9. 110:7. Pr 18:4. Is 15:7. Je 31:40. Jn 18:1. **rejoice**. Dt 12:7, 11, 12, 18. 14:26. *16:11, 14, 15. 26:11. 27:7. ●28:47. Ne *8:10. Ps *5:11. 9:2. 66:6. *72:16-19. *96:7-13. 105:43. Is *35:1, 2, 10. 65:13. 66:10. Jl 2:26. Jn *11:52. 16:22. Ro 5:11. Ph 3:3. 4:4. 1 P 1:8. **before**. ♪144A1, Ge +11:8.

41. **ye shall**. Nu 29:12. Ne 8:18. **for ever**. Heb. *olam*, Ex +*12:24.

42. **dwell in**. Ge 33:17. Nu 24:2, 5. Ne 8:14-17. Je 35:10. 2 C 5:1. He 11:13-16. **booths**. ♪66, Ge +9:3. Ne 8:17. Ho *12:9. Zc *14:16. Mt=17:4. Mk=9:5. Lk=*9:27, 33. Jn *7:2, 3, 6, 14, 37-39. 2 P 1:16. **Israelites born**. or, natives in Israel. as in Ex 12:19, but not strangers, sojourners, or settlers (Young).

43. **your generations**. Ex 13:14. Dt 31:10-13. Ps 78:5, 6. **may know**. Dt *8:2-9, 14-16. Ps *78:5, 6. **brought them out**. Ro *8:22, 23. 2 C *4:17, 18. 2 T *1:12. He *11:14. *12:11. 1 P *5:10.

44. **declared**. ver. 1, 2. Le 21:24. Mt 28:20.

LEVITICUS 24

Laws concerning the oil for the lamps of the golden candlestick, and the ordering of them, 1-4; and concerning the showbread, 5-9. Shelomith's son stoned for blasphemy, 10-12. Some laws repeated on that occasion: the law of blasphemy, 13-16; the law of murder, 17; of damage, 18-22. The blasphemer is stoned, 23.

2. **that they**. Ex 27:20, 21. 39:37. 40:24, 25. Nu 8:2-4. 1 S 3:3, 4. **the lamps**. 2 Ch 13:11. Ps 119:*105, *130, 140. Pr 6:23. Is √8:20. 11:2. Mt 4:16. 5:16. 25:1-8. Lk 1:79. 12:35. Jn 1:4, 9. 5:35. *8:12. Ac 26:18. 2 C 4:6. Ep 1:17, 18. 5:8-14. Ph 2:15, 16. **burn continually**. Heb. ascend. Ex 25:37.

3. **Without the vail**. Ex 27:21. 39:37. Zc 4:2, 3, 10-14. Col 2:9. He 9:2. Re 1:12-14. 2:18. 4:5. **continually**. Ex 27:20. Mt 25:1-4. Jn=*5:39. =16:13-15. Ac=17:11, 12. 1 J 1:5, 6, 7. 2:27. **forever**. Heb. *olam*, Ex +12:24.

4. **the pure**. Ex 25:31-39. 31:8. 37:17-24. 39:37. Nu 3:31. 4:9. 1 K 7:49. 1 Ch 28:15. Ps 119:*105, 130, *140. Je 52:19. Zc 4:2, 3, 11-14. He 9:2. 2 P 1:19. Re 1:20. 2:1, 5. 11:4.

5. The loaves of bread which the officiating priest placed every sabbath day upon the golden table in the *Sanctum*, before the Lord, were twelve in number, representing the twelve tribes of Israel. The loaves must have been large, since two tenth deals (about six pints) of flour were used for each, Le 24:3, 6, 7. They were served up hot on the sabbath day in the *Sanctum*, when the stale ones, which had been exposed the whole week, were taken away, and none but the priests were allowed to eat them. In an extraordinary extremity, David and his men partook of the showbread (see 1 S 21:6), the urgent necessity alone justifying the act. The Hebrew signifies *bread of faces*, or, *of the face*. **fine**. Ex +27:20. Is=53:5. He +=2:10. **twelve cakes**. Ex 25:30. 40:23. 1 K 18:31. 1 S 21:4, 5. Mt 12:4. Ac 26:7. Ja 1:1.

6. **in two rows**. 1 C 14:40. **row**. 1 Ch +9:32. **pure**. Ex 25:23, 24. 37:10-16. 39:36. 40:22, 23. 1 K 7:48. 2 Ch 4:19. 13:11. He 9:2, 9, 23.

7. **pure**. Le 2:2. Ep 1:6. He 7:25. Re 8:3, 4. **the bread**. Jn 6:33, 35. =50, =51. **a memorial**. Ge 9:16.

Ex 12:14. 13:9. 17:14. Ac 10:4, 31. 1 C 11:23-25.

8. **sabbath**. ♪84, Ge +6:17. Nu 4:7. 1 Ch 9:32. 23:29. 2 Ch 2:4. Ne 10:33. Mt 12:3-5. **everlasting**. Heb. *olam*, Ge +17:7. **covenant**. Ge +9:16.

9. **Aaron's**. Le 8:31. 1 S 21:6. Ml 1:12. Mt 12:4. Mk 2:26. Lk 6:4. **they shall**. Le 6:16. 8:3, 31. 10:17. 21:22. Ex 29:32, 33. **eat**. Jn=6:50, 51. **in the**. Mt 17:5. Jn 19:5. **holy place**. Ep=2:6. **perpetual**. Heb. *olam*, Ge +9:12.

10. **Israelitish**. i.e. *a female descendant of Israel*, ✳S#3482h. Le 24:10, 10, 11. **father was**. Ex 12:38. Nu 11:4.

11. **blasphemed**. ver. 15, 16. Ex 20:7. 2 S 12:14. 1 K 21:10, 13. 2 K 18:30, 35, 37. 19:1-3, 6, 10, 22. 2 Ch 32:14-17. Ps 74:18, 22. Mt 26:65. Ac 6:11-13. Ro 2:24. 1 T 1:13. Re 16:11, 21. **the name**. Houbigant and others think that *the name* which this man blasphemed was the name of the god of his native land. But that *hashshem, the name*, denotes Jehovah, appears from its being used in the latter part of verse 16, as equivalent to *the name of Jehovah*, in the former part. The Jews also frequently use *hashshem* for Jehovah. **cursed**. Jb 1:5, 11, 22. 2:5, 9, 10. Is 8:21. **brought him**. Ex 18:22, 26. Nu 15:33-35. **Shelomith**. i.e. *peaceable*, ✳S#8019h. 1 Ch 3:19. 23:18. 26:28. 2 Ch 11:20. Ezr 8:10. Also 1 Ch 23:9. 26:25. (1) A woman of the tribe of Dan, Le 24:11. (2) One of the daughters of Zerubbabel, 1 Ch 3:19. (3) A descendant of Gershon, the son of Levi, 1 Ch 23:9. (4) One of the Kohathite Levites, 1 Ch 23:18, called Shelomoth, 1 Ch 24:22. (5) One who had charge of dedicated things, 1 Ch 26:25, 26. (6) One of the sons of Rehoboam, 2 Ch 11:20. (7) A Jew whose sons returned with Ezra, Ezr 8:10. **Dibri**. i.e. *eloquent; promise*, ✳S#1704h.

12. **that the mind of the Lord might be showed them**. Heb. to expound unto them according to the mouth of the Lord. Ex 18:15, 16, 23. Nu 27:5. 36:5, 6.

14. **without**. Le 13:46. Nu 5:2-4. 15:35. **all that**. Dt 13:9. 17:7. **let all the**. Le 20:2, 27. Nu 15:35, 36. Dt 13:10. 21:21. 22:21. Jsh 7:25. Jn 8:59. 10:31-33. Ac 7:58, 59.

15. **Whosoever curseth**. Ex 20:7. 23:20, 21. Mt 12:31, 32. Ac 7:51. Ep *4:30. 1 Th 5:19. **bear his sin**. Le 5:1. 20:16, 17. Nu 9:13.

16. **blasphemeth**. As the word *nakav* not only signifies to *curse*, or *blaspheme*, but also to *express*, or *distinguish by name* (Nu 1:17. 1 Ch 12:31. Is 62:2), hence the Jews, at a very early period, understood this law as prohibiting them from uttering the name Jehovah, on any other than sacred occasions. The Septuagint, which was made at least 250 years before Christ, renders it "Whosoever nameth the name of the Lord, let him die;" from which we see that the Jews at this time were accustomed to pronounce *adonay*, or *Lord*, instead of *Jehovah;* for in place of it the Septuagint always put *o Kurios*. Philo, who lived in the time of Christ, explains the passage, connecting it with the preceding verse, in the following terms: "Strange gods are not to be blasphemed, lest men should be accustomed to think meanly of the Deity. But if any one (I do not say *blaspheme*, for that is not here the question, but) even so much as *utter* unseasonably the name of the LORD of men and gods, he shall die" (*Opera*, Vol. II, p. 166). This explanation, whether it please us or not, cannot therefore be looked

upon as a piece of superstition originating with the Jews who lived after the destruction of Jerusalem. Ex +*20:7. 1 K 21:10-13. Ps 74:10, 18. 139:20. Mt 12:31. Mk 3:28, 29. Jn 8:58, 59. 10:33-36. Ac 26:11. 1 T 1:13. Ja 2:7. **surely.** ∫147B, Ge +2:16. **stone him.** Jn +*10:32n.

17. **And he.** Ge 9:5, 6. Ex 21:12-14. Nu 35:31. Dt 19:11, 12. Jn 8:44. **killeth.** Heb. smiteth the life of a man. ver. 18. **any man.** Heb. *nephesh*, soul. Ge +37:21. **surely.** ∫147B, Ge +2:16.

18. **that killeth.** ver. 21. **a beast.** Heb. the soul (*nephesh*, Ge +√2:19) of a beast. Ex 21:34-36. **beast for beast.** Heb. *nephesh*, life for life, Ge +√2:19. T#987‡. Re 16:3.

19. **as he.** Dt 19:21. Mt 5:38. 7:2. Ro 5:8. 13:10. 1 J 4:16.

20. **Breach for.** Ex 21:23-25. Dt 19:21. Mt ▶5:38, 39. 7:1, 2. 1 P 2:19, 21, 22.

21. **a beast.** Heb. *behemah*, no word for "soul" here as there is in ver. 18. Ex 21:33. **a man.** ver. 17.

22. **one manner.** Le 17:10. 19:34. Ex 12:49. Nu 9:14. 15:15, 16, 29.

23. **that they.** See on ver. 14-16. Nu 15:35, 36. He 2:2, 3. 10:28-31. **and stone.** Jn 10:32n.

LEVITICUS 25

The law of the sabbatical year, 1-7. That of the jubilee in the fiftieth year, 8-13. Various laws, relating to the due observance of the sabbatical year, and the year of jubilee: against oppression, 14-17. The redemption of land, 23-28. Of houses, 29-34. Compassion to the poor, 35-38. The usage of bondmen, 39-46. The redemption of servants, 47-55.

1. **the Lord spake.** Ex 19:1. Nu 1:1. 10:11, 12. Ga 4:24, 25.

2. **When ye.** See on Le 14:34. Dt 32:8, 49. 34:4. Ps 24:1, 2. 115:16. Is 8:8. Je 27:5. **keep.** Heb. rest. Le 23:32mg. **a sabbath.** Le 26:34, 35. Ex 20:10, 11. 23:10, 11. 2 Ch 36:21.

3. **six years.** Mt=*21:33-41. Lk *13:6-9.

4. **in the seventh.** ver. 20-23. Le 26:34, *35, 43. Ex *23:10, 11. 2 Ch 36:21. **sabbath of rest.** Ps *96:11, 12. Is *11:6-10. *65:25. He *4:10, 11.

5. **groweth.** 2 K 19:29. Is 37:30. **thy vine undressed.** Heb. thy separation. ver. 11.

6. **for thee.** Ex 23:11. Ac 2:44. 4:32, 34, 35.

8. **thou shalt number.** Le 23:15. Ge 2:2.

9. **of the jubilee to sound.** Heb. loud of sound. Nu 10:10. Ps 89:15. Is √27:12, 13. Ac 13:38, 39. Ro 10:18. 15:19. 2 C 5:19-21. 1 Th 1:8. **jubilee.** ver. 10-12, *52n. Le 27:17, 24. Nu 10:1-3, 7, 8, 10. 36:4. Is *35:1-10. 61:2. 63:4. Ac=3:21. Re 7:13-17. =21:1. F. W. Grant (*Numerical Bible*, vol. 1, p. 366) notes that "Upon a passover, the antitype of the passover was fulfilled (Le 23:11n. Dt 16:1n. Lk 23:44n), as we well know; upon a pentecost came what we still call Pentecost (Le 23:2n, 16. Ac 2:1): so assuredly will come a jubilee yet that shall be in the full meaning 'jubilee' " (references added). See further on ver. 52n. **tenth day of.** Le 23:27. Is 27:13. 35:1-10. Re 7:13-17. **the day of atonement.** Le 16:20, 30. 23:24, +*27. **throughout all.** Ps *68:11. Mk *16:15. 2 C +*6:2.

10. **proclaim liberty.** T#683. Ex 20:2. Ezr 1:3. Ps 146:7. Is 49:9, 24, 25. 61:1-3. 63:4. Je 34:8, 13-17. Zc 9:11, 12. Lk 1:74. 4:16-21. Jn 8:32-36. Ro 6:17,

18. 8:21. 2 C 3:17. Ga 4:25-31. 5:1, 13. 1 P 2:16. 2 P 2:19, 20. **every man.** ver. 13, 26-28, 33, 34. Le 27:17-24. **ye shall return.** Le 27:24. Nu 36:2-9. Ac +*3:21.

11. **A jubilee.** Respecting the literal meaning of the word *yobel*, or *yovel*, critics are not agreed. Some derive it from *Jubal*, who was the inventor of musical instruments (Ge 4:21), because this year was one of mirth and joy, on which music is a common attendant, or else because it was ushered in by the musical sound of the trumpet. Others tell us that this year was so called because it was proclaimed with trumpets made of ram's horns. The most natural derivation, however, of the word seems to be from *hovil*, the Hiphil form of *yaval*, to recall, restore, or bring back, because this year restored all slaves to their liberty, and brought back all alienated estates to their primitive owners. Accordingly, the LXX. render it her *aphesis*, a *remission;* and Josephus says it signifies *eleutherian, liberty.* **jubilee.** Le 27:17. **ye shall.** ver. 5-7.

12. **ye shall.** ver. 6, 7.

13. **In the year of.** ver. 10. Le 27:17-24. Nu 36:4. Is *61:2. *63:4.

14. **not oppress.** ver. 17. Ex +18:21. Le +*19:13. Dt 16:19, 20. Jg 4:3. 1 S 12:3, 4. 2 Ch 16:10. Ne 9:36, 37. Jb 20:19, 20. Ps 10:18. Pr 14:31. 21:13. 22:16. *28:3, 8, 15, 16. Ec 5:8. Is 1:17. 3:12-15. 5:7. 33:15. 58:6. Je *22:16, 17. Ezk 22:7, 12, 13. Am 5:11, 12. 8:4-7. Mi 2:2, 3. 6:10-12. 7:3. Lk 3:14. *12:15. 1 C 6:8. He *13:5. Ja *5:1-5. 2 P *2:14.

15. **According to.** Le 27:18-23. Ph 4:5.

17. **shall not.** ver. +*14. Ex *18:21. Je 22:16, 17. Lk 12:15. He 13:5. 2 P 2:14. **fear.** ver. 43. Le 19:14, 32. Ge 20:11. 22:12. 39:9. 42:18. Ex 20:20. Dt 25:18. 1 S 12:24. 2 Ch 19:7. Ne 5:9, 15. Ps 19:9. Pr 1:7. Je 22:16. Ml +*3:5. Lk 12:5. Ac 9:31. 10:2, 35. Ro 3:18. 11:20.

18. **Wherefore.** Le 19:37. Ps 103:18. **and ye.** Le 26:3-12. Dt 12:10. 28:1-14. 33:12, 28. Jb 5:22-24. Ps 4:8. Pr 1:33. Je 7:3-7. 23:6. 25:5. 33:16. Ezk 33:24-26, 29. 34:25-28. 36:24-28. Mt *6:33. Ro 8:31, 32. 1 C 3:21-23. **in safety.** ver. 19. Dt 28:7, 10. ◐25. 33:27, 28. Ps 127:1. Pr 21:31. +*22:3.

19. **the land shall.** Le 26:5. Ps 67:6. 85:12. Is 30:23. 65:21, 22. Ezk 34:25-28. 36:30. Jl 2:24, 26.

20. **What shall.** Nu 11:4, 13. 2 K 6:15-17. 7:2. 2 Ch 25:9. Ps 78:19, 20. Is 1:2. Mt *6:25-34. 8:26. Lk 12:29. Ph 4:6. He 13:5, 6.

21. **I will.** As it is here graciously promised, that the sixth year was to bring forth fruits for *three* years, not merely for *two*, it is evident that both the sabbatical year and the year of jubilee were distinctly provided for. They were not to sow from the sixth year to the eighth year, omitting *two seed times;* nor reap from the sixth to the ninth, omitting *two harvests.* No legislator, unless conscious of being divinely commissioned, would have committed himself to enacting such a law as this; nor would any people have submitted to receive it, except in consequence of the fullest conviction that a divine authority had dictated it. It therefore stands as a proof that Moses acted by the express direction of the Almighty, and that the people were fully persuaded of the reality of his divine mission by the miracles he wrought. Ge 26:12. 41:47. Ex 16:29. Dt 28:3, 8. Jb *5:22-24. Ps 4:8. *34:10. 133:3. Pr 1:33. 10:22. Je 23:6. Ml *3:10. Mt *6:33. Ro=8:31, 32. 1 C 3:21-

23. 2 C 9:10. Ph *4:6, 7. He 11:1. 1 P *5:7. **three years**. ver. 4, 8-11.

22. **eighth**. 2 K 19:29. Is 37:30. **old fruit**. Jsh 5:11, 12.

23. **The land**. See on ver. 10. 1 K 21:3. Is 62:4. Ezk 48:14. Jl 2:18. **forever**. *or*, to be quite cut off. Heb. for cutting off. ver. 30. **for the land is mine**. Le 27:24. Dt +*32:43. 2 Ch 7:20. Ps 24:1. 85:1. Is 8:8. 62:4. Ezk +*38:16. Ho 9:3. Jl *2:18. 3:2. The land was held as belonging to Jehovah, and if sold, or redeemed, the price must be reckoned according to the number of years to the next Jubilee, when all possessions returned to their former owners (*Concise Bible Dictionary*, London, Geo. Morrish, n.d., p. 455). **for ye are**. Ge 49:7. 1 Ch *29:15. Ps *39:12. 119:19. He *11:9-13. 1 P *2:11.

24. **redemption**. ver. 26, 27, 29, 31, 32, 48, 51-53. Ru 4:6-8. Ezk 11:15. Jb *19:25. Pr *23:10, 11. Is *47:4. Ro 8:23. 1 C *1:30. Ep *1:7, 13, 14. *4:30. 1 P *1:3-5. **his kin**. lit. redeemer, as in ver. 26, applied alike to God and to man; see Ge 48:16. Nu 5:8. 35:12, 19, 21, 24, 25, 27. Dt 19:6, 12. Jb 19:25 (Young, *Concise Critical Comments*).

25. **and if**. Ru *2:20. *3:2, 9, 12. *4:4-6. Je *32:7, 8. 2 C 8:9. He 2:13, 14. Re 5:9.

26. **himself be able to redeem it**. Heb. his hand hath attained, and found sufficiency. ver. 28, 47. Le 5:7mg. Nu 6:21. Jg 9:33mg.

27. **let him count**. ver. 50-53.

28. **and in the**. ver. 13. **he shall**. See on Is 35:9, 10. Je 32:15. 1 C *15:52-54. 1 Th *4:13-18. 1 P *1:4, 5.

29. **house in**. A very proper difference is here made between houses in a city and houses in the country. Houses in a city might be redeemed any time in the course of a year; but after that time could not be redeemed, or go out with the jubilee: houses in the country might be redeemed at any time; and if not redeemed must go out with the jubilee. The reason in both cases is sufficiently evident; the house in the city might be built merely for purposes of trade or traffic—the house in the country was much builded on, or attached to, the *inheritance* which God had divided to the respective families. It was therefore necessary that the same law should apply to the house as to the inheritance; which necessity did not exist with regard to the house in the city. And, as the house in the city might be purchased for the purpose of trade, it would be very inconvenient for the purchaser, when his business was established, to be obliged to remove. **year**. Heb. days. √171T2C, Ge +24:55. *Days* is put for a whole year of days. ver. 30.

31. **they may be redeemed**. Heb. redemption belongeth unto it. ver. 32, 48. Ps 49:7, 8.

32. **the cities**. As the Levites had *no inheritance* in Israel, but only *cities* to dwell in; and consequently the *houses* in these cities were all they could call *their own*, therefore they could not be ultimately alienated. Nu 35:2-8. Jsh 21. **at any time**. Heb. *olam*, ✝S#5769h. Rendered "any more," Ezk 27:36. 28:19. "long," Ps 143:3. Ec 12:5. "world," Ps 73:12. Ec 3:11. "continuance," Is 64:5. "eternal," Is 60:15. "lasting," Dt 33:15. "long time," Is 42:14. "at any time," Le 25:32. "since the beginning of the world," Is 64:4.

33. **a man purchase of the Levites**. *or, one* of the Levites redeem them. **shall go**. ver. 28. **for the houses**. Nu 18:20-24. Dt 18:1, 2.

34. **the field of**. ver. 23. Ac *4:36, 37. **perpetual**. Heb. *olam*, Ge +9:12. **possession**. Nu *35:2, 5. Jn *10:28. *14:2. Ro 6:23. √11:29. 2 C *5:1. He *6:20. 1 P 1:4. 1 J 5:11-13.

35. **thy brother**. ver. 25. Dt √15:7, 8. Pr 14:20, 21. 17:5. 19:17. Mk 14:7. Jn 12:8. 2 C 8:9. Ja 2:5, 6. **fallen in decay**. Heb. his hand faileth. **thou shalt**. Ps 37:26. 41:1. 112:5, 9. Pr 14:31. Lk 6:35. Ac *11:29, 30. Ro 12:13, 18, 20. 2 C 9:1, 12-15. Ga 2:10. 1 J *3:17. **relieve**. Heb. strengthen. T#526. Le 19:9, 10. Dt 15:7, 8, 10, 11. Jb +6:14 (T#7). Pr +21:13 (T#687). Ezk +*16:49. Da 4:27. Mt *10:8. Lk *6:35. Ja *1:27. *2:1-9, 15, 16. 1 J *3:17. **a stranger**. Le 19:34. Ex 23:9. Dt 10:18, 19. Mt 25:35. He 13:2.

36. **usury**. Ex 22:25. Dt 23:19, 20. Ne *5:7-10. Ps 15:5. Pr *28:8. Is +*24:2. Ezk 18:8, 13, 17. 22:12. Mt *25:27n. **fear**. ver. 17. Ne 5:9, 15.

38. **which**. Ex 20:2. **and to be**. Le 11:45. 22:32, 33. Nu 15:41. Je 31:1, 33. 32:38. He 11:16.

39. **be sold**. Ex 21:2. 22:3. Dt 15:12. 1 K 9:22. 2 K 4:1. Ne 5:5. Je 34:14. **compel him to serve as**. Heb. serve thyself with him with the service of, etc. ver. 46mg. Ex 1:14. Je 25:14. 27:7. 30:8.

40. **as an hired**. Ex 21:2, 3.

41. **then shall**. Ex 21:3. Jn 8:32. Ro 6:14. T 2:14. **shall return**. See on ver. 10, 28.

42. **my servants**. ver. 55. Ro 6:22. 1 C 7:21-23. **as bondmen**. Heb. with the sale of a bondman.

43. **not rule**. ver. 46, 53. Ex 1:13, 14. 2:23. 3:7, 9. 5:14. 1 K *9:22. Is 47:6. 58:3. 1 C *6:19, 20. *7:22. Ga *5:1. Ep +*6:9. Col +*4:1. **but shalt**. See on ver. 17. Ex 1:17, 21. Dt 25:18. Ml +*3:5.

44. **thy bondmen**. Ex 12:44. Ps 2:8, 9. Is 14:1, 2. Re 2:26, 27. **the heathen**. T#677-3.

45. **of the children**. Dt *9:5, 6. Is *14:2. 56:3-6. *61:5.

46. **And ye shall**. Is 14:2. **they shall be your bondmen for ever**. Heb. ye shall serve yourselves with them. Heb. *olam*, Ex +*12:24. See on ver. 39. **ye shall not rule**. ver. 43.

47. **sojourner or stranger wax rich**. Heb. the hand of a stranger, etc. obtain, etc. ver. 26. 1 S 2:7, 8. Ja +*2:5.

48. **one of his**. See on ver. 25, 35. Ne 5:5, 8. Ga 4:4, 5. He 2:11-13.

49. **or if he be**. See on ver. 26. Ps *49:6-8, 14, 15. Is *41:13, 14. *49:24-26. +*59:20. Je *50:33, 34. Jn=8:36. Ro +*8:16, 17, 23. Ep +*5:30.

50. **reckon**. ver. 27. **price of his sale**. This was a very equitable law, both to the sojourner to whom the man was sold, and to the Israelite who had been sold. The Israelite might redeem himself, or one of his kindred might redeem him; but this must not be done to the prejudice or disadvantage of his master. They were therefore to reckon the years he must have served, from that time till the jubilee; and then taking the current wages of a servant, per year, at that time, multiply the remaining years by that sum, and the aggregate was to be given to his master for his redemption. The Jews hold that the kindred of such a person were bound, if in their power, to redeem him, lest he should be swallowed up among the heathen; and we find (Ne 5:8) that this was done by the Jews on their return from the Babylonish captivity. **according to the time**. ver. 40, 53. Dt 15:18. Jb 7:1, 2. 14:6. Is 16:14. 21:16.

52. **jubilee**. The jubilee was a wonderful institution, and of great service to the religion, freedom, and independence of the Hebrews. It was calculated to prevent the rich from oppressing the poor, and reducing them to perpetual slavery; and to hinder their obtaining possession of all the lands by purchase, mortgage, or usurpation. It was further intended, that *debts* should not be multiplied too much, lest the poor should be entirely ruined; that slaves should not always continue in servitude; that personal liberty, equality of property, and the regular order of families might, as much as possible, be preserved; and that the people might thus be strongly attached to their country, lands, and inheritances. The *Concise Bible Dictionary* notes (p. 456) that "There is no record of the Sabbatical year and the year of Jubilee ever being kept. Lev. 26:34, 35 predicts what would happen if the Israelites did not let the land keep the sabbaths. It reads almost like a prophecy: the land should lie desolate 'because it *did not* rest in your sabbaths.' In Jer. 25:11, 12; 29:10; Dan 9:2 the actual desolation is said to be seventy years. And as the land was to have rested one year in every seven, it follows that the 70 answer to 70 X 7= 490 years. Now the kingdom began B.C. 1095, and Jerusalem was taken in 606, which is just 490 years, and seems to confirm the silence in the history of Israel as to their giving the land the prescribed sabbaths. Apparently in this, as in everything else, they failed to obey; but the Jubilee will be made good to them in grace when they own their Messiah." The jubilee is a type of the millennium. It speaks of a time, never yet celebrated, when Israel shall be restored to God's favor, and shall return to the undisturbed possession (Is 11:11; Am *9:15; Mi 4:6, 7) of her land, when the great jubilee trumpet will recall them to worship in Jerusalem (Is *27:12, 13). See ver. 9n.

53. **shall not**. See on ver. 43.

54. **in these years**. *or*, by these means. **then**. ver. 40, 41. Ex 21:2, 3. Is 49:9, 25. 52:3. **he shall go**. Ps *37:7, 11. Is √26:3, 4. 2 P *3:9, 10, 13-15. Re *22:7, 20.

55. **my servants**. ver. 42. Ex 13:3. 20:2. Ps 116:16. Is 43:3. Lk 1:74, 75. Ro 6:14, 17, 18, 22. 1 C 7:22, 23. 9:19, 21. Ga 5:13. Ep *6:5-8.

LEVITICUS 26

Idolatry again forbidden, and regard to the Lord's sabbaths and sanctuary required, 1, 2. Blessings ensured to the people while obedient, 3-13. Judgments threatened in case of disobedience, and still more and more severe as long as they persisted in it, 14-39. Encouragements, if at length they should repent, 40-46.

1. **Ye shall**. Le 19:4. Ex 20:4, 5, 23. 23:24. 34:17. Dt 4:16-19. 5:8, 9. 16:21, 22. 27:15. 1 K 11:4, 5. Ps 97:7. 115:4-8. Is 2:20. 44:9-20. 45:5. 48:5-8. Je 10:3-8. Ac 17:29. Ro 2:22, 23. 1 C 10:19, 20. Re 13:14, 15. 22:15. **standing image**. *or*, pillar. **image of stone**. *or*, figured stone. Heb. a stone of picture.

2. **keep**. See on Le 19:30. Is 56:4-7.

3. **If**. Ge +*4:7. **ye walk**. Le 18:4, 5. Dt 11:13-15. 28:1-14. Jsh 23:14, 15. Jg 2:1, 2. Ps 81:12-16. Is 1:19. 48:18, 19. Mt 7:24, 25. Ro 2:7-10. Re 22:14.

4. **Then I**. Dt 28:12. 1 K 17:1. Jb 5:10. 37:11-13. 38:25-28. Ps 65:9-13. 68:9. 104:13. Is 5:6. 30:23. Je

14:22. Ezk 34:26, 27. Jl 2:23, 24. Am 4:7, 8. Mt +*5:45. Ac 14:17. Ja 5:7, 17, 18. Re 11:6. **the land**. Le 25:21. Ps 67:6. 85:12. Ezk 34:27. 36:30. Hg 2:18, 19. Zc 8:12.

5. **threshing**. Am 9:13. Mt 9:37, 38. Jn 4:35, 36. **eat your**. Le 25:19. Ex 16:8. Dt 11:15. Jl 2:19, 26. Ac 14:17. 1 T 6:17. **dwell**. Le 25:18. 1 K 4:25. Jb 11:18, 19. Ps 46:1-7. 90:1. 91:1-14. Pr 1:33. 18:10. Is 48:17-19. Je 23:6. Ezk 34:25-28. Mt 23:37. 1 P 1:5.

6. **I will**. 1 Ch 22:9. Ps 29:11. 147:14. Is 9:7. 45:7. Je 30:10. Ho 2:18. Mi 4:4. Hg 2:9. Zc 9:10. Jn 14:27. Ro 5:1. Ph 4:7-9. **ye shall**. Jb 11:19. Ps 3:5. 4:8. 121:4-7. 127:1, 2. Pr 3:24. 6:22. Is 35:9. Je 30:10. 31:26. Ezk 34:25. Zp 3:13. Ac 12:6. **rid**. Heb. cause to cease. Ex 23:29. 2 K 2:24. 17:25, 26. Jb 5:23. Is 35:9. Ezk 5:17. 14:15, 21. **shall the sword**. i.e. war. √121B, Ex +5:3. Ezk 14:17.

7. **chase**. 1 S *14:6. 2 Ch 20:5-7, 12, 14-17. Zc *12:8.

8. **five of**. Nu 14:9. Dt 28:7. 32:30. Jsh 23:10. Jg 7:19-21. 1 S 14:6-16. 17:45-52. 1 Ch 11:11, 20. Ps 81:14, 15.

9. **For I**. Ex 2:25. 2 K 13:23. Ne 2:20. Ps 89:3. 138:6, 7. Je 33:3. He 8:9. **make you**. Ge 17:6, 7, 20. 26:4. 28:3, 14. Ex 1:7. Dt 28:4, 11. Ne 9:23. Ps 107:38. **establish**. Ge 6:18. 17:7. Ex 6:4. Is 55:3. Ezk 16:62. Lk 1:72.

10. **eat old**. Le 25:22. Jsh 5:11. 2 K 19:29. Lk 12:17.

11. **I will**. Ex 25:8. 29:45. Jsh 22:19. 1 K 8:13, 27. Ps 76:2. 78:68, 69. 132:13, 14. Ezk 37:26-28. Mt=1:23. Jn=1:14. 2 C 6:16. Ep 2:22. Re 21:3. **soul**. Heb. *nephesh*, Ge +34:3. ver. 30. Jg 10:16. 1 S 2:35. Jb 23:13. Ps 11:5. 24:4mg. Pr 6:16mg. SS 6:12. Is 1:14. 42:1. Je 5:9, 29. ?6:8. 9:9. ?12:7. 14:19. 15:1. 32:41. 51:14mg. La 3:20. Ezk 23:18. Am 6:8. Mt 12:18. He 10:38. Note that in all the preceding references, "soul" is ascribed to God. √22A1. Anthropopatheia or Anthropomorphism B872. A soul is attributed to God. For other instances of this figure see the preceding references. **abhor**. Le 20:23. Dt 32:19. Ps 78:59. 106:40. Je 14:21. La 2:7. Zc 11:8.

12. **I will**. Ge 3:8. 5:22, 24. 6:9. Dt 23:14. 2 C ▶6:16. Re 2:1. **walk**. √22C17. Anthropomorphism B888. Human actions are attributed to God: walking. For other instances of this figure see ver. 24, 28. Dt 23:14. 2 C 6:16. **will be**. Ge 17:7. Ex 3:6. 6:7. 19:5, 6. Ps 50:7. 68:18-20. Is 12:2. 41:10. Je 7:23. 11:4. 30:22. 31:33. 32:38. Ezk 11:20. 36:28. Jl 2:27. Zc 13:9. Mt 22:32. He 11:16. Re 21:7.

13. **I am**. Le 25:38, 42, 55. See on Ex 20:2. Ps 81:6-10. 1 C 6:19, 20. **and I have**. Ps 116:16. Is 51:23. Je 2:20. Ezk 34:27. Lk 13:13. Jn 8:36. Ro 8:21. Ga 5:1.

14. **if**. Ge +*4:7. **ye will not**. ver. 18. Dt 28:15-68. Je 17:27. La 1:18. 2:17. Ml 2:2. Ac 3:23. He 12:25.

15. **if**. Ge +*4:7. **despise**. ver. 43. Nu 15:31. 2 S 12:9, 10. 2 K 17:15. 2 Ch 36:16. Pr 1:7, 30. Je 6:19. Am 3:1-3. Zc 7:11-13. Ac 13:41. 1 Th 4:8. **soul**. Heb. *nephesh*, Ge +34:3. Le 17:11. 1 S 1:26. Ps +50:17. Pr 5:12. Ro 8:7. 2 C +*12:15mg. **break**. Ge 17:14. Ex 19:5. 24:7. Dt 31:16. Is 24:5. Je 11:10. 31:32. Ezk 16:59. He 8:9.

16. **appoint**. Ps 109:6. **over you**. Heb. upon you. **terror**. Dt 28:65-67. 32:25. Jb 15:20, 21. 18:11. 20:25. Ps 73:19. Is 7:2. Je 15:8. 20:4. He 10:31. **consumption**. Ex +15:26. Dt 28:21, 22, 35. **consume**. Dt 28:32, 34, 67. 1 S 2:33. Ps 78:33. Ezk 33:10. Zc 14:12. **heart**. Heb. *nephesh*, soul. Ex +23:9. **and ye shall**. Dt 28:33,

51. Jg 6:3-6, 11. Jb 31:8. Is 65:22-24. Je 5:17. 12:13. Mi 6:15. Hg 1:6. **for your.** Is 10:4.

17. **set.** See on Le 17:10. 20:5, 6. Ps 68:1, 2. **ye shall be.** Dt 28:25. Jg 2:14. 1 S 4:10. 31:1. Ne 9:27-30. Ps 106:41, 42. Je 19:7. La 1:5. 2:17. **shall flee.** ver. 36. Ps 53:5. Pr 28:1.

18. **if.** Ge +*4:7. **seven times.** ver. 21, 24, 28. 1 S 2:5. Ps 119:164. Pr 24:16. Da 3:19.

19. **will break.** 1 S 4:3, 11. Is 2:12. 25:11. 26:5. Je 13:9. Ezk 7:24. 30:6. Da 4:37. Zp 3:11. **make.** Dt 11:16, 17. 28:23. 1 K 17:1. Is 5:1-7. Je 14:1-6. Lk 4:25.

20. **your strength.** Ps 127:1. Is 49:4. Hab 2:13. Ga 4:11. **for your land.** See on ver. 4. Dt 11:17. 28:18, 38-40, 42. Jb 31:40. Ps 107:34. Ho 2:8, 9. Hg 1:9-11. 2:16. 1 C 3:6.

21. **if.** Ge +*4:7. **contrary unto me.** *or,* at all adventures with me; and so ver. 24.

22. **wild.** ver. 6. Dt 32:24. 1 K *13:21-24. 20:35, 36. 2 K 2:24. 17:25. Je 2:15. 8:17. 15:3. Ezk 5:17. 14:15, 21. Re 6:7, 8. **rob you.** 2 K 2:24. Ezk 5:17. **your high.** Jg 5:6. 2 Ch 15:5. Is 24:6. 33:8. La 1:4. Ezk 14:15. 33:28. Mi 3:12. Zc 7:14.

23. **if.** Ge +*4:7. **ye will not.** Pr 29:1. Is 1:16-20. Je 2:30. 5:3. Ezk 24:13, 14. Am 3:6-12. 4:6-12.

24. **will I also.** 2 S 22:27. Jb 9:4. Ps 18:26. Is 63:10. Ml 2:2. Re ch. 8. **walk.** ╱22C17, Le +26:12.

25. **will I bring.** Dt 32:25, 41. Jg 2:14-16. Ps 78:62-64. Is 34:5, 6. Je 9:16. 14:12, 13. 15:2-4. La 2:21. Ezk 5:17. 6:3. 14:17. 21:4-17. 29:8. 33:2. Re 6:3, 4. **covenant.** Ps 111:5. Je 31:31-33. 34:13. Ezk 16:8. 17:19. **avenge.** Dt 32:35. Ps 94:1. Ezk 20:37. He 10:28-30. **send the pestilence.** Nu 14:12. 16:49. Dt 28:21. 2 S 24:15. Je 14:12. 24:10. 29:17, 18. Ezk 24:16n. +*38:22. Am 4:10. Lk 21:11.

26. **I have broken.** Ps 105:16. Is 3:1. 9:20. Je 14:12. La 4:3-9. Ezk 4:10, 16. 5:16. 14:13. Ho 4:10. Mi 6:14. Hg 1:6.

27. **if.** Ge +*4:7. **ye.** ver. 21, 24.

28. **walk.** ╱22C17, Le +26:12. **in fury.** Ex 20:5, 6. Dt 4:24. Is 27:4. 59:18. 63:3. 66:16. Je 21:5. Ezk 5:13, 15. 8:18. Na 1:2, 6. Re 15:1.

29. This was literally fulfilled at the siege of Jerusalem. Josephus gives a dreadful detail respecting a woman named Mary, who, in the extremity of the famine, during the siege, killed her sucking child, roasted, and had eaten part of it, when discovered by the soldiers! (*De Bell. Jud.* I.vii. c.2). Dt 28:53, 57. 2 K 6:28, 29. Is ◑*49:15. Je 19:9. La 2:20. 4:10. Ezk 5:10. Mt 24:19. Lk 23:29. He 10:31.

30. **I will destroy.** 1 K 13:2. 2 K 23:8, 16, 20. 2 Ch 14:3-5. 23:17. 31:1. 34:3-7. Is 27:9. Je 8:1-3. Ezk 6:3-6, 13. **high places.** 2 K +*21:3. **images.** lit. sun images. 2 Ch +14:5mg. 34:4mg, 7. Is 17:8. 27:9. Ezk 6:4, 6. **the carcases.** ╱46A. Catachresis; or, Incongruity B675: Of two words, where the meanings are remotely akin. Here the word "carcase" is changed from its strictly correct application to flesh and blood, and its use applied to the fragments of wood or stone of an idol. For other instances of this figure see Nu 9:18. Dt 16:8. 32:14. 2 S 23:17. Jb 4:12mg. Ps 74:1. 80:4mg. 88:5. Is 62:5. Ho 14:2. Mt 12:5. Ro 7:23. 1 C 1:25. Col 3:5. **my soul.** Heb. *nephesh,* Ge +34:3. See on ver. +√11n, 15. **abhor.** Le 20:23. Dt 32:19. Ps 78:58, 59. 89:38. Je 14:19.

31. **And I will make.** 2 K 25:4-10. 2 Ch 36:19. Ne 2:3, 17. Is 1:7. 24:10-12. Je 4:7. 9:11. La 1:1. 2:7.

Ezk 6:6. 21:15. Mi 3:12. **and bring.** Ps 74:3-8. Is 16:12. Je 22:5. 26:6, 9. 52:13. La 1:10. Ezk 9:6. 21:2. 24:21. Am 7:9. Mt *23:37, 38. 24:1, 2. Lk 21:5, 6, 24. Ac 6:14. **I will not smell.** See on Ge 8:21. Is 1:11-14. 66:3. Am 5:21-23. He 10:26.

32. **And I.** Dt 29:23. Is 1:7, 8. 5:6, 9. 6:11. 24:1. 32:13, 14. 64:10. Je 9:11. 25:11, 18, 38. 44:2, 22. La 5:18. Ezk 33:28, 29. Da 9:2, 18. Hab 3:17. Lk 21:20. **and your.** Dt 28:37. 29:24-28. 1 K 9:8. Je 18:16. 19:8. La 4:12. Ezk 5:15.

33. **I will scatter.** Dt 4:7. 28:64-66. Ps 44:11. Je 9:16. La 1:3. 4:15. Ezk 12:14-16. 20:23. 22:15. Am 9:8, 9. Zc 7:14. Lk *21:24. Ja 1:1.

34. This was fulfilled during the Babylonish captivity: for, from Saul to the captivity are about 490 years, during which period there were 70 sabbaths of years neglected by the Hebrews. Now the Babylonish captivity lasted 70 years, and during that time the land of Israel *rested.* **Then shall.** Le 25:2-4, 10. 2 Ch *36:21.

35. **because it.** Is 24:5, 6. Ro 8:22.

36. **I will send.** Ge 35:5. Dt 28:65-67. Jsh 2:9-11. 5:1. 1 S 17:24. 2 K 7:6, 7. 2 Ch 14:14. Jb 15:21, 22. Is 7:2, 4. Ezk 21:7, 12, 15. Am 5:3. **and the.** ver. 7, 8, 17. Dt 1:44. Jb 15:21. Pr 28:1. Is 30:17. **shaken.** Heb. driven. ❋S#5086h. Jb 13:25. 32:13 (thrusteth him down). Ps 1:4. 68:2, 2. Pr 21:6 (tossed to and fro). Is 19:7. 41:2. **none pursueth.** Pr 28:1.

37. **they shall.** Jg 7:22. 1 S 14:15, 16. Is 10:4. Je 37:10. **and ye shall.** Nu 14:42. Jsh 7:12, 13. Jg 2:14.

38. **ye shall.** Dt 4:27. 28:48, 68. Is 27:13. Je 42:17, 18, 22. 44:12-14, 27, 28.

39. **shall pine.** Dt 28:65. 30:1. Ne 1:9. Ps 32:3, 4. Je 3:25. 29:12, 13. La 4:9. Ezk 4:17. 6:9. 20:43. 24:23. 33:10. 36:31. Ho 5:15. Zc 10:9. **and also.** Ex 20:5. 34:7. Nu 14:18. Dt 5:9. 2 Ch 36:16. Ps 76:7. Je 31:29. Ezk 18:2, 3, 19. Mt 23:35, 36. Ro 11:8-10.

40. **If.** Ge +*4:7. **confess.** Nu 5:7. Dt 4:29-31. 30:1-3. Jsh 7:19. 2 S 12:13. 1 K 8:33-36, 47. Ne 9:2, etc. Jb 33:27, 28. Ps *32:5. Pr *28:13. Je 3:13. 29:12, 13. 31:18-20. Ezk 36:31. Da 9:3-20. Ho 5:15. 6:1, 2. Zc 10:9. Lk 15:18, 19. 1 J √1:8-10. **and that.** ver. 21, 24, 27, 28. Ezk 20:43.

41. **their uncircumcised.** Dt 30:6. Je 4:4. 6:10. 9:25, 26. Ezk 44:7. Ac 7:51. Ro 2:28, 29. Ga 5:6. Ph 3:3. Col 2:11. **if then.** 1 K 8:47-50. Lk 15:18. 1 J 1:9. **humbled.** Ex 10:3. 1 K 21:29. 2 Ch 12:6, 7, 12. 32:26. 33:12, 13, 19, 23. Ezk 6:9. 20:43. Mt 23:12. Lk 14:11. 18:14. Ja 4:6-9. 1 P 5:5, 6. **and they.** Ezr 9:4-9, 13, 15. Ne 1:9. 9:33. Ps 39:9. 51:3, 4. 79:1-5. 80:1-7. 85:4-7. Da 9:7-14, 18-25.

42. **remember my covenant.** Ge 9:16. Ex 2:24. 6:5. Dt 4:31. Ps +*89:34. 106:45. 136:23. Je 3:13. Ezk 16:60. Ho 11:8, 9. Ml +*3:6. Lk 1:72. **with Abraham.** Ge +*15:18. Ac +*7:5. Ro +*4:13. **remember the land.** Ps 85:1, 2. 136:23. Ezk 36:1-15, 33, 34. Jl +*2:18.

43. **shall enjoy.** See on ver. 34, 35. 2 Ch 36:19-21. Je 25:11. **and they.** See on ver. 41. 1 K 8:46-48. 2 Ch 33:12. Jb 5:17. 34:31, 32. Ps 50:15. 119:67, 71, 75. Is 26:16. Je 31:19. Da 9:7-9, 14. He 12:5-11. **they despised.** See on ver. 15. 2 K 17:7-17. 2 Ch 36:14-16. **their soul.** Heb. *nephesh,* Ge +34:3. ver. 15, 30. Ps 50:17. Am 5:10. Zc 11:8. Jn 7:7. 15:23, 24. Ro 8:7.

44. **I will.** Dt 4:29-*31. 2 K 13:23. Ne 9:31. Ps +*94:14. 98:2. Je +*4:27. Ezk 14:22, 23. Am 9:*9, 11-15. Ro 11:+√2, 26. **abhor.** See on ver. 11. **break.** Ps 89:33. Je 14:21. 33:20, 21. Ezk 16:60.

45. **for their**. Ge 12:2. 15:18. 17:7, 8. Ex 2:24. 19:5, 6. Lk 1:72, 73. Ro 11:12, 23-26, 28, 29. 2 C 3:15, 16. **whom I**. Le 22:33. 25:38. See on Ex 20:2. **in the sight**. Ps 98:2, 3. Ezk 20:9, 14, 22.

46. As this verse appears to be the proper concluding verse of the whole book, Dr. A. Clarke thinks that the 27th chapter originally followed the 25th. Others suppose that the 27th chapter was added after the book was finished; and, therefore, there is apparently a double conclusion, one at the end of this, and another at the end of the 27th chapter. All the ancient versions agree in concluding both chapters in nearly the same way. **the statutes**. Le 27:34. Dt 6:1. 12:1. 13:4. Jn 1:17. **in mount Sinai**. Le 25:1. Dt +*33:2. Jn 1:17. **by the hand**. Le 8:36. Ex +24:4. Nu 4:37. Ps 77:20.

LEVITICUS 27

He that maketh a singular vow must be the Lord's, 1, 2. The estimation of a person, 3-8; of a beast given by vow, 9-13; of a house, 14, 15; of a field, and the redemption thereof, 16-27. No devoted thing may be redeemed, 28, 29. The tithe may not be changed, 30-34.

2. **When**. Ge 28:20-22. Nu 6:2. 21:2. Dt 23:21-23. Jg 11:30, 31, 39. 1 S 1:11, 28. 2:11, 19, 25-28. Ps 4:3. 116:12-14. Ro 12:1. **a singular vow**. A vow is a religious promise made to God, for the most part with prayer, and paid with thanksgiving. Vows were either of abstinence (Nu chs. 6, 30.), or the devoting of something to the Lord, as sacrifices (Le 7:16), or the value of persons, beasts, houses, or lands, concerning which the law is here given. A man might vow or devote himself, his children, his domestics, his cattle, his goods, etc.; and respecting the redemption of all these, rules are laid down in this chapter. But if, after consecrating these things, he refused to redeem them, they then became the Lord's property for ever. The *persons* continued all their lives devoted to the sanctuary; the *goods* were sold for the profit of the temple, or the priests; and the *animals*, if clean, were offered in sacrifice; and if not proper for sacrifice, were sold, and the proceeds devoted to sacred uses. This is a general view of the different laws relative to vows, mentioned in this chapter. Ec 5:4, 5. **for the Lord**. Sometimes a person in his zeal for the Lord might wish to devote himself, or some of his family to His service, but as this would have unduly increased the number of those employed in divine service, while they were allowed thus to devote themselves, they were required also to redeem themselves by paying an equivalent for the services in money. The generous spirit of self-dedication was thus cherished and yet restrained at the same time (Young). **persons**. Heb. *nephesh*, Ge +12:5. **thy estimation**. or, thy valuation. ver. 3, 4, *18. Le 5:15, 18. 6:6. Jb 28:13, 17. Ps 55:13. lit. arrangement, ordering; this was according to the probable value of the person's services and position, and was expressly defined to prevent an exorbitant overcharge on the one hand, or a rash vow on the other (Young).

3. **And thy estimation**. ver. 14. Le 5:15. 6:6. Nu 18:16. 2 K 12:4mg. **after the**. ver. 25. Ex 30:13. 38:24. **shekel of the sanctuary**. or, holy shekel, having always the same value (Young).

4. **thirty shekels**. A little more than one-half the value of a man; for this obvious reason, that a woman,

if employed, would not be of so much use in the sanctuary as the man. Ex 21:32. Zc 11:12, 13. Mt 26:15. 27:9, 10. Ph=2:5-7.

6. **from**. Nu 3:40-43. 18:14-16. **the male**. The male five shekels, the *female* three shekels. Being both in infancy they were nearly of an equal value.

7. **from**. Ps 90:10. **fifteen**. The old man and the old woman, being almost past labor, were nearly of an equal value; the former being estimated at 15 shekels, and the latter at 10.

8. **poorer**. Le 5:7. 12:8. 14:21, 22. Mk 14:7. Lk 21:1-4. 2 C 8:9, 12. He 10:5-9. **according**. ver. 16, 18. Le 25:51. Je 5:7. **his ability**. Le 25:26. **that vowed**. A rich person might make a vow of some poorer person over whom he had authority, and this poor person might be unable to redeem himself by his poverty, and might claim a reduction thereupon, but the law here declares that the valuation is to be reckoned not by the ability of him who is vowed, but of him who is vowing (Young).

9. **all...is holy**. i.e. separated and devoted; it cannot be redeemed like a human being, a house, or a field (Young).

10. **He shall not**. ver. 15-33. Ja *1:8. **alter**. Heb. *halaph*, +S#2498h. Ge 31:41 (changed). Jb 14:7 (sprout). 29:20 (renewed. mg, changed). Ps 102:26. Is 9:10. 40:31 (renew. mg, change). 41:1. This Hebrew word often means to change for the better; another Hebrew word (*mur*) frequently signifies change for the worse, Mi +2:4n. Ge 35:2. Ps 55:19. **nor change**. Heb. *mur*, S#4171h, Mi +2:4. As in Ge 31:7, 41; an ox for a sheep, or a sheep for an ox. **the exchange**. As in Ps *15:4; 106:20, an old for a young one, or a young one for an old one.

11. **unclean beast**. Dt 23:18. Ml 1:14. For sacrifice or food; it might be sold, but if its owner wished to redeem it, he had to pay a fifth more than its valuation. These regulations would tend to prevent rash vows, and this shows how very far the spirit of the Mosaic legislation was from being allied to what is commonly called *priest-craft* (Young).

12. **or bad**. Ps 66:13:15. 76:11. Jon 2:9. Ml *1:14. **as thou valuest it, who art the priest**. Heb. according to thy estimation, O priest, etc. ver. 14.

13. **then he shall add**. ver. 10, 15, 19. Le 5:16. 6:4, 5. 22:14.

14. **sanctify**. ver. 21. Le 25:29-31. Nu 18:14. Ps 101:2-7. **as the priest**. ver. 12.

15. **then he shall add**. See on ver. 13. Dt 23:21-23. Ec 5:4, 5.

16. **some part**. Though the words *some part* are not expressed, yet it is generally allowed that they should be supplied here; as it was not lawful for a man to alienate in this manner his whole patrimony: he might express his good will for the house of God but he must not impoverish his own family. **of a field**. Ac 4:34-37. 5:4. **an homer**. or, the land of an homer, etc. i.e. as much land as required a homer of barley to sow it. The *homer* was very different from the *omer*; the latter held about three quarts, the former seventy-five gallons three pints. Is 5:10. Ezk 45:11-14. Ho 3:2. **possession**. i.e. derived from his parents, or by marriage, in opposition to "the field of his purchase," noticed in ver. 22 (Young). **fifty shekels**. The same as that of a full grown male, see ver. 3 (Young).

18. **after the jubilee**. Le 25:15, 16, 27, 51, 52.

19. **then he shall add**. See on ver. 13. **assured to him**. He 9:12.

21. **when**. Le 25:10, 28, 31. **devoted**. It is *cherem*, a thing so devoted to God, as never more to be capable of being redeemed. ver. 28, 29. Ex 22:20. Dt 13:17. Jsh 6:17. Ezr 10:8. Ezk 44:29mg. The original word denotes an object irrevocably devoted to God, either for preservation or destruction, more generally the latter. ❋S#2764h. Le 27:21, 28, 28, 29. Nu 18:14. Dt 7:26 (cursed thing), 26. 13:17 (cursed thing; mg, devoted). Jsh 6:17 (accursed; mg, devoted), 18, 18, 18. 7:1, 1, 11, 12, 12, 13, 13, 15. 22:20. 1 S *15:21 (things which should have been utterly destroyed). 1 K 20:42 (appointed to utter destruction). 1 Ch 2:7. Ec 7:26 (nets). Is 34:5 (curse). 43:28. Ezk 26:5 (nets), 14. 32:3. 44:29 (dedicated thing; mg, devoted). 47:10 (nets). Mi 7:2 (net). Hab 1:15, 16, 17 (net). Zc 14:11 (utter destruction). Ml *4:6 (a curse). **priest's**. Nu 18:14. Ezk 44:29.

22. **his possessions**. Le 25:10, 25.

23. **thy estimation**. ver. 12, 18.

24. **return**. Le 25:10. Ac 3:21. **to him**. ver. 20. Le 25:28. **land**. Le +25:23. Dt +32:43.

25. **And all**. ver. 3. **to the shekel**. A standard shekel; the standard being kept in the sanctuary, to try and regulate all the weights in the land by. 1 S 2:3. Pr 16:11. Is 26:7. Ac 4:34-37. 5:1-5. **twenty**. Ex 30:13. Nu 3:47. 18:16. Ezk 45:12.

26. **the firstling**. Heb. first born, etc. ❋S#1060h. Ge 10:15. 22:21. 25:13. +√27:19, 32. 35:23. 36:15. 38:6, 7. 41:51. 43:33. +√48:14, 18. *49:3. Ex √4:22, 23. 6:14. 11:5. 12:12, 29. 13:2, 13, 15. 22:29. 34:20. Le 27:26 (firstling; mg, firstborn). Nu 1:20 (eldest son). 3:2, 12, 13, 40, 41, 42, 43, 45, 46, 50. 8:16, 17, 18. 18:15, 17. 26:5. 33:4. Dt 15:19. 21:15, +√16, 17. 25:6. 33:17. Jsh 6:26. 17:1. Jg 8:20. 1 S 8:2. 17:13. 2 S 3:2. 1 K 16:34. 2 K 3:27 (eldest). 1 Ch 1:13, 29. 2:3, 13, 25, 27, 42, 50. 3:1, 15. 4:4. *5:1, 3. 6:28. 8:1, 30, 39. 9:5, 31, 36. 26:2, 4, +√10. 2 Ch 21:3. Ne 10:36. Jb 1:13, 18 (eldest). *18:13. Ps 78:51. +√89:27. 105:36. 135:8. 136:10. Is 14:30. Je +√31:9. Mi 6:7. Zc 12:10. See on Col +√1:15. See also on ❋S#1061h, firstfruits, Ex +23:16. As these firstlings were the Lord's before, it would have been a solemn mockery to pretend to make them a matter of a singular vow; for they were already appointed, if clean, to be sacrificed. **which**. Ex 13:2, 12, 13. 22:30. Nu 18:17. Dt 15:19.

27. **and shall add**. This was probably intended to prevent rash vows and covetous redemptions. The

priest alone was to value the thing; and to whatever his valuation was, a fifth part must be added by him who wished to redeem it. ver. 11-13.

28. **no devoted**. This is the *cherem*, the absolute, irredeemable grant to God. ver. +21n. Ex 22:20n. Nu 21:2, 3. Dt 7:1, 2. 13:15, 16. 20:16, 17. 25:19. Jsh 6:17-19, 26. 7:1, 11-13, 25. Jg *11:30, 31. 21:5, 11, 18. 1 S 14:24-28, 38-45. 15:3, 18, 32, 33. Mt 25:41. Ac 23:12-14. Ro 9:3. 1 C 16:22. Ga 3:10, 13. **most holy**. 1 Ch 29:1-9. 2 Ch 5:1.

29. **None**. Ex 17:14-16. Nu 21:2, 3. Jsh 6:17-19. 1 S 15:9, 18-23, 26, 33. 1 K 20:42. 1 C 10:2. **which shall be devoted**. That is, either that every person devoted to the service of God shall not be redeemed, but die in that devoted state, or, that such as were devoted to death by the appointment and law of God, as the Canaanites were, shall be put to death. **of men**. i.e. *out of men*; the reference is to such cases as that of the Amalekites, and the Canaanites, who were thus devoted not by men, but by God *out of men*, and not at all to the case of a person vowed to the Lord, as in ver. 2-8, who were to be all redeemed, being not *devoted*, but simply *vowed*. The original words are quite different. This applies to the case of Jephthah's daughter (Young). Jg 11:30-40. 21:11. **surely**. ƒ147B, Ge +2:16.

30. **all the tithe**. Ge +14:20. 28:22. Nu 18:21-24. Dt 12:5, 6. 14:22, 23. 2 Ch 31:5, 6, 12. Ne 10:37, 38. 12:44. 13:5, 12. Ps 56:12. Ml 3:8-10. Mt +*23:23n. Lk +*11:42n. 18:12. He 7:5-9.

31. **at all redeem**. ver. 13.

32. **passeth under the rod**. The Rabbins say, that when a man gave the tithe of his sheep or calves, he shut them in one fold, in which was a narrow door, to let out but one at a time. He then stood by the door, with a rod dipped in vermilion in his hand, and as they passed he counted them with the rod; and when the **tenth** came he touched it, by which it was distinguished as the tithe calf, sheep, etc. Young states, "The allusion is to the practice of shepherds, who in counting their flocks caused them to pass by a narrow opening, where with their crooks they could easily number them in succession." Je 33:13. Ezk 20:37. Mi 7:14. **the tenth shall be holy**. Nu 18:21. 31:30, 37-41.

33. **neither shall**. ver. 10.

34. **commandments**. Le 26:46. Dt 4:45. Jn 1:17. **Moses**. Ps 77:20. **in mount**. Le 25:2. 26:46. Nu 1:1. Ga 4:24, 25. He 12:18-25.

NUMBERS

NUMBERS 1

The Lord commands Moses to number Israel, 1-4; and appoints by name a prince from each tribe to assist him, 5-16. The number of every tribe, 17-46. The Levites are not numbered with the rest, being exempted to serve at the tabernacle, 47-54.

1. A.M. 2514. B.C. 1490. **wilderness**. Nu 10:11, 12, 33. Ex *18:5. *19:1. Le 27:34. Ac *7:30. Ga *4:25. He *12:18. **tabernacle**. Ex 25:22. Le 1:1. **on the first day**. As the tabernacle was erected on the first day of the first month, in the second year of their departure

from Egypt (Ex 40:17), and this happened on the first day of the second month, in the same year, it is evident that the transactions related in the preceding book must all have taken place in the space of *one month*, and during the time the Israelites were encamped at Mount Sinai. Nu 9:1. 10:11. Ex 40:17. 1 K 6:1.

2. **Take ye the sum**. This numbering was probably intended to illustrate the Divine faithfulness in thus increasing the seed of Abraham; to prepare them to preserve due order in their march; and to distinguish the tribes and families. Nu 26:2-4, 63, 64. Ex 30:12. 38:26. 2 S 24:1-3. 1 Ch 21:1, 2. 27:23, 24. **the children**.

Ge 49:1-3. Ex 1:1-5. **after.** ver. 18, 22, 26, etc. Ex 6:14-19.

3. **twenty.** Nu 14:29. 32:11. Ex 30:14. **able.** Nu 26:2. Dt 3:18. 24:5. 2 S 24:9. 2 Ch 17:13-18. 26:11-13. **by their.** Nu 33:1. Ex *12:17, 51. *13:18. Ps *105:37.

4. **every one.** ver. 16. Nu 2:3-31. 7:10-83. 10:14-27. 13:2-15. 17:3. 25:4, 14. 34:18-28. Ex *18:25, 26. Jsh 22:14. 1 Ch 27:1-22.

5. **stand with.** Ge 29:32-35. 30:5-20. 35:17-26. 46:8-24. ch. 49. Ex 1:2-5. Dt ch. 33. Re 7:4-8. **tribe of Reuben.** ver. 21. Nu 2:10, 10, 16. 7:30. 10:18. 13:4. 32:1, 2, 6, 25, 29, 31, 33, 37. 34:14. Dt 27:13. 33:6. Jsh 4:12. 13:15, 23, 23. 18:7. 20:8. 21:7, 36. 22:9, 10, 11, 13, 15, 21, 25, 30, 31, 32, 33, 34. Jg 5:15, 16. 1 Ch 5:18. 6:63, 78. Ezk 48:6, 7, 31. Re 7:5. **Elizur.** i.e. *my God is a rock,* ✳S#468h. Nu 1:5. 2:10. 7:30, 35. 10:18. **Shedeur.** i.e. *the Mighty One is light; spreading of light,* ✳S#7707h. Nu 1:5. 2:10. 7:30, 35. 10:18.

6. **of Simeon.** ver. 22, 23. Nu 2:12, 12. 7:36. 10:19. 13:5. 26:12. 34:20. Dt 27:12. Jsh 19:1, 1, 8, 9, 9. 21:4, 9. Jg 1:3, 3, 17. 1 Ch 2:1. 4:24, 42. 6:65. 12:25. 2 Ch 15:9. 34:6. Ezk 48:24, 25, 33. Re 7:7. **Shelumiel.** i.e. *my friend is God; at peace with God,* ✳S#8017h. Nu 2:12. 7:36, 41. 10:19. **Zurishaddai.** i.e. *my rock is the Mighty One,* ✳S#6701h. Nu 2:12. 7:36, 41. 10:19.

7. **Nahshon.** i.e. *serpent; diligent observer.* Nu 2:3. 7:12. 10:14. Ru 4:18-26. 1 Ch 2:+10, 11. Mt 1:2-5. Lk *3:32, Naasson.

8. **Nethaneel.** i.e. *given by God,* ✳S#5417h. Nu 2:5. 7:18, 23. 10:15. 1 Ch 2:14. 15:24. 24:6. 26:4. 2 Ch 17:7. 35:9. Ezr 10:22. Ne 12:21, 36. (1) One of the captains of Issachar in the wilderness, Nu 1:8; 10:15. (2) A son of Jesse, 1 Ch 2:14. (3) A priest in the time of King David, 1 Ch 15:24. (4) One of the Levites, 1 Ch 24:6. (5) A son of Obed-edom, 1 Ch 26:4. (6) One of the princes in the reign of Jehoshaphat, 2 Ch 17:7. (7) A Levite in the time of King Josiah, 2 Ch 35:9. (8) A Jew who took a foreign wife, Ezr 10:22. (9) A priest in the time of Joiakim, Ne 12:21. (10) One of the players on musical instruments when the wall of Jerusalem was dedicated, Ne 12:36. **Zuar.** i.e. *smallness; restraint,* ✳S#6686h. Nu 2:5. 7:18, 23. 10:15.

9. **Of Zebulun.** ver. 30, 31. Nu 2:7, 7. 7:24. 10:16. 13:10. 26:26. 34:25. Dt 27:13. 33:18. Jsh 19:10, 16, 27, 34. 21:7, 34. Jg 1:30. 4:6, 10. 5:14, 18. 6:35. 12:12. 1 Ch 6:63, 77. 12:33, 40. 27:19. 2 Ch 30:10, 11, 18. Ps 68:27. Is 9:1. Ezk 48:26, 27, 33. **Eliab.** i.e. *my God is father,* ✳S#446h. Nu 2:7. 7:24, 29. 10:16. 16:1, 12. 26:8, 9. Dt 11:6. 1 S 16:6. 17:13, 28, 28. 1 Ch 2:13. 6:27. 12:9. 15:18, 20. 16:5. 2 Ch 11:18. (1) A captain of Zebulun, Nu 1:9; 10:16. (2) Father of Dathan and Abiram, Nu 16:1; Dt 11:6. (3) A brother of David, 1 S 16:6; 1 Ch 2:13. Supposed to be the same as Elihu, who is named as one of the brethren of David in 1 Ch 27:18. (4) A name given in one place as that of the grandfather of Elkanah, but in 1 Ch 6:34 it is given as Eliel, 1 Ch 6:27. (5) A valiant man of the Gadites, 1 Ch 12:9. (6) A musician for the service of the Tabernacle, 1 Ch 15:18; 16:5. **Helon.** i.e. *strong,* ✳S#2497h. Nu 2:7. 7:24, 29. 10:16.

10. **of Joseph.** ver. 32. Nu 13:11. 26:28, 37. 36:1, 5. Dt 33:13, 16. Jsh 17:17. 18:5, 11. 24:32. Jg 1:22, 23, 35. 2 S 19:20. 1 K 11:28. 1 Ch 5:1. 7:29. Ps 77:15. 78:67. 80:1. 81:5. Ezk 37:16, 19. 47:13. 48:32. Am 5:6, 15. 6:6. Ob 18. Zc 10:6. Re 7:8. **Elishama.** i.e. *my God hath heard,* ✳S#476h. Nu 2:18. 7:48, 53.

10:22. 2 S 5:16. 2 K 25:25. 1 Ch 2:41. 3:6, 8. *7:26. 14:7. 2 Ch 17:8. Je 36:12, 20, 21. (1) A captain of Ephraim, Nu 1:10; 1 Ch 7:26. (2) A son of David, 2 S 5:16; 1 Ch 14:7. (3) Grandfather of Ishmael, who slew Gedaliah, 2 K 25:25; Je 41:1. (4) An Israelite of Judah, 1 Ch 2:41. (5) Another son of David, 1 Ch 3:6, called Elishua in the lists given in 2 S 5 and 1 Ch 14. (6) A priest in the time of Jehoshaphat, 2 Ch 17:8. (7) A scribe in the time of Jehoiakim, Je 36:12, 21. **Ammihud.** i.e. *my people is honorable,* 2 S +13:37. **of Manasseh.** ver. 34, 35. Nu 2:20, 20. 7:54. 10:23. 13:11. 26:34. 32:33. 34:14, 23. 36:12. Dt 3:13. 29:8. 33:17. 34:2. Jsh 1:12. 4:12. 12:6. 13:7, 29, 29. 14:4. 16:4, 9. 17:1, 2, 5, 6, 7, 8, 8, 9, 9, 11, 12, 17. 18:7. 20:8. 21:5, 6, 25, 27. 22:1, 7, 9, 10, 11, 13, 15, 21, 30, 31. Jg 1:27. 6:15, 35. 7:23. 11:29. 1 Ch 5:18, 23, 26. 6:61, 62, 70, 71. 7:29. 9:3. 12:19, 20, 20, 31, 37. 26:32. 27:20, 21. 2 Ch 15:9. 30:1, 10, 11, 18. 31:1. 34:6, 9. Ps 60:7. 80:2. 108:8. Is 9:21, 21. Ezk 48:4, 5. **Gamaliel.** i.e. *my rewarder is God,* ✳S#1583h. Nu 2:20. 7:54, 59. 10:23. **Pedahzur.** i.e. *the ransomed of the Rock; God delivers,* ✳S#6301h. Nu 2:20. 7:54, 59. 10:23.

11. **Abidan.** i.e. *my father is judge.* Nu 2:22. +7:60. 10:24. **Gideoni.** i.e. *the cutter down; warlike,* ✳S#1441h. Nu 2:22. 7:60, 65. 10:24.

12. **Of Dan.** ver. 38, 39. Nu 2:25, 25, 31. 7:66. 10:25. 13:12. 26:42, 42. 34:22. Ex 31:6. 35:34. 38:23. Le 24:11. Dt 27:13. 33:22. Jsh 19:40, 47, 47, 48. 21:5, 23. Jg 1:34. 5:17. 13:25. 18:2, 16, 22, 23, 25, 26, 30, 30. 1 Ch 27:22. 2 Ch 2:14. **Ahiezer.** i.e. *my brother is a help.* Nu 2:25. 7:66. 10:25. **Ammishaddai.** i.e. *my people is mighty; people of the Almighty,* ✳S#5996h. Nu 2:25. 7:66, 71. 10:25.

13. **Of Asher.** ver. 40, 41. Nu 2:27, 27. 7:72. 10:26. 13:13. 26:44, 47. 34:27. Dt *27:13. *33:24. Jsh 19:24, 31, 34. 21:6, 30. Jg 1:31. 5:17. 6:35. 7:23. 1 Ch 6:62, 74. 12:36. 2 Ch 30:11. Ezk 48:2, 3, 34. **Pagiel.** i.e. *he who meeteth me is God; event of God,* ✳S#6295h. Nu 2:27. 7:72, 77. 10:26. **Ocran.** i.e. *the troubled* or *the troubler; afflicted,* ✳S#5918h. Nu 2:27. 7:72, 77. 10:26.

14. **Of Gad.** ver. 24, 25. Nu 2:14, 14. 7:42. 10:20. 13:15. 26:15, 18. 32:1, 2, 6, 25, 29, 31, 33, 34. 34:14. Dt 27:13. 33:20, 20. Jsh 4:12. 13:24, 24, 28. 18:7. 20:8. 21:7, 38. 22:9, 10, 11, 13, 15, 21, 25, 30, 31, 32, 33, 34. 1 S 13:7. 2 S 24:5. 1 Ch 2:2. 6:63, 80. 12:14. Je 49:1. Ezk 48:27, 28, 34. Re 7:5. **Eliasaph.** i.e. *my God gathers; protector,* ✳S#460h. Nu 7:42, 47. 10:20. Son of Reuel, Nu 2:14. (1) A captain of the tribe of Gad, Nu 1:14; 10:20. (2) A descendant of Gershon, Nu 3:24. **Deuel.** i.e. *known of God; invocation of God,* ✳S#1845h. Nu 2:14, Reuel, i.e. *a friend of God.* 7:42, 47. 10:20.

15. **Of Naphtali.** ver. 42, 43. Nu 2:29, 29. 7:78. 10:27. 13:14. 26:48, 50. 34:28. Dt 27:13. 33:23. 34:2. Jsh 19:32, 32, 39. 20:7. 21:6, 32. Jg 1:33. 4:6, 10. 5:18. 6:35. 7:23. 1 K 4:15. 7:14. 15:20, 29. 1 Ch 6:62, 76. 12:34, 40. 27:19. 2 Ch 16:4. 34:6. Ps 68:27. Is 9:1. Ezk 48:3, 4. **Ahira.** i.e. *my brother is evil; brother of evil,* ✳S#299h. Nu 2:29. 7:78, 83. 10:27. **Enan.** i.e. *having eyes; great fountain,* ✳S#5881h. Nu 2:29. 7:78, 83. 10:27.

16. **the renowned.** *Keruey haaidah,* literally, "the called of the congregation," those who were summoned by *name* to attend. Nu 2:3-31. 7:2, 10-83. 10:14-27.

11:17. 16:2. 26:9. Jg 6:15. 1 Ch 27:16-22. **heads.** ver. 4. Ex 18:+*21, 25. Dt 1:15. 1 S 22:7. 23:23. Mi +*5:2.

17. **these men.** ver. 5-15. Is *43:1. Jn +*10:3. Re *7:4, etc.

18. **their pedigrees.** Ezr 2:59. Ne 7:61. He 7:3mg, 6mg. **by the.** See on ver. 2. **according.** ver. 20, etc. Is 43:1. Jn 10:3. Re 7:4. **from twenty.** In this census no women were reckoned, nor children, nor minors, nor strangers, nor Levites, nor old men; which, collectively, must have formed an immense multitude: the Levites alone amounted to 22,300 men.

19. **As the.** ver. 2. Nu 26:1, 2. 2 S 24:1-10.

20. **Reuben, Israel's son.** Nu 2:10, 11. 26:5-7. Ge *29:32. *46:8, 9. 49:3, 4. 1 Ch 5:1. Re 7:5.

21. **were forty and.** Nu 2:10, 11. 26:7.

22. **Simeon.** Nu 2:12, 13. 26:12-14. Ge *29:33. 34:25-30. 42:24. *46:10. 49:5, 6. Re 7:7.

23. **were fifty and.** Nu 2:13. 25:8, 9, 14. 26:14.

24. **Gad.** Nu 2:14, 15. 26:15-18. Ge *30:10, 11. *46:16. 49:19. Re 7:5.

25. **forty and.** Nu 2:15. 26:18.

26. **Judah.** Nu 2:3, 4. 26:19-22. Ge *29:35. 46:12. *49:8-12. 2 S 24:9. 1 Ch 5:2. 2 Ch 17:14-16. Mt 1:2. He 7:14. Re 7:5.

27. **tribe of Judah.** ver. 7, 26. Nu 2:3, 3, 9. 7:12. 10:14. 13:6. 26:20, 22. 34:19. Ge +*49:10. Ex 31:2. 35:30. 38:22. Dt 27:12. 33:7, 7. 34:2. Jsh 7:1, 16, 17, 18. 11:21. 14:6. 15:1, 12, 13, 20, 21, 63, 63. 18:5, 11, 14. 19:1, 9, 9, 34. 20:7. 21:4, 9, 11. Jg 1:2, 3, 4, 8, 9, 10, 16, 16, 17, 18, 19. 10:9. 15:9, 10, 11. 17:7. 18:12. 20:18. Ru 1:7. 1 S 11:8. 15:4. 17:1, 52. 18:16. 22:5. 23:3, 23. 27:6, 10. 30:14, 16, 26. 2 S 1:18. 2:1, 4, 4, 7, 10, 11. 3:8, 10. 5:5, 5. 6:2. 11:11. 12:8. 19:11, 14, 15, 16, 40, 41, 42, 43, 43. 20:2, 4, 5. 21:2. 24:1, 7, 9. 1 K 1:9, 35. 2:32. 4:20, 25. 1 Ch 6:55, 57, 65. 9:3. 12:16, 24. 13:6. 27:18. 28:4, 4. 2 Ch 2:7. 9:11. Ezr 1:2, 3, 5, 8. 4:4, 6. 5:1. 7:14. 9:9. 10:7, 9. Ne 1:2. 2:5, 7. 4:10, 16. 5:14. 6:7, 17, 18. 7:6. 11:3, 4, 4, 20, 25, 36. 12:31, 32, 44. 13:12, 15, 16, 17. Est 2:6. Ps 48:11. 60:7. 63. 68:27. 69:35. 76:1. 78:68. 97:8. 108:8. 114:2. He 8:8. **three score and.** Nu 2:3, 4. 26:22. 2 S 24:9. 2 Ch 17:14-16.

28. **Issachar.** ver. 8, +29. Nu 2:5, 6. 23:23-25. Ge *30:17, 18. *46:13. 49:14, 15. Re 7:7.

29. **tribe of Issachar.** ver. 8, 28. Nu 2:5, 5. 7:18. 10:15. 13:7. 23:23, 25. 34:26. Dt 27:12. 33:18. Jsh 17:10, 11. 19:17, 17, 23. 21:6, 28. Jg 5:15, 15. 10:1. 1 K 4:17. 15:27. 1 Ch 6:62, 72. 7:5. 12:32, 40. 27:18. 2 Ch 30:18. Ezk 48:25, 26, 33. Re 7:7. **fifty and.** Nu 2:6. 26:25.

30. **Zebulun.** Nu 2:7, 8. 26:26, 27. Ge *30:20. *46:14. 49:13. Re 7:8.

31. **fifty and seven.** Nu 2:8. 26:27.

32. **Joseph.** Nu 2:18, 19. 26:35-37. Ge *30:24. ch. 37, 39. 46:20. *48:8-14, 20. 49:22-26. Dt 33:17. **children of Ephraim.** ver. +33. Ge 48:5. Dt 33:17.

33. **the tribe of Ephraim.** ver. 10, 32. Nu 2:18, 18, 24. 7:48. 10:22. 13:8. 26:35, 37. 34:24. Dt 33:17. 34:2. Jsh 14:4. 16:4, 5, 8, 9. 17:8, 9, 17. 21:5, 20. Jg 1:29. 5:14. 7:24. 8:1, 2. 10:9. 12:1, 4, 4, 4, 15. 12:15. 2 S 2:9. 1 Ch 6:66. 9:3. 12:30. 15:9. 17:2. 25:7, 10. 27:10, 14, 20. 28:7, 12. 30:1, 10, 18. 31:1. 34:6, 9. Ps 60:7. 78:9, 67. 80:2. 108:8. Is 7:2, 5, 8, 9, 17. 9:9, 21, 21. 11:13, 13. 17:3. 28:1, 3. Je 7:15. 31:9, 18, 20. Ezk 37:16, 19. 48:5, 6. Ho 4:17. 5:3, 3, 5, 9, 11, 12, 13, 13, 14. 6:4, 10. 7:1, 8, 8, 11. 8:9, 11. 9:3, 8, 11,

13, 13, 16. 10:6, 11, 11. 11:3, 8, 9, 12. 12:1, 8, 14. 13:1, 12. 14:8. Ob 19. Zc 9:10, 13. 10:7. **were forty.** Nu 2:19. 26:37.

34. **Manasseh.** Nu 26:34. Ge 41:51. 46:20. 48:1. 50:23. Dt 33:17. Jsh 4:12. 17:1. 1 Ch 7:14. Re 7:6.

35. **thirty and two.** Nu 2:21. 26:34. Ge 48:19, 20.

36. **Benjamin.** Ge *35:16-18. 44:20. *46:21. 49:27.

37. **tribe of Benjamin.** ver. 11, 36. Nu 2:22, 22. 7:60. 10:24. 13:9. 26:38, 41. 34:21. Ge 49:27. Dt 27:12. 33:12. Jsh 18:11, 20, 21, 28. 21:4, 17. Jg 1:21, 21. 5:14. 10:9. 19:14. 20:3, 4, 10, 12, 13, 14, 15, 17, 18, 20, 21, 23, 24, 25, 28, 30, 31, 32, 35, 36, 39, 41, 44, 46, 48. 21:1, 6, 13, 14, 15, 16, 17, 18, 20, 21, 23. 1 S 4:12. 9:1, 16, 21. 10:2, 20, 21. 13:2, 15, 16. 14:16. 2 S 2:9, 15, 25, 31. 3:19, 19. 4:2, 2. 19:17. 21:14. 23:29. 1 K 4:18. 12:21, 23. 15:22. 1 Ch 6:60, 65. 8:40. 9:3, 7. 11:31. 12:2, 16, 29. 21:6. 27:21. 2 Ch 11:1, 3, 10, 12, 23. 14:8. 15:2, 8, 9. 17:17. 25:5. 31:1. 34:9, 32. Ezr 1:5. 4:1. 10:9. 11:4, 7, 31, 36. Ps 68:27. 80:2. Je 1:1. 6:1. 17:26. 32:8, 44. 33:13. 37:12. 48:22, 23, 24, 32. Ho 5:8. Ob 19. Ac 13:21. Ro 11:1. Ph 3:5. Re 7:8. **thirty and five.** Nu 2:23. 26:41. Jg 20:44-46. 2 Ch 17:17.

38. **Dan.** Nu 26:42, 43. Ge *30:5, 6. *46:23. 49:16, 17. Dt 33:22. Jsh 19:40-48. Jg 1:34. 13:2. 18:2. Je 4:15. 8:16. Ezk 48:1.

39. **threescore and two.** Nu 2:26. 26:43.

40. **Asher.** Ge *30:12, 13. +46:17. 49:20. Dt *33:24. Jsh 19:24. Re 7:6.

41. **forty and one.** Nu 2:28. 26:47.

42. **Naphtali.** Ge *30:7, 8. *46:24. 49:21. Re 7:6.

43. **fifty and three.** Nu 2:30. 26:50.

44. **are those.** ver. 2-16. Nu 26:64.

45. **all.** i.e. except the Levites, ver. 47. √ʃ171B, Synecdoche (of the Genus), Ge +24:10. **house of.** Nu 2:32. **twenty years.** ver. 3. Nu 14:29.

46. **six hundred thousand.** What an astonishing increase from seventy persons who went down into Egypt 215 years before, where they had latterly endured the greatest hardships! Such was the effect of God's promise, which cannot fail. Nu 2:32. 23:10. 26:51. Ge 12:2. 13:16. 15:5. 17:6. 22:17. 26:3. 28:14. 46:3, 4. Ex *12:37. 38:26. Dt 10:22. 1 K 4:20. 2 S 24:9. 1 Ch 21:5. 2 Ch 13:3. 17:14-19. He 11:11, 12. Re 7:4-9.

47. **the Levites.** ver. 3, 50. Nu 2:33. 3:14-29. ch. 4, 8. 26:57-62. Ge *29:34. *46:11. 1 Ch ch. 6. 21:6.

49. **Only thou.** Nu 2:33. 26:62. **tribe of Levi.** Nu 3:6, 15. 4:2. 16:7, 8, 10. 17:3, 8. 18:2, 21. Ge 46:11. Ex 2:1, 1. 6:19. 32:26, 28. Dt 10:8, 9. 18:1. 21:5. 27:12. 31:9. 33:8. Jsh 13:14, 33. 21:10. 1 K 12:31. 1 Ch 2:1. 6:1, 16. 9:18. 12:26. 21:6. 23:6, 14, 24. 24:20. Ezr 8:15. Ne 10:39. 12:23. Ps 135:20. Ezk 40:46. 48:31. Zc 12:13. Ml 2:4, 8. 3:3. He 7:5, 9. Re 7:7.

50. **thou shalt.** Nu 3:1-10. 4:15, 25-33. Ex 31:18. 32:26-29. 38:21. 1 Chs. 23. 25, 26. Ezr 8:25-30, 33, 34. Ne 12:8, 22, 47. 13:5, 10-13, 22. **the tabernacle.** ver. 53. Nu 20:11. Ex 31:18. *38:21. Ps 122:4. **shall encamp.** Nu 2:17. 3:23-38. 10:21. **round about.** 1 Ch 9:27. Mt =18:20. Ac=11:23. Re=1:13.

51. **the Levites.** Nu 4:5-33. 10:11, 17-21. **tabernacle.** Nu 10:17, 21. Ac=5:42. 1 C 12:4-6, 20, 21. **the stranger.** Nu 3:10, 38. 16:40. 18:22. Le 22:10-13. 1 S 6:19. 2 S 6:7. **shall be.** Nu *16:23, 24, 31-33, 35. 1 S *6:19. 2 S *6:6, 7.

52. **pitch.** Nu 2:2, 34. ch. 10. *24:2, 5, 6.

53. **shall pitch.** ver. 50. Nu 3:7. 18:3. 1 T 4:13-16.

2 T 4:2. **there be.** Nu 8:19. 16:46. 18:5. Le 10:6. 1 S 6:19. Je 5:31. 23:15. Ac 20:28-31. **and the.** Nu 3:7, 8. 8:24-26. 18:3-5. 31:30, 47. 1 Ch 23:32. 2 Ch *13:10, 11.

54. **according to.** Nu 2:34. Ezk 23:21, 22. 39:32, 43. 40:16, 32. Dt 32:32. 1 S 15:22. Ps *19:8, 11. Mt 28:20.

NUMBERS 2

A command that the people should encamp according to their tribes, 1, 2. Judah, Issachar, Zebulun, on the east; the first division, 3-9. Reuben, Simeon, Gad, on the south; the second division, 10-16. The Levites around the tabernacle in the midst, 17. Ephraim, Manasseh, Benjamin, on the west; the third division, 18-24. Dan, Asher, Naphtali, on the north, and in the rear, 25-31. A general recapitulation, 32-34.

2. **shall pitch.** ver. 3, 10. Nu 1:52. 10:14, 18, 22, 25. **the ensign.** Is 11:10-12. 18:3. Zc 9:16. **far off.** Heb. over against. Jsh *3:3, 4. Pr 14:7. SS *6:4, 10. Je 16:17. Am 9:3. **about the.** Nu 1:50, 53. Ps 76:11. Is 12:6. Ezk 43:7. 1 C 14:23, 40. Ph 1:27. Col 2:19. Re *4:2-5.

3. **the standard.** Ge *49:8-10. Jg 1:1, 2. 1 Ch 5:2. **Nahshon.** Nu 1:7. 7:12, 17. 10:14-16. 26:19-22. Ru 4:20. 1 Ch *2:10. Mt 1:4. Lk 3:32, 33, Naasson. **Judah.** Ge 49:8-10. Re *5:5. *22:16.

4. **threescore and fourteen.** Nu 1:27. 26:22.

5. **Issachar.** Ge *49:14. **and Nethaneel.** Nu 1:8, 28, 29. 7:18, 23. 10:15. 26:23-25.

6. **fifty and four.** Nu 1:29. 26:25.

7. **Zebulun.** Ge *49:13. **Eliab.** Nu 1:9, 30, 31. 7:24, 29. 10:16.

8. **fifty and seven.** Nu 1:31. 26:26, 27.

9. **These shall.** Nu 10:14.

10. **camp of Reuben.** Ge *49:3, 4. 1 Ch +*5:1, 2. **Elizur.** Nu 1:5. 7:30, 35. 10:18.

11. **forty and six.** Nu 1:21. 26:7.

12. **Simeon.** Ge *49:5, 7. **Shelumiel.** Nu 1:6. 7:36, 41. 10:19.

13. **fifty and nine.** Nu 1:23. 26:14.

14. **Gad.** Ge *49:19. **Eliasaph.** Nu 1:14. 7:42, 47. 10:20. Son of Deuel.

15. **forty and five.** Nu 1:25. 26:18.

16. **an hundred.** ver. 9, 24, 31. **they shall.** Nu 10:18.

17. **tabernacle.** ver. 2. Nu 1:50-53. 3:38. 10:17, 21. 2 S *7:5, 6. Jn=*2:21. 1 C *14:40. Col 2:5. Re=21:3. **in the midst.** Mt=18:20. Re=1:13.

18. **camp of Ephraim.** Nu 1:32. 10:22. Ge 48:5, 14-20. Dt 33:17. Ps 80:1, 2. **Elishama.** Nu 1:10. 7:48, 53. 10:22. 1 Ch 7:26, 27.

19. **forty thousand and.** Nu 1:33. 26:37.

20. **Gamaliel.** Nu 1:10. 7:54, 59. 10:23.

21. **his host.** Ge *49:22. **thirty and two.** Nu 1:35. 26:34.

22. **Benjamin.** Ge *49:27. **Abidan.** Nu 1:11. 7:60, 65. 10:24.

23. **thirty and five.** Nu 1:37. 26:41.

24. **Ephraim.** Ge +*48:17-19, 20. **an hundred.** ver. 9, 16, 31. **And.** Nu 10:22.

25. **Dan.** Ge *49:16, 17. **Ahiezer.** Nu 1:12. 7:66, 71. 10:25.

26. **threescore and.** Nu 1:39. 26:43.

27. **Asher.** Ge *49:20. **Pagiel.** Nu 1:13. 7:72, 77. 10:26.

28. **forty.** Nu 1:41. 26:47.

29. **the tribe.** Nu 1:42, 43. 26:48-50. **Naphtali.** Ge *49:21. **Ahira.** Nu 1:15. 7:78, 83. 10:27.

30. **fifty and three.** Nu 1:42, 43. 26:50.

31. **Dan.** Nu *10:25. **an hundred.** ver. 9, 16, 24. **They.** Nu 10:25.

32. **six hundred.** ver. 9. Nu 1:46. 11:21. 26:51. Ex 12:37. 38:26.

33. **not numbered.** Nu 1:47-49.

34. **according.** Nu 1:54. Ex 39:42. 1 Ch *6:32. Ps 119:6. Lk 1:6. 1 C *14:40. Col *2:5. **so they.** ver. 2. Nu 10:28. 23:9, 10, 21. 24:2, 5, 6.

NUMBERS 3

The sons of Aaron, 1-4. The Levites are given to the priests instead of the firstborn, 5-13. The Levites are numbered according to the three families of Gershon, Kohath, and Merari, 14-20. The families, number, and charge of the Gershonites, 21-26; of the Kohathites, 27-32; of the Merarites, 33-37. The place and charge of Moses and Aaron, 38, 39. The firstborn are freed by the Levites, 40-43. The overplus are redeemed, 44-51.

1. **generations.** Ge 2:4. 5:1. 10:1. Ex 6:16, 20. Mt 1:1. **spake.** Nu 1:1. Le 25:1. 27:34.

2. **the names.** Nu 26:60. Ex *6:23. 28:1. 1 Ch 6:3. 24:1.

3. **the priests.** Ex *28:41. 40:13, 15. Le 8:2, 12, 30. **whom he consecrated.** Heb. whose hand he filled. √121S3P, Ex +28:41. Ex 29:1-37. Le ch. 8, 9. He 7:28.

4. **Nadab.** Nu 26:61. Le *10:1, 2. 1 Ch *24:2. **in the sight.** 1 Ch 24:1-6. 1 J=3:22.

6. **Bring.** Nu 1:49-53. 2:17, 33. 8:6-15, 22-26. 16:9-11. 18:2-6. Ex *32:26-29. Dt 33:8, 9. Ps 119:91. Is 42:1. Ml 2:4. Jn *12:26. **near.** Ep=2:13. The word *hakraiv*, here rendered *bring near*, is properly a sacrificial word, and signifies the presenting of a sacrifice or offering to the Lord. As an offering, the tribe of Levi was entirely given up to the service of the sanctuary, to be no longer their own, but the Lord's. **present.** Ep=5:27. **minister unto.** Mt=25:40. =27:55. He=6:10.

7. **keep.** Nu 3:32. 8:26. 31:30. 1 Ch 23:28-32. 26:20, 22, 26. 2 T=1:14. =4:7. **to do the.** Nu 1:50. 8:11, 15, 24-26. **service.** Col=3:24.

8. **they shall keep.** Nu 4:15, 28, 33. 10:17, 21. 1 Ch 26:20-28. Ezr 8:24-30. Is 52:11. **to do the service.** Ex 32:26-28. Ps 119:91. Is 42:1. Jn 12:26.

9. **thou shalt.** Nu 8:19. 18:6, 7. Ep 4:8, 11. **wholly given.** Jn=17:24.

10. **appoint.** Ps *105:26. He √5:4. **they shall.** Nu 18:7. 1 Ch 6:49. Ezk 44:8. Ac 6:3, 4. Ro 12:7. 1 T 4:15, 16. **wait.** Ge 30:30. Ro=12:7. **priest's office.** 1 P=2:5, 9. Re=1:6. **and the stranger.** ver. 38. Nu 1:51. 16:35, 40. 18:3. 1 S 6:19. 2 S 6:7. 2 Ch 26:16-21. Ep 2:19. He 8:4. 10:19-22.

12. **I have taken.** ver. 41, 45. Nu 8:16, 18. 18:6. **firstborn.** Le +27:26. He=12:23.

13. **Because.** Nu 8:16, 17. 18:15. Ex *13:2, 12. 22:29. 34:19. Le 27:26. Ps *89:27. Ezk 44:30. Lk *2:23. Col +√1:13-15. He *12:23. Ja *1:18. Re *1:5. **on the day.** Ex 12:29, 30. *13:2, 12, 15. Ps *78:51. 105:36.

15. **Number.** Ps 147:4. Lk 12:7. **by their families.** Dt 32:8, 9. **every male.** ver. 22, 28, 34, 39, 40, 43. Nu 18:15, 16. 26:62. Pr 8:17. Je 2:2. 31:3. Mk 10:14. 2 T 3:15.

16. **word**. Heb. mouth. ✠121BA, Ge +45:21. ver. 39, 51. Nu 4:27, 37, 41, 45, 49. Ge 45:21. Dt +21:5.

17. **And these**. Nu 26:57, 58. Ge 46:11. Ex 6:16-19. Jsh 21. 1 Ch 6:1, 2, 16-19, Gershom. 15:5-23. 23:6-23. ch. 24-26. Ne 11, 12.

18. **Libni**. ver. 21. Ex 6:17-19. 1 Ch 6:17, 20, 21. 23:7-11. 23:12, 13, 18-20, Izhar. 25:4. ch. 26. Ne 12:1-26.

19. **Amram**. ver. 27. Ex 6:18, 20. 1 Ch 6:18, 38. 15:5, 8-10, 17-21. 23:12, 13, 18-20. **Izehar**. i.e. *oil*, ✱S#3324h. Nu 16:1. Ex 6:18, 21. 1 Ch 6:2, 18, 38. 23:12, 18.

20. **Mahli**. i.e. *sickly; my sickness, infirmity, disease*, ✱S#4249h. ver. 33. Ex 6:19. 1 Ch 6:19, 29, 47. 15:6. 23:21, 21, 23. 24:26, 28, 30. 25:3. Ezr 8:18. (1) A son of Merari, the son of Levi, Nu 3:20; 1 Ch 6:19. Called Mahali in Ex 6:19. (2) A son of Mushi, the son of Merari, 1 Ch 6:47; 23:23.

21. **of the Libnites**. See ver. 18. ✱S#3846h. Nu 26:58. **Shimites**. ✱S#8097h. Zc 12:13, Shimei. **Gershonites**. ✱S#1649h. ver. 23, 24. Nu 4:24, 27, 28. 26:57. Jsh 21:33. 1 Ch 23:7. 26:21, 21. 29:8. 2 Ch 29:12.

22. **according to**. Dt *32:8, 9. Ps *147:4. Lk *12:7. **seven thousand and**. Nu 4:38-40.

23. **behind**. Nu 1:53. 2:17.

24. **Lael**. i.e. *unto, by, because of God*, ✱S#3815h.

25. **the charge**. ver. 7. Nu 4:24-28. 7:7. 10:17. 1 Ch 9:14-33. 23:32. 26:21, 22. 2 Ch 31:2, 11-18. Ezr 8:28-30. Mk 13:34. Ro *12:6-8. 1 C *12:6. Col 4:17. 1 T 1:18. From this and the next chapter (See on Nu 4:44n), we see the very severe labor which the Levites were to perform, while the journeyings of the Israelites lasted. When we consider, that there was not less than 14 tons 266 pounds of metal employed in the tabernacle (see note on Ex 38:24), besides the immense weight of the skins, hangings, cords, boards, and posts, we shall find it was no easy matter to transport this movable temple from place to place. The *Gershonites*, who were 7500 in number, had to carry the tent, coverings, vail, hangings of the court, cords, etc. (ver. 25, 26); the *Kohathites*, who were 8600, the ark, table, candlestick, altars, and instruments of the sanctuary (ver. 31); and the *Merarites*, who were 6200, the boards, bars, sockets, and all matters connected with these belonging to the tabernacle, with the pillars of the court, their sockets, pins, and cords (ver. 36, 37; Nu 4:44n). **the tabernacle and**. Ex 25:9. *26:1-14. 36:8-19. 40:19. **and the hanging**. Ex *26:36, 37. 36:37, 38. 40:28.

26. **the hangings**. Ex *26:1, 7, 14, 36. *27:9-16. 38:9-16. **the cords**. Ex *35:18.

27. **of Kohath**. See on ver. 19. 1 Ch 23:12. 26:23. **Amramites**. ✱S#6020h. 1 Ch 26:23. **Izharites**. ✱S#3324h. 1 Ch 24:22. 26:23, 29. **Hebronites**. ✱S#2276h. Nu 26:58. 1 Ch 26:23, 30, 31, 31. **Uzzielites**. ✱S#5817h. 1 Ch 26:23. **Kohathite**. ✱S#6956h.

28. **eight thousand**. Nu 4:35, 36. **keeping**. ver. 7, 31.

29. **southward**. ver. 23. Nu 1:53. 2:10.

30. **Elizaphan**. i.e. *God is protector; whom God hides*, ✱S#469h. Nu 34:25. Ex 6:22. Le 10:4. 1 Ch 15:8. 2 Ch 29:13. (1) A Levite of the sons of Kohath, Nu 3:30; 1 Ch 15:8. See Elzaphan. (2) Prince of Zebulun in the time of Moses, Nu 34:25.

31. **the ark**. Nu 4:4-16. Ex *25:10-40. ch. 31-35. 37:1-24. 39:33-42. 40:2-16, 30. **the altars**. Ex 27:1-8.

*30:1-10. 37:25-29. 38:1-7. **and the hanging**. Ex *26:31-33. 36:35, 36.

32. **Eleazar**. Nu 4:16, 27. 20:25-28. 2 K 25:18. 1 Ch 9:14-20. 26:20-24. **chief over**. ✠147H, Ge +9:25. 1 C *12:18-21.

33. **of Merari**. ✠66, Ge +9:3. **the family**. See on ver. 20. 1 Ch 6:19. 23:21. **Mahlites**. ✱S#4250h. Nu 26:58. **Mushites**. ✱S#4188h. Nu 26:58.

34. **six thousand and**. Nu 5:43, 44.

35. **Zuriel**. i.e. *my rock is God*, ✱S#6700h. **Abihail**. i.e. *father of might; father of valor*, ✱S#32h. 1 Ch 2:29. 5:14. 2 Ch 11:18. Est 2:15. 9:29. (1) A Levite of the family of Merari, who was the father of Zuriel, the chief of the Merarites in the time of Moses, Nu 3:35. (2) The wife of Abishur, a descendant of Hezron, of the tribe of Judah, 1 Ch 2:29. (3) Head of a family in the tribe of Gad, 1 Ch 5:14. (4) A daughter of Eliab, David's brother, who became wife of Rehoboam, the son of Solomon, 2 Ch 11:18. (5) Father of Esther the Jewess, whom Ahasuerus, king of Persia, made queen instead of Vashti, Est 2:15; 9:29. **shall**. ver. 28, 29. Nu 1:53. **northward**. Nu 2:25.

36. **under the custody and charge**. Heb. the office of the charge. ver. 32. Nu 4:16. 1 C *12:11. *14:33. **the boards**. Nu 4:29-33. *7:8. Ex *26:15-29, 32, 37. 27:9-19. 35:11, 18. 36:20-34, 36. 38:17-20. 39:33.

38. **toward**. ver. 23, 29, 35. Nu 1:53. 2:3. **keeping**. ver. 10. Nu 18:1-5. 1 Ch 6:48, 49. **for the charge**. See on ver. 7, 8, 10. Ps *93:5.

39. **commandment**. ✠121BA, Ge +45:21. **twenty and two thousand**. Nu 4:47, 48. 26:62. Mt 7:14.

40. **Number all**. See on ver. 12, 15, 45. Ex 32:26-29. Ps 87:6. Is 4:3. Lk 10:20. Ph 4:3. 2 T 2:19. He 12:23. Re 3:5. 14:4.

41. **shalt take**. ver. 12, 45. Nu 8:16. 18:15. Ex 24:5, 6. 32:26-29. Mt *20:28. 1 T *2:6.

43. **a month old**. Le 27:6, 25. Ep 1:4-7. 1 P 1:18, 19. **were twenty and two**. ver. 39.

45. **the Levites instead**. ver. 12, 40, 41. **be mine**. Je *18:1-6. Ro *9:21.

46. **redeemed**. Nu 18:15. Ex 13:13. 1 P 1:18, 19. **which are**. ver. 39-43.

47. **five shekels**. Nu 18:16. Le 27:6. **the shekel**. ver. 50. Ex 30:13. Le 27:25. Ezk 45:12.

50. **a thousand three**. ver. 46, 47. Mt 20:28. Ep *1:4-7. 1 T 2:5, 6. T 2:14. He 9:12. 1 P *1:18. 3:18.

51. **Moses**. ver. 48. Nu 16:15. 1 S 12:3, 4. Ac 20:33. 1 C 9:12. 1 P 5:2. **as the Lord**. Le *27:6, 25. Ml 4:4.

NUMBERS 4

A command to number the family of Kohath from thirty to fifty years old, 1-3. The most holy things to be carried by them, having been prepared and covered by the priests, 4-15. The charge of Eleazar, 16. Moses and Aaron solemnly charged about covering the holy things, 17-20. The service and burden of the sons of Gershon, from thirty to fifty, 21-28; and of the Merarites, 29-33. The number of the Kohathites, 34-37; of the Gershonites, 38-41; and of the Merarites, 42-44. The sum total, 45-49.

2. **Kohath**. See on Nu 3:19, 27.

3. **thirty years**. Nu 8:24-26. Ge 41:46. 1 Ch 23:3, 24-27. 28:12, 13. Lk 3:23. 1 T 3:6. **enter**. 2 K 11:4-12. 2 Ch 23:1-11. 2 C 10:3, 4. Ep 6:10-18. 1 T 1:18. **to do**. Nu 3:7, 8. 16:9. 1 Ch 6:48. 23:4, 5, 28-32. 1 T 3:1.

4. **the service**. ver. 15, 19, 24, 30. Nu 3:30, 31. Mk 13:34.

5. **And when**. Nu 2:16, 17. 10:14. **Aaron shall come**. The law prohibiting any person, except the high priest on one day in the year, to enter into the most holy place, must have admitted an exception while the Israelites were in the wilderness: that exception, therefore, is here expressly made; and the directions given respecting it must be religiously observed, or the service could not be safely performed. While the cloud rested on the tabernacle, the general rule was in force; but when it was removed, then the priests might enter, to prepare the sacred vessels for removal. ver. 15. Nu 3:27-32. **they shall**. Ex 26:31-33. 36:35. 40:3. Is 25:7. Mt 27:51. He 9:3. *10:19, 20, 22. **and cover**. Ex 25:10-22. 37:1-9. 2 S 6:2-9.

6. **badgers' skins**. This was not the covering of badgers' skins made for the tabernacle, which was carried by the Gershonites (ver. 24, 25), but one made for the purpose of concealing and sheltering the ark when it was to be carried. **a cloth**. ver. 7, 8, 11-13. Ex 35:19. 39:1, 41. **and shall put**. Rather, "and adjust the staves thereof;" i.e. dispose them rightly under the covering, that they might be laid on their shoulders: for the staves were never taken out of the rings. **the staves**. Ex 25:13-15. 1 K 8:7, 8.

7. **the table**. Ex 25:23-30. 37:10-16. Le 24:5-8. **showbread**. Ex +25:30. 1 Ch ◑+9:32. **cover withal**. or, pour out withal. Ge 35:14. Ex 25:29. 29:40. 30:9. 37:16. **the continual**. The Israelites, without doubt, were able to procure corn enough from the adjacent countries, even when in the wilderness, to make the showbread, and to present the daily meat offerings.

8. **cloth of scarlet**. ver. 6, 7, 9, 11-13.

9. **the candlestick**. Ex 25:31-39. 37:17-24. Ps 119:105. Re 1:20. 2:1.

10. **within a covering**. ver. 6, 12.

11. **the golden altar**. Ex 30:1-10. 37:25-28. 39:38. 40:5, 26, 27.

12. **the instruments of**. ver. 7, 9. Nu 3:8. Ex 25:9. 31:10. 2 K 25:14, 15. 1 Ch 9:29. 2 Ch 4:11, 16, 19, 22.

13. **they shall take**. The embers of the sacred fire seem to have been removed in the grate, which was carried apart from the brazen altar; both being covered from view by purple cloths. **the ashes**. Ex 27:3-5. Le 6:12, 13. **purple cloth**. ver. 6-9, 11, 12. Ex 39:1, 41. Ezk *27:7.

14. **all the vessels thereof**. Ex 38:1-7. 2 Ch 4:19. **basons**. or, bowls. Nu 7:13. Ex 27:3.

15. **after that**. Nu 7:9. *10:21. Dt 31:9. Jsh 4:10. 2 S 6:3. 1 Ch *15:2, 4, 5, 12-15. **come to bear**. Nu *10:21. Dt *31:9. Jsh 3:9, 11-13. 1 Ch 13:6-10. **they shall**. Nu 3:38. Ex 19:12. 1 S 6:19. 2 S 6:6, 7. 1 Ch 13:9, 10. He *12:18-29. **These things**. Nu 3:30, 31.

16. **the office**. Eleazar himself, perhaps with the other priests, was required to carry the oil for the light, the incense, and the flour for the daily meat offering, and the holy ointment; besides superintending the Levites. It may be supposed, that he himself carried no more of the oil than for present use (see ver. 9). Nu 3:32. **the oil**. Ex *25:6. 27:20, 21. Le 24:2. **the sweet**. Ex 30:34-38. 37:29. **the daily**. Ex 29:39-41. **meat offering**. Le +23:13. **the anointing**. Ex *30:23-33. **the oversight**. Lk 4:18. Ac *20:28. 1 C 4:1. 1 T 2:5. He 3:1, 6. 1 P 2:25. 5:2.

18. **Cut ye not off**. Eleazar and the priests would be chargeable with the death of the Kohathites, if they failed to give them proper cautions and directions; or permitted them to gaze with irreverence or curiosity upon the holy things, which they might carry, but not see (ver. 20). Nu 16:32. 17:10. 18:5. Ex 19:21. Le 10:1, 2. 1 S 6:19. 2 S 6:6, 7. Je 38:23.

19. **the most holy**. ver. 4. **appoint**. Mk=13:34.

20. **they shall**. ver. 15, 19. Ex *19:21. Le 10:2. 1 S *5:1-3, 6, 10, 11. *6:19. He 10:19, 20. Re 11:19. **the holy things**. *Hakkodesh, the holy*, or *sanctuary*, i.e. the *ark*, as the Jews generally understand it; and with good reason, as any one may be convinced, who compares 1 K 8:8 with 2 Ch 5:9, where that which is called *the holy* in the former, is called *the ark* in the latter.

22. **the sum**. See on Nu 3:18, 21, 24.

23. **thirty years**. See on ver. 3. **to perform the service**. Heb. to war the warfare. *147D, Ge +1:29. ver. 3, 30. Nu 8:24. Ex 38:8. Is 63:1-4. Ro 7:14-24. 1 C 9:7. 2 C 6:7. 10:3-5. Ga 5:17, 24. Ep *6:10-19. 1 T 1:18. 2 T *2:3, 4. √4:7.

24. **burdens**. or, carriage. ver. 15, 19, 27, 31, 32, 47, 49.

25. **the curtains**. See on Nu 3:25, 26. 7:5-7. **the covering**. Ex 26:14.

26. **the hangings**. Ex 27:9. **and their cords**. Ex 35:18n.

27. **appointment**. Heb. mouth. ver. 37, 41, 45, 49. Nu 3:16. The Levites were under the command of the priests. Eleazar exercised this authority in general, as next in succession to Aaron; and he in particular was placed over the Kohathites; while Ithamar, his younger brother, commanded the Gershonites and Merarites (ver. 33). Mt=25:14, 15. Mk=13:34. Lk 1:70. =19:12, 13. 1 C 11:2. Ep=2:10. 1 Th =5:18. **burdens**. Ga=6:5.

28. **under the hand**. ver. 33. 1 C 12:5, 6.

29. **sons of Merari**. See on Nu 3:33-35.

30. **service**. Heb. warfare. See on ver. 3, +23mg, 35, 39, 43. Nu 31:3, 4, 5. Ps 110:1-7. 1 T 6:11, 12. 2 T *2:4. √4:7, 8.

31. **the charge**. See on Nu 3:36, 37. 7:8, 9. **the boards**. Ex 26:15.

32. **and by name**. An inventory was taken of every particular, even to the very pins belonging to each part, that nothing might be wanting when the tabernacle was set up. **the instruments**. Nu 3:8. 7:1. Ex 25:9. 38:17, 21. 1 Ch 9:29.

33. **under the hand**. ver. 28. Jsh 3:6. Is 3:6.

34. **Moses and**. ver. 2.

35. **thirty years old**. ver. 3, 23, 30, 39, 43, 47. Nu 8:24-26. 1 Ch 23:3, 24, 26, 27. 28:13. Lk 3:23. 1 T 3:6.

40. **two thousand and**. Nu 3:32.

41. **were numbered**. ver. 22.

44. The family of Merari, though smaller than either of the other families of Levi, yet had a greater number of able men than any of them; for out of 6200 males of a month old and upwards, we find 3200 who were neither too young nor too old for the service of the sanctuary; which was more than one half of their whole number. In this the wisdom and providence of God appear most conspicuously; for the Merarites were charged with the heaviest part of the sanctuary, as

the boards, bars, sockets, etc.; and though wagons were afterwards provided for them, yet the loading and unloading of the sockets, and other things of great weight, would require much strength, both bodily and numerical (compare ver. 36, 40, with Nu 3:22, 23, 24, *25n). Thus God ever manifests his wisdom, in fitting men for the work to which they are appointed, whether with respect to number or gifts: "For to one is given, by the Spirit, the word of wisdom; to another, the word of knowledge, by the same Spirit," etc., "...dividing to every man severally as he will" (See 1 C 12:8-11). **three thousand and**. Nu 3:34. Dt 33:25. 1 C 10:13. 12:8-12. 2 C 12:9, 10.

45. **according**. ver. 29.

47. **From thirty**. ver. 3, 23, 30. 1 Ch 23:3, 27. **every one**. ver. 15, 24, 37. Ro *12:6-8. 1 C *12:4-31. He *2:4. 1 P *4:10.

48. **were numbered**. Nu *4:3. 1 Ch *23:27-32. **were eight thousand and**. Nu 3:39. Mt 7:14. 20:16. 22:15.

49. **According to the**. ver. 37, 41, 45. Nu 1:54. 2:33. 3:51. 7:5, 6. 18:31. 1 C=3:8. He=6:10. **every one**. ver. 15, 24, 31. Is 11:2-4. 42:1-7. 49:1-8. Ro √12:4-8. **as the Lord**. ver. 1, 21. Ps *103:21, 22.

NUMBERS 5

The lepers and unclean to be excluded from the camp, 1-4. The law of restitution enforced, 5-10. The trial to be made of a woman suspected by her husband of adultery, 11-31.

2. **put out of the camp**. Nu *12:14. Le *13:46. Dt 24:8, 9. 2 K *7:3. 2 Ch 26:21. Mk *1:40-42. Lk *17:12-14. **and every**. Le *15:2-27. **and whosoever**. Nu 9:6-10. 19:11-16. *31:19. Le 21:1. **the dead**. Heb. *nephesh*, soul, Le +19:28. Lk ◐8:4.

3. **without**. 2 K 7:3. 1 C 5:7-13. 2 C 6:17. 2 Th 3:6. T 3:10. He 12:15, 16. 2 J 10, 11. Re 21:27. **defile not**. Nu 19:22. Hg 2:13, 14. **in the midst**. Le 26:11, 12. Ex *25:8. 29:45, 46. Dt 23:14. Ps 68:18. Is 12:6. 2 C 6:16. Re 21:3. **I dwell**. Ex 25:8. 29:45, 46. 2 C *6:16. 2 C *7:1.

6. **When**. Le 5:1-4, 17. 6:2, 3. **person**. Heb. *nephesh*, soul, Ge +27:31.

7. **confess**. Le 5:5. 26:40. Jsh *7:19. Jb 33:27, 28. Ps √32:5. Pr √28:13. Da *9:4. Mt *3:5, 6. 1 J √1:8-10. **and he shall**. Not only confession, but restitution, in every possible case, is necessary in order to obtain forgiveness. **with the principal**. Le 5:15. *6:4-7. 7:7. Lk +*19:8.

8. **have no**. Le 25:25, 26. **beside the ram**. Le *6:6, 7. 7:7. **an atonement**. Le +23:27.

9. **offering**. *or*, heave offering. Nu 18:8, 9, 19. Ex 29:28. Le 6:17, 18, 26. 7:6-13, +*14. *10:13. 22:2, 3. Dt 18:3, 4. Ezk 44:29, 30. Ml *3:8-10. 1 C *9:7-14.

10. **hallowed things**. 1 C *3:21-23. 1 P *2:5, 7, 9.

12. **If any**. ver. 19, 20. Pr 2:16, 17.

13. **lie with**. Le *18:20. 20:10. Ex +*20:14. Pr *7:18, 19. 30:20.

14. **spirit**. Heb. *ruach*, Ge +41:8. *Ruach kinah*, either a supernatural diabolic influence, exciting him to jealousy, or, rather the passion or affection of jealousy. ver. 30. Pr *6:26-35. SS 8:6. Zp 3:8. 1 C 10:22.

15. **her offering for her**. Le 5:11. Ho 3:2. **bringing**. 1 K *17:18. Ezk 29:16. He *10:3.

16. **bring her near**. or, rather, *bring it near*; i.e. her offering. **set her**. Rather, *set it*, i.e. the offering;

for the woman is afterwards ordered to be set before the Lord (ver. 18). Le 1:3. Je 17:10. He 13:4. Re 2:22, 23.

17. **holy water**. That is, water from the laver; called *holy*, because separated from common to sacred uses. This is the most ancient account of the trial by *ordeal*, which obtained so generally among various nations; and it was calculated to fortify the minds of the Israelitish women in the hour of temptation, and to render them watchful against all occasions of exciting suspicion in the breasts of their husbands (1 Th 5:22). Nu *19:2-9, 17. Ex 30:18. **of the dust**. Jb 2:12. Je 17:13. La 3:29. Jn 8:6, 8.

18. **the priest**. He 13:4. Re 2:19-23. **uncover**. Le 13:45. 1 C 11:15. He *4:12, 13. **and put**. ver. 15, 25, 26. **the bitter water**. So called from the *bitter* effects which it had upon the guilty. Compare ✝121G, Metonymy of the Effect, where the effect is put for the thing or action causing or producing it, Ge +31:1. ver. 17, 22, 24. Dt 29:18. 1 S 15:32. Pr 5:4. Ec 7:26. Is 38:17. Je 2:19. Re 10:9, 10.

19. **charge her**. Mt 26:63. **with another**. *or, being* in the power of thy husband. Heb. under thy husband. ver. 20, 29. Nu 3:12, 41, 45. 32:14. Ro 7:2g.

21. **an oath**. Jsh *6:26. 1 S *14:24. Ne 10:29. Mt 26:74. **The Lord make**. Is 65:15. Je 29:22. **thigh**. ✝88, Ge +24:2. **rot**. Heb. fall. 2 Ch 21:15. Pr 10:7.

22. **the curse**. He *13:4. Ja *1:14, 15. **go into**. ver. 27. Ps *109:18. Pr 1:31. Ezk 3:3. **the woman**. Dt 27:15-26. Jb 31:21, 22, 39, 40. Ps 7:4, 5. **Amen**. Ps 41:13. 72:19. 89:52. Jn 3:3, 11. 5:24, 25. 6:53g.

23. **write these**. Ex 17:14. Dt 31:19. 2 Ch 34:24. Jb 31:35. Je 51:60-64. 1 C 16:21, 22. Re 20:12. **blot**. Ps 51:1, 9. Is 43:25. 44:22. Ac *3:19.

24. **the water**. Zc *5:3, 4. Ml +*3:5. 2 C *5:21. Ga *3:13.

25. **priest**. ver. 15, 18. **wave**. Ex 29:*24, 27n. Le *8:27. Le +23:15.

26. **the memorial**. Le 2:2, 9. 5:12. 6:15.

27. **if she be defiled**. ver. 20. Pr 5:4-11. Ec 7:26. Ro 6:21. 2 C 2:16. He 10:26-30. 2 P 2:10. **the woman**. Ex *34:14. Dt 28:37. Ps 83:9-11. Is 65:15. Je *24:9. 29:18, 22. 42:18. Zc 8:13. 2 C *11:2.

28. **And if**. ver. 19. Mi 7:7-10. 2 C 4:17. 1 P 1:7. **and shall**. Ps +*113:9.

29. **the law**. He 7:11. 11:46. 13:59. 14:54-57. 15:32, 33. **when a wife goeth**. ver. 12, 15, 19. Is 5:7, 8.

30. **spirit**. Heb. *ruach*, Ge +41:8.

31. **be guiltless**. Ps 37:6. **bear**. Nu 9:13. Le 20:10, 17-20. Ezk *18:4. Ro 2:8, 9. **iniquity**. ✝121C1E, Ge +19:15.

NUMBERS 6

The Nazarite's vow, 1-8. His rule, in case he unavoidably contracted uncleanness, 9-12. His sacrifices and observances at the expiration of his vow, 13-21. The blessing which the priests were to pronounce on the people, 22-27.

2. **When**. ver. 5, 6. Ex 33:16. Le 20:26. Pr *18:1. Ro 1:1. 2 C *6:17. Ga 1:15. He 7:27. **separate themselves**. The word *yaphli*, rendered "shall separate themselves," signifies "the doing of something extraordinary," and is the same word as is used concerning the making "a singular vow" (Le 27:2); it seems to convey the idea of a person's acting from extraordinary

zeal for God and religion. **to vow.** Le 27:2. Jg 13:5. 1 S 1:28. Am 2:11, 12. Lk 1:15. Ac 21:23, 24. **Nazarite.** i.e. *separated one,* ***S#5139h.** ver. 13, 18, 19, 20, 21. Ge 49:26 (separate from). Le 25:5 (undressed. mg, separation), 11. Dt 33:16 (separated). Jg 13:5, 7. 16:17. La 4:7. Am 2:11, 12. **to separate themselves.** *or,* to make *themselves* Nazarites. *Lehazzir,* from *nazar, to be separate;* hence *nazir,* a *Nazarite,* i.e. a person separated; one peculiarly devoted to the service of God by being separated from all servile employments. The Nazarites were of two kinds: such as were devoted to God by their parents in their infancy, or even sometimes before they were born; and such as devoted themselves. The former were Nazarites for life; the latter commonly bound themselves to observe the laws of the Nazarites for a limited time. The Nazarites for life were not bound to the same strictness as the others, concerning whom the laws relate.

3. **from wine.** Le 10:9. Jg *13:4, 5. 14. Pr 31:4, 5. Je 35:6-8. Am *2:12. Lk ❭1:15. 7:33, 34. 21:34. Ep *5:18. 1 Th 5:22. 1 T 5:23. The sobriety and temperance which the Nazarites were obliged to observe were very conducive to health. Accordingly, they were celebrated for their fair and ruddy complexion; being said to be both whiter than milk, and more ruddy than rubies (La 4:7).

4. **separation.** *or,* Nazariteship. ver. 5, 8, 9, 12, 13, 18, 19, 21. **vine tree.** Heb. vine of the wine. Jg 13:14.

5. **razor.** Jg 13:5. *16:17, 19. 1 S *1:11. La 4:7, 8. 1 C 11:10-15.

6. **he shall come.** Nu *19:11-16. Le 19:28. Je 16:5, 6. Ezk 24:16-18. Mt 8:21, 22. Lk 9:59, 60. 2 C 5:16. **dead body.** Heb. *nephesh,* soul, Le +19:28.

7. **unclean.** Nu 9:6. Le 21:1, 2, 10-12. Ezk 44:25. **consecration.** Heb. separation. ver. 4. Ex 29:6. 39:30. Le 8:9. 1 C 11:10. This expression, "the consecration, or separation, of God is on his head," denotes his *hair,* which was the proof and emblem of his separation, and of his subjection to God through all the peculiarities of his Nazarate. Paul probably alludes to this circumstance in 1 C 11:10; by considering a married woman as a Nazarite for life, i.e. *separated* from all others, and united to her husband, to whom she is *subject.* ƒ121M, Ex +8:23. Metonymy of the Subject B586, the thing signified is put for the sign. Here, "separation" is put for the hair, which was the sign and symbol of his separation.

8. **All the days.** Jn *17:15-19. Ro *1:1. 2 C *6:17, 18.

9. **and he.** Nu 19:14-19. **shave.** ver. 18. Ac 18:18. 21:23, 24. Ph 3:8, 9.

10. **eighth day.** Le 1:14. 5:7-10. 9:1-21. 12:6. 14:22, 23, 31. 15:14, 29. Jn 2:1, 2. Ro 4:25.

11. **offer.** Le 5:8-10. 14:30, 31. **sin offering.** Le +*23:19. **burnt offering.** Le +*23:12. **the dead.** Heb. *nephesh,* soul, Le +19:28. **and shall.** ver. 5. Is *52:11. 2 C *7:1. Re *18:4.

12. **a trespass.** Le +5:6. 14:24. **but the.** Ezk 18:24. Mt 3:15. 24:13. Jn 8:29-31. Ja 2:10. 2 J 8. **lost.** Heb. fall. 1 K 20:25. S#5307h. Ge 4:5 (fell), 6 (fallen). 15:12 (fell). 25:+18 (died; mg, fell). Ex 19:21 (perish). 1 K 1:52 (fall). Ps 5:10. 35:8. *37:24. 91:7. 141:10. Je 6:15.

13. **are fulfilled.** Ac 21:26. **door of.** Le *1:2, 3.

14. **one he.** Le *1:4, 10-13. 1 Ch 15:26, 28, 32. **burnt offering.** Le +*23:12. **one ewe.** Le *4:2, 3, 27,

32. Ml 1:13, 14. 1 P 1:19. **sin offering.** Le +*23:19. **one ram.** Le 3:6. **peace offerings.** Le *3:1. +*23:19.

15. **a basket.** Le 2:4. 8:2. 9:4. Jn 6:50-59. **anointed.** Ex 29:2. **meat offering.** Le *2:1, 2. +*23:13. **drink offering.** Nu *15:5, 7, 10. Le +*23:13. Is 62:9. Jl 1:9, 13. 2:14. 1 C 10:31. 11:26.

16. **sin offering.** Le +*23:19. **burnt offering.** Le +*23:12.

17. **peace offerings.** Le +*23:19. **meat offering.** Le +*23:13. **drink offering.** Le +*23:13.

18. **shave the head.** The *hair,* which was permitted to grow for this purpose, was shaven off, as a token that the vow was accomplished. ver. 5, 9. Ac *18:18. *21:23, 24, 26. **and put it.** Lk 17:10. Ep 1:6.

19. **the sodden.** Le 8:31. 1 S 2:15. **put them.** Ex *29:23-28. Le 7:30. 8:27.

20. **the priest shall.** Nu 5:25. Ex 29:27, 28. Le 9:21. 10:15. 23:11. **wave offering.** Le +*23:15. **with the wave.** Nu 18:18. Le 7:31, 34. **and after.** Ps *16:10, 11. Ec 9:7. Is 25:6. *35:10. 53:10-12. Zc 9:15, 17. 10:7. Mt 26:29. Mk 14:25. Jn 17:4, 5. 19:30. 2 T 4:7, 8.

21. **the law.** See on Nu 5:29. **beside that.** Ezr 2:69. Ga 6:6. He 13:16.

23. **Aaron and.** Le *9:22. 1 Ch *23:13. **ye shall bless.** Ge 14:19, 20. 24:60. 27:27-29. 28:3, 4. 47:7, 10. 48:20. Le 9:22, 23. Dt 10:8. 21:5. 33:1. Jsh 8:33. 1 Ch 23:13. Lk 24:50, 51. Ro 1:7. 1 C 1:3. 2 C 13:14. He 7:1, 7. 11:20, 21. 1 P 1:2. 2 P 1:2, 3. 2 J *3.

24. **The Lord.** Ru 2:4. Ps *5:12. *115:12. 133:3. *134:3. Pr +*10:22. 1 C 14:16. Ep 6:24. Ph 4:23. Re 1:4, 5. **keep thee.** Ps 91:11. *121:3-8. Is *27:3. 42:6. Jn *17:11. Ph *4:7. 1 Th *5:23. 1 P *1:5. Ju √24.

25. **The Lord.** Ps 21:6. *31:16. 67:1. 80:1-3, 7, 19. *119:135. Da *9:17. 2 C *4:4. **face.** ƒ22A4, Ge +19:13. **shine.** ƒ22J, Ps +*27:1. **be gracious.** T#1509. Ge ◐31:49. 43:29. Ex 33:19. +√34:6, 7. Ps *30:7. 77:9. Is *30:19. 33:2. Ml 1:9. Lk *18:13. Jn *1:17. 2 C √13:14. He *13:20, 21.

26. **lift up.** Ps *4:6. 42:5. *89:15. Ac 2:28. ƒ121S3E3. Metonymy of the Adjunct B606. The sign is put for the thing signified in connected words and phrases. Here, "to lift up the face" is put for boldness and courage. For other instances of this figure see Dt 28:50mg. Ec 8:1mg. Da 8:23. **countenance.** ƒ22A4, Ge +19:13. Ps 21:6. 89:15. **give thee.** Ps *16:11. 29:11. Is *26:3, 12. 57:19. Mi 5:5. Lk 2:14. Jn *14:27. 16:33. 20:21, 26. Ac *10:36. Ro *5:1. 15:13, 33. Ep 2:14-17. 6:23. Ph √4:6, 7. 2 Th *3:16. **peace.** ƒ17I19A, Ge +43:23.

27. **put my name.** Ge 48:16. Ex 3:13-15. 6:3. 34:5-7. Dt *28:10. 1 K 11:36. 14:21. 2 K 21:4. 2 Ch +√7:14. Ezr 6:12. Ne 1:9. Ps +*9:10. Is 4:1. 43:7. Je 14:9. Da *9:18, 19. Mt +*28:19. Jn 17:26. Ac 15:14. Re 3:12. 22:4. **and I will.** Nu 23:20. Ge 12:2, 3. 32:26, 29. 1 Ch 4:10. Ps 5:12. 67:7. 115:12, 13. Ga *3:14. Ep *1:3-5. *2:19.

NUMBERS 7

The princes of Israel present, at the dedication of the sanctuary, six covered wagons and twelve oxen, which the Lord directs to be given to the Levites, 1-9. Each of the twelve princes, on twelve succeeding days, brings oblations and sacrifices, 10-88. The Lord speaks to Moses from the mercy seat, 89.

1. **had fully.** Ex *40:2, 17-19. **anointed it.** Ex 30:23-

30. **Le** *8:10, 11. **ch.** 9. **He** *9:2. **sanctified them.** Ge 2:3. Ex 13:2. 1 K 8:64. Mt 23:19.

2. **the princes.** Nu *1:4-16. **ch.** 2, 10. **and were over,** etc. Heb. who stood. **offered.** Ex 35:27. 1 Ch 29:6-8. 2 Ch 35:8. Ezr 2:68, 69. Ne 7:70-72.

3. **covered wagons.** The Hebrew *egloth tzav*, signifies *tilted wagons;* so LXX. *amaxas lampanikas*, with which the Coptic agrees. These were given for the more convenient exporting of the heavier parts of the tabernacle.

5. **Take it.** Ex 25:1-11. 35:4-10. Ps 16:2, 3. Is 42:1-7. 49:1-8. Ep 4:11-13. T 3:8. **give them.** i.e. *distribute them among the Levites as they need them;* giving most to those who have the heaviest burdens to bear. **according.** Nu 4:9. 18:31. 1 C=3:8. He=6:10.

7. **Two wagons.** Nu 3:25n, 26. 4:24-28. **sons of Gershon.** The Gershonites being fewest in number of able men, had the less burdensome things to carry; for they carried only the curtains, coverings, and hangings (Nu 4:25, 40). And although this was a cumbersome carriage, and they needed wagons, yet it was not a heavy one, and they needed few. Nu *4:25.

8. **four wagons.** Nu 3:36, 37. *4:28-33. **the sons.** Though the Merarites were the most numerous, yet they had the greatest burden, namely, the boards, bars, pillars, and sockets, to carry (Nu 4:31, 32, 44n, 48). Therefore they had double the number of wagons to what the Gershonites had assigned them.

9. **unto the.** Because they had the charge of the ark, table, candlestick, altars, etc. (Nu 4:4-15), which were to be carried upon their shoulders, for those sacred things must not be drawn by beasts. **because.** Nu 3:31. *4:4-16. 2 S 6:6, 13. 1 Ch 15:3, 13. 23:26. **shoulders.** Mt=11:29, 30.

10. **princes.** Every prince, or chief, offered in the behalf, and doubtless at the expense, of his whole tribe. **dedicating.** Dt 20:5. 1 K 8:63. 2 Ch 7:5, 9. Ezr 6:16, 17. Ne 12:27, 43. Ps 30, title. Jn 10:22.

11. **shall offer.** 1 Ch 29:6-10, 13-16. **on his day.** 1 C 14:33, 40. Col 2:5.

12. **Nahshon.** Nu 1:7. 2:3. 10:14. Ge 49:8, 10. Ru 4:20. Mt 1:4. Lk 3:32, Naasson.

13. **charger.** Ex 25:29. 37:16. 1 K 7:43, 45. 2 K 25:14, 15. Ezr 1:9, 10. 8:25. Je 52:19. Da 5:2. Zc 14:20. Mt 14:8, 11. **the shekel.** Ex *30:13. Le 27:3, 25. **a meat offering.** Le *2:1.

14. **spoon.** Nu 4:7. Ex 37:16. 1 K 7:50. 2 K 25:14, 15. 2 Ch 4:22. 22:14. **incense.** Ex *30:7, 8, 34-38. 35:8.

15. **One young.** Nu ch. 25, 28, 29. Le ch. 1. Is 53:4, 10, 11. Mt 20:28. Jn 17:19. Ro 3:24-26. 5:6-11, 16-21. 8:34. 10:4. 1 T 2:6. T 2:14. He 2:10. 1 P 1:18, 19. 2:24. 3:18. **burnt offering.** Le +*23:12.

16. **sin offering.** Le *4:23, 25. +*23:19.

17. **peace offerings.** Le ch. 3. +*23:19. 2 C 5:19-21. **this was the offering.** It is worthy of remark, that the different tribes are represented here as bringing their offerings precisely in the same order in which they encamped about the tabernacle (see Nu ch. 2, 10), beginning at the East, then proceeding to the South, then to the West, and ending with the North, according to the course of the sun. Thus God evinces that he "is not the author of confusion, but of peace" (1 C 14:33).

18. **Nethaneel.** Nu 1:8. 2:5.

19. **He offered.** See on ver. 12-17.

21. **burnt offering.** Ge 8:20. Le +*23:12. Ro 12:1. Ep 5:2.

23. **peace offerings.** Le 7:11-13. +*23:19. 1 K 8:63. Pr 7:14. Mt *10:8. Col 1:20.

24. **Eliab.** Nu 1:9. 2:7.

27. **young bullock.** Ps 50:8-14. 51:16. Is 1:11. Je 7:22. Am 5:22.

29. **the offering.** 2 S *24:22, 23. Is *32:8.

30. **Elizur.** Nu 1:5. 2:10.

31. **offering.** ver. 13, etc. **charger.** Evidently a large deep bowl for the use of the altar of burnt offerings in the outer court, for all the vessels of the sanctuary were of gold. It was probably used for receiving the flesh of the sacrifices upon which the priests feasted, or the fine flour for the meat offerings. **bowl.** *Mizrak*, from *zarak*, to sprinkle, a bowl or basin, used in sprinkling the blood of the sacrifice (Ex 27:23).

32. **spoon.** A pan or censer, on which the incense was put. Both the metal of which it was made, and that which it contained, show that it was for the use of the golden altar in the sanctuary. **incense.** Ps 66:15. Ml 1:11. Lk 1:10. Re 8:3.

35. **the offering.** Ac +*20:35.

36. **Shelumiel.** Nu 1:6. 2:12.

37. **His offering.** ver. 13, etc.

39. **one lamb.** Ex 12:5. Jn 1:29. Ac 8:32. 1 P 1:19. Re 5:6.

41. **the offering.** 2 C *9:5-7.

42. **Eliasaph.** Nu 1:14. 2:14. Son of Reuel.

43. **offering.** ver. 13, etc. **mingled with oil.** Le 2:5. 14:10. He 1:9. 1 J 2:27.

45. **young bullock.** Ps 40:6. Is 53:4. 2 C 5:21.

47. **the offering.** Ex *35:29.

48. **Elishama.** Nu 1:10. 2:18.

49. **His offering.** ver. 13, etc.

53. **the offering.** Ex *35:20-24.

54. **Gamaliel.** Nu 1:10. 2:20.

55. **His offering.** ver. 13, etc.

59. **the offering.** 2 Ch *24:8-11.

60. **Abidan.** i.e. *father of judgment,* *S#27h. ver. 65. Nu 1:11. 2:22. 10:24.

61. **His offering.** ver. 13, etc.

62. **incense.** Ps 141:2. Is 66:20. Da 9:27. Ro 15:16. Ph 4:18. He 13:15.

65. **the offering.** Mk *12:41-44.

66. **Ahiezer.** Nu 1:12. 2:25.

67. **His offering.** ver. 13, etc.

71. **the offering.** 2 C *8:1-4.

72. **Pagiel.** Nu 1:13. 2:27.

73. **His offering.** ver. 13, etc.

77. **the offering.** Ph +*4:17, 18.

78. **Ahira.** Nu 1:15. 2:29.

79. **His offering.** ver. 13, etc.

83. **the offering.** Ro *11:35, 36.

84. **the dedication.** See on ver. 10. 1 Ch 29:6-8. Ezr 2:68, 69. Ne 7:70-72. Is 60:6-10. He 13:10. Re 21:14. **the princes.** Jg 5:9. Ne 3:9.

85. **two thousand.** 1 Ch 22:14. 29:4, 7. Ezr 8:25, 26. **after the shekel.** See on ver. 13.

88. **dedication.** 2 Ch *7:5, 9. Ezr *6:16. Ne *12:27. **that it was anointed.** ver. 1, 10, 84.

89. **to speak.** Nu *12:7, 8. Ex 33:9-11. **him.** i.e. *God.* **he heard.** Nu 1:1. Ex *25:22. Le 1:1. He *4:16. **two cherubims.** Ex 25:18-21. 1 S 4:4. 1 K 6:23. Ps 80:1. 1 P 1:12.

NUMBERS 8

The lamps of the candlestick lighted, 1-4. The Levites consecrated, 5-22. The age and time of their service, 23-26.

2. **lightest.** Ex 25:37. 37:18, 19, 23. 40:25. Le 24:1, 2. Ps *119:105, 130. Is +*8:20. Mt 5:14. Lk 2:32. Jn 1:9. *3:19. *8:12. 9:5. 2 C 4:6. Ep 5:8. 1 P 2:9. 2 P *1:19. 1 J *1:5. Re 1:12, 20. 2:1. 4:5.

3. **as the Lord commanded.** Ps 40:7, 8. Jn *8:28, 29. He *3:1-6.

4. **this work.** Ex 25:31-39. 37:17-24. **candlestick.** Zc *4:2, 3, 11-14. Re *4:5. **beaten gold.** Ex +27:20. Is=53:5. He +=2:10. **beaten work.** Ex 25:18. 37:7, 17, 22. **the pattern.** Ex 25:9, 40. 1 Ch 28:11-19. He 8:5. 9:23.

6. **cleanse them.** Nu 4:23. 19:17, 18. Ex 19:15. Mt +*3:15. 21:23, 24, √25, 27. Mk +1:8. Lk √7:30. Jn 1:28, 29. 3:23, 25. Ac +*1:5n. ❍21:24, 25. 1 C=11:28. 2 C=7:1. He *7:13, 14. Ja 4:8.

7. **Sprinkle.** Le 8:6. 14:7. Is *52:15. Ezk *36:25. 1 C *6:11. T 3:5, 6. He *9:10. +*10:22. **water.** Nu *19:9, 10, 13, 17-19. Ps 51:7. He 9:13. =10:22. **let them shave.** Heb. let them cause a razor to pass over, etc. Le 14:8, 9. **wash their.** Nu 19:7, 8, 10, 19. 31:20. Ge 35:2. Ex 19:10. Le 15:6, 10, 11, 19, 27. 16:28. 31:20. Ps 51:2. Je 4:14. Mt 23:25, 26. Ep *5:26, 27. Ja 4:8. 1 P 3:21. Re 7:14.

8. **a young.** Ex 29:1, 3. Le *1:3. 8:2. **his meat offering.** Nu 15:8, 9. Le *2:1. Le +*23:13. **another.** Le *4:3, 14. 16:3. Is 53:10. Ro 8:3. 2 C 5:21. **sin offering.** ⨍121L5, Ge +4:5. Le +*23:19.

9. **thou shalt bring.** Ex 29:4, etc. 40:12. **shalt gather the whole.** The words *kol adath*, which are rendered "the whole assembly," often signify *all the elders*, or principal persons in the several tribes (Nu 15:4. 25:7. 35:12). And they cannot well have any other sense here; for it would be impossible for all the children of Israel to put their hands on the Levites, as stated in the next verse. **shalt gather.** Le 8:3. **whole.** √⨍171B. Synecdoche of the Genus, Ge +24:10. See also ⨍102. Hyperbole or Overstatement, Ge +7:19.

10. **and the children.** Nu 3:45. Le 1:4. Ac 6:6. 13:2, 3. 1 T 4:14. 5:22.

11. **offer.** Heb. wave. **offering.** Heb. wave offering. ver. 13, 15, 21. Nu 5:25. Ex 28:27n. Le +*23:15. Ro=15:16. Not that they were actually *waved*, but they were presented to God, as the God of heaven, and the Lord of the whole earth, as the wave offerings were: and in calling them *wave offerings*, it was intimated to them that they must move to and fro with readiness in the business of their profession (Ro 12:11). Nu 6:20. Ex 29:24. Le 7:30. 8:27, 29. **they may execute.** Heb. they may be to execute, etc. Nu 1:49-53. 3:5-43. 1 Ch *23:27-32.

12. **Levites.** ⨍66, Ge +9:3. Ex 29:10. Le *1:4. 8:14. 16:21. **the one.** ver. 8. Nu 6:14, 16. Le 5:7, 9, 10. 8:14, 18. 9:7. 14:19, 20, 22. He 10:4-10. **sin offering.** Le +*23:19. Ga =2:20. **burnt offering.** Le +*23:12. Ep =1:6. **atonement.** Le *1:4. 4:20, 35. 8:34. 16:6, 11, 16-19. He *9:22.

13. **offer them.** ver. 11n, 21. Nu 18:6. Ro =▶12:1. 15:16.

14. **separate.** Nu 6:2. Dt 10:8. Ro 1:1. 2 C=6:17. Ga 1:15. He 7:26. **and the Levites.** ver. 17. Nu 3:45. 16:9, 10. 18:6. Ml *3:17. **mine.** Jn=17:9, 10.

15. **go in.** ver. 11. Nu 3:23-37. 4:3-32. 1 Ch ch. 23, 25, 26. **and offer.** See on ver. *11, *13. Nu 3:12.

16. **wholly given.** *Nethunim, nethunim, given, given.* ⨍84. Epizeuxis, Ge +6:17. Nu 3:9. Ro=14:8. **instead of such.** Houbigant, on the authority of the Samaritan, reads "instead of every firstborn of the children of Israel, who openeth the womb." Nu 3:12, 45. Young notes that the firstborn, having been spared to the children of Israel while those of the Egyptians were slain, were Jehovah's by right of redemption; afterwards He thought fit to take the whole of the males of the tribe of Levi for His ministering servants in their stead, as noted in Nu 3:12, 13 (*Concise Critical Comments*). **taken.** Ac=15:14.

17. **all the.** Nu 3:13. Ex *13:2, 12-15. Lk 2:23. **on the day.** Ex 12:29. Ps 78:51. 105:36. 135:8. He 11:28. **I sanctified.** Ex 13:14, 15. 29:44. Le 27:14, 15, 26. Ezk 20:12. Jn 10:36. 17:19. He 10:29. Ja 1:18.

18. **I have taken.** Nu *16:8, 9. Mt *1:23-25. Lk *2:23.

19. **I have given.** Nu 3:6-9. 18:2-6. 1 Ch 23:28-32. Ezk 44:11-14. Jn=17:6, 9, 10, 15. **a gift.** Heb. given. **that there.** Nu 1:53. 16:46. 18:5. 1 S 6:19. 2 Ch 26:16-20.

21. **were purified.** See on ver. 7. Nu 19:12, 19. T=2:14. **offered.** See on ver. 11-13, 15. Nu 3:12. **offering.** Ju=24. **Aaron made.** ver. 12. **atonement.** Ro=5:11.

22. **after that.** ver. 15. 2 Ch 30:15-17, 27. 31:2. 35:8-15. Ro=6:18. **before Aaron.** Lk=1:74, 75. 1 C *9:19. Ga *1:10. **as the Lord.** ver. 5, etc.

24. **from twenty.** In Nu 4:3, the Levites are appointed to the service of the tabernacle at the age of 30 years; and in 1 Ch 23:24, they are ordered to commence their work at 20 years of age. In order to reconcile this apparent discrepancy, it is to be observed, (1) At the time of which Moses speaks in Nu 4:3, the Levitical service was exceedingly *severe*, and consequently required full grown, robust men, to perform it: the age of 30 was therefore appointed as the period for commencing this service, the weightier part of which was probably intended. (2) In this place God seems to speak of the service in a general way, hence the age of 25 is fixed. (3) In David's time, and afterwards, in the fixed tabernacle and temple, the laboriousness of the service no longer existed, and hence 20 years was the age appointed. **from twenty and five.** Nu 4:3, 23. 1 Ch 23:3, 24-27. 28:12, 13. **wait upon.** Heb. war the warfare of, etc. Nu +4:23mg. 1 C 9:7. 2 C 10:4. Ep 6:11-18. Ph=1:17. 1 T=1:18. 6:12. 2 T=2:3-5. **service of.** Is *42:1. Ph *2:5-7.

25. **cease waiting upon the service thereof.** Heb. return from the warfare of the service. Nu 4:23. 2 T *4:7.

26. **to keep.** Nu 1:53. 3:32. 18:4. 31:30. 1 Ch 23:32. 26:20-29. Ezk 44:8, 11. **and shall.** 1 T 4:15.

NUMBERS 9

The passover is again commanded, 1-5. The case of some who were unclean, 6-8. A second passover for the unclean or absent to be observed in the second month, 9-14. The cloud directs the removals and encampments of Israel, 15-23.

1. A.M. 2514. B.C. 1490. **in the first month.** See on Nu 1:1. Ex 40:2.

2. **keep**. Ex *12:1-3, etc. **passover**. Le +23:5. **his appointed**. Nu 28:16. Ex 12:6, 14. Le 23:5. Dt 16:1, 2. Jsh 5:10. 2 Ch 35:1. Ezr 6:19. Mk 14:12. Lk 22:7. 1 C 5:7, 8.

3. **the fourteenth**. 2 Ch 30:2, 15. **at even**. Heb. between the two evenings. Ex 12:6mg, n. He 9:26. **according to all the rites**. ver. 11, 12. See on Ex *12:7-11.

4. **keep the passover**. Ex *12:1-11. Le *23:5. Dt *16:1. Jsh *5:10.

5. **they kept**. Jsh *5:10. **according**. Nu 8:20. 29:40. Ge 6:22. 7:5. Ex 39:32, 42. Dt 1:3. 4:5. Mt 28:20. Jn 15:14. Ac 26:19. He 3:5. 11:8.

6. **defiled**. Nu 5:2. 6:6, 7. *19:11, 16, 18. Le 21:11. Jn *18:28. **dead body**. Heb. *nephesh*, soul, Le +19:28. ver. 7, 10. **they came**. Nu 15:33. 27:2, 5. Ex 18:15, 19, 26. Le 24:11.

7. **dead body**. Heb. *nephesh*, soul, Le +19:28. ver. 6, 10. **we may not offer**. ver. 2. Ex 12:27. Dt 16:2. 2 Ch 30:17-19. 1 C 5:7, 8.

8. **Stand**. Ex 14:13. 1 S *9:27. 12:7. 2 Ch 20:17. Jb 37:14. Ps 46:10. Is 30:18. Je 23:18. Hab 2:1. **I will**. Nu 27:5. Ex *18:15, 16. Ps 25:14. *85:8. Pr *3:5, 6. Ezk 2:7. 3:17. Jn *7:17. 17:8. Ac 20:27. 1 C 4:4. 11:23. He 3:5, 6.

10. **be unclean**. ver. 6, 7. Ro 15:8-19. 16:25, 26. 1 C 6:9-11. Ep 2:1, 2, 12, 13. 3:6-9. **dead body**. Heb. *nephesh*, soul, Le +19:28. ver. 6, 7. **yet he shall keep**. Mt 5:24. Ro *5:8. 1 C 11:28. Ep *2:4, 5.

11. **fourteenth**. ver. 3. Ex 12:2-14, 43-49. 2 Ch 30:2-15. Jn 19:36. **and eat it**. Ex 12:8. Ps *69:21. 1 C *5:6-8.

12. **shall leave**. Ex 12:10. Ac=2:30, 31. **break any bone**. Ex 12:46. Ps=✻34:20. Jn ✻±19:36. As this passage is cited in Jn 19:36 as a fulfillment of *prophecy*, it may well be urged as proof that the study of types is as valid a study as the study of fulfilled messianic prophecy, for the Scripture there does not distinguish between the two. **according**. ver. 3. Ex 12:43.

13. **forbeareth**. Nu 15:30, 31. 19:13. Ge 17:14. Ex 12:15. Le 17:4, 10, 14-16. He 2:3. 6:6. *10:26-29. 12:25. **soul**. Heb. *nephesh*, Ge +17:14. **because**. See on ver. 2, 3, 7. **bear his sin**. ſ121C1E, Ge +19:15. Nu 5:31. Le 20:20. 22:9. Ezk 23:49. He +*9:28.

14. **if a stranger**. Ex 12:48, 49. Le 19:10. 22:25. 24:22. 35:15. Dt 29:11. 31:12. Is 56:3-7. Ep 2:19-22. **one ordinance**. Ex 12:49. 1 C √12:13. Ep *2:17-19. √4:4. Re *22:17.

15. **on the day**. Ex 40:2, 18. **the cloud**. ſ22D3J5, Ex +13:21. Nu 14:14. Ex 14:19, 20, 24. 33:9, 10. *40:34. Ne 9:12, 19. Ps 78:14. 105:39. Is 4:5. Ezk 10:3, 4. 1 C *10:1. **at even**. Ex 13:21. 40:38.

16. **alway**. ver. 18-22. Ex 13:21, 22. *14:19, 20. *33:14. 40:38. Dt 1:33. Ne 9:12, 19. Ps 78:14. *80:1. 105:39. Is 4:5, 6. 1 C *10:1. 2 C 5:19. Re 21:3.

17. **when the cloud**. Nu 10:11, 33, 34. Ex *33:9, 10. 40:36-38. Ps 80:1, 2. Is 49:10. Jn 10:3, 4, 9. **and in the**. Ex 33:14, 15. Ps *32:8. 73:24. Jn 10:3, 4, 9.

18. **At the commandment**. ſ70, Ex +16:35. ſ46A, Le +26:30. ver. 20. Nu 10:13. Ex 17:1. 2 J 6. **as long as**. 1 C *10:1. There is no time lost, while we are waiting God's time. It is as acceptable a piece of submission to the will of God, to sit still contentedly when our lot requires it, as to work for him when we are called to it (Nu +9:8. Is 30:18).

19. **tarried long**. Heb. prolonged. ver. 22. **kept the**. See on Nu 1:52, 53. 3:8. Zc 3:7.

20. **few**. Ge 34:30. Jb 16:22. Is +10:19mg. **according to**. ſ113. Mesarchia; or, Beginning and middle repetition B260. For other instances of this figure see Ec 1:2. Je 22:10. Ezk 37:25. Zp 1:15, 16. Mt 10:40, 41.

21. **abode**. Heb. was. Ne *9:12, 19.

22. **a year**. or, days. This term is not necessarily to be understood of *a year*, as is done in the A.V.; it probably is equal to: *any number of days*, beyond a month (Young). Ge 21:34. 26:8. 37:34. 38:12mg. Jg ❍21:19mg. 1 S 7:2. 29:3. **abode**. See on ver. 17. Nu 1:54. 8:20. 23:21, 22. Ex *13:21, 22. 39:42. 40:16, 36, 37. Dt 1:6, 7. 2:3, 4. Ps *32:8. 48:14. 73:24. 77:20. *78:14. 107:7. 143:10. Pr *3:5, 6. Ac 1:4.

23. **they kept**. ver. 19. Ge 26:5. Jsh 22:3. Ps *77:20. Ezk 44:8. Zc 3:7.

NUMBERS 10

Directions for making and using the silver trumpets, 1-10. The Israelites journey from Sinai to Paran, 11-13. The order in which they marched, 14-28. Moses entreats Hobab to continue with them, 29-32. The prayer and blessing of Moses at the removing and the resting of the ark, 33-36.

2. **two trumpets**. A single alarm was a signal for the *eastward* division to march; *two* such alarms the signal for the *south*; and probably *three* for the west, and *four* for the *north*. There appears, therefore, a deficiency in the Hebrew text, which is thus supplied by the LXX.: "And when ye blow a third alarm, or signal, the camps on the west shall march; and when ye blow a fourth alarm, the camps on the north shall march." This addition, however, is not acknowledged by the Samaritan, nor any other version than the Coptic, nor any MS. yet collated. Le +23:24. 2 K 12:13. 1 Ch 15:28n. 2 Ch 5:12. **silver**. Ex 30:12-15. 36:24. 1 C=6:20. T 2:14. **of a whole piece**. Ex 25:18, 31. Ep 4:5. **the calling**. ver. 7. Ps 81:3. 89:15. Is *1:13. Ho 8:1. Jl 1:14.

3. **they shall blow**. Je *4:5. Jl *2:15, 16.

4. **heads of**. Nu 1:4-16. *7:2. Ex *18:21n. Dt 1:15.

5. **blow**. ver. 6, 7. Le 25:8, 9. Is 27:13. 58:1. Jl 2:1. **camps**. Nu *2:3-9.

6. **an alarm**. Nu 31:6. **the camps**. Nu *2:10-16.

7. **gathered**. Le *25:8, 9. Is √27:13. 1 C *15:51. 1 Th √4:16. 2 Th √2:1. **ye shall blow**. ver. 3, 4. **sound**. Jl *2:1. 1 Th *1:8.

8. **the sons of**. Nu *31:6. Jsh 6:4-16. 1 Ch 15:24. 16:6. 2 Ch 13:12-15. **trumpets**. 1 C=14:8. 1 Th=1:8. **for ever**. Heb. *olam*, Ex +12:24. Ge +9:16.

9. **if ye go**. Nu *31:6. Jsh *6:5. 2 Ch *13:14. **war**. 1 C=14:8. **oppresseth**. Jg 2:18. 3:27. 4:2, 3. 6:9, 34. *7:16-21. 10:8, 12. 1 S 10:18. Ps 106:42. **then ye shall**. Ne *4:18-20. Is 18:3. 58:1. Je 4:5, 19, 21. 6:1, 17. Ezk 7:14. 33:3-6. Ho 5:8. Am *3:6. Zp 1:16. 1 C *14:8. **alarm**. 1 C=14:8. **remembered**. Ge 8:1. Ps 106:4. 136:23. Lk 1:70-74.

10. **in the day**. Nu 29:1. Le *23:24. 25:9, 10. 1 Ch *15:24, 28. 16:42. 2 Ch *5:12, 13. 7:6. 29:26, 28. Ezr 3:10. Ne 12:35. Ps *81:3. 89:15. 98:5, 6. 150:3. Is *27:13. *55:1-4. Mt 11:28. 1 C *15:52. 1 Th √4:16-18. Re *8:2, 6. 22:17. **gladness**. Ps +*118:24. **the beginnings**. Nu +28:11. 2 Ch +2:4. Is 66:23. **blow with**. 1 Ch 15:24. **burnt offerings**. Le +23:12. **sacrifices of**.

Le +7:11. **peace offerings**. Le +23:19. **a memorial**. ver. 9. Ex 28:29. 30:16. Jsh 4:7. Ac 10:4. 1 C 11:24-26.

11. **on the twentieth**. Nu 1:1. 9:1, 5, 11. Ex 40:2. **the cloud**. See on Nu 9:17-23. Ex *40:36.

12. **took**. Nu 33:16. Ex 13:20. 40:36, 37. Dt 1:19. **out of the**. Nu 1:1. 9:1, 5. 33:15. Ex *19:1, 2. **the wilderness**. Nu *12:16. 13:3, 26. Ge *21:21. Dt 1:1. +*33:2. 1 S 25:1. Hab +*3:3.

13. **first took**. Nu *2:34. *9:23.

14. **the first**. Nu *2:3-9. 26:19-27. Ge 49:8. **Nahshon**. See on Nu 1:7. 7:12.

15. **Issachar**. Nu 1:8. 7:18.

16. **Zebulun**. Nu 1:9. 7:24.

17. **the tabernacle**. Nu *1:51. He 9:11. 12:28. 2 P 1:14. **the sons**. Nu 3:25, 26, 36, 37. 4:24-33. *7:6-8. **bearing**. Nu 1:51. 1 C 11:4-6, 20, 21.

18. **the camp**. Nu *2:10-16. 26:5-18. **Elizur**. Nu 1:5. 7:35.

19. **Simeon**. Nu 1:6. 7:36.

20. **Eliasaph**. Nu 1:14. 2:14, a son of Reuel. 7:42.

21. **the Kohathites**. Nu 2:17. 3:27-32. 4:4-16. *7:9. 1 Ch 15:2, 12-15. **bearing**. Nu 1:51. Ac=5:42. **the other did**. that is, *the Gershonites and the Merarites*. ver. 17. Nu 1:51.

22. **the camp**. Nu *2:18-24. 26:23-41. Ge 48:19. Ps 80:1, 2. **Elishama**. Nu 1:10. 7:48.

23. **Gamaliel**. Nu 1:10. 7:54.

24. **Abidan**. Nu 1:11. 7:60.

25. **the camp**. Nu *2:25, 28-31. 26:42-51. Ge 49:16, 17. **the rereward**. Dt 25:17, 18. Jsh *6:9. Is 52:12. 58:8. **Ahiezer**. Nu 1:12. 7:66.

26. **Pagiel**. Nu 1:13. 7:72.

27. **Ahira**. Nu 1:15. 7:78.

28. **Thus were**. Heb. These. **according**. ver. 35, 36. Nu *2:34. 24:4, 5. SS *6:10. 1 C *14:33, 40. Col *2:5.

29. **Hobab**. i.e. *loving; cherished*, ❋S#2246h. Jg 4:11. Called Reuel in Ex 2:18. **Raguel**. i.e. *friend of God*, ❋S#7467h. Nu 2:14. Ge 36:+4, 10, 13, 17, 17. Ex 2:18. 1 Ch 1:35, 37. 9:8. This person is also called Reuel in Ex 2:18; but the Hebrew is the same in both places. The reason of this difference is, that the letter *ayin* is sometimes pronounced according to the vowel which is attached to it, and sometimes as a strong guttural, which scarcely any European can enunciate; therefore, as an approach to its sound, represented by g, gn, or ng. Most probably Reuel was the same person as Jethro, and that Hobab was his son. Ex 2:18. 3:1. 18:1, 27. **the Midianite**. ❋S#4084h. Nu 25:6, 14, 15, 17. 31:2. Ge 37:28. **the Lord**. Ge 12:7. 13:15. 15:18. Ac 7:5. **come**. Jg 1:16. 4:11. 1 S 15:6. Ps 34:8. Is 2:3. Je 50:5. Zc 8:21-23. Re 22:17. **for the Lord**. Nu 23:19. Ge 32:12. Ex 3:8. 6:7, 8. T 1:2. He 6:18.

30. **will not**. Ge ◐24:58. Mt *21:28, 29. **I will depart**. Ge 12:1. 31:30. Ru 1:15-17. Ps 45:10. Lk 14:26. 2 C 5:16. He 11:8, 13.

31. **forasmuch**. As the Israelites were under the immediate direction of God himself, and were guided by the pillar of cloud and fire, it might be supposed that they had no need of Hobab. But it should be remembered, that the cloud directed only their general journeys, not their particular excursions. Parties took several journeys while the grand army lay still (Nu ch. 13, 20, 31, 32); and, therefore, they needed such a person as Hobab, well acquainted with the desert,

to direct these excursions; to point out the watering places, and where they might meet with fuel, etc. See some valuable observations on this subject in Harmer, ch. V, Observation 34, and Dr. A. Clarke. **instead of eyes**. Jb 29:15. Ps 32:8. 1 C 12:14-21. Ga 6:2.

32. **what goodness**. Ge √12:7. *32:12. Ex *3:8. *6:7, 8. Jg *1:16. *4:11. 1 S *15:6. Mk=16:15. 2 T=4:2. 1 J 1:3.

33. **the mount**. Ex 3:1. 19:3. 24:17, 18. **the ark**. Dt 9:9. 31:26. Jsh 4:7. Jg 20:27. 1 S 4:3. Je 3:16. He 13:20. **went before**. Ex 33:14, 15. Dt *1:33. Jsh *3:2-6, 11-17. Je 31:8, 9. Ezk 20:6. Jn=10:4. **a resting place**. Ps 95:11. Is 28:12. 66:1. Je 6:16. Mt *11:28-30. He *4:3-11.

34. **the cloud**. Ex *13:21, 22. Ne *9:12, 19. Ps 105:39.

35. **Rise up, Lord**. Ps *68:1, 2. *114:1-8. *132:8. Is 51:9. ʃ22C21. Anthropomorphism B889. Human actions are attributed to God: rising up. For other instances of this figure see Ps 12:5. 44:26. 68:1. 102:13. Is 2:12, 21. 33:10.

36. **Return, O Lord**. Ex *29:45, 46. *33:14-16. Ps 90:13-17. Is *63:8, 9. **many thousands of Israel**. Heb. ten thousand thousands. Ge 24:60. Dt *1:10.

NUMBERS 11

The people complain, and the fire of the Lord burns among them, but is quenched through Moses's prayer, 1, 2; the place is called Taberah, 3. The people grow weary of manna, and lust for flesh, 4-9. Moses complains, 10-15. God promises to give him seventy assistants; and flesh to the people for a month, 16-20. Moses's faith is staggered, 21-23. God gives of his Spirit to seventy elders, 24, 25. Two prophesy in the camp: Joshua would forbid them; but Moses reproves him, 26-30. The quails are sent in vast abundance, but in wrath, at Kibroth-hattaavah, 31-35.

1. **And when**. Nu 10:33. 20:2-5. 21:5. Ex 15:23, 24. 16:2, 3, 7, 9. 17:2, 3. Dt *9:22. Jb 15:11-13. Ps 106:25. 144:14. Pr +*19:3. Ec *7:10. Is √29:24. ◐58:13. La 3:39. Jn 6:43. Ro *9:19, 20. 1 C 10:10. Ph +*2:14. Ja 5:9. Ju +*16. **complained**. *or*, were as it were complainers. Ru +*1:13. Ps +*77:3. Ezk +*18:25. Pr +*19:3. Is ◐+√29:24. Ph ◐+*4:11. He ◐+*13:5. **as**. ʃ160B, Ge +25:31. **it displeased the Lord**. Heb. it was evil in the ears of the Lord. Nu +22:34mg. Ge 38:10. 2 S 11:27mg. Ja 5:4. **and the fire**. Nu 16:35. Le 10:2. Dt 32:22. 2 K 1:12. Jb 1:16. Ps *78:21. *79:5. 106:18. Pr 24:18mg. Is 30:33. 33:14. Na 1:5. Mk 9:43-49. He 12:29. **the uttermost**. Dt 25:18.

2. **cried**. Nu 21:7. 1 S *7:9. Ps 78:34, 35. Je ◐15:1. 37:3. 42:2. Ac 8:24. **prayed**. Nu 14:13-20. Ge 18:23-33. Ex 32:10-14, 31, 32. 34:9. Dt 9:19, 20. Ps 106:23. Is 37:4. Je 15:1. Am 7:2-6. Ja +*5:16. 1 J *5:16. **the fire**. Nu 16:45-48. Ge 19:24. Le 10:2. 1 K 18:38. 2 K 1:12. Jb 1:16. He 7:26. 1 J 2:1, 2. **was quenched**. Heb. sunk. Je 51:64.

3. **Taberah**. that is, *a burning*. ❋S#8404h, Dt 9:22. Is 4:4. 30:27. √33:14. He *12:29.

4. **the mixed**. Ex *12:38. Le 24:10, 11. Ne 13:3. **fell a lusting**. Heb. lusted a lust. ʃ147D, Ge +1:29. Nu 11:34. Dt 5:21. 2 S 23:15. 1 Ch 11:17. Ps 45:11. √106:14, 15. Pr 13:4. 21:26. 23:3, 6. 24:1. Ec 6:2. Je

17:16. Am 5:18. Ro *1:18. 1 C *10:6. Ep *5:6, 7. Col *3:5, 6. Ja *1:13-15. **the children**. 1 C 15:33. **wept again**. Heb. returned and wept. Je 18:4mg. **who shall**. Ps 78:18-20. 106:14. Ro *13:14. 1 C *10:6.

5. **the fish**. Ex 16:3. Ps 17:14. Ph 3:19. **cucumbers**. Is 1:8. **leeks**. lit. grass, as in 1 K 18:5. 2 K 19:26. Jb 8:12 (herb). 40:15. Ps 37:2. 90:5. 103:15. 104:14. 129:6. 147:8. Pr 27:25 (hay). Is 15:6 (hay). 35:7. 37:27. 40:6, 7, *8. 44:4. 51:12, being all the passages where it occurs (Young; *S#2682h).

6. **our**. Nu *21:5. Ex *16:3. 2 S 13:4. Ps *81:10-13. *106:21, 22, 25. Ro *3:9, 10, 22, 23. Ro *5:12. **soul**. Heb. *nephesh*. Here, *nephesh* is used of man as possessing animal appetites and desires, rendered *soul* (as here) at Nu 21:5. Dt 12:15, 20, 20, 21. 14:26, 26. 1 S 2:16. Jb 6:7. 33:20. Ps 107:18. Pr 6:30. 13:25. Is 29:8, 8. Mi 7:1. In this sense rendered elsewhere by "pleasure," Dt 23:24; "lust," Ps 78:18; "appetite," Pr 23:2. Ec 6:7; "greedy," Is 56:11. For the other uses of *nephesh* see Ge +2:7. For the equivalent New Testament use of *psyche*, see Re +*18:14.

7. **the manna**. Ex *16:14, 15, 31. 1 C 1:23, 24. Re 2:17. **color thereof as the color of**. Heb. eye of it as the eye of. ♪121R1, Le +13:55. **bdellium**. Ge *2:12.

8. **the people**. Ex 16:16-18. Jn 6:27, 33-58. **beat**. Ex +27:20. Is 28:28. =53:5. He +=2:10. **baked it**. Ex 16:23. **taste of it**. Ex 16:31.

9. **dew fell**. Ge *27:28. Ex *16:13, 14. Dt 32:2. Ps 78:23-25. 105:40. *133:3. Ho *14:5. Jn *6:32-35, 48-51.

10. **weep throughout**. Nu 14:1, 2. 16:27. 21:5. Ps 106:25. **the anger**. ver. 1. Dt 32:22. Ps 78:21, 59. *95:8-11. Is 5:25. Je 17:4. **Moses**. Nu *12:3. 20:10-13. Ps 106:32, 33. 139:21. Mk 3:5. 10:14.

11. **Wherefore hast thou**. ver. 15. Ex 17:4. Dt 1:12. Je 15:10, 18. 20:7-9, 14-18. Ml 3:14. 2 C 11:28. **wherefore have**. Jb 10:2. Ps 130:3. 143:2. La 3:22, 23, 39, 40.

12. **Carry them**. Is *40:9, 11. Ezk 34:23. Jn 10:11. **thy bosom**. ♪22A19, Ps 74:11. **as a nursing**. Is 49:15, 23. Ga 4:19. 1 Th 2:7. **the land**. Ge 13:15. 22:16, 17. 26:3. 50:24. Ex 13:5.

13. **Whence**. Mt 15:33. Mk 8:4. 9:23.

14. **not able**. Ex 18:18. Dt 1:9-12. Jb *5:1. Ps 89:19. Is 9:6. Zc 6:13. 2 C 2:16. **bear**. ♪147D, Ge +1:29. **it is**. ♪63E1, Le 4:2.

15. **kill me**. 1 K *19:4. Jb 3:20-22. 6:8-10. 7:15. Jon *4:3, 8, 9. Ph 1:20-24. Ja 1:4. **let me not**. Je 15:18. 20:18. Zp 3:15. **my wretchedness**. Two of Dr. Kennicott's manuscripts read, *"their* wretchedness." The Jerusalem Targum has the same, and adds, by way of explanation, "who are thine own people." ♪182. Emendations of the Sopherim B1018, Ge +18:22. lit. **my evil**. The primitive text was "Thy evil," "evil" being put by Metonymy for the punishment or evil which God would inflict on the people.

16. **seventy**. Ge 46:27. Ex 4:29. ◗+18:21n. *24:1, 9. Ezk 8:11. Lk=10:1, 17. **officers**. Dt 1:15. 16:18. 31:28.

17. **I will come**. ver. 25. Nu 12:5. Ge 11:5. 18:21. Ex 19:11, 20. 34:5. Jn *3:13. **talk with**. Nu 12:8. Ge 17:3, 22. 18:20-22, 33. **I will take**. Nu 27:18. 1 S *10:6. 2 K 2:9, 15. Ne *9:20. Is 44:3. 59:20, 21. Jl 2:28. Jn 7:39. Ro 8:9. 1 C 2:12. 12:4-11. 1 Th 4:8. 1 P 1:22. Ju 19. **spirit**. Heb. *ruach*, Ge +41:38. ♪121A3. Metonymy of the Cause B542. The *Spirit* is put for special

operations of the Spirit acting externally in various ways, publicly or privately. For other instances of this figure see 2 K 2:9. Da 5:12. 6:3. Lk 1:17, 80. Jn 7:39. Ac 1:5. 7:51. 2 C 3:6. **they shall**. Ex 18:22. Dt *16:18. Ac *6:3, 4.

18. **Sanctify**. Ge 35:2. Ex *19:10, 15. Jsh 7:13. **ye have wept**. ver. 1, 4-6. Ex 16:3-7. Jg 21:2. **in the ears**. Ex *16:7. **flesh to eat**. T#1496. Ps *78:27-29. **it was well**. See on ver. 4, 5. Nu 14:2, 3. Ac 7:39.

20. **whole month**. Heb. month of days. Ex 16:8, 13. **and it**. Nu 21:5. Ps 78:27-30. *106:15. Pr 27:7. **despised**. 1 S 2:30. 2 S 12:10. Ml 1:6. Ac *7:39. 13:41. 1 Th 4:8.

21. **six hundred thousand footmen**. Nu 1:46. 2:32. Ge 12:2. Ex *12:37. 38:26.

22. **the flocks**. 2 K 7:2. Mt *15:33. Mk 6:37. *8:4. Lk 1:18, 34. Jn 6:6, 7, 9.

23. **Is the Lord's**. Ge *18:14. Ps *50:10-12. 78:41. Is *50:2. *59:1. Mi 2:7. Mt 19:26. Lk 1:37. **hand**. ♪22A14.1. Anthropomorphism B878. A hand is attributed to God, as manifesting his power and miraculous operation. For other instances of this figure see Jb 10:8. 12:9, 10. Ps 8:6. 95:5. Is 11:11. **thou shalt**. Nu √23:19. 2 K *7:2, 17-19. Je 44:28, 29. Ezk *12:25. 24:14. Mt *24:35. **my word**. Ps √119:89-91. *138:2. **shall come**. Is √55:8-11. Je *32:17-21, 27.

24. **gathered**. See on ver. 16, 26. **seventy**. Ex ◗+18:21n. Lk=10:1.

25. **came down**. ver. 17. Nu 12:5. Ex 34:5. 40:38. Ps 99:7. Lk 9:34, 35. **took**. See on ver. 17. 2 K *2:15. Ja 1:17. **spirit**. Heb. *ruach*, Ge +41:38. **gave it**. 1 S *10:5, 6, 10. 19:20-24. Je 36:5, 6. Jl 2:28, 29. Ac *2:17, 18. 11:28. 21:9-11. 1 C 11:4, 5. *14:1-3, 31-33. 2 P 1:21. **spirit**. Heb. *ruach*, Ge +41:38.

26. **Eldad**. i.e. *God has loved*, *S#419h. ver. 27. **Medad**. i.e. *would be loving*, *S#4312h. ver. 27. **spirit**. Heb. *ruach*, Ge +41:38. **were written**. Ex 31:18. **went not out**. Ge 3:11. 4:13, 14. 1 S 10:22. 20:26. Je 1:6. *23:24. 36:5.

28. **Joshua**. See on Ex 17:9. **My lord**. Mk 9:38, 39. Lk *9:49, 59. Jn *3:26.

29. **Enviest**. 1 C 3:3, 21. 13:4. Ph 2:3. Ja 3:14, 15. 4:5. 5:9. 1 P 2:1. **would**. Ac 26:29. 1 C *14:5. Ph 1:15-18. **that the**. Mt 9:37, 38. Lk 10:2. **spirit**. Heb. *ruach*, Ge +41:38.

31. **a wind**. Ex 10:13, 19. 15:10. Ps 135:7. **and brought**. Ex *16:13. Ps *78:26-29. 105:40. **quails**. Ex 16:13. Ps 78:27, 28. **a day's journey**. Heb. the way of a day. **and as it were two cubits**. That is, the quail flew in the air at a height of two cubits above the ground. **face**. Ge +1:2.

32. **homers**. Ex x16:36. Le ◗27:16n. Ezk *45:11. *S#2563h. Ge 11:3 (mortar). Ex 1:14. 8:14 (heaps; lit. heaps heaps). Le 27:16n (homer). Nu 11:32. Jb 4:19 (clay). 10:9. 13:12. 27:16. 30:19 (mire). 33:6. 38:14. Is 5:10 (homer). 10:6 (mire). 29:16 (clay). 41:25 (mortar). 45:9. *64:8. Je 18:4, *6. Ezk 45:11 (homer), 11, 13, 13, 14. Ho 3:2 (homer). Na 3:14 (mortar). Hab 3:15 (heap; mg, mud).

33. **And while**. Ps *78:30, 31. 106:14, 15. Ho *13:11. Ro *6:23. He *3:17-19. **smote**. Nu 16:49. 25:9. Dt 28:27.

34. **Kibroth-hattaavah**. i.e. *graves of lust*, *S#6914h. ver. 35. Nu *33:16, 17. Dt *9:22. **Kibroth**, Heb. *qeber*, Ge +23:4. that is, *the graves of lust*. Nu 33:16. Dt 9:22. 1 C 10:6.

35. **journeyed.** Nu 33:17. **Kibroth.** Heb. *qeber*, Ge +23:4. **unto Hazeroth.** i.e. *yards, enclosures,* ✳S#2698h. Nu 12:16. 33:17, 18. Dt 1:1. **abode at.** Heb. they were in, etc.

NUMBERS 12

Miriam and Aaron speak against Moses, 1, 2. His singular meekness, 3. God vindicates Moses, and punishes Miriam with a leprosy, 4-10. Aaron submits, and Moses intercedes for Miriam, 11-13. The Lord directs that she should be shut out of the camp seven days; and afterwards the people march to the wilderness of Paran, 14-16.

1. **Miriam.** Ex *15:20. Mi *6:4. Mt 10:36. 12:48. Jn 7:5. 15:20. Ga 4:16. **against.** Jn=7:5. **Ethiopian.** or, Cushite. Matthew Poole notes that this is probably Zipporah, who is here called an *Ethiopian*, in the Hebrew a Cushite, because she was a Midianite; the word Cush being generally used in Scripture, not for Ethiopia properly so called below Egypt, but for Arabia, as some late learned men have evidently proved from 2 K 19:9; 2 Ch 21:16; Ezk 29:10; 30:8, 9; Hab 3:7, and other places. Nu 10:29. Ge 25:1-4. Ex 2:16, *21. 3:1. 4:24-26. *18:1-6. Jg 1:16. 4:11. ✳S#3569h. Nu 12:1, 1. 2 S 18:21, 21, 22, 23, 31, 31, 32, 32. 2 Ch 12:3. 14:9, 12, 12, 13. 16:8, 21:16. Je 13:23. 36:14. 38:7, 10, 12. 39:16. Da 11:43. Am 9:7. Zp 1:1. 2:12. For ✳S#3568h, see Ge +2:13. **married.** Heb. taken. Nu +36:6. Ge ◑+21:21. 24:3, 37, +*57, 58. 26:34, 35. 27:46. 28:6-9. 34:14, 15. 41:45. Ex +2:21. 34:16. Le 21:14. Jsh *15:16, 17. Jg ◑14:2. 1 S *18:27.

2. **Hath the Lord.** Nu 16:3. Ex 4:30. 5:1. 7:10. 15:20, 21. Mi 6:4. **hath he not.** Nu 11:29. Pr 13:10. Ro *12:3, 10. Ph +*2:3, 14. 1 P 5:5. **And the.** Nu 11:1. Ge 29:33. 2 S 11:27. 2 K *19:4. Ps *94:7-9. Is 37:4. Ezk *35:12, 13. Ro 12:19.

3. **very meek.** Ps 147:6. *149:4. Mt *5:5. =*11:29. 21:5. 2 C *10:1. 1 Th 2:7. Ja *3:13. 1 P *3:4. **above.** Nu 11:10-15. 20:*10-12. Ps *106:32, 33. 2 C *11:5. 12:11. Ja *3:2, 3. **face.** Ge +1:2.

4. **the Lord.** Ps *76:7-9. **Come out.** Nu 16:16-21.
5. **in the pillar.** Nu 11:25. *16:19. Ex 34:5. 40:38. Ps 99:7.
6. **a prophet.** Ge 20:7. Ex 7:1. Ps 105:15. Mt 23:31, 34, 37. Lk 20:6. Ep 4:11. Re 11:3, 10. **in a vision.** Ge *15:1. *46:2. Jb 4:13. *33:15. Ps 89:19. Ezk 1:1. Da 8:2. 10:8, 16, 17. Lk 1:11, 22. Ac 10:11, 17. 22:17, 18. **a dream.** Ge 31:10, 11. 1 K 3:5. Je 23:28. Da 7:1. Mt 1:20. 2:12, 13, 19.
7. **My servant.** Dt *18:18. Ps √103:7. *105:26. Mt 11:9, 11. Ac 3:22, 23. 7:31. **faithful.** 2 Ch *19:9. 34:12. Pr 25:13. 1 C 4:2. 1 T *3:15. He *3:2-6. 1 P 2:4, 5. 3 J 5.
8. **mouth.** Nu 14:14. Ex *33:11. Dt *34:10. Ps √103:7. 1 C *13:10. 1 T 6:16. ⨍22A10. Anthropomorphism B876. Mouth, lips, and a tongue are attributed to God. For other instances of this figure see Dt 8:3. Jsh 9:14. Jb 11:5. Is 11:4. 30:27. 55:11. **dark speeches.** Ps 49:4. Ezk 17:2. 20:49. Mt *13:35. Jn 15:15. 1 C 13:12. or, riddles. ✳S#2420h. Jg 14:12, 13, 14, 15, 16, 17, 18, 19. 1 K 10:1. 2 Ch 9:1. Ps 49:4. 78:2. Pr 1:6. Ezk 17:2. Da 8:23. Hab 2:6. **similitude.** Ex 24:10, 11. 33:19, 23. 34:5-7. Dt 4:15. Is 40:18. 46:5. Jn *1:18. 14:*7-10. 15:*24. 2 C 3:18. 4:4-6. Col +√1:15. He √1:3. **wherefore.** Jn=5:23. **were ye.** Ex 34:30. Lk 10:16. 1 Th 4:8. 2 P 2:10. Ju 8.

9. **the anger.** Nu 11:1. Ho 5:15. Na *1:2, 3, 5, 6.
10. **the cloud.** Ex 33:7-10. Ezk 10:4, 5, 18, 19. Ho 9:12. Mt 25:41. **behold.** Dt *24:9. **leprous.** Le 13:2, 3, etc. 2 K *5:27. *15:5. 2 Ch *26:19-21.
11. **I beseech thee.** Ex 12:32. 1 S 2:30. 12:19. 15:24, 25. 2 S 24:10. 1 K 13:6. Je 42:2. Ac 8:24. Re 3:9. **lay not.** 2 S 19:19. 24:10. 2 Ch 16:9. Ps *38:1-7. Pr 30:32. **foolishly.** 2 S *24:10. Ps *69:5. Pr 24:10.
12. **as one dead.** Le *13:44, 46. Ps 88:4, 5. Ep *2:1-5. Col *2:13. 1 T 5:6. **of whom.** Jb 3:16. Ps 58:8. 1 C 15:8. **the flesh.** ⨍182, Ge +18:22. **his mother's.** ⨍182, Ge +18:22.
13. **cried unto.** Nu 14:2, 13-20. 16:41, *46-50. Ex *32:10-14. 1 S √12:23. 15:11. Mt *5:44, 45. Lk 6:28. *23:34. Ac 7:60. Ro *12:21. Ja *5:15, 16. **Heal.** Ex 15:26. +23:25. Mt ◐=8:2, 3. **God.** Heb. *El*, Ex +15:2.
14. **spit.** Dt 25:9. Jb 30:10. Is 50:6. Mt 26:67. He 12:9. **let her be.** Nu *5:2, 3. Le *13:4-6, 45, 46. 14:8. 2 Ch 26:20, 21. Ps *103:2-4, 8-14.
15. **shut out.** Dt 24:8, 9. Ro *15:1-4. 2 C *11:29. Ga *6:1, 2. **and the.** Ge 9:21-23. Ex 20:12. **till Miriam.** La 3:32. Mi 6:4. 7:8, 9. Hab 3:2.
16. **afterward.** Nu 11:35. 33:18. **Hazeroth.** Dt 2:23. **the wilderness.** Nu 10:12. 13:4, 26. Ge 21:20, *21. 1 S 25:1. Hab +*3:3.

NUMBERS 13

Moses sends twelve men to search the land, 1-16. He instructs them, 17-20. They return after forty days; and ten of them bring a discouraging report, from which Caleb and Joshua dissent, 21-33.

2. **Send thou.** Nu 32:8. Dt 1:22-25. Jsh ch. 2. **of every.** Nu 1:4. 34:18. **a ruler.** Nu 11:16. Ex 18:25. Dt 1:15.
3. **from the.** See on Nu 12:16. 32:8. Dt 1:19, 23. 9:23.
4. **Shammua.** i.e. *a rumor; renowned; a hearkener,* ✳S#8051h. 2 S 5:14. 1 Ch 14:4. Ne 11:17. 12:18. (1) One of the spies sent out by Moses to search the land of Canaan, Nu 13:4. (2) One of the Levites, Ne 11:17. (3) A priest of the family of Bilgah, Ne 12:18. (4) A son of David, 1 Ch 14:4, called also Shammuah. **Zaccur.** i.e. *mindful.* 1 Ch +25:2.
5. **Shaphat.** i.e. *he judged.* 1 Ch +3:22. **Hori.** i.e. *a worker in linen; freeman of Jah; my freeman.* Ge +36:22.
6. **Caleb.** i.e. *capable; dog; firmly bound; determination,* ✳S#3612h. ver. 30. Nu 14:6, 24, 30, 38. 26:65. 27:15-23. 33:12. 34:19. Dt 1:36. 31:7-17. Jsh 14:6, 13, 14. 15:13, 14, 16, 17, 18. 21:12. Jg 1:12, 13, 14, 15, 20. 3:9. 1 S 30:14. 1 Ch 2:18, 19, 42, 46, 48, 49, 50. 4:15. 6:56. (1) A son of Hezron, 1 Ch 2:18, 42. Called also Chelubai in 1 Ch 2:9. He was the father of Hur. (2) The son of Jephunneh, Nu 13:6, one of the twelve chiefs, one from each tribe, sent by Moses to spy out the land of Canaan. (3) Caleb, the son of Hur, is mentioned in 1 Ch 2:50. He may be Caleb the spy. (4) The region between Hebron and Carmel assigned to Caleb, 1 S 30:14. **Jephunneh.** i.e. *may he be regarded with favor; for whom a way is prepared,* ✳S#3312h. Nu 14:6, 30, 38. 26:65. 32:12. 34:19. Dt 1:36. Jsh 14:6, 13, 14. 15:13. 21:12. 1 Ch 4:15. 6:56. 7:38. (1) A man of the tribe of Judah, father of Caleb the spy, Nu 13:6; Jsh 14:14; 1 Ch 4:15. (2) Head of a family in Asher, 1 Ch 7:38.

8. **Oshea**. i.e. *safety*, S#1954h. ver. 16, Jehoshua. Ex 17:9-13. 24:13. 32:17. Dt 31:7, 8, 14, 23. 34:9. Jsh 1:1-9, 16. 24. Mi 11:28, 27:18–22.

9. **Palti**. i.e. *deliverance of Jehovah; escape of Jah; my escape*, ✳S#6406h. 1 S 25:44. **Raphu**. i.e. *healed; comforted*, ✳S#7505h.

10. **Gaddiel**. i.e. *troop of God; fortune of God*, ✳S#1427h. **Sodi**. i.e. *counsel of God; my counsel*, ✳S#5476h.

11. **Gaddi**. i.e. *troop of Jah; my troop; fortune*, ✳S#1426h. **Susi**. i.e. *horse of Jah; my horse; swallow*, ✳S#5485h.

12. **Ammiel**. i.e. *people of God*. **Gemalli**. i.e. *deed of Jah; my deed; camel driver*, ✳S#1582h.

13. **Sethur**. i.e. *hidden, mysterious*, ✳S#5639h.

14. **Nahbi**. i.e. *hidden; hidden of the Lord*, ✳S#5147h. **Vophsi**. i.e. *my addition; addition of Jah; diminished*, ✳S#2058h.

15. **Geuel**. i.e. *excellency of God; majesty of God*, ✳S#1345h. **Machi**. i.e. *my lowness; decrease*, ✳S#4352h.

16. **Oshea**. Ho 1:1. Ro 9:25. **Jehoshua**. i.e. *Jehovah is salvation*, S#3091h. See on ver. 8. Nu 14:6, 30. Ex 17:9. Mt 1:21-23. Ac 7:45. He 4:8, Jesus.

17. **southward**. ver. 21, 22. Ge 12:9. 13:1. Jsh 15:3. Jg 1:15. **the mountain**. Nu 14:40. Ge 14:10. Dt 1:44. Jg 1:9, 19.

18. **the land**. Ex 3:8. Is 64:4. Ezk 34:14. 1 C 2:9, 10.

19. **strong holds**. ✳S#4013h. Nu 32:17, 36 (fenced). Jsh 10:20. 19:29 (strong), 35. 1 S 6:18. 2 S 24:7. 2 K 3:19. ✳8:12. 10:2. 17:9. 18:8. 2 Ch 17:19. Ps 89:40. 108:10. Is 17:3 (fortress). 25:12. 34:13. Je 1:18 (defenced). 4:5. 5:17. 6:27. 8:14. 34:7. 48:18. La 2:2, 5. Da 11:15, 24, 39. Ho 10:14. Am 5:9. Mi 5:11. Na 3:12, 14. Hab 1:10.

20. **whether it be**. Ne 9:25, 35. Ezk 34:14. **good courage**. ver. 30, 31. Dt 31:6-8, 23. Jsh 1:6, 9. 2:3, 22, 23. 1 Ch 22:11. He 13:6. **the firstripe**. ver. 23, 24. Mi 7:1.

21. **from the wilderness of Zin**. i.e. *a thorn; coldness*, ✳S#6790h. The wilderness of Zin is different from that called *Sin* (Ex 16:1). The latter was near Egypt, but the former was near Kadesh Barnea, not far from the border of Canaan. Nu 20:1. 27:14, 14. 33:36. 34:3, 4. Dt 32:51. Jsh 15:1, 3. 2 K 3:8n. **Rehob**. i.e. *a broad place*, ✳S#7340h. Jsh 19:28, 30. 21:31n. Jg 1:31. 2 S 8:3, 12. 10:8. 1 Ch 6:75. Ne 10:11. Compare Jg 18:28; Am +5:16. (1) The extreme northern limit reached by the spies sent by Moses, Nu 13:21. It is called Beth-rehob in 2 S 10:6, 8. (2) A place in Asher, Jsh 19:28. (3) Another place in Asher, Jsh 19:30; 21:31. (4) The father of Hadadezer, king of Zobah, 2 S 8:3, 12. (5) One of the Levites who sealed the covenant with Nehemiah, Ne 10:11. **Hamath**. i.e. *a walled place; citadel*, ✳S#2574h. Nu 34:8. Jsh 13:5. Jg 3:3. 2 S 8:9. 1 K 8:65. 2 K 14:25, 28. 17:24, 30. 18:34. 19:13. 23:33. 25:21. 1 Ch 13:5. 18:3, 9. 2 Ch 7:8. 8:3, 4. Is 10:9. 11:11. 36:19. 37:13. 38:9. 49:23. 52:9, 27. Ezk 47:16, 16, 17, 20. 48:1, 1. Am 6:2, 14. Zc 9:2.

22. **Ahiman**. i.e. *brother of gift*. Jsh 11:21, 22. 15:13, 14. Jg 1:10. **Sheshai**. i.e. *whitish*, ✳S#8344h. Jsh 15:14. Jg 1:10. **Talmai**. i.e. *brotherly; suspending the waters; furrows*, ✳S#8526h. Jsh 15:14. Jg 1:10. 2 S 3:3. 13:37. 1 Ch 3:2. (1) A son of Anak, Nu 13:22; Jsh 15:14. (2) A king of Geshur whose daughter was a wife of David,

2 S 3:3; 1 Ch 3:2. **the children**. ver. 33. **Hebron**. Ge 13:18. 23:2. 35:27. 37:14. Jsh 11:21, 22. 14:13-15. 15:13, 14. 21:11, 13. 2 S 2:1, 11. 1 Ch 6:57. **Zoan**. i.e. *a low region; removal, motion*, ✳S#6814h. Ps 78:12, 43. Is 19:11, 13. 30:4. Ezk 30:14.

23. **brook**. or, valley. ver. 24. Nu 21:12. 32:9. Dt 1:24, 25. 2:13mg. Jg +16:4mg. 1 S 17:40mg. 2 S 17:13. 22:30mg. 24:5mg. 1 Ch 11:32. 2 Ch 20:16mg. **Eschol**. i.e. *a cluster; cluster of grapes*, ✳S#812h. ver. 24. Nu 32:9. Ge ◐14:13, 24. Dt 1:24. (1) An Amorite, brother of Mamre, in whose plain Abram dwelt when he rescued Lot, Ge 14:13, 24. (2) A valley, and a brook which flowed through it. From this valley a cluster of grapes was taken by the Israelite spies as a specimen of the fruit of Canaan, Nu 13:23, 24; 32:9; Dt 1:24.

24. **brook**. or, valley. ver. 23. **Eshcol**. **that is**, a cluster of grapes. Ge 14:21-24.

25. **forty days**. Nu 14:33, 34. Ex 24:18. 34:28.

26. **unto the wilderness**. ver. 3. **Kadesh**. Nu 20:1, 16. 32:8. 33:36. Dt 1:19. Jsh 14:6.

27. **floweth with**. Nu 14:8. Ex 3:8, 17. 13:5. 33:3. Le 20:24. Dt 1:25, etc. 6:3. 11:9. 26:9, 11-15. 27:3. 31:20. Jsh 5:6. Je 11:5. 32:22. Ezk 20:6, 15. **milk and**. ∫174, Ge +18:27. **honey**. ∫171l17, Ex +3:8.

28. **strong**. Dt 1:28. 2:10, 11, 21. 3:5. 9:1, 2. Pr 26:13. **saw the**. ver. 22, 23, 33. Jsh 11:22. 15:14. Jg 1:20.

29. **Amalekites**. Nu 14:43. 24:20. Ge 14:7. Ex 17:8-16. Jg 6:3. 1 S 14:48. 15:3, etc. 27:8. 30:1. Ps 83:7. **the Hitites**. See on Ge 15:19-21. Ex 3:8, 17.

30. **Caleb stilled**. Nu 14:6-9, 24. Jsh 14:6-8. Ps 27:1, 2. 60:12. 118:10, 11. Is 41:10-16. Ro 8:31, 37. Ph 4:13. He 11:33.

31. **not able**. Nu 32:9. Dt 1:28. Jsh 14:8. He 3:19.

32. **brought**. Nu 14:36, 37. Dt 1:28. Mt 23:13. **a land**. See on ver. 28. Ezk 36:13. Am 2:9. **men of a great stature**. Heb. men of statures. 2 S 21:20h. 1 Ch 20:6mg.

33. **saw the giants**. ver. 22. Dt 1:28. 2:10, +20. 3:11. 9:2. 1 S 17:4-7. 2 S 21:20-22. 1 Ch 11:23. Am 2:9. **Anak**. i.e. *neck chain; long-necked*, ✳S#6061h. ver. 22, 28. Dt 9:2. Jsh 15:13, 14, 14. 21:11. Jg 1:20. **and we were**. 1 S 17:42. Is 40:22. **as**. ∫111, Ge +18:27.

NUMBERS 14

The people murmur at the news, and propose returning to Egypt, 1-5. The people threaten to stone Caleb and Joshua, while they in vain attempt to pacify them, 6-10. God threatens to destroy them at once, 11, 12. Moses intercedes, and prevails for their rescue, and obtains their pardon, 13-25. Yet that generation of murmurers is debarred from entering into the land, and doomed to fall in the wilderness, Caleb and Joshua excepted, 26-35. The men who raised the evil report died by the plague, 36-38. The people attempt to march to Canaan against the will of God, but are warned by Moses, and smitten by their enemies, 39-45.

1. **lifted up**. Nu 11:1-4. Dt 1:45.

2. **murmured**. Nu +11:1. 16:41. Ex 15:24. 16:2, 3. 17:3. Dt 1:27. Ps 106:24, 25. 1 C 10:10. Ph 2:14, 15. Ju 16. **Would**. ver 28, 29. Nu 11:15. 1 K 19:4. Jb 3:11. 7:15, 16. Jon 4:3, 8.

3. **the Lord**. Ps 78:40. Je 9:3. **our wives**. ver. 31, 32.

4. **Let us make.** Dt 17:16. 28:68. Ne 9:16, 17. Lk 17:32. Ac 7:39. He *10:38, 39. 11:15. 2 P 2:21, 22.

5. **fell on.** Nu 16:4, 22, 45. Ge 17:3. Le 9:24. Jsh 5:14. 7:10. 1 K 18:39. 1 Ch 21:16. Ps 105:26. Ezk 9:8. Da 10:9. Mt 26:39. Re 4:10. 5:14. 7:11.

6. **Joshua.** ver. 24, 30, 38. Nu 13:6, 8, 30. **rent their clothes.** Ge 37:29, 34. 44:13. Jsh 7:6. Jg 11:35. 2 S 3:13. 2 K 18:37. Jb 1:20. Jl 2:12, 13. Mt 26:65.

7. **an exceeding good land.** Nu 13:27. Dt 1:25. 6:10, 11. 8:7-9.

8. **bring.** Ge 48:21. **delight.** Dt 10:15. 2 S 15:25, 26. 22:20. 1 K 10:9. Ps 22:8. 147:10, 11. Is 62:4. Je 32:41. Zp 3:17. Ro 8:31. **a land which.** Nu 13:27. **milk and.** ♪174, Ge +18:27. **honey.** ♪17I17, Ex +3:8.

9. **Only rebel.** Dt 9:7, 23, 24. Is 1:2. 63:10. Da 9:5, 9. Ph 1:27. **neither.** Dt 7:18. 20:3. **are.** ♪63B, Ge +2:10. **bread.** Nu 24:8. Dt 32:42. Ps 14:4. 74:14. **defence.** Heb. shadow. Ps 91:1. 121:5. Is 30:2, 3. 32:2. Je 48:45. **the Lord.** Ge 48:21. Ex 33:16. Dt 7:21. 20:1-4. 31:6, 8. Jsh 1:5. Jg 1:22. 1 K 10:9. 2 Ch 13:12. 15:2. 20:17. 32:8. Ps 46:1, 2, 7, 11. 144:1, 2, 15. 146:5. Pr 16:20. Is 8:9, 10. 41:10. Mt 1:23. Ro √8:31. **is.** ♪63B, Ge +2:10. **fear them not.** Is 41:14.

10. **But all.** Ex 17:4. 1 S 30:6. Mt 23:37. Ac 7:52, 59. **And the.** Nu 16:19, 42. 20:6. Ex 16:7, 10. 24:16, 17. 40:34. Le 9:23.

11. **How long will this.** ver. 27. Ex 10:3. 16:28. Pr 1:22. Je 4:14. Ho 8:5. Zc 8:14. Mt 17:17. **provoke.** ver. 23. Dt 9:7, 8, 22, 23. Ps 78:22, 32, 37-41. 95:8. 106:43. He 3:8, 16-19. **believe me.** Dt 1:32. Ps 78:22, 32, 41, 42. 106:24. Mk 9:19. Jn 10:38. 12:37. 15:24. He 3:18.

12. **smite.** Nu 16:46-49. 25:9. Ex 5:3. Dt 28:15, 20, 21. 2 S 24:1, 12-15. **will make.** See on Ex 32:10.

13. **Then the.** Ex 32:12. Dt 9:26-28. 32:27. Jsh 7:8, 9. Ps 106:23. Ezk 20:9, 13-15, 17. **from among.** lit. out of the midst of them. ♪144A6, Ge +45:6.

14. **they have.** Ex 15:14. Jsh 2:9, 10. 5:1. **among.** Dt +23:14. **art seen.** Nu 12:8. Ge 32:30. Ex 33:11. Dt 5:4. 34:10. Jn 1:18. 14:9. 1 C 13:12. 1 J 3:2. **thy cloud.** Nu 9:15-21. 10:34. Ex 13:21, 22. 40:38. Ne 9:12, 19. Ps 78:14. 105:39.

15. **as one.** Jg 6:16.

16. **not able.** Dt 9:28. 32:26, 27. Jsh 7:9.

17. **let the power.** Mi 3:8. Mt 9:6, 8.

18. **longsuffering.** See on Ex 34:6, 7. Ps 103:8. 145:8. Jon 4:2. Mi 7:18. Na 1:2, 3. Ro 3:24-26. 5:21. 2 C 5:21. Ep 1:7, 8. **visiting.** Ex 20:5. 34:7. Je 23:2.

19. **Pardon.** Ex 32:32. 34:9. 1 K 8:34. Ps 51:1, 2. Ezk 20:8, 9. Da 9:16-19. **according.** Is *55:7. T 3:4-7. **greatness.** ♪22I2, Ex +15:16. **and as thou.** Ex 32:10-14. 33:17. Ps 78:38. 106:7, 8, 45. Jon 3:10. 4:2. Mi *7:18. Ja 5:15. 1 J *5:14-16. **until now.** or, hitherto. 1 S 7:12.

20. **pardoned.** Ps 78:37-43. 106:45. Is 48:9, 11. Ep=4:32. **according.** Ja 5:16. 1 J 5:14, 15.

21. **as truly.** Dt 32:40. Is 49:18. Je 22:24. Ezk 5:11. 18:3. 33:11, 27. Zp 2:9. **all the.** Ps 72:19. Hab 2:14. Mt 6:10.

22. **which have.** ver. 11. Dt 1:31-35. Ps 95:9-11. 106:26. He 3:17, 18. **tempted.** Ex 17:2. Ps 95:9. 106:14. Ml 3:15. Mt 1:7. 1 C 10:9. He 3:9. **ten times.** Ge 31:7, 41. Jb 19:3.

23. **Surely they shall not see.** Heb. If they see. Nu 26:64. 32:11. Dt 1:35, etc. Ne 9:23. Ps 95:11. 106:26. Je 15:1. Ezk 20:15. He 3:17, 18. 4:3.

24. **But.** ♪171C, Synecdoche of the Genus, Ex +20:10. ❶♪171B, Ge +24:10. ver. 30. Jsh 14:1. 22:13. **my servant.** ver. 6-9. Nu 13:30. 26:65. Dt 1:36. Jsh 14:6-14. **another.** Nu 12:7. 1 K 19:18. Ne 7:2. 1 C 4:17. Col 1:7. 4:9. Re 17:14. **spirit.** Heb. *ruach*, Ge +41:8. ♪121A10, Ge +26:35. Mt 21:28-32. Mk 10:38, 39. Lk 9:55. 1 C 2:11, 12. **followed me fully.** Nu 32:11, 12. Dt 6:5. Jsh 14:+*8, 9. 1 Ch +22:16 (T#1). 29:9, 18. 2 Ch 25:2. Ps 119:80, 145. Pr 23:26. Lk *16:10. Ac 11:23. Ro 12:11. Ep 6:6, 7. Col *3:23. Re 14:4, 5.

25. **the Amalekites.** Nu 13:29. Ge +14:7. **Canaanites.** Ge +10:18. **turn you.** ver. 4. Dt 1:40. Ps 81:11-13. Pr 1:31.

27. **How long.** See on ver. 11. Ex 16:28. Mt 17:17. Mk 9:19. **I have heard.** Ex 16:12. 1 C 10:10.

28. **As truly.** See on ver. 21, 23. Nu 26:64, 65. 32:11. Dt 1:35. Ps 90:8, 9. He 3:17. **as ye have.** ver. 2.

29. **carcases.** ver. 32, 33. 1 C 10:5. He 3:17. Ju 5. **all that were.** Nu 1:45. 26:63-65.

30. **sware.** Heb. lifted up my hand. Ge +14:22. Ex 6:8. Dt 32:40. Ps 106:24-26. Is 3:7mg. Ezk 20:5, 6. Da 12:7. Re 10:5, 6. **save Caleb.** ver. 38. Nu 26:65. 32:12. Dt 1:36-38.

31. **little ones.** Nu 26:4, 64. Dt 1:39. **ye said.** ver. 3. **know.** Their children, by possessing Canaan, *knew* what a good land their fathers had despised. **the land.** Ge 25:34. Ps 106:24. Pr 1:25, 30. Mt 22:5. Ac 13:41. He 12:16, 17.

32. **your carcases.** See on ver. 29. 1 C 10:5. He 3:17.

33. **shall wander in the wilderness.** or, feed. This implies that they should move from place to place in the deserts, as the Bedouin Arabs, who have no certain dwelling, but rove about, seeking pasture for their flocks. Nu 32:13. Ex 34:7. Jsh 14:10. Ps 107:4, 40. **forty years.** Nu 33:38. Dt 1:3. 2:14. **bear.** ♪121C1E, Ge +19:15. Nu 5:31. Je 3:1, 2. Ezk 23:35, 45-49. Ho 9:1.

34. **After.** Nu 13:25. 2 Ch 36:21. **the number.** Ps 95:10. Ezk 4:6. Da 9:24. Re 11:3. **shall ye bear.** Nu 18:23. Le 20:19. Ps 38:4. Ezk 14:10. **ye shall.** 1 K 8:56. Ps 77:8. 105:42. Je 18:9, 10. La 3:31-33. He 4:1. **breach of promise.** or, altering of my purpose. Jb 33:10. *Tenooathi*, rather, my *failure*, or *disannulling*, from *noo*, to *fail*, *disannul*; for as they had broken their engagements, God was no longer held by his covenant. Dt 31:16, 17. 1 S 2:30. Zc 11:10.

35. **I will surely.** Nu 23:19. He 6:13. **this evil.** ver. 27-29. Nu 26:65. 1 C 10:5, 11. He 3:19.

36. **the men.** Nu 13:31-38. Ml 3:18. 1 C 10:10.

37. **those men.** Thus *ten* of the twelve who searched out the land were struck dead, by the justice of God, on the spot. In commemoration of this event, the Jews, to this day, celebrate a fast, on the seventh day of the month *Elul*. **died.** ver. 12. Nu 16:49. 25:9. Je 28:16, 17. 29:32. 1 C 10:10. He 3:17. Ju 5.

38. **Joshua.** Nu 26:65. Jsh 14:6-10.

39. **mourned greatly.** Ex 33:4. Pr 19:3. Is 26:16. Mt 8:12. He 12:17.

40. **rose up.** Dt 1:41. Ec 9:3. Mt 7:21-23. 25:11, 12. Lk 13:25. **for we have sinned.** We are sensible of our sin, and repent of it; and are now ready to do as Caleb and Joshua exhorted us. Or, *though we have sinned*, yet we hope God will make good his promise.

41. **do ye**. ver. 25. 2 Ch 24:20. **but it shall**. Jb 4:9. Je 2:37. 32:5.

42. **Go not**. Dt 1:42. Jsh 7:8, 12. 2 Ch *15:2. *24:20. Ps 44:1-11.

43. **Amalekites and**. ver. 25. Nu 13:29. Le 26:17. Dt 28:25. **because**. Jg 16:20. 1 Ch 28:9. 2 Ch 15:2. Is 63:10. Ho 9:12.

44. **they presumed**. Nu 15:30. Dt 1:43. Ps 19:13. 2 P 2:9. **the ark**. Nu 10:33. 1 S 4:3-11.

45. **the Amalekites**. See on ver. 43. Ex 17:16. Dt 1:44. 32:30. Jsh 7:5, 11, 12. *S#6003h. ver. 25, 43. Jg 12:15. 1 S 15:6, 15. 27:8. 30:1, 13. 2 S 1:8, 13. **Hormah**. i.e. *place desolated; destruction,* *S#2767h. Nu 21:3. Dt 1:44. Jsh 12:14. 15:30. 19:4. Jg 1:17. 1 S 30:30. 1 Ch 4:30.

NUMBERS 15

The law of the meat offering, and the drink offering to be brought with the sacrifices, 1-13; in which strangers are included under the same law, 14-16. The law of the first of the dough for an heave offering, 17-21. The sin offerings of the congregation, and of private persons for sins of ignorance, 22-29. The punishment of presumption, 30, 31; exemplified in the stoning of a sabbath breaker, 32-36. The law of fringes, 37-41.

1. It is very probable that the transactions recorded in this and the four following chapters took place during the time the Israelites abode in Kadesh (Dt 1:46).

2. **When ye be come**. ver. 18. Ex 3:17. Le 14:34. 23:10. 25:2. Dt 7:1, 2. 8:7-9. 12:1, 9.

3. **will make**. Ex 29:18, 25, 41. Le 1:2, 3, 9, 13, 17. 10:13. **a burnt offering**. Le 1:1, etc. +23:12. **a sacrifice**. Le 7:+11, 16. 22:18-23. +23:38. Dt 12:11. Pr 7:14. **performing**. Heb. separating. ver. 8. Le 22:21. 27:2. **or in a freewill offering**. Le 22:21, 23. +23:38. Dt 12:6, 17. 16:10. **in your**. Nu 28:16-19, 27. 29:1, 2, 8, 13, etc. Le 23:8, 12, 36. Dt 16:1-17. **a sweet**. Ge 8:21. Ex 29:18. Mt 3:17. Ep 5:2. Ph 4:18. **the herd**. Under the term *bakar*, are comprehended the ox, heifer, etc.; and under *tzon*, are included sheep and goats. The animals enjoined in the Levitical law are the very same which God commanded Abraham to offer (Ge 15:9). Hence it is evident that God delivered to the patriarchs an epitome of that law which was afterwards given in detail to Moses, the essence of which consisted in its sacrifices; and these sacrifices were of clean animals, the most perfect, useful, and healthy of all that are brought under the immediate government of man. Gross feeding and ferocious animals were all excluded, as well as all birds of prey. **sweet savor**. Nu 28:27. Ge 8:20, 21. 2 C 2:15. Ep 5:2.

4. **a meat offering**. Ex 29:40. Le 2:1. 6:14, 15. 7:9, 10. +23:13. Is 66:20. Ml 1:11. Jn 4:34. Ro 15:16. He 10:7. 13:16. **the fourth**. Nu 28:5, etc. Ex 29:40. Le 2:15. 14:10. 23:13. Jg 9:9. Ezk 46:14. Ro 11:24.

5. **the fourth**. Nu 28:7, 14. **of wine**. Ge 49:11, 12. Jg 9:13. Ne 8:10. Ps 100:2. 104:15. 116:13. SS 1:4. Is 35:10. Zc 9:17. Mt 26:28, 29. Jn 15:1. Ph 2:17. 2 T 4:6. **drink offering**. Le +23:13. **burnt offering**. Le +23:12.

6. **for a ram**. ver. 4. Nu 28:12-14. Ps 45:7. SS 3:11.

8. **preparest**. Le 22:21. **burnt offering**. Le +23:12.

vow. Le +23:38. Ps 50:14. Pr 7:14. Jon 2:9. **peace offerings**. See on Le 3:1. 7:11-18. +*23:19.

9. **with a**. Nu 28:12, 14. **a meat**. Nu 29:6. Le 6:14. 7:37. 14:10. 1 Ch 21:23. Ne 10:33. Ezk 42:13. 46:5, 7, 11, 15. Jl 1:9. 2:14.

10. **drink offering**. See on ver. 5. Nu 6:15.

11. **Thus shall**. Nu ch. 28.

12. **according to the number**. Mt 9:29. 25:14, 15. 2 C 8:12-15. 9:6, 7.

15. **One**. ver. 29. Nu 9:14. Ex 12:49. Le 24:22. Ga 3:28. Ep 2:11-22. Col 3:11. **an ordinance**. Nu 10:8. 18:8. Ex 12:14, 24, 43. 1 S 30:25. **for ever**. Heb. *olam*, Ex +12:24.

16. **One law**. Nu 9:14. Ex 12:49. Jn 3:17. 10:16. 14:6. Ac 4:12. Ro 3:29, 30. 1 C *12:13. Ep 2:11-18. +√4:4. 1 T *2:3, 4. Re ●x?7:4, 9.

18. **When ye come**. See on ver. 2. Dt 26:1, etc.

19. **when ye**. Jsh 5:11, 12. **heave offering**. Le +7:14.

20. **a cake**. Nu 18:12. Ex 23:19. Dt 26:2-10. Jsh 5:11, 12. Ne 10:37. Pr 3:9, 10. Ezk 44:30. Mt 6:33. Ro 11:16. 1 C 15:20. Ja 1:18. Re 14:4. **the heave offering**. Le 2:14. +*7:14. 23:10, 16, 17.

21. **an heave offering**. Nu 18:26. Ex 29:28. Le +*7:14.

22. **if ye have erred**. Le 4:2, 13, 14, 22, 27. 5:13, 15-17. Ps 19:12. Mk +*12:24. Lk 12:48. 23:34. Jn 16:3. Ac 2:36-39. 3:17-19. 1 C 2:8.

24. **if ought**. See on Le 4:13. **without**. Heb. from the eyes. Le 4:13. **one young bullock**. See on Le 4:14-21. **burnt offering**. Le +*23:12. with his. ver. 8-10. **meat offering**. Le +*23:13. **drink offering**. Le +*23:13. **manner**. *or*, ordinance. ver. 16. **one kid**. Nu 28:15. Le 4:23. 2 Ch 29:21-24. Ezr 6:17. 8:35. **sin offering**. Le +*23:19.

25. **the priest**. See on Le 4:20, 26. Ro 3:25. 1 J 2:2. **forgiven them**. Lk 23:34. Ac 13:39.

27. **if any**. See on Le 4:27, 28. Ac 3:17. 17:30. 1 T 1:13. **soul**. Heb. *nephesh*, Ge +27:31.

28. **the priest**. Le 4:35. **soul**. Heb. *nephesh*, Ge +27:31.

29. **one law**. See on ver. 15. Nu 9:14. Le 16:29. 17:15. Ro 3:29, 30. 11:13. **sinneth**. Heb. doeth. Nu 11:15 (deal).

30. **soul**. Heb. *nephesh*, Ge +27:31. **doeth ought**. Nu 9:13. 14:44. Ge 17:14. Ex 21:14. Le 20:3, 6, 10. Dt 1:43. 17:12. 29:19, 20. Ps 19:13. Mt 12:32. He 10:26, 29. 2 P 2:10. **presumptuously**. Heb. with a high hand. Ex 14:8. That is, bold, daring, deliberate acts of transgression against the fullest evidence, and in despite of the Divine authority. Such conduct "reproacheth the Lord," as if his commands were needless, unreasonable, and inimical to the happiness of man; his favor were not desirable, or his wrath not to be feared: in short, as if it were more advantageous to rebel against him than to serve him. Such acts admitted of no atonement (He 10:26): the person was condemned to bear his own iniquity, and to be cut off. **reproacheth**. Ps 69:9. 74:18, 22. 79:12. 89:15. Pr 14:31. Is 37:23, 24. **soul**. Heb. *nephesh*, Ge +17:14.

31. **despised**. Le 26:15, 43. 2 S 12:9. 2 Ch 36:16. Ps 119:126. Pr 13:13. Is 30:12. Jn 12:48. 1 Th 4:8. He 4:12, 13. 10:28, 29. Re 19:11-16. **soul**. Heb. *nephesh*, Ge +17:14. **his iniquity**. Le 5:1. Ps 38:4. Is 53:6. Ezk 18:20. 1 P 2:24. 2 P 2:21.

32. **they found a man**. This example seems to have

been evidently introduced to illustrate the foregoing law. The man despised the word of the Lord, presumptuously broke his commandment, and on this ground was punished with death. Ex 16:23, 27, 28. +*20:8-10. 31:14, 15. 35:2, 3.

33. **brought him.** Ex 18:19. Jn 8:3, etc.

34. **put him in ward.** Le 24:12.

35. **Moses.** ♪132G, Ge +3:19. **The man.** Ex 31:14, 15. **surely.** ♪147, Ge +2:16. **stone him.** See on Le 24:14, 23. 1 K 21:13. Ac 7:58. He 13:11, 12.

36. **all the congregation.** Jsh 7:25.

38. **fringes in the borders.** The word *tzitzith* properly denotes an ornament resembling a flower. From ver. 39, we learn that these were emblematical of the commands of God. That there is any analogy between a *fringe* and a *precept*, it would be bold to assert; but when a thing is appointed to *represent* another, no matter how different, that first object becomes the legitimate representative or sign of the other. Dt 22:12. Mt 9:20. 23:5. Lk 8:44.

39. **remember.** Ex 13:9. Dt 6:6-9. 11:18-21, 28-32. Pr 3:1. **ye seek not.** Dt 29:19. Jg 17:5, 6. Jb 31:7. Pr 28:26. Ec 11:9. Je 9:14. Ezk 6:9. **go a whoring.** Ex 34:15, 16. Ps 73:27. 106:39. Ezk 6:9. Ho 2:2. Ja *4:4.

40. **be holy.** Le 11:44, 45. 19:2. Ro *12:1. Ep 1:4. Col 1:2. 1 Th 4:7. 1 P 1:15, 16.

41. **brought you.** Le 11:44, 45. 22:33. 25:38. Ps 105:45. Je 31:31-33. 32:37-41. Ezk 36:25-27. Ro *12:1. 1 Th 4:7. He 11:16. 1 P 1:15, 16. 2:9, 10.

NUMBERS 16

Korah, Dathan, and Abiram, openly rebel; and Moses falls down before God, 1-4. Moses remonstrates with Korah for seeking the priesthood; and sends for Dathan and Abiram, who refuse to come, 5-15. Korah and his company burn incense, and draw together the congregation. The glory of the Lord appears, 16-19. He threatens to consume them; but is stayed by the prayer of Moses and Aaron, 20-22. By divine command, Moses calls the people away from the tents of the rebels, and denounces their doom, 23-30. The earth opens and swallows up Korah, and a fire consumes those who burnt incense, 31-35. Their censers are reserved to cover the altar, for a memorial to posterity, 36-40. The rebellion is renewed; fourteen thousand and seven hundred are slain by a plague, for murmuring against Moses and Aaron, 41-45. The plague is stopped by Aaron burning incense, 46-48. The number that died, 49, 50.

1. **Korah.** i.e. *bald.* He was cousin to Moses and Aaron, being great-grandson of Levi, Ex 6:16-21. Nu 26:9, 10. 27:3. Ex 6:18, 21. Ju 11. **Izhar.** i.e. *oil.* He was younger brother of Amram. **Kohath.** i.e. *obedience.* **Dathan.** i.e. *law; of a fountain.* *S#1885h. Nu 16:1, 12, 24, 25, 27, 27. 26:9, 9. Dt 11:6. Ps 106:17. **Abiram.** i.e. *father of elevation; my father is high; lofty.* *S#48h. Nu 16:1, 12, 24, 25, 27, 27. 26:9, 9. Dt 11:6. 1 K 16:34. Ps 106:17. (1) A son of Eliab a Reubenite, who with Korah and others undertook to overthrow the authority of Moses and Aaron in the wilderness. (2) Son of Hiel the Bethelite, who attempted to rebuild Jericho, 1 K 16:34. **Eliab.** i.e. *my God is father.* He was son of Pallu, the second son of Reuben, Nu 26:5, 8. Nu 1:9. **On.** i.e. *strength; iniquity.* He is not mentioned again elsewhere, probably he repented and left

them (Young). *S#203h. (1) One of the sons of Peleth. He joined in a conspiracy against Moses, Nu 16:1-3. (2) *S#204h. i.e. *sun, light.* A famous city of Lower Egypt. It was on the east side of the river Nile, a few miles north of Memphis. Ge 41:45, 50. 46:20. It is called Beth-shemesh (*house of the sun*) in Je 43:13, and was known to the Greeks as Heliopolis. **Peleth.** i.e. *escape; separation; swiftness.* *S#6431h. Nu 16:1. 1 Ch 2:33. He, with Dathan and Abiram were sons of Reuben, and therefore, it may be, dissatisfied with the presidency of Judah, while Korah was dissatisfied with the superior authority of his cousins (Young). (1) A Reubenite whose son On joined the conspiracy against Moses, Nu 16:1. (2) A descendant of Pharez, the son of Judah, 1 Ch 2:33. **sons of Reuben.** Ge 49:3, 4. 1 Ch 5:1, 2. **men.** ♪63K, Ge +37:13.

2. **famous.** Nu 26:9. Ge 6:4. 1 Ch 5:24. 12:30. Ezk 16:14. 23:10.

3. **gathered.** ver. 11. Nu 12:1, 2. 14:1-4. Ps 106:16. Ac 7:39, 51. **Ye take too much upon you.** Heb. *It is much for you.* ver. 7. ◆Ex 18:13-23. **all the.** Ex 19:6. Ezr 9:2. Is 1:11-16. Je 7:3-12. Mt 3:9, 10. Ro 2:28, 29. **the Lord.** Nu 14:14. 35:34. Ex 29:45, 46. Ps 68:17.

4. **he fell.** ver. 45. Nu 14:5. 20:6. Jsh 7:6. 2 P 2:9, 10.

5. **the Lord.** Ml *3:18. 2 T ▶2:19. **who is holy.** ver. 3. Le 21:6-8, 12-15. Is 61:5, 6. 1 P 2:5-9. Re 1:6. 5:9, 10. **will cause.** Ex 28:43. Le 10:3. Ps 65:4. Ezk 40:46. 44:15, 16. Ep 2:13. He *10:19-22. *12:14. **even him.** Nu 17:5. Ex 28:1. Le 8:2. 21:12. 1 S 2:28. Ps 105:26. Jn *15:16. Ac 1:2, 24. 13:2. 15:7. 22:14. 2 T 2:3, 4, 19.

6. **Take.** ver. 35-40, 46-48. Le 10:1. 16:12, 13. 1 K 18:21-23.

7. **that the man.** See on ver. 3, 5. Ep 1:4. 2 Th 2:13. 1 P 2:9. **too much.** ver. 3. 1 K 18:17, 18. Mt 21:23-27.

9. **Seemeth it but.** ver. 13. Ge 30:15. Jsh 22:17. 1 S 18:23. 2 S 7:19. Jb 15:11. Is 7:13. 29:17. Ezk 16:20. 34:18. 1 C 4:3. A strong way of implying a negative answer (Young). **separated.** Nu 1:53. 3:10, 38, 41-45. 4:17-20, 49. 8:14-16. 18:2-6. Dt 10:8. 2 Ch 35:3. Ne 12:44. Ezk 44:10, 11. Ac 13:2. 2 C=6:17.

10. **near.** Ep=2:18. **and seek.** Pr 13:10. Mt 20:21, 22. Lk 22:24. Ro 12:10. Ph +*2:3. 3 J 9.

11. **gathered.** Ex 25:22. 29:42, 43. 30:6, 36. **against.** ver. 3. 1 S 8:7. Lk 10:16. Jn 12:48. 13:20. Ro 13:2. **what is Aaron.** Ex 16:7, 8. 17:2. Ac 5:4. 1 C 3:5.

12. **which said.** Ex 2:14. Pr 29:9. Is 3:5. Mt 21:29. Lk 19:14, 27. Jn *5:40. Ac 7:35. 1 P 2:13, 14. Ju 8.

13. **a small.** See on ver. 9. **out of a.** Nu 11:5. Ex 1:11, 22. 2:23. **milk and.** ♪174, Ge +18:27. **honey.** ♪171I7, Ex +3:8. **to kill.** Nu 20:3, 4. Ex 16:3. 17:3. **thou make.** Ex 2:14. Ps 2:2, 3. Lk 19:14. Ac 7:25-27, 35.

14. **Moreover.** Nu 45:8-10. See on Ex 3:8, 17. Le 20:24. 2 P 2:21, 22. 3:3, 4, 9. **milk and.** ♪174, Ge +18:27. **put out.** Heb. bore out. Jg +16:21. 1 S 11:2. Pr 30:17. Is 51:1. A horrible custom of abusing prisoners or suspected persons in ancient times (Young).

15. **very wroth.** Nu 12:3. Ge 4:5, 6. Ex 32:19. Mt 5:22. Mk 3:5. Ep 4:26. **Respect not.** ver. 6, 7. Nu 14:25 (turn you). Ge 4:4, 5. 18:22 (turned their faces). Is 1:10-15. **I have not.** 1 S 12:3, 4. Ac 20:33, 34. 24:16. 1 C 9:15. 2 C 1:12. 7:2. 12:14-17. 1 Th 2:10. **one ass.** Though this animal is generally respectfully spoken

of in the Scriptures, yet here it appears to be considered of little or no value, as Sampson evidently considered it in Jg 15:16.

16. **Be thou.** See on ver. 6, 7. **before.** Ex 25:22. 1 S 12:3, 7. 2 T 2:14.

17. **and bring.** 1 S 12:7.

18. **every man.** 1 C 3:13. Re 8:3-5.

19. **Korah.** ver. 1, 2. **and the glory.** ver. 42. Nu 12:5. 14:10. Ex 16:7, 10. Le 9:6, 23. Ezk 1:28. 2:1-5.

21. **Separate.** Ge 19:15-22. 1 Ch 12:8. 23:13. Ezr 6:21. 9:1. 10:8, 11, 16. Ne 9:2. 10:28. Je 51:6. Ac 2:40. 2 C 6:17. Ep 5:6, 7. Re 18:4. **that I may.** ver. 45. Nu 14:12, 15. Ex 32:10. 33:5. Ps 73:19. Is 37:36. He 12:28, 29.

22. **they fell.** ver. 4, 45. Nu 14:5. **the God.** Nu 27:16n. Jb 12:10. Ec +*12:7. Is 57:16. Zc +*12:1n. He +*12:9. **spirits.** Heb. *ruach*, ✣S#7307h. Here *ruach* has reference to the invisible psychological part of man given to him by God at man's formation at birth, and returning to God at his death. Nu √27:16n. Jb 27:3. 34:14. Ps 31:5. 104:30. Ec *3:21, 21. 8:8, 8. 11:5. *12:7. Is 42:5. Ezk 37:9 (wind). Zc 12:1. For the other uses of *ruach*, see Ge 6:3n. For the equivalent New Testament Greek category of *pneuma*, see Mt 27:50n. He +12:9. **all flesh.** Jb 12:10. Ac 17:24-26. **one man sin.** Ge *18:23-25, 32. 20:4. Jsh 7:1, etc. 2 S 24:1, 17. Ro *5:18. 1 C 13:7. **wilt thou.** T#1129. Ge *18:23-32. Jsh 7:6, 7. 2 S 24:17. 2 Ch 20:10-12. Ezk 9:8. Jon 1:14.

24. **Get you up.** See on ver. 21. It should seem that Dathan and Abiram had set up a spacious tabernacle in the midst of the tents of their families, where they kept court, met in council, and hung out their flag of defiance against Moses; it is here called the tabernacle of Korah, Dathan, and Abiram (Ex ☾33:7n). There, as in the place of rendezvous, Dathan and Abiram stayed, when Korah and his friends went up to the tabernacle of the Lord, waiting the issue of their trial; but here we are told how they had their business done, before that trial was over. God will take what method he pleases in his judgments.

25. **went unto.** Imitating Him who willeth all men to be saved (Young). 1 T *2:4. **the elders.** Nu 11:16, 17, 25, 30. **followed him.** That they might also bear witness to the truth (Young). Nu 35:30. Jsh *22:13. Mt *18:16. 1 T 5:20.

26. **Depart, I pray you.** The rebels, with all that belonged to them, were, as *an accursed thing*, devoted to utter destruction (Le 27:28, 29. Jsh 7:13-15, 23-26). The people therefore were forbidden to touch any thing belonging to them; that they might enter a solemn protest against their wickedness, acknowledge the justice of their punishment, and express their fear of being involved in it. See on ver. 21-24. Ge 19:12-14. Dt 13:17. Is 52:11. Je 51:6. Mt 10:14. Ac 2:40. 8:20. 13:51. 2 C 6:17. 1 T 5:22. Re 18:4.

27. **and stood.** Ex 32:26-28. 2 K 9:30, 31. Jb 9:4. 40:10, 11. Pr 16:18. 18:12. Is 28:14. **little children.** or, infants. ✣S#2945h. Ge 34:29. 43:8. 45:19. 46:5. 47:12mg. 50:8, 21. Ex 10:10, 24. 12:37. Nu 14:3, 31. 16:27. 31:9, 17, 18. 32:16, 17, 24, 26. Dt 1:39. 2:34. 3:6, 19. 20:14. +*29:11n. 31:12. Jsh 1:14. 8:35. Jg 18:21. 21:10. 2 S 15:22. 2 Ch 20:13. 31:18. Ezr 8:21. Est 3:13. 8:11. Je 40:7. 41:16. 43:6. Ezk 9:6.

28. **Hereby.** Ex 3:12. 4:1-9. 7:9. Dt 18:22. 1 S 12:15-18. Zc 2:9. 4:9. Jn 5:36. 11:42. 14:11. **for I have.** Kee

lo millibbee, "and that not out of my heart." It was not of my own device or contrivance. It was not out of an ambitious desire to be great myself that I took upon me the government, nor out of private affection to my brother, that I appointed him and his family to the priesthood. *J*63B, Ge +25:28. **of mine.** Nu 24:13. 1 K 12:33. 18:36. Ne 6:8. Jb 8:10. Je 14:14. 23:16, 26. Ezk 13:2, 17. Jn 5:30. 6:38.

29. **the common,** etc. Heb. as every man dieth. Ge 3:19. **visited.** Ex 20:5. 32:34. Jb 35:15. Is 10:3. Je 5:9. La 4:22. **the Lord.** 1 K 22:28. 2 Ch 18:27.

30. **make a new thing.** Heb. create a creature. *J*147D, Ge +1:29. *weim beriah yivra Yeowah,* "And if Jehovah should create a creation," i.e. do such a thing as was never done before. Young notes, "The idea involved is rather that of being out of the ordinary currents of events, than of a merely *new* event." Jb 31:3. Is 28:21. 43:19. 45:7, 12. Je 31:22. **quick.** or, alive. ver. 33. Ps 55:15. Pr 1:12. **pit.** Heb. *sheol,* Ge +37:35. Sheol is rendered *pit* only here, at ver. 33, and Jb 17:16. The fact that they went down alive into Sheol, together with their goods and all that pertained to them, shows that Sheol does not always refer exclusively to a place where man's soul goes upon death. See especially in this regard Ezk √32:27. **have provoked.** Nu 14:11, 23. Dt 9:7, 8. 31:29. 32:19 (mg, despised). Ps 95:8. He 3:8, 16.

31. **the ground clave.** Nu 26:10, 11. 27:3. Dt 11:6. Jb 31:3. Ps 55:15. 106:17, 18. Is 28:21. Ju 11.

32. **the earth.** ver. 30. Ge 4:11. Is 5:14. Re 12:16. **all.** *J*171A, Ex +9:6. The terrible judgment here recorded would seem to have included the *households* as well as the leaders, yet from Nu 26:11, it appears that the *children* (more lit. *sons*) of Korah did not die. The orientals appear generally to have used much more indeterminate language than the westerns, so that what happened to the greater part, or any large number, is said to have happened to ALL. A similar remark appears necessary in the case of Achan, recorded in Jsh 7:24-26. The *sons of Korah* were authors of many of the Psalms in later ages. ver. 17. Nu √26:11n. 27:3. 1 Ch 6:22, 37. Ps ch. 84, 85, 88 titles. *J*171A. Figure of speech Synecdoche of the Genus: universals for particulars; "All" is put for the greater part, Ex +9:6.

33. **into the.** Ps 9:15. 55:23. 69:15. 143:7. Is 14:9, 15. Ezk 32:18, 30. **pit.** Heb. *sheol,* Ge +37:35n. ver. 30n. **they perished.** Ju 11.

34. **fled.** Is 33:3. Am 1:1. Zc 14:5. He 11:7. Re 6:15-17. **Lest.** Nu 17:12, 13.

35. **And there.** Nu 11:1. 26:10. Ex 22:6. Le 9:24. 10:2. Jb 4:8, 9. Ps 106:18. Is 33:10-12, *14. **two hundred.** See on ver. 2, 17.

37. **the censers.** See on ver. 7, 18. **hallowed.** *kadashoo, consecrated,* i.e. to the service of God, though in this instance, improperly employed. See on Le 27:28.

38. **sinners.** 1 K 2:23. Pr 1:18. 8:36. 20:2. Hab 2:10. **souls.** Heb. *nephesh,* Ge +12:13. **a sign.** ver. 40. Nu 17:10. 26:10. Ezk 14:8. 1 C 10:11. 2 P 2:6.

40. **that no.** Nu 3:10, 38. 18:4-7. Le 22:10. 2 Ch 26:18-20. Ju 11. **come near.** 1 K 13:1-3. 2 Ch 26:16-21.

41. **on the morrow.** It is not unlikely, that the people persuaded themselves that Moses and Aaron had used some *cunning* in this business, and that the *earthquake*

and *fire* were artificial; for, had they discerned the hand of God in this punishment, they would scarcely have dared the anger of the Lord in the very face of his justice. And while they thus absurdly imputed this judgment to Moses and Aaron, they impiously called the persons, thus perishing in their rebellion, "the people of the Lord!" **all the.** See on ver. 1-7. Nu 14:2. Ps 106:13, 23, 25, etc. Is 26:11. **Ye have killed.** ver. 3. 2 S 16:7, 8. 1 K 18:17. Je 37:13, 14. 38:4. 43:3. Am +√3:6. 7:10. Mt 5:11. Ac 5:28. 21:28. 2 C 6:8. The reduplication of the pronoun ("Ye—ye have" in the original) shows the bitterness of the people; they thought that Moses and Aaron might have interceded with the Lord, and He would have spared even the guilty; they, not doing so, were held as having "put them to death." So, also, because Jeremiah (1:10) was commissioned to foretell the desolation of nations, he is said to do it himself; and God, because he foretold (Ex 3:19) the obstinacy of Pharaoh, is said (in Ex 4:21) to have produced it. The Hiphil (or causative) form of the Hebrew verb found here is often only *permissive* (Young).

42. when the. ver. 19. **the glory.** ver. 19. Nu 14:10. 20:6. Ex 16:7, 10. 24:16. 40:34, 35. Le 9:23.

45. Get you up. See on ver. 21, 24, 26. or, be lifted up. Jb 24:24. Ps 118:16. Is 33:3, 10. Ezk 10:15, 17, 19. **that.** Ex 20:5. 32:34. Je 5:9. **And they.** ver. 22. Nu 20:6. 1 S *12:23-25. 1 Ch 21:16. Mt 26:39.

46. from off. Le 9:24. 10:1. 16:12, 13. Is 6:6, 7. Ro 5:9, 10. He 7:25-27. 9:25, 26. Re 8:3-5. **and put.** Ps 141:2. Ml 1:11. **an atonement.** Ex 30:7-10. Le 16:11-16. 1 J 2:1, 2. **there is wrath.** Nu 1:53. 8:19. 11:33. 18:5. Le 10:6. 1 Ch 27:24. Ps 106:29. **the plague is begun.** God now punished them by a *secret blast*, so as to put the matter beyond dispute—His hand, and His alone, was seen, not only in the plague, but in the *manner* in which the mortality was arrested. It was necessary that it should be done in *this way*, that the whole congregation might see that these men who had perished were not "the people of the Lord," and that God, not *Moses* and *Aaron*, had destroyed them. T#1641. Nu 11:1, 2. 21:7. Ex 8:12, 29. 9:28. 10:17. 1 K 8:37-39. 2 Ch 7:13, 14. Am 7:1-3.

47. as Moses. Ps 103:7. **and ran.** Mt 5:44. Ro 12:21. **and behold.** Ps 106:29. **and he put.** See on ver. 46. Dt 33:10, 11. Is 53:10-12.

48. What the plague was we know not; but it seems from this to have begun at one part of the camp, and to have proceeded regularly onward. **he stood between.** ver. 18, 35. Nu 25:8-11. 2 S 24:16, 17, 25. 1 Ch 21:26, 27. Is 53:12. 1 Th 1:10. 1 T 2:5, 6. He 7:24, 25. Ja 5:16. 1 J 5:14. **was stayed.** ver. 50. Nu 25:8. 1 S 21:7 (detained). 2 S 24:21, 25. 1 K 8:35 (shut up). 1 Ch 21:22. 2 Ch 6:26. Ps 106:30.

49. fourteen thousand. ver. 32-35. Nu 25:9. 1 Ch 21:14. 27:24. He 2:1-3. 10:28, 29. 12:25.

50. returned. ver. 43. 1 Ch 21:26-30. Ps 68:18-20.

NUMBERS 17

The Lord commands twelve rods, one from each tribe, with the name written on it, to be laid up before the ark, 1-5. Aaron's rod alone buds, blossoms, and bears almonds, 6-9. It is laid up for a memorial, 10, 11. The people are affrighted, and despond, 12, 13.

2. a rod. The word *matteh* signifies a *staff*, or *scepter*, which the prince or chief of each tribe bore, and which was the sign of office or royalty among almost all the people of the earth. **all their princes.** Nu 1:4-16. 2:3-30. 10:14-27. **twelve rods.** Ge *49:10. Ex 4:2, 17. Ps 110:2. 125:3. Ezk 19:14. 21:10, 13. 37:16-20. Mi 7:14.

3. the head. Nu 3:2, 3. 18:1, 7. Ex 6:16, 20. 1 C 11:3. Ep 4:15. Col 1:17, 18.

4. before the. Ex 25:16-22. 29:42, 43. 30:6, 36.

5. whom I. See on Nu 16:5. **blossom.** ver. 8. Is 5:24. 11:1. 27:6. 35:1, 2. 42:1. Ho 14:5. Zc 6:12, 13. **I will.** ver. 10. Is 13:11. Ezk 16:41. 23:27. **they murmur.** See on Nu 16:11.

6. a rod apiece, for each prince one. Heb. a rod for one prince, a rod for one prince. ℐ84, Ge +6:17. See on ver. 2.

7. tabernacle. Nu 18:2. Ex 38:21. Ac 7:44. He 9:23.

8. the rod of Aaron. This fact was so unquestionably miraculous, that no doubt could remain on the minds of the people, or the envious chiefs, of the divine appointment of Aaron: and as there were buds, blossoms, and fruit on the rod at the same time, which was never the case with branches in the natural and ordinary course, this evidently *proved* the miracle, and took away all suspicion of the fraud which has been impiously suggested, that Moses had taken away Aaron's rod in the night time, and put a living branch of an almond tree in the room of it. A scepter or staff of office resuming its vegetative life, was considered an absolute impossibility among the ancients; and as they were accustomed to swear by their scepters, this circumstance was added to confirm the oath. **budded.** See on ver. 5. Ge 40:10. Ps 110:2. 132:17, 18. SS 2:3. Is 4:2. Ezk 17:24. 19:12, 14. Jn 12:24. 15:1-6. Ro 1:3, 4. =8:11. 1 C=6:14. =15:20. Ep 1:18-23. Col 3:3, 4. 2 T 1:10.

10. Bring Aaron's. He 9:4. **for a token.** Nu 16:38, 40. Ex 16:32. Dt 31:19-26. Ac 17:30, 31. He 9:3, 4. **rebels.** Heb. children of rebellion. 1 S 2:12. 30:22. Ps 57:4. Is 1:2. Ho 10:9. Ep 2:2, 3. 5:6. **and thou.** ver. 5.

11. Moses did. Ge 6:22. 12:4. *18:19. Jsh 11:15. Mt 7:21. He 5:8, *9.

12. Behold. Nu 26:11. Jb 14:1, 2. Ps 90:7. Pr 19:3. Is 57:16. 64:6. Ro 5:12. 6:23. He 12:5. Ja 1:13-15. 4:14. **we die.** *Gawanoo, we expire*: it signifies not so much to *die* simply, as to *feel an extreme difficulty in breathing*, which producing *suffocation*, ends at last in death. See the folly and extravagance of this sinful people, in thus rebelling against the authority of those whom Jehovah had appointed to be their rulers. S#1478h, Ge +49:33. Nu +16:12. Lk 19:14. **perish.** ℐ84, Ge +6:17.

13. Whosoever. Nu 1:51-53. 18:4-7. **any thing.** Ge 3:3. Ex 23:20, 21. 34:14. Le 10:3. 1 S 6:19-21. 2 S 6:6-12. 1 Ch 13:11-13. 15:13. Ps 85:5. 130:3, 4. Is 63:9, 10. Ac 5:5, 11-14. Ep 2:13. He 10:19-22. **near.** ℐ84, Ge +6:17. **consumed.** Nu 16:26. 32:13. Dt 2:16. Jb 34:14, 15. Ps 90:7. Is 28:22. **dying.** ℐ84, Ge +6:17. S#1478h, Ge +49:33.

NUMBERS 18

The charge of the priests and Levites, 1-7. The portion of the priests, 8-20. The tithes assigned to the

Levites, 21-24. The tithe of that tithe of the heave offering assigned to the priests out of the Levite's portion, 25-32.

1. **Aaron, Thou.** Nu 17:3, 7, 13. He 4:15. **shall bear.** ver. 22. Nu 14:34. Ex 28:38. Le 22:9. Jb 33:24. Ps 89:19. Is 53:6, 11, 12. Ezk 3:18, 19. Ac 20:26, 27. Ro 4:5-8, 23-25. He 7:26-28. 8:1, 2. 13:17. 1 P 2:24.

2. **father.** Jn=20:17. He=2:11. **bring.** He=2:10. 1 P=3:18. **joined unto thee.** There is a fine paronomasia (♪140, Ge +4:25) in the original. *Levi* is derived from *lawah*, to join, couple, associate; hence Moses says, the *Levites yillawoo*, "shall be joined," or *associated*, with the priests: they shall conjointly perform the sacred office, but the priests shall be *principal*, the Levites their *associates* or assistants. ver. 4. Ge 29:34. 1 C=6:17. Ep=5:30. **minister.** See on Nu 3:6-9. 8:19, 22. **but thou.** Nu 3:10, etc. 4:15. 16:40. 17:7. 1 Ch 16:39, 40. 2 Ch 30:16. Ezk 44:15.

3. **only they.** See on Nu 3:25, 31, 36. 4:19, 20. 16:40. **neither.** Nu 4:15, 17-20.

4. **a stranger.** Nu 1:51. 3:10. 1 S 6:19. 2 S 6:6, 7.

5. **And ye.** Nu 8:2. Ex 27:21. 30:7, etc. Le 24:3. 1 Ch 9:19, 23, 33. 24:5. 1 T 1:18. 3:15. 5:21. 6:20. **no wrath.** Nu 8:19. 16:46. Je 23:15. Zc 10:3.

6. **And I.** Ge 6:17. 9:9. Ex 14:17. 31:6. Is 48:15. 51:12. Ezk 34:11, 20. **I have.** See on Nu 3:12, 45. **given.** Nu 3:9. 8:16-19. **for the Lord.** Jn=17:12.

7. **Therefore thou.** ver. 5. Nu 3:10. **within.** Le 16:2, 12-14. He 9:3-6. **have given.** ♪96C9, Ge +2:10. **as a service.** Nu 16:5-7. 1 S 2:28. Ps 65:4. Jn 3:27. Ro 15:15, 16. Ep 3:8. He 5:4. **of gift.** Ro 11:29. 1 C 7:7. 12:4-6. 14:1, 12. Ep 4:7, 8, 11, 12. 1 T 4:14. 2 T 1:6. Ja 1:16, 17. 1 P 4:10, 12. **the stranger.** ver. 4. Nu 3:38. 16:40.

8. **the charge.** Nu 5:9. Le 6:16, 18, 20, 26. 7:6, 32-34. 10:14, 15. Dt 12:6, 11. 26:13. **heave offerings.** Le +7:14. **by reason.** Ex 29:21, 29. 40:13, 15. Le 7:35. 8:30. 21:10. Is 10:27. He 1:9. 5:1-6. 7:23, 24. 1 J 2:20, 27. **anointing.** ♪121S1, Ge +49:10. Here, the anointing is put for the Priesthood, of which it was the sign. **for ever.** Heb. *olam*, Ex +12:24.

9. **every meat offering.** Le 2:2, 3. 10:12, 13. +*23:13. **every sin offering.** Le 4:22, 27. 6:25, 26. 10:17. +*23:19. **every trespass offering.** Le 5:1, +*6. 7:1, 7. 10:12. 14:13. **most holy.** Le 2:3. Nu 5:9. He 8:3-5.

10. **In the.** Ex 29:31, 32. Le 6:16, 26, 29. 7:6. 10:13, 17. 14:13. **every male.** Le 6:18, 29. 7:6. 21:22.

11. **the heave offering.** ver. 8. Ex 29:27, 28. Le 7:+*14, 30-34. **wave offerings.** Le +*23:15. **unto thee.** Le 10:14. Dt 18:3. **for ever.** Heb. *olam*, Ex +12:24. **every one.** Le 22:2, 3, 11-13. 1 P=2:2-5.

12. **best of the oil.** Heb. fat. ver. 29. **the firstfruits.** Nu 15:19-21. Ex 22:29. 23:19. 34:26. Le 2:14. 23:17, 20. Dt 18:4. 26:2. Ne 10:35-37. Pr 3:9. SS 5:1. Jn 6:48-58.

13. **whatsoever.** Ex 22:29. Je 24:2. Ho 9:10. Mi 7:1. **first ripe.** Ro=4:25. 1 C=15:20, 23. **every one.** ver. 11.

14. **devoted.** Le 27:28. Ezk 44:29mg. Lk 10:7. 1 C=3:21-23. 9:7-11.

15. **openeth.** Nu 3:13. Ex 13:2, 12. 22:29. 34:20. Le 27:26. **the firstborn.** Ex 13:13. 34:20. Le 27:27.

16. **according.** Nu 3:47. Le 27:2-7. **which is.** Ex

30:13. Le 27:25. Ezk 45:12. 1 P 1:18, 19.

17. **the firstling.** Dt 15:19-22. **thou shalt.** See on Ex 29:16. Le 3:2-5. Ep 5:2.

18. **as the wave.** Ex 29:26-28. Le 7:31-34.

19. **the heave offerings.** ver. 8, 11. Nu 15:10-21. 31:29, 41. Le +*7:14. Dt 12:6. 2 Ch 31:4. **for ever.** Heb. *olam*, Ex +12:24. **covenant of salt.** Le 2:13. 2 Ch 13:5. **for ever.** Heb. *olam*, Ex +12:24.

20. **Thou shalt have.** The principal part of what was offered to God was the portion of the priests; who had no inheritance of land in Israel. The Rabbins say, 24 gifts were given to the priests; all of which are expressed in the law. Eight were only eaten in the sanctuary: (1) The flesh of the sin offering, Le 6:25, 26; (2) The flesh of the trespass offering, Le 7:1, 6; (3) The peace offering of the congregation, Le 23:19, 20; (4) The remainder of the sheaf, Le 23:10; (5) The remnants of the meat offerings, Le 6:16; (6) The two loaves, Le 23:17; (7) The show bread, Le 24:9; (8) The log of oil offered by the leper, Le 14:10. Five they ate only at Jerusalem: (1) The breast and shoulder of the peace offerings, Le 7:31, 34. (2) The heave offering of confession, Le 7:12-14; (3) The heave offering of the Nazarite's ram, Le 6:17-20; (4) The firstling, Nu 18:15; (5) The firstfruits, Nu 18:13. Five were due to them only in the land of Israel: (1) The heave offering of firstfruits, Nu 18:12; (2) Of the tithe, Nu 18:28; (3) The cake, Nu 15:20; (4) The first of the fleece, Dt 18:4; (5) The field of possession, Nu 35. Five were due both within and without the land: (1) The gifts of slain beasts, Dt 18:3; (2) The redemption of the firstborn, Nu 18:15; (3) The lamb for a firstling ass, Ex 4:20; (4) That taken by violence from a stranger, Nu 5:8; (5) All devoted things. One was from the sanctuary, the skins, etc., Le 7:8. **no inheritance.** ver. 23, 24. Nu 26:62. Dt 10:9. 12:12. 14:27, 29. Jsh 14:3. Col=3:24. **any part.** 2 C=6:15. **I am thy part.** Dt 18:1, 2. Jsh 13:14, 33. 14:3. 18:7. Ps 16:5. 73:25, 26. 142:5. SS 2:16. La 3:24. Ezk 44:28. 1 C 3:21-23. Re 21:3. **inheritance.** Dt 10:9. 14:27. 18:1, 2. Ezk 44:28. Ro=8:17. Ep=1:11. 1 P=1:4.

21. **the tenth.** ver. 24-26. Le 27:30-32. Dt 12:17-19. 14:22-29. 2 Ch 31:5, 6, 12. Ne 10:37-39. 12:44. 13:12. He 7:5-9. **even the service.** ver. 6. Nu 3:7, 8. 1 C 9:13, 14. Ga 6:6.

22. **come nigh.** ver. 7. Nu 1:51. 3:10, 38. **bear sin.** Le 20:20. 22:9. **and die.** Heb. to die.

23. **do the service.** See on Nu 3:7. **for ever.** Heb. *olam*, Ex +12:24. **among.** See on ver. 20.

24. **the tithes.** Ge +14:20. Le 27:30, 32. Ml 3:8-10. Mt 22:21. +*23:23. Ro 13:7. He 7:5. **heave offering.** Le +*7:14.

26. **then ye shall.** See on ver. 19. **offer.** 1 C=16:1, 2. 2 C=9:7. **heave offering.** Le +*7:14. **a tenth part.** Ne 10:38.

27. **heave offering.** Le +*7:14. **as though.** Le 6:19-23. **the corn.** ver. 30. Nu 15:20. Dt 15:14. 2 K 6:27. Ho 9:1, 2.

28. **heave offering.** Le +*7:14. **and ye shall.** Ge 14:18. He 6:20. 7:1-10.

29. **heave offering.** Le +*7:14. **best.** Heb. fat. ver. 12.

30. **the best.** ver. 28. Ge 43:11. Dt 6:5. Pr *3:9, 10. Ml 1:8. Mt 6:33. 10:37-39. Ph 3:8, 9. **then it shall.** ver. 27.

31. **in every.** Dt 14:22, 23. **your reward.** Nu 4:49.

7:5. Je 31:14. Mt 10:10. Lk 10:7. 1 C=3:8. 9:10-14. 2 C 12:13. Ga 6:6. 1 T 5:17, 18. He=6:10.

32. **bear.** ver. 22. Le 19:8. **pollute.** Le 22:2, 15. Ml 1:7. Mt 21:33-41. 1 C 11:27, 29.

NUMBERS 19

The water of separation directed to be made with the ashes of a red heifer; and all who prepared these must be cleansed from pollution, 1-10. The cases in which the water was to be used, and how; the soul that neglected it to be cut off; and the person that sprinkled it to be cleansed, 11-22.

2. **the ordinance.** Nu 31:21. He 9:10. **commanded.** ∫144C1, Ge +21:1. **a red heifer.** The following curious particulars have been remarked in this ordinance: (1) A *heifer* was appointed for sacrifice, in opposition to the Egyptian superstition, which held these *sacred*, and worshipped their goddess Isis under this form; and this appears the more likely, because *males* only were chosen for sacrifice. So Herodotus says, they sacrifice males, both old and young; but it is not lawful for them to offer females. (2) It was to be a *red* heifer, because the Egyptians sacrificed *red bulls* to the evil demon Typhon. (3) It was to be *without spot*, having no mixture of any other color. Plutarch says, the Egyptians "sacrifice red bulls, and select them with such scrupulous attention, that if the animal has a single black or white hair, they reckon it *athuton*, unfit to be sacrificed." (4) *Without blemish.* This law is so founded on the nature of the thing itself, that it has been in force among all nations that sacrificed victims to their deities. (5) *On which never came yoke:* because an animal which had been used for a common purpose was deemed improper for sacrifice. ver. 6. Le 14:6. Is 1:18. Re 1:5. **no blemish.** See on Ex 12:5. Le 22:20-25. Ps 45:2. SS 4:7. Ml 1:13, 14. Lk *1:35. He 7:26. 9:13, 14. 1 P 1:19. 2:22. **upon which.** Dt 21:3. 1 S 6:7. La 1:14. Mt 17:25, 26. Jn *10:17, 18. Ph 2:6-8.

3. **without the camp.** Nu 5:2. 15:36. Le 4:12, 21. 13:45, 46. 16:27. 24:14. He 13:11-13.

4. **sprinkle.** Le 4:6, 17. 16:14, 19. He 9:13, 14. 12:24. 1 P 1:2.

5. **her skin.** Ex 29:14. Le 4:11, 12, 21. Ps 22:14. Is 53:10.

6. **cedar wood.** Le 14:4, 6, 49. Ps 51:7. Is 1:18. He 9:19-23.

7. **wash.** ver. 8, 19. Le 11:25, 40. 14:8, 9. 15:5. 16:26-28. **come into.** Jn 13:3-10. He 10:22. 1 P 3:21.

9. **clean.** ver. 18. Nu 9:13. 2 C 5:21. He 7:26. 9:13. **lay them up.** ver. 17. **a water of separation.** That is, water prepared by being mixed with the ashes of the heifer, and set apart for the special purpose of being sprinkled on those who had contracted any legal defilement. To this rite the apostle Paul, in his Epistle to the Hebrews (He 9:13, 14), pointedly alludes. ver. 13, 20, 21. Nu 6:12. 31:23, 24. Le 15:20. Zc 13:1. Jn 19:34. 2 C 7:1. 1 J 1:7. **purification for sin.** Heb. sin offering. Le +*23:19. Is 52:14, 15. 53:6. Je 33:8.

10. **wash his.** See on ver. 7, 8, 19. Is 52:11. 1 T 5:22. Ju 23. Re 3:4. **it shall be.** Nu 15:15, 16. Ex 12:49. Ro 3:29, 30. Col 3:11. **for ever.** Heb. *olam*, Ex +12:24.

11. **toucheth the dead.** He who touched a dead beast was only unclean for one day (Le 11:12, 27, 39); but

he who touches a *dead man* is unclean for *seven days*. This was certainly designed to show the peculiar impurity and sinfulness of man, and the hatefulness of sin—seven times worse than the vilest animal! ver. 16. Nu 5:2. 9:6, 10. 31:19. Le 11:31. 21:1, 11. La 4:14. Hg 2:13. Ro 5:12. 2 C 6:17. Ep 2:1. He 9:14. **man.** Heb. soul (Heb. *nephesh*, Le +19:28) of man. ver. 13. Nu 6:6. 9:6, 7, 10. Le 21:11. Hg 2:13.

12. **He shall purify.** *Yithchatta*, literally, "he shall sin himself," i.e. not *add sin*, but take it away—*purify*. So we say to "fleece," and to "skin," which do not signify to "add a fleece," or a "skin," but to take one away. ver. 17, 18. Ps 51:7. Is 1:16. Ezk 36:25. Ac 15:9. 24:16. 2 C 1:12. 1 Th 4:3, 4. 1 T 3:9. Ja 1:27. 1 J 3:3. Re 7:14. **third day.** Nu 31:19. Ex 19:11, 15. Le 7:17. Ho 6:2. 1 C +√15:3, 4.

13. **dead body.** Heb. *nephesh*, soul, Le +19:28. **purifieth.** Nu 15:30. Le 5:3, 6, 17. 15:31. 1 C 3:16, 17. 6:19, 20. He 2:2, 3. 10:29. Re 21:8. 22:11, 15. **soul.** Heb. *nephesh*, Ge +17:14. Le 7:20. **the water.** ver. 9, 18. Nu 8:7. **sprinkled.** Heb. *zaraq*, *S#2236h. Kal, Preterite: Ex 9:8. 24:6. 29:16, 20. Le 1:5, 11. 3:2, 8, 13. 17:6. Ezk *36:25. Ho 7:9 (here and there; mg., sprinkled). Kal, Infinitive: Ezk 43:18. Kal, Imperative: Ezk 10:2. Kal, Future: Ex 9:10. 24:8. Ve 7:2. 8:19, 24. 9:12, 18. Nu 18:17. 2 K 16:13, 15. 2 Ch 29:22, 22, 22. 34:4. 35:11. Jb 2:12. Is 28:25 (scatter). Kal, Participle: Le 7:14. 2 Ch 30:16. Pual, Preterite: Nu 19:13, 20. This passage is cited in the Old Testament Apocrypha by the son of Sirach, Ecclesiasticus 34:25, "He that washeth himself after the touching of a dead body, if he touch it again, what availeth his washing." In the Greek of the Septuagint, this passage has *baptidzomenos* where the English has "washeth," and *loutro* for "washing." Fairfield remarks "The entire process of cleansing from a dead body to which the son of Sirach refers, was by sprinkling, and yet he calls it baptism" (Edmund B. Fairfield, *Letters on Baptism*, p. 73). ver. 17-19. He ʔ9:13, 14. +*10:22. **his uncleanness.** Le 7:20. 22:3. Pr 14:32. Jn 8:24.

14. **unclean.** Jb *15:14-16. Hab *1:13.

15. **open vessel.** Nu 31:20. Le 11:32. 14:36.

16. **toucheth.** ver. 11. Nu 31:19. 1 S 20:25, 26. **a bone.** Ezk 39:11-16. **a grave.** Heb. *qeber*, Ge +23:4. Mt 23:27. Lk 11:44.

17. **ashes.** Heb. dust. ver. 9, 10. **purification for sin.** Heb. sin offering. Le +*23:19. **running water shall be put thereto.** Heb. living waters shall be given. Running water is a reference to water in motion. No bathing tub for immersion was ever used. There is not a single requirement for immersion in the whole Mosaic code. When such a tub was used in connection with the bathing of the whole person, the bather used it simply for a receptacle of the water after it had been sprinkled or poured upon the body (Is 44:3). The water was then defiled and unfit for further use (Fairfield, *Letters on Baptism*, p. 106). Ge +26:19mg. Le 14:5, 6, 50-52. 15:13. SS +*4:15. Jn 4:10, 11. *7:38. Re 7:17. 22:1.

18. **a clean.** ver. 9. Ps 51:7. Ezk 36:25-27. Jn 15:2, 3. 17:17, 19. 1 C 1:30. He 9:14. **grave.** Heb. *qeber*, Ge +23:4.

19. **shall sprinkle.** Ep 5:25-27. T 2:14. 3:3-5. 1 J 1:7. 2:1, 2. Ju 23. Re 1:5, 6. **purify.** Nu 31:20, 23. Ps 51:7. Ezk 36:25. 1 C 6:11. **on the seventh day.** ver. 12. Nu 31:19. Ge 2:2. Le 14:9. **he shall purify himself.**

This is *not* spoken of the person who had touched a dead body, but of the administrator of the ritual of purification, as is similarly required of the administrator in ver. 7, 8, 10.

20. **shall not**. See on ver. 13. Nu 15:30. Ge 17:14. Mk 16:16. Ac 13:39-41. Ro 2:4, 5. 2 P 3:14. Re 22:11. **soul**. Heb. *nephesh*, Ge +17:14. **water of**. Nu 8:5-7. 1 T 1:5, 19.

21. **perpetual**. Heb. *olam*, Ge +9:12. Fairfield notes, "This form of making a statute perpetual seems never to be used *except* when the statute has been previously announced. But unless we understand it to be announced in the latter half of the 19th verse, it is not found at all" (*Letters on Baptism*, p. 79). Ex 12:14, 17. 29:9. 31:16. Le 3:17. 24:3. Nu 18:8, 19. 19:10. **he that**. Le 11:25, 40. 16:26-28. He 7:19. 9:10, 13, 14. 10:4. Ja 1:17. **sprinkleth**. Heb. *nazah*, *S#5137h. Kal, Future: Le 6:27, 27. 2 K 9:33. Is 63:3. Hiphil, Preterite: Ex 29:21. Le 4:6, 17. 5:9. 14:7, 16, 27, 51. 16:14, 15, 19. Nu 19:4, 18, 19. Hiphil, Imperative: Nu *8:7. Hiphil, Future: Le 8:11, 30. 16:14. Is *52:15. Hiphil, Participle: Nu 19:21. **wash**. Heb. *kabas*, *S#3526h. Kal, Participle: 2 K 18:17 (fuller's). Is 7:3. 36:2. Piel, Preterite: Ge 49:11. Ex 19:10. Le 13:6, 34, 54. 14:8, 9. 15:8, 11, 13, 27. 17:15. Nu *8:7. 19:7, 10, 19. 31:24. 2 S 19:24. Piel, Imperative: Ps 51:2. Je 4:14. Piel, Future: Ex 19:14. Le 6:27. 11:25, 28, 40, 40. 13:58. 14:47, 47. 15:5, 6, 7, 10, 21, 22. 16:26, 28. 17:16. Nu 8:21. 19:8, 21. Ps 51:7. Je 2:22. Piel, Participle: Ml 3:2. Pual, Preterite: Le 13:58. 15:17. Hothpael, Infinitive: Le 13:55, 56.

22. **whatsoever**. Le 7:19. Ps 19:7-11. 119:140. Hg 2:13. Ph 4:8. T 1:15. Ja 3:17. **the soul**. Heb. *nephesh*, Ge +27:31. Le 15:5. Mt 15:19, 20. Mk 7:21-23.

NUMBERS 20

The people come to Zin, where Miriam dies, 1. They murmur for water, 2-6. Moses speaks to the people in anger and unadvisedly, and smites the rock, instead of speaking to it, as ordered; water is given, but Moses and Aaron are doomed to die in the wilderness, 7-13. Edom refuses Israel a passage through their land, 14-21. At mount Hor, Aaron resigns his priesthood to Eleazar, and dies, 22-29.

1. A.M. 2552. B.C. 1452. **Then**. This was the first month of the fortieth year after the departure from Egypt. (Compare Nu 33:38 with ver. 28 of this chapter and Dt 1:3.) This year was the last of their journeyings, for from the going out of the spies (Nu ch. 13) unto this time, was about thirty-eight years. Dt 1:22, 23. 2:14. **into**. Nu 13:21. 27:14. 33:36. Dt 32:51. **Kadesh**. This Kadesh in the wilderness of Zin, is different from Kadesh-barnea, lying in, or adjoining to the wilderness of Paran, about eight leagues south of Hebron (See Nu 34:3, 4. Jsh 15:1, 3). Kadesh is called *Rekam* by the Targumists, *Rekem*, in the Syriac, and *Rakim* in the Arabic. *Rekem* is on the east, meaning of the land of Israel. ver. 16. Ps 29:8. **Miriam**. Nu 12:1, 10, 15. 26:59. Ex 2:4, 7. 15:20. Mi 6:4.

2. **no**. Ex 15:23, 24. 17:1-4. **gathered**. Nu 11:1-6. 16:3, 19, 42. 21:5. Ex 16:2, 7, 12. 1 C 10:10, 11.

3. **God**. Nu 14:1, 2. Ex 16:2, 3. 17:2. Jb 3:10, 11. **died**. S#1478h, Ge +49:33. **when**. Nu 11:1, 33, 34.

14:36, 37. 16:31-35, 49. La 4:9. **died**. S#1478h, Ge +49:33.

4. **why**. Nu 11:5. Ex 5:21. 17:3. Ps 106:21. Ac 7:35, 39, 40. **that we**. Nu 16:13, 14, 41. Ex 14:11, 12. 16:3.

5. **this evil**. Nu 16:14. Dt 8:15. Ne 9:21. Je 2:2, 6. Ezk 20:36. **no place of**. i.e. "no place for *sowing*." **neither**. Nu 11:1, 3. 14:2, 37. 16:32, 35, 42, 49. Ex 17:1-3.

6. **they fell**. Nu 14:5. 16:4, 22, 45. Ex 17:4. Jsh 7:6. 1 Ch 21:16. Ps 109:3, 4. Mt 26:39. **the glory**. Nu 12:5. 14:10. 16:19, 42. Ex 16:10.

8. **the rod**. Nu 21:15, 18. Ex 4:2, 17. 7:20. 14:16. 17:5, 9. **speak**. Ge 18:14. Jsh 6:5, 20. Ps 33:9. Mt 21:21. Mk 11:22-24. Lk 11:9, 13. Jn 4:10-14. 16:24. Ac 1:14. 2:1-4. Re 22:1, 17. **bring forth**. ver. 11. Ne 9:15. Ps 78:15, 16. 105:41. 114:8. Is 41:17, 18. 43:20. 48:21.

9. **before the Lord**. Nu 17:10.

10. **ye rebels**. Dt 9:24. Ps 106:32, 33. Mt 5:22. Lk 9:54, 55. Ac 23:3-5. Ep 4:26. Ja 3:2. **we fetch**. Nu 11:22, 23. Ge 40:8. 41:16. Da 2:28-30. Ac 3:12-16. 14:9-15. Ro 15:17-19. 1 C 3:7.

11. **smote**. ver. 8. Le 10:1. 1 S 15:13, 14, 19, 24. 1 K 13:21-24. 1 Ch 13:9, 10. 15:2, 13. Is 50:5, 6. 53:4, 5, 8, 10. Mt 28:20. Ac 2:23. Ga 3:1. Ja 1:20. **the water**. Ex 17:6. Dt 8:15. Is 55:1. Ho 13:5. Jn 4:10. 7:37. 1 C 10:4. Re 22:17.

12. **Because ye believed**. Nu 11:21, 22. 2 Ch 20:20. Is 7:9. Mt 17:17, 20. Lk 1:20, 45. Ro 4:20. **sanctify**. Nu 27:14. Le 10:3. Dt 1:37. 32:51. Ps 99:8. Is 8:13. Ezk 20:41. 36:23. 38:10. 1 P 3:15. **ye shall**. ver. 24. Nu 11:15. Dt 3:23-26. 32:49, 50. 34:4. Jsh 1:2. Jn 1:17.

13. **the water**. Dt 33:8. Ps 81:7. 95:8. 99:5. 106:32, etc. **Meribah**. i.e. Strife. Ex 17:7. Dt 32:51, Meribah-Kadesh. **he was**. Is 5:16. Ezk 20:41. 36:23. 38:16.

14. **Moses**. Jg 11:16, 17. **thy brother**. Ge 25:29-34. 32:3, 4. 36:40-43. Dt 2:4, etc. 23:7. Ob 10-12. Ml 1:2. **befallen us**. Heb. found us. ⌐155F, Ge +4:7. Ge 44:34. Ex 18:8. 2 K 9:21mg.

15. **our fathers**. Ge 46:6. Ac 7:15. **dwelt**. Ge 15:13. Ex 12:40. **vexed us**. Nu 11:5. 16:13. Ex 1:11-14, 16, 22. 5:14. Dt 26:6. Ac 7:19.

16. **we cried**. Ex 2:23, 24. 3:7-9. 6:5. 14:10. **sent an**. Ex 3:2-6. 14:19. 23:20. 33:2. Is 63:9.

17. **through thy**. Nu 21:1, 22-24. Dt 2:1-4, 27, 29. **wells**. Heb. *be-er*, Ge +16:14. **king's high way**. Nu 21:22. **turn to**. Dt 2:27. 5:32. Pr 4:27.

19. **We will go**. Dt 2:6, 28.

20. **Thou shalt**. ver. 18. Ge 27:41. 32:6. Jg 11:17, 20. Ps 120:7. Ezk 35:5-11. Am 1:11. **And Edom**. Ob 10-15.

21. **refused**. Dt 2:27, 29. **wherefore**. Dt 2:4-8. 23:7. Jg 11:18, 24. Lk 9:56.

22. **Kadesh**. ver. 1, 14, 16. Nu 13:26. 33:36, 37. Ezk 47:19. 48:28. **mount Hor**. i.e. *who shows*, *S#2023h. ver. 23, 25, 27. Nu 21:4. 33:37, 38, 39, 41. 34:7, 8. Dt 32:50. (1) A mountain "in the edge of the land of Edom," Nu 33:37. Edom, or Mount Seir, included the range of mountains which extends nearly from the south end of the Dead Sea to the Gulf of Akabah. About the middle of this range is its highest mountain, which is probably Mount Hor, on which Aaron died, Nu 20:24-29; 33:38, 39; Dt 32:50. (2) A mountain on the northern boundary of the Promised Land. It is mentioned only in Nu 34:7, 8, is probably the extreme northern summit of the Lebanon range,

has an elevation of 10,000 feet, and is the highest mountain in Syria.

24. **gathered.** Nu 27:13. 31:2. Ge 15:15. 25:8, 17. 35:29. 49:29, 33. Dt 32:50. Jg 2:10. 2 Ch 34:28. **because ye.** See on ver. 11, 12. **word.** Heb. mouth. ✓121BA, Ge +45:21. Nu 4:27mg. Dt 32:50.

25. **Take Aaron.** Nu 33:38, 39.

26. **strip Aaron.** Ex 29:29, 30. Is 22:21, 22. He 7:11, 23, 24.

28. **Moses.** ver. 26. Nu 33:38, etc. Ex 29:29, 30. **put them.** Nu 27:16-23. Dt 31:7, 8. 34:9. 1 Ch 22:11, 12, 17. 28:5-9. Ac 20:25-29. 2 P 1:15. **died there.** Nu 33:38, 39. Dt 10:6. 32:49, 50. 34:5. He 7:23-25.

29. **dead.** S#1478h, Ge +49:33. **mourned.** Ge 50:10. Dt 34:8. 2 S 3:38. 2 Ch 35:24, 25. Ac 8:2.

NUMBERS 21

Israel is assaulted by a Canaanitish king, and utterly destroys him, his people, and his cities at Hormah, 1-3. The people murmur, and are punished with fiery serpents; but, confessing their sin, they are healed by means of a brazen serpent, 4-9. They go forward several stages; and compose a song on finding water, 10-20. They conquer Sihon and Og, kings of the Amorites, 21-35.

1. **Arad.** Nu 33:40. Jsh 12:14. Jg 1:16. **the way of the spies.** Nu 13:21, 22. 14:45. **then.** Dt 2:32. Jsh 7:5. 11:19, 20. Ps 44:3, 4.

2. **vowed.** Ge 28:20. Jg 11:30. 1 S 1:11. 2 S 15:7, 8. Ps 56:12, 13. 116:18. 132:2. **I will.** Le 27:28, 29. Dt 13:15. Jsh 6:17, 26. 1 C 16:22.

3. **hearkened.** Ps 10:17. 91:15. 102:17. **Canaanites.** Ge +10:18. **and they utterly.** *wyyacharem*, rather, with the LXX. *kai anethematisen*, "and they anathematised, or devoted them to destruction"; for it is certain that these Canaanites and *Arad* were not utterly destroyed till the time of Joshua (Jsh 12:14). **the name.** Nu 14:45. Dt 1:44. Jg 1:17. 1 S 30:30. **Hormah.** *that is,* utter destruction. **Chormah**, rather a devoting to destruction: so LXX. *Anathema.*

4. **mount Hor.** Nu 20:22, 23, 27. 33:41. **by the way.** Nu 14:25. Dt 1:40. **compass.** Nu 20:18-21. Dt 2:5-8. Jg 11:18. **the soul.** Heb. *nephesh*, Ge +34:3. Nu 32:7, 9. Ex 6:9. Dt 11:13. Mt +*22:37. Ac 14:22. 1 Th 3:3, 4. **discouraged.** *or,* grieved. Heb. shortened. Nu 11:23. Ex 6:9. Ps 107:4-7. He 12:1-7.

5. **spake.** Nu 11:1-6. 14:1-4. 16:13, 14, 41. 17:12. Ex 14:11. 15:24. 16:2, 3, 7, 8. 17:2, 3. Ps 68:6. 78:19. **and our soul.** Heb. *nephesh*, Nu +11:6. Nu 11:6-9. Ex 16:15, 31. Ps 78:24, 25. Pr *27:7.

6. **fiery serpents.** Ge 3:14, 15. Dt 8:15. Is 14:29. 30:6. Je 8:17. Am 9:3, 4. 1 C 10:9.

7. **We have.** Ex 9:27, 28. 1 S 12:19. 15:24, 30. Ps 78:34. Mt 27:4. **pray.** Ex 8:8, 28. 1 K 13:6. Je 37:3. Ac 8:24. Ro 8:34. Ja 5:16. **take away.** T#1589. Nu 11:1, 2. Ex 32:11, 12. 2 Ch 20:9. Da 9:18. **serpents.** ✓96, Ge +3:8. **And Moses.** Nu 11:2. 14:17-20. Ge 20:7. Ex 32:11, 30. Dt 9:20, 26-29. 1 S 12:20-23. Jb 42:8, 10. Ps 106:23. Je 15:1. Ro 10:1.

8. **the Lord.** Ps 106:43-45. 145:8. **looketh.** Is 45:22. He 12:2.

9. **a serpent of.** Ge 3:1-5. 2 K 18:4. Jn 3:14, 15. 8:28. 12:31, 32. Ro 8:3. 2 C 5:21. Re 12:9. **when he.** Is 45:22. Zc 12:10. Jn 1:29. He 12:2. 1 J 3:8. **he lived.** Jn 6:40. Ro 1:17. 5:20, 21.

10. **set forward.** Nu 33:43-45. **Oboth.** i.e. *hollow passes.* S#88h. Nu 21:10, 11. 33:43, 44.

11. **Oboth.** Probably Oboda, a city of Arabia Petraea, mentioned by Ptolemy. **Ije-abarim.** *or,* heaps of Abarim. Nu 33:44, 47, 48. Ps 79:1.

12. **the valley of Zared.** Dt 2:13, 14, the brook Zered. **Zared.** i.e. *the bond subdued.* S#2218h. Nu 21:12. Dt 2:13, 13, 14.

13. **on the other side.** ver. 14. Nu 22:36. Dt 2:24. Jg 11:18. Is 16:2. Je 48:20. **Arnon.** i.e. *a brawling stream.* S#769h. Nu 21:13, 13, 14, 24, 26, 28. 22:36. Dt 2:24, 36. 3:8, 12, 16. 4:48. Jsh 12:1, 2. 13:9, 16. Jg 11:13, 18, 18, 22, 26. 2 K 10:33. Is 16:2. Je 48:20. In Nu 33:45 it is called Dibon-Gad, whence they removed to Almon-diblathaim, according to 33:46, 47.

14. **in the book.** Jsh 10:13. 2 S 1:18. 2 Ch 16:11. **What he did.** *or,* Vaheb in Suphah. The following seems to be the sense of this passage: "From Vaheb in Suphah, and the torrents of Arnon, even the effusion of the torrents, which goeth down to the dwelling of Ar, and lieth for the boundary of Moab; even from thence to the well; (which is the well of which Jehovah spake unto Moses, Gather the people, and I will give them water. Then sang Israel this song: Spring up, O well! Answer ye to it. The well, the princes digged it; even nobles of the people digged it, by a decree, upon their borders); and from the wilderness (or the *well*, as in LXX.) to Mattanah; and from Mattanah," etc. The whole of this, from ver. 14-20, is a fragment from "the book of the wars of Jehovah," probably a book of remembrances or directions written by Moses for the use of Joshua, and describes the several boundaries of the land of Moab. This rendering removes every obscurity, and obviates every difficulty.

15. **stream.** or, spring. Compare the plural form in Dt 3:17mg. 4:49. Jsh 10:40. 12:3mg, 8. 13:20mg. **Ar.** i.e. *awaking.* ✱S#6144h: ver. 28. Dt 2:9, 18, 29. Is 15:1. **lieth.** Heb. leaneth. **Moab.** 2 K 3:15-27.

16. **Beer.** i.e. *a halting place.* S#876h. Jg 9:21. **well.** Heb. *be-er*, Ge +16:14. **Gather.** Nu 20:8. Ex 17:6. Is 12:3. 41:17, 18. 43:20. 49:10. Jn 4:10, 14. 7:37-39. Re 21:6. 22:1, 17.

17. **sang.** Ex 15:1, 2. Jg 5:1. Ps 105:2. 106:12. Is 12:1, 2, 5. Ja 5:13. **Spring up.** Heb. ascend. Jn=4:14. **well.** Heb. *be-er*, Ge +16:14. **sing ye.** *or,* answer.

18. **princes.** 2 Ch 17:7-9. Ne 3:1, 5. 1 T 6:17, 18. **well.** Heb. *be-er*, Ge +16:14. **the lawgiver.** Ge *49:10. Dt 5:31. 33:4. Is 33:22. Jn 1:17. Ja 4:12. **And from.** Nu 33:45, 47. **Mattanah.** i.e. *gift.* S#4980h. Nu 21:18, 19.

19. **Nahaliel.** i.e. *valley* or *stream of God.* S#5160h. Nu 21:19, 19. **Bamoth.** i.e. *heights; high places.* S#1120h. Nu 21:19, 20. Compare Nu 22:41.

20. **country.** Heb. field. Nu 22:1. 26:63. 33:49, 50. Dt 1:5. **to the.** Nu 23:14. Dt 3:27. 4:49. 34:1. **Pisgah.** *or,* the hill. i.e. *a sight, or view.* S#6449h. Nu 21:20. 23:14. Dt 3:17, 27. 4:49. 34:1. Jsh 12:3. 13:20. **Jeshimon.** *or,* the wilderness. i.e. *the waste.* S#3452h, only here. Nu 23:28. Dt 32:10. 1 S 23:19, 24. Ps 68:7. 78:40. 106:14. 107:4. Is 43:19, 20.

21. **sent messengers.** Nu 20:14-19. Dt 2:26-28. Jg 11:19-21. **Sihon.** i.e. *a sweeping away; tempestuous.* S#5511h. Nu 21:21, 23, 23, 26, 27, 28, 29, 34. 32:33. Dt 1:4. 2:24, 26, 30, 31, 32,. 3:2, 6. 4:46. 29:7. 31:4. Jsh 2:10. 9:10. 12:2, 5. 13:10, 21, 21, 27. Jg 11:19,

20, 20, 21. 1 K 4:19. Ne 9:22. Ps 135:11. 136:19. Je 48:45.

22. **Let**. Nu 20:17. **well**. Heb. *be-er*, Ge +16:14.

23. **Sihon would**. Dt 2:30-32. 29:7, 8. **not**. ſ175B, Ge +21:16. **Jahaz**. i.e. a *trodden down* place. Jg 11:20. Is 15:4. Je 48:34. S#3096h. Nu 21:23. Dt 2:32. Jg 11:20. In latter times it was in the possession of the Reubenites, and given to the Levites, see Dt 2:32. Jsh 13:18. Is 15:4. Je 48:21, 34 (Young).

24. **Israel**. Nu 32:1-4, 33-42. Dt 2:31-37. 29:7. Jsh 9:10. 12:1-3. 13:8-10. 24:8. Jg 11:21-23. 12:1, 2. 24:8. Ne 9:22. Ps 135:10-12. 136:19. Am 2:9. **Arnon**. See on ver. 13. Ge 32:22. Dt 3:16.

25. **dwelt**. ver. 31. Nu 32:33-42. Dt 2:12. **in Heshbon**. i.e. *intelligence; reason, or device.* SS 7:4. Is 15:4. 16:8, 9. Je 48:2, 34, 45. S#2809h: Nu 21:25, 26, 27, 28, 30, 34. 32:3, 37. Dt 1:4. 2:24, 26, 30. 3:2, 6. 4:46. 29:7. Jsh 9:10. 12:2, 5. 13:10, 17, 21, 26, 27. 21:39. Jg 11:19, 26. 1 Ch 6:81. Ne 9:22. SS 7:4. Is 15:4. 16:8, 9. Je 48:2, 34, 45, 45. 49:3. **villages**. Heb. daughters. ver. 32. Nu 32:42. Ge 49:22mg. Jsh 17:11. Jg 11:26. 2 S 20:19. 1 Ch 7:28mg. 2 Ch 13:19. 28:18. Ne 11:25. SS 7:4. Je +49:2. Ezk 16:27mg, 46, 49, 53. ſ155E5. Prosopopoeia; or, Personification B868. Cities and villages are spoken of as daughters. For other instances of this figure see Jsh 15:45, 47. 17:11, 16. Jg 11:26. 1 Ch 7:28mg, 29. 18:1. Ps 45:12. 137:8. Is 1:8. 10:32. 16:1. 23:12. 37:22. 47:1. Je 4:31. 6:2. 18:13. 31:4, 21. 46:11. La 1:6. 2:1, 2, 13. Am 5:2. Zc 9:9.

26. **Heshbon**. ver. 25. Nu 32:3, 37. **Sihon**. ver. 21. Nu 32:33. **Moab**. Nu 22:3. Ex 15:15. **Arnon**. ver. 13. Nu 22:36.

27. **they that**. ver. 14. Is 14:4. Hab 2:6. **proverbs**. or, similes. i.e. *those comparing* one thing with another, as in Nu +*23:7n. 1 S 10:12. 24:12, *13. 1 K 4:32. Jb 30:19 (become like). Ps 28:1. 49:12, 20. 143:7. Is 14:10. 46:5. Ezk 12:23. 16:44. 17:2. 18:2, 3. 20:49. 24:3. **say**. ſ138A, Ge +10:9.

28. **a fire**. Jg 9:20. Ps 29:7. Is 10:16. Je 48:45, 46. Am 1:4, 7, 10, 12, 14. 2:2, 5. **Ar of Moab**. See on ver. 15. Dt 2:9, 18. Is 15:1, 2.

29. **O people**. Jg 11:24. 1 K 11:7, 33. 2 K 23:13. Je 48:7, 13, 46. 1 C 8:4, 5. **Chemosh**. i.e. *subduer, vanquisher*. The national deity of Moab and Ammon, Jg 11:24. 1 K 11:7, 33. 2 K 23:13. Je 48:7, 13, 46. S#3645h.

30. **have shot**. Ge 49:23. 2 S 11:24. Ps 18:14. **Dibon**. i.e. *pain, grief, waster*. Called Dibon-gad in Nu 33:45, because rebuilt by the Gaddites; given to the Reubenites in Jsh 13:9, 17, and afterwards occupied by the Moabites, Is 15:2. Je 48:18, 22. Doubtless it is the same place that is called *Dimon* in Is 15:19; another town of the same name belonging to Judah is noticed in Ne 11:25, which in Jsh 15:22 is called *Dimonah* (Young). Nu 32:34. Jsh 13:17. Is 15:2, 9. Je 48:18, 22, 45, 46. **Nophah**. i.e. *a gust, blast*. S#5302h, only here. Not mentioned elsewhere unless it is to be identified with Nebo in Is 15:2 (Young). **Medeba**. i.e. *water of strength; waters of rest*. S#4311h: Nu 21:30. Jsh 13:9, 16. 1 Ch 19:7. Is 15:2. A city in a plain of the same name, afterwards belonging to the Reubenites (Young).

31. **Israel dwelt**. Nu 32:33-42. Dt 3:16, 17. Jsh 12:1-6. 13:8-32. **Amorites**. ſ96, Ge +3:8.

32. **Jaazer**. i.e. *helpful*. S#3270h: Nu 21:32. 32:1,

3, 35. Jsh 13:25. 21:39. 2 S 24:5. 1 Ch 6:81. 26:31. Is 16:8, 9. Je 48:32, 32, Jazer. **villages**. ver. +25.

33. **they turned**. Dt 3:1-6. 29:7. Jsh 13:12. **Bashan**. i.e. *light sandy soil*. S#1316h. Nu 21:33, 33. 32:33. Dt 1:4. 3:1, 1, 3, 4, 10, 10, 11, 13, 13, 14. 4:43, 47. 29:7. 32:14. 33:22. Jsh 9:10. 12:4n, 5. 13:11, 12, 30, 30, 30, 31. 17:1, 5. 20:8. 21:6, 27. 22:7. 1 K 4:13, 19. 2 K 10:33. 1 Ch 5:11, 12, 16, 23. 6:62, 71. Ne 9:22. Ps *22:12. 68:15, 15, 22. 135:11. 136:20. Is 2:13. 33:9. Je 22:20. 50:19. Ezk 27:6. 39:18. Am 4:1. Mi 7:14. Na 1:4. Zc 11:2. The northern part of the region beyond Jordan, and afterwards occupied by the half-tribe of Manasseh; it is celebrated for its oaks (Is 2:13. Ezk 27:6. Zc 11:2); its fertility and cattle (Dt 32:14. Ps 22:13. Ezk 39:18. Am 4:1). **Og**. i.e. *hearth-cake; one who goes in a circle,* or rolls about, from fatness it may be. S#5747h. Nu 21:33. 32:33. Dt 1:4. 3:1, 3, 4, 10, 11, 13. 4:47. 29:7. 31:4. Jsh 2:10. 9:10. 12:4. 13:12, 30, 31. 1 K 4:19. Ne 9:22. Ps 135:11. 136:20. **Edrei**. i.e. *goodly pasture; mighty, strong.* S#154h. Nu 21:33. Dt 1:4. 3:1, 10. Jsh 12:4. 13:12, 31. 19:37. Afterwards occupied by Manasseh; another place of the same name belonging to Naphtali is mentioned in Jsh 19:37 (Young).

34. **Fear him**. Nu 14:9. Dt 3:2, 11. 20:3. 31:6. Jsh 10:8, 25. Is 41:13. **for I have**. Dt 3:3. 7:24. Jsh 8:7. Jg 11:30. 1 S 23:4. 2 S 5:19. 1 K 20:13, 28. 2 K 3:18. **thou shalt**. ver. 24. Ps 135:10, 11. **as thou**. ver. 24, 25.

35. **smote him**. Dt 3:3-17. 29:7, 8. Jsh 12:4-6. 13:12. Ne 9:22. Ps 135:10-12. 136:17-21. Ro 8:37.

NUMBERS 22

Israel encamps in the plains of Moab, 1. Balak king of Moab sends for Balaam to curse the people, 2-7. He, forbidden by the Lord, refuses to go, 8-14. On a second message he extorts permission, and goes, 15-21. An angel opposes him, and he is rebuked by his ass, whose mouth God opens; he beholds the angel, and obtains leave to proceed, 22-35. Balak meets him, and sacrifices, 36-41.

1. **the children**. Nu 21:20. 33:48-50. 36:13. Dt 34:1, 8. **the plains**. Heb. Arabah. Nu 26:3, 63. 31:12. 33:48-50. 35:1. 36:13. Dt +*11:30. 34:1, 8. Jsh 23:32. **on this side**. Nu 32:19. 34:15. Dt 1:5. 3:8. Jsh 3:16. **Jericho**. i.e. *place of fragrance*, *S#3405h. Nu 22:1. 26:3. 31:12. 33:48, 50. 34:15. 35:1. 36:13. Dt 32:49. 34:1, 3. 2 S 10:5. 2 K 25:5. 1 Ch 6:78. 19:5. 2 Ch 28:15. Ezr 2:34. Ne 3:2. 7:36. Je 39:5. 52:8. Also *S#3405h. Jsh 2:1, 2, 3. 3:16. 4:13, 19. 5:10, 13. 6:1, 2, 25, 26. 7:2. 8:2. 9:3. 10:1, 28, 30. 12:9. 13:32. 16:1, 1, 1, 7. 18:12, 21. 20:8. 24:11, 11. 2 K 2:4, 4, 5, 15, 18. Also *S#3405. 1 K 16:34.

2. **Balak**. i.e. *a waster*, *S#1111h. Nu 22:2, 4, 7, 10, 13, 14, 15, 16, 18, 18, 35, 36, 37, 38, 39, 40, 41. 23:1, 2, 3, 5, 7, 11, 13, 15, 16, 17, 18, 25, 26, 27, 28, 29, 30. 24:10, 10, 12, 13, 25. Jsh 24:9. Jg 11:25. Mi 6:5. **Zippor**. i.e. *bird; hopping*, *S#6834h. Nu 22:2, 4, 10, 16. 23:18. Jsh 24:9. Jg 11:25. **saw all**. Nu 21:3, 20-35. Jg 11:25.

3. **Moab**. Ex 15:15. Dt 2:25. Jsh 2:10, 11, 24. 9:24. Ps 53:5. Is 23:5.

4. **elders**. ver. 7. Nu 25:15-18. 31:8. Ge 25:1, 2. Jsh 13:21, 22. **Now shall**. Nu 24:17. Ge 15:2-5. 17:19-21. Je 48:38. **round about**. lit. circuit. ſ121J1. Meton-

ymy of the Subject B573. "Circuit" is put for what is contained in it. For other instances of this figure see Ezr 1:6. **And Balak.** ver. 2. Jg 11:25.

5. **sent.** Dt 23:4. Jsh 13:22. 24:9. Ne 13:1, 2. Mi 6:5. 2 P 2:15, 16, son of Bosor. Ju 11. Re 2:14. **Balaam.** i.e. *destruction of the people; glutton,* *S#1109h. Nu 22:5, 7, 8, 9, 10, 12, 13, 14, 16, 18, 20, 21, 23, 25, 27, 27, 28, 29, 30, 31, 34, 35, 35, 36, 37, 38, 39, 40, 41. 23:1, 2, 2, 3, 4, 5, 11, 16, 25, 26, 27, 28, 29, 30. 24:1, 2, 3, 10, 10, 12, 15, 25. 31:8, 16. Dt 23:4, 5. Jsh 13:22. 24:9, 10. Ne 13:2. Mi 6:5. **Beor.** i.e. *shepherd; burning, torch, fire,* *S#1160h. Ge 36:32. Nu 22:5. 24:3, 15. 31:8. Dt 23:4. Jsh 13:22. 24:9. 1 Ch 1:43. Mi 6:5. (1) Father of Bela, king of Edom, Ge 36:32; 1 Ch 1:43. (2) Father of Balaam the prophet, Nu 22:5; Jsh 13:22. He is called Bosor in 2 P 2:15. **Pethor.** i.e. *interpretation of dreams,* *S#6604h. Nu 22:5. Dt 23:4. **his people.** or, *Ammon,* as Syriac and Vulgate, agreeing with Dt 23:4. Calmet is of opinion, that it was situated towards Thapsacus, beyond the Euphrates. Nu 23:7. Dt 23:4. **they cover.** Ge 13:16. Ex 1:7-10. Ps 105:24. **face.** Heb. eye. ver. 11. Ge +1:2.

6. **curse me.** Nu 23:7, 8. 24:9. Ge 12:3. 27:29. Dt 23:4. Jsh 24:9. 1 S 17:43. Ne 13:2. Ps 109:17, 18. Je 17:5. Mi 6:5. **we.** ϟ96D4, Ge +29:27. **I wot.** 1 K 22:6, 8, 13. Ps 109:28. Pr 26:2. Is 47:12, 13. Ezk 13:6. Ac 8:9, 10. 16:16.

7. **rewards of divination.** Ge +30:27. Dt 18:9-14. 1 S 6:2. 9:7, 8. 2 K 17:7-9, 17, 18. Is 56:11. Je 27:9, 10. 29:8, 9. Ezk 13:19. Mi 3:11. Ro 16:18. 1 T 6:9, 10. T 1:11. 2 P 2:15. Ju 11. Re 2:14. ϟ121C1G. Metonymy of the Cause B551. "Divination" is put for the money received for it.

8. **this night.** ver. 19, 20. Nu 12:6. 23:12. Je 12:2. Ezk +*33:31.

9. **God.** ver. 20. Ge 20:3. 31:24. 41:25. Da 2:45. 4:31, 32. Mt 7:22. 24:24. Jn 11:51. **What men.** ϟ22, Ge +3:9. Ge 3:9-11. 4:9. 16:8. Ex 4:2. 2 K 20:14, 15.

10. **Balak.** See on ver. 4-6.

11. **face.** Ge +1:2. **able to overcome them.** Heb. prevail in fighting against him.

12. **Balaam, Thou shalt.** ver. 20. Jb 33:15-17. Mt 27:19. **thou shalt not curse.** ver. 19. Nu 23:3, 13-15, 19, 23. Mi 6:5. **for they.** Nu 23:20. Ge 12:2. 22:16-18. Dt 23:5. 33:29. Ps 144:15. 146:3-6. Ro 4:6, 7. 11:29. Ep 1:3.

13. **for the Lord.** ver. 14. Dt 23:5. Ps 29:4.

14. **Balaam refuseth.** ver. 13, 37.

15. **princes.** ver. 7, 8. Ac 10:7, 8.

16. **Let nothing,** etc. Heb. Be not thou letted from, etc.

17. **I will promote.** Nu 24:11. Dt 16:9. Est 5:11. 7:9. Mt 4:8, 9. 16:26. **very great.** ϟ147B, Ge +2:16. **and I will do.** Nu 23:2, 3, 29, 30. Mt 14:7. **come.** ver. 6. **curse me.** An erroneous opinion prevailed, both in those days and in after ages, that some men had the power, by the help of their gods, to devote, not only particular persons, but cities and whole armies, to destruction. This they are said to have done by words of imprecation; of which there was a set form among some people, which Aeschines calls "the determinate curse." See on Pr 26:2.

18. **If Balak.** Nu 24:13. T 1:16. **I cannot.** Nu 23:26. 24:13. 1 K 22:14. 2 Ch 18:13. Da 5:17. Ac 8:20. **word.** Da 4:35. He 4:12, 13.

19. **tarry.** See on ver. 7, 8. Je 42:4-6, 19-21. 1 T 6:9, 10. 2 P 2:3, 15. Ju 11.

20. **God.** See on ver. 9. **If the men.** 1 S 8:5-9. 12:12-19. Ps 81:12. Ezk 14:2-5. 2 Th 2:9-12. **but yet.** ver. 35. Nu 23:12, 26. 24:13. Ps 33:10, 11. 78:30, 31. Is 37:29. 46:9-11. Ho 13:11.

21. **rose up.** Pr 1:15, 16.

22. **God's.** 1 S 2:3. 16:7. 2 K 10:30. Ho 1:4. **and the angel.** ver. 35. See on Ge 48:15, 16. Ex 3:2-6. Ho 12:4, 5. **stood.** ver. 32. Ex 4:24. Is 37:28, 29. La 2:4. Ezk 38:3, 4.

23. **the ass saw.** 2 K 6:17. 1 Ch 21:16. Da 10:7. Ac 22:9. 1 C 1:27-29. 2 P 2:16. Ju 11. **the ass turned.** Je 8:7.

25. **crushed Balaam's.** Jb 5:13-15. Is 47:12.

26. **where was no way.** Is 26:11. Ho 2:6.

27. **and Balaam's anger.** Pr 12:10. 14:16. 27:3, 4.

28. **the Lord opened.** And where is the wonder of all this? If the ass had opened her own mouth, and reproved the rash prophet, we might well be astonished; but when God opens the mouth, an ass can speak as well as a man. It is to no purpose to speak of the construction of the ass's mouth, of the formation of the tongue and jaws being unfit for speaking; for an adequate cause is assigned for this wonderful effect— "The Lord opened the mouth of the ass"; and no one who believes in a God, can doubt of his power to do this and much more. Ex 4:11. Lk 1:37. 1 C 1:19. 2 P 2:14-16. **What have I.** Ro 8:22.

29. **for now would.** Pr 12:10, 16. Ec 9:3.

30. **the ass said.** 2 P 2:16. **upon which thou hast ridden.** Heb. who hast ridden upon me. **ever since I was thine.** or, ever since thou *wast,* unto, etc. 1 C 1:27, 28.

31. **opened.** Nu 24:4mg, 16. Ge +3:7. 21:19. 2 K 6:17-20. 1 Ch 21:15, 16, 20. Lk 24:16, 31. Ac 26:18. **bowed down.** Ex 34:8. Ps 9:20. Jn 18:6. **fell flat on his face.** or, bowed himself.

32. **Wherefore.** ver. 28. Dt 25:4. Ps 36:6. 145:9. 147:9. Jon 4:11. **withstand thee.** Heb. be an adversary unto thee. ver. 22. Zc 3:1mg. **thy way.** Dt 23:4. Pr 28:6. Mi 6:5. Ac 13:10. 2 P 2:14, 15. **before me.** See on ver. 20, 22, 35. Ex 3:2-6. Pr 14:2. 28:18.

33. **surely.** Nu 14:37. 16:33-35. 1 K 13:24-28. Re 19:11-15.

34. **I have sinned.** Ex 9:27. 10:16, 17. Jsh 7:20. 1 S 15:24, 30. 24:17. 26:21. 2 S ◐+12:13. 19:20. 1 K 8:38, 39. 1 Ch 28:9. Jb 34:31, 32. Ps 7:9. 78:34. Je 17:9, 10. Mt 15:7, 8. 27:4, 5. **if it displease thee.** Heb. be evil in thine eyes. See on ver. 12. Nu 11:1. Ge +28:8. 1 S +8:6. 18:8. 1 Ch 21:7. Pr 24:18, margins. **I will get.** Jb 34:31, 32.

35. **Go.** See on ver. 20. Ps 81:12. √106:15. Is 37:26-29. Ro 9:17-22. 2 Th 2:9-12. **I shall speak.** See on ver. 20, 21.

36. **went.** Ge 14:17. 18:2. 46:29. Ex 18:7. 1 S 13:10. Ac 28:15. **the border.** Nu 21:13, 14. Dt 2:24. 3:8. Jg 11:18. Is 16:2. Je 48:20.

37. **earnestly send.** ϟ147B, Ge +26:28. **am I not able.** ver. 16, 17. Nu 24:11. Ps 75:6. Mt 4:8, 9. Lk 4:6. Jn 5:44.

38. **have I.** ver. 18. Ps 33:10. 76:10. Pr 19:21. Is 44:25. 46:10. 47:12. **the word.** Nu 23:16, 26. 24:13. 1 K 22:14. 2 Ch 18:13.

39. **Kirjath-huzoth.** or, a city of streets. *S#7155h, only here. Probably Rabbath-Moab, now called Rabba,

the capital of the Moabites; and being the royal city, distinguished by its streets.

40. offered oxen. Nu 23:2, 14, 30. Ge 31:54. Pr 1:16. Ezk 21:21-23.

41. high places. *Bamoth baal,* "the high places of Baal," probably the same as *Bamoth* mentioned in Nu 21:19, 20; evidently not far from *Baal-meon,* in the mountains of Abarim: for the Israelites were now encamped in the plains of Moab, which these mountains overlook. Baal, which signifies a lord or governor, was a name common to many idols; and probably here was the same as *Chemosh,* the god of Moab. Nu 25:2, 3. Dt 12:2. 2 Ch 11:15. Je 48:35. **utmost.** Nu 23:13.

NUMBERS 23

Balak builds seven altars, and offers sacrifices on them, 1, 2. *Balaam goes to meet the Lord, and returning blesses Israel: Balak remonstrates, and Balaam excuses it,* 3-12. *Balak sacrifices in another place, Balaam blesses Israel still more; Balak cannot hinder him,* 13-26. *Balak sacrifices on the top of Peor,* 27-30.

1. Build me. ver. 29. Ezk 33:31. Ju 11. **seven altars.** Ex 20:24. 27:1, etc. 1 S 15:22. 2 K 18:22. Ps 50:8, 9. Pr 15:8. Is 1:11-15. Mt 23:14. **seven oxen.** Nu 29:32. 1 Ch 15:26. 2 Ch 29:21. Jb 42:8. Ezk 45:23.

2. offered. ver. 14, 30. Ps *50:16, 17.

3. Stand. ver. 15. **burnt.** Ge 8:20. 22:2, 7, 8, 13. Ex 18:12. Le ch. 1. **peradventure.** ver. 15. Nu 22:8, 9, 31-35. 24:1. **went to a high place.** *or,* went solitary. Is 41:18. Je 3:2.

4. God. ver. 16. Nu 22:9, 20. **met.** ∫22C19. Anthropomorphism B888. Human actions are attributed to God: meeting. For another instance of this figure see Nu 23:16. **I have prepared.** See on ver. 1. Ps 50:21, 22. Is 58:3, 4. Mt 20:12. Lk 18:12. Jn 16:2. Ro 3:27. Ep 2:9.

5. put a word. ver. 16. Nu 22:35. Dt *18:18. Pr 16:1, 9. Is 51:6. 59:21. Je 1:9. Lk 12:2. Jn 11:51.

6. he stood. ver. 3.

7. he took. ver. 18. Nu 24:3, 15, 23. Jb 27:1. 29:1. Ps 78:2. Ezk 17:2. 20:49. Mi 2:4. Hab 2:6. Mt 13:33, 35. Mk 12:12. **parable.** The word *mashal,* which as a verb is to "rule, have authority," and also to "compare," as a noun signifies whatever is expressed in *parabolic* or *figurative* language. All these oracular speeches of Balaam are in hemistic meter in the original. They are highly dignified and sublime; and may be considered as immediate poetic productions of the Spirit of God (Nu 24:2). ver. 7-12, 18-24. Nu +*21:27. 23:18. 24:3, 15, 20, 21, 23. Jb 27:1. 29:1. Ps 49:4. 78:2. Pr 26:7, 9. Ezk 17:2. 20:49. 24:3. Mi 2:4. Hab 2:6. **Aram.** Nu 22:5. Ge 10:22. 28:2, 7. Dt 23:4. **Come.** Nu 22:6, 11, 17. Pr 26:2. **defy Israel.** 1 S 17:10, 25, 26, 36, 45. 2 S 21:21. 23:9.

8. How shall. ∫85H, Jg +11:12. ver. 20, 23. Jb 34:29. Is 44:25. 47:12, 13.

9. the people. They shall ever be a *distinct* nation. This prophecy has been literally fulfilled, through a period of 3300 years, to the present day (not to mention its continued fulfillment for nearly two hundred more years since this note was originally composed, and the establishment of Israel as a nation in her own land in 1948). **dwell alone.** Ex 19:5, 6. 33:16. 34:12, 13, 15, 16. Dt 33:28. Est 3:8. 2 C 6:17. T 2:14. 1 P 2:9. **shall not.** Ex 8:22, 23. Dt 32:8. 33:28. Ezr 9:2. Je 46:28.

Am 9:9. Ro 15:8-10. Ep 2:12-14.

10. can count. Ge 13:16. 22:17. 28:14. **the dust.** ∫138B, Ge +13:16. i.e. the posterity of Jacob, which was to be so numerous as to resemble the dust. **the fourth.** Nu 2:9, 16, 24, 31. **me.** Heb. my soul, *or,* my life. ∫171Q2. Synecdoche of the Part B641. "My soul," "his soul," becomes by Synecdoche the idiom for *me, myself, himself.* For other instances of this figure see Jg 16:30mg. Jb 36:14. Ps 3:2. 16:10. 25:13. 35:13. 103:1. Is 58:5. Lk 12:19. Ac 2:31. Ro 16:4. 1 P 1:9. Here *nephesh* is used of man as being mortal, subject to death of various kinds, from which it can be saved and delivered and life prolonged. Rendered "me" here, and at Jg 16:30. 1 K 20:32. Rendered "ghost," Jb 11:20, Je 15:9; "person," 2 S 14:14; "tablets," Is 3:20 (R.V. perfume boxes), Heb. "houses of the soul," i.e. boxes of scent for the nose; "deadly," Ps 17:9 (Heb. "enemies against my *nephesh*"); "himself," 1 K 19:4, Am 2:14, 15; "they," Jb 36:14; "themselves," Is 47:14; "yourselves," Dt 4:15, Jsh 23:11. For the rendering "soul," see Ge +12:13; for "life, lives," see Ge +44:30. For *nephesh* used of man as actually dead, see Le +19:28. For *nephesh* spoken of as going to *sheol,* etc., see Ps +30:3. For the equivalent New Testament use of *psyche* to emphasize the personal pronoun in the first person, see Mt +*12:18. **Let me.** T#1464. **the death.** Nu 31:8. Ps 37:37. 116:15. Pr ❂11:7. 14:32. Is 57:1, 2. Lk 2:29, 30. 1 C 3:21, 22. 15:53-57. 2 C 5:1. Ph 1:21-23. 2 T 4:6-8. 2 P 1:13-15. Re √14:13.

11. I took. See on ver. 7, 8. Nu 22:11, 17. 24:10. Ge 27:29, 33. Ps 109:17-20. **altogether.** ∫147B, Ge +2:16.

12. Must. ver. 20, 26. Nu 22:38. 24:13. Pr 26:25. Jn 19:11. Ro 16:18. T 1:16.

13. with me. Jg 17:5, 13. **unto.** 1 K 20:23, 28. Mi 6:5. **utmost.** Nu 22:41. **and curse me.** Jsh 24:9. Ps 109:17. Ja 3:9, 10.

14. Zophim. i.e. *watchers, watchmen,* ✱S#6839h, only here. **Pisgah.** *or,* the hill. Nu 21:20. Dt 3:27mg. 4:49. 34:1mg. **built seven.** ver. 1, 2, 29. Is 1:10, 11. 46:6. Ho 12:11.

15. while I meet. ver. 3. Nu 22:8.

16. met. ∫22C19, Nu +23:4. **put a word.** See on ver. 5. Nu 22:35. 24:1.

17. What. ver. 26. Jg 3:20. 1 S 3:17. Je 1:9. 37:17.

18. Rise up. Jg 3:20.

19. God. 1 S 15:29. Jb 23:13. Ps 89:35. Hab 2:3. Ml 3:6. Lk 21:33. Ro 11:29. T 1:2. He 6:18. Ja 1:17. **or hath he.** Ex 9:16. 1 Ch 17:17. Pr 16:4. Mi 7:20.

20. he hath. Nu 22:12. Ge 12:2. 22:17. **I cannot.** Nu 22:18, 38. Jn 10:27-29. Ro 8:38, 39. 1 P 1:5.

21. hath not. Ps 103:12. Is 1:18. 38:17. Je 50:20. Ho 14:2-4. Mi *7:18-20. Jn +17:6. Ro 4:7, 8. 6:14. 8:1. 2 C 5:19. **Jacob.** ∫121T3, Ge +9:27. **perverseness.** Jb 4:8. 15:35. Ps 7:14. 10:7, 14. **Israel.** ∫121T3, Ge +9:27. **the Lord.** Ex 13:21. 29:45, 46. 33:14-16. 34:9. Jg 6:13. 2 Ch 13:12. Ps 23:4. 46:7, 11. Is 8:10. 12:6. 41:10. Ezk 48:35. Mt 1:23. 2 C 6:16. **the shout.** Ps 47:5-7. 89:15, 18. 97:1. 118:15. Is 33:22. Lk 19:37, 38. 2 C 2:14.

22. God. Nu 22:5. 24:8. Ex 9:16. 14:18. 20:2. Ps 68:35. **the strength.** Dt 33:17. Jb 39:10, 11. Ps 22:21. **unicorn.** The *reaim,* most probably denotes the *rhinoceros,* so called from the horn on its nose. In size he is only exceeded by the elephant; and in strength and power inferior to none. He is at least twelve feet in length, from the snout to the tail; six or seven feet in height; and the circumference of the body is nearly equal to his length. He is particularly distinguished from all other animals by the remarkable and offensive weapon he carries on his nose; which is very hard horn, solid throughout, directed forward. He principally feeds upon large succulent plants, prickly shrubs, and branches; and delights in marshy places. Ps 29:6. 92:10. Is 34:7.

23. **no enchantment.** T#779. Nu 22:6. 24:1. Ge 3:15. Ex 7:10-12. 8:16-19. Pr *21:30. Ezk 21:21-23. Mt 12:25, 27. 16:18. Lk 10:18, 19. Ro 16:20. Re 12:9. **against.** *or*, in. **according.** Ps 44:1-3. 136:13-20. Is 63:9-12. Da 9:15. Mi 6:4, 5. 7:15. **What hath.** Ps 31:19. 44:1. 64:9. 126:2, 3. Is 41:4. Jn 11:47. Ac 4:16. 5:12, 14. 10:38. 15:12. Ga 1:23, 24. 1 Th 1:8, 9.

24. **as a great.** Nu 24:8, 9. Ge 49:9. Dt 33:20. Jg 14:18. Ps 17:12. Pr 28:1. 30:29, 30. Is 31:4. Je 50:43-46. Am 3:8. Re 5:5. **he shall.** Nu 24:17. Ge 49:27. Da 2:44. Mi 5:8, 9. Zc 10:4, 5. 12:6. Re 19:11-21.

25. **Neither curse.** Ps 2:1-3.

26. **All that.** ver. 12, 13. Nu 22:18, 38. 24:12, 13. 1 K 22:14. 2 Ch 18:13. Jl 3:1. Am 3:4-8. Ac 4:19, 20. 5:29.

27. **Come.** ver. 13. **peradventure.** See on ver. 19, 20. Jb 23:13. Pr 16:25. 19:21. 21:30. 29:1. Is 14:27. 46:10, 11. Ml 3:6. Ro 11:29.

28. **Peor.** i.e. *cleft, opening.* S#6465h. Nu 23:28. 25:18. 31:16. Jsh 22:17. **Jeshimon.** Nu 21:20. 33:49.

29. **Build me.** See on ver. 1, 2.

30. **every altar.** See on ver. 1, 2.

NUMBERS 24

Balaam desists from enchantments, and predicts the happiness of Israel and the destruction of his enemies, 1-9. Balak, being greatly enraged, dismisses Balaam, 10-13. Balaam prophesies of the Star of Jacob, the ruin of several nations, and very remote events, 14-25.

1. **saw.** Nu 22:13. 23:20. 31:16. 1 S 24:20. 26:2, 25. Re 2:14. **at other times.** Nu 23:3, 15. **to seek for enchantments.** Heb. to the meeting of enchantments. Nu 23:23. 2 K 19:21, 23. Is 44:24-26. Ezk 13:22, 23. Ac 16:16-18.

2. **lifted.** ∫144A12, Ge +22:13. **abiding.** ver. 5. Nu 2:2, etc. 3:38. 23:9, 10. SS 6:4, 10. **the spirit.** Heb. *ruach,* Ge +41:38. Nu 11:25-29. 1 S 10:10. 19:20, 23, 24. 2 Ch 15:1. Mt 7:22. 10:4, 8. Lk 10:20. Jn 11:49-51.

3. **he took up.** See on Nu 23:7, 18. **whose eyes are open hath said.** Heb. who had his eyes shut, *but now opened.* ver. 4, 16. Nu 22:31.

4. **saw.** See on Nu 12:6. Ge 15:12. Ps 89:19. Da 8:26, 27. Ac 10:10, 19. 22:17. 2 C 12:1-4. **falling.** Nu 22:31. 1 S 19:24. Ezk 1:28. Da 8:17, 18. 10:15, 16. Re 1:10, 17.

5. **How goodly.** ∫176. Thaumasmos; or, Wondering B923. An expression of feeling by way of wonder. For other instances of this figure see Mt 8:10. Ro 11:33. Ga 1:6. **tents.** Nu 1:52. 2:2. 2 S 20:1. 1 K 12:16. Je 4:20. 30:18. Ml 2:12. **Jacob.** ∫121A5, Ge +9:27. Ex 6:3. Ru 1:20, 21. **Israel.** ∫121A5, Ge +9:27.

6. **as gardens.** Ge 2:8-10. 13:10. 27:27. SS 4:12-15. 6:11. Is 58:11. Je 31:12. Jl 3:18. **as the trees.** Ps 1:3.

Je 17:8. **which the.** Ps 104:16, 17. Is 41:19. 61:3. **as cedar.** Ps 92:12-14. Ezk 31:3, 4. 47:12.

7. **pour.** Heb. *nazal,* *S#5140h. Kal, Preterite: Jg 5:5 (melted; mg., flowed). Kal, Future: Nu 24:7. Dt 32:2 (distill). Jb 36:28 (drop). Ps 147:18 (flow). SS 4:16. Is 45:8 (pour down). Je 9:18 (gush out). Kal, Participle, Poel: Ex 15:8 (floods). Ps 78:16 (streams), 44 (floods). Pr 5:15 (running waters). SS 4:15 (streams). Is 44:3 (floods). Je 18:14 (flowing). Hiphil, Preterite: Is 48:21 (flow). **many waters.** Ps 68:26. Pr 5:16-18. Is 48:1. **many waters.** Ps 93:3, 4. Je 51:13. Jn +3:23. Re 17:1, 15. **his king.** Ezr 4:20. Ps 2:6-10. 18:43. Jn 1:49. Ph 2:10, 11. Re 19:16. **Agag.** i.e. *flame, blazing; sublime,* *S#90h. Nu 24:7. 1 S 15:8, 9, 20, 32, 33. **his kingdom.** Ge 17:4-8, 15, 16. 2 S 5:12. 1 K 4:21. 1 Ch 14:2. Is 2:2. 9:6, 7. Da 2:44. Lk 1:31-33. Ac 5:30, 31. Re 11:15.

8. **God.** Nu 21:5. 23:22. **shall eat.** Nu 14:9. 23:24. Dt 7:1. **break.** Ps 2:9. 110:2. Is 38:13. Je 50:17. Da 6:24. **pierce.** Dt 32:23, 42. Ps 21:12. 45:5. Je 50:9. 1 C 15:25.

9. **couched.** Ge 49:9. Jb 38:39, 40. **who shall.** See on Nu 23:24. Jb 41:10. Ps 2:12. Re 5:5. **Blessed.** Ge 12:3. 22:17, 18. 27:28, 29. Ps 122:6. Mt 25:40, 45. Ac 9:5.

10. **he smote.** Jb 27:23. Ezk 21:14, 17. 22:13. **I called.** Nu 22:6, 11, 17. 23:11. Dt 23:4, 5. Jsh 24:9, 10. Ne 13:2. **altogether blessed.** ∫147B, Ge +2:16.

11. **I thought.** Nu 22:17, 37. **the Lord.** Mt 19:28-30. Ac 8:20. Ph 3:8. He 11:24-26. 1 P 5:2, 3. 2 J 8.

12. **Spake I.** See on Nu 22:18, 38. Mt 24:25.

13. **If.** Nu 22:18. Is 33:15. **I cannot go.** Nu 22:18. 23:26. 1 K 22:14. 2 K 17:13. 2 Ch 18:13. **good or.** Ge 24:50. 31:24. 2 S 13:22. Is 41:23. Je 10:5. Zp 1:12. **of mine own mind.** Nu 16:28. Jb 38:36. Je 23:16, 26. Ezk 13:2, 17. **but what.** Nu 22:18, 20, 38. Je 1:7, 17. 23:13, 18, *21, 22, *28, 29. Ezk *2:7. 3:17. Ac 5:20. 8:18-23. 2 T 4:2. T 2:15. 2 P 2:15, 16. Ju 11.

14. **I will advertise.** ver. 17. Nu 31:7-18. Mi 6:5. Re 2:10, 14. **the latter.** Ge 49:1. Is 24:22. Je 48:47. 49:39. Da 2:28. 10:14. Ho 3:5. Ac 2:17. 2 T 3:1.

15. **took up.** ver. 3, 4. Nu 23:7, 18. Jb 27:1. Mt 13:35. Jn 11:51.

16. **which heard.** See on ver. 4. 2 S 23:1, 2. 1 C 8:1. 13:2.

17. **I shall see him.** The Targum of Onkelos translates this passage in the following manner: "I shall see him, but not now; I shall behold him, but he is not near. When a king shall arise from the house of Jacob, and the Messiah be anointed from the house of Israel; he shall slay the princes of Moab, and rule over all the children of men." The marginal references will direct the reader to the fulfillment of these remarkable prophecies. Jb 19:25-27. Zc 12:10. Ju 11, 14, 15. Re 1:7. **come.** Mt 16:27. 24:30. 26:64. Mk 13:25, 26. Re 6:13-17. **a Star.** Da 12:3. Mt 2:2-9. Lk 1:78. 2 P 1:19. Re 22:16. **out of Jacob.** T#1878. Ge 35:10-12. Mt *1:2. Lk *1:33. *3:23, *34. ∫121A5. ∫121T3, Ge +9:27. **a Sceptre.** Ge +*49:10. Ps 45:6. 78:70-72. 110:2. Is 9:7. Lk 1:32, 33. 24:27. He 1:8. **Israel.** ∫121A5. ∫121T3, Ge +9:27. **smite the corners of Moab.** *or*, smite through the princes of Moab. 1 S 14:38mg. Zc 10:4. **Moab.** Nu 21:29. 2 S 8:2. 2 K 3:5, 26, 27. 1 Ch 18:2. Is 15:1. 16:11-14. Je 48:45. **all the children.** Ge 4:25, 26. 5:3-29, Seth. Ps 72:8-11. Re 11:15. **Sheth.** i.e. *set, appointed; tumult,* *S#8352h. Ge 4:25, 26. 5:3, 4, 6, 7, 8. Nu 24:17. 1 Ch 1:1.

18. **Edom**. Ge +25:30. 27:29, 40. 2 S 8:14. 1 Ch 18:12, 13. Ps ch. 60, Title, 8-12. Is 34:5. 63:1-4. Ezk 25:12-14. Am 9:12. **Seir**. Ge +32:3.

19. **of Jacob**. Ge 49:10. Ps 2:1-12. 72:10, 11. Is 11:10. Mi 5:2, 4. Mt 28:18. 1 C 15:25. Ep 1:20-22. Ph 2:10, 11. He 1:8. 1 P 3:22. Re 19:16. **shall come**. ver. +17. Da 7:13, 14. **shall destroy**. Ps 21:7-10. Mt 25:46. Lk 19:12, 27.

20. **the first of the nations**. or, the first of the nations that warred against Israel. Ex 17:8, 14-16. **his latter end**. Jg 6:3. 1 S 14:48. 15:3-8. 27:8, 9. 30:1, 17. 1 Ch 4:43. Est 3:1. 7:9, 10. 9:14. **shall be that he perish for ever**. or, shall be even to destruction. Ex 17:14. 1 S 15:3, 8. *J*79, Ge +21:16.

21. **the Kenites**. Ge 15:19. Jg 1:16. 1 S 15:6. 1 Ch 2:55. Je 35:5-11. **puttest**. *J*96B. Heterosis of Moods B515. Imperative for Subjunctive. The sense is subjunctive, thou mayest put. For other instances of this figure see 2 S 18:23. 1 K 22:22. 2 K 2:17. Ps *4:4. Na 3:14. Mt 8:32. Lk 10:28. 1 C 7:15. 11:6. **nest**. Jb 29:18.

22. **the Kenite**. Heb. Kain. i.e. a smith; a fabricator; a nest, *S#7014h. Nu 24:22. Jg 4:11. **until Asshur shall carry thee away captive**. or, how long shall it be ere Asshur carry thee away captive? Ge 10:11. 2 Ch 36:17-20. Ezr 4:2. Ps 83:8. Ho 14:3.

23. **when God**. Nu 23:23. 2 K 5:1. Je 9:1. La 1:15, 16. Ml 3:2.

24. **Chittim**. i.e. subduers, hidden, *S#3794h. Ge 10:4. Nu 24:24. 1 Ch 1:7. Is 23:1, 12. Je 2:10. Ezk 27:6. Da 7:19, 20. 8:5-8, 21. 10:20. *11:30. **afflict Asshur**. Is 10:12. **and shall afflict Eber**. Ge 10:21-25. 14:13. Da 9:26, 27. Mt 24:15. Lk 20:24. 23:29-31. Jn 11:48. **and he also**. Da 2:35, 45. 7:23-26. 11:45. Re 18:2-24.

25. **returned to**. ver. 11. Nu 31:8. Jsh 13:22.

NUMBERS 25

The Israelites at Shittim commit whoredom and idolatry, being tempted by the women of Moab and Midian, 1-3 God commands the criminals to be slain, 4, 5. Phinehas kills Zimri and Cosbi, and the plague which wasted Israel is stayed, 6-9. God approves his zeal, and gives him the covenant of a perpetual priesthood, 10-15. Moses commanded to make war against the Midianites, 16-18.

1. **Shittim**. i.e. thorns; acacias, *S#7851h. Nu 33:49. Jsh 2:1. 3:1. Jl 3:18. Mi 6:5. **the people**. Nu 31:15, 16. Ec 7:26. 1 C 10:8. **with**. *J*63H, Ge +12:5.

2. **they called**. Ex 34:15, 16. Jsh 22:17. 1 K 11:1-8. Ps 106:28. Ho 9:10. 1 C 10:20, 27, 28. 2 C 6:16, 17. Re 2:14. **bowed**. Ex 20:5. 23:24. Jsh 23:7, 16. 1 K 19:18. Ps *16:4.

3. **joined**. ver. 5. Ex 20:5. Dt 4:3, 4. Jsh 22:17. Ps 106:28, 29. Ho 9:10. 1 C 10:20. **unto**. Nu 23:28. **Baal-peor**. i.e. lord of the opening, *S#1187h. ver. 5. Dt 4:3, 3. Ps 106:28. Ho 9:10. **the anger**. Jsh 22:17. Jg 14, 20. Ps 90:11. Je 17:4.

4. **all the heads**. ver. 14, 15, 18. Ex 18:25. Dt 4:3. Jsh 22:17. 23:2. **and hang**. Dr. Kennicott remarks that the Samaritan and Hebrew texts must be united to make the sense of this verse complete: "And the Lord said unto Moses, **Speak** unto all the heads of the people; **and let them slay the men that were joined to Baal-peor**; and hang them up before the Lord, against the sun," etc. Dt 13:6-9, 13, 15. 21:22, 23.

2 S 21:6, 9. Est 7:9, 10. **that the fierce**. ver. 11. Dt 13:17. Jsh 7:25, 26. Ps 85:3, 4. Jon 3:9.

5. **judges**. Ex 18:21, 25, 26. **Slay ye**. Ex 22:20. 32:27, 28. Dt 13:6, 9, 13, 15. 17:3-5. 1 K 18:40. Mt 10:37.

6. **a Midianitish**. S#4084h. ver. 14, 15. Nu ●22:4. 31:2, 9-16. **in the sight of Moses**. Nu 15:30, 31. Dt 29:19-21. Je 3:3. 8:12. 36:23. 42:15-18. 43:4-7. 44:16, 17. 2 P 2:13-15. Ju 13. **weeping**. Jg 2:4. Ezr 9:1-4. 10:6-9. Is 22:12. Ezk 9:4-6. Jl 2:17.

7. **Phinehas**. Ex 6:25. Jsh 22:30, 31. Jg 20:28. **a javelin**. 1 S 18:10, 11. 19:9.

8. **thrust**. ver. 5, 11, 14. Ps 106:29-31. **So the plague**. Nu 16:46-48. 2 S 24:25. 1 Ch 21:22.

9. **St. Paul reckons only 23,000**: Moses includes in the 24,000 he names, the 1000 men who were slain in consequence of the judicial examination (ver. 4), as well as the 23,000 who died of the plague; while St. Paul only refers to the latter. ver. 4, 5. Nu 16:49, 50. 31:16. Dt 4:3, 4. 1 C 10:8.

11. **turned my**. Jsh 7:25, 26. 2 S 21:14. Ps 106:23. Jn 3:36. **for my sake**. Heb. with my zeal. 2 C 11:2. **that I**. Ex 20:5. 22:5. 34:14-16. Dt 4:24. 29:20. 32:16, 21. Jsh 24:19. 1 K 14:22. Ps 78:58. Ezk 16:38. Na 1:2. Zp 1:18. 3:8. 1 C 10:22. **jealousy**. *J*22B, Ex +20:5.

12. **I give**. Nu ●18:1. Ne 13:29. Ml 2:4, 5. 3:1. Ro=5:11. Ep=2:13, 14. He=2:17.

13. **his seed**. 1 S 2:30. 1 K 2:27. 1 Ch 6:4-15, 50-53. **an everlasting**. Heb. olam, Ge +17:7. Ex 40:15. Is 61:6. Je 33:17, 22. He 7:11, 17, 18. 1 P 2:5, 9. Re 1:6. **zealous**. 1 K 19:10, 14. Ps 69:9. 106:31. 119:139. Jn 2:17. Ac 22:3-5. Ro 10:2-4. **atonement**. Ex 32:30. Jsh 7:12. 2 S 21:3. He 2:17. 1 J 2:2.

14. **Israelite**. S#3481h. Le 24:10. 2 S 17:25. **Zimri**. i.e. praised. **Salu**. i.e. valued; weighed, *S#5543h. 1 Ch 9:7 & Ne 11:7, Sallu. Ne 12:7, Sallu. Ne 11:8 & 12:20, Sallai. ver. 4, 5. 2 Ch 19:7. **chief house**. Heb. house of a father. ver. 15. Dt 28:41. **the Simeonites**. *S#8099h. Nu ●1:23. 26:14. Jsh 21:4. 1 Ch 27:16.

15. **Cozbi**. i.e. lying; false, *S#3579h. ver. 18. **Zur**. i.e. a rock; to besiege, *S#6698h. Nu 31:8. Jsh 13:21. 1 Ch 8:30. 9:36. (1) A prince of Midian who was slain by Phinehas, Nu 25:15; 31:8; Jsh 13:21. (2) A Benjamite and an ancestor of Saul, 1 Ch 8:30; 9:36.

17. Balaam's counsel seems to have been first given to Balak, king of Moab; but probably the Midianitish women, especially of the higher ranks, as Cozbi was, were the principal tempters; and the nation of Midian seems to have come into the execrable measure more generally and heartily than that of Moab: they were therefore first selected to be made examples of, for a warning to the Moabites, who were spared at this time. Nu 31:2. Re 18:6.

18. **vex you**. Nu 31:15, 16. Ge 26:10. Ex 32:21, 35. Re 2:14. **beguiled**. Ge 3:13. 2 C 11:3. 2 P 2:14, 15, 18. **which**. ver. 8. Peor's. Nu 23:28.

NUMBERS 26

The people are numbered by divine command: the number of each tribe, and the sum total, 1-51. The law for the division of the promised land, 52-56. The Levites are numbered, 57-62. None left of those before numbered, but Caleb and Joshua, 63-65.

1. **after the plague**. Nu 25:9.

2. **Take the sum**. The plague having swept away

the last of that devoted generation, which provoked the Lord to "swear in his wrath that they should not enter" Canaan; he now, after an interval of 38 years, commands another census of the Israelites to be made, to preserve the distinction of families, and to regulate the tribes previous to their entry into the promised land, as well as to ascertain the proportion of land which should be allotted to each tribe. For, though the whole was divided by lot, yet the portions were so disposed, that a numerous tribe did not draw where the lots assigned small inheritances, or the contrary. See on Nu 1:2, 3. Ge 24:44n. Ex 30:12. 38:25, 26. Jsh *14:2n.

3. **plains of Moab.** ver. 63. Nu 22:1. 31:12. 33:48. 35:1. Dt 4:46-49. 34:1, 6, 8.

4. **Take the sum.** *✓*63I1D. Ellipsis: Repetition of preceding connected words B96. Here, repetition of words expressed in ver. 2. For other instances of this form of ellipsis as given by EWB in B, see Jsh 24:19. Jb 3:23. Ps 84:3. Pr 21:1. Ec 7:11, 12. Zc 14:18. Mt 2:10. 13:32. Mk 5:23. Jn 1:18. 9:3. Ro 4:12. 5:3, 11. 7:7. 8:23. 9:10. 10:8. 1 C 15:42. 2 C 8:19. Col 3:4. 2 T 1:7. 1 J 2:19. 5:15. **commanded.** Nu 1:1-3. Ex 30:12-16. 1 Ch 21:1.

5. **the eldest.** Ge 29:32. 49:2, 3. 1 Ch 5:1. **the children.** Ge 46:8, 9. Ex 6:14. 1 Ch 5:1-3. **Hanoch.** i.e. *trained, dedicated.* Ge +25:4. Ex 6:14. **Hanochites.** *✱S#2599h.* **Pallu.** i.e. *wonderful; distinguished; separated,* *✱S#6396h.* ver. 8. Ge 46:9. Ex 6:14. 1 Ch 5:3. **Palluites.** *✱S#6384h.*

6. **Hezronites.** *✱S#2697h.* ver. 21. **Carmites.** *✱S#3757h.*

7. **Reubenites.** *✱S#7206h.* Nu 34:14. Dt 3:12, 16. 4:43. 29:8. Jsh 1:12. 12:6. 13:8. 22:1. 2 K 10:33. 1 Ch 5:6, 26. 11:42, 42. 12:37. 26:32. 27:16. **forty and three.** ver. 1, 21. Nu 2:11. Ge 46:8, 9.

9. **famous.** Nu 1:16. 16:1, 2, etc. Ps 106:17. Ju 11.

10. **earth opened.** Nu 16:2, 31-35, 38. 27:3. Ex 16:35. Ps 106:17, 18. **together.** The Samaritan text does not intimate that Korah was swallowed up, but that he was burnt, as appears to have been the fact; and the Psalmist also (Ps 106:17), only mentions Dathan and Abiram as having been swallowed up: "And the earth swallowed them up, what time that company died; and the fire devoured Korah with the 250 men, who became a sign." **they became a sign.** Nu 16:38. 1 S 2:34. Je 29:22. Ezk 14:8. 1 C 10:6-10. 2 P 2:6. Ju 7.

11. **died not.** It seems to be intimated in Nu 16:27, 31-33, that the *sons and the little ones* of Korah, Dathan, and Abiram, were swallowed up; but the text *here* expressly affirms, that the children of Korah "died not"; and their descendants were famous even in David's time. On a close inspection, however, of ver. 27, we shall find, that "the sons and the little ones" of Dathan and Abiram alone are mentioned. Nu 16:5. Ex 6:24. 1 Ch 6:22-28. Ps ch. 42, 44, 45, etc. Titles.

12. **Nemuel.** i.e. *day of God; circumcised of God,* *✱S#5241h.* ver. 9. Ge 46:10. Ex 6:15, Jemuel. 1 Ch 4:24. (1) A descendant of Reuben, Nu 26:9. (2) One of the sons of Simeon, Nu 26:12; 1 Ch 4:24. He is called Jemuel in Ge 46:10; Ex 6:15. **Nemuelites.** *✱S#5242h.* **Jamin.** i.e. *the right hand.* Ge +46:10. **Jamites.** *✱S#3228h.* **Jachin.** 1 K 7:21. 1 Ch 4:24, Jarib. **Jachinites.** *✱S#3200h.*

13. **Zerah.** Ge 46:10, Zohar. **Zarhites.** *✱S#2227h.*

ver. 20. Jsh 7:17, 17. 1 Ch 27:11, 13. **Shaulites.** *✱S#7587h.*

14. **Simeonites.** The immense decrease of this tribe, no less than 37,100, renders it highly probable, that, influenced by the bad example of Zimri, the Simeonites had been peculiarly criminal in the late wickedness, and that multitudes of them had died of the plague. It is remarkable that Moses, in Dt ch. 33, bestows no blessing upon this tribe. Nu 1:22, 23. 2:12, 13. 1 Ch 4:24-27, 42, 43.

15. **Zephon.** i.e. *watchfulness; watching, looking out,* *✱S#6827h.* Nu 2:14. Ge 46:16, Ziphion, Haggai, Shuni, Ezbon, Eri, Arodi, Areli. **Zephonites.** *✱S#6831h.* **Haggites.** *✱S#2291h.* **Shunites.** *✱S#7765h.*

16. **Ozni.** *or,* Ezbon. i.e. *hearing; having ears,* *✱S#244h.* Ge ●46:16. **Oznites.** *✱S#244h.* **Erites.** *✱S#6180h.*

17. **Arod.** i.e. *a wild ass; I shall subdue; I shall roam,* *✱S#720h.* Ge 46:16, Arodi. **Arodites.** *✱S#722h.* Ge 46:16, Arodi. **Arelites.** *✱S#692h.* Ge 46:16, Areli.

18. **forty thousand and.** Nu 1:24, 25. 2:14, 15. 1 Ch 5:11-17.

19. **Er and Onan.** Ge 38:1-10. 46:12. 1 Ch 2:3, etc.

20. **Shelah.** Ge 38:5, 11, 14, 26-30. 1 Ch 4:21. **Shelanites.** *✱S#8024h.* **Pharez.** Ge 38:27-29. 46:12. Ru 4:18-22. 1 Ch 2:3, etc. Ne 11:4, 6, 24, Perez. Mt 1:3. Lk 3:33, Phares. **Pharzites.** Some editions read **Pharezites.** *✱S#6558h.* **Zerah.** Ge 38:30. 46:12, Zarah. 1 Ch 2:4. Ne 11:24.

21. **Hamulites.** *✱S#2539h.*

22. **threescore and.** Nu 1:26, 27. 2:3, 4. Ge 49:8. 1 Ch 5:2. Ps 115:14. He 7:14.

23. **sons of Issachar.** Nu 2:5. Ge 30:17, 18. 46:13. 1 Ch 7:1-5. **Tolaites.** *✱S#8440h.* **Pua.** *or,* Phuvah. i.e. *mouth,* *✱S#6312h.* Ge 46:13. **Punites.** *✱S#6324h.*

24. **Jashub.** *or,* Job. i.e. *inhabited; he turns; he will return,* *✱S#3437h.* Ge ●46:13. 1 Ch 7:1. Ezr 10:29. (1) A son of Issachar and founder of the Jashubites, Nu 26:24; 1 Ch 7:1. Called Job in Ge 46:13. (2) A Jew who married a foreign wife, Ezr 10:29. **Jashubites.** *✱S#3432h.* **Shimronites.** *✱S#8117h.*

25. **threescore.** Nu 1:28, 29. 2:5, 6.

26. **sons of Zebulun.** Ge 30:19, 20. 46:14, 15. **Sered.** i.e. *fear, humbling,* *✱S#5624h.* Ge 46:14. **Sardites.** i.e. *dissension,* *✱S#5625h.* **Elonites.** *✱S#440h.* **Jahleelites.** *✱S#3178h.*

27. **Zebulunites.** *✱S#2075h.* Jg 12:11, 12. **threescore thousand.** Nu 1:30, 31. 2:7, 8.

28. **sons of Joseph.** Ge 41:51, 52. 46:20. 48:5, 13-20.

29. **Manasseh.** Ge 46:20. **Machir.** Nu 32:39, 40. 36:1. 48:14. Dt 3:15. Jsh 17:1. Jg 5:14. 1 Ch 7:14-19. **Machirites.** *✱S#4354h.* **Gilead.** i.e. *heap of testimony,* *✚S#1568h.* ver. 30. Nu 27:1. 36:1. Jsh 17:1, 3. 1 Ch 2:21, 23. 7:14, 17. **Gileadites.** *✱S#1569h.* Jg 10:3. 11:1, 40. 12:7. 2 S 17:27. 19:31. 1 K 2:7. 2 K 15:25. Ezr 2:61. Ne 7:63.

30. **Jeezer.** i.e. *where is help?* or *there is no help, helpless,* *✱S#372h.* **called** Abiezer. Jsh 17:2. Jg 6:11, 24, 34. 8:2. **Jeezerites.** *✱S#373h.* **Helek.** i.e. *a portion, share,* *✱S#2507h.* Jsh 17:2. **Helekites.** *✱S#2516h.*

31. **Asriel.** i.e. *a binding of God; vow of God,* *✱S#844h.* Jsh 17:2. 1 Ch 7:14. **Asrielites.** *✱S#845h.* **Shechemites.** *✱S#7930h.*

32. **Shemida.** i.e. *fame of knowledge,* ✳S#8061h. Jsh 17:2. 1 Ch 7:19. **Shemidaites.** ✳S#8062h. **Hepher.** i.e. *a digging; pit; well,* ✳S#2660h. ver. 33. Nu 27:1. Jsh 17:2, 3. 1 Ch 4:6. 11:36. Also Jsh 12:17. 19:13. 1 K 4:10. 2 K 14:25. (1) A descendant of Manasseh, Nu 26:32; Jsh 17:2. (2) A descendant of Judah, 1 Ch 4:6. (3) A captain of David's army, 1 Ch 11:36. (4) A district of Palestine, probably in Judah; taken by Joshua, Jsh 12:17. **Hepherites.** ✳S#2662h.

33. **Zelophehad.** i.e. *first rupture; first breach; being burnt,* ✳S#6765h. Nu 27:1, 7. 36:2, 6, 10, 11. Jsh 17:3. 1 Ch 7:15, 15. **Mahlah.** i.e. *disease, sickness,* ✳S#4244h. Nu 27:1. 36:11. Jsh 17:3. 1 Ch 7:18. **Noah.** i.e. *wandering,* ✳S#5270h. Nu 27:1. 36:11. Jsh 17:3. **Hoglah.** i.e. *a partridge,* ✳S#2295h. Nu 27:1. 36:11. Jsh 17:3. **Milcah.** i.e. *queen; counsel,* Ge +11:29. **Tirzah.** i.e. *pleasure; charm; she will delight; willing,* ✳S#8656h. Nu 27:1. Jsh 12:24. 17:3. 1 K 14:17. 15:21, 33. 16:6, 8, 17. 2 K 15:14, 16. SS 6:4. (1) A daughter of Zelophehad, Nu 26:33; Jsh 17:3. (2) A city of the Canaanites taken by Joshua, Jsh 12:24. It was the capital of the northern kingdom of Israel from the time of Jeroboam till the reign of Omri, 1 K 14:17; 15:21, 33; 16:6-17.

34. **fifty and two thousand.** Nu 1:34, 35. 2:20, 21.

35. **Shuthalhites.** ✳S#8364h. **Becher.** i.e. *a young camel.* 1 Ch 7:20, 21. Bered. Tahath. Eladah. Tahath. **Tahan.** i.e. *a camp.* 1 Ch +7:25. **Tahanites.** ✳S#8470h.

36. **Eran.** i.e. *watcher; watchful,* ✳S#6197h. **Eranites.** ✳S#6198h.

37. **thirty and two thousand.** Nu 1:32, 33. 2:18, 19.

38. **sons of Benjamin.** Ge 46:21. 1 Ch 7:6-12. **Bela.** i.e. *devouring, swallowing.* Ge +46:21. **Belaites.** ✳S#1108h. **Ashbel.** i.e. *opinion of God.* Ge +46:21. **Ashbelites.** ✳S#789h. **Ahiram.** i.e. *my brother is high,* ✳S#297h. Ge 46:2. **Ahiramites.** ✳S#298h. **Ehi.** 1 Ch 8:1, Aharah.

39. **Shupham.** i.e. *serpent-like; bareness,* ✳S#8197h. **Hupham.** i.e. *inhabitant of a haven,* ✳S#2349h. Ge ◐46:21, Muppim, and Huppim. **Huphamites.** ✳S#2350h.

40. **Ard.** i.e. *a fugitive,* S#714h. He is called son of Benjamin in Ge +46:21, and grandson of Benjamin in Nu 26:40. In 1 Ch 8:3 he is called Addar. **and Naaman.** i.e. *pleasant.* Ge +46:21. **Ardites.** ✳S#716h. **Naamites.** ✳S#5280h.

41. **forty and five.** Nu 1:36, 37. 2:22, 23. Ge 46:21.

42. **Shuham.** i.e. *pit digger; sink humbly,* ✳S#7748h. Ge ◐46:23, Hushim. **Shuhamites.** ✳S#7749h. ver. 43.

43. **threescore and four.** Nu 1:38, 39. 2:25, 26.

44. **the children of Asher.** Ge 46:17, Jimnah. Ishuah. Isui. 1 Ch 7:30, Imnah. Isuah. Ishuai. **Jimnah.** i.e. *prosperity,* ✚S#3232h. Ge 46:17, Jimnah. **Jimnites.** ✚S#3232h. **Jesui.** i.e. *equal, level,* ✳S#3440h. Ge 46:17. 1 S 14:49. 1 Ch 7:30. **Jesuites.** ✳S#3441h. **Beriah.** i.e. *in evil.* 1 Ch +7:23. **Beriites.** ✳S#1284h.

45. **Heberites.** ✳S#2277h. **Malchielites.** ✳S#4440h.

46. **Sarah.** Ge 46:17, Serah.

47. **fifty and three.** Nu 1:40, 41. 2:27, 28.

48. **the sons of Naphtali.** Ge 46:24. 1 Ch 7:13. **Jahzeel.** i.e. *God divides* or *halves.* Ge +46:24. **Jahzeelites.** ✳S#3184h. **Guni.** i.e. *colored; painted*

with colors; my garden. Ge +46:24. **Gunites.** ✳S#1477h.

49. **Jezer.** i.e. *frame, formation.* Ge +46:24. **Jezerites.** ✳S#3340h. 1 Ch 25:11, Izri. **Shillem.** i.e. *recompense.* Ge +46:24. 1 Ch 7:13, Shallum. **Shillemites.** ✳S#8016h.

50. **forty and five.** Nu 1:42, 43. 2:29, 30.

51. **six hundred thousand and.** Nu 1:44-46. 2:32. Ge ◐46:26, 27. Ne 9:23. Jb 12:9, 10, 14, 20-23. Ps 77:20.

53. **Unto these.** Ge *12:2, 7. Jsh 11:23. 14:4. Ps 49:14. 105:44. Ezk 47:22. Da 7:27. Mt +*5:5. Re +*5:10. 21:27.

54. **many.** Nu 32:3, 5. 33:54. Jsh 17:14. **give the more.** Heb. multiply his. **give the less.** Heb. diminish his. Nu 33:54. 35:8. **according to.** Ex 16:18. Jsh 11:23. Mt 25:15-28. Lk 19:13-25. 1 C 15:41. 2 C 8:15.

55. **by lot.** ver. 56. Nu 33:54. 34:13. Jsh 11:23. 14:2. 17:14. 18:6, 10, 11. 19:1, 10, 17, 24, 32, 40. Pr 16:33. 18:18. Ac 1:26. Col 1:12. Re 7:4-8.

56. **the lot.** lit. mouth of the lot. ʄ144A2, Ge +34:26. Ge +24:44n. Jsh 14:1. *18:10. 21:8. Pr *16:33. Ro 11:7. 1 C 12:4.

57. **these are.** Nu 35:2, 3. Ge 46:11. Ex 6:16-19. 1 Ch 6:1, 16, etc. **of Gershon.** See on Nu 3. 4. **Merarites.** ✳S#4848h.

58. **Libnites.** Nu 3:17-21. 16:1. **Korathites.** ✳S#7145h. Ex +6:24, Korhites. 1 Ch 9:19, Korahites. 9:31, Korahite.

59. **Jochebed.** Ex 2:1, 2. 6:20. Le 18:12.

60. **unto Aaron.** Nu 3:2, 8.

61. **Nadab and.** Nu 3:4. Le 10:1, 2. 1 Ch 24:1, 2.

62. **those that.** Nu 1:49. 3:39. 4:47, 48. 18:20-24. 35:2-8. Dt 10:9. 14:27-29. 18:1, 2. Jsh 13:14, 33. 14:3. **they were not.** See on Nu 1:49. **because.** Nu 18:20-24. 35:2-8. Dt 10:9. 14:27-29. 18:1, 2. Jsh 13:14, 33. 14:3.

63. **numbered by.** See on ver. 3.

64. **there was not.** Nu ch. 1, 2. Dt 2:14, 15. 4:3, 4. 1 C 10:5.

65. **They shall.** Nu 14:23, 24, 28-30, 35, 38. Ex 12:37. Dt 2:14, 15. 32:49, 50. Ps 90:3-7. Ro 11:22. 1 C 10:5, 6. He 3:17, 18. Ju 5. **surely.** 147B, Ge +2:16. **save Caleb.** See on Nu 14:30, 38. Is 46:11. 55:11. Ml *3:18.

NUMBERS 27

The daughters of Zelophehad ask for their father's inheritance, 1-5. The law of inheritance, 6-11. Moses is warned of his approaching death; and, in answer to his prayer, Joshua is appointed to succeed him, 12-23.

1. **the daughters.** In the orders for the division of the land, just given, no provision had been made for females, in the case of failure of male issue. The five daughters of Zelophehad, therefore, considered themselves as destitute, having neither father nor brother, and being themselves entirely overlooked; and they agreed to refer the case to Moses and the rulers, whether it were not equitable that they should inherit their father's portion. This led to the enactment of an additional law to the civil code of Israel, which satisfactorily ascertained and amply secured the right of succession in cases of inheritance. This law, which is as reasonable as it is just, stands thus: (1) On the

demise of the *father*, the estate descends to the *sons*. (2) If there be no *son*, the *daughters* succeed. (3) If there be no *daughter*, the *brothers* of the deceased inherit. (4) If there be no *brethren*, or paternal *uncles*, the estate goes to the *grand uncles*, or *brothers* of his *father*. (5) If there be no *grand uncles*, then the *nearest of kin* succeeds to the inheritance. Beyond this *fifth* degree the law does not extend, because there must always have been some among the Israelites who could be called *kinsmen*. **Zelophehad**. Nu 26:33. 36:1-12. Jsh 17:3-6. 1 Ch 7:15. Ga 3:28. **these are the names**. Is 49:14-16. Jn 10:3. He 12:23.

2. **they stood**. Nu 15:33, 34. Ex 18:13, 14, 19-26. 28:29. Dt 17:8-10. He 12:23.

3. Rosenmuller translates this verse as follows: "Our father died in the wilderness, leaving no sons; nor was he among those who rebelled against the Lord with Korah, who died on account of his own sin." Professor Dathe, however, understands by "his own sin," that sin which was common to all the Israelites, who died on account of their unbelief. **died in the.** Nu 14:35. 26:64, 65. Ju 5. **in the company**. Nu 16:1-3, 19, 32-35, 49. 26:9, 10. **died in his**. Ezk 18:4. Jn 8:21, 24. Ro 5:12, 21. 6:23.

4. **Why**. Ex 32:11. Ps 109:13. Pr 13:9. **done away**. Heb. diminished. Nu 36:3. **Give**. Jsh 17:4.

5. **Moses brought**. Nu 15:34. Ex 18:15-19. 25:22. Le 24:12, 13. Jb 23:4. Pr 3:5, 6. 1 J=2:1.

6. **the Lord spake**. Ps 68:5, 6. Ga 3:28.

7. **thou shalt**. Nu 36:1, 2. Jsh 17:4. Ps 68:5. Is 56:4-7. Je 49:11. Jn 17:12. Ac 20:32. 26:18. Ga 3:28, 29. Ep 1:9-11, 13, 14. 2:12, 13. Col 1:12. He 9:15. 1 P 1:*4, 5.

11. **kinsman**. Le 25:25, 49. Ru 4:3-6. Je 32:8. **a statute**. Nu 35:29. 1 S 30:25. **as the Lord commanded**. Ps 2:7, 8. He 1:1, 2.

12. **mount**. Nu 33:47, 48. Dt 3:27. 32:49. 34:1-4. **Abarim**. i.e. *the places beyond; the passages; regions beyond*, *S#5682h. Nu 33:47, 48. Dt 32:49. Je 22:20. Young notes, a mountain range, of which Nebo is one part (whose top is Pisgah).

13. **And when**. Dt 31:2. 34:4. **thou also**. Nu 31:2. See on Ge 25:8, 17. **as Aaron**. Nu 20:24-28. 33:38. Dt 10:6. 32:50.

14. **ye rebelled**. Nu 20:8-13. Dt 1:37. 32:51, 52. Ps 106:32, 33. **commandment**. ♪121BA, Ge +45:21. **Mirabah**. Nu 20:1, 13, 24. Ex 17:7.

16. **the Lord**. *Yehowah elohey haroochoth lechol basar*, "Jehovah, the God of the spirits of all flesh." This address sufficiently proves, that this holy man believed man to be compounded of flesh and spirit, and that these principles are perfectly distinct. Either the materiality of the soul is a human fable, or, if it be a true doctrine, Moses did not pray under the influence of the Divine Spirit. There is a similar form of expression in Nu 16:22: "O God, the God of the spirits of all flesh"; and in Jb 12:10, "In whose hand is the soul (nephesh) of all living; and the spirit (ruach) of all flesh of man." These seem decisive proofs, among many others, that the Old Testament teaches that there is an immortal spirit in man; for though *ruach* sometimes denotes *breath* or *wind*, yet it certainly has not that signification *here*, nor in the other passages cited. **the God**. Nu +*16:22. Ec +*12:7. Zc +*12:ln. He +12:9. **spirits**. Heb. *ruach*, Nu +16:22. **set a man**. T#1599. Nu 13:8, 16. Dt 31:14. 1 S 12:13. 1 K 5:5.

Je 3:15. 23:4, 5. Ezk 34:11-16, 23. 37:24. Mt 9:38. Jn 10:11. Jn=14:16-18. Ac 20:28. 1 P 5:2-4.

17. **go out**. Dt 31:1, 2. 1 S 8:20. 18:13. 2 S 5:2. 1 K 3:7. 2 Ch 1:10. Jn 10:3, =4, 9. 2 P 1:14, 15. ♪171J3. Synecdoche of the Species B630. To *go out* and *come in* is used of official actions or of life in general. For other instances of this figure see Nu 27:21. 2 Ch 1:10. Ps 121:8. Is 37:28. Jn 10:9. Ac 1:21. **lead**. Ps 77:20. 78:52. Jn=14:16-18. **as sheep**. Ge 49:22-24. 1 K 22:17. 2 Ch 18:16. Ps 80:1. Is 40:11. Ezk 34:5. Zc 10:2. 13:7. Mt ⅃9:36. 10:6. 15:24. Mk ⅃6:34. Jn 10:11-16. He 4:8. 13:20. 1 P 2:24, 25. 5:4.

18. **Take thee**. See on Nu 11:28. 13:8, 16. Ex 17:9. Dt 3:28. 31:7, 8, 23. 34:9. **a man**. Nu 11:17. Ge 41:38. Jg 3:10. 11:29. 1 S 16:13, 14, 18. Is 63:11. Da 5:14. Jn 3:34. Ac 6:3. 1 C 12:4-11. **spirit**. Heb. *ruach*, Ge +41:38. **lay**. ver. 23. Dt 34:9. Ac 6:6. 8:15-19. 13:3. 19:6. 1 T *4:14. 5:22. He 6:2.

19. **give him**. Dt 31:7. Lk 9:1-5. 10:2-11. Ac 20:28-31. Col 4:17. 1 T 5:21. 6:13-17. 2 T 4:1-6.

20. **put some**. Nu 11:17, 28, 29. 1 S 10:6, 9. 2 K 2:9, 10, 15. 1 Ch 29:23, 25. **may be**. Jsh 1:16-18.

21. **he shall**. Jsh 9:14. Jg 1:1. 20:18, 23, 26-28. 1 S 22:10. 23:9. 28:6. 30:7. **Eleazar**. Jsh 14:1. 21:1, 2. **shall ask**. Jsh 9:14. 1 S 23:9-12. Ps 73:24. Pr 3:5, 6. Is 28:29. **Urim**. Ex 28:30. Le 8:8. Dt 33:8. 1 S 28:6. Ezr 2:63. Ne 7:65. **at his word**. See on ver. 17. Jsh 9:14. 1 S 22:10-15. **go out**. ♪171J3, ver. 17. Jg 1:1. 20:18, 23.

23. **gave**. See on ver. 19. Dt 3:28. 31:7, 8. Jsh 1:1-9. 3:7.

NUMBERS 28

Laws for the daily burnt offerings, and those of the sabbath, 1-10; those of the new moons, 11-15; those of the Passover, and the feast of unleavened bread, 16-25; and those for the feast of Pentecost in the day of first-fruits, 26-31.

2. **my bread**. ♪171, Ge +3:19. Le 2:1, 2. 3:11. 21:6, 8. Ml 1:7, 12. ♪22D5M. Anthropopatheia or Anthropomorphism B894. Bread is attributed to God. For other instances of this figure see Jn 6:35, 48. **for a sweet savor unto me**. Heb. savor of my rest. ♪22C15, Ge +8:21. Nu 15:3, 7, 24. Ge 8:21. Ex 29:18. Le 1:9, 13, 17. 3:11. Ezk 16:19. 20:41mg. 2 C 2:15. Ep 5:2. Ph 4:18. **in their due season**. The stated sacrifices and service of the tabernacle having, probably, been greatly interrupted for several years, and a new generation having arisen, who were children or minors when the law was given respecting these ordinances; and as they were now about to enter into the promised land, where they must be established and constantly observed; God commands Moses to repeat them to the people in the following order: (1) DAILY: the *morning* and *evening* sacrifices; a lamb each time (ver. 3, 4). (2) WEEKLY: the *sabbath* offerings; two lambs of a year old (ver. 9, 10). (3) MONTHLY: at the beginning of each month, two young bullocks, one ram, and seven rams of a year old, and a kid for a sin offering (ver. 11-15). (4) ANNUAL: 1. The *Passover* to last seven days; the offerings, two young bullocks, one ram, seven lambs of a year old, and a he-goat (ver. 16-25); 2. The day of *first-fruits*: the sacrifices the same as on the beginning of the month (ver. 26-31). Nu 9:2, 3, 7, 13. Ex 23:15. Ps 81:3. **due season**. Ge +17:21 (✦S#4150h). Mt +√24:45. Lk 12:42. 1 C 11:20-26. *14:40.

3. **two lambs**. Ge *22:8. Ex 29:38, 39. Le 1:1, 2, 10-13. 6:9. Is *53:7. Ezk 46:13-15. Jn *1:29. 8:46. *14:30. 1 P *1:19, 20. 2:22. He *4:15. 9:14. Re 13:8. **day by day**. Heb. in a day. ver. 24. Ex 29:36, 38. Da 8:13. 11:31. 12:11.

4. **one lamb**. Jn 1:29. Re 13:8. 21:23. **and the other**. 1 K 18:29, 36. Ezr 9:4, 5. Ps 141:2. Da 9:21. **at even**. Heb. between the two evenings. ver. 8. Nu 9:3. Ex 12:6mg&n. 1 K 18:29, 30. 2 Ch 13:10, 11. Ps 55:17. 141:2.

5. **a tenth**. Nu 15:4, 5. Ex 16:36. 29:38-42. Le 2:1. **meat offering**. Le +*23:13.

6. **a continual**. Ex 29:38-42. Le 6:9. 2 Ch 2:4. 31:3. Ezr 3:4. Ps 50:8. Ezk 46:14. Am 5:25. **was ordained**. Ex 24:18. 29:38-42. 31:18.

7. **drink offering**. Le +*23:13. **in the holy**. Ex 29:42. **to be poured**. ver. 14, 31. See on Nu 15:5, 7, 10. Ex 29:40. 30:9. Le 23:13. Is 57:6. Jl 1:9, 13. 2:14. Ph 2:17g.

8. **sacrifice**. He 7:24-27. 1 P 1:18, 19.

9. **sabbath**. Ex +*20:8-11. 34:21. Le 19:3. 23:3. Ne 13:15-22. Ps 92:1-4. Is 56:2. +*58:13n, 14. Ezk 20:12. 46:4. Mt 12:5. Mk 2:23-28. He 4:3-5, 9. Re ◐+*1:10n.

10. **the burnt offering**. Le +*23:12. Ezk 46:4, 5. **the continual**. ver. 23. Nu 29:6, 11, 16, 19, 22, 25, 31, 34, 38, 39. **drink offering**. Le +*23:13.

11. **in the beginnings**. Nu 10:10. 15:3-11. 1 S 20:5. 2 K *4:23. 1 Ch 23:31. 2 Ch +2:4. Ezr 3:5. Ne 10:33. Ps 40:6-8. 81:3. Is 1:13, 14. 66:23. Ezk 45:17, 18. 46:1, 6. Ho 2:11. Am 8:5. Ga 4:10. Col 2:6, 16n. **two young**. ver. 19. He 10:10-14.

12. **three tenth deals**. Nu 15:4-12. 29:10. Ezk 46:5-7.

13. **for a burnt**. See on ver. 2.

15. **one kid**. ver. 22. Nu 15:24. Le 4:23. 16:15. Ro 8:3. 2 C 5:21. **sin offering**. Le 4:1-3, 13, 14, 22, 23, 27, 28. +*23:19. **beside**. See on ver. 3, 10, 11. **burnt offering**. Le +*23:12. Zc 13:7. Lk 24:46. **drink offering**. Le +*23:13.

16. **the fourteenth**. Nu 9:3-5. Ex 12:2-11, 18, 43-49. Le 23:5-8. Dt 16:1-8. Ezk 45:21-24. Mt 26:2, 17. Lk 22:7, 8. Ac 12:3, 4. 1 C 5:7, 8. **passover**. Le +*23:5.

17. **the fifteenth**. Ex 12:15-17. 13:6. 34:18. Dt 16:1-8. **unleavened**. Le +*23:6. Mt 26:2, 19, 26-29. 1 C 5:7, 8.

18. **the first**. Ex 12:16. Le 23:7, 8. **holy convocation**. Ge 49:10. Le 23:1, 2. He 12:23. Re 7:9.

19. **two young**. Ezk 45:21-25. **they shall**. ver. 31. Nu 29:8. Le 22:20. Dt 15:21. Ml 1:13, 14. 1 P 1:19.

22. **one goat**. See on ver. 15.

23. **beside**. See on ver. 3, 10.

25. **on the seventh**. Ex 12:16. 13:6. Le 23:8. **ye shall do**. ver. 18, 26. Nu 29:1, 12, 35. Le 23:3, 8, 21, 25, 35, 36.

26. **in the day**. Ex 23:16. 34:22. **firstfruits**. Nu 15:19-21. Ex 34:26. Le 23:+*10, 15-21. Dt 16:9-11. Ac 2:1, etc. 1 C 15:20. Ja 1:18. **after your weeks**. Dt 16:9, 10. Ac 2:1-4, 41. Re 14:1-4. **convocation**. He 10:25.

27. **two young**. ver. 11, 19. Le 23:18, 19. Bishop Patrick observes that no *peace offerings* are appointed in this chapter, which were chiefly for the benefit of the offerers, and therefore in them they were left more to themselves; but *burnt offerings*, which were purely for the honor of God, and confessions of his dominion, and which figured evangelical piety and devotion, by which the soul is wholly offered up to God, in the flames of holy love; and *sin offerings*, which were typical of Christ's sacrifice of himself, by which we and our services are perfected and sanctified. **sweet savor**. Ep 5:2. **seven**. Ge 4:15. 8:20, 21. Ps 79:12. Pr 6:31.

30. **one kid**. ver. 15, 22. Nu 15:24. 2 C *5:19, 21. Ga *3:13. 1 P *2:24. *3:18.

31. **without blemish**. ver. 19. Ml 1:13, 14.

NUMBERS 29

The sacrifices to be offered at the feast of trumpets, 1-6; on the day of atonement, 7-11; and on the eight days of the feast of tabernacles, 12-40.

1. **the seventh**. That is, the month *Tisri*, the *seventh* month of their ecclesiastical year, but the *first* of their civil year, answering to our *September*. This, which was their *new year's day*, was a time of great festivity, and ushered in by the blowing of trumpets; whence it was also called *the feast of blowing the trumpets*. Le *23:24, 25. Ezr 3:6. Ne 7:73. **the first day of the month**. The monthly sacrifices were regulated by the new moons; and it is probable that the solemn sacrifices were appointed by God, to prevent the idolatry which was usual among the heathen at this period; who expressed the most extravagant rejoicings on the first appearance of the new moon. Moses, however, used the return of the moon only as one of the most natural and convenient measures of time; and appointed sacrifices to *Jehovah*, to prevent the Israelites from falling into the idolatries of their heathen neighbors. In the serene climate of Arabia and Judea, its first faint crescent is, for the most part, visible to all. **blowing**. Nu 10:1-10. 1 Ch 15:28. Ps 81:3. 89:15. Is 27:13. Zc 9:14. Mk 16:15, 16. Ro 10:14-18. 15:16-19. He 12:25. **trumpets**. Le +*23:24.

2. **sweet savor**. Ge 8:21. Ep 5:2. Ph 4:18. **one young**. ver. 8, 36. Nu 28:19, 27. Le 1:2-13. He 10:10-14. **lambs**. Re 5:6. **without blemish**. 1 P 1:19.

3. **meat offering**. Le 2:1, 2. +*23:13. **flour**. Nu 28:5. **mingled with oil**. Ps 45:7, 8. Ac 10:4. Ep 2:18. He 9:14. **tenth deals**. Ex 16:36.

5. **one kid**. See on Nu 28:15, 22, 30. Le 4:1-12, 22, 23, 27, 28. Zc 13:1. Jn 19:16-18. He 13:11, 12.

6. **the burnt offering**. See on Nu 28:11-15. Le +*23:12. **of the month**. Nu 28:11-15. **meat offering**. Le +*23:13. Jn 4:34. 6:51. **the daily**. See on Nu 28:3-8. Ex 29:38-42. Le 6:9. **drink offerings**. Le +*23:13. Ps 104:15. Jn 15:1. **according**. ver. 18, 21. Nu 9:14. 15:11, 12, 24. Ezr 3:4. **sweet savor**. Ep 5:2. **a sacrifice**. He 9:22. **by fire**. Nu 28:3-7.

7. **on the tenth**. Le 16:29-31. 23:27. **afflict**. Le 16:29. Ezr 8:21. Ps 35:13. 126:5, 6. Is 22:12. 53:6. 58:3-5. Zc 7:3. 12:10. Mt 5:4. Lk 13:3, 5. Ac 27:9. Ro 6:6. 1 C 9:27. 15:56, 57. 2 C 7:9-11. Ga 2:20. 5:24. Ph 3:10. Ja 4:8-10. 1 P 4:13. 1 J 2:2. **souls**. Heb. *nephesh*, Ge +27:31.

8. **without blemish**. ver. 2, 13. Nu 28:19.

9. **meat offering**. See on Nu 15:3-12. Le +*23:13.

11. **sin offering**. Le +*23:19. **beside**. Le 16:3, 5, 9. Is 53:10. Da 9:24-26. He 7:27. 9:25-28. **atonement**. Le +*23:24. Jn 10:18. Ro 8:32. Ga 2:20. **the continual**. See on ver. 6. Nu 28:3-8. **burnt offering**. Le +*23:12. **meat offering**. Le +*23:13. **drink offerings**. Le +*23:13.

12. **the fifteenth day**. Le +*23:34. This was the *feast of Tabernacles*, kept in commemoration of their dwelling in tents in the wilderness for forty years. Ex 23:16. 34:22. Le 23:33-43. Dt 16:13, 14. Ne 8:14, 18. Ezk 45:25. Zc 14:16-19. Jn 1:14. 7:2, 3, 6, 14, 37-39. He 11:9-13.

13. **thirteen young bullocks**. ver. 2, 8. Nu 28:11, 19, 27. Ezr 3:4. He 10:12-14.

14. **oil**. Ezr 3:4. Ezk 45:25. He +=2:10.

16. **one kid**. See on ver. 11.

17. **twelve**. ver. 13, 20, etc. Ps 40:6. 50:8, 9. 51:16, 17. 69:31. Is 1:11. Je 7:22, 23. Ho 6:6. Ro 12:1. He 8:13. 9:3-14.

18. **after the manner**. That is, *after the manner* already prescribed. ver. 3, 4, 6, 9, 10. Nu 15:4-12. 28:7, 14. Ezr 3:4.

19. **sin offering**. ver. 11, 22, 25. Am 8:14. Mk 10:45. 1 P 3:18. **continual**. He 13:15.

20. **without blemish**. Jb 33:24. Ro 4:7, 8. 2 C 5:21.

21. **after the manner**. ver. 18.

22. **drink offering**. Ps 16:4. Jl 1:9, 13. 2:14.

23. **without blemish**. Ps 32:1. 1 T 2:5, 6.

25. **continual burnt**. See on ver. 11. Jn 8:31. Ac 13:43. Ro 2:7. Ga 2:5. 6:9. 2 Th 3:13. He 3:14. 10:39. 13:15.

26. **without spot**. Jb 15:15. He 1:2, 3. 1 J 2:1, 2.

29. **without blemish**. Ac 4:27, 28.

32. **without blemish**. Jn *1:29. Ga 1:4. He 9:26-28.

35. **eighth day**. Though this day was properly a distinct festival, and esteemed the chief or high day of the feast, yet fewer sacrifices are appointed for it than for any of the foregoing seven. On every one of them two rams and fourteen lambs were offered; but on this day there were but half as many; and whereas seven bullocks were the fewest that were offered on any of those days, on this there was only one. At this feast there was an extraordinary ceremony of which the rabbins inform us, namely, the drawing water out of the pool of Siloam, and pouring it, mixed with wine, on the sacrifice as it lay on the altar. This they are said to have done with such expressions of joy, that it became a common proverb, "He that never saw the rejoicing of drawing of water, never saw rejoicing in all his life" (*Mishnah*, "Succah," c. V. sec. I). The Jews pretend to ground this custom on the following passage of Isaiah (Is 12:3), "With joy shall ye draw water out of the wells of salvation;" and to this ceremony Jesus is supposed to refer, when "in the last day, the great day of the feast, he stood and cried, saying, If any man thirst, let him come unto me, as the Scripture saith, out of his belly shall flow rivers of living water" (Jn 7:37, 38): thereby calling off the people from their carnal mirth and festive and pompous ceremonies, to seek spiritual refreshment for their minds. See related note (1 S 7:6n). Le 23:36. Is 12:3. Jn 7:37-39. Ga 4:4. 1 T 3:16. Re 1:5, 6. 7:9-17. 13:8.

39. **do**. *or*, offer. He 9:11-14. 10:10-12. 1 J 1:7. **in your set feasts**. Le 23:2. 1 Ch 23:31. 2 Ch 31:3. Ezr 3:5. Ne 10:33. Is 1:14. Da 9:24. **beside your vows**. Nu 6:21. Le 7:11, 16, etc. 22:21-23. +*23:38. Dt 12:6. 1 C 10:31. **freewill offerings**. Le +*23:38. **burnt offerings**. Le +*23:12. **meat offerings**. Le +*23:13. **drink offerings**. Le +*23:13. **peace offerings**. Le +*23:19.

40. **Moses told**. Ex 40:16. Dt 4:5. Mt 28:20. Jn 1:17. Ac 20:27. 1 C +*15:3. He 3:2, 5.

NUMBERS 30

Vows not to be broken, 1, 2. Those of a minor daughter might be disallowed by her father, 3-5. Those of a wife by her husband, 6-8. The vows of a widow, and of a divorced woman, 9-16.

1. **the heads**. Nu 1:4-16. 7:2. 34:17-28. Ex 18:25. Dt 1:3-17.

2. **If a man**. The preceding chapters had treated of sacrifices required by law; and in the laws here delivered in respect to vows must have been very useful, as they both *prevented* and *annulled* rash vows, and provided a proper sanction for the support and performance of those which were rationally made, and which were made to the Lord (Le 27:2n). **vow a vow**. Nu 21:2. Ge 28:20-22. Le 27:2, etc. Dt 23:21, 22. Jsh 9:3-6, 14, 15. Jg 11:11, 30, 31, 35, 36, 39. 1 S 14:24-27, 37-44. Ps 15:3. 22:25. 50:14. 56:12. 66:13, 14. 76:11. 116:14. 119:106. Pr 20:25. Ec 5:4-6. Mt 14:9. Ac 23:14. **swear**. Ex +*20:7. Le 5:4. Mt 5:33, 34. 14:7-9. Ac +*23:12. 2 C 1:23. 9:9-11. **to bind**. ver. 3, 4, 10. Mt 23:16, 18g. Ac 23:12, 14, 21. **soul**. Heb. *nephesh*, Ge +27:31. **break**. Heb. profane. Ps 55:20mg. **he shall do**. Jb 22:27. Ps 22:25. 50:14. 66:13, 14. 116:14, 18. Ec *5:4, 5. Ezk 17:18n. Na 1:15.

3. **woman**. Est 1:17-20. Pr ●7:14. 1 C +14:34.

4. **her father**. Ep 6:1-3. Col 3:20. 1 T 3:4. He 12:5, 6. **hear**. ver. 2n. Le 27:2n. **her bond**. See on ver. 2. **soul**. Heb. *nephesh*, Ge +27:31.

5. **her father**. Ho 6:6. Mt 15:4-6. Mk 7:10-13. Ep 6:1. **disallow**. ver. 8, 12, 15. *S#5106h. Nu 30:5, 8, 11. 32:7 (discourage), 7, 9. Ps 33:10 (maketh of none effect). 141:5 (shall break). **soul**. Heb. *nephesh*, Ge +27:31.

6. **she vowed**. Heb. her vows *were* upon her. ver. 8. Ps 56:12. **soul**. Heb. *nephesh*, Ge +27:31.

7. **held his peace**. 1 S 1:21-23. **soul**. Heb. *nephesh*, Ge +27:31.

8. **her husband**. Ge 3:16. 1 C 7:4. 14:34. Ep 5:22-24, 33. Col 3:18. 1 T 2:11-14. **soul**. Heb. *nephesh*, Ge +27:31.

9. **a widow**. Le 21:7. Lk 2:37. Ro 7:2. **souls**. Heb. *nephesh*, Ge +27:31.

10. **soul**. Heb. *nephesh*, Ge +27:31.

11. **soul**. Heb. *nephesh*, Ge +27:31.

12. **utterly**. ƒ147B, Ge +2:16. **her husband hath made**. 1 C 11:3. **soul**. Heb. *nephesh*, Ge +27:31. **and the Lord**. ver. 5, 8. Nu 15:25, 28.

13. **and every**. Ge 3:16. 1 C 11:3, 9. 1 P 3:1-6. **to afflict**. See on Nu 29:7. Le 16:29. 23:27, 32. Ezr 8:21. Ps 35:13. Is 58:5. 1 C 7:5. **soul**. Heb. *nephesh*, Ge +27:31.

14. **her husband**. ver. 7.

15. **he shall bear**. ver. 5, 8, 12. Le 5:1, 4-10. Ga 3:28. He 9:22.

16. **the statutes**. Nu 5:29, 30. Le 11:46, 47. 13:59. 14:54-57. 15:32, 33.

NUMBERS 31

The Israelites, by divine command, war against the Midianites, slay the men, with their kings, and Balaam; and take the women and children with much spoil, 1-12. Moses is wroth with the officers for sparing the women; and orders them with the male children to be slain, 13-18. The warriors, captives, and spoil are purified, 19-24. *The partition of the cattle and the captives*, 25-47. *The voluntary oblation unto the treasury of the Lord by the officers and soldiers*, 48-54.

2. **Avenge.** ver. 3. Nu 25:17, 18. Dt 32:35. Jg 16:24, 28-30. Ps 94:1-3. Is 1:24. 34:8. 47:3. 63:4. Na 1:2. Lk 21:22. Ro 3:5, 6. 12:19. 13:4. 1 Th 4:6. He 10:30. Re 6:10. 18:20. 19:2. **the Midianites.** Nu 25:6, 14-18. Ge 25:1-4. Ex 2:16. **gathered.** Nu 20:24. 27:13. Ge 15:15. 25:8, 9, 17. 49:33. Dt 32:50. Jg 2:10. Ac 7:59. 13:36. 2 T 4:6, 7.

3. **Arm some.** Ex 17:9-13. Je 25:31. Lk +*22:36, 38. **avenge the Lord.** Nu 25:11, 13. Ex 17:16. Le 26:25. Jg 5:2, 23. 2 K 9:7. 10:30. Je 46:10. 50:28. Ho *4:1, 2.

4. **Of every tribe a thousand.** Heb. A thousand of a tribe, a thousand of a tribe. **a thousand.** Le 26:8. Jg 7:2. 1 S 14:6.

6. **Phinehas.** Nu 25:7-13. **the holy instruments.** Nu 14:44. 33:20-22. Ex 25:9. Jsh 6:4-6, 13-15. 1 S 4:4, 5, 17. 14:18. 23:9. 2 S 11:11. **to blow.** Nu 10:2, 8, 9. 2 Ch 13:12-15.

7. **all.** Dt 20:13, 14. Jg 21:11. 1 S 27:9. 1 K 11:15, 16. **the males.** Jg 6:1, 2, 33.

8. **the kings.** Nu 22:4. Jsh 13:21, 22. **Evi.** i.e. *desire*, *S#189h. Jsh 13:21. **Zur.** Nu 25:15, 18. **Reba.** i.e. *a fourth part*, *S#7254h. Jsh 13:21. **Balaam.** Nu 22:10. 24:25. Jsh 13:21, 22. Ps 9:16. 10:2. 34:21. 37:7-10, 12-15, 20, 34-36. 119:118, 119. 139:19. Pr 10:25. 11:5-7. 1 T 6:9, 10. 2 P 2:15. Ju 11. Re 2:14. 19:20.

9. **the women.** ver. 15, 16. Dt 20:14. 2 Ch 28:5, 8-10.

10. **burnt all.** Jsh 6:24. 1 S 30:1. 1 K 9:16. Is 1:7. Re 18:8.

11. **took.** Dt 20:10-18. Jsh 8:2.

12. **the plains of Moab.** See on Nu 22:1.

13. **went forth.** Ge 14:17. 1 S 15:12. 30:21. **without the camp.** ver. 12, 22-24. Nu 5:2. 19:11.

14. **wroth.** Nu 12:3. Ex 32:19, 22. Le 10:16. 1 S 15:13, 14. 1 K 20:42. 2 K 13:19. Ep 4:26. **battle.** Heb. host of war.

15. **Have ye saved.** Dt 2:34. 20:13, 16-18. Jsh 6:21. 8:25. 10:40. 11:14. 1 S 15:3. Ps 137:8, 9. Je 48:10. Ezk 9:6.

16. **these caused.** Nu 24:14. 25:1-3. Pr 23:27. Ec 7:26. 2 P 2:15. Re 2:14. **in the matter.** Nu 25:18. Dt 4:3. Jsh 22:17. **and there.** Nu 25:9.

17. **kill every male.** Ge 18:25. Jg 21:11, 12. **known.** Ge +4:1, 17. Ex +34:15. **him.** Heb. a male.

18. **keep alive for yourselves.** Le 25:44. Dt 20:14. 21:10-14. 2 Ch 28:8-10. Is 14:2. **known.** Ge +4:1, 17. Ex +34:15.

19. **abide.** Nu 5:2. 19:11-18. 1 Ch 22:8. **any person.** Heb. *nephesh*, Jsh +10:28.

20. **raiment.** Nu 19:14-16, 22. Ge 35:2. Ex 19:10. **that is made.** Heb. instrument, *or*, vessel.

21. **the ordinance.** See on Nu 30:16.

23. **abide.** Is 43:2. Zc 13:9. Ml 2:2, 3. Mt 3:11. 1 C 3:13-15. 1 P 1:7. 4:12. 2 P 3:5-7. Re 3:18. **it shall be purified.** Nu 8:7. 19:9, 17. **ye shall make.** Le 11:32. 15:17. Ep 5:26. T 3:5, 6. 1 P 3:21.

24. **wash.** Nu *19:19, 20. Le 11:25. 14:9. 15:13.

26. **that was taken.** Heb. of the captivity. Is +49:25mg. Am 4:10mg.

27. **two parts.** Jsh 22:8. 1 S 30:4, *24, 25. Ps 68:12.

28. **levy.** Ge 14:20. Jsh 6:19, 24. 2 S 8:11, 12.

1 Ch 18:11. 26:26, 27. Pr 3:9, 10. Is 18:7. 23:18. 60:9. Mt 22:21. **one soul.** Heb. *nephesh*, Ge +2:19. T#986‡. ver. 30, 47. Nu 18:26. Ge ‡1:21, 24. +*2:19. 9:4.

29. **an heave offering.** Nu 18:8, 19, 26. Ex 29:27. Le +*7:14. Dt 12:12, 19.

30. **one portion.** See ver. 42-47. **flocks.** *or*, goats. ver. 28. Ex 12:21. **and give.** ver. 28. Nu 18:24-28. 1 C 9:13, 14. **keep the.** Nu 3:7, 8, 25, 31, 36, etc. 18:1-5, 23, 26. 1 Ch 9:27-29. 23:32. 26:20-27. Ac *20:28. 1 C 4:2. Col 4:17. He 13:17.

32. **the prey.** Nu 23:24. Dt 32:35, 39-43. Na 1:2, 3.

35. **persons.** Heb. *nephesh*, souls, Ge +12:5.

40. **the persons.** Heb. *nephesh*, souls, Ge +12:5. ℐ66, Ge +9:3. **two persons.** Heb. *nephesh*, souls, Ge +12:5.

41. **heave offering.** Le +7:14. **Eleazar.** ver. 29-31. Nu 18:8, 14, 19, 20. Mt 10:10. 1 C 9:10-14. Ga 6:6. 1 T 5:17. He 7:4-6, 9-12.

46. **persons.** Heb. *nephesh*, souls, Ge +12:5.

47. **the Levites.** Nu 18:21-24. Dt 12:17-19. Lk 10:1-8. 1 Th 5:12, 13. **kept the charge.** See on ver. 30. Ps 134:1. Is 56:10, 11.

49. **charge.** Heb. hand. **lacketh.** Nu 23:23. 1 S 30:18, 19. Ps 72:14. Is 49:24, 25. Mi 5:15. Jn 18:9.

50. **therefore brought an oblation.** Ps 107:15, 21, 22. 116:12, 17. **gotten.** Heb. found. **an atonement.** Ex 30:12, 15, 16. Le 17:11. **souls.** Heb. *nephesh*, Ge +12:13.

51. **took the gold.** Nu 7:2-6.

52. **offering.** Heb. heave offering. Le +7:14.

53. **men of war.** Dt 20:14. Jg 8:24-26.

54. **a memorial.** Nu 16:40. Ex 30:16. Jsh 4:7. Ps 18:49. 103:1, 2. 115:1. 145:7. Zc 6:14. Mt 26:6-13. Lk 22:19. Ac 10:4.

NUMBERS 32

The tribes of Reuben and Gad request an inheritance eastward of Jordan, 1-5. Moses sharply remonstrates with them, 6-15. They explain; Moses is satisfied; and a conditional grant is made to them and half the tribe of Manasseh, 16-33. They rebuild the cities, etc., 34-42.

1. **the children.** Nu 2:10-15. 26:5-7, 15-18. Ge 29:32. 30:10, 11. **cattle.** ℐ66, Ge +9:3. **Jazer.** i.e. *helpful*, *S#3270h. ver. 3, 35. Nu 21:32, Jaazer. Jsh 13:25. 21:39. 2 S 24:5. Is 16:8, 9. Je 48:32, 32. **the place.** ver. 26. Ge 13:2, 5, 10, 11. 47:1-4. Ex 9:6, 7. 10:8, 9, 24-26. 12:31, 32. Je 50:19. Mi 7:14. 1 J *2:16.

3. **Ataroth.** i.e. *crowns*, *S#5852h. ver. 1, 34-38. Jsh 13:17. *16:2, 7. Is 15:2-4. Je 48:22, 23. (1) A town of Gad, east of Jordan, Nu 32:3, 34, now *Attarus*, a ruin. (2) A town of Ephraim, Jsh 16:2. It may be the same as Ataroth-adar and Ataroth-addar, Jsh 18:13. (3) Ataroth (house of Joab, is found in the genealogy of Judah, 1 Ch 2:54. **Nimrah.** i.e. *leopardess*, *S#5247h. ver. 36, Beth-nimrah. Is 15:6, Nimrim. **Heshbon.** Nu 21:25, 26, 28. Jg 11:26. Ne 9:22. Is 15:4. 16:8, 9. Je 48:2, 34, 45. **Elealeh.** i.e. *the exalted God*, *S#500h. ver. 37. Is 15:4. 16:9. Je 48:34. **Shebam.** i.e. *fragrance; their hoar head*, *S#7643h. ver. 38, Shibmah. Jsh 13:19. Is 16:8, 9. Je 48:32, Sibmah. **Nebo.** i.e. *interpreter*, *S#5015h. ver. 38. Nu 33:47. Dt 32:49. 34:1. 1 Ch 5:8. Ezr 2:29. 10:43. Ne 7:33. Is 15:2. 46:1. Je 48:1, 22. (1) A city on the east side of

the river Jordan. It was rebuilt by the Gadites, Nu 32:3, 38, and was captured by the Moabites, Is 15:2; Je 48:1. (2) A town of Benjamin, Ne 7:33. (3) A mountain on the east side of the river Jordan, and part of the range of Abarim. It is in the land of Moab and "over against Jericho," and from it Moses beheld the land of Canaan, Dt 32:49. See Pisgah, Nu +21:20. (4) An Assyrian god, Is 46:1. **Beon.** i.e. *in the dwelling; indwelling,* *S#1194h. ver. 38, Baal-meon.

4. **the country.** Nu 21:24, 34. Dt 2:24-35. 1 Ch 5:18-22.

5. **if we have.** Ge 19:19. Ru 2:10. 1 S 20:3. 2 S 14:22. Est 5:2. Je 31:2. **bring us.** Dt 1:37. 3:25, 26. Jsh 7:7.

6. **shall ye sit here.** 2 S 11:11. 1 C 13:5. Ph 2:4.

7. **wherefore.** ver. 9. Nu 21:4. Dt 1:28. **discourage.** Heb. break. Ac 21:13.

8. **when I sent:** See on Nu 13:2-26. 14:2. Dt 1:22, 23. Jsh 14:6, 7.

9. **valley of Eschol.** Nu 13:23-33. 14:1-10. Dt 1:24-28.

10. **anger.** Nu 14:11, 21, 23, 29. Dt 1:34-40. Ps 95:11. Ezk 20:15. He 3:8-19.

11. **none.** Nu 26:64, 65. Dt 1:34-36. **from twenty.** Nu 14:28, 29. 26:2, 64, 65. Dt 1:35. 2:14, 15. **because.** Nu 14:24, 30. Jsh 14:8, 9. **wholly followed me.** Heb. fulfilled after me. ver. 12. Nu 14:24. Dt 1:36. Jsh +*14:8, 9.

12. **Kenezite.** i.e. *hunter,* *S#7074h. Ge 15:19. Jsh 14:6, 14. **wholly followed** Nu 14:24, 30. 26:65. Dt 1:36. Jsh +*14:8, 9.

13. **wander.** Nu 14:33-35. Dt 2:14. Ps 78:33. **until all.** Nu 26:64. Dt 2:15. 1 C 10:5. He 3:16-19.

14. **an increase.** Ge 5:3. 8:21. Ne 9:24-26. Jb 14:4. Ps 51:5. 78:57. Is 1:4. 57:4. Ezk 20:21. Mt 23:31-33. Lk 11:48. Ac 7:51, 52. Ep 2:3. **to augment.** Dt 1:34, 35. Ezr 9:13, 14. 10:10. Ne 13:18. Is 65:6, 7.

15. **if ye turn.** Le 26:14-18. Dt 28:15, etc. 30:17-19. Jsh 22:16-18. 2 Ch 7:19-22. *15:2. **he will yet.** Nu 14:30-35. ye shall. Je 38:23. Mt 18:7. Ro 14:15, 20, 21. 1 C 8:11, 12.

16. **and said.** Jg 8:1-3. Pr 15:1, 2. 25:15. **We will.** ver. 34-42. Ge 33:17.

17. **we ourselves.** ver. 29-32. Dt 3:18-20. Jsh 4:12, 13.

18. **not return.** Jsh 22:4, 5.

19. **we will.** Ge 13:10-12. 14:12. 2 K 10:32, 33. 15:29. 1 Ch 5:25, 26. Pr 20:21. **because.** ver. 33. Jsh 12:1-6. 13:8. **on this side.** ver. 32. Nu 34:15. Jsh 1:14, 15. 22:4, 9.

20. **Moses said.** Dt 3:18-20. Jsh 1:13-15. 4:12, 13. 22:2-4.

22. **land.** Dt 3:20. Jsh 10:30, 42. 11:23. 18:1. Ps 44:1-4. 78:55. **ye shall.** Jsh 22:4, 9. **be guiltless.** Jsh 2:19. 2 S 3:28. **this land.** Dt 3:12-18. Jsh 1:15. 13:8, 29-32. 22:9.

23. **if ye will.** Le 26:14, etc. Dt 28:15, etc. **be sure your sin.** If the persons concerned prevaricated, and so imposed on men, or if they afterwards refused to fulfill their engagement, God would most certainly detect and expose their wickedness, and inflict condign punishment upon them. Of all the ways, says Dr. South, to be taken for the prevention of that great plague of mankind, Sin, there is none so rational and efficacious as to confute and baffle those motives by which men are induced to embrace it; and among all

such motives, the heart of man seems to be chiefly overpowered and prevailed upon by two, *viz.* secrecy in committing sin and impunity with respect to its consequences. Accordingly, Moses, in this chapter, having to deal with a company of men suspected of a base and fraudulent design, though couched under a very fair pretence, as most such designs are, endeavors to quash it in its very conception, by secretly applying himself to encounter those secret motives and arguments, which he knew were the most likely to encourage them in it. And this he does very briefly, but effectually, by assuring them, that how covertly and artificially soever they might carry on their dark project, yet their sin would infallibly find them out. Though the subject and occasion of these words are indeed particular, yet the design of them is manifestly of an universal import, as reaching the case of all transgressors, in their first entrance on any sinful act or course. **will find.** T#733. Ge 4:7. +6:13 (T#566). +29:25. 44:16. Ex +22:20 (T#362). 1 S +3:13 (T#497). 1 K *13:1-32. 1 Ch +28:9 (T#555). 2 Ch 28:19. Jb 21:17-20. 27:13-17. Ps 1:4-6. *7:11-16. 9:15, 16. 34:+16 (T#303), 21. +37:9 (T#87). 55:23. 58:8n, +11 (T#630). 73:12, 18, 19. 90:8. 139:11. 140:11. Pr 3:33. 5:22. *13:5, 15, 21. 15:3. +16:18 (T#551). +21:7 (T#489). 26:27. 28:8, 18. *30:17. Ec 10:8. Is 3:11. 59:1, 2, 12. Je +*6:19. *17:11. +20:11 (T#513). 22:17-19. Ezk *14:10. *22:12-14. 28:15, 16. +39:23 (T#486). Zc +10:11 (T#381). Mt +15:14 (T#478). +16:27 (T#556). Ro 1:27. 2:9. √14:12. 1 C 4:5. +*6:9, 10. Ga +*6:7. Ep +5:5 (T#138). He 4:12, 13. Ja +1:20 (T#735). 5:3, 4. 2 P 2:5, 6.

24. **Build.** ver. 16, 34, etc. Jsh 1:13-15.

25. **spake.** ✗96D5. Heterosis of Person and Number B525: the singular for the plural. Here, "spake" is singular: *he spake,* and is put for the plural, *they spake.* As this figure is not directly observable in English translation, it is unmarked at the following passages where instances of this figure occur: 1 S 16:4. Est 9:23. Jb 12:7. Ps 73:7. Pr 14:1, 9. **Thy servants.** Jsh 1:13, 14.

27. **thy servants.** Jsh 4:12, 13. **armed.** ver. 17. 2 C 10:4, 5. Ep 6:10-18. 2 T 4:7, 8. **as my lord.** Nu 11:28. 12:11. 36:2.

28. **concerning them.** Jsh 1:13.

29. **If the children.** See on ver. 20-23.

30. **have possessions.** Jsh 11:23. 21:43-45. 22:19.

32. **possession.** Jsh 22:4.

33. **Moses.** See on ver. 1. Dt 3:12-17. 29:8. Jsh 12:1, 6. 13:8, etc. 22:4. **half the.** Nu 34:14. 1 Ch 5:18. 12:31. 26:32. **the kingdom of Sihon.** Nu 21:23-35. Dt 2:30-33. 3:1-8. Ps 135:10, 11. 136:18-21.

34. **Dibon.** See on ver. 3. Nu 21:30. 33:45, 46. **A-roer.** i.e. *ruins; destitute,* *S#6177h. Dt 2:36. 3:12. 4:48. Jsh 12:2. 13:9, 16, 25. Jg 11:33. 1 S 30:28. 2 S 24:5. 2 K 10:33. 1 Ch 5:8. Is *17:2. Je 48:19. (1) A city of the Gadites near Rabbah, Nu 32:34; Jsh 13:25. (2) A city of the Amorites, Dt 2:26; Je 48:19. (3) A town in the south of Judah, 1 S 30:28, 11 miles southeast of Beersheba. It is now called *Ararah.* (4) Aroer, in Is 17:2, must be a region near Damascus if it is a proper name.

35. **Atroth.** i.e. *crown,* *S#5855h. **Shophan.** *hidden; their bruising,* *S#5855h. **Jaazer.** ver. 1, 3, Jazer. **Jogbehah.** i.e. *elevated,* *S#3011h. Jg 8:11.

36. **Beth-nimrah.** See on ver. 3, Nimrah. Probably the same as *Nimrim* in Je 48:34. **Bethharan.** i.e. *house*

of their mount; house of the joyful shouter, *S#1028h.

37. **Heshbon.** See on ver. 3. Nu 21:27. Is 15:4.
Kirjathaim. i.e. *double city,* *S#7156h. Jsh 13:19.
1 Ch 6:76. Je 48:1, 23. Ezk 25:9.

38. **Nebo.** Is 46:1. **Baal-meon.** i.e. *lord of the dwelling,* *S#1186h. Nu ❶22:41. 1 Ch 5:8. Ezk 25:9. **Shibmah.** i.e. *spice; why hoary?* *S#7643h. Jsh 13:19. Is 16:8, 9. Je 48:32. **gave other names unto the cities.** Heb. they called by names the names of the cities. ver. 3. Ge 26:18. Ex 23:13. Jsh 23:7. Ps 16:4. Is 46:1.

39. **Machir.** Nu 26:29. Ge 50:23. Jsh 17:1.

40. **gave Gilead.** Dt 3:13-15. Jsh 13:29-31. 17:1. 1 Ch 5:23-26.

41. **Jair.** i.e. *whom Jehovah enlightens; illuminated,* *S#2971h. Dt 3:14, 14. Jsh 13:30. Jg 10:3, 4, 5. 1 K 4:13. 1 Ch 2:22, 23. Est 2:5. ✓66, Ge +9:3. (1) A prominent warrior under Moses; was a descendant of the most powerful family of Judah and Manasseh. He conquered all the country of Argob east of Jordan; also villages in Gilead which he named Havoth-jair, Nu 32:41; Dt 3:14; 1 Ch 2:21-23. (2) One of the judges of Israel, Jg 10:3-5. He judged Israel 22 years. (3) A Jew of the tribe of Benjamin, whose son Mordecai was cousin to Esther, Est 2:5. (4) Father of Elhanan, 1 Ch 20:5, called Jaare-oregim in 2 S 21:19. **Havoth-jair.** i.e. *villages of Jair,* *S#2334h. Jg 10:3, 4. 1 K 4:13.

42. **Nobah.** i.e. *a barking,* *S#5025h. Jg 8:11. (1) An Israelite, the conqueror of Kenath, a city of the Amorites, Nu 32:42. (2) The name given by Nobah to Kenath and its adjacent villages when he conquered that place, Nu 32:42; Jg 8:11. **Kenath.** i.e. *possession,* *S#7079h. 1 Ch 2:23. **villages.** Nu +21:25mg.

NUMBERS 33

A record of forty-two journeys of Israel, 1-49. A charge to destroy the Canaanites and their idols, 50-56.

1. **with their armies.** Ex 12:37, 51. 13:18. **under the hand.** Jsh 24:5. 1 S 12:8. Ps 77:20. Mi 6:4.

2. **Moses wrote.** Ex +√24:4. **journeys.** Nu 9:17-23. 10:6, 13. Dt 1:2. 8:2. 10:11.

3. **they departed.** Ge 47:11. Ex 1:11. 12:37. **in the first.** Ex 12:2. 13:4. **passover.** Le +*23:5. **with an high.** Ex 14:8. Ps 105:38. Is 52:12. Mi 2:13.

4. **Egyptians.** ✓16, Ge +1:27. **buried.** Ex 12:29, 30. Ps 105:36. **upon their gods.** Ex 12:12. 18:11. Is 19:1. Zp 2:11. Re 12:7-9.

5. **removed.** Ex 12:37. **Rameses.** ver. 3. Ex 12:37.

6. **departed.** Ex 13:20, 21. **Succoth.** Ex 12:37. **Etham.** Ex 13:20.

7. **they removed.** ver. 8. Ex 14:2, 9. **Baal-Zephon.** Ex 14:2n, 9.

8. **departed.** Ex 14:21, 22, etc. 15:22-26. **passed.** Ex 15:10. Dt 11:4. **three days.** Nu 10:33. Ex 15:22. Jon 3:3. **Etham.** Called *Shur* in Exodus; but Dr. Shaw says that Shur is a particular district of the wilderness of *Etham.* **Marah.** Ex 15:22, 23.

9. **they removed.** Ex 15:27.

10. **Elim.** Ex 16:1. 17:1. **Red sea.** Nu 21:4. Ex 10:19. Dt 1:40. *Lit. Sea of Suph;* so called after the name of some Egyptian king; there is really no foundation whatever for the idea that the name was derived from the abundance of *weeds* (see Ex 2:3, 5) which grew in it; it has no more weeds than any other inland sea. *Red*

is, of course, a translation of *Edom,* whose descendants were the leading tribe or nation on its Arabian side, from whom it derived the appellation, *Sea of Edom* (Young, *Concise Critical Comments* at Ex 10:19).

11. **wilderness of Sin.** Ex 17:1.

12. **Dophkah.** i.e. *beating or knocking,* *S#1850h.

13. **Allush.** i.e. *mingling together,* *S#442h.

14. **Rephidim.** Ex 17:1-8, 13. 19:2.

15. **they departed.** Ex 16:1. 19:1, 2.

16. **they removed.** Nu 10:11-13, 33. Dt 1:6. **Kibroth-hattaavah.** Heb. *qeber,* Ge +23:4. *That is,* the graves of lust. Nu 11:4, 31-34.

17. **Kibroth.** Heb. *qeber,* Ge +23:4. **Hazeroth.** Nu 11:35.

18. **they departed.** Nu 12:16. **Rithmah.** i.e. *binding; broom copse,* *S#7575h. Rithmah was a place in the wilderness of Paran, near Kadesh Barnea; probably so called from the great number of juniper trees, as the name signifies, growing in that district. Not mentioned elsewhere, some suppose it the same as Kadesh-Barnea. Nu 2:16. 13:1, 26. 32:8. Dt 2:19. Jsh 14:7.

19. **Rimmon-parez.** lit. *pomegranate of the breach,* *S#7428h, not mentioned elsewhere. Probably the same as **Rimmon,** a city of Judah and Simeon, Jsh 15:32. 19:7.

20. **Libnah.** i.e. *whiteness,* *S#3841h. ver. 21. Jsh 10:29, 29, 31, 32, 32. 12:15. 15:42. 21:13. 2 K 8:22. 19:8. 23:31. 24:18. 1 Ch 6:57. 2 Ch 21:10. Is 37:8. Je 52:1. (1) The sixteenth encampment of the Israelites after they left Egypt, Nu 33:20, 21. (2) A city of Judah. It was nearly south of Jerusalem, and had been a chief royal city of the Canaanites. It became a Levitical city, Jsh 10:29; 15:42; 2 K 19:8.

21. **Libnah.** Dt 1:1, Laban. **Rissah.** lit. *a drop,* not mentioned elsewhere.

22. **Kehelathah.** lit. *an assembly.* Not mentioned elsewhere.

23. **Shapher.** i.e. *beauty; pleasantness,* *S#8234h. ver. 24.

24. **Shapher.** lit. *beauty,* not mentioned elsewhere. **Haradah.** lit. *fear and trembling,* *S#2732h, not mentioned elsewhere. ver. 25.

25. **Makheloth.** lit. *assemblies,* *S#4722h, not mentioned elsewhere. ver. 26.

26. **Tahath.** lit. *place; station; depression,* only here. 1 Ch 6:24, 37. 7:20, 20. (1) One of the camping stations in the wilderness, Nu 33:26, 27. (2) A descendant of Kohath, the son of Levi, 1 Ch 6:24, 37. (3, 4) Two Ephraimites, 1 Ch 7:20.

27. **Tarah.** lit. *delay,* *S#8646h, only here. ver. 28.

28. **Mithcah.** lit. *sweetness,* *S#4989h, only here. ver. 29.

29. **Hashmonah.** lit. *fatness,* *S#2832h, only here. ver. 30.

30. **Moseroth.** lit. *bonds,* *S#4149h. ver. 31. Dt 10:6, Mosera.

31. **Bene-Jaakan.** lit. *sons of Jaakan,* *S#1142h. ver. 32. In Dt 10:6 more fully "Beeroth (i.e. wells) of the sons of Jaakan." Ge 36:27. Dt 10:6. 1 Ch 1:42, 43.

32. **Hor-hagid-gad.** i.e. *hole of the cleft,* *S#2735h. ver. 33. Dt 10:7, Gudgodah.

33. **Jotbathah.** i.e. *goodness,* *S#3193h. ver. 34. Mr. Taylor, who imagines the Israelites to be now in

the track of the Mecca pilgrims, supposes Jotbathah, which is described as "a land of brooks of water," to be *Callah Nahar*, a torrent, said to be good water by Dr. Shaw. Dt 10:7, Jotbath.

34. **Ebronah**. lit. *a passage, gateway*, ✱S#5684h, only here. ver. 35.

35. **Ezion-gaber**. i.e. *the backbone of man*, ✱S#6100h. Nu 14:25. Dt 2:8. 1 K 9:26. 22:48, Ezion-geber. 2 Ch 8:17. 20:36.

36. **wilderness of Zin**. Nu 13:21. 20:1. 27:14. 34:3. Dt 32:51.

37. **Kadesh**. Nu 20:22, 23. 21:4.

38. **Aaron**. Nu 20:24-28. Dt 10:6. 32:50.

40. **king Arad**. See on Nu 21:1-3, etc. **Canaanite**. Ge +10:18.

41. **departed**. Nu 21:4. **Zalmonah**. i.e. *shady; imagery*, ✱S#6758h. ver. 42.

42. **Punon**. lit. *distraction, pining away*, ✱S#6325h. ver. 43.

43. **pitched in Oboth**. lit. *bottles*, see Nu 21:10, 11.

44. **Ije-abarim**. or, heaps of Abarim. i.e. *ruins of further regions*, ✱S#5863h. Nu 21:11.

45. **Iim**. lit. *heaps, ruins*, ✱S#5864h. Jsh 15:29. **Dibon-gad**. lit. *pain or grief of Gad*, ✱S#1769h. ver. 46. Nu 21:30. 32:34.

46. **Dibon-gad**. Nu 32:34. Is 15:2. Je 48:18. **Almon-diblathaim**. lit. *a concealment of branches of figs*, ✱S#5963h, only here. ver. 47. Je 48:22, Beth-diblathaim. Ezk 6:14, Diblath.

47. **the mountains of Abarim**. Nu 21:20. Dt 32:49-52. 34:1. lit. *places beyond*, or *passages*, Nu 27:12. **Nebo**. lit. *prophecy*, Nu 32:3. 1 Ch 5:8. Is 15:2. Je 48:1, 22.

48. **in the plains**. See on Nu 22:1. 31:12. 35:1.

49. **Beth-jesimoth**. lit. *house of the deserts*, ✱S#1020h. Jsh 12:3. 13:20. Ezk 25:9. **Abel-shittim**. or, the plains of Shittim. lit. *meadow or mount of shittim wood; mourning of the acacias*, ✱S#63h. Nu 25:1-9. Ex 25:5, 10, 23. Jsh 2:1. Mi 6:5.

50. **in the plains**. ver. 48, 49.

51. **When**. Dt 7:1. 9:1. Jsh 3:17.

52. **drive out**. Ex 23:24, 31-33. 34:12-17. Dt 7:2-5, 25, *26. 12:2, 3, 30, 31. 20:16-18. Jsh 11:11, 12. 23:7. Jg 2:2. **pictures**. or, figured stones. Le 26:1. Ezk 8:12. **destroy all**. Ex 34:13. Dt 7:5, 25. **molten images**. Ex 32:4, 8. **pluck down**. or, lay waste. Dt 26:30.

53. **have given**. Ex 23:27-31. Dt 32:8. Ps 24:1, 2. 115:16. Je 27:5, 6. Da 4:17, 25, 32. Mt 20:15.

54. **ye shall divide**. See on Nu 26:53-56. 34:13. **give the more inheritance**. Heb. multiply his inheritance. Nu 26:54. 35:8. **give the less inheritance**. Heb. diminish his inheritance. Nu 26:54. 35:8. Ex 30:15. **in the place**. Jsh 15:1-12. 16:1, etc. 17:1, etc. 18:11, etc. 19:1-48. **lot falleth**. Ge ◐24:44n.

55. **shall be pricks**. Ex 23:33. Dt 7:4, 16. Jsh 23:12, 13. Jg 1:21-36. 2:3. Ps 106:34-36. Ezk 28:24.

56. **do unto you**. Le 18:28. 20:23. Dt 28:63. 29:28. Jsh 23:15, 16. 2 Ch 36:17-20. Ezk 12:11. 33:24-29. Zc 1:6. Lk 21:23, 24.

NUMBERS 34

The boundaries of Canaan, 1-15. The names of the men who were chosen to divide the land, 16-29.

2. **is the land**. Nu 33:51, 53. Ge 12:6, 7. 13:15-17.

15:16-21. *17:8. Dt 1:7, 8. Ps 78:55. 105:11. Ezk 47:14. Ac 17:26. **an inheritance**. Ps 16:5, 6. Je 3:19. Ac 26:18. Ep 1:14, 18. 1 P 1:3, 4.

3. **south quarter**. Ex 23:31. Jsh 15:1-12. Ezk 47:13, 19, etc. **salt sea eastward**. Ge 14:3. Jsh 3:16. 15:2. Ezk 47:8, 18.

4. **Akrabbim**. i.e. *scorpions*, ✱S#6137h; ✱S#4610h. Jsh 15:3. Jg 1:36. **Zin**. ver. 3. Nu 13:21n. 20:1. 33:36, 37. **Kadesh-barnea**. i.e. *desert of wandering*, ✱S#6947h. Nu ◐13:26. 32:8. Dt 1:2, 19. 2:14. 9:23. Jsh 10:41. 14:6, 7. 15:3. **Hazar-addar**. i.e. *village of springs*, ✱S#2692h. Jsh 15:3, 4. **Azmon**. i.e. *strong; bone*, ✱S#6111h. ver. 5. Jsh 15:4.

5. **the river**. Ge 15:18. Jsh 15:4, 47. 1 K 8:65. Is 27:12. **the sea**. ver. 6, 7.

6. **the great sea**. Jsh 1:4. 9:1. 15:12, 47. 23:4. Ezk 47:10, 15, 20.

7. **north border**. ver. 3, 6, 9, 10. **mount Hor**. Nu 33:37.

8. **the entrance**. Nu 13:21. Jsh 13:5, 6. 2 S 8:9. 2 K 14:25. Je 39:5. Ezk 47:15-20. **Zedad**. i.e. *steep place*, ✱S#6657h. Ezk 47:15.

9. **Ziphron**. i.e. *sweet smell*, ✱S#2202h. **Hazar-enan**. Ezk 47:17.

10. **Shepham**. i.e. *high, sticking out; bareness*, ✱S#8221h. ver. 11.

11. **Riblah**. i.e. *fertility; fruitful*, ✱S#7247h. 2 K 23:33. 25:6, 20, 21. Je 39:5, 6. 52:9, 10, 26, 27. **Ain**. lit. *eye* or *fountain*, ✱S#5871h. Jsh 15:32. 19:7. 21:16. 1 Ch 4:32. (1) A place west of Riblah, in the northern part of Canaan, Nu 34:11. "Ain," meaning *a fountain*, is spelled "En" in compound words like En-rogel, in the English Bible. (2) A city in the tribe of Judah. It was subsequently assigned to Simeon, Jsh 15:32. This city was given to the priests, and is called Ashan in 1 Ch 6:59. Jn +3:23n. **reach unto**. Heb. smitten against. lit. *to wipe or blot out*, as in Ge 6:7. 7:4, 23, etc. **side**. Heb. shoulder. Ex 26:14, 15. 28:7, 12, etc. **sea of Chinnereth**. lit. *harps*. Dt 3:17. Jsh 11:2, Chinneroth. 13:27. 19:35. Ezk 47:18, *the east sea*. Mt 14:22, 34. Lk 5:1, Gennesaret. Jn 6:1, Sea of Tiberias.

12. **Jordan**. Jsh 3:14-16. **the salt sea**. ver. 3. Ge 13:10. 14:3. 19:24-26.

13. **This is the land**. ver. 1. Jsh 14:1, 2. **by lot**. Nu 26:56. Ge +24:44n.

14. **of Reuben**. Nu 32:23, 33. Dt 3:12-17. Jsh 13:8-12. 14:2, 3.

15. **on this side Jordan**. Nu 32:32.

17. **are the names**. It is worthy of remark, that Moses does not follow any order hitherto used in arranging the tribes, but places them exactly in the order in which they possessed the land, and according to their *fraternal* relationship. *Judah* is first, having the first lot, in the South (Jsh 15); and next him is *Simeon*, because his inheritance was "within the inheritance of the children of Judah" (Jsh 19:1). *Benjamin*, the third, had his portion between "Judah and the children of Joseph" (Jsh 18:11). *Dan* was the fourth, and his lot was westward of Benjamin (Jsh 19:40, 41). *Manasseh* and his brother *Ephraim* had their inheritances behind that of Benjamin (Jsh 16:7). Next these dwelt *Zebulun* and *Issachar* (Jsh 19:10-17); and then *Asher* and *Naphtali* (Jsh 19:24-32). **Eleazar**. Jsh 14:1. 19:51. **Joshua**. See on Nu 13:8, 16.

18. **one prince**. See on Nu 1:4-16.

19. **Caleb**. Nu 13:30. 14:6, 24, 30, 38. 26:65.

20. **tribe of the children of Simeon**. Nu 2:12. 10:19. 13:5. Ge 49:12. Dt 27:12. **Shemuel**. lit. *heard of God*, *S#8050h. 1 Ch 6:33. 7:2. See 1 S 1:20. (1) A chief of Simeon, Nu 34:20. (2) The prophet Samuel, 1 Ch 6:33. (3) One of the chieftains of Issachar, 1 Ch 7:2. **Ammihud**. Nu 1:10.

21. **the tribe of Benjamin**. Nu 2:22. 10:24. 13:9. Ge 49:27. Dt 27:12. **Elidad**. lit. *my God is beloved*, *S#449h, only here. **Chislon**. lit. *folly, confidence*, *S#3692h, only here.

22. **children of Dan**. Nu 2:25. 10:25. 13:12. Ge 49:16, 17. Dt 27:13. **Bukki**. lit. *mouth of Jehovah; my emptiness*, *S#1231h. 1 Ch 6:5, 5, 51. Ezr 7:4. (1) A chief of Dan appointed to divide the land west of Jordan, Nu 34:22. (2) A grandson of Eleazar, 1 Ch 6:5; Ezr 7:4. **Jogli**. lit. *exiled*, *S#3020h, only here.

23. **children of Manasseh**. Nu 2:20. 10:23. 13:11. 36:12. Dt 33:17. **Hanniel**. lit. *grace of God*, *S#2592h. 1 Ch 7:39. **Ephod**. lit. *a girdle*, *S#641h, not mentioned elsewhere.

24. **children of Ephraim**. Nu 2:18. 10:22. 13:8. Dt 33:17. **Kemuel**. lit. *helper; gathered of God*, *S#7055h. Ge 22:21. 1 Ch 27:17. (1) A son of Nahor, the brother of Abraham, Ge 22:21. (2) A prince of Ephraim, one of those who divided Canaan, Nu 34:24. (3) A Levite, the father of Hashabiah, 1 Ch 27:17. **Shiphtan**. lit. *judicial*, *S#8204h, only here.

25. **children of Zebulun**. Nu 13:10. Dt 27:13. **Elizaphan**. lit. *my God hath hidden*, Ex 6:22. Le 10:4. Nu 3:30. 1 Ch 15:8. 2 Ch 29:13. **Parnach**. lit. *delicate*, *S#6535h, only here.

26. **children of Issachar**. Nu 13:7. Dt 27:12. **Paltiel**. lit. *an escape of God, deliverance of God*, *S#6409h. 2 S 3:15. **Azzan**. lit. *strength*, *S#5821h, only here.

27. **children of Asher**. Nu 2:27. 10:26. 13:13. Ge *49:20. Dt 27:13. *33:24. Jb *29:6. **Ahihud**. lit. *my brother is honor, brother of majesty*, *S#282h, only here. **Shelomi**. lit. *my peaceful one*, *S#8015h, only here.

28. **children of Naphtali**. Nu 13:14. Dt 27:13. **Pedahel**. lit. *ransom of God, redeemed of God*, *S#6300h, only here. **Ammihud**. ver. 20.

29. **These are**. ver. 18. Jsh 19:51.

NUMBERS 35

Forty-eight cities with their suburbs to be given to the Levites, and the measure thereof, 1-5. Six of them are to be cities of refuge, 6-8. The laws of murder and manslaughter, 9-30. No satisfaction for murder, 31-34.

1. **the plains**. Nu 22:1. 26:63. 31:12. 33:50. 36:13. Dt 34:1, 8.

2. **the children of**. Le 25:32, 33. Jsh 14:3, 4. 21:2, etc. Ezk 45:1-8. 48:8, 22. 1 C 9:10-14.

3. **and the suburbs**. Jsh 21:11. 2 Ch 11:14. Ezk 45:2.

4. **suburbs**. Le 25:34. **thousand cubits**. i.e. nearly half a mile, or half a sabbath day's journey, according to Gill.

5. **two thousand cubits**. It is not easy to reconcile this verse with the preceding; it looks like an interpolation; some think the first thousand included in the 2000, others consider the whole suburb to have consisted of 3000 cubits. The explanation of Maimonides is the only one that is intelligible, and appears perfectly

satisfactory. "The suburbs," says he, "of the cities are expressed in the law to be 3000 cubits on every side, from the wall of the city and outwards. The first 1000 cubits are the suburbs; and the 2000, which they measured without the suburbs, were for fields and vineyards." Thus the city is innermost, surrounded by the suburbs, and the whole surrounded by fields and vineyards. **to them**. Le 25:32-34.

6. **six cities for refuge**. ver. 13, 14. Dt 4:41-43. Jsh 20:2-9. 21:3, 13, 21, 27, 32-36, 38. 1 Ch 6:57, 67. Ps 9:9. 62:7, 8. 142:4, 5. Pr 14:26. Is 4:6. Mt 11:28. He 6:8, =18, 19. **to them ye shall add**. Heb. above them ye shall give.

7. **forty and eight**. Jsh 21:3-42. 1 Ch 6:54-81.

8. **possession**. Ge 49:7. Ex 32:28, 29. Dt 33:8-11. Jsh 21:3. **from them**. Nu 26:54. 33:54. Ex 16:18. 2 C 8:13, 14. **he inheriteth**. Heb. they inherit.

10. **When ye**. Nu 34:2. Le 14:34. 25:2. Dt 12:9. 19:1, 2.

11. **ye shall appoint**. As the *goel*, or *kinsman*, had a right to avenge the death of his relation, by slaying the murderer wherever he found him, the appointment of these cities was a humane institution for the protection of the involuntary homicide; for they were designed only for the protection of such. See on ver. 6. Jsh 20:2. **refuge**. Pr 14:26. He=6:18. **any person**. Heb. *nephesh*, Jsh +10:28. ver. 15, 30. **unawares**. Heb. by error. ver. 22, 23. Ex 21:13. Dt 4:42. 19:4, 5.

12. **from the avenger**. ver. 19, 25-27. Dt 19:6. Jsh 20:3-6, 9. 2 S 14:7. **until he stand**. ver. 24. Dt 19:11, 12. Jsh 20:4-6.

13. **six cities**. ver. 6.

14. **three cities**. Dt 4:41-43. 19:2, 8-10. Jsh 20:2, 7-9.

15. **both for**. Nu +*15:16. Ex 12:49. Le 24:22. Ro 3:29. Ga *3:28. **any person**. Heb. *nephesh*, Jsh +10:28. ver. 11, 30.

16. **if he smite**. ver. 22-24. Dt 19:11-13. **the murderer**. ver. 30-33. Ge 9:5, 6. Ex 21:12-14. Le 24:17. 1 K 2:29-34. **surely**. ∫147B, Ge +2:16.

17. **throwing a stone**. Heb. a stone of the hand. Ex 21:18. **shall surely**. ∫147B, Ge +2:16. Le 24:17.

18. **surely**. ∫147B, Ge +2:16.

19. **revenger of blood**. 12:21, 24, 27. Dt 19:6, 11, 12. Jsh 20:3, 5.

20. **if he thrust**. Ge 4:5, 8. 2 S 3:27. 13:22, 28, 29. 20:10. 1 K 2:5, 6, 31-33. Pr 26:24. 28:17. Lk 4:29. **by laying**. Ex 21:14. Dt 19:11. 1 S 18:10, 11, 25. 19:9-12. 20:1. 23:7-9. 24:11. Ps 10:7-10. 11:2. 35:7, 8. 57:4-6. Pr 1:18, 19. Mk 6:19, 24-26. Ac 20:3. 23:21.

21. **in enmity**. Ge 4:8. 1 J 3:12, 15. Ju 11. Re 22:15. **surely**. ∫147B, Ge +2:16.

22. **without enmity**. ver. 11. Ex 21:13. Dt 19:4, 5. Jsh 20:3, 5.

24. **the congregation**. See on ver. 12. Jsh 20:6.

25. **shall deliver**. Jn 8:36. Ro 8:1. Col 1:21, 22. **abide in it**. ver. 28. Jsh 20:6. Ro 3:24-26. Ep 2:16-18. He 4:14-16. 7:25-28. 9:12-15. 10:19-22. **anointed**. Ex 29:7. Le 4:3. 8:12. 21:10.

26. **But if**. After the manslayer had been received into the city of refuge, the avenger of blood could only act as prosecutor; and the magistrates, in the presence of the people, were appointed to decide on the cause according to the rules here laid down. Probably the accused person was tried at or near the place where the deceased had been slain, and where evidence could

most easily be brought: and in case he was acquitted by the decision of the judges, and with the approbation of the people, he was conveyed back to the city of refuge, where he was protected as a kind of prisoner at large, till the death of the high priest; when the public loss, and the grief occasioned by it, might be supposed to swallow up all personal regrets and resentments: and then he was permitted to return to his house and estate. But if, in the mean while, he ventured to leave the city, and the avenger met him and slew him, he was supposed to merit his doom by thus neglecting the appointment of God for his preservation, and the avenger must not be punished. This shows that in other cases, if the avenger slew an innocent man on surmise, he was liable to the punishment of a murderer; but if, by the testimony of *two* credible witnesses, the man who had fled to the city of refuge was adjudged guilty, he must without fail be put to death. **come without.** 1 K 2:42-46.

27. **he shall not be guilty of blood.** Heb. no blood *shall be* to him. Ex 22:2. Dt 19:6, 10. Jn 8:36. Ro 8:1.

28. **he should.** Jn 15:4-6. Ac 11:23. 27:31. He 3:14. 6:4-8. 10:26-30, 39. **after the death.** He 7:22-24. 9:11, 12, 15-17.

29. **a statute.** See on Nu 27:1, 11.

30. **any person.** Heb. *nephesh,* Jsh +10:28. ver. 11, 15. **the mouth.** ♪121B, Dt +17:6. Dt 17:6, 7. 19:15. Mt 18:16. Jn 8:17, 18. 2 C 13:1. 1 T 5:19. He 10:28. Re 11:3. **any person.** Heb. *nephesh,* Jsh +10:28. ver. 11, 15.

31. **Moreover.** Ge 9:5, 6. Ex 21:14. Dt 19:11-13. 2 S 12:13. 1 K 2:28-34. Ps 51:14, 16. **satisfaction.** Ex 30:12. 1 S 12:3. **life.** Heb. *nephesh,* soul, Ge +44:30. **guilty of death.** Heb. faulty to die. Ezk *18:20. Mt 26:66. Mk 14:64. **surely.** ♪147B, Ge +2:16.

32. **no satisfaction.** Ac *4:12. Ga 2:21. 3:10-13, 22. He 6:17-20. Re 5:9. The region east of Jordan was nearly as long as that on the west, and therefore three cities were appointed in each division. One or other of these cities would be within half a day's journey of every part of the land; and as it would rarely happen that the avenger of blood would be on the spot, and none had a right to assault or detain the manslayer, at least if no malicious intention was manifest, the unhappy men would, therefore, get the start of their adversaries, and very few of them be overtaken before they gained the place of refuge. But then they must forsake their families, employments, most important interests, and dearest comforts; and they must neither loiter nor yield to weariness, nor regard difficulties, nor slacken their pace, till they had got safe within the walls of the city. The Jewish writers inform us, that, to afford every facility to those who thus fled for their life, the road to these cities was always preserved in good repair; and way-posts, upon which was inscribed "refuge," were placed wherever needful, that they might not so much as hesitate for a moment. Ezk 21:19mg.

33. **it defileth.** Le 18:25. Dt 21:1-8, 23. 2 K 23:26. 24:4. Ps *106:38. Is 26:21. Ezk 22:24-27. Ho 4:2, 3.

Mi 4:11. Mt 23:31-35. Lk 11:50, 51. **the land cannot be cleansed.** Heb. there can be no expiation for the land. Dt *32:43. Is +*27:9. Da +√9:24n. Jl √3:21. Zc √13:1. **but by.** Ge 4:9-11. *9:6. Jb 16:18. He 12:22, 24.

34. **Defile not.** Nu 5:3. Le 18:25. 20:24-36. Dt *21:23. Ps 78:58. Je 2:7. **I dwell.** Ps 135:21. Is 57:15. Ho 9:3. 2 C 6:16, 17. Re 21:3, 27. **dwell among.** Nu 5:3. Ex 25:8. 29:45, 46. 1 K 6:13. Ps 132:14. 135:21. Is 8:12.

NUMBERS 36

A difficulty shown by the Manassites respecting daughters inheriting, 1-5. Such must marry in their own tribe, 6-9. Zelophehad's daughters are married to the sons of their father's brother, 10-13.

1. **Gilead.** Nu 26:29-33. 27:1, 7. Jsh 17:2, 3. 1 Ch 7:14-16.

2. **The Lord commanded.** To one division of the tribe of Manasseh, a portion had been assigned eastward of Jordan; but Zelophehad was of that division to which an inheritance was afterwards allotted west of Jordan; yet, expecting the promised land, the elders of the Manassites now propose a difficulty, upon the adjudged case of Zelophehad's daughters (Nu 27:1-11). If the females should inherit, in defect of male issue, and should intermarry with other tribes, they would diminish the interest and weaken the influence of their own tribes, and give occasion to future confusion, and perhaps contention. The Manassites therefore referred the case to Moses; and he, by the authority of God, annexed a clause, which would effectually keep the tribes and inheritances distinct, as long as it was observed. Heiresses were not allowed to marry out of their own tribe, though within those bounds they might consult their own inclinations. Nu 26:55, 56. 27:1-7. 33:54. Jsh 13:6. 14:1, 2. 17:3. **to give.** Nu 27:1, 7. Jsh 17:3-6. Jb 42:15.

3. **whereunto they are received.** Heb. unto whom they shall be. **the lot of.** Nu 26:55. 33:54. Ge +24:44n.

4. **the jubilee.** Le 25:10-18, 23. Is 61:2. Lk 4:18, 19.

5. **hath said well.** Nu 27:7. Dt 5:28.

6. **marry.** Heb. be wives. ver. 3, 8, 11, 12. Nu +12:1. **to whom.** 1 C 7:39. **only to the family.** ver. 12. Ge 24:3, *4, 57, 58. 2 C 6:14.

7. **for every one.** That is, *he shall not endeavor to obtain any part of the inheritance of another tribe by marrying an heiress.* **keep himself.** Heb. cleave. ver. 9. 1 K 21:3.

8. **every daughter.** 1 Ch 23:22.

9. **his own.** 1 K 21:3.

10. **as the Lord.** Ex 39:42, 43. Le 24:23. 2 Ch 30:12. Mt 28:20.

11. **Mahlah.** Nu 27:1.

12. **into the families.** Heb. to some that were of the families. 1 Ch 23:22.

13. **the commandments.** Le 7:37, 38. 11:46. 13:59. 14:54-57. 15:32, 33. 27:34. Ps 103:7. **in the plains of Moab.** Nu 26:3. 33:50. 35:1.

DEUTERONOMY

DEUTERONOMY 1

Moses, toward the end of the fortieth year of Israel's continuance in the wilderness, addresses the people, 1-5. He relates how the Lord directed them to leave Horeb, 6-8; and appointed him assistants in the government, 9-18; of sending the spies to search the land, 19-33; of his anger for their incredulity, 34-40; and disobedience, 41-46.

1. **on this.** Nu 32:5, 19, 32. 34:15. Jsh 9:1, 10. 22:4, 7. **the plain.** Heb. the Arabah. Dt 2:8mg. 4:49mg. +11:30mg. **Red sea.** *or,* Zuph. Or rather, Suph. This could not have been the Red sea, not only because the word *yam, sea,* is not joined with it as usual, but because they were now east of Jordan, and farther from the Red sea than ever. It seems to be the same which is called *Suphah* in Nu 21:14; which must necessarily signify some place in or adjoining to the plains of Moab, and not far from the Jordan and Arnon. **Paran.** Dt +*33:2. Ge 21:21. Nu 10:12. 12:16. 13:3, 26. 1 S 25:1. Hab +*3:3. **Tophel.** i.e. *quagmire,* *S#8603h. **Hazeroth.** Nu 11:35. 33:17, 18. **Dizahab.** i.e. *sufficiency of gold,* *S#1774h.

2. **eleven days'.** Nu ❶14:25, 33, 34. **by the way.** ver. 44. Dt 2:4, 8. Nu 20:17-21. **Seir.** ♪146, Ge +10:10. **unto.** Nu 2:14. 9:23. Nu 13:26. 32:8. Jsh 14:6.

3. **in the fortieth.** Nu 20:1. 33:38. **Moses.** Lk *16:31. 24:27. Jn 1:17, 45. *5:39, 45. 9:28, 29.

4. **he had slain.** Dt 2:26-37. 3:1-11. Nu 21:21-35. Jsh 12:2-6. 13:10-12. Ne 9:22. Ps 135:11. 136:19, 20. **Astaroth.** i.e. *accessions,* S#6252h.

5. **to declare.** Dt 4:8. 17:18, 19. 31:9, 11. 32:46.

6. **in Horeb.** Dt 5:2. Ex 3:1. 17:6. 1 K 19:8. **Ye have.** Ex 19:1, 2. Nu 10:11-13.

7. **the mount.** Nu *15:16-21. Ex 23:31. Nu 34:3-12. Jsh 24:15. Am 2:9. **Amorites.** Ge +10:16. **all the places.** Heb. all his neighbors. Dt 12:5. **in the plain.** Dt 11:11. Jsh 10:40. 11:16, 17. Zc +*7:7. **Canaanites.** Ge +10:18. **Lebanon.** i.e. *very white,* *S#3844h. Dt 3:25. 11:24. Jsh 1:4. 9:1. 11:17. 12:7. 13:5, 6. Jg 3:3. 9:15. 1 K 4:33. 5:6, 9, 14. 7:2. 9:19. 10:17, 21. 2 K 14:9, 9. 19:23. 2 Ch 2:8, 8, 16. 8:6. 9:16, 20. 25:18, 18, 18. Ezr 3:7. Ps 29:5, 6. 72:16. 92:12. 104:16. SS 3:9. 4:8, 8, 11, 15. 5:15. 7:4. Is 2:13. 10:34. 14:8. 29:17. 33:9. 35:2. 37:24. 40:16. 60:13. Je 18:14. 22:6, 20, 23. Ezk 17:3. 27:5. 31:3, 15, 16. Ho 14:5, 6, 7. Na 1:4. Hab 2:17. Zc 10:10. 11:1. **the great river.** Dt 11:24. Jsh 1:4. 2 S 8:3. 1 Ch 5:9. 18:3.

8. **set.** Heb. given. **which.** Ge 12:7. 13:14, 15. 15:16, 18. 17:7, 8. 22:16-18. 26:3, 4. 28:13, 14.

9. **I am not.** Ex 18:18. Nu 11:11-14, 17.

10. **your God.** Dt 10:22. 28:62. Ge 15:5. 22:17. 26:4. 28:14. Ex 12:37. 32:13. Nu 1:46. 1 Ch 27:23. Ne 9:23. **ye are this day.** This was the promise made by God to Abraham (Ge 15:5, 6), which Moses considers now as amply fulfilled. Many suppose this expression to be hyperbolical; and others, no friends to revelation, think it a vain, empty boast, because the stars, in their apprehension, amount to innumerable millions. But, as this refers to the number of stars which appear to the *naked eye,* which only amount to about 3010 in

both hemispheres, the number of the Israelites far exceeded this; for independently of women and children, at the last census, they amounted to more than 600,000. **as the stars.** ♪138B, Ge +13:16.

11. **make you.** 2 S 24:3. 1 Ch 21:3. Ps 115:14. **and bless you.** Dt 33:1, 29. Ge 15:5. 22:17. 26:4. 49:25. Ex 32:13. Nu 6:27. 22:12.

12. **bear your cumbrance.** ver. 9. Ex 18:13-16. Nu 11:11-15. 1 K 3:7-9. Ps 89:19. 2 C 2:16. 3:5. **wise men.** 1 K 3:7-9. **rulers.** Ex *18:17, 18, 21. Nu 11:16, 17. Ac 6:1-4.

13. **Take.** Heb. Give. Ex 18:21. Nu 11:16, 17. Ac 1:21-23. 6:2-6.

15. **I took.** Dt 16:18. Ex 18:25, 26. **made.** Heb. gave. Ep 4:11. **captains over thousands.** Nu 31:14. 1 S 8:12. 17:18. 22:7.

16. **charged.** Dt 27:11. 31:14. Nu 27:19. 1 Th 2:11. 1 T 5:21. 6:17. **Hear.** Dt 16:18, 19. Ex 23:2, 3, 7, 8. Le 19:15. 2 S 23:3. 2 Ch 19:6-10. Ps 58:1. Jn 7:24. **the stranger.** Dt 10:18, 19. 24:14. +26:11. Ge +23:4 (*S#1616h). Ex 12:48. 22:21. 23:9. Le 24:22. Jsh +20:9. Mt +25:35.

17. **shall not.** Dt 10:17. 16:19. Le 19:15. 1 S 16:7. 2 S 14:14. 2 Ch 19:6. Ps 82:1. Pr 24:23. Ec 5:8. Lk 20:21. Jn 7:24. Ac 10:34, 35. Ro 2:11. Ep 6:9. Col 3:25. Ja 2:1, 3, 9. 1 P 1:17. **respect persons.** Heb. acknowledge faces. ♪121C2A1, Jb +19:25. That is, let not the bold, daring countenances of the rich or mighty induce you to give an unrighteous decision; and let not the abject look of the poor man induce you either to favor him in an unrighteous cause, or to give judgment against him at the demand of the oppressor. Dt 10:17. Jb 34:19. Ml 2:9mg. **ye shall hear.** Ex ❶18:22, 26. 23:3, 6, 7. 1 S 12:3, 4. Jb 22:6-9. 29:11-17. 31:13-16. Ps 82:3, 4. Pr 22:22, 23. Je 5:28, 29. Am 5:11, 12. Mi 2:1-3. 3:1-4. 7:3, 4. Ja 2:2-4, 6. **ye shall not.** 1 K 21:8-14. Jb 31:34. Pr 29:25. Je 1:17. Mt 22:16. Mk 12:14. 1 Th 2:4. **the judgment.** 2 Ch 19:6. **the cause.** Dt 17:8-10. Ex 18:18, 22, 26.

18. **I commanded.** Dt 4:5, 40. 12:28, 32. Mt 28:20. Ac 20:20, 27.

19. **through.** Dt 8:15. 32:10. Nu 10:12. Je 2:6. **Amorites.** Ge +10:16. **we came.** See on ver. 2. Nu 13:26.

20. **the mountain.** See on ver. 7, 8.

21. **fear not.** Dt 20:1. Nu 13:30. 14:8, 9. Jsh 1:9. Ps 27:1-3. 46:1, 7, 11. Is 41:10. 43:1, 2. Lk 12:32. He 13:6.

22. **We will send.** The people proposed this measure through unbelief; Moses, mistaking their motive, approved of it; and God, being justly displeased, permitted them to follow their own counsel, which proved injurious to them only through their sin and folly. See on Nu 13:1-20.

23. **I took.** Nu 13:3, etc. **twelve.** Mk=3:13, 14.

24. **they turned.** See on Nu 13:21-27. Jsh 2:1, 2.

26. **ye would not.** Nu 14:1-4. Ps 106:24, 25. Is 63:10. Ac 7:51. **rebelled.** ver. 43. Jsh 1:18. Ps 107:11. **commandment.** ♪121BA, Ge +45:21.

27. **the Lord hated us.** Dt 9:28. Ex 16:3, 8. Nu 14:3. 21:5. Mt 25:24. Lk 19:21.

28. **discouraged.** Heb. melted. Dt 20:8mg. Ex

15:15. Jsh 2:9, 11, 24mg. 14:8. Is 13:7. Ezk 21:7. **The people.** Dt 9:1, 2. Nu 13:28-33. **walled.** ℐ102, Ge +2:24. That is, with very high walls, which could not be easily scaled. **we have seen.** Dt 9:2. Jsh 11:22. 15:14. Jg 1:10, 20. 2 S 21:16-22. **Anakims.** i.e. *descendants of Anak,* ✱S#6062h. Dt 1:10, 11, 21. 9:2. Jsh 11:21, 22. 14:12, 15.

29. **Dread not.** See on ver. 21.

30. **he shall.** Dt 20:1-4. Ex 14:14, 25. Jsh 10:42. 1 S 17:45, 46. 2 Ch 14:11, 12. 32:8. Ne 4:20. Ps 46:11. Is 8:9, 10. Ro 8:31, 37. **according.** Ex 7-15. Ps 78:11-13, 43-51. 105:27-36.

31. **in the wilderness.** Ex 16. 17. Ne 9:12-23. Ps 78:14-28. 105:39-41. **bare thee.** Dt 32:11, 12. Ex 19:4. Nu 11:11, 12, 14. Is 40:11. 46:3, 4. 63:9. Ho 11:3, 4. Ac 13:18mg. He 12:5-7. **all the way.** Mt=28:20.

32. **did not believe.** 2 Ch +*20:20. Ps 78:22. 106:24. Is 7:9. He 3:12, 18, 19. Ju 5.

33. **Who went.** Ex 13:21. Nu 10:33. Ps 77:20. Ezk 20:6. **in fire.** Ex 13:21, 22. 14:19, 20, 24. 40:34-38. Nu 9:15-22. 10:11, 12. 14:14. Ne 9:12. Ps 78:14. 105:39. Is 4:5, 6. Zc 2:5.

34. **and sware.** Dt 2:14, 15. Nu 14:22-30. 32:8-13. Ps 95:11. Ezk 20:15. He 3:8-11.

35. **Surely.** Nu 14:22, 23, 29. Ps 95:11.

36. **Caleb.** Nu 13:6, 30. 26:65. 32:12. 34:19. Jsh 14:6-14. Jg 1:12-15. **wholly followed.** Heb. fulfilled to *go* after. Nu 14:24. 32:11. Jsh 14:9.

37. **the Lord.** Dt 3:23-26. 4:21. 34:4. Nu 20:12. 27:13, 14. Ps 106:32, 33.

38. **Joshua.** See on Nu 13:8, 16. 14:30, 38. 26:65. **which standeth.** Ex 17:9-14. 24:13. 33:11. 1 S 16:22. Pr 22:29. **encourage him.** Dt 3:28. 31:7, 8, 14, 23. Nu 27:18-23. Jsh 1:1, 6-9.

39. **your little.** Nu 14:3, 31. **which in.** Is 7:15, 16. Jon 4:11. Ro 9:11. Ep 2:3.

40. **turn you.** See on Nu 14:25.

41. **We have sinned.** See on Nu 14:39, 40, etc. 22:34. Pr 19:3.

42. **Go not up.** Ex 33:15, 16. Nu 14:41, 42. **for I am not.** Le 26:17. Jsh 7:8-13. 1 S 4:2, 10. Is 30:17. 59:1, 2. Ho 9:12. **among you.** Dt +*23:14.

43. **but rebelled against.** T#1795. 1 S 8:18. 28:4-6. Pr *1:24-28. Is +*63:10. Ac 7:51. Ro 8:7, 8. **commandment.** ℐ121BA, Ge +45:21. **went presumptuously up.** Heb. ye were presumptuous and went up. Nu 14:44.

44. **Amorites.** Ge +10:16. **chased you.** Dt 28:25. 32:30. Ps 118:12. Is 7:18. **Seir.** ℐ146, Ge +10:10. **unto Hormah.** Nu 14:45. 21:3.

45. **ye returned.** Ps 78:34. He 12:17. **not hearken.** Pr 1:24-31. Zc 7:11, 13.

46. **abode in Kadesh.** Nu 14:25, 34. 20:1, 22. Jg 11:16, 17. Ps 29:8.

DEUTERONOMY 2

Moses reminds the people of the command given them not to meddle with Edom, 1-8; Moab, 9-15; or Ammon, 16-19; he introduces some fragments of very ancient history, and touches on the continuance of Israel during forty years in the wilderness, till the rebellious generation was dead, 20-23. The grant and conquest of the kingdom of Sihon, 24-37.

1. **we turned.** Dt 1:40. Nu 14:25. **we compassed.** Dt 1:2. Nu 21:4. Jg 11:18.

3. **long enough.** ver. 7, 14. Dt 1:6.

4. **Ye are to pass.** Dt 23:7. Nu 20:14-21. Ob 10-13. **they shall.** Ex 15:15. Nu 22:3, 4. 24:14-18. **take ye.** Mt 5:16. Lk 12:15. Ep 5:15. Ph 2:15. Col 4:5.

5. **no, not so much as a foot breadth.** Heb. even to the treading of the sole of the foot. Ac 7:5. **because.** Dt 32:8. Ge 33:16. 36:8. Jsh 24:4. 2 Ch 20:10-12. Je 27:5. Da 4:25, 32. Ac 17:26.

6. **buy meat.** ver. 28, 29. Nu 20:19. Mt 7:12. Ro 12:17. 2 Th 3:7, 8.

7. **blessed.** Ge 12:2. 24:35. 26:12. 30:27. 33:8-11. 39:5. Ps 90:17. **he knoweth.** Dt 8:4. Jb 23:10. Ps 1:6. 31:7. Jn 10:27. **these forty.** Dt 8:2-4. 29:5. Ne 9:21. Lk 22:35.

8. **And when.** Nu 20:20, 21. 21:4. Jg 11:18. **Seir.** ℐ146, Ge +10:10. **the plain.** Heb. the Arabah. Dt 1:1mg. 3:17mg. +11:30mg. **Elath.** i.e. *palm grove,* ✱S#359h. 1 K 9:26, Eloth. 2 K 14:22. 16:6, 6. 2 Ch 8:17. 26:2.

9. **Distress not the Moabites.** *or,* Use no hostility against Moab. Nu 22:4. Jg 11:17. 2 Ch 20:10. **Ar.** ver. 5. Nu 21:15, 28. **the children.** ver. 19. Ge 19:36, 37. Ps 83:8.

10. All the nations here mentioned appear to have been the posterity of Ham, who lay under the prophetical curse of Noah, which was thus executed upon this part of them by the Moabites and Edomites. ver. 11. Ge 14:5.

11. **giants.** ver. +*20. **as the Anakims.** See on Dt 1:28. 9:2. Nu 13:22, 28, 33.

12. **Horims.** i.e. *cave dwellers,* ✚S#2752h. ver. 22. Ge 14:6. 36:20-30. 1 Ch 1:38-42. **succeeded them.** Heb. inherited them. ver. 21, 22. Ge 36:31-43. 1 Ch 1:43-54. **stead.** *or,* room. ver. 21-23. **as Israel did.** Israel had, at the time when Moses spake this, conquered Sihon and Og, and taken possession of their countries, as Edom had done to the Horims. ver. 22, 32-37. Dt 3:1-11. Ge 36:20. Nu 21:21, etc.

13. **brook.** *or,* valley. Nu 13:23mg. **Zered.** i.e. *luxuriant growth of trees,* ✱S#2218h. ver. 14. Nu 21:12, Zared.

14. **Kadesh-barnea.** Dt 1:2, 19, 46. Nu 13:26. **until all the generation.** Dt 1:34, 35. Nu 14:28-35. 26:64, 65. 32:11. Ps 90:3, 9. 95:11. Ezk 20:15. He 3:8-19. Ju 5.

15. **the hand of the.** Jg 2:15. 1 S 5:6, 9, 11. 7:13. Ps 32:4. 78:33. 90:7-9. 106:26. Is 66:14. 1 C 10:5.

18. **pass over.** See on Nu 21:15, 23. Is 15:1.

19. **distress them not.** See on ver. 5, 9. Ge 19:36-38. Jg 11:13-27. 2 Ch 20:10. **children of Ammon.** Dt *23:3.

20. **land of giants.** Dt 3:13. Jsh 12:4. *15:8. 17:15. 18:16. 1 Ch 11:15. 14:9. Is 17:5. **giants.** ver. 11. Dt 3:8-11, 13. Ge 6:4. Nu 13:28-33. Jsh 11:21. 12:4. 13:12. 17:15. 1 S 17:4. 2 S 5:18, 22. 21:15-22. 23:13. 1 Ch 20:5. Jb 16:14. **Zamzummims.** i.e. *noisy tribes,* ✱S#2157h. Ge 14:5, Zuzims.

21. **great.** See on ver. 10, 11. Dt 1:28. 3:11. **but the Lord.** These fragments of ancient history seem to be introduced to encourage the Israelites. If the Lord destroyed these gigantic people before the posterity of Lot and of Esau, what cause had the posterity of Abraham, Isaac, and Jacob, his chosen servants and friends, to fear the Anakims, or the Canaanites? especially as Israel acted by commission from God, and had his promise as their security of success, and the

pledge of it in his presence, and the wonders which he had already wrought for them; and as they were the only nation of worshippers of the Lord, in the ordinances of his institution, which could be found on earth. This is so often repeated to possess the minds of the Israelites with a sense of God's providence, which rules every where; displacing one people, and placing another in their stead; and fixing their bounds also, which they cannot pass without his leave. ver. 22. Dt 32:7-9. Jg 11:24. Je 27:7, 8. Hab 1:10, 11. Ac 17:26.

22. **Esau.** Ge 36:8. **the Horims.** ver. 12. Ge 14:6. 36:20-30. 1 Ch 1:38, etc. **unto this day.** Dt +29:4. Ge +19:38.

23. **the Avims.** i.e. *accumulated evils; subverters,* ✱S#5757h. Jsh 13:3, Avites. 18:23. 2 K 17:31. **Hazerim.** i.e. *inclosures; courts,* ✱S#2699h. **Azzah.** i.e. *fortified,* ✤S#5804h. 1 K 4:24. Je 25:20. Zp 2:4, Gaza. Zc 9:5. **the Caphtorims which came.** ✱S#3732h. Ge 10:14. 1 Ch 1:12. Je ◐47:4. Am ◐9:7. **dwelt in their stead.** Ac *17:26.

24. **the river Arnon.** ver. 36. Nu 21:13-15. Jg 11:18-21. **behold.** Jsh 6:16. 2 Ch 36:23. Ezr 1:2. Je 27:5. Ezk 29:20. Da 2:38. 4:17. **begin to possess it.** Heb. begin, possess. ver. 31.

25. **the dread.** Dt 11:25. 28:10. Ex 15:14-16. 23:27. Nu 22:3. Jsh 2:9-12. 9:24. 2 K 7:6, 7. Ps 105:38. Je 33:9. Re 3:9.

26. **Kedemoth.** Jsh 13:18. 21:37. **with words.** Dt 20:10, 11. Est 9:30. Mt 10:12-15. Lk 10:5, 6, 10-12.

27. **pass through.** ver. 6. Nu 21:21-23. Jg 11:19.

28. **only will I pass.** Nu 20:19.

29. **As the children.** It appears to have been only the Edomites of Kadesh-Barnea, south of Canaan, who denied the Israelites a passage; for those of mount Seir are here expressly said to have granted it them; and this, in fact, was the very road by which they arrived at Canaan. Dt 23:3, 4. Nu 20:18. Jg 11:17, 18. **into the land.** Dt 4:1, 21, 40. 5:16. 9:6. 25:15. Ex 20:12. Jsh 1:11-15.

30. **Sihon.** Nu 21:23. **for the Lord.** See on Ex 4:21. 11:10. Nu 21:23. Jsh 11:19, 20. Jg 11:20. Ro 9:17-23. **God hardened.** Ex +*4:21. 7:3. 9:12. 10:1. 14:8, 17. Jsh 11:19, +*20. Jg 7:22. 2 S *24:1. 1 K *22:23. Jb 17:4. Ps 28:3. 105:25. +*115:3. 119:36. 141:4. Is 19:14. *29:10. *44:18. *45:7. 63:17. Ezk 14:9. Zc 8:10. Lk 10:21. Jn *12:39-41. Ro *9:18. 11:7, 8. 2 Th √2:10-12. Re √17:17. **obstinate.** Is 48:4. **deliver.** Dt 9:3-5. Ge 15:13-16.

31. **give Sihon.** See on ver. 24. Dt 1:8.

32. **Sihon.** Nu 21:23-30. Jg 11:20-23. Ne 9:22. Ps 120:7. 135:11. 136:19.

33. **the Lord.** Dt 3:2, 3. 7:2. 20:16. Ge 14:20. Jsh 21:44. Jg 1:4. 7:2. **we smote.** Dt 29:7, 8. Nu 21:23, 24. Jsh 10:30-42. 11:21.

34. **utterly destroyed.** Dt 7:2, 26. 20:16-18. Le 27:28, 29. Nu 21:2, 3. Jsh 7:11. 8:25, 26. 9:24. 11:14. 1 S 15:3, 8, 9. **the men, and the women, and the little ones, of every city.** Heb. every city of men, and women, and little ones. Dt 3:6.

35. **the cattle.** Dt 3:7. 20:14. Nu 31:9-11. Jsh 8:27.

36. **Aroer.** Dt 3:12. 4:48. Jsh 13:9. Is 17:2. Je 48:19. **Arnon.** Dt 3:16. Nu 21:24. **not.** Jsh 1:5. Is 41:15, 16. **God delivered.** Nu 14:9. Ps 44:3. 118:6. Ro *8:31.

37. **unto the land.** ver. 5, 9, 19. Dt 3:16. Jg 11:15. **Jabbok.** Ge 32:22. Nu 21:24. Jsh 12:2.

DEUTERONOMY 3

Israel's victory over Og king of Bashan, 1-10. The size of his bed, 11. His kingdom and that of Sihon are given to the two tribes and a half, 12-17. The command given to them and to Joshua, 18-22. Moses prays to enter the promised land, but is refused, 23-25. He is permitted to see it, 26-29.

1. **Bashan.** Famous for its pastures and its oaks. Nu +21:33. **Og.** Dt 1:4. 4:47. 29:7. 31:4. Nu 21:33-35. Jsh 9:10. 12:4. 13:30. 1 K 4:19. Ne 9:22. Ps 135:10, 11. 136:20. **Edrei.** Said to have been six miles from Ashteroth, his capital city. ver. +10. See Dt 1:4. Nu 21:33.

2. **Fear.** ver. 11. Dt 20:3. Nu 14:9. 2 Ch 20:17. Is 41:10. 43:5. Ac 18:9. 27:24. Re 2:10. **as thou didst.** Dt 2:24-37. Nu 21:23-25.

3. **God delivered.** Dt 2:33, 34. Nu 21:35. Jsh 13:12, 30.

4. **all his cities.** Nu 32:33-42. Jsh 12:4. 13:30, 31. **all the region.** lit. line. ꭓ121B, Jsh +17:14. 1 K 4:13.

5. **fenced.** Dt 1:28. Nu 13:28. He 11:30.

6. **we utterly.** Dt 2:34. 20:16-18. Le 27:28, 29. Nu 21:2. Jsh 11:14. **as we did.** ver. 2. Dt 2:24, 34. Ps 135:10-12. 136:19-21.

7. **all the cattle.** Dt 2:35. Jsh 8:27. 11:11-14.

8. **the land.** Nu 32:33-42. Jsh 12:2-6. 13:9-12. **Hermon.** i.e. *strong fortress,* ✱S#2768h. ver. 9. Dt 4:48. Jsh 11:3, 17. 12:1, 5. 13:5, 11. 1 Ch 5:23. Ps 89:12. 133:3. SS 4:8.

9. **Hermon.** Dt 4:48, 49. Ps 29:6. 89:12. 133:3. SS 4:8. **Sidonians.** ✱S#6722h. Jsh 13:4, 6. Jg 3:3. 10:12. 18:7, 7. 1 K 5:6. 11:5, 11, 33. 16:31. 2 K 23:13. 1 Ch 22:4. Ezr 3:7. Ezk 32:30. **Sirion.** i.e. *coat of mail; breastplate; sheeted with snow,* ✱S#8303h. Ps 29:6. **Shenir.** i.e. *an apron; bear the lamp,* ✱S#8149h. Dt ◐4:48. 1 Ch 5:23. Ezk 27:5, Senir. SS 4:8.

10. **the cities.** Dt 4:49. **Salchah.** i.e. *a walk; firmly bound, straitened basket,* ✱S#5548h. Jsh 12:5. 13:11. 1 Ch 5:11. **Edrei.** ver. 1. Nu 21:33. Jsh 12:4, 5. 13:11, 12, 31.

11. **giants.** Dt +*2:20. Ge 14:5. 1 Ch 20:4-8. **Rabbath.** i.e. *great or populous place,* ✤S#7237h. 2 S 12:26. Je 49:2. Ezk *21:20. Am 1:14, Rabbah. **nine cubits.** 1 S 17:4. Am 2:9. **cubit of a man.** Re 21:17.

12. **from Aroer.** Dt 2:36. 4:48. Nu 32:33-38. Jsh 12:2-6. 13:8-12, 14-28. 2 K 10:33. **Gadites.** ✱S#1425h. ver. 16. 4:43. 29:8. Nu 34:14. Jsh 1:12. 12:6. 13:8. 22:1. 2 S 23:36. 2 K 10:33. 1 Ch 5:18, 26. 12:8, 37. 26:32.

13. **the rest.** Nu 32:39-42. Jsh 13:29-32. 1 Ch 5:23-26. **which was called.** Michaelis says, "The tradition that giants formerly dwelt in this part, still remains in Arabia, only that it makes them rather *taller* than Moses does Og, and calls the land in which they lived, not Bashan, but Hadrach, which name occurs in Zc 9:1. I received this information from the verbal communication of a credible Arab, who was born on the other side of Jordan, about three days' journey from Damascus." **land of giants.** ver. 11. Dt 2:11, 20. Jsh 12:4. 13:12. 15:8. 17:15. 18:16.

14. **Jair.** Nu 32:41. 1 Ch 2:21-23. **Argob.** See on ver. 4. **Geshuri.** ✱S#1651h. Jsh 12:5. 13:*2, 11, 13. 1 S 27:8. 2 S ◐3:3. 10:6. 13:37. (1) The inhabitants of Geshur, Dt 3:14; Jsh 12:5. (2) An ancient tribe bordering on the Philistines, Jsh 13:2. **Bashan-havoth-jair.**

i.e. *Bashan of the villages of Jair,* *S#2333h, 2334h. Nu 32:41. Jsh 13:30. Jg 10:4. 1 K 4:13. 1 Ch 2:23. **unto this day.** Dt +29:4.

15. **Machir.** Ge 50:23. Nu 26:29. 32:29, 39, 40. Jsh 17:1-3. 22:7.

16. **Reubenites.** Nu 32:33-38. 2 S 24:5. **river Jabbok.** Dt 2:37. Ge 32:22. Nu 21:24. Jsh 12:2, 3.

17. **The plain.** Heb. Arabah. Dt 1:1mg. 4:49mg. +11:30mg. **Chinnereth.** i.e. *a harp,* *S#3672h. See on Nu 34:11. Jsh 11:2. 12:3. 13:27. 19:35. 1 K 15:20. **the sea.** Dt 4:49. Ge 13:10. 14:3. 19:28, 29. Nu 34:11, 12. Jsh 3:16. 12:3. 15:2, 5. 18:19. **Ashdoth-pisgah.** *or,* the springs of Pisgah, *or,* the hill. *S#798h. Dt 4:49. Nu ◐23:14. Jsh 10:40 (springs). 12:3mg, 8. 13:20mg.

18. **I commanded.** Nu 32:20-24. Jsh 1:12-15. 4:12, 13. 22:1-9. **meet for the war.** Heb. sons of power. Jg 18:2mg. 21:10. 1 S 18:17. 2 S 2:7mg. 13:28. 17:10. 2 K 2:16. 1 Ch 5:18. 2 Ch 28:6, etc.

20. **return.** Jsh 22:4, 8.

21. **I commanded.** Nu 27:18-23. **so shall.** Jsh 10:25. 1 S 17:36, 37. Ps 9:10. 2 C 1:10. 12:10. Ep 3:20. 2 T 4:17, 18.

22. **shall not.** Is 43:1, 2. **for the Lord.** Dt 1:30. 20:4. Ex 14:14. Nu 21:34. Jsh 10:42. 2 Ch 13:12. 20:17, 29. Ps 44:3.

23. **I besought.** 2 C 12:8, 9.

24. **thy greatness.** ♪22I2, Ex +15:16. Dt 5:24. 11:2. 1 Ch 29:11. Ne 9:32. Ps 106:2. 145:3, 6. Je 32:18-21. **what.** Ex 15:11. 2 S 7:22. Ps 35:10. 71:19. 86:8. 89:6, 8. Is 40:18, 25. Je 10:6. Da 3:29. **God.** Heb. *El,* Ex +15:2.

25. **the good land.** Dt 4:21, 22. 11:11, 12. Ex 3:8. Nu 32:5. Ezk 20:6. **Lebanon.** Dt 1:7. 11:24. Jsh 1:4. 9:1. 11:17. 12:7. 13:5, 6. Jg 3:3. 1 K 5:14. 9:19. 2 Ch 8:6. Ps 104:16. SS 4:11. Is 2:13.

26. **the Lord.** Dt 1:37. 31:2. 32:51, 52. 34:4. Nu 20:7-12. 27:12-14. Jb 23:13, 14. Ps 106:32, 33. Is 53:5, 6. Mt 26:39. **not hear.** Is 59:1, 2. Jn +*9:31. **Let it.** 1 Ch 17:4, 12, 13. 22:7-9. 28:2-4. Mt 20:22. 2 C 12:8. **speak no more.** Ex 32:10. 33:20. 2 S 12:16-23. Je 7:16. 11:14. Ezk 14:3. 20:3. Jn *17:9. 1 J *5:16.

27. **thee up.** Dt 34:1-4. Nu 27:12. **Pisgah.** *or,* the hill. ver. 17. **lift up.** ♪144A12, Ge +22:13. Ge 13:14, 15. **not go.** Dt 1:37. 31:2. 32:51, 52. 34:1-4. Ps 106:32. Lk ◐=9:31.

28. **charge Joshua.** Dt 1:38. 31:3, 7, 23. Nu 27:18-23. 1 Ch 22:6, 11-16. 28:9, 10, 20. 1 T 6:13, 14. 2 T 2:1-3. 4:1-6. **for he shall.** Jsh 1:2. 3:7-17. Jn 1:17. Ac 7:45. He 4:8, Jesus.

29. **the valley.** Dt 4:3, 46. 34:6. Nu 25:3. 33:48, 49. **Bethpeor.** i.e. *house of the opening,* *S#1047h. Dt 4:46. 34:6. Jsh 13:20.

DEUTERONOMY 4

Earnest exhortations to obedience, and dissuasives from idolatry, 1-24. Prophetical warnings of the consequences of disobedience, and promises of mercy to the penitent, 25-31. The Lord's special care of Israel, and his wonderful works for them, 32-40. Three cities of refuge appointed eastward of Jordan, 41-43. An introduction to the following exhortations, 44-49.

1. **unto the statutes.** *Statutes,* everything that concerned morals and the rites and ceremonies of religion; *judgments,* all matters of civil right and wrong. ver. 8, 45. Dt 5:1. 6:1, 2. 8:1. 11:1, 32. Le 19:37. 20:8.

22:31. Ps 105:45. 119:4. Ezk 11:20. +*36:27. 37:24. Mt 28:20. Lk 1:6. Jn 14:21, 24. 15:14. 1 J 2:3-5. **that ye may.** Le 18:5. Ezk 20:11, 21. Ro 10:5.

2. **not add.** Dt *12:32. 18:20. Jsh 1:7. Pr *30:6. Ec 12:13. Je 26:2. Mt 5:*18, 43. *15:2-9. Mk *7:1-13. Ga 3:15. Re √22:18, 19.

3. **what the.** Nu 25:1-9. 31:16. Jsh 22:17. Ps 106:28, 29. Ho 9:10. **for all the men.** It appears from this appeal, that the pestilence, as well as the sword of the magistrates, singled out the guilty persons and spared the rest (Ps 91:6-8). The legislator, in order to deter the Jews from idolatry, alludes to this fact, but he notices no circumstances but one, which, though in the original narrative was not stated, was infinitely the most important to advert to on this occasion; but which no persons, but spectators of the fact, and perfectly acquainted with every individual concerned in it, could possibly feel the truth of. Nu 26:64.

4. **cleave unto.** Dt 10:20. 13:4. 30:20. Nu 14:30-33. 25:10-13. 26:63-65. Jsh 22:5. 23:8. Ru 1:14-17. Ps 63:8. 143:6-11. Is 26:20. Ezk 9:4. Jn 6:67-69. Ac 11:23. Ro 12:9. Re 14:4. 20:4.

5. **I have taught.** ver. 1. Pr 22:19, 20. Mt 28:20. Ac 20:27. 1 C 11:23. 15:3. 1 Th 4:1, 2. He 3:5. The people had been often ready to conclude that Moses taught them by his own authority; but at the close of his life he solemnly assured them that he had instructed them exactly as the Lord had commanded him, neither more, nor less, nor otherwise. This is a most express declaration that he was divinely inspired, and utterly incompatible with his integrity of character, if he was not (Scott).

6. **this is your.** Jb 28:28. Ps 19:7. 111:10. 119:98-100. Pr 1:7. 4:5-7. 9:10. 14:8. Je 8:9. Ep 5:17. 2 T 1:13, 14. *3:15. Ja 3:13. **in the sight.** Je 20:10, 11. 1 C 4:9. **Surely.** 1 K 4:34. 10:6-9. Ps 119:99. Da 1:20. 4:9. 5:11-16. Zc 8:20-23. Ml 3:12.

7. **what nation.** Nu 23:9, 21. 2 S 7:23. Is 43:4. **who hath.** Dt 5:26. Ps 46:1. 73:28. 86:5. *145:18. 148:14. Is *55:6. Ep 2:12-22. Ja 4:8. **nigh.** Ps 4:5.

8. **statutes.** Dt 10:12, 13. Ps *19:7-11. 119:2-8, 86, 96, 127, 128, 160, 164. 147:19, 20. Ro 7:12-14. 2 T √3:16, 17.

9. **keep thy.** ver. *15, *23. Pr *3:1, 3. *4:20-23. Mt 15:19, 20. Lk *8:18. Ep 5:15. He *2:3. Ja *2:22. 2 P 3:11. 1 J 5:18. Ju 21. Re 16:15. **soul.** Heb. *nephesh,* Ge +34:3. **lest they.** Jsh 1:18. Ps *119:11. Pr 3:1-3, 21. *4:4. 7:1. He *2:1. Re 3:3. **teach them.** Dt *6:7. 11:19. *29:29. *31:19. Ge *18:19. Ex 13:+*8, 9, 14-16. Jsh 4:6, 7, 21. Ps *34:11-16. 71:18. *78:3-8. Pr *1:8. *4:1-13. +*22:6. 23:26. Is 38:19. Ep +*6:4. 2 T *1:5. +*3:15.

10. **the day.** Dt 5:2. Ex 19:9, 16. 20:18. He 12:18, 19, 25. **fear me.** Dt 5:29, 33. Ex 20:20. 1 S *12:23, 24. Ec 12:13. Lk 1:50. Re 19:5.

11. **stood.** Dt 5:23. Ex 19:16-18. 20:18, 19. He 12:18. **midst.** Heb. heart. Ex 15:8. 2 S 18:14. **clouds.** Ge +9:13. **thick darkness.** Dt 5:22. Ex +*10:22. 2 S 22:10. 1 K 8:12. 2 Ch 6:1. Jb 38:9. Pr +*20:20. Mt 27:45.

12. **the Lord.** Dt 5:4, 22, 23. Ex 20:22. **no similitude.** ver. 15. Nu 12:8. Is 40:18. Col *1:15. **only ye heard a voice.** Heb. save a voice. ver. 33, 36. Ge 4:10. Dt 3:16. 20:18, 22. 1 K 19:12, 13. Jb 4:10. Is 30:21. 40:3, 6. Mt 3:3, 17. 17:5. Lk 1:64. Jn 12:28-30. 2 P *1:17, 18. **heard.** ♪180A, Ge +4:20. Notice that the Zeugma

consists of the verb "saw" being applied to *voice*. Compare the figure ♪171J15, Ge +42:1.

13. **And he.** Dt 5:1-21. Ex 19:5. 24:7, 8. He 9:19, 20. **ten.** Dt 10:4. Ex 34:28. **he wrote.** Dt 9:9-11. 10:1-5. Ex 24:12. 31:18. 34:28. 2 C 3:3, 7. He 9:4.

14. **at that time.** Ex ch. 21-23. Ps 105:44, 45. Is 28:10, 13. Ml 4:4. He 3:5.

15. **Take ye.** See on ver. 9, 23. Jsh 23:11. 1 Ch 28:9, 10. Ps *119:9. Pr 4:23, 27. Je 17:21. Ml 2:15. **yourselves.** Heb. *nephesh*, Nu +23:10. **of similitude.** See on ver. 12. Ex 33:20. Is 40:18. Jn 1:18. Ac 17:29. 2 C 4:4-6. Col 1:15. 1 T 6:16. He 1:3.

16. **corrupt.** Dt 5:9. Ex 20:4, 5. 32:7. Ps 106:19, 20. Je 7:18. Ro 1:22-24. **the likeness.** Such as Baalpeor, the Roman Priapus; *Ashtaroth* or *Astarte*, the Greek and Roman Venus, and many others. ver. 23. Is 40:18. +*66:17n. Ezk +*16:17. +*23:14, 20. Jn *4:24. Ac 17:29. 20:4, 5. 1 T 1:17.

17. **likeness.** Jsh 22:28. Ezk 8:3. Ro 1:22, 23, 25.

19. **lift.** ♪144A12, Ge +22:3. **when thou.** Dt 17:3. 2 K 23:4, 5, 11. Jb 31:26, 27. Je 8:2. Ezk 8:16. Am 5:25, 26. **the host.** Ge 2:1. 2 K 17:16. 21:3. 23:5, 11. Je 19:13. Zp 1:5. Ac 7:42. Ro 1:25. **which the Lord.** Ge 1:16-18. Jsh 10:12, 13. Ne 9:6. Ps 74:16, 17. 136:7-9. 148:3-5. Je 31:35. 33:25. Mt 5:45. **divided.** *or*, imparted. Dt 29:26mg. **nations.** or, peoples.

20. **the iron.** 1 K 8:51. Je 11:4. **furnace.** Ge 15:17. **out of Egypt.** Ex 1:11-14. 5:7-9, 18, 19. **a people.** Dt 9:26, 29. 32:9. Ex 19:5, 6. Ps 28:9. 33:12. 135:4. Is 63:17, 18. Ep 1:18. T *2:14. 1 P *2:9.

21. **angry with me.** See on Dt 1:37. 3:26. 31:2. Nu 20:12. Ps 106:32, 33.

22. **I must die.** Dt 3:25, 27. 34:4. 1 K 13:21, 22. Am 3:2. He 12:6-10. 2 P 1:13-15.

23. **heed.** See on ver. 9, 15, 16. Dt 27:9. Jsh 23:11. Mt 24:4. Lk 12:15. 21:8. He 3:12. **lest ye forget.** Dt 6:12. 29:25. 31:20. Jsh 23:16. 1 Ch 16:15. Is 24:5. Je 31:32. Ezk 16:59. **make you.** See on ver. 16. Ex 20:4, 5.

24. **thy God.** Dt 9:3. 32:22. Ex 24:17. Ps 21:9. Is 30:33. *33:14. Je 21:12-14. Na 1:6. Zp 1:18. He 12:)29. **consuming.** Ml 4:1. **fire.** ♪22K1. Anthropomorphism B896. God is spoken of as a Fire. For other instances of this figure see Dt 9:3. 29:20. Ps 74:1. 80:4. Is 10:17. He 12:29. **a jealous.** Dt 6:15. 29:20. 32:16, 21. Ex 20:5. 34:14. Ps 78:58. Is 42:8. Na 1:2. Zp 3:8. 1 C 10:22. **God.** Heb. *El*, Ex +15:2.

25. **beget.** Dt 31:16-18. Jg 2:8-15. **corrupt.** See on ver. 16. Dt 31:29. Ex 32:7. Ho 9:9. **do evil.** 2 K 17:17-19. 21:2, 14-16. 2 Ch 36:12-16. 1 C 10:22.

26. **I call heaven.** Dt 8:19. 30:18, 19. 31:28. 32:1. Ps 50:4. Is 1:2. Je 2:12. 6:19. 22:29. Ezk 36:4. Mi 1:2. 6:2. **this day.** ♪121I2, Ge +2:17. ver. 39, 40. Dt 5:1. 6:6. 7:11. 8:1, 11, 19. 9:1, 3. 10:13. 11:2, 8, 13, 26, 27, 28, 32. 13:18. 15:5, 15. 19:9. 26:3, 16, 17, 18. 27:1, 4, 10. 28:1, 13, 14, 15. 30:2, 8, 11, 15, 16, 18, 19. 32:46. Je 42:21. Lk +*23:43n. Ac 20:26. **ye shall.** Dt 29:28. Ge +4:7. Le 18:28. 26:31-35. Jsh 23:16. Is 6:11. 24:1-3. Je 44:22. Ezk 33:28. Lk *21:24.

27. **scatter you.** Dt 28:62-64. Le *26:33. Ne 1:3, 8, 9. Ezk 12:15. 32:26.

28. **ye shall.** Dt 28:36, 64. 1 S 26:19. Je 16:13. Ezk 20:32, 39. Da 3:1-7. Ac 7:42. **the work of men's hands.** Dt 27:15. Ps 115:4. Is 17:8. 31:7. 40:19. 44:9. 46:6. Ho 13:2. Mi 5:13. Ac 19:26. **neither see.** 1 K 18:26. Ps 115:4-7. 135:15, 16. Is 41:22. *44:7, 9, 10. 45:20,

21. 46:6, 7. 48:5. Je 10:3, 9. Hab 2:18. 1 C 12:2. Re 9:20.

29. **But if.** Dt *30:10. Ge +*4:7. Le *26:39-42. 2 Ch *15:4, 15. Ne *1:9. Is √55:6, 7. Je *3:12-14. *29:12-14. **with all.** Dt *30:1-3. 1 K 8:47, 48. 2 K 10:31. 23:3. 2 Ch 15:4, 12. *31:21. Ps *119:2, 10, 58, 145. Je 3:10. Da 9:3-18. Jl 2:12. **soul.** Heb. *nephesh*, Ge +34:3.

30. **in tribulation.** T#1417. 1 S 26:24. Jb 38:23. Is 2:19. 48:10. Je 23:20. √30:7. Ezk 20:37. Da +*12:1. Ho *5:15. Jl 2:11, 31. Na 1:7. Zp +*1:15. Zc 10:11. 13:8, 9. Mt 24:8, +*21, 29. Re 7:4-8. 12:1, 2, 17. **all these.** 1 K 8:46-53. 2 Ch 6:36-39. Da 9:11-19. **are come upon thee.** Heb. have found thee. Dt 31:17. Ge 44:34. Ex 18:8mg. Ne 9:32. **in the latter days.** Dt 31:29. Ge 49:1. Nu 24:20. Je 23:20. Da 10:14. Ho +*3:5. He 1:2. **if thou.** Dt 30:10. La 3:40. Ho *14:2, 3. Jl 2:12, 13. Ac +√3:19. 26:20. **obedient.** Is 1:19. Je 7:23. Zc 6:15. He *5:9.

31. **the Lord.** Ex 34:6, 7. Nu 14:18. 2 Ch 30:9. Ne 1:5. 9:31. Ps 78:34-40. 86:5, 15. 116:5. 145:8, 9. Jon 4:2. Mi 7:18. Na 1:7. Ml 4:2. **not forsake.** Je 31:36. 33:25, 26. Ro +*11:1. **forget.** Le 26:42, 45. Ps 105:8. 111:5, 9. Je 14:21. Lk 1:72.

32. **ask now.** Dt 32:37. Jb 8:8. Ps 44:1. Is *41:22. Jl 1:2. **the days.** ♪121P4. Metonymy of the Adjunct B594. Day, or days, is put for what transpires in them. Here, for what has transpired in the days of past history. For other instances of this figure see Jb 18:20. 24:1. Ps 37:13. 137:7. Is 13:6. Ezk 21:29. 22:4. Ho 1:11. Jl 1:15. Ob 12. Mi 7:4. Lk 17:22, 26. 19:42. 1 C 4:3mg. Ep 5:16. **from the one.** ♪121Q3, 2 S +22:8. Dt 30:4. Mt 24:31. Mk 13:27.

33. **hear the voice.** Dt 5:24-26. 9:10. Ex 19:18, 19. 20:18, 19. 24:11. 33:20. Jg 6:22.

34. **take him.** Ex 1:9. 3:10, 17-20. 6:6. **temptations.** Dt 7:19. 29:3. Ex 9:20, 21. 10:7. **by signs.** Ex 7:3. Ps 78:12, 48-53. Je 32:21. **by a mighty.** Dt 5:15. 6:21. 7:8, 9. 26:8. Ex 6:6. 13:3. 1 P 5:6. **and by great.** Dt 26:8. 34:12. Ex 12:30-33. Je 32:21.

35. **showed.** Dt 5:24, 26. Ex 24:11. 33:20. **know.** 1 S 17:45-47. 1 K 18:36, 37. 2 K 19:19. Ps 58:11. 83:18. **none else.** Dt 32:39. Ex 15:11. 1 S 2:2. 2 S 22:32. Is 44:6, 8. 45:5, 18, 22. 46:9. Mk 12:29, +*)32, 43. 1 J 5:20, 21.

36. **Out of heaven.** ver. 33. Ex 19:9, 19. 20:18-22. 24:16. Ne 9:13. He 12:18, 25.

37. **because.** Dt 7:7-9. 9:5. 10:15. Ps 105:6-10. Is 41:8, 9. Je 31:1-3. Ml 1:2, 3. Lk 1:72, 73. Ro 9:5. 11:28, 29. **and brought.** Ex 13:3, 9, 14. **in his sight.** 2 Ch 16:9. Ps 32:8. 34:15. **with his.** See on ver. 34. Ps 114. 136:10-15. Is 51:9-11. 63:11, 12.

38. **drive.** Dt 7:1. 9:1-5. 11:23. Ex 23:27, 28. Jsh 3:10. Ps 44:2, 3. **as.** Dt 2:31-37. 3:1-16. 8:18.

39. **and consider.** Dt 32:29. 1 Ch 28:9. Is 1:3. 5:12. Ho 7:2. **the Lord.** See on ver. 35. Jsh 2:11. 1 Ch 29:11. 2 Ch 20:6. Ps 115:3. 135:6. Da 4:35. **in heaven.** Ec 5:2. Mt 3:16, 17. 6:9. Jn 12:28-30. 17:1. **none else.** Dt +32:39. Mk +*12:32.

40. **keep.** See on ver. *1, *6. Dt 28:1-14. Le *22:31. 26:1-13. Je 11:4. Jn *14:15, 21-24. **it may go.** Dt *5:16. *6:3, 18. 11:9. 12:25, *28. *22:7. Pr 10:27. Is 38:1-5. Ep *6:3. 1 T *4:8. **prolong.** Dt +*5:16. 11:9. 17:20. Ex 20:12. Ps +*91:16mg. Pr 10:27. Ec ◐+*8:13. Je 35:7. Ep 6:3. **for ever.** or, all the days. i.e. continually. Dt 5:29. 6:24. 11:1. 14:23. 18:5. 19:9. 28:29, 32, 33.

31:13. Ge 6:5. 43:9. 44:32. Jsh 4:24. Jg 16:16. 1 S 2:32.

41. **severed three cities**. Nu 35:6, 14, 15. Jsh 20:2-9.

42. **the slayer**. Dt 19:1-10. Ex 21:12, 13. Nu 35:6, 11, 12, 15-28. He *6:18.

43. **Bezer**. i.e. *stronghold; an inaccessible spot,* *S#1221h. *Bezer* is the same as *Bozra,* formerly a royal city of Edom. See on Ge ○36:33. Jsh 20:8. 1 Ch 6:78. 7:37. (1) A city of refuge in the wilderness east of Jordan, Dt 4:43; Jsh 21:36. (2) An Israelite of Asher, 1 Ch 7:37. **Ramoth**. Jsh 21:38. 1 K 4:13. 22:3, 4. 1 Ch 6:80. **Golan**. i.e. *great exodus; captive; rejoicing,* *S#1474h. Jsh 20:8. 21:27. 1 Ch 6:71. **Bashan**. Nu 32:4, 33. Ps 22:12. Am 4:1. **Manassites**. *S#4520h. Dt 29:8. Jg ○12:4. 2 K *10:33. 1 Ch 26:32.

44. **this is the law**. This is evidently an introduction to the discourse of the subsequent chapters. Moses having practically improved some particulars in the history of Israel, proceeded to repeat and enforce the laws which he had before delivered, with additions and explanations, beginning with the ten commandments. Dt 1:5. 17:18, 19. 27:3, 8, 26. 33:4. Le 27:34. Nu 36:13. Ml 4:4. Jn 1:17.

45. **These**. Dt 6:17, 20. 1 K 2:3. Ps 119:2, 14, 22, 24, 111. **statutes**. See on ver. 1. Ps 119:5. **judgments**. Ps 119:7.

46. **On this side**. ver. 47. See on Dt 1:5. 3:29. Nu 32:19. **over**. Dt 3:29. **Beth-peor**. Beth-peor was a city which was situated, according to Eusebius, opposite Jericho, and six miles above Livias. As the name signifies *the house of Peor,* it is probable that there was a temple to Peor, situated in this place, full in view of the people, while Moses was pressing upon them the worship of Jehovah alone; and perhaps the very temple where so many had sinned to their own destruction. Dt 3:29. 34:6. Jsh 13:20. **Moses**. Dt 1:4. 2:30-36. 3:8. Nu 21:21-32. **smote**. Ps 136:16-22.

47. **land of Og**. See on Dt 3:1-14. 29:7, 8. Nu 21:33-35. Ps 68:14, 15.

48. **Aroer**. Dt 2:36. 3:12. Jsh 13:24, etc. **even unto**. The Samaritan interpreter has, "unto the mountain of snow, which is Hermon." The Chaldee Targumist, who places it at Caesarea, and Samaritan interpreter, call it "the mountain of snow," because of its being always covered with snow; and Jerome informs us that in the summer time snow used to be carried from thence to Tyre. See on Dt 3:9. **Sion**. i.e. *lofty; peak,* *S#7865h, only here. Dt 3:9, Shenir. Ps 133:3. (1) One of the names of Mount Hermon, Dt 4:48. (2) The Greek form of Zion, designating a district of Jerusalem, Ps 65:1; Mt 21:5; Jn 12:15; Re +14:1. **Hermon**. Ps 133:3.

49. **plain**. Heb. Arabah. Dt 1:1mg. 2:8mg. 3:17mg. +11:30mg. **sea**. Nu 34:3. **under the springs**. or, slopes. Dt 3:17. 34:1. Jsh 10:40. 13:20.

DEUTERONOMY 5

Moses shows that God made a covenant with Israel at Horeb, 1-5. He sets the ten commandments before them, 6-21. He relates how, at the people's request, he had received the law from God for them, 22-31. He exhorts them to obedience, 32, 33.

1. **all Israel**. Dt 1:1. 29:2, 10. **Hear**. See on Dt 4:1. Ps 81:8, 9. 85:8. Is 55:3. Lk 9:35. Re 2:7. **keep, and**. Heb. keep to. Mt 23:3.

2. **our God**. Dt 4:23. Ex 19:5-8. 24:8. He 8:6-13. 9:19-23.

3. **made not**. Dt 29:10-15. Ge 17:7, 21. Ps 105:8-10. Je 32:38-40. Mt 13:17. Ro 4:23, 24. Ga 3:17-21. He 8:8, 9.

4. **The Lord talked**. ver. 24-26. Dt 4:33, 36. 34:10. Ex 19:9, 18, 19. 20:18-22. 33:11. Nu 12:8. **face**. ✓22A4, Ge +19:13.

5. **stood**. ver. 27. Ge 18:22. Ex 19:16. 20:18-21. 24:2, 3. Nu 16:48. Ps 106:23. Je 30:21. Zc 3:1-5. Ga 3:19. He 9:24. 12:18-24. **to show**. He=1:2.

6. **I am the**. Dt +*6:4. See on Ex *20:2-17. ○32:7. ○33:1. Le 26:1, 2. Is 42:8. **brought**. Ps 81:5-10. **bondage**. Heb. servants. Dt 6:12. Ex 13:3. 20:2.

7. **The First Commandment**. **Thou shalt have none other gods before me**. Dt *6:4. See on Ex 20:3. Mt *4:10. Jn *5:23. 1 C 8:5. Col *3:5. 1 J 5:21.

8. The Second Commandment. **Thou shalt not make thee any graven image**. **graven image**. See on Dt 4:15-19. Ex *20:4. **likeness**. Dt 4:12, 15, 16, 23. Ex *20:4n. Jb 4:16. Ps *17:15. Is 40:18-25. 46:5-7.

9. **shalt not**. See on Ex 20:4-6. **the Lord**. On the import of the word *yehowah,* which we translate Lord, see Note on Ex 3:15. The word *elohim,* which is rendered God, in the singular *eloah,* and in Arabic *allah,* is derived from the Arabic *alaha,* he worshipped, adored, was struck with astonishment, fear or terror: and hence, he adored with sacred horror and veneration: it also signifies, he succoured, liberated, kept in safety, or defended. Hence we learn that *elohim* denotes the sole object of adoration; the perfections of whose nature must astonish all who contemplate them, and fill with horror all who rebel against him; that consequently he must be worshipped with reverence and religious fear; and that every sincere worshipper may expect help in all his weaknesses, etc., freedom from the power, guilt, and consequences of sin, and support and defence to the uttermost. **a jealous God**. See on Ex 34:14. **visiting**. Ex +20:5. 34:7. Je 32:18. Da 9:4-9. Mt 23:35, 36. Ro 11:28, 29.

10. **showing**. Ex +*34:6, 7. Is 1:16-19. Je 32:18. Da 9:4. Mt 7:21-27. Ga 5:6. 1 J 1:7. **love me**. Dt 6:5, 6. 10:12, 13. Jn 14:15, 21-23. +*15:14. Ro ✓8:28. Ja 1:25. 1 J 5:2, 3.

11. The Third Commandment. **Thou shalt not take the name of the Lord thy God in vain**. Dt 6:13. See on Ex 20:7. Le 19:12. 24:10-16. Ps 139:20. Je 4:2. Mt 5:33, 34. Jn 10:30-36. Ja 5:12.

12. The Fourth Commandment. **Keep the sabbath day to sanctify it**. See on Ex 20:8-11. Le 26:2. Is 56:6. +*58:13n.

13. **Six days**. Ex 23:12. 35:2, 3. Ezk 20:12. Lk 13:14-16. 23:56.

14. **the sabbath**. Ge 2:2. Ex 16:29, 30. He 4:4, 9-11. **not do any work**. Ex 23:12. 35:2. 2 Th ○3:6, 11, 12. **thy stranger**. Ne 13:15-21. **thy manservant**. Ex 23:12. Le 25:44-46. Ne 5:5.

15. **remember**. Dt 15:15. 16:12. 24:18-22. Is 51:1, 2. Ep 2:11, 12. **the Lord**. See on ver. 6. Ps 116:16. Is 63:9. Lk 1:74, 75. T 2:14. **through**. See on Dt 4:34-37.

16. The Fifth Commandment. **Honor thy father and thy mother**. See on Ex *20:12. Le 19:3. Dt 27:16. Pr 1:8, 9. 30:17. Mt 15:4-6. Mk 7:10-13. Ep 6:1-3. Col 3:20. **that thy days**. ver. 33. Dt +*4:40. 6:2. 27:16. 1 K 3:14. Jb 5:26. Ps 34:12, 14. +*91:16mg. Pr 3:2,

16. 4:10, 20-22. 9:11. 10:27. Is 65:22. Je 35:7. Zc 8:4. Ep *▶6:1-3. 1 P 3:10.

17. The Sixth Commandment. **Thou shalt not kill.** See on Ex *20:13. Ps 51:14. Mt ▶5:21, 22. Jn 8:44. Ja ▶2:11. 1 J 3:10-12, 15. Re 21:8.

18. The Seventh Commandment. **Neither shalt thou commit adultery.** See on Ex *20:14. Pr 6:32, 33. Mt ▶5:27, 28. Lk 18:20. Ja 2:10, 11. He 13:4.

19. The Eighth Commandment. **Neither shalt thou steal.** See on Ex *20:15. Jn 12:4-6. Ro ▶13:9. Ep 4:28.

20. The Ninth Commandment. **Neither shalt thou bear false witness against thy neighbor.** Dt 19:16-21. See on Ex *20:16. 23:1. 1 K 21:12, 13. Ps 50:19, 20. Pr 6:19. 19:5, 9. Ml 3:5. **bear.** or, answer, in reply to the questions of a judge. **false.** or, empty, worthless testimony.

21. The Tenth Commandment. **Neither shalt thou desire thy neighbor's wife, neither shalt thou covet.** See on Ex *20:17. 1 K 21:1-4. Mi 2:2. Hab 2:9. Lk 12:15. 18:20. Ro ▶7:7, 8. 13:9, 10. 1 T 6:9, 10. He 13:5. **desire.** Dt 7:25. Ex 20:17. 34:24. **covet.** Nu 11:*4, 34. 2 S 23:15. 1 Ch 11:17. Ps 45:11. *106:14. Pr 13:4. 21:10, 26. 23:3, 6. 24:1. Ec 6:2. Is ◐*26:9. Je 17:16. Am 5:18.

22. **These words.** See on ver. 4. Dt 4:12-15, 36. Ex 19:18, 19. **added no more.** 1 J 2:7, 8. **he wrote.** See on Dt 4:13. Ex 24:12. 31:18.

23. **when ye heard.** Ex 19:19. 20:18, 19. He 12:18-21.

24. **we have heard.** ver. 4, 5. Ex 19:19. **he liveth.** Dt 4:33. Ge 32:30. Ex 33:20. Jg 13:22. Notwithstanding all this; the common impression being that death would ensue; compare the feelings of Hagar (Ge 16:13), Jacob (Ge +*32:30), Moses (Ex 3:6), Manoah (Jg *13:22), Elijah (1 K 19:13), Daniel (Da 10:9), John (Re 1:17).

25. **this great.** Dt 18:16. 33:2. 2 C 3:7-9. Ga 3:10, 21, 22. He 12:29. **hear.** Heb. add to hear. Is 29:14mg.

26. **who is.** It seems to have been a general opinion, that if God *appeared* to men, it was for the purpose of destroying them. And indeed most of the extraordinary manifestations of God were in the way of judgment; but here it was widely different. God did appear in a sovereign and extraordinary manner; but it was for the instruction, direction, deliverance, and support of his people. 1. They heard this voice speaking with them in a distinct, articulate manner. 2. They saw the fire, the symbol of his presence, the appearances of which demonstrated it to be supernatural. 3. Notwithstanding God appeared so terrible, yet no person was destroyed; for he came not to destroy but to save. See on ver. 24n. Dt 4:33. **all flesh.** Ge 6:12. Is 40:6. Ro 3:20. **living.** Jsh 3:10. Ps 42:2. 84:2. Je 10:10. Da 6:26. Mt 26:63. Ac 14:15. 2 C 6:16. 1 Th 1:9.

27. **hear all.** Ex *20:19. He 12:19.

28. **they have well said all.** Dt *18:17. Nu 27:7. 36:5. He 1:1-3. 2:1-4. 3:3.

29. The language of the original is very emphatic: *Mee yittain wehayah levavom zeh lahem,* literally, "Who will give that there may be such a heart in them?" They refuse to receive such a heart from *me,* who then can supply it? **O that there.** Dt 32:29, 30. Ps 81:13-15. Is 48:18. Je 44:4. Ezk 33:31, 32. Mt 23:37. Lk 19:42. 2 C 5:20. 6:1. He 12:25. √124. Oeonismos; or, Wishing B922. An expression of feeling by way of wishing or hoping for a thing. For other instances of this figure see Dt 32:29. Ps 55:6. 81:13. Is 48:18. 64:1.

Mt 23:37. Ga 5:12. **keep all.** Dt 11:1. Ps 106:3. 119:1-5. Lk 11:28. Jn 15:14. Re 22:14. **that it might.** ver. +*16. Dt +*4:40. 6:3, 18. 12:25, 28. 19:13. 22:7. Ru 3:1. Ps 19:11. Is 3:10. Je 22:14, 15. Ep 6:3. Ja 1:25. **forever.** Heb. *olam,* Ex +12:24. Ge +9:12.

31. **by me.** Ex 33:21. Lk 15:1. **I will.** See on ver. 1. Dt 4:1, 5, 45. 6:1. 11:1. 12:1. Ezk 20:11. Ml 4:4. Ga 3:19.

32. **observe.** Dt *6:3, 25. 8:1. 11:32. 24:8. 2 K *21:8. Ezk 37:24. **ye shall not.** Dt *4:1, 2. 12:32. *17:20. 28:14. Jsh 1:7. 23:6. Ps *125:5. Pr *4:27. Is *30:21. 2 P *2:21.

33. **walk.** Dt *10:12. Ps 119:6. Ec 12:13, 14. Je 7:23. Lk 1:6. Ro *2:7. **well.** ver. 29. Dt +*4:40. Je *7:23. 1 T *4:8. **prolong.** ver. +*16. Dt +*4:40. Pr 10:27.

DEUTERONOMY 6

The end of the law is obedience, 1, 2. An exhortation thereto, with various instructions and cautions, 3-19. What they are to teach their children, 20-25.

1. **the commandments.** Dt 4:1, 5, 14, 45. 5:31. 12:1. Le 27:34. Nu 36:13. Ezk 37:24. **go to possess it.** Heb. pass over. Dt 7:1. Ge 15:7. 28:4. Le 20:24. Ps 37:24.

2. **fear.** See on Dt 4:10. 10:12, 13, 20. 13:4. Ge 22:12. Ex 20:20. Jb 28:28. Ps 111:10. 128:1. Pr 16:6. Ec 12:13. Lk 12:5. 1 P 1:17. **and thy son.** ver. 7. Ge +*18:19. Ps √78:4-8. **thy days.** Dt +*4:40. 5:+*16, 33. 22:7. Pr 3:1, 2, 16. 10:27. 1 P 3:10, 11.

3. **and observe.** Dt 4:6. 5:32. Ec 8:12. Is 3:10. **that ye may.** Ge *12:2. 13:16. 15:5. 22:17. 26:4. 28:14. Ex 1:7. Ac 7:17. **in the land.** Ex 3:8. **milk and.** √174, Ge +18:27. **honey.** √17117, Ex +3:8.

4. *Shema Yisrael, Yehowah, Elohainoo, Yehowah aichod,* "Hear, Israel, Jehovah, our God, is one Jehovah." On this passage the Jews lay great stress; and it is one of the four passages which they write on their phylacteries. On the word *Elohim,* Simeon Ben Joachi says; "Come and see the mystery of the word Elohim: there are *three degrees,* and each degree is by itself *alone,* and yet they are all *one,* and *joined together* in *one,* and are not *divided* from each other" (Zohar. Lev. Sect. 16. Col 116). **the Lord.** Dt 4:35, 36. 5:6. 1 K 18:21. 2 K 19:5. 1 Ch 29:10. Is 42:8. 44:6, 8. 45:5, 6. Je 10:10, 11. Mk ▶12:29-32. Jn 17:3. 1 C 8:4-6. 1 T 2:5. **God.** Dt 32:39. Ge ◐+1:26. √2:24. Is 45:5. Jn 17:3. 1 C 8:6. **one.** Heb. *ehad,* S#259h, a compound unity, one made up of others: Ge 1:5, one of seven; 2:11, one of four; 2:21, one of twenty-four; 2:24, one made up of two; 3:22, one of the three; 49:16, one of twelve; Nu 13:23, one of a cluster; Ps 34:20. Je +10:8mg. Contrast *yahed,* *S#3173h, unique, a single or only one: Ge 22:2, 12, 16. Jg 11:34. Ps +22:20. 25:16. 35:17. 68:6. Pr 4:3. Je 6:26. Am 8:10. Zc 12:10. See Ps 133:1.

5. **thou shalt.** Dt *10:12. *11:13. *30:6. Mt *▶22:37. Mk *▶12:30, 33. Lk *▶10:27. 1 J *5:3. **God with all.** Dt *4:29. 2 K *23:25. Jl 2:12▶𝒫. Mt *10:37. Jn *14:20, 21. 2 C *5:14, 15. **soul.** Heb. *nephesh,* Ge +34:3.

6. **shall be.** Dt 11:18. 32:46. Ps 37:31. 40:8. 119:*11, 98. Pr 2:10, 11. 3:1-3, 5. 7:3. Is 51:7. Je 31:33. Ps 2:51. 8:15. 2 C 3:3. Col 3:16. 2 J 2.

7. **And thou shalt.** ver. 2. Dt *4:9, 10. *11:19. Ge +*18:19. Ex 12:26, 27. 13:14, 15. Ps *78:4-6. Ep *6:4. **teach.** Heb. whet, *or* sharpen. or, repeat. Dt +32:41.

diligently. Jsh √1:8. children. Ex +*13:8. 2 T +*3:15.
shalt talk. T#1073. Ru 2:4, 12. 4:11. Ps *37:30. *40:9,
10. √107:2. 119:46. 129:8. Pr *6:22. *10:21. *15:2, 7.
Ml √3:16. Mt *12:35. Lk *6:45. Ep *4:29. Col *4:6.
1 P √3:15.

8. **bind them.** Dt 11:18. Ex 13:9, 16. Nu 15:38,
39. Pr 3:3. 6:21. 7:3. Mt 23:5. He 2:1.

9. **write them.** Dt 11:20. Ex 12:7. Jb 19:23-25. Is
30:8. 57:8. Hab 2:2.

10. **land.** Ge 13:15-17. 15:18. 26:3. 28:13. **great.**
Jsh 24:13. Ne 9:25. Ps 78:55. 105:44.

11. **wells.** Heb. bor, Ge +37:20. **when thou.** Dt
7:12-18. 8:10, etc. 32:15. Jg 3:7. Pr 30:8, 9. Je 2:31,
32. Ezk 16:10-20. Mt 19:23, 24.

12. **bondage.** Heb. bondsmen, or servants. Dt 5:6.
7:8. 8:14. 13:5, 10. Ex 13:3mg. 20:2. Jg 6:8.

13. **fear.** See on ver. 2. Dt 5:29. 10:12, 20. 13:4.
Ex +34:14. Mt ₭4:10. Lk ₭4:8. **and serve him.** Our
Savior quotes these words thus: "And him *only* (*auto
mono*) shalt thou serve;" from which it would appear,
that the word *levaddo* was anciently in the Hebrew
text, as it was in the Septuagint, Coptic, Vulgate (*illi
soli*), and Anglo-Saxon. Dr. Kennicott argues that without the word *only*, the text would not have been conclusive for the purpose for which our Lord advanced it.
It is proper, however, to observe, that the word *levaddo*
is not found in any MS. yet collated, though retained
in the above versions. **shalt swear.** Dt 10:20. Le 19:12.
Jsh 2:12. Ps *15:4. 63:11. Is 45:23. 48:1. 65:16. Je
4:2. 5:2, 7. 12:16.

14. **not go.** Dt 8:19. 11:28. Ex 34:14-16. Je 25:6.
1 J 5:21. **of the gods.** Dt 13:7.

15. **is a jealous.** See on Dt 4:24. Ex 20:5. Am 3:2.
1 C 10:22. **lest.** Dt 7:4. 11:17. Nu 32:10-15. 2 Ch
36:16. Ps 90:7, 11. **destroy.** Ge 7:4. Ex 32:12. 1 K
13:34. Am 9:8. **face.** Ge +1:2.

16. **tempt.** Mt ₭4:7. Lk ₭4:12. **tempted him.** Ex 17:2,
7. Nu 20:3, 4, 13. 21:4, 5. Ps 95:8, 9. 1 C 10:9. He
3:8, 9.

17. **diligently.** ver. 1, 2. Dt 11:13, 22. Ex +*15:26.
Ps *119:4. 1 C √15:58. T 3:8. He 6:11. 2 P √1:5-10.
*3:14.

18. **shalt do.** Dt 8:11. 12:25, 28. 13:18. Ex 15:26.
Ps 19:*11. Is 3:10. Ezk 18:5, 19, 21, 27. 33:14, 16,
19. Ho 14:9. Jn 8:29. Ro *12:2. **that it may.** See on
Dt +*4:40. 5:+16, 29, 33.

19. **cast out.** Ex 23:28-30. Nu 33:52, 53. Jg 2:1-3.
3:1-4.

20. **when thy son.** See on ver. +*7. Dt 4:9. 32:7.
Ge +*18:19. 35:2. Ex 12:26. +*13:8, 14. Jsh 4:6, 7,
21-24. 6:13. Jb +*1:5. 8:8, 10. 15:18. Ps 44:1. 48:13.
√78:3, 5-8. 145:4. Pr +*22:6. Ml +*4:6. Ep +*6:4.
in time to come. Heb. tomorrow. Ge +30:33mg. Ex
8:10. 13:14. Jsh +4:6mg. +22:24mg.

21. **We were.** Dt 5:6, 15. 15:15. 26:5-9. See on
Ex 20:2. Ne 9:9, 10. Ps 136:10-12. Is 51:1. Je 32:20,
21. Ro 6:17, 18. Ep 2:11, 12. **with a mighty.** Ex 3:19.
13:3.

22. **showed.** See on Dt 4:34. Ex 7-12. 14. Ps 135:9.
sore. Heb. evil. Dt 1:35, 39. 4:25. 24:7. 28:35, 59.
Ge 2:9, 17. 3:5, 22. 6:5. Jb 1:1, 8. 2:3. 2:7, 10, 11.
5:19. Ps 23:4. 71:20. **before.** Dt 1:30. 3:21. 4:3. 7:19.
Ps 58:10, 11. 91:8.

23. **to give us.** ver. 10, 18. Dt 1:8, 35. See on Ex
13:5. 2 Ch 20:11.

24. **to fear.** ver. 2. **for our good.** Dt 10:13. Jb 35:7,

---

8. Pr 9:12. Is 3:10. Je 32:39. Mt *6:33. Ro 6:21, 22.
he might. Dt 4:1, 4. 8:1, 3. Ps 41:2. 66:9. Pr 22:4.
Ro 10:5. **at this day.** Dt 2:22. +29:4, 28. Ge +19:38.

25. **it shall.** Dt 24:13. Le 18:5. Ps 106:30, 31. 119:6.
Pr 12:28. Ezk 20:11. Lk 10:28, 29. Ro 10:3, 5, 6. Ga
3:12. Ja *2:10. **righteousness.** Is *64:6. Je *23:6. **to
do.** Le +*18:5. Ps 71:16. 106:30, 31. Ro *10:3.

DEUTERONOMY 7

*The nations of Canaan must be utterly destroyed,
and no leagues or communion be made with them, 1,
2; no intermarriage with them allowed, 3; for fear of
idolatry, 4, 5; for the holiness of the people, 6-8; for
the nature of God in his mercy and justice, 9-16;
for the assuredness of victory which God will give
over them, 17-24. Images to be utterly destroyed, 25,
26.*

1. **the Lord.** See on Dt 4:38. 6:1, 10, 19, 23. 9:1,
4. 11:29. 31:3, 20. Ex 6:8. 15:17. Nu 14:31. Ps 44:2,
3. 78:55. **the Hittites.** Ge 15:18-19, +20, 21. Ex 23:23,
28. 33:2. **Girgashites.** Ge +10:16. **Amorites.** Ge
+10:16. **Canaanites.** Ge +10:18. **Perizzites.** Ge +13:7.
Hivites. Ge +10:17. **Jebusites.** Ge +10:16. **greater.**
See on Dt 4:38. 4:1-3. 20:1.

2. **deliver.** ver. 23, 24. Dt 3:3. 23:14. Ge 14:20.
Jsh 10:24, 25, 30, 32, 42. 21:44. Jg 1:4. **utterly.** Dt
20:16, 17. Le 27:28, 29. Nu 33:52. Jsh 6:17-25. 8:24.
9:24. 10:28, 40. 11:11, 12. **make no.** Dt 20:10, 11.
Ex 23:32, 33. 34:12-16. Jsh 2:14. 9:18-21. Jg 1:24. 2:2.
2 S 21:2.

3. **make marriages.** Ge 6:2, 3. Ex 34:15, 16. Jsh
23:12, 13. Jg 3:6, 7. 1 K 11:2. Ezr 9:1, 2. Ne 13:23-
27. 1 C √7:39. 2 C √6:14-17.

4. **so will.** Ex 6:15. 32:16, 17. Ex 20:5. Jg 2:11,
20. 3:7, 8. 10:6, 7. Pr 29:1.

5. **destroy.** Dt 12:2, 3. Ex 23:24. 34:13. 2 K 23:6-
14. **images.** Heb. statues, or pillars. Dt 16:22. Le 26:1.
and cut. Jg 6:25, 26. **burn.** ver. 25. Dt 9:21. Ex 32:20.
2 Ch 33:22n. Ac 19:19.

6. **an holy.** Dt 14:2. 26:18, 19. 28:9. Ex 15:16. 19:5,
6. +33:19. Ps 50:5. 135:4. Je 2:3. Am 3:2. 1 C √6:19,
20. T *2:14. 1 P *2:5, 9. **chosen thee.** Ps +*33:12. **to
be a special.** Dt +*32:43. Ex 19:5. Ezk 38:14. Am
*3:2. Ml *3:17. T *2:14. 2 P 2:9. **face.** Ge +1:2.

7. **The Lord.** Ps 115:1. Ro 9:11-15, 18, 21. 11:6.
1 J 3:1. 4:10. **ye were.** Dt 10:22. 26:5. Is 51:2. Mt
7:14. Lk 12:32. Ro 9:27-29.

8. **because.** Dt 4:37. 9:4, 5. 10:15. 1 S 12:22. 2 S
22:20. Ps 37:4. 44:3. Is 43:4. Je 31:3. Zp 3:17. Mt
11:26. Ep 2:4, 5. 2 Th 2:13, 14. T 3:3-7. 1 J 4:19.
oath. Ge 22:16-18. Ex 32:13. Ps 105:8-10, 42. Lk 1:55,
72, 73. He 6:13-17. **Lord brought.** See on Dt 4:20,
31. Ex 12:41, 42. 13:3, 14. 20:2.

9. **the faithful.** Ex 34:6, 7. Ps 119:75. 146:6. Is 49:7.
La 3:23. 1 C 1:9. 10:13. 2 C 1:18. 1 Th 5:24. 2 Th
3:3. 2 T 2:13. T 1:2. He 6:18. 10:23. 11:11. 1 J 1:9.
God. Heb. El, Ex +15:2. **which keepeth.** Dt 5:10.
Ge +9:16. 17:7. Ex 20:6. Ne 1:5. Da 9:4. Ro √8:28.
1 C 8:3. Ja 1:12. **covenant and.** ſ174, Ge +18:27. **a
thousand.** 1 Ch 16:15.

10. **repayeth.** Dt 5:9. 32:35, 41. Ex 23:22. Ps 21:8,
9. Pr 11:31. Is 59:18. 63:3-6. Na 1:2. Ro 12:19. **slack.**
Dt 32:35. 2 P 3:9, 10. **hateth.** Ex 20:5. Jn 15:23, 24.

11. **keep.** See on Dt 4:1. 5:32. Is *26:9. Jn +*14:15.

12. **if.** Heb. because. Dt 8:20. 28:1. Le 26:3. Mt

6:33. Jn 14:21. 1 T 4:8. **Lord**. See on ver. 9. Ps 105:8-10. Mi 7:20. Lk 1:55, 72, 73.

13. **he will love**. See on ver. 7. Dt 28:4. Ex 23:25. Ps 1:3. 11:7. 144:12-15. Jn 14:21. 15:10. 16:27. **he will also**. Dt 28:3-5, 8, 11, 15-18. Le 26:3-5, 9, 10. Jb 42:12. Ps +*127:3. Pr 10:22. Hg 2:15-19. Ml 3:10, 11. Mt 6:33.

14. **blessed**. Dt 33:29. Ge 25:8. 35:29. 1 Ch 23:1. Jb 5:26. 42:17. Ps *55:23. 107:38. 115:15. 147:19, 20. Ml 3:10, 11. Ac 1:18. **male or**. Dt 28:4, 11. Ex 23:26, etc. Le 26:9. Ps +*127:3.

15. **from thee**. Dt 28:27. Ex 9:11. Le 26:3, 4. These promises of temporal blessings were given for the nation as a whole; for though godliness often secures the most solid temporal advantages, yet temporal blessings were not, even among them, uniformly dispensed to *individuals* according to their obedience; but they were to the *nation*, with an exactness which is not observed towards any other people. This principle of promises applying to the group as a whole, but not necessarily infallibly to every individual in the group, is seen throughout Scripture. In the New Testament this principle is often seen by noting that personal pronouns, which in English translation are ambiguous as to whether they are singular or plural (especially the second person "you"), are most frequently in the Bible languages plural. This principle has important doctrinal bearing on passages pertaining to the security of the believer versus the possibility of apostasy. **will put none**. Dt 28:27, 60. Ex 9:11. *15:26. +*23:25. Ps 105:36, 37. **diseases of Egypt**. Dt 28:27. 1 S 4:8. 5:10-12. **but will**. Dt +*30:7.

16. **consume**. See on ver. 2. **thine eye**. Dt 13:8. 19:13, 21. 25:12. Je 21:7. **for that will**. Dt 12:30, 31. Ex 23:33. 34:12-16. Nu 33:55. Jsh 23:13-16. Jg 2:3, 12. 3:6. 8:27. Ps 106:34-38. 1 C 15:33. 2 C 6:14, 15.

17. **thou shalt**. Dt 8:17. 15:9. 18:21. Is 14:13. 47:8. 49:21. Je 13:22. Lk 9:47. **These nations**. Nu 13:32. 33:53. Jsh 17:16-18. **how**. ƒ85C, Ge +18:14.

18. **shalt not**. See on Dt 1:29. 3:6. 31:6. Ps 27:1, 2. 46:1, 2. Is 41:10-14. **remember**. Ex 8-14. Jg 6:8-10, 13. Ps 77:11. 78:11, 42-51. 105:5, 26-36. 135:8-10. 136:10-15. Is 51:9, 10. 63:11-15.

19. **great**. See on Dt 4:34. 11:2-4. 29:3. Ne 9:10, 11. Je 32:20, 21. Ezk 20:6-9. **so shall**. Jsh 3:10.

20. **the hornet**. Ex 23:28-30. Jsh 24:12.

21. **not be affrighted**. Jsh 10:8. **the Lord**. Ex 17:7. Nu 11:20. 14:9, 14, 42. 16:3. 23:21. Jsh 3:10. 2 Ch 32:8. Ps 46:5, 7, 11. Is 8:9, 10. Zc 2:10, 11. 1 C 14:25. **a mighty**. Dt 2:25. 10:17, 25. 26:8. Ge 35:5. 1 S 4:8. Ne 1:5. 4:14. 9:32. Zc 12:2-5. **God**. Heb. *El*, Ex +15:2.

22. **put out**. Heb. pluck off. ver. 1. Pr 2:22mg. **thou mayest**. Ex 23:29, 30. Jsh 15:63. Jg 14:5. Je 49:19.

23. **the Lord**. See on ver. 2. Jg 1:4. 7:23-25. 11:21. **unto thee**. Heb. before thy face. Dt 9:3. **shall destroy**. Dt 2:15. 8:20. Is +*13:6. Je 17:18. Jl *1:15. 2 Th *1:9.

24. **he shall**. Jsh 10:24, 25, 42. 12:1, etc., 7-24. 21:44. **destroy their name**. Dt 9:14. 25:19. 29:20. Ex 17:14. 1 S 24:21. Ps 9:5. 109:13. Pr 10:7. Is ●56:5. ●65:15. Je 10:11. Zp 1:4. **there shall**. Dt 11:25. Jsh 1:5. 10:8. 23:9. 2 S 8:3, 5, 13. 1 K 4:21, 24. Is 54:17. Ro 8:37. 1 C 15:57.

25. **graven**. See on ver. 5. Dt 12:3. Ex 32:20. Jsh 22:5. 24:14, 15, 21. 1 Ch 14:12. Is 30:22. **thou shalt**. Jsh 7:1, 21. **snared**. Jg 8:24-27. Zp 1:3. 1 T 6:9, 10. **an abomination**. Dt 17:1. 23:18. Re 17:5.

26. **shalt**. Dt 13:17. Le 27:28, 29. Jsh 6:17-24. 7:1, etc., 11-26. Jg 8:27. Ezk 14:7. Hab 2:9-11. Zc 5:4. **but thou shalt**. Is 2:20. 30:22. Ezk 11:18. Ho 14:8. Ro 2:22.

DEUTERONOMY 8

Exhortations and cautions, enforced by arguments drawn from the Lord's former dealings with Israel, and the good land intended for them; from the dangers to which they would be exposed; and from the effects of disobedience, 1-20.

1. **observe to do**. See on Dt 4:1. 5:32, 33. 6:1-3. Ps 119:4-6. 1 Th 4:1, 2. 1 J 3:21-24. Re 22:14.

2. **remember**. See on Dt 7:18. Ps 77:10-12. 106:7. Ep 2:11, 12. 2 P 1:12, 13. 3:1, 2. **led thee**. Dt 1:3, 33. 2:7. 29:5. Ps 136:16. Am 2:10. **to humble**. 2 Ch 32:25, 26. 33:12, 19, 23. Jb 33:17. 42:5, 6. Is 2:17. Lk 18:14. Ja 4:6, 10. 1 P 5:5, 6. **prove thee**. ver. 16. Dt 13:3. Ge 22:1. Ex 15:25. 16:4. 20:20. Jg 3:1, 4. 2 Ch 32:31. Ps 81:7. Pr 17:3. Ml 3:2, 3. Ja 1:3. 1 P 1:7. **to know**. ƒ22C1, Ge +18:21. Je *17:9, 10. Jn +*2:25. Re 2:23. **whether**. T#4. 2 Ch 33:12, 13. Jb 5:17. *23:10. Ps 78:34, 35. 94:12, 13. 119:67, 71, 75. Pr 3:11, 12. Is *26:9. 27:7, 9. *48:10. Je 24:5. La 3:27. Da *11:35. 12:10. Ho *5:15. Zc *13:9. Jn +10:28 (T#515). Ro *5:3, 4. 1 C 11:32. 2 C *4:17, 18. 12:10. 2 T +2:12 (T#512). He 2:10. 12:10, 11. Ja 1:2, 3, 12. 1 P 1:7, 19. Re +3:19 (T#508). **wouldest keep**. Ex 19:8. 32:7, 8.

3. **fed thee**. Ex 16:2, 3, 12-35. Ps 78:23-25. 105:40. Mt 4:4. Jn 6:30-35, 41, 48-51, 57, 58, 63. 1 C 10:3. **doth**. Ps 37:3. 104:27-29. Mt ▶4:4. Lk ▶4:4. 12:29, 30. He 13:5, 6. **bread**. ƒ171, Ge +3:19. **proceedeth**. Je √15:16. Jn 1:1, 14, 45. 6:52-55. 2 T +√3:16. **mouth**. ƒ22A10, Nu +12:8.

4. **raiment**. Ex 3:22. 12:35. **waxed not old**. Dt *29:5. Ne *9:21. Mt 6:25-30.

5. **consider**. Dt 4:9, 23. Is 1:3. Ezk 12:3. 18:28. **as a man**. 2 S 7:14. Jb 5:17, 18. Ps 89:32. 94:12. Pr 3:12. 1 C 11:32. He 12:5-11. Re 3:19.

6. **walk**. Dt 5:33. 10:12, 13. Ex 18:20. 1 S 12:24. 2 Ch 6:31. Ps 128:1. Lk 1:6. **fear him**. Ps 111:10. Is 8:13. Ro 13:7. He 12:28.

7. **land of brooks**. Dt 6:10, 11. 11:10-12. Ex 3:8. Jg 1:12-15. Ne 9:24, 25. Ps 65:9-13. Ezk 20:6. 31:4.

8. **land of**. Nu ●11:5. **wheat**. Dt 32:14. Jg 6:11. Ru 2:23. 2 S 4:6. 1 K 5:11. Ps 81:16. 147:14. Ezk 27:17. **barley**. 2 Ch 2:10-15. Jn 6:9, 13. **vines**. 1 K 4:25. 2 Ch 26:10. SS 2:11-13. Is 7:23. Je 5:17. 31:5. Ho 2:8, *12, 22. Mi 4:4. Hab 3:17. **oil olive**. Heb. olive tree of oil. Ex 30:24. Le 24:2. **honey**. ƒ171I7, Ex +3:8. Dt 6:3. 11:9. 26:9, 15. 27:3. 31:20. *32:13. Ge 43:11. Ex 3:8, 17. 13:5. 16:31. 33:3. Le 2:11. 20:24. Nu 13:27. 14:8. 16:13, 14. Jsh 5:6. Je 11:5. 32:22. Ezk 20:6.

9. **whose stones**. Dt 33:25. Jsh 22:8. 1 K 7:9-12. 1 Ch 22:14. Jb 28:2.

10. **thou hast**. Dt 6:11, 12. Ps 103:1-5, 22. Mt 14:19. Jn 6:23. Ro 14:6. 1 C 10:31. 1 Th 5:18. 1 T 4:4, 5. **then thou**. T#1240. 1 S 1:9, 10. 1 Ch 29:14. Ps 103:2. 106:48. Pr 3:9. Lk +24:30 (T#1270).

11. **Beware**. Ps 106:21. Pr 1:32. 30:9. Ezk 16:10-15. Ho 2:8, 9.

12. **Lest when**. Dt 28:47. 31:20. 32:15. Pr 30:9. Ho

13:5, 6. **and hast built**. Ec 2:4. Je 22:14, 15. Ezk 11:3. Am 5:11. Hg 1:4. Lk 12:18. 17:28.

13. **thy herds**. Ge 13:1-5. Jb 1:3. Ps *39:6. Lk *12:13-21.

14. **thine heart**. Dt 17:20. 2 Ch 26:16. 32:25. Je 2:31. 1 C 4:7, 8. **thou forget**. See on ver. 11. Ps 106:21. Je 2:6.

15. **led thee**. Dt 1:19. Ps 136:16. Is 63:12-14. Je 2:6. **fiery serpents**. Nu 21:6. Ho 13:5. **no water**. Je 2:6. Ho 13:5. **who brought**. Ex 17:6. Nu 20:11. Ps 78:15, 16. 105:41. 114:8. Is 35:7. 1 C 10:4. **water out**. Ps 87:7.

16. **fed thee**. ver. 3. Ex 16:15. **he might**. See on ver. 2. **to do thee**. Je 24:5, 6. La 3:26-33. Ro *8:28. 2 C 4:17. He 12:10, 11. Ja 1:12. 1 P 1:7.

17. **thou say**. See on Dt 7:17. **My power**. Dt 9:4. Is 10:8-14. Da 4:30. Ho 12:8. Hab 1:16. Lk 12:19. 2 C 4:7. **wealth**. ʃ121N2, Ge +34:29.

18. **he that**. Ge 26:12, 13. 1 S 2:7. 1 K 3:13. 1 Ch 29:12. Ps 112:3. 127:1, 2. 128:1-6. 144:1. Pr 8:18. *10:22. Ec 2:24. 5:19. Ho 2:8. **that he may**. Dt 7:8, 12.

19. **if**. Ge +4:7. **I testify against**. Dt 4:26. 28:58-68. 29:25-28. 30:18, 19. Jsh 23:13. 1 S 12:25. Da 9:2. Am 3:2. Zp 1:18. 3:6. Lk *12:46-48. *13:3, 5.

20. **so shall ye perish**. 2 Ch 36:16, 17. Da 9:11, 12. Lk 13:1-5. **obedient**. 1 S √15:22, 23. Mt 7:21. Lk *6:46. Jn 3:36g. 2 Th *1:7-9. He *5:9. 1 J *2:3. **voice**. Dt +13:4. 26:17. 28:2. Jn 10:4, 5, *27.

DEUTERONOMY 9

Israel assured of victory, not for their righteousness, but through the wickedness of their enemies, 1-6; reminded of their rebellions, and of the Lord's mercies, 7-29.

1. **to pass**. Dt 3:18. 11:31. 27:2. Jsh 1:11. 3:6, 14, 16. 4:5, 19. **this day**. ʃ12112, Ge +2:17. The Hebrew *hyyom, this day*, frequently denotes, as here, *this time*. They had come, 38 years before this, nearly to the verge of the promised land, but were not permitted, because of their unbelief and rebellion, at *that day* or *time*, to enter; but this time they shall certainly pass over. This was spoken in the eleventh month of the fortieth year of their journeying; and it was on the first month of the following year they passed over: and during this interval Moses died. The time was so short (less than two months), that it is regarded as if *today*. See Dt 1:3. Jsh 4:19. Jn 8:56. 1 C 4:5. Re 16:14. **nations**. See on Dt 4:38. 7:1. 11:23. ʃ121K1. Metonymy of the Subject B582. The possessor is put for the thing possessed. Nations are put for countries. For other instances of this figure see 2 S 8:2. Ps 79:7. Mk 5:35. **cities**. Dt 1:28. Nu 13:22, 28-33. **fenced**. ʃ102, Ge +2:24.

2. **great**. See on Dt 2:11, 12, 21. **children**. ʃ144A3, Ge +11:5. **Who can stand**. Dt 7:24. Ex 9:11. Jb 11:10. Da 8:4. 11:16. Na 1:6.

3. **Understand**. ver. 6. Mt 15:10. Mk 7:14. Ep 5:17. **goeth over**. Dt 1:30. 20:4. 31:3-6. Jsh 3:11, 14. Mi 2:13. Re 19:11-16. **a consuming fire**. ʃ22K1, Dt 4:24. Dt 4:24. Is 27:4. 30:27, 30, 33. 33:14. Na 1:5, 6. 2 Th *1:8. He ▸12:29. **he shall**. Dt 7:1, 2, 16, 23, 24. Ex 23:29-31. Is 41:10-16. Ro *8:31.

4. **Speak not**. ver. 5. Dt 7:7, 8. 8:17. Ezk 36:22, 32. Ro ▸10:6. 11:6, 20. 1 C 4:4, 7. Ep 2:4, 5. 2 T

*1:9. T *3:3-5. **for the wickedness**. Dt 12:31. 18:12. Ge 15:16. Le 18:24, 25. Mt 6:31, 32.

5. **Not for**. Though the Canaanites were expelled for their wickedness, it does not follow, that the Israelites were established in their room on account of any distinguished virtue, or because they deserved it. On many occasions, it may be seen in the history of the world, that God punishes the wicked by the instrumentality of other men, who are as wicked as themselves. Not the Israelites' righteousness, but the wickedness of the inhabitants, and the promise of God to their fathers, was the cause of their obtaining Canaan. Ps 115:1-3. T 3:5. **that he may**. Ge 12:7. 13:15. 15:7. 17:8. 26:4. 28:13. Ex 32:13. Ps *119:89. Is *55:10, 11. Je *1:12. Ezk 20:14. 36:22. Mi 6:20. Lk 1:54, 55. Jn 17:17. Ac 3:25. 13:32, 33. Ro 11:28. 15:8.

6. **Understand**. See on ver. 3, 4. Ezk 20:44. **giveth thee**. Moses repeats this a third time, that, if it were possible, he might root out of the Israelites the opinion of their own deserts, before God rooted out the Canaanites from their country. **a stiffnecked**. ver. 13. Dt 10:16. 31:27. Ex 32:9. 33:3. 34:9. 2 Ch 30:8. 36:13. Ps 78:8. Is 48:3, 4. Ezk 2:4. Zc 7:11, 12. Ac 7:51. Ro 3:9-12. 5:20, 21.

7. **Remember**. In order to destroy the opinion which the Israelites had of their own righteousness, it was necessary to call to mind some of their most notorious provocations and rebellions, which Moses exhorts them to preserve in their mind, as a means to keep them humble. Dt 8:2. Ezk 16:61-63. 20:43. 36:31, 32. 1 C 15:9. Ep 2:11. 1 T 1:13-15. **from the day**. Dt 31:27. 32:5, 6. Ex 14:11. 16:2. 17:2. Nu 11:4. 14:1, etc. 16:1, etc. 20:2-5. 21:5. 25:2. Ne 9:16-18. Ps 78:8, etc. 95:8-11. Is *48:8. Da 9:8.

8. **Also in Horeb**. Or rather, *Even at Horeb*, for there is a peculiar emphasis here—even there where they had lately received the law, attended with the most astonishing appearances and circumstances. Ex 32:1-6. Ps 106:19-22.

9. **I was**. Ex 24:12, 15, 18. **the tables**. ver. 15. Ex 31:18. 34:28. Je 31:31, 32. Ga 4:24. **then I**. Ex 24:18. 34:28. 1 K 19:8. Mt 4:2. **I neither**. ver. 18. 1 K 13:8, 9. 2 K 6:22.

10. **the Lord**. Ex 31:18. **written with**. ʃ22C43, Ex +31:18. Dt 10:4. Mt 12:28. Lk 11:20. 2 C 3:3. He 8:10. **all the words**. Dt 4:10-15. 5:6-21. 18:16. Ex 19:17-19. 20:1-18. Ac 7:36-38.

11. **the tables of the covenant**. See on ver. 9. Nu 10:33. He 8:6-10. 9:4. Ps 40:7, 8.

12. **Arise**. See on Ex 32:7, 8. **corrupted**. Dt 4:16. 31:29. 32:5. Ge 6:11, 12. Ju 10. **are quickly**. ver. 16. Jg 2:17. Ps 78:57. Je 17:9. Ho 6:4. 7:16. Ro 7:18. Ga 1:6. **molten image**. Is ◑40:18.

13. **I have**. Ge 11:5. 18:21. Ex 32:9, 10. Ps 50:7. Je 7:11. 13:27. Ho 6:10. Ml 3:5. **stiffnecked**. See on ver. 6. Dt 10:16. 31:27. Ex 32:9, 10. 2 K 17:14.

14. **Let me**. Ex 32:10-13. Is 62:6, 7. Je 14:11. 15:1. Lk 11:7-10. 18:1-8. Ac 7:51. **blot**. Dt 29:20. Ex 32:32, 33. Ps 9:5. 109:13. Pr 10:7. Re 3:5. **and I will**. Nu 14:11, 12. Je 18:7-10. Da 4:34, 35.

15. **I turned**. Ex 32:14, 15, etc. **the mount**. Dt 4:11. 5:23. Ex 9:33. 19:18. He 12:18.

16. **I looked**. Ex 32:19. Ac 7:40, 41.

17. **cast them**. Moses might have done this through distress and anguish of spirit, on beholding their abominable idolatry and dissolute conduct; or probably he

did it emblematically, and perhaps by the direction of God; intimating thereby, that as by this act of his the tables were broken in pieces, on which the Law of God was written, so they, by their present conduct, had made a breach in the covenant, and broken the laws of their Maker and Sovereign. Ex 32:19. **brake.** Ps ◑=40:8.

18. **I fell down.** See on ver. 9. Ex 32:10-14. 34:28. 2 S 12:16. Ps 106:23. **forty days.** T#1761. ver. 25.

19. **For I.** ver. 8. Ex 32:10, 11. Ne 1:2-7. Lk 12:4, 5. He ▶12:21. **to destroy.** 1 Ch 13:9-12. 21:30. Ps 106:23. **But the.** Dt 10:10. Ex 32:14. *33:17. Ps 99:6. 106:23. Am 7:2, 3, 5, 6. Ga 3:19. Ja *5:16, 17.

20. **very angry.** Ex 32:2-5, 21, 35. He 7:26-28.

21. **I took.** See on Ex 32:20. Is 2:18-21. 30:22. 31:7. 44:22. Je 50:20. Ho 8:11. Mi 7:18, 19. 1 J 1:7. **the brook.** This was the stream which flowed from the rock that Moses smote with his rod (Ex 17:6), and to which the Psalmist alludes in Ps 78:16-20. 105:41.

22. **Taberah.** Nu 11:1-5. **Massah.** Ex 17:7. Ps 78:16-20. 105:41. **Kibroth-hattaavah.** Nu 11:4, 34. Heb. *qeber,* Ge +23:4.

23. **Likewise.** Dt 1:19, etc. Nu 13:1-3. **ye rebelled.** See on Nu 14:1-4, 10-41. Is 63:10. **ye believed.** Dt 1:32, 33. 2 K 17:14. Ps 78:22, 32. 106:24, 25. He *3:18, 19. 4:2.

24. **rebellious.** ver. 6, 7. Dt 31:27. Ex 14:10-12. Ac 7:51.

25. **I fell.** See on ver. 16, 18.

26. **prayed.** Ex 32:11-13. 34:9. Nu 14:13-19. Ps 99:6. 106:23. Je 14:21. **thy people.** Ex ◑+*32:7. 33:13. 1 S 12:22. **thine inheritance.** 1 K 8:51. **which thou hast redeemed.** ver. 29. Dt 32:9. Ps 74:1, 2. Is 63:19. **which thou hast brought forth.** Dt 7:8. 13:5. 15:15. 21:8. 26:7, 8. Ex 15:13. 2 S 7:23. Ne 1:10. Ps 77:15. 107:2. Is 44:23. Mi 6:4. T *2:14. He 9:12. Re 5:9.

27. **Remember.** Ex 3:6, 16. 6:3-8. 13:5. 32:13. Je 14:21. **look not.** Ex 32:31, 32. 1 S 25:25. Ps 78:8. Pr 21:12. Is 43:24, 25. Je 50:20. Mi *7:18, 19.

28. **the land.** Ge 41:57. Ex 6:6-8. 1 S 14:25. **Because.** Dt 32:26, 27. Ex 32:12. Nu 14:15, 16. Jsh 7:7-9. Ps 115:1, 2. Is 43:25. 48:9-11. Je 14:7-9. Ezk 20:8, 9, 14. Da 9:18, 19.

29. **Yet they.** ver. 26. Dt 4:20. 1 K 8:51. Ne 1:10. Ps 95:7. 100:3. Is 63:19. **which thou.** See on ver. 26. Dt 4:34. 28:9. Nu 23:+*21, 22. 1 K 8:51. Je 14:9. 1 J *2:1, 2.

DEUTERONOMY 10

Moses relates the mercy of God, in again giving the tables of the law, 1-5; in continuing the priesthood, 6, 7; in separating the tribe of Levi, 8, 9; in hearing the prayer of Moses for the people, 1-11. Hence he exhorts them to obedience, 12-22.

1. **Hew.** ver. 4. Ex 34:1, 2, 4. **make thee.** ver. 3. Ex 25:10-15. He 9:4.

2. **thou shalt.** ver. 5. Ex 25:16-22. 40:20. 1 K 8:9. He 9:4.

3. **I made.** Ex 25:5, 10. 37:1-9. **hewed.** ver. 1. Ex 34:4.

4. **he wrote.** See on Dt 9:10. Ex 34:28. **the ten.** Dt 4:13. Ex 34:28. **commandments.** Heb. words. Ex 34:28mg. **which.** Dt 5:4-21. Ex 20:1-17. **out of the.** Dt 4:11-15. 5:22-26. Ex 19:18. He 12:18, 19. **in the day.** Dt 9:10. 18:16. Ex 19:17.

5. **I turned.** Dt 9:15. Ex 32:15. 34:29. **put the.** See on ver. 2. Ex 25:16. 40:20. **there they.** Jsh 4:9. 1 K 8:8, 9. Ro 3:1, 2. He 9:4.

6. **took.** Nu 10:6, 12, 13. 33:1, 2. **Beeroth of.** i.e. *wells,* *S#885h, only here. For *S#881h, Beeroth, see Jsh +9:17. **Jaakan.** i.e. *necessity; strait,* ✛S#3292h. **Mosera.** i.e. *discipline,* *S#4149h. Nu 33:30, 31, Moseroth. Hor-ha-gid-gad. Jotbatha. **there Aaron.** Nu 20:23-28. 33:38. **in his stead.** He ◑7:23-25.

7. **From thence.** Nu 33:32, 33. **Gudgodah.** i.e. *incision,* *S#1412h. **Jotbath.** i.e. *goodness,* *S#3193h. Nu 33:33, 34.

8. **time the Lord.** Ex 29:1, etc. Le 8:9. Nu 1:47-53. ch. 3, 4, 8. 16:9, 10. 18. Jn 15:16. Ac 13:2. Ro 1:1. 2 C 6:17. Ga 1:15. **separated.** Ac=4:13. **bear.** Nu 3:31. 4:15. 1 K 8:3, 4, 6. 1 Ch 15:12-15, 26. 23:26. 2 Ch 5:4, 5. Ac=9:15. 2 C=4:10. **to stand.** ♪121S2, Ge +21:6. Dt 18:5. 2 Ch 29:11. Ps 134:2. 135:2. Je 15:19. Ezk 44:11, 15. Ro 12:7. **unto him.** 1 C=7:22. Ep=6:7. **to bless.** Dt 21:5. Le 9:22. Nu *6:23-27. 2 Ch 30:27. **his name.** Ac=3:16. =4:29, 30. **unto this day.** Dt +29:4.

9. **Levi.** Dt 18:1, 2. Nu 18:20-24. 26:62. Jsh 14:3. Ezk 44:28. **no part.** He =13:14. **Lord.** ♪121K4, Jsh 13:33. **inheritance.** Dt 32:9. Nu 18:20. 35:1-4. Ezk 44:28. Ro=8:17. Ep=1:11. 1 P=1:4.

10. **I stayed.** Dt 9:18, 25. Ex 24:18. 34:28. **first time.** *or,* former days. **the Lord hearkened.** Dt 3:23-27. 9:19. Ex 32:14, 33, 34. *33:17. Ps 106:23. Mt 27:42.

11. **Arise.** Ex 32:34. 33:1. Mi 2:10. **take thy.** Heb. go in.

12. **what doth.** Je *7:22, 23. Mi +*6:8. Mt *11:29, 30. 1 J 5:3. **fear.** Dt *6:13. Ps *34:9. *128:1. Je *32:39, 40. Ac 9:31. 1 P 1:17. **to walk.** See on Dt *5:33. Jsh *22:5. Ps 81:13. Ezk *11:20. T *2:11, 12. 1 P 1:15, 16. **to love.** See on Dt *6:5. *11:13. *30:16, 20. Ps *18:1. *145:20. Mt *22:37. Mk *12:29-33. Lk 10:27. *11:42. Ro *8:28. 1 J *2:15. *4:19, 20. *5:2, 3. **to serve.** Jb *36:11. Zp 3:9. Ro *1:9. He *12:28. **God with all.** See on Dt *4:29. **soul.** Heb. *nephesh,* Ge +34:3.

13. **for thy.** Dt 6:24. Pr 9:12. Je 32:39. 1 T 4:8. Ja 1:25.

14. **the heaven.** 1 K 8:27. 2 Ch 6:18. Ne 9:6. Ps 115:16. 148:4. Is 66:1. **heaven of.** 2 C +*12:2. **the earth.** Ge 14:19. Ex 9:29. 19:5. Ps 24:1. 50:12. Je 27:5, 6. 1 C 10:26, 28.

15. **had.** See on Dt *4:37. 7:7, 8. Nu 14:8. Ro 9:13-23. **delight.** Dt 7:8. Ps 37:4. **chose.** Ps 33:12. 65:4. 106:5. Hg 2:23. Mt 11:27. 22:14. 24:22, 24, 31. Lk 18:7. Ro 8:28-30, 33. 11:28. Col 3:12. 1 Th 5:9. T 1:1. 1 P 1:1, 2. 2:8, 9. Re 17:14.

16. **Circumcise.** Dt *30:6. Le *26:41. Je *4:4, 14. Ro *2:28, 29. Col *2:11. **be no more.** Is *30:18, 19. Lk 13:6-9. Ja 5:7. 2 P *3:9, 15. **stiffnecked.** See on Dt *9:6, 13. *31:27. Pr *29:1. Ja *4:6, 7.

17. **God is.** Re 17:14. 19:16. **God of gods.** ♪147H, Ge +9:25. Jsh 22:22. 1 Ch 16:25, 26. Ps 136:2. Da 2:47. 11:36. **Lord of lords.** ♪147H, Ge +9:25. Ps 136:3. Re 17:14. 19:16. **a great.** Dt 7:21. Ne 1:5. 4:14. 9:32. Jb 37:22, 23. Ps 99:3. Je 20:11. **God.** Heb. *El,* Ex +15:2. **regardeth.** 2 Ch 19:7. Jb 34:19. Mk 12:14. Ac 10:34. Ro 2:11. Ga 2:6. Ep 6:9. Col 3:25. 1 P 1:17.

18. **doth.** Ps 68:5. 103:6. 146:9. Is 1:17. Je 49:11. Ho 14:3. **fatherless and.** ♪171I14, Ex +22:22. T#782. Ge +11:28. 24:53n. Ex +*22:22-24. Ps 10:14, 17, 18.

68:5. *146:9. Pr 15:25. *23:10, 11. Je *49:11. Ho *14:3. Ml +*3:5. **loveth**. Ps 145:9. Mt *5:45. Ac 14:17. **stranger**. ver. 19. Dt +26:11. Ge +23:4 (＊S#1616h). Ex 12:48. Jsh +20:9. Mt +25:35.

19. **Love**. Ex 22:21. 23:9. Le 19:33, 34. Lk *6:35. 10:28-37. 17:18. Ga 6:10. 1 T 6:18. Ja *2:15, 16. 1 J *3:17, 18. **stranger**. ver. +18. Ex 12:48, 49. **ye were**. 1 C 6:11. Ep 2:19.

20. **fear**. Dt 6:13. 13:4. Ex +34:14. Mt *4:10. Lk 4:8. **cleave**. Dt 4:4. 11:22. 13:4. Jsh 23:8. Ac *11:23. Ro 12:9. **swear**. See on Dt 6:13. Ge 21:23. 31:53. Ps *63:11. Is *45:23. Mt❍*5:33-37. ❍23:16-22. Ja❍*5:12.

21. **thy praise**. Ex 15:2. Ps 22:3. Is 12:2-6. 60:19. Je 17:14. Lk 2:32. Re 21:23. **that hath**. Dt 4:32-35. 1 S 12:24. 2 S 7:23. Ps 106:21, 22. Is 64:3. Je 32:20, 21.

22. **with threescore**. And now, from so small a beginning, they are multiplied to more than 600,000 men, besides women and children; and this, indeed, in the space of 40 years; for the 603,000 which came out of Egypt were at this time all dead, except Moses, Joshua, and Caleb. How easy can God increase and multiply, as well as diminish and bring low! In all things, by his omnipotence, he can do whatever he will, and he will do whatsoever is right. Ge 46:27. Ex 1:5. Ac 7:14. **persons**. Heb. *nephesh*, souls, Ge +12:5. **as the stars**. ∫102B, ∫138B, Ge +13:16. Dt 1:10. 28:62. Ge 15:5. Nu 26:51, 62. Ne 9:23. He 11:12.

DEUTERONOMY 11

An exhortation to obedience, 1; by their own experience of God's great works, 2-7; by promise of God's great blessings, 8-15; and by threatenings, 16, 17. A careful study is required of God's words, 18-25. The blessing and curse set before the people, with orders to publish them from mount Gerizim and mount Ebal, 26-32.

1. **thou shalt**. This verse is the practical improvement of the conclusion of the foregoing chapter; while the next verse begins another view of the subject. See on Dt 6:5. 10:12. 30:16-20. Ps 116:1. **keep**. Le 8:35. Zc 3:7. Jn *14:21. 15:8-10. 2 J 6. Re 22:14. **his statutes**. See on Dt 4:1, 5, 40. 6:1. Ps 105:45. Lk 1:74, 75. **judgments**. Ps 9:16. **commandments**. Ps *19:7-10. 112:1.

2. **And know**. Ro 7:1. He 12:5-7. **ye this**. Moses seems here to have addressed himself particularly to the elders, who had in their youth witnessed the wonderful works which Jehovah had wrought both for them and among them; and who were bound to remember them for their own warning, and testify them to the rising generation who had not been eye-witnesses. Dt 8:19. 29:10. Pr 22:19. Jn 20:29. Ac 1:21, 22. *26:22. 2 P 1:16. **children**. ver. 19. Ex +13:8. Dt +6:20. **have not known**. Lk 12:47, 48. Jn 20:29. Ro 2:12. **the chastisement**. See on Dt 8:2-5. **his greatness**. See on Dt 5:24. 9:26. **his mighty**. See on Dt 7:19.

3. **his miracles**. See on Dt 4:34. 6:22. 7:8, 19. 26:8. Ex 15:12. Ps 78:12, 13, 43-51. 105:27, etc. 135:9. 136:10-12. Je 32:20, 21.

4. **how he made**. Ex 14:23-31. 15:4, 9, 10, 19. Ps 106:11. He 11:29. **unto this day**. Dt +29:4.

5. **what he did**. Ps 77:20. 78:14, etc., 50-53. 105:39-41. 106:12, etc.

6. **he did unto**. Nu 16:1, 31-33. 26:9, 10. 27:3. Ps

106:17. Ju 11. **substance**. *or*, living substance which followed them. Ge 7:4, 23. **in their possession**. Heb. at their feet. Dt 28:57. *33:3. Ge 30:30mg. 33:14mg. *49:10. Ex +11:8. Jg 5:15mg, 27mg.

7. **your eyes**. ver. +2. Dt 5:3. 7:19. Ps 106:2. 145:4-6, 12. 150:2. 1 C 15:5-8. 2 P 1:16. 1 J 1:1.

8. **therefore**. See on Dt 8:10, 11. 10:12-15. 26:16-19. 28:47. Ps 116:12-16. 119:97-100. **that ye may**. Dt 31:23. Jsh 1:6, 7. Ps 138:3. Is 40:31. Da 10:19. 2 C 12:9, 10. Ep *3:16. 6:10. Ph *4:13. Col 1:11.

9. **prolong**. Dt +*4:40. 5:16. 6:2. Ps 34:12, etc. Pr 3:2, 16. 9:11. *10:27. Is 48:18. **sware**. See on Dt 6:18. 9:5. **a land**. Dt +8:8. See on Ex 3:8. Ezk 20:6. **milk and**. ∫174, Ge +18:27. **honey**. ∫171I7, Ex +3:8.

10. **wateredst it with thy foot**. Rain seldom falls in Egypt; the land being chiefly watered by the inundations of the Nile. In order to water the grounds where the inundations do not extend, water is collected in ponds, and directed in streamlets to the different parts of the field where irrigation is necessary. It is no unusual thing in the East to see a man, with a small mattock, making a little trench for the water to run into; and, as he opens the passage, the water following, he uses his foot to raise up the mould against the side of this little channel, to prevent the water from being shed unnecessarily, before it reaches the place of its destination. Hence, he may justly be said to "water the ground with his foot." Ps 1:3. Pr *21:1. Is 19:7. 37:25. 43:19. Je 17:8. Zc 14:18.

11. **the land**. See on Dt 8:7-9. Ge 27:28. Ps 65:12, 13. 104:10-13. Is 28:1. Je 2:7. He 6:7.

12. **careth for**. Heb. seeketh. or searcheth. 1 Ch +*28:9. Ps +√9:10. 14:2. 119:2. **the eyes**. 1 K 9:3. 2 Ch *16:9. Ezr 5:5. Ps 33:18. 34:15. Je 24:6. ∫22A7. Anthropomorphism B875. Eyes are used of God's grace and favor. For other instances of this figure see Dt 32:10. 1 K 9:3. 2 Ch 16:9. Ps 31:22. *32:8. Ezk 5:11. 7:4. 20:17. 1 P 3:12. **always**. Is +*58:11 (continually).

13. **diligently**. ver. 8, 22. See on Dt 6:17. Ps 119:4, 33-35. **to love**. See on Dt 4:29. 6:5, 6. 10:12. **soul**. Heb. *nephesh*, Ge +34:3. Mt +*22:37.

14. **I will**. Dt 28:12. Le 26:3-5. Jb 5:10, 11. 37:11-13. Ps 65:9-13. Je 14:22. Ezk 34:26. Jl 2:22, 23. Mt 5:45. Ja 5:7. **first rain**. Ps 84:6mg. Je 5:24. Ho 6:3. Jl 2:23. Zc 10:1. **latter rain**. Jb 29:23. Pr 16:15. Je 3:3. 5:24. Ho 6:3. Ac 2:16-18. 3:19-26.

15. **And I will**. 1 K 18:5. Ps 104:14. Je 14:5. Jl 1:18. 2:22. **send**. Heb. give. Ge 1:29. 3:12. 1 S 12:17. 1 K 18:1. 2 K 19:7. 2 Ch 6:27. Ps 68:33. Ec 12:7. SS 1:12. 2:13. 7:13. **eat and be full**. Dt 6:11. 8:10. Jl 2:19. Hg 1:6. Ml 3:10, 11.

16. **Take heed**. See on Dt 4:9, 23. Lk 21:8, 34, 36. He *2:1. √3:12. *4:1. *12:15. **your heart**. Dt 13:3. 17:20. 29:18. Jb 31:27. Is 44:20. Je *17:9. Ja 1:26. 1 J 5:21. Re 12:9. 13:14. *20:4. **turn aside**. Dt 28:14. **serve other**. Dt 8:19. 30:17. Le 26:1. 1 C *8:5, 6. 10:14. **worship**. Ex +34:14.

17. **the Lord's wrath**. See on Dt 6:15. 30:17, 18. **shut up**. Dt 28:23, 24. Le 26:23, 24, 26. 1 K 8:35. 17:1. 2 Ch 6:26. *7:13, 14. Je 14:1-6. Am 4:7. Hg 1:9-11. Ja 5:17, 18. **ye perish**. Dt 4:26. 8:19, 20. 30:18. Jsh 23:13-16.

18. **ye lay up**. See on Dt 6:6-9. 32:46. Ex 13:9, 16. Ps 119:√11, 129-131. Pr *3:1. 6:20-23. *7:2, 3. Col *3:16. He *2:1. 2 P 1:12. 3:1, 2. **soul**. Heb. *nephesh*, Ge +34:3. **a sign**. Mt *23:5.

19. **shall teach.** Dt 4:9, 10. 6:7, +*20. Ge *18:19. Ex +*13:8. 1 Ch 28:9. Ps 34:11. *78:3-6. Pr 1:8, 9. 2:1. 4:1, 10-13. 22:6. Is *38:19. Mt 28:20. Ep 6:4. Col 3:16. 2 T 1:5. +√3:15. **speaking.** Ps 119:46-48. Je √23:28.

20. **write.** Dt 6:9. Ha 2:2.

21. **your days.** See on Dt *4:40. 5:16. 6:2. *32:46, 47. Ps 89:29. Pr 3:2, 16. 4:10. 9:11. **as the days.** Ps 72:5. 89:28, 29. +*118:24. Is *65:20. Re *20:6. **of heaven upon.** Mt *6:10. He +√11:13.

22. **if.** Ge +4:7. **ye shall.** See on ver. 13. Dt 6:17. **diligently.** Jsh 22:5. Ps 119:4. Ac 11:23. He 11:6. 2 P 1:10. 3:14. **to love.** See on ver. 13. Mt 22:37. 2 T 4:8. 1 J 5:2, 3. **to cleave.** See on Dt 10:20. 30:20. Ge 2:24. Ac *11:23. 2 C 11:2, 3.

23. **drive out.** Dt 4:38. 7:1, 2, 22, 23. 9:1, 5. Ex 23:27-30. 34:11. Lk 11:21. 1 J 4:4.

24. **Every place.** Ge 15:18-21. Ex 23:31. Nu 34:3, etc. Jsh 1:3, 4. 14:9. 2 S 8:3, 6, 14. 1 K 4:21, 24. 9:17-19. 2 Ch 9:26.

25. **There shall.** See on Dt 2:25. 7:24. 28:10. Ex 23:27. Jsh 1:5. 2:9. 5:1. **and.** ƒ174, Ge +18:27. **as he hath.** Ex 23:27. Nu *23:19.

26. **I set before.** Dt 30:1, 15-20. Nu 22:6. Ps 37:22. Ga 3:10, 13, 14.

27. **A blessing.** Dt 28:1-14. Le 26:3-13. Ps *19:11. Is 1:19. 3:10. Mt 5:3-12. 25:31, etc. Lk 11:28. Jn 13:17. 14:21-23. Ro 2:7. Ja 1:25. Re 22:14. **if.** Ge +4:7.

28. **a curse.** Dt 28:15, etc. 29:19-28. Le 26:14, etc. Is 1:20. 3:11. Mt 25:41. Ro 2:8, 9. Ga 3:10. **to go after.** Dt 6:14. **other gods.** ver. 16. Dt 8:19. 30:17. **not known.** Ga 1:8.

29. **put the blessing.** Dt 27:12-26. Jsh 8:30-35. **Gerizim.** i.e. *the cutters off,* ✳S#1630h. Dt 27:12. Jsh 8:33. Jg 9:7. Jn 4:20.

30. **Are.** ƒ85B, Ge +13:9. **Canaanites.** Ge +10:18. **champaign.** Heb. *Arabah.* Dt 1:1mg. 2:8mg. 4:49mg. Nu +22:1. Jsh 3:16. +4:13. 8:14. 11:2, 16. 12:8. 18:18. 1 S 23:24. 2 S 2:29. 4:7. +15:28. 2 K 14:25. 25:4. Je 39:4. 52:7. Ezk 47:8. Am +*6:14. Zc 14:10. **Gilgal.** Ge 12:6. Jsh 4:19, 20. 5:9. 9:6. 10:6. 12:23. 14:6. 15:7. Jg 2:1. 3:19. 1 S 7:16. 10:8. 11:14. 13:4. 15:12. **the plains.** or, oaks, or terebinths. Ge 13:18. 35:4, 8. Jsh 24:26. **Moreh.** Ge 12:6. Jg 7:1.

31. **pass over Jordan.** Dt 9:1. Jsh 1:2, 11. 3:13-17. 11:23.

32. **observe to do.** See on Dt 5:32, 33. *12:32. Ps 119:6. Mt √7:21-27. 28:20. Lk 1:6. Jn +*15:14. 1 Th *4:1, 2.

DEUTERONOMY 12

Monuments of idolatry must be destroyed, 1-3. The place of God's service to be kept, 4-14. Blood is forbidden, 15, 16, 20-25. Holy things must be eaten in the holy place, 17, 18, 26-28. The Levite is not to be forsaken, 19. Idolatry is not to be enquired after, 29-31. God's Word to be obeyed, not added to nor diminished, 32.

1. **the statutes.** See on Dt 4:1, 2, 5, 45. 6:1, 2. **all the days.** ver. 19. Dt 4:10. Nu 15:37-41. 1 K 8:40. Jb 7:1. Ps 104:33. 146:2.

2. **utterly.** See on Dt 7:5, 25, 26. Ex 23:24. 34:12-17. Nu 33:51, 52. Jg 2:2. **possess.** *or,* inherit. Nu 22:41. 2 K 16:4. 17:10, 11. 23:13-15. Je 3:6. Ezk 20:28, 29. Ho 4:13. **high mountains.** 1 K 14:23. 2 K 16:4. 17:10.

Je 3:6. **the hills.** 2 K 16:4n. +*17:10. **green tree.** 2 K 16:4n. +*17:10.

3. **ye shall.** Nu 33:52. Jg 2:2. 2 Ch 31:1. **overthrow.** Heb. break down. Dt 7:5. Ex 34:13. Jg 2:2. **and burn.** 1 K 15:13. 2 K 18:4. 23:14. 2 Ch 14:3. 19:3. 34:3. Je 17:2. Mi 5:14. **images.** ƒ100, Ge +10:9. **and destroy.** Ex 23:13. Ps 16:4. Ho 2:17. Zc 13:2. Re 13:1.

4. **not do so.** ver. 30, 31. Dt 6:13-19. 16:21, 22. 20:18. Le 20:23. Mt *4:10.

5. **But unto.** ver. 11. Dt 16:2. 26:2. Jsh 9:27. 18:1. 1 K 8:16, 20, 29. 14:21. 1 Ch 22:1. 2 Ch 7:12. Ps 78:68. 87:2, 3. Jn 4:20-22. He 12:22. Re 14:1. **habitation.** Ex 15:2. 25:22. Nu 7:89. 1 K 8:27, *29. Ps 132:13, 14. Is 66:1, 2. Ac 7:48-50. Ep 2:20-22. Col 2:9.

6. **your burnt offerings.** Le 17:3-9. +*23:12. Ezk 20:40. **sacrifices.** Le +*7:11. +*23:19. **tithes.** ver. 11, 17. Dt 14:22-26. 15:19, 20. 26:2. Ge +*14:20. Le 27:32, 33. Nu 18:15-17. Ml *3:8, 10. Mt +*23:23n. Lk +*11:42n. 18:12. **heave offerings.** Le +*7:14. **vows.** Le +*23:38. **freewill offerings.** Le +*23:38.

7. **And there.** ver. 18. Dt 14:23, 26. 15:20. 1 K 4:20. Ne *:10. Ec 9:7-9. Is 23:18. **ye shall.** ver. 12, 18. Dt 16:11-15. 26:11. 27:7. Le 23:40. Ps 16:11. 128:1, 2. Ml 2:13. Ac 2:46. Ph 3:1. *4:4. **put your hand.** ƒ121R7, Ge +43:11.

8. **every man.** Nu 15:39. Jg 17:6. 21:25. Pr 21:2. Am 5:25. Ac 7:42. **right.** Dt ⬤13:18. Jg 21:25. 1 K 12:33. Pr √14:12.

9. **not as yet.** He 2:8. 1 J *3:2. **rest.** Dt 25:19. 1 K 8:56. 1 Ch 23:25. Mi 2:10. He *4:8, 9. 1 P *1:3, 4.

10. **But when.** Dt 3:27. 4:22. 9:1. 11:31. Jsh 3:17. 4:1, 12. **ye dwell.** Dt 33:12, 28. Le 25:18, 19. 1 S 7:12. 1 K 4:25. Ps 4:8. Pr 1:33. Je *23:6. 32:37. 33:11. Ezk 28:26. 34:25, 28. 38:8. **rest from.** Jsh 21:43-45.

11. **a place.** See on ver. 5, +*14, 18, 21, 26. Dt 14:23. 15:20. 16:2, 6, 7, 11, 15, +*16. 17:8. 18:6. 23:16. 26:2. 31:11. Ex +20:24. +23:20. +29:24. Jsh 9:27. 18:1. √22:27. 1 K 8:13, 29. 2 Ch 7:12. Ps 78:68. Je 7:12. Mt 18:20. Jn 4:20-23. He 10:25. **burnt offerings.** Le +*23:12. **sacrifices.** Le +*7:11. +*23:19. **your tithes.** ver. +6. Ge +*14:20. **heave offering.** Le +*7:14. **your choice.** Heb. the choice of your vows. **vows.** Le +*23:38.

12. **And ye.** See on ver. 7. Dt 14:26, 27. 1 K 8:66. 2 Ch 29:36. 30:21-26. Ne 8:10-12. Ps 100:1, 2. 147:1. 1 J 1:3, 4. **the Levite.** ver. 19. Dt 14:27, 29. 16:11, 14. 18:6. 26:12. **gates.** ƒ171S6, Ge +14:7. **forasmuch.** Dt 10:9. 18:1, 2. See on Nu 18:20, 23, 24, 26. Jsh 13:14, 33. 14:4.

13. **Take heed.** This was directly opposed to the customs of the heathen idolaters, in offering their sacrifices on the tops of hills and mountains. ver. 6. Le 17:2-5. 1 K 12:28-32. 15:34. 2 Ch 15:17. **every place.** Jsh *22:16, √29.

14. **place.** ver. 5, +*11. Dt 16:+6, 16. Le 17:3-9. 23:4. Ps 5:7. 9:11. 2 C 5:19. He 10:19-22, *25. 13:15.

15. **whatsoever.** Dt 14:26. **soul.** Heb. *nephesh,* Nu +11:6. **lusteth.** ƒ108K40B, Ex 15:9. **the unclean.** ver. 21, 22. Dt 14:5. 15:22, 23. Le 17:3-5. Of the propriety of eating clean animals there could be no question, but the blood must be poured out: yet there were cases when they might kill and eat in all their gates such as the roebuck and the hart, or all clean *wild* beasts; for these being taken in hunting, and frequently shot by arrows, their blood could not be poured out at the altar.

16. **not eat.** ver. 23, 24. Dt 15:23. Ge 9:4. See on Le 7:26, 27. 17:10-13. Jn ●6:51-56. Ac *15:29. 1 T 4:4.

17. **the tithe.** See on ver. +*6, 11. Dt 14:22-29. 26:12, 14. Le 27:30-32. Nu 18:21, etc. **thy corn.** Ne 10:39. **vows.** Le +*23:38. **freewill offerings.** Le +*23:38. **heave offering.** Le +*7:14.

18. **thou must.** See on ver. 11, 12, 19. Dt 14:23. 15:20. **rejoice.** See on ver. 7. Ps 32:11. 68:3. Pr 3:17. Is 12:3. Ac *2:46. 16:34. 1 C *10:31. Ga *5:22. Ph 3:1-3.

19. **take.** Dt 14:27-29. 2 Ch 11:13, 14. 31:4-21. Ne 10:34-39. 1 C 9:10-14. **as long**, etc. Heb. all thy days. See on ver. 1. Jsh 4:24mg. **earth.** or, thy ground.

20. **shall.** 1 Ch 4:10. **as he hath.** See on Dt 11:24. 19:8. Ge 15:18-21. 28:14. Ex 23:31. 34:24. **I will.** See on ver. 15. Ge 31:30. Nu 11:4, 20, 34. 2 S 13:39. 23:15. Ps 63:1. 84:2. 107:9. 119:20, 40, 174. 2 C 9:14. Ph 1:8. 2:26. **soul.** Heb. *nephesh*, Nu +11:6.

21. **to put.** ver. 5, 11. Dt 14:23, 24. 16:6, 11. 26:2. Ex 20:24. 1 K 14:21. 2 Ch 12:13. Ezr 6:12. **soul.** Heb. *nephesh*, Nu +11:6.

22. **roebuck.** See on ver. 15, 16.

23. **sure.** Heb. strong. Dt 31:6, 7, 23. Jsh 1:6, 7, 9, 18. 10:25. Is 41:6mg. **the blood is.** Ge 9:4. Le 3:16, 17n. 17:*11, 14. Mt 20:28. Re 5:9. **life.** Heb. *nephesh*, soul, Ge +√2:19. Pr 12:10. **not eat.** ver. 16. Le *3:16, 17n. 7:26. 17:10. 1 S 14:33. Ezk 33:25. Ac 15:29.

24. **shalt pour.** ver. 16. Dt 15:23.

25. **that it.** ver. 28. See on Dt 4:40. 5:16. Ps 112:2. Is 3:10. 48:18, 19. Ezk 33:25. **when.** See on Dt 6:18. 13:18. Ex 15:26. 1 K 11:38. Ec 2:26. 1 T 4:8.

26. **holy.** See on ver. 6, 11, 18. Nu 5:9, 10. 18:19. **thy vows.** See on Ge 28:20. Le 22:18, etc. +*23:38. 1 S 1:21-24. Ps 66:13-15.

27. **thy burnt.** See on Le 1:5, 9, 13. 17:11. **and the blood.** Le 3:16, 17n. 4:30. *17:11. **poured out.** ver. 16.

28. **Observe.** Dt 24:8. See on Ex 34:11. Le 19:37. 2 Ch 7:17. Ne 1:5. Ps 105:45. Ezk 37:24. Jn 15:*3, 10, 14. **and hear.** Is 48:18, 19. Mk 4:24. Lk 8:18. **that it may.** See on ver. 25. **for ever.** Heb. *olam*, Ex +12:24.

29. **cut off.** Dt 9:3. 19:1. Ex 23:23. Jsh 23:4. Ps 78:55. **succeedest.** Heb. inheritest, *or*, possessest. ver. 2. Dt 19:1.

30. **Take heed.** Ac 20:28. **that thou.** Dt 7:16. Ex 23:31-33. Le 18:3. Nu 33:52. Jg 2:2, 3. 2 K 17:15. Ps 106:34-38. Ezk 20:28. **by following.** Heb. after. Dt 1:4, 8, 36mg. 4:3. Ge 5:4, etc. 6:4. 9:9, 28. Jsh 6:8. Jg 9:3mg. Ps 73:24. Pr 7:22. 24:27. 28:23. **How did.** Je 10:2. Ezk 20:32. Ro *12:2. Ep 4:17. 1 P 4:3, 4.

31. **Thou.** ver. 4. Dt 18:9. Ex 23:2. Le 18:3, 26-30. 2 K 17:15-17. 21:2. 2 Ch 33:2. 36:14. **abomination to the.** Heb. abomination of the. Dt 7:25. 17:1. 18:12. 22:5. 23:18. 25:16. 27:15. **even their sons.** Dt 18:10. Le 18:21. 20:2. Je 7:31. 32:35. Ezk 20:31. 23:37. Mi 6:7.

32. **observe.** Mt 28:20. Mt 7:21. Lk *6:46. *8:21. Ja 1:22. **thou shalt not.** Dt *4:2. *13:18. Jsh 1:7. 8:30-35. Pr 19:27. *30:6. Mt 28:20. Re *22:18, 19.

DEUTERONOMY 13

Enticers to idolatry must be put to death, 1-5. Even the nearest relations must accuse them, 6-8; and lead the way in stoning them, 9-11. Idolatrous cities are not to be spared, but must be utterly destroyed, 12-18.

1. **a prophet.** That is, one pretending to the divine inspiration and authority of the prophetic office—or "a dreamer of dreams," one who pretends that some deity has spoken to him in the night season—"and giveth thee a sign," *oth*, what appears to be a miraculous proof of his mission, "or a wonder," *mopheth*, some "portentous sign," such as an eclipse, which he, who knew when it would happen, might predict to the people, who knew nothing of the matter, and thereby accredit his pretensions. But no pretended miracles must be admitted as a proof that the people might violate the first and great commandment. 1 K 13:18. Is 9:15. Je 6:13. 23:11. Ezk 13:2, 3, 23. Zc 13:4. Mt 7:15. 24:11. Lk 6:26. 2 P 2:1. 1 J 4:1. **a dreamer.** Je 23:25-28. 27:9. 29:8, 24mg. Zc 10:2.

2. **the sign.** Dt 18:22. Ex 7:22. 1 K 13:3-5, √7-32. Je *28:9. Mt *7:22, 23. *24:24. 2 C *11:13-15. 2 Th *2:9-11. Re *13:13, 14.

3. **hearken.** Is +√8:20. Ac +*17:11. Ep +*4:14. 1 J *4:1. **proveth.** See on Dt 8:2. Ex 16:4. 20:20. Ps 66:10. 81:7. Mt 24:24. 1 C +*11:19. 2 Th 2:11. Ja 1:12. 1 J √2:19. 4:4. 1 P 1:6, 7. Re 13:14. **ye love the Lord your God.** See on Dt 6:5. 2 C 8:8. **soul.** Heb. *nephesh*, Ge +34:3.

4. **walk.** See on Dt 6:13. 2 K 23:3. 2 Ch 34:31. Mi +*6:8. Lk 1:6. Col +√1:10. 1 Th 4:1, 2. **fear.** ʃ173, Ge +27:44. Dt 10:20. **and obey.** Dt 30:20. Je *7:23. Mt 7:21. Lk *6:46. He *5:9. **his voice.** Dt 8:20. 30:20. Jn 10:4, 5, *27. **and cleave.** See on Dt 10:20. 30:20. Ro 6:13. 1 C 6:17. +√15:2mg.

5. **prophet.** Dt 18:20. 1 K 18:40. Is 9:14, 15. 28:17, 18. Je 14:15. 28:15-17. 29:21, 22. Zc 13:3. Re 19:20. **spoken.** Heb. spoken a revolt against the Lord. Is 1:5mg. Je +28:16mg. **turn you.** ver. 10. Dt 7:4. Je 50:6. Ac 13:8. 2 T 4:4, 5. 2 J 9-11. **put the evil away from the midst.** Dt 17:7. 19:19. 22:21, 24. 24:7. 1 C 5:13. He *12:14, 15.

6. **thy brother.** Dt 17:2, 3. 28:54. Ge 16:5. Pr 5:20. 18:24. Mi 7:5-7. Zc 13:2, 3. Mt 12:48-50. 2 C 5:16. **which is.** 1 S 18:1, 3. 20:17. 2 S 1:26. **soul.** Heb. *nephesh*, Ge +27:31. **entice.** Jb 31:27. Ga 2:4. Ep *4:14. Col 2:4. 2 P 2:1. 1 J 2:26, 27. Re 12:9. 13:14. 20:3. **which thou.** Dt 32:16-18. Jg 2:13. 5:8. 10:6. 1 K 11:5-7. 2 K 17:30, 31.

7. **gods of the people.** Dt 6:14. 1 Ch 16:26. Is 2:8. Je 2:11, 28. 16:20. Da 5:4. Jn 10:34. 1 C √8:5. 12:2. Ga 4:8.

8. **consent.** Ex 20:3. Pr *1:10. Ga *1:8, 9. 1 J 5:21. **shall thine.** See on Dt 7:16. 19:13. Ezk 5:11. 9:5, 6. **eye.** ʃ155A, Ge +31:35.

9. **But.** Dt 17:2-7. Ex 22:20. Mt 10:37. Lk 14:26. **thine hand.** Dt 17:7. Zc 13:2, 3. Jn 8:7. Ac 7:58.

10. **stone him.** Dt 21:21. Le 20:2, 27. 24:14-16, 23. Nu 15:35, 36. Jsh 7:25. 2 Ch 24:21. By this law, every Israelite was bound in conscience to inform against, to prosecute, and to assist at the execution of anyone, even the nearest relation or friend, who attempted to persuade him to idolatry; yet it is observable that parents and husbands are not expressly mentioned in the list of those who were thus to be publicly accused (Scott). **which brought.** See on Ex 20:2. **bondage.** Heb. bondmen. Dt +6:12.

11. **all Israel.** Dt 17:13. 19:20. Pr *19:25. 21:11. 1 T 5:20.

12. **shalt hear**. Jsh 22:11, etc. Jg 20:1, 2, etc.

13. **the children**. *or*, naughty men. Jg 19:22. 20:13. 1 S 2:12. 10:27. 25:17, 25. 2 S 16:7. 20:1. 23:6. 1 K 21:10, 13. 2 Ch 13:7. Jn *8:44. 2 C 6:15. 1 J 3:10. **Belial**. i.e. *wicked; vile; perverse; worthlessness*, *S#1100h. Dt 15:9 (wicked). Jg 19:22. 20:13. 1 S 1:16. 2:12. 10:27. 25:17, 25. 30:22. 2 S 16:7. 20:1. 22:5. 23:6. 1 K 21:10, 13, 13. 2 Ch 13:7. Jb 34:18 (wicked). Ps 18:4mg. 41:8mg. 101:3mg. Pr 6:12 (naughty). 16:27mg. 19:28mg. Na 1:11mg, 15 (wicked). **are gone**. Dt 4:19. 2 K 17:21. 1 J *2:19. Ju 19. **Let us**. ver. 2, 6.

14. **inquire**. Dt 17:4. 19:18. Nu 35:30. Is 11:3, 4. Jn 7:24. 1 T 5:19.

15. **edge**. ⌐144A2, Ge +34:26. **destroying it utterly**. Dt 2:34. 7:2, 16. Ex 22:20. 23:24. Le 27:28. Jsh 6:17-21, 24. Jg 20:48. Re 17:16. 18:18-24. 19:2, 3.

16. **burn with**. Jsh 6:24. an heap. Nu 21:2, 3. Jsh 6:26. 7:26. 8:28. Is 17:1. 25:2. Je 49:2. Mi 1:6. **for ever**. Heb. *olam*, Ex +12:24.

17. **cleave**. See on Dt 7:26. Jsh 6:18. 7:1. **cursed**. *or*, devoted. See on Le 27:28, 29. 1 C 16:22. **the Lord**. Jsh 6:26. 7:26. 22:20. Ps 78:38. 85:3. **and show**. Ex 20:6. La 3:32. **compassion**. Dt 30:3. La 3:32. **and multiply**. Ezk 37:26. **as he hath**. Ge 22:16, 17. 26:4, 24. 28:14.

18. **to keep**. See on Dt 12:25, 28, 32. Ps 119:6. Mt *6:33. *7:21, 24.

DEUTERONOMY 14

God's children must be distinguished from other nations in their mourning, and are not to disfigure themselves, 1, 2. What may, and what may not be eaten, 3; of beasts, 4-8; of fishes, 9, 10; of fowls, 11-20. That which dieth of itself may not be eaten, 21. True tithing commanded, 22. A tithe of their increase to be eaten before the Lord, or the price of it to be spent at the appointed place in religious feasting, 23-27; but every third year's tithe of alms to be given in works of charity and piety for the maintenance of the Levites and the poor, 28, 29.

1. **the children**. Ge 6:2, 4. Ex 4:22, 23. Ps 82:6, 7. Je 3:19. Ho 1:10. Jn *1:12. 11:52. Ro *8:16. 9:8, 26. 2 C 6:18. Ga √3:26. He 2:10. 1 J *3:1, 2, 10. 5:2. **ye shall not**. The heathen nations not only did these things in honor of their gods, but in grief for the death of a relative. Le 19:27, 28. 21:5. Je +*10:2. *16:6. 41:5. 47:5. 1 Th *4:13.

2. **For thou**. ver. 21. See on Dt 7:6. 26:18, 19. 28:9. Ex 15:16. 19:5, 6. Le 11:45. 19:2. 20:26. 2 S 7:24. Ps 135:4. Is 6:13. 62:12. Je 31:31-34. Ezk 21:2. Da 8:24. 12:7. Ho 1:10. T *2:14. 1 P *2:9.

3. **not eat**. Le 11:43. 20:25. Is 65:4. Ezk 4:14. Ac 10:12-14. Ro 14:14. 1 C *10:28. 1 T ◑4:3-5. T *1:15.

4. **the beasts**. See on Le 11:2-8. 1 K 4:23.

5. **The hart**. Dt 12:15, 22. 15:22. 1 K 4:23. Ps *42:1. SS 2:9, 17. 8:14. Is *35:6. La 1:6. **pygarg**. *or*, bison. Heb. *dishon*. **wild ox**. or, antelope. Is 51:20mg. **the chamois**. or, mountain sheep.

6. **parteth the hoof**. Le 11:+*3, 4. Ps *1:1, 2. 34:14. Pr 18:1. 2 C 6:17. On this verse remark, that the clean beast must both chew the cud and part the hoof: two distinct characteristics, or general signs, by which the possibility of error arising from the misinterpretation of names is obviated. When God directs, his commands

are not of doubtful interpretation (See on Ge +22:15. *41:32. Dt 17:6). **cheweth the cud**. Jsh=1:8. Ps=1:1, 2. Ph=4:8. 1 T=*4:15, 16.

7. **ye shall not eat**. Mt *7:22, 23, 26. 2 T *3:5. T 1:16. 2 P 2:18-22. **unclean**. Ge 7:1, 2. Le 11:2-8. Is 52:11. 1 Th *5:22.

8. **the swine**. Is 65:4. 66:3, 17. Lk 15:15, 16. 2 P 2:22. **unclean unto you**. ver. 7. Ro ◑14:14, 17. 1 C ◑8:8. Col 2:16, 17. 1 T ◑*4:3. He 9:9, 10. **touch**. Le 11:26, 27.

9. **shall eat**. Le 11:9-12. Lk 24:42, 43.

10. **hath not fins**. Le 11:10. Da *1:8. Ho 9:3.

11. **clean birds**. Le 14:4. Ezk 22:26. 44:23.

12. **not eat**. See on Le 11:13-19.

13. **the glede**. Heb. *raah*, probably the same as *daah*, rendered *vulture* in Le 11:14. **after his kind**. Ge 1:11. 6:20. 7:14. Le 11:14. Ezk 47:10.

14. **raven**. Le +11:15. 1 K 17:4, 6.

15. **the owl**. or, ostrich. Le 11:16. Jb 30:29. **night hawk**. Le 11:16. **cuckoo**. Heb. *Shachaph*, probably the sea-gull or mew. Le 11:16. **hawk**. Le 11:16. Jb 39:26.

16. **little owl**. Le 11:17. Ps 102:6. **great owl**. Le 11:17. Is 34:11. **the swan**. *Tinshemeth*, probably the goose. Le 11:18, 30.

17. **the pelican**. Le 11:18. Ps 102:6. **the gier**. *Rachamah*, probably a species of vulture. **the cormorant**. *Shalach*, probably the cataract or plungeon, a sea fowl. Is 34:11. Zp 2:13, 14. Re 18:2.

18. **the stork**. Le 11:19. Ps 104:17. **lapwing**. *Doocheephath*, the upupa, or hoop, a beautiful but very unclean bird. **the bat**. Le 11:19. Is 2:20.

19. **every creeping**. Le 11:20-23. Ph 3:19. or, teeming or swarming. Ge 1:20. The original word is expressive of fecundity (Young). Ge 7:21. 8:17. 9:7. Ex 1:7. 8:3. Le 11:29, 41, 42, 43. Ps 105:30. **unclean**. ver. 7, 8. 1 C 8:13. 1 J 3:4.

20. **clean fowl**. ver. 11. Ac 15:18-20. Ro 14:2, 3.

21. **any thing**. Le 17:15. 22:8. Ezk 4:14. Ac 15:20. **the stranger**. Ex 12:43-45. Le 19:33, 34. **an holy**. See on ver. 2. Dt 7:6. 26:18, 19. Le 20:6. Da 8:24. 12:7. 1 P 1:16. **Thou shalt**. Ex ◑16:23. 23:19. 34:26. Ps 145:9. Ro 12:2. Forbidden, being a heathen practice for incantations (Young).

22. **truly tithe**. Dt 12:6, 17. 26:12-15. Ge +*14:20. Le 27:30-33. Nu 18:21. Ne 10:37.

23. **eat before**. Dt 12:5-7, 17, 18. **place**. Dt 16:+6, +16. **the firstlings**. Dt 15:19, 20.

24. **if the place**. Dt 11:24. 12:21. Ex 23:31. **which**. See on Dt 12:5.

25. **turn**. Mt 21:12. Mk 11:15. Lk 19:45. Jn 2:14. **bind up the money**. Ge 23:16. 2 K 5:23. 12:10.

26. **bestow**. Ezr 7:15-17, 22. Mt 21:12. Mk 11:15. Jn 2:14-16. **thy soul**. Heb. *nephesh*, Nu +11:6. Dt 12:15, 20, 21. Ps 106:14. 1 C 6:12, 13. 10:6. **soul**. Heb. *nephesh*, Nu +11:6. **desireth**. Heb. asketh of thee. Dt 6:20. Ge 24:47, 57. Jsh 4:6, 21. **eat**. Dt 12:7, 12, 18. 26:11. **rejoice**. Ne 8:10. Ps 128:1, 2. Ec 9:7. Ac 2:44-47.

27. **the Levite**. ver. 29. Dt 12:12, 18, 19. Ga 6:6. 1 T 5:17. **gates**. ⌐171S6, Ge +14:7. **he hath no**. ver. 29. Dt 18:1, 2. Nu 18:20.

28. **the end**. See on ver. 22. Dt 26:12-15. Am 4:4. **thou shalt bring**. Ml 3:10. Pr 3:9, 10. 11:24, 25. As the Levites had no inheritance, the Israelites were not to forget them, but truly tithe their increase. For

their support, the Levites had: (1) The tenth of all the productions of the land. (2) Forty-eight cities, each forming a square of 4000 cubits. (3) Two thousand cubits of ground round each city; total of land, 53,000 acres. (4) The firstfruits, and certain parts of all the animals killed in the land. But though this was a very small proportion for a whole tribe that had consented to annihilate its political existence, that it might wait upon the service of God, yet, let it be considered, that what they possessed was the best of the land: and while it was a slender remuneration for their services, yet their portion was such as rendered them independent, and kept them comfortable; so that they could wait on God, and labor in his work, without distraction.

29. **he hath**. ver. 27. Dt 12:12. 15:10. 18:1, 2. 26:11. Nu +18:20. **the stranger**. Dt 16:11, 14. 24:19-21. 26:12, 13. Ex 22:21-24. Le 19:34. Jb 31:16-22. Lk 14:12-14. He 13:2. Ja 1:27. **fatherless**. Dt +10:18. Ge +11:28. Ps 10:14. 68:5. Je 49:11. Ho 14:3. Ja 1:27. **that the Lord**. Dt 15:10. Ps 41:1. Pr *3:9, 10. 11:24. 14:21. 19:17. Is 58:7-12. Ml *3:10, 11. Lk *6:35. 11:41. 2 C 6:9-11.

DEUTERONOMY 15

On the seventh year the debts of the poor must be remitted, 1-6. Nevertheless the people must give and lend liberally, 7-11. Hebrew servants must be released in the seventh year, unless unwilling to depart, 12-18. All firstling males of the cattle are to be sanctified unto the Lord, 19-23.

1. **seven**. Dt 31:10. Ex 21:2. 23:11. Le 25:2-4. Is 61:1-3. Je 34:8-18. Lk 4:18, 19. Ro 6:17, 18. 1 C 6:20. Ga 5:1.

2. **creditor that lendeth**. Heb. master of the lending of his hand. Ge 37:19. **exact it**. Ne 5:7-11. Is 58:3. Am 8:4-6. Mt 6:12, 14, 15. 18:25-35. Lk 6:34-38. 7:42. Ja 2:13.

3. **foreigner**. Dt 23:20. Ex 46:16, 17. Mt 17:25, 26. Jn 8:35. 1 C 6:6, 7. Ga *6:10. Ep 2:19. **brother**. 1 Th 4:9. He 13:1.

4. **save**, etc. *or*, To the end that there be no poor among you. ver. 11. Houbigant follows this marginal reading, to which he joins the end of the third verse, considering it as explanatory of the law; as if he had said, "Thou shalt not exact the debt that is due from thy brother, but *thy hand shall release* him, for this reason, *that there may be no poor among you* through your severity." He justly contends that the phrase *ephes kee*, can here only mean, *to the end that*. **greatly bless**. See on Dt 14:29. 28:1-8, 11. Pr 11:24, 25. 14:21. 28:27. Is 58:10, 11.

5. **Only**. See on Dt 4:9. 11:13-15. 28:1-15. Le 26:3-14. Jsh 1:7. Ps 19:11. Is 1:19, 20. Ph 1:27. **if**. Ge +4:7.

6. **thou shalt lend**. Dt 28:12, 44. Ps 37:21, 26. 112:5. Pr *22:7. Lk 6:35. **thou shalt reign**. Dt 28:13. 1 K 4:21, 24. 2 Ch 9:26. Ezr 4:20. Ne 9:27.

7. **there be**. ver. 11. Mt 26:11. Lest the preceding law might render the Israelites cautious in lending to the poor, Moses here warns them against being led by so mean a principle; but to lend liberally, and God would reward them. **harden**. Dt 2:30. 24:12, 13. Ex 23:6. Pr 22:22. Zc *7:10. 1 J 3:17. **brother**. 2 P 1:5, 7. 8. **shalt open**. ver. 9, 11. Le 25:35. Est 9:22. Jb 29:16. Ps 37:21. *41:1. 81:10. 112:5-9. 145:16. Pr 11:24,

25. *19:17. *21:13, 26. 22:9. *28:8, 27. Ec 11:1, 2, 6. Mt 5:42. ◐*18:30. Lk *6:34, 35. Ac 24:17. 2 C 8:7-9. 9:5-13. Ga 2:10. Ja *2:15, 16. 1 J *3:16, 17. **lend**. ver. 6. Dt 23:19, 20. Le 25:35-37. **sufficient**. Ex 36:6, *7. **his need**. Mt ◐+*5:42. Lk ◐+*6:30. Ja 2:15, 16. 1 J 3:17, 18. **wanteth**. Jg 18:10. 19:19, 20. Ps *34:9. Pr 6:11. *11:24. 14:23. *21:5, 17. 22:16. 24:34. *28:27.

9. **Beware**. Pr *4:23. Je *17:10. Mt *15:19. Mk *7:21, 22. Ro 7:8, 9. Ja 4:5. **thought**, etc. Heb. word with thine heart of Belial. Dt 13:13. 1 S 1:16. 2 S 22:5mg. 23:6. Ps 18:4mg. 41:8mg. *101:3mg. Na 1:11mg. **release**. Mt √6:12. Lk 11:4. **thine eye**. Dt 28:54-56. Pr 23:6. 24:9. *28:22. Mt 20:15. Ja *5:9. 1 P *4:9. **he cry**. +√24:15. Ex 3:7. *22:23. Jb 34:28. Ps *9:12. Pr *21:13. Ja *5:4. **sin unto thee**. Mt 25:41-45. Ja *4:17. 1 J *3:15-17.

10. **thine heart**. Mt *25:40. Ac *20:35. Ro 12:8-10. 2 C *9:5-7. Ep 5:3. 1 T *6:18, 19. 1 P 4:11. **because**. See on ver. *4. Dt *14:29. *24:19. Ps *41:1, 2. Pr *11:24, 25. 22:9. Is 32:8. *58:10, 11. Ro *12:13. 2 C *9:8-11. Ph *4:18, 19. He *13:16.

11. **the poor**. Although Moses, by the statutes relative to the division of the land, and inheritance, and the inalienable nature of it, had studied to prevent any Israelite from being born poor, yet he exhorts them to the tenderest compassion and most benevolent actions; and not to refuse assistance to the decayed Israelite, though the sabbatical year drew nigh. Ex ◐+23:3. Pr 22:2. Mt *26:11. Mk *14:7. Jn 12:8. **Thou shalt**. See on ver. +8. Mt +*5:42. 25:41, 42. Lk *12:33. Ac 2:45. *4:32-35. 11:28-30. 2 C *8:2-9. 1 J *3:16-18.

12. **if thy brother**. See on ver. 1. Ex 21:2-6. Le 25:39-41. Ne 5:5. Je 34:14. Jn 8:35, 36. **or an**. ʃ63G, Ge +50:23. There is an ellipsis which may be supplied after "brother," namely, "or thy sister," an instance where the omitted word is to be supplied by analogous or related words.

13. **shalt not**. This is a most humane and merciful addition to the law in Ex 21:2-11; enforced upon the Israelites by the consideration of their Egyptian bondage. As a faithful servant has made no property for himself while honestly serving his master, so now, when he quits his service, he has nothing to begin the world with except what the kindness of his master may bestow upon him as a remuneration for his zeal and fidelity. Though what was to be bestowed upon servants is not fixed, yet they were to be liberally supplied (ver. 14). Ge 31:42. Ex 3:21. Le 25:42-44. Pr 3:27, 28. Je 22:13. Ml 3:5. Col 4:1.

14. **the Lord**. Ne 8:10. Ps 68:10. Pr 10:22. Ac 20:35. 1 C 16:2. 2 C 9:5-7.

15. **shalt remember**. Dt 5:14, 15. 16:12. Ex 20:2. Is 51:1. Mt 6:14, 15. 18:32, 33. Ep *1:7. 2:12. 4:32. 5:1, 2. T *2:14. 1 J *3:16. 4:9-11.

16. **if he say**. See on Ex 21:5, 6. Ps 40:6, 8.

17. **ear**. Ex +21:6. Jb 33:16. *36:10, 15. Ps *40:6mg. Is ◐48:8. **forever**. Heb. *olam*, Ex +12:24. Ex +21:6. Le 25:39-42. 1 S 1:22.

18. **shall not**. ver. 10. **a double**. ʃ121L9, Ge +43:12. Is 16:14. 21:16. Lk 17:7, 8. 1 T=5:17, 18. **bless**. Pr *10:22. 11:24.

19. **the firstling**. Ex 13:2, 12. 22:29, 30. 34:19. Le 27:26. Nu 3:13. 18:17. Lk 2:23. Ro 8:29. 1 C=15:20. Col +=*1:15. He 12:23. **thou shalt do**. Dt 12:5-7. 17. 14:23. 16:11, 14. Nu 18:15.

20. **shalt eat**. See on Dt 12:5-7, 17. **place**. Dt

+*16:6, +16. **choose**. Jsh 18:1. Ps 78:60, 68. 132:13, 14.

21. **if there be**. Dt 17:1. Le 22:20-24. Ml 1:7, 8. He 9:14. 1 P 1:19.

22. **the unclean**. Dt 12:15, 21, 22. **roebuck**. Dt 14:5. 2 S 2:18. 1 K 4:23n. **hart**. Dt +14:5.

23. **not eat the blood**. See on Dt 12:16, 23. Ge 9:4. Le 3:17n. 7:26. 17:10. 1 S 14:32, 33. 1 Ch 11:18, 19. Ezk 33:25. Mt 26:28. Mk 14:24. Jn ⬤6:53. 19:34. Ac *15:20. Ro 3:25. 5:9. Ep *1:7. Col 1:14, 20. He 9:22. 1 J *1:7. Re *1:5. **pour**. Dt 12:16, 24. Le *17:13.

DEUTERONOMY 16

The laws concerning the three great annual feasts recapitulated: the feast of the passover, 1-7, and to eat unleavened bread, 8. The seven weeks or pentecost, and their feasts, 9-12. The feast of tabernacles to be observed by them and their family seven days, 13-15. All the males to appear before the Lord three times a year, and at these three feasts, with an injunction that every one should then offer according to his ability 16, 17. Judges and officers are appointed, 18-20, and are prohibited to set up groves and images, 21, 22.

1. **The month**. Ex 12:2, etc. 13:4. 23:15. 34:18. Le 23:5. Nu 9:2-5. 28:16. **the passover**. Le 23:5-8. Nu 28:16-25. 2 K 23:23. 2 Ch 35:13. Mt 26:2, 19, 26-29. 1 C 5:7, 8. This word comes from the Hebrew verb *pasach*, to pass, to leap or skip over. The destroying angel *passed over* the houses marked with the blood of the paschal lamb, so the wrath of God passes over those whose souls are sprinkled with the blood of Christ, 1 C 5:7. As the paschal lamb was killed before Israel was delivered, so by the death of Christ, we have redemption through his blood, Ep 1:7. It was killed before the tables of the law were delivered to Moses, or Aaron's sacrifices were enjoined; thus deliverance comes to men, not by the works of the law, but by the only true passover, the Lamb of God, Jn 1:29. Ro 3:25. He 9:14. It was killed the first month of the year, which prefigured that Christ should suffer death in that month, Jn 18:28. 1 C +15:4. It was killed in the evening, Ex 12:6. Christ suffered at that time of day, Mt 27:46. Lk 23:44n. He 1:2. At even the sun sets; at Christ's passion, universal darkness was upon the whole earth. The passover was roasted with fire, denoting the sharp and dreadful pains that Christ should suffer, not only from men, but from God also. It was to be eaten with bitter herbs, Ex 12:8; not only to put them in remembrance of their bitter bondage in Egypt, but also to testify our mortification to sin, and readiness to undergo afflictions for Christ, Col 1:24; and likewise to teach us the absolute necessity of true repentance in all that would profitably feed by faith on Christ, the true paschal lamb. **for in**. Ex 12:29-42. 13:4. 23:15. 34:18.

2. **sacrifice**. Ex 12:5-7. Nu 28:16-19. 2 Ch 35:7. Mt 26:2, 17. Mk 14:12. Lk 22:8, 15. 1 C *5:7. **in the place which**. ver. +6, +16. See on Dt 12:5, 11, 14, 18, 26. 15:20.

3. **eat no**. Ex 12:15, 19, 20, 39. 13:3-7. 34:18. Le +*23:6. Nu 9:11. 28:17. 1 C 5:8. **the bread of**. ſ121M, Ex +8:23. Metonymy of the Subject, the thing signified is put for the sign. Here, the reference is to the bread which was the sign and symbol of their affliction in Egypt. 1 K 22:27. Ps 102:9. 127:2. Zc 12:10. 2 C 7:10,

11. 1 Th 1:6. **for thou camest**. Ex 12:32, 33, 39. **mayest**. Ex 12:14, 26, 27. 13:7-9. Ps 111:4. Lk 22:19. 1 C 11:24-26.

4. **there shall**. Ex 12:15. 13:7. 34:25. **neither**. See on Ex 12:10.

5. **sacrifice**. *or*, kill. See on ver. 2. Dt 12:5, 6. **gates**. ſ171S6, Ge +14:7.

6. **place**. ver. +16. Dt +12:14. Le 23:4. Mt 18:20. **passover**. Le +*23:5. **at even**. Ex 12:6-9. Nu 9:3, 11. Mt 26:20. Ac 20:7. 1 C 11:20. He 1:2, 3. 9:26. 1 P 1:19, 20.

7. **roast**. lit. cook. ſ46A, Le +26:30. Ex 12:8, 9. 2 Ch 35:13. Ps 22:14, 15. **in the place**. ver. 2, +6, +16. 2 K 23:23. Jn 2:13, 23. 11:55.

8. **Six days**. Ex 12:15, 16. 13:7, 8. Le 23:6-8. Nu 28:17-19. **unleavened**. Le +*23:6. **solemn assembly**. Heb. restraint. Le 23:36. 2 Ch 7:9. Ne 8:18. Jl 1:14mg.

9. **Seven weeks**. ver. 10, 16. Ex 23:16. 34:22. Le 23:15, 16. Nu 28:26-30. 2 Ch 8:13. Ac 2:1. 1 C 16:8. He 2:1.

10. **feast of weeks**. Le +*23:10. Ac 2:1-4, 41. Re 14:1-4. **a tribute**. *or*, sufficiency. ver. 16. Le 5:7mg. 12:8mg. 25:26mg. Nu 31:28, 37. Pr *3:9, 10. **freewill offering**. Le +*23:38. **according**. ver. 17. Pr 10:22. Jl 2:14. Hg 2:15-19. Ml *3:10, 11. 1 C √16:2. 2 C 8:10, *12. *9:5-11.

11. **shalt rejoice**. See on ver. 14. Dt 12:7, 12, 18. Is 64:5. 66:10-14. Hab 3:18. Ro 5:11. 2 C 1:24. Ph *4:4. **and thy**. ſ148, Ge +8:22.

12. **remember**. See on ver. 15. Dt 15:15. La 3:19, 20. Ro 6:17, 18. Ep 2:1-3, 11. **observe and do**. Dt +*26:16, 18. Ezr +*7:10. Jn +*13:17. 1 J +√2:3.

13. **shalt observe**. Ps 126. Zc 14:18. **the feast**. Dt 31:10. Ex 23:16. 34:22. Le 23:+*34, 35-36, 42, 43. Nu 29:12, etc. 2 Ch 5:3. 7:8-10. 8:13. Ezr 3:4. Ne 8:14-18. Zc 14:16-18. Jn 7:2. **gathered**. Dt 32:11. Mt 23:37. **corn and thy wine**. Mt 13:30. Jn=12:24. 1 C=15:23. Re=14:14-16. =20:5. Heb. floor and thy winepress. Dt 15:14. Ge +50:10. Nu 15:20. 18:27, 30. Jg *6:37. Ru *3:2. 1 S 23:1. 2 S *6:6. 24:16, *24. 1 K 22:10mg. 2 K 6:27. 1 Ch 13:9. 21:15. 2 Ch 3:1. 18:9. Jb 39:12. Is 21:10. Je 51:33. Da 2:35. Ho 9:1, 2. Jl 2:24. Mi 4:12. Mt 3:12. Lk 3:17. **wine**. Re=14:17-20.

14. **rejoice**. See on Dt 12:12. 26:11. Ne 8:9-12. Ec 9:7. Is 12:1-6. 25:6-8. 30:29. 35:10. 2 C 6:10. 1 Th *5:16. **fatherless**. Dt +10:18. **gates**. Ge +14:7.

15. **Seven days**. Ex 23:36-42. Nu 29:12-38. **because**. See on ver. 10. Dt 7:13. 28:8-12. 30:16.

16. **Three times**. Ex 23:14-17. 34:22, 23. 1 K 9:25. Lk 2:40-42. Jn 2:13. 7:2-10. 11:55. **place**. ver. +6. Dt +12:14. 26:2. Ge 22:3. Ex +20:24. +23:20. +29:24. Jsh *22:11, 16, 21-29. **unleavened**. Le +*23:6. **and they shall**. Ex 23:15. 34:20. 1 Ch 29:3-9, 14-17. Ps 96:8. Pr *3:9, 10. Is 23:18. 60:6-9. Hg 1:9. Mt 2:11. Mk 12:3. **empty**. Dt 26:2. Ex +*23:15. 29:24. 34:20. Le 16:12. 1 S 9:7, 8. 2 S 24:24. 1 Ch 21:24. Lk 21:4. 1 C +*16:2.

17. **as he is able**. Heb. according to the gift of his hand. See on ver. 10. Le 27:8. Ezr 2:63. Mk 12:41-44. Lk +*11:41mg,n. 1 C +*16:2. 2 C √8:12. *9:6, 7.

18. **Judges**. Dt 1:15-17. 17:9, 12. 19:17, 18. 21:2. Ex 18:25, 26. 21:6. 1 Ch 23:4. 26:29. 2 Ch 19:5-11. Ps 82:2, 3. Ro 13:1-6. **in all thy gates**. ſ171S7B, Ge +14:7. This expression may refer to the gate of the city, as the forum or place of public concourse among

the Israelites, where a court of judicature was held, to try all causes and decide all affairs. ver. 14. Dt 17:8. 21:19. 22:15. 25:7. Ge +*14:7n. 2 S 15:2. Jb 31:21. Is 29:21. Am *5:15. Zc 8:16. **they shall.** T#313. ver. 19. Dt 1:16, 17. 17:15, 18-20. 19:18, 19. 25:1, 2. Ps *82:2-4. Pr *16:12. 20:28. *29:14. *31:4, 5. Je 22:2, 3, *15, *16. Ezk 45:9, 10. *46:18.

19. **wrest.** or, incline, or, stretch out. Ex 23:2, 6. Ps 56:5. **judgment.** Dt 24:17. 27:19. Ex 23:2, 6-8. Le 19:15. 1 S 8:3. 12:3. Jb 31:21, 22. Pr 17:23. 18:5. Ec 7:7. Is 1:17, 23. 10:2. 33:15. Je 5:28. La 3:35. Ezk 22:12. Mi 7:3. Hab 1:4. Zp 3:3-5. Ac 16:37. 23:3. **respect.** See on Dt 1:16, 17. 10:17. Ex 23:7, 8. Pr 24:23, 28. *28:21. Ac 10:34. **pervert.** Ex 23:8. Pr 13:6. *19:3. 21:12. 22:12. **words.** or, matters. Pr 22:12mg.

20. **That which,** etc. Heb. Justice, justice. ſ84, Ge +6:17. The repetition denotes the intensity of the command. Dt +*25:13-16. Mi +*6:8. Ph *4:8. **altogether just.** Le +*19:15. Ec +*5:8. Lk +*16:10. Jn +*7:24, 51. 1 T +*5:19n. **follow.** Jg 8:4. Ps 23:6. *34:14. 38:20. Pr *21:21. Is 51:1. Ho *6:3. **live.** See on Dt 4:1. Ezk *18:5, 7-9. Ro 10:5. **inherit.** Mt +*5:5. Ro +*4:13.

21. **plant.** Ge 2:8. Ex 34:13. Jg 3:7. 1 K 14:15. 16:33. 2 K 17:16. 21:3. 2 Ch 33:3. **grove.** Ex 34:13. Dt 7:5.

22. **image.** or, statue, or pillar. Ge 28:18, 22. 31:13. Ex +*20:4. Le 26:1. Ps 10:3. Col *3:5. 1 J 5:21. **which.** Dt 12:31. Je 44:4. Zc 8:17. Re 2:6, 15. **hateth.** Ps 5:5. 11:5. Pr *6:16.

DEUTERONOMY 17

The sacrifices are required to be unblemished, 1. Idolaters to be punished with death, 2-7. Difficult cases must be referred to the priests and judges at the sanctuary, 8-11. Such as refused to submit to their decision must be put to death, 12, 13. A king to be chosen of their own brethren, and not a stranger, 14, 15. The duty of their king, 16-20.

1. **Thou shalt.** Dt 15:21. See on Ex 12:5. Le 22:20-25. Ml 1:8, 13, 14. He 9:14. 1 P 1:19. **sheep.** or, goat. Ex 12:3n. **any evil favoredness.** Ge 41:3, 4, 19. **for that.** Dt 23:18. 24:4. 25:16. Pr 6:16. 11:1. 15:8. 20:10.

2. **within any of thy gates.** The expression denoted all residing in the cities, and all who went in and came out at the gates of them; so that it included the inhabitants of the whole land. Dt 13:12. Ge +14:7. **man.** ver. 5. Dt 13:6-14. 29:18. **in transgressing.** Dt 4:23. 29:25. 31:20. Le 26:15, 25. Jsh 7:11, 15. 23:16. Jg 2:20. 2 K 18:12. Je 31:32. Ezk 16:38. Ho 6:7. 8:1. He 8:9, 10. **covenant.** Ex 34:27.

3. **the sun.** See on Dt 4:19. 2 K 21:3. Jb 31:26-28. Je 8:2. Ezk 8:16. **which.** Je 7:22, 23, 31. 19:5. 32:35.

4. **enquired.** Dt 13:12-14. 19:18. Pr 25:2. Jn 7:51.

5. **stone them.** Dt 13:10, 11. 21:21. 22:21, 24. Le 24:14, 16. Jsh 7:25. **till they die.** 1 K 15:11-13. 2 K 10:23-28. 11:18-20. Jn *10:30-33.

6. **the mouth.** Dt 19:15. Nu 35:30. Mt *18:16. Jn 8:17, 18. 2 C 13:1. 1 T 5:19. He 10:28. ſ121B. Metonymy of the Cause B545: The organic cause or instrument is put for the thing effected by it. The organs of speech are put for the testimony borne. The mouth is put for the witness or the testimony borne by it. For other instances of this figure see Dt 19:15. Nu 35:30. Ho 14:2. Mt 18:16. 2 C 13:1. **two.** Dt +14:6n. Ge +22:15. *41:32. Mt 18:19.

7. **of the witnesses.** Dt 13:9. 1 K 21:12, 13. Ac 7:57-59. **all the people.** Jsh 7:25, 26. **So thou.** ver. 12. Dt 13:5. 19:19. 24:7. Jg 20:13. 1 C)5:13.

8. **arise.** Dt 1:17. Ex 18:26. 1 K 3:16-28. 2 Ch 19:8-10. Hg 2:11. Ml 2:7. **between blood.** Dt 19:4, 10, 11. Ex 21:12-14, 20, 22, 28. 22:2. Nu 35:11, 16, 19, etc. **gates.** ſ171S7B, Ge +14:7. **get thee up.** See on Dt 12:5. +16:6, +16. 19:17. Ps 68:16. *122:3-5. 132:13, 14.

9. **the priests.** Nu 27:21. Is +*66:21. Je 18:18. Hg 2:11. Ml 2:7. **the judge.** ver. 12. Dt 19:17. ſ96F1. Heterosis of Number, Ge +3:8. The singular is put for the plural, as at Ge 3:2, 7. 49:6. 1 S 31:1. 1 K 10:22. 2 K 11:10 w 2 Ch 9:21. 23:9. 1 Ch 4:42h. **they shall.** Dt 19:17-21. Ezk 44:24.

10. **do according.** Mt 22:2, 3.

11. **According to.** Jsh 1:7. 1 K 2:23-25. 3:28. Ml 2:8, 9. Ro *13:1-6. T 3:1. 1 P *2:13-15. 2 P *2:10. Ju 8. **they shall teach thee.** Dt 33:10. Le 10:11. 1 Ch 25:7n, 8n. 26:32n. 2 Ch +15:3. *35:3n. Ezr *7:10. Je 18:18. Hg 2:11, 12. Ml *2:7. **to the right.** ver. *20. Dt *5:32. 28:14. Jsh *1:7. 23:6. 2 S 14:19. Pr *4:27.

12. **will do.** Dt 13:5, 11. Nu 15:30. Ezr *10:8. Ps 19:13. Ho 4:4. Mt 10:14. He 10:26-29. **and will not hearken.** Heb. not to hearken. Je 25:3, etc. **the priest.** Dt 10:8. 18:5, 7. Lk 10:16. Jn 12:48. 20:23. 1 Th 4:2, 8. **that man.** He 10:28. **thou shalt.** See on ver. 7. Dt 13:5. Pr 21:11. 1 T 5:20.

13. **shall hear.** See on Dt 13:11. 19:20. **presumptuously.** See on Nu 15:30, 31. 2 P *2:10.

14. **When thou.** Dt 7:1. 12:9, 10. 18:9. 26:1, 9. Le 14:34. Jsh 1:13. **I will set.** 1 S 8:5-7, 10, 19, 20. 12:19.

15. **king.** 1 S)8:18. **whom.** 1 S 9:15-17. 10:24, 25. 16:11-13. 2 S 5:2. 1 Ch 12:23. 22:10. 28:5. Ps 2:2, 6. 78:70, 71. **from among.** Dt 18:15, 18. Ge +*49:10. Ps 89:18-21. Je *30:21. Mt ●22:17. **not set.** Je 2:25. **stranger.** Dt 14:21. ●+26:11. Ex 12:19, 43mg. 29:33. Le 22:10. Nu 1:51. 3:10, 28. 16:40. 18:4, 7.

16. **multiply horses.** 1 S 8:11. 2 S 8:4. 1 K ●4:26. 8:9. ●10:26, 28. 2 Ch 9:25. Ps *20:7. Is 30:16. Ho 14:3. **cause.** Is *31:1-3. Je 42:14. Ezk 17:15. **Ye shall henceforth.** Dt 28:68. Ex 13:17. 14:13. Nu 14:3, 4. Jsh 3:4. Je 42:13-16. Ho 11:5.

17. **multiply wives.** Ge 2:24. +4:19. 2 S 3:2-5. ●5:13. 1 K 11:1-4. Ne 13:26. Ml 2:15. Mt *19:5. **neither shall he.** 2 S 8:6, 7, 10, 11. 1 K 10:21, 27. Ps 62:10. Pr 30:8, 9. Is 2:7. Mt *6:19, 20. 13:22. 19:23, 24. Lk 12:15. 1 T *6:9, 17.

18. **that he shall.** 2 K 11:12. **a copy.** Mishneh hattorah hazzoth, "a duplicate of this law;" translated by the Septuagint, to deuteronomion touto, this Deutronomy. From this version, both the Vulgate and all the modern versions have taken the name of this book; and from the original word, the Jews call it Mishneh. **out of that which.** Dt 31:9, 25, 26. 2 K 11:12, 17. 22:8, 10, 11, 13. 2 Ch 34:15.

19. **read therein.** Dt *6:6-9. 11:18. Jsh *1:8. Ps *1:2. *119:97-100. Jn √5:39. 2 T +*3:15-17. **all the days.** Ac *17:11. **fear.** Dt *10:12. Pr +1:7. 2 C 5:11. He 10:31. Re 19:5. **keep.** Dt 4:10. 14:23. **to do.** T#1043. Dt +*26:16, 18.

20. **his heart.** Dt *8:2, 13, 14. 11:16. 2 K 14:10. 2 Ch 25:19. *26:16. 32:25, 26. *33:12, 19, 23. *34:27. Ps *131:1, 2. Is 2:12. Da 5:20-23. Hab 2:4. 2 C *12:7. 1 P *5:5. **he turn.** See on Dt *4:2. *5:32. 12:25, 28, 32. 1 K 15:5. **not aside.** Dt 11:16. *28:14. **right hand.**

See on ver. *11. 1 S *13:13, 14. *15:23. 1 K 11:12, 13, 34, 36. 2 K 10:30. Ps *19:11. 132:12. **that he**. Dt +4:40. Pr *10:27. *27:24. Ec *8:13. **in his kingdom**. Ge 49:10. 2 S 23:1, 5. Ac 13:32-34.

DEUTERONOMY 18

The LORD is the priests and Levites' inheritance, 1, 2. The priests' due, 3-5. The Levites' portion, 6-8. All unlawful arts such as idolatry and witchcraft prohibited, 9-14. A promise is given them of the spirit of prophecy to continue among them, and to center at last in Christ the great prophet "like unto Moses," 15-18. Wrath threatened against those that despise prophecy, 19; or counterfeit it, 20. How false prophets were to be known, 21, 22.

1. **shall have**. Dt 10:9. 12:19. Nu 18:20. 26:62. Jsh 13:14, 33. 18:7. Ezk 44:28. 1 P 5:2-4. **they shall**. Nu 18:8, 9. Jsh 13:14. 1 C 9:13, 14. Ga 6:6.

2. **the Lord**. ſ121K4, Jsh 13:33. Ge 15:1. Ps 16:5. 73:24-26. 84:11. 119:57. Is 61:6. La 3:24. 1 P 2:5, 9. Re *1:5, 6.

3. **due**. Ml 3:8-10. 1 C *9:13. **offer a sacrifice**. Dt 12:27. Le 7:30-34.

4. **firstfruit**. Dt 26:9, 10. Ex 22:29. 23:19. Le 23:10, 17. Nu 18:12-24. 2 Ch 31:4-10. Ne 12:44-47. Pr *3:9, 10. Ml 3:10. **the fleece**. Jb 21:20.

5. **chosen him**. Dt 10:8. 17:12. Ex 28:1, etc. Nu 3:10. 16:5, 9, 10. 17:5-9. 25:13. Jn=15:19. **in the name**. Col=3:17.

6. **come**. See on Nu 35:2, 3. **and come with**. 1 S 1:24-28. 2:18. Ps 26:8. 27:4. 63:1, 2. 84:5, 10. 1 T 3:1. 1 P 5:2. **mind**. Heb. *nephesh*, soul, Ge +23:8. **unto the place**. Dt 12:5. 16:2, +6, +16.

7. **as all his brethren**. 2 Ch 31:2-4.

8. **like portions**. Le 7:8, 9, 14. Nu 31:30, 47. Ne 12:44, 47. Lk 10:7. 1 C 9:7-14. 1 T 5:17, 18. **that which cometh of the sale of his patrimony**. Heb. his sales by the fathers.

9. See on Dt 12:29-31. Le 18:26, 27, 30.

10. **maketh**. Dt 12:31. Le 18:21, etc. 20:2-5. 2 K 16:3. 17:17. 21:6. 2 Ch 28:3. Ps 106:37, 38. Je 19:4-6. 32:35. **that useth divination**. Ge +30:27. The precise import of the terms here used to express these unhallowed practices cannot be clearly ascertained: he "that useth divination," *kosaim, kesamim*, seems a general term for the various species after specified; "observer of times," *meonain*, one who pretends to foretell by the clouds, planets, etc.; "enchanter," *menachesh*, a diviner, either by means of serpents, or by inspecting the entrails of beasts, the flight of birds, etc.; "a witch," *mecashsheph*, one who used magical fumigations, etc.; "a charmer," *chover chaver*, one who uses spells, or a peculiar conjunction of words, or tying knots, etc.; "a consulter with familiar spirits," *shoel ov*, a pythoness; a "wizard," *yidoni*, a cunning man; "necromancer," *doresh el hammaithim*, one who seeks enquiries of the dead. Ex 22:18. Le 19:26, 31. 20:26, 27. 1 S 28:3, 7, 9. 1 Ch 10:13. 2 Ch 33:6. Is *8:19, 20. *47:13. Ac 16:16-18. *19:19. Ga *5:20. Re *21:8. **witch**. Ex 22:18. Ml +*3:5 (sorcerers).

11. **a charmer**. lit. one that charms a charming. Ps 58:5. Is +*47:12. **or a necromancer**. 1 S 28:11-14.

12. **because of**. Dt 9:4, 5. Le 18:24, 25, 27.

13. **Thou shalt**. Ge 6:9. *17:1. Jb 1:1, 8. Ps 37:37. Mt 5:48. Ph 3:12, 15. Re 3:2. **perfect**. *or*, upright,

or, sincere. 1 K 8:61. 2 K 20:3. 2 Ch 15:17. Ps 101:2.

14. **possess**. *or*, inherit. Dt 12:2. **hath not suffered**. ver. 10. Ge 20:6. Le 20:23. Ps 147:19, 20. Je *10:2. Ezk 21:21, 22. Ac 14:16.

15. **a Prophet**. ſ171E12, Ge +14:22. T#1885. ver. *18, *19. Mk 9:7. Lk *7:16. Jn 1:25, +*45. 6:14. Ac *)3:22, 23. *)7:37. He 2:14-17. **midst**. Dt +*17:15. Ge +49:10. **like unto me**. Dt *5:5. 34:10. Lk 24:19. 1 T *2:5. He 1:1, 2. *2:1-3. *3:2-6. **unto him**. Mt *17:5. Lk 9:35. *10:16. Jn *6:29. He *1:2. 2:1-3. 1 J *3:23. **hearken**. Mt 11:15. 17:5.

16. **in Horeb**. Dt 9:10. **Let me not hear**. Dt 5:24-28. Ex 20:19. He *12:19.

17. **well spoken**. See on Dt 5:28.

18. **raise them**. ver. *15. Jn *1:45. **Prophet**. ſ171E12, Ge +14:22. Dt 32:36. Ps 80:17. +*102:16. 118:22, 26. Is *49:5, 6. 63:17, 18. Ezk *34:11, 12. Ho *3:4, 5. Am 9:11. Mi *5:3-7. Mt 13:57, 58. 16:13, 14. 21:10, 11. Jn 1:19, 21. 4:19, 25. *6:14. Ac +√3:19-21. 15:16. Ro +*11:26. **from among**. Dt +17:15. **like unto**. Dt *5:5. 33:5. Ex 32:19, 20, 26, 27. 40:26-29. Nu 12:*3, *6-8, 13. Ps 2:6. 110:4. Is *9:6, 7. Zc 6:12, 13. Ml 3:1. Mt 11:29. Lk *24:19. Jn 2:13-17. Ga 3:19, 20. 1 T *2:5. He *3:2-6. *7:22. *12:24, 25. **will put**. Is *50:4. *51:16. Jn 17:18. **he shall**. Jn *4:25. *8:28. *12:49, 50. *15:15.

19. **whosoever will not**. Mk *16:16. Jn 3:18. *5:45-47. *8:24. 12:44-48. Ac *3:22,)23. He *2:3. 3:7. *10:26. *12:25, 26. Re 19:11-15. **come to pass**. ſ144A11, Ge +38:1. **require**. Dt 23:21. Ge 9:5. Jb 3:4h. Ps 10:13. Ezk 20:40. 33:6, *8. Lk 19:27, 44. Ep 6:17. He 4:12.

20. **the prophet**. Dt 13:1-5. Je 2:8. 14:14, 15. 23:13-15, 31. 27:15. Ezk 13:6. Mt 7:15. 2 P 2:12. **in the name**. Dt 13:1, 2. 1 K 18:19, 27, 40. Je 2:8. 28:15-17. Zc 13:3. Re 19:20.

21. **How shall we know**. Je 28:9. 1 Th *5:21, 24. 1 J *4:1-3. Re 2:2.

22. **speaketh**. Is 41:22. Je 28:1-14. **if the thing**. Dt 13:2. 2 K 20:1. Jon 3:4. 4:2. Zc 1:5, 6. **the Lord hath not spoken**. Je 18:7-10. 28:3. The credentials of a true prophet are the fulfillment of his words. Unlike any other work of literature, the Bible stakes its credibility upon the truthfulness of its predictive prophecy. The Bible is the only source of such true prophecy, distinguished from all other such claims by the great specificity with which the predictions are made, all of which come true precisely as predicted, and by the fact that the predictions were well publicized before the events came to pass. **presumptuously**. ver. 20. Je 28:15-17. 29:30-32. **shalt not**. Pr 26:2. 29:25.

DEUTERONOMY 19

The cities of refuge, 1-3. The privilege thereof for him that killeth his neighbor ignorantly, 4-10; but he that hateth and killeth his neighbor, though fled into one of these cities, must die, 11-13. The old landmark is not to be removed, 14. Two witnesses at the least are required in a criminal cause, 15. How the false witness must be punished, 16-21.

1. **hath cut**. Dt 6:10. 7:1, 2. 12:1, 29. 17:14. **succeedest**. Heb. inheritest, *or* possessest. Dt 12:2, 29. 18:14.

2. **separate three**. Dt 4:41-43. Ex 21:13. Nu 35:10-15. Jsh 20:2-7. He 6:18.

3. **prepare**. Is 35:8. 57:14. 62:10. He 12:13.

4. **the slayer.** Dt 4:42. Nu 35:15-24. **in time past.** Heb. from yesterday the third day. ver. 6. Ge +31:2mg. Ex 4:10mg. 21:29. Jsh 3:4mg. 1 Ch 11:2mg. Is 30:33mg.

5. **As when.** 171K1. Synecdoche of the Species B634. One example or specimen is put for all kinds of similar things in human actions. Here, one kind of homicide is mentioned as an example of every kind. For other instances of this figure see Jb 9:5. Ps 112:5. Pr 20:10. 27:14. Je 15:10. Zc 5:3. Mt 5:22. 6:1, 5, 16. Mk 11:23. He 13:9. **head.** Heb. iron. 2 K 6:5-7. **helve.** Heb. wood. **lighteth.** Heb. findeth. **he shall flee.** Nu 35:25. Pr 27:12. Is 32:2.

6. **the avenger.** Nu 35:12. Jsh 20:5. 2 S 14:7. **slay him.** Heb. smite him in life. Heb. *nephesh,* Jsh +10:28. Je +40:14mg. **not worthy.** Dt 21:22. 1 S 24:4, 9, 10, 17, 18. Je 26:15, 16. Mt 10:29, 30. **in time past.** Heb. from yesterday the third day. ver. +4.

8. **enlarge.** Dt 11:24, 25. 12:20. Ge 15:18-21. 26:3. 28:13, 14. Ex 23:31. 34:24. 1 K 4:21. Ezr 4:20.

9. **If.** Ge +4:7. **thou shalt.** See on Dt 11:22-25. 12:32. **then shalt thou.** Jsh 20:7, 8.

10. **innocent blood.** ver. 13. Dt 21:8. 1 K 2:31. 2 K 21:16. 24:3, 4. Ps 94:21. 106:37, 38. Pr 6:17. Is 59:7. Je 7:6, 7. Jl 3:19. Jon 1:14. Mt 27:4, 5. **blood.** *f*171I12, Le 20:9.

11. **But if any.** Dt 27:24. Ge 9:6. Ex 21:12-14. Nu 35:16-21, 24. Pr 28:17. Mt *26:52. **mortally.** Heb. in life. Heb. *nephesh,* Jsh +10:28. Dt 22:26.

12. **fetch him.** 1 K 2:5, 6, 28-34. **avenger.** Jsh 20:3. **of blood.** *f*171I11. Synecdoche of the Species B628. Blood (often plural in Hebrew) is put for murder or cruelty, or death generally. For other instances of this figure see Ps 9:12. Ho 1:4. Mt 23:35. 27:24.

13. **Thine eye.** Dt 7:16. 13:8. 25:12. Ezk 16:5. **but thou.** Dt 21:9. Ge 9:6. Le 24:17, 21. Nu 35:33, 34. 2 S 21:1, 14. 1 K 2:31.

14. **shalt not remove.** Before the extensive use of fences, landed property was marked out by stones or posts, set up so as to ascertain the divisions of family estates. It was easy to remove one of these landmarks, and set it in a different place; and thus a dishonest man might enlarge his own estate by contracting that of his neighbor. Hence it was a matter of considerable importance to prevent this crime among the Israelites; among whom, removing them would be equivalent to forging, altering, destroying, or concealing the title-deeds of an estate among us. Accordingly, by the Mosaic law, it was not only prohibited in the commandment against covetousness, but we find a particular curse expressly annexed to it in Dt 27:17. Josephus considers this law a general prohibition, intended not only to protect private property, but also to preserve the boundaries of kingdoms and countries inviolable. Dt *27:17. Jb 24:2. Pr *22:28. *23:10. Ho 5:10.

15. **at the mouth.** *f*121B, Dt +17:6. Dt 17:6. Nu 35:30. 1 K 21:10, 13. Mt ⟩18:16. 26:60, 61. Jn 8:17. 2 C ⟩13:1. 1 T 5:19. He 10:28. Re 11:3-7. **two.** Dt +14:6n. +17:6. Ge +22:15. *41:32.

16. **a false witness.** Ex 23:1-7. 1 K 21:10-13. Ps 27:12. 35:11. Pr 19:5, 9. Mk 14:55-59. Ac 6:13. **that which is wrong.** *or,* falling away. Dt 13:5.

17. **before the priests.** Dt 17:9. 21:5. Ml 2:7. Mt 23:2, 3.

18. **diligent.** See on Dt 13:14. 17:4. 2 Ch 19:6, 7. Jb 29:16.

19. **Then shall.** Pr 19:5, 9. Je 14:15. Da 6:24. **so shalt.** Dt 13:5. 17:7. 19:20. 21:20, 21. 22:21, 24. 24:7. 1 C ⟩5:13.

20. **shall hear.** Dt 13:11. 17:7, 13. 21:21. Pr 21:11. Ro 13:3, 4. 1 T 5:20. **commit no more.** Ge 2:17. Pr 19:25. 21:11. 26:3. Ec √8-11. Is *26:9. 1 T +*5:20.

21. **thine eye.** See on ver. 13. **life shall.** Ex 21:23-25. Le 24:17-21. Mt ⟩5:38, 39. **life.** Heb. *nephesh,* soul. Ge +44:30.

DEUTERONOMY 20

The priest required to exhort the soldiers before they engage in battle, 1-4. What persons the officers must exempt from the war, 5-9. How the cities which accept or refuse peace, must be treated, 10-15. The devoted nations to be extirpated, 16-18. Fruit trees must be spared in a siege, 19, 20.

1. **goest out.** Dt 3:21, 22. 7:1. **horses.** Jsh 10:5-8. 11:4-6, 9. Jg 4:3-9. 2 Ch 14:11. 20:12. Ps 20:7. 33:16, 17. Is 31:1. 37:24, 25. **the Lord.** Dt 2:7. 31:6, 8. Ge 26:3. Nu 23:21. Jsh 1:5, 9. Jg 6:12. 2 K *6:16. 2 Ch *32:7, 8. Ps 46:7, 11. 118:6. Is 7:14. 8:9, 10. 43:2. Ro 8:31.

2. **the priest.** Nu 10:8, 9. 31:6. Jg 20:27, 28. 1 S 14:18. 30:7, 8. 2 Ch 13:12.

3. **let not.** Ps 27:1-3. Is 35:3, 4. 41:10-14. Mt 10:16, 28, 31. Ep *6:11-18. 1 Th 5:14. He 12:12, 13. Re 2:10. **faint.** Heb. be tender. *f*173, Ge +27:44. ver. 8. **tremble.** Heb. make haste. Jb 40:23. Is 28:16. **be ye terrified.** Ps 3:6. Is 8:12, 13. 57:7, 8. Mt 8:26. Mk 16:6, 18. Ac 18:9, 10. 27:24. 1 T 6:12. He 13:6.

4. **to fight.** Dt 1:30. 3:22. 11:25. 32:30. Ex 14:14. Jsh 10:42. *23:10. 2 Ch 13:12. 32:7, 8. Ps 144:1, 2. Ro 8:37.

5. **the officers.** Dt 1:15. 16:18. Nu 31:14, 48. 1 S 17:18. **dedicated.** Ne 12:27. 1 K 8:63. 2 Ch 7:5. Ps 30, Title.

6. **eaten of it.** Heb. made it common. Dt 28:30. Le 19:23-25. Je 31:5. **lest he die.** Is 65:22. Zp 1:13.

7. **betrothed a wife.** It was customary among the Jews to contract matrimony, espouse, or betroth, and for a considerable time to leave the parties in the houses of their respective parents; and when the bridegroom had made proper preparations, then the bride was brought home to his house, and the marriage consummated. The provisions in this verse refer to a case of this kind; though the Jews extend it to him who had newly consummated his marriage, and even to him who had married his brother's wife. It was deemed a peculiar hardship for a person to be obliged to go to battle, who had left a house unfinished, newly purchased land half tilled, or a wife with whom he had just contracted marriage. Dt 22:23-25. 24:5. Mt 1:18. Lk *14:20. **lest he die.** Dt 28:30. Lk 14:18-20. 2 T 2:4.

8. **fearful.** Dt 1:28. 23:9. Jg *7:3. Lk 9:62. Ac 15:37, 38. Re 3:16. 21:8. **lest his brethren's.** Nu 13:31-33. 14:1-3. 32:9. 1 C 15:33. **faint.** Is 40:30, 31. Ml 1:13. Ro 2:7. 1 C *15:58. Ga *6:9. 2 Th 3:13. Heb. melt. Dt 1:28mg. Ex 15:15. Jsh 2:11. 5:1. 7:5. Jg 15:14mg. 2 S 17:10. Ps 22:14. Is 13:7. Is 19:1. Je 49:23mg. Ezk 21:7.

9. **to lead the people.** Heb. to be in the head of the people. 1 S 23:8-29.

10. **then proclaim.** 2 S 20:18-22. Is 57:19. Zc 9:10. Lk 10:5, 6. Ac *10:36. 2 C 5:18-21. 6:1. Ep 2:17.

11. **tributaries.** Le 25:42-46. Jsh 9:22, 23, 27. 11:19, 20. 16:10. Jg 1:28, 30-35. 1 K 9:21, 22. Ps 120:7. Lk *19:14.

12. **And if.** Nu 21:21-24.

13. **thou shalt smite.** See on Nu 31:7-9, 17, 18. 1 K 11:15, 16. Ps 2:6-12. 21:8, 9. 110:1. Lk *19:27. 2 Th 1:7-9.

14. **the women.** Nu ◐31:9, 12, 18, 35, etc. Jsh 8:2. 11:14. 2 Ch 14:13-15. 20:25. Ps 68:12. Ro 8:37. **spoil.** Ge 49:27. **take unto thyself.** Heb. spoil. Ge 34:27. **thou shalt eat.** Jsh 22:8.

15. **Thus shalt.** Nu 21:33-35.

16. **the cities.** Dt 7:1-4, 16. Nu 21:2, 3, 35. 33:52. Jsh 6:17-21. 8:1, 2. 9:24, 27. 10:28, 40. 11:11, 12, 14. **breatheth.** Heb. *nephesh*, soul. Ge +2:7. Jsh 10:40. 11:14.

17. **thou shalt.** Jsh ◐17:13. Is 34:5, 6. Je 48:10. 50:35-40. Ezk 38:21-23. Re 19:18. **Hittites.** i.e. *descendants of Heth*, *S#2850h. See on Dt 7:1. Ge +15:20. 23:10. 25:9. 26:34, 34. 36:2. 49:29, 30. 50:13. Ex 3:8, 17. 13:5. 23:23, 28. 33:2. 34:11. Nu 13:29. Jsh 1:4. 3:10. 9:1. 11:3. 12:8. 24:11. Jg 1:26. 3:5. 1 S 26:6. 2 S 11:3, 6, 17, 21, 24. 12:9, 10. 23:39. 1 K 9:20. 10:29. 11:1. 15:5. 2 K 7:6. 1 Ch 11:41. 2 Ch 1:17. 8:7. Ezr 9:1. Ne 9:8. Ezk 16:3, 45. **Amorites.** i.e. *mountaineers*, *S#567h. Dt 1:4, 7, 19, 20, 27, 44. 2:24. 3:2, 8, 9. 4:46, 47. 7:1. 20:17. 31:4. Ge +10:16. 14:7, 13. 15:16, 21. 48:22. Ex 3:8, 17. 13:5. 23:23. 33:2. 34:11. Nu 13:29. 21:13, 13, 21, 25, 26, 29, 31, 32, 34. 22:2. 32:33, 39. Jsh 2:10. 3:10. 5:1. 7:7. 9:1, 10. 10:5, 6, 12. 11:3. 12:2, 8. 13:4, 10, 21. 24:8, 11, 12, 15, 18. Jg 1:34, 35, 36. 3:5. 6:10. 10:8, 11. 11:19, 21, 22, 23. 1 S 7:14. 2 S 21:2. 1 K 4:19. 9:20. 21:26. 2 K 21:11. 1 Ch 1:14. 2 Ch 8:7. Ezr 9:1. Ne 9:8. Ps 135:11. 136:19. Ezk 16:3, 45. Am 2:9, 10. **Canaanites.** Ge +10:18. **Perizzites.** Ge +13:7. **Hivites.** Ge +10:17. **Jebusites.** Ge +10:16.

18. **teach.** Dt 7:4, 5. 12:30, 31. 18:9. Ex 23:33. 34:11-17. Jsh 23:13. Jg 2:3. Ps 106:34-40. Je +*10:2. 1 C 15:33. 2 C 6:17. Ep *5:11. 2 Th 3:14. 1 T 6:5. 2 T 2:17, 18. Re 18:3-5.

19. **not destroy the trees.** Mt 3:10. 7:15-20. 21:19. Lk *13:7-9. Jn *15:2-8. Re 6:6n. **for the tree,** etc. *or*, for, O man, the tree of the field *is* to be employed in the siege. The original is exceedingly difficult. However rendered, the sense is sufficiently clear: and it is a merciful provision to spare all the fruit trees for the support of both the besieged and the besiegers. Dt 26:6. Le 27:12. Mt 5:45. 10:29. Lk 6:35. 1 P 5:7. **to employ,** etc. Heb. to go from before thee. Dt 8:7, 8. Ge 2:9.

20. **thou shalt build.** Dt 1:28. 2 Ch 26:15. Ec 9:14. Is 37:33. Je 6:6. 33:4. Ezk 17:17. **be subdued.** Heb. come down.

DEUTERONOMY 21

Expiation to be made for the land from murder, when the murderer was concealed, 1-9. How the marriage of an Israelite with a captive maid must be regulated, 10-14. The firstborn, though the son of the hated, is not to be disinherited to please the beloved wife, 15-17. The rebellious son to be stoned, 18-21. Malefactors not to remain all night on a tree, 22, 23.

1. **found slain.** Ps 5:6. 9:12. Pr 28:17. Is 26:21. Ac 28:4.

2. **thy elders.** See on Dt 16:18, 19. Ro 13:3, 4.

3. **an heifer.** Nu 19:2. Je 31:18. Mt 11:28-30. Ph 2:8.

4. **a rough valley.** or, valley with ever-running water. T#1213. Ex 14:27. Am 5:24. Ac 8:26, 36, 38, 39. As the word *nachal* signifies both a torrent and the valley or glen through which it flows, *nachal aithan* may be rendered a "rapid torrent." Many torrents in Judea are dry during a great part of the year; when not only their banks but their beds may be plowed, and yield a crop. Hence there is no impropriety in specifying that such a place should be one that "is neither eared nor sown;" while the circumstance that the elders were to wash their hands over the heifer, whose head had been struck off into the stream, confirms this interpretation. The spot of ground where this sacrifice was made must be uncultivated, because it was considered as a sacrifice for the atonement of murder, and consequently, would pollute the land. **shall strike.** or, break. ver. 6. Ex 13:13. 34:20. Is 53:6. 66:3. Ep 1:7. He *9:22. 1 P 2:21-24. 3:18.

5. **for them.** See on Dt 10:8. 18:5. Nu 6:22-27. 1 Ch 23:13. **chosen to minister.** 1 P=2:9. **to bless.** Dt 10:8. **by their.** See on Dt 17:8-12. 19:17. Ml 2:7. **word.** Heb. mouth. Dt 34:5. Nu +3:16mg. 4:27mg. *20:24mg. 27:21. Jsh 9:2mg. 1 S 12:14mg. 2 S 13:32mg. 17:5mg. 2 Ch 18:12mg. Ezr 8:17mg. Jb 33:6mg. 39:27mg. Ps 49:13mg. Ec 10:13mg. La 1:18mg. Ob 12mg. i.e. decision. **tried.** or, settled and decided.

6. **wash their hands.** Washing the hands was anciently a symbolical action, denoting that the person was innocent of the crime in question. Jb 9:30. Ps 19:12. 26:6. *51:2, 7, 14. 73:13. Is 1:15, 16. Je 2:22. Mt *27:24, 25. He 9:10.

7. **Our hands.** Nu 5:19-28. 2 S 16:8. Jb 21:21-23, 37-40. Ps 7:3, 4.

8. **Be merciful.** or, forgive. Heb. cover. Dt 32:43. Ex 29:33. Ezk 16:63mg. **lay not.** Nu 35:33. 2 S 3:28. 2 K 24:4. Ps 19:12. Je 26:15. Ezk 22:3, 24, 25. Jon 1:14. Mt 23:35. ◐*27:25. Lk 11:50. Ac *5:28. 1 Th 2:15, 16. Re 18:24. **unto thy people.** Heb. in the midst. **blood.** ƒ171I12, Le +20:9.

9. **shalt thou.** See on Dt 19:12, 13. **innocent blood.** ƒ171I12, Le +20:9. 2 K 24:3, 4. **when thou shalt.** Dt 13:18. 2 K 10:30, 31.

10. **thou goest.** Dt 20:10-16.

11. **desire.** Ge 6:2. 12:14, 15. 29:18-20. 34:3, 8. Jg 14:2, 3. Pr 6:25. 31:10, 30. **that.** Nu 31:18.

12. **and she shall.** This was in token of renouncing her religion, and becoming a proselyte to that of the Jews. 1 C 11:6. Ep 4:22. **pare her nails.** or, suffer to grow. Heb. make, or dress. Probably neither paring nor letting them grow, but dressing or beautifying them as the Eastern women still do by tinging them with the leaves of an odoriferous plant called *alhenna*. The leaves are pulverized and made into a paste with water: they bind this paste on the nails of their hands and feet, and keep it on all night. This gives them a deep yellow, which is greatly admired by Eastern nations. The color lasts for three or four weeks before there is occasion to renew it. The custom is so ancient in Egypt, says Hasselquist, that "I have seen the nails of mummies dyed in this manner." 2 S 19:24n.

13. **shall remain.** Ps 45:10. **and bewail.** Ps 45:10, 11. Lk 14:26, 27.

14. **she will.** Heb. *nephesh*, Ex +15:9. **thou shalt.**

Ex 21:7-11. **because thou**. Dt 22:19, 24, 29. Ge 34:2. Jg 19:24. 1 C 7:3. Ep 5:25.

15. **two wives**. Ge +4:19. 29:18, 20, 30, 31, 33. Le 18:18. 1 S 1:4, 5. One after the other, not necessarily at the same time (Young). **hated**. ♪121C2C2, Ge +29:31. i.e. the one loved more than the other, as in the case of Rachel and Leah. In scripture language that which is loved less is said to be *hated* (Young). Ge 29:31, 33. Lk +√14:26. **firstborn**. Ge +27:32. +√41:51. Le +27:26. Jb 18:13. Col +√1:15.

16. **when**. ♪171, Ge +2:17. Ge 43:33. 1 Ch 5:2. 26:10. 2 Ch 11:19-22. 21:3. Ro *8:29. Ph *4:8. He 12:16, 17. **make**. Ge 48:14-19. 1 Ch *26:10.

17. **by giving**. Ge 25:5, 6, 32, 34. 1 Ch 5:1, 2. **double portion**. 1 S 1:2, 4, *5mg. 2 K 2:9. **that he hath**. Heb. that is found with him. **the beginning**. Ge 49:3. Ps 78:51. 105:36. **the right**. Ge 25:31-34.

18. **have a stubborn**. or, apostatizing. lit. *turning aside*, as in ver. 20. ✸S#5637h, Ho +9:15. Ne 9:29. Ps 66:7. 68:6, *18. √78:8. Pr 7:11. Is 1:23. *30:1. *65:2. Je 5:23. 6:28. Ho 4:16. 9:15. Zc √7:11. **rebellious son**. ver. +20. 1 S √15:23. Pr 28:24. *30:11, 17. Is 1:2. **obey the voice**. Dt 27:16. Ex +*20:12. 21:15, 17. Le 19:3. 21:9. Pr *15:5. *20:20. Ezk *22:7. **when they**. Dt 8:5. 2 S 7:14. Pr √13:24. *19:18. *22:15. *23:13, 14. *29:17. He *12:9-11. **will not hearken**. Pr ◑1:8. Is *1:5. Je √5:3. 31:18. Ezk *24:13. Am *4:11, 12. Zc *7:11.

19. **Then**. Ec *8:11. **lay hold**. Dt 22:28. Ge 4:21. 39:12. **and bring**. ver. 2. Dt *16:18. 25:7. Zc 13:3. **gate**. ♪171S7B, Ge +14:7. Ge +14:7. 19:1. 23:10, 18. The public place of judgment in the east.

20. **rebellious**. ✛S#4784h. ver. 18. Nu 20:10. 2 K 14:26 (bitter). Ps *78:8. Je 5:23. Ho +13:16 (✛S#4784h). **he will not obey**. Pr ◑29:17. **he is a glutton**. Nu 11:32. Pr *19:26. 20:1. 23:1-3, 19-21, 29-35. 28:7mg. Ph +*3:19. **a drunkard**. Pr *23:20, 21. Ezk 23:42mg. 1 C √6:9, 10.

21. **all the men**. Dt 13:10, 11. 17:5. Le 24:16. Nu 15:35. **so shalt thou**. Dt 13:5, 11. 19:19, 20. 22:21, 24. **all Israel**. Dt *13:11. +19:20. Ro 6:23. He 12:9.

22. **worthy of death**. Heb. of the judgment of death. Dt 19:6. The Hebrews understand this not of putting to death by hanging, but of hanging a man up after he was stoned to death; which was done more ignominiously of some heinous malefactors. We have the examples of Rechab and Baanah, who, for murdering Ishbosheth, were slain by David's commandment, their hands and feet cut off, and *then* hanged up. 2 S 4:12. See also Jsh 8:29. 10:26. So Nu 25:4, we read, "And the Lord said unto Moses, Take all the heads (chief men) of the people, and hang them up before the Lord against the sun, that the fierce anger of the Lord may be turned away from Israel." Among the Romans, in after ages, they hanged, or rather fastened to the tree ALIVE; and such was the cruel death of our blessed Lord and Saviour Jesus Christ. Dt 19:6. 22:26. 1 S 26:10. Mt 26:66. Ac 23:29. 25:11, 25. 26:31. **thou hang**. 2 S 21:6, 9. Lk 23:33. Jn 19:31-38. **tree**. 121D8, Ge 40:19.

23. **tree**. ♪121D8, Ge +40:19. **he that is hanged**. 2 C 5:21. Ga ◗3:13. **is accursed of God**. Heb. the curse of God. Dt 7:26. Nu 5:21. 25:4. Jsh 7:12. 2 S 21:6. Ps 102:8mg. Je 29:22. Ro 9:3. 1 C 16:22. 2 C 5:21. Ga ◗3:13. That is, it is the highest degree of reproach that can attach to a man, and proclaims him

under the curse of God as much as any external punishment can. They that see him thus hanging between heaven and earth, will conclude him abandoned of both, and unworthy of either. Bp. Patrick observes, that this passage is applied to the death of Christ; not only because he bare our sins and was exposed to shame, as these malefactors were that were accursed of God, but because he was in the evening taken down from the cursed tree and buried (and that by the particular care of the Jews, with an eye to this law, Jn 19:31), in token, that now the guilt being removed, the law was satisfied, as it was when the malefactors had hanged till sunset: it demanded no more. Then he, and those that are his, ceased to be a curse. And as the land of Israel was pure and clean when the body was buried, so the church is washed and cleansed by the complete satisfaction which Christ thus made. **thy land**. Le 18:25. Nu 35:33, 34. **defiled**. Ge 34:5. Nu 35:34.

DEUTERONOMY 22

Strayed cattle and lost property to be restored, and another's ass or ox, if fallen, to be lifted up, 1-4. The sexes to be distinguished by apparel, 5. The mother bird not to be taken with her young, 6, 7. Railings or battlements to be placed on every house, 8. Improper mixtures to be avoided: of seeds sown, 9; plowing with an ox and ass together, 10; garments of mixed fabrics, 11. Fringes to be worn on garments, 12. The case of a woman accused of unchastity before marriage if false, 13-19; if true, 20, 21. Adultery to be punished with death, the betrothed virgin being adjudged a wife, 22-24. Rapes to be punished with death, 25-27. Of fornication, 28, 29. Incest forbidden, 30.

1. **Thou shalt**. Ex 23:4. Ezk 34:4, 16. Mt 10:6. 15:24. 18:12, 13. Lk 15:4-6. Ja 5:19, 20. 1 P 2:25. **not**. ♪19. Anastrophe; or, Arraignment B699: the position of one word changed so as to be set over against the other; the inversion or reversal of words. The word thus put out of its usual place receives great emphasis. Here, the *negative* is put with "see" instead of with "hide," in order to emphasize the command, which would otherwise tamely read "If thou shalt see...thou shalt not hide," etc. For other instances of this figure see Mi 6:10. Ac 7:48. **hide thyself**. ♪121S2, Ge +21:6. ver. 3, 4. Le 20:4. Pr 24:11. 28:27. Is 8:17. 58:7. Lk 10:31, 32. Ja 2:8.

2. **thou shalt restore**. Mt 7:12. Ga 5:14. 1 Th 4:6. He 10:24. 13:1. Ja 2:8. 1 J 3:11, 18.

3. **ass**. Ex 23:4. **lost things**. Ex 22:9. Le 6:3, 4. **hide thyself**. ver. 1. Jb 6:16. Ps 55:1. Is 58:7.

4. **thou shalt surely**. Ex 23:4, 5. Mt 5:44. Lk 10:29-37. Ro 15:1. 2 C 12:15. Ga 6:1, 2. 1 Th 5:14. He 12:12, 13.

5. **woman shall not**. 1 C 11:4-15. 1 T 2:9. T 2:4, 5. 1 P 3:3-5. This prohibition was no doubt intended to exclude the idolatrous customs of the heathen, as well as to prevent the evil which would be produced by the introduction of such customs. Nothing was more common among idolaters, than for men, in the worship of several of their gods, to put on the garments worn by women; particularly in the worship of Venus, to which that of Ashtaroth among the Canaanites bore a striking resemblance, the women were accustomed to appear in armor before her, and the men in women's apparel. But independently of this, the practice has

produced the greatest confusion in society, and has been productive of the grossest crimes. Hence Clodius, who dressed himself as a woman, that he might mingle with the Roman ladies in the feast of the *Bona dea*, was universally justly execrated. Je +10:2. **abomination**. See on Dt 18:12.

6. **young ones**. Lk 12:6. **thou shalt not**. Ge 8:17. 32:11. Le 22:28. Pr 12:10. Ho 10:14.

7. **But thou shalt**. Ge 1:22. Ps *145:9. Mt 23:37. The extirpation of any species of birds, whether edible or birds of prey, is often attended with serious consequences, and is always productive of evil; to prevent which was the object of this law. Palestine is situated in a climate producing poisonous snakes and scorpions, and between deserts and mountains, from which it would be inundated by them, as well as with immense swarms of flies, locusts, and mice, if the birds which feed upon them were extirpated. In a moral point of view, it may have been intended to inculcate a spirit of mercy and kindness, and to prevent the exercise of cruelty even towards a sparrow; for he who is guilty of such cruelty will, if circumstances be favorable, be cruel to his fellow creatures. Lk 12:6, 7. 16:10. **that it may**. See on Dt +4:40. **thou mayest**. Pr 22:4.

8. **then thou shalt**. The eastern houses being built with flat roofs, which were used for various purposes, as walking, sleeping, etc., it was therefore necessary to have a sort of battlement, or balustrade, to prevent accidents, by people falling off. Ex 21:28-36. 22:6. Ro 14:13. 1 C 10:32. Ph 1:10. 1 Th 5:22. **thy roof**. 2 S 11:2. Is 22:1. Je 19:13. Mt 10:27. Mk 2:4. Ac 10:9. **thou bring**. Ge 9:5. Ps 119:156. Ezk 3:18, 20. 32:2-9. Mt 18:6, 7. Ac 20:26, 27. Ja 5:11. 1 J 4:16.

9. **shalt not sow**. Ge 1:11. Le 19:19. Mt 6:24. 9:16. *13:24, 25. Ro 11:6. 2 C 1:12. 6:14-16. 11:3. Ja 1:6-8. 3:10. **fruit of thy seed**. Heb. fulness of thy seed. Ex 22:29mg. Nu 18:27.

10. **together**. 2 Ch 18:1. 2 C 6:14. Two different species cannot associate comfortably together, nor pull pleasantly either in cart or plow; and the ass being lower than the ox, when yoked, he must bear the principal part of the weight. 2 C 6:14-16. Matthew Poole remarks also because the one was a clean beast, the other unclean; whereby God would teach men to avoid polluting themselves by the touch of unclean persons or things, 2 C 6:14.

11. **not wear**. Le 19:19. Mt 6:22, 24. Ga 2:17, 18. 4:21-23.

12. **fringes**. Nu 15:38, 39. 1 K 7:17. Mt 23:5. **quarters**. Heb. wings. ver. 30. **coverest**. Ge 20:16. Ex 21:10. *22:27.

13. **go in**. Ge +4:1. 6:4. 29:21, 23, 31. Jg 15:1, 2. **and hate**. ver. 16. Dt +*21:15. 24:3. 2 S 13:15. Ml 2:14-16. Ep ◐5:28, 29, 33.

14. **give occasions**. ver. 19. Ex 20:16. 23:1. Pr 18:8, 21. 1 T 5:14. or, ascribed **or** laid actions. ver. 17. 1 S 2:3. 1 Ch 16:8. Ps 9:11. **of speech**. Heb. of words. i.e. of discourses or defamations. **evil name**. ver. 19. Ne 6:13. Lk 6:22. **found**. Ps 26:1, 2, 6. a maid. S#1331h, Le +21:13. Ge 24:14, +16 (S#1330h), 28. Ru 2:6. 4:12.

15. **tokens of … virginity**. ꟻ121M, Ex +8:23. ver. 16, 17, 20. Le +*21:13. Jg 11:37, 38. Ezk 23:3, 8. Lk *15:8-10. **elders**. Dt 21:2. **gate**. ꟻ171S7B, Ge +14:7. Dt 21:19. Ge +14:7.

16. **hateth**. ver. +13. Ml 2:15, 16.

17. **occasions of**. ver. 14. Ge 38:24. Ps 141:4. Ho 1:2. **spread**. Nu 4:7, 11. **tokens**. ꟻ121M, Ex +8:23. **the cloth**. or, the garment. That worn by day often serves for night in the east (Young). F. Delitzsch at this place comments that the parents were to "establish the chastity and innocence of their daughter by spreading the bed-clothes" before the elders of the city by showing the marks of a first intercourse upon the bed-clothes or dress.

18. **the elders**. Dt 1:13. 16:18. Ex 18:21, 22. **chastise**. Dt 25:2. Pr 10:13. 19:29. 20:30.

19. **amerce**. or, fine. Ex 21:22. 2 Ch 36:3. Pr 17:26. 21:11. 22:3. 27:12. Am 2:8mg. **because**. Ex 23:7. Jb 22:19. **he may not put**. ver. 29. Dt 24:1-4. Mt 19:8, 9.

20. **this thing**. Dt 17:4. **tokens of virginity**. ver. +15.

21. **stone her**. ver. 22, 24. Dt 13:10. 17:5. 21:21. Le 24:16, 23. Nu 15:35, 36. **she hath wrought**. Ge +34:7. Le 21:9. Jsh +7:15. Jg 20:6, 10. 2 S 13:12, 13. **to play**. Le 19:29. Dt 23:17. He +*13:4. **shalt thou**. Dt 13:5. 17:7. 19:19. 1 C ◐5:13.

22. **a man**. Ex *20:14. Le 20:10. Nu 5:22-27. Pr 6:27-29. Ezk 23:45-47. Jn *8:4, 5. He +*13:4.

23. **betrothed**. See on Dt 20:7. Mt 1:18, 19.

24. **both**. Nu *32:23. Ps 34:15-17. 2 C 5:10. **and ye shall stone**. In these laws, the betrothed damsel was considered as the wife of the man to whom she was engaged, though they had not come together; and therefore the crime was adjudged adultery. But a charitable supposition is admitted in the damsel's favor, in case she was found in a solitary place. **he hath humbled**. Dt 21:14. Ge 29:21. Mt 1:20, 24. **so shalt thou put**. ver. 21, 22, 24. Dt 13:5. 1 C 5:2, ◗13.

25. **force her**. or, take strong hold of her. 2 S 13:14.

26. **no sin**. See on Dt 21:22. **slayeth him**. Heb. *nephesh*, Jsh +10:28.

27. **cried**. 1 C 13:7. **none**. *Nu 32:23. 1 S 2:3. 2 Ch 16:9. Pr 15:3.

28. **a damsel**. See on Ex 22:16, 17.

29. **shall give**. Ge 34:12. Ex 22:16, 17. **because he hath humbled**. ver. 19, 24. Dt 21:14.

30. **a man shall**. This is to be understood as referring to the case of a *stepmother*. A man in his old age may have married a young woman, and on his dying, his son by another, or a former wife, may desire to espouse her; which is here forbidden. Dt 27:20. Ge 35:22. 49:3, 4. Le 18:8. 20:11. 1 Ch 5:1. 1 C 5:1, 13. **discover**. Ru 3:9. Ezk 16:8. **skirt**. Heb. wing. ver. 12mg.

DEUTERONOMY 23

What Israelites must not enter into the congregation, 1, 2. An Ammonite, or Moabite, is excluded to the tenth generation; an Edomite or Egyptian to the third, 3-8. The camps of Israel to be kept pure from moral, ceremonial, and natural pollution, 9-14. Fugitive slaves to be protected, 15, 16. Whoredom, sodomy, and usury, to be strictly guarded against, 17-20. Vows must be performed, 21-23. The liberty that was lawful in a neighbor's vineyard and cornfield, 24, 25.

1. **wounded**. ✱S#1795h, only here. lit. wounded by bruising. See ✱S#1794h, Ps +10:10. Le 21:17-21. 22:22-24. 1 K 20:37. SS 5:7. Ga 3:28. Young's *Literal Translation* adds here "or bruised." Ps 10:10mg. 38:8.

44:19. 51:*8, √17. **stones**. Jb 40:17. **member**. ❋S#8212h, only here. Not mentioned elsewhere, from a root signifying *to pour out*. Ho ◗2:10 (❋S#5040h). **cut**. Le *22:24. 1 S 5:4. **shall not enter**. It is evident that this law was not meant to exclude mutilated Israelites, either from the common benefits of civil society, or any essential religious advantages; but merely to lay them under a disgraceful distinction. This would tend to discourage parents from thus mutilating their children; a practice which was exceedingly common in those ages and countries. To this they might often be induced by the custom which prevailed, of employing eunuchs in the houses of the great and the courts of princes: so that they often rose to the highest posts of honor and authority (2 K 20:17, 18. Da 1:3-7). Some expositors therefore consider the phrase, "shall not enter into the congregation of the Lord," as meaning, that they should be incapable of bearing any office in that government, which was placed over the people of God, who must thus enter a protest against this custom, and deliver selfish parents from this temptation. But others think, that the persons intended might not enter the inner court of the sanctuary, or join in celebrating the sacred feasts, as in full communion with the congregation of the Lord; but must be contented to worship without, as uncircumcised Gentiles were allowed to do. Indeed it is probable that the exclusion related to both these particulars: for, as the blemished priests might not officiate at the altar (Le 21:17, 23), it is reasonable to conclude, that the blemished Israelite must neither enter the inner court of the sanctuary, nor fill up any public office in the congregation; in order that the people and ordinances of God might be preserved in purity and honor. **shall not**. ver. 2, 3, 8. Ne 13:1-3. Ps ◗65:4. Is 56:3, 4. La 1:10. Mt 19:12. Ac ◗*8:27, 38, 39. 2 C 13:9. **congregation of the Lord**. This term signifies here not the body of the people, as it usually does, but the society of the elders or rulers of the people, who, as they represent the whole congregation, and act in their name, and for their service and good, so they are sometimes called by the name of *the congregation*, as Nu 35:12, 24, 25. Jsh 20:6, 9. 1 K *8:1-3, 5. 1 Ch 13:1, 2, 4. 29:1, 10, 20. 28:1. 29:6. Ps 82:1.

2. **bastard**. Ex 34:6, 7. Is 57:3. Je 31:29, 30. Ezk 18:1-4. Zc 9:6. Jn 8:41. He 12:8. **tenth generation**. This round number implies that they can never obtain this privilege (Young). Ge 31:7, 41.

3. **Ammonite**. These nations were subjected for their impiety, wickedness, and enmity to Israel (ver. 4, 5) to peculiar disgrace; and on this account were not permitted to hold any office among the Israelites. This did not, however, disqualify them from becoming proselytes (Ex 12:48. Le 22:18. Nu 9:14. 15:15); for Ruth, who was a Moabitess, was married to Boaz, and became one of the progenitors of our Lord. Ru 4:6, 10-22. Ne 4:3, 7. 13:1, 2, 23. Is 56:3. **Moabite**. ❋S#4125h. Dt 2:11, 29. Ru 1:4, 22. 2:2, 6, 21. 4:5, 10. 1 K 11:1. 1 Ch 11:46. 2 Ch 24:26. Ezr 9:1. Ne 13:1, 23. **tenth generation**. ver. 2n. **for ever**. lit. to the age. i.e. *never*, but some say, "till the age of Messiah" (Young). Heb. *olam*, Ex +12:24. 2 S 5:14. 7:12-16. 1 Ch 3:17, 18. Je 22:24-30. Mt. 1:6, 11, 12. Lk ◗3:23-28.

4. **Because they met**. Dt 2:28, 29. Ge 14:17, 18. 1 S 25:11. 1 K 18:4. Is 63:9. Zc 2:8. Mt *25:45. Ac

9:4. **because they hired**. See on Nu 22:5, 7, 17. Ne 13:2.

5. **Nevertheless**. Nu 22:35. 23:5-12, 16-26. 24:9. Mi 6:5. Ro 8:31. 2 C 4:17. **turned**. Pr *26:2. Ro 8:28. **because the**. T#1804. Dt 7:7, 8. 33:3. Ps 73:1. Je 31:3. Ezk 16:8. Ml 1:2. Ro 9:13. 11:28. Ep 2:4, 5.

6. **Thou shalt**. 2 S 8:2. 12:31. Ezr 9:12. Ne 13:23-25. **prosperity**. Heb. good. ver. 16mg. Jg 9:2mg. 1 S 9:10mg. 1 S 12:23. 15:22. **for ever**. Heb. *olam*, Ex +12:24.

7. **Edomite**. Ge ◗+36:9. 1 S 21:7. 22:9, 18, 22. 1 K 11:14. Ps 52:t. **he is thy**. Ge 25:24-26, 30. Nu 20:14. Ob 10-12. Ml 1:2. **because thou**. Dt 10:19. Ge 45:17, 18. 46:7. 47:6, 12, 27. Ex 22:21. 23:9. Le *19:34. Jb 31:32. Ps 105:23. Mt *25:34, 35. Ac 7:10-18.

8. **enter into**. See on ver. 1. Ro 3:29, 30. Ep 2:12, 13. **third generation**. ver. 2, 3. Ex 20:5, 6.

9. **keep thee**. Jsh 6:10, *18, 19. 7:11-13. Jg 20:26. 2 Ch 19:4. 20:3-13. 31:20, 21. 32:1-22. Lk 3:14. Re 19:11-14.

10. **that is**. Le 15:16. Nu 5:2, 3. 1 C 5:11-13. 2 C 7:1.

11. **when evening**. Le 11:25. 15:17-23. **cometh on**. Heb. turneth toward. Ge 24:63. **wash himself**. Le ◗+11:32. 14:9. 15:5, 11, 13. 22:6. Ps 51:2, 7. Ezk *36:25. Mt *3:11. Mk 7:2-5. Lk *11:38, 39. Ep *5:26, 27. He *9:9, 10. √10:22. 1 P *3:21. Re *1:5.

12. **a place**. lit. hand. Nu 2:17. Ezk 21:19mg. In such a vast camp as that of the Israelites (See notes on Numbers chapter 1 and 2) and indeed, as in every well regulated camp, cleanliness is considered as indispensably necessary. Hence every person who had any disease, and those who were reputed unclean, were forbidden to enter it. Those who have the health of men confided to them, are not ignorant that diseases may easily be produced by putrid exhalations from excrementitious matter. Hence these regulations, though they may appear trifling to some, were essentially necessary to preserve the health of the people.

13. **paddle**. Heb. nail *or* pin *or*, shovel. Ex 27:19. 35:18. 38:20, 31. 39:40. Nu 3:37. 4:32. Jg 4:21, 22. **wilt ease thyself**. Heb. sittest down. Jg 3:24mg. 1 S 24:3. **dig**. Ge 21:30. **cover that**. Ezk 24:6-8. **which cometh**. Ezk 4:12.

14. **walketh**. ♪22C17, Le +26:12. Ge 3:8. 17:1. Le 26:11, 12. 2 C 6:16. 1 P ◗5:8. **in the midst**. Dt 1:42. 6:15. 7:21. 31:17. Ex +17:7. 33:3. 34:9. Nu 11:20. 14:14, 42. 16:3. **to deliver**. Ex *3:8. **to give**. Dt 7:2, 23. **holy**. ♪108B. Idiom B830. Special idiomatic usages of nouns and verbs: "holy" means primarily that which is ceremonially clean and free from defilement. **unclean thing**. Heb. nakedness of any thing. Dt 24:1mg. **turn away**. Le 26:17. 2 P *3:14.

15. **shalt not**. 1 S 23:11, 12. 30:15. Ob 14. Phm 10-19. We cannot suppose that this law required the Israelites to entertain slaves who had robbed their masters, or left their service without cause; but such only as were cruelly treated, and fled to them for protection, especially from the neighboring nations. To such they were commanded to afford shelter, and show great kindness; both in order to recommend their religion, and to give them an opportunity of learning it. **escaped**. Ge 32:30. 2 K 19:11.

16. **shall dwell**. Is 16:3, 4. Lk 15:15-24. T 3:2, 3. **gates**. Ge +14:7. **liketh him best**. Heb. is good for

him. Est 1:19mg. **thou shalt not.** Ex 22:21. 23:9. Le 19:33. 25:14, 17. Je 7:6. Zc 7:10. Ml 3:5. Ja 2:6.

17. **There shall be,** etc. The prohibition in the text, like many others, has no direct application to practices that were common among the Israelites at that time; but was intended to guard them against the enormities which were practiced among the surrounding nations. The words *kaidesh* and *kedaishah,* properly denote persons dedicated or consecrated to the worship of some abominable god or goddess (See note on Ge 38:21); whose impure earnings were applied to the support of their execrable worship. Dt 22:21, 29. Le 18:22. *19:29. Pr 2:16. **whore.** *or,* sodomitess. Ge 38:21, 22. Ho 4:14. Ro 1:26. **sodomite.** Ge 19:4, 5. 34:7. Le 18:9, 11. 20:13, 17. Jg 19:22, 23. 20:6. 2 S 13:12. 1 K 14:24. 15:12. 22:46. 2 K 23:7. Jb 36:14mg. Ro 1:27, 28. 1 C 6:9, 10. 1 T 1:9, 10. ⁕S#6945h: Dt 23:17. 1 K 14:24. 15:12. 22:46. 2 K 23:7. Jb 36:14mg.

18. **hire.** Ps 93:5. Is 23:17, 18. Ezk 16:31, *33, 34, 41. Ho 9:1. Mi 1:5, 7. **dog.** Ps 22:16. Pr 26:11. Is 56:10, 11. Mt 7:6. Ph 3:2. 2 P 2:22. Re 22:15. **any vow.** See on ver. 21. Dt 12:6. Le 7:16. +*23:38. Ps 5:4-6. Is 61:8. Hab 1:13. Ml 1:14.

19. **shalt not.** Dt 15:7, 8. 24:10-13. 28:*12, ◑44. Ex 22:25. Le 25:35-37. Ne 5:1-7. Ps 15:5. Ezk 18:7, 8, 13, 16-18. 22:12. Lk 6:34, 35. **lend upon usury.** Heb. *noshak,* S#5391h. lit. bite, as in Ge 49:17 (an adder that biteth the horse heels). Pr 23:32 (biteth). Ec 10:8, 11. Is +24:2. **usury of.** Heb. *neshek,* ⁕S#5392h. Ex 22:25. Le 25:36, 37. Ps 15:5. Pr 28:8. Ezk 18:8, 13, 17. 22:12.

20. **a stranger.** Heb. *nokri,* Ge +31:15. Dt 14:21. 15:3. Le 19:33, 34. **mayest lend.** S. C. Mooney argues, "Usury exacted from the foreigner does not imply that usury is not inherently evil, just as the carrying out of the death penalty does not imply that killing is not inherently evil. The command to execute a murderer is not to be taken as an 'exception' to, or 'qualification' of the commandment 'you shall not kill.'" In the same way, usury is an inherent evil that is not 'qualified' by permission to practice on foreigners" (*Usury: Destroyer of Nations,* p. 151). Mooney cites Erskine and Fisher's commentary on the Westminster Shorter Catechism, "Q. How do you prove from Scripture, that moderate usury, or common interest, is not oppression in itself? A. From the express command laid upon the Israelites not to oppress a stranger, Ex 23:9; and yet their being allowed to take usury from him, Dt 23:20; which they would not have been permitted to do, if there had been an intrinsic evil in the thing itself" (Mooney, p. 149). Mooney argues that this argument, though it sounds conclusive, "ignores the distinction that is evident in the Hebrew between the *Ger* in Ex 23:9 and the *Nokri* in Dt 23:20" (Mooney, p. 149). See related note, Ge 31:15. **may bless.** See on Dt 15:10. Pr *19:17. Is 1:19. Lk +*6:34-36. +*14:14. 1 C *15:58.

21. **When.** ver. 18. Ge 28:20. 35:1-3. Le 27:2, etc. Nu 30:2, etc. Ps 56:12. 66:13, 14. 76:11. 116:18. Ec 5:4, 5. Jon 1:16. 2:9. Na 1:15. **vow.** Le +*23:38. **slack.** *or,* delay *or* be behind. Ge 32:4. 34:19. Ex *22:29. Ec *5:4. 2 P ◑*3:9.

22. **forbear.** Ge 11:8. 18:11. 41:49. **to vow.** Le +*23:38. 27:2n. **no sin.** Ac 5:1-4.

23. **That which.** Nu 30:2. Jg 11:30, 31, 35. 1 S 1:11. Ps *66:13, 14. 116:18. Pr 20:25. Ec *5:4, 5. **hast vowed.**

1 S 14:24. Je 44:25-27. Mk 6:22, 23. Ac 23:12, 21. **freewill offering.** Le +*23:38.

24. **thou mayest.** Ro 12:13. 1 C 10:26. He 13:5. **grapes.** Ge 40:10. **thy fill.** or, sufficiency. Ex *16:3. Le 25:19. 26:5. **pleasure.** or, desire. Heb. *nephesh,* soul, Nu +11:6. ♪121A9, Ge +23:8. Ps 105:22. Je 2:24. **vessel.** Bag, or anything with which travellers in the east are generally provided (Young). Dt 28:5n. Le 11:32. 1 S 17:40mg. Mt +10:10.

25. **standing corn.** Dt 16:9. Ex 22:6. **then thou mayest.** Mt 12:1, 2. Mk 2:23. Lk 6:1, 2. **pluck.** Jb 8:12. 30:4. Ezk 17:4, 22. **move.** or, wave. Dt 27:5. Ex 20:25. Jsh 8:31. **sickle.** Dt 16:9.

DEUTERONOMY 24

The law of divorces, 1-4. Newly married men exempted for one year from war and public services, 5. Laws for the punishment of menstealers; concerning pledges, and the separation of lepers, 6-13. The hire of servants not to be detained, 14, 15. Parents and children not punishable for each other's crimes, 16. Justice must be done to the widows, fatherless, and friendless, 17, 18. Liberal gleanings to be left for the poor, 19-22.

1. **hath taken.** Dt 21:15. 22:13. Ex 21:10. **uncleanness.** Heb. matter of nakedness. Dt 23:14. **then let him.** ver. 3. Ezr 10:3. Je 3:8. Mt ▶5:31, 32. ▶19:7-9. Mk 10:▶4-12. **divorcement.** Heb. cutting off. Is 50:1. **send her.** Dt 22:19, 29. Ml 2:16. Mt 1:19. Lk 16:18. 1 C 7:11, 12.

2. **she may go.** Le 21:7, 14. 22:13. Nu 30:9. Ezk 44:22. Mt 5:32. Mk 10:11. 1 C 7:15.

3. **hate.** Dt +*21:15n. 22:13, 16. 2 S 13:15. Lk *14:26. **bill of.** Mt ▶19:7. Mk ▶10:4. **die.** Ro 7:2.

4. **Her former.** Ps 107:33, 34. Je *3:1. Ml 2:14-16. **after that she is defiled.** Not simply and absolutely, as if her second marriage were a sin, but respectively, or as to her first husband, to whom she is as a defiled or unclean woman, that is, forbidden; for things forbidden are accounted and called unclean, Jg 13:7, because they may no more be touched or used than an unclean thing (Matthew Poole). **thou shalt.** Le 18:24-28. Jsh 22:17, 18.

5. **a man.** See on Dt 20:7. Ge 2:24. Mt 19:4-6. Mk 10:6-9. 1 C 7:10-15. Ep 5:28, 29. T 2:4, 5. **neither,** etc. Heb. not any thing shall pass upon him. **cheer up.** Pr 5:18. Ec 9:9. 1 C 7:29.

6. **shall take.** Ex 22:26, 27. Re 18:22. **the nether.** Ex 11:5. Nu 11:8. Is 47:2. Je 25:10. **upper.** Jg 9:53. 2 S 11:21. Mt 18:6. Mk 9:42. Lk 17:2. Re 18:21, 22. Small handmills, which ground at one time only a sufficient quantity for a day's consumption; hence they were forbidden to take either of the stones to pledge, because if they did, they would be deprived of the means of preparing their necessary food, and the family be without bread. Under this one kind is to be understood the taking away all other things necessary to get a livelihood, the taking away whereof is against the laws both of charity and prudence, seeing by those things alone he can be enabled both to subsist and to pay his debts. This is an instance of ♪171I15. Synecdoche of the Species B625, whereby a species of a thing is put for the whole genus; here, one means of livelihood is put for any means of livelihood, as the preceding note explains. Compare ♪171I8, Ge +3:19;

*171I14, Ex +22:22. **to pledge**. Ge 47:19. Ex 22:26. Ne 5:3. Jb 22:6. 24:9. Pr 20:16. 22:27. Am 2:8. Ja 2:5-8. **life**. Dt 20:19. Ge 44:30. Lk 12:15. **a man's life**. Heb. *nephesh*, soul, Ge +44:30. *121F, Ge +49:6. Metonymy of the Effect: the thing effected by an instrument for the instrument or organic cause of it B563. Here, "life," the effect, is put for the means of livelihood by which the life is preserved. i.e. his livelihood, or the necessary supports of his life. Dt 20:19. Ge 44:30. Lk *12:15.

7. **found**. Ge 37:28. 44:16. Ex *21:16. Ezk 27:13. 1 T 1:10. Re 18:13. **any**. Heb. *nephesh*, soul, Ge +12:5. **then that**. See on Ex 21:16. 22:1-4. **maketh merchandise**. Dt 21:14. **and thou shalt**. Dt 13:5. See on 19:19. 1 C)5:13.

8. **the plague of**. Le 13, 14. 2 Ch 26:19. Mt 8:4. Mk 1:44. Lk 5:14. 17:14.

9. **remember**. Lk 17:32. 1 C 10:6, 11. **Miriam**. Nu 5:2. 12:10-15. 2 K 7:3. 2 Ch 26:20, 21.

10. **When**. See on Dt 15:8. **lend thy brother anything**. Heb. lend the loan of anything to thy brother. Dt 15:2. **loan**. or debt, or burden. Pr 22:26. **pledge**. ver. 11-13.

12. **man be poor**. ver. 17. Jb 22:6. 24:3, 9.

13. **deliver**. Ex 22:26, 27. Jb 24:7, 8. 29:11-13. 31:16-20. Ezk 18:7, 12, 16. 33:15. Am 2:8. 2 T 1:16-18. **the sun**. ver. 15. 2 C 9:13, 14. Ep 4:26. **in his own raiment**. The raiment here referred to was most likely the same as the *hyke* of the Arabs, a long kind of blanket, resembling a Highland plaid, generally about six yards in length, and five or six feet broad; in which they often carry their provisions, as well as wrap themselves in, in the day, and sleep in at night, it being their only substitute for a bed. How necessary, then, it was to restore the *hyke* to a poor man before the going down of the sun, that he might have something to repose on, will sufficiently appear from these considerations. **shall be**. Dt 6:25. 15:9, 10. Ge √15:6. Ps 106:30, 31. 112:9. Is 58:8. Da *4:27. Ja *1:27. *2:13-23.

14. **not oppress**. *108J, Ge +43:18. Le *25:40-43. Jb 24:10, 11. *31:13-15. Ps +*12:5. Pr *14:31. 22:16. Ezk +*16:49. 22:7. Am *2:7. 4:1. 8:4. Ml +*3:5. Lk *10:7.

15. **At his**. Le +*19:13. Pr *3:27, 28. Je 22:13. Mt 20:8. Mk 10:19. Ja *5:4. **setteth his heart upon it**. Heb. lifteth his soul (Heb. *nephesh*, Ex +23:9) unto it. Ps 24:4. 25:1. 86:4. **lest he**. Dt √15:9. Ex √22:+23, 24. 1 S 25:*17, 39. Jb 31:16, 21-23, 38. 34:28. 35:9. Ps 12:5. *35:10. 43:1. 68:5. *140:12. Pr √22:22, 23. *23:10, 11. Is 5:7. 33:10. Je *22:13, 16. Ep *6:9. Ja √5:4. **cry**. Ge *4:10. 18:20, 21. Ex 3:9. Jb *34:28. Hab 2:9-11. Lk *18:7.

16. **fathers**. 2 K *14:5, 6. 2 Ch 25:4. Je 31:29, 30. Ezk *18:20. This law is given to men, not to God; and though God do visit the father's sins upon the children, Ex 20:5, yet he will not suffer men to do so (Matthew Poole). **his own**. Ezk *18:4n.

17. **pervert**. Dt 16:19. 27:19. Ex 22:21, 22. 23:2, 6, 9. Le 25:35. 1 S 12:3, 4. Jb 22:8, 9. 29:11-17. Ps 82:1-5. 94:3-6, 20, 21. Pr 22:22, 23. 31:5. Ec 5:8. Is 1:17, 23. 3:15. 33:15. Je 5:28. 22:3. Ezk 22:7, 29. Am 5:7-12. Mi 2:1, 2. 7:3. Zc 7:10. Ml 3:5. Lk 3:14. Ja 2:6. **stranger**. Dt 10:19. Le 25:35. **fatherless**. Dt +10:18. Ps 10:14. 68:5. Is 1:17. 10:2. Ja 1:27. **nor take**. See on Ex 22:26, 27. Jb 24:3.

18. **thou shalt**. See on ver. 22. Dt 5:15. 15:15. 16:12.

19. **When thou**. Le 19:9, 10. 23:22. Ru 2:16. Ps 41:1. **harvest**. *121P10. Metonymy of the Adjunct B597. Harvest is put for the fruits of the harvest. For other instances of this figure see Is 17:5. Jl 3:13. **it shall be**. ver. 20, 21. See on Dt 14:29. 26:13. **may bless**. Dt 15:10. Jb 31:16-22. 42:12. Ps 41:1-3. 112:9. Pr 11:24, 25. 14:21. 19:17. Is 32:8. 58:7-11. Lk *6:35, 38. 14:13, 14. 2 C 9:6-8. 1 J 3:17-19.

20. **beatest**. Jg 6:11. Ru 2:17. Pr 19:17. Is 27:12. 28:27. **go over the boughs again**. Heb. bough *it* after thee. Is 10:33. Ezk 17:6. 31:5, 6, 8, 12, 13.

21. **gatherest**. See on ver. 19. Lk 19:9, 10. 25:5. **afterward**. Heb. after thee. Dt 15:10. Ps 41:1.

22. **thou shalt remember**. ver. 18. See on Dt 5:14, 15. 7:8. Is 51:1. 2 C 8:8, 9. Ep 5:1, 2. 1 J 4:10, 11.

DEUTERONOMY 25

Judges must do justly, 1, 2. Not more than forty stripes must be inflicted on malefactors, 3. Oxen treading out the corn not to be muzzled, 4. The widow of him who died childless to be married by his brother, who if he refused to take her, must be disgraced, 5-10. The punishment of an immodest woman, 11, 12. Just weights and measures to be used, 13-16. The memory of Amalek to be blotted out, 17-19.

1. **a controversy**. Dt 16:18-20. 17:8, 9. 19:17-19. Ex 23:6, 7. 2 S 23:3. 2 Ch 19:6-10. Jb 29:7-17. Ps 58:1, 2. 82:2-4. Pr 17:15. 31:8, 9. Is 1:17, 23. 5:23. 11:4. 32:1, 2. Je 21:12. Ezk 44:24. Mi 3:1, 2. Hab 1:4, 13. Ml 3:18. Mt 3:10.

2. **worthy**. Mt 10:17. 27:26. Lk *12:47, 48. Ac 5:40. 16:22-24. 1 P 2:20, 24.

3. **not exceed**. 2 C *11:24, 25. **vile unto thee**. Dt 27:16. Jb 18:3. Pr 12:9. Is 3:5. 16:14. *52:14, 15. *53:3. Lk 15:30. 18:9-12. 1 C 4:9, 11-13. Ja 2:2, 3. That is, be beaten so cruelly, that, by retaining the marks, he become contemptible in the eyes of his brethren. Amendment, and not this, was the object of the punishment. We should hate and despise the sin, but not the sinner. Pr 17:10. 19:25. 27:22.

4. **Thou**. 138C, Ge +22:14. **muzzle**. or, stop. Pr 12:10. Ezk 39:11. 1 C)9:9, 10. 1 T 5:17,)18. **treadeth out**. Heb. thresheth. Is 28:27. Ho 10:11.

5. **If. Heb**, when. So Dt 21:1, 18, 22. 22:6, 8, 13, 22, 23. 23:9, 10. **brethren**. Mt)22:24. Mk)12:19. Lk 20:28. **husband's brother**. or, next kinsman. Ge 38:8, 9. Ru 1:12, 13. 3:9, 10n. 4:5.

6. **the firstborn**. Ge *38:8-10. **that his name**. Dt 9:14. 29:20. Ru 4:10, etc. Ps 9:5. 109:13.

7. **brother's wife**. or, next kinsman's wife. Ru 1:15. **go up**. Dt 21:19. Ru 4:1-7. **gate**. *171S7B, Ge +14:7.

8. **I like not**. Ru 4:6.

9. **loose his shoe**. Pulling off the shoe seems to express his being degraded to the situation of slaves, who generally went barefoot; and spitting in, or rather before (*biphney*) his face, was a mark of the utmost ignominy. Ru 4:7, 8, 11. Is 20:2. Mk 1:7. Jn 1:27. **spit**. Nu 12:14. Jb 30:10. Is 50:6. Mt *26:67. *27:30. Mk 10:34. **So shall**. Ge 38:8-10. Ru 4:10, 11. 1 S 2:30. **build up**. Ge 16:2. Ex 1:21. 1 K 11:38. 1 Ch 17:25.

10. **his name**. i.e. His person, *names* often being put for *persons*, and his posterity also. So it was a lasting blot (Matthew Poole). *121T2, Ac +1:15.

11. **strive**. 2 T 2:5. **to deliver her husband**. Ro 3:8. 1 T 2:9. **secrets**. lit. *shameful things*, only here.

12. **thine eye.** See on Dt 19:13, 21.

13. **in thy bag.** Le 19:35, 36. Pr 1:14. 11:1. 16:11. 20:10. Is 46:6. Ezk 45:10, 11. Ho 12:7, 8. Am 8:5. Mi 6:11, 12. 1 Th *4:3, 6. **divers weights.** Heb. a stone and a stone. ⨍121D7, Ex +7:19. i.e. divers stones or weights of different value for cheating customers, because weights were anciently made of stone.

14. **divers measures.** Heb. an ephah and an ephah. Ex 16:36. Le 19:35, 36. Pr 11:1. 16:11. Ezk 45:10. Ho 12:7, 8. 1 Th *4:3, 6. This was the most common measure among the Israelites, by which all the others were made and adjusted. They are not only forbidden to use divers weights and measures, one large or heavy to buy with, and another small or light to sell with, but they were not even allowed to keep such in the house. It is observable also, that these too common but dishonest actions are branded as "an abomination to the Lord," equally with idolatry, and other scandalous crimes.

15. **that thy days.** Dt +*4:40. 5:16, 33. 6:18. 11:9. 17:20. Ex 20:12. Ps 34:12. Ep 6:3. 1 P 3:10.

16. **all that do.** Dt 18:12. 22:5. Pr 11:1. 20:23. Am 8:5-7. 1 C 6:9-11. 1 Th 4:6. Re 21:27.

17. **what Amalek.** ⨍121T3, Ge +9:27. Ge 36:12, 16. Ex 17:8, etc. Nu 24:20. 25:17, 18.

18. **feared.** Ne 5:9, 15. Ps 36:1. Pr 16:6. Ro 3:18.

19. **when the.** Jsh 23:1. **thou shalt.** Dt 9:14. Ex 17:14, 16. Jg 6:3. 7:12, 22-25. 1 S 14:48. 15:3, 32, 33. 27:8. 30:1-7. 1 Ch 4:42, 43. Est 3:1. 7:10. 9:7-10, 12, 13. Ps 83:7-17.

DEUTERONOMY 26

The thankful acknowledgments to be made at presenting the firstfruits, 1-11. A profession and prayer for every third year respecting the second tithe, 12-15. A summary of the covenant between God and Israel, 16-19.

1. **when.** Dt 5:31. 6:1, 10. 7:1. 12:1, 9. 17:14. 18:9. Nu 15:2, 8.

2. **That thou shalt.** Dt 16:10. 18:4. Ex 23:16, 19. 34:26. Le 2:12, 14. Nu 18:12, 13. 2 K 4:42. 2 Ch 31:5. Ne 10:35-37. 12:44. 13:31. Pr *3:9, 10. Je 2:3. Ezk 20:40. 44:30. 48:14. Ro 8:23. 11:16. 16:5. 1 C 15:20, 23. 16:2. Ja 1:18. Re 14:4. **first.** Le +*23:10. **go unto.** See on Dt 12:5, 6. Jsh 18:1. 2 Ch 6:6. **place.** Dt +16:16. Ex 29:24. Le 16:12.

3. **the priest.** Dt 19:17. He 7:26. 10:21. 13:15. 1 P 2:5. **which the.** Ge 17:8. 26:3. Ps 105:9, 10. Lk 1:72, 73. He 6:16-18.

4. **before the.** Mt 5:23, 24. 23:19. He 13:10-12.

5. **A Syrian.** Jacob being called a Syrian from his long residence in Padan-aram. Ge 24:4. 25:20. 28:5. 31:20, 24. Ho 12:12, 13. **ready.** Ge 27:41. 31:40. 43:1, 2, 12. 45:7, 11. Is 51:1, 2. **he went down.** Ge 42:1, 2. 46:1-7. 47:11. Ps 105:23, 24. Ac 7:15. **a few.** Dt 7:7. Ge 46:27. Ex 1:5. **became.** See on Dt 10:22. Ge 47:27. Ex 1:7, 12. Nu 23:10.

6. **the Egyptians.** Dt 4:20. Ex 1:11, 14, 16, 22. 5:9, 19, 23.

7. **we cried.** Ex 2:23-25. 3:9. 4:31. 6:5. Ps 50:15. 103:1, 2. 116:1-4. Je *33:3. Ep 3:20, 21. **looked.** Ex 4:31. 1 S 9:16. 2 S 16:12. Ps 102:19, 20. 119:132.

8. **the Lord.** See on Dt 4:34. 5:15. Ex 12:37, 41, 51. 13:3, 16. 14:16, etc. Nu 23:22. Ps 78:12, 13. 105:27-38. 106:7-10. Is 63:12. **with great.** Dt 4:34.

9. **he hath.** Jsh 23:14. 1 S 7:12. Ps 78:52-54. 105:44. 107:7, 8. Ac 26:22. **a land.** Ex 3:8. Ezk 20:6, 15. 1 C *2:9, 10. **milk and.** ⨍174, Ge +18:27. **honey.** 171I7, Ex +3:8.

10. **I have.** See on ver. 2. Dt 16:17. 1 Ch 29:14. Ro *12:1. 1 P 4:10, 11. **And thou.** ver. 4. Dt 18:4. Ex 22:29. Nu 18:11-13. **and worship.** Dt 6:10-13. Ps 22:27, 29. 86:9. 95:6. 115:1. Pr *3:9. Is 66:23. 1 C *10:31. Re 5:13, 14. 22:9.

11. **rejoice.** See on Dt 12:7, 12, 18. 16:11. 28:47. Ne 8:10. Ps 63:3-5. 96:7-9. 100:1, 2. Is 65:14. Zc 9:17. Ac 2:46, 47. Ph 3:1. *4:4. 1 Th *5:16. 1 T 6:17, 18. **the Levite.** Dt 18:6. 1 C 9:11. **the stranger.** Dt 10:19. 14:29. ◐+*17:15. Ex 12:19, ◐43mg, 48mg, 49. 20:10. 22:21. 23:9, 12. Le 16:29. 17:8. 18:26. 19:10, 34. 23:22. 25:35. Nu 9:14. Jsh +*20:9. Jb 31:32. 1 T 3:2. 5:10. T 1:8. He *13:2. 1 P 4:9. 3 J 5.

12. **the tithes.** Ge +14:20. Le 27:30. Nu 18:24. **the third.** See on Dt 14:22-29. **hast given it.** Dt 12:17-19. 16:14. Pr 14:21. Ph 4:18, 19.

13. **Levite.** ver. 12. Dt 14:29. 24:19-21. Jb 31:16-20. **I have not.** Ps 18:21-24. 26:1-3, 6. Ac 24:16. 2 C 1:12. 11:31. 1 Th 2:10. 1 J 3:17-22. **forgotten.** 2 K 20:1-3. Ps 119:93, 139, 141, 153, 176. Pr 3:1.

14. **eaten.** ⨍108H4, Is +58:7. Dt 16:11. Le 7:20. 21:1, 11. Ho 9:4. Ml 2:13. **the dead.** Ps 106:28. Ezk 24:17. **hearkened.** ver. 16, +17. Ne 5:13, 19.

15. **Look down.** See on ver. 7. Ex ◐14:24. 1 K 8:27, 43. Ps 14:2. 53:2. 85:11. 102:19, 20. Is 57:15. 61:1. 63:15. 66:1, 2. La 3:50. Zc 2:13. Mt 6:9. Ac 7:49. **habitation.** 2 Ch 30:27mg. Ps 68:5. Je 25:30. Zc 2:13mg. **bless thy.** Nu *6:22-27. Ps 28:9. 51:18. 90:17. 115:12-15. 137:5, 6. Pr *10:22. Je 31:23. **as thou.** Jsh *21:45. 1 C 1:9. He 6:13-18. 10:23. **milk and.** 174, **Ge +18:27. honey.** ⨍17117, Ex +3:8.

16. **This day.** See on Dt 4:1-6. 6:1. 11:1, 8. 12:1, 32. Mt 28:20. **keep.** Dt 6:5, 17. 8:2. 13:3, 4. Lk *11:28. Jn 14:15, 21-24. 1 J 5:2, 3. **and do.** Ezr +*7:10. Mt *5:19. Ja *1:22. **with all.** Mt 22:36, 37. **soul.** Heb. *nephesh*, Ge +34:3.

17. **avouched.** Dt 5:2, 3. Ex 15:2. 20:19. 24:7. 2 Ch 34:31. Is 12:2. 44:5. Zc 13:9. Ac 27:23. Ro 6:13. 1 C 6:19, 20. 2 C 8:5. **and to.** See on Dt 10:12, 13. 13:4, 5. 30:16. Jsh 22:5. 1 K 2:3, 4. Col +*1:10. **to keep.** Dt 13:18. Ps 147:19, 20. Lk 11:28. **hearken.** Dt 13:18. 15:5. Mk 4:24. Lk 8:18. **voice.** Dt 8:20. Jn 10:3, 4, *5, *27.

18. **And the.** Dt 7:6. 14:2. 28:9. Ex 6:7. 15:16. 19:5, 6. Ps 135:4. Je 31:32-34. Ezk 36:25-27. T *2:14. 1 P 2:9. **keep.** ver. +17. Ps 119:6. Mt 5:19. Jn 14:15. Ro 16:26. 1 J *2:3.

19. **high above.** Dt 4:7, 8. 28:1. Ps 148:14. Is 62:12. 66:20, 21. Je 13:11. 33:9. Ezk 16:12-14. Zp 3:19. 1 P 2:5. Re 1:5, 6. **an holy.** Dt 7:6. 28:9. Ex 19:6. 1 P *2:9.

DEUTERONOMY 27

A command to set up stones for a remembrance on mount Ebal, and to write the law upon them, 1-4. They must build the altar of the Lord with whole stones, 5-8. Israel urged to obedience, 9, 10. Six tribes are directed to stand to bless on mount Gerizim, and six to curse, on mount Ebal, 11-13. Curses to be pronounced by the Levites, and confirmed by the people, 14-26.

1. **Keep all.** See on Dt 4:1-3. 11:32. 26:16. Lk *11:28. Jn *15:14. 1 Th 4:1, 2. Ja *2:10.

2. **on the day.** Dt 6:1. 9:1. 11:31. Jsh 1:11. 4:1, 5, etc. **unto the.** ver. 3. Dt 26:1. **great stones.** Ezk 11:19. 36:26. **and plaister.** Is 33:12. Am 2:1. Houbigant and others are of the opinion that the original words, *wesadta othom beseed*, should be rendered "thou shalt cement them with cement," because this was intended to be a durable monument. Some suppose that the writing was to be in *relievo*, and that the spaces were to be filled up by the mortar or cement; as is frequently the case with eastern inscriptions.

3. **thou shalt.** Jsh 8:32. Je *31:31-33. 2 C 3:2, 3. He 8:6-10. 10:16. **this law.** See on Dt 6:3. "This law" probably means only the blessings and curses mentioned in this and the following chapter; which indeed contain an epitome of the whole law. **a land.** Dt 26:9, 15. Ex +3:8. Le 20:24. Nu 13:27. 14:8. Jsh 5:6. Je 11:5. 32:22. **milk and.** ſ174, Ge +18:27. **honey.** ſ171I7, Ex +3:8.

4. **in mount Ebal.** The Samaritan text has "in mount Gerizim"; which has given rise to a violent controversy. Dr. Kennicott supposes that the Jews corrupted this passage out of their enmity to the Samaritans, who had their temple on mount Gerizim (Jg 9:7. Jn 4:9, 20); while Dr. Parry and H. Verschuir defend the present reading: to the writings of these authors the reader is referred. Dt 11:29, 30. Jsh 8:30-33.

5. **And there.** Ex 24:4. Jsh 8:30, 31. 1 K 18:31, 32. **thou shalt not.** Ex 20:25.

6. **burnt offerings.** See on Le 1. +*23:12. Ep 5:2.

7. **peace offerings.** See on Le 3. 7:11-17. +*23:19. Ac 10:36. Ro 5:1, 10. Ep 2:16, 17. Col 1:20. He 13:20, 21. **rejoice.** See on Dt 12:7, 12. 16:11, 14. 26:10, 11. 2 Ch 30:23-27. Ne 8:10. Ps 100:1, 2. Is 12:3. 61:3, 10. Hab 3:18. Ph 3:3. *4:4.

8. **thou shalt.** See on ver. 3. Jsh 8:34, 35. **very plainly.** Ps *119:130. Pr +*8:9. Is 35:8. Hab *2:2. Jn 7:17. *16:25. 2 C 3:12. 2 P ●3:16. 1 J 2:20, 27.

9. **this day.** See on Dt *26:16-18. Ro 6:17, 18, 22. 1 C *6:9-11. Ep 5:8, 9. 1 P *2:10, 11. 2 P 3:11, 14. **art become.** 1 C 6:20. *15:57, 58.

10. **obey.** See on Dt 10:12, 13. 11:1, 7, 8. +*26:16. Le 19:2. Mi 4:5. +*6:8. Mt 5:48. Ep 4:17-24. 1 P 1:14-16. 4:1-3. **voice.** Dt +26:17. Jn 10:27.

12. **upon mount Gerizim.** Dt 11:26-29. Jsh 8:33, 34. Jg 9:7. **Simeon.** Ge 29:33-35. 30:18, 24. 35:18.

13. **mount Ebal.** See on ver. 4. Dt 11:29. Jsh 8:33. **to curse.** Heb. for a cursing. **Reuben.** Ge 29:32. 30:6-13, 20. 49:3, 4.

14. **the Levites.** Dt 33:9, 10. Jsh 8:33. Ne 8:7, 8. Da 9:11. Ml 2:7-9.

15. **Cursed be.** Dt 28:16-19. Ge 9:25. 1 S 26:19. Je 11:3. **maketh.** See on Dt 4:16-23. 5:8. Ex 20:4, 23. 32:1-4. 34:17. Le 19:4. 26:1. Jg 17:4, 5. Is 44:9, 10, 17. Ho 13:2, 3. **an abomination.** Dt 29:17. 1 K 11:5-7. 2 K 23:13. 2 Ch 33:2. Is 44:19. Ezk 7:20. Da 11:31. Mt 24:15. Re 17:4, 5. **and putteth.** Ge 31:19, 34. 2 K 17:19. Ps 44:20, 21. Je 23:24. Ezk 8:7-12. 14:4. **And all.** See on Nu 5:22. Je 11:5. 28:6. Mt 6:13. 1 C 14:16. **Amen.** ſ76, Ge +13:6. Je 11:5. To each of the curses the people were to say Amen, as well as to the blessings; to denote a profession of their faith in the truth of them, that they were the real declarations of the wrath of God, and an acknowledgment of the equity of these curses. It was such an imprecation

upon themselves, as strongly obliged them to have nothing to do with those evil practices on which the curse is entailed. We read of those who entered into a curse "to walk in God's law" (Ne 10:29). All the people, by saying this *Amen*, became bound one for another, that they would observe God's laws, by which every man was obliged, as far as he could, to prevent his neighbor from breaking these laws, and to reprove those that had offended, lest they should bear sin and the curse for them (Le 19:17).

16. **setteth light.** Dt 21:18-21. Ex +*20:12. 21:17. Le 19:3. Pr 20:20. 30:11-17. Ezk 22:7. Ml +*4:6. Mt 15:4, 6. **father or.** T#54. Dt 21:18, 21. Ex 21:15, 17. Pr 20:20. 30:17. **Amen.** ſ76, Ge +13:6.

17. **removeth.** Dt 19:14. Jb 24:2. Pr 22:28. 23:10, 11. Ho 5:10.

18. **the blind.** See on Le *19:14. Jb 29:15. Pr 28:10. Is 56:10. Mt 15:14. Re 2:14.

19. **perverteth the judgment.** See on Dt 10:18. 24:17. Ex 22:21-24. 23:2, 8, 9. Ps 68:5. 82:2-4. Pr 17:23. 31:5. Mi 3:9. Ml +*3:5. **widow.** ſ171I14, Ex +22:22.

20. **lieth with.** Dt 22:30. Ge 35:22. 49:4. Le 18:8. 20:11. 2 S 16:22. 1 Ch *5:1. Ezk 22:10. Am 2:7. 1 C *5:1.

21. **of beast.** Ex 22:19. Le 18:23. 20:15.

22. **his sister.** Le 18:9. 20:17. 2 S 13:1, 8-14. Ezk 22:11.

23. **lieth with.** Le 18:17. 20:14.

24. **smiteth.** Dt 19:11, 12. Ge 9:5, 6. Ex 20:13. 21:12-14. Le 24:17. Nu 35:31. 2 S 3:27-30. 11:15-17. 12:9-12. 13:28. 20:9, 10. 1 K 2:5, 6. Ps 51:14.

25. **taketh reward.** Dt 10:17. 16:19. Ex 23:7, 8. Ps 15:5. Pr 1:11-29. Ezk 22:12, 13. Da 9:11. Mi 3:10, 11. 7:2, 3. Mt 26:15. 27:3, 4. Ac 1:18. **person.** Heb. *nephesh*, Jsh +10:28.

26. **Cursed.** See on ver. 15. Dt 28:15, etc. Ps 119:21. Mt 25:41. 1 C 16:22. **confirmeth.** Je 11:3-5. Ezk 18:24. Ro 3:19, 20. 10:5. Ga ▶3:10. **all.** Ja 2:10. **words.** 2 K 22:13.

DEUTERONOMY 28

Blessings promised to Israel, while obedient, 1-14; and awful curses, of every kind imaginable, denounced if they were disobedient, 15; including curses of urban blight and agricultural disaster, 16, 17; lack of fruitfulness and success, 18, 19; adversity, 20; pestilence, 21; disease, 22; drought, 23, 24; military defeats, 25, 26; incurable diseases, 27; insanity, blindness, despair, 28; oppression, 29; lack of allies, 29; deterioration of the family structure, economic and military adversity, slavery, captivity, idolatry, 30-36; loss of reputation, 37; agricultural disaster, blight, harvest failures, 38-40; captivity of children, 41; insect damage to crops, 42; foreign oppression, national decline, 43; mounting national debt, national economic declension, 44; all of which curses result from disobedience to God, 45-47; curse of poverty, bondage, 48; national military defeat, famine resulting in cannibalism, 49-57; destructive diseases, 58, 59; decimation of the population, 62; removal from own land, 63, 64; unsettledness, adversity, fear, sorrow of mind, terror, insecurity, unrest, 65-67; captivity and bondage, 68.

1. **If.** ver. ●15. Ge +*4:7. Je +*7:5. 2 P +*1:10. **thou shalt.** See on Dt *11:13. 15:5. 27:1. Ex *15:26. Le 26:3, etc. Ps *106:3. Is 1:19. 3:10. *34:16. *55:2,

3. Je 11:4. 12:16. 17:24. Lk *11:28. **to do all**. Ps *111:10. 119:6, *128. Lk 1:6. Jn *15:14. Ga 3:10. Ja 2:*10, 11. **will set**. See on Dt 26:19. Ps *91:14. 148:14. Is 33:16. Lk 9:48. Ro *2:7.

2. **these blessings**. ſ105, Ml +4:2. Ge 22:18. Ps 128:1, 4. Pr *10:22. 1 T 4:8. **come on thee**. ver. 15, 45. Zc 1:6. 1 T 4:8. **if**. Ge +4:7. **hearken**. Dt +26:17. Mk 4:24. Lk 8:18. **voice**. Dt +26:17. Jn +10:27.

3. **Blessed**. ſ43. Benedictio; or, Blessing B919. An expression of feeling by way of benediction or blessing. For other instances of this figure see Ge 1:22, 28. 2:3. Ps 1:1. 2:12. 32:1, 2. 33:12. 34:8. 40:4. 41:1. 65:4. 84:4, 5, 12. 89:15. 94:12. 106:3. 112:1. 119:1, 2. 127:5. 128:1. 137:8, 9. 144:15. 146:5. Ec 10:17. Is 30:18. Ep 1:3. Re 1:3. 14:13. 16:15. 19:9. 20:6. 22:7, 14. **in the city**. Ps 107:36, 37. 128:1-5. 144:12-15. Is 65:21-23. Zc 8:3-5. **in the field**. Ge 26:12. *39:5. Le 26:3. Am 9:13, 14. Hg 2:19. Ml *3:10, 11.

4. **Blessed**. ſ18. Anaphora; or, Like sentence beginnings B199. The repetition of the same word at the beginning of successive sentences. For other instances of this figure see 2 S 23:5. Ps 3:1, 2. 94:3, 4. 115:12, 13. 118:8, 9. 118:10, 11, 12. 121:7, 8. (122:6, 7). 123:2, 3. 124:1, 2. 124:3, 4, 5. 126:2. 127:1. 128:5, 6. 129:1, 2. 148:1-4. Is 51:1, 4, 7. Je 1:18. 4:23-26. 5:17. 50:35, 36. 51:20-23. Ho 3:4. Mi 5:9-13. 7:11, 12. Zp 1:2, 3. Mt 5:3-11. 5:22. 11:7, 8, 9. 11:18, 19. Ro 8:33, 34, 35. 1 C 3:9. 6:11, 12. 11:3. 12:8-11. 13:4, 7. 2 C 7:11. 11:26. Ga 1:9. Ep 6:12. Ph 3:2. 4:2. 4:8. 1 J 1:1-3. Ja 5:7, 8. 5:13, 14. 1 J 3:5, 8. Re 7:6. **fruit of thy body**. ver. *11, ◗+18. Dt 7:13. Ge 22:17. +29:31. *49:25. Le 26:9. Ps 107:38. +*127:3. 128:3. Pr 10:22. 13:22. *20:7. 1 T *2:15. 4:8.

5. **Blessed**. Ex 23:25. Is 55:2. **thy basket**. Dt 26:2, 4. ſ121J2, Metonymy of the Subject B573. Basket is put for its contents. Here, probably, the "basket" is put for the seed, and "kneading trough" for the meal; the beginning and end of their labors. Mr. Harmer thinks that *taine*, in this place, means their traveling baskets; and *mishaireth* (store), their leather bags (Dt +23:24. 1 S 17:40); in both of which they were wont to carry things in traveling; and that, "understood in this manner, the passage promises Israel success in their commerce, as the next verse (the 6th) promises them personal safety in their going out and in their return. In this view, the passage appears with due distinctness, and a noble extent" (Observations, vol. 2, p 178n). By "basket" may be understood the olive-gathering and vintage, in which it was employed; and by the "store" or "remainder" all laid up for future use, or prepared for present consumption. **store**. *or*, dough, *or* kneading troughs. ver. 17. Ex 8:3. 12:34.

6. **Blessed**. Ge 49:28. **comest in**. Dt 31:2. Nu 27:17. 2 S 3:25. 2 Ch *1:10. Ps 121:8. Young remarks, "To thine own house and family." Pr 3:33. **goest out**. Young remarks, "To transact business of any kind."

7. **shall cause**. ver. *25. Dt 32:30. Le 26:7, 8. 2 S 22:38-41. Ps 89:23. Pr +*16:7. **one way**. Jsh 23:10. 1 S 14:6. **flee before**. Jsh 8:22. *10:10, 11, 42. Jg 7:22. 1 S 7:3, 4, 10, 11. 2 Ch 14:2-6, 9-15. 19:4. 20:22-25. *31:20, 21. 32:21, 22. Zc 12:8.

8. **command**. ver. ◗45. Le 25:21. Ps *42:8. 44:4. *133:3. **storehouses**. *or*, barns. Le 26:4, 5, 10. 2 K 6:27. Ps 144:13. Pr *3:9, 10. Hg 2:19. Ml *3:10, 11. Mt *6:26. 13:30. Lk 12:18, 24, 25. **in all**. 2 C 8:9.

*9:8. **settest thine hand**. ſ121R7, Ge +43:11. Dt 15:7, 10.

9. **establish**. See on Dt 7:6. 26:18, 19. 29:13. Ge 17:7. Ex +*19:5, 6. Ps 87:5. Is 1:26. 62:12. 2 Th 3:3. T *2:14. 1 P 2:9-11. 5:10. **sworn**. See on Dt 7:8. 13:17. 29:12. Ex 19:5, 6. Je 11:5. He 6:13-18.

10. **And all**. Ml 3:12. **called**. Nu 6:27. 2 Ch *7:14. Is 4:1. 63:19. Da 9:18, 19. **and they shall**. See on Dt 4:6-8. 11:25. Ex 12:33. 14:25. 23:22. Jsh 2:10, 11. 5:1. 1 S 18:12-15, 28, 29. 1 Ch 14:17. Je 33:9. Re 3:9.

11. **plenteous**. See on ver. 4. Dt 30:9. Le 26:9. Pr 10:22. **in goods**. *or*, for good. **fruit of thy**. Ge +29:31. **body**. Heb. belly. ver. 4, 18, 53. Dt 30:9. Jb 19:17mg. Ps 132:11mg. Mi 6:7mg. **the Lord sware unto**. Ex 2:25. 2 K 13:23. Ne 9:23.

12. **open**. ſ22C30, Ps +78:23. Dt 11:14. Le 26:4. Jb 38:22. Ps 65:9-13. 135:7. Jl 2:23, 24. **treasure**. i.e. of rain. Dt 32:34. Le 26:4. Jb 38:22. Ps 33:7. 135:7. ſ22D5o. Anthropomorphism B894. "Treasure" is attributed to God. For other instances of this figure see Dt 32:34. Ps 135:7. Is 33:6. Je 10:13. 50:25. 51:16. Mt 6:20. 19:21. Mk 10:21. Lk 12:33. 18:22. Ro 2:5, 9, 10. 2 C 4:7. **season**. Ps 67:6. Ezk 34:26. Zc 8:12. **to bless all**. Dt 14:29. 15:10. Is 48:17-19. **shalt lend**. ver. ◗√44. Dt 15:6. Is +√58:7. **unto many nations**. Ezr ◗4:20. Ro +*11:25n. **not borrow**. 2 K 4:7n. 2 Ch √26:5. Ps √37:21. Pr 17:18. +√22:7. *27:23, 24. Lk *14:28. Ro +*13:8.

13. **the head**. Ge +*22:17. Nu 24:18, 19. Ps +*18:43. Is 9:14, 15. Ro +*11:25n. **shalt not**. ſ144D, Ge 40:23. **if**. ver. +*1. **thou hearken**. See on ver. 1. Dt 4:6-9. Lk +*8:18. Ph 1:27.

14. **thou shalt**. See on Dt 5:32. 11:16, 26-28. 17:20. Jsh 23:6. 2 K 22:2. Pr 4:26, 27. **the right**. Is 30:21. **other gods**. T#361. Dt 6:14, 15. Ex 20:3-5. 34:17. Le 19:4. 26:1.

15. **But**. ver. ◗1. **if thou wilt**. Le 26:14, etc. La 2:17. Da 9:11-13. Ml 2:2. Ro 2:8, 9. **not hearken**. Je +*6:19. *29:19. Lk +*8:18. **all these curses**. ſ105, Ml +4:2. The same variety of expression is used in these terrible curses, as in the preceding blessings, to intimate every kind of prosperity or adversity, personal, relative, and public. The succeeding history of the Israelites shows, that as long as they adhered to the service of God, they were uniformly prosperous; but when disobedient, these awful curses have "overtaken them," even to the present day. Consulting the marginal references will generally lead to the best exposition of the terms employed; and will frequently point out the fulfillment of the promises and threatenings. While these blessings and curses are specifically addressed to national Israel, the principles they are designed to inculcate are undoubtedly valid for all nations and individuals (Ps +*9:17. Ac 10:34. Ro +*15:4. 2 T +*2:15n. +√3:15-17). See on ver. 2. Dt √27:15-26. 29:20. Ps +*119:21. Pr +*3:33. Is 3:11. Je 11:3-5. Da +*9:11. Zc +*5:3. Mt +*25:41. Ga 3:10.

16. **Cursed**. ſ110, Ezk +34:2. **in the city**. See on ver. 3, etc. Pr 3:33. Is 24:6-12. 43:28. Je 9:11. 26:6. 44:22. La 1:1. 2:11-22. 4:1-13. Ml 2:2. 4:6. **in the field**. ver. 55. Ge 3:17, 18. 4:11, 12. 5:29. 8:21, 22. 1 K 17:1, 5, 12. Je 14:2-5, 18. La 5:10. Jl 1:4, 8-18. 2:3. Am 4:6-9. Hg 1:9-11. 2:16, 17. Ml 3:9-12.

17. **thy basket**. See on ver. 5n. Ps 69:22. Pr 1:32. Hg *1:6. Zc 5:3, 4. Ml 2:2. Lk 16:25.

18. **the fruit of thy body**. See on ver. 4. Ge +11:30.

Dt 5:9. Jb 18:16-19. Ps 109:9-15. La 2:11, 12, 20. Ho 9:11-14. Ml 2:3. Lk 23:29, 30. **thy land**. See on ver. 16. Le 26:19, 20, 26. Hab 3:17.

19. **comest in**. See on ver. 6. Jg 5:6, 7. 2 Ch 15:5.

20. **send**. Ps 7:11. **cursing**. or, the curse. Ps 37:22. Pr +*3:33. 28:27. Zc +*5:3, 4. Ml 2:2. 3:9. **vexation**. or, the trouble. 1 S 14:20. Ps 80:4-16. Is 28:19. 30:17. 51:20. 66:15. Zc 14:12, 13. Jn *3:36. 1 Th 2:16. ❋S#4103h. Dt 7:23 (destruction). 1 S 5:9, 11. 14:20 (discomfiture). 1 Ch 15:5. Pr 15:16. Is 22:5. Ezk 7:7. 22:5. Am 3:9 (tumults). Zc 14:13. **rebuke**. or, the rebuke. 2 S 22:16. Ps 80:16. **for to do**. Heb. which thou wouldest do. **until thou be**. See on Dt 4:26. 7:23. 12:30. 32:30. Le 26:31-33, 38. Jsh 23:16. Ps 92:7. **quickly**. Ex 32:8.

21. **pestilence**. Ex 5:3. 9:3, 15. Le 26:25. Nu 14:12. 16:46-49. 25:9. 2 S 24:15. Ps 73:27. Je 15:2. 16:4. 21:6, 7. 24:10. Ezk 24:16n. +*38:22. Am 4:10. Mt 24:7. Ro +*1:27.

22. **a consumption**. See on Le 26:16. 2 Ch 6:28. Je 14:12. **sword**. or, drought. Dt 32:24. Ge 3:24. Le +*26:25. Je +29:17. Hg 1:11. **blasting**. 1 K 8:37. 2 K 19:26. 2 Ch 6:28. Am 4:9. Hg 2:17. **mildew**. ❋S#3420h. 1 K 8:37. 2 Ch 6:28. Je 30:6 (paleness). Am 4:9. Hg 2:17. **perish**. Je 44:7, 8.

23. **thy heaven**. The language here is remarkable: "Thy heaven;" that part of the atmosphere which was over Judea, instead of being replenished with aqueous vapours, should become, with respect to moisture, like brass: and consequently their land would become as hard as iron, and wholly incapable of cultivation; while the clouds might give showers in abundance, and the earth be moist and fruitful in other regions. Ge +9:13. Le 26:19. 1 K 17:1. 18:2. Je 14:1-6. Am 4:6-8. Ja 5:17, 18.

24. **make the rain**. This was a natural consequence of their heaven's being *brass*, or yielding no rain; for the surface of the earth being reduced to powder, and frequently taken up by strong winds, would fall down in showers instead of rain. These showers of sand (compare Ge 29:2n) frequently, in the East, bury whole caravans. ver. 12. Ge 19:24. Jb 18:15-21. Is 5:24. Am 4:11.

25. **cause thee**. See on ver. 7. Dt 32:30. Le 26:17, 25, 36, 37. Is 30:1, 17. **removed**. Heb. for a removing. Je 15:2-9. 24:9. 29:18. 34:17mg. La 1:18mg. Ezk 23:46mg. Lk *21:24.

26. **thy carcass**. 1 S 17:44-46. Ps 79:1-3. Is 34:3. Je 7:33. 8:1. 16:4. 19:7. 34:20. Ezk 39:17-20.

27. **the botch**. ver. 35. Ex 9:9, 11. *15:26. **emerods**. 1 S 5:6, 9, 12. Ps 78:66. **scab**. Le 13:2-8. 21:20. Is 3:17. **canst not be healed**. Ezk 24:16n. Ro +*1:27.

28. **with madness**. 1 S 16:14. 2 K 9:20mg. Ps 60:3. Is 6:9, 10. 19:11-17. 42:19. Je 4:9. Ezk 4:17. Zc 12:4. Lk 21:25, 26. Ac 13:41. 2 Th 2:9-11. 2 T ●*1:7.

29. **grope**. Ge 27:12, 22. 31:34, 37. Ex 10:21. Jb 5:14. 12:25. Ps 69:23, 24. Is 59:10. La 5:17. Zp 1:17. Ro 11:7-10, 25. 2 C *4:3, 4. **darkness**. Ex 10:22. **not prosper**. 2 Ch 13:12. Pr 28:13. Is 51:17-20. Je 2:37. 32:5. **thou shalt be**. Jg 3:14. 4:2, 3. 6:1-6. 10:8. 13:1. 1 S 13:5-7, 19-22. Ne 9:26-29, 37. Ps 106:40-42. La 5:8. Lk *21:24. **oppressed**. ver. 33. Ps 103:6. 146:7. Pr 28:17h. Ec 4:1. Je 50:33. Ho 5:11. **spoiled**. ver. 31. Je 21:12. 22:3. Ml 1:3. **save**. Dt 22:27.

30. **betroth**. Dt 20:6, 7. 2 Ch 29:8, 9. Jb 31:10. Je 8:10. Ho 4:2. **build**. Jb 31:8. Is 5:9, 10. 65:21, 22. Je

12:13. La 5:2. Am 5:11. Mi 6:15. Zp 1:13. **gather**. Heb. profane, or, use it as common meat. Dt 20:6mg. Am 4:9, 10.

31. **ox**. Jg 6:4. Jb 1:14, 15. **be restored to thee**. Heb. return to thee.

32. **sons and**. Regarded as such blessings in the East (Ps +127:3). ver. 18, 41. Nu 21:29. 2 Ch 29:9. Ne 5:2-5. Je 15:7-9. 16:2-4. Ezk 24:25. Jl 3:6. Am 5:27. Mi 4:10. **given**. In several countries, particularly in Spain and Portugal, the children of the Jews have been taken from them, by order of the government, to be educated in the Roman Catholic faith. There have been some instances of such cruelty even in Protestant countries. **fail**. ver. 65. Jb 11:20. 17:5. Ps 69:3. 119:82, 123. Is 38:14. Je 5:17. 24:8-10. La 2:11. 4:17. 5:17. **no might in thine hand**. Young renders, "thy hand is not to God!" i.e. thou hast no power even to pray for them to God. Ge 31:29. Ex 32:10. Ne *5:5. Pr 3:27. Je *7:16. *11:14. Mi 2:1. Jn *17:9. 1 J *5:16.

33. **The fruit**. See on ver. 30, 51. Le 26:16. Ne 9:36, 37. Is 1:7. Je 5:17. 8:16. 32:2. **labors**. ♫121C1H. Metonymy of the Cause B551. Labor is put for that which is produced by it, the fruit of thy labors. For other instances of this figure see Ps 78:46. 105:44. 128:2. Pr 5:10. Ec 2:19. Is 45:14. Je 3:24. 20:5. Ezk 23:29. Mt 26:9. **thou shalt be**. See on ver. 29. Je 4:17. **crushed**. or, bruised. Jg +10:8mg. 2 K 18:21. Is 36:6. *42:3. 58:6. Ho 5:11.

34. **mad**. See on ver. 28. 1 S 21:15. 2 K 9:11. Is 33:14. Je 25:15, 16. 29:26. Ho 9:7. Re 16:10, 11.

35. **botch**. ver. 27. Jb 2:6, 7. Is 1:6. 3:17, 24. or, ulcer. Jb 2:7. **the sole**. 2 S 14:25. Jb 2:7. Is 1:6. Lk 16:20, 21.

36. **bring thee**. 2 K 17:4-6. 24:12-15. 25:6, 7, 11. 2 Ch 33:11. 36:6, 17, 20. Is 39:7. Je 22:11, 12, 24-27. 24:8-10. 39:5-7. 52:8-11. La 4:20. Ezk 12:12, 13. **there shalt thou**. ver. 64. See on Dt 4:28. Je 16:13. Ezk 20:32, 33, 39.

37. **become**. See on ver. 28. Dt 4:30, 31. 29:22-28. 1 K 9:7, 8. 2 Ch 7:20. Ps 44:13, 14. Je 24:9. 25:9, 18. 42:18. 44:22. Jl 2:17mg. Zc 8:13. 12:10. Ro ●11:26. **a proverb**. or, simile. Nu 23:+7, 18. 24:3, 15, 20, 21, 23. 1 S 10:12. 24:13. 1 K 4:32. *9:7, 8. 2 Ch 7:20, etc. Ezk 14:8. **byword**. 1 K 9:7. 2 Ch 7:20. Ps 44:14. Je 24:9. **among**. Is 18:2, 7. **lead**. i.e. captive.

38. **shalt carry**. Is 3:1. 5:10. Ezk 4:16. 14:13. Mi 6:15. Hg 1:6. **for the locust**. Ex 10:14, 15. Jl 1:4. 2:3, 25. Am 4:9. 7:1, 2.

39. **wine**. Ho 2:8, 9. **for the worms**. Jl 1:4-7. 2:2-4. Jon 4:7.

40. **but**. Hg 1:5, 6. **anoint thyself**. Ps *23:5. 104:15. Mi 6:15.

41. **but**. Ge ●18:19. Ml 4:5, 6. **thou shalt not enjoy them**. Heb. they shall not be thine. **for**. See on ver. 32. 1 K 24:14. La 1:5.

42. **thy trees**. See on ver. 38, 39. Am 7:1, 2. **consume**. or, possess. Jg 14:15.

43. **shall get**. Jg 2:3, 11-15. 4:2, 3. 10:7-10. 14:4. 15:11, 12. 1 S 13:3-7, 19-23. 2 K 17:20, 23. 24:14-16. Jn 18:31. 19:15. **high**. ♫84, Ge +6:17. **low**. ♫84, Ge +6:17.

44. **lend to thee**. See on ver. ●+√12. **not lend**. ver. 48n. Hg *1:6. **be the tail**. ver. ●/13. Ps ●+*18:43. La ❋1:5.

45. **Moreover**. See on ver. 5, 15. Dt 29:20, 21. Le 26:28. 2 K 17:20. Pr 13:21. Is 1:20. 65:14, 15. Je

24:9, 10. 26:2-7. La 2:15-17. Ezk 7:15. 14:21. **all**. ver. ◐8. 2 C *8:9. ◐9:8. **shall come**. Ps 37:22. Pr 26:2. Mt 25:41. Ga 3:10, 13. Re 22:3. **because**. See on Dt 11:27, 28. Ps 119:21. Je 7:22-25. **hearkenedst**. ver. +2. Dt +26:17. **voice**. ver. +2. **to keep**. Dt +26:16.

46. **a sign**. ver. 37, 59. Dt 29:20, 28. Is 8:18. Je 19:8. 25:18. Ezk 14:8. 23:32, 33. 36:20. 1 C 10:11. **for ever**. Heb. *olam*, Ex +12:24.

47. **servedst not**. See on Dt 12:7-12. 16:11. 32:13-15. Ne 9:35. 1 T 6:17-19. **with joyfulness**. Ne 8:10. Ps 100:2. Lk 1:74.

48. **serve**. 2 Ch 12:8. Ne 9:35-37. Je 5:19. 17:4. Ezk 17:3, 7, 12. Ro 1:20, 21. 2 P 2:13, 14. **in hunger**. Je 44:17, 18, 22, 27. La 5:2-6. Ezk 4:16, 17. **in want of all things**. This might well be termed the "poverty curse," which Christ exhausted on the Cross for us. Many of the following references contain significant cause/effect relationships pertaining to poverty (Ps +√9:10n). 2 Ch ◐√26:5n. Jb 15:23. 30:3. Pr 6:10, 11. 11:24. *13:4. *19:15. 20:4. 21:17. 23:21. 24:33, 34. 28:19. 2 C *8:9. ◐9:8. Ga 3:10, 13. Re 22:3. **a yoke**. Is 47:6. Je 27:12, 13. 28:13, 14. Mt *11:29.

49. **shall bring**. √105. Ml +4:2. **a nation**. Though the Chaldeans are frequently described under the figure of an eagle, yet these verses especially predict the desolations brought on the Jews by the Romans; who came from a country far more distant than Chaldea; whose conquests were as rapid as the eagle's flight, and whose standard bore this very figure; who spake a language to which the Jews were then entire strangers, being wholly unlike the Hebrew, of which the Chaldee was merely a dialect; whose appearance and victories were terrible; and whose yoke was a yoke of iron, and the havoc which they made tremendous. Nu 24:24. Is 5:26-30. Je 5:15-17. 6:22, 23. Da 9:26. Hab 1:6, 7. Lk 19:43, 44. Jn 11:48. **as the eagle**. Je 4:13. 48:40. 49:22. La 4:19. Ezk 17:3, 12. Da 7:2-4. Ho 8:1. Mt *24:28. **a nation whose**. Is 28:13. Je 5:15. Ezk 3:6. 1 C *14:21. **understand**. Heb. hear.

50. **of fierce countenance**. Heb. strong of face. √121S3E3, Nu +6:26. Pr 7:13mg. Ec 8:1mg. Da 7:7. 8:23. **shall not**. 2 Ch 36:17. Is 47:6. Ho 13:16. Lk 19:44. *21:23, 24.

51. **the fruit**. See on ver. 33. Is 1:7. 12:8. 62:8. **which also**. Le 26:26. Je 15:13. 17:3. Ezk 12:19. Hab 3:16, 17. **not leave**. Dt 2:34. 3:3. **corn**. Ge 27:28, 37. **wine**. or, new wine. Ge 27:28, 37. **oil**. Nu 18:12. **increase of**. Je 28:14.

52. **besiege**. Le 26:25. 2 K 17:1-6. 18:13. 24:10, 11. 25:1-4. Is 1:7. 62:8. Je 21:4-7. 37:8. 39:1-3. 52:4-7. Ezk 4:1-8. Da *9:26. Zc 12:2. 14:2. Mt 22:7. *24:15, 16. Lk 19:43, 44. *21:20-24. Re 6:7, 8.

53. **eat the fruit**. ver. 18, 55, 57. Le 26:29. 2 K 6:28, 29. Is 49:15. Je *19:9. La 2:20. 4:10. Ezk 5:10. Mt *24:19. **body**. Heb. belly. ver. 4, 11, 18. **straitness**. ver. 55, 57. 1 S 22:2. Ps 119:143. Je *19:9.

54. **tender**. 1 Ch 22:5. 29:1. 2 Ch 13:7. Pr 4:3. **his eye**. Dt 15:9. Pr 23:6. 28:22. Mt 20:15. **and toward**. Dt 13:6. 2 S 12:3. Mi 7:5. The Roman armies at length besieged, sacked, and utterly desolated Jerusalem: and during this siege, the famine was so extreme, that even rich and delicate persons, both men and women, ate their own children, and concealed the horrible repast, lest others should tear it from them! "Women snatched the food out of the very mouths of their husbands, and sons of their fathers, and (what is most miserable) mothers of their infants." "In every house, if there appeared any semblance of food, a battle ensued, and the dearest friends and relations fought with one another; snatching away the miserable provisions of life." "A woman distinguised by birth and wealth, after she had been plundered by the tyrants (or soldiers) of all her possessions, —boiling her own sucking child, ate half of him, and concealing the other half, reserved it for another time!" Josephus, De Bel. l. v. c. 10.3. l. vi. c. 3.3. l. vi. c. 3.4. **his children**. Ps 103:13. Is 49:15. Mt 7:9-11. Lk 11:11-13.

55. **in the siege**. Je 5:10. 34:2. 52:6.

56. **tender**. ver. 54. **and delicate**. Is 3:16. La 4:3-6. **her eye shall be evil**. See on ver. 54.

57. **young one**. Heb. afterbirth. or, her seed. Ge 49:10. **cometh out**. Ge 49:10. Is 49:15. **feet**. Ezk ◐16:25. **for she shall**. ver. 53.

58. **If thou wilt**. See on ver. 15. Le 26:14, 15. 2 K 17:15. Je 7:9, 10, 26-28. Ja 2:10. **book**. ver. +61. Dt 31:26. Ex 24:7. Le 26:15. **fear this**. Dt 6:13. Ex 3:14, 15. 6:2, 3. 20:2. 34:5-7. Ne 9:5. Ps 18:26. 50:7. 72:19. 83:18. Ps 99:1-3. Is 41:10. 42:8. Je 5:12. Am 3:1-3. Mt *10:28. He *10:30, 31. 12:28, 29. **glorious**. or, honored. Ge 34:19. Ex 14:4. Le 10:3. Nu 22:15. Ps 72:19. **fearful**. Dt 10:17. Ge *28:17. Ex 15:11. Ne 1:5. Ps 99:3. Is 29:23. **name**. Ex 6:3. Ps √9:10. 83:18. 99:3. 113:3. Pr 18:10. √121T1. Metonymy of the Adjunct B608. The name of a person is put for the person himself: the person, when that person is Divine. For other instances of this figure see Ps 20:1. 115:1. Pr 18:10. Is 30:27. Je 10:25. Mi 5:4. Jn 1:12. 3:18. 17:6. 20:31. Ac 3:16. 4:12. 5:41. 10:43. 1 J 2:12. **the Lord**. Ex *3:15. *6:3. 20:2. Ps 83:18. Is 42:8. Ml *2:2.

59. **thy plagues**. ver. 46. Dt 29:20-28. 31:17, 18. 32:22, 26. 1 K 9:7-9. 16:3, 4. La 1:9, 12. 4:12. Da 9:12. Ho 3:4. Mk 13:19. **wonderful**. Le 27:2 (singular). Nu 6:2h. Jg 13:19. **long continuance**. Ho *3:4, 5. Mt +*25:19.

60. **all the diseases**. See on Dt 7:15. Ex ◐*15:26.

61. **book of this law**. ver. 58. Dt *17:18, 19. 29:21. 30:10. 31:10, 11, 26. Jsh *1:8. 8:34. 23:6. 24:26. 2 K 14:6. 22:8. 23:2. 2 Ch 17:9. 25:4. 34:14. Ne 8:1, *3, 18. Ml 4:4. **bring upon thee**. Heb. cause to ascend. **destroyed**. Dt 4:25, 26. He 10:31.

62. **few in number**. Dt 4:27. 26:5. Le 26:22. 2 K 13:7. 24:14. Ne 7:4. Is 1:9. 24:6. Je 42:2. 52:28-30. Am 5:3. Mk 13:20. Ro 9:27-29. **as the stars**. √102B, √138B, Ge +13:16. See on Dt 10:22. Ge 15:5. Ne 9:23. Ro 9:27.

63. **rejoiced over**. √22B, Dt 30:9. Ps 104:31. Is 62:5. Je 32:41. Mi 7:18. Zp 3:17. Lk 15:6-10, 23, 24, 32. **will rejoice over**. Pr 1:26. Is 1:24. Ezk 5:13. 33:11. **bring you**. Ezk 21:7. 24:23. Am *5:3. **plucked from**. Dt 7:22mg. Ps 52:5. Pr 2:22mg. 15:25h. Je 12:14, 15. 18:7. 24:6. 31:28, 40. 42:10. Da 7:8.

64. **scatter**. See on Dt 4:27, 28. Le 26:33. Ne 1:8. Je 16:13. 50:17. Ezk 11:16, 17. Am 9:4. Lk *21:24. **all**. √171A, Ex +9:6. **there thou shalt**. ver. 36. Je 16:13.

65. **among**. After the conquest of their country by the Romans, Hadrian, by a public decree, ratified by the senate, forbade any Jew to come even within sight of Judea; and hence they were dispersed over every quarter of the globe, where they found no alleviation or respite from misery. In no country are they treated as denizens: all suspect them as enemies, and behave

to them as aliens; if they do not, as has been too fre-quently the case, harass, oppress, and persecute them, even unto death. **shalt thou.** Ge 8:9. Jg 2:14. 2 Ch 36:16. Ps 76:7. Pr 29:1. Is 57:21. Je 2:30. 5:3. Ezk 5:12-17. 20:32-35. Am *3:6-12. 9:4, 9, 10. **the Lord.** Le 26:36. Is 51:17. Ezk 12:18, 19. Ho 11:10, 11. Hab 3:16. Lk 21:26. **trembling.** or, raging. Dt 2:25. Ge 45:24. **failing of eyes.** or, consumption of eyes. Le 26:16. Is 10:22 (consumption). 65:14. La 3:65. Mt 24:8. Ro 11:10. **sorrow.** or, grief. Jb 41:22. **mind.** Heb. *neph-esh,* soul. Ge +23:8.

66. **hang in doubt.** 2 S 21:12h. Ho 11:7h. **thou shalt fear.** ver. 67. Pr ❍+*34:4. La 1:13. He 10:27. Re 6:15-17.

67. **the morning.** See on ver. 34. Jb 7:3, 4. Pr 28:1. Re 9:6. **Would God.** ♪87, Ps 118:25.

68. **bring thee into Egypt.** This verse seems espe-cially to point out an event, which took place subse-quently to the destruction of Jerusalem by Titus, and the desolation made by Hadrian. Numbers of the cap-tives were sent by sea into Egypt (as well as into other countries), and sold for slaves at a vile price, and for the meanest offices; and many thousands were left to perish from want; for the multitude was so great, that purchasers could not be found for them all at any price! Dt 17:16. Je 43:7. 44:12, 14. Ho 8:13. 9:3. **with ships.** Ge 49:13. **there ye shall.** Ex 20:2. Ne 5:8. Est 7:4. Jl 3:3-7. Lk *21:24. **be sold.** ♪108A1, Ex +8:18. 1 K 21:20, 25. 2 K 17:17.

DEUTERONOMY 29

The manifold works and mercies of God a motive to obedience by the memory of the works they had seen, 1-9. Moses solemnly engageth them to keep cov-enant with God, 10-17. Unbelief, careless contempt, and breach of covenant shall be severely punished, 18-28. The end and use of the revealed, as opposed to the secret or unrevealed, will of God, 29.

1. **the words.** ver. 12, 21-25. Le 26:44, 45. 2 K 23:3. Je 11:2, 6. 34:18. Ac 3:25. **beside the.** Dt 4:10-13, 23. 5:2, 3. Ex 19:3-5. 24:2-8. Je 31:32. He 8:9.

2. **Ye have seen all.** See on Ex 8:12. 19:4. Jsh 24:5, 6. Ps 78:43-51. 105:27-36. Ac 1:21, 22. 2 P 1:16. 1 J 1:1-3.

3. **temptations.** See on Dt 4:32-35. 7:18, 19. Ne 9:9-11.

4. **not given.** See on Dt +*2:30. Pr 20:12. Is 6:9, 10. 63:17. Ezk 36:26. Mt 13:11-15. Jn *8:43. 12:37-40. Ac 28:26, 27. Ro ▸11:7-10. 2 C 3:15. Ep 4:18. 2 Th √2:10-12. 2 T +*2:25. Ja 1:13-17. **unto this day.** ver. +28. Dt *34:6. Ge +19:38. Jsh +4:9.

5. **I have led.** Dt 1:3. 8:2. **your clothes.** See on Dt *8:4. Ne 9:21. Mt 6:31, 32. **and thy shoe.** Jsh 9:5, 13. Mt 10:10.

6. **eaten bread.** See on Dt *8:3. Ex 16:12, 35. Ne 9:15. Ps 78:24, 25. **neither have.** Nu 16:14. 20:8, 11. Ps 78:15, 16. 1 C 9:25. 10:4. Ep *5:18.

7. **Sihon.** Dt 2:24-37. 3:1-17. Nu 21:21-35. 32:33-42. Ps 135:10-12. 136:17-22.

8. **and gave.** Dt 3:12, 13. Nu 32:33.

9. **Keep.** See on ver. 1. Dt 4:6. +26:16. Jsh 1:7. 1 K 2:3. Ps 25:10. 103:17, 18. Is 56:1, 2, 4-7. Je 50:5. Lk *11:28. He 13:20, 21. **and do.** Dt +26:16. Lk *6:46. Ja 1:22. **prosper.** Ge +*39:3, 23. Jsh *1:8. 2 Ch +*20:20. *31:21. 32:30. Ps *1:3. *122:6. Is 44:4. Col

1:6. 3 J 2. Heb. deal wisely. S#7919h. Dt 32:29 (under-stood). Jsh 1:7 (prosper; mg, do wisely), 8 (have good success; mg, do wisely). 1 S 18:5mg. 1 K 2:3mg. 2 K 18:7. Ps *32:8 (instruct thee). 94:8 (be wise). 101:2 (behave myself wisely). Pr 16:23 (teacheth; mg, maketh wise). *17:8. Is 41:20 (understand). 52:13 (deal pru-dently; mg, prosper). Da 9:25 (understand).

10. **stand.** Dt 4:10. 31:12, 13. 2 Ch 23:16. 34:29-32. Ne 8:2. 9:1, 2, 38. 10:28. Jl 2:16, 17. Re 6:15. 20:12.

11. **little ones.** S#2945h, Nu +16:27. i.e. infants, they also being in the covenant, as they had previously been in the Adamic and Abrahamic ones (Young). ver. +29. Dt 31:12. Ge 6:18. *12:7. 13:15. 17:7, 8. 21:13. 26:3-5, 24. Ex 12:37. Le 26:44, 45. Jsh 8:35. 2 Ch 20:13. Ne +*12:43. Jb 5:25. Ps *25:13. 37:25, 26. 69:36. 102:28. 112:2. Pr 11:21. 14:26. *20:7. Is *65:23. Je 32:39. Mt 19:13-15. Mk *9:36, 37. 10:14. Lk *18:15. Ac *2:39. +16:15. 1 C √7:14. **wives.** Jsh +8:35. **stranger.** Dt 5:14. Ex 12:38, 48, 49. Nu 11:4. **the hewer.** Jsh 9:21-27. Ga *3:28. Col *3:11.

12. **thou shouldest.** Dt 5:2, 3. Ex 19:5, 6. Jsh 24:25. 2 K 11:17. 2 Ch 15:12-15. **enter.** Heb. pass. Ge 15:17. Jsh 9:6. Ezr 10:3. Je 34:+*18n, 19. This is an allusion to the solemn ceremony used by several ancient na-tions, when they entered into a covenant with each other. The victims, slain as a sacrifice on this occasion, were divided, and the parts laid asunder: the contract-ing parties then passed between them, imprecating, as a curse on those who violated the sacred compact, that they might in like manner be cut asunder (Ge 15:10). Thus Homer says, "They cut the quarters and cover them with the fat: dividing them into two, they place the raw flesh upon them." St. Cyril, in his work against Julian, shows that "passing between the divided parts of a victim" was used also among the Chaldeans, and other people. **into his oath.** ver. 14. 2 Ch 15:12-15. Ne 10:28, 29.

13. **establish.** See on Dt 7:6. 26:18, 19. 28:9. **he may be.** See on Ge 17:7. 26:3, 4. 28:13-15. Ex 6:7. Je 31:31-33. 32:38. He 11:16.

14. **do I make.** Je 31:31-34. Ac 2:39. He 8:7-12.

15. **also with him.** See on Dt 5:3. Je 32:39. 50:5. Mt 13:17. Jn 17:20. 20:29. Ac *2:39. 1 C *7:14.

16. **through the nations.** Dt 2:4, 9, 19, 24. 3:1, 2. Ex 12:12.

17. **abominations.** Heb. detestable things. 1 K 11:5, 7. **idols.** Heb. dungy gods. Le 26:30. Nu 25:2. 1 K 21:26. Ezk 20:8. 22:3. 30:13. **wood and.** Dt 4:28. 28:64. 2 K 18:34, 35. **silver and gold.** Ex 20:23.

18. **among you man.** Dt *11:16, 17. 13:1-15. *17:2-7. He *3:12. **heart turneth away.** Lk 8:13. Ac 8:20-23. He *3:12-14. He 12:15. **among you a root.** Je *9:15. Ho 10:4. Am *6:12. Ac *8:23. He √12:15. **gall.** or, a poisonful herb. Heb. *rosh.* Dt 32:32, 33. Jb 20:16. Ps *69:21. Je 8:14. 9:15. 23:15. La 3:5, 15. Ho 10:4. Am 6:12. **wormwood.** Pr 5:4. Je 9:15. 23:15. La 3:15, 19. Am 5:7. 6:12.

19. **this curse.** ver. 12. Ge 2:17. **that he bless.** Dt 17:2. Ge 22:18h. 26:4. Nu 15:30, 39. Ps 10:4-6, 11. 49:18. 72:17. 94:6, 7. Pr *29:1. Is 65:16h. Je 4:2h. 5:12, 13. 7:3-11. 28:15-17. 44:16, 17, 27. Ezk 13:16, 22. Ep 5:6. **I shall.** Ge *3:4. Is 48:22. Ezk +13:22. Re ❍14:13. **though I walk.** Nu 15:30. Ec 11:9. Ro 1:21. 2 C 10:5. Ep 4:17. **imagination.** or, stubbornness. Ps 81:12. Je 3:17mg. 7:24mg. 9:14. 11:8. *13:10. 16:12.

*18:12. 23:17. **to add**. Jb 15:16. 34:7. Is 30:1. 56:12. Ro 2:5. Ep 4:19. A very forcible metaphor, denoting the natural progress and increasing avidity of sinful passions and depraved inclinations; which lead men to drink down iniquity as the drunkard does his liquor, without regard to consequences. Some render, "to add thirst to drunkenness;" and then it implies the insatiableness of men's sinful passions, which hanker for more and more indulgence after the greatest excesses. **drunkenness**. or, fulness. This word is generally used of liquids. Ps 36:8. 65:10. Pr 5:19. 7:18. *11:25. **to thirst**. 2 S 17:29. Ps 107:5. Pr *25:21. Is 21:14. *29:8. 32:6. *44:3. *55:1. Je 2:25. Heb. the drunken to thirsty.

20. **will not spare**. 2 K 24:4. Ps 52:5. 78:50. Pr 2:22. 6:34. Is 27:11. Je 13:14. Ezk 5:11. 7:4, 9. 8:18. 9:10. 14:7, 8. 24:14. Ro 8:32. 11:21. 2 P 2:4, 5. **the anger**. Ps 74:1. **his jealousy**. Ex 20:5. 34:14. Ps 78:58. 79:5. SS 8:6. Ezk 8:3, 5. 23:25. 36:5. Na 1:2. Zp 1:18. 1 C 10:22. **smoke**. ✓22K1, Dt +4:24. Ps 18:8. 74:1. 80:4mg. He 12:29. **all the curses**. Dt 27:15-26. 28:15-68. **blot out**. See on Dt 9:14. 25:19. Ex 32:32, 33. Ps 69:28. Ezk 14:7, 8. Re +*3:5. 13:8.

21. **separate**. Jsh ch. 7. Ezk 13:9. *14:7, 8. Ml 3:18. Mt 24:51. 25:32, 41, 46. **are written**. Heb. is written. Dt 30:10.

22. **shall say**. ver. 24. **sicknesses**. 2 Ch 21:19. Ps *103:3. Je 14:18. 16:4. **which the Lord hath laid upon it**. Heb. wherewith the Lord hath made it sick. Dt 28:59. Je 19:8. 49:17. 50:13.

23. **brimstone**. Jb 18:15. Is 34:9. Lk 17:29. Re 19:20. **salt**. Jg 9:45. Ps 107:34. Je 17:6. Ezk 47:11. Zp 2:9. Lk 14:34, 35. **nor beareth**. Ps 107:33, 34. **like the**. Ge 14:2. 19:24, 25. Je 20:16. Ho 11:8, 9. Am 4:11. Ju 7.

24. **Wherefore**. 1 K 9:8, 9. 2 Ch 7:21, 22. Je 22:8, 9. La 2:15-17. 4:12. Ezk 14:23. Ro 2:5.

25. **Because**. Is 47:6. Je 40:2, 3. 50:7. **they have forsaken**. 1 K 19:10-14. Is 24:1-6. Je 22:9. 31:32. Da 9:11, 13, 14. He 8:9.

26. **they went**. Jg 2:12, 13. 5:8. 2 K 17:7-18. 2 Ch 36:12-17. Je 19:3-13. 44:2-6. **gods whom**. Dt 28:64. **whom he had**, etc. _or_, who had not given to them any portion. **given**. Heb. divided. or, apportioned. Dt 4:19. The ancients had the notion that each nation was bound to worship its own deity, and not that of another country (Young). Jg 11:24n. 1 K 20:23n. Is 36:18n. Ac ◑17:26, 29-31.

27. **kindled**. Dt 6:15. 7:4. 11:17. Ps 79:5. **all the curses**. ver. 20, 21. Dt 27:15, etc. 28:15, etc. Le 26:14, etc. Is 43:27, 28. Da 9:11-14. Mk 11:20-22. 2 C 5:11.

28. **rooted them**. Dt 28:25, 36, 64. 1 K 14:15. 2 K 17:18, 23. 2 Ch 7:20. Ps 52:5. Pr 2:22. Je 42:10. Lk 21:23, 24. **cast**. Dt 28:64. 30:1, 3. Ps 74:1. Is 22:17, 18. Je 7:15. 22:26. **as it is this day**. ver. +4. Dt 6:24. 8:18. Ge +19:38. Ezr 9:7. Da 9:7.

29. **secret**. Jb *11:6, 7. *28:28. Ps *25:14. Pr *3:32. Is 48:8. Je *23:18. Da *2:18, 19, 22, 27-30. 4:9. Am *3:7. Mt *13:35. Jn *15:15. 21:22. Ac *1:7. Ro *11:33, 34. *16:25, 26. 1 C *2:10, 16. **things**. ✓63K, Ge 37:13. EWB in B114, 115 gives this as an instance of false ellipsis, which, while it makes excellent sense in English, does not accord with the meaning of the Hebrew. The passage is one of fifteen examples in the Massorah where the words are dotted, and which are therefore to be cancelled in reading. When this is done, the sense is "The secret things and the revealed things

are for us and for our children forever, that we may do all the words of this law." The secret things have reference to things which have not been, but will yet be revealed. Dt 30:11-14. **revealed**. T#51. Ge 18:17-19. Ex 33:13. Nu 12:7, 8. Ps +19:7 (T#47). +36:9 (T#279). *78:2-7. 103:7. Is +/3:8:20. Am *3:7. Mt *11:27-30. *13:11. Lk +16:31 (T#433). Jn 15:15. *20:31. Ro 11:33. *16:26. 2 T 1:5. +✓3:16, 17. Re 22:18, 19. **and to our**. ver. +*11n. See on Dt *6:7. *30:2. **for ever**. Heb. _olam_, Ex +12:24.

DEUTERONOMY 30

A promise of gracious deliverance to Israel upon their repentance, in future times, 1-10. The law of God manifest and just, 11-14. Life and death solemnly set before the people, 15-20.

1. **And**. The several great covenants of Scripture may be found at the following passages: (1) Edenic, Ge 1:28. (2) Adamic, Ge 3:14, 15. (3) Noahic, Ge 8:21. (4) Abrahamic, Ge 15:18. (5) Mosaic, Ex 19:25. (6) Palestinian, Dt 30:1. (7) Davidic, 2 S 7:10, 12, 15, 16. Is +*55:3. (8) New, He 8:8. **it shall come**. See on Dt 4:30. Le 26:40-46. **these things**. Dt 28:2. Ne 9:36. Da 9:13. **the blessing**. ver. 15, 19. Dt 11:26-28. ch. 27, *28. *29:18-23. Le ch. ✓26. **the curse**. Dt 11:28. 28:15-45. **thou shalt call**. Dt 4:29. 1 K 8:47, 48. Is 46:8. Ezk 18:28. Lk 15:17. **mind**. Dt 4:29-31. **whither**. Ge 4:14. Je 8:3.

2. **return unto**. Dt 4:28-31. 2 S +7:3. 1 K 8:47, 48. 2 Ch 6:37, 38. 15:4. Ne 1:9. Is 55:6, 7. Je 4:1, 2. *29:12, 13. 30:8-10. La 3:32, 40. Ho 3:5. 6:1, 2. 14:1-3. Jl 2:12, 13. Zc 12:10. Ro 11:23, 24. 2 C 3:16. 1 J *1:9. **obey**. Dt 15:5. 28:1. Jg 3:4. 1 S 12:14. 1 K 11:38. Jb *36:11. Ps 81:8. 95:7. Is 1:19. Je 17:24. 26:3. Zc 6:15. **with all thine heart**. Dt 4:29. 6:5. 13:3. 1 Ch 29:9, 17. Ps 41:12. 119:80. Je 3:10. 4:14. 29:13. Ep 6:24. **soul**. Heb. _nephesh_, Ge +34:3.

3. **That then**. Ps *106:44-46. 126:1-4. Ac +✓3:19-21. **will turn**. Ge 28:15. 48:21. Jb 42:10. Ps 14:7. 53:6. 85:1-3. 106:45-47. 126:1-4. Is 56:8. Je 29:14. 30:3, 18. 31:10. 33:11. La 3:22, 32. Ezk 16:53. 39:25. Ho 6:11. Jl 3:1. Am 9:14. Zp 2:7. Ro 11:23, 26, 31. Ep 4:8. **return and**. Ps 2:9. 24:10. 50:3. *96:13. 110:1. Is *9:7. *11:10-12. Je *23:5, 6. Ezk 37:21, 22. Da *7:13, 14, 22. Ho 3:4, 5. Am +*9:11. Mi +*4:7. Zc *2:10-12. *6:12, 13. 12:10. 13:6. *14:4, 5. Mt *19:28. +*23:39. *24:30, 39. +*25:31. Mk 13:26. Lk 12:40. 17:30. +*18:8. 21:27. 24:25, 26. Jn 14:2, 3. Ac *1:11. *15:14-17. Ro +*11:25, 26. 1 C 15:23, 51, 52. Ph 3:20, 21. 1 Th 1:9, 10. 2:19. 3:13. 4:14-17. 2 Th 1:7-10. 2:8. 1 T 6:14, 15. T +*2:13. He 10:37. Ja 5:7, 8. 2 P 3:3, 4. 1 J *3:2. Ju 14, 15. Re 1:7, 8. 2:25. 16:15. 19:11. *20:4. 22:7, 12, 20. **have compassion**. Dt 13:17. La *3:32. Jl 2:25. Mi +*7:20. Zc *10:6. **gather thee**. This seems to refer to a more extensive captivity than that which the Jews suffered in Babylon. Ge *15:16. 48:21. 1 Ch 16:35. Ezr 1:1-4. Ne 1:9. Ps 107:3. +*147:2. Is ✓11:11n. Je 12:15. *16:15. 24:6. 29:14. *30:3. *31:8, 9. *32:37-42. 48:47. 49:6. Ezk *20:33-37. 34:12, 13. 36:24. Mi *2:12. Zp *3:13-20. Zc *8:7, 8. *10:6-12. Jn 11:51, 52. Ro 11:1-32. **scattered**. Dt 4:27. 28:64. Ge 11:4. 1 K 22:17. Est 3:8. Ps 44:11. 60:1. Je 31:10. Ezk 6:8. Jl 3:2. Mt 9:36.

4. **driven out**. 2 S 14:13, 14. Ne 1:9. Is 16:3, 4. 27:13. Je 30:17. 49:36. Ezk 34:4, 16. Mi 4:6. Zp 3:19.

unto. Dt 28:64. Ne 1:9. Ps 19:6. Is 11:11-16. 62:11. Ezk 39:25-29. Zp 3:19, 20. Re 7:1-3. 20:7-10. **of heaven.** ʃ121Q3, 2 S +22:8. **thence will the.** Ne 1:9. Is 43:6. 48:20. Je 31:8, 10. Am *9:9. Zp 3:20. Zc 8:7. As this promise refers to a return from a captivity among all nations, consequently it cannot be exclusively the Babylonish captivity which is intended; and the repossession of their land must be different from that which was consequent on their return from Babylon. Nor at that period could it be said that they were "multiplied more than their fathers," or, as the Hebrew imports, "made greater than their fathers," when after their return they were tributary to the Persians, and afterwards fell under the power of the Greeks, under whom they suffered much; nor have their hearts, as a nation, yet been *circumcised* (ver. +6). Is +*11:11n. **gather thee.** Is 27:12. 40:11. 49:5mg. *56:8. Je *23:3. Ezk 20:34, 41. 28:25. √36:24. 37:21, 22.

5. **bring thee.** Ne 1:9. Je 29:14. 30:3. **possess it.** Is 11:11, 12. Je 23:3-8. 32:6-15, 44. Ezk 37:21-25. Ho 11:10, 11. Mi *4:4. **he will do thee good.** ver. 9. Dt *8:16. 28:63. Ezk 34:24-31. Zc 8:13-15. **multiply thee.** ver. 16. Dt 1:11. 7:13. 13:17. 28:63. Ge 17:6. Ex 1:7. Le 26:9. 2 S 24:3. Ne 9:23. Ps 107:38. Is 27:6. **fathers.** Ho 1:10, 11.

6. **And.** or, For (denoting the reason of a thing). 1 K 1:21. 18:3, 4. Ps 1:3. *5:12. Is 16:2. 64:5. **God will.** T#594. Ps 51:10. Je 24:7. 31:33. Ezk 11:19, 20. 36:25-27. Jn √1:12, 13. Ro 9:15, 16. 15:16. 1 C 3:5-7. 4:7. Ga +4:6 (T#347-4). Ep 2:4, 5, *8, *10. *4:24. Col 1:12, 13. 2 Th 2:13. 2 T +2:25 (T#434). T *3:5. He 13:20, 21. Ja 1:18. **circumcise thine heart.** T#506. Dt 10:16. Is +60:21 (T#441). Je 4:4. 9:26. 31:33. 32:39, 40. *50:20. Ezk 11:19, 20. 36:26, 27. Ho 2:14-16. Jn *3:3-7. Ro 2:28, 29. 11:26. 2 C 5:17. Col 2:11. **to love the Lord.** Dt 6:5. 11:1. 13:3. 19:9. Ex 20:6. Jsh 22:5. 23:11. Ps 31:23. Mt 22:37. Ro *8:28. 1 C 8:3. Ja 1:12. 2:5. 1 J 4:7, 16-19. 5:3, 4. **soul.** Heb. *nephesh,* Ge +34:3.

7. **put all.** Dt *7:15. 33:11. Ge *12:3. 22:17. 24:60. Nu 24:14. Jb *8:22. Ps 35:26. *71:13. 109:29. 137:7-9. Is 10:12. 11:14. 14:1-27. 19:1. 34:1, 2. 54:15-17. Je 25:12-16, 29. *30:16, 20. 46:1, 2. 47:1. 50:33, 34. 51:24-26, 34-37. La 3:54-66. 4:21, 22. Ezk 25:3, 6, 8, 12, 15. 38:1. 39:1. Da 12:1. Jl 3:1-8. Am 1:3, 6, 9, 11, 13. Ob 10. Zp 2:8, 9. 3:19. Zc 12:3. Mt 25:31-46.

8. **thou shalt return.** See on ver. 2. Pr 16:1. Is 1:25, 26. Je 31:33. 32:39, 40. Ezk 11:19, 20. 36:27. 37:24. Ho 6:1. 14:1. Zp 3:20. Ro 11:26, 27. Ep 2:16. Ph *2:13.

9. **make thee.** Dt *28:4, 11-14. Le *26:4-6, 9, 10. Ps 37:25. Je 31:27, 28. Am *9:13-15. **every work.** Is 65:21. Ml 3:10. Mt *6:33. Ph *4:19. **thy body.** Ge +29:31. Ps +*127:3. **thy cattle.** Dt 7:14. 28:4. Ps 107:38. **thy land.** Dt 26:4. Ps *67:6. Je 1:10. 31:28. Ro 8:19-23. 2 C 9:10. **for good.** Dt 15:4. 1 K 10:7. Pr 10:22. Je 24:5-7. Ezk 34:27. Ml 3:10-12. **rejoice over thee.** ʃ22B, Ps +104:31. Dt 28:63. Is 62:5. 65:19. Je 24:6. 32:41. 33:9. Zp 3:17. Lk 15:6-10, 32. Jn 15:11.

10. **If.** Ge +4:7. **hearken unto.** See on ver. 2, 8. Is 55:2, 3. 1 C 7:19. **to keep.** Dt 26:16, 17. 30:2. 1 C 7:19. Re 22:14. **book of.** Dt 29:21. Ex 17:14. 2 K 22:8. 23:25. **law.** Dt 33:4. Pr 3:1, 2. **turn unto.** ver. 2. Ne 1:9. Is 55:2. La 3:40, 41. Ezk 18:21. 33:11, 14, 19. Ac *3:19. 26:20. **with all.** Dt *4:29. **soul.** Heb. *nephesh,* Ge +34:3.

11. **it is not hidden.** Dt 10:12. 17:8. *29:29. Pr +√8:9. 30:18. Is 30:21. *48:16. Je 32:17mg. Or, as the word *niphlaith* implies, not too wonderful for thee to comprehend or perform; but easily to be acquainted with, and understood, because clearly revealed: *neither is it afar off*; it was proclaimed in your ears from mount Sinai, and is now proclaimed in the sanctuary: *it is not in heaven*; for it has already been revealed: *neither is it beyond the sea*; that you need travel for instruction, as the ancient philosophers did, or seek instruction from men, at immense labor and expense; *but the word is nigh to thee*; brought to thy very doors; in *thy mouth, and in thy heart*; made so familiar as to afford a topic of common discourse, that it might be laid up in the memory and reduced to practice. Ps 119:11, 50, *105, 162, 172. 147:19, 20. Pr 6:22, 23. *8:9. Is +*8:20n. 45:19. Je *15:16. Ro 16:25, 26. Ga 1:8n. Col 1:26, 27. **far off.** Ec 7:24.

12. **not in heaven.** Pr 30:4. Jn 3:13. Ro ▶10:6, 7.

13. **sea.** Jb 28:14. **Who shall.** Ac 10:22, 33. 16:9. Ro 10:14, 15. **go over the sea.** Pr 2:1-5. 3:13-18. 8:11. 16:6. Mt 12:42. Jn 6:27. Ac 8:27, etc.

14. **the word.** Ps 138:2. Pr 8:22. Is 55:10, 11. Jn 1:1, 14. **very nigh.** Dt 4:7, 8. Is 51:5. Ezk 2:5. 33:33. Lk 10:11, 12. Jn 5:46. Ac 13:26, 38-41. 28:23-28. He *2:1-3. **mouth.** Jsh 1:8. Je 12:2. Ezk 33:31. Mt 7:21. Ro *10:8-10. 1 Th 1:8. **heart.** He 8:10. **do.** Dt 26:16. Mt 7:21. Ja 1:22, 25.

15. **I have set.** ver. 1, *19. Dt *11:26. *28:1, etc. *32:47. Ps 1:6. Je 21:8. Mk *16:16. Jn *3:16. Ga *3:13, 14. *5:6. 6:8. 1 J *3:23. *5:11, 12. **life.** Dt 11:26. *32:47. Ne *9:29. Pr 4:22. 10:16. *11:19. 12:28. Je *21:8. **good.** Dt 28:11mg. Jb 36:11. Ps 25:13mg. 106:5. **life and good.** i. e. a good or a happy life; a figure called Hendiadys (ʃ93A, Ge +1:26): or, life, and all the blessings of life, as *good* is often used, as Jb 7:7. Ps 4:6. 128:5. Ec 2:24. 4:8. 6:3. **death.** ʃ121G, Ge +*2:17. +31:1. **evil.** Dt 11:26. Am 5:14.

16. **to love.** See on ver. 6. Mt 22:37, 38. 1 C 7:19. 13:4. 1 J 5:2, 3. **to keep.** Pr 19:16. Jn 14:21. 1 C 7:19. **judgments.** Dt 4:45. Le 25:18. Ps 19:9. **live.** ver. 19. Dt 4:1. *32:47. Le *18:5. Ne 9:29. Ezk 20:11, 13, 21. Ro 7:10. 10:5. 2 C 3:7. Ga 3:12. **possess.** ver. 5.

17. **if.** Ge +4:7. **thine.** See on Dt 29:18-28. 31:29. Jg 2:17. 1 S 12:25. Ml 2:8. Jn 3:19-21. **heart turn away.** Dt 17:17. 1 K 11:2. Pr 1:32. 14:14. Lk +*8:13. 2 T 4:4. He √3:12. *12:25. **not hear.** Mt 13:11-17. 2 Th *2:10-12. **drawn away.** Dt 31:29. **other gods.** Dt 5:9. 6:14. *12:30. 16:22. 28:14. 29:18. Ex +*20:5. 23:24. 34:14-16. Jsh *23:7. Jg 6:10. 1 K 11:2, 10. 2 K 17:35, 38. Ps 81:9. 96:5. Je 7:6. 25:6. *35:15. Ezk 20:7, 18. 1 C 8:4-7. 10:7. 1 J 5:21. **serve.** Dt 4:19. Jsh 24:16-22. Mt ◐4:10.

18. **denounce.** or, declare. Dt 4:26. 8:19, 20. 29:27. 31:17, 18, 29. Jsh 23:15, 16. 1 K 9:7. 14:15. 2 K 24:3. Is 63:17, 18. Je 10:18. 25:9. 44:11. **perish.** Dt 4:26. **prolong.** Dt 4:26. Ex 20:12. Ec 8:13. **passest.** Dt 9:1. 11:31. 12:10. 27:2. 31:13. Nu 33:51. 35:10. **Jordan.** Jsh 1:14.

19. **I call heaven.** See on Dt *4:26. 31:28. 32:1. Ps 50:4. Is 1:2. Je *2:12, 13. 6:19. 22:21, 29, 30. Ezk 36:4. Mi 1:2. 6:1, 2. 1 T *5:21. **record.** Jsh 24:27. **that I have.** See on ver. *15. Dt *11:26. **life.** Dt 32:47. Pr 8:35. Jn *14:6. Ro *6:23. **death.** Ezk *18:31, 32. *33:11. 2 P √3:9. **blessing.** Dt 11:26. 28:2. **cursing.** Dt 27:26. 28:15, 20. **choose.** T#271. Ex 8:32. 9:27.

10:16, 17. Jsh *24:15. 2 S +15:6 (T#329). 24:1, 10. Ps +58:5 (T#373). +119:59 (T#600). Pr 1:29-31. 16:9. 23:26. SS 1:4. Is 66:3. Ho 13:9. Mt 13:15. +16:27 (T#556). 18:7. Lk 22:22. Jn *5:40. Ac +3:19 (T#601). 4:27, 28. Ro 2:15. +3:19 (T#128). Ph *2:12, 13. **life**. Jsh *24:15-22. 1 K *18:21. Ps 119:*30, 111, 173. Pr *1:29. *8:36. Is 56:4. Lk *10:42. Jn 5:40. Re *3:20. **that both thou**. Dt 6:2. Je *32:39. Ac *2:39.

20. love. See on ver. 6, 16. Dt 10:12. 11:22. **cleave**. Dt 4:4. 10:20. 11:22. 13:4. Jsh 22:5. 23:8. Ac *11:23. Ro 12:9. **thy life**. Dt 4:1. 8:3. 32:47. Ps 27:1. 30:5. 36:9. 66:9. 133:3. Pr 3:22. Jn 5:26. 11:25, 26. √14:6. √17:3. Ac 17:25, 28. Ga *2:20. Col 3:3, 4. Re 21:6. 22:1, 17. **length of thy days**. Dt +*4:40. 5:*16, 33. 6:2. 11:9. 17:20. 22:7. 25:15. 32:47. 1 K 3:14. Ps 21:4. 61:6. *91:16. Pr *3:2, 16. 4:10. 9:11. **thou mayest**. See on Dt 4:40. 5:16. 11:9. 12:10. **land**. Ps 37:3. **sware unto**. Dt 4:31. 7:13. 8:1. 10:11. 11:9, 21. 13:17. 26:3, 15. 28:11. Ge 12:7. 15:18. 26:2, 3. 28:13. 50:24. Jsh 1:6. 5:6. 21:43. Jg 2:1. 2 K 13:23. Ne 9:8. Ps 106:45. 136:23. Ro 11:+√1, *2, 28, 29.

DEUTERONOMY 31

Moses declares to the people his approaching death, and encourages them, 1-6. He encourages Joshua, 7, 8. He delivers the law to the priests, and orders it to be publicly read every seventh year, 9-13. The Lord informs Moses and Joshua of the future apostasy and calamities of Israel; and orders a song to be made to testify against them, 14-22. Moses gives Joshua a charge, 23. Moses finishes the book of the law, 24. Moses delivers the book of the law to the Levites to keep beside the ark of the covenant, 24-27. The elders convened and the congregation assembled to hear the song, 28-30.

2. **I am an**. The life of Moses, the great prophet of Jehovah and lawgiver of the Jews, was exactly the same in length as the time Noah employed in preaching righteousness to the antediluvian world. These one hundred and twenty years were divided into three remarkable periods. Forty years he lived in Egypt, in the court of Pharaoh, acquiring all the learning and wisdom of the Egyptians (Ac 7:20, 23); forty years he sojourned in Midian, in a state of preparation for his great and important mission (Ac 7:29, 30); and forty years he guided, led, and governed the Israelites under the express direction and authority of God: in all 120 years. Dt 34:7. Ex 7:7. Jsh 14:10, 11. Ps 90:10. Ac 7:23. **I can no more**. See on Dt 34:7. Nu 27:15-17. 2 S 21:17. 1 K 3:7. **Thou shalt not**. Dt 3:26, 27. 4:21, 22. 32:48-52. Nu *20:12. 27:13, 14. Ac 20:25. 2 P 1:13, 14.

3. **The Lord**. √66, Ge +9:3. **thy God**. See on Dt 9:3. Ge 48:21. Ps 44:2, 3. 146:3-6. **and Joshua**. ver. 7, 8, 14, 23. Dt 3:28. 34:9. Nu 27:18-21. Jsh 1:2. 3:7. 4:14. Ac 7:45. He 4:8, Jesus.

4. **the Lord**. √16, Ge +1:27. **shall do**. Dt 2:33. 3:3-11, 21. 7:2, 16. Ex 23:28-31. See on Nu 21:24-35.

5. **And the Lord**. Dt 3:21. 7:2, 18. **according**. Dt 7:23-25. 20:16, 17. Ex 23:32, 33. 34:12-16. Nu 33:52-56.

6. **Be strong**. ver. 7, 23. Dt 20:4. Jsh *1:6, 7, 9. 10:25. 1 Ch *22:13. 28:10, 20. 2 Ch *32:7. Ps 27:14. Is *43:1-5. Hg 2:4. Zc 8:13. 1 C 16:13. Ep 6:10. 2 T 2:1. **fear not**. Dt 1:29. 7:18. 20:1, 3, 4. Nu 14:9. Ps

*27:1. Is *41:10. 51:12. Lk 12:32. Re *21:8. **with thee**. Ex 13:21, 22. 33:14. He 13:5. **he will not fail**. Dt 4:31. Jsh *1:5. 1 Ch 28:20. Is *41:13-17. He *▶13:5.

7. **Be strong**. See on ver. 6, 23. Dt 1:38. 3:28. Jsh 1:6. 1 Ch 28:20. Da 10:19. Ep 6:10. **for thou must**. See on ver. 3. Dt 1:38. 3:28. Jn 1:17.

8. **he it is that**. ver. 3. Dt 9:3. Ex 13:21, 22. 33:14. **before**. Jsh 3:11. **he will be**. See on ver. 6. Jsh 1:5, 9. 1 Ch 28:20. Is 8:9, 10. 43:1, 2. Ro 8:31. **he will not**. He ▶13:5. **neither forsake**. ver. ❶+*17. **fear not**. Jsh 1:6, 7, 9.

9. **Moses wrote**. ver. 22-24, 28. Ex +*24:4. Nu 33:2. Da 9:13. Ml 4:4. Mk 10:4, 5. 12:19. Lk 20:28. Jn 1:17, 45. 5:46. **delivered**. ver. 24-26. Dt *17:18. **the priests**. Ho 4:6. Ml 2:7. **which bare**. Nu 4:15. Jsh 3:3, 14-17. 6:12. 1 K 8:3. 1 Ch 15:2, 12-15.

10. **at the end**. Dt 15:1, 2. See on Le 23:34-43.

11. **to appear**. Dt 16:16, 17. Ex 23:16, 17. 34:24. Ps 84:7. **in the place**. See on Dt 12:5. 16:2, +6, +16. **thou shalt read**. Jsh 8:34, 35. 2 K 23:2. Ne 8:1-8, 18. 9:3. Lk 4:16, 17. Ac 13:15. 15:21. Ph=2:16. 2 T=4:2.

12. **Gather**. ver. 28. See on Dt 4:10. Le 8:3. 20:8. Jsh 8:34, 35. Ne *8:1-3. 2 K 23:2. **men**. Dt 6:6, 7. Ezr 10:1. Ps *19:7-11. Jn √5:39. 2 T √3:15-17. **women and children**. Their presence was not generally required at the three great festivals in the other six years (Young). **that they may**. Dt 29:29. Ps 34:11-14. 78:6, 7. **hear...learn**. Since faith comes by hearing, and hearing by the word of God. Ro 10:17. **fear...observe to do**. Reverence to God is the basis of obedience. **this law**. Evidently the Scriptures do not regard ignorance as the mother of devotion (Young).

13. **their children**. See on Dt 6:7. 11:2. Ps 78:4-8. Pr 22:6. Ep 6:4.

14. **that thou must die**. See on ver. 2. Dt 34:5. Ge 3:19. Nu 27:13. Jsh 23:14. 2 K 1:4. Ec 9:5. Is 38:1. **I may give**. ver. 23. See on Nu 27:19, 20. Ac 20:28-31. 2 T 4:1-4. **presented**. Ex 8:20. 9:13. 14:13. 34:2. Jsh 24:1. 1 S 10:19. Jb 1:6. 2:1. Ro *12:1. Ju *24. **tabernacle of**. Ex 27:21, etc.

15. **the Lord appeared**. See on Ex 33:9, 10. 40:38. Ps 99:7.

16. **thou shalt**. Dt 34:5. Ge +*25:8n. Nu 27:13. 2 S 7:12. Is *57:2. Ac 13:36. 15:18. **sleep**. Heb. lie down. 2 S 7:12. *Shochaiv*, lying down: it signifies to rest, take rest in sleep, and metaphorically, to die. Though much stress cannot be safely laid upon this expression to prove the immortality of the soul, or that the people, in the time of Moses, had a distinct notion of its separate existence; yet it was understood in this sense by Jonathan, who paraphrases the words thus: "Thou shalt lie down in the dust with thy fathers; and thy soul (*nishmatoch*) shall be laid up in the treasury of the life to come, with thy fathers." Jb 20:11. The death of men, both good and bad, is oft called a *sleep*, because they shall certainly awake out of it by resurrection (Matthew Poole). 1 K +*11:43. Ps 76:5. Da +*12:2n. 1 Th *4:13, etc. 2 P 3:4. **and go a**. Ex 32:6. 34:15. Le 20:3-6. Jg 2:17-20. Ps 73:27. 106:39. Is 57:3-8. Je 3:1-3. Ezk 16:15, 25-36. 23:5-8, etc. Ho 2:2-5. Ac *20:29, 30. Re 17:2-5. 19:2. **whoring**. √155E3, Is 32:9. **strangers**. Dt 32:12. Ex 12:43 (❋S#5236h). Le 22:13. Jsh 24:20, 23. **forsake me**. Dt 32:15. Jg 2:12. 10:6, 13. Is 1:4. Je *2:11-13. **break my**. Le 26:15. Jg 2:20. Ps ❶89:34. Je 31:32.

17. **my anger**. See on Dt 29:20. 32:21, 22. Jg 2:14,

15. Ps *2:12. *90:11. **I will forsake.** ver. ◑+*8. Jsh 24:20. 1 Ch 28:9. 2 Ch 12:5. *15:2. 24:20. Ezr 8:22. Ps ◐*9:10. Je 23:33, 39. Ho 9:12. 2 T *2:12. He 12:25. ◐13:5, 6. **hide my face.** Though this may allude to the withdrawing of the Shechinah, or visible appearance of Jehovah, yet the general meaning of the expression in Scripture is, the withdrawing of his approbation and protection, of which his visible appearance was formerly the sign and pledge. Dt 32:20. Jb 13:24. Ps 27:9. 30:7. 89:46. 104:29. Is 8:17. 64:7. Ezk 39:23, 24, 29. **befall them.** Heb. find them. ✝155F, Ge +4:7. ver. 21. Dt 4:30. Ge 44:34. Jsh 2:23. Jg 6:13. Ne 9:32mg. Jb 34:11. **Are not these.** See on Dt 29:24-27. Nu 14:42. Jg 6:13. Is 63:17.

18. **surely hide.** See on ver. 16, 17n. Nu 14:42. Jg 6:13. Ps 73:27. Is 8:17. 64:7.

19. **this song.** ver. 22, 30. Dt 32:1, etc., 44, 45. **and teach it.** See on Dt 4:9, 10. 6:7. 11:19. **put it in their.** Ex 4:15. 2 S 14:3. Is 51:16. 59:21. Je 1:9. **a witness.** T#347-3. ver. 21, 26. Ex 3:15-17. Ne *9:20. Ezk 2:5. Mt 10:18. 24:14. Lk 2:26. 12:11, 12. Jn 12:48. *14:26. Ac 11:28. 1 J 5:8, 9.

20. **when.** See on Dt 6:10-12. 7:1. 8:7. **floweth.** See on Ex 3:+8, 17. **milk and.** ✝174, Ge +18:27. **honey.** ✝17117, Ex +3:8. **eaten.** Dt 8:10-14. Ne 9:25, 26. **waxen fat.** Dt 32:15. Ne 9:25, 26, 35. Ps 17:10. 73:7. 119:70. Je 5:28. 50:11. Ezk 34:16, 20. Ho *13:6. **then.** See on ver. *16, 17. Dt +30:17. Jg 2:17.

21. **this song.** See on ver. 19. The inimitable song which follows in the next chapter. Things of great importance and general concern, were, among the ancients, put into verse; as this was found not only attractive and agreeable, but the best method of fixing and retaining them in the memory; especially in those early times, when writing was but little practiced. For this purpose, Jehovah was pleased to adapt his instructions. A sacred song, containing the substance of the preceding addresses, was appointed to be composed by Moses, doubtless under divine inspiration; which the people were required to learn, and teach to their children from generation to generation. This song would, when its predictions were verified, testify that they had been sufficiently warned; bear witness to the justice of God; and form a powerful call to repentance. **testify.** ✝155F, Ge +4:7. **against.** Heb. before. **I know.** Ge 6:5. 8:21. Ps 14:2, 3. 139:2. Is 46:10. Ezk 38:10, 11. Ho 5:3. 13:5, 6. Am 5:25, 26. Jn *2:24, +25. Ac 2:23. 4:28. 7:43. **go about.** Heb. do.

22. **Moses therefore wrote.** See on ver. 9, 19. Ex +*24:4.

23. **he gave Joshua.** See on ver. 7, 8, 14. Jsh 1:5-9. **shalt bring.** See on ver. 3. Dt 3:28. Ac 7:45.

24. **writing the words.** See on ver. 9. Dt 17:18. Ex +*24:4.

25. **bare the ark.** See on ver. 9.

26. **in the side.** Ex 25:16. 1 K 8:9. 2 K 22:8-11. 2 Ch 34:14, 15. **a witness.** See on ver. 19. 2 K 22:8, 13-19. Ro 3:19, 20. Ga 2:19.

27. **I know.** ver. 21. Dt 32:20. **stiff neck.** See on Dt 9:6. 32:20. Ex 32:9. 2 Ch 30:8. Ps 78:8. Is 48:4. Ac 7:51. **ye have been.** See on Dt 9:6, *24.

28. **Gather unto me.** See on ver. 12. Dt 29:10. Ge 49:1, 2. Ex 18:25. Nu 11:16, 17. **call heaven.** Dt 4:26. See on Dt +30:19. 32:1. Is 1:2. Lk 19:40.

29. **after.** Ac 20:29. **corrupt yourselves.** Dt 32:5. Jg 2:19. Ps 106:34, 35, 43. Is 1:4. Ho 9:9. Ac 20:30.

2 T 3:1-6. 2 P 1:14, 15. 2:1, 2. **and evil.** Dt 28:15, etc. 29:18-28. Le 26:14, etc. 2 Ch 34:24. Lk 19:42-44. *21:24. **befall.** ✝155F, Ge +4:7. **the latter days.** Dt *4:30. Ge *49:1. Jb *19:25. Ezk +*38:8. 1 T *4:1. 2 T *3:1. He 1:2. 2 P 3:3.

30. **Moses spake.** See on Dt 4:5. Jn *12:49. Ac *20:27. He 3:2, 5.

DEUTERONOMY 32

The song of Moses, contrasting the perfections of God, and his special goodness to Israel, with Israel's ingratitude and apostasy, 1-18. God's wrath and future judgments on them for their sins, 19-26. Yet the idolatrous nations to be destroyed, and they at last to be enlarged in mercy, 27-43. Moses exhorts them to set their hearts on these words for their good, 44-47. The Lord orders him to go up to mount Nebo, to view the promised land, and die, 48-52.

1. **Give ear.** Dt 4:26. +30:19. 31:28. Ps 49:1, 2. 50:4. Is 1:2. Je 2:12. 6:19. 22:29. **heavens.** ✝38G. Apostrophe: a turning aside from the direct subject matter to address others. Here, apostrophe to inanimate things B904. For other instances of this figure see 2 S 1:21. 1 K 13:2. Ps 114:5. 148:3-5. Is 1:2. Je 2:12. 22:29. 47:6. Ezk 13:11. 36:4, 8. Ho 13:14. Jl 2:21. Mi 6:2. Zc 11:1, 2.

2. **doctrine.** Jb 11:4. Pr 1:5. *4:2. *9:9. 16:21, 23. Is *29:24. **drop.** Dt 33:28. 2 S 23:4. Jb 29:22, 23. Ps 72:6. Is *55:10, 11. Ho 6:4. 14:5. 1 C *3:6-8. He 6:7. **rain.** Dt 11:11, 14, 17. Is *44:10, 11. **distil.** Nu 24:7. Jg 5:5mg. Jb 36:28. Ps 147:18. SS 4:16. Is 45:8. Je 9:18. **dew.** Ge 27:28, 39. Ps 110:3. 133:3. Pr 19:12. Is +*26:19n. Ho 14:5. **small rain.** or, storms. The original word is not found elsewhere in this sense; it means *heavy, rough, tempestuous* (Young). Ho 6:3. **tender herb.** Ge 1:11, 12. Ps 72:6. **as the showers.** Ps 65:10. 72:6. Je 3:3. 14:22. Ezk 34:26. Mi 5:7. Zc 10:1. **grass.** Ge 1:11, 12, 29, 30.

3. **Because.** Ex 3:13-16. 6:3. 20:24. 34:5-7. Ps 29:1, 2. 89:16-18. 105:1-5. 145:1-10. Je 10:6. *23:6. Mt 1:23. *6:9. Jn 17:6, 26. **publish.** Ps 22:22. Jn 17:26. **name.** Dt 28:58. Ps 68:4. Ac 3:16. Ph 2:9-11. Re 19:11-13. **greatness.** Dt 9:26. 11:2. **ascribe.** Dt 5:24. 1 Ch 17:19. *29:11. Ps 29:1, 2. 96:2-8. 145:3. 150:2. Je 10:6. Ep 1:19.

4. **the Rock.** ver. 15, 18, 30, 31. 1 S 2:2. 2 S 22:2, 3, 32, 47. 23:3. Ps 18:2, 31, 46. 61:2-4. 92:15. Is 17:10. =26:4mg. 28:16. 32:2. Hab 1:12. Mt=*16:16-18. 1 C=*10:4. He 13:8. 1 P 2:6. **his work.** T#249. Ge 1:31. 2 S *22:31. Ps 18:30, 31. 19:7. 138:8. Ec *3:14. Mt 5:48. Jn 17:4. Ep +3:11 (T#304). Ja 1:17. **all his.** Dt 10:18. Ge +*18:25. 1 S 2:3. Jb 8:3. 35:14. Ps 9:16. 77:13, 19. 97:2. 99:4. 103:6. Is *30:18. Je 9:24. Da 4:37. Jn 5:22. Ro 1:32. 2:2, 5. Ja 4:12. Re *15:3, 4. **judgment.** Ps 33:5. 67:4. Ne 9:33. **a God.** Heb. *El*, Ex +15:2. **of truth.** Ex +34:6. Ps 31:5. 61:7. 85:10. 98:3. 100:5. 146:6. Is 25:1. Je 10:10. Jn *1:14, 17. √14:6. T *1:2. or, stedfastness. Ex 17:12. 1 S 26:23. 2 K 12:15. *22:7. Ps 89:1, 2, 5, 8, 24, *33. or, faithfulness. Dt 7:9. He 10:23. 1 P 4:19. **without.** Dt 25:16. Jb 34:10-12. Ps 92:15. Hab *1:12, 13. Ro 3:5. **right.** Ge +*18:25. Ps *25:8. 92:15. 99:4. Ho *14:9.

5. **They have corrupted themselves.** Heb. He hath corrupted to himself. Dt 4:16. 9:12. 31:29. Ge 6:12. Ex 32:7. Jg 2:19. Ps 14:1. Is 1:4. Ho 9:9. Zp 3:7. Mt

7:16-18. 2 C 11:3. Re ◐14:1. **their spot**, etc. *or*, that they are not his children, that is their blot. Jn *8:41, 44. 2 C 7:1. 1 J 3:8-10. Ju 23. **a perverse**. Dt 9:24. 2 S 22:27. Ps 18:26. 78:8. *101:4. 125:5. Pr 2:15. *8:8. 11:20. 17:20. *19:1. 22:5. *28:6. Is 1:4. Mt 3:7. 16:4. 17:17. Lk 9:41. Ac 7:51. Ph=2:15. **crooked**. This Hebrew word is not found elsewhere. Jb 5:13. Pr 8:8. Is 42:16. **generation**. Ps 95:10. Ph 2:15.

6. **requite**. ver. 18. Ge 50:15, 17. Ps 116:12. Is 1:2. 2 C *5:14, 15. T *2:11-14. **O foolish**. Ps 74:18. Je 4:22. 5:21. Ga *3:1-3. **and unwise**. ♪144D, Ge +40:23. **thy father**. ver. 18. Ex 4:22. Is *63:16. Ml 1:6. Lk 15:18-20. Jn 8:41. Ro 8:15. 1 C 1:21. Ga 3:26. 4:6. 1 J 3:1. **hath bought**. Ex 15:16. Ps 74:2. 78:54. Is 43:3, 4. Ac +√20:28. 1 C 6:19, 20. 7:23. 2 P 2:1. **made thee**. ♪144C1, Ge +21:1. ver. 15. Jb 10:8. Ps 95:6. 100:3. 149:2. Is 27:11. 43:7. 44:2. or, advanced. 1 S 12:6. Est 6:6. **established**. Ps *55:22.

7. **Remember**. Ex *13:14. Jb 20:4. Ps 44:1. 77:5. 119:52. Is 51:1-3. 63:11. La 5:21. **days**. Is *63:9. Je 2:20. Am 9:11. Mi *5:2. 7:14. Ml 3:4. **of old**. Heb. *olam*, Ge +6:4. **many generations**. Heb. generation and generation. ♪84, Ge +6:17. Ps 10:6mg. 77:8mg. Jl 2:2mg. **ask**. Dt 4:32. Ex 12:26. 13:14. Jg 6:13. Jb 8:8-10. Ps 44:1. 77:5, 6, 11, 12. 78:3, 4. Is 46:9.

8. **most High**. Ge +√14:18. Nu 24:16. Ps +7:17. 50:14. 82:6. 91:1. 92:8. Is 14:14. Da 4:17, 24, 25. 5:18. *7:18, 22, 25, 27. Ac 7:48. **divided**. Dt 2:5, 9. 21:16. Ge 10:5, 25, 32. 11:9. Ps 115:16. Pr *16:33. Am 9:7. Zc 9:2. Ac 15:18. *17:26. **inheritance**. Ps 115:16. **separated**. Ge *11:8, 9. Ex 33:16. Nu 23:9. **he set**. Ge 10:15-19. 15:18-21. **bounds**. Dt 2:5, 19. Ps 48:2. 100:1. Ro 11:12-16. **according to**. Ge 15:18. Ex 23:31. Ps 105:44.

9. **the Lord's**. Dt 7:6. 26:18, 19. Ex 15:16. 19:5, 6. 1 S 10:1. Ps 78:71. 135:4. Is 43:21. Je 10:16. 51:19. Am 3:2. Ep 1:18. T 2:14. 1 P 2:9, 10. **portion**. Ex 34:9. 1 K 8:51, 53. Ps 16:5. Is 19:24, 25. La 3:24. **his people**. ver. +*43. Ps +33:12. **lot**. Heb. cord. or, line. ♪121B, Jsh 17:14. S#2256h. Dt 3:4 (region), 13. Jsh 2:15. 17:5 (portion), 14. 19:9, 29. 1 Ch 16:18mg. Jb 18:10 (snare). 21:17 (sorrows). *36:8. Ps 16:6. 18:4, 5 (sorrows). 78:55. 105:11mg. 116:3. 119:61 (bands). 140:5. Pr 5:22. Ec 12:6. Is 5:18. 13:8 (sorrows). 26:17 (pangs). *66:7 (pain). Je 13:21. 22:23. 38:6. Ezk 27:24. 47:13. Ho 13:13. Am 7:17. Mi *2:5, 10 (destruction). Zp 2:5 (coast), 6, 7. Zc 2:1. **his inheritance**. Dt 10:9. Ex 19:5. Jsh 13:33. 1 S +√10:1. Ps 47:4. 74:2. 78:71. Lk +*1:32, 33.

10. **found**. Dt 8:15, 16. 2 S 9:4. Ne 9:19-21. Ps 107:4, 5. SS 8:5. Je 2:6. Ho 13:5. Jn *15:16. **desert**. Dt 26:5. Ps 107:4. SS 3:6. 8:5. Je 2:6. Ezk 16:4. Ho 9:10. *13:9. **waste**. or, void. Ge 1:2. **howling**. Is 15:8. 43:20. Mi 1:8. **wilderness**. Dt 8:15. Nu 21:20mg. Jb 12:24. Je 2:6. Ho 13:5. Ac 7:38. **led him**. or, compassed him. S#5437h. Ex 13:18. Jsh 6:3. Ne 9:19. Ps 7:7. 26:6. 32:7, 10. 55:10. 59:6, 14. SS 3:2. Je *31:22. Jon 2:3, 5. Ezk 47:2. **about**. Ex 13:21, 22. Ps 32:7, 8. 107:7. **he instructed**. Dt 4:36. Ne 9:20. Ps 32:7-10. 147:19, 20. Ro 2:18. 3:2. **he kept**. Ps 17:8. Pr 7:2. Is *26:3. Zc 2:8. Ph *4:7. 1 P 5:7. **him**. ♪76, Ge +13:6. **apple**. lit. *little man*. Ps *17:8. Pr 7:2, 9h. 20:20h.

11. **an eagle**. Ex 19:4. Is 31:5. +*40:31. 46:4. 63:9. Ho 11:3. Mt ◐+*24:28. Lk ◐+*17:37n. Re 12:14. **nest**. ♪121J11. Metonymy of the Subject B577. Nests are put for the birds in them. **stirreth**. Dt 1:6, 7.

1 Ch 5:26. **fluttereth**. Ge 1:2. Mt *23:37. **beareth**. Ex 19:4. Is 31:5. *40:31. *46:4. *63:9. Ho 11:3. **wings**. ♪22G2, Ps 91:4. Jb 39:13. Ps 68:13. *91:4.

12. **the Lord**. Dt 1:31. Ne 9:12. Ps 27:11. 78:14, 52, 53. 80:1. 103:13, 14. 136:16. Is 46:4. 63:9-13. **lead him**. ♪76, Ge +13:6. Dt 1:31. Ex 13:17, 21. 15:13. Ps 23:1. Is 48:17. **no strange**. Dt 31:16. Ex 12:43 (❋S#5236h). Le 22:25. Jsh 24:20, 23. **god**. Ps 81:9, 10. Is 43:11, 12. 44:7, 8.

13. **ride on**. Dt 33:26, 29. Ex 14:8. Is 58:14. Ezk 36:2. Ho 10:11. i.e. subdue or conquer. Ps 45:4. 66:12. Re 6:2. 19:11, 14. **high**. Ps 18:33. Ep=2:6. **places**. Dt 1:28. 2:36. 33:29. Is *58:14. Hab 3:19. **eat**. Dt 8:8. Ps 81:16. **honey**. ♪171I7, Ex +3:8. Ex 3:8. Jb 29:6. Ps 81:16. Is 48:21. Ezk 27:17. **and oil**. Dt 8:8. 28:40. 33:24. Ge +*28:18. **flinty**. Dt 8:15. Jb 28:9. Ps 114:8. Is 50:7. The olive trees grow and fructify most in rocky or hilly places (Matthew Poole).

14. **Butter**. Ge 18:8. Jg 5:25. 2 S 17:29. Jb 20:17. 29:6. Is 7:15, 22. **kine**. Ge 12:6. **sheep**. Ge 4:2. **fat of lambs**. Le 3:9, 10. **of Bashan**. Nu +21:33. 32:4, 33. Ps *22:12. Ezk 39:18. Am 4:1. Mi 7:14. **goats**. Ge 31:10, 12. **the fat of kidneys of wheat**. i.e. with the finest of the grains or kernels of wheat, compared to kidneys for their shape, and plumpness, and largeness (Matthew Poole). Ps 81:16. 147:14. **blood**. ♪46A, Le +26:30. Wine not mixed with water, but pure as it comes from the grape, which was of a red or bloody color (Poole). Ge 49:10-12. Ps 75:8. 104:15. Is 27:2. Mt 26:28, 29. Lk 22:18. Jn 6:55, 56.

15. **Jeshurun**. i.e. *upright*, ❋S#3484h. Dt 33:5, 26. Is 44:2. **kicked**. 1 S 2:29. Ac 9:5. **waxen fat**. Dt 31:20. Jb 15:27. Ps 17:10. 73:7. 119:70. Is 6:10. Je 5:28. Ac 28:27. Ro 2:4, 5. **thick**. 1 K 12:10. 2 Ch 10:10. **covered with**. Jb 15:27. Ps 17:10. 73:7. 119:70. **forsook God**. Dt 6:10-12. 8:10-14. 31:16, 20. Jg 2:11, 12. 10:6. 2 Ch 7:22. 26:15. Ne 9:25, 26. Is 1:4. Je 2:5. 5:7, 28, 29. 15:6. Ho 13:6. **made him**. ver. 6. Is 51:13. **lightly esteemed**. Je 14:21. Mi 7:6. Na 3:6. **the Rock**. See on ver. 4. 2 S 22:47. Ps 18:46. 89:26. 95:1.

16. **provoked**. ♪132G, Ge +3:19. Dt 5:9. 1 K 14:22, 23. Ps *78:58. Na 1:1, 2. 1 C 10:22. **to jealousy**. ♪22B, Ex +20:5. Ex 34:14. Ps 78:58. Pr 6:34. SS 8:6, 7. Ezk 8:3-6. **with strange**. Jg 2:12. **abominations**. Dt 7:25. Le 18:27. 2 K 23:13. Ezk 8:17. **anger**. Ps 106:29.

17. **sacrificed unto devils**. Le +17:7. Ps 106:37, 38. 1 C ▶10:20. 1 T 4:1. Re 9:20. **not to God**. Ps 90:2. or, which were not God. ver. 21. Je 10:15. 1 C *8:4. 10:19. **to gods**. Dt 28:64. Is 44:8. Je 2:26-28. **knew not**. Ps 1:6. Ho 13:5. **to new gods**. Jg 5:8. Da ◐7:9. Mt ◐19:8. Ac 7:42, 43.

18. **the Rock**. ver. 4, 15. Is 17:10. 44:8mg. **unmindful**. Dt 8:19. Is 17:10. Je 2:32. **forgotten**. Dt 6:12. 8:11, 14, 19. Ps 9:17. 44:20-22. 106:21. Is 17:10. 22:10, 11. Je 2:32. 3:21. Ho 8:14. **formed thee**. Dt 4:34. Mt 24:8.

19. **And when**. Le 26:11. Jg 2:14. Ps *5:4, 5. 10:3. 78:59. *106:40. Am *3:2, 3. Zc 11:8. Re *3:16. **abhorred them**. or, despised. Le 26:30. Ps 10:3. 106:40. Pr *22:14. La 2:6. Am 6:8. **provoking**. Je 44:21-23. of his sons. Ps *82:6, 7. Is *1:2. Je 11:15.

20. **I will hide**. Dt 31:17, 18. Jb 13:24. 34:29. Ps 30:7. 104:29. Is 64:7. Je 18:17. Ho *5:15. 9:12. Ro 11:20. He 3:19. **their end**. Dt *31:29. **a very**. See on ver. 5. Is 65:2-5. Mt 11:16, 17. Lk 7:31, 32. **froward**. Pr 2:12, 14. 6:14. 8:13. 10:31, 32. 16:28, 30. 23:33.

children. 2 Ch 20:20. Pr 13:17. 14:5. 20:6. Is 7:9. 26:2. *30:9. Mt 17:17. Mk 9:19. Lk 18:8. 2 Th 3:2. He *11:6. **no faith.** Is 30:9. Lk 18:8.

21. **moved me.** ver. 16. Ps 78:58. Je 8:19. **jealousy.** ſ132D, Ge +19:25. ſ22B, Ex +20:5. **not God.** ver. 17mg. Ps 96:5. Is *44:10. 1 C *8:4. 10:20. or, no gods. Ac 19:26. Ga 4:8. **with their vanities.** ſ121N1, Ge +31:54. 1 S 12:21. 1 K 16:13, 26. 2 K 17:15. Ps 31:6. Is 41:29. 44:9. Je 2:5. 8:19. 10:8. 14:22. 51:18. Jon *2:8. Zc 10:12. Ac 14:15. **I will.** Ho 1:10. 2:23. Ro 9:25. ▶10:19. 11:11-14, 25. 1 P 2:9, 10. **move them.** Mt 21:43-46. Ac 11:2, 3. *22:21-23. 1 Th 2:15, 16. **foolish nation.** Ps 74:18. Je 10:8. Ro *1:22. 1 C 12:2.

22. **For a fire.** Dt 4:24. 29:20. Nu 16:35. Ps 18:7, 8. 21:9. 83:14. 97:3. Is 66:15, 16. Je 4:4. 15:14. 17:4. La 2:3. 4:11. Ezk 30:8. 36:5. Am 2:2, 5. Na 1:6. Ml 4:1, 2. Mk 9:43-48. 2 Th *1:8. He 12:29. Ju 7. **mine anger.** Ps 7:11. **shall burn.** or, hath burned. **lowest.** Ps 63:9. 86:13. 88:6. Is 30:33. Am *9:2. Zp 3:8. Mt +√10:28. 18:9. 23:33. Ep 4:9. +❋S#8482h: Ge 6:16 (lower). Ex 19:17 (nether). Jsh 15:19. Jg 1:15. 2 S 24:6 (Tahtim-hodshi; mg, nether land, etc.). Ne 4:13 (lower). Jb 41:24. Ps *63:9 (lower parts). *86:13 (lowest). 88:6. 139:15. Is 44:23. La 3:55. Ezk 26:20. 31:14, 16, 18. 32:18, 24. **hell.** Heb. *sheol*, Ge +37:35. 2 S 22:6. Jb 11:8. +26:6. Ps +16:10. Is30:33. +66:24. **shall consume.** or, hath consumed. Dt 29:23. Le 26:20. Is 24:6, 19, 20. Am 7:4. Zp 3:8. **foundations.** Jb 9:5, 6. Ps 46:2. 144:5. Is 54:10. Mi 1:4. Na 1:5. Hab 3:10. **mountains.** Ps 83:14.

23. **heap mischiefs.** Dt 28:15. Le 26:18, 24. Is 24:17, 18. 26:15. 40:2. Je 15:2, 3. Ezk 14:21. Mt 24:7, 8. 1 Th 2:16. **spend.** Ps 7:12, 13. La 3:13. Ezk 5:16. **arrows.** Ps 18:14. 45:5. Zc 9:14. ſ22D5B. Anthropomorphism B893. Bow and arrow are attributed to God. For other instances of this figure see ver. 42. Jb 6:4. Ps 21:12. 38:2. 64:7. La 2:4. 3:12, 13. Zc 9:14.

24. **burnt.** Dt 28:53. Je 14:18. La 4:4-9. 5:10. **burning heat.** Heb. burning coals. ❋S#7565h. Dt 28:22. Jb 5:7h. Ps 18:12-14. 76:3h (arrows). 78:48h. 120:4. SS 8:6h. Hab 3:5h. **destruction.** Ps 91:6. Is 28:2. Ho *13:14. **the teeth.** Le 26:22. Je *15:3, 4. 16:4. Ezk 5:16, 17. 14:15, 21. **of beasts.** Ps 80:13. **poison.** ver. 33. Jb 6:4. Ps 58:4. 140:3. **serpents.** Ge 3:14. 49:15, 17. Nu 21:6. Is 8:17. Am 9:3. or, fearful things. Jb 32:6. Mi *7:17.

25. **sword.** Le 26:36, 37. 1 Ch *21:11, 12. Ezr 9:7. Is 30:16. Je 9:16, 21. La 1:20. Ezk 7:15. 2 C 7:5. **within.** Heb. from the chambers. Ge 43:30. Je 9:21. Ezk 7:15. **destroy.** Heb. bereave. Ge 27:45. 42:36. 43:14. 1 S 15:33. Je 50:9mg. Ezk 14:15mg. Ho 9:14mg. **the young.** 2 Ch 36:17. Ps 78:62, 63. Je 9:21. La 2:19-22. 4:4. Am 4:10. **virgin.** S#1330h, Ge +24:16. **suckling.** Dt +29:11n. S#3243h. 33:19h. Nu 11:12. 1 S 15:3. 22:19. Ps *8:2. SS 8:1. Is *11:8. Je 44:7. La 2:11. 4:4. Jl *2:16. **gray hairs.** ❋S#7872h. Ge 15:15 (old age). 25:8. Ge 42:38. 44:29, 31. Le 19:32 (hoary head). Jg 8:32. Ru 4:15. 1 K 2:6, 9. 1 Ch 29:28. Jb 41:32. Ps 71:18 (greyheaded). *92:14. Pr 16:31. 20:29. Is *46:4. Ho 7:9.

26. **scatter.** Dt 28:25, 37, 64. Le 26:33, 38. Is 63:16. Ezk 20:13, 14, 23. Lk *21:24. **cease.** Dt 9:14. Jb 18:17. Ps 34:16.

27. **not.** Ps 115:1. **I feared.** Dt 1:17. 18:22. Jsh +*7:9. Ezk 20:9. 36:22, 23. This is spoken of course after the manner of men (Young). **wrath.** Is 37:28,

29. **lest their.** 1 S 12:22. Is 37:28, 29, 35. 47:7. Je 19:4. La 1:9. Ezk 20:13, 14, 20-22. Zc 1:14, 15. **they should.** Dt 9:28. Ex 32:12. Nu 14:15, 16. Jsh 7:9. Ps 115:1, 2. *140:8. Is 10:8-15. 37:10, 12-23. Da 4:30-37. **Our hand,** etc. or, Our high hand and not the Lord hath done all this. **high.** Ps 44:3. 115:2. 137:7-9. *140:8. Je 50:17, 18. **hath not.** Is 10:13. Je ◐40:2, 3.

28. **a nation.** ver. 6. Jb 28:28. Ps 81:12. Pr 1:7. Is *27:11. 29:14. Je *4:22. 8:9. Ho 4:6. Mt 13:14, 15. Ro 11:25. 1 C 3:19. **counsel.** Ps 106:13. *107:11. Lk 7:30. **neither.** Is 6:10. Mt 13:15. **understanding.** ver. 6. Is 1:3. 1 C *2:14.

29. **O that.** ſ124, Dt +5:29. Ps 81:13. 107:15, *43. Is 48:18, 19. Ho 14:9. Lk 19:41, *42. 20:41-44. Ro 16:19. **wise.** Ps 107:43. Pr 1:5. 27:11. Lk 19:42. **understood.** Dt +*29:9h. Ps 47:7. 101:2. **they would consider.** Pr +6:6. Is 10:3. 47:7. Je 5:31. 17:11. La 1:9. Lk 12:20. 16:19-25. 1 T 4:15.

30. **one chase.** Le 26:8. Jsh 23:10. Jg 7:22, 23. 1 S 14:15-17. 2 Ch 24:24. Is 30:17. **sold them.** Jg 2:14. 3:8. 1 S *12:9. Ps 44:12. Is 50:1. 52:3. Mt 18:25. **shut them.** Jg 6:1. Jb 11:10. 16:11. Ps 31:8. Je 21:7.

31. **their rock.** Ex 14:25. Nu 23:8, 23. Jsh 5:1. 1 S *2:2. 4:8. Ezr 1:3. 6:9-12. 7:20, 21. Je 40:3. Da 2:47. 3:29. 6:26, 27. **our Rock.** ſ22L3. Anthropomorphism B897. God is figured by things which pertain to the earth: a rock. For other instances of this figure see Ps 18:2. 31:2mg, 3. 42:9. 73:26mg. Is 26:4mg. Mt 16:18. **our enemies.** 1 S 4:8. Je 40:3. Mk 1:24, +25.

32. **of the vine of Sodom.** Is 5:1, 2. or, worse than the vine of Sodom, etc. Proverbially worthless. (ſ138A, Paroemia; or, Proverb. Ge +10:9.) Is 1:10. Je 2:21. La 4:6. Ezk 16:45-51. Mt 11:24. **fields of Gomorrah.** Which were barren and useless. **grapes of gall.** Dt +29:18. La 3:15, 19. Is 5:4. Am 5:7. 6:12. He *12:15.

33. **the poison.** ver. 24. Jb 20:14-16. Ps 58:4. 140:3. Je 8:14mg. Ro 3:13. **dragons.** Ge 1:21. Ex 7:9, 10, 12. Ps *74:13. **venom.** Dt *29:18. **asps.** Jb 20:14, 16. Ps 58:4.

34. **laid up.** Jb 14:17. Je *2:22. Ho 13:12. Ro 2:5. 1 C 4:5. Re 20:12, 13. **treasures.** ſ22D5o, Dt +28:12.

35. **To me.** T#248. ver. 41, *43. Ps *94:1. Pr 24:29. Na *1:2, 6. Ro *12:19, 21. 13:4. He +*10:30 (T#558). **belongeth.** ſ63K, Ge +37:13. **their foot.** Ps 9:15. *73:17-19. Pr *4:19. Is 6:21. *13:16. 1 P *2:8. **shall slide.** Ps 38:16. *94:18. **for the day.** 2 P *2:3. **calamity.** 2 S *22:19. Jb 18:12. *21:17. Is 2:10-21. Je 10:15. Lk 19:44. Re 22:10, 11. **the things.** Is 5:19. *30:12, 13. 60:22. Hab *2:3. Lk *18:7, 8. 2 P *2:3. *3:8-10. **that shall come.** or, prepared. ❋S#6264h. Est 3:14 (ready). 8:13. Jb 3:8. 15:24. Is 10:13 (treasures). **haste.** Nu 32:17 (ready). Jb 20:2.

36. **For the.** Ps 7:8. 50:4-6. 96:13. 135:14. **shall judge.** i.e. *shall plead their cause.* Ps 7:8. 10:18. Is 1:17. 11:4. Je 5:28. *22:16. **repent.** Ge 27:42h (comfort himself). 37:35h (comforted). Nu *23:19. Jg 2:18. 10:15, 16. Ps 85:1-3. 90:13. 106:45. 119:52h (comforted). 135:14. Je 31:20. Jl 2:13, 14. Am 7:3, 6. **power.** Heb. hand. ſ121BA. Metonymy of the Cause B547. The hand is put for the actions performed by it. For other instances of this figure see 1 S 22:17. 2 S 3:12. 14:19. 1 K 10:29mg. Ps 7:3. Is 1:15. Of the hand as being the seat of power. Jb 1:12mg. Ps 79:8. 85:25n. 88:3, 4. Is 57:10. 2 C 12:10. **none.** 1 K 14:10. 21:21. 2 K 9:8. 14:26. **left.** 2 K 25:12.

37. **Where**. Jg 10:14. 2 K 3:13. Je 2:28. **rock**. ✒60A, Ge +3:22. ver. 31.

38. **Which**. Ex ●34:13. Ps *106:28. 1 C 10:20. **eat the fat**. Ge 4:4. Ex 23:18. Le 21:21. Ps 50:13. Eze 16:18, 19. Ho 2:2. Zp 2:11. **wine**. Ho 2:8. 1 C 10:21. **drink offerings**. Ge 35:14. Ex 29:40. **let them**. Jg *10:14. Je 2:28. **your protection**. Heb. an hiding for you. lit. *secret place*, but the original word is not found elsewhere. Am 9:2.

39. **I, even I**. Ps 102:27. Is *41:4. 45:5, 18, 22. 46:4. *48:12. Zp 2:15. He 1:12. Re 1:11. 2:8. **am he**. Compare LXX (ego eimi) w Jn 8:24, 58. Jn 13:19 w Is 43:10. 46:4. *44:6, 8. ●47:8. **no god**. Dt ●*4:35. +6:4. Is 45:√5, 18, 22. **with me**. Jn ●√1:1. **I kill**. or, put to death. i.e. *I am the cause of death to every one* (Young). 1 S *2:6. 2 K *5:7. Jb 5:18. Ps 68:20. Is 43:13. Ho 6:1. Am +√3:6. Jn *8:24. Re 1:17, 18. **make alive**. i.e. I give, preserve, or restore life. 1 S +*2:6. Is +*26:19n. Je *31:17. **I wound**. 2 Ch 21:18. Ps 51:8. Je ●8:11. Ho 6:1. **I heal**. Ex +15:26. Nu 12:13. Ps *103:3. Je *17:14. Ho 6:1. **neither**. Jb 10:7. Ps 50:22. Is 43:13. Mi 5:8. **deliver**. Is 43:13. Jn ●10:28.

40. **I lift**. ✒22A14.8K, Ex +6:8. The usual form of an oath. Ge 14:22. Ex 6:8. Nu 14:28-30. Is 45:23. Je 4:2. He 6:*13, 17, 18. Re 10:5, 6. **live for ever**. Ps *90:2. Is 49:18. Je 22:24. 46:18. Ezk 5:11. 14:16. 16:48. 17:16, 19. 18:3. 20:3. *33:11. 34:8. 35:6, 11. Zp 2:9. Jn 14:19. 1 T 1:17. 6:15, 16. Re 10:5, 6. **for ever**. Heb. *olam*, Ex +12:24.

41. **whet**. or, sharpen. Dt *6:7mg. Ps 7:12. 45:5. 64:3. 120:4. 140:3. Pr 25:18. Is 5:28. 27:1. *34:5, 6. *66:16. Ezk 21:9-15, 20. Zp 2:12. Re 19:11-19. **glittering**. or, brightness of. or, lightning. Ex 19:16. 2 S 22:15. **sword**. Zc 13:7. Re 19:15. ✒22D5D. Anthropomorphism B893. A sword is attributed to God. For other instances of this figure see Jg 7:20. Ps 17:13. Is 27:1. 34:5, 6. Ezk 21:9. Zc 13:7. **on judgment**. Na 1:3. **I will**. See on ver. 35. Is 1:24. 59:18. 66:6. Na 1:2. **render vengeance**. Is 34:8. +*61:2. Ezk 25:14. Na +*1:2. **them that hate**. Dt 5:9. 7:10. See on Ex 20:5. 2 Ch *19:2. Ps 68:1. 81:15. 83:2. 139:21. Jn 15:23, 24. Ro 1:30. 8:7. 2 T 3:4.

42. **make mine**. See on ver. 23. Ps 45:5. 68:23. Is 34:6-8. Je 46:10. Ezk 35:6-8. 38:21, 22. **arrows**. ✒22D5B, ver. 23. **drunk**. or, merry. ✒155D, Ge +4:10. Ge 43:34. i.e. *it is satiated with blood*. **blood**. ✒132D, Ge +19:25. **my sword**. Is 34:5, 6. Je 12:12. 46:10, 14. **devour**. 2 S 2:26. 11:25. 18:8. Is *1:20. Je 2:30. Ezk 36:14. Na 2:13. 3:15. Zc 11:1. **slain**. or, pierced. Ge 34:27. **revenges**. Jsh 10:17, 26. 1 S 15:33. Ps 68:21. ✒24J. Antimereia: a noun for an adjective B497. For other instances of this figure see Le 19:24. 2 S 23:17. Ps 99:4. Ezk 2:7mg. 1 C 14:12mg, *32. Ga 1:14. He 12:11. 1 J 5:6. or, freeman. Jg 5:2. The word *paroth*, rendered *revenges*, a sense in which it never seems to be used, has rendered this passage very obscure. As the word *paira* signifies the "hair of the head," both in Hebrew and in Arabic, Mr. Parkhurst and others render *mairosh paroth*, "from the hairy head;" but to have this sense, the words should rather have been *mipparoth rosh*, according to the Hebrew idiom. The word *faron*, in Arabic, however, denotes a *prince* or *chief*; and the words may be literally rendered, with the LXX, "from the head of the chiefs of the enemies." The *hyperbaton* (✒101. Hyperbaton; or Transposition: the placing of a word out of its usual

order in a sentence. For other instances of this figure see Is 34:4. Je 14:1. 17:3. Mt 5:3-11. *7:13. Lk 16:11. Jn √1:1. 4:19, *24. 6:60. 7:4. 9:31. *17:5. Ac 17:23. Ro 1:3. 5:8. 8:18. 9:13. 12:19. 14:1. 1 C 3:9. 1 C 13:1. 2 C *13:5. Ep 6:8. 1 T 1:15. 3:1, *16. 4:9. 6:5, 12. 2 T 2:11. T 3:8. He 6:16. 7:4. 10:30. 1 P 2:7. *3:21. 1 J *2:24, 27. Re 13:8) or transposition of words from their grammatical order, is very observable in this verse; the third member forming a continuation of the first, and the fourth of the second. Jb 13:24. Je 30:14. La 2:5. ✒24J. Antimereia: or, Exchange of Parts of Speech; here, a noun is put for an adjective. "The revenges of the enemy" is put for "the revengeful enemy," just as at Ge 17:5, "a multitude of nations" is put for "many nations," as Ro ▶4:17; Ge 45:22, "changes of raiment" is put for changeable raiment; and Ps 99:4, "the king's strength" is put for the strong and mighty king. For other instances of this figure see Le 19:24. Ac 10:45 (circumcision). 11:2 (circumcision). Ro 2:26 (uncircumcision). Ro 4:9 (uncircumision). 1 C 14:12, 32. 16:22 (anathema). Ga 1:14. Ep 2:11 (uncircumcision). Col 3:11 (uncircumcision). 4:11 (circumcision). T 1:10 (circumcision). He 12:11. 1 J *5:6.

43. **Rejoice**. Ex 18:9. Ps 67:3-7. ch. 100. Is 2:2-4. or, Praise his people, ye nations; or, Sing ye. Is +*35:10. Ro ▶15:10. **O ye nations**. Ge 12:3. 1 K 8:43. Ps 22:27. Is 11:10. 19:23, 25. Lk 2:10, 11, 32. Ac 13:47, 48. Ro 3:29. 15:9-13. Re 5:9, 10. **with**. Le 26:42. Ro *12:15. **for he**. T#237. Ps 28:+4, 5. *48:11. 58:9, *10. 97:8. 136:1, 10, 11. Je 11:19, +*20. Ezk 5:13. Zp +3:14 (T#88). Lk +23:41 (T#571). **avenge**. See on ver. 35. 2 K 9:7. Jb 13:24. Je 13:14. La 2:5. Lk *18:7, 8. 19:27, 43, 44. 21:22-24. Ro *12:19. Re *6:10. 15:2, 4. 18:2, 20. 19:2. **render vengeance**. ver. 41. Mi 5:15. Lk 21:22. **will be merciful**. Dt 21:8mg. Ex 29:33. Nu +*35:33. 2 Ch 30:18. Ps 65:3. Ps 79:9. Is 6:7. +*27:9. +*41:9. √54:7, 8. +*55:3. Da +√9:24n. Jl *3:21. Mi +*7:18, 20. Hab *3:2. Zc √10:6. √13:1. or, pardon. lit. cover. Ge *6:14h (pitch). 32:20h (appease). Ex 30:10h (make an atonement). 2 Ch *30:18. Ps 78:38 (forgave). Pr 16:14. Da 9:24h (reconciliation). or, purge. Ps 65:3. 79:9. **unto his land**. Le +*25:23. Dt 11:12. Jsh 22:19. 2 Ch 7:20. √20:7. Ps *85:1. Is +*19:25. +*60:21n. Je 2:7. Ezk +*38:16. Ho 9:3. Jl 2:18. **his people**. ver. *9. Dt 7:6. 14:2. 26:18. Ex *19:5. 2 Ch √20:7. Ps 83:3. Is 1:24-27. *25:8. Ezk *38:14. Jl 2:18. Am *3:2. Lk *2:32. Ro 11:15, 26.

44. **spake**. See on Dt 31:22, 30. Re 15:3. **Hoshea**. or Joshua. Dt 31:23. Nu 11:28. See on Nu 13:8, 16.

46. **Set your hearts**. i.e. Think seriously upon. See on Dt 6:6, 7. 11:18. 1 Ch 22:19. Jb 22:22. *23:12. Ps 37:31. 40:8. *119:11. Pr 3:1-4. Is 51:7. Je *15:16. *31:33. Ezk 40:4. 44:5. Lk 9:44. 2 C 3:3. He *2:1. **words**. Jsh *1:8. Ps 32:8. Mt 4:4. Jn 5:24. +√5:39. 6:63. 15:3. Ac *17:11, 12. Ro *1:16. √10:17. Col 1:5, 6. *3:16. 1 Th 1:5. *2:13. 2 T *2:15. +√3:15, 16. 4:2. He 11:6. Ja 1:18. **command your children**. Dt 4:9. 6:7. 11:19. Jsh 24:15. Ps 78:1-8. Pr *22:6. Ep 6:4.

47. **not a vain**. Dt +30:19. Le 18:5. Pr 3:1, 2, 18, 22. *4:22. Is *45:19. Mt *6:33. Ro 10:5, 6. 1 T 4:8. 6:6-8. 2 T *3:16. He 4:12. 1 P 3:10-12. 2 P 1:3, 16. Re 22:14. **your life**. ✒121G, Ge +31:1. Dt 5:16, *33. *8:3. 30:20. Le 18:5. Ga 3:12. **prolong**. Dt +*4:40. *33:25. **go over Jordan**. Dt +30:19. 31:13.

48. **the Lord spake**. A.M. 2553. B.C. 1451. An.

Ex. Is. 40. Adar. Nu 27:12, 13. **selfsame.** Ge 7:13. 17:23. Ex 12:17. Le 23:14. Jsh 5:11.

49. **mountain Abarim.** Dt 34:1. Nu 21:11. 27:12, 13. See on Nu 33:47, 48. **Nebo.** Dt 3:27. 34:1. Nu 32:38. *Nebo* was a ridge or top of the mountains of Abarim. The whole tract of mountains was called *Abarim,* Nu 33:47, whereof one of the highest was called *Nebo,* Dt 32:49, and the top of that, *Pisgah,* Dt 34:1 (Matthew Poole). **and behold.** Dt 34:2-5. Is 33:17. 2 C 5:1. **possession.** Ge 10:19. 15:18. Jsh 1:3.

50. **And die.** Dt 34:5. **be.** *J*96B, Ge +20:7. **gathered unto.** Dt +*31:16n. Ge 15:15. +*25:8n, 9, 17. 35:29. 49:29, 33. Nu 20:24, 26. 27:13. 31:2. Da 12:13. **as Aaron.** Nu 20:24-29. 33:38.

51. **ye trespassed.** Dt 3:23-27. Nu 20:11, 12, 24. 27:14. Ps *106:32, 33. **Meribah-Kadesh.** *or,* strife at Kadesh. S#6946h. Not the *Meribah* referred to in Ex 17:7, but in Nu 20:13, 14. **Zin.** Nu 13:21n. **because ye.** See on Le 10:3. 22:32. 1 K 13:21-26. Is 6:3. 8:13. Ezk 20:41. Mt 6:9. 1 P 4:17.

52. **thou shalt see.** ver. 49. Dt 3:27. 34:1-4. Nu 27:12. He 11:13, 39.

DEUTERONOMY 33

Moses records the displays of the Lord's majesty, and his love to Israel, 1-5. He pronounces a prophetical blessing on each of the tribes, 6-25; and shows in general their felicity as the people of God, 26-29.

1. **the blessing.** Ge 27:4, 27-29. 49:1, 28. Nu 6:23-27. Lk=24:50, 51. Jn 14:27. 16:33. ch. 17. **the man.** Jsh 14:6. Jg 13:6. 1 S 2:27. 9:6, 7. 1 K 13:1, 6. Ps 90, title,mg. 1 T 6:11. 2 T 3:17. 2 P 1:21.

2. **The Lord came.** Ps +√68:7. Is *63:1-4. Hab +*3:3. Ac +*1:11. **from Sinai.** Ex 19:18-20. Jg 5:4, 5. Ps *68:7-10, 21, 23. Je +*31:2. Hab +*3:3. **rose up.** 1 C 15:20. **from Seir.** Jg 5:4, 5. **from mount Paran.** Hab +*3:3. **came with.** Zc +*14:5. Mk +*8:38. Jn +*14:2, 3. Ro +*8:19. 1 Th +*4:16, 17. 2 Th +*2:1. **ten thousands.** Ps 68:7, 17. Da 7:9, 10. Ac 7:53. Ga 3:19. 2 Th 1:7. He 2:2. Ju +*14. Re 5:11. **saints.** Ps +*149:5-9. Zc +*14:5. **a fiery law.** Heb. a fire of law. Dt 5:22. Da 7:9, 10. Mt +*3:11, 12. 2 C *3:7, 9. Ga 3:10, 19. He 2:2. 12:20, 29. 2 P +*3:7. **for.** Jn 15:14.

3. **he loved.** Dt 7:7, 8. 10:15. Ex 19:5, 6. Ps 47:4. 147:19, 20. Je 31:3. Ho 11:1. Ml 1:2. Jn 13:1. Ro 9:11-13. Ep 2:4, 5. 1 J 4:19. **all his saints.** Dt 7:6. 1 S 2:9. Ps 31:15. 50:5. 148:14. +*149:9. Je 32:40. Jn *10:28, 29. 17:11-15. Ro 8:35-39. Col 3:3, 4. 1 P 1:5. **they sat.** 2 S 7:18-27. SS 2:3. Is 30:7. Lk 2:46. *8:35. +*10:39. Ac *22:3. Ep 2:6. **shall receive.** Ps 106:12. Pr 2:1. Lk +*11:28. Jn *8:47. 17:8. Ac 13:7. Ro *10:17. 1 Th 1:6. 4:1.

4. **Moses.** Jn 1:17. 7:19. Ro 3:1, 2. **the inheritance.** Dt 9:26-29. Ps 119:72, 111.

5. **king.** Ge 36:31. Ex 18:16, 19. Nu 16:13-15. Jg 8:22. 9:2. 17:6. Ps 45:1. 72:1. Ac 7:35. **Jeshurun.** See on Dt 32:15. **gathered.** Ac=17:7.

6. **Reuben live.** Ge 17:18. 49:3, 4, 8. Nu 32:31, 32. Jsh 22:1-9. Is 6:13. **not die.** *J*144D, Ge +40:23. **not.** *J*63I1C1, Ge +2:6. **few.** Is +*10:19mg. Je 23:3. Ezk 5:3. Ro 9:27.

7. **Judah.** Ge 49:8-12. He 7:14. Re 22:16. *J*171R, Ex +12:40. Only "Judah" is named in the blessing, but in company with him Simeon is understood. For their inheritance and blessing was one. Jsh 19:1. Jg

1:3. **and bring.** Ge 49:8-12. Jg 1:1, etc. Ps 78:68, 70. Is 11:12-14. Je 3:18. 30:3. Ezk 37:15-22. Ho 1:11. Mi *5:2. Ml *3:1. He 7:14. **let his hands.** 2 S 3:1. 5:1, 19, 24. 1 Ch 5:2. 12:22. 2 Ch 17:12-19. Is *9:7. Re 19:13-16. **and be thou.** 2 S 7:9-12. Ps 2. 20:2. 21:1, 8. 110:1, 2. 146:5. Lk 19:27. 1 C 15:25. Re 20:10-15.

8. **Levi.** Ge 49:5-7. **Let thy.** T#1723. Ex 28:30, 36. Le 8:8. Nu 27:21. 1 S 28:6. Ezr 2:63. Ne 7:65. **Thummim.** Jn=8:12. Col=2:3. **with thy.** Le 21:7. Nu 16:5. 2 Ch 23:6. Ezr 8:28. Ps *16:10. 106:16. He 7:26. Re 3:7. **prove at.** Dt 6:16. 8:2, 3, 16. Ex 17:7. 32:26. Nu 20:13. Ps 81:7.

9. **Who said.** Ex 32:25-29. Le 10:6. 21:11. Nu 25:11-13. Ml 2:5. Mt 10:37. 12:48. 22:16. Lk 14:26. 2 C 5:16. Ga 1:10. 1 Th 2:4. 1 T 5:21. **I have not.** Ge 29:32. 1 Ch 17:17. Jb 37:24. **neither.** Mt=19:29. Lk=14:26. **acknowledge his brethren.** Ex 32:29. Mt 10:37. 3 J 9. **knew.** *J*121C2A2, Ge +39:6. **for they have.** T#672. Nu 23:21. Jb 7:17. +36:7 (T#585). Ps 50:2. +119:1 (T#504). SS 4:7. Is 43:4. 46:13. 62:3, 5. Je 18:18. Ml 2:5-7. Mt *13:43. Lk 7:42, 43, 47. 15:7, 22. Jn +1:12 (T#584). 14:21-23. 15:9, 15. +*17:6. 20:17. Ro 8:29. 1 C +2:9 (T#340). 6:3. 2 C 8:23. Ep 5:+25 (T#94), 26, 27. Col 1:21, 22. He 12:23. Re 1:6. 14:3. 21:9. **observed.** Ml 2:4-6. Mt=28:20. Re 3:8. **kept.** Jn=14:23. Jn +17:6.

10. **They shall teach.** *or,* Let them teach, etc. Dt 17:9-11. 24:8. Le 10:11. 2 Ch 17:8-10. 30:22. Ne 8:1-9, 13-15, 18. 9:4, etc. Je 18:18. Ezk 44:23, 24. Ho 4:6. Ml 2:6-8. Mt 23:2, 3. Jn 21:15, 16. **they shall put incense.** *or,* let them put incense. Ex 30:7, 8. Nu 16:6, 7, 40, 46. 1 S 2:28. 2 Ch 26:18. Ps 141:2. Lk 1:9, 10. 2 C=2:15. He *7:25. *9:24. Re=5:8. 8:3-5. **before thee.** Heb. at thy nose. *J*22A9, Ex +15:8. **whole.** Le 1:9, 13, 17. 9:12, 13. 2 Ch 29:20-35. Ps 51:19. Ezk 43:27. Ro=12:1. 2 P=2:5.

11. **his substance.** Dt 18:1-5. Nu 18:8-20. 35:2-8. Mt=*6:33. Ro=8:32. **accept.** 2 S 24:23. Ps 20:3. 90:17. Ezk 20:40, 41. 43:27. Ml 1:8-10. Ro=14:18. 2 C=5:9. Ph *4:18. **smite.** Is 29:21. Je 15:10. Am 5:10. Mt 10:14, 15. Lk 10:10-12, 16. Ro=8:37. 1 C=*15:57. 1 Th 4:8. **rise not.** Ps 18:37, 38.

12. **Benjamin.** Ge 49:27. **The beloved.** See on ver. 27-29. Jsh 18:11-28. Jg 1:21. 1 K 12:21. 2 Ch 11:1. 15:2. 17:17-19. Ps 45:1. 60:5. 108:6. *127:2. 132:14. Is 5:1. 37:22, 35. 62:4, 5. Je 11:15. Ezk 48:35. **dwell.** Ps *4:8. Is 32:18. **in safety.** Ge ◑+19:30. **cover him.** Ps 91:4. Is 51:16. Mt 3:16, 17. 23:37.

13. **Joseph.** See on Ge 48:5, 9, 15-20. 49:22-26. **Blessed.** Ps=45:7. **his land.** Young notes, comprising Gilead, Bashan, and Samaria. Dt 8:7-10. +*32:43. Ps 65:9-13. **heaven.** Ge 27:28. 49:25. **the dew.** Dt +32:2. Ge 27:28, 29. Jb 29:19. Ps 110:3. Pr 3:20. 19:12. Is 18:4. Ezk 34:26. Ho 14:5. Mi 5:7. Zc 8:12. **deep.** *❋S#8415h, Jon +*2:5. Ge √49:25. Hab 3:10. **coucheth.** *✦S#7257h. Ge 4:7 (lieth). 29:2. 49:14, √25 (lieth). Ex 23:5. Dt 22:6 (sitting). Ezk 29:3. **beneath.** S#8478h. Ge 35:8. Ex 20:4. 32:19. Dt 4:18, 39. 5:8, 8. Jsh 2:11. Jg 7:8. 1 K 4:12. 7:29. *8:23. Jb 18:16. Is *14:9. 51:6. Am 2:9. Matthew Poole notes "the springs of water bubbling out of the earth."

14. **precious things.** ver. 14-16. Dt 28:8. Le 26:4. 2 S 23:4. Ps 65:9-13. 74:16. *84:11. SS 4:13, 16. 7:13. Ml 4:2. Mt *5:45. Ac 14:17. 1 T 6:17. **put forth.** Heb. thrust forth. **moon.** Heb. moons. Ps 8:3. 104:19. Re 22:2.

15. **ancient.** Heb. *kedem*, Mi +*5:2. **chief things.** Ge 49:26. Hab 3:6. Ja 5:7. **lasting.** Le +*25:32.

16. **the earth.** Dt 28:3-5. Ps 24:1. 50:12. 89:11. Je 8:16mg. 1 C 10:26, 28. Ep ●1:3. **the good.** Ex 3:2-4. Mk 12:26. Lk 2:14. Ac 7:30-33, 35. 2 C 12:7-10. **and upon the top.** Ge 37:28, 36. 39:2, 3. 43:32. 45:9-11. See on Ge 49:26. **separated.** He=7:26.

17. **the firstling.** Ge 48:14, 18-20. 1 Ch +*5:1. **his horns.** Nu 23:22. 24:8. Jb 39:9, 10. Ps 22:21. 29:6. 89:17, 24. *92:10. Is 34:7. Mi 4:13. **unicorns.** Heb. an unicorn. **he shall push.** 1 K 22:11. 2 Ch 18:10. Ps 44:5. **the ten thousands.** Ge 48:19. Nu 26:34, 37. Ho 5:3. 6:4. 7:1. **of Ephraim.** Nu 1:33, 35. Ho 11:8, 9.

18. **Zebulun.** Ge 49:18. **Rejoice.** Ge 49:13-15. Jsh 19:10, 11, 17, 22. Jg 4:10. 5:14. 1 Ch 12:32, 33. Ps 89:12. Je 46:18. **going out.** Dt 28:6. Ps *121:8.

19. **call the people.** Is 2:3. Je 50:4, 5. Mi 4:2. Zc 14:16. **they shall.** Ps 4:5. 50:13-15. 51:16, 17. 107:22. He 13:15, 16. 1 P 2:5. **suck of.** Dt 32:13. Is 44:22, 23. 60:3-5, 16. 66:11, 12. **hid.** *144B. Pleonasm B414. Literally, "hidden things hidden of the sand," referring to hidden things of the earth, in contrast with the treasures of the sea. For other instances of this figure see Ps 40:7. Is 33:23. Da 12:2. Ro 1:23. 2 C 5:1. Ep 4:23. 1 Th 2:13. Re 16:19. **in the sand.** ver. ●24. Jsh 7:21, 22.

20. **Blessed.** Ge 9:26, 27. Jsh 13:8, 10, 24-28. 1 Ch 4:10. 12:8, 37, 38. Ps 18:19, 36. **he dwelleth.** 1 Ch 5:18-21. 12:8-14. **lion.** Ge 49:19. **teareth.** Ge 49:27. Ps 149:6-9. Mi 5:8.

21. **Gad.** Jsh 13:24. 1 Ch 5:18, 20, 21. 12:8. **the first part.** Nu 32:1-6, 16, 17, etc. **a portion.** Nu 32:33. Jsh 1:14. 22:4. **lawgiver.** Ge +*49:10. Nu 21:18. Jg 5:14. Ps *60:7. 108:8. Is 33:22. **seated.** Heb. cieled. or, covered. 1 K 6:9. 7:3, 7. Je 22:14. Hg 1:4. **he came.** Nu 32:16, 21. Jsh 4:12, 13. Jg 5:2, 11.

22. **Dan is.** Ge 49:9, 16, 17. Jsh 19:47. Jg 13:2, 24, 25. 14:5, 6, 19. 15:8, 15. 16:30. 18:27. 1 Ch 12:35. **leap.** Jsh 19:47. Jg 18:27.

23. **O Naphtali.** Ge 49:21. Ps 36:8. 90:14. Is 9:1, 2. Je 31:14. Mt 4:13, 16. 11:28. **satisfied.** Ps 22:26. 36:8. Je 50:19, 20. **with favor.** Ps 5:12. **possess.** Jsh 19:32-39. Ph 3:12, 13. 2 P 3:18.

24. **Asher be blessed with children.** Ge +46:17. 49:20. Nu 26:47. Ps 115:15. 128:3, 6. Lk 2:36-38. **let him be.** Pr 3:3, 4. Ec 12:10. Ac 7:10. Ro 14:18. 15:31. **let him dip.** ver. ●19. Dt +32:13n. 1 K 17:12n. Jb *29:6. So indicating that he shall have such plenty of oil, that he may not only wash his face, but his feet also, in it (Matthew Poole). A reference to olive trees and olive oil in great plenty. **oil.** ✣S#8081h. Ge +*28:18. 35:14. Ex 25:6. 27:20. Dt 8:8. 28:40. *32:13n. Jb 29:6. Is +1:6mg. 5:1mg. Ezk 32:14. Ho 2:5. 12:1. Am 6:6. Mi 6:7, 15. Hg 2:12. Mt 26:23, 26.

25. **Thy shoes,** etc. or, Under thy shoes shall be iron. Dt 8:9. Jg 5:21. Lk 15:22. Ro 16:20. Ep 6:15. **and as thy.** 1 K 8:59. 2 Ch 16:9. Ne 6:11. Ps 138:3. Is 27:8. 40:29. *41:10. Mk 13:11. 1 C √10:13. 2 C √12:9, 10. Ep 6:10. Ph *4:13. Col 1:11. He 13:5, 6.

26. **none like.** Ex 15:11. 2 S +7:22. 1 K 8:23. Ps 86:8. Is 40:18, 25. 43:11-13. 86:8. Je 10:6. **Jeshurun.** See on Dt 32:15. **rideth.** *22C18. Anthropomorphism B888. Human actions are attributed to God: riding. For other instances of this figure see Ps *18:10. 68:4, *33, 34. 104:3. Is *19:1. Na 1:3. Hab 3:8.

27. **eternal.** Heb. *kedem*, Mi +5:2. T#212. Ge

+*21:33n. 1 S 15:29. Ps *90:1, 2. 93:2. 102:24-27. Is *9:6. 44:6. 48:12. *57:15. Je *10:10. Mi *5:2. Hab 1:12. Ro +*16:26. 1 T *1:17. 6:15, 16. He *9:14. 13:8. Re 1:11. **refuge.** Ps 9:9. 14:6. *18:2. 27:5. 36:7. 46:*1, 7, 11. 48:3. *57:1, 2. 59:16, 17. 71:3, 7. *91:1, 2, 9, 15. 94:22. Pr *18:10. Is *25:4. 32:2. Je 16:19. Lk 13:34. Ph 3:9. He *6:18. **underneath.** Ge 49:24. Ex ●17:12. Pr *10:25. SS 2:6. Is *26:4. He 13:5. 1 P 1:5. Ju *24. **everlasting.** Heb. *olam*, Ge +17:7. **arms.** Ps 103:17. Is 26:4. *40:28, 29. Je 31:3. 1 Th *2:16, 17. **thrust.** See on Dt *9:3-5. Ex 23:28. Ps 80:8. Jn *10:28, 29. Ro *8:2. 16:20. Re *20:2, 3, 10.

28. **Israel.** *121T3, Ge +9:27. **dwell in safety.** Ex 33:16. Nu 23:9. 1 K 4:25. Is 11:6-9. Je 23:6. 33:16. Ezk 34:25. Mi 4:4. Re 21:27. 22:14, 15. **the fountain.** Dt 8:7, 8. Ps 68:26. Pr 5:15-18. Is 48:1. **corn.** *121D4, Ge +27:28. **and.** *174, Ge +18:27. Ge 27:28. Ps 65:9. 104:16. Ho 2:22. Jl 2:19. **wine.** *121D13, Ge +27:28. **his.** See on ver. 13. Dt 8:7, 8. 11:11. 32:2. Ge 27:28. **dew.** Ps 133:3. Ho 14:5.

29. **Happy.** Dt 4:7, 8. Nu 23:20-24. 24:5. 2 S 7:23. 1 K 10:8. Ps 33:12. 144:15. 146:5. 148:14. Ep 1:3. **who.** Dt 4:7. 2 S 7:23. Ps 147:20. **saved.** Is 12:2. 45:17. 1 T 4:10. **the shield.** *22D5F, Ge +15:1. Ps 5:12. 33:20. 35:1, 2. *84:11, 12. 115:9-11. Pr *30:5. Ep 6:16. **the sword.** Jg 7:20. Ps 7:12. 45:3. Is 27:1. 34:5, 6. 41:2-4. 66:16. Je 12:12. 47:6. Ep 6:17. He *4:12. Re 1:13, 16. 19:21. **found liars.** *or,* subdued. Ge 22:17. 2 S 22:45mg. Ps 18:44mg. 47:3. 66:3mg. 81:15mg. Je 3:10mg. 1 C *15:25, 26. **thou shalt.** Dt 9:3. 32:13. Jsh 10:24, 25. Hab 3:19.

DEUTERONOMY 34

Moses ascends mount Nebo, and views the promised land, 1-4. His death, 5; his burial, 6; and age, 7. Israel's mourning for him thirty days, 8. Joshua succeeds him, 9. The praise of Moses, no prophet arose like to him, 10-12.

1. **Moab.** Ps 108:8. **the mountain.** See on Dt 32:49n. Nu 27:12. 33:47. **Pisgah.** or, the hill. See on Nu 21:20mg. **showed him.** ver. 4. Dt 3:27. Nu 32:33-40. Ezk 40:2. Re 21:10. **Gilead.** Nu 32:29. 1 K 17:1. **Dan.** Ge 14:14. Jsh 19:47. Jg 18:29.

2. **unto the utmost sea.** Dt 11:24. Ex 23:31. Nu 34:6. Jsh 15:12.

3. **the south.** Nu 34:3. **the city of palm.** Jg 1:16. 3:13. 2 Ch 28:15. **Zoar.** Ge 14:2, 8. 19:22. Nu 34:3.

4. **This is the land.** Ge 12:7. 13:15. 15:18-21. 26:3. 28:13. Ps 105:9-11. **I have caused.** Dt 3:26, 27. 32:52. Nu 20:12. Jn 1:17.

5. **So Moses.** Jsh 1:1. Ps 90 title, mg. Ml 4:4. Jn 8:35, 36. 2 T 2:24, 25. He 3:3-6. 2 P 1:1. Re 15:3. **died there.** Dt 31:14. 32:50. Jsh 1:1, 2. **the word.** *121BA, Ge +45:21.

6. **he buried him.** Ju 9. **sepulchre.** S#6900h, *qeburah*, Ge +35:20. **no man knoweth.** Ac ●2:29.

7. **And Moses.** 1 S ●4:18. 1 K ●1:1. ●11:4. **an hundred and twenty.** Dt 31:2. Ps ●90:10. Ac 7:23, 30, 36. **his eye.** Ge 27:1. 48:10. Jsh 14:10, 11. Jb 17:7. **natural force.** Heb. moisture. or, freshness, greenness. 1 K ●1:1. Is 40:30, 31. **abated.** Heb. fled. Jg 6:11mg. Ps 104:7. 114:3, 5. SS 2:17. 4:6. Is 35:10. 51:11.

8. **wept for Moses.** Ge 50:3, 10. Nu 20:29. 1 S 25:1. 2 S 3:35, 38. Is 57:1. Ac 8:2. **mourning.** 2 S 11:27.

9. **full of the spirit.** Heb. *ruach*, Ge +41:38. Ex

31:3. Nu 11:17. 1 K 3:9, 12. 2 K 2:9, 15. Is 11:2. Da 6:3. Jn *3:34. Col *2:3. **Moses**. Ge 48:10. Nu 8:10. 27:18-23. Ac 6:6. 8:17-19. 1 T 4:14. 5:22. **the children.** Jsh 1:16-18. 3:7. 4:14.

10. **there arose.** Dt 18:15-18. Mt 17:1-8. Lk 16:29-31. Ac 3:22, 23. 7:37. He 3:5, 6. **prophet.** ✶171E12, Ge +14:22. **the Lord.** Dt 5:4, 5. Ex 33:11. Nu 12:6-8. **knew.** Jn=10:15. **face to face.** ✶22A4, Ge +19:13. Ex 24:9-11. Nu 12:8. 14:14.

11. **In all the signs.** Rather, "with respect to all the signs and wonders," etc. Dt 4:34. 7:19. Ne 9:6-10. Ps 78:43-58. 105:26-38. Jn=15:24. **to Pharaoh.** Ex 11:3.

12. **mighty hand.** Ex 3:19. 6:1. 13:3, 9, 14, 16. Jsh 4:24. 1 K 8:42. 2 Ch 6:32. Ne 1:10. Ps 136:12. Is 40:10. Je 21:5. 32:21. Ezk 20:33. Da 9:15. Lk 24:19. **great terror.** Dt 4:34. 26:8. Je 32:21. 2 C 5:11.

JOSHUA

JOSHUA 1

The Lord appoints Joshua to succeed Moses, 1, 2. The borders of the promised land, 3, 4. God promises to assist Joshua, 5-7. He gives him instructions, 8, 9. Joshua prepares the people to pass over Jordan, 10, 11. He puts the two tribes and a half in mind of their promise to Moses, 12-15. The people promise obedience, 16-18.

1. **the death.** Jsh 12:6. See on Dt 33:1. 34:5. Ac 13:36, 37. Ro 1:1. T 1:1. Ja 1:1. Re 1:18. **Joshua.** Ex 17:9-13. See on Nu 13:8, 16. 27:18-20. Dt 1:38. 31:3, 23. 34:9. Ac 7:45, Jesus. **Moses' minister.** Ex 24:13. Nu 11:28. 1 K 19:16. 2 K 3:11. 4:27-29. 5:25-27. Mt 20:26, 27. Lk 16:10.

2. **Moses.** See on ver. 1. Is 42:1. He 3:5, 6. 7:23, 24. **servant.** Re 1:1. **arise.** Nu 27:15-21. Dt 3:28. 31:7.

3. **Every.** 1 C 3:22. **the sole.** Jsh 14:9. Dt 11:24, 25. T 1:2.

4. **From the wilderness.** That is, their utmost limits should be from the Desert of Arabia Petraea on the south, to Lebanon on the north; and from the Euphrates on the east, to the Great sea, or the Mediterranean, on the west. The Israelites did not possess the full extent of this grant until the time of David. T#376. Ge 12:7. 13:14-17. 15:18-21. 17:8. Ex 6:4. 23:31. 32:13. Nu 34:2-18. Dt 1:7. 3:25. 11:24. 32:8, 9. 1 K +*4:21n. 1 Ch 5:9. 18:3. **Hittites.** Ge +15:20.

5. **There shall.** Dt 7:24. 20:4. Ps 46:11. Ro 8:31, 37. **as I was.** ver. 9, 17. Jsh 3:7. 6:27. Ex 3:12. Dt 31:8, 23. Mt 28:20. Ac 18:9, 10. 2 T 4:17. **be with.** ver. 17. Jsh 3:7. 4:14. Dt 31:6. 1 Ch 28:20. **I will not.** Dt 31:6-8. Is 41:10-16. 43:2-5. Ro 8:31, 37. He *13:5.

6. **Be strong.** ver. 7, 9. Dt 31:6, 8. 1 S 4:9. 1 K 2:2. 1 Ch 22:13. 28:10. 2 Ch 32:7, 8. Ps 27:14. Is 35:3, 4. Da 10:19. Hg 2:4. Zc 8:9. 1 C 16:13. Ep 6:10. 2 T 2:1. **good courage.** 2 Ch 19:11. **unto this people,** etc. *or,* thou shalt cause this people to inherit the land. **divide.** Nu 34:17-29. **which I sware.** Ge 26:3.

7. **which Moses.** See on ver. 1. Jsh 11:15. Nu 27:23. Dt 31:7. **turn not.** Dt 4:2. 5:32. 12:32. 28:14. Pr 4:27. 8:20. *30:6. **that.** Dt 29:9. 1 K 2:3. 1 Ch 22:13. **prosper.** *or,* do wisely. ver. 8mg. Dt +29:9. 1 K 2:3.

8. **book.** Dt *6:6-9. *11:18, 19. *17:18, 19. 30:14. 31:11. Ps *37:30, 31. 40:10. *119:11, 42, 43. Is 59:21. Mt 12:35. Ep *4:29. **not depart.** Dt 6:7. **thou shalt meditate.** T#48, 891. Dt 11:18-21. Ps *1:+2, 3. *19:14. +36:9 (T#279). *37:31. 63:5, 8. 103:17, 18. *119:11, 15, 97, 99. Pr *2:1-5. 3:1. 4:13, 20, 21, 22, 26. 14:22. Is 64:5. Mt *22:+6 (T#493), 29. +28:19 (T#458). Jn +*5:39. Ac +*17:11. Ro +*15:4. Col *3:16. 1 Th 5:27.

1 T *4:14-16. He 2:1. 1 P *2:2. Re 1:3. **observe.** See on Dt *5:29, 32, 33. 6:1-3. Mt √7:21, 24. *28:20. Lk *11:28. Jn *13:17. *14:21. Ja *1:22-25. Re *22:14. **to do.** Jsh 22:5. Dt 30:6. **thy way.** Pr 2:6, 7. **prosperous.** Ge 39:3, 23. Dt +29:9. Ps *1:3. Is 44:4. Col 1:6. **have good success.** *or,* do wisely. ver. 7mg.

9. **Have.** Dt 31:7, 8, 23. Jg 6:14. 2 S 13:28. Ac *4:19. **Be strong.** ver. 6, 7. Dt 31:6, 8. Ps 71:16. 2 T 2:1. **courage.** T#134. Dt 31:6. 1 Ch 28:20. 2 Ch 19:11. Ezr 10:2-5. Ne 6:11. Ps 27:14. 31:24. Ph +1:20(T#460). 1 T +5:20 (T#461). **be not afraid.** Jsh 8:1. See on Ge 28:15. Dt 20:1. Ps *27:1, 2. Je *1:7, 8. **for the Lord.** Ps 46:7. Is 43:1, 5. **with thee.** Ge *28:15. Ps 46:7. Mt 28:20.

10. **the officers of the people.** The *shoterim,* or officers, were different from the *shophetim,* who were the judges among the people. The *shoterim* have been supposed to be subordinate officers, whose business it was to see the decisions of the *shophetim* carried into effect. Calmet conjectures that the *shoterim* here may have been the heralds of the army.

11. **three days.** Jsh 3:2. Ex 19:11. 2 K 20:5. Ho 6:2. **ye shall.** See on Dt 9:1, 5. 11:31. **pass over.** Is 43:1-3.

12. **Reubenites.** Jsh 4:12, 13. Nu 32:33. Re 22:1-4.

13. **Remember.** ✶96B, Ex +20:8. Jsh 22:1-4. Nu 32:20-28. Dt 3:18.

14. **little ones.** Jsh 8:35. Dt +*29:11. **armed.** Heb. marshalled by five. Ex 13:18. **the mighty.** Dt 20:8. Re 17:4.

15. **Until.** Nu 32:17-22. Ga 5:13, 14. 6:2. Ph 1:21-26. 2:4. **then ye shall.** Jsh 22:4, etc. 1 C 12:26. 13:5.

16. **All that.** Nu 32:25. Dt 5:27. 2 S 15:15. Ro *13:1-5. T 3:1. 1 P *2:13-15. **whithersoever.** Mt 8:19. Re 14:4. **will go.** Nu 32:17, 18. 1 S 15:22.

17. **as we hearkened.** ver. 5. Jsh 3:7. 4:14. **only the Lord.** ver. 5. 1 S 20:13. 1 K 1:37. 1 Ch 28:20, 21. Ps 20:1, 4, 9. 118:25, 26. Mt 21:9. 1 T 2:1, 2.

18. **that doth rebel.** Dt 17:12. 1 S 11:12. Ps 2:1-6. Lk *19:27. He *10:28, 29, 31. *12:25. **he shall be.** Ro *13:1-5. **only be.** See on ver. 6, 7, 9. Ezr 10:4. 1 C 16:13. Ep *6:10.

JOSHUA 2

Two spies, sent by Joshua, enter Jericho, and are concealed by Rahab, 1-7. She informs them of the terror which had seized the Canaanites, 8-11; and covenants with them, 12-21. They return and make their report, 22-24.

1. **sent.** *or,* had sent. **Shittim.** Nu 25:1. 33:49. **to**

spy secretly. Nu 13:2, 17-21. Jg 18:2, 14, 17. Mt 10:16. Ep 5:15. even Jericho. Jsh 5:10. 6:1-24. harlot's house. Though the word *zonah* generally denotes a prostitute, yet many very learned men are of opinion that it should be here rendered an *innkeeper*, or *hostess*, from *zoon*, to furnish or provide food. In this sense it was understood by the Targumist, who renders it *ittetha pundekeetha*, "a woman, a tavern-keeper," and so St. Chrysostome, in his second sermon on Repentance, calls her *pandokeutria*. The Greek *porna*, by which the LXX. render it, and which is adopted by the Apostles, is derived from *pernao*, "to sell," and is also supposed to denote a tavern keeper. Among the ancients, women generally kept houses of entertainment. Herodotus says, "Among the Egyptians, the women carry on all commercial concerns, and *keep taverns*, while the men continue at home and weave" (Euterp. c. 35). The same custom prevailed among the Greeks. Jsh 6:17, 25. Jg 11:1n. 16:1n. 1 K 3:16n. Mt 1:5, Rachab. 21:31. He 11:31. Ja 2:25. **Rahab**. i.e. *spacious, wide; breadth,* *✻S#7343h*. ver. 3. Jsh 6:17, 23, 25. **lodged**. Heb. lay. ver. 8.

2. **told the king**. Ps 127:1. Pr 21:30, 31. Is 43:13. Da 4:35.

3. **Bring**. Jsh 10:23. Ge 38:24. Le 24:14. Jb 21:30. Jn 19:4. Ac 12:4, 6. **to search**. Ge 42:9-12, 31. 2 S 10:3. 1 Ch 19:3.

4. **took**. Ex 1:19. 2 S 16:18, 19. 17:19, 20. 2 K 6:19.

5. **of shutting**. ver. 7. Ne 13:19. Is 60:11. Ezk 46:1, 2, 12. Re 21:25. **the men went out**. Je 50:20. Ro 3:7, 8.

6. **to the roof**. ver. 8. Ex 1:15-21. Dt 22:8. 2 S 11:2. Mt 24:17. **hid them**. Ex 2:2. 2 S 17:19. 1 K 18:4, 13. 2 K 11:2. Je 36:26. Col 3:3. He 11:23. **flax**. *✻100*, Ge +10:9.

7. **Jordan**. i.e. *descending*, *✻S#3383h*. ver. 10. Jsh 1:2, 11, 14, 15. 3:1, 8, 8, 11, 13, 13, 14, 15, 15, 17, 17. 4:1, 2, 5, 7, 7, 7, 8, 8, 9, 10, 16, 17, 18, 18, 19, 20, 22, 23. 5:1, 1. 7:7, 7. 9:1, 10. 12:1, 7. 13:8, 23, 27, 27, 32. 14:3. 15:5, 5. 16:1, 7. 17:5. 18:7, 12, 19, 20. 19:22, 33, 34. 20:8. 22:4, 7, 10, 10, 11, 25. 23:4, 8, 11. Ge 13:10, 11. 32:10. 50:10, 11. Nu 13:29. 22:1. 26:3, 63. 31:12. 32:5, 19, 19, 21, 29, 32. 33:48, 49, 50, 51. 34:12, 15. 35:1, 10, 14. 36:13. Dt 1:1, 5. 2:29. 3:8, 17, 20, 25, 27. 4:21, 22, 26, 41, 46, 47, 49. 9:1. 11:30, 31. 12:10. 27:2, 4, 12. 30:18. 31:2, 13. 32:47. Jg 3:28. 5:17. 7:24, 24, 25. 8:4. 10:8, 9. 11:13, 22. 12:5, 6. 1 S 13:7. 31:7. 2 S 2:29. 10:17. 17:22, 22, 24. 19:15, 15, 17, 18, 31, 31, 36, 39, 41. 20:2. 24:5. 1 K 2:8. 7:46. 17:3, 5. 2 K 2:6, 7, 13. 5:10, 14. 6:2, 4. 7:15. 10:33. 1 Ch 6:78, 78. 12:15, 37. 19:17. 26:30. 2 Ch 4:17. Jb 40:23. Ps 42:6. 114:3, 5. Is 9:1. Je *12:5. 49:19. 50:44. Ezk 47:18. Zc 11:3. **the fords**. Jg 3:28. 12:5. **they shut**. ver. 5. Ac 5:23.

9. **I know**. Ex 18:11. 2 K 5:15. Jb *19:25. Ec 8:12. He *11:1, 2. **that the Lord**. Ge 13:14-17. 15:18-21. Ex 23:6-8. Dt 32:8. Ps 115:16. Je 27:5. Mt 20:15. **your terror**. Ge 35:5. Ex 15:15, 16. 23:27. Dt 2:25. 11:25. 28:7, 10. Jg 7:14. 1 S 14:15. 2 K 7:6. **faint**. Heb. melt. ver. 11. 1 S 14:16. 2 S 17:10. Ps 112:10. Is 19:1. Na 2:10.

10. **For we**. Jsh 4:24. Ex 14:21-31. 15:14-16. **what ye did**. Nu 21:21-35. Dt 2:30-37. 3:1-8.

11. **had heard**. Ex 15:14. **our hearts**. See on Jsh 5:1. 7:5. 14:8. Dt 1:28. 20:8. Is 13:7. Na 2:10. **did there remain**. Heb. rose up. Re 6:16. **courage**. Heb. *ruach*, spirit, Ge +26:35. **for the Lord**. Dt 4:39. 1 K

8:60. 1 Ch 16:31. Ps 83:18. 99:1. 102:15. Je 16:19-21. Da 4:34, 35. 6:25-27. Zc 8:20-23. 2 P 3:10. Re 19:6.

12. **swear**. Jsh 9:15, 18-20. 1 S 20:14, 15, 17. 30:15. 2 Ch 36:13. Je 12:16. He 6:16, 18. **that ye will**. 1 S 20:14-17. 24:21, 22. Est 8:6. 2 T 1:16-18. Ja 2:13. **my father's**. ver. 13. Ge 24:3, 9. Ro 1:31. 1 T 5:8. **give me a true token**. ver. 18. Ge +17:11. Ex *12:13. Ezk *9:4-6. Mk 14:44. Ro 4:11. 2 T *2:19.

13. **my father**. It is observable that in this enumeration of her kindred, there is no mention made of a husband. It is most likely that she was a single woman or a widow, who obtained an honest livelihood by keeping a house for the entertainment of strangers; and not a woman of ill fame, as some have supposed. The spies sent on this occasion were certainly some of the most confidential persons that Joshua had in his host, and their errand was of the greatest importance; is it then not most likely that they lodged at an inn? **lives**. Heb. *nephesh*, souls, Ge +44:30.

14. **life**. Heb. *nephesh*, soul. Ge +44:30. **for your's**. Heb. instead of you to die. 1 K 20:39. **it shall be**. *✻144A11*, Ge +38:1. **when the Lord**. Jsh 6:17, 25. Ge 24:49. Nu 10:29-32. Jg 1:24, 25. 1 S 20:8. 2 S 9:1. Pr 18:24. Mt 5:7.

15. **she let them**. 1 S 19:12-17. Ac 9:25. 2 C 11:32, 33. **for her house**. Jsh 6:20.

16. **Get you**. ver. 22. 1 S 23:14, 29. Ps 11:1.

17. **We will be**. ver. 20. Ge 24:3-8. Ex 20:7. Le 19:11, 12. Nu 30:2. 2 S 21:1, 2, 7.

18. **scarlet**. ver. 21. Le 14:4. Nu 4:8. 19:6. He 9:19. **thread**. Ezk 9:4, 6. Ro 4:11. 2 T 2:19. He 11:28. 12:24. **bring**. Heb. gather. **thy father**. ver. 13. Jsh 6:23. Ge 7:1. 12:2. 19:12-17. Ex 20:12. Est 8:6. Lk 19:9. Ac 10:27, 33. 11:14. 2 T 1:16. **all thy**. Ge *7:1. Ex 12:22. 1 K 17:15. Ac 11:14. 16:15, 31.

19. **whosoever**. Ex 12:13, 23. Nu 35:26-28. 1 K 2:36-42. Ezk 33:4, 5. Mt 24:17. Ac 27:31. Ph 3:9. He 10:29, 31. 1 J 2:27, 28. **go out**. Ex 12:22. **street, his blood**. Le 20:9-11. 2 S 1:16. 3:28, 29. Ezk 33:4, 5. Mt 27:24. Ac 18:6. 20:26. **in the house**. ver. *13. Jsh 6:23. Ge 7:1. 12:2. 19:12-17. Est 8:6. Lk 19:9. Ac 10:27, 33. *11:14. *16:31. 2 T 1:16. **his blood**. ver. 14. 2 S 4:11. 1 K 2:32. Mt 27:25.

20. **And if thou**. Pr 11:13. **we will be quit**. See on ver. 17.

21. **According**. 2 Ch 32:8. **and she bound**. See on ver. 18. Ex 12:13. Mt 7:24. Jn 2:5.

22. **found them not**. 1 S 19:10-12. 2 S 17:20. Ps 32:6, 7, 10.

23. **told him**. Pr 25:13.

24. **Truly the Lord**. Jsh 1:8. 21:44, 45. Ex 23:31. Nu 13:32, 33. Pr 25:13. **all the inhabitants**. See on ver. 9-11. Ps 48:5, 6. Re 6:16, 17. **faint**. Heb. melt. ver. 9, 11. Jsh 5:1. Ex 15:15.

JOSHUA 3

Israel arrives at Jordan, 1. The officers give orders concerning the passage: and Joshua directs both priests and people, 2-6. The Lord encourages and instructs Joshua, 7-9. Joshua encourages the people, assuring them that the waters would be divided before the ark, 10-13. The waters are divided, and Israel passes the river, while the priests bearing the ark stand in the midst of it, 14-17.

1. **rose early**. Archbishop Usher supposes, that this

was upon Wednesday, the 28th of April, A.M. 2553, the fortieth year of the Exodus from Egypt. Ge +22:3. Ps 119:60. Je 7:13. 25:3. 26:5. Mk 1:35. **Shittim**. Jsh 2:1. Nu 25:1. Mi 6:5. **Jordan**. Dt 32:47.

2. **three days**. See on Jsh 1:10, 11.

3. **When ye see**. ver. 11. See on Nu 10:33. **the priests**. ver. 6, 8, 14-17. Jsh 4:10. 6:6. Nu 4:15. Dt 31:9, 25. 2 S 6:3, 13. 1 Ch 15:11, 12. **ye shall remove**. Ex 13:21, 22. Mt 8:19. 16:24. Re 14:4. it. *J*63I2. Ellipsis from succeeding clause B103. By ellipsis, supply "the priests and Levites bearing it (going before), then ye shall remove from your place, and go after it." Here the words *going before* are necessitated, and are to be supplied from the words that follow, "go after." EWB suggests the following passages may exhibit this same form of ellipsis: Jg 16:13, 14. 1 S *16:7. 1 K 3:12. 14:15. 1 Ch 4:7. Ne 5:2. Jb 20:17. 38:19. Ps 35:16. Pr *13:1. Is 19:11. 31:5. Hab 2:3. Lk 1:17. 22:36. Jn 6:32, 35. 9:2. *12:25. Ac 2:3. *7:59. Ro 2:12. (2:28, 29). (4:13). (5:16). 1 C 1:26, 27. 5:4, 5. 6:12. 14:22. 15:47. 2 C *5:10. Ep 2:1. Ph 3:13. 2 T 1:5. T 2:2. He (8:1). **go after it**. He=12:1, 2.

4. **a space**. Ex 3:5. 19:12. 33:7. Ps 89:7. He 12:28, 29. **have not passed**. Dt 17:16. **heretofore**. Heb. since yesterday and the third day. Ge 31:2. Ex +4:10mg. Ru 2:11. 1 Ch 11:2mg. Is *30:33mg.

5. **Sanctify**. Jsh 7:13. Ex 19:10-15. Le 10:3. 20:7, 8. Nu 11:18. 1 S 16:5. Jb 1:5. Jl 2:16. Jn 17:19. **the Lord**. ver. 13, 15. Ps 86:10. 114:1-7.

6. **Take up**. See on ver. 3. Nu 4:15. 10:33. Mi 2:13. Jn 14:2, 3. He 6:20.

7. **magnify thee**. Jsh 4:14. 1 Ch 29:25. 2 Ch 1:1. Jb 7:17. Ps 18:35. Lk 1:32. Jn 17:1. Ac 5:31. Ph 1:20. 2:9-11. **that, as I was**. See on Jsh 1:5, 17. 4:14.

8. **to the brink**. Heb. to the extremity. i.e. so far as the river then spread itself, which was now more than ordinary, ver. 15. **command**. See on Jsh 1 Ch 15:11, 12. 2 Ch 17:8, 9. 29:4-11, 15, 27, 30. 30:12. 31:9, 10. 35:2-6. Ne 12:24-28. 13:22, 28. **ye shall stand**. ver. 17. Ex 14:13. La 3:26. **in**. This expression signifies not the exact middle of a place, but any part within it, as appears from Ge 45:6. Ex 8:22. 24:18. Jsh 7:13. 10:13. Pr 30:19. Thus, within the waters of Jordan, in the first entrance into the river; where they stood for a season, till the river was divided, and then they went into the midst of it, as is implied, ver. 17, and there abode till all the people were passed over, as it follows in the history (Matthew Poole).

9. **Come hither**. 1 S *9:27. 12:7. **hear the words**. Dt 4:1. 5:26. 12:8.

10. **Hereby ye**. Nu 16:28-30. 1 K 18:36, 37. 22:28. Ps 9:16. Is 7:14. 2 C 13:2, 3. He *11:6. **living**. Dt 5:26. 1 S 17:26. 2 K 19:4. Je 10:10. Ho 1:10. Mt 16:16. Jn 6:69. 1 Th 1:9. He 10:31. **God**. Heb. *El*, Ex +15:2. **among**. Jsh 22:31. Ex 17:7. Dt 31:17. Jg 6:12, 13. **drive out from**. See on Jsh 21:45. Ge 15:15-18. Ex 3:8. 23:27-30. 33:2. Dt 7:1. Ps 44:2, 3. **Canaanites**. Ge +10:18. **Hittites**. Ge +15:20. **Hivites**. Ge +10:17.. **Perizzites**. Ge +13:7. **Amorites**. Ge +10:16. **Jebusites**. Ge +10:16. **Girgashites**. Ge +10:16.

11. **the Lord**. ver. 13. Ps 24:1. *47:2. Is 54:5. Je 10:7. Mi 4:13. Zp 2:11. Zc 4:14. 6:5. 14:9. **passeth**. ver. 3-6. Is 3:12. **over before**. Dt 31:8. Ps 23:4. Lk 19:28. Jn *10:4.

12. **take you twelve**. Jsh 4:2, 9.

13. **the soles**. ver. 15, 16. Ex 14:19-22. **in the waters**.

Ro=6:3, 4. Col=3:1-4. **of the Lord**. ver. 11. **stand upon**. ver. 16. Ex 15:8. Ps 33:7. 78:13. 114:3-5. Hab 3:15.

14. **bearing the ark**. See on ver. 3, 6. Jsh 6:6. Nu 10:35. Dt 31:26. Je 3:16. Ac 7:44, 45. 1 C 1:24, 25. He 9:4.

15. **the feet**. ver. 13. Is 26:6. **Jordan overfloweth**. The ordinary current of the Jordan, near where the Israelites crossed, is said by Maundrell, to be about twenty yards across, deeper than a man's height, and so rapid that there is no swimming against it. It has, however, two banks; the first, or inner one, is that of the river in its natural state, and the second, or outer one, about a furlong distant, is that of its overflowings, which it does when the summer's sun has melted the snow on mount Lebanon and Hermon, in the months of March and April. And this was the time which God chose that the Israelites should pass over it; that a miraculous interposition might be necessary; and that, by the miracle, they might be convinced of his omnipotence. Jsh 4:18. 1 Ch 12:15. Je √12:5. 49:19. Mk √1:5n. **all the time**. Jsh 5:10-12. Le 23:10-16. Dt 16:1-9.

16. **rose up**. See on ver. 13. Ps 29:10. 77:19. 114:3. Mt 8:26, 27. 14:24-33. **Adam**. i.e. *red earth*, ✱S#121h. This city is not mentioned elsewhere. 1 Ch ●1:1. **Zaretan**. i.e. *narrowness of dwelling place; their distress*, ✱S#6891h. 1 K 4:12, Zartanah. 7:46, Zarthan. **the plain**. Dt +11:30. 1 K 7:46. 2 K 14:25. **the salt sea**. Jsh 15:2. Ge 14:3. Nu 34:3. Dt 3:17. The passage through the Red Sea took place in the night, when the Israelites were fleeing from the Egyptians with great trepidation (Ex 14:19-31): but they passed Jordan in the daytime, with previous warning, leisurely, directly opposite Jericho, and with a triumphant defiance of the Canaanites (compare Mt 26:55. Ac 26:26); this passage into the promised land evidently typifying the believer's passage through death to heaven. **against Jericho**. Jsh 5:10, 12.

17. **the priests**. ver. 3, 6. **stood firm**. Jsh 4:3. 2 K 2:8. **in the midst**. *J*144A6, Ge +45:6. Jsh 4:3, 8. In the middle and deepest part of the river. See Jsh 4:16. **all the Israelites**. Ex 14:22, 29. Ps 66:6. Is 25:8. He 11:29.

JOSHUA 4

Twelve men are appointed to take twelve stones for a memorial out of Jordan, 1-8. Twelve other stones are set up in the midst of Jordan, 9. The people pass over, 10-13. God magnifies Joshua, 14. The priests are ordered to bring the ark out of Jordan, which then overflows as before, 15-18. The date of this event, 19. The twelve stones are set up in Gilgal, where Israel encamped, 20-24.

1. **were clean passed**. Jsh 3:17. Dt 27:2.

2. **twelve men**. Jsh 3:12. Nu 1:4-15. 13:2. 34:18. Dt 1:23. 1 K 18:31. Mt 10:1-5.

3. **the priest's feet**. See on Jsh 3:13. **twelve stones**. Jsh 24:27. Ge 28:22. Dt 27. 1 S 7:12. Ps 103:2. 111:4. Lk 19:40. **leave them**. ver. 8, 19, 20.

4. **prepared**. ver. 2. Mk 3:14-19.

6. **a sign**. Jsh 22:27. 24:27. Ge 31:51, 52. Ex 12:14. 13:9. 31:13. Nu 16:38. Is 55:13. Ezk 20:12, 20. **when your**. ver. 21. Ex 12:26, 27. 13:14. Dt 6:20, 21. 11:19. Ps 44:1. 71:18. 78:3-8. Is 38:19. Ac 2:39. **in time to**

come. Heb. tomorrow. ver. 21. Jsh 3:5. +22:24mg. Dt +6:20mg.

7. **the waters**. Jsh 3:13-16. **passed over**. Ex 12:13. **memorial**. See on ver. 6. Ex 12:14. 28:12. 30:16. Nu 16:40. Ps 111:4. Is 66:3mg. 1 C 11:24. **for ever**. Heb. *olam*, Ex +12:24.

8. **did as Joshua**. ver. 2-5. Jsh 1:16-18.

9. **set·up twelve**. Ex 24:12. 28:21. 1 K 18:31. Ps 111:2-4. **in the midst**. Jsh 3:8, *17. **and they are there**. These words might be written by Joshua at the close of his life, or perhaps be added by some later prophet. It seems from this verse, that there were two sorts of stones erected as a memorial of this great event: twelve at Gilgal (ver. 20), and twelve in the bed of the Jordan; which last might have been placed on a base of strong stone work, so high as always to be visible, and serve to mark the very spot where the priests stood with the ark. Drs. Kennicott and Shuckford, however, would read here with the Syriac, *mittoch*, "*from* the midst," instead of *bethoch*, "*in* the midst;" and render, "And Joshua took up the twelve stones (taken) from the midst of Jordan," etc. But this reading is unsupported by any MS. yet collated; and it appears wholly unnecessary. **unto this day**. Jsh 7:26. 8:28, 29. 9:27. 10:27. 13:13. 14:14. 15:63. Ge +19:38. 26:33. Dt +29:4. 34:6. Jg 1:21n, 26. 6:24. 15:19. 18:12. 1 S 27:6. 30:25. 2 S 4:3. 2 Ch 5:9. Mt 27:8. 28:15. Ep 4:8-10. 1 C 3:21-23.

10. **the ark**. Ac 7:44, 45. **stood in the midst**. See on Jsh 3:8, 13, 16, *17. Is 28:16. **Moses**. Nu 27:21-23. Dt 31:9. **hasted**. Ex 12:39. Ps 119:60. Pr 27:1. Ec 9:10. 2 C 6:2. He 3:7, 8.

11. **clean passed over**. Ex 10:26. 1 C 10:1. He=1:3. **that the ark**. ver. 18. Jsh 3:8, 17.

12. **the children**. Jsh 1:14. Nu 32:20-32.

13. **prepared for war**. *or*, ready armed. Jsh 6:7, 9, 13. Nu 31:5. 32:27. Ep *6:11. **passed over**. Ps 116:9. **to the plains**. Jsh 5:10. Dt +11:30. 2 K 25:5. Je 39:5. 52:8.

14. **magnified**. Jsh 1:16-18. See on Jsh 3:7. 1 C 10:2. **they feared him**. Ex 14:31. 1 S 12:18. 1 K 3:28. 2 Ch 30:12. Pr 24:21. Ro 13:4. **as they**. Jsh 1:5, 17. 3:7.

16. **the priests**. See on Jsh 3:3-6. Ex 25:16-22. Re 11:19. **come up out of Jordan**. Jsh 3:8, 17. Mt 3:11, 16. Mk 1:9, 10. Lk 3:16, 21. Jn 1:28, 31-33. 3:23. 10:40.

17. **Come ye up**. Ge 8:16-18. Da 3:26. Ac 16:23, 35-39.

18. **the soles**. See on Jsh 3:13, 15. **lifted up**. Heb. plucked up. Jsh 8:6, 16. **that the waters**. As soon as the priests and the ark were come up out of Jordan, the waters of the river, which had stood on a heap, flowed down according to their natural and usual course, and again soon filled the channel. This makes it abundantly evident, that the miraculous change which had been given to the river was not from any secret natural cause, but solely by the power of God, and for the sake of his chosen people; for when Israel's hosts had passed through, and the token of his presence was removed, immediately the waters went forward again:—so that if it be asked, "What ailed thee, O Jordan, that thou wast driven back?" it must be answered, it was in obedience to the God of Israel, and in kindness to the Israel of God. Ex 14:26-28. **and flowed**. Heb. went. **over all**. Jsh 3:15. 1 Ch 12:15. Is 8:8. Je 12:5. **before**. Heb. yesterday, the third day.

*S#8543h. Jsh 3:4mg. 20:5. Ge 31:+2mg, 5mg. Ex 4:10mg. 5:7, 8, 14. 21:29, 36. Dt 4:42. 19:4mg, 6mg. Ru 2:11. 1 S 20:27. 21:5. 2 S 3:17mg. 15:20. 2 K 13:5mg. 1 Ch 11:2mg. Jb 8:9.

19. **first month**. Ex 12:2, 3. **Gilgal**. i.e. *rolled; rolling; a wheel*, *S#1537h. ver. 19, 20. Jsh 5:9, 10. 9:6. 10:6, 7, 9, 15, 43. 12:23. 14:6. 15:7. Jg 2:1. 3:19. 1 S 7:16. 10:8. 11:14, 15, 15. 13:4, 7, 8, 12, 15. 15:12, 21, 33. 2 S 19:15, 40. 2 K 2:1. 4:38. Ho 4:15. 9:15. 12:11. Am 4:4. 5:5, 5. Mi 6:5. That is, the place afterwards called Gilgal; for it is so called here by anticipation (𝒥151. Prolepsis (Ampliato); or, Anticipation. +Ge 1:28). (1) A place on the west side of Jordan, not far from Jericho, in Benjamin, and where the Israelites first encamped after miraculously passing over Jordan, Jsh 3:13-17. (2) A place supposed to have been in the west part of Canaan, in the territory afterward possessed by the tribe of Dan; but it seems not quite certain that this Gilgal was not, as well as the other, in the east part of the land, near the Jordan, Jsh 12:23. (3) It is apparently agreed among the authorities of the present day that there was a place called Gilgal near the sea, a little to the north of Joppa, and to this reference is supposed to be made in Jsh 9:6; 10:6, 7, 9, 15, 43. Supposed to be the modern *Jidjuleh*, near the ancient *Antipatris*. (4) Some think another place bore the same name, Gilgal, about twelve miles south of Ebal and Gerizim, and that this is the place referred to in 2 K 2:1; 4:38. Supposed to be the modern *Jiljilia*.

20. **those twelve**. See on ver. 3, 8.

21. **When your**. See on ver. 6. Ps 105:2-5. *145:4-7. **in time to come**. Heb. tomorrow. ver. 6.

22. **saying**. See on Jsh 3:17. Ex *14:29. 15:19. Ps 66:5, 6. Is 11:15, 16. 44:27. *51:10. Re 16:12.

23. **as the Lord**. The parents must take that occasion to tell their children of the drying up of the Red Sea forty years before:—"As the Lord your God did to the Red Sea." It greatly magnifies later mercies to compare them with those before enjoyed; for, by making the comparison, it appears that God is the same yesterday, today, and forever. Later blessings should also bring to remembrance former mercies, and revive thankfulness for them. **which he dried**. Ex *14:21. Ne 9:11. Ps 77:16-19. 78:13. Is 43:16. 63:12-14. **until we**. Jn 8:51. 11:26. 1 C 15:54, 55, 57.

24. **That**. Jn +11:42. **all the people**. Ex *9:16. Dt 28:10. 1 S 17:46. 1 K 8:42, 43. 2 K *5:15. 19:19. 1 Ch 5:25. 2 Ch *6:33. 13:9. *32:19. Ezr 3:3. 9:1, *2, 11. *10:11. Ps 106:7, 8. Da 3:26-29. 4:34, 35. *6:26, 27. **that it is**. Ex 15:16. 1 Ch *29:12. Ps 89:13. **mighty**. Ps 89:19. Is 63:1. Zp 3:17. Ep 1:18-20. **ye might**. Ex *14:31. 20:20. Dt 6:2. Ps 76:6-8. *89:7. Je 10:6, 7. *32:40. Re 15:4. **forever**. Heb. all days. Dt 12:19mg.

JOSHUA 5

The Amorites and Canaanites hear of the miraculous crossing of Jordan, and are afraid, 1. Joshua, at God's command, circumcises the males born in the wilderness, 2-8. The place is called Gilgal, 9. The passover is kept at Gilgal, 10. They eat of the corn of the land, and the manna ceases, 11, 12. One appears to Joshua, calling himself "The Captain of the Lord's host," in form of a man of war; Joshua worships him; the place of his presence holy ground, 13-15.

1. **all the kings.** Jsh 12:9-24. 24:15. Ge 10:15, +16, 17-19. 15:18-21. 48:22. Nu 13:29. Jg 11:23. 2 S 21:2. Ezk 16:3. Am 2:9. **Canaanites.** Jsh 17:12, 18. Ge +10:18. 12:6. Ex 23:28. Jg 1:1. 4:2. Ezr 9:1. Ps 135:11. **which were by.** Nu 13:29. Jg 3:3. Zp 2:4-6. **heard.** See on Jsh 2:9-11. Ex 15:14, 15. Ps 48:4-6. Lk 21:25, 26. Re 18:10. **neither was.** 1 S 25:37. 1 K 10:5. Is 13:6-8. Ezk 21:7. Da 5:6. **spirit.** Heb. *ruach*, Ge +41:8.

2. **sharp knives.** *or*, knives of flints. Ex +4:25. Before the use of iron was common, all the nations of the earth had their edge tools made of stones, flints, etc. Our ancestors had their arrows and spearheads made of flint; which are frequently turned up by the plow. And even when iron became more common, stone knives seem to have been preferred for making incisions in the human body. The Egyptians used such to open the bodies for embalming; and the tribe of Alajab in Ethiopia, to follow the Mosaic institution, perform the rite of circumcision, according to Ludolf, *cultris lapidibus*, with knives made of stone. **circumcise.** Ge 17:10-14. Dt 10:16. 30:6. Ro 2:29. 4:11. Col 2:11.

3. **Joshua.** Ge 17:23-27. Ex *12:48. Mt 16:24. **the hill of the foreskins.** *or*, Gibeah haaraloth. **hill.** Ge 49:26. Ex 17:6. **foreskins.** ✱S#6190h. Ge 17:11, 14, 23, 24, 25. 34:14. Ex 4:25. Le 12:3. 19:23. Dt 10:16. 1 S 18:25, 27. 2 S 3:14. Je 4:4. 9:25.

4. **All the.** Nu 14:29. 26:64, 65. Dt 2:16. Ps 95:10, 11. 1 C 10:5. He 3:17-19.

5. **they had not.** Dt 12:8, 9. Ho 6:6, 7. Mt 12:7. Ro 2:26. 1 C 7:19. Ga 5:6. 6:15.

6. **walked.** Nu 14:32-34. Dt 1:3. 2:7, 14. 8:4. Ps 95:10, 11. Je 2:2. **because they obeyed not.** Dt +*26:17. 28:45. **sware that.** Nu 14:22, 23. He 3:11. **a land.** See on Ex 3:+8, 17. Ezk 20:6, 15. Jl 3:18. **milk and.** ✱174, Ge +18:27. **honey.** ✱17117, Ex +3:8.

7. **their children.** Nu 14:31. Dt 1:39. **had not.** Ex *4:25. Lk 7:30. Ac *16:3. 19:1-7.

8. **when they**, etc. Heb. when the people had made an end to be circumcised. Ga 5:1. Ph 3:3. **till they were whole.** Ge 34:25.

9. **I rolled away.** Jsh 10:18. *24:14. Ge 34:14. Le 24:14. 1 S 14:6. 17:26, 36. Ps 119:22, 39. Je 9:25. Ezk 20:7, 8. 23:3, 8. Ep 2:11, 12. **reproach.** Ge 30:23. *34:14. Ex 6:5, 6. 13:3. *15:26. Dt 5:6. *28:27. 1 S 11:2. **Gilgal. That is,** rolling. Jsh 4:19.

10. **kept the passover.** Ex 12:3, 6, etc. Nu 9:1-5.

11. **old corn.** Jn=12:24. This original word is not found elsewhere. The people would find abundance of old corn in the deserted granaries of the affrighted inhabitants; the corn of the last year, which the inhabitants of those parts had left in their barns, being doubtless fled for fear of the Israelites into their strong cities, or other remoter and safer parts. **on the morrow after the passover.** Le *23:10, +*11n, 14. i.e. *on the sixteenth day;* for the passover was killed between the two evenings of the fourteenth day, and was eaten in that evening or night, which, according to the Jewish computation, whereby they begin their days at the evening, was a part of the fifteenth day, all which was the feast of the passover; and so the morrow of the sixteenth day was "the morrow after the passover," when they were obliged to offer unto God the first sheaf, and then were allowed to eat of the rest (Matthew Poole). **unleavened cakes.** Ex 12:18-20. 13:6, 7. Le 23:6, 14. **parched.** or, roasted. Le 2:14. of that year's

corn, which was most proper and customary for that use. **in the selfsame day.** Dt +32:48. Having an eager desire to enjoy the fruits of the land, the barley harvest being ripe, after offering the sheaf of firstfruits, they ate also new parched corn; and thus the manna being no longer necessary, ceased, after having been sent them regularly for almost forty years. To Christians the manna for *their* souls shall never fail, till they arrive at the Canaan above, to feast on its rich and inexhaustible provisions.

12. **the manna.** Ex 16:35. Ne 9:20, 21. Re 7:16, 17. **ceased.** Ph 4:19. **but they did eat.** Dt 6:10, 11. Pr 13:22. Is 65:13, 14. Jn 4:38.

13. **he lifted.** Ge 33:1, 5. Ps 121:1. 123:1. Da 8:3. *10:5. **a man.** Jsh 6:2. Ge *18:2. *32:24-30. Ex 23:23. Jg 13:8, 9, 11, 22. Da 10:5. Ho *12:3-5. Zc 1:8. Ac *1:10. Ro 8:31. Re 1:13. **his sword.** Nu *22:23, 31. 1 Ch 21:*16, *17, 27, 30. **Art thou for us.** 1 Ch 12:17, 18.

14. **but as the captain.** *or*, Prince. Ex 23:20-22. Is 55:4. Da 10:13, 21. *12:1. He 2:10. *12:2. Re 12:7. 19:11-14. **fell on his.** Ge 17:3, 17. Ex 3:6. Le 9:24. Nu 16:22, 45. Da 10:9. Mt 8:2. Lk 5:12. Ac *10:25, 26. Re 1:17. *4:9-11. *5:13, 14. +*19:10. *22:8, 9. **What saith.** 1 S *3:9, 10. Is *6:8. Ac 9:6. **my lord.** Ex ◑4:10, 13. Ps *110:1. Mt 22:44. Lk 1:43. 20:42. Jn +√20:28. Ph *3:8.

15. **Loose.** Ex *3:5. Ac 7:32, 33. 2 P 1:18. **And Joshua.** Many persons have been puzzled to know what was intended by this extraordinary appearance of the angel to Joshua, because they supposed that the whole business ends with the chapter; whereas it is continued in the succeeding one, the first verse of which is a mere parenthesis (✱137, Parenthesis. Ge +13:13), simply relating to the state of Jericho at the time when Joshua was favored with this encouraging vision; by which he was shown that their help came from God alone, and that it was not by human might or power, but by the *Lord of hosts* they were to obtain the victory.

JOSHUA 6

Jericho is shut up by the Israelites, 1. The Lord instructs Joshua how to conduct the siege, 2-5. Joshua directs the priests to carry the ark round the city, preceded by other priests, sounding with trumpets, and attended by the people, 6, 7. They thus march around the city daily for six days, and seven times on the seventh day, 8-16. The city and all in it (except Rahab and those with her) are devoted to destruction, 17-19. The people shout, the walls fall down, and the city is taken and destroyed; but Rahab is preserved, 20-25. A curse is pronounced on him who should rebuild Jericho, 26. Joshua becomes renowned, 27.

1. **was straitly.** Heb. did shut up, and was shut up. Jsh 2:7. 2 K 17:4. **because.** Jsh 2:9-14, 24. Ps 127:1.

2. **the Lord.** See on Jsh 5:13-15. **See, I have.** ver. 9:24. Jsh 2:9, 24. 8:1. 11:6-8. Jg 11:21. 2 S 5:19. Ne 9:24. Da 2:21, 44. 4:17, 35. 5:18. **the king.** Dt 7:24. Jg 11:24.

3. **ye shall.** ver. 7, 14. Nu 14:9. 1 C 1:18, 21-25, 27, 28. 2 C 4:7. *12:9. **six days.** Jn ◑11:39.

4. **trumpets of rams**'. The words *shopertoth hyyovelim*, should rather be rendered "jubilee trumpets," i.e. such as were used on the jubilee, which were

probably made of horn or silver: for the entrance of the Israelites into Canaan was indeed a *jubilee* to them (See Note on Le 25:11n): instead of the dreadful trumpet of war, they were ordered to sound the trumpet of joy, as already conquerors. Le 25:9. Nu 10:1-10. Jg 7:7, 8, 15-22. 2 Ch 13:12. 20:17, 19, 21. Is 27:13. Zc 4:6. **seven times**. Ge 2:3. 7:2, 3. Le 4:6. 14:16. 25:8. Nu 23:1. 1 K 18:43. 2 K 5:10. Jb 42:8. Zc 4:2. Re 1:4, 20. 5:1, 6. 8:2, 6. 10:3. 15:1, 7. 16:1.

5. **make a long**. ver. 16, 20. Ex 19:19. 2 Ch 20:21, 22. **the people**. Jg 7:20-22. 1 S 4:5. 17:20, 52. 2 Ch 13:14, 15. Je 50:15. **and the wall**. The words *wenaphelah chomath hair tachteyha*, are literally, "and the wall of the city shall fall down under itself;" which appears simply to mean, that the wall shall fall down from its very foundation; which was probably the case in every part, though large breaches in different places might have been amply sufficient first to admit the armed men, after whom the host might enter to destroy the city. There is no ground for the supposition that the walls sunk into the earth. Is 25:12. 30:25. 2 C 10:4, 5. He 11:30. **flat**. Heb. under it. ver. 20.

6. **Take up the ark**. ver. 8, 13. See on Jsh 3:3, 6. Ex 25:14. Dt 20:2-4. Ac 9:1.

7. **that is armed**. ver. 3. Jsh 1:14. 4:13.

8. **before the Lord**. See on ver. 3, 4. Nu 32:20.

9. **and the rereward**. Heb. gathering host. ver. 13. Nu 10:14, 18, 21, 22, *25. Is 52:11, 12. 58:8.

10. **not shout**. Ps 4:4, 5. 46:10, 11. Is 30:15. La 3:26. **any noise with your voice**. Heb. your voice to be heard. Is 42:2. Mt 12:19. **until the day**. 2 S 5:23, 24. Is 28:16. Lk 24:49. Ac 1:7.

12. **Joshua rose**. See on Jsh 3:1. Ge 22:3. 28:18. Ex 24:4. Ps 57:8. Pr 8:17. Mk 1:35. **the priests**. See on ver. 6-8. Dt 31:25. Jn 2:5-8. 6:10, 11. 9:6, 7. He 11:7, 8.

13. **went on**. 1 Ch 15:26. Mt 24:13. Ga *6:9.

14. **the second**. ver. 3, 11, 15.

15. **about the dawning**. Ps 119:147. Mt 28:1. 2 P 1:19. **only on that day**. See on ver. 4.

16. **Shout**. See on ver. 5. Jg 7:20-22. 2 Ch 13:15. 20:22, 23. **hath given**. 2 C=10:5. Ph=3:21. 1 J=5:5.

17. **accursed**. or, devoted. Jsh 7:1. Le 27:28, 29. Nu 21:2, 3. Dt 2:34. 1 Ch 2:7. Ezr 10:8mg. Is 34:6. Je 46:10. Ezk 39:17. Mi 4:13. 1 C 16:22. Ga 3:10, 13. **only Rahab**. See on Jsh 2:1. **because**. ver. 22, 23. Jsh 2:4-6, 22. Ge 12:3. 1 S 15:6. Mt 10:41, 42. 25:40. He 6:10. 11:31. Ja 2:25.

18. **in any wise**. Ro 12:9. 2 C *6:17. Ep *5:11. Ja 1:27. 1 J 5:21. **lest ye make**. Jsh 7:1, 11, 12, 15. Dt 7:26. 13:15-17. **make the camp**. Jsh 7:11, 12. 22:18-20. 1 S 14:28-42. Ec 9:18. Jon 1:12. **and trouble it**. Jsh 7:25. 2 S 21:1. 1 K 18:17, 18. Ga 5:12.

19. **all the silver**. 2 S 8:11. 1 Ch 18:11. 26:20, 26, 28. 28:12. 2 Ch 15:18. 31:12. Is 23:17, 18. Mi 4:13. **consecrated**. Heb. holiness. Le 19:24mg. Zc 14:20, 21. **the treasury**. 1 K 7:51. 14:26. 2 K 24:13. 1 Ch 26:20. Ne 7:70, 71. 10:38. Je 38:11. Mt 27:6. Mk 12:41.

20. **the sound of the trumpet**. 1 Th *4:16. **the wall**. See on ver. 5. Is 2:12, 15. 2 C 10:4, 5. He 11:30. Re 14:8. 18:21. **flat**. Heb. under it. ver. 5.

21. **And they**. The Canaanites were ripe for destruction; and God was pleased, instead of destroying them by a pestilence, a famine, or an earthquake, to employ the Israelites as the executioners of his vengeance. Had an angel been commissioned to slay them, who

would have charged him with iniquity or cruelty? In all public calamities infants are involved; and tens of thousands of infants die in great agony every year. Now, either God is not the agent of these calamities (which opinion, though often implied in men's reasonings on these subjects, is not far from atheism), or they must consist with the most perfect justice and goodness. Am +√3:6. **utterly**. Jsh 9:24, 25. 10:28, 39. 11:14. Dt 2:34. 7:2, 3, 16. 20:16, 17. 1 S 15:3, 8, 18, 19. 1 K 20:42. Ps 137:8, 9. Je 48:18. 2 C 7:11. Col 3:5, 6. Re 18:21. **all**. *ʄ171A, Ex +9:6. **and old**. ʄ174, Ge +18:27.

22. **Joshua**. ver. 17. Jsh 2:1, etc. **as ye sware unto her**. Jsh 2:12-14, 17-20. 9:15, 18-20. 2 S 21:2, 7. Ps 15:4. Ezk 17:13, 16, 18, 19. He 11:31.

23. **out Rahab**. Jsh 2:18. Ge 12:2. 18:24. 19:29. Ac 27:24. He 11:7. **kindred**. Heb. families. **left them**. Nu 5:2, 3. 31:19. Ac 10:28. 1 C 5:12. Ep 2:12.

24. **burnt**. Jsh 8:28. Dt 13:16. Nu 31:10. 2 K 25:9. Re 17:16. 18:8, 9. **only the silver**. See on ver. 19. **the treasury**. ver. 19.

25. **saved**. Lk 5:32. **Rahab**. Jsh 11:19, 20. Jg 1:24, 25. Ac 2:21. He 11:31. **she dwelleth**. Mt 1:5. Lk 3:32. **unto**. See on Jsh 4:9. **because**. Ja 2:25.

26. **adjured**. This is to be regarded as a prediction, that he who rebuilt the city should lose his children in the interim between the laying all of the foundation to the completion of the walls. Nu 5:19-21. 1 S 14:24, etc. 1 K 22:16. Mt 26:63. Ac 19:13. **Cursed**. 1 K ✱16:34. Ml 1:4.

27. **the Lord**. Jsh 1:5, 9. Ge 39:2, 3, 21. Dt 31:6. Mt 18:20. 28:20. Ac 18:9, 10. 2 C 13:14. 2 T 4:17, 22. **his fame**. Jsh 9:1, 3, 9. 1 S 2:30. 2 S 7:9. Mt 4:24. 14:1. Lk 5:15, 16.

JOSHUA 7

Achan takes of the accursed and devoted thing, and God is angry with Israel, 1. Joshua sends three thousand men against Ai, and Israel is defeated; they flee, and thirty-six are slain, 2-5. Joshua, with the elders, humbles himself, and complains before God, 6-9. God shows the cause, directs him how to proceed, and enjoins a lot, 6-15. Achan, taken by lot, confesses his crime, 16-21. He and all belonging to him are stoned, burned, and destroyed, 22-25. The place named the valley of Achor, 26.

1. **committed**. ver. 20, 21. Jsh 22:16. 2 Ch 24:18. Ezr 9:6. Da 9:7. **for Achan**. i.e. *a troubler*, ✱S#5912h. ver. 18, 19, 20, 24. Jsh 22:20. 1 Ch ◑2:6, 7, Achar, Zimri. Ho ◑2:15. **Zabdi**. i.e. *gift of Jehovah; my dowry; giving*, ✱S#2067. ver. 17, 18. 1 Ch 8:19. **Zerah**. Ne 11:17. (1) Grandfather of Achan, Jsh 7:1, 17, 18. (2) A son of Shimhi, a Benjamite, 1 Ch 8:19. (3) One who had charge of David's wine cellars, 1 Ch 27:27. (4) One of the Levites, Ne 11:17. **took**. See on Jsh 6:17, 18. **the anger**. Jsh 22:18. 2 S 24:1. 1 Ch 21:7. Ec 9:18. Jon 1:7. 1 C 5:1-6. He 12:15, 16.

2. **to Ai**. i.e. *a heap of ruins*, ✛S#5857h. ver. 3, 4, 5. Jsh 8:1, 2, 3, 9, 10, 11, 12, 14, 16, 17, 18, 20, 21, 23, 24, 25, 26, 28, 29. 9:3. 10:1, 2. *12:9. Ge 12:8. Hai. Ezr 2:28. Ne 7:32. 11:31, Aija. Je 49:3. **Bethaven**. i.e. *house of iniquity, vanity, sorrow*, ✱S#1007h. Jsh 18:12. Ge 28:19. 1 S 13:5. 14:23. Ho 4:15. 5:8. 10:5. **Go up**. Jsh 2:1. Pr 20:18. 24:6. Mt 10:16. Ep 5:15.

3. **about two.** Heb. about 2000 men, or about 3000 men. **labor.** Pr 13:4. 21:25. Lk 13:24. He 4:11. 6:11, 12. 2 P 1:5, 10. **few.** 1 K *20:11. Ps 34:2.

4. **fled.** Le 26:14, 17. Dt 28:15, 25. 32:30. Is 30:17. 59:2.

5. **for they.** Dt 1:44. **Shebarim.** i.e. *broken places, fractures, terrors,* *S#7671h. **the going down.** *or,* Morad. **wherefore.** See on Jsh 2:9, 11. 5:1. Le 26:36. Ps 22:14. Is 13:7. **melted.** T#1350. Jsh 2:11.

6. **rent.** Ge 37:29, 34. Nu 14:6. 2 S 13:31. Ezr 9:3-5. Est 4:1. Jb 1:20. Jl 2:12, 13. Ac 14:14. **fell.** Nu 16:22, 45. 2 S 12:16. **before the ark.** He=4:16. **until the eventide.** Jg 20:23, 26. 21:2. 2 S 1:12. **put dust.** Rending the clothes, beating the breast, tearing the hair, throwing dust upon the head, and falling prostrate, were usual signs of deep affliction and distress among the ancient Israelites. In illustration of this custom, see 1 S 4:12, when the messenger brought tidings to Eli of the discomfiture of the armies of Israel by the Philistines; again, in the case of Tamar, 2 S 13:19, and in Ne 9:1, when a whole nation "assembled with fasting, and with sackcloth, and earth upon them." See also the case of Mordecai, Est 4:1, and Job, Jb 2:12, where his friends abased themselves to comfort him; refer also to Ezk 27:30. Jon 3:6. Mi 1:10. In each of these instances it is worthy of remark, that putting dust on the head generally follows rending the clothes, and was the usual mode of evincing poignant sorrow.

7. **Alas.** J59, Ge +28:16. **wherefore.** Ex 5:22, 23. 32:12. Nu 14:3. 2 K 3:10. 2 Ch 20:9, 11. Ps 116:11. Je 12:1, 2. He 12:5. **to deliver.** Ex 14:11, 12. 17:3. Nu 20:4, 5. Mt 17:17, 20. Mk 8:17, 18. **would to.** Ex 16:3. **and dwelt.** See on Jsh 1:2-4. He 10:38. 11:15.

8. **what shall.** Ezr *9:10. Hab *2:1. Ro 3:5, 6. **backs.** Heb. necks. ver. 12. Ge 49:8. Ex 23:27.

9. **Canaanites.** Ge +10:18. **shall hear.** Ex 32:12. Nu *14:13, 15, 16. 1 Ch 20:9, 11. **environ.** Ps 83:4. *124:2, 3. **what wilt thou.** Dt *32:26, 27. Ps 106:6-8. Ezk *20:9. *36:22, 23. Jl 2:17. Jn *12:28.

10. **wherefore.** Ex 14:15. 1 S *15:22. 16:1. 1 Ch 22:16. **liest.** Heb. fallest. ver. 6. Ge +17:2, 17. 1 S 5:3, 4. Mt *26:39. Mk 3:11. 5:22. 7:25. 14:35. Lk 5:12. Jn 11:32.

11. **Israel.** ver. 1, 20, *21. **and.** J148, Ge +8:22. **transgressed.** Jsh 23:16. Dt 17:2. Jg 2:20. 2 K *18:12. Is *24:5. 50:1, 2. Je *31:32. Ho 6:7. **the accursed.** See on ver. *21. Jsh 6:17-19. **stolen.** Ml *3:8, 9. Mt *22:21. **dissembled.** 2 K *5:25, 26. Jn *12:5, 6. Ac *5:1, 2, 9. He *4:13. **among.** Le 5:15. Hab *2:6. Zc +*5:3, 4.

12. **the children.** Jsh 22:18-20. Nu 14:45. Jg 2:14. Ps *5:4, 5. Pr 28:1. Is *59:2. Hb *1:13. **they were.** Jsh 6:18. Dt 7:26. Hg 2:13, 14. 1 J 5:21. **neither.** Je 6:8. 23:33. Ho 9:12.

13. **sanctify.** Jsh 3:5. Ex 19:10-15. La 3:40, 41. Jl 2:16, 17. Zp 2:1, 2. **an accursed.** See on ver. 11. 2 Ch 28:10. Mt 7:5. **take away.** 1 C 5:1-6, 11-13.

14. **the tribe.** ver. 17, 18. Ge ◑24:44n. 1 S 10:19-21. 14:38-42. Pr *16:33. Jon 1:7. Ac 1:24-26.

15. **he that is.** ver. 25, 26. Dt 13:15, 16. 1 S 14:38, 39. 1 C *3:16, 17. **he hath.** See on ver. 11. **wrought.** Ge 34:7. Jg 20:6, 10. 1 S 26:21. 2 S 13:12, 13. **folly.** *or,* wickedness. Ge +*34:7. Dt *22:21. Jg 20:6. 1 S +*25:+17, *25. 2 S *13:12, 13. Jb *42:8. Is +9:16 (*S#5039h).

16. **rose up.** See on Jsh +3:1. Ge +22:3. Ps 119:60. Ec *9:10. **and brought.** See on ver. 14.

17. **the family of.** See on Ge 38:30, Zarah. Nu 26:20. 1 Ch 2:4-7.

18. **was taken.** Ge +24:44n. Nu √32:23. 1 S 14:42. Pr *13:21. *16:33. Je 2:26. Ac 5:1-10.

19. **My son.** 2 T 2:25. T 2:2. Ja 1:20. 1 P 3:8, 9. **give.** 1 S 6:5. Is 43:12. Je 13:16. Lk 17:18. Jn 9:24. Re 16:9. **make.** Nu 5:6, 7. 2 Ch 30:22. 33:12, 13. Ezr 10:10, 11. Ps *32:5. *51:3. Pr *28:13. Je 3:12, 13. Da 9:4. Ro *10:10. Ja *5:16. 1 J √1:8-10. **tell me.** 1 S 14:43. Jon 1:8-10.

20. **Indeed.** Ge 42:21. Ex 9:27. 10:16. Nu 22:34. 1 S 15:24, 30. Jb 7:20. 33:27. Ps 38:18. Mt 27:4.

21. **I saw.** Ge *3:6. 6:2. 2 S 11:2. Jb *31:1. Ps *119:◑18, 37. Pr *23:31. *28:22. Mt *5:28, 29. 1 J *2:15, 16. **Babylonish garment.** ✧S#8152h. ver. 24. Ge 25:25. *Addereth shinar,* "a splendid or costly robe of Shinar," the plain in which Babylon stood. Bochart and Calmet have shown at large, that Babylonish robes were very splendid, and in high reputation. Calmet says, they are generally allowed to have been of various colors, though some suppose they were woven thus; others, that they were embroidered with the needle; and others, that they were painted. Silius Italicus seems to think they were woven; Martial supposes them to have been embroidered with the needle; and Pliny and Apuleius speak of them as painted. Ge 10:10mg. 11:2. 14:1, 9, etc. **wedge.** Heb. tongue. **I coveted.** Ge 2:9. *3:6. Ex +*20:17. Dt 7:25. 1 K 21:1, 2. 2 K 5:20-27. Ps 119:36. Hab 2:9. Lk +*12:15. Ro 7:7, 8. Ep 5:3. Col +*3:5. 1 T +*6:9, 10. He *13:5. 2 P 2:15. **took them.** Pr +*4:23. Mi 2:1, 2. Ja *1:15. **they are hid.** ver. 22. Dt 33:19. 2 S 11:6-17. 2 K 5:24, 25. Jb 3:16h. 18:10. Is 28:15. 29:15. Lk 12:2.

23. **laid them out.** Heb. poured. 2 S 15:24. Ps 45:2.

24. **And.** J148, Ge +8:22. **took Achan.** See on ver. 1. Jb 20:15. Pr 15:27. Ec 5:13. Ezk 22:13, 14. 1 T *6:9, 10. **the son.** J171G, Ge +13:8. **his sons, and his daughters.** Jsh 6:18, 21. Ge +√18:25. Ex *20:5. Nu 16:27-31. Dt ◑*24:16. Jb 20:23-28. **and all that he had.** Ge 20:7. Nu 16:32, 33. Ezk 32:27. Da 6:24. **the valley.** ver. 26. Jsh 15:7. Is 65:10. Ho 2:15. **Achor.** i.e. *troubled,* *S#5911h. ver. 26. Jsh 15:7. Is 65:10. Ho 2:15.

25. **Why hast.** ver. 11-13. Jsh 6:18. Ge 34:30. 1 K 18:17, 18. 1 Ch 2:7. Hab 2:6-9. Ga 5:12. 2 Th 1:6. He +*12:15. **all Israel.** Le 20:2. 24:14. Dt 13:10. *17:2-5. 21:21. 22:21-24. **burned them.** ver. 15, 24. Ge 38:24. Le 20:14. 21:9. Dt ◑*24:16. 1 S 31:12. 2 K 23:20. 2 Ch 34:5. Am 2:1. 6:10. Ep 5:11. 1 T *5:22. 2 J 11. If his family was included, it was doubtless because they were sharers of his guilt (Young).

26. **raised.** Jsh 8:29. 10:27. 2 S 18:17. La 3:53. **So the Lord.** Ex 32:12. Nu 25:4. Dt 13:17. 2 S 21:14. Is 40:2. Jl 2:13, 18. Jon 3:9, 10. Zc 6:8. **The valley.** ver. 24. Jg 14:14. Is 65:10. Ho *2:15. **Achor.** that is, *Trouble.* See on ver. 25. Jsh 15:7. **unto this day.** i.e. when the author was writing. Jsh +4:9. Ge +19:38. Dt +29:4.

JOSHUA 8

God puts new courage into Joshua; commands him to go and besiege Ai, promising he should take it, 1,

2. *The stratagem whereby Ai was to be taken, 3-8. The city is taken and destroyed with the inhabitants, 9-22. Its king hanged up, and its spoil divided, 23-29. Joshua builds an altar on Ebal, 30. Sacrifices are offered, 31. The law is written on stones, 32. The law and its blessings and curses are read before the people, as Moses had commanded, 33-35.*

1. **Fear not.** See on Jsh 1:9. 7:6, 7, 9. Dt 1:21. 7:18. 31:8. Ps 27:1. 46:11. Is 12:2. 41:10-16. 43:2. Je 46:27. Mt 8:26. **see, I have.** See on Jsh 6:2. Ps 44:3. Da 2:21, 37, 38. 4:25, 35.

2. **do to Ai.** ver. 24, 28, 29. See on Jsh 6:21. 10:1, 28. Dt 3:2. **only the spoil.** ver. 27. Dt 20:13, 14. Jb 27:16, 17. Ps 39:6. Pr 13:22. 28:20. Je 17:11. Lk 12:20, 21. **lay thee.** ver. 7, 9, 12, 14, 19. Jg 20:29-33. 2 Ch 13:13. 20:22. Je 51:12. **behind.** Ex 3:1.

3. **by night.** Mt 24:39, 50. 25:6. 1 Th 5:2. 2 P 3:10.

4. **lie in wait.** ver. 16. Jg 9:25. 20:29, 33, 36. 1 S 15:2, 5. Ac 23:21. **go not.** Ec 7:19. 9:16. **all ready.** 2 T 2:21.

5. **as at.** Jsh 7:5. **that we will.** Jg 20:31-33. Mt 10:16.

6. **drawn.** Heb. pulled. ver. 16. **They flee.** Ex 14:3. 15:9. Jg 20:32. Ec 8:11. 9:12.

7. **for the Lord.** See on ver. 1. 2 K 5:1. Pr 21:30, 31. **will deliver.** 1 C 15:57.

8. **set the city.** ver. 28. Jg 6:24. **see, I have.** Jsh 1:9, 16. Jg 4:6. 2 S 13:28.

9. **between.** ver. 12. Jg 7:2. Ge 12:8, Hai. Ezr 2:28. Ne 7:32. **lodged.** Ge 32:21.

10. **rose up.** See on Jsh +3:1. 6:12. 7:16. Ps 119:60.

11. **all the.** See on ver. 1-5.

12. **five thousand.** See on ver. 2, 3. **of the city.** *or,* of Ai.

13. **liers in wait.** Heb. lying in wait. ver. 4. Jg 20:29. **on the west.** ver. 8, 12.

14. **Ai saw it.** ver. 5, 16. **he wist not.** Jg 20:34, etc. Ec 9:11, 12. Is 19:11, 13. Da 4:31. Mt 24:39, 50. 1 Th 5:1-3. 2 P 2:3.

15. **by the way.** Jsh 18:12.

16. **called together.** Jg 20:36-39. **drawn away.** ver. 5, 6. Jg 20:31. Ps 9:16. Ezk 38:11-22. Re 16:14. 19:19-21.

17. **a man.** ver. 3, 24, 25. Jsh 11:20. Dt 2:30. Jb 5:13. Is 19:11-13.

18. **Stretch.** ver. 7, 26. Ex 8:5. 17:11. Jb 15:25. **the spear.** The word *keedon* is rendered *clypeum,* a shield or buckler, by the Vulgate; but the LXX translate it *gaison,* which Suidas says, signifies a kind of weapon *oion doratos,* "like a spear." It may denote a short spear, javelin, or lance; for it is evident that it signifies neither the larger spear nor the shield, because it is distinguished from both, 1 S 17:6, 41, 45. Jb 39:23. Joshua may have had a flag or ensign at the end of the spear, which might be seen at a considerable distance when extended, which was the sign agreed upon between him and the ambush.

19. **the ambush.** ver. 6-8.

20. **the smoke.** Ge 15:17. *19:28. Ex 19:18. Is 34:10. Re 18:9. 19:3. **and they had.** Jb 11:20. Ps 48:5, 6. 76:5. Am 2:14-16. **power.** Heb. hand. Jg 18:10. **this way or.** 1 K 20:40.

22. **let none.** Jsh 6:21. 10:28. 11:11, 12. Dt 7:2. Jg 20:36-43. Jb 20:5. Is 8:15. 28:13. Lk 17:26-30. 21:34, 35. 1 Th 5:3.

23. **the king.** ver. 29. Jsh 10:17. 1 S 15:8. Re 19:20.

24. **returned unto Ai.** This must refer to the women

and children, and old persons left behind; for it seems that all the effective men had sallied out when they imagined the Israelites had fled (ver. 16). Jsh 10:30-41. 11:10-14. Nu 21:24. **smote it.** Dt 13:16. Re 18:19, 21-23.

26. **Joshua.** Joshua seems to have been not only the general but the standard-bearer of the army (ver. 18); and continued in this employment, by holding up or extending his spear, during the whole of the battle; and did not slacken from the pursuit till the forces of Ai were utterly discomfited. Some commentators, however, understand this action in a figurative sense, like the holding up of Moses' hands (Ex 17:11), as if it implied that Joshua continued in prayer for the success of his troops, nor ceased till the armies of Ai were annihilated, and the city taken and destroyed. **drew not.** ver. 18. Ex *17:11, 12. **utterly destroyed.** Jsh 2:10. 6:21. 10:1. 11:11. Nu 21:3. Dt 2:34. 3:6. 7:2. 20:17. Jg 1:17. 21:11. 1 S 15:3. 1 K 9:21. 2 K 19:11. 1 Ch 4:41. 2 Ch 20:23. 32:14. Is 11:15. 34:2. 37:11. Je 25:9. 44:11.

27. **the cattle.** ver. 2. Jsh 11:14. Nu 31:22, 26. Ps 50:10. Mt 20:15. **he commanded.** ver. 2.

28. **an heap.** Dt 13:16. 2 K 19:25. Is 17:1. 25:2. Je 9:11. 49:2. 50:26. Mi 3:12. Re 18:19, 21-23. **for ever.** Heb. *olam,* Ex +12:24. **unto this day.** See on Jsh +*4:9.

29. **the king.** The kings of Canaan lay under the same curse as their subjects, and probably were more deeply criminal. The reserving of the king of Ai for a solemn execution, would tend to strike terror into the other kings, contribute to the success of Israel, and give their proceedings the stamp of a judicial process, and of executing the vengeance of God upon his enemies. Jsh 10:26-28, 30, 33. Dt 21:22, 23. Est 7:10. Ps 107:40. 110:5. 149:7-9. Ac 12:23. Re 19:17, 18. **hanged on a tree.** The most disgraceful mode of punishment in ancient times (Young). Jsh 10:26. Dt *21:22n, 23n. **until eventide.** Dt 21:23. **the tree.** ✧121D8, Ge +40:19. **as soon.** Jsh 10:27. **a great heap.** Jsh 7:26. 2 S 18:17. **that.** ✧63H, Ge +12:15. **unto this day.** ver. 28. See on Jsh +*4:9.

30. **built an altar.** Ge +8:20. 12:7, 8. +13:18. **in mount Ebal.** Moses himself had twice given express orders for this solemnity; once Dt 11:29, 30, in which he pointed out the very place where it was to be performed; and again, at the 27th chapter, there is a renewal of the instructions to Joshua, with special reference to minute particulars. It was a federal transaction: the covenant was now renewed between God and Israel upon their taking possession of the land of promise, that they might be encouraged in the conquest of it, and might know upon what terms they held it, and come under fresh obligations to obedience. ver. 33.

31. **as it is.** ver. 34, 35. Jsh *1:8. 2 K 14:6. 22:8. 2 Ch 25:4. 35:12. Ezr 6:18. Ne 13:1. Mk 12:26. **altar.** Ex 20:24, 25. Dt 27:5, 6. 1 K 18:31, 32. **and they offered.** Ex 18:12. 24:5. Dt 27:6, 7. **burnt offerings.** Le +*23:12. **peace offerings.** Le +*23:19.

32. **wrote.** Dt 27:2, 3, 8. Jg 9:6, 7. **copy.** or, duplicate. Dt 17:18.

33. **all Israel.** Jsh 23:2. 24:1. Dt 27:12, 13. 29:10, 11. **priests.** Jsh 3:3, 6, 14. 4:10, 18. 6:6. Dt 31:9, 25. 1 Ch 15:11-15. **stranger.** ver. 35. Ex 12:48, 49. Le 24:22. Nu 15:16, 29. Dt +26:11. 31:12. **Gerizim.** Dt 27:11, 12. **Ebal.** Dt 27:13-15. **Moses.** See on ver. 30-32. Dt 11:29. 27:12.

34. **he read**. Dt 31:10-12. Ne *8:2, 3. *9:3. *13:1. **blessings**. Le ch. 26. Dt 11:26-30. 27:14-26. *28:1-3, etc. 29:20, 21. 30:15-20. **cursings**. Dt 27:13-15. 28:*15, 16, 45. 29:20, 21. *30:19.

35. **was not**. Dt *4:2. Je 23:22. *26:2. Ac *20:26, 27. **Moses commanded**. Dt 31:9-13. **women**. Ex 15:20. 35:22. Dt +*29:11. *31:12. Ezr 10:1. Ne 8:2. Jl 2:16. Mk 10:14. Ac *21:5. **little ones**. or, infants. Jsh 1:14. Dt +*29:11. **strangers**. ver. 33. Ex 12:48. Dt +*26:11. **were**. Heb. walked. **conversant**. The word *conversant*, from the Latin *conversor*, is here used in the classical sense of "having intercourse with;" i.e. living among, dwelling in their midst.

JOSHUA 9

The kings of Canaan hear of Joshua's exploits; consult together, and conclude to fight against Israel, 1, 2. The Gibeonites, feigning themselves to be of a far country, obtain a league, 3-15. The fraud is detected: yet their lives are spared on account of the oath sworn to them, and the promise which was confirmed with an oath remains firm, 16-20. But for a punishment they are condemned to perpetual slavery, and willingly submit, 21-27.

1. **all the kings**. Jsh 10:2-5, 23, 28-39. 11:1-5, 10, 11. 12:7-24. **on this**. Jsh 1:15. 3:17. 5:1. 22:4, 7. Dt 4:49. **of the great**. Jsh 1:4. 15:12. 23:4. Ge 15:18-21. Nu 34:6. **Lebanon**. Jsh 11:17. 12:7. 13:5. Dt 3:25. **Hittite**. Jsh 24:11. Ge +15:20. Ex 3:17. 23:23, 31. 34:11. Dt 7:1. **Amorite**. Ge +10:16. **Canaanite**. Ge +10:18. **Perizzite**. Ge +13:7. **Hivite**. Ge +10:17. **Jebusite**. Ge +10:16.

2. **gathered**. 2 Ch 20:1, etc. Ps 2:1, 2. 83:2-8. Pr 11:21. Is 8:9, 10, 12. 54:15. Jl 3:9-13. Ac 4:26-28. Re 16:14. 20:8, 9. **accord**. Heb. mouth. 2 Ch 18:12mg.

3. **Gibeon**. ver. 17. Jsh 10:1, 2. *11:19. 2 S 21:1, 2. **Jericho**. Jsh 6. 8.

4. **work wilily**. Ge 34:18. Ex 21:14h. 1 K 20:31-33. Pr 1:4h. 8:5, 12mg. Mt 10:16. Lk 16:8. **as if**. Ge +27:16. **ambassadors**. Pr 13:17. 25:13. **wine bottles**. ✳S#4997h. ver. 13. Jg 4:19. 1 S 16:20. Ps 56:8. 119:83. These bottles being made of skin, were consequently liable to be rent, and capable of being mended; which is done, according to Chardin, by putting in a piece, or by gathering up the wounded piece in the manner of a purse; and sometimes by inserting a flat piece of wood. Ps 119:83. Mt *9:17. Mk 2:22. Lk 5:37, 38. **bound up**. with new skin. Ex 12:34. 1 S 25:29. 2 S 20:3mg. Ho 13:12.

5. **old shoes**. ver. 13. Dt 29:5. 33:25. Lk 15:22. **clouted**. or, patched. lit. spotted. Ge 30:32. **provision**. lit. hunting. Ge 25:28. **mouldy**. or, crumbs. ver. 12. 1 K 14:3.

6. **the camp**. Jsh 5:10. 10:43. **We be**. ver. 9. Dt *20:11-15. 1 K 8:41. 2 K 20:14. Lk 14:32. **make ye**. *kirthoo lanoo berith*, "cut or divide with us a covenant," or rather the covenant sacrifice offered on these occasions (See Note on Dt 29:12n).

7. **Hivites**. Jsh 11:19. Ge +10:17. 34:2. Ex 3:8. **how shall**. Ex *23:31-33. 34:12. Nu 33:52. Dt *7:2, 3. *20:16, 17. Jg 2:2. 2 C 6:14. Ep 5:11.

8. **We are**. ver. 11, 23, 25, 27. Ge 9:25, 26. Dt 20:11. 1 K 9:20, 21. 2 K 10:5. **Who are**. Compare the anxiety of Isaac before conferring the blessing of the birthright, in Ge 27:18-26.

9. **From a**. Dt 20:15. **because**. 1 K 8:41. 2 Ch 6:32, 33. Ne 9:5. Ps 72:19. 83:18. 148:13. Is 55:5. Ac 8:7. **we have**. ver. 24. Jsh 2:9, 10. Ex 9:16. *15:14. Nu 14:15. 21:33, 34. Is 66:19.

10. **two kings**. Nu 21:24-35. Dt 2:30-37. 3:1-7. **Ashtaroth**. Jsh 12:4. Dt 1:4. 1 Ch 6:71.

11. **our elders**. Est 8:17. **Take**. Jsh 1:11. Mt 10:9, 10. Lk 9:3. **with you**. Heb. in your hand. Ge 43:12. **We are your**. See on ver. 8. Est 8:17.

12. **our bread**. See on ver. 4, 5.

13. **bottles of wine**. rather, wine bottles.

14. **the men took of their victuals**. *or*, they received the men by reason of their victuals. **asked not**. T#1820. Ge 24:57. Ex 28:30. Nu 27:21. Jg 1:1. 20:18, 28. 1 S 14:18, 19. 22:10. 23:9-12. 30:7, 8. 2 S 2:1. 5:19. 1 K 22:7. 1 Ch 10:13, 14. 15:13. +√28:9. 2 Ch 15:1, 2. 16:12, 13. Ezr 8:21, 22. Jb 15:4, 20, 21. 21:13-20. 36:13, 14. Ps 9:17. *10:4, 5. 33:11. 50:22. 73:24. 79:6. 81:11, 12. 106:13. Pr *1:24-28. √3:5, 6. *12:15. 19:20. Is 11:2, 3. *30:1, 2. 31:1. 65:11, 12. *66:4. Je 7:13-16. +*10:25 (T#548). 21:2. 42:2, 20. Da *9:13, 14. Am 4:6-13. Zp 1:4-6. Lk ◐24:30 (T#1270). 2 C 6:14. He 12:25. Ja √1:5. +*4:2, 3. **mouth**. √22A10, Nu +12:8.

15. **made peace**. Jsh 2:12-19. 6:22-25. 11:19. Dt 20:10, 11. 2 S 21:2. Je 18:7, 8. **and the**. 2 S 21:2.

16. **that they heard**. Pr 12:19. **neighbors**. Ge 45:10.

17. **Gibeon**. Jsh 10:2. 18:25-28. 2 S *21:2. 1 Ch 21:29. 2 Ch 1:3. Ezr 2:25. Ne 7:29. **Chephirah**. i.e. *a village; a young lioness; covert*, ✳S#3716h. Jsh 18:26. Ezr 2:25. Ne 7:29. **Beeroth**. Heb. wells. ✳S#881h. Jsh 18:25. Ge ◐+16:14. 2 S 4:2. Ezr 2:25. Ne 7:29. Compare ✳S#885h, Dt 10:6. **Kirjath-jearim**. lit. city of forests. ✳S#7157h. Jsh 15:9, 60. 18:14, 15. Jg 18:12, 12. 1 S 6:21. 7:1, 2. 1 Ch 2:50, 52, 53. 13:5, 6. 2 Ch 1:4. Ne 7:29. Je 26:20.

18. **had sworn**. 2 S 21:7. Ps *15:4. 24:4. Ec 5:2, 6. 9:2. Ezk *17:18n.

19. **We have**. ver. 20. Ec 8:2. 9:2. Je 4:2. **we may not touch them**. Jg +*11:35. 2 S 21:1-3. Ezk *17:18n. Ro *11:29. Ga 3:15.

20. **lest wrath**. 2 S 21:1-6. 2 Ch 36:13. Pr 20:25. Ezk √17:12-21. Zc +*5:3, 4. Ml +*3:5. Ro 1:31. 1 T 1:10.

21. **let them**. ver. 23, 27. Dt *29:11, 12. 2 Ch 2:17, 18. Is +61:5. **as the princes**. See on ver. 15.

22. **Wherefore**. Ge 3:13, 14. 27:35, 36, 41-45. 29:25. 2 C 11:3. **We are**. ver. 6, 9, 10. **ye dwell**. ver. 16.

23. **cursed**. This may refer to the original curse pronounced against the descendants of Canaan: both of them seem to have implied nothing else than perpetual slavery. The Gibeonites were brought, no doubt, under tribute; performed the meanest offices for the Israelites; being in the same condition as the servile class of Hindoos, called the *Chetrees*; had their national importance annihilated, and yet were never permitted to incorporate themselves with the Israelites. See on Ge 9:25, 26. Le 27:28, 29. **none of you be freed**. Heb. not be cut off from you. **hewers**. ver. 27. 1 Ch 9:2 (Nethinims). Ezr 2:43. 8:20. In the East, collecting wood for fuel, and carrying water, are the peculiar employment of females. The Arab women of Barbary, and the daughters of the Turcomans, are thus employed. Hence Mr. Harmer concludes, that the bitterness of the doom of the Gibeonites does not seem to have consisted in the laboriousness of the service enjoined them, but its disgracing them from the characteristic employment

of men, that of bearing arms, and condemning them and their posterity forever to the employment of females. Compare 2 S 3:29n. ver. 21, 27.

24. **the Lord.** Ex 23:31-33. Nu 33:51, 52, 55, 56. Dt 7:1, 2, 23, 24. 20:15-17. **we were sore.** Ex 15:14-16. Jb 2:4. Mt +√10:28. **lives.** Heb. *nephesh*, our souls. Ge +44:30.

25. **we are.** Ge 16:6. Jg 8:15. 2 S 24:14. Is 47:6. Je 26:14. 38:5. **as it seemeth.** Jg 10:15. 1 S 3:18. Mt 11:26. **good and right.** 2 Ch 14:2. 31:20.

26. **delivered.** Jsh 24:10.

27. **made them.** Heb. gave, *or*, delivered to be. ver. 21, 23. 1 Ch 9:2. Ezr 2:43. 8:20. Ne 7:60. 11:3, Nethinim. **for the altar.** Ps 84:10. Lk 15:19. Ga 4:1, 3. **unto this day.** Jsh +4:9. **in the place.** Jsh 18:1. Dt 12:5. 16:2, +6, +16. 2 Ch 6:6. Ps 78:68. 132:13, 14. Is 14:32. whether at Gilgal, Shiloh, or Jerusalem (Young).

JOSHUA 10

Five of the kings of Canaan, afraid of Joshua, are angry with the Gibeonites, and wage war against them, 1-5. At the request of the Gibeonites, Joshua goes to assist them; and being encouraged by God, he routes the enemy with great slaughter, 6-9. God casts down hailstones upon the enemy, 10, 11. Joshua prays to God, and commands the sun to stand still, which it does for about the space of a day, 12-15. The five kings are discovered in a cave, and shut up there, 16-21. At length they are brought forth, 22, 23; scornfully used, 24, 25; and hanged, 26, 27. Seven kings more are conquered, 28-42. The army returns to Gilgal, 43.

1. **Adoni-zedec.** i.e. *lord of righteousness.* S#139h. Ge 14:18. He 7:1, 2. **Jerusalem.** i.e. *possession or foundation of peace; the abode of harmony,* S#3389h. ver. 3, 5, 23. 12:10. 15:8, 63, 63. 18:28. Ps 51:18. 122:2, 3, 6. Zc 14:2, 4, 8, 10, 11, 12, 14, 16, 17, 21. Ml 2:11. 3:4. **as he had.** Jsh 6:21. 8:2, 22-29. **how the.** Jsh 9:15-27. 11:19, 20. 1 Th 1:8-10.

2. **they feared.** Jsh 2:9-13, 24. Ex 15:14-16. Dt 11:25. 28:10. Ps 48:4-6. Pr 1:26, 27. 10:24. Ac 5:11. He 10:27, 31. Re 6:15-17. **Gibeon.** Gibeon was situated on an eminence, as its name imports, 40 furlongs north from Jerusalem, according to Josephus. Jsh 9:3, 17. 11:19. 18:25. 21:17. 2 S 2:12. 3:30. 20:8. 1 K 3:4, 5. 9:2. 1 Ch 8:29. 9:35. 14:16. 16:39. 21:29. 2 Ch 1:3, 13. Ne 3:7. 7:25. Is 28:21. Je 28:1. 41:12, 16. **the royal cities.** Heb. cities of the kingdom. 1 S 27:5. 2 S 12:26.

3. **king of Jerusalem.** ver. 1, 5. Jsh 12:10-13. 15:35, 39, 54, 63. 18:28. **Hoham.** i.e. *he impels,* ✻S#1944h. **Hebron.** Hebron was situated on an eminence, 20 miles south of Jerusalem, and the same distance north of Beersheba. Jsh 14:15. Ge 23:2. 37:14. Nu 13:22. 2 S 2:11. **Piram.** i.e. *a wild ass; indomitable,* ✻S#6502h. **Japhia.** i.e. *beautiful; splendid; illustrious,* ✻S#3309h. Jsh 19:12. 2 S 5:15. 1 Ch 3:7. 14:6. (1) The Amorite king of Lachish who, with the neighboring kings, laid siege to Gibeon, but was defeated by Joshua, Jsh 10:3. (2) A son of David, born in Jerusalem, 2 S 5:15; 1 Ch 3:7; 14:6. (3) A town of Zebulun, Jsh 19:12. **Lachish.** i.e. *captured; invincible,* ✻S#3923h. ver. 5, 23, 31, 32, 33, 34, 35. Jsh 12:11. 15:39. 2 K 14:19, 19. *18:14, 17. 19:8. 2 Ch *11:9. 25:27, 27. 32:9. Ne 11:30. Is

36:2. 37:8. Je 34:7. Mi *1:13. **Debir.** i.e. *sanctuary; oracle,* ✻S#1688h. ver. 38, 39. Jsh 11:21. 12:13. 13:26. 15:7, 15, 15, 49. 21:15. Jg 1:11, 11. 1 Ch 6:58. (1) King of Eglon, Jsh 10:3, was one of the five kings who fought against Gibeon, and was slain, with his companions, by Joshua, Jsh 10:26. (2) A place in Judah, near Hebron. It was taken by Joshua, Jsh 10:38, 39, and was first called Kirjath-sepher, Jsh 15:15, and Kirjath-sannah, Jsh 15:49. (3) A place near the valley of Achor, Jsh 15:7. (4) A place on the border of Gad, east of Jordan, Jsh 13:26. May be the same as Lo-debar.

4. **and help.** Is 8:9-13. 41:5-7. Ac 19:24-27. 21:28. Re 16:14. 20:8-10. **we may.** ver. 1. Jsh 9:15. Mt 16:24. Jn 15:19. 16:2, 3. Ac 9:23. 2 T 3:12. Ja 4:4. 1 P 4:4. **for it.** Ps 120:6, 7. Pr 11:21.

5. **five kings of.** ver. 6. See on Jsh 9:1, 2. Ge 15:16. Is 8:9, 10.

6. **to the camp.** Jsh 5:10. 9:6. **Slack.** 2 K 4:24. **from thy.** Jsh 9:15, 24, 25. Is 33:22. **mountains.** Jsh 21:11. Dt 1:15. Ps 125:2. Lk 1:39.

7. **Joshua ascended.** Is 8:12, 13.

8. **Fear them not.** Jsh *1:5-9. 8:1. 11:6. Dt 1:29. 3:2. 20:1-4. Jg 4:14, 15. Ps *27:1, 2. Is √41:10-15. Ro *8:31.

9. **all night.** 1 S 11:9-11. Pr 22:29. 24:11, 12. Ec 9:10. 2 T 2:3. 4:2.

10. **the Lord.** Jsh 11:8. Ex 14:14. Dt 1:30. 3:22. Jg 4:15. 1 S 7:10-12. 2 Ch 14:12. Ps 18:13, 14. 44:3. 78:55. **at Gibeon.** Is 28:21. **Beth-horon.** i.e. *house of the little cave,* ✻S#1032h. ver. 11. Jsh 16:3, 5. 18:13, 14. 21:22. 1 S 13:18. 1 K 9:17. 1 Ch 6:68. 7:24. 2 Ch 8:5, 5. 25:13. Young notes there are two places of the same name, the upper (Jsh 16:5; 21:22) and the lower (Jsh 16:3; 18:13; 2 Ch 25:13). **Azekah.** i.e. *a fenced place.* S#5825h. ver. 11. Jsh 15:35. 2 Ch 11:9. Ne 11:30. Je 34:7. **Makkedah.** i.e. *place of shepherds,* ✻S#4719h. ver. 16, 17, 21, 28, 28, 29. Jsh 12:16. 15:41.

11. **the Lord.** Ge 19:24. Ex 9:22-26. Jg 5:20. Jb 38:22, 23. Ps 11:6. 18:12-14. 77:17, 18. 148:8. Is 28:2, 17, 18. 30:30. Ezk 13:11. 38:22, 23. Re 11:19. 16:21.

12. **Sun.** Joshua doubtless acted, on this occasion, by an immediate impulse upon his mind by the Spirit of God. The terms here employed to record the miracle, agree with the accustomed manner in which the motions of the earth and sun are described in our own day. The sun apparently moves, but really is stationary; while the diurnal movement of the earth on its axis is by us unnoticed, and would not have been known except by astronomical science. The sun appeared to the Israelites over Gibeon, and the moon over the valley of Ajalon, and there they stayed in their course for "about a whole day." Many vain enquiries have been made concerning the way in which this miracle was wrought, and many difficulties and objections have been urged against understanding it literally. But the fact is authenticated by the Divine testimony; and the manner in which it was accomplished lies entirely out of our province, because beyond our comprehension. See on ver. *13. Dt *4:19. 17:3. Jb *9:7. 31:26, 27. Ps 19:4. 74:16. 148:3. Is *28:21. *38:8. 60:20. Am 8:9. Hab *3:11. **stand thou.** Heb. be silent. T#1717. Ps +37:7mg. Hab *2:20mg. Zc 2:13. **Ajalon.** i.e. *a little hind; deer field.* S#357h. Jsh 19:42. 21:24. Jg 1:35. 12:12, Aijalon. 1 S 14:31. 1 Ch 6:69. 8:13. 2 Ch 11:10. 28:18.

13. **stood still**. Heb. was silent. i.e. still, as this phrase is commonly used, as 1 S 14:9. Ps 4:4. Jon 1:12; the cessation of the tongue's motion being put synecdochically (*171G3, Synecdoche of the Species: words of a limited and special sense are used with a wider and more universal meaning. Compare *171G2, Ge +13:8.) for the cessation of any other motion or action (Matthew Poole). **until**. Nu 31:2. Jg 5:2. *16:28. Est 8:13. Lk 18:7. Re *6:10. **Jasher**. *or*, the upright. i.e. *straight*, ✢S#3477h. Nu 21:14. 2 S *1:18. 2 Ch 16:11. **So the sun**. ver. 11, 14. Ps 19:4. 74:16, 17. 136:7-9. 148:3. Is 24:23. *38:8. Jl *2:10, 31. 3:15. Mt *5:45. *24:29. Ac 2:20. Re 6:12. 8:12. 16:8, 9. *21:23.

14. **there was**. 2 K 20:10, 11. Is √38:8. Zc 14:7. **the Lord**. Zc 4:6, 7. Mt 21:21, 22. Mk *11:22-24. Lk 17:6. **hearkened**. Jg 13:9. **for the Lord**. ver. 42. Jsh 23:3. Ex 14:4. Dt 1:30.

15. **Joshua returned**. ver. 6, 43. Jn 17:4.

16. **and hid**. Ps 48:4-6. 139:7-10. Is 2:10-12. Am *9:2, 3. Re *6:15. **in a cave**. Jg 6:2. 1 S 13:6. 24:3, 8. Is *2:19-22. 24:21, 22. Mi 7:17.

17. This information brought to Joshua, is an evidence that there were those of the country, who knew the holes and fastnesses of it, that were in his interests. And the care Joshua took to secure them there, as it is an instance of his policy and presence of mind, even in the heat of action; so, in the success of their project, it shows how they who think to hide themselves from God (He ◐11:38. Re 6:15, 16), not only deceive, but destroy themselves. Their refuge of lies will but bind them over to God's judgment (Nu 32:23).

18. **Roll**. ver. 22. Jg 9:46-49. Jb 21:30. Am 5:19. 9:1. Mt 27:66.

19. **stay ye**. Ps 18:37-41. Je 48:10. **smite**. Heb. cut off the tail. Dt 25:18. Is 9:14, 15. **suffer them**. ver. 20. 2 S 17:13. 20:6. Je 8:14.

20. **had made**. ver. 10. Jsh 8:24. 2 Ch 13:17. **fenced cities**. 2 S 20:6. Je 8:14.

21. **to the camp**. ver. 15-17. **none**. Ex 11:7. Is 54:7. 57:4.

22. **Open**. See on ver. 16-18. 1 S 15:32.

23. **the king of**. See on ver. 1, 3, 5.

24. **put your feet**. Dt 33:29. Jg 8:20. 2 S 22:43. Ps 2:8-12. 18:40. 91:13. 107:40. 110:1, 5. 149:8, 9. Pr 16:5. Is 26:5, 6. 28:18. 60:11, 12. Ezk 21:28, 29. Ml 4:3. Ro 16:20. Re 2:26, 27.

25. **Fear not**. See on Jsh *1:9. Dt 31:6-8. 1 S 17:37. Ps 63:9. 77:11. Lk 12:32. 2 C 1:10. 2 T 4:17, 18. **be strong**. Ep 6:10. **thus shall**. See on Dt 3:21, 22. 7:19. Ro 8:37.

26. **Joshua**. Jg 8:21. 1 S 15:33. **hanged**. Jsh 8:29. Nu 25:4. Dt *21:22n, 23n. 2 S 21:6, 9. Est 2:23. 7:9, 10. Mt 27:25. Ga 3:13.

27. **they took**. Jsh 8:29. Dt 21:23n. 2 S 18:17. **which**. *63H, Ge +12:15. **until this very day**. See on Jsh +*4:9. 7:26. Ge +19:38. Dt +29:4.

28. **Makkedah**. *171R, Ex +12:40. Situated, according to Eusebius, 8 miles east from Eleutheropolis. It was afterwards assigned to the tribe of Judah. Jsh 15:21, *41, 42. **them**. ver. 32, 35, 37, 39. Jsh 6:21. Dt 7:2, 16. 20:16, 17. Ps 21:8, 9. 110:1. Lk 19:27. 1 C 15:25. **souls**. Heb. plural of *nephesh*. Here, *nephesh* is used of man being slain or killed by man. In this use *nephesh* may be rendered *everyone*, *individuals*, *persons*, *person*, as it has no essential reference to *soul* as a separate, immaterial, conscious constituent

part of man which survives the dissolution of the body (Mt +√10:28). ver. 30, 32, 35, 37, 37, 39. Jsh 11:11. Je 2:34. Ezk 13:19. 22:25, 27. Rendered "person," Jsh 20:3, 9. Dt 27:25. 1 S 22:22. Pr 28:17. Ezk 17:17. any, Le 24:17. any person, Nu 31:19. 35:11, 15, 30, 30. Ezk 33:6. him, Ge +37:21. Dt 19:6. 22:26. mortally, Dt 19:11. life, 2 S 14:7. thee, Je 40:14, 15. Compare Ge +17:14, where *nephesh* is used of man as being cut off by God. For the other uses of *nephesh* see Ge +2:7. **and he did**. ver. 30. Jsh 8:2. **as he did**. Jsh 6:2, 21.

29. **Libnah**. i.e. whiteness. Jsh 12:15. 15:42. 21:13. 2 K 8:22. 19:8. 23:31. It fell to the tribe of Judah. This city was situated in the south of Judah, and in the district of Eleutheropolis, according to Eusebius and Jerome. It is probably the Libnah in the neighborhood of which the Israelites encamped. Nu 33:20. Je 52:1. **as he did**. ver. 28. Jsh 6:21. 8:2, 29.

30. **all the souls**. i.e. the human souls, for all the cattle they had for a prey (Matthew Poole). ver. +*28. plural of *nephesh*. Jsh 6:21. 8:2, 29.

31. **Lachish**. Lachish was also situated in the south of Judah, seven miles south from Eleutheropolis, according to Eusebius and Jerome. It appears to have been anciently a very strong place; for though the people were panic struck, and the Israelites flushed with success, yet Joshua could not reduce it until the second day; and the king of Assyria afterwards was obliged to raise the siege. ver. 3, 5. Jsh 12:11. 15:21, *39. 2 K 19:8. 2 Ch 11:9. Is 37:8. Mi 1:13.

32. **souls**. Heb. *nephesh*, ver. +*28. **to Libnah**. ver. 30.

33. **Horam**. i.e. *height; very high*, ✢S#2036h. **Gezer**. Gezer was situated on the confines of Ephraim and Manasseh, between Beth-horon and the sea; and is evidently the village of Gazara mentioned by Eusebius, 4 miles north from Nicopolis or Emmaus. Jsh 12:12. 16:3, 10. 21:21. Jg 1:29. 1 K 9:16, 17. 1 Ch 6:67. 14:16. 20:4.

34. **Eglon**. This town appears to have been no great distance from Lachish, with which it is mentioned, Jsh 15:39, as one of the cities given to Judah. ver. 3. Jsh 12:12. 15:39.

35. **on that day**. ver. 32. **souls**. Heb. *nephesh*, ver. +*28. **utterly**. ver. 37. Jsh +8:26. Le 26:44. Jb 19:10.

36. **Hebron**. ver. 3, 5. Jsh 14:13-15. 15:13, 14, 54. 21:13. Ge 13:18. Nu 13:22. Jg 1:10. 2 S 5:1-5. 15:9, 10. 1 Ch 12:23, 28.

37. **the king**. From ver. 23, we learn that the king of Hebron was one of the five whom Joshua slew and hanged on five trees at Makkedah. This slaying of the king of Hebron, therefore, must either refer to what had already been done, or the Hebronites had set up another king, whom Joshua now slew when he took the city. **souls**. Heb. *nephesh*, ver. +*28. **according**. ver. 35. **utterly**. Jsh +8:26. **souls**. i.e. *nephesh*, ver. +*28.

38. **Debir**. Debir was situated in the south of the tribe of Judah, near Hebron. The expression of Joshua's "returning" to Debir probably denotes that having carried his conquests in the southern part as far as Gaza (ver. 41), which was in the southwest angle of Canaan, he then marched back to besiege Debir. Jsh 12:13. 15:15-17, 49. 21:15. Jg 1:11-15.

39. **souls**. Heb. *nephesh*, ver. +*28. **he left none**. ver. 33, 37, 40. Jsh 11:8. Dt 3:3. 2 K 10:11. Ob 18.

40. **all the country**. Jsh 15:21-63. 18:21-28. 19:1-8,

40-48. **springs**. Jsh 12:3, 8. Dt 3:17. 4:49. 8:7. **utterly**. ver. 35, 37. Jsh +8:26. Dt 20:16, 17. 1 K 15:29. Ps 9:17. 2 Th *1:7-9. **all that breathed**. Jsh 11:11, 14. Ge +√2:7 (✱S#5397h). 7:22. Dt 20:*16. i.e. all mankind, by a synecdoche (𝑓171R. Synecdoche of the Part: an integral part of men, "all that breathed," is put for the whole, "all mankind." See Ex +12:40); for they reserved the cattle for their own uses (ver. 30). **as the Lord God of Israel commanded**. 𝑓171R, Jsh 6:17. 8:2, 27. 9:24. Ex +12:40. 23:31-33. 34:12. Dt 7:2, 16. 20:16, 17. Am +*3:6. Matthew Poole notes that this is added for the vindication of the Israelites, whom God would not have to suffer in their reputation for executing his commands; and therefore he acquits them of that implacable hatred and heinous cruelty which they might be thought guilty of, and ascribes it to himself and his own just indignation against this most wicked people.

41. **Kadesh-barnea**. Jsh 14:6, 7. Nu 13:26. 32:8. 34:4. Dt 1:19. 9:23. **Gaza**. Ge 10:19. Jg 16:1, 21. 1 S 6:17. Zc 9:5. Ac 8:26. **all the country of Goshen**. i.e. *drawing near*, ✱S#1657h. (1) The name of a district of Lower Egypt which lay apparently to the east of the Pelusiac, or eastern branch of the Nile, near to On or Heliopolis, and which Joseph assigned as the residence of his father and his brethren: Ge 45:10. 46:28, 28, 29, 34. 47:1, 4, 6, 27. 50:8. Ex 8:22. 9:26. (2) A district in the hill country of Judah. Not that Goshen in Egypt, but another in Judah, Jsh 11:16. (3) A town enumerated among the cities of Judah, Jsh 15:51. The country of Goshen, mentioned here, seems to have been in the south of Judah; and to have taken its name from the city Goshen, situated in the same tribe. **Gibeon**. ver. +*2, 12. 1 K 3:5.

42. **because**. ver. 14. Ex 14:14, 25. Dt 20:4. Ps 44:3-8. 46:1, 7, 11. 80:3. 118:6. Is 8:9, 10. 43:4. Ro *8:31-37. Ep 6:10-12. Ph *4:13. Col 2:15. 1 T 6:12.

43. **unto the camp**. ver. 15. Jsh 4:19. 1 S 11:14.

JOSHUA 11

The remaining kings and cities of Canaan gather themselves to fight against Israel, 1-5. God encourages Joshua, promising him victory, 6. Joshua attacks and conquers them at the waters of Merom, 7-9. He burns Hazor, and takes the cities of the other kings, and destroys the inhabitants in obedience to the Lord, 10-15. A general account of all the country taken by Joshua, 16-18. The hearts of the Canaanites hardened, 19, 20. The Anakims destroyed, except for those in Gaza, Gath, and Ashdod, 21, 22. The land rests from war, 23.

1. **Jabin**. i.e. *whom God observes; he understands*, ✱S#2985h. ver. 10. Jsh 12:19. 19:36. Jg 4:2, 7, 17, 23, 24, 24h. Ps 83:9h. (1) A king of Hazor who was defeated by Joshua near the lake Merom, Jsh 11:1. (2) Another king of the same name and place, who oppressed the Israelites twenty years in the time of the judges, Jg 4:2, 7, 17, 23, 24; Ps 83:9. **he sent**. Jsh 10:3, 4. Ps 2:1-4. 83:1-3. Is 26:11. 43:2, 5-7. **Madon**. i.e. *contention*, ✱S#4068h. Jsh 12:19. The LXX. read *Maron*, which, if legitimate, Calmet thinks may be the same as *Maronia* or *Marath* in Phoenicia, to the north of mount Lebanon. Jsh 12:19, 20. 19:15, 25. **Shimron**. Supposed to be the same with *Symira*, in Coele-Syria, joined to Maron or Marath by Pliny and Pomponius Mela. **Achshaph**. i.e. *enchantment*, ✱S#407h. Jsh 12:20. 19:25. Supposed by some to be the same as *Achzib* or *Ecdippa*; from which, however, it is distinguished in Jsh 19:25, 29. It was in the northern part of the tribe of Asher.

2. **on the north**. ver. 21. Jsh 10:6, 40. Lk 1:39. **Chinneroth**. i.e. *harps*, ✱S#3672h. Jsh 12:3. Dt ◐3:16, 17. 1 K 15:20. Jerome and others suppose this city to be the same as was afterwards called *Tiberias*, now *Tabaria*, situated on the western shore of the lake of the same name. Jsh 12:3. See on Nu 34:11, Chinnereth, 12. Lk 5:1, Gennesaret. **Dor**. Jsh 12:23. 17:11. Jg 1:27. 1 K 4:11.

3. **Canaanite**. Ge +10:18. **Amorite**. Ge +10:16. **Hittite**. Ge +15:20. **Perizzite**. Ge +13:7. **the Jebusite**. Jsh 15:63. Ge +10:16. Nu 13:29. 2 S 24:16. **Hivite**. ver. ◐19. Ge +10:17. Jg 3:3. The "Hivite under Hermon" is to be differentiated from those Hivites who lived in Gibeon, Jsh 9:3-15. **Hermon**. Jsh 13:11. Dt 4:48. Ps 89:12. 133:3. SS 4:8. **land of Mizpeh**. Jsh 18:26. Ge *31:49. Jg 11:11n, 29. 20:1. 21:5, 8. 1 S 7:5-7. 10:17. 1 K 15:22. Je 40:6, 10. 41:3, 14. Matthew Poole notes that there were other cities called by the name *Mizpeh*, which signifying a watching-place, might be easily applied to several places of good prospect. Besides Mizpeh of Gilead, there is one Mizpeh of Judah, Jsh 15:38; another of Benjamin, Jsh 18:26; a third in Moab, 1 S 22:3.

4. **as the sand**. 𝑓102B, 𝑓138B, Ge +13:16. Ge 22:17. 32:12. Jg 7:12. 1 S 13:5. 2 S 17:11. 1 K 4:20. 2 Ch *20:15. Re 20:9.

5. **all these**. Ps 3:1. 118:10-12. Is 8:9. Re 16:14. **met together**. Heb. assembled by appointment. Ec +*3:8. **Merom**. i.e. *high place*, ✱S#4792h. ver. 7.

6. **Be not**. See on Jsh 10:8. Ps 20:7, 8. *27:1, 2. 33:16, 17. 46:11. Is *8:12, 13. **tomorrow**. Jsh 3:5. Jg 20:28. 1 S 11:9. 2 Ch 20:16. **hough**. ver. 9. 2 S 8:4. **horses**. Dt 17:16. Ps 20:7, 8. 46:9. 147:10, 11. Pr 20:7. Is 30:16. 31:1. Ho 14:3.

7. **suddenly**. Jsh 10:9. Pr 6:15. Is 29:5. 1 Th 5:2, 3.

8. **the Lord**. Jsh 21:44. **great Zidon**. or, Zidon-rabbah. Jsh 19:28. Ge 10:15. 49:13. Zc 9:2. **Misrephothmaim**. or, salt pits. Heb. burning of waters. i.e. boilings. ✱S#4956h. Jsh 13:6. Calmet identified it with the Sarepta in Lk 4:26. **Mizpeh**. ver. +3. Ge *31:49. Jg 11:29. 1 S 7:5.

9. **he houghed**. ver. 6. 2 S 8:4. Ps 46:9. Ezk 39:9, 10.

10. **Hazor**. ver. 1. Jg 4:2. **the head of all those kingoms**. Not of all Canaan, but of all those who were confederate with him in this expedition (Matthew Poole). 𝑓171B. Synecdoche of the Genus: when "all" and "every," as universal affirmations, extend not to all the individuals, but to all that are specified or implied, Ge +*24:10. Compare Ge 41:57; 1 K √18:10.

11. **smote**. T#982‡. Jsh 10:32. Ezk +18:4 (T#981‡). **souls**. Heb. plural of *nephesh*. Jsh +*10:28. Mt ◐+√10:28. **edge of**. 2 C 10:4. He 4:12. **not any**. i.e. *no human person*. 𝑓171B, Ge +24:10. See ver. 10n. **any left to breathe**. Heb. any breath. T#989‡. ver. +14. Ge +*2:7 (✱S#5397h). Jsh +10:40. Jb x7:15.

12. **all the**. Jsh 10:28, 30, 32, 35, 37, 39, 40. **utterly destroyed**. Jsh +8:26. **as Moses**. ver. 15. Jsh 8:8, 31. 9:24. *10:40. Nu 33:52, 53. Dt 7:2. *20:16, 17.

13. **in their.** Heb. on their heap. The Vulgate, Syriac, Onkelos and Waterland render *al tillom,* "on their hills." As the cities of the plain might be easily attacked and carried, Joshua destroyed them; but as those on mountains, hills, or other eminences, might be retained by him with little trouble, prudence would dictate their preservation. Je 30:18.

14. **the spoil.** Jsh 8:27. Nu 31:9. Dt 6:10, 11. 20:14. **neither.** ver. 11. Ge +*2:7 (*S#5397h). Jsh +10:40.

15. **the Lord.** See on ver. 12. Ex 34:11-13. **so did Moses.** Ex 34:11, 12. Dt 7:2. 31:7. **and so did Joshua.** Jsh 1:7. Ex 39:42, 43. Dt 4:5. 2 Ch 30:12. **he left nothing undone.** Heb. removed nothing. Dt *4:2. *12:32. 1 S 15:1-3, 8, 9, 11, 19-22. Mt *23:23. Lk 11:42. Ac *20:20, 27.

16. **all that land.** Ge 15:18-21. Nu 34:2-13. Dt 34:2, 3. **hills.** Jsh 9:1. 12:8. **the south.** Jsh 10:40. 12:8. 18:5. Nu 13:22, 29. 21:1. **the land.** Jsh 10:41. **the mountain.** ver. 21. Ezk 17:23. 36:1-3, 8.

17. **the mount Halak.** *or,* the smooth mountain. i.e. *smooth, bare,* *S#2510h. Jsh 12:7. **that goeth.** Ge 32:3. Dt 2:1. 33:2. **Seir.** ver. 3. Jsh 1:4. 12:7. 13:5. **Baalgad.** i.e. *lord of a troop or fortune,* *S#1171h. Jsh 12:7. 13:5. **all their.** Jsh 12:7-24. Dt 7:24. Ep 6:12. Col 2:15.

18. **a long time.** Caleb was forty years old when sent from Kadesh-barnea to spy the land, and he was eighty-five at the conclusion of this war (Jsh 14:10). Almost thirty-nine years of this time were spent before Israel passed Jordan; which leaves between six and seven years for the term of Joshua's wars. ver. 23. Jsh 14:7-10. Dt 7:22.

19. **the Hivites.** See on Jsh 9:3-27.

20. **it was.** See on Ex 4:21. 7:13. 9:12, 16. 14:17. Dt +*2:30. Jg 14:4. 1 S 2:25. 1 K 12:15. 22:20-23. 2 Ch 25:16. Is *6:9, 10. Ro 9:*18, 22, 23. **as the Lord.** ver. 12-15. Dt *20:16, 17.

21. **the Anakims.** Jsh 14:12-14. 15:13, 14. Nu 13:22, 28, +*33. Dt 1:28. 2:+*20, 21. 9:2. Jg 1:10, 11, 20. Je 3:23. 9:23. Am 2:9. **Anab.** i.e. *a grape,* *S#6024h. Jsh 15:50. **from the mountains.** Heb. mountain. or, hill country. The singular number is put for the plural. *96F.1. Heterosis of Number, the Singular for the Plural, Ge +3:8. **Joshua destroyed.** Jsh +8:26. 10:40n, 42. 24:11, 12. Ps 110:5, 6. *149:6-9. Re 6:2. 19:11-21. **Judah, and from.** Matthew Poole notes: "It doth not follow from hence, which some conclude, that this book was written by some other person long after Joshua's death, even after the division of the Israelites into two kingdoms, of Israel and Judah; but only that this was one of those clauses which were added or altered and suited to the style of the present times by Ezra, or some other prophet, though that be not necessary; for since it was evident to Joshua, from Ge 49:9, etc. that the tribe of Judah was to be the chief of all the tribes, and some dawnings of its eminency appeared in that time, in their having the first lot in the land of Canaan, Jsh 15:1, and the largest inheritance, Jsh 19:9, it is no wonder that it is mentioned apart, and distinguished from the rest of the tribes of Israel, though that also be one of them; even as 'the daughter of Pharaoh' is distinguished from 'the strange women,' 1 K 11:1, and Saul from *all* David's *enemies,* Ps 18, title, and *Peter* from the *disciples,* Mk 16:7, though they were each of the same nature and quality with the rest."

22. **only.** Jsh 23:13. Nu *33:55. **in Gaza.** Jg 3:3. 1 S 17:4. 2 S 21:16-22. 1 Ch 18:1. 20:4-8. **Gath.** i.e. *a wine trough; winepress,* *S#1661h. Jsh 19:13. 1 S 5:8. 6:17. 7:14. 17:4, 23, 52. 21:10, 12. 27:2, 3, 4, 11. 2 S 1:20. 15:18. 21:20, 22. 1 K 2:39, 39, 40, 40, 41. 2 K 12:17. 14:25. 1 Ch 7:21. 8:13. 18:1. 20:6, 8. 2 Ch 11:8. 26:6. Ps 56:t. Am 6:2. Mi 1:10. **Ashdod.** i.e. *fortified,* *S#795h. Jsh 15:46, 47. 1 S 5:1, 5, 6, 7. 6:17. 2 Ch 26:6, 6. Ne 13:23, 24. Is 20:1, 1. Je 25:20. Am 1:8. 3:9. Zp 2:4. Zc 9:6.

23. **the whole land.** Synecdochically (*171A. Synecdoche of the Genus: All is put for the greater part. Ex +9:6), i.e. the greatest and best part of it, for some parts and places are expressly excepted in the following history. **according to all.** Ex 23:27-31. 34:11. Nu 34:2-13. Dt 11:23-25. 34:1-4. **according to their.** Jsh 14-19. Nu 26:52-55. **And the land.** ver. 18. Jsh 14:15. 21:44, 45. 22:4. 23:1. Ps 46:9. 2 T 4:7, 8. He 4:8, 9.

JOSHUA 12

A catalog of the kings, and their possessions, out of which they were driven by the Israelites; first in the time of Moses on the other side, or eastward of Jordan, 1-6; and afterwards the kings which Joshua smote on this side or westward of Jordan, 7-23; in all thirty-one kings, 24.

1. **on the other.** Jsh 1:15. 22:4. **from the.** Nu 21:13, 24. Dt 2:24. Jg 11:18. Is 16:2. **unto mount Hermon.** Jsh 11:3, 17. Dt 3:8, 9. 4:48. Ps 133:3.

2. **Sihon.** Nu 21:23-30. Dt 2:24-37. 3:6-17. Ne 9:22. Ps 135:11. 136:19, 20. **Jabbok.** Ge 32:22. Jg 11:13, 22.

3. **sea of Chinneroth.** This inland sea, or rather lake, derives its several names, the Lake of Tiberias, Sea of Galilee, Lake of Gennesareth, from the territory which forms its western and southwestern border. See on Jsh 11:2. Dt 3:17. Jn 6:1, Sea of Tiberias. **the sea.** Jsh 3:16. 15:2, 5. Ge 14:3. 19:25. Dt 3:17. **Beth-jeshimoth.** i.e. *house of the deserts,* *S#1020h. Jsh 13:20. Nu 33:49. Ezk 25:9. **the south.** *or,* Teman. Jsh 11:16. 13:4. Jb 9:9. Ezk 47:19. Hab 3:3mg. **Ashdoth-pisgah.** *or,* the springs of Pisgah, *or,* the hill. Nu 21:20mg. Dt 3:17mg. 4:49.

4. **the coast.** Nu 21:33-35. Dt 3:1-7, 10, 11, 13. **Bashan.** Nu +21:33. Dt 32:14. Ps 22:12. lit. the Bashan, famous for pasturage. lit. soft, sandy. The northern part of the region beyond Jordan, and afterwards occupied by the half-tribe of Manasseh; it is celebrated for its oaks (Is 2:13. Ezk 27:6. Zc 11:2); its fertility and cattle (Dt 32:14. Ps 22:12. Ezk 39:18. Am 4:1). **the remnant.** Jsh 13:12. Dt +*2:20. 3:11. **dwelt.** See on Dt 1:4. **and at.** To wit, successively; sometimes at the one, sometimes at the other city; both being his royal mansions (Matthew Poole).

5. **Hermon.** See on ver. 1. Jsh 11:3. Dt 3:8, 9. 4:47, 48. **Salcah.** Jsh 13:11. Dt 3:10. **unto the border.** Jsh 13:13. Dt 3:14. 1 S 27:8. 2 S 3:3. 13:37. 15:8. 23:34. 2 K 25:23. **Geshurites.** +S#1651h. Jsh 13:11, 13, 13. 1 S 27:8.

6. **did Moses.** Nu 21:24-35. **gave it.** Jsh 13:8-32. Nu 32:29-42. Dt 3:11-17.

7. **on this side.** ver. 1. Dt 3:17. 9:1. **Baal-gad.** Jsh 11:17. 13:5. **Seir.** Ge 14:6. 32:3. 36:8, 20, 30. Dt 2:1, 4. **Joshua gave.** Jsh 1:3, 4. 11:23. 13-19. Dt 11:23, 24.

8. **the mountains.** Jsh 10:40. 11:16. **the wilderness.** This word here and elsewhere in Scripture notes not a land wholly desert and uninhabited, but one thin of inhabitants, as 1 K 2:34. 9:18. Mt 3:1, 3. **the Hittites.** Jsh 9:1. Ge 15:18, 19, +*20, 21. Ex 3:8. 23:23, 28-31. Dt 7:1. 9:1. **Amorites.** Ge +10:16. **Canaanites.** Ge +10:18. **Perizzites.** Ge +13:7. **Hivites.** Ge +10:17. **Jebusites.** Ge +10:16.

9. **Jericho.** Jsh 6:2-21. **Ai.** Jsh 8:1, 17, 29, etc. **which is beside Bethel.** This is added to distinguish it from Ai of the Ammonites, Je 49:3. Similarly, at Mi 5:2, *Bethlehem Ephratah* (Ge 35:19) is to be distinguished from Bethlehem in Zebulun, Jsh 19:15.

10. **Jerusalem.** See on Jsh 10:23. **Hebron.** Jsh 10:3, 23, 36, 37.

11. **Jarmuth.** Jsh 10:3-23. **Lachish.** Jsh 10:3, 23, 31, 32.

12. **Eglon.** Jsh 10:3, 23. 15:39. **Gezer.** Jsh 10:33.

13. **Debir.** Jsh 10:3, 38. **Geder.** i.e. *a wall*, *S#1445h. Jsh ⬤15:36.

14. **Hormah.** Nu 14:45. 21:3. **Arad.** Nu 21:1.

15. **Libnah.** Jsh 10:+29, 30. **Addullam.** i.e. *justice of the people; a testimony to them; retreat; hiding place,* *S#5725h. Jsh 15:35. 1 S 22:1. 2 S 23:13. 1 Ch 11:15. 2 Ch 11:7. Ne 11:30. Mi 1:15.

16. **Makkedah.** Jsh 10:28. **Bethel.** Jsh 8:17. Ge 12:8. 28:19. Jg 1:22.

17. **Tappuah.** Jsh 15:34. **Hepher.** Jsh 19:13. 1 K 4:10.

18. **Aphek.** i.e. *strength; strong or fortified place,* *S#663h. Jsh 13:4. 19:30. 1 S 4:1. 29:1. 1 K 20:26, 30. 2 K 13:17. (1) A royal city of the Canaanites. Its king was slain by Joshua, Jsh 12:18. Probably the same as Aphekah, Jsh 15:53. (2) A city of Asher, Jsh 19:30, near Sidon. Probably the same as Aphik, Jg 1:31. (3) A place northwest of Jerusalem where the Philistines encamped before the ark was taken, 1 S 4:1. It is now called *Belled el-Foka.* (4) A place in Issachar where the Philistines were before they defeated Saul, 1 S 29:1. (5) A walled city of Syria, 1 K 20:26, 30, about six miles east of the Sea of Galilee. It is now called *Fik.* **Lasharon.** or, Sharon. S#8289h. Is 33:9.

19. **Madon.** Jsh 11:1. **Hazor.** Jsh 11:1, 10, 11. Jg 4:2.

20. **Shimron-meron.** i.e. *guardian of arrogance; guard of lashing,* *S#8112h, only here. Jsh 11:1. 19:15. **Achshaph.** Jsh 11:1. 19:25. Achshaph, a place in the tribe of Asher (Jsh 19:25, 31), the furthest part of the land toward the north and west.

21. **Taanach.** Jsh 17:11. Jg 5:19. **Megiddo.** i.e. *gathering; place of multitudes,* *S#4023h. Jsh +17:11. Jg 1:27. 5:19. 1 K 4:12. 9:15. 2 K 9:27. 23:29, 30. 1 Ch 7:29. 2 Ch 35:22. Zc 12:11, Megiddon.

22. **Kedesh.** Jsh 15:23. 19:35, 37, 39. 21:32. **Jokneam.** i.e. *possessed by the people,* *S#3362h. Jsh 19:11. 21:34. **Carmel.** i.e. *a fruitful place.* Jsh 15:55. 19:26. 1 S 15:12. 25:2, 5, 7, 40. 1 K 18:19, 20, 42. 2 K 2:25. 4:25. Is 35:2.

23. **Dor.** i.e. *habitation, circuit, circle; generation; dwelling,* *S#1756h. Jsh 11:2. 17:11. Jg 1:27. 1 K 4:11. 1 Ch 7:29. **the nations.** Ge 14:1, 2. Is 9:1. **Gilgal.** Jsh 4:19. 5:9, 10. Not of that Gilgal where Joshua first lodged after his passage over Jordan, where it doth not appear that there was either king or city; but of another city of the same name (as was frequent in those parts: see Jsh 12:9n), probably in Galilee towards

the sea, whither divers people might possibly resort for trade and merchandise, over whom this was king, as formerly Tidal seems to have been, Ge 14:1 (Matthew Poole).

24. **Tirzah.** i.e. *pleasantness.* 1 K 14:17. 15:21, 33. 16:6, 8, 15, 23. 2 K 15:14. SS 6:4.

JOSHUA 13

God makes known to Joshua the bounds of the land not yet conquered, 1-6. Joshua is directed to divide the whole by lot, 7. The inheritance of the two tribes and a half on the other side of Jordan, 8-13. The Lord and his sacrifices are the inheritance of Levi, 14. The borders of Reuben, 15-23; of Gad, 24-28; of the half tribe of Manasseh, 29-32. No inheritance assigned to Levi, 33.

1. A.M. 2560. B.C. 1444. An. Ex. Is. 47. **Joshua.** Jsh 14:10. 23:1, 2. 24:29. Ge 18:11. 1 K 1:1. Lk 1:7. **there remaineth.** Ph 3:13. **land.** Dt 32:9. Ps 16:5. **to be possessed.** Heb. to possess it. Dt 31:3.

2. **the land.** Ex 23:29-31. Dt 11:23, 24. Jg 3:1. Am 9:7. **borders.** Ge 10:14. 26:1. Jl 3:4. **Geshuri.** ver. 11, 13. Jsh 12:5. 1 S 27:8. 2 S 3:3. 13:37, 38. 15:8.

3. **Sihor.** i.e. *black; turbid,* *S#7883h. 1 Ch 13:5. Is 23:3. Je 2:18. **Ekron.** i.e. *uprooting,* *S#6138h. Jsh 15:11, 45, 46. 19:43. Jg 1:18. 1 S 5:10, 10. 6:16, 17. 7:14. 17:52, 52. 2 K 1:2, 3, 6, 16. Je 25:20. Am 1:8. Zp 2:4. Zc 9:5, 7. **which is counted.** Ge 10:15-19. Nu 34:2-14. Dt 2:23. Am 9:7. **five lords.** Jg 3:3. 1 S 6:4, 16, 17. Zp 2:4, 5. The Philistines were not descended from Canaan, but from Mizraim, the son of Ham (compare Ge 10:6 with ver. 13); yet they were numbered with the Canaanites in this distribution. **Gazathites.** *S#5841h. Jg 16:2, Gazites. **Ashdothites.** *S#796h. 1 S 5:3, 6. Ne 4:7. 13:23. **Eshkalonites.** *S#832h. Jg +1:18 (Askelon). **Gitites.** *S#1663h. 2 S 6:10, 11. 15:18, 19, 22. 18:2. 21:19. 1 Ch 13:13. 20:5. **Ekronites.** *S#6139h. 1 S 5:10. **Avites.** Dt 2:23, Avims.

4. **the land of.** Jsh 10:40. 11:3. 12:7, 8. **Canaanites.** Ge +10:18. **Mearah.** or, the cave. *S#4632h. **Aphek.** This is probably the Aphek spoken of in 1 K 20:26. 2 K 13:18, as the capital of the kings of Syria, celebrated for the infamous temple of Venus the Aphacite. This is not the Aphek of Judah of Jsh 15:53, but the Aphek in the tribe of Asher, Jsh 12:18; Jg 1:31. Jsh 19:30, 31. Jg 1:31. 1 S 4:1. **the Amorites.** Ge +10:16. Jg 1:34-36.

5. **Giblites.** i.e. *stone-squarer,* see 1 K 5:18mg. Ps 83:7. Ezk 27:9. *S#1382h. 1 K 5:18h. Probably the inhabitants of the country around Gebal (Ezk 27:9), or Byblos, as the LXX. render, a city of Phoenicia, situated on the Mediterranean, between Sidon and Tripoli, on the north of the river Adonis. Its walls are about a mile in circumference, with square towers about every forty yards' distance. Anciently it must have been a place of no mean extent and of considerable beauty, from the ruins still visible. **Lebanon.** Dt 1:7. 3:25. **Baal-gad.** Jsh 12:7. **under mount.** Jsh 11:17. **unto the.** Nu 34:8. Is 10:9. Am 6:2.

6. **hill country.** lit. mountain. ⌐121J7A. Metonymy of the Subject B575. Mountain is put for mountainous region. For other instances of this figure see Jg 3:27. 7:24. **Misrephoth-maim.** Jsh 11:8. **them.** Jsh 23:11-13. Ge 15:18-21. Ex 23:30, 31. Jg 2:21-23. **only divide.**

See on Jsh 14:1, 2. Nu 26:55, 56. 33:54. **by lot.** Ge +24:44n.

7. **this land.** Nu 26:53-56. 33:54. 34:2-14. Ezk 47:13-23. 48:23-29.

8. **Moses gave.** Jsh 4:12. 22:4. Nu 32:33-42. Dt 3:12-17.

9. **Aroer.** ver. 16. Jsh 12:2. Dt 2:36. 3:12, 16. 4:48. Is 17:2. **all the plain.** Nu 21:30. 33:45, 46. Is 15:2. Je 48:18, 22.

10. **the cities of.** Nu 21:24-26. Ps 136:19.

11. **Gilead.** Jsh 12:2-5. Dt 3:12, 13. 4:47, 48. 1 Ch 2:23. **Salchah.** i.e. *extension; straitened basket,* ✳S#5548h. Jsh 12:5. Dt 3:10. 1 Ch 5:11.

12. **Og.** Jsh 12:4. Dt 3:10, 11. **these did.** Jsh 14:3, 4. Nu 21:23-35. Not all now mentioned, as appears from ver. 13, but Sihon and Og, and their people, and the generality of them, which he had now named, some of them being excepted. ʃ171A, Ex +9:6. Synecdoche of the Genus: All or the whole put for the greater part. See Jsh 11:23.

13. **expelled.** ver. 11. Jsh 23:12, 13. Nu *33:55. Jg *2:1-3. 2 S 3:3. 13:37, 38. **until this day.** Jsh +*4:9.

14. **Levi.** See the Note on ver. 33. Jsh 14:3, 4. Nu 18:20-24. Dt 10:9. 12:12, 19. 18:1, 2. **Sacrifices of the Lord...made by fire.** Which by a synecdoche are here put for all those sacrifices and oblations, including first-fruits and tithes, which were assigned to the Levites. ʃ171S10, Synecdoche of the Part: a part of a thing is put for the whole of the thing. Ge +14:7.

15. Heshbon, Dibon, and Ataroth were upon the borders of Reuben and Gad, and therefore sometimes are ascribed to Reuben, as here, and Nu 32:37, sometimes to Gad, as Nu 32:34; 1 Ch 6:80, 81, by whom Heshbon is said to be given to the Levites, Jsh 21:39. Possibly it and the rest were jointly inhabited by both tribes, as Jerusalem was by Jews and Benjamites (Matthew Poole).

16. **from Aroer.** ver. 9. Jsh 12:2. Nu 21:28-30. 32:33-38. Dt 3:12. Is 15:1, 2, 4. 16:7-9. Je 48:21-24.

17. **Heshbon.** Jsh 21:38, 39. Nu 32:37, 38. 1 Ch 6:80, 81. **Dibon.** Eusebius says the city was situated in the plain of the Arnon. **Bamoth-baal.** *or,* the high places of Baal, and the house of Baal-meon. ✳S#1120h. Nu 21:19, 20. 22:41h. 32:37, 38. **Beth-baal-meon.** i.e. *house of habitation of Baal,* ✳S#1010h.

18. **Jahaza.** i.e. *trodden down,* ✳S#3096h. Jsh 21:36, 37. Nu 21:23, Jahaz. Dt 2:32. 1 Ch 6:78, 79, Jahzah. Je 48:21. **Kedemoth.** i.e. *beginnings,* ✳S#6932h. Dt 2:26. 1 Ch 6:79. Supposed to have been situated east of the Arnon, from the wilderness of which Moses sent messengers to Sihon, Dt 2:26; given to the Levites. **Mephaath.** i.e. *beauty; splendor,* ✳S#4158h. Situated near the desert, east of Moab, given to the Levites, as in Jsh 21:36, 37. 1 Ch 6:79. Je 48:21.

19. **And Kirjathaim.** Nu 32:37, 38. **Sibmah.** Called "Shibmah," Nu 32:38, and celebrated for its vines, Je 48:32. Is 16:8, 9; on which last place, Jerome says, there were scarcely 500 paces between it and Heshbon. **Zareth-shahar.** i.e. *the beauty of dawn, brightness of the dawn,* ✳S#6890h.

20. **Beth-peor.** Nu 25:3. Dt 4:46. **Ashdoth-pisgah.** *or,* springs of Pisgah, *or,* the hill. Jsh 12:3mg. Dt 3:17. **Beth-jeshimoth.** Nu 33:49. Ezk 25:9.

21. **And all the kingdom of Sihon.** Dt 3:10. A synecdochical expression, for a great part of it (ʃ171A, Synecdoche of the Genus: All or the whole is put for the greater part; as Jsh 11:23; 13:12. Ex +9:6); in which sense we read of "all Judea," and "all the region round about Jordan," Mt 3:5, "and all Galilee," Mt 4:23, and many others. **whom Moses.** Nu 21:24-35. Dt 2:30-36. **with the.** Nu 31:8.

22. **Balaam.** Nu 22:5-7. 24:1. 31:8. Dt 23:4. Mi 6:5. 2 P *2:15. Ju *11. Re 2:14. 19:20. **soothsayer.** *or,* diviner. Ge +30:27. Dt 18:*10, 14.

23. **and the border thereof.** i.e. those cities or places which bordered upon Jordan. ʃ121L10, Metonymy of the Subject: the object is put for that which pertains or relates to it; here, "border" is put for the cities which are upon the border.

24. **Gad.** Nu 32:34-36.

25. **their coast.** Nu 32:35. **Jazer.** A city near a brook of the same name, now called *Wady Szyr;* and probably the present Szyr occupies its site. Nu 21:32. 32:1, 35. 2 S 24:5. Is 16:8. Je 48:32. **and all the cities of Gilead.** i.e. all the cities of note and eminency; all cities properly so called, which it seems lay in that part of Gilead. (ʃ171A, Synecdoche of the Genus: universals put for particulars, all or the whole put for the greater part. Jsh 11:23. 13:12. Ex +9:6.) And so this may well agree with ver. 31, where half the country of Gilead is said to be given to the Manassites; but there is no mention of any cities there (Matthew Poole). **half.** Nu 21:26-30. Dt 2:19. Jg 11:13-27. **Rabbah.** i.e. *contentious; populous,* ✳S#7237h. Jsh 15:60. Dt 3:11. 2 S 11:1. 12:26, 27, 29. 17:27. 1 Ch 20:1, 1. Je 49:2, 3. Ezk 21:20, Rabbath. 25:5. Am 1:14.

26. **Ramath-mizpeh.** i.e. *the watchtower height,* ✳S#7434h, only here. Jsh 11:3n. 20:8. Ge *31:49. Jg 10:17. 11:11, 29. 1 K 22:3. i.e. *Ramath-Gilead.* Jsh 20:8. **Betonim.** i.e. *nuts,* ✳S#993h. **Mahanaim.** Jsh 21:38. Ge 32:1, 2. 2 S 2:8. 17:27. **Debir.** Jsh 10:38, 39. 2 S 9:5. 17:27, 30, Lodebar.

27. **Beth-aram.** i.e. *mountain house,* ✳S#1027h, only here. Nu 32:34, 36, Beth-haran. **Beth-nimrah.** i.e. *house of the leopardess,* ✳S#1039h. Nu 32:3, 36h. Is 15:6. **Succoth.** Ge 33:17. Jg 8:5, 6, 14-16. 1 K 7:46. **Zaphon.** i.e. *north,* ✳S#6829h. **Chinnereth.** Jsh 11:2n. 12:3n, Chimneroth. Nu 34:11. Dt 3:17. Lk 5:1, Gennesaret.

30. **their coast.** ver. 26. Nu 32:39-41. Dt 3:13-15. 1 Ch 2:21-23. **Jair.** Nu 32:41. Dt 3:14. **Bashan.** Jsh 12:4n. Nu +21:33. Dt 3:13. Ps 22:12.

31. **Ashtaroth.** See on Jsh 12:4. Dt 1:4. **Og.** Jsh 12:4. **the children of Machir by.** Jsh 17:1, 2. Nu 32:39, 40.

33. **gave not.** At verse 14, as well as here, notice is taken, that to the tribes of Levi, "Moses gave no inheritance," for so God had appointed. Nu 18:20. If they had been appointed to a lot entire by themselves, Moses would have served them first, not because it was his own tribe, but because it was God's. But they must be provided for in another manner; their habitation must be scattered in all the tribes, and God himself was the portion both of their inheritance and of their cup. **God.** ʃ121K4. Metonymy of the Subject B583. See ver. √14. *God* is put for the sacrifices offered to Him. For other instances of this figure see Dt 10:9. 18:2. **their inheritance.** Dt 32:9. Ps *16:5. 33:12. 47:4. **as he said.** Jsh 18:7. Dt 10:9. 18:1, 2.

JOSHUA 14

The country west of Jordan to be divided by lot to the nine tribes and a half, 1-5. Caleb having on his return from spying the land encouraged the people, Moses then promised him the land of Hebron, which he now claims of Joshua, 6-12. Joshua grants his request, 13-15.

1. **which Eleazar**. Jsh 19:51. See on Nu 34:17-29. Mt 25:34. 1 P *1:4.

2. **lot**. Though God had sufficiently pointed out by the predictions of Jacob and Moses what portions he designed for each tribe, yet we readily discern an admirable proof of His wisdom, in the orders he gave to decide them by lot. By this means, the false interpretations which might have been given to the words of Jacob and Moses were prevented; and by striking at the root of whatever might occasion jealousies and disputes among the tribes, he evidently secured the honesty of those appointed to distribute the conquered lands of Canaan. Besides, the success of this method gave a fresh proof of the divinity of the Jewish religion, and the truth of its oracles. Each tribe finding itself placed by lot exactly in the spot where Jacob and Moses foretold, it was evident that Providence had equally directed both the predictions and that lot; and it would be the greatest insolence and stupidity not to acknowledge the inspiration of God in the words of Jacob and Moses; the direction of his hand in the lot, and his providence in the event. Ge ❶24:44n. Nu 26:2n, 55, 56. 33:54. 34:13. Ps *16:5, 6. Pr *16:33. 18:18. Mt 25:34.

3. **Moses**. Jsh 13:8. Nu 32:29-42. Dt 3:12-17. **but unto**. See on Jsh 13:14, 32, 33.

4. **the children**. Ge 48:5, 22. 1 Ch +*5:1, 2. **save cities**. Jsh 21:2-42. Nu 35:2-8. 1 Ch 6:54-81.

6. **Judah**. Jsh 15:17. Nu 13:6. 32:12. The fourth son of Jacob, but now reckoned the "first-born," as in 1 Ch +*5:2. **Gilgal**. Jsh 4:19. 10:43. **Caleb**. Nu 13:6. 14:6. **Kenezite**. ver. 14. Jsh 15:17. Nu 32:12. **Thou knowest**. Nu 14:24, 30. Dt 1:36-38. **the man**. Nu 12:7, 8. Dt 33:1. 34:5, 10. Jg 13:6-8. 1 K 13:1, 14. 2 K 4:9, 16, 42. 8:7, 11. Ps 90, title. 1 T 6:11. 2 T 3:17. **concerning me**. Nu *14:24. **Kadesh-barnea**. Nu 13:26. 32:8. Dt 1:19.

7. **sent me**. Nu 13:6, 16-20. **I brought**. Nu 13:26-33. 14:6-10. Ps 112:7, 8. Pr 16:23.

8. **made the heart**. Nu 13:31. Dt 1:28. **wholly followed**. ver. 14. Nu +*14:24. 32:12. Dt 1:36. 2 K 23:3, 25. 1 Ch +22:16 (T#1). 2 Ch 15:15. 17:3-6. Ps 37:18n. 119:69. Pr 20:6. 25:13. 28:20. Mt *7:21. Lk *6:46. 18:28-30. Jn *8:31. Ac *11:23. 13:43. *14:22. Ro *10:9, 10. 12:1, 2, *11. 1 C 7:35. *12:3. √15:58. Ph 3:7, 8, *13, *14. Col +*1:23. 1 Th *5:23. 1 T +*4:15. 2 T 4:7. He 3:14. 5:9. 6:12. 10:39. +*11:6. 2 P *1:3-10. Re 14:4.

9. **Surely**. Jsh 1:3. Nu 13:22. 14:22-24. **for ever**. Heb. *olam*, Ex +12:24. **because**. ver. +8, 14. Nu *14:24. Dt 1:34, *36. Pr 12:14. Je 51:56. Ga *6:7. He *10:35.

10. **hath kept**. Jsh 23:14. 1 Th 5:24. **forty**. Jsh 11:18. Nu 14:33, 34. **wandered**. Heb. walked. Nu 14:33. Dt 1:3. 2:1. Ps 95:10, 11.

11. **As yet**. Dt 31:2. 34:7. Ps *90:10. 102:27, 28. 103:5. Mt 28:20. **go out**. Nu 27:16, 17.

12. **this mountain**. Jsh 20:7. Nu 13:22, 28, 30. 14:8.

the Anakims. Jsh 11:21, 22. Nu 13:28, +*33. Dt +*2:20. **if so be**. Nu 14:8, 9. 21:34. 1 S 14:6. 2 Ch 14:11. Ps 18:32-34. 27:1-3. 44:3. 60:12. 118:10-12. Ro *8:31. 1 C 15:57. Ph *4:13. He 11:33. **I shall**. Jsh 15:14. Jg 1:20. **drive them out**. Jsh 17:12.

13. **blessed**. Jsh 22:6. Ge 47:7, 10. 1 S 1:17. SS 6:9. **gave unto**. Jsh 10:36, 37. 15:13, 14. 21:11, 12. Jg 1:20. 1 Ch 6:55, 56.

14. **Hebron**. Jsh 21:11, 12. 1 Ch 6:55, 56. **unto this day**. Jsh +*4:9. **because**. ver. +√8, 9. 1 C *15:58.

15. **And the name**. Jsh 15:13. Ge 23:2. 35:27. **And the land**. Jsh 11:23. Jg 3:11, 30. 5:31. 8:28.

JOSHUA 15

The boundaries of the lot of Judah, 1-12. Caleb takes Hebron, drives thence the three sons of Anak, 13-15. Caleb promises to give his daughter in marriage to him who should smite Kirjath-sepher; which Othniel does, and obtains her, 16, 17. She requests of her father some land for a dowry, which he grants, 13-19. The cities in the lot of Judah, 20-62. The Jebusites could not be conquered by them, retain Jerusalem, 63.

1. A.M. 2561. B.C. 1443. An. Ex. Is. 48. **This then was the lot**. The geography of the sacred writings presents many difficulties, occasioned by the changes which Canaan has undergone, especially for the last 2000 years. Many of the ancient towns and villages have had their names so totally changed that their former appellations are no longer discernible; several lie buried under their own ruins, and others have been so long destroyed that not a vistage of them remains. On these accounts it is very difficult to ascertain the precise situation of many places mentioned in these chapters; but this cannot in any measure affect the *truth* of the narrative. Jsh 14:2. Nu 26:55, 56. **children of Judah**. Jsh 14:6. 18:5. **even to the**. Nu 33:36, 37. 34:3-5. Ezk 47:19. **wilderness of Zin**. Dt 32:51.

2. **south border**. Nu 34:3. Ezk 47:19. **the salt sea**. Jsh 3:16. 12:3. 18:19. Ge 14:3. Nu 34:3. Ezk 47:8, 18. **bay**. Heb. tongue. ver. 5. Jsh 7:21mg, 24mg. 10:21. 18:19mg. Is 11:15.

3. **Maaleh-acrabbim**. i.e. *ascent of scorpions*. or, the going up to Acrabim. *S#4610h. Nu 34:4. Jg 1:36. **Zin**. i.e. *a low palm tree*. Ge 14:7. Nu 13:21. 20:1. 32:8. **Kadesh-barnea**. i.e. *the son of wandering was set apart*. Jsh 14:6, 7. Nu 34:4. Dt 1:19, 20. Jg 11:16, 17. **Hezron**. i.e. *enclosed wall; courtyard; arrow of song*. Ge 46:9. Nu 34:4. Name of a place, as well as two individuals. **Adar**. i.e. *exceeding glorious*. *S#146h. 1 Ch 8:3. Probably the same as **Hazar-addar**, Nu 34:4. (1) A city, called also Hazar-Addar, in the south of Judah near Edom, Jsh 15:3. (2) Son of Bela and grandson of Benjamin, 1 Ch 8:3. (3) S#143h. i.e. *fire god*. The sixth month in the civil year of the Jews. It included part of February and March. The celebrated feast of Purim occurred on the fourteenth and fifteenth of this month. Adar was the twelfth month of the sacred year of the Jews. It was doubled every second year to make the lunar year agree with the solar year, Ezr 6:15; Est +3:7. **Karkaa**. i.e. *floor, bottom*, *S#7173h.

4. **Azmon**. i.e. *the mighty*. The last city they possessed towards Egypt; east of the River of Egypt or Rhinocolura. Nu 34:5. **river**. ver. 47. Jsh 13:3. Ge 15:18. Ex 23:31. Nu 34:5. 1 K 8:65. Is 27:12.

5. **the east border.** Nu 34:10, 12. Ezk 47:18.
6. **Beth-hogla.** i.e. *house of a partridge*, *S#1031h. Jsh 18:19, 21. Probably the Bethagla mentioned by Jerome is the same as "the threshing-floor of Atad" (Ge 50:10), situated three miles from Jericho, and two from Jordan; and belonging to the tribe of Benjamin, though serving as a frontier to the tribe of Judah. Jsh 18:19-21. **Beth-arabah.** i.e. *house of the desert*. Jsh 18:18, 22. **the stone.** Jsh 18:17. **Bohan.** i.e. *thumb*. *S#932h. Jsh 18:17. **the son of.** Dt 11:6. 1 Ch 5:3.
7. **Debir.** ver. 15. Jsh 10:38, 39. 11:21. 13:26. 21:15. Jg 1:11. **the valley.** Jsh *7:26. Is 65:10. Ho 2:15. **Gilgal.** *rolling; a wheel.* Jsh 4:19. 5:9, 10. 10:43. 14:6. 18:17, Geliloth. Jg 2:1. **Adummim.** i.e. *ruddy; quieted ones.* *S#131h. A town and mountain of Benjamin (Jsh 18:17), near Jericho, towards Jerusalem. **En-shemesh.** i.e. *fountain of the sun,* *S#5885h. Jsh 18:17. Situated east of Jerusalem, on the confines of Judah and Benjamin. **En-rogel.** i.e. *fountain of the spy,* *S#5883h. Supposed to be the same as the fountain of *Siloam* (Jn 9:7, 11), east of Jerusalem, at the foot of mount Zion. Jsh 18:16. 2 S 17:17. 1 K 1:9.
8. **valley of the son of Hinnom.** i.e. *to make drowsy; behold them; full of goodness,* *S#2011h. A valley near to Jerusalem, a very pleasant place, but afterwards made infamous, 2 K *23:10. Jsh 18:16, 16. 2 K *23:10. 2 Ch 28:3. 33:6. Ne 11:30. Je 7:31, 32. 19:2, 6, 11, 14. 31:40. 32:35. This valley was desecrated by offering human sacrifices to Molech. It later became a refuse dump where fires were continually kept burning, and as such, became a symbol of the eternal fires of hell, or gehenna, mentioned in the New Testament as the place of future eternal torment for the punishment of the wicked (Mt 5:22, 29, 30. +√10:28. *18:9. 23:15, 33. Mk 9:43, 45, 47. Lk 12:5. Ja 3:6). In Scripture it is the same place as the "lake of fire," Re 19:20. 20:11-15. *21:8. "furnace of fire," Mt 8:12. 13:42, 50. 22:13. 24:51. 25:30. Lk 3:17. It is a place of eternal "fire and brimstone," Mt *25:41, √46. Re 14:9-11. 19:20. 20:10-15. 21:8. See Is 66:22-24. **the Jebusite.** ver. 63. Jsh 18:28. Jg 1:8, 21. 19:10. **the same is Jerusalem.** According to later usage. ∫151, Prolepsis; or, Anticipation. Ge +1:28. It may seem hence, and from Dt 33:12; Jsh 18:28; Jg 1:21, that Jerusalem, properly, or at least principally, belonged to Benjamin; and yet it is ascribed to Judah also here, ver. 63, and elsewhere, either because a part of the city was allotted to Judah; or because the Benjamites needed or desired the help and conjunction of this powerful tribe of Judah, for the getting and keeping of this most important place. And when the Benjamites had in vain attempted to drive out the Jebusites, this work was at last done by the tribe of Judah, who therefore had an interest in it by the right of war; as Ziklag, which belonged to the tribe of Simeon, being gotten from the Philistines by David, was adjoined by him to his tribe of Judah, 1 S 27:6 (Matthew Poole). **valley of the giants.** Situated apparently west of Jerusalem and mount Moriah. Jsh 18:16. 2 S 5:18, 22. Is 17:5, the valley of Rephaim.
9. **drawn.** or, marked out. ver. 11. Jsh 18:14, 17. Is 44:13. **fountain.** Heb. *mayan*, S#4599h, Ge +7:11. **Nephtoah.** i.e. *waters of the opening.* *S#5318h. Jsh 18:15. **Ephron.** i.e. *a little calf.* **Baalah.** i.e. *mistress.* *S#1173h. A city near Bethshemesh, and, according to Eusebius, nine miles from Jerusalem, in going towards Diospolis. ver. 10, 11, 29. 2 S 6:2. 1 Ch 13:6.

(1) A name sometimes given to Kirjath-jearim, Jsh 15:9; 1 Ch 13:6. (2) A hill of Judah, Jsh 15:11. (3) A city of Judah, Jsh 15:29. Probably the same as Balah, Jsh 19:3, and Baal in 1 Ch 4:33. **Kirjath-jearim.** i.e. *city of forests.* Jsh 9:17. Jg 18:12. Called Kirjath-baal, ver. 60; Jsh 9:17. 18:14, 15. Jg 18:12. 1 S 6:21. 7:2.
10. **mount Seir.** Jsh 12:7. Jg 5:4. **Jearim.** i.e. *forests.* *S#3297h. **Chesalon.** i.e. *confidence, hope,* *S#3693h. **Beth-shemesh.** i.e. *house of the sun.* Placed by Eusebius ten miles east from Eleutheropolis, towards Nicopolis. 1 S 6:12-21. There were several cities of this name; this in Judah here, and Jsh 21:13, 16; 2 K 14:11, another in Issachar, and a third in Naphtali, Jsh 19:22, 38 (Matthew Poole). **Timnah.** ver. *57. Ge 38:12, 13. Jg 14:1, 5. 2 Ch 28:18.
11. **Ekron.** i.e. *uprooting.* ver. 45. Jsh 13:3. 19:43. 1 S 5:10. 6:17. 7:14. 2 K 1:2, 3, 6, 16. **Shicron.** i.e. *merriment; drunkenness,* *S#7942h. **mount Baalah.** i.e. *mistress.* ver. 9. Jsh 19:44. **Jabneel.** i.e. *built of God.* *S#2995h. Jsh 19:33. (1) A town of Judah, Jsh 15:11, called also Jabneh in 2 Ch 26:6. It was captured by Uzziah from the Philistines. (2) A border town of Naphtali; location uncertain, Jsh 19:33.
12. **west border.** Nu 34:6. Ezk 47:20. **the great sea.** ver. 47. Jsh 1:4. 9:1. 23:4. Nu 34:6, 7. Dt 11:24. Ezk 47:10, 20. 48:28mg.
13. **Caleb.** Jsh 14:6-15. Nu 13:30. 14:23, 24. Dt 1:34-36. **the city of Arba.** Arba. i.e. *four,* *S#704h. Jsh 14:15. 21:11. *or,* Kirjath-arba. ver. 54. Jsh 14:15. Not the city, which was the Levites', but the territory of it, Jsh 21:13. **Hebron.** i.e. *communion.* Jsh 14:13, 15. 20:7.
14. **thence.** i.e. from the said territory, from their caves and forts in it: compare Jsh 14:12. **the three sons.** Jsh 10:36, 37. 11:21. Nu 13:22, 23. Jg 1:10, 20.
15. **went up.** Jsh 10:3, 38. Jg 1:11-13. **Kirjath-sepher.** i.e. *city of books,* compare ver. 49. *S#7158h. ver. 16. Jg 1:11, 12. 2 T=4:13.
16. **He that.** Jg 1:6, 12, 13. **will I give.** 1 S 17:25. **Achsah.** i.e. *tinkling ornament,* *S#5915h. ver. 17. Jg 1:12, 13. 1 Ch 2:49. **my daughter.** 1 Ch 2:48, 49.
17. **Othniel.** i.e. *lion of God; force of God,* *S#6274h. Jg 1:13. 3:9, 11. 1 Ch 4:13, 13. 27:15. **Kenaz.** i.e. *hunting.* Jsh 14:6. Nu 32:12. 1 Ch 4:13. **Achsah.** i.e. *tinkling ornament.* 1 Ch 2:49.
18. **she came.** Jg 1:14. Mt 1:18. **to ask.** Ex 22:17. Jg 1:14, 15. **she lighted.** Ge 24:64. 1 S 25:23.
19. **Give me.** Jg 1:14, 15. Mt 7:7, 8. 1 C 12:31. **a blessing.** Ge 33:11. Dt 33:7. 1 S 25:27. Jn 4:10, 14. 2 C 9:5mg. Re 7:17. *or,* "pool," as in 2 S 2:13. **south land.** a dry hill country (Young). i.e. a dry land, which was much exposed to the south wind, which in those parts was very hot and drying, as coming from the deserts of Arabia (Matthew Poole). **springs of waters.** ∫121.O, Ge +28:22. So necessary in eastern lands. **nether springs.** Jg 1:15.
20. **the inheritance.** Ge 49:8-12. Dt 33:7.
21. **southward.** Dt 1:7. Jg 1:9. **Kabzeel.** i.e. *gathering of God,* *S#6909h. 2 S 23:20. Ne 11:25. 1 Ch 11:22. **Eder.** i.e. *drove, arrangement.* Ge 35:21. **Jagur.** i.e. *a lodging,* *S#3017h, only here.
22. **Kinah.** i.e. *lamentation,* *S#7016h. **Dimonah.** i.e. *the quieter: silence; sufficient numbering.* *S#1776h. i.e. Dibon, Ne 11:25. **Adadah.** i.e. *a great company.* *S#5735h.
23. **Kedesh.** i.e. *a sanctuary.* *S#6943h. Jsh 12:22.

19:37. 20:7. 21:32. Nu 33:37. Dt 1:19. Jg 4:6, 9, 10, 11. 2 K 15:29. 1 Ch 6:72, 76. (1) A town in the south of Judah, Jsh 15:23. (2) A city of Issachar assigned to the Levites, 1 Ch 6:72. Called Kishon in Jsh 21:28. (3) A city of Naphtali assigned to the Levites. It became a city of refuge and was the residence of Barak, Jg 4:6, where it is called Kedesh-naphtali. It was the place where the tribes of Zebulun and Naphtali were assembled by Deborah, Jg 4:11. Tiglath-pileser captured it, 2 K 15:29. The city of the Canaanites mentioned in Jsh 12:22; 19:37 is probably the same place. Kedesh is now called *Kades*. **Hazor**. i.e. *enclosed; castle*. *S#2674h. ver. 25. Jsh 11:1, 10, 10, 11, 13. 12:19. 19:36. Jg 4:2, 17. 1 S 12:9. 1 K 9:15. 2 K 15:29. Ne 11:33. Je 49:28, 30, 33. The LXX. read *Asorionain*, for Hazar-Ithnan, regarding these two as one city. (1) A royal city of the Canaanites situated in the north part of the land; afterward a city of Naphtali, Jsh 11:1; 1 S 12:9. (2) A city of Judah, Jsh 15:23. (3) A town of Judah, Jsh 15:25, called Hazor-Hadattah or New Hazor. (4) A city of Judah, Jsh 15:25. Same as Hezron. (5) A town of Benjamin, Ne 11:23. (6) A name given to certain countries in the east of Arabia, Je 49:28, 30, 33. **Ithnan**. i.e. *a gift*, *S#3497h.

24. **Ziph**. i.e. *a flowing*, *S#2128h. ver. 55. 1 S 23:14, 15, 24. 26:2, 2. 1 Ch 2:42. 2 Ch 11:8. Eusebius and Jerome say, that Ziph was a village in their time, eight miles east from Hebron. 1 S 23:14, 19, 24. Ps 54, title. **Telem**. i.e. *covering them: casting them out.* 1 S 15:4. **Bealoth**. i.e. *mistresses.* *S#1175h. 1 K 4:10.

25. **Hazor**. *ƒ*66, Ge +9:3. Or rather, *Hazar-hadattah*. i.e. *enclosure of rejoicing: new enclosure, trumpeting of joy, trumpeting anew.* Or, as the LXX. Alexandrian, and Vulgate render, *Asor nova*, "New Hazor," to distinguish it from the preceding and following (ver. 28) *Hazor*. Eusebius and Jerome say it was a village in their time, on the eastern confines of Askelon. **Kerioth**. i.e. *cities.* *S#7152h. Je 48:24, 41. Am 2:2. Or, rather, *Kerioth-Hezron*, "the cities of Hezron." Kerioth is supposed to be the birth place of Judas Iscariot, i.e. the man of Kerioth (Young).

26. **Amam**. their mother; metropolis. *S#538h. **Shema**. i.e. *rumor.* *S#8090h. Compare *S#8087h, 1 Ch +2:43, also rendered *Shema*. **Moladah**. i.e. *birth; birthplace, lineage*, as in Jsh 19:2. *S#4137h. Jsh 19:2. 1 Ch 4:28. Ne 11:26. Probably the same as *Malatha*, a city frequently mentioned by Eusebius; from whom it appears to have been situated in the southern border of Judah, about twenty miles from Hebron.

27. **Hazar-gaddah**. i.e. *village of the troop or fortune*, *S#2693h. This is apparently the city which Eusebius calls Aser; which he says, was, in his time, a town situated between Askalon and Ashdod. **Heshmon**. i.e. *little fertile place.* *S#2829h. **Beth-palet**. i.e. *house of escape.* *S#1046h. Ne 11:26.

28. **Hazar-shual**. i.e. *village of a fox.* *S#2705h. Jsh 19:3. 1 Ch 4:28. Ne 11:27. **Beer-sheba**. well of the oath. Jsh 19:2. Ge 21:14, 31n-33. 26:33. 46:1, 5. **Bizjoth-jah**. i.e. *contempt of Jah*, *S#964h. not mentioned elsewhere. Instead of Bizjothjah, the LXX. read, "and their towns and villages."

29. **Baalah**. i.e. *mistress*, given to Simeon, Jsh 19:3. 1 Ch 4:29. ver. 9-11. Jsh 19:3. **Iim**. i.e. *ruinous heaps*. **Azem**. i.e. *strength.* *S#6107h. Jsh 19:3. 1 Ch 4:29.

30. **Eltolad**. i.e. *the generation*, in 1 Ch 4:29, Tolad.

*S#513h. Jsh 19:4. **Chesil**. i.e. *confidence*, *S#3686h, only here. LXX. reads *Baithel*, see Jsh 19:4; 1 Ch 4:30. **Hormah**. i.e. *destruction*, the same as Zephath in Jg 1:17. Jsh 12:14. 19:4. These three cities were given to Simeon, Jsh 19:4. Nu 14:45. Dt 1:44. Jg 1:17.

31. **Ziklag**. i.e. *outpouring of a spring; winding; enveloped in grief*, *S#6860h. Jsh 19:5. 1 S 27:6, 6. 30:1, 1, 1, 14, 26. 2 S 1:1. 4:10. 1 Ch 4:30. 12:1, 20. Ne 11:28. **Madmannah**. i.e. *dung hill*, *S#4089h. 1 Ch 2:48, 49. Is 10:31, Madmenah. Compare the similar meaning of Dimnah, Jsh 21:35. **Sansannah**. i.e. *bushes* or *boughs.* *S#5578h.

32. **Lebaoth**. i.e. *lionesses*, *S#3822h, perhaps the same as Beth-lebaoth in Jsh 19:6. **Shilhim**. i.e. *S#7978h, *presents*, only here. **Ain**. i.e. *fountain*, compare Nu 34:11. Probably the Bathanin of Eusebius, four miles from Hebron. **Rimmon**. i.e. *pomegranate.* Jg 20:45, 47. 21:13. Ne 11:29, Enrimmon.

33. **Eshtaol**. i.e. *request*, *S#847h. This town is placed by Eusebius ten miles from Eleutheropolis, towards Nicopolis: and it is supposed to be a wretched village, called Esdad, about 15 miles south of Yebna. Jsh 19:41. Nu 13:23. Jg 13:25. 16:31. 18:2, 8, 11. **Zoreah**. i.e. *hornet*, *S#6881h, Jsh 19:41. Jg 13:2, 25. 16:31. 18:2, 8, 11. 2 Ch 11:29. A town near to Eshtaol, placed at ten miles' distance north of Eleutheropolis by Eusebius. **Ashnah**. i.e. *fortification; strong, mighty*, *S#823h, only here. (1) A town of Judah, about sixteen miles north-west of Jerusalem, Jsh 15:33. (2) A town of Judah, sixteen miles south-west of Jerusalem, Jsh 15:43.

34. **Zanoah**. i.e. *marsh; a rejected place*, *S#2182h, only here. ver. 56. 1 Ch 4:18. Ne 3:13. 11:30. (1) In 1 Ch 4:18 Jekuthiel is called "the father of Zanoah," that is, he was the founder of a village of that name, a town in the hill country of Judah, Jsh 15:56. (2) A town in the lowlands of Judah, Jsh 15:34; Ne 3:13; 11:30. **En-gannim**. i.e. *fountain of gardens.* **Tappuah**. i.e. *an apple.* ver. 53. Jsh 12:17. 16:8. 17:8. **Enam**. i.e. *fountains; double fountain*, *S#5879h.

35. **Jarmuth**. i.e. *a high place.* Jsh 10:3, 23. 12:11. Ne 11:29. **Adullam**. i.e. *a testimony to them; justice of the people; retreat; hiding place; struck with terror; their ornament.* Jsh 12:15. 1 S 22:1. 2 Ch 11:7. Ne 11:30. Mi 1:15. **Socoh**. i.e. *bough*, *S#7755h. ver. 48. 1 S 17:1, 1. 1 K 4:10. 1 Ch 4:18. 2 Ch 11:7. 28:18. Eusebius says, there were two cities of Socoh, an upper and lower, nine miles from Eleutheropolis, towards Jerusalem. ver. 48. 1 S 17:1. 1 Ch 4:18. **Azekah**. i.e. *fence, signet.* Eusebius and Jerome say there was a town of this name in their time, between Jerusalem and Eleutheropolis. Jsh 10:10. 1 S 17:1.

36. **Sharaim**. i.e. *two gates*, 1 S 17:52. 1 Ch 4:31. **Adithaim**. i.e. *two ornaments; double prey*, *S#5723h. Eusebius mentions two cities called *Adatha*, one towards Gaza, and the other east of Lydda. **Gederah**. i.e. *the fence*, *S#1449h. Jsh 12:13. Perhaps the same as the next mentioned place. **and**. *or, or.* **Gederothaim**. i.e. *two fences; two sheepfolds*, *S#1453h. **fourteen cities**. There are fifteen in all; but the two last seem to be only two names of the same city.

37. **Zenan**. i.e. *a thorn*, *S#6799h, perhaps the same as *Zaanan*, in Mi 1:11. **Hadashah**. i.e. *the new one; new city*, *S#2322h, only here. **Migdal-gad**. i.e. *tower of Gad*, *S#4028h, only here.

38. **Dilean**. i.e. *brought low in affliction; large*

gourd, *S#1810h. **Mizpeh**. i.e. *the watchtower*, *S#4708h. Jsh 11:3n. Ge *31:48, 49. Jg 20:1. 21:5. 1 S 7:5, 6, 16. 10:17. **Joktheel**. i.e. *subdued of God; obedient to God; subdued*, *S#3371h. 2 K 14:7. (1) A city in the plain country of Judah, Jsh 15:38. (2) The name given by Amaziah to Selah, a chief city of Edom. Perhaps the same place now called *Petra*. 2 K 14:7n.

39. **Lachish**. i.e. *obstinate*. Jsh 10:3, 31, 32. 12:11. 2 K 14:19. 18:14, 17. 19:8. **Bozkath**. i.e. *a swelling*, *S#1218h. 2 K 22:1. **Eglon**. i.e. *a little calf*. Jsh 10:3. 12:12.

40. **Cabbon**. i.e. *to heap up; cake*, *S#3522h. **Lahmam**. i.e. *bread*, *S#3903h. **Kithlish**. i.e. *wall of a man*, *S#3798h.

41. **Gederoth**. i.e. *fences*, *S#1450h. 2 Ch 28:18. **Beth-dagon**. i.e. *house of Dagon*, *S#1016h. Jsh 19:37h. 1 S 5:2. (1) A town of Judah, Jsh 15:41. (2) A town of Asher, Jsh 19:27. **Naamah**. i.e. *pleasantness*. **Makkedah**. i.e. *branding (spotting) place*. Jsh 10:21, 28. 12:16.

42. **Libnah**. Jsh +10:29. 12:15. 2 K 8:22. **Ether**. i.e. *abundance, supplicant*. Jsh 19:7. **Ashan**. i.e. *smoke; anger*, *S#6228h. Jsh 19:7. 1 Ch 4:32. 6:59.

43. **Jiphtah**. i.e. *he opens*, *S#3316h, only here. **Ashnah**. i.e. *I will cause change*. ver. 33. **Nezib**. i.e. *a pillar; a garrison*, *S#5334h.

44. **Keilah**. i.e. a *fortress; voice of God*, *S#7084h. 1 S 23:1, 2, 3, 4, 5, 5, 6, 7, 8, 10, 11, 12, 13, 13. 1 Ch 4:19. Ne 3:17, 18. (1) A city of Judah, Jsh 15:44; 1 S 23:1; Ne 3:17, 18. (2) A descendant of Judah, 1 Ch 4:19. **Achzib**. i.e. *a lie*, *S#392h. Jsh 19:29. Ge ●38:5. Jg 1:31. Mi 1:14. (1) A town in the mouth of Judah, Jsh 15:44; Mi 1:14. Perhaps the same as Chezib in Ge 38:5. (2) A city of Asher, now called Ezzib, on the Mediterranean, 9 miles N. of Acre, Jsh 19:29; Jg 1:31. **Mareshah**. i.e. *the chief place; summit*, *S#4762h. 1 Ch 2:42. 4:21. 2 Ch 11:8. 14:9, 10. 20:37. Mi 1:15. (1) i.e. *possession*. A descendant of Caleb, the son of Hezron, 1 Ch 2:42. (2) i.e. *top of a hill*. A fortified city of Judah, Jsh 15:44; 2 Ch 11:8.

45. **Ekron**. i.e. *a little root*. Jsh 13:3. 1 S 5:10. 6:17. Am 1:8. Zp 2:4. Zc 9:5-7. **villages**. ♪155E5, Nu +21:25.

46. **near**. Heb. by the place of. **Ashdod**. i.e. *I will spoil*. Jsh 11:22. 1 S 5:1, 6. 2 Ch 26:6. Ne 13:23, 24. Is 20:1. Am 1:8. Zp 2:4. The same as *Azotus* in the New Testament, its Greek form. Ac 8:40.

47. **villages**. ♪155E5, Nu +21:25. **Gaza**. i.e. *strength*. Jsh 11:22. Ge +10:19. Jg 1:18. 6:4. 16:1, 21. 1 S 6:17. 1 K 4:24 (Azzah). 2 K 18:8. Je 25:20 (Azzah). 47:1, 5. Am 1:6, 7. Zp 2:4. Zc 9:5. Ac 8:26. **the river**. ver. 4. Jsh 13:3. Ex 23:31. Nu 34:5, 6. Young comments it is absurd to suppose that it refers to the Nile. **great sea**. i.e. the Mediterranean. ver. 12. Jsh 1:4. 9:1. 23:4. Nu 34:6, 7. Ezk 47:10.

48. **Shamir**. i.e. *a brier, diamond*. LXX. *Sophir*. **Jattir**. i.e. *excellent, abundant*, *S#3492h. Jsh 21:14. 1 S 30:27. 1 Ch 6:57. **Socoh**. i.e. *hedge, fence*. different from that in ver. 35.

49. **Dannah**. i.e. *a low place*, or *judgment*, *S#1837h, only here. **Kirjath-sannah**. i.e. *city of the bush*, or *study*, which agrees with its other name, ver. *15. *S#7158h. ver. 15, 16. Jg 1:11, 12. 1 T=4:13. 2 T=2:15. =4:13. **Debir**. i.e. *an oracle*. Jsh 11:21.

50. **Anab**. i.e. *a grape*. Jsh 11:21. **Eshtemoh**. i.e. *obedience*, *S#851h. Jsh 21:14. 1 S 30:28. 1 Ch 4:17,

19. 6:57, Eshtemoa. **Anim**. i.e. *fountains*, *S#6044h, only here.

51. **Goshen**. i.e. *drawing near*. Jsh 10:41n. 11:16. **Holon**. i.e. *sandy*, *S#2473h. Jsh 21:15. Je 48:21. Perhaps the same as Hilen in 1 Ch 6:58. (1) A city in the mountains of Judah, Jsh 15:51; 21:15, called Hilen in 1 Ch 6:58. (2) A city of Moab, east of the Jordan, Je 48:21. **Giloh**. i.e. *exile*, *S#1542h. 2 S 15:12.

52. **Arab**. i.e. *ambush*, *S#694h, only here. **Dumah**. i.e. *silence*. Ge 25:14. Is 21:11. It is the name of a person and of a place in Arabia. (1) A son of Ishmael, Ge 25:14; 1 Ch 1:30. (2) A town of Judah ten miles southwest of Hebron; is now *ed Domeh*, Jsh 15:52. (3) A city or a tribe, Is 21:11. **Eshean**. i.e. *a prop, support*, *S#824h, only here.

53. **Janum**. i.e. *sleep*, *S#3241h. or, Janus. i.e. *slight*. only here. **Beth-taphuah**. i.e. *house of the apple*, *S#1054h. **Aphekah**. i.e. *restraint*, *S#664h, only here. For places with the same name see Jsh 12:18. 13:4.

54. **Humtah**. i.e. *place of lizards*, *S#2547h, only here. **Kirjath-arba**. i.e. *city of four*, *S#7153h. ver. 13. Jsh 14:15. 20:7. 21:11. Ge 23:2. 35:27. Jg 1:10. Ne 11:25. **Zior**. i.e. *a little one*, *S#6730h.

55. **Maon**. i.e. *habitation*, *S#4584h. Jg 10:12. 1 S 23:24, 25, 25. 25:2, 7. 1 Ch 2:45, 45. 2 Ch ●26:10. Is ●35:2. (1) A descendant of Caleb, the son of Hezron, 1 Ch 2:45. (2) A city of Judah, Jsh 15:55; 1 S 25:2. **Carmel**. i.e. *fruitful place; fruitful field*, S#3760h. Jsh +12:22. 19:26. 1 S 15:12. *25:2, 2, 5, 7, 40. 1 K 18:42. (1) The name of that mountain-ridge, twelve miles long, which from the western highlands of Palestine juts out into the Mediterranean Sea. It is noted as the scene of the most remarkable events in the history of Elijah and Elisha. (2) A town where Saul set up a monument, 1 S 15:12; 25:2, 5, 7, 40, and Uzziah had his vineyards, 2 Ch 26:10. It was situated in the mountains of Judah, ten miles sout-east of Hebron. It is now called *Kurmul*. **Ziph**. i.e. *flowing*. ver. 24. 1 S 23:14, 15. 26:1, 2. 2 Ch 11:8. **Juttah**. i.e. *stretched out*, *S#3194h. Jsh 21:16.

56. **Jezreel**. i.e. *God sows*. 1 S 25:43. 29:1. **Jokdeam**. i.e. *burning of the people: let the people kindle*, *S#3347h. **Zanoah**. i.e. *a rejected place*. Different from that in ver. 34.

57. **Cain**. i.e. *the acquisition*. **Gibeah**. i.e. *height*. **Timnah**. i.e. *thou wilt number: a portion*. ver. 10. Ge 38:12. Jg 14:1. 2 Ch 28:18.

58. **Halhul**. i.e. *very sandy* or *very painful; travail-pain*, *S#2478h. **Beth-zur**. i.e. *house of a rock*, *S#1049h. 1 Ch 2:45. 2 Ch 11:7. Ne 3:16. **Gedor**. i.e. *hedge, fence*, *S#1446h. Jsh ●12:13. 1 Ch 4:39. 12:7. (1, 2) Two names in the genealogy of Judah, 1 Ch 4:4, 18. (3) A Benjamite name in the genealogy of Saul, 1 Ch 8:31; 9:37. (4) A town in the hill country of Judah, Jsh 15:58. (5) Apparently a town of Benjamin, 1 Ch 12:7. Probably the same as Geder of Jsh 12:13. (6) Gedor of 1 Ch 4:39 was probably between Judah and Mount Seir. It is called Gerar in the Septuagint.

59. **Maarath**. i.e. *a cave* or *naked place; treeless place*, *S#4638h. **Beth-anoth**. i.e. *house of answers*, *S#1042h, a reference to echoes. Compare Jsh 19:38, Beth-anath. **Eltekon**. i.e. *the straight* or *right place*, *S#515h. Compare Elteken, Jsh 19:44.

60. **Kirjath-baal**. i.e. *city of Baal*, *S#7154h. ver. 9. Jsh 18:14. 1 S ●7:1, 2. **Kirjath-jearim**. i.e. *city of*

forests. **Rabbah**. i.e. *the great place*.
61. **wilderness**. or pasture land of Judea. **Beth-arabah**. i.e. *house of the desert*, *S#1026h. ver. 6. Jsh 18:☉18, 22. **Middin**. i.e. *measures; judging*, *S#4081h. **Secacah**. i.e. *enclosure*, *S#5527h.
62. **Nibshan**. i.e. *soft or sandy soil; level soft soil*, *S#5044h. **the city of Salt**. This city was situated somewhere in the vicinity west of the lake Asphaltites; and supposed by some to be the same as *Zoar*. Ge 19:22. **En-gedi**. i.e. *fountain of the kid*, *S#5872h. En-gedi, or Hazazon-Tamar, was situated, according to Eusebius, in the desert west of the Dead Sea. Josephus says it was 300 stadia from Jerusalem, and not far from the lake Asphaltites; and consequently it could not have been far from Jericho and the mouth of the Jordan. It was celebrated for the abundance of its palm trees. Ge 14:7. 1 S 23:29. 24:1. 2 Ch 20:2. SS 1:14. Ezk 47:10.
63. **the Jebusites**. Ge +10:16. Jg 1:8, 21. 19:11. 2 S 5:6-9. 1 Ch 11:4-8. Ro 7:14-21. **could not drive them out**. Jsh 7:12. 13:13. 16:10. 17:12, 13. Le 26:37. Dt *28:32. Jg 1:19, 21, 28. 2:14. 16:17. 1 S 17:24. Je 51:30. Mt *13:58. Mk *6:5, 6. 9:18. Jn *15:5. Ro *6:12-14. **dwell with**. Jg 1:21. To which of the tribes did Jerusalem belong? whether Benjamin, Ge 49:27; Dt 33:12; Je 6:1. or Judah, as implied here; Ps 78:68, 69. Some think that Jerusalem being in the borders of both, it was common to both, and promiscuously inhabited by both; and it is certain that after the captivity it was possessed by both, Ne 11:4 (Matthew Poole). **unto this day**. Jsh +*4:9.

JOSHUA 16

The borders of Joseph's posterity, west of Jordan, 1-4. The border of the inheritance of Ephraim, 5-9. The Canaanites of Gezer not conquered but placed under tribute, 10.

1. **fell**. Heb. went forth. **the water**. Jsh 8:15. 15:61. 18:12. 2 K 2:19-21. **the wilderness**. Jsh 18:12.
2. **Bethel**. Jsh 18:13. Ge 28:19. 48:3. Jg 1:22-26. **Archi**. i.e. *lengthy*, *S#757h. 2 S 15:32. 16:16. 17:5, 14. 1 Ch 27:33.
3. **Japhleti**. i.e. *it frees; delivered*, *S#3311h. 1 Ch 7:32, 33. **Beth-horon**. i.e. *house of the hollow*. Eusebius says that the two "Beth-horons" were twelve miles from Jerusalem, towards Nicopolis or Emmaus: of which the one, called upper Beth-horon, from its situation, was built (rebuilt) by Solomon, and the other, called nether Beth-horon, was given to the Levites. Josephus places Beth-oron about 100 furlongs from Jerusalem. Dr. Clarke mentions an Arab village called Bethoor, about twelve miles from Jerusalem, a small distance from Rama, which he supposes, from its situation on a hill, to be Beth-horon the upper. Jsh 10:10, 11. 18:13. 1 K 9:15-17. 1 Ch 7:24, 28. 2 Ch 8:5. **Gezer**. i.e. *piece* or *part*. Probably the Gadara of Eusebius, four miles from Nicopolis. Jsh 10:33. 12:12. 1 K 9:15. 1 Ch 7:28. The same as *Gadara*, 1 K 9:15. 1 Ch 7:28. **the sea**. Jsh 17:9. Nu 34:6.
4. **the children of Joseph**. Jsh 17:14. **Manasseh**. i.e. half Manasseh, by a synecdoche (♪171.O.13, Synecdoche of the Whole: a place is put for a part of it). Jsh 14:4. **Ephraim**. Jsh 14:4. 17:14-18.
5. **Ataroth-addar**. i.e. *crowns of Addar*. ver. 2. Jsh 18:13.

6. **Michmethah**. i.e. *hiding place*, *S#4366h. Jsh 17:7. **Taanath-shiloh**. i.e. *meeting of Shiloh*, *S#8387h. Placed by Eusebius ten miles east of Neapolis or Shechem. Jsh 18:1. **Janohah**. i.e. *rest*, *S#3239h. ver. 7. Eusebius calls it Iano in Acrabatene, twelve miles east from Neapolis.
7. **Ataroth**. i.e. *crowns*. ver. 5. 1 Ch 7:28. **Naarath**. i.e. *damsel; maiden place*, *S#5292h. 1 Ch 4:5, 6, 6, Naarah. 7:28, Naaran. **Jericho**. Jsh 3:16. 6:1, 26. 18:21. Nu 33:48.
8. **Tappuah**. i.e. *apple*. Jsh 12:17. 15:34. 17:8. **river Kanah**. i.e. *reed*, *S#7071h. Jsh 17:9. 19:28. (1) A town in Asher, Jsh 19:28. (2) A river, part of the boundary-line between Ephraim and Manasseh, Jsh 16:8; 17:9. **the sea**. ver. 3-6. Nu 34:6.
9. **separate cities**. Jsh 17:9.
10. **they drave not**. Jsh +*15:63. Ex 23:31-33. Dt 7:2. Jg 1:29. 1 K 9:16, 21. **the Canaanites dwell**. Ge +10:18. Nu 33:52-55. Dt 7:1, 2. **Ephraimites**. ✛S#669h. Jg 12:4, 5, 5, 6. **unto this day**. Jsh +*4:9. **under tribute**. or, task work. Ge 9:26. 49:15. Dt 20:11. Jsh 17:13. Jg 1:28, 30, 33, 35. 1 K 9:16.

JOSHUA 17

The lot of the half tribe of Manasseh, 1, 2. The case of Zelophehad's daughters, 3-6. The borders of Manasseh, 7-11. The Canaanites unexpelled, but under tribute, 12, 13. The sons of Joseph petition for another lot, which Joshua refuses them, but promises them the subduing of the Canaanites whose land they should then have, 14-18.

1. **the firstborn**. Ge +41:51. 46:20. *48:18. Dt *21:17. Col +√1:15n. **Machir**. Ge 50:23. Nu 26:29. 27:1. 32:39, 40. Dt 3:13, 15. Jg 5:14. 1 Ch 2:23. 7:14, 15. **Gilead**. i.e. *the heap of witness*. Nu 26:29. 32:33, 40. Dt 3:13-15. **man of war**. or, of battle. Ex 15:3. Nu 31:21, 28, 49. **Bashan**. Jsh 12:4n. Nu +21:33. Ps 22:12.
2. **the rest**. Nu 26:29-32. **the children**. Jg 6:11. 8:2. 1 Ch 7:18. **Abiezer**. i.e. *father of help*, *S#44h. Nu ☉26:30, Jeezer. Jg 6:34. 8:2. 2 S 23:27. 1 Ch 7:18. 11:28. 27:12. (1) Head of a family descended from Manasseh, probably the same as Jeezer, the son of Gilead (Nu 26:30), Jsh 17:2; 1 Ch 7:18. (2) A district in Manasseh inhabited by the Abiezrites, Jg 6:34; 8:2. (3) One of David's valiant men, an inhabitant of Anathoth, in the tribe of Benjamin, 2 S 23:27; 1 Ch 11:28. **Helek**. i.e. *a portion*. **children of Asriel**. i.e. *vow of God*. Nu 26:31. 1 Ch 7:14, Ashriel. **Shechem**. i.e. *a shoulder*. **children of Hepher**. i.e. *a pit*. Nu 26:32. 27:1. **Shemida**. i.e. *fame of knowledge*. Nu 26:32. 1 Ch 7:19.
3. **Zelophehad**. i.e. *fracture; first rupture, i.e. firstborn; shadow of fear; being burnt*. Nu 26:33. 27:1. *36:2-11. **Mahlah**. i.e. *disease; infirmity; pardon*. **Noah**. i.e. *motion; wandering; movable; commotion; agitation; flattering*. **Hoglah**. i.e. *a partridge; the feast has languished*. **Milcah**. i.e. *a queen* or *a woman of counsel*. **Tirzah**. i.e. *pleasantness; she will delight; his delight; well pleasing; willing*.
4. **Eleazar**. Jsh 14:1. Nu 34:17-29. **the Lord commanded Moses**. Nu 27:6, 7. Ga 3:28.
5. **ten portions**. As there were six sons and five daughters among whom this division was to be made, there should be eleven portions: but Zelophehad, son of Hepher, having left five daughters in his place, nei-

ther he nor Hepher is reckoned. The lot of Manasseh therefore was divided into ten parts; five for the five sons of Gilead: Abiezer, Helek, Asriel, Shechem, and Shemida; and five for the five daughters of Zelophehad: Mahlah, Noah, Hoglah, Milcah, and Tirzah. ver. 2, 3, 14. **beside.** Jsh 13:29-31. Nu 32:30-42.

6. **the daughters.** Nu 27:8. An exception to the general rule. **sons.** i.e. the Machirites and the Gileadites. Nu 26:29.

7. **Asher.** i.e. *happy*. A city not mentioned elsewhere. Eusebius says this was a town in his time not far from Neapolis, towards Scythopolis or Bethshan; between which towns it is also placed by the old Jerusalem Itinerary. **Michmethah.** i.e. *a hiding place; the poverty of the dead; the poverty of the reward; concealment.* Jsh 16:6. Situated, probably, east of Shechem; though its precise situation, as well as that of many others, cannot, at this distance of time, be ascertained. Many of these towns were small, and we may rationally conclude, slightly built; and consequently have perished more than two thousand years ago. It would therefore be useless **now** to look for such places; though in many instances, their ancient names have been preserved, and their sites identified. Several towns even in England, mentioned by Caesar and other ancient writers, are no longer discernible: several have changed their names, and not a few their situation. Jsh 16:6-8. **Shechem.** ver. 2. Jsh 20:7. 21:21. 24:1, 32. Ge 34:2. 37:12, 14. Jg 9:1. 1 K 12:1, 25. 1 Ch 6:67. **En-tappuah.** i.e. *fountain of the apple,* *S#5887h.

8. **of Tappuah.** i.e. *an apple.* Jsh 12:17. 15:34, 53. 16:8.

9. **river Kanah.** or, brook of reeds. The brook *Kanah* seems to be what is now called *Nahr el Kasab,* which falls into the Mediterranean a few miles south of Caesarea of Palestine. Jsh 16:8. **these cities.** Jsh 16:9. **the outgoings.** Jsh 16:3, 8. 19:29. **the sea.** The Mediterranean. Jsh 15:47. Nu +34:6.

11. **Manasseh.** Jsh 16:9. 1 Ch 7:29. **Beth-shean.** i.e. *house of rest; house of quiet,* *S#1052h. The *Scythopolis* of the Greek and Roman writers, was situated in the plain of Jordan, west of that river, 120 furlongs south from Tiberias, according to Josephus, and 600 furlongs north from Jerusalem (2 Mac 12:29). It was the largest city of the Decapolis (see Mt 4:25. Mk 5:20. 7:31), and the only one on that side of Jordan. It is now called *Bisan,* 8 hours or 24 miles from Tiberias; and described by Dr. Richardson, exclusive of its ruins, as "a collection of miserable hovels, containing 200 inhabitants." ver. 16. Jg 1:27. 1 S ◖31:10, 12, Bethshan. 2 S ◖21:12. 1 K 4:12, 12. 1 Ch 7:29. **and her towns.** Heb. daughters. ♪155E5, Nu +21:25. **Ibleam.** i.e. *swallowing up a people.* Jg 1:27. 2 K 9:27. 1 Ch 6:70, Bileam. **Dor.** i.e. *habitation,* Dor, according to Eusebius, was situated on the Mediterranean, nine miles from Caesarea Palestine, towards Carmel. The village of *Tortura,* four leagues north of Caesarea, is supposed to nearly occupy its site. Jsh 12:23. Jg 1:27. 1 K 4:11. **Endor.** i.e. *fountain of Dor or habitation,* *S#5874h. 1 S *28:7. Ps 83:10. **Taanach.** i.e. *wandering through; she will afflict thee; humbling thee; sandy,* *S#8590h. Jsh 12:21. 17:11. Jg 1:27. 5:19. 1 K 4:12. 1 Ch 7:29. **Megiddo.** i.e. *place of multitudes; invading; gathering for cutting; his cutting place; rendezvous.* Jg 1:27. 5:19. 1 K 4:12. 9:15. 2 K 9:27. 23:29n, 30. 2 Ch 22:9mg. 35:22. Zc 12:11. Re *16:16.

12. **could not drive out.** Jsh 14:12. +*15:63. 16:10. Ex 23:29-33. Nu 33:52-56. Jg 1:27, 28. Ro *6:12-14. **would dwell.** Jg 1:27, 35.

13. **waxen strong.** Jg 1:28. 2 S 3:1. 2 Ch 26:15. Ep *6:10. Ph *4:13. 2 P √3:18. **put the.** Jsh 16:10. Dt 20:11-18. Jg 1:30, 33, 35. 2 Ch 8:7, 8. **utterly drive.** Dt 20:17.

14. **one lot.** Jsh 16:4. Ge 48:22. Nu 26:34-37. Dt 33:13-17. ♪121B. Metonymy of the Cause B548. A line is used for the territory divided up or marked out by it. For other instances of this figure see Dt 3:4. 32:8, 9. Ps *16:6. 19:4. 105:11mg. Am 7:17. Mi 2:5. 2 C *10:13, 16mg. **a great.** Ge 48:19. 49:22-26. **the Lord hath.** 1 S 7:12. Ps 115:12. **blessed.** Ge 48:19. Nu 26:34, 37. Ep=1:3.

15. **If thou be.** Lk *12:48. *16:10. **the Perizzites.** Jsh 3:10. 9:1. 11:3. 12:8. Ge +13:7. Ex 33:2. Ezr 9:1. **giants.** or, *Rephaim.* Jsh 12:4. 13:12. 15:8. 18:16. Ge 14:5. 15:20. Dt +*2:20. 2 S 5:18, 22. Is 17:5. **Ephraim.** ✚S#669h. Jsh 19:50. 20:7. 21:21. 24:30, 33. Jg 2:9. 3:27. 4:5. 7:24. 10:1. 17:1, 8. 18:2, 13. 19:1, 16, 18. 1 S 1:1. 9:4. 14:22. 2 S 20:21. 1 K 4:8. 12:25. 2 K 5:22. 1 Ch 6:67. 2 Ch 13:4. 15:8. 19:4. Je 4:15. 31:6. 50:19.

16. **chariots of iron.** ver. 18. Jg 1:19. 4:3. **Beth-shean.** ver. 11. 1 K 4:12. **towns.** ♪155E5, Nu +21:25. **valley of Jezreel.** Jsh 15:56. 19:18. Jg 6:33. 1 K 4:12. 18:46. 21:1, 23. 2 K 8:29. 9:10, 15, 37. 10:6, 7. 2 Ch 22:6. Ho 1:4, 5.

17. **Thou art a great.** See on ver. 14. **great power.** Ph=4:13.

18. **the mountain shall be thine.** ver. 15. Jsh 15:9. 20:7. Mt 17:20. **for thou shalt.** Jsh 11:4-6. 13:6. Nu 14:6-9. Dt 20:1-4. Ps *27:1, 2. Is *41:10-16. 51:12, 13. Ro *8:31, 37. 1 C 15:57. Ph 4:13. He *13:6. **iron chariots.** ver. 16. Jg 1:19. **strong.** Dt 20:1.

JOSHUA 18

The tabernacle is set up at Shiloh, 1. The remainder of the land described, and divided into seven parts, for the seven tribes which as yet had no inheritance, 2-9. Joshua casts the lot at Shiloh for the distribution of the land, 10. The first comes out for Benjamin, whose borders are described, 11-20. The cities of Benjamin, 21-28.

1. **assembled.** Dt 12:5. **Shiloh.** Shiloh was situated on a hill in the tribe of Ephraim, though near the borders of Benjamin, about fifteen miles north of Jerusalem, and, according to Eusebius, twelve, or according to Jerome, ten miles south from Shechem or Nablous. It was but a little north from Bethel or Ai, and near the road from Shechem to Jerusalem (Jg 21:19). In Jerome's time, Shiloh was ruined; and nothing remarkable was extant, but the foundations of the altar of burnt offerings which had been erected when the tabernacle stood there. Jsh 19:51. 21:2. 22:9. Jg 7:12. **set up.** Jg 18:31. 1 S 1:3, 24. 4:3, 4. 1 K 2:27. 14:2, 4. Ps 78:60. Je 7:12-14. 26:6. **tabernacle.** Jsh 4:19.

3. **How long are.** Jg 18:9. Pr 2:2-6. 10:4. 13:4. 15:19. Ec 9:10. Zp 3:16. Mt 20:6. Jn 6:27. Ph 3:13, 14. 2 P 1:10, 11. **slack.** or, remiss. lit. show yourselves feeble. Pr 12:27. *18:9. *24:10. He *6:12.

4. **three.** ver. 3. Jsh 3:12. 4:2. Nu 1:4. 13:2. Ec 4:12. **describe.** ver. 6, 9.

5. **Judah shall**. Jsh 15:1, etc. 19:1-9. **the house**. Jsh 16. 17. **abide**. Jn=15:4.

6. **that I may cast**. ver. 8, 10. Jsh +14:2n. Ge +24:44n. Nu 26:54, 55. 33:54. 34:13. Ps 105:11. Pr *16:33. 18:18. Ac 13:19.

7. **the Levites**. Jsh 13:14, 33. Nu 18:20, 23. Dt 10:9. 18:1, 2. **and Gad**. Jsh 13:8-31. Nu 32:29-41. Dt 3:12-17. 4:47, 48.

8. **Go**. Ge +*13:17. **that I may here**. ver. 6, 10. Jsh 7:16-18. 13:7. 14:1, +*2n. 15:1. Ge ◑+*24:44n. 1 S 14:41. Pr *16:33. 18:18. Ac 1:24-26. Ro 14:19.

9. **described**. The surveyors seem to have formed some kind of map of the country, as well as a description of it in writing. The Egyptians, from the situation of their fields, as annually overflowed by the Nile, acquired great skill in mensuration and land surveying; and some of the Israelites had, no doubt, learned these from them, without a knowledge of which they could not properly have divided the land. This is probably the first act of surveying on record. **into seven**. Ac 13:19. **in a book**. or, on a book. Jsh 10:13. Dt 17:18. 31:24. 1 P 1:4.

10. **cast lots**. ver. 6, 8. Jsh 14:2n. Ge +*24:44n. Pr *16:33. 18:18. Ezk 47:22. 48:29. Mt 27:35. Ac 13:19. **before the Lord**. Ps 16:5, 6. 47:4. 61:5. Jn 17:2. Ac 26:18. Col 1:12.

11. **of Benjamin**. Dt 33:12. **came up**. Jsh 14:2n. 19:1 (came forth), 17 (came out). Le 16:9mg. **came forth**. Jsh 19:1 (came forth), 17 (came out). An evident reference to how the lot was drawn out of the bag containing the Urim and Thummin which was in or behind the breastplate worn by Eleazar the high priest. See Pr 16:33. The Urim and Thummin were probably two precious stones which were drawn out as a lot to give Jehovah's judgment. **between the children**. Jsh 15:1-8. 16:1-10. Dt 10. 13:12.

12. **Jericho**. Jsh 2:1. 3:16. 6:1. 16:1. **the wilderness**. Jsh 7:2. Ho 4:15. 5:8. 10:5. **Beth-haven**. Near Bethel and Ai. Jsh *7:2. 8:20.

13. **side of Luz**. Jsh 16:2. Ge +*28:19. Jg 1:22-26. **Atroth-addar**. i.e. *crowns of glory*, ✳S#5853h. Jsh 16:2, *5. 1 Ch 2:54. **nether Beth-horon**. Jsh 10:11. 16:3. 21:22. Lower Beth-horon as distinct from "upper Beth-horon," Jsh 16:5. It was rebuilt by Solomon, 1 K 4:17.

14. **was drawn**. ver. 17. Jsh 15:9. **corner of the sea**. or, west corner. Benjamin had no sea coast; so in last clause of this verse (Young). **Kirjath-baal**. Jsh 15:9, 60. 1 S 7:1, 2. 2 S 6:2. 1 Ch 13:5, 6.

15. **well**. Heb. *mayan*, S#4599h, Ge +7:11. **Nephtoah**. Jsh 15:9.

16. **valley of the son of Hinnom**. Jsh +*15:8n. 2 K *23:10. 2 Ch 28:3. 33:6. Is 30:33. Je 7:31, 32. 19:2, 6, 11. 32:35. **the valley of the giants**. See on Jsh 15:8. 1 Ch 14:9. **Jebusi**. i.e. *threshing floor*, ✳S#2983h. Mount Zion, south of Jerusalem; for *Jebusi* or *Jebus* was the ancient name of that city. ver. *28. Jsh +*15:63. Jg 1:8, 21. 19:10. **En-rogel**. Jsh 15:7. 2 S 17:17. 1 K 1:9.

17. **En-shemesh**. The fountain of the Sun; whether a town, or simply a fountain, is uncertain. Jsh 15:7. **Geliloth**. i.e. *borders*, ✳S#1553h. Jsh 15:7. Geliloth is probably the same as Gilgal; though as the word may signify *borders* or *limits*, some think that it is probably not the proper name of a place: "And went forth towards the borders which are over against the

ascent to Adummim." Others render Geliloth *circuits* or *roundings*, or the *hills* about Jordan. **the stone**. Jsh 15:6.

18. **Arabah**. *or*, the plain. S#6160h. Jsh 3:16. +4:13. 15:6, 61. Nu +22:1. Dt +11:30mg. Am +6:14.

19. **Bethhogla**. i.e. *house of a partridge*, ✳S#1031h. ver. 21. Jsh 15:6. **bay**. Heb. tongue. Jsh +*15:2mg. Is 11:15. **the salt sea**. Jsh 3:16. 12:3. Ge 14:3. 19:25. Nu 34:3. Dt 3:17. **this was the**. The borders of this tribe on the north were the same as those of Ephraim on the south, and his southern boundaries the same as the northern borders of Judah; but drawn from west to east, instead of from east to west (Jsh 15:1-12. ch. 16). As the inheritance of Benjamin did not extend to the Mediterranean sea, and no other sea or lake is known to have been in those parts, perhaps this expression, "compassed the corner of the sea southward" (ver. 14), should be rendered, "made a circuit on the side next the sea towards the south"; for it seems to connect the northern border, in the preceding verses, with the southern which follows.

20. **the inheritance**. ver. 11.

21. **Jericho**. ver. 12. Jsh 2:1. 6:1. Lk 10:30. 19:1. **Beth-hoglah**. ver. 19. Jsh 15:6. **Keziz**. i.e. *cuttings off; extremity*, ✳S#7104h.

22. **Beth-arabah**. ver. 18. Jsh 15:6. **Zemaraim**. i.e. *two cuttings off; double woolens; double fleece; cold; double mountain forest*, ✳S#6787h. Ge ◑10:18. 2 Ch 13:4. **Beth-el**. Jsh 15:6. 1 K 12:29-32.

23. **Avim**. i.e. *perverse places; perverters; villagers*, ✳S#5761h. Jsh 13:3, Avites. Dt 2:23, Avims. 2 K 17:31, Avites. (1) A tribe of the Philistines, Dt 2:23; Jsh 13:3. (2) A city of Benjamin, Jsh 18:23. (3) A tribe transported to Samaria, 2 K 17:31. **Parah**. i.e. *the cow*, ✳S#6511h. **Ophrah**. i.e. *a fawn*. Situated, according to Eusebius, five miles east of Bethel. 1 S 13:17. Mi 1:10, Bethophrah.

24. **Chepher-haammoni**. i.e. *village of the Ammonites*, ✳S#3726h. **Ophni**. i.e. *becoming moldy; flying; darkness; folding together; weariness*, ✳S#6078h. Probably the same as *Gophna*; which, according to Josephus, was about fifteen miles from Jerusalem, towards Shechem, says Eusebius. **Gaba**. i.e. *hill, gently rising; elevation; hillock*, ✚S#1387h. Ezr 2:26. Ne 7:30. The same as Gibeah. Jg 19:12. Ho 5:8. Gaba or Geba, according to Josephus, was not far from Rama, forty stadia from Jerusalem, and, according to Eusebius, five miles from Gophna, towards Shechem. Jsh +21:17. 1 S +13:3, Geba. Ezr 2:26. Ne 7:30.

25. **Gibeon**. Jsh 9:17. +*10:2. 1 K 3:4, 5. 9:2. Is 28:21. **Ramah**. i.e. *the lofty place; the height*. Situated, according to Eusebius, six miles from Jerusalem towards Bethel; though Jerome places it near Gaba, seven miles from Jerusalem. 1 S 1:1, Ramathaimzophim. 7:17. 15:34. Je *31:15. Ho 5:8. Mt 2:17, *18. 27:57, Arimathea. **Beeroth**. i.e. *wells*. Jsh 9:17. Dt 10:6. 2 S 4:2. Ezr 2:25. Ne 7:29. Eusebius says Beeroth was seven miles from Jerusalem, towards Nicopolis or Emmaus. Jerome, however, reads Neapolis or Shechem; but Reland prefers the former.

26. **Mizpeh**. i.e. *watchtower; lofty place*. Situated not far from Rama, forty stadia from Jerusalem. Jsh 11:3n. Jg 10:17. 21:1. **Chephirah**. lit. *a village*. Jsh 9:17. Ezr 2:25. Ne 7:29. **Mozah**. i.e. *an outlet; bubbling waters; a spring; fountain, the place from which one goes forth; origin; drained*, ✳S#4681h.

27. **Rekem**. i.e. *variegated, embroidered; vain.* **Irpeel**. i.e. *God heals; God will restore; the health, medicine, or exalting of God,* ✱S#3416h. Ps=103:3. Pr=4:22mg. **Taralah**. i.e. *a reeling; trembling; release the curse; searching out of a slander; his increase,* ✱S#8634h.

28. **Zelah**. i.e. *a rib; limping; one-sided,* ✱S#6762h. 2 S 21:14. **Eleph**. i.e. *the thousand* or *chief; learning,* ✱S#507h. **Jebusi**. ver. 16. Jsh +*15:8, 63. 2 S 5:8. **Jerusalem**. As in Jsh 15:63; it belonged partly to Benjamin, and partly to Judah; Moriah to the former, and Zion to the latter (Young). **Gibeath**. i.e. *a high place,* S#1394h. Jsh 15:57. Jg 19:12-15. 20:4, 5. 1 S 10:26. 11:4. 13:15, 16. 14:16. 2 S 21:6. 1 Ch 11:31. 12:3. Is 10:29. Ho 5:8. 9:9. 10:9, Gibeah. **Kirjath**. i.e. *a city,* S#7157h. **according**. Nu 26:54. 33:54.

JOSHUA 19

The second lot falls to Simeon; his borders among the tribe of Judah, whose inheritance was too great for them, 1-9. The third lot falls to Zebulun, 10-16. The fourth to Issachar, 17-23. The fifth to Asher, 24-31. The sixth to Naphtali, 32-39. The seventh to Dan, 40-48. The children of Israel give an inheritance to Joshua, 49, 50. The division of the land finished, 51.

1. **second lot**. Jsh 18:6-11. **within the**. ver. 9. Ge 49:5-7. Jg 1:3.

2. **Beer-sheba**. i.e. *well of an oath.* Jsh 15:28. Ge 21:31. **Sheba**. i.e. *oath.* This word is omitted in the enumeration in 1 Ch 4:28. **and Moladah**. Jsh 15:26. 1 Ch 4:28-30. Bilhah. Ezem. Tolad. Bethuel. Ne 11:26-30.

3. **Hazar-shual**. Jsh 15:28, 29. **Balah**. i.e. *decayed; worn out,* ✱S#1088h, only here. Jsh 15:29, Baalah. **Azem**. Jsh 15:29, i.e. Ezem.

4. **Eltolad**. Jsh 15:30. 1 Ch 4:29. **Bethul**. i.e. *separated,* ✱S#1329h, only here. Jsh 15:30, Chesil. 1 Ch 4:29, 30, Bethuel. **Hormah**. Jsh 15:30. Jg 1:17.

5. **Ziklag**. Jsh 15:31. 1 S 27:6. 30:1. **Beth-marcaboth**. i.e. *a house of chariots.* **Hazar-susah**. i.e. *a house of horses,* ✱S#2701h. 2 K 23:11. 1 Ch 4:31, Hazar-susim.

6. **Beth-lebaoth**. i.e. *house of lions,* ✱S#1034h. Jsh 15:32. **Sharuhen**. i.e. *a beginning of grace; gracious house,* ✱S#8287h.

7. **Ain**. Jsh 15:32. **Remmon**. i.e. *elevation; pomegranate,* ✱S#7417h, so rendered only here. Jsh 15:32. Nu 33:19, 20. 1 Ch 4:32, Rimmon. **Ether**. i.e. *abundance,* ✱S#6281h. Jsh 15:42. **Ashan**. Jsh 15:42.

8. **Baalath-beer**. i.e. *mistress of a well,* ✱S#1192h. 1 Ch 4:33. **Ramath of the south**. i.e. *the height; height of the south,* ✱S#7418h, only here. 1 S 30:27, Ramoth.

9. **too much**. Ex 16:18. 2 C 8:14, 15. **therefore**. ver. 1.

10. **third**. Jsh 18:6, 11. **Zebulun**. Ge 49:13. Dt 33:18, 19. **Sarid**. i.e. *a remnant; survivor,* ✱S#8301h. ver. 12.

11. **toward the sea**. ver. 13, 14. Ge ✱49:13. **Maralah**. i.e. *trembling, shaking; earthquake,* ✱S#4831h. **Dabbasheth**. i.e. *a hump of a camel;* he whispered shame; or eminence, like a bee-hive; flowing with honey, ✱S#1708h. **the river**. The river *Kishon,* which empties itself into the Mediterranean near Mount Carmel, in the vicinity of which Jokneam was situated. **Jokneam**. i.e. *the people will be purchased; the people*

will be lamented. Jsh 12:22. 1 K 4:12. 1 Ch 6:68, Jokmeam.

12. **Chisloth-tabor**. i.e. *confidence of Tabor (i.e. choice, purity),*" ✱S#3696h. Called *Chasalus* by Eusebius and Jerome, and placed at the foot of mount Tabor, eight miles east of Diocaesarea. ver. 22. Jg 4:6, 12. Ps 89:12. **Daberath**. i.e. *led, submissive, obedient,* ✦S#1705h. Jsh ●21:28, Dabareh. 1 Ch *6:72. Josephus, who calls this town *Dabaritta,* or *Darabitta,* places it in the plain of Jezreel, or Esdraelon, on the confines of Samaria and Galilee. It is probably the *Dabira* which Jerome places towards mount Tabor, in the district of Diocaesarea; and the *Debora* or *Daboura* mentioned by travellers as a village at the foot of mount Tabor. **Japhia**. i.e. *beautiful.* Jsh 10:3. Probably *Japha,* a city of Galilee, near Jotapata, mentioned by Josephus.

13. **Gittah-hepher**. i.e. *wine press of the well,* ✱S#1662h. Placed by Jerome two miles from Sephoris, or Diocaesarea, towards Tiberias. 2 K 14:25, Gath-hepher. **Ittah Kazin**. i.e. *time of the captain,* ✱S#6278h. **-methoar**. *or,* which is drawn. 1 Ch 6:77. i.e. *Rimmon that is marked out; the marked out pomegranate,* S#7417h. **Neah**. i.e. *moving, shaking,* ✱S#5269h.

14. **Hannathon**. i.e. *gracious,* ✱S#2615h. **Jiphthahel**. i.e. *God opens,* ✱S#3317h. ver. 27.

15. **Kattath**. ✱S#7005h, only here. i.e. *very small; littleness. Kitron, a bond,* as in Jg 1:30. Jsh 21:34, 35. **Nahallal**. i.e. *pasture land,* ✱S#5096h. Jsh 21:35. Jg 1:30, Nahalol. **Shimron**. i.e. *a little watchtower.* Jsh 11:1. 12:20. **Idalah**. i.e. *what God exalts,* ✱S#3030h. **Beth-lehem**. i.e. *house of bread,* S#1035h. Different from that in Judah (see Jsh 12:9n). Ru 1:19. 2 S 23:15. 2 Ch 11:6. (1) A village of Judah, originally called Ephrath, Ge 35:19, and which is more fully named Bethlehem Judah or Bethlehem Ephratah. Ge 35:19. 48:7. Jg +17:7. Ru 1:19, 19, 22. 2:4. 4:11. 1 S 16:4. 17:15. 20:6, 28. 2 S 2:32. 23:14, 15, 16, 24. 1 Ch 11:16, 17, 18, 26. 2 Ch 11:6. Ezr 2:21. Ne 7:26. Mi *5:2. (2) A town in Zebulun, six miles west of Nazareth, Jsh 19:15. (3) A town in Ephraim, Jg 12:8, 10. (4) A descendant of Caleb, 1 Ch 2:51, 54; 4:4.

17. **Issachar**. Ge 49:14, 15.

18. **Jezreel**. Jsh 17:16. 1 K 21:1, 15, 16. 2 K 8:29. 9:15, 30. Ho 1:4, 5. **Chesulloth**. i.e. *the confident places; foolish confidences,* ✱S#3694h. Probably the same as **Chisloth-tabor**, ver. 12. **Shunem**. i.e. *resting places,* ✱S#7766h. 1 S 28:4h. 1 K 1:3. 2:17, 21. 2 K 4:8h, 12.

19. **Haphraim**. i.e. *two pits,* ✱S#2663h. A town called *Aiphraim,* in the time of Eusebius, six miles north of Legio. **Shihon**. i.e. *wall of strength; a waste; a ruin,* ✱S#7866h. A town called *Seon* by Eusebius, at the foot of mount Tabor. **Anaharath**. i.e. *groaning, roaring; the groaning of fear,* ✱S#588h.

20. **Rabbith**. i.e. *multitude,* ✱S#7245h. **Kishion**. i.e. *sharpness* or *hardness,* ✱S#7191h. Jsh 21:28. **Abez**. i.e. *tin,* ✱S#77h.

21. **Remeth**. i.e. *a high place,* ✱S#7432h, only here. Jsh 21:29. 1 Ch 6:73. **En-gannim**. i.e. *fountain of gardens,* ✱S#5873h. Jsh 15:34. 21:29. Different from that in Jsh 15:34. **En-haddah**. i.e. *fountain of sharpness,* ✱S#5876h. **Beth-pazzez**. i.e. *house of dispersion,* ✱S#1048h.

22. **Tabor**. i.e. *thou wilt purge; stone quarry;*

choice; separated; purity. ver. 12. Jg 4:6. 8:18. 1 Ch 6:77. Ps 89:12. Je 46:18. Ho 5:1. **Shahazimah.** i.e. *to strut proudly,* *S#7831h. **Beth-shemesh.** i.e. *house of the sun.* ver. 38. Jsh 21:16. 1 S 6:9, etc. 1 K 4:9. 2 K 14:11-13. Je 43:13.

24. The lot of Asher lay upon the coast of the great sea. We read of only one remarkable person of this tribe, and that was Anna, the prophetess, the daughter of Phanuel, a widow of about fourscore and four years, which departed not from the temple, but served God with fastings and prayers night and day. Lk 2:36-38.

25. **Helkath.** i.e. *a portion, field,* *S#2520h. Jsh 21:31. 2 S 2:16. **Hali.** i.e. *ornament,* *S#2482h. **Beten.** i.e. *belly or womb; valley,* *S#991h. Probably the same as *Bebeten* or *Batnai,* mentioned by Eusebius, eight miles from Ptolemais; and perhaps the *Ecbatana* which Pliny places not far from Ptolemais. **Achsaph.** i.e. *enchantment; sorcery.* Jsh 11:1. 12:20.

26. **Alammelech.** i.e. *the king's oak,* *S#487h. **Amad.** i.e. *people of old; eternal people,* *S#6008h. **Misheal.** i.e. *a request,* *S#4861h. Situated, according to Eusebius, near mount Carmel, on the sea coast. Jsh 21:30h. 1 Ch 6:74, Mashal. **Carmel.** i.e. *a fruitful place.* Different from that in Jsh 15:55. 1 S 15:12. 25:2. 1 K 18:19, 20, 42. 2 K 2:25. 4:25. SS 7:5. Is 33:9. 35:2. 37:24. Je 46:18. 50:19. Am 1:2. Mi 7:14. Na 1:4. **Shihor-libnath.** i.e. *blackness of whiteness,* *S#7884h.

27. **Beth-dagon.** Jsh 15:41. 1 S 5:2. **Zebulun.** i.e. *wished for dwelling.* Situated on the sea coast, near Ptolemais. **valley of.** ver. 14. **Beth-emek.** i.e. *house of the valley,* *S#1025h. **Neiel.** i.e. *motion of God; we shall be shaken of God; the moving of God,* *S#5272h. **Cabul.** i.e. *sandy; a border,* *S#3521h. Supposed to be the same town which Josephus calls Xoboulo, and which he says was situated near the sea side, near Ptolemais. 1 K 9:13. (1) A border city of Asher, Jsh 19:27. (2) The name given by Hiram to the land containing twenty cities of Galilee which Solomon gave him, 1 K 9:13.

28. **Hebron.** i.e. *one who has crossed.* Not the same as Jsh 15:54; identified with Abdon in Jsh 21:30. 1 Ch 6:74. **Rehob.** i.e. *broad place; square, plaza.* See on ver. 30. **Hammon.** i.e. *warm, sunny; hot spring,* *S#2540h. 1 Ch 6:76. Different from that in 1 Ch 6:76. (1) A town of Asher, Jsh 19:28. (2) A city of Naphtali which was assigned to the Levites, 1 Ch 6:76, probably the same as Hammath and Hamoth-dor. **Kanah.** i.e. *place of reeds; he has purchased.* This seems a different Cana from that in Lower Galilee; and to be that which is placed in some maps east of Tyre, between Libanus and Antilibanus, and south of the river Cassimer, or Leitani. Jn 2:1, 11. 4:46, Cana. **great.** Jsh 11:8. Jg 1:31. Is 23:2, 4, 12. **great Zidon.** i.e. *a hunting; fishery; ship of judgment.* So called because of its great size and importance in those days. Jsh 11:8. Jg 1:31. Is 23:2, 4. Zc 9:2.

29. **Ramah.** i.e. *the high place.* Different from that in ver. 36. Probably the *Rama* mentioned by Theodoret as a city of Syria; and placed in some maps between Sarepta and Sidon, eastward, near Lebanon. **strong city.** or, fenced city. Nu 13:19. 2 S *24:7. **Tyre.** Heb. Tzor. i.e. *a rock.* 2 S 5:11. 24:7. 1 K 5:1. 7:13. 9:11, 12. 1 Ch 14:1, 2. 2 Ch 2:3, 11. Ps 45:12. 83:7. Is ch. 23. Ezk ch. 26-28. Some think it another place of the same name. **Hosah.** i.e. *a refuge.* **Achzib.** i.e. *a lie.*

As in Jg 1:31. Different from Jsh 15:44; Mi 1:14. Ge 38:5.

30. **Ummah.** i.e. *over against, near; association,* *S#5981h. **Aphek.** i.e. *strength.* Jsh 12:18. 13:4. 1 S 4:1. 1 K 20:30. **Rehob.** i.e. *street,* Jsh 21:31. Nu 13:21. Jg 1:31. 2 S 10:6, 8. 1 Ch 6:71, 74, 75.

31. **the inheritance.** Ge 49:20. Dt 33:24, 25.

33. **Heleph.** i.e. *an exchange,* *S#2501h. **Allon.** i.e. *an oak.* **Zaanannim.** i.e. *removings; wanderings,* *S#6815h. Jg 4:11, Zaanaim. **Adami.** i.e. *human.* Different from Adam of Jsh 3:16. **Nekeb.** i.e. *a cavern,* *S#5346h. **Jabneel.** i.e. *God builds.* Different from that in Jsh 15:11. **Lakum.** i.e. *the rising up; stopping by the way; fortified place,* *S#3946h.

34. **turneth.** Dt 33:23. **Aznoth-tabor.** i.e. *ears (summits) of Tabor,* *S#243h. Apparently the same as *Azanoth,* which Eusebius places in the plain not far from Diocaesarea or Sephoris. ver. 12, 22. **Hukkok.** i.e. *things decreed; appointed portion,* *S#2712h. Jsh 21:31, Helkath. 1 Ch 6:75. **south side.** Dt 33:23. **Judah.** As it is certain that the tribe of Naphtali did not border upon that of Judah, there being several tribes between, we should probably omit Judah, with the Septuagint; though it may have been a town so called.

35. **Ziddim.** i.e. *the sides,* *S#6661h. **Zer.** i.e. *strait; flint,* *S#6863h. **Hammath.** i.e. *warm baths; warm springs,* *S#2575h. 1 Ch 2:55h. For other places with the same name see Jsh 19:35. 21:32. Ge 10:18. Nu 13:21. 34:8. 1 K 8:65, Hamath. **Rakkath.** i.e. *a shore or river bank; leanness; her spitting; empty; vain,* *S#7557h. **Chinnereth.** i.e. *a harp.* Jsh 11:2, Chinneroth. 12:3n. 13:27. Nu 34:11. Dt 3:17. Ezk 47:18, the east sea. In the New Testament called *sea of Tiberias* (Jn 6:1, 23. 21:1), and *sea of Gennesaret* (Mt 14:34. Mk 6:53. Lk 5:1).

36. **Adamah.** i.e. *earth,* *S#128h. Different from *Adami* in ver. 33. **Ramah.** i.e. *the high place.* Different from that in ver. 13. **Hazor.** i.e. *village, hamlet.* Jsh 11:1, 10, 13. 12:19. Jg 4:2. 1 K 9:15. 2 K 15:29.

37. **Kedesh.** i.e. *a place set apart; a sanctuary; consecrated.* Jsh 12:22. 20:7. 21:32. Jg 4:6, 9, 10. 1 Ch 6:76. Not the same as Jsh 15:23. **Edrei.** i.e. *strong.* Not the same place mentioned in Nu 21:23. **En-hazor.** i.e. *fountain of the village,* *S#5877h.

38. **Iron.** i.e. *the little fearful one,* *S#3375h. **Migdal-el.** i.e. *tower of God,* *S#4027h. Probably the Magdala of Mt 15:39. **Horem.** i.e. *devoted; banned; separated; dedication,* *S#2765h. **Beth-anath.** i.e. *the house of answers, responses, replies, echoes,* *S#1043h. Jg 1:33, 33. Not the same place as Jsh 15:59. Eusebius mentions a town of the name of Batanaian, fifteen miles from Caesarea (Diocaesarea or Sephoris, probably). **Beth-shemesh.** i.e. *house of the sun.* Different place from that in ver. 22. Jsh 21:16. Jg 1:33.

40. **Dan.** Dt 33:22.

41. **Zorah.** i.e. *leprosy,* *S#6881h. Situated on the frontiers of Dan and Judah, ten miles north from Eleutheropolis, towards Nicopolis, according to Eusebius, not far from Caphar-Sorek. Jsh 15:33, Zoreah. Jg 13:2, 25. 16:31. 18:2, 8, 11. 1 Ch ❶2:53. 2 Ch 11:10. Ne 11:29. **Eshtaol.** Jsh 15:33. **Ir-shemesh.** i.e. *city of the sun,* *S#5905h. Supposed by some to be the same as *Beth-shemesh* in the tribe of Judah; but this latter city is evidently distinguished from it by being assigned by the tribe of Judah to the Levites (Jsh 21:16). **Ir-shemesh,** rendered *polis Sammaus* by

the LXX., seems to be the same as *Emmaus* or *Nicopolis*, 22 miles southeast from Lydda, according to the Old Jerusalem Itinerary.

42. **Shaalabbin.** i.e. *place of foxes*, *S#8169h. Jg 1:35, Shaalbim. 1 K 4:9, Shaalbim. Eusebius calls it *Salaba*, and places it in Samaria: and Jerome calls it *Salebi* (Ezk 48), and joins it to Ajalon and Emmaus. **Ajalon.** i.e. *little hind.* This appears to be the Ajalon which Jerome places two miles from Nicopolis or Emmaus, in the road to Jerusalem. Jsh *10:12. 21:24. Jg 1:35. 1 S 14:31. 1 Ch 6:69. **Jethlah.** i.e. *lofty place,* *S#3494h.

43. **Elon.** i.e. *an oak.* **Thimnathah.** i.e. *portion assigned, divided allotment; a portion there,* S#8553h. Ge 38:12. Jg 14:1, 2, Timnath. 2 Ch 28:18, Timnah. **Ekron.** i.e. *eradication.* Ekron is placed by Eusebius between Ashdod and Jamnia, eastward; and probably the ruined village of *Tookrair,* mentioned by Dr. Richardson, situated on the top of a hill, and which he says seems to have been a place of considerable consequence, occupies its site. Jsh 15:45. Jg 1:18. 1 S 5:10. 7:14. Am 1:8. Zc 9:7.

44. **Eltekah.** i.e. *the object of fear.* Jsh 15:59. 21:23. **Gibbethon.** i.e. *a lofty place,* *S#1405h. Jsh 21:23. 1 K 15:27, 27. 16:15, 17. **Baalath.** i.e. *mistress,* *S#1191h. Different place from Jsh 15:29. 1 K 9:18. 2 Ch 8:6.

45. **Jehud.** i.e. *praised,* *S#3055h. **Bene-berak.** i.e. *sons of lightning,* *S#1139h. **Gath-rimmon.** i.e. *wine press of the pomegranate.* Jsh 21:24. 1 Ch 6:69.

46. **Me-jarkon.** i.e. *waters of paleness; yellow water; water of great greenness,* *S#4313h. **Rakkon.** i.e. *thinness,* *S#7542h. **before.** *or,* over against. **Japho.** i.e. *beauty,* *S#3305h. *or,* Joppa. 2 Ch 2:16, Joppa. Ezr 3:7. Jon 1:3. Ac 9:36, 38, 43. 10:8.

47. **the coast.** Jg 1:34, 35. 18:1-29. **called Leshem.** i.e. *unto desolation; precious stone; fortress,* *S#3959h, only here. Jg 18:7, 27, 29, Laish (i.e. *a lion; strong; crushing; destructive blows*).

49. **gave.** Ezk 45:7, 8.

50. **Timnath-serah.** i.e. *outspread portion; fruitful portion,* *S#8556h. Jsh 24:30h. Jg 2:9, Timnath-heres. 1 Ch 7:24.

51. **These are.** Jsh 14:1. Nu 34:17-29. Ps 47:3, 4. Mt 20:23. 25:34. Jn 14:2, 3. 17:2. He 4:8, 9. **in Shiloh.** Jsh 18:1, 10. Ge *49:10. Jg 21:19, 21. 1 S 1:3. Ps 78:60. Je 7:12-14.

JOSHUA 20

God commands Joshua to appoint six cities of refuge for those who unawares should slay a man, 1-4. The right use of them, 5, 6. The children of Israel appoint three cities on the west, and three on the east side of the river Jordan, 7-9.

1. **spake.** Jsh 5:14. 6:2. 7:10. 13:1-7. **saying.** Ex 21:13. Nu 35:6, 11, 14. Dt 19:2, 9.

2. **Appoint.** Ex 21:13, 14. Nu 35:6, 11-14. Dt 4:41-43. 19:2-13. Ro 8:1, 33, 34. He 6:18, 19.

3. **person.** Heb. *nephesh,* Jsh +10:28. ♪171Q1, Ge +12:5. **unawares** and **unwittingly.** Heb. through ignorance, *or* error, *or* mistake, *and* without knowledge. The same thing twice repeated, to cut off all the claims and expectations that willful murderers might have of protection here; God having declared that such should be taken even from his altar, that they might

be killed, Ex 21:14; and accordingly Joab was by Solomon's order killed even at the altar, 1 K 2:28-31, 34. It is the more strange and impudent that any Christians should make their sanctuaries give protection to such persons whom God hath so expressly excepted from it (Matthew Poole). Le 4:2, 13, 22, 27. 5:15, 18. Dt 4:42. 19:4, 5. **your refuge.** Nu 35:15-24. Dt 19:5, 6. He=*6:18. **avenger of blood.** The kinsman, who had right or power to demand or take vengeance of the slaughter (Matthew Poole). Nu 35:12, 19, 25. Dt 19:6, 12, 13. 2 S 14:11.

4. **shall stand.** Ex 33:21. Nu 35:12, 14. **at the entering.** Ru 4:1, 2. Jb 5:4. 29:7. Pr 31:23. Je 38:7. **the gate.** Ge +14:7. Dt 25:7. **shall declare.** Is 1:18. 41:21. 56:5. **the elders.** Jsh 24:1. Ex +*18:21. Dt 5:23. 31:28. Jg 21:16. Ru 4:2. 1 S 4:3. 8:4. 15:30. 30:26. 2 S 3:17. 5:3. 17:4, 15. 19:11. 1 K 8:1, 3. 20:7. 2 K 23:1. 1 Ch 11:3. 15:25. *21:16. 2 Ch 5:2, 4. 34:29. Je 19:1. 26:17. 29:1. Ezk 8:1, 12. 14:1. 20:1, 3. Jl 1:14. 2:16. Lk 22:66. Ac 4:5. 22:5. 23:14. 24:1. 25:15. **take.** Jsh 2:18mg. 24:1. Ps 26:9. **a place.** Zc 3:7. **that he may.** Ep 2:13, 19. He *6:18.

5. **if the avenger.** Nu 35:12, 25. **shall not deliver.** Jb 33:24, 28. Ps 46:1. 48:3. 57:1. Jn=√10:28.

6. **until.** Nu 35:12, 24, 25, 28. 2 K 12:10. He 5:1. 7:27, 28. 8:3. 9:7, 25, 26. 13:11. **he stand.** Standing was the posture of the accused and accusers, Ex 18:13. Is 50:8. Zc 3:1. **before the congregation.** The council appointed to judge these matters: not the council of the city of refuge, for they had examined him before, ver. 4; but of the city to which he belonged, or in or nigh which the fact was committed, as appears from Nu 35:25. **until the death of the high priest.** Nu 35:25. Ps 1:5. He *7:23-25.

7. **appointed.** Heb. sanctified. Nu 16:37, 38. Dt 19:3. Jg 17:3. **Kedesh.** i.e. *a thing set apart.* Jsh 19:37. 21:32. Jg 4:6. **Kedesh,** called *Cadesa,* or *Caidesa,* by Josephus, was situated in Upper Galilee, twenty miles southeast from Tyre, according to Eusebius. The cities of refuge were distributed through the land at proper distances from each other, that they might be convenient to every part of the land; and it is said they were situated on eminences, that they might be easily seen at a distance; the roads leading to them being broad, even, and always kept in good repair; and way posts (Nu 35:32n. Dt 27:8. Is 35:8. Je 31:21. Hab *2:2), upon which was inscribed "refuge," were placed wherever needful, that they might not so much as hesitate for a moment (Nu 35:32n). Kedesh and Hebron were at the two extremities of the land—the former being in Galilee, and the latter in Judah, both in mountainous districts, and Shechem was in mount Ephraim, nearly in the center. Bezer was east of Jordan, in the eastern part of the plain opposite Jericho; Ramoth was about the midst of the country of the two tribes and a half, being about the middle of the mountains of Gilead; and Golan, the capital of Gaulonitis, was situated in the tribe of Manasseh, in the land of Bashan. As this institution is considered as a type of Christ (He 6:18-20), some expositors observe a significancy in the names of these cities with application to Him as our Refuge. *Kedesh* signifies "holy," and our refuge is in the holy Jesus (Lk +*1:35). *Shechem,* "a shoulder," "and the government shall be upon his shoulder" (Is 9:6). *Hebron,* "fellowship," and believers are called into the fellowship of Christ Jesus our Lord (1 C 1:9. 1 J 1:3).

Bezer, "a fortification," for he is a stronghold to those who trust in him (He 6:18-20). *Ramoth*, "high," or "exalted," for him hath God exalted with his own right hand (Ac 2:33. *5:31. Ph 2:9). *Golan*, "joy," or "exultation," for in him all the saints are justified, and shall glory (Lk 1:47. Ac 10:43. *13:39. Ga 6:14). Jsh 21:32. 1 Ch 6:76. **Galilee**. i.e. *a circuit*, *S#1551h. Jsh 21:32. 1 K 9:11. 2 K 15:29. 1 Ch 6:76. Is 9:1. **Shechem**. i.e. *back, shoulder*. Jsh 21:21. Ge 12:6, Sichem. 33:18, 19. 37:12, 14. 1 Ch 6:67. 2 Ch 10:1. Ps 60:6. Jn 4:5, Sychar. **Kirjath-arba**. Jsh 14:15. 21:11, 13. Jg 1:10. The city, not the country, which was given to Caleb, Jsh 14:13. 21:31n. **which is Hebron**. Jsh 14:15. 21:11, 13. Jg 1:10, 20. 1 K 2:11. 1 Ch 6:57. **mountain of Judah**. Mt *5:14. Lk 1:39, 65.

8. the other side Jordan. Dt 19:9. **assigned**. Dt 4:41. **Bezer**. i.e. *gold ore; defense; stronghold*. Jsh 21:36. Dt 4:43. 1 Ch 6:78. **Ramoth**. i.e. *heights; eminences*. Jsh 21:38. Dt 4:43. 1 K 22:3, 4, 6, 29. 2 K 8:28. 1 Ch 6:80. **Golan**. i.e. *great exodus; their captivity; their rejoicing*. Jsh 21:27. Dt 4:43. 1 Ch 6:71.

9. the cities. Nu 35:15. **and for the stranger**. Jsh 8:33, 35. Ex 12:+√48mg, 49. *20:10. Le *20:2. 22:18. 24:16. 25:6. Nu 9:14. 15:14, 30. 19:10. 35:15. Dt 1:16. 5:14. 16:11. +√26:11. 29:11. *31:12. 2 Ch 30:25. Ep 2:19. **person**. Heb. *nephesh*, Jsh +10:28. **until he stood**. See on ver. 4, 6.

JOSHUA 21

The Levites require their cities, 1, 2. Forty-eight cities given by lot, out of the other tribes, unto the Levites, 3-8. The cities of the priests, 9-19; of the other Kohathites, 20-26; of the Gershonites, 27-33; of the Merarites, 34-40. In all, forty-eight cities, with their suburbs, 41, 42. God giveth the land, and rest unto the Israelites, 43, 44. An acknowledgment that the promise of God to Israel was fulfilled, 45.

1. the heads. Jsh 19:51. Ex 6:14, 25. **Eleazar**. Jsh 14:1. 17:4. Nu 34:17-29.

2. Shiloh. See on Jsh 18:1. **The Lord**. Nu 35:2-8. Ezk 48:9-18. Mt 10:10. Ga 6:6. 1 T 5:17, 18.

3. unto the Levites. Ge 49:7. Dt 33:8-10. 1 Ch 6:54-81.

4. Kohathites. Ex 6:18. Nu 3:17, 27. **the children**. ver. 8-19. Jsh 24:33. Ex 6:20. Nu 3:2-4, 19. 1 Ch 6:54-60. **the tribe**. These tribes furnished more habitations to the Levites, in proportion, than any of the other tribes, because they possessed a more extensive inheritance, agreeably to what Moses commanded (Nu 35:8). It is worthy of remark, that the principal part of this tribe, whose business was to minister at the sanctuary, which sanctuary was afterwards established at Jerusalem, had their appointment nearest to that city; so that they were always within reach of the sacred work which God had appointed them.

5. the rest. ver. 20-26. Ge 46:11. Ex 6:16-25. Nu 3:27. 1 Ch 6:18, 19, 61, 66-70.

6. of Gershon. ver. 27-33. Ex 6:16, 17. Nu 3:21, 22. 1 Ch 6:62, 71-76.

7. of Merari. ver. 34-40. Ex 6:19. Nu 3:20, 33. 1 Ch 6:63, 77-81.

8. by lot. ver. 3. Jsh 14:2n. 18:6. Ge ◖+*24:44n. Nu 33:54. 35:3. Pr +*16:33. 18:18. **as the Lord**. Nu 35:2.

9. of Simeon. Jsh 19:1. **these cities**. ver. 13-18.

1 Ch 6:65. **mentioned**. Heb. called.

10. of Aaron. See on ver. 4. Ex 6:18, 20-26. Nu 3:2-4, 19, 27. 4:2.

11. And they. 1 Ch 6:55. **the city of Arba**. *or*, Kirjath-arba. Jsh 14:15. 15:13, 14, 54. Ge 23:2. 35:27. Jg 1:10. **is Hebron**. Jsh 20:7. 2 S 2:1-3. 5:1-5. 15:7. **in the hill**. Jsh 20:7, etc. Lk 1:39.

12. fields of. Jsh 14:13-15. 1 Ch 6:55-57. Ne 12:44. **the city**. Jsh 20:7n. **his possession**. Jsh 14:6, *13, +*14. 15:13.

13. they gave. 1 Ch 6:56. **Hebron**. Jsh 10:3, 5. 15:54. **a city**. Jsh 20:7. Nu 35:6. **Libnah**. Jsh 10:29. 12:15. 15:42. 2 K 8:22. 19:8. 1 Ch 6:57. 2 Ch 21:10. Is 37:8.

14. Jattir. Jattir or Jether, according to Eusebius, was situated in the district of Daroma, or the southern part of Judah, 20 miles south from Eleutheropolis, towards the city of Malatha. Jsh 15:48. 1 S 30:27, 28. **Eshtemoa**. Eusebius says Eshtemoa, or Esthema, was a great city in the south of Judah, and in the district of Eleutheropolis, north of the city. Jsh 15:50, Eshtemoh. 1 S 30:26, 28. 1 Ch 4:17, Eshtemoa. 6:57.

15. Holon. Jsh 15:51. 1 Ch 6:58, Hilen. **Debir**. Jsh 10:38. 11:21. 12:13. 15:49. Jg 1:11.

16. Ain. Jsh 15:32, 42, Ashan. 19:7. 1 Ch 6:59, Ashan. **Juttah**. Eusebius says Juttah was a great town 18 miles south from Eleutheropolis. Jsh 15:55. **Beth-shemesh**. Jsh 15:10. 1 S 6:9, 12. 2 K 14:11, 13. 1 Ch 6:59. 2 Ch 25:21.

17. Gibeon. Jsh 9:3. +10:2. 18:25. 1 Ch 6:60. **Geba**. Jsh +18:24n, Gaba. 1 S 13:3. Ne 11:31. Is 10:29.

18. Anathoth. i.e. *answers*. Anathoth was situated about three miles northward from Jerusalem, according to Eusebius and Jerome (in Je. ch. 1. and ch. 30.); or twenty furlongs, according to Josephus (Ant. l. vii.c.10). 2 S 23:27. 1 K 2:26. Ne 11:32. Is 10:30. Je 1:1. 32:9. **Almon**. i.e. *hidden*, *S#5960h. 1 Ch 6:60, Alemeth.

19. cities of. 1 Ch 6:54, 60.

20. the families. ver. 5. 1 Ch 6:66.

21. Shechem. Jsh 20:7. Ge 33:19. Jg 9:1. 1 K 12:1. **Gezer**. Jsh 10:33. 16:10. Jg 1:29. 1 K 9:15-17. 1 Ch 6:67.

22. Kibzaim. i.e. *two gatherings*, *S#6911h. Perhaps the same as Jokdeam, 1 Ch 6:68. **Beth-horon**. Jsh 10:10, 11. 16:3, 5. 18:13, 14. 1 Ch 6:68. 2 Ch 8:5.

23. Dan. ver. 5. Jsh 19:40, 44. **Eltekeh**. i.e. *God-fearing*, *S#514h. Jsh 19:44, 45. **Gibbethon**. Probably the *Gabatha* mentioned by Eusebius and Jerome, as situated in the south of Judah, 12 miles from Eleutheropolis, where the prophet Habakkuk's sepulchre was shown. Jsh 19:44.

24. Aijalon. i.e. *deer field; a large stag*, ✢S#357h. Jsh 10:12. 19:42, Ajalon. Jg 1:35. 1 Ch 6:69. (1) The name of a valley in the land of Dan, Jsh 10:12. (2) A Levitical city of Dan, in or near the valley of Ajalon, Jsh 19:42; 21:24; Jg 1:35. (3) A place in the land of Zebulun, Jg 12:12. (4) A town in the land of Benjamin or Judah, though there may be doubt whether it is not the same with Ajalon in Dan, or whether the texts cited here all refer to the same city, 1 S 14:31; 1 Ch 8:13; 2 Ch 11:10; 28:18. (5) A Levitical city supposed to be in the land of Ephraim, 1 Ch 6:69, but is probably the same as number 2. **Gathrimmon**. Gathrimmon is said by Jerome to be a great town 10 miles from Diospolis, or Lydda, towards Eleutheropolis. Jsh 19:45.

25. Tanach. i.e. *afflicting thee,* *S#8590h. Jsh 17:11. Jg 1:27. 5:19. 1 Ch 7:29h. Aner and Bileam are mentioned in Chronicles, instead of Tanach and Gath-rimmon (1 Ch 6:70). Either the cities had at this time different names, or afterwards their names were changed—or the Levites, being by some means dispossessed of the cities first assigned them, received others from their brethren. A careful examination of the marginal references will discover other variations of this kind, which may be accounted for in the same manner. **Gath-rimmon.** i.e. *winepress of the pomegranate,* *S#1667h. ver. 24. Jsh 19:45. 1 Ch 6:69. (1) A city of Dan, Jsh 19:45. (2) A city of the Levites, apparently on the boundary between Ephraim and Manasseh, Jsh 21:25; 1 Ch 6:69, called Bileam in 1 Ch 6:70.

26. children of Kohath. ver. 5.

27. And unto. ver. 6. **Golan.** Jsh 20:8. Dt 1:4. 4:43. 1 Ch 6:71. **in Bashan.** Jg 12:4n. Nu +21:33. **Beesh-terah.** i.e. *house or temple of Ashtoreth,* *S#1203h. It is very probable that *Beesh-terah* is a contraction of *baith ashtaroth,* "the house of Ashtaroth," and the same as *Ashtaroth,* which is the reading in 1 Ch 6:71. Dt 1:4.

28. Kishon. i.e. *tortuous, winding.* Jsh 19:20, Kishion. 1 Ch 6:72, Kedesh. **Dabareh.** i.e. *manner of speech,* *S#1705h. Jsh 19:12, Daberath. 1 Ch 6:72, 73.

29. Jarmuth. i.e. *height; elevated, high; he will be lifted up; casting down death,* *S#3412h. Jsh 10:3, 5, 23. 12:11. 15:35. Ne 11:29. This seems to be the same city with *Remeth,* Jsh 19:19, 21, and *Ramoth,* 1 Ch 6:73, mentioned with Engannim. Jsh 10:3, 23. 12:11. (1) A town of Judah, Jsh 15:35; Ne 11:29. (2) A Levitical city of Issachar, Jsh 21:29, called Remeth in Jsh 19:21, and Ramoth in 1 Ch 6:73. **En-gannim.** Jsh 19:21. 1 Ch 6:73, Anem. **Abdon.** i.e. *rigorous slavery; servitude.* Perhaps the same as Hebron in Jsh 19:28, Helkath. Jsh 19:25, 34, Hukkok. 1 Ch 6:75, Hukok.

30. Mishal. i.e. *prayer, sentence, similitude; inquiry; request,* *S#4861h. Jsh 19:26h. Jsh 19:25-28, Misheal (i.e. *who is that which God is?*). 1 Ch 6:74, 75, Mashal (i.e. *a parable, a parabolist; intreaty*).

31. Rehob. Rehob was a city, afterwards given to the tribe of Asher, situated near Mount Lebanon, at the northern extremity of the Promised Land on the road which leads to Hamath, and west of Laish or Dan. Jsh 19:28, +30. Nu 13:21. Jg 1:31. 18:28. 1 Ch 6:75.

32. Kedesh. Jsh 19:37. +20:7n. Jg 4:6, 10. 2 K 15:29. 1 Ch 6:76. **Hammoth-dor.** i.e. *hot places of the dwelling,* *S#2576h. Supposed by many to be the same as *Tiberias;* so called from the hot baths, as the word *Chammoth* may denote, in its vicinity. Jsh 19:35, Hammath. Nu 13:21, Hamath. 1 Ch 6:76, Hammon. **Kartan.** i.e. *two cities; their hap; their meeting place,* *S#7178h. Supposed to be the same as *Kirjathaim,* 1 Ch 6:76. Different from that in Nu 32:37.

33. Gershonites. ver. 6.

34. And unto. ver. 7. 1 Ch 6:77. **Jokneam.** Jsh 12:22. 19:11, 15. **Kartah.** i.e. *city; meeting; her hap; her meeting place,* *S#7177h. Perhaps the same as Kattah, Jsh 19:15.

35. Dimnah. i.e. *dunghill,* *S#1829h. Compare the similar meaning of *Madmannah,* Jsh 15:31. Perhaps the same as Rimmon, 1 Ch 6:77. This and the following

verse are wholly omitted by the Masora, and many Hebrew Bibles which are esteemed very highly; though, without them, neither the twelve cities of the Merarites in particular (ver. 40), nor the forty-eight Levitical cities in general (ver. 41), nor the six cities of refuge, can be made up. But these two verses, thus absolutely necessary for the truth and consistency of this chapter, are happily preserved in no less than 149 MSS. collated by Dr. Kennicott, and upwards of 40 collated by De Rossi. **Nahalal.** i.e. *pasture, place of leading out,* *S#5096h. Jsh 19:15, Nahallal. Jg 1:30, Nahalol.

36. Bezer. Jsh +20:8. Dt 4:43. 1 Ch 6:78, 79. **Jahazah.** i.e. *strife,* +S#3096h. Jsh 13:18. Nu 21:23, Jahaz. 1 Ch 6:78, Jahzah. Je 48:21.

37. Kedemoth. i.e. *beginnnings, ancients; confrontings.* Jsh 13:18. Dt 2:26. 1 Ch 6:79. **Mephaath.** *beauty.* Jsh 13:18. Je 48:21.

38. Ramoth. Jsh *20:8. 1 K 22:3. 1 Ch 6:80. **Mahanaim.** i.e. *two hosts, two camps.* Jsh 13:26. Ge 32:2. 2 S 2:8. 17:24. 19:32. 1 K 2:8.

39. Heshbon. Jsh 13:17, 21. Nu 21:26-30. 32:37. 1 Ch 6:81. **Jazer.** Nu 21:32. 32:1, 3, 35, Jaazer. Is 16:8, 9. Je 48:32.

40. of Merari. ver. 7.

41. within. Ge 49:7. Nu 35:1-8. Dt 33:10. **forty and eight.** At the last census, the tribe of Levi amounted only to 23,000 (Nu 36:62); and it is thought by some that forty-eight cities was too great a proportion for this tribe. But it should be considered, that cities in ancient times were little more than villages.

42. These cities. Nu 35:3, 4.

43. gave unto. Ge 12:7. 13:15. 15:18-21. 26:3, 4. 28:4, 13, 14. Ex 3:8, 17. 23:27-31. Ps 44:3. 106:42-45. **all the land.** *√171A. Synecdoche of the Genus: All is put for the greater part, Ex +9:6. See Jsh 11:23n. He gave them the right to all, and the actual possession of the greatest part of it, and power to possess the rest as soon as it was needful and convenient for them, which was by degrees, when their numbers were increased, and the absolute dominion of all the people remaining in it (Matthew Poole). Some Amillennialists cite this text (as well as Jsh 23:14. 1 K 4:21. 2 Ch 9:26. He 11:10) to prove that the promise of God to Abraham of the land has thus been completely fulfilled (See, e.g., R. Bradley Jones, *What, Where, and When Is the Millennium?* pp. 47, 48). But the question is not, did Israel possess the land, but did Abraham, Isaac, and Jacob, to whom the promise was personally given and confirmed, personally receive or experience the fulfillment? The answer to this question is absolutely not, as Scripture plainly declares (Ac +*7:5. He √11:13, 39). Fulfillment must take place, therefore, in the future, in the land of Israel, upon their resurrection from the dead (Mt +*8:11). Jesus did not come to change, replace, redefine, or abrogate the Old Testament covenants and promises, but to confirm them (Mt +*5:17, 18. Ro 15:4, +*8). Ex *23:29, 30. Mt +*8:11. Ro +*15:8. He ◐+*11:13, 39.

44. gave them rest. Jsh 1:15. 11:23. 22:4, 9. Dt 7:22-24. 31:3-5. He ◐√4:8-10. **delivered all.** Dt 7:24. Ps 78:55.

45. failed not. Jsh 23:14, 15. Nu *23:19. 1 K 8:56. Ps *16:5, 6. 34:10. 1 C 1:9. 1 Th 5:24. T *1:2. He *6:18.

JOSHUA 22

Joshua dismisses Reuben, Gad, and Manasseh, with his commendation, counsel, strict charge to fear the Lord, and blessing; and with a large booty, 1-9. They build an altar of testimony at the brink of Jordan, 10. The other tribes are offended, and assemble to wage war against them, 11, 12. They first send Phinehas and ten princes ambassadors to reprove them, 13-20. They explain and vindicate their conduct, to the satisfaction of their brethren, 21-33. The name of the altar or the inscription on it, 34.

1. **Joshua.** See on Nu 32:18-33. Dt 29:7, 8. **Reubenites.** Jsh 1:12-15. We have already seen, that a detachment of 40,000 men, of the tribes of Reuben and Gad, and the half tribe of Manasseh, had passed over Jordan armed, with their brethren, according to their agreement with Moses. The war now being concluded, the land divided, and their brethren settled, Joshua assembles these warriors; and with commendations for their services and fidelity, he dismisses them, having first given them the most pious and suitable instructions. They had now been about seven years absent from their respective families; and though there was only the river Jordan between the camp at Gilgal and their own inheritance, yet it does not appear that they had, during that time, ever revisited their home, which they might have done at any time of the year, except the harvest, as the river was at other times easily fordable.

2. **Ye have.** Nu 32:20-29. Dt 3:18-20. **obeyed.** Jsh 1:12-18.

3. **have not left.** Ph 1:23-27.

4. **given rest.** See on Jsh 21:43, 44. Dt 12:9. **as he promised.** Ro 4:21. **get.** Jsh 13:8, 15-33. 14:1-5. Nu 32:33-42. Dt 3:1-17. 29:8.

5. **take.** See on Ex 15:26. Dt 4:1, 2, 6, 9. 6:6-9, 17. 11:22. 1 Ch 28:7, 8. Ps 106:3. 119:4-6. Pr *4:23. Is 55:2. Je 12:16. He +*6:11, 12. 12:15. 2 P √1:5-10. **love.** Ex 20:6. Dt 6:5. *10:12, 13. 11:1, 13. Mt 22:37. Jn 14:15, 21-23. 21:15-17. Ro *8:28. Ja 1:12. 2:5. 1 J 5:2, 3. Ju +21. **cleave.** Jsh 23:8. Dt 4:4. 10:20. 13:4. Ac *11:23. Ro 12:9. **serve.** Jsh *24:14, 15. 1 S 7:3. 12:20, 24. Mt *4:10. 6:24. Lk 1:74. Jn 12:26. Ac 27:23. Ro 1:9. **soul.** Heb. *nephesh*, Ge +34:3.

6. **blessed them.** ver. 7, 8. Jsh 14:13. Ge 14:19. +31:49. 47:7, 10. Ex 39:43. 1 S 2:20. 2 S 6:18, 20. 2 Ch 30:18. Lk 2:34. 24:50, 51. He 7:6, 7.

7. **Now to.** Jsh 13:29-31. 17:1-12. Nu 32:33.

8. **Return.** Dt 8:9-14, 17, 18. 2 Ch 17:5. 32:27. Pr 3:16. *10:4, 22. 1 C *15:58. He 11:26. **divide.** Nu 31:27. 1 S √30:24. Ps 68:12. Ro 8:37.

9. **the country of Gilead.** Jsh 13:11, 25, 31. Nu 32:1, 26, 39, 40. Dt 3:15, 16. Ps 60:7. **according.** Nu 32:20, 22.

10. **the children.** This verse should probably be rendered, "And when they came to the borders of Jordan, that *are* in the land of Canaan, the children of Reuben, and the children of Gad, and the half tribe of Manasseh, then built an altar by (or *beyond*) Jordan, a great altar to the view." It would appear, that when they came to the river, they formed the purpose of building the altar; and when they crossed it they put that purpose into execution. It is evident that they did not build it west of Jordan, for that was not in their territories, and the next verse expressly says that it was "built

over against the land of Canaan." **built.** ver. 25-28. Jsh 4:5-9. 24:26, 27. Ge 28:18. 31:46-52.

11. **heard.** Le 17:8, 9. Dt 12:5-7. *13:12-14. Jn 20:1, 12. **at the passage.** Jsh 2:7. 3:14-16. Jg 12:5. Jn 1:28.

12. **the whole.** Supposing they had built this altar for sacrifice, in opposition to the command of God, they considered them as rebels against God, and the Israelitish constitution. Dt 13:15. Jg 20:1-11. Ac 11:2, 3. Ro 10:2. Ga 4:17, 18.

13. **sent.** Nu 16:25. Dt 13:14. Jg 20:12. Pr 20:18. Mt *18:15. **Phinehas.** Ex 6:25. Nu 25:7, 11-13. Jg 20:28. Ps 106:30, 31. Pr 25:9-13.

14. **with him.** Dt 17:6. Mt 18:16. 2 C 13:1. **chief house.** Heb. house of the father. **an head.** Ex 18:25. Nu 1:4. 13:2. **among the thousands.** ver. +√21.

16. **the whole.** ver. 12. Jsh 18:1. Mt +*18:17. 1 C 1:10. 5:4. Ga 1:1, 2. **trespass.** Le 5:19. 26:40. Nu 5:6. 1 Ch 21:3. 2 Ch 26:18. 28:13. Ezr 9:2, 15. Mt 6:14, 15. **to turn.** ver. 18. Ex 32:8. Nu 14:43. 32:15. Dt 7:4. 30:17. 2 Ch 10:19. 25:27. He 12:25. **rebel.** Le 17:8, 9. Dt 12:4-6, √13, *14. 1 S √15:23. Ps 78:8. Is 63:10.

17. **Is the iniquity.** Nu 25:3, 4, etc. Dt 4:3, 4. Ps 106:28, 29. **Peor.** Nu 23:28. 31:16. **from which.** Jsh 24:23. Ezr *9:13, 14. Ac 20:29, *30. 1 C *10:8, 11. **not cleansed.** or, "have not cleansed ourselves." Nu 8:7, 21. 2 K 5:14. 2 Ch *30:18. Ezr 6:20. Ne 12:30.

18. **following.** See on ver. 16. Dt 7:4. 1 S 12:14, 20. 1 K 9:6. 2 K 17:21. 2 Ch 25:27. 34:33. **and it will.** Ezr 9:13, 14. **he will be.** ver. 20. Jsh 7:1, 11, 12. Nu 16:22. 2 S 24:1. 1 Ch 21:1, 14, 17. 1 C 12:26.

19. **unclean.** Ex 15:17. Le 18:25-28. Am 7:17. Ac 10:14, 15. 11:8, 9. **the land of the possession of the Lord.** Le 25:23. Dt +*32:43. Mi 2:10. **wherein.** Jsh 18:1. Le 17:8, 9. Dt 12:5, 6. 2 Ch 11:13, 16, 17.

20. **Did not Achan.** Jsh 7:1, 5, 18, 24. 1 C 10:6. 2 P 2:6. Ju 5, 6. **perished.** S#1478h, Ge +49:33.

21. **Then the children.** The conduct and answer of these Reubenites and their associates are worthy of admiration and imitation. Though conscious of their innocence, they permitted Phinehas to finish his speech, though composed of little else than accusations, without any interruption; and, taking in good part the suspicions, reproofs, and even harshness of their brethren, with the utmost meekness and solemnity they explain their intention, give all the satisfaction in their power, and with great propriety and reverence, appeal to God against whom they were supposed to have rebelled. 1 S ❶+√25:17. Pr *18:13. **answered.** Pr *15:1. *16:1. 18:13. 24:26. Ac 11:4. Ja 1:19. 1 P *3:15. **heads.** ver. 14. Ex +*18:21-25. Nu 1:16. 10:4. 1 S 8:12. 22:7. 2 S 18:1. 1 Ch 12:32. 13:1. 15:25. 26:26. 27:1. 28:1. 29:6. 2 Ch 1:2. 17:14. 25:5. Mi *5:2.

22. **The Lord God of gods.** *El Elohim Yehowah,* literally, "The strong God, Elohim Jehovah." **God.** Heb. *El,* Ex +15:2. Ex 18:11. Dt 10:17. Ps +*82:1. 95:3. 97:7. 136:2. Da 2:47. 11:36. Jn +*10:33-36. 1 T 6:16. Re 19:16. **he knoweth.** 1 K 8:39. Jb 10:7. 23:10. Ps 7:3. 44:20, 21. *139:1-12. Je 12:3. 17:10. Jn +*2:24, 25. 21:17. Ac 1:24. 2 C 11:11, 31. He *4:13. Re 2:18, 19, 23. **Israel.** Ps 37:6. Mi 7:9. Ml 3:18. Ac 11:2-18. 2 C 5:11. **if it be.** 1 S 15:23. Jb 31:5-8, 38-40. Ps 7:3-5. Ac 25:11.

23. **burnt offering.** Le +*23:12. **meat offering.** Le +*23:13. **peace offering.** Le +*23:19. **let the Lord.**

Ge 9:5. Dt 18:19. 1 S 20:16. 2 Ch 24:22. Ps 10:13, 14. Ezk 3:18. 33:6, 8.

24. **for fear.** Ge +*18:19. **In time to come.** Heb. Tomorrow. Jsh +4:6mg. Ge +*30:33mg. Ex 13:14mg. Dt +6:20mg. **What have.** √85H, Jg +11:12.

25. **ye have no part.** ver. 27. 2 S 20:1. 1 K 12:16. Ezr 4:2, 3. Ne 2:20. Ac 8:21. **make.** 1 S 26:19. 1 K 12:27-30. 14:16. 15:30. Mt √18:6.

27. **a witness.** ver. 10, 34. Jsh 24:27. Ge 31:48, 52. Dt 4:26. 1 S 7:12. **that we.** Dt 12:5, 6, 10, +*11, 17, 18, 26, 27.

28. **Behold.** Ex 25:40. 2 K 16:10. Ezk 43:10, 11. He 8:5.

29. **God forbid.** Jsh 24:16. Ge 44:7, 17. 1 S *12:23. 1 K 21:3. Ro 3:6. 6:2. 9:14. **to build.** ver. 23, 26. Dt 12:13, 14. 2 K 18:22. 2 Ch 32:12. **for burnt offerings.** ver. +23. Ex 40:6, 9.

30. **it pleased them. it was good in their eyes.** ver. 33. Ge 16:6mg. ◑28:8mg. +45:16mg. Jg 8:3. 1 S ◑8:6mg. 25:32, 33. 29:6mg. 2 S 3:36mg. 1 K 3:10. 21:2mg. 2 Ch 30:4mg. Est 1:21mg. Pr 15:1. Zc 11:12mg. Ac 11:18.

31. **the Lord is.** See on Jsh 3:10. Le 26:11, 12. Nu 14:41-43. 2 Ch *15:2. Ps 68:17. Is 12:6. Zc 8:23. Mt 1:23. 1 C 14:25. **not committed.** 1 C 11:31. 2 C *7:11. **now.** Heb. then.

32. **and brought.** ver. 12-14. Pr 25:13.

33. **the thing.** See on ver. 30. Ac 15:12, 31. 2 C 7:7. 1 Th 3:6-8. **blessed.** 1 S 25:32, 33. 1 Ch 29:20. Ne 8:5, 6. Ps 68:35. Da 2:19. Lk 2:28. Ep *1:3.

34. **Ed.** i.e. *a witness.* S#5707h. The word *witness*, or *testimony*, is not found here in the common editions of the Hebrew Bible; and is supplied in italics by our venerable translators, at least in our modern copies; for in the first edition of this translation (the Authorized or King James Version), it stands in the text without any note of this kind; but it is found in several of Kennicott's and De Rossi's MSS., and also in the Syriac and Arabic. Several also of the early printed editions of the Hebrew Bible have the word *ed,* either in the text or in the margin; and it must be allowed to be necessary to complete the sense. It is very probable that an inscription was put on this altar, signifying the purpose for which it was erected. Thus was this affair most happily terminated. ver. 27. Jsh 24:27. 1 K 18:39. Is 43:10. Mt *4:10. **the Lord is God.** Several MSS. read more emphatically, *Yehowah hoo Elohim,* "Jehovah *he* is God."

JOSHUA 23

Joshua, now grown old, convenes the elders of Israel, 1, 2 He exhorts them by the mercies of God, 3, 4; and the prospects of future blessings, to be stead-fast in his service, 5-10. He warns them against connec-tions with idolaters; and protests, that the threatenings of God, in case of their disobedience, would as certainly be fulfilled, as his promises had been, 11-16.

1. **the Lord.** Jsh 11:23. 21:44. 22:4. Ps 46:9. He 4:8, 9. **waxed old.** Jsh 13:1. Ge 25:8. Dt 31:2. Phm 9. **stricken in age.** Heb. come into days.

2. **Joshua called.** Ge 49:1. **all Israel.** Jsh 24:1. Dt 31:28. 1 Ch 28:1. Ac *20:17-35. **and for their elders.** Or, "*even* for their elders," etc.; for it is probable that Joshua gave the following charge only to the elders, judges, etc., to communicate to the people. Nu 10:4.

Dt 31:28. 1 K 8:1. 1 Ch 28:1. Ps 40:9. Ac 15:6. 1 C 5:4.

3. **And ye.** Dt 4:9. Ps 44:1, 2. Mal 1:5. **for the.** Jsh 10:14, 42. Ex 14:14. Dt 20:4. 2 Ch 20:17. Ps 44:3. 2 C *15:57.

4. **Behold.** Jsh 13:2, 6, 7. 18:10. **by lot.** Jsh 14:2n. **westward.** Heb. at the sunset. Jsh 1:4. 15:12. Nu 34:6. Ps 80:11.

5. **he shall.** ver. 12, 13. Jsh 13:6. Ex 23:30, 31. 33:2. 34:11. Dt 11:23. **as the Lord.** Nu 33:52, 53.

6. **very.** Jsh 1:7-9. Je 9:3. 1 C 16:13. Ep *6:10-19. He 12:4. Re *21:8. **that ye.** Dt 5:32. *12:32. 17:20. 28:14. Pr 4:26, 27.

7. **That ye come.** Have no civil or social contracts with them, as these will infallibly lead to spiritual affini-ties—in consequence of which, ye will make honorable "mention of the name of their gods," "swear by them," and "serve them" in their abominable rites; and "bow yourselves unto them," as your creators and preservers. All this will follow by simply coming among them. He who walks in the counsel of the ungodly, will soon stand in the way of sinners, and sit in the seat of scor-ners. ver. 12. Ex 23:33. Dt 7:2, 3. Ps 119:115. Pr 4:14, 15. 1 C 15:33. 2 C *6:14-17. Ep *5:11. **neither.** Ex *23:13. Nu 32:38. Ps *16:4. Ho 2:17. **to swear.** Je 5:7. Zp 1:5.

8. **But cleave.** *or,* For if ye will cleave, etc. Jsh 22:5. Dt 4:4. 10:20. 11:22. 13:4. 2 K 18:6. Ps 119:31. Ac *11:23.

9. **For the Lord.** *or,* Then the Lord will drive. ver. 5. Jsh 21:43, 44. Dt 11:23. Ps 44:2. **no man.** Jsh 1:5, 8, 9. 15:14.

10. **One man.** Le 26:8. Dt 28:7. 32:30. Jg 3:31. 7:19-22. 15:15. 1 S 14:6, 12-16. 2 S 23:8. He 11:32-34. **Lord.** Jsh 10:42. Ex 14:14. 23:27, etc. Dt 3:22. 20:4. Ps 35:1. 44:4, 5. 46:7. Ro 8:31.

11. **Take good heed.** Jsh 22:5. Dt 2:4. 4:9. 6:5-12. Pr *4:23. Lk 21:34. 1 C 16:22. Ep 5:15. He *12:15. Ju 21. **yourselves.** Heb. your souls. Heb. *nephesh,* Nu +23:10. Dt 4:15. **love.** Ex 20:6. Mt 22:37, 38. Ro *8:28. 1 C 8:3. 16:22. Ju 20, 21.

12. **go back.** Ps 36:3. 125:5. Is 1:4. Ezk 18:24. Zp 1:6. Mt 12:45. Jn 6:66. He 3:12. *10:38, 39. 2 P *2:18-22. 1 J 2:19. **cleave.** Ge 2:24. 34:3. 1 S 18:1-3. 1 K 11:2. Lk 12:52. Ro 12:9. **shall make.** Ge 34:9. Ex 34:12-16. Dt 7:3. 1 K 11:4. Ezr 9:1, 2, 11, 12. Ne 13:23-26. 1 C 7:39. 2 C *6:14-17.

13. **will no.** Ex 23:33. Nu 33:55. Dt 7:16. Jg 2:2, 3. Ps 106:35-39. **snares.** Dt 7:16. Jg 2:3. 1 K 11:4. Ps 69:22. 2 T 2:26. Re 2:20. or, gins. Jb 18:9. 22:10. Ps 11:6. **traps.** or, snares. Ex 10:7. 23:33. 34:12. **scourges.** 1 K 12:11, 14. 2 Ch 10:11, 14. Jb 5:21. 9:23. Pr 26:3. Is *10:26. *28:15, 18. Na 3:2. **your sides.** Nu 33:55. **until ye perish.** Le 26:31-35. Dt 4:26. 28:63-68. 29:28. 30:18. 2 K 17:22, 23. 25:21, 26. Lk *21:24.

14. **I am going.** 1 K 2:2. Jb 30:23. Ec 9:10. 12:5. Ro 5:17. 2 T 4:6. He *9:27. 2 P 1:13, 14. **souls.** Heb. *nephesh,* Ge +34:3. **not one thing.** Jsh 14:10. 21:43-45. Ex 3:8. 23:27-30. Le 26:3-13. Nu 33:19. Dt 28:1-14. 1 S 3:19. 1 K 8:56. Lk 16:17. 21:33. 1 Th 5:24. He 10:23.

15. **so shall.** Le 26:14, 21, 23, 24, etc. Dt 28:15-68. Jg 3:8, 12. 4:1, 2. 6:1. 10:6, 7. 13:1. 2 Ch 36:16, 17. Lk 21:22-24. 1 Th 2:16.

16. **and bowed.** √15G, Ge +35:3. **then shall.** 2 K 24:20. Is 6:11, 12. Je 4:25-27. **perish.** ver. 13. Ps 2:12.

JOSHUA 24

Joshua assembles the tribes at Shechem, 1. He lays before them a brief history of the Lord's kindness to their ancestors from the days of Terah, and exhorts them faithfully to serve the true God, 2-13. He renews the covenant between them and God, promising for himself and his house to choose the service of God, the people likewise promising for themselves, 14-25. He writes this in the book of the law, and sets up a stone for a witness, 26-28. Joshua's age, death, and burial, 29-30. Israel serves the Lord till some time after Joshua's death, 31. Joseph's bones are buried, 32. Eleazar dies, 33.

1. **Joshua.** This must have been a different assembly from that mentioned in the preceding chapter, though probably held not long after the former. **Shechem.** As it is immediately added, that "they presented themselves before God," which is supposed to mean at the tabernacle; some are of opinion that Joshua caused it to be conveyed from Shiloh to Shechem on this occasion, to give the greater solemnity to his last meeting with the people. The Vatican and Alexandrian copies of the Septuagint, however, read *Shiloh*, both here and in verse 25; which many suppose to have been the original reading. Dr. Shuckford supposes that the covenant was made at *Shechem*, and that the people went to Shiloh to confirm it. But the most probable opinion seems to be that of Dr. Kennicott, that when all the tribes were assembled at Shechem, Joshua called the chiefs to him on that mount, which had before been consecrated by the law, and by the altar which he had erected. Jsh 8:30, 31. Ge 12:6. 33:18, 19. 35:4. Jg 9:1-3. 1 K 12:1. 2 Ch 10:1. Jn 4:5, 20. **called.** Jsh 23:2. Ex 18:25, 26. **presented.** 1 S 10:19. Ac 10:33.

2. **Your fathers.** Ge 11:26, 31. 12:1. 31:53. Dt 26:5. Is 51:2. Ezk 16:3. **the flood.** ♪171E12, Ge +14:22. ♪32, Ge +31:21. 2 Ch *9:26. Is +*27:12. **in old time.** Heb. *olam*, ✚S#5769h. Je 2:20. Ezk 26:20. For other renderings and uses of *olam*, see Ex +12:24. **Nachor.** i.e. *snorter*, ✚S#5152h. Ge +11:22, Nahor. **served other gods.** In the case of Abraham this was probably the case, till he was called to the knowledge of God, when above 70 years old. ver. 15. Ge 31:19, 30, 32, 53. 35:4.

3. **I took.** Ge 12:1-4. Ne 9:7, 8. Ac 7:2-4. He 11:8, 9. **gave.** Ge 21:2, 3. Ps +*127:3. He 11:11, 12.

4. **unto Isaac.** Ge 25:21, 24-26. **unto Esau.** Ge 32:3. 36:8. Dt 2:5. **Jacob.** Ge 46:1-7. Ps 105:23. Ac 7:15.

5. **sent.** Ex 3:10. 4:12, 13, 28. 5:1. Ps 105:26. **plagued.** Ex ch. 7-12. Ps 78:43-51. 105:27-36. 135:8, 9. 136:10.

6. **I brought.** Ex 12:37, 41, 51. Mi 6:4. **Egyptians.** Ex ch. 14, 15. Ne 9:11. Ps 77:15-20. 78:13. 136:13-15. Is 63:12, 13. Ac 7:36. He 11:29.

7. **And when.** Ex 14:10. **he put.** Ex 14:20. **brought.** Ex 14:27, 28. **your eyes.** Ex 14:31. Dt 4:34. 29:2. **ye dwelt.** Jsh 5:6. Nu 14:33, 34. Ne 9:12-21. Ps 95:9, 10. Ac 13:17, 18. He 3:17.

8. **I brought.** Jsh 13:10. Nu 21:21-35. Dt 2:32-37. 3:1-8. Ne 9:22. Ps 135:10, 11. 136:17-22.

9. **Then Balak.** Nu 22:5, 6, etc. Dt 23:4, 5. Jg 11:25. Mi 6:5.

10. **I would not.** Nu 22:11, 12, 18-20, 35. 23:3-12, 15-26. 24:5-10. Dt 23:5. Is 54:17. **blessed.** ♪147B, Ge +2:16.

11. **And ye.** Jsh 3:14-17. 4:10-12, 19, 23. Ps 114:3, 5. **the men.** Jsh ch. 6, 10, 11. Ne 9:24, 25. Ps 78:54, 55. 105:44. Ac 7:45. 13:19. **the Amorites.** Ge +10:16. **Perizzites.** Ge +13:7. **Canaanites.** Ge +10:18. **Hittites.** Ge +15:20. **Girgashites.** Ge +10:16. **Hivites.** Ge +10:17. **Jebusites.** Ge +10:16.

12. **I sent.** Ex 23:28. Dt 7:20. **not.** Ps 44:3-6.

13. **And I.** Jsh 21:45. **for which.** Jn 4:38. **cities.** Jsh 11:13. Dt 6:10-12. 8:7. Pr 13:22.

14. **fear.** Dt 10:12. 1 S 12:24. Jb 1:1. 28:28. Ps 111:10. 130:4. Ec +12:13. Ho 3:5. Ac 9:31. **serve him.** ver. 23. Ge 17:1. 20:5, 6. Ex +34:14. Dt 18:13. 2 K 20:3. Ps 119:1, 80. Lk 8:15. Jn 4:23, 24. ◐+10:28. 2 C 1:12. Ep 6:24. Ph 1:10. **in sincerity.** Ps +*37:18n. 1 C 5:8. 2 C *1:12. *2:17. 8:8. Ph 1:10. **in truth.** Ps +*15:2. Jn *4:23. **put.** From this exhortation of Joshua, we not only learn that the Israelites still retained some relics of idolatry, but to what gods they were attached. (1) Those whom their fathers worshiped on the other side of the flood, or the river Euphrates, i.e. the gods of the Chaldeans, fire, light, the sun, etc. (2) Those of the Egyptians, Apis, Anubis, serpents, vegetables, etc. (3) Those of the Amorites, Moabites, Canaanites, etc. Baal-peor, Astarte, etc. How astonishing is it, that after all that God had done for them, and all the miracles they had seen, there should still be found among them both idols and idolaters! ver. 2, 23. Ge 35:2. Ex 20:3, 4. Le 17:7. Ezr 9:11. Ezk 20:18. Am 5:25, 26. **in Egypt.** Ezk 20:7, 8. 23:3.

15. **choose.** Dt +*30:19. Ru *1:15, 16. 1 K *18:21. Ezk 20:39. Mt *6:24. Lk 16:13. Jn *1:12. 6:67. Ro 6:16. 2 C +*6:2. He *2:3. Re *3:20. **whether the gods.** ver. 14. **or the gods.** Ex 23:24, 32, 33. 34:15. Dt *13:7. *29:18. Jg 6:10. **as for me.** Ge +*18:19. Ps 101:2. 119:106, 111, 112. Mt 26:33, 35. Jn *6:68. Ac 11:23. **my house.** Ex +13:8. Ac +16:31.

16. **God forbid.** 1 S 12:23. Ro 3:6. 6:2. He *10:38, 39.

17. **he it is.** ♪63K, Ge +37:13. **that brought.** ver. 5-14. Ex 19:4. Dt 32:11, 12. Is 46:4. 63:7-14. Am 2:9, 10. **house of bondage.** Ex +13:3. 20:2. Jg 6:8. **great signs.** Ps 78:12, 43, 52, 55. 105:44. **in our sight.** Ac *26:26. 2 P *1:16. 1 J *1:1.

18. **drave out.** Ps 105:44. **will we also.** Ex 10:2. 15:2. Ps 116:16. Mi 4:2. Zc 8:23. Lk 1:73-75. **our God.** Ps 48:14.

19. **Ye cannot.** ver. 23. Ru 1:15. Mt *6:24. Lk 14:25-33. **Lord.** ♪63I1D, Nu +26:4. Supply ellipsis, "Ye cannot serve the Lord (unless ye put away your idols), for he (*is*) a holy God," etc. **holy.** Le 10:3. 19:2. 1 S 6:20. Ps 99:5, 9. Is 5:16. 6:3-5. 30:11, 15. Hab 1:13. **a jealous.** Ex +*20:5. 34:14. Dt 4:24. 1 C 10:20-22. He 12:29. **God.** Heb. *El*, Ex +15:2. **he will not.** Ex 23:21. 34:7. 1 S 3:14. 2 Ch 36:16. Is 27:11.

20. **If.** Ge +4:7. **strange.** ver. 23. Ex 12:43 (✱S#5236h). Dt 32:12. Jg 10:16mg. **he will turn.** Jsh 23:12-15. 1 Ch *28:9. 2 Ch *15:2. Ezr *8:22. Is 1:28. 63:10. 65:11, 12. Je 17:13. Ezk 18:24. Ac 7:42. He *10:26, 27, 38. **after that.** Jsh 23:15. Ps 78:58-60, 62, 63.

21. **Nay.** Ex 19:8. 20:19. 24:3, 7. Dt 5:27, 28. 26:17. Is 44:5.

22. **Ye are witnesses.** Ye have been sufficiently apprised of the difficulties in your way—of God's holiness, and the nature of his service—your own weakness, inconstancy, and insufficiency—your need of Divine

help, and the hope of assistance held out in the law— and the awful consequences of apostasy: and now ye make your choice. Remember then that ye are witnesses against yourselves; and your own conscience will be witness, judge, and executioner. Dt 26:17. Jb 15:6. Lk 19:22. **ye have.** Ps 119:111, *173. Lk 10:42. Jn *15:16.

23. **put away.** ver. 14. Ge 35:2-4. Ex 20:23. Jg 10:15, 16. 1 S 7:3, 4. Ho 14:2, 3, 8. 1 C 10:19-21. 2 C 6:16-18. **strange.** ver. 20. **incline.** Ps 119:36. Pr 2:2. He 12:28, 29.

24. **people said.** ver. 21. Dt 5:28, 29. 23:21-23. Ec *5:4-7. Jn *15:5. Ph *4:13.

25. **made.** Ex 15:25. 24:3, 7, 8. Dt 5:2, 3. 29:1, 10-15. 2 K 11:17. 2 Ch 15:12, 15. 23:16. 29:10. 34:29-32. Ne 9:38. *10:28, 29. **in Shechem.** ver. 1, 26.

26. **Joshua wrote.** Ex 24:4. 34:27. Dt 31:24-26. Is *30:8. Ezk 43:11. **took.** Jg 9:6. **great stone.** Ge 28:18. 1 S *7:12. Zc 3:9. **set it.** Jsh 4:3-9, 20-24. Ge 28:18-22. **under.** Ge 35:4, 8. Jg 9:6.

27. **this stone.** Jsh 22:27, 28, 34. Ge 31:44-52. Dt 4:26. 30:19. 31:19, 21, 26. 1 S 7:12. **it hath.** Dt 32:1. Is 1:2. Je 22:29. Hab 2:11. Lk *19:40. **heard.** ♪155D, Ge +4:10. **deny.** Jb 31:23. Pr 30:9. Mt 10:33. 2 T 2:12, 13. T 1:16. Re 3:8.

28. **Joshua let.** Jg 2:6.

29. **After these.** Dt 34:5. Jg 2:8. Ps 115:17. 2 T 4:7, 8. Re *14:13. **an hundred and ten.** Ge 50:22, 26.

30. **Timnath-serah.** Jsh 19:50. Jg 2:9. **Gaash.** i.e. shaking, *S#1608h. Jg 2:9. 2 S 23:30. 1 Ch 11:32.

31. **served.** Dt 31:29. Jg 2:7. 2 Ch 24:2, 17, 18. Ac *20:29. Ph 2:12. **overlived Joshua.** Heb. prolonged their days after Joshua. **which had.** Dt 11:2, 3, 7. 31:13.

32. **bones.** Ge 50:25. Ex 13:19. Ac 7:16. He 11:22. **buried.** Ge 33:19, 20. 48:22. **pieces of silver.** or, lambs.

33. **Eleazar.** Jsh 14:1. Ex 6:23, 25. Nu 3:32. 20:26-28. **died.** Jb 30:23. Ps 49:10. Is 57:1, 2. Zc 1:5. Ac 13:36. He 7:24. 9:26, 27. **Phinehas.** Jg 20:28. **mount Ephraim.** Jsh 21:20, 21.

JUDGES

JUDGES 1

Judah and Simeon war against the Canaanites, defeat Adoni-bezek, and retaliate on him his cruelty to captive kings, 1-7. Jerusalem is taken, 8, 9. The sons of Anak slain, 10. Othniel takes Debir, and marries Caleb's daughter, 11-15. The Kenites dwell with Judah, 16. Hormah, Gaza, Askelon, and Ekron, are taken by Judah and Simeon: and Hebron is given to Caleb, 17-20. Benjamin is unable to drive the Jebusites from Jerusalem, 21. Ephraim and Manasseh take Bethel, 22-25. A Canaanite builds a city called Luz, 26. The Canaanites are not wholly expelled by Manasseh, 27, 28; by Ephraim, 29; by Asher, 31, 32; by Naphtali, 33. The Amorites force Dan into the mountain, 34-36.

1. **Now.** Jsh 24:29, 30. **asked.** Jg 20:18, 28. Ex 28:30. Nu 27:21. 1 S 22:9, 10. 23:9, 10. **Canaanites.** Ge +10:18.

2. **Judah shall.** Ge 49:8-10. Nu 2:3, 9. 7:12. Ps 78:68-70. He 7:14. Re 5:5. 19:11-16.

3. **Simeon.** Ge 29:33. Jsh 19:1. **I likewise.** ver. 17. 2 S 10:11. Ph 1:27, 30.

4. **Lord.** Ex 23:28, 29. Dt 7:2. 9:3. Jsh 10:8-10. 11:6-8. 1 S 14:6, 10. 17:46, 47. 1 K 22:6, 15. **Perizzites.** Ge 13:7. **Bezek.** i.e. a flash of lightning, *S#966h. ver. 5. 1 S 11:8. Eusebius and Jerome mention two villages of this name, near each other, about seventeen miles from Shechem, towards Scythopolis. 1 S 11:8.

5. **Adoni-bezek.** i.e. lord of Bezek, *S#137h. ver. 6, 7.

6. **cut off.** ver. 7. Dt 25:12. 2 S 4:12. **thumbs, etc.** lit. "thumbs of his hands and of his feet." Ex 29:20. Le 8:23, 24. 14:14, 17, 25, 28. The one loss prevented his fighting, the other his running (Young).

7. **their thumbs.** Heb. the thumbs of their hands and of their feet. ver. 6. This was not an unusual act of cruelty in ancient times towards enemies. Aelian informs us, that in after ages "the Athenians, at the instigation of Cleon, son of Cleaenetus, made a decree that all the inhabitants of the island of Aegina should have the thumb cut off from the right hand, so that

they might ever after be disabled from holding a spear, yet might handle an oar." It was a custom among those Romans who did not like a military life, to cut off their thumbs, that they might be incapable of serving in the army; and for the same reason, parents sometimes cut off the thumbs of their children. **gathered.** or, gleaned. Ru 2:2, 7. Lk 16:21. **as I have.** Ex 21:23-25. Le 24:19-21. Dt 19:19. 1 S 15:33. Est 9:25. Ps *7:16. Is 33:1. Je 51:56. Da 6:24. Mt 7:1, 2. Lk 6:37, 38. Ro 2:15. Ga 6:7. Ja 2:13. Re 13:10. 16:6.

8. **children of Judah.** ver. 21. Jsh +*15:63. **set the city.** Jg 20:48.

9. **afterward.** Jsh 10:36, 37. 11:21. 15:13-20. **valley.** or, low country. Dt 1:7. Jsh 9:1. 10:40. 11:2, 16. 12:8. 15:33. Zc +*7:7.

10. **Kirjath-arba.** Jsh 14:15. **Sheshai.** ver. 20. Nu 13:22, 33. Jsh 15:13, 14. Ps 33:16, 17. Ec 9:11. Je 9:23.

11. **Debir.** Jsh 10:38, 39. 15:15. **Kirjath-sepher.** i.e. city of the book. Jsh +15:15, 16.

12. **And Caleb.** The whole of this account is found in Jsh 15:13-19, and seems to be inserted here by way of recapitulation. Jsh 15:16, 17. 1 S 17:25. 18:23. **to him.** In ancient times fathers assumed an absolute right over their children, especially in disposing of them in marriage; and it was customary for a king or great man to promise his daughter to him who should take a city, etc. **Achsah.** Jsh 15:16.

13. **Othniel.** i.e. lion of God. Jg 3:9. **Kenaz.** i.e. hunting.

14. **And it came.** Jsh 15:18, 19. **moved him.** Dt 13:6. **and she lighted.** Watitznach, "she hastily or suddenly alighted," as if she had forgotten something, or was about to return. Ge 24:64. 1 S 25:23. Jsh 15:18. **ass.** Jg 19:28. Ex 4:20. Jsh 15:18.

15. **a blessing.** Ge 33:11. 1 S 25:18, 27. Pr 10:22. 1 C 12:31. 2 C 9:5mg. He 6:7. 1 P 3:9. or, pool. Ps 84:6. Ec 2:6. **a south land.** Which was probably dry, or very ill watered. **give me also springs of water.** Let me have some fields with brooks or wells already digged.

16. **the Kenite.** Jg 4:11, 17. Nu 10:29-32. 24:21, 22. 1 S 15:6. 1 Ch 2:55. Je 35:2. **Moses.** Ex 3:1. 4:18. 18:1, 7, 12, 14-17, 27. Nu 10:29. **city of palm.** Jg 3:13. Dt 34:3. 2 Ch 28:16. **which.** Nu 21:1. Jsh 12:14. **Arad.** i.e. *wild ass.* Nu 21:1. 33:40. Jsh 12:14. 1 Ch ❿8:15. **they went.** Nu 10:29-32. 1 S 15:6.

17. **And Judah.** See on ver. 3. **Zephath.** i.e. *a watch-tower,* *S#6857h. 2 Ch 14:10, Zephathah. **Hormah.** i.e. *devotion* or *destruction.* Nu 14:45. 21:3. Jsh 12:14. 19:4.

18. **Also Judah.** There is the following remarkable variation here in the Septuagint: "But Judah did *not* possess Gaza, nor the coasts thereof; nor Askelon, nor the coasts thereof; nor Ekron, nor the coasts thereof; nor Ashdod, nor the coasts thereof." Procopius and Augustine read the same; and Josephus (Ant. l. v. c. 2) says that the Israelites only took Askelon and Ashdod, but not Gaza or Ekron: and from Jg 3:3, and the whole succeeding history, it appears that these cities were not in the possession of the Israelites, but of the Philistines. **Gaza.** Jg 3:3. 16:1, 2, 21. Ex 23:31. See on Jsh 11:22. 13:3. 15:45-47. 1 S 6:17. **Askelon.** i.e. *migration* or *a weighing out,* *S#831h. Jg 14:19. Jsh 13:3. 1 S 6:17. 2 S 1:20. Je 25:20. 47:5, 7. Am 1:8. Zp 2:4, 7. Zc 9:5, 5. **Ekron.** Jsh 13:3. 15:+11, 45. 19:43. 1 S 17:52. 2 K *1:2. Je 25:20. Am 1:8. Zp 2:4. Zc 9:5, 7.

19. **the Lord.** ver. 2. Jg 6:12, 13. Ge 39:2, 21, 23. Jsh 1:5, 9. 14:12. 1 S 18:14. 2 S 5:10. 2 K 18:7. Ps 46:7, 11. 60:12. Ec 9:11. Is 7:14. 8:10. 41:10, 14, 15. Mt 1:23. 28:20. Ro 8:31. **he drave,** etc. *or,* he possessed the mountain. **mountain.** Jsh 17:18. **but could.** Not because the iron chariots were too strong for Omnipotence, or because he refused to help them; but because their courage and faith failed when they saw them. ver. 27-32. Jsh 7:12. Mt 14:30, 31. 17:19, 20. Ph *4:13. **chariots.** Ex 14:7, etc. Jsh 11:1-9. 17:16-18. Ps 46:9.

20. **they gave.** Nu 14:24. Dt 1:36. Jsh 14:9-14. 15:13, 14. 21:11, 12. **the three sons.** ver. 10. Nu 13:22.

21. **Benjamin did not.** Jg 19:10-12. Jsh +*15:63. 18:11-28. 2 S 5:6-9. **Jebusites.** Ge +10:16. 15:21. Zc 9:7. **unto this day.** ver. 26. Jg 6:24. Ge +18:38. Dt +29:4. Jsh +4:9. This phrase shows that the book was composed before the time of David, who entirely dispossessed them (Young), 2 S 5:7.

22. **the house.** Nu 1:10, 32. Jsh 14:4. 16:1-4. 1 Ch 7:29. Re 7:8. **Bethel.** Jsh 8:17. 16:1, 2. **the Lord.** See on ver. 19. Ge 49:24. 2 K 18:7.

23. **sent.** Jg 18:2. Jsh 2:1. 7:2. **Luz.** i.e. *a nut.* Ge 28:19. 35:6. 48:3.

24. **we will.** Jsh 2:12-14. 1 S 30:15.

25. **they smote.** Jsh 6:22-25.

26. **the land.** 2 K 7:6. 2 Ch 1:17. **unto this day.** ver. +21. Jg 15:19. 18:12. Ge +19:38. Dt +29:4. Jsh +4:9. Je +25:18.

27. **Manasseh.** Jsh 17:11-13. **Beth-shean.** i.e. *house of rest.* Jsh 17:11, 16. 1 S 31:10. 1 K 4:12. **Taanach.** Jg 5:19. Jsh 12:21. 17:11. 21:25. 1 S 15:9. Ps 106:34, 35. Je 48:10. **Ibleam.** i.e. *swallowing up a people,* *S#2991h. Jsh 17:11. 2 K 9:27. **Megiddo.** Jsh 12:21. +17:11. **would dwell.** ver. 35. Jsh 17:12.

28. **when Israel.** Ex 23:32. Dt 7:2. 1 S 15:9. Ps 106:34, 35. Je 48:10.

29. **Neither did Ephraim.** See on Jsh ❿10:33. +16:10. 1 K 9:16. **Gezer.** Jsh 10:33.

30. **Zebulun.** Jsh 19:16. **Kitron.** i.e. *knotty,* *S#7003h. The Talmudists say *Kitron* is *tzippor,* that

is, *Sepphoris,* or *Diocaesarea,* a celebrated city of Galilee, now the village *Safoury;* situated in the plain of Esdraelon, twenty miles northwest from Tiberias, according to Benjamin of Tudela. Not mentioned elsewhere, but supposed to be the same as Kattah in Jsh 19:15, or Kartah, Jsh 21:34. **Nahalol.** i.e. *pasture,* *S#5096h. Jsh 19:15, Nahalal. 21:35.

31. **Asher.** Jsh 19:24-30. **Accho.** i.e. *sand-heated,* *S#5910h. Ac 21:7, Ptolemais. *Accho,* the *Ptolemais* of the Greeks and Romans, and called *Saint John of Acre* by the Crusaders, is situated on the Mediterranean, in a fine plain, at the north angle of a bay to which it gives name, and which extends in a semicircle of three leagues as far as Carmel, and nine leagues from Tyre. **Zidon.** Jsh 11:8. 19:28. Another celebrated city of Phoenicia, now *Saide,* situated in a fine country on the Mediterranean, 400 stadia from Berytus, and 200 north from Tyre, according to Strabo, one day's journey from Paneas, according to Josephus, and sixty-six miles from Damascus, according to Abulfeda. **Ahlab.** i.e. *fertility; fatness, fat.* **Ahlab.** i.e. *fatness,* *S#303h. **Achzib.** i.e. *a lie. or,* **Ecdippa,** now **Zib,** nine miles north from Accho. Ge 38:5, Chezib. Jsh 15:44. 19:29. Mi *1:14. **Helbah.** i.e. *fat, fatness,* *S#2462h. **Aphik.** i.e. *strength,* *S#663h. Jsh 12:18, Aphek. 13:4. 15:53, Aphekah. 19:30. 1 S 4:1. 29:1. 1 K 20:26, 30. 2 K 13:17. **Rehob.** Jsh +19:24, 25, *30.

32. **Asherites.** *S#843h. **dwelt among.** Ps *106:34, 35.

33. **Naphtali.** Jsh 19:32-38. **Beth-shemesh.** Jsh +19:38. **Beth-anath.** Jsh 19:38. **he dwelt.** ver. 29, 30, 32. **became.** ver. 30, 35. Ps 18:24.

34. **the Amorites forced.** Jg 18:1. Jsh 19:47. **children of Dan.** Jsh 19:40-42. **the mountain.** Seir or Baalah: see Jsh 15:10, 11.

35. **would dwell.** ver. 27. Jsh 17:12. **Heres.** i.e. *heat* or *the sun,* *S#2776h, only here. Jg 2:9. Jsh 19:41. **Aijalon.** i.e. *a little hind.* Jg 12:12. Jsh *10:12. 19:42. **Shaalbim.** i.e. *place of foxes,* *S#8169h. Jsh 19:42. 1 K 4:9. **prevailed.** Heb. was heavy.

36. **from the going.** *or,* Maaleh-akrabbim. Nu 34:4. Jsh 15:3. **the rock.** Young suggests "perhaps the city of Petra in Edumea is meant by this phrase." 2 K 14:7n.

JUDGES 2

An angel rebukes the people for disobedience; and the place is called Bochim, from their weeping, 1-5. They serve the Lord until Joshua and the elders die, but in the next generation run into shameful idolatries, 6-13. God is angry with them; yet pities their distresses, and raises up judges to deliver them, 14-18. Their ingratitude provokes him to permit the Canaanites to remain, in order to prove Israel, 19-23.

1. **And an angel.** *or,* messenger. Jg 6:12. 13:3. Ge 16:7-10, 13. 22:11, 12. 48:16. Ex 3:2-6. 14:19. 23:20. 33:14. Jsh 5:13, 14. Ec 5:6. Is 42:19. *63:9. Ho 12:3-5. Hg 1:13. Zc 3:1, 2. Ml 2:7. *3:1. Ac 7:30-33. **made.** ℐ96C8, Ex +15:5. **Bochim.** i.e. *weepers,* *S#1066h. ver. 5. A place so called here by anticipation (ℐ151. Prolepsis; or, Anticipation, Ge +1:28), for the reason expressed in ver. 5. It seems to be no other than Shiloh, where it seems probable that the people were met together upon some solemn festival, as this was the proper and usual place of sacrificing, ver. 5. **I made.**

Ex 3:7, 8. 14:14. 20:2. Dt 4:34. Ps 78:51-53. 105:36-38. 1 P 2:9. **have brought.** Ge 12:7. 22:16, 17. 26:3, 4. Jsh 3:10. Ps 105:44, 45. **I will never.** See on Ge 17:7, 8. Le 26:42. Nu 14:34. Ps √89:28, 34. Je 14:21. +√33:20, 21. Zc 11:10. Ro *11:29.

2. **And ye shall.** Ex 23:32, 33. 34:12-16. Nu 33:52, 53. Dt 7:2-4, 16, 25, 26. 12:2, 3. 20:16-18. 2 C 6:14-17. **but ye have.** ver. 20. Ezr 9:1-3, 10-13. Ps 78:55-58. 106:34-40. Je 7:23-28. 2 Th 1:8. 1 P 4:17. **why have.** Ge 3:11, 12. 4:10. Ex 32:21. Je 2:5, 18, 31-33, 36.

3. **I also said.** ver. 21. Nu 33:55. Jsh 23:13. **their gods.** Jg 3:6. Ex 23:33. 34:12. Dt 7:16. 1 K 11:1-7. Ps 106:36.

4. **the people.** 1 S 7:6. Ezr 10:1. Pr 17:10. Je 31:9. Zc 12:10. Lk 6:21. 7:38. 2 C 7:10. Ja 4:9.

5. **Bochim.** *that* i.e. Weepers. Ge 35:8. Jsh 7:26. **they sacrificed.** Jg 6:24. 13:19. 1 S 7:9.

6. **Joshua.** Jsh 22:6. 24:28, etc.

7. **the people.** Jsh 24:31. 2 K 12:2. 2 Ch 24:2, 14-22. Ac 20:29. Ph 2:12. **outlived.** Heb. prolonged days after.

8. **Joshua.** Jsh 24:29, 30.

9. **Timnath-heres.** i.e. *image of the sun,* ✳S#8556h. This was his own inheritance; and Eusebius says it was celebrated in his time for the tomb of Joshua. Jsh 19:50. 24:30, Timnath-serah. **Gaash.** Jsh 24:30.

10. A.M. cir. 2590. B.C. cir. 1414. An. Ex. Is. cir. 77. **gathered.** Ge 15:15. 25:8, 17. 49:33. Nu 27:13. Dt 31:16. 2 S 7:12. Ac 13:36. **knew not.** ✶121C2A2, Ge +39:6. Ex 1:8. *5:2. 1 S 2:12. 1 Ch 28:9. Jb 21:14. Ps 92:5, 6. Is 5:12. Je 9:3. 22:16. 31:34. Ga 4:8, 9. 2 Th 1:8. T 1:16. 1 J 5:21.

11. **did evil.** Jg 4:1. 6:1. 13:1. Ge 13:13. 38:7. 2 Ch 33:2, 6. Ezr 8:12. **and served Baalim.** i.e. *the lords (idols),* ✦S#1168h. Baalim, or *lords,* seems to have been the common appellation of the Syrian gods; whence we have Baal-peor, Baal-zebub, etc. Jg 3:7. 8:33. 10:6, 10. 1 S 7:4. 12:10. 1 K 18:18. 2 Ch 17:3. 24:7. 28:2. 33:3. 34:4. Je 2:23. 9:14. Ho 2:13, 17. 11:2.

12. **forsook.** See on Dt 13:5. 29:18, 25. *31:16, 17. 32:15. 33:17. **other gods.** Jg 5:8. Dt 6:14, 15. **bowed.** See on Ex 20:5. Dt 5:9.

13. **forsook the Lord.** Dt 32:15. 2 Ch 15:2-4. 27:2. 30:1-12. Je 17:13. Ho 11:7. Jn 6:66. 1 C 10:11, 12. 2 C 12:20, 21. Ga 4:9-11. 5:7. 1 T 1:19. 6:21. He *3:12, 13. 4:11. *12:15. **served.** ver. 11. Jg 3:7. 10:6. 1 S 31:10. 1 K 11:5, 33. 2 K 23:13. Ps 78:58. 106:36. 1 C 8:5. 10:20-22. **Baal.** A Phenician idol supposed to denote the sun (Young). **Ashtaroth.** ✳S#6252h. (1) A city of Bashan. It was east of the Jordan, Dt 1:4. Jsh 9:10. 12:4. 13:12, 31. Same as Beeshterah, Jsh 21:27. (2) An idol, a Syrian goddess, commonly identified with Astarte, the goddess of the moon. A Phoenician female goddess, supposed to be Venus. Jg 10:6. 1 S 7:3, 4. 12:10. 31:10. 1 K 11:5. 2 K 23:13. 1 Ch 6:71.

14. **the anger.** Jg 3:7, 8. 10:7. Le 26:28. Nu 32:14. Dt 28:20, 58. 29:19, 20. 31:17, 18. 2 Ch 36:16. Ps 78:59. 106:40-42. **he delivered.** 2 K 17:20. 2 Ch 15:5. **spoilers.** 1 S 17:53. 2 K 17:20. Ps 89:41. Is *13:16. Je *30:16. Zc *14:2. **sold them.** Jg 3:8. 4:2. Dt 32:30. Ps 44:12. Is 50:1. **could not.** Jg 1:19, 34. Le 26:37. Dt 32:30. Jsh 7:12, 13. Ps 44:9, 10. Je 37:10.

15. **against.** Je 18:8. 21:10. 44:11, 27. Mi 2:3. **had said.** Le 26:15, etc. Dt 4:25-28. 28:15, etc. Jsh 23:15, 16. Ps 78:62-64. **had sworn.** Dt 32:40, 41. **greatly.** Jg 10:9. Ge 32:7. 1 S 13:6. 14:24. 30:6. 2 C 4:8.

16. A.M. 2591-2909. B.C. 1413-1095. **the Lord.** Jg 3:9, 10, 15. 4:5. 6:14. 1 S 12:10, 11. Ac 13:20. **judges.** The *shophetim* were not judges in the usual sense of the term; but were heads or chiefs of the Israelites, raised up on extraordinary occasions, who directed and ruled the nation with sovereign power, administered justice, made peace or war, and led the armies over whom they presided. Officers with the same power, and nearly the same name, were established in New Tyre, after the termination of the regal state; and the Carthaginian *Suffetes,* the Athenian *Archons,* and the Roman *Dictators,* appear to have been nearly the same. **delivered.** Heb. saved. ver. 18. Jg 3:9, 31. 10:1mg. Ne 9:27. Ps 106:43-45.

17. **they would.** 1 S 8:5-8. 12:12, 17, 19. 2 Ch 36:15, 16. Ps 106:43. **whoring.** ✓155E3, Is +32:9. Ex 34:15, 16. Le 17:7. Ps 73:27. 106:39. Ho 2:2. Re 17:1-5. **quickly.** Ex 32:8. Dt 9:12, 16. Ga 1:6. **which their.** ver. 7. Jsh 24:24, 31.

18. **then the Lord.** Ex 3:12. Jsh 1:5. Ac 18:9, 10. **it repented.** Jg 10:16. Ge 6:6, 7. Dt 32:36. 2 Ch *7:14. Ps 90:13. 106:44, 45. 135:14. Je 18:7-10. Ho 11:8. Jon 3:10. **their groanings.** Ex 2:24. 6:5. 2 K 13:4, 22, 23. Ps 12:5. Ezk 30:24. **oppressed.** Jg 6:9. Ex 3:9. 1 S 10:18. Is *19:20. Je 30:20. **vexed.** Jl 2:8 (thrust).

19. **when the.** See on ver. 7. Jg 3:11, 12. 4:1. 8:33. Jsh 24:31. 2 Ch 24:17, 18. **corrupted.** *or,* were corrupt. Dt 31:29. **more.** Je *16:12. Mt 23:32. 2 T *3:13. **ceased not from.** Heb. let nothing fall of. Is ◖1:16. **stubborn.** 1 S 15:23. Ps 78:8. Je 3:17. 23:17.

20. **the anger.** ver. 14. Jg 3:8. 10:7. Ex 32:10, 11. Dt 32:22. **transgressed.** Ex 24:3-8. Dt 29:10-13. Jsh 23:16. 24:21-25. Je 31:32. Ezk 20:37.

21. **will not.** ver. 3. Jg 3:3. Jsh 23:12, 13. Ezk 20:24-26.

22. **through.** See on Jg 3:1-4. **prove.** Ge 22:1. Dt 8:2, 16. 13:3. 2 Ch 32:31. Jb 23:10. Ps 66:10. Pr 17:3. Ml 3:2, 3.

23. **left.** *or,* suffered. Jg 3:1. 1 P 1:7. 4:12.

JUDGES 3

The nations which were left to prove Israel, 1-4. The people are seduced into idolatry by marrying their daughters and serving their gods, 5-7. The people are sold into the hand of Chushan-rishathaim, king of Mesopotamia, but delivered by Othniel, 8-11. Continuing to do evil, they are again punished and oppressed by Eglan, the king of the Moabites, but delivered by Ehud, 12-30. They are afterwards delivered from the Philistines by Shamgar, who slays six hundred Philistines with an ox-goad, 31.

1. A.M. 2561. B.C. 1443. An. Ex. Is. 48. **the nations.** Jg 2:21, 22. Dt 7:22. **prove.** Ex 16:4. 20:20. Dt 8:2, 16. 2 Ch 32:31. Jb 23:10. Pr 17:3. Je 6:27. *17:9, 10. Zc 13:9. Jn *2:24. 1 P 1:7. 4:12. Re 2:23. **as had not.** Jg 2:10.

2. **might know.** Ge 2:17. 3:5, 7. 2 Ch 12:8. Mt 10:34-39. Jn 16:33. 1 C 9:26, 27. Ep 6:11-18. 1 T 6:12. 2 T 2:3. 4:7. **to teach.** 2 S 22:35. Ps 144:1. Lk *22:36. Their fathers fought by a divine power. God taught their hands to war and their fingers to fight, that they might be the instruments of destruction to the wicked nations on whom the curse rested; but now that they had forfeited his favor, they must learn what it is to fight like other men.

3. **five lords.** Jg 10:7. 14:4. Jsh 13:3. 1 S 4:1, 2. 6:4, 16, 18. 13:5, 19-23. 29:2. Zp 2:5. **Canaanites.** Jg 4:2, 23, 24. Ge 10:15-17, +18, 19. Nu 13:29. **Sidonians.** Jg 10:12. 18:7. Ge 49:13. Jsh 11:8-13. 19:28. **Hivites.** Ge +10:17. **in mount.** Nu 34:8. Dt 1:7. 3:9. Jsh 11:3. 13:5. **Baal-hermon.** i.e. *place of the nose; having a fortress,* ✱S#1179h. 1 Ch 5:23. **Hamath.** i.e. *fortress.* Nu 13:21. 34:8. Jsh 13:5. 2 K 14:25, 28. 17:24. 18:34. 19:13. Is 10:9. Am 6:2.

4. **to prove.** See on ver. 1. Jg 2:22. Ex 15:25. Dt 8:2. 33:8. 1 C 11:19. 2 Th 2:9-12.

5. **dwelt among.** Jg 1:29-32. Ps *106:34-38. **Canaanites.** Ge 10:15-17, +18. 15:19-21. Ex 3:8, 17. Dt 7:1. Jsh 9:1. Ne 9:8. **Hittites.** Ge +15:20. **Amorites.** Ge +10:16. **Perizzites.** Ge +13:7. **Hivites.** ver. 3. Ge +10:17. **Jebusites.** Ge +10:16.

6. **took their daughters.** Ex *34:16. Dt √7:3, 4. 1 K 11:1-5. Ezr 9:11, 12. Ne 13:23-27. Ezk 16:3.

7. **did evil.** ver. 12. Jg 2:11-13. or, the evil thing; a reference to idolatry. ver. 12. **and served.** Jg 2:13. **Baalim.** Jg +2:11. **the groves.** Jg 6:25. Ex 34:13. Dt 7:5. 16:21. 1 K 16:33. 18:19. 2 K 23:6, 14. 2 Ch 15:16. 24:18. 33:3, 19. 34:3, 7.

8. A.M. 2591. B.C. 1413. An. Ex. Is. 78. **was hot.** Jg 2:14, 20. Ex 22:24. Dt 29:20. Ps 6:1. 85:3. **he sold.** Jg 2:14. 4:9. Dt +*32:30. 1 S *12:9. Is 50:1. Ro 7:14. **Chushan-rishathaim.** i.e. *a Cushite most wicked or of double wickedness,* ✱S#3573h. ver. 10. *Aram-naharayim,* "Syria of the two rivers," is a famous province situated between the Tigris and Euphrates. It is called by Arabian geographers, *Maverannaher,* "the country beyond the river;" and is now called Diarbek. Hab 3:7.

9. A.M. 2599. B.C. 1405. An. Ex. Is. 86. **cried.** ver. 15. Jg 4:3. 6:7. 10:10. 1 S 12:10. Ne 9:27. Ps 22:5. 78:34. 106:41-44. 107:13-19. **raised up.** See on Jg 2:16. **deliverer.** Heb. savior. ver. 15. Jg 2:16. Dt 22:27. 28:29. 1 S 11:3. **who delivered.** Ex 2:17. **Othniel.** See on Jg 1:13.

10. **the Spirit.** Heb. *ruach,* Ge +41:38. Jg 6:34. 11:29. 13:25. 14:6, 19. 15:14. Nu 11:17. 27:18. 1 S 10:6. 11:6. 16:3, 13, 16. 2 Ch 15:1. 20:14. Ps 51:11. Is 61:1. 1 C 12:4-11. He 6:4. **came.** Heb. was. Nu 24:2. 1 S 4:1mg. 10:11. **Mesopotamia.** Heb. Aram. Ge 11:2. 14:1. Dt 23:4. 1 Ch 19:6, 7.

11. **the land.** ver. 30. Jg 5:31. 8:28. Jsh 11:23. Est 9:22. **Othniel.** ver. 9. Jsh 15:17. 1 Ch 4:13.

12. A.M. 2662. B.C. 1342. An. Ex. Is. 148. **did evil.** ver. 7. Jg 2:19. Ho 6:4. **and the Lord.** Ex 9:16. 2 K 5:1. Is 10:15. 37:26. 45:1-4. Ezk 38:16. Da 4:22. 5:18. Jn 19:11. **Eglon.** i.e. *a little calf,* ✱S#5700h. ver. 14, 15, 17, 17. (1) A royal city of the Amorites (or Canaanites) which was taken by Joshua, Jsh 10:3, 5, 23, 34, 36, 37. 12:12. 15:39. (2) A king of Moab who oppressed the Israelites, Jg 3:12, 17. **the king.** 1 S 12:9.

13. **Ammon.** Jg 5:14. Ps 83:6-8. **the city.** Jg 1:16. Dt 34:3. Ps 83:7.

14. **served.** Le 26:23-25. Dt 28:40, *47, *48.

15. A.M. 2679. B.C. 1325. An. Ex. Is. 166. **cried unto.** ver. 9. Ps 50:15. 78:34. 90:15. Je 29:12, 13. 33:3. **Ehud.** i.e. *united.* **Gera.** i.e. *a grain.* **a Benjamite.** or, the son of Jemini. 1 S 9:1mg. 2 S 16:1. 19:16. 1 K 2:8. **left-handed.** Heb. shut of his right hand. or, restrained, as in Jg 20:16. Ps 69:15 (shut). This Hebrew phrase intimates that, either through disease or disuse,

he made little or no use of the right hand, but of his left only, and so was the less fit for war, because he would most likely wield a dagger awkwardly: yet God chose this left-handed man to be the minister of his retributive justice. It was God's right hand that gained Israel the victory, Ps 44:3; not the right hand of the instruments he employed. Jg 20:16. Ge +48:13. 1 Ch 12:2. **sent a present.** Ge 4:5. 32:13, 18, 20, 21. 1 S 10:27. Pr 18:16. 19:6. 21:14. Is 36:16.

16. **two edges.** Heb. mouths. Ps 149:6. Is 41:15mg. He *4:12. Re 1:16. 2:12. **raiment.** or, long robe. Le 6:10. **upon.** ver. 21. Ps 45:3. SS 3:8.

17. **a very fat.** ver. 29mg. Ge 41:2, etc. 1 S 2:29. Jb 15:27. Ps 73:4mg, 7, 19. Je 5:28. 50:11. Ezk 34:20.

19. **quarries.** or, graven images. ver. 26. Dt 7:5, 25. 12:3. Jsh 4:20. **a secret.** ver. 20. 2 K 9:5, 6. Ac 23:18, 19. **Keep silence.** Ne 8:11. Am 6:10. 8:3. Hab *2:20. Zp 1:7. Zc 2:13. **And all that.** Ge 45:1.

20. **a summer parlor.** Heb. a parlor of cooling. The *aleeyah,* or upper chamber, seems to have been of the same description as the *oleah* of the Arabs, but properly ventilated, described by Dr. Shaw, who says, that to most of their houses there is a smaller one annexed, which sometimes rises one story higher than the house; at other times, it consists of one or two rooms only, and a terrace; while others that are built, as they frequently are, over the porch or gateway, have, if we except the ground floor, which they want, all the conveniences that belong to the house itself. There is a door of communication from them into the gallery of the house; besides another, which opens immediately from a private staircase, down into the porch or street, without giving the least disturbance to the house. In these back houses strangers are usually lodged and entertained; and to them likewise the men are wont to retire from the noise and hurry of their families, to be more at leisure for meditation or diversions. or, upper chamber. ver. 23, 24, 25. Jsh 2:6. 2 S 18:33. 1 K *17:19, 23. 2 K 1:2. 4:10n, 11. 23:12. 1 Ch 28:11. 2 Ch 3:9. 9:4. Ne 3:31, 32. Ps 104:3, 13. Je 22:13, 14. Am 3:15. Mk 2:4. 14:15. Lk 17:31. 22:12. Ac 1:13. 9:37, 39. 10:9. 20:8, 9. **I have.** ver. 19. 2 S 12:1, etc. 24:12. Mi 6:9. **he arose.** Ps 29:1. Je 10:7. **seat.** or, throne. Ge 41:40. Ex 11:5. 12:29. Dt 17:18. 1 S 1:9. 2:8. 4:13, 18.

21. **thrust it.** Nu 25:7, 8. 1 S 15:33. Jb 20:25. Zc 13:3. 2 C 5:16.

22. **blade.** lit. flame. Jg 13:20. Jb 39:23. 41:21. Is 13:8. 29:6. 30:30. 66:15. Jl 2:5. **the dirt came out.** or, it came out at the fundament.

23. **shut the doors.** Jg 9:51. Ge 7:16. Jn 20:19, 26. **locked them.** 2 S 13:17, 18. Ne 3:3. SS 4:12.

24. **covereth,** etc. or, doeth his easement. 1 S 24:3. 2 K 18:27mg. ♪88, Ge +15:15. ♪121S3Q. Metonymy of the Adjunct B607. "To cover the feet" is put for performing the duty of nature. For another instance of this figure see 1 S 24:3.

25. **ashamed.** 2 K 2:17. 8:11. Je 6:15. 8:12. **key.** 1 Ch +9:27 (opening). Pr 8:6 (opening). Is 22:22.

26. **escaped.** 1 S 23:13. **tarried.** Jg 19:18. Ge 19:16. 43:10. Ex 12:39. 2 S 15:28. Ps 119:60. Is 29:9. Hab 2:3. **the quarries.** ver. 19. **Seirath.** lit. *a hairy or rough place; the hairy she-goat,* ✱S#8167h.

27. **he blew.** Jg 5:14. 6:34. 1 S 13:3. 2 S 20:22. 2 K 9:13. Jl 2:1, 15. 1 C 14:8. **mountain.** ♪121J7A. Jsh 13:6. Jg 7:24. 17:1. 19:1. Jsh 17:15, 18.

28. **Follow**. Jg 4:10. 7:17. **the Lord**. Jg 7:9, 15. 1 S 17:47. **the fords**. Jg 12:5, 6. Jsh 2:7.

29. **lusty**. Heb. fat. or, robust. lit. oily, fat, shining. See on ver. 17. Ge 49:20. Dt 32:15. Ne 9:25, 35. Jb 15:27. Ps 17:10. Is 30:23. Ezk 34:14, 16. Hab 1:16. **valor**. Ge 47:6. Ex *18:21, 25. Jsh 1:14. 6:2. 8:3. 10:7.

30. **subdued**. or, humbled. Jg 8:28. 11:23. **And the land**. ver. 11. Jg 5:31.

31. **Shamgar**. i.e. *destroyer*, *S#8044h. Jg 5:6. **Anath**. i.e. *afflicted; answered*, *S#6067h. Jg 5:6. **an ox goad**. This implement, Mr. Maundrell informs us, in Palestine and Syria is of an extraordinary size. He measured several, and "found them about eight feet long; and at the bigger end about six inches in circumference. They were armed at the lesser end with a sharp prickle for driving the oxen; and at the other end with a small paddle of iron, strong and massive, for cleansing the plow from the clay." In the hand of a powerful man such an instrument must be more dangerous and fatal than a sword. Jg 15:15. 1 S 13:19-22. 17:47, 50. Zc 4:6. 1 C 1:27. **also**. Jg 2:16. **Israel**. So part is called Israel. Jg 2:16. 4:1, 3, etc. 5:6, 8. 10:7, 17. 11:4, etc. 1 S 4:1. 13:19, 22. It seems to concern only the country next to the Philistines.

JUDGES 4

Israel, again revolting, is oppressed by Jabin and Sisera, 1-3. The prophetess Deborah from the Lord stirs up Barak for their deliverance, 4-9. Barak destroys the army of Jabin, 10-16. Jael the Kenite hides Sisera in her tent and slays him while he sleeps, 17-22. Jabin subdued and destroyed, 23, 24.

1. A.M. 2699. B.C. 1305. An. Ex. Is. 186. **did evil**. Jg 2:11, 19, 20. 3:7, 12. 6:1. 10:6. Le 26:23-25. Ne 9:23-30. Ps 78:56, 57. *106:43-45. Je 5:3. **dead**. Jg 2:9, 10, 19. 3:11, 12.

2. **sold**. See on Jg 2:14, 15. 3:8. 10:7. 1 S 12:9. Is 50:1. Mt 18:25. "It seems to concern only north Israel." **Jabin**. i.e. *he understands*. **Hazor**. Jsh 11:1, 10, 11. 19:36. **Sisera**. i.e. *battle-array; binding in chains*, *S#5516h. ver. 7, 9, 12, 13, 14, 15, 15, 16, 17, 18, 22, 22. Jg 5:20, 26, 28, 30. 1 S 12:9. Ezr 2:53. Ne 7:55. Ps 83:9. (1) The commander of the army of Jabin, king of Canaan, Jg 4:2-22; 5:20. (2) A Jew whose descendants returned with Zerubbabel, Ezr 2:53; Ne 7:55. **Harosheth**. i.e. *carving; city of crafts*, *S#2800h. ver. 13, 16.

3. **cried**. Jg 3:9, 15. 10:10, 16. 1 S 7:8. Ps 50:15. 78:34. Je 2:27, 28. **chariots of iron**. Jg 1:19. Jsh 17:16. **mightily**. Jg 5:8. Dt *28:29, 33, 47, 48. Ps 106:42. 107:10-13, 39.

4. A.M. 2719. B.C. 1285. An. Ex. Is 206. **Deborah**. i.e. *a bee*. Ge 35:8. Ex 15:20. 2 K 22:14. 2 Ch 34:22. Ne 6:14. Is 8:3. Jl 2:28, 29. Mi 6:4. Lk 2:36. Ac 21:9. 1 C 11:5. Ga 3:28. **Lapidoth**. i.e. *lamps; enlightened*, *S#3941h. Perhaps she was a maker of lamps (Young).

5. **the palm**. Ge 35:8. **between Ramah**. Jsh 16:2. 18:22, +*25. 1 S 1:1, 19. 7:16, 17. 25:1. Je 31:15. **Bethel**. Ge 12:8. **in mount Ephraim**. Jsh 24:33. **came up**. Ex 18:13, 16, 19, 26. Dt 17:8-12. 2 S 15:2-6.

6. **Barak**. i.e. *lightning*, *S#1301h. ver. 8, 9, 10, 12, 14, 14, 15, 16, 22. Jg 5:1, 12, 15. He 11:32. **Abi-noam**. i.e. *my father is pleasant*, or *father of pleasantness*, *S#42h. ver. 12. Jg 5:1, 12. **Kedesh-naphtali**.

i.e. *my wrestling*, *S#5321h. Jsh 19:32, 37. *20:7. 21:32. **Hath**. Jsh 1:9. Ps 7:6. Is 13:2-5. Ac 13:47. **Tabor**. i.e. *mound, height; thou wilt purge; purity*, *S#8396h. ver. 12, 14. Jg 8:18. Jsh 19:22. 1 S 10:3. 1 Ch 6:77. Ps 89:12. Je 46:18. Ho 5:1. (1) A famous mountain on the north-east edge of the great plain of Esdraelon, and on the border between Zebulun and Issachar, is six miles south-east of Nazareth, Jsh 19:22; Ps 89:12. Barak gathered his army there to overthrow Sisera, Jg 4:6-14. It is now called *Jebel et Tor*, and its summit is about two thousand feet above the Mediterranean Sea. It rises from the plain as an isolated mass in the shape of a dome. Tradition makes it the Mount of Transfiguration, but the majority of modern scholars place that event on Mount Hermon, since it occurred only a few days after Christ's arrival in that region. (2) A city of Zebulun, 1 Ch 6:77. **ten thousand**. ver. 10. Jg 5:14-18.

7. **And I will draw**. Ex +*4:21. *14:4. Jsh 11:20. Ezk 38:10-16. Jl 3:11-14. **Kishon**. i.e. *bending*. Jg 5:21. 1 K 18:40. Ps 83:9, 10. **deliverer**. ver. 14. Ex 21:13. Jsh 8:7. 10:8. 11:6. 1 S 24:10, 18.

8. **If thou**. Ex 4:10-14. Mt 14:30, 31. **wilt go**. Is *31:1.

9. **notwithstanding**. 1 S 2:30. 2 Ch 26:18. **not be**. Ps 115:1. Je 17:5. **sell Sisera**. See on Jg 2:14. **into the hand of a woman**. ver. 17-22. Jg 5:24-27. *9:54. 2 S 20:21, 22.

10. **called**. ver. 13mg. **Zebulun**. ver. 6. Jg 5:18. **at his**. Jg 5:15mg, 27mg. Ge 30:30mg. Ex +11:8. Dt +11:6mg. 1 S 25:27. 1 K 20:11mg.

11. **Heber**. i.e. *a companion*, or *charm*. ver. 17. Jg 1:16. Nu 10:29. 24:21. **Hobab**. Ex 2:18. 3:1. 18:1. Nu 10:29. **Zaanaim**. i.e. *changing; wandering*, *S#6815h. Jsh 19:33, 37, Zaanannim. **Kedesh**. ver. 6. Jsh 19:37.

12. **mount Tabor**. ver. 6. Jsh 19:12, 34. Ps 89:12. Je 46:18. Ho 5:1.

13. **gathered**. Heb. gathered by cry, *or* proclamation. Jg 6:34. 1 S 10:17. 2 S 20:4, 5. Jb 35:9. Jon 3:7. Zc 6:8. **chariots**. ver. 13. Jsh 11:6. **nine hundred**. See on ver. 2, 3, 7. **chariots of iron**. ver. 3. Probably chariots armed with iron scythes, projecting from the axle on each side, by which the infantry might be easily cut down or thrown into confusion. The ancient Britons are said to have had such chariots.

14. **Up**. Jg 19:28. Ge 19:14. 44:4. Jsh 7:13. 1 S 9:26. **for this**. This is exactly the purpose for which the Septuagint states, ver. 8, that Barak wished Deborah to accompany him: "Because I know not the day in which God will send his angel to give me prosperity." **is not**. Dt 9:3. 2 S 5:24. Ps 68:7, 8. Is 52:12. Mi 2:13. Zc 14:3. **mount Tabor**. Jsh 19:12. Mount Tabor, called by the Arabs *Djebel Tour*, is almost entirely insulated, and rises up in the plain of Esdraelon, about six miles from Nazareth, in a conical form, somewhat like a sugarloaf. Josephus states its height to be thirty stadia, with a plain of 26 stadia in circumference on its top, on which was formerly a city, which was used as a military post. It is described as an exceedingly beautiful mountain, having a rich soil, producing excellent herbage, and adorned with groves and clumps of trees.

15. **the Lord discomfited**. Jg 5:20, 21. Jsh 10:10. 2 K 7:6. 2 Ch 13:15-17. Ps *20:7, 8. 33:16, 17. 83:9, 10. Pr *21:31. He 11:32.

16. **pursued**. Le 26:7, 8. Jsh 10:19, 20. 11:8. Ps

104:35. Ro 2:12. Ja 2:13. **there.** Is 43:17. **a man left.** Heb. unto one.

17. **fled.** Jb 12:19-21. 18:7-12. 40:11, 12. Ps 37:35, 36. 107:40. Pr 29:23. Am 5:19, 20. **Jael.** i.e. *a roe*, ✻S#3278h. ver. 18, 21, 22. Jg 5:6, 24. **peace.** Ps 69:22. Is 57:21.

18. **Jael.** 2 K 6:19. **mantle.** *or*, rug *or* blanket.

19. **Give me.** Jg 5:25, 26. Ge 24:43. 1 K 17:10. Is 41:17. Jn 4:7. **a bottle.** Not "a bottle," for they were made of skins, as in Jsh 9:4, 13. 1 S 16:20. Ps 56:8. 119:83.

20. **Is there.** Jsh 2:3-5. 2 S 17:20.

21. **took.** Jg 3:21, 31. 5:26. 15:15. 1 S 17:43, 49, 50. 1 C 1:19, 27. **a nail.** Jg 16:14. One of the spikes of the tent. See Note on Ex 35:18. **and took.** Heb. and put. **hammer.** 1 K 6:7. Is 44:12. Je 10:4. **went softly.** 2 S 18:5 (gently). 1 K 21:27. Jb 15:11 (secret thing. or, gentle word). Is 8:6. **smote.** Ps 3:7. **temples.** ver. 22. Jg 5:26. SS 4:3. 6:7. **fast asleep.** Ps 76:6. Pr 10:5. Da 8:18. 10:9. Jon 1:5, 6. **weary.** 1 S 14:28mg. **he died.** Jg 5:27.

22. **and I will.** 2 S 17:3, 10-15.

23. **God subdued.** 1 Ch 22:18. Ne 9:24. Ps 18:39, 47. 47:3. 81:14. 1 C 15:28. He 11:33.

24. **prospered**, etc. Heb. going, went and was hard against. 1 S 3:12.

JUDGES 5

The song of Deborah and Barak introduced, 1. A call to kings and people to consider this and other works of God for Israel, 2-5. The sin and misery of Israel shown, 6-8. Praises rendered to God, 9-13. commendations bestowed on some Israelites who went forth willingly to this battle, and censures on the unwilling who tarried at home, 14-18. The victory described in all its circumstances, 19-22. Meroz cursed for not coming to their assistance, 23. The conduct of Jael celebrated, 24-27. The disappointment of Sisera's mother represented, 28-30. A prayer added for victory to the people of God, and ruin to their enemies, 31.

1. **sang Deborah.** This verse briefly recites the subject of this inspired song, which consists of eight stanzas: The first opens with a devout thanksgiving. The second describes the magnificent scenes at Mount Sinai, etc. The third states the apostasy and consequent punishment of the Israelites. The fourth contrasts their present happy state. The fifth censures the recreant tribes of Reuben, Gad, etc. The sixth records the defeat of the confederate kings of Canaan. The seventh contains a panegyric on Jael. And the eighth describes the fond anticipations and disappointment of the mother of Sisera. Ex 15:1, 21. Nu 21:17. 1 S 2:1. 2 Ch 20:21, 27. Jb 38:7. Ps 18, title. Is 12:1-6. 25:1. 26:1. Lk 1:46, 67, 68. Re 15:3, 4. 19:1-3.

2. **for the avenging.** Dt 32:43. 2 S 22:47, 48. Ps 18:47. 48:11. 94:1. 97:8. 136:15, 19, 20. *149:6-9. Re 6:10. 16:5, 6. 18:20. 19:2. **when.** ver. 9. Jg 5:18. 2 Ch 17:16. Ne 11:2. Ps 110:3. 1 C 9:17. 15:57. 2 C 8:5, 12. 9:7. Ph 2:13. Phm 14.

3. **O ye kings.** Dt 32:1, 3. Ps *2:10-12. 49:1, 2. 119:46. 138:4, 5. **I, even I.** ver. 7. Ge 6:17. 9:9. Ex 31:6. Le 26:28. 1 K 18:22. 19:10, 14. Ezr 7:21. **will sing.** 2 S 22:50. Ps 7:17.

4. **Lord.** Dt 33:2. Ps 68:7, 8. 97:4. Hab 3:3-6. **Seir.** Ge 36:8. **the earth trembled.** ✔102, Ge +2:24. Dt

2:25. Jsh 5:1. 2 S 22:8. Jb 9:6. Ps 18:7-15. **the clouds.** Ge +9:13. Ex 19:9. 2 S 22:12. **dropped.** Ps 68:8. *77:17. SS 5:5.

5. **mountains.** Dt 4:11. Ps 97:5. 114:4. Is 64:1-3. Na 1:5. Hab 3:10. **melted.** Heb. flowed. ✔102, Ge +2:24. Dt 32:2. Ps 147:18. SS 4:16. Is 64:1, 3. **that Sinai.** Ex 19:18. 20:18. Dt 4:11, 12. 5:22-25. He 12:18.

6. **Shamgar.** Jg 3:31. **Jael.** Jg 4:17, 18. **the highways.** Le 26:22. 2 Ch 15:5. Is 33:8. La 1:4. 4:18. Mi 3:12. Zc 7:14. **unoccupied.** ✔63F, Ge +33:10. **travelers.** Heb. walkers of paths. Jb 19:8. **byways.** Heb. crooked ways. Ps 125:5.

7. **the villages.** ✔121J17, Ge +6:11. Est 9:19. **a mother in Israel.** Jg 4:4-6. 2 S 20:19. Is 49:23. Ro 16:13.

8. **chose.** ✔96C8, Ex 15:5. **new gods.** Jg 2:12, 17. Dt 32:16, 17. Je 2:11, 13. **was there.** Jg 4:3. 1 S 13:19-22.

9. **offered.** See on ver. 2. 1 Ch 29:9. 2 C 8:3, 4, 12, 17. 9:5.

10. **Speak.** *or*, Meditate. 1 Ch 16:9. Jb 12:8. Ps 105:1, 2. 145:5, 6, 11. Is 12:4. **ride.** ✔132A, Ge +4:23. Jg 10:3, 4. 12:13, 14. Zc *9:9. Mt *21:5. **on white.** ✔142, Ge +20:16. **ye that sit.** Ps 107:32. Is 28:6. Jl 3:12.

11. **the noise.** La 5:4, 9. **in the places.** Dr Shaw mentions a beautiful rill of water in Barbary, which runs into a large basin, called *shrub we krub*, "drink and be off," because of the danger of meeting with robbers and assassins in this place, who fall upon those who come to drink. Ge 24:11, 13, 19, 20, 43-45. 26:20-22. Ex 2:17-19. Is 12:3. **rehearse.** 1 S 12:7. **righteous acts.** Heb. righteousnesses. 1 S 12:7mg. Ps 145:7. Is 33:15mg. 45:24mg. Mi 6:5. **villages.** See on ver. 7. **go down.** Dt 22:24. Jb 29:7. Is 28:6. Je 7:2.

12. **awake, Deborah.** Ps 57:8. 103:1, 2. 108:2. Is 26:19. 51:9, 17. 52:1, 2. 60:1. Je 31:26. 1 C 15:34. Ep 5:14. **utter a song.** Ep 5:19. Re 15:3. **lead.** Ps 68:18. Is 14:2. 33:1. 49:24-26. Ep *4:8. 2 T 2:26.

13. **he made.** Ps 49:14. 149:8. Is 41:15, 16. Ezk 17:24. Da 7:18-27. Ro 8:37. Re 2:26, 27. 3:9. **the Lord.** Ps 75:7.

14. **of Ephraim.** Jg 3:15, 26, 27. 4:5, 6. **Amalek.** See on Jg 3:13. Ex 17:8-16. **after.** Jg 4:10, 14. **Machir.** Nu 32:39, 40. Jsh 17:1. **Zebulun.** Jg 4:6. **handle the pen.** Heb. draw with the pen. Ps 45:1.

15. **the princes.** See on 1 Ch 12:32. **Barak.** See on Jg 4:6, 14. **foot.** Heb. his feet. *Beraglaiv*, rather, "with his footmen": so LXX. Alex. *pedous auto*. Ac 20:13. **For the.** *or*, In the divisions, etc. 2 Ch 35:5. Ac 15:39. **thoughts.** Heb. impressions. Pr 22:13. 2 C 11:2.

16. **sheepfolds.** Nu 32:1-5, 24. Ph 2:21. 3:19. **For.** *or*, In. ver. 15mg. **great.** Ps 4:4. 77:6. La 3:40, 41. **Reuben.** Ge 49:4. **searchings.** Jb 5:9. 8:8. 9:10. *11:7. 36:26. 38:16. Ps 145:3. Pr 25:3mg, 27. Is *40:28.

17. **Gilead.** Nu 26:29. Jsh 13:25, 31. **Dan.** Jsh 19:46, 48. **Asher.** Jsh 19:24-31. **sea shore.** *or*, sea port. **breaches.** *or*, creeks.

18. **Zebulun.** See on Jg 4:10. **jeoparded.** Heb. exposed to reproach. **their.** Est 4:16. Ac 20:24. 1 J 3:16. Re *12:11. **lives.** Heb. *nephesh*, souls, Ge +44:30. **in the high.** Jg 4:6, 10, 14.

19. **kings.** Jsh 10:22-27. 11:1, etc. Ps 48:4-6. 68:12-14. 118:8-12. Re 17:12-14. 19:19. **Taanach.** Jg 1:27. Jsh 12:21. 17:11. 1 K 4:12. **waters of Megiddo.** Jsh

12:7, 21. 17:11. Zc 12:11. Re *16:16. **they took**. ver. 30. Ge 14:22. 4:16. Ps 44:12.

20. **fought**. Jsh 10:11. 1 S 7:10. Ps 18:12-14. 77:17, 18. **the stars**. Jg 4:15. **courses**. Heb. paths. Nu 20:19 (high way). **fought**. ∫155D, Ge +4:10.

21. **Kishon**. i.e. *winding; ensnarer,* *S#7191h. Jg 4:7, 13. 1 K 18:40. Ps 83:9, 10. **O my soul**. Heb. *nephesh,* Ge +27:31. Ge 49:18. Ps 44:5. Is 25:10. Mi 7:10. **hast**. lit. wilt tread. ∫96C10. Heterosis of Tenses B523: the future of the indicative is put for the imperative. EWB suggests the following as additional instances of this figure: Ps (5:11). 1 C 5:13. 1 T 6:8. **trodden**. Dt 33:29. Ps 91:13.

22. **horsehoofs**. Anciently, horses were not shod; nor are they at the present day in some parts of the East. The flight was so rapid, that the hoofs of their horses were splintered and broken by the roughness of the roads; in consequence of which they became lame, and could not carry off their riders. Ge 49:17. Ps 20:7. 33:17. 147:10, 11. Is 5:28. Je 47:3. Mi 4:13. **broken**. or, hammered. ver. 26. 1 S 14:16. Ps 74:6. 141:5. Pr 23:35. Is 16:8. *28:1mg. 41:7. **pransings**. *or,* tramplings, *or* plungings. ∫84, Ge +6:17. Na 3:2. **mighty ones**. 1 S 21:7. Jb 24:22. 34:20. Ps 22:12. 76:5. 78:25mg. 103:20mg. Is 10:13. 46:12. Je *8:16. 46:12, 15. *47:3. 50:11. La 1:15. *or,* as Dr. Waterland renders, "mighty horses," or "strong steeds," as Dr. Kennicott, i.e. *their war horses,* which gives great energy to the text and renders it perfectly intelligible.

23. **Curse ye**. 1 S 26:19. Je 48:10. 1 C 16:22. **Meroz**. i.e. *leanness,* *S#4789h. This city of Meroz seems to have been, at this time, a place of considerable importance, since something great was expected from it: but probably after the angel of the Lord had pronounced this curse, it dwindled, and, like the fig tree which Christ cursed (Mt 21:19), withered away, so that we never read of it after this Scripture. **the angel**. Jg 2:1. 4:6. 6:11. 13:3. Mt 25:41. **they came**. Jg 21:9, 10. Ne 3:5. Ps 78:9. **to the help**. 1 S 17:47. 18:17. 25:28. Ro 15:18. 1 C 3:9. 2 C 6:1.

24. **Blessed above women**. Jg 4:17. Ge 14:19. Pr 31:31. Lk *1:28, 42. √11:27, 28.

25. **asked**. See on Jg 4:19-21. **butter**. *Chemah* may signify *buttermilk,* which is made by the Arabs by agitating the milk in a leather bag; and is highly esteemed because of its refreshing and cooling qualities. Ge 18:8. Dt 32:14. 2 S 17:29. Jb 20:17. Pr 30:33. Is 7:*15, 22. **dish**. Jg 6:38.

26. **nail**. Jg 4:21. **workmen's**. Jb 3:20. 20:22. Pr 16:26. Ec 2:18, 22. 3:9. *4:8. 9:9. **with the**. Heb. she hammered. **she smote off**. Or rather, "she smote his head, then she struck through and pierced his temples": which is more consonant to the original, and to fact, as it does not appear that she smote off his head. 1 S 17:49-51. 2 S 20:22.

27. **At**. Heb. Between. Ge 49:10. Dt +11:6mg. **he fell**. ∫41, Ge +10:1. **at her**. ∫70, Ex +16:35. **where**. Ps 52:7. Mt 7:2. Ja 2:13. **dead**. Heb. destroyed. Ps 137:8. Is 33:1. Je 4:30.

28. **looked out**. 2 S 6:16. 2 K 9:30. 1 Ch 15:29. Pr 7:6. **through**. 2 K 1:2. SS 2:9. **Why is**. Jg 4:15. SS 8:14. Ja 5:7.

29. **wise ladies**. 2 S 20:16. 1 K 11:3. Est 1:18. Is 49:23mg. La 1:1. **answer**. Heb. her words. ∫37C, Ge +25:22. Pr 7:5.

30. **Have they not sped**. Ex 15:9. Jb 20:5. **every**

man. Heb. the head of a man. ∫171Q12. Synecdoche of the Part B645. The head is put for the man himself. For other instances of this figure see 2 S 1:16. 1 K 2:37. 2 K 2:3. Ps 3:3. 7:16. 66:12. Pr 10:6. Is 35:10. Ezk 33:4. Mt 27:25. Ac 18:6. **a damsel**. or, female. lit. a womb. Ge 49:25. Pr 30:16. Is 46:3. Ezk 20:26. ∫171Q19. Synecdoche of the Part B648. The womb is put for a female, in respect to her being marriageable. **of divers**. Ge 37:3. 2 S 13:18. Ps 45:14. **needlework**. 1 Ch 29:2. Ps *45:14. Ezk 16:10, 13, 18. 17:3. 26:16. 27:7, 16, 24.

31. **So let**. Ps 48:4, 5. 58:10, 11. 68:1-3. 83:9-18. 92:9. 97:8. Re 6:10. 18:20. 19:2, 3. **O Lord**. ∫74. Epiphonema; or, Exclamation B464. Addition of conclusion by way of exclamation; an exclamation at the conclusion of a sentence. For other instances of this figure see Ps 2:12. 3:8. 14:7. 134:21. Jon 2:9. Mt 11:15. 17:5. 20:16. 22:14. 24:28. Re 22:20. **them that**. Ex 20:6. Dt 5:10. 6:5. Ps 91:14. 97:10. *122:6. Ro *8:28. 1 C 8:3. Ep 6:24. Ja 1:12. 2:5. 1 P 1:8. 1 J 4:19-21. 5:2, 3. **the sun**. 2 S 23:4. Ps 19:4, 5. 37:6. Pr *4:18. Da *12:3. Ho 6:3. Mt 13:43. **And the land**. The victory here celebrated in this song, was of such happy consequence to Israel, that for the principal part of one age, they enjoyed the peace to which it had been the means of opening the way. *The land had rest forty years,* that is, *so long it was from this victory to the raising up of Gideon.* And well would it have been for the Israelites, if while the tribes had rest, they had taken advantage of the cessation from war, and had walked in the fear of the Lord. Jg 3:11, 30.

JUDGES 6

Israel, relapsing into sin, is oppressed by Midian, 1-7. A prophet rebukes them, 8-10. The Angel of the Lord appoints Gideon to deliver them, 11-16. The angel confirms his commission by consuming his oblation with fire, 17-21. Gideon knows who the Angel is, and is alarmed; but when encouraged, he builds an altar, and calls it Jehovah Shalom, 22-24. By divine command Gideon destroys Baal's altar and grove, and offers a sacrifice to Jehovah, 25-27. His citizens purpose to put him to death, but his father defends him, and calls him Jerubbaal, 28-32. Gideon raises an army, 33-35. Gideon is encouraged by a twofold sign involving fleece and dew, 36-40.

1. **did evil**. Jg 2:13, 14, 19, 20. Le 26:14, etc. Dt 28:15, etc. Ne 9:26-29. Ps 106:34-42. **delivered**. When God judges, he will overcome; and sinners shall be made either to bend or break before him. See the ensuing history. **Midian**. Ge 25:1, 2. Nu 25:17, 18. Hab 3:7.

2. **the hand**. Le 26:17. Dt 28:47, 48. **prevailed**. Heb. was strong. **dens**. Dr. Shaw says that a great way on each side Joppa, on the sea coast, there is a range of mountains and precipices; and in these high situations are generally found the dens, holes, or caves, which are so frequently mentioned in Scripture; and which were formerly the lonesome retreats of the distressed Israelites. Young renders *flowings,* stating "of water in trenches; this original word is not found elsewhere." **caves**. 1 S 13:6. 14:11. He 11:38. Re 6:15. **strongholds**. 1 S 23:14, 19, 29. 1 Ch 11:7. 12:8, 16. Is 33:16. Je 48:41. 51:30. Ezk 33:27.

3. **when Israel.** Le 26:16. Dt 28:30-33, 51. Jb 31:8. Is 65:21, 22. Mi 6:15. **Amalekites.** Ge 36:12. Jg 3:13. **children.** ver. 33. Jg 7:12. 8:10. Ge 25:6. 29:1. Nu 23:7. 1 K 4:30. Jb 1:3. Je 49:28. Ezk 25:4, 10.

4. **destroyed.** Le 26:16. Dt 28:30, 33, 51. Mi 6:15. **till thou come.** The Midianites dwelt beyond the eastern borders of the land of Canaan, east of the Dead Sea, and Gaza was on the Mediterranean, on the west: so that these invaders ravaged the whole breadth of the land. Ge 10:19. 13:10. **left no.** Pr 28:3. Je 49:9, 10. Ob 5. **sustenance.** Jg 17:10. **sheep.** or, goat. Ex 12:3n.

5. **tents.** SS 1:5. Is 13:20. **as grasshoppers.** Jg 7:12. 8:10. Je 46:23. **their camels.** Jg 8:21. 1 S 30:17. Is 60:6. Je 49:29, 32. **to destroy.** Ps 83:4-12.

6. **impoverished.** Ps 79:8. 106:43mg. Is 17:4. Je 5:17. Ml 1:4. **cried.** See on Jg 3:9, 15. Ps 50:15. 78:34. 106:44. 107:13. Is 26:16. Ho 5:15.

8. A.M. 2759. B.C. 1245. An. Ex. Is. 246. **a prophet.** Heb. a man, a prophet. Is +40:13mg. **Thus saith.** See on Jg 2:1-3. Ne 9:9-12. Ps 136:10-16. Is 63:9-14. Ezk 20:5, etc.

9. **drave them.** See on Ps 44:2, 3.

10. **I am the.** See on Ex 20:2, 3. **fear not.** 2 K 17:33, 35-39. Je +*10:2. **ye have.** Jg 2:2. Pr 5:13. Je 3:13, 25. 9:13. 42:21. 43:4, 7. Zp 3:2. Ro 10:16. He *5:9.

11. **an angel of.** ſ171E12, Ge +48:16. ver. 14-16. Jg 2:1-5. 5:23. 13:3, 18-20. Ge 48:16. Jsh 18:23. Is *63:9. **an oak.** ver. 19. 1 K 13:14. **in Ophrah.** Jg 8:27. 9:5. Different from that in Jsh 18:23, which belonged to Benjamin (Young). **Joash.** i.e. *Jehovah has become man; whom Jehovah bestowed,* *S#3101h. ver. 29, 30, 31. Jg 7:14. 8:13, 29, 32, 32. 1 K 22:26. 2 K 11:2. 12:19, 20. 13:1, 9, 10, 12, 13, 13, 14, 25. 14:1, 3, 17, 23, 23, 27. 1 Ch 3:11. 4:22. 12:3. 2 Ch 18:25. 22:11. 24:1, 2, 4, 22, 24. 25:17, 18, 21, 23, 23, 25, 25. Ho 1:1. Am 1:1. (1) The father of Gideon, Jg 6:11. (2) A son of Ahab, 1 K 22:26; 2 Ch 18:25. (3) Son and successor of Ahaziah, king of Judah, 2 K 11:2, 3. (4) Son of Jehoahaz, whom he succeeded as king of Israel, 2 K 14:12-16. (5) A descendant of Judah, 1 Ch 4:22. (6) One of David's heroes, 1 Ch 12:3. **Abi-ezrite.** *S#33h. ver. 24. Jg 8:2, 32h. Nu 26:30. Jsh 17:2. 1 Ch 7:17, 18. **Gideon.** i.e. *a cutter down,* *S#1439h. ver. 13, 19, 22, 24, 27, 29, 34, 36, 39. Jg 7:1, 2, 4, 5, 7, 13, 14, 15, 18, 19, 20, 24, 25. 8:4, 7, 11, 13, 21, 22, 23, 24, 27, 27, 28, 30, 32, 33, 35. He 11:32. **Gedeon. threshed.** or, beating out. Dt 24:20. Ru *2:17. Is 27:12. 28:27. **wheat.** 1 Ch 21:20. **winepress.** S#1660h. Ne 13:15. Is 63:2 (winefat), 3. La 1:15. Jl 3:13. Mt 26:26. Re 14:19. 19:15. **hide it.** Heb. cause it to flee. Jg 7:21. Ex 9:20. Dt 32:30. +34:6.

12. **the angel.** Jg 13:3. Lk 1:11, 28. **The Lord.** Jg 2:18. Ex 3:12. Jsh 1:5, 9. Ru 2:4. Mt 1:23. 28:20. Lk 1:28. Ac 18:9, 10. **with thee.** Jsh 1:5. **valor.** Jg 11:1. Jsh 1:14. 6:2. 8:3. 10:7. 1 S 16:18. 2 S +2:7mg. 1 Ch 9:13mg. 26:6n.

13. **if the Lord.** Ge 25:22. Ex 34:14-16. Nu 14:14, 15. Ro *8:31. **why then.** Dt 29:24. 30:17, 18. Ps 77:7-9. 89:49. Is 59:1, 2. 63:15. **our fathers.** Ps 13:1. 44:1. 78:3, 4, 12. 89:49. **from Egypt.** Ps 80:8, 12-14. **forsaken us.** Dt 31:17. 2 Ch √15:2. Ps 27:9. Is 41:17. Je 23:33.

14. **the Lord.** See on ver. 11. **Go in.** Jg 4:6. Jsh *1:5-9. 1 S *12:11. 1 Ch 14:9, 10. He 11:32, 34. **have not I.** Jg 4:6. Jsh 1:9.

15. **wherewith.** Ex 3:11. 4:10. Je 1:6. Lk 1:34. **my family is poor.** Heb. my thousand is the meanest. Ex *18:21-25. 1 S 9:21. 18:23. Mi +*5:2. **the least.** Ge 32:10. Ps 68:27. Je 50:45. 1 C 15:9. Ep 3:8.

16. **Surely.** ver. 12. Ex 3:12. Jsh *1:5. Is *41:10, 14-16. Mt *28:20. Mk 16:20. Ac 11:21.

17. **If now.** See on Ex 33:13, 16. **sight.** Ge 18:3. **show.** ver. 36-40. Ge 15:8-17. Ex 4:1-9. 2 K 20:8-11. Ps 86:17. Is 7:11. **sign.** or, token. Jsh +2:12. Lk ◖11:29. 2 C √5:7. **thou.** ſ63C, Ge +25:32. Supply ellipsis, "Thou (art Jehovah Who) talkest."

18. **Depart not.** Ge 18:3. Nu 14:44. **bring.** Jg 13:15. Ge 18:3, 5. 19:3. **present.** or, meat offering. Ge 4:3-5. Le +*23:13.

19. **and made.** Dr. Shaw observes, "Besides a bowl of milk, and a basket of figs, raisins, or dates, which upon our arrival were presented to us, to stay our appetite, the master of the tent fetched us from his flock, according to the number of our company, a kid or a goat, a lamb or a sheep; half of which was immediately seethed by his wife, and served up with cucasoe: the rest was made *kab-ab*, i.e. cut to pieces and roasted, which we reserved for our breakfast or dinner next day." May we not suppose, says Mr. Harmer, that Gideon presented some slight refreshment to the supposed prophet, according to the present Arab mode, and desired him to stay till he could provide something more substantial; that he immediately killed a kid, seethed a part of it, and when ready brought the stewed meat in a pot, with unleavened cakes of bread, which he had baked; and the other part, the *kab-ab*, in a basket, for him to carry with him for some after repast in his journey? Jg 13:15-19. Ge 18:6-8. **a kid.** Heb. a kid of the goats. Jg 13:15, 19. 15:1. **unleavened cakes.** Le 2:4. **an ephah of flour.** 1 S 1:24. **basket.** Ge 40:16-18. Ex 29:3, 23, 32. Le 8:2, 26, 31. Nu 6:15, 17, 19. **broth.** ver. 20. Is 65:4. **pot.** Nu 11:8. 1 S 2:14.

20. **lay them.** Jg 13:19. **pour out.** Ex 4:9. Le 14:41. 1 K *18:33, 34.

21. **rose up.** Jg 13:20. Le 9:24. 1 K 18:38. 1 Ch 21:26. 2 Ch 7:1. **out of.** Jb 29:6. Ps 81:16. **rock.** Ex 17:6.

22. **perceived.** Jg 13:21. Lk 24:31. **Alas.** Jg *11:35. Jsh 7:7. 2 K 3:10. 6:5, 15. Je 1:6. 4:10. 14:13. √30:7. *32:17. Ezk 4:14. 9:8. 11:13. 20:49. Jl *1:15. **O Lord.** 1 S 20:12. Jn *20:28. **God.** Jg 16:28. Ge 15:2, 8. Dt 3:24. 9:26. Jsh 7:7. 2 S 7:18. **because.** Jg 13:22, 23. Ge 16:13. 32:30. Ex 33:20. Dt 5:5, 24-26. Is 6:5-8. Jn 1:18. 12:41. **face to face.** Ge 32:30n. Ex 33:11. Dt 34:10.

23. **Peace be.** Ge 32:30. 43:23. Ps 85:8. Da 10:19. Jn 14:27. 20:19, 21, 26. Ro 1:7.

24. **built.** Jg 21:4. Ge 33:20. Jsh 22:10, 26-28. **altar.** Ge +8:20. +13:18. **Jehovah-shalom.** *S#3073h, only here. Ex +*15:26. that is, *the Lord send peace.* Ge 22:14. Ex 17:15. Je 23:6. 33:16. Ezk 48:35. **Shalom.** Le 3:1. 7:11. Is 9:6. *26:3. Lk 2:14. Jn 14:27. 16:33. Ro 5:1. 15:13. Ph *4:7. Ep 2:14, 15, 17. Col *1:20. He 7:1, 2. **unto this day.** Jg 1:21. Ge +*19:38. Dt +29:4. Jsh +4:9. **Ophrah.** Jg 8:32.

25. **Take thy father's.** Ge 35:2. Jb 22:23. Ps 101:2. **even.** or, and. **throw.** 1 K 18:21, 30. 19:10, 14. Mt 6:24. 2 C 6:15-17. **Baal.** i.e. *possessor, owner,* *S#1168h. ver. 28, 30, 31, 32. Jg 2:11, 13. 3:7. 8:33. 10:6, 10. 1 S 7:4. 12:10. 1 K 16:31, 32, 32. 18:18, 19, 21, 22, 25, 26, 26, 40. 19:18. 22:53. 2 K 3:2. 10:18,

19, 19, 19, 20, 21, 21, 21, 22, 23, 23, 23, 25, 26, 27, 27, 28. 11:18, 18. 17:16. 21:3. 23:4, 5. 1 Ch 4:33. 5:5. 8:30. 9:36. 2 Ch 17:3. 23:17, 17. 24:7. 28:2. 33:3. 34:4. Je 2:8, 23. 7:9. 9:14. 11:13, 17. 12:16. 19:5, 5. 23:13, 27. 32:29, 35. Ho 2:8, 13, 17. 11:2. 13:1. Zp 1:4. **thy father.** Mt 10:37. Ac 4:19. 5:29. **cut down.** Jg 3:7. Ex 34:13. Dt 7:5.

26. **build.** 2 S 24:18. **altar.** Ge +13:18. **rock.** Heb. strong place. Da 11:7, 10, 31. Na 1:7. **the ordered place.** *or*, an orderly manner. Ex 39:37. Le 24:6. 1 S 4:2. 1 Ch 12:38. 1 C 14:33, 40.

27. **and did.** Dt 4:1, 2. Mt 16:24. Jn *2:5. 15:14. Ga 1:16. 1 Th 2:4. **he did it.** Ps 112:5. Jn 3:2.

28. **cast down.** ver. 30, 31, 32.

29. **they said, Gideon.** i.e. *they*, some of the people who may have noticed the operations.

30. **Bring.** Je 26:11. 50:38. Jn 16:2. Ac 26:9. Ph 3:6.

31. **Will ye plead.** The words are very emphatic: "Will ye plead in earnest (*tereevoon*) for Baal? Will ye really save (*tosheeoon*) him? If he be God (*Elohim*), let him contend for himself, seeing his altar is broken down." Ex 23:2. Nu 14:6. Ep *5:11. **let him be.** Dt 13:5, etc. 17:2-7. 1 K 18:40. **if he be.** 1 K 18:27, 29. Ps 115:4-7. Is 41:23. 46:1, 7. Je 10:5, 11. 1 C 8:4.

32. **Jerubbaal. that is,** Let Baal plead. *S#3378h. Jg 7:1. 8:29, 35. 9:1, 2, 5, 5, 16, 19, 24, 28, 57. 1 S *12:11. 2 S ●11:21. Jerubbesheth: that is, Let the shameful thing plead. Je 11:13. Ho 9:10.

33. **Then all.** Ps 3:1. 27:2, 3. 118:10-12. Is 8:9, 10. Ro 8:35-39. **children.** ver. 3. Jg 8:10, 11. 1 Ch 5:19, 20. Jb 1:3. **went over.** Jg 7:24. Jsh 3:16, 17. **the valley.** Jsh 17:16. 19:18. 1 S 29:1, 11. 2 S 4:4. 1 K 18:45. 21:1.

34. **the Spirit.** Heb. *ruach*, Ge +41:38. Jg 3:10. 13:25. 14:19. 15:14. 1 S 10:6. 11:6. 16:14. 1 Ch 12:18. 2 Ch 24:20. Ps 51:11. 1 C 12:8-11. **came upon.** Heb. clothed. 1 Ch 12:18. 2 Ch 24:20. Ro *13:14. Ga *3:27. **blew.** Jg 3:27. Nu 10:3. **Abiezer.** ver. 11. Jg 8:2. Jsh 17:2. **was gathered.** Heb. was called. Jg 4:13. 7:23, 24. 18:22, 23. 1 S 14:20.

35. **messengers.** 2 Ch 30:6-12. **Manasseh.** The tribe to which Gideon himself belonged. **Naphtali.** These three tribes lay nearest to him on the north.

36. **If thou wilt.** ver. 14, 17-20. Ex 4:1-9. 2 K 20:8, 9. Ps 103:13, 14. Mt 16:1. or, art savior of Israel. 1 S 14:39. 2 K 13:5. Is *43:3. 45:15.

37. **Behold.** Dt 32:2. Ps 72:6. Ho 6:3, 4. 14:5. **floor.** or, threshing floor. Ge 50:10. **dew.** Ge 27:28, 39. **only.** Ps 147:19, 20. Mt 10:5, 6. 15:24. **dry.** or, drought. Ge 31:40. **all the earth.** i.e. upon all that spot of ground which adjoineth to and encompasseth the fleece (Matthew Poole). ʃ171.O.3. Synecdoche of the Whole, Ge +41:57. **then shall I know.** 1 S 14:8-10. Lk 2:12. ●11:29.

38. **thrust.** or, presseth. Jb 39:15. Is 1:6. **wringed.** Ps 75:8. Is 51:17. Ezk 23:34. **a bowl.** Jg 5:25. Is 35:7.

39. **Let not thine.** Ge 18:32. Ex 32:22. **prove.** Ge 22:1. Ec 2:1. **let it now.** Ge +22:15. 1 S 10:22. **dry.** Ps 107:33-35. Is 35:6, 7. 43:19, 20. 50:2. Mt 8:12. 21:43. Ac 13:46. 22:21. 28:28. Ro 11:12-22.

40. **did so.** To satisfy the soul of his servant who trusted in him (Young). Nowhere else in Scripture is there an example of what is popularly called "putting out the fleece" as a means of discerning God's guidance. It would be especially wrong to specify to God that if a certain thing happens in a particular way, that would

be His indication that a particular course of action is in accordance with His will. As Scripture nowhere else recommends this procedure to obtain a knowledge of God's direction in a matter, it would be foolhardy—though many godly sincere persons have testified to God's leading them by this means—to do so. Such a procedure violates the whole tenor of the rest of Scripture. Guidance is to be sought from God's written word (Ps 119:105. 2 T 3:16, 17), which provides basic principles for making wise decisions (Pr 1:4. 3:5, 6. Je 10:23), not the caprice of circumstance (Ge 24:44n), however contrived (Ro 10:17. 2 C *5:7). See related notes (2 K 12:7n, 10n. 13:9n, 18n).

JUDGES 7

Gideon's army of thirty-two thousand is tried by divine directions, and reduced to three hundred men, 1-8. He is sent into the enemy's camp by night, and encouraged by hearing a dream interpreted, 9-15. He divides his army into three companies, giving each man a trumpet, and a lamp in a pitcher, 16-18. The Midianites are thrown into confusion and put to flight, 19-22. The Israelites intercept their flight, and take their princes Oreb and Zeeb, whom they put to death, 23-25.

1. **Jerubbaal.** It appears that *Jerubbaal* had now become the surname of Gideon. Jg 6:32. **rose up.** Ge 22:3. Jsh 3:1. 6:12. Ec 9:10. **Harod.** i.e. *trembling*, *S#5878h, only here. 2 S 23:8, 25. **Midianites.** Jg 6:33. **Moreh.** Ge 12:6. Dt 11:29, 30.

2. **too many.** 1 S 14:6. 2 Ch 14:11. Is 40:29. Zc *4:6. 12:7. 1 C 1:27-29. 2:4, 5. 2 C 4:7. 10:4, 5. *12:10. **Israel.** Dt 32:27. Is 2:11, 17. Je 9:23. Ro 3:27. 11:18. 1 C 1:29. 2 C 4:7. Ep 2:9. Ja 4:6. **Mine own.** Dt 8:17. Is 10:13. Ezk 28:2, 17. Da 4:30. Hab 1:16. Zc *4:6.

3. **Whosoever.** Dt *20:8. Mt 13:21. Lk 14:25-33. Re 17:14. *21:8. **mount Gilead.** Gideon was certainly not at mount Gilead, east of Jordan, at this time; but rather near mount **Gilboa**, west of Jordan. 1 S 31:1. 2 S 1:21. Calmet thinks there must either have been two Gileads, which does not appear from Scripture to have been the case, or that the Hebrew text is corrupt, and that for *Gilead* we should read *Gilboa*. This reading, though adopted by Houbigant, is not confirmed by any MS. or version. Dr. Hales endeavors to reconcile the whole, by the supposition that in Gideon's army there were many eastern Manassites from mount Gilead, near the Midianites; and therefore proposes to read "Whosoever from mount Gilead is fearful and afraid, let him return (home) and depart early." **twenty.** Mt 20:16.

4. **people.** Ps 33:16. **I will.** Ge 22:1. 1 S 16:7. Jb 23:10. Ps 7:9. 66:10. Je 6:27-30. Ml 3:2, 3.

5. **lappeth.** The original word *yalok*, is precisely the sound which the dog makes in lapping. It appears that it is not unusual for the Arabs to drink water out of the palms of their hands; and, from this account, we learn that the Israelites did so occasionally. From the letters of Busbequius we learn, that the Eastern people are not in the habit of drinking standing. The 300 men, who satisfied their thirst in the most expeditious manner, by this sufficiently indicated their spirit, and alacrity to follow Gideon in his dangerous enterprise; while the rest showed their love of ease, self-indulgence, effeminacy, and want of courage. Lk 16:10.

7. **By the.** ver. 18-22. 1 S 14:6. Is 41:14-16.

8. **trumpets.** Jg 3:27. Le 23:24. +25:9. Nu 10:9. Jsh 6:4, 20. Is *27:13. 1 C *15:52. **unto his tent.** Jg 19:9mg. **in the valley.** Jg 6:32.

9. **the same.** Ge 46:2, 3. Jb 4:13. 33:15, 16. Mt 1:20. 2:13. Ac 18:9, 10. 27:23. **Arise.** Jsh 1:5-9. Is 41:10-16. 43:1, 2. **I have delivered.** Jg 3:10, 28. 4:14, 15. 2 Ch 16:8, 9. 20:17.

10. **if thou fear.** Jg 4:8, 9. Ex 4:10-14. **Phurah.** i.e. *a branch or bough; fruitful, foliage,* *S#6513h. ver. 11. **thy servant.** ver. 13. Jg 6:27.

11. **thou shalt.** ver. 13-15. Ge +18:10. 24:14. 27:5, 6. 1 S 14:8-12. **thine hands.** 1 S 23:16. Ezr 6:22. Ne 6:9. Is 35:3, 4. 2 C 12:9, 10. Ep 3:16. 6:10. Ph *4:13. **armed men.** *or,* ranks by five. Ex 13:18mg.

12. **the Midianites.** Jg 6:3, 5, 33. 1 K 4:30. **grasshoppers.** Jg 8:10. 2 Ch 14:9-12. Ps 3:1. 33:16. 118:10-12. Is 8:9, 10. **for multitude.** Is 60:6. **as the sand.** /102B, /138B, Ge +13:16. Ge 22:17. Is 48:19.

13. **lo, a cake.** Jg 3:15, 31. 4:9, 21. 6:15. Is 41:14, 15. Ho 12:10. 1 C 1:27.

14. **his fellow.** Nu 22:38. 23:5, 20. 24:10-13. Jb 1:10. **into his hand.** Ex 15:14, 15. Jsh 2:9, 24. 5:1. 2 K 7:6, 7.

15. **interpretation thereof.** Heb. breaking thereof. Ge 40:8. 41:11. S#7667h. Le 21:19 (broken). 24:20 (breach). Jb 41:25 (breakings). Pr 15:4. 16:18 (destruction). Is +51:19mg. **worshipped.** Ge 24:26, 27, 48. Ex 4:30, 31. 2 Ch 20:18, 19. **Arise.** Jg 4:14. 2 C 10:4-6.

16. **three companies.** This small number of men, thus divided, would be able to encompass the whole camp of the Midianites. Concealing the lamps in the pitchers, they would pass unobserved to their appointed stations; then, in the dead of the night, when most of the enemy were fast asleep, all at once breaking their pitchers one against another, with as much noise as they could, and blowing the trumpets and shouting, they would occasion an exceedingly great alarm. The obedience of faith alone could have induced such an expedient, which no doubt God directed Gideon to employ (Scott). **a trumpet.** Heb. trumpets in the hand of all of them. **empty.** 1 C 1:27, 28. 2 C 4:7. **lamps.** *or,* fire-brands, *or* torches. Jg 15:4, 5. Ge 15:17. Jb 12:5.

17. **Look on.** Jg 9:48. Mt 16:24. 1 C *11:1. He 13:7. 1 P 5:3. **do likewise.** Jn 13:15.

18. **blow ye.** ver. 20. **The sword.** The word *cherev,* sword, necessarily implied, and rightly supplied by our venerable translators from ver. 20, is found in this place, in the Chaldee, Syriac, and Arabic, and in eight MSS.; and evidently appears to be genuine. 1 S 17:47. 2 Ch 20:15-17.

19. **in the beginning.** Ex 14:24. Mt 25:6. 1 Th 5:2, 3. Re 16:15. **they blew.** ver. 8. **brake.** ver. 16. Ps 2:9. Je 13:13, 14. 19:1-11.

20. **blew.** How astonishing and overwhelming must the effect be, in a dark night, of the sudden glare of 300 torches, darting their splendor in the same instant on the half-awakened eyes of the terrified Midianites; accompanied with the clangor of 300 trumpets, alternately mingled with the thundering shout of *cherev yehowah oolegidon,* "The sword of Jehovah and of Gideon!" Nu 10:1-10. Jsh 6:4, 16, 20. Is 27:13. 1 C 15:52. 1 Th 4:16. **brake.** 2 C 4:7. He 11:4. 2 P 1:15. **sword.** /22D5D, Dt +32:41.

21. **stood.** Ex 14:13, 14. 2 Ch 20:17. Is 30:7, 15. **all the host.** Ex 14:25. 2 K 7:6, 7. Jb 15:21, 22. Pr 28:1.

22. **blew.** Jsh 6:4, 16, 20. 2 C 4:7. **the Lord.** 1 S 14:16-20. 2 Ch 20:23. Ps 83:9. Is 9:4. 19:2. **against his.** Zc 14:13. **Bethshittah.** i.e. *house (or place) of shittim wood; the acacia house; house of the scourge,* *S#1029h. **in.** *or,* toward. **Zererath.** i.e. *cooling; straitness,* *S#6888h. Probably the same as *Zartanah,* 1 K 4:12. **border.** Heb. lip. Ge 11:1mg. Ex 39:19. 1 K 9:26mg. 2 K +2:13mg. Jb 2:10. 11:2mg. Pr 10:8mg, 10mg. 17:7mg, 28. Is 19:18mg. 36:5mg. 57:19. Ezk 3:5mg. 47:7mg. Da 12:5mg. Zp 3:9mg. **Abelmeholah.** i.e. *a meadow of dancing; mourning of dancing,* *S#65h. Situated, according to Eusebius, 16 miles south from Scythopolis, or Bethshan. 1 K 4:12. 19:16. **Tabbath.** i.e. *good,* *S#2888h. Probably the town of Thabas, mentioned by Eusebius, 13 miles from Neapolis, or Shechem, towards Scythopolis.

23. **gathered.** Jg 6:35. 1 S 14:21, 22.

24. **sent.** Jg 3:27. Ro 15:30. Ph 1:27. **mount.** /121J7A, Jsh +13:6. **take before.** Jg 3:28. 12:5. **Bethbarah.** i.e. *house or place of passage,* *S#1012h. Probably the same as *Bethabara,* beyond Jordan, and at the ford where the Hebrews passed under the direction of Joshua. Jn 1:28.

25. **two princes.** Jg 8:3. Ps 83:11, 12. **rock.** Jsh 7:26. Is 10:26. **Oreb.** i.e. *a raven,* *S#6159h. Jg 8:3. Ps 83:11. Is 10:26. Eusebius and Jerome speak of a small place called Araba, three miles west from Scythopolis, which is supposed by some to have had its name from Oreb. (1) One of the princes of Midian whom Gideon defeated, and who was slain by the Ephraimites near the river Jordan, Jg 7:25; 8:3; Ps 83:11. (2) A rock named after Oreb, a prince of Midian, Jg 7:25; Is 10:26. **Zeeb.** i.e. *a wolf,* *S#2062h. Jg 8:3. Ps 83:11. **the rock.** Jg 6:21. **winepress.** Jg 6:11. Nu 18:27, 30. Dt 16:13. 2 K 6:27. **and brought.** 1 S 17:51, 54. 2 K 10:6, 7. Mt 14:8, 11. Among the ancient nations, the head of the conquered chief was usually brought to the conqueror. Thus Pompey's head was brought to Caesar, Cicero's head to Mark Antony, and the heads of Ahab's children to Jehu (2 K 10:6, 7). These barbarities are seldom practiced now, except among the Mohammedans or the savages of Africa and America; and for the credit of human nature, it is to be wished that such atrocities had never been committed. **on the other side.** The words *maiaiver lyyarden* may denote at the passage of Jordan or from beyond Jordan. Gideon does not appear to have yet passed the Jordan. Jg 8:4.

JUDGES 8

The Ephraimites take offence, but are pacified by Gideon, 1-3. He pursues the Midianites: the men of Succoth and Penuel insolently refuse relief to his company: he threatens to chastise them; which he does, after he has taken Zebah and Zalmunna, 4-17. He puts Zebah and Zalmunna to death, because they had slain his brethren, 13-21. He refuses the government offered him: but asks the earrings out of the spoil, and of these he makes an ephod, which proves an occasion of idolatry, 22-27. Midian is subdued, 28. Gideon's family and death; and Israel's idolatry and ingratitude, 29-35.

1. **the men.** Jg 12:1-6. 2 S 19:41. Jb 5:2. Ec 4:4.

Ja 4:5, 6. **Why**, etc. Heb. What thing *is* this thou hast done unto us? **sharply.** Heb. strongly. Pr *15:1. 25:15.

2. **What.** 1 C 13:4-7. Ga 5:14, 15. Ph 2:2, 3. Ja 1:19, 20. 3:13-18. **Is not the.** That is, the Ephraimites have performed more important services than Gideon and his men had achieved. Jg 6:15. **Abi-ezer.** Jg 6:11, 34.

3. **God.** Jg 7:24, 25. Ps 44:3. 115:1. 118:14-16. Jn 4:37. Ro 12:3, 6. 15:18, 19. 1 C 4:7. Ph +*2:3. **Then.** Pr *15:1. 16:32. 25:11, 15. **anger.** Heb. spirit. Heb. *ruach*, Ge +26:35. √121A10, Ge +26:35.

4. **faint.** 1 S 14:28, 29, 31, 32. 30:10. 2 C 4:8, 9, 16. Ga 6:9. He 12:1-4.

5. **Succoth.** Ge 33:17. Ps 60:6. **loaves.** Ge 14:18. Dt 23:4. 1 S 25:5, 8, 18. 2 S 17:28, 29. 3 J 6-8. **Zebah.** i.e. *a sacrifice*, ✻S#2078h. ver. 6, 7, 10, 12, 12, 15, 15, 18, 21, 21. Ps 83:11. **Zalmunna.** i.e. *a shadow withheld; shelter is denied*, ✻S#6759h. ver. 6, 7, 10, 12, 12, 15, 15, 18, 21, 21. Ps 83:11.

6. **Are the.** Jg 5:23. Ge 25:13. 37:25, 28. 1 S 25:10, 11. 1 K *20:11. 2 K 14:9. Pr 18:23. Ph 2:21.

7. **tear.** Heb. thresh. ver. 16.

8. **Penuel.** Ge 32:30, 31. 1 K 12:25.

9. **I come.** 1 K 22:27, 28. **I will break.** ver. 17.

10. **Karkor.** i.e. *soft, level ground; battering down; excavation*, ✻S#7174h. If this were the name of a place, it is no where else mentioned. Some contend that *karkor* signifies *rest*; and the Vulgate renders it *requiescebant, rested*. This seems the most likely; for it is said (ver. 11) that Gideon "smote the host: for the host was secure." **children.** Jg 7:12. **fell an hundred,** etc. *or,* an hundred and twenty thousand, every one drawing a sword. Jg 7:22. 20:2, 15, 17, 25, 35, 46. 2 K 3:26. 2 Ch 13:17. 28:6, 8. Is 37:36.

11. **Nobah.** *Nobah* took its name from an Israelite who conquered it; and is said by Eusebius to have been, in his time, a forsaken place eight miles south from Heshbon. 1 Ch 2:23n. **Jogbehah.** *Jogbehah* was probably near Nobah. Nu 32:+35, 42. **secure.** Jg 18:27. 1 S 15:32. 30:16. 1 Th 5:3.

12. **took.** Jsh 10:16-18, 22-25. Jb 12:16-21. 34:19. Ps 83:11. Am 2:14. Re 6:15, 16. 19:19-21. **discomfited.** Heb. terrified. 2 S 17:2.

13. **before.** The words *milmaaleh haichaires* should, most probably, be rendered "from the ascent of Chares;" which is the reading of the LXX., Syriac, Arabic, and Houbigant.

14. **caught.** Jg 1:24, 25. 1 S 30:11-15. **described.** Heb. writ.

15. **upbraid.** ver. 6, 7. Is 32:5, 6. 58:10.

16. **the elders.** ver. 7. Pr 10:13. 19:29. Ezr 2:6. **thorns.** Mi 7:4. **taught.** Heb. made to know. 1 S 14:12. 16:3. Pr 26:3. Ro 13:4. Instead of *wyyoda*, Houbigant, Le Clerc, and others read *wyyadosh*, "and he tore or threshed;" and this is not only agreeable to what Gideon threatened (ver. 7), but is supported by the LXX., Vulgate, Chaldee, Syriac, and Arabic. The Hebrew text might easily have been corrupted simply by the change of the letter *shin* into the letter *ayin*, letters very similar to each other.

17. **he beat.** ver. 9. 1 K 12:25. Pr 16:18.

18. **Tabor.** Jg 4:6. Jsh 19:22. Ps 89:12. **As thou art.** Ps 12:2. Ju 16. **resembled.** Heb. according to the form of, etc. 1 S 16:18.

19. **sons of my mother.** Ge 27:29. Ps *69:8. SS 1:6.

as the Lord liveth. Ru 3:13. Je 4:2.

20. **Up and slay.** Jsh 10:24, 25. 1 S 15:33. Ps 149:9.

21. **Rise thou.** It was disgraceful to fall by the hands of a child; and death by the blows of such a person must be much more lingering and tormenting. Some have employed children to dispatch captives. Jg 9:54n. 1 S 31:3, 5. Re 9:6. **his strength.** Dt 33:25. Ps 83:11, 12. **slew.** Ps 83:1. **ornaments.** *or,* ornaments like the moon. ver. 26. Is 3:18.

22. **Rule thou.** Jg 9:8-15. Dt 17:14, 15. 1 S 8:5, 7. 10:19. 12:12. Jn 6:15.

23. **I will.** Jg 2:18. 10:18. 11:9-11. Lk 22:24-27. 2 C 1:24. 1 P 5:3. **the Lord.** 1 S 8:6, 7. 10:19. 12:12. Is 33:22. 63:19.

24. **give me.** Ge 24:22, 53. Ex 12:35. 32:3. 1 P 3:3-5. **because.** Ge 16:10, 11. 25:13. 37:25, 28. 1 S 25:11. 1 K 20:11.

26. **collars.** *or,* sweet jewels. **purple.** Est 8:15. Je 10:9. Ezk 27:7. Lk 16:19. Jn 19:2, 5. Re 17:4. 18:12, 16. **chains.** ver. 21.

27. **an ephod.** Jg 17:5. 18:14, 17. Ex 28:6-12. 1 S 23:9, 10. Is √8:20. Ho 3:4. **Ophrah.** ver. 32. Jg 6:11, 24. Dt 12:5. **a whoring.** ver. 33. Jg 2:17. Ex 23:33. +34:15. Le 17:7. Ps 73:27. 106:39. Ho 2:2. 4:12-14. **a snare.** ver. 33. Dt 7:16.

28. **was Midian.** Ps 83:9-12. Is 9:4. 10:26. **lifted.** √121S3E2. Metonymy of the Adjunct B606. Connected words and phrases: "to lift up the head" is put for lifting up the soul, taking courage, or rejoicing. For other instances of this figure see Ps 83:2. Lk 21:28. **forty years.** Jg 3:11, 30. 5:31.

29. **Jerubbaal.** Jg 6:32. 1 S 12:11. **in his own house.** Ne 5:14, 15.

30. **threescore.** Jg 9:2, 5. 10:4. 12:9, 14. Ge 46:26. Ex 1:5. 2 K 10:1. **of his body begotten.** Heb. going out of his thigh. √88, Ge +24:2n. Ge 35:11. 46:26mg. Ex 1:5mg. **many wives.** Ge 2:24. +4:19. 7:7. Le 18:18. Dt 17:17. 2 S 3:2-5. 5:13-16. 1 K 11:3. Ml *2:15. Mt *19:5-8. Ep 5:31-33.

31. **concubine.** Jg 9:1-5. Ge 16:15. 22:24. **Shechem.** Ge 12:6. Jsh +*20:7. **called.** Heb. set. Da 1:7. **Abimelech.** i.e. *my father is king*, or *father of a king.* Jg 9:18. Ge 20:2.

32. **died in.** Ge 15:15. 25:8. Jsh 24:29, 30. 1 Ch 29:28. Jb 5:26. 42:17. **sepulchre.** Heb. *qeber*, Ge +23:4. **Ophrah.** ver. 27. Jg 6:24.

33. **as soon.** Jg 2:7-10, 17, 19. Ge +40:23. Jsh 24:31. 2 K 12:2. 2 Ch 24:17, 18. Ps 31:12. **went.** ver. 27. Jg 2:17. Ex 34:15, 16. Je 3:9. **Baal-berith.** Literally, *the lord of the covenant*, ✻S#1170h. Jg 9:4h, 46.

34. **remembered.** Ps 78:11, 42. 106:13, 21. Ec 12:1. Je 2:32.

35. **showed.** Jg 9:5, 16-19. Ec 9:14, 15. **Jerubbaal.** Rather, *Jerubbaal Gideon*; as we say, *Simon Peter*, or call a person by his Christian and surname. Gideon was a mighty man of valor, a true patriot, evidently disinterested and void of ambition. He loved his country, and hazarded his life for it; but refused the kingdom, when it was offered to him and his heirs. The act of making the ephod was totally wrong; yet, probably it was done with no reprehensible design.

JUDGES 9

Abimelech, son of Gideon by a concubine, conspires with the Shechemites, murders his brethren, and is made king, 1-6. Jotham, by a parable, exposes their ingratitude, and foretels their ruin, 7-21. The Shechemites conspire with Gaal against Abimelech; Zebul sends him word; he overcomes them, and sows their city with salt, 22-45. They retire to the temple of Baalberith, and are burnt in it, 46-49. Abimelech is slain at Thebez by a woman with a piece of a millstone, and Jotham's curse is fulfilled, 50-57.

1. **Abimelech**. Jg 8:31. 2 S 11:21. **Shechem**. Ge 33:18. 34:2. 1 K 12:1. **brethren**. ☞171G, Ge +13:8. **communed**. 2 S 15:6. 1 K 12:3, 20. Ps 83:2-4. Je 18:18.

2. **Whether**, etc. Heb. What is good? whether, etc. **threescore**. Jg 8:30. **your bone**. Ge 29:14. 2 S 5:1. 19:13. 1 Ch 11:1. Ep +*5:30. He 2:14.

3. **spake**. Ps 10:3. Pr 1:11-14. **to follow**. Heb. after. **our brother**. Ge 29:15.

4. **house**. ver. 46-49. Jg 8:33. **vain**, etc. *anashim raikim oophochazim*, "worthless and dissolute men;" persons who were living on the public, and had nothing to lose. Such was the foundation of his Babel government. By a cunning management of such unprincipled men most revolutions are brought about. Jg 11:3. 1 S 22:2. 2 Ch 13:7. Jb 30:8. Pr 12:11. Ac 17:5.

5. **at Ophrah**. Jg 6:24. **slew**. 2 K 10:17. 11:1, 2. 2 Ch 21:4. Mt 2:16, 20. **Jotham**. i.e. *Jehovah is perfect*, ✻S#3147h. ver. 7, 21, 57. 2 K 15:5, 7, 30, 32, 36, 38. 16:1. 1 Ch 2:47. 3:12. 5:17. 2 Ch 26:21, 23. 27:1, 6, 7, 9. Is 1:1. 7:1. Ho 1:1. Mi 1:1. (1) The youngest son of Gideon, who escaped when his brothers were slain by Abimelech, Jg 9:5, 7, 21, 57. (2) A son of Azariah (or Uzziah), king of Judah, who ruled during part of his father's life (because he had been smitten with leprosy), and on his death succeeded him as king, 2 K 15:5, 7, 30, 32, 36, 38. He reigned twenty-three years, including seven years he ruled during his father's life. (3) A descendant of Judah, 1 Ch 2:47.

6. **the house**. 2 S 5:9. 2 K 12:20. **Millo**. Probably the name of a person of note in Shechem. **plain**. *or*, oak. Jsh 24:26. 1 K 12:1, 20, 25.

7. **mount Girizim**. Dt 11:29. 27:12. Jsh 8:33. Jn 4:20. **lifted**. ☞144A12, Ge +22:13. **Hearken**. Ps 18:40, 41. 50:15-21. Pr 1:28, 29. 21:13. 28:9. Is 1:15. 58:6-10. Mt 18:26-34. Ja 2:13.

8. **The trees**. ☞. Allegory: by continued Hypocatastasis B749, Ga +4:24. This is the most ancient fable or *aplogne* extant; and is extremely beautiful, apposite, and intelligible. 2 K 14:9. Ezk 17:3, etc. Da 4:10, etc. **olive tree**. The *zayith* or olive tree was the most useful of all the trees of the forest; as the *bramble* was the meanest and most worthless. **Reign**. Jg 8:22, 23.

9. **fatness**. Ps 23:5. Ro 11:17. **wherewith**. Ex 29:2, 7, 40. 35:5, 8, 14. Le 2:1. 1 K 19:15, 16. Ps 89:20. 104:15. Ac 4:27. 10:38. 1 J 2:20. **God**. Heb. *elohim*, rather *gods*; the parable being adapted to the idolatrous Shechemites. **to be promoted over the trees**. Heb. up and down for other trees. Jb 1:7. 2:2.

11. **Should I**. Lk 13:6, 7.

13. **cheereth**. Nu 15:5, 7, 10. 28:7. Ps 104:15. Pr 31:6, 7. Ec 10:19. SS 1:2. Is 55:1. Zc 10:7.

14. **bramble**. *or*, thistle. 2 K 14:9.

15. **shadow**. Is 30:2. Da 4:12. Ho 14:7. Mt 13:32. **let fire**. ver. 20, 49. Nu 21:28. Is 1:31. Ezk 19:14. Ga 5:15. **the cedars**. 2 K 14:9. Ps 104:16. Is 2:13. 37:24. Ezk 31:3.

16. **according**. Jg 8:35.

17. **fought**. Jg 7:20. 8:4-10. **adventured his life**. Heb. cast his life. Jg 5:18. 12:3. Est 4:16. Ro *5:8. 16:4. Re 12:11. **life**. Heb. *nephesh*, soul. Ge +44:30. ☞121A7, Ge +9:5.

18. **are risen**. ver. 5, 6. Jg 8:35. Ps 109:4. **Abimelech**. ver. 6, 14. Jg 8:31.

19. **rejoice**. Is 8:6. Ph 3:3. Ja 4:16.

20. **let fire come out**. ver. 15, 23, 56, 57. Jg 7:22. 2 Ch 20:22, 23. Ps 21:9, 10. 28:4. 52:1-5. 120:3, 4. 140:10.

21. **Beer**. Probably the *Beer* mentioned by Mr. Maundrell, three hours and a half, or about ten miles, north of Jerusalem, towards Shechem. It is situated toward the south, on an easy declivity; and has a fountain of excellent water at the bottom of the hill, from which it has taken its name. Close to the well are the mouldering walls of a ruined khan; and on the summit of the hill two large arches still remain of a ruined convent. Dr. Richardson says, that it seems to have been once a place of considerable consequence. Nu 21:16. Jsh 19:8. 2 S 20:14.

23. A.M. 2771. B.C. 1233. An. Ex. Is. 258. **God sent**. That is, God permitted the evil spirit of jealousy, treachery, and discord, to break out between Abimelech and the Shechemites. ver. 15, 20. 1 S 16:14-16. 18:9, 10. 1 K 12:15. 22:22, 23. 2 Ch 10:15. 18:19-22. Is 19:2, 14. Am +√3:6. 2 Th 2:11, 12. Ja √1:13, 14. **dealt**. ver. 16. Is 33:1. Mt 7:2. **evil spirit**. Heb. *ruach*, used here of an evil spirit being, whether evil angel or demon. For the other uses of *ruach*, see Ge 6:3n. 1 S 16:14, 15, 16, 23, 23. 18:10. 19:9. 1 K 22:21, 22, 23. 2 Ch 18:20, 21, 22. Mt +*8:16.

24. **That the**. 1 S 15:33. 1 K 2:32. Est 9:25. Ps 7:15, 16. Pr 26:27. Je *51:56. Mt 7:2. 23:34-36. **aided him in the killing of**. Heb. strengthened his hands to kill. Sooner or later, God will make inquisition for blood, and will return it on the heads of those that shed it. Accessaries will be reckoned with, as well as principals, in that and other sins. The Shechemites who countenanced Abimelech's pretensions, aided and abetted him in his bloody project, and avowed the fact by making him king after he had done it, must fall with him—fall by him—and fall first. Those that combine together to do wickedly, are justly dashed in pieces one against another. Blood cannot be a lasting cement to any interest. Ge +*6:13 (T#566).

25. **set liers**. Jsh 8:4, 12, 13. Pr *1:11, 13.

26. **Gaal**. i.e. *a loathing*, ✻S#1603h. ver. 28, 30, 31, 35, 36, 37, 39, 41. **brethren**. Ge 13:8. 19:7.

27. **merry**. *or*, songs. Ps *4:7. Is 16:9, 10. 24:7-9. Je 25:30. Am 6:3-6. **the house**. ver. 4. Jg 16:23. Ex 32:6, 19. Da 5:1-4, 23. **did eat**. Is 22:12-14. Lk 12:19, 20. 17:26-29. **cursed**. Le 24:11. 1 S 17:43. Ps 109:17.

28. **Who is Abimelech**. 1 S 25:10. 2 S 20:1. 1 K 12:16. **Zebul**. i.e. *habitation; abiding*, ✻S#2083h. ver. 30, 36, 36, 38, 41. **Hamor**. Ge 34:2, 6.

29. **would to God**. The very words and conduct of a sly, hypocritical demagogue. 2 S 15:4. 1 K 20:11. Ps 10:3. Ro 1:30, 31. **And he said**. Rather, "and I would say to Abimelech," as the LXX. renders; for, as Dr. Wall observes, this was probably not said in the presence of Abimelech; but at an intemperate feast, in his absence, when he boasted he would challenge him. **Increase thine army**. 2 S 2:14-17. 2 K 14:8. 18:23. Is 36:8, 9.

30. **kindled**. *or*, hot. Jg 10:7.

31. **privily.** Heb. craftily, or, to Tormah. Ps 119:118. Tormah is supposed to be the same place as Arumah in ver. 41. **they fortify.** Under pretense of repairing the walls and towers, they were actually putting the place in a state of defence, intending to seize on the government as soon as they found Abimelech coming against them.

32. **by night.** Jb 24:14-17. Ps 36:4. Pr 1:11-16. 4:16. Ro 3:15.

33. **as thou shalt find.** Heb. as thine hand shall find. Le 25:26mg. 1 S 10:7. 25:8. Ec 9:10.

35. **Gaal.** Of this person we know no more than is here recorded. He was probably one of the descendants of the Canaanites, who hoped, from the state of the public mind and their disaffection to Abimelech, to cause a revolution, and thus to restore the ancient government as it was under Hamor, the father of Shechem. Josephus says he was a man of authority, who sojourned with them, with his armed men and kinsmen; and that the Shechemites desired that he would allow them a guard during the vintage. **the people.** ver. 44.

36. **seest the shadow.** Doubdan states, that in some parts of the Holy Land there are many detached rocks scattered up and down, some growing out of the ground, and others fragments broken off from rocky precipices, the shadow of which, it appears, Josephus thought might be most naturally imagined to look like troups of men at a distance, rather than that of the mountains; for he represents Zebul as saying to Gaal, that he mistook the shadow of the rocks for men. Ezk 7:7. Mk 8:24.

37. **middle.** Heb. navel. Ezk 38:12mg. **Meonenim.** or, the regarders of the times. Dt 18:14. i.e. observers of clouds, *S#6049h (2 K +21:6), not mentioned elsewhere. 1 Ch ◐+*12:32n. Ps ◐74:9.

38. **Where is.** ver. 28, 29. 2 S 2:26, 27. 2 K 14:8-14. Je 2:28.

39. **Shechem.** 1 K 12:25.

40. **he fled before.** 1 K 20:18-21, 30.

41. **Arumah.** i.e. a high place; exalted, *S#725h. This place appears from the next verse to have been near Shechem; and is perhaps the same as Ruma (2 K 23:36), a village of Galilee, mentioned by Josephus, Bel. l. iii. c. 9. ver. 31n. **Zebul.** ver. 28, 30.

44. **rushed forward.** ver. 15, 20. Ga 5:15.

45. **he took.** ver. 20. **beat.** Dt 29:23. 1 K 12:25. 2 K 3:25. Ps 107:34mg. Ezk 47:11. Zp 2:9. Ja 2:13. **sowed.** Je 17:16. Salt in small quantities renders land extremely fertile; but too much destroys vegetation. Every place, says Pliny, in which salt is found is barren, and produces nothing. Hence the sowing of a place with salt was a custom in different nations to express permanent desolation. Sigonius observes, that when Milan was taken, A.D. 1162, the walls were razed, and it was sown with salt. And Brantome informs us, that it was an ancient custom in France, to sow the house of a man with salt, who had been declared a traitor to his king. Charles IX, king of France, the most base and perfidious of human beings, caused the house of Admiral Coligni (whom he and the Duke of Guise caused to be murdered, with thousands more of Protestants, on the eve of St. Bartholomew, 1572), to be sown with salt!

46. **tower.** Ge 11:4, 5. **an hold.** or, high place. Young notes, a "place for crying out" war (Is 42:13. Zp 1:14).

ver. 4, 27, 49. Jg 8:33. 1 S 13:6. 1 K 18:26. 2 K 1:2-4. Ps 115:8. Is 28:15-18. 37:38. **Berith.** i.e. covenant; to eat together, *S#1286h, only here. ver. 4. Jg 8:33.

48. **Zalmon.** i.e. a great shade. Ps 68:14. **What ye.** Jg 7:17, 18. Pr 1:11, 12. **me do.** Heb. I have done.

49. **put them.** ver. 15, 20. Ga 5:15. Ja 3:16.

50. **Thebez.** i.e. brilliancy; he gushed out, *S#8405h. 2 S 11:21. According to Eusebius, thirteen miles from Shechem, towards Scythopolis.

52. **Abimelech came.** ver. 48, 49. 2 K 14:10. 15:16.

53. **woman.** ver. 15, 20. 2 S 11:21. 20:21. Jb 31:3. Je 49:20. 50:45. **and all to.** An antiquated expression, meaning "full intention" to complete an object. "All to," observes Dr. Johnson, "is a particle of mere enforcement." The original is wattaritz eth gulgalto, which is simply, as the LXX. render, kai eklase to kranion auton, "and she brake his skull." Plutarch relates, that Pyrrhus was killed at the siege of Thebes, by a piece of a tile, which a woman threw upon his head. **brake.** S#7533h. Jg 10:8mg. Dt +28:33.

54. **Draw thy.** 1 S 31:4, 5. **And his young man.** It was a disgrace to be killed by a woman (compare Jg 8:21n). On this account, Seneca, the Tragedian, thus deplores the death of Hercules: "O turpe fatum! foemina Herculeae necis autor feritur"; "O dishonorable fate! a woman is reported to have been the author of the death of Hercules." Abimelech might also have been afraid, that if he fell thus mortally wounded into the hands of his enemies, they might treat him with cruelty and insult.

55. **when the men.** 2 S 18:16. 20:21, 22. 1 K 22:35, 36. Pr 22:10.

56. **God rendered.** ver. 24. Jb 31:3. Ps 9:12. 11:6. 58:10, 11. 94:23. Pr 5:22. Mt 7:2. Ac 28:4. Ga √6:7. Re 19:20, 21. Both the fratricide Abimelech and the unprincipled men of Shechem had the iniquity visited upon them of which they had been guilty. Man's judgment may be avoided; but there is no escape from that of God. How many houses have been sown with salt in France, by the just judgment of God, for the massacre of the Protestants on the eve of St. Bartholomew! See Note on ver. 45.

57. **upon them.** ver. 20, 24, 45. Jsh 6:26. 1 K 16:34. Jb 31:3. Ps 94:23. Pr *5:22.

JUDGES 10

Tola judges Israel in Shamir, 1, 2; and Jair, whose thirty sons had thirty cities, 3-5. The Israelites, relapsing into idolatry, are oppressed by the Philistines and Ammonites, 6-9. They cry to God, who sends them for help to their idols, 10-14. They deeply repent and he pities them, 15, 16. They consult about choosing a leader, 17, 18.

1. A.M. 2772. B.C. 1232. An. Ex. Is. 259. **arose.** Jg 2:16. 3:9. **defend.** or, deliver. Heb. save. ver. 12, 13. Jg 2:16. **Shamir.** Jsh 15:48. 1 K 16:23, 24, Shemer.

3. A.M. 2795. B.C. 1209. An. Ex. Is. 282. **a Gileadite.** Ge 31:48. Nu 26:29. 32:29, 39-41.

4. **rode.** Jg 5:10. 12:14. **called.** Nu 32:41. Dt 3:14. **Havoth-jair.** or, the villages of Jair.

5. **Camon.** i.e. abounding in stalks; an elevation; standing, *S#7056h.

6. A.M. 2817. B.C. 1187. An. Ex. Is. 304. **did evil.** Jg 2:11-13. 4:1. 6:1. 13:1. 1 S 12:10. A.M. 2799. B.C. 1205. An. Ex. Is. 286. **Baalim.** Jg 2:11-14. 3:7. 2 Ch

28:23. Ps 106:36. **the gods of Zidon**. 1 K 11:5, 7, 33. 16:31. 2 K 17:16, 29-31. 23:13. **the gods of the Philistines**. Jg 16:23. 1 S 5:2. 2 K 1:2, 3. Je 2:13. Ezk 16:25, 26.

7. **was hot**. Jg 2:14. Dt 29:20-28. 31:16-18. 32:16-22. Jsh 23:15, 16. Ps 74:1. Na 1:2, 6. **he sold**. Jg 4:2. 1 S 12:9, 10. Ps 44:12. Is 50:1.

8. **that year**. ver. 5. Is 30:13. 1 Th 5:3. **vexed**. *S#7492h. Ex 15:6 (dashed in pieces). **oppressed**. Heb. crushed. S#7533h. Jg 9:53. Dt +28:33 (crushed). 1 S 12:3, 4. 2 Ch 16:10. Jb *20:19mg. Is *42:3 (bruised). 58:6. La 1:15.

9. **passed**. Jg 3:12, 13. 6:3-5. 2 Ch 14:9. 20:1, 2. **distressed**. Dt 28:65. 1 S 28:15. 2 Ch 15:5.

10. **cried**. Jg 3:9. 1 S 12:10. Ps 106:43, 44. 107:13, 19, 28.

11. **did not I**. Jg 2:1-3. **Egyptians**. Ex 14:30. 1 S 12:8. Ne 9:9-11. Ps 78:51-53. 106:8-11. He 11:29. **Amorites**. Nu 21:21-25, 35. Ps 135:10, 11. **children**. Jg 3:11-15. **Philistines**. Jg 3:31.

12. **Zidonians**. *S#6722h. Jg ●5:19, etc. 18:7, 7. 1 K 11:1, 5, 33. 16:31. 2 K 23:13. 1 Ch 22:4. Ezk 32:30. **Amalekites**. Jg 6:3. **the Maonites**. ✛S#4584h. The LXX. have "the Midianites," which Dr. Wall thinks the true reading. But the Maonites might be a tribe of Arabs, inhabitants of Maon (Jsh 15:55. 1 S 23:24, 25. 25:2), which assisted Moab. 2 Ch 26:6, 7. Ps 106:42, 43.

13. **have forsaken me**. Jg 2:12. Dt 32:15. 1 Ch √28:9. Je *2:13. Jon 2:8.

14. **Go**. ♪60A, Ge +3:22. **cry unto**. Dt 32:26-28, 37, 38. 1 K *18:27, 28. 2 K 3:13. Jb 12:1. Pr 1:25-27. Ec 11:9. Is 10:3. Je *2:28.

15. **We have sinned**. 2 S 12:13. 24:10. Jb 33:27. Pr *28:13. 1 J √1:8-10. **do thou**. Jsh 9:25. 1 S 3:18. 2 S 10:12. 15:26. 24:17. Jb 1:21. 2:10. Jon 2:4. 3:9. Lk 15:18, 19. 23:40, 41. **seemeth**, etc. Heb. is good in thine eyes. 1 S 1:23. 3:18. 2 S 10:12. 15:26. 2 K 20:19. 1 Ch 19:13. Ps 39:9. Is 39:8. **deliver**. 2 S 24:14. Jb 34:31, 32.

16. **they put**. 2 Ch *7:14. 15:8. 33:15. Je 18:7, 8. Ezk 18:30-32. Ho 14:1-3, 8. **strange gods**. Heb. gods of strangers (S#5236h, Ex 12:43mg. Dt +*17:15). Ge 35:2, 4. Jsh 24:20. 1 S 7:3. **his soul**. Ge 6:6. Ps 78:38, 39. 106:44, 45. Is *63:9, +*10. Je 31:20. Ho 11:8. Lk 15:20. 19:41. Jn 11:34. Ep *4:30. He 3:10. 4:15. Heb. *nephesh*, Ge +34:3. Le +26:11. **grieved**. Heb. shortened. ♪22B, Ge +6:6. Jg 16:16. Nu 21:4. Jb 21:4. Pr 14:17, 29. Mi 2:7mg. Zc 11:8mg. Not that there is any grief in God; he has infinite joy and happiness in himself, which cannot be broken in upon by either the sins or the miseries of his creatures. Not that there is any change in God; for he is of one mind, and who can turn him? But his goodness is his glory; by it he proclaims his name, and magnifies it:—and as he is pleased to put himself into the relation of a father to his people, so he is pleased to represent his goodness to them by the compassion of a father to his children; for as he is the Father of lights (Ja 1:17), so is he the Father of mercies (Ex +*34:6, 7. Ps 62:12. 86:5, 15. 2 C *1:3).

17. **children**. ♪132F. Parallelism: Extended Alternation B356. The alternation is extended to consist of three or more lines. Here the pattern is ABC/ABC, involving the key words children/gathered/encamped; children/assembled/encamped. For another example

of this figure see Mt 6:19, 20, where the key words involved are treasures/moth and rust/thieves; treasures/moth nor rust/thieves. This figure abounds in the Scripture, and may be found displayed in the margins of the Companion Bible. **gathered together**. Heb. cried together. Jg 7:23. **Mizpeh**. Jg 11:3n, 11, 29. Ge +*31:49.

18. **What man**. Jg 1:1. 11:5-8. Is 3:1-8. 34:12. **he shall be**. Jg 11:11. 12:7. 1 S 17:25.

JUDGES 11

Jepthah, the base born son of Gilead, thrust out by his brethren, is chosen commander against the Ammonites, 1-11. He sends an embassy to their king, but in vain, 12-28. His rash vow, 29-31. He conquers the Ammonites, 32, 33. He is met by his only daughter, and is deeply distressed; she piously submits, and he performs his vow, 34-40.

1. **Jephthah**. ♪66, Ge +9:3. i.e. *he opens; whom God sets free*, *S#3316h. ver. 2, 3, 3, 5, 6, 7, 8, 9, 10, 11, 11, 12, 13, 14, 15, 28, 29, 30, 32, 34, 40. 12:1, 2, 4, 7, 7. Jsh ●15:43, Jiphtah. 1 S 12:11. He 11:32, called Jephthae. **a mighty**. Jg +6:12. 2 K 5:1. **son of**. Dt 23:2. **an harlot**. Heb. a woman, an harlot. Is +40:13mg. Je 3:3. Probably *zonah* should be rendered, as in Jsh 2:1n, a *hostess*, or *inn-keeper*: so Targum of Jonathan, *wehoo bar ittetha pundekeetha*, "and he was the son of a woman, a *tavern-keeper*." She was very probably a Canaanite, as she is called, ver. 2, a strange woman, *ishah achereth*, "a woman of another race;" and on this account his brethren drove him from the family, as not having a full right to the inheritance. Jg 16:1n. Ge ●38:21n. 1 K 3:16n.

2. **thrust out**. Ge 21:10. Dt 23:2. Ga 4:30. **a strange**. Pr 2:16. 5:3, 20. 6:24-26.

3. **from his brethren**. Heb. from the face of. ♪144A1, Ge +11:8. **Tob**. i.e. *good; goodness*, *S#2897h. ver. 5. Probably the same as *Ish-tob*; and appears to have been a part of Syria, near Zobah, Rehob, and Maachah, east of Jordan, and in the most northern part of the portion of Manasseh. If so, it could not be far from Gilead, the country of Jephthah. This country is called *Tobie* or *Tubin*, 1 Mac 5:13; and the Jews who inhabited this district, *Tubieni*, 2 Mac 12:17. 2 S 10:6, 8. **vain men**. Jg 9:4. 1 S 22:2. 27:2. 30:22-24. Jb 30:1-10. Ac 17:5.

4. A.M. 2817. B.C. 1187. An. Ex. Is. 304. **in process of time**. Heb. after days. Jg 10:8. 1 K 18:1. 2 Ch 21:19.

5. **made war**. Jg 10:9, 17, 18. **to fetch**. 1 S 10:27. 11:6, 7, 12. Ps 118:22, 23. Ac 7:35-39. 1 C 1:27-29.

7. **Did ye not hate**. Ge 26:27. 37:27. 45:4, 5. Pr 17:17. Is 60:14. Mt 23:37-39. Lk 13:25. Ac 7:9-14. Re 3:9.

8. **the elders**. Ex 8:8, 28. 9:28. 10:17. Jsh +20:4. 1 K 13:6. Lk 17:3, 4. **we turn**. Jg 10:18.

9. **If ye bring**. Nu 32:20-29.

10. **The Lord**. Ge 21:23. 31:50. 1 S 12:5. Je 29:23. 42:5. Ro 1:9. 2 C 11:31. **be witness**. Heb. be the hearer between us. Ge 16:5. *31:48, 50, 52, 53. Dt 1:16. 1 S 24:12. Je 42:5. **if we do**. Ex 20:7. Zc 5:4. Ml +*3:5.

11. **head**. ver. 8. **uttered**. 1 S 23:9-12. 1 K 3:7-9. 2 C 3:5. Ja *1:5, 17. **Jephthah uttered**. That is, upon his elevation, he immediately retired to his devotion, and in prayer spread the whole matter before God,

both his choice to the office, and his execution of the office, as one that had his eye ever toward the Lord, and would do nothing without him, —that leaned not to his own understanding or courage, but depended on the Almighty God, and his favor. This is an example worthy of universal imitation; in all our ways, whether great or apparently subordinate, let us acknowledge God and seek his direction. So shall we make our way prosperous, and obtain that peace which passeth all understanding (Jsh 1:8. Pr 3:5, 6. Ph 4:6, 7). Jephthah opened his campaign with prayer. Ex +*19:8. **before**. Jg 10:17. 20:1. 1 S 10:17. 11:15. **Mizpeh**. This *Mizpeh* was east of Jordan, in the mountains of Gilead (Ge +*31:49); and hence called Mizpeh of Gilead (ver. 29), to distinguish it from another place of the same name, west of Jordan, in the tribe of Judah, Jsh 15:38. Jsh 11:3n.

12. **sent messengers**. In this Jephthah acted in accordance with the law of Moses; and hence the justice of his cause would appear more forcibly to the people. Nu 20:14. 21:21. Dt 2:26. *20:10, 11. Pr 25:8, 9. Mt *18:15, 16. **What hast**. 2 S 16:10. 19:22. 1 K 17:18. 2 K 3:13. 9:18. 14:8-12. 2 Ch 35:21. Jn +*2:4. ✓85H. Erotesis; or, Interrogating: in refusals and denials B953. For other instances of this figure see Nu 23:8. Jsh 22:24. 2 S 16:10. 19:22. 1 K 17:18. 2 K 3:13. 2 Ch 35:21. Ho 14:8. Mt 8:29. Mk 1:24. 5:7. Lk 4:34. 8:28. Jn 2:4.

13. **Ammon**. Jsh 13:25. **Because Israel**. Nu 21:24-26. Pr 19:5, 9. **from Arnon**. That is, all the land which had belonged to the Amorites and the Moabites. **Jabbok**. Ge 32:22. Dt 2:37. 3:16.

14. **again unto**. Ps 120:7. Ro 12:18. He 12:14. 1 P 3:11.

15. **Israel took not**. Nu 21:13-15, 27-30. Dt 2:9, 19. 2 Ch 20:10. Ac 24:12, 13.

16. **But when**. The whole of these messages show, that Jephthah had well studied the book of Moses. His arguments are also very clear and cogent, and his demands reasonable; for he only required that the Ammonites should cease to harass a people who had neither injured them, nor intended to do so. **walked**. Nu 14:25. Dt 1:40. Jsh 5:6. **came to Kadesh**. Ge 14:7. Nu 13:26. 20:1. 33:36. Dt 1:46.

17. **sent messengers**. Nu 20:14-21. Dt 2:4-8, 29. **the king**. Dt 2:9. **abode**. Nu 20:1, 16.

18. **went**. Nu 20:22. 21:10-13. 33:37-44. Dt 2:1-8. **compassed**. Nu 21:4, etc. **came by**. Nu 21:11. **pitched**. Nu 21:13. 22:36.

19. **Israel sent**. Nu 21:21-35. Dt 2:26-34. 3:1-17. Jsh 13:8-12.

20. **Sihon trusted not**. Nu 21:23. Dt 2:32.

21. **Lord God**. Ne 9:22. Ps 135:10-12. 136:17-21. **they smote**. Nu 21:24, 25. Dt 2:33, 34. **so Israel**. Jsh 13:15-32.

22. **And they**. Dt 2:36. **from the wilderness**. From Arabia Deserta on the east, to Jordan on the west.

23. Jephthah shows that the Israelites did not take the land of the Moabites or Ammonites, but that of the *Amorites*, which they had conquered from Sihon their king; and although the Amorites had taken the lands in question from the Ammonites, yet the title by which Israel held them was good, because they took them, not from the Ammonites, but from the Amorites.

24. **Wilt not thou possess**. This is simply an *argu-*

mentum ad hominem ("an argument against the man," an appeal to the emotions, beside the point, and a logical fallacy; used here, however, in the sense of arguing on his own ground. This is the argument *a fortiori*, "with stronger reason, more conclusively"); in which Jephthah argues on the principles recognized by the King of Ammon. As if he had said, "You suppose that the land which you possess was given you by your god Chemosh; and therefore will not relinquish what you believe you hold by a divine right. Now, we know that Jehovah, our God, has given us the land of the Israelites; and therefore, we will not give it up." 1 K 20:23n. 2 K 17:26. Is 36:18n. **Chemosh**. Nu 21:29. 1 K 11:7. Je 48:7, 46. **whomsoever**. Dt 9:4, 5. Jsh 3:10. Ps 44:2. 78:55. Mi 4:5.

25. **Balak**. Nu 22:2, etc. Dt 23:3, 4. Jsh 24:9, 10. Mi 6:5.

26. **Heshbon**. Nu 21:25-30. Dt 2:24. 3:2, 6. Jsh 12:2, 5. 13:10. **her towns**. Heb. daughters. ✓155E5, Nu +21:25. **Aroer**. Dt 2:36. **three hundred**. Jg 3:11, 30. 5:31. 8:28. 9:22. 10:2, 3, 8. Jsh 11:18. 23:1. Matthew Poole notes "not precisely, but about that time; either from their coming out of Egypt, or from their first conquest of those lands; and thus numbers are oft expressed: see Nu 1:46. 2:32. 11:21. Jg 20:46."

27. **the Judge**. Ge +*18:25. 1 S 2:10. Jb 9:15. 23:7. Ps 7:11. 50:6. 75:7. 82:8. 94:2. 98:9. Ec 11:9. 12:14. Jn *5:22, 23. Ro 14:10-12. 2 C 5:10. 2 T 4:8. He 12:23. **be judge**. Ge 16:5. 31:53. 1 S 24:12, 15. Ps 7:8, 9. 2 C 11:11.

28. **hearkened not**. 1 S +*25:17. 2 K 14:11. Pr 16:18.

29. **the Spirit**. Heb. *ruach*, Ge +41:38. Jg 3:10. 6:34. 13:25. Nu 11:25. 1 S 10:10. 16:13-15. 1 Ch 12:18. **Jephthah**. "Jephthah seems to have been judge only of northeast Israel." **over Mizpeh**. ver. +11n. Jg 10:17.

30. **Jephthah vowed a vow**. Ge *28:20. Ge 31:32n. Le +*23:38. 27:29n. Nu 30:+*2n, etc. 1 S 1:11. Ec ✓5:1, 2, 4, 5. Ezk +*17:18n. Ac +*23:12.

31. **whatsoever**, etc. Heb. that which cometh forth, which shall come forth. Ge 14:17. 18:2. 24:17. Lk 15:20. The marginal references show that this is a common phrase in Scripture which speaks of one person meeting another, and never of any brute creature. **shall surely**. Le 27:2, 3, 28, 29. 1 S 1:11, 28. 2:18. 14:24, 44. Ps 68:13, 14. **and I will**. *or*, or I will, etc. *Wehaaleetheehoo olah*, rather, as Dr. Randolph and others contend, "and I will offer Him (or to Him, i.e. *Jehovah*) a burnt offering;" for *hoo* may with much more propriety be referred to the person to whom the sacrifice was to be made, than to the thing to be sacrificed. Unless understood in this way, or as the marginal reading, it must have been a vow of a heathen or a madman. If a dog, or other unclean animal had met him, he could not have made it a burnt offering; or if his neighbor's wife, sons, etc., his vow gave him no right over them. Nevertheless, the context may support the view that Jephthah's vow was rash (Nu 30:2n), and that he, though apparently well acquainted with Scripture (ver. 16n), mistakenly believed that he must fulfill its demands, not being able to redeem his daughter by the provisions given in Le 27:2-5, but required to fulfill the vow by what is written in Le 27:28, 29. Such misunderstandings of the text of Scripture (2 P 3:16) are not unheard of in our own day, witness news accounts of self-mutilation by individuals who misunderstand the words of Mt 5:29. Le 27:2-5, 11, 12, ◐28, ◐29. Dt 23:18. Ps

66:13. Is 66:3. **and.** The conjunctive particle *and* may be here put for the disjunctive *or*, as it often is, as Ex 21:16, 17. Le 6:3, 5. 2 S 2:19, etc.; yet it is not to be so considered without necessity, which seems not to be in this place; nor is it very proper to distinguish two sentences in this manner, where the one is more general, and the other being more special, is comprehended in it, which is the case here; for it "shall surely be the Lord's," is the general; and its being "offered up for a burnt offering," is the particular way or manner how it was to be the Lord's; therefore, in all the alleged instances where "and" is properly put for "or," they are two distinct persons or things, and not one comprehended within the other, as Ex 21:17, "father or mother"; 2 S 2:19, "right hand or left" (adapted from Matthew Poole).

32. **the Lord.** Jg 1:4. 2:18. 3:10.

33. **Aroer.** Dt 2:36. 3:12. **Minnith.** i.e. *allotment*, ✻S#4511h. Situated, according to Eusebius, four miles from Heshbon, towards Philadelphia or Rabbath. Ezk 27:17. **the plain.** *or*, Abel. 1 S +6:18.

34. **Mizpeh.** ver. +*11n. Jg 10:17. **his daughter.** Jg 5:1, etc. Ex 15:20. 1 S 18:6, 7. Ps 68:25. 148:11, 12. 150:4. Je 31:4, 13. **beside her.** *or*, he had not of his own either son or daughter. Heb. of himself. **neither.** Zc 12:10. Lk 7:12. 8:42. 9:38.

35. **rent his clothes.** Ge 37:29, 30, 34, 35. 42:36-38. 2 S 13:30, 31. 18:33. Jb 1:20. **Alas.** Jg +*6:22. **have opened.** Le *27:28, 29. Nu 30:2-5. Ps *15:4. Ec *5:2-6. Mt *5:33. ♪108H6A. Idiom B842. To "open the mouth" is a Hebraism, used for speaking at length or with great solemnity, liberty, or freedom. For other instances of this idiom see Jb 3:1. 33:2. Ps 78:2. Pr 31:26. Ezk 24:27. Da 10:16. Mt 5:2. 13:35. Lk 1:64. Ac 8:35. 10:34. 2 C 6:11. Re 13:6. Contrast ♪108H6B, Ps +38:13, where the opposite, "not to open the mouth," is a Hebraism for silence. **I cannot.** Jg 21:1-7, 18. Jsh +9:19. 1 S 14:44, 45. Ps +*15:4. Ezk +*17:18n. Mt 14:7-9. Ac 23:14. Ro 11:29. Ga 3:15.

36. **according to.** Ps 22:25. 76:11. **forasmuch.** Jg 16:28-30. 2 S 18:19, 31. 19:30. Ac 20:24. 21:13. Ro 16:4. Ph 2:30.

37. **go up and down.** Heb. go and go down. **bewail.** 1 S 1:6. Lk 1:25. **virginity.** Ge +11:30. ◖+29:31. *30:23n. Ps 127:3. 1 C 7:32. 2 C 11:2.

39. **did with.** That Jephthah did not sacrifice his daughter, but consecrated her to the service of God in the tabernacle, in a state of celibacy, may be argued as evident from the following considerations: (1) Human sacrifices were ever an abomination to Jehovah, of which Jephthah could not be ignorant; and consequently he would neither have made such a vow, nor carried it into execution. (2) We are expressly told (ver. 29) that Jephthah was under the influence of the Spirit of God, which would effectually prevent him from embruing his hands in the blood of his own child. (3) He had it in his power to redeem his daughter (Le 27:4); and surely his only child must have been of more value than thirty shekels. (4) Besides, who was to perform the horrid rite? Not Jephthah himself, who was no priest, and in whom it would have been most unnatural and inhuman; and the priests would certainly have dissuaded him from it. (5) The sacred historian informs us that "she bewailed her virginity," that "she knew no man," and that the Israelite women went yearly to comfort or lament with her, ver. 40mg.

It may be argued to the contrary, however, that: (1) Though human sacrifices are an abomination, yet this seems to have been a time of spiritual darkness (Jg 10:6), and though they seem now to have repented and forsaken their idols (Jg 10:16), there seems to have been retained part of the old leaven, for though they were not to offer human sacrifices to Molech, as they had done, yet here it appears they did so to the Lord. Perhaps such misconception of the will of God led to a change in the priesthood (1 S 2:35, 36). (2) Though Jephthah was under the influence of the Spirit of God, yet with him, as in our own day, it is possible to grieve the Holy Spirit by the intrusion of our own fleshly will, expressed here by the rashness of his vow, despite such provisions that God has made in his Word to discourage such vows (Nu 30:2n). The Spirit was not given to Jephthah to impart to him spiritual wisdom and discernment, but to empower him to be a man of valor (ver. 1), and make possible his victory over the Ammonites. (3) Though Jephthah had it in his power to redeem his daughter by the gracious provision of the law (Le 27:4), yet here again he may have been influenced by a misinterpretation and misapplication of Le 27:28, 29, as explained above, ver. 31n, just as there are those today who misinterpret such a passage as Mt 5:29. (4) As to who would perform the rite, if the priest was under the same misconception as Jephthah, the question is answered. (5) That the sacred historian informs us that she bewailed her virginity is no argument against the specific provisions of the vow in verse 31; rather, it would have been inappropriate to bewail her death since she so generously and cheerfully accepted, because attended and occasioned by the public good, and her father's honor and happiness, ver. 36; the mention that "she knew no man" is plainly distinguished from the execution of her father's vow, which is here mentioned before; and this is added, not as an explication of the vow, but as an aggravating circumstance. Furthermore, there is no example in all the Scripture of any woman that was obliged to perpetual virginity by any vow of her own, much less by the vow of her parents; the express words of the vow (ver. 31) mention nothing of her virginity, but only that she should "surely be the Lord's," i.e. devoted to the service of the Lord, which might be without any obligation to perpetual virginity; for even Samuel, who was as fully devoted to the Lord by his parents as she could be, 1 S 1:11; and Samson, who was devoted not only by his parents but by God himself, and that in the highest degree, even to be a perpetual Nazarite, Jg 13:5, 7; yet were not prohibited marriage. Therefore, if she were not offered up as a burnt offering, but was only consecrated to God, there was no occasion to bewail her virginity, which, for anything that appears, she was not tied to (adapted chiefly from Matthew Poole). ver. 31. Le √27:28, 29n. Dt 12:31. Is 66:3. **to his vow.** 1 S 1:11, 22, 24, 28. 2:18. **knew no man.** Ge +4:1. 19:8. **custom.** *or*, ordinance. Le 18:30. 2 Ch 35:25. Je 10:3mg. 32:11.

40. **yearly.** Heb. from year to year. ♪171T2C, Ge +24:55. Jg 17:10. +21:19mg,n. Ge 4:3mg. +*24:55mg. 1 S 1:3mg. **lament.** *or*, to talk with. Jg 5:11. Or, to discourse of (so the Hebrew *lamed* is sometimes used), to celebrate her praises, who had so willingly yielded up herself for a sacrifice (Matthew Poole). **four.** 1 K 9:25. **days.** ♪145. Antanaclasis; or, Word-clashing B287.

Repetition of the same word in the same sentence, with different meanings. Here, "yearly" is literally "days to days," where "days" is first used synecdochally to mean for a year, i.e., year to year. In the second instance, "four days," "days" is used literally for days of twenty-four hours. For other instances of this figure see Jg 15:16. 1 S 1:24. Ps 141:5. Is 37:18. 58:10. 66:3, 4. Je 7:18, 19. 8:14. 34:17. Ezk 20:24-26. Mt 8:22. Jn 1:10, 11. 2:23, 24. 3:√6, 31. 4:31, 32. 19:22. Ro 2:12, 26. 3:21, 27. 7:13, 23. 9:6. 12:13, 14. 1 C 11:24. 15:28. 2 C *5:21. Ep 1:3. 1 T 5:6. 6:5, 6. He 2:14. 1 P 3:1.

JUDGES 12

The Ephraimites quarrel with Jephthah, and discerned by Shibboleth, are smitten by the Gileadites, and slain in very great numbers at the passage of Jordan, 1-6. Jephthah dies, 7. Ibzan, who had thirty sons and thirty daughters, judges Israel, 8-10; and after him Elon, 11, 12; and then Abdon, who had forty sons and thirty grandsons, 13-15.

1. **gathered.** Heb. were called. Jg 6:+34, 35. 7:23. 10:17. **Wherefore.** Jg 8:1. 2 S 19:41-43. Ps 109:4. Ec 4:4. Jn 10:32. **we will burn.** Jg 14:15. 15:6. Pr 27:3, 4. Ja 3:16. 4:1, 2.

2. **I and my.** Jg 11:12, etc.

3. **put my life.** Jg 9:17. 1 S 19:5. 28:21. Jb 13:14. Ps 119:109. Ro 16:4. Re *12:11. Heb. *nephesh,* soul, Ge +*44:30. **wherefore.** Jg 11:27. 2 Ch 13:12.

4. **and the men.** Jg 11:10. Nu 32:39, 40. Dt 3:12-17. **fugitives.** 1 S 25:10. Ne 4:4. Ps 78:9. Pr 12:13. 15:1.

5. **the passages.** Jg 3:28. 7:24. Jsh 2:7. 22:11.

6. **Say now.** Jg 18:3n. Ne 13:24. Zp 3:9. Mt *26:73. Mk *14:70. **Shibboleth.** *S#7641h. Ge 41:5 (ears of corn), 6, 7, 22, 23, 24, 26, 27. Ru 2:2. Jb 24:24. Ps 69:2 (floods), 15. Is 17:5, 5. 27:12. Zc 4:12. Which signifieth a stream, or flood. Ps 69:2, 15. Is 27:12. Heb. *Shibboleth* also means an *ear of corn,* Jb 24:24, and *sibboleth* signifies a *burden,* Ex 6:6; and a heavy burden were they obliged to bear who could not pronounce this test letter. It is well known that several nations cannot pronounce certain letters. The sound of *th* cannot be pronounced by the Persians, no more than by some of our Continental neighbors. Jg 18:3n. 2 K 8:21n. 1 Ch 6:36n. Ne 13:24. Mt *26:73. Mk 14:70. Ac 2:6, 7. **sibboleth.** i.e. *a burden; old age,* *S#5451h, only here. **there fell.** Pr 17:14. 18:19. Ec 10:12. Mt 12:25. Ga 5:15. **forty and two thousand.** *Arbaim ooshenayim aleph,* "forty and two thousand." Here the Hebrew letter *vau* "and," may mean simple addition; and this number may denote 2040, and not 42,000. At the last census of the Israelites (Nu 26:37) the whole tribe of Ephraim only amounted to 32,500, compared with which this last number appears far too great. Young renders "chiefs," commenting "not 'thousands,' as in the Common Version; compare Mi 5:2, etc." Jg 6:15. Ex +18:21. Jsh 22:21. 1 K 20:30n.

7. **Jephthah.** He 11:32. **cities.** J96F3, Ge +8:4.

8. **Ibzan.** i.e. *tin; great fatigue; beautiful,* *S#78h. ver. 10. A.M. 2823. B.C. 1181. An. Ex. Is. 310. "He seems to have been only a civil judge to do justice in northeast Israel." **Bethlehem.** Ge 35:19. 1 S 16:1. Mi *5:2. Mt *2:1.

9. **thirty sons.** ver. 14. Jg 10:4.

11. A.M. 2830. B.C. 1174. An. Ex. Is. 317. **Elon.**

i.e. *an oak.* "A civil judge in North-east Israel." **Zebulonite.** *S#2075h. ver. 12. Nu 26:27.

12. **Aijalon.** Jsh 19:42. 1 Ch 6:69. 8:13. A city different from that in Jg 1:35 (Young).

13. A.M. 2840. B.C. 1164. An. Ex. Is. 327. **Abdon.** i.e. *servile; service; servitude,* *S#5658h. ver. 15. 1 Ch 8:23, 30. 9:36. 2 Ch 34:20. "A civil judge also in northeast Israel." (1) A city of Asher which was afterwards assigned to the Levites, Jsh 21:30; 1 Ch 6:74. (2) A man of Ephraim who was one of the judges of Israel, Jg 12:13, 15. (3) A descendant of Benjamin, 1 Ch 8:23. (4) The eldest son of the father of Gibeon, 1 Ch 8:30; 9:36. (5) The name apparently of one of the priests in the time of Josiah, king of Judah, whom the king sent to enquire of the Lord when the book of the law had been found, 2 Ch 34:20. **Hillel.** i.e. *praising,* *S#1985h. ver. 15.

14. **nephews.** Heb. sons' sons. Ge 21:23. Jb 18:19. Is 14:22. 1 T 5:4. **rode.** Jg 5:10. 10:4.

15. A.M. 2848. B.C. 1156. An. Ex. Is. 335. **Pirathonite.** *S#6553h. ver. 13. 2 S 23:30. 1 Ch 11:31. 27:14. **Pirathon.** i.e. *just revenge,* *S#6552h. **in the mount.** Jg 3:13, 27. 5:14. Ge 14:7. Ex 17:8. 1 S 15:7.

JUDGES 13

Israel offends God and is reduced to serve the Philistines forty years, 1. An angel appears to Manoah's wife, and promises her a son, who should be a perpetual Nazarite, 2-5. She informs her husband; who prays that the angel may again appear to instruct them, 6-8. The angel appears, and by his conduct, especially by ascending in the flame of Manoah's sacrifice, discovers who he is, 9-20. Manoah is greatly alarmed, as having seen God; but is encouraged by his wife, 21-23. Samson is born, and is moved by the Spirit of God, 24, 25.

1. **did.** Heb. added to commit, etc. Jg 2:11. 3:7. 4:1. 6:1. 10:6. Ro 2:6. **in the sight.** Je 13:23. **delivered.** "This seems a partial captivity." **into the.** 1 S 12:9.

2. **Zorah.** Jsh 15:33. 19:41. **Danites.** *S#1839h. Jg 18:1, 11, 30. Ge ●49:16. 1 Ch 12:35. **Manoah.** i.e. *rest,* *S#4495h. ver. 8, 9, 9, 11, 12, 13, 15, 16, 16, 17, 19, 19, 20, 21, 21, 22. Jg 16:31. **barren.** Ge +11:30. 16:1. 25:21. 1 S 1:2-6. Lk 1:7.

3. **the angel.** Jg 2:1. 6:11, 12. Ge 16:7-13. Lk 1:11, 28, etc. **but thou.** Ge 17:16. 18:10. 1 S 1:20. 2 K 4:16. Lk 1:13, 31.

4. **drink not.** ver. 14. Nu 6:2, 3. Lk 1:15. **eat not.** Le 11:27, 47. Ac 10:14.

5. **no razor.** Nu 6:2, 3, 5. 1 S 1:11. La 4:7. Am 2:11. Mt 2:23. **begin.** 1 S 7:13. 2 S 8:1. 1 Ch 18:1.

6. **A man.** Dt 33:1. Jsh 14:6. 1 S 2:27. 9:6. 1 K 17:18, 24. 2 K 4:9, 16. 1 T 6:11. **countenance was.** Mt 28:3, 4. Lk 9:29. Ac 6:15. Re 1:16. **terrible.** ver. 22. Ge 28:16, 17. Ex 3:2-6. Da 8:17. 10:5-11. Jl 2:11. Mt 28:4. Re 1:17. **but I asked**, etc. The Vulgate renders this clause very differently, the negative NOT being omitted: "Whom when I asked who he was, and whence he came, and by what name he was called, would not tell me: but this he said," etc. The negative is also wanting in the Septuagint, as it is in the Complutensian Polyglott: "And I asked him whence he was, and his name, but he did not tell me." This is also the reading of the Codex Alexandrinus; but the Septuagint in the London Polyglott, the Chaldee, Syriac,

and Arabic, read the negative particle with the Hebrew text: "I asked *not* his name," etc. **his name**. ver. 17, 18. Ge 32:29. Lk 1:19.

7. **conceive**. Ge 16:11. **wine**. ver. 4. **strong drink**. or, sweet drink. **womb**. *or*, belly. ver. 5.

8. **intreated**. Ge 25:21. **my Lord**. Ge 15:2, 8. **man of God**. ver. 6. **teach us**. T#*1449*. Ge 46:28 (direct). Ex +*13:8. Jb 34:32. Pr *3:5, 6. Ac 9:6. Ep +*6:4. 2 T +*3:15. **what we shall**. Ex 2:9.

9. **hearkened**. Ge 30:17. Jsh 10:14. Ps 65:2. Mt 7:7-11.

10. **Behold**. Jn 1:41, 42. 4:28, 29. **the other day**. *Byyom*, rather, "in this day," or "today;" for the word *other* is not in the original, and it is probable that the angel appeared in the morning and evening of the same day.

12. **How shall we order the child**. Heb. what shall be the manner of the child? *ʃ181E*, Ge +3:24. Ge +*18:19. 40:13 (manner). Pr 4:4. *22:6. Ep *6:4. **how shall we do unto him**. or, what shall he do? Heb. what shall be his work? Ge 5:29.

14. **neither**. ver. 4. Nu 6:3-5. **all that I**. Dt 12:32. Mt 28:20. Jn 2:5. 15:14. 2 Th 3:4.

15. **let us**. Jg 6:18, 19. Ge 18:3-5. **until**. Manoah, not knowing the quality of his guest, wished to do this as an act of hospitality. **a kid**. Ge 27:9, 16. **for thee**. Heb. before thee.

16. **I will not**. As I am a spiritual being, I subsist not by earthly food; and cannot partake of your bounty. 1 S 28:23. **bread**. *ʃ171I8*, Ge +3:19. **and if**, etc. Rather, "but if thou wilt offer," etc. **unto the**. ver. 23. Jg 6:26.

17. **thy name**. ver. 6. Ge 32:27. Ex *3:13. **do thee honor**. 1 S 9:7, 8. 1 K 14:3. Jn 5:23.

18. **Why askest**. ver. 6. Ge 32:29. **secret**. *or*, wonderful. It was because his name was secret that Manoah wished to know it. But the angel does not say it was secret, but *hoo pailee*, "it is *wonderful*;" the very character given to the Messiah: "His name shall be called *pailai*, wonderful," Is 9:6. Ex 15:11. Dt 29:29. Ps 77:11, 14. 88:10, 12. *119:129. 139:6. Pr 30:4. Is *9:6. Da ❶+*8:13mg.

19. **took**. Jg 6:19, 20. 1 K 18:30-38. **did wonderously**. He acted according to His name: He, being wonderful, performed wonders; probably causing fire to arise out of the rock and consume the sacrifice, and then ascended in the flame. Jg 6:21. 1 K 18:38.

20. **when the flame**. 2 K 2:11. Ps 47:5. He 1:3. **fell on**. Ge 17:3. Le 9:24. 1 Ch 21:16, 26. Ezk 1:26, 28. Da 10:9. Mt 17:6.

21. **knew**. Jg 6:22. Ho 12:4, 5.

22. **We shall**. Jg 6:22, 23. Ge 32:30. Ex 33:20. Dt 4:38. 5:26. Is 6:5. **surely**. *ʃ147B*, Ge +2:16. **we have**. Jn *1:18. 5:37.

23. **his wife**. Ec 4:9, 10. 1 C 12:21. **were pleased to**. Jsh 11:20. 1 S 2:25. 2 S 15:26. **he would not**. Ge 4:4, 5. Ps 86:17. **burnt offering**. Le +*23:12. **meat offering**. Le +*23:13. **he have showed**. Ps 25:14. 27:13. Pr 3:32. Jn 14:20, 23. 15:15.

24. A.M. 2849. B.C. 1155. An. Ex. Is. 336. **Samson**. i.e. *a little sun* or *servant*. He 11:32. **the child**. 1 S 3:19. Lk 1:80. *2:52.

25. **the Spirit**. Heb. *ruach*, Ge +41:38. Jg 3:10. 6:34. 11:29. 1 S 11:6. Mt 4:1. Jn 3:34. **move**. Ge 41:8. Ps 77:4 (troubled). **the camp of Dan**. Heb. Mahanehdan, as Jg 18:12. **between**. Jg 18:11. Jsh 15:33. **Eshtaol**. Jsh 15:33. 19:41.

JUDGES 14

Samson desires a woman of the Philistines to wife, 1-4. Going to see her he slays a lion; and afterwards finds honey in its carcass, 5-9. At his marriage feast he proposes a riddle, which the guests explain by means of his wife, 10-18. He kills thirty Philistines, gives their spoil to those who explained the riddle, and departs in anger, 19. His wife is given to his companion, 20.

1. **Timnath**. Ge 38:12, 13. Jsh 15:10. 19:43. 2 Ch 28:18. **saw**. Ge 6:2. 34:1, 2. 2 S 11:2. Jb *31:1. Ps 119:37. 1 J *2:16.

2. **get her**. Ge +21:21. 24:2, 3. 34:4. 38:6. 2 K 14:9.

3. **thy brethren**. Ge 13:8. 24:3, 4, 27. 27:46. Dt 7:3. 2 C *6:14. **uncircumcised**. Jg 15:18. Ge 34:14. Ex 34:12-16. Dt 7:2, 3. 1 S 14:6. 16:26, 36. 31:4. 2 S 1:20. **she pleaseth me well**. Heb. she is right in mine eyes. ver. 7. Nu 23:27. 1 S 18:20, 26. 2 S 17:4. 19:6. 1 K 9:12. 2 Ch 30:4.

4. **it was of the Lord**. That is, God *permitted* it, that it might be a means of bringing about the deliverance of Israel. Such marriages were forbidden to the Israelites, to keep them separate from the idolatrous nations. Jsh 11:20. 1 K 12:15. 2 K 6:33. 2 Ch 10:15. 22:7. 25:20. Ps 115:3. Am +*3:6. **had dominion**. Jg 13:1. 15:11. Dt 28:47, 48.

5. **lion roared**. 1 P 5:8. **against him**. Heb. in meeting him. Jg 15:14.

6. **the Spirit**. Heb. *ruach*, Ge +41:38. Jg 3:10. 11:29. 13:25. 1 S 11:6. **came mightily**. 2 C 10:4. **rent him**. Now it is not intimated that he did this by his own natural strength; but by the supernatural strength communicated by the "Spirit of the Lord coming mightily upon him"; which strength was not at his own command, but was, by the will of God, attached to his hair and *nazarate*. Jg 15:8, 15. 16:30. 1 S 17:34-37, 46. Zc 4:6. 1 J 3:8. **he told**. Is 42:2. Mt 11:29.

8. **to take her**. Ge 29:21. Mt 1:20. **a swarm**. It is probable, that the flesh had been entirely consumed off the bones, which had become dry; and the body having been thrown into some private place (for Samson turned aside to visit it), a swarm of bees had formed their combs in the cavity of the dry ribs, or region of the thorax: nor was it a more improper place than a hollow rock.

9. **he took**. 1 S 14:25-30. Pr 25:15.

10. **made there**. Ge 29:22. Est 1:7, etc. Ec 10:19. Mt 22:2-4. Jn 2:9. Re 19:9.

11. **saw him**. 1 S 10:23. 16:6. **thirty**. Mt 9:15. Jn 3:29.

12. **a riddle**. 1 K 10:1. Ps 49:4. Pr 1:6. Ezk 17:2. 20:49. Mt 13:13, 34. Lk 14:7. Jn 16:29. 1 C 13:12mg. **the seven**. Ge 29:27, 28. 2 Ch 7:8. **sheets**. *or*, shirts. Pr 31:24. Is 3:23. Mt 27:28. Mk 14:51, 52. **change**. ver. 19. Ge 45:22. 2 K 5:5, 22. Mt 6:19. Ja 5:2.

14. **Out of the eater**. *ʃ3*, Ge +49:10. Ac 3:15. Dt 8:15, 16. 1 K 17:6. 2 Ch 20:2, 25. Is 53:10-12. Ro 5:3-5. 8:37. 2 C 4:17. 12:9, 10. Ph 1:12-20. He 2:14, 15. 12:10, 11. Ja 1:2-4. 1 P 2:24. **came forth**. Is 55:10. **they could**. Pr 24:7. Mt 13:11. Ac 8:31.

15. **on the seventh day**. The LXX. reads "on the fourth day;" with which the Syriac and Arabic agree. This, as Dr. Wall observes, is certainly right; for it appears from ver. 17, that she wept the remainder of the seven days; for which there could have been no

time, if they did not threaten her till the seventh. **Entice.** Jg 16:5. Ge 3:1-6. Pr 1:11. 5:3. 6:26. Mi 7:5. **lest we burn.** Jg 12:1. 15:6. **take that we have.** Heb. possess us, *or*, impoverish us. Dt 28:42mg.

16. **Thou dost.** Jg 16:15. **I have not.** Ge 2:24. Mi *7:5.

17. **the seven.** *or*, the rest of the seven days. **he told.** Jg 16:16, 17. **she lay.** Jg 16:6, 13, 16. Ge 3:6. Jb 2:9. Pr 7:21. Lk 11:8. 18:4, 5. **and she told.** Pr 2:16, 17.

18. **What is.** *ƒ*21. Anteisagoge; *or*, Counter Question B964. For other instances of this figure see Mt 21:23-26. Ro 9:19, 20.

19. **the Spirit.** Heb. *ruach*, Ge +41:38. ver. 6. Jg 3:10. 13:25. 15:14. 1 S 11:6. **Ashkelon.** i.e. *weight; balance*, ✛S#831h. Je 25:20. 47:5, 7. Am *1:8. Zp 2:4, 7. Zc 9:5, 5. **spoil.** *or*, apparel. 2 S 2:21. **change of garments.** ver. 13. Ge 45:22. 2 K 5:5, 22, 23.

20. **given to.** Jg 15:2. **his friend.** Ps 55:12, 13. SS 5:1. Je 9:5. Mi 7:5. Mt 26:49, 50. Jn 3:29. 13:18.

JUDGES 15

Samson, returning to visit his wife, finds her given to another, 1, 2. He sets fire, with foxes and fire brands, to the corn of the Philistines; who burn his wife and her father, 3-6. Samson smites them, and retires to the rock Etam, 7, 8. The men of Judah, by his consent, deliver him bound to the Philistines; and he kills a thousand of them with the jawbone of an ass, 9-17. Being ready to perish by thirst, he cries to the Lord, who opens for him a fountain in Lehi, 18, 19. He judges Israel, 20.

1. **a kid.** Ge 38:17. Lk 15:29. **I will go.** Ge 6:4. 29:21. **suffer.** *ƒ*108A4, Ge +31:7.

2. **I verily.** Jg 14:16, 20. Ac 26:9. **I gave.** Jg 14:20. Ge 38:14. **take her.** Heb. let her be thine.

3. **Now shall**, etc. *or*, Now shall I be blameless from the Philistines, though, etc. Jg 14:15.

4. **caught three hundred.** Ps 63:10. SS 2:15. La 5:18. **firebrands.** *or*, torches. Jg 7:16mg.

5. **he let them go.** Ex 22:6. 2 S 14:30.

6. **Timnite.** i.e. *one from Timnah*, ✻S#8554h. **and burnt.** Jg 12:1. 14:15. Pr 10:24. 22:8. Ho 8:7. 1 Th 4:6.

7. **Though.** Jg 14:4, 19. Ro 12:19.

8. **smote them.** Is 25:10. 63:3, 6. **Etam.** 2 Ch 11:5, 6.

9. **Lehi.** i.e. a *jawbone*, ✻S#3896h. ver. 14, ◐17mg, 19.

11. **went.** Heb. went down. **the rock Etam.** Probably near the town *Etam*, mentioned in 1 Ch 4:32. **Philistines.** Jg 13:1. 14:4. Dt 28:13, 47, 48. Ps 106:41.

12. **to bind thee.** Mt 27:2. Ac 7:25. **fall.** Jg 8:21. 1 K 2:25, 34.

13. **surely.** *ƒ*147B, Ge +2:16.

14. **the Philistines.** Jg 5:30. 16:24. Ex 14:3, 5. 1 S 4:5. Jb 20:5. Mi 7:8. **the Spirit.** Heb. *ruach*, Ge +41:38. Jg 3:10. 14:6, 19. Zc *4:6. **came mightily.** Jg ◐16:20. Ac 5:3, 4. **the cords.** Jg 16:9, 12. 1 S 17:35. Ps 18:34. 118:11. Ph 4:13. **loosed.** Heb. were melted. Dt +20:8mg.

15. **new.** Heb. moist. Is 1:6. **jawbone.** Dt 18:3. 1 K 22:24. **slew.** or, smiteth. ver. 16. Jg 3:31. 4:21. 7:16. Le 26:8. Jsh 23:10. 1 S 14:6, 14. 17:49, 50. 1 C 1:27, 28. **a thousand.** Some would render the words

aileph ish, "a chief"; but it is *alluph*, and not *aileph*, which signifies a chief; besides which, the Hebrew idiom would, even in that case, require it to be *ish alluph*, "a man, a chief," and not *alluph ish*, "a chief, a man." Add to which, that every version renders it "a thousand men." Jg 3:31. ◐12:6mg,n. 1 Ch 11:11.

16. **with the jawbone.** There is a fine paronomasia (*ƒ*140. Paronomasia; or, Rhyming Words, Ge +4:25) upon the word *chamor*, "an ass," which also signifies a heap: *bilchee hachamor, chamor chamorathayim*, "With the jawbone of an ass, a heap upon two heaps." Nu 16:15n. **ass.** *ƒ*145, Jg 11:40. **heaps upon heaps.** Heb. an heap, two heaps.

17. **Ramath-lehi.** i.e. *the high place of the jawbone. that is*, the lifting up of the jawbone, *or*, the casting away of the jawbone, ✻S#7437h.

18. **he was sore.** Jg 8:4. Ge *21:17, +19. Ps 22:14, 15. Is *40:29, 31. Jn 19:28. 2 C 4:8, 9. **Thou hast given.** Ps 3:7, 8. 18:31-40. **shall.** Ge 32:31. 2 C 12:7, 8. **and fall.** Ge 12:12, 13. 20:11. 1 S 27:1. 2 S 24:14. 2 C 1:8, 9. He 11:32. **the uncircumcised.** 1 S 17:26, 36. 2 S 1:20.

19. **the jaw.** *or*, Lehi. This reading is certainly preferable: it was in the place called Lehi where a spring was supernaturally opened. **there came.** Is 44:3. **his spirit.** Heb. *ruach*, Ge +41:8. 45:27. 1 S 30:12. Is 40:26. **En-hakkore.** i.e. *fountain of the calling* or *the called* or *of him that called*, as upon God in distress, ✻S#5875h. Samson gave this expressive name to the miraculously springing water, to be as a memorial of the goodness of God to him. En-hakkore, "the well of him that cried," which kept him in remembrance both of his own distress which caused him to cry, and the favor of Jehovah to him in answer to his cry. Many a spring of comfort God opens to his people, which may fitly be called by the name *En-hakkore*: and this instance of Samson's relief should encourage us to trust in God, for when he pleases he can "open rivers in high places." Is 41:17, 18. Samson at first gave the name of *Ramoth-lehi* "the lifting up of the jawbone", which denoted him great and triumphant: but now he gives it another name, *En-hakkore*, which denotes him wanting and dependent. **called the name.** Ge 16:13. 22:14. 28:19. 32:30. Ex 17:15. Ps 34:6. 120:1. **unto this day.** Jg 1:26. Jsh +4:9.

20. **he judged.** Jg 13:1, 5. 16:31. "He seems to have judged South-west Israel during twenty years of their servitude of the Philistines."

JUDGES 16

Samson, ensnared by a harlot at Gaza, is in imminent danger, but escapes by carrying off the gates of the city, 1-3. He loves Delilah; who bribed by the Philistines, repeatedly, but in vain, tries to discover in what his strength lay, 4-15. Overcome by her importunity he discloses the secret; and the Philistines, shaving his head while asleep, bind and imprison him, having put out his eyes, 16-21. His hair grows again, and his strength returns, 22. The Philistines, at the feast of Dagon, make sport of him: he pulls down the house, and dies with great multitudes of his enemies, 23-30. He is buried by his friends, 31.

1. **Gaza.** Ge 10:19. Jsh 15:47. Gaza, a city of great antiquity, was situated between Raphia and Askelon, twenty-two miles north of the former, and sixteen south

of the latter, according to the Antonine Itinerary; three miles from the sea, according to Arrian, and thirty-four from Ashdod or Azotus, according to Diodorus Siculus. It was a place of great strength and importance; and successively belonged to the Philistines, Hebrews, Chaldeans, and Persians; which latter defended it for two months against Alexander the great, who finally took and destroyed it. It was afterwards rebuilt, and alternately possessed by the Egyptians, Syrians, and Jews. The present town, which the Arabs call *Razza*, is situated on an eminence, and is rendered picturesque by the number of fine minarets which rise majestically above the buildings, with beautiful date trees interspersed. It contains upwards of 2000 inhabitants. **an harlot**. Heb. a woman an harlot. Jg 11:1n. Jsh 2:1n. 6:22. 1 K 3:16n. Is +40:13mg. Je 3:3. Young notes "The Targum reads an 'innkeeper,' as in Jsh 2:1." **and went**. Ge 38:16-18. Ezr 9:1, 2.

2. **Gazites**. i.e. *inhabitants of Gaza*, *S#5841h. Jsh 13:3, Gazathites. **compassed**. 1 S 19:11. 23:26. Ps 118:10-12. Ac 9:23, 24. 2 C 11:32, 33. **quiet**. Heb. silent. Jg 18:19. Ge 24:21. 1 S *10:27mg. 2 S 19:10mg. 1 K 20:2mg. Pr 17:28. **kill him**. Jg 15:18. Mt 21:38. 27:1. Ac 23:15.

3. **took**. Ps 107:16. Is 63:1-5. Mi 2:13. Ac 2:24. **doors**. 1 S 21:13. 1 Ch 22:3. Ezk 8:3, 14. 11:1. Ac 12:13. **gate**. Ge +14:7. **posts**. Dt 11:20. 1 S 1:9. 1 K 6:31, 33. **bar and all**. Heb. with the bar. Dt 3:5. 1 S 23:7. 1 K 4:13. 2 Ch 8:5. 14:7. Ne 3:3, 6, 13-15. Jb 38:10. Ps 107:16. 147:13. Pr 18:19. Is 45:2. Je 49:31. 51:30. La 2:9. Ezk 38:11. Am 1:5. Jon 2:6. Na 3:13. **Hebron**. Jsh 14:14.

4. **he loved**. 1 K 11:1. Ne 13:26. Pr 22:14. 23:27. 26:11. 27:22. 1 C 10:6. **in the valley**. *or*, by the brook. Ge 32:23. Nu 13:23. Dt 2:13mg. 2 S 23:30mg. 24:5mg. 1 Ch 11:32. **Sorek**. i.e. *a hisser*, *S#7796h. **Delilah**. i.e. *lean, poor, weak; delicate; languishing*, *S#1807h. ver. 6, 10, 12, 13, 18.

5. **the lords**. Jg 3:3. Jsh 13:3. 1 S 29:6. **Entice**. Jg 14:15. Pr 2:16-19. 5:3-11, 20. 6:24-26. 7:21-27. 1 C 6:15-18. **afflict**. *or*, humble. ver. 6, 19. **we will**. Jg 17:2. Ge 38:16. Nu 22:17, 18. Mi 7:3. Mt 26:15. 1 T 6:9, 10.

6. **Tell me**. Ps 12:2. Pr 6:26. 7:21. 22:14. 26:28. Je 9:2-5. Mi *7:2, 5.

7. **If they bind**. ver. 10. 1 S 19:17. 21:2, 3. 27:10. Pr 12:19. 17:7. Ro 3:8. Ga 6:7. Col 3:9. **green withs**. *or*, new cords. Jb 30:11. Ps 11:2. Heb. moist. Ge 30:37. Ezk 17:24. 20:47. **another**. Heb. one. ver. 11.

8. **bound him**. Ec 7:26.

9. **broken**. Jg 15:14. **toucheth**. Heb. smelleth. Ps 58:9.

10. **now tell me**. ver. 7, 13, 15-17. Pr 23:7, 8. 24:28. Ezk 33:31. Lk 22:48.

11. **If they bind me**. Pr 13:3, 5. 29:25. Ep 4:25. **that never**, etc. Heb. wherewith work hath not been done.

13. **with the web**. √63I2, Jsh +3:3. It is evident that this verse ends abruptly, and does not contain a full sense. Houbigant has particularly noticed this, and corrected the text from the Septuagint; which adds after these words, "and shall fasten them with the pin in the wall, I shall become weak like other men: and so it was, that when he slept, Dalida took the seven locks of his head, and wove them with the web," etc. This is absolutely necessary to complete the sense;

else Delilah would appear to do something she was not ordered to do, and to omit what she was commanded. Dr. Kennicott very judiciously observes, that the omission, for such it appears to be, begins and ends with the same word; and that the same word occurring in different places, is a very common cause of omission in Hebrew manuscripts. This form of omission is called *Homoeoteleuton*, of which another example given by EWB in B1004 is 1 K 8:16, "*I chose* (Jerusalem that my name might be there, and *I chose*) David to be over my people Israel."

14. **went away**. Ezr 9:13, 14. Ps 106:43.

15. **How canst**. Jg 14:16. Pr 2:16. 5:3-14. **when thine**. Ge 29:20. Dt 6:5. 1 S 15:13, 14. 2 S 16:17. Pr 23:26. SS 8:6, 7. Jn 14:15, 21-24. 15:10. 2 C 5:14, 15. 1 J *2:15, 16. 5:3.

16. **she pressed**. Pr 7:21-23, 26, 27. Lk 11:8. 18:5. **soul**. Heb. *nephesh*, Ge +34:3. **vexed**. Heb. shortened. Jg +10:16mg. Jb 21:4mg. Jon 4:9. Mk 14:34.

17. **all his heart**. Pr 12:23. 29:11. Mi *7:5. **There hath**. Jg 13:5. Nu 6:5. Ac 18:18. **from my**. Ps 22:10.

18. **Come up**. Ps 62:9. Pr 18:8. Je 9:4-6. **brought money**. ver. 5. Nu 22:7. 1 K 21:20. Mt 26:15. Ep 5:5. 1 T 6:10.

19. **she made**. Pr 7:21-23, 26, 27. 23:33, 34. Ec 7:26.

20. **I will go**. ver. 3, 9, 14. Dt *32:30. Is *42:25. Ho *7:9. **as at other times**. Jg 20:30, 31. Nu 24:1. 1 S 20:25. **shake myself**. Ex 14:27. Ne 5:13. Jb 38:13. Ps 109:23. 136:15mg. Is 33:9, 15. 52:2. Je 51:38mg. **the Lord**. Nu 14:9, 42, 43. Jsh 7:12. 1 S 16:14. *18:12. 28:14-16. 2 Ch *15:2. Is *59:1, 2. Je *9:23, 24. Mt *17:16, 20. 2 C *3:5. **was departed**. Jg ●15:14. Ac 5:3, 4. ●7:9.

21. **and put out**. Heb. and bored out. Nu 16:14mg. 1 S 11:2. Pr 5:22. 14:14. 30:17. Is 51:1. Je 2:19. **bound him**. 2 K 25:7. 2 Ch 33:11. Ps 107:10-12. 149:8. **fetters of brass**. lit. two brasses. √121D2. Metonymy of the Cause B558. Brass is put for fetters. For other instances of this figure see 2 S 3:34. La 3:7. **grind**. Ex 11:5. Is 47:2. Mt 24:41.

22. **the hair**. Le 26:44. Dt 32:26. Ps 106:44, 45. 107:13, 14. **after he was shaven**. *or*, as when he was shaven.

23. **Dagon**. i.e. *a little fish*, the lower part of the image being that of a fish, and the upper part that of a man (Young). Jsh 15:41. 19:27. 1 S 5:2-5, 7. 1 Ch 10:10. Je 2:11. Mi 4:5. Ro 1:23-25. 1 C 8:4, 5. 10:20. **to rejoice**. Jb 30:9, 10. Ps 35:15, 16. Pr 24:17. √24H. Antimereia of the Noun: A noun for a verb B496. lit. for a great rejoicing. For other instances of this figure see Is 7:1. Mk *12:38.

24. **praised**. Dt 32:27. Is 37:20. Ezk 20:14. Da 5:4, 23. Hab 1:16. Re 11:10. **and the**. √15G, Ge +35:3. **which slew many of us**. Heb. and who multiplied our slain. Jg 15:8, 16.

25. **their hearts**. Jg 9:27. 18:20. 19:6, 9. 2 S 13:28. 1 K 20:12. Est 3:15. Is 22:13. Da 5:2, 3. Mt 14:6, 7. **them**. Heb. before them. **sport**. 2 S 2:14. Jb 30:9, 10. Ps 35:15, 16. 69:12, 26. Pr 24:17, 18. Mi 7:8-10. Mt 26:67, 68. 27:29, 39-44. He 11:36.

27. **was full**. 2 K 10:21mg. **and there**. "Samson, therefore," says Dr. Shaw, "must have been in a court or area below; and consequently the temple will be of the same kind with the ancient *temena*, or sacred enclosures, which were only surrounded either in part,

or on all sides, with some plain or cloistered buildings. Several palaces, *doutwanas*, (as the courts of justice are called in those countries) are built in this fashion. On their public festivals and rejoicings, the roofs of these cloisters are crowded with spectators. I have often seen numbers of people diverted in this manner on the roof of the dey's palace at Algiers; which, like many others, has an advanced cloister, over against the gate of the palace, like a long penthouse, supported by one or two contiguous pillars in front or center." **the roof.** Jg 9:51. Dt 22:8. Jsh 2:6, 8. 1 S 9:25. 2 S 11:2.

28. **called.** 2 Ch 20:12. Ps 50:15. 91:15. 116:4. La 3:31, 32. He 11:32. **remember me.** Ps 74:18-23. Je 15:15. Jon 2:1, 2, 27. **that I may.** Jg 5:31. Ps 58:10, 11. 143:12. 2 T 4:14. Re 6:10.

29. **took hold.** Ru 3:8mg. Jb 6:18 (turned aside). **on which it was borne up.** *or*, he leaned on them. 2 K 18:21. Is 36:6.

30. **me.** Heb. my soul, *nephesh*, Nu +23:10. ♪171Q2, Nu +23:10. 1 K 20:32. Mt +*12:18. **die.** Mt 16:25. Ac 20:24. 21:13. Ph 2:17, 30. He 12:1-4. **and the house.** Jb 20:5. 31:3. Ps 62:3. Ec 9:12. Mt 24:38, 39. 1 Th 5:2. **So the dead.** Jg 14:19. 15:8, 15. Ge 3:15. Ph 2:8. Col 2:15. He 2:14, 15.

31. **his brethren.** Jn 19:39-42. **between Zorah.** Jg 13:2, 25. 18:2. Jsh 19:41. **burying place.** Heb. *qeber*, Ge +23:4. **And he judged.** Jg 13:25. 15:20.

JUDGES 17

Micah, an Ephraimite, steals money from his mother, which he restores, and she makes images from it, 1-4 Micah's idolatry, 5, 6. He hires a Levite to be his priest, 7-13.

1. A.M. 2585. B.C. 1419. An. Ex. Is. 72. **there was.** It is extremely difficult to fix the chronology of this and the following transactions. Some think them to be here in their natural order; others that they happened in the time of Joshua, or immediately after the ancients who outlived him. All that can be said with certainty is, that they happened when there was no king in Israel; that is, about the time of the judges, or in some time of the anarchy (ver. 6). **mount.** Jg 10:1. Jsh 15:9. 17:14-18. **Micah.** i.e. *who is like Jah?*, *S#4319h. ver. 4.

2. **eleven hundred.** Young notes "which seem to have made 'a bag,' as at Jg 16:5. **about,** etc. Houbigant renders thus, "and for which you put me to my oath." **cursedst.** Jg 5:23. Dt 27:16. 1 S 14:24, 28. 26:19. Ne 13:25. Je 48:10. Ho 4:2. 10:4. Mt 26:74. Ro 9:3. 1 C 16:22. **I took it.** Pr 28:24. **Blessed.** Ge 14:19. 24:30, 31. Ex 20:7. Ru 3:10. 1 S 23:21. Ne 13:25. Ps 10:3. 2 J 11.

3. **I had wholly.** ver. 13. Jg 18:5. Is 66:3. **a graven image.** Ex 20:4, 23. 32:4, 5. Le 19:4. Dt 12:3. Ps 115:4-8. Is 40:18-25. 44:9-20. Je 10:3-5, 8. Hab 2:18, 19. Jn 16:2.

4. **two hundred.** Is 46:6, 7. Je 10:9, 10. **the founder.** *or*, a refiner. Is 40:19. 41:7mg. 46:6.

5. **an house of gods.** *or*, as *baith Elohim* may also signify, "a house of God." Jg 18:24. Ge 31:30. Ezr 1:7. Ho 8:14. **ephod.** Jg 8:27. 18:14. Ex 28:4, 15. 1 S 23:6. **teraphim.** Ge 31:19, 30mg. Ho 3:4. **consecrated.** Heb. filled the hand. ♪121S3P, Ex +28:41mg. Ex 29:9. 1 K 12:31. 13:33, 34. He 5:4. **his sons.** Ex 24:5.

6. **no king.** Jg 18:1. 19:1. 21:3, *25. Ge 36:31. Dt 33:5. 1 S 12:12. **right.** Dt *12:8. Ps *12:4. Pr *12:15. *14:12. 16:2. Ec 11:9. Je *44:16, 17.

7. **Beth-lehem-judah.** ver. 8, 9. Jg 19:1, 2, 18, 18. Ge ◑35:19. Jsh ◑19:15. Ru 1:1, 2. 1 S 17:12. Mi ◑+*5:2. Mt *2:1, 5, 6. **of the family.** That is, of the tribe of *Judah* by his mother; and of that of *Levi* by his father.

8. **departed.** ver. 11. Ne 13:10, 11. **as he journeyed.** Heb. in making his way.

10. **a father.** ver. 11. Jg 18:19. Ge 45:8. 2 K 6:21. 8:8, 9. 13:14. Jb 29:16. Is 22:21. **I will give.** Jg 18:20. 1 S 2:36. Ezk 13:19. Mt 26:15. Jn 12:6. 1 T 6:10. 1 P 5:2. **year.** ♪171T2C, Ge +24:55. **a suit of apparel.** *or*, a double suit, etc. Heb. an order of garments.

12. **consecrated.** ♪121S3P, Ex +28:41. ver. 5. **his priest.** Jg 18:30. Nu 16:5, 8-10. 1 K 12:31. 13:33, 34.

13. **Now know.** Pr *14:12. Is 44:20. 66:3, 4. Mt 15:9, 13. Jn 16:2. Ac 26:9. Ro 10:2, 3.

JUDGES 18

The Danites send five men to seek an inheritance for them, 1, 2. Meeting with Micah's Levite, they consult him, and are encouraged to proceed, 3-6. They search Laish, and bring back an encouraging report, 7-10. Six hundred men are sent to surprise the place, 11, 12. They rob Micah of his idols, and entice away his priest, 13-21. Micah pursues them, but is frightened back by threats, 22-26. They take Laish, and call it Dan, 27-29. They set up idolatry; and Micah's Levite, who was called Jonathan, and his sons after him, become the priests, 30, 31.

1. **no king.** The word *mailech*, which generally means a *king*, is sometimes taken for a supreme ruler, governor, or judge (see Ge 36:31. Dt 33:5); and it is probable it should be so understood here, and in the parallel passages. Jg 17:6. 19:1. 21:25. **the tribe.** Jsh 19:40-48. **for unto.** Jg 1:34.

2. **men.** Heb. sons. Dt 3:18mg. 1 S 18:17. **Zorah.** ver. 8, 11. Jg 13:2, 25. 16:31. Ge 42:9. Jsh 19:41. **to spy.** Nu 13:17. Jsh 2:1. Pr 20:18. Lk 14:31. **mount.** Jg 17:1. 19:1, 18. Jsh 17:15-18.

3. **they knew.** They knew by his dialect or mode of pronunciation, that he was not an Ephraimite: see the parallel texts. Jg +*12:6n. Ge 27:22. Mt *26:73. **and what hast.** Is 22:16.

4. **hired me.** Jg 17:10. Pr 28:21. Is 56:11. Ezk 13:19. Ho 4:8, 9. Ml 1:10. Jn 10:12, 13. Ac 8:18-21. 20:33. 1 T 3:3. T 1:11. 2 P 2:3, 14, 15.

5. **Ask counsel.** T#1458. Jg 20:18, 23, 26-28. 1 S 8:21, 22. 14:36, 37. 1 K 22:5. 2 K 16:15. Is 30:1. Ezk 21:21. Ho 4:12. Ac 8:10. **of God.** ver. 14. Jg 17:5, 13.

6. **Go in peace.** 1 K 22:6, 12, 15. Je 23:21, 22, 32. **before.** Dt 11:12. Ps 33:18. 1 Th 3:11. **the Lord.** As the Levite uses the word Jehovah, and as the Danites succeeded according to the oracle delivered by him, some learned men are of the opinion, that the worship established by Micah was not of an idolatrous kind.

7. **Laish.** Jsh 19:47, called Leshem. **how they.** ver. 27, 28. Re 18:7. **magistrate.** Heb. possessor, *or*, heir, of restraint. ver. 28. 1 S 3:13. 1 K 1:6. Ro 13:3. 1 P 2:14. **and had no.** In the most correct copies of the LXX. this clause reads "and they had no transactions with *Syria*"; evidently reading instead of *adam*, "man,"

aram, "Syria"; words so nearly similar that the only difference between them is in the Hebrew letter *raish* and *daleth*, which in both MSS. and printed books is sometimes indiscernible. Laish was situated on the frontiers of Syria.

8. **Zorah and Eshtaol.** ver. 2, 11. Jg 13:2. 16:31.

9. **Arise.** Nu 13:30. 14:7-9. Jsh 2:23, 24. **are ye still.** 1 K 22:3. **be not.** Jsh 18:3. 1 S 4:9. 2 S 10:12. Jn 6:27. He 6:11, 12. 2 P 1:10, 11.

10. **secure.** ver. 7, 27. **God hath.** Dt 2:29. 4:1. Jsh 6:16. **where there.** Ex 3:8. Dt 8:7-9. 11:11, 12. Ezk 20:6. 1 T 6:17.

11. **appointed.** Heb. girded. ver. 16. Ex 12:11.

12. **Kirjath-jearim.** A city of Judah, on the confines of Benjamin; distant nine miles from Aelia or Jerusalem, in going towards Diospolis or Lydda, according to Eusebius. Jsh 15:9, 60. 1 S 7:1. 1 Ch 13:5, 6. 2 Ch 1:4. **Mahaneh-dan.** i.e. *camp of Dan*, *S#4265h, only here. Jg 13:25mg. **unto this day.** Jg 1:26. Ge +19:38. Jsh +4:9. **behind.** Ex +3:1.

13. **mount Ephraim.** ver. 2, 3. Jg 17:1. 19:1. Jsh 24:30, 33.

14. **Then.** 1 S 14:28. **in these.** ver. 3, 4. Jg 17:5. **houses.** ♪96F3, Ge +8:4. **now therefore.** Pr 19:27. Is 8:19, 20.

15. **saluted him.** Heb. asked him of peace. Ge +29:6mg. 37:14mg. 43:27mg. Ex 18:7mg. 1 S 10:4. 17:22mg. 2 K 4:23mg, 26. 10:13mg. Je 15:5mg. Mt 10:12, 13. Lk 10:4-6. 1 m 14:27.

16. **six hundred.** ver. 11.

17. **five men.** ver. 2, 14. **the graven.** Jg 6:31. 17:4, 5. Ex 32:20. 1 S 4:11. 6:2-9. 2 K 19:18, 19. Is 46:1, 2, 7.

19. **lay thine hand.** Jb 21:5. 29:9. 40:4, 5. Pr 30:32. Mi 7:16. or, keep silent. Heb. be deaf. Jg 16:2. 1 S 10:27mg. Mi 7:16. ♪121S3N. Metonymy of the Adjunct B607: Connected words and phrases. "To put the hand" or "hands on the mouth" is put for silence, or having no answer. For other instances of this figure see Jb 21:5. 29:9. 40:4. Mi 7:16. These men were evidently very ignorant; and absurdly concluded that they should, by taking Micah's gods, secure the presence and favor of the God of Israel, in their expedition and settlement. They perhaps supposed the piety of their motives, and the goodness of their end (Ro 3:8), would justify the means. But it was a base robbery of Micah, aggravated by the Levite's ingratitude, and their menaces. **a father.** Jg 17:10. 2 K 6:21. 8:8, 9. 13:14. Mt 23:9.

20. **heart.** Jg 17:10. Pr 30:15. Is 56:11. Ezk 13:19. Ho 4:8. Ac 20:33. Ph 3:19. 2 P 2:3, 15, 16. **went.** He was glad of his preferment among the Danites; and went into the crowd, that he might not be discovered by Micah or his family. Lk +4:30. Jn 10:12, 13.

21. **and put,** etc. These men were so confident of success, that they removed their whole families, household goods, cattle, and all. **the carriage.** Heb. *Kevoodah*, from *kavad*, to be heavy, denotes the luggage or baggage.

23. **What aileth.** Ge 21:17. 1 S 11:5. 2 S 14:5. 2 K 6:28. Ps 114:5. Is 22:1. **comest.** Heb. art gathered together.

24. **what have.** Jg 17:13. Ps 115:8. Is 44:18-20. Je 50:38. 51:17. Ezk 23:5. Hab 2:18, 19. Ac 19:26. Re 17:2.

25. **angry.** Heb. bitter of soul. Heb. *nephesh*, Ex +15:9. 1 S 1:10. 22:2mg. +30:6mg. 2 S 17:8. 2 K

4:27mg. Jb 3:5mg. 27:2mg. Pr 31:6mg. He 12:15. **life.** Heb. *nephesh*, soul, Ge +44:30. **lives.** Heb. *nephesh*, or, souls. Ge +44:30.

27. **Laish.** ver. 7, 10. **quiet and secure.** 1 Th 5:3. **they smote.** Ge 49:17. Dt 33:22. Jsh 19:47. **burnt.** Jsh 11:11.

28. **And there.** 2 S 14:6mg. Ps 7:2. 50:22. Da 3:15-17. **far from.** Probably the people of Laish were originally a colony of the Zidonians; who being an opulent people, and in possession of a strong city, lived in a state of security, not being afraid of their neighbors. In this the Leshemites imitated them, though they appear not to have had the same reason for their confidence; and though they might naturally expect help from their countrymen, yet as they lived at a considerable distance from Sidon, the Danites saw they could strike the blow before the news of the invasion could reach that city. ver. 1, 7. Jsh 11:8. Is 23:4, 12. **Bethrehob.** Nu 13:21, Rehob. 2 S 10:6.

29. **Dan.** Jg 20:1. Ge 14:14. Jsh 19:47. 2 S 17:11. 1 K 12:29, 30. 15:20. **who was.** Ge 30:6. 32:28. *Laish*, or *Dan*, was situated at the northern extremity of the land of Canaan, in a beautiful and fertile plain, at the foot of Mount Lebanon, on the springs of Jordan, and, according to Eusebius, four miles from Caesarea Philippi or Paneas, now Banias (with which some have confounded it), towards Tyre. Burckhardt says, that the source of the river El Dhan, or Jordan, is at an hour's distance from Banias, which agrees with Eusebius.

30. **set up.** Ex 20:4. Le 26:1. Dt 17:2-7. 27:15. 31:16, 29. Jsh 19:40-48. Ps 78:58-61. God had graciously performed his promise in putting these Danites in possession of that which fell to their lot, obliging them thereby to be faithful to him who had been so to them; they inherited the labor of the people, that they might observe his statutes, Ps 105:44, 45. But the first thing they do after they are settled is to break his laws by setting up the graven image, attributing their success to that idol, which, if God had not been infinitely patient, would have been their ruin. Thus a prosperous idolater goes on to offend, imputing this his power unto his God. Instead of *Manasseh*, some would read *Moses*; as it is found in some MSS., in the Vulgate, and in the concessions of the most intelligent Jews. But Bp. Patrick takes this to be an idle conceit of the Rabbins, and supposes this Jonathan to be of some other family of the Levites. **Gershom.** Ex 2:21, 22. **until.** Jg 13:1. 1 S 4:2, 3, 10, 11. Ps 78:60-62. **the land.** Houbigant contends that instead of *haaretz*, "the land," we should read *haaron*, "the ark," for the *wav*, and *noon* final, might easily be mistaken for *tzadday* final; which is the only difference between the two words. This conjecture is the more likely, as the next verse tells us, that Micah's graven image continued at Dan "all the time that the house of God was at Shiloh;" which was till the ark was taken by the Philistines.

31. **all the time.** Jg 19:18. 21:12. Jsh 18:1. 1 S 1:3. 4:3, 4. Je 7:12.

JUDGES 19

A Levite's concubine commits adultery, and returns to her father, 1, 2. The Levite goes to take her back, and is kindly entertained, 3-9. They depart at a late hour and lodge at Gibeah, being entertained by an old man of Ephraim, who sojourned there, 10-21. The men of the city beset the house, with a vile intent; the Levite yields up his concubine, who is abused till she dies, 22-28. He divides her body into twelve parts, and sends one to each tribe, 29, 30.

1. **when there**. Jg 17:6. 18:1, 7. 21:25. **mount Ephraim**. Jg 17:1, 8. Jsh 24:30, 33. **a concubine**. Heb. a woman, a concubine, *or*, a wife, a concubine. Ge 22:24. 25:6. 2 S 3:7. 5:13. 16:22. 19:5. 20:3. 1 K 11:3. 2 Ch 11:21. Est 2:14. SS 6:8, 9. Is +40:13mg. Da 5:3. Ml 2:15. **Beth-lehem-judah**. Jg 17:8. Ge 35:19. Mt 2:6.

2. **played**. Le 21:9. Dt 22:21. Ezk 16:28. **four whole months**. *or*, a year and four months. Heb. days, four months. Jg 11:40. ℐ144A10, Ge +29:14.

3. **went**. Jg 15:1. **speak**. Ge 50:21. Le 19:17. 20:10. Ho 2:14. Mt 1:19. Jn 8:4, 5, 11. Ga *6:1. **friendly unto her**. Heb. to her heart. Ge 34:3mg. Ho 2:14mg. **to bring**. Je 3:1. **his servant**. Nu 22:22.

5. **Comfort**. Heb. Strengthen. ver. 8. Ge 18:5. 1 S 14:27-29. 30:12. 1 K 13:7. Ps 104:15. Jn 4:34. Ac 9:19. **with a morsel**. ver. 22.

6. **let thine heart**. ver. 9, 21. Jg 9:27. 16:25. Ru 3:7. 1 S 25:36. Est 1:10. Ps 104:15. Lk 12:19. 1 Th 5:3. Re 11:10, 13.

8. **until afternoon**. Heb. till the day declined. 2 K 20:10. Ps 109:23. Merely that they might avoid the heat of the day, which would have been very inconvenient in traveling.

9. **the day**. Lk 24:29. **draweth**, etc. Heb. is weak. **the day groweth to an end**. Heb. it is the pitching time of the day, Je 6:4. Nu 1:51. 10:31, 33. Dt 1:33. Ezk 20:6. That is, it was near the time in which travelers ordinarily pitched their tents, to take up their lodging for the night. In the latter part of the afternoon, eastern travelers begin to look out for a place for this purpose. So Dr. Shaw observes, "Our constant practice was to rise at break of day, set forward with the sun, and travel to the middle of the afternoon; at which time we began to look out for encampments of Arabs; who, to prevent such parties as ours from living at free charges upon them, take care to pitch in woods, valleys, or places the least conspicuous." **tomorrow**. Pr 27:1. Ja 4:13, 14. **home**. Heb. to thy tent. Jg 7:8. 20:8.

10. **over against**. Heb. to over against. **Jebus**. i.e. *threshing floor*, *S#2982h. Jg 1:8. Jsh 15:8, 63. 18:28. 2 S 5:6. 1 Ch 11:4, 5h.

11. **the Jebusites**. ver. 10. Jg 1:21. Ge +10:16. Jsh 15:63. 2 S 5:6.

12. **Gibeah**. i.e. *height; a hill*, ✛S#1390h. ver. 13, 14, 15, 16. Jg 20:4, 5, 9, 10, 13, 14, 15, 19, 20, 21, 25, 29, 30, 31, 33, 34, 36, 37, 43. Jsh 15:57. ◗21:17. 1 S 10:26. 11:4. 13:2, 15, 16. 14:2, 5, 16. 15:34. 22:6. 23:19. 26:1. 2 S 6:3, 4. 21:6. 23:29. 1 Ch 11:31. 2 Ch 13:2. Is 10:9. Ho 5:8. *9:9. 10:9, 9. Gibeah, a city of Benjamin, and the birth-place of Saul, was situated near Rama and Gibeon, according to Josephus, thirty furlongs north from Jerusalem; or, according to Jerome, about two leagues. (1) A town in the hill country of Judah, Jsh 15:57. (2) Gibeah of Benjamin. The tribe of Benjamin was nearly destroyed by a dreadful crime of some of its people. See Jg ch. 19-21. This town is generally considered to be the same as Gibeah of Saul. (3) Gibeah of Saul, 1 S 10:26; 11:4, the home of Saul, is held by many authorities to be the same

as Gibeah of Benjamin. (4) Gibeah in Kirjath-jearim; doubtless a hill in that city, 2 S 6:3, 4. (5) Gibeah in the field, Jg 20:31. It was probably the same as Geba. (6) Gibeah-haaraloth, in the marginal notes, Jsh 5:3. See Gilgal.

13. **Gibeah**. Jsh 18:25, 26, 28. 1 S 10:26. Is 10:29. Ho 5:8.

15. **no man**. There was probably no inn, or house of public entertainment in this place; and therefore they could not have a lodging unless furnished by mere hospitality. But these Benjamites seem to have added to their other vices, avarice and inhospitality, like the inhabitants of Akoura in mount Lebanon, mentioned by Burckhardt. ver. 18. Ge 18:2-8. 19:2, 3. Mt 25:35, 43. He *13:2.

16. **his work**. Ge 3:19. Ps 104:23. 128:2. Pr 13:11. 14:23. 24:27. Ec 1:13. 5:12. Ep 4:28. 1 Th 4:11, 12. 2 Th 3:10.

17. **lifted**. ℐ144A12, Ge +22:13. **wayfaring man**. 2 S 12:4. Je *14:8. **Whither**. Ge 16:8. 32:17. **in the street**. Young renders, "broad place," as ver. 15, where travellers often encamped. Ge 19:2.

18. **I am now**. The LXX. read, "I am going to my own house;" which is probably the true reading, as we find (ver. 29) that he really went home; yet he might have gone previously to Shiloh, or to "the house of the Lord," because that was also in mount Ephraim. **the house**. Jg 18:31. 20:18. Jsh 18:1. 1 S 1:3, 7. **receiveth**. Heb. gathereth. ver. 5. Ps 26:9. Jn *15:6.

19. **straw and provender**. In those countries principally devoted to pasturage, they made little or no hay: but as they raised corn, they took great care of their straw for their cattle, which by their mode of threshing was chopped very small. See Note on Ge 24:32. **bread**. ℐ171I8, Ge +3:19. **and**. ℐ174, Ge +18:27. **wine**. ℐ121D13, Ge +27:28.

20. **Peace be**. Jg 6:23. Ge 43:23, 24. 1 S 25:6. 1 Ch 12:18. Lk 10:5, 6. Jn 14:27. 1 C 1:3. **let all thy wants**. Here was genuine hospitality: "Keep your bread and wine for yourselves, and your straw and provender for your asses; you may need them before you finish your journey: I will supply all your wants for this night; only do not lodge in the street." Ro 12:13. Ga 6:6. He *13:2. Ja 2:15, 16. 1 P 4:9. 1 J 3:18. **lodge not**. Ge 19:2, 3. 24:31-33. Young comments, "because of the cold, and of the people."

21. **So he brought**. Ge 24:32. 43:24. **they washed**. Ge 18:4. 1 S 25:41. 2 S 11:8. Lk 7:44. Jn 13:4, 5, 14, 15. 1 T 5:10.

22. **they were**. ver. 6, 7. Jg 16:25. **the men**. Jg 20:5. Ge 19:4. Ho 9:9. 10:9. Ro 1:24. **sons of Belial**. Dt 13:13. +15:9. 1 S 1:16. 2:12. 10:27. 25:25. +30:22. 2 S 23:6, 7. 2 C 6:15. **Bring forth**. Ge 19:5. Ro 1:26, 27. 1 C *6:9. Ju 7.

23. **the man**. Ge 19:6, 7. **do not this folly**. Jg 20:6. Ge 34:7. Jsh 7:15. 2 S 13:12. Is +9:16 (*S#5039h).

24. **Behold**. The rites of hospitality are regarded as sacred and inviolable in the East: and a man who has admitted a stranger under his roof, is bound to protect him even at the expense of his life. On these high notions only, the influence of which an Asiatic mind alone can appreciate, can the present transaction be either excused or palliated. **them**. Ge 19:8. Ro 3:8. **humble ye**. Ge +34:2mg. Dt 21:14. **so vile a thing**. Heb. the matter of this folly. ver. 23. Dt 22:21. Is +9:16 (*S#5039h).

25. **knew her**. Ge +4:1. **and abused**. Nu 22:29 (mocked; Young renders "rolled thyself against me"). 1 S 31:4. Je 5:7, 8. Ho 7:4-7. 9:9. 10:9. Ep 4:19. or, rolled themselves upon her (Young). **the day began**. Ge 19:15. +32:24mg.

26. **the dawning**. Ex 14:27. **where her lord was**. ver. 3, 27. Ge 18:12. 1 P 3:6.

27. **to go**. Young notes, "to his own dwelling, glad to escape with his life, intending to leave her behind." **threshold**. 1 K 14:17. 2 K 12:9mg. 22:4. 23:4. 25:18mg. 1 Ch 9:19mg, 22.

28. **But none answered**. Jg 20:5. 1 K 18:26, 29. Is 50:2. 66:4.

29. **knife**. Ge 22:6, 10. Pr 30:14. **divided her**. It is probable, that with the pieces he sent to each tribe a circumstantial account of the barbarity of the men of Gibeah; and that they considered each of the pieces as expressing an execration. That a similar custom prevailed in ancient times is evident from 1 S 11:7. It had an inhuman appearance, thus to mangle the corpse of this unhappy woman; but it was intended to excite a keener resentment against so horrible a crime, which called for a punishment proportionably severe. Jg 20:6, 7. Ro 10:2. **with her bones**. Dt 21:22, 23.

30. **consider**. Jg 20:7. Pr 11:14. 13:10. 15:22. 20:18. 24:6. Is 8:10. He +*13:4.

JUDGES 20

Israel assembles at Mizpeh, and the Levite states his wrong, 1-7. The assembly resolve to punish the men of Gibeah, 8-11. The Benjamites, when required, refuse to deliver them up, and prepare for war, 12-17. By divine direction Judah goes first to fight with them; yet the Israelites are defeated twice with great loss, 18-25. They humble themselves before God, with fasting and sacrifices, and are promised success, 26-28. They employ a stratagem, and destroy all the tribe of Benjamin, except six hundred men, who flee to the rock Rimmon, 29-48.

1. **Then all**. *107, Ge +10:5. ver. 2, 8, 11. Jg 21:5. Dt 13:12, etc. Jsh 22:12. **as one man**. 1 S 11:7, 8. 2 S 19:14. Ezr 3:1. Ne 8:1. **from Dan**. Jg 18:29. 1 S 3:20. 2 S 3:10. 24:2. 1 K 4:25. 1 Ch 21:2. 2 Ch 30:5. **with the**. Nu 32:1, 40. Jsh 17:1. 2 S 2:9. **unto the**. ver. 18, 26. Jg 11:11. **in Mizpeh**. Jg 10:17. 11:11. Jsh 15:38. 18:26. 1 S *7:5, 6, 16. 10:17. 2 K 25:23. It does not appear that the Israelites on this occasion, were summoned by the authority of any common head; but they came together by the consent and agreement, as it were, of one common heart, fired with a holy zeal for the honor of God and Israel. The place of their meeting was Mizpeh; they gathered together unto the Lord there; for Mizpeh was so very near to Shiloh, that their encampment might very well be supposed to reach from Mizpeh to Shiloh. Shiloh was a small town, and therefore, when there was a general meeting of the people to present themselves before God, they chose Mizpeh for their head quarters, which was the next adjoining city of note; perhaps, because they were not willing to give that trouble to Shiloh, which so great an assembly would occasion; it being the residence of the priests that attended the tabernacle.

2. **chief**. Heb. corners. Dt 1:15. 1 S 14:38. Is 19:13. Zc 10:4. **presented themselves**. Jg 5:10. 12:14. **drew sword**. ver. 15, 17. Jg 8:10. 2 S 24:9. 2 K 3:26.

3. **the children of Benjamin**. Pr 22:3. Mt 5:25. Lk 12:58, 59. 14:31, 32. **how was**. Jg 19:22-27.

4. **the Levite**. Heb. the man the Levite. Ex 2:14. **I came**. Jg 19:15-28.

5. **And the men**. or, masters. Jg 9:2, 6, 7, 18, 20, 23, 24, 25, 26, 39. 19:22. Jsh 24:11. **beset**. Ge 19:4-8. **and my concubine**. Jg 19:25, 26. **forced**. Heb. humbled. Jg 19:24. Dt 22:24. Ezk 22:10, 11.

6. **cut her**. Jg 19:29. **folly in Israel**. ver. 10. Jg 19:23. Ge 34:7. Jsh 7:15. 2 S 13:12, 13.

7. **ye are all**. Ex 19:5, 6. Dt 4:6. 14:1, 2. 1 C 5:1, 6, 10-12. **give here**. Jg 19:30. Jsh 9:14. Pr 20:18. 24:6. Ja *1:5. **counsel**. Pr 8:14. Is 8:10.

8. **as one man**. See on ver. 1, 11. **We will not**. Jg 21:1, 5. Pr 21:3. Ec 9:10.

9. **by lot against it**. Jsh *14:2n. 1 S 14:41, 42. 1 Ch 24:5. Ne 11:1. Pr 16:33. Jon 1:7. Ac 1:26.

10. **ten thousand**. or, myriad. Ge 24:60.

11. **knit**. 1 S 18:1. 1 Ch 12:17. 2 Ch 5:13. **together as one man**. Heb. fellows. or, companions. Ps 45:7. +*119:63. Pr 28:24. Ec 4:10. SS 1:7. 8:13. Is 1:23. 44:11. Ezk 37:16, 19.

12. **sent men**. Dt 13:14-16. 20:10, 12. Jsh 22:13-16. Mt 18:15-18. Ro 12:18.

13. **deliver**. 2 S 20:21, 22. **children of Belial**. Jg +19:22. Dt 13:13. +15:9. 1 S 30:22. 2 S 20:1. 23:6. 1 K 21:13. 2 Ch 13:7. **put away**. Dt 17:7, 12. 19:19. 21:21. 22:21, 24. 24:7. Ec 11:10. **would not**. 1 S 2:25. 2 Ch 25:16, 20. Pr *29:1. Ho 9:9. 10:9. Ro 1:32. Re 18:4, 5. The conduct of the Israelites was very equitable in this demand; but perhaps the rulers or elders of Gibeah ought previously to have been applied to, to deliver up the criminals to justice. However, the refusal of the Benjamites, and their protection of those who had committed this horrible wickedness, because they were of their own tribe, prove them to have been deeply corrupted, and (all their advantages considered) as ripe for divine vengeance as the inhabitants of Sodom and Gomorrah had been. Confiding in their own valor and military skill, they seem to have first prepared for battle in this unequal contest with such superior numbers.

14. **to go**. Nu 20:20. 21:23. 2 Ch 13:13. Jb 15:25, 26.

15. **twenty and six thousand**. ver. 25, 35, 46, 47. Nu 26:41.

16. **left-handed**. *Itter yad yemeeno*, "obstructed in his right hand;" so the Chaldee Targum, *gemid beedaih deyammeena*, "contracted or impeded in his right hand." Le Clerc observes, that the 700 men left-handed seem therefore to have been made slingers, because they could not use the right hand, which is employed in managing heavier arms; and they could discharge the stones from the sling in a direction against which their opponents were not upon their guard, and thus do the greater execution. Jg 3:15n. Ge +48:13. 1 Ch 12:2. **sling stones**. The sling was a very ancient warlike instrument; and, in the hands of those who were skilled in the use of it, produced astonishing effects. The inhabitants of the islands of *Baleares*, now Majorca and Minorca, were the most celebrated slingers of antiquity. They did not permit their children to break their fast, till they had struck down the bread they had to eat from the top of a pole, or some distant eminence. Vegetius tells us, that slingers could in general hit the mark at 600 feet distance. 1 S 17:40, 49, 50. 25:29.

2 Ch 26:14. Je 10:18. **hair.** ƒ102, Ge +2:24. ƒ79, Ge 21:16. 1 S 14:45. **not miss.** or, err. lit. sin, by missing the mark (Young).

17. **four hundred thousand.** ver. 2. Nu 1:46. 26:51. 1 S 11:8. 15:4. 1 Ch 21:5. 2 Ch 17:14-18.

18. **house of God.** Jg 18:31. 19:18. Jsh 18:1. Jl 1:14. **asked counsel.** ver. 7, 23, 26, 27. Jg 1:1. Nu 27:5, 21. Jsh 9:14. **Judah.** Jg 1:1, 2. Ge 49:8-10. Nu 10:14.

19. **rose up.** Jsh 3:1. 6:12. 7:16.

21. **the children of Benjamin.** Ge 49:27. Ho 10:9. **destroyed.** Dt 23:9. 2 Ch 28:10. Ps 33:16. 73:18, 19. 77:19. Ec 9:1-3. Je 12:1. Ga 5:15.

22. **encouraged.** Heb. strengthened. ver. 15, 17. Ge 48:2. 1 S 30:6. 2 S 11:25. Ps 64:5. **in the place.** Hereby showing their freedom from that heathenish superstition, whereby they might have been apt to have rejected that as an unlucky place (Matthew Poole). Compare 1 K 20:23, 28. See Note on Ge 24:44. Jsh 14:2n.

23. **wept.** ver. 26, 27. Ps 78:34-36. Ho 5:15. **asked counsel.** Is 1:12, 16. Ho 7:14. **And the.** It seems most evident that the Israelites did not seek the protection of God. When they "went to the house of God" (ver. 18), it was not to enquire concerning the expediency of the war, nor of its success, but which of the tribes should begin the attack: and here the question is, "Shall I go up again to battle against the children of Benjamin my brother?" Having so much right on their side, they had no doubt of the justice of their cause, and the propriety of their conduct; and having such a superiority of numbers, they had no doubt of success. But God humbled them, and delivered them into the hands of their enemies; and showed them that the race was not to the swift, nor the battle to the strong. Ja 4:2.

25. **destroyed.** ver. 21. Ge 18:25. Jb 9:12, 13. Ps 97:2. Ro 2:5. 3:5. 11:33.

26. **all the children of Israel.** ver. 18, 23. **wept.** 1 S 7:6. 2 Ch *20:3. Ezr 8:21. 9:4, 5. Jl 1:14. 2:12-18. Jon 3:5-10. **and sat.** Young notes, "in prayer, as David did in 1 Ch 17:16; here we have a congregation, there an individual, worshipping God in a sitting posture; the mode is nothing, if the spirit be right." Jg 21:2. 2 S 7:18. 1 K 19:4. 1 Ch 17:16. Ne 1:4. Ezk 14:1-3. 20:1. **and fasted.** 1 S 7:6. Ezr 8:21. Ne 1:4. Est 4:3, 16. Is *58:3-7. Je 36:9. Da 9:3. Jl 2:12, 15. Mt +4:2. +6:16. Lk ◐+18:12. Ac 14:23. This is the first occasion in which a voluntary fast is mentioned in the Bible. The only fast appointed by Moses was that of the seventh month, Zc 8:19. Le 16:29. 23:27, 29, 32. Ps *35:13. 69:10. Fasting is God's appointed means of our humbling ourselves before Him. 2 Ch +√7:14. Ps *35:13. **until even.** T#1764. ver. 23. Jg 21:2. Jsh 7:6. **burnt offerings.** Le +*23:12. **peace offerings.** Le +*23:19.

27. **enquired.** ver. 18, 23. Nu 27:21. **the ark.** Jsh 18:1. 1 S 4:3, 4. Ps 78:60, 61. Je 7:12. The loss of two battles at length brought this stiff-necked people to enquire of the Lord: for all the company at this time met at Shiloh, and kept a day of fasting and prayer with great earnestness and solemnity. Is 59:1.

28. **Phinehas.** Nu 25:7-13. Jsh 22:13, 30-32. 24:33. It is evident from this mention of Phinehas, that the son of Eleazar, that these transactions must have taken place not long after the death of Joshua. Thus this history did not take place in the chronological order in which it is here placed, after Samson's death, but

long before. See notes on the Figure Hysterologia at Jg 19:1 and 20:1, and the Figure Hysteresis at Jg 18:1. **stood.** Dt 10:8. 18:5, 7. 2 K 25:8. Pr 22:29. Je 52:12. That is, ministered, as the word stand often signifies, because standing is the usual posture of servants (Matthew Poole). **Shall I yet.** Jsh 7:7. 1 S 14:37. 23:4-12. 30:8. 2 S 5:19-24. 6:3, 7-12. Pr *3:5, 6. Je 10:23. **Go up.** Jg 1:2. 7:9. 2 Ch 20:17.

29. **Israel.** Though God had promised them success, they knew they could expect it only by the use of proper means. Hence they used all prudent precaution, and employed all their military skill. **liers.** ver. 34. Jsh 8:4. 2 S 5:23.

31. **drawn.** Jsh 8:14-16. **smite of the people, and kill, as at.** Heb. smite of the people wounded as at, etc. ver. 39. **the house of God.** or, Bethel. ver. 18, 26, 27. Jg 18:31. 21:2, 12, 19. 1 S 10:3. **Gibeah.** Jg 19:13, 14. Is 10:29. **in the field.** So called to differentiate from the other Gibeah which was upon a hill, where it is constantly said that they ascend or go up against it, ver. 23, 30. See Jsh 18:24, 28. **thirty men.** Jsh 7:5.

32. **Let us flee.** This was done, not only because they had placed an ambuscade behind Gibeah, which was to enter and burn the city as soon as the Benjamites left it; but it would seem, that the slingers, by being within the city and its fortifications, had great advantage over the Israelites by their slings, when they could not come among them with their swords, unless they got them in the country. Jsh 8:15, 16.

33. **rose up.** Jsh 8:18-22. **put themselves.** There appears to have been three divisions of the Israelitish army: one at Baal-tamar (which was situated, says Eusebius, near Gibeah); a second behind the city in ambush; and a third, who skirmished with the Benjamites before Gibeah. **Baal-tamar.** i.e. possessing palms; lord of the palm, *S#1193h. **meadows.** lit. a naked place, or perhaps cave, as in 1 S 13:6.

34. **ten thousand.** ver. 29. **knew not.** Jsh 8:14. Jb 21:13. Pr 4:19. 29:6. Ec 8:11, 12. 9:12. Is 3:10, 11. 47:11. Mt 24:44. Lk 21:34. 1 Th 5:3.

35. **the Lord smote.** Dt 32:35. **twenty and five thousand and.** ver. 15, 44-46. Jb 20:5. Though the numbers of the Israelites were immensely superior to those of Benjamin—though the stratagem was well laid and ingeniously executed, and the battle bravely fought—yet the inspired historian ascribes the victory to the hand of the Lord, as entirely as if he had smitten the Benjamites by a miracle.

36. **for the men.** Jsh 8:15, etc.

37. **the liers in wait hasted.** Jsh 8:15, 19. **drew themselves along.** or, made a long sound with the trumpets. Ex 19:13. Jsh 6:5. or, marched or went. Heb. drew their feet. So this verb is often used, as Ge 37:28. Ex 12:21. Jg 4:6. Jb 21:33. Here, a reference to marching in rank and file, as armies do (Matthew Poole).

38. **Now there.** From this verse to the end of the chapter, we have the details of the same operations which are mentioned, in a general way, in the preceding verses of this chapter. **sign.** or, time. Ge +17:21 (✦S#4150h). 2 K 4:16mg. **and.** Heb. with. **flame.** Heb. elevation.

39. **And when.** ver. 31. **smite and kill.** Heb. smite the wounded.

40. **a pillar.** Ge 19:28. SS 3:6. Jl 2:30. Re 19:3.

looked. Jsh 8:20. **flame.** Heb. whole consumption.
41. **were amazed.** Ge +*45:3mg. Ex 15:9, 10. Is
13:8, 9. 33:14. Lk 17:27, 28. 21:26. 1 Th 5:3. 2 P
2:12. Re 6:15-17. 18:8-10. **was come upon them.** Heb.
touched them.
42. **the battle.** La 1:3. Ho 9:9. 10:9. i.e. *the men
of battle or war;* the abstract for the concrete, as poverty, 2 K 24:14; pride, Ps 36:11; deceit, Pr 12:5; dreams,
Je 27:9; election, Ro 11:7, are put for persons that
are poor, proud, deceitful, dreamers, elect. ƒ121N1.
Metonymy of the Adjunct, Ge 31:54mg.
43. **inclosed.** Jsh 8:20-22. **with ease.** or, from Menu-
chah, etc. Nu 10:33. 1 Ch 2:52. Je 51:59. Mi 2:10.
over against. Heb. unto over against.
45. **Rimmon.** i.e. *pomegranate.* Jsh 15:32. 1 S 14:2.
1 Ch 6:77. Zc 14:10. **gleaned.** Dt 24:21. **Gidom.** i.e.
a *cutting down,* *S#1440h.
46. **twenty and five thousand.** ver. 15, 35. Besides
the odd hundred expressed (ver. 35); but here only
the great number is expressed, the less being omitted,
as inconsiderable; which way of numbering is frequent
in Scripture, as Jg 11:26; 2 S 5:5, and in other authors,
and in vulgar use; as when they are called seventy
interpreters, who in truth and exactness were seventy-
two. Here are also a thousand more omitted, because
here he speaks only of them who fell in that third
day of battle (Matthew Poole).
47. **six hundred.** Jg 21:13. Ps 103:9, 10. Is 1:9. Je
14:7. La 3:32. Hab 3:2. **rock of Rimmon.** The rock of
Rimmon was doubtless a strong place; but it is uncertain
where situated. It is probable however, that it was
near, and took its name from, the village *Remmon,*
mentioned by Eusebius, fifteen miles north from Jerusalem. It appears that rocks are still resorted to in
the East, as places of security; and some of them are
even capable of sustaining a siege. De La Roque says,
that "The Grand Seignior, wishing to seize the person
of the emir (Fakr-eddin, prince of the Druzes), gave
orders to the pacha to take him prisoner: he accordingly
came in search of him, with a new army, in the district
of Chouf, which is part of mount Lebanon, wherein
is the village of Gesin, and close to it, the rock which
served for a retreat to the emir. It is named in Arabic,
Magara Gesin, i.e. the cavern of Gesin, by which name
it is famous. The pacha pressed the emir so closely,
that this unfortunate prince was obliged to shut himself
up in the cleft of a great rock, with a small number
of officers. The pacha besieged him there several
months; and was going to blow up the rock by a mine,
when the emir capitulated."
48. **smote them.** Dt 13:15-17. 2 Ch 25:13. 28:6-9.
Pr 18:19. **the men.** Comprehensively taken, so as to
include women and children. Jg 21:5, 10. Ge +*6:5n.
Nu 31:17. Dt 13:15, 16. Jsh 7:15. 1 S 15:3. **came to
hand.** Heb. was found. 2 K 19:4mg. 2 Ch +29:29mg.
they came to. Heb. were found. Ge 19:15mg. 1 S
9:8. 13:15, 16. 21:3. 1 Ch 29:17. 2 Ch +29:29mg.
34:32. Ezr 8:25. Est +*1:5mg.

JUDGES 21

*The people lament over Benjamin, are in difficulty,
having sworn not to give a wife to any of that tribe;
and inquire after such as had not joined them, having
sworn also to put them to death, 1-7. On that account
they destroy the inhabitants of Jabesh-Gilead, except*

*four hundred virgins, whom they give to that number
of the remaining Benjamites, 8-15. The elders consult,
how to find wives for the rest consistently with their
oath; and by their advice they carry off the virgins
who danced at Shiloh, 16-23. The people separate and
return home, 24, 25.*

1. **Now.** ƒ107, Ge +10:5. **had sworn.** Jg 20:1, 8,
10. Je 4:2. **There.** ver. 5. Jg 11:30, 31. 1 S 14:24, 28,
29. Ec 5:2. Mk 6:23. Ac 23:12. Ro 10:2. **his daughter.**
Ex 34:12-16. Dt 7:2, 3.
2. **the house of God.** ver. 12. Jg 20:18, 23, 26. Jsh
18:1. **abode there.** or, sat (in prayer). Jg +*20:26n.
lifted. ƒ144A12, Ge +22:13. Jg 2:4. Ge 27:38. 1 S
30:4. **wept sore.** Jg 20:23, 26. 2 S 13:36mg. 2 K *20:3mg.
Is 38:3mg.
3. **why is.** Dt 29:24. Jsh 7:7-9. Ps 74:1. 80:12. Pr
19:3. Is 63:17. Je 12:1. **one tribe.** T#1727.
4. **rose early.** Ps 78:34, 35. Ho 5:15. **built there.**
Jg 6:26. Ex 20:24, 25. 1 S 7:9, 17. 11:15. 16:2, 5. 2 S
24:18, 25. 1 K 8:64. He 13:10. **an altar.** Ge +13:18.
burnt offerings. Le +*23:12. **peace offerings.** Le
+*23:19.
5. **came not.** ver. 8. Jg 5:23. **a great oath.** ver. 1,
18. Jg 5:23. Le 27:28, 29. 1 S 11:7. Je 48:10. **to Mizpeh.**
Jg 20:1. Ge +31:49. Jsh +11:3n. **surely.** ƒ147B, Ge
+2:16.
6. **repented them.** ver. 15. Jg 11:35. 20:23. 2 S
2:26. Ho 11:8. Lk 19:41, 42.
7. **sworn.** ver. 1, 18. 1 S 14:28, 29, 45.
8. **came not up.** ver. 5. 1 S 11:7. **Jabesh-gilead.**
i.e. "Jabesh in the territory of Gilead," S#1568h. 1 S
11:1-3. 31:11-13. 2 S 2:5, 6. A city in Gilead, and in
the tribe of Manasseh, east of Jordan. Eusebius and
Jerome say it was a great town in their time, standing
upon a hill, six miles south from Pella, in the way to
Gerasa, now Djerash. The *Wady Yabes,* mentioned
by Burckhardt, which empties itself into the Jordan,
in the neighborhood of Bisan, or Bethshan (see 1 S
31:11), and upon which Pella was situated (celebrated
by Pliny, l. v. c. 18, for its fine waters), seems to
have taken its name from *Jabesh.* Near this spot, we
must therefore look for its site; and the place called
Kalaat Rabbad seems to correspond, very nearly, to
the spot; though it probably still retains among the
Arabs its ancient name.
10. **go and smite.** As they had sworn to destroy
those who would not assist in the war (ver. 5), they
determined to destroy the men of Jabesh, and to leave
none except the virgins; and to give these to the 600
Benjamites who had escaped to the rock of Rimmon.
The whole account is dreadful. The crime of the men
of Gibeah was of the deepest dye; the punishment
involving both the guilty and the innocent, was extended to the most criminal excess; and their mode
of remedying the evil they had occasioned was equally
abominable. ver. 5. Jg 5:23. Dt 13:15. Jsh 7:24. 1 S
11:7. 15:3. **women and the children.** Who in such
public and scandalous crimes were, for the greater
terror of such transgressors, and prevention of the like
sins, oft involved in the same punishment with the
men, as Dt 13:15; Jsh 7:24, etc.
11. **utterly destroy.** or, devote. Le 27:29n. **every
male.** Nu 31:17, 18. Dt 2:34. **hath lain by man.** Heb.
knoweth the lying with man. ver. 12. Ge +*4:1. Nu
31:17, 18.
12. **virgins.** Heb. women, virgins. Ge +*24:16. Is

+40:13mg. **Shiloh**. Jg 20:18, 23. Jsh 18:1. Ps 78:60. Je 7:12. **Canaan**. West of Jordan (Young).

13. **to speak**. Heb. and spake and called. **the rock Rimmon**. Jg 20:47. Jsh 15:32. **call peaceably**. or, proclaim peace. Dt 20:10. Is 57:19. Lk 10:5. Ep 2:17.

14. **sufficed them not**. ver. 12. Jg 20:47. 1 C 7:2.

15. **repented**. See on ver. 6, 17. **the Lord had made**. The Benjamites were the only authors of the sin, but God was the chief author of the punishment, and the Israelites were but his executioners (Matthew Poole). Am +√3:6. **a breach**. 1 Ch 13:11. 15:13. Is 30:13. 58:12.

16. **the elders**. Ex +18:21. Jsh +20:4. 24:1. 1 S 4:3. **How**. ver. 7.

17. **an inheritance**. Nu 26:55. 36:7. Jsh 12:6, 7. **be escaped**. Ex 10:5. **destroyed**. or, blotted out. Ge 6:7.

18. **not give**. Jg +*11:35. **sworn**. See on ver. 1. Jg 11:35.

19. **a feast**. Ex 10:9. 23:14-16. Le 23:2, 4, 6, 10, 34. Nu 10:10. 28:16, 26. 29:12. Dt 16:1, 10, 13. Ps 81:3. Jn 5:1. 7:2. **Shiloh**. i.e. *his peace, prosperity,* *S#7887h. ver. 12, 21, 21. Jsh 18:1, 8, 9, 10. 19:51. 21:2. 22:9, 12. Jg 18:31. 1 S 1:3, 9, 24. 2:14. 3:21, 21. 4:3, 4, 12. 14:3. 1 K 2:27. 14:2, 4. Ps 78:60. Je 7:12, 14. 26:6, 9. 41:5. **yearly**. Heb. from year to year. lit. from days to days. ♪171T2C, Ge +24:55. S#3117h. Jg +11:40mg. Ge +4:3mg. +*24:55mg. Nu +*9:22n. 1 S 1:3. Yearly; on the three solemn feasts, in which they used some honest and holy recreations; among which dancing was one, Ex 15:20; 1 S 18:6; 2 S 6:14; and probably it was the feast of tabernacles, which they did celebrate with more than ordinary joy, Dt 16:13-15 (Matthew Poole). **which is on**. ♪178, Ge 25:18. **the east side**. or, toward the sun-rising. Jg 20:43. **of the highway**. or, on. **Lebonah**. i.e. *frankincense,* *S#3829h. Maundrell supposes, that either *Khan Leban,* which is situated on the eastern side of a delicious vale, four leagues south from Shechem, and two leagues north from Bethel, or the village of Leban, which is on the opposite side, occupies the site of the ancient **Lebonah**. It is eight hours, or about 24 miles, from Jerusalem, according to Dr. Richardson.

21. **daughters of Shiloh come**. Poole notes that these may be not only the settled inhabitants of the region, but all the women who came to the feast, for though only the men were obliged to attend, the devout women usually came upon special reasons or occasions: see 1 S 1:7, 21, 22, 24; 1 Ch 15:20n. Lk 2:22, 23, 41-43. **dance**. Jg 11:34. Ex +15:20n. 1 S 18:6. 2 S 6:14, 21. Ps 149:3. 150:4. Ec 3:4. Je 31:13. Mt 10:17. Lk 15:25. **catch you**. Take them away by force or violence; which they might the better do, because mixed dances were not used by the people of God in their solemnities, but the women danced by themselves, and therefore were more liable to this rape (Matthew Poole).

22. **Be favorable unto them**. or, Gratify us in them. Ps 123:3. Is 33:2. Phm 9-12. **each man**. ver. 14. Ge 1:27. 7:13. Mk 10:6-8. 1 C 7:2. **give unto**. ver. 1, 7, 18. Pr 20:25.

23. **according to their number**. ver. 22. By which we may see they had no very favorable opinion of polygamy, because they did not allow it in this case, when it might seem most necessary for the reparation of a lost tribe (Matthew Poole). **they caught**. or, took violently away. ver. 21. **and they went**. It appears that the Benjamites acted in the most honorable way to the women they had thus violently carried off, and we may rest assured, that they took them to an inheritance more than equal to their own. But this transaction, as well as the indiscriminate massacre of the people of Jabesh-gilead, as Dr. Gray observes, was certainly stamped with injustice and cruelty; and must be condemned on those principles which the Scriptures elsewhere furnish. **repaired**. Jg 20:48.

24. **departed thence**. Dt 33:4, 5. Nu 27:15-17. 1 K 22:17.

25. **no king**. Jg *17:6. 18:1. 19:1. **did**. lit. will do. ♪96C8, Ex 15:5. Heterosis of tenses, the future for the past. **right**. Jg 18:7. Dt *12:8. Ps *12:4. Pr *3:5. *14:12. 16:2. 23:4. 26:12. Ec *11:9. Is 5:21. Mi *2:1, 2.

RUTH

RUTH 1

Elimelech induced by famine to sojourn in Moab dies there, 1-3. His two sons, having married women of Moab, die without children; and Naomi, Elimelech's widow, prepares to return to Israel, 4-6. Orpah and Ruth, her daughters-in-law, propose to accompany her; she dissuades them, and Orpah returns back, 7-14. Ruth determines to go with her, 15-18. They arrive at Bethlehem, and Naomi answers the inquiries of her neighbors, 19-22.

1. **the judges**. Jg 2:16. 12:8. Ac 13:20. **ruled**. Heb. judged. Jg 2:16. **a famine**. Ge 12:10. 26:1. 43:1. Le 26:19. Dt 28:23, 24, 38. Jg 6:3, 4. 2 S 21:1. 1 K 17:1-12. 18:2. 2 K 8:1, 2. Ps *105:16. *107:33, 34. Je 14:1. Ezk 14:13, 21. Jl 1:10, 11, 16-20. Am 4:6. Lk 15:14. **Beth-lehem-judah**. Jg 17:8. 19:1, 2. Jsh 19:15.

2. **Elimelech**. i.e. *my God is king,* *S#458h. ver. 3. Ru 2:1, 3. 4:3, 9. The Rabbins say, that Elimelech was the son of Salmon, who married Rahab; and that

Naomi was his niece. **Naomi**. i.e. *my pleasant one,* *S#5281h. ver. 3, 8, 11, *20, 21, 22. 2:1, 2, 6, 20, 20, 22. 3:1. 4:3, 5, 9, 14, 16, 17. **Mahlon**. i.e. *sickness,* *S#4248h. ver. 5. Ru 4:9, 10. **Chilion**. i.e. *consumption,* *S#3630h. ver. 5. Ru 4:9. It is imagined, and not without probability, that Mahlon and Chilion are the same with *Joash* and *Saraph,* mentioned in 1 Ch 4:22. **Ephrathites**. *S#673h. Ge ❶35:19. Jg 12:5. 1 S 1:1. 17:12. 1 K 11:26. Mi ❶5:2. **continued**. Heb. were.

3. **husband died**. Ge 11:32. Ac 7:4. **and she was**. 2 K 4:1. Ps 34:19. He 12:6, 10, 11. **left**. ver. 4. Ge 7:23.

4. **they took**. The Targum says, "they transgressed the decree of the word of the Lord, and took to them strange women." **wives**. Dt *7:3. *23:3. 1 K 11:1, 2. **Orpah**. i.e. *a neck* or *hind,* *S#6204h. ver. 14. **Ruth**. i.e. *appearance* or *friend; beauty,* *S#7327h. ver. 14, 16, 22. 2:2, 8, 21, 22. 3:9. 4:5, 10, 13. Mt 1:5.

5. A.M. 2696. B.C. 1308. An. Ex. Is. 183. **Mahlon**.

Dt 32:39. Ps 89:30-32. Je 2:19. **died**. The Targum adds, "And because they transgressed the decree of the word of the Lord, and joined affinity with strange people, therefore their days were cut off." **and the woman**. Is 49:21. Mt 22:25-27. Lk 7:12.

6. **visited**. or, looked after. Ge 21:1. 50:25. Ex +*3:16. *4:31. 13:19. 1 S 2:21. Jb *10:12. Ps 65:9. 107:35-37. Is 24:22. Lk 1:68. 19:44. 1 P 2:12. **in giving**. Ge 28:20. 48:15. Ex 16:4-6. Ps 37:25. 104:14, 15. 111:5. *132:15. 145:15. 146:7. 147:14. Pr 30:8. Is 55:10. Mt *6:11. 1 T 6:8.

7. **she went**. 2 K 8:3. **they went**. ver. 10, 14. Ex 18:27.

8. **Go**. Jsh 24:15, etc. Lk 14:25, etc. **the Lord**. Ph 4:18, 19. 2 T 1:16-18. **the dead**. ver. 5. Ru 2:20. Ep 5:22. 6:2, 3. Col 3:18, 24.

9. **rest**. Ru 3:1. **she kissed**. Ge 27:27. 29:11. 45:15. Ac 20:37. **lifted**. ♪144A12, Ge +22:13.

10. **Surely**. Ps 16:3. +*119:63. Zc 8:23.

11. **are there**. This alludes to the custom that when a married brother died, without leaving posterity, his brother should take his widow; and the children of such marriages were accounted those of the deceased brother. This address of Naomi to her daughters-in-law is exceedingly tender, persuasive, and affecting. **womb**. or, bowels. Ps 71:6. **that they**. Ge 38:*8, 11. Dt *25:5.

12. **too old**. Ge 17:17. 1 T 5:9. **to have an husband**. rather, "to be to a husband," for the wife in the Old Testament is always represented as belonging to the husband, but never vice versa (Young). **I should have**. or, I were with.

13. **tarry**. Heb. hope. Ge 38:8, *11. **it grieveth me much**. Heb. I have much bitterness. ver. 20. 1 S 30:6mg. 2 K 4:27mg. He +*12:15. *S#4843h: Kal, Preterite: Ru 1:13. 1 S 30:6mg. 2 K *4:27mg. Is 38:17. La 1:4. Kal, Future: Is 24:9. Piel, Future: Ge 49:23. Ex 1:14. Is 22:4mg. Hiphil, Preterite: Ru *1:20. Jb 27:2mg. Hiphil, Infinitive: Zc *12:10. Hiphil, Future: Ex 23:21 (provoke). Hithpalpel, Future: Da 8:7 (choler). 11:11. **for your sakes**. ver. 8. 1 J 4:7. **the hand**. Ex 7:5. Dt 2:15. Jg 2:15. 1 S 5:6, 11. Jb +*2:10. 19:21. *30:20, 21. Ps 32:4. ◐+√37:24. 38:2. 39:9, 10. +*77:3. Is ◐√29:24. Ezk +*18:25. Mt +*5:45. Lk +*6:35. Ac 13:11. Ja +*1:13, 17. **against me**. Ge 42:36. 2 K +*6:33. Pr +√19:3. Je ◐+√29:11.

14. **lifted**. ♪144A12, Ge +22:13. **Orpah**. Ge 31:28, 55. 1 K 19:20. Mt 10:37. 19:22. Mk 10:21, 22. 2 T 4:10. **but Ruth**. The LXX. add, "and returned to her own people." The Vulgate, Syriac, and Arabic, are to the same purpose. It seems a very natural addition, and agrees with the assertion in the next verse; and is accordingly adopted by Houbigant as a part of the text. Dt 4:4. 10:20. Pr 17:17. 18:24. Is 14:1. Zc 8:23. Mt 16:24. Jn 6:66-69. Ac 17:34. He 10:39.

15. **gone back**. Ps 36:3. 125:5. Zp 1:6. Mt 13:20, 21. He 10:38. 1 J 2:19. **and unto**. They were probably both idolaters at this time. That they were *proselytes* is an unfounded conjecture; and the conversion of Ruth now only commenced. **her gods**. Nu 21:29. 25:3. Jsh 24:15. Jg 11:24. 2 K 5:18, 19n. Mi 4:5. **return**. Jsh *24:15, 19. 2 S 15:19, 20. 2 K 2:2. Lk 14:26-33. 24:28.

16. **Ruth**. A more perfect surrender of friendly feelings to a friend was never made. This was a most extraordinary and disinterested attachment. **Intreat me**

not. or, Be not against me. Ru 2:22. Jg 15:12. 18:25. **to leave**. 2 K 2:2-6. Lk 5:28. 24:28, 29. Jn 1:38, 39. Ac 21:13. **whither**. 2 S 15:21. Mt 8:19. Jn *13:37. Re *14:4. **will lodge**. Ru 2:12. Ps 91:1. **thy people**. Ru 2:11, 12. Ps 45:10. Is *14:1. **thy God**. Jsh 24:18. Da 2:47. *3:29. *4:37. Ho *13:4. 2 C *6:16-18. 1 Th 1:9. **my God**. Ru 2:11, 12.

17. **the Lord**. 1 S 3:17. 14:44. 20:13. 25:22. 2 S 3:9, 35. 19:13. 1 K 2:23. 19:2. 20:10. 2 K 6:31. **do so**. ♪110, Ezk +34:2. **but death**. Ac *11:23. *20:24. **part**. 2 K 2:11. Pr 18:18. Ro 8:35, 38, 39.

18. **When**. Ac 21:14. **was steadfastly minded**. Heb. strengthened herself. 1 K 12:18. 2 Ch 10:18. 13:7. Ac 2:42. Ep *6:10. Ja 1:6, 8.

19. **all the city**. From this it would appear that Naomi was not only well known, but also highly respected at Bethlehem: a proof that Elimelech was of high consideration at that place. Mt 21:10. **was moved**. or, sounded, as in 1 S 4:5. 1 K *1:45. Mt 21:10. **Is this Naomi**. Is 23:7. La 2:15.

20. **Naomi**. that is, *Pleasant*. 2 S 1:26. SS 7:6. **Mara**. that is, *Bitter*. *S#4755h, only here. Ex 15:23. Jb 13:26. **the Almighty**. Ge 17:1. 43:14. Jb 5:17. 11:7. Re *1:8. *21:22. **dealt**. Jb 6:4. 19:6. 27:2mg. Ps 73:14. 88:15. Is 38:13. La 3:1-20. He 12:11. **very bitterly**. ver. +√13. Pr +√19:3. **with me**. Ps +*40:17. 103:14. Is +√29:24. Je ◐+√29:11. 1 C +*10:13. 2 C √1:3, 4.

21. **and the**. 1 S 2:7, 8. Jb 1:21. **the Lord**. Jb 10:17. 13:26. 16:8. Ml +*3:5. **empty**. Jb 1:21. **hath afflicted**. or, done evil. Jb 10:17mg. 16:8. Je ◐+√29:11. Am +√3:6.

22. **Moabitess**. ✛S#4125h. Ru 2:2, 21. 4:5, 10. 2 Ch 24:26. **in the beginning**. At the beginning of spring; for the barley harvest began immediately after the passover, and that festival was held on the 15th of *Nisan*, corresponding nearly with our *March*. Ru 2:23. Ex 9:31, 32. Le 23:10, 14. 2 S 21:9. 2 Ch 30:21. Lk 15:23.

RUTH 2

Ruth is led, without design, to glean in the field of Boaz, 1-3. He comes to see his reapers, and piously salutes them, and is saluted by them, 4. He shows kindness to Ruth; who behaves respectfully towards him, 5-10. He states what he had heard of her, prays for her, and shows her further kindness, 11-17. She returns to Naomi, and informs her of what had passed, 18-23.

1. **kinsman**. Ru 3:2, 12. Pr 7:4. **a mighty**. Dt 8:17, 18. Jb 1:3. 31:25. Ep 3:16. **Boaz**. i.e. *fleetness, strength*, *S#1162h. ver. 3, 4, 5, 8, 11, 14, 15, 19, 23. Ru 3:2, 7. 4:1, 1, 5, 8, 9, 13, 21, 21. 1 K 7:21. 1 Ch 2:11, 12. 2 Ch 3:17. Boaz, according to the Targumist, was the same as Ibzan. ver. 3. Ru 4:21. Jg 12:8-10. 1 Ch 2:10-12. Mt 1:5. Lk 3:32, Booz. (1) A Bethlehemite of Judah, husband of Ruth the Moabitess, and an ancestor of David, Ru 2:1; 1 Ch 2:11; Mt 1:5; Lk 3:32. (2) The name which Solomon gave to a brazen pillar he erected in the porch of the Temple, 1 K 7:21; 2 Ch 3:17.

2. **glean ears**. Le 19:9, 10, 16. 23:22. Dt 24:19-21. **find grace**. Ge 6:8.

3. **gleaned**. 1 Th 4:11, 12. 2 Th 3:12. **reapers**. ver. 4, 5, 6, 7, 14. 1 S 6:13. 2 K 4:18. Ps 129:7. Je 9:22. Am 9:13. **hap was**. Heb. happened. Ge ◐+24:44n. 1

S 6:9. 20:26. 2 K 8:5. Est 6:1, 2. Ec 2:14, 15mg. 3:19. 9:2, 3. Mt 10:29. Lk 10:31. **part.** Ru 4:3.

4. **The Lord.** Ps 118:26. *129:7, 8. Lk 1:28. 2 Th 3:16. 2 T 4:22. 2 J 10, 11. **And they.** Ru 4:11. Ge 18:19. Jsh *24:15. Ps 133:1-3. 1 T 6:2.

5. **Boaz.** Ru 4:21. 1 Ch 2:11, 12.

6. **the servant.** This seems to have been a kind of steward, who had the under-management of the estate. Ge 15:2. 24:2. 39:4. Mt 20:8. 24:45. **It is the.** Ru 1:16, 19, 22. **Moabitish.** ✛S#4125h, so rendered only here.

7. **I pray.** Pr 15:33. 18:23. Mt 5:3. Ep 5:21. 1 P 5:5, 6. **sheaves.** ver. 15. Dt 24:19. Jb 24:10. **continued.** Pr 13:4. 22:29. Ec 9:10. Ro 12:11. Ga *6:9. **in the house.** It seems that the reapers were now resting in a tent, erected for that purpose; and that Ruth had just gone in with them, to take her rest also.

8. **my daughter.** 1 S 3:6, 16. 2 K 5:13. Mt 9:2, 22. **neither.** SS 1:7, 8. **abide.** Mt 10:7-11. Ph *4:8.

9. **not touch thee.** ♪108B, Ge +26:29. Ge 20:6. 26:11. Jb 19:21. Ps 105:15. Pr 6:29. 1 C *7:1. 1 J 5:18. **go.** Ge 24:18-20. Mt 10:42. Jn 4:7-11.

10. **fell.** Ge 18:2. 33:3. 42:6. 1 S 25:23, 24. Mt 2:11. 8:2. **Why have.** ver. 2, 13. 2 S 9:8. 19:28. Lk 1:43, 48. Ro 12:10. **seeing.** Is 56:3-8. Mt 15:22-28. 25:35. Lk 7:6, 7. 17:16-18.

11. **all that.** Ru 1:11, 14-24. Ps 37:5, 6. **and how.** Ps 45:10. Lk 5:11, 28. 14:33. 18:29, 30. He 11:8, 9, 24-26. **heretofore.** Heb. yesterday, third day. Ex +4:10mg. 5:7, 8, 14. Jsh +3:4mg. 1 Ch 11:2mg. Is *30:33mg.

12. **recompense.** 1 S 24:19. Ps 19:11. 58:11. Pr 11:18. 23:18mg. Mt 5:12. 6:1. 10:41, 42. Lk *6:35. 14:12-14. Col 2:18. 2 T 1:18. 4:8. He 6:10. 11:6, 26. **under.** Ps 91:1. Mt 11:28. Lk 10:42. **wings.** Ru 1:16. Ex 25:20. Dt 32:11. Ps 17:8. 36:7. 57:1. 61:4. 63:7. 91:4. Mt 23:37. **trust.** Ps 91:4. 118:9, 10. Is 30:2.

13. **Let me find.** or, I find favor. Ge 33:8, 10, 15. 43:14. 1 S 1:18. 2 S 16:4. **comforted.** Is 40:1, 2. **friendly.** Heb. to the heart. Ge 34:3. Jg 19:3. **not like.** 1 S 25:41. Pr 15:33. SS 1:5, 6. Ph 2:3.

14. **At meal-time.** Jb 31:16-22. Pr 11:24, 25. Is 32:8. 58:7, 10, 11. Lk 14:12-14. **dip.** 1 S 14:27. **thy morsel.** Pr 17:1. Vinegar, robb of fruits, etc., are used for this purpose in the East to the present day; into which, says Dr. Shaw, they dip the bread and hand together. **vinegar.** Nu 6:3. Ps 69:21. **parched corn.** Le 2:14. 23:14. 1 S 17:17. 25:18. 2 S 17:27, 28. **she did.** Dt 8:10. 11:15. 2 K 4:43, 44. Mt 14:20. **was sufficed.** ver. 18. Ps 23:5.

15. **glean.** The word *glean* comes from the French *glaner*, to gather ears or grains of corn. **reproach.** Heb. shame. Ja *1:5. or, cause to blush. Jg 18:7. 1 S 20:34.

16. **let fall.** Dt *24:19-21. Ps 112:9. Pr *19:17. Mt 25:40. Ro 12:13. 2 C 8:5-11. Phm 7. He 6:10. 1 J 3:17, 18. **rebuke.** Ge 37:10.

17. **she gleaned.** Pr 31:27. 2 Th 3:10. **beat out.** Dt 24:20. Jg 6:11. Is 27:12. 28:27. **ephah.** Ex 16:36. Le 5:11. Jg 6:19. Ezk 45:11, 12.

18. **she had reserved.** ver. 14. Jn 6:12, 13. 1 T 5:4.

19. **blessed.** ver. 10. Ps *41:1. Pr *22:9. 2 C 9:13-15. **Boaz.** 1 K 7:21.

20. **Blessed.** Ru 3:10. 2 S 2:5. Jb 29:12, 13. 2 T 1:16-18. **hath not.** 2 S 9:1. Pr 17:17. Ph 4:10. **one of our.** or, one that hath right to redeem. Ru 3:9. 4:6. Le 25:25. Dt *25:5-7. Jb *19:25.

21. **Thou shalt.** ver. 7, 8, 22. SS 1:7, 8. **young men.** The word *hannearim* should have been translated "the servants"; both male and female being included in it, the latter especially: see ver. 8, 22, 23.

22. **Ruth.** Ruth is said, by the Targumist, to have been the daughter of Eglon, king of Moab. **It is good.** Pr 27:10. SS 1:8. **meet.** or, fall not upon thee. Ru 1:16.

23. **kept fast by.** Pr 6:6-8. 13:1, 20. 1 C 15:33. Ep 6:1-3. **wheat harvest.** Ge 30:14. The wheat harvest began at Pentecost. **dwelt with.** Pr ◖7:11, 12.

RUTH 3

By Naomi's instruction, 1-4, Ruth lies down in the night at the feet of Boaz, 5-7. He acknowledges that he owes the duty of a kinsman, but shows that another has a prior claim, 8-13. He sends her away in the morning with six measures of barley, and she confers with Naomi, 14-18.

1. **shall I not.** ♪85B, Ge +13:9. Ru 1:9. 1 C 7:36. 1 T 5:√8, 14. **may be.** Ge 40:14. Dt +*4:40. Ps 128:2. Je 22:15, 16.

2. **is not Boaz.** Ru 2:20-23. Dt *25:5, 6. He 2:11-14. **kindred.** Ru 2:1. **with whose.** Ru 2:8, 23. **he winnoweth.** It is probable that the winnowing of grain was effected by taking up a portion of the corn in a sieve, and letting it down slowly in the wind; thus the grain would, by its own weight, fall in one place, while the chaff, etc., would be carried to a distance by the wind. It is said here that this was done at night; probably what was threshed out in the day was winnowed in the evening, when the sea breeze set in, which was common in Palestine. Mt 3:12. **threshing floor.** Ge +50:10. Jg *6:37. 2 S 6:6. 24:16. 2 Ch 3:1.

3. **anoint thee.** 2 S 14:2. Ps 104:15. Ec 9:8. Mt 6:17. **put thy.** Est 5:1. Is 49:18. 52:1. Je 2:32. 1 T 2:9, 10. Re 19:7. 21:2. **the floor.** ver. 2.

4. **uncover his feet.** or, lift up the clothes that are on his feet. ver. 7, 8, 14. Da 10:6. 1 Th 5:22.

6. **the floor.** ver. +2, 3. **and did.** Ex 20:12. Pr 1:8. Jn *2:5. *15:14.

7. **eaten and drunk.** Jg 9:27. Ps *4:7. Is 9:3. **his heart.** Ge 43:34. Jg 16:25. 19:6, 9, 22. 2 S 13:28. Est 1:10. Ps 104:15. Ec 2:24. 3:12, 13. 8:15. 9:7. 10:19. 1 C 10:31. Ep *5:18. **went to lie.** Such was the simplicity of those early times, that the most wealthy persons looked after their own affairs, both at home and in the field. These threshing floors were covered at top to keep off the rain, but lay open on all sides, that the wind might come in freely, for winnowing the corn; which being done, it is probable they were shut up at night, with doors fitted to them, that if any one lay there he might be kept warm, and the corn be secured from robbers. **came softly.** Jg 4:21. 1 S 18:22. 24:4.

8. **afraid.** Ge +27:33mg. **turned.** or, took hold on. Jg 16:29. Jb 6:18.

9. **Ruth.** Ru 2:10-13. 1 S 25:41. Lk 14:11. **handmaid.** Not now merely a "maidservant," as she had called herself in Ru 2:13 (Young). **spread therefore.** Heb. spread thy wing: the emblem of protection; and a metaphor taken from the young of fowls, which run under the wings of their mother from birds of prey. Even to the present day, when a Jew marries a woman, he throws the skirts of his *talith* over her, to signify that

he has taken her under his protection. *88, Ge +15:15. Ru 2:12. Ge 20:16. Dt 22:30. 27:20. Ezk *16:8. 1 C 11:5, 6, 10. **a near kinsman**. *or*, one that has right to redeem. ver. 12. Ru 2:20.

10. **Blessed**. Ru 2:4, 20. 1 C 13:4, 5. **at the beginning**. Ru 1:8. **followedst not**. She preferred obedience to God's command (Dt 25:5) before the pleasing of herself (2 C *6:14. 1 T 5:11, 12). **poor**. lit. lean, thin. Ge 41:19. Ex 23:3. 30:15. Le 14:21. 19:15. Jg 6:15. 1 S 2:8. Jb 5:16. 20:10, 19. 31:16. 34:19, 28. Ps 41:1. 72:13. 82:3, 4. 113:7. Pr 10:15. 14:31. 19:4, 17. 21:13. 22:9, 16, 22. 28:3, 6, 8, 11, 15. 29:7. 29:14. Is 11:4. 14:30. 25:4. Je 5:4. 39:10. Am 2:7. 4:1. 5:11. 8:6. Zp 3:12. **rich**. Pr 10:15. *14:20. 18:11, 23. 22:2.

11. **fear not**. Mt 9:22. Mk 5:34. Lk 8:48. **city**. Heb. gate. *171S7, Ge +14:7. Ru 4:1. Ge +14:7. **virtuous woman**. Pr 12:4. *31:10, 29-31.

12. **there is**. Ru 4:1. Mt 7:12. 1 Th 4:6.

13. **Tarry**. Ge 19:2. **if he will**. Ru 2:20. *4:5. Dt *25:5-9. Mt 22:24-27. Mt 22:24. **the Lord liveth**. Jg 8:19. Je 4:2. 2 C 1:23. He 6:16. **the morning**. Ps 30:5. 46:5. 143:8.

14. **could know**. While it was yet so dark that one person could not discern another; or, before they were carnally known (Ge +4:1) to one another (Matthew Poole). **Let it not**. Ec 7:1. Ac 24:16. Ro *12:17. 14:16. 1 C 10:32. 2 C 8:21. 1 Th √5:22. 1 P 2:12.

15. **vail**. *or*, sheet, *or* apron. Is 3:22. But compare ver. 9 and 1 C 11:5, 6, 10. Not a veil for the face, but a covering for the head (Young). The word *mitpa-chath* has been variously rendered. The LXX. translate it *peridzoma*, an apron, and Vulgate, *pallium*, a cloak. By the circumstances of the story, it must have been of a considerable size; and accordingly Dr. Shaw thinks it was no other than the *hyke*, the finer sort of which, such as are still worn by ladies and persons of distinction among the Arabs, he takes to answer to the *peplos*, or robe, of the ancient Greeks. **he measured**. Is 32:8. Ga 6:10. **six measures**. The quantity of this barley is uncertain. The Targum renders it *shith sein, six seahs*. A seah contained about two gallons and a half, six of which must have been a very heavy load for a woman; and so the Targumist thought, for he adds, "And she received strength from the Lord to carry it."

16. **Who art thou**. Or, as the Vulgate renders, *Quid egisti filia?* "What hast thou done, my daughter?"

18. **Sit still**. Ps 4:4. *37:3-5. 46:10. Is 23:2. 28:16. *30:7. *50:10. **thou know**. Ph 1:6.

RUTH 4

Boaz proposes to the kinsman of whom he had spoken to redeem Elimelech's land, and to marry Ruth; which he declines to do, 1-8. Boaz buys the inheritance and marries Ruth, 9-12. She bears Obed the grandfather of David, 13-17. The genealogy from Pharez to David, 18-22.

1. **to the gate**. Ge +14:7. 23:10, 18. Dt 16:18. 17:5. 21:19. *25:7. Jb 29:7. 31:21. Pr ◑24:7. 31:23. Am 5:10-12, 15. **and sat**. Pr 31:23. **the kinsman**. Ru 3:12. **of whom**. Ru 3:11, 12. **Ho, such**. 1 S 21:2. 2 K 6:8. Is 55:1. Zc 2:6.

2. **ten men**. This being probably the legal number of witnesses in such cases as the present (Young). 1 K 21:8. **the elders**. Ex 18:+21, 22. 21:8. Dt 29:10. 31:28. Jsh +20:4. 1 K 21:8. Pr 31:23. La 5:14. Ac 6:12.

3. **he said**. Ps 112:5. Pr 13:10. **selleth a parcel**. Le 25:25.

4. **I thought**. Heb. I said I will reveal *in* thine ear. 1 S 9:15mg. 20:2mg, 12mg, 13. 22:8mg, 17. 2 S 7:27. 1 Ch 17:25mg. **Buy it**. Je 32:7-9, 25. Ro 12:17. 2 C 8:21. Ph 4:8. **before the inhabitants**. Ge 23:17, 18. Je 32:10-12. **for there is none**. Le 25:25-29.

5. **What day**. Or, rather, according to the emendations proposed by Houbigant and Dr. Kennicott, and which have been confirmed by a great many MSS. since collated, and agreeably to the ancient versions, "In the day thou purchasest the land from the hand of Naomi, thou wilt also acquire Ruth, the Moabitess, the wife of the dead," etc. This is Boaz's statement of the case to his kinsman, before the people and elders. **to raise up**. Ru 3:12, 13. Ge *38:8. Dt *25:5, 6. Mt 22:24. Lk 20:28.

6. **I cannot**. The Targum seems to give the proper sense of this passage: "I cannot redeem it, because I have a wife already; and it is not fit for me to bring another into my house, lest brawling and contention arise in it; and lest I hurt my own inheritance. Do thou redeem it, for thou hast no wife; which hinders me from redeeming it." **mar**. or, destroy. By bringing in additional heirs and claimants to his property (Young).

7. **in former time**. This shows that the composition of this narrative was considerably after the occurrence of the events (Young). **changing**. Le 27:10, 13. **a man plucked off**. This custom does not refer to the law about refusing to marry a brother's widow (Dt 25:9), but was usual in the transfer of inheritances: for this relative was not a brother, but simply a kinsman; and the shoe was not pulled off by Ruth, but by the kinsman himself. The Targumist, instead of "his shoe," renders "his right hand glove," it probably being the custom, in his time, to give that instead of a shoe. Jarchi says, "When we purchase any thing new, it is customary to give, instead of a shoe, a handkerchief or veil." Dt 25:7-10. Ps 60:8. **testimony**. Is 8:16, *20.

9. **Ye are witnesses**. Ge 23:16-18. Je 32:10-12.

10. **have I**. Ge 29:18, 19, 27. Pr 18:22. 19:14. 31:10, 11. Ho 3:2. 12:12. Ep 5:25. **the name**. Ge 48:5. Jsh 7:9. Ps 34:16. 109:15. Is 48:19. Zc 13:2. **gate**. *171S7, Ge +14:7. **ye are witnesses**. Is 8:2, 3. Je 32:25. Ml 2:14. He 13:4.

11. **The Lord**. Ge 24:60. Ps 127:3-5. 128:3-6. **Rachel**. Ge 29:32-35. 30:1-24. 35:16-20. 46:8-27. Nu ch. 26. **build**. Dt 25:9. Pr 14:1. **two**. Ge +4:19. **did build**. Ge 16:2mg. Ex 1:21. Ps *127:1, +*3. 128:3. **do thou worthily**. *or*, get thee riches, or power. Ru 2:1. 1 S 9:1. **Ephratah**. i.e. *the fruitful place*. Ru 1:2. Ge 35:16, 19. Ps 132:6. Mi +*5:2. Mt *2:6. **be famous**. Heb. proclaim *thy* name. ver. 14. Le 24:11, 16. Dt 28:58. **Bethlehem**. i.e. *the house of bread*. Ge 35:19. Mi +*5:2.

12. **the house**. Ge 46:12. Nu 26:20-22. **whom Tamar**. Ge 38:29. 1 Ch 2:4. Mt 1:3. Lk 3:33. **of the seed**. 1 S 2:20. Ga 3:16.

13. A.M. 2697. B.C. 1307. An. Ex. Is. 184. **Boaz took**. Ru 3:11. **went in**. Ge 6:4. 16:2. 30:3, 9. Jg 15:2. **the Lord**. ver. 12. Ge ◑+*11:30. 20:17, 18. 21:1-3. 25:21. +*29:31. 30:2, 22, 23n. 33:5. Dt 7:14. 28:4. 1 S 1:27. 2:5. Ps *113:9. +*127:3.

14. **the women**. Lk 1:58. Ro 12:15. 1 C *12:26. **Blessed**. Ge 29:35. Ps *34:1-3. 103:1, 2. 1 Th 5:18.

2 Th 1:3. **which hath**. Ge *24:27. **not left thee**. Heb. caused to cease unto thee. **kinsman**. *or*, redeemer. Ru 2:20. **that his**. ver. *21, *22. Ge *12:2. Is *11:1-4. Mt *1:5-20.

15. **restorer**. 1 S 2:6. La 1:16mg. Is 58:12. **life**. Heb. *nephesh*, soul. Ge +44:30. **a nourisher**, etc. Heb. to nourish thy grey hairs. Ge 45:11. 47:12. 1 K 17:4, 9. Ps *55:22. Is *46:4. **for thy**. Ru 1:16-18. **better**. 1 S 1:8. Pr 18:24. **seven sons**. Seven, the number of perfection (Young). 1 S 2:5. Jb 1:2. Je 15:9. **born him**. or, to wit, a son: the pronoun for noun understood; or, hath born to him, i.e. *to thy kinsman*, to wit, a son, which is easily understood; and so the pronoun affix is put for the separate, of which other instances include Jsh 15:19; 1 K 19:21; Jb 31:37; Ezk 29:3 (Matthew Poole).

16. **child**. Ex 2:9. **bosom**. 1 K 3:20. **nurse**. lit. supporter. Nu 11:12. 2 S 4:4. 2 K 10:1mg, 5. Est 2:7mg. Is 49:23mg.

17. **the women**. Lk 1:58-63. **Obed**. i.e. *serving; servant*, ✻S#5744h. ver. ◐15, 21, 22. 1 Ch 2:12, 12, 37, 38. 11:47. 26:7. 2 Ch 33:1. (1) A son of Boaz and Ruth and father of Jesse, Ru 4:17, 21, 22; 1 Ch 2:12. He was an ancestor of Joseph, the husband of Mary, Mt 1:5; Lk 3:32. (2) A son of Ephlal, who was a descendant of Judah, 1 Ch 2:37, 38. (3) One of David's valiant men, 1 Ch 11:47. (4) A porter for the Tabernacle in the time of David, 1 Ch 26:7. (5) The father of Azariah, who was one of the captains who aided Jehoiada the priest in making Joash king of Judah, 2 Ch 23:1. **Jesse**. i.e. *my substance*, or *wealthy*. **David**. i.e. *beloved*.

18. **the generations**. Ge 2:4. Nu 3:1. Ezr 7:2 w 1 Ch 6:3 w Mt 1:1, *8. **Pharez**. Ge 38:29mg. 1 Ch 2:4, etc. 4:1. Mt 1:3. Lk 3:33, Phares. **Hezron**. Ge 46:12. Mt 1:3. Lk 3:33, Esrom.

19. **begat Ram**. 1 Ch 2:9, 10. Mt 1:4, Aram. Lk 3:33. **Amminidab**. Ex 6:27. Mt 1:4. Lk 3:33, Aminadab.

20. **Nahshon**. Nu 1:7. 2:3. 7:12. Mt 1:4. Lk 3:32, Naasson. **Salmon**. *or*, Salmah. i.e. *garment; peaceable*, ✻S#8009h, only here. 1 Ch 2:11.

21. **Salmon**. 1 Ch 2:11, Salma. Mt 1:5. Lk 3:32. **and Boaz**. 1 Ch 2:12. Mt 1:5. Lk 3:32, Booz.

22. **Jesse**. 1 S 16:1. Is 11:1. **David**. 1 Ch 2:15. Mt 1:6. Lk 3:31.

1 SAMUEL

1 SAMUEL 1

Elkanah a Levite has two wives, 1, 2. He goes yearly to worship at Shiloh, 3. He favors and comforts Hannah, when insulted by Peninnah on account of her barrenness, 4-8. Hannah in grief prays for a son, and vows to devote him to God as a perpetual Nazarite, 9-11. Eli through mistake at first rebukes, but afterwards blesses her, 12-18. She bears Samuel, stays till he is weaned, and then presents him to God, according to her vow, 19-23.

1. **Ramathaim-zophim**. i.e. *the two high places of the watchers*, ✻S#7436h. This ancient town, now called *Ramla*, is, according to Phocas, about thirty-six miles west of Jerusalem, and, according to modern travelers, about nine miles from Joppa and a league from Lydda, between which it is situated. It is built on a rising ground, on a rich plain, and contains about two thousand families. ver. 19. Jsh +*18:25. Mt 27:57, Arimathea. **mount Ephraim**. Jg 17:1. 19:1. **Elkanah**. i.e. *God has brought*. He had an ancestor by the same name, 1 Ch 6:23. 1 Ch 6:25-27, 34. **Jeroham**. i.e. *he is loved; who finds mercy*, ✻S#3395h. 1 Ch 6:27, 34. 8:27. 9:8, 12. 12:7. 27:22. 2 Ch 23:1. Ne 11:12. (1) Grandfather of the prophet Samuel, 1 S 1:1; 1 Ch 6:27, 34. (2, 3) Benjamites, 1 Ch 8:27; 9:8. (4) A priest, father of Adaiah, 1 Ch 9:12. May be the same person as in Ne 11:12. (5) Father of some of David's warriors, 1 Ch 12:7. (6) Father of Azareel, prince of Dan, 1 Ch 27:22. (7) Father of a captain who assisted Jehoiada to place Joash on the throne of Judah, 2 Ch 23:1. **Elihu**. i.e. *my God is he*, ✻S#453h. 1 Ch *6:26, Eliab. 12:20. 26:7. 27:18. Jb 32:2, 4, 5, 6. 34:1. 35:1. 36:1. (1) A descendant of Kohath, 1 S 1:1. (2) A man of Manasseh who joined David in Ziklag, 1 Ch 12:20. (3) A descendant of Kohath, 1 Ch 26:7. (4) One of the brethren of David who was made ruler over the tribe of Judah, 1 Ch 27:18. Supposed to be same as Eliab, 1 S 16:6. (5) A person who apparently had accompanied the friends of Job when they visited him, Jb 32:2; 36:1. **Tohu**. i.e. *they sank down*, ✻S#8459h. 1 Ch 6:26, Nahath. 6:34, Toah. **Zuph**. i.e. *dropping of honey; honeycomb*, ✻S#6689h. 1 S 9:5. 1 Ch 6:26, Zophai. 6:35, Zuph, or Ziph. **Ephrathite**. 1 S 17:12. Jg 12:5. Ru 1:2. 1 K 11:26.

2. **two wives**. Ge 4:+19, 23. 29:23-29. Jg 8:30. Ru 4:11. Mt 19:8. **Hannah**. ƒ132G, Ge +3:19. i.e. *gracious*, ✻S#2584h. ver. 5, 5, 8, 9, 13, 15, 19, 20, 22. 1 S 2:1, 21. **Peninnah**. i.e. *pearl* or *coral*, ✻S#6444h. ver. 4. **but**. Ge 16:1, 2. 25:21. 29:31. Jg 13:2. Lk 1:7. **no children**. Ge +11:30.

3. **yearly**. Heb. from year to year. ƒ171T2C, Ge +24:55mg. Ex 23:14, 17. 34:23. Dt 16:16. Jg +11:40mg. Lk 2:41. **to worship**. Dt 12:5-7, 11-14. **Lord of hosts**. Ex +15:26. Ps +24:10. Ro 9:29. Ja 5:4. **Shiloh**. ver. 9. Jsh 18:1. Jg 18:31. Ps 78:60. Je 7:12-14. **And the**. ver. 9. 1 S 2:12-17, 34. 3:13. 4:4, 11, 17, 18. **Eli**. i.e. *going up* or *pestle*, ✻S#5941h. ver. 9, 12, 13, 14, 17, 25. 1 S 2:11, 12, 20, 22, 27. 3:1, 2, 5, 6, 8, 8, 9, 12, 14, 14, 15, 16. 4:4, 11, 13, 14, 14, 15, 16. 14:3. 1 K 2:27. **Hophni**. i.e. *a boxer; fighter*, ✻S#2652h. 1 S 2:34. 4:4, 11, 17.

4. **offered**. Le 3:4. 7:15. Dt 12:5-7, 17. 16:11. 2 S 6:18, 19.

5. **a worthy portion**. *or*, a double portion. The Hebrew phrase, *manah achath appayim*, is correctly rendered by Gesenius, "a portion for two persons, a double portion;" for *aph* in Hebrew, and *prosopon* in Greek, which literally mean "a face," are used for a person. Ge 43:34. 45:22. **he loved**. Ge 29:30, 31. Dt 21:15. **shut up**. Ge +11:30. 20:18. ◐29:31. 30:2.

6. **adversary**. Le 18:18. Jb 6:14. or, adversity. Ge 35:3. **provoked her**. Heb. angered her. Dt 31:29. 32:21. **had shut**. ver. +5. Jb 24:21. Ps +*127:3.

7. **year**. 1 S 2:19. **when she**. *or*, from the time that she. Heb. from her going up. **not eat**. Ps 42:3.

8. **why weepest**. 2 S 12:16, 17. 2 K 8:12. Jb 6:14. Jn 20:13, 15. 1 Th 5:14. **am not**. Ru 4:15. Ps 43:4. Is

54:1, 6. **ten sons**. That is, any number of sons (Young). Ne 4:12n. Jb 19:3.

9. **the temple**. 1 S 3:3, 15. 2 S 7:2. Ps 5:7. 27:4. 29:9. From this application of *haychahl yeowah*, "the temple of Jehovah," to the tabernacle, some are of the opinion that the books of Samuel were not compiled till the first temple was built; but as the same expression was used in the time of David, nothing certain can be inferred from this. See the marginal references.

10. **in bitterness of soul**. Heb. bitter of soul. Heb. *nephesh*, 1 S +30:6mg. Jg +18:25mg. Ru *1:20. 2 S 17:8. Jb 7:11. 9:18. 10:1. Is 38:15. 54:6. La 3:15. **prayed**. Ps 50:15. 91:15. Lk 22:44. He 5:7. **wept sore**. Ge 50:10. Jg 21:2. 2 S 13:36. 2 K 20:3. Je 13:17. 22:10.

11. **vowed**. Ge 28:20. Le +*23:38. Nu 21:2. 30:3-8. Jg 11:30. Ec 5:4. **look**. Ge 29:32. Ex 4:31. 2 S 16:12. Ps 25:18. **remember**. ✗22C3, Ge +8:1. ver. 19. Ge 8:1. 30:22. Ps 132:1, 2. 136:23. **not forget**. 144D, Ge +40:23. **a man child**. Heb. seed of men. A phrase not found elsewhere. Ge ◑3:15. **I will give**. Samuel, as a descendant of Levi, was the Lord's property, from twenty-five years of age till fifty; but the vow here implies that he should be consecrated to the Lord from his infancy to his death, and that he should not only act as a *Levite*, but as a *Nazarite*. **there**. Nu 6:5. Jg 13:5. 16:17.

12. **continued praying**. Heb. multiplied to pray. 2 K 21:6h (wrought much). 2 Ch 33:6 (lit. he multiplied to do evil). 36:14mg (very much). Ps 78:38 (many a time). Lk *11:8-10. 18:1. Ro 15:30. Ep 6:18. Col 4:2, 12. 1 Th *5:17. Ja *5:16.

13. **spake**. Ge 24:42-45. Ne 2:4. Ps 25:1. Ro 8:26. **not heard**. T#532, 1282. Ge 24:42-45. Ne 2:4, 5. Ro 8:26. **she had**. Zc 9:15. Ac 2:13. 1 C 13:7. **drunken**. 1 S 25:36. 1 K 16:9. 20:16. Jb 12:25. Ps 107:27. Pr 26:9. Is 19:14. 24:20. 28:1, 3. Je 23:9. Jl 1:5.

14. **How long**. Jsh 22:12-20. Jb 8:2. Ps 62:3. Pr 6:9. Mt 7:1-3. **put away**. 1 S 7:3. Ge 35:2. Jsh 24:14, 23. 1 K 20:24. Jb 11:14. 22:23. Ps 39:10. 119:29. Pr 4:24, 27. Ec 11:10. Ep 4:25, 31.

15. **No, my lord**. Pr 15:1. 25:15. **of a sorrowful spirit**. Heb. hard of spirit. Heb. *ruach*, Ge +41:8. **poured**. Ps 42:4. *62:8. 142:2, 3. 143:6. La 2:19. ✗12I1, Ge +3:7. **soul**. nephesh, Ge +34:3.

16. **a daughter of Belial**. 1 S 2:12. 10:27. 25:25. Dt +13:13. +15:9. Jg +19:22. 2 C 6:15. **out of**. Jb 6:2, 3. 10:1, 2. Mt 12:34, 35. **complaint**. or, meditation. ✱S#7879h: 1 S 1:16. 1 K 18:27mg. 2 K 9:11. Jb 7:13. 9:27. 10:1. 21:4. 23:2. Ps 55:2. 64:1. 102:title. *104:34. 142:2. Pr 23:29 (babbling). **grief**. Dt 32:19 (provoking).

17. **Go in peace**. 1 S 25:35. 29:7. Jg 18:6. 2 S 15:9. 2 K 5:19. Mk 5:34. Lk 7:50. 8:48. **the God**. Nu 6:24-26. 1 Ch 4:10. Ps 20:1, 3-5.

18. **Let thine**. Ge 32:5. 33:8, 15. Ru 2:13. 1 Th 1:3, 10. 1 P 5:7. **find grace**. Ge *6:8. 18:3. **went her way**. Ec 9:7. Jn 16:24. Ro 15:13. Ph *4:6, 7. **countenance**. Ps 34:5.

19. **they rose**. 1 S 9:26. Ps *5:3. 55:17. 119:147. Mk +*1:35. **knew**. Ge +4:1. **and the Lord**. ver. 11. Ge 8:1. 21:1. 30:22. Ps 25:7. +113:9. 136:23. Lk 23:42. **remembered**. ✗22C3, Ge +8:1. ✗103, Ge +3:13.

20. **when the time was come about**. Heb. in revolution of days. Ex 34:22mg. 2 Ch 24:23mg. Ps 19:6. **Samuel**. i.e. *God hath heard. that is,* Asked of God. **Because**. Ge 4:25. 5:29. 16:11. 20:32-35. 30:6-21. 41:51, 52. Ex 2:10, 22. Mt 1:21.

21. **and all**. Ge *18:19. Jsh *24:15. Ps 101:2. Ac +16:31. **went up**. ver. 3.

22. **then**. Dt 16:16. Lk 2:22, 41, 42. **be weaned**. In the East weaning is often delayed till a much later period than it is in the West (Young); in ancient Israel the period extended for about three years. Ge 21:8. 1 K 11:20. Ps 131:2. Is 11:8. *28:9. Ho 1:8. The Hebrew word (✤S#1580h) is elsewhere translated "rewarded," 1 S 24:17; Ps 103:10; "dealt bountifully," Ps 13:6; 116:7; 119:17. **and there**. ver. 11, 28. 1 S 2:11, 18. 3:1. Ps 23:6. 27:4. **for ever**. Heb. *olam*, Ex +12:24. Ge +9:16. Ex 21:6. Le 25:23. Jsh 4:7. 2 S 7:29. 22:51. Ps 110:4. Is 9:7.

23. **Do what**. Nu 30:6-11. **the Lord**. 2 S 7:25. Is 44:26. **son suck**. Ge 21:7, 8. Ex 2:7. Ps 22:9. Mt 24:19. Lk 11:27.

24. A.M. 2839. B.C. 1165. An. Ex. Is. 326. **she took**. Nu 15:9, 10. Dt 12:5, 6, 11. 16:16. **three bullocks**. The LXX. Syriac, and Arabic, read "a bullock of three years old;" which is probably correct, as we read (ver. 25) that they slew *eth happar*, "the bullock." **bottle**. 1 S 10:3. 25:18. 2 S 16:1. Je +*13:12n. **house of the Lord**. 1 S 4:3, 4. Jsh 18:1. **young**. ✗145, Jg +11:40.

25. **brought**. Ex 13:2. Lk 2:22, 23. 18:15, 16.

26. **as thy soul**. 1 S 17:55. 20:3. Ge 42:15. Le 17:11. 26:15. 2 S 11:11. 14:19. 2 K 2:2, 4, 6. 4:30. 2 C +*12:15mg. Heb. *nephesh*, Ge +27:31.

27. **For this**. ver. 11-13. Mt 7:7. **and the Lord**. Ps 66:19. 116:1-5. 118:5. 1 J *5:15. **petition**. ✗121R7, Ge +43:11.

28. **lent him**. or, returned him, whom I have obtained by petition, to the Lord. The word *hishilteehoo*, "I have lent him," is the Hiphil conjugation of *shaal*, "he asked," (ver. 27), and refers to the name of Samuel. Ex 12:36. **he shall be**. or, he whom I have obtained by petition shall be returned. Ex 3:22. 2 K 6:5. **he worshipped**. Ge 24:26, 48, 52. 2 T 3:15.

1 SAMUEL 2

Hannah's thankful song of praise, 1-10. The sin of Eli's sons, 11-17. Samuel ministers before God, 18, 19. Eli blesses Elkanah; and Hannah, who bears more children, 20, 21. Eli reproves his sons, but far too gently, 22-26. A prophet foretells the ruin of Eli's house, 27-36.

1. **prayed**. Ne 11:17. Hab 3:1. Ph 4:6. **My heart**. T#657, 1356. Ex 15:2. Jb +13:15 (T#294). Ps 16:5, 8. 18:2. +23:4 (T#6). 34:2. 38:15, 21. 32:22. 39:7. 42:1, 2. 43:4. 51:11. *63:1-3, 8. *73:25. 119:57. Is 12:2. 26:8, 9. 61:10. Je 14:8, 9. La 3:24. Hab *3:17, 18. Lk 1:46, 47, etc. Ro 5:2, 11. 1 C 1:9. Ph 3:3. 4:4, 6. 1 P 1:8. 1 J 1:3. **mine horn**. Ps 18:2. 89:17. 92:10. 112:8, 9. Lk 1:69. **my mouth**. Ex 15:1, 21. Jg 5:1, 2. Ps 51:15. 71:8. Re 18:20. **I rejoice**. Ps 9:14. 13:5. 20:5. 34:2. 35:9. 118:14. Is 12:2, 3. Hab 3:18. Lk 1:46-48.

2. **none holy**. Ex 15:11. Dt 32:4. Ps 99:5, 9. 111:9. Is 6:3. 57:15. 1 P 1:16. Re 4:8. 15:4. **none beside**. Dt 4:35. 2 S 22:32. Ps 73:25. Is 43:10, 11. 44:6, 8. **rock**. Dt 3:24. 32:30, 31, 39. Ps 18:2. 71:3, 19. 86:8. 89:6, 8. Is 40:18. Je 10:6.

3. **Talk no more**. Ps *12:3, 4. **proudly**. ✗84, Ge +6:17. **let not**. ✗63, Ge +2:6. **arrogancy**. Heb. hard. Ps 31:18. 94:4. Pr 8:13. Is 37:23. Da 4:30, 31, 37. Ml 3:13. Ju 15, 16. **a God**. Heb. *El*, Ex +15:2. **of knowledge**. 1 K 8:39. Ps 44:21. 94:7-10. 147:5. Je *17:10.

He *4:12. Re 2:23. **by him.** Jb 31:6. Pr 16:2. Is 26:7. Da 5:27.

4. **The bows.** Ps 37:15, 17. 46:9. 76:3. **stumbled.** Ps *37:24. 145:14. Is 10:4. Je 37:10. Mi *7:8. 2 C 4:9, 10. *12:9, 10. Ep 6:14. Ph *4:13. He 11:34. **girded with strength.** Is +*40:29. Zc *12:8.

5. **full.** Ps 34:10. Lk 1:53. 16:25. **the barren.** 1 S 1:20. Ps 68:6. 107:41. +*113:9. Is +*54:1. **borne seven.** Ru 4:15n. Jb 1:2. Je 15:9. **waxed feeble.** 1 S 1:6. Is 54:1. Je 15:9. Ga 4:27.

6. **killeth.** T#147. ver. 7 (T#3). Dt +*32:39n. 2 K 5:7. Jb *5:18. Ps 68:20. Da 5:23. Ho 6:1, 2. Jn *5:25-29. *11:25. Re 1:18. **grave.** Heb. *sheol,* Ge +37:35. **he bringeth up.** 1 S 20:3. Jb +33:28. Ps 27:13n. 41:8, 10. 56:13. +*71:20. 116:3, 8, 9, 16. 118:17, 18. 142:5, 7. Is +*26:19n. Je +*31:17. Ezk *37:12. Jon *2:2-6. Zc 9:11, 12. Mt *12:40. 27:52. Jn 6:54, 58. 11:41, 44. Ro 6:5. +*8:11, 23. 1 C 6:14. 15:42-44. 2 C *1:9, 10. Ph 3:21. 2 T 2:18.

7. **maketh poor.** T#3. ver. +6 (T#147). Dt *8:17, 18. Ru 1:21. Jb *1:21. 5:6, 11, 18. Ps 39:9. 66:11. 89:30-32. 102:10, 23. 2 C *12:7. Ep +1:11 (T#260). **bringeth.** Ps 75:7. Is 2:12. Ja *1:9, 10. *4:10.

8. **the poor.** Jb *2:8. 42:10-12. Ps +*113:7, 8. Da *4:17. Lk *1:51, 52. Ja +*2:5. **dust.** √138B, Ge 13:16. **set them.** Ps *45:7, 16. 1 S *15:17. Ge 41:14, *40. 2 S 7:8. Jb *36:6, 7. Ec 4:14. Da 2:48. *6:3. Ja +*2:5. Re *1:6. *3:21. *5:10. 22:5. **inherit the throne.** Da +*7:14, 22, 27. Mt +*19:28. 1 C +*6:2. **the pillars.** Jb 38:4-6. Ps 24:2. 102:25. 104:5. He *1:3.

9. **will keep.** Jb *5:24. Ps *37:23, 24. 56:13. *91:1 1, 12. 94:18. 116:8. √119:105. *121:3, 5, 8. Pr *16:9. 1 P *1:5. **the feet.** Ps √31:8. 56:13. **his saints.** Dt *33:3. Ps *37:28. *97:10. Pr *2:8. Is +*26:19n. Ju *1, +*3. **the wicked.** Jb +*21:30. Pr 20:20. **be silent.** Jb 5:16. 27:19. 40:12, 13. Ps *31:17. 52:5. +*115:17. +*146:4. 147:6. Pr 12:7. Ec *5:17. Is +*24:22. √26:14. Je *8:14. Zp *1:15. Mt *8:12. *22:12, 13. 25:30. Ro *3:19. 2 P *2:17. Ju *13. **in darkness.** Ps 49:19. Col +*1:13. Ju 6, 13. **by strength.** 1 S *17:49, 50. Ps *33:16, 17. +*49:14mg. +*146:3. Ec *9:11. Je *9:23. Zc *4:6.

10. **adversaries.** Ex 15:16. Jg 5:31. Ps *2:9. 21:8, 9. 68:1, 2. 92:9. Lk *19:27. **out of heaven.** The LXX. insert, "Let not the wise glory in his wisdom, nor the strong glory in his strength, nor the rich glory in his riches; but let him who glorieth glory in this, that he understandeth and knoweth the Lord, and executeth judgment and righteousness in the midst of the earth." **he thunder.** 1 S 7:10. *12:18. Jb 40:9. Ps 18:13, 14. **judge.** Ps *50:1-6. 96:13. 98:9. Ec 11:9. *12:14. Mt *25:31, 32. Jn *5:21, 22. Ro *14:10-12. 2 C *5:10. Re *20:11-15. **he shall.** 1 S 12:13. *15:28. *16:1. 2 S 7:8, 13. Ps *2:6. 21:1, 7. Is 32:1. *45:24. Mt *25:34. 28:18. Lk 1:51. **exalt.** Ps 89:17, 24. 92:10. 148:14. Lk *1:69. **the horn.** Ps 92:10. 132:17, 18. **anointed.** 1 S 12:3. Ps *2:2. 18:50. 20:6. 28:8. *45:7. Ac *4:27. *10:38.

11. **minister.** ver. 18. 1 S 1:28. 3:1, 15.

12. **the sons.** Ho 4:6-9. Ml 2:1-9. **sons of Belial.** 1 S 10:27. 25:17. Dt *13:13. +*15:9. Jg +19:22. 1 K 21:10, 13. 2 C 6:15. **knew not the Lord.** 1 S 3:7. Jg 2:10. Je 2:8. 22:16. Jn *8:55. *16:3. *17:3. Ro 1:21, 28-30. T 1:16. 1 J √2:4.

14. **all that the flesh-hook.** ver. 29. Ex 29:27, 28. Le 7:31-35. Is 56:11. Ml 1:10. 2 P 2:13-15.

15. **before they.** Le 3:3-5, 16, 17. 7:23, 25, 30, 31. Ro 16:18. Ph 3:19. Ju 12.

16. **presently.** Heb. as on the day. Le 3:16. 7:23-25. **soul.** Heb. *nephesh,* Nu +11:6. **I will take.** Jg 18:25. Ne 5:15. Mi 2:1, 2. 3:5. 1 P 5:2, 3.

17. **before.** Ge 6:11. 10:9. 13:13. 2 K 21:6. Ps 51:4. Is 3:8. **abhorred.** Ezk 22:8. Ml 1:6. 2:*8, 13. Mt 18:7.

18. **ministered.** ver. 11. 1 S 3:1. **a linen ephod.** 1 S 22:18. Ex 28:4n. Le 8:7. 2 S 6:14.

19. **a little coat.** *Meil katon,* a little cloak or surtout; an upper garment: see note on Ex 28:4. **from year to year.** 1 S 1:+3, 21. Ex 23:14.

20. The natural place for this verse seems to be before the 11th, after which the 21st should probably come in; and after the 21st, perhaps the 26th should follow. **blessed.** Ge 14:19. 27:27-29. Nu 6:23-27. Ru 2:12. 4:11. **loan.** or, petition which she asked, etc. 1 S 1:27, 28.

21. **visited.** 1 S 1:19, 20. Ge 21:1. Lk 1:68. **grew.** ver. 26. 1 S 3:19. Jg 13:24. Lk 1:80. *2:40, 52.

22. **Now.** 1 S 8:1. **did unto.** ver. 13-17. Je 7:9, 10. Ezk 22:26. Ho 4:9-11. **women.** It is probable that these were persons who had some employment about the tabernacle: see note on Ex 38:8. **assembled.** assembled by troops. Ex 38:8.

23. **Why.** 1 K 1:6. Ac 9:4. 14:15. **I hear,** etc. or, I hear evil words of you. **by all.** Is 3:9. Je 3:3. 8:12. Ph 3:19.

24. **no good.** Ac 6:3. 2 C 6:8. 1 T 3:7. 3 J 12. **ye make.** ver. 17, 22. Ex 32:21. 1 K 13:18-21. 15:30. 2 K 10:31. Ml 2:8. Mt 18:6. 2 P 2:18. Re 2:20. **transgress.** or, cry out. or, pass over the command of the Lord (Young).

25. **sin against.** Dt 17:8-12. 25:1-3. **if a man.** 1 S 3:14. Nu 15:30, 31. Ps 51:4, 16. He 10:26. Mt *2:1. **who shall.** √85C, Ge +18:14. 1 T √2:5. He *7:25. **hearkened.** Dt 2:30. Jsh 11:20. 2 Ch 25:16. Pr 15:10. 29:1. Jn 12:39, 40. Ro *9:22. **because.** Rather, "therefore," as the particle *kee* also signifies (see Ps 116:10): so Noldius, *Ideo voluit Jehova eos interficere,* "Therefore Jehovah purposed to destroy them."

26. **grew on.** ver. 21. **was in favor.** T#1890. Pr 3:3, 4. Is *40:5. Lk 1:80. 2:40, +*52. Ac 2:47. Ro 14:18.

27. **a man.** 1 S 9:6. Dt 33:1. Jg 6:8. 13:6. 1 K 13:1. 1 T 6:11. 2 T *3:17. 2 P *1:21. **Did I.** Ex 4:14, 27.

28. **And did I.** Ex 28:1, 4, 6-30. 29:4, etc. 39:1, etc. Le 8:7, 8. Nu 16:5. 17:5-8. 18:1-7. 2 S 12:7. 2 Ch *29:11. **did I give.** Le 2:3, 10. 6:16. 7:7, 8, 32, 34, 35. 10:14, 15. Nu 5:9, 10. 18:8, 19. Dt 18:1-8.

29. **kick ye.** ver. 13, 17. Dt 32:15. Ml 1:12, 13. **and at mine.** They disdained to take the *part* allowed by the law; and would take for themselves *what* part they pleased, and as *much* as they pleased. ver. 13-16. **habitation.** Dt 12:5, 6. Jsh 18:1. **and honorest.** By permitting his sons to deal thus with the sacrifices, and to be served *first,* by taking their part *before* the fat, etc. was burnt to the Lord, Eli thus honored his sons *above* God. Le 19:15. Dt 33:9. Mt 10:37. 22:16. Lk 14:26. 2 C 5:16. Ja 3:17. **make.** ver. 13-16. Is 56:11, 12. Ezk 13:19. 34:2. Ho 4:8. Mi 3:5. Ro 16:18.

30. **I said.** Ex 28:43. 29:9. Nu 25:11-13. **for ever.** Heb. *olam,* Ex +12:24. **Be it far.** Nu 45:34mg. 2 Ch 15:2. Je *18:9, 10. **them that honor me.** Ex +20:12. Jg 9:9. Est 6:9, 10. 8:15. Ps 50:23. Pr *3:9, 10. Is 29:13. Da 4:34. Ml 1:6. Jn √5:23. *8:49. 13:31, 32. *17:4, 5. S#3513h: 1 S 2:30. 2 S 10:3. 1 Ch 19:3. Pr

14:31. La 1:8. **I will honor.** Ps 18:20. 91:14. Mt 6:33. Jn *5:44. *12:26. 1 C 4:5. 1 P 1:7. S#3513h: Nu 22:17 (promote, honor). 24:11. Jg 9:9. 1 S 2:29, 30. 6:6 (harden). Ps 15:4. 50:15 (glorify), 23. 86:9, 12. 91:15. Pr 4:8. Is 25:3. 43:20. 60:13. Da 11:38. Ml *1:6. **that despise.** Nu 11:20. 2 S 12:9, 10. Ml *2:8, 9. **lightly esteemed.** Lk 16:15.

31. **I will cut.** lit. have cut. ✓96C2, Ge +45:9. That is, I will destroy the strength, power, influence, and authority of thee and thy family; of which the arm of man being the instrument, is used as the emblem. 1 S 4:2, 11, 17-20. 14:3. 22:17-20. 1 K 2:26, ✱27, 35. Jb 22:9. Ps 37:17. Ezk 30:21-24. 44:10.

32. **an enemy,** etc. *or,* the affliction of the tabernacle, for all the wealth which God would have given Israel. This appears to be the right translation; for agreeably to this prediction, he *did* see the tabernacle deprived of the ark, which was its glory, and lived to hear that it was captured by the Philistines. 1 S 4:4, 11, 22. Ps 78:59-64. **an old man.** Zc 8:4.

33. **to consume.** 1 S 22:21-23. 1 K 1:7, 19. 2:26, 27. Mt 2:16-18. **heart.** Heb. *nephesh,* Ex +23:9. **in the flower,** etc. Heb. men.

34. **a sign.** 1 S 3:12. 1 K 13:3. 14:12. **in one day.** 1 S 4:✱11, 17.

35. **I will raise.** 1 K 1:8, 45. 2:35. 1 Ch 29:22. Ezk *34:23. 44:15, 16. He *2:17. *7:26-28. **mind.** Heb. *nephesh,* soul, Ge +23:8. Le +26:11n. **I will build.** 1 S *25:28. Ex 1:21. Nu 25:13. 2 S *7:11, 27. 1 K *11:38. 1 Ch 6:8-15. Ne 12:10, 11. **mine.** Ps *2:2. *18:50.

36. **is left.** 1 K 2:27. Ezk 44:10-12. **Put.** Heb. Join. Or, admit. 1 S 26:19. Jb 30:7. Is *14:1. Hab *2:15. **one of the priest's offices.** Heb. somewhat about the priesthood. Ex 29:9. **eat.** ver. 29, 30. Ml 1:13.

1 SAMUEL 3

The Lord reveals himself to the child Samuel, and informs him of his purposes against the house of Eli, 1-14. Samuel, adjured by Eli, tells him the vision; and Eli answers submissively, 15-18. Samuel is established to be a prophet of the Lord, 19-21.

1. **the child.** ver. 15. 1 S *2:11, 18. **the word.** ver. 21. Ps *74:9. Is 13:12. Ezk 7:26. Am *8:11, 12. **precious.** ✱S#3368h. 2 S 12:30. 1 K 5:17 (costly). 7:9, 10, 11. 10:2, 10, 11. 1 Ch 20:2. 29:2. 2 Ch 3:6. 9:1, 9, 10. 32:27. Jb 28:16. 31:26 (brightness). Ps 36:7 (excellent. mg, precious). 37:20 (fat). 45:9 (honorable). 116:15. Pr 1:13. 3:15. 6:26. 12:27. 17:27. 24:4. Ec 10:1 (reputation). Is 28:16. Je *15:19. La 4:2. Ezk 27:22. 28:13. Da 11:38. Zc 14:6 (clear. mg, precious).

2. **his eyes.** 1 S 2:22. 4:14. Ge 27:1. 48:10. Ps 90:10. Ec 12:3.

3. **ere.** Before sunrise; for it is probable the lamps were extinguished before the rising of the sun: see the Parallel Passages. **the lamp.** Ex 27:20, 21. 30:7, 8. Le 24:2-4. 2 Ch 13:11. **went out.** Ex +30:8. **the temple.** 1 S 1:9. Ps 5:7. 27:4. 29:9.

4. **called Samuel.** Ge 22:1. Ex 3:4. Ps 99:6. Ac 9:4. 1 C 12:6-11, 28. Ga 1:15, 16.

6. **my son.** 1 S 4:16. Ge 43:29. 2 S 18:22. Mt 9:2.

7. **Now Samuel.** *or,* Thus did Samuel before he knew the Lord, and before the word of the Lord was revealed unto him. **did not yet.** Samuel was not destitute of the knowledge of God, in that sense which

implies the total absence of true piety, as Eli's sons were; for he knew and worshipped the God of Israel: but he did not know him as communicating special revelations of his will to him, in the manner in which he made it known to the prophets. Je 9:24. Ac 19:2.

8. **the third.** Jb 33:14, 15. Although Samuel did not apprehend the way in which God reveals himself to his servants the prophets—by the "still small voice"—yet when this direct communication from the Almighty was made the third time, in a way altogether new and strange to him, it seems astonishing that he did not immediately apprehend. Perhaps he would have been sooner aware of a divine revelation, had it come in a dream or a vision. Those who have the greatest knowledge of divine things, should remember the time when they were as babes, unskilful in the works of righteousness. 1 C 13:11, 12. **child.** T#55. 2 Ch 34:1, 3. Pr 8:17. +*22:6. Ec *12:1. Is 28:9. 2 T *3:15.

9. **Speak.** Ex 20:19. Ps 85:8. Is 6:8. Da 10:19. Ac 9:6.

10. **the Lord came.** This seems to imply a visible appearance, as well as an audible voice. **as at other.** ver. 4-6, 8. Samuel did not now rise and run as before, when he thought Eli called, but lay still and listened. All must be silent, when God speaks. Observe, however, Samuel in his reply left out one word: he did not say, "Speak, Lord," but only, "Speak, for thy servant heareth; perhaps, as Bp. Patrick suggests, out of uncertainty, whether it was God who spake to him or not. However, by this answer way was made for the message he was now to receive, and Samuel was brought acquainted with the words of God and visions of the Almighty. **Samuel.** ✓84, Ge +22:11.

11. **I will do.** Is 29:14. Am 3:6, 7. Hab 1:5. Ac 13:41. **both the ears.** 2 K 21:12. Is 28:19. Je 19:3. Lk 21:26.

12. **I will perform.** 1 S 2:27-36. Nu 23:19. Jsh 23:15. Zc 1:6. Lk 21:33. **when I begin,** etc. Heb. beginning and ending.

13. **For I have told him.** *or,* And I will tell him, etc. 1 S 2:27-30, etc. **I will judge.** 2 Ch 20:12. Ezk 7:3. 18:30. Jl 3:12. **his house.** Ge ◐18:19. **for ever.** Heb. *olam,* Ex +12:24. **which he knoweth.** 1 K 2:44. Ec 7:22. 1 J 3:20. **his sons.** 1 S 2:12, 17, 22, 23, etc. **vile.** *or,* accursed. ✓182, Ge +18:22. **restrained them not.** Heb. frowned not upon them. T#497. Ex +*20:5. Nu 14:33. Nu +*32:23 (T#733). 1 S 2:23-25. 1 K *6:3. 2:24. 16:3. 21:21. Jb *17:5. *21:17-19. Pr +*19:18. *22:15. +*23:13, 14. *29:15, 17. Is 14:21. Je 32:18. Ho *4:6. Mt 10:37. ✱S#3543h: Kal, Preterite: Dt 34:7 (dim). Kal, Infinitive: Zc 11:17 (utterly. lit. darkening). Kal, Future: Ge 27:1 (dim). Jb 17:7. Is 42:4 (fail). Zc 11:17 (darkened). Piel, Preterite: Ezk 21:7 (shall faint).

14. **the iniquity.** Ex 17:16. 20:5. 1 S 2:25. Nu 15:30, 31. Ps 51:16. Is 22:14. 48:22. Je 7:16. 15:1. Ezk 24:13. He 10:4-10, 26-31. **for ever.** Heb. *olam,* Ex +12:24.

15. **opened.** 1 S 1:9. Ps 84:10. Ml 1:10. **Samuel.** Samuel reverenced Eli as a father, and feared to distress him by showing what God had purposed to do. It does not appear that God commanded Samuel to deliver this message; he therefore did not attempt it till adjured by Eli. It might be supposed that Samuel would have been so full of ecstacy as to have forgotten his ordinary service, and run amongst his friends to tell them of the converse he had had with God in the

night: but he modestly keeps it to himself. Our secret communion with God is not to be proclaimed on the housetop. **feared**. Je 1:6-8. 1 C 16:10, 11.

17. **I pray thee**. Ps 141:5. Da 4:19. Mi 2:7. **God**. 1 S 20:13. Ru 1:17. 2 S 3:35. 19:13. 1 K 22:16. Mt 26:63. **do so**. ♪110, Ezk 34:2. **more also**. Heb. so add. Ru 1:17. **thing**. *or*, word.

18. **Samuel told**. Mt 26:62-64. **every whit**. Heb. all the things, *or* words. *Whit*, or *wid*, comes from the Anglo-Saxon *wiht*, which signifies *person*, *thing*, etc.: equivalent to *every jot*. **It is the Lord**. Ge 18:25. Le 10:3. Jg 10:15. 2 S 16:10-12. Jb 1:21. 2:10. Ps 39:9. Is 39:8. La 3:39. 1 P 5:6. **let him**. 2 S 15:26. Jb 1:21. 2:10. Ps 39:9. Jn 18:11. Ac +21:14.

19. **grew**. 1 S 2:21. Jg 13:24. Lk 1:80. *2:40, 52. **the Lord**. 1 S 18:14. Ge 39:2, 21-23. Is 43:2. Mt 1:23. Lk 1:28. 2 C 13:11, 14. 2 T 4:22. **let none**. 1 S 9:6. 1 K 8:56. Est 6:10. Is 44:26. 55:11.

20. **Dan**. Jg 20:1. 2 S 3:10. 17:11. **established**. *or*, faithful. 1 T 1:12. **prophet**. Dt 18:22. Ac 3:24. He 11:32.

21. **And the Lord**. *Wyyoseph yehowah lehairaoh*, "And Jehovah added to appear;" that is, He *continued* to reveal himself to Samuel at Shiloh. **appeared**. Ge 12:7. 15:1. Nu 12:6. Am *3:7. He 1:1. **the word**. ver. 1, 4.

1 SAMUEL 4

The Israelites, smitten by the Philistines, send for the ark, 1-4. The Philistines are affrighted on account of it; but encourage one another, 5-9. Israel is again smitten, with great slaughter; the ark is taken, and Eli's two sons are slain, 10, 11. On hearing these tidings Eli falls and breaks his neck, 12-18. The wife of Phinehas travails, names the child Ichabod, and dies, 19-22.

1. A.M. 2863. B.C. 1141. An. Ex. Is. 350. **came**. *or*, came to pass. Heb. was. 1 S 3:11. Jg 3:10. 1 K 6:11. **Ebenezer**. i.e. *stone of help*, *S#72h. That is, the place afterwards so called. See the Parallel Texts. 1 S 5:1. *7:12. **Aphek**. This *Aphek* was situated in the tribe of Judah, and is probably the same as *Aphekah*, Jsh 15:53. It must be carefully distinguished from that near Jezreel, and another in Asher. 1 S 29:1. Jsh 19:30. 1 K 20:30.

2. **put**. 1 S 17:8, 21. **they joined battle**. Heb. the battle was spread. *or* is left. 1 S 10:2. 12:22. 17:20, 22, 28. *30:16. **Israel**. Jsh 7:5-8, 12. Ps 44:9, 10. **and they**. Ps 79:7, 8. 106:40, 41. La 3:40. **the army**. Heb. the array. ver. 12, 16. 1 S 17:20mg. Jg +6:26.

3. **the elders**. Jsh +20:4. **Wherefore**. Dt 29:24. Ps 74:1, 11. 78:56. Is 50:1. 58:3. **Let us**. 1 S 14:18. Nu 31:6. Jsh 6:4, 5. 2 S 15:25. 1 K +20:23n. Is 1:11-15. 55:8. Je 7:4, 8-15. Mt 3:9, 10. **fetch**. Heb. take unto us. **the ark**. Nu 10:33. Dt 31:26. Jsh 4:7. 1 Ch 17:1. Je 3:16. He 9:4. **it may save**. Je 7:8-11. Am 5:21, 22. Mt 23:25-28. Ro 2:28, 29. 1 C 10:1-5. 2 T 3:5. 1 P 3:21. Ju 5.

4. **Lord of hosts**. Jb 25:3. Ps 46:7. **which dwelleth**. 2 S 6:2. 2 K 19:15. Ps 80:1. 99:1. **the cherubims**. Ex 25:18-22. Nu 7:89. **Zophni**. 1 S 2:12-17, 22. Ps 50:16, 17. Ml 1:9. Ac 19:15, 16. **with the ark**. Nu 4:5, 15.

5. **all Israel**. They vainly supposed that the ark would save them, when the God of it had departed

from them because of their wickedness. Jg 15:14. Jb 20:5. Je 7:4. Am 6:3. Mi 2:11. **shouted**. ♪147D, Ge +1:29. Ps 47:1-3.

6. **What meaneth**. Ex 32:17, 18.

7. **were afraid**. Ex 14:25. 15:14-16. Dt 32:30. **heretofore**. Heb. yesterday *or* the third day. 1 S 10:11. 14:21. 19:7. 21:5. Ex +4:10mg. Jsh 3:4.

8. **smote**. Ex 7:5. 9:14. 14:27. Ps 78:43-51. **wilderness**. Ex 13:20.

9. **Be strong**. 2 S 10:12. Lk *16:8. 1 C *16:13. Ep 6:10, 11. **as they have**. Dt 28:47, 48. Jg 10:7. 13:1. Is 14:2. 33:1. **quit yourselves like men**. Heb. be men. 1 K 2:2.

10. **Israel**. ver. 2. Le 26:17. Dt 28:25. Ps 78:9, 60-64. **fled**. Mk=14:50. **every man**. 2 S 20:1. 1 K 12:16. 22:36. 2 K 14:12. **a very great**. 2 S 18:7. 2 Ch 13:17. 28:5, 6. Is 10:3-6.

11. **the ark**. 1 S 2:32. Ps 78:61. **was taken**. 1 S 2:32mg. Ps 78:60, 61. Mk=14:46. Ac=2:23. **the two sons**. 1 S 2:34. Ps 78:64. Is 3:11. **were slain**. Heb. died.

12. **with his clothes rent**. These, as we have already remarked (Jsh +7:6n), were the general signs of sorrow and distress among all nations. When the Trojan fleet was burnt, Aeneas is represented as tearing his robe from his shoulders, and invoking the aid of the gods (Virgil, *Aenead*. l.v.v.685). We have the same custom in one line by Catullus (*Epith. Pelei et Thetidos*, v. 224), "dishonoring her hoary locks with earth and sprinkled dust." 2 S 1:2. **with earth**. Jsh 7:6n. 2 S 13:19. 15:32. Ne 9:1. Jb 2:12.

13. **sat upon**. 1 S 1:9. **his heart**. Jsh 7:9. Ne 1:3, 4. Ps 26:8. 79:1-8. 137:4-6.

14. **What meaneth**. ver. 6.

15. **ninety**. 1 S 3:2. Ps 90:10. **and his eyes**. See on Ge 27:1. **were dim**. Heb. stood. 1 K 14:4mg.

16. **What is there done**. Heb. What is the thing. 2 S 1:4. **my son**. See on 1 S 3:6. Jsh 7:19.

17. **Israel**. ver. 10, 11. 1 S 3:11.

18. **when he made**. ver. 21, 22. Ps 26:8. 42:3, 10. 69:9. La 2:15-19. **his neck**. 1 S 2:31, 32. 3:12, 13. Le 10:3. 1 C 11:30-32. 1 P 4:17, 18. **And he had**. "He seems to have been a judge to do justice only, and that in south-west Israel."

19. **with child**. *S#2030h: Ge 16:11. 38:24, 25. Ex 21:22. Jg 13:5, 7. 2 S 11:5. 2 K 8:12. 15:16. Is 7:14. 26:17. Je 20:17. 31:8. Am 1:13. **be delivered**. *or*, cry out. **bowed herself**. Ge 4:7. 49:9. 1 K 8:54. Is 45:23. **travailed**. Je 30:6. 50:43. Ho 13:13. Mi 4:9, 10. **pains**. Is 21:3. **came upon her**. Heb. were turned. 1 S 10:6. Da 10:16.

20. **Fear not**. Ge 35:17, 18. Jn 16:21. **neither did she regard it**. Heb. and set not her heart. 1 S 9:20. 25:25. Ex 7:23. 2 S 13:20mg. Ps 48:13mg. *62:10. *77:2. Pr 22:15, 17. 24:32mg. 27:23mg.

21. **Ichabod**. that is, *Where is the glory? or, There is no glory*. ♪32, Ge +31:21. *S#350h. 1 S 14:3. **The glory**. Ps 26:8. 63:1, 2. 78:61, 64. 106:20. Je 2:11. Ho 9:12.

22. **The glory**. Nu 12:10. Ps 137:5, 6. Ezk 10:18. 11:23. Jn 2:17.

1 SAMUEL 5

The Philistines place the ark in the temple of Dagon at Ashdod, 1, 2. Dagon falls down before it and is broken in pieces, 3-5. The Philistines are smitten with emerods at Ashdod, Gath, and Ekron, when the ark is brought to those cities, 6-12.

1. **took.** 1 S 4:11, 17, 18, 22. Ps 78:61. **Ebenezer.** 1 S 4:1. 7:12. **Ashdod.** *Ashdod,* called *Azotus* by the Greeks, was one of the five satrapies of the Philistines, and a place of great strength and consequence. It was situated near the Mediterranean, between Askelon and Jamnia, thirty-four miles north of Gaza, according to Diodorus Siculus, and the Antonine and Jerusalem Itineraries. It is now called *Shdood;* and Dr. Richardson says they neither saw nor heard of any ruins there. "The ground," he observes, "around Ashdod is beautifully undulating, but not half stocked with cattle. The site of the town is on the summit of a grassy hill; and, if we are to believe historians, was anciently as strong as it was beautiful." Jsh 11:22. Ac 8:40, Azotus.

2. **of Dagon.** Jg 16:23. 1 Ch 10:10. Da 5:2, 23. Hab 1:11, 16.

3. **Dagon was.** Ex 12:12. Ps 97:7. Is 19:1. 46:1, 2. Zp 2:11. Mk 3:11. Lk 10:18-20. 2 C 6:14-16. **fallen.** Lk=11:22. Jn=18:6. 1 J=5:21. **set him.** Is 19:1. 40:20. 41:7. 44:17-20. 46:1, 2, 7. Je 10:8.

4. **fallen.** ver. +3. **the head.** Is 2:18, 19. 27:9. Je 10:11. 50:2. Ezk 6:4-6. Da 11:8. Mi 1:7. **of Dagon.** The name of this idol, *Dagon,* signifies *a fish:* and it is supposed to be the *Altergatis* of the Syrians, corruptly called *Derceto* by the Greeks, which had the upper part like a woman, and the lower part like a fish; as Lucian informs us: "In Phoenicia I saw the image of *Derceto;* a strange sight truly! For she had the half of a *woman,* but from the thighs downwards a fish's tail." Diodorus (l. ii.) describing the same idol, as represented at Askelon, says "It had the head of a woman, but all the rest of the body a fish's." Probably Horace alludes to this idol, in *De Art. Poet.* v. 4: "The upper part a handsome woman, and the lower part a fish." If such was the form of this idol, then every thing that was human was broken off from what resembled a fish. **the stump.** *or,* the fishy part. Jg 16:23. **Dagon.** *J*171N, Ge +8:13.

5. **neither.** Ps 115:4-7. 135:15-18. **tread.** Jsh 5:15. Zp 1:9.

6. **the hand.** ver. 7, 11. Ex 9:3. Ps 32:4. Ac 13:11. **emerods.** ver. 9, 11. 1 S 6:5. Dt 28:27. Jb 31:3. Ps 78:66. **thereof.** The LXX. and Vulgate add: "And (the cities and fields in *Vulgate*) the midst of that region produced mice; (*Vulg.* burst up, and mice were produced); and there was the confusion of a great death in the city." See 1 S 6:4, 5.

7. **saw.** 1 S 4:8. Ex 8:8, 28. 9:28. 10:7. 12:33. **The ark.** 1 S 6:20. 2 S 6:9. 1 Ch 13:11-13. 15:13. **sore.** or, hard. Ge 49:7. Dt 1:17. 15:18. 2 S 8:1. 19:43. **upon Dagon our god.** See on ver. 3, 4. Je 46:25. 48:7.

8. **What shall.** Zc 12:3. **Gath.** 1 S 17:4. 1 Ch 18:1. Am 6:2.

9. **the hand.** ver. 6. 1 S 7:13. 12:15. Dt 2:15. Am 5:19. 9:1-4. **with a very.** ver. 11. **and they had emerods.** ver. 6. 1 S 6:4, 5, 11. Ps 78:66.

10. **God to Ekron.** Jsh 15:45. Jg 1:18. 2 K 1:2. Am 1:8. **us, to slay us and our people.** Heb. me, to slay me and my people. 1 S 7:13.

11. **that it slay.** Ex 14:20. Ho 14:9. Mt 21:44. 1 P 2:6-8. **us not, and our people.** Heb. me not, and my people. **a deadly.** 2 S ◑6:11. Is 13:7-9. Je 48:42-44. 2 C=2:15, 16. **the hand.** ver. 6, 9.

12. **died.** 1 K 19:17. Am 5:19. **the cry.** 1 S 9:16. Ex 12:30. Is 15:3-5. Je 14:2. 25:34. 48:3. **went.** *J*102, Ge +2:24.

1 SAMUEL 6

At the end of seven months the Philistines consult about sending back the ark, 1-9. They bring it on a new cart, with oblations, to Beth-shemesh, 10-18. The Beth-shemites are smitten for looking into it, 19, 20. They send to the men of Kirjath-jearim to fetch it, 21.

1. A.M. 2864. B.C. 1140. An. Ex. Is. 351. **the ark.** 1 S 5:1, 3, 10, 11. Ps 78:61.

2. **called.** Ge 41:8. Ex 7:11. Is 47:12, 13. Da 2:2. 5:7. Mt 2:3, 4. **wherewith.** Mi 6:6-9.

3. **empty.** Ex 23:15. 34:20. Dt 16:16. **a trespass offering.** Le 5:+6, 15-19. 6:6. 7:1-7. **known.** ver. 9. 1 S 5:7, 9, 11. Jb 10:2. 34:31, 32.

4. **Five golden.** ver. 5, 17, 18. 1 S 5:6, 9. Ex 12:15. Jsh 13:3. Jg 3:1, 3. **you all.** Heb. them.

5. **mice.** Ex 8:5, 17, 24. 10:14, 15. Jl 1:4-7. 2:25. **give glory.** Jsh 7:19. Ps 18:44. 66:3mg. Is 42:12. Je 3:13. 13:16. Ml 2:2. Jn 9:24. Re 11:13. 16:9. **lighten.** 1 S 5:6, 11. Ps 32:4. 39:10. *J*22A14.8E. Anthropomorphism B879: in idiomatic expressions. Here, "to make the hand light" means to reduce the chastisement. **off your.** 1 S 5:3, 4, 7. Ex 12:12. Nu 33:4. Is 19:1.

6. **harden.** Jb 9:4. Ps 95:8. Ro 2:5. He 3:13. **the Egyptians.** Ex 7:13. 8:15. 9:16, 34. 10:3. 14:17, 23. 15:14-16. **wonderfully.** or, reproachfully. Ex 10:2. **did they not.** Ex 12:31-33. **the people.** Heb. them.

7. **new cart.** Ge 45:19. 2 S 6:3. 1 Ch 13:7. **milch.** or, suckling. ver. 10. Ge 33:13. Ps 78:71. Is 40:11mg. **and tie.** *J*96C2, Ge +45:9. **on which.** Nu 19:2.

8. **jewels.** ver. 4, 5.

9. **Beth-shemesh.** i.e. *house of the sun.* Jsh 15:10. 21:16. **he.** *or,* it. Am 3:6. **we shall.** ver. 3. **not his hand.** Is 26:11. **a chance.** Here the term is used by Philistine diviners. Ge +*24:44n. 2 S 1:6. Ec 9:11. Lk 10:31. or, accident. Ru 2:3. 1 S 20:26. Ec 2:14, 15. 3:9. 9:2, 3.

11. **they laid.** 2 S 6:3. 1 Ch 13:7. 15:13-15.

13. **lifted.** 144A12, Ge +22:13.

14. **Bethshemite.** *S#1030h. ver. 18. **offered.** 1 S 7:9, 17. 11:5. 20:29. Ex 20:24. Jg 6:26. 21:4. 2 S 24:18, 22, 25. 1 K 18:30-38. 19:21. **burnt offering.** Le +*23:12.

16. **the five.** ver. 4, 12. Jsh 13:3. Jg 3:3. 16:5, 23-30. **they returned.** 1 S 5:10.

17. **these.** ver. 4. **Ashdod.** 1 S 5:1. 2 Ch 26:6. Je 25:20. Zc 9:6. **Gaza.** Jg 16:1, 21. Am 1:7, 8. **Askelon.** Jg 1:18. Zc 9:5. **Gath.** 1 S 5:8. 2 S 1:20. 21:22. Am 6:2. **Ekron.** 1 S 5:10. 2 K 1:2. Am 1:8.

18. **the five lords.** ver. 16. Jsh 13:3. **great stone of.** *or,* great stone. **Abel.** i.e. *meadow,* *S#59h. Nu 33:49. Jg 11:33mg. 2 S 20:14, 15, 18. 1 K 15:20. 2 K 15:29. **unto this day.** Ge +19:38. Dt +29:4, 28.

19. **he smote.** Ex 19:21. Le 10:1-3. Nu 4:4, 5, 15, *20. Dt 29:29. 2 S 6:7. 1 Ch 13:9, 10. Col 2:18. 1 P 4:17. **looked into.** 2 S 6:6, 7. Mt=11:27. Col=2:18. **the ark.** Ex 25:21. 40:20. 2 C 3:7. **fifty thousand.** As it is very improbable that the village of Beth-shemesh should contain, or be capable of employing, 50,070 men in the fields at wheat harvest, much less that they could all peep into the ark, and from the uncommon manner in which it is expressed in the original,

it is generally allowed that there is some corruption in the text, or that some explanatory word is omitted. The Hebrew is *shivim ish, chamishim aileph ish*, literally, "seventy men, fifty thousand men": so LXX. Vulgate, "70 (chief) men, and 50,000 (common) people." Targum, *besabey amma*, "of the elders of the people 70 men, *ovekahala*, and in the congregation 50,000 men." But the Syriac, *chamsho alphin weshivin gavrin*, "5000 and 70 men"; with which the Arabic agrees; while Josephus has only *ebdomakonta*, seventy men; and three reputable MSS. of Dr. Kennicott's also omit "50,000 men." Some learned men, however, would render, by supplying the Hebrew *mem*, "70 men; fifty out of a thousand"; which supposes about 1400 present, and that a twentieth part were slain. or, fifty chief men, as the original word *eleph* means in Mi +*5:2, compared with Mt 2:6; it was only a small village (Young). **lamented.** Ge 37:34. **a great slaughter.** Le 26:21.

20. **Who is able.** Nu 17:12, 13. 2 S 6:7, 9. 1 Ch 13:11-13. Ps 76:7. Ml 3:2. Mt 8:34. Mk 10:32. Lk 5:8. 8:37. **whom shall.** 1 S 5:8-12.

21. **Kirjath-jearim.** or Kirjath-Baal, see Jsh 15:9. 18:14. Jg 18:12. 1 Ch 13:5, 6. Ps 78:60. Je 7:12, 14.

1 SAMUEL 7

The ark is removed to Kirjath-jearim, and remains there a long time, 1, 2. At Samuel's exhortation the Israelites repent, and humble themselves before God at Mizpeh, 3-6. The Philistines prepare to assault them: but, while Samuel prays and sacrifices, the Lord discomfits them with thunder before Israel, 7-11. Samuel calls the place Ebenezer, and sets up a stone for a memorial, 12. The Philistines are subdued, and Samuel judges Israel, 13-17.

1. **Kirjath-jearim.** 1 S 6:21. Jsh 18:14. 2 S 6:2. 1 Ch 13:5, 6. Ps 132:6. **Abinadab.** i.e. *my father is noble.* 2 S 6:3, 4. 1 Ch 13:7. Is 52:11. **Eleazar.** i.e. *God is help.*

2. **lamented.** Jg 2:4. Je 3:13, 22-25. 31:9. Zc 12:10, 11. Mt 5:4. 2 C *7:10, 11.

3. A.M. 2884. B.C. 1120. An. Ex. Is. 371. **If.** Ge +4:7. **return.** Dt 30:2-10. 1 K 8:48. 2 K +17:13. 2 Ch 30:6, 9. Jb 22:23. Is 44:22. 55:7. Je 3:12. 4:1. Ezk 14:6. 18:30. Ho 6:1, 2. 12:6. 14:1, 2. Jl 2:12, 13. Zc 1:3. Ml 3:7. **put away.** Ge 35:2. Jsh 24:14, 23. Jg 2:13. 10:6. **strange.** Ex 12:43 (*S#5236h). Jg 10:16mg. 2 S 22:45, 46. **prepare.** Dt 30:6. 1 Ch 22:19. 28:9. 29:16. 2 Ch *12:14. 19:3. 30:19. Ezr *7:10. Jb 11:13, 14. Ps 10:17. *78:8mg. Pr 16:1. Je 4:3, 4. Ezk 18:31. Mt 15:8. Jn 4:24. **serve him.** Dt 6:13. 10:20. 13:4. Mt *4:10. 6:24. Lk 4:8.

4. **Baalim.** lit. lords, masters, possessors. Jg 2:11, 13. 3:7. 10:15, 16. 1 K 11:33. Ho 14:3, 8.

5. **Gather.** Ne 9:1. Jl 2:16. **Mizpeh.** ver. 12, 16. 1 S 10:17. Jsh 15:38. Jg *20:1. 2 K 25:23. This is the Mizpeh of Benjamin, westward of Jordan (Young). **I will pray.** 1 S √12:23.

6. **drew water.** √102, Ge +2:24. Grotius says, that the pouring out of water means the shedding of tears; and the Targum reads, "And they poured out their hearts in penitence, as waters, before the Lord." Others suppose that it was done emblematically, to represent the contrition of their hearts, and their desire to *wash away* their past offences. But some learned men con-

ceive that it was poured out as a libation, in token of joy, after they had fasted and confessed their sin, as they were wont to do in the feast of tabernacles (See note on Nu 29:35). 1 S 1:15. 2 S 14:14. Jb 16:20. Ps 6:6. 42:3. 119:136. Je 9:1. La 2:11, 18. 3:49. **poured.** T#1295. 2 S 14:14. 23:16, 17. 1 Ch 11:18. Ps 22:14. **fasted.** Jg 20:26n. 2 Ch *7:14. 20:3. Ezr 8:21-23. Ne 9:1-3. Da 9:3-5. Jl 2:12. Jon ch. 3. **We have sinned.** Le 26:40. Jg 10:10. 1 K 8:47. Ezr 9:5-10. Jb 33:27. 40:4. 42:6. Ps 38:3-8. 106:6. Je 3:13, 14. 31:19. Da 9:3-5. Jl 2:12. Lk 15:18. **judged.** Jg 3:10. Ne 9:27. Ezk 20:4.

7. **afraid.** 1 S 13:6. 17:11. Ex 14:10. 2 Ch 20:3.

8. **Cease,** etc. Heb. Be not silent from us from crying. T#1367. 1 S 12:19-24. Ge 18:32. 32:24-26. 1 S +*23:4. Jb 13:13mg. Ps 28:1. 35:22. 39:12. 50:3. 83:1. *86:3, 6. 88:1, 2, 9, 13. 102:1-11, +*17. 109:1. +*119:145-147. Is 37:4. *62:1, 6, 7. Je 38:27mg. Ho 12:4. Lk *11:5-9. +*18:1-6. Ac 12:5. Ja +*5:16.

9. **a sucking lamb.** ver. 17. 1 S 6:14, 15. 9:12. 10:8. 16:2. Jg 6:26, 28. 1 K 18:30-38. Is 65:25. **burnt offering.** Le +√23:12. **cried unto.** Ps 50:15. 99:6. Je 15:1. Ja *5:16. **heard.** *or*, answered. 1 S 8:18. Ps 20:1, 3, 5, 6. 99:6. Je ◑15:1. Mi 3:4.

10. **thundered.** 1 S 2:10. 12:17. Ex 9:23-25. Jg 5:8, 20. 2 S 22:14, 15. Ps 18:11-14. 77:16-18. *81:7. 97:3, 4. Re 16:18-21. **discomfited.** Dt 20:3, 4. Jsh 10:10. Jg 4:15. 5:20. Zc 4:6.

11. **Beth-car.** i.e. *house of Car* or *a lamb,* *S#1033h. This place was probably situated in the tribe of Dan. Josephus calls it *korraioi*; The LXX. *Baithxor*; Targum, *Beth-saron*; Syriac and Arabic, *Beth-jasan*; by which Houbigant supposes is meant *Beth-shan.*

12. **took a stone.** Ge 28:18, 19. 31:45-52. 35:14. Jsh 4:9, 20-24. 24:26, 27. Is 19:19. 28:16. **Mizpeh.** ver. 5n, 6. Jsh 11:3n. **Shen.** i.e. *a tooth.* **Ebenezer.** that is, *The stone of help.* 1 S 4:1. 5:1. Ge 22:14. Ex 17:15. **Hitherto.** Ps 71:6, 17. Is 46:3, 4. Ac 26:22. 2 C 1:10.

13. **subdued.** Jg 13:1. **came no more.** 1 S 13:1-5. **against.** 1 S 14:6-16, 20-23. 17:49-53. 28:3-5. 31:1-7.

14. **peace.** 1 S 12:11. Dt 7:2, 16. Jg 4:17. Ps 106:34.

15. A.M. 2873-2947. B.C. 1131-1057. **judged.** ver. 6. 1 S 12:1. 25:1. Jg 2:16. 3:10, 11. Ac 13:20, 21.

16. **he went.** When he was at *Bethel*, the tribe of Ephraim and all the northern parts of the country could attend him; when at *Gilgal*, the tribe of Benjamin and those beyond Jordan could have easy access to him; and when at *Mizpeh*, he was within the reach of Judah, Simeon, and Gad: but at *Ramah* was the place of his ordinary abode; here he held his court, for "there he judged Israel": and as it is probable Shiloh was destroyed, it is said (ver. 17) that "there," i.e. at *Ramah*, "he built an altar to the Lord." **year to year.** 1 S 1:7. 1 K 5:11. 10:25. **in circuit.** Heb. and he circuited. 1 S 9:6, 11, 12. Jg 5:10. 10:4. 12:14. Ps 75:2. 82:3, 4.

17. **his return.** 1 S 1:1, 19. 8:4. 19:18-23. **he built.** 1 S 11:15. Ge 12:7, 8. +13:18. 33:20. 35:7. Jg 21:4. 1 K 18:30-36.

1 SAMUEL 8

Samuel, when old, makes his sons judges; who behave ill, and give the people an occasion of desiring a king, 1-5. Samuel is displeased, and prays concerning it; but the Lord requires him to comply, and to show them the manner of a king, 6-18. They persist in their request; and Samuel by divine direction yields to them, 19-22.

1. A.M. 2892. B.C. 1112. An. Ex. Is. 379. **made his.** Dt 16:18, 19. Jg 8:22, 23. 2 Ch 19:5, 6. Ne 7:2. 1 T 5:21. **sons judges.** Jg 5:10. 10:4. 12:14.

2. **Joel.** i.e. *the Lord is God,* *S#3100h. 1 Ch 4:35. 5:4, 8, 12. 6:◑28, 33, 36, ◐38, Vashni. 7:3. 11:38. 15:7, 11, 17. 23:8. 26:22. 27:20. 2 Ch 29:12. Ezr 10:43. Ne 11:9. Jl 1:1. (1) The eldest son of the prophet Samuel, 1 S 8:2; 1 Ch 6:33; 15:17, erroneously called Vashni in 1 Ch 6:28. (2) A descendant of Simeon, 1 Ch 4:35. (3) A descendant of Reuben, 1 Ch 5:4, 8. (4) Head of a Gadite family, 1 Ch 5:12. (5) A Levite of the family of Kohath, 1 Ch 6:36, probably a corruption of Shaul in 1 Ch 6:24. (6) A descendant of Issachar, 1 Ch 7:3. (7) One of David's valiant men, 1 Ch 11:38, called Igal in 2 S 23:36. (8) A chief of the family of Gershom, 1 Ch 15:7, 11. (9) One of the keepers of the treasure of the house of the Lord, 1 Ch 23:8; 26:22. (10) A prince of Manasseh, 1 Ch 27:20. (11) A descendant of Kohath in the time of Hezekiah, 2 Ch 29:12. (12) A Jew who had a foreign wife, Ezr 10:43. (13) An overseer of the Benjamites that dwelt in Jerusalem, Ne 11:9. (14) One of the minor prophets, a son of Pethuel; lived in Judah under the reign of Uzziah, but nothing further is known of his personal history, Jl 1:1. **Abiah.** i.e. *the Lord is my father,* ✛S#29h. 1 Ch 2:24. 6:28. 7:8. (1) Samuel's second son, 1 S 8:2; 1 Ch 6:28. (2) The wife of Hezron, the grandson of Judah by Pharez, 1 Ch 2:24. (3) The name given in Chronicles to the son of Rehoboam who succeeded his father as king of Judah, 1 Ch 3:10; Mt 1:7, and who is called Abijam in 1 K 15. (4) One of the sons of Becher, the son of Benjamin, 1 Ch 7:8. (5) A priest in the time of David, set over a particular course of service in the tabernacle, Lk 1:5.

3. **his sons.** 2 S 15:4. 1 K 12:6-11. 2 K 21:1-3. Ec 2:19. Je 22:15-17. **but turned.** Ex ◐*18:21, 22. Dt 16:19. Ps 15:5. 26:10. Is 33:15. Je 22:15-17. 1 T 3:3. 6:10.

4. **the elders.** Ex 3:16. +18:21. 24:1. Jsh +20:4. 2 S 5:3.

5. **now make.** ver. 6-8, 19, 20. 1 S 12:17. Ex 32:1. Nu 23:9. Dt 17:14, 15. Ho 13:10, 11. Ac 13:21.

6. **displeased.** Heb. was evil in the eyes of. 1 S 12:17. 18:8. Ge 28:8mg. 38:10. 48:17. Nu +11:1mg. +22:34mg. Jsh ◐+22:30mg. 2 S 11:25mg, 27mg. 1 Ch 21:7. Pr 24:18mg. Is 59:15. Jon 4:1. **prayed.** 1 S 15:11. Ex 32:31, 32. Nu 16:15, 22, 46. Ezr 9:3-5. Ps 109:4. Lk 6:11, 12. Ph *4:6. Ja *1:5.

7. **Hearken.** Nu 22:20. Ps *81:11, 12. Is *66:4. Ho *13:9-11. **they have not.** 1 S *10:19. *12:17-19. Ex 16:8. Mt *10:24, 25, 40. Lk *10:16. *19:14, 27. Jn 5:23. 13:16. *15:20, 21. **rejected me.** Ex 16:8. Ps 51:4. Ac 5:4.

8. **to all.** Ex 14:11, 12. 16:3. 17:2. 32:1. Nu 14:2-4. 16:2, 3, 41. Dt 9:24. Jg 2:2, 3, 20. 4:1. 6:1. 13:1. Ps 78:56-59. 95:10. 106:14-21, 34-40. Ac 7:51-53. **forsaken me.** Is *1:4. Je *2:13.

9. **hearken unto.** or, obey. ver. 7, 22. **howbeit,** etc. or, notwithstanding when thou hast solemnly protested against them, then thou shalt show, etc. Ezk 3:18. **the manner.** ver. 11-18. 1 S 2:13. 10:25. 14:52. Ezk 45:7, 8. 46:18.

11. **This will.** 1 S 10:25. Dt 17:14-20. **He will take.**

1 S 14:52. 1 K 9:22, 23. 10:26. 12:4, 10. 2 Ch 26:10-15. **his chariots.** 1 K 4:26. **run.** 2 S 15:1. 1 K 1:5. 18:46.

12. **appoint.** 1 Ch 27:1-22. **and will set.** 1 K 4:7, 22, 23, 27, 28. 2 Ch 32:28, 29.

14. **will take.** 1 S 22:7. 1 K 21:7, 19. Ezk 46:18.

15. **give to.** 1 K 4:7, 22, 23. **officers.** Heb. eunuchs. Ge +37:36mg. 2 K +8:6mg. Is 39:7. Da 1:3, 7-10, 18.

18. **cry out.** Is 8:21. **your king.** Dt 17:15. 1 K 12:4, 14, 15. **and the Lord.** "Hitherto," says Puffendorf, "the people of Israel had lived under governors raised up by God, who had exacted no tribute of them, nor put them to any charge; but little content with this form of government, they desire to have a king like other nations, who should live in magnificence and pomp, keep armies, and be able to resist any invasion. Samuel informs them what it was they desired; that, when they understood it, they might consider whether they would persist in their choice. If they would have a king splendidly attended, he tells them that he would take their sons for his chariots, etc.: if they would have him keep up constant forces, then he would appoint them for colonels and captains; and employ those in his wars who were accustomed to follow their family business; and since, after the manner of other kings, he must keep a stately court, they must be content that their daughters should serve in several offices, which the king would think below the dignity of his wives and daughters (ver. 13). In one word, that, to sustain his dignity, their king would exact the tenth of all they possessed, and be maintained in a royal manner out of their estates." **will not hear.** Jb 27:9. Ps 18:41. Pr *1:24-28. 21:13. Is *1:15. Mi 3:4. Lk 13:25.

19. **refused to obey.** Ps 81:11. Je 7:13. *44:16. Ezk 33:31.

20. **we also.** ver. 5. Ex 33:16. Le 20:24-26. Nu 23:9. Dt 7:6. Ps 106:35. Jn 15:19. Ro 12:2. 2 C 6:17. Ph 3:20. 1 P 2:9. **fight our.** 2 Ch 32:8.

21. **he rehearsed.** Ex +19:8. Jg 11:11n.

22. **Hearken.** ver. 7. Ps 106:15. Ho 4:17. 13:11.

1 SAMUEL 9

The ancestry and personal qualifications of Saul, 1, 2. He is sent to seek his father's asses; but not finding them, he, by the counsel of his servant, purposes going to Samuel, 3-10. He is directed by young maidens where to find him, 11-14. Samuel, prepared by a revelation from God, expects him, and entertains him with great respect, 15-24. On the morrow he privately discourses with him, and brings him on his way, 25-27.

1. **Kish.** i.e. *laying a snare* or *bending; a bow,* *S#7027h. ver. 3. 1 S 10:11, 21. 14:51. 2 S 21:14. 1 Ch 8:30, 33, 33. 9:36, 39, 39. 12:1. 23:21, 22. 24:29, 29. 26:28. 1 Ch 29:12. Est 2:5. Ac 13:21, Cis. (1) Father of King Saul, 1 S 9:1, 3; 10:11, 21, called Cis, Ac 13:21. (2) A Levite, the grandson of Merari, 1 Ch 23:21; 24:29. (3) A Benjamite, 1 Ch 8:30; 9:36. (4) A Levite, 2 Ch 29:12. (5) A Benjamite who was an ancestor of Mordecai, Est 2:5. **Abiel.** i.e. *my father is strong* or *is God,* *S#22h. 1 S 14:51. 1 Ch 11:32. (1) An Israelite of the tribe of Benjamin, who was the grandfather of Saul, the first king of Israel, 1 S 9:1; 14:51. (2) One of David's valiant men, 1 Ch 11:32. He is called Abi-

albon in 2 S 23:31. **Zeror**. i.e. a *bundle* or *bag*, *S#6872h. **Bechorath**. i.e. a *first-born*, *S#1064h. **Aphiah**. i.e. *blown* or *inflamed; rekindled, refreshed*, *S#647h. **a Benjamite**. *or*, the son of a man of Jemini. **power**. *or*, substance. 1 S 25:2. 2 S 19:32. Jb 1:3.

2. **Saul**. i.e. *asked; prayed for; desired*, S#7586h. (1) One of the kings of Edom, Ge 36:37, 38. He is called Shaul in 1 Ch 1:48, 49. (2) The first king of Israel, the son of Kish, of the tribe of Benjamin. **choice**. Ex 14:7. Jg 20:15, 16, 34. 1 S 16:7. Ge 6:2. 2 S 14:25, 26. Je 9:23. **from his shoulders**. 1 S 10:23. 17:4. Nu 13:33.

3. **the asses**. 1 S 10:2. Ge 12:16. 32:15. 45:23. 49:11. Nu 22:21-33. Jg 5:10. 10:4.

4. **mount**. Jg 17:1. 19:1. **Shalisha**. i.e. *triangular; a third*, *S#8031h. 2 K 4:42, Baal-shalisha. **Shalim**. i.e. *place of foxes*, *S#8171h, only here. Ge 33:18. Jn 3:23.

5. **Zuph**. 1 S 1:1. **leave**. *or*, cease. Ge 11:8. 18:11. **take thought**. *or*, sorrow. *S#1672h. 1 S *10:2h. Ps 38:18h. Is 57:10, 11h. Je 17:8h. 38:19h. 42:16h. Mt 6:25, 28, 34. Lk 12:11, 22.

6. **man of God**. 1 S 2:27. Dt 33:1. Jsh 14:6. Jg 13:6, 8. 1 K 12:22. *13:1, etc. 2 K 4:9. 6:6. 23:17. 1 T 6:11. **an honorable**. 1 Th 2:10. 5:13. **all that he saith**. 1 S 3:19, 20. Is 44:26. Zc 1:5, 6. Mt 24:35.

7. **what shall**. Dt +16:16. Jg 6:18. 13:15-17. 2 S 24:24. 1 K 14:3. 2 K 4:42. 5:5. 8:8. Lk 21:4. **spent in**. Heb. gone out of, etc. **there is not**. We are not to suppose from this that the prophets took money to predict future events: Saul only refers to an invariable custom, that no man approached a superior without some present or another, however small in value. Dr. Pococke tells us of a present of *fifty radishes!* Other authors mention a flower, an orange, or similar trifles; and Mr. Bruce says, that one who wished to solicit a favor from him, presented him with about a score of dates! "I mention this trifling circumstance," says Mr. B., "to show how essential to human and civil intercourse presents are considered to be in the East; whether it be dates, or whether it be diamonds, they are so much a part of their manners, that without them, an inferior will never be at peace in his own mind, or think that he has hold of his superior for protection. But superiors give no presents to their inferiors." Presents then are tokens of honor; not intended as offers of payment or enrichment. **bring to**. Ga *6:6. 1 T *5:17. He 13:16. **have we**. Heb. is with us.

8. **I have here at hand**. Heb. there is found in my hand.

9. **enquire**. Ge 25:22. Jg 1:1. **Prophet**. Nu 12:6. 24:4. **a Seer**. 2 S +24:11. 2 K 17:13. 1 Ch 26:28. 29:29. 2 Ch 16:7, 10. Is 29:10. 30:10. Am 7:12.

10. **Well said**. Heb. Thy word *is* good. 2 K 5:13, 14.

11. **the hill to the city**. Heb. in the ascent of the city. **found**. Ge 24:11, 18-20. Ex 2:16. Jg 5:11.

12. **he is**. 1 S 7:17. **sacrifice**. *or*, feast. lit. the sacrifice of the day. 1 S 16:2. Ge 31:54. Dt 12:6, 7. 1 C 5:7, 8. **the high place**. 1 S 10:5, 13. 1 K 3:2-4. 1 Ch 16:39.

13. **he doth bless**. Ex 23:25. Ps *132:15. Mt 26:26. Mk 6:41. Lk 24:30. Jn 6:11, 23. 1 C 10:30. 1 T 4:4. **this time**. Heb. today. ver. 27mg.

15. **the Lord**. ver. 17. 1 S 15:1. Ps 25:14. Am 3:7. Mk 11:2-4. 14:13-16. Ac 13:21. 27:23. **told Samuel in**

his ear. Heb. revealed the ear of Samuel. ver. 17. 1 S 15:22. 20:2. Ge 18:17. Ru +4:4. 2 S 7:27. Jb 33:16mg. Ps 78:1. Is 50:4.

16. **thou shalt**. 1 S 10:1. 15:1. 16:3. 1 K 19:15, 16. 2 K 9:3-6. **captain**. i.e. *one in the foreground*. *S#5057h; 1 S 9:16. 10:1. 13:14. 25:30 (ruler). 2 S 5:2. 6:21. 7:8. 1 K 1:35. 14:7 (prince). 16:2. 20:5. 1 Ch 5:2. 9:11, 20. 11:2. 12:27 (leader). *13:1. 17:7. 26:24. 27:4, 16. 28:4. 29:22. 2 Ch 6:5. 11:11, 22. 28:7. 31:12, 13. 32:21. 35:8. Ne 11:11. Jb 29:10 (nobles). 31:37. Ps 76:12. Pr 8:6 (excellent things). 28:16. Is 55:4. Je 20:1 (chief). Ezk 28:2. Da *9:25, 26. 11:22. **save**. 1 S *14:23. 18:7. **looked upon**. Ex 2:23-25. 3:7-9. Ps 25:18. 106:44.

17. **Behold**. 1 S 16:6-12. Ho 13:11. **reign over**. Heb. restrain in. 1 S 3:13. 2 S 23:6, 7. Ne 13:19, 25. Jb 29:9. Ac 13:21. Ro 13:3, 4.

18. **gate**. *or*, city. ver. 14. Ge +14:7.

19. **the Seer**. The word *roaih* literally signifies *one who sees;* particularly preternatural sights. A seer and a prophet were the same in most cases; only with this difference, the seer was always a prophet, but the prophet was not always a seer. A seer seems to imply one who frequently met with and saw some symbolical representation of God. All prophets, true or false, profess to see God (see Nu 24:4, 16. Je 14:4); and diviners, in their enthusiastic flights, boasted that they had those things exhibited to their sight which would come to pass. **and will tell**. Jn 4:29. 1 C 14:25.

20. **three days ago**. Heb. today three days. ver. 3. **set not**. 1 S +4:20mg. 1 Ch 29:3. Ps 62:10. Col 3:2. **on whom**. 1 S 8:5, 19. 12:13, 15. **desire**. ♪121R5, Ge +27:15.

21. **Am**. ♪85E, Ge +17:17. **a Benjamite**. Jg 20:46-48. Ps 68:27. **the smallest**. Mi 5:2. **my family**. 1 S 10:27. *15:17. 18:18, 23. Jg 6:14, 15. Ho 13:1. Lk 14:11. Ep 3:8. **so to me**. Heb. according to this word.

22. **the parlor**. Perhaps a place for reclining at food (Young). 2 K 23:11. 1 Ch 9:26, 33. 23:28. 28:12. 2 Ch 31:11. Ezr 8:29. **in the chiefest**. Ge 43:32. Lk *14:10.

23. **cook**. lit. slaughter man. Ge 37:36mg. Je 39:9mg. **Bring**. 1 S 1:5. Ge 43:34. **portion**. Ex 29:26.

24. **cook**. ver. +23. **the shoulder**. Probably the shoulder was set before Saul, not because it was the best part, but because it was an emblem of the government to which he was now called (See Is 9:6). Le 7:32, 33. Ezk 24:4. **left**. *or*, reserved. Ge 14:10 (remained). **this time**. or, appointed season. Young notes, Of the festival, as Ex 13:10.

25. **And when**. ver. 13. **the top**. ver. 26. Dt +22:8n. 2 S 11:2. Ne 8:16. Je 19:13. Mt 10:27. Ac 10:9.

26. **Samuel**. Saul had no doubt slept there all night, as is usual in the East; and now, being the break of day, "Samuel called to Saul on the top of the house": there was no calling him to the top of the house a second time; he was already sleeping there, and Samuel called him up. **top of the house**. ver. 25. Dt +22:8n. Jsh 2:6, 8. Jg 16:27. 2 S 16:22. Is 15:3. Mt 24:17. **Up**. Ge 19:14. 44:4. Jsh 7:13. Jg 19:28.

27. **Bid the servant**. 1 S 20:38, 39. Jn 15:14, 15. **but stand**. 1 S 12:7. 23:16. Da 10:19. **a while**. Heb. today. ver. 13. **that I may**. 1 S 15:16. 2 K 9:5, 6. Da *10:21.

1 SAMUEL 10

Samuel anoints Saul, and dismisses him with directions, and with tokens which came to pass accordingly, 1-13. Saul answers the inquiries of his uncle, but conceals the matter of the kingdom, 14-16. Samuel convenes the people at Mizpeh, where Saul is chosen king by lot, 17-25. A few honorably attend him, but others despise him, 26, 27.

1. **a vial.** 1 S 2:10. 9:16. 16:13. 24:6. 26:11. Ex 30:25. 2 K 9:3-6. Ac 13:21. Re 5:8. **kissed him.** 2 S 19:39. 1 K 19:18. Ps 2:12. Ho 13:2. 1 Th 5:26. **captain.** 1 S 8:9, 19. 13:14. Jsh 5:14, 15. 2 S 5:2. 2 K 20:5. He 2:10. **his inheritance.** 1 S 26:19. Ex 19:5, 6. Dt +*32:9. 2 S 20:19. 21:3. 1 K 8:51, 53. 2 K 21:14. Ps 2:8. 28:9. 78:71. +*94:14. *132:11, 13. 135:4. Is 63:17. 65:9. Je 10:16. Zc *2:12. Lk +*1:32, 33. Ep 1:18. Col +*3:24. He 1:2.
2. **shalt find.** ⌐96C2, Ge +45:9. **Rachel's.** Ge 35:19, 20. Je 31:15. **sepulchre.** S#6900h, *qeburah*, Ge +35:20. **Zelzah.** i.e. *shade from heat; a clear shadow*, ❋S#6766h. Jsh 18:28. **The asses.** ver. 16. 1 S 9:3-5. **care.** Heb. business.
3. **Tabor.** Jsh 19:12, 22. Jg 4:6, 12. 8:18. Ps 89:12. **Bethel.** Ge 28:19, 22. 35:1, 3, 6, 7. **three kids.** Le 1:10. 3:6, 12. 7:13. 23:13. Nu 15:5-12. **a bottle.** 1 S 1:24. Je +*13:12n.
4. **salute thee.** Heb. ask thee of peace. Jg +18:15mg.
5. **hill of God.** ver. 10. 1 S 13:3. **garrison.** 1 S 13:3. 2 S 5:7. Ps 2:6. 68:15, 16. **a company.** 1 S 19:20. 2 K 2:3, 5, 15. 4:38. 6:1. Ps 119:61mg. **high place.** 1 S 9:12, 13. **a psaltery.** Ex 15:20, 21. 2 S 6:5. 1 K 10:12. 2 K 3:15. 1 Ch 13:8. 15:16, 19-21, 27, 28. 16:5, 42. *25:1-6. 2 Ch 5:12. 9:11. 20:28. 29:25-27. Ps 49:4. 150:3-6. **tabret.** Ge 31:27. Ex 15:20. 2 K 3:15. **pipe.** 1 K 1:40. Is 5:12. *30:29. Je 48:36. **harp.** Ge 4:21. **prophesy.** 1 C 14:1.
6. **Spirit.** Heb. *ruach*, Ge +41:38. ver. 10. 1 S 16:13. 19:23, 24. Nu 11:25. Jg 3:10. Jl 2:28. Mt 7:22. **another man.** ver. 9-12.
7. **let it be.** Heb. it shall come to pass that, etc. **signs.** Ex 4:8. Lk 2:12. Jn 16:4. **that thou do as occasion,** etc. Heb. do for thee as thine hand shall find. 1 S 18:14. Jg +9:33. **God.** Ge 21:20. Dt 20:1. Jg 6:12. Is 7:14. 45:1, 2. Mt 1:23. 28:20. Ac 18:10.
8. **to Gilgal.** 1 S 11:14, 15. 13:4, 8-15. 15:33. **burnt offerings.** Le +*23:12. **sacrifices of.** Le +*7:11. **peace offerings.** Le +*23:19.
9. **back.** Heb. shoulder. 1 S 9:2. Ge 49:15. Ps 21:12. **gave.** Heb. turned. **another heart.** ver. 6. Nu 14:24. **and all those signs.** ver. 2-5. Jg 6:21, 36-40. 7:11. Is 38:7, 8. Mk 14:16.
10. **they came.** ver. 5. 1 S 19:20-24. **Spirit.** Heb. *ruach*, Ge +41:38. **came upon.** T#347-2. Lk 1:67. Ac 2:4. 10:45, 46. 11:15.
11. **when all.** Jb 42:11. Jn 9:8, 9. Ac 3:10. **beforetime.** lit. "from yesterday, third day." Jsh +*4:18mg. **one to another.** Heb. a man to his neighbor. Je 13:14mg. **What is this.** Mt 13:54, 55. Ac 2:7, 8. 4:13. 9:21. **Is Saul.** 1 S 19:24. Mt *13:54, 55. Jn 7:15. Ga 1:23.
12. **of the same place.** Heb. from thence. **who is their.** Is 54:13. Jn 6:45. 7:16. Ja 1:17. **proverb.** ⌐138A, Ge +10:9. Nu +*21:27.
14. **And he said.** 1 S 9:3-10. **no where.** 2 K 5:25.
16. **matter.** 1 S 9:27. Ex 4:18. Jg 14:6. Pr 29:11.

17. **unto the Lord.** 1 S *7:5, 6. Jg 20:1.
18. **Thus saith.** Jg *2:1. 6:8, 9. Ne 9:9-12, 27, 28. **brought up.** Ge 50:24. Ex 17:3. **and delivered.** Ex *18:8. Jsh 24:10.
19. **And ye have.** 1 S 8:*7-9, 19. 12:12, *17-19. **saved you.** Jg 3:9mg, 15. 6:36. **present yourselves.** 1 S 12:7, 16. Jsh *24:1. **by your tribes.** Nu 17:2. Jsh 7:14, etc. **your thousands.** Mi +*5:2.
20. **caused.** 1 S 14:41. Jsh 7:16-18. Ac 1:24-26. **was taken.** Jsh 14:2n. 1 S 14:41. Ac 1:24, 26.
21. **Matri.** i.e. *rainy; rain of Jehovah*, ❋S#4309h.
22. **enquired.** 1 S 23:2-4, 11, 12. Nu 27:21. Jg 1:1. 20:18, 23, 28. **further.** 1 S 16:11. 23:4. **hid.** 1 S 9:21. 15:17. Jsh 2:6. Lk 14:11.
23. **he was higher.** 1 S 9:2. 16:7. 17:4.
24. **See ye him.** Dt 17:15. 2 S 21:6. **God save the king.** Heb. Let the king live. 1 K 1:25, 31, 39. 2 K 11:12. Mt 21:9. ⌐108B. Idiom B829. "To live" is used of having all that makes life worth living, flourishing, and prospering. For other instances of this idiom see 1 S 25:6. 1 K 1:25. Ps 22:26. 34:12. 69:32. Ec 6:8. 1 Th 3:8. 1 P 3:10.
25. **the manner.** 1 S 8:11-18. Dt 17:14-20. Ezk 45:9, 10. 46:16-18. Ro 13:1-7. 1 T 2:1, 2. T 3:1. 1 P 2:13, 14. **wrote.** Dt 17:18, 19.
26. **Gibeah.** i.e. *height* or *hill*. 1 S 11:4. 15:34. Jsh 18:28. Jg 19:12-16. 20:14. 2 S 21:6. **band.** Ex 14:4, 9, 28. **whose hearts.** Ezr 1:5. Ps 110:3. Ac 7:10. 13:48. 16:14.
27. **children of Belial.** 1 S 2:12. 11:12. Dt 13:13. +15:9. Jg +19:22. 2 S 20:1. 2 Ch 13:7. Ac 7:35, 51, 52. **brought him.** 1 S 9:7n. Ge 43:11. Jg 3:15. 2 S 8:2. 1 K 4:21. 10:25. 2 Ch 17:5. Ps 72:10. Mt 2:11. **he held his peace.** *or,* he was as though he had been deaf. Ps 38:13. Is 36:21. Mt 27:12-14.

1 SAMUEL 11

Nahash, the Ammonite, encamps against Jabeshgilead, and offers the inhabitants most cruel and disgraceful terms; who obtain seven days' respite, 1-3. They send messengers to Gibeah, and Saul delivers them, and smites the Ammonites, 4-11. Saul will not allow his despisers to be punished, 12, 13. He is made king in Gilgal, 14, 15.

1. **Nahash.** i.e. *a serpent*, as in Ge 3:1. ❋S#5176h. In the Vulgate this chapter begins thus: *Et factum est quasi post mensem*, "And it came to pass about a month after;" which is also the reading of the principal copies of the Septuagint; and is also found in Josephus, though it appears to be of little authority. ver. 2. 1 S 12:12. Jg ◑10:7. ◑11:8, etc. 2 S 10:2. 17:25, 27. 1 Ch 19:1, 2. (1) One of the Ammonite kings, 2 S 10:2. (2) A man (or woman) whose daughter Abigail was the mother of Amasa, 2 S 17:25. **the Ammonite.** A descendant of Lot, as in Ge 19:38. 1 S 12:12. Dt 2:19. Jg 3:13. 2 S 10:1. 1 K 11:1. **Jabesh-gilead.** 1 S 31:11-13. Jg 21:8, 10, etc. **Make.** Ge 26:28. Ex *23:32. Dt 23:3. 1 K 20:34. Jb 41:4. Is 36:16. Ezk 17:13.
2. **On this.** 2 K 18:31. **thrust.** Nu 16:14mg. Jg 16:21. Est 3:6. Jb 30:17. Pr 12:10. *30:17. Is 51:1. Je 39:7. **right eyes.** So that they would be unfit for shooting in battle (Young). **reproach.** 1 S 17:26. Ge 34:14. Ps 44:15, 16.
3. **elders.** Who ruled in every city (Young). Jsh +20:4. **Give us.** Heb. Forbear us.

4. **to Gibeah.** 1 S 10:26. 14:2. 15:34. 2 S 21:6. **lifted up.** ƒ144A12, Ge +22:13. 1 S 30:4. Jg 2:4. 21:2. Ro 12:15. 1 C 12:26. Ga *6:2. He *13:3.

5. **after the herd.** 1 S 9:1. 1 K 19:19. Ps 78:71. **What aileth.** Ge 21:17. Jg 18:23. Is 22:1.

6. **Spirit of God.** Heb. *ruach*, Ge +41:38. 1 S 10:10. 16:13. Jg 3:10. 6:34. 11:29. 13:25. 14:6. **his anger.** Ex 32:19. Nu 12:3. Mk 3:5. Ep 4:26. Ja 1:20.

7. **he took.** The sending the pieces of the oxen was an act similar to that of the Levite, Jg 19:29, where see Note. **hewed.** Jg 19:29. 20:6. **Whosoever.** Jg 21:5-11. **the fear.** Ge 35:5. Jg 5:23. 2 Ch 14:14. 17:10. **with one consent.** Heb. as one man. Jg 20:1.

8. **he numbered.** Lest any of the tribes and families might be missing (See Jg *21:5-11). Nu 31:48, 49. 1 S 14:17. 2 S 18:1, 2. 20:4. 24:1-9. 1 K 20:15, 26. 2 K 25:19. 1 Ch 21:5, 6. 2 Ch 25:5. Is 13:4. **Bezek.** Jg 1:4, 5. **the children.** 1 S 13:15. 15:4. 2 S 24:9. 2 Ch 17:12-19.

9. **help.** *or*, deliverance. Ps 18:17.

10. **Tomorrow.** ver. 2, 3.

11. **on the morrow.** Ge 22:14. Ps 46:1. **in three.** Jg 7:16. 9:43. **morning.** Ex 14:24. **slew.** ver. 2. Jg 1:7. Mt 7:2. Ja 2:13. **Ammonites.** *S#5984h. Dt 2:20. 23:3. 1 S 11:1, 2. 2 S 23:37. 1 K 11:1, 5. 14:21, 31. 1 Ch 11:39. 2 Ch 12:13. 20:1. 24:26. 26:8. Ezr 9:1. Ne 2:10, 19. 4:3, 7. 13:1, 23. **so that two.** 1 S 30:17, 18. Jg 4:16.

12. **Who is he.** 1 S 10:27. Ps 21:8. Lk *19:27.

13. **There shall.** 1 S 14:45. 2 S 19:22. **the Lord.** 1 S 19:5. Ex 14:13, 30. Ps 44:4-8. Is 59:16. 1 C 15:10. **wrought salvation.** 1 S 14:45.

14. **let us go.** 1 S 7:16. 10:8. **renew.** 1 S 10:24. 2 S 5:3. 1 Ch 12:38, 39.

15. **king.** 1 Ch 11:3. **before the Lord.** 1 S 10:17. **sacrificed.** 1 S 10:8. Ex 24:5. 1 Ch 29:21-24. **sacrifices.** Le +*7:11. **peace offerings.** Le +*23:19. **rejoiced greatly.** 1 S 8:19. 12:13-15, 17. Ho 13:10, 11. Ja 4:16.

1 SAMUEL 12

Samuel, before Israel, avows his integrity, and the people fully justify him, 1-5. He expostulates with them, for their ingratitude, in rejecting the government of God, and warns them against disobedience, 6-15. To show their guilt in asking a king, he calls for thunder and rain in time of harvest, which greatly dismays them, 16-19. He promises to instruct and pray for them, and encourages them to cleave to the service of God, and to trust in his mercy, 20-25.

1. **Behold.** 1 S 8:5-8, 19-22. **have made.** 1 S 10:1, 24. 11:14, 15.

2. **walketh.** 1 S 8:20. Nu 27:17. **I am old.** 1 S 8:1, 5. Ps 71:18. Is 46:3, 4. 2 T 4:6. 2 P 1:14. **grayheaded.** Jb 15:10. **my sons.** 1 S 2:22, 29. 3:13, 16. 8:3. **I have walked.** 1 S 3:19, 20.

3. **his anointed.** ver. 5. 1 S 10:1. 24:6. 2 S 1:14-16. Mt 22:21. Ro 13:1-7. **whose ox.** Nu *16:15. Jg 15:16. Ac 20:33. 24:16. 2 C 12:14. 1 Th 2:5, 10. 1 P 5:2. **bribe.** Dt 16:19. Heb. ransom. lit. a covering. *S#3724h: Ge 6:14 (with pitch). Ex 24:30 (sum of money). 30:12. Nu 35:31, 32 (satisfaction). 1 S 6:18 (villages). 12:3. Jb *33:24 (ransom; mg, or, atonement). 36:18. Ps *49:7. Pr 6:35. 13:8. 21:18. SS 1:14 (camphire). 4:13. Is 48:3. Am 5:12. **blind mine eyes.** *or*, that I should hide mine eyes at him. Ex 23:8. Le 20:4.

Dt 16:19. Pr *28:27. Is *1:15. Ezk *22:26. **I will.** Ex 22:4. Le 6:4. Lk 19:8.

4. **hast not.** Ps 37:5, 6. Da 6:4. 3 J 12.

5. **The Lord.** Jb 31:35-40. 42:7. **his anointed.** 1 S 26:9. **ye have.** Jn 18:38. Ac 23:9. 24:16, 20. 1 C 4:4. 2 C 1:12. 1 Th 2:10. **in my hand.** Ex 22:4. Ps 17:3.

6. **It is the Lord.** Ex 6:26. Ne 9:9-14. Ps 77:19, 20. 78:12, etc. 99:6. 105:26, 41. Is 63:7-14. Ho 12:13. Mi 6:4. **advanced.** *or*, made.

7. **stand still.** 1 S 9:27. **reason.** Is √1:18. 5:3, 4. Ezk 18:25-30. Mi 6:2, 3. Ac *17:3. **righteous acts.** Heb. righteousness, *or* benefits. Jg +5:11, **to.** Heb. with.

8. **Jacob.** Ge 46:5-7. Nu 20:15. Ac 7:15. **cried.** Ex 2:23, 24. 3:9. **sent Moses.** See on ver. 6. Ex 3:10. 4:14-16, 27-31. 6:26. Ps 77:20. **brought.** Ex 12:51. 14:30, 31. **made them.** Jsh 1:2-4, 6. 3:10-13. Ps 44:1-3. 78:54, 55. 105:44.

9. **forgat.** Dt 32:18. Jg 3:7. Ps 10:4. 106:21. Je 2:32. **he sold.** Dt 32:30. Jg 2:14. 3:8. 4:2. Is 50:1, 2. **of the Philistines.** Jg 10:7. 13:1. **into the.** Jg 3:12. Is 63:10.

10. **And they.** 1 S 7:2. Jg 3:9, 15. 4:3. 6:7. 10:10, 15. Ps 78:34, 35. 106:44. Is 26:16. **Baalim.** Jg 2:13. 3:7. **deliver.** Jg 10:15, 16. Is 33:22. Lk 1:74, 75. 2 C 5:14, 15.

11. **Jerubbaal.** Jg 6:14, 32. *7:1. 8:29, 35. **Bedan.** He 11:32. *Bedan*, whose name occurs no where else as a judge of Israel, Bp. Patrick and others suppose to be a contraction of *ben Dan*, "the son of Dan;" by which they suppose *Samson* is meant, as the Targum reads. The LXX., Syriac, and Arabic, however, instead of *Bedan* read *Barak*; and the two latter versions, instead of *Samuel* have *Samson*. These readings are adopted by Houbigant, and appear to be genuine; for it is not probable that Samuel would enumerate himself. Jg ch. 13-16. **Jepthah.** Jg 11:1, etc. **Samuel.** 1 S 7:13.

12. **saw.** ƒ106, Ge +31:7. **Nahash.** 1 S 11:1, 2. **Nay.** 1 S 8:3, 5, 6, 19, 20. Jg 9:18, 56, 57. **when the Lord.** 1 S *8:7. *10:19. Ge *17:7. Ex *19:5, 6. Nu 23:21. Jg 8:23. Ps 74:12. Is 33:22. Ho 13:10.

13. **behold.** 1 S 10:24. 11:15. **whom ye.** 1 S 8:5. 9:20. **have desired.** Ps 78:29-31. *106:15. Ho 13:11. Ac 13:21.

14. **If.** Ge +4:7. **ye will.** Le 26:1-13. Dt 28:1-14. Jsh 24:14, 20. Ps 81:12-15. Is 3:10. Ro 2:7. **commandment.** Heb. mouth. **continue.** Heb. be after.

15. **But if ye.** Le 26:14-30. Dt *28:15-68. Jsh 24:20. Is 1:20. 3:11. Ro 2:8, 9. **against.** See on ver. 9.

16. **stand.** ver. 7. 1 S 15:16. Ex 14:13, 31.

17. **Is it.** In northern latitudes, thunder and rain are far from being uncommon during harvest. But rain is hardly ever known in Palestine during that season, which commences about the end of June, or beginning of July. This fact is abundantly confirmed by modern travelers, and is demonstrative to every unprejudiced reader of the Holy Scriptures, that the thunder and rain, which at Samuel's invocation, was sent at this season of the year, was a miraculous interposition of the power of God; for we read in ver. 16, it was a "great thing which the Lord will do." Thus were the Israelites warned of their sin in having asked a king, and of the omnipotence of that God, whose gracious promises they virtually neglected by this act. Pr 26:1. **wheat harvest.** 1 S 6:13. Ru 2:23. **I will call.** 1 S 7:9, 10. Jsh 10:12. Ps 99:6. Je 15:1. Ja *5:16-18. **your wickedness.** See on 1 S 8:7.

18. **sent thunder**. Ex 9:23-25. Re 11:5, 6. **feared**. Ex 14:31. Ezr 10:9. Ps 106:12, 13.

19. **Pray for thy**. 1 S 7:5, 8. Ge 20:7. Ex 9:28. 10:17. 1 K 13:6. Jb 42:8. Ps 78:34, 35. Is 26:16. Ml 1:9. Ac 8:24. Ja 5:15. 1 J 5:16.

20. **Fear not**. Ex 20:19, 20. 1 P 3:16. **turn not**. Dt 11:16. 31:29. Jsh 23:6. Ps 40:4. 101:3. 125:5. Je 3:1.

21. **vain things**. Dt 32:21. Je 2:5, 13. 10:8, 15. 14:22. 16:19. Jon *2:8. Hab 2:18. 1 C *8:4. **cannot profit**. Ps 115:4-8. Is 41:23, 24. 44:9, 10. 45:20. 46:7. Je *10:5. 16:19. Hab 2:18. 1 C *8:4. **nor deliver**. Dt 32:30.

22. **not forsake**. Dt 31:17. 2 S +*7:15. 1 K 6:13. 2 K 21:14. 1 Ch +*28:9. 2 Ch 15:2. Ps √94:14. Is *41:9, 17. 42:16. +*54:7. +√55:3. Je +*4:27. +√33:24-26. La 3:31, 32. 5:20. Ro +√)11:2. He +*13:5. **for his great**. Ex 32:12. Nu 14:13-19. Dt 32:26, 27. Jsh 7:9. Ps 106:8. Is 37:35. 43:25. 48:11. Je 14:7, 21. Ezk 20:9, 14. Ep 1:6, 12. **it hath**. Ex 19:5, 6. Dt 7:7, 8. 9:5. 14:2. Ml 1:2. Mt 11:26. Jn *15:16. Ro 9:13-18. *11:29. 1 C 4:7. Ep 1:3. Ph 1:6. T 3:5.

23. **God forbid**. Ge *18:25. Ac 12:5. Ro 1:9. Col 1:9. 1 Th 3:10. 2 T 1:3. **in ceasing**. Heb. from ceasing. Je 44:18 (left off). **pray for**. T#1815. Ge 20:7, 17. Dt 9:20. 2 Ch 30:18-20. Jb *42:8-10. Ps 2:8. Je 42:4. La 2:18, 19. Mt *5:44. 9:38. 18:18, √19. Lk 23:34. Jn 17:9, *20, 21. Ac 8:14, 15. 20:36, 37. Ro *1:9. 10:1. 2 C 1:11. Ep *6:18, 19. Ph 1:19. Col 4:2, 3. 2 Th 1:11, 12. 1 T √2:1-4. Ja *5:14, 15. 1 J 5:16. **I will teach**. Ps *34:11. Pr 4:11. Ec 12:10. Ac 20:20. Col 1:28. **the good**. 1 K 8:36. 2 Ch 6:27. Je *6:16.

24. **fear the Lord**. Jb *28:28. Ps *110:10. Pr *1:7. Ec *12:13. He 12:29. **in truth**. Ps 119:80. Jn 1:47. **consider**. Ezr 9:13, 14. Is 5:12. Ro *12:1. **how great things**. *or*, what a great *thing*, etc. Dt 10:21. Ps 126:2, 3.

25. **But if**. Dt 32:15, etc. Jsh 24:20. Is 3:11. **ye and**. 1 S 31:1-5. Dt 28:36. Ho 10:3.

1 SAMUEL 13

Saul chooses a select band, and dismisses the people, 1, 2. Jonathan, his son, smites a garrison of the Philistines, and Saul summons the people to Gilgal, 3, 4. The Philistines gather a great army; and Israel is distressed and scattered, 5-7. Saul, weary of waiting for Samuel, sacrifices, 8, 9. Samuel comes and reproves him, and shows that God has rejected him; while Saul in vain excuses himself, 10-14. A small company attend Saul; and three bands of Philistines waste the land, 15-18. The policy of the Philistines, who suffer no smith in Israel, 19-23.

1. A.M. 2911. B.C. 1093. An. Ex. Is. 398. **reigned one year**. Heb. the son of one year in his reigning. This verse is variously interpreted; but probably it only means, according to the Hebrew idiom, that during the first year nothing remarkable occurred; but after two years, (or in the second year of his reign), the subsequent events took place. Ex 12:5. Mi 6:6mg.

2. **chose**. 1 S 8:11. 14:52. **Michmash**. i.e. *treasure*, *S#4363h. ver. 5, 11, 16, 23. 1 S 14:5, 31. Ne 11:31. Is 10:28. **Bethel**. Ge 12:8. **Jonathan**. i.e. *Jah hath given*, *S#3129h. ver. 3, 16, 22, 22. 14:1, 3, 4, 12, 12, 13, 13, 14, 17, 21, 27, 29, 39, 40, 41, 42, 43, 43, 44, 45, 45, 49. 19:1. 1 K 1:42, 43. 1 Ch 2:32, 33. 10:2. 11:34. Ezr 8:6. 10:15. Ne 12:11, 11, 14, 35. Je 40:8. For *S#3083h, see 1 S +14:6. (1) An Israelite of the

tribe of Levi, who became a priest of the idol set up by Micah in Mount Ephraim, and which was afterward taken away and set up at Laish by the Danites, Jg 17:7-13; 18:30. (2) One of the sons of Saul, the first king of Israel, famous for his piety and valor, 1 S 13:2; 14:6-14; 18:1; 31:6; 2 S 1:17-27. (3) A son of Abiathar, one of the high priests in the time of David, 2 S 15:27; 1 K 1:42, 43. (4) A son of Shimeah, one of the brothers of David, 2 S 21:21; 1 Ch 20:7. (5) One of David's valiant men, 2 S 23:32; 1 Ch 11:34. (6) A descendant of Jerahmeel, 1 Ch 2:32, 33. (7) An uncle of David, 1 Ch 27:32. (8) A chief man of the Jews, whose son returned with Ezra to Babylon, Ezr 8:6. (9) A Jew who aided Ezra in the investigation of mixed marriages, Ezr 10:15. (10) A high priest for thirty-two years, Ne 12:11, called Johanan in Ne 12:22, 23. (11) A priest, the descendant of Melicuh, Ne 12:14. (12) Another priest, a descendant of Shemaiah, Ne 12:35, called Jehonathan in Ne 12:18. (13) A scribe in whose house the prophet Jeremiah was imprisoned by the princes of Judah, Je 37:15, 20; 38:26. (14) A son of Kareah, Je 40:8. **in Gibeah**. 1 S 10:26. 15:34. Jsh 18:28. Jg 19:12. 2 S 21:6. Is 10:29.

3. **the garrison**. 1 S 10:5. 14:1-6. 2 S 23:14. **Geba**. *or*, the hill. i.e. *a height*, *S#1387h. ver. 16. Jsh 18:24, Gaba. 21:17. Jg 20:10, 33. 2 S 5:25. 1 K 15:22. 2 K 23:8. 1 Ch 6:60. 8:6. 2 Ch 16:6. Ezr 2:26. Ne 7:30. 11:31. 12:29. Is *10:29. Zc *14:10. **blew**. Jg 3:27. 6:34. 2 S 2:28. 20:1.

4. **was had in abomination**. Heb. did stink. Ge 34:30. 46:34. Ex 5:21. Zc 11:8. **to Gilgal**. 1 S 10:8. 11:14, 15. Jsh 5:9.

5. **thirty thousand chariots**. The Philistines had no doubt collected troops in this emergency, from all the surrounding nations; but the number of chariots is immensely large beyond any example, and wholly disproportioned to the number of their cavalry. It is probable, therefore, that for *sheloshim aileph*, "thirty thousand," we should read *shelosh aileph*, "three thousand," with the Syriac and Arabic. Young notes "or *charioteers*, as in 2 S 10:18; 1 K 20:21; 1 Ch 19:18; or *thirty chief chariots*; Syr. and Ar. read '3000 chariots,' but even Pharaoh had only 600 (Ex 14:7); Jabin 900 (Jg 4:3); Zerah 300 (2 Ch 14:9)." **as the sand**. Ɩ102B, Ge +13:16. Ge 22:17. Jsh 11:4. Jg 7:12. 2 Ch 1:9. Is 48:19. Je 15:8. Ro 9:27. **Beth-aven**. 1 S 14:23. Jsh 7:2. 18:11, 12. Ho 4:15. 5:8. 10:5.

6. **in a strait**. Ex 14:10-12. Jsh 8:20. Jg 10:9. 20:41. 2 S 24:14. Ph 1:23. **in caves**. 1 S 14:11. 23:19. 24:3. Jg 6:2. Is 42:22. He 11:38. **pits**. Heb. *bor*, Ge +37:20.

7. **the Hebrews**. Le 26:17, 36, 37. Dt 28:25. **Gad**. Nu 32:1-5, 33-42. Dt 3:12. Jsh 13:24-31. **followed him trembling**. Heb. trembled after him. Dt 20:8. Jg 7:3. Ho 11:10, 11.

8. **tarried**. 1 S 10:8. **had appointed**. Ɩ63E2. Ellipsis (Relative: of cognate words) B57: where the verb is to be supplied from the noun. Here, the verb "appointed" is supplied from the noun "set time." For other instances of this form of ellipsis identified by EWB in Bsee 1 Ch 17:18. Ps 94:10. Ho 1:2. Mi 7:3. Ro 12:6-8. 13:7. 1 C 1:26. 2 C 5:17. Ep 3:16.

9. **burnt offering**. Le +*23:12. **peace offerings**. Le +*23:19. **he offered**. ver. 12, 13. 1 S 14:18. 15:21, 22. Dt 12:6. 1 K 3:4. Ps 37:7. Pr 15:8. 20:22. 21:3, 27. Is 66:3.

10. **Saul.** 1 S 15:13. **salute him.** Heb. bless him.
1 S 15:13. Ru 2:4. Ps 129:8.

11. **What hast.** Ge 3:13. 4:10. 20:9. 31:26. Jsh 7:19.
2 S 3:24. 2 K 5:25. Jn 18:35. **Michmash.** ver. 2, 5,
16, 23. 1 S 14:5. Is 10:28.

12. **said I.** 1 K 12:26, 27. **made supplication unto.**
Heb. intreated the face of, etc. Ex 32:11mg. 1 K
13:6mg. 2 K 13:4. Jb +11:19mg. Ps 45:12mg. Je
+26:19mg. **I forced.** 1 S 21:7. Ps 66:3. Am 8:5. 2 C
9:7.

13. **Thou hast done.** 2 S *12:7-9. 1 K 18:18. 21:20.
2 Ch *16:9. *19:2. 25:15, 16. Jb *34:18. Pr 19:3. Mt
14:3, 4. **hast not kept.** 1 S 15:11, *22, 28. Ps 50:8-
15. 2 T 2:13. **for ever.** Heb. olam, Ex +12:24.

14. **But now.** 1 S *2:30. 15:28. **the Lord.** 1 S 16:1,
12. 2 S *7:15, 16. Ps 78:70. 84:2. 89:19, 20, etc. Ac
▶13:22. **heart.** ʃ22A17, Ge 6:6. **captain over.** 1 S 9:16.
2 S 5:2. 2 K *20:5. He *2:10. **not kept.** Jn 14:15. Re
22:14.

15. **Samuel.** The LXX. have, "Samuel arose and
went away from Gilgal, and the remainder of the people
went up along with the men of war after Samuel from
Gilgal to Gibeah of Benjamin." This is probably the
true reading; for it does not appear that Samuel went
to Gibeah, which was Saul's usual residence; and the
Hebrew copyist, as Dr. Wall observes, seems to have
missed a line, and added to the sentence concerning
Samuel, that which ended the sentence concerning
Saul. One MS instead of *Samuel*, in the beginning of
the sentence, reads *Saul*. **present.** Heb. found. ʃ171J5.
Synecdoche of the Species B631. To *find* is used of
to *have*, or to be *present with*. For other instances of
this figure see Lk 9:36. Ro 7:18. Ph 2:8. 3:9. He 11:5.
about six. ver. 2, 6, 7. 1 S 14:2.

16. **Gibeah.** Heb. Gebah. See on ver. 3.

17. **in three companies.** 1 S 11:11. **Ophrah.** Jsh
18:23. **Shual.** Jsh 19:3.

18. **Beth-horon.** Jsh 10:11. 16:3, 5. 18:13, 14. 1 Ch
6:68. 2 Ch 8:5. **Zeboim.** Ge 14:2. Ne 11:34. Ho 11:8.

19. **there was no.** It is probable that the Philistines
in the former wars had carried away all the smiths
from Israel. Jg 5:8. 2 K 24:14. Is 54:16. Je 24:1.

21. **a file.** Heb. a file with mouths. **sharpen.** Heb.
set.

22. **there was neither.** 1 S 17:47, 50. Jg 5:8. Zc
4:6. 1 C 1:27-29. 2 C 4:7.

23. **garrison.** *or*, standing camp. ver. 3. 1 S 14:4.
passage. ver. 2, 5. 1 S 14:1, 4, 5. Is 10:28.

1 SAMUEL 14

*Jonathan, attended only by his armor-bearer, smites
the garrison of the Philistines, 1-14; who are seized
with terror, and destroy one another, 15, 16. Saul,
seeing the tumult, inquires of God: but without waiting
for an answer, he assaults the Philistines; being joined
by the Hebrews who had deserted or hid themselves,
17-23. His rash curse, against such as ate that day,
hinders the completion of the victory; and Jonathan,
not knowing what had passed, violates it, 24-30. The
people fly upon the spoil, and are hardly restrained
from eating with the blood, 31-34. Saul builds an altar;
and asks counsel of God, but is not answered, 35-37.
Jonathan, taken by lot and sentenced to die, is rescued
by the people, 38-46. Saul's victories and family, 47-
52.*

1. A.M. 2917. B.C. 1087. An. Ex. Is. 404. **it came
to pass upon a day.** *or*, there was a day. **Jonathan.**
ver. 39-45. 1 S 13:2, 22. 18:1-4. 2 S 1:4, 5, 25, 26.
he told not. 1 S 25:19. Jg 6:27. 14:6. Mi 7:5.

2. **in the uttermost.** 1 S 13:15, 16. Is 10:28, 29. **a
pomegranate.** Jg 4:5. 20:45, 47. **Migron.** i.e. *place of
great conflict; precipice*, *S#4051h. Is 10:28.

3. **Ahiah.** i.e. *brother of Jah.* 1 S 22:9-12, 20, called
Ahimelech. i.e. *brother of a king.* **Ahitub.** i.e. *brother
of goodness,* *S#285h. 1 S 22:9, 11, 12, 20. 2 S 8:17.
1 Ch 6:7, 8, 11, 12, 52. 9:11. 18:16. Ezr 7:2. Ne 11:11.
(1) A grandson of Eli and son of Phinehas. He succeeded
Eli as high priest, Phinehas having been killed in battle,
1 S 14:3; 22:11. (2) Father of Zadok, who was high
priest in David's time. Sometimes supposed to be the
same as number 1. (3) Another priest, who lived in
the seventh generation after number 2, 1 Ch 6:11,
12. (4) Perhaps the same as number 3. He was a priest
and the ruler of God's house in Nehemiah's time,
1 Ch 9:11; Ne 11:11. **Ichabod's.** 1 S 4:21. **wearing.**
1 S 2:28. Ex 28:26-32.

4. **the passages.** 1 S 13:23. **Bozez.** i.e. *shining; white,*
*S#949h. **Seneh.** i.e. *bush* or *tooth; bramble,*
*S#5573h.

5. **forefront.** Heb. tooth. ver. 4. **Bozez.** i.e. *shining.*
Seneh. i.e. a *bush* or *tooth.*

6. **Jonathan.** i.e. *whom Jehovah gave,* *S#3083h.
ver. 8. 1 S 18:1, 1, 3, 4. 19:1, 2, 4, 6, 7, 7, 7. 20:1,
3, 4, 5, 9, 10, 11, 12, 13, 16, 17, 18, 25, 27, 28, 30,
32, 33, 34, 35, 37, 37, 38, 38, 39, 40, 42, 42. 23:16,
18. 31:2. Jg 18:30. 2 S 1:4, 5, 12, 17, 22, 23, 25, 26.
4:4, 4. 9:1, 3, 6, 7. 15:27, 36. 17:17, 20. 21:7, 7, 12,
13, 14, 21. 23:32. 1 Ch 8:33, 34. 9:39, 40. 20:7. 27:25,
32. 2 Ch 17:8. Ne 12:18. Je 37:15, 20. 38:26. For
*S#3129h, see 1 S +13:2. **Come.** This action of Jonathan's was totally contrary to the laws of war; no military
operation should be undertaken without the knowledge
and command of the general. But it is highly probable,
that this gallant man was led to undertake the hazardous
enterprise by an immediate divine impulse; and by
the same influence was kept from informing the soldiers, and even from consulting his father, who might
have opposed his design. **uncircumcised.** 1 S 17:26,
36. Ge 17:7-11. Jg 15:18. 2 S 1:20. Je 9:23-26. Ep
2:11, 12. Ph 3:3. **it may be.** 2 S 16:12. 2 K 19:4. Am
5:15. Zp 2:3. **for there is no restraint.** Where there
is a promise of defence and support, the weakest, in
the face of the strongest enemy, may rely upon it with
the utmost confidence. Dt 32:30. Jsh 14:12. Jg 7:4-7.
2 Ch *14:11. Ps 115:1-3. Zc *4:6. Mt 19:26. Ro *8:31.

7. **Do all.** 1 S 10:7. 2 S 7:3. Ps 46:7. Zc 8:23.

8. **we will pass.** Jg 7:9-14.

9. **they.** Ge 24:13, 14. Jg 6:36-40. **Tarry.** Heb. Be
still. Jsh 10:12.

10. **this shall be a sign.** 1 S 10:7. Ge 24:14. Jg 7:11.
Is 7:11-14.

11. **out of the holes.** ver. 22. 1 S 13:6. Jg 6:2.

12. **Come up to us.** Meaning, that they would cause
them to repent of their audacity. This was the favorable
sign which Jonathan had requested. ver. 10. 1 S 17:43,
44. 2 S 2:14-17. 2 K 14:8. **Come up after me.** Ge
24:26, 27, 42, 48. Jg 4:14. 7:15. 2 S 5:24.

13. **climbed up.** Ps 18:29. He 11:34. **fell.** Le 26:7,
8. Dt 28:7. 32:30. Jsh 23:10. Ro 8:31.

14. **an half acre of land.** *or*, half a furrow of an
acre of land. The original is very obscure and variously

understood; but it is probably a proverbial expression for a small space.

15. **there was trembling**. Jsh 2:9. Jg 7:21. 2 K 7:6, 7. Jb 18:11. Ps 14:5. **the spoilers**. 1 S 13:17, 23. **the earth quaked**. Ex 19:18. Mt 24:7. 27:50, 51. **very great trembling**. Heb. trembling of God. Ge +*23:6. 35:5. Le 26:36, 37. 2 S 5:24. 1 Ch 12:22. Ps 36:6mg. Da 5:6. ſ108C4. Idiom B834. "of God" is used as an adjective. Here, "trembling of God" means a very great trembling, meaning an earthquake. For another instance of this figure see Ps 36:6mg. God will in some way or other direct the steps of those who acknowledge him in all their ways, and seek unto him for direction with full purpose of heart. Sometimes we find most comfort in that which is least our own doing, and into which we have been led by the unexpected, but well observed, turns of Providence.

16. **melted away**. Ps 58:7. 68:2. Is 40:15. **beating down**. ver. 20. Jg 7:22. 2 Ch 20:22-25. Is 19:2.

17. **Number**. 1 S +11:8.

18. **Bring hither**. The Septuagint reads, "Bring hither the *ephod*; for he bore the *ephod* on that day before Israel:" which Houbigant and others think is the true reading. Finding that his son Jonathan and his armor-bearer were absent (ver. +17), Saul wished to consult the high-priest; but the tumult increasing, he says to him, 'Withdraw thine hand:' i.e. desist from consulting the ephod on the present occasion; and immediately hastened to make the best use he could of this astonishing victory. 1 S 4:3-5. 30:8. Nu 27:21. Jg 20:18, 23, 28. 2 S 11:11. 15:24-26. **For the ark**. 1 S 5:2. 7:1.

19. **talked unto**. Nu 27:21. **noise**. *or*, tumult. **Withdraw**. ver. 24. 1 S 13:11. Jsh 9:14. Ps 106:13. Is 28:16.

20. **assembled themselves**. Heb. were cried together. **every man's**. ver. 16. Jg 7:22. 2 Ch 20:23. Is 9:19-21. 19:2.

21. **the Hebrews**. Probably such as they held in bondage, or who were their servants. Instead of *haivrim*, 'the Hebrews,' the LXX. evidently read *haavdim*, for they have *oi douloi*, 'the slaves;' but this reading is not countenanced by any other version, nor by any MS. 1 S 29:4. Jg 7:23.

22. **hid themselves**. 1 S 13:6. 31:7. **the battle**. The LXX. and Vulgate add here, "And (all the people who were, LXX) there were with Saul about ten thousand men;" but this is supported by no other authority.

23. **the Lord**. Ex 14:30. Jg 2:18. 2 K 14:27. Ps 44:6-8. Ho 1:7. **Beth-aven**. 1 S 13:5.

24. **Cursed**. ver. 27-30. Le 27:29. Nu 21:2. +*30:2n. Dt 27:15-26. Jsh 6:17-19, 26. Jg *11:30, 31. 21:1-5. Pr 11:9. Ro 10:2. 1 C 16:22. **food**. ſ171I8, Ge +3:19. **I may be**. Jg 5:2. 16:28. Ps 18:47.

25. **all they**. Dt 9:28. Mt 3:5. **honey**. This was wild honey, which to this day abounds in Judea; and bursting from the comb, runs down the hollow trees, rocks, etc. Ex 3:8. Nu 13:27. Mt 3:4. **upon**. ſ144A1, Ge 11:8.

26. **the people**. Ec 9:2.

27. **his eyes**. ver. 29. 1 S 30:12. Pr 25:26.

28. **adjured**. Jsh 6:26. **Cursed**. See on ver. 24, 43. **faint**. *or*, weary.

29. **My father**. 1 K 18:18. **land**. ſ121J17, Ge +6:11. **see**. It is well known, that hunger and fatigue produce faintness and dim the sight; and on taking a little food, this affection is immediately removed.

30. **had there**. Ec 9:18.

31. **from Michmash**. The distance, Calmet states to be three or four leagues. **Aijalon**. Jsh 10:12. 19:42. 21:23, 24.

32. **flew**. 1 S 15:19. **the people**. The people having abstained from food the whole of the day, and being now faint through hunger and fatigue, they flew upon the cattle, and not taking time to bleed them properly, they eagerly devoured the flesh with the blood, directly contrary to the law—another bad effect of Saul's rash adjuration. **did eat**. Ge 9:4. Le 3:17n. 7:26, 27. 17:10-14. 19:26. Dt 12:16, 23, 24. Ezk 33:25. Ac 15:20, 29.

33. **transgressed**. *or*, dealt treacherously. Mt 7:5. Ro 2:1.

34. **with him**. Heb. in his hand.

35. **built**. It is probable that Saul converted the great stone, on which the cattle had been slaughtered, into an altar, on which sacrifices were offered, before the people attempted to proceed any further. This we are told was the first he had built. Samuel, as a prophet and a priest, had hitherto erected the altars; but Saul seems to have thought he had sufficient authority to erect one himself, without the prophet, as he had once offered sacrifice without him. 1 S 7:9, 17. Jg 21:4. Ho 8:14. 2 T 3:5. Ju 12. **the same**, etc. Heb. that altar he began to build unto the Lord. **altar**. Ge +13:18.

36. **Let us go**. Jsh 10:9-14, 19. Je 6:5. **let us not leave**. 1 S 11:11. Jsh 11:14. **Then said the priest**. It is evident that Ahiah, who had before been interrupted by Saul's impatience, doubted of the propriety of pursuing the Philistines that night, and properly counseled them to enquire of the Lord. Nu 27:21. Ps *73:28. Is 48:1, 2. *58:2. Ho +*6:1. Ml *2:7. Ja *4:8.

37. **Shall I go**. 1 S 23:4, 9-12. 30:7, 8. Jg 1:1. 20:18, 28. 2 S 5:19, 23. 1 K 22:5, 6, 15. **he answered him not**. 1 S *28:6. Dt 1:45. Ezk 14:3-5. 20:3.

38. **Draw ye near**. 1 S 10:19, 20. Jsh 7:14, etc. **chief**. Heb. corners. Nu 24:17. Jg 20:2. 2 S 18:3. Ps 47:9. Is 19:13mg. Zc 10:4. Mt 21:42. Ep 2:20.

39. **the Lord liveth**. ver. 24, 44. 1 S 19:6. 20:31. 22:16. 28:10. 2 S 12:5. Ec 9:2. **surely**. ſ147B, Ge +2:16.

40. **Do what seemeth**. ver. 7, 36. 2 S 15:15.

41. **Give a perfect lot**. *or*, Show the innocent. Jsh +14:2n. Pr *16:33. Ac 1:24. **And Saul**. 1 S 10:20, 21. Jsh 7:16-18. Jon 1:7. **escaped**. Heb. went forth.

43. **Tell me**. Jsh 7:19. Jon 1:7-10. **I did but**. ver. 27.

44. **God**. 1 S 25:22. Ru 1:17. 2 S 3:9, 35. 19:13. **thou shalt**. See on ver. 39. Ge 38:24. 2 S 12:5, 31. Pr 25:16. **surely**. ſ147B, Ge +2:16.

45. **who hath wrought**. ver. 23. 1 S 11:13. 19:5. Ne 9:27. **there shall not**. The people judged rightly, that the guilt was contracted by Saul, and not by Jonathan; and therefore they rescued him from the hands of his rash and severe father. 2 S 14:11. 1 K 1:52. Mt 10:30. Lk 21:18. Ac 27:34. **one hair**. ſ138B, Ge +13:16. **he hath**. 2 Ch 19:11. Is 13:3. Ac 14:27. 15:12. 21:19. Ro 15:18. 1 C 3:9. 2 C 6:1. Ph 2:12, 13. Re 17:14. 19:14. **the people**. Is 29:20, 21.

47. **Saul**. 1 S 13:1. **fought**. 2 K 14:27. **Ammon**. 1 S 11:11. 12:2. **Zobah**. i.e. *depression; standing*, *S#6678h. 2 S 8:3, 5, 12. 10:6, 8. 23:36. 1 K 11:23. 1 Ch 18:3, 5, 9. 19:6. 2 Ch 8:3. Ps 60:t.

48. **gathered an host**. *or*, wrought mightily. ſ121N2, Ge +34:29. **smote**. 1 S 15:3-7. Ex 17:14. Dt 25:19.

49. **Jonathan**. 1 S +13:2. 31:2. 1 Ch 8:33. 9:39.

Ishui. i.e. *he is equal*, *S#3440h, so rendered only here. Nu 26:44, Jesui. 1 Ch 7:30, Ishuai. The same as Abinadab in 1 Ch 8:33; 9:39. **Melchishua.** i.e. *my king is rich; king of wealth*, *S#4444h. 1 S 31:2. Ishbosheth (or Eshbaal) in 2 S 2:18; 1 Ch 8:33, was probably not then born; see also 2 S 21:8. **name of the firstborn.** 1 S 18:7-21. 25:44. 2 S 3:13-16. 6:20-23. **Merab.** i.e. *multiplication*, *S#4764h. 1 S 18:17, 19. **Michal.** i.e. *a brook*, who afterwards became wife of David, as in 1 S 18:27. *S#4324h. 1 S 18:20, 27, 28. 19:11, 12, 13, 17, 17. 25:44. 2 S 3:13, 14. 6:16, 20, 21, 23. 21:8. 1 Ch 15:29.

50. **Ahinoam.** i.e. *my brother is pleasant; brother of grace*, *S#293h. 1 S 25:43. 27:3. 30:5. 2 S 2:2. 3:2. 1 Ch 3:1. (1) The wife of Saul, 1 S 14:50. (2) A woman of Jezreel. She was the wife of David and the mother of Amnon, 1 S 25:43; 2 S 2:2; 3:2; 1 Ch 3:1. **Ahimaaz.** i.e. *powerful brother; my brother is angry*, *S#290h. 2 S 15:27, 36. 17:17, 20. 18:19, 22, 23, 27, 28, 29. 1 K 4:15. 1 Ch 6:8, 9, 53. (1) Father of Ahinoam, wife of King Saul, 1 S 14:50. (2) The son and successor of Zadok; probably became high-priest in Solomon's reign. In the reign of David Ahimaaz made known to him the counsels of Absalom and his advisers in rebellion, and carried to David the news of Absalom's defeat. (3) An officer of Solomon, 1 K 4:15. **the name of the captain.** 1 S 17:55. 2 S 2:8. 3:27. **Abner.** Heb. Abiner. i.e. *my father is light; father of light*, *S#74h. 1 S 17:55, 55, 55, 57. 20:25. 26:5, 7, 14, 14, 14, 15. 2 S 2:8, 12, 14, 17, 19, 19, 20, 21, 22, 23, 24, 25, 26, 29, 30, 31. 3:6, 7, 8, 9, 11, 12, 16, 17, 19, 19, 20, 20, 21, 21, 22, 23, 24, 25, 26, 27, 28, 30, 31, 32, 32, 33, 33, 37. 4:1, 12. 1 K 2:5, 32. 1 Ch 26:28. 27:21. **Ner.** i.e. *light.* 1 Ch +9:36.

51. **Kish.** 1 S 9:1, 21. **Abiel.** i.e. *my father is strong or God.* 1 S 9:1.

52. **sore.** 2 S 11:15. **strong.** 1 S 9:1. **valiant.** Dt 3:18. Jg 21:10. **when Saul.** 1 S 8:1, 11.

1 SAMUEL 15

Saul is sent to destroy Amalek, 1-3. He gathers a large army, favors the Kenites, and smites the Amalekites, 4-7. He spares Agag and the best of the spoil, 8, 9. Samuel is sent to declare unto him, that God has rejected him for his disobedience; and Saul in vain attempts to excuse himself, 10-21. He is convicted of rebellion; and partially humbles himself, but cannot get the sentence reversed, 22-31. Samuel kills Agag, and finally leaves Saul, 32-35.

1. **A.M.** 2925. **B.C.** 1079. **An. Ex. Is.** 412. **The Lord.** ver. 17, 18. 1 S 9:16. 10:1. **hearken.** ver. 16. 1 S 12:14. 13:13. 2 S 23:2, 3. 1 Ch 22:12, 13. Ps 2:10, 11.

2. **Lord of hosts.** Is 47:4. 48:2. 51:15. 54:5. **I remember.** Je 31:34. Ho 7:2. Am 8:7. **Amalek.** Ge 36:1, 2, 4. Ex *17:8-16. Nu *24:20. Dt *25:17-19. 1 Ch 1:36.

3. **Now go.** The Amalekites, a people of Arabia Petraea, who inhabited a tract of country on the frontiers of Egypt and Canaan, had acted with great cruelty towards the Israelites on their coming out of Egypt, and God then purposed that Amalek, as a nation, should be blotted out from under heaven; but it had been spared until it had filled up the measure of its iniquities, and now this purpose is carried into effect by Saul, upwards of 400 years afterwards! Nothing could justify such an exterminating decree but the absolute authority

of God; and this was given: all the reasons of it we do not know; but this we know well, "the Judge of all the earth doeth right." Ge +*18:25. **utterly destroy.** T#244. ver. ◐8. Ge *22:2. Le *27:28, 29. Nu 24:20. Dt 13:15, 16. *20:16-18. Jsh *6:17-21. **slay.** Ex 20:5. Nu 31:17. Is 14:21, 22. **ox and sheep.** Ge 3:17, 18. Ro 8:20-22.

4. **Telaim.** i.e. *young lambs*, *S#2923h. Jsh ◐15:24, Telem. **two.** 1 S 11:8. 13:15.

5. **laid wait.** *or*, fought.

6. **the Kenites.** 1 S 27:10. Ex 18:10, 19. Nu 10:29, 32. 24:21, 22. Jg *1:16. *4:11. 5:24. 1 Ch 2:55. **Go, depart.** ſ41, Ge +10:1. Ge *18:25. 19:12-16. Nu 16:26, 27, 34. Pr 9:6. Is 52:11. Ac 2:40. 2 C *6:17. Re *18:4. **ye showed.** Ex 18:9, 10, 19. Nu 10:29-32. 2 T 1:16.

7. **smote.** 1 S 14:48. Jb 21:30. Ec 8:13. **Havilah.** This *Havilah* was probably situated in Arabia, and the district of *Chaulon* may mark the spot. It seems different from that encompassed by the river Pison, one of the rivers of Eden. Ge 2:11. 25:18. **Shur.** 1 S 27:8. Ge 16:7. Ex 15:22.

8. **Agag.** ver. 3. Nu 24:7. 1 K 20:30, 34-42. Est 3:1. **utterly.** ver. 3. 1 S 27:8. 30:1. Jsh 10:39. 11:12.

9. **the best.** ver. 3, 15, 19. Jsh 7:21. **the fatlings.** *or*, the second sort. 2 S 6:13.

11. **repenteth me.** ver. 35. Ge 6:6, 7. 2 S 24:16. Ps 110:4. Je 18:7-10. Am 7:3. Jon 3:10. 4:2. Ro ◐11:29. **turned back.** T#19. Jsh 22:16. 1 K 9:6, 7. 11:4 (T#23). 1 Ch 28:9. Ezr 8:22 (T#27). Ps 36:3. 78:41, 57. 125:5. Ezk 3:20. 13:18. 18:13, 24. Ho 6:4. Zp 1:6. Mt 24:13. 25:8. Lk *9:62. Jn 6:66. Ga 5:4. 1 T 1:19. 2 T 1:15. He 10:38. 2 P √2:20-22. **hath not performed.** ver. 3, 9. 1 S *13:13. **it grieved.** ver. 35. 1 S 16:1. Ps 119:136. Je 9:1, 18. 13:17. Lk 19:41-44. Ro 9:1-3. **he cried.** 1 S 12:23. Ps 109:4. Mt 5:44. Lk 6:12.

12. **Carmel.** 1 S 25:2. Jsh 15:55. 1 K 18:42. **he set him.** 1 S 7:12. Jsh 4:8, 9. 2 S 18:18. **a place.** *Yad*, literally, as the LXX. render *xeira*, a "hand;" probably because the trophy or monument of victory was in the shape of a large hand, the emblem of power, erected on a pillar. These memorial pillars were anciently much in use; and the figure of a hand, by its emblematical meaning, was well adapted to preserve the remembrance of a victory. 2 S 18:18. Is 56:5.

13. **Blessed.** 1 S 13:10. Ge 14:19. Jg 17:2. Ru 3:10. **I have performed.** ver. 9, 11. Ge 3:12. Nu +*32:23. Pr *27:2. √28:13. *30:13. 31:31. Lk √17:10. *18:11, 12.

14. **What meaneth.** Ps 36:2. 50:16-21. Je 2:18, 19, 22, 23, 34-37. Ml 3:13-15. Lk *19:22. Ro 3:19. 1 C 4:5.

15. **for.** ver. 9, 21. Ge 3:12, 13. Ex 32:22, 23. Jb 31:33. Pr *28:13. **to.** Mt 2:8. Lk 10:29.

16. **Stay.** 1 S 9:27. 12:7. 1 K 22:16.

17. **When thou.** 1 S 9:21. 10:22. Jg 6:15. Ho 13:1. Mt *18:4. **the Lord.** ver. 1-3. 1 S 10:1.

18. **the sinners.** Ge 13:13. 15:16. Nu 16:38. Jb 31:3. Pr 10:29. 13:21. **they be consumed.** Heb. they consume them.

19. **fly upon.** Pr 15:27. Je 7:11. Hab 2:9-12. 2 T 4:10. **didst evil.** 2 Ch 33:2, 6. 36:12.

20. **Yea.** ver. 13. Jb 33:9. 34:5. 35:2. 40:8. Mt 19:20. Lk 10:29. 18:11. Ro 10:3. 2 C *10:18. **have brought.** ver. 3, 8.

21. **the people.** ver. +15. Ge *3:12, 13. Ex *32:22, 23.

22. **Samuel said.** 1 S 9:15, 17. Ps 78:1. Is 50:4. **Hath the Lord.** Le *23:2. Ps 50:8, 9. *51:16, 17. Pr *15:8. *21:3. Is *1:11-17. *66:3. Je *7:22, 23. Ho *6:6. Am 5:21-24. Mi *6:6-8. Mt *9:13. *12:7. *23:23. He 10:4-10. **to obey.** Ex 19:5. Ec *5:1. Je 7:23. 11:4, 7. *26:13. Ezk +*33:31, 32. Ho *6:6. Zc +*6:15. Mt *5:24. *7:21. Mk *12:33. Lk +*6:46. Jn √14:15. 2 C 8:5. He +*5:9. 1 J +√2:3n. **to hearken.** Dt 28:1, 2, 15. Lk +*8:18. +*11:28.

23. **rebellion.** 1 S 8:7. 12:14, 15. Nu 14:9, 41-45. Dt 9:7, 24. √21:20, 21. Jsh 22:16-19. Jg 6:10. Ne 9:16, 17, 26. Jb +*21:14, 15. √34:37. Ps 66:7. 68:6, 18. √78:5-8. 107:11. Pr 17:11. Is 1:5. 7:13. 30:1. *59:12, 13. *63:10. 65:2. Je 5:5. *28:16. 29:32. 44:24-30. Ezk 2:5-8. 11:15. 12:2. Ho 7:14. Zc *7:11, 12. Col 1:21. 2 Th 3:14, 15. **sin.** Heb. *chata*, S#2403h. To miss the mark (as in Jg 20:16); to stumble and fall (Pr 19:2). Morally, a coming short, blameworthiness, not necessarily willful. An act of thought, word, or deed, not a condition. Ge 4:7. 2 S 12:13. Pr 20:9. Da 9:20, 24. Mi 7:19. Zc 14:19mg. **witchcraft.** Heb. divination. Ex 22:18. Le 20:6, 27. Dt +*18:10, 11. Is *8:19. 19:3. Ga 3:1. Re 22:15. **stubbornness.** Dt √21:20. Ps 32:9. 58:3-5. *78:8. Pr *29:1. Is 46:12. Je 4:3. *32:33. 44:16. Ezk 33:31, 32. Zc *7:11, 12. Ml +*2:2. Mt 21:28-32. Ac 7:51. 2 C 6:16. Ga 5:20. 2 P 2:10. Re *21:8. **iniquity.** Heb. *aven*, S#205h. Iniquity, especially connected with idolatry. Used because an idol is nothing and vanity (Ho 4:15; 5:8; 10:5, 8. Am 5:5mg). Hence, *aven* comes to mean vanity (Jb 15:35. Ps 10:7. Pr 22:8). *Aven* is rather a course of bad conduct flowing from the evil desires of fallen nature, than breaches of the law as such. Ps 5:5. 14:4. 36:3, 4mg. *66:18. 119:133. Is 55:7mg. **idolatry.** Ezk +*14:3. Col 3:5. 1 J 5:21. **thou hast rejected.** 1 S 2:30. 8:7. 13:14. 16:1. 2 K 17:15-20. 1 Ch +*28:9. 2 Ch 36:16. Pr 1:7. 5:12. **rejected thee.** 2 K *17:20. Mt *7:21-23. *25:12. Lk *13:27. He *3:12, 13, 19. *12:17.

24. **I have sinned.** ver. 30. Ex *9:27. 10:16. Nu +22:34. 2 S 12:13. Mt 27:4. Ac 8:24. **I feared.** ver. 9, 15. Ex *23:2. Jb 31:34. Pr *29:25. Is *51:12, 13. Lk 23:20-25. Ga 1:10. Re *21:8. **obeyed.** 1 S 2:29. Ge 3:12, 17. Je 38:5.

25. **pardon.** Ex 10:17. Ac 8:24.

26. **I will not.** ver. 31. Ge 42:38. 43:11-14. Lk 24:28, 29. 2 J 11. **for thou.** See on ver. 23. 1 S *2:30. 13:14. 16:1. Je 6:19. Ho 4:6.

27. **he laid hold.** 1 K 11:30, 31.

28. **The Lord.** 1 S *28:17, 18. 1 K 11:30, 31. **hath given.** 1 S 2:7, 8. Je 27:5, 6. Da 4:17, 32. Jn 19:11. Ro 13:1. **a neighbor.** 1 S 13:14. 16:12. Ac 13:22.

29. **Strength.** or, Eternity, or, Victory. √121N1, Ge +31:54. Dt 33:27. Jb 4:20 (*S#5331h). Ps 29:11. 68:35. Is 25:8. 45:24. Jl 3:16. 2 C *12:9. Ph *4:13. **will not lie.** Nu 14:28, 29. 23:19. Ps 95:11. Ezk 24:14. 2 T 2:13. T *1:2. He *6:18. **nor repent.** Nu 23:19. Ezk 24:14. He 13:8. Ja *1:17.

30. **honor me now.** Hab 2:4. Jn *5:44. *12:43. **that I may worship.** Is 29:13. Lk 18:9-14. 2 T 3:5.

32. **Agag said.** Je 48:44. 1 Th 5:3. Re 18:7.

33. **As thy sword.** Ge 9:6. Ex 17:11. Nu 14:45. Jg 1:7. Mt 7:2. 26:52. Ja 2:13. Re 16:6. 18:6. **Samuel.** It has been a matter of wonder to many, how Samuel could thus slay a captive prince, even in the presence of Saul, who from motives of clemency had spared him; but it should be remarked, that what Samuel

did here, he did in his magisterial capacity; and that Agag had been a cruel tyrant, and therefore was cut off for his merciless cruelties. Farther, it is not likely that he did it by his own sword, but by that of the executioner. What kings, magistrates, and generals do, in an official way, by their subjects, servants, or soldiers, they are said to do themselves: *qui facit per alterum, facit per se.* **hewed.** Nu 25:7, 8. 1 K 18:40. Is 34:6. Je 48:10.

34. **Ramah.** 1 S 19:23, 24. **Gibeah.** 1 S 11:4.

35. **Samuel.** 1 S 19:24. **Samuel mourned.** ver. 11. 1 S 16:1. Ps 119:136, 158. Je 9:1, 2. Ro 9:2, 3. Ph 3:18. **repented.** ver. 11. Ge *6:6.

1 SAMUEL 16

God sends Samuel to Bethlehem, to anoint a king out of Jesse's sons, and directs him to conceal his business by a sacrifice, 1-5. Seven of Jesse's sons pass by, and are not approved, 6-10. David is called from the flock, and anointed, 11-13. An evil spirit troubles Saul; who, counselled by his servants, sends for David, and is relieved by his music, 14-23.

1. A.M. 2941. B.C. 1063. An. Ex. Is. 428. **And.** √107, Ge +10:5. **How long.** 1 S 15:11, 35. Je 7:16. 11:14. **thou mourn.** Le 10:3, 6. **seeing.** ver. 15, 23. 1 S 13:13, 14. 15:23, 26. Je 6:30. 14:11, 12. 15:1. 1 J 5:16. **horn with oil.** 1 S 9:16. 10:1. 2 K 9:1, 3, 6. **Jesse.** 1 S 13:14. Ge 49:8-10. Ru 4:18-22. 1 Ch 2:10-15. Ps 78:68-71. 89:19, 20. Is 11:1, 10. 55:4. Ac *13:21, 22. Ro 15:12. **Bethlehemite.** *S#1022h. ver. 18. 1 S 17:58. 2 S 21:19. **I have.** Ge 22:8.

2. **How can I go.** Ex 3:11. 4:1. 1 K 18:9-14. Je 1:6. Mt 10:16. Lk 1:34. **kill me.** 1 K 18:14. **Take an heifer.** For the prudent management of the affair, and to avoid suspicion, Samuel was directed to go to Bethlehem to sacrifice, as he probably did from time to time in many different places; and the answer which he was instructed to return was strictly true though he did not tell the principal design of his coming; for though no man in any circumstances should tell a lie, yet, in all circumstances, he is not bound to tell the whole truth, though he must tell nothing but the truth, and so tell that truth that the hearer shall not believe a lie by it; Samuel was not bound to divulge all his intentions (Compare 1 S ●21:2n. Je *38:24-28. Pr 29:11). **with thee.** Heb. in thine hand. 1 S 9:12. **I am come.** 1 S 9:12. 20:29. Je *38:26, 27.

3. **call Jesse.** 1 S 9:12, 13. 20:29. 2 S 15:11. Mt 22:1-4. **and I will show.** Ex 4:15. Ac 9:6. **anoint.** ver. 12, 13. 1 S 9:16. Dt 17:14.

4. **trembled.** 1 S 21:1. 2 S 6:9. 1 K 17:18. Ho 6:5. 11:10. Lk 5:8. 8:37. **coming.** Heb. meeting. **Comest.** √96D5, Nu 32:25. 1 K 2:13. 2 K 9:22. 1 Ch 12:17, 18.

5. **sanctify yourselves.** Ex 19:10, 14, 15. Le 20:7, 8. Nu 11:18. Jsh 3:5. 7:13. 2 Ch 30:17-20. Jb 1:5. Ps 26:2-6. Jl 2:16. 1 C 11:28.

6. **Eliab.** i.e. *my God is father.* 1 S 17:13, 28. 1 Ch 2:13. 27:18, Elihu. **Surely.** Jg 8:18. 1 K 12:26.

7. **Look not.** 1 S 9:2. 10:23, 24. 2 S 14:25. 2 K 5:1. Ps 147:10, 11. Pr 31:30. Is 55:8. 2 C 10:7. **refused him.** Ps 75:6, 7. **the Lord.** √63I2, Jsh +3:3. **seeth not.** Jb 10:4. Is 55:8, 9. Mt 7:21, 23. Lk 16:15. 1 P 2:4. 3:4. **looketh.** Jn 7:24. 2 C 10:7, 10. **outward appearance.** Heb. eyes. **on the heart.** T#333. Dt 26:16.

1 K *8:39. 1 Ch *28:9. 2 Ch 6:8. 16:9. Ps 7:9. 66:18. 139:2. Ps 145:18 (T#542). Pr 15:11. 16:2. Je 11:20. *17:10. 20:12. *29:13. Mt 22:37. 23:26. Lk *16:15. Jn 4:24. Ac 1:24. 8:21, 37. Ro 2:28, 29. *10:10. Col *3:16 (T#529). 1 T 1:5. He *4:13. Re 2:23.

8. **Abinadab.** i.e. *my father is noble; source of liberality,* ***S#41h.** 1 S 7:1. *17:13. 31:2. 2 S 6:3, 3, 4. 1 K 4:11. 1 Ch *2:13. 8:33. 9:39. 10:2. 13:7. (1) An Israelite who lived near Kirjath-jearim and in whose house the ark of God was left after it had been returned by the Philistines, 1 S 7:1; 2 S 6:3, 4. (2) The second son of Jesse, the father of David, 1 S 16:8; 1 Ch 2:13. (3) A son of King Saul, slain at Gilboa by the Philistines with his brother Jonathan, 1 S 31:2; 1 Ch 8:33. (4) Father of one of Solomon's officers, set over Dor in territory of Issachar, 1 K 4:11. **chosen.** ✒22C13, Ge +16:13.

9. **Shammah.** i.e. *desolation* or *hearkening,* ***S#8048h.** 1 S *17:13. Ge 36:13, 17. 2 S ◐*13:3, Shimeah. 23:11, 25, 33. 1 Ch 1:37. ◐*2:13, Shimma. (1) One of the sons of Reuel, the son of Esau, Ge 36:13, 17; 1 Ch 1:37. (2) A son of Jesse, 1 S 16:9; 17:13, called also Shimeah and Shimma. (3) One of the chief among David's valiant men, 2 S 23:11, 33. (4) One of David's valiant men, 2 S 23:25, called also Shammoth the Harorite in 1 Ch 11:27, and Shamhuth the Izrahite in 1 Ch 27:8.

10. **seven.** 1 Ch 2:13-15. Seven in all, including Nathanael, Raddai, and Ozem (1 Ch 2:14, 15); the seventh is not mentioned by name (Young).

11. **Are here all.** 1 S 10:22. **thy.** lit. Are the young men finished? or, Are the young men finished passing by? ✒63BB. Ellipsis (Absolute: of infinitive) B36: When the infinitive of the verb is wanting: after the verb *to finish.* For other instances of this form of ellipsis see Mt 10:23. 13:53. **There remaineth.** 1 S 17:12-15, 28. Ge 4:2. 2 S 7:8. 1 Ch 17:7. Ps 78:70, 71. **down.** Heb. round.

12. **ruddy.** 1 S 17:42. SS 5:10. La 4:7. Ac 7:20. He 11:23. **of a beautiful countenance.** Heb. fair of eyes. ver. 7. Ps 45:2. Da 1:15. **And the Lord.** 1 S 9:17. **anoint him.** Ps 2:2, 6. 89:19, 20. Ac 4:27.

13. **anointed.** 1 S 10:1. 2 K 9:6. Ps 89:20. 92:10. Is 61:1. 1 J 2:20, 27. **the Spirit.** Heb. *ruach,* Ge +41:38. ver. 18. 1 S 10:6, 9, 10. Nu 11:17. 27:18. Jg 3:10. 11:29. 13:25. 14:6. Is 11:1-3. Jn *3:34. He 1:9.

14. **the Spirit.** Heb. *ruach,* Ge +41:38. 1 S ◐11:6. 18:12. 28:15. Jg 16:29. Ps 51:11. Ho 9:12. **departed.** 1 S 18:12. 28:15. Ps 51:11. **evil spirit.** Heb. *ruach,* Jg +9:23. Mt +*8:16. The evil spirit was either sent immediately from the Lord, or permitted to come; but whether this was a diabolic possession, or a mere mental malady, is not agreed: it seems to have partaken of both. That Saul had fallen into a deep melancholy, there is little doubt; and that an evil spirit might work more effectually on such a state of mind, there can be little question. His malady appears to have been of a mixed kind, natural and diabolical. There is too much of apparent nature in it to permit us to believe it was all spiritual; and there is too much of apparently supernatural influence, to suffer us to believe it was all natural. 1 S 16:23. 18:10. 19:9, 10. Jg 9:23. 1 K 22:22. Ac 19:15, 16. **from the Lord.** 1 S 18:10n. Je ◐+*29:11. Am +√3:6. **troubled.** *or,* terrified. ver. 15. 2 S 22:5. Jb 3:5. 7:14. 9:34.

15. **evil spirit.** Heb. *ruach,* Jg +9:23. Mt +*8:16.

16. **before thee.** ver. 21, 22. Ge 41:46. 1 K 10:8. **evil spirit.** Heb. *ruach,* Jg +9:23. Mt +*8:16. **play.** ver. 23. 1 S 10:5. 16:23. 2 K 3:15.

18. **playing.** ✢S#5059h: 1 S 18:10. 19:9. 2 K 3:15. Ps 33:3. 68:25. Is 23:16. 38:20. **a mighty.** 1 S 17:32-36. Jg +6:12. 2 S 17:8, 10. **and prudent.** 2 S 14:20. **matters.** *or,* speech. Jb 29:22. Col *4:6. T 2:8. **a comely.** ver. 12. **the Lord.** 1 S *3:19. 10:7. 18:12-14. Ge *39:2, 23. Mt 1:23. *28:20.

19. **David.** i.e. *beloved,* S#1732h. **with the sheep.** ver. 11. 1 S 17:15, 33, 34. Ex 3:1-10. 1 K 19:19. Ps 78:70-72. 113:8. Am 1:1. 7:14, 15. Mt 4:18-22.

20. **an ass laden.** *Chamor lechem,* literally, "an ass of bread," rendered by the LXX. *gomor arton,* "a gomer of bread"; meaning, probably, not an animal, but a vessel containing a certain measure of bread. 1 S 10:27. 17:18. 25:18. Ge 43:11. 2 S 16:1, 2. Pr *18:16.

21. **stood before him.** Ge 41:46. Dt 1:38. 10:8. 1 K 10:8. Pr *22:29. **loved him.** Ps 62:9. 118:9. 146:3.

23. **the evil spirit.** Heb. *ruach,* Jg +9:23. See on ver. 14, 16. Mt +*8:16. **Saul.** 1 S 18:10, 11. Mt 12:43-45. Lk 11:24-26. **evil spirit.** Heb. *ruach,* Jg +9:23. Mt +*8:16.

1 SAMUEL 17

The armies of Israel and of the Philistines are drawn out to battle, 1-3. Goliath challenges, defies, and dismays the Israelites, 4-11. David is sent to the army to visit his brethren, 12-19. He hears the challenge of Goliath and expresses indignation at it, 20-27. Eliab rebukes him, and he answers mildly, 28-30. He is brought before Saul, accepts the challenge, and states the grounds of his confidence, 31-37. He refuses Saul's armor; and takes only his staff, a sling, and stones, 38-40. Goliath disdains and curses him, 41-44. David answers, expressing his assured confidence in God, 45-47. He kills Goliath, and cuts off his head, 48-51. The Philistines are routed, 52, 53. David returns with Goliath's head in his hand; and answers Saul's inquiries concerning him, 54-58.

1. **gathered.** 1 S 7:7. 13:5. 14:46, 52. Jg 3:3. **Shochoh.** i.e. *hedge; to entwine,* ***S#7755h.** Jsh 15:35, 48, Shocho. 1 K 4:10. 2 Ch 11:7. 28:18. **Azekah.** Jsh 10:10, 11. 15:35. Je 34:7. **Ephes-dammim.** *or,* the coast of Dammim. i.e. *extremity of Dannim; limit of bloods,* ***S#658h.** 1 Ch 11:13, Pas-dammim.

2. **the valley.** ver. 19. 1 S 21:9. **set the battle in array.** Heb. ranged the battle.

4. **Goliath.** i.e. *an exile,* ***S#1555h.** ver. 23. 1 S 21:*9, 10. 2 S 21:19. 1 Ch 20:5. **of Gath.** 1 S 27:4. Jsh *11:22. 2 S 21:16-22. 1 Ch 20:4-8. **whose height.** Dt 3:11. 1 Ch 11:23. Am 2:9. **six cubits.** According to Bp. Cumberland's calculation, the height of Goliath was about eleven feet ten inches; but Parkhurst, estimating the ordinary cubit at seventeen inches and a half, calculates that he was nine feet six inches high. Few instances can be produced of men who can be compared with him. Pliny says, "The tallest man that hath been seen in our days was one named Gabara, who, in the days of Claudius, the late Emperor, was brought out of Arabia: he was nine feet nine inches." Josephus mentions a Jew, named Eleazar, whom Vitellius sent to Rome, who was seven cubits, or ten feet two inches, high. Becanus saw a man near ten feet, and a woman that was full ten feet. And, to mention

no more, a man of the name of John Middleton, born at Hale, near Warrington, in Lancashire, in the reign of James the First, was more than nine feet high. Dr. Plott, in his history of Staffordshire, says, that "his hand, from the carpus to the end of his middle finger, was seventeen inches, his palms eight inches and a half broad, and his whole height was nine feet three inches; wanting but six inches of the height of Goliath of Gath."

5. **armed**. Heb. clothed. ver. 38.

6. **target of brass**. or, gorget. 1 K 10:16. 2 Ch 9:15.

7. **the staff**. 2 S 21:19. 1 Ch 11:23. *20:5. **and one**. ∫164. Syllogismus: or, omission of the conclusion B165. Here, the description of Goliath's armor and weapons is given; and it is left for us to conclude how great his strength must have been. For other instances of this figure see Is 2:3, 4. 4:1. 49:20, 21. Mt 10:30. 24:20. Lk 7:44. 1 C 11:6. 2 Th 3:10.

8. **servants to Saul**. ver. 26. 1 S 8:17. 2 S 11:11. 1 Ch 21:3.

9. **and serve us**. 1 S 11:1. Ro 6:16.

10. **I defy**. ver. 25, 26, 36, 45. Nu 23:7, 8. 2 S 21:21. 23:9. Ne 2:9. **give me**. Jb 40:9-12. Ps 9:4, 5. Pr 16:18. Je 9:23. Da 4:37.

11. **dismayed**. Dt 31:8. Jsh 1:9. Ps 27:1. Pr 28:1. Is 51:12, 13. 57:11.

12. **David**. ver. 58. 1 S 16:1, 18. Ru 4:22. Mt 1:6. Lk 3:31, 32. **Ephrathite**. Ge 35:19. Ps 132:6. Mi *5:2. Mt 2:1, 6. **eight sons**. 1 S 16:10, 11. 1 Ch 2:13-16.

13. **the names**. ver. 28. 1 S 16:6-9. 1 Ch 2:13. **Shammah**. 2 S 13:3, 32. 21:21, Shimeah.

14. **the youngest**. lit. the small one. 1 S 16:11. Ge 25:23. ∫96E2. Heterosis of Degree: the positive for the superlative B527. Here, "the small one" is put for "the smallest." For other instances of this figure see 2 Ch 21:17. Jon 3:5. Mt 5:19. He 10:21. 13:20.

15. **returned**. 1 S 16:11, 19-23.

16. **forty days**. Mt 4:2. Lk 4:2.

17. **Take now**. Mt 7:11. Lk 11:13. **an ephah**. Ex 16:16, 36. **parched corn**. 1 S 25:18. Ru 2:14. 2 S 17:28.

18. **carry**. 1 S 16:20. **cheeses**. Heb. cheeses of milk. 2 S 17:29. Jb 10:10. **captain of**. Jg 6:15. Mi 5:2. **their thousand**. Heb. a thousand. **look**. Ge 37:14. Ac 15:36. 1 Th 3:5, 6.

19. **the valley**. Dr. Richardson says, that in about twenty minutes, in an easterly direction, from the cave of St. John (which is about two hours or six miles, in a westerly direction, from Jerusalem), they came to the *valley of Elah*; which position seems to agree with that of Shocoh and Azekah. He describes it as "a small valley, and the place of their encampment is pointed out where it narrows into a broad, deep ravine; part of it was in crop, and part of it was under the plow, which was drawn by a couple of oxen. A small stream, which had shrunk almost under its stony bed, passes through it from east to west, from which we are informed that David chose out five smooth stones, and hasted and ran to meet the haughty champion of Gath. A well of water under the bank, with a few olive trees above, on the north side of the valley, are said to mark the spot of the shepherd's triumph over his boasting antagonist. Saul and his men probably occupied the side of the valley which is nearest to Jerusalem, on which the ground is higher and more rugged than on the other side."

20. **left the sheep**. ver. 28. Ep 6:1, 2. **trench**. or,

place of the carriage. 1 S 26:5. Lk 19:43. **fight**. or, battle array, **or** place of fight.

22. **his carriage**. Heb. the vessels from upon him. Jg 18:21. **saluted his brethren**. Heb. asked his brethren of peace; as Ge +37:14mg. 1 S 10:4. Jg +18:15mg. 2 S 11:7. 2 K 4:26. Mt 10:12, 13. Lk 10:5, 6.

23. **according**. ver. 4-10.

24. **him**. Heb. his face. 1 S 13:6, 7. **sore afraid**. ver. 11. Le *26:36. Nu 13:33. Dt 32:30. Is 7:2. 30:17.

25. **the king**. 1 S 18:17-27. Jsh 15:16. Re 2:7, 17. 3:5, 12, 21. **free in Israel**. Ezr 7:24. Mt 17:26.

26. **reproach**. 1 S 11:2. Jsh 5:9. 7:8, 9. 2 K 19:4. Ne 5:9. Ps 44:13. 74:18. 79:12. Da 9:16. Jl 2:19. Ro 8:33. **uncircumcised**. ver. 36. 1 S 14:6. **defy**. ver. 10. Dt 5:26. Jsh 3:10. Is 31:3. Je 10:10. 1 Th 1:9. 1 J 5:20.

27. **So shall it**. ver. 25.

28. **Eliab's anger**. 1 S 16:13. Ge 37:4, 8, 11. Pr 18:19. 27:4. Ec 4:4. Mt 10:36. 27:18. Mk 3:21. **with**. ver. 20. **I know**. 1 S 16:7. Ps 35:11. Ju 10.

29. **What have**. Pr *15:1. Ac *11:2-4. 1 C *2:15. 1 P *3:9. **Is there not**. Ps 74:10.

30. **manner**. Heb. word. ver. 26, 27.

31. **sent for him**. Heb. took him. Pr 22:29. The preceding twenty verses, from the 12th to the 31st inclusive, the 41st, and from the 54th to the end of this chapter, with the five first verses and the 9th, 10th, 11th, 17th, 18th, and 19th of ch. 18, are all wanting in the Vatican copy of the LXX.; and they are supposed by Dr. Kennicott, and others, to be an interpolation. But, as Bp. Horsley observes, it appears, from many circumstances of the story, that David's combat with Goliath was many years prior to Saul's madness, and David's introduction to him as a musician. In the first place, David was quite a youth when he engaged with Goliath (ver. 33, 42): when introduced to Saul he was of full age, 1 S 16:18. Again, this combat was his first appearance in public life, and his first military exploit (ver. 36, 38, 39): when introduced as a musician, he was a man of established character, and a man of war (1 S 16:18). Now the just conclusion is, that the last ten verses of chapter 16 have been misplaced; their true place being between the ninth and tenth verses of chapter 18. Let them be removed there, and the whole apparent disorder will be removed.

32. **Let**. Nu 13:30. 14:9. Dt 20:1-4. Is 35:3. He 12:12. **thy**. 1 S 14:6. 16:18. Jsh 14:12. Ps 3:6. 27:1-3.

33. **Thou art not**. Nu 13:31. Dt *9:2. Ps 11:1. Re 13:4. **for thou art but**. ver. 42, 56.

34. **and**. ∫148, Ge +8:22. **lamb**. or, kid. Ex 12:3n.

35. **And**. ∫148, Ge +8:22. **smote him**. Jg 14:5, 6. 2 S 23:20. Ps 91:13. Da 6:22. Am 3:12. Ac 28:4-6. 2 T 4:17, 18.

36. **and**. ∫148, Ge +8:22. **this**. ver. 26. Ezk 32:19, 27-32. Ro 2:28, 29. **seeing**. ver. 10. Is 10:15. 36:8-10, 15, 18. 37:22, 23, 28, 29. Zc 2:8. 12:3. Ac 5:38, 39. 9:4, 5. 12:1, 2, 22, 23.

37. **The Lord**. 1 S *7:12. Ps 11:1. 18:16, 17. 22:21. 63:7. 77:11. *138:3, 7, 8. Da 6:22. 2 C *1:9, 10. 2 T 4:17, *18. **paw**. ∫144A5, Ge +9:5. **will deliver**. Ps 91:13, 14. 2 C 1:10. **Go**. 1 S 20:13. 24:19. 26:25. 2 S 10:12. 1 Ch *22:11, 16.

38. **armed David with his armor**. Heb. clothed David with his clothes, ver. 5.

39. **I cannot go**. Is 31:1. **put them off**. Ps 44:5, 6.

Ho 1:7. Zc *4:6. Ro 13:12. 2 C *10:4, 5.

40. staff. Jg 3:31. 7:16-20. 15:15, 16. 20:16. Ps 144:1. 1 C 1:27-29. **brook.** *or,* valley. Nu 13:24. Jg +16:4. **bag.** Heb. vessel. ver. 49. Dt 23:24. **even.** √93A, Ge +1:26. **scrip.** Mt 10:10. Mk 6:8. Lk 22:35, 36.

41. the man. ver. 7. Ge 15:1. Ps 3:3. 144:2.

42. and saw. Ne 4:2, 6. **disdained.** 1 K 20:18. 2 K 18:23, 24. Ne 4:2-4. Ps 123:4, 5. 2 C *1:27-29. **a youth.** ver. 33. 1 S 16:12.

43. Am I a dog. 1 S 24:14. 2 S 3:8. 9:8. 16:9. 2 K 8:13. **cursed.** Ge 27:29. Nu 22:6, 11, 12. Jg 9:27. Ps 10:7. Pr 26:2.

44. Come to me. 1 K √20:10, 11. Ps 10:5. Pr 18:12. Ec 9:11, 12. Je 9:23. Ezk 28:2, 9, 10. 39:17-20. **I will give.** Parallel instances of vaunting occur in some writers of a more recent date: The conspirators against the emperor Maximinus having slain him, his son, and several of his best friends, threw out their bodies to be devoured by dogs and the fowls of the air. This custom appears to have been frequently threatened; and, however shocking to human feelings, was often carried into effect. **unto the fowls.** Ezk √39:4, 17. Mt +*24:28. Lk +*17:37n.

45. thou comest. Ps 44:6. **in the name.** 2 S 22:33-35. 2 Ch 32:8. Ps 3:8. 18:2. 20:5-7. 44:6. 116:4. 118:10, 11. 124:8. 125:1. Pr 18:10. 2 C 3:5. 10:4. Ph *4:13. He 11:33, 34. **defied.** ver. 10, 26, 36. Is 37:23, 28.

46. will the Lord. Dt 7:2, 23. 9:2, 3. Jsh 10:8. **deliver thee.** Heb. shut thee up. 1 S 23:11, 12, 20. 24:18. 26:8. 2 S 18:28. Ps 31:8. **take thine.** ver. 51. **carcases.** ver. 44. Dt +*28:26. Is 56:9. Mt +*24:28. Lk +*17:37n. Re 19:17, 18. **fowls of the air.** ver. +*44. Dt +*28:26. **all the earth.** Ex 9:16. 15:14, 15. Jsh 4:24. 1 K 8:43. 18:36, 37. 2 K *19:19. Ps 46:10. 58:10, 11. Is 52:10. Da 2:47. 3:29. 6:26, 27.

47. the Lord. Ps 46:11. **saveth not.** Ps 33:16, 17. 44:6, 7. Pr 21:30, 31. Ho 1:7. **the battle.** 1 S 14:6. Ex 15:3. 2 Ch *20:15-17. Ps 46:11. Is 9:7. Zc *4:6. Ro *8:31, 37.

48. David hasted. Ps 27:1. Pr 28:1.

49. smote. 1 K 22:34. 2 K 9:24. 1 C 1:27, 28.

50. So David prevailed. The tradition of the combat between David and Goliath, in which the latter was killed, is preserved among the Arabs; for he is mentioned in the Koran, where he is called *Galut,* or *Jalut.* The Arabs also call the dynasty of the Philistine kings, who reigned in Palestine when the Hebrews came there, *Galutiah,* or *Jalutiah.* Achmed Al Fassi says, "Those kings were as well known by the name of *Jalaut,* as the ancient kings of Egypt by that of Pharaoh. David killed the *Jalaut* who reigned in his time, and entirely rooted out the Philistines, the rest of whom fled into Africa, and from them descended the Brebers or Berbers, who inhabit the coast of Barbary." It is remarkable that the Berbers themselves should acknowledge their descent from the Philistines. "The name Goliath, which they pronounce *Sghiatud,* is very common among the Brebers, and the history of the champion of the Philistines is very well known to the Moors. When children quarrel, and the bigger one challenges the smaller to fight, the latter answers, "Who will fight with you? (Enta men ulid Sgialud). You are of the race of Goliath." The Jews who dwell among them, on the mountains, all call them Philistines" (Host's Account of Morocco and Fez, p. 133). 1 S 21:9. 23:21. Jg 3:31. 15:15. 2 C *12:9. **but there was.** ver. 39. 1 S 13:22.

51. his sword. 1 S 21:9. 2 S 23:21. Est 7:10. Ps 7:15, 16. He 2:14. **cut off.** ver. 46. **head.** Jg +7:25. **fled.** He 11:34.

52. the men of Israel. 1 S 14:21, 22. Jg 7:23. 2 S 23:10. **valley.** Jsh 15:33-36, 45, 46. **Shaaraim.** i.e. *double gate; goats; demons,* *S#8189h. Jsh 15:36. 1 Ch 4:31.

53. they spoiled. 2 K 7:7-16. Je 4:20. 30:16.

54. took the head. 1 S 21:9. Ex 16:33. Jsh 4:7, 8. Jg +7:25. Col 2:15.

55. whose son. ver. 58. 1 S 16:21, 22. Ec 2:16. 9:15. **soul.** Heb. *nephesh,* Ge +27:31.

56. stripling. 1 S 20:22.

57. the head. ver. 54.

58. Whose son. To account for the apparent inconsistency of Saul not knowing David, see the Note at the end of verse 31. **I am the son.** ver. 12. 1 S 16:18, 19.

1 SAMUEL 18

Jonathan loves David, and covenants with him, 1-4. David gains favor with the people and the servants of Saul, 5. The praises bestowed on David excite Saul's envy, 6-9. Saul attempts to kill him, 10, 11. David's prudence and success make Saul afraid of him, 12-16. He offers to give him his elder daughter, hoping to ensnare him; but gives her to another, 17-19. He promises him Michal, his younger daughter, finding that she loved him; and David brings two hundred foreskins of the Philistines, being double the stipulated dowry, and marries her, 20-27. Saul's hatred and David's reputation increase, 28-30.

1. the soul. Heb. *nephesh,* Ge +34:3. **of Jonathan.** The modesty, piety, and courage of David were so congenial to the character of the amiable Jonathan, that they attracted his most cordial esteem and affection; so that the most intimate friendship subsisted between them from that time, and they loved each other with pure hearts fervently. Their friendship could not be affected by the common vicissitudes of life; and it exemplifies by fact what the ancients have written on the subject; "Friendship is an entire sameness, and one soul: a friend is another self." 1 S 14:1-14, 45. Ge 44:30. Jg 20:11. 1 Ch 12:17. Ps 86:11. Col 2:2. **was knit.** Jg 20:11. 1 Ch 12:17. 2 Ch 5:13. **the soul.** Heb. *nephesh,* Ge +34:3. **loved him.** ver. 3. 1 S 19:2. 20:17. Dt 13:6. 2 S *1:26. Pr 18:24. **own soul.** Heb. *nephesh,* Ge +27:31.

2. took him. 1 S 16:21-23. 17:15.

3. made a covenant. 1 S 20:8-17, 42. 23:18. 2 S 9:1-3. 21:7. **soul.** Heb. *nephesh,* Ge +27:31.

4. stripped himself. Presents of clothes or rich robes, as tokens of respect or friendship, are frequent in the East. Ge 41:42. Est 6:8, 9. Is 61:10. Lk 15:22. 2 C 5:21. Ph 2:7, 8.

5. behaved. *or,* prospered. ver. *14, 15, 30. Ge 39:2, 3, 23. Ps *1:3. Ac 7:10. **wisely.** Mt 10:16. Ep *5:17. Col *4:5. **the men of war.** 1 S 13:2. 14:52.

6. Philistine. *or,* Philistines. **the women.** Ex 15:20. Jg 11:34. Ps 68:25. Je 31:11-13. **instruments of music.** Heb. three stringed instruments. The original *shalishim* is rendered by the Vulgate *sistris.* The *sistrum* was an ancient Egyptian instrument made of brass, with three, and sometimes more brass rods across; which, being loose in their holes, made a jingling noise when shaken.

7. **answered**. Ex 15:21. Ps 24:7, 8. **Saul**. ♪171R, Ex 12:40. 1 S 21:11. 29:5. **David**. ♪171R, Ex +12:40.
8. **the saying**. Est 3:5. Pr 13:10. 27:4. Ec 4:4. Ja 4:5. **displeased him**. Heb. was evil in his eyes. 1 S +8:6mg. 15:11. Ge 28:8mg. Nu 11:1mg. +22:34mg. Jg ◑+14:3mg. Pr 24:18mg. **and what**. 1 S 13:14. 15:28. 16:13. 20:31. 1 K 2:22.
9. **eyed David**. Ge 4:5, 6. 31:2. Pr 23:6-8. Mt 20:15. Mk 7:22. Ep 4:27. Ja 5:9.
10. **the evil spirit**. Heb. *ruach*, Jg +9:23. 1 S 16:14n, 15. 19:9. 26:19. Mt +*8:16. **from God**. It is evident, both from Scripture and experience, that God hath permitted some men to be really acted upon and dis-quieted by the devil; and why not Saul as well as others? "from God," i.e. *by God's permission or judg-ment*, delivering him up to Satan (Matthew Poole on 1 S 16:14). 1 S 16:14n. 19:9. Dt +2:30 (T#267). Jg 9:23. Am +*3:6. Ep +1:11 (T#260). **and he prophe-sied**. *Wyyithnabbai*, rather, "and he pretended to prophesy"; for the verb is in Hithpael, the signification of which conjugation is not only reflex action, but also affectation of that action: Je 29:26, 27. The meaning seems to be, that Saul, influenced by the evil spirit, feigned to be prophesying, the better to conceal his murderous intentions, and render David unsuspicious. 1 S 19:24. 1 K 18:29. 22:12, 20-23. Je 28:2-4, 11. Zc 13:2-5. Ac 16:16. 2 Th 2:11. **played**. 1 S 16:16, 23. **and there was**. *Wehuchanith beyad shaool*, rather, "and the javelin was in the hand of Saul"; for the javelin or spear was the emblem of regal authority; and kings had it always in their hand, as may be seen represented on ancient monuments. In ancient times, says Justin, kings used a spear instead of a sceptre.
11. **cast the javelin**. 1 S 19:9, 10. 20:33. Pr 27:4. Is 54:17. **And David**. Ps 37:32, 33. Is 54:17. Lk 4:30. Jn 8:59. 10:39.
12. **afraid**. ver. 15, 20, 29. 1 S 16:4. Ps 14:5. 48:3-6. 53:5. Mk 6:20. Lk 8:37. Ac 24:25. **the Lord**. 1 S 16:13, 18. 22:13. Ac 7:9. **departed**. 1 S 16:14. 28:15. Ps 51:11. Ho 9:12. Mt 25:41.
13. **removed**. ver. 17, 25. 1 S 8:12. 22:7. **thousand**. 1 S 6:19n. 10:19. Mi +5:2. **he went out**. Saul was sensible that the Lord was departed from him; while he perceived, with evident sorrow of heart, that the Lord had given David peculiar wisdom, and that he was with him to prosper all his undertakings. This increased the disquietude of his malevolent mind, and his dread of David as a prevailing rival: he therefore removed him from his presence. This impolitic step, however, served the more to ingratiate David with the people, by affording him the opportunity of leading them forth to victory over their enemies. ver. 16. Nu 27:16, 17. 2 S 5:2. Ps 121:8.
14. **behaved**. or, prospered. See on ver. 5. Mk 6:20. Lk 8:37. Ac 24:25. **the Lord**. 1 S 10:7. 16:18. Ge 39:2, 3, 23. Jsh 6:27. Mt 1:23. 28:20. Ac 18:10.
15. **wisely**. Ps *112:5. Da *6:4, 5. Col *4:5. Ja 1:5. *3:17.
16. **all Israel**. ver. 5. Lk 19:48. 20:19. **he went**. Nu 27:17. 2 S 5:2. 1 K 3:7.
17. **her will I give**. 1 S 17:25. Ps 12:2. 55:21. **valiant**. Heb. a son of valor. 1 S 14:52. Jg +6:12. 18:2. 21:10. **the Lord's**. 1 S 17:47. 25:28. Nu 32:20, 27, 29. **Let not mine**. ver. 21, 25. Dt 17:7. 2 S 11:15. 12:9.
18. **Who am I**. ver. 23. 1 S *9:21. Ex 3:11. Ru 2:10. 2 S *7:18. Pr 15:33. 18:12. Je 1:6.

19. **was given**. Jg 14:20. **Adriel**. lit. drove of God; flock of God, *S#5741h. 2 S 21:8. **Meholathite**. i.e. *mirth; dancing; writhing*, *S#4259h. Jg ◑7:22. 2 S 21:8.
20. **loved David**. ver. 28. Ge 29:18, 20. 34:3. Jg 16:4, 15. 2 S 33:1. 1 K 11:1, 2. Ho 3:1. **they told**. Ge +24:57. **pleased him**. Heb. was right in his eyes. ver. 26. Jg +14:3mg.
21. **a snare**. Ex 10:7. Ps 7:14-16. 38:12. *119:110. 140:5. 142:3. Pr 26:24-26. 29:5. Je 5:26. 9:8. **the hand**. ver. 17. 1 S 19:11, 12. **this day**. ver. 26. **twain**. ♪96F3, Ge +8:4.
22. **commanded**. Ps 36:1-3. 55:21. **servants**. 2 S 13:28, 29. Pr 29:12.
23. **a light**. 1 J 3:1. **a poor man**. 1 S 9:21. Pr 14:20. 19:6, 7. Ec 9:15, 16. **and lightly**. Ps 119:141.
24. **On this manner**. Heb. According to these words.
25. **dowry**. Ge 29:18. 34:12. Ex 22:16, 17. **but an hundred**. That is, Thou shalt slay one hundred Philis-tines, and thou shalt produce their foreskins, as a proof, not only that thou hast killed one hundred men, but that these are of the uncircumcised Philistines. **fore-skins**. 1 S 17:26, 36. Ge 17:11-14. Jsh 5:3. **to be avenged**. 1 S 14:24. **thought**. ver. 17. 2 S 17:8-11.
26. **the days**. ver. 21. **expired**. Heb. fulfilled. 1 Ch 17:11.
27. **his men**. ver. 13. **slew**. Jg 14:19. 2 S *3:14. Is 43:1, 4. **two hundred men**. The Septuagint has only *ekaton andras*, "one hundred men"; and as Saul cov-enanted for an hundred, and as David himself says (2 S 3:14), that he espoused Michal for an hundred, it is very probable that this is the true reading.
28. **Saul saw**. 1 S 24:20. 26:25. Ge 30:27. 37:8-11. 39:3. Re 3:9.
29. **yet the**. ver. 12, 15. Ps 37:12-14. Ec 4:4. Ja 2:19. **Saul became**. Ge 4:4-8. Jn 11:53. 1 J 3:12-15.
30. **the princes**. Of this war we know no more than that David, whose military skill was greater, was more successful in it, than all the other officers of Saul. **went forth**. 2 S 11:1. **behaved himself**. ver. 5. Ps 119:99. Da 1:20. Lk 21:15. Ep 5:15. Ph 1:9. **his name**. SS 1:3. Ph 2:9. **set by**. Heb. precious. 1 S 2:30. 26:21. 2 K 1:13. Ps 72:14. 116:15. Is 43:4. 1 P 2:4, 7.

1 SAMUEL 19

Saul orders David to be slain. Jonathan informs David; and, pleading for him with Saul, effects a recon-ciliation, 1-7. David's success in war renders Saul again jealous; he seeks to kill David, who escapes by flight, 8-10. Saul sends to kill him in his house; but Michal favors his escape, and deceives Saul by an image in the bed, 11-17. David goes to Samuel, 18. Saul sends messengers after him to Naioth; and then goes himself: but first his messengers are seized by the Spirit of prophecy, and afterwards he also, 19-24.

1. **And Saul**. Saul's enmity now burst forth, in the avowed purpose of putting David to death; and nothing less than the especial interposition of Providence could have saved David's life, when every officer about the king's person, and every soldier, had positive orders to dispatch him. 1 S 18:8, 9. Pr 27:4. Ec 9:3. Je 9:3. 2 T 3:13.
2. **delighted**. 1 S 18:1-3. Ps 16:3. Jn 15:17-19. 1 J 3:12-14. **Jonathan**. 1 S 20:2. Pr 17:17. Ac 9:24. 23:16.

3. **and what.** 1 S 20:9, 13. **I see.** ♪63B, Ge 25:28. Supply by ellipsis, (what he replies), that will I tell thee.

4. **spake good.** 1 S 20:32. 22:14. Pr 24:11, 12. *31:8, 9. Je 18:20. **sin against.** 1 S 2:25. Ge 9:6. 42:22. 2 Ch 6:22. 1 C 8:12. 1 J 3:15. **because his works.** Ps 35:12. 109:4, 5. Pr *17:13. Je 18:20. Jn 10:32.

5. **put his.** 1 S 28:21. Jg 9:17. 12:3. Ps 119:109. Ac 20:24. Ph 2:30. **life.** Heb. *nephesh,* Ge +44:30. **slew.** 1 S 17:49-51. **wrought.** 1 S 11:13. 14:45. 17:52, 53. Ex 14:13. 1 Ch 11:14. He 2:3. **sin against innocent.** 1 S 20:32. Je 26:15. Mt 27:4, 24. **without a cause.** Ps 25:3. 35:19. 69:4. 119:161. Jn 15:25.

6. **sware.** 1 S 14:39. 28:10. Ps 15:4. Pr 26:24, 25. Je 5:2. **he shall not.** ver. 10, 11.

7. **in times past.** Heb. yesterday, third day. 1 S 16:21. 18:2, 10, 13. Ge +*31:2mg. Ex +4:10mg. Jsh +4:18mg. 2 S 5:2. 1 Ch 11:2mg. Is 30:33mg.

8. **David.** Ps 18:32, etc. 27:3. **him.** Heb. his face.

9. **the evil spirit.** Heb. *ruach,* Jg +9:23. 1 S *16:14n. +*18:10n, 11. Mt +*8:16. **from the Lord.** 1 S +*18:10n.

10. **sought.** ver. 6. Ho 6:4. Mt 12:43-45. Lk 11:24-26. 2 P 2:20-22. **he slipped.** 1 S 20:33. Jb 5:14, 15. Ps 18:17. 34:19. Pr 21:30. Is 54:17. Lk 4:30. Jn 10:39. **and escaped.** Ps 124:7. Mt 10:23.

11. **sent messengers.** Ps 59, title, 3, 4, 6, 15, 16. **to watch him.** Jg 16:2. Ps *37:32. Mk 6:20. Lk 20:20. **life.** Heb. *nephesh,* Ge +44:30. **thou shalt be.** ♪63, Ge +2:10.

12. **Michal.** Ps 34:19. **let David.** Jsh 2:15. Ac 9:24, 25. 2 C 11:32, 33.

13. **took.** Ge 27:16. **an image.** Heb. teraphim. Ge +*31:19mg. Jg 17:5. 18:14, 17. Ho 3:4. **a pillow.** Rather, "the network of goats' hair at its (the Tera-phim's) pillow;" for the *kevir,* (whence the Chaldee and Syriac *kavreetho,* a honeycomb, from its net-like form), seems to have been a kind of mosquito net, which, says Dr. Shaw, is "a close curtain of gauze, used all over the East, by people of fashion, to keep out the flies." That they had such anciently cannot be doubted. Thus when Judith had beheaded Holo-fernes in his bed (ch. 13:9, 15), "she pulled down the *canopy* (or the mosquito net, *to konopeion,* from *ko-nops,* a gnat, or mosquito, whence our word *canopy)* wherein he did lie in his drunkenness, from the pillars." 2 K 8:15n.

14. **she said.** Jsh 2:5. 2 S 16:17-19. 17:20.

15. **Bring him.** The eastern beds consist merely of two thick cotton quilts, one of which, folded double, serves as a mattress, the other as a covering. Such seems to have been the bed of David, which could easily have been carried, with himself in it, to the presence of Saul. ver. 6. Jb 31:31. Ps 37:12. Pr 27:3, 4. Ro 3:15.

16. **And when.** It is highly probable that David, when supposed to be sick, was thought to be hid in the harem or chamber of Michal. "The harems," says De La Motraye, "are sanctuaries, as sacred and inviola-ble, for persons pursued by justice for any crime, debt, etc. as the Roman Catholic churches in Italy, Spain, Portugal, etc." Thus we find, that to effect his purpose, Saul sent messengers to Michal, but they treated her harem with too much respect to enter it at first; but being authorized by Saul, they entered even into her chamber; and during the delay occasioned by respect

for the privacy of Michal, David escaped. Compare the Note at Ge 24:67.

17. **Why hast.** 1 S 22:17. 28:12. Mt 2:16. **mine en-emy.** 1 K 21:20. Ga 4:16. **And Michal.** 2 S 17:20. **He said.** ver. 14. Ex 1:17-19. **why should.** ♪85L, Ge +27:45. 2 S 2:22.

18. **and escaped.** Ps 35:27. 52:6, 7. 59:16, 17. **to Samuel.** 1 S 7:17. 15:34. 28:3. Ps 116:11. Ja *5:16. **Naioth.** i.e. *habitations; dwellings,* *S#5121h. ver. 19, 22, 23, 23. 1 S 20:1.

19. **it was told.** 1 S 22:9, 10. 23:19. 26:1. Pr 29:12.

20. **sent messengers.** ver. 11, 14. Jn 7:32, 45. **when they.** 1 S 10:5, 6, 10. Nu 11:25, 26. Jl 2:28. Jn 7:32, 45, 46, etc. 1 C 14:3, 24, 25. **and Samuel.** Ps 14:5. *125:2, 3. **Spirit.** Heb. *ruach,* Ge +41:38.

21. **sent messengers.** 2 K 1:9-13. Pr 27:22. Je 13:23. **prophesied also.** Jl 2:28.

22. **went he also.** Pr 21:1. **well.** Heb. *bor,* Ge +37:20. **Sechu.** i.e. *watchtower; an observatory; they hedged up; a bough,* *S#7906h.

23. **the Spirit.** Heb. *ruach,* Ge +41:38. ver. 20. 1 S 10:16. Nu 23:5. 24:2. Mt 7:22. Jn 11:51. 1 C 13:2. **until he came.** Pr 16:9. 21:1.

24. **stripped.** 2 S 6:14, 20n. Is 20:2. Mi 1:8. **lay.** Heb. fell. Nu 24:4. **naked.** ♪171N, Ge +8:13. Jn 21:7. **Is Saul.** 1 S 10:10-12. Mt *7:22, 23. Ac 9:21.

1 SAMUEL 20

David consults with Jonathan how to provide for his safety, 1-10. They renew the covenant of friendship, and confirm it by oath, 11-17. They agree on a token, 18-23. David absents himself from the king's table, and is excused by Jonathan, whom Saul abuses and at-tempts to kill, 24-34. Jonathan shows David his danger, and most affectionately takes leave of him, 35-42.

1. **fled.** 1 S 19:19-24. 23:26-28. Ps 124:6-8. 2 P 2:9. **What have.** 1 S 12:3. 24:11, 17. Ps 7:3-5. 18:20-24. 2 C 1:12. 1 J 3:21. **life.** Heb. *nephesh,* soul, Ge +44:20.

2. **God forbid.** 1 S 14:45. Ge 44:7. Jsh 22:29. 24:16. Lk 20:16. **show it me.** Heb. uncover mine ear. ver. 12. 1 S +9:15mg. 22:8, 17. Ru +4:4mg. Ps 40:6. Is 50:5. Jn 15:15. 17:8.

3. **sware.** Dt 6:13. Je 4:2. He 6:16. **but truly.** 1 S 25:26. 27:1. 2 S 15:21. 2 K 2:2, 4, 6. **and as thy.** 1 S 1:26. 17:55. Je 38:16. **soul.** Heb. *nephesh,* Ge +27:31. **but a step.** 1 S 27:1. Dt 28:66. Ps 88:3, 4. 116:3. 143:7. Is 27:4h. Ac 12:4, 6. 1 C 15:30, 31. 2 C 1:9, 10.

4. **Whatsoever,** etc. *or,* Say what is thy mind, and I will do, etc. **soul.** Heb. *nephesh,* Ge +34:3. **desireth.** Heb. speaketh, *or* thinketh. Jn 14:13.

5. **the new moon.** The months of the Hebrews were lunar months, and they reckoned from one new moon to another: and, as their feasts, particularly the pass-over, were reckoned according to this, they were very scrupulous in observing the first appearance of each new moon. On these new moons, they offered sacri-fices, and feasted together: but the gathering together of all the families of a tribe on such occasions seems to have taken place only once in the year. ver. 6. Nu 10:10. 28:11. 2 K 4:23. Ps 81:3. Col 2:16. **that I may.** ver. 19. 1 S 19:2. Ps 55:12. Pr +*22:3. Jn 8:59. Ac 17:14.

6. **at all miss.** lit. missing shall miss. ♪147B, Ge +26:28. **Bethlehem.** 1 S 17:58. Jn 7:42. **sacrifice.** *or,* feast. 1 S 9:12. 16:2-5.

7. **It is well**. Dt 1:23. 2 S 17:4. **evil**. ver. 9. 1 S 25:17. Est 7:7.

8. **deal kindly**. Ge 24:49. 47:29. Jsh 2:14. Ru 1:8. Pr 3:3. **thou hast**. ver. 16. 1 S 18:3. 23:18. **if there be**. Jsh 22:22. 2 S 14:32. Ps 7:4, 5. Ac 25:11. **why shouldest**. 1 Ch 12:17. Ps 116:11.

9. **then would**. ver. 38, 42. 1 S 19:2.

10. **answer thee**. ver. 30-34. 1 S 25:10, 14, 17. Ge 42:7, 30. 1 K 12:13. Pr 18:23.

12. **O Lord**. This verse is evidently deficient. The LXX. have *Kurios o theos Israal oiden*, "The Lord God of Israel doth know;" the Syriac and Arabic, "The Lord God of Israel is witness;" either of which makes a good sense. But two of Dr. Kennicott's MSS. supply the word *chai, liveth;* and the text reads thus: "As the Lord God of Israel liveth, when I have sounded my father, if there be good unto David, and I then send not unto thee," etc.; which is a still better sense. Jsh 22:22. Jg 6:22. Jb 31:4. Ps 17:3. 139:1-4. Jn 20:28. **sounded**. Heb. searched. Pr 20:5. 25:2, 3. **show it thee**. Heb. uncover thine ear. ver. 2. Ru +4:4mg.

13. **The Lord do**. 1 S 3:17. 25:22. Ru 1:17. 2 S 3:35. 19:13. 1 K 19:2. 20:10. **I will show**. ver. 2, 12. Ru +4:4mg. **the Lord be**. 1 S 17:37. Jsh 1:5. 1 Ch 22:11, 16. Mt *28:20. Ph 4:9. **he hath been with my father**. 1 S 10:7. 11:6-13. 14:47. 2 S 7:15.

14. **the kindness**. 2 S 9:3. Ep 5:1, 2.

15. **thou shalt**. 1 S 24:21. 2 S 9:1-7. 21:7. **for ever**. Heb. *olam*, Ex +12:24. **face of**. Ge +1:2.

16. **made**. Heb. cut. 1 S 18:3. Ge 15:18. **Let the Lord**. 1 S 25:22. 31:2. 2 S 4:7, 8. 21:8. Je 51:56.

17. **because he loved him**. *or*, by his love toward him. **for he loved**. 1 S 18:1, 3. Dt 13:6. 2 S 1:26. Pr 18:24. SS 2:14. **soul**. Heb. *nephesh*, Ge +27:31.

18. **new moon**. See on ver. 5. **and thou shalt**. Among the forms of salutation and compliment used in Persia, one was "according to my mode of notation in italics, *Ja i shama khali bud pish yaran*, signifying, Thy place or seat was empty among thy friends. This phrase, or the greater part of it, was frequently addressed to myself when coming into a circle of Persian acquaintances, after an absence of several days or weeks. It reminded me of a passage in the First Book of Samuel (ch. 20:18), *And thou shalt be missed, because thy seat will be empty*. And again, *David's place was empty*" (Sir W. Ouseley's Travels, vol. 1. preface, p. 16). **empty**. Heb. missed. ver. 6, 25, 27. 1 S 25:7, 15, 21. Is 34:16.

19. **quickly**. *or*, diligently. Heb. greatly. **hide thyself**. ver. 5. 1 S 19:2. **when the business**. Heb. in the day of business. **Ezel**. *or*, that showeth the way. i.e. *going away*; or as in ver. 41 *Etzel*, i.e. *near* (Young). *S#237h.

21. **no**. Heb. not any thing. **as the**. Je 4:2. 5:2. 12:16. Am 8:14.

23. **the matter**. ver. 14, 15. **the Lord**. ver. 42. Ge 16:5. *31:49, 50, 53. **for ever**. Heb. *olam*, Ex +12:24.

24. **the king**. Ps 50:16-21. Pr 4:17. 15:17. 17:1. 21:3, 27. Is 1:11-15. Zc 7:6. Jn 18:28. **meat**. ʃ171l8, Ge +3:19.

25. **as at other times**. Jg 16:20.

26. **not anything**. ʃ171C, Ex +20:10. **he is not clean**. Le 7:21. 11:24, 27, 31, 40. 15:5, 16, 17, 19-21. Nu 19:16.

27. **Wherefore**. 1 S 18:11. 19:9, 10, 15. **the son**. 1 S 22:7-9, 13, 14. 25:10. Is 11:1, 2. Mt 13:55. 1 P 2:4. **meat**. ʃ171l8, Ge +3:19.

28. **answered Saul**. ver. 6.

29. **my brother**. 1 S 17:28.

30. **Saul's**. Jb 5:2. Pr 14:29. 19:12, 19. 21:24. 25:28. 27:3. Ja 1:19, 20. **Thou**, etc. *or*, Thou perverse rebel. Heb. Son of perverse rebellion. Pr 15:2. 21:24. Mt 5:22. Ep 4:31. 6:4. **and unto the**. This reflection on the mother of Jonathan, by the passionate monarch, at the close of his speech, is just as gross as our translation represents it to be at the beginning; and certainly reflects more dishonor on himself than on his brave and noble minded son. It should be remembered that Saul was subject to a disease which weakened his mental powers; of which we need no stronger proof than that before us—his calling names. Mungo Park gives an instance of the prevalence of the same principles in Africa; and if we suppose king Saul, unable to vilify Jonathan to his own satisfaction by personal reproaches, had outstepped the ordinary abuse of his day, and proceeded to that which was designed to produce unusual vexation, we do little injury to his character or his general deportment. "Maternal affection," says Mr. Park (Travels in Africa, p. 264), "is everywhere conspicuous among the Africans, and creates a correspondent return of tenderness in the child. 'Strike me,' said my attendant, 'but do not curse my mother.' I found the same sentiment to prevail universally in all parts of Africa."

31. **send**. ver. 8. 1 S 19:6, 11-15. **shall surely die**. Heb. is the son of death. 1 S 26:16. 2 S 12:5. 19:28. Ps 79:11mg. ʃ108B. Idiom B833. "Son of death" means devoted to death. For other instances of this idiom see 1 S 26:16. Ps 102:20. Jon 4:10mg. Mt 9:15. 13:38. 23:15. Lk 5:34. Jn 17:12. Ac 13:10. Ep 2:2, 3. 5:6. 2 Th 2:3.

32. **Wherefore**. 1 S 19:5. Pr 24:11, 12. 31:8, 9. Jn 7:51. **what hath**. Mt 27:23. Lk 23:22. **cast**. 1 S 18:11. 19:10, 11. Pr 22:24. Ec 9:3. Je 17:9. **whereby**. ver. 7. Ec 7:9.

34. **in fierce**. Ec *7:20. Ep 4:26. **he was grieved**. Mk 3:5.

35. **at the time**. ver. 19. 2 S 20:5.

36. **Run**. ver. 20, 21. **beyond him**. Heb. to pass over him. ver. 21, 22.

38. **Make speed**. Ps 55:6-9. Pr 6:4, 5. Mt 24:16-18. Mk 13:14-16. Lk 17:31, 32.

39. **knew not**. 2 S 15:11. Ec 9:5.

40. **artillery**. Heb. instruments. 1 S 21:8. Rather, *weapons*, as the word *kelim* also denotes; and here means the bow, quiver, and arrows. This is probably the only place in our language in which the word *artillery* is not applied to *cannon* or *ordnance*, but simply to *weapons* of war. **his lad**. Heb. the lad that was his. 1 S 24:4.

41. **and fell**. 1 S 25:23. Ge 43:28. 2 S 9:6. **and they kissed**. 1 S 10:1. Ge 29:11, 13. 45:15. 2 S 19:39. Ac 20:37. **and wept**. Ps 6:6, 7. 39:12. 56:8. **David exceeded**. 1 S 18:3. 2 S 1:26.

42. **Go in peace**. ver. 22. 1 S 1:17. Nu 6:26. Lk 7:50. Ac 16:36. **forasmuch as**. *or*, The Lord be witness of that which, etc. ver. 23. **The Lord be between**. Ge 31:49. **And he arose**. 1 S 23:18. The separation of two such faithful friends was equally grievous to them both, but David's case was the more deplorable: for when Jonathan was returning to his family and friends, David was leaving all his comforts, even those of God's sanctuary, and therefore his grief exceeded Jonathan's;

or, perhaps it was because his temper was more tender and his passions stronger. They referred each other to the covenant of friendship that was between them, both of them being comforted thereby in this very mournful separation: "We have sworn both of us in the name of the Lord, for ourselves and our heirs, that we and they will be faithful and kind to each other from generation to generation." ver. 23. Ge 31:49. **for ever**. Heb. *olam*, Ex +12:24.

1 SAMUEL 21

David comes to Nob, and obtains from Ahimelech hallowed bread, 1-6. Doeg, an Edomite, is present, 7. David takes also Goliath's sword, 8, 9. He flees to Gath, and feigns himself mad, and is sent away, 10-15.

1. **Nob**. i.e. *fruit*. Nob appears to have been a sacerdotal city of Benjamin or Ephraim. Jerome says, that in his time the ruins of it might be seen not far from Diospolis or Lydda. But the rabbins assert that Jerusalem might be seen from this town. The tabernacle resided some time at Nob; and after it was destroyed, it was removed to Gibeon; "and the days of Nob and Gibeon were fifty-seven years." Maimonides in *Beth-habbechirah*, c. 1. 1 S 22:19. Ne 11:32. Is 10:24, 32. **to Ahimelech**. i.e. *brother of the king*, he was brother of Ahijah, son of Ahitub (Young). 1 S 14:3, **called** Ahiah. 1 S 22:9-19. 2 S 8:17. called also Abiathar, Mk 2:26. **afraid**. 1 S 16:4.

2. **The king**. The whole of this is a gross falsehood; and which was attended with the most fatal consequences. It is well known that from all antiquity it was held no crime to tell a lie in order to save a life. Thus Diphilon, "I hold it right to tell a lie for safety: nothing should be avoided to save life." A heathen may say or sing thus: but no Christian can act thus and save his soul, though he may save his life. 1 S ●16:2n. 19:17. 22:22. Ge 27:20, 24. 1 K 13:18. Ps 119:28, 29. Ga 2:12. Col 3:9.

3. **under thine**. ver. 4. Jg 9:29. Is 3:6. **present**. Heb. found. Jg 20:48.

4. **hallowed bread**. ver. 6. Ex 25:30. Le 24:5-9. Mt 12:3, 4. **if the young**. Ex 19:15. Le 15:18. Zc 7:3. 1 C 7:5.

5. **the vessels**. Ac 9:15. 2 C 4:7. 1 Th 4:3, 4. 2 T 2:20, 21. 1 P 3:7. **in a manner**. Le 24:9. yea, **though it were sanctified this day in the vessel**. *or*, especially when this day there is other sanctified in the vessel. Le 8:26.

6. **gave him**. Mt 12:3, 4. Mk 2:25-27. Lk 6:3, 4. **hot bread**. Le 24:5-9.

7. **detained**. Je 7:9-11. Ezk 33:31. Am 8:5. Mt 15:8. Ac 21:26, 27. **Doeg**. i.e. *sorrowful, fearful*, ✳S#1673h. 1 S 22:9, 18, 18, 22. Ps 52, title. **an Edomite**. Dt 23:7, 8. **herdmen**. 1 S 11:5. Ge 13:7, 8. 26:20. 1 Ch 27:29. 2 Ch 26:10.

8. **business**. Lk 2:49. Jn 9:4.

9. **The sword**. 1 S 17:51-54. Mk 4:4-10. Ep 6:17. He *4:12. Re 19:15. **the valley**. 1 S 17:2, 50. **behold**. 1 S 31:10. **behind**. Ex 28:6, etc.

10. **fled**. 1 S 27:1. 1 K 19:3. Pr +*22:3. Je 26:21. **Achish**. *or*, Abimelech. i.e. *object of fear or reverence*, ✳S#397h. ver. 11, 12, 14. 1 S 27:2, 3, 5, 6, 9, 10, 12. 28:1, 2. 29:2, 3, 6, 8, 9. 1 K 2:39, 40. Ps 34, title,mg. **Gath**. Jerome says there was a large town

called *Gath*, in the way from Eleutheropolis to Gaza; and Eusebius speaks of another *Gath*, five miles from Eleutheropolis, towards Lydda (and consequently different from that mentioned by Jerome); and also of another *Gath*, between Jamnia and Antipatris. It appears to have been the extreme boundary of the Philistine territory in one direction, as Ekron was on the other (1 S 7:14. 17:52), and lay near Mareshah (2 Ch 11:8. Mi 1:14), which agrees pretty well with the position assigned it by Jerome. But Reland and Dr. Wells agree with Eusebius; and the authors of the Universal History (b. i. c. 7) place it about six miles from Jamnia, fourteen south of Joppa, and thirty-two west of Jerusalem.

11. **the servants**. Ps 56, title. **the king**. 1 S 16:1. 18:7, 8. 29:5.

12. **laid up**. Ps *119:11. Lk 2:19, 51. **sore**. ver. 10. Ge 12:11-13. 26:7. Ps 34:4. 56:3.

13. **changed**. Jb 14:20. Ps 34, title. Pr 29:25. Ec 7:7. **behavior**. lit. taste, as in Ex 16:31. Nu 11:8. 1 S 25:33. Jb 6:6. 12:20. Ps 34:1. 119:66. Pr 11:22. 26:16. Je 48:11. Jon 3:7. **scrabbled**. *or*, made marks. Ezk 9:4. **spittle**. Jb 6:6. **fall down**. Ps 78:16. La 2:18. **beard**. Reckoned an unfallible sign of madness (Young).

14. **is mad**. *or*, playeth the madman. Ge +27:16. 1 S 16:2n. 2 K 9:11. Ps 34:6, 17-19. Pr +*22:3. Ec 7:7. Is 59:15mg.

15. **need**. or, lack. ✳S#2638h. 2 S 3:29. 1 K 11:22. *17:16. Pr 6:32. 7:7. 9:4, 16. 10:13, 21. 11:12. 12:9, 11. 15:21. 17:18. 24:30. 28:16. Ec 6:2. 10:3.

1 SAMUEL 22

David escapes to Adullam, whither his kindred and others resort to him, 1, 2. At Mizpeh he commends his parents to the protection of the king of Moab, 3, 4. Admonished by the prophet Gad, he returns to the land of Judah, 5. Saul complains that his servants are unfaithful, 6-8. Doeg accuses Ahimelech; who is sent for with the priests, and answers the charge, 9-16. Saul's soldiers refusing to slay the priests at his command, Doeg executes it; and destroys their city with their wives and children, 17-19. Abiathar escapes to David, who blames himself, and assures him of protection, 20-23.

1. **David**. 1 S 21:10-15. Ps 34 and 57, titles. **the cave**. Jsh 12:15. 15:35. 2 S 23:13, 14. 1 Ch 11:15-17. Ps 142, title. Mi 1:3, 15. He 11:38. **Adullam**. Jsh 15:35. Adullam was a city of Judah; and according to Eusebius, ten miles (Jerome says eleven) eastward from Eleutheropolis. **they went**. Ps 42:1.

2. **distress**. Jg 11:3. Mt 11:12, 28. **was in debt**. Heb. had a creditor. Mt 18:25-34. **discontented**. Heb. bitter of soul. Heb. *nephesh*, Ex +15:9. 1 S 1:10. 30:6. Jg +18:25mg. 2 S 17:18. Pr 31:6mg. **a captain**. 1 S 9:16. 25:15, 16. 30:22-24. 2 S 5:2. 2 K 20:5. 1 Ch 11:15-19. Ps 72:12-14. Mt 9:12, 13. 11:19. Lk 15:2. He 2:10.

3. **Mizpeh**. Jg 11:29. **the king**. 1 S 14:47. Ru 1:1-4. 4:10, 17. **Let my father**. Ge 47:11. Ex 20:12. Mt 15:4-6. 1 T 5:4. **till I know**. 1 S 3:18. 2 S 15:25, 26. Ph 2:23, 24.

4. **Moab**. Is 16:4. **in the hold**. 2 S 23:13, 14. 1 Ch 12:16.

5. **Gad**. 2 S 24:11, 13, 14, 18, 19. 1 Ch 21:9, 11, 13, 18, 19. 29:29. 2 Ch 29:25. **depart**. 1 S 23:1-6. Ne

6:11. Ps 11:1. Is 8:12-14. **David departed**. Mt 10:23. **Hareth**. i.e. *forest; cutting of wood; engraving*, ✱S#2802h.

6. **tree**. *or*, grove in a high place. 1 S 31:13. Ge 21:33. 35:8. 1 Ch 10:12. **spear**. 1 S 18:10. 19:9. 20:33.

7. **the son of Jesse**. ver. 9, 13. 1 S 18:14. 20:27, 30. 25:10. 2 S 20:1. 1 K 12:16. Is 11:1, 10. **give**. 1 S 8:14, 15. **captains**. 1 S 8:11, 12.

8. **showeth me**. Heb. uncovereth mine ear. ver. 17. 1 S +9:15mg. +20:2mg. Ru +4:4mg. Jb 33:16mg. **that my son**. 1 S 18:3. 20:8, 13-17, 30-34, 42. 23:16-18.

9. **Then**. *∫*106, Ge +31:7. **Doeg**. He is also said to be "the chiefest of the herdsmen that belonged to Saul;" and the Septuagint intimates that he was over the mules of Saul. He may have been what we call the king's *equerry* or *groom*. 1 S 21:7. Ps 52, title, 1-5. Pr 19:5. 29:12. Ezk 22:9. Mt 26:59-61. **the Edomite**. One of a nation whose hatred of Israel was unbending (Young on 1 S 21:7). **Ahimelech**. 1 S 21:1, etc. **Ahitub**. 1 S 14:3.

10. **he enquired**. ver. 13, 15. 1 S 21:6, 9. 23:2, 4, 12. 30:8. Nu 27:21. Ps 52:2-4. **him victuals**. 1 S 21:6-9.

11. **sent to call**. Ro 3:15. **Nob**. i.e. *fruit; high place*, ✱S#5011h. ver. 9, 19. 1 S 21:1. Ne 11:32. Is 10:32.

12. **thou son**. ver. 7, 13. **Here I am**. Heb. Behold me. 1 S 3:4-6. 2 S 9:6. Is 65:1.

13. **Why have**. ver. 8. Ps 119:69. Am 7:10. Lk 23:2-5.

14. **And who**. 1 S 19:4, 5. 20:32. 24:11. 26:23. 2 S 22:23-25. Pr 24:11, 12. 31:8, 9. **the king's**. ver. 13. 1 S 17:25. 18:27. **goeth**. 1 S 18:13. 21:2.

15. **Did I then**. He seems to intimate, that his enquiring now for David was no new thing, having often done so before, without ever being informed it was wrong in itself or displeasing to the king. **thy servant**. Ge 20:5, 6. 2 S 15:11. 2 C 1:12. 1 P 3:16, 17. **less or more**. Heb. little or great. 1 S 25:36.

16. **Thou shalt**. 1 S 14:44. 20:31. 1 K 18:4. 19:2. Pr 28:15. Da 2:5, 12. 3:19, 20. Ac 12:19. **surely**. *∫*147B, Ge +2:16. **thou, and**. Dt 24:16. Est 3:6. Mt 2:16.

17. **footmen**. *or*, guard. Heb. runners. 1 S 8:11. 20:36. 2 S 15:1. 18:22, 24, 26. 1 K 1:5. 14:27mg, 28. 2 K 10:25. 11:4, 6. 2 Ch 12:10. +30:6n. **slay the priests**. ver. 13. 1 S 20:33. 25:17. 1 K 18:4. **hand**. *∫*121BA, Dt 32:36. **show**. ver. 8. Ru +4:4mg. **would not**. 1 S 14:45. Ex +1:17. 2 K 1:13, 14. Ac +*4:19. +*5:29.

18. **Doeg**. See on ver. 9. **he fell**. 2 Ch 24:21. Ho 5:11. 7:3. Mi 6:16. Zp 3:3. Ac 26:10, 11. **fourscore**. The LXX. read, *triakosious kai pente andras*, "three hundred and five men;" and Josephus, "three hundred and eighty-five men." Probably the eighty-five were priests, and the three hundred the families of the priests; three hundred and eighty-five being the whole population of Nob. 1 S 2:30-33, 36. 3:12-14. **a linen ephod**. 1 S 2:18, 28. Ex 28:40. 39:27.

19. **Nob**. ver. 9, 11. 1 S 21:1. Ne 11:32. Is 10:32. **the city**. *∫*121J19. Metonymy of the Subject B579. Here, the city is put for its inhabitants. For other instances of this figure see Is 14:31. Je 4:29. 26:2. 48:8. 49:23. Mi 6:9. Mt 11:21, 23. 23:37. Mk 1:5, 33. Ac 8:25. **men**. 1 S 2:33. 4:11, 12. 15:3, 9. Jsh 6:17, 21. 2 S 21:1. Ps 53:4. 137:7. Ho 10:14. Ja 2:13. **with the edge**. This is one of the worst acts of Saul's life:

his malice was implacable, and his wrath cruel; and there is no motive of justice or policy by which such a barbarous massacre can be justified.

20. **one**. 1 S 23:6. 30:7. 2 S 20:25. 1 K 2:26, 27. **Abiathar**. i.e. *father of abundance*, ✱S#54h. ver. 21, 22. 1 S 23:6, 9. 30:7, 7. 2 S 8:17. 15:24, 27, 29, 35, 35, 36. 17:15. 19:11. 20:25. 1 K 1:7, 19, 25, 42. 2:22, 26, 27, 35. 4:4. 1 Ch 15:11. 18:16. 24:6. 27:34. **escaped**. 1 S 2:33. 4:12. Jb 1:15-17, 17, 19.

22. **I have occasioned**. 1 S 21:1-9. Ps 44:22. **persons**. Heb. *nephesh*, Jsh +10:28.

23. **with me**. Jn 14:19. Col 3:2. **he that seeketh**. 1 K 2:26. Mt 24:9. Jn 15:20. 16:2, 3. He 12:1-3. **life**. Heb. *nephesh*, soul, Ge +44:30. **but with me**. Jn *10:28-30. 17:12. 18:9.

1 SAMUEL 23

David, inquiring of God by Abiathar, defends Keilah and smites the Philistines, 1-6. Saul purposes to besiege him in Keilah; but the Lord showing David the treachery of the men of Keilah, he flees to Ziph, where Jonathan meets and comforts him, 7-18. The Ziphites inform Saul concerning him, who closely pursues him to Maon; but is called off by an invasion of the Philistines, 19-28. David dwells at En-gedi, 29.

1. **Keilah**. Keilah was a city of Judah, situated, according to Eusebius, eight miles from Eleuteropolis, towards Hebron. Sozomen says that the prophet Habakkuk's tomb was shown there. Jsh 15:44. Ne 3:17, 18. **rob the**. Le 26:16. Dt 28:33, 51. Jg 6:4, 11. Mi 6:15. **threshingfloors**. Ge 50:+10, 11. Dt +*16:13mg. Jg 6:11.

2. **enquired**. In what way David made this enquiry we are not told; but it was probably by means of Abiathar; and therefore it would seem, that with Houbigant, we should read the sixth verse immediately after the first. This adventure was truly noble and patriotic. Had not David loved his country, and been above all motives of private and personal revenge, he would have rejoiced in this invasion of Judea, as producing a strong diversion in his favor, and embroiling his inveterate enemy. In most cases, a man with David's wrongs would have joined with the enemies of his country, and avenged himself on the author of his calamities; but he thinks of nothing but succouring Keilah, and using his power and influence in behalf of his brethren. ver. 4, 6, 9-12. 1 S 30:8. Nu 27:21. Jsh 9:14. Jg 1:1. 20:18. 2 S 5:19, 23. 1 Ch 14:10. Ps *32:8. Pr *3:5, 6. Je 10:23.

3. **Behold**. ver. 15, 23, 26. Ps 11:1. Je 12:5. Jn 11:8.

4. **inquired**. Is 37:14. **yet again**. 1 S 10:22. 16:11. 28:6. Ge 18:29. +22:15. Jg 6:39. 2 K=13:18, 19. Ec ◐+*5:2. Mt *26:42, 44. Lk +*11:9. *18:1-8. **for I will**. Jsh 8:7. Jg 7:7. 2 S 5:19. 2 K 3:18.

6. **when Abiathar**. 1 S 22:20. **an ephod**. 1 S 14:3, 18, 36, 37. Ex 28:28, 30, 31.

7. A.M. 2943. B.C. 1061. An. Ex. Is. 430. **God hath**. ver. 14. 1 S 24:4-6. 26:8, 9. Ps 71:10, 11. **he is shut**. Ex 14:3. 15:9. Jg 16:2, 3. Jb 10:5. Lk 19:43, 44.

9. **David**. Ps 10:9. 37:12, 13. Je 11:18, 19. Ac 9:24. 14:6. 23:16-18. **Bring**. ver. 6. 1 S 14:18. 30:7. Nu 27:21. Je 33:3.

10. **destroy the city**. ver. 8. 1 S 22:19, *22. Ge 18:24. Est 3:6. Ps *69:6. Pr 28:15. Jn *18:8. Ro 3:15, 16.

11. **And the Lord**. Ps 50:15. Je 33:3. Mt 7:7, 8.

12. **deliver**. Heb. shut up. ver. 7, 11, 20. 1 S 17:46. +24:18mg. 30:15. Dt 32:30. Jsh 20:5. Ps 31:8. **They will**. ver. 7. Ps 35:12. 41:9. 62:1. 118:8. Ec 9:14, 15. Is 29:15. Mi 7:5. He 4:13.

13. **six hundred**. 1 S 22:2. 25:13. 30:9, 10.

14. **a mountain**. 1 S 26:20. Jsh 15:48, 55. Ps 11:1-3. 54:3, 4. 124:7. **the wilderness**. *Ziph* is mentioned in *Joshua* with Carmel and Maon, near which it seems to have been situated; and as we have mention of Carmel and Maon in the history of David, as adjoining to Ziph, it cannot be doubted that by the Ziph, in the wilderness of which David now lay, and where was the hill of Hachilah, is to be understood Ziph near Carmel and Maon. Jsh 15:24, 48, 55. **Saul**. 1 S 27:1. Ps 54:3, 4. Pr 1:16. 4:16. **but God**. ver. 7. Ps 32:7. 37:32, 33. 54:3, 4. Pr 21:30. Je 36:26. Ro 8:31. 2 T 3:11. 4:17, 18.

15. **life**. Heb. *nephesh*, soul. Ge +44:30.

16. **strengthened**. 1 S +9:27. Dt 3:28. Ne 2:18. Jb *4:3, 4. 16:5. Pr 27:9, 17. Ec 4:9-12. Is 35:3, 4. Ezk *13:22. Da *10:19, 21. Lk 22:32, 43. Ac 13:43. Ep *6:10. 2 T 2:1. He 10:24, 25. 12:12, 13.

17. **Fear not**. Is 41:10, 14. He 13:6. **shall not**. Jb 5:11-15. Ps 27:1-3. 46:1, 2. 91:1, 2. Pr 14:26. Is 54:17. **thou shalt be**. 1 S 15:28. Lk 12:32. **I shall be**. Pr 19:21. Ac 28:16. Ro 15:24. **that also Saul**. 1 S 20:31. *24:20. Ac 5:39.

18. **they two**. 1 S 18:3. 20:12-17, 42. 2 S 9:1. 21:7.

19. **the Ziphites**. i.e. *smelters*, *S#2130h. 1 S 22:7, 8. *26:1h. Jsh 15:24. Ps *54, title, 3, 4. Pr 29:12. **Gibeah**. Jsh 18:28. **hide himself**. 1 S 26:1. Ps 54:1. Is 45:15. **strong holds**. ver. 14, 29. 1 S 22:4. 24:22. **Hachilah**. i.e. *red; darksome*, *S#2444h. 1 S 26:1, 3. Calmet states, that *Hachilah* was a mountain about ten miles south of Jericho, where Jonathan Maccabeus built the castle of Massada, west of the Dead sea, and not far from En-gedi. 1 S 26:1, 3. **on the south**. Heb. on the right hand. Ge 14:15. **Jeshimon**. *or*, the wilderness. ver. 24. Nu 21:20. Ps 63, title. Eusebius places *Jeshimon* ten miles south of Jericho, near the Dead sea; which agrees extremely well with the position of Hachilah, as stated by Calmet.

20. **all the desire**. Dt 18:6. 2 S 3:21. Ps 112:10. Pr 11:23. **soul**. Heb. *nephesh*, Ge +34:3. **our part**. 1 K 21:11-14. 2 K 10:5-7. Ps 54:3. Pr 29:26.

21. **Saul said, Blessed**. 1 S 22:8. Jg 17:2. Ps 10:3. Is 66:5. Mi 3:11.

22. **haunt is**. Heb. foot shall be. Jb 5:13.

23. **take knowledge**. Mk 14:1, 10, 11. Jn 18:2, 3. **I will search**. 2 S 17:11-13. 1 K +√18:10. Pr 1:16. Ro 3:15, 16. **the thousands**. 1 S 6:19n. 10:19. Ex +18:21. Nu 10:36. Jg 12:6mg,n. 15:15n. Mi +*5:2.

24. **Ziph**. Jsh 15:24. **the wilderness**. *Maon*, from which the adjoining mountainous district derived its name, was a city in the most southern parts of the tribe of Judah, and a neighboring town to Carmel. Hence Nabal (1 S 25:2) is described as a man of Maon, whose possessions were in Carmel; and though he might dwell generally in Maon, yet he is styled Nabal the Carmelite, from the place where his estate lay. Calmet supposes it to be the city *Minois*, which Eusebius places in the vicinity of Gaza; and the *Maenaemi Castrum*, which the Theodosian code places near Beersheba. **Maon**. 1 S 25:2. Jsh 15:55. **the south**. ver. 19.

25. **into a rock**. *or*, from the rock. ver. 28. Jg 15:8. Afterwards called "the rock of division."

26. **David made haste**. 1 S 19:12. 20:38. 2 S 15:14. 17:21, 22. Ps 31:22. **away**. 2 Ch 20:12. Ps 17:8, 9, 11. 22:12, 16. 31:2-4, 15. *32:7. 118:11-13. 140:1-9. 2 C 1:8. Re 20:9.

27. **there came**. Ge 22:14. Dt 32:36. 2 K 19:9. Ps 116:3. **the Philistines**. 2 K 19:9. Re 12:16. **invaded**. Heb. spread themselves upon. 1 S 27:8, 10. 30:1, 14. Jg 9:44. 1 Ch 14:13.

28. **Sela-hammahlekoth**. that is, *the rock of divisions*. *S#5555h. Because, says the Targum, "the heart of the king was divided to go hither and thither." Here Saul was obliged to separate himself from David, in order to go and oppose the invading Philistines; which deliverance of David was of such a nature as made the Divine interposition fully visible.

29. **strong holds**. ver. 14, 19. The district around *En-gedi*, near the western coast of the Dead sea, is reported by travelers to be a mountainous territory, filled with caverns; and consequently, proper for David in his present circumstances. Dr. Lightfoot thinks this was the wilderness of Judah, in which David was when he penned the 63rd Psalm, which breathes as much pious and devout affection as almost any of his Psalms; for in all places and in all conditions he still kept up his communion with God. If Christians knew their privileges better, and acted up thereto, there would be less murmuring at the dark dispensations of Divine Providence. **En-gedi**. 1 S 24:1. Ge 14:7. Jsh 15:61, 62. 2 Ch 20:2. SS 1:14. Ezk 47:10.

1 SAMUEL 24

David in a cave, having Saul entirely in his power, cuts off his skirt, but spares his life, 1-7. He proves his innocency to Saul, 8-15. Saul owns his fault, requires an oath of David, and departs, 16-22.

1. **when Saul**. 1 S 23:28, 29. **following**. Heb. after. **it was told**. 1 S 23:19. Pr 25:5. 29:12. Ezk 22:9. Ho 7:3. **the wilderness**. 1 S 23:29.

2. **Saul took**. 1 S 13:2. **and went**. Ps 18:36, 43, 48. 37:32. 38:12. **the rocks**. Ps 104:18. 141:6.

3. **the sheepcotes**. Caves in the rocks, in which it is still common for shepherds and their flocks to lodge. Dr. Pococke observes, "Beyond the valley (of Tekoa), there is a very large grotto, which the Arabs call *El-Maama*, a hiding place: the high rocks on each side of the valley are almost perpendicular; and the way to the grotto is by a terrace formed in the rock, which is very narrow. There are two entrances into it; we went by the farthest, which leads by a narrow passage into a very large grotto, the rock being supported by natural pillars: the top of it rises in several places like domes; the grotto is perfectly dry. There is a tradition, that the people of the country, to the number of 30,000, retired into this grotto to avoid a bad air. This place is so strong, that one would imagine it to be one of the strong holds of *En-gedi*, to which David and his men fled from Saul: and possibly it may be that very cave in which he cut off Saul's skirt; for David and his men might, with good ease, lie hid there and not be seen by him" (*Travels*, vol. ii. P. I. p. 41). **and Saul**. Ps 141:6. **to cover**. √88, Ge +15:15. √121S3Q, Jg +3:24. Jg *3:24mg. 2 K 18:27mg. **David**. Ps 57, title. 142, title.

4. **the men.** 1 S *26:8-11. Nu 31:16. 2 S 4:8. 1 K 12:10, 28. 2 Ch 10:10. 22:3. Jb 2:9. 31:31. **I will deliver.** ver. 10, 18. 1 S 23:7. 26:23. David's men urged very plausibly, that God had brought his enemy into his power, in order to fulfil his promises to him: yet they were greatly mistaken; as in reality the Lord intended to give David an opportunity of exercising faith, patience, and generous kindness; of showing the tendency and efficacy of his religious principles, the tenderness of his conscience, and the stedfastness of his loyalty; for the confutation of his accusers, a rebuke to Saul, and an example to all who read it. David had a promise of the kingdom, but no command to slay the reigning king, or promise that God would deliver Saul into his hand (Scott). See related note (1 K 13:18n) regarding circumstances not being a sure sign of God's leading or providence. **Saul's robe.** Heb. the robe which was Saul's. ver. 5. 1 S 20:40. 1 K 1:33.

5. **David's heart.** 2 S 12:9. *24:10. 2 K *22:19. 1 J *3:20, 21. **cut off.** 2 S 10:4.

6. **The Lord forbid.** 1 S *26:9-11. 2 S *1:14. 1 K 21:3. Jb *31:29, 30. Mt *5:44. Ro *12:14-21. *13:1, 2. 1 Th *5:15.

7. **stayed.** Heb. cut off. Le 1:17. Jg 14:16. Ps *7:3-5. Pr 31:8. Mt 5:44. Ro 12:17-21. **suffered.** ♪108A4, Ge +31:7. 1 S 25:33.

8. **My lord.** 1 S 26:17. **David stooped.** 1 S 20:41. 25:23, 24. Ge 17:3. Ex 20:12. Ro 13:7. 1 P 2:17.

9. **Wherefore hearest.** 1 S 26:19. Le 19:16. Ps 101:5. 141:6. Pr *16:28. 17:*4, 9. 18:8. 25:23. 26:20-22, 28. 29:12. Ec 7:21, 22. Ja 3:6.

10. **bade me.** ver. 4. 1 S 26:8. **mine eye.** ♪63K, Ge +37:13. **not put forth.** 1 T=5:19, ◐20. **the Lord's.** 1 S *26:9. Ps 105:15.

11. **my father.** 1 S 18:27. 2 K 5:13. Pr 15:1. **neither evil.** 1 S 26:18. Ps 7:3, 4. 35:7. Jn 15:25. **thou huntest.** 1 S 23:14, 23. 26:20. Jb 10:16. Ps 109:2-5. 140:11. La 4:18. Ezk 13:18. Mi 7:2. **soul.** Heb. *nephesh*, Ge +12:13.

12. **Lord judge between.** T#1510. 1 S 26:10, 23. Ge 16:5. 31:48-53. Jg 11:27. Jb 5:8. Ps 7:8, 9. 35:1. 43:1. 94:1. Ro 12:19. 1 P 2:23. Re 6:10. **but mine hand.** 1 S 26:10, 11.

13. **proverb.** or, simile. ♪138A, Ge +10:9. Nu +21:27. 23:7. **ancients.** or "eastern," as in Jb 18:20 (went before). Is 43:18. Ezk 10:19. 11:1. 38:17. 47:18. Jl 2:20. Zc 14:8. Ml 3:4. (*S#6931h). **Wickedness.** Mt *7:16-18. *12:33, 34. 15:19.

14. **the king.** 2 S 6:20. 1 K 21:7. **a dead dog.** ♪111, Ge +18:27. 1 S 17:43. 2 S 3:8. 9:8. 16:9. **a flea.** 1 S 26:20. Jg 8:1-3.

15. **be judge.** See on ver. 12. 2 Ch 24:22. Mi 1:2. **plead.** Ps 35:1. 43:1. 119:154. Mi *7:9. **deliver.** Heb. judge. 1 S 26:4.

16. **Is this.** 1 S 26:17. Jb 6:25. Pr 15:1. 25:11. Lk 21:15. Ac 6:10. **Saul lifted.** ♪144A12, Ge +22:13. Ge 33:4.

17. **Thou art.** 1 S *26:21. Ge *38:26. Ex 9:27. Ps *37:6. Mt *5:20. *27:4. **thou hast.** Mt *5:44. Ro *12:20, 21. **rewarded.** 1 S +1:22n (✛S#1580h).

18. **Lord.** ver. *10. 1 S 23:7. 26:23. **delivered me.** Heb. shut me up. 1 S +17:46mg. 23:12mg. 26:8mg. Jb 16:11mg. Ps *31:8.

19. **the Lord.** 1 S 23:21. 26:25. Jg 17:2. Ps 18:20. Pr 25:21, 22.

20. **I know well.** 1 S 20:30, 31. 23:17. 2 S 3:17, 18. Jb 15:25. Mt 2:3-6, 13, 16.

21. **Swear.** 1 S 20:14-17. Ge *21:23. 31:48, 53. He 6:16. **that thou.** 2 S 21:6-8.

22. **David and.** Pr 26:24, 25. Mt 10:16, 17. Jn 2:24. **the hold.** 1 S 23:29.

1 SAMUEL 25

Samuel dies, and is lamented and buried by all Israel; and David goes to Paran, 1. The character of Nabal, and of his wife Abigail, 2, 3. David sends to Nabal most respectfully requesting some provisions; but provoked by his answer, sets out to destroy him, 4-13. A servant warns Abigail, 14-17. She meets David with a present, and wisely pacifies him, 18-31. David blesses God for her interposition, and courteously dismisses her, 32-35. Nabal, hearing of the danger to which he had been exposed, is terrified, and dies, 36-38. David marries Abigail and also Ahinoam, 39-41. Michal is given to Phalit, 44.

1. A.M. 2944. B.C. 1060. An. Ex. Is. 431. **Samuel.** 1 S 28:3. **lamented.** Ge 50:11. Nu 20:29. Dt 34:8. Ac 8:2. **in his house.** 1 S 7:17. 1 K 2:34. 2 Ch 33:20. Is 14:18. **at Ramah.** 1 S 1:19. **the wilderness.** Ge 14:6. 21:21. Nu 10:12. 12:16. 13:3, 26. Ps 63:1. 120:5. 143:6.

2. **Maon.** 1 S 23:24. **possessions were.** or, business was. Ge 47:3. **Carmel.** Not the famous mount Carmel, in the north of Canaan, and in the tribe of Asher; but a city, on a mountain of the same name, in the south of Judah, which seems to have given name to the surrounding territory. Eusebius and Jerome inform us, that there was in their time a town called *Carmelia*, ten miles east from Hebron, where the Romans kept a garrison, whose position well agrees with this Carmel. **man.** Ge 26:13. 2 S 19:32. Ps 17:14. 73:3-7. Lk 16:19-25. **three thousand.** Ge 13:2. Jb 1:3. 42:12. **shearing.** This was a very ancient custom, and appears to have been always attended with festivity. The ancient Romans, however, used to pluck off the wool from the sheeps' backs; and hence a fleece was called *vellus, a vellendo*, from plucking it off. Pliny says, that in his time sheep were not shorn every where, but in some places the wool was still plucked off. Ge 38:13. 2 S 13:23, 24. **Carmel.** 1 S 30:5. Jsh 15:55.

3. **Nabal.** i.e. *folly; foolish*, *S#5037h. ver. 4, 5, 9, 10, 14, 19, 25, 25, 26, 34, 36, 36, 37, 38, 39, 39, 39. 27:3. 30:5. 2 S 2:2. 3:3. **Abigail.** i.e. *cause of delight; father of joy; source of joy*, *S#26h. ver. 14, 18, 23, 32, 36, 39, 40, 42. 27:3. 30:5. 2 S 2:2. 3:3. 17:25. 1 Ch 2:16, 17. 3:1. (1) The wife of Nabal of Carmel, and afterward of David. (2) A sister or a niece of Zeruiah and mother of Amasa, 2 S 17:25; 1 Ch 2:16, 17. **good.** Pr 14:1. 31:26, 30, 31. **understanding.** *S#7922h: 1 S 25:3. 1 Ch 22:12. 26:14. 2 Ch 2:12. 30:22. Ezr 8:18. Ne 8:8. Jb 17:4. Ps 111:10. Pr 3:4. 12:8. 13:15. 16:22. 19:11. 23:9. Da 8:25. **beautiful countenance.** Ge 29:17. **was churlish.** ver. 10, 11, 17. Ps 10:3. Is 32:5-7. **and he was.** *Wehoo calibbee*, literally, "and he was a Calebite;" but as the word *cailev* signifies *a dog*, the Septuagint has understood it as implying a man of a canine disposition, and translated it, *kai anthropos kunikos*, "and he was a doggish man." It is understood in the same way by the Syriac and Arabic.

4. **did shear.** Ge 38:13. 2 S 13:23.

5. **greet him**, etc. Heb. ask him in my name of peace. 1 S 17:22mg. Ge 43:23. Jg +18:15mg.

6. **liveth**. *108B, 1 S +10:24. 1 Th 3:8. 1 T 5:6. **Peace be both.** 2 S 18:28mg. 1 Ch 12:18. Ps 122:6, 7. Mt 10:12, 13. Lk 10:5, 6. Jn 14:27. 2 Th 3:16.

7. **thy shepherds.** In those times, and at the present day, wandering Arabs, under their several chiefs, think that they have a right to exact contributions of provisions, etc. wherever they come. But David, though he lived in the wilderness like the Arab emirs, had not adopted their manners: one of them, at the head of 600 men, would have demanded, from time to time, some provision or other present from Nabal's servants, for permitting them to feed at quiet; and would have driven them away from the watering place upon any dislike. David had done nothing of this kind; but had protected them against those who would. **we hurt.** Heb. we shamed. ver. 15, 16, 21. 1 S 20:34. 22:2. Is 11:6-9. Lk 3:14. Ph 2:15. 4:8.

8. **a good day.** Ne 8:10-12. Est 9:19. Ec 11:2. Mt 5:42. Lk 11:41. 14:12-14. **thy son.** 1 S 3:6. 24:11.

9. **ceased.** Heb. rested. or, became quiet. Ge 8:4. 2 K 2:15. 2 Ch 14:7.

10. **Who is David.** 1 S 20:30. 22:7, 8. Ex 5:2. Jg 9:28. 2 S 20:1. 1 K 12:16. Ps 14:1, 6. 73:7, 8. 123:3, 4. Is 32:5, 7. **there be.** 1 S 22:2. Ec 7:10. **many servants.** Ex 21:5.

11. **Shall I then.** ver. 3. 1 S 24:13. Dt 8:17. Jg 8:6. Jb 31:17. Ps 73:7, 8. 1 P 4:9. **flesh.** Heb. slaughter. Ge 43:16. **give it.** Ec 11:1, 2. Ga 6:10. **whom.** ver. 14, 15. Jn 9:29, 30. 2 C 6:9.

12. **came.** 2 S 24:13. Is 36:21, 22. He 13:17.

13. **Gird ye.** Jsh 9:14. Pr 14:29. 16:32. 19:2, 11. 25:8. Ja 1:19, 20. **David also.** 1 S 24:5, 6. Ro 12:19-21. **two hundred.** 1 S 30:9, 10, *21-24.

14. **railed on them.** Heb. flew upon them. 1 S 14:32. 15:19. Mk 15:29.

15. **very good.** ver. 7, 21. Ph 2:15. **hurt.** Heb. shamed. ver. 7.

16. **a wall.** Ex 14:22. Jb 1:10. Je 15:20. Zc 2:5.

17. **evil.** 1 S 20:7, 9, 33. 2 Ch 25:16. Est 7:7. **a son of Belial.** ver. 25. 1 S 2:12. Dt *13:13. +15:9. Jg +19:22. 2 S 23:6, 7. 1 K 21:10, 13. 2 Ch 13:7. **that a man cannot speak to him.** T#1853. ver. ◑√33. 1 S 20:32, 33. Jsh *22:21n. Jg 11:28. 2 S ◑*19:8n. 1 K 12:8, 13. 2 K ◑*5:13, 14. 2 Ch 10:8, 13. +*25:16. Jb ◑31:13. Ps *25:9, 12. Pr ◑*1:5. 8:33. *9:8, 9. √12:15. *13:+1, 10. 15:22. ◑17:10. ◑*18:13. +*19:20. 21:29. Ec 4:13. Je *36:25. Zp +*3:2. Mt +*7:6. 18:17. T 3:10, 11.

18. **made haste.** ver. 34. Ge 32:20. Nu 16:46-48. Pr 6:4, 5. 18:16. *21:14. Mt 5:25. **took two hundred loaves.** The Eastern bread is generally both thin and small; and answers to our cakes. Ge 32:13-20. 43:11-14. 2 S 17:28, 29. Pr 18:16. 21:14. **two bottles.** That is, two goat-skins' full. 1 S 1:24. Je ◑*13:12n. **five sheep.** Not one sheep to one hundred men. **clusters.** Heb. lumps. 1 S 30:12. 2 S 16:1. 1 Ch 12:40. Raisins dried in the sun. **cakes of figs.** Figs cured and then pressed together. 1 S 30:12. 2 K 20:7. 1 Ch 12:40. Is 38:21. Now all this provision was a matter of little worth; and had it been granted in the first instance, it would have perfectly satisfied David, and secured his good offices.

19. **Go.** Ge 32:16, 20. **But.** Pr 31:11, 12, 27.

20. **rode.** 2 K 4:24. **she came down.** David was coming down mount Paran; Abigail was coming down from Carmel.

21. **Surely.** ver. 13. Jb 30:8. Ps 37:8. Ep 4:26, 31. 1 Th 5:15. 1 P 2:21-23. 3:9. **he hath requited.** Ge 44:4. Ps 35:12. 38:20. *109:3-5. Pr *17:13. Je 18:20. Ro 12:21. 1 P 2:20. 3:17.

22. **So and more.** Nothing can justify this conduct of David, which was rash, unjust, and cruel in the extreme. David himself condemns it, and thanks God for being prevented from executing this evil (ver. 32-34). 1 S 3:17. 14:44. 20:13, 16. Ru *1:17. **if I leave.** ver. *34. **any that pisseth**, etc. This seems to have been a proverbial expression among the Israelites; and may with the utmost propriety be read "any male." 1 K *14:10. *16:11. *21:21. 2 K *9:8.

23. **lighted.** Jsh 15:18. Jg 1:14. **fell.** 1 S 20:41. 24:8.

24. **fell.** 2 K 4:37. Est 8:3. Mt 18:29. **Upon.** ver. 28. Ge 44:33, 34. 2 S 14:9. Phm 18, 19. **let thine.** Ge 44:18. 2 S 14:9, *12. **audience.** Heb. ears.

25. **regard.** Heb. lay it to his heart. 1 S +4:20mg. 2 S 13:33. Is 42:25. Ml 2:2. **man of Belial.** See on ver. 17, 26. **Nabal.** that is, *fool.* **folly.** Ge +34:7. Jsh +7:15. Jb 42:8. Pr 12:15. Ec 10:2, 3. Is +9:16 (*S#5039h).

26. **as the Lord liveth.** ver. 34. 1 S 20:3. 2 K 2:2, 4, 6. **and as thy.** See on 1 S 1:26. **soul.** Heb. *nephesh,* Ge +27:31. **the Lord hath withholden.** ver. 33. Ge *20:6. **from.** Ro 12:19, 20. **avenging thyself.** Heb. saving thyself. ver. 31, 33. Ps 18:47, 48. 44:3. Is 59:16. 63:5. Ro *12:19. **now let.** 2 S *18:32. Je 29:22. Da 4:19.

27. **blessing.** *or*, present. *108B, Ge +33:11. 1 S 30:26. Ge *33:11. 2 K 5:15. 18:31. 2 C 9:5. **follow.** Heb. walk at the feet of. ver. 42mg. Ex 11:8. Jg 4:10. 2 S 16:2.

28. **forgive.** ver. 24. **the Lord.** 1 S 15:28. 2 S 7:11, 16, 27. 1 K 9:5. 1 Ch *17:10, 25. Ps 89:29. **fighteth.** 1 S 17:47. 18:17. 2 S 5:2. 2 Ch 20:15. Ep 6:10, 11. **evil hath.** 1 S 24:6, 7, 11, 17. 1 K 15:5. Ps 119:1-3. Mt 5:16. Lk 23:41, 47.

29. **to pursue.** Ac 9:4. **soul.** Heb. *nephesh,* Ge +12:13. **bound.** The metaphors in this verse are derived from the consideration, that things of value are collected together, and often tied up in bundles, like sheaves of corn, to prevent their being scattered and lost; and that whatever is put into a sling is not intended to be preserved, but to be thrown away. 1 S 2:9. Ge 15:1. Dt 33:29. Ps 66:9. 116:15. Ml 3:17. Mt 10:29, 30. **bundle.** Ge 42:35. Mt 13:30. **with the Lord.** Jn *10:27-30. 14:19. 17:21, 23. Col *3:3, 4. 1 P *1:5. 1 J 5:20. **souls.** Ge +12:13. **sling out.** Je 10:18. **as out of the middle of a sling.** Heb. in the midst of the bow of a sling.

30. **according.** 1 S 13:14. 15:28. 23:17. Ps 89:20.

31. **grief.** Heb. staggering, *or* stumbling. Pr 5:12, 13. Ro 14:21. 2 C 1:12. **causeless.** *24E, Ge +30:33. **avenged.** ver. 33. 1 S 24:15. 26:23. 2 S 22:48. Ps 94:1. Ro 12:19. **remember.** ver. 40. Ge 40:14. Lk 23:42.

32. David overlooks the rich and seasonable present of Abigail, though pressed with hunger and wearied with travel; but her advice, which disarmed his rage, and calmed his revenge, draws forth these high and affectionate gratulations. These were his joyful and glorious trophies; not over his enemies, but over himself. **Blessed.** Ge 24:27. Ex 18:10. Ezr 7:27. Ps 41:

12, 13. 72:18. Lk 1:68. 2 C 8:16.

33. **blessed**. Ps *141:5. Pr *9:9. *17:10. 25:12. *27:21. *28:23. **which hast**. ver. 26. **avenging**. See on ver. 26, 31. 1 S *24:19. *26:9, 10. Le 19:18. Pr 20:22.

34. **kept me back**. ver. 26. **hasted**. ver. 18. 1 S 11:11. Jsh 10:6, 9. **there had**. See on ver. 22.

35. **Go up**. 1 S 20:42. 2 S 15:9. 2 K 5:19. Lk 7:50. 8:48. **I have hearkened**. Pr 16:32. 1 C 13:4, 5, 7. Ja 3:17. **accepted**. Ge 19:21. Jb 34:19. Ec 9:7. Ep 1:6.

36. **a feast**. 2 S 13:23. Est 1:3-7. Lk 14:12. **merry**. 2 S 13:28. 1 K 20:16. Pr *20:1. *23:29-35. Ec 2:2, 3. 10:19. Is 28:3, 7, 8. Je 51:57. Da 5:1-5. Na 1:10. Hab *2:15, 16. Lk 21:34. Ro 13:13. Ep *5:18. 1 Th 5:7, 8. **very drunken**. or, drunk unto excess. lit. unto might, as in 2 Ch 16:14. Ps 119:107. La 5:22. Da 8:8. **she told him**. ver. 19. Ps 112:5. Mt 10:16. Ep 5:15.

37. **had told him**. ver. 22, 34. **his heart died**. ✝102, Ge +2:14. Dt 28:28. Jb 15:21, 22. Pr 23:29-35. **as a stone**. lit. "hath become a stone;" compare the language in Ge 19:26. Ex 4:3. 7:9-12.

38. **the Lord**. ver. 33. 1 S 6:9. Ex 12:29. 2 K 15:5. 19:35. 2 Ch 10:15. Lk *12:20, 21. Ac 12:23.

39. **Blessed**. ver. 32. Jg 5:2. 2 S 22:47-49. Ps 58:10, 11. Re 19:1-4. **pleaded**. Pr 22:23. La 3:58-60. Mi 7:9. **kept his servant**. ver. 26, 34. Ho 2:6, 7. 2 C 13:7. 1 Th 5:23. 2 T 4:18. **hath returned**. 2 S 3:28, 29. 1 K 2:44. Est 7:10. Ps 7:16. Ezk 17:19. **to take her**. It is probable that David had heard that Saul, to cut off his pretensions to the throne, had married Michal to Phalti; and this justified him in taking Abigail, it not being then unlawful for a man to have several wives. This conduct of David's corresponds with the manner in which the Oriental princes generally form their matrimonial alliances. "The king of Abyssinia," says Mr. Bruce, "sends an officer to the house where the lady lives, who announces to her that it is the king's pleasure she should remove instantly to the palace. She then dresses herself in the best manner, and immediately obeys. Thenceforward he assigns her an apartment in the palace, and gives her a house elsewhere, in any part she chooses." Pr 18:22. 19:14. 31:10, 30.

40. **spake**. Ge +24:57. **David sent**. Ge 24:37, 38, 51.

41. **thine**. Ru 2:10, 13. Pr 15:33. 18:12. **to wash**. ✝171K2, Ex 23:4. Ge *18:4. 2 K *3:11. Jn *13:3-5. 1 T 5:10.

42. **Abigail**. Ge 24:61-67. Ps 45:10, 11, 14. **after her**. Heb. at her feet. ver. 27.

43. **Ahinoam**. i.e. *brother of pleasantness*. Compare 2 S 3:2, 3, where she seems to have been married before Abigail (Young). **Jezreel**. Jsh 15:56. 2 S 3:2. **both**. Ge ❍2:24. +4:19. 32:22. Mt 19:5, 8. **his wives**. 1 S 27:3. 30:5. 2 S 5:13-16.

44. **But Saul**. Rather, "For Saul," etc. as the particle *wav* frequently signifies; this being the cause why David took another wife. **Michal**. 1 S 18:20, 27. **Phalti**. i.e. *escape of God*, ✲S#6406h. Nu +13:9h, Palti. 2 S 3:14, 15, Phaltiel. **Laish**. i.e. *a lion*, ✲S#3919h. Jg 18:7, 14, 27, 29. 2 S *3:15. Is 10:30. (1) Father of Phalti, 1 S 25:44; called Phaltiel in 2 S 3:15, to whom King Saul gave David's wife Michal. (2) A town in the north border of Canaan, Jg 18:7. It is called Leshem in Jsh 19:47, and was afterwards called Dan. (3) The

Laish mentioned in Is 10:30 is probably not the same place as number 2. Its situation is uncertain. **Gallim**. i.e. *billows*, ✲S#1554h. Is 10:30. This town appears to have been situated in the tribe of Benjamin, as it is mentioned in Is 10:30 with Michmash, Geba, etc.

1 SAMUEL 26

Saul, informed by the Ziphites, pursues David to Hachilah, 1-4. David by night comes to Saul's tent, with Abishai, whom he hinders from slaying Saul; but he takes away his spear and cruse, 5-12. David at a distance reproves Abner's negligence, protests his own innocency, and expostulates with Saul, 13-20. Saul owns his sin, and returns home, 21-25.

1. **Ziphites**. Jsh 15:24, 55. **Doth not**. ver. 3. 1 S 23:19. Ps 54, title.

2. **Saul arose**. 1 S 23:23-25. 24:17. Ps 38:12. 140:4-9. **three thousand**. 1 S 24:2.

3. **Hachilah**. ver. 1. 1 S 23:19.

4. **sent out spies**. Jsh 2:1. Mt 10:16.

5. **Abner**. 1 S 9:1. 14:50, 51. 17:55. 2 S 2:8, etc. 3:7, 8, 27, 33-38. 1 Ch 9:39. **trench**. *or*, midst of his carriages. ver. 7. 1 S 17:20. The word *maugal* never signifies a ditch or rampart, but a chariot or wagon way. Nor does it seem to denote a ring of carriages, as Buxtorf and others interpret the word; for it is not probable that Saul would encumber his army with baggage in so rapid a pursuit, nor that so mountainous a country was practicable for waggons. It appears simply to mean here, the circular encampment (from *agal, round*) which these troops formed, in the midst of which, as being the place of honor, Saul reposed. An Arab camp, D'Arvieux informs us, is always circular, when the disposition of the ground will permit, the prince being in the middle, and the troops at a respectful distance around him. Add to which, their lances are fixed near them in the ground all the day long, ready for action.

6. **Ahimelech**. i.e. *brother of the king*. **Hittite**. Ge 10:15. 15:20. 2 S 11:6, 21, 24. 12:9. 23:39. **to Abishai**. i.e. *father of presents; generous*, ✲S#52h. ver. 7, 8, 9. 2 S 2:18, 24. 3:30. 10:10, 14. 16:9, 11. ◐18:2, *5, 12. 19:21. 20:6, 10. 21:17. 23:18. 1 Ch 2:16. 11:20. 18:12. 19:11, 15. **Zeruiah**. i.e. perhaps a *cleft*, as in 2 S 2:13, 18. 3:39. 8:16. 14:1. 16:9, 10. 17:25. 18:2. 19:21. 1 Ch *2:15, 16. **Joab**. i.e. *whose father is Jehovah*, ✲S#3097h. 2 S 2:13, 14, 14, 18, 22, 24, 26, 27, 28, 30, 32. 3:22, 23, 23, 24, 26, 27, 29, 30, 31. 8:16. 10:7, 9, 13, 14. 11:1, 6, 6, 7, 11, 14, 16, 17, 18, 22, 25. 12:26, 27. 14:1, 2, 3, 19, 19, 20, 21, 22, 22, 23, 29, 30, 31, 32, 33. 17:25, 25. 18:2, 2, 5, 10, 11, 12, 14, 15, 16, 16, 20, 21, 22, 29. 19:1, 5, 13. 20:7, 8, 9, 9, 10, 10, 11, 11, 11, 13, 15, 16, 17, 20, 21, 22, 22, 23. 23:18, 24, 37. 24:2, 3, 4, 4, 9. 1 K 1:7, 19, 41. 2:5, 22, 28, 28, 28, 29, 30, 31, 33. 11:15, 16, 21. 1 Ch 2:16. 4:14. 11:6, 8, 20, 26, 39. 18:15. 19:8, 10, 15. 20:1, 1. 21:2, 3, 4, 4, 5, 6. 26:28. 27:7, 24, 34. Ezr 2:6. 8:9. Ne 7:11. Ps 60:t. (1) A son of Zeruiah, the sister of David, and the "chief and captain," of his army, 1 Ch 11:6. (2) A grandson of Kenaz, 1 Ch 4:14. (3) One whose descendants returned from Babylon, Ezr 2:6; 8:9. (4) A descendant of Caleb, the son of Hur, 1 Ch 2:54. **Who will go**. 1 S 14:6, 7. Jg 7:10, 11.

7. **sleeping**. 1 Th 5:2, 3. **bolster**. or, pillow. ver. 11, 16. 1 S 19:13, 16. Ge 28:11, 18. 1 K 19:6mg.

8. **God**. ver. 23. 1 S 23:14. 24:*4n, 18, 19. Jsh 21:44. Jg 1:4. 1 K 13:18n. **delivered**. Heb. shut up. 1 S +17:46mg. 24:18. Dt 32:30. Ps 31:8. Ro 11:32mg. Ga 3:22, 23. **the second time**. Na 1:9.

9. **who can stretch**. 1 S *24:6, 7. 2 S *1:14, 16. Ps *105:15. **anointed**. 1 S 24:6, +*10. 1 T ◑5:19, 20.

10. **the Lord liveth**. 1 S 24:15. 25:26, 38. Ps 94:1, 2, 23. Lk 18:7. Ro 12:19. Re 18:8. **shall smite**. 1 S 25:38. Ps 10:15, 17, 18. 140:9-11. **his day**. Ge 47:29. Dt 31:14. Jb 7:1. 14:5, 14. Ps 37:10, *13. Ec 3:2. He 9:27. **he shall descend**. 1 S *31:6. Dt 32:35.

11. **that I should**. 1 S 24:6, 12. 2 S 1:14, 16.

12. **So David**. ver. 7. 1 S 24:4. **a deep sleep**. Ge 2:21. 15:12. Est 6:1. Is 29:10.

13. **the top**. 1 S 24:8. Jg 9:7. David, by retiring to a place of safety before he called to Abner, seems to have manifested more distrust of Saul than he had done on a former occasion. Yet he desired that Saul and all Israel should be informed of his conduct at this time. Abner and his soldiers, by neglecting to guard Saul when he slept, had exposed his life, and merited to be treated as his enemies, though he confided in them as friends; for, although their sound sleep was undoubtedly supernatural, yet there might be a neglect of placing sentinels, arising from contempt of David's small company. Saul also deemed David his enemy, though David had before spared and protected his life.

15. **Art**. ſ60B, Ge +20:16. **there came**. ver. 8.

16. **worthy to die**. Heb. the sons of death. ſ108B, 1 S +20:31. 1 S 20:31mg. 2 S *12:5mg. 19:28mg. 1 K 2:26mg. Ps 79:11mg. 102:20mg. Ep 2:3. **Lord's anointed**. ver. 9, 11. 1 S 24:6.

17. **Is this thy**. 1 S 24:8, 16.

18. **Wherefore**. 1 S 24:9, 11-14. Ps 7:3-5. 35:7. 69:4. **what have I**. 1 S 17:29. Jn 8:46. 10:32. 18:23.

19. **let my lord**. 1 S 25:24. Ge 44:18. **stirred**. 1 S 16:14-23. 18:10. 2 S 16:11. 24:1. 1 K 22:22. 1 Ch 21:1. **accept**. Heb. smell. Ge 8:21. Le 26:31. Ps 119:1-8. **cursed**. Pr 6:16-19. 30:10. Ga 1:8, 9. 5:12. 2 T 4:14. **they have driven**. Dt 4:27, 28. Jsh 22:25-27. Ps 42:1, 2. 120:5. Is 60:5. Ro 14:15. **abiding**. Heb. cleaving. 1 S 2:36. **the inheritance**. Dt 32:9. 2 S 14:16. 20:19. Ps 42:2. 84:1, 2.

20. **let not my**. 1 S 2:9. 25:29. Ge 4:10. **the king**. 1 S 24:14. Mt 26:47, 55. **a flea**. 1 S 24:14. *Parosh*, (in Arabic *borghooth*, Syriac, *poorthano*), the well-known little contemptible and troublesome insect, the flea, seems to be so called from its agility in leaping and skipping, from *para*, "free," and *raash*, "to leap, bound." David, by comparing himself to this insect, seems to import, that while it would cost Saul much pains to catch him, he would obtain but very little advantage from it. **a partridge**. Je 17:11. *Korai* certainly denotes the partridge, which is called in Arabic *kirua*. It seems to be so called from the cry or *cur* which it utters when calling its young.

21. **I have sinned**. 1 S 15:*24, 30. *24:17. Ex 9:27. Nu 22:34. Mt 27:4. **I will no**. 1 S 27:4. **my soul**. Heb. *nephesh*, Ge +12:13. ſ121A7, Ge +9:5. **was precious**. ver. 24. 1 S 18:30. 2 K 1:13, 14. Ps 49:8. 72:14. 116:15. 139:17. **played the fool**. Ge 31:28. **have erred**. Le 4:13. Mk *12:24, 27.

23. **Lord**. ſ66, Ge +9:3. **render**. 1 K 8:32. Ne 13:14. Ps 7:8, 9. 18:20-26. **I would not**. ver. 9, 11. 1 S 24:6, 7.

24. **as thy life**. Heb. *nephesh*, soul, Ge +44:30. Ps 18:25. Mt 5:7. 7:2. **mine eyes**. Ps 17:8. 33:18, 19. **my life**. Heb. *nephesh*, soul, Ge +44:30. **let him deliver**. T#1728. Ge 48:16. Dt *4:29-31. Ps 18, title, 48. 25:20-22. 34:17, 18. 144:2. Ac 14:22. 2 C 1:9, 10. 2 Th 3:2. Re 7:14.

25. **Blessed**. 1 S 24:19. Nu 24:9, 10. **prevail**. Ge 32:28. Is 54:17. Ho 12:4. Ro 8:35, 37. **So David**. 1 S 24:22. Pr 26:25.

1 SAMUEL 27

David escapes to Gath, and is received by Achish, 1-3. Saul seeks him no more, 4. He asks Ziklag of Achish, 5-7. He invades the adjacent countries, and disingenuously leads Achish to suppose that he warred against Judah, 8-12.

1. **A.M. 2946. B.C. 1058. An. Ex. Is. 433. And David**. 1 S 16:1, 13. 23:17. 25:30. Ps 116:11. Pr 13:12. Is 40:27-31. 51:12. Mt 14:31. Mk 4:40. 2 C 7:5. **I shall**. This was a rash conclusion: God had caused him to be anointed king of Israel, and promised his accession to the throne, and had so often interposed in his behalf, that he was authorised to believe the very reverse. 2 S ◑22:1. **perish**. Heb. be consumed. 1 S 26:10. **there is nothing**. 1 S 22:5. Ex 14:12. Nu 14:3. Pr *3:5, 6. Is 30:15, 16. La 3:26, 27. **into the land**. ver. 10, 11. 1 S 21:10-15. 28:1, 2. 29:2-11. 30:1-3. **despair**. Jb 6:26. Ec 2:20. Is 57:10. Je 2:25mg. 18:12. **so shall**. 1 K 19:2, 3. Ps +√34:4. Pr +*22:3. 29:25. He *13:5, 6.

2. **David**. This measure of David's, in uniting himself to the enemies of his God and people, was highly blameable; was calculated to alienate the affections of the Israelites; and led to equivocation, if not downright falsehood. **the six hundred**. 1 S 25:13. 30:8. **Achish**. 1 S 21:10. 1 K 2:40. **Maoch**. i.e. *bruising; breast band*, *S#4582h.

3. **with his two**. 1 S 25:3, 18-35, 42, 43. 30:5. Ge +4:19. **Jezreelitess**. *S#3159h. 1 S 30:5. 2 S 2:2. 3:2. 1 Ch 3:1. **Carmelitess**. *S#3762h. 1 Ch 3:1.

4. **he sought**. 1 S 26:21.

5. **some town**. Ge 46:34. 2 C 6:17.

6. **Ziklag**. *Ziklag* was at first given to the tribe of Judah, but was afterwards ceded to that of Simeon; but as it bordered on the Philistines, if they had ever been expelled, they had retaken it. Eusebius simply says it was situated in the south of Canaan. 1 S 30:1, 14. Jsh 15:31. 19:5. 2 S 1:1. 1 Ch 4:30. 12:1, 20. Ne 11:28. **unto this day**. 1 S 6:18. Ge +19:38. Dt +29:4, 28. Jsh +4:9. Jg 1:21, 26.

7. **the time**. Heb. the number of days. Ps 94:14, 17, 18. Is +10:19mg. **country**. ſ171S1, Ge +14:7. **a full year**. Heb. a year of days. ſ171T2C, Ge +24:55. 1 S 29:3. Ge +*24:55mg.

8. **A.M. 2948. B.C. 1056. An. Ex. Is. 435. the Geshurites**. Dt 3:14. Jsh 13:2, 11, 13. 2 S 3:3. 10:6. 13:37, 38. 14:23, 32. 15:8. 1 Ch 2:23. **Gezrites**. or, Gerzites. These people seem to be the Gerrhenians (2 Mac 13:34) whose chief city, Gerrha, is mentioned by Strabo as lying between Gaza and Pelusium in Egypt. Inhabitants of Gezer (Young). *S#1511h, only here. Jsh 10:33. 12:12. 16:3, 10. 21:21. Jg 1:29. 2 S 5:25. 1 K 9:15-17. 1 Ch 6:67. 7:28. 14:16. 20:4. **the Amalekites**. Ex 17:16. Jsh 16:10. Jg 1:29. 1 K 9:15-17. **of old**. Heb. *olam*,

Ge +6:4. **as thou goest.** 1 S 15:7, 8. 30:1. Ge 25:18. Ex 17:14-16.

9. **left neither.** 1 S 15:7. Ge 16:7. 25:18. Ex 15:22. 17:14. Le 27:28. Dt *7:2. 25:19. Ps 139:21, 22. **and the camels.** 1 S 15:3. Dt 25:17-19. Jsh 6:21.

10. **Whither.** etc. **or,** Did you not make a road. 1 S 23:27. **And David.** 1 S 21:2. Ge 27:19, 20, 24. Jsh 2:4-6. 2 S 17:20. Ps 119:29, 163. Pr 29:25. Ga 2:11-13. Ep 4:25. **Against.** David here meant the Geshurites, and Gezrites, and Amalekites, which people occupied that part of the country which lies to the south of Judah. But Achish, as was intended, understood him in a different sense, and believed that he had attacked his own countrymen. David's answer, therefore, though not an absolute falsehood, was certainly an equivocation intended to deceive, and therefore incompatible with that sense of truth and honor which became him as a prince, and a professor of true religion. From these, and similar passages, we may observe the strict impartiality of the Sacred Scriptures. They present us with the most faithful delineation of human nature; they exhibit the frailties of kings, priests, and prophets, with equal truth; and examples of vice and frailty, as well as of piety and virtue, are held up, that we may guard against the errors to which the best men are exposed. **the Jerahmeelites.** *S#3397h. 1 S 30:29h. 1 Ch 2:9, 25. **Kenites.** 1 S 15:6. Nu 24:21. Jg 1:16. 4:11. 5:24.

11. **Lest.** 1 S 22:22. Pr 12:19. 29:25.

12. **believed. or,** remained steadfast. Ge 15:6. **utterly to abhor.** Heb. to stink. 1 S 13:4. Ge 34:30. **for ever.** Heb. *olam,* Ex +12:24. **or,** age-during. That is, during his life-time, as in Dt 15:17. Jn √6:54n.

1 SAMUEL 28

Achish, preparing war against Israel, places confidence in David, 1, 2. Saul, after having destroyed those who had familiar spirits, at length, fearing the Philistines and being forsaken by God, goes to the witch of Endor and engages to indemnify her, 3-10. She, by his desire, calls up Samuel, who predicts his ruin, 11-19. Saul falls down in despair; but, being prevailed upon to take food, he returns to his army, 20-25.

1. **that the.** 1 S 7:7. 13:5. 17:1. 29:1. **Philistines.** Jg 3:1-4. **thou shalt go.** 1 S 27:12. 29:2, 3.

2. **Surely.** 1 S 27:10. 2 S 16:16-19. Ro 12:9.

3. **Samuel.** 1 S 25:1. Is 57:1, 2. **Ramah.** 1 S 1:19. **even.** √93A, Ge +1:26. lit. in Ramah and his own city. By Hendiadys, signifying "in Ramah, even in his own city." **put away.** ver. 9. Ex 22:18. Le 19:31. 20:6, 27. Dt +*18:10, 11. Ac 16:16-19. **familiar spirits.** Le 19:31. 20:6, 27. **wizards.** Le 19:31. 20:6, 27.

4. **Shunem.** Jsh 19:18. 1 K 1:3. 2 K 4:8. **Gilboa.** i.e. *bubbling up of a fountain,* *S#1533h. 1 S 31:1, 8. 2 S 1:6, 21. 21:12. 1 Ch 10:1, 8.

5. **he was afraid.** 1 S 17:11. Jb 15:21. 18:11. Ps 48:5, 6. 73:19. Pr 10:24. Is 7:2. 21:3, 4. 24:17. 57:20, 21. Da 5:6. **trembled.** 1 S 4:13. 14:15. Ge 27:33mg. Jb 37:1.

6. **enquired.** 1 S 14:37. 1 Ch 10:14. Pr 1:27, 28. La 2:9. Ezk 20:1-3, 31. Jn 9:31. Ja 4:3. **by dreams.** T#1768. ver. 15. Ge 20:5-7. 28:12-15. 46:2-4. Nu 12:6. 1 K 3:11-15. 2 K 9:1-3. Jb 33:14-16. Je +*23:28n. Mt 1:20. **by Urim.** T#1779. Ex 28:30. Nu 27:21. Dt 33:8.

The Lord answered him not by Urim and Thummim which were in the ephod, which Saul by his cruelty to the priests had lost, 1 S 23:6 (Matthew Poole). **by prophets.** T#1776. ver. 15. Nu 12:6. Dt 5:27, 28. Jg 4:2-6. 6:7, 8. 2 S 24:10-12, 17-19. 1 K 21:27-29. 2 K 19:15, 16, 20. 20:2-5. 2 Ch 20:3-6, 14, 15. Ps 74:9. La 2:9. Ezk 20:1-3. Mi 3:6, 7.

7. **Seek me.** 2 K 1:2, 3. 6:33. Is *8:19, 20. La 3:25, 26. Hab 2:3. **a familiar spirit.** ver. 3. Dt +*18:11. 2 Ch 33:6. Is 19:3. 29:4. Ac 16:6. **that I may.** Le 19:31. 1 Ch 10:13. Is 8:19. **En-dor.** *En-dor,* a city of Manasseh, was situated in the plain of Jezreel; and Eusebius and Jerome inform us, that it was a great town in their days, four miles south from mount Tabor, near Nain, towards Scythopolis. This agrees with Maundrell, who says, that not many miles eastward of Tabor, you see mount Hermon, at the foot of which is seated Nain and *Endor*; and Burckhardt says, that in two hours and a half from Nazareth, towards Scythopolis or Bisan, they came to the village of Denouny, near which are the ruins of *Endor*; where the witch's grotto is shown. Jsh 17:11. Ps 83:10.

8. **disguised.** Ge +27:16. 1 K 14:2, 3. 20:38. 22:30, 34. 2 Ch 18:29. Jb 24:13-15. 30:18. Je 23:24. Jn *3:19, 20. **by night.** 1 S 14:36. 26:7. 31:12. To save time, and that he might not be known (Young). **I pray thee, divine.** Dt *18:10, 11, 14. 1 Ch *10:13, 14. Is *8:19. Ezk 21:21, 23, 29. **bring me.** ver. 15.

9. **how he hath.** See on ver. 3. **wherefore.** 2 S 18:13. 2 K 5:7. **snare.** Dt 12:30. Ps *9:16. 38:12. 109:11. **life.** Heb. *nephesh,* soul, Ge +44:30.

10. **sware.** 1 S 14:39. 19:6. Ge 3:5. Ex 20:7. Dt *18:10-12. 2 S 14:11. Mt 26:72. Mk 6:23. **no punishment.** lit. *iniquity.* Ge 4:13. 15:15. 19:15. 44:16. 2 K 7:9.

11. **bring up.** Out of Sheol, the state of the dead, supposed to be beneath the ground (Young).

12. **the woman saw.** Before she had time to commence her incantations (Young). **loud voice.** From terror, as the word implies, and for help (Young). Her surprise reveals her duplicity, and the falsehood of all pretended communication with the dead. For had what she expected to happen transpired, it would not have occasioned such surprise and terror. This circumstance also proves that this was a real appearance of Samuel, not a demonic imitation. This incident, though unique in Scripture, coupled with the decided belief in necromancy on the part of the Hebrews, and God's forthright commands against its practice, shows that the Hebrews believed that the dead have a conscious existence after death, and Saul's experience with Samuel clearly proves this belief is correct. Is 14:9. Ezk 32:21n. Mt 12:40. Lk +*16:23. **deceived me.** ✛S#7411h: 1 S 19:17. Ge 29:25. Jsh 9:22. 2 S 19:26. 1 Ch 12:17 (betray). Pr 26:19. La 1:19. **thou art Saul.** ver. 3. 1 K 14:5.

13. **gods ascending.** Ex 4:16. 22:28. Ps 82:6, 7. Jn 10:34, 35. i.e. A god, a divine person, glorious, and full of majesty and splendor, exceeding not only mortal men, but common ghosts. She uses the plural number, *gods,* either after the manner of the Hebrew language, which commonly uses that word of one person; or after the language and custom of the heathens. But the whole coherence shows that it was but one. For Saul desired but one, ver. 11, and he inquires and the woman answers only of one, ver. 14 (Matthew Poole). The Hebrew term *elohim* is sometimes, as here, used

of human judges (Ps 82:6n).

14. **What form is he of**? Heb. What is his form? Jg 8:18mg. Is 52:14. 53:2. La 4:8. **cometh up**. Ec ◐12:7. Is ◐57:2. Lk ◐16:22. Re ◐14:13. **a mantle**. or, upper robe. 1 S 15:27. 24:4, 11. 2 K 2:8, 13, 14. Zc 13:4. **and bowed himself**. Re 19:10. 22:8, 9. Since the spirit received without objection worship from Saul, it must have been an evil spirit, argues Matthew Poole.

15. **Why hast**. ver. 8, 11. **disquieted**. Jb 9:6. 12:6 (provoke). Is 13:13 (shake). 14:16. 23:11. Je 50:34. **I am sore**. Pr 5:11-13. 14:14. Je 2:17, 18. **distressed**. 2 S 24:14. **the Philistines**. ver. 4. **God**. 1 S 16:13, 14. *18:12. Jg 16:20. Ps 51:11. Ho 9:12. Mt 25:41. **answereth**. ver. 6. 1 S 23:2, 4, 9, 10. **prophets**. Heb. the hand of prophets. ver. 17. **therefore**. Lk 16:23-26.

16. **Wherefore**. Jg 5:31. 2 K 6:27. Ps 68:1-3. Re 18:20, 24. 19:1-6. **and is become**. Ps 139:20. La 2:5. Mi 5:14.

17. **to him**. or, for himself. The LXX. read *soi*, and the Vulgate *tibi*, "to thee"; which is the reading of five of Dr. Kennicott's and De Rossi's MSS., as well as both the Bibles printed in Venice in 1518, where we read *lecha*, "to thee," for *lo*, "to him;" and as the words are spoken *to* Saul, this seems to be evidently the correct reading. Pr 16:4. **as he spake**. 1 S 13:13, 14. 15:27-29. **me**. Heb. mine hand. ver. 15. **thy neighbor**. 1 S 15:28. 16:13. 24:20. **hath rent**. 1 S 15:28. 1 K 11:31.

18. **obeyedst**. 1 S 13:9. 15:9, 23-26. 1 K *20:42. 1 Ch 10:13. Je 48:10. **wrath**. ∫121C1C, Ps +79:6. **hath the Lord**. Ps 50:21, 22.

19. **the Lord**. 1 S 12:25. 31:1-6. 1 K *22:20, 28. **and tomorrow**. Matthew Poole notes that this word may be understood not of the very next day, but indefinitely of some short time after this, as it is taken in Ex 13:14mg. Dt 6:20mg. Jsh 4:6mg, 21mg. There is considerable diversity of opinion, both among learned and pious men, relative to this appearance to Saul. But the most probable opinion seems to be, that Samuel himself did actually appear to Saul, not by the power of enchantment, but by the appointment and especial mercy of God, to warn this infatuated monarch of his approaching end, that he might be reconciled with his Maker. There is not the smallest intimation of chicanery or satanic influence given in the text; but on the contrary, from the plain and obvious meaning of the language employed, it is perfectly evident that it was *Samuel himself*, (*Shemooel hoo*), as it is expressed in ver. 14. Indeed the very soul of Samuel seems to breathe in his expressions of displeasure against the disobedience and wickedness of Saul; while the awful prophetic denunciations which accordingly came to pass, were such as neither human nor diabolical wisdom could forsee, and which could only be known to God himself, and to those to whom he chose to reveal them. Ex 9:18. Je 28:16, 17. Da 5:25-28. Mt 26:24. Ac 5:5, 9, 10. **with me**. 2 S ◐7:14, 15. +*12:23. Is 14:9-11. Lk 23:43. **deliver**. Da 5:25-28.

20. **fell straightway**. Heb. made haste and fell with the fulness of his stature. 1 S 9:2. 10:23. Ge 48:19. 2 S 8:2. **sore afraid**. ver. 5. 1 S 25:37. Jb 15:20-24. 26:2. Ps 50:21, 22. **no strength**. 1 S 30:4. Le 26:20. 2 K 19:3. 2 Ch *14:11. *20:12. **bread**. ∫17I18, Ge +3:19.

21. **I have put**. 1 S 19:5. Jg 12:3. Jb 13:14. **life**. Heb. *nephesh*, soul, Ge +44:30. **hand**. 1 S 19:5. Jg

12:3. Jb 13:14. 1 C 15:30, 31.

22. **morsel of bread**. 1 S 2:36. Ge 18:5. Jg 19:5. 2 S 12:3mg. 1 K 17:11. Jb 31:17. Pr 17:1. 23:8. 28:21. Ezk 13:19.

23. **I will**. 1 K 21:4. Pr 25:20. **compelled him**. 2 S 13:25, 27. 2 K 4:8. 5:23. Lk 14:23. 24:29. Ac 16:15. 2 C 5:14. **bed**. 1 S 19:13, 15, 16. Est 1:6.

24. **a fat calf**. Ge 18:7, 8. Je 46:21. Am 6:4. Ml 4:2. Lk 15:23. **flour**. 1 S 1:24. Ge 18:6. Nu 5:15. Jg 6:19. 2 S 17:28. 1 K 4:22. 17:12, 14, 16. 2 K 4:41. 1 Ch 12:40. Is 47:2. Ho 8:7. **kneaded**. Ge 18:6. 2 S 13:8. Je 7:18. Ho 7:4.

25. **that night**. ver. 8.

1 SAMUEL 29

David attends Achish, which offends the lords of the Philistines, 1-5. Achish dismisses him with commendations, 6-11.

1. **the Philistines**. 1 S 28:1, 2. **Aphek**. 1 S 4:1. Jsh 19:30. 1 K 20:26, 30. **Jezreel**. 1 S 28:4. Jsh 17:16. 19:18. Jg 6:33. 1 K 18:45, 46. 21:1, 13. 2 K 9:36. Ho 1:4-11.

2. **the lords**. ver. 6, 7. 1 S 5:8-11. 6:4. Jsh 13:3. Jg 16:5, 30. **but David**. 1 S 28:1, 2.

3. **Is not this David**. These words seem to mark no definite time; and may be understood thus: "Is not this David, the servant of Saul the king of Israel, who has been with me for a considerable time?" **these days**. 1 S 27:7. **found**. 1 S 25:28. Da 6:5. Jn 19:6. Ro 12:17. 1 P 3:16.

4. **Make this fellow**. The princes reasoned wisely, according to the common practice of mankind; and it was well for David that they were such good politicians: it was ordered by a gracious Providence that they refused to let David go with them to this battle, in which he must have been either an enemy to his country, or false to his friends and to his trust. Had he fought for the Philistines, he would have fought against God and his country; and had he in the battle gone over to the Israelites, he would have deceived and become a traitor to the hospitable Achish. God therefore delivered him from such disgrace; and by the same kind Providence he was sent back to rescue his wives, and the wives and children of his people, from captivity. 1 S 14:21. 1 Ch 12:19. Lk 16:8.

5. **Is not**. 1 S 18:6, 7. 21:11. Pr 27:14.

6. **the Lord**. 1 S 20:3. 28:10. Dt 10:20. Is 65:16. Je 12:16. **thou hast**. Mt 5:16. 1 P 2:12. 3:16. **thy going**. Nu 27:17. 2 S 3:25. 2 K 19:27. Ps 121:8. **I have not**. ver. 3. **the lords favor**, etc. Heb. thou art not good in the eyes of the lords. Ge 16:6. Jsh +22:30mg.

7. **displease**. Heb. do not evil in the eyes of the lords. Nu 22:34.

8. **But what have**. 1 S 12:3. 17:29. 20:8. 26:18. **with**. Heb. before. **that I may not**. 1 S 28:2. 2 S 16:18, 19. Ps 34:13, 14. Mt 6:13.

9. **as an angel**. 2 S 14:17, 20. 19:27. Ga 4:14. **the princes**. ver. 4.

10. **now rise**. 1 S 30:1, 2. Ge 22:14. Ps 37:23, 24. 1 C √10:13. 2 P 2:9.

11. **And the Philistines**. See on ver. 1. Jsh 19:18. 2 S 4:4. **Jezreel**. Jezreel, or Esdraelon, was a city of Issachar, afterwards celebrated as the residence of the kings of Israel, delightfully situated in the extensive and fertile plain of the same name, which extends from

Scythopolis or Bethshan on the east to Mount Carmel on the west. Eusebius and Jerome inform us, that it was in their time a place of considerable consequence, lying between Scythopolis on the east and Legio on the west; and the latter (on Ho 1) informs us that it was pretty near Maximianopolis. The Jerusalem Itinerary places it ten miles west from Scythopolis; and William of Tyre says it was called *Little Gerinum* in his time, and that there was a fine fountain in it, whose waters fell into the Jordan near Scythopolis. See ver. 1.

1 SAMUEL 30

David on his return finds that the Amalekites had burnt Ziklag, and carried captive the women and children, 1-3. David and his men are greatly distressed, 4, 5; but inquiring of God, he is encouraged to pursue them, 6-10. He obtains intelligence from an Egyptian slave, 11-15. He smites them, recovers all, and takes much spoil, 16-20. His law to divide the spoil equally between them that fight and them that keep the stuff, 21-25. He sends presents to his friends, 26-31.

1. **were come**. 1 S 29:11. 2 S 1:2. **on the third**. This was the third day after he had left the Philistine army at Aphek, from which place, Calmet supposes, Ziklag was distant more than thirty leagues. **the Amalekites**. 1 S 15:7. 27:8-10. Ge 24:62. Jsh 11:6.

2. **slew not**. ver. 19. 1 S 27:11. Jb 38:11. Ps 76:10. Is 27:8, 9.

3. **burned**. Ps 34:19. He 12:6. 1 P 1:6, 7. Re 3:9.

4. **lifted up**. ℐ144A12, Ge +22:13. 1 S 4:13. 11:4. Ge 37:33-35. Nu 14:1, 39. Jg 2:4. 21:2. Ezr 10:1.

5. **two wives**. 1 S 1:2. 25:42, 43. 27:3. Ge +4:19. 2 S 2:2. 3:2, 3. **wife**. ℐ11, Ge +2:23. **Carmelite**. *S#3761h. 2 S 2:2. 3:3. 23:35. 1 Ch 11:37.

6. **was greatly**. Ge *32:7. Ps *25:17. 42:7. *116:3, 4, 10. 2 C *1:8, 9. *4:8. *7:5. **the people**. Ex *17:4. Nu 14:10. Ps 62:9. Mt *21:9. *27:22. **soul**. Heb. *nephesh*, Ge +34:3. **grieved**. Heb. bitter. 1 S *1:10mg. Jg *18:25mg. 2 S *17:8mg. 2 K *4:27mg. **David**. Jb *13:15. Ps *18:6. *26:1, 2. *27:1-3. *34:1-8. *40:1, 2. *42:5, 10, 11. *56:3, 4, 11. *62:1, 5, 8. 0:4, 5. 118:8-13. Pr *18:10. Is *25:4. *37:14-20. Je *16:19. Hab *3:17, 18. Ro *4:18. *8:31. 2 C *1:6, 9, 10. 2 T 1:15. 4:16, 17. He *13:6.

7. **Abiathar**. 1 S 22:20, 21. 23:2-9. 1 K 2:26. Mk 2:26. **bring me hither the ephod**. T#1769. 1 S 23:9-12. ◐28:6. Nu 27:2.

8. **enquired**. 1 S 23:2, 4, 10-12. Jg 20:18, 23, 28. 2 S 5:19, 23. Pr *3:5, 6. **he answered him**. 1 S 14:37. 28:6, 15, 16. Nu 27:21. Ps 50:15. 91:15.

9. **the six hundred**. 1 S 25:13. 1 Ch 12:21. **brook Besor**. i.e. *cold water; tidings,* *S#1308h. ver. 10, 21. Nu ◐13:23.

10. **for two hundred**. ver. 21. **so faint**. 1 S 14:30, 31. Jg 8:4, 5. **the brook Besor**. This brook or torrent, it is evident from the circumstances of the history, must be in the southwest part of Judea, and must empty itself into the Mediterranean Sea. In the more particular situation of it writers are not agreed. Some suppose it to be between Gaza and Rhinocurura; but Jerome places it between Rhinocurura and Egypt. It is supposed by some to be the same as the river of the wilderness (Am 6:14), and the river of Egypt, Jsh 15:4.

11. **gave him**. Dt 15:7-11. 23:7. Pr 25:21. Mt 5:44.

25:35. Lk 10:33, 36, 37. Ro 12:20, 21.

12. **cake of figs**. 1 S 25:18. 2 K 20:7. 1 Ch 12:40. Is 38:21. **his spirit**. Heb. *ruach*, Ge +41:8. 1 S 14:27. Jg 15:19. Is 40:29-31. **came again**. Ge +*2:7n. La ◐1:11. **three days**. ver. 13. Est 4:16. Jon 1:17. Mt 27:63. ℐ108H12. Idiom B845. "Three days and three nights" is an idiom which covers any part of three days and three nights. For other instances of this idiom see Est 4:16. Jon 1:17. Mt *12:40. 27:63. Lk 24:21. Jn 2:19. 1 C 15:4, which is to be understood synecdochically (ℐ171T8. Synecdoche of the Part: A part of time is put for the whole time, compare 1 K 2:11) of one whole day, and part of two others, as the same phrase is taken in Mt 12:40, as appears from the next verse, where he says, "three days agone I fell sick," but in the Hebrew it is, "this is the third day since I fell sick" (Matthew Poole).

13. **my master**. Though they had booty enough, and this poor sick slave might have been carried on an ass or a camel, yet they inhumanly left him to perish; but, in the righteous providence of God, this cruelty was the occasion of their destruction; while David's kindness to a perishing stranger and slave was the means of his success, and proved the truest policy. Jb 31:13-15. Pr 12:10. Ja 2:13.

14. **the Cherethites**. Calmet and others suppose that these people, who inhabited the same district as the Philistines, were the aborigines of the island of Crete, from which they derived their name. ver. 16. 2 S 8:18. 1 K 1:38, 44. 1 Ch 18:17. Ezk 25:16. Zp 2:5. **Caleb**. A district in the south of Judea, in which were the cities of Kirjath-Arba or Hebron, and Kirjath-sepher, belonging to the family of Caleb. Jsh 14:13. 15:13. **we burned**. ver. 1-3.

15. **Swear**. 1 S 29:6. Jsh 2:12. 9:15, 19, 20. Ezk 17:13, 16, 19. **nor deliver**. Dt 23:15, 16.

16. **when he**. Jg 1:24, 25. **spread abroad**. Jg 7:12. 1 Th 5:3. **eating**. 1 S 25:36-38. Ex 32:6, 17-19, 27, 28. Jg 16:23-30. 2 S 13:28. Is 22:13. Da 5:1-4, 30. Lk 12:19, 20. 17:27-29. 21:34, 35. 1 Th 5:3. Re 11:10-13. **because of all**. Jb 20:5.

17. **twighlight**. 2 K 7:5, 7. Jb 3:9. 7:4. 24:15. Ps 119:147. Pr 7:9. Is 5:11. 21:4. 59:10. Je 13:16. **the next day**. Heb. their morrow. **and there**. 1 S 11:11. Jg 4:16. 1 K 20:29, 30. Ps 18:42. **camels**. 1 S 15:3. 27:9.

18. **recovered**. ver. 8. **had carried away**. ver. 2. **two wives**. ver. 5. Ge +4:19.

19. **nothing lacking**. ver. 8. Ge 14:14-16. Nu 31:49. 2 S 17:22. 1 K 4:27. Jb 1:10. Ps 34:9, 10. 91:9, 10. Is *34:16. 40:26. 59:15. Zp 3:5. Mt *6:33. Ro *8:37.

20. **drave**. Ge 31:18. **This is David's spoil**. ver. 26. Ge 49:27. Nu 31:9-12. 2 Ch 20:25. Is 53:12. Ro 8:37.

21. **two hundred men**. ver. 10. **came near**. He 13:1. 1 P *3:8. **saluted them**. Heb. asked them how they did. Jg +18:15mg.

22. **wicked**. 1 S 22:2. 25:17, 25. **men of Belial**. Dt *13:13. +15:9. Jg +19:22. 2 S 22:5mg. 23:6. 1 K 21:10, 13. Jb 34:18. Ps 18:4mg. 41:8mg. √101:3mg. Na 1:15mg. **those**. Heb. the men. **Because**. Mt 7:12. **not give**. 1 S 25:11. Est 6:6. Is 56:11. Mk 10:37. Lk 10:31, 32. Ph 2:21. Ja 2:16.

23. **my brethren**. Ge 19:7. Jg 19:23. Ac 7:2. 22:1. **which the Lord**. ver. 8. 1 S 2:7. Nu 31:49-54. Dt 8:10, 18. 1 Ch 29:12-14. Hab 1:16. **who hath**. Ps 44:2-7. 121:7, 8.

24. but as his part. This equitable edict was somewhat different from that which had so long obtained in Israel, and by which the spoil of the Midianites was divided: *that* related to the whole people: *this* only to the soldiers, some of whom went to battle, while others guarded the baggage. Nu 31:27. Jsh 22:8. Ps 68:12. 1 C *12:26. **tarrieth.** 1 S 25:13. 3 J 8. **part alike.** 2 S 8:15. Ps √149:9. Ph +*4:17.

25. forward. Heb. and forward. 1 S 16:13.

26. to his friends. 1 Ch 12:1, etc. Ps 35:27. 68:18. Pr 18:16, 24. Is 32:8. **present.** Heb. blessing. 1 S 25:27. Ge 33:11. 2 K 5:15. 2 C 9:5.

27. Beth-el. Probably not the celebrated city of this name, but *Bethul* a city of Simeon (Jsh 19:4), supposed by some to be the same as *Bethelia*, mentioned by Sozomen as belonging to Gaza, well peopled, and having several temples remarkable for their structure and antiquity; and which Jerome says, in his life of Hilarion, was five short days' journey from Pelusium. Young identifies it with Kirjath-Jearim, where the ark was, as in 1 S 7:1; 9:3; also called Baalah, Jsh 15:9. Ge 28:19. Jsh 16:2. Jg 1:22, 23. 1 K 12:29. **south Ramoth.** A city of Simeon; so called to distinguish it from *Ramoth Gilead* beyond Jordan. Jsh 19:8, Ramath. **Jattir.** A city in Judah. Jsh 15:48. 21:14.

28. Aroer. Jsh 13:16. **Siphmoth.** i.e. *coverings,* *S#8224h. Supposed to be the same with *Shepham* (Nu 34:10), on the eastern borders of Canaan. **Eshtemoa.** i.e. *obedience,* *S#851h. Jsh 15:50, Eshtemoh. 21:14. 1 Ch 4:17, 19. 6:57.

29. Rachal. i.e. *traffic,* *S#7403h. Supposed by Calmet to be the same as *Hachilah,* 1 S 23:19. **Jerahmeelites.** The descendants of Jerameel, son of Hezron (1 Ch 2:9, 25-27), who inhabited a district in the south of Judah. 1 S 27:10. **Kenites.** These people inhabited a small tract west of the Dead Sea. Jg 1:16.

30. Hormah. Jsh 15:30. 19:4. Jg 1:17. **Chorashan.** i.e. *a furnace of smoke; smoking furnace; anger,* *S#3565h. Probably the same as *Ashan* in Simeon, Jsh 15:42. 19:7, which Eusebius says was sixteen miles west from Jerusalem. 1 Ch 4:32. 6:59. **Athach.** i.e. *a lodging place; thy due season,* *S#6269h.

31. Hebron. Ge 13:18. Jsh 14:13, 14. 2 S 2:1. 4:1. 15:10.

1 SAMUEL 31

Saul's army being defeated, and his sons slain, he and his armorbearer kill themselves, 1-6. The Philis-

tines seize the towns which the Israelites forsake; and insult over the dead bodies of Saul and his sons, 7-10. The men of Jabesh-gilead rescue and burn them, and bury the bones, 11-13.

1. the Philistines. 1 S 28:1, 4, 15. 29:1. **fled.** Le 26:36. Dt 28:25. **fell down.** 1 S 12:25. 1 Ch 10:1-12. **slain.** Heb. wounded. ver. 8. 2 S 1:19, 22, 25. 23:8, 18. **Gilboa.** Eusebius and Jerome place this mountain six miles west from Bethshan, where was a large place called *Gelbus.* The natives still call it Djebel *Gilbo.* 1 S 28:4. 2 S 1:21.

2. followed. 1 S 14:22. 2 S 1:6. **Jonathan.** 1 S 13:2, 16. 14:1-14, 49. 18:1-4. 23:17. 1 Ch 8:33. 9:39. **Saul's sons.** Ex 20:5. 2 K 25:7.

3. went sore. 2 S 1:4, 6. Am 2:14. **archers hit him.** Heb. shooters, men with bows, found him. Ge 49:23. 1 K 22:34.

4. Draw. Jg *9:54. 1 Ch 10:4. **uncircumcised.** 1 S 14:6. 17:26, 36. 2 S 1:20. Je 9:25, 26. Ezk 44:7-9. **abuse me.** *or,* mock me. Je +38:19. **he was sore.** 2 S 1:14. **Saul.** 2 S 1:9, 10. 17:23. 1 K 16:18. 1 Ch 10:13, 14. Mt 27:4, 5. Ac 1:18. 16:27. **a sword.** *Eth hacherev,* rather, "the sword," i.e. his armorbearer's, who according to the Jews, was Doeg; and if so, then Saul and his executioner fell by the same sword with which they massacred the priests of God. **fell upon.** 2 S 1:10. *3:29.

5. when his. 1 Ch 10:5.

6. Saul died. 1 S 4:10, 11. 11:15. 12:17, 25. *28:19. 1 Ch 10:6, *13, *14. Ec 9:1, 2. Ho 13:10, 11.

7. they forsook the cities. 1 S 13:6. Le 26:32, 36. Dt 28:33. Jg 6:2.

8. to strip. 1 Ch 10:8. 2 Ch 20:25.

9. cut off. ver. 4. 1 S 17:51, 54. 1 Ch 10:9, 10. **to publish.** Jg 16:23, 24. 2 S 1:20.

10. they put. The Philistines placed the armor of Saul in the temple of Ashtaroth as a trophy of victory, and a testimony of their gratitude, in the same manner as David placed the sword of Goliath in the tabernacle. 1 S 5:2. 21:9. **Ashtaroth.** Jg 2:13. **Bethshan.** i.e. *house of rest, peace, or ease,* *S#1052h. ver. 12. Jsh 17:11. Jg 1:27. 2 S *21:12-14.

11. Jabesh-gilead. 1 S 11:1. 2 S 2:4. **of that.** *or,* concerning him, that which, etc.

12. valiant. Jsh 1:14. Jg +6:12. **burnt them there.** 2 Ch 16:14. Je 34:5. Am 6:10.

13. their bones. Ge 35:8. 2 S 2:4, 5. 21:12-14. **a tree.** 1 S 22:6. Ge 21:33. 1 Ch 10:12. **fasted.** 2 S 12:16. **seven.** Ge 50:10.

2 SAMUEL

2 SAMUEL 1

An Amalekite brings Saul's crown and bracelet to David, informs him of the event of the battle, and asserts that he slew Saul, 1-10. David rends his clothes, weeps, and orders the messenger to be put to death as a murderer, 11-16. His poetical lamentation for Saul and Jonathan, 17-27.

1. A.M. 2949. B.C. 1055. An. Ex. Is. 436. **when David.** 1 S 30:17-26. **Ziklag.** 1 S 27:6.

2. the third. Ge 22:4. Jsh 5:11n. 1 S *30:12n. Est 4:16. 5:1. Ho 6:2. Mt *12:40. 16:21. **a man.** 2 S 4:10.

clothes. Ge 37:29, 34. Jsh 7:6. 1 S 4:12, 16. Jl 2:13. **and earth.** 2 S 15:32. See on 1 S 4:12. **he fell.** 2 S 14:4. Ge 37:7-10. 43:28. 1 S 20:41. 25:23. Ps 66:3. Re 3:9.

3. From. 2 K 5:25. **am I.** Jb 1:15-19.

4. How went. Heb. What was, etc. 1 S 4:16mg. **the people.** 1 S 31:1-6. 1 Ch 10:1-6.

5. How knowest. ♪96C1, Ge +4:1. Pr 14:15. 25:2.

6. As I happened. lit. "meeting I met" (S#7136h). 2 S 18:9. *20:1. Ex 5:3. Dt *22:6. 1 S +6:9. Je 32:23 (hast caused to come). **by chance** (S#7122h). Ge +24:44n. Jsh 14:2n. Jg 20:22n. 1 S +6:9. Je 44:23.

The story of this young man appears to be wholly a fiction, formed for the purpose of ingratiating himself with David, as the next probable successor to the crown. There is no fact in the case, except the bringing of the diadem and bracelets of Saul, as a sufficient evidence of his death, which, as he appears to have been a plunderer of the slain, he seems to have stripped from the dead body of the unfortunate monarch. It is remarkable, that Saul, who had forfeited his crown by his disobedience and ill-timed clemency with respect to the Amalekites, should now have the insignia of royalty stripped from his person by one of those very people. Ru 2:3. 1 S 6:9. Lk 10:31. **mount**. ver. 21. 1 S 28:4. 31:1. **Saul**. 1 S 31: 2-7.

7. **Here am I**. Heb. Behold me. 2 S 9:6. Jg 9:54. 1 S 22:12. Is 6:8mg. 65:1.

8. **an Amalekite**. Ge 14:7. Ex 17:8-16. Nu 24:20. Dt 25:17-19. 1 S 15:3. 27:8. 30:1, 13, 17.

9. **anguish**, etc. *or*, my coat of mail, *or* my embroidered coat hindereth me, that my, etc. Ex 28:20, 39. **life**. Heb. *nephesh*, soul, Ge +44:30.

10. **slew**. Jg 1:7. 9:54. 1 S 22:18. 31:4, 5. Mt 7:2. **crown**. 2 S 12:30. La 5:16. **bracelet**. This was probably worn as an ensign of royalty, as is frequently the case in the East. When the Khalif Cayem Bemrillah granted the investiture of certain dominions to an Eastern prince, the ceremony was performed by sending him letters patent, a crown, chain, and bracelets. The bracelets, says Mr. Morier, are ornaments fastened above the elbows, composed of precious stones of great value, and are only worn by the king and his sons.

11. **rent**. 2 S 3:31. 13:31. Ge 37:29, 34. Ac 14:14. **likewise**. Ro 12:15.

12. **mourned**. Ps 35:13, 14. Pr 24:17. Je 9:1. Am 6:6. Mt 5:44. 2 C 11:29. 1 P 3:8.

13. **Whence art**. ver. 8. **stranger**. Ge 23:4 (✱S#1616h). Ex 12:48mg. Dt +26:11. Jsh +20:9. Mt +25:35. **an Amalekite**. Dt 25:19.

14. **How**. Nu 12:8. 1 S 31:4. 2 P 2:10. **stretch forth**. 1 S 24:6. 26:9. Ps 105:15. **to destroy**. 2 S 14:11. 24:16. **anointed**. Heb. *Messiah*, as in ver. 16, 21.

15. **Go near**. 2 S *4:10-12. Jg 8:20. 1 S 22:17, 18. 1 K 2:25, 34, 46. Jb 5:12. Pr 11:18.

16. **Thy blood**. Ge 9:5, 6. Le 20:9, 11-13, 16, 27. Dt 19:10. Jsh 2:19. Jg 9:24. 1 S 26:9. 1 K 2:32, 33, 37. Ezk *18:13. 33:5. Mt 27:25. Ac *20:26. **head**. ʃ171Q12, Jg +5:30. **mouth**. ver. 10. Jb 15:6. Pr 6:2. Lk 19:22. Ro 3:19.

17. **lamented**. ver. 19. 2 S 3:33. Ge 50:11. 2 Ch 35:25. Je 9:17-21. Ezk 27:32. 32:16.

18. **teach**. Ge 49:8. 1 S 11:3. 31:3. **the use**. ʃ63K, Ge +37:13. An example of false ellipsis; supply the ellipsis (this song of) "The Bow." See the following note. **bow**. *Kasheth*, or "the bow," was probably the title of the following threnody; so called, in the Oriental style, because Saul's death was occasioned by that weapon, and because the bow of Jonathan, out of which "the arrow was shot beyond the lad" (1 S 20:6), is celebrated in this song. **written in**. Nu 21:14. Jsh 10:13. 2 Ch 16:11. **the book**. Jsh 10:13, 33. **Jasher**. *or*, the upright. So LXX. *epi bibliou tou euthous*; Targum, *siphra deooritha*, "the book of the law;" the Arabic, "the book of Ashee: this is the book of Samuel." This book was probably a collection of divine odes, written

to commemorate remarkable events.

19. **beauty**. ver. 23. Dt 4:7, 8. 1 S 31:8. Is 4:2. 53:2. La 2:1. Zc 11:7, 10. **how are**. ver. 25, 27. La 5:16. ʃ53. Cycloides; or, Circular Repetition B342: the repetition of the same phrase at regular intervals. For other instances of this figure see Ps 42:5, 11. 43:5. 46:7, 11. 56:4, 10. 80:3, 7, 19. Je 3:12, 22. Ezk 32:20, 21, 22, 23, 24, 25, 26, 28, 29, 30, 31, 32.

20. **Tell**. Dt 32:26, 27. Jg 14:19. *16:23, 24. 1 S 17:4. 31:9. Mi 1:10. **Askelon**. Jg 1:18. 14:19. 16:23. 1 S 6:17. Je 25:20. **Philistines**. Ex 15:20, 21. Jg 11:34. 1 S 18:6. Ezk 16:27, 57. **uncircumcised**. 1 S 17:26, 36. 31:4, 9. **triumph**. Ps 28:7 (rejoiceth). 60:6 (rejoice). 68:4 (rejoice). 94:3. 96:12 (joyful). 108:7. 149:5. Pr 23:16. Is 23:12. Is 11:15. 15:17. 50:11. 51:39. Hab 3:18. Zp 3:14.

21. **mountains**. ʃ38G, Dt +32:1. 1 S 31:1. 1 Ch 10:1, 8. **no dew**. Jg 5:23. Jb 3:3-10. Is 5:6. Je 20:14-16. **offerings**. Ex 29:27n, 28. Le +*23:15. Ezr +8:25. Jl 1:9. 2:14. **as though**. ʃ63K, Ge +37:13. An example of false ellipsis, the verse should read as in the note below, supplying by ellipsis *weapons*. **not**. Instead of *belee*, "not," we should probably, with Dr. Delaney and others, read *keley*, "weapons," as it is found in one MS. and in the first edition of the Hebrew Bible, printed at Soncini, 1488: "the shield of Saul; the weapons of the anointed with oil." **anointed**. 1 S 10:1. Is 21:5.

22. **the bow**. 1 S 14:6-14. 18:4. Is 34:6, 7.

23. **lovely**. 1 S 9:2. **pleasant**. *or*, sweet. 2 S 23:1. 1 S *18:1. 20:2. Jb 36:11. Ps *16:6, 11. 81:2. 133:1. 135:3. 147:1. Pr 22:18. 23:8. 24:4. SS 1:16. **they were**. 1 S 31:1-5. **swifter**. ʃ102B, Ge +13:16. 2 S 2:18. Dt 28:49. 1 Ch 12:8. Jb 9:26. Je 4:13. La 4:19. Hab 1:8. **stronger**. ʃ102B, Ge +13:16. 2 S 23:20. Jg *14:18. Pr 30:30.

24. **Ye daughters**. Jg *5:30. Ps 68:12. Pr 31:21. Is *3:16-26. Je *2:32. 1 T *2:9, 10. 1 P *3:3-5. ʃ38B. Apostrophe B902: to men, either living or dead; to certain definite persons, here, the daughters of Israel. For other instances of this figure see 2 S 7:23. Is 2:10-12. 6:8. Is 1:4, 5. Je 5:10. 11:18. Ac 15:10. Ro 11:13, 14. Ja 5:1-6.

25. **How are**. ʃ53, 2 S 1:19. ver. 19, 27. La 5:16. **O Jonathan**. ʃ38B, 2 S 1:24. **thou wast**. Jg 5:18. 1 S 14:13-15.

26. **my brother**. Pr 27:10. **thy love**. 1 S *18:1-4. 19:2. *20:17, 41. *23:16. Pr 5:19.

27. **How are**. ver. 19, 25. **weapons**. 2 K 2:12. 13:14. Ps 46:9. 76:6. Ezk *39:9, 10.

2 SAMUEL 2

David, by divine direction, goes with his company to Hebron, and is anointed king over Judah, 1-4. He commends the men of Jabesh-gilead for their kindness to Saul, 5-7. Abner sets up Ish-bosheth as king over Israel, 8-11. Twelve of Abner's men, and twelve of Joab's, engage in a fatal contest, which brings on a battle, in which Israel is vanquished, 12-17. Asahel, Joab's brother, is slain by Abner, 18-24. At Abner's desire Joab sounds a retreat, 25-29. The number of the slain, 30, 31. Asahel's burial, 32.

1. **enquired**. 2 S 5:19, 23. Nu 27:21. Jg 1:1. 1 S 23:2, 4, 9-12. 30:7, 8. Ps 25:4, 5. 27:4. 143:8. Pr *3:5, 6. Ezk 36:37. **Hebron**. ver. 11. 2 S 5:1-3. 15:7. Ge

23:2. Nu 13:22. Jsh 14:14, 15. 20:7. 1 S 30:31. 1 K 2:11. 1 Ch 29:7.

2. his two wives. 1 S 25:42, 43. 30:5. Lk 22:28, 29.

3. his men. 1 S 22:2. 27:2, 3. 30:1, 9, 10. 1 Ch 12:1, 22, etc. **the cities.** Jsh 21:11, 12.

4. the men of Judah. ver. 11. 2 S 19:11, 42. Ge 49:8-10. **anointed.** ver. 7. 2 S 5:3, 5, 17. 1 S 16:13. 1 Ch 11:3. **the men of Jabesh-gilead.** 1 S 31:11-13.

5. David. This was a generous and noble act, highly indicative of the grandeur of David's mind. He respected Saul, though he had been greatly injured by him, as the anointed king of Israel, and once his legitimate sovereign; and he loved Jonathan as his most intimate friend. **Blessed.** Ru 1:8. 2:20. 3:10. 1 S 23:21. 24:19. 25:32, 33. Ps 115:15.

6. the Lord. 2 S 15:20. Ps 57:3. Pr 14:22. Mt 5:7. 2 T 1:16-18. **I also.** 2 S 9:3, 7. 10:2. Mt 5:44. 10:16. Phm 18, 19.

7. let your. 2 S 10:12. Ge 15:1. 1 S 4:9. 31:7, 12. 1 C 16:13. Ep 6:10. **valiant.** Heb. the sons of valor. 2 S 13:28mg. 17:10. Dt 3:18mg. Jg +6:12. 21:10. 1 S 18:17mg. 2 K 2:16mg. 1 Ch 5:18mg. 9:13mg. 26:6n. 2 Ch 28:6mg.

8. Abner. 1 S 14:50. 17:55. 26:14. **Saul's host.** Heb. the host which was Saul's. Ge 32:1, 2. 1 S 24:4. **Ish-bosheth.** 2 S 3:7, 8. 4:5, 6. 1 Ch 8:33. 9:39, Esh-baal. **Mahanaim.** 2 S 17:26, 27. Ge 32:2.

9. Gilead. Nu 32:1, etc. Jsh 13:8-11. Ps 108:8. **Ashurites.** i.e. *guided, blessed,* *S#843h. Jg 1:32, Asher-ites. Ezk 27:6. The LXX. read *ton Thasiri, Thasiri;* and the Vulgate *Gessuri,* "Geshurites;" but it is probable that for *ashuri,* "Ashurites," we should read *ashairi,* "Asherites," or those of the tribe of *Asher.* Ge 30:13. Nu 1:40. **over Jezreel.** Jsh 19:18.

10. two years. Houbigant proposes to read *shesh shanah,* "six years," instead of *shetayim shanim,* "two years," of the text, which he contends is a solecism; for, in pure Hebrew, the words should be *shetayim shanah;* and this is the reading of twenty MSS.; but "two" is acknowledged by all the versions and MSS. yet collated. **Judah followed.** 1 K 12:20.

11. time. Heb. number of days. 2 S 5:4, 5. 1 K 2:11. 1 Ch 3:4. 29:27. Is +10:19mg.

12. A.M. 2951. **B.C.** 1053. **An. Ex. Is.** 438. **Mahanaim.** 2 S 17:14. Ge 32:2. **Gibeon.** Jsh 9:3. 10:2, 4, 12. 18:25.

13. Joab. ver. 18. 2 S 8:16. 20:23. 1 K 1:7. 2:28-35. 1 Ch 2:16. **together.** Heb. them together. **pool.** Je 41:12.

14. play before. ver. 17, 26, 27. Pr *10:23. 17:14. 20:18. 25:8. *26:18, 19.

16. by the head. Probably by the beard or hair of the head. Plutarch, in his *Apophthegms,* informs us, that all things being ready for a battle, Alexander's captains asked him whether he had anything else to command them, "Nothing," said he, "but that the Macedonians shave their beards." Parmenio wondering what he meant, "Dost thou not know," said he, "that in fight, there is no better hold than the beard?" **Helkath-hazzurim.** that is, *the field of strong men.* i.e. *portion or place of the sharp weapons,* *S#2521h.

17. Abner. 2 S 3:1.

18. three. 1 Ch 2:15, 16. 11:26. **was as light.** 2 S 1:23. 22:34. 1 Ch 12:8. Ps 147:10, 11. Ec 9:11. Am 2:14. **foot.** Heb. his feet. **a wild roe.** Heb. one of the

roes that *is* in the field. Ps 18:33. SS 2:17. 8:14. Hab 3:19. The word *tzevee,* rather denotes the *gazelle* or *antelope* (See Note on 1 K 4:23).

19. turned. ver. 21. Jsh 1:7. 23:6. 2 K 22:2. Pr 4:27. **following Abner.** Heb. after Abner.

21. and take thee. It seems that Asahel wished to get the armor of Abner as a trophy. **armor.** *or,* spoil. Jg 14:19.

22. wherefore. ʃ85L, Ge +27:45. 1 S 19:17. 2 K 14:10-12. Pr 29:1. Ec 6:10. **how then.** 2 S 3:27.

23. the fifth rib. 2 S 3:27. 4:6. 5:6. 20:10. **stood still.** 2 S 20:12, 13.

24. Ammah. i.e. *cubit* or *pedestal; beginning; head,* *S#522h. 2 S ◐8:1. **Giah.** i.e. *breaking forth of a fountain,* *S#1520h.

26. Shall. ver. 14. Ac 7:26. **sword.** 2 S 11:25. Is 1:20. Je 2:30. 12:12. 46:10, 14. Ho 11:6. **for ever.** Jb +4:20 (*S#5331h). **it will be.** ver. 16. Pr 17:14. **how long.** Jb 18:2. 19:2. Ps 4:2. Je 4:21.

27. As God. This was spoken in allusion to the proposal of Abner (ver. 14), which led to the slaughter of twelve young men of each party, and thus provoked the battle. It is probable that Joab had orders simply to act on the defensive, and would not have attacked the Israelites that day unless compelled: therefore the blame lay upon Abner and Israel. 1 S 25:26. Jb 27:2. **unless.** ver. 14. Pr 15:1. *17:14. 20:18. 25:8. Is 47:7. Lk 14:31, 32. **spoken.** ʃ63D2, Ge +30:27. Supply by ellipsis (the words which caused the provocation). **in the morning.** Heb. from the morning. **gone up.** *or,* gone away.

29. the plain. lit. the Arabah. 2 S 4:7. Dt +11:30. **Bithron.** i.e. *separation,* *S#1338h. *Bithron* or *Bether* is probably the same as *Betarus,* which is placed in the Antonine Itinerary between Caesarea of Palestine and Diospolis or Lydda, 18 miles from the former, and 22 from the latter. The Jerusalem Itinerary mentions a place called *Bethar,* 16 miles from Caesarea, and 20 from Diospolis, which is probably the same. The Talmudists say that it was four miles distant from the sea. SS 2:17, Bether. **Mahanaim.** ver. 12.

30. nineteen. So that only seven appear to have been killed in the general conflict, see ver. 16 (Young).

31. three hundred. The slain of Israel, though greatly exceeding those of Judah, were not great. This might be owing to the directions given by David, to be as lenient as possible; but the death of Asahel seems to have stopped the pursuers, and greatly favored the escape of the vanquished. 1 S 3:1. 1 K 20:11.

32. buried. 1 S 17:58. 1 Ch 2:13-16. 2 Ch 16:14. 21:1. **sepulchre.** Heb. *qeber,* Ge +23:4. **went.** 2 S 5:1. Pr 22:29.

2 SAMUEL 3

David grows stronger, and Ish-bosheth weaker, during the war, 1. Six sons are born to David in Hebron, 2-5. Abner quarrels with Ish-bosheth, and offers his services to David, 6-12. David demands and receives back Michal, 13-16. Abner communes with the Israelites, goes to David, and is feasted by him, and sent away in peace, 17-21. Joab is angry with David, and murders Abner, 22-27. David protests against his wickedness, and denounces a curse upon him, 28-30. David mourns for Abner, 31-39.

1. long war. 1 K 14:30. 15:16, 32. **between.** Ge

3:15. Ps 45:3-5. Mt 10:35, 36. Ga 5:17. Ep 6:12. **Saul.** *ʃ*132G, Ge +3:19. **David waxed.** 2 S 2:17. Est 6:13. Jb 8:7. 17:9. Ps 84:5, 7. Pr +*4:18, 19. 10:29, 30. 24:3, 5. Da 2:34, 35, 44, 45. Re 6:2.

2. **sons born.** 1 Ch 3:1-4. **Amnon.** i.e. *steadfast,* ✱S#550h. 2 S 13:1, 2, 2, 3, 4, 6, 6, 7, 8, 9, 10, 10, 15, 15, 22, 22, 26, 27, 28, 28, 29, 32, 33, 39. Once called *Aminon,* in 2 S 13:20. Ge ◐49:3, 4. 1 Ch 3:1. 4:20. (1) The eldest son of David by Ahinoam of Jezreel, 2 S 3:2. (2) The son of Shimon, 1 Ch 4:20. **Ahinoam.** 1 S 25:43.

3. **Chileab.** i.e. *the father hath completed,* ✱S#3609h. 1 Ch 3:1, Daniel. **Abigail.** 2 S 2:2. 1 S 25:3, 42. **wife.** *ʃ*11, Ge +2:23. **Absalom.** i.e. *father of peace.* 2 S 13:20-28. 14:24-33. 15:1-18. 17:1-14. 18:9-18, 33. **Maacah.** i.e. *oppression,* S#4601h, 1 K +2:39, Maachah. (1) A wife of King David and the mother of Absalom, 2 S 3:3; 1 Ch 3:2, Maachah. (2) A small district of Syria on the northeast of Palestine, 2 S 10:8; 1 Ch 19:6, 7, Maachah. (3) A king of Maacah, 2 S 10:6. **Talmai.** i.e. *full of furrows.* 2 S 13:37, 38. **Geshur.** i.e. *expulsion; proud beholder; a bridge,* ✱S#1650h. 2 S 13:37, 38. 14:23, 32. 15:8. Dt ◐3:14. Jsh 13:13. 1 S 27:8. 1 Ch 2:23. 3:2.

4. **Adonijah.** i.e. *the Lord is Jah.* 1 K 1:5, etc. 2:13-25. **Haggith.** i.e. *festive,* ✱S#2294h. 1 K 1:5, 11. 2:13. 1 Ch 3:2. **Shephatiah.** i.e. *Jah hath judged,* ✱S#8203h. 1 Ch 3:3. 9:8. Ezr 2:4, 57. 8:8. Ne 7:9, 59. 11:4. Je 38:1. Also 1 Ch 12:5. 27:16. 2 Ch 21:2. (1) David's fifth son, 2 S 3:4; 1 Ch 3:3. (2) A Benjamite who joined David at Ziklag, 1 Ch 12:5. (3) Prince of Simeon, 1 Ch 27:16. (4) One of the sons of Jehoshaphat, 2 Ch 21:2. (5, 6) Two Jews whose descendants returned with Zerubbabel, Ezr 2:4, 57; Ne 7:9, 59. (7) A descendant of Judah, Ne 11:4. (8) A prince of Judah in the time of Zedekiah, Je 38:1-4. **Abital.** i.e. *father of dew,* ✱S#37h. 1 Ch 3:3.

5. **Ithream.** i.e. *abundance* or *remnant of a people,* ✱S#3507h. 1 Ch 3:3. **Eglah.** i.e. *a calf,* ✱S#5698h. 1 Ch 3:3.

6. **Abner.** 2 S 2:8, 9. 2 K 10:23. 2 Ch 25:8. Pr 21:30. Is 8:9, 10. Jl 3:9-13. Mt 12:30. **himself strong.** 1 Ch 11:10. Da *10:21mg. **for.** or, in.

7. **had.** Ge +4:19. **concubine.** 2 S 21:8, 11. Ge 22:24. **Rizpah.** i.e. *a burning coal,* ✱S#7532h. 2 S 21:8, 10, 11. **Aiah.** i.e. *kite* or *vulture,* ✱S#345h. 2 S 21:8, 10, 11. 1 Ch 1:40. **Ishbosheth.** *ʃ*63A1, Ge +14:20. **Wherefore.** This action of Abner's seems a most evident proof that he intended to seize on the government; and it was so understood by Ish-bosheth: see Parallel Texts. **gone in.** 2 S 12:8. 16:21, 22. Ge 6:4. 1 K 2:17, 21, 22.

8. **Abner.** Ps 76:10. Mk 6:18, 19. **Ishbosheth.** i.e. *man of shame,* ✱S#378h. ver. 10, 12, 15. 2 S 3:8, 14, 15. 4:5, 8, 8, 12. **Am I a dog's head.** This was a proverbial expression among the Hebrews to denote whatever was deemed worthless and contemptible. Something similar to this was the answer of the Turkish commander at Beer, on the Euphrates, to a request made to see the castle. "Do they," said he, "take me for a child, or an ass's head, that they would feed me with sweetmeats, and dupe me with a bit of cloth? No, they shall not see this castle." 2 S 9:8. 16:9. Dt *23:18. 1 S 24:14, 15. 2 K 8:13. **do show.** ver. 9, 18. 2 S 5:2. 1 S 15:28. Ps 2:1-4. Is 37:23. Ac 9:4, 5.

9. **So do God.** ver. 35. 2 S 19:13. Ru 1:17. 1 S

3:17. 14:44. 25:22. 1 K 19:2. 2 K 6:31. **as the Lord.** 1 S 15:28. 16:1-13. 28:17. 1 Ch 12:23. Ps 89:3, 4, 19, 20, 35-37. *132:11.

10. **translate the kingdom from.** 1 Ch 12:23. **from** Dan. 2 S 17:11. 24:2. Jg 20:1. 1 K 4:25.

11. **because.** ver. 39.

12. **Whose.** 2 S 19:6. 20:1-13. **Make.** Ps 62:9. Lk 16:5-8. **my hand.** *ʃ*121BA, Dt +32:36. ver. 21, 27. 2 S 5:1-3. 19:14, 41-43. 20:1, 2. 1 Ch 11:1-3. 12:38-40. Mt 21:8-10.

13. **that is.** Heb. saying. **Thou shalt.** Ge 43:3. 44:23, 26. **except.** As Michal was not divorced, but violently separated from David, he had a legal right to demand her, and was justified in receiving her again. It is probable, also, that her marriage with Phaltiel was a force upon her inclinations; and whatever affection he might have for her, it was highly criminal for him to take another man's wife. David required Michal probably both out of affection for her and to strengthen his interest, by asserting his affinity with the house of Saul. **Michal.** ver. 20-23. 1 S *18:20-28. 19:11-17. 1 Ch 15:29.

14. **Ish-bosheth.** 2 S 2:10. **an hundred.** 1 S 18:25, 27.

15. **Phaltiel.** i.e. *escape of God; deliverance of God,* ✱S#6409h. Nu 34:26. 1 S ◐25:44, Phalti.

16. **along weeping.** Heb. going and weeping. Pr 9:17, 18. **Bahurim.** i.e. *choice youths,* ✱S#980h. 2 S 16:5. 17:18. 19:16. 1 K 2:8. A city of Benjamin. The Targum reads *Almuth,* perhaps the same as Almon, in Jsh 21:18, and Alemeth in 1 Ch 6:68 (Young).

17. **Ye sought.** 2 S 5:1, 2. Ezk 21:27. 1 P 4:3. **in times past.** Heb. both yesterday and the third day. 2 S 5:2. Ge +31:2mg. Ex +4:10mg. Jsh +4:18mg. 1 S +19:7mg.

18. **for the Lord.** ver. 9. 1 S 13:14. 15:28. 16:1, 12, 13. Jn 12:42, 43. **By the hand.** Ps 89:3, 4, 19-23. 132:17, 18. **save.** *ʃ*96B, Ge +8:5.

19. **Benjamin.** 1 S 10:20, 21. 1 Ch 12:29. Ps 68:27.

20. **David.** Ge 26:30. 31:44, 46, 54. Est 1:3.

21. **will gather.** ver. 10, 12. 2 S 2:9. Ph 2:21. **reign over.** 1 K 11:37. Ps 20:4. **heart.** Heb. *nephesh,* Ex +23:9.

24. **What hast.** Joab and his brother Abishai, David's nephews, had been very faithful and highly useful to him in his distresses; and from gratitude and natural affection, he had inadvertently permitted them to assume almost as much ascendency over him as Abner had over the pusillanimous Ishbosheth: he trusted and feared them too much, and allowed them all the importance they claimed; which had emboldened them, especially Joab, to a high degree of presumption. ver. 8, 39. 2 S 19:5-7. Nu 23:11. Jn 18:35.

25. **that he came.** ver. 27. 2 K 18:32mg. Jn 7:12, 47. Ro 2:1. **and to know.** 2 S 10:3. Ge 42:9, 12, 16. Nu 27:17. Dt 28:6. 1 S 29:4-6. Ps 121:8. Is 37:28.

26. **he sent.** Pr 26:23-26. 27:4-6. **well.** Heb. *bor,* Ge +37:20. **Sirah.** i.e. *the turning aside; departure; a pot, hook,* ✱S#5626h.

27. **took him.** 2 S 20:9, 10. Dt 27:24. 1 K 2:5, 32. **quietly.** or, peaceably. Je 41:2, 6, 7. **and smote.** Joab was afraid that Abner, after rendering such essential service to David, would be made the general over the army; and therefore, under pretence of avenging the death of his brother, he treacherously assassinated the unsuspecting and too-confiding Abner: and such

was the power of this cool-blooded and nefarious murderer, that the king dared not bring him to justice for his crime. But, while Joab's conduct cannot be too severely reprobated, the justice of God is apparent in Abner's punishment; who, from ambition, had pertinaciously, against his conscience, opposed the declared will of God; and was induced by base resentment to desert Ishbosheth, and offer his services to David: see ver. 6-10. 2 S 4:6. **fifth rib**. 2 S 2:23. **for the blood**. 2 S 2:19-23.

28. **guiltless**. Ge *9:6. Ex 21:12. Nu 35:33. Dt 21:1-9. Mt 27:24. **for ever**. Heb. *olam*, Ex +12:24. **blood**. Heb. bloods. ♪96F2, Ge +4:10. Ge 4:10mg. 2 K +9:26mg.

29. **rest**. 2 S 1:16. Jg 9:24, 56, 57. 1 K 2:31-34. Pr 6:16, 17. Is 24:16-18. Ac 28:4. Re 16:6. **and let there**. 1 S 2:32-36. 2 K 1:10. 5:27. Ne 4:5. Ps 10:15. 55:15. 58:6. 68:2. 69:22. 83:11. 109:6, 8-19. 137:7. Je +√10:25. Ac 23:3. Ga 1:9. **fail**. Heb. be cut off. Je 30:23mg. **an issue**. Le 15:2. **leper**. Le 13:44-46. 14:2. 2 K 5:1. **leaneth on a staff**. i.e. *does the work belonging to women*, taking *staff* to mean "spindle," the curse of effeminacy. Keil and Delitzsch (*Samuel*, p. 306) take this to mean "a lame person or cripple" (Ex 21:19). An alternate view takes the phrase to curse his posterity to a life employed in women's work (compare Jsh 9:23n). This curse was placed on Joab for the treacherous act of assassination (ver. 30. 2 S 2:23, compare 2 S 20:10). Le 21:18. Dt 22:5. 23:1. Pr *31:19. Is ◑+*56:3-5. 1 C +√6:9. **falleth on**. ♪142, Ge +20:16. A circumlocution for being put to death by the public executioner. 1 S 31:4, 5. **the sword**. Le 26:25, 33. Dt 28:22. 32:25. **lacketh bread**. Ps ◑*37:25. 109:10.

30. **slew Abner**. Dt *27:24. Pr 28:17. Ac 28:4. **because**. 2 S 2:19-23.

31. **And David**. David, intending no doubt to punish Joab, and to lessen his authority with the people, commanded him to take upon him the office of chief mourner; but, as his revenge was gratified, his rival removed, and no heavier punishment inflicted, it is probable his hardened mind would feel but little objection to the ceremony. **Rend**. 2 S 1:2, 11. Ge 37:29, 34. Jsh 7:6. Jg 11:35. 2 K 19:1. **bier**. Heb. bed. Lk 7:14.

32. **lifted**. ♪144A12, Ge +22:13. 2 S 1:12. 18:33. 1 S 30:4. Jb 31:29. Pr 24:17. Lk 19:41, 42. **grave**. Heb. *qeber*, Ge +23:4.

33. **Died**. ♪96C8, Ex 15:5. **as a fool dieth**. That is, as a bad man, as the word frequently signifies in Scripture. 2 S 13:12, 13, 28, 29. Jb 5:2. Pr 18:7. Ec 2:15, 16. Je 17:11. Lk 12:19, 20.

34. **hands**. The hands of malefactors were usually secured with cords, and their feet with fetters; a custom to which David affectingly alludes in his lamentation over the dust of Abner: "Thy hands, O Abner, were not bound, as found to be a malefactor, nor thy feet put in fetters; thou wast treated with honor by him whose business it was to judge thee, and thy attachment to the house of Saul was esteemed rather generous than culpable: as the best of men may fall, so thou fellest by the sword of treachery, not of justice." Jg 16:21. Ps 107:10, 11. **fetters**. lit. brasses. ♪121D2, Jg +16:21. **wicked men**. Heb. children of iniquity. 2 S 7:10. 1 Ch 17:9. Jb 24:14. Ps 89:22. Ho 6:9. **wept**. 2 S 1:12.

35. **cause**. 2 S 12:17. Je 16:7. Ezk 24:17, 22. **So do**. ver. 9. Ru 1:17. **till the**. 2 S 1:12. Jg 20:26.

36. **took notice**. Mk 7:37. **pleased them**. Heb. was good in their eyes. 2 S 19:18mg, 27, 37, 38. Jsh +22:30mg. **as**. 2 S 15:6, 13. Ps 62:9. Mk 7:37. 15:11-13.

38. **a prince**. ver. 12. 2 S 2:8. 1 S 14:50, 51. Jb 32:9.

39. **I am**. Ex 21:12. 2 Ch 19:6, 7. Ps 75:10. 101:8. Pr 20:8. 25:5. **weak**. Heb. tender. 1 Ch 22:5. Is 7:4mg. Ro 13:4. **the sons**. 2 S 16:10. 1 Ch 2:15, 16. **too hard**. 2 S 19:6, 7, 13. **the Lord**. Ge +*6:13 (T#566). 1 K 2:5, 6, 33, 34. Ps *7:16. 28:4. 62:12. 2 T +*4:14.

2 SAMUEL 4

Ish-bosheth and Israel are troubled at Abner's death, 1. After Saul's death, changes took place, and Mephibosheth, Jonathan's son, was lamed, 2-4. Rechab and Baanah slay Ishbosheth, and bring his head to David, 5-8. David causes them to be put to death, and Ish-bosheth's head to be buried, 9-12.

1. **his hands**. 2 S 17:2. Ezr 4:4. Ne 6:9. Is 13:7. 35:3. Je 6:24. 50:43. Zp 3:16. **and all**. Mt 2:2, 3.

2. **captains**. 2 S 3:22. 2 K 5:2. 6:23. **Baanah**. i.e. *son of affliction*. **other**. Heb. second. **Rechab**. i.e. *a rider; horseman; charioteer*, *S#7394h. ver. 5, 6, 9. 2 K 10:15, 23. 1 Ch 2:55. Ne 3:14. Je 35:6, 8, 14, 16, 19. (1) An ancestor of Jehonadab, the founder of the Rechabites, 2 K 10:15, 23; 1 Ch 2:55; Je 35:6-19. (2) One of Ish-bosheth's captains, 2 S 4:2. (3) The father of Malchiah, Ne 3:14. **Rimmon**. i.e. *a pomegranate*. 2 K +5:18. **Beerothite**. *S#886h. ver. 3, 5, 9. 2 S 23:37. **Beeroth**. Jsh 9:17. 18:25.

3. **fled**. 1 S 31:7. Ne 11:33. **Gittaim**. i.e. *two winefats; double winepress*, *S#1664h. 2 S ◑6:10, 11. Ne 11:33h.

4. **Jonathan**. 2 S 9:3. **when the tidings**. 1 S 29:1, 11. 31:1-10. **Mephibosheth**. 1 Ch 8:34. 9:40, Meribaal.

5. **Baanah**. i.e. *son of response; answering; affliction; son of grief*, *S#1196h. ver. 2, 6, 9. 2 S 23:29. 1 Ch 11:30. Ezr 2:2. Ne 7:7. 10:27. (1) The father of one of David's valiant men, 2 S 23:29; 1 Ch 11:30. (2) One of Ishbosheth's captains, 2 S 4:2, 5, 6, 9. (3) An Israelite who returned from Babylon, Ezr 2:2; Ne 7:7. (4) Perhaps same as number 3, Ne 10:27. **went**. 2 Ch 24:25. 25:27. 33:24. **lay on a bed**. It is customary, in all hot countries, to travel or work very early and very late, and to rest at noon, at which time the heat most prevails. 2 S 11:2. 1 K 16:9. Pr 24:33, 34. 1 Th 5:3-7.

6. **as though**. It is still the custom of the East, according to Dr. Perry, to allow the soldiers a certain quantity of corn, with other articles of provision, together with some pay: and as it was the custom also to grind the corn, as needed at the break of day, these two captains very naturally went the day before to the palace, where the king's stores appear to have been kept, to fetch wheat, in order to distribute it to the soldiers under them, to be ground at the accustomed hour in the morning. The princes of the East, in those days, as appears from the history of David, reposed on their couches till the cool of the evening: they therefore came in the heat of the day, when they knew their master would be resting on his bed; and as it was necessary to have the corn before it was needed, their coming at this time, though it might be earlier than

usual, excited no suspicion. **under.** 2 S 2:23. 3:27. 20:10.

7. **took his head.** 1 S 17:54. 31:9. 2 K 10:6, 7. Mt 14:11. Mk 6:28, 29. When those difficulties dispirit us which should rather invigorate us and sharpen our endeavors, we betray a carelessness of character which is soon taken advantage of by our more watchful neighbors. Love not sleep, lest we come to poverty and ruin. The idle soul is an easy prey to the destroyer.

8. **sought.** 1 S 18:11. 19:2-11, 15. 20:1. 23:15. 25:29. Ps 63:9, 10. 71:24. Mt 2:20. **life.** Heb. *nephesh*, soul, Ge +44:30. **the Lord.** 2 S 18:19, 31. 22:48. 1 S +24:4n. Lk 18:7, 8. Re 6:10. 18:20.

9. **As the Lord liveth.** Ru 3:13. **who hath.** Ge 48:16. 1 K 1:29. Ps 31:5-7. 34:6, 7, 17, 22. 71:23. 103:4. 106:10. 107:2. 2 T 4:17, 18. **soul.** Heb. *nephesh*, Ge +12:13.

10. **one.** 2 S 1:2-16. **thinking,** etc. Heb. he was in his own eyes, as a bringer, etc. **who thought,** etc. *or*, which was the reward I gave him for his tidings. **thought.** ʃ63B, Ge +25:28.

11. **when wicked.** Dt 27:24. 1 K 2:32. Pr 25:26. Hab 1:4, 12. 1 J 3:12. **require.** 2 S 3:27, 39. Ge 9:5, 6. Ex 21:12. Nu 35:31-34. Ps 9:12. **from.** Ge 4:11. 6:13. 7:23. Ex 9:15. Ps 109:15. Pr 2:22. Je 10:11.

12. **slew them.** 2 S 1:15. Ps 55:23. Mt 7:2. **hanged.** 2 S 21:9. Dt 21:22, 23. **in the sepulchre.** Heb. *qeber*, Ge +23:4. **of Abner.** 2 S 3:32.

2 SAMUEL 5

The elders of the tribes, at Hebron, anoint David king over all Israel, 1-3. His age at the beginning of his reign, and the length of his reign, 4, 5. He takes Zion from the Jebusites, and calls it the city of David, 6-10. Hiram sends him timber and workmen to build him a house, 11. He prospers, and takes more wives; and eleven sons are born to him, 12-16. By divine direction, he gains victories over the Philistines at Baal-perazim, 17-21; and again at the mulberry trees, 22-25.

1. **came.** 1 Ch 11:1-3. 12:23-40. **we are.** 2 S 3:17, 18. 19:13. Ge 29:14. Dt 17:15. Jg 9:2. Ezk 21:27. Ep 5:30. He 2:14. 1 P 4:3.

2. **time past.** lit. "yesterday, the third day." 2 S +3:17mg. Ge +*31:2mg. 1 S +19:7mg. **leddest out.** ver. 24. Nu 27:17. 1 S 18:13, 16. 25:28. Is 55:4. Jn *10:4. **feed.** 2 S 7:7. 1 S 16:1, 12, 13. 25:30. Ps 78:70-72. Is 40:11. Ezk 34:23. 37:24, 25. Mi 5:4. Mt 2:6. Jn 10:3, 4, 11. **a captain.** 1 S 9:16. 13:14. 18:13. 2 K 20:5. Is 55:4. He 2:10.

3. **So all.** Ex 3:16. Jsh +20:4. 1 Ch 11:3. **made.** 1 S 11:15. 2 K 11:17. 2 Ch 23:16. Ne 9:38. **before.** Jg 11:11. 1 S 23:18. **anointed.** 2 S 2:4. 1 S 16:13.

4. **thirty.** Nu 4:43. Lk *3:23. **forty.** 1 Ch 26:31. 29:27. 2 Ch 9:30. Ac 13:21.

5. **seven years.** 2 S 2:11. 1 K 2:11. 1 Ch 3:4.

6. **Jerusalem.** Ge 14:18. Jsh 10:3. Jg 1:8. He 7:1. **the Jebusites.** Jsh *15:63. 18:28. Ge +10:16. Jg 1:8, 21. 19:10-12. 1 Ch 11:4, 5. **which spake,** etc. Dr. Kennicott's amended translation is as follows: "Who spake unto David, saying, Thou shalt not come in hither; for the blind and the lame shall drive thee away, by saying, David shall not come in hither." ver. 8. "And David said, Whosoever smiteth the Jebusites, and through the subterraneous passage reacheth the lame

and the blind, who hate the life of David (because the blind and the lame said, he shall not come into the house), shall be chief and captain. So Joab, the son of Zeruiah, went up first, and was chief." **Except.** Je 37:10. **thinking, David cannot.** *or*, saying, David shall not, etc.

7. **David took.** 1 Ch 11:5. **Zion.** i.e. *the dry or sunny part of Jerusalem, at the south; spiritual illumination,* ✻S#6726h. Ps *2:6. 9:*11, 14. 14:7. 20:2. *48:2, 11, 12. 50:2. 51:18. 53:6. 65:1. 69:35. 74:2. 76:2. 78:68. 84:7. 87:2, 5. 97:8. 99:2. 102:13, 16, 21. 110:2. 125:1. 126:1. 128:5. 129:5. 132:13. 133:3. 134:3. 135:21. 137:1, 3. 146:10. 147:12. 149:2. SS 3:11. Is 1:8, 27. 2:3. 3:16, 17. 4:3, 4, 5. 8:18. 10:12, 24, 32. *12:6. 14:32. 16:1. 18:7. 24:23. 28:16. 29:8. 30:19. 31:4, 9. 33:5, 14, 20. 34:8. 35:10. 37:22, 32. 40:9. 41:27. 46:13. 49:14. 51:3, 11, 16. 52:1, 2, 7, 8. *59:20. 60:14. 61:3. 62:1, 11. 64:10. 66:8. Je 3:14. 4:6, 31. 6:2, 23. 8:19. 9:19. 14:19. 26:18.30:17. 31:6, 12. 50:5, 28. 51:10, 24, 35. La 1:4, 6, 17. 2:1, 4, 6, 8, 10, 13, 18. 4:2, 11, 22. 5:11, 18. Jl 2:1, 15, 23, 32. 3:16, 17, 21. Am 1:2. 6:1. Ob 17, 21. Mi 1:13. 3:10, 12. 4:*2, 7, 8, 10, 11, 13. Zp 3:14, 16. Zc 1:14, 17. 2:7, 10. 8:2, 3. 9:9, 13. Ro 9:33. He 12:22. Re 14:1. **the same.** ver. 9. 2 S 6:10. 1 K 2:10. 3:1. 8:1. 1 Ch 11:7. 2 Ch 5:2. 24:16.

8. **Whosoever.** Jsh 15:16, 17. 1 S 17:25. **the gutter.** Ps 42:7. ʃ84:6. **Jebusites.** Ge +10:16. **soul.** Heb. *nephesh*, Ge +34:3. **he shall be.** ʃ37A, Ex +32:32. 1 Ch 11:6-9. **Wherefore,** etc. *or*, Because they had said, even the blind and the lame, he shall not come into the house. Ac 3:2, 8.

9. **city.** ver. 7. **Millo.** i.e. *a bastion; a filling up; a rampart, mound,* ✻S#4407h. Jg 9:6, 20, 20. 1 K 9:15, 24. 11:27. 2 K 12:20. 1 Ch 11:8. 2 Ch 32:5. (1) A part of the citadel or fortress of Jerusalem, 2 S 5:9; 1 K 9:15. (2) Those who lived in the fortress of Shechem, Jg 9:6, 20. (3) The place where Joash was murdered, 2 K 12:20. See Number 1.

10. **went on, and grew great.** Heb. went going and growing. 2 S 3:1. 1 Ch 11:9. Jb 17:9. Pr *4:18. Is 9:7. Da 2:44, 45. Lk *2:52. **the Lord.** Ge 21:22. Ps 46:7, 11. Is 8:9, 10. Ro 8:31.

11. **Hiram.** i.e. *noble; freeman; height of life,* ✻S#2438h. (1) The king of Tyre in the time of David and Solomon. 1 K 5:1, 1, 2, 7, 8, 10, 11, 11, 12. 9:11, 11, 12, 14, 27. 10:11, 22. 1 Ch 14:1. (2) A famous artificer from Tyre who was employed by Solomon for the furniture of the Temple, 1 K 7:13, 40, 40, 45. He is called Huram in 2 Ch 4:11, 16. **Tyre.** Jsh 19:24, 25, 28, 29. **masons.** Heb. hewers of stone of the wall. **they built.** 2 S 7:2. 1 K 7:1-12. Ec 2:4-11. Je 22:14-16.

12. **David.** 2 S 7:16. 1 Ch 14:2. **his people.** 1 K 10:9. 2 Ch 2:11. Est 4:14. Is 1:25-27. Da 2:30.

13. **David took.** Ge 25:5, 6. Le 18:18mg. Dt 17:17. 1 Ch 3:9. 14:3-7. 2 Ch 11:18-21. 13:21. **more concubines.** 2 S 16:21. **and wives.** Ge +4:19.

14. **the names.** 1 Ch 3:5-9. 14:4. **Shammuah.** i.e. *rumor; a hearkener; heard,* ✻S#8051h. Nu 13:4. 1 Ch 14:4. Ne 11:17. 12:18. *or*, Shimea, as 1 Ch 3:5. **Shobab.** i.e. *a bringer back.* 1 Ch 3:5. 14:4. **Nathan.** i.e. *he gave.* 2 S 12:1-7. Lk 3:31. **Solomon.** i.e. *peace,* S#8010h. 2 S 12:24, 25. Mt 1:6.

15. **Ibhar.** i.e. *he chooses; whom God chooses,* ✻S#2984h. 1 Ch 3:6. 14:5. **Elishua.** i.e. *my God saves; God of supplication* or *riches,* ✻S#474h. *or,* Elishama,

as 1 Ch 3:6. 1 Ch *14:5. **Nepheg.** i.e. *a going forth; sprout*, *S#5298h. Ex 6:21. 1 Ch 3:7. 14:6. (1) One of the brothers of Korah, Ex 6:21. (2) One of David's sons, 2 S 5:15; 1 Ch 14:6. **Japhia.** i.e. *he breathes.*

16. **Elishama.** i.e. *God hears.* **Eliada.** i.e. *God knows*, *S#450h. 1 K 11:23. 1 Ch 3:8. 2 Ch 17:17. (1) A son of David, 2 S 5:16; 1 Ch 3:8. (2) The father of Rezon, 1 K 11:23. (3) The chief captain of Benjamin in the time of Jehoshaphat, 2 Ch 17:17. *or*, Beeliada, as 1 Ch 14:7. **Eliphalet.** i.e. *God escapes; God of salvation*, *S#467h. 1 Ch 3:6, 8, Eliphelet. 14:5, *7.

17. **But when.** 1 Ch 14:8, 9. Ps 2:1-5. Re 11:15-18. **the hold.** 2 S 23:14. 1 Ch 11:16.

18. **the valley.** 2 S √23:13, 15, 16. Ge 14:5. Jsh 15:8. 1 Ch 11:15-18. 14:9. Is 17:5. **Rephaim.** i.e. *the dead; healers; giants*, *S#7497h. Ge 14:5. 15:20. Dt 2:11, 20, 20. 3:11, 13. Jsh 12:4. 13:12. 17:15. 18:16. Is 17:5.

19. **enquired.** 2 S 2:1. 1 S 23:2, 4. 30:7, 8. 1 Ch 14:10. Ja 4:15. **And the Lord.** ver. 23. Jg 20:28. 1 S 28:6. 30:8. 1 K 22:6, 15-23. Pr *3:6.

20. **Baal-perazim.** that is, *the plain of breaches.* i.e. *lord of breaches*, *S#1188h. 1 Ch 14:11mg. Is 28:21. La 2:13. **broken forth.** 2 Ch 20:37. 24:7. ♪22C41. Anthropomorphism B890: human actions are attributed to God: breaking forth. For another instance of this figure see 2 S 6:8mg.

21. **David.** Dt 7:5, 25. 1 S 5:2-6. 1 Ch 14:11, 12. Is 37:19. **burned them.** *or*, took them away. or, lifted them up. Is 46:1, 2. Je 43:12.

22. **came up.** 1 K 20:22. 1 Ch 14:13. **spread themselves.** Jg 15:9. **valley of Rephaim.** ver. 18. Jsh 15:8. A valley at the west of Jerusalem (Young).

23. **enquired.** ver. 19. **fetch.** Jsh 8:2, 7. 1 Ch 14:14. Mt 9:29, 30. Mk 8:23-25. Jn 9:6, 7. **the mulberry trees.** ver. 24. 1 Ch 14:14, 15. Ps *84:6. The word *bechaim*, rendered *mulberry trees*, is rendered by Aquila, *apion*, "pear-trees," as the LXX. also render it in 1 Ch 14:14, 15; and so the Vulgate in both places has *pyrorum*. The Rabbins, however, believe *bacha* signifies the mulberry tree: with whom Ursinus agrees. It more probably denotes a large shrub which the Arabs still call *baca*, from its distilling an odoriferous gum, from *bachah*, "to distill," as tears. Of this opinion is Celsius, who quotes a passage from *Abulfadi*, who describes it as a balsam shrub, having longish leaves, and bearing a large fruit with an acrid taste. M. Forskal mentions a tree by the name of *baeca*, with leaves rather ovated, smooth, entire: its berries are poisonous to the sheep. Robert Dick Wilson wrote of this term in his pamphlet, *Is Higher Criticism Scholarly?* He wrote, "You will have observed that the critics of the Bible who go to it in order to find fault have a most singular way of claiming to themselves all knowledge and all virtue and all love of truth. One of their favorite phrases is, 'all scholars agree.' When a man writes a book and seeks to gain a point by saying 'All scholars agree,' I wish to know who the scholars are and why they agree. Where do they get their evidence from to start with? I remember that some years ago I was investigating the word *Baca*, which you have in the English Bible— "Passing through the valley of Baca, make it a well" (Ps 84:6). I found in the Hebrew dictionary that there was a traveler named Burkhart, who said that *Baca* meant mulberry trees. That was not very enlightening. I could not see how mulberries had anything to do

with water. I looked up all the authority of the scholars in Germany and England since Burkhart's time and found they had all quoted Burkhart. Just one scholar at the back of it! When I was traveling in the orient, I found that we had delicious water here and there. The water sprang up apparently out of the ground in the midst of the desert. I asked my brother who was a missionary where this water came from. He said, 'They bring this water from the mountains. It is an underground aqueduct. They cover it over to prevent it from evaporating.' Now the name of that underground aqueduct was *Baca*. My point is that you ought to be able to trace back this agreement among scholars to the original scholar who propounded the statement, and then find out whether what that scholar said is true. What was the foundation of his statement?" The valley of Rephaim has been connected by some with the valley of Baca mentioned in Ps 84:6. Thus John D. Davis in his *A Dictionary of the Bible*, notes "possibly the valley of Rephaim, where such trees were found (2 S 5:22, 23, R.V. margin). Perhaps, however, the expression is figurative, as the Greek and Syrian translators believed, like 'valley of the shadow of death,' and denotes any vale of tears." Though *baca* has been identified by many, as in Davis, as "a balsam tree, so named from its shedding, as it were, tears of gum; possibly also a noun meaning weeping," yet the identification is conjectural, as Willis J. Beecher notes in ISBE (1929 ed.), "Conjecturally the word is, by variant spelling, of the stem which denotes weeping." Wilson's correction of the identification of *baca* as an underground acqueduct is more probable than the admittedly conjectural identification with the balsam tree or mulberry tree, for it suits the context, since such an aqueduct is mentioned in ver. 8, by means of which David's men gained access to the previously unconquerable stronghold of the Jebusites, now Jerusalem. Furthermore, the valley of Rephaim was known for its good water (2 S 23:13, 15, 16).

24. **sound.** 2 K 7:6. 19:7. **a going.** or, a stepping. *S#6807h. 1 Ch 14:15. Is 3:20. Since "mulberry trees" should be an underground aqueduct, when they heard the sound of footsteps through the aqueduct, they would know that the Jebusite security had been breached successfully by ascending the shaft which ascended from the valley to the top of the hill of the Jebusite stronghold, and it was time to launch their attack. **thou shalt bestir.** Ex 11:7h. Jg 4:14. 7:15. 1 S 14:9-12. 1 Ch 14:15. Ph 2:11, 12. **go out before.** ver. +2. Jg 4:14. Ps 60:12. Ezk 46:10. Jn *10:4.

25. **Geba.** 1 Ch 14:16, Gibeon. **Gazer.** i.e. *a portion*, ✠S#1507h. Jsh ◑16:10. 1 Ch 14:16.

2 SAMUEL 6

David fetches the ark from Kirjath-jearim on a new cart, 1-5. Uzzah is smitten, David is disconcerted, and the ark is left with Obed-edom, whose house is blessed on account of it, 6-11. David brings the ark to Zion with sacrifices; and dances before it, for which Michal despises him, 12-16. He places it in a tabernacle with joy and feasting, 17-19. Michal, deriding David for his religious joy, continues childless, 20-23.

1. **gathered.** 2 S 5:1. 1 K 8:1. 1 Ch 13:1-4. Ps 132:1-6.

2. **Baale of Judah.** i.e. *possessors of Judah*, called

Baalah in Jsh 15:9, 10, and Kirjath Jearim in 1 Ch 13:6; and Kirjath-Baal in Jsh 15:60. 1 S 7:1. 1 Ch 13:5, 6. **whose name**, etc., *or,* at which the name, even the name of the Lord of hosts, was called upon. Le 24:11-16. Is 47:4. 54:5. **hosts.** 2 S 5:10. 1 S 1:3, 11. 15:2. 17:45. **dwelleth.** Ex 25:18-22. 1 S 4:4. 1 K 8:6, 7. Ps 80:1. 99:1. 1 P 1:12.

3. **set**, etc. Heb. made the ark of God to ride. Nu 4:5-12, *15. √7:9. 10:21. 1 S 6:7, 8, 14. **Gibeah.** *or*, the hill. 1 S 7:1. **Uzzah.** i.e. *strength*, *S#5798h. 2 K 21:18, 26. 1 Ch 8:7. 13:7, 9, 10, 11. Ezr 2:49. Ne 7:51. Also ver. 6, 7, 8. 1 Ch 6:29. **Ahio.** i.e. *his brother; brotherly*, *S#283h. ver. 4. 1 Ch 8:14, 31. 9:37. 13:7. (1) A son of Abinadab, 2 S 6:3, 4; 1 Ch 13:7. (2) One of the tribe of Benjamin, 1 Ch 8:14. (3) A Benjamite of the family of Gibeon, from which Saul descended, 1 Ch 8:31; 9:37.

4. **the house.** 1 S 7:1, 2. 1 Ch 13:7. **accompanying.** Heb. with.

5. **David.** 1 S 10:5. 16:16. 2 K 3:15. 1 Ch *13:8. 15:10-24. Ps 47:5. 68:25-27. 150:3-5. Da 3:5, 7, 10, 15. Am 5:23. 6:5. **all.** *√171A, Ex +9:6. **played.** 1 S 18:7. 1 Ch 13:8. 15:29. **on all manner.** This place should doubtless be corrected from the parallel place, 1 Ch 13:8; where, instead of *bechol atzey beroshim*, which is literally, "with all trees or wood of fir," we read *bechol oz oovesheerim*, "with all their might, and with songs." This makes good sense, while the former makes none: the LXX. have the same reading here, *en isxui, kai en odais*. But see following note on the figure of speech involved here. **fir wood.** *√121D1*. Metonymy of the Cause B557: *Trees* are put for *arms* or *instruments* made from them. For another instance of this figure see Na 2:3. **harps.** Ge 4:21. 31:27. 1 S 10:5. **psalteries.** 1 S 10:5. **timbrels.** Ge 31:27. **cymbals.** Ps 150:5.

6. **Nachon's.** i.e. *smitten; established*, *S#5225h. 1 Ch 13:9, he is called Chidon. **threshingfloor.** Ge +50:10. Dt +*16:13mg. **put forth.** Even the Kohath-ites, who were appointed to carry the ark, after it was covered by the priests, were forbidden to touch it on pain of death; but Uzzah, who certainly was no priest, probably with some degree of irreverence, hav-ing presumed to lay his hand upon the ark, which perhaps was not covered, thus incurred the penalty due to his rashness. Nu 4:15, 19, 20. 1 S 6:19. Mt=11:27. Col=2:18. **his hand.** 1 Ch 13:9. *√63A2*. Ellipsis (Absolute: of Accusative) B8: Omission of the object or accusative after the verb. Here, "his hand" must be supplied by ellipsis. For other instances of this figure see 1 Ch 16:7. Jb 24:6. Ps 21:12. 44:10. 57:2. 94:10. 103:9. 119:126n. 137:5. Pr 24:24. Is 53:12. Je 3:5, 12. 8:4. 16:7. Na 1:2. Mt 11:18. Lk 9:52. Jn 15:6. Ac 9:34. 10:10. Ro 15:28. 1 C 3:1. 7:17. 10:24. 2 C 5:16, 20. 11:20. Ph 3:13. 1 Th 3:1. 2 Th (2:6, 7). Ja 5:3. 1 P 2:23. **shook it.** *or*, stumbled. 2 K 9:33.

7. **God smote.** Le 10:1-3. 1 S 6:19. 1 Ch 13:10. 15:2, 13. 1 C *11:30-32. **error.** *or*, rashness.

8. **displeased.** 1 Ch 13:11, 12. Jon 4:1, 9. **made.** Heb. broken. 2 S 5:20. **a breach.** *√22C41*, 2 S +5:20. **Perez-uzzah.** that is, *the breach of Uzzah*. *S#6560h. 1 Ch 13:11. **to this day.** Jsh +4:9.

9. **afraid.** Nu 17:12, 13. 1 S 5:10, 11. 6:20. Ps 76:7. 119:120. Is 6:5. Lk=5:8, 9. 1 P 3:6. **How shall.** 1 K 8:27. 1 Ch 13:11, 12. Jb 25:5, 6.

10. **Obed-edom.** i.e. *servant of Edom*, *S#5654h. ver. 11, 11, 12, 12. 1 Ch 13:13, 14, 14. 15:18, 21,

24, 25. 16:5, 38, 38. 26:4, 8, 8, 15. 2 Ch 25:24. (1) A Gittite in whose house the ark of God was kept three months after the Lord slew Uzzah for putting his hand on it, 2 S 6:6-10; 1 Ch 13:13. (2) A Levite who had charge of the vessels of the sanctuary in the time of King Amaziah, 2 Ch 25:24. **Gittite.** i.e. *winepress*, *S#1663h. ver. 11. Jsh 13:3. 2 S ◑4:3. 15:18, 19, 22. 18:2. 21:19. 1 Ch 13:13. 15:18, 21, 24. 16:5, 6. 20:5. Perhaps he was of Gath-Rimmon, a Levitical city, as in Jsh 21:24 (Young).

11. **the Lord blessed.** Ge 30:27. 39:5, 23. 1 Ch 13:14. Pr 3:9, 10. 10:22. Ml *3:10. Jn=14:23. 2 C=2:15, 16.

12. **because.** Mt 10:42. **So David.** 1 Ch 15:1-4, 11-14, 16, 25. Ps 24:7-10. 68:24-27. 132:6-8.

13. **when they.** Nu 4:15. 7:9. Jsh 3:3. 1 Ch 15:2, 15, 25, 26. **oxen.** 1 K 8:5. 2 Ch 5:6.

14. **danced.** Ex 15:20. Jg 11:34. 21:21. Ps 30:11. 149:3. 150:4. Lk 15:25. **with all his.** Dt 6:5. Ec 9:10. Col 3:23. **girded.** 1 S 2:18, 28. 22:18. 1 Ch 15:27. Ps 110:4. Zc 6:13.

15. **David.** Ps 132:28. **all.** *√171A, Ex +9:6. **with shouting.** 1 Ch 15:16, 24, 25, 28. Ezr 3:10, 11. Ps 47:1, 5, 6. 68:24-27. 1 Th *4:16. **the sound.** Nu 10:1-10. Jsh 6:4, 5. Ps 150:3. 1 Th *4:16.

16. **And as.** 1 Ch 15:29. **Michal.** See on 2 S 3:14. **looked through.** Jg 5:28. 2 K 9:30. **despised.** 1 Ch 15:29. Ps 69:7. Is *53:2, 3. Ac 2:13. 1 C 1:28. *2:14.

17. **they brought.** 1 Ch 15:1. 16:1. 2 Ch 1:4. Ps 132:1-8. **pitched.** Heb. stretched. Ge 12:8. 26:25. **of-fered.** 1 K 8:5, 62-65. 2 Ch 5:6. 7:5-7. Ezr 6:16, 17. **burnt offerings.** Le +*23:12. **peace offerings.** Le +*23:19. 1 K 8:63.

18. **as soon.** 1 K 8:55. 1 Ch 16:2. 2 Ch 6:3. 30:18, 19, 27. Ac 3:26. **burnt offerings.** Le +*23:12. **peace offerings.** Le +*23:19. **he blessed.** Ge 14:19. Ex 39:43. Le 9:22, 23. 2 Ch 30:27. He 7:1-7.

19. **he dealt.** 1 Ch 16:3. 2 Ch 30:24. 35:7, 8, 12, 13. Ne 8:10. Ezk 45:17. Ac 20:35. Ep 4:8. **So all the.** 1 K 8:66. 2 Ch 7:10.

20. **bless.** ver. 18. Ge *18:19. Jsh *24:15. 1 Ch 16:43. Ps 30, title. 101:2. **Michal.** ver. 16. Ps 69:7-9. Mk 3:21. **How.** *√60D, Ge +37:19. *√91. Exouthenismos; or, Contempt B939: An expression of feeling by way of contempt. For other instances of this figure see Jb 26:2. Je 22:23. **glorious.** Ne 4:3, 4. Is 53:2, 3. Jn 13:6. 1 C 4:10-13. Ro 2:7, 8. **uncovered.** We are only to understand by this expression that David had divested himself of his royal robes, in order to appear humble before the Lord, by assimilating himself to the condi-tion of one of the priests or Levites: for we find that he was "girded with a linen ephod;" and consequently no part of his body was exposed, having only put off his outer garments. The terms *uncovered* or *naked* frequently mean no more than this in Scripture. ver. 14, 16. Ex 32:25n. 1 S 19:23, 24. Jb 24:10. Mt 25:43. Jn 21:7n. **vain fellows.** Jg 9:4. Jb 30:8. **shamelessly.** *or*, openly. 1 P 4:14.

21. **before.** ver. 14, 16. 1 C 10:31. Col *3:23. 2 T 1:7. **chose.** 1 S 13:14. 15:28. 16:1, 12. Ps 78:70-72. 89:19, 20. Ac 13:22. **play.** ver. 5. 1 Ch 15:29. Ps 69:7-9. 123:4.

22. **more vile.** Ps 51:5. 69:5. Is 50:6. 51:7. Mt 5:11, 12. Ac 5:41, 42. He 12:2. 1 P *4:14. **in mine.** Ge 32:10. Jb 40:4. 42:6. 1 T 1:15. 1 P 5:6. **maid-servants.** *or*, handmaids. **I be had.** 1 S 2:30.

23. **Michal.** 1 S 1:6-8. Is 4:1. Ho 9:11. Lk 1:25. **no

child. Ge +*11:30. Le 20:20. Ps +*127:3. Je 22:30.
unto the day. 1 S 15:35. Is 22:14. Mt 1:25.

2 SAMUEL 7

David purposes to build a temple, and Nathan encourages him, 1-3. God, by Nathan, forbids it, but with promises of special blessings to Israel, to David, and to his seed, 4-17. David's prayer and thanksgiving, 18-29.

1. **the king.** 1 Ch 17:1, etc. Da 4:29, 30. **the Lord.** Jsh 21:44. 23:1. 1 K 5:4. 2 Ch 14:6. Ps 18, title. Pr *16:7. Lk 1:74, 75.

2. **Nathan.** 2 S 12:1. 1 Ch 29:29. **I dwell.** 2 S 5:11. 1 Ch 14:1. *17:1. Je 22:13-15. Hg 1:4. **the ark.** Ps 132:5. Jn 2:17. Ac 7:46. **curtains.** 2 S 6:17. Ex 26:1-14. 40:21. 1 Ch 16:1. 2 Ch 1:4. √121D3. Metonymy of the Cause B558. Curtains are put for tents. For other instances of this figure see Je 4:20. Hab 3:7.

3. **Go, do.** 2 K 4:27. **all that.** 1 S +*16:7. 1 K √8:17, 18. ◐*10:24. 1 Ch 22:7. 28:2. Ps 20:4. 37:4. **for the.** 1 S 10:7. 1 J 2:27.

4. **that night.** Nu 12:6. 1 Ch 17:3. Am 3:7.

5. **my servant David.** Heb. to my servant, to David. 1 Ch 17:7. **Shalt.** 1 K 5:3. 8:16-19. 1 Ch 17:4. *22:7, 8. *28:3, etc. **me.** √84, Ge +6:17.

6. **I have not.** Jsh 18:1. 1 K 8:16. 1 Ch 17:5, 6. **walked.** Ex 33:14, 15. 40:35-38. Le 26:23, 24, 27, 28. Nu 10:33-36. Dt 23:14. 2 C 6:16. Re 2:1. **tent.** Ex 40:18, 19, 34. Ac 7:44.

7. **walked.** Le 26:11, 12. Dt 23:14. 2 C 6:16. **any of the tribes.** 1 Ch 17:6, any of the judges. Instead of *shivtey*, "tribes," we should probably read, with Houbigant, Drs. Waterland and A. Clarke, and others, *shophtey*, "judges;" which is the reading in the parallel passage. Indeed there is but one letter of difference between them, and letters which might be easily mistaken for each other; the apex under the upper stroke of the *pay*, being the only mark to distinguish it from the *baith*. Compare ver. 11. **feed.** 2 S 5:2. Ps 78:71, 72. Is 40:11. Je 3:15. 23:4. Ezk 34:2, 15, 23. Mi 5:4. Mt 2:6mg. Jn *21:15-17. Ac *20:28. 21:28. 1 P *5:2.

8. **the Lord.** 2 C ▶6:18. **I took thee.** 1 S 16:11, 12. 1 Ch 17:7. Ps 78:70. **following.** Heb. after. Ps 78:71mg. Je +17:16mg. Am 7:15mg. **ruler.** 2 S 6:21. 12:7. 1 S 9:16. 10:1.

9. **And I was.** 2 S 5:10. 8:6, 14. 22:30, 34-38. 1 S 18:14. 1 Ch 17:8. Ps 121:8. **cut off.** 2 S 22:1. 1 S 31:6. Ps 18:37-42. 89:23. 132:18. **out of thy sight.** Heb. from thy face. Is 5:21mg. **a great name.** Ge *12:2. 1 S 2:8. 1 Ch 17:8. Ps 113:7, 8. Lk 1:52. **like unto.** Ps 87:3-6.

10. **I will.** Ps 89:3, 4. **plant them.** 1 Ch 17:9. Ps 44:2. 80:8. Je +11:17. 18:9. 24:6. Ezk 37:25-27. Am √9:15. **a place.** Jn 14:2, 3. 1 P 1:4. Re 3:12. **neither.** Ps 89:22, 23. Is 60:18. Ezk 28:24. Ho 2:18. Re 21:4. **move no more.** 2 K *21:8. Is *60:21. Je *24:6. *32:41. *33:19-22. Ezk 34:28. √37:25. Jl √3:20. Am +√9:15. Mi 4:4. **children of wickedness.** 2 S 3:34mg. Ps 89:22. **as beforetime.** Ex 1:13, 14, 22. Jg 4:3. 6:2-6. 1 S 13:17.

11. **since.** Jg 2:14-16. 1 S 12:9-11. Ps 106:42. **have caused.** ver. 1. Jb 5:18, 19. 34:29. Ps 46:9. **he will make.** ver. 27. Ex 1:21. 1 K 2:24. 11:38. 1 Ch 17:10. 22:10. Ps 89:3, 4. 127:1. Pr 14:1. He *3:6. **house.** √121J4, Ge +7:1.

12. **And when.** 1 K 2:1. *8:20. Jb 7:1. **sleep.** Ge

+*25:8n. Dt *31:16n. 1 K 1:21. +*11:43. +14:20. Da +*12:2n. Ac 13:36. 1 C *15:51. 1 Th *4:14. **I will set.** Ge 15:4. Jsh 17:14. 1 K *8:20. 1 Ch *17:11. Ps *89:29. 115:12. *132:11, 12. Is *9:7. *11:1-3, 10. Mt 22:42-44. Ac 2:30. Ro 1:3. 2 T 2:8. **thy seed.** T#1881. Ps 16:8-10. 89:3, 4, 35-37. Is +*9:6, 7. +*55:3, 4. Am *9:11, 12. Mt +1:1. Lk 1:32, 69. Ac 2:25-28. +*13:23. 15:15-18.

13. **He shall.** 1 K 5:5. *6:12. *8:19. 1 Ch 17:11, 12. *22:9, 10. 28:6, 10. Zc 6:13. Mt *16:18. Lk *1:31-33. He 3:3. 1 P *2:5. **an house.** 1 K *11:38, 39. Am √9:11. Ac +*15:16. **I will stablish.** ver. +*16. 1 K 2:45. 8:25. 9:5. 1 Ch 22:10. *28:7. Ps 21:4, 7. 89:*4, 21, *27-29, *35-37. 132:11-18. Is *9:7. 49:8. +*55:3. Lk √1:32, 33. **the throne.** He +*1:8. **his kingdom.** Da +*7:14. He +*1:8. **for ever.** Heb. *olam*, Ex +12:24. Ge +9:16. Da +*7:14. He +*1:8. Re √11:15.

14. **I will be.** 1 Ch 17:13. 28:6. Ps 89:20-37. Mt 3:17. 2 C *6:16, 18. He ▶1:5. Re ▶21:7. **If he.** Ps 89:30-35. **I will.** Dt 8:5. Jb 5:17. Ps 94:12, 13. Pr 3:11, 12. Je 30:11. 1 C 11:32. He 12:5-11. Re 3:19. **with the rod.** T#265. 2 K 5:1. 1 Ch 6:15. Jb 1:15, 17, 21. Ps 17:13, 14. +39:9 (T#278). Is 10:5-7, 12, 15. 13:5. 37:7. Je 27:8. 50:9. Ezk 25:14. Hab 1:6, 12.

15. **But my mercy.** ver. 14, 16. 1 S 19:24. Ps 89:28, *33, 34. Is 38:5. +√55:3. Ac 13:34-37. **not depart.** 1 S ◐+28:19. 1 K +*11:39. 1 Ch ◐*28:9. Ps *89:28, 33, 37. +√132:11. **as I took.** 1 S *15:23, 28. 16:14. 1 K 11:13, 34-36. Is 9:7. 37:35.

16. **thine house.** ver. +*13. Ge *49:10. 1 K 1:48. 2 K 19:34. 1 Ch 17:13, 14. Ps 45:6. 72:*5, 8, *17-19. 89:36, 37. Is *9:7. Da *2:44. +*7:14. Mt *16:18. Lk √1:32, 33. Jn 12:34. **for ever.** Heb. *olam*, Ex +12:24. Ps 145:13. Da *7:14. Jn *12:34. **thy throne.** He √1:8. Re 11:15. **for ever.** Heb. *olam*, Ex +12:24.

17. **According to.** 1 Ch 17:15. Ac 20:20, 27. 1 C *15:3.

18. **sat.** Jg +*20:26n. 1 Ch 17:16. Is 37:14. **Who am I.** √85F, Ps +8:4. Ge *32:10. Ex 3:11. Jg 6:15. 1 S 9:21. 15:17. 18:18. Ps 8:4. Ep 3:8.

19. **And this.** 2 S 12:8. Nu 16:9, 13. **but thou.** ver. 11-16. 1 Ch 17:17. Ps 103:17. **And is this.** √85F, Ps +8:4. Ps 36:7. Is √55:8, 9. Ep 2:7. 3:19, 20. **manner.** Heb. law. 1 Ch 17:17. **of.** √181E, Ge +3:24.

20. **knowest.** Ge *18:19. 1 S *16:7. 1 Ch 17:19. Ps *139:1. Jn +*2:25. 21:17. He *4:13. Re 2:23.

21. **thy word's.** Nu 23:19. Dt 9:5. Jsh 23:14, 15. Ps 115:1. 138:2. Is 43:25. Je 14:7. Ezk 36:22. Mt 24:35. Lk 1:54, 55, 72. **according.** Mt 11:26. Lk 10:21. 12:32. 1 C 1:1. Ep 1:9. 3:11.

22. **Wherefore.** Dt 3:24. 1 Ch 16:25. 2 Ch 2:5. Ps 48:1. 86:10. 96:4. 135:5. 145:3. Ezk 36:22, 32. **great.** √12112, Ge +2:17. **none.** Ex 15:11. Dt 4:35. 32:39. 1 S 2:2. Ps 86:8. 89:6, 8. Is 40:18, 25. 45:5, 18, 22. Je 10:6, 7. Mi 7:18.

23. **what one.** Dt 4:7, 8, 32-34. 33:29. Ps 147:20. Ro 3:1, 2. **went.** Ex 3:7, 8. 19:5, 6. Nu 14:13, 14. Ps 111:9. Is 63:7-14. T 2:14. 1 P 2:9. Re 5:9. **make him.** Ex 9:16. Jsh 7:9. 1 Ch 17:21. Is 63:12, 14. Ezk 20:9. Ep 1:6. **and to do.** √38B, 2 S +1:24. **great things.** Dt 10:21. Ps 40:5. 65:5. 66:3. 106:22. 145:6. **thy people.** Dt 9:26. 15:15. Ne 1:10. **nations and their gods.** Ex 12:12.

24. **confirmed.** Ge 17:7. Dt 26:18. **art become.** ver. 23. Ex 15:2. Dt 27:9. 1 Ch 17:22. Ps *48:14. Is *12:2. Je 31:1, 33. 32:38. Ho 1:10. Zc 13:9. Jn √1:12. Ro

9:25, 26. 1 P 2:10. **for ever.** Heb. *olam*, Ex +12:24. Ge +9:12. Je +√31:36. Ro +√11:1.

25. **his house.** T#1488. 2 S 12:15, 16. Ge 17:18. 27:26-28. 28:1-4. 32:9-12. 48:14-16. 1 K 8:25, 26. 2 K 4:1. 1 Ch 22:11, 12. 2 Ch 1:9. Ps 72:1. 144:12. La 2:19-21. Mt 9:18. 15:22. 19:13-15. 20:20, 21. Lk 16:27-30. Jn 4:46, 47. **establish it.** Ge 32:12. Ps 119:49. Je 11:4, 5. Ezk 36:37. **for ever.** Heb. *olam*, Ex +12:24. Ge +9:12. **and do.** Ge 32:12. Ex 32:13. 1 K *8:25. Ps *119:58.

26. **let thy.** 1 Ch 17:23, 24. 29:10-13. Ps 72:18, 19. 115:1. Mt *6:9. Jn 12:28. **for ever.** Heb. *olam*, Ex +12:24. **before thee.** Ge 17:18. 1 Ch 17:23, 24. Ps 89:36.

27. **revealed.** Heb. opened the ear. Ru +4:4mg. 1 S 9:15mg. Ps 40:6. **I will.** ver. 11. **found.** 1 Ch 17:25, 26. Ps 10:17.

28. **thy words.** Nu +*23:19. Jn *17:17. 2 C 1:20. T +*1:2n.

29. **let it please thee to bless.** Heb. be thou pleased and bless. Nu *6:24-26. 2 K 5:23. 1 Ch 17:27. Ps *115:12-15. **for ever.** Heb. *olam*, Ex +12:24. 2 S *22:51.

2 SAMUEL 8

David subdues the Philistines and Moabites, 1, 2. He smites Hadadezer and the Syrians, 3-8. Toi, king of Hamath, sends his son to David with presents, which he dedicates to God, with the spoils that he had taken, 9-13. He puts garrisons in Edom, 14. He reigns in equity, 15. The names of his chief officers, 16-18.

1. A.M. 2964. B.C. 1040. An. Ex. Is 451. **And after.** 2 S 7:9. 21:15-22. **Metheg-ammah.** *or*, the bridle of Ammah. i.e. *the bridle of the arm*, *S#4965h, only here. 2 S 2:24. 1 Ch 18:1, etc., Gath. In the parallel passage of Chronicles, we read, "David took Gath and her towns;" and it is probable that *Gath* and its districts were called *Metheg-ammah* in David's time; which, being unusual or becoming obsolete, in the time of the author of the Chronicles, led him thus to explain it.

2. **he smote.** Nu *24:17. Jg 3:29, 30. 1 S 14:47. Ps 60:8. 83:6. 108:9. **measured.** 2 S 12:31. Is 18:2. 28:17. **them.** ʃ121K1, Dt 9:1. **And so.** ver. 6, 12-14. 2 K 1:1. 3:4-27. 1 Ch 18:2. **brought gifts.** 1 S 10:27. 2 Ch 26:8. Ps 72:10, 11. Is 36:16. Mt 2:11.

3. **Hadadezer.** i.e. *Hadad is help; noisy helper*, *S#1909h. ver. 5, 7, 8, 9, 10, 10, 12. 1 K 11:23. 1 Ch ◐18:3, Hadarezer. **Rehob.** i.e. *broad*. ver. 12. 2 S 10:8. Nu +13:21. Compare *S#7339h, Am +5:16n. **Zobah.** i.e. perhaps *a station*. 2 S 10:6. 1 S 14:47. K 11:23, 24. Ps 60, title. Called also *Aram-Zobah*, Ps 60, title. **at the river.** Ge *15:18. Ex 23:31. Dt 11:24. 1 K 4:21. Ps 72:8.

4. **from him.** *or*, of his. **chariots.** As 1 Ch 18:4. See another elipsis supplied from Chronicles at 2 S 5:8. **seven hundred.** In the parallel place in Chronicles it is *"seven thousand horsemen,"* a far more probable number. The letter *zayin*, with a dot upon it, stands for *seven thousand*, and the final letter, *noon*, for *seven hundred*: the great similarity of these letters might easily cause the one to be mistaken for the other, and so produce an error in this place. **David houghed.** Dt 17:16. Jsh *11:6, 9. Ps 20:7. 33:16, 17. **reserved.** 1 K 10:26.

5. **And when.** 1 K 11:23-25. 1 Ch 18:5, 6. Is 7:8. **came.** Jb 9:13. Ps 83:4-8. Is 8:9, 10. 31:3. **Zobah.** From 2 Ch 8:3, we learn that *Zobah* was the district in which *Tadmor* or *Palmyra* was situated; and consequently lay between the land of Israel and the Euphrates. The capital was probably the same as the *Sabe* mentioned by Ptolemy as a city of Arabia Deserta.

6. **garrisons.** ver. 14. 2 S 23:14. 1 S 13:3. 14:1, 6, 15. 2 Ch 17:2. Ps 18:34-46. **became.** ver. 2. **the Lord.** ver. 14. 2 S 7:9. 1 Ch 18:13. Ps 5:11, 12. 121:7, 8. 140:7. 144:1, 2. Pr 21:31.

7. **shields.** 1 K 10:16, 17. 14:26, 27. 1 Ch 18:7. 2 Ch 9:15, 16.

8. **Betah.** i.e. *confidence; security; refuge*, *S#984h, only here. In 1 Ch 18:8 it is called Tibhath, i.e. *slaughter*. Probably the same as *Bathne* in Syria, between Beroaea and Hierapolis. 1 Ch 18:8, Tibhath. **Berothai.** i.e. *my wells*, *S#1268h. 1 Ch 18:8, Chun. Ezk 47:16h, Berothah. Berothai is probably the *Barathena* of Ptolemy, which he mentions, along with *Sabe*, as a city of Arabia Deserta, in the confines of the Palmyrenian district. **exceeding.** 1 Ch 22:14, 16. 29:7. 2 Ch 4:1-18.

9. **Toi.** i.e. *erring; wandering*, *S#8583h. ver. 10, 10. 1 Ch 18:9, Tou. **Hamath.** Nu 34:8. Am 6:2.

10. **Joram.** 1 Ch 18:10, Hadoram. **salute him.** Heb. ask him of peace. Ge 29:6mg. 43:27. 2 K 4:23mg, 26. Is 39:1. **to bless him.** 1 S 13:10mg. 1 K 1:47. Ps 129:8. **had wars.** Heb. was a man of wars. 1 Ch 18:10mg. Is 42:13. **brought with him.** Heb. in his hand were. 11. **Which.** 1 K *7:51. 1 Ch 18:11. 22:14-16. 26:26-28. 29:2. Mi 4:13.

12. **Syria.** 2 S 10:11, 14. 12:26-31. 1 Ch 18:11.

13. **gat him.** 2 S 7:9. 1 Ch 18:12. Ps 60, title. **smiting.** Heb. his smiting. **the valley of salt.** 2 K 14:7. 2 Ch 25:11. **being.** *or*, slaying. 1 Ch 18:12.

14. **all they.** Ge 25:23. 27:29, 37, 40. Nu *24:18. 1 K 22:47. 1 Ch 18:13. Ps 60:8, 9. 108:9, 10. **the Lord.** See on ver. 6. Ps 121:4-8. Pr 20:26, 28.

15. **over all Israel.** 2 S 3:12. 5:5. **David executed.** 2 S 23:3, 4. 1 Ch 18:14. Ps 45:6, 7. 72:2. 75:2. 78:71, 72. 89:14. 101:1-8. 119:121. Pr 8:15. Is 9:7. Je 22:15, 16. 23:5, 6. Am 5:15, 24.

16. **Joab.** 2 S 19:13. 20:23. 1 Ch 11:6. 18:15-17. **Jehoshaphat.** i.e. *whom Jehovah judges; Jehovah is judge*, *S#3092h. 2 S 20:24. 1 K 4:*3, 17. 15:24. 22:2, 4, 4, 5, 7, 8, 8, 10, 18, 29, 30, 32, 32, 41, 42, 44, 45, 48, 49, 49, 50, 51. 2 K 1:17. 3:1, 7, 11, 12, 12, 14. 8:16, 16. 9:2, 14. 12:18. 1 Ch 3:10. 18:15. 2 Ch 17:1, 3, 5, 10, 11, 12. 18:1, 3, 4, 6, 7, 7, 9, 17, 28, 29, 31, 31. 19:1, 2, 4, 8. 20:1, 2, 3, 5, 15, 18, 20, 25, 27, 30, 31, 34, 35, 37. 21:1, 2, 2, 12. 22:9. Jl 3:2, 12. (1) The royal recorder under David and Solomon, 2 S 8:16; 1 K 4:3. (2) One of Solomon's purveyors, 1 K 4:17. (3) The son of Asa who succeeded his father as king of Judah. He reigned B.C. 914-890, and was pious and prosperous, 2 Ch 17:3-6. (4) The father of King Jehu, 2 K 9:2, 14. (5) A priest in the time of David, 1 Ch 15:24. (6) A valley named only in Joel 3:2, 12, usually identified with the valley of the brook Kedron. **Ahilud.** i.e. *brother of one born*, *S#286h. 2 S 20:24. 1 K 4:8, 12. 1 Ch 18:15. **recorder.** *or*, remembrancer, *or* writer of chronicles. Ge 41:9. Nu 5:15. 2 S 20:24. 1 K 4:3mg. 2 K 18:18mg, 37. 1 Ch 18:15mg. 2 Ch 34:8. Is 36:3mg, 22. 62:6mg. 66:3mg. Ezk 21:23. 29:16.

17. **Zadok**. i.e. *just*, *S#6659h. 2 S 15:24, 25, 27, 29, 35, 35, 36. 17:15. 18:19, 22, 27. 19:11. 20:25. 1 K 1:8, 26, 32, 34, 38, 39, 44, 45. 2:35. 4:2, 4. 2 K 15:33. 1 Ch 6:8, 8, 12, 12, 53. 9:11. 12:28. 15:11. 16:39. 18:16. 24:3, 6, 31. 27:17. 29:22. 2 Ch 27:1. 31:10. Ezr 7:2. Ne 3:4, 29. 10:21. 11:11. 13:13. Ezk 40:46. 43:19. 44:15. 48:11. (1) One of the two high priests in David's time, 2 S 20:25. (2) A priest in King Ahaziah's time, 1 Ch 6:12. (3) Father of Jerusha, King Uzziah's wife, 2 K 15:33; 2 Ch 27:1. (4) One of the Jews who repaired the wall of Jerusalem, Ne 3:4. (5) A priest, Ne 3:29. (6) A Jew who sealed the covenant, Ne 10:21. (7) A scribe in charge of the treasuries, Ne 13:13. **Ahitub**. i.e. *brother of good*. **Ahimelech**. i.e. *brother of the king*, *S#288h. 1 S 21:1, 1, 2, 8. 22:9, 11, 14, 16, 20. 23:6. 26:6. 30:7. 1 Ch 24:3, 6, 31. Ps 52:t. (1) The son of Ahitub and brother of Ahiah. He succeeded the latter as high priest, and received David at the tabernacle in Nob when fleeing from Saul, and gave him the showbread and Goliath's sword. Saul caused Ahimelech to be put to death for this act. (2) A Hittite, an officer of David's army when pursued by Saul, 1 S 26:6. **Abiathar**. or rather perhaps "Abiathar, son of Ahimelech," see 1 S 21:2; 22:9; Ps 52:2; but compare 1 Ch 24:3, 6, 31 (Young). **and Seraiah**. i.e. *Jah's prince; warrior of Jehovah*, *S#8304h. 2 S 20:25, Sheva. 1 K 4:3, Shisha. 2 K 25:18, 23. 1 Ch 4:13, 14, 35. 6:14, 14. 18:16, Shavsha. Ezr 2:2. 7:1. Ne 10:2. 11:11. 12:1, 12. Je 40:8. 51:59, 59, 61. 52:24. (1) David's scribe or secretary, 2 S 8:17. He is called Sheva in 2 S 20:25, Shisha in 1 K 4:3, and Shavsha in 1 Ch 18:16. (2) The chief priest in the reign of Zedekiah, 2 K 25:18; 1 Ch 6:14. (3) An Israelite of Nopha, 2 K 25:23; Je 40:8. (4) A son of Kenaz, 1 Ch 4:13, 14. (5) A descendant of Simeon, 1 Ch 4:35. (6) A priest who returned with Zerubbabel, Ezr 2:2; Ne 10:2. (7) An ancestor of Ezra, Ezr 7:1; Ne 11:11. (8) A chief man under Jehoiakim, Je 36:26. (9) One of the princes of Jerusalem who accompanied King Zedekiah to Babylon, Je 51:59, 61. **scribe**. or, secretary. That is, *writer*, as in Jg 5:14. 1 K 4:3mg. 2 K 18:18mg.

18. **Benaiah**. 1 K 1:44. 2:34, 35. 1 Ch 18:17. **Jehoiada**. 1 Ch 18:17. **the Cherethites**. i.e. *cutters off*, that is, *executioners*. *S#3774h. It is a gentile name in 1 S 30:14; Ezk 25:16; Zp 2:5 (Young). 2 S 15:18. 20:7, 23. 23:20-23. 1 S 30:14. Ezk 25:16. Zp 2:5. **Pelethites**. i.e. *runners*, S#6432h, as in 2 S 15:18; 20:7, 23. 1 K 1:38. **chief rulers**. or, princes. 2 S 20:26. Is +24:2mg.

2 SAMUEL 9

David inquires after Saul's family and is informed, by Ziba, of Mephibosheth the son of Jonathan, 1-4. He sends for him and entertains him at his table for Jonathan's sake, 5-8. He restores to him the family estate, intrusting the management to Ziba, 9-13.

1. **show him**. 2 S 1:26. 1 S 18:1-4. 20:14-17, 42. 23:16-18. 1 K 2:7. Ps 24:3, 4. Pr *27:10. Mt 10:42. 25:40. Mk 9:41. Jn 19:26, 27. Phm 9-12. 1 P 3:8.

2. **a servant**. Ge 15:2, 3. 24:2. 39:6. **was Ziba**. i.e. *a thing planted*, *S#6717h. ver. 3, 4, 9, 10, 11, 12. 2 S 16:1, 2, 2, 3, 4, 4. 19:17, 29.

3. **the kindness of God**. ʃ24L, Ge +6:2. That is, the *highest degree of kindness*; as "the hail of God" is very great hail; the "mountains of God" exceeding high mountains; besides which, this kindness was ac-

cording to the covenant of God made between him and Jonathan. Ge +23:6. Dt 4:37. 10:15. 1 S 20:14-17. Mt 5:44, 45. Lk 6:36. T 3:3, 4. **yet a son**. 2 S 4:4. 19:26.

4. **Where**. Dt 32:10. **Machir**. i.e. *sold*. 2 S 17:27-29. Ge 50:23. Nu 26:29. 32:39. Jg 5:14. **Ammiel**. i.e. *people of God*. ver. 5. 2 S 17:27. Nu 13:12. **Lo-debar**. lit. *without anything* or *without pasture*, as 2 S 17:27. This place appears to have been situated beyond Jordan; and was probably, as Reland supposes, the same as *Debir* or *Lidbir*, Jsh 13:26.

5. **sent, and**. Ps 63:1. 68:9.

6. **Mephibosheth**. 1 Ch 8:34. 9:40, called Meribbaal. **he fell**. Ge 18:2. 33:3. 1 S 20:41. 25:23.

7. **Fear not**. Ge 43:18, 23. 50:18-21. 1 S 12:19, 20, 24. Is 35:3, 4. Mk 5:33, 34. Lk 1:12, 13, 29, 30. **for I will**. See on ver. 1, 3. Ru 2:11, 12. 2 T 1:16-18. **kindness**. T#320. 2 S 19:32, 33. Mt 25:34-36. **father**. ʃ171G, Ge +13:8. Here, father is put for grandfather. 1 K +15:10n. **eat bread**. ver. 11. 2 S 19:28, 33. 1 K 2:7. Ps 41:9. Je 52:33, 34. Mt *6:11. Lk 22:30. Re *3:20.

8. **a dead dog**. 2 S 3:8. 16:9. 1 S 24:14, 15. 26:20. Mt 15:26, 27.

9. **I have given**. 2 S 16:4. 19:29. 1 S 9:1. Is 32:8.

10. **shall eat bread**. The eating at courts was of two kinds; the one public and ceremonious, the other private. Sir John Chardin understands those passages which speak of a right to eat at the royal table, as pointing out a right to a seat there, when the repast was public and solemn. So in a MS. Note on 1 K 2:7, he tells us that it was to be understood of the *majlis*, (the term for an assembly of lords, or a public feast), and not of the daily and ordinary repast. Hence, though Mephibosheth was to eat at all public times at the king's table, yet he would heed the produce of his lands for food at other times, which it was necessary for Ziba to understand. ver. 7, 11-13. 2 S 19:28. 1 K 2:7. 2 K 25:29. Lk 14:15.

11. **Ziba**. 2 S 19:17. **According**. 2 S 16:1-4. 19:26. **said the king**. ʃ63BA, Ge +26:7. Ex 18:4.

12. **Mephibosheth**. ʃ66, Ge +9:3. **son**. 1 Ch 8:8, 34-40. 9:40-44, Micah. **Micha**. i.e. *humble*, *S#4316h. 1 Ch 9:15. Ne 10:11. 11:17, 22. (1) A Levite who sealed the covenant made by Nehemiah, Ne 10:11. See Micah, Number 5, 1 Ch 9:15. (2) The son of Merib-baal, 2 S 9:12. See Micah, Number 4, 1 Ch 8:34, 35. **servants**. Mi 7:5, 6.

13. **Mephibosheth**. ʃ16, Ge +1:27. **he did eat**. ver. 7, 10, 11. **was lame**. ver. 3.

2 SAMUEL 10

David sends ambassadors to comfort Hanun, the king of Ammon, on the death of his father; who grossly insults them, 1-4. David counsels and comforts them, 5. The Ammonites, assisted by the Syrians, are overcome by Joab and Abishai, 6-14. Hadarezer sends another army, which David conquers, slaying Shobach, its general, 15-18. The kings of Syria submit to David, 19.

1. A.M. 2967. B.C. 1037. An. Ex. Is. 454. **king**. Jg 10:7-9. 11:12-28. 1 S 11:1-3. 1 Ch 19:1-3. **Hanun**. i.e. *gracious; favored*, *S#2586h. ver. 2, 3, 4. 1 Ch 19:2, 2, 3, 4, 6. Ne 3:13, 30. (1) A king of the Ammonites who insulted the messengers whom David sent to comfort him after the death of his father, 2 S 10:2; 1 Ch

19:4. (2) A Jew who aided in repairing the walls of Jerusalem, Ne 3:13. (3) A Jew who, with Hananiah, repaired part of the walls of Jerusalem, Ne 3:30.

2. **show kindness**. Dt 23:3-6. Ne 4:3-7. 13:1-3. **Nahash**. 1 S 11:1. **as his father**. 1 S 22:3, 4.

3. **Thinkest thou that David doth**. Heb. In thine eyes doth David. **not**. Ge 42:9, 16. 1 C 13:5, 7.

4. **and shaved**. The beard is held in high respect and greatly valued in the East: the possessor considers it as his greatest ornament; often swears by it; and, in matters of great importance, pledges it; and nothing can be more secure than such a pledge; for its owner will redeem it at the hazard of his life. The beard was never cut off but in mourning, or as a sign of slavery. It is customary to shave the Ottoman princes, as a mark of their subjection to the reigning emperor (DelaMotraye, p. 247). The beard is a mark of authority and liberty among the Mohammedans. The Persians who clip the beard, and shave above the jaw, are reputed heretics. They who serve in the seraglios have their beards shaven, as a sign of servitude; nor are they allowed to let them grow till the sultan has set them at liberty. Among the Arabians, it is more infamous for anyone to appear with his beard cut off, than among us to be publicly whipped or branded; and many would prefer death to such a punishment (Niebuhr, ch. vii). See Note on Is 50:6. 2 S 19:24. Le *19:27. 1 Ch 19:3, 4. Ezr 9:3. Ps 109:4, 5. Is 15:2. Je 41:5. 48:37. Lk 22:64. Jn 18:22. **cut off**. Is 20:4. 47:2, 3. Je 41:5. Re 3:18.

5. **Jericho**. Jsh 6:24-26. 1 K 16:34. 1 Ch 19:5.

6. **stank**. Ge 34:30. Ex 5:21. 1 S 13:4. 27:12. 1 Ch 19:6, 7. Is 65:5. **Syrians of Beth-rehob**. i.e. *house of the broad way*, *S#1050h. 2 S 8:3, 5, 12, Zobah. Jg 18:28h. Pr 25:8. Is 8:9, 10. **Zobah**. i.e. *army*, *S#6678h. ver. 8. **Maacah**. Jsh 13:11-13. **Ish-tob**. or, the men of Tob. Jg 11:3, 5.

7. **all the host**. 2 S 23:8, etc. 1 Ch 19:8, etc.

8. **at the entering**. This was at the city of *Medeba*, a city upon the borders of the Ammonites, and in their possession. 1 Ch 19:7. **Rehob**. ver. 6. Nu 13:21. Jsh 19:28. Jg 1:31. **Ishtob**. *S#382h. i.e. *good man*, *S#382h. ver. 6.

9. **the front**. Jsh 8:21, 22. Jg 20:42, 43.

11. **If**. 1 Ch 19:9-12. Ne 4:20. Lk 22:32. Ro 15:1. Ga 6:2. Ph 1:27, 28.

12. **Be of good**. This is a very fine military address, and equal to any thing of the kind in ancient or modern times. Ye fight *pro aris et focis*; for every good, sacred and civil; for God, for your families, and for your countries. Such harangues, especially in very trying circumstances, are very natural, and may perhaps be found in the records of every nation. Several instances might be quoted from Roman and Grecian history; but few are more remarkable than that of Tyrtaeus, the lame Athenian poet, to whom the command of the army was given in one of the Messenian wars. The Spartans had at that time suffered great losses, and all their stratagems proved ineffectual, so that they began to despair of success; when the poet, by his lectures on honor and courage, delivered in moving verse to the army, ravished them to such a degree with the thoughts of dying for their country, that, rushing on with a furious transport to meet their enemies, they gave them an entire overthrow, and by one decisive battle brought the war to a happy conclusion (See Potter,

vol ii. p. 76). Nu 13:20. Dt 31:6. Jsh 1:6, 7, 9, 18. 1 S 14:6, 12. 17:32. 2 Ch 32:7. Ne 4:14. He *13:6. **play**. 1 S 4:9. 1 Ch 19:13. 1 C *16:13. **the Lord**. 2 S 16:10, 11. Jg 10:15. 1 S 3:18. Jb 1:21.

13. **they fled**. 1 K 20:13-21, 28-30. 1 Ch 19:14, 15. 2 Ch 13:5-16.

14. **Abishai**. 1 S 26:6.

15. A.M. 2968. B.C. 1036. An. Ex. Is. 455. **gathered**. Ps 2:1. Is 8:9, 10. Mi 4:11, 12. Zc 14:2, 3. Re 19:19-21.

16. **Hadarezer**. i.e. *majesty of help*, *S#1928h. ver. 19. 2 S ●8:3-8. 1 Ch 18:3, 5, 7, 8, 9, 10, 10. 19:16, 19. **the river**. i.e. Euphrates. 2 S 8:3. **Helam**. i.e. *fortress*, *S#2431h. **Shobach**. i.e. *enlarging; turning back*, *S#7731h. ver. 18. or, Shophach. i.e. *pouring out*. 1 Ch 19:16.

17. **he gathered**. 1 Ch 19:17.

18. **fled**. 2 S 8:4. Ps 18:38. 46:11. **horsemen**. 1 Ch 19:18, footmen. **Shobach**. Jg 4:2, 22. 5:26.

19. **servants**. Ge 14:1-5. Jsh 11:10. Jg 1:7. 1 K 20:1. Da 2:37. **and served**. By paying a tribute, so that Ge *15:18 was now fulfilled (Young). **feared**. 2 S 8:6. 1 Ch 19:19. Ps 18:37, 38. 48:4, 5. Is 26:11. Re 18:10.

2 SAMUEL 11

Joab besieges Rabbah, 1. David commits adultery with Bath-sheba, the wife of Uriah, 2-4. She informs David that she is pregnant, 5; who sends for Uriah, and in vain tries to induce him to visit his wife, 6-13. He sends by Uriah a letter to Joab, according to which Uriah, with others, is slain by the Ammonites, 14-17. Joab sends word to David, and he answers the messengers in very improper language, 18-25. David marries Bath-sheba, who bears him a son; but God is displeased, 26, 27.

1. A.M. 2969. B.C. 1035. An. Ex. Is. 456. **after the year**, etc. Heb. at the return of the year. 1 K 20:22, 26. 2 Ch 36:10. Ec 3:8. **at the time**. The sacred historian seems to intimate that there was one particular time of the year to which military operations were limited; and Josephus informs us that this took place in the beginning of spring. In another part of his works he says that as soon as spring was begun, Adad levied and led forth his army against the Hebrews. Antiochus also prepared to invade Judea at the first appearance of spring; and Vespasian marched to Antipatris at the commencement of the same season. The kings and armies of the East, says Chardin, do not march except when there is grass and when they can encamp, which is in April. This rule, however, seems to be disregarded in modern times. 1 K 20:22, 26. 1 Ch *20:1. Jb 7:1mg. Ec 3:8. Is 40:2mg. **David sent**. 1 Ch 20:1. Zc 14:3. **Rabbah**. 2 S 12:26. Dt 3:11. 1 Ch 20:1. Ezk 21:20. **David tarried**. Ro *12:11. He 6:11, 12. 1 P *5:8.

2. **arose from**. 2 S 4:5, 7. Pr 19:15. 24:33, 34. Ezk *16:49. Mt 26:40, 41. 1 Th 5:6, 7. 1 P 4:7. **the roof of**. 2 S 16:22. Dt 22:8. Je 19:13. Mt 10:27. Ac 10:9. **he saw**. Ge *3:6. 6:2. 34:2. Jb √31:1. Ps +*101:3. 119:37. Mt *5:28. 1 J *2:16. **washing**. Heb. *rahats*, Ex +29:4. **very beautiful**. Ge *24:16. 26:7. 39:6. Pr 6:25. 31:30.

3. **sent**. Je 5:8. Ho 7:6, 7. Ja *1:14, 15. **Bath-sheba**. or, Bath-shua. i.e. *daughter of an oath*, *S#1339h. 2 S 12:24. 1 K 1:11, 15, 16, 28, 31. 2:13, 18, 19. 1 Ch 3:5, Bath-shua. Ps 51:t. **Eliam**. i.e. *God is gath-*

erer; God of the people, *S#463h. 2 S 23:34. *or,* Ammiel. 1 Ch 3:5. **Uriah.** i.e. *light of Jah,* ✛S#223h. (1) The husband of Bathsheba: ver. 6, 6, 7, 8, 8, 9, 10, 10, 11, 12, 12, 14, 15, 16, 17, 21, 24, 26, 26. 2 S 12:9, 10. 23:8, 39. 1 K 15:5. 1 Ch 11:41. (2) A rebuilder of Jerusalem's wall, Ezr 8:33. (3) A priest whom Isaiah took as a witness, Is 8:2.

4. **sent messengers.** Ge 39:7. Jb 31:9-11. Ps 50:18. **he lay.** Ps 51, title. Ga 5:19, 21. Ja *1:14, 15. **she was,** etc. *or,* and when she had purified herself, etc., she returned. Pr 30:20. Is 66:17. **purified.** Le 12:2-5. *15:19-28, etc. 18:19.

5. **I am with child.** Dt 22:22. Nu +*32:23. Pr 6:34. 7:23.

6. **Send me.** Ge 4:7. 38:18-23. 1 S 15:30. Jb 20:12-14. Pr *28:13. Is 29:13. Mt 26:70, 72, 74.

7. **how Joab did.** Heb. of the peace of Joab. Ge 29:6. 37:14. 1 S 17:22.

8. **go down.** Ps 44:21. Is 29:15. Lk 12:2. He *4:13. **wash.** Ge 18:4. 19:2. **there followed him.** Heb. there went out after him. Ps 12:2. 55:21. **a mess.** or, gift. A token of respect. Ge 43:34. 2 Ch 24:6, 9. Est 2:18.

9. **Uriah slept.** Jb 5:12-14. Pr 21:30.

11. **The ark.** 2 S 7:2, 6. 1 S 4:4. 14:18. **my lord.** 2 S 20:6. Mt 10:24, 25. Jn 13:14. 1 C 9:25-27. 2 T 2:3, 4, 12. He *12:1, 2. **shall I then.** Is 22:12-14. **as thou livest.** 2 S 14:19. 1 S 1:26. 17:55. 20:3. 25:26. **soul.** Heb. *nephesh,* Ge +27:31. **I will not.** ver. ◖1.

12. **Tarry.** Je 2:22, 23, 37.

13. **made him drunk.** lit. made him merry. Ge 9:21. 19:32-35. 43:34. Ex 32:21. SS 5:1. Hab *2:15. **with the servants.** ver. 9.

14. **wrote a letter.** It was resolved in David's mind that Uriah must die—that innocent, valiant, and gallant man, who was ready to sacrifice his life for the honor of his prince; and, worst of all, by being himself made the bearer of letters to Joab which prescribed the mode by which he was to be murdered. This was the greatest treachery and villany on the part of David; while Joab appears to enter as fully upon the execution of the murder, being perhaps pleased to have this opportunity of further enthralling his king and thus increasing his own power. 1 K 21:8-10. Ps 19:13. 52:2. 62:9. Je 9:1-4. 17:9. Mi 7:3-5.

15. **Set ye.** ver. 17. 1 S 18:17, 21, 25. Ps 51:4, 14. Je 20:23. **hottest.** Heb. strong. **from him.** Heb. from after him. **and die.** 2 S 12:9.

16. **he assigned.** ver. 21. 2 S 3:27. 20:9, 10. 1 S 22:17-19. 1 K 2:5, 31-34. 21:12-14. 2 K 10:6. Pr 29:12. Ho 5:11. Ac 5:29.

17. **there fell.** 2 S 12:9. Ps 51:14.

21. **Abimelech.** Jg 9:53. **Jerubbesheth.** ♪121G, Ge +31:1. i.e. *he will contend with shame,* *S#3380h, only here. Jg 6:32. 7:1, Jerubbaal. **Thy servant.** 2 S 3:27, 34. Ps 39:8. Is 14:10. Ezk 16:51, 52.

22. **the messenger.** Pr 25:13.

25. **displease thee.** Heb. be evil in thine eyes. 1 S 8:6mg. **for the sword.** Jsh 7:8, 9. 1 S 6:9. Ec 9:1-3, 11, 12. **one.** Heb. so and such. What abominable hypocrisy! He knew well that the death of this noble and gallant man was no chance-medley: he was by his own order killed. **make.** 2 S 12:26.

26. **she mourned.** 2 S 3:31. 14:2. Ge 27:41.

27. **And when,** etc. The whole of her conduct indicates that she observed the form, without feeling the power of sorrow. She lost a captain and got a king

for her husband; therefore, *Lacrymas non sponte cadentes effudit; gemitusque expressit pectore laeto;* "She shed reluctant tears; and forced out groans from a joyful breast!" **fetched her.** 2 S 3:2-5. 5:13-16. 12:9. Dt 22:29. **But the thing.** Ge 38:10. 1 Ch 21:7. **displeased.** Heb. was evil in the eyes of. ver. 25. Le 20:10. Ps 5:6. 50:18, 19, 21, 22. 51:4, 5. Pr 24:18mg. He *13:4.

2 SAMUEL 12

Nathan by a parable causes David to pass sentence on himself, 1-6. David, convicted by Nathan, confesses his guilt and is pardoned, but told that the child shall die, 7-14. The child is smitten and dies, though David fasted and prayed for him while he lived, 15-18. Finding that the child is dead, David worships God and takes comfort, 19-23. Solomon is born and named Jedidiah, 24, 25. David takes Rabbah and treats the Ammonites with severity, 26-31.

1. A.M. 2970. B.C. 1034. An. Ex. Is. 457. **the Lord.** 2 S 7:1-5. 24:11-13. 1 K 13:1. 18:1. 2 K 1:3. **unto David.** 2 S 11:10-17, 25. 14:14. Is 57:17, 18. **he came.** Ps *51, title. **There were.** There is nothing in this parable which requires illustration. Its bent is evident; and it was wisely constructed, by not having too near a resemblance, to make David unwittingly pass sentence on himself. The parable was in David's hand what his own letter was in the hands of the brave Uriah. Nathan at length closed in with him in the application of it. In beginning with a parable he showed his prudence, and great need there is in prudence in giving reproof; but now he speaks as an ambassador from God. He reminds David of the great things God had designed and done for him, and then charges him with a high contempt of the divine authority, and threatens an entail of judgments upon his family for this sin. Those who despise the word and law of God, despise God himself, and will assuredly suffer for such contempt. 2 S 14:5-11. Jg 9:7-15. 1 K 20:35-41. Is 5:1-7. Mt 21:33-45. Lk 15:11, etc. 16:19, etc.

2. **exceeding.** ver. 8. 2 S 3:2-5. 5:13-16. 15:16. Jb 1:3.

3. **one little.** 2 S 11:3. Pr 5:18, 19. **did eat.** ♪96C8, Ex +15:5. **meat.** Heb. morsel. Ge 18:5. **lay in his.** Dt 13:6. Mi 7:5.

4. **a traveller.** Ge 18:2-7. Ja 1:14. **took the.** 2 S 11:3, 4.

5. **David's.** 2 S 24:14. Ge 38:24. 1 S 25:21, 22. Lk 6:41, 42. 9:55. 19:22. Ro 2:1. **As the Lord.** 1 S 14:39. **shall surely die.** *or,* is worthy to die. Heb. *is a son of death.* 1 S 20:31. 26:16mg.

6. **restore.** Ex 22:1. Pr 6:31. Lk 19:8. **because.** Ja 2:13.

7. **Thou art.** 1 S 13:13. 1 K 18:18. 21:19, 20. Mt 14:4. **I anointed.** 2 S 7:8. 1 S *15:17. 16:13. **I delivered.** 2 S 22:1, 49. 1 S 18:11, 21. 19:10-15. 23:7, 14, 26-28. Ps 18, title.

8. **thy master's wives.** ver. 11. Ge +4:19. 1 K 2:22. **gave thee.** 2 S 2:4. 5:5. 1 S *15:19. **I would.** 2 S 7:19. Ps *37:4. *84:11. *86:15. Ro *8:32.

9. **never depart.** Pr +*17:13. **despised.** ver. 10. 2 S *11:4, 14-17. Ge *9:5, 6. Ex *20:13, 14. Nu *15:30, 31. 1 S *15:19, 23. Pr 5:21. *13:13. 19:16. Is 5:24. Am 2:4. He *10:28, 29. **to do evil.** 2 Ch *33:6. Ps *51:4. *90:8. *139:1, 2. Je 18:10. **thou hast.** 2 S 11:15-27.

10. **the sword.** ⨍121S1, Ge +49:10. "Sword" is put for manifested hostility. 2 S 13:28, 29. 18:14, 15, 33. 1 K 2:23-25. Am 7:9. Mt *26:52. **because.** Nu 11:20. 1 S *2:30. Ml 1:6, 7. Mt 6:24. Ro *2:4. 1 Th *4:8. **hast taken.** Ge 20:3. Pr *6:32, 33.

11. **I will raise.** 2 S 13:1-14, 28, 29. 15:6, 10. 16:11. **I will take.** That is, *in the course of my providence I will permit this to be done.* Such phrases in Scripture do not mean that God either does or can do evil himself; but only that he *permits* such evil to be done as he foresaw would be done, and which, had he pleased, he might have prevented. 2 S 16:21, 22. Dt 28:30. 1 S +18:10n. 1 K 1:5. Je ◐+*29:11. Ezk 14:9. 20:25, 26. Ho 4:13, 14. Am +√3:6.

12. **secretly.** 2 S 11:4, 8, 13, 15. Jb 24:15. Ec 12:14. Mk 4:22. Lk 12:1, 2. 1 C 4:5.

13. **David.** 1 S 15:20, 24. 1 K 13:4. *21:20. *22:8. 2 K 1:9. 2 Ch 16:10. *24:20-22. 25:16. Mt 14:3-5, 10. **I have sinned.** 2 S 24:10. Ge 39:9. Le *26:40, 42. Nu +22:34. 1 S *15:24, 25, 30. Ne 9:33. Jb 7:20. *33:27. 40:4. 42:6. Ps *32:3-5. *51:4. Pr *25:12. *28:13. Is 6:5. Je *3:13. 14:7, 20. Da 9:5. Mi 7:9. Lk *15:21. 23:41. Ac 2:37. 1 J √1:8-10. **The Lord.** 2 S 24:10. Jb 7:21. Ps *32:1, 2. 51:9. *130:3, 4. Is 6:5-7. *38:17. *43:25. *44:22. La *3:32. Mi *7:18, 19. Zc 3:4. Jn 8:11. He *9:26. 1 J *1:7, 9. *2:1. Re *1:5. **thou.** Le *20:10. Nu *35:31-33. Ps *51:16. Ac *13:38, 39. Ro *8:33, 34. **not die.** Ge +*2:17. Le 20:10. Ps 51:6. Pr 14:12. 16:25. Ezk 18:4. Ac 13:38, 39. Ro 8:33, 34. 1 J +*5:16.

14. **by this deed.** Ne *5:9. Ps 74:10. Is 52:5. Ezk 36:20-23. Mt 18:7. Ro 2:24. **thou.** ⨍182, Ge +18:22. The primitive text was, "Thou hast greatly blasphemed the Lord." This was altered to soften the sin of David, and constitutes one of the emendations of the Sopherim. **given great.** 2 Ch +*19:2. **occasion.** Ps 39:1. Pr +*25:26. **the child.** Ps 89:31-33. *94:12. Pr 3:11, 12. Am 3:2. 1 C *11:32. He 12:6. Re *3:19. **surely.** ⨍147B, Ge +2:16.

15. **struck the child.** Dt 32:29. 1 S 25:38. 26:10. 2 K 15:5. 2 Ch 13:20. Ps 104:29. Ac 12:23.

16. **besought.** ver. 22. Ps 50:15. Is 26:16. Jl 2:12-14. Jon 3:9. **fasted.** Heb. fasted a fast. ⨍147D, Ge +1:29. 1 S 31:13. 1 K 21:27. Est 4:16. Ps 69:10. Is 22:12. Ac 9:9. **lay all night.** 2 S 13:31. Jb 20:12-14. Ps 32:4. 88:1, 2.

17. **the elders.** 2 S 3:35. Jsh +20:4. 1 S 28:23. 1 K 12:6.

18. **seventh day.** T#1762. **vex.** Heb. do hurt to. Nu 20:15.

20. **arose.** Jb 1:20. 2:10. Ps 39:9. La 3:39-41. **and washed.** Ru 3:3. **anointed.** Ru 3:3. Ec 9:8. **and changed.** Ps 51:12, 14, 15. **the house.** 2 S 6:17. 7:18. Jb 1:20.

21. **What thing.** 1 C 2:15.

22. **I fasted.** Ps 107:17-20. Is *38:1-3, 5. Jl *1:14. 2:14. Am *5:15. Jon *1:6. *3:9, 10. Ja *4:9, 10.

23. **I shall go.** Ge +√37:35n. 1 S 28:19. Jb *30:23. Je √31:15-17. Am +*9:2n. Lk *23:43. 2 C +*5:8. **he shall not.** Jb *7:8-10. +*16:22. Jn 11:25, 26. He +*9:27.

24. **A.M.** 2971. **B.C.** 1033. **An. Ex. Is.** 458. **she bare.** 2 S 7:12. 1 Ch 3:5. 22:9, 10. 28:5, 6. 29:1. Mt 1:6. **Solomon.** in Heb. *Shelomoh,* as in 2 S 5:14.

25. **Nathan.** ver. 1-14. 2 S 7:4. 1 K 1:11, 23. **Jedidiah.** *that is,* Beloved of the Lord. i.e. *dearly beloved of Jah,* ✻S#3041h, only here. Ne 13:26. Mt 3:17. 17:5.

26. **Joab.** 2 S 11:25. 1 Ch 20:1. **Rabbah.** Rabbah,

or *Rabbath-Ammon,* also called *Philadelphia,* from Ptolemy Philadelphus, king of Egypt, was situated east of Jordan, and, according to Eusebius, ten miles east from Jazer. It is sometimes mentioned as belonging to Arabia, sometimes to Caelo-Syria; and was one of the cities of the Decapolis east of Jordan. Josephus extends the region of Perea as far as Philadelphia. It is now, says Burckhardt, called *Amman,* distant about 19 miles to the Southeast of Szalt, and lies along the banks of a river called Moiet Amman, which has its source in a pond at a few hundred paces from the southwestern end of the town, and empties itself into the Zerka, or Jabbok, about four hours to the north. This river runs in a valley bordered on both sides by barren hills of flint, which advance on the south side close to the edge of the stream. The edifices which still remain, though in a decaying state, from being built of a calcareous stone of moderate hardness, sufficiently attest the former greatness and splendor of this metropolis of the children of Ammon. Dt 3:11.

27. **Rabbah.** 2 S 11:1. Dt 3:11. Ezk 21:20. **the city of waters.** ⨍100, Ge +10:9. Probably that part of the city situated near the pond, from which the rest received their water.

28. **it be called after my name.** Heb. my name be called upon it. Jn 7:18.

30. **took.** 1 Ch 20:2. **their king's.** or, Malcam. 2 K +23:13. Je 49:1mg. Zp 1:5. **the weight.** If this talent were only seven pounds, as Whiston says, David might have carried it on his head with little difficulty; but this weight, according to common computation, would amount to nearly 114 pounds! Some therefore think that *mishkelah* should be taken for its value, not weight, which renders it perfectly plain. J. Finnis Dake in his *Annotated Reference Bible* suggests that the crown weighed 131 lbs. troy, valued at $29,085.00, adding "How a crown weighing this much could be worn by a man is hard to understand." The ancients mention several such large crowns, made more for sight than use. Athenaeus describes a crown of gold that was 24 feet in circumference; and mentions others that were two, some four, and others five feet deep. Pliny takes notice of some that were no less than eight pounds weight. Besides the crown usually worn, it was customary for kings, in some nations, to have such large ones as described either hung or supported over the throne, where they sat at their coronation or other solemn occasions. **in great abundance.** Heb. very great. ver. 2. 2 S 8:8. Ps 21:3.

31. **and put them.** Rather, as the Hebrew particle used here frequently signifies, "And he put them to saws, and to harrows, and to axes," etc. as we say "to put a person to the plow, to the anvil, to the last," etc. See on 1 Ch 20:3. 2 S 8:2. Ps 21:8, 9. Am 1:3. **pass through.** Je 43:11. Mt 25:32. **brickkiln.** Je *43:9n. Rather, a platform upon which the king sat upon his throne and reviewed the captives, and decided upon their destiny. Mt 25:31-33.

2 SAMUEL 13

Amnon, David's son, loves his sister Tamar, 1, 2; and by Jonadab's advice he feigns sickness, that Tamar might wait on him; and taking that opportunity he ravishes her, 3-14. He hates her and drives her away, and she in grief and shame retires to Absalom, 15-

20. *David is angry; but Absalom conceals his hatred,*
21, 22. Absalom invites his brethren to a feast; where
Amnon at his command is murdered, 23-29. David
grieves vehemently, supposing that all his sons are
slain; but is comforted by Jonadab and learns the truth,
30-36. Absalom flees to Geshur; but David longs after
him, 37-39.

1. A.M. 2972. B.C. 1032. An. Ex. Is. 459. **Absalom**.
*S#53h. ver. 4, 20, 20, 22, 22, 23, 23, 24, 25, 26,
27, 28, 29, 29, 30, 32, 34, 37, 38, 39. 2 S 3:3. 14:1,
21, 23, 24, 25, 27, 28, 29, 30, 31, 32, 33, 33. 15:1,
2, 2, 3, 4, 6, 6, 7, 10, 10, 11, 12, 12, 13, 14, 31, 34,
37. 16:8, 15, 16, 16, 17, 18, 20, 21, 22, 22, 23. 17:1,
4, 5, 6, 6, 7, 9, 14, 14, 15, 18, 20, 24, 25, 26. 18:5,
5, 9, 9, 10, 12, 14, 15, 17, 18, 18, 29, 32, 33, 33.
19:1, 4, 4, 6, 9, 10. 20:6. 1 K 1:6. 2:7, 28. 15:2, 10.
1 Ch 3:2. 2 Ch 11:20, 21. Ps 3:t. **a fair sister**. 2 S
11:2. Ge 6:2. 12:11, 14. 39:6, 7. Pr 6:25. 31:30. **Tamar**.
i.e. *a palm tree*. 2 S 14:27. 1 Ch 3:9. **Amnon**. 2 S
3:2, 3. **loved her**. ver. 15. Ge 29:18, 20. 34:3. 1 K
11:1.

2. **vexed**. 1 K 21:4. SS 5:8. 2 C 7:10. **Amnon, etc.**
Heb. it was marvellous, *or* hidden, in the eyes of Amnon. Zc 8:6. **hard**. Ge 18:14.

3. **a friend**. Ge 38:1, 20. Jg 14:20. Est 5:10, 14.
6:13. Pr 19:6. **Jonadab**. i.e. *Jah made willing*. **Shimeah**.
*S#8093h. ver. 32. 1 S 16:9, Shammah. 1 S 17:13.
subtil man. 2 S 14:2, 19, 20. Ge 3:1. Pr *19:27. Je
*4:22. Ro *16:19. 1 C 3:19. Ja 3:15.

4. **Why art**. 1 K 21:7. Est 5:13, 14. Lk 12:32. **lean**.
Heb. thin. 2 S 3:1. **from day to day**. Heb. morning
by morning. Ex 16:21. 30:7. 36:3. Le 6:12. 1 Ch 9:27.
23:30. 2 Ch 13:11. Is 28:19. *50:4. Ezk 46:13mg, 14,
15. Zp 3:5mg. **I love**. Is 3:9. Je 8:12. Mi 7:3. **my brother**.
Le 18:9. 20:17.

5. **Lay thee**. 2 S 16:21-23. 17:1-4. Ps 50:18, 19. Pr
19:27. Mk 6:24, 25. Ac 23:15.

6. **make me**. Ge 18:6. Mt 13:33. **cakes**. Young notes,
"in the shape of 'hearts,' as the original word implies;
so in ver. 8."

8. **she took**. Dr. Russell says, "The Eastern ladies
often wash their own hands, prepare cakes, pastry,
etc. in their apartments; and some few particular dishes
are cooked by themselves, but not in their apartments:
on such occasions, they go to some room near the
kitchen" (MS. note, cited by the editor of Harmer,
vol. I, p. 487). **flour**. *or*, paste. Ex 12:34, 39. Je 7:18.
Ho 7:4. **and make cakes**. Rather, as Mr. Parkhurst
renders, "and *tossed* it (*wattelabbaiv*) in his sight, and
dressed *the tossed cakes* (*halleveevoth*)." This will receive illustration from the account which Mr. Jackson
(p. 50) gives of the Arabian manner of kneading and
baking. "They have a small place built with clay, between two and three feet high, having a hole at the
bottom for the convenience of drawing out the ashes,
something similar to that of a brick-kiln. The oven is
usually about fifteeen inches wide at top, and gradually
grows wider to the bottom. It is heated with wood;
and when sufficiently hot, and perfectly clear from
smoke, having nothing but clear embers at bottom,
which continue to reflect great heat, they prepare the
dough in a large bowl, and mould the cakes to the
desired size on a board or stone placed near the oven.
After they have kneaded the cake to a proper consistence, they pat it a little, then *toss it about* with great
dexterity in one hand till it is as thin as they choose

to make it. They then wet one side of it with water,
at the same time wetting the hand and arm with which
they put it into the oven."

9. **And Amnon**. 2 S 12:12. Ge 45:1. Jg 3:19. Jn
*3:20. Ep *5:12.

11. **Come lie**. Ge 39:7, 12.

12. **force me**. Heb. humble me. ver. 14, 22, 32.
Ge 34:2. Dt 21:14. 22:29. **no such thing ought**. Heb.
it ought not so. Le 18:9, 11. 20:17. **folly**. Ge 34:7. Jg
19:23. 20:6. Pr 5:22, 23. 7:7.

13. **shame**. Ge 30:23. **fools**. Dt 32:6, 21. **Now therefore**. Ge 19:8. Jg 19:24.

14. **forced her**. 2 S 12:11. Dt 22:25-27. Jg 20:5.
Est 7:8.

15. **hated her**. Ezk 23:17. **exceedingly**. Heb. with
great hatred greatly. ver. 36mg.

16. **cause**. Ge 21:11, 25. Je 3:8. **would not hearken**.
Dt *22:28, 29. 1 S +25:17.

17. **bolt**. Jg 3:23.

18. **a garment**. Ge 37:3, 23, 32. Jg 5:30. Ps 45:13,
14. **robes**. Ex 28:4, 31, 34. Ps 45:14. Ezk 16:10, 13.
virgins. Ge 24:16 (*S#1330h).

19. **put ashes**. 2 S 1:2. Jsh 7:6. Jb 2:12. 42:6. Is
61:3. **laid her hand**. 𝒥121S3M. Metonymy of the Adjunct B607. To put hands on the head is put for grief.
For another instance of this figure see Je 2:37.

20. **Amnon**. Heb. Aminon. **but hold**. Pr 26:24. Ro
12:19. **regard not**. Heb. set not thine heart on. 2 S
18:3mg. Ex 7:23. 1 S +4:20mg. **desolate**. Heb. and
desolate. Ge 34:2. 46:15. Without society; as in Is 49:8,
19. 54:1. 61:4. La 1:4, 13, 16. 3:11. Ezk 36:4. Da
8:13. 9:18, 26, 27. 12:11.

21. **heard**. Ge 35:22. **he was very wroth**. The Septuagint and Vulgate add, "But he would not grieve the
soul of Amnon his son, for he loved him because he
was his firstborn." The same addition is found in Josephus; and it is probable that it once formed a part
of the Hebrew text. 2 S 3:28, 29. 12:5, 10, √11. Ge
4:5. 34:7. +44:30. 1 S 2:22-25, 29. Ps 101:8. Pr 17:25.
19:13.

22. **spake**. Le √19:17, 18. Pr 25:9. Mt 18:15. **neither
good**. Ge 24:50. 31:24, 29. **hated**. Le *19:17, 18. Pr
10:18. 26:24. 27:4-6. Ec 7:9. Ep 4:26, 31. 1 J 3:15.

23. A.M. 2974. B.C. 1030. An. Ex. Is. 461. **sheep-
shearers**. Ge 38:12, 13. 1 S 25:2, 4, 36. 2 K 3:4.
2 Ch 26:10. Is 53:7. **Baal-hazor**. i.e. *possessor of Hazor;
having a village*, *S#1178h, only here. Jsh 15:25. **invited**. 1 K 1:9, 19, 25.

24. **let the king**. 2 S 11:8-15. Ps 12:2. 55:21. Je
41:6, 7.

25. **pressed**. Ge 19:2, 3. Jg 19:7-10. 1 S 28:23.
2 K 5:23. Lk 14:23. 24:29. Ac 16:15. **blessed**. 2 S
14:22mg. Ru 2:4.

26. **let my brother**. He urged this with the more
plausibility because Amnon was the first-born, and presumptive heir to the crown; and he had dissembled
his resentment so long and so well, that he was not
suspected. 2 S 3:27. 11:13-15. 20:9. Ps 55:21.

27. **Absalom**. Pr *26:24-26.

28. **commanded**. 2 S 11:15. Ex 1:16, 17. 1 S 22:17,
18. Ac 5:29. **heart is merry**. 2 S 11:13. Ge 9:21. 19:32-
35. Jg 19:6, 9, 22. Ru 3:7. 1 S 25:36-38. 1 K 20:16.
Est 1:10. Ps 104:15. Ec 9:7. 10:19. Da 5:2-6, 30. Na
1:10. Lk 21:34. Ep *5:18. Ja 5:13. **fear not**. Nu 22:16,
17. 1 S 28:10, 13. **have not I**. *or*, Will you not, since
I have, etc. Jsh 1:9. **valiant**. Heb. sons of valor. 2 S

+2:7mg. Dt 3:18mg. Jg 21:10.

29. **servants.** 1 S 22:18, 19. 1 K 21:11-13. 2 K 1:9-12. Pr 29:12. Mi 7:3. **gat him up.** Heb. rode. **mule.** 2 S 18:9. Ge 36:24. Le 19:19. 1 K 1:33. 10:25. 18:5. 2 K 5:17. 1 Ch 12:40. 2 Ch 9:24. Ezr 2:66. Ne 7:68. Ps 32:9. Is 66:20. Ezk 27:14. Zc 14:15.

30. **tidings.** 2 S 4:4, 10. 18:19. Ex 33:4. 1 S 4:19. 11:4, 5. 27:9-11. Ps 112:7. **slain all.** 2 S *12:10. Jg *9:5.

31. **arose.** 2 S 12:16. Ge 37:29, 34. Jsh 7:6. Jb 1:20. **all his servants.** 2 S 1:11. 3:31.

32. **Jonadab.** ver. 3-5. **Shimeah.** 1 S 16:9, Shammah. **David's brother.** This man had given his cousin Amnon the most detestable advice; and here speaks coolly of a most bloody tragedy of which he had been the cause. **appointment.** Heb. mouth. **determined.** or, settled. Ge 27:41. Ps 7:14. Pr 24:11, 12.

33. **let not my lord.** 2 S 19:19.

34. **Absalom fled.** ver. 38. Ge 4:8-14. Pr 28:17. Je 47:44. Am 5:19. **lifted.** /144A12, Ge +22:13.

35. **as thy servant said.** Heb. according to the word of thy servant.

36. **lifted.** /144A12, Ge +22:13. **very sore.** Heb. with a great weeping greatly. /147D, Ge +1:29. ver. 15mg. 2 S 12:21. 18:33. Jg 21:2. 2 K 20:3mg. Is 38:3mg.

37. **Absalom fled.** As Absalom had committed willful murder, he could not avail himself of a city of refuge but went to Talmai, king of Geshur, his maternal grand-father. **Talmai.** 2 S 3:3. 1 Ch 3:2. **Ammihud.** i.e. *my people is honorable; people of majesty,* *S#5989h. or,* Ammihur. Nu 1:10. 2:18. 7:48, 53. 10:22. 34:20, 28. 2 S 13:37. 1 Ch 7:26. 9:4. (1) An Ephraimite whose son was appointed by the Lord chief of the tribe, Nu 1:10; 1 Ch 7:26. (2) A Simeonite whose son Shemuel was appointed to divide the land, Nu 34:20. (3) A man of Naphtali whose son Pedahel was appointed to divide the land, Nu 34:28. (4) Father of Talmai, king of Geshur, 2 S 13:37. (5) A man of Judah, a descendant of Pharez, 1 Ch 9:4.

38. A.M. 2974-2977. B.C. 1030-1027. An. Ex. Is. 461-464. **Geshur.** This was not the Geshur lying be-tween Philistia and Egypt (Jsh 13:13. 1 S 27:8), but another in Syria; probably the same as that beyond Jordan, whose inhabitants are joined with those of Maa-chathi, Dt. 3:14. Jsh 12:5. 2 S 3:3. 14:23, 32. 15:8. **three years.** Until his recall, as in 2 S 14:23 (Young).

39. **the soul of.** Ge 31:30. Dt 28:32. Ph 2:26. **longed.** *or,* was consumed. Ps 84:2. 119:20. **comforted.** 2 S 12:23. Ge 24:67. 37:35. 38:12.

2 SAMUEL 14

Joab instructs a woman of Tekoah and sends her to David, 1-3. With a feigned tale and artful manage-ment she induces him to recall Absalom, 4-20. Joab is sent to bring him to Jerusalem; yet he is not allowed to see the king, 21-24. Absalom's beauty, 25, 26. His children, 27. After two years, he prevails with Joab to introduce him to David, 28-33.

1. A.M. 2977. B.C. 1027. An. Ex. Is. 464. **Joab.** 2 S 2:18. 1 Ch 2:16. **toward Absalom.** 2 S 13:39. 18:33. 19:2, 4. Pr 29:26.

2. **to Tekoah.** i.e. *a trumpet blast,* *S#8620h. Tek-oah was a city of Judah, situated, according to Eusebius and Jerome, twelve miles south of Jerusalem. Josephus says it was not far from the castle of Herodium; and

Jerome (*Prologue to Amos*) says it stood on a hill six miles south from Bethlehem. Dr. Pococke places it at the same distance and says there are still considerable ruins on the top of a hill, which is about half a mile long and a furlong broad. 1 Ch 2:24. 4:5. 2 Ch 11:6. 20:20. Ne ●3:5, 27. Je 6:1. Am 1:1, Tekoa. **mourning.** 2 S 11:26. Ru 3:3. Ps 104:15. Ec 9:8. Mt 6:17.

3. **put the words.** ver. 19. Ex 4:15. Nu 23:5. Dt 18:18. Is 51:16. 59:21. Je 1:9.

4. **fell on her.** 2 S 1:2. 1 S 20:41. 25:23. **Help.** Heb. Save. 2 K 6:26-28. Jb 29:12-14. Lk 18:3-5.

5. **I am indeed.** It is very possible that the principal incidents mentioned here were real; and that Joab found a person whose circumstances bore a near resem-blance to that which he wished to represent. She did not make the similitude too plain and visible, lest the king should see her intention before she had obtained a grant of pardon; and thus her circumstances, her mournful tale, her widow's dress, her aged person (for Josephus says she was advanced in years), and her impressive manner, all combined to make one united irresistible impression on the heart of the aged mon-arch. 2 S 12:1-3. Jg 9:8-15.

6. **and they two.** Ge 4:8. Ex 2:13. Dt 22:26, 27. **none to part.** Heb. no deliverer between. Dt 32:39. Jg 8:34. 18:28. Jb 5:4. 10:7. Ps 7:2. 35:10. 50:22. 71:11. Pr 14:25. Is 5:29. 42:22. 43:13. Da 8:4, 7. Ho 5:14. Mi 5:8.

7. **the whole.** Ge 4:14. Nu *35:19. Dt *19:12. **the life.** Heb. *nephesh,* Jsh +10:28. Le 17:11. Est 8:11. Mt +*2:20. Lk 12:22. **so they.** Ge 27:45. Dt 25:6. **quench.** 2 S 21:17. **upon the earth.** Heb. upon the face of the earth.

8. **I will give.** 2 S 12:5, 6. 16:4. Jb 29:16. Pr 18:13. Is 11:3, 4.

9. **the iniquity.** Ge 27:13. 1 S 25:24. Mt 27:25. **and the king.** 2 S 3:28, 29. Nu 35:33. Dt 21:1-9. 1 K 2:33.

11. **let the king.** Ge 14:22. 24:2, 3. 31:50. 1 S 20:42. **thou,** etc. Heb. the revenger of blood do not multiply to destroy. **the revengers.** Nu 35:19, 27. Dt 19:4-10. Jsh 20:3-6. **As the Lord.** 1 S 14:45. 28:10. Je 4:2. **not one hair.** /138B, Ge +13:16. 1 K 1:52. Mt 10:30. Lk 21:18. Ac 27:34.

12. **Let thine.** 1 S 25:24. **speak one word.** Ge 18:27, 32. 44:18. Je 12:1. **Say on.** Ac 26:1.

13. **Wherefore.** 2 S 12:7. 1 K 20:40-42. Lk 7:42-44. **people.** 2 S 7:8. Jg 20:2. He 11:25. **in that the king.** 2 S 13:37, 38.

14. **we must.** 2 S 11:25. Jb 30:23. 34:15. Ps 90:3, 10. Ec 3:19, 20. 9:5. He *9:27. **as water spilt.** 1 S 7:6. Jb 14:7-12, 14. Ps 22:14. 79:3. **neither,** etc. *or,* because God hath not taken away his life, he hath also devised means, etc. **person.** Heb. *nephesh,* soul, Nu +23:10. **God.** Dt 10:17. Jb 34:19. Mt 22:16. Ac 10:34. Ro 2:11. 1 P 1:17. **he devise.** Ex 21:13. Le 26:40. Nu 35:15, 25, 28. Is 50:1, 2. Ml 2:16.

16. **hand.** Ge 20:5. **the inheritance.** 2 S 20:19. 1 S 26:19.

17. **comfortable.** Heb. for rest. **as an angel.** This is very much like the hyperbolical language which is addressed by the Hindus to an European when they desire to obtain something from him: "Sahib," say they, "can do everything. No one can prevent the execution of Sahib's commands. Sahib is God." Though this ex-pression may be imputed to the hyperbolical genius of these countries, yet there was, perhaps, more of

real persuasion than we are apt to suppose. Sir John Chardin states that having found fault with the king of Persia's evaluation of a rich trinket, the grand master told him that if a Persian had dared to have done such a thing, it would have been as much as his life was worth. "Know," said he, "that the kings of Persia have a general and full knowledge of matters, as sure as it is extensive; and that, equally in the greatest and smallest things, there is nothing more just and sure than what they pronounce." ver. 20. 2 S 19:27. Ge +17:1. 1 S 29:9. Pr 27:21. 29:5. **to discern.** Heb. to hear. 1 K 3:9, 28. Jb 6:30. 1 C 2:14, 15mg. He 5:14.

18. **Hide not.** 1 S 3:17, 18. Je 38:14, 25.

19. **the hand.** ſ121BA, Dt +32:36. **of Joab.** 2 S 3:27, 29, 34. 11:14, 15. 1 K 2:5, 6. **As thy soul.** Heb. *nephesh*, Ge +27:31. 2 S 11:11. 1 S 1:26. 17:55. 20:3. 25:26. 2 K 2:2. **turn.** Nu 20:17. Dt 5:32. 28:14. Jsh 1:7. Pr 4:27. **he put.** See on ver. 3. Ex 4:15. Lk 21:15.

20. **fetch.** 2 S 5:23. **according.** ver. 17. 2 S 19:27. Jb 32:21, 22. Pr 26:28. 29:5. **to know.** Ge 3:5. Jb 38:16, etc. 1 C 8:1, 2.

21. **I have done.** ver. 11. 1 S 14:39. Mk 6:26.

22. **thanked.** Heb. blessed. 2 S 19:39. Ne 11:2. Jb 29:11. 31:20. Pr 31:28. **I have found.** Ge 6:8. Ex 33:16, 17. Ru 2:2. 1 S 20:3. **his.** *or*, thy.

23. **Geshur.** 2 S 3:3. 13:37.

24. **let him not.** ver. 28. 2 S 3:13. Ge 43:3. Ex 10:28. Pr 16:15. Re 22:4.

25. **But in all Israel,** etc. Heb. And as Absalom there was not a beautiful man in all Israel to praise greatly. 1 S 9:2. *16:7. Pr 31:30. Mt 23:27. **from the sole.** Dt *28:35. Jb *2:7. Is *1:6. Ep *5:27.

26. **when he polled.** 2 S 18:9. Is 3:24. 1 C 11:14. Re 9:8. **two hundred shekels.** If the shekel be allowed to mean the common shekel, the amount will be utterly incredible; for Josephus says that "two hundred shekels make five minae:" and the mina, he says, "weighs two pounds and a half;" which calculation makes Absalom's hair weigh twelve pounds and a half! But it is probable that the *king's shekel* was that which Epiphanius and Hesychius say was the *fourth part of an ounce,* half a stater, or two drachms: the whole amount, therefore, of the 200 shekels is about 50 ounces, which make 4 lb. 2 oz. troy weight, or 3 lb. 2 oz. avoirdupois. This need not be accounted incredible, especially as abundance of oil and ointment was used by the ancients in dressing their heads. Josephus also informs us, that the Jews also put gold dust in their hair. Ge 23:16. Le 19:36. Ezk 45:9-14.

27. **born.** 2 S 18:18. Jb 18:16-19. Is 14:22. Je 22:30. **one daughter.** Whom Rehoboam afterwards married, see 1 K 15:22; 2 Ch 11:20 (Young). **Tamar.** 2 S 13:1. Named after his sister in 2 S 13:1. **fair countenance.** 2 S 11:2. Ge 29:17. 1 S 25:3. 1 K 1:4. Est 1:11. 2:7. Jb 42:15.

28. A.M. 2977-2979. B.C. 1027-1025. An. Ex. Is. 464-466. **and saw not.** ver. 24.

29. **but he would.** ver. 30, 31. Est 1:12. Mt 22:3.

30. **near mine.** Heb. near my place. 2 S 19:43. **go and set.** 2 S 13:28, 29. Jg 15:4, 5. **And Absalom's.** 1 K 21:9-14. 2 K 9:33. 10:6, 7.

32. **it had been.** Ex 14:12. 16:3. 17:3. **if there.** Ge 3:12. 1 S 15:13. Ps 36:2. Pr 28:13. Je 2:22, 23. 8:12. Mt 25:44. Ro 3:19.

33. A.M. 2979. B.C. 1025. An. Ex. Is. 466. **kissed**

Absalom. 2 S 15:5. 19:39. 20:9. Ge 27:26. 29:13. 31:55. 33:4. 45:15. Ex 18:7. Lk 15:20. 22:47.

2 SAMUEL 15

Absalom, by fair speeches and affected courtesy, steals the hearts of the people, 1-6. Under pretence of a vow, he obtains leave to go to Hebron, where he raises rebellion, 7-12. David hearing it retires from Jerusalem, 13-18. Ittai the Gittite faithfully adheres to him, and the people weep over him, 19-23. Zadok and Abiathar are sent back with the ark, 24-29. David and his company ascend Mount Olivet weeping, 30. Hearing that Ahithophel had joined Absalom, he prays that his counsel may be turned into foolishness, 31. Hushai is sent back with instructions, 32-37.

1. A.M. 2980. B.C. 1024. **Absalom.** 2 S 12:11. Dt 17:16. 1 S 8:11. 1 K 1:5, 33. 10:26-29. Ps 20:7. Pr 11:2. *16:18. *17:19. Je 22:14-16.

2. **rose up.** Jb 24:14. Pr *4:16. Mt 27:1. **gate.** ſ171S7B, Ge +14:7. **came.** Heb. to come. Ex 18:14, 16, 26. 1 K 3:16-28.

3. **thy matters.** Nu 16:3, 13, 14. Ps 12:2. Da 11:21. 2 P 2:10. **there is,** etc. *or*, none will hear thee from the king downward. 2 S 8:15. Ex 20:12. 21:17. Pr 30:11, 17. Ezk 22:7. Mt 15:4. Ac 23:5. 1 P 2:17.

4. **Oh that I.** Jg 9:1-5, 29. Pr 25:6. Lk 14:8-11. **I would do.** Pr 24:15, 16. 27:2. 2 P 2:19.

5. **took him.** Ps 10:9, 10. 55:21. Pr 26:25. **and kissed.** 2 S 14:33.

6. **stole.** T#329. Ex 8:15. Dt *30:19 (T#271). 1 Ch ◐12:32. 2 Ch 18:31 (T#264). 30:18. Ezr 7:10. Est 7:5. Ps 10:10. 73:13. 119:12, 59 (T#600). Pr +*4:23. ✓11:9. 23:26. Mt 5:28. Jn 3:6 (T#592). Ro *16:18. Ep +*4:14. 2 T 2:16, 17. 3:2, 3, 6, 8, 9. 2 P 2:3. **hearts.** ſ171Q20, Ge +31:20. Pr +*4:23.

7. A.M. 2983. B.C. 1021. An. Ex. Is. 470. **forty years.** As David reigned in the whole only forty years, this reading is evidently corrupt, though supported by the commonly printed Vulgate, LXX. and Chaldee. But the Syriac, Arabic, Josephus, Theodoret, the Sixtine edition of the Vulgate, and several MSS. of the same version, read *four years*; and it is highly probable that *arbaim,* "forty," is an error for *arba,* "four," though not supported by any Hebrew MS. yet discovered. Two of those collated by Dr. Kennicott, however, have *yom,* "day," instead of *shanah,* "year," i.e. *forty days* instead of forty years; but this is not sufficient to outweigh the other authorities. 2 S 13:38. 1 S 16:1, 13. **let me go.** 2 S 13:24-27. **pay.** 1 S 16:2. Pr 21:27. Is 58:4. Mt 2:8. 23:14. **vow.** Le +*23:38.

8. **thy servant.** Ge 28:20, 21. 1 S 1:11. 16:2. Ps 56:12. Pr 21:27. Ec 5:4. **vowed.** Le +*23:38. **Geshur.** 2 S 13:37, 38. 14:23, 32. **If.** Ge +28:20. **I will serve.** Jsh 24:15. Is 28:15. Je 9:3-5. 42:20.

10. **spies.** 2 S 13:28. 14:30. **reigneth.** 2 S 19:10. Jb 20:5, etc. Ps 73:18, 19. **Hebron.** 2 S 2:1, 11. 3:2, 3. 5:5. 1 Ch 11:3. 12:23, 38.

11. **called.** 1 S 9:13. 16:3-5. **their simplicity.** Ge 20:5. 1 S 22:15. Pr *14:15. *22:3. Mt 10:16. Ro 16:18, 19. **knew not.** 1 S 20:39. Ec 9:5.

12. **Ahithophel.** i.e. *brother of folly,* ✱S#302h. ver. 31. 2 S 15:12, 31, 31, 34. 16:15, 20, 21, 22, 23, 23. 17:1, 6, 7, 14, 14, 15, 21, 23. 23:34. 1 Ch 27:33, 34. **Gilonite.** ✱S#1526h. 2 S 23:34. **David's.** Ps *41:9. *55:12-14. Mi 7:5, 6. Jn 13:18. **Giloh.** Jsh 15:51. **while**

he offered. Nu 23:1, 14, 30. 1 S 16:3, 5. 1 K 21:9, 12. Ps 50:16-21. Pr 21:27. Is 1:10-16. T 1:16. the people. Ps 3:1, 2. 43:1, 2.

13. The hearts. ver. 6. 2 S 3:36. Jg 9:3. Ps 62:9. Mt 21:9. 27:22.

14. Arise. 2 S 19:9. 1 S 27:1. Ps 3, title. bring. Heb. thrust. 2 S 14:14. Ezk 46:18. Mt 11:12mg. Lk 10:15. and smite. 2 S 23:16, 17. Ps 51:18. 55:3-11. 137:5, 6.

15. Behold. Pr 18:24. Lk 22:28, 29. Jn 6:66-69. 15:14. are ready. Jsh 1:16. 2 Ch 34:16. Mt 8:19. Lk 22:23. Jn 2:5. Re 14:4. appoint. Heb. choose.

16. the king. Ps 3, title. after him. Heb. at his feet. Jg 4:10. 1 S 25:27, 42mg. ten women. 2 S 12:11. 16:21, 22. 20:3. Ro 12:2.

17. went forth. Ps 3, title, 2. 66:12. Ec 10:7.

18. Cherethites. 2 S 8:18. 20:7, 23. 1 S 30:14. 1 K 1:38. 1 Ch 18:17. Gittites. ver. 19-22. 2 S 6:10. 18:2. 1 S 27:3.

19. Ittai. i.e. living being, *S#863h. 2 S 15:19, 21, 22, 22. 18:2, 5, 12. 23:29. Ru ❶1:11-13. 1 Ch 11:31. (1) One of David's valliant men, a native of Gath, 2 S 18:2. He was greatly attached to David, 2 S 15:19-22. (2) A valiant Benjamite in David's army, 2 S 23:29. See Ithai, 1 Ch +11:31.

20. go up and down. Heb. wander in going. Ps 56:8. 59:15. Am 8:12. Mt 8:19, 20. He 11:37, 38. seeing. 1 S 23:13. mercy. 2 S 2:6. Ps 25:10. 57:3. 61:7. 85:10. 89:14. Pr 14:22. Jn 1:17. 2 T 1:16-18. and truth. J174, Ge +18:27.

21. As the Lord. 1 S 20:3. 25:26. 2 K 2:2, 4, 6. 4:30. surely. Ru 1:16, 17. Pr 17:17. 18:24. Mk 8:19, 20. Jn *6:66-69. Ac 11:23. 21:13. 2 C 7:3. there also. Jn 12:26.

22. and all the little. Sir John Chardin informs us in a MS. note on this place (mentioned by Harmer, ch. ix. Ob. 80), that it is usual with the greatest part of the eastern people, especially the Arabs, to take their whole family with them when they go to war.

23. all. *J171.O.3, Ge +41:57. the country. J121J17, Ge +6:11. wept. Ro 12:15. the brook. The brook Kidron, which is but a few paces broad, runs along the valley of Jehoshaphat, east of Jerusalem, to the south-west corner of the city, and then, turning to the south-east, empties itself into the Dead Sea. Like the Ilisus, it is dry at least nine months in the year, being only furnished with water in the winter; and after heavy rains its bed is narrow and deep, which indicates that it must formerly have been the channel for waters which have found some other, probably subterranean course. Kidron. i.e. gloomy, full of darkness, *S#6939. 1 K *2:37. 15:13. 2 K 23:4, 6, 6, 12. 2 Ch 15:16. 29:16. 30:14. Je 31:40. Jn=*18:1, Cedron. the wilderness. 2 S 16:2. Mt 3:1, 3. Lk 1:80.

24. Zadok. ver. 27, 35. 2 S 8:17. 20:25. 1 K 1:8. 2:35. 4:2-4. 1 Ch 6:8-12. Ezk 48:11. bearing. 2 S 6:13. Nu 4:15. 7:9. Jsh 3:3, 6, 15-17. 4:16-18. 6:4, 6. 1 S 4:3-5, 11. 1 Ch 15:2.

25. Carry back. 2 S 12:10, 11. 1 S 4:3-11. Je 7:4. if I shall. 2 S 6:22. he will bring. Ps 26:8. 27:4, 5. 42:1, 2. 43:3, 4. 62:5. 63:1, 2. 84:1-3, 10. 122:1, 9. Is 38:22. habitation. 2 S 6:17. 7:2.

26. I have no. 2 S 22:20. Nu 14:8. 1 K 10:9. 2 Ch 9:8. Ps 18:19. Is 42:1. 62:4. Je 22:28. 32:41. Ml 1:10. let him. Jg 10:15. 1 S 3:18. Jb 1:20, 21. Ps 39:9. Ac +21:14.

27. Art not. J85B, Ge +13:9. a seer. 2 S 24:11. 1 S 9:9. 1 Ch 25:5. return. ver. 34, 36. 2 S 17:17.

28. I will tarry. ver. 23. 2 S 16:2. 17:1, 16. in the plain. Heb. arabah. 2 S 2:29. *17:16. Dt +*11:30. Jsh 5:10.

30. the ascent. Zc 14:4. Lk 19:29, 37. 21:37. 22:39. Ac 1:12. mount Olivet. i.e. olive yard, S#2132h. Mount Olivet, so called from its abounding with olive trees, is situated east of Jerusalem, being separated from it only by the valley of Jehoshaphat and the brook Kidron. Josephus says it is five stadia, i.e. 625 geometrical paces, from Jerusalem; and St. Luke (Ac 1:12) says it is a Sabbath day's journey, or about eight stadia distant, i.e. to the summit. It forms part of a ridge of limestone hills, extending from north to south for about a mile; and it is described as having three, or, according to others, four summits; the central and highest of which overlooks the whole of the city, over whose streets and walls the eye roves as if in the survey of a model. and wept as he went up. Heb. going up and weeping. Ps 42:3-11. 43:1, 2, 5. Lk 19:41. his head covered. This custom was only practiced by persons in great distress or when convicted of great crimes. Thus Darius, when informed by Tyriotes, the eunuch, that his queen was dead, and that she had suffered no violence from Alexander, "covered his head" and wept for a long time; then throwing off the garment that covered him, he thanked the gods for Alexander's moderation and justice. 2 S 19:4. Est 6:12. Je 14:3, 4. barefoot. Is 20:2, 4. Ezk 24:17, 23. covered. J121S3F2. Metonymy of the Adjunct B606. To cover the head is put for self-condemnation or condemnation. For other instances of this figure see 2 S 19:4. Est 7:8. Jb 9:24. Je 14:4. weeping. Ps 51:17. *126:5, 6. Mt *5:4. Ro *12:15. 1 C 12:26. 1 P 5:6.

31. Ahithophel. ver. 12. Ps 3:1, 2. 37:12, 13. 41:9. 55:12, 14, 21, 23. Mt 26:14, 15. Jn 13:18. O Lord. Ps 55:15-17. 109:3, 4. turn the counsel. 2 S 16:23. 17:14, 23. Jb 5:12. 12:16-20. Pr +*21:30. Is 19:3, 11-41. Je *8:8, 9. 1 C 1:20. 3:18-20. Ja *3:15.

32. the top. ver. 30. 1 K 11:7. Lk 19:29. Jn 8:1. he worshipped. 1 K 8:44, 45. Jb 1:20, 21. Ps 3:3-5, 7. 4:1-3. 50:15. 91:15. Hushai. i.e. hastening of the Lord, *S#2365h. ver. 37. 2 S 16:16, 16, 17, 18. 17:5, 6, 7, 8, 14, 15. 1 K 4:16. 1 Ch 27:33. Archite. *S#757h. 2 S 16:16. 17:5, 14. Jsh 16:2. 1 Ch 27:33. coat rent. 2 S 1:2. 13:19.

33. then thou. 2 S 19:35.

34. return. ver. 20. Jsh 8:2. Mt 10:6. as I have been. 2 S 16:16-19. mayest. 2 S 17:5-14.

35. thou shalt tell. 2 S 17:15, 16.

36. their two sons. ver. 27. 2 S 17:17. 18:19, etc.

37. friend. 2 S 16:16. 1 Ch 27:33. Absalom. 2 S 16:15.

2 SAMUEL 16

Ziba imposes on David and obtains a grant of Mephibosheth's estate, 1-4. Shimei a Benjamite curses and slanders David, who bears it humbly and meekly, 5-14. Hushai insinuates himself into Absalom's counsels, 15-19. By Ahithophel's advice, Absalom openly goes in to his father's concubines, 20-23.

1. little past. 2 S 15:30, 32. Ziba. 2 S 9:2, 9-12. with a couple. 2 S 17:27-29. 19:32. 1 S 17:17, 18. raisins. 1 S 25:18. 30:12. 1 Ch 12:40. Pr 18:16. 29:4,

5. **summer**. *121P9, Is +16:9. These were probably
pumpions, cucumbers, or watermelons; the two latter
being extensively used in the East to refresh travelers
in the burning heat of the summer; and probably, as
Mr. Harmer supposes, called "summer fruits" on this
very account. Is 16:9. 28:4. Je 40:10, 12. 48:32. Am
8:1. Mi 7:1. **a bottle**. 1 S 1:24. 10:3. 16:20. Je +*13:12n.
wine. 1 S 1:24. 10:3. 25:18.

2. **What meanest**. Ge 21:29. 33:8. Ezk 37:18. **The
asses**. This is the eastern mode of speaking when presenting any thing to a great man: "This is for the slaves
of the servants of your majesty;" when at the same
time the presents are intended for the sovereign himself, and it is so understood. 2 S 15:1. 19:26. Jg 5:10.
10:4. **for the young**. 1 S 25:27. **that such**. 2 S 15:23.
17:29. Jg 8:4, 5. 1 S 14:28. Pr 17:23. 31:6, 7.

3. **where is**. 2 S 9:9, 10. Ps 88:18. Mi 7:5. **Today**.
2 S 19:24-30. Ex 20:16. Dt 19:18, 19. Ps 15:3. 101:5.
Pr 1:19. 21:28. 1 T 6:9, 10. Ju 11.

4. **Behold**. 2 S 14:10, 11. Ex 23:8. Dt 19:15. Pr
*18:13, 17. 19:2. **I humbly beseech thee**. Heb. I do
obeisance. 2 S 14:4, 22.

5. **Bahurim**. This place is supposed to be the same
as *Almon* (Jsh 21:18), and *Alemeth* (1 Ch 6:60), a city
of Benjamin, north of Jerusalem, and apparently not
far from Olivet. ver. 14. 2 S 3:16. 17:18. **whose name**.
2 S 19:16, etc. 1 K 2:8, 9, 36-44, etc. **Shimei**. i.e.
famous, heard of, *S#8096h. ver. 7, 13. Ex 6:17. Nu
3:18. 2 S 19:16, 18, 21, 23. 1 K 1:8. 2:8, 36, 38, 38,
39, 39, 40, 40, 41, 42, 44. 4:18. 1 Ch 3:19. 4:26, 27.
5:4. 6:17, 29, 42. 8:21. 23:7, 9, 10, 10. 25:17. 27:27.
2 Ch 29:14. 31:12, 13. Ezr 10:23, 33, 38. Est 2:5. (1)
A son of Gershon, the son of Levi, Nu 3:18; 1 Ch
6:17, called also Shimi, Ex 6:17. (2) A Benjamite, of
the family of Saul, who cursed David when he fled
from Absalom, 2 S 16:5-13; 19:23. (3) An officer of
David who remained faithful when Adonijah rebelled,
1 K 1:8. (4) One of the provision officers of Solomon,
1 K 4:18. (5) A grandson of Jeconiah, 1 Ch 3:19. (6)
A descendant of Simeon, 1 Ch 4:26, 27. (7) A descendant of Reuben, 1 Ch 5:4. (8) A descendant of Merari,
the son of Levi, 1 Ch 6:29, 42. (9) The head of the
tenth course in the service of song, 1 Ch 25:17. (10)
An overseer of David's vineyards, 1 Ch 27:27. (11) A
descendant of Heman, 2 Ch 29:14. (12) A Levite in
charge of offerings, 2 Ch 31:12, 13. (13) A Levite who
took a foreign wife, Ezr 10:23. (14, 15) Two Jews who
took foreign wives, Ezr 10:33, 38. (16) An ancestor of
Mordecai, Est 2:5. **he came**, etc. *or*, he still came
forth and cursed. **cursed**. Ex 22:28. 1 S 17:43. Ps 69:26.
109:16-19, 28. Pr 26:2. Ec 10:20. Is 8:21. Mt 5:11,
12.

7. **bloody man**. Heb. man of blood. *96F2, Ge
+4:10. 2 S 3:37. 11:15-17. 12:9. Ps 5:6. 26:9mg. 51:14.
55:23mg. **man of Belial**. Dt 13:13. +15:9. Jg +19:22.
1 S 2:12. 25:17, 25. 1 K 21:10, 13.

8. **returned**. Jg 9:24, 56, 57. 1 K 2:32, 33. Ac 28:4,
5. Re 16:6. **the blood**. 2 S 1:16. 3:28, 29. 4:8-12. Ps
3:2. 4:2. **thou**, etc. *or*, thee in thy evil. **bloody**. *96F2,
Ge +4:10.

9. **Abishai**. 2 S 3:30. 1 S 26:6-8. **dead dog**. 2 S
3:8. 9:8. 1 S 24:14. *28. Antiprosopopoeia; or, Anti-
personification B870. Persons represented as inanimate
things. A dog does not curse, still less a dead dog,
but this figure says in few words what would take a
whole paragraph to state literally what this figure im-

plies. **curse**. See on Ex *22:28. Ac *23:5. 1 P *2:17.
let me go. 1 S 26:6-11. Jb 31:30, 31. Je 40:13-16.

10. **What have**. *85H, Jg +11:12. 2 S 3:39. *19:22.
Jg +*11:12. 1 K 2:5. Mt 16:23. Lk 9:54-56. Jn +*2:4.
1 P *2:23. *108H8. Idiom B842. "What to me and to
thee" means "what is there between thee and me,"
"what have in common." For other instances of
this figure see 2 S 19:22. 1 K 17:18. 2 K 3:13. Mt
8:29. Mk 1:24. Lk 4:34. Jn 2:4. **so let him**. Ge 50:20.
1 K 22:21-23. 2 K 18:25. La 3:38, 39. Jn 18:11. **Who
shall**. 1 S +18:10n. Jb 2:10. 9:12. Ec 8:4. Da 4:35.
Am +*3:6. Ro 9:20. Ep +1:11.

11. **Behold**. 2 S *12:11, 12. **came forth**. 2 S 7:12.
Ge 15:4. **seeketh**. 2 S 17:1-4. 2 K 19:37. 2 Ch 32:21.
Mt 10:21. **life**. Heb. *nephesh*, soul, Ge +44:30. **the
Lord**. Is 10:5-7. Ezk 14:9. 20:25.

12. **the Lord**. Ge 29:32, 33. Ex 2:24, 25. 3:7, 8.
1 S 1:11. Ps 25:18. **affliction**. *or*, tears. Heb. eye. *182,
Ge +18:22. Ps 39:12. 42:3. **requite**. Dt 23:5. Is 27:7.
Mt *5:11, 12. Ro *8:28. 2 C 4:17. 2 Th *1:7. He 12:10.
1 P 4:12-19.

13. **cursed**. ver. 5, 6. Ps 109:17, 18, 26-28. **cast
dust**. Heb. dusted him with dust. Ac 22:23. It was
an ancient custom, in those warm and arid countries,
to lay the dust before a person of distinction by sprinkling the ground with water. Dr. Pococke and the
consul were treated with this respect when they entered Cairo (vol. i. p. 17). The same custom is alluded
to in the well known fable of Phaedrus, in which a
slave is represented as going before Augustus and offi-
ciously laying the dust. To throw dust in the air while
a person was passing was therefore an act of great
disrespect; to do so before a sovereign prince, an indecent outrage. But it is probable that Shimei meant
more than disrespect and outrage to this afflicted king.
Sir John Chardin informs us, that in the East in general,
those who demand justice against a criminal throw
dust upon him, signifying that he ought to be put in
the grave: hence the common imprecation among the
Turks and Persians, "Be covered with earth," or, "Earth
be upon thy head."

14. **there**. ver. 5. Ps 3:5. 4:8.

15. **Absalom**. 2 S 15:37.

16. **David's friend**. 2 S 15:37. **God save the king**.
Heb. Let the king live. 1 S 10:24. 1 K 1:25, 34. 2 K
11:12. Pr 27:14. Da 2:4. 5:10. 6:6, 21. Mt 21:9.

17. **Is this thy**. Dt 32:6. **why wentest**. 2 S 15:32-
37. 19:25. Pr 17:17. 18:24.

18. **whom the Lord**. 2 S 5:1-3. 1 S 16:13.

19. **should I not serve**. 2 S 15:34. 1 S 28:2. 29:8.
Ps 55:21. Ga 2:13.

20. **Give counsel**. Ex 1:10. Ps 2:2. 37:12, 13. Pr
+*21:30. Is 8:10. 29:15. Mt 27:1. Ac 4:23-28. **we**.
*96D4, Ge +29:27.

21. **Go in**. Ge 6:4. 38:16. **unto thy**. 2 S 12:11. 15:16.
20:3. Ge 35:22. Le 18:8. 20:11. 1 K 2:17, 22. 1 C
5:1. **abhorred**. Ge 34:30. 1 S 13:4. **thy father**. Ge
49:3, 4. **then shall**. 1 S 27:12. **the hands**. 2 S 2:7. Zc
8:13.

22. **the top**. 2 S 11:2. **went in**. 2 S 12:11, 12. 15:16.
*20:3. Nu 25:6. Is 3:9. Je 3:3. 8:12. Ezk 24:7. Ph 3:19.
in the sight. 2 S *12:11, 12. *22A5. Anthropomorphism
B874: eyes are attributed to God. For another instance
of this figure see Zc 2:8. **of all**. *171A, Ex +9:6.

23. **the counsel**. 1 Ch 27:33. **as if**. Nu 27:21. 1 S
30:8. Ps 28:2. 1 P 4:11. **oracle of God**. Heb. word of

God. Ps 19:7. **so was**. The first counsel of this sagacious but wicked man to Absalom was more like an oracle of Satan, both for subtlety and atrocity. He advised the shameless measure just detailed, in order to establish Absalom and preclude the possibility of a reconciliation with David. The wives of a conquered king were always the property of the conqueror; and in possessing these he appeared to possess the right to the kingdom. **all the counsel**. 2 S 17:14, 23. Jb *5:12. *28:28. Je 4:22. *8:9. Mt 11:25. Lk *16:8. Ro 1:22. 1 C *3:19, 20. Ja *3:13-18. **both**. 2 S 15:12. Ec 10:1.

2 SAMUEL 17

Hushai's counsel is preferred to the politic but desperately wicked counsel of Ahithophel, by the secret appointment of God, 1-14. Hushai sends intelligence to David, who hastily passes over Jordan, 15-22. Ahithophel returns home and hangs himself, 23. David comes to Mahanaim, 24. Amasa is made captain of Absalom's army, which is encamped at Gilead, 25, 26. David's friends bring him provisions, 27-29.

1. **I will arise**. Pr 1:16. 4:16. Is 59:7, 8. **this night**. Ps 3:3-5. 4:8. 109:2-4.

2. **weary**. 2 S 16:14. Dt 25:18. **I will smite**. 1 K 22:31. Zc 13:7. Mt 21:38. 26:31. Jn 7:7. 11:50. 18:4-8.

3. **I will bring**. 2 S 3:21. **shall be**. Is 48:22. 57:21. 1 Th 5:3.

4. **the saying**. 1 S 18:20, 21. 23:21. Est 5:14. Ro 1:32. **pleased Absalom well**. Heb. was right in the eyes of Absalom. Jg 14:3mg. 2 Ch 30:4mg. Est 1:21mg.

5. **Hushai**. 2 S 15:32-37. 16:16-19. **he saith**. Heb. is in his mouth.

6. **saying**. Heb. word.

7. **given**. Heb. counselled. **not good**. Pr 31:8.

8. **mighty men**. 2 S 15:18. 21:18-22. 23:8, 9, 16, 18, 20-22. Ge 6:4. 10:8, 9. Dt 10:17. Jsh 1:14. 1 S 16:18. 17:34-36, 50. 1 Ch 11:25-47. He 11:32-34. **chafed in their minds**. Heb. bitter of soul. Heb. *nephesh*, Ge +23:8. Jg +18:25mg. 1 S 1:10. 22:2. +30:6mg. **as a bear**. 2 K 2:24. Pr 17:12. 28:15. Da 7:5. Ho 13:8. **thy father is**. Ex 15:3. 1 S 23:23.

9. **he is hid**. Jg 20:33. 1 S 22:1. 24:3. **some**. Jsh 7:5. 8:6. Jg 20:32. 1 S 14:14, 15. **pit**. Heb. *pachath*, *S#6354h. 2 S 18:17. Is 24:17, 18. Je 48:28, 43, 44. La 3:47. **overthrown**. Heb. fallen.

10. **valiant**. or, son of valor. 2 S 2:7mg. Dt 3:18. **heart**. 2 S 1:23. 23:20. Ge 49:9. Nu 24:8, 9. Pr 28:1. **utterly melt**. Ex 15:15. Dt 1:28. Jsh 2:9-11. Is 13:7. 19:1. **thy father**. 1 S 18:17. He 11:34. **and they which**. SS 3:7.

11. **all Israel**. 2 S 24:2. Jg 20:1. **from Dan to**. 2 S 3:10. **as the sand**. ſ102B, 138B, Ge +13:16. Ge 13:16. *22:17. Jsh 11:4. 1 K 4:20. 20:10. **thou go**. Heb. thy face, or presence, go, etc. ſ171Q, Ge +3:19. **in thine**. 2 S 12:28. Ps 7:15, 16. 9:16.

12. **in some place**. 1 S 23:23. **we will**. Ps 12:2. 2 P 2:18. **light upon**. This is a very beautiful and expressive figure. The dew in Palestine and other warm climates falls fast, sudden, and heavy; and it falls upon every spot of earth, so that not a blade of grass escapes it. It is therefore no inept emblem of a numerous and active army; and it was, perhaps, for this reason that the Romans called their light armed forces *rorarii*. 1 K 20:10. 2 K 18:23. 19:24. Is 10:13, 14. Ob 3. **dew**.

Dt 32:2. Ps 133:3. Pr 19:12. Is 18:4. Ho 14:5. Mi 5:7.

13. **bring ropes**. In the same manner the king of Maturan, in Java, proposed pulling down a tower which the Dutch had built by making his people and elephants pull at a number of chains and ropes of cocoa-nut bark thrown around it. 2 S 8:2. Jsh 2:15. 1 K 20:31, 32. Est 1:8. Jb 41:1. **draw**. or, *tear*. Je 15:3. 22:19. 49:20. 50:45. **river**. or, brook *or* valley. Ge 26:17, 19. Jg +16:4. 1 S 17:40. **not one**. ſ102, Ge +2:24. **small stone**. Am 9:9. Mt 24:2.

14. **the Lord**. 2 S 15:31. Ge 32:28. Ex 9:16. Dt 2:30. 2 Ch 25:16, 20. **appointed**. Heb. commanded. Ps 7:6. 33:9, 10. La 3:37. Am 9:3. **to defeat**. 2 S 15:*31, 34. 16:23. Jb 5:12-14. Pr 19:21. 21:30. Is 8:10. 1 C 1:19, 20. 3:19. **good counsel**. Lk 16:8. **the Lord**. Am +*3:6. **bring evil**. Is +*45:7.

15. **Zadok**. 2 S 15:35.

16. **Lodge**. 2 S 15:28. **but speedily**. ver. 21, 22. 2 S 15:14, 28. 1 S 20:38. Ps 55:8. Pr 6:4, 5. Mt 24:16-18. **be swallowed**. 2 S 20:19, 20. Ps 35:25. 56:2. 57:3. 1 C 15:54. 2 C 5:4.

17. **Jonathan**. 2 S 15:27, 36. **stayed**. Jsh 2:4, etc. En-rogel. Jsh 15:7. 18:16. 1 K 1:9. **wench**. or, the maid servant. Of the household, most probably (Young).

18. **Bahurim**. 2 S 3:16. 16:5. 19:16. **well**. Heb. *be-er*, Ge 14:10. +16:14. **court**. Ge 25:16. 1 S 6:26.

19. **spread a covering**. Nu 4:6, 7, etc. Jsh 2:4-6, etc. Ps 105:39. Is 22:8. **well's**. Heb. *be-er*, Ge +16:14. **spread**. Nu 11:32. Jb 12:23. Ps 88:9. Je 8:9. **ground corn**. Pr 27:22. **the thing**. Ex 1:19.

20. **They be gone**. 2 S 15:34. Ex 1:19. Jsh 2:4, 5. 1 S 19:14-17. 21:2. 27:11, 12. **when they had sought**. Jsh 2:22, 23.

21. **well**. Heb. *be-er*, Ge +16:14. **Arise**. See on ver. 15, 16. **thus hath Ahithophel**. ver. 1-3.

22. **and they passed**. ver. 24. Pr 27:12. Mt 10:16. **there lacked**. Nu 31:49. Jn 18:9.

23. **saw**. Pr 16:18. 19:3. **followed**. Heb. done. his city. 2 S 15:12. **put his household in order**. Heb. gave charge concerning his house. 2 K 20:1mg. Is 38:1mg. **and hanged himself**. 2 S 15:31. 1 S 31:4, 5. 1 K 16:18. +19:4. Jb 31:3. Ps 5:10. 35:8. *37:7, 35, 36. 55:23. Mt 27:5. Ac 1:18. or, strangled. Na 2:12. **buried**. 2 S 2:32. Jg 8:32. **sepulchre**. Heb. *qeber*, Ge +23:4.

24. **Mahanaim**. 2 S 2:8. Ge *32:2. Jsh 13:26. **all**. *ſ171A, Ex +9:6.

25. **Amasa**. i.e. *a load, burden; burden bearer*, *S#6021h. 2 S 19:13. 20:4, 5, 8, 9, 9, 10, 12, 12. 1 K 2:5, 32. 1 Ch 2:17, 17. 2 Ch 28:12. (1) David's nephew, the son of David's sister, Abigail, and Jether, an Ishmaelite, 2 S 20:4-10; 1 Ch 2:17. (2) A chief of Ephraim, 2 Ch 28:12. **Ithra**. i.e. *super-abundance*, *S#3501h. 1 K 2:5, Jether. 1 Ch 2:16, 17, Jether the Ishmaelite. **Abigail**. Heb. Abigal. i.e. *father of joy*. **Nahash**. i.e. *a serpent*. or, *Jesse*. 1 Ch 2:13, 16. **Zeruiah**. i.e. *perhaps a cleft*. 1 S +26:6. David's only sister, apparently (Young).

26. **land of Gilead**. Nu 32:1, etc. Dt 3:15. Jsh 17:1.

27. **Shobi**. i.e. *one leading away captive*, *S#7629h. **the son of Nahash**. 2 S 10:1, 2. 12:29, 30. 1 S 11:1. **Machir**. i.e. *sold*. 2 S 9:4. **Ammiel**. i.e. *my people is strong*. **Lo-debar**. i.e. *barren*, *S#3810h. 2 S 9:4, 5. This person brought up Mephibosheth. **Barzillai**. i.e. *iron*. 2 S 19:31, 32. 1 K 2:7. Ezr 2:61. **Rogelim**. i.e. *footmen; treaders; fullers*, *S#7274h. 2 S 19:31.

28. beds. These no doubt consisted of skins of beasts, mats, carpets, and such like. 2 S 16:1, 2. Ge 49:4. 1 S 25:18. Is 32:8. **basons.** or, cups. Ex 12:22. *Sappoth,* probably wooden bowls, such as the Arabs still eat out of, and knead their bread in. **earthen vessels.** *Keley yotzair,* literally, "vessels of the potter." Ps 2:9. Is 29:16. 30:14. Je 19:1, 11. So when Dr. Perry visited the temple of Luxor in Egypt, he says, "We were entertained by the Caliph here with great civility and favor; he sent us, in return of our presents, several sheep, a good quantity of eggs, *bardacks,* etc. (p. 346, 347). The *bardacks,* he informs us, were earthen vessels used to cool and refresh their water in, by means of which it drinks very cool and pleasant in the hottest seasons of the year. See Harmer, ch. vi. Ob. 3, (p. 339, 340). **wheat.** Mr. Jones says, 'Travelers use *zumeet, tumeet,* and *limereece. Zumeet* is flour mixed with honey, butter, and spice; *tumeet* is flour done up with organ oil; and *limereece* is flour mixed with water, for drink. This quenches thirst much better than water alone; satisfies a hungry appetite; cools and refreshes tired and weary spirits," etc. **wheat.** Ge 30:14. **barley.** Ex 9:31. **flour.** Ge 18:6. **parched.** or, roasted. Le 23:14. **beans.** Ezk 4:9. **lentiles.** Ge 25:34.

29. honey. Ge 43:11. **butter.** Ge 18:8. **sheep.** Ge 4:2, 4. **cheese of kine.** 1 S 17:18. **for David.** Lk 8:3. Ph 4:15-19. **to eat.** 2 S 17:2. Ps 34:8-10. 84:11. **The people.** Jg 8:4-6. Ec 11:1, 2. Is 21:14. 58:7. **in the wilderness.** 2 S 16:2, 14. Ps 107:4-6.

2 SAMUEL 18

David musters his troops under three commanders and charges them to spare Absalom, 1-5. Absalom's army is routed; he flees, and, his head being entangled in an oak, he is slain by Joab, and cast into a pit, 6-17. Absalom's place, 18. Ahinoam and Cushi carry tidings to David, 19-32. He laments most bitterly, 33.

1. numbered. Ex 17:9. Jsh 8:10. 1 S +11:8. **captains of thousands.** 1 S 8:12.

2. a third part. Jg 7:16, 19. 9:43. **the hand of Joab.** 2 S 10:7-10. **Ittai.** 2 S 15:19-22. **I will surely.** 2 S 17:11. Ps 3:6. 27:1-3. 118:6-8.

3. Thou shalt. 2 S *21:17. **if we flee.** 2 S 17:2. 1 K 22:31. Zc 13:7. **care for us.** Heb. set their heart on us. 2 S 13:20. **but now.** The particle *attah,* "now," is doubtless a mistake for the pronoun *attah,* "thou:" and so it appears to have been read by the LXX., Vulgate, and Chaldee, and by two of Kennicott's and De Rossi's MSS. **worth,** etc. Heb. as ten thousand of us. SS 5:10. La 4:20. **succor.** Heb. be to succor. 2 S 10:11. 11:1. Ex 17:10-12.

4. by the gate. ver. 24. Is 28:6. **by hundreds.** David's small company, by this time, was greatly recruited; but what its number was we cannot tell. Josephus says it amounted only to four thousand men. ver. 1. 1 S 29:2.

5. Deal gently. 2 S 16:11. 17:1-4, 14. Dt 21:18-21. Ps 103:13. Lk 23:34. **all the people.** ver. 12.

6. wood of Ephraim. The wood of Ephraim was evidently beyond Jordan and apparently not far from Mahanaim; it is supposed to be the place where the Ephraimites were slain by Jepthah. Jsh 17:15, 18. Jg 12:4-6.

7. the people. 2 S 2:17. 15:6. 19:41-43. **a great.**

Pr 11:21. 24:21, 22. **twenty thousand men.** 2 S 2:26, 31. 2 Ch 13:16, 17. 28:6.

8. the wood. That is, probably, many more were slain in pursuit through the wood than in the battle, by falling into swamps, pits, etc. and being entangled and cut down by David's men. Such is the relation of Josephus; but the Chaldee, Syriac, and Arabic state, that they were devoured by wild beasts in the wood. Ex 15:10. Jsh 10:11. Jg 5:20, 21. 1 K 20:30. Ps 3:7. 43:1. **devoured more.** Heb. multiplied to devour. lit. eat. Ge 31:15. Nu 26:10. 2 Ch 7:13.

9. his head. Riding furiously under the thick boughs of a great oak, which hung low and had never been cropped, either the twisted branches or some low forked bough of the tree caught him by the neck, or, as some think, by the loops into which his long hair had been pinned, which had been so much his pride and was now justly made a halter for him. He may have hung so low from the bough, in consequence of the length of his hair, that he could not use his hands to help himself, or so entangled that his hands were bound, so that the more he struggled the more he was caught. This set him up as a fair mark to the servants of David; and although David would have spared his rebellious son, if his orders had been executed, yet he could not turn aside the sword of divine justice, in executing the just, righteous sentence of death on this traitorous son. ver. 14. 2 S 14:26. 17:23. Mt 27:5. **taken up.** Dt 21:23. 27:16, 20. Jb 18:8-10. 31:3. Ps 63:9, 10. Pr 20:20. 30:17. Je 48:44. Mk 7:10. Ga 3:13.

12. receive, etc. Heb. weigh upon mine hand. **in our hearing.** ver. 5. **Beware,** etc. Heb. Beware, whosoever *ye be,* of the, etc. **touch.** 63B, Ge +25:28.

13. wrought. 2 S 1:15, 16. 4:10-12. **life.** Heb. *nephesh,* soul, Ge +44:30. **for there is no.** 2 S 14:19, 20. He *4:13.

14. with thee. Heb. before thee. **thrust them.** ver. 5. Jg 4:21. 5:26, 31. Ps 45:5. 1 Th 5:3. **midst.** Heb. heart. Dt 4:11. Ps 46:2. Jon 2:3. Mt 12:40.

15. and slew. Ps 109:6, 12.

16. blew the trumpet. 2 S 2:28. 20:22. Nu 10:2-10. 1 C 14:8.

17. laid. This was the ancient method of burying, whether heroes or traitors; the heap of stones being designed to perpetuate the memory of the event, whether good or bad. The Arabs in general make use of no other monument than a heap of stones over a grave. Thus, in an Arabic poem it is related that Hatim, the father, and Adi the grandfather of Kais, having been murdered at a time before Kais was capable of reflection, his mother kept it a profound secret; and in order to guard him against having any suspicion, she collected a parcel of stones on two hillocks in the neighborhood, and told her son, that the one was the grave of his father, and the other of his grandfather. The ancient cairns in Ireland and Scotland and the *tumuli* in England are of this kind. **heap.** properly a "round heap," as in Ge 31:46-52. Jsh 7:26. 8:29. 10:27. Pr 10:7. Je 22:18, 19. **fled.** 2 S 19:8. 20:22. 1 S 4:10. 13:2. 1 K 8:66. 2 K 8:21. 13:5. **tent.** 2 S 19:8. 1 S 4:10.

18. reared up. 1 S 15:12. **pillar.** Ge 28:18. 35:14, 20. **the king's.** Ge 14:17. Jl 3:2. **I have no son.** 2 S 14:27. Jb 18:16, 17. Ps 109:13. Je 22:30. **he called.** Ge 11:4. 1 S 15:12. Ps 49:11. Da 4:30. **unto this day.**

Jsh +4:9. **Absalom's place**. or, monument. lit. hand, as in 1 S 15:12. Is 56:5. Josephus (Ant. I. vii. c. 9. par. 3) says there was in his time, about two furlongs from Jerusalem, a marble pillar called *Absalom's hand*, as it is in the Hebrew (See Note on 1 S 15:12); and there is one shown to the present day, in the valley of Jehoshaphat, which, though comparatively a modern structure, probably occupies the site of the original one set up by Absalom. Ge 11:9. Ac 1:18, 19.

19. **Ahimaaz**. ver. 23, 27-29. 2 S 15:36. 17:17. **avenged him**. Heb. judged him from the hand, etc. Ps 7:6, 8, 9. 9:4, 16. 10:14, 18. Ro 12:19.

20. **bear tidings**. Heb. be a man of tidings. 2 S 17:16-21. **because**. ver. 5, 27, 29, 33.

22. **howsoever**. Heb. be what may. ver. 23. **ready**. or, convenient. Ro 1:◑15, 28. Ep 5:4.

23. **Run**. ♪96B, Nu 24:21. **overran Cushi**. Jn 20:4.

24. **between**. ♪143, Ge +19:2. ver. 4. 1 S 4:13. **the watchman**. 2 K 9:17-20. Is 21:6-9, 11, 12. Ezk 33:2-7. **lifted**. ♪144A12, Ge +22:13.

26. **porter**. 1 Ch +23:5.

27. **Methinketh**. Heb. I see. 2 K 9:20. **He is a good**. 1 K 1:42. Pr 25:13, 25. Is 52:7. Ro 10:15.

28. **All is well**. or, Peace be to thee. Heb. Peace. **he fell down upon his face**. This act was not only in reverence to the king but in humble adoration of God, whose name he praises for this victory. The more our hearts are fixed and enlarged, in thanksgiving to God for our mercies, the better disposed we shall be to bear with patience the afflictions mixed with them. 2 S 1:2. 14:4. 1 S 25:6. **Blessed**. 2 S 22:47. Ge 14:20. 24:27. 2 Ch 20:26. Ps 115:1. 124:6. 144:1, 2. Re 19:1-3. **delivered up**. Heb. shut up. 1 S 17:46. 24:18. 26:8. Ps 31:8.

29. **Is the young man Absalom safe?** Heb. is there peace to, etc.? ver. 32. 2 S 20:9. **I saw a great**. ver. 19, 20, 22.

31. **Tidings**. Heb. Tidings is brought. **the Lord**. ver. 19, 28. 2 S 22:48, 49. Dt 32:35, 36. Jg 5:31. Ps 18:47, 48. 58:10. 94:1-4. 124:2, 3. Lk 18:7, 8. Cushi was the man Joab ordered to carry the tidings to David. He was an Ethiopian, as his name signifies, and some think he was so by birth—a black, who waited on Joab, probably one of the ten that had helped to dispatch Absalom; though it was dangerous for one of those to bring the news to David, lest his fate be the same with theirs that reported the death of Saul and Ishbosheth to him.

32. **The enemies**. Thus Cushi obliquely and slowly informs David of the death of his son Absalom. Jg 5:31. Ps 68:1, 2. Da 4:19. **be as**. ♪88, Ge +15:15.

33. **much moved**. or, troubled *or* angry. 2 S 7:10. 22:8. Ge 45:24. **the chamber over the gate**. Jg 3:20, 23, 24, 25. 1 K 17:19, 23. 2 K 1:2. 4:10, 11. 23:12. 1 Ch 28:11. **O my son**. 2 S 19:4. **son**. ♪84, Ge +6:17. **would God**. 2 S 12:10-23. Ps 103:13. Pr 10:1. *17:25. Zc 12:10. Ja *5:17.

2 SAMUEL 19

The people being greatly disappointed and discouraged by David's conduct, Joab, by rude expostulations, induces him to restrain his grief and come forth to them, 1-8. The men of Israel dispute about bringing back David; who sends to the priests to incite the men of Judah to take the lead in this; and they readily comply, 9-15. Shimei submitting is not punished, 16-23. Mephibosheth meets David; complains that Ziba had deceived and slandered him, and has half his land restored, 24-30. Barzillai attends David over Jordan, and his son is taken into the king's family, 31-40. The Israelites expostulate with the men of Judah for bringing back the king without them, 41-43.

1. **it was told**. 2 S 18:5, 12, 14, 20, 33. Pr 17:25.

2. **victory**. Heb. salvation, or, deliverance. 2 S 23:10, 12. 1 S 11:9, 13. 1 Ch 11:14. **turned**. Pr 16:15. 19:12.

3. **into the city**. ver. 32. 2 S 17:24. **steal**. Ge 31:27.

4. **covered**. ♪121S3F2, 2 S +15:30. See on 2 S 15:30. Ps 69:7. **O my son**. It is allowed by competent critics that the lamentation of David over his son, of which this forms a part, is exceedingly pathetic; and Calmet properly remarks that the frequent repetition of the name of the deceased is common in the language of lamentation. 2 S 18:33.

5. **Thou hast**. Everyone must admit that David's immoderate grief for his rebellious son was imprudent, and that Joab's firm and sensible reproof was necessary to arouse him to a sense of his duty to his people: but, in his manner, Joab far exceeded the bounds of that reverence which a servant owes to his master, or a subject to his prince. **saved**. Ne 9:27. Ps 3:8. 18:47, 48. **life**. Heb. *nephesh*, soul, Ge +44:30. **lives**. Heb. *nephesh*, Ge +44:30.

6. **In that**, etc. Heb. By loving, etc. Jn *3:16. Ro *5:8, 10. *8:32. **thou regardest**, etc. Heb. princes or servants are not to thee. ♪108B. Idiom B827. "To be" is an idiom which means to be in high esteem, or of great value. Here, the figure is translated, but the margin gives "are not to thee," rendered by the R.V. "Are nought unto thee." For another instance of this idiom see 1 C 1:28. **then it had**. 2 S 3:24, 25. Jb 34:18. Pr 19:9, 10. Ac 23:5.

7. **Now**. ♪66, Ge +9:3. **arise**. Pr +*19:15. **comfortably unto thy**. Heb. to the heart of thy. Ge +34:3mg. Is 40:2mg. Ho 2:14mg. **there**. Pr 14:28. **all the evil**. Ps 71:4-6, 9-11, 18-20. 129:1, 2. Mt 27:64.

8. **sat in the gate**. ♪171S7B, Ge +14:7. How prudently and mildly David took the reproof and counsel given him! He shook off his grief, anointed his head, and washed his face, that he might not appear to men to mourn, and then made his appearance at the gate of the city, which was the public place of resort for the hearing of causes and giving judgment as well as a place to ratify special bargains. The people flocked to congratulate him on his and their safety, and that all was well. When we are convinced of a fault, we must amend, though we are told of it by our inferiors in a way which is peculiarly painful to our natural feelings (1 S ◑+*25:17. 2 K +*5:13). This ancient custom still exists in the East; for when Dr. Pococke returned from viewing the town of ancient Byblus, he says, "The sheik and the elders were sitting in the gate of the city, after the ancient manner, and I sat awhile with them" (Travels, vol. ii., p. 98). 2 S ◑15:2. 18:6-8. Ge +14:7. 2 K 7:1n. Je 38:7. 39:3. **for Israel**. ver. 3. 2 S 18:6-8. 1 K 22:36. 2 K 14:12.

9. **strife**. Ge 3:12, 13. Ex 32:24. Ja 3:14-16. **The king**. 2 S 8:10. 1 S 17:50. 18:5-7, 25. 19:5. **he is fled**. 2 S 15:14.

10. **whom**. 2 S 15:12, 13. Ho 8:4. **is dead**. 2 S 18:14.

speak ye not a word. Heb. are ye silent? Jg +16:2mg. 18:9. 1 K 20:2mg.

11. king. ✗16, Ge +1:27. sent. 2 S 15:29, 35, 36. 1 K 2:25, 26, 35. Speak. 2 C 5:20. Why are. Mt *5:16. 2 Th 3:9.

12. my bones. 2 S *5:1. Ge 2:23. Jg 9:2. Ep +*5:30.

13. Amasa. 2 S 17:25. 1 Ch 2:16, 17. 12:18. God. 2 S 3:39. Ru 1:17. 1 K 19:2. room of Joab. ver. 5-7. 2 S 3:29, 30. 8:16. 18:11.

14. he bowed. The measures that he pursued were the best calculated that could be adopted for accomplishing this salutary end. David appears to take no notice of their infidelity but rather to place confidence in them, that their confidence in him might be naturally excited; and to oblige them yet further, purposes to make Amasa general of the army, instead of Joab. even. Jg 20:1. Ps 110:2, 3. Je 32:39. Ezk 11:19. Ac 4:32.

15. Gilgal. Jsh 5:9. 1 S 11:14, 15.

16. Shimei. It appears that Shimei was a powerful chieftain in the land, for he had here in his retinue no less than a thousand men. 2 S 16:5-13. 1 K 2:8, 36-46. hasted. Jb 2:4. Pr 6:4, 5. Mt 5:25.

17. Ziba. ver. 26, 27. 2 S 9:2, 10. 16:1-4.

18. And there. The LXX. connecting this with the preceding verse, render "and they made ready Jordan before the king, and did the necessary service to bring over the king;" and the Vulgate has, "and breaking into Jordan, they passed the fords before the king, to bring over the king's household." Josephus says they prepared a bridge over the Jordan, to facilitate his passage. what he thought good. Heb. the good in his eyes. ver. 27, 37, 38. 2 S 24:22. Jsh 22:30. fell down. Ps 66:3. 81:15. Re 3:9.

19. And said. Ec 10:4. Let not. 1 S 22:15. Ps 32:2. Ro 4:6-8. 2 C 5:19. remember. Ps 79:8. Is 43:25. Je 31:34. did perversely. 2 S 16:5-9, etc. Ex 10:16, 17. 1 S 26:21. Mt 27:4. take it. 2 S 13:20, 33. 1 S 25:25.

20. I am come. Ps 78:34-37. Je 22:23. Ho 5:15. Joseph. ver. 9. 2 S 16:5. 19:16. Ge 46:19. 48:14, 20. 1 K 12:20, 25. Ho 4:15-17. 5:3.

21. Shall not. Ex *22:28. 1 K 21:10, 11. Ec *10:20. cursed. 2 S 16:5, 7, 9, 13. 1 S 24:6. 26:9.

22. What have. ✗85H, Jg +11:12. ✗108H8, 2 S +16:10. 2 S +*3:39. 16:10. Jg +*11:12. 1 S 26:8. Mt 8:29. Jn +*2:4. shall there any man. 1 S 11:13. 25:32, 33. Is 16:5. Lk 9:54-56.

23. Thou shalt. 1 K 2:8, 9, 37, 46. sware. 1 S 28:10. 30:15. He 6:16.

24. Mephibosheth. 2 S 9:3, 6. 16:3. the son. Young notes, or rather grandson, being son of Jonathan. ✗171G2. Synechdoche of the Species, Ge +13:8. 1 K +15:10n. dressed his feet. Literally, "made his feet," which seems to mean washing the feet, paring the nails, and perhaps anointing or otherwise perfuming them, if not tinting the nails with henna: see Note on Dt 21:12. Sir John Chardin, in his MS. note on this place, informs us, that it is customary in the East to have as much care of the feet as the hands; and that their barbers cut and adjust the nails with a proper instrument, because they often go barefoot. The nails of the toes of the mummies inspected in London in 1763, of which an account is given in the *Philosophical Transactions* for 1764, seem to have been tinted with some reddish color. 2 S 15:30. Is 15:2. Je 41:5. Mt 6:16. Ro 12:15. He 13:3. trimmed. Literally, "made his beard," which may mean combing, curling, and

perfuming it. But Mr. Morier (Journey through Persia, p. 247) says that they almost universally dye the beard black, by successive layers of a paste made of henna and another made of the leaf of the indigo: the first tinting it with an orange color and the next with a dark bottle green, which becomes jet black when exposed to the air for twenty-four hours.

25. Wherefore. 2 S 16:17.

26. I will saddle. 2 S 16:2, 3. thy servant. 2 S 4:4.

27. slandered. 2 S 16:3. Ex 20:16. Ps 15:3. 101:5. Je 9:4. as an angel. 2 S 14:17, 20. 1 S 29:9.

28. father's. ✗171G, Ge +13:8. were. Ge 32:10. dead men. Heb. men of death. 2 S 12:5mg. 1 S 26:16mg. didst thou. 2 S 9:7, 8, 10, 13. to cry. 2 K 8:3.

29. Why speakest. Jb 19:16, 17. Pr 18:13. Ac 18:15. Thou. 2 S 16:4. Dt 19:17-19. Ps 82:2. 101:5.

30. Yea. 2 S 1:26. Ac 20:24. Ph 1:20.

31. Barzillai came. 1 K 2:7. Ezr 2:61. Ne 7:63.

32. fourscore. Ge 5:27. 9:29. 25:7. 47:28. 50:26. Dt 34:7. Ps *90:3-10. Pr 16:31. provided. 2 S 17:27. 1 P 4:9. for he was. 1 S 25:2. Jb 1:3.

33. Come thou. 2 S 9:11. Mt 25:34-40. Lk 22:28-30. 2 Th 1:7.

34. How long have I to live? Heb. How many days are the years of my life? ✗144A10, Ge +29:14. Ge 47:8mg, 9. Jb *14:14. Ps 39:5, 6. 1 C 7:29. Ja *4:14.

35. can I discern. Jb 6:30. 12:11. He 5:14. 1 P 2:3. taste. Ec 12:1-5. I hear. Ezr 2:65. Ne 7:67. Ec 2:8. 12:4. a burden. 2 S 13:25. 15:33.

36. the king. Lk 6:38.

37. Let thy. The whole of this little episode is extremely interesting and contains an affecting description of the infirmities of old age. The venerable and kind Barzillai was fourscore years old; his ear was become dull of hearing, and his relish for even royal dainties was gone: the evil days had arrived in which he was constrained to say, "I have no pleasure in them" (Ec 12:1). As he was too old either to enjoy the pleasures of a court or to be of any further service to the king, he finishes his affecting address to the aged monarch with the request that he would suffer him to enjoy what old men naturally desire, to "die in mine own city, and be buried by the grave of my father and my mother;" at the same time commending his son Chimham to his kind offices. I may die. Ge 48:21. Jsh 23:14. Lk 2:29, 30. 2 T 4:6. 2 P 1:14. by the grave. Heb. qeber, Ge +23:4. 47:30. 49:29-31. 50:13. 1 K 13:22. Chimham. i.e. *a longing.* ver. 38. It is spelled *Chimhan* in ver. 40. 1 K 2:7. Je 41:17.

38. require. Heb. choose.

39. the king. The kiss was the token of friendship and farewell; the blessing a prayer to God for his prosperity: probably a prophetical benediction. kissed Barzillai. Ge 31:55. 45:15. Ru 1:14. 1 K 19:20. Ac 20:37. 1 Th 5:26. blessed. 2 S 6:18, 20. 13:25. Ge 14:19. 28:3. 47:7, 10. Lk 2:34. returned. Ge 31:55. Nu 24:25. 1 S 24:22.

40. Chimham. Heb. Chimhan. i.e. *longing, pining,* ✱S#3643h. ver. 37, 38. Je 41:17. all the people. ver. 11-15. Ge *49:10. Mt 21:9. Mk 11:9, 10. ◐15:14.

41. Why have. Jg 8:1. 12:1. Jn 7:5, 6. stolen. ver. 3. Ge 31:26, 27.

42. Because. ver. 12. 2 S 5:1. 1 Ch 2:3-17.

43. We have. 2 S 20:1, 2, 6. 1 K 12:16. ten parts. 2 S 5:1. Ge 47:24. Pr 13:10. despise us. Heb. set us

at light. Ge 16:4, 5. Is 9:1. 23:9. Ezk 22:7. **our advice**. ver. 9, 14. Ga 5:20, 26. Ph +*2:3. **the words**. Jg 8:1. 9:23. 12:1-6. Pr √15:1. 17:14. *18:19. Ro *12:21. Ga 5:15, 20. Ja *1:20. 3:2-10, 14-16. 4:1-5. Whatever value or respect the men of Israel at this time professed for their king, they would not have quarrelled so fiercely about their own credit and interest in recalling him if they had been truly sorry for their former rebellion. **Judah**. Jg 8:1. 12:1. Is 9:21. 11:13. **were fiercer**. or, harder. Ge 49:7. Dt 1:17. 15:18. 1 S 5:7.

2 SAMUEL 20

Sheba draws the men of Israel into a revolt, 1, 2. David shuts up his ten concubines, 3. Amasa, being sent to call together the men of Judah, is murdered by Joab, who resumes the command and pursues Sheba, 4-13. He besieges Abel, whither Sheba had fled, 14, 15. Through the interposition of a wise woman, Sheba's head is thrown over the wall, and the revolt is terminated, 16-22. David's officers, 23-26.

1. **And there**. 2 S 19:41-43. Ps 34:19. **happened**. 2 S +1:6. **a man of Belial**. 2 S 23:6. Dt 13:13. +15:9. Jg +19:22. 1 S 2:12. 30:22. Ps 17:13. Pr 26:21. Hab 1:12, 13. **Sheba**. i.e. *an oath*, *S#7652h. ver. 2, 6, 7, 10, 13, 21, 22. 1 Ch 5:13. Also Jsh 19:2. (1) A man of Benjamin who raised a rebellion against David, 2 S 20:1. (2) One of the chiefs of Gad, 1 Ch 5:13. (3) A town of Simeon, Jsh 19:2. **Bichri**. i.e. *first fruits; youthful*, *S#1075h. ver. 2, 6, 7, 10, 13, 21, 22. **he blew**. 2 S 15:10. Jg 3:27. Pr 24:21, 22. 25:8. **We have**. 2 S 19:43. 1 K 12:16. 2 Ch 10:16. Lk 19:14, 27. Ac 8:21. **every man to**. ver. 22. 1 S 4:10. 1 K 12:16. 2 Ch 10:16. **tents**. ƒ182, Ge +18:22.

2. **every man**. 2 S 19:41. Ps 62:9. 118:8-10. Pr *17:14. **the men**. Jn 6:66-68. Ac *11:23. **from Jordan**. 2 S 19:15, 40, 41. 2 Ch 10:17.

3. **ten women**. 2 S 15:16. 16:21, 22. **and put**. The confinement and retired maintenance of these women was the only measure which in justice and prudence could be adopted. In China, when an emperor dies, all his women are removed to an edifice called the *palace of chastity*, situated within the palace, in which they are shut up for the remainder of their lives. **ward**. Heb. an house of ward. Ge 40:3. **shut**. Heb. bound. **living in widowhood**. Heb. in widowhood of life.

4. **Amasa**. 2 S 17:25. 19:13. 1 Ch 2:17. **Assemble**. Heb. Call. ver. 5. Jg 4:13. 1 S +11:8.

5. **So Amasa**. 2 S 19:13. **tarried**. 1 S 13:8.

6. **Abishai**. 2 S 2:18. 3:30, 39. 10:9, 10, 14. 18:2, 12. 21:17. 23:18. 1 S 26:6. 1 Ch 11:20. 18:12. **do us**. 2 S 19:7. **thy lord's**. 2 S 11:11. 1 K 1:33. **escape us**. Heb. deliver himself from our eyes.

7. **Joab's men**. ver. 23. 2 S 8:16, 18. 15:18. 23:22, 23. 1 K 1:38, 44.

8. **in Gibeon**. 2 S 2:13. 3:30. **Amasa**. ver. 4, 5.

9. **Art thou**. Ps 55:21. Pr 26:24-26. Mi 7:2. **took Amasa**. Thevenot (P. i. p. 30) says, that among the Turks it is a great affront to take one by the beard unless it be to kiss him, in which case they often do it. D'Arvieux (*Voy. dans la Pal.* p. 71), describing an assembly of Arab emirs at an entertainment, says, "After the usual civilities, caresses, *kissings of the beard*, and of the hand, which every one gave and received according to his rank and dignity, they sat down upon mats." This act by the Arab emirs corresponds with

the conduct of Joab and illustrates this horrid assassination. 2 S 10:4n. **to kiss him**. Pr 6:34. 27:4. Mt 26:48, 49. Lk 22:47, 48.

10. **in Joab's**. ver. 9. Jg 3:21. 1 Ch 12:2. **he smote**. 2 S 2:23. 3:27. 4:6. Ge 4:8. 1 K 2:*5, 6, 31-34. **and shed**. Ac 1:18, 19. **struck him not again**. Heb. doubled not his stroke. 1 S 26:8.

11. **He that**. ver. 6, 7, 13, 21. **for David**. ver. 4. 2 K 9:32.

12. **Amasa wallowed**. 2 S 17:25. Ps 9:16. 55:23. Pr 24:21, 22.

13. **the highway**. Nu 20:19.

14. **Abel**. Or rather, probably, *Abel of Beth-Maachah*, as in the next verse. It appears, from Joab having marched "through all the tribes of Israel," to have been situated in the northern confines of the land of Israel, and in the half tribe of Manasseh, east of Jordan, as that was the situation of Maachah, to which it belonged. This agrees with the situation of the *Abela* which Eusebius and Jerome place between Paneas, or Caesarea Philippi, and Damascus. Josephus (Ant. I. vii. c. 10) says it was a fortified city, and a metropolis of the Israelites; and (Ant. I. viii. c. 6) also that it belonged to the ten tribes, having been taken from the king of Damascus. Jsh 18:21, 25. 1 K 15:20. 2 K 15:29. 2 Ch 16:4. **Bethmaachah**. i.e. *house of oppression*, *S#1038h. ver. 15. 2 K 15:29. **Berites**. *S#1276h, only here. Jsh 18:25, Beeroth.

15. **cast up**. 2 K 19:32. Is 29:3. 37:33. Je 6:6. 32:24. 33:4. Ezk 4:2. 26:8. Lk 19:43. **a bank**. So LXX. generally render *solelah*, by *prosxoma* or *xoma*; which latter is described by Potter (vol. ii. b. iii. c. 10) as "a *mount*, which was raised so high as to equal, if not exceed, the top of the besieged walls. The sides were walled in with bricks or stones, or secured with strong rafters; the fore part only, being by degrees to be moved near the walls, remained bare." Je 32:24n. **it stood in the trench**. or, it stood against the outmost wall. 1 K 21:23. Is 26:1. La 2:8. Na 3:8. **battered**, etc. Heb. marred to throw down.

16. **wise woman**. ver. 22. 2 S *14:2. Jg +5:29. 1 S 19:11-18. 25:3, 18, 23-25, *32, *33. 1 K 12:7n. Pr 11:16. 12:4. 14:1. 31:10, 30. Ec 9:14-18. Ac *18:26. 23:16. Ro 16:3, 4.

17. **Hear the words**. 2 S 14:12. 1 S 25:24.

18. **They were wont**, etc. or, They plainly spake in the beginning, saying, Surely they will ask of Abel, and so make an end. 2 S 2:1. *16:23. Dt 20:10, 11. 1 S 23:2. 30:8. Pr *12:15. **saying**. ƒ138A, Ge +10:9. **at Abel**. ver. 18. 2 K 15:29.

19. **peaceable**. Ge 18:23. Ro 13:3, 4. 1 T +*2:2. **faithful**. ƒ121N1, Ge +31:54. **a city**. 108C6. Idiom B834. Idiomatic degrees of comparison: two nouns conjoined. By using a noun instead of an adjective, not in regimen, but (by *Hendiadys*) in the same case and number, and joined to the other noun by a conjunction. Here, "a city and a mother" is an idiom for a metropolitan city. For another instance of this idiom see Ac 14:13. **and**. ƒ93A, Ge +1:26. **a mother**. Nu 21:25, 32. 32:42. Jsh 17:11. Jg 5:7. 11:26. Ezk 16:45-49. ƒ155E4. Prosopopoeia; or, Personification B868. A city spoken of as a mother (i.e. a metropolitan city). By this figure a city or people is spoken of as a mother. For instances of this figure see Is 50:1. Ezk 23:2. Ho 2:2. Ga 4:26. **swallow**. 2 S 17:16. Nu 16:32. 26:10. Ps 124:3. Je 51:34, 44. La 2:2, 5, 16. 1 C 15:54. 2 C

5:4. **the inheritance**. 2 S 21:3. Ex 19:5, 6. Dt 32:9. 1 S 26:19.

20. **Far be it**. 2 S 23:17. Jb 21:16. 22:18. **that I should**. ver. 10. Pr 28:13. Je 17:9. Lk 10:29.

21. **a man**. ver. 1. Jg 2:9. 7:24. 2 K 5:22. Je 4:15. 50:19. **by name**. Heb. by his name. **lifted**. 2 S 23:18. 1 S 24:6. 26:9. **his head**. 2 S 17:2, 3. 2 K 10:7. Jn 18:4-8.

22. **in her wisdom**. ver. +*16. Ec 7:19. 9:14-18. **he blew**. ver. 1. 2 S 2:28. 18:16. **retired**. Heb. were scattered. **every man to**. ver. 1. 1 S 4:10. **And Joab**. 2 S 3:28-39. 11:6-21. Ec 8:11. **Cherethites**. ver. 7. 2 K 11:4.

23. **Now Joab**. 2 S 8:16-18. 1 Ch 18:15-17. **and Benaiah**. See on ver. 7.

24. **Adoram**. i.e. *high honor; their glory*, ✻S#151h. 1 K ●4:6. 12:18. (1) An officer of David who was set over the tribute, 2 S 20:24. (2) An officer of Rehoboam, 1 K 12:18. **tribute**. 1 K 4:6. Exacted from all Israel for civil and sacred purposes (Young). **Jehoshaphat**. 2 S 8:16. 1 K 4:5. **recorder**. *or*, remembrancer. 2 S 8:16. 1 K 4:3.

25. **Sheva**. i.e. *Jehovah contends; habitation; vanity; guile*, ✻S#7724. 2 S 8:17. 1 K 4:4. 1 Ch 2:49h. 18:16, Shavsha. (1) A son of Maachah, the concubine of Caleb, the son of Jephunneh, 1 Ch 2:49. (2) David's scribe or secretary, 2 S 20:25, same as Seraiah, 2 S +8:17.

26. **Ira**. i.e. *stirring; watchfulness*, ✻S#5896h. 2 S 23:26, 38. 1 Ch 11:28, 40, Ithrite. 27:9. (1) One of David's chief rulers after the rebellion of Sheba was quelled, 2 S 20:26. (2, 3) Two of David's valiant men, 2 S 23:26, 38; 1 Ch 11:28, 40; 27:9. **Jairite**. ✻S#2972h, only here. Nu 32:41. Jg 10:4, 5. **chief ruler**. *or*, prince. 2 S 8:18. Ge 41:43, 45. Ex 2:14, 16. Is +24:2mg. The Hebrew is *cohen ledawid*, which might be rendered, "a priest of David;" and so the Septuagint, Vulgate, Syriac, and Arabic. The Chaldee has *rav*, a "chief" or "prince;" probably he was a kind of domestic chaplain or seer to the king. See 2 S 24:11. 2 Ch 35:15.

2 SAMUEL 21

A famine prevails for three years; as a judgment on the land for Saul's cruelty to the Gibeonites, who being asked, require seven of his descendants and hang them up before the Lord, 1-9. Rizpah watches their bodies; David buries their bones with those of Saul and Jonathan in the sepulchre of Kish; and the famine ceases, 10-14. In several battles with the Philistines four of David's mighty men slay four giants, 15-22.

1. A.M. 2986. B.C. 1018. An. Ex. Is. 473. **a famine**. Ge 12:10. 26:1. 41:57. 42:1. 43:1. Le 26:19, 20, 26. 1 K 17:1. 18:2. 2 K 6:25. 8:1. Je 14:1, etc. **enquired**. Heb. sought the face, etc. ♪22A4, Ge +19:13. Nu 27:21. **of the Lord**. 2 S 5:19, 23. Nu 27:21. 1 S 23:2, 4, 11. Jb 5:8-10. 10:2. Ps 50:15. 91:15. **It is**. Jsh 7:1, 11, 12. **Saul**. 1 S 22:17-19. **Gibeonites**. ✻S#1393h. ver. 2, 2, 3, 4, 9. 1 Ch 12:4. Ne 3:7.

2. **now the**. Jsh 9:3-21. **the Amorites**. The Gibeonites were *Hivites*, not Amorites, as appears from Jsh 6:19; but *Amorites* is a name often given to the Canaanites in general. Ge 15:16. Am 2:9, 10. **in his zeal**. Dt 7:16. 1 S 14:44. 15:8, 9, 22, 23. 2 K 10:16, 31. Lk 9:54, 55. Jn 12:43. 16:2. Ro 10:2. Ga 4:17, 18.

3. **wherewith**. Ge 32:20. Ex 32:30. Le 1:4. 1 S 2:25. Mi 6:6, 7. He 9:22. 10:4-12. **bless**. 2 S 20:19.

4. **We will**, etc. *or*, It is not silver nor gold that we have to do with Saul, or his house; neither pertains it to us to kill, etc. **no silver**. Ps 49:6-8. 1 P 1:18, 19.

5. **The man**. ver. 1. Est 9:24, 25. Mt 7:2. **devised**. *or*, cut us off. Jg 20:5. Ps 50:21. Da 9:26. Ho 4:5, 6.

6. **Let seven**. As God accepted the expiation here demanded, we must suppose that both the enquiry of David, and the answer of the Gibeonites, were directed by some open or secret intimation from him. **hang**. 2 S 17:23. 18:10. Ge 40:19, 22. Nu 25:4, 5. Dt 21:22, 23. Jsh 8:29. 10:26. Ezr 6:11. Est 9:10, 13, 14. Mt 27:5. **in Gibeah**. 1 S 10:26. 11:4. **whom the Lord did choose**. *or*, the chosen of the Lord. 1 S 9:16, 17. 10:1, 24. Am 3:2. Ac 13:21.

7. **Mephibosheth**. 2 S 4:4. 9:10. 16:4. 19:25. **because**. 1 S 18:3. 20:8, 15, 17, 42. 23:18.

8. **Rizpah**. 2 S 3:7. **Armoni**. i.e. *palatial; my palace*, ✻S#764h. **Mephibosheth**. i.e. *exterminating the idol or shame; idol breaker*, ✻S#4648h. ver. 7. 2 S 4:4. 9:6, 6, 10, 11, 12, 12, 13. 16:1, 4. 19:24, 25, 30. (1) A son of King Saul. David delivered him into the hands of the Gibeonites, who hanged him, 2 S 21:8, 9. (2) A son of Jonathan and grandson of King Saul, 2 S 4:4; 9:6; 21:7. He is called Meribaal in 1 Ch 8:34; 9:40. **and the five sons**. This Adriel did not marry Michal, Saul's younger daughter, but *Merab*, 1 S 18:19; Michal being married to David, and afterwards to Phaltiel; though it is here said "she bore" (*yaledah*), not "brought up," as falsely rendered, five sons to Adriel. Two of Dr. Kennicott's MSS., however, have *Merab*, instead of Michal; the Syriac and Arabic have *Nadab*; and the Chaldee renders the passage thus: "And the five sons of *Merab* which Michal the daughter of Saul brought up, which she brought forth to Adriel the son of Barzillai." **Michal**. *or*, Michal's sister. 1 S 18:19. **brought up for**. Heb. bare to. Ge 50:23. 1 S 18:19. **Barzillai**. i.e. *strong; iron of the Lord; he is iron*, ✻S#1271h. 2 S 17:27. 19:32, 33, 33, 34, 39. 1 K 2:7. Ezr 2:61, 61. Ne 7:63, 63. (1) A Gileadite who helped David when he was fleeing from Absalom, 2 S 17:27; 19:31; 1 K 2:7. (2) An Israelite, father of Adriel, 2 S 21:8. (3) A priest whose descendants returned from Babylon with Ezra, Ezr 2:61; Ne 7:63. **the Meholathite**. Jg 7:22. 1 K 4:12.

9. **before the Lord**. See on ver. 6. 2 S 6:17, 21. Ex 20:5. Nu 35:31-34. Dt 21:1-9. 1 S 15:33. 2 K 24:3, 4. **in the beginning**. This happened in Judea about the vernal equinox, or 21st of March. Ru 1:22. **barley harvest**. Le 23:10, 11. Young states that the harvest began on the 16th of Nisan, or the beginning of April.

10. **Rizpah**. ver. 8. 2 S 3:7. **took sackcloth**. 1 K 21:27. Jl 1:13. **from the**. See on ver. 9. Dt 21:13, 23. **until water**. Some suppose that this means a providential supply of rain, in order to remove the famine; but from the manner in which it is introduced, it seems to denote the autumnal rains, which commence about October. For five months did this brokenhearted woman watch by the bodies of her sons! Dt 11:14. 1 K 18:41-45. Je 5:24, 25. 14:22. Ho 6:3. Jl 2:23. Zc 10:1. **suffered**. ♪108A4, Ge 31:7. **the birds**. Ge 40:19. Ezk 39:4.

11. **told David**. 2 S 2:4. Ru 2:11, 12.

12. **the bones of Saul**. 2 S 2:5-7. 1 S 31:11-13. **Bethshan**. Jsh 17:11, Beth-shean. 1 S 31:10. **when**. ♪171, Ge +2:17. **in Gilboa**. 2 S 1:6, 21. 1 S 28:4. 31:1. 1 Ch 10:1, 8.

14. **buried.** 2 S 3:32. 4:12. **Zelah.** Jsh 18:28. 1 S 10:2, Zelzah. **sepulchre.** Heb. *qeber*, Ge +23:4. **God.** 2 S 24:25. Ex 32:27-29. Nu 25:13. Jsh 7:26. 1 K 18:40, 41. Je 14:1-7. Jl 2:18, 19. Am 7:1-6. Jon 1:15. Zc 6:8.

15. **the Philistines.** 2 S 5:17, 22. 1 Ch 20:4. **and David waxed faint.** Jsh 14:10, 11. Jg 4:21. 1 S 14:28mg, 31. Ps 71:9, 18. 73:26. Ec 12:3. Is 40:28-30. Je 9:23, 24. 1 P 1:24, 25.

16. **Ishbi-benob.** i.e. *whose seat is in Nob or on high*, ✻S#3430h. **of the sons.** Ge 6:4. Nu 13:32, 33. Dt 1:28. 2:10, 21. 3:11. 9:2. 1 S 17:4, 5. **the giant.** *or*, Rapha. ver. 18, 20mg, 22. 2 S 5:18. Ge 14:5. Dt +2:20. Jsh +17:15. **whose spear.** Heb. the staff, *or* the head. **brass.** Just half the weight of Goliath's, as in 1 S 17:7 (Young). **thought.** 1 S 17:45-51.

17. **Abishai.** 2 S 20:6-10. 1 S 26:6. **succored.** 2 S 22:19. Ps 46:1. 144:10. **Thou shalt.** 2 S 18:3. **quench.** 2 S 14:7. 1 K 11:36. 15:4. Ps 132:17. Jn 1:8, 9. 5:35. **light.** Heb. candle, *or* lamp. Ex 25:37. 1 K 11:36mg. Jb 21:17mg. Ps +18:28mg. 132:17mg. Jn 8:12.

18. **And it came.** 1 Ch 20:4-8. **Gob.** i.e. *a pit*, ✻S#1359h. ver. 19. In l Ch 20:4, it is Gezer. **Sibbechai.** i.e. *thicket of Jehovah; my thicket*, ✻S#5444h. 2 S 23:27, Mebunnai. 1 Ch 11:29. 20:4. 27:11. **Hushathite.** 2 S 23:27. 1 Ch 4:4. 11:29. 20:4. **Saph.** i.e. *bason; threshold*, ✻S#5593h. 1 Ch 20:4, Sippai. **the giant.** *or*, Rapha. ver. 16mg, 20mg.

19. **Elhanan.** i.e. *God is kind*, ✻S#445h. 2 S 23:24. 1 Ch 11:26. 20:5. (1) A man who slew Goliath's brother, 2 S 21:19; 1 Ch 20:5. (2) One of David's mighty men, 2 S 23:24; 1 Ch 11:26. **Jaare-oregim.** i.e. *forest of the weavers*, ✻S#3296h. *or*, Jair. 1 Ch 20:5, Jair. **Goliath.** 1 S 17:4, etc. **staff.** lit. wood. ᒧ121D8, Ge +40:19. **beam.** 1 S 17:7. 1 Ch 11:23. 20:5.

20. **yet a battle.** 1 Ch 20:6. **Gath.** 1 S 17:4. **stature.** or, of contention. Nu 13:32mg. 1 Ch 20:6mg. Pr 26:21. Je 15:10. **toes.** lit. fingers, as in Ex 8:19. 1 Ch 20:6. **the giant.** *or*, Rapha. ver. 16mg, 18mg.

21. **defied.** *or*, reproached. Jg 8:15. 1 S 17:10, 25, 26, 36, 45. 2 K 19:13. **Jonathan.** Brother of Jonadab, 2 S 13:3. 1 Ch 27:32. **Shimeah.** i.e. *the hearing—that is, answering—prayer; astonishment; desolation*, ✛S#8092h. 1 S 16:9. 17:13, Shammah. 1 Ch 2:13, Shimma. (1) A brother of David, 2 S 21:21, called also Shammah and Shimma. (2) A son of David and Bathsheba, 1 Ch 3:5, called also Shammua and Shammuah. (3) A descendant of Merari, the son of Levi, 1 Ch 6:30. (4) A son of Gershon, the son of Levi, 1 Ch 6:39. (5) A man of Benjamin, 1 Ch 8:32.

22. **the giant.** ver. 16, 18, 20mg. **four.** 1 Ch 20:8. **fell by.** Jsh 14:12. Ps 60:12. 108:13. 118:15. Ec 9:11. Je 9:23. Ro *8:31, 37.

2 SAMUEL 22

The introduction to David's psalm of thanksgiving, 1. He professes his confidence and joy in God, 2, 3. He states his trials and dangers and celebrates the praises of God for surprising deliverances, 4-20. He avows his integrity and shows the method of the Lord's dealings with men, 21-28. He ascribes to God all the glory of his victories, 29-36. He exults, with grateful praises, in the destruction or subjection of all his enemies, 37-44. He anticipates the submission of the nations and glories in the salvation of God and his mercies to him and to his Seed forever, 45-51.

1. **David.** Ps 50:14. *103:1-6. *116:1, etc. **words.** Ex *15:1. Jg 5:1. **in the day.** ver. 49. Ps *18, title. *34:19. Is 12:1, etc. 2 C 1:10. 2 T *4:18. Re 7:9-17. **and out.** 1 S 23:14. 24:15. 25:29. *26:24. 27:1.

2. **The Lord.** Dt *32:4. 1 S 2:2. Ps *18:2, etc. 31:3. 42:9. 71:3. *91:2. 144:2. Mt *16:18.

3. **in him.** Ps 18:2. Is 8:17. 12:2. He ᒧ*2:13a. **shield.** Ge *15:1. Dt 33:29. Ps 3:3. 5:12. 28:7. 84:9, *11. 115:9-11. Pr *30:5. **the horn.** Nu 23:22. 24:8. 1 S 2:1. Lk 1:69. **my high.** ver. 51. Ps 61:3. 144:2. Pr *18:10. **my refuge.** Ps 9:9. 14:6. *18:2. *27:5. *32:7. 46:1, 7, 11. 59:16. 71:7. 142:4. Is *32:2. Je *16:19. **my savior.** Is *12:2. 45:21. Lk 1:47, 71. T *3:4, 6. **thou savest.** ver. 49. Ps 55:9. *72:14. 86:14. *140:1, 4, 11.

4. **I will.** Ps 116:2, 4, 13, 17. **worthy.** Ne 9:5. Ps *18:3. 66:2. 106:2. 148:1-4. Re *4:11. *5:12. **so shall.** Ps *34:6. *50:15. 55:16. 56:9. 57:1-3. Ro *10:13.

5. **waves.** *or*, pangs. Ps 42:7. 88:7. 93:4. Jon 2:3. 1 Th *5:3. **the floods.** Ps 18:4. 69:14, 15. 93:3, 4. Is 59:19. Je 46:7, 8. Re 12:15, 16. 17:1, 15. **ungodly men.** Heb. Belial. 1 S +30:22. Ps 18:4mg. Pr 19:28mg.

6. **sorrows.** *or*, cords. Jb 36:8. Ps 18:5. 116:3. 140:5. Pr 5:22. Jon 2:2. Ac 2:24. **hell.** Heb. *sheol*, Ge +37:35. **the snares.** Pr 13:14. 14:27.

7. **my distress.** Ps 116:4. 120:1. Jon 2:2. Mt 26:38, 39. Lk 22:44. **He** 5:7. **did hear.** Ex 3:7. Ps 34:6, 15-17. **out.** 1 K 8:28-30. Ps 18:6. 27:4. Jon 2:4, 7. Hab *2:20. **my cry.** Ja +*5:4.

8. **the earth.** Ex 19:16, 18. Jg 5:4. Ps 18:7. 77:18. 97:4. Hab 3:6-11. Mt 27:51. 28:2. Ac 4:31. **foundations.** 2 S 22:16. Dt 32:22. Jb 26:11. 38:4. Ps 18:7, 15. 82:5. Pr 8:29. Na 1:5. He 12:26. ᒧ121Q3. Metonymy of the Adjunct B598. The appearance of a thing, or an opinion about it, is put for the thing itself, in connected words or sentences. Mountains are here spoken of as the "foundations of heaven" upon which the heavens appear to rest. This is a very significant feature of biblical language, which is not technical and scientific but expressed in the language of appearance, just as we commonly speak of the sun rising and setting, though we are not thereby denying a known contrary scientific fact by so speaking. Had the Scriptures been written in the language of God's absolute scientific knowledge, no doubt such language could not have been understood by the original audience, nor by us, even to this day. One of the amazing marks of the divine inspiration of Scripture is the things the Bible does not say, for it does not contain the many contemporary scientific misconceptions of the time and culture that produced the Bible. It can be safely asserted that, though the Bible is not a textbook of science, yet there are no proven scientific errors in its teaching. There are many things taught or commanded in the Bible which anticipated the findings of modern science and medicine, such as the dietary laws and requirements for purification found in the law of Moses. For other instances of this figure see Dt 4:32. 30:4. Ne 1:9. Jb 26:11. Ps 72:9. Is +*13:5. Mt 24:31.

9. **went.** ver. 16. Ex 15:7, 8. 19:18. 24:17. Dt 32:22. Jb 4:9. 41:20, 21. Ps 18:8, 15. 97:3-5. Is 30:27, 33. Je 5:14. 15:14. Da 7:9, 10. He 12:29. **out of his.** Heb. by his, etc. **coals.** Hab 3:5.

10. **bowed.** Ps 144:5. Is 64:1-3. **darkness.** ver. 12. Ex 20:21. Dt 4:11. 1 K 8:12. Jb 38:9. Ps 18:9, 11. 97:2. 104:3. Mt 27:45. Lk 23:44, 45.

11. **a cherub**. Ge 3:24. Ex 25:19. 1 S 4:4. Ps 18:10. 68:17. 80:1. 99:1. Ezk 9:3. 10:2-14. He 1:14. **did fly**. *√*22F3. Anthropomorphism B895: the actions of certain animals are attributed to God: flying. For another instance of this figure see Ps 18:10. **upon the**. Ps 104:3. 139:9.

12. **made**. ver. 10. Ps 18:11, 12. 27:5. 97:2. **darkness**. 2 S 22:10. Ex 20:21. Jb 38:9. **dark waters**. Heb. binding of waters. **thick clouds**. Ge +9:13. Ex 19:9. Jg 5:4. Ps 18:11. **skies**. Dt 33:26.

13. **brightness**. 2 S 23:4. Ps 18:12. Pr *4:18. Is 4:5. 50:10. 60:3, 19. 62:1. Ezk 1:4, 13, 27, 28. 10:4. Jl 2:10. 3:15. Am 5:20. Hab 3:4, 11. **coals of fire**. ver. 9. Le 16:5. Ps 18:12, 13. Ezk 1:13. 10:2. **kindled**. ver. 9. Ex 3:2, 3.

14. **thundered**. Ex 9:28. 19:16. Jg 5:20. 1 S 2:10. 7:10. 12:17, 18. Jb 37:2-5. 40:9. Ps 18:13. 29:3-9. 77:16-19. Is 30:30. Ezk 10:5. Re 11:19.

15. **arrows**. Dt 32:23. Jsh 10:10. Ps 7:12, 13. 18:14. 45:5. 144:6, 7. Hab 3:11.

16. **the channels**. Ex 14:21-27. 15:8-10. Ps 18:15-17. 114:3-7. Ezk 31:12 (✛S#650h). **rebuking**. Ex 15:8. Jb 38:11. Ps 106:9. Na 1:4. Hab 3:8-10. Mt 8:26, 27. **blast**. Heb. *neshamah*, Ge +2:7. **breath**. Heb. *ruach*, Ex +15:8. **nostrils**. *or*, anger. ver. 9. Ps 74:1.

17. **sent**. Ps 18:16. 144:7. **he drew**. Ex 2:10. Ps 18:16. 32:6. 59:1, 2. 93:3, 4. 124:4, 5. 130:1. Is 43:2. La 3:54. Jon 2:3. Re 17:15. **many**. *or*, great. Ps 42:7. 69:1, 2.

18. **delivered**. ver. 1. Ps 3:7. 56:9. 2 C 1:10. 2 T 4:17.

19. **prevented**. 2 S 15:10-13. 1 S 19:11-17. 23:26, 27. Ps 18:18, 19. 118:10-13. Mt 27:39-44. **the Lord**. Ps 71:20, 21. Is 26:34. 50:10.

20. **brought**. Ge 26:22. 1 Ch 4:10. Ps 31:8. 118:5. Ho 4:16. **delighted**. 2 S 15:26. Ps 22:8. 147:11. 149:4. Is 42:1. Mt *3:17. 17:5. 27:43. Ac 2:32-36.

21. **rewarded**. ver. 25. 1 S *26:23. 1 K *8:32. Ps 7:3, 4, 8. 18:20-25. 19:11. 1 C *15:58. **cleanness**. Ex=30:18. Jb 17:9. Is 24:4. Ja 4:8. **hands**. Jb 17:9. Ps 24:3, 4. 26:6. Ja 4:8.

22. **I have kept**. Nu 16:15. 1 S 12:3. Jb 23:10-12. 2 C 1:12. **the ways**. Ge *18:19. Ps 119:1, 3. 128:1. Pr 8:32. **have not**. Ps 36:3. 125:5. Zp 1:6. Jn 15:10. He 10:38, 39.

23. **For all**. Ps 119:6, 86, 128. Lk 1:6. Jn 15:14. **judgments**. Dt 6:1, 2. 7:12. Ps 19:8, 9. 119:13, 30, 102. **I did not**. Dt 8:11.

24. **upright**. Ge 6:9. 17:1. Jb 1:1. Ps 51:6. *84:11. Jn 1:47. 2 C 5:11. **before him**. Heb. to him. Ps 18:23. **kept**. 1 S 24:11. Pr *4:23. He 12:1.

25. **recompensed**. ver. 21. Is 3:10. Ro 2:7, 8. 2 C 5:10. **cleanness**. ver. +21. **in his eye sight**. Heb. before his eyes. Pr 5:21.

26. **the merciful**. Mt *5:7. Ja 2:13.

27. **the pure**. Mt 5:8. **froward**. Le 26:23-28. Dt 28:58-61. Ps 125:5. **show thyself unsavory**. *or*, wrestle. Ex 18:11. Ps 18:26. Is 45:9.

28. **afflicted**. Ex 3:7, 8. Ps 12:5. 18:27. *72:12, 13. 113:7, 8. 140:12. Is 61:1-3. 63:9. Mt 5:3. **but thine**. Ex 9:14-17. 10:3. 18:11. Jb 40:11, 12. Ps 138:6. Pr 21:4. Is 2:11, 17. 5:15. 37:23, 28, 29. Da 4:37. Lk 1:51. Ja 4:6, 7. 1 P 5:5, 6. **haughty**. Jb 9:4. Pr 16:18. Da 5:20.

29. **lamp**. *or*, candle. Jb 29:3. Ps 27:1. *84:11. Pr 13:9. Jn *8:12. Re 21:23. *√*22K2. Anthropomorphism

B896. God is spoken of as a lamp. For other instances of this figure see Ps 18:28. *119:105. Pr 6:23. 2 P 1:19. **lighten**. Ps 4:6. 18:28. 97:11. 112:4. Is 50:10. 60:19, 20. Mi 7:9. Ml 4:2. Jn 12:46. Ep *5:8.

30. **run through**. *or*, broken. Ps 18:29. 118:10-12. Ro 8:37. Ph *4:13.

31. **God**. Heb. *El*, Ex +15:2. **his way**. Dt *32:4. Da 4:37. Mt 5:48. Re 15:3. **the word**. Ps 12:6. 18:30. 119:140. Pr *30:5. **tried**. *or*, refined. Ps 12:6. **a buckler**. ver. 3. Ge 15:1. Dt 33:29. Ps 35:2. 91:4. Pr 2:7. **that trust**. Ps 2:12. 5:11. 17:7. 18:30. 31:19. 34:22. Pr 14:32h. 30:5. Is 57:13. Na 1:7.

32. **For who**. Dt 32:31, 39. 1 S 2:2. Is 42:8. 44:6, 8. 45:5, 6, 21. Je 10:6, 7, 16. **God**. Heb. *El*, Ex +15:2. **a rock**. ver. 2, 3.

33. **God**. Heb. *El*, Ex +15:2. **strength**. Ex 15:2. Ps 18:32. 27:1. 28:7, 8. 31:4. 46:1. Is 41:10. Zc 10:12. 2 C 12:9. Ep *6:10. Ph *4:13. **maketh**. Heb. riddeth, *or* looseth. **my way**. He 13:21. **perfect**. Dt 18:13. Jb 22:3. Ps 101:2, 6. 119:1.

34. **maketh**. Heb. equalleth to. Pr 26:7. **like hinds'**. 2 S 2:18. Dt 33:25. Hab 3:19. **setteth**. Dt 32:13. Is 33:16. 58:14. Ep 2:6.

35. **teacheth**. Ps 18:33, 34. 144:1. **to war**. Heb. for the war. 2 C 10:4, 5. Ep 6:13. **a bow**. Ps 46:9. Ezk 39:3, 9, 10.

36. **the shield**. Ge 15:1. Ps *84:11. Ep *6:16. **gentleness**. Ps 18:35. **made me great**. Heb. multiplied me. Ge 12:2. 22:17. Ps 115:14.

37. **enlarged**. Ps 4:1. 18:36. Pr 4:12. **feet**. Heb. ankles. 1 S 2:9. Ps 17:5. 94:18. 119:117. 121:3.

38. **pursued**. 2 S 5:18-25. 8:1, 2, 13, 14. 10:14. Ps 18:37. 21:8, 9. Ro 8:37.

39. **consumed**. Ps 18:37, 38. 110:1, 5, 6. 118:10-12. Ml 4:1, 3. Ro 16:20.

40. **girded**. 1 S 17:49-51. 23:5. Ps 18:32, 39. Is 45:5. Col 1:11. **them**. Ps 44:5. 144:2. **subdued**. Heb. caused to bow. Is 60:14. Re 3:9.

41. **necks**. Ge 49:8. Ex 23:7. Jsh 10:24. 11:23. Ps 18:40, 41. 1 C 15:25. **I might**. Ps 21:8, 9. Lk 19:14, 27. 2 Th 1:8, 9.

42. **unto the Lord**. 1 S 28:6. Jb 27:9. Pr *1:28. Is *1:15. Ezk 20:3. Mi *3:4. Mt √7:22, 23. Lk *13:25, 26. **answered them not**. T#1797. ver. 41. Ps *18:41. Pr +*1:28. 15:29. 21:13. Is 8:21. Je *7:16. 11:14. 14:11. Jn +*9:31.

43. **as small**. 2 K 13:7. Ps 35:5. Da 2:35. Ml 4:1. **as the mire**. Ps 18:42. Is 10:6. Mi 7:10. Zc 10:5. **did spread**. Dt 32:26. Is 26:15. Zc 2:6. Lk 21:24.

44. **delivered**. 2 S 3:1. 5:1. 18:6-8. 19:9, 14. 20:1, 2, 22. Ps *2:1-6. 18:43. Ac 4:25-28. 5:30, 31. **head**. 2 S 8:1-14. Dt 28:13. Ps 2:8. 60:8, 9. 72:8, 9. 110:6. Is 60:12. Da 7:14. Ro 15:12. Re 11:15. 19:16. **a people**. Is 55:5. 65:1. Ho 2:23. Ro 9:25.

45. **Strangers**. Heb. Sons of the stranger. ver. 46. Ge 17:12, 27. 35:2, 4. Ex 12:43 (*S#5236h). 1 S 7:3. 2 Ch 14:3. Is 56:3, 6. **submit themselves**. *or*, yield feigned obedience. Heb. lie. Dt 33:29mg. Ps 18:44mg, 45. +66:3mg. 81:15mg. Je 3:10mg. Ezk *33:31, 32. Ac 8:13, 21-23.

46. **fade away**. Ps ◑*1:3. Is *64:6. Ja 1:11. **out**. Is 2:19, 21. Am 9:3. Mi 7:17. Re 6:15, 16.

47. **Lord**. Dt 32:39, 40. Jb *19:25. **the rock of**. Ps 18:46. 89:26. 95:1. Lk 1:47.

48. **God**. Heb. *El*, Ex +15:2. **avengeth me**. Heb. giveth avengement for me. 2 S 18:19, 31. 1 S 25:30.

Ps 18:47. 94:1. **that bringeth.** Ps 110:1. 144:2. 1 C 15:25.

49. **thou also.** 2 S 5:12. 7:8, 9. Nu 24:7, 17-19. 1 S 2:8. Ps 18:48. **the violent.** Ps 52:1. 140:1.

50. **Therefore.** Ps ‖18:49. Ro ▸15:9. **among.** Ro 15:9. **I will sing.** Ps 18:49. 103:1. 138:1. 145:1, 2. 146:1, 2. Is 12:1-6.

51. **the tower.** ƒ22L6, Ps +61:3. ver. 2. Ps 3:3. 21:1. 48:3. 89:26. 91:2. 144:10. **his anointed.** Ps 18:50. 89:20. **seed.** 2 S *7:12, 13. Ps 18:50. *89:29, 36. Is 8:18. Je 30:9. Lk +*1:31-33. Ac 4:27. He 2:13. Re +*11:15. **evermore.** Ps +*18:50.

2 SAMUEL 23

David's last words, in which he professes his faith in God's promises to be beyond sense or experience, 1-5. The different state of the wicked, 6, 7. The names and exploits of his chief warriors, 8-39.

1. A.M. 2989. B.C. 1015. An. Ex. Is. 476. **Now.** ƒ107, Ge +10:5. **the last.** Ge 49:1. Dt 33:1. Jsh ch. 23. 24. Ps 72:20. 2 P 1:13-15. **raised.** 2 S 7:8, 9. Ps 78:70, 71. 89:27. **the anointed.** 1 S 2:10. 16:12, 13. 24:6. Ps +*2:2, 6mg. 89:20. La 4:20. **sweet psalmist.** 1 Ch 16:4, 5, 7, 9. Am 6:5. Lk 20:42. 24:44. Ep 5:19, 20. Col *3:16. Ja 5:13.

2. **The Spirit.** Heb. *ruach,* Is +48:16. Mt 22:43. Mk 12:36. Lk 24:44. Ac 2:25-31. 4:25. √5:3, 4. He 3:7, 8. 2 P √1:21.

3. **God.** Ge *33:20. Ex *3:15. *19:5, 6. 20:2. **the Rock.** 2 S *22:2, 32. Dt *32:4, 30, 31. Ps *42:9. **He that ruleth.** *or,* Be thou ruler, etc. Ps *110:2. **must be just.** Ex *23:6-8. Dt 16:18-20. Ps *82:3-4. Pr *31:9. Is *11:4, 5. *32:1. Je *23:5. Zc *9:9. He *1:8. **ruling.** Ex +*18:21. 2 Ch *19:7-9. Ne 5:15.

4. **he shall.** Is 11:4. **as the light.** Jg 5:31. Ps 89:36. *110:3. Pr *4:18. Is 60:1, 3, 18-20. Ho *6:5. Ml *4:2. Lk *1:78, 79. Jn *1:7. **morning.** Ho *6:3. **clouds.** Ge +9:13. **tender.** Dt *32:2. Ps 72:6. Is 4:2. Mi 5:7.

5. **Although.** 2 S 7:18. 12:10. 13:14, 15, 28. 18:14, 15. 1 K 1:5. 2:24, 25. 11:6-8. 12:14. **God.** Heb. *El,* Ex +15:2. **he hath made.** 2 S *7:14-16. 1 Ch 17:11-14. Ps *89:3, 28. Is 9:6, 7. 55:3. 61:8. Je *32:40. +√33:20, 21, 25, 26. Ezk 37:26. Ro 3:3, 4. He 13:20. **everlasting.** Ge +9:16. +*17:7. **covenant.** T#830. 2 S 7:15, 16. Ps *89:22. Is +√55:3. Ho 2:19, 20. **ordered.** *or,* arranged. Jsh 2:6. Is *30:33. Je 6:23. 50:42. Ezk 23:41. Jl 2:5. 1 C 14:33, 40. **and sure.** 1 S 2:35. 25:28. 1 K 11:38. Is +*55:3. Ac √13:34. He *6:19. **for.** ƒ18, Dt +28:4. According to the Hebrew, each line in this verse begins with the word *kee,* "for." "For is not my house thus with God? For He hath made with me an everlasting covenant, ordered in all things and sure, For this is all my salvation, and all my desire. For shall He not make it to prosper?" These four lines are in the form of an introversion: (a) Question. (b) Answer and Reason. (b) Answer and Reason. (a) Question. In (a) and (a), the question is concerning David's house; while in (b) and (b) the subject is Jehovah's covenant. **all my salvation.** Ps 62:2. 119:81. **desire.** Ps 27:4. 63:1-3. 73:25, 26. **to grow.** Is 4:2. *7:14. *9:6, 7. *11:1. 27:6. Am *9:11. 1 C 3:6, 7.

6. **the sons of Belial.** 2 S 20:1. 22:5mg. Dt 13:13. +15:9. Jg +19:22. 1 S 2:12. +30:22. Jb 34:18. Ps 18:4mg. Na 1:15mg. **thorns.** Ge 3:18. SS 2:2. Is 9:18. 33:12. Ezk 2:6. Mi 7:4. **thrust away.** Jb 20:8. Ps 64:8.

7. **fenced.** Heb. filled. **and they shall be.** 2 S 22:8-10. Is 27:4. Mt *3:10-12. 13:42. Lk 19:14, 27. Jn *15:6. 2 Th *1:8. 2:8. He *6:8. **utterly burned.** Is 9:5. Re 19:20.

8. A.M. 2949-2989. B.C. 1055-1015. An. Ex. Is. 436-476. **The Tachmonite.** i.e. *wise,* ✻S#8461h. *or,* Josheb-basebet, the Tachmonite, head of the three. 1 Ch 11:11, 12. 27:2, 32. It is highly probable that in this verse, instead of *yoshaiv bashshaiveth tachkemoni,* we should read *yoshavam ben chachmoni,* "Joshebeam, son of Hachmoni;" and instead of *hoo adino haetzni, hoo orair eth chanitho,* "he lift up his spear," which are the readings in the parallel place in Chronicles, where it is also "three hundred," instead of "eight hundred." **chief among.** Je +13:18mg. **Adino.** i.e. *a spear; his delight,* ✻S#5722h. **Eznite.** i.e. *sharp or strong,* ✻S#6112h. **he lift up.** Supplied from 1 Ch 11:11. **whom he slew.** Heb. slain.

9. **Eleazar.** 1 Ch 11:12-14. 27:4, Dodai. **Ahohite.** i.e. *descendant of Ahoah* (i.e. *brother of the Lord,* 1 Ch +8:4), ✻S#266h. ver. 28. 1 Ch ◉8:1, 3, +4. 11:12, 29. 27:4. **defied.** Nu 23:7, 8. 1 S 17:10, 26, 36, 45, 46. **the men.** Is 63:3, 5. Mk 14:50.

10. **and smote.** 1 Ch 11:13, 14. **the Lord.** Jsh 10:10, 42. 11:8. Jg 15:14, 18. 1 S 11:13. 14:6, 23. 19:5. 2 K 5:1. Ps 108:13. 144:10. Ro 15:18. 2 C 4:5. Ep 6:10-18. **and the people.** Ps 68:12. Is 53:12.

11. **Shammah.** 1 Ch 11:27, Shammoth the Harorite. **Agee.** i.e. *fugitive,* ✻S#89h. **Hararite.** i.e. *mountaineer; the curser,* ✻S#2043h. ver. 33. 1 Ch 11:34, 35. **the Philistines.** 1 Ch 11:13, 14. **into a troop.** *or,* for foraging. Heb. *chay,* ver. 13.

12. **the Lord.** See on ver. 10. Ps 3:8. 44:2. Pr 21:31.

13. **three,** etc. *or,* the three captains over the thirty. 1 Ch 11:15-19. *Shalishim,* "captains," should most probably be read instead of *shaloshim:* thirty *shalishim,* as it is in ver. 8, and Ex 14:7: where LXX. render *tristatas,* which Jerome (on Ezk 33) says "among the Greeks is the name of the second rank after the royal dignity." **the cave.** Jsh 12:15. 15:35. 1 S 22:1. Mi 1:15. **troop.** Heb. *chay,* ver. 11mg. **the valley.** 2 S 5:18, 22. 1 Ch 11:15. 14:9. Is 17:5.

14. **an hold.** 2 S 5:17. 1 S 22:1, 4, 5. 24:22. 1 Ch 12:16. **garrison.** 1 S 10:5. 13:4, 23. 14:1, 6.

15. **longed.** Nu 11:4, 5. Ps 42:1, 2. 63:1. 119:81. Is 41:17, 18. 44:3. Jn 4:10, 14. 7:37, 38. **Oh that.** ƒ85G, Is 6:8. **well.** Heb. *bor,* Ge +37:20. **Bethlehem.** Bethlehem signifies the "house of bread," and the place was likewise noted for excellent water. There Christ was born, who is the "bread of life" and who also gives us the "water of life." "The water that I shall give him shall be in him a well of water springing up into everlasting life," Jn 4:14.

16. **the three.** ver. 9. 1 S 19:5. Ac 20:24. Ro 5:7. 2 C 5:14. **well.** Heb. *bor,* Ge +37:20. **poured.** Heb. *nasak,* ✻S#5258h. Kal, Preterite: Ps 2:6 (set. mg, anointed). Is 29:10. 40:19 (melteth). 44:10 (molten). Kal, Infinitive: Is 30:1 (cover). Kal, Future: Ge 30:9. Ho 9:4 (offer). Niphal, Preterite: Pr 8:23 (set up). Piel, Future: 1 Ch 11:18. Hiphil, Preterite: Je 32:29. Hiphil, Infinitive: Je 7:18. 19:13. 44:17, 18, 19, 19, 25. Hiphil, Imperative: Nu 28:7. Hiphil, Future: Ge 35:14. 2 S 23:16. 2 K 16:13. Ps 16:4 (offer). Ezk 20:28. Hophal, Future: Ex 25:29 (cover. mg, pour). 37:16mg. **it unto.** Nu 28:7. 1 S 7:6. La 2:19. Ph 2:17.

17. **Be it far.** 2 S 20:20. Ge 44:17. 1 S 2:30. 26:11.

1 K 21:3. 1 Ch 11:19. **is not this.** ſ63B, Ge +25:28. **the blood.** ſ46A, Le +26:30. Ge 9:4. Le 17:10. Ps 72:14. Mt 26:28. Mk 14:24. Jn 6:52-54. 2 C 5:14. **jeopardy.** ſ24J, Dt +32:42. Jg 5:18. 1 C 15:30. **lives.** Heb. *nephesh*, *souls*, Ge +44:30. **therefore he would not.** We have an almost similar account in Arrian's *Life of Alexander* (l. vi.): "When his army was greatly oppressed with heat and thirst, a soldier brought him a cup of water: he ordered it to be carried back; saying, I cannot bear to drink alone, while so many are in want; and this cup is too small to be divided among the whole." The example was noble in both cases, but David added piety to bravery: he poured it out to the Lord.

18. **Abishai.** 2 S 2:18. 3:30. 10:10, 14. 18:2. 20:10. 1 S 26:6-8. 1 Ch 2:16. 11:20, 21. **and slew them.** Heb. slain.

19. **he attained.** ver. 9, 13, 16. 1 Ch 11:25. Mt 13:8, 23. 1 C 15:41.

20. **Benaiah.** 2 S 8:18. 20:23. 1 K 1:8, 26, 38. 2:29-35, 46. 1 Ch 18:17. 27:5, 6. **Kabzeel.** Jsh 15:21. **who had done many acts.** Heb. great of acts. **he slew.** Ex 15:15. **lion-like men.** Heb. lions of God. 2 S 1:23. 1 Ch 11:22-24. 12:8. Is 29:1, 2, 7. Ezk 43:15. ſ63A1, Ge +14:20. or, Ariel. Supply "sons" by ellipsis of the nominative, to get "He slew the two (sons of) Ariel of Moab." **slew a lion.** Jg 14:5, 6. 1 S 17:34-37. **pit.** Heb. *bor*, Ge +37:20. **snow.** 1 Ch 11:22. Jb 6:16. 37:6. 38:22. Ps 68:14. 147:16. 148:8. Pr 25:13. 26:1. 31:21. Je 18:14.

21. **a goodly man.** Heb. a man of countenance, *or* sight, **called,** 1 Ch 11:23, a man of great stature. **slew him.** 1 S 17:51. Col 2:15.

23. **more honorable.** *or*, honorable among the thirty. 1 Ch 27:6. **over his guard.** *or*, over his council. Heb. at his command. or, listeners. ſ121N1, Ge +31:54. 2 S 8:18. 20:23. 1 S 22:14. Is 11:14.

24. **Asahel.** 2 S 2:18. 1 Ch 11:26. 27:7. **Dodo.** i.e. *his love* or *uncle; amatory; his beloved,* ✱S#1734h. ver. 9. Jg 10:1. 1 Ch 11:12, 26. (1) Grandfather of Tola, Jg 10:1. (2) Father of Eleazar, 2 S 23:9; 1 Ch 11:12. (3) Father of Elhanan, 2 S 23:24; 1 Ch 11:26.

25. **Shammah.** 1 Ch 11:27, 28, Shammoth the Harorite. **Harodite.** i.e. *trembling, terror,* ✱S#2733h. Jg 7:1. **Elika.** i.e. *God of the congregation* or *rejected,* ✱S#470h.

26. **Paltite.** i.e. *my escape,* ✱S#6407h. 1 Ch 11:27. 27:10, Pelonite. **Ira.** i.e. *watchful.* ver. 38. 1 Ch 11:28. 27:9. **Ikkesh.** i.e. *perverse,* ✱S#6142h. 1 Ch 11:28. 27:9. **Tekoite.** ✱S#8621h. See on 2 S 14:+2, 4, 9. 1 Ch 11:28. 27:9. Ne 3:5, 27.

27. **Abiezer.** i.e. *father of help.* 1 Ch 11:28, Antothite. 27:12, Anetothite. **Anethothite.** S#6069h, only here. Jsh 21:18. 1 Ch 11:28. 12:3. 27:12, Anetothite. Je 29:27. **Mebunnai.** i.e. *built up; buildings of the Lord,* ✱S#4012h, only here. 2 S 21:18. 1 Ch 11:29, Sibbecai. 27:11. **Hushathite.** i.e. *sensuality,* ✱S#2843h. 2 S 21:18. 1 Ch 4:4. A descendant of Judah. 11:29. 20:4. 27:11.

28. **Zalmon.** i.e. *shady; his image,* ✱S#6756h. 1 Ch 11:29, Ilai. (1) One of David's valiant men, 2 S 23:28, called Ilai in 1 Ch 11:29. (2) A high hill near Shechem, Jg 9:48, probably same as *Salmon*, Ps 68:14. **Ahohite.** ver. 9. 1 Ch 8:4. 11:12. A descendant of Benjamin. **Maharai.** i.e. *hasting,* ✱S#4121h. 1 Ch 11:30. 27:13. **Netophathite.** i.e. *distillation; an inhabitant of*

Netophah (Ezr 2:22), *a city of Judah,* ✱S#5200h. ver. 29. 2 K 25:23. 1 Ch 2:54. 9:16. 11:30, 30. 27:13, 15. Ne 7:26. 12:28. Je 40:8.

29. **Heleb.** i.e. *fatness,* ✱S#2460h. 1 Ch 11:30, Heled. 27:15, Heldai. **Baanah.** i.e. *son of affliction.* 1 Ch 11:30. **Ittai.** 1 Ch 11:31, Ithai. Not the Gittite in 2 S 15:19. **Ribai.** i.e. *my striving,* ✱S#7380h. 1 Ch 11:31. **Gibeah.** Jsh 18:28. Jg 19:13.

30. **Benaiah.** 1 Ch 11:31. 27:14. **Pirathonite.** Jg 12:15. **Hiddai.** i.e. *echo; chief,* ✱S#1914h. 1 Ch 11:32, Hurai. **brooks,** *or*, valleys. Dt 1:24. Jg 2:9. +16:4. **Gaash.** Jsh 24:30. Jg 2:9.

31. **Abi-albon.** i.e. *valiant,* ✱S#45h. 1 Ch 11:32, Abiel. **Arbathite.** ✱S#6164h. Jsh 15:6, 7. Jsh 18:18, 22. 1 Ch 11:32h. **Azmaveth.** i.e. *strong to death; strength of death,* ✱S#5820h. 1 Ch 8:36. 9:42. 11:33. 12:3. *27:25. Ezr 2:24. Ne 12:29. (1) Probably a place in Benjamin, Ezr 2:24; Ne 12:29, called also Bethazmaveth, Ne 7:28. (2) One of David's valiant men, 2 S 23:31; 1 Ch 11:33. (3) A descendant of Jonathan, 1 Ch 8:36; 9:42. (4) A Benjamite, 1 Ch 12:3. (5) A treasurer of David, 1 Ch 27:25. **Barhumite.** i.e. *son of the blackened; a native of Bahurim,* ✱S#1273h. 2 S 16:5. 19:16. 1 Ch 11:33, Baharumite.

32. **Eliahba.** i.e. *God hides,* ✱S#455h. 1 Ch 11:33. **Shaalbonite.** ✱S#8170h. Jsh 19:42. 1 K 4:9. 1 Ch 11:33h. **Jashen.** i.e. *sleepy; ancient,* ✱S#3464h. 1 Ch 11:34, Hashem, the Gizonite.

33. **Shammah.** i.e. *desolation, astonishment.* 1 Ch 11:27. **Hararite.** i.e. *mountaineer.* **Ahiam.** i.e. *brother of a mother,* ✱S#279h. 1 Ch 11:35. **Sharar.** i.e. *hostile; an observer,* ✱S#8325h. 1 Ch 11:35, Sacar.

34. **Eliphelet.** 1 Ch 11:35, Eliphal son of Ur. **Ahasbai.** i.e. *brother of my encompassers; I will take refuge in my arms; I flee to the Lord,* ✱S#308h. **Maachathite.** ✱S#4602h. 2 S 10:6, 8. Dt 3:14. Jsh 12:5. 13:11, 13. 2 K 25:23. 1 Ch 4:19. Je 40:8. **Eliam.** 2 S 11:3. 15:31. 17:23. 1 Ch 27:33, 34. Perhaps the same as Ahijah the Pelonite, in 1 Ch 11:36 (Young). **Ahithophel.** 2 S 15:12, 31.

35. **Hezrai.** i.e. *my court* or *village,* ✱S#2695h. 1 Ch 11:37, Hezro. **Carmelite.** Jsh 15:55. 1 S 25:2. **Paarai.** i.e. *my openings,* ✱S#6474h. Perhaps the same as Naarai, son of Ezbai. **Arbite.** ✱S#701h. Jsh 15:52.

36. **Igal.** i.e. *whom God redeems; God will revenge,* ✱S#3008h. Nu 13:7. 1 Ch 3:22. 11:38, Joel. (1) One of the spies whom Moses sent to search the land of Canaan, Nu 13:7. (2) One of David's guard, 2 S 23:36, called Joel in 1 Ch 11:38. **Nathan.** i.e. *he gave.* **Zobah.** 2 S 8:3. **Bani.** 1 Ch 11:38, Mibhar, son of Haggeri.

37. **Zelek.** i.e. *a cleft,* ✱S#6768h. 1 Ch 11:39. **Nahari.** i.e. *my snorting; snorer,* ✱S#5171h. 1 Ch 11:37, 39. **Beerothite.** 2 S 4:2. Jsh 18:25. **armorbearer.** 2 S 18:15.

38. **Ira.** 2 S 20:26. 1 Ch 2:53. 11:40. **Ithrite.** i.e. *remaining,* ✱S#3505h. 1 Ch 2:50, 53. 4:15, 17. 11:40, 40. **Gareb.** i.e. *reviler; scrabby; scabby; leprous,* ✱S#1619h. 1 Ch 11:40. Je 31:39. (1) One of David's valiant men, 2 S 23:38; 1 Ch 11:40. (2) A hill near Jerusalem, Je 31:39.

39. **Uriah.** 2 S 11:3, 6, etc. 12:9. 1 K 15:5. 1 Ch 11:41. Mt 1:6. **thirty and seven in all.** From the number of these officers being thirty-seven, it is almost self-evident that *shalishim* cannot denote "the thirty," as rendered in ver. 13, etc., but some particular description of men, or officers; for it can scarcely be said,

with propriety, that we have thirty-seven out of thirty; and besides, in the parallel place in 1 Chronicles, there are sixteen added!

2 SAMUEL 24

David requires Joab to number the people, who very reluctantly complies, 1-8. Joab delivers the number to the king, 9. He repents after being warned by Gad the prophet, and obliged to choose one plague out of three proposed to him, he fixes on three days' pestilence, 10-14. After seventy thousand die in Israel, the angel is stayed from destroying Jerusalem in answer to David's prayer, 15-17. David, directed by God, purchases Araunah's threshing floor, builds an altar, and sacrifices; and the plague is stayed, 18-25.

1. A.M. 2987. B.C. 1017. An. Ex. Is. 474. **And.** ſ107, Ge +10:5. **again.** 2 S 21:1, etc. **he.** That is, Satan, 1 Ch 21:1. ſ63A1, Ge +14:20. This verse, when read without reference to any other part of the word of God is very difficult to understand, and has been used by those who desire to undermine the justice of God to show that he sought occasion to punish—that he incited David to sin; and when he had so incited him, gave the dreadful alternative of choosing one of three scourges by which his people were to be cut off. On the face of the passage these thoughts naturally arise, because "the Lord" is the antecedent to the pronoun "he,"—he moved David. But to those who "search the Scriptures," this exceedingly difficult passage receives a wonderful elucidation. By referring to 1 Ch 21:1, the reader will there find that Satan was the mover, and that the Lord most righteously punished David for the display of pride he had manifested. Oh, that Christians, who sometimes have their minds harassed with doubts, would remember the promise, that what they know not now they shall know hereafter (Jn 13:7); and if no other instance of elucidation than this passage occurred to them to remove their doubts, let this be a means of stirring them up to dig deeper than ever into the inexhaustible mines of the Inspired Word. Ja *1:13, 14. **moved.** 2 S 12:11. 16:10. Ge 45:5. 50:20. Ex *7:3. Dt +2:30. 1 S 26:19. 1 K 22:20-23. Ezk 14:9. 20:25. Ac 4:28. 2 Th 2:11. David's thought and purpose of numbering the people, sprang from his remaining depravity, excited by Satan's suggestions: and as this "was of the Lord," (in the same manner, that it was of him that the Canaanites should be hardened and that Ahab should be deceived), he withdrew every internal or external restraint, and left him to follow his own counsels (see the preceding Marginal References). Thus, by a manner of expression common in Scripture, the Lord is said to have "moved David against Israel;" for certainly this is the most natural construction of the words. But other passages prove that the sinful disposition and resolution could not be from God, though he both permitted and overruled them to accomplish his own wise and righteous purposes. This example throws light upon the doctrine of God's providential government of the world and suggests many practical instructions (Scott). See Note and References at 1 S 18:10n. 2 S 12:11n. Am +√3:6. **Go, number.** 1 S +11:8. 1 Ch 27:23, 24.

2. **Joab.** 2 S 2:13. 8:16. 20:23. 23:37. **Go now,** etc. *or,* Compass now all. 1 Ch 21:2. **from Dan.** ver. 15. 2 S 3:10. 17:11. Jg 20:1. **and number.** We know not in what the sinfulness of this action consisted. Some think it was a contempt of the promise that the Israelites should be innumerable, and that they ought not to have been numbered without an express command, as in the days of Moses. Others suppose with Josephus that it was a kind of sacrilege in omitting to collect the half shekel apiece for the use of the sanctuary. It however would appear that pride, ambition, and a desire of conquest induced David to this measure, and rendered it so displeasing to God. **that I may.** Dt 8:13, 14. 2 Ch 32:25, 26, 31. Pr 29:23. Je *17:5. 2 C 12:7.

3. **Now the Lord.** 2 S 10:12. 1 Ch *21:3, 4. 27:23. Ps 115:14. Pr 14:28. Is 60:5.

4. **the king's.** 1 S +*25:17. 1 Ch 21:4. Ec *8:4. **went out.** Ex 1:17. Ac +*5:29. **to number.** Nu 1:2-4. 1 Ch 27:1.

5. **Aroer.** Nu 32:34. Dt 2:36. Jsh 13:9, 16. 1 S 30:28. Is 17:2. **river.** *or,* valley. Nu +*13:23mg. Jg +16:4mg. **Jazer.** Nu 32:1, 3, 35. Is 16:8, 9.

6. **Gilead.** Ge 31:21, 47, 48. Nu 32:1, 39. 1 Ch 5:10. **land of Tahtim-hodshi.** *or,* nether land newly inhabited. i.e. *my new places; under the new moon,* *S#8483h. **Dan-jaan.** i.e. *judge of purpose,* *S#1842h. Jsh 19:47. Jg 18:29. **Zidon.** Ge 10:15. Jsh 11:8. 19:28. Jg 18:28.

7. **Tyre.** Jsh 19:29. **to Beer-sheba.** ver. 2. Ge 21:31-33. **the Hivites.** Ge +10:17. **the Canaanites.** Ge +10:18. Jsh 11:3. Jg 3:3.

8. **Jerusalem.** 1 Ch 21:4.

9. **eight hundred thousand.** Nu 1:45, 46. 26:51. 1 Ch 21:5, 6. 27:23, 24.

10. **David's heart.** 1 S 24:5. Jn 8:9. 1 J 3:20, 21. **I have sinned.** 2 S 12:13. 1 Ch 21:8. 2 Ch 32:26. Jb 33:27, 28. Ps *32:5. Pr *28:13. Mi 7:8, 9, 18, 19. 1 J *1:9. **take away.** Jb 7:21. Ho 14:2. Jn *1:29. **foolishly.** 2 S 12:13. Dt 32:6. 1 S 13:13. 26:21. 1 Ch 21:7, 8. 2 Ch 16:9. Pr *24:9. Mk 7:22. T 3:3.

11. **Gad.** i.e. *a troop.* 1 S 22:5. 1 Ch 21:9. 29:29. **seer.** 1 S *9:9. 2 K 17:13. 1 Ch 21:9. 25:5. 26:28. 29:29. 2 Ch 9:29. 12:15. 16:7, 10. 19:2. 29:25, 30. Is 29:10. 30:10. Am 7:12.

12. **I offer.** 1 Ch 21:10, 11. **that I may.** 2 S 12:9, 10, 14. Le 26:41, 43. Jb 5:17, 18. Pr 3:12. He 12:6-10. Re 3:19.

13. **seven.** 2 S 21:1. Le 26:20. 1 K 17:1, etc. 1 Ch 21:10-12. Ezk 14:13, 21. Lk 4:25. **flee.** Le 26:17, 36, 37. Dt 28:25, 52. **three days.** Le 26:16, 25. Dt 28:22, 27, 35. Ps 91:6. Ezk 14:19-21.

14. **I am in.** 1 S 13:6. 2 K 6:15. 1 Ch 21:13. Jn 12:27. Ph +*1:23. **let us fall.** T#1528. Ex +*34:6, 7. Is +*55:3. Je +*29:11. **for his.** Ex 34:6, 7. 1 Ch 21:13. Ps 51:1. 86:5, 15. *103:8-14. 119:156. ch. 136. 145:9. Is 55:7. Jon 4:2. Mi 7:18. Ja 2:13. **great.** *or,* many. Ps 119:156. **let me not.** T#1615. 2 K 13:3-7. 2 Ch 28:5-9. Ps 106:41, 42. Pr 12:10. Is 47:6. Zc 1:15.

15. **the Lord.** Ex *30:12. Nu 16:46-49. 25:9. 1 S 6:19. 1 Ch 21:14. 27:24. Mt *24:7. Re 6:8. **from Dan.** See on ver. 2. **seventy thousand men.** Is 37:36.

16. **the angel.** T#12. Ex 12:23. 2 K 19:35. 1 Ch 21:15, 16. 2 Ch 32:21. Jb 38:7. Ps 35:6. 91:11, 12. Da 6:22. 9:21, 22. Mt 13:39, 41. 18:10. Lk 16:22. Ac 12:23. He 1:14. **the Lord repented.** ſ22B, Ge +6:6. Ge +6:6. 1 S 15:11. Ps 78:38. 90:13. 135:14. Je 18:7-10. Jl 2:13, 14. Am 7:3, 6. Jon +3:10 (T#608). Hab 3:2. **It is enough.** Ex 9:28. 1 K 19:4. Is 27:8. 40:1, 2.

57:16. Jl 2:13, 14. Mk 14:41. 2 C 2:6. **Araunah.** i.e. *make ye to shine; I shall shout for joy,* *S#728h. ver. 18, 20, 20, 21, 22, 23, 23, 24. 1 Ch 21:15. 2 Ch 3:1, Ornan. **the Jebusite.** 2 S 5:8. Ge +10:16. Jsh 15:63. Jg 1:21. 19:11. Zc 9:7.

17. **spake.** 1 Ch *21:16, 17. **Lo, I have sinned.** ver. 10. Jb 7:20. 42:6. Ps 51:2-5. Is 6:5. **these sheep.** 1 K 22:17. Ps 44:11. 74:1. Ezk 34:2-6, 23, 24. Zc 13:7. **let thine.** Ge 44:33. Jn 10:11, 12. 1 P 2:24, 25.

18. **Gad.** ver. 11. 1 Ch 21:18, etc. 2 Ch 3:1. **threshing floor.** These, among the ancient Jews, were only round, level plats of ground in the open air, as they are to this day in the East, where the corn was trodden out by oxen. Ge +50:10. Dt +*16:13mg. **Araunah.** Heb. Araniah. i.e. *joyful shouting of Jah.* See on ver. 16. **Jebusite.** Ge +10:16.

19. **as the Lord.** Ge 6:22. 1 Ch 21:19. 2 Ch 20:20. 36:16. Ne 9:26. He 11:8.

20. **bowed.** 2 S 9:8. Ge 18:2. Ru 2:10. 1 Ch 21:20, 21.

21. **Wherefore.** ver. 3, 18. **To buy.** Ge 23:8-16. 1 Ch 21:22. Je 32:6-14. **the plague.** 2 S 21:3-14. Nu 16:47-50. 25:8. Ps 106:30.

22. **Araunah.** i.e. *Jehovah is firm.* **Let my lord.** Ge 23:11. 1 Ch 21:22. **be oxen.** 1 S 6:14. 1 K 19:21.

23. **as a king.** Ps 45:16. Is 32:8. **give unto.** Ge 23:11. 1 Ch 21:23. **The Lord.** Jb 42:8, 9. Ps 20:3, 4. Is 60:7. Ezk 20:40, 41. Ho 8:13. Ro 15:30, 31. 1 T 2:1, 2. He *7:7. 1 P 2:5.

24. **Nay.** Ge 23:13. *29:15. 1 Ch *21:24. Is 43:23, 24. Ml *1:12-14. Ro *12:17. **that which.** Ex 23:15. Dt 16:16. Pr *3:9. Mt 19:27. Mk +*10:28-30. Lk 5:28. *21:4. Jn 12:3. Ac 20:24. Ph 3:7, 8. **doth cost me nothing.** Had Araunah's offer been accepted, the sacrifice would have been Araunah's, not David's (*Annotated Paragraph Bible*). Matthew Poole notes: "For this would be both dishonorable to God, as if I thought him not worthy of a costly sacrifice; and a disparagement to myself, as if I were unable and unwilling to offer a sacrifice of my own goods; and unsatisfactory to the command of God, which obliges all offenders, and me in a particular manner, to offer sacrifice of their own estate." Ge +*29:15. Ex 23:15. 1 S 9:7, 8. 1 Ch +*‖21:24n. 1 C +*16:2. **So David.** 1 Ch 21:25. 22:1.

25. **built there.** Ge +8:20. +13:18. 22:9. 1 S 7:9, 17. 1 Ch 21:26-30. **and offered.** Jg 20:26. 21:4. **burnt offerings.** Le +*23:12. **peace offerings.** Le +*23:19. **So the Lord.** ver. 14. 2 S 21:14. 1 Ch 21:26, 27. La √3:32, 33. **the plague.** Nu 25:8. Ps 106:30.

1 KINGS

1 KINGS 1

Abishag is procured to cherish David, in his old age and sickness, 1-4. Adonijah gains over Joab and Abiathar, and aspires to the throne, 5-10. Nathan counsels Bathsheba, who speaks to David, and is seconded by Nathan, 11-27. David assures Bathsheba, by an oath, that Solomon shall succeed him; and gives orders that he should, that day, be anointed and proclaimed king, 28-37. Zadok, Benaiah, and Nathan zealously execute these orders, and the people rejoice, 38-40. Jonathan informs Adonijah and his company; and they hastily disperse, 41-49. Adonijah flees to the horns of the altar, and obtains from Solomon a conditional pardon, 50-53.

1. A.M. 2989. B.C. 1015. An. Ex. Is. 476. **old.** David was probably now about *sixty-nine* years of age. He was *thirty* years old when he began to reign, reigned *forty* years, and died in his *seventieth* year; and the transactions mentioned here are supposed to have taken place about a year before his death. Sixty-nine was not an advanced age; but he had been exhausted with various fatigues, and especially family afflictions, so that he was much older in constitution than in years. 2 S 5:4. 1 Ch 23:1. 29:27, 28. Ps *90:10. Ec 12:1. **and stricken in years.** Heb. and entered into days. Ge 18:11. 24:1. Jsh 23:1, 2. Lk 1:7. **clothes.** Ge 24:53. 27:15, 27. **heat.** Dt 19:6. Ec *4:11. Ezk 24:11.

2. **Let there be sought.** Heb. Let them seek. **a young virgin.** Heb. a damsel, a virgin. Jg 21:12. **stand.** Dt 10:8. 1 S 16:21, 22. 2 Ch 29:11. **cherish him.** Heb. be a cherisher unto him. or, companion. ver. 4. Jb 15:3 (unprofitable). 22:2, 21 (acquaint...thyself). 34:9. 35:3 (advantage). Ps 139:3 (acquaint). Is 22:15 (trea-

surer). **lie.** Ge 16:5. Dt 13:6. 2 S 12:3. Mi 7:5. **get heat.** Ec *4:11.

3. **So.** Est 2:2-4. **coasts.** Jg 19:29. 1 S 11:7. 2 S 21:5. **Abishag.** i.e. *father of error,* *S#49h. ver. 15. 1 K 2:17, 21, 22. **Shunamite.** i.e. *perfect,* *S#7767h. ver. 15. 2 K 2:17, 21, 22. Jsh ●19:18. 1 S ●28:4. 2 K 4:●8, 12, 25, 36.

4. **very.** lit. "unto might." 1 S 25:36. **fair.** Ge 12:11. *24:16. 26:7. 29:17. 1 S 25:3. 2 S 11:2. 13:1. 14:27. Est 1:11. **knew.** Ge +4:1. Mt 1:25.

5. **Adonijah.** i.e. *Jehovah is my Lord,* *S#138h. ver. 7, 18. 1 K 2:28. 2 S 3:4. 1 Ch 3:2. Ne 10:16. (1) Fourth son of David, put to death by Solomon for aspiring to the throne. (2) One of the Levites sent by Jehoshaphat to teach the law, 2 Ch 17:8. (3) A chief of the people that with Nehemiah sealed the covenant, Ne 10:16. **Haggith.** 2 S +3:4. **exalted.** ver. 11. 1 K 2:24. Ex 9:17. Pr 16:18. 18:12. Lk 14:11. 18:14. **I will.** Dt 17:15. Jg 9:2. 1 Ch 22:5-11. 28:5. 29:1. **be king.** Heb. reign. **and he.** Dt 17:16. 2 S *12:10. 15:1. Is 2:7.

6. **his father.** Ge +*44:30. 2 S 13:21n. **had not.** 1 S +*3:13mg. Pr +*19:18. *22:15. +*23:13, 14. *29:15. He *12:5, 6. **at any time.** Heb. from his days. **very goodly.** 1 S *9:2. 10:23. 2 S *14:25. **his mother.** or, Haggith. √6311A, Ex +12:4. **bare him.** 2 S *3:3, 4. 1 Ch 3:2.

7. **And he conferred.** Heb. his words were. 2 S *15:12. Ps 2:2. **Joab.** 1 K 2:28. 2 S 8:16. 20:23. **Abiathar.** 1 S 22:20-23. 2 S 15:24-29, 35. 20:25. **following Adonijah helped him.** Heb. helped after Adonijah. 1 K 2:22, 26-35.

8. **Zadok.** 1 K 2:35. 2 S 8:17, 18. 20:25. 1 Ch 27:5, 6. Ezk 44:15. **Nathan.** 2 S 7:2-4. 12:1-15. **Shimei.**

1 K 4:18. Zc 12:13. **Rei.** i.e. *my friend*, *S#7472h. **the mighty.** 2 S 23:8-39. 1 Ch 11:10-47.

9. **Adonijah.** The Oriental banquet, in consequence of the intense heat, is often spread upon the verdant turf, beneath the shade of a tree, where the streaming rivulet supplies the company with wholesome water, and excites a gentle breeze to cool their burning temples. **slew.** 2 S 15:12. Pr 15:8. **Zoheleth.** i.e. *fearful, creeping thing,* *S#2120h. **En-rogel.** *or,* the well Rogel. Jsh 15:7. 2 S 17:17. **called.** 2 S 13:23-27. 15:11.

10. **But Nathan.** ver. 8, 19. 2 S 12:1, etc.

11. **Nathan.** 2 S 7:12-17. 12:24, 25. 1 Ch 22:9, 10. 28:4, 5. 29:1. **Adonijah.** See on ver. 5. **Haggith.** 2 S 3:4.

12. **let me.** Pr *11:14. 20:18. 27:9. Je 38:15. **save.** ver. 21. Ge 19:17. Ac 27:31. **the life.** Heb. *nephesh,* soul, Ge +44:30. Jg 9:5. 2 K 11:1. 2 Ch 21:4. 22:10. Mt 21:38.

13. **Assuredly.** See on ver. 11, 17, 30. 1 Ch 22:6-13. 28:5. 29:1. Ps 2:6, 7. **sit.** ver. 17, 24, 30, 35, 48. 1 K 2:12. Dt 17:18. 1 Ch 29:23. Ps 132:11, 12. Is 9:7. Je 33:21. Lk 1:32, 33.

14. **I also.** ver. 17-27. 2 C 13:1. **confirm.** Heb. fill up.

15. **very old.** ver. 2-4.

16. **bowed.** ver. 23. 1 S 20:41. 24:8. 25:23. **And the.** 1 K 2:20. Est 7:2. Mt 20:21, 32. **What wouldest thou?** Heb. What to thee? Est 5:2, 3.

17. **My lord.** Ge 18:12. 1 P 3:6. **thou swarest.** It is not recorded when or upon what occasion David sware to Bathsheba that Solomon should succeed him; but it is supposed, with some degree of probability, that it took place after Absalom's rebellion; and as God himself had settled the succession, he might very properly give her this assurance. ver. 13, 30.

18. **Adonijah.** ver. 5, 24. 2 S 15:10. **thou knowest.** ver. 11, 24, 27. Ac 3:17.

19. **he hath slain.** ver. 7-10, 25.

20. **the eyes.** 2 Ch 20:12. Ps 25:15. 123:1, 2. Zc 3:9. **that thou.** At this time the monarchy of Israel was *unsettled*: no man knew who was to succeed to the crown; and the minds of the people were as unsettled as the succession. It was neither *hereditary* nor *elective*: the king, as was anciently the case in most countries, *named* his successor; but in this instance, God had already assigned the throne to Solomon. 2 S 23:2. 1 Ch 22:8-10. 28:5, 6, 10. 29:1.

21. **sleep.** See on 1 K 2:10. +11:43. Ge 15:15. Dt 31:16. **that I.** That is, when Adonijah is established on the throne, I and my son Solomon shall be put to death as state criminals. The history of the world demonstrates that the lust of dominion has tempted men to commit the most enormous crimes. A father has destroyed his son, a son deposed a father, and a brother murdered a brother, in order to obtain a crown! **offenders.** Heb. sinners. 1 K 2:15, 22-24.

22. **while she.** Ge 24:15. Jb 1:16-18. Da 9:20.

23. **he bowed.** See on ver. 16. Ro 13:7. 1 P 2:17.

24. **hast thou.** ver. 14, 18. **reign.** ver. 5, 13, 17.

25. **slain.** See on ver. 9, 19. 1 S 11:14, 15. 1 Ch 29:21-23. **God save king Adonijah.** Heb. Let king Adonijah live. ∫108B, 1 S +10:24. ver. 34. 1 S 10:24mg. 2 S 16:16mg. 2 K 11:12mg. 2 Ch 23:11mg. Mt 21:9. Mk 11:9, 10. Lk 19:38.

26. **me thy.** ver. 8, 19. 2 S 7:2, 12-17. 12:25.

27. **and thou.** ver. 24. 2 K 4:27. Jn 15:15.

28. **Call me.** She appears to have gone out when Nathan entered; and he retired when she was readmitted. **into the king's presence.** Heb. before the king.

29. **As the.** 1 K 2:24. 17:1. 18:10. Jg 8:19. 1 S 14:39, 45. 19:6. 20:21. 2 S 12:5. 2 K 4:30. 5:16, 20. **hath.** Ge 48:16. 2 S 4:9. Ps 34:19-22. 72:14. 136:24. 138:7. **soul.** Heb. *nephesh,* Ge +12:13.

30. **Even as I sware.** See on ver. 13, 17.

31. **did reverence.** 2 S 9:6. Est 3:2. Mt 21:37. Ep 5:33. He 12:9. **Let my.** See on ver. 25. Ne 2:3. Da 2:4. 3:9. 5:10. 6:6, 21. **for ever.** Heb. *olam,* Ex +12:24.

32. **Zadok.** See on ver. 8, 26, 38.

33. **Take.** 2 S 20:6. **and cause.** Maimonides informs us, that it was a capital offence for any one to ride on the king's mule, to sit on his throne, or to handle his sceptre, without permission; and as David ordered Solomon to ride on his own mule, etc., it was ample evidence that he had appointed him his successor. **to ride.** ver. 5, 38, 44. Ge 41:43. Est 6:6-11. **mine own mule.** Heb. the mule which *belongeth* to me. Le 19:19. **Gihon.** ver. 38, 45. 2 Ch 32:30. 33:14.

34. **Zadok.** 1 K 19:16. 1 S 10:1. 16:3, 12, 13. 2 S 2:4. 5:3. 2 K 9:3, 6. 11:12. 2 Ch 23:11. Ps 45:7. *89:20, 36. Is 45:1. Ac 10:38. 2 C 1:21, 22. **blow ye.** 2 S 15:10. 2 K 9:13. 11:14. Ps 98:5-7. **God.** See on ver. 25. 2 K 11:12.

35. **sit.** See on ver. 13, 17. 1 K 2:12. **I have.** 1 K 2:15. 1 Ch 23:1. 28:4, 5. Ps 2:6. 72, title, 1, 2.

36. **Amen.** Dt 27:15-26. Ps 72:19. Je *11:5. *28:6. Mt *6:13. 28:20. 1 C 14:16. **the Lord.** 1 S 25:29. 1 Ch 17:27. Ps *18:2. *63:1. 89:20, 26.

37. **As the.** 1 K 3:7-9. Ex 3:12. Jsh *1:5, 17. 1 S 20:13. 1 Ch 28:20. 2 Ch 1:1. Ps 46:7, 11. Is 8:10. Mt 1:23. Ro *8:31. **and make.** ver. 47. 2 S 24:3. 2 K 2:9. Ps 72:8, 17-19. 89:27. Da 7:14.

38. **Zadok.** See on ver. 8, 26. **the Cherethites.** 1 S 30:14. 2 S 8:18. 15:18. 20:20-23. 1 Ch 18:17. Zp 2:5. **king David's.** See on ver. 33.

39. **an horn.** See on 1 S 16:3. **out.** Ex 30:23-33. Ps 89:20. **anointed.** 1 Ch *29:22. **all the people.** See on ver. 25. 1 S 10:24. 2 K 11:12. 2 Ch 23:11, 13.

40. **piped.** ∫147D, Ge +1:29. **pipes.** *or,* flutes. Da 3:5. **rejoiced.** ∫147D, Ge +1:29. 1 S 11:15. 2 K 11:14, 20. 1 Ch 12:38-40. Ps 97:1. Zc 9:9. Lk 19:37. Re 11:15-18. **the earth rent.** ∫102, Ge +2:24. We use a similar expression in precisely the same sense: "They *rent the air* with their cries."

41. **as they.** Jb *20:5. Pr 14:13. Ec 7:4-6. Mt 24:38, 39. Lk 17:26-29. **Wherefore.** Ex 32:17. Jb 15:21, 22. Ps 73:18-20. **the city.** Mt 21:9-11, 15. Ac 21:31.

42. **Jonathan.** 2 S 15:36. 17:17. **a valiant.** 1 K 22:18. 2 S 18:27. 2 K 9:22. Is 57:21. 1 Th 5:2, 3.

43. **Verily.** See on ver. 32-40.

44. **Cherethites.** ver. 38. **ride upon.** ver. 32, 33, 38.

45. **Gihon.** This was a fountain on the west of Jerusalem, (consequently in an opposite direction to En-rogel on the east, where Adonijah was proclaimed king), of which there were two pools, an upper and a lower (2 Ch 32:30). There is a large square cistern in the ravine west of the city, mentioned by Dr. Richardson as a little to the south of the Jaffa gate, which Dr. Pococke describes as a basin about 250 paces long and 100 broad. It is commonly called the pool of Bathsheba, but seems to be the lower pool of Gihon. "Nearly a mile to the N.N.W. is the pool of Gihon, which I

suppose to be the upper pool. It is a very large basin, and, if I mistake not, is cut down about ten feet into the rock, there being a way down to it by steps. It was almost dry at that time, and seems designed to receive the rain waters which come from the hills about it. There is a canal from the pool to the city, which is uncovered part of the way, and, it is said, goes to the pool in the streets near the holy sepulchre. The fountain of Gihon arose either in the upper pool, or out of the high ground above it" (*Travels*, book i. ch. 6). See Note on 2 S 5:23. **the city.** ver. 40. 1 S 4:5. Ezr 3:13. **This is.** 1 K 14:6. 1 S 28:29. Da 5:26-28.

46. **Solomon sitteth.** ver. 13. 1 Ch 29:23. Ps 132:11. Hag 2:22.

47. **bless.** Ex 12:32. 2 S 8:10. 21:3. Ezr 6:10. Ps 20:1-4. **God.** ver. 37. Lk 19:38. **bowed.** Ge 47:31. He 11:21.

48. **Blessed.** Ge 14:20. 1 Ch 29:10, 20. Ne 9:5. Ps 34:1. 41:13. 72:17-19. 103:1, 2. 145:2. Da 4:34. Lk 1:46, 47, 68, 69. Ep 1:3. 1 P 1:3. **which.** 1 K 3:6. 1 Ch 17:11-14, 17. Ps *132:11, 12. Pr 17:6. **mine eyes.** 2 S 24:3. Ps 128:5, 6.

49. **all the guests.** Pr 28:1. Is 21:4, 5. Da 5:4-6.

50. **caught.** 1 K 2:28. Ex 21:14. 38:2. Ps 118:27.

52. **there shall.** 1 S 14:45. 2 S 14:11. Mt *10:29, 30. Lk 21:18. Ac 27:34. **not an hair.** ♪138B, Ge +13:16. **wickedness.** 1 K 2:21-25. Jb 15:22. Pr *13:6. *21:12.

53. **bowed himself.** See on ver. 16, 31. 2 S 1:2. **Go to.** 1 K 2:36. 2 S 14:24, 28. Pr 24:21.

1 KINGS 2

David charges Solomon to serve God; and directs him how to act towards Joab, the sons of Barzillai, and Shimei, 1-9. His death and the years of his reign, 10, 11. Solomon succeeds him, 12. Adonijah persuades Bath-sheba to ask Solomon to give him Abishag as his wife; and is put to death, 13-25. Abiathar's life is spared, but he is deprived of the high priesthood, 26, 27. Joab, having fled to the altar, is there put to death, 28-34. Beniah succeeds Joab, and Zadok, Abiathar, 35. Shimei is, by Solomon, required to reside in Jerusalem, and engages by oath to do so: but breaking his engagement, he is put to death, 36-46.

1. **the days.** Ge 47:29. Dt 31:14. 33:1. 2 T 4:6. 2 P 1:13-15. **charged.** Nu 27:19. Dt 3:28. 31:23. Ac 20:28-31. 1 T 1:18. 6:13. 2 T 4:1.

2. **I go.** Jsh 23:14. Jb 16:22. 30:23. Ps 89:48. He 9:27. **be thou.** Dt 17:19, 20. 31:6. Jsh 1:6, 7. 1 Ch 28:20. Ep 3:16. 6:10. Col 1:11. 2 T 2:1. 1 P 1:13. 2 P 1:5. **and show.** 1 K 3:7. 2 S 10:12. Ec 12:13. 1 C 16:13. 1 T 4:12.

3. **And keep.** Dt 29:9. Jsh 1:7. 22:5. 1 Ch 22:12, 13. 28:8, 9. 29:19. **statutes.** See on Dt 4:1, 5, 8. 5:1. 6:1, 2. **testimonies.** Dt 4:45. Ps 19:7. 119:2, 111, 138. **written.** Dt *17:18-20. Ml 4:4. **that thou.** Dt 29:9. **prosper.** *or*, do wisely. Jsh *1:7, 8, mg. 1 S 18:5, 14, 30. 2 Ch 31:20, 21. Ps 1:2, 3. 119:98-100. Pr 3:1-4. **whithersoever.** 2 S 8:6, 14. 2 K 18:7.

4. **That the Lord.** Ge 18:19. Dt 7:12. 1 Ch 28:9. Jn 15:9, 10. Ju 20, 21, 24. **his word.** 2 S 7:11-16, 25. 1 Ch 17:11-15. 22:9-11. 28:5-7. Ps 89:29-37. 132:11, 12. **walk.** 1 K 3:3, 14. 8:23. Ge 17:1. Le 26:3. 2 K 20:3. 23:3, 25. 2 Ch 17:3. Lk 1:6. **with all their heart.** Dt 6:5. 10:12. 11:13. Mt 22:37. **soul.** Heb. *nephesh*, Ge +34:3. **fail,** etc. Heb. be cut off from thee from

the throne. 1 K 8:25. 2 S 7:12, 13, 16. Ps 37:9, 22. Zc 14:2.

5. **Joab.** 1 K 1:7, 18, 19. 2 S 3:27, 39. 18:5, 12, 14. 19:5-7. **Abner.** 2 S 3:27. **Amasa.** 2 S 20:10. **Jether.** 2 S 17:25, Ithra. **shed.** Heb. put. Je 2:34. 6:15. Ezk 24:7, 8.

6. **according.** ver. 9. Pr *20:26. **let.** This ought by no means to be imputed to personal resentment, but to David's regard for justice. Joab, for two most atrocious murders, according to the law of God should die; and it would have been a flagrant breach of that law, and an insult to justice, not to have taken his life. David was culpable in delaying it so long; and without giving this order to Solomon, could not have died in the approbation of his Maker. ver. 28-34. Ge 9:6. Nu 35:33. Pr 28:17. Ec *8:11. Is 65:20. **grave.** Heb. *sheol*, Ge +37:35. **in.** Ge 42:38. 2 K 22:20. Ps *37:37. Is 48:22. 57:2, 21.

7. **Barzillai.** 2 S 17:27-29. 19:31-40. Pr 27:10. **eat.** 2 S 9:7, 10. 19:28. Lk 12:37. 22:28-30. Re *3:20, 21. **when I fled.** 2 S 15:13-15.

8. **Shimei.** ver. 36-46. 2 S 16:5-8. **grievous.** Heb. strong. Jb 6:25. Mi 2:10. **he came.** 2 S 19:16-23. Je 4:2.

9. **hold him.** Do not consider him as an innocent man; for, as thou art a wise man, and knowest how to treat such persons, treat him as he deserves; only, as I have sworn to him that I would not put him to death, "bring NOT his hoar head down to the grave with blood." So Solomon understood David; for, after he had commanded Joab to be slain, in obedience to his father, he sent for Shimei, and knowing he ought to be well watched, he confined him to Jerusalem for the rest of his life: and so it appears David should be understood; for the negative particle *lo*, in the former clause—"hold him *not* guiltless," should be repeated in the latter clause, though not expressed; instances of which frequently occur in the Hebrew Scriptures (See Jg 5:30. 1 S 2:3. Ps 1:5. 9:18. 38:1. 75:5. Pr 5:16. 24:12, etc.). This is the view taken of the subject by Dr. Kennicott, and it seems the best and most correct mode of interpreting the text. ♪63I1C1, Ge +2:6. Ex 20:7. 22:28. Jb 9:28. **wise.** 1 K 3:12, 28. Mt 5:43, 44. **his.** ver. 6. Ge 42:38. 44:31. **down.** ♪63, Ge +2:6. **grave.** Heb. *sheol*, Ge +37:35. **with.** Nu 32:23.

10. **So David.** See on 1 K 1:21. +11:43. 1 Ch 29:28. Ac 2:29. 13:36. **the city.** 1 K 3:1. 11:43. 2 S 5:7. 1 Ch 11:7.

11. **reigned over.** 2 S 5:4. 1 Ch 29:26, 27. **seven years.** ♪171T7. Synecdoche of the Part B656. In chronology a part of a time or period is sometimes put for the whole of such period. Here, "seven years" is put for seven and a half years. Compare 2 S 2:11. For another instance of this figure see 2 K 24:8.

12. A.M. 2990. B.C. 1014. An. Ex. Is. 477. **sat Solomon.** 1 K 1:46. 1 Ch 29:23-25. 2 Ch 1:1. Ps 132:12. **his kingdom.** 2 S 7:12, 13, 29. Ps 72:8, etc. 89:36, 37.

13. **Adonijah.** See on 1 K 1:5-10, 50-53. **Comest.** 1 S 16:4, 5. 2 K 9:18-22. 1 Ch 12:17, 18. Lk 10:5, 6.

14. **I have.** 2 S 14:12. Lk 7:40.

15. **Thou knowest.** 1 K 1:5, 25. 2 S 15:6, 13. 16:18. **for it was.** 2 S 7:12. 12:24. 1 Ch 22:9, 10. 28:5-7. Pr *21:30. Je 27:5-8. Da 2:22.

16. **deny me not.** Heb. turn not away my face.

ſ171Q, Ge +3:19. ver. 17, 20. 2 Ch 6:42. Ps 132:10. Pr 30:7.

17. **say.** ſ171Q, Ge +3:19. **Abishag.** 1 K 1:2-4. 2 S 3:7. 12:8.

18. **Well.** Pr 14:15.

19. **rose up.** Ex 20:12. Le 19:3, 32. **she sat.** Ps 45:9. 110:1. Mt 25:33.

20. **I desire.** Mt 20:20, 21. Jn 2:3, 4. **say.** ſ171Q, Ge +3:19. **Ask on.** Mt 7:7-11. 18:19. Mk 10:35, 36. 11:24. Lk *11:9, 10. Jn 14:13, 14. *15:16. **say.** ſ171Q, Ge +3:19.

21. **Let Abishag.** Ge 49:3. 2 S 16:21, 22.

22. **why dost.** Mt 20:22. Mk 10:38. Ja 4:3. **the kingdom.** 1 K 1:5-7, 11, 24, 25.

23. **God.** 1 K 20:10. Ru 1:17. 1 S 14:44. 2 S 3:9, 35. 19:13. 2 K 6:31. **if Adonijah.** We have already seen, that the whole regal succession (See note on 2 S 16:23); and it was treason for a subject to claim any wife or virgin who had once formed a part of it. Solomon evidently considered the request of Adonijah in this light; and was convinced that he was still aiming to seize the crown, to which he considered this as one step. But it is very doubtful, how far the plea either of policy or state necessity can justify Solomon in thus embruing his hands in his brother's blood, whatever might have been his treasonable intentions or conduct. **spoken.** Ps 64:8. 140:9. Pr 18:6, 7. Ec 10:12. Lk 19:22. **life.** Heb. *nephesh*, soul, Ge +44:30. ſ121A7, Ge +9:5.

24. **as the Lord.** See on 1 K 1:29. **set me.** 1 K 3:6, 7. 10:9. 1 Ch 29:23. 2 Ch 1:8, 9. **made me.** Ex 1:21. 1 S 25:28. 2 S 7:11-13, 27. 1 Ch 17:10, 17, 23. Ps 127:1. **as he promised.** 1 Ch 22:10. **put.** 1 K 1:52. Ec 8:11-13.

25. **he fell.** ver. 31, 34, 46. Jg 8:20, 21. 1 S 15:33. 2 S 1:15. 4:12.

26. **Abiathar.** ver. 35. 1 K 1:7, 25. **Anathoth.** Jsh 21:18. Is 10:30. Je 1:1. **worthy of death.** Heb. a man of death. 1 S 26:16. 2 S 12:5mg. **barest.** 1 S 22:20-23. 23:6-9. 2 S 15:24, 29. 1 Ch 15:11, 12. **hast been.** 2 S 15:24-29. Mt 10:42. Lk 22:28. Ga 3:4.

27. **So Solomon.** This was for having taken part with Adonijah; but by it a remarkable prophecy was fulfilled. God had told Eli (1 S 2:30-36), that the priesthood should depart from his house; Abiathar was the last of the priests of *Ithamar*, of which family was Eli the high priest. Zadok, who succeeded, was of the family of Eleazar; and by this change the priesthood reverted to its ancient channel. **that he.** 1 S 2:30-36. 3:12-14. Mt 26:56. Jn 12:38. 19:24, 28, 36, 37. **Shiloh.** Jsh 18:1. Ps 78:60. Je 7:12-14.

28. **Joab had.** 1 K 1:7. Ex 21:14. Dt 32:35. 2 S 18:2, 14, 15. **caught.** See on 1 K 1:50. Ex 27:2.

29. **he is by.** Ex 21:14. Ezk 9:6. 1 P 4:17. **Go.** ver. 25, 31, 46.

31. **Do.** Ex 21:14. **that thou.** Ge 9:5, 6. Nu 35:33. Dt 19:12, 13. 21:8, 9. 2 K 9:26. ◐24:4. Pr 28:17. Ac 28:4. **which.** ver. 5. **and from.** 2 S 3:28.

32. **return.** ver. 44. Ge 4:11. Jg 9:24, 57. Ps 7:16. **two men.** 2 S 3:27. 20:10. **more righteous.** 1 S 15:28. 2 S 4:11. 2 Ch 21:13. Est 1:19. **my father.** 2 S 3:26, 37. **Abner.** 2 S 3:27. **Amasa.** 2 S 20:10. **Jether.** ver. 5. 2 S 17:25, Ithra.

33. **return upon.** See on ver. 32. 2 S 3:29. 2 K 5:27. Ps 101:8. 109:6-15. Mt 27:25. **for ever.** Heb.

olam, Ex +12:24. **upon David.** 2 S 3:28. Pr 25:5. **his house.** Ps 89:29, 36, 37. 132:12. Is 9:6, 7. 11:1-9. Lk 1:31-33. 2:14. **for ever.** Heb. *olam*, Ex +12:24.

34. **Benaiah.** ver. 25, 31, 46. **and fell.** It appears that he slew him at the very altar. The altar was so sacred among all people, that, in general, even the vilest wretch found safety, if he once reached it. This led to many abuses, and the perversion of public justice; and God decreed (Ex 24:14) that the presumptuous murderer, who had taken refuge at his altar, should be dragged thence and put to death. **buried.** 2 K 21:18. 2 Ch 33:20. **in the.** Jsh 15:61. Mt 3:1.

35. **in his room.** Jb 34:24. **Zadok.** See on ver. 27. Nu 25:11-13. 1 S 2:35. 1 Ch 6:4-15, 50-53. 24:3. 29:22. Ps 109:8. Ac 1:20.

36. **Shimei.** ver. 8, 9. 2 S 16:5-9. Pr 20:8, 26. **Build.** No doubt Solomon suspected that Shimei's influence would be dangerous upon his own estate and among his numerous dependents in different parts of the land; and therefore he proposed to him, as the condition of his indemnity for former crimes, that he should live in Jerusalem under his eye, and by no means remove thence. These terms Shimei readily agreed to, and solemnly swore to observe them; and for three years he lived unmolested and in affluence. But growing secure, in contempt of Solomon's authority and of the oath of God, upon an unnecessary business he took a journey, which according to his own engagement forfeited his life. Thus the Lord left him to be infatuated, that due punishment might be inflicted upon him; in order that every ringleader of opposition to Solomon's kingdom might be crushed, and others be intimidated by their examples. Solomon's throne by the death of this man was established in peace, and became a type of the Redeemer's kingdom of peace and righteousness (Scott). 1 K 1:53. 2 S 14:24, 28.

37. **on the day.** ſ171, Ge +2:17. **over the.** 1 K 15:13. 2 S 15:23. 2 K 23:6. 2 Ch 29:16. Je 31:40. Jn 18:1, Cedron. **surely die.** ſ147B, Ge +2:16. **thy blood.** See on ver. 31, 33. Le 20:9. Jsh 2:19. 2 S 1:16. Ezk 18:13. **head.** ſ171Q12, Jg +5:30.

38. **The saying.** 1 K 20:4. 2 K 20:19.

39. **A.M.** 2993. **B.C.** 1011. **An. Ex. Is.** 480. **Achish.** 1 S 21:10. 27:2, 3. **Maachah.** i.e. *oppression*, *S#4601h. 1 K 15:2, 10, 13. Ge 22:24. 2 S 3:3. 1 Ch 2:48. 3:12. 7:15, 16. 8:29. 9:35. 11:43. 19:6. 27:16. 2 Ch 11:20, 21, 22. 15:16. Also Jsh 13:13. 2 S 10:6, 8. 1 Ch 19:7. (1) A daughter of Nahor, the brother of Abraham, Ge 22:24. (2) The father of Achish, king of Gath, 1 K 2:39. He is called Maoch in 1 S 27:2. (3) The mother of King Abijah, wife of King Rehoboam, 1 K 15:2; 2 Ch 11:20. (4) The concubine of Caleb, the son of Hezron, 1 Ch 2:48. (5) A Benjamitess who became the wife of Machir, 1 Ch 7:15, 16. (6) The wife of Jehiel, the founder of Gibeon, 1 Ch 8:29; 9:35. (7) The father of Hanan, who was one of David's warriors, 1 Ch 11:43. (8) The father of Shephatiah, a ruler of the Simeonites, 1 Ch 27:16. (9) A small district of Syria on the northeast of Palestine, 2 S 10:6; 1 Ch 19:6, 7. (10) A wife of King David and the mother of Absalom, 2 S 3:3, Maacah; 1 Ch 3:2. (11) Mother of King Asa, 1 K 15:13; 2 Ch 15:16.

40. **arose.** Pr *15:27. Lk *12:15. 1 T +*6:10.

42. **Did I not.** ver. 36-38. Ps 15:4. Lk 19:22. **on the day.** ſ171, Ge +2:17. **surely die.** ſ147B, Ge +2:16. **and thou saidst.** Lk 15:22.

43. **Why.** 2 S 21:2. Ezk 17:18, 19. **commandment.** 2 Ch 30:12. Ec 8:2. Ro 13:5.

44. **Thou knowest.** 2 S 16:5-13. Jn 8:9. Ro 2:15. 1 J 3:20. **return.** See on ver. 32, 33. Ps 7:16. Pr 5:22. Ezk 17:19. Ho 4:9mg.

45. **blessed.** Ps 21:6. 72:17. **the throne.** See on ver. 24, 33, 34. Pr *25:5. Is 9:6, 7. **for ever.** Heb. *olam*, Ex +12:24.

46. **the kingdom.** ver. 12, 45. 2 Ch 1:1. Pr 29:4.

1 KINGS 3

Solomon marries Pharaoh's daughter, 1. The people sacrifice in high places, 2, 3. Solomon offers a thousand burnt-offerings at Gibeon, 4. God appears to him in a dream; and he asks and obtains from him wisdom, together with riches and honor, 5-15. His sagacious decision of a perplexing cause between two harlots renders him celebrated for wisdom, 16-28.

1. A.M. 2990. B.C. 1014. An. Ex. Is. 477. **affinity.** 2 Ch 18:1. Ezr 9:14. **and took.** 1 K 7:8. 9:24. 11:1. **the city.** 2 S 5:7. 1 Ch 11:7. **his own.** 1 K 7:1-12. **the house.** 1 K ch. 6. 7:13-51. 2 Ch ch. 2-4. Ezr 5:11. **the wall.** 1 K 9:15-19.

2. **the people.** It was not right to offer sacrifices in any place but where the tabernacle and ark were; and wherever they were, whether on a high place or plain, sacrifices might be lawfully offered, previously to the building of the temple. The tabernacle was now at Gibeon (2 Ch 1:3), which was therefore called the great high place; whither we find Solomon, without censure, repaired to sacrifice. 1 K 22:43. Le 17:3-6. 26:30. Dt *12:2-5. 2 Ch 33:17. **was no.** 1 K 5:3. 1 Ch 17:4-6. 28:3-6. Ac 7:47-49.

3. **loved.** Dt 6:5. 10:12. 30:6, 16, 20. 2 S 12:24, 25. Ps 31:23. Mt 22:36, 37. Mk 12:29, 30. Ro *8:28. 13:10. 1 C 8:3. 2 C 5:14. Ja 1:12. 2:5. 1 J 4:19, 20. 5:2, 3. **walking.** See on ver. 6, 14. 1 K 2:3, 4. 11:34. 15:3. 1 Ch 28:8, 9. 2 Ch 17:3-5. Jn 14:15, 21. **only he.** 1 K 15:14. 22:43. 2 K 12:3. 14:4. 15:4, 35. 18:4, 22.

4. **Gibeon.** 1 K 9:2. Jsh 9:3. 10:2. 1 Ch 16:39. 21:29. 2 Ch 1:3, 7, etc. **a thousand.** 1 K 8:63. 2 Ch 1:6. 7:5. 29:32-35. 30:24. Is 40:16. Mi 6:6, 7.

5. **the Lord.** 1 K 9:2. **in a dream.** Ge 28:12, 13. Nu *12:6. Jb 33:14, 15. Mt 1:20. 2:13, 19. **Ask what.** 2 Ch 1:7-12. Mt *7:7, 8. Mk 10:36-38, 51. *11:24. Lk *11:9. Jn 14:13, 14. *15:16. *16:23, 24. Ja √1:5, 6. 1 J *5:14, 15.

6. **thy servant.** Nu 12:7. 2 S 7:5. **great.** 2 S 7:8-12. 12:7, 8. 22:47-51. 1 Ch 29:12-14. Ps 78:70-72. **mercy.** *or,* bounty. Ps 13:6. 116:7. 119:17. 2 C 9:5, 11. **according.** 1 K 2:4. 9:4. 15:5. 2 K 20:3. Ps 15:2. 18:20-24. **that.** See on 1 K 1:48.

7. **thou hast.** Da 2:21. 4:25, 32. 5:18, 21. **a little.** Ex 4:10. 1 Ch 29:1. 2 Ch 1:8, 9. Jb 32:6-8. Ec 10:16. Je 1:6. Mt 18:3, 4. **know not.** Ps 32:8. **to go.** Nu 27:15-17. Dt 31:2. 1 S 18:16. 2 S 5:2. Ps 121:8. Jn 10:3, 4, 9.

8. **thy people.** Ex 19:5, 6. Dt 7:6-8. 1 S 12:22. Ps 78:71. **cannot.** Ge 13:16. 15:5. 22:17. 1 Ch 21:2, 5, 6. 27:23, 24.

9. **Give therefore.** 1 Ch 22:12. 29:19. 2 Ch 1:10. Ps 119:34, 73, 144. Pr 2:3-9. 3:13-18. 16:16. Ja *1:5. 3:17. **understanding.** Heb. hearing. T#1551. Pr 20:12. **to judge.** ver. 28. Ps 72:1, 2. Pr 14:8. Ec 7:11, 19.

9:15-18. Jn 5:30. **discern.** 2 S 14:17. Is 11:2-4. 1 C *2:14, 15. Ep 5:17. Ph *1:10g. He +*5:14. **who is able.** Ex 3:11, 12. 4:10-13. Je 1:6. Mt 3:11, 14. 2 C 2:16. 3:5.

10. **pleased.** Pr 15:8.

11. **hast not.** Ps 4:6. Pr 16:31. Mt 20:21, 22. Ro 8:26. Ja *4:2, 3. **long life.** Heb. many days. 2 Ch 1:11. **the life.** Heb. *nephesh*, soul, Ge +44:30. **discern.** Heb. hear. ver. 9mg.

12. **I have done.** Ps 10:17. Pr 2:1-9. Is *65:24. Ro *8:26, 27. 1 J 5:14, 15. **I have given.** ver. 28. 1 K 2:6, 9. 4:29-34. 5:12. 10:3-8, 23, 24. 1 Ch 29:25. 2 Ch 1:11, 12. 2:12. 9:5-8, 22. Ec 1:13, 16. 2:9. Lk *21:15. **neither.** Mt *12:42. Col *2:3. **thee.** ∫6312, Jsh +3:3. Supply ellipsis from succeeding clause (ver. 13), "among the kings." 1 K 10:23.

13. **And I.** Ps *84:11, 12. Mt *6:33. Ro *8:32. 1 C 3:22, 23. Ep 3:20. **riches.** 1 K 4:21-24. 10:23-29. Pr *3:13, 16. **shall not be.** *or,* hath not been.

14. **if thou.** 1 K 2:3, 4. 1 Ch 22:12, 13. 28:9. 2 Ch 7:17-19. Ps 132:12. Zc 3:7. **as thy.** See on ver. 3. 1 K 9:4, 5. 15:5. 2 Ch 17:3, 4. 29:2. 34:2. Jn +*17:6. Ac 13:22. **I will lengthen.** Dt +5:16. 25:15. Ps 21:4. *91:14, 16. Pr 3:2, 16. 1 T +*4:8.

15. **awoke.** Ge 41:7. Je 31:26. **before.** 2 S 6:17. 1 Ch 16:1, 2. **burnt offerings.** Le +*23:12. **peace offerings.** 1 K 8:63, 65. Le ch. 3. 7:11-19. +*23:19. 2 S 6:18, 19. 2 Ch 7:5, 7-10. 30:22-26. **a feast.** Ge 31:54. 40:20. Est 1:3. Da 5:1. Mk 6:21.

16. **two women.** Le 19:29. Dt 23:17. Jsh 2:1. **harlots.** The word *zanoth*, rendered *harlots*, is here translated by the Targumist, the best judge in this case, *pundekon*, "tavern-keepers;" see on Jsh 2:1n. Jg 11:1n. Compare Ge 38:21n. Had these women been harlots, it is not likely that they would have dared to appear before Solomon; nor is it likely that such persons would have been permitted in the reign of David. Their *husbands* might at this time have been following their necessary occupations in distant parts. **stood.** Ex 18:13, 16. Nu 27:2.

17. **O my Lord.** Ge 43:20. Ro 13:7.

20. **midnight.** Jb 24:13-17. Ps 139:11. Mt 13:25. Jn *3:20. **took.** ver. 21.

21. **give.** Ge 21:7. 1 S 1:23. La 4:3, 4.

22. **Nay.** ver. 23, 24. **spake.** ∫63A4. Ellipsis (Absolute: of connected words) B20. lit. "they talked (very much) before the king." It is not to be supposed that two women under these exciting circumstances would confine themselves to the few concise words of this verse. For other instances of this figure see 2 K 6:25. 25:3. Ps 119:56. Je 51:31. Ezk (13:18). Mt 19:17. Mk 6:14-16. Lk 14:18. Jn 3:13. Ac (10:36). 18:22. Ro (2:27). 11:11. 12:19. 14:2. 1 C 9:9. EWB in B gives further instances of possible ellipsis of this class for the following passages, which have not been referenced in the *Treasury*: Ro 14:5, 20, 23. 1 C 7:6. 9:9, 10. 12:6. 14:27. 15:28. 2 C 1:6. 5:5. Ga 5:10. Ep 1:23. Ph 1:18. Col 3:11. 1 Th 3:7. 4:1. He 13:25. 1 J 5:15, 19.

25. **Divide.** This was apparently a very strange decision; but Solomon saw that the only way to discover the real mother was by the affection and tenderness she would necessarily show to her offspring. The plan was tried, and succeeded; and it was a proof of his sound judgment, penetration, and acquaintance with the human heart, or rather, of his extraordinary and supernatural wisdom. See ver. 28. The two following

instances are in some faint manner to be compared to Solomon's decision, inasmuch as they also work upon the human sympathies. Suetonius, in his Life of the emperor Claudian (c. xv.), tells us, that this emperor discovered a woman to be the real mother of a young man, whom she refused to acknowledge, by commanding her to marry him, the proofs being doubtful on both sides; for, rather than commit incest, she confessed the truth. Diodorus Siculus also informs us, that Ariopharnes, king of Thrace, being appointed to decide between three young men, each of whom professed to be the son of the deceased king of the Cimmerians, and claimed the succession, discovered the real son by ordering each to shoot an arrow into the dead body of the king: two of them did this without hesitation; but the real son of the deceased monarch refused. Pr 25:8.

26. **her bowels**. ♪121G1, Is +63:15. Ge 43:30. Is *49:15. Je 31:20. Ho 11:8. Ph 1:8. 2:1. 1 J *3:17. **yearned**. Heb. were hot. Ps *39:3. **give her**. Ro 1:31. 2 T 3:3.

28. **feared**. Ex 14:31. Jsh 4:14. 1 S *12:18. 1 Ch 29:24. Pr *24:21. **saw**. Ge 30:27. **the wisdom**. ver. 9-12. Ezr *7:25. Ec *7:19. Da 2:21, 47. 5:11. 1 C 1:24, *30. Col 2:3. **in him**. Heb. in the midst of him. ♪144A6, Ge +45:6. **to do**. Ps *72:2, 4.

1 KINGS 4

Solomon's princes, 1-6. Twelve officers who provided for his household, each in his month, 7-19. The prosperity and grandeur of his kingdom, 20-25. His horses and chariots, 26-28. His wisdom and reputation, 29-34.

1. **over all Israel**. 1 K 11:13, 35, 36. 12:19, 20. 2 S 5:5. 1 Ch 12:38. 2 Ch 9:30. Ec 1:12.

2. **the princes**. That is, great, chief, or principal men; for none of them were princes in the common acceptation of the word. Ex +*18:21. 2 S 8:15-18. 20:23-26. 1 C 12:28. **Azariah**. 1 Ch 6:8-10. 27:17. **priest**. *or,* chief officer. Ge 41:45. 1 Ch 6:10.

3. **Elihoreph**. i.e. *God of my maturity; God of autumn,* ✻S#456h. **Shisha**. i.e. *whiteness,* ✻S#7894h, only here. 2 S 8:17, Seraiah. 20:25, Sheva. 1 Ch 18:16, Shavsha. **scribes**. *or,* secretaries. 2 S 8:17mg. 20:25. 2 K 12:10mg. 18:18mg. Est 3:12mg. **recorder**. *or,* remembrancer. 2 S 8:16mg. 20:24mg. 1 Ch 18:15mg. Is 62:6mg.

4. **Benaiah**. See on 1 K 2:35. **Zadok**. See on 1 K 2:26, 27, 35.

5. **son of Nathan**. 1 K 1:10, etc. 2 S 7:2. 12:1-15, 25. **the officers**. ver. 7. **Zabud**. i.e. *endowed,* ✻S#2071h. **the principal**. 2 S 8:18. 20:26. **the king's**. 2 S 15:37. 16:16. 19:37, 38. 1 Ch 27:33. Pr 22:11. Lk 22:29. Jn 13:23. 15:14, 15. Ja 2:23.

6. **Ahishar**. i.e. *brother of a singer* or *of the upright,* ✻S#301h. **household**. 2 S 20:24. **Adoniram**. i.e. *Lord of height,* ✻S#141h. 1 K 5:14. ◐12:18. 2 S 20:24, Adoram. 2 Ch 10:18, Hadoram. **Abda**. i.e. *servant.* **tribute**. *or,* levy. 1 K 5:13, 14. 9:15, 21.

7. **officers**. ver. 5, 27. 1 K 5:16. 9:23. 2 Ch 8:10. These are doubtless to be considered as general receivers; for, as Sir John Chardin observes, "the revenues of the princes of the East are paid in the fruits and productions of the earth: there are no other taxes on

the peasants." **each man**. 1 Ch 27:1-15.

8. **The son of Hur**. *or,* Ben-hur. i.e. *son of whiteness.* Jg 17:1. 19:1.

9. **The son of Dekar**. *or,* Ben-dekar. i.e. *son of piercing through,* ✻S#1857h. **Makaz**. i.e. *extremity; end,* ✻S#4739h. **Shaalbim**. Jsh 19:42, Shaalabbin. **Beth-shemesh**. See on 1 S 6:12, 20. **Elon-beth-hanan**. i.e. *oak of the house of grace,* ✻S#358h. Jsh ◐19:43.

10. **The son of Hesed**. *or,* Ben-hesed. i.e. *son of kindness,* ✻S#2618h. **Aruboth**. i.e. *windows,* ✻S#700h. **Sochoh**. i.e. *his branch; to entwine,* ✻S#7755h. See on Jsh 15:35, 48. 1 S 17:1, 1. **Hepher**. Jsh 12:17. 17:2.

11. **The son of Abinadab**. *or,* Ben-abinadab. **Dor**. Jsh 12:23. 17:11. Jg 1:27. **Taphath**. i.e. *a drop* or *dropping,* ✻S#2955h.

12. **Baana**. i.e. *son of affliction,* ✻S#1195h. ver. 16. Ne 3:4. (1) A provider for Solomon, 1 K 4:12. (2) Another provider for Solomon, 1 K 4:16. (3) Father of Zadok, Ne 3:4. **Taanach**. See on Jsh 17:11. Jg 5:19. **Megiddo**. Jsh +17:11. 2 K 23:29, 30. Re 16:16. **Beth-shean**. 1 S 31:10, 12. **Zartanah**. i.e. *perplexity; their distress,* ✻S#6891h. 1 K 7:46, Zarthan. Jsh 3:16, Zaretan. But Young notes "not that referred to in Jsh 3:16." **Jezreel**. 1 K 18:46. **Abel-meholah**. 1 K 19:16. Jg 7:22. **Jokneam**. Jsh 19:11. 1 Ch 6:68.

13. **The son of Geber**. *or,* Ben-geber. i.e. *the son of a mighty one.* **Ramoth-gilead**. i.e. *perpetual spring,* ✻S#7433h. 1 K 22:4, 6, 12, 15, 20, 29. Dt 4:43. Jsh *20:8. 21:38. 2 K 8:28. 9:1, 4, 14. 2 Ch 18:2, 3, 5, 11, 14, 19, 28. 22:5. **the towns**. Nu 32:41. Dt 3:14. **Argob**. i.e. *stony; lion's den; clod heap; cursed heap,* ✻S#709h. Dt 3:4, 8, 13, 14. 2 K 15:25. Ps 22:12. 68:15. **Bashan**. i.e. *the soft, sandy soil.* Nu +21:33. 32:33. Jsh 12:4n. Ps 22:12. **threescore great cities**. These were fortified cities; their gates and bars being covered with plates of brass. Such were the gates in Priam's palace: "Pyrrhus himself in the front, snatching up a battle-axe, beats through the stubborn gates, and labors to tear the brazen posts from the hinges" (Virgil, Aen. l. II. v. 479). **with walls**. Dt 3:4. 2 Ch 8:5. **brasen bars**. Dt 3:5. 1 S 23:7. 2 Ch 8:5. 14:7.

14. **Ahinadab**. i.e. *brother of liberality,* ✻S#292h. **Mahanaim**. *or,* to Mahanaim. 1 K 2:8. Ge 32:2. Jsh 13:26, 30. 21:38. 2 S 2:8, 12, 29. 17:24, 27. 19:32. 1 Ch 6:80.

15. **Ahimaaz**. 2 S 15:27. **Naphtali**. Jsh 19:32-39. **Basmath**. i.e. *spicy,* S#1315h. Ge +36:3, Bashemath. **the daughter**. ver. 11. 1 S 18:18.

16. **Hushai**. 2 S 15:32, 37. **Asher**. Jsh 19:24-31. **Aloth**. i.e. *ascents,* ✻S#1175h. Jsh 15:24.

17. **Paruah**. i.e. *flourishing,* ✻S#6515h. **Issachar**. Jsh 19:17-23.

18. **Shimei**. 1 K 1:8. Zc 12:13. **Elah**. i.e. *a terebinth.* **Benjamin**. Jsh 18:20-28.

19. **Geber**. i.e. *strong; a valiant man,* ✻S#1398h. (1) Father of one of Solomon's officers or purveyors, 1 K 4:13. (2) An officer or purveyor of Solomon, 1 K 4:19. **Uri**. i.e. *my light.* Probably father of the officer mentioned in ver. 13. **the country of Sihon**. Nu 21:21-35. Dt 2:26-37. 3:1-17. Jsh 13:9-12. **Bashan**. ver. +13.

20. **many**. Zc 10:8. **as the sand**. ♪102B, ♪138B, *+13:16. 1 K 3:8. Ge 13:16. 15:5. *22:17. Pr 14:28. **eating**. 1 S 30:16. 1 Ch 12:39. Jb 1:18. Ps 72:3-7. Ec 2:24. Is 22:13. Mi 4:4. Zc 3:10. 9:15. Ac 2:46.

21. **Solomon reigned**. ver. 24. Ge 15:18. Ex 23:31. Dt 11:24. Jsh 1:4. √21:43n. 2 Ch 9:26, etc. Ezr 4:20. Ps 72:8-11. **over all kingdoms**. Referring to this passage, Thomas Hartwell Horne states, "In the reign of (Solomon) was realized the Abrahamic covenant in its full extent" (*Introduction*, vol. 2, p. 14 of 2 vol. edition; vol. 3, p. 5 of the 5 vol. edition). George N. H. Peters answers, "Some indeed (Horne's *Intro*. vol. 2, p. 12) think that in David's and Solomon's reign this was the extent, but others more accurately narrow their dominion in actual possession. Whatever may be the fact in reference to past fulfillment, three things are very evident, (a) that a portion was not held by the Jews, excepting by a precarious tributary arrangement; (b) that it was only thus possessed for a short time, and hence is in no way commensurate with the promise; (c) that the predictions relating to the future take it as a matter of course that at the future restoration this will be effected, seeing that all the covenant promises are *then* to be realized" (*Theocratic Kingdom*, vol. 2, p. 144). See related notes (Jsh 21:43n. Je 33:21n. Ac 7:5n). Ge 15:18. Ex 23:31. Dt 11:24. Jsh 1:3, 4. Is +*26:15. Je +7:7. Ac +*3:19-21. He √11:13, 39. **brought**. 1 S 10:27. 2 K 17:3. 2 Ch 17:5. 32:23. Ps 68:29. 72:10, 11. 76:11.

22. **provision**. Heb. bread. **measures**. Heb. *cors*. 1 K 5:11. 2 Ch 2:10. 27:5. Ezk *45:14. A dry and liquid measure containing ten ephahs or baths (Young).

23. **Ten fat**. Ne 5:17, 18. **harts**. Dr. Shaw understands *ayil* as the name of the *genus*, including all the species of the *deer* kind, whether they are distinguished by round horns, as the stag, or by flat ones, as the fallow deer, or by the smallness of the branches, as the roe. **roebucks**. Dt 15:22. *Tzevee*, in Arabic *zaby*, Chaldee and Syriac *tavya*, denotes the *gazelle* or *antelope*, so called from its *stately beauty*, as the word imports. In size it is smaller than the roe, of an elegant form, and its motions are light and graceful. It bounds seemingly without effort, and runs with such swiftness that few creatures can exceed it (2 S 2:18). Its fine eyes are so much celebrated as even to become a proverb; and its flesh is much esteemed for food among eastern nations, having a sweet, musky taste, which is highly agreeable to their palates (1 K 4:23). If to these circumstances we add, that they are gregarious, and common all over the East, whereas the *roe* is either not known at all, or else very rare in these countries, little doubt can remain that the *gazelle* and not the *roe* is intended by the original word. **fallow-deer**. *Yachmur*, rendered *bubalus* by the Vulgate, probably the *buffalo*; and though "the flesh of a buffalo does not seem so well tasted as beef, being harder and more coarse," yet in our times, "persons of distinction, as well as the common people, and even the European merchants, eat a good deal of it, in the countries where that animal abounds" (Niebuhr, Descrip. de l'Arab. p. 146).

24. **the river**. Ge 15:18. Jsh 1:4. Is +*27:12. **Tiphsah**. i.e. a *passage over*, as in 2 K 15:16, on the western bank of the Euphrates, mentioned by Xenophon, Arrian, Strabo (Young). **Azzah**. Ge 10:19. Jg 16:1, Gaza. **all the kings**. See on ver. 21. Ps 68:29. 72:8, 10, 11. **had peace**. 1 K 5:4. 1 Ch 22:9. Ps 72:3, 7. Is 9:7. Lk 2:14. He 7:1, 2.

25. **safely**. Heb. confidently. Is 60:18. Je 23:5, 6.

33:15, 16. Ezk *28:26mg. +*38:11mg. **every man**. 2 K 18:31. Mi 4:4. Zc 3:10. **from Dan**. Jg 20:1. 2 S 17:11. 24:15.

26. **forty thousand**. 1 K 10:25, 26. Dt 17:16. 2 S 8:4. 2 Ch 1:14. 9:25. Ps 20:7. In 2 Ch 9:25 it is four thousand.

27. **those officers**. ver. 7-19. **lacked nothing**. Ne 9:21. Lk 22:35.

28. **dromedaries**. or, mules, or swift beasts. Est 8:10, 14. Mi 1:13.

29. **God**. See on 1 K 3:12, 28. 10:23, 24. 2 Ch 1:10-12. Ps 119:34. Pr 2:6. Ec 1:16. 2:26. Ja *1:5, 17. 3:17. **largeness**. Is 60:5. **as the sand**. ʃ102B, ʃ138B, Ge +13:16. See on ver. 20. Ge 41:49. Jg 7:12. Je 33:22. Hab 1:9.

30. **the children**. Ge 25:6. Jb *1:3. Da 1:20. 4:7. *5:11, 12. Mt 2:*1, 16. **east**. ʃ171.O.6. Synecdoche of the Whole B639. The *east* is put for Persia, Media, and other countries east of Jerusalem. For other instances of this figure see Is 2:6. Ezk 25:4. Mt 2:1. **the wisdom of Egypt**. Is 19:11, 12. Ac *7:22.

31. **wiser**. See on 1 K 3:12. Mt 12:42. Lk 11:31. Col 2:3. **Ethan**. 1 Ch 15:19. Ps 89, title. **Ezrahite**. i.e. *sprung up*, ✳S#250h. Ps 88, title. 89, title. **Heman**. 1 Ch 2:6. 6:33. 15:17. 16:41, 42. 25:1. Ps 88, title. **Chalcol**. i.e. *nourished; comprehended*, ✳S#3633h. 1 Ch 2:6. **Darda**. i.e. *pearl of knowledge; bearer*, ✳S#1862h. 1 Ch 2:6, Dara. **Mahol**. i.e. *a dance*, ✳S#4235h. 1 Ch 2:6, Zerah. **his fame**. 1 K 5:7. 10:1, 6. 2 Ch 9:23. Mt 4:24.

32. **he spake**. Pr ch. 1, etc. Ec 12:9. Mt 13:35. **proverbs**. or, similes. Nu +*21:27. Pr 1:1, 6. 10:1. 25:1. Ec 12:9. **songs**. SS 1:1, etc. Two of them are Ps 72 and 127 (Young).

33. **the cedar tree**. the word *airez*, whence the Chaldee and Syriac *arzo*, and the Arabic and Ethiopic *arz*, and the Spanish *alerze*, unquestionably denotes the *cedar*; it is thus rendered by the LXX. and other versions, *kedros*, and by the Vulgate *cedrus*; and the inhabitants of mount Lebanon still call it *ars*. The cedar is a large and noble evergreen tree, and grows on the most elevated part of the mountain, is taller than the pine, and so thick that five men together could scarcely fathom one. It shoots out its branches at ten or twelve feet from the ground; they are large and distant from each other, and are perpetually green. The wood is of a brown color, very solid and incorruptible, if preserved from wet. The tree bears a small cone like that of the pine. Nu 24:6. 2 K 19:23. Ps 92:12. **the hyssop**. Ex 12:22. Nu 19:18. Ps 51:7. He 9:19. **of beasts**. See on Ge 1:20-25.

34. **there came**. 1 K *10:1. 2 Ch *9:1, 23. Is 2:2. Zc *8:23.

1 KINGS 5

Hiram, king of Tyre, sends to congratulate Solomon; who informs him that he intends to build a temple, and desires him to furnish the timber, 1-6. Hiram blesses God for Solomon's wisdom, and engages for the timber, requiring in return food for his household, 7-9. The mutual good offices between Hiram and Solomon, 10-12. The number of Solomon's workmen and laborers, 13-18.

1. A.M. 2990. B.C. 1014. An. Ex. Is. 477. **Hiram**. ver. 10, 13. 1 K 9:12-14. 2 Ch 2:3, Huram. **sent**. 2 S

8:10. 10:1, 2. Ps 45:12. **for Hiram**. 2 S 5:11. 1 Ch 14:1. Pr *27:10. Am 1:9.

2. **Solomon sent**. 2 Ch 2:3.

3. **could not**. 2 S 7:5-11. 1 Ch 22:4-6. 2 Ch 6:6-8. **the wars**. 1 Ch 22:8. 28:3. 2 Ch 2:3. **put**. Jsh 10:24. Ps 8:6. 110:1. Ml 4:3. 1 C 15:25. Ep 1:22.

4. **hath given**. See on 1 K 4:24. 1 Ch 22:9. Ps 72:7. Is 9:7. Ac 9:31.

5. **behold**. 2 Ch 2:1-4, etc. **purpose**. Heb. say. 2 Ch 2:1. **as the Lord**. 2 S *7:12, 13. 1 Ch 17:12. 22:10. 28:6, 10. Zc *6:12, 13.

6. **cedar trees**. 1 K 6:9, 10, 16, 20. 2 Ch 2:8, 10, 16. Ps 29:5. **will I give hire**. Ro 12:17. Ph 4:8. **appoint**. Heb. say. 1 K 11:18. **that there is not**. 1 C 12:14-21. Ep 4:7. **Sidonians**. Ge 10:15. Ezr 3:7. 1 Ch 22:4.

7. **Blessed**. 1 K 10:9. 2 Ch 2:11, 12. 9:7, 8. Ps 122:6, 7. 137:6. **which hath**. 1 K 1:48. Ge 33:5. Is 8:18. 9:6. **a wise son**. See on 1 K 3:9. 2 Ch 2:11. Pr 10:1. 13:1. 15:20. 23:24.

8. **considered**. Heb. heard. **timber of fir**. 1 K 6:15, 34. 2 S 6:5. 2 Ch 3:5.

9. **Lebanon**. Dt 3:25. **and I will**. 2 Ch 2:16. **appoint**. Heb. send. **in giving food**. 2 Ch 2:15. Ezr 3:7. Ezk 27:17. Ac *12:20.

10. **measures**. Heb. *cors*. 1 K +4:22mg. 2 Ch 2:10. **twenty measures**. "Twenty thousand *baths* of oil" are mentioned in Chronicles; and the Syriac, Arabic, and Septuagint also have here "twenty thousand measures." But as *barley* and wine are also spoken of *there*, it is probable, that the *wheat* mentioned *here*, and the small quantity of fine *oil*, were intended for the use of Hiram's own family, while that in Chronicles was for his workmen.

12. **as he promised him**. 1 K 3:12. 4:29. 2 Ch 1:12. He 10:23. Ja *1:5. **they two**. 1 K 15:19. Ge 21:32. Am 1:9.

13. **levy**. Heb. tribute *of men*. 1 K 4:6. **the levy**. 1 K 9:15.

14. **a month**. 1 K 4:7-19. 1 Ch 27:1-15. **Adoniram**. See on 1 K 4:6.

15. **threescore and ten thousand**. These were all *strangers*, or *proselytes*, dwelling among the Israelites, as we learn from the parallel place in 2 Chronicles. 1 K 9:20-22. 2 Ch 2:17, 18. 8:7-9. Ezr 2:58. Ne 7:57, 60.

16. **three thousand three hundred**. In the parallel passage of Chronicles, it is "three thousand *six* hundred," which is also the reading of the Septuagint here. 1 K 9:23. 2 Ch 2:2.

17. **costly stones**. 1 K 6:7. 7:9. 1 Ch 22:2. Ps 144:12. Is 28:16. 1 C 3:11, 12. 1 P 2:6, 7. Re 21:14-21.

18. **the stone-squarers**. *or*, Giblites. Jsh 13:5. Ps 83:7. Ezk 27:9.

1 KINGS 6

The building of the temple is begun, 1. The dimensions of the house, and its porch, 2, 3. The windows, 4. The chambers, 5-10. The promise of God concerning the temple, 11-13. Its walls, ceiling, floor, and ornaments, 14-18. The Oracle and Cherubim, 19-30. The doors of the Oracle, and of the house, 31-35. The inner court, 36. The time in which the whole was completed, 37, 38.

1. A.M. 2993. B.C. 1011. An. Ex. Is. 480. **And it**

came. Jg 11:26. 2 Ch 3:1, 2. **in the month Zif**. i.e. *brightness, beauty*, ✱S#2099h. ver. 37. Nu 1:1. **began**. Heb. built. Ac 7:47. **build**. 1 Ch 29:19. Zc 6:12, 13, 15. Jn √2:19-21. 1 C 6:19. 2 C 6:16. Ep 2:20-22. Col *2:7. He 3:6. 9:11. 11:10. 1 P 2:5.

2. **the house**. Ezk ch. 40. 41. **the length**. According to Bp. Cumberland's estimation of the cubit, its length was 36 yds. 1 ft. 5.28 inch; its breadth, 12 yds. 5.76 inch; and its height, 18 yds. 8.64 inch. This constituted what is properly called the temple; but, besides this, there were the courts and colonnades, where the people might assemble to perform their devotions, without being exposed to the open air. **threescore**. Ezr 6:3, 4. Ezk 41:1, etc. Re 21:16, 17.

3. **the porch**. 1 Ch 28:11. 2 Ch 3:3, 4. Ezk 41:15. Mt 4:5. Jn 10:23. Ac 3:10, 11.

4. **windows of narrow lights**. *or*, windows broad within, and narrow without; *or*, skewed and closed. See on 1 K 6:4. SS 2:9. Ezk 40:16. 41:16, 26.

5. **against**. *or*, upon, *or* joining to. **built**. 1 Ch 9:26. 23:28. 28:11. 2 Ch 31:11. Ne 10:37. 12:44. 13:5-9. SS 1:4. Je 35:4. Ezk 40:44. 41:5-11. 42:3-12. **chambers**. Heb. floors. These appear to have been what we should now call corridors or galleries; in which were apartments for the use of the priests. They consisted of three stories, and increased one cubit in breadth in every story, the wall of the temple being two cubits thicker at the bottom than at the top; and where the wall diminished, a rest was thus formed for the beams of the chambers to lodge upon. **oracle**. ver. 16n, 19-21, 31. Ex 25:22. Le 16:2. Nu 7:89. 2 Ch 4:20. 5:7, 9. Ps 28:2. **chambers**. Heb. ribs. ver. 8. 1 K 7:3. Ezk 41:5-9, 11, 26.

6. **narrowed rests**. *or*, narrowings, *or* rebatements. **the beams**. Ezk 41:6.

7. **built of stone**. 1 K 5:17, 18. Dt 27:5, 6. Pr 24:27. Ro 9:23. 2 C 5:5. Col 1:12. 1 P 2:5. **neither hammer**. Is 42:2. Ac 9:31. Ja 1:20. 3:17, 18.

8. **side**. Heb. shoulder. **went up**. Ezk 41:6, 7.

9. **he built**. ver. 14, 38. **with beams and boards of cedar**. *or*, the vault beams and the ceilings with cedar.

12. **if thou wilt**. 1 K 2:3, 4. 3:14. 8:25. 9:3-6. Ge +4:7. 1 S 12:14, 15. *13:13, 14. 1 Ch 28:9. 2 Ch 7:17, 18. Ps 132:12. Zc 3:7. Col 1:23. **then will I perform**. 2 S *7:13. 1 Ch 22:10.

13. **I will dwell**. 1 K 8:27. Ex 25:8. Le 26:11. Ps 68:18. 132:12-14. Is 57:15. Ezk 37:26-28. 2 C 6:16. Re 21:3. **will not forsake**. See on Dt 31:6, 8. 1 S 12:22. 1 Ch 28:9, 20. He +*13:5.

14. A.M. 2993-3000. B.C. 1011-1004. **Solomon built**. ver. 9, 38. Ac 7:47, 48.

15. **he built**. That is, he lined or wainscoted the walls with cedar, the floor being covered with planks of fir: the marginal reading in this verse is preferable, as it removes every difficulty and obscurity. **both the floors of the house, and the walls**. *or*, from the floor of the house, unto the walls, etc. and so ver. 16.

16. **built them**. ver. 5, 19, 20. 1 K 8:6. Ex 25:21, 22. 26:23. Le 16:2. 2 Ch 3:8. Ezk 45:3. He 9:3, 8, 11, 24. **the oracle**. The *oracle* was the *sanctuary*, or *holy of holies*, in which there was nothing but the ark of the covenant, including the tables of the law, and into which the high priest alone was to enter but once a year. ver. +5. 2 Ch +3:16.

18. **knops**. *or*, gourds. *Pekaim*, "artificial knops," in the shape of "colocynths," or "wild gourds," as the

word denotes (See Note on 2 K 4:39); the full-blown flowers of which must have been very ornamental. **open flowers**. *or*, openings of flowers. **no stone**. *ſ*144D, Ge +40:23. 1 P=2:5.

19. **the oracle**. See on ver. 5, 16. 2 Ch 4:20. Ps 28:2. **to set**. 1 K 8:6-10. Ex 40:20, 21. 2 Ch 5:7. He 9:3, 4.

20. **twenty cubits**. See on ver. 2, 3. **pure**. Heb. shut up. ver. 21. 1 K 7:49, 50. 10:21. 2 Ch 4:20, 22. 9:20. **the altar**. ver. 22. 1 K 7:48. Ex 30:1-3.

21. **overlaid**. Ex 26:29, 32. 36:34. 2 Ch 3:7-9. **by the chains**. ver. 5. Ex 26:32, 33. 2 Ch 3:14-16.

22. **the whole house**. It is impossible to calculate this expense, or the quantity of gold employed in this sacred building; but both must have been immense. **also**. See on ver. 20. Ex 30:1, 3, 5, 6. 36:34. 2 Ch 3:7, etc. **the whole altar**. This was the altar of incense without the vail, in the *holy place*, which was twice the length of the *most holy place*.

23. **two cherubims**. These were distinct from, and much larger than those which covered the mercy seat. Ge 3:24. Ex 25:18-22. 37:7-9. 2 Ch 3:10-13. Ps 18:10. 80:1. Is 37:16. Ezk 10:2, etc. He 1:14. 1 P 1:12. **olive trees**. *or*, oily trees. Heb. trees of oil. ver. 31-33. Ne 8:15. Is *41:19.

27. **they stretched forth the wings of the cherubims**. *or*, the cherubims stretched forth their wings. Ge 3:24. Ex 25:18, 20. 37:9. 2 Ch 3:11. 5:8. Ezk 10:2-5.

29. **carved figures**. Ex 36:8. 2 Ch 3:14. 4:2-5. Ps 103:20. 148:2. Lk 2:13, 14. Ep 3:10. Re 5:11-14. **palm trees**. *Tamar*, in Ethiopic, *tamart*, the *palm tree*, is so called, says Parkhurst, from its *straight*, *upright* growth, for which it seems more remarkable than any other tree; and it sometimes rises to the height of more than 100 feet. The trunk is remarkably straight and lofty; and it is crowned at the top with a large tuft of spiring leaves, about four feet long, which never fall off, but always continue in the same flourishing verdure. The stalks are generally full of rugged knots, which are vestiges of decayed leaves: for the trunk of the tree is not solid, but its center is filled with pith, round which is a tough bark full of strong fibers when young, which when the tree becomes old, hardens and becomes ligneous. To this bark the leaves are closely joined, which in the center rise erect, but after they are advanced above the vagina which surrounds them, they expand very wide on every side of the stem, and as the older leaves decay, the stalk advances in height. The leaves, when the tree has grown to a size for bearing fruit, are six or eight feet long, and very broad when expanded. The fruit, called the *date*, grows below the leaves in clusters. Ps 92:12-15. Re 7:9. **open flowers**. Heb. openings of flowers. ver. 18, 32.

30. **the floor**. Is 54:11, 12. 60:17. Re 20:18-21. 21:18.

31. **doors**. Jn *10:9. 14:1, √6. Ep 2:18. He 10:19, 20. **a fifth part**. *or*, five square.

32. **two doors**. *or*, leaves of the doors. Ge +19:6n. Ezk 41:23-25. **olive tree**. Ge 8:11. Lk 3:22. **open flowers**. Heb. openings of flowers. ver. 18, 29.

33. **a fourth part**. *or*, four square.

34. **fir tree**. 1 K 5:8. **the two leaves**. Ezk 41:23-25.

36. **the inner**. Ex 27:9-19. 38:9-20. 2 Ch 4:9. 7:7. Re 11:2.

37. **the fourth year**. ver. 1. 2 Ch 3:2. Among chro-nologists there is a great diversity of opinion respecting the time of the building of the temple. The Septuagint has 440 years; Glycas, 330; Josephus and Maeslinus, 592; Melchius Canus, 590; Sulpicius Severus, 588; Clemens Alexandrinus, 570; Cedrenus, 672; Codomus, 598; Vossius and Capellus, 580; Serarius, 680; Nicholas Abraham, 527; Petavius and Valtherus, 520. After all, that in the common Hebrew text is more likely to be the true one, than any of the others.

38. **Bul**. i.e. *changeable*, *S#945h, only here. **finished**. Ezr 6:14, 15. Zc 4:9. 6:13-15. **throughout**, etc. *or*, with all the appurtenances thereof, and with all the ordinances thereof. **finished**. Is 66:9. Ph 1:6. **seven years**. ver. 1, 9. 1 K 7:1. Ezr 3:8-13. 6:15. Jn *2:20.

1 KINGS 7

Solomon builds himself an house, 1; and the house of the forest of Lebanon, 2-5; the porch of the pillars, 6; the porch of judgment, 7; the house of Pharaoh's daughter, 8. The costly materials of these structures, and of the great court, 9-12. Hiram, a skilful artificer, is fetched from Tyre, 13, 14. He casts two pillars of brass, 15-22; and the brazen sea; with ten bases, and ten lavers, and other vessels for the temple, 23-47. The furniture and sacred vessels of gold are made for the temple, 48-50. The dedicated treasures are brought into it, 51.

1. **thirteen years**. 1 K 9:10. 2 Ch 8:1. Ec 2:4, 5. Mt 6:33.

2. **the house**. 1 K 9:19. 10:17. 2 Ch 9:16. SS 7:4.

3. **beams**. Heb. ribs. 1 K 6:5mg.

4. **windows**. ver. 5. 1 K 6:4. Is 54:12. Ezk 40:16, 22, 25, 29, 33, 36. 41:26. **light was against light**. Heb. sight against sight.

5. **doors and posts were square**, with the windows. *or*, spaces and pillars *were* square in prospect. Ex 27:1. Ezk 41:21. 43:16.

6. **before them**. *or*, according to them. Ezk 41:25, 26. **thick**. 2 Ch 4:17. Ezk 41:25. **before them**. *or*, according to them.

7. **a porch**. 1 K 6:3. **for the throne**. 1 K 10:18-20. Ps 122:5. Is 9:7. **of judgment**. 1 K 3:9, 28. Pr 20:8. **from one side of the floor to the other**. Heb. from floor to floor.

8. **another court**. 2 K 20:4. **an house**. See on 1 K 3:1. 9:24. 2 Ch 8:11.

9. **costly stones**. ver. 10, 11. 1 K 5:17. **saw**. 2 S 12:31. 1 Ch 20:3. **coping**. lit. hand-breadth. *ſ*121N2, Ge +34:29. Heb. spans, put by Metonymy for the height: i.e. from the foundation to the summit. ver. 26. 2 Ch 4:5. Ps 39:5.

10. **the foundations**. Is 28:16. 54:11. 1 C 3:10, 11. Re 21:19, 20. **stones of ten cubits**. Reckoning the cubit at 21 inches, the ten cubits are 17 feet and a half, and the eight cubits are 14 feet. The magnitude of these stones was certainly extraordinary; but let us hear M. Volney, and our surprise will no longer be fixed on these stones, but be transferred from Solomon's house to the ruins of Balbec: "What is still more astonishing is the enormous stones which compose the sloping wall. To the west, the second layer is formed of stones which are from 28 to 35 feet long, by about 9 in height. Over this layer, at the north-west angle, there are three stones, which alone occupy a space

of 175 feet and a half; *viz.* the first, 58 feet 7 inches; the second, 58 feet 11 inches; and the third, exactly 58 feet; and each of these is 12 feet thick. These stones are of white granite, with large shining flakes, like gypsum: there is a quarry of this kind of stone under the whole city, and another in the adjacent mountains, which is open in several places. On the right, as we approach the city, there is still lying there a stone hewn on three sides, which is 69 feet 2 inches long, 12 feet 10 inches broad, and 13 feet 3 inches in thickness" (*Travels*, vol. ii. p. 241).

11. **above were.** Ep 2:20-22. 1 P 2:5.

12. **three rows.** See on 1 K 6:36. **the porch.** Jn 10:23. Ac 3:11. 5:12.

13. **Hiram.** ver. 40. 2 Ch 2:13. 4:11, Huram. **Tyre.** i.e. *rock, strength*, *S#6865h. 1 K 5:1. 9:11, 12. Jsh 19:29. 2 S 5:11. 24:7. 1 Ch 14:1. 2 Ch 2:3, 11. Ps 45:12. 83:7. 87:4. Is 23:1, 5, 8, 15, 15, 17. Je 25:22. 27:3. 47:4. Ezk 26:2, 3, 4, 7, 15. 27:2, 3, 3, 8, 32. 28:2, 12. 29:18, 18. Ho 9:13. Jl 3:4. Am 1:9, 10. Zc 9:2, 3.

14. **a widow's son.** Heb. the son of a widow woman. **tribe.** The mother of Hiram (not the Tyrian king mentioned before, but an intelligent coppersmith, of Jewish extraction by her mother's side) in Chronicles is said to have been of "the daughters of *Dan*;" and she might have been of *Naphtali* by her father, and of Dan by her mother; or she might originally be of the tribe of Dan, and have been first married to a man of the tribe of Naphtali; and, in either case, she might be indifferently called "of the tribe of Naphtali," or of "the daughters of Dan." **Naphtali.** 2 Ch 2:14. **his father.** 2 Ch 4:16. **worker.** or, plower, graver. 1 K 19:19. Jb 1:14. **in brass.** Ezk 27:13. **he was filled.** Ex 31:2-6. 35:30-35. 36:1, 2, 8. 2 Ch 2:13, 14. 4:11. Is 28:26. Da 1:17.

15. **cast.** Heb. fashioned. By cutting and carving. Ex 32:4. **two pillars.** ver. 21. 2 K 25:16, 17. 2 Ch 3:15-17. 4:12, etc. Je 52:21-23. **eighteen cubits.** That is, nearly thirty feet, English measure. But in the parallel place in Chronicles, these pillars are said to be thirty-five cubits high. Tremellius reconciles this difference by observing, that the common cubit was but one half of the cubit of the sanctuary; so that eighteen of the one would make thirty-six of the other; from which, if we deduct one cubit for the base, there will remain thirty-five. Notwithstanding the *names* of these pillars, they seem to have supported no part of the building, and appear to have been formed for ornament; and were no doubt also emblematical. The right pillar was called *Jachin*, which signifies, "He will establish;" while that on the left was named *Boaz*, "In it is strength." Some think they were intended for memorials of the pillar and cloud of fire, which led Israel through the wilderness; but Henry supposes them designed for memorandums to the priests and others that came to worship at God's door. 1st. To depend upon God only, and not upon any sufficiency of their own, for strength and establishment in all their religious exercises. 2nd. It was a memorandum to them of the strength and establishment of the temple of God among them. When the temple was destroyed, particular notice is taken of the breaking up and carrying away of these brazen pillars, 2 K 25:13, 17, which had been the tokens of its establishment, and would have been still so, if they had not forsaken God. **eighteen cubits.**

2 Ch 3:15. **line.** or, cord. Ge 14:23. Jsh 2:18. Jg 16:12. Ec 4:12. SS 4:3. Je 52:21.

16. **two chapiters.** or, crowns. ver. 17, 18, 19, 20, 31, 41, 42. Ex 36:38. 38:17, 19, 28. 2 K 25:17. 2 Ch 4:12, 13. Je 52:22. **molten.** or, cast. ver. 23, 33. 2 K 4:5h (poured out). 2 Ch 4:2. Jb 11:15h (steadfast). 37:18.

17. **checker work.** ver. 18, 20, 41, 42. 2 K 1:2. 25:17. 2 Ch 4:12, 13. Jb 18:8. Je 52:22, 23. **wreaths.** Ex 28:14, 22, 24, 25. 39:15-18. Dt 22:12. 2 K 25:17. **chainwork.** Ex 28:14. 39:15. 2 Ch 3:5, 16.

19. **lily work.** ver. 22, 26. 1 K 6:18, 32-35. Ps 45, title (Shoshannim). 69, title. 80, title. SS 2:16. 4:5. 5:13. 6:2, 3. 7:2.

20. **and the pomegranates.** 2 K 25:17. 2 Ch 3:16. 4:13. Je 52:22, 23.

21. **And he set the pillars.** Ex 36:38. 38:17, 19, 28. 2 Ch 3:17. Je 52:17. Ga 2:9. Re 3:12. **the porch.** ver. 12. 1 K 6:3. Ezk 40:48, 49. **Jachin.** i.e. *he prepares* or *establishes.* 2 S 7:12. Is 9:7. **Boaz.** i.e. *fleetness.* Ru 4:21. 2 Ch 3:17. Is 45:24. Mt 16:18.

23. **he made.** Ex 30:18-21. 38:8. **a molten sea.** 2 K 25:13. 2 Ch 4:2. Je 52:17, 20. **the one brim to the other.** Heb. his brim *to* his brim. This laver was thus of immense size. Ditzler suggests it was eight feet, nine inches deep, stating it was "placed upon twelve molten oxen, which made it twenty-one feet from the level of the floor to the top of the laver" (*Baptism*, p. 62). Ditzler says "The water was brought in aqueducts under ground some four miles from a distant fountain, and made to rise up through the hollow pedestal into the basin, and then there were, first two, later twelve cocks at the basis out of which the water ran, at which the priests baptized. The laver was thus made twenty-one feet high to keep any unclean person from touching the water by which it would be defiled" (p. 62). Ditzler then notes that "If a person got into the vessel, then, he had, 1. To violate the express precept to 'wash out of it' (Ex √30:19, *thereat.* lit. out of it); 2. He would violate all the facts in Leviticus and Numbers cited about not using defiled water (Le 11:29-36. Nu 31:23, 24. 19:21, 22); 3. He would violate the repeated precepts of the rabbins, who taught it 'was better to die of thirst than disobey' the laws of rabbins. Lightfoot gives us many such facts. 4. He would have to leap *twenty-one feet* high to get to the top; 5. When in the vessel he would have to swim or drown, as it 'contained' the amount of water named in 2 Ch 4; 6. He would have to leap down twenty-one feet on the solid stone pavement; 7. The vessel would then have to be emptied of all its water, burnt out, and cleansed for seven days before it could be used. All this is involved in the immersion theory; 8. All this must be done in the presence of multitudes of men and women—of course the clothes retained on the person" (p. 62). Thus it is absurd to suppose that any one or any thing was ever immersed in the laver; rather, the priests washed their hands or feet at the spouts provided at the foot or base of the huge laver, this being done by means of sprinkling or pouring. The whole person is spoken of as being washed, anointed, etc., when only a given part of the person is literally washed (Nu 8:7, LXX. Jb 9:30. Mt 26:6-12. Jn 2:6. *13:5-10). See related notes (Ex 30:21n. 40:12n).

24. **knops.** 1 K 6:18. Ex 25:31-36. 37:17-22. **compassing the sea.** 2 Ch 4:3.

25. **upon twelve.** 2 Ch 4:4, 5. Je 52:20. Ezk 1:10. Mt 28:19. Mk 16:15, 16. Lk 24:47. 1 C 9:9. Re 4:6, 7.

26. **an hand breadth.** ♪79, Ge +21:16. Je 52:21. **with flowers.** ver. 19. 1 K 6:18, 32, 35. **cup.** Ge 40:11. 2 Ch 4:5. **it contained.** This immense laver, called a *sea* from its magnitude, held, at a moderate computation, 16,000 gallons. Besides this great brazen laver, there were in the temple ten lavers of brass of a less size, which moved on wheels, and were ornamented with the figures of various animals, having, probably, always some relation to the cherubim. These lavers were to hold water for the use of the priests in their sacred office, particularly to wash the victims that were to be offered as a burnt offering, as we learn from 2 Ch 4:6; but the *brazen sea* was for the priests to wash in. The *knops* are supposed to have been in the form of an ox's head (2 Ch 4:3); and some think the water flowed out at their mouths. **two thousand.** ver. 38. 2 Ch *4:5n. Ezk 45:14.

27. **ten bases.** These highly ornamental bases appear to have been square stands, or immense pedestals, for the purpose of supporting the lavers. 2 K 25:13, 16. 2 Ch 4:14. Je 52:17, 20.

28. **bases was on.** It seems evident that these bases or pedestals rose with steps, and that the ornaments mentioned in the next verse appeared in front, forming so many entablatures. But the description of these bases is very difficult to comprehend: many of the original words are seldom, if at all, used elsewhere; and it would be impossible to give an explanation of each particular, without a labor and prolixity disproportioned to its importance to us. **borders.** Ex 25:25, 27. 37:12, 14. 2 S 22:46. 2 K 16:17. Ps 18:45. Mi 7:17h (out of their holes).

29. **lions.** See on ver. 25. 1 K 6:27. Ezk 1:10. 10:14. 41:18, 19. Ho 5:14. Re 4:6, 7. 5:5. **cherubims.** Ge 3:34. Ex 25:18. 37:7. He 9:5. **certain additions.** 1 P 2:5.

30. **wheels.** Ex 14:25. Pr 20:26. 25:11mg. Is 28:27. Ezk 1:15-21. 3:13. 10:10-13. Na 3:2. **had undersetters.** It is probable that these *undersetters* were so many strong legs, somewhat shorter than the wheels, and were intended to prevent the laver from tilting, or falling, in case of any accident.

31. **gravings.** or, carvings. 1 K 6:18, 29, 32.

32. **joined to the base.** Heb. in the base.

33. **And the work.** Ezk 1:16, 18.

36. **plates.** or, tablets. Ex 24:12. **graved cherubims.** ver. 29. 1 K 6:29, 32, 35. Ezk 40:31, 37. 41:18-20, 25, 26. **proportion.** Heb. nakedness. Na 2:5.

37. **casting.** ver. 16, 23. **measure.** Ex 26:2. **one size.** 1 K 6:25.

38. **ten lavers.** Ex 30:17-21, 28. 38:8. 40:11, 12. 2 Ch 4:6, etc. Zc 13:1. He 9:10. 10:22. Jn 1:7. Re 7:14. **baths.** ver. 26. 2 Ch 2:10. 4:5. Is 5:10. Ezk 45:10. *11, *14.

39. **side.** Heb. shoulder. 1 K 6:8. **he set.** 2 Ch 4:6, 10. **the sea.** Zc 13:1. Lk 24:47. Jn 13:8. T 3:5, 6. He 9:10. +√10:22. Re 7:13, 14.

40. **Hiram.** Heb. Hirom. ver. 13. **the lavers.** ver. 38. 2 K 25:14, 15. 2 Ch 4:6, 11-16. Je 52:18, 19. **the shovels.** ver. 45. **the basons.** or, sprinkling bowls. ver. 45, 50. Ex *24:6. *S#4219h: Ex 27:3. 38:3. Nu 4:14. 7:13, 19, 25, 31, 37, 43, 49, 55, 61, 67, 73, 79, 84, 85. 2 K 12:13. 25:15. 1 Ch 28:17. 2 Ch 4:8, 11, 22.

Ne 7:70. Je 52:18, 19. Am *6:6. Zc 9:15. 14:20. **So Hiram.** Ex 39:32-43.

41. **two pillars.** See on ver. 15-22. 2 Ch 4:12. **bowls.** ver. 42. 2 Ch 4:12, 13. Ec 12:6. Zc 4:3. **two networks.** ver. 17, 18.

42. **the pillars.** Heb. the face of the pillars.

43. **ten bases.** ver. 27-39.

44. **one sea.** See on ver. 23-26.

45. **the pots.** Ex 27:3. 38:3. Le 8:31. 1 S 2:13, 14. 2 Ch 4:16. Ezk 46:20-24. Zc 14:20, 21. **bright brass.** Heb. brass made bright, *or* scoured. Is 18:2h (peeled), 7. Ezk 21:10h (furbished), 11.

46. **plain.** *or*, circuit. Ge 13:10, 11. **the clay ground.** Heb. the thickness of the ground. **Succoth.** Ge 33:17. **Zarthan.** i.e. *narrowness of dwelling place; their distress,* *S#6891h. Zarthan is supposed to have been situated in the tribe of Manasseh, *west* of Jordan, near Jezreel and Bethshan or Scythopolis, and not far from the Jordan. Succoth we know was situated *east* of Jordan, in the tribe of Gad, and according to Jerome, in the district of Scythopolis: hence the "plain of Jordan," where Hiram cast the brazen vessels, must be the plain in which that river runs, Zarthan and Succoth being probably nearly opposite each other; but whether the precise spot of his operations was on *this* side or on the *other* side, is uncertain. In this place he found that particular *clay* that was proper for his purpose; and it being a considerable distance from Jerusalem, that city would not be annoyed by the smoke and noxious vapors necessarily occasioned by the process. 1 K 4:12, Zartanah. Jsh 3:16, Zaretan. 2 Ch ◐4:17, Zeredathah.

47. **unweighed.** ♪63BC, Ge +9:20. **because they were exceeding many.** Heb. for the exceeding multitude. 2 Ch 4:18. Jn 14:2. Ro 9:23, 24. **found out.** Heb. searched. 1 Ch 22:3, 14, 16. Je +*31:37. 46:23.

48. **the altar.** Ex 30:1-5. 37:25-28. 39:38. 40:26. 2 Ch 4:19. **of gold.** That is, covered with it. 1 K 6:20. Re 8:3. **the table.** Ex 25:23-30. 37:10-16. 39:36. 40:22, 23. Le 24:5-9. 2 Ch *4:8. Ezk 40:39, 42. 41:22. 44:16. Ml 1:12. 1 C 10:21. He 9:2. **the showbread.** Ex 25:30.

49. **the candlesticks.** Ex 25:31, etc. 37:17, etc. 39:37. 40:24, 25. 2 Ch 4:7. Zc 4:1-3, 11-14. Mt 5:14-16. Re 1:20. 2:1. **pure gold.** 1 K 6:20, 21. **before the oracle.** See on 2 Ch 4:20. **the tongs.** Ex 25:38. Nu 4:9. 2 Ch 4:21. Is 6:6.

50. **bowls.** Ex 12:22. 2 S 17:28. **snuffers.** 2 K 12:13. 25:14. 2 Ch 4:22. Je 52:18. **basons.** or, sprinkling bowls. ver. +40, 45. **spoons.** Ex 25:29. Nu 7:86. **censers.** Heb. ash pans. Ex 25:38. Le 16:12. 2 Ch 4:21, 22. **the temple.** Ex 25:29, 38. 2 Ch 4:21, 22. 1 C 12:4-7.

51. **was ended.** Ex 40:33. Ezr 6:15. Zc 4:9. **Solomon brought.** It appears, therefore, that Solomon did not use any of the gold and silver in the structure of the temple which his father had provided. **things which David his father had dedicated.** Heb. holy things of David. 2 S 8:7-11. 1 Ch 18:7, 8, 10, 11. 26:26-28. 28:11-18. 29:2-8. 2 Ch 5:1. **treasures.** Dt 28:12. 32:34.

1 KINGS 8

Solomon assembles the elders and princes; and the priests carry the ark into the most holy place, 1-9. The glory of the Lord fills the house, 10, 11. Solomon blesses Israel; and praises God for performing his word to David, 12-21. He prays, that God would answer the supplications of Israel, and of strangers, in all ages, and in all cases, in which they should call upon him, towards this his holy temple, 22-53. He again praises God, and blesses the people, 54-61. He offers very numerous sacrifices, keeps the feast fourteen days; and dismisses the people, who return home joyful and thankful, 62-66.

1. A.M. 3000. B.C. 1004. **Solomon**. This did not take place, according to Abp. Usher, till the year after the temple was finished, because that year was a *jubilee*. "The 8th day of the 7th month, *viz.* the 30th of our October, being Friday, was the first of the seven days of dedication; the 10th day, Saturday, November 1, the fast of expiation or atonement was held; whereon, according to Levitical law, the jubilee was proclaimed by sound of trumpet. The 15th day, Friday, was the feast of tabernacles, which was always very solemnly kept; and the day following, November 14, being our Saturday, when the Sabbath was ended, the people returned home." 2 Ch 5:2, etc. **assembled**. Jsh 23:2. 24:1. 1 Ch 28:1. 2 Ch 30:1. Ezr 3:1. **elders**. Ex +18:21. Jsh +20:4. **chief of the fathers**. Heb. princes. Nu +1:16. 7:3. **that they might bring**. 2 S 6:1, 2, 6, 12. 1 Ch 13:1-5. 15:3, 25. **out of the city**. 1 K 3:15. 2 S 5:7-9. 6:12-17. 1 Ch 11:7. 15:29. 16:1. Ps 9:11. 102:21. Is 28:16. 46:13. 1 P 2:6. **Zion**. i.e. *the sunny place.* 2 S 5:7. 2 K 19:21, 31. 1 Ch 11:5. 2 Ch 5:2. Ps 2:6. *78:68, 69. He 12:22. 1 P 2:5, 7, 9.

2. **at the feast**. Le 23:34. Nu 29:12, etc. Dt 16:13. 2 Ch 5:3. 7:8-10. Ezr 3:4. Ne 8:14-18. Zc 14:16-19. Jn 7:2, 37. **Ethanim**. i.e. *perennial streams, *S#388h, only here, the same as Tisri, part of September and October (Young).

3. **came**. 2 S 6:17. **the priests took up**. Nu 4:15. Dt 31:9. Jsh 3:3, 6, 14, 15. 4:9. 6:6. 1 Ch 15:2, 11-15. 2 Ch 5:4-8. Is 52:11.

4. **and the**. 1 K 3:4. 2 Ch 1:3. **tabernacle of the congregation**. Ex +25:9n. 26:1n. 27:21n. 33:7n. See on 40:2-33. **holy vessels**. Nu 31:6.

5. **assembled unto**. The original word indicates met by agreement (Young). Nu 14:35. 16:11. 27:3. 2 Ch 5:6. **sacrificing sheep**. ver. 62, 63. 2 S 6:13. 1 Ch 16:1. He 9:28. 10:14. **could not be told**. 1 K 3:8. Ge 16:10. 32:12. 1 Ch 23:3. 2 Ch 5:6. Je 33:22. Ho 1:10.

6. **And the priests**. ver. 4. 2 S 6:17. 2 Ch 5:7. **his place**. 1 K 6:19. Ex 26:33, 34. 40:20, 21. **the oracle**. ver. 8. 1 K 6:5, 16, 19, 20, 21, 22, 23, 31. 7:49. 2 Ch 3:16. 4:20. 5:7, 9. Ps 28:2. **under the wings**. ver. 7. 1 K 6:24, *27. Ex 25:20-22. 37:9. Ru 2:12. 1 S 4:4. 2 S 6:2. 1 Ch 3:11-13. 5:7, 8. Ps 80:1. 99:1. Is 37:16. Ezk 10:5.

7. **two wings**. Ps 80:1. 99:1. He 9:5, 24.

8. **drew out the staves**. Ex 25:14, 15. 37:4, 5. 40:20. 2 Ch 5:9. **ends**. Heb. heads. holy place. *or*, ark, as 2 Ch 5:9. **unto this day**. Jsh +*4:9. Mt 28:15.

9. **nothing**. Ex 25:21. Dt 10:2. 2 Ch 5:10. **in the ark**. Ex 16:33. Nu 17:10. He 9:3, 4. **put there at Horeb**. Ex 25:21. 40:20. Dt 10:2, 5. 31:26. when. *or*, where. ver. 21. Ex 24:8. 34:27, 28. Dt 4:13. **the cloud**. Ex 13:21. 14:24. 16:10. 24:16-18. 40:34, 35. Le 16:2. Nu 9:15. 2 Ch 5:13, 14. 7:1-3. Ezk 10:4. Re 15:8.

10. **the cloud**. The usual symbol of the Divine Presence (Young). Ex 40:34, 35. Le 16:2. 2 Ch 5:13, 14. 7:2. **filled**. Ezk 10:3, 4.

11. **for the glory**. Le 9:6, 23. Ezk 43:2, 4, 5. 44:4.

Jn 1:14. Ac 7:55. 2 C 3:18. 4:6. Re 21:11, 23. **filled**. 2 Ch +5:14.

12. **The Lord**. Le 16:2. Dt 4:11. 2 Ch 6:1, 2, etc. Ps 18:8-11. 97:2. **the thick**. Ex 20:21. Le 16:2. Dt 5:22. Ps 139:12. Is 45:15. He 12:18. **darkness**. Ex +20:21. Dt 4:11. 5:22. 2 S 22:10. 2 Ch 6:1. Jb 22:13. +38:9. Ps 18:9. 97:2. Is 60:2. Je 13:16. Ezk 34:12. Jl 2:2. Zp 1:15.

13. **surely built**. 2 S 7:13. 1 Ch 17:12. 22:10, 11. 28:6, 10, 20. 2 Ch 6:2. Ps 49:14. Is 63:15. Hab 3:11. **a settled**. Ex 15:17. Ps 78:68, 69. 132:13, 14. Jn 4:21-23. Ac 6:14. He 8:5-13. 9:11, 12, 24. **for ever**. Heb. *olam*, plural, Ps +61:4.

14. **blessed all**. ver. 55, 56. Jsh 22:6. 2 S 6:18. 1 Ch 16:2. 2 Ch 6:3. 30:18-20. Ps 118:26. Lk 24:50, 51. **all the congregation**. 2 Ch 7:6. Ne 8:7. 9:2. Mt 13:2.

15. **Blessed**. 1 Ch 29:10, 20. 2 Ch 6:4. 20:26. Ne 9:5. Ps 41:13. 72:18, 19. 115:18. 117:1, 2. Lk 1:68. Ep 1:3. 1 P 1:3. **which spake**. 2 S 7:5, 25, 28, 29. 1 Ch 17:12. Is 1:20. Lk 1:70. **hath**. Jsh 21:45. 23:15, 16. Ps 138:2. Mt 24:35. Lk 1:54, 55, 72.

16. **since**. See on 2 S 7:6, 7. 2 Ch 6:5, etc. **I chose**. 1 Ch 17:5, 6. Ps 132:13. **my name**. See on ver. 29. 1 K 11:36. Dt 12:11. 2 K 23:27. Ne 1:9. Je 7:12. Da 9:19. **I chose David**. 1 S 16:1. 2 S 7:8. 1 Ch 28:4. Ps 78:70. 89:19, 20.

17. **it was**. 2 S 7:2, 3. 1 Ch 17:1, 2, etc. 22:7. 28:2.

18. **Whereas**. 2 Ch 6:7-9. 2 C 8:12. **in thine heart**. T#331. 2 Ch 32:26. Ps 55:21. 78:72. *95:10. Pr 6:14. *23:7. Ec *9:3. Is 10:7. Je 48:29. Mt 5:8. *15:18, 19. Ro *10:10. He *3:12.

19. **shalt not**. 1 K 5:3-5. 2 S 7:5, 12, 13. 1 Ch 17:4, 11, 12. 22:8-10. 28:6.

20. **hath performed**. See on ver. 15. Ne 9:8. Is 9:7. Je 29:10, 11, 29. Ezk 12:25. 37:14. Mi 7:20. Ro 4:21. Ph *1:6. **as the Lord**. 1 Ch 28:5, 6.

21. **And I have**. See on ver. 5, 6. **the covenant**. ver. 9. Ex 34:28. Dt 9:9, 11. 31:26. ✓121L7. Metonymy of the Subject B585: *covenant* is put for the two tables of stone. For another instance of this figure see Ro 9:4.

22. **stood before the altar**. See ver. 54. 2 K 11:14. 23:3. 2 Ch 6:12, 13, etc. **spread forth**. Ex 9:29, 33. See on 2 Ch 6:12. Ezr 9:5. Jb 11:13. Ps 28:2. 63:4. Is *1:15. 1 T *2:8.

23. **Lord God**. Ge 33:20. Ex *3:15. **no God**. Ex *15:11. 1 S 2:2. 2 S *7:22. Ps 35:10. 86:8. *89:6-8. 113:5. Is 40:18, 25. Je 10:6, 16. Mi *7:18. **who keepest**. Dt *7:9. Ne *1:5. 9:32. Ps 36:5. 89:3-5. Da *9:4. Mi *7:19, 20. Lk *1:72. **and mercy**. ✓174, Ge +18:27. **walk before**. 1 K *2:4. 3:6. 6:12. Ge *17:1. 2 K *20:3.

24. **thou spakest**. See on ver. *15. 2 S *7:12, 16. 2 Ch *6:14, 15. **as it is**. Ezr 9:7. Ne +9:32. Je +25:18.

25. **keep with thy**. 1 K *2:4. Ge 32:12. Ex 32:13. 2 S 7:25, 27-29. 1 Ch *17:23-27. Ps 119:58. Lk 1:68-72. **There shall not**, etc. Heb. There shall not be cut off unto thee a man from my sight. 2 S 7:25. 2 Ch 21:7. Ps *89:33-37. 132:12. Je 33:17-26. Lk 1:32, 33. **so that**. Heb. only if. **thy children**. 1 K *2:4. *9:4-6. 1 Ch *28:9. 2 Ch 6:16, 17. Ps 132:12.

26. **And now**. ver. 23. Ex 24:10. 1 S 1:17. Ps 41:13. Is 41:17. 45:3. **let thy word**. 2 S 7:25-29. 2 Ch 1:9. Ps 119:49. Je 11:5. Ezk 36:36, 37.

27. **But will**. Ge 18:13. Nu 22:32. 2 Ch 6:18. Ps 58:1. Is 66:1. Jn 1:14. Ac 7:48, 49. 17:24. 2 C 6:16.

1 J 3:1. **dwell**. Ps 139:7, 12. Je 23:23, 24. Am 9:2. **the heaven**. ſ147H, Ge +9:25. Dt 10:14. 2 Ch 2:6. 6:18. Ps 113:4. 139:7-16. Je 23:24. 2 C 12:2.

28. **Yet have thou**. 2 Ch 6:19. Ps 141:2. Da 9:17-19. Lk 18:1, 7. **respect**. The original word signifies to "turn the face toward," as in Ge 18:22. **prayer**. ver. 29, 38, 45, 49, 54. 1 K 9:3. 2 S 7:27. 2 K 19:4. 20:5. 2 Ch 6:19, 20, 29, 35, 39, 40. **supplication**. Jsh 11:20 (no favor; grace, or supplication). Ezr 9:8. **hearken**. Ps 4:1. 5:1. 86:3, 6, 7. 88:1, 2. **cry**. *S#7440h. 1 K 22:36. 2 Ch 6:19. 20:22 (sing). Ps 17:1. 30:5 (joy). 42:4. 47:1 (triumph). 61:1. 88:2. 105:43 (gladness). 106:44. 107:22 (rejoicing). 118:15. 119:169. 126:2 (singing), *5 (joy), *6 (rejoicing). 142:6. Pr 11:10 (shouting). Is 14:7 (singing). 35:10 (songs). 43:14. 44:23. 48:20. 49:13. 51:11. 54:1. 55:12. Je *7:16. 11:14. 14:12. Zp 3:17.

29. **That thine**. ver. 52. 2 K 19:16. 2 Ch 6:20, 40. 7:15. 16:9. Ne 1:6. Ps 34:15. Da 9:18. **open**. Ne 1:6. Zc 12:4. Lk 22:61. **My name**. ver. 16, 43mg. 1 K 11:36. Ex 20:24. Dt 12:11. 16:2, 6. 26:2. 2 K 21:4, 7. 23:27. 2 Ch 6:5, 6, 20. 7:16. 20:8. 33:4, 7. Ne 1:9. Jn 14:13, 14. **toward this place**. or, in this place. Da +*6:10.

30. **when they shall**. 2 Ch 20:8, 9. Ne 1:5, 6. **toward this place**. or, in this place. ver. 29. Da +*6:10. Jon 2:4. **and hear**. ver. 34, 36, 39, 43, 49. 2 Ch 6:21. Ps 33:13, 14. 113:5, 6. 123:1. Ec 5:2. Is 57:15. Mt 6:9. **forgive**. ver. 34, 36, 39. 2 Ch +√7:14. Ps 130:3, 4. Da 9:19. Mt 6:12.

31. **If**. Ge +4:7. **any man**. Solomon here puts *seven cases*, in all of which the mercy and intervention of God would be indispensably requisite; and he earnestly bespeaks that mercy and intervention, on condition that the people pray towards that holy place, and with a feeling heart make earnest supplication to the throne of mercy. **trespass**. 2 Ch 6:22, 23. **an oath be laid upon him**. Heb. he require an oath of him. Ex 22:8-11. Le 5:1. Pr 30:9. **the oath**. Ge 24:41. Nu 5:16-22. Mt 23:18.

32. **hear thou**. See on ver. 30. **condemning the wicked**. T#1751. Ex 22:9. 34:7. Nu 5:27. Dt 25:1. Ne 13:28, 29. Ps 10:13-15. 28:4, 5. 31:17, 18. 40:14, 15. 59:12-15. 79:6-12. 109:4-13. 140:8-11. 144:5-8. Pr 1:31. Is 3:10, 11. Je +√10:25. 17:18. Ezk 18:13, 30. Ro 2:6-10. **his way**. Ge +*6:13 (T#566). Nu +*32:23. 2 Ch 6:23. **justifying**. Ex 23:7. Pr 17:15. Is 3:10. Ezk 18:20. Ro 2:13. 7:9. **to give**. 1 T +*4:8.

33. **smitten down**. Le 26:17, 25. Dt 28:25, 48. Jsh 7:8. 2 Ch 6:24, 25. Ps 44:10. **because they have**. Jsh 7:11, 12. Jg 6:1, 2. 2 K 17:7-18. 18:11, 12. 2 Ch 36:14-17. **turn again**. Le 26:39-42. Ne 1:8, 9. Jon 3:10. **pray**. Ezr 9:5, etc. Ne 9:1-3, etc. Is 63:15-19. ch. 64, etc. Da 9:3, etc. **in**. or, toward. ver. 30.

34. **forgive the sin**. T#1623. ver. 30, 44-53. Ge 20:3, 4. Ex 32:11-13. 32:30-32. 34:8, 9. Nu 11:1, 2. 14:13-19. 16:20-22, 44-46. 21:6, 7. Dt 9:18, 19. 21:8. Jg 3:9, 15. 4:2, 3. 6:6. 10:15, 16. *20:26. 21:2, 3. 1 S 7:5-7. 12:19-23. 2 S 24:17. 2 K 13:3-5. 19:15-19. 1 Ch 21:16, 17. 2 Ch 12:5, 6. 15:10-15. 20:4-12. Ezr 1:1-6. 9:4-15. Ne 1:4-11. 9:32-38. Ps 74:2-10. 79:1-13. 80:4-7. 85:1-8. 106:47. Is 63:15-19. 64:1-12. Je 14:19. 31:4-9, 27. 32:37. 33:10-13. 42:1, 2. 50:4, 5. La 1:9-11. Ezk 9:8. Da 9:2, 16-19, 25. Ho +*3:4, 5. 14:1-3. Jl *2:15-19. Am 7:2. Zc *1:12. *12:10-14. *13:8, 9. **which thou gavest**. Ge 13:15. Ex 6:8. Jsh 21:43.

35. **heaven**. 1 K 17:1. Le 26:19. Dt 11:17. 28:12,

23, 24. 2 S 24:13. Je 14:1-7. Ezk 14:13. Ml 3:10. Lk 4:25. Re 11:6. **if they pray**. ver. 33. 2 Ch 6:24, 26. Ro √10:9. 15:9. **confess**. ver. 29, 30. Jl 1:13-20. 2:15-17. **and turn**. ver. 33. Is *1:15, 16. 9:13. Ezk 18:30-32. Ho 14:1.

36. **thou teach**. Ps *25:4, 5, 8, √9, 12. 27:11. *32:8. 94:12. 119:33. 143:8. Is 35:8. Mi 4:2. **the good way**. 1 S *12:23, 24. 2 Ch 6:26, 27. Is 30:21. Je 6:16. 42:3. Mt 22:16. **give rain**. 1 K 18:1, 27-40, 45. Ps 68:9. 147:8. Je 14:22. Ja 5:17, 18.

37. **in the land famine**. T#1489. Ge 12:10. 26:1. Le 26:16, 25, 26, etc. Dt 28:21, 22, 25, 38-42, 52-61. 2 K 6:25-29. 1 Ch 21:12. 2 Ch 6:28-31. 20:9. Ps 105:34, 35. Je 32:2. 39:1-3. Ezk 14:21. Jl 1:4-7. 2:25, 26. **pestilence**. Ex 5:3. 9:3, 15. **blasting**. Dt 28:22. 2 Ch 6:28. Am 4:9. Hg 2:17. **mildew**. Dt 28:22. 2 Ch 6:26. Je 30:6. Am 4:9. Hg 2:17. **locust**. Ex 10:4, 12, 13, 14, 19. Le 11:22. Dt 28:38. Jg 6:5. 7:12. 2 Ch 6:28. Jb 39:20. Ps 78:46. **caterpiller**. 2 Ch 6:28. Ps 78:46. Is 33:4. Jl 1:4. 2:25. **cities**. or, jurisdiction. or, gates. Ge +14:7. 19:1. Dt 28:52, 55, 57. 2 S 19:8n. 2 Ch 6:28mg. **sickness**. Ex *15:26. +*23:25. 2 Ch 6:28.

38. **prayer**. 2 Ch 20:5-13. Ps 50:15. 91:15. Is 37:4, 15-21. Jl 2:17. Am 7:1-6. **the plague**. 2 Ch 6:29. Jb 7:11. Ps 32:3, 4. 42:6, 9, 11. 73:21, 22. 142:3-5. Pr 14:10. Ro 7:24. Ph *4:6. **spread forth**. ver. 22. Is *1:15.

39. **Then hear**. See on ver. 32, 36. Ps 94:9. 139:2, 4. Is 40:13, 14. **in heaven**. ſ22D3A. Anthropomorphism B892. God is spoken of being in circumstances which have to do with *place*. Here, *heaven* is his dwelling place. For other instances of this figure see Ps 2:4. 24:3. Is 26:21. Mi 1:3. **give to every man**. Ps 18:20-26. 28:4. Je *17:10. 32:19. Ezk 18:30. Re 22:12. **for thou**. ſ81, Ge +15:13. **knowest**. 1 S +*16:7. 1 Ch *28:9. 2 Ch 6:30. Ps 11:4, 5. 139:1, 2. Je *17:10. Mt 9:4. Jn +√2:24, 25. +16:30. 21:17. Ac 1:24. He √4:12, 13. 1 J 3:20. Re 2:18, +23. **children**. ſ144A3, Ge 11:5.

40. **fear thee**. Ge 22:12. Ex 20:20. Dt 6:2, 13. 1 S 12:24. Ps 115:13. *130:4. Je 32:39, 40. Ho 3:5. Ac 9:31. 10:2. He 12:28. Re 15:4. 19:5.

41. **a stranger**. 1 K 10:1, 2. Ge 31:15. Ru 1:16. 2:11. 2 Ch 6:32. Is 56:3-7. Mt 8:5, 10, 11. 15:22-28. Lk 17:18. Jn 12:20. Ac 10:1-4. **cometh out**. 1 K 10:1, 2. Ex 18:8-12. 2 K 5:1-7, 16, 17. Is 60:1-10. Mt 2:1. 12:42. Ac 8:27, etc.

42. **For they shall**. ſ81, Ge +15:13. Ex 15:14. Dt 4:6. Jsh 2:10, 11. 9:9, 10. 2 Ch 32:31. Da 2:47. 3:28. 4:37. **great name**. Ex 3:13-16. 34:5-7. Jsh 7:9. Ps 86:8, 9. Ezk 20:9. **thy strong hand**. Ex 3:19. 9:15. 13:14. Dt 3:24. 4:34. 11:2, 3. 2 K 17:36. Ps 89:13. 136:12. Is 51:9. 63:12. Je 31:11. 32:17. **when he shall**. Ps 2:8. Is 66:19, 20. Je 3:19. Zc 14:16. Ac 8:27.

43. **in heaven**. ſ22D3A, ver. +39. **thy dwelling place**. or, settled place of thy dwelling. Ex 15:17. **that all the people**. 1 S 17:46. 2 K 19:19. 2 Ch 6:33. Ps 22:27. 67:2. 72:10, 11. 86:9. Is 11:9. Re 11:15. **fear thee**. Ps 102:15. ch. 117. **this house**. Heb. thy name is called upon this house. ver. 29. 2 Ch 6:33. Je 7:10, 11, 14, 30. 32:34. 34:15.

44. **go out to battle**. Dt 20:1-4. 31:3-6. Jsh 1:2-5. 2 Ch 6:34. **whithersoever**. Nu 31:1, etc. Jsh 6:2-5. 8:1, 2. Jg 1:1, 2. 4:6. 6:14. 1 S 15:3, 18. 30:8. 2 S 5:19, 23. **shall pray**. 2 Ch 14:9-12. 18:31. 20:6-13. 32:20. **toward the city**. Heb. the way of the city. See on ver. 16. Ps 78:67-69. 132:13, 14. Da *6:10. 9:17-19.

45. **cause.** *or,* right. Ge +*18:25. Ps 9:4. Je 5:28. lit. done their judgment. ver. 49, 59. 2 Ch 6:35, 39.
46. **If.** Ge +4:7. **they sin.** The second clause of this verse, as it is here translated, renders this *supposition* entirely nugatory; for if there be *no man that sinneth not,* it is useless to say IF *they sin:* but this objection is removed by rendering the original "If they shall sin against thee (for there is no man that, *lo yechetai, may* not sin)"; i.e. there is no man *impeccable* or *infallible*; none that is not liable to transgress. Ph 3:12. **for.** ✓138C, Ge +22:14. **there is no man.** 2 Ch ||6:36. Jb 14:4. 15:14-16. Ps 19:12. 130:3. *143:2. Pr ✓20:9. Ec ✓7:20. Is *53:6. ✓64:6. Ro 3:9-12, 19, ✓23. Ga 3:22. Ja 3:2, 8. 1 J ✓1:8-11. **angry.** 2 Ch 6:36. Ezr 9:14. Ps 2:12. 60:1. 79:5. 85:5. Is 12:1. **deliver them to the enemy.** Le 26:34, 44. Dt 28:36, 64. 2 Ch 28:8. Je 40:1. **captives.** Ge 34:29. Dt 21:10. 2 Ch 6:36. 28:11. Ps 68:18. **unto the land.** Le 26:34-39. Dt 4:26, 27. 28:36, 64-68. 29:28. 2 K 17:6, 18, 23. 25:21. Da 9:7-14. Lk *21:24.
47. **Yet if they.** Le 26:40-45. Dt 4:29-31. 30:1, 2. 2 Ch 6:37. 33:12, 13. Ezk 16:61, 63. 18:28. Hg 1:7. Lk 15:17. **bethink themselves.** Heb. bring back to their heart. Dt 4:39. 30:1. **saying.** Ezr 9:6, 7. Ne 1:6, etc. 9:26-30. Ps 106:6. Is 64:6-12. Da *9:5-11. Zc 12:10. **done perversely.** Jb 33:27, 28. Je 31:18-20. Lk 15:18.
48. **And so return.** Dt 4:29. 6:5, 6. Jg 10:15, 16. 1 S 7:3, 4. Ne 1:9. Ps 119:2, 10, 145. Pr 23:26. Is 55:6, 7. Je 3:10. 24:7. *29:12-14. Da 9:13. Ho 14:1, 2. Ac 8:37. Ro ✓10:10. **soul.** Heb. *nephesh,* Ge +34:3. **pray unto.** See on ver. 29, 30. Da 6:10. **the city.** See on ver. 44.
49. **Then hear.** See on ver. 30. **cause.** *or,* right. ver. 45. 2 K 19:19. Zc 1:15, 16.
50. **and give them.** 2 Ch 30:9. Ezr 7:6, 27, 28. Ne 1:11. 2:4-8. Ps 106:46. Pr ✓16:7. Da 1:9, 10. Ac 7:9, 10.
51. **thy people.** ver. 53. Ex 32:11, 12. Nu 14:13-19. Dt 9:26-29. 2 Ch 6:39. Ne 1:10. Is 63:16-18. 64:9. Je 51:19. **the furnace.** Dt 4:20. Pr 17:3. 27:21. Is 48:10. Je *11:4. Ezk 22:18, 20, 22.
52. **That thine.** ver. 29. 2 Ch 6:40. **in all that.** Ps 86:5. 145:18. **they call.** ✓24A, Ge +32:24.
53. **separate.** Ex 19:5, 6. 33:16. Nu 23:9. Dt 4:34. 7:6-8. 9:26, 29. 10:15. 14:2. 32:9. 2 C *6:14-18. T *2:14. 1 P *2:9. **thine inheritance.** Dt +*32:9. 1 S +✓10:1. Ne 1:10. Je 10:16. Ep 1:18. 1 P 2:9, 10. **as thou spakest.** Ex 19:5, 6. 33:16. Dt 9:26, 29. 14:2. 33:1-3, 26-29. **by the hand.** ✓144A5, Ge +9:5.
54. **when Solomon.** Lk 11:1. 22:45. **kneeling.** See on 2 Ch 6:13. Ps 95:6. Lk 22:41, 45. Ac 20:36. 21:5. **with his hands.** See on ver. 22. 2 Ch 6:12.
55. **blessed.** See on ver. 14. Nu *6:23-26. 2 S 6:18. 1 Ch 16:2.
56. **Blessed be.** See on ver. 15. **hath given rest.** Dt 3:20. 12:10, 12. Jsh 21:44. 2 Ch 14:6. He 4:3-9. **there.** Jsh 21:45. 23:14, 15. Lk 1:54, 55, 72, 73. 21:33. **failed.** Heb. fallen. Jsh 21:45. 23:14. 1 S 3:19. 2 K 10:10.
57. **The Lord.** Dt 31:6, 8. Jsh *1:5, 9. 1 Ch 28:9. 2 Ch 32:7, 8. Ps 46:7, 11. Is 8:10. 41:10. Mt *1:23. ✓28:20. Ro *8:31. He +*13:5.
58. **incline.** Jsh 24:23. 2 S 19:14. Ps 110:3. 119:36. 141:4. Pr 2:2. 21:1. SS 1:4. Je +*31:33. Ezk 36:26, 27. Ph *2:13. He *13:21. **his commandments.** See on Dt 4:1, 45. 6:1. 1 J *2:3.

59. **let these my words.** This and the following verse are a sort of supplement to the prayer; and there is an important addition to this prayer in 2 Ch 6:41, 42, apparently taken from one of the Psalms. **nigh.** Ps 102:1, 2. 141:2. Jn 17:9, 20-24. 1 J 2:2. **at all times.** Heb. the thing of a day in his day. Ex 16:4mg. 2 Ch 31:16. Ezr 3:4mg. Ne 11:23. Je 52:34mg. Da 1:5. Lk 11:3. **as the matter.** Ex 5:11. 16:4. Dt 33:25. 2 Ch 8:13. Ezr 3:4.
60. **That all.** See on ver. 43. Jsh 4:24. 1 S 17:46. 2 K 19:19. **the Lord.** 1 K 18:39. Dt 4:35, 39. Is 44:6, 8, 24. 45:5, 6, 22. Je 10:10-12. Jl 2:27. **God.** lit. "the God," that is, the only true one (Young). 1 K 18:21. Ge 5:22. 6:9, 11. 17:18. 20:6, 7. Dt 4:35. Da 9:11. **none else.** Dt 4:35, 39.
61. **perfect.** 1 K 11:4. 15:3, 14. Ge *17:1. Dt 18:13. 2 K 20:3. 1 Ch 12:38. ✓28:9. 29:9, 19. 2 Ch 15:17. *16:9. 19:9. 25:2. Jb *1:1, 8. Ps 37:37. Is *38:3. 2 C *7:1. Ph *3:12-16. Ju 24, 25.
62. **the king.** 2 S 6:17-19. 2 Ch 7:4-7.
63. **a sacrifice.** Le ch. 3. +*7:11. 1 Ch 29:21. 2 Ch 15:11. 29:32-35. 30:24. 35:7-9. Ezr 6:16, 17. Ezk 45:17. Mi 6:7. **peace offerings.** Le +*23:19. **two and twenty thousand.** We are not to suppose that all these victims were sacrificed in one day, or on one altar; for this was the whole amount of those that had been offered during the *fourteen days* which the feast of tabernacles lasted; and there appears to have been an altar erected in the middle of the court, which was set apart for that purpose, in consequence of the great altar of burnt offering being not sufficient for the multitude of sacrifices then offered. **dedicated.** lit. "to make narrow," hence to "set apart." Nu 7:10, 11, 84-88. Dt 20:5. 2 Ch 2:4. 7:5. Ezr 6:16, 17. Ne 12:27. Pr ✓22:6. Jn 10:22.
64. **hallow.** 2 Ch 7:7. **burnt offerings.** Le +*23:12. **meat offerings.** Le +*23:13. **peace offerings.** Le +*23:19. **the brazen.** 2 Ch 4:1.
65. **held.** ver. 2. Le 23:34-43. 2 Ch 7:8, 9. **a great.** 2 Ch 30:13. Ps 40:9, 10. **from the entering.** 1 K 4:21, 24. Ge 10:18. Nu 13:21. 34:5, 8. Jsh 13:5. Jg 3:3. 2 S 8:9. 2 K 14:25. 1 Ch 1:16. 18:3, 9. 2 Ch 7:8. 8:3, 4. Is 10:9. Je 39:5. 49:23. Ezk 47:16, 20. Am 6:2, 14. Zc 9:2. **the river.** Ge 15:18. Ex 23:31. Nu 34:5. Jsh 13:3. Is +*27:12. **seven days.** 2 Ch 7:8, 9. 30:23.
66. **the eighth day.** In the parallel passage of Chronicles this is termed "the three and twentieth day of the seventh month;" that is, the *ninth* day of the dedication; which Jarchi reconciles by supposing that Solomon gave them leave to return on the *eighth* day, and many of them did return; and that he dismissed the remainder on the *ninth,* or twenty-third of the seventh month: see Note on ver. 1. 2 Ch 7:10. 31:1. **blessed.** *or,* thanked. ver. 1, 47. **joyful.** Dt 12:7, 12, 18. 16:11. 2 Ch 29:36. 30:26, 27. Ne 8:10. Ps 81:1. 95:1, 2. 100:1, 2. 106:4, 5. 122:6, 9. 149:2, 5. Is 61:9, 10. 66:13, 14. Je 31:12-14. Zp 3:14. Zc 9:9, 17. Ac 2:46. Ga 5:22. Ph 4:4. **tents.** 2 S 18:17. **glad of heart.** 1 S 25:36. 2 S 13:28. 2 Ch 7:10. **David.** ✓171R, Ex +12:40. David is named, but Solomon, his son, is understood together with him; see 2 Ch 7:10, where it is expressly added; and 1 K 10:9.

1 KINGS 9

God appears again to Solomon, and makes a covenant with him, 1-9. Transactions between Solomon and Hiram, 10-14. Solomon builds or rebuilds several cities, 15-19. He subjects the remnant of the Canaanites to bond-service, and employs the Israelites in more honorable offices, 20-23. Pharaoh's daughter removes to her house, 24. Solomon sacrifices thrice every year, 25. His navy fetches gold from Ophir, 26-28.

1. A.M. 3013. B.C. 991. **it came.** 1 K 6:37, 38. 7:1, 51. 2 Ch 7:11, etc. **the house.** 2 Ch 8:1-6. Ec 2:4. **all Solomon's desire.** ver. 11, 19. 2 Ch 8:6. Ec 2:10. 6:9. Is 21:4. **pleased.** Ge 34:19. 2 Ch 7:11. Ec 2:4-6.

2. **as he.** 1 K 3:5. 11:9. 2 Ch 1:7-12. 7:12.

3. **I have heard.** 2 K *20:5. Ps 10:17. 66:19. 116:1. Da *9:23. Jn *11:42. Ac 10:31. 1 J √5:14. **I have hallowed.** 1 K 8:10, 11. Ex 20:11. Nu 16:38. Mt *6:9. **to put.** 1 K 8:29. Dt 12:5, 11, 21. *16:11. **for ever.** Heb. *olam,* Ex +12:24. **mine eyes.** ✧22A7, Dt +11:12. Dt *11:12. 2 Ch 6:40. *7:15, 16. Ps 132:13, 14. SS 4:9, 10. Is ◐3:8. Je *15:1.

4. **And if.** Ge +4:7. **thou wilt walk.** 1 K *3:14. 8:25. 11:4, 6, 38. 14:8. *15:5. Ge *17:1. Dt *28:1. 2 Ch 7:17, 18. Jb *23:11, 12. Ps 15:2. 26:1, 11. Pr 20:7. Zc 3:7. Lk 1:6. 1 Th 4:1, 2. **in integrity.** Ge 20:5, 6. Ps *78:72. *101:2. Pr 10:9. 28:18.

5. **I will establish.** 1 K *2:4. 6:12. 8:15, 20. 2 S *7:12, 16. 1 Ch 22:9, 10. Ps *89:28-39. *132:11, 12. **for ever.** Heb. *olam,* Ex +12:24.

6. **if ye.** 1 S 2:30. 2 S 7:14-16. 1 Ch *28:9. 2 Ch 7:19-22. 15:2. Ps √89:30-37. **go.** 1 K 11:4-10. Jsh 23:15, 16.

7. **I will cut.** Le 18:24-28. Dt 4:26. 29:26-28. 2 K 17:20-23. 25:9, 21. Je 7:15. 24:9. Ezk 33:27-29. Lk *21:24. **this house.** See on ver. 3. 2 K 25:9. 2 Ch 7:20. 36:19. Je 7:4-14. 26:6, 18. 52:13. La 2:6, 7. Ezk 24:21. Mi 3:12. Mt 24:2. Lk *21:24. **name.** Dt 12:11. **and Israel.** Dt 28:37. Ne 4:1-4. Ps 44:14. Is 65:15. Je 24:9. La 2:15, 16. Jl 2:17. **proverb.** Nu +21:27. Dt 28:37. **byword.** Dt 28:37. 2 Ch 7:20. Ps 44:14. Je 24:9.

8. **at.** 2 Ch 7:21. Is 64:11. Je 19:8. 49:17. 50:13. Da 9:12. **hiss.** Jb 27:23. Is 5:26. 7:18. Je 19:8. 49:17. 50:13. La 2:15, 16. Ezk 27:36. Zp 2:15. Zc 10:8. **Why.** Dt 29:24-26. Je 2:11. 22:8, 9, 28.

9. **Because.** Dt 29:25-28. 2 Ch 7:22. Je 2:10-13, 19. 5:19. 16:10-13. 50:7. La 2:16, 17. 4:13-15. Ezk 36:17-20. Zp 1:4, 5. **therefore.** Je 12:7, 8.

10. **at the end of twenty.** ver. 1. 1 K 6:37, 38. 7:1. 2 Ch 8:1, etc.

11. **Now Hiram.** See on 1 K 5:6-10. 2 Ch 2:8-10, 16. **King Solomon.** 2 Ch 8:2. **of Galilee.** See on Jsh +*20:7n.

12. **they pleased him not.** Heb. were not right in his eyes. Nu 22:34mg. Jg 14:3mg.

13. **What cities.** ✧85N. Erotesis; or, Interrogating B954. The asking of questions without waiting for the answer: in disparagements. For another instance of this figure see Is 2:22. **my brother.** 1 K 5:1, 2. Am 1:9. **Cabul.** *that is,* Displeasing, *or* dirty. Jsh 19:27. Josephus (Ant. l. viii. c.2) says that *Cabul,* in the Phoenician language, signifies *ouk areskon,* "displeasing;" and that these cities were situated in the neighborhood of Tyre. Most commentators are persuaded that the city *Cabul* in the tribe of Asher was one; and probably from this Hiram took occasion to give this name to all the other cities which Solomon had ceded to him. Jsh 19:27.

14. **Hiram sent.** ver. 11, 28. 1 K 10:10, 14, 21.

15. A.M. 2989-3029. B.C. 1015-975. **the reason.** ver. 21. See on 1 K 5:13. **to build.** ver. 10. 1 K 6:38. 7:1. 2 Ch 8:1. **Millo.** Millo is said to have been a deep valley, between the ancient city of Jebus and the city of David on mount Zion. This Solomon filled up, and built upon; and it became a fortified place, and a place for public assemblies. ver. 24. 1 K 11:27. Jg 9:6, 20. 2 S 5:9. 2 K 12:20. 2 Ch 32:5. **the wall.** Ps 51:18. **Hazor.** Probably the city of *Hazor* in Naphtali, and the famous capital of Jabin, situated on the lake Merom or Semechon, and placed by Josephus south of Tyre, near Ptolemais. Jsh 11:1. 19:36. Jg 4:2. 2 K 15:29. **Migiddo.** 1 K 4:12. Jsh +17:11. Jg 5:19. 2 K 9:27. 23:29, 30. 2 Ch 35:22. Zc 12:11. Re 16:16. **Gezer.** ver. 16, 17. Jsh 10:33. 16:10. 21:21. Jg 1:29. 1 Ch 6:67. 20:4.

16. **Gezer.** i.e. *precipice,* ✱S#1507h. ver. 15, 17. Jsh 10:33. 12:12. 16:3, 10. 21:21. Jg 1:29, 29. 1 Ch 6:67. 7:28. 20:4. **Canaanites.** Ge +10:18. **daughter.** See on ver. 24. 1 K 3:1.

17. **Gezer.** Jsh 16:10. 21:21. Jg 1:29. 1 S 27:8. **Beth-horon.** Jsh 16:3. 19:44. 21:22. 2 Ch 7:4-6, etc. 8:5.

18. **Baalath.** Jsh 19:44. **Tadmor.** or, "Tamor," a palm tree, in Greek, *Palmyra,* 2 Ch 8:3, 4. Ezk 47:19.

19. **the cities of store.** 1 K 4:26-28. Ex 1:11. 2 Ch 8:4, 6. 16:4. 17:12. 32:28. **chariots.** 1 K 4:26. 10:26. 2 Ch 1:14. 8:6. 9:25. **that which Solomon desired.** Heb. the desire of Solomon which he desired. See on ver. 1. Ec 2:10. 6:9. **Lebanon.** 1 K 7:2. 2 Ch 8:6. 9:16.

20. **left.** 2 Ch 8:7, 8, etc. **Amorites.** Ge +10:16. 15:19-21. Ex 23:23, 28-33. 34:11, 12. Dt 7:1-3. **Hitites.** Ge +15:20. **Perizzites.** Ge +13:7. **Hivites.** Ge +10:17. **Jebusites.** Ge +10:16. Jsh 15:63. 17:12. Jg 1:21. 3:1.

21. **left.** Jg 1:21, 27-35. 2:20-23. 3:1-4. Ps 106:34-36. **not.** Jsh 15:63. 17:12, 16-18. **levy.** ver. 15. 1 K 5:13. Jg 1:28, 35. **tribute.** He made them do the most laborious parts of the public works, the *Israelites* being exempt from all but the more honorable employments. Ge 9:25, 26. Le 25:39. Jg 1:28. **bondservice.** Ge 9:25, 26. 49:15. 2 S 12:31. 2 Ch 8:7, 8. Ezr 2:55-58. Ne 7:57. 11:3.

22. **of the children.** Le *25:39. **but they were men.** 1 K 4:1-27. 1 S 8:11, 12. 2 Ch 8:9, 10.

23. **chief.** 1 K 5:16. 2 Ch 2:18. 8:10.

24. **Pharaoh's.** ver. 16. 1 K 3:1. 7:8. 2 Ch *8:11. **the city of David.** 2 S 5:9. **Millo.** ver. 15. 1 K 11:27. 2 Ch 32:5.

25. **three times.** Ex 23:14-17. 34:23. Dt 16:16. 2 Ch 8:12, 13. At the Passover, Pentecost, and Tabernacle festivals (Young). **burnt offerings.** Le +*23:12. **peace offerings.** Le +*23:19. **he burnt.** Ex 30:7. 1 Ch 23:13. 2 Ch 26:16-21. 29:11. 34:25. **upon the altar that was before.** Heb. upon it which *was* before. **So he finished the house.** 1 K 6:38. 2 Ch 8:16.

26. **made a navy.** ver. 27. 1 K 10:11, 22. 2 Ch 8:12, 17, 18, etc. Is 33:21. **Ezion-geber.** i.e. *the giant's backbone,* ✱S#6100h. 1 K 9:26. 22:48. Nu 33:35, 36. Dt 2:8. 2 Ch 8:17. 20:36. **Eloth.** i.e. *grove,* ✱S#359h. 2 K 14:22. 16:6. 2 Ch 8:17. 26:2. **shore.** Heb. lip. Jg +7:22mg. 2 K 2:13mg.

27. **his servants.** 1 K 5:6, 9. 22:49. 2 Ch 20:36, 37.

28. **Ophir.** 1 K 10:11. 22:48. Ge 10:29. 1 Ch 1:23. 29:4. 2 Ch 8:18. 9:10. Jb 22:24. 28:16. Ps 45:9. Is 13:12. The locality of Ophir is unknown; some say,

in Arabia, near Aden, others India, and others Mozambique, in Africa (Young). **four hundred and twenty.** In 2 Ch 8:18, it is 450.

1 KINGS 10

The queen of Sheba comes to visit Solomon and to propose hard questions to him, 1, 2. He answers her questions, and she greatly admires his piety, wisdom, and magnificence, 3-9. Their presents to each other, 10-13. Solomon's yearly revenue, 14, 15. His golden targets and shields, 16, 17. His throne of ivory, 18-20. His rich vessels, and lucrative commerce; and the presents brought him, by such as came to hear his wisdom, 21-25. His chariots and horsemen, 26. The plenty of silver and cedar in his time, 27. Horses, chariots, and linen-yarn, brought out of Egypt, 28, 29.

1. A.M. 3014. B.C. 990. **And when.** 2 Ch 9:1, etc. Mt *12:42. Lk 11:31. **Sheba.** i.e. *seven; oath,* ✻S#7614h. ver. 4, 10, 13. Ge 10:7, 28. 25:3. 1 Ch 1:9, 22, 32. 2 Ch 9:1, 3, 9, 12. Jb 1:15. 6:19. Ps 72:10, 15. Is 60:6. Je 6:20. Ezk 27:22, 23. 38:13. **heard.** 1 K 4:31, 34. **concerning.** Jb 28:28. Pr 2:3-6. Jn *17:3. 1 C 1:20, 21. **prove him.** Jg 14:12-14. Ps 49:4. Pr *1:5, 6. Mt 13:11, 35. Mk 4:34. **hard questions.** Nu +12:8. Da 8:23.

2. **a very great train.** 2 K 5:5, 9. Is 60:6-9. Ac 25:23. **spices.** Ex 25:6. 2 K 20:13. **communed.** Ge 18:33. Jb 4:2. Ps 4:4. 62:8. Da 1:19. Lk 24:15. Jn 1:39.

3. **told her.** 2 Ch 9:2. Pr 1:5, 6. 13:20. Is 42:16. Mt 13:11. Jn *7:17. 15:15. 1 C 1:30. Col *2:3. **questions.** Heb. words. **hid from the king.** See on ver. 1. 1 K 3:12. 2 S 14:17, 20. Da 2:20-23. Jn +*2:24, 25. Col 2:2, 3. He *4:12, 13.

4. **Solomon's.** 1 K 3:28. 4:29-31. 2 Ch 9:3, 4. Ec 12:9. Mt 12:42. **the house.** 1 K ch. 6. 7.

5. **the meat.** 1 K 4:22, 23. **attendance.** Heb. standing. **cupbearers.** *or,* butlers. Ge 40:1. **ascent.** The LXX. and Vulgate render the original *weolatho asher yaaleh baith yehowah* by "And the burnt offerings (or holocausts) which he offered in the house of the Lord;" with which the Chaldee, Syriac, and Arabic agree; and this seems to be the true sense of the passage. 2 K 16:18. 1 Ch 9:18. 26:16. 2 Ch 23:13. Ezk 44:3. 46:2. **there was no.** ✓102, Ge +2:24. Jsh 5:1. 2 Ch 9:4. **spirit.** Heb. *ruach,* Ge +41:8.

6. **report.** Heb. word. 2 Ch 9:5, 6mg. **acts.** *or,* sayings.

7. **I believed not.** Is 64:4. Zc 9:17. Mk 16:11. Jn 20:25-29. 1 C 2:9. 1 J 3:2. **came.** Jn 1:39. **thy wisdom and prosperity exceeded the fame.** Heb. thou hast added wisdom and goodness to the fame.

8. **happy are these.** 2 Ch 9:7, 8. Pr 3:13, 14. 8:34. 10:21. 13:20. Mt 13:16, 17. Lk 10:23, 24, 39-42. 11:28, 31. **continually.** Is 40:31. +*58:11. Ho 12:6.

9. **Blessed.** See on 1 K 5:7. Ps 72:17-19. **delighteth.** Ps 18:19. 22:8. Is 42:1. 62:4. **to set thee.** Pr 8:15. **because the.** Dt 7:8. 1 Ch 17:22. 2 Ch 2:11. **for ever.** Heb. *olam,* Ex +*12:24. **to do.** 2 S 8:15. 23:3. Ps 72:2. Pr 8:15, 16. Is 9:7. 11:4, 5. 32:1, 2. Je 23:5, 6. Ro 13:3, 4.

10. **she gave.** See on ver. 2. 1 K 9:14. Ps 72:10, 15. Mt 2:11. **an hundred.** Dake (*Annotated Reference Bible*) notes that 120 talents of gold at $29,085 would be $3,490,000. **spices.** Ge 43:11. Ex 30:34. **and pre-**

cious. Pr 3:13-15. 20:15. Re 21:11.

11. **Hiram.** ✓171R, Ex +12:40. The navy of Hiram is named, but Solomon is included; see 1 K 9:26, 27. **from Ophir.** See on 1 K 9:27, 28. 2 Ch 8:18. Ps 45:9. **almug.** 2 Ch 2:8. 9:10, 11, algum trees.

12. **pillars.** *or,* rails. Heb. a prop. 2 Ch 9:11. **harps.** 1 Ch 23:5. 25:1, etc. Ps 92:1-3. 150:3-5. Re 14:2, 3.

13. **all her desire.** ver. 2. 1 K 9:1. Ps 20:4. 37:4. Ml 3:10. Mt 15:28. Jn 14:13, 14. Ep 3:20. **which Solomon gave her of his royal bounty.** Heb. which he gave her, according to the hand of king Solomon.

14. A.M. 2989-3029. B.C. 1015-975. **was six hundred threescore and six.** ver. 14. Re 13:18. At the rate in ver. 14, this would be $19,370,610. This was what he got annually in bullion. See on 1 K 9:28.

15. **all the kings.** 1 Ch 9:24. 2 Ch 9:13, 14. 17:11. Ps 72:10. Is 21:13. Ga 4:25. **governors.** *or,* captains. 1 K 20:24. 2 K 18:24. 2 Ch 9:14. Ezr 5:14. 8:36. Ne 2:7, 9. 3:7. 5:14, 15, 18. 12:26. Est 3:12. 8:9. 9:3. Is 36:9. Je 51:23, 28, 57. Ezk 23:6, 12, 23. Hg 1:1, 14. 2:2, 21. Ml 1:8.

16. **two hundred.** Dake notes that 200 targets, 600 shekels each, would be 120,000; and these at $9.69 1/2 a shekel, would be worth $1,163,400. 1 K 14:26-28. 2 Ch 9:15, 16. 12:9, 10.

17. **three hundred shields.** The 300 shields were worth $872,550. Combined, targets and shields were worth $2,035,950. These shields were taken away by Shishak, king of Egypt in the reign of Rehoboam, son of Solomon (1 K 14:26). **in the house.** See on 1 K 7:2.

18. **a great throne.** 2 Ch 9:17-19. Ps 45:6. 110:1. 122:5. He 1:3, 8. Re 20:11. **ivory.** ver. 22. 1 K 22:39. Ps 45:8. Ezk 27:6. Am 6:4. Re 18:12.

19. **behind.** Heb. on the hinder part thereof. **stays.** Heb. hands.

20. **lions.** Ge 49:9. Nu 23:24. 24:9. Re 5:5. **the like made.** Heb. so made.

21. **drinking.** 2 Ch 9:20-22. **the house.** ver. 17. 1 K 7:2. **none were of silver.** *or,* there was no silver in them.

22. **Tharshish.** 1 K 22:48. Ge +10:4. 2 Ch 9:21. 20:36, 37. Ps 48:7. 72:10. Is 2:16. 23:1, 6, 10. 60:9. 66:19. Je 10:9. Ezk 27:12. Jon 1:3, Tarshish. **ivory.** *or,* elephants' teeth. ver. 18. Am 3:15. **apes.** rather, monkeys. **peacocks.** Jb 39:13.

23. **exceeded.** 1 K 3:12, 13. 4:29-34. 2 Ch 9:22, 23. Ps *89:27. Ep 3:8. Col *1:18, 19. *2:2, 3.

24. **sought to.** Heb. sought the face of. ✓171Q, Ge +3:19. **which God.** See on 1 K 3:9, 12, 28. Pr 2:6. Da 1:17. 2:21, 23. 5:11. Ja *1:5.

25. **every man.** ver. 10. Jg 3:15. 1 S 10:27. 2 S 8:2, 10. 2 Ch 26:8. Jb 42:11. Ps 72:10, 15. Is 36:16. Mt 2:11. **and mules.** 1 K 1:33. 18:5. Ge 36:24. Ezr 2:66. Est 8:10, 14. Is 66:20. Ezk 27:14. **a rate.** 2 K 17:4. 2 Ch 9:24.

26. **Solomon.** See on 1 K 4:26. Dt 17:16. 2 Ch 1:14. 9:25. Is 2:7. **in the cities.** 2 Ch 9:25.

27. **the king.** 2 Ch 1:15-17. 9:27. Jb 22:24, 25. **made.** Heb. gave. **as stones.** ✓102B, Ge +13:16.

28. **Solomon,** etc. Heb. the going forth of the horses which *was* Solomon's. **horses brought.** Dt 17:16. 2 Ch 1:16, 17. 9:28. Is *31:1-3. 36:9. Ho 14:3. **and linen yarn.** Ge 41:42. Pr 7:16. Is 19:9. Ezk 27:7.

29. **for six hundred.** This was the ordinary price of a *chariot,* as 150 shekels was that of a *horse.* It

seems that neither horses nor chariots came out of Egypt but by means of Solomon's servants. **the kings.** Jsh 1:4. 2 K 7:6. **Hittites.** 1 K 11:1. Ge +15:20. Jg 1:26. **their means.** Heb. their hand. ⌐121BA, Dt +32:36. Nu 15:23. 2 Ch 7:6mg. 8:18. Ho 12:10mg. Ml +1:1mg, 9mg.

1 KINGS 11

Solomon, having taken very many wives and concubines, even strange women, is in his old age seduced by them into idolatry, 1-8. The Lord threatens to rend the greater part of the kingdom from his family, 9-13. Solomon finds an adversary in Hadad the Edomite, who had been entertained in Egypt, 14-22; and in Rezon, who reigned in Damascus, 23-25; and in Jeroboam, to whom Ahijah foretold that he should reign over ten tribes, and whom Solomon in vain attempts to kill, 26-40. Solomon dies and is buried, and Rehoboam succeeds him, 41-43.

1. **A.M.** 3020-3029. B.C. 984-975. **loved.** ver. 8. Ge 6:2-5. Dt *17:17. Ne 13:23-27. Pr 2:16. 5:3-20. 6:24. 7:5. 22:14. 23:33. **together with.** *or,* beside. 1 K 3:1. Le 18:18. **Moabites.** Nu 24:17. 2 S 8:2. Je 48:45. **Ammonites.** 1 K 14:21, 31. **Edomites.** Ge 25:26, 30. 36:1. Nu 24:18. Am 1:11. 9:12. **Zidonians.** 1 K 16:31. Jg 18:7. **Hittites.** 1 K 10:29. Ge +15:20.

2. **Ye shall not go in.** Ex 23:32, 33. 34:16. Dt *7:3, 4. Jsh 23:12, 13. Ezr 9:12. 10:2, etc. Ml 2:11. **surely.** 1 K 16:31-33. Nu 25:1-3. Jg 3:6, 7. 2 Ch 21:6. 2 C *6:14-16. **Solomon.** Ge 2:24. 34:3. Jg 16:4-21. 2 Ch 19:2. Ps 139:21. Ro 1:32. 12:9. 1 C 15:33. Re 2:4.

3. **seven hundred.** Jg 8:30, 31. 9:5. 2 S 3:2-5. 5:13-16. 2 Ch 11:21. Ec 7:28. **wives.** Ge +4:19.

4. **when Solomon.** ver. 42. 1 K 6:1. 9:10. 14:21. **his wives.** See on ver. 2. Dt *7:4. *17:17. Ne *13:26, 27. **turned away.** T#23. Ex 32:1-6. 1 S 15:11 (T#19). 2 S 12:7. 2 Ch 16:7-10. Je 8:5. Ho 11:7. Mt 16:6. Lk 19:14 (T#695). **his heart.** ver. 6, 38. 6:12, 13. 8:61. 9:4. *15:3, 14. 2 K *20:3. 1 Ch *28:9. 29:19. 2 Ch 17:3. 25:2. *31:20, 21. 34:2.

5. **Ashtoreth.** i.e. *queen of heaven,* *S#6253h. ver. 33. Jg 2:13. 10:6. 1 S 7:3, 4. 12:10. 2 K 23:13. Je *2:10-13. Je ◑7:18. **Milcom.** i.e. *high king,* *S#4445h. ver. 7, 33. Le *18:21. *20:2-5, Molech. 2 K 23:13. Zp *1:5, Malcham.

6. **went not fully after.** Heb. fulfilled not after. Nu *14:24. Jsh 14:8, *14h.

7. **build an high.** Le 26:30. Nu 33:52. 2 K 21:2, 3. 23:13, 14. Ps 78:58. Ezk 20:28, 29. **Chemosh.** Nu 21:29. Jg 11:24. Je 48:13. **Molech.** Le 18:21. 20:2. 2 K 23:13, 14. Je 32:35. 48:13. **abomination.** Dt 13:14. 17:3, 4. 27:15. Is 44:19. Ezk 18:12. Da 11:31. 12:11. Re 17:4, 5. **the hill.** This was the *mount of Olives,* which lay *east* of Jerusalem; and that the Hebrews would consider *before it*; for the very term used to denote the *east, kedem,* means "before," while *acharon,* "behind," sometimes signifies the *west.* Ge 33:2. 2 S 15:30. 2 K 23:13. Zc 14:4. Mt 26:30. Ac 1:9, 12.

8. **all his strange wives.** ver. 1. Ezk 16:22-29. Ho 4:11, 12. 1 C 10:11, 12, 20-22.

9. **angry.** Ex 4:14. Nu 12:9. Dt 3:26. 9:8, 20. 2 S 6:7. 11:27. 1 Ch 21:7. Ps 78:58-60. 90:7, 8. **his heart.** ver. 2, 3. Dt 7:4. Pr +*4:23. Is *29:13, 14. Ho 4:11. 2 T *4:10. **which had appeared.** 1 K 3:5. 9:2. **twice.** T *3:10.

10. **commanded.** 1 K 6:12, 13. 9:4-7. 2 Ch 7:17-22.

11. **is done of thee.** Heb. is with thee. **thou hast not.** Is 29:13, 14. **I will surely.** ver. 31. 1 K 12:15, 16, 20. Nu 14:23, 35. 1 S 2:30-32. 13:13, 14. 15:26-28. 2 S 12:9-12.

12. **in the days.** 1 K 21:29. 2 K 20:17, 19. 22:19, 20. **for David.** 1 K 9:4, 5. Ge 12:2. 19:29. **I will rend it out.** See on Ex 20:5. **the hand.** ⌐144A5, Ge +9:5.

13. **Howbeit.** ver. 39. 2 S *7:15, 16. 1 Ch 17:13, 14. 2 Ch 6:6. Ps 89:33-37. **one tribe.** ver. 35, 36. 1 K 12:20. **for David.** See on 1 K 11:12, 32. Dt 9:5. 2 K 13:23. 19:34. Ps 89:49. 132:1, 17. Is 9:7. Je 33:17-26. Lk 1:32, 33. **for Jerusalem's.** Dt 12:5, 11. 2 K 21:4. 23:27. Ps 132:13, 14. Is 14:32. 62:1, 7. Je 33:15, 16.

14. **the Lord.** 1 K 12:15. 1 S 26:19. 2 S 24:1. 1 Ch 5:26. Is 10:5, 26. 13:17. Am ◑+*3:6. **an adversary.** lit. "a satan." ver. 23, 25. 1 K 5:4h. Nu 22:22h. 1 S 29:4h. 2 S 7:14. Ps 89:30-34. 1 P 5:8. **Edom.** Am 1:11.

15. **when David.** 2 S 8:14. 1 Ch 18:12, 13. Ps 60, title. 108:10. **after he had.** Ge 25:23. 27:40. Nu 24:18, 19. Dt 20:13. Ml 1:2, 3. **every male.** Nu 31:17.

16. **Joab remain.** 1 Ch 11:6. **all.** *⌐171A, Ex +9:6.

17. **Hadad.** Ex 2:1-10. 2 S 4:4. 2 K 11:2. Mt 2:13, 14. **a little child.** *Nuur katon,* rather, "a little boy;" one who was apprehensive of his danger, and could, with his father's servants, make his escape.

18. **Midian.** Probably not the *Midian* east of the Red sea, to which Moses fled (Ex 2:15, etc.), but the *Midian* east of the Dead sea, and south of Moab. These Midianites, whose daughters seduced the Israelites to commit idolatry (Nu 22:4, 7. 25:15. 31:2, etc.), were descendants of *Midian,* son of Abraham (Ge 25:2). Their capital city was called *Midian,* and its remains were to be seen in the time of Eusebius and Jerome: it was situated on the Arnon, south of the city Ar, or Areopolis. Ge 25:2, 4. Nu 22:4. 25:6, 14, 18. **Paran.** Probably the city of *Paran,* or the district around it, situated in the south of Idumea, and according to Eusebius, three days' journey east from Elah or Elath, at the head of the eastern branch, or Elamitic gulf of the Red sea. Ge 14:6. 21:21. Nu 10:12. Dt 1:1. 33:2. Hab 3:3.

19. **found.** Ge 39:4, 21. Ac 7:10, 21. **that he gave.** Ge 41:45. **Tahpenes.** i.e. *head of the age,* according to Gesenius. *S#8472h. ver. 20, 20. Je 43:7-9. **queen.** 1 K 15:13. 2 K 10:13. 2 Ch 15:16. Je 13:18. 29:2.

20. **Genubath.** i.e. *theft,* *S#1592h. **weaned.** Ge 21:7. 1 S 1:+22n, 24.

21. **Hadad.** 1 K 2:10, 34. Ex 4:19. Mt 2:20. **Let me depart.** Heb. Send me away. Ge 45:24. Jsh 2:21. 1 S 9:26. 2 S 3:21.

22. **But.** Je 2:31. Lk 22:35. **Nothing.** Heb. Not. **let me go.** Je 18:22, 23. Ps 37:8. Mk 14:31.

23. **God.** See on ver. *14. 2 S 16:11. Ezr 1:1. Is 13:17. 37:26. 45:5. Ezk 38:16. **Rezon.** i.e. *to wax lean; a prince,* *S#7331h. **Eliadah.** i.e. *God knows,* *S#450h. 2 S 5:16. 1 Ch 3:8. 2 Ch 17:17. **Hadadezer.** 2 S 8:3, 6. 10:8, 15-18. 1 Ch 18:3-9. 19:6, 16-19, Hadarezer. Ps 60, title.

24. **to Damascus.** 1 K 19:15. 20:34. Ge 14:15. Ac 9:2. **in Damascus.** *Damascus,* called also "Damesk," but generally "El Sham," by the Arabs, is situated in a delightful plain, well watered by the Barrada, at the eastern foot of Antilibanus, being surrounded by

the hills in the form of a triumphal arch, 136 miles north of Jerusalem, 195 miles south of Antioch, and 276 miles S.S.W. of Diarbekir. It is a city of the highest antiquity, being at least as ancient as the time of Abraham: it has been often captured, and several times demolished, but has always risen to splendor and dignity. The modern town is described by Maundrell as of a long, straight figure, its ends pointing nearly N.E. and S.W. It is very slender in the middle, but swells bigger at each end, especially at that to the N.E. According to Niebuhr, the walls are something less than a league and a half in circumference; and the population is estimated at from 100,000 to 150,000.

25. **an adversary.** ver. 14. **all the days.** 1 K 5:4. 2 Ch 15:2. **did.** √63B, Ge +25:28. **abhorred.** Ge 34:30. Dt 23:7. 2 S 16:21. Ps 106:40. Zc 11:8.

26. **Jeroboam.** i.e. *whose people is many; the people will contend*, ✱S#3379h. (1) Founder of the kingdom of Israel, a son of Nebat, B.C. 975-954. ver. 11, 28, 29, 31, 40, 40. 1 K 12:2, 2, 3, 12, 15, 20, 25, 26, 32. 13:1, 4, 33, 34. 14:1, 2, 2, 4, 5, 6, 7, 10, 10, 10, 11, 13, 13, 14, 16, 17, 19, 20, 30. 15:1, 6, 7, 9, 25, 29, 29, 30, 34. 16:2, 3, 7, 19, 26, 31. 21:22. 22:52. 2 K 3:3. 9:9. 10:29, 31. 13:2, 6, 11. 14:24. 15:9, 18, 24, 28. 17:21, 21, 22. 23:15. 1 Ch 5:17. 2 Ch 9:29. 10:2, 2, 3, 12, 15. 11:4, 14. 12:15. 13:1, 2, 3, 4, 6, 8, 13, 15, 19, 20. (2) Son of Joash and great grandson of Jehu, reigned B.C. 825-784. 2 K 13:13. 14:16, 23, 27, 28, 29. 15:1, 8. 1 Ch 5:17. Ho 1:1. Am 1:1. 7:9, 10, 11. **Nebat.** i.e. *regard*, ✱S#5028h. 1 K 12:2, 15. 15:1. 16:3, 26, 31. 21:22. 22:52. 2 K 3:3. 9:9. 10:29. 13:2, 11. 14:24. 15:9, 18, 24, 28. 17:21. 23:15. 2 Ch 9:29. 10:2, 15. 13:6. **an Ephrathite.** Ge 35:16. Ru 1:2. 1 S 1:1. 17:12. 1 Ch 2:19. **Solomon's servant.** 1 K 9:22. 2 Ch 13:6. **Zeruah.** i.e. *leprous; a hornet*, ✱S#6871h.

27. **lifted up.** 2 S 20:21. Pr 30:32. Is 26:11. **Solomon.** See on 1 K 9:15, 24. **repaired.** Heb. closed. Ge 2:21. 7:16. 19:6, 10. Am 9:11. **the breaches.** Ne 4:7. Ps 60:2. Is 22:9. Ezk 13:5. **the city.** See on 2 S 5:7.

28. **was industrious.** Heb. did work. Pr 22:29. **he made.** 1 K 5:16. **charge.** Heb. burden. Dt 1:12. Is 14:25. Mt *11:30. **the house.** Jsh 18:5. Jg 1:22, 23. 2 S 19:20. Am 5:6. Zc *10:6.

29. **Ahijah.** i.e. *brother of Jah.* 1 K 12:15. 14:2, 6, 18. 2 Ch 9:29. 10:15. **Shilonite.** ✱S#7888h. 1 K 12:15. 15:29. Jsh ◗18:1. 1 Ch 9:5. 2 Ch 9:29. 10:15. **and they two.** Ge 4:8. 2 S 14:6.

30. **rent it.** 1 S 15:27, 28. 24:4, 5. **twelve pieces.** 1 K 18:31. Ex 24:4.

31. **thus saith.** See on ver. 11, 12. 1 K 14:2.

32. **he shall.** See on 1 K 12:20. **one tribe.** √171R, Ex +12:40. "One tribe" is mentioned; but, by Synecdoche, Simeon and Benjamin are included, as well as the Levites and others who joined the tribe. See 2 Ch 15:9. 1 K 12:23. 2 Ch 11:13. All these are included, by Synecdoche, in 1 K 12:20. **for Jerusalem's sake.** See on ver. 13.

33. **they have forsaken.** ver. 9. 1 K 3:14. 6:12, 13. 9:5-7. 1 Ch *28:9. 2 Ch 15:2. Je 2:13. Ho 4:17. **Ashtoreth.** See on ver. 5-8.

34. **Howbeit.** See on ver. 12, 13, 31. Jb 11:6. Ps 103:10. Hab 3:2. **for David.** Is 55:3. **he kept.** Jn +*17:6. Ja 4:11. 1 J *2:3.

35. **I will take.** Ex 20:5, 6. **will give.** 1 K 12:15-17, 20. 2 Ch 10:15-17.

36. **one tribe.** 1 K 12:16, 17. 2 K 8:19. **David.** 1 K 15:4. 2 S 7:16, 29. 21:17. 2 K 8:19. 2 Ch 21:7. Ps 132:17. Je +√33:17-21. Am *9:11, 12. Lk 1:69, 70, 78, 79. Ac 15:16, 17. **light.** Heb. lamp, *or* candle. 2 S 21:17mg. Ps +18:28mg. 132:17mg. **the city.** see on ver. 13. 1 K 9:3. Ga 4:25, 26. He 12:22. Re 21:10.

37. **according.** ver. 26. Dt 14:26. 2 S 3:21. **soul.** Heb. *nephesh*, Ge +34:3.

38. **if thou wilt.** 1 K 3:14. 6:12. 9:4, 5. Ex 19:5. Dt 15:5. Zc 3:7. **that I will.** See on Dt 31:8. Jsh *1:5. **build thee.** 1 K 14:7-14. 2 S *7:11, 16, 26-29. 1 Ch 17:10, 24-27. **sure house.** Is +√55:3. Am +*9:11. Ac 1:6. 15:16.

39. **afflict.** 1 K 12:16. 14:8, 25, 26. Ps 89:*38-45, 49-51. **not for ever.** See on ver. 36. 1 S +*12:22. Ps 89:30-34. Is *7:14. *9:7. *11:1-10. +√41:9. 60:20. Je +*4:27. *23:5, 6. √30:11. La *3:31, 32. Zc √10:6. Ml +*3:6. Lk *1:32, 33. 2:4, 11. Ro +*11:1, 2, 29.

40. **Solomon sought.** 2 Ch 16:10. Pr 21:30. Is 14:24-27. 46:10. La 3:37. **Shishak.** i.e. *greedy of fine linen; he who will give drink*, ✱S#7895h. This is the first time we meet with the proper name of an Egyptian king in Scripture, *Pharaoh* being the general appellation for all the sovereigns of that country. Some are of opinion that *Shishak* is the same with the celebrated *Sesostris* of the Greek historians; but it is probable that this king lived long before Solomon's time. Usher thinks him to be *Sesonchis*, and places the beginning of his reign, A.M. 3026. B.C. 978. 1 K 14:25. 2 Ch 12:2, 5, 5, 9.

41. **rest.** 2 Ch 9:29-31. **acts.** *or*, words, *or* things.

42. **time.** Heb. days. **forty years.** Josephus says *fourscore years*; which is sufficiently absurd. Calmet supposes him to have been 18 years old when he came to the throne, and 58 when he died. 1 K 2:11.

43. A.M. 3029. B.C. 975. **slept with.** 1 K 1:21. +*14:20. 15:8, 24. 16:6. Ge +*25:8n. 35:29. +√49:33 w 50:13. Dt 31:16n. 2 K 16:20. 20:21. 21:18. ◗√24:6n. 2 Ch +*28:27n. **buried.** 1 K 2:10. 14:31. 2 K 21:18, 26. 2 Ch 21:20. 26:23. 28:27. Je 22:19. **Rehoboam.** 1 Ch 3:10. 2 Ch 9:31. 13:7. Mt 1:7, Roboam.

1 KINGS 12

The Israelites, assembled at Shechem to make Rehoboam king, with Jeroboam now returned from Egypt, demand redress of their grievances, 1-5. Rehoboam, rejecting the counsel of the old men, and following that of the young, answers them roughly, 6-15. Ten tribes revolt, stone Adoram, and make Jeroboam king, 16-20. Rehoboam raises an army to subdue them; but is forbidden by the prophet Shemaiah, 21-24. Jeroboam builds Shechem and Penuel, 25; and to establish his kingdom, he sets up the worship of the golden calves in Bethel and Dan, 26-33.

1. A.M. 3029. B.C. 975. **Rehoboam.** See on 1 K 11:43. 2 Ch 10:1, etc. **Shechem.** Ge 12:6, Sichem. 33:18, 19. Jsh +*20:7. 24:1, 32. Jg 9:1. Ps 60:6. Ac 7:16, Sychem.

2. **Jeroboam the son of Nebat.** 1 K 11:26-31, 40. 2 Ch 10:2, 3.

4. **our yoke.** 1 K 4:7, 20, 22, 23, 25. 9:15, 22, 23. 1 S *8:11-18. 2 Ch 10:4, 5. Mt *11:29, 30. 23:4. 1 J 5:3.

6. **consulted with.** 2 S 16:20. 17:5. Jb *12:12. *32:7.

Pr 11:14. 12:15. √13:10. 15:22. *20:18. 24:6. *27:10. Je 42:2-5. 43:2. **old men.** or, elders. Ge 50:7. 2 S 12:17.

7. they spake. ver. ◐+*10. Ex 18:19. 1 S 19:11. 2 S *20:16-22. *25:33. Da 4:27. Mt 27:19. Ac 5:35. Re 3:18. Scripture furnishes a number of suggestions for sources of wise counsel: (1) The Lord, Pr 16:9. (2) God's written word, Ps 119:105. (3) Pastors and elders, He 13:7, 17. (4) Mature men, 1 K +*12:7. (5) Parents, Col 3:20. (6) Wise women, 2 S +*20:16. (7) Wife, 1 S 19:11. 25:33. (8) Servants or employees, 2 K +*5:13. (9) The lowliest servants of Christ, 1 C 6:4. (10) Individuals who are faithful in even the smallest of matters, Lk +*16:10. Pr 20:6. (11) Individuals who are well grounded in Bible doctrine, 1 T +*4:16. (12) Those whom God has placed in authority over us, Ge +*16:9. (13) Those believers who manifest the Biblical pattern of relationships to others, Ro +*12:3; Ph +*2:3; 1 P √5:5. (14) Those individuals who by their successes demonstrate the qualities of character and special talent in the area of needed advice, Pr 13:20; Lk 16:8; Ac +*6:3. See related notes on sources of true guidance (1 K +√13:9n). **If thou wilt.** 2 Ch ∥10:6, 7. Mk *10:43, 44. Ph 2:7-11. **be a servant.** Ex +*18:21. Mt √20:25-27. *23:11. Mk 9:35. Lk 22:24-27. 2 C +*1:24. **serve them.** Ro +*12:3, 16. Ga √5:13. Ph +*2:3. **answer them.** 1 S ◐+√25:17. 2 K +√5:13. 2 Ch +*∥10:7. Pr *15:1. *25:15. Ep +*6:9. Col +*4:1. 1 T *5:19n. **speak good.** ver. 13. 2 S 15:3-6. Ec 10:4. Zc 1:13.

8. forsook the counsel. ver. 13. 1 K 13:15-22. 1 S +*25:17. 2 Ch +*∥10:8n. *25:15, 16. Pr 1:2-5, 25, 30. *19:20. 25:12. Ec 10:2, 3. **consulted with.** Pr *29:12. 1 T 5:19. **young men that.** 2 Ch +*10:8n. *13:7.

9. What counsel. It is very unwise procedure to go shopping around for counsel until you find the counsel you want to hear. 1 K 22:6-8. 2 S 17:5, 6. 2 Ch 10:9n. 18:5-7. 2 T 4:3.

10. spake unto. ver. ◐+*7, 28. Nu 31:16. 2 Ch 10:10. 22:3. Jb 2:9. Scripture furnishes suggestions that warn us of sources of unwise counsel: (1) Immature advisors, often young, lacking in judgment and experience, 1 K 12:10. (2) Members of our own peer group, 2 Ch *13:7. (3) Individuals who, though they claim to have spiritual insight, offer advice contrary to the already revealed will of God as found in his written word, 1 K *13:18. (4) Individuals prompted by false spiritual gifts, Je +*23:28n. (5) False teachers, Ezk 14:10n. (6) Those who have an unstable character, Pr 22:24. (7) Unfaithful individuals, Pr 25:19. (8) The proud and boastful, Pr 20:6. (9) Those who lack integrity, or compromise justice, Lk +*16:10. (10) Those who compromise the truth and receive falsehood, Pr 29:12. (11) The generality of opinion expressed by the crowd, or majority opinion, when not in accordance with the principles of God's word, Ex *23:2. (12) Feelings and emotions, Ge 49:4; Je 23:17; 2 C 5:7; Ja 1:6, 8; 2 P 2:14. (13) Conscience, when not informed by the written word of God, Pr 14:12; Ac ◐24:16. (14) The occult, Is +*8:19, 20. (15) Misunderstood or misapplied Scripture, Jg 6:40n; 11:39n; Mt 4:6; 2 T 2:15n; 2 P √3:16. See related notes on sources of false guidance (1 K +√13:18n). **Thus shalt thou.** 2 S 17:7-13. **My little finger.** A proverbial mode of expression: "My little finger is thicker than my father's thigh." As much as the *thigh* surpasses the *little finger* in thickness, so much does my power exceed that of my father; and

the use I shall make of it to oppress and tax you shall be in proportion. 2 Ch 10:10, 11. Pr 10:14. 18:6, 7. 28:25. 29:23. Is 47:6.

11. I will add. Ex 1:13, 14. 5:5-9, 18. 1 S 8:18. 2 Ch 16:10. Is 58:6. Je 27:11. 28:13, 14. **but I will chastise.** Should you rebel or become disaffected, my father's *whip* shall be a *scorpion* in my hand. His was *chastisement*, mine shall be *punishment.* Celsius and Hiller conjecture that *ukrabbim* denotes a thorny kind of shrub, whose prickles are of a venomous nature, called by the Arabs "scorpion thorns," from the exquisite pain which they inflict. But the Chaldee renders it *margenin*, and the Syriac *moragyai*, i.e. *maragnai*, "scourges;" and in the parallel place of Chronicles the Arabic has *saut*, a *scourge.* Isidore, and after him Calmet and others, assert that the *scorpion* was a sort of severe *whip*, the lashes of which were armed with knots or points that sunk into and tore the flesh. **scorpions.** ver. 14. Ezk 2:6. Re 9:3-10.

12. Come to me again. ver. 5. 2 Ch 10:12-14.

13. answered. 1 K 20:6-11. Ge 42:7, 30. Ex 5:2. 10:28. Jg 12:1-6. 1 S 20:10, 30, 31. 25:10, 11. 2 S 19:43. Pr 10:11, 32. 15:1. 18:6, 7, 23. Ec 10:12. Ja 3:17. **roughly.** Heb. hardly. Ge 16:6. 1 S 20:10. **forsook.** ver. +*8. Pr *13:20. *22:28. 23:10.

14. the counsel. 2 Ch 22:4, 5. Est 1:16-21. 2:2-4. Pr *12:5. Is 19:11-13. Da 6:7. **My father made.** ver. 10, 11. Pr 13:10. 16:18. 17:14. Ec 7:8. Ja 3:14-18. 4:1, 2.

15. the cause. The *cause* of all this confusion and anarchy was Rehoboam's folly, cruelty, and despotic tyranny, and this was certainly *not* "from the Lord," nor does the original text speak this doctrine. See an elucidation of a similar passage at 2 S 24:1. It says *sibbah*, (from *savav*, to "turn, change"), "the *change* or *revolution* was from the Lord;" which is consistent with all the preceding declarations. God stirred up the people to revolt from a man who had neither skill nor humanity to govern them. God serves his own wise and righteous purpose by the imprudences and iniquities of men, and snares sinners in the work of their own hands. "He maketh the wrath of man to praise him." ver. 24. 1 K 22:23. Dt 2:30. Jg 14:4. 2 Ch 10:15. 22:7. 25:16, 20. Ps 5:10. Am +√3:6. Ac 2:23. 4:28. **that he might.** See on 1 K 11:11, 29-38. 1 S 15:29. 2 S 17:14. 2 K 9:36. 10:10. Is 14:13-17. 46:10, 11. Da 4:35. Jn 19:23, 24, 28, 29, 32-37. Ac 3:17. 13:27-29.

16. What portion. See on 2 S 20:1. 2 Ch 10:16. **to your tents.** ƒ182, Ge +18:22. 1 K 22:17, 36. 2 S 20:1. **now see.** 1 K 11:13, 34, 36, 39. 2 S 7:15, 16. Ps 2:1-6. 76:10. 89:29-37. 132:17. Is 7:2, 6, 7. 9:6, 7. Je 23:5, 6. 33:15, 16, 21. Lk 19:14, 27. **So Israel.** Jg 8:35. 2 S 15:13. 16:11.

17. the children. 1 K 11:13, 36. 2 Ch 10:17. 11:13-17.

18. Adoram. 1 K 4:6. 5:14, Adoniram. 2 S 20:24. 2 Ch 10:18, Hadoram. **all Israel.** Ex 17:4. Nu 14:10. 2 Ch 24:21. Ac 5:26. 7:57, 58. **made speed.** Heb. strengthened himself. Ru 1:18. 2 Ch ∥10:18mg. 13:7. **flee to Jerusalem.** 1 K 20:18-20. Pr 28:1, 2. Am 2:16.

19. Israel. 1 S 10:19. 2 K 17:21. 2 Ch 10:19. 13:5-7, 17. Is 7:17. **rebelled.** *or*, fell away. 2 K 1:1. 3:5, 7. He 6:6. **unto this day.** 1 K 8:8. See on Jsh +4:9.

20. and made him. 1 S 10:24. Ho 8:4. **none that followed.** See on ver. 17. 1 K 11:13, *32n. Ho 11:12.

Judah. ✗171R, Ex +12:40. See 1 K 11:32n. **only.** ver. ◑21, 23. 1 K 11:13, *32n, 36.

21. **when Rehoboam.** 2 Ch 11:1-3. **an hundred.** 1 Ch 21:5. 2 Ch 14:8, 11. 17:14-19. Pr 21:30, 31.

22. **Shemaiah.** i.e. *heard of Jah.* 2 Ch 11:2. 12:5, 7. **the man.** 1 K 13:1, 4, 5, 11. 17:18, 24. See on Dt 33:1. 2 K 4:16, 22, 25, 27. 1 T 6:11.

24. **Ye shall not go up.** Nu 14:42. 2 Ch 11:4. 25:7, 8. 28:9-13. **for this thing.** See on ver. 15. 1 K 11:29-38. Ho 8:4. **They hearkened.** 2 Ch 25:10. 28:13-15.

25. **built.** 1 K 9:15, 17, 18. 15:17. 16:24. 2 Ch 11:5-12. **Shechem.** See on ver. 1. Jg 9:1, 45-49. **Penuel.** Ge 32:30, 31. Jg 8:8, 17.

26. **said in his heart.** Ps 14:1. Mk 2:6-8. Lk 7:39. **Now shall.** 1 K 11:38. 1 S 27:1. 2 Ch +*20:20. Is 7:9. Je 38:18-21. Jn 11:47-50. 12:10, 11, 19. Ac 4:16, 17.

27. **go up.** 1 K 8:29, 30, 44. 11:32. Dt 12:5-7, 14. 16:2, 6. **and they shall.** Ge 12:12, 13. 26:7. Pr *29:25. 1 C 1:19, 20.

28. **took counsel.** See on ver. 8, 9. Ex 1:10. Is *30:1. **two calves of gold.** He invented a political religion, and instituted feasts in his own times, different from those appointed by Jehovah; gave the people certain objects of adoration, and pretended to think that it would be both inconvenient and oppressive to them to go up to Jerusalem to worship. These calves were doubtless of the same kind as the calf which was set up by Aaron; and it is remarkable, that in pointing them out to the people he should use the same words that Aaron used on that occasion, when they must have heard what terrible judgments fell upon their forefathers for this idolatry. Solomon's idolatry, however, had prepared the people for Jeroboam's abominations. Ex 20:4. Dt 4:14-18. 2 K 10:29. 17:16. 2 Ch 11:15. Ho 8:4-7. 10:5, 6. **It is too much.** Is 30:10. 2 P 2:19. **behold.** See on Ex 32:4, 8. Ps 106:20.

29. **Bethel.** Ge 12:8. 28:19. 35:1. Ho 4:15. **Dan.** Ge 14:14. Dt 34:1. Jg 18:29-31. 20:1. 2 K 10:29. Je 8:16. Am 8:14.

30. **became a sin.** 1 K 13:34. 2 K 10:31. 17:21.

31. **an house.** 1 K 13:24, 32. Dt 24:15. Ezk 16:25. Ho 12:11. **priests.** 1 K 13:33. Nu 3:6, 10. 2 K 17:32. 2 Ch 11:14. 15. 13:9. Ezk 44:6-8.

32. **like unto.** 1 K 8:2, 5. Le ◑*23:33, 34, etc. Nu 29:12, etc. Ezk 43:8. Da 7:25. Mt 15:8, 9. **offered upon the altar.** *or,* went up to the altar. ver. 33. 1 K 13:1. **sacrificing.** *or,* to sacrifice. **he placed.** Am 7:10-13.

33. **offered upon the altar.** *or,* went up to the altar, etc. ver. 32. **in the month.** Nu 15:39. Ps *106:39. Is 29:13. Da 7:25. Mt *15:6. Mk 7:13. **own heart.** Nu +16:28. Dt 12:8. **he offered.** 1 K 13:1. 1 S 13:12. 2 Ch *26:16. **and burnt incense.** Heb. to burn incense. 1 K 13:1.

1 KINGS 13

A man of God sent from Judah prophesies to Jeroboam, while burning incense, that Josiah of David's race should defile the altar at Bethel; and he gives him a sign, 1-3. Jeroboam's hand, stretched forth against him, withers; and the altar is rent, 4, 5. Jeroboam's hand is restored at the prophet's prayer, 6. He refuses entertainment and a reward, and leaves

Bethel, 7-10. He is seduced, and brought back, by the lie of an old prophet, who afterwards denounces the judgment of God against him for his disobedience, 11-22. A lion kills him on his way home, 23-25. The old prophet fetches his body, buries it with lamentations, and confirms his prophecy, 26-32. Jeroboam persists in his evil ways, 33, 34.

1. **there came.** See on 1 K 12:22. 2 K 23:17. 2 Ch 9:29. Je 25:4. **by the word.** ver. 5, 9, 26, 32. 1 K 20:35. Je 25:3. 1 Th 4:15. **Jeroboam.** 1 K 12:32, 33. 2 Ch 26:18. **burn.** *or,* offer. Nu 16:40. Je 11:12. 32:29. Ml 1:11. Re 8:3.

2. **altar.** ✗38G, Dt +32:1. **O altar.** Dt 32:1. Is 1:2. 58:1. Je 22:29. Ezk 36:1, 4. 38:4. Lk 19:40. **a child shall.** 2 K 4:16. Is 9:6. Mt 1:21. **Josiah.** i.e. *sustained of Jehovah.* *S#2977h: 1 K 13:2. 2 K 21:24, 26. 22:1, 3. 23:16, 19, 23, 24, 28, 29, 30, 34, 34. 1 Ch 33:25. 34:1, 33. 35:1, 7, 16, 18, 19, 20, 20, 22, 23, 24, 25, 25, 26. 36:1. Je 1:2, 3, 3. 3:6. 22:11, 11, 18. 25:1, 3. 26:1. 27:1. 35:1. 36:1, 2, 9. 37:1. 45:1. 46:2. Zp 1:1. Zc 6:10. **by name.** 2 K 22:1, 2. 23:15-18. 2 Ch 34:1, 4-7. Is 42:9. *44:26-28. 45:1. 46:10. 48:5-7. This prediction was delivered considerably more than three hundred years before Josiah was born; yet during all those years no one of the house of David gave his son this name, or attempted to fulfill the prophecy, until the appointed time was arrived; and then Amon, a wicked prince, named his son Josiah (Scott). 2 K 23:16n. **offer.** 2 K 23:15-17.

3. **he gave.** Ex 4:3-5, 8, 9. 7:10. Dt 13:1-3. 1 S 2:34. 2 K 20:8. Is 7:11-14. 38:6-8, 22. Je 44:29. Mt 12:38-40. Jn 2:18. 1 C 1:22.

4. **Lay hold.** 2 Ch 16:10. 18:25, etc. 25:15, 16. Ps 105:14, 15. Je 20:2-4. 26:8-11, 20-23. 38:4-6. Am 7:10-17. Mt 25:40. 26:57. Mk 14:44-46. Jn 13:20. Ac 6:12-14. **his hand.** Ge 19:11. 2 K 6:18-20. Je 20:4-6. Lk 3:19, 20. 6:10. Jn 18:6. Ac 9:4, 5. 13:8-11. Re 11:5.

5. **according to.** ver. 3. 1 K 22:28, 35. Ex 9:18-25. Nu 16:23-35. Dt 18:22. Je 28:16, 17. Mk 16:20. Ac 5:1-10.

6. **now.** Ex 8:8, 28. 9:28. 10:17. 12:32. Nu 21:7. 1 S 12:19. Je 37:3. 42:2-4. Ac 8:24. Ja *5:16. Re 3:9. **my hand.** T#1544. **besought.** Ex 8:12, 13. Nu 12:13. 1 S *12:23. Mt 5:44. Lk 6:27, 28. 23:34. Ac 7:60. Ro 12:14, 21. Ja 5:16-18. 1 J 2:1. **Lord.** Heb. face of the Lord. Ex 32:11mg. 1 S +13:12mg. Jb +11:19mg. Je +26:19mg.

7. **refresh.** Ge 18:5. Jg 13:15. 19:21. **I will give.** As great men of the East make no presents to equals or inferiors when visited, Sir John Chardin thinks that the king intended by this to treat the prophet as his superior. 1 S 9:7, 8. 2 K 5:15. Je 40:5. Ml 1:10. Ac 8:18-20. 1 P *5:2.

8. **If.** Nu *22:18. 24:13. Est 5:3, 6. 7:2. Mk 6:23. **go.** 2 K 5:16, 26, 27. Mk 6:11. 2 C 11:9, 10.

9. **For.** See on ver. 1, 21, 22. 1 S 15:22. Jb 23:12. Jn 13:17. 15:9, 10, 14. **by the word.** ver. ◑+*18. Scripture by example and precept suggests several sources of true guidance: (1) The written word of God found in the Bible, Ps 119:105; Is +*8:20. (2) God speaking to us through our thoughts, 1 K 8:18; Pr +*4:23; √16:3, 9. Thoughts must be tested as to their source, 1 K 8:17, 18; *10:24; Je 23:16; Ac ◑5:3. Thoughts may be correct and good, 1 K *8:18; 2 Ch 31:20, 21; Da 1:8; Ac 7:60; 26:29. But thoughts may be evil, Dt 15:9; Pr 23:7; 1 T 4:1, 2; Ja 1:14, 15. Even diet may affect

our judgment, Is 7:15, 22. (3) Circumstances, 1 S 14:15n; Pr *16:33. But care must be exercised in interpreting circumstances, 1 S 24:4n. (4) Steadfast, committed obedience to the already revealed will of God, Ro 12:1, 2; 2 C 6:14. (5) Our enlightened understanding as we study God's word, Ep 1:18, 19; 5:17; Col 1:9. (6) Obedience to the direct commands of Scripture, 1 S +*15:22. (7) Judgment as to needs, Ac 15:36. (8) By checks in the way, Ge 24:27; Nu 22:22, 26; Pr 30:19; Ac 16:6; Ro 1:13; 15:22; 1 Th ◐2:18. (9) By faith and by bridle, Ps 32:8, 9. (10) Wise counsel, 1 S 9:27; 1 K +√12:7n; Pr 11:14; 15:22; *24:6; 27:17. (11) The peace of God, wrought by the Holy Spirit, Jn 14:27; Ro 15:13; Ph 4:6, 7; Col 3:15. But feelings are subjective, not objective, may be mistaken (whether by a misinformed conscience, a mistaken interpretation of Scripture, a misreading of apparently favorable circumstances, etc.) or counterfeited, affected by mood and temperament, and are based upon an "experience centered" rather than a Bible or Christ centered approach to the Christian life (Is 65:5n). Great caution must be exercised in evaluating any feeling of peace, lest one be misled by false peace, ver. 18n; Ezk +*13:10. (12) The voice of the church, Ac 13:1-3; 1 T +*4:16. He 13:7, 17. (13) Through chastening, He 12:6. (14) Pastors and elders, He 13:7, 17. (15) Parents, Pr 12:15; 13:10; 1 C 7:37, 38; Col 3:20. (16) Wife or husband, 1 S 19:11; 25:33; Mt 27:19; Ep 5:22, 23; 1 P 3:7, 8. See related note on sources of wise counsel (1 K +√12:7n). **Eat no bread.** Nu 16:26. Dt 13:13-18. Ps 141:4. Ro 16:17. 1 C 5:11. Ep *5:11. 2 J *10, 11. Re 18:4.

11. **an old prophet.** ver. 20, 21. Nu 23:4, 5. 24:2. 1 S 10:11. 2 K 23:18. Ezk 13:2, 16. Mt *7:22. 2 P 2:16. **sons.** Heb. son. **came.** 1 T 3:5.

13. **Saddle me.** ver. 27. Nu 22:21. Jg 5:10. 10:4. 2 S 19:26.

14. **sitting.** 1 K 19:4. Jn 4:6, 34. 1 C 4:11, 12. 2 C 11:27. Ph 4:12, 13. **Art thou.** See on ver. 1.

16. **I may not.** ver. 8, 9. Ge 3:1-3. Nu 22:13, 19. Mt *4:10. 16:23.

17. **It was.** Heb. a word *was.* **by the word.** See on ver. 1. 1 K 20:35. 1 Th 4:15.

18. **a prophet also.** ver. +*9. Scripture warns against the dangers of false guidance from various sources: (1) Careless handling, and incorrect understanding and application of God's written word, Jg 6:40n; 11:35n. Mk 9:43; 2 T 2:15n; 2 P 3:17. Do not seek for guidance by opening the Bible at random and hoping for a verse to speak to you, Ge 24:44n; Jn ◐+*5:39. (2) Itching ear syndrome: seeking guidance until you find the advice you wanted to hear, 1 K 12:9n; 2 T 4:3. (3) Wrong friends, 2 Ch *13:7; 1 C 15:33. (4) Inexperienced and unqualified individuals, often young, who lack the necessary discernment, 1 K +√12:10; 2 T 3:14; He 5:14; 13:7. (5) Requiring God to specially engineer circumstances or signs, Jg 6:40n. Be especially wary of looking to signs or circumstances to confirm guidance when what is sought is contrary to the written word of God, 2 C 6:14. (6) Basing our thinking on artificial categories either imposed upon Scripture or Christian experience, such as the distinction of sacred and secular, or of "called" and "voluntary" Christian service, distinctions not taught in the word of God, 2 T 2:15n. (7) Wrongly weighting factors in determining God's guidance. Certain factors are readily

subject to misinterpretation, such as circumstances, 1 S 24:4n; 2 S 4:8. Others, such as the feeling of peace (ver. 9n. Ezk ◐+*13:10), are extremely subjective, and can be affected by our present physical state of health, Pr 17:22; Ro 15:13; 2 C 5:7. Guidance must be based upon wisdom and sound principles, properly weighted, and applied without haste, Pr 19:2; 28:22; Col 1:10; Ja 1:5. (8) Occult practices, Is *8:19. (9) Dreams, Je +*23:28n. (10) Exclusive reliance upon our own resources in understanding God's word without seeking the assistance of the godly, consecrated scholarship of other men available to us in books and Bible study tools, Ac 8:31n. (11) Resolutely holding to a favorite set of prooftexts from Scripture, rather than adhering to the whole counsel of God, 2 K 22:8n; Ac 2:38n; 1 J 2:19n; 2 P 1:20n. (12) In doctrinal matters, failing to genuinely accept the Bible as the sufficient, perspicuous, sole and final authority, Pr +*8:9; 18:1n; Is +*8:20n; Je +*23:28n; Ga 1:8n; 2 T +*3:15-17. (13) False teachers, false cults and religions, Je 14:14n; Ezk 14:10n. (14) Any plan or scheme that lacks wisdom, prudence, and good judgment (sanctified common sense), Pr +*22:3; Lk 14:28-32. (15) Guidance from an individual who falsely claims possession of a spiritual gift, or possesses a false gift, 1 K 13:18. (16) Guidance which conflicts with genuine guidance previously received, 1 K 13:18. It is wise to commit to writing a record of God's leading in our lives, recording the specific reasons which originally committed us to a given course of action or life direction. Then, should mixed signals, conflicting advice, or doubts later arise, we can return to that record for confirmation of the original guidance. See related notes on sources of unwise counsel (1 K +√12:10n). **an angel.** Nu 22:35. Jg 6:11, 12. 13:3. 2 C √11:14. Ga √1:8n. **But.** Ge 3:4, 5. Is *9:15, 16. Je 5:12, 31. 23:14, *16, *17, *32. 28:15, 16. Ezk 13:6, 7, 9, 10, 22. Mt 7:15. 24:24. Ro 16:18. 2 C 11:3, 13-15. Ga 1:8. 2 P 2:1. 1 J *4:1. Re 19:20.

19. **he went back.** ver. 9. Ge *3:6. Dt 13:1, 3, 5. 18:20. Ac 4:19. 2 P 2:18, 19.

20. **the word of the Lord.** "A great clamor," says Dr. Kennicott, "has been raised against this part of the history, on account of God's denouncing sentence on the *true* prophet by the mouth of the *false* prophet; but if we examine with attention the original words here, they will be found to signify either, *he who brought him back,* or, *whom he had brought back;* for the very same words, *asher heshivo,* occur again, ver. 23, where they are now translated, "whom he had brought back;" and where they cannot be translated otherwise. This being the case, we are at liberty to consider the words of the Lord as delivered to the *true* prophet, thus brought back; and then the sentence is pronounced by God himself, calling to him out of heaven, as in Ge 22:11. And that this doom was thus pronounced by God, not by the false prophet, we are assured in ver. 26. "The Lord hath delivered him unto the lion, according to the word of the Lord, which HE spake unto him." Josephus (and also the Arabic) asserts, that the sentence was declared by God to the *true* prophet." Nu 23:5, 16. 24:4, 16-24. Ps +*50:16. Mt *7:22. Jn 11:51. 1 C 13:2.

21. **Thus saith.** ver. 17. Ge 3:7. Est 6:13. Je 2:19. Ga *1:8, 9. **thou hast disobeyed.** Le 10:3. Nu 20:12, 24. 1 S 4:18. *13:13, 14. *15:19, 22-24. 2 S 6:7. 12:9-11. 24:13. Re *3:19.

22. camest back. Jb ❶*23:12. Jn 13:17. **eaten.** ver. 19. **of the.** ver. 9. **carcase.** ver. 30. 1 K 14:13. 2 Ch 21:19, 20. Is 14:18-20. Je 22:18, 19. **not come.** Nu 20:12, 24. Dt 32:50, 51. **sepulchre.** Heb. *qeber*, Ge +23:4.

24. a lion. 1 K 20:36. 2 K 2:24. Pr 22:13. 26:13. Am 5:19. 1 C 11:31, 32. 1 P 4:17, 18. **slew him.** 2 S 6:7. Pr 11:31.

26. the man. Le 10:3. 2 S 12:10, 14. Ps 119:120. Pr 11:31. Ezk 9:6. 1 C 11:30. He 12:28, 29. 1 P 4:17. **torn.** Heb. broken. ver. 28. **which he spake.** ver. 9.

28. the lion had. All here was supernatural. The lion, though he had killed the man, yet, contrary to his nature, did not devour him, nor tear the ass, nor meddle with the travellers that passed by; while the ass stood quietly by, not fearing the lion, nor betaking himself to flight; both stood as guardians of the fallen prophet, till this extraordinary intelligence was carried into the city, which rendered the miracle the more illustrious, and plainly showed that this event did not happen by chance. This concatenation of miracles marked the death of the man of God as a Divine rebuke for his disobedience in eating bread at idolatrous Bethel; and here we see, as in various other cases, that "often judgment begins at the house of God." The true prophet, for suffering himself to be seduced by the old prophet, and for receiving that as a revelation from God which was opposed to the revelation which he himself had received, and which was confirmed by so many miracles, is slain by a lion, and his body deprived of the burial of his fathers; while the wicked king and the fallen prophet are both permitted to live. 1 K 17:4, 6. Le 10:2, 5. Jb 38:11. Ps 148:7, 8. Je 5:22, 23. Da 3:22, 27, 28. 6:22-24. Ac 16:26. He 11:33, 34. **torn.** Heb. broken. ver. 26.

30. grave. Heb. *qeber*, Ge +23:4. **mourned over.** 1 K 14:13. Je 22:18. Ac 8:2.

31. sepulchre. Heb. *qeber*, Ge +23:4. **lay my bones.** Nu 23:10. Ps 26:9. Ec 8:10. Lk 16:22, 23.

32. the saying. ver. 2. 2 K 23:16-19. **the houses.** 1 K 12:29, 31. Le *26:30. **in the cities.** 1 K 16:24. 2 Ch 25:13. Ezr 4:10. Jn 4:4, 5.

33. A.M. 3030-3050. **B.C.** 974-954. **Jeroboam.** 1 K 12:31-33. 2 Ch 11:15. 13:9. Am 4:6-11. **made again.** Heb. returned and made. Ne 9:28. Ps 78:34. Je 18:4mg. 2 T 3:13. **whosoever.** Nu 1:51. *3:10. 17:5, 12, 13. **consecrated him.** Heb. filled his hand. ſ121S3P, Ex +28:41. Ex 28:41mg. 29:9mg. Jg 17:5mg, 12.

34. became sin. 1 K 12:30. 2 K 10:31. 17:21. Ps 78:32. 2 T 3:13. **to cut it off.** 1 K 12:26. 14:10. 15:29, 30. Pr 13:6. **the face.** Ge +1:2.

1 KINGS 14

Jeroboam sends his wife, disguised, to Ahijah, the prophet, to inquire concerning his son Abijah, who was sick, 1-4. Ahijah, forewarned by God, denounces to her the destruction of Jeroboam's family, the death of her son, and the rejection of Israel, 5-16. Abijah dies and is buried, 17, 18. Jeroboam dies and is succeeded by Nadab, 19, 20. Rehoboam reigns over Judah; and they provoke the Lord by their wickedness, 21-24. Shishak carries away much treasure, and the golden shields, from Jerusalem, 25, 26. Rehoboam makes brazen shields in their stead, 27, 28. His acts, and wars with Jeroboam, 29, 30.

1. Abijah. i.e. *my father is Jah,* ✠S#29h. (1) A son of Jeroboam who died young, 1 K 14:1. (2) A priest in the time of David who was at the head of the eighth course in the temple service, 1 Ch 24:10; Lk 1:5, Abiah. (3) One of the sons of Rehoboam, the son of Solomon, by Maachah, the daughter of Absalom: 2 Ch 11:20, 22. 12:16. 13:1, 2, 3, 4, 15, 17, 19, 20, 21, 22. 14:1. (4) The mother of Hezekiah, king of Judah, 2 Ch 29:1. (5) A priest that sealed the covenant made by Nehemiah and the people to serve the Lord, Ne 10:7. (6) A priest that went up from Babylon with Zerubbabel, Ne 12:4, 17. May be the same as number 5. **that time.** 1 K 13:33, 34. **the son.** ver. 12, 13. Ex 20:5. 1 S 4:19, 20. 31:2. 2 S 12:15.

2. disguise thyself. ver. 5, 6. 22:30. Ge +27:16. 1 S 28:8. 2 S 14:2, 3. 2 Ch 18:29. Lk 12:2. **Ahijah.** See on 1 K 11:29-38.

3. And take. 1 K 13:7. 1 S 9:7, 8. 2 K 4:42. 5:5, 15. 8:7-9. **with thee.** Heb. in thine hand. Ge 24:10. **cracknels.** or, cakes. Jsh ❶9:5. 2 S 13:6. *Nikkoodim,* "spotted," or "perforated cakes;" either, as some suppose, thin cakes pierced through with holes, the same as is called "Jew's bread" to the present day, and used by them at the passover; or, as Mr. Harmer imagines, cakes *spotted* with seeds, as with sesamum, Roman coriander, etc., such as he proves from Rauwolff, Russell, and Hanway, are still used in the East. This was certainly not a present that proclaimed royalty; but it does not appear to have been, in the estimation of the East, a present only fit for a country woman to have made, as Bp. Patrick supposes: for D'Arvieux informs us, that when he waited on an Arab emir, his mother and sisters sent him a present of pastry, honey, and fresh butter with a basin of sweetmeats of Damascus (See Harmer, ch. VI. Ob 2). **cruse.** or, bottle. Je 19:1, 10. **he shall tell.** 2 K 1:2. 8:8. Lk 7:2, 3. Jn 4:47, 48, ❶50. 11:3.

4. Shiloh. 1 K 11:29. Jsh 18:1. 1 S 4:3, 4. Je 7:12-14. **for his eyes.** Ge 27:1. 48:10. Dt 34:7. 1 S 3:2. 4:15. Ps 90:10. Ec 12:3. **were set by reason of his age.** Heb. stood for his hoariness. 1 S 4:15.

5. the Lord. 2 K 4:27. *6:8-12. Ps 139:1-4. Pr 21:30. Am *3:7. Ac 10:19, 20.

6. Ahijah. i.e. *Jehovah is brother,* ✠S#281h. (1) The name of a prophet who foretold to Jeroboam the revolt of the ten tribes from Rehoboam: 1 K 11:29, 30. 12:15. 14:2, 4, 4, 5, 6, 18. 15:29. 2 Ch 9:29. 10:15. (2) An Israelite whose son, Baasha, conspired against Nadab, the son of Jeroboam, and reigned in his stead: 1 K 15:27, 33. 21:22. 2 K 9:9. (3) Son of Jerahmeel, 1 Ch 2:25. (4) One of David's mighty men, 1 Ch 11:36. (5) A Levite set over the treasures of God's house in David's time, 1 Ch 26:20. (6) A Levite who, in the time of Nehemiah, sealed a covenant to serve the Lord, Ne 10:26. **sound of her feet.** 2 K 6:32. **thou wife.** Jb 5:13. Ps 33:10. **why feignest.** ver. 2, 5. Ps 139:1-6. Pr 21:30. Ezk 14:3-5, 7, 8. Lk 12:2. 20:20-23. Ac 5:3-5, 9, 10. He 4:13. **for I am.** ver. 10, 11. 13:20-22. 20:42. 21:18-24. 22:8. 1 S 15:16, 26. 28:18. Je 21:2-7. Ezk 2:4, 5. Da 4:19-25. 5:17-28. Mk 14:21. **heavy.** Heb. hard. 1 K 12:4, 13. **tidings.** ſ63B, Ge +25:28.

7. Forasmuch. 1 K 12:24. 16:2. 1 S 2:27-30. 15:16. 2 S 12:7, 8.

8. rent. 1 K 11:30, 31. **my servant David.** 1 K 3:14. 11:33-38. 15:5. 2 Ch 17:3. 28:1. Ac 13:22, 36.

9. hast done. ver. 16. 1 K 12:28. 13:33, 34. 15:34.

16:31. **thou hast gone.** Dt 32:16, 17, 21. Jg 5:8. 2 Ch 11:15. Ps 106:19, 20. 115:4-8. Is 44:9-20. Je 10:14-16. **to provoke.** ver. 22. Dt 9:8-16, 24. 2 K 21:3. 23:26. 2 Ch 33:6. Ps 78:40, 56. 106:29. Je 7:9, 10. Ezk 8:3, 17. 1 C 10:22. **cast me.** Ne *9:26. Ps *50:17. Ezk *23:35.

10. **I will bring.** 1 K 15:25-30. Am 3:6. **him that pisseth.** 1 K 16:1. 21:21. 1 S 25:22n, 34. 2 K 9:8, 9. **him that is shut up.** Dt 32:36. 2 K 14:26. **as a man taketh.** 1 S 2:30. 2 K 9:37. 21:13. Jb 20:7. Ps 83:10. Is 5:25. 14:19, 23. Je 8:2. Ezk 26:4. Zp 1:17. Ml 2:3. Lk 14:34, 35.

11. **that dieth.** 1 K 16:4. 21:19, 23, 24. Is 66:24. Je 15:3. Ezk 39:17-19. Re 19:17, 18.

12. **when thy feet.** ver. 3, 16, 17. 2 K 1:6, 16. Jn 4:50-52.

13. **shall mourn.** Nu 20:29. Je 22:10, 18. **grave.** Heb. *qeber*, Ge +23:4. **there is found.** 1 K 19:18. 2 Ch 12:12. 19:3. Jb 19:28. Ezk 18:14, etc. Phm 6. 2 P 2:8, 9.

14. **the Lord.** 1 K 15:27-29. **but what.** ƒ10. Amphidiorthosis; or, Double Correction B912: a setting both hearer and speaker right by a correction which acts both ways. Here, "But what, even now"; as if the prophet meant (being led of the Spirit) to say, first, "that day"; and then to add shock upon shock by going on, "But what am I saying? 'that day?' even now." For another instance of this figure see 1 C 11:22. **even now.** Ec 8:11. Ezk 7:2-7. 12:22-28. Ja 5:9. 2 P 2:3.

15. **the Lord.** 1 S 12:25. 2 K 17:6, 7. **as a reed.** ƒ63I2, Jsh +3:3. Supply by ellipsis from succeeding clause, "(shaking him) as a reed is shaken in the water." Mt 11:7. Lk 7:24. **root up Israel.** Dt 29:28. Ps 52:5. Pr 2:22. Am 2:9. Zp 2:4. Mt 15:13. **this good land.** Le 26:32-34, 43. Dt 4:26, 27. 28:36, 63-68. 29:24-28. Jsh 23:15, 16. **shall scatter.** 2 K 15:29. 17:6, 23. 18:11, 12. Am 5:27. Ac 7:43. **beyond the river.** i.e. *beyond the river Euphrates.* 2 K 15:29. 17:6, Gozan. **because.** Ex 34:13, 14. Dt 12:3, 4. Is 1:28, 29. **provoking.** See on ver. 9, 23, 24. 1 K 16:33.

16. **he shall give Israel.** Jsh 23:15, 16. Ps 52:5. 81:12. Is 40:24. Ho 9:11, 12, 16, 17. **who did sin.** 1 K 12:30. 13:34. 15:30, 34. 16:2. Ex 32:21, 35. 2 K 15:29. 17:6. Je 5:31. Ho 5:11, 12. Mi 6:16. Mt 18:7. Ro 14:13. **who made.** ƒ108A5, Ge +42:38. 1 K 15:26. 2 K 3:3. 10:29. 13:2.

17. **Tirzah.** *Tirzah* was a city of Ephraim, to which tribe Jeroboam belonged; and appears to have been pleasantly situated, as it is said in SS 6:4, "Thou art beautiful, O my love, as Tirzah," though its precise situation cannot now be ascertained. It seems to have been the *royal city*, and the seat of government for a long time after the revolt of the ten tribes, till Omri built Samaria. 1 K 15:21, 33. 16:6, 8, 9, 15, 23. Jsh 12:24. SS 6:4. **when she came.** See on ver. 12, 13. 1 S 2:30-34. 4:18-20. **threshold.** *S#5592h. Ex 12:22 (bason). Jg *19:27. 2 S 17:28 (basons; mg, cups). 1 K 7:50 (bowls). 2 K 12:9mg. 22:4mg. 23:4. 25:18mg. 1 Ch 9:19mg, 22 (gates). 2 Ch 3:7 (posts). 23:4mg. 34:9 (doors). Est 2:21mg. 6:2mg. Is 6:4mg. Je 35:4mg. 52:19 (basons), 24mg. Ezk 40:6, 7. 41:16 (door posts). 43:8. Am 9:1 (posts). Zp 2:14. Zc 12:2 (cup). **the child died.** Jn ◑4:51.

19. A.M. 3029-3050. B.C. 975-954. **how he warred.** ver. 30. 2 Ch 13:2-20. **book.** ver. 29. 1 K 15:31. 16:5, 15, 20, 27. 22:39. 1 Ch 27:24. Est 6:1.

20. **slept.** Heb. lay down. ver. 31. 1 K 2:10. +*11:43. 15:8, 24. 16:6, 28. 22:40, 50. 2 K 8:24. 10:35. 13:9, 13. 14:16, 29. 15:7, 22, 38. 16:20. 20:21. 21:18. 24:6. 2 Ch 9:31. 12:16. 14:1, etc. Jb 7:21. 11:18. 14:12. Ps 3:5. 4:8. **Nadab.** i.e. *liberal, impulsive.* 1 K 15:25-31.

21. **Rehoboam.** i.e. *enlargement of the people,* *S#7346h. 1 K *11:43. 12:1, 3, 6, 12, 17, 18, 18, 21, 23, 27, 27. 14:21, 21, 25, 27, 29, 30, 31. 15:6. 1 Ch 3:10. 2 Ch 9:31. 10:1, 3, 6, 12, 13, 17, 18, 18. 11:1, 1, 3, 5, 17, 18, 21, 22. 12:1, 2, 5, 10, *13, 13, 15, 15, 16. *13:7, 7. **forty and one years.** Being born one year before Solomon ascended the throne. 2 Ch 22:13. **the city.** See on 1 K 8:16, 44. 11:36, Ps 78:68, 69. 87:1, 2. 132:13, 14. Is 12:6. **to put his name.** See on Ex 20:24. Dt 12:5, 21. **Naamah.** i.e. *pleasantness.* ver. 31. Dt 23:3. 2 Ch 12:13. ◑22:3.

22. **Judah.** Jg 3:7, 12. 4:1. 2 K 17:19. 2 Ch 12:1. Je 3:7-11. **they provoked.** See on ver. 9. Dt 4:24. 29:28. 32:16-21. Ps 78:58. Pr 6:34, 35. Is 65:3, 4. 1 C 10:22. **to jealousy.** ƒ22B, Ex +20:5. **above all.** 1 K 16:30. 2 K 21:11. Ezk 16:47, 48.

23. **they also.** 2 Ch 14:3. Pr 16:7. **built.** 1 K 3:2. Dt 12:2. Is 57:5. Ezk 16:24, 25. 20:28, 29. **images.** *or,* standing images, *or* statues. Le 26:1. 2 K +10:26mg. +*17:10. **groves.** Ex 34:13. Dt 12:2, 3. 2 K 17:9, 10. 21:3-7. 2 Ch 28:4. Je 17:2. Mi 5:14. **high hill.** 2 K +*17:10. Je 2:20. **under every.** 2 Ch 28:4. Is 57:5. Je 3:13. 13:27. **green tree.** 2 K 16:4n. +*17:10.

24. **And there.** 1 K 15:12. 22:46. Ge 19:5. Dt 23:17. Jg 19:22. 2 K 23:7. Ro 1:24-27. 1 C 5:1. 6:9, 10. Ju 7.

25. A.M. 3034. B.C. 970. **Shishak.** 1 K 11:40n. 2 Ch 12:2-4.

26. **he took away.** See on 1 K 7:51. 15:18. 2 K 24:13. 2 Ch 12:9-11. Ps 39:6. 89:35-45. **the shields of gold.** 1 K 10:16, 17. 2 Ch 9:15, 16. Pr 23:5. Ec 2:18, 19.

27. **made.** La 4:1, 2. **guard.** Heb. runners. ver. 1, 5. 1 K 18:46. 1 S 8:11. 22:17. 2 S 15:1.

28. **the guard chamber.** 2 Ch 12:11. Ezk 40:7.

29. A.M. 3029-3046. B.C. 975-958. **are they not written.** See on ver. 19. 1 K 11:41. 15:23. 22:45. 2 Ch 12:15.

30. **there was war.** 1 K 12:24. 15:6, 7. 2 Ch 12:15.

31. A.M. 3046. B.C. 958. **Rehoboam.** See on ver. 20. 1 K 11:43. 15:3, 24. 22:50. 2 Ch 12:16. **his mother's.** See on ver. 21. **Abijam.** 1 Ch 3:10, Abia. 2 Ch 12:16, Abijah. Mt 1:7, Abia. Dr. Kennicott observes that the name of this king of Judah is now expressed *three* ways; here, and in four other places, it is *Abijam*; in two others (2 Ch 13:20, 21) it is *Abijahu*; but in *eleven* others it is *Abijah* or *Abiah*, as it is expressed by St. Matthew, (ch. 1:7) "Abia;" and this is the reading of thirteen of Kennicott's and De Rossi's MSS., and of thirteen respectable editions of the Hebrew Bible. The Syriac is the same. The Septuagint in the London Polyglott has *Abiou*, "Abihu;" but in the Complutensian and Antwerp Polyglotts it has *Abia*, "Abiah:" and in the Editio Princeps of the Vulgate, some MSS. and the text in these two Polyglotts, instead of *Abiam*, have *Abia*.

1 KINGS 15

Abijam's wicked reign, 1-7. He dies, and is succeeded by Asa, 8. Asa's good reign, 9-15. In his war with

Baasha, he makes a league with Benhadad, king of Syria; compels Baasha to desist from building Ramah; and with the materials builds Geba and Mizpah, 16-22. He dies, and is succeeded by Jehoshaphat, 23, 24. Nadab's wicked reign over Israel, 25, 26. Baasha slays him, seizes the kingdom, and executes Ahijah's prophecy against Jeroboam's family, 27-32. Baasha's wicked reign, 33, 34.

1. **Now in the**. See on 1 K 14:31. 2 Ch 13:1, 2, etc. **Abijam**. i.e. *father of the sea; seaman,* ✻S#38h. ver. 7, 7, 8. 1 K 14:31.

2. **his mother's**. ✓171G, Ge +13:8. By *Synecdoche of Genus,* "mother" is put for "grandmother." ver. 13. 2 Ch 11:20-22. **Maachah**. i.e. *oppression*. 2 Ch 13:2, Michaiah the daughter of Uriel. **Abishalom**. i.e. *father of peace,* ✚S#53h. ver. 10. 2 Ch 11:21, Absalom.

3. **all the sins**. 1 K 14:21, 22. **and his heart**. See on 1 K 3:14. 11:4, 33. 2 K 20:3. 2 Ch 25:2. 31:20, 21. Ps 119:80.

4. **for David's**. 1 K 11:12, 32. Ge 12:2. 19:29. 26:5. Dt 4:37. 2 S *7:12-16. Is 37:35. Je 33:20-26. Ro 11:28. **give him**. 1 K 11:36. 2 Ch 21:7. Ps 132:17. Lk 1:69-79. 2:32. Jn 8:12. Re 22:16. **lamp**. *or*, candle. 1 K *11:36. 2 S 21:17. Ps 18:28. **and to establish**. Ps 87:5. Is 9:7. 14:32. 62:7. Je 33:2. Mi 4:1, 2. Mt *16:18.

5. **David**. See on ver. 3. 1 K +3:14. 11:4, +34. 14:8. 2 K 22:2. 2 Ch 34:2. Ps 119:6. Lk 1:6. Ac 13:22, 36. **save only**. 2 S 11:4, 15-17. 12:9, 10. Ps 51, title.

6. **there was war**. Instead of *Rehoboam,* fourteen MSS., the Arabic, and some copies of the Targum, read *Abijam*. The Syriac has "Abia, the son of Rehoboam;" and the Editio Princeps of the Vulgate has *Abia*. This is doubtless the true reading, as otherwise it would be an unnecessary repetition of 1 K 14:30, and a repetition which interrupts the history of Abija (see 2 Ch 13:3, etc.). See on 1 K 14:30.

7. **the rest**. See on 1 K 14:29. 2 Ch 13:2, 21, 22. **there was war**. 2 Ch 13:3-20.

8. A.M. 3049. B.C. 955. **Abijam**. See on 1 K 14:1, 31. 2 Ch 14:1. **Asa**. 1 Ch 3:9. Mt 1:7, 8.

10. A.M. 3049-3090. B.C. 955-914. **mother's**. *that is,* grandmother's. ✓171G, Ge +13:8. ver. 2, 13. 2 K 8:21mg,n, 26. 2 Ch 11:20, 21. 13:2. And so the names of *father,* and *mother,* and *sons,* and *daughters* are often taken, both in sacred and profane authors, for grandparents and grandchildren. And his grandmother's name may be here mentioned rather than his mother's, because his mother was either an obscure person, or was long since dead, or indisposed or unwilling to take care of the education of her son, and so he was educated by the grandmother, who, though she did poison his father Abijam with her idolatrous principles, ver. 12, yet could not infect Asa, nor withhold him from prosecuting his good purposes of reforming religion; which is here remembered to his praise (Matthew Poole). Ge 28:13. 2 S 9:7. 19:28. 2 K 14:3. 1 Ch 7:6n. 2 Ch 11:18n. 15:16mg. 34:1, 2. Je 27:7. Da 5:*2mg, 11.

11. **Asa**. ver. 3. 2 Ch 14:2, 11. 15:17. 16:7-10.

12. **the sodomites**. See on 1 K 14:24. 22:46. Ro 1:26, 27. Ju 7. **all the idols**. ver. 3. 1 K 11:7, 8. 14:23. 2 Ch 14:2-5. Ezk 20:18, 19. Zc 1:2-6. 1 P 1:18.

13. **Maachah**. ver. 2, 10. 2 Ch 15:15, 16, etc. **his mother**. ✓171G, Ge +13:8. By *Synecdoche of Genus,* "mother" is put for "grandmother." Dt *13:6-11. 33:9. Zc 13:3. Mt *10:37. 12:46-50. 2 C 5:16. Ga 2:5, 6,

14. **destroyed**. Heb. cut off. Le 26:30. Dt 7:5. 2 K 18:4. 23:12-15. 2 Ch 34:4. **and burnt**. Ex 32:20. Dt 9:21. Jsh 6:24. **the brook**. 2 S 15:23. 2 K 23:6. Jn 18:1, Cedron.

14. **the high places**. 1 K 22:43. 2 K 12:3. 14:4. 15:4. 2 Ch 14:3, 5. **was perfect**. ver. 3. 1 K 8:61. 11:4. 2 Ch 12:14. 15:17, 18. 16:9. 25:2. 27:6. Ps 7:9. 66:18.

15. **he brought**. See on 1 K 7:51. 1 Ch 26:26-28. 2 Ch 14:13. 15:18. **things**. Heb. holy. 2 K 12:4. 1 Ch 26:20. 2 Ch 5:1.

16. **there was war**. ver. 6, 7, 32. 1 K 14:30. 2 Ch 16:1, etc. **Baasha**. i.e. *evil; offensive,* ✻S#1201h. ver. 17, 19, 21, 22, 27, 27, 28, 32, 33. 16:1, 3, 4, 5, 6, 7, 8, 11, 12, 13. 21:22. 2 K 9:9. 2 Ch 16:1, 3, 5, 6. Je 41:9.

17. A.M. 3074. B.C. 930. **Baasha**. ver. 27. 2 Ch 16:1, etc. **Ramah**. i.e. *the lofty place*. By *building* Ramah is here meant *fortifying* it, in order to prevent all intercourse with the kingdom of Judah: for *Ramah* was a city of Benjamin, situated on the confines of both kingdoms, probably on a *hill,* as the name imports, commanding a narrow defile between the mountains, through which lay the principal road to Jerusalem; so that a fortification being erected here, no communication could be held between the people of Israel and Judah, without Baasha's permission. ver. 21. Jsh 18:25. 1 S 7:17. 15:34. Je 31:15. **he might not suffer**. 1 K 12:27. 2 Ch 11:13-17.

18. **Asa**. ver. 15. 1 K 14:26. 2 K 12:18. 18:15, 16. 2 Ch 15:18. 16:2-6. **Ben-hadad**. i.e. *son of shouting,* ✻S#1130h. ver. 20. 1 K 20:1, 2, 5, 9, 10, 16, 20, 26, 30, 32, 33, 33. 2 K 6:24. 8:7, 9. 13:3, 24, 25. 2 Ch 16:2, 4. Je 49:27. Am 1:4. The title of kings of Syria. (1) King of Damascus in the time of Asa, king of Judah, 1 K 15:18; 2 Ch 16:4. (2) A king of Damascus in the time of Ahab, 1 K 20:1; 2 K 6:24. (3) Son of Hazael, 2 K 13:3; Am 1:4. (4) A general name of kings of Syria who reigned in Damascus, Je 49:27. **Damascus**. 1 K 11:23, 24. Ge 14:15. 15:2. Je 49:27. Am 1:4. **Tabrimon**. i.e. *good is the pomegranate,* or *good is Rimmon,* the Syrian deity. ✻S#2886h. **Hezion**. i.e. *vision,* ✻S#2383h. Perhaps the same as Rezon in 1 K 11:25 (Young). **Damascus**. 1 K 11:23, 24. Ge 14:15. 15:2. Je 49:27. Am 1:4.

19. **There is a league**. 2 Ch 19:2. Is 31:1. **break thy league**. 2 S 21:2. 2 Ch 16:3. Ezk 17:13-16. Ro 1:31. 3:8. **depart**. Heb. go up. 2 Ch 16:3.

20. **Ijon**. i.e. *ruin,* ✻S#5859h. 2 K 15:29. 2 Ch 16:4. Probably the same as *Hazar-enan,* a frontier town to Damascus (Ezk 48:1); and perhaps the *Inna* of Caele-Syria, long. 68 degrees and a half, lat. 33, according to Ptolemy. 2 K 15:29. **Dan**. 1 K 12:29. Ge 14:14. Jsh 19:47. Jg 18:29. **Abel-beth-maachah**. i.e. *mourning of the house of oppression,* ✻S#62h. 2 S 20:14, 15. 2 K 15:29. Compare 2 S 20:18. 2 Ch 16:4. **Cinneroth**. i.e. *lyres,* ✻S#3672h. Nu 34:11. Dt 3:17. Jsh 11:2. 12:3. 13:27. 19:35.

21. **when Baasha**. 2 Ch 16:5. **Tirzah**. 1 K 14:17. 16:15-18. SS 6:4.

22. **made a proclamation**. 2 Ch 16:6. **exempted**. Heb. free. **Geba**. Jsh 18:24, Gaba. 21:17. **Mizpah**. Jsh 18:26. 1 S 7:5, Mizpeh. Je 40:6, 10.

23. **The rest of all**. ver. 7, 8. 1 K 14:29-31. **in the time**. 2 Ch 16:12-14. Ps *90:10.

24. A.M. 3090. B.C. 914. **was buried**. Of his splen-

did and costly funeral we read in 2 Ch 16:14. **Jehosha-phat.** i.e. *Jehovah has judged.* 1 K 22:41-43. 2 Ch 17:1, etc. Mt 1:8, Josaphat.

25. A.M. 3050-3051. B.C. 954-953. **Nadab.** i.e. *liberal.* 1 K 14:12, 20. **began to reign.** Heb. reigned. ver. 33. 1 K 14:21. 16:8, 11, 23, 29. 22:41. 2 K 8:16. **two years.** Or nearly so, see ver. 28 (Young). ver. 33.

26. **he did evil.** 1 K 16:7, 25, 30. **walked.** 1 K 12:28-33. 13:33, 34. 22:52. 2 Ch 22:3. Je 9:14. Ezk 20:18. Am *2:4. Mt 14:8. **in his sin.** ver. 30, 34. 1 K 14:16. 16:19, 26. 21:22. 22:52. Ge 20:9. Ex 32:21. 1 S 2:24. 2 K 3:3. 21:11. 23:15. Je 32:35. Ro 14:15. 1 C 8:10-13.

27. **Baasha the son.** See on ver. 16, 17. 1 K 14:14. **conspired.** 1 K 16:9. 1 S 22:8. 2 K 12:20. **Gibbethon.** 1 K 16:15, 17. Jsh 19:44. 21:23.

28. **in the third year.** ver. 25, 33. Dt 32:35.

29. **all the house.** That he might have no rival (Young). **he left not.** 1 K 14:9-16. 2 K 9:7-10, 36, 37. 10:10, 11, 31. 19:25. **any that.** Dt 20:16. Jsh 10:40. 11:11. **breathed.** Heb. *neshamah*, Ge +2:7.

30. **the sins.** See on ver. 26. 1 K 14:9-16. **by his provocation.** 1 K 14:22.

31. A.M. 3050-51. B.C. 954-953. **are they not written.** 1 K 14:19. 16:5, 14, 20, 27.

32. A.M. 3051-3074. B.C. 953-930. **there was war.** That is, there was a constant spirit of hostility kept up between the two kingdoms, and no doubt frequent skirmishing between the bordering parties; but there was no open war till Baasha king of Israel began to build Ramah, which was, according to 2 Ch 15:19. 16:1, in the *thirty-sixth* year of Asa; but according to 1 K 16:8-10, his son was killed by Zimri in the *twenty-sixth* year of Asa, and consequently he could not make war upon him in the *thirty-sixth* year of his reign. Chronologers endeavor to reconcile this, by saying that the years should be reckoned, not from the beginning of Asa's reign, but from the separation of the kingdoms of Israel and Judah. We must either adopt this mode of solution, or admit that there is a mistake in some of the numbers, probably in the parallel places in Chronicles, but which we have no direct means of correcting. See on ver. 16.

33. **twenty and four years.** 1 K 16:8.

34. **he did evil.** ver. 26. **walked.** See on ver. 26. 1 K 12:28, 29. 13:33, 34. 14:16. Is *1:4.

1 KINGS 16

Jehu the prophet predicts the ruin of Baasha's family, 1-4. Baasha dies, and is succeeded by his son Elah, 5-7. Zimri slays Elah, succeeds him, and fulfils Jehu's prophecy, 8-14. Omri usurps the kingdom, and besieges Zimri in Tirzah, who burns himself in the palace, 15-20. Tibni opposes Omri, who prevails against him, 21, 22. Omri builds Samaria, reigns very wickedly, dies, and is succeeded by Ahab, 23-28. Ahab's excessive wickedness and idolatry, as instigated by his wife Jezebel, 29-33. Joshua's curse on him that should rebuild Jericho, is fulfilled on Hiel, 34.

1. A.M. 3073. B.C. 931. **the word of the Lord.** 1 K 13:1, 20. **Jehu.** i.e. *he is.* He reproved Asa in 2 Ch 16:7; and Jehoshaphat in 2 Ch 19:2; and wrote a history, as in 2 Ch 20:34 (Young). ver. 7. 2 Ch *19:2. 20:34. **Hanani.** 1 K 15:33. 2 Ch 16:7-10.

2. **I exalted thee.** 1 K 14:7. 1 S 2:8, 27, 28. *15:17-19. 2 S 12:7-11. Ps 113:7, 8. Lk 1:52. **dust.** ⨍111, Ge +18:27. **thou hast walked.** See on 1 K 13:33, 34. 15:34. **hast made my people.** See on 1 K 14:16. 15:26. Ex 32:21. 1 S 2:24. 26:19. Mt 5:19.

3. **will make thy house.** ver. 11, 12. 1 K 14:10. 15:29, 30. 21:21-24. Is *66:24. Je 22:19.

4. **shall the dogs eat.** See on 1 K 14:11.

5. A.M. 3051-3074. B.C. 953-930. **the rest.** See on 1 K 14:19. 15:31. 2 Ch 16:1, etc.

6. A.M. 3074. B.C. 930. **Baasha slept with.** 1 K +11:43. +14:20. 15:24. Being one of the few kings of Israel who died a natural death (Young). **Tirzah.** 1 K 14:17. 15:21. **Elah.** i.e. *a terebinth tree.* ver. 8, 13, 14.

7. **the hand.** See on ver. 1, 2. **and against his house.** Ex 20:5. **in provoking.** ver. 13. **with the work.** Ps 115:4. Is 2:8. 44:9-20. **because he killed them.** This the Vulgate understands of *Jehu the prophet*; some think *Baasha* is intended; others *Nadab* the son of Jeroboam; and others *Jeroboam*, whom Baasha destroyed in his posterity by cruelly murdering them all. 1 K 14:14. 15:27-29. 2 K 10:30, 31. Is 10:6, 7. Ho 1:4. Ac 2:23. 4:27, 28.

8. A.M. 3075. B.C. 929. **In the twenty and sixth year.** ⨍171T9. Synecdoche of the Part B656. In chronology a part of a time or period is sometimes put for the whole of such period: a part of a year is accounted a whole year. Baasha began to reign in the third year of Asa, and reigned 24 years; yet he died and was succeeded by Elah in the 26th year of Asa; and, in like manner, Elah, who began to reign in the 26th year of Asa, and was killed in the 27th, is said to have reigned *two* years. Thus it is evident that a *part* of a year is calculated as a whole year. In the Chinese annals, the whole year in which a king dies is ascribed to his reign, the years of the succeeding king being reckoned only from the beginning of the following year (Jackson's Chr. Ant. Vol. II. p. 443). 1 K 15:25. Compare the notes on 1 S 30:12n and Jsh 5:11n, where a part of a day is counted as a whole day. Compare 1 K 2:11 (⨍171T7), where "seven years" is put for seven years and a half.

9. **his servant.** 2 K 9:31. **conspired.** 1 K 15:27. 2 K 9:14. 12:20. 15:10, 25, 30. **drinking.** 1 K 20:16. 1 S 25:36-38. 2 S 13:28, 29. Pr *23:29-35. Je *51:57. Da 5:1-4, 30. Na 1:10. Hab *2:15, 16. Mt 24:49-51. Lk *21:34. **Arza.** i.e. *earth; earthiness,* ✱S#777h. **steward of.** Heb. which *was* over. 1 K 18:3. Ge 15:2. 24:2, 10. 39:4, 9. 43:16.

10. **Zimri.** i.e. *my song.* 2 K 9:31. **reigned.** ver. 15. But only for seven days; see ver. 15 (Young).

11. **he slew.** 1 K 15:29. Jg 1:7. **he left not.** See on 1 K 14:10. 1 S 25:22n, 34. **neither of his kinsfolks, nor of his friends.** *or,* both his kinsmen and his friends. kinsmen, or redeemers. Ge 48:16. Ex 6:6. Le *25:25.

12. **according.** See on ver. 1-4. **by Jehu the prophet.** Heb. by the hand of Jehu the prophet. ver. 1, 7, 34. 14:18. 15:29. 17:16. 2 K 9:36mg. 10:10mg. 14:25. 17:13mg. 19:23mg. 24:2mg. 1 Ch 11:3mg. 25:2mg. 29:8. 2 Ch 10:15. 23:18mg. *29:25mg. 33:8. √34:14mg,n. Ezr 9:11mg. Ps 63:10mg. 77:2mg. Pr 26:6.

13. **in provoking.** 1 K 15:30. **vanities.** Dt 32:21. 1 S 12:21. 2 K 17:15. Is 41:29. Je 8:19. 10:3-5, 8, 15. Jon 2:8. Ro 1:21-23. 1 C 8:4. 10:19, 20.

14. **they not written.** See on ver. 5.

15. **seven.** ver. 8. 2 K 9:31. Jb *20:5. Ps 9:16. 37:35. **And the people were encamped.** 1 K 15:27. Jsh 19:44. 21:23.

16. **Omri.** i.e. *my sheaf; servant of the Lord; pupil of Jehovah,* *S#6018h. ver. 17, 21, 22, 22, 23, 25, 27, 28, 29, 29, *30. 2 K *8:26. 1 Ch 7:8. 9:4. 27:18. 2 Ch *22:2. Mi *6:16. (1) A captain of the host of Israel. He was made king instead of Zimri, who had conspired against Elah and slain him, 1 K 16:16-30; 2 K 8:26; 2 Ch 22:2; Mi 6:16. He founded the city of Samaria. (2) A son of Becher, the son of Benjamin, 1 Ch 7:8. (3) One of the descendants of Judah, 1 Ch 9:4. (4) Prince of the tribe of Issachar in David's time, 1 Ch 27:18.

17. **besieged Tirzah.** Jg 9:45, 50, 56, 57. 2 K 6:24, 25. 18:9-12. 25:1-4. Lk 19:43, 44.

18. **palace.** *S#759h. 2 K 15:25. 2 Ch 36:19. Ps 48:3, 13. 122:7. Pr *18:19 (castle). Is 23:13. 25:2. 32:14. 34:13. Je 6:5. 9:21. 17:27. 30:18. 49:27. La 2:5, 7. Ho 8:14. Am 1:4, 7, 10, 12, 14. 2:2, 5. 3:9, 10, 11. 6:8. Mi 5:5. **and burnt the king's house.** Jg 9:54. 1 S 31:4, 5. 2 S +*17:23. Jb 2:9, 10. Mt 27:5.

19. **in doing.** ver. 7, 13. 1 K 15:30. Ps 9:16. 58:9-11. **in his.** See on 1 K 12:28. 14:16. 15:26, 34.

20. **the rest.** ver. 5, 14, 27. 1 K 14:19. 15:31. 22:39. **treason.** 2 K 11:14. 2 Ch 23:13.

21. **divided.** ver. 8, 29. 1 K 15:25, 28. Pr *28:2. Is 9:18-21. 19:2. Mt *12:25. 1 C 1:12, 13. Ep 4:3-5. **Tibni.** i.e. *my structure; building of Jah,* *S#8402h. ver. 22, 22. **Ginath.** i.e. *a garden; protection,* *S#1527h. ver. 22.

22. **Omri.** ⌐132G, Ge +3:19.

23. A.M. 3079-3086. B.C. 925-918. **the thirty and first.** As it is stated in verses 10 and 15, that Zimri began to reign in the 27th year of Asa; and as he reigned only *seven days,* and Omri *immediately* succeeded him, this could not be in the 31st, but in the 27th year of Asa. Jarchi, from *Sedar Olam,* reconciles this, by stating that Tibni and Omri began to reign *jointly* in the 27th year of Asa; and that Tibni dying about *five* years afterwards, Omri began to reign *alone* in the 31st year of Asa. 2 Ch 22:2. **began Omri.** Mi 6:16. **twelve years.** ver. 8, 29.

24. **Shemer.** i.e. *dregs.* **the name of the city.** 1 K 13:32. 18:2. 20:1. 22:37. 2 K 17:1, 6, 24. Jn 4:4, 5. Ac 8:5-8. **Samaria.** Heb. Shomerⱥn, from Shemer, i.e. *dregs.* i.e. *an adamant stone; guardianship,* S#8111h. ver. 28, 29, 32. 1 K 18:2. 20:1, 10, 17, 24, 43. 21:1, 18. 22:10, 37, 37, 38, 51. 2 K 1:2, 3. 2:25. 3:1, 6. 5:3. 6:19, 20. 2 Ch 18:2, 9. 22:9. 25:13, 24. 28:8, 9, 15. Ne 4:2. Is 7:9, 9. 8:4. 9:9. 10:9, 10, 11. 36:19. Je 23:13. 31:5. 41:5. Ezk 16:46, 51, 53, 55. 23:4, 33. Ho 7:1. 8:5, 6. 10:5, 7. 13:16. Am 3:9, 12. 4:1. 6:1. 8:14. Ob 19. Mi 1:1, 5, 6. *Samaria* was situated on an agreeable and fertile hill in the tribe of Ephraim, twelve miles from Dothaim and four from Atharoth, according to Eusebius, and one day's journey from Jerusalem, according to Josephus. **Shemer.** i.e. *dregs; a thorn; guardianship,* *S#8106h.

25. **did worse.** ver. 30, 31, 33. 1 K 14:9. Mi 6:16.

26. **he walked.** ver. 2, 7, 19. 1 K 12:26-36. 13:33, 34. **their vanities.** See on ver. 13. Ps 31:6. Je 8:19. 10:3, 8. 14:22. 16:19. 18:15. Ac 14:15. Ro 1:21-23.

27. **the rest.** ver. 5, 14, 20. 1 K 15:31.

28. **So Omri slept.** See on ver. 6. **Ahab.** i.e. *father's brother; uncle,* *S#256h. ver. 29, 29, 30, 33. 1 K

17:1. 18:1, 2, 3, 5, 6, 9, 12, 16, 16, 17, 17, 20, 41, 42, 44, 45, 46. 19:1. 20:2, 13, 14. 21:1, 2, 3, 4, 8, 15, 16, 16, 18, 20, 21, 24, 25, 27, 29. 22:20, 39, 40, 41, 49, 51. 2 K 1:1. 3:1, 5. 8:16, 18, 18, 25, 27, 27, 27, 28, 29. 9:7, 8, 8, 9, 25, 29. 10:1, 1, 10, 11, 17, 18, 30. 21:3, 13. 2 Ch 18:1, 2, 2, 3, 19. 21:6, 6, 13. 22:3, 4, 5, 6, 7, 8. Je 29:21, 22. Mi 6:16.

29. A.M. 3086-3107. B.C. 918-897. **Samaria.** See on ver. 24.

30. **above.** ver. 25, 31, 33. 1 K 14:9. 21:25. 2 K 3:2.

31. **as if it had been a light thing.** Heb. was it a light thing. Ge 30:15. Nu 16:9. Is 7:13. Ezk 8:17. 16:20, 47. 34:18. **took to wife.** Ge 6:2. Dt 7:3, 4. Jsh 23:12, 13. Ne 13:23-29. **Jezebel.** i.e. *without habitation; a dunghill; without cohabitation; unchaste,* *S#348h. 1 K 18:4, 13, 19. 19:1, 2. 21:5, 7, 11, 14, 15, 15, 23, 23, 25. 2 K 9:7, 10, 22, 30, 36, 37, 37. Re 2:20. **Ethbaal.** i.e. *with Baal,* *S#856h. **the Zidonians.** 1 K 11:1. Jg 10:12. 18:7. **and went.** See on 1 K 11:4, 8. **served Baal.** 1 K 21:25, 26. Jg 2:11. 3:7. 10:6. 2 K 10:18. 17:16.

32. **the house of Baal.** 2 K 10:21, 26, 27.

33. **made a grove.** Ex 34:13. 2 K 13:6. 17:16. 21:3. Je 17:1, 2. **did more to provoke.** ver. 30. 1 K 21:19, 25. 22:6, 8.

34. **Hiel.** i.e. *God liveth,* *S#2419h. **Bethelite.** *S#1017h. **build Jericho.** 2 K 2:4, 19-22. **Abiram.** i.e. *my father is high.* **Segub.** i.e. *set on high.* i.e. in the beginning of his building God took away his firstborn, and others successively in the progress of the work, and the youngest when he finished it (Matthew Poole). Poole also notes that Hiel undertook the construction of buildings at Jericho, not so much for his own advantage, as out of a contempt of the true God, and of his threatenings, which he designed to convince of falsehood by his own experience. And so he found by his own sad experience the truth of God's word, and how vain it was to contend with him. Je 52:10. **according to.** Jsh ⚫*6:26. 23:14, 15. Zc 1:5. Mt *24:35.

1 KINGS 17

Elijah foretells to Ahab a long and excessive drought; and is sent by God to the brook Cherith, and fed by ravens, 1-7. He is afterwards sent to Zarephath, and sustained by a widow woman, whose barrel of meal and cruse of oil do not fail, 8-16. Her son dies, but is restored to life in answer to Elijah's prayer, whom she fully believes to be sent by God, 17-24.

1. A.M. 3094. B.C. 910. **Elijah.** Heb. Elijahu. i.e. *My God is He,* *S#452h. ver. 13, 15, 16, 18, 22, 23, 24. 1 K 18:1, 2, 7, 7, 8, 11, 14, 15, 16, 17, 21, 22, 23, 25, 27, 30, 31, 36, 40, 40, 41, 42, 46. 19:1, 2, 9, 13, 13, 19, 20, 21. 21:17, 20, 28. 2 K 1:10, 13, 15, 17. 2:1, 1, 2, 4, 6, 9, 11, 13, 14, 14, 15. *3:11. 9:36. 10:10, 17. 2 Ch 21:12. Mt 11:14. 16:14. *17:3, 4, 10, 11, 12. 27:47, 49. Lk *1:17. *4:25, 26. *9:30, 33, 54. Jn 1:21, 25. Ro 11:2, Elias. **the Tishbite.** i.e. *captivity; recourse,* *S#8664h. 1 K 21:17, 28. 2 K 1:3, 8. 9:36. From Tishbe, a city of Naphtali in Galilee (Young). **inhabitants.** Ge 23:4 (S#8453h). Nu 35:15. 1 Ch 29:15. **As the Lord God.** 1 K 22:14. 2 K 3:14. 5:16. Is 49:18. Mt 7:29. Lk 1:17. **before whom.** Dt 10:8. Je *15:19. Pr 8:34. Lk 1:19. *21:36. Ac 27:23.

dew nor rain. Lk *4:25. Ja *5:17. Re *11:6.

2. **the word.** 1 K 12:22. 1 Ch 17:3. Je 7:1. 11:1. 18:1. Ho 1:1, 2.

3. **hide thyself.** 1 K 22:25. Ps *31:20. +*83:3. Pr +*22:3. Je 36:19, 26. Jn *8:59. Ac 17:14. He 11:38. Re *12:6, 14. **Cherith.** i.e. *a cutting off; piercing; slaying,* *S#3747h. ver. 5.

4. **I have commanded.** ver. 9. 1 K *19:5-8. Nu 20:8. Jb 34:29. 38:8-13, 41. Ps 33:8, *9. 147:9. Am *9:3, 4. Mt *4:4, 11. **feed.** Ru +4:15.

5. **did according.** 1 K 19:9. Pr *3:5, 6. Mt *16:24. Jn *15:14. Many learned men have raised doubts on those parts of the Inspired Word, which may, by the perverseness of their argument and the ingenuity of their surmises, be made *to appear* inconsistent with fact. In this case, they are not satisfied with being expressly told by God that the ravens supplied Elijah with food, while the brook gave him drink—but apparently to mystify a manifest miracle, they suggest whether these ravens might not be *merchantmen*, or *the inhabitants of a neighboring town.* Let any unprejudiced reader and lover of the Bible take the whole history of Elijah, and he will find that his life was almost a daily illustration of the power of God in his miraculous interpositions. Instance the supply of provision in the unwasting barrel of meal and cruse of oil, after the prophet had removed to Zarephath: the power communicated to him to raise the widow's son from death: the wonderful interposition of the Lord to prove the folly of Baal's worshippers, in sending down fire from heaven to consume Elijah's sacrifice and lick up the water, although the sacrifice had been saturated therewith, and the altar surrounded by a deep trench to prevent its running away. The prayer for rain is another instance; the sojourn in Horeb forty days and forty nights, after having eaten of the cake; the destruction of Ahaziah's messengers twice; the smiting of the waters at Jordan; the fall of the mantle on Elisha; and finally, in the closing scene of life, he was taken to glory without tasting the pains of death—the sting was taken away.

6. **the ravens.** Ex 16:35. Nu 11:23. Jg 14:14. 15:18, 19. Ps *34:9, 10. *37:3, 19. 78:15, 16, 23, 24. Is *33:16. Je 37:21. 40:4. Hab 3:17, 18. Mt 4:4. *6:31-33. *14:19-21. *19:26. Lk *22:35. He *6:18. *13:5, 6. Some have thought that the prophet Elijah, instead of being fed by *ravens*, was supplied by *merchants*, or *Arabians*, or the inhabitants of the city *Arbo.* But, (1) *orevim* is never used singly to denote merchants; nor would God have said, generally, that he had commanded the *merchants*, but would have specified *what* merchants he had commanded. (2) The word is not read *orevim* but *arevim* when it signifies *Arabs*; nor is it likely that they should be found in that district. (3) The inhabitants of *Arbo*, or *Orbo*, if any city of that name then existed, must have been called, according to the genius of the Hebrew language, *arboyim* or *arbonim*, not *orevim.* (4) The solemn declaration of good Obadiah, that Ahab took an oath of *every people*, that he was not concealed among them, shows that his situation required the utmost privacy, even to solitude, and that it was impossible for him to remain concealed among the inhabitants of the country. (5) When the brook was dried up, the prophet was obliged to quit his asylum, which he needed not to have done had a people been his suppliers, as they could have brought him water as well as

food. (6) Hence we may justly conclude, that these *orevim* were true *ravens*, as it is rendered in nearly every version. **bread and flesh.** ♪174, Ge +18:27. **he drank.** Ps 110:7.

7. A.M. 3095. B.C. 909. **after a while.** Heb. at the end of days. ♪171T2C, Ge +24:55. ver. 15. Ge +4:3mg. +*24:55mg. Jg +11:40mg. Ne 13:6mg. **the brook.** Is 40:30, 31. 54:10.

8. **the word.** ver. 2. Ge 22:14. Is 41:17. He 13:6.

9. **Zarephath.** i.e. *a refining place; smelting house,* *S#6886h. ver. 10. Ob 20. Lk 4:26, Sarepta. **Zidon.** 1 K 16:31. 2 S 24:6. 1 Ch 1:13. **widow woman.** ver. 4. Jg 7:2, 4. 2 S 14:5. Ro 4:17-21. 2 C 4:7. **sustain.** Ge 45:11. Ru +4:15. Is 54:10. Mt 15:21, 22. Lk 4:25, 26.

10. **he arose.** Ro 4:20, 21. **the gate.** Ge +14:7. 2 S 19:8n. **Fetch me.** Ge 21:15. 24:17. Jn 4:7. 2 C 11:27. He 11:37.

11. **as she was going.** Ge 24:18, 19. Mt *10:41, 42. *25:35-40. He 13:2. **a morsel.** ver. 9. 1 K 18:4. Ge 18:5.

12. **As the Lord.** ver. 1. 1 S 14:39, 45. 20:3, 21. 25:26. 26:10. 2 S 15:21. Je 4:2. 5:2. **liveth.** Jg 8:19. **have not.** Mk 12:44. **cake.** Ps 35:16h. **but an handful.** Ex 9:8. Le 2:2. 2 K 4:2-7. Mt 15:33, 34. **meal.** Ge 18:6. **barrel.** or, pitcher. ver. 14, 16. 18:33. Ge 24:14, 15, 16, 17, 18, 20, 43, 45, 46. Jg 7:16, 19, 20. Ec 12:6. **oil.** Ge 28:18. Ge 49:20. Dt 33:24, Asher had abundance of oil, though water was scarce (Companion Bible note). Jsh 19:24-28, Zidon fell to the lot of Asher. **cruse.** or, dish. ver. 14, 16. 1 K 19:6. 1 S 26:11, 12, 16. **gathering.** Nu 15:32, 33. **two sticks.** Is 17:6. Je 3:14. That is, a few (Young). **that we may eat it.** Ge 21:16. Je 14:18. La *4:9. Ezk 12:18, 19. Jl 1:15, 16.

13. **Elijah.** Lk 4:26. **Fear not.** Ex 14:13. 2 K 6:16. 2 Ch 20:17. Is 41:10, 13. Mt 28:5. Ac 27:24. **make me thereof.** Ge 22:1, 2. Jg 7:5-7. Mt 19:21, 22. He 11:17. 1 P 1:7. **first.** Pr *3:9, 10. Ml *3:10. Mt √6:33. *10:37. *15:33-38.

14. **thus saith.** 2 K 3:16. *7:1. 9:6. **The barrel of meal.** ♪100, Ge +10:9. i.e. the meal in the barrel. ver. *4. 2 K *4:2-7, 42-44. Mt *14:17-20. 15:36-38. **sendeth.** Heb. giveth.

15. **did according.** Ge 6:22. 12:4. *22:3. 2 Ch *20:20. Mt *15:28. Mk *12:43. Jn *11:40. Ro 4:19, 20. He *11:7, 8, 17. **many days.** or, a full year. ♪171T2C, Ge +24:55. ver. 7.

16. **the barrel.** Mt 9:28-30. 15:28. *19:26. Lk *1:37, 45. Jn *4:50, 51. 11:40. **according.** See on 1 K 13:5. **by Elijah.** Heb. by the hand of Elijah. 1 K +*16:12mg.

17. A.M. 3096. B.C. 908. **the son of the woman.** Ge 22:1, 2. 2 K 4:18-20. Zc 12:10. Jn 11:3, 4, 14. Ja 1:2-4, 12. 1 P 1:7. 4:12. **mistress.** lit. "lady," as in 1 S 28:7. Na 3:4. **that there was.** Jb 12:10. 34:14. Ps 104:29. Da 5:23. Ja 2:26mg. **breath.** Heb. *neshamah*, Ge +2:7.

18. **What have I.** ♪85H, Jg +11:12. ♪108H8, 2 S +16:10. Dt 32:39. Jg +*11:12. 2 S 16:10. 19:22. Ja 3:13. 2 Ch 35:21. Jb 3:6. Am +*3:6. Lk 4:34. 5:8. 8:28. Jn +*2:4. **O thou man.** See on 1 K 13:1. **art thou come.** 1 K 18:9. Ge 42:21, 22. 50:15, 17. 1 S 16:4. Jb 13:23, 26. Ezk 21:23, 24. Mk 5:7, 15-17. 6:16. **to call.** Nu 5:15. Ezk 29:16. Lk 5:8.

19. **into a loft.** or, chamber. T#1198. ver. 23. Jg 3:20. 2 S +18:33. 2 K 4:10, 21, 32. Ac 9:37.

20. **he cried.** 1 K 18:36, 37. Ex 17:4. 1 S 7:8, 9.

2 K 19:4, 15. Ps 99:6. Mt 21:22. Ja 5:15-18. **hast thou also**. Ge 18:23-25. Jsh 7:8, 9. Ps 73:13, 14. Je 12:1.

21. **stretched himself**. Heb. measured himself. 2 K 4:33-35. Ac 20:10. **O Lord my God**. Ac 9:40. He 11:19. **soul**. Heb. *nephesh*, Ge +12:13. Mt +√10:28. Ac 2:27. **into him**. Heb. into his inward parts.

22. **soul**. Heb. *nephesh*, Ge +12:13. 25:+*8n, 9, 17. 35:18. Jb 14:22. 33:18, 22. Ps 88:3. Mt +√10:28. Ac 2:37. +*7:59. **into him**. Heb. into his inward parts. Ge 18:12 (within), 24 (within). **and he revived**. Dt 32:39. 1 S 2:6. 2 K 13:21. Lk 7:14, 15. 8:54-56. Jn 5:28, 29. 11:43, 44. Ac 9:40. 20:12. Ro 14:9. He *11:35. Re 11:11.

23. **chamber**. ver. 23. 2 S +18:33. **See, thy son liveth**. 2 K 4:36, 37. Lk 7:15. Ac 9:41. He *11:35.

24. **Now by this**. Jn 2:11. 3:2. 4:42-48. 11:15, 42. 15:24. 16:30. **the word**. Ec 12:10. 1 Th √2:13. 1 J 2:21.

1 KINGS 18

Elijah is sent to meet Ahab, 1, 2. Ahab and pious Obadiah go different ways, to search the land for pasture, 3-6. Elijah meets Obadiah and sends him to call Ahab, 7-16. Ahab, at Elijah's word, convenes Israel, with the prophets of Baal, at Carmel, 17-20. Elijah proposes to decide, whether JEHOVAH or Baal be God, by proving which would answer by fire, 21-24. Baal's prophets invoke him in vain, 25-29. Elijah prepares a sacrifice, causes much water to be poured upon it, and calls on JEHOVAH, who answers by fire consuming the altar with the sacrifice; the people are convinced that JEHOVAH is God; and at Elijah's word they slay Baal's prophets, 30-40. Elijah gives Ahab notice of abundant rain, which he obtains by prayer; and then he runs before Ahab's chariot to Jezreel, 41-46.

1. A.M. 3098. B.C. 906. **after many days**. √171T2C, Ge +24:55. 1 K 17:1. Lk 4:25. Ja 5:17. Re 11:2, 6. **in the third year**. This form of expression, both in Hebrew and Latin, means "after the third year," i.e. some time between the third and fourth year. Hence this statement agrees with that of our Lord (Lk 4:25) and St. James (Ja 5:17), who say that the drought lasted *three years and six months*; and the fact itself is attested to by Menander, who, as cited by Josephus, says it happened in the time of Ithobalus, the father of Jezebel. 1 K 17:1, 7, 15. Lk 4:25. Ja 5:17. **Go**. ver. 2, 15, etc. **I will send rain**. Le 26:4. Dt 28:12. Ps 65:9-13. Is 5:6. Je 10:13. 14:22. Jl 2:23. Am 4:7.

2. **went to show**. Ps 27:1. 56:4. Pr 28:1. Is 51:12. He 13:5, 6. **a sore**. Le 26:26. Dt 28:23, 24. 2 K 6:25. Je 14:2-6, 18. Jl 1:15-20.

3. **Obadiah**. Heb. Obadiahu. i.e. *servant of Jah*. **the governor of his house**. Heb. over *his* house. Ge 24:2, 10. 39:4, 5, 9. 41:+40, 41. **feared the Lord**. ver. 12. Ge 22:12. 42:18. 2 K 4:1. Ne 5:15. 7:2. Pr 14:26, 27. Ml *3:16. Mt *10:28. Ac 10:2, 35.

4. **Jezebel**. Heb. Izabel. ver. 13, 19. 1 K 16:31. **cut off the prophets**. 1 K 19:18. Ne 9:26. Mt 21:35. Re 17:4-6. **hid**. Jsh 6:17. **in a cave**. He 11:38. **fed them**. ver. 13. 2 K 6:22, 23. Mt 10:40-42. 25:35, 40. **bread and water**. √174, Ge +18:27. 1 K 13:8, 9, 16.

5. **fountains**. Heb. *mayan*, Ge +7:11 (S#4599h). **grass**. Ps 104:14. Je 14:5, 6. Jl 1:18, 20. 2:22. Hab 3:17. Ro 8:20-22. **we lose not all the beasts**. Heb. we cut not off *ourselves* from the beasts.

6. **Ahab went**. Je 14:3.

7. **was in the way**. 1 K 11:29. **he knew**. 2 K 1:6-8. Mt 3:4. 11:8. **fell on**. Ge 18:2. 50:18. 1 S 20:41. 2 S 19:18. Is 60:14. **my lord Elijah**. Ge 18:12. 44:16, 20, 33. Nu 12:11.

8. **thy lord**. ver. 3. Ro 13:7. 1 P 2:17, 18.

9. **What have I sinned**. ver. 12. See on 1 K 17:18. Ex 5:21. **deliver**. √121E2, Ge +42:38.

10. **the Lord**. ver. 15. 1 K 1:29. 2:24. 17:1, 12. 1 S 29:6. **no nation or kingdom**. √102. Hyperbole/Overstatement, Ge +√7:19. 2 K *20:13. Mt √5:29. **whither my lord**. Ps 10:2. Je 26:20-23. **they found thee not**. 1 K 17:5, 9. Ps 12:7, 8. 31:20. 91:1. Je 36:26. Jn 8:59.

11. **Go, tell thy lord**. ver. 8, 14.

12. **the Spirit of the Lord**. 2 K 2:11, 16. Is 48:16. Ezk 3:12-14. 8:3. 11:24. 37:1. 40:1, 2. Mt 4:1. Ac 8:39. 2 C 12:2, 3. **he shall slay me**. 1 S 22:11-19. Da 2:5-13. Mt 2:16. Ac 12:19. **from my youth**. 1 S 2:18, 26. 3:19, 20. 2 Ch 34:3. Ps 71:17, 18. Pr 8:13. Ec 7:18. Is 50:10. Lk 1:15. 2 T *3:15.

13. **what I did**. ver. 4. Ge 20:4, 5. Ps 18:21-24. Ac 20:34. 1 Th 2:9, 10. **I hid an hundred**. Mt 10:41, 42. **fed them**. Mt 25:35. **bread and water**. √174, Ge +18:27.

14. **tell**. Ex 4:1. 1 S 16:2. Je 1:6. **and he shall slay me**. Mt *10:28.

15. **As the Lord**. See on ver. 10. He 6:16, 17. **of hosts liveth**. Ge 2:1. Dt 4:19. Jb 25:3. Ps 24:8-10. 103:21. 148:2, 3. Is 6:3. Je 8:2. Lk 2:13, 14. **before whom I**. See on 1 K 17:1. Dt 1:38. Lk 1:19. **I will surely**. Ps 27:1. Pr 28:1. Is 51:7, 8. He 13:5, 6.

17. **he that troubleth**. 1 K 21:20. Jsh 7:25. Je 26:8, 9. 38:4. Am 7:10. Ac 16:20. 17:6. 24:5. **Israel**. √121A5, √121T3, Ge +9:27.

18. **I have not**. Ezk 3:8. Mt 14:4. Ac 24:13, 20. **Israel**. √121A5, √121T3, Ge +9:27. **but thou**. √120. Metastasis; or, counter-blame B967: A transferring of the blame from one's self to another; from one person or thing to another. For other instances of this figure see Ge 3:12, 13. 2 K 9:19. Ro 7:14. **in that ye have**. 1 K 9:9. 2 Ch 15:2. Pr 11:19. 13:21. Is 3:11. Je 2:13, *19. Ro 2:8, 9.

19. **Mount Carmel**. *Mount Carmel* is situated north of Dora and south of Ptolemais or Acre, from which it is distant, according to Josephus, 120 stadia, or, according to Thevenot, 10 miles; one of its principal points advancing considerably into the Mediterranean, and forming an elevated promontory. It is described as a flattened cone, about 2000 feet (some say 1500) in height, very rocky, its sides steep and rugged, and the soil neither deep nor rich. Captain Mangles says it is now quite barren, though at the northeastern foot of it there are some pretty olive grounds. ver. 42, 43. Jsh 19:26. 1 S 15:12. 2 K 2:25. Je 46:18. Am 1:2. 9:3. **the prophets of Baal**. 1 K 22:6. 2 P 2:1. Re 19:20. **prophets of the groves**. 1 K 15:13. 16:33. 2 K 13:6. Though *ashairah* certainly denotes in some places a *grove*, yet it is equally certain, that in others, as here, it must signify an idol; and it is thought by learned men to be the same as *Ashtoreth*, or *Astarte*, the Syrian *Venus*. **eat at Jezebel's table**. 1 K 19:1, 2. 2 K 9:22. Re 2:20.

20. **gathered**. 1 K 22:9.

21. **How long**. Dt *4:35. Jsh *24:15. 2 K 17:41. Zp 1:5. Mt *6:24. Lk 16:13. Jn *1:12. Ro *6:16-22. 1 C *10:21, 22. 2 C *6:14-16. He *2:3. Re *3:15, 16,

20. **opinions.** *or,* thoughts. Ps 119:113. **if the Lord.** ver. *39. Ex 5:1, 2. Jsh *24:15, 23, 24. 1 S *7:3. 1 Ch 17:26. 2 Ch 33:13. Ps *100:3. **answered.** Ge *24:50. 44:16. Jb *40:4, 5. Mt *22:12, 34, 36. Ro *3:19. 6:21.

22. **I only.** 1 K 19:10, 14. 20:13, 22, 35, 38. 22:6-8. Ro *11:3. **Baal's prophets.** ver. 19, 20. Mt *7:13-15. 2 T *4:3, 4. 2 P *2:1-3.

24. **answereth by fire.** T#1495. ver. *38. Le *9:24. Jg *6:21. 1 Ch *21:26. 2 Ch *7:1, 3. Is 31:9. **and said.** 2 S 14:19. **It is well spoken.** Heb. The word is good. Is *39:8.

26. **from morning.** Mt *6:7. **saying.** ♪42. Battologia; or, vain repetition B404. For another instance of this figure see Ac 19:34. **hear.** *or,* answer. ver. 37. **no voice.** ver. 24. Ps 115:4-8. 135:15-20. Is 37:38. 44:17. 45:20. Je 10:5. Da 5:23. Hab 2:18. 1 C 8:4. 10:19, 20. 12:2. **answered.** *or,* heard. **leaped upon the altar.** *or,* leaped up and down at the altar. Zp 1:9.

27. **Elijah.** 1 K 22:15. 2 Ch 25:8. Ec 11:9. Is 8:9, 10. 44:15-17. Ezk 20:39. Am 4:4, 5. Mt 26:45. Mk 7:9. 14:41. **Cry.** ♪60B, Ge +20:16. **aloud.** Heb. with a great voice. **for he is a god.** Is 41:23. **either.** Such were the absurd and degrading notions which the heathens entertained of their gods. "Vishnoo sleeps four months in the year; and to each of the gods some particular business is assigned. Vayoo manages the winds; Vuroonu the waters, etc. According to a number of fables in the pooranus, the gods are often out on journeys or expeditions" (Ward's *View of the Hindoos*, vol ii. p. 324). **he is talking.** *or,* he meditateth. 1 S +1:16 (❋S#7879h). 2 K 9:11. Jb 7:13. 9:27. 10:1. 21:4. 23:2. Ps 55:2. 64:1. 102, title. 104:34. 142:3. Ps 23:29. **is pursuing.** Heb. hath a pursuit. **must be awaked.** Ps 44:23. 78:65, 66. 121:4. Is 51:9. Mk 4:38, 39.

28. **cut themselves.** Le 19:28. Dt 14:1. Mi 6:7. Mk 5:5. 9:22. **the blood gushed out upon them.** Heb. they poured out blood upon them. 1 S 25:31. Pr 1:16. Is 59:7. Je 6:11. 22:17. Ezk 9:8. 17:17 (casting up). 20:8, 13, 21. 21:22. 22:6, 9, 12, 27. Zp 3:8.

29. **prophesied.** 1 K 22:10, 12. 1 S 18:10. Je *28:6-9. Ac 16:16, 17. 1 C 11:4, 5. **offering.** Heb. ascending. See on ver. 36. **voice.** See on ver. 26. Ga 4:8. 2 T *3:8, 9. **that regarded.** Heb. attention. 2 K 4:31. Is 21:7. 1 C *8:4. Ga 4:8.

30. **he repaired.** 1 K 19:10, 14. 2 Ch *33:16. Ro 11:3. **the altar of the Lord.** This altar of Jehovah was probably built in the time of the judges; and it was even known among the heathen by the name of the *altar of Carmel.* Both Tacitus and Suetonius mention an altar on mount Carmel, which Vespasian went to consult: there was no temple nor statue, but simply an altar, venerable for its antiquity.

31. **twelve stones.** Ex 24:4. Jsh 4:3, 4, 20. Ezr 6:17. Je 31:1. Ezk 37:16-22. 47:13. Ep 2:20. 4:4-6. Re 7:4-8. 21:12. **saying.** Ge 32:28. 33:20. 35:10. 2 K 17:34. Is 48:1.

32. **And with.** Ex 20:24, 25. Jg 6:26. 21:4. 1 S 7:9, 17. **an altar.** Ge +8:20. +13:18. **in the name.** 1 C 10:31. Col 3:17.

33. **he put.** Ge 22:9. Le 1:6-8. **Fill four.** Da 3:19-25. Jn 11:39, 40. 19:33, 34. **pour it.** Jg 6:20.

34. **Do it the second.** 2 C *4:2. *8:21.

35. **ran.** Heb. went. **the trench.** ver. 32, 38.

36. **at the time.** ver. 29. Ex 29:39-41. Ezr 9:4, 5. Ps 141:2. Da 8:13. 9:21. 12:11. Ac 3:1. 10:30. **Lord**

God of Abraham. ver. 21. Ge 26:24. 31:53. 32:9. 46:3. Ex 3:6, 15, 16. 32:13. 1 Ch 29:18. 2 Ch 20:6, 7. Lk +√20:37, 38. Ep 1:17. 3:14. **let it.** 1 K 8:43. 1 S 17:46, 47. 2 K 1:3, 6. 5:15. 19:19. Ps 67:1, 2. 83:18. Ezk 36:23. 39:7. **and that I have.** 1 K 22:28. Nu *16:28-30. Jn 11:42. 1 C *10:31. Col *3:17.

37. **Hear me.** ver. 24, 29, 36. Ge *32:24, 26, 28. 2 Ch *14:11. 32:19, 20. Is 37:17-20. Da *9:17-19. Lk *11:8. Ja *5:16, 17. **may know.** Jn +11:42. **that thou art.** 2 K 19:19. Ps 83:18. **thou hast turned.** Je 31:18, 19. Ezk *36:25-27. Ml *4:5, 6. Lk *1:16, 17.

38. **Then the.** Ge 15:17. Le *9:24. Jg *6:21. 1 Ch *21:26. 2 Ch *7:1. **fire.** ver. *24. Le *10:2. 2 K *1:12. Jb *1:16. Is 31:9.

39. **they fell.** Jg 13:20. 1 Ch 21:16. 2 Ch *7:3. **The Lord.** ver. *21, *24. Jn 5:35. *20:28. Ac 2:37. *4:16.

40. **Take.** *or,* Apprehend. 2 K 10:25. **Kishon.** See on Jg 5:21. **slew them there.** Dt 13:5. 18:20. Je 48:10. Zc 13:2, 3. Re 19:20. 20:10.

41. **Get.** Ec *9:7. Ac *27:34. **a sound,** etc. *or,* a sound of a noise of rain. See on ver. 1. 1 K 17:1.

42. **Elijah.** ver. 19. Mt 14:23. Lk 6:12. Ac 10:9. **he cast himself.** Ge 24:52. Jsh 7:6. 2 S 12:16. Da 9:3. Mk 14:35. Ja 5:16-18. **put his face.** 1 K 19:13. Ezr 9:6. Ps 89:7. Is 6:2. 38:2. Da 9:7.

43. **Go up.** Ps 5:3. Lk 18:1. **Go again.** Ge 32:26. Ezk 36:37. Hab 2:3. Lk 18:7. Ep 6:18. He 10:36, 37.

44. **a little cloud.** Heb. *Kekaphish,* "like the *hollow* of a man's hand;" in the form of a hand bent, the concave side downmost. A similar phenomenon is noticed by Homer (Il. l. iv. 275); and was observed by Mr Bruce (Travels, vol. iii. p. 666) in Abyssinia, as attending the inundation of the Nile. "Every morning, about nine, a small cloud, not above four feet broad, appears in the east, whirling violently round, as if upon an axis; but arrived near the zenith, it first abates its motion, then loses its form, and extends itself greatly, and seems to call up vapors from all opposite quarters. These clouds, having attained nearly the same height, rush against each other with great violence, and put me always in mind of Elijah foretelling rain on Mount Carmel." Ge +9:14. Jb 8:7. Zc *4:10. **Prepare.** Heb. Tie, *or,* Bind. 1 K 20:14mg. 1 S 6:7, 10. 2 K 9:21mg. 2 Ch 13:3mg. Ps 118:27. Je 46:4. Mi 1:13.

45. **black.** Je 4:28. **clouds.** Ge +9:13. **there was.** ver. 39, 40. Nu 25:8. 2 S 21:14. Ezk 36:37. Ja 5:18. **Ahab.** 1 K 21:1, 23. Jsh 19:18. 2 S 2:9. 2 K 9:16.

46. **the hand.** 2 K 3:15. Is 8:11. Ezk 1:3. 3:14. ♪22A14.8L. Anthropomorphism B880. The "hand of the Lord upon" a man denotes the power of the prophetic spirit. For other instances of this figure see 2 K 3:15. Ezk 1:3. 8:1. 33:22. **he girded.** 2 K 4:29. 9:1. Jb 38:3. Je 1:17. Ep 6:14. 1 P 1:13. **ran before.** Mt 22:21. 1 P 2:17. **to the entrance of.** Heb. till thou come to. **Jezreel.** Jsh 17:16.

1 KINGS 19

Ahab shows Jezebel, that Elijah had slain Baal's prophets, and she sends to Elijah, threatening to take away his life, 1, 2. He flees to the wilderness; is weary of living; but being twice strengthened with food brought by an angel, he fasts forty days, and arrives at Horeb, 3-8. There God meets him, preceded by a strong wind, an earthquake, and fire; and, speaking to him in a still small voice, commissions him to anoint

Hazael, Jehu, and Elisha, 9-17. Elijah is informed that seven thousand worshippers of JEHOVAH still remain in Israel, 18. Elijah casts his mantle on Elisha, who takes leave of his friends, and follows him, 19-21.

1. **Ahab.** 1 K 16:31. 21:5-7, 25. **how he had slain.** See on 1 K 18:40.

2. **So let.** 1 K 2:28. 20:10. Ru 1:17. 2 K 6:31. **if I.** Ex 10:28. 15:9. 2 K 19:10-12, 22, 27, 28. Da 3:15. **life.** Heb. *nephesh*, soul, Ge +44:30. **tomorrow.** Pr *27:1. Ac 12-4-6. Ja *4:13, 14.

3. **saw.** ♪171J15, Ge +42:1. **he arose.** Ge 12:12, 13. Ex 2:15. 1 S 27:1. Is 51:12, 13. Mt 26:56, 70-74. 2 C 12:7. **and went.** Pr +*22:3. **life.** Heb. *nephesh*, soul, Ge +44:30. ♪121A9, Ge +23:8. **Beer-sheba.** 1 K 4:25. Ge 21:31. Am 7:12, 13.

4. **sat down.** 1 K 13:14. Ge 21:15, 16. Jg +20:26. Jn 4:6. **juniper tree.** Jb 30:4. Ps 120:4. **he requested.** T#24. ver. 3. Ge 42:36. Nu 11:15. 2 K 2:11. Jb 3:1, 20-22. 7:15. Ps 73:2, 3, 7, 8. Pr 12:25 (T#171). Is 9:13 (T#9). 49:14. Je 8:3. 20:14-18. La 3:2, 3, 7, 8. Ezk 33:20 (T#272). Jon 4:1-4, 8. Ph 1:21-24. Ju 16 (T#700). Re 9:6. **for himself.** Heb. for his life. Heb. *nephesh*, soul, Nu +23:10. **life.** Heb. *nephesh*, soul, Ge +44:30. **might die.** Jb +*6:9. **take away.** T#1463. Nu 11:11, 14, 15. Jg 16:28-30. Jb 6:8, 9. 14:13. Jon 4:1-3. Lk *2:25-30. **better.** Am 6:2. Na 3:8. Mt 6:26. Ro 3:9.

5. **as he lay.** Ge 28:11-15. **an angel.** Ps 34:7, 10. Da 8:19. 9:21. 10:9, 10. Ac 12:7. He *1:14. 13:5. **Arise.** Pr 20:13.

6. **cake.** 1 K 17:6, 9-15. Ge 18:6. Ex 12:39. Nu 11:8. Ps 37:3. Is 33:16. Ezk 4:12. Ho 7:8. Mt 4:11. 6:32. Mk 8:2, 3. Jn 21:5, 9. **the coals.** or, burning stones. Is 6:6. **cruse.** 1 K 17:12, 14, 16. 1 S 26:11, 12, 16. **head.** Heb. bolster. Ge 28:11, 18. 1 S 19:13, 16. 26:+7, 11, 16.

7. **the angel.** See on ver. 5. Lk 22:43. **because the journey.** Dt 33:25. Ps 103:13, 14. Mk 8:2, 3.

8. **in the strength.** Da 1:15. 2 C 12:9. **forty days.** Ex 24:18. 34:28. Dt 9:9, 18. Mt 4:2. Mk 1:13. Lk 4:2. **Horeb.** See on Ex 3:1. 19:18. Ml 4:4, 5.

9. **unto a cave.** T#1181. Ge 19:30. Ex *33:21, 22. Je 9:2. He *11:38. **What doest thou.** ♪22C2, Ge +3:9. ver. 13. Ge *3:9. *16:8. Je 2:18. Jon 1:3, 4.

10. **very jealous.** Ex *20:5. *34:14. Nu 25:11, 13. Dt 5:9, 10. 2 S 21:2 (zeal). Ps *69:9. 119:139. Jn *2:17. **thrown down.** ver. 14. 1 K 18:4, 30. Je *2:30. Ho 5:11. Mi 6:16. 7:2. Ro ▶11:3. **altars.** ♪121S1, Ge +49:10. i.e. given up thy worship (of which the altars were the sign and symbol). **I only.** 1 K 18:4, 20, 22. 20:13, 22, 35, 41, 42. 22:8. Ro *11:2-4. **they seek my.** ver. *2. 1 K 18:*10, 17. **life.** Heb. *nephesh*, soul, Ge +44:30.

11. **stand upon the mount.** Ex 19:20. 24:12, 18. 34:2. Mt *17:1-3. 2 P *1:17, 18. **the Lord passed.** Ex *33:21-23. *34:6. Hab 3:3-5. **and a great.** Ex *19:16. 20:18. Jb 38:1. Ps 50:3. Is 30:30. Ezk 1:4. 37:7. Na 1:3, 6. He 12:18-21. Re *20:11. **but the Lord was not in the wind.** Zc *4:6. **an earthquake.** ✳S#7494h. 1 S 14:15. Ps 68:8. Na 1:5. Zc *14:5. Mt *24:7. *27:51-54. *28:2. He 12:26. Re 11:19. *16:18. or, shaking. ver. 12. Jb 39:24 (fierceness). 41:29. Is 9:5 (confused noise). 29:6. Je 10:22 (commotion). 47:3 (rushing). Ezk 3:12, 13. 12:18. 37:7. 38:19. Am 1:1. Na 3:2 (rattling). Zc 14:5.

12. **a fire.** 1 K 18:38. Ge 15:17. Ex *3:2. Dt 4:11, 12, *33. 2 K 1:10. *2:11. He *12:29. **a still.** Ex *34:6.

Jb *4:16. 33:7. Zc *4:6. Ac *2:2, 36, 37.

13. **he wrapped his face.** This he did to signify his *reverence*; for *covering the face* was a token of respect among the Asiatics, as *uncovering* the head is among Europeans. See on 1 K 18:42. Ex 3:5, 6. 33:18, 19, 23. 1 S 21:9h. Is 6:2, 5. 25:7h (cast). **mantle.** or, robe. Ge 25:25 (garment). Jsh *7:21n, 24. 2 K 2:8, 13, 14. Ezk 17:8 (goodly; lit. a vine of *magnificence*). Jon 3:6. Zc 11:3 (glory). 13:4 (garment). **What doest.** ♪22C2, Ge +3:9. ver. 9. Ge 16:8. Jn 21:15-17.

14. **I have been.** See on ver. 9, 10. Is 62:1, 6, 7. **forsaken.** Dt 29:25. 31:20. Ps 78:37. Is 1:4. Je 22:9. Da 11:30. Ho 6:7. He 8:9. **thrown down.** Ro ▶11:3.

15. **wilderness of Damascus.** The *wilderness of Damascus* seems to have been that part of Arabia Deserta which lay on the south-east of that city, and east of the Trachonites, or the Djebel Haouran and El Ledja; at which place the prophet could arrive without meeting Jezebel or any of his enemies. Ge 14:15. 2 K 8:7. Ac 9:2, 3. **anoint.** Is 45:1. Je 1:10. 27:2, etc. **Hazael.** i.e. *God has seen.* 2 K 8:8-15, 28. 9:14. Am 1:4.

16. **Jehu.** i.e. *he is.* See on 2 K 9:1-3, 6-14. **Nimshi.** i.e. *drawn out, saved,* ✳S#5250h. 2 K 9:2, 14, 20. 2 Ch 22:7. **Elisha.** i.e. *God of safety; thy God is salvation,* ✳S#477h. ver. 17. See on ver. 19-21. 2 K 2:1, 2, 3, 4, 5, 9, 9, 12, 14, 15, 19, 22. 3:*11, 13, 14. 4:1, 2, 8, 17, 32, 38. 5:8, 9, 10, 20, 25. 6:1, 12, 17, 17, 18, 19, 20, 21, 31, 32. 7:1. 8:1, 4, 5, 7, 10, 13, 14, 14. 9:1. 13:14, 15, 16, 17, 20, 21, 21. Lk 4:27, Eliseus. **Shaphat.** i.e. *he judged.* **Abel-meholah.** 1 K 4:12. Jg 7:22.

17. **him that escapeth.** 2 K 9:24, 33. 10:1-7, 33. Is 24:17, 18. Am 2:14. 5:19. **the sword of Hazael.** 2 K 8:12, 13. 10:32. 13:3, 22. **the sword of Jehu.** 2 K 9:14, 24. 10:6, 7, 9, 10. **Elisha slay.** 2 K 2:23, 24. 6:11, 12. Is 11:4. Je 1:10. Ho 6:5. Re 19:21.

18. **Yet I have left.** *or,* Yet will I leave. Is *1:9. 10:20-22. Ro *11:▶4, 5. **the knees.** Ex *20:5. Ps 95:6. Is 49:23. Ro *14:10-12. Ph *2:10. **every mouth.** Idolaters often *kissed their hand* in honor of their idols; and hence the origin of *adoration*, from *ad*, to, and *os, oris*, the *mouth*. "In the act of adoration, we kiss the right hand" (Pliny, l. xviii. c.2). Cicero mentions a statue of Hercules, the chin and lips of which were considerably *worn* by the *kissing* of his worshippers (Orat. in Verrem). Ge +41:40mg. Jb 31:27. Ps *2:12. Ho 13:2. **kissed.** ♪121S2, Ge +21:6.

19. **Elisha.** See on ver. 16. **he with.** Ex 3:1. Jg 6:11. Ps 78:70-72. Am 7:14. Zc 13:5. Mt 4:18, 19. **his mantle.** ver. 13. 1 S 28:14. 2 K 2:8, 13, 14.

20. **he left.** Mt 4:20, 22. 9:9. 19:27-29. **Let me, I pray.** Mt 8:21, 22. Lk 9:61, 62. Ac 20:37. **Go back again.** Heb. Go, return.

21. **boiled their flesh.** 2 S 24:22. **gave unto.** Lk 5:28, 29. **ministered.** 1 K 18:43. Ex 24:13. Nu 27:18-20. 2 K 2:3. 3:11. Ac 13:5. 2 T 4:11. Phm 13.

1 KINGS 20

Ben-hadad king of Syria, not satisfied with Ahab's submission, leads a powerful army against Samaria, and wars against it, 1-12. Ahab, directed by a prophet, gains a complete victory over him, 13-21. A prophet warns Ahab to prepare for another assault, 22. The Syrians come again, the next year, with very great preparations; and are opposed by a very small com-

pany, 23-27. A prophet assures Ahab of victory, because the Syrians thought JEHOVAH the God of the hills, but not of the valleys, 28. The Syrians are smitten with immense slaughter, and Ben-hadad flees and hides himself, 29, 30. He submissively sues to Ahab, who makes a league with him, 31-34. A prophet, by a parable, leads Ahab to condemn himself, and then denounces the judgment of God against him for his unseasonable lenity, 35-43.

1. A.M. 3103. B.C. 901. **Ben-hadad.** 1 K 15:18, 20. 2 K 8:7-10. 2 Ch 16:2-4. Je 49:27. Am 1:4. **thirty and two.** ver. 16, 24. Ge 14:1-5. Jg 1:7. Ezr 7:12. Is 10:8. Ezk 26:7. Da 2:37. **and horses.** Ex 14:7. Dt 20:1. Jg 4:3. 1 S 13:5. Is 37:24. **besieged.** Le 26:25. Dt 28:52. 2 K 6:24-29. 17:5, 6.

2. **he sent.** 2 K 19:9. Is 36:2, etc. 37:9, 10.

3. **Thy silver and.** Ex 15:9. Is 10:13, 14.

4. **I am thine.** Le 26:36. Dt 28:48. Jg 15:11-13. 1 S 13:6, 7. 2 K 18:14-16.

6. **and they shall search.** 1 S 13:19-21. 2 S 24:14. 2 K 18:31, 32. **pleasant.** Heb. desirable. Ge 27:15. Ezr 8:27. Is 44:9. Je 25:34. La 1:7, 10. Ho 9:6. 13:15. Jl 3:5, margins. 1 J *2:16. **eyes.** ʃ155A, Ge +31:35. **and take.** Ex 15:9. Is 10:13, 14.

7. **all the elders.** 1 K 8:1. 2 K 5:7. 1 Ch 13:1. 28:1. Pr 11:14. **Mark.** 2 K 5:7. **seeketh mischief.** Jb 15:35. Ps 7:14. 36:4. 62:3. 140:2. Pr 6:14. 11:27. 24:2. Da 11:27. Ro 3:13-18. **denied him not.** Heb. kept not back from him. ver. 4.

8. **the elders.** 1 K 8:1. Jsh +20:4. **Hearken not.** Pr 11:14.

10. **and said.** ʃ102C, Mt +5:29. **The gods.** 1 K 19:2. Ac 23:12. **if the dust.** 2 S 17:12, 13. 2 K 19:23, 24. Is 10:13, 14. 37:24, 25. **handfuls.** Is 40:12. **follow me.** Heb. *are* at my feet. Ge 30:30mg. Ex 11:8mg. Jg 4:10. 2 K +3:9mg.

11. **Let not him,** etc. ʃ138C, Ge +22:14. This was no doubt a proverbial mode of expression. Jonathan renders it: "Let not him who girds himself, and goes down to the battle, boast as he who has conquered and returned from it." 1 S 14:6, 12, 13. 17:44-47. Pr *27:1. Ec 9:11. Is 10:15, 16. Mt 26:33-35, 75. **harness.** The word *harness* is an obsolete word for *armor,* derived from the French *harnois;* see Ex 13:18.

12. **message.** Heb. word. **drinking.** ver. 16. 1 K 16:9. 1 S 25:36. 2 S 13:28. Pr 31:4, 5. Da 5:2, 30. Lk 21:34. Ep *5:18. **pavilions.** *or,* tents. The word "pavilion," from *papilio,* "a butterfly," here signifies a *tent,* so called because when spread out it resembles such insects. That even persons of regal dignity regaled themselves in this manner, we may learn from Dr. Chandler (*Travels in Asia Minor,* p. 149) who, when he went to visit the Aga of Suki, after his return from hawking, found him vexed and tired; and "a couch was prepared for him beneath a shed made against a cottage, and covered with green boughs to keep off the sun. He entered as we were standing by, and fell down on it to sleep, without taking any notice of us." Je 43:10. **Set yourselves in array. And they set,** etc. *or,* Place *the engines.* And they placed *engines.* 1 S 15:2.

13. **came.** Heb. approached. **Hast thou.** 2 K 6:8-12. 7:1. 13:23. Is 7:1-9. Ezk 20:14, 22. **and thou shalt.** ver. 28. 1 K 18:37. Ex 14:18. 16:12. Ps 83:17, 18. Is 37:20. Ezk 6:7. Jl 3:17.

14. **young men.** *or,* servants. Ge 14:14-16. Jg 7:16-

20. 1 S 17:50. 1 C 1:27-29. **order.** Heb. bind, or tie. See on 1 K 18:44. 2 K 9:21mg. 2 Ch 13:3mg. Ps 118:27. Je 46:4.

15. **numbered.** 1 S +11:8. **two hundred and.** Jg 7:7, 16. 1 S 14:6. 2 Ch 14:11. **seven thousand.** 1 K 19:18. 1 S 14:2. 2 K 13:7. Ps 106:40-43.

16. **Ben-hadad.** See on ver. 11, 12. 1 K 16:9. Pr *23:29-32. 31:4, 5. Ec *10:16, 17. Ho 4:11. **the thirty and two.** Is 54:15. The Syrians, the besiegers, had their directions from a drunken king, who gave orders over his cups while he was drinking at noon. Drunkenness is a sin which is most detestable in all, but more so in a king than in a private individual, inasmuch as the greater weight a man's situation carries, whether from accumulated riches, family connections, hereditary authority, or invested command, so is the influence which his vices must have on those around him. Perhaps it may be said, from past experience, that drunkenness, which is a most heinous sin in the sight of God, may be charged on those who indulge *only now and then* in that which may eventually lead them into drunkenness; for they shut their eyes against the most palpable facts, and rather than give up the paltry gratification of a debauch, involve thousands by their example to positive harm. Benhadad's drunkenness was the forerunner of his fall. Belshazzar also, we read, drank wine with his princes, his wives, and his concubines, and praised the gods of gold, silver, brass, iron, wood, and stone: and in *the same hour* came forth the finger of a man's hand and wrote his doom on the plaster of the wall. Those who fancy themselves perfectly secure, and above the possibility of falling, are commonly nearest their destruction: there is always an Ahab ready to take advantage of and improve the self-imposed imbecility.

17. **the young men.** ver. 14, 15, 19.

18. **Whether they.** 1 S 2:3, 4. 14:11, 12. 17:44. 2 K 14:8-12. Pr *18:12.

20. **they slew.** 2 S 2:16. Ec 9:11. **the Syrians.** Le 26:8. Jg 7:20-22. 1 S 14:13-15. 2 K 7:6, 7. Ps 33:16. 46:6. **fled.** They were doubtless seized with a supernatural fear, which the strongest mind could not reason down, nor the firmest heart resist. This fear the Greeks and other heathen nations called a *panic;* because Pan, one of their gods, was believed to be the author of it. Bacchus, in his Indian expedition, led his army into some defiles, where he was surrounded by his enemies, and reduced to the last extremity. By the advice of Pan, his lieutenant general, he made his army give a sudden shout, which struck the enemy with so great astonishment and terror, that they fled with the utmost precipitation. Hence it was ever afterwards called a *panic,* and supposed to come directly from heaven. It is thus expressed by Pindar: "When men are struck with divine terrors, even the children of the gods betake themselves to flight." **escaped.** 1 S 30:16, 17. 2 K 19:36.

21. **went out.** Jg 3:28. 7:23-25. 1 S 14:20-22. 17:52. 2 K 3:18, 24.

22. **the prophet.** ver. 13, 38. 1 K 19:10. 22:8. 2 K 6:12. **strengthen.** 2 Ch 25:8, 11. Ps 27:14. Pr 18:10. 20:18. Is 8:9. Jl 3:9, 10. Ep 6:10. **at the return.** ver. 26. 2 S 11:1mg,n. 1 Ch 20:1mg. 2 Ch 36:10mg. Ps 115:2, 3. Is 26:11. 42:8.

23. **Their gods.** It was a general belief in the heathen world, that each *district* had its tutelary and protecting

deity, who could do nothing out of his own province. ver. 28. 1 K 14:23. Jg 11:24n. 1 S 4:8. 2 K +*17:25, 26. 19:12. 2 Ch 32:13-19. Ps 50:21, 22. 121:1, 2. Is 42:8.

24. **Take the.** ver. 1, 16. 1 K 22:31. Pr +*21:30.

25. **thou hast lost.** Heb. was fallen. **and surely.** Ps *10:3.

26. **return of the year.** ver. 22. **numbered.** 1 S +11:8. **Aphek.** Supposed to be the *Aphek* near the river Adonis, between Heliopolis and Biblos, and probably the same place that Paul Lucas (vol. i. c. 20) mentions in his Voyage to the Levant. It was swallowed up by an earthquake, and formed a lake about nine miles in circumference, in which he says there were several houses still to be seen entire, under water. ver. 30. Jsh 13:4. 19:30. Jg 1:31, Aphik. 1 S 4:1. 29:1. 2 K 13:17. **to fight against Israel.** Heb. to the war with Israel.

27. **were all present.** or, were victualled. 1 K 4:7, 27. Jsh 1:11. Jg 7:8. **like two.** Dt 32:30. Jg 6:5. 1 S 13:5-8. 14:2. 2 Ch *14:11. *32:7, 8. Ec 9:11.

28. **there came.** ver. 13, 22. 1 K 13:1. 17:18. 2 Ch 20:14-20. **Because.** See on ver. 23. Is 37:29-37. **therefore will.** ver. 13. Dt 32:27. Jsh 7:8, 9. Jb 12:16-19. Ps 58:10, 11. 79:10. Is 37:29, 35. Je 14:7. Ezk 20:9, 14. 36:21-23, 32. **ye shall know.** See on ver. 13. Ex 6:7. 7:5. 8:22. Dt 29:6. Ezk 6:14. 11:12. 12:16. 36:22. 39:7.

29. **seven days.** Jsh 6:15. 1 S 17:16. Ps 10:16. **an hundred thousand.** Dt 32:30. 2 S 10:18. 2 Ch 13:17. 20:23-25. 28:6. Is 37:36.

30. **the rest.** Ps 18:25. **a wall.** Is *24:18. Je 48:44. Am 2:14, 15. *5:19. 9:3. Lk 13:4. **thousand.** Young notes this should be understood as "chief men, not thousand men." 1 S 6:19n. +23:23. Mi +*5:2. **fled.** ver. 10, 20. Da 4:37. **into an inner chamber.** or, from chamber to chamber. Heb. into a chamber within a chamber. 1 K 22:25mg. Ge 43:30. 2 K 9:2. 2 Ch 18:24.

31. **his servants.** ver. 23. 2 K 5:13. **merciful kings.** Pr 20:28. Is 16:5. Ep 1:7, 8. **let us, I pray thee.** Six of the citizens of Calais are reported to have acted nearly in the same manner, when they surrendered their city to Edward the Third, king of England, in 1346. See the whole story circumstantially related by Sir John Froissart (ch. clxiv) who lived in that time, with that simplicity and detail that give it every appearance of truth. **put sackcloth.** 1 K 21:27-29. Ge 37:34. 2 S 3:31. 14:2. 2 K 19:1, 2. Est 4:1-3. Is 22:12. 37:1. Jon 3:5, 6. Re 11:3. **peradventure.** 2 K 7:4. Est 4:16. Jb 2:4. Mt +*10:28. **life.** Heb. *nephesh*, soul, Ge +44:30.

32. **Thy servant.** ver. 3-6. Jb 12:17, 18. 40:11, 12. Is 2:11, 12. 10:12. Da 5:20-23. Ob 3, 4. **me.** Heb. *nephesh*, soul, Nu +23:10. **he is my brother.** ver. 42. 1 S 15:8-20.

33. **the men.** Pr 25:13. Lk 16:8. **diligently observe.** lit. divined and hasted. ♪93A, Ge +1:26. By Hendiadys, the emphasis is placed upon *diligently*. Ge 30:27 (S#5172h, "divine"). **any.** ♪63K, Ge +37:13. **and he caused.** 2 K 10:15. Ac 8:31.

34. **The cities.** 1 K 15:20. 2 Ch 16:4. **said Ahab.** ♪63BA, Ge +26:7. **So he made a covenant.** One of the conditions of this covenant, we learn, was, that Ahab should have "*streets* (*chutzoth*) in Damascus;" a proposal better relished by Ahab than understood by the generality of commentators. This, however, is well

illustrated by Mr. Harmer (Observations, ch. ix. Ob. 77) from William of Tyre (Gesta Dei, p. 791, 830, 831), the great historian of the Crusades; from whom it appears that it was customary to give those nations which were engaged in them, churches, *streets*, and great jurisdiction therein, in those places which they assisted to conquer. The Genoese and Venetians had each a *street* in Acon, or Acre, in which they had their own jurisdiction, with liberty to have an oven, mill, baths, weights and measures, etc. So Knolles, in his history of the Turks, relates, that in the treaty of peace granted by Bajazet, the Turkish emperor, to Emanuel, the Greek emperor, it was stipulated, that the latter should grant free liberty to the Turks to dwell together, in one *street* of Constantinople, with the free exercise of their own religion, laws, etc. ver. 42. 1 K 22:31. 2 Ch 18:30. Is 8:12. 26:10.

35. **of the sons.** ver. 38. 1 S 10:12. 2 K 2:3, 5, 7, 15. 4:1, 38. Am 7:14. **in the word.** 1 K 13:1, 2, 17, 18. **smite me.** ver. 37. Is 8:18. 20:2, 3. Je 27:2, 3. Ezk 4:3. Mt 16:24.

36. **Because thou.** 1 K 13:21-24, 26. 1 S *15:22, 23.

37. **Smite me.** ver. 35. Ex 21:12. **so that**, etc. Heb. smiting and wounding.

38. **the prophet.** Is 8:18. 20:2, 3. Je 27:2, 3. Ezk 4:3. **disguised.** 1 K 14:2. 22:30. Ge +27:16. 1 S 28:8. 2 S 14:2. Mt 6:16.

39. **Thy servant.** Jg 9:7-20. 2 S 12:1-7. 2 S 12:1-7. 14:5-7. Mk 12:1-12. **thy life.** Heb. *nephesh*, soul, Ge +44:30. ver. 42. 2 K 10:24. **or else.** Ex 21:30. Jb 36:18. Ps 49:7, 8. Pr 6:35. 13:8. 1 P 1:18, 19. **pay.** Heb. weigh. Ex 22:17. Est 3:9. 4:7.

40. **he was gone.** Heb. he *was* not. Je 31:15. **So shall thy judgment be.** 2 S *12:5-7. Jb 15:6. Mt 21:41-43. 25:24-27. Lk 19:22.

41. **the ashes away.** ver. 38. 2 S 13:19. Jb 2:8. Je 6:26.

42. **Because.** ver. 34. 1 K 22:31-37. 1 S 15:9-11. **let go.** Is 26:10. **thy life.** Heb. *nephesh*, soul, Ge +44:30. **shall go.** 1 K 22:31-37. 2 K 6:24. 8:12. 2 Ch 18:33, 34.

43. **went.** 1 K 21:4. 22:8. Est 5:13. 6:12, 13. Jb 5:2. Pr +*19:3.

1 KINGS 21

Ahab covets Naboth's vineyard, and is greatly displeased because Naboth refuses to part with it, 1-4. Jezebel discovering this, by letters, in Ahab's name, to the elders of Jezreel, causes Naboth to be stoned, as a blasphemer, 5-14. She excites Ahab to take possession of his vineyard, 15, 16. Elijah is sent to meet Ahab, and to denounce the judgment of God against him, and his family, and Jezebel, 17-24. Ahab's enormous wickedness, 25, 26. He externally humbles himself before God, and the judgments on his family are deferred to his son's days, 27-29.

1. A.M. 3105. B.C. 899. **after.** 1 K 20:35-43. 2 Ch 28:22. Ezr 9:13, 14. 1s 9:13. Je 5:3. **Naboth.** i.e. increase, produce, *S#5022h. ver. 2, 3, 4, 6, 7, 8, 9, 12, 13, 14, 15, 15, 15, 16, 16, 18, 19. 2 K 9:21, 25, 26. **Jezreelite.** *S#3158h. ver. 4, 6, 7, 15, 16. 2 K 9:21, 25. **Jezreel.** 1 K 18:45. Jsh 19:18. Jg 6:33. 1 S 29:1. Ho 1:4, 5.

2. **Give me.** The request of Ahab, at first view, appears fair and honorable. But, as he most evidently

wished Naboth to *alienate* it *finally*, which was expressly forbidden and provided against in the law of God (Le 25:14-28), it was high iniquity in Ahab to tempt him to do it, and to covet it showed the depravity of his soul. Ge *3:6. Ex 20:17. Dt 5:21. 1 S 8:14. Je 22:17. Hab 2:9-11. Lk 12:15. 1 T 6:9. Ja 1:14, 15. **a garden of herbs.** 2 K 9:27. Dt 11:10. Ec 2:5. SS 4:15. **seem good to thee.** Heb. be good in thine eyes. Ge 16:6mg. 1 S +8:6mg. 29:6mg. Zc 11:12mg.

3. **The Lord.** Ge 44:7, 17. Jsh 22:29. 24:16. 1 S *12:23. 24:6. 26:9-11. 1 Ch 11:19. Jb 27:5. Ro 3:4, 6, 31. 6:2, 15. 7:7, 13. 1 C 6:15. Ga 6:14. **I should give.** Le *25:23. Nu *36:7. Ezk *46:18.

4. **heavy.** 1 K 20:43. Jb 5:2. Pr *14:30. +*19:3. Is *57:20, 21. Jon 4:1, 9. Hab 2:9-12. **I will not.** ver. 3. Nu 22:13, 14. **And he laid him.** Ge 4:5-8. 2 S 13:2, 4. Ec √6:9. *7:8, 9. Ep *4:27. Ja √1:14, 15.

5. **Jezebel.** ver. 25. 1 K 16:31. 18:4. 19:2. Ge 3:6. **Why is thy.** 2 S 13:4. Ne 2:2. Est 4:5. **spirit.** Heb. *ruach*, Ge +41:8.

6. **Because.** ver. 2. Est 5:9-14. 6:12. Pr 14:30. 1 T *6:9, 10. Ja 4:2-7. **I will not give.** See on ver. 3, 4.

7. **Dost thou now.** 1 S *8:14. 2 S 13:4. Pr *30:31. Ec *4:1. *8:4. Da 5:19-21. **I will give thee.** ver. 15, 16. Mi √2:1, 2. *7:3.

8. **she wrote.** 2 S 11:14, 15. 2 Ch 32:17. Ezr 4:7, 8, 11. Ne 6:5. Est 3:12-15. 8:8-13. **the elders.** Nu 11:16. Dt 16:18, 19. 21:1-9. **the nobles.** ver. 1. 2 K 10:1-7, 11.

9. **Proclaim a fast.** Ge 34:13-17. Is 58:4. Mt 2:8. 23:14. Lk 20:47. Jn 18:28. **on high among.** Heb. in the top of. ver. 12. Je 13:18mg.

10. **two men.** Dt 19:15. Mt 26:59, 60. Ac 6:11. **sons of Belial.** Dt 13:13. +15:9. Jg +19:22. 1 S +30:22. 2 S +16:7. **Thou didst blaspheme.** Some, with Parkhurst, would render the original, *bairachta elohim wamailech*, "Thou hast blessed the gods and Molech;" a sense, however, which seems extremely forced, and is not acknowledged by any of the ancient versions, though the LXX. and Vulgate render *bairachta* by *eulogase, benedixit*, "blessed." It is no unusual thing for a word to have opposite senses. However, this is one of the places affected by the emendations of the Sopherim (Ge +18:22), where the word *gadaph* meaning "to blaspheme" was replaced by *berech*, "to bless," in order to avoid having to pronounce the word "blaspheme" in connection with God. The same substitution was made at 2 S 12:14; 1 K 21:13; Jb 1:5, 11; 2:5, 9. Ps 10:3; and commentators, ignorant of the real fact of the emendations, have labored to prove that *berech* means both "to bless" and "to curse," which is not the case (See Bullinger's *Figures of Speech Used in the Bible*, p. 1021). Ex 22:28. Le 24:15, 16. Mt 26:59-66. Jn 10:33. Ac 6:13.

11. **did as Jezebel.** Ex 1:17, 21. 23:1, 2. Le 19:15. 1 S 22:17. 23:20. 2 K 10:6, 7. 2 Ch 24:21. Pr 29:12, 26. Da 3:18-25. Ho 5:11. Mi 6:16. Mt 2:12, 16. Ac 4:19. 5:29.

12. **proclaimed a fast.** ver. 8-10. Is 58:4.

13. **children of Belial.** 1 S +30:22. 2 S +16:7. **the men of Belial.** Ex *20:16. Dt 5:20. 19:16-21. Ps 27:12. 35:11. Pr 6:16, 19. 19:5, 9. 25:18. Ml 3:5. Mk 14:56-59. **blaspheme God.** ver. +10n. Jb 1:5, 11. 2:9. Mt 9:3. Jn 10:33. Ac 6:11, 13. 7:57-59. **the king.** Ec *10:20. Is 8:21. Am 7:10. Lk 23:2. Jn 19:12. Ac 24:5. **they carried him.** Le 24:11-16. Nu 15:35, 36. Dt 13:10.

21:21. 22:21, 24. Jsh 7:24, 25. 2 K 9:26. Ec 4:1. Ac 7:57-59.

14. **Naboth is stoned.** 2 S 11:14-24. Ec *5:8. *8:14.

15. **Arise.** See on ver. 7. Pr 1:10-16. 4:17.

16. **Ahab rose up.** 2 S 1:13-16. 4:9-12. 11:25-27. 23:15-17. Ps 50:18. Is 33:15. Ob 12-14. Ro 1:32. 2 P 2:15.

17. **the word.** 2 K 1:15, 16. 5:26. Ps 9:12. Is 26:21.

18. **which is in Samaria.** 1 K 13:32. 2 Ch 22:9.

19. **Hast thou killed.** Ge 3:11. 4:9, 10. 2 S 12:9. Mi 3:1-4. Hab 2:9, 12. **In the place.** This punishment, on Ahab's humiliation and repentance, was transferred from him to his son Jehoram (ver. 29), in whom it was literally accomplished: see the parallel texts. 1 K ✦22:38. Jg 1:7. 2 S 12:11. 2 K 9:25, 26, ✦36. Est 7:10. Ps 7:15, 16. 9:16. 58:10, 11. Mt 7:2.

20. **Hast thou found me.** 1 K 18:17. 22:8. 2 Ch 18:7, 17. Ps 10:8. Pr 1:18. Am 5:10. Mk 12:12. Ga 4:16. Re 11:10. **thou hast sold.** ver. 25. 2 K 17:17. Is 50:1. 52:3. Ro 7:14. **to work.** 1 K 16:30. Nu 32:13. 2 K 21:2. 2 Ch 33:6. Ro 7:14. Ep 4:19.

21. **Behold.** See on 1 K 14:10. Ex 20:5, 6. 2 K 9:7-9. 10:1-7, 11-14, 17, 30. **him that pisseth.** 1 S *25:22n, 34. **him that is shut up.** 1 K 14:10. Dt 32:36. 2 K 9:8, 9. 14:26.

22. **make thine.** 1 K 15:29. 16:3, 4, 11. **made Israel to sin.** See on 1 K 14:16. 15:30, 34. 16:26.

23. **Jezebel.** See on ver. 25. 2 K 9:10, 30-37. **the dogs.** Shocking as this must appear to minds that have been humanized by the kindly influence of Christianity, we still find similar instances in the accounts of modern travelers. Mr. Bruce (*Travels*, vol. iv. p. 81) says, that when at Gondar, "the bodies of those killed by the sword were hewn to pieces and scattered about the streets, being denied burial. I was miserable, and almost driven to despair, at seeing my hunting dogs, twice let loose by the carelessness of my servants, bringing into the courtyard the heads and arms of slaughtered men, and which I could no way prevent, but by the destruction of the dogs themselves." **wall.** or, ditch. 2 S 20:15. 2 K 9:36. Ps 122:7. Is 26:1. La 2:8. Na 3:8.

24. **that dieth.** 1 K 14:11. 16:4. Is 14:19. Je 15:3. Ezk 32:4, 5. 39:18-20. Re 19:18.

25. **But there.** ver. 20. 1 K 16:30-33. 2 K 23:25. **sell himself.** ver. 20. Dt 28:68. 2 K 17:17. Is 50:1. 52:3. Ro 6:19. 7:14. **whom Jezebel.** ver. 7. 1 K 11:1-4. 16:31. 18:4. 19:2. Pr 22:14. Ec 7:26. Mk 6:17-27. Ac 6:12. 14:2. **stirred up.** or, incited. Dt 13:6. Jsh 15:18. Jg 1:14. 1 S 26:19. 2 S *24:1. 1 Ch *21:1. 2 Ch 18:2, 31.

26. **very abominably.** 2 Ch 15:8. Is 65:4. Je 16:18. 44:4. Ezk 18:12. 1 P 4:3. Re 21:8. **following idols.** 1 K 15:12. Dt 29:17. 2 K 17:12. *21:11. **according to.** Ge 15:16. Le 18:25-30. 20:22, 23. Dt 12:31. 2 K 16:3. 21:2, 11. 2 Ch 33:2, 9. 36:14. Ezr 9:11-14. Ps 106:35-39. Ezk 16:47. **Amorites.** Ge +10:16.

27. **that he.** 2 Ch 12:7. Ja 4:10. 1 P 5:6. **rent.** Ge 37:34. 2 K 6:30. 18:37. Jon 3:6. **lay in sackcloth.** 2 S 12:17. Jb 16:15. Is 22:12. 58:5-8. Jl 1:13. **went softly.** Is 38:15.

29. **Seest thou.** Je 7:17. Lk 7:44. **Ahab.** Ex 10:3. Ps 18:44. 66:3. 78:34-37. **I will not.** Ps 86:15. Ezk 33:10, 11. Mi 7:18. Ro 2:4. 2 P 3:9. **the evil in.** See on ver. 21-23. **in his son's days.** 2 K 9:25, 26, 33-37. ✦10:1-7, 11.

1 KINGS 22

Ahab persuades Jehoshaphat to go with him against Ramoth-gilead, 1-4. Jehoshaphat proposes to inquire of the Lord; and the false prophets assure Ahab of success, 5-7. At Jehoshaphat's request Micaiah, whom Ahab hates, is sent for, 8-12. The messenger's advice to Micaiah, and his answer, 13, 14. Micaiah, adjured by Ahab to declare the truth, predicts his death, and shows that his prophets are deceived by a lying spirit, 15-23. He is reviled, smitten, and sent to prison, 24-28. Jehoshaphat goes to battle in his robes, but Ahab in disguise, 29, 30. Jehoshaphat, mistaken for Ahab, narrowly escapes; Ahab is mortally wounded; and the people are dispersed by proclamation, 31-36. Ahab dies; and dogs lick his blood, 37, 38. The acts of Ahab, who is succeeded by Ahaziah, 39, 40. Jehoshaphat's good reign, and acts, 41-49. He dies and is succeeded by Jehoram, 50. Ahaziah's wicked reign, 51-53.

1. A.M. 3104-3107. B.C. 900-897. **they continued**. See on 1 K 20:34.

2. A.M. 3107. B.C. 897. **in the third**. ver. 1. Mt 12:40. 16:21. **Jehoshaphat**. ver. 41, 44. See on 1 K 15:24. 2 K 8:18. 2 Ch 18:1, 2, etc.

3. **Ramoth**. 1 K 4:13. Dt 4:41-43. Jsh *20:7n, 8. **still**. Heb. silent from taking it. Jsh 18:3. Jg 16:2mg. 18:9. 2 S 19:10mg.

4. **Wilt thou go**. 2 K 3:7. 2 Ch 18:3. **with me**. Ec 4:9, 10. **I am as thou**. 2 Ch 19:2. Ps 139:21, 22. Pr 13:20. 1 C 15:33. 2 C 6:16, 17. Ep *5:11. 2 J 11. Re 2:2, 6.

5. **Enquire**. Nu *27:21. Jsh 9:14. Jg 1:1. 20:18, 23, 28. 1 S 14:18, 19. 23:2, 4, 9-12. 30:8. 2 K 1:3. 3:11. 1 Ch 10:13. 2 Ch 18:4, 5. Pr *3:5, 6. Je 21:2. 42:2-6. Ezk 14:3. 20:1-3.

6. **the prophets together**. 1 K 18:19. 2 T 4:3. **Go up**. ver. 15, 22, 23. 2 Ch 18:14. Je 5:31. 8:10, 11. 14:13, 14. 23:14-17. 28:1-9. Ezk 13:7-16, 22. Mt *7:15. 2 P 2:1-3. Re 19:20. **the Lord**. This prophecy is couched in the *ambiguous terms* in which the heathen oracles were delivered. It may mean either "The Lord will deliver *it* (Ramoth Gilead) into the king's (Ahab's) hand;" or, "The Lord will deliver (Israel) into the king's (of Syria) hand." So in the famous reply of the Delphian oracle to Pyrrhus: "I say to thee, Pyrrhus the Romans shall overcome: thou shalt go, thou shalt return never in war shalt thou perish." Compare Na 3:18n.

7. **Is there not**. 2 K 3:11-13. 2 Ch 18:6, 7.

8. **yet one man**. 1 K 18:4. *19:10, 14. 20:41, 42. **Micaiah**. i.e. *who is like God? who is like him*, ✚S#4321h. ver. 9, 13, 14, 15, 24, 25, 26, 28. 2 Ch 18:7, 8, 12, 13, 14, 23, 24, 25, 27. **Imlah**. i.e. *he fills; whom God makes full*, ✳S#3229h. ver. 9. 2 Ch 18:7, 8, Imla. **but I hate him**. ver. *27. 1 K 20:43. 21:20. Ge *37:8. 2 Ch *36:16. Ps *34:21. Pr *9:8. 15:12. Is 49:7. Je *18:18. 20:10. 43:3, 4. Am *5:10. Zc 11:8. Mt *10:22. Jn *3:19-21. 7:7. *15:18, 19. 17:14. Ga *4:16. Re *11:7-10. **good**. ver. *13. Is 30:10. Je 38:4. Mi 2:11. **concerning me**. 1 K *20:35-42. 2 K 9:22. Is 3:11. *57:19-21. **Let not the**. 1 K 21:27-29. Pr 5:12-14. Mi *2:7.

9. **officer**. *or*, eunuch. Ge +37:36mg. 2 K +8:6mg. 9:32mg. 2 Ch 18:8mg. Is 39:7. Da 1:18. **Hasten**. ver. 26, 27.

10. **having put**. ver. 30. Est 5:1. 6:8, 9. Mt 6:20. 11:8. Ac 12:21. 25:23. **void place**. Heb. floor. Ge

50:+10, 11. Dt +16:13mg. Jg 6:37. Ru 3:2. **gate**. ♪171S7B, Ge +14:7. **of Samaria**. 1 K 16:24. **all the prophets**. 1 K 18:29. 2 Ch 18:9-11. Je 27:14-16. Ezk 13:1-9.

11. **Zedekiah**. i.e. *justice of Jehovah; righteousness of Jehovah*, ✳S#6667h. 1 Ch 3:16. Ne 10:1. Je 27:12. 28:1. 29:3. Also 1 K 22:24. 2 K 24:17, 18, 20. 25:2, 7, 7. 1 Ch 3:15. 2 Ch 18:10, 23. 36:10, 11. Je 1:3. 21:1, 3, 7. 24:8. 27:3. 29:21, 22. 32:1, 3, 4, 5. 34:2, 4, 6, 8, 21. 36:12. 37:1, 3, 17, 18, 21. 38:5, 14, 15, 16, 17, 19, 24. 39:1, 2, 4, 5, 6, 7. 44:30. 49:34. 51:59. 52:1, 3, 5, 8, 10, 11. (1) The last king of Judah, 2 Ch 36:11. (2) A false prophet who encouraged Ahab to attack the Syrians, 1 K 22:11, 24; 2 Ch 18:10, 23. (3) A false prophet, Je 29:21, 22. (4) A prince of Judah, Je 36:12. (5) A grandson of Jehoiakim, 1 Ch 3:16. **horns of iron**. Je 27:2. 28:10-14. Zc 1:18-21. Ac 19:13-16. 2 C 11:13-15. 2 T 3:8. **Thus saith**. Je 23:17, 25, 31. 28:2, 3. 29:21. Ezk 13:6-9. 22:27, 28. Mi 3:11.

12. **Go up**. See on ver. 6-15, 32-36. 2 Ch 35:22.

13. **Behold now**. Ps 10:11. 11:1. 14:1. 50:21. Is 30:10, 11. Ho 7:3. Am 7:13-17. Mi 2:6, 7, 11. 1 C 2:14-16.

14. **what the Lord**. Nu 22:38. 24:13. 2 Ch 18:12, 13. Je 23:28. 26:2, 3. 42:4. Ezk 2:4-8. 3:17-19. Ac *20:20, 26, 27. 2 C *2:17. *4:1, 2. Ga *1:10.

15. **shall we go**. See on ver. 6. **Go, and prosper**. ♪60B, Ge +20:16. This was strong *irony*; they were the precise words of the false prophets; but were spoken by Micaiah in such a tone and manner as at once showed Ahab that he did not believe, but ridiculed these words of uncertainty. The reply of the Delphian oracle to Croesus was as ambiguous as that returned to Pyrrhus: "If Croesus crosses the Halys, he will overthrow a great empire." This he understood of the empire of Cyrus; the event proved it to be his own: he was deluded, yet the oracle maintained its credit. ver. 6n. 1 K 18:27. Jg 10:14. 2 K 3:13. 2 Ch 18:14. Ec 11:9. Na 3:18n. Mt 26:45. **for**. ♪83. Epitrope; or, Admission B972. Admission of wrong in order to gain what is right. Micaiah (by *Epitrope* and *Irony*) admitted what was in Jehoshaphat's heart, and thus exposed and condemned it. For other instances of this figure see Ec 11:9. Je 2:28. Am 4:4, 5. Mt 23:32. Jn 13:27. Ro 11:19, 20.

16. **shall I adjure**. Jsh 6:26. 1 S 14:24. 2 Ch 18:15. Mt *26:63. Mk 5:7. Ac 19:13. **that thou tell**. Je 42:3-6. Mt 22:16, 17.

17. **I saw**. 1 S 9:9. Je 1:11-16. Ezk 1:4. Ac 10:11-17. **as sheep**. ver. 34-36. Nu 27:17. 2 Ch 18:16, 17. Je 23:1, 2. 50:6, 17. Ezk 34:4-6. Zc 10:2. 13:7. Mt *9:36.

18. **Did I not tell**. See on ver. 8. Pr *10:24. 27:22. 29:1. Lk 11:45.

19. **Hear thou**. Is 1:10. 28:14. Je 2:4. 29:20. 42:15. Ezk 13:2. Am 7:16. **I saw the Lord**. 1 K 19:11-18. Ge 17:22. 18:1, 2, 22. 19:1. 26:2-4, 24. 28:12-15 w 35:1. 32:24-32. 35:9-15. Ex 3:1-4. 19:11-24. 24:12-18. *33:11, 23. 34:5. Le 9:23, 24. 10:1, 2. Nu 12:4, 5. 22:20, 34, 35. Dt 5:4, 22-29. 31:2, 15, 16. Jsh 5:13-15. Jg 2:1-5. 6:11, 14, 16. 13:3-7, *22. 1 S 3:10, 21. 1 Ch 21:16, 17 w 2 Ch 3:1. Jb 42:5. Micaiah evidently gives here an account of what appeared to him in a vision: many of the circumstances must be considered as *parabolical*; for *truth*, rather than *fact*, is revealed in such representations. Nevertheless, as the references preceding this note indicate, there is strong sup-

port in Scripture for those who choose to regard these many instances in Scripture as actual appearances of God to man in visible form, despite the charge by some that this is "gross anthropomorphism." 2 Ch 18:18-22. Is 6:1-3. Ezk 1:26-28. Da 7:9, 10. Ac 7:55, 56. Re 4:2, 3. **all the host**. Jb 1:6. 2:1. Ps *103:20, 21. Is 6:2, 3. Da 7:10. Zc 1:10. Mt 18:10. 25:31. He 1:7, 14. 12:22. Re 5:11. **standing by**. Zc +*3:7.

20. **persuade**. or, deceive. ver. 21, 22. Ex 22:16. Jb 12:16. Pr 25:15. Je 4:10. 20:7mg. Ezk 14:9. **And one**. Zc 1:10. He 1:7, 14.

21. **there came**. ver. 23. Jb 1:6, 7. 2:1. **a spirit**. Heb. ruach, Jg +9:23.

22. **a lying spirit**. Heb. ruach, Jg +9:23. Jb 1:8-11. 2:4-6. 12:16. Jn *8:44. Ac *5:3, 4. 2 Th √2:9, 10. 1 T *4:1, 2. 1 J 4:6. Re 12:9, 10. 13:14. 16:13, 14. 20:3, 7, *8, 10. **Thou shalt**. ver. 20. Jg 9:23. Jb 12:16. Ps 109:17. 2 Th √2:10-12. Re 17:17. **go forth**. √96B, Nu +24:21.

23. **behold, the Lord**. Ex 4:21. 10:20. Dt +*2:30. 2 Ch 25:16. Is 6:9, 10. 44:20. Ezk 14:3-5, 9. Mt 13:13-15. 24:24, 25. 2 Th *2:11, 12. **spirit**. Heb. ruach, Jg +9:23. **and the Lord**. See on ver. 8-11. 1 K 20:42. 21:19. Nu 23:19, 20. 24:13. Is 3:11.

24. **Zedekiah**. ver. 11. **smote Micaiah**. 2 Ch 18:23, 24. Is 50:5, 6. La 3:30. Mi 5:1. Mk 14:65. 15:19, 20. Jn 15:18, 20. Ac 23:2. **Which way**. Je 28:10, 11. 29:26, 27. Mt 26:68. 27:42, 43. **Spirit**. Is +48:16.

25. **Behold**. Nu 31:8. Is 9:14-16. Je 23:15. 28:16, 17. 29:21, 22, 32. Am 7:17. 2 P 2:1. Re 19:20. **into an inner chamber**. or, from chamber to chamber. Heb. a chamber in a chamber. 1 K +20:30mg.

26. **the king of Israel said**. Pr *29:1. **carry him back**. ver. 9.

27. **Put this fellow**. 2 Ch 16:10. 18:25-27. Je 20:2. 29:26. 37:15. 38:6. La 3:53-55. Mk 6:17-28. Lk 3:20. Ac 5:18. 16:23, 24. 24:25-27. 26:10. Ep 3:1. Re 2:10. **bread of affliction**. Dt 16:3. Ps 80:5. 102:9. 127:2. Is 30:20. **until I come in peace**. Lk 12:45, 46. 1 Th 5:2, 3. Ja 4:13, 14.

28. **If thou return**. Nu *16:29. Dt *18:20-22. 2 K 1:10, 12. Is *44:25, 26. Je 28:8, 9. Ac 13:10, 11. **Hearken**. 1 K 18:21-24, 36, 37. 2 Ch 18:27. Am 3:1. Mi 1:2. Mk 7:14-16. 12:37.

29. **the king**. ver. 2-6. 2 Ch 18:28.

30. **I will**, etc. or, when he was to disguise himself, and enter into battle. **put thou on**. ver. 10. Ps 12:2. **disguised himself**. √96B, Ge +8:5. 1 K 14:2. 20:38. Ge +27:16. 1 S 28:8. 2 S 14:2. 2 Ch 18:29. 35:22. Pr +*21:30. Je 23:24.

31. **thirty and two**. 1 K 20:24. 2 Ch 18:30. **Fight**. See on 1 K 20:33-42. **small or great**. See on Ge 19:11. 1 S 30:2. Je 16:6.

32. **they turned**. Pr 13:20. **Jehoshaphat**. Ex 14:10. 2 Ch 18:31. Ps *50:15. 76:10. 91:15. 116:1, 2. 130:1-4. Jon 2:1, 2.

33. **that they turned**. ver. 31. Ps 76:10.

34. **at a venture**. Heb. in his simplicity. The marginal rendering is more accurate, and, as Carr observes, "only implies the unconsciousness of the agent in carrying out the divine purpose, and certainly conveys no thought of chance, for never was weapon more divinely guided in its aim" (Horae Biblicae, p. 37). Ge +24:44n. 2 S 15:11. **and smote**. 1 S *17:49. 2 K 9:24. **joints of the harness**. Heb. joints and the breastplate. 1 K 20:11. Re 9:9. **wounded**. Heb. made sick. 2 K 8:29mg. 2

Ch 18:33mg. 35:23mg. Mi 6:13.

35. **increased**. Heb. ascended. Ezk 41:7. **died at even**. ver. 28. 1 K 20:42. **midst**. Heb. bosom.

36. **there went**. ver. 17, 31. 1 K 12:16. 2 K 14:12. **Every man**. 1 K 12:24. Jg 7:7, 8. 21:24. 1 S 4:10. 2 S 19:8. 2 K 14:12. **to**. √63B, Ge +25:28. By ellipsis, supply "every man (return) to his city."

37. **was brought**. Heb. came.

38. **and the dogs**. See on 1 K 21:19. Jsh 23:14, 15. Is 44:25, 26. 48:3-5. Je 44:21-23. Zc 1:4-6. Mt *24:35.

39. A.M. 3086-3107. B.C. 918-897. **the rest**. 1 K 14:19. 15:23, 31. 16:5, 20, 27. **the ivory house**. That is, probably, decorated with ivory in such abundance as to merit the appellation of an "ivory house." 1 K 10:18, 22. Ps 45:8. Ezk 27:6, 15. Am 3:15. 6:4.

40. **slept with his fathers**. See on 1 K 2:10. 11:21, +*43. 14:+20, 31. 16:28. Ge +25:8n. Dt 31:16n. 2 S 7:12. **Ahaziah**. i.e. laid hold of by Jah; possessed of Jehovah, *S#274h. ver. 49, *51. 2 K 1:*2, *17, 18. 8:24, 25, 26, 29. 9:16, 21, 23, 27, 29. 10:13, 13. 11:1, 2. 12:18. 13:1. 14:13. 1 Ch 3:11. 2 Ch 20:*35, 37. 22:1, 1, 2, 7, 8, 8, 9, 9, 10, 11, 11. (1) The son and successor of Ahab; was the eighth king of Israel. He reigned two years, including the time in which he was associated with his father, which commenced B.C. 896. He was idolatrous like his father. Elijah the prophet foretold his speedy death. 1 K 22:40, 49, 51. 2 K 1:2, 18. 1 Ch 3:11. 2 Ch 20:35, 37. (2) Azariah or Jehoahaz, fifth king of Judah, son of Jehoram and Athaliah. He succeeded his father B.C. 885, and reigned only one year. He was idolatrous, and was killed by Jehu. He is called Jehoahaz in 2 Ch 21:17. 2 K 8:24.

41. A.M. 3090. B.C. 914. **Jehoshaphat**. ver. 2. 1 Ch 3:10. 2 Ch 17:1. 20:31. **began to reign**. "Began to reign alone, ver. 51."

42. **thirty and five**. 2 K 1:17. 8:16. **And his mother's**. 1 K 14:21. 15:2, 10. **Azubah**. i.e. a forsaken woman, *S#5806h. 1 Ch 2:18, 19. 2 Ch 20:31. (1) Mother of Jehoshaphat, 1 K 22:42; 2 Ch 20:31. (2) Wife of Caleb, 1 Ch 2:18, 19. **Shilhi**. i.e. my shoot or dart; armed, *S#7977h. 2 Ch 20:31.

43. **he walked**. 1 K 15:11, 14. 2 Ch 14:2-5, 11. 15:8, 17. 17:3. **he turned**. 1 K 15:5. Ex 32:8. 1 S 12:20, 21. 2 Ch 16:7-12. Ps 40:4. 101:3. 125:5. Pr 4:27. **doing**. 2 Ch 17:3-6. 19:3, 4. 20:3, etc. **the high**. 1 K 14:23. 15:14. 2 K 12:3. 14:3, 4. 15:3, 4. 18:22.

44. **made peace**. ver. 2. 2 K 8:18. 2 Ch 19:2. 21:6. 2 C √6:14. By intermarriage.

45. **Now**. ver. 39. **are they not written**. 1 K 11:41. 14:29. **the chronicles**. 2 Ch 20:34.

46. **the remnant**. 1 K 14:24. 15:12. Ge 19:5. Dt 23:17. Jg 19:22. Ro 1:26, 27. 1 C *6:9. 1 T 1:10. Ju 7.

47. **no king**. √66, Ge +9:3. Ge 25:23. 27:40. 36:31, etc. 2 S 8:14. 2 K 3:9. 8:20. Ps 108:9, 10. **Edom**. 2 S 8:14. 2 K 8:20. **a deputy**. 1 K 4:5.

48. **Jehoshaphat**. 2 Ch *20:35, 36, etc. **made ships**. or, had ten ships. 1 K 10:22. 2 Ch 9:21. Ps 48:7. Is 2:16. 60:9. Jon 1:3. **Tharshish**. Josephus and the Chaldee and Arabic paraphrasts explain this place of Tarsus in Cilicia; the LXX., Theodoret, and Jerome, understand it of Carthage; but the learned Bochart makes it Tartessus, an island in the straits of Gades. Ibn Haukal describes Tarsousa as belonging to Andalus, or Andalusia; and Festus Avienus expressly says, "the

city of Cadiz was formerly called *Tartessus.*" Ge +10:4. **to Ophir**. See on 1 K 9:28n. Ps 45:9. **they went not**. 2 Ch 20:37. 25:7. **Ezion-geber**. See on 1 K 9:26. Nu 33:35, 36.

50. A.M. 3115. B.C. 889. **slept with his fathers**. *f*151, Ge +1:28. See on ver. +40. 1 K 2:10. 2 Ch 21:1. **in the city**. See on 1 K 11:43. 14:31. 15:24. **Jehoram**. i.e. *Jah is high*. 2 K 8:16-18. 2 Ch 21:5-7.

51. A.M. 3107-3108. B.C. 897-896. **began**. "*Now*

he begins to reign alone, ver. 40." **two years**. 1 K 15:25. 2 K 1:17. Young notes "not complete; see 2 K 3:1." 1 K 16:8n.

52. **he did evil**. See on 1 K 15:26. 16:30-33. 2 K 1:2-7. **in the way**. 1 K 21:25. 2 K 8:27. 9:22. 2 Ch 22:3. Mk 6:24. Re *3:20. **and in the way**. See on 1 K 12:28-33. 14:9-16. 15:34. 2 K 3:3.

53. **he served Baal**. 1 K 16:31. Jg 2:1-11. 2 K 1:2. 3:2. **provoked**. 1 K 16:7. Ps 106:29. Is 65:3. Ezk 8:3. **according to all**. 1 K 21:29. Ezk 18:14-18.

2 KINGS

2 KINGS 1

Moab rebels against Israel, 1. Ahaziah, being sick, sends to inquire of Baal-zebub; and Elijah is sent by an angel to order the messengers to inform him, in the name of Jehovah, that he should surely die, 2-4. Ahaziah sends to apprehend Elijah, who twice calls down fire to consume those who came against him, 5-12. The captain of the third company sues for mercy; and Elijah, encouraged by an angel, goes to Ahaziah, and assures him that he would die at that time, 13-16. Ahaziah dies, and is succeeded by Jehoram, 17, 18.

1. A.M. 3108. B.C. 896. **Moab**. Nu 24:17. 2 S 8:2. 1 Ch 18:2. Ps 60:8. **after the**. 2 K 3:4, 5. 8:20, 22.

2. **a lattice**. The flat roofs of the eastern houses are generally surrounded by a parapet wall breast high; but, instead of this, some terraces are guarded with balustrades only, or latticed work. Of the same kind, probably, was the lattice, or net, as the term *shevacha* seems to import, through which Ahaziah fell into the court. This incident proves the necessity of the law for the formation of battlements for the roof (Dt 22:8), which God graciously dictated from Sinai, which furnishes a beautiful example of his paternal care and goodness; for the terrace was a place where many offices of the family were performed, and business frequently transacted. Jg 3:20n. 5:28. SS 2:9. Ac 20:9. **upper chamber**. 2 S 18:33. **was sick**. 1 K 22:34mg. 2 Ch 21:14, 15. Jb 31:3. **Baal-zebub**. i.e. *lord of the fly*, *S#1176h. ver. 3, 6, 16. Mt 10:25. 12:24-27. Mk 3:22. Lk 11:15, Beelzebub. **god**. Jg 11:24. 1 S 5:10. 1 K 11:33. Is 37:12, 19. **whether**. 2 K 8:7-10. 1 K 14:3.

3. **angel**. ver. 15. 1 K 19:5, 7. Ac 8:26. 12:7-11. **Elijah**. ver. 8. 1 K 17:1. **Arise**. 1 K 18:1. **Is it not**. ver. 6, 16. 2 K 5:8, 15. 1 S 17:46. 1 K 18:36. Ps 76:1. **ye go**. Je *2:11-13. Jon 2:8. Mk 3:22.

4. **Thou shalt**, etc. Heb. The bed whither thou art gone up, thou shalt not come down from it. ver. 6, 16. **but shalt**. Ge 2:17. 3:4. Nu 26:65. 1 S 28:19. 1 K 14:12. Pr 11:19. 14:32. Ezk *18:4. Jon 2:8.

6. **Thus saith**. Is 41:22, 23. **therefore**. ver. 3, 4. 1 Ch 10:13, 14. Ps 16:4.

7. **What manner of man was he?** Heb. What *was* the manner of the man? Jg 8:18. 1 S 28:14.

8. **an hairy man**. That is, he wore a rough garment, either made of camels' hair, as that of John the Baptist, or of a skin, dressed with the *hair* on. Sir J. Chardin informs us, in a MS. note on this place, cited by Mr. Harmer, that the eastern dervishes and fakeers are clothed just as Elijah was, with a *hairy* garment, girded

with a leathern girdle. Is 20:2. Zc 13:4mg. Mt 3:4. 11:8. Lk 1:17. Re 11:3.

9. **sent unto**. 2 K 6:13, 14. 1 K 18:4, 10. 19:2. 22:8, 26, 27. Mt 14:3. **he sat**. 1 K 18:42. Lk 6:11, 12. **Thou man of God**. Am 7:12. Mt 26:68. 27:29, 41-43. Mk 15:29, 32. He 11:36.

10. **If I be a man of God**. 2 K 2:23, 24. Nu 16:28-30. 1 K 18:36-38. 22:28. 2 Ch 36:16. Ps 105:15. Mt 21:41. 23:34-37. Ac 5:3-10. **let fire**. Or, rather, as the original literally imports, and the LXX. render, *katabusetai pur,* "*fire shall come down;*" Elijah's words being simply *declarative,* and not *imprecatory.* Nu 11:1. 16:35. Jb 1:16. Ps 106:18. Je +10:25. Lk 9:54. He 12:29. Re 11:5. **consumed**. Da 3:22, 25. 6:24. Ac 12:19.

11. **Again**. Nu 16:41. 1 S 6:9. Is 26:11. Je 5:3. Jn 18:5-12. Ac 4:16, 17. **O man**. 1 S 22:17-19. Pr 29:1. Is 32:7. Mt 2:16. Lk 22:63, 64.

12. **If I**. See on ver. 9, 10. **let fire**. T#1494.

13. **he sent again**. Jb 15:25, 26. Pr *27:22. Ec 9:3. Is 1:5. **fell on**. Heb. bowed. 1 K 19:18. Is 66:2. **besought**. Ex 11:8. Nu 12:11-13. 1 K 13:6. Is 60:14. Re 3:9. **O man of God**. Ps *102:17. Ja 4:7. **life**. Heb. *nephesh,* soul, Ge +44:30. **be precious**. ver. 14. 1 S 18:30. 26:21. Ps 72:14.

14. **Behold**. ver. 10, 11. **let my**. 1 S 26:21, 24. Ps 49:8. 72:14. 116:15. Pr 6:26. Mt 16:25, 26. Ac 20:24. **life**. Heb. *nephesh,* soul, Ge +44:30.

15. **be not afraid of him**. Ge 15:1. 1 K 18:15. Ps 27:1. Is 51:12, 13. Je 1:17. 15:20. Ezk 2:6. Mt +*10:28. He 11:27.

16. **Forasmuch**. See on ver. 3, 4, 6. Ex 4:22, 23. 1 K 14:6-13. 21:18-24. 22:28. **Baal-zebub**. Literally, "the lord of flies;" or, as the LXX. render, *Baal mnian theon,* "Baal the fly god." See note on Ex 8:24. **on which thou art gone up**. In the East there is usually at the end of each chamber a little gallery, raised three or four feet above the floor, with a balustrade in front, to which they *go up* by a few steps: here they place their beds; an allusion to which situation is involved in this declaration of Elijah's, and frequently referred to in the Sacred Scriptures: see Ge 49:4. 2 K 5:21, 34. Ps 132:3. **surely**. *f*147B, Ge +2:16.

17. **Jehoram**. i.e. *the Lord exalts,* *S#3088h. (1) The eldest son of Jehoshaphat, and his successor as king of Judah, 1 K 22:50. 2 K 1:17. 8:16, 25, 29. 12:18. 2 Ch 21:1, 3, 4, 5, 9, 16. 22:1, 6, 11. (2) A son of Ahab, king of Israel, who succeeded to the throne on the death of Ahaziah, who had no son. 2 K 1:17. 3:1, 6. 9:24. 2 Ch 22:5, 6, 7. (3) A priest employed by Jehoshaphat to instruct the people, 2 Ch 17:8. As it is said in 2 K 3:1, that he began his reign in the *eigh-*

teenth of Jehoshaphat, it is supposed that Jehoshaphat admitted his son Jehoram to reign with him eight or nine years before his death. "The second year that *Jehoram* was *Prorex*, and the eighteenth of *Jehosha-phat.*" **in the second**. 2 K 3:1. 8:16, 17. 1 K 22:51.

18. **in the book**. See on 1 K 14:19. 22:39.

2 KINGS 2

Elijah when about to be translated, cannot induce Elisha not to attend him in his progress, 1-7. With his mantle he divides Jordan, and they pass over, 8. Elijah allows conditionally of Elisha's request of a double measure of the Spirit, and is taken to heaven in a fiery chariot, 9-11. Elisha takes up Elijah's mantle; smites and divides Jordan with it, and passes over; and is received as Elijah's successor, 12-15. The sons of the prophets in vain seek for Elijah, 16-18. Elisha heals with salt the bad waters of Jericho, 19-22. Bears destroy the children that mock him, 23-25.

1. **take up**. Ge 5:24. 1 K 19:4. Lk 9:51. Ac 1:9. He 11:5. Re 11:12. **by a whirlwind**. ver. 11. 1 K 18:12. 19:11. Jb 38:1. *40:6. Ps 107:25, 29. 148:8. Is 21:1. 29:6. 40:24. 41:16. Je 23:19. 25:32. 30:23. Ezk *1:4. 13:11, 13. Zc 9:14. **Elisha**. 1 K 19:16-21. **Gilgal**. Jsh 4:19. 5:9.

2. **Tarry here**. Ru 1:15, 16. 2 S 15:19, 20. Jn 6:67, 68. **As the Lord**. ver. 4, 6. 2 K 4:30. 1 S 1:26. 17:55. 25:26. Je 4:2. **soul**. Heb. *nephesh*, Ge +27:31. **I will not**. Ru 1:16-18. 2 S 15:21. 1 J √2:19. **Bethel**. Ge 28:19. 1 K 12:29, 33. 13:1, 2.

3. **And the sons**. ver. 5, 7, 15. 2 K 4:1, 38. 9:1. 1 S 10:10-12. 19:20. 1 K 18:4. 20:35. Is 8:18. **thy master**. Dt 33:3. Ac 22:3. **thy head**. √171Q12, Jg +5:30. **hold**. Ec 3:7.

4. **Jericho**. Jsh 6:26. 18:21. 1 K 16:34. Lk 19:1. **As the Lord**. ver. 2. 2 K 4:30. Ac 2:42. 11:23. **soul**. Heb. *nephesh*, Ge +27:31.

5. **the sons**. i.e. as the Targumist renders, *talmeedey neveeya*, "disciples of the prophets." ver. 5, 7, 15. 2 K 4:1, 38. 5:22. 6:1. 9:1, 4. 1 S 10:10. 19:20. 1 K 20:35. **thy master**. See on ver. 3. Jsh 1:1, 2. Lk 24:51. Jn 17:5-7. Ac 1:2, 11. 20:25. **Yea, I know it**. Ge 48:19. Ec 3:7. Is 41:1. Hab *2:20.

6. **As the Lord**. ver. 4. 1 S 20:3. **soul**. Heb. *nephesh*, Ge +27:31.

7. **fifty men**. ver. 17. 1 K 18:4, 13. **to view afar off**. Heb. in sight, *or* over against. Young indicates strong preference for "over against." ver. 15. 2 K 4:25.

8. **his mantle**. *Tan malotan autou*, "his sheep skin," says the Septuagint; the skins of sheep being formerly worn by prophets as the simple insignia of their office: see Note on 2 K 1:8. 1 K 19:13, 19. or, robe. *S#155h: ver. 13, 14. Ge 25:25. Jsh 7:21n, 24. 1 K 19:13, 19. Ezk 17:8 (goodly; lit. "a vine of *magnificence*"). Jon 3:6. Zc 11:3 (glory). 13:4. **were**. ver. 14. Ex 14:21, 22. Jsh 3:14-17. Ps 114:5-7. Is 11:15. He 11:29. Re 16:12.

9/ **Ask what**. 2 K 13:14-19. Nu 27:16-23. Dt 34:9. 1 Ch 29:18, 19. Ps 72:1, 20. Lk *24:45-51. Jn *17:9-13. Ac √1:8. 8:17. *20:25, 36. **before**. Not *after*, for the intercession of saints is only on earth (Young). Is +*63:16. **Elisha said**. Nu *11:17, 25. 1 K *3:9. 2 Ch 1:9, 10. Jn *14:12-14. 16:7. 1 C 12:31. **a double portion**. lit. "two mouths," as in Dt 21:17. Zc 13:8. This probably refers to the law respecting the firstborn, who had a

double portion of the property of his father (Dt *21:17). As Elisha may have considered himself as the first-born of Elijah, so he requested a double portion of his spiritual influence. T#1710. Nu 27:20. Dt *21:17. Zc 9:12. *12:8. 1 T *5:17. **spirit**. Heb. *ruach*, Ge +41:38. √121A3, Nu +11:17.

10. **Thou hast**. Mk *11:22-24. Jn *16:24. **asked a hard thing**. Heb. done hard in asking. Lk 21:36. Ac 1:6, 7. **if thou see**. ver. *12. Ac *1:9, 10. **it shall be**. Zc 12:8. Mk *11:22-24. Jn *16:24. 1 C 12:31. 14:12.

11. **a chariot**. i.e. a chariot and horses of the most resplendent glory, which manifesting itself in corruscations or shooting rays, seemed to be like blazing fire, or the sun in his strength. Some think that this circumstance gave rise to the fable of Apollo, or the sun, being seated in a blazing chariot, drawn by horses breathing fire. 2 K *6:17. Ps 68:17. 104:3, 4. Ezk 1:4, etc. 10:9, etc. Hab 3:8. Zc 6:1-8. He *1:14. **parted**. Ge 30:40 (separate). Dt 32:8 (separated). Ru 1:17. Pr 16:28. 17:9. 18:18. **by a whirlwind**. See on ver. +1. **into heaven**. Mk *16:19. Lk 9:51. Ac 1:9.

12. **And**. √148, Ge +8:22. **saw it**. ver. 10. **My father**. 2 K 13:14. Jb 22:30. Pr *11:11. Ec *7:19. 9:16-18. Is 37:4, 15, 21. Ac 27:24. **he saw him**. Pr 30:4. Mk *16:19. Lk 2:15. 24:51. Jn *3:13. Ac *1:9. 2 C 5:2, 4. Ep *4:8. Re 11:12. **rent them**. Ge 37:29, 34. Jb 1:20, 21. Is 57:1, 2. Ac 8:2.

13. **the mantle**. ver. +*8. 1 K 19:+13, 19. **bank**. Heb. lip. 1 K 9:26mg. Ge 41:17. Dt 4:48. Jsh 13:9, 16. Jg +7:22mg. Ezk 47:7mg. Da 12:5mg.

14. **And**. √148, Ge +8:22. **smote**. See on ver. 8-10. Jsh 1:1-9. Mk 16:20. Jn 14:12. Ac 2:33. 3:12, 13. **Where is**. Jg 6:13. 1 K 18:36-39. Ps 42:2, 10. 115:2. Jl 2:17.

15. **to view**. See on ver. 7. **The spirit**. Heb. *ruach*, Ge +41:38. Nu 11:25-29. 27:20. Jsh 3:7. Is *11:2. 59:21. Jn 15:26, 27. Ac *1:8. 2 C *12:9. 1 P *4:14. **bowed**. ver. 19. 2 K 4:1-4, 37. 6:1-7. Jsh 4:14.

16. **strong men**. Heb. sons of strength. Jg 18:2mg. 2 S +2:7mg. 1 Ch 26:7, 9. **the Spirit**. 1 K 18:12. Ezk 3:14. 8:3. 11:24. 40:2. Ac 8:39. 2 C 12:2, 3. **some mountain**. Heb. one of the mountains.

17. **they urged**. 2 K 5:16. Ge 19:3 (pressed), 9. 33:11. Jg 19:7. 2 S 18:22, 23. Lk 11:8. Ro 10:2. **ashamed**. 2 K 8:11. Jg 3:25. **Send**. √96B, Nu +24:21. **found him not**. He 11:5.

18. **Go not**. Ro 10:2.

19. **my lord seeth**. Nu 12:11. 1 K 18:7, 13. 1 T 5:17. **the water**. Ex 7:19. 15:23. Jsh 6:17, 26. 1 K 16:34. **barren**. Heb. causing to miscarry. ver. 21. Ge 31:38. Ex 23:26. Dt 28:2-4, 11, 15-18. Jb 21:10. Ho 9:14. Ml 3:11.

20. **cruse**. 2 K 21:13. 2 Ch +35:13. Pr 19:24. 26:15. **salt therein**. Jg 9:45. Ezk 47:11. Zp 2:9.

21. **spring**. or, source. 2 Ch 32:20 (cause). Ps 107:33, 35. Is 41:18. 58:11. **cast**. 2 K 4:41. 5:10. 6:6. Ex 7:19. 15:25, 26. Le 2:13. Mt 5:11, 13. Mk 7:33. 8:23. 9:50. Jn 9:6. **I have healed**. Ezk 47:8-11. 1 C 1:18-28. Re 22:2, 3. **there shall**. Ps 107:33-38. Re 21:4.

22. **healed**. T#1547. Ex 15:23-25. **unto this day**. Jsh +4:9. 1 K 8:8. 12:19.

23. **Bethel**. 1 K 12:28-32. Ho 4:15. 10:5, 15. Am 3:14. 4:4. 5:5. 7:13. **little**. Ge 44:20. 1 S 20:35. **children**. The words "neurim ketannim" not only signify *little children*, but *young men*; for "katon" signifies not only *little*, but *young*, in opposition to *old*; and "naar" signi-

fies not only a *child*, but a *young man*, grown to years of maturity: thus Isaac is called "naar" when *twenty-eight* years old, Joseph when *thirty-nine*, and Rehoboam when *forty*. These idolatrous young men, having heard of the ascension of Elijah, without believing it, blasphemously bade Elisha follow him. The venerable prophet, from a divine impulse, pronounced a *curse* "in the name of the Lord," which was immediately followed by the most terrible judgment; thus evincing the Source from which it flowed. Ge 22:5, 12. 41:12. 43:8. Ru 2:15. 2 S 18:5. 2 Ch 12:13. 13:7. Jb +*19:18. 30:1, 8, etc. Ps 148:12. Pr 20:11. 22:6, 15. Ec 11:10. Is 1:4. 3:5. Je 7:18. **mocked**. Ge 21:9. 2 Ch 36:16. Jb 30:1, 8, 9. Ps 35:15. Pr 17:5. 30:17. Is 57:3, 4. Ezk 22:5. Hab 1:10. Ga 4:29. He 11:36. **Go up**. ver. 11. Mt 27:29-31, 40-43. **baldhead**. Le 13:40. 21:5. Dt 14:1.

24. **cursed them**. 2 K 1:10-12. Ge 8:21. 12:3. 9:25. Ex 21:17mg. 22:28. Dt 28:15-26. Jg 9:20, 57. Ne 13:25. Je 28:16. 29:21-23. La 3:65. Am 7:17. Mk 11:14, 21. Ac 5:5, 9. 8:20. 13:9-11. 2 C 10:6. **she bears**. 1 S 17:34, 36, 37. 2 S 17:8. Pr 17:12. 28:15. Is 11:7. 59:11. La 3:10. Ho 13:8. Am 5:19. **and tare**. 2 K 8:12 (ripped). 15:16. Ge 22:3 (clave). 1 S 6:14. Jb 28:10. Ps 78:15. Is 59:5. Ezk 13:11, 13. Ho 13:8. Hab 3:9. **children**. S#3206h, Da +*1:4n. Ge 21:14n, 15, 16. **of them**. Ge 4:23. Ex 20:5. 1 K 13:24. 19:17. 20:36.

25. **Mount Carmel**. 2 K 4:25. 1 K 18:19, 42.

2 KINGS 3

Jehoram reigns wickedly, 1-3. Mesha king of Moab revolts, 4, 5. Jehoram, Jehoshaphat, and the king of Edom, march against him; and being greatly distressed for lack of water, they apply to Elisha, who sharply reproves Jehoram, but shows respect to Jehoshaphat, 6-14. He promises them water, and victory, 15-19. Plenty of water is sent; the Moabites are deceived by the appearance, and are entirely defeated, 20-24. The allied kings destroy the cities, spoil the country, and besiege Kir-haraseth, 25. The king of Moab, sacrificing his eldest son, causes them to raise the siege, 26, 27.

1. **Jehoram**. 2 K 1:17. 8:16, Joram. 1 K 22:51.

2. **wrought evil**. 2 K 6:31, 32. 21:6, 20. See on 1 S 15:19. 1 K 16:19. **but not**. 1 K 16:33. 21:20, 25. **and like**. 2 K 9:22, 34. 1 K 21:5-15, 25. **image**. Heb. statue. 2 K 10:26. Ge 28:18, 22. Ex 23:24. **Baal**. 2 K 10:18, 26-28. 1 K 16:31, 32.

3. **he cleaved**. 2 K 10:20-31. See on 1 K 12:28-33. **which made**. See on 1 K 14:16. 15:26, 34. 16:31. **he departed**. 2 K 13:2, 6, 11. 14:24. 15:9, 18. 17:22. 1 K 12:26-28. 13:33. 1 C 1:19, 20. **therefrom**. ✓96F1, Ge +3:8.

4. **Mesha**. i.e. safety, *S#4337h. **a sheepmaster**. Ge 13:2. 26:13, 14. 2 Ch 26:10. Jb 1:3. 42:12. **rendered**. 2 S 8:2. 1 Ch 18:2. Ps 60:8. 108:9, 10. **lambs**. Is 16:1.

5. **that the king**. See on 2 K 1:1. 8:20. 2 Ch 21:8-10.

6. A.M. 3109. B.C. 895. **numbered**. 1 S 11:8. 15:4. 2 S 24:1, etc. 1 K 20:27.

7. **wilt thou go**. See on 1 K 22:4, 32, 33. 2 Ch 18:3, 29-32. 19:2. 21:4-7. 22:3, 4, 10-12.

8. **wilderness of Edom**. The "wilderness of Edom" was probably the same as that of Zin or Kadesh, through which the children of Israel passed; extending southward from the Dead sea, to the eastern branch of the

Red sea. See Note on Nu 13:21. Nu 21:4, 5. Ml 1:2, 3.

9. **Edom**. See on 1 K 22:47. **no water**. Ex 15:22. 17:1. Nu 20:2, 4. 21:5. 33:14. **that followed them**. Heb. at their feet. Ge 30:30mg. Ex 11:8mg. Jg 4:10. 1 K 20:10mg.

10. **the Lord**. 2 K 6:33. Ge 4:13. Ps 78:34-36. Pr 19:3. Is 8:21. 51:20.

11. **Is there not here**. See on 1 K 22:7. Ps 74:9. Am 3:7. **that we may**. ver. 1, 3. Jsh 9:14. Jg 20:8-11, 18, 23, 26-28. 1 Ch 10:13. 14:10, 14. 15:13. **poured**. ✓96C1, Ge +4:1. ✓121S3.O. Metonymy of the Adjunct B607. To "pour water on the hands" is put for serving. Heb. *yatsaq*, *S#3332h. Kal, Preterite: Ex 25:12 (cast). 26:37. 29:7 (pour). Le 2:1, 6. 8:15. 9:9. 14:15. 1 K 7:46 (cast). 2 K 4:4. 9:3. 2 Ch 4:17 (cast). Kal, Infinitive: Ex 38:27 (cast). Jb 38:38 (groweth). Kal, Imperative: 1 K 18:33. 2 K 4:41. Ezk 24:3. Kal, Future: Ge 28:18. 35:14. Ex 36:36 (cast). 37:3, 13. 38:5. Le 8:12. 14:26. Nu 5:15. 1 S 10:1. 2 S 13:9. 1 K 22:35 (ran out). 2 K 4:40. 9:6. Is 44:3, 3. Kal, Participle, Paul: 1 K 7:24 (cast), 30 (molten). 2 Ch 4:3. Jb 41:23 (firm), 24, 24 (hard). Ps 41:8 (cleaveth fast). Hiphel, Future: Jsh 7:23 (laid them out). 2 S 15:24 (set down). Hophel, Preterite: Ps 45:2. Hophal, Future: Le 21:10. Jb 22:16 (overflown). Hophal, Participle: 1 K 7:16 (molten), 23, 33. 2 K 4:5. 2 Ch 4:2 (molten). Jb 11:15 (stedfast). 37:18. **water**. That is, was his constant and confidential servant. Mr. Hanway (*Travels*, vol. I. p. 223), speaking of a Persian supper, says, "Supper being now brought in, a servant presented a basin of water, and a napkin hung over his shoulders; he went to every one in the company, and *poured water* on their hands to wash." This text has an important bearing upon the mode of washing, for it shows that washing was accomplished by pouring water on the hands, not placing the hands into the water, as is our custom. Water was poured upon the hands by a servant, and the waste water was received by a basin, over which the hands were held. See related notes (Ex 30:19n. Is 44:3n. Lk 7:44n). Ge 18:4. Jsh 1:1. 1 K 19:21. Lk 22:26, 27. Jn *13:4, 5, 13, 14. Ph 2:22. 1 T 5:10.

12. **The word**. 2 K 2:14, 15, 21, 24. 1 S 3:19-21. **Israel**. 2 K 2:25. 5:8, 9, 15. Is 49:23. 60:14. Re 3:9.

13. **What have**. ✓85H, Jg +11:12. ✓108H8, 2 S 16:10. Jg +*11:12. Ezk 14:3-5. Mt 8:29. Jn +*2:4. 2 C 5:16. 6:15. **get**. Jg 10:14. Ru 1:15. Pr 1:28-30. Je 2:27, 28. Ezk ✓14:3. **the prophets**. Of Baal, whom he and his parents patronized (Young). 1 K 18:19. 22:6, 10, 11, 20-25. **Nay**. See on ver. 10. Dt 32:37-39. Ho 6:1.

14. **As the Lord**. 2 K 5:16. 1 K 17:1. 18:15. **I regard**. Ge 19:21. 2 Ch 17:3-9. 19:3, 4. Ps *15:4. **I would not look**. 1 S 15:26-31. 1 K 14:5, etc. 21:20. Je 1:18. Da 5:17-23. Mt 22:16.

15. **bring me**. This was evidently intended to soothe and tranquilize the prophet's mind, which had been agitated and discomposed with holy indignation by the presence of the idolatrous king, and the recollection of his abomination. The soothing influence of music is generally acknowledged in every civilized nation. Cicero, in his *Tusculan Questions* (lib. iv.) says, that "The Pythagoreans were accustomed to calm their minds, and soothe their passions, by singing and playing on the harp." 1 S 10:5, 6. *16:23. 18:10. 1 Ch 25:1-3. Ep *5:18, 19. **the hand**. ✓22A14.8L, 1 K

+18:46. 1 K 18:46. Ezk 1:3. 3:14, 22. 8:1. 37:1. 40:1. Ac 11:21.

16. **make this valley.** 2 K 4:3. Nu 21:8, 16-18. **ditches.** lit. ditches ditches. 1 K 6:9 (beams; mg, vault-beams). Is 10:31 (Gebim. *or*, the ditches). Je 14:3 (pits).

17. **Ye shall not.** 1 K 18:36-39. Ps 84:6. 107:35. Is 41:17, 18. 43:19, 20. 48:21. **that ye may.** Ex 17:6. Nu 20:8-11.

18. **And this.** 1 K 3:13. Je 32:17, 27. Lk 1:27. Ep 3:20. **a light thing.** 2 K 20:10. 1 K 16:31. Is 7:13. 49:6. Ezk 8:17. **he will.** 1 K 20:13, 28. Is 7:1-9.

19. **And ye.** 2 K 13:17. Nu 24:17. Jg 6:16. 1 S 15:3. 23:2. **fenced city.** Nu 13:19. 32:17, 36. Jsh 10:20. 19:29, 35. 1 S 6:18. 2 S 24:7. **choice.** 2 K 19:23. **fell.** 2 K 6:5. Dt 20:19, 20. **stop.** With dust and stones, as in ver. 25. 2 Ch 32:3, 4, 30. **wells.** Heb. *mayan*, Ge +7:11 (S#4599h). Ge 8:2. Le 11:36. Jsh 15:9. 18:15. 1 K 18:5. **mar.** Heb. grieve. lit. pain. ✦155D, Ge +4:10. ver. 25. Jb 5:18 (sore). Is 5:2. Ezk 13:22 (sad). 28:24.

20. **when the meat offering.** On the altar of God in Jerusalem (Young). Ex 29:39, 40. Le +*23:13. 1 K 18:36. Da 9:21. **there came water.** This supply was altogether miraculous; for there was neither wind nor rain, nor any other natural means to furnish it. **filled.** See on Ps 78:15, 16, 20. Is 35:6, 7.

21. **gathered.** Heb. were cried together. Jsh 8:16. Jg 7:23. **put on armor.** Heb. gird himself with a girdle. Ex 12:11. 1 K 20:11. Ep *6:14.

22. **shone.** lit. "arisen." Ge 32:31. **red.** Ge 25:30. Nu 19:2. SS 5:10. Is 63:2. Zc 1:8. 6:2.

23. **This is blood.** 2 K 6:18-20. 7:6. **surely.** ✦147B, Ge +2:16. **slain.** Heb. destroyed. lit. "dried up." Ge 8:13. Ezk 26:19. 30:7. **now therefore.** Ex 15:9. Jg 5:30. 2 Ch 20:25. Is 10:14. **spoil.** Ge 49:27.

24. **smote the.** Jsh 8:20-22. Jg 20:40-46. Is 16:7, 11. 1 Th 5:3, 4. **went forward.** *or,* smote it in even smiting.

25. **beat down.** ver. 19. Jg 9:45. 2 S 8:2. Is 37:26, 27. **stopped.** ver. 19. Ge 26:15, 18. 2 Ch 32:4. **wells.** Heb. *mayan*, Ge +7:11. ver. 19. **and felled.** Dt 20:19, 20. **only in**, etc. Heb. until he left the stones thereof in Kir-haraseth. ✦63I1A, Ex +12:4. Supply ellipsis from the preceding clause, ver. 24, "Until in Kirharaseth (only) they left the stones thereof (to the Moabites)." **Kir-haraseth.** i.e. *wall of clay*, *S#7025h. Supposed to be the same as *Ar*, or *Areopolis*, the capital of Moab. See on Dt 2:9. Is 15:1. 16:7, 11. Je 48:31, 36, Kir-heres. **slingers.** 1 S *17:40, 50. *25:29. 2 Ch 26:14mg. Jb 41:28. Je 10:18. Zc 9:15mg.

26. **that drew swords.** Jg 8:10. 20:2. **break through.** Is 7:6. Je 39:2. **unto the king of Edom.** ver. 9. Am 2:1.

27. **eldest son.** *or,* first born. Dt 12:31. 21:15-17. Mi 6:7. **offered him.** In cases of great extremity, it was customary in various heathen nations, to offer *human* sacrifices, and even their own *children*. This was frequent among the Phoenicians, Greeks, Romans, Scythians, Gauls, Africans, and others; and was the natural fruit of a religious system, which had for the objects of its worship cruel and merciless divinities. The king of Moab, in this case, sacrificed his son to obtain the favor of Chemosh, *his god*, who, being a devil, delighted in blood and murder, and the destruction of mankind. The dearer anything was to them, the more acceptable those idolaters thought the sacrifice, and therefore burnt their children in the fire to

their honor. Ge 22:2, 13. Dt 12:31. Jg 11:31, 39. Ps 106:37, 38. Ezk 16:20. Mi 6:7. **burnt offering.** Jg 11:31, 39. **upon the wall.** Of the capital city, in the sight of friend and foe (Young). **they departed.** 1 S 14:36-46. 1 K 20:13, 28, 43. **returned.** 2 Ch 20:1, 22, 23.

2 KINGS 4

At Elisha's word the oil of a poor prophet's widow is increased, to enable her to pay her debt, 1-7. He is hospitably entertained by a woman of Shunem, who is rewarded by having a son in her old age, 8-17. The child dies, but is restored to life in answer to Elisha's prayer, 18-37. Elisha heals the pottage made with poisonous herbs, 38-41; and feeds a hundred men with twenty small barley loaves, 42-44.

1. **A.M. 3110. B.C. 894. there cried.** T#1448. **sons.** ver. 38. See on 2 K 2:3, 5. 1 K 20:35. **thy servant did fear.** Ge 22:12. 1 K 18:3. Ne 7:2. Ps 103:11, 17. 112:1, 2. 115:13. 147:11. Ec 8:12. 12:13. Ml *3:16. 4:2. Ac 13:26. Re 15:4. 19:5. **the creditor.** T#1556. Le 25:39, 40, 48. Ne 5:2-5. 10:31. Is 34:14. Mt 18:25, 30, 35. Ja 2:13. **to take.** Children, according to the Hebrew laws, were considered the property of their parents, who had a right to dispose of them for the payment of their debts. The Romans, Athenians, and Asiatics in general, had the same authority over their children: they sold them in time of poverty; and their creditors seized them as they would sheep or oxen, or household goods. The same laws still exist among the Georgians (Tavernier, l. III. c.9).

2. **What shall I.** 2 K 2:9. 6:26, 27. Ps 81:10. Mt 15:34. Jn 6:5-7. *16:24. Ac 3:6. 2 C 6:10. **save a pot of oil.** 1 K 17:12. Ja 2:5.

3. **empty vessels.** 2 K 3:16. Jn 2:7. **borrow not a few.** Heb. scant not. 2 K 13:18, 19. Ps 81:10. Jn 16:24.

4. **thou shalt shut.** ver. 32, 33. 1 K 17:19, 20. Is 26:20. Mt 6:6. Mk 5:40. Ac 9:40. **and shalt pour.** Mk 6:37-44. 8:5-9. Jn 2:7-9. 6:11. Ep 3:20.

5. **she went.** 2 K 5:11. 1 K 17:15, 16. Lk 1:45. He 11:7, 8.

6. **when the vessels.** ver. 43, 44. Mt 9:29. 13:58. 14:20. 15:37. Lk 6:19. 2 C 6:12, 13. **And the oil.** 2 K 13:19. Ex 16:18. Jsh 5:12. 1 K 17:14. Jn 6:12.

7. **pay.** Implicit in the prophet's directive is the very wisest of economic counsel: make it your first priority to get out of debt. As to spending priorities, Scripture teaches our primary responsibility is to (1) meet the necessities of our own family (1 T +*5:8); (2) pay our debts, and become debt free (2 K 4:7n. Pr +✓22:7. Ro *13:8); (3) assist our immediate family financially if needed (Is +*58:7); (4) give to the Lord as he enables (Lk +*11:41n), after the preceding primary obligations have been met. See related notes (Dt 28:48n. Mk 7:11n. Jn 4:8n. Lk 11:41n). Ps +*37:21. Ro *12:17. *13:8. Ph *4:8. 1 Th 2:9, 10. 4:12. 2 Th 3:7-12. **debt.** *or,* creditor. **thy children.** Is +*58:7. 1 T +*5:8.

8. **it fell on.** Heb. there was. ver. 11, 18. Jb 1:6, 13. 2:1. **Shunem.** This city was situated in the tribe of Issachar, five miles south from mount Tabor, according to Eusebius; and is probably the place which he calls *Sanim*, in Acrabatene, in the neighborhood of Samaria or Sebaste. ver. 12. Jsh 19:18. 1 S 28:4. 1 K 1:3. **a great woman.** 2 S 19:32. Jb 1:3. 32:9. Lk 1:15. That is, in station, wealth, goodness, etc. (Young). **she**

constrained him. she laid hold on him. Ge 19:3. Jg 19:20. Pr 7:21. Lk 14:23. 24:29. Ac *16:15.

9. **she said**. Pr 31:10, 11. 1 P 3:1. **this is**. Mt 5:16. 1 Th 2:10. T 1:8. 2 P 1:21. 3:2. **man of God**. See on Dt 33:1. 1 K 13:1. 17:18, 24. 1 T 6:11.

10. **Let us**. Is 32:8. Mt 10:41, 42. 25:40. Mk 9:41. Lk 8:3. Ro *12:13. He 10:24. *13:2. 1 P *4:9, 10. **a little chamber**. An *aleeyah*, or *oleah*, as the Arabs call it; a small back house annexed to the principal dwelling, in which the prophet could live in as great privacy as in his own house, and to which he could retire at pleasure, without breaking in upon the private affairs of the family, or being in his turn interrupted by them in his devotions. ver. 11. See the Note on Jg 3:20. 2 S 18:33. 1 K 17:19. **bed**. lit. "a thing stretched out." Ge 47:31. **table**. Ex 25:23. **stool**. or, high seat. lit. "a throne." Ge *41:40. Ex 11:5. 12:29. Dt 17:18. Jg 3:20. 1 S 1:9. 2:8. 4:13, 18.

11. **it fell on a day**. Jb 1:6, 13. **chamber**. ver. 10n. Jg 3:20n. 2 S 18:33.

12. **Gehazi**. i.e. *valley of vision*, *S#1522h. ver. 12, 14, 25, 27, 29, 31, 36. 2 K 5:20, 21, 25. 8:4, 5. **servant**. 2 K 3:11. 1 K 18:43. 19:3. Ac 13:5.

13. **thou hast**. Mt *10:40-42. Lk 9:3-5. Ro 16:2, 6. Ph *4:18, 19. 1 Th *5:12, 13. 2 T 1:16-18. He *6:10. **careful**. ſ147D, Ge +1:29. 1 S 16:4. **to the king**. 2 K 3:15-18. 8:3-6. Ge 14:24. 2 S 19:32-38. **to the captain**. 2 K 9:5. 2 S 19:13. 1 K 2:32. **I dwell**. Je 6:2mg. 1 T 6:6-8. He 13:5. **among**. lit. in the midst. ſ144A6, Ge +45:6. **mine own**. 2 K 8:1. Ru 1:1-4. Ps 37:3.

14. **she hath no child**. Ge +11:30. 15:2, 3. 17:17. 18:10-14. 25:21. 30:1. Jg 13:2. 1 S 1:2, 8. Lk 1:7.

16. **About this**. Ge 17:21. 18:10, 14. **season**. Heb. set time. ver. 17. Ge +*17:21 (✛S#4150h). Jg 20:38mg. **thou shalt**. Ge 17:16, 17. Lk 1:13, 30, 31. **my lord**. See on 2 K 2:19. **do not lie**. ver. 28. 2 K 5:10, 11. Ge 18:12-15. 1 K 17:18. 18:9. Ps 116:11. Lk 1:18-20.

17. **the woman**. Ge 21:1. 1 S 1:19, 20. Ps +*113:9. Lk 1:24, 25, 36. He 11:11.

18. **to the reapers**. Ru 2:4.

19. **My head**. From this peculiar exclamation, and the season of the year, it is probable he was affected by the *coup de soleil*, or stroke of the sun, which is by no means uncommon in that climate, and often proves fatal. During the Crusades, the army of King Baldwin IV suffered considerably by this circumstance near Tiberias; and Egmont and Heyman, in the 18th century, found the air about Jericho extremely hot; and say that the year before they were there, it destroyed many persons. Jb 14:1, 2. Je 4:19. **head**. ſ84, Ge +6:17.

20. **his mother**. Is 49:15. *66:13. Lk 7:12. **and then died**. Ge 22:2. 37:3, 35. 1 K 17:17. Ezk 24:16-18. Lk 2:35. Jn 11:3, 5, 14.

21. **went up**. 2 K 1:16n. **the bed**. ver. 10. 1 K 17:19. **of the man of God**. Jg 13:6. 1 K 17:16. **and shut**. or, made secure. **the door**. ver. 4, 5, 33.

22. **I may run**. ver. 24, 26. Jn 11:3. Ac 9:38.

23. **go to him**. Jg 13:8. 2 Ch 17:9. **new moon**. When the monthly festival was held. Nu 10:10. 28:11. 1 Ch 23:31. 2 Ch +*2:4. Is 1:13-15. Col *2:16. **nor sabbath**. When the prophets and Levites instructed the people (Young). **she said**. Ex +*15:20n. Jg +*21:21n. 1 Ch 15:20n. **well**. Heb. peace. ver. 26. 2 K 5:21mg, 22. 9:11, 17, 18, 19, 22. Ge +29:6mg.

24. **Then she**. Ex 4:20. 1 S 25:20. 1 K 13:13, 23. **an ass**. These animals were not anciently, as now, used only by the lower classes, but were in general use among the noble and chief personages of the East, and it was not unusual for even the husband to walk by the side of his wife while thus riding; the driver, as was the custom, following. The Shunammite, when she went to the prophet, did not desire so much attendance; but only requested her husband to send her an ass and its driver. **Drive**. 1 S 25:19. **slack not thy riding for me**. Heb. restrain not for me to ride.

25. **to mount Carmel**. 2 K 2:25. Jsh 19:26. 1 K 18:19, 42. Is 35:2. Sixteen miles from Shunem (Young).

26. **Run now**. Zc 2:4. **Is it well with thee**. Ge +29:6mg. 37:14mg. Jg 18:15mg. 1 S 17:18, 22mg. Mt 10:12, 13. Ac 15:36. **It is well**. ver. 23. Le 10:3. 1 S 3:18. Jb 1:21, 22. Ps 39:9.

27. **him by the feet**. Heb. by his feet. Mt 28:9. Lk 7:38. **thrust**. Mt 15:23. 20:31. Mk 10:13. Jn 4:27. 12:4-6. **Let her alone**. Mk 14:6. Jn 12:7. **soul**. Heb. *nephesh*, Ge +34:3. Ge 35:18. Jb +*14:22. Mt +√10:28. 1 Th *5:23. **vexed**. Heb. bitter. 1 S 1:10mg. +30:6. Jb 3:20. 7:11. 10:1. Pr 14:10mg. 18:14. **hid it from me**. 2 K 6:12. Ge 18:17. 2 S 7:3. Am 3:7. Jn 15:15.

28. **Did I desire**. Ge 30:1. **Do not**. See on ver. 16.

29. **said to**. ſ121S4. Metonymy of the Adjunct B608. The whole utterance, which may consist of admonition, instruction, etc., sometimes consists of sign or symbol, and the signs are thus put for the things signified. Here, in what Elisha said in his instructions to Gehazi, the signs given are put by the figure Metonymy of Adjunct for the things symbolized by them. For other instances of this figure see Is 2:4. Je 9:17, 18. 10:18. Ezk 39:9, 10. Am 5:16. Mt 24:20. Lk 22:36. **Gird up thy loins**. 2 K 9:1. 1 K 18:46. Ep 6:14. 1 P 1:13. **take my**. 2 K 2:14. Ex 4:17. **salute him not**. ſ108B. Idiom B827. "Salute" is used by Hebrew idiom for stopping to talk, or hold familiar intercourse. For other instances of this idiom see 1 S 13:10mg. Lk 10:4. Ac 18:22. 21:7, 19. 25:13. **answer him not**. To prevent loss of time (Young). **lay my staff**. 2 K 2:8, 14. Ex 7:19, 20. 14:16. Jsh 6:4, 5. Ac 3:16. *19:12.

30. **As the Lord**. See on 2 K 2:2, 4. 1 S 1:26. 20:3. **soul**. Heb. *nephesh*, Ge +27:31. **I will not**. Ex 33:12-16. Ru 1:16-18.

31. **neither voice**. 1 S 14:37. 28:6. Ezk 14:3. Mt 17:16-21. Mk 9:19-29. Ac 19:13-17. **hearing**. Heb. attention. 1 K 18:26, 29. Is 21:7. **not awaked**. S 26:12. Jb 14:12. Ps 3:5. 17:15. 35:23. 44:23. 59:4, 5. 73:20. 139:18. Pr 6:22. 23:35. Is *26:19. 29:8. Je 31:26. *51:39, 57. Ezk 7:6mg. Da *12:2. Jl 1:5. Hab *2:19. Mk 5:39. Jn *11:11, 43, 44. Ep 5:14.

32. **the child**. 1 K *17:17. Lk *8:52, 53. Jn *11:17.

33. **shut the door**. ver. *4. Mt *6:6. **prayed**. 2 K 5:11. 6:17, 18, 20. 1 K *17:20, 21. 18:26, 27. Jn *11:41, 42. Ac *9:40. Ja *5:13-18.

34. **went up**. 2 K 1:16n. **lay upon**. 1 K *17:21. Ac *20:10. **stretched himself**. ver. 35. 1 K 18:42. **waxed warm**. Ex 16:21. 1 K 1:2. Ps 39:3. Ec 4:11. Is 44:15, 16. 47:14.

35. **to and fro**. Heb. once hither and once thither. **and the child opened**. 2 K 8:1, 5. *13:21. 1 K *17:22. Lk *7:14, 15. *8:55. Jn *11:43, 44. Ac *9:40. **eyes**. Ge +*21:19.

36. **Call this Shunammite**. ver. 12. **Take up**. 1 K 17:23. Lk 7:15. He *11:35.

37. **fell at his feet**. ver. *27. 2 K 2:15. 1 K *17:24. **took up her son**. 2 K 8:1, 5. 1 K 17:23. He 11:35.

38. **Elisha**. 2 K 2:1. 1 S 7:16, 17. Ac *10:38. 15:36. **Gilgal**. 2 K 2:1. **a dearth**. 2 K 8:1. Le 26:26. Dt 28:22-24, 38-40. 2 S 21:1. Je 14:1-6. Ezk 14:13. Lk 4:25. **the sons**. 2 K 2:3. 1 S 19:20. **were sitting**. Dt 33:3. Pr 8:34. Lk 2:46. 8:35, 38. *10:39. Ac 22:3. **Set on the great pot**. Ex 16:3. Ezk 24:3. Mk 6:37. 8:2-6. Lk 9:13. Jn 21:5, 9. **pottage**. Ge 25:29, 34. Hg 2:12.

39. **herbs**. Is 26:19. **a wild vine**. Is 5:4. Je 2:21. Mt 15:13. He 12:15. **wild gourds**. The word *pakkuoth*, from *peka*, in Chaldee, to *burst*, and in Syriac, to *crack*, *thunder*, is generally supposed to be the fruits of the *coloquintida*, or *colocynth;* whose leaves are large, placed alternately, very much like those of the *vine*, whence it might be called a *wild vine:* the flowers are white, and the fruit of the gourd kind, of the size of a large apple, and when ripe, of a yellow color, and a pleasant and inviting appearance. It ranks among vegetable *poisons*, as all intense bitters do; but, judiciously employed, it is of considerable use in medicine. It is said that the fruit, when ripe, is so full of wind that it *bursts*, and throws its liquor and seeds to a great distance: and if touched, before it breaks of itself, it flies open with an explosion, and discharges its fetid contents in the face of him who touched it (See Celsius, *Hierobot*. P. I. p. 393).

40. **O thou**. ver. 9. 2 K 1:9, 11, 13. Dt 33:1. 1 K 17:18. **death**. ♪121G1, Ge +31:1. By Metonymy of the Effect, "death" is put for that which produces death as the effect of eating it. How forcible is this Metonymy, by the use of which time is saved, and perhaps life too (EWB, B564). Ex 10:17. 15:23. Mk 16:18.

41. **he cast**. 2 K 2:21. 5:10. 6:6. Ex 15:25. Jn 9:6. 1 C 1:25. **meal**. Ge 18:6. **there**. Ac 28:5. **harm**. Heb. evil thing.

42. **Baal-shalisha**. i.e. *lord of the third part*, ✱S#1190h, only here. 1 S 9:4, 7. **bread**. ver. 38. Ex 23:16. Dt 12:6. 26:2-10. 1 S 9:7. 2 Ch 11:13, 14. Pr *3:9, 10. 1 C *9:11. Ga *6:6. **of barley**. 2 K 7:1, 16-18. Dt 8:8. 32:14. Jn 6:9, 13. **the husk thereof**. *or*, his scrip, *or* garment. Note: Parched corn, or corn to be parched; full ears before they are ripe, parched on the fire: a very frequent food in the East. The loaves were probably extremely small, as their loaves still are in eastern countries. But small as this may appear, it would be a considerable present in the time of famine; though very inadequate for the number of persons. *Baal-shalisha*, of which the person who made this seasonable present was an inhabitant, was situated, according to Eusebius and Jerome, fifteen miles north of Diospolis, or Lydda.

43. **his servitor**. See on ver. 12. 2 K 6:15mg. Ex 24:13. **What**. Mt 14:16, 17. 15:33, 34. Mk 6:37-39. 8:4. Lk 9:13. Jn 6:9. **They shall eat**. Mt 14:20. 15:37. 16:8-10. Mk 6:42, 43. 8:20. Lk 9:17. Jn 6:11-13. **shall leave**. Ex 36:7. Ru 2:14. 2 Ch 31:10. Je 44:7.

44. **and left**. ver. 43.

2 KINGS 5

Naaman, captain of the host of Syria, is a leper, 1. By the report of a captive maid of Israel, concerning the prophet, he comes to the king of Israel at Samaria to be healed, 2-7. Elisha sends for him; Naaman goes to him, and is ordered to wash seven times in Jordan: he is angry; but, persuaded by his servants, he complies and is cleansed, 8-14. He acknowledges the true God; offers presents to Elisha, who refuses them; and is sent away in peace, resolving to worship the LORD alone, 15-19. Gehazi, by a lie, obtains presents from Naaman, and is punished by leprosy, entailed also on his descendants, 20-27.

1. A.M. 3110. B.C. 894. **Naaman**. i.e. *pleasantness*. Ge 46:21. Nu 26:40. Lk 4:27. **a great**. 2 K 4:8. Ex 11:3. 1 S 16:7. Est 9:4. 10:3. **with**. Heb. before. ver. 3. **honorable**. *or*, gracious. Heb. lifted up, *or* accepted in countenance. 2 K 3:14. Jb 22:8mg. Is 3:3mg. 9:15. **by him**. Pr *21:31. Is 10:5, 6. Je 27:5, 6. Da 2:37, 38. Jn 19:11. Ro 15:18. **deliverance**. *or*, victory. **but**. *520*. Anesis; or, Abating B463: addition of conclusion by way of lessening the effect. Thus, all his grandeur and importance counted for nothing. **a leper**. ver. 27. 2 K 7:3. Le 13:2, 3, 44-46. Nu 12:10-12. 2 S 3:29. 2 Ch 26:19-23. 2 C 12:7.

2. **by companies**. 2 K 6:23. 13:20. Jg 9:34. 1 S 13:17, 18. **waited on**. Heb. was before. Ps 123:2.

3. **mistress**. Ge 16:4, 8, 9. **Would God**. Nu 11:29. Ac 26:29. 1 C 4:8. **with**. Heb. before. ver. 1. **he would**. ver. 8. Mt 8:2, 3. 11:5. Lk 17:12-14. **recover him of**. Heb. gather in. ver. 6, 7, 11.

4. **and told his lord**. 2 K 7:9-11. Mk 5:19. 16:9, 10. Jn 1:42-46. 4:28, 29. 1 C 1:26, 27.

5. **Go to**, go. Ge 11:3, 7. Ec 2:1. Is 5:5. Ja 4:13. 5:1. **and took**. 2 K 8:8, 9. Nu 22:7, 17, 18. 24:11-13. 1 S 9:8. 1 K 13:7. 45:3. Ac 8:18-20. **with him**. Heb. in his hand. 2 K 8:8, 9. **ten talents of silver**. Ten talents at ✱1,920 each would be ✱19,200. **six thousand**. At ✱9.69 1!2 each would be ✱58,170. **gold**. ♪121D5, Ge +23:9. **ten changes**. Ge 45:22. Jg 14:12. Ja 5:2, 3.

6. **the king of Israel**. 1 K 20:7.

7. **that he rent**. 2 K 11:14. 18:37. 19:1. Nu 14:6. Je 36:24. Mt 26:65. Ac 14:14. **Am I God**. Ge 30:2. Dt *32:39. 1 S *2:6. Da *2:11. Ho 6:1. **see how**. 1 K 20:7. Lk 11:54.

8. **rent his clothes**. ver. 7. 2 S 3:31. **let him come**. ver. 3, 15. 2 K 1:6. 1 K 17:24. 18:36, 37. **and he shall**. Ex 11:8. Ro 11:13. Ezk 2:5. Ho 12:13.

9. **Naaman came**. 2 K 3:12. 6:32. Is 60:14. Ac 16:29, 30, 37-39.

10. **sent a messenger**. Mt *15:23-26. **wash**. Heb. *rahats*, Ex +29:4 (✱S#7364). ver. 12, 13. 2 K 2:21. 3:√11n, 16. *4:41. Ge 18:4 (wash. Gr. *nipto*). 19:2. 24:32. 43:24, 31. Ex 2:5 (wash. Gr. *louo*). 29:4. 30:19 (wash. Gr. *nipto*), 20, 21. 40:12, 32 (Gr. *nipto*). Le 8:6 (wash. Gr. *louo*). 14:8. 15:5, 6, 7, 8, 10, 11, 13, 16, 18, 21, 22, 27. 16:4, 24, 26, 28. 17:15, 16. 22:6. Nu 19:7, 19. Dt 21:6 (wash. Gr. *nipto*). 23:11 (wash. Gr. *louo*). Jg 19:21 (washed. Gr. *nipto*). Ru 3:3 (wash. Gr. *louo*). 1 S 25:41 (wash. Gr. *nipto*). 2 S 11:2 (washing. Gr. *louo*), 8 (wash. Gr. *louo*). 12:20 (washed. Gr. *louo*). 1 K 22:38. 2 K 5:10, 12, 13. 2 Ch 4:6 (washed. Gr. *pluno*). Jb 9:30 (wash. Gr. *louo*). 29:6 (washed. Gr. *cheo*). Ps 26:6 (wash. Gr. *nipto*). 58:10. 73:13. SS 5:3 (washed. Gr. *nipto*), 12 (washed. Gr. *louo*). Is 1:16. 4:4 (washed. Gr. *pluno*). Ezk 16:4 (washed. Gr. *louo*), 9. 22:40. Jn *9:7. 1 C *6:11. Hibbard notes that the Hebrew *rahats* is rendered with some latitude into several Greek terms: *louo*, which denotes the washing

of the body; *nipto*, used to denote washing of hands or feet; *pluno*, which denotes the washing of clothes; and once by *cheo*, which denotes "to flow, to pour forth, to shed." Furthermore, *rahats* "is never used as a synonym of *bathe*. It properly denotes *wash*. The washing, it is true, might be performed by *bathing*; but then it might be performed equally well without it, and where bathing might have been practiced it was not itself sufficient. The force of the word implies some effort made to cleanse, as by rubbing with the hand. And, as President Beecher has well said, bathing fulfilled the command, not because it was a bathing, but solely because it was a washing. Besides, in many cases, as in the washing of hands, the water was poured. At other times it was simply taken out of the vase or vessel by one hand, and applied to the body. This was *washing*, and this mode was included in the *baptisms* (*baptismon*) of He 9:10" (*Christian Baptism*, pp. 210-213). 2 K √3:11n. **seven times**. Le *14:7, 16, 51. *16:14, 19. Nu *19:4, 19. Jsh *6:4, 13-16. **thy flesh**. ver. *14. Ex *4:6, 7.

11. **Naaman**. Pr *13:10. Mt 8:8. 15:27. Lk *14:11. **wroth**. Ge 40:2. Ac 26:9. **went away**. Pr *1:32. Mt *19:22. Jn *6:66-69. *13:20. He *12:25. **Behold**. Pr *3:7. Is *55:8, 9. Jn 4:48. 1 C *1:21-25. *2:14-16. 3:18-20. **I thought**, etc. Heb. I said, etc. *or*, I said with myself, He will surely come out, etc. **strike**. Heb. move up and down. Ex 20:25. 29:24mg, 26, 27n. 35:22. Jb 31:21. Is 11:15.

12. **Abana**. i.e. *a stone; constancy; a sure ordinance*, *S#71h. SS 4:8, Amana. **and Pharpar**. i.e. *swift; producing fruit*, *S#6554h, only here. *or*, Amana. This river is evidently the *Barrada*, or *Barda*, as the Arabic renders, the *Chrysorrhoas* of the Greeks, which taking its rise in Antilibanus, runs eastward towards Damascus, where it is divided into three streams, one of which passes through the city, and the other two through the gardens; which reuniting at the east of the city, forms a lake about five or six leagues to the southeast, called *Behairat el Marj*, or, Lake of the Meadow. Pharpar was probably one of the branches. **rivers**. S#5104h. Heb. *nahar*, a perennial river. Used of the Euphrates (Ge +15:18. 2 Ch +9:26. Is +*27:12) and the great rivers of Mesopotamia (Ge 2:10, 13, 14. Ps 137:1), but it is not used of the river Jordan (unless it, or the Dead Sea is intended in Ps 56:6. 74:15. Hab 3:8, 9). Ezk +32:2. **better**. ver. 17. 2 K 2:8, 14. Jsh 3:15-17. Ezk 47:1-8. Zc *13:1. 14:8. Mk 1:9. **waters**. Heb. *mayim*, S#4325h. Natural use: Ge 1:2. Jsh 3:13. 11:5. Da 12:6, 7. Ritual use: Nu 8:7. 19:7, *17. Ezk 36:25. Metaphorical use: Ps 1:3. Is 58:11. Je 2:13. Eschatalogical use: Ezk 47:1. Zc 14:8. **rage**. Ge 27:44.

13. **his servants**. ver. 3. Jsh *22:21n. 1 S ❂+√25:17. 2 S 19:8n. 1 K 12:7. 20:24, 31. Jb 31:13. *32:8, 9. Pr *18:13. Je 38:7-10. Mt +*18:31. Lk 22:26. 1 C 6:4, 5. **and spake**. Pr +*9:8, 9. +*13:18. 1 T +*5:19n. **My father**. 2 K 2:12. 6:21. 13:14. Ge 41:43. Ml *1:6. Mt *23:9. 1 C 4:15. **how much rather**. Pr 3:7. 1 C *1:21, 27. **Wash**. See on ver. 10. Ps *51:2, 7. Is *1:16. Jn *13:8. Ac *22:16. Ep *5:26, 27. T *3:5. He +*10:22. 1 P *3:21. Re *7:14.

14. **Then**. Pr 17:10. **went he down**. Jb *31:13. Pr *9:9. *25:11, 12. Ezk 47:1-9. Zc *13:1. 14:8. Jn 5:4. Ac 8:38. **and dipped**. Heb. *tabal*, *S#2881h. 2 K 8:15. Ge 37:31. Ex 12:22. Le 4:6, 17. 9:9. 14:6, 16, 51. Nu 19:18. Dt 33:24. Jsh 3:15. 1 S 14:27. Ru 2:12. Jb +9:31.

See *S#2882h, 1 Ch *26:11n. The Hebrew *tabal* is rendered by *baptidzo* by the Septuagint in this place only. "This passage contains the only instance of the use of the word *baptidzo* (as a rendering of *tabal*) in the canonical books of the Old Testament. This passage is of peculiar importance as the oldest Scriptural use of the word *baptidzo*" (Thomas Gallaher, *Baptism*, p. 70). Naaman's leprosy was local, ver. 11. Had his leprosy been over all his body, he would have been clean (Le 13:12, 13). The prophet Elisha commanded Naaman to do what the law of God required for the cleansing of leprosy, and that law required that the leper be sprinkled seven times (Le 14:7). The law did not require anything to be done seven times except the sprinkling; the "shaving, and washing his flesh with water," was done but once. Thus, the translators of the Septuagint chose to render *tabal* here alone by *baptidzo*, for in their mind the word *baptidzo* referred to ceremonial cleansing, which was accomplished by sprinkling (Nu 19:13n). Fairfield notes that the Hebrew word *tabal* which occurs here is used sixteen times in the Hebrew Scriptures. Fourteen times it is translated into Greek by the Septuagint translators by *bapto*, once by *moluno* (Ge 37:31, to defile or stain), once by *baptidzo* (*Letters on Baptism*, p. 54). The action "dipped" (Heb. *tabal*) in this verse answers to what Elisha commanded in the 10th verse by the use of the Hebrew *rahats* (Greek *louo*), "Go and *wash* in Jordan seven times, and thou shalt be clean." "There is no necessity of supposing that Naaman plunged into the river, but, rather, made a sevenfold application of the water to his person" (Thomas O. Summers, *Baptism*, p. 224). **seven times**. Ps 12:6. **in Jordan**. Mt *3:6. Mk +*1:5n, 9n. **according to**. ver. *10. 2 Ch *20:20. Jn *2:5. He 11:7, 8. **his flesh**. ver. 10. Jb *33:25. **and he was clean**. Lk *4:27. 5:13. T *2:14.

15. **he returned**. Lk *17:15-18. **now I know**. ver. 8. Jsh 2:9-11. 9:9, 24. 1 S 17:46, 47. 1 K 18:36. Is 43:10, 11. 44:6, 8. 45:6. Je 10:10, 11. 16:19-21. Da 2:47. 3:29. *4:34, 35. 6:26, 27. Ro *10:10. **a blessing**. Ge 33:11. 1 S 25:27. 2 C 9:5.

16. **As the Lord**. See on 2 K 3:14. 1 K 17:1. 18:15. **I will receive none**. ver. 20, 26. Ge 14:22, 23. 1 K 13:8. Da 5:17. Mt *10:8. Ac *8:18-20. 20:33-35. 1 C 6:12. 10:32, 33. 2 C 11:9, 10. 12:14. **he urged**. 2 K 2:17. Ge 19:3, 9, 11. Jg 19:7. **he refused**. Ge *37:35. 39:8. 48:19.

17. **two mules'**. 2 K 9:25. Jg 19:3, 10. 1 S 11:7. 14:14. 2 S 16:1. 1 K 19:19, 21. Jb 1:3. 42:12. Is 5:10. 21:7, 9. Je 51:23. **of earth**. ver. 12. Ex 20:24. Ro 14:1. **will henceforth**. 1 K *18:21. Ac 26:18. 1 Th *1:9. 1 P 4:3.

18. **Rimmon**. i.e. *pomegranate*, *S#7417h. (1) An idol of the Syrians, 2 K 5:18. Ac 7:43, Remphan. (2) A Benjamite whose sons were captains in the army of Ish-bosheth, 2 S 4:2, 5, 9. (3) A town of Judah afterward given to Simeon, Jsh 15:32; 1 Ch 4:32; Zc 14:10. It is also called Remmon in Jsh 19:7. (4) A city of Zebulun, 1 Ch 6:77. It is called Remmon-methoar in Jsh 19:13. It is now the village of Rummaneh, near Nazareth. (5) A rocky region near Gibeah in Benjamin, called "the rock Rimmon," to which the surviving Benjamites retreated after the slaughter of most of their tribe, Jg 20:45, 47; 21:13. **and he leaneth**. This verse should probably, as many learned men have supposed, be read in the *past*, and not in the *future* tense: "In

this thing the Lord pardon thy servant, that when my master *went* into the house of Rimmon to worship there, and he *leaned* on my hand, and I *worshipped* in the house of Rimmon; in that I have *worshipped* in the house of Rimmon, the Lord pardon thy servant in this thing." *Rimmon* is supposed by Selden to be the same with *Elion*, a god of the Phoenicians, borrowed undoubtedly from the *Elyon* of the Hebrews, one of the names of God. 2 K 7:2, 17. **on my hand**. Or, arm, as the word sometimes signifies, or, shoulder, upon which the king leaned, either for state or for support. 1 K 7:2. **and I bow**. Not in honor to the idol, which I do here, and shall there, openly renounce; but only in compliance with the king's infirmity and conveniency, who cannot well bow if I stand upright. 2 K 17:35. Ex *20:5. 1 K 19:18. **when I bow**. T#1682. See preceding and succeeding notes and references. Ru 1:15. Mi 4:5. **the Lord pardon**. Because there seemed to be an appearance of evil in this action, though done with an honest mind, he desires the prophet's prayers that God would not charge it upon him as idolatry, nor be displeased with him for that practice (Matthew Poole). Ru ❍1:15. 2 Ch 30:18, 19. Je 50:20. Am ❍4:5. Ro 14:1, 3, 4, 10-14. Ga 6:1.

19. **he said**. Mt 9:16, 17. Jn 16:12. 1 C 3:2. He 5:13, 14. **Go**. ♪9. Amphibologia; or, Double Meaning B804: A word or phrase susceptible of two interpretations. Elisha's answer was an amphibologia. If Elisha had said, "Yes, you may bow," that would have been to sanction idolatry. And if he had said, "No, you must not bow," that would have been to put Naaman's conscience under a yoke of bondage to Elisha (EWB, B804). For other instances of this figure see Ezk 12:13. Jn 19:22. Ac 17:22. **in peace**. Ex 4:18. 1 S 1:17. 25:35. Mk 5:34. Lk 7:50. 8:48. **little way**. Heb. a little piece of ground. Ge 35:16mg. 48:7.

20. **Gehazi**. 2 K 4:12, 31, 36. Mt 10:4. Jn 6:70. 12:6. 13:2. Ac 8:18, 19. **my master**. Pr 26:16. Lk 16:8. Jn 12:5, 6. Ac *5:2. **as the Lord liveth**. Ex *20:7. 1 S 14:39. **and take**. Ex *20:17. Ps 10:3. Je 22:17. Hab 2:9. Lk 12:15. 1 T 6:9-11. 2 T 4:10. T 1:7. 1 P 5:2. 2 P 2:14, 15.

21. **he lighted**. Lk 7:6, 7. Ac 8:31. 10:25, 26. **Is all well**. Heb. Is there peace? ver. 22. 2 K 4:+23mg, 26. 9:11, 17-22. Ge +29:6mg.

22. **My master**. Lk 13:18. Is 59:3. Je 9:3, 5. Jn *8:44. Ac *5:3, 4. Re +*21:8. **the sons**. See on 2 K 2:3. 1 K 20:35. **give them**. 2 C 12:16-18. **a talent**. See on ver. 5. Ex 38:24-28. 1 K 20:39.

23. **Be content**. 2 K 6:3. Jg 19:6. 2 S 7:29mg. 1 K 20:7. 2 Ch 17:27mg. Jb 6:28. Lk 11:54. **And he urged him**. ver. 16. 2 K 2:17. 1 S 28:23. 2 S 13:25, 27. **bound**. 2 K 12:10mg. Dt 14:25. **bags**. or, purses. Is 3:22. **and they bare**. Is 30:6.

24. **tower**. *or*, secret place. Heb. *Ophel*. Nu 14:14. 2 Ch 27:3mg. 33:14mg. Ne 3:26mg, 27. 11:21mg. Is 32:14mg. Mi 4:8. Hab 2:4. **and bestowed**. Jsh 7:1, 11, 12, 21. 1 K 21:16. Is 29:15. Hab 2:6. Zc 5:3, 4.

25. **stood before**. Pr 30:20. Ezk 33:31. Mt 26:15, 16, 21-25. Jn 13:2, 26-30. **Whence**. 2 K 20:14. Ge 3:8, 9. 4:9. 16:8. **Thy servant**. ver. 22. Ac *5:3, 4. **no whither**. Heb. not hither or thither.

26. **he said**. Ps 63:11. Pr 12:19, 22. Ac 5:9. **Went**. 2 K 6:12. 1 C 5:3. Col 2:5. **Is it a time**. ver. 16. Ge 14:23. Ec 3:1-8. Mt 10:8. Ac 20:33, 35. 1 C 9:11, 12.

2 C 11:8-12. 2 Th 3:8, 9. **and**. ♪148, Ge +8:22.

27. **leprosy**. See on ver. 1. Jsh 7:25. Is 59:2, 3. Ho 10:13. Ml 2:3, 4, 8, 9. Mt 27:3-5. Ac 5:5, 10. 8:20. 1 T *6:10. 2 P 2:3. **cleave**. Ge 2:24. **unto thy seed**. 1 S 2:30-36. 2 S 3:29. **for ever**. Heb. *olam*, Ex +12:24. **a leper**. 2 K 15:5. Ex 4:6. Nu 12:10. **as snow**. Ex 4:6. Nu 12:10. 2 S 23:20. 1 Ch 11:22. Jb 6:16. 9:30. 24:19. 37:6. 38:22. Ps 51:7. 147:16. 148:8. Pr 25:13. 26:1. 31:21. Is *1:18. 55:10. Je 18:14. La 4:7.

2 KINGS 6

The sons of the prophet prepare to enlarge their dwelling, and Elisha causes iron to swim, 1-7. He discloses to Jehoram the councils of the Syrian king, who sends troops to apprehend him, 8-14. Elisha's servant is terrified; but is encouraged by seeing horses and chariots of fire round his master, 15-17. The Syrians, at Elisha's prayer, are partially blinded; and he conducts them into Samaria, where they regain their sight, and by the prophet's proposal are entertained, and dismissed in peace, 18-23. Ben-hadad besieges Samaria, and reduces it to extreme famine, 24, 25. Women contest about eating their own children; and appeal to the king, who in a rage resolves to kill Elisha, 26-33.

1. **the sons**. See on 2 K 2:3. 4:1. 1 K 20:35. **the place**. 2 K 4:38. 1 S 19:20. **too strait for us**. Jsh 17:14. 19:47. Jb 36:16. Is 49:19, 20. 54:2, 3.

2. **and take thence**. Jn 21:3. Ac 18:3. 20:34, 35. 1 C 9:6. 1 Th 2:9. 2 Th 3:8. 1 T 6:6.

3. **Be content**. 2 K 5:23. Jg 19:6. Jb 6:28. **go with thy**. Jg 4:8.

4. **they cut down wood**. Dt 19:5. 29:11.

5. **ax head**. Heb. iron. Ec 10:10. Is 10:34. ♪121D6. Metonymy of the Cause B559. *Iron* is put for things made of it. For another instance of this figure see Ps 105:18. **Alas, master**. ver. 15. 2 K 3:10. Re 18:10, 16, 19. **for it was borrowed**. 2 K 4:7. Ex 22:14, 15. Ps 37:21.

6. **he cut down**. This could have no natural tendency to raise the iron and to cause it to swim: it was only a sign, or ceremony, which the prophet chose to employ on the occasion. 2 K 2:21. 4:41. Ex 15:25. Mk 7:33, 34. 8:23-25. Jn 9:6, 7. **the iron**. This was a real miracle; for the gravity of the metal must otherwise still have kept it at the bottom of the river.

7. **Take it up**. 2 K 4:7, 36. 2 Ch 20:20. Lk 7:15. Ac 9:41. **put out**. Ex 4:4.

8. **the king**. ver. 24. 1 K 20:1, 34. 22:31. **took**. 1 K 20:23. Jb 5:12, 13. Pr 20:18. +*21:30. Is 7:5-7. 8:10. Je 23:23, 24. **camp**. *or*, encamping.

9. **Beware**. 2 K 3:17-19. 1 K 20:13, 28. **thither the Syrians**. 2 K 4:27. Am 3:7. Re 1:1.

10. **sent to the place**. To see if it were so. But the Vulgate renders, "the king of Israel sent to the place, and pre-occupied it;" which is very likely, though not expressed in the Hebrew text. 2 K 5:14. Ex 9:20, 21. 1 K 20:15. Pr 27:12. Mt 24:15-17. **warned him**. Ezk 3:18-21. Mt 2:12. 3:7. He 11:7. **saved**. 2 K 2:12. 13:14. 2 Ch 20:20. Am 7:1-6. Ac 27:24.

11. **Therefore**. 1 S 28:21. Jb 18:7-11. Ps 48:4, 5. Is 57:20, 21. Mt 2:3, etc. **Will ye not**. 1 S 22:8.

12. **None**. Heb. No. **Elisha**. 2 K 5:3, 8, 13-15. Am *3:7. **telleth**. See on ver. 9, 10. Is 29:15. Je 23:23, 24. Da 2:22, 23, 28-30, 47. 4:9-18. **thy bedchamber**.

2 K 1:16n. Ps 139:1-4. Ec *10:20.

13. **spy where.** 1 S 23:22, 23. Ps 10:8-10. 37:12-14, 32, 33. Je 36:26. Mt 2:4-8. Jn 11:47-53. Ac 23:12-27. **Dothan.** Ge 37:17. This is supposed to be the same place where Joseph was sold by his brethren; and it is placed 12 miles north of Samaria.

14. **sent he thither horses.** It is strange the Syrian monarch did not think, that he who could penetrate his secrets with respect to the Israelitish army, could inform himself of all the machinations against his own life. 2 K 1:9-13. 1 S 23:26. 24:2. Mt 26:47, 55. Jn 18:3-6. **great.** Heb. heavy. 2 K 18:17mg. Ge 50:9. 1 K 3:9. 10:2. 2 Ch 9:1. Is 36:2.

15. **servant.** or, minister. See on 2 K 3:11. 4:43mg. 5:20, 27. Ex 24:13. 1 K 19:21. Mt *20:26-28. Ac *13:5. **Alas.** ver. 5. 2 Ch *20:12. Ps *53:5. Mt *8:26.

16. **Fear not.** Ex *14:13. Ps 3:6. 11:1. 27:3. 118:11, 12. Is 8:12, 13. *41:10-14. Mk 16:6. Ac *18:9, 10. Ph *1:28. **they that be.** 2 Ch 13:12. *16:9. *32:7, 8. Ps 46:7, 11. 55:18. Is *8:10. Mt *26:53. Ro *8:31. 1 J *4:4.

17. **prayed.** Ps *91:15. Ja *5:16-18. **open his eyes.** ver. 18-20. Ge +*3:7. Ps *119:18. Is 42:7. Ac *26:18. Ep 1:18. Re *3:7. **full of horses.** 2 K +*2:11. Ps *34:7. 68:17. *91:11. 104:3. Ezk 1:13-16. Zc 1:8. 6:1-7. Mt *26:53. He *1:14. Re *19:11, 14. **chariots.** ƒ22D5G, Ps +68:17.

18. **Smite this people.** Confound their sight, so that they may not know what they see; and so mistake one place for another. The word *sanverim*, rendered *blindness*, occurs only here and in Ge +*19:11, on which see the Note. Dt 28:28. Jb 5:14. Zc 12:4. Jn 9:39. 12:40. Ac 13:11. Ro 11:7. **blindness.** ƒ96F2, Ge +4:10.

19. **follow me.** Heb. come ye after me. ver. 32. Mt 16:24. Mk 8:34. Lk 9:23. **I will bring.** 2 S 16:18, 19. Lk 24:16.

20. **open the eyes.** See on ver. 17. Lk 24:31. **opened.** Jg 20:40-42. Lk 16:23.

21. **My father.** This was dastardly: the utmost he ought to have done with these men, when thus brought into his hand, was to make them prisoners of war. 2 K 2:12. 5:13. 8:9. 13:14. **shall.** 1 S 24:4, 19. 26:8. Lk 9:54-56. 22:49. Ro 12:21.

22. **shalt not.** Ro 12:21. **wouldest.** Dt 20:11-16. 2 Ch 28:8-13. **thy sword and.** ƒ174, Ge +18:27. Ge 48:22. Jsh 24:12. Ps 44:6. Ho 1:7. 2:18. **set bread.** Pr 25:21, 22. Mt 5:44. Ro 12:20, 21. **and water.** ƒ174, Ge +18:27.

23. **he prepared.** 1 S 24:17, 18. 2 Ch 28:15. Pr 25:21, 22. Mt 5:47. Lk *6:35. 10:29-37. **So the bands.** That is, for a considerable time. What is mentioned in the next verse was more than a year afterwards. See on ver. 8, 9. 2 K 5:2. 13:20. 24:2. 2 Ch 22:1. 25:9, 10, 13. 26:11. Mt 4:11. Lk 4:13.

24. **gathered.** 2 K 17:5. 18:9. 25:1. Dt 28:52. 1 K 20:1. 22:31. Ec 9:14.

25. **a great famine.** ver. 28, 29. 2 K 7:4. 25:3. Le 26:26. 1 K 18:2. Je 14:13-15, 18. 32:24. 52:6. **an ass's head.** If the pieces of silver were worth 64 cents each, then 80 of them would total *51.20 for an ass's head, which was a great price for so mean a part of this unclean animal. Ezk 4:13-16. **dove's dung.** This probably denotes, as Bochart, Scheuchzer, and others suppose, a kind of *pulse*, or *vetches*, which the Arabs still call *pigeon's dung.* "They never," says Dr. Shaw

(*Travels*, p. 140), "constitute a dish by themselves, but are strewed singly as a garnish over *cuscasowe*, *pillowe*, and other dishes. They are besides in the greatest repute after they are parched in pans and ovens; then assuming the name *leblebby*," and he thinks they were so called from being pointed at one end, and acquiring an ash color in parching. **pieces.** ƒ63A4, 1 K +3:22.

26. **Help, my lord.** 2 S 14:4. Is 10:3. Lk 18:3. Ac 21:28.

27. **If the Lord,** etc. or, Let not the Lord save thee. 2 K 7:2. **whence.** Ps 60:11. 62:8. 118:8, 9. 124:1-3. 127:1. 146:3. Is 2:22. Je 17:5. **barnfloor.** Nu 18:27, 30. 1 K 22:10. 1 Ch 13:9. **winepress.** Jg 7:25. Jb 24:11.

28. **What aileth thee.** Ge 21:17. Jg 18:23. 1 S 1:8. 2 S 14:5. Ps 114:5. Is 22:1. **Give thy son.** Le 26:29. Dt 28:53-57. Is 9:20, 21. 49:15. La 4:10. Ezk 5:10. Mt 24:18-21. Lk 23:29.

29. **next.** Heb. other. Ge 17:21. **she hath hid.** 1 K 3:26. Is 49:15. 66:13.

30. **he rent his clothes.** 2 K 5:7. 19:1. 1 K 21:27. Is 58:5-7.

31. **God do so.** Ru 1:17. 1 S 3:17. 14:44. 25:22. 2 S 3:9, 35. 19:13. 1 K 2:23. **if the head.** 1 K 18:17. 19:2. 22:8. Je 37:15, 16. 38:4. Jn 11:50. Ac 23:12, 13.

32. **the elders.** Ezk 8:1. 14:1. 20:1. 33:31. **ere the messenger.** ver. 12. 2 K 5:26. **See ye how.** Lk 13:32. **son of a murderer.** 1 K 18:4, 13, 14. 21:10, 13. Is 1:21. **the sound.** 2 K 7:17. 1 K *14:6.

33. **this evil is.** ƒ63B, Ge +2:10. **of the Lord.** Ge 4:13. Ex 16:6-8. Dt +*2:30. Ru +*1:13. 1 S 28:6-8. 31:4. Jb 1:11, 21. 2:5, 9. Pr ◖/19:3. Is 8:21. ◖/29:24. +*45:7. Je 2:25. Ezk +*18:25. 33:10. Am +√3:6. Mt 27:4, 5. Ro ◖+*9:14. 2 C 2:7, 11. Ja ◖+*1:13, 17. Re 16:9-11. **wait for the.** Ps 27:14. +√37:7, 9. 62:5. Is 8:17. √26:3. √29:24. 50:10. La 3:25, 26. Hab *2:3. Lk 18:1.

2 KINGS 7

Elisha predicts great plenty in Samaria, and the death of an unbelieving lord, 1, 2. Four lepers venture into the Syrian camp, and bring word that it is entirely deserted, a terror from God having driven away the army, 3-11. Jehoram fears a stratagem, and sends messengers to examine, and finds the report true, 12-15. The people spoil the Syrian camp; the predicted plenty takes place; and the unbelieving lord, having charge of the gate, is trodden to death, 16-20.

1. **Elisha said.** See on 2 K 6:33. 20:16. 1 K 22:19. Is 1:10. Ezk 37:4. **Tomorrow.** ver. 18, 19. Ex 8:23. 9:5, 6. 14:13. 16:12. Jsh 3:5. 1 S 11:9. Ps 46:5. **a measure of fine flour.** A *seah* of flour: the *seah* was about two gallons and a half. A shekel was worth about 64 cents. A wide difference in price from that of the ass's head (2 K 6:25). 2 K 6:25. Re 6:6. **of barley.** 2 K 4:42. Jn 6:9. **in the gate of Samaria.** ƒ171S7B, Ge +14:7. From this it appears that the *gates* were not only used as courts of judicature, but as market places. So Mr. Morier (*Journey through Persia,* p. 189) observes: "In our rides we usually went out of the town at the *Derwazeh Shah Abdul Azeem,* or the *gate* leading to the village of Shah Abdul Azeem, where a *market* was held every morning, particularly of horses, mules, asses, and camels. At about sunrise, the owners of the animals assemble and exhibit them for sale. But besides, here were

sellers of all sorts of goods, in temporary shops and tents: and this, perhaps, will explain the custom alluded to in 2 K 7:18." Ge +14:7. 2 S 19:8n.

2. **a lord**, etc. *or*, a lord which *belonged* to the king, leaning on his hand. 2 K 5:18. **if the Lord**. Ge 18:12-14. Nu 11:21-23. Ps 78:19-21, 41. **windows**. Ge 7:11. Ml 3:10. **might this**. Mt 19:26. Mk 11:23. **thou shalt see it**. ver. 17-20. Dt 3:27. 2 Ch 20:20. Is 7:9. Ro 3:3. 2 T 2:13. He 3:17-19.

3. **four leprous**. See on 2 K 5:1. 8:4. Le *13:46. Nu 5:2-4. 12:14. **Why**. ver. 4. Je 8:14. 27:13.

4. **we will enter**. Je 14:18. **let us fall**. 1 Ch 12:19. Je 37:13, 14. **if they save us**. Est 4:16. Je 8:14. Jon 3:9. Lk 15:17-19. **we shall but die**. 2 S 14:14. He +*9:27.

5. **in the twilight**. 1 S 30:17. Ezk 12:6, 7, 12. **behold**. Le 27:8, 36. Dt 28:7. 32:25, 30.

6. **the Lord**. 2 K 3:22, 23, etc. 19:7. 2 S 5:24. Jb *15:21. Ps 14:5. Je 20:3, 4. Ezk 10:5. Re 6:15, 16. 9:9. **the kings of the Hittites**. Ge +15:20. Jsh 1:4. Jg 1:26. 1 K 10:29. At one time skeptics scoffed at the Biblical comparison here of the Hittites with the Egyptians and Syrians as a military power to be reckoned with, for they understood the references in the Bible to suggest that the Hittites were merely a Canaanitic tribe of no great significance. How wrong such critics were has since been discovered by archeologists, who have shown that the Hittites were a powerful people who once ruled a great empire. The Hittite empire at its height might well be compared in vastness and influence to the later Roman empire. **the kings of the Egyptians**. 2 Ch 12:2, 3. Is 31:1. 36:9.

7. **they arose**. Jb *18:11. Ps 48:4-6. 68:12. Pr 21:1. *28:1. Je *20:4. 48:8, 9. **and fled**. Ps 53:5. **their horses**. Ps 20:7, 8. 33:17. Am 2:14-16. **and fled for their**. Nu 35:11, 12. Pr 6:5. Is 2:20, 21. Mt 24:16-18. He 6:18. **life**. Heb. *nephesh*, soul, Ge +44:30.

8. **hid it**. 2 K 5:24. Jsh 7:21. Je 41:8. Mt 13:44. 25:18.

9. **they said one**. ver. 3. Hg 1:4, 5. **this day**. ver. 6. Is 41:27. 52:7. Na 1:15. Lk 2:10. Ph 2:4. **some mischief will come upon us**. Heb. we shall find punishment. 2 K 5:26, 27. Ge 4:13. Nu +*32:23. Pr 24:16. **go and tell**. Is 52:7. Jn 1:41, 45. 4:29. Re 22:17.

10. **the porter**. ver. 11. 2 S 18:26. Ps 127:1. Mk 13:34, 35. **no man there**. See on ver. 6, 7. **as they were**. Jn 4:6.

12. **unto his servants**. 2 K 6:8. Ge 20:8. 41:38. 1 K 20:7, 23. **I will now**. ver. 1. 2 K 5:7. **They know that we be hungry**. This was a very natural conclusion; and in the History of the revolt of Ali Bey, we have an account of a stratagem very similar to that supposed to have been practiced by the Syrians. The pasha of Damascus having approached the sea of Tiberias, found sheik Daher encamped there; but the sheik, deferring the engagement till the next morning, during the night divided his army into three parts, and left the camp with great fires blazing, all sorts of provisions, and a large quantity of spiritous liquors. In the middle of the night the pasha, thinking to surprise the sheik, marched in silence to the camp, which, to his astonishment, he found entirely abandoned; and imagining the sheik had fled with so much precipitation that he could not carry off his baggage and stores, he stopped in the camp to refresh his soldiers. They soon fell to plunder, and drunk so freely of the liquors, that, over-

come with the fatigue of the day's march, and the fumes of the spirits, they ere long sunk into profound repose. At that time, two sheiks, who were watching the enemy, came silently into the camp, and being rejoined by Daher, they all rushed into the camp, and fell upon the sleeping foe, 8000 of whom they butchered on the spot; and the pasha, with the remainder, escaped with much difficulty to Damascus, leaving all their baggage in the hands of the victorious Daher. 2 K 6:25-29. **hide themselves**. Jsh 8:4-12. Jg 20:29-37.

13. **And one**. See on 2 K 5:13. **Let some take**. Ex +18:17, 23. 1 S *25:17-25. Pr 13:16. 14:8, *15. 18:15. *22:3. *27:12. Ho 14:9. Mt +*7:6. **five**. Ge 43:34n. 1 S 1:8n. Is 4:1. *19:18. Am 1:3, 6, 9, 11. Zc 8:23. **in the city**. Heb. in it. **they are even**. ver. 4. 2 K 6:33. Je 14:18. La 4:9.

15. **vessels**. Est 1:7. Is 22:24. **had cast away**. Jb 2:4. Is 2:20. 10:3. 31:7. Ezk 18:31. Mt 16:26. 24:16-18. Ph 3:7, 8. He 12:1.

16. **spoiled the tents**. 1 S 17:53. 2 Ch 14:12-15. 20:25. Jb 27:16, 17. Ps 68:12. Is 33:1, 4, 23. **according to**. ver. 1. Nu 23:19. Is *44:26. Mt *24:35.

17. **the lord**. See on ver. 2. **the people trode upon him**. 2 K 9:33. Jg 20:43. Is 25:10. Mi 7:10. He 10:29.

18. **as the man**. See on ver. 1, 2. 2 K 6:32. Ge 18:14. **in the gate**. ver. 1n. Ge +14:7. 2 S 19:8n.

19. **that lord answered**. ver. 2.

20. **so it fell**. Nu 20:12. 2 Ch +*20:20. Jb 20:23. Is 7:9. Je 17:5, 6. He 3:18, 19.

2 KINGS 8

The Shunammite, by Elisha's advice, to avoid a famine of seven years, goes to sojourn in Philistia, 1, 2. On her return, she applies to the king, who is conversing with Gehazi on Elisha's miracles; and he restores her land, 3-6. Elisha goes to Damascus: Hazael is sent by Ben-hadad to inquire of him concerning his sickness: he predicts Hazael's cruelty to Israel, as destined to be king of Syria, 7-13. Hazael murders Ben-hadad and succeeds him, 14, 15. Jehoram reigns wickedly in Judah, 16-19. Edom and Libnah revolt, 20-22. Jehoram is succeeded by Ahaziah, who reigns wickedly, 23-27. He assists the king of Israel against Syria, and when wounded visits him at Jezreel, 28, 29.

1. A.M. 3113. B.C. 891. **whose son**. See on 2 K 4:18, 31-35. **sojourn**. Ge 12:10. 26:1. 47:4. Ru 1:1. **the Lord**. Ge 41:25-28, 32. Le 26:19, 20, 26. Dt 28:22-24, 38-40. 1 K 17:1. 18:2. Ps 105:16. 107:34. Hg 1:11. Lk 21:11, 22. Ac 11:28. **called for a famine**. Je 25:29. **seven years**. Ge 41:27. 2 S 21:1. 24:13. Lk 4:25.

2. **with**. 1 T 5:8. **land**. Jg 3:3. 1 S 27:1-3.

3. A.M. 3119. B.C. 885. **she went forth**. ver. 6. 2 K 4:13. 6:26. 2 S 14:4. Ps 82:3, 4. Je 22:16. Lk 18:3-5.

4. **the king**. As it appears not likely that the king would hold conversation with a leprous man; or, that, knowing Gehazi had been dismissed with the highest disgrace from the prophet's service, he would talk with him concerning his late master; some have supposed that this happened *before* the cleansing of Naaman. But it agrees better with the chronology to consider it as having taken place *after* that event; the king, probably, having an insatiable curiosity to know the private history of a man who had done such astonishing

things. As to the circumstance of Gehazi's disease, he might overlook that, and converse with him, keeping a reasonable distance, as nothing but actual contact could defile. **Gehazi**. 2 K 5:20-27. 7:3, 10. **Tell**. Mt 2:8. Lk 9:9. 23:8. Jn 9:27. Ac 24:24. **all the great**. 2 K 2:14, 20-22, 24. 3:14-16. 4:3-6, 16, 17. 5:14, 27. 6:6, 9-12, 17-20, 32. 7:1, 16-20.

5. **he had restored**. 2 K 4:35. **behold, the woman**. Ru 2:3. Est 5:14. 6:11, 12. Pr 16:9. Ec 9:11. Mt 10:29, 30. Ac 8:27, etc. Ro *8:31. **My lord**. 2 K 6:12, 26. 1 S 26:17. Ps 145:1.

6. **officer**. *or*, eunuch. 2 K 9:32mg. Ge 37:36mg. 39:1. 40:2, 7. 1 S 8:15mg. 1 K 22:9mg. 1 Ch 28:1mg. Je +29:2mg. **Restore all**. Dt 22:2. Jg 11:13. 2 S 9:7. Pr *16:7. 21:1.

7. **Damascus**. Ge 14:15. 1 K 11:24. Is 7:8. **Ben-hadad**. 2 K 6:24. 1 K 15:18. 20:1, 34. 22:31. **The man of God**. 2 K 1:9, 10. 2:15. 6:12. See on Dt 33:1. 1 K 13:1. **is come**. Jg 16:2. Ac 17:6.

8. **Hazael**. i.e. *God has seen*, *S#2371h. ver. 9, 12, 13, 15, 28, 29. 2 K 9:14, 15. 10:32. 12:17, 17, 18. 13:3, 3, 22, 24, 25. 1 K 19:15, 17. 2 Ch 22:5, 6. Am 1:4. **Take**. See on 2 K 5:5. 1 S 9:7. 1 K 14:3. **enquire**. 2 K 1:2, 6. 3:11-13. 1 K 14:1-4. Lk 13:23. Ac 16:30.

9. **Hazael**. See on 1 K 19:15. **with him**. Heb. in his hand. 2 K 5:5. **every**. √171B, Ge +24:10. **Thy son Ben-hadad**. 2 K 6:21. 13:14. 16:7. 1 S 25:8. Phm 10.

10. **Thou mayest**. ♪60B, Ge +20:16. 1 K 22:15. **the Lord**. ver. 13. Ge 41:39. Je 38:21. Ezk 11:25. Am 3:7. 7:1, 4, 7. 8:1. Zc 1:20. Re 22:1. **he shall surely die**. ♪147B, Ge +2:16. ver. 15. 2 K 1:4, 16. Ge 2:17. Ezk 18:13.

11. **stedfastly**. Heb. and set *it*. 2 K 12:17. Lk 9:51. **wept**. Ge 45:2. Ps 119:136. Je 4:19. 9:1, 18. 13:17. 14:17. Lk 19:41. Jn 11:35. Ac 20:19, 31. Ro 9:2. Ph 3:18.

12. **my lord**. See on 2 K 4:28. 1 K 18:13. **the evil**. 2 K 10:32, 33. 12:17. 13:3, 7. Am 1:3, 4. **strongholds**. Nu 13:19. **set on fire**. Jsh 8:8. **wilt dash**. 2 K 15:16. Ps 137:8, 9. Is 13:16, 18. Ho 10:14. 13:16. Am 1:3-5, 13. Na 3:10. **children**. or, sucklings. 1 S 15:3. 22:19. Jb 3:16. Ps 8:2. 17:14. 137:9. **rip up**. 2 K 15:16. Ho 13:16. Am 1:13. **with child**. Ge 16:11. 38:24, 25.

13. **a dog**. 1 S 17:43. 2 S 9:8. Ps 22:16, 20. Is 56:10, 11. Mt 7:6. Ph 3:2. Re 22:15. **he should do**. Je *17:9. Mt *26:33-35. **The Lord**. See on ver. 10. 1 K 19:15. Mi 2:1.

14. **He told me**. ver. 10. 2 K 5:25. Mt 26:16.

15. **And it came**. ver. 13. 1 S 16:12, 13. 24:4-7, 13. 26:9-11. 1 K 11:26-37. **on the morrow**. Ps 36:4. Mi 2:1. **that he took a thick cloth**. There is a considerable degree of ambiguity in this passage. The pronoun *he* is generally referred to *Hazael*; but Dr. Geddes and others are decidedly of opinion, that we should understand by it *Ben-hadad*; who, encouraged by the favorable answer of Elisha, as reported by Hazael, adopted a violent remedy to allay the heat of his fever, and put over his face the *keveer*, or *fly-net* (See Note on 1 S 19:13), dipped in water, which suddenly checked the perspiration, and occasioned his death. **so that he died**. 2 K 9:24. 15:10-14, 25, 30. 1 K 15:28. 16:10, 18. Is 33:1. **Hazael**. ver. 13. 1 K 19:15.

16. A.M. 3112. B.C. 892. **Jehoram**. 2 K 1:17. 1 K 22:50. 2 Ch 21:1-20. **began to reign**. Heb. reigned. 1 K 15:25. "Began to reign in concert with his father."

17. A.M. 3112-3119. B.C. 892-885. **Thirty and two**. 2 Ch 21:5-10.

18. **in the way**. 2 K 3:2, 3. 1 K 22:52, 53. **the house**. 2 K 9:7, 8. 21:3, 13. 2 Ch 21:13. Mi 6:16. **the daughter**. ver. 26. 1 K 21:25. 2 Ch 18:1. 19:2. 21:6. 22:1-4. **his wife**. Ge 6:1-5. Dt 7:3, 4. See on 1 K 11:1-5. Ne 13:25, 26.

19. **for David**. 2 K 19:34. 2 S 7:12, 13, 15. 1 K 11:36. 15:4, 5. 2 Ch 21:7. Is *7:14. 37:35. Je 33:25, 26. Ho 11:9. Lk 1:32, 33. **light**. Heb. candle, *or* lamp. 2 S 21:17mg. See on 1 K 11:36mg.

20. **Edom**. ver. 22. 2 K 3:9, 27. Ge 27:40. 2 Ch 21:8-10. **made a king**. 2 S 8:14. 1 K 22:47.

21. **Zair**. i.e. *little, small; in tribulation*, *S#6811h. *Zair* is supposed by Calmet and others to be the same as *Seir*, the country of *Seir* the Horite, inhabited by the Edomites or Idumeans. Probably the former was a dialectical pronunciation of the latter. Compare Jg *12:6n. Ne 13:24. Mt *26:73. Mk *14:70. Ac 2:6, 7.

22. **Yet**. "And so fulfilled Ge ✱27:40." See ver. 20. **Edom**. 1 K 22:47. **unto this day**. Thus the book of Kings was written before the captivity of Judah to Babylon. 2 K 2:22. Jsh +4:9. 1 S 6:18. 27:6. 2 S 6:8. 1 K 8:8. 12:19. **Libnah**. 2 K 19:8. Jsh 10:29. 21:13. 2 Ch 21:10.

23. **the rest of**. 2 K 15:6, 36. See on 1 K 11:41. 14:29. 15:23. 2 Ch 21:11-20.

24. **slept with his fathers**. Ge +*25:8n. Dt 31:16n. See on 1 K 2:10. +*11:43. 14:+20, 31. **Ahaziah**. i.e. *laid hold of by Jah*. 1 Ch 3:11. 2 Ch 21:1, 17. 25:23, Jehoahaz. 22:1, 6, Azariah.

25. A.M. 3119-3120. B.C. 885-884. **In the twelfth year**. See on ver. 16, 17. 2 K 9:29. 2 Ch 21:20. **Ahaziah**. Ahaziah, Joash, and Amaziah are all omitted in Mt 1:8; all died violent deaths. 2 K 9:27. 12:20. 14:19.

26. **Two and twenty**. In the parallel passage of Chronicles (2 Ch 22:2), it is said, "*forty and two* years old was Ahaziah when he began to reign;" but this is evidently a mistake, as it makes the son two years older than his own father! For his father began to reign when he was *thirty-two* years old, and reigned *eight* years, and so died, being *forty* years old. See ver. 17, and the Note on 2 Ch 22:2. **one year**. 2 K 9:21-27. 2 Ch 22:5-8. **Athaliah**. i.e. *afflicted of Jah*. 2 Ch 11:1, 2, 13-16. **daughter**. *or*, grand-daughter. ver. 18. Athaliah was the daughter of Ahab and Jezebel, but she is spoken here as being the "daughter" of Omri, her grandfather, the father of Ahab, thus indicating that Omri is considered greater than Ahab. Scott suggests that Omri may have adopted and educated Athaliah. So, in Mt 1:1, David is actually mentioned before Abraham. See 1 K +15:10n.

27. **he walked**. See on ver. 18. **the son in law**. ver. 18. 2 Ch 22:3, 4. Ec 7:26. 2 C 6:14-17.

28. A.M. 3120. B.C. 884. **he went**. 2 K 3:7. 9:15. 1 K 22:4. 2 Ch 18:2, 3, 31. 19:2. 22:5. **Hazael**. ver. 12, 13. 1 K 19:17. **Ramoth-gilead**. Jsh 21:38. 1 K 4:13. 22:3.

29. **Joram**. 2 K 9:15. **which the Syrians had given**. Heb. wherewith the Syrians had wounded. **Ramah**. "Called *Ramoth*, ver. 28." **Ahaziah**. 2 K 9:16. 2 Ch 22:6, 7. **sick**. Heb. wounded. 1 K +22:34mg.

2 KINGS 9

A young prophet, by Elisha's orders, goes to Ramoth-gilead; anoints Jehu as king over Israel, and directs him to extirpate Ahab's family, 1-10. Jehu acquaints the captains, is proclaimed king, and marches in haste to Jezreel against Joram, 11-16. Joram sends messengers to Jehu, who detains them, 17-20. He and Ahaziah meet Jehu: who kills Joram, and casts him into the field of Naboth, 21-26. Ahaziah is slain at Gur and buried at Jerusalem, 27-29. Jezebel, by Jehu's orders, is thrown out of the window, and trampled under foot, 30-33. She is eaten by dogs, as Elijah had predicted, 34-37.

1. **one.** The Jews say that this was *Jonah* the prophet, the son of Amittai. **the children.** 2 K 2:3. 4:1. 6:1-3. See on 1 K 20:35. **Gird up thy loins.** As the upper garments of the Orientals were long and flowing, it was indispensably necessary to tuck up the skirts with a girdle about their loins, in order to use any expedition in their work or on a journey. 2 K 4:29. 1 K 18:46. Je 1:17. Lk 12:35-37. 1 P 1:13. **box of oil.** ver. 3. 1 S 10:1. 16:1. 1 K 1:39. **Ramoth-gilead.** 2 K 8:28, 29. Dt 4:1, 3. 1 K 22:4, 20.

2. **Jehu.** i.e. *he is; Jehovah is he,* *S#3058h. Jehoram having retired from the army, Jehu seems to have been left first in command, having been long employed by Ahab's family. ver. 5, 11, 13, *14, 15, 16, 17, 18, 19, 20, 21, 22, 22, 24, 27, 30, 31. 2 K 10:1, 5, 11, 13, 18, 18, 19, 20, 21, 23, 24, 25, 28, 29, 30, 31, 34, 35, 36. 12:1. 13:1. 14:8. 15:12. 1 K *19:16, 17. 1 Ch 2:38, 38. 4:35. 12:3. 2 Ch 19:2. 20:34. 22:7, 8, 9. 25:17. Ho 1:4. (1) The son of Hanani the seer, 1 K 16:1, 7, 12; 2 Ch 19:2; 20:34. (2) The son of Jehoshaphat and grandson of Nimshi, whom Elisha was commanded to anoint king over Israel, 1 K 19:16, 17; 2 K 9:1-10. (3) A descendant of Jerahmeel, the son of Hezron, 1 Ch 2:38. (4) One of the tribe of Simeon, 1 Ch 4:35. (5) A Benjamite who was with David at Ziklag, 1 Ch 12:3. **among his brethren.** ver. 5, 11. **inner chamber.** Heb. chamber in a chamber. 1 K 20:30mg. 22:25mg.

3. **pour it.** Ex 29:7. Le 8:12. 1 S 16:13. 1 K 19:16. **I have anointed.** 2 K 8:13. 1 S 9:16. 15:1, 17. 16:12. 1 K 1:39. 19:16. Ps 75:6, 7. Pr 8:15, 16. Je 27:5-7. Da 2:21. 4:35. 5:18. Jn 19:10, 11. **and flee.** 1 S 16:2. Mt 2:13. 10:16.

4. **the young man.** *Hannaar hannavee,* not as some would render, "the servant of the prophet," but correctly rendered by our venerable translators, "the young man, the prophet;" for *hannaar,* "the young man," is not in *regimine,* but in *appositione,* with *hanavee,* "the prophet." Is +40:13mg. **the prophet.** 2 K 2:3.

5. **I have an errand.** Jg 3:19.

6. **he arose.** Ac 23:18, 19. **I have anointed.** See on ver. 3. 1 K 1:34. 19:16. 2 Ch *22:7. Ps 2:6mg. 75:6. Is 45:1. Da 2:21. 4:17, 32. 5:20, 21. **over the people.** 1 K 3:8. 10:9. 14:7. 16:2.

7. **I may avenge.** Dt 32:35, 43. Ps 94:1-7. 116:15. Mt 23:35. Lk 18:7, 8. Ro 12:19. 13:4. He 10:30. Re 6:9, 10. 18:20. 19:2. **at the hand.** ver. 32-37. 1 K 18:4. 21:15, 21, 25.

8. **I will cut off.** See on 1 K 14:10, 11. 21:21, 22. **him that pisseth.** 1 S 25:22n. **him that is shut up.** 2 K 14:26. Dt 32:36.

9. **like the house.** 1 K 14:10, 11. 15:29. 21:22. **and like the house.** 1 K 16:3-5, 11, 12.

10. **the dogs.** ver. 35, 36. 1 K 21:23. Je 22:19. **he opened.** ver. 3. Jg 3:26.

11. **all is well.** ver. 17, 19, 22. 2 K 4:23mg, 26.

5:21. Ge +29:6mg. **this mad fellow.** It is probable there was something peculiar in the young prophet's manner and address, similar to the vehement actions sometimes used by the prophets when under the Divine influence, which caused the bystanders to use this contemptuous language. Dt 28:34. 1 S 21:14mg, 15. Is 59:15mg. Je 29:26. Ho 9:7. Mk 3:21. Jn 10:20. Ac 17:18. 26:24. 1 C 4:10. 2 C 5:13. **communication.** 1 S 1:16. 1 K *18:27mg. Jb 7:13. 9:27. 10:1. 21:4. 23:2. Ps 55:2. 64:1. 102:1. 104:34. 142:2. Pr 23:29.

12. **false.** Je 37:14. 40:16. **thus and thus.** See on ver. 6-10.

13. **and took every.** The spreading of garments in the street, before persons to whom it was intended to show particular honor, was an ancient and very general custom; the garments in these cases being used for carpets. In the *Agamemnon* of Aeschylus, the hypocritical Clytemnestra commands the maids to spread carpets before her returning husband, that on his descending from his chariot he may place his foot on "a purple-covered path." We also find this custom among the Romans. Plutarch relates, that when Cato of Utica left the Macedonian army, where he had become legionary tribune, the soldiers spread their clothes in the way. Mt 21:7, 8. Mk 11:7, 8. **on the top.** The ancient fortified cities were generally strengthened with a citadel (Jg 9:46, 51), commonly built on an eminence, to which they ascended by a *flight of stairs* (Ne 3:15). It is extremely probable, therefore, that Ramoth-gilead, being a frontier town of Israel and Syria, had a tower of this nature; and that Jehu was proclaimed king on the *top of the stairs* by which they ascended the hill on which the tower stood, i.e. in the area before the door of the tower, and consequently the most public place in the city. lit. "bone." *S#1634h, 1635h. Ge 49:14 (strong). 2 K 9:13 (top). Jb 40:18. Pr 17:22. 25:15. Da 6:24. **blew with trumpets.** 2 S 15:10. 1 K 1:34, 39. Ps 47:5-7. 98:6. **is king.** Heb. reigneth.

14. **conspired.** ver. 31. 2 K 8:12-15. 10:9. 15:30. 1 K 15:27. 16:7, 9, 16. **kept Ramoth-gilead.** 2 K 8:28. 1 K 22:3.

15. **Joram.** Heb. Jehoram. **returned.** 2 K 8:29. 2 Ch 22:6. **had given.** Heb. smote. **minds.** Heb. *nephesh,* soul, Ge +23:8. **none go forth.** Heb. no escaper go forth. 1 S 27:9-11.

16. **And Ahaziah.** 2 K 8:28, 29. 2 Ch 22:6, 7.

17. **a watchman.** 2 S 13:34. 18:24. Is 21:6-9, 11, 12. 56:10. 62:6. Ezk 33:2-9. Ac 20:26-31. **Take an horseman.** 2 K 7:14. **Is it peace.** ver. 19. 2 K 5:21mg. Ge +29:6mg. 1 S 16:4. 17:22mg. 1 K 2:13. Lk 10:5, 6.

18. **What hast.** *J*120, 1 K +18:18. Jg +*11:12. Jn +*2:4. **thou to do.** ver. 19, 22. Is 48:22. 59:8. Je 16:5. Ro 3:17.

20. **driving.** *or,* marching. Hab 1:6. 3:12. **for he driveth.** 2 K 10:16. Ec 9:10. Is 54:16. Da 11:44. **furiously.** Heb. in madness. ver. 11. Dt 28:28. Zc 12:4.

21. **Make ready.** Heb. bind. 1 K 18:44mg. 20:14mg. 2 Ch 13:3mg. Je 46:4. Mi 1:13mg. **Joram.** 2 Ch 22:7. **met.** Heb. found. 2 K 10:13mg, 15mg. Ge 44:34mg. Nu 20:14mg. Ne 9:32mg. **the portion of Naboth.** ver. 25. 1 K 21:1-7, 15, 18, 19.

22. **Is it peace.** See on ver. 17. **What peace.** ver. 18. Is *48:22. 57:19-21. 59:8. Je *16:5. Ro 3:17. **the whoredoms.** Ex 7:11. 1 K 16:30-33. 18:4. 19:1, 2. 21:8-10, *25. 2 Ch 21:13. Na 3:4. Re 2:20-23. 17:4, 5. 18:3,

23. **witchcrafts.** Is *47:9, 12. Mi *5:12. Na *3:4.

23. **There is treachery.** 2 K 11:14. 2 Ch 23:13.

24. **drew a bow with his full strength.** Heb. filled his hand with a bow. **smote.** 1 K *22:34. Jb 20:23-25. Ps 50:22. Pr 21:30. Ec 8:12, 13. 1 Th 5:3. **sunk.** Heb. bowed. Ge 49:9.

25. **Bidkar.** i.e. *son of piercing through; stabber; assassin,* *S#920h. **the Lord.** 1 K 21:19, 24-29. Is 13:1. Je 23:33-38. Na 1:1. Ml 1:1. Mt 11:30.

26. **blood of Naboth.** Heb. bloods. Ge 4:10mg. 2 S 3:28mg. 1 Ch 28:3mg. Ps 5:6mg. 51:14mg. 55:23mg. Is 1:15mg. 26:21mg. Ezk 16:9mg. 18:13mg. Ho 4:2mg. 12:14mg. Mi 3:10mg. Na 3:1mg. Hab 2:8mg, 12mg, 17. Zc 9:7mg. **of his sons.** Dt 24:16. 2 Ch 24:25. 25:4. **I will requite.** Ex *20:5. Dt 5:9. Ezk 18:19. **plat.** *or*, portion. ver. 21, 25. 1 K 21:19.

27. **Ahaziah.** 2 K 8:29. Nu 16:26. 2 Ch 22:7-9. Pr 13:20. 2 C 6:17. **garden house.** 1 K 21:2. **And they did.** 2 Ch 22:9. **Gur.** i.e. a *whelp* or *sojourner*, *S#1483h. **Ibleam.** Jsh 17:11. Jg 1:27. **Megiddo.** "In the kingdom of Samaria." 2 K 23:29, 30. Jsh +17:11. Jg 1:27. 5:19. 1 K 4:12. 2 Ch 22:9.

28. **his servants carried.** 2 K 12:21. 14:19, 20. 23:30. 2 Ch 25:28. 35:24. **sepulchre.** Heb. *qeburah*, Ge +35:20 (*S#6900h).

29. **in the eleventh.** 2 K 8:16, 24, 25. 2 Ch 21:18, 19. 22:1, 2. **began Ahaziah.** "Then he began to reign as viceroy to his father in his sickness, 2 Ch 21:18, 19. But in Joram's twelfth year, he began to reign alone. 2 K 8:25."

30. **Jezebel.** 1 K 19:1, 2. **painted her face.** Heb. put her eyes in painting. Pr 6:25. Je √4:30mg. Ezk *23:40. **tired her head.** Is 3:18-24. Je 13:18mg. Ezk 24:17. 1 T 2:9, 10. 1 P 3:3. **looked out.** Jg +5:28.

31. **Zimri.** 1 K 16:9-20. **peace.** See on ver. 18-22.

32. **Who is on my side?** Ex 32:26. 1 Ch 12:18. 2 Ch 11:12. Ps 118:6. 124:1, 2. **eunuchs.** *or*, chamberlains. 2 K 8:6mg. Ge +*37:36mg. Est 1:10mg. 2:15, 21. Je +29:2mg. Ac 12:20.

33. **Throw her down.** See on 1 K 21:11. *S#8058h: Ex 23:11 (let it rest). Dt 15:2 (release), 3. 2 S 6:6 (shook; mg, stumbled). 2 K 9:33 (Throw), 33 (threw). 1 Ch 13:9 (stumbled; mg, shook). Ps 141:6 (overthrown). Je 17:4 (discontinue). **sprinkled.** Le 6:27. Is 63:3. This terrible mode of punishment appears to have been but rarely used, though we occasionally meet with it during this and subsequent periods. The same punishment, it is well known, obtained among the Romans, who used to throw certain malefactors from the Tarpeian rock (Livy, l.vi. c. 20). This practice obtains among the Moors at Constantia, a town of Barbary (Pitt, pp. 311, 312); and is also of frequent occurrence in Persia (See Sir R. K. Porter's *Travels in Persia*, vol. ii. pp. 28-30). **and he trode.** ver. 26. 2 K 7:20. Is 25:10. La 1:15. Mi 7:10. Ml 4:3. Mt 5:13. He 10:29.

34. **he did eat.** 1 K 18:41. Est 3:15. Am 6:4. **this cursed woman.** 1 K 21:25. Pr 10:7. Is 65:15. Mt 25:41. **she is a king's daughter.** 1 K 16:31.

35. **but they found.** Jb 31:3. Ec 6:3. Is 14:18-20. Je 22:19. 36:30. Ac 12:23. **skull.** Ex 16:16. 38:26. Nu 1:2, 18, 20, 22. 3:47. Jg 9:53. 1 Ch 10:10. 23:3, 24. **the palms.** Le 14:15, 26. 1 S 5:4.

36. **This is.** See on 1 K 21:23. **by his.** Heb. by the hand of his. 2 K 10:10. 14:25. Le 8:36. 2 S 12:25. 1 K +*16:12mg.

37. **the carcase.** Ps 83:10. Ec 6:3. Is 14:18-20. Je

8:2. 16:4. 22:19. 36:30. Ezk 32:23-30. **as dung.** Je 9:22. 25:33.

2 KINGS 10

Jehu, by letters to the elders, causes Ahab's seventy sons to be slain at Samaria, and their heads brought to Jezreel, 1-7. He shows this to be a fulfilment of Elijah's prophecy, and destroys all Ahab's kindred in Jezreel, 8-11. In his way to Samaria he slays forty-two of Ahaziah's brethren, 12-14. Attended by Jehonadab, he slays all that remained to Ahab in Samaria, 15-17. He assembles all the worshippers of Baal by stratagem; puts them to death, and breaks down Baal's images and temple, 18-28. He follows the sins of Jeroboam; yet the kingdom to the fourth generation is promised him, for destroying the house of Ahab, 29-31. Hazael smites Israel, 32, 33. Jehu dies, and Jehoahaz succeeds him, 34-36.

1. **seventy sons.** Young notes, including grandsons, doubtless. ✓171G2. Synecdoche of the Species, Ge +13:8. Jg 8:30. 10:4. 12:14. **in Samaria.** 2 K 5:3. 1 K 13:32. +15:10n. 16:28. 2 Ch 22:9. **the rulers.** See on Dt 16:18. 1 K 21:8-14. **them.** Heb. nourishers. ver. 5. Est 2:7.

2. **as soon.** See on 2 K 5:6.

3. **Look even.** Dt 17:14, 15. 1 S 10:24. 11:15. 2 S 2:8, 9. 1 K 1:24, 25. 12:20. **fight for.** 2 S 2:12-17. 1 K 12:21. Jn 18:36.

4. **Behold.** 2 K 9:24, 27. **how then shall.** Is 27:4. Je 49:19. Na 1:6. Lk 14:31.

5. **We are thy servants.** 2 K 18:14. Jsh 9:11, 24, 25. 1 K 20:4, 32. Je 27:7, 8, 17. Jn 12:26.

6. **If ye be mine.** Heb. If ye *be* for me. See on 2 K 9:32. Mt 12:30. Lk 9:50. **take ye.** Nu 25:4. See on 1 K 21:8-11. **your master's sons.** Dt 5:9. Jsh 7:24, 25. Jb 21:19. Is 14:21, 22. Re 2:20-23. **which brought them up.** "The rich," says Mr. Morier (*Second Journey through Persia*, p. 110), "hire a *dedeh*, or wet nurse for their children. If a boy, the father appoints a steady man from the age of two years to be his *leleh*, who, I conjecture, must stand in the same capacity as the bringers up of children mentioned in the catastrophe of Ahab's sons. But if it be a daughter, she has a *gees sefeed*, or white head, attached to her for the same purpose as the *laleh*."

7. **slew.** Ge 22:10. 37:31. Ex 12:6. **seventy men.** ver. 9. 2 K 11:1. Jg 9:5, etc. 1 K 21:21. 2 Ch 21:4. Mt 14:8-11. **heads.** Jg +7:25. **baskets.** *S#1731h. 1 S 2:14 (kettle). 2 Ch 35:13 (cauldrons). Jb 41:20 (pot). Ps 81:6mg. Je 24:2.

8. **there came.** 2 S 11:18-21. 1 K 21:14. Mk 6:28. **Lay ye them.** Such barbarities are by no means uncommon in the East. 'It has been known to occur,' says Mr. Morier (*Second Journey*, p. 186), 'after the combat was over, that prisoners have been put to death in cold blood, in order that the heads, which are immediately despatched to the king, and deposited in heaps at the palace gates, might make a more considerable show.' **until the morning.** Dt 21:23.

9. **Ye be righteous.** 1 S 12:3. Is 5:3. **I conspired.** See on 2 K 9:14-24. Ho 1:4.

10. **fall unto the earth.** 1 S 3:19. 15:29. Je 44:28, 29. Zc 1:6. Mk 13:31. **the Lord hath done.** 2 K 9:7-10. 1 K 21:19, 21-24, 29. **by.** Heb. by the hand of. 2 K 9:36mg. 1 K +16:12mg.

11. **and**. Ps 125:5. Pr 13:20. **kinsfolks**. *or*, acquaintance. Ru 2:1. Jb 19:14. Ps 31:11. 55:13. 88:8, 18. Is 12:5 (known). **his priests**. 2 K 23:30. 2 S 20:26. 1 K 18:19, 40. 22:6. Re 19:20. 20:10. **he left**. Jsh 10:30. 11:8. 1 K 14:10. 15:29. 16:11. 21:21, 22. Jb 18:19. Ps 109:13. Is 14:21, 22. Jn 10:35.

12. **shearing house**. Heb. house of shepherds binding *sheep*. ver. 14.

13. **met with**. Heb. found. ver. 15. 2 K 9:21mg. **the brethren**. 2 K 8:24, 29. 9:21-27. 2 Ch 21:17. 22:1-10. **salute**. Heb. the peace of, etc. Jg +18:15mg. **queen**. 1 K 11:19. 15:13. 2 Ch 15:16. Je 13:18. 29:2.

14. **Take them alive**. ver. 6, 10, 11. Ge 39:12 (caught). 1 K 20:18. **pit**. Heb. *bor*, Ge +37:20. **neither left**. 2 K 8:18. 11:1. 2 Ch 22:8, 10.

15. **lighted on**. Heb. found. ver. 13mg. 2 K +9:21mg. **Jehonadab**. i.e. *The Lord gave freely*, ✠S#3082h. ver. 23. Je 35:+6, 8h, 14h, 16h, 18h, 19, Jonadab. **Rechab**. i.e. *a rider, charioteer*. 2 Ch 2:55. **saluted**. Heb. blessed. Ge 4:29. See on Ge 31:55. 47:7, 10. 1 S 13:10mg. **Is thine heart right**. 1 Ch 12:17, 18. Jn 21:15-17. Ga 4:12. **give me**. Ezr 10:19. Ezk 17:18. Ga 2:9. **he took him**. Jehu asked for the hand of Jehonadab not merely for the purpose of assisting him into the chariot, but that he might give him an assurance that he would assist him in the prosecution of his desires; for "giving the hand" is considered as a pledge of friendship and fidelity, or a form of entering into a contract, among all nations. Mr. Bruce relates (*Travels*, vol. I. p. 148), that when he entreated the protection of a *sheikh*, the great people who were assembled came, "and after *joining hands*, repeated a kind of prayer, of about two minutes long; by which they declared themselves and their children accursed, if ever they lifted their hands against me in the *tell* (or field), in the desert, or on the river; or, in case that I, or mine, should fly to them for refuge, if they did not protect us at the risk of their lives, their families, and their fortunes, or, as they emphatically expressed it, to the death of the last male child among them." Another striking instance occurs in Ockley's *History of the Saracens* (vol. i. p. 36). Telha, just before he died, asked one of Ali's men if he belonged to the emperor of the faithful; and being informed that he did, "Give me then," said he, "your hand, that I may put mine in it, and by this action renew the oath of fidelity which I have already made to Ali." Ac 8:31.

16. **Come with me**. ver. 31. 2 K 9:7-9. Nu 23:4. 24:13-16. 1 K 19:10, 14, 17. Pr 27:2. Ezk 33:31. Mt 6:2, 5. Ro 10:2.

17. **he slew**. See on ver. 11. 2 K 9:8. 2 Ch 22:8. Ps 109:8, 9. Ml 4:1. **according**. See on ver. 10. 2 K 9:25, 26. 1 K 21:21.

18. **Ahab served Baal**. 2 K 3:2. 1 K 16:31, 32. 18:19, 22, 40. **Jehu**. Jb 13:7. Ro 3:8. Ph 4:8.

19. **all the prophets of Baal**. 2 K 3:13. 1 K 22:6. **all his servants**. ver. 21. **all his priests**. ver. 11. **But Jehu**. See on ver. 18. Jb 13:7. Pr 29:5. 2 C 4:2. 11:3, 13-15. 12:16-18. 1 Th 2:3.

20. **Proclaim**. Heb. Sanctify. 1 K 18:19, 20. 21:12. Jl 1:14. **solemn assembly**. Le 23:36. **they proclaimed**. Ex 32:5.

21. **And they came**. Jl 3:2, 11-14. Re 16:16. **the house of Baal**. 1 K 16:32. **full from one end to another**. *or, so* full *that they stood* mouth to mouth. Jg 16:27.

22. **vestments**. Ex 28:2. Mt 22:11, 12.

23. **Jehonadab**. ver. 15. **Search**. Ge 31:35. 44:12. 1 S 23:23. 1 K 20:6, etc. **none of**. Ge 19:22. Ezk 9:6. Am 9:9. Re 7:3. **the worshippers**. Mt 13:30, 41. 25:32, 33.

24. **If any of the men**. 1 K 20:30-42. **his life**. Heb. *nephesh*, soul, Ge +44:30. 1 K 20:39.

25. **Go in**. Ex 32:27. Dt 13:6-11. Ezk 9:5-7. **guard**. or, runners. 1 S 22:17mg. **let**. Dt 13:9-11. Ezk 22:21, 22. Re 16:6, 7. **edge**. Heb. mouth. Ge +34:26mg.

26. **images**. Heb. statues. or, standing pillars. 2 K 3:2. Ge 28:18, 22. 31:13, 45, 51, 52. 35:14, 20. Ex 23:24. 24:4. 34:13. Le 26:1. 1 K 14:23mg. **and burned them**. 2 K 19:18. 2 S 5:21.

27. **brake down the image**. 2 K 18:4. 23:7-14. Le 26:30. Dt 7:5, 25. 1 K 16:32. 2 Ch 34:3-7. **made it a draught house**. or, latrine. This was an ancient mode of degradation, which still continues in the East; and we are informed, that Abbas the Great, king of Persia, having conquered Bagdad, treated the tomb of Hanifah, one of the fathers of the church among the Turks, in a similar manner. Ezr 6:11. Da 2:5. 3:29.

29. A.M. 3120-3148. B.C. 884-856. **the sins**. 2 K 13:2, 11. 14:24. 15:9, 18, 24, 28. 17:22. 1 K 12:28-30. 13:33, 34. 14:16. **who made Israel to sin**. Ge 20:9. Ex 32:21. 1 S 2:24. Mk 6:24-26. 1 C 8:9-13. Ga 2:12, 13. **the golden calves**. Ex 32:4. 1 K 12:28, 29. Ho 8:5, 6. 10:5. 13:2. **in Beth-el**. 1 K 12:29.

30. **Because thou hast**. 1 K 21:29. Ezk 29:18-20. Ho 1:4. **according to all that**. 1 S 15:18-24. 1 K 20:42. 21:22. **thy children**. ver. 35. 2 K 13:1, 10. 14:23. 15:8-12. **fourth**. 2 K ✳15:12. Ge 15:16.

31. **took no heed**. Heb. observed not. Nu 23:12. Dt 4:15, 23. 1 K 2:4. Ps 39:1. 119:9. Pr 4:23. He *2:1. *12:15. **walk**. Dt 5:33. 10:12, 13. 2 Ch 6:16. Ne 10:29. Ps 78:10. Ezk 36:27. Da 9:10. **he departed**. ver. 29. 2 K 3:3. 1 K 14:16.

32. **cut**. Heb. cut off the ends of. Pr 26:6. Hab 2:10. **Hazael**. 2 K ✳8:12. 13:22. 1 K 19:17.

33. **eastward**. Heb. toward the rising of the sun. **the land of Gilead**. Nu 32:33-42. Dt 3:12-17. Jsh 13:9-12. **even**. *or*, even to. Am 1:3, 4. **Bashan**. Nu +21:33. Jsh 12:4n. 1 K 4:13. Ps 22:12. Young notes that these were the first conquered and the first lost.

34. **the rest of**. 2 K 12:19. 13:8. See on 1 K 11:41. 14:19, 29.

35. A.M. 3148. B.C. 856. **Jehu slept**. Ge +*25:8n. Dt 31:16n. 2 S 7:12. 1 K 1:21. 2:10. +*11:43. 14:+20, 31. **Jehoahaz**. i.e. *Jah has taken hold; whom Jehovah holds*, ✳S#3059h. 2 K 13:1, 4, 7, 8, 9, 10, 22, 25, 25. 14:8, 17. 23:30, 31, 34. 2 Ch 21:17. 25:17, 23, 25. 36:1. Reigned 17 years, as 2 K 13:1. (1) Son and successor of Jehu, king of Israel, 2 K 10:35. (2) One of the sons of Josiah, king of Judah, whom the people made king after his father's death, 2 K 23:30, 31, 34; 2 Ch 36:1, 2, 4. (3) The son of Jehoram, king of Judah, who succeeded his father on the throne, 2 Ch 21:17. Same as Ahaziah and Azariah, 1 K +22:40; 1 Ch +6:36.

36. **the time**. Heb. the days *were*. **twenty and eight years**. Thus Jehu's reign was longer than any other king of Israel.

2 KINGS 11

Athaliah murders the seed royal of Judah: but Joash, the infant son of Ahaziah, is preserved by Jehosheba in the temple, 1-3. Jehoiada the high priest, in the seventh year, having taken proper measures, anoints and crowns him, 4-12. Athaliah, pressing into the temple, is seized and slain, 13-16. Jehoiada renews the covenant between the LORD, the king, and the people, restoring the worship of God; and destroys the worship of Baal, 17, 18. Joash reigns in peace, and the people rejoice, 19-21.

1. A.M. 3120. B.C. 884. **Athaliah.** 2 Ch 22:10. 24:7. **the mother.** 2 K 8:18, 26. 9:27. **and destroyed.** A similar history is related by Mr. Bruce (*Travels*, vol. iii. p. 526), as having occurred in Abyssinia. Judith "surprised the rock Damo, and slew the whole of the princes, to the number, it is said, of about 400;" while the infant king, Del Naad, was conveyed for safety to a loyal province, and afterwards restored. Mt 2:13, 16. 21:38, 39. **seed royal.** Heb. seed of the kingdom. 2 K 25:25mg. Jsh 10:2. 1 S 27:5. 1 K 11:14. 2 Ch 22:10. Est 1:7. Je 41:1. Ezk 17:13. Da 1:3.

2. **Jehosheba.** i.e. *sworn of Jehovah*, *S#3089h. 2 Ch 22:11, Jehoshabeath. **Joram.** i.e. *Jehovah is high.* 2 K 8:16, Jehoram. **Joash.** i.e. *Jehovah is foundation.* 2 K 12:1, 2, Jehoash. **stole him.** 2 Ch 22:11. **they hid him.** 2 K 8:19. Pr 21:30. Is 7:6, 7. 37:35. 65:8, 9. Je 33:17, 21, 26. **his nurse.** Ge 24:59. 32:15 (milch). 35:8. Ex 2:7. 2 Ch 22:11. Is 49:23. **in the bedchamber.** *Bachadar hammittoth*, "in a chamber of beds," which Sir J. Chardin thinks does not mean a room to sleep in, but a chamber used as a repository for beds; for, in the East, they sleep upon cotton mattresses, "of which they have several in great houses, against they should have occasion, and a room on purpose for them" (See Harmer, ch. xi. Ob. 86). 1 K 6:5, 6, 8, 10. Je 35:2. Ezk 40:45.

3. A.M. 3120-3126. B.C. 884-878. **hid.** 1 S 14:22. 1 Ch 21:20. 2 Ch 22:9, 12. Pr +*22:3. Col 3:3. **And Athaliah.** 2 Ch 22:12. Ps 12:8. Ml 3:15.

4. A.M. 3126. B.C. 878. **the seventh.** 2 Ch 23:1, etc. **Jehoiada.** i.e. *Jehovah hath known; whom Jehovah knows*, *S#3077h. (1) The father of Benaiah, one of David's chief officers: 2 S 8:18. 20:23. 23:20, 22. 1 K 1:8, 26, 32, 36, 38, 44. 2:25, 29, 34, 35, 46. 4:4. 1 Ch 11:22, 24. 18:17. 27:5. This Jehoiada was the chief priest, 1 Ch 27:5. By a copyist's error Benaiah is said to have been the father of Jehoiada instead of the son, 1 Ch 27:34. (2) The high priest who made Joash king after Athaliah had usurped the kingdom seven years: 2 K 11:4, 9, 15, 17. 12:2, 7, 9. 2 Ch 22:11. 23:1, 8, 8, 9, 11, 14, 16, 18. 24:2, 3, 6, 12, 14, 14, 15, 17, 20, 22, 25. (3) The second priest in the reign of Zedekiah, Je 29:26. (4) A Jew who repaired a gate at Jerusalem, Ne 3:6. (5) The leader of the Aaronites who went to Ziklag to help David, 1 Ch 12:27. **rulers.** ver. 9. 1 Ch 9:13. **over hundreds.** Ex 18:21, 25. **the captains.** or, executioners. ver. 19. 2 S 20:23 (Cherethites). Ac 5:24, 26. **guards.** or, runners. 2 K 11:13mg. 1 S 22:17mg. 1 K 14:27mg. **made a covenant.** ver. 17. 2 K 23:3. Jsh 24:25. 1 S 18:3. 23:18. 2 Ch 15:12. 29:10. 34:31, 32. Ne 9:38. **took an oath.** Ge 50:25. 1 K *18:10. Ne 5:12. 10:29.

5. **that enter.** 1 Ch 9:25. 23:3-6, 32. 24:3-6. Lk 1:8, 9. **the watch.** ver. 19. 2 K 16:18. 1 K 10:5. Je 26:10. Ezk 44:2, 3. 46:2, 3.

6. **the gate of Sur.** i.e. *turning aside; deteriorated*, *S#5495h, only here. 1 Ch 26:13-19. 2 Ch 23:4, 5. In 2 Ch 23:5 it is "the foundation," by changing a Hebrew letter (Young). **the guard.** or, runners. In

2 Ch 23:4mg, called "of the thresholds" (Young). **that it be not broken down.** or, from breaking up.

7. **parts.** or, companies. Heb. hands. Ge 47:24. 2 S 19:43. Ne 11:1. Da 1:20. **go forth.** ver. 5. 2 Ch 23:6.

8. **compass.** 2 K 6:14. Jsh 6:3, 11. **he that cometh.** ver. 15. Ex 21:14. 1 K 2:28-31. 2 Ch 23:7. **the ranges.** ver. 15. 1 K 6:9. 2 Ch 23:14.

9. **the captains.** See on ver. 4. 1 Ch 26:26. 2 Ch 23:8.

10. **king David's spears.** Josephus (Ant. l. ix. c.7 par. 2) states that, for fear of creating suspicion, they came *unarmed*, "and Jehoiada having opened the arsenal in the temple which David had prepared, he divided among the centurions, priests, and Levites, the spears (arrows), and quivers, and all other kinds of weapons which he found there." 1 S 21:9. 2 S 8:7. 1 Ch 26:26, 27. 2 Ch 5:1. 23:9, 10.

11. **every man.** ver. 8, 10. **corner.** Heb. shoulder. Ex 26:14, 15. 28:7, 12, 25, 27. **by the altar.** Ex 40:6. 2 Ch 6:12. Ezk 8:16. Jl 2:17. Mt 23:35. Lk 11:51.

12. **he brought.** ver. 2, 4. 2 Ch 23:11. **put the crown.** 2 S 1:10. 12:30. Est 2:17. 6:8. Ps 21:3. 89:39. 132:18. Mt 27:29. He 2:9. Re 19:12. **gave.** ſ180A, Ge +4:20. **the testimony.** 2 K +*14:6n. Ex 16:34. 25:16. 31:18. Dt √17:18-20. Ps 78:5. Is 8:16, *20. **anointed him.** 2 K 9:3. 1 S 10:1. 16:13. 2 S 2:4, 7. 5:3. 1 K 1:39. La 4:20. Ac 4:27. 2 C 1:21. He 1:9. **and they clapped.** *Wyyakkoo kaph*, "they clapped the hand," which Mr. Harmer thinks was similar to the mode in which Oriental females express their respect for persons of high rank, by gently applying one of their hands to their mouth. So Pitts (p. 85) relates, that in some of the towns of Barbary, the leaders of the sacred caravan being received with loud acclamations, "the very women get upon the tops of the houses to view the parade, or fine show, where they keep striking their four fingers on their lips, as fast as they can, making a joyful noise all the while." Nu 24:10. Jb 27:23. Ps 47:1. 98:8. Is 55:12. **and said.** 1 K 1:34. Ps 72:15-17. Pr 29:2. Da 3:9. 6:21. Mt 21:9. **God save the king.** Heb. Let the king live. 1 S 10:24mg. 2 S 16:16mg.

13. **when Athaliah.** 2 Ch 23:12-15.

14. **stood by.** The Orientals considered a seat by a pillar or column as particularly honorable. Thus Homer (*Od.* xxiii.) places Ulysses on a lofty throne by a pillar; and in the eighth book of the *Odyssey* he twice alludes to the same custom. See the parallel texts. **a pillar.** 2 K 23:3. 2 Ch 34:31. Called "his pillar" in 2 Ch 23:13 (Young). **trumpeters.** or, trumpets. 2 K 12:13. Nu 10:2, 8, 9, 10. 31:6. 1 Ch 13:8. 15:24, 28. 16:6, 42. **the princes.** ver. 10, 11. See on Nu 10:1-10. **all the people.** 1 K 1:39, 40. 1 Ch 12:40. Pr 29:2. Lk 19:37. Re 19:1-7. **Treason.** ver. 1, 2. 2 K 9:23. 1 K 18:17, 18. or, Conspiracy. 2 K 12:20. 14:19. 15:15, 30. 17:4. 1 K 16:20. 2 Ch 15:12. 23:13mg. 25:27. Is 8:12. Je 11:9. Ezk 22:25.

15. **captains.** ver. 4, 9, 10. 2 Ch 23:9, 14. **officers.** or, inspectors. Nu 31:14, 48. 2 Ch 23:14. **Have.** Ge 9:6. Ex *21:14. Mt 7:2. Ja 2:13. **followeth.** See on ver. 8. **Let.** Ezk 9:7.

16. **by the which.** 2 Ch 23:15. **there was she slain.** Ge 9:6. Jg 1:7. Mt 7:2. Ja 2:13. Re 16:5-7.

17. **made a covenant.** See on ver. 4. Dt 5:2, 3. 29:1-15. Jsh 24:25. 2 Ch 15:12-14. 29:10. 34:31. Ezr 10:3. Ne 5:12, 13. 9:38. 10:28, 29. 2 C 8:5. **between**

the king. 1 S 10:25. 2 S 5:3. 1 Ch 11:3. 2 Ch 23:16. Ro 13:1-6.

18. **went**. 2 K 9:25-28. 10:26. 18:4. 23:4-6, 10, 14. 2 Ch 23:17. 34:4, 7. **brake they**. 2 K 18:4. Ex 32:20. Dt 12:3. 2 Ch 12:17. Is 2:18. Zc 13:2. **images**. Nu 33:52. 1 S 6:5, 11. 2 Ch 23:17. **and slew**. Dt 13:5, 9. 1 K 18:40. 2 Ch 23:17. Zc 13:2, 3. **Mattan**. i.e. *a gift*, *S#4977h. 2 Ch 23:17. Je 38:1. **appointed**. 2 Ch 23:18-20. **officers**. Heb. offices. 1 Ch 26:30. 2 Ch 24:11.

19. **took**. See on ver. 4-11. 2 Ch 23:20. **by the way**. See on ver. 5. 2 Ch 23:5, 19. **he sat**. 1 K 1:13. 1 Ch 29:23. Je 17:25. 22:4, 30. Mt 19:28. 25:31.

20. **rejoiced**. See on ver. 14. 2 Ch 23:21. Pr 11:10. 29:2. **slew Athaliah**. See on ver. 15.

21. **Seven years old**. ver. 4. 2 K 22:1. 2 Ch 24:1, etc.

2 KINGS 12

Jehoash reigns well so long as Jehoiada lives, 1-3. He gives orders that the temple should be repaired; yet the priests neglect the service; but he devises a plan for defraying the expense, and completes the work, 4-16. He gives the consecrated treasures to Hazael, to divert him from assaulting Jerusalem, 17, 18. He is slain by his servants, and succeeded by his son Amaziah, 19-21.

1. **the seventh**. 2 K 9:27. 11:1, 3, 4, 21. 2 Ch 24:1, etc. **Jehoash**. i.e. *whom Jehovah bestowed; Jehovah is foundation*, *S#3060h. ver. 2, 4, 6, 7, 18. 2 K 11:2mg, 21. 13:10, 25. 14:8, 9, 11, 13, 13, 15, 16, 17. 1 Ch 3:11, Joash. The original form of Joash, and applied to two kings. See Joash, Number 3 and 4, 1 Ch +7:8. **forty years**. Like David and Solomon. **Zibiah**. i.e. *a roe*, *S#6645h. 2 Ch 24:1. **Beer-sheba**. Jsh 15:28.

2. **Jehoash did**. 2 K 14:3. 2 Ch 24:2, 17-22. 25:2. 26:4. **instructed**. or, directed. Ge 46:28. Ex 4:12, 15.

3. **high places**. 2 K 14:4. 18:4. 1 K 15:14. 22:43. 2 Ch 31:1. Je 2:20.

4. A.M. 3148. B.C. 856. **said to the priests**. 2 K 22:4. 2 Ch 29:4-11. 35:2. **the money**. 121D5, Ge +23:9. ver. 18. Ge 23:16. 1 K 7:51. 1 Ch 18:11. 2 Ch 15:18. 31:12. **dedicated things**. *or*, holy things. Heb. holinesses. Le 5:15, 16. 27:12-27, 31. **even the money**. Ge 22:4. Ex 30:12-16. 2 Ch 24:9, 10. **that every man is set at**. Heb. of the souls of his estimation. **man**, Heb. *nephesh*, soul, Ge +12:5. Le 27:2-8. **and all the money**. Ex 25:1, 2. 35:5, 22, 29. 36:3. 1 Ch 29:3-9, 17. Ezr 1:6. 2:69. 7:16. 8:25-28. Lk 21:4. **cometh**, etc. Heb. ascendeth upon the heart of a man. Ex 35:5. 1 Ch 29:9. Je +3:16mg. 7:31mg. 171J1. Synecdoche of the Species B629. "To ascend" is used for "to come," or "to enter into the thoughts," or the mind. For other instances of this figure see Je 7:31mg. Ezk 38:10. 1 C 2:9.

5. **Let the priests**. 2 Ch 24:5. **let them repair**. ver. 12. 2 K 22:5, 6. 1 K 11:27. 2 Ch 24:7. Is *58:12.

6. **three and twentieth year**. Heb. twentieth year and third year. **the priests**. 1 S 2:29, 30. 2 Ch 29:24. Is *56:10-12. Ml 1:10. Ph *2:21. 1 P 5:2.

7. **king Jehoash**. 2 Ch 24:5, 6, etc. **Jehoiada**. ver. 2. 2 K 11:4. 2 Ch 23:1. 24:16. **Why repair ye**. 1 Ch 21:3.

8. **consented**. Ge 34:15, 22, 23.

9. **took a chest**. Ge 50:26. Ex 25:10. 2 Ch 24:8,

10, 11. Mk 12:41. **bored**. 2 K 18:21. **hole**. 1 S 14:11. **beside**. 2 Ch 24:10. **the priests**. 2 Ch 22:4. 23:4. 25:18. 1 Ch 15:18, 24. Je 35:4. 52:24. **door**. Heb. threshold. 2 K 23:4. 25:18mg. Jg +19:27. 1 K +14:17. 1 Ch 9:19mg. 2 Ch 34:9. Est 2:21mg. 6:2mg. Ps 84:10mg. Is 6:4mg. Je 35:4mg. 52:24mg.

10. **the king's**. 2 K 19:2. 22:3, 12. 2 S 8:17. 20:25. **scribe**. *or*, secretary. 1 K +4:3mg. **put up**. Heb. bound up. 2 K 5:23. Dt 14:25. **in bags**. Sir J. Chardin informs us (in a MS. note on Tobit 9:5), cited by Mr. Harmer (ch. 18. Ob 89), "it is a custom of Persia always to seal up bags of money; and the money of the king's treasure is not told, but is received by bags sealed up." These are what are called in the East *purses*; each of which, as Maillet informs us, contains money to the amount of 1500 livres, or about 63 *l* of our money. The money thus collected for the reparation of the temple, seems, in like manner, to have been reckoned in bags of equal value to each other; as we can scarcely imagine the placing it in bags would otherwise have been mentioned. The value of a Jewish purse is unknown; but the bags mentioned in 2 K 5:23, amounted to a talent. **and told**. Ge 13:16.

11. **gave the money**. 2 K 22:5, 6. 2 Ch 24:11, 12. 34:9-11. **being told**. or, weighed. Jb 28:25. Ps 75:3. Is *40:12. **laid it out**. Heb. brought it forth. **carpenters**. 2 S 5:11.

12. **masons**. 1 K 5:17, 18. Ezr 3:7. 5:8. Lk 21:5. **was laid out**. Heb. went forth.

13. **there were not**. That is, there were no vessels made for the service of the temple till all the outward repairs were completed; but, when this was done, "they brought the rest of the money before the king and Jehoiada, whereof were made vessels of gold and silver" (2 Ch 24:14), to replace those which had been taken away by Athaliah and her sons. 2 Ch 24:14. **bowls**. Ex 12:22. See on Nu 7:13, 14. 1 K 7:48-50. Ezr 1:9-11. **snuffers**. 1 K 7:50. **basons**. Ex 27:3. 1 K +7:40. **trumpets**. See on Nu 10:2.

15. **they reckoned not**. 2 K 22:7. **for they dealt**. Ex *18:21. 2 Ch 34:12. Ne 7:2. Pr 28:20. Is 52:11. Mt +*24:45. 25:21. Lk 16:1, √10, 11. Ac +*6:3. 1 C +*4:2, 3. 2 C *7:2. √8:20, 21. Ph +*2:12. 2 T *2:2. 3 J *5. **faithfully**. S#530h. 2 K 22:7. Ex 17:12 (steady). +*18:21. Dt 32:4 (truth). 1 S 26:23. 2 Ch 31:12. Ne 5:15. Pr 28:20. La 3:23. Hab *2:4 (by his faith).

16. **trespass money**. Le 5:+*6, 15-18. 7:7. Nu 5:8-10. 18:8, 9. Ho 4:8. **sin money**. or, sin offering money. Ge 4:7. Le +*23:19. **it was**. Le 7:7. Nu 18:9.

17. A.M. 3164. B.C. 840. **Hazael**. See on 2 K 8:12-15. **against Gath**. 1 S 27:2. 1 K 2:39, 40. 1 Ch 8:13. 18:1. **set his face**. Ge 31:21. Je 42:15. Lk 9:51, 53. **to Jerusalem**. 2 Ch 24:23, 24.

18. **took all the hallowed**. He dearly bought, by such unhallowed means, a peace which was of *short duration*; for the next year Hazael returned, and Jehoash having no more treasures, was obliged to hazard a battle, which he lost, and the principal part of his nobility, so that Judah was totally ruined, and Jehoash soon after slain in his bed by his own servants. 2 K 16:8. 18:15, 16. 1 K *15:18. 2 Ch 16:2. **went away**. Heb. went up.

19. **the rest of the acts**. 2 K 8:23. 1 K 11:41. 14:19, 29.

20. **his servants**. 2 K 14:5. 2 Ch 24:24, 25. 25:27. 33:24. **conspiracy**. 2 K +11:14. 1 K 15:27. 2 Ch

24:21. **the house of Millo**. *or*, Beth-millo. Jg 9:6. 2 S 5:9. 1 K 11:27. **Silla**. i.e. *a basket; weighing place*, *S#5538h, only here. 2 Ch 26:16.

21. **Jozachar**. i.e. *Jehovah has remembered*, *S#3108h. This person is called *Zabad* in Chronicles, and Shimeath his mother is said to be an *Ammonitess*; and *Jehozabad* is said to be the son, not of *Shomer*, but of *Shimrith*, a *Moabitess*. Who the fathers of these two persons were we know not; they were probably foreigners and aliens. Some suppose that they belonged to the king's *chamber*, and therefore could have easy access to him. 2 Ch 24:26, Zabad. **Shimeath**. i.e. *hearing; fame, report*, *S#8100h. 2 Ch 24:6. **Jehozabad**. i.e. *Jehovah has endowed*. **Shomer**. i.e. *a keeper; guarding*, *S#7763h. (1) A great-grandson of Asher, 1 Ch 7:32. He is called Shamer in 1 Ch 7:34. (2) A Moabitess whose son Jehozabad was one of the conspirators against King Joash, 2 K 12:21. She is called Shimrith in 2 Ch 24:26, Shimrith. **Amaziah his son**. i.e. *strengthened by Jah*. 2 Ch 24:27.

2 KINGS 13

Jehoahaz reigns wickedly over Israel, 1, 2. Israel is oppressed by Hazael, but relieved in answer to Jehoahaz's prayer, 3-7. Jehoahaz reigns wickedly, dies, and is succeeded by his son Jeroboam, 10-13. An account of a visit paid by Joash to Elisha on his death-bed, who by a sign assured him of three victories over the Syrians, 14-19. Elisha dies; the Moabites invade the land; and a dead man is raised to life, on touching his bones, 20, 21. Hazael, who had oppressed Israel, dies, and Joash gains three victories over his son Ben-hadad, 22-25.

1. **three and twentieth year**. Heb. twentieth year, and third year. 2 K 8:26. 10:36. 11:4, 21. 12:6mg. **Jehoahaz**. i.e. *Jehovah has laid hold*. 2 K 10:35.

2. A.M. 3148-3165. B.C. 856-839. **followed**. Heb. walked after. ver. 11. See on 2 K 10:29. 1 S 17:13, 14. 2 S 3:31. 1 K 12:26-33. 14:8, 16. Ho 5:11.

3. **and he delivered**. Le 26:17. Dt 4:24-27. 27:25. Jg 2:13, 14. 3:7, 8. 10:7-14. Is 10:5, 6. He 12:29. **Hazael**. ver. 22. See on 2 K 8:12, 13. 12:17. 1 K 19:17. **Ben-hadad**. i.e. *son of shouting*. ver. 24, 25. **all their days**. Rather, "all *his* days;" for Joash son of Jehoahaz delivered Israel from Ben-hadad, ver. 25.

4. **Jehoahaz**. Nu 21:7. Jg 6:6, 7. 10:10. Ps *78:34. Is 26:16. Je 2:27. **the Lord**. 2 K *14:26. Ge 21:17. Ex 3:7. Jg 10:15, 16. 2 Ch 33:12, 13, 19. Ps 50:15. 106:43, 44. Je 33:3. **he saw**. Ge 31:42. Ex 3:9. Is 63:9. **because the king**. ver. 22. 2 K 14:26.

5. **a savior**. This *savior* was undoubtedly *Joash*, whose successful wars are subsequently detailed. Houbigant recommends to read the seventh verse after the fourth. ver. 25. 2 K 14:25, 27. Ne *9:27. Is *19:20. Ob *21. Lk 2:11. **beforetime**. Heb. yesterday *and* third day. Ge +*31:2mg. Ex 4:10mg. Dt 19:4mg. Jsh +4:18mg. 1 S 4:7mg. +19:7mg. 2 S 5:2. 1 Ch 11:2mg.

6. **departed**. See on ver. 2. 2 K 10:29. 17:20-23. Dt 32:15-18. **walked**. Heb. he walked. 1 K 15:3. 16:26. **and there remained**. Heb. and there stood. 2 K 17:16. 18:4. 23:4. Dt 7:5. 1 K 16:33. Ec 2:9. **grove**. or, shrine. Made by Ahab, 1 K 16:33, and Jehu had spared (Young).

7. **fifty horsemen**. 1 S 13:6, 7, 15, 19-23. 1 K 20:15, 27. Is 36:8. **the king**. 2 K 8:12. 10:32. **like the dust**.

Ps 18:42. Is 41:2, 15, 16. Jl 3:14mg. Am 1:3.

8. **the rest of the acts**. 2 K 10:34, 35. See on 1 K 11:4. 14:19, 20, 29, 31.

9. A.M. 3165. B.C. 839. **slept with**. 1 K +*11:43. **buried him**. ver. 13. 2 K 10:35. 1 K 14:13. **Joash**. ver. 10. 2 K 14:8, Jehoash. **reigned in his stead**. "Alone."

10. **In the thirty**. Joash, the son of Jehoahaz, was associated with his father in the government two years before his death. It is this association that is spoken of here. Joash reigned *sixteen* years, which include the years he governed conjointly with his father. **began Jehoash**. "In consort with his father, 2 K 14:1."

11. **he departed**. See on ver. 2, 6. 2 K 3:3. 10:29.

12. A.M. 3163-3179. B.C. 841-825. **the rest**. ver. 14-25. 2 K 14:15, 25. **his might**. 2 K 14:8-16. 2 Ch 25:17-24.

13. **slept with his fathers**. Ge +*25:8n. Dt 31:16n. 2 S 7:12. 1 K 1:21. 2:10. 11:31, +*43. +14:20. **Jeroboam**. 2 K 14:28, 29. **was buried**. See on ver. 9.

14. A.M. 3166. B.C. 838. **fallen sick**. ſ147D, Ge +1:29. 2 K 20:1. Ge 48:1. Is +*38:1. Jn 11:3. Ph 2:26, 27. 2 T *4:20. **sickness**. Dt 7:15. **he died**. Ps 12:1. Is 57:1. Zc 1:5. Ac 13:36. **O my father**. 2 K *2:12. 6:21. Pr 11:11. Ezk 14:14. 22:30. Mk 6:20. **the chariot**. 2 K +2:11n.

16. **Put thine hand**. Heb. make thine hand to ride. 2 S 6:3. **Elisha**. 2 K 4:34. Ge 49:24. Ps 144:1.

17. **Open**. 2 K 5:10-14. Jn 2:5-8. 11:39-41. **eastward**. Ge 13:14. **The arrow**. ſ121M, Ex +8:23. i.e. the sign of the future deliverance which the Lord would work for His People (EWB, B586). This was a *symbolical action*, indicative of the deliverance of Israel from Syria. It was an ancient custom to shoot an arrow or cast a spear into a country before the commencement of hostilities. Virgil (Aen. l. ix. v.51) represents Turnus as giving the signal of attack by *throwing* a spear; upon which Servius shows that it was a custom to proclaim war in this way. The *pater patratus*, or chief of the *Feciales*, a sort of herald, went to the confines of the enemy's country; and, after some solemnities, said with a loud voice, "I wage war with you, for such and such reasons," and then *threw a spear*. If the parties defied did not come to some accommodation within thirty days, the war was begun. Ex 4:2, 17. Jg 7:9-20. 2 S 5:24. Ps 144:1. 1 C 1:18. **Aphek**. 1 S 4:1. 1 K 20:26, 30.

18. **Smite**. Is 20:2-4. Ezk 4:1-10. 5:1-4. 12:1-7. **he smote thrice**. 2 K 4:6. Ex 17:11. **and stayed**. Lk ●+=11:9. Ja=1:6, 7. 4:2.

19. **the man of God**. 2 K 1:9-15. 4:16, 40. 6:9. **was wroth**. Le 10:16. Nu 16:15. Mk 3:5. 10:14. **shouldest have**. 1 S +*23:4. Is *62:6, 7. Lk +*11:9. **then hadst**. Mt 11:23n. Lk 19:42. Jn=4:10. Ep +=3:20. **now thou shalt**. ver. 25. Mk 6:5.

20. A.M. 3167. B.C. 837. **buried him**. 2 Ch 24:16. Ac 8:2. **the bands**. 2 K 5:2. 6:23. 24:2. **the Moabites**. 2 K 3:5, 24-27. Jg 3:12. 6:3-6.

21. **sepulchre**. Heb. *qeber*, Ge +23:4. **was let down**. Heb. went *down*. **touched**. 2 K 4:35. Is 26:19. Ezk 37:1-10. Mt 27:52, 53. Jn +*5:25, 28, 29. 11:44. Ac 5:15, 16. 19:12. Re 11:11.

22. A.M. 3148-3165. B.C. 856-839. **Hazael**. ver. 3-7. 2 K 8:12. Ps 106:40-42.

23. **the Lord**. 2 K 14:27. Ex 33:19. 34:6, 7. Jg 10:16. Ne 9:31. Ps 86:15. Is 30:18, 19. Je 12:15. La 3:32.

Mi 7:18, 19. **had respect**. Ex 2:24, 25. 1 K 8:28. **because of his covenant**. Ge 13:16, 17. 17:2-5, 7, 8. Ex 3:6, 7. 32:13, 14. Le 26:42. Dt 32:36. Ne 9:32. Ps 105:8. Mi *7:18-20. Lk 1:54, 55, 72, 73. **neither cast he**. 2 K 17:18. 24:20. Ps 51:11. La *3:31, 32. Mt 25:41. Ro +*11:1. 2 Th 1:9. **presence**. Heb. face. Ge 3:8. 6:3.

24. **Hazael**. Ps 125:3. Lk 18:7.

25. A.M. 3168. B.C. 836. **took again**. Heb. returned and took. 2 Ch 19:4. **Three times**. ver. 18, 19. Am 1:4.

2 KINGS 14

Amaziah reigns well, yet not like David, 1-4. He justly punishes his father's murderers, 5, 6. He gains a victory over Edom, 7. He rashly challenges Jehoash king of Israel, and, obstinately persisting, is vanquished and taken prisoner by him; the wall of Jerusalem is broken down, and the treasures of the temple spoiled, 8-14. Jehoash dies, and is succeeded by Jeroboam, 15, 16. Amaziah is slain by conspirators, 17-20. His son Azariah is made king, and builds Elath, 21, 22. Jeroboam's wicked reign, 23, 24. He restores the coast of Israel, 25-27. He dies and is succeeded by his son Zachariah, 28, 29.

1. A.M. 3165. B.C. 839. **Joash**. ver. 15. 2 K 13:10. **reigned Amaziah**. 1 Ch 3:12. 2 Ch 25:1, etc.

2. **Jehoaddan**. i.e. *Lord of pleasure* (*S#3086h). 2 Ch 25:1.

3. A.M. 3165-3194. B.C. 839-810. **he did**. 2 K 12:2. 1 K 11:4. 15:3. 2 Ch 25:2, 3. **he did according**. 2 Ch 24:2, 17. 25:14-16. Je 16:19. Zc 1:4-6. 1 P 1:18.

4. **the high places**. 2 K 12:3. 15:4, 35.

5. A.M. 3166. B.C. 838. **that he slew**. Ge 9:6. Ex 21:12-14. Nu 35:33. **his servants**. 2 K 12:20, 21. 2 Ch 25:3, 4.

6. **The fathers**. Dt)24:16. Je 2:8n. Ezk +*18:4n, 20n. These references to the very words of the law, as they now stand in the books of Moses, should not be unnoticed. Undoubtedly these books were extant, and well known, when this history was written (Scott). 2 K 11:12. 2 Ch 14:4. 17:9. 25:4. 34:14n. **for his own sin**. T#159. Dt 24:16. 2 Ch 25:4. Jb 19:4. Ezk *18:2, 20. Is 3:11. Je 31:29, *30. Ga 6:5.

7. A.M. 3177. B.C. 827. **slew**. 2 K 8:20-22. 2 Ch 25:11, 12. **the valley of salt**. Some suppose that the *Valley of Salt* was south of the Dead, or Salt sea, towards the land of Edom; and others suppose it to be the Valley of Salt, about three or four miles south-east of Palmyra, which now supplies, in a great measure, the surrounding country with salt. 2 S 8:13. 1 Ch 18:12. Ps 60, title. **Selah**. *or*, the rock (*S#5554h). Jsh ◐15:38. Jg 1:36n. 2 Ch 25:12. Is 16:1h. *Selah* is generally supposed to be the same as *Petra*, which in Greek signifies a *rock*, the celebrated capital of Arabia Petraea. Strabo (l. xvi.) places it three or four days' journey from Jericho, and five days' journey from the forest of palm trees on the Red sea. Pliny (l. vi. c. 28) places it 600 miles from Gaza, and 125 from the Persian gulf; but Cellarius and Reland very justly consider that the numbers have been changed, and that we ought to read 125 miles from Gaza, and 600 from the Persian gulf. Eusebius places Beerothbene-jaakan 30 miles west from *Petra*, and Elath ten miles east; and Burckhardt (*Travels in Syria*, etc., pp. 429-433) discovered the

ruins of this ancient city in a valley called *Wady Mousa*. **Joktheel**. Jsh 15:38. **unto this day**. 2 K 2:22. 8:22n. 16:6. Jsh +*4:9.

8. A.M. 3178. B.C. 826. **Amaziah**. 2 Ch 25:17-24. **Come**. ver. 11. 2 S 2:14-17. Pr 13:10. 17:14. 18:6. 20:18. 25:8. **look**. ♪108B. Idiom B827. "To see another" is used for making war with him, or of meeting him in battle. For other instances of this idiom see ver. 11. 2 K 14:11. 23:29.

9. **The thistle**. Jg 9:8-15. 2 S 12:1-4. 1 K 4:33. Ezk 20:49. The word *choach*, which is rendered here, and in 2 Ch 25:18. Jb 31:18, *thistle*, in 1 S 13:6, *thicket*, in Is 34:13, *bramble*, and in 2 Ch 33:11. Pr 26:9. SS 2:2. Ho 9:6, *thorn*, is probably the *black thorn*, or *sloe tree*, the *prunus spinosa* of Linnaeus, as the same word signifies in Arabic (See Celsius, *Hierbot*. P. I. p. 477). There is a vast deal of insolent dignity in this remonstrance of Jehoash; but it has nothing conciliatory; no proposal of making amends for the injury his army had done to the unoffending inhabitants of Judah (2 Ch 25:10-13). The comparatively useless thorn, which may by chance lacerate the incautious passenger, is made the emblem of the house of Judah and David, while the house of Jehu is represented by the stately cedar.

10. **thine heart**. Dt 8:14. 2 Ch 26:16. 32:25. Pr 16:18. Ezk 28:2, 5, 17. Da 5:20-23. Hab 2:4. Ja 4:6. **glory of this**. Ex 8:9. Je 9:23, 24. Ja 1:9. **home**. Heb. thy house. **why shouldest**. 2 Ch 35:21. Pr 3:30. 15:18. *17:14. *20:3. *25:8. 26:17. Lk *14:31, 32.

11. **Amaziah**. 2 Ch 25:16, 20. **looked**. ♪108B, ver. 8. **Beth-shemesh**. Jsh 15:10. 19:38. 21:9, 13, *16. 1 S 6:9, 12.

12. **was put to the worse**. Heb. was smitten. 1 S 4:10. Pr *16:18. 29:23. **they fled**. 1 S 4:10. 2 S 18:17. 1 K 22:36.

13. **took Amaziah**. 2 K 25:6. 2 Ch 33:11. 36:6, 10. Jb 40:11, 12. Pr 16:18. 29:23. Is 2:11, 12. Da 4:37. Lk 14:11. **the gate of Ephraim**. 2 Ch 25:23, 24. Ne 8:16. 12:39. **the corner**. 2 Ch 26:9. Ne 3:13. Je 31:38. Zc 14:10.

14. **all the gold**. 2 K 24:13. 25:15. 1 K 7:51. 14:26. 15:18. **and hostages**. 2 K 18:23mg. 2 Ch 25:4.

15. A.M. 3163-3179. B.C. 841-825. **the rest**. 2 K 10:34, 35. 13:12. 1 K 14:19, 20. **conspiracy**. 2 K +11:14.

16. A.M. 3179. B.C. 825. **Jehoash slept with**. See on 2 S 7:12. 1 K 1:21. +*11:43. **was buried**. See on 2 K 13:9. **Jeroboam**. 2 K 13:13. Ho 1:1. Am 1:1. 7:10, 11.

17. A.M. 3779-3194. B.C. 825-810. **Amaziah**. ver. 1, 2, 23. 2 K 13:10. 2 Ch 25:25, etc.

18. **the rest**. 2 K 13:8, 12. 1 K 11:41. 14:29.

19. A.M. 3194. B.C. 810. **they made**. 2 K 12:20, 21. 15:10, 14, 25, 30. 21:23. 2 Ch 25:27, 28. **conspiracy**. 2 K +11:14. **fled to Lachish**. Jsh 10:31. Mi 1:13.

20. **he was buried**. 2 K 8:24. 9:28. 12:21. 1 K 2:10. +*11:43. 2 Ch 21:20. 26:23. 33:20.

21. **Azariah**. i.e. *help of Jah*. 2 K 15:13. 2 Ch 26:1, Uzziah. i.e. *strength of Jah*. Is 1:1. 6:1. Mt 1:8, 9, Ozias. **made him king**. 2 Ch 21:24. 1 Ch 3:12.

22. **Elath**. *Elath*, the *Aela* or *Elana* of the Greek and Roman writers, was a celebrated port situated at the extremity of the eastern branch of the Red sea, hence called the "Elanitic gulf," ten miles east from Petra, according to Eusebius, and 150 Roman miles from Gaza, according to Pliny, but 1260 stadia, or 157

miles, according to Strabo and Marcianus Herecleota. It is now called *Akaba*, and is nothing but a tower or castle, surrounded by a large grove of date trees, the residence of a governor dependent on him of Grand Cairo (See Burckhardt's *Travels in Syria*, etc. pp. 509-511). 2 K 16:6. Dt 2:8. 1 K 9:26. 2 Ch 26:2, Eloth.

23. A.M. 3179-3220. B.C. 825-784. **the fifteenth**. ver. 17. **Jeroboam**. ver. 27. Ho 1:1. Am 1:1. 7:9-11. **began to reign**. "Now he begins to reign alone."

24. **in the sight**. 2 K 21:6. Ge 38:7. Dt 9:18. 1 K 21:25. **he departed**. See on 2 K 13:2, 6, 11. 1 K 12:28, etc. Ps 106:20. **who made**. 1 K 14:16.

25. **from the entering of Hamath**. Nu 13:21. 34:7, 8. Dt 3:17. 1 K 8:65. Ezk 47:16-18. Am 6:14. **unto the sea**. Ge 14:3. Dt 3:17. **of the plain**. Dt +*11:30. Jsh 3:16. **by the hand**. 2 K 9:36mg. 10:10mg. 19:23mg. 1 K +16:12mg. **Jonah**. i.e. *a dove*. Jon 1:1. Mt 12:39, 40. 16:4, Jonas. **Amittai**. i.e. *true, steadfast*. *S#573h: 2 K 14:25. Jon 1:1. **Gath-hepher**. i.e. *wine-press of the well*. S#1662h. Jsh 19:13, Gittah-hepher. Jn 7:52. In Zebulun, in Galilee.

26. **saw the affliction**. 2 K 13:4. Ex 3:7, 9. Jg 10:16. Ps 106:43-45. Is 63:9. **bitter**. lit. "rebellious." Nu 20:10. Dt *21:18, 20. Ps 78:8. Je *5:23. **not any shut**. Dt 32:36. 1 K 14:10. 21:21. **any helper**. Jb *29:12. 30:13. Ps 22:11mg. 72:12. Is 63:5. La 1:7. Da 11:45.

27. **said not**. 2 K *13:23. Ho 1:6. **blot out**. Ex 32:32, 33. Dt 9:14. 25:19. 29:20. Ps 69:28. Ro *11:+√1, 2, etc. Re 3:5. **he saved**. 2 K 5:1. 13:5. Ho 1:7. T 3:4-6.

28. **the rest**. See on ver. 15. **Damascus**. 2 S 8:6. 1 K 11:24. 1 Ch 18:5, 6. 2 Ch 8:3, 4. **which belonged to Judah**. These places belonged to Judah by David's conquest (2 S 3:11), but had been repossessed by the Syrians.

29. A.M. 3220. B.C. 784. **Jeroboam slept with**. 1 K +*11:43. **Zachariah**. i.e. *remembered by Jah*. (1) A king of Israel, the son of Jeroboam II, killed by Shallum after a reign of six months, B.C. 773. 2 K 15:8-11. (2) A prophet who lived after the Babylonish captivity. Son of Barachiah, grandson of Iddo the prophet, Zc 1:1, 7. Ezr 5:1. 6:14. (3) A son of Barachiah, contemporary with Isaiah, Is 8:2. (4) A prophet, the son of Jehoiada, slain in the court of the temple, in the reign of Joash, 2 Ch 24:20. (5) A prophet living at Jerusalem in the reign of Uzziah, 2 Ch 26:5. *S#2148h: rendered "Zachariah," "Zechariah." 2 K 14:29. 15:11. 1 Ch 9:21, 37. 15:20. 16:5. 2 Ch 17:7. 24:20. 34:12. Ezr 8:3, 11, 16. 10:26. Ne 8:4. 11:4, 5, 12. 12:16, 35, 41. Zc 1:1, 7. 7:1, 8. **reigned**. "After an interregnum of eleven years."

2 KINGS 15

Azariah's good reign, 1-4. He is smitten with leprosy, and Jotham his son governs for him, and succeeds him, 5-7. Zachariah, the last of Jehu's generation, reigns ill, and is slain by Shallum; and the fulfillment of the word of God to Jehu is noticed, 8-12. After one month, Shallum is slain, and succeeded by Menahem; who treats his opposers with savage cruelty; reigns wickedly; becomes tributary to Pul, king of Assyria; dies, and is succeeded by his son Pekahiah, 13-22. Pekahaiah reigns ill, and is slain and succeeded by Pekah, 23-26. Pekah imitates the sins of his predecessor; Tiglath-pileser of Assyria, carries captive part of Israel; and Hoshea kills and succeeds Pekah, 27-31.

Jotham reigns well in Judah, 32-35. He dies, and is succeeded by his son Ahaz, 36-38.

1. A.M. 3194. B.C. 810. **In the**. ver. 8. 2 K 14:16, 17. **twenty and seventh**. "This is the twenty-seventh year of Jeroboam's partnership in the kingdom with his father, who made him consort at his going to the Syrian wars. It is the sixteenth year of Jeroboam's monarchy." **Azariah**. ver. 13, 30, etc. 2 K 14:21. 2 Ch 26:1, 3, 4, Uzziah.

2. **Sixteen years old**. 2 Ch 26:3, 4.

3. **he did that which was right**. 2 K 12:2, 3. 14:3, 4. 2 Ch 26:4.

4. **the high places**. ver. 35. 2 K 14:4. 18:4. 1 K 15:14. 22:43. 2 Ch 17:6. 32:12. 34:3.

5. A.M. 3239-3246. B.C. 765-758. **the Lord**. 2 S 3:29. 2 Ch *26:16-20. Jb 34:19. **so that**. 2 K 5:27. Nu 12:10. **and dwelt**. 2 K 7:3. Le 13:46. Nu 12:14. Dt 24:8. **Jotham**. 2 Ch 26:21, 23. **judging**. 2 S 8:15. 15:2-4. 1 K 3:9, 28. Ps 72:1.

6. **the rest**. 2 Ch 26:22, 23. **Azariah**. Dr. Kennicott complains loudly here of "the corruption in the name of this king of Judah, who is expressed by *four* different names in this chapter: *Ozriah, Oziah, Ozrihu*, and *Ozihu*." Our oldest Hebrew MS. relieves us here, by reading truly, in verses 1, 6, 7, *Uzziah*, where the printed text is differently corrupted. This reading is called *true*, (1) Because it is supported by the Syriac and Arabic versions in these three verses. (2) Because the printed text itself has it so in ver. 32 and 34 of this very chapter. (3) Because it is so expressed in the parallel place in Chronicles; and (4) because it is not "Adzarias," *Azarias*, but "Odzias," *Ozias* (Uzziah) in St. Matthew's genealogy. **they not written**. See on 2 K 14:18. 2 Ch 26:5-15.

7. A.M. 3246. B.C. 758. **Azariah**. 2 Ch 26:23. Is 6:1, Uzziah. **slept with**. 1 K +*11:43.

8. A.M. 3231. B.C. 773. **the thirty**. "There having been an interregnum for eleven years." ver. 1. 2 K 14:16, 17, 21. **Zachariah**. 2 K 14:29. .

9. **as his**. See on 2 K 10:29, 31. 13:2, 11. 14:24.

10. A.M. 3232. B.C. 772. **Shallum**. i.e. *recompense; restitution; retribution*, *S#7967h. (1) An Israelite who slew Zachariah, king of Israel, and reigned in his stead: 2 K 15:10, 13, 14, 15. (2) The husband of Huldah the prophetess, 2 K 22:14; 2 Ch 34:22. (3) A descendant of Jerahmeel, 1 Ch 2:40, 41. (4) A son of Josiah, king of Judah, 1 Ch 3:15; Je 22:11. Called Jehoahaz in 2 K 23:31-34; 2 Ch 36:1-4. (5) A grandson of Simeon, the son of Jacob, 1 Ch 4:25. (6) A priest whose son Hilkiah found the book of the law in the Temple, 1 Ch 6:12, 13; Ezr 7:2. (7) One of the sons of Naphtali, 1 Ch 7:13. See Shillem. (8) Head of a family of Levite porters in the Tabernacle: 1 Ch 9:17, 19. Ezr 2:42. Ne 7:45. (9) A Levite porter in the Tabernacle, 1 Ch 9:19, 31. (10) One of the chief Ephraimites, 2 Ch 28:12. (11) A Levite porter who had taken a foreign wife, Ezr 10:24. (12) A Jew who had taken a foreign wife, Ezr 10:42. (13) A Jew who repaired part of the wall of Jerusalem, Ne 3:12. (14) A Benjamite, uncle of Jeremiah the prophet, Je 32:7. (15) One of the Temple doorkeepers, Je 35:4. **Jabesh**. i.e. *dry; shame*, *S#3003h. ver. 13, 14. **smote him**. "As prophesied, Am 7:9." **slew him**. ver. 14, 25, 30. 2 K 9:24, 31. 1 K 15:28. 16:9, 10. Ho 1:4, 5.

11. **the rest**. See on 2 K 14:28.

12. A.M. 3120. B.C. 884. **the word**. 2 K 10:30.

Thy son. 2 K 13:1, 10, 13. 14:29. **And so.** 2 K 9:25, 26, 36, 37. 10:10. Nu 23:19. Zc 1:6. Mk 13:31. Jn *10:35. 19:24, 36, 37. Ac 1:16.

13. A.M. 3232. B.C. 772. **Uzziah.** ver. 1, Azariah. Mt 1:8, 9, Ozias. **a full month.** Heb. a month of days. Ge 41:1. Dt 21:13. 1 K 16:15. Jb 20:15. Ps 55:23. Pr 28:2, 17. Da 10:2.

14. **Menahem.** i.e. *a comforter,* ✳S#4505h. ver. 16, 17, 19, 20, 21, 22, 23. **Gadi.** i.e. *a Gadite; troop of God,* ✳S#1424h. ver. 17. **Tirzah.** Jsh 12:24. 1 K 14:17. 15:21, 33. 16:8, 9, 15, 17. **and smote.** See on ver. 10.

15. **the rest.** See on ver. 11. 1 K 14:19, 29. 22:39.

16. **Tiphsah.** i.e. *a passage over; ford,* ✳S#8607h. 1 K 4:24. **all the women.** 2 K 8:12. Ho 13:16. Am 1:13.

17. A.M. 3232-3243. B.C. 772-761. **nine and thirtieth.** ver. 13.

18. **evil in the sight.** See on ver. 9. **who made Israel.** 1 K 14:16.

19. A.M. 3233. B.C. 771. **Pul.** i.e. *a lord, elephant,* or bean, ✳S#6322h. Prideaux supposes that this *Pul* was the father of the famous *Sardanapalus,* who was called *Sardan* with his father's name annexed, as was frequent in those times, making "Sardanpul;" thus Merodach, king of Babylon, was Merodach-Baladan, because he was the son of Baladan. This *Pul* began to reign, according to Usher, A.M. 3237, the fifth year of Menahem; and he is supposed to be the same that reigned in Nineveh, when Jonah preached in that city. 1 Ch 5:25, 26. Is ❍*9:1. 66:19. **Menahem.** 2 K 12:18. 16:8. 17:3, 4. 18:16. Ho 5:13. 8:9, 10. 10:6. **to confirm.** 2 K 14:5. Je 17:5.

20. **Menahem.** 2 K 23:35. **exacted.** Heb. caused to come forth. **the mighty.** Ru 2:1. 2 S 19:32. Jb 1:3. **of each man,** etc. Or rather, as Bishop Patrick renders, "to give to the king of Assyria fifty shekels of silver for each man," i.e. in his army. It may be supposed, that Menahem compelled "the mighty men of wealth" to give much more a piece than this sum, and each of them in some proportion to his affluence. **stayed not.** ver. 29. 2 K 17:3, 4. 2 K 18:14-17.

21. A.M. 3232-3243. B.C. 772-761. See on ver. 15.

22. **Menahem slept with.** 1 K +*11:43. **Pekahiah.** i.e. *opened by Jah,* ✳S#6494h. ver. 23, 26.

23. A.M. 3243. B.C. 761. **and reigned two years.** 2 K 21:19. 1 K 15:25. 16:8. 22:51. Jb 20:5.

24. A.M. 3243-3245. B.C. 761-759. **evil in.** See on ver. 9, 18.

25. A.M. 3245. B.C. 759. **Pekah.** i.e. *opening; open-eyed,* ✳S#6492h. ver. *27, 29, 30, 31, 32, 37. 2 K 16:1, 5. 2 Ch *28:6. Is *7:1. **Remaliah.** i.e. *whom Jehovah adores,* ✳S#7425h. ver. 27, 30, 32, 37. 2 K 16:1, 5. 2 Ch 28:6. Is 7:1, 4, 5, 9. 8:6. **a captain.** 2 K 9:5. 1 K 16:9. **conspired.** ver. 10. 2 K 9:14. **in the palace of.** 1 K 16:18. 2 Ch 36:19. **with Argob.** From the construction of the Hebrew text, it would appear that Argob and Arieh were slain with the king, and that the fifty Gileadites were conspirators with Pekah. **Arieh.** i.e. *the lion,* ✳S#745h.

26. **the rest.** See on ver. 15.

27. A.M. 3245-3265. B.C. 750-739. **the two and fiftieth.** ver. 2, 8, 13, 23. **Pekah.** ver. 25, 37. Is 7:1, 4, 9.

28. **evil.** or, the evil thing. That is, idolatry. See on ver. 9, 18. 2 K 13:2, 6. 21:2.

29. **Tiglath-pileser.** i.e. *lord of the Tigris,* ✳S#8407h. Some suppose Tiglath-pileser to be the son of Sardanapalus: but the learned Prideaux makes him the same as *Arbaces* the Mede, called by Aelian (Hist. Anim. l. xii. c. 12), Thelgamus, and by Castor, Ninus Junior, who, with Belesis, headed the conspiracy against Sardanapalus, and fixed his royal seat at Nineveh, as *Belesis,* called in Scripture *Baladan* (Is 39:1), did his at Babylon. He reigned nineteen years, from A.M. 3257 to A.M. 3276. 2 K 16:7, 10. 1 Ch 5:6, 26. 2 Ch 28:20, 21, Tiglath-pilneser. Is 9:1. **Ijon.** 1 K 15:20. 2 Ch 16:4. **Abel-beth-maachah.** 2 S 20:14, 15. 1 K 15:20. **Janoah.** i.e. *rest,* ✳S#3239h. Jsh 16:6, 7, Janohah. **Kedesh.** Jsh 19:37. +20:7n. **Hazor.** Jsh 11:1, 10, 13. 12:19. Jg 4:2. **Gilead.** Nu 32:1, 40. Dt 3:15. Am 1:3, 13. **Galilee.** Jsh 20:7n. 1 K 9:11. Is 9:1, 2. Mt 4:15, 16. **carried them.** 2 K 17:6, 23. Le *26:32, 38, 39. Dt *4:26, 27. *28:25, 64, 65. Is 1:7. 7:20. Thus beginning the threatened captivity of the ten tribes (Young).

30. A.M. 3265. B.C. 739. **Hoshea.** i.e. *ease, safety,* ✢S#1954h. (1) The name which Joshua, the servant and successor of Moses, bore before Moses changed it to Joshua, Dt 32:44. See Oshea, Nu +13:8. (2) The last of the kings of Israel, who was subdued and imprisoned by Shalmaneser, king of Assyria: 2 K 15:30. 17:1, 3, 4, 6. 18:1, 9, 10. (3) A ruler of the tribe of Ephraim, 1 Ch 27:20. (4) A Jew who sealed the covenant, Ne 10:23. **Elah.** i.e. *an oak.* **made.** See on ver. 10, 25. **conspiracy.** 2 K +11:14. **and smote.** Ho 10:3, 7, 15. **reigned.** "After an anarchy for some years, 2 K 17:1. Ho 10:3, 7, 15." **in the twentieth.** "In the fourth year of Ahaz, in the twentieth year after Jotham had begun to reign: Usher." ver. 32, 33. 2 K 16:1. 17:1. 2 Ch 27:1. 28:4-6, 16. Is 7:1-9. 8:6.

32. A.M. 3246. B.C. 758. **Jotham.** ver. 7. 1 Ch 3:12. 2 Ch 27:1, etc. Mt 1:9, Joatham. **Uzziah.** See on ver. 1, 7, 13, 17, 23, 27. 2 K 14:21. 1 Ch 3:12, Azariah.

33. A.M. 3246-3262. B.C. 758-742. **Jerusha.** i.e. *a possession,* ✳S#3387h. 2 Ch 27:1, Jerushah. **Zadok.** i.e. *righteous.*

34. **according.** ver. 3, 4. 2 Ch 26:4, 5. 27:2.

35. **Howbeit.** See on ver. 4. 2 K 18:4. 2 Ch 32:12. **the higher gate.** 2 Ch 23:20. 27:3.

36. **the rest.** See on ver. 6, 7. 2 Ch 27:4-9.

37. A.M. 3262. B.C. 742. **In those days.** "At the end of Jotham's reign." This Jotham died at forty-one. He was too great a blessing to be continued long to such an unworthy people. His death was a judgment, especially considering the character of Ahaz, his son and successor: for we read (2 K 16:3) Ahaz made his son pass through the fire. This son may have been Hezekiah, who served the Lord, and whose prayer in sickness was most graciously heard and answered. Is ch. 38. **began.** 2 K 10:32. 1 S 3:12. Je 25:29. Lk 21:28. **to send.** Dt 28:48. Ps 78:49. Is 10:5-7. Je 16:16. 43:10. **Rezin.** i.e. *a prince; stable, firm,* ✳S#7526h. 2 K 16:5, 6, 9. 2 Ch ❍28:6. Ezr 2:48. Ne 7:50. Is 7:1, 4, 8. 8:6. 9:11. Ho ❍5:12, 13. (1) A king of Syria, 2 K 15:37; Is 7:1. (2) An Israelite some of whose descendants returned with Zerubbabel, Ezr 2:48; Ne 7:50. **Pekah.** See on ver. 27.

38. **Jotham.** See on 2 S 7:12. 1 K 1:2. 14:20, 31. 2 Ch 27:9. **Ahaz.** i.e. *he laid hold.* 2 K 16:1. 1 Ch 3:13. 2 Ch 28:1. Mt 1:9, Achaz.

2 KINGS 16

Ahaz reigns very wickedly, 1-4. Rezin and Pekah war against him; and Rezin takes Elath, 5, 6. Ahaz hires Tiglath-pileser against them, who takes Damascus and slays Rezin, 7-9. Ahaz sends a pattern of an altar from Damascus; and Urijah, the high priest, makes one like it for burnt offerings; reserving the brazen altar for Ahaz to inquire by, 10-16. Ahaz robs and defaces the temple for the king of Assyria, 17, 18. He dies, and is succeeded by his son Hezekiah, 19, 20.

1. **seventeenth.** 2 K 15:27-30, 32, 33. **Ahaz.** See on 2 K 15:38. 2 Ch 28:1, etc. Is 1:1. 7:1. Ho 1:1. Mi 1:1.

2. **did not.** 2 K 14:3. 15:3, 34. 18:3. 22:2. 1 K 3:14. 9:4. 11:4-8. 15:3. 2 Ch 17:3. 29:2. 34:2, 3.

3. **he walked.** (T#359). 2 K 8:18. 1 K 12:28-30. 16:31-33. 21:25, 26. 22:52, 53. 2 Ch 22:3. 28:2-4. Ro 1:21-24, 29-31. Ep 4:17-19. **made his son.** 2 K 17:17. +21:6. 23:10. Le *18:21. 20:2. Dt *12:31. +*18:10. 2 Ch 33:6. Ps *106:37, 38. Je 32:35. Ezk 16:21. 20:26, 31. **according.** 2 K 21:2, 11. Dt 12:31. 1 K 14:24. 2 Ch 33:2. Ps 106:35. Ezk 16:47. **abominations.** Ge 43:32. 46:34. Ex 8:26. **cast out.** Ex 34:24.

4. **he sacrificed.** 2 K 14:4. **high places.** 2 K +21:3. 1 K 3:2. **on the hills.** 2 K +*17:10. Dt 12:2. 1 K 14:23. Is 57:5-7. 65:4. 66:17. Je 17:2. Ezk 20:28, 29. Such places were frequented for pagan worship by the ancient Greeks, Romans, etc. (Young). **green tree.** Dt 12:2. Is +1:29. The *oak* anciently was reckoned sacred to Jupiter, the *laurel* to Apollo, the *ivy* to Bacchus, the *olive* to Minerva, the *myrtle* to Venus, etc. (Young).

5. A.M. 3262. B.C. 742. **Rezin.** 2 K 15:37. 2 Ch 28:5-15. Is 7:1, 2, etc. **but could not.** 1 K 11:36. 15:4. Is 7:4-6, *14. 8:6, 9, 10. *9:6, 7.

6. **recovered.** 2 K 14:22. Dt 2:8. **and drave.** Ex 3:5. Dt 7:1, 22. 28:40. **Elath.** Heb. Eloth. 1 K 9:26. 2 Ch 26:2. **unto this day.** 2 K 2:22. 8:22n. 14:7. Jsh +*4:9.

7. **Tiglath-pileser.** Heb. Tilgath-pileser. See on 2 K 15:29. 1 Ch 5:26, etc. 2 Ch 28:20, Tilgath-pilneser. **I am thy servant.** 1 K 20:4, 32, 33. **and save.** Ps 146:3-5. Je *17:5. La 4:17. Ho 5:13. 7:11. 8:9. 11:5. 12:1. 14:3.

8. **the silver.** ver. 17, 18. 2 K 12:17, 18. 18:15, 16. 2 Ch 16:2. 28:20, 21. **to the king.** Ps 7:15, 16. Is 7:17. 8:7, 8. **for a present.** or, bribe. Ex 23:8. 1 K 15:19.

9. A.M. 3264. B.C. 740. **went up.** 2 Ch 28:5. Foretold Am 1:3-5. **Damascus.** Heb. Dammesek. ver. 10, 11. 1 K 11:24. 1 Ch 18:5. 2 Ch 28:5. **Kir.** Josephus informs us that this place was in Upper Media; and it is clear that it must be understood of some city or country in the dominions of the king of Assyria. It is highly probable that it was the country on the banks of the river *Kuros, Cyrus,* or *Kyrus,* now called *Kur,* or *Kura;* and we find cities called *Cyropolis, Cyrena,* and *Carine,* mentioned by writers as lying in these parts; and a part of Media, called *Syromedia,* as it is thought, from the Syrians who were carried captive thither (See Michaelis, *Supplement.* p. 2191). Is 22:6. Am 1:5. 9:7. **slew Rezin.** Is 7:16. 9:11.

10. **saw an altar.** Dt *12:30. 2 Ch 28:23-25. Je +√10:2. Ezk 23:16, 17. Ro *12:2. 1 P 1:18. **Urijah.** i.e. *light of Jah.* Is 8:2. **the pattern.** Ex 24:4. 39:43.

1 Ch 28:11, 12, 19. Ps 106:39. Ezk 43:8, 11. Mt 15:6, 9.

11. **built an altar.** Contrary to the law of God, and apparently without hesitation (Young). 1 K 21:11-13. 2 Ch 26:17, 18. Je 23:11. Ezk 22:26. Da 3:7. Ho 4:6. 5:11. Ml 2:7-9. Ga 1:10. **Urijah.** Is 8:2.

12. **approached.** 1 K 13:1. 2 Ch 26:16-19. 28:23, 25. **offered thereon.** Nu 18:4-7.

13. **he burnt.** Le ch. 1-3. **burnt offering.** Le +*23:12. **meat offering.** Le +*23:13. **drink offering.** Le +*23:13. **sprinkled.** Ex 9:8, 10. 24:6, 8. 29:16, 20. **of his peace offerings.** Heb. of the peace offerings which *were* his. Le +*23:19. 1 S 24:4.

14. **the brasen.** Ex 40:6, 29. 2 Ch 1:5. 4:1. Mt 23:35. **the altar.** ver. 10-12. **on the north side.** Young notes, out of view.

15. **the morning.** 2 K *3:20. Ex 29:39-41. Nu 28:2-10. Da 9:21, 27. 11:31. 12:11. **the king's burnt offering.** Le 4:13-26. +*23:12. 2 S 6:17, 18. 1 K 3:4. 8:64. 2 Ch 7:4, 5. 29:21-24, 32, 35. Ezk 46:4-7, 12-14. **meat offering.** Le +*23:13. **drink offerings.** Le +*23:13. **brasen altar.** 2 Ch 4:1. **for me to enquire by.** 2 K 18:4. Ge 44:5. 2 Ch 33:6. Is 2:6. Ho 4:12.

16. **Thus did Urijah.** See on ver. 11. Ac ❶*4:19. ❶*5:29. 1 Th 2:4. Ju 11.

17. A.M. 3265. B.C. 739. **cut off.** 2 Ch 28:24. 29:19. **borders.** 1 K 7:23, 27-39. 2 Ch 4:14. **sea.** 2 K 25:13-16. 1 K 7:23-26. 2 Ch 4:15. Je 52:20.

18. **the covert.** There are a great number of conjectures concerning this covert; but it is probable that it was either, as Locke supposes, a sort of shelter or *canopy* erected for the people on the sabbath, when the crowd was too great for the porch to contain them; or, as Dr. Geddes supposes, a seat, covered with a *canopy,* placed on an elevation, for the king and his court, when they attended public worship. 2 K 11:5. 1 K 10:5. Ezk 46:2.

19. A.M. 3262-3278. B.C. 742-726. 2 K 15:6, 7, 36, 38. 20:20, 21. 1 K 14:29.

20. A.M. 3278. B.C. 726. **Ahaz slept with.** 1 K +*11:43. **buried.** 2 K 21:18, 26. 2 Ch 28:27. **Hezekiah.** i.e. *strength of Jah; the might of Jehovah.* 2 K 18:1. 1 Ch 3:13. 2 Ch 29:1. Is 1:1. Ho 1:1. Mi 1:1. Mt 1:9, Ezekias. (1) A king of Judah (728-699 B.C.). 2 K 18:1, 10. Is 1:1. Ho 1:1. (2) A successor of Jeconiah, 1 Ch 3:23. (3) One whose children returned from Babylon, Ne 7:21. (4) One who sealed the covenant, Ne 10:17. (5) An ancestor of the prophet Zephaniah, supposed to be the same as king Hezekiah, Zp 1:1. ✶S#2396h: 2 K 16:20. 18:9, 13, 17, 19, 22, 29, 30, 31, 32, 37. 19:1, 3, 5, 9, 10, 14, 14, 15, 20. 20:1, 3, 5, 8, 12, 12, 13, 13, 14, 14, 15, 16, 19, 20, 21. 21:3. 1 Ch 3:13. 2 Ch 29:18, 27. 30:24. 32:15. Is 36:1, 2, 4, 7, 14, 15, 16, 18, 22. 37:1, 3, 5, 9, 10, 14, 14, 15, 21. 38:1, 2, 3, 5, 9, 22. 39:1, 2, 2, 3, 3, 4, 5, 8. Je 26:18, 19. Another form of the same Hebrew name with the same Strong number, ✶S#2396h: 2 K 18:1, 10, 14, 14, 15, 16, 16. 1 Ch 3:23. Ne 7:21. 10:17. Pr 25:1. Zp 1:1.

2 KINGS 17

Hoshea becomes tributary to Shalmaneser, conspires with the king of Egypt against him, and is shut up in prison by the king of Assyria, 1-4. Shalmaneser besieges Samaria; and after three years takes it, and carries Israel captive into Assyria and Media, 5, 6. The crimes, which brought this punishment from God on his people, 7-23. The strange nations planted in the land, are plagued by lions, 24, 25: but, instructed by a priest of Israel, in the worship of the Lord, they serve him along with their own idols, 26-41.

1. A.M. 3274. B.C. 730. **In the twelfth year.** In 2 K 15:30, this is said to be "in the twentieth year of Jotham," which Calmet thus reconciles: "Hosea conspired against Pekah, the 20th year of the reign of this prince, which was the 18th of Jotham, king of Judah. Two years after this, that is, the fourth of Ahaz and the 20th of Jotham, Hosea made himself master of a *part* of the kingdom, according to 2 K 15:30. Finally, in the 12th year of Ahaz, Hosea had peaceable possession of the *whole* kingdom, agreeably to 2 K 17:1." **Hoshea.** "After an interregnum, 2 K 15:30. 18:9."

2. **but not as the kings.** 2 K 3:2. 10:31. 13:2, 11. 15:9, 18, 24. 2 Ch 30:5-11.

3. **Shalmaneser.** i.e. *retribution; their peace offering of bondage,* *S#8022h. This was the son and successor of **Tiglath-pileser**: he reigned 14 years, from A.M. 3276 to 3290. 2 K 18:9. Ho 10:14, Shalman. **king of Assyria.** 2 K 15:19, 29. 16:7. 18:13. 19:36, 37. Is 7:7, 8. 10:5, 6, 11, 12. **and Hoshea.** 2 K 16:8. 18:14-16, 31. **gave.** Heb. rendered. **presents.** *or,* tribute. Jg 3:15. 1 S 10:27. 2 S 8:2, 6.

4. A.M. 3279. B.C. 725. **found conspiracy.** 2 K +11:14. 24:1, 20. Ezk 17:13-19. **So.** i.e. *conspicuous; lifted up,* *S#5471h. **king of Egypt.** 2 K 18:21. Is 30:1-4. 31:1-3. Ezk 17:15. **brought.** 2 K 18:14, 15. **bound him.** 2 K 25:7. 2 Ch 32:11. Ps 149:7, 8.

5. A.M. 3281-3283. B.C. 723-721. **the king.** 2 K 18:9. **three years.** 2 K 25:1-3. Je 52:4, 5.

6. A.M. 3283. B.C. 721. **the king of Assyria.** 2 K 18:10, 11. Ho 1:6, 9. 13:16, foretold. **carried.** Le 26:32, 33, 38. Dt 4:25-28. 28:36, 64. 29:27, 28. 30:18. 1 K 14:15, 16. Am 5:27. **Halah.** i.e. *painful; fresh anguish,* *S#2477h. 2 K 18:12. ◐19:12. 1 Ch 5:26. Is ◐37:12, 13. Probably Calachene, north of Asshur, next to Armenia (Young). **Habor.** i.e. *a joining together,* *S#2249h. A river in Aram Naharaim, falling into the Euphrates at Circesium, as in 2 K 18:11. 1 Ch 5:26. **Gozan.** i.e. *cut off; quarry,* *S#1470h. 2 K 18:11. 19:12. 1 Ch 5:26. Is 37:12. **Medes.** 1 Ch 5:26. Is 13:17. 21:2. Da 5:28.

7. **sinned.** Dt 31:16, 17, 29. 32:15, etc. Jsh 23:16. Jg 2:14-17. 2 Ch 36:14-16. Ne 9:26. Ps 106:35-41. Ezk 23:2, etc. Ho 4:1-3. 8:5-14. **the Lord.** 2 K 16:2. 1 K 11:4. 15:3. 2 Ch 36:5. **which had.** See on Ex 20:2. **and had feared.** ver. 35. Je 10:5.

8. **walked.** 2 K 16:3, 10. 21:2. Le 18:3, 27-30. Dt 12:30, 31. 18:9. 1 K 12:28. 16:31-33. 21:26. 106:35. Je +√10:2. **of the kings of Israel.** Ho 5:11. Mi 6:16.

9. **secretly.** Dt 13:6. 27:15. Jb 31:27. Ezk 8:12. Mt 6:4, 18. **from the tower.** 2 K 18:8. Ho 12:11.

10. **they set.** 2 K 16:4. Ex 34:13. Le 26:1. 1 K 14:23. Is 57:5. **images.** Heb. statues. or, standing pillars. 2 K 3:2. 10:26, 27. 18:4. 23:14. Ge 35:14, 20. Ex 23:24. 34:13. Le 26:1. Dt 7:5. 12:3. 16:22. 1 K 14:23. 2 Ch 14:3. 31:1. Je 43:13. Ezk 26:11h. Ho 3:4. 10:1, 2. Mi 5:13. **groves.** Ex 34:13. Dt 7:5. 16:21. Jg 3:7. 6:25. Mi 5:14. **in every.** 2 K 16:4n. Dt 12:2, 3. 1 K 14:23. 2 Ch 28:4. **high hill.** 2 K 16:4n. Dt 12:2. 1 K 14:23. 2 Ch 28:4. Is 57:5, 7. 65:7. Je 2:20. 3:6, 9. 12:12. **green tree.** 2 K 16:4n. Dt 12:2. Is +1:29. 57:5. Je 2:20. 3:6, 13. Ezk 6:13. Ho 4:13.

11. **burnt.** 1 K 13:1. 2 Ch 28:25. Je 44:17. **to provoke.** 2 K 21:6. Ps 78:56-58.

12. **whereof.** Ex *20:3-5. 34:14. Le 26:1. Dt 4:19. 5:7-9. **Ye shall not.** Dt 4:15-19, 23-25. 12:4.

13. **testified.** Dt *8:19. *31:21. Ne 9:2-30. Ps 50:7. 81:8, 9. Je 42:19. Ac 20:21. **and against Judah.** 2 Ch 36:15, 16. Je 3:8-11. 42:19. Ho 4:15. **all.** Heb. the hand of all. √144A5, Ge +9:5. ver. 23. 2 K 24:2. Dt 4:26. Jsh 23:16. Jg 6:10. 10:11-14. 1 S 12:7-15. 1 K +16:12mg. Is 1:5-15, 21-24. Je 5:29-31. *35:15. Zc 1:3-6. **seers.** See on 1 S 9:9. 1 Ch 29:29. **Turn ye.** 2 Ch √7:14. Is *1:16-20. *55:6, 7. Je 7:3-7. *18:11. *25:4, 5. 35:15. Ezk 18:31. Ho 14:1. 2 P 3:9. **keep.** Je 7:22, 23. 26:4-6.

14. **would not hear.** 1 S +*25:17. Pr *29:1. **but hardened.** Dt 31:27. 2 Ch 36:13. Pr *29:1. Is 48:4. Je 7:26. Ro 2:4-5. He 3:7, 8. **like to.** √63E1, Le +4:2. Supply ellipsis, "the hardness of." **and did not believe.** Dt 1:32. Ps 78:22, 32. 106:24. He 3:12.

15. **they rejected.** Je 8:9. **his covenant.** Ex 24:6-8. Dt 29:10-15, 25, 26. Je 31:32. **testimonies.** Dt 6:17, 18. 2 Ch 36:15, 16. Ne 9:26, 29, 30. Je 44:4, 23. **vanity.** Dt 32:21, 31. 1 S 12:21. 1 K 16:13. Ps 115:8. Je +*8:19. 10:8, 15. Jon 2:8. **became vain.** Ps *115:8. Je +*2:5. Ro *1:21-23. 1 C *8:4. **concerning whom.** ver. 8, 11, 12. Dt 12:30, 31. 2 Ch 33:2, 9. Je +*10:2. **not do like them.** Ex +*23:2. 1 S 8:19, 20. Je +*10:2. Mt *6:8. 23:2, 3.

16. **molten images.** Ex 32:4, 8. 1 K *12:28. Ps 106:18-20. Is 44:9, 10. **a grove.** ver. +*10. 1 K 14:15, 23. 15:13. 16:33. **worshipped.** Dt 4:19. Je 8:2. **Baal.** 2 K 10:18-28. 11:18. +23:4. 1 K 16:31. 22:53.

17. **they caused.** 2 K 16:3. +21:6. Le *18:21. 2 Ch 28:3. Ps 106:37, 38. Ezk 20:26, 31. 23:37, 39. **used divination.** 2 K 21:6. Dt +*18:10-12. 2 Ch 33:6. Is 8:19. 47:9, 12, 13. Je 27:9. Mi 5:12. Ac 16:16. Ga 5:20. **enchantments.** Ge 30:27. Le 19:26. **sold.** 1 K 21:20, 25. Is 50:1. Ro 7:14. **in the sight.** ver. 11. 2 K 21:6.

18. **removed.** 2 K 13:23. 23:27. Dt 29:20-28. 32:21-26. Jsh 23:13, 15. Je 15:1. Ho 9:3. **the tribe.** 1 K 11:13, 32, 36. 12:20. Ho 11:12. **Judah.** √171R, Ex +12:40. The Levites and Benjamites, etc., are included. See 1 K 11:32n.

19. **Also Judah.** 1 K 14:22, 23. 2 Ch 21:11, 13. Je 2:28. 3:8-11. Ezk 16:51, 52. 22:2-16. 23:4-13. **walked.** 2 K 8:18, 27. 16:3.

20. **rejected.** ver. 15. 1 S 15:√23, 26. 16:1. Je 6:30. Ro ◐11:+√1, 2. **all the seed.** 1 Ch 16:13. Ne 9:2. Is 45:25. Je ◐+√31:36, 37. 33:24-26. 46:28. **delivered.** 2 K 13:3, 7. 15:18-20, 29. 18:9. 2 Ch 28:5, 6. Ne 9:27, 28. **until he had cast.** See on ver. 18. Dt 11:12. Jon 1:3, 10. Mt 25:41. 2 Th 1:9.

21. **For he rent.** 1 K 11:11, 31. 14:8. Is 7:17. **they made.** 1 K 12:19, 20. 2 Ch 10:15-19. **Jeroboam drave.** Dt 13:13. See on 1 K 12:20, 28-30. 14:16. 2 Ch 11:14, 15. **a great sin.** Ge 20:9. Ex 32:21. 1 S 2:17, 24. Ps 25:11. Jn 19:11.

22. **walked in all the sins.** See on 2 K 3:3. 10:29, 31. 13:2, 6, 11. 15:9.

23. **the Lord.** See on ver. 18, 20. **as he had said.** See on ver. 13. 1 K 13:2. 14:16. Ho 1:4-9. Am 5:27. Mi 6:1. **So was Israel.** ver. 6. 2 K 18:11, 12.

24. A.M. 3326. B.C. 678. **the king.** Ezr 4:2-10. **Babylon.** i.e. *confusion,* S#894h. ver. 30. 2 Ch 33:11. **Cutha.** i.e. *place of crushing,* *S#3575h. Ge 10:6.

2 K 17:30. **Ava.** i.e. *perverted*, *S#5755h. ver. 31. 2 K 18:34. 19:13. Dt 2:23. Is 37:13, Ivah. **Hamath.** 2 K 19:13. Nu 34:8. Is 10:9. 36:19. **Sepharvaim.** i.e. *city of the sun; two-fold enumeration*, *S#5617h. ver. 31. 2 K 18:34. 19:13. Is 36:19. 37:13. **in the cities thereof.** ver. 6. Mt 10:5.

25. **they feared.** ver. 28, 32, 34, 41. Jsh 22:25. Je 10:7. Da 6:26. Jon 1:9. **the Lord sent.** 2 K 2:24. Jg 14:5. 1 S 17:34. 1 K 13:24. 20:36. Je 5:6. 15:3. Ezk 14:15, 21. Am 3:12.

26. **and placed.** See on ver. 24. **know not.** ver. 27. 1 S 8:9. 10:25. Am 3:14. **God of the land.** Jg 11:24n. 1 K 20:23n.

27. **one of the priests.** Jg 17:13. 1 K 12:31. 13:2. 2 Ch 11:15.

28. **in Bethel.** 1 K 12:29-32. **taught them.** Is 29:13. Mt 15:14.

29. **made gods.** Ps 115:4-8. 135:15-18. Is 44:9-20. Je 2:28. *10:2-5. Ho 8:5, 6. Mi 4:5. Ro 1:23. **the houses.** ver. 32. 2 K 23:19. 1 K 12:31. 13:32. **high places.** Le 26:30. 1 K 12:31. 13:32. **in their cities.** Je *11:13.

30. **Babylon.** ver. 24. **Succoth-benoth.** i.e. *booths of daughters.* Literally, "the tents of the daughters," *S#5524h, only here. 2 K 5:18. 19:37. 21:7. Ge 24:67n. **Cuth.** i.e. *burning, crushing*, *S#3575h, only here. *Cuth* is probably the Cush watered by the Gihon, or Araxes, now Aras (Ge 2:13), the ancient country of the *Scythians* (Herodotus, l. i. c. 201. l. iv. c. 11) where we meet with the *Quitians, Coethians,* or *Coetae,* and *Cytheans,* and the cities of *Cotatis, Cetemane, Cythanum, Cyta, Cethena,* etc. **Nergal.** i.e. *the lamp rolled*, *S#5370h, only here. Supposed to denote the *solar orb*; the emblem of which, according to the Rabbins, was *a cock,* which we know was sacred to Apollo, "because," says Helidorus (Aethiop. l. i.), "by a natural sensation of the sun's revolution to us, they are incited to salute the god." **Ashima.** i.e. *guiltiness*, *S#807h, only here. Jarchi says this idol was of the form of a goat.

31. **the Avites.** ver. 24. Ezr 4:9. **Nibhaz.** i.e. *to speak*, *S#5026h, only here. Supposed to be the same as the *Anubis* of the Egyptians; and was in form partly a dog and partly a man. **Tartak.** i.e. *intense darkness; a flat basket*, *S#8662h, only here. **Sepharvites.** i.e. *inhabitants of Sepharvaim*, *S#5616h, only here. **burnt their children.** See on ver. 17. Le *18:21. Dt *12:30, 31. **Adrammelech.** i.e. *honor of the king.* 2 K 19:37. **Anammelech.** i.e. *the affliction of the king*, *S#6048h.

32. **made unto themselves.** 1 K 12:31. 13:33. **the lowest.** Young renders, "the extremities." Ge 47:2 (some). Ex 25:18 (ends). Jg 18:2 (from their coasts). 1 K *12:31. *13:33. Is 40:28 (ends). **the houses.** ver. 29. 2 K 23:19. 1 K 13:32.

33. **They feared.** ver. 41. 1 K 18:21. Ho 10:2. Zp 1:5. Mt √6:24. Lk 16:13. **whom they carried,** etc. *or*, who carried them away from thence. The new inhabitants of the land imitated the idolatrous Israelites, by associating their idols with Jehovah, as the objects of worship. The remainder, however, of the verses seem to relate to the Israelites after they were carried captive. They still persevered in idolatry and disobedience; and not being purified, were left to be consumed in the furnace. It is said that the Israelites "did not fear the Lord," yet the heathens, who followed their example, are said "to have feared the Lord." The Israelites did

not so much as fear the wrath of Almighty God; but, on the other hand, the poor pagans feared the power of his wrath, and to avert it paid some ignorant worship, according to the wretched instructions given them. As this was an external acknowledgment of his power and Godhead, and a homage paid to him, he was pleased in consequence to withdraw his judgments from them (Scott).

34. **fear not.** See on ver. 25, 27, 28, 33. **whom he named Israel.** Ge 32:28. 33:20. 35:10. 1 K 11:31. 18:31. Is 48:1.

35. **With whom.** ver. 15. Ex 19:5, 6. 24:6-8. Dt 29:10-15. Je 31:31-34. He 8:6-13. **charged them.** Ex *20:4, 5. 34:12-17. Dt 4:23-27. 13:1, etc. Jsh 23:7, 16. **not fear other gods.** Jg 6:10. Je 10:5. **nor bow.** Mt 28:9. Col 3:24.

36. **a stretched.** See on Ex 6:6. 9:15. Dt 5:15. Je 32:21. Ac 4:30. **him shall ye fear.** Le 19:32. Dt 6:13. 10:20. 12:5, 6, 11, 12. Mt +*10:28. Re 15:4.

37. **the statutes.** Le 19:37. Dt 4:44, 45. 5:31-33. 6:1, 2. 12:32. 1 Ch 29:19. Ps 19:8-11. 105:44, 45. **wrote for you.** Ex +24:4. Dt 31:9, 11. Ne 9:13, 14. 2 T √3:16. **and ye shall not.** See on ver. 35.

38. **the covenant.** 1 K 8:9. **ye shall not forget.** Dt 4:23. 6:12. 8:11, 14-18. **neither shall.** ver. 35. Jg 6:10.

39. **the Lord.** See on ver. 36. Dt 6:13. 10:20. 1 S *12:24. Is 8:12-14. Je 10:7. Mt +√10:28. Lk 1:50. **he shall deliver.** Ne 9:27. Lk 1:71, 74, 75.

40. **they did not.** Je 13:23. **but they did.** See on ver. 8, 12, 34. Dt 4:28.

41. **these nations.** ver. 32, 33. Jsh 24:14-20. 1 K 18:21. Zp 1:5. Mt *6:24. Re 3:15, 16. **unto this day.** 2 K 8:22n. 16:6. Jsh +4:9. Ezr 4:1-3.

2 KINGS 18

Hezekiah reigns well, abolishes idolatry, and prospers, 1-8. In his time Samaria is taken, and Israel carried captive, 9-12. Sennacherib invades Judah, and Hezekiah pays him tribute, 13-16. Rabshakeh, sent by Sennacherib, in an insulting and blasphemous speech, aims to induce the people to revolt, 17-35. Hezekiah's servants hold their peace, and rend their clothes, 36, 37.

1. A.M. 3278. B.C. 726. **in the third.** ver. 9. 2 K 15:30. 17:1. **Hezekiah.** i.e. *strength of Jah.* 2 K 16:20. 1 Ch 3:13. 2 Ch 28:27. 29:1. Mt 1:9, 10, Ezekias.

2. **Twenty and five years old.** As Ahaz was 20 years old when he began to reign, and died when he had reigned 16 years, his whole age only amounted to 36 years; and as Hezekiah was, at least, entering on his 25th year when he began to reign, then Ahaz must have been under twelve years of age when his son was born! This is not at all impossible: and there are well-attested facts of men having children at as early a period, especially in eastern countries. A.M. 3278-3306. B.C. 726-698. **Abi.** i.e. *my father* *S#21h. 2 Ch 29:1, Abijah.

3. **right in the sight.** An expression used of no other king before him (Young). 2 K 20:3. Ex 15:26. Dt 6:18. 2 Ch 31:20, 21. Jb 33:27. Ps 119:128. Ro 7:12. Ep *6:1. **according.** 2 K 22:2. 1 K 3:14. 11:4, 38. 15:5, 11. 2 Ch 29:2.

4. **removed.** 2 K 12:3. 14:4. 15:4, 35. Le 26:30. 1 K 3:2, 3. 15:14. 22:43. Ps 78:58. Ezk 20:28, 29. **brake.** 2 K 23:4. Dt 7:5. 12:2, 3. Jg 6:25, 28. 1 K

15:12, 13. 2 Ch 19:3. 31:1. 33:3. **images**. Heb. statues. 2 K 3:2. 10:26. +*17:10. Ex 23:24. **the brasen serpent**. Nu 21:8, 9. Jn 3:14, 15. **unto those days**. 2 K 16:15. **Nehushtan**. that is, a *piece of brass* (S#5180h).

5. **trusted**. 2 K 19:10. 2 Ch 32:7, 8. Jb 13:15. Ps 13:5. *27:1, 2. 46:1, 2. 84:12. 146:5, 6. Je *17:7, 8. Mt 27:43. Ep 1:12. **after him**. 2 K 19:15-19. 23:25. 2 Ch 14:11. 16:7-9. 20:20, 35.

6. **he clave**. None of the kings of Judah, from the time of the division of the kingdom, equalled Hezekiah in the steadfastness and simplicity of his dependence upon the Lord; in which he aspired to an equality with his progenitor David, who had reigned over the whole land. Even Asa, through weakness of faith, sought the assistance of a heathen prince; and Jehoshaphat formed an alliance with idolatrous Ahab; but Hezekiah clave to the Lord, in entire confidence and unreserved obedience, to the end of his life. Dt 10:20. Jsh 23:8. Ac *11:23. **from following him**. Heb. from after him. 2 K 17:21. **kept**. 2 K 17:13, 16, 19. Je 11:4. Jn *14:15, 21. *15:10, 14. 1 J *2:3. 5:3.

7. **And the Lord**. Ge 21:22. 39:2, 3. 1 S 18:14. 2 Ch 15:2. Ps 46:11. 60:12. Mt 1:23. *28:20. Ac 7:9, 10. **he prospered**. Ge 39:2. 1 S 18:5, 14mg. 2 S 8:6, 14. 2 Ch 31:21. 32:30. Ps *1:3. 60:12. Ro *8:31. **rebelled**. ver. 20. 2 K 16:7.

8. **the Philistines**. 1 Ch 4:41. 2 Ch 28:18. Is 14:29. **Gaza**. Heb. Azzah. Ge 10:19. Jsh 15:47. **from the tower**. 2 K 17:9. 2 Ch 26:10. Is 5:2.

9. A.M. 3281. B.C. 723. **the fourth year**. ver. 1. 2 K 17:4-6. **Shalmaneser**. 2 K 17:3, etc. Ho 10:14, Shalman.

10. A.M. 3283. B.C. 721. **they took it**. Ho 13:16. Am 3:11-15. 4:1-3. 6:7. 9:1-4. Mi 1:6-9. 6:16. 7:13.

11. **the king**. 2 K 17:6. 19:11. 1 Ch 5:26. Is 7:8. 8:4. 9:9-21. 10:5, 11. 37:12. Ho 8:8, 9. 9:3. Am 5:1-3, 6, 25-27. Ac 7:43. **Halah**. It is thought, with much probability, that *Halah*, or *Chalach*, is Ptolemy's *Calachene*, the northern part of Assyria; that *Habor*, or *Chabor*, is the mountain, or mountainous country, between Media and Assyria, called by Ptolemy *Xaboras*, *Chaboras*; and that *Gozan* is the *Gauzanitis* of Ptolemy, situated between that mountain and the Caspian sea, and between the two channels of the river Cyrus.

12. **they obeyed not**. 2 K *17:7-23. Dt 8:20. 11:28. 29:24-28. 31:17. Ne *9:17, 26, 27. Ps *107:17. Is 1:19. Je 3:8. Da *9:6-11. Mi 3:4. 2 Th √1:8. 1 P 2:8. 4:17. **Moses**. Nu 12:7. Dt 34:5. Jsh 1:1. 2 T 2:24. He 3:5, 6.

13. A.M. 3291. B.C. 713. **the fourteenth**. 2 Ch 32:1, etc. Is 36:1, etc. **Sennacherib**. Heb. Sanherib. i.e. *the thorn laid waste*. Is 20:1. *S#5576h: 2 K 18:13. 19:16, 20, 36. 2 Ch 32:1, 2, 9, 10, 22. Is 36:1. 37:17, 21, 37. **come up**. Is 7:17, etc. 8:7, 8. 10:5. Ho 12:1, 2.

14. **I have offended**. ver. 7. 1 K 20:4. Pr *29:25. Lk *14:31, 32.

15. **Hezekiah gave**. 2 K 12:18. 16:8. 1 K 15:15, 18, 19. 2 Ch 16:2.

16. **gold**. 1 K 6:31-35. 2 Ch 29:3. **it**. Heb. them.

17. A.M. 3294. B.C. 710. **the king**. 2 Ch 32:9. Is 20:1. 36:2. **Tartan**. i.e. *commander-in-chief; release the dragon*. *S#8661h: 2 K 18:17. Is 20:1. Calmet remarks, that these are not the names of *persons*, but of *offices*: *Tartan* signifies "he who presides over gifts or tribute;" *Rabsaris*, "the chief of the eunuchs;" and

Rabshakeh, "the chief cup-bearer." **Rabshakeh**. *S#7262h: 2 K 18:17, 19, 26, 27, 28, 37. 19:4, 8. Is 36:2, 4, 11, 12, 13, 22. 37:4, 8. **great**. Heb. heavy. 2 K 6:14mg. **the conduit of the upper pool**. If the *Fuller's field* were near *En-Rogel* (i.e. *fountain of the fuller*. A well near Jerusalem, to the south-east. Jsh 15:7. 18:16. 2 S 17:17. 1 K 1:9), or the *Fuller's fountain*, east of Jerusalem, as is generally supposed, then the "conduit of the upper pool" may have been an acqueduct that brought the water from the *upper* or *eastern* reservoir of that fountain, which had been seized in order to distress the city. 2 K 20:20. 2 S 5:23n. Is 7:3. 22:9-11. 36:2. Ezk +47:1n.

18. **Eliakim**. i.e. *God is setting up; God raises up*. 2 K 19:2. Is 22:20-24. 36:3, 22. 37:2. *S#471h: 2 K 18:18, 26, 37. 19:2. 23:34. 2 Ch 36:4. Ne 12:41. Is 22:20. 36:3, 11, 22. 37:2. (1) The master of the king's household at Jerusalem in the time of Hezekiah, 2 K 18:18; Is 37:2. (2) A son of King Josiah, 2 K 23:34; 2 Ch 36:4. His name was changed to Jehoiakim (1 Ch +3:15). (3) A priest who officiated in purifying the rebuilt wall of Jerusalem, Ne 12:41. (4) An ancestor of Joseph, the husband of Mary, as given by Matthew, Mt 1:13. (5) An ancestor of Joseph in the line given by Luke, Lk 3:30. **Hilkiah**. i.e. *the Lord is my portion; portion of Jah*. *S#2518h: 2 K 18:18, 26. 22:4, 8, 14. 23:4, 24. 1 Ch 26:11. 2 Ch 34:9, 14, 15, 15, 18, 20, 22. Is 22:20. 36:3, 22. Je 1:1. (1) The father of Eliakim, 2 K 18:18; Is 22:20. (2) The high priest in the reign of Josiah. He found the book of the law, 2 K 22:8, and is also mentioned in 2 K 23:4, 24; 2 Ch 34:9, 14, 15, etc. (3, 4) Two descendants of Merari, 1 Ch 6:45; 26:11. (5) A priest who stood beside Ezra while he read the book of the law to the people, Ne 8:4; 11:11. (6) A priest who returned with Zerubbabel, Ne 12:7, 21. (7) A priest who was the father of Jeremiah the prophet, Je 1:1. (8) Father of an ambassador from Zedekiah to Nebuchadnezzar, Je 29:3. **Shebna**. i.e. *youth, tenderness, or tender age*. Prefect of the palace, Is 22:15; afterwards secretary of Hezekiah, 2 K 18:18, 26, 37; Is 36:22. Is 22:15-19. *S#7644h: 2 K 18:18, 26. **the scribe**. *or*, secretary. ver. 37. 2 K 12:10. 19:2. Jg 5:14. 2 S 8:17mg. 1 K 4:3. **Joah**. i.e. *Jah is brother; whose brother (i.e. helper) is Jehovah*. A son of Asaph, Hezekiah's recorder, 2 K 18:18; Is 36:3. Recorder of king Josiah, 2 Ch 34:8. Name used also of others. **Asaph**. i.e. *a gatherer; collector*. Six persons have this name: (1) A Levite, chief of the singers appointed by David. 1 Ch 16:5. 2 Ch 29:30, to whom Ps 50, 70-83 are ascribed, whose descendants are mentioned as having occupied themselves with sacred verse and song. 1 Ch 25:1. 2 Ch 20:14. 29:13. Ezr 2:41. 3:10. Ne 7:44. 11:22. (2) Here, a recorder for Hezekiah, 2 K 18:18. Is 36:3. (3) An officer appointed by the king of Persia to keep the forests in Judea, Ne 2:8. (4) A Levite, an ancestor of Mattaniah, Ne 11:17. Perhaps the same as Number 1. (5) A Levite whose descendants dwelt in Jerusalem after the captivity, 1 Ch 9:15. (6) A descendant of Kohath, 1 Ch 26:1. *S#623h: 2 K 18:18, 37. 1 Ch 6:39, 39. 9:15. 15:17, 19. 16:5, 5, 7, 37. 25:1, 2, 2, 2, 6, 9. 26:1. 2 Ch 5:12. 20:14. 29:13, 30. 35:15, 15. Ezr 2:41. 3:10. Ne 2:8. 7:44. 11:17, 22. 12:35, 46. Ps 50, title. 73:t. 74:t. 75:t. 76:t. 77:t. 78:t. 79:t. 80:t. 81:t. 82:t. 83:t. Is 36:3, 22. **the recorder**. 2 S 8:16mg. 20:24mg. 1 K 4:3mg. 2 Ch 34:8.

19. **Rab-shakeh**. i.e. *chief of the cup-bearers*. A

captain of Sennacherib, 2 K 18:17; Is 36:2. He was the chief speaker, being a very eloquent man, and, according to the Hebrews, whom Procopius follows, an apostate Jew; which is not improbable, as he spoke Hebrew so fluently; and when he blasphemed the Divine Majesty, the king and nobles rent their clothes, which was not usual unless the blasphemer were an Israelite. **Thus saith**. 2 Ch 32:10. Is 10:8-14. 36:4. 37:13. Da 4:30. **What confidence**. ver. 22, 29, 30. 2 K 19:10. 2 Ch 32:7, 8, 10, 11, 14-16. Ps 4:2. Is 36:4, 7. 37:10.

20. **sayest**. or, talkest. **vain words**. Heb. word of the lips. **I have counsel and strength for the war**. or, but counsel and strength *are* for the war. Pr +*21:30, 31. **rebellest**. ver. 14.

21. **trustest**. Heb. trustest thee. ver. 24. **the staff**. Is 36:6. Ezk 29:6, 7. **bruised**. ∫24C. Antimereia; or, Exchange of Parts of Speech B494: The passive participle for the adjective. i.e. this broken reed. For other instances of this figure see Ps 12:6. 18:3. Pr 21:20. Is 33:19. Zp 2:1. Ga 2:11. He 12:27. **upon Egypt**. Is 30:2, 7. 31:1-3. **so is Pharaoh**. 2 K 17:4. Je *46:17.

22. **We trust**. ver. 5. Da 3:15. Mt 27:43. **whose high places**. ver. 4. 2 Ch 31:1. 32:12. Is 36:7. 1 C 2:15.

23. **pledges**. Heb. hostages. 2 K 14:14. **I will deliver**. 1 S 17:42-44. 1 K 20:10, 18. Ne 4:2-5. Ps 123:3, 4. Is 10:13, 14. 36:8, 9.

24. **How then**. Is 10:8. Da 2:37, 38. 4:22, 37. **thy trust**. ver. 21. See on Dt 17:16. Is 31:1, 3. 36:6, 9. Je 37:7. 42:14-18. Ezk 17:15, 17. **chariots**. Ps 20:7, 8.

25. **Am I now**. 2 K 19:6, 22, etc. 1 K 13:18. 2 Ch 35:21. Is 10:5, 6. Am +√3:6. Jn 19:10, 11.

26. **Speak**. Perceiving that the object of this blasphemous caitiff was to stir up the people to sedition, they mildly and reasonably required him to make his proposals in the Syrian language. **in the Syrian language**. Ezr 4:7. Is 36:11, 12. Da 2:4. **on the wall**. Watching and hearing the interview (Young). Ge +18:10.

27. **eat**. 2 K *6:25. Dt 28:53-57. Ps 73:8. La 4:5. Ezk 4:13, 15. **their own piss**. Heb. the water of their feet. Jg 3:24mg. 1 S 24:3. This is a reference to the hardhips they would undergo during a threatened siege.

28. **Rab-shakeh**. 2 Ch 32:18. Is 36:13-18. **the king of Assyria**. ver. 19. Ezr 7:12. Ps 47:2. Is 10:8-13. Ezk 29:3. 31:3-10. Re 19:16.

29. **saith**. Ps 73:8, 9. **Let not**. 2 Ch 32:11, 15. Da 3:15-17. 6:16. Jn 19:10, 11. 2 Th 2:4, 8. **deceive you**. ver. 32mg. 2 K 19:10. Ge 3:13.

30. **make you**. ver. 22. 2 K 19:10, 22. Ps 4:2. 11:1. 22:7, 8. 71:9, 11. 125:1, 2. Mt 27:43. Lk 23:35. **this city**. 2 K 19:32-34.

31. **Make an agreement with me**. or, Seek my favor. Heb. Make with me a blessing. Ge 32:20. *33:11. Jg 1:15. 1 S +25:27mg. 30:26mg. Pr 18:16. **eat ye**. 1 K 4:20, 25. Zc 3:10. **cistern**. or, pit. Heb. bor, Ge +37:30. 2 K 10:14. Ne 9:25. Pr 5:15. Ec 12:6.

32. **I come**. ver. 11. 2 K 17:6, 23. 24:14-16. 25:11. Pr 18:16. **like your own**. Ex 3:8. Nu 13:26, 27. 14:8. Dt 8:7-9. 11:12. 32:13, 14. **corn**. ∫121D4, Ge +27:28. **and wine**. ∫174, Ge +18:27. ∫121D13, Ge +27:28. **and vineyards**. ∫174, Ge +18:27. **honey**. ∫17I17, Ex +3:8. **persuadeth**. or, deceiveth. ver. 29. 2 Ch 32:11, 15.

33. **Hath any**. 2 K 19:12, 13, 17, 18. 2 Ch 32:14-17, 19. Is 10:10, 11. 36:18-20. Da 3:15. **gods of the nations**. 2 K 17:26. Jg 11:24n. 1 K 20:23n.

34. **the gods**. 2 K 19:13. Nu 13:21. 2 S 8:9. Je 49:23. **Hamath**. 2 K 17:24. 1 K 8:65. *Hamath*, there is little doubt, was the *Epiphania* of the Greeks, as Josephus (Ant. l. i. c.7.), Theodoret, and Jerome expressly assert. It was a celebrated city of Syria, situated on the Orontes, and the present *Hamah* doubtless occupies its site; as Abulfeda, who was prince or emir of *Hamah* states, in his *Description of Syria* (pp. 108, 109), that *Hamah* is an ancient city mentioned in the writings of the Israelites. It is still a considerable town, situated on both sides of the Orontes, about three days' journey and a half from Tripoli; and must contain, Burckhardt says (*Travels in Syria*, etc. pp. 146-148), at least 30,000 inhabitants. **Arpad**. i.e. *spread out* or *supported*. 2 K 19:13. Is 10:9. 36:19. 37:13. Je 49:23. Ezk ●27:8, 11. *S#774h: 2 K 18:34. 19:13. Is 10:9. 36:19. 37:13. Je 49:23. *Arpad* is probably the town of *Arphas*, mentioned by Josepus (Bell. l. III. c.2) as limiting the province of Gamalitis, Gaulanitis, Batanea, and Trachonitis, to the N.E.; and the *Raphan*, or *Raphanea*, which Stephanus places near Epiphania. **the gods**. ver. +33. **Sepharvaim**. 2 K 17:24. 19:13. **Hena**. 2 K 19:13. **Ivah**. i.e. *overturning*. 2 K 17:24-33, Ava. 19:13. 36:18, 19. 37:11, 12, 18, 19. *S#5755h: 2 K 18:34. 19:13. Is 37:13. **have they delivered**. 2 K 17:6, 23, *24, 30, 31. 19:12, 13.

35. **Who are**. 2 K 19:17. Da 3:15. **that the Lord**. Ex 5:2. 2 Ch 32:15. Jb 15:25, 26. Is 10:15. 37:23-29.

36. **held their peace**. Ex 34:5. Ps 38:13, 14. 39:1. Pr *9:7. 26:4. Ec 3:7. Am *5:13. Mt 7:6. 27:12.

37. **Eliakim**. ver. 18, 26. 2 K 19:2. **the scribe**. ver. 18mg. 2 S 8:17mg. **the recorder**. 2 S 8:16mg. **with their clothes rent**. 2 K 5:7. 22:11, 19. Ge 37:29, 34. Jb 1:20. Is 33:7. 36:21, 22. Je 36:24. Mt 26:65.

2 KINGS 19

Hezekiah in distress sends to desire Isaiah's prayers, and receives an encouraging answer, 1-7. Sennacherib, going to oppose the king of Ethiopia, sends a blasphemous letter to Hezekiah, 8-13. His prayer on the receipt of it, 14-19. Isaiah, in the name of God, rebuking the proud blasphemies of Sennacherib, foretells his overthrow, and the prosperity of Zion, 20-34. An angel destroys the Assyrian army, 35. Sennacherib is slain by his own sons, in the temple of his idol, 36, 37.

1. A.M. 3294. B.C. 710. This chapter is nearly identical to Isaiah 37. **when king**. Is 37:1, etc. **he rent**. 2 K 5:7. 18:37. 1 S 4:12. Ezr 9:3. Jb 1:20. Je 36:24. Mt 26:65. **covered**. 2 K 6:30. Ge 37:34. 1 K 21:27, 29. Est 4:1-4. Ps 35:13. Jon 3:8. Mt 11:21. **went into**. 2 Ch 7:15, 16. Jb 1:20, 21.

2. **he sent Eliakim**. 2 K 18:18. 22:13, 14. Is 37:2-5. **the elders of the priests**. Is 37:2. Je 19:1. **covered with sackcloth**. 1 K 20:31. As a mark of humiliation (Young). **to Isaiah**. i.e. *safety of Jah*. 2 Ch 26:22. Mt 4:14. Lk 3:4, Esaias. **the son of Amoz**. i.e. *a strong one*, *S#531h. ver. 20. 2 K 20:1. 2 Ch 26:22. 32:20, 32. Is *1:1. *2:1. 13:1. 20:2. 37:2, 21. 38:1.

3. **This day**. 2 K 18:29. Ps 39:11. 123:3, 4. Je 30:5-7. Ho 5:15. 6:1. **blasphemy**. or, provocation. Nu 14:11. 16:30. Ne 9:18, 26. Ps 95:8. Ezk 35:12. He 3:15, 16. **for the children**. Is 26:17, 18. 66:9. Ho 13:13.

4. **the Lord**. Ge 22:14. Dt 32:36. Jsh 14:12. 1 S 14:6. 2 S 16:12. **whom the king**. 2 K 18:17-35. **reprove**. ver. 22. 1 S 17:45. Ps 50:21. 74:18. **lift up**. 2 Ch 32:20. Ps 50:15. Je 33:3. Ezk 36:37. Ro 9:27. Ja 5:16, 17. **the remnant**. 2 K 17:5, 6. 18:13. 2 Ch 28:5, 6. Is 8:7, 8. 10:6. **left**. Heb. found. Jg +20:48mg.

6. **Isaiah**. Is 37:6, 7, etc. **Be not afraid**. 2 K 6:16. Ex 14:13. Le 26:8. Dt 20:1, 3, 4. Jsh 11:6. 2 Ch 20:15, 17. Is 41:10-14. 51:7, 12, 13. **the servants**. 2 K 18:17, 35. Ps 74:18, 23. Re 13:6.

7. **a blast**. Heb. *ruach*, Ex +15:8. ver. 35-37. Jb 4:9. Ps 11:6. 18:14, 15. 50:3. Is 10:16-18. 11:4. Je 51:1. **hear a rumor**. *f*147D, Ge +1:29. 2 K 7:6. Jb 15:21. Je 49:14. 51:46. Ob 1. **I will cause**. ver. 36, 37. 2 Ch 32:21. **his own land**. *f*115. Mesoteleuton; or, Middle and End Repetition B262. The repetition of the same word or words in the middle and at the end of successive sentences. For other instances of this figure see Is 8:12. Mk 5:2, 3.

8. **returned**. 1 S 23:27. **Libnah**. 2 K 8:22. Jsh 10:29. 12:15. 15:42. **Lachish**. 2 K 18:14. Jsh 12:11. 15:39. Is 37:8, 9. Mi 1:13.

9. **when he heard**. When Sennacherib had levied contributions on Hezekiah, he marched his army into Egypt; where, after several successes, he laid siege to Pelusium (Josephus, Ant. l. x. c.1), and spent much time in it; but hearing that Tirhakah, king of Ethiopia, whom Strabo (l. i) calls *Therchon*, was marching against him with a great army, to assist his kinsman *Sevechus*, or *Sethon*, the king of Egypt, he durst not abide his coming, but raised the seige; and returning to Judea, he encamped against Lachish, and afterwards against Libnah. But finding that Tirhakah pursued him as a fugitive, he marched back to encounter him; and having totally routed his army, he returned to wreak his vengeance on Hezekiah. 1 S 23:27, 28. Is 37:9. **Tirhakah**. i.e. *inquirer; beholder*, *S#8640h. Is 37:9. **Ethiopia**. i.e. *black*, *S#3568h. (1) The land south of Egypt: Ge 2:13. Est 1:1. 8:9. Jb 28:19. Ps 87:4. Is 18:1. Ezk 29:10. Zp 3:10. Ac 8:37. (2) Inhabitants of Ethiopia: 2 K 19:9. Ps 68:31. Is 20:3, 5. 37:9. 43:3. 45:14. Ezk 30:4, 5. Ezk 38:5. Na 3:9. **thee**. *f*63C, Ge +25:32. Supply the Ellipsis (Absolute: Brachylogia), "(he turned his army against him; and, having conquered him, he returned to Jerusalem, and) he sent messengers again unto Hezekiah." **sent**. 2 K 18:17.

10. **Let not**. 2 K 18:5, 29, 30. 2 Ch 32:15-19. Is 37:10-14.

11. **thou hast heard**. ver. 17, 18. 2 K 17:5, etc. 2 Ch 32:13, 14. Is 10:8-11.

12. **Have the gods**. 2 K 18:33, 34. **Gozan**. 2 K 17:6. 1 Ch 5:26. **Haran**. Ge 11:31. 29:4. Ac 7:4, Charran. **Rezeph**. i.e. *heated stone*, *S#7530h. Rezeph was probably either *Rezapha*, which Ptolemy places in the Palmyrene, west of the Euphrates; or rather, *Rezipha*, in Mesopotamia, east of the Euphrates. Is 37:12. **Eden**. Ge 2:8. Is 37:12. Ezk 27:23. **Thelasar**. i.e. *hill of Assur; weariness of the prince*, *S#8515h. Is 37:12, Telassar.

13. **the king**. 2 K 17:24. Nu 13:21. 34:8. Is 11:11. Je 39:5. 49:23. Zc 9:2. **Arpad**. 2 K 18:34. Is 37:13, etc., Arphad.

14. **Hezekiah**. Is 37:14. **spread it**. T#1260. 1 K 8:28-30. Ezr 9:5. Ps 74:10, 11. 91:1, 2. 123:1-4.

15. **prayed**. 2 S 7:18, etc. 2 Ch 14:11. 20:6. 32:20. Da 9:3, 4. **O Lord God**. Ge 32:28. 33:20. 1 K 8:23. 1 Ch 4:10. Is 41:17. **dwellest**. Ex 25:22. 1 S 4:4.

2 Ch 5:7, 8. Ps 80:1. 99:1. **thou art the God**. 2 K 5:15. 1 K 18:39. Is 43:10. 44:6, 8. 45:22. Da 4:34, 35. **thou alone**. Is +*37:16. **of all**. Jg ●11:24n. 1 K ●20:23n. Is ●36:18n. **thou hast made**. Ge 1:1. 2:4. Ps 33:9. 102:25. 146:6. Je 10:10-12. Jn 1:1-3.

16. **bow down**. Ps 31:2. Is 37:17. **open**. 1 K 8:29. 2 Ch 6:40. Da 9:18. **which hath sent**. ver. 4. Ps 79:12. Is 37:4, 17. He 11:26.

17. **Of a truth**. Jb 9:2. Is 5:9. Je 26:15. Da 2:47. Mt 14:33. Lk 22:59. Ac 4:27. 1 C 14:25. **the kings**. 2 K 16:9. 17:6, 24. 1 Ch 5:26. Is 7:17, 18. 10:9-11.

18. **have cast**. Heb. have given. 2 S 5:21. Is 46:1, 2. **for they were**. Ps 115:4-8. Is 37:18, 19. 44:9-20. Je 10:3-9, 14-16. Ac *17:29. **no gods**. Is +*37:19.

19. **O Lord**. Ex 9:15, 16. Jsh 7:9. 1 S 17:45-47. 1 K 8:43. 18:36, 37. 20:28. Ps 67:1, 2. 83:18. Da 4:34-37. **that thou art**. 1 K 18:39. **thou only**. Is +*37:20. 44:6.

20. **which thou hast**. 2 S 15:31. 17:23. **I have heard**. 2 K 20:5. 2 Ch 32:20, 21. Jb 22:27. Ps 50:15. 65:2. Is 58:9. 65:24. Je *33:3. Da 9:20-23. Jn *11:42. Ac 10:4, 31. 1 J √5:14, 15.

21. **the word**. Ps 126:1-3. **The virgin**. Is 23:12. 37:21, 22, etc. 47:1. Je 14:17. 18:13. 31:4. La 1:15. 2:13. Am 5:2. **the daughter**. Ps 9:14. 137:8. Is 1:8. 23:10. 47:5. Je 46:11. La 2:13. 4:21. Mi 4:8. Zc 9:9. **shaken her head**. Jb 16:4. Ps 22:7, 8. Is 37:22. La 2:15. Mt 27:39.

22. **Whom**. 2 K 18:28-35. Ex 5:2. Ps 73:9. 74:22, 23. **exalted thy voice**. Ex 9:17. Pr 30:13. Is 10:15. 14:13, 14. Ezk 28:2-9. Da *5:20-23. 2 C 10:5. 2 Th *2:3, 4. **the Holy One**. Ps 71:22. Is 5:24. 30:11, 12, 15. Je 51:5.

23. **By**. Heb. By the hand of. 2 K 14:25. 1 K +16:12mg. **messengers**. 2 K 18:17. 2 Ch 32:17. **With the multitude**. 2 K 18:23, 33, 34. Ps 20:7. Is 10:7-11, 14. 37:24, 25. Ezk 31:3, etc. Am 9:3. **tall cedar trees thereof**. Heb. tallness of the cedar trees thereof. **the forest of his Carmel**. or, the forest, *and* his fruitful field. Is 10:18.

24. **I have digged**, etc. *f*102, Ge +2:24. I have conquered *strange countries*, and marched through the driest places, in which I have digged wells for my army. **with the sole**. My infantry have been so numerous, that they alone have been sufficient to dry up all the rivers of besieged places, either by drinking them, or by diverting their course into other channels. Ex 15:9. 2 S 17:13. 1 K 20:10. Da 4:30. **besieged places**. or, fenced places. Ps 31:21mg. 60:9mg. Is +37:25mg.

25. **Hast thou not**, etc. or, Hast thou not heard *how* I have made it long ago, and formed it of ancient times? should I now bring it to be laid waste, *and* fenced cities *to be* ruinous heaps? **I have done it**. Ps 33:11. 76:10. Is 10:5, 6, 15. 37:26, 27. +*45:7. 46:10, 11. 54:16. Ac 4:27, 28. **ancient times**. Heb. *kedem*, Mi +5:2.

26. **of small power**. Heb. short of hand. Nu 11:23. 14:9. Ps 48:4-7. 127:1. Je 37:10. 50:36, 37. 51:30, 32. **they were**. Ps 92:7. 102:11. Is 40:6-8. Ja 1:10, 11. 1 P 1:24. **the grass**. Ps 129:6-8.

27. **I know**. Ps 139:1-11. Je 23:23, 24. **abode**. or, sitting. Ex 15:17. **thy going out**. Dt 28:6, 19. Ps 121:8. Is 37:28, 29.

28. **thy rage**. Ps 2:1-5. 7:6. 10:13, 14. 46:6. 93:3, 4. Lk 6:11. Jn 15:18, 23, 24. Ac 7:51. **thy tumult**. Ps 65:7. 74:4, 23. 83:2. **I will put**. This alludes to the

method by which the common people manage their beasts in the East, especially the dromedaries, which are governed by a bridle fastened to a ring, which runs through the nostril of the beast. Jb 41:2. Ps 32:9. Ezk 29:4. 38:4. Am 4:2. Ja 3:3. **by the way.** ver. 33, 36, 37.

29. **a sign.** ver. 21, 31-34. 2 K 20:8, 9. Ex 3:12. 1 S 2:34. Is 7:11-14. Lk 2:12. **Ye shall eat.** Le 25:4, 5, 20-22. Is 37:30.

30. **the remnant that,** etc. Heb. the escaping of the house of Judah that remaineth. ver. 4. 2 Ch 32:22, 23. Is 1:9. 10:20-22. **shall yet again.** Ps 80:9. Is 27:6. 37:31, 32.

31. **For.** ver. 4. Je 44:14. Ro 9:27. 11:5. **they that escape. the escaping.** Ge 32:8. 45:7. **the zeal.** ✻22B, Is +9:7. Is 9:7. 59:17. 63:15. Ezk 5:13. 20:9. Zc 1:14. Jn 2:17.

32. **He shall not come.** Is 8:7-10. 10:24, 25, 28-32. 37:33-35. **cast a bank.** 2 S 20:15. Ezk 21:22. Lk 19:43, 44.

33. **By the way.** ver. 28, 36.

34. **I will defend.** 2 K 20:6. Ps 46:5, 6. 48:2-8. Is 31:5. 38:6. **for mine.** Dt 32:27. Is 43:25. 48:9, 11. Ezk 36:22. Ep 1:6, 14. **my servant.** 1 K 11:12, 13. 15:4. Is 9:7. Je 23:5, 6. 33:20, +√21, +√25, 26.

35. **that night.** Ex 12:29. Da 5:30. 1 Th 5:2, 3. **the angel.** Ex 12:29, 30. 2 S 24:16. 1 Ch 21:12, 16. 2 Ch 32:21, 22. Ps 35:5, 6. Ac 12:23. **and smote.** Is 10:16-19, 33. 30:30-33. 37:36. Ho 1:7. **when they arose.** Ex 12:30. Ps 76:5-7, 10.

36. **Sennacherib.** ver. 7, 28, 33. **Nineveh.** Ge 10:11, 12. Jon 1:2. 3:2, etc. Na 1:1. 2:8. Mt 12:41.

37. **Nisroch.** i.e. *great eagle,* ✻S#5268h. ver. 10. 2 K 18:5, 30. Dt 32:31. 2 Ch 32:14, 19. Is 37:37, 38h. **Adrammelech.** i.e. *honor of the king; splendor,* ✻S#152h. 2 K 17:31. Is 37:38. (1) An idol of the people of Sepharvaim whom Shalmaneser brought to Samaria after he had carried away the inhabitants into captivity, 2 K 17:31. (2) Son of Sennacherib, king of Assyria, who, along with his brother Sharezer, killed their father in the temple of Nisroch, an idol of the Assyrians, 2 K 19:37; Is 37:38. **Sharezer.** i.e. *prince of fire,* ✻S#8272h. Is 37:38. Zc 7:2. **his sons smote.** ver. 7. 2 Ch 32:21. **the land.** *Armenia* or *Ararat* is a province of Asia, comprising the modern Turcomania and part of Persia; having Georgia on the north, Curdistan, or the ancient Assyria, on the south, and Asia Minor, now Natolia, on the west. **Armenia.** Heb. Ararat. ✻S#780h. Ge 8:4. Is 37:38. Je 51:27. **Esarhaddon.** i.e. *gift of fire,* ✻S#634h. Ezr 4:2. Is 37:38.

2 KINGS 20

Hezekiah, when sick, is warned by Isaiah to prepare for death, 1; but praying, he receives the promise of fifteen years added to his life, and of deliverance from the Assyrians, 2-7. In confirmation, the shadow on Ahaz's dial goes back ten degrees, 8-11. The king of Babylon sends to congratulate Hezekiah, who shows the ambassadors all his treasures, 12, 13. Isaiah reproves him for this, and foretells the Babylonish captivity, 14-19. Hezekiah dies, and is succeeded by Manasseh, 20, 21.

1. A.M. 3291. B.C. 713. **In those days.** ✻171, Ge +2:17. **was Hezekiah sick.** 2 K ✻13:14. 2 Ch 32:24, etc. Is 38:1, etc. Jn ✻11:1-5. Ph ✻2:27, 30. 2 T +✻4:20.

the prophet. 2 K 19:2, 20. **Set thine house in order.** Heb. Give charge concerning thine house. 2 S 17:23mg. Is 38:1mg. **thou shalt die.** Je 18:7-10. Jon 3:4-10. **not live.** ✻144D, Ge +40:23.

2. **he turned.** 1 K 8:30. 1 S 20:25. Ps 50:15. Is 38:2, 3. Mt 6:6.

3. **remember.** Ge 8:1. Ne 5:19. 13:14, 22, 31. Ps 25:7. 89:47, 50. 119:49. Is 63:11. **I have walked.** 2 K 18:3-6. Ge 5:22, 24. 17:1. 1 K 2:4. 3:6. Jb 1:1, 8. Lk 1:6. Col +√1:10. **in truth.** 2 Ch 31:20, 21. Ps 32:2. 145:18. Je 4:2. Jn 1:47. 2 C 1:12. 1 J 3:21, 22. **perfect.** Ps √37:18n. ✻S#8003h: Ge 15:16 (full). 34:21 (peaceable). Dt 25:15. 27:6 (whole). Jsh 8:31 (whole). Ru 2:12 (full). 1 K 6:7 (made ready, lit. perfected). 8:61. 11:4. 15:3, 14. 2 K 20:3. 1 Ch 12:38. 28:9. 29:9, 19. 2 Ch 8:16 (perfected). 15:17. ✻16:9. ✻19:9. ✻25:2. Pr 11:1 (just; mg, perfect). Is 38:3. Am 1:6 (whole), 9 (whole). Na 1:12 (quiet; mg, at peace). **heart.** Jsh 14:8, 9. 14:14. 1 K 8:61. 11:4. 15:3, 14. 1 Ch 12:38n. 2 Ch 15:17. ✻16:9. 19:9. ✻25:2. Ps 119:2, 34. Pr 3:5. Is 38:3. Je ✻29:13. Jl 2:12. Mt 5:8. 22:37. Ac 8:37. 16:14. **have done.** Jb 23:11. He ✻6:10. **wept sore.** Heb. wept with a great weeping. Jg 21:2. 2 S 12:21, 22. +13:36mg. Ps 6:6. 102:9. Is 38:14. He ✻5:7.

4. **afore.** T#1783. Ge 21:16, 17. 24:12-15. Nu 16:28-33. Jg 15:18, 19. 16:28-30. 1 K 13:6. ✻18:36-38. 2 Ch 13:14-16. 14:10-12. 20:3-7, 12-17. Ne 2:4-8. Ps ✻138:3. Is ✻65:24. Da 9:20-23. 10:2-6, 11, 12. Jon 1:13-15. Zc 1:12, 13. Mt 8:5-7, 24-26. 9:18, 19, 23-25, 27-29. 17:14-18. 20:30-34. Mk 1:40-42. 7:32-34. 8:22-25. 10:46-52. Lk 3:21, 22. 17:12-14. Jn 4:49-53. Ac 9:39, 40. **court.** *or,* city. 2 K 22:14. 1 K 7:8.

5. **Turn again.** 2 S 7:3-5. 1 Ch 17:2-4. **the captain.** Jsh 5:14, 15. 1 S 9:16. 10:1. 2 S 5:2. 2 Ch 13:12. He 2:10. **the God.** 2 Ch 34:3. Is 38:5. 55:3. Mt 22:32. **I have heard.** 2 K 19:20. Ps 65:2. 66:19, 20. Lk 1:13. **I have seen.** Ps 39:12. 56:8. 126:5. Re 7:17. **I will heal.** ver. 7. Ex ✻15:26. +✻23:25. Dt 32:39. Jb 33:19, 26. Ps +41:3. +✻103:3. 147:3. Mt ✻8:2, 3, 17. Ac ✻10:38. Ph 2:27. Ja ✻5:14, 15. 3 J √2. **thou shalt go.** ver. 8. Ps 66:13-15, 19, 20. 116:12-14. 118:17-19. Is 38:22. Jn 5:14.

6. **I will add.** Jb ✻14:5, 6. Ps 116:15. Ac 27:24. **I will defend.** See on 2 K 19:34. 2 Ch 32:22. Is 10:24.

7. **Take a lump.** 2 K 2:20-22. 4:41. Is 38:21. Jn 9:6. **the boil.** The word *shechin,* from the Arabic *sachana,* to be *hot,* signifies an *inflammatory tumor,* or *burning boil;* and some think that Hezekiah's malady was a *pleurisy;* others, that it was the *plague;* and others, the *elephantiasis,* a species of *leprosy,* as one of the Hexapla versions renders in Job 2:7. A poultice of figs might be very proper to maturate a boil, or dismiss any obstinate inflammatory swelling, and the propriety of such an application is expressly mentioned by Pliny (l. xxii. c.25. l. xxiii. c.7), but we cannot discuss its propriety in this case, unless we were certain of the nature of the malady. It was, however, the natural means which God chose to bless for his recovery, as was the clay which Christ moistened to anoint the eyes of the blind man (Jn 9:6); for in both cases, without Divine interposition the cure would not have been effected.

8. **What shall be.** ver. 5. 2 K 19:29. Jg 6:17, 37-40. Is 7:11, 14. 38:22. Ho 6:2.

9. **This sign.** Is 38:7, 8. Mt 16:1-4. Mk 8:11, 12. Lk 11:29, 30. **shadow.** Jb 7:2. Is 38:8.

10. **It is a light**. 2 K 2:10. 3:18. Is 49:6. Mk 9:28, 29. Jn 14:12. Comparatively speaking it might be deemed an accident or overlooked entirely (Young). **go down**. S#5186h, Heb. gram. form, *Kal, infinitive:* Ex 7:5 (stretch forth). 23:2 (decline). Nu 22:26 (turn). Jsh 8:19 (stretched out). Jg 19:8 (mg, declined). Ps 17:11 (bowing down; lit., to bend). *109:23 (when it declineth). **backward**. Ge 9:23.

11. **cried unto**. Ex 14:15. 1 K 17:20, 21. 18:36-38. Ac 9:40. **he brought**. Jsh *10:12-14. 2 Ch 32:24, 31. Is 38:8. **dial**. Heb. degrees. lit. goings up or steps, as in Ex 20:26; 1 K 10:19, 20. What these degrees were, or how dials were then constructed, is wholly uncertain. It is probable that this miracle was effected by refraction, rather than by arresting the motion of the earth. There has been much speculation regarding this miracle. Many tie it to the long day of Joshua (Jsh 10:13), where the sun is said to have not gone down for "about a whole day;" the ten degrees here are then taken to be equivalent to fifteen minutes, and the two miracles account for a so-called "missing day" in alleged astronomical calculations. But the documentation for the apparently apocryphal story is shaky, and defies scholarly efforts to track it down. So while this speculation about the miracle is interesting, it is not true, and like the speculation about Charles Darwin repenting of his belief in evolution and turning to Christ for salvation upon his death bed, is apocryphal, and like similar speculation in prophetic sensationalism, does more harm than good to the cause of truth. That God performed the miracle is not questioned; how the miracle was effected is unrevealed.

12. A.M. 3292. B.C. 712. **Berodach-baladan**. Is 39:1, etc., Merodach-baladan. i.e. *the mighty lord,* ✱S#1255h. **Baladan**. i.e. *having power and riches,* ✱S#1081h. Is 39:1. **king**. 2 Ch *32:31. **Babylon**. Ge 10:10. 11:9. Is 13:1, 19. 14:4. **sent letters**. 2 S 8:10. 10:2. **for he had heard**. Is 39:1.

13. **hearkened**. Dt 7:25, 26. Pr *1:10. 4:14, 15. Is 33:15, 16. Mt *26:41. 1 C *10:13. Ep 6:11-18. Ja 1:12. *4:7. 1 P *5:8, 9. **showed**. Ec 5:11. Ex 5:2. 2 Ch 26:16. *32:25, 27. Est 3:5. Pr 11:2. 15:33. *16:18. 18:12. Is 10:13. 14:13. *39:2. 47:10. Da 4:30. *5:23. Ob 3. Lk *12:15-21. **precious things**. or, spicery. Ge 37:25. 43:11. 1 K 10:2, 10, 15, 25. **armor**. or, jewels. Heb. vessels. 2 Ch 32:27. Is 39:2mg. **there was nothing**. 2 Ch 32:25, 26. Pr *23:5. Ec *7:20. **nor in all**. Ge +√7:19 (√102, Hyperbole/Overstatement). 1 K √18:10. Mt √5:29. **dominion**. 2 K 20:13. 2 Ch 8:6.

14. **came Isaiah**. Is 39:3-8. **What said**. √22C2, Ge +3:9. 2 K 5:25, 26. 2 S 12:7, etc. 2 Ch 16:7-10. 25:7-9, 15, 16. Ps 141:5. Pr 25:12. Je 26:18, 19. Am 7:12, 13. Mk 6:18, 19. **a far country**. Dt 28:49. Jsh 9:6, 9. Is 13:5.

15. **What**. √22C2, Ge +3:9. **All the things**. ver. *13. Nu +*32:23. Jsh *7:19. Jb *31:33. Pr *28:13. 1 J √1:8-10.

16. **Hear**. 2 K 7:1. 1 K 22:19. Is 1:10. Am 7:16.

17. **shall be carried**. 2 K 24:13. 25:13-15. Le 26:19. 2 Ch 36:10, 18. Je 27:21, 22. 52:17-19.

18. **thy sons**. 2 K 24:12. 25:6. 2 Ch 33:11. **they shall be**. "Fulfilled, Da 1:3-7." Ge 37:36mg.

19. **Good**. Le 10:3. 1 S 3:18. Jb 1:21. Ps 39:9. La *3:22, 31-33, 39. **Is it not good**, etc. or, Shall there not be peace and truth, etc. **peace and truth**. Est 9:30. Je 33:6. Zc 8:19. Lk 2:10, 14. 1 T *2:1, +2.

20. **he made a pool**. 2 Ch 32:4, 30, 32. Ne 3:16. Is 22:9-11. **a conduit**. 2 K 18:17n. 2 S 5:23n. **the book**. 2 K 8:23. 15:6, 26. 16:19. 1 K 14:19. 15:7, 23.

21. A.M. 3306. B.C. 698. **slept with his fathers**. 2 K 21:18. Ge +*25:8n. Dt 31:16n. 1 K 2:10. +*11:43. 14:+20, 31. 2 Ch 26:23. 32:33. **Manasseh**. i.e. *causing to forget*. 2 K 21:1. Ge +41:51mg. Is 38:19n.

2 KINGS 21

Manasseh reigns very wickedly and idolatrously, 1-9. Prophets are sent to predict judgments upon Judah because of his wickedness, 10-16. He dies and is succeeded by Amon, 17, 18. Amon reigns wickedly, 19-22. He is slain by his servants; the people put the conspirators to death, and make his son Josiah king, 23, 24. Amon's acts and burial, 25, 26.

1. A.M. 3306-3361. B.C. 698-643. **was twelve**. 2 K 20:21. 1 Ch 3:13. 2 Ch 32:33. 33:1, etc. Mt 1:10, Manasses. **Hephzi-bah**. i.e. *my delight is in her*. Pr 5:19. Is 62:4mg.

2. **And he did**. ver. 7, 16. 2 K 16:2-4. 22:17. 2 Ch 33:2-4. **after the abominations**. Le 18:25-29. Dt 12:31. 2 Ch 36:14. Ezk 16:51.

3. **high places**. 2 K 12:3. 14:4. 15:4, 35. 16:4. 17:9. Le 26:30. Nu 21:28. 33:52. 1 K 3:2. *11:7. 12:31, 32. 13:33. *14:23. 15:14. 22:43. 2 Ch *11:15. 15:17. *20:33n. *21:11. 28:4. 33:3. Ps 78:58. Is 15:2. 16:12. Je *7:31. 17:3. *19:5. 32:35. Ezk 16:16. 20:29. 36:2. *43:7. Mi 1:5. **which**. 2 K 18:4, 22. 2 Ch 32:12. 34:3. **he reared**. 2 K 10:18-20. 1 K 16:31-33. 18:21, 26. **a grove**. Rather, as we have before remarked, *Asherah* or *Astarte*. So Castell defines *Asherah* to be "A wooden image dedicated to *Astarte*." 2 K 13:6. 17:+10, 16. 18:4. 23:4. 1 K 18:19n. Is +*66:17n. **Ahab**. 2 K 8:18, 27. Mi 6:16. **and worshipped**. 2 K 17:16. 23:4. Dt 4:19. 17:3. 2 Ch 33:3-5. Jb 31:26. **the host of heaven**. 2 K 17:16. 23:4. Dt 4:19. 17:3. 2 Ch 33:5. Jb 31:26, 28. Je *7:18. 8:2. *19:13. 44:17, 19. Ezk 8:15, 16. Zp 1:5. Ac 7:42.

4. **he built**. 2 K 16:10-16. Je 32:34. **In Jerusalem**. Ex 20:24. Dt 12:5. 2 S 7:13. 1 K 8:29. 9:3. Ps 78:68, 69. 132:13, 14.

5. **in the two courts**. 2 K 23:4, 6. 1 K 6:36. 7:12. 2 Ch 33:5, 15. Ezk 40:28, 32, 37, 47. 42:3. 43:5. 44:19.

6. A.M. 3321. B.C. 683. **pass through the fire**. 2 K 3:27. 16:3. 17:17. 23:10. Le 18:21. 20:2, 3, 5. Dt 12:31. *18:10. 2 Ch 28:3. 33:6. Ps *106:37, 38. Is 65:3. Mi 6:7. **observed times**. or, observed clouds. ✱S#6049h: Ge 9:14h (bring a cloud). Le 19:26h, 31. Dt +*18:10, 14. Jg 9:37mg. 2 Ch 33:6. Is 2:6h (soothsayers). 57:3h (sorceress). Je 27:9h (enchanters). Mi 5:12h (soothsayers). **enchantments**. ✱S#5172h. Le 17:17. Ge +30:27h (learned by experience). 44:5, 15. Le *19:26. Nu 23:23h. 24:1. Dt +*18:10. 1 K 20:33h (observe). 2 Ch *33:6mg. **familiar spirits**. ✱S#178h. 2 K 23:24. Le *19:31. *20:6, 27. Dt +*18:11. 1 S 28:3, 7-9. 1 Ch 10:13. Jb 3219h (like bottles). Is 8:19. 19:3. 29:4. Ac 16:16. **wizards**. ✱S#3049h. 2 K 23:24. Le 19:31. 20:6, 27. Dt +*18:11. 1 S 28:3, 9. 2 Ch 33:6. Is 8:19. 19:3. **wrought**. 2 K 24:3, 4. Ge 13:13.

7. A.M. 3306-3327. B.C. 698-677. **he set**. 2 K 23:6. 2 Ch 33:7, 15. **graven image**. Ex *20:4. Le 26:1. **In this house**. ver. 4. 2 K 23:27. 2 S 7:13. 1 K 8:29, 44. 9:3, 7. 2 Ch 7:12, 16, 20. Ne 1:9. Ps 74:2. 78:68, 69. 132:13, 14. Je 32:34. **for ever**. Heb. *olam*, Ex +12:24.

8. **will I make.** 2 K 18:11. 2 S 7:10. 1 Ch 17:9. 2 Ch 33:8. **only if they.** Le 26:3, etc. Dt 5:28, 29. 28:1, etc. Jsh 23:11-13. Ps *37:3. 81:11-16. Is 1:19. Je 7:3-7, 23. 17:20-27. Ezk 22:2-16. 33:25-29.

9. **they hearkened not.** 2 Ch 36:16. Ezr 9:10, 11. Ne 9:26, 29, 30. Ps 81:11. Da 9:6, 10, 11. Lk 13:34. Jn 15:22. Ja *4:17. **seduced.** 1 K 14:16. 2 Ch 33:9. Ps 12:8. Pr *29:12. Ho 5:11. Re 2:20. **more evil.** Je 2:10, 11. Ezk 16:47, 51, 52.

10. **the Lord spake by.** 2 Ch 33:10. 36:15. Ne 9:26, 30. Mt 23:34-37. In the following verses the doom of Judah and Jerusalem is passed, and it is a heavy doom. The prophets were sent in the first place to teach them the knowledge of God, to remind them of their duty, and direct them in it: if they succeeded not in that, their next work was to reprove them for their sins, and to set them in view before them, that they might repent and reform, and return to their duty: if in this they prevailed not, their next work was to foretell the judgments of God, that the terror of them might awaken to repentance those who would not be made sensible of the obligations of his love; or else that the execution of them, in their season, might be a demonstration of the divine mission of the prophets who foretold them. They were made *judges* to those who would not hear and receive them as *teachers* (Henry).

11. **Because.** 2 K 23:26, 27. 24:3, 4. Je 15:4. **above all.** ver. 9. 1 K 21:26. Ezk 16:3, 45. **Amorites.** Ge +10:16. **made Judah.** ver. 9. 1 K 14:16. 15:30. 16:19.

12. **I am bringing.** 2 K 22:16. Da 9:12. Mi 3:12. **whosoever.** 1 S 3:11. Is 28:16. Je 19:3. Am 3:2. Mt 24:21, 22. Lk 23:28, 29. Re 6:15-17.

13. **I will stretch.** This metaphor is taken from the custom of using a *line* in measuring land, and in dividing portions of it among several persons. Samaria was taken, pillaged, and ruined, and its inhabitants carried into captivity: Jerusalem shall have the same measure. 2 K 17:6. Is 10:22. 28:17. 34:11. La 2:8. Ezk 23:31-34. Am 7:7, 8. Zc 1:16. **the plummet.** 2 K 10:11. 1 K 21:21-24. **I will wipe.** 𝑓147A, Ge +50:24. I will empty Jerusalem of all its wealth and inhabitants, as truly as a dish turned up and wiped is emptied of its contents. 1 K 14:10. Is 14:23. Je 25:9. Ezk 24:10, 11. Re 18:21-23. **wiping it, and turning it upside down.** Heb. he wipeth and turneth *it* upon the face thereof.

14. **And I will.** Dt 31:17. 2 Ch 15:2. Ps 37:28. 89:38, etc. Je 12:7. 23:33. La 5:20. Am 5:2. **the remnant.** 2 K 19:4, 30, 31. 24:2. 2 Ch 36:16, 17. 23:33. **deliver.** Le 26:17, 36-38. Dt 4:26, 27. 28:25, 31-33, 48. Jg 2:14, 15. Ne 9:27-37. Ps 71:1-7. 106:40-43. Is 10:6. La 1:5, 10.

15. **have provoked.** Is 65:3. **since the day.** Dt 9:24. 31:27, 29. Jg 2:11-13. Ps 106:34-40. Ezk 16:15, etc. 20:4, 13, 21, 23, 30. 23:3, 8, etc. Da 9:5-11.

16. **Manasseh.** 2 K 24:3, 4. Nu 35:33. Dt 21:8, 9. Je 2:34. 7:6. 15:4. 19:4. Mt 23:30, 31. 27:6. Lk 13:34. He 11:37. **one end to another.** Heb. mouth to mouth. 2 K +10:21mg. **beside his sin.** ver. 7, 11. Ex 32:31. 1 K 14:15, 16. 2 Ch 33:9.

17. **the rest.** See on 2 K 20:20, 21. 2 Ch 33:1-20.

18. A.M. 3361. B.C. 643. **slept with his fathers.** 2 K √24:6n. 1 K +*11:43. **and was buried.** 2 Ch 21:20. 24:16, 25. 28:27. 32:33. 33:20. Je 22:19. **the garden.** Jn 19:41. **Uzza.** i.e. *strength; goat.* ver. 26. 2 S 6:6-8. (1) A Levite who presumptuously touched the ark, and was slain by Jehovah, 2 S 6:3, 6, 7, Uzzah. (2) A

chief man of Benjamin, 1 Ch 8:7. (3) One whose children returned from Babylon, Ezr 2:49. Ne 7:51. (4) One of the inhabitants of Jerusalem, who owned the garden in which Manasseh, king of Judah, and his son Amon were buried, 2 K 21:18, 26. (5) A descendant of Merari, the son of Levi, 1 Ch 6:29. (6) A son of Abinadab, 1 Ch 13:7-11. *S#5798h: 2 S 6:3, 6, 7, 8. 2 K 21:18, 26. 1 Ch 6:29. 8:7. 13:7, 9, 10, 11. Ezr 2:49. Ne 7:51. **Amon.** i.e. *an artificer.*

19. A.M. 3361-3363. B.C. 643-641. **Amon.** 1 Ch 3:14. 2 Ch 33:21-25. Mt 1:10. **two years.** 2 K 15:23, 25. 16:8. 22:51. **Meshullemeth.** i.e. *one recompensed,* *S#4922h. **Haruz.** i.e. *sharp pointed, diligent,* *S#2743h. **Jotbah.** i.e. *goodness; pleasantness,* *S#3192h. See *S#3193h: Nu 33:33, 34. Dt 10:7.

20. **as his father.** ver. 2-7. Nu 32:14. 2 Ch 33:22, 23. Mt 23:32. Ac 7:51.

22. **he forsook.** 2 K 22:17. Dt 32:15. 1 K 11:33. 1 Ch *28:9. Je 2:13. Jon 2:8.

23. A.M. 3363. B.C. 641. **the servants.** 2 K 12:20. 14:19. 15:25, 30. 1 K 15:27. 16:9. 2 Ch 33:24, 25.

24. **the people of the land slew.** 2 K 14:5. **made Josiah.** 2 K 11:17. 14:21. 1 S 11:15. 2 S 5:3. 1 K 12:1, 20. 2 Ch 22:1. 26:1. 33:25.

25. **the rest.** ver. 17. 2 K 20:20.

26. **sepulchre.** Heb. *qeburah,* Ge +35:20 (*S#6900h). **in the garden.** See on ver. 18. 2 S 6:6-8. **Josiah.** 1 K 13:2. Mt 1:10, Josias.

2 KINGS 22

Josiah reigns well, 1, 2. He provides for the repairs of the temple, 3-7. Hilkiah finds the book of the law, which is read to the king; who is alarmed by God's threatenings against backsliders, and sends to inquire of God by Huldah the prophetess, 8-14. She foretells the destruction of Jerusalem, but speaks peace to Josiah, 15-20.

1. A.M. 3363-3394. B.C. 641-610. **Josiah.** This prince was one of the best, if not the best, of all the Jewish kings since the time of David. He began well, continued well, and ended well. 1 K 13:2. 2 Ch 34:1, 2, etc. Je 1:2. Zp 1:1. Mt 1:10, Josias. **eight years old.** 2 K 11:21. 21:1. Ps 8:2. Ec 10:16. Is 3:4. **Jedidah.** i.e. *beloved; amiable,* *S#3040h. **Adaiah.** i.e. *adorned of Jah.* **Boskath.** i.e. *loftiness; stony region,* *S#1218h. Jsh 15:39, Bozkath. This was a city in the plain country of the tribe of Judah; and is mentioned in the parallel passage (Jsh 15:39) along with Lachish and Eglon.

2. **walked.** 2 K 16:2. 18:3. 2 Ch 17:3. 29:2. Pr 20:11. **walked.** 1 K 3:6. 11:38. 15:5. **turned.** Dt 5:32. Jsh 1:7. Pr 4:27. Ezk 18:14-17.

3. A.M. 3380. B.C. 642. **in the.** 2 Ch 34:3-8, etc. **Shaphan.** i.e. *a coney.* ver. 12. Je 36:10. Ezk 8:11. (1) A scribe of Josiah, 2 K 22:3, 12. Je 36:10 w Ezk 8:11. (2) Father of Ahikam, and comtemporary with the first Shaphan, 2 K 22:12. 25:22. Je 26:24. 39:14. *S#8227h: 2 K 22:3, 8, 9, 10, 10, 12, 12, 14. 25:22. 2 Ch 34:8, 15, 15, 16, 18, 18, 20, 20. Je 26:24. 29:3. 36:10, 11, 12. 39:14. 40:5, 9, 11. 41:2. 43:6. Ezk 8:11. **Azaliah.** i.e. *kept back by Jah.* **Meshullam.** i.e. *recompensed.*

4. **Hilkiah.** i.e. *portion of Jah.* 1 Ch 6:13. 9:11. 2 Ch 34:9-18. Je 1:1, 2. **that he may.** Ten years seem to have elapsed since the people began to present the accustomed offerings; yet no one had taken an

account of them, nor were they applied to the purpose for which they were given. **sum the silver.** 2 K 12:4, 8-11. 2 Ch 24:8-12. Mk 12:41, 42. **the keepers.** 1 Ch 9:19. 26:13-19. 2 Ch 8:14. Ne 11:19. Ps 84:10. **door.** Heb. threshold. 2 K 12:9mg. 1 K +14:17mg. Is 6:4.

5. **deliver.** 2 K 12:11-14. **to repair.** 2 K 12:5. 2 Ch 24:7, 12, 13, 27. Ezr 3:7. **the breaches.** 2 K 12:8, 12.

6. **carpenters.** or, artificers. Ex 28:11. 35:35. 38:23. **builders.** 2 K 12:11. Ge 4:17. 1 K 5:18. 6:12. **masons.** or, repairers of the wall. 2 K 12:12. Is 58:12. Ezk 22:30.

7. **Howbeit.** 2 K 12:15. 2 Ch 24:14. **they dealt faithfully.** 2 K +*12:15. Ex 36:5, 6.

8. **I have found.** This certainly was a genuine copy of the divine law, and probably the *autograph* of Moses, as it is said, in the parallel place of Chronicles (2 Ch *34:14mg), to be the book of the *law of the Lord by Moses*. It is not probable that this was the *only* copy of the law in the land, or that Josiah had never before seen the book of Moses; but the fact seems to be, that this was the original of the covenant renewed by Moses in the plains of Moab, and now being unexpectedly found, its *antiquity*, the *occasion* of its being made, the present *circumstances* of the people, the *imperfect state* in which the reformation was as yet, after all that had been done, would all concur to produce the effect here mentioned on the mind of the pious Josiah. Scott further suggests that it is highly probable, that copies of the law were at that time very scarce, through the idolatry of the former reigns, and the lamentable ungodliness of the people. It might also be reasonably conjectured, that the priests had made abstracts from it, of the outlines of their worship, without specifying particulars, or inserting the solemn sanctions annexed to each of them. This would spare them the trouble of transcribing, or studying, or reading to the people, the whole book; and, as these abstracts would come into common use, few people would look any further. But had not a universal traditional recollection of the law, and in general of its contents, prevailed in the nation; how could the book, when found, have obtained proper and implicit credit as the word of God by Moses? In the dark ages this was precisely the case: the liturgies and rituals contained a few selected portions of Scripture; and not only were the *people* kept in the dark as to the entire contents of the Bible, but few even of the *priests* had ever read it through, and numbers of these had never seen a complete copy of it. The same naturally becomes the case still, (notwithstanding the multiplication of copies of the Bible by the art of printing, and its public allowance in the vulgar tongue, and the commendable pains by pious persons to disperse them) whenever any set of men become strenuous for one part of religion in preference to the rest. They, who are the oracles of each party, insert in their writings those portions of Scripture, which are supposed to inculcate the doctrines for which they contend; but keep out of sight, perhaps without design, those passages which as strongly declare, what they undervalue, overlook, or are prejudiced against. And these writings form the religion of the zealous friends of that party, while the rest of Scripture is comparatively neglected or forgotten. Indeed we all are disposed to have favorite passages of Scripture, to which we are more attentive than to the rest; so that without great

care we shall be led into this error.—And may it not be hinted with propriety, that some text-books, which were well designed, are yet capable of a dangerous abuse? I mean those books, which give a text of Scripture for every day, with pious observations upon it. Many read these in family worship, instead of the Bible itself; and others, it is likely, do the same in their closets: but numbers are thus undesignedly led to substitute a part for the whole; the abstract with an exposition, instead of the book of the law: whereas "all Scripture is given by inspiration of God, and is profitable for doctrine, for reproof, for correction, for instruction in righteousness; that the man of God may be perfect, throughly furnished unto all good works" (2 T *3:16). The proper use of such books is to suggest subjects for pious meditations and ejaculations, in the intervals of conversation and business.—The scarcity of the written word did not *excuse* Israel's degeneracy and idolatry, because it was the *effect* of it; "the people loved to have it so" (Je 5:31); but the abundance of Bibles, with which this land is favored, will exceedingly aggravate the guilt of our national impiety, infidelity, and licentiousness: for what greater contempt of God can we show, than to refuse to read his word, when put into our hands; or, reading it, to refuse to believe and obey it? 2 K 14:6n. Dt 31:24-26. 2 Ch 34:14, 15, etc. Je 2:8n.

9. **Shaphan.** ver. 3, 12. 2 K 25:22. Je 26:24. 29:3. 36:10-12. 39:14. 40:11. 41:2. Ezk 8:11. **the scribe.** See on 2 K 18:18. **gathered.** Heb. melted. Ezk 22:20. or, poured out. 2 Ch 34:17. Jb 10:10.

10. **Shaphan.** Dt 31:9-13. 2 Ch 34:18. Ne 8:1-7, 14, 15, 18. 13:1. Je 36:6, 15, 21. **the king.** Dt *17:18-20. Je 13:18. 22:1, 2.

11. **that he rent.** ver. 19. 2 Ch 34:19. Je 36:24. Jl 2:13. Jon 3:6, 7.

12. **the king.** 2 K 19:2, 3. 2 Ch 34:19-21. Is 37:1-4. **Ahikam.** i.e. *brother of a withstander* or *the enemy*. ver. 9. Je 26:22, 24. Father of Gedaliah, governor of Judea, 2 K 25:22. Je 39:14. 40:5. *S#296h: 2 K 22:12, 14. 25:22. 2 Ch 34:20. Je 26:24. 39:14. 40:5, 6, 7, 9, 11, 14, 16. 41:1, 2, 6, 10, 16, 18. 43:6. **Achbor.** i.e. *a mouse.* 2 Ch 34:20, Abdon. **Michaiah.** i.e. *who is like Jah.* or, Micah. Jg 17:1. 2 Ch 34:20. Father of Abdon, or Achbor, employed by king Josiah, 2 Ch 34:20. Called Michaiah, 2 K 22:12. *S#4320h: 2 K 22:12. Ne 12:35, 41. Je 26:18. **Asahiah.** i.e. *doing of Jah.*

13. **enquire.** 2 K 3:11. 1 K 22:7, 8. 1 Ch 10:13, 14. Ps 25:14. Pr *3:6. Je 21:1, 2. 37:17. Ezk 14:3, 4. 20:1-3. Am 3:7. **great.** Ex *20:5. Dt 4:23-27. *29:23-28. 31:17, 18. Ne 8:8, 9. 9:3. Ps 76:7. Da 9:5, 6. Na 1:6. Ro 3:20. 4:15. 7:9. Re 6:17. It is supposed that the portion, which was first read to Josiah, was the 28th and 29th chapters of Deuteronomy: and these were doubtless well suited to convince him, that the guilt and danger of his people was much greater than he had apprehended, and to induce the expressions of fear, sorrow, and humiliation, which he showed. It is probable his reformation had hitherto been conducted by such abstracts, as have been mentioned, or by traditional knowledge. If the kings of Judah had observed the rule of transcribing the law with their own hands, very salutary effects might have been produced; but it seems to have been entirely neglected, as well as the command to read the law publicly to

the people, every year at the feast of tabernacles (Scott). "No revival is more to be desired than that of systematic, personal Bible study!" Dt 17:18. 31:9-13. Ne 8:1-18. 9:3. **because our fathers.** 2 Ch 29:6. 34:21. Ps 106:6. Je 16:12. 44:17. La 5:7. Da 9:8, 10. Ja 1:22-25. **not hearkened.** Dt 27:26. Ja 2:10.

14. **Asahia.** i.e. *wrought of Jah.* (1) A man of Simeon, 1 Ch 4:36. (2) A son of Merari, of Levi, 1 Ch 6:30; 15:6, 11. (3) A Shilonite, one of the first who dwelt in their possessions, 1 Ch 9:5. (4) A servant sent by king Josiah to enquire about the book found, 2 Ch 34:21; 2 K 22:12, 14. ✻S#6222h: 2 K 22:12, 14. 1 Ch 4:36. 6:30. 9:5. 15:6, 11. 2 Ch 34:20. **Huldah.** i.e. *a mole* or *weasel,* ✻S#2468h. 2 Ch 34:22. **prophetess.** Ex 15:20n. Jg 4:4. 2 Ch 34:22. Ne 6:14. Is 8:3. Mi 6:4. Lk 1:41, etc. 2:36. Ac 21:9. 1 C 11:5. **Shallum.** i.e. *recompense.* **Tikvah.** i.e. *expectation; hope.* 2 Ch 34:22, Tikvath. ✻S#8616h: 2 K 22:14. 2 Ch 34:22. Ezr 10:15. (1) The father of Shallum, the husband of Huldah the prophetess. (2) The father of Jahaziah, Ezr 10:15. **Harhas.** i.e. *extremely poor; glittering* ✻S#2745h. 2 Ch 34:22, Hasrah. **wardrobe.** Heb. garments. 2 K 10:22. Ne 7:72. **college.** or, second part. 2 Ch 34:22mg,n. Ne 11:9. Zp 1:10.

15. **Thus saith.** 2 K 1:6, 16. Je 23:28.

16. **Behold.** 2 K 20:17. 21:12, 13. 2 Ch 34:24, 25. **all the words.** 2 K 25:1-4. Le 26:15, etc. Dt 28:15, etc. 29:18-23. 30:17, 18. 31:16-18. 32:15-26. Jsh 23:13, 15. Da 9:11-14.

17. **have forsaken.** 2 K ◖12:15. Ex 32:34. Dt *29:24-28. 32:15-19. Jg 2:12-14. 3:7, 8. 10:6, 7, 10-14. 1 K 9:6-9. 2 Ch ◖31:12. Ne 9:26, 27. Ps 106:35-42. Je 2:11-13, 27, 28. Da 9:11-14. Lk ◖*16:10. 1 C ◖4:2. 3 J ◖5. **the works.** Ps 115:4-8. Is 2:8, 9. 44:17-20. 46:5-8. Mi 5:13. **therefore.** 1 Th 2:16. **shall not be.** Dt 32:22. 2 Ch 36:16. Is 33:14. Je 7:20. 17:27. Ezk 20:47, 48. Zp 1:18.

18. **the king.** 2 Ch 34:26-28. **thus shall ye.** Is 3:10. Ml *3:16, 17. **As touching.** ♪63C, Ge +25:32.

19. **heart was tender.** T#1360. 1 S 24:5. Ps *51:17. 119:120. Is 46:12. +*57:15. 66:2, 5. Je 36:24, 29-32. Ezk *9:4. Ro 2:4, 5. Ja 4:6-10. **humbled.** Ex 10:3. Le 26:40, 41. 1 K 21:29. 2 Ch 33:12, 19, 23. Mi *6:8. 1 P 5:5, 6. **a desolation.** Le 26:31, 32. Dt 29:23. Je 26:6. 44:22. **hast rent.** ver. 17. **wept.** Nu 25:6. Jg 2:4, 5. 20:26. Ezr *9:3, 4. *10:1. Ne 1:4. 8:9. Ps 119:136. Je 9:1. 13:17. 14:17. Lk 19:41. Ro 9:2, 3. **I also have.** 2 K 19:20. 20:5.

20. **I will gather.** ♪88, Ge +15:15. Ge +*25:8n. Dt 31:16n. 1 Ch 17:11. 2 Ch 34:28. **thou shalt.** During thy life, none of *these calamities* shall fall upon thee nor thy people; no *adversary* shall be permitted to disturb the peace of Judea; and thou shalt at last "be gathered into thy grave in peace." Now, though it is stated that Pharaoh-Necho slew him at Megiddo (2 Ch 35:22-24), yet the Assyrians and the Jews were at peace; and though Josiah might feel it his duty to oppose the Egyptian king's going against his friend and ally, and that, in his endeavors to oppose him, he was mortally wounded at Migiddo, yet certainly he was not killed *there*, but was brought to Jerusalem, where he died in peace. Young notes "his encounter with the king of Egypt was more a personal than a national act." Scott notes, "Though he was slain in battle, yet he died in peace with God, and went to glory. As he was not forty years old when he died, and the total

destruction of Jerusalem took place within twenty-three years after, he might have lived to that time, according to the ordinary course of nature. But as his piety and zeal could not avail to prevent that catastrophe, he was mercifully 'taken away from the evil to come'" (Is 57:1). **be gathered.** 2 K 23:29, 30. Ps *37:37. Is *57:1, 2. Je *22:10, 15, 16. **grave.** Heb. *qeber,* Ge +23:4.

2 KINGS 23

Josiah reads the law in a solemn assembly gathered for that and similar purposes, 1, 2. He enters into covenant with God; and abolishes idolatry in Judah, 3-14. He burns men's bones on the altar at Bethel; fulfills the prediction of the prophet sent to Jeroboam, destroys the high places in Samaria, and slays the priests, 15-20. He celebrates a solemn passover, 21-23. He puts away wizards, etc., 24: and excels all his predecessors, 25. The wrath of God against Judah is yet unappeased, 26-28. Josiah is slain in battle by Pharaoh-necho, and succeeded by Jehoahaz, 29, 30; who reigns wickedly three months, is led away prisoner by Pharaoh into Egypt, and succeeded by Jehoiakim, 31-34; who taxes the land for Pharaoh's tribute, and reigns wickedly, 35-37.

1. **the king sent.** Dt 31:28. 2 S 6:1. 2 Ch 29:20. 30:2. *34:29, 30, etc. **elders.** Jsh +20:4. 1 K 8:1.

2. **both small and great.** Heb. from small even unto great. Ge 19:11. 1 S 5:9. 30:2. 2 Ch 15:13. Est 1:5. Jb 3:19. Ps 115:13. Ac 26:22. Re 20:12. **he read.** Dt 31:10-13, 28. 2 Ch *17:9. Ne *8:1-8. 9:3. 13:1. **the book.** 2 K 22:8n. Dt 31:26. 1 K 8:9.

3. **stood.** 2 K 11:14, 17. 2 Ch 23:13. 34:31, 32. **made a covenant.** Ex 24:7, 8. Dt 5:1-3. 29:1, 20-15. Jsh 24:25. 2 Ch 15:12-14. 23:16. 29:19. Ezr 10:3. Ne 9:38. 10:28, etc. Je 50:5. He 8:8-13. 12:24. 13:20. **to walk.** 2 K 20:3. Dt 8:19. 13:4. **his commandments.** Dt 4:45. 5:1. 6:1. Ps *19:7-9. **with all their heart.** Dt 6:5. 10:12. 11:13. Mt 22:36, 37. **And all.** Ex 24:3. Jsh 24:24. 2 Ch 34:32, 33. Ec 8:2. Je 4:2. **soul.** Heb. *nephesh,* Ge +34:3.

4. **priests of the second order.** These were either such as occasionally supplied the high priest's office, or those of the *second course* or *order* established by David. See the References. 1 Ch 24:14-19. Mt 26:3. 27:1. **the keepers.** See on 2 K 22:4. 1 Ch 26:1-19. **door.** 2 K 12:9mg. 1 K +14:17. **to bring.** 2 K 21:3, 7. 2 Ch 33:3, 7. 34:3, 4. **Baal.** 2 K 17:16. Jg 2:13. 1 K 16:31. 18:19, 26, 40. 19:18. Is 27:9. Je 7:9. **Kidron.** 2 S 15:23. Jn 18:1, Cedron. **Bethel.** 1 K 12:29. Ho 4:15. Am 4:4.

5. **put down.** Heb. caused to cease. **the idolatrous priests.** Heb. Chemarim. Ho 10:5mg. "Foretold, Zp 1:4, 5." **planets.** or, twelve signs, or constellations. So the Vulgate *duodecim signa,* "the twelve signs," i.e. the *zodiac;* which is the most probable meaning of the word *mazzaloth,* from the Arabic *manzeel,* a caravanserai, house, or dwelling, as being the apparent *dwellings* of the sun in his annual course; and the Targumists and Rabbins often employ the words *tereysar mazzalaya,* to denote the signs of the *zodiac.* Jb 38:32mg,n. **all the host.** See on 2 K 21:+3, 4. Je 8:1, 2. 44:17-19. Zp 1:4, 5.

6. **the grove.** Or rather, *Ashera,* or Astarte. 2 K +17:10. 21:7. Jg 3:7. 1 K 14:23. 16:33. 2 Ch 34:4. Je

17:2. **to powder**. Ex 32:20. **and burned**. Ex 32:20. Dt 7:25. 9:21. **the graves**. Heb. *qeber*, Ge +23:4. 2 K 10:27. 2 Ch 34:4. **the children**. Probably the common people.

7. **the sodomites**. Ge 19:4, 5. Dt 23:17mg. 1 K 14:24. 15:12. 22:46. 2 Ch 34:33. Jb 36:14mg. Ro 1:26, 27. **where**. Ex 35:25, 26. Ezk 8:14. 16:16. Ho 2:13. **hangings**. Heb. houses.

8. **from**, etc. The northern and southern borders of Judah. **Geba**. Jsh 21:17. 1 K 15:22. 1 Ch 6:60. Is 10:29. Zc 14:10. **Beer-sheba**. Ge 21:31. 26:23. Jg 20:1. 1 K 19:3.

9. **the priests**. Ezk 44:10-44. Ml 2:8, 9. **but they did**. 1 S 2:36. Ezk 44:29-31.

10. **Topheth**. i.e. *the wonder*, S#8612h. Le +18:21. 1 K 11:7, 33. Ps 106:37, 38. Is *30:33 (✱S#8613h). Je 7:31h, 32h. 19:6, 11-14h, Tophet. Ezk 20:31. 23:37. Am 5:26. Ac 7:43. **the valley of the children of Hinnom**. Jsh +*15:8n. 18:16. Ne 11:30. 2 Ch 28:3. 33:6. Je 7:31. 19:2, 6, 11. 32:35. Mt 5:22g. **might make**. 2 K 16:3. 17:17. 21:6. Le 18:21. Dt +*18:10. Je 32:35. Ezk 16:21. 20:26, 31. 23:37-39. **to Molech**. ver. 13, Milcom. 1 K 11:7.

11. **the sun**. ver. 5. 2 Ch 14:5. 34:4. Ezk 8:16. **house of the Lord**. Throughout the East, the *horse*, because of his swiftness and utility, was dedicated to the *sun*; and the Greeks and Romans feigned that the *chariot* of the sun was drawn by four horses, Pyrous, Eous, Aithou, and Phlegon; and hence also *chariots* were dedicated to that luminary. Jarchi says, that those who adored the sun had *horses*, which they mounted every morning, to go out to meet him at his rising. The kings of Judah had imitated these idolatrous customs, and kept the horses of the sun even at the entrance of the temple of the Lord! **chamber**. 1 S 9:22. 1 Ch 9:26, 33. 2 Ch 31:11. Ezr 8:29. 10:6. Ne 10:37-39. **Nathan-melech**. i.e. *ruled by conscience*, ✱S#5419h. **chamberlain**. *or*, eunuch, *or* officer. 2 K +8:6mg. 24:12mg, 15mg. 25:19mg. Ge +*37:36mg.

12. **on the top**. Dt 22:8. Je 19:13. 32:29. Zp 1:5. **upper chamber**. Jg +3:20n. 2 S 18:33. **which Manasseh**. 2 K 21:5, 21, 22. 2 Ch 33:5, 15. **brake them down from thence**. *or*, ran from thence. **cast**. See on ver. 6.

13. **the mount of corruption**. that is, *the mount of Olives*. J146, Ge +10:10. Houbigant, deriving the Hebrew *mashchith* from *mashach*, "to anoint," reads "the Mount of *Olives*." Jarchi, following the Chaldee, also says this was the Mount of Olives; for this is the mount *hammishcha*, of *unction*; but because of the idolatrous purposes for which it was used, the Scripture changed the appellation to "the mount of hammashchith," *corruption*. 1 K 11:7. **Solomon**. 1 K 11:7. Ne 13:26. **Ashtoreth**. ✱S#6252h. Jg 2:13. 10:6. 1 S 7:3, 4. 12:10. 31:10. 1 K 11:5, 33. 1 Ch 6:71. **Chemosh**. ✱S#3645h. Nu 21:29. Jg 11:24. 1 K 11:7, 33. Je 48:7, 13, 46. **Milcom**. ✱S#4445h. 2 S 12:30rmg. 1 K 11:5, 33. 1 Ch 8:9. Je 49:1mg. Zp 1:5, Malcham.

14. **he brake**. Ex *23:24. Nu 33:52. Dt *7:5, 25, 26. 2 Ch 34:3, 4. Mi 1:7. **images**. Heb. statutes. Ex 23:24. **groves**. Dt 7:5. **the bones of men**. ver. 16. Nu *19:11, 16, 18. Je *8:1, 2. Ezk *39:12-16. Mt *23:27, 28.

15. **the altar**. 2 K 10:31. 1 K 12:28-38. 14:16. 15:30. 21:22. **stamped**. See on ver. 6.

16. **sepulchres**. Heb. *qeber*, Ge +23:4. **in the**

mount. Young notes, "where people often were buried, as in Jsh 24:30, 33." **burned**. 1 K ✱*13:1, 2, 32. Mt *24:35. Jn +*10:35. **who proclaimed**. The Septuagint and Hexaplar Syriac at Paris insert, "when Jeroboam stood by the altar at the feast. And turning about, he cast his eyes on the sepulchre of the man of God." On this occasion Josiah exactly accomplished the prediction of the man of God concerning him, delivered about three hundred and sixty years before: and though *he* may be supposed to have designed that accomplishment; yet so wicked a man as his father Amon (2 K 21:19-22, 24) could have had no such intentions, in giving his son the name of *Josiah*.

17. **What title**. Je 31:21. Ezk 39:15. **It is the sepulchre**. Heb. *qeber*, Ge +23:4. **of the man of God**. 1 K *13:1, 30, 31.

18. **alone**. Heb. to escape. 1 S 20:29. **the bones of the prophet**. 1 K 13:1-22, 31.

19. **the houses**. 2 K 17:9. 1 K 12:31. 13:32. **the cities**. 2 Ch 30:6-11. 31:1. 34:6, 7. **the kings**. 2 K 8:18. 1 K 16:33. Mi 6:16. **to provoke the Lord**. 2 K 17:16-18. 21:6. Ps 78:58. Je 7:18, 19. Ezk 8:17, 18.

20. **he slew**. *or*, he sacrificed. 2 K 10:25. 11:18. Ex 22:20. Dt 13:5. 1 K 13:2. *18:40. Is 34:6. Zc 13:2, 3. **burned**. 2 Ch *34:5.

21. **Keep**. 2 Ch 35:1, etc. **passover**. Le +*23:5. **as it is written**. Ex 12:3, etc. Le 23:5-8. Nu 9:2-5. 28:16-25. Dt 16:1-8.

22. **Surely**. 2 Ch 35:18, 19. **passover**. Le +*23:5. **of the kings**. 2 Ch 30:1-3, 13-20. 35:3-17.

24. A.M. 3381. B.C. 623. **Moreover**. "His eighteenth year ending." **the workers**. 2 K 21:3, 6. 1 S 28:3-7. Is *8:19. 19:3. Ac 16:16-18. Re 22:15. **familiar spirits**. 2 K +21:6. Le 19:31. 20:6, 27. **wizards**. 2 K +21:6. Le 19:31. 20:6, 27. **images**. *or*, teraphim. Ge 31:+19mg, 34, 35. Jg 17:5. 18:17, 18. 1 S 19:13. Ezk +21:21mg. Ho 3:4. Zc 10:2mg. **idols**. 2 K 17:12. 21:11, 21. Le 26:30. Dt 29:17. 1 K 15:12. 21:26. Je 50:2. Ezk 6:4. **abominations**. Dt 29:17. **that he might**. Le 19:31. 20:27. Dt 18:10-12. Is √8:20. Ro 3:20. Ja 1:25. **the book**. 2 K +*22:8n-13. 2 Ch +*34:14n-19.

25. A.M. 3363-3394. B.C. 641-610. **like**. J66, Ge +9:3. **unto him**. 2 K 18:5. **that turned**. ver. 3. Dt 4:29. 6:5. 1 K 2:4. 8:48. 15:5. Je 29:13. **soul**. Heb. *nephesh*, Ge +34:3. **according**. Ne 10:29. Ml 4:4. Jn 1:17. 7:19.

26. **Notwithstanding**. 2 K 21:11-13. 22:16, 17. 24:2, 4. Ex 32:34. 2 Ch 36:16. Je 3:7-10. 15:1-4. **fierceness**. 2 Ch +*24:18. 30:8. **provocations**. Heb. angers. 1 K 21:22.

27. **I will remove**. 2 K 17:18, 20. 18:11. 21:13. 24:3. 25:11. Dt 29:27, 28. Je *2:19. 3:11. Ezk 23:32-35. **out of my sight**. Ps 51:11. Je 31:37. 33:24. La 2:7. **My name**. See on 2 K 21:4, 7. 1 K 8:29. 9:3.

28. **the rest**. See on 2 K 20:20. 2 Ch 35:26, 27.

29. A.M. 3394. B.C. 610. **Pharaoh-nechoh**. The Targum reads "Pharaoh the lame." *Pharaoh-nechoh*, called *Nekos*, the son of Psammiticus, by Herodotus (l. i. c. 17, 18, 25. and l. ii. c. 159), was now marching "to make war upon the Medes and Babylonians, who had dissolved the Assyrian empire" (Josephus, Ant. l. x. c.6); the king of the latter being the famous *Nabopollasar*, who had also become king of Assyria. ✱S#6549h. ver. 33, 34, 35h. 2 Ch 35:20-24. Je 46:2h. **Euphrates**. 2 K 24:7. 2 Ch 35:20. Je 46:2. **Josiah went**.

2 Ch 35:20-23. **slew him**. 2 K *22:20n. Ec 8:14. 9:1, 2. Is *57:1, 2. Ro *11:33. **Migiddo**. *Migiddo*, called "Magdolon," *Magdolum*, by Herodotus, was situated in the tribe of Manasseh, west of Jordan, in the valley of Jezreel, and not far from Hadad-Rimmon, or Maximianopolis. This shows that Josiah reigned over the country formerly possessed by the ten tribes; and it is also probable, that Nechoh had landed his troops at or near Caesarea of Palestine. 2 K 9:27. Jsh +17:11. Jg 1:27. 5:19. 1 K 4:12. Zc 12:11, Megiddon. Re 16:16, Armageddon. **he had seen him**. ♪108B, 2 K +14:8. 2 K 14:8, 11.

30. **servants**. 2 K 9:28. 1 K 22:33-38. 2 Ch *35:24. **sepulchre**. Heb. *qeburah*, Ge +35:20 (✳S#6900h). **the people**. 2 K 14:21. 21:24. 2 Ch 36:1, 2, etc. **Jehoahaz**. 1 K 13:3, etc. 1 Ch 3:15, Shallum. Je 22:11, Shallum. **anointed**. 1 S 9:14-16.

31. **Jehoahaz**. 1 Ch 3:15. Je 22:11, Shallum. **Hamutal**. i.e. *kinsman of the dew*, ✳S#2537h. 2 K 24:18. Je 52:1. **Libnah**. Jsh 10:29. 15:42.

32. **he did**. 2 K 21:2-7, 21, 22.

33. **put him**. 2 Ch 36:3, 4. Ezk 19:3, 4. **Riblah**. 2 K 25:6. Nu 34:11. Je 39:5, 6. 52:9, 10, 26, 27. Theodoret (in Je 46) expressly affirms that *Riblah* or *Reblatha* was in his time called *Emesa*. *Koma de estin a Reblatha tas nun kaloumenas Emesas*. *Emesa* was a city of Syria, situated on the Orontes, and according to the *Antonine Itinerary*, 18 miles from Laodicea ad Libanum. It is now called *Homs*, or *Hems*, about eight hours, or twenty-four miles S.E. of Hamah or Hamath, in the road to Damascus. The present town only occupies about one quarter of the space contained within the ancient walls, which apparently date from the time of the Saracens. Here is nothing remarkable, except a Roman sepulchre, and a large castle in ruins. **Hamath**. Nu 13:21. 1 K 8:65. **that he might not reign**. *or*, because he reigned. **put**, etc. Heb. set a mulct upon the land. or, a fine. 2 K 18:14. Ex 21:22. 2 Ch 36:3. Pr 19:19.

34. **Eliakim**. Jsh 18:18. 2 Ch 36:3, 4. **the son**. 1 Ch 3:15. **turned**. 2 K 24:17. Ge 41:45. Da 1:7. **Jehoiakim**. i.e. *Jah raises up*. Mt 1:11, Jakim. **he came**. Je 22:11, 12. Ezk 19:3, 4.

35. **the silver**. ver. 33. **taxed**. 2 K 15:19, 20. Le 27:8, 12, 14. **exacted**. Ex 3:7.

36. A.M. 3394-3405. B.C. 610-599. **Jehoiakim**. 1 Ch 3:15. 2 Ch 36:5. Je 1:3. **twenty and five years old**. Thus two years older than his brother Jehoahaz, as in ver. 31; B.C. 610 (Young). **Zebudah**. i.e. *endowed*, ✳S#2080h. **Pedaiah**. i.e. *whom Jehovah delivers; ransomed; whom Jehovah redeemed*. (1) The grandfather of Josiah, king of Judah, 2 K 23:36. (2) Son or grandson of Jeconiah, of David's line, king of Judah, 1 Ch 3:18, 19. (3) One who helped to build the wall of Jerusalem, Ne 3:25. (4) A Levite who stood on the left of Ezra when he read the law to the people, Ne 8:4. (5) A man of Benjamin named in the genealogies, Ne 11:7. (6) A Levite in the time of Nehemiah set over the treasuries, Ne 13:13. (7) Father of Joel, prince of the half tribe of Manasseh west of Jordan, 1 Ch 27:20. ✳S#6305h: 2 K 23:36. 1 Ch 3:18, 19. 27:20. Ne 3:25. 8:4. 11:7. 13:13. **Rumah**. i.e. *height*, ✳S#7316h. Josephus here reads *Abuma*; but he also speaks of *Ruma*, a village of Galilee (De Bell. l. iii. c. 9).

37. **he did**. Je 22:13-17. 26:20-23. 36:23-26, 31. Ezk 19:5-9. **all that**. 2 Ch 28:22-25. 33:4-10, 22, 23.

2 KINGS 24

Jehoiakim submits to Nebuchadnezzar, but afterwards rebels, 1. God hastens the fulfillment of his predictions against Judah, 2-4. Jehoiakim dies, and is succeeded by Jehoiachin, 5, 6. The king of Babylon prevails against the king of Egypt, 7. Jehoiachin reigns wickedly, 8, 9. Jerusalem is taken; and the king, with his family and treasures, and the sacred vessels, and chief persons of Judah, is carried captive to Babylon, 10-16. Zedekiah is made king, reigns wickedly, and rebels against the king of Babylon, 17-20.

1. **his days**. 2 K 17:5. 2 Ch 36:6, etc. Je 25:1, 9. 46:2. Da 1:1. **Nebuchadnezzar**. i.e. *Nebo is prince of gods*, or *god of fire*, or *prince of the god Mercury*. Sometimes spelled "Nebuchadrezzer," as in Je 39:1, 11. 43:10. Ezk 29:18. This prince, so famous in the writings of the prophets, was the son of Nabopollasar, king of Babylon; who, being old and infirm, associated his son with him in the government, and sent him against Carchemish and the provinces which had revolted from him to Pharaoh-Nechoh. ✳S#5019A: 2 K 24:1, 10, 11. 25:1, 8, 22. 1 Ch 6:15. 2 Ch 36:6, 7, 10, 13. Ezr 2:1. Je 27:6, 8, 20. 28:3, 11, 14. 29:1, 3. 34:1. 39:5. Da 1:1. See also ✳S#5019B: Ezr 1:7. Ne 7:6. Est 2:6. Da 1:18. 2:1, 1. Also ✳S#5019C: Je 21:2, 7. 22:25. 24:1. 25:1, 9. 29:21. 32:1, 28. 51:31. 37:1. 39:1, 11. 43:10. 44:30. 46:2, 13, 26. 49:28, 30. 50:17. 51:34. 52:4, 12, 28, 29, 30. Ezk 26:7. 29:18, 19. 30:10. See also ✳S#5020h: Ezr 5:12, 14. 6:5. Da 2:28, 46. 3:1, 2, 2, 3, 3, 5, 7, 9, 13, 14, 16, 19, 24, 26, 28. 4:1, 4, 18, 28, 31, 33, 34, 37. 5:2, 11, 18.

2. **the Lord**. 2 K 6:23. 13:20, 21. Dt 28:49, 50. 2 Ch 33:11. Jb 1:17. Is 7:17. 13:5. Je 35:11. Ezk 19:8. **bands**. or, troops. Ge 49:19. **Chaldees**. 2 K 25:4. Ge 11:31. 15:7. Je 35:11. **Syrians**. 2 K 6:23. Je 35:11. **Ammon**. 1 S 11:1. **according**. 2 K *20:17. 21:12-14. 23:27. Is 6:11, 12. Je *25:9. 26:6, 20. *32:28. Mi 3:12. **his**. Heb. the hand of his. 2 K 14:25. 19:23mg. 1 K +16:29mg.

3. **Surely**. 2 K 18:25. Ge *50:20. 2 Ch 24:24. 25:16. Is 10:5, 6. 45:7. 46:10, 11. Am +*3:6. **remove them**. 2 K 23:26, 27. Le 26:33-35. Dt 4:26, 27. *28:63. 29:28. Jsh 23:15. Je 15:1-4. Mi 2:10. **for the sins**. 2 K *21:2-11. Ex *20:5.

4. **for the innocent**. 2 K 21:16. Nu 35:33. Dt 19:10. Je 2:34. 19:4. **he filled**. Ps 106:38. **blood**. ♪171I12, Le +20:9. **which**. Je 15:1, 2. La 3:42. Ezk 33:25.

5. **the rest**. 2 Ch 36:8. Je 22:13-17. ch. 26. 36.

6. A.M. 3405. B.C. 599. **slept**. Ge +*25:8n. Dt 31:16n. 1 K +*11:43. +14:20. 2 Ch +*28:27n. As Jehoiakim was "buried with the burial of an ass," by being "drawn and cast forth beyond the gate of Jerusalem" (Je 22:19) without interment, the expression "slept with his fathers" can only mean that he died, without determining what became either of his soul or body. In the East, a body exposed during the night would be a prey to wild animals; if any of it were left (2 K 9:35) till the morning, the carnivorous birds would devour it. Notice also that "burial" is used without meaning actual interment, a fact fatal to the usual interpretation given to the term in Ro 6:4. 2 Ch 36:6, 8. Je *22:18, 19. 36:30. **Jehoiachin**. i.e. *Jah establishes*. As this man reigned only *three months*, and was a mere *vassal* of the king of Babylon, his reign is scarcely reckoned; and therefore Jeremiah (Je 35:30) says of

Jehoiakim, "he shall have none to sit upon the throne of David."

7. **the king**. Je 37:5-7. 46:2. **from the river**. Ge 15:18. Nu 34:5. Jsh 15:4. 1 K 4:21. Is 27:12. **Euphrates**. Ge 2:14.

8. **Jehoiachin**. i.e. *the Lord will establish*. 1 Ch 3:16. Je 24:1, Jeconiah. Je 22:24, 28. 37:1, Coniah. Mt 1:11, 12, Jechonias. **eighteen years**. In the parallel place (2 Ch 36:9), he is said to be only *eight* years old; but this must be a mistake, for we find that having reigned only *three months*, he was carried captive to Babylon, and there had *wives* (2 K 24:15); and had he been of such a tender age, it could scarcely have been said that, as a king, "he did that which was evil in the sight of the Lord." 2 Ch 36:9n. ✱S#3078h: 2 K 24:6, 8, 12, 15. 25:27, 27. 2 Ch 36:8, 9. Je 52:31, 31. **three months**. ⌐171T7, 1 K +2:11. 2 Ch ◐36:9. **Nehushta**. i.e. *brass*, ✱S#5179h. ver. 15. **Elnathan**. i.e. *God hath given*. (1) Grandfather of Jehoiachin, 2 K 24:8. Perhaps the same mentioned in Je 26:22; 36:12, 25. (2) Three Levites in the time of Ezra, Ezr 8:16. ✱S#494h: 2 K 24:8. Ezr 8:16, 16, 16. Je 26:22. 36:12, 25.

9. **evil**. Young renders, "the evil thing," noting, "that is, idolatry." **according**. ver. 19. 2 Ch 36:12.

10. **At that time**. Da 1:1, 2. **was besieged**. Heb. came into siege. 2 K 25:2. Dt 20:19, 20.

12. **Jehoiachin**. 2 Ch 36:10. Je 24:1. 29:1, 2. 38:17, 18. Ezk 17:12. **officers**. *or*, eunuchs. 2 K +8:6mg. Ge +*37:36mg. **took him**. 2 K 25:27. Je 52:28, 31. **eighth year**. "Nebuchadnezzar's eighth year." Je 25:1. 52:28.

13. **he carried**. 2 K 20:17. Is *39:6, 7. Je 20:5. **and cut**. 2 K 16:17. 25:13-15. Ezr 1:7-11. Je 27:16-21. 28:3, 4, 6. Da *5:2, 3. **which Solomon**. 1 K 7:48-50. 2 Ch 4:7-22. **as the Lord had said**. 2 K *20:17. Je 20:5.

14. **all**. ⌐171B. Figure of speech Synecdoche of the Genus; where universals are put for particulars: here, "all" is put not for all things or individuals, but to all that are specified or implied. Ge +7:19 (⌐102, hyperbole/overstatement). +24:10 (⌐171B). That is, all the chief men, the nobles, and the artificers. Among these were 7000 mighty men, and 1000 craftsmen and smiths. **Jerusalem**. 2 Ch 39:9, 10. Je 24:1-5. 52:28. Ezk 1:1, 2. **ten thousand**. Je ◐52:28. **craftsmen**. Ex 28:11h. So 1 S 13:19-22. Je 24:1. **and smiths**. ver. 16. Je 24:1. 29:2. **the poorest sort**. 2 K 25:12. Je 39:10. 40:7. 52:16. Ezk 17:14.

15. **he carried**. See on ver. 8. 2 Ch 36:10. Est 2:6. Je 22:24-28. **officers**. *or*, eunuchs. 2 K +8:6mg. +23:11mg. Ge +*37:36mg.

16. **seven thousand**. Je 29:2. 52:28. **apt for war**. Dt 20:20. 1 K 12:21. **brought captive to Babylon**. Je 24:1. 29:1, 2. 52:28. Ezk 17:12.

17. **the king**. 2 Ch 36:10, 11. Je 37:1. 52:1. **Mattaniah**. i.e. *gift of Jah*, third son of Josiah (Young). (1) The original name of king Zedekiah, 2 K 24:17. (2) A Levite singer named in the genealogies, 1 Ch 9:15. (3) A singer, son of Heman, who had the ninth lot, 1 Ch 25:4, 16. (4) A progenitor of Jahaziel, who spake by the Spirit, 2 Ch 20:14. (5) One of the Levites who sanctified themselves under Hezekiah, 2 Ch 29:13. (6) Four of those that married strange wives, Ezr 10:26, 27, 30, 37. (7) One of the Levites who dwelt at Jerusalem, Ne 11:17; 12:8, 25; and whose grandson Hanan was made treasurer, Ne 13:13. ✱S#4983h: 2 K 24:17.

1 Ch 9:15. 25:4, 16. 2 Ch 20:14. 29:13. Ezr 10:26, 27, 30, 37. Ne 11:17, 22. 12:8, 25, 35. 13:13. **his father's brother**. Le 10:4. He was the son of Josiah, brother to Jehoiakim, and uncle of Jehoiachin. 1 Ch 3:15, 16. 2 Ch 36:10. **changed**. 2 K 23:34. Ge 41:45. 2 Ch 36:4. Da 1:7. The *change* of name was to show Nebuchadnezzar's *supremacy*, and that Zedekiah was only his *vassal* or *viceroy*. The custom of changing names, we are assured by travelers, still exists in the East. **Zedekiah**. i.e. *righteousness of Jah*.

18. A.M. 3405-3416. B.C. 599-588. **Zedekiah**. 2 Ch 36:11. Je 37:1, 2. 52:1, etc. **Hamutal**. 2 K 23:31. **Libnah**. 2 K 23:31.

19. **And he did**. 2 K 23:37. 2 Ch 36:12. Je 24:8. ch. 37; 38. Ezk 21:25.

20. **through**. 2 K 22:17. Ex 9:14-17. Dt +√2:30. Is 19:11-14. 1 C 1:20. 2 Th *2:9-11. **Zedekiah**. 2 Ch 36:13. Je 27:12-15. 38:17-21. Ezk 17:15-20.

2 KINGS 25

Jerusalem is besieged and taken; Zedekiah flees, and is made prisoner; his sons are slain, his eyes are put out, and he is carried in chains to Babylon, 1-7. The temple, palaces, and city are burned, the walls are broken down, and the remnant of the people led captive, except a small number of the poor, 8-12. The residue of the sacred vessels and treasures are carried away, 13-17. The nobles are slain at Riblah, 18-21. Gedaliah, who is left governor, being treacherously slain, the rest flee into Egypt, 22-26. After many years, Evil-merodach shows great kindness to Jehoiachin, 27-30.

1. A.M. 3414. B.C. 590. **in the ninth**. This, according to the calculation of Archbishop Usher, was on Thursday, January 30, A.M. 3414, which was a sabbatical year; wherein they proclaimed liberty to their servants, according to the law, but soon enthralled them again (See Je 34:8-10). 2 Ch 36:17, etc. Je 34:2, 3, etc. 39:1, etc. 52:4, 5, etc. Ezk 24:1, 2, etc. **Nebuchadnezzar**. 2 K 24:1, 10. 1 Ch 6:15. Je 27:8. 32:28. 43:10. 51:34. Ezk 26:7, Nebuchadrezzar. Da 4:1, etc. **pitched**. Is 29:3. Je 32:24. Ezk 4:1-8. 21:22-24. Lk 19:43, 44.

3. A.M. 3416. B.C. 588. **the ninth day**. Je 39:2. 52:6. Zc 8:19. **fourth**. ⌐63A4, 1 K +3:22. Je *39:2. **the famine**. Le 26:26. Dt 28:52, 53. La 4:4-10. Ezk 4:7-17. 5:10, 12. 7:15. 14:21. **there was no**. Je 37:21. 38:2.

4. **the city**. This being the ninth day of the fourth month, corresponded to Wednesday, July 27. Je 5:10. 39:2, 3. 52:6, 7, etc. Ezk 33:21. **fled**. ⌐63B, Ge +25:28. Le 26:17, 36. Dt 28:25. 32:24, 25, 30. Je 39:4-7. **by**. ⌐143, Ge +19:2. **and the king**. ver. 5. Ex 12:12.

5. **Chaldees pursued**. 2 Ch 36:17. **and overtook**. Is 30:16. Je 24:8. 39:5. 52:8. Am 2:14-16.

6. **they took**. 2 Ch 33:11. Je 21:7. 34:21, 22. 38:23. La 4:19, 20. Ezk 17:20, 21. 21:25-27. **Riblah**. 2 K 23:33. Je 52:9. **gave judgment upon him**. Heb. spake judgment with him. Je +4:12mg.

7. **they slew**. Ge 21:16. 44:34. Dt 28:34. Je 22:30. 39:6, 7. 52:10, 11. **and put out**. Heb. and made blind. Thus were fulfilled the apparently contradictory prophecies of Jeremiah and Ezekiel—that his eyes should *see* the king of Babylon (Je 32:4), but Babylon he should *not see*, though he should die there (Ezk 12:13). Je 32:4, 5. 34:3. Ezk 12:13, etc. **bound him**. Jg 16:21.

2 Ch 33:11. 36:6. Ps 107:10, 11. 149:8. Ezk 7:27. 17:16-20.

8. in the fifth month. This answered to Wednesday, August 24; and three days after he reduced the temple to ashes, and carried Judah captive; in the 11th year of Zedekiah; the 19th of Nebuchadnezzar; 424 years, 3 months, and 8 days from the foundation of the temple; 468 years from the beginning of the reign of David; 388 years from the division of the ten tribes; and 134 years from their captivity. Je 52:12-14. Zc 7:3. 8:19. **the nineteenth.** ver. 27. 2 K 24:12. **Nebuzar-adan.** i.e. *whom Nebo favors.* ver. 11, 20. Je 39:9-14. 40:1-4. 43:6. 52:12-16. La 4:12. *S#5018h: 2 K 25:8, 11, 20. Je 39:9, 10, 11, 13. 40:1. 41:10. 43:6. 52:12, 15, 16, 26, 30. **captain.** *or,* chief marshal. or, executioner. Ge 37:36mg.

9. he burnt. 1 K 9:8. 2 Ch 36:19. Ps 74:3-9. 79:1. Is 64:10, 11. Je 7:14. 26:9. La 1:10. 2:7. Mi 3:12. Lk 21:5, 6. Ac 6:13, 14. **the king's.** Je 34:22. 37:8, 10. 39:8. 52:13. Am *2:5.

10. brake. Ne 1:3. Je 5:10. 39:8. 52:14, etc.

11. the rest. Je 15:1, 2. 39:9. 52:15. Ezk 5:2. 12:15, 16. 22:15, 16. **fugitives.** Heb. fallen away.

12. left of the poor. 2 K 24:44. Je 39:10. 40:7. 52:16. Ezk 33:24. Mt 26:11.

13. the. 2 K 20:17. 2 Ch 36:18. Je 27:19-22. 52:17-20. La 1:10. **pillars.** Ex 27:3. 1 K 7:15, 27. 2 Ch 4:12, 13. **bases.** 1 K 7:23-45. 2 Ch 4:2-6, 14-16.

14. the pots. Ex 27:3. 38:3. 1 K 7:47-50. 2 Ch 4:20-22. 24:14. **the shovels.** Ex 27:3. **the snuffers.** 1 K 7:50. **the spoons.** 1 K 7:50.

15. firepans. Ex 27:3. 1 K 7:45. **bowls.** 1 K +7:40. **and such things.** Ex 27:3. Nu 7:13, 14. 1 K 7:48-51. 2 Ch 24:14. Ezr 1:9-11. Da *5:2, 3.

16. one sea. Heb. the one sea. **the brass.** 1 K 7:47. **without weight.** 1 K 7:47.

17. one pillar. 1 K 7:15, 16. 2 Ch 36:18. Je 27:19, 22. 52:21-23.

18. captain. ver. 24, 25, etc. **Seraiah.** i.e. *soldier of Jehovah.* 1 Ch 6:14. Ezr 7:1. Je 52:24. **Zephaniah.** i.e. *hidden of Jah.* Je 21:1. 29:25, 29. **the second priest.** Called by the Jews *sagan,* who officiated for the high priest in case of any temporary incapacity. **door.** Heb. threshold. 2 K 12:9mg. Jg +19:27. 1 K +14:17.

19. officer. *or,* eunuch. 2 K +8:6mg. +23:11mg. Ge +*37:36mg (*S#5631h). Je 52:25. **was set.** S#6496h, Ge +41:34mg. **were in the king's presence.** Heb. saw the king's face. ♪22A4, Ge +19:13. Est 1:14. **principal.** *or,* scribe of the captain of the host. **mustered.** 1 S +11:8.

20. and brought. Je 52:26, 27. La 4:16.

21. the king. These men were put to death as accessaries to Zedekiah's rebellion; for the king of Babylon had no doubt found that they had counselled him to revolt. **So Judah.** 2 K 17:20. 23:27. Le *26:33-35. Dt 4:26. *28:36, 64. Je 24:9, 10. 25:9-11. Ezk 12:25-28. 24:14. Am 5:27. ◐+√9:14, 15.

22. the people. Je 40:5, 6, etc. **Gedaliah.** i.e. *greatness of Jah.* ver. 25. Je 39:14. 41:2. **Ahikam.** i.e. *my brother has risen.* 2 K 22:12. 2 Ch 34:20. Je 26:24. **Shaphan.** i.e. *a coney.*

23. And when. Je 40:7-9, 11, 12. **Mizpah.** There were several places of the name of *Mizpah,* or *Mizpeh,* and we do not certainly know which of them this was; but it is probable that it was that situated *east* of Jordan, in the mountains of Gilead (Ge 31:49), and most con-

tiguous to Babylon; and therefore the most proper for the residence of Gedaliah. Ge +31:49. Jsh +11:3n. 18:25. **Ishmael.** i.e. *God hears.* **Nethaniah.** i.e. *given of Jah.* **Johanan.** i.e. *Jah is gracious.* (1) A captain of Gedaliah, 2 K 25:23. Je 40:8. (2) The eldest son of king Josiah, 1 Ch 3:15. (3) Two of David's officers, 1 Ch 12:4, 12. (4) A member of the high-priestly line, 1 Ch 6:10. (5) A son of Elioenai, 1 Ch 3:24. (6) A son of Hakkatan who accompanied Ezra from Babylon, Ezr 8:12. (7) Son of Eliashib, Ezr 10:6. (8) Son of Tobiah, the Ammonite, in the days of Nehemiah, Ne 6:18. (9) A high priest, grandson of Eliashib, Ne 12:22, 23. *S#3110h: 2 K 25:23. 1 Ch 3:15, 24. 6:9, 10. 12:4, 12. Ezr 8:12. Ne 12:22, 23. Je 40:8, 13, 15, 16. 41:11, 13, 14, 15, 16. 42:1, 8. 43:2, 4, 5. **Careah.** i.e. *bald.* *S#7143h: 2 K 25:23. Je 40:8, 13, 15, 16. 41:11, 13, 14, 16. 42:1, 8. 43:2, 4, 5. **Seraiah.** ver. 18. **Tanhumeth.** i.e. *consolation,* *S#8576h: 2 K 25:23. Je 40:8. **the.** Je 40:8. **Netophathite.** 2 S 23:28, 29. 1 Ch 2:54. 9:16. 11:30. Ezr 2:22. Ne 7:26. 12:28. **Jaazaniah.** i.e. *Jah gives ear,* *S#2970h: 2 K 25:23. Ezk 8:11. (1) A captain of the Jewish army, 2 K 25:23. (2) A chief man of the Rechabites in the time of Jeremiah, Je 35:3. (3) One of the seventy "men of the ancients" seen by Ezekiel in a vision, Ezk 8:11. (4) A prince seen in a vision by Ezekiel, Ezk 11:1, against whom he was directed to prophesy. **Maachathite.** Dt 3:14. 2 S 20:14.

24. sware to them. 2 S 14:11. 19:23. Je 40:9, 10. Ezk 33:24-29. **and it shall be.** Je 27:5, 6, 11. 31:2. 40:9. 42:6.

25. seventh. Zc 7:5. 8:19. **Ishmael.** ver. 23. Je 40:15, 16. 41:1-15. **Elishama.** i.e. *my God has heard.* **royal.** Heb. of the kingdom. 2 K 11:1. 2 S 12:26. Est 1:7. Is 62:3. Je 41:1. Ezk 17:13. Da 1:3. **Mizpah.** ver. +23n. Jsh 18:25.

26. all the people. Je 41:16-18. 42:14-22. *43:4-7. **Chaldees.** S#3778h. Ge 11:28, 31. 2 K 24:2. 25:4, 5, 10, 13, 24, 25, 26. 2 Ch 36:17. Ne 9:7. Jb 1:17. Is 13:19. 23:13. 43:14. 47:1, 5. 48:14, 20. Je 21:4, 9. 22:25. 24:5. 25:12. 32:4, 5, 24, 25, 28, 29, 43. 33:5. 35:11. 37:5, 8, 9, 10, 11, 13, 14. 38:2, 18, 19, 23. 39:5, 8. 40:9, 10. 41:3, 18. 43:3. 50:1, 8, 10, 25, 35, 45. 51:4, 24, 35, 54. 52:7, 8, 14, 17. Ezk 1:3. 12:13. 23:14, 15, 23. Da 1:4. 2:2, 4. 5:30. 9:1. Hab 1:6. Also Ezk 11:24. 16:29. 23:16.

27. A.M. 3442. B.C. 562. **it came to pass.** Je 24:5, 6. 52:31-34. **seven and thirtieth.** Being 55 years of age (Young). **the captivity of Jehoiachin.** 2 K 24:12, 15. **seven and twentieth day.** Je ◐52:31. **Evil-merodach.** i.e. *the fool of Merodach,* *S#192h: Je 52:31. **king of Babylon.** Pr 21:1. **lift up the head.** Ge 40:13, 20. **prison.** or, house of restraint. ver. 29. 2 K 17:4. 1 K 22:27. 2 Ch 18:26. Is 42:*7, 22. Je 37:15, 18. 52:33.

28. kindly to him. Heb. good things with him. Nu 10:29. 1 K 12:7. Ps 78:38, 39. 106:46. Je 12:6mg. Da 11:34. **the throne.** Je 27:6-11. Da 2:37. 5:18, 19.

29. changed. 2 K 24:12. Ge 41:14, 42. Est 4:4. 8:15. Is 61:3. Zc 3:4. Lk 15:22. **he did eat bread.** 2 S 9:7. **continually.** Is +*58:11.

30. continual. Is +*58:11. **a daily rate.** Ne 11:23. 12:47. Pr 15:17 (dinner). Je 40:5. 52:34. Da 1:5. Mt 6:11. Lk 11:3. Ac 6:1. **every day.** or, a day in its day. Ex +5:13mg. +16:4mg. 2 Ch 31:16mg. **all the days of his life.** Ge 48:15, 16.

1 CHRONICLES

The genealogy, from Adam to Noah and his sons, 1-4. The sons of Japheth, 5-7; of Ham, 8-16; and of Shem, 17-23. A genealogy from Shem to Abraham and his sons, 24-28. The sons of Ishmael, 29-31; and of Keturah, 32, 33. The posterity of Abraham by Esau, 34-37. The sons of Seir, 38-42. The kings and dukes of Edom, 43-54.

1. **Adam.** Ge 2:19. **Sheth.** Ge 4:+25, 26. 5:3, 8. Lk 3:38, Seth. **Enosh.** i.e. *a mortal*, *S#583h. Ge 4:26. 5:6, 7, 9, 10, 11. Lk 3:38, Enos.

2. **Kenan.** i.e. *owner; fixed*, *S#7018h. Ge 5:9, 10, 12, 13, 14. Lk 3:37, Cainan. **Mahalaleel.** Ge +5:12. Lk 3:37, Maleleel. **Jered.** i.e. *a descent*, *S#3382h. Ge 5:15, 16, 18, 19, 20. 1 Ch 4:18. Lk 3:37, Jared. (1) Elsewhere called Jared, the son of Mahalaleel, of the family of Seth, Ge 5:15-20; Lk 3:37. He was the father of Enoch and the grandfather of Methuselah. (2) A descendant of Judah, 1 Ch 4:18.

3. **Henoch.** i.e. *disciplined; initiated*, *S#2585h. Ge 4:17, 17, 18. 5:18, 19, 21, 22, 23, 24. 25:4. 46:9. Ex 6:14. Nu 26:5. 1 Ch 1:3, 33. 5:3. (1) Eldest son of Cain, whose name was given to the city which his father built, Ge 4:17. (2) Father of Methuselah, translated to heaven, Ge 5:18-24. He 11:5. Ju 14, Enoch. **Methuselah.** Ge 5:+21, 25-27. Lk 3:37, Mathusala. **Lamech.** Ge +4:18. 5:28-31. Lk 3:36.

4. **Noah.** Ge 5:+29, 32. 6:8, 9. 7:1. 9:29. Is 54:9, 10. Ezk 14:14. Mt 24:37, 38. Lk 3:36. 17:26, Noe. He 11:7. 2 P 2:5. **Shem.** Ge +5:32. 6:10. 9:18.

5. **the sons of Japheth.** Ge 10:1-5. Ezk 27:13. 38:2, 3, 6. 39:1. **Gomer.** Ge +10:2. **Magog.** Ge +10:2. **Madai.** Ge +10:2. **Javan.** Ge +10:2. **Tubal.** Ge +10:2. **Meshech.** Ge +10:2. **Tiras.** Ge +10:2.

6. **Ashchenaz.** Ge +10:3, Ashkenaz. **Riphath.** *or,* Diphath, as it is in some copies. Ge +10:3.

7. **Tarshish.** Ge +10:4. Ps 72:10. Is 66:19. **Kittim.** These, and other words ending in *im*, forming the Hebrew plural, are not the names of individuals, but of nations. Ge +10:4. Nu 24:24. Is 23:1, 12. Je 2:10. Ezk 27:6, Da 11:30, Chittim. **Dodanim.** *or,* Rodanim, according to some copies. Ge +10:4.

8. **sons of Ham.** Ge 10:6, 7. **Put.** Ge 10:6, Phut.

9. **Sabta.** i.e. *he compassed the chamber; to surround*, *S#5454h. Ge 10:7. **Sabtechah.** i.e. *terror*, *S#5455h. Ge 10:7.

10. **Cush.** Ge +10:6. **begat Nimrod.** Ge 10:+8-12. Mi 5:6.

11. **Mizraim.** Ge +10:6. **Ludim.** Ge +10:13. **Anamim.** Ge +10:13. **Lehabim.** Ge +10:13. **Naphtuhim.** Ge +10:13.

12. **Pathrusim.** Ge +10:14. **Caphthorim.** i.e. *a native of Caphtor*, *S#3732h. Ge 10:14. Dt 2:23. 1 Ch 1:12. Je 47:4. Am 9:7.

13. **Canaan.** Ge 9:22, 25, 26. 10:15-19, Sidon. **Heth.** Ge 23:3, 5, 20. 27:46. 49:30-32. Ex 23:28. Jsh 9:1. 2 S 11:6.

14. **Jebusite.** Ge +10:16. 15:21. Ex 33:2. 34:11. Jg 1:21. 19:11. 2 S 24:16. Zc 9:7. **Amorite.** Ge 48:22. Nu 21:21-32. Dt +20:17. Jsh 3:10. 24:15. 2 S 21:2.

2 K 21:11. Am 2:9. **Girgashite.** Ge +15:21. Dt 7:1. Jsh 3:10. Ne 9:8.

15. **Hivite.** Ge +10:17. Ex 3:+8, 17. 13:5. 1 K 9:20.

16. **Arvadite.** i.e. *a refuge for the roving*, *S#721h. Ge 10:18. **Zemarite.** *S#6786h. Ge 10:18. **Hamathite.** i.e. *one from Hamath* (Nu +13:21), *S#2577h. Ge 10:18. Nu 34:8. 1 K 8:65.

17. **sons of Shem.** Ge 10:22-32. 11:10. **Elam.** Ge +10:22. 14:1. Is 11:11. 21:2. 22:6. Je 25:25. Ezk 32:24. Da 8:2. **Asshur.** Ge +10:22. Nu 24:22-24. Ezr 4:2. Ps 83:8, Assur. Ezk 27:23. 32:22. Ho 14:3. **Lud.** Ge +10:22. Is 66:19. Ezk 27:10. **Aram.** Ge +22:21. Nu 23:7. **Meshech.** Ge 10:+2, 23, Mash.

18. **Shelah.** Ge +10:24. 11:12-15, Salah.

19. **Eber.** Ge 10:21, +24, 25. 11:16, 17. Nu 24:24. **Peleg.** *that is, Division.* Ge +10:25.

20. **Joktan.** Ge +10:25. **Hazarmaveth.** Ge 10:+26, 27.

21. **Hadoram.** Ge +10:27.

22. **Ebal.** Ge 10:28, Obal. +36:23.

23. **Ophir.** Ge +10:29. 1 K 9:28. 10:11. 1 Ch 29:4. Jb 22:24. Ps 45:9. Is 13:12. **Havilah.** Ge 2:11. +10:7. 25:18. 1 S 15:7.

24. **Shem.** Ge +5:32. 11:10-26. **Shelah.** Lk 3:35, Sala.

25. **Eber.** Lk 3:35, Heber. **Peleg.** Lk 3:35, Phalec. **Reu.** Ge +11:18. Lk 3:35, Ragau.

26. **Serug.** Ge +11:20. Lk 3:35, Saruch. **Nahor.** Ge +11:22, 29. Lk 3:34, Nachor. **Terah.** Ge +11:26. Lk 3:34, Thara.

27. **Abram.** Ge 11:+26, 27-32. 17:5. Jsh 24:2. Ne 9:7.

28. **Isaac.** Ge 17:+19, 20, 21. 21:2-5, 12. **Ishmael.** Ge 16:+11, 12-16. 21:9, 10.

29. **The firstborn.** Ge 25:12-16. **Nebaioth.** Ge +25:13, Nebajoth. 28:9. Is 60:7. **Kedar.** Ge +25:13. Ps 120:4. SS 1:5. Is 21:17.

30. **Dumah.** Ge +25:14. Is 21:11. **Hadad.** *or,* Hadar. Ge 25:15.

31. **Jetur.** Ge +25:15.

32. A.M. 2151. B.C. 1853. **the sons.** Ge 25:1-4. **Midian.** Ge +25:2. 37:28. Ex 2:15, 16. Nu 22:4-7. 25:6. 31:2. Jg 6:1-6. **Sheba.** 1 K +10:1. Jb 6:19. Ps 72:10, 15. Is 60:6. **Dedan.** Ge +10:7. Is 21:13. Je 25:23. 49:8. Ezk 25:13. 27:20.

33. **Ephah.** Ge +25:4. Is 60:6. **Abida.** i.e. *father of knowledge*, *S#28h. Ge 25:4.

34. **Abraham.** Ge 21:2, 3. Mt 1:2. Lk 3:34. Ac 7:8. **The sons of Isaac.** Ge 25:24-28. Ml 1:2-4. Ro 9:10-13. **Israel.** Ge +32:28.

35. **sons of Esau.** Ge 36:4, 5, 9, 10.

36. **Teman.** ver. 53. Ge 36:+11, 12-15. Je 49:7, 20. Am 1:12. Ob 9. Hab *3:3. **Omar.** i.e. *eloquent*, *S#201h. Ge 36:11, 15. **Zephi.** i.e. *expectation; watch thou*, *S#6825h. Ge 36:11, 15. The various reading of "Zephi" and "Zepho" is caused simply by the mutation of the Hebrew letter *yood*, and *waw*. Ge 36:15, Zepho.

37. **Reuel.** Ge +36:4.

38. **the sons of Seir.** Ge 36:20, 29, 30. **Dishon.** i.e. *a thresher; antelope*, *S#1787h. 1 Ch 1:38, 41, 41.

Ge 36:21, 25, 30. **Ezar.** i.e. *treasure*, *S#687h. 1 Ch 1:38, 42. Ge 36:21, 27, 30. The variation here is only in the translation. Ge 36:21, Ezer.

39. **Hori.** Ge +36:22. Dt 2:12, 22. **Homam.** i.e. *destruction*, *S#1950h. This variation is simply the mutation of *yood* and *wav*, that in Genesis being properly "Hemam," and this, "Homam." Ge 36:22, Hemam.

40. **Alian.** i.e. *lofty*, *S#5935h. Both these variations are also caused by the mutation of *yood* and *wav*. The former being written "Alvan," and "Alian;" and the latter, "Shepho," and "Shephi." Ge 36:23, Alvan, Shepho. **Shephi.** i.e. *my bareness; my prominence*, *S#8195h. **Aiyah.** Ge 36:24, Ajah.

41. **The sons.** ⌐171E13, Ge +46:7. **Dishon.** ver. +38. Ge 36:25. **Amram.** This variation is only caused by the mutation of a *daleth* and a *raish*; the original being in Genesis "Hemdan," and here "Hamran." Ge 36:26, Hemdan.

42. **Zavan.** i.e. *disquiet*, *S#2190h. Ge 36:27. The former of these is the same in the original, *Zauvan*, and the latter, is an error for *weakan*, "and Achan." Ge 36:27, Zaavan, Achan. **Jakan.** i.e. *let him oppress them*, *S#3292h. **Uz.** Ge +10:23. 36:28. La 4:21.

43. **the kings.** Ge 36:31-39. 49:10. Nu 24:17-19.

44. **Bozrah.** Ge +36:33. Is 34:6. 63:1. Je 49:13. Am 1:12. Mi 2:12.

45. **Jobab.** Ge +10:29. **Husham.** Ge +36:34. **Temanites.** ver. 36, 53. Ge 36:34. Jb 2:11. Je 49:7, 20. Ezk 25:13. Am 1:12. Ob 9. Hab 3:3.

46. **Hadad.** Ge +36:35. **Bedad.** Ge +36:35. **Midian.** Ge +25:2. **Avith.** Ge +36:35.

47. **Samlah.** Ge +36:36. **Masrekah.** Ge +36:36.

48. **Shaul.** The original is uniformly "Shaul." Ge 36:37, Saul.

49. **Baal-hanan.** Ge +36:38. **Achbor.** Ge +36:38.

50. **Hadad.** This variation is occasioned simply by the mutation of *raish*, and *daleth*, being in Genesis "Hadar," and here, "Hadad." Ge 36:39, Hadar. **Pai.** i.e. *sighing*, *S#6464h. This simply depends on the interchange of *yood* and *wav*; being written in Genesis "Pau," and here, "Pai." Ge 36:39, Pau.

51. **Aliah.** i.e. *moral perverseness*, *S#5933h. This is another instance of the mutation of *yood* and *wav*; in the former instance being "Alvah," and here, "Aliah," though the Keri also reads "Alvah." Ge 36:40, Alvah.

52. **Duke Aholibamah.** Ge +36:41.

53. **Kenaz.** Ge +36:11. **Teman.** Ge +36:11. **Mibzar.** Ge +36:42.

54. **Magdiel.** Ge +36:43. **These are.** Ge 36:41-43.

1 CHRONICLES 2

The sons of Israel, 1, 2; of Judah, 3-12; of Jesse, 13-17; of Caleb, the son of Hezron, 18-20; of Hezron, by the daughter of Machir, 21-24; and of Jerahmeel, Hezron's son, 25-33. The posterity of Shesham, by his daughter, 34-41. Another branch of Caleb's posterity, 42-49. The sons of Caleb, the son of Hur, 50-54. The families of the Kenites, 55.

1. A.M. 2252, etc. B.C. 1752, etc. **Israel.** *or*, Jacob. Ge +25:26. +32:28. 49:2. **Reuben.** Ge 29:+32, 33-35. 30:5-24. 35:18, 22-26. 46:8, etc. 49:4-28. Ex 1:2-4. Nu 1:5-15. 13:4-15. 26:5, etc. Re 7:5-8. **Simeon.** Ge +29:33. **Levi.** Ge +29:34. **Judah.** Ge +35:23. **Issa-**

char. Ge +30:18. **Zebulun.** Ge +30:20.

2. **Dan.** Ge +30:6. **Joseph.** Ge +30:24. **Benjamin.** Ge +35:18. **Naphtali.** Ge +30:8. **Gad.** Ge +30:11. **Asher.** Ge +30:13. 35:26. 46:17. 49:20. Nu 1:40, 41. Dt +*33:24n. Jsh 19:24-31.

3. **Er, and.** 1 Ch 9:5. Ge 38:2-10. 46:12. Nu 26:19. **Onan.** Ge +38:4. **Shelah.** Ge +38:5. **Shua.** i.e. *riches; a cry; salvation*, *S#7770h. Ge 38:2. **Canaanites.** Ge +10:18. **firstborn.** Le +27:26.

4. **Tamar.** Ge 38:+6, 13-30. Ru 4:12. Mt 1:3, Thamar. **Pharez.** 1 Ch 9:4. Ge +46:12. Nu 26:21. Ru 4:18. Ne 11:4, Perez. Mt 1:3. Lk 3:33, Phares. **Zerah.** 1 Ch 9:6. Ge +36:13. Nu 26:13, 20. Ne 11:24. Mt 1:3, Zara.

5. **Hezron.** Ge 46:+9, 12. Nu 26:21. Ru 4:18. Mt 1:3. Lk 3:33, Esrom.

6. **Zimri.** i.e. *snug; my song; my field*, *S#2174h. Nu 25:14. 1 K 16:9, 10, 12, 15, 16, 18, 20. 2 K 9:31. 1 Ch 2:6. 8:36, 36. 9:42, 42. Je 25:25. (1) Captain of Elah king of Israel, whom he slew and succeeded, B.C. 930. 1 K 16:9, 10. 2 K 9:31. (2) Captain of the Simeonites, Nu 25:14. (3) Descendant of Judah by Tamar, 1 Ch 2:4. (4) Of the stock of Saul, 1 Ch 8:36. 9:42. (5) A son of Zerah, the son of Judah, 1 Ch 2:6, called Zabdi in Jsh 7:1, 17, 18. *Zabdi* is apparently here called "Zimri," in consequence of a *baith* being mistaken for a *mem*, and a *daleth* for a *raish*. Jsh 7:+1, 17, 18, Zabdi. (6) A name applied to a tribe and supposed to refer to people in Eastern Arabia, Je 25:25. **Ethan.** i.e. *perennial, constant; ancient*, *S#387h. 1 Ch 2:6, 8. 6:42, 44. 15:17, 19. 1 K 4:31. Ps 89, title. (1) An Israelite known for his wisdom, an Ezrahite, to whom Psalm 89 is attributed in its title, 1 K 4:31. (2) A son of Zerah, the son of Judah, 1 Ch 2:6, 8. (3) A descendant of Gershon, the son of Levi, 1 Ch 6:42. (4) A descendant of Merari, the son of Levi, 1 Ch 6:44; 15:19. **Heman.** i.e. *faithful*, *S#1968h. 1 Ch 2:6. 6:33. 15:17, 19. 16:41, 42. 25:1, 4, 4, 5, 5, 6. 1 K 4:31. 2 Ch 5:12. 29:14. 35:15. Ps 88, title. (1) A wise man, who flourished before Solomon, 1 K 4:31; 1 Ch 2:6. (2) A Levite of the Kohathites, a leader of David's choir, 1 Ch 15:17; 16:41, 42; Ps 88:1. See also *Homam*, 1 Ch 1:39. **Calcol.** i.e. *sustenance; comprehended*, *S#3633h. 1 K 4:31. **Dara.** i.e. *pearl of wisdom*, *S#1873h. "Darda" is here called "Dara," by the elision of a *daleth*. 1 K 4:+31, Darda.

7. **the sons.** ⌐171E13, Ge +46:7. **Carmi.** 1 Ch +4:1. **Achar.** i.e. *troublesome*, *S#5917h. *Achan* is probably called *Achar*, from the *trouble* he occasioned. Jsh 7:1-5, Achan. **accursed.** Dt 7:26. 13:17. Jsh 6:18. 7:11-15, 25. 22:20.

8. **Ethan.** ver. +6. **Azariah.** 1 Ch +6:36.

9. **Jerahmeel.** i.e. *on whom God has mercy*, *S#3396h. 1 Ch 2:9, 25, 26, 27, 33, 42. 24:29. Je 36:26. (1) A son of Hezron, the grandson of Judah, 1 Ch 2:9, 25, 26, 27, 33, 42, founder of the Jerahmeelites. (2) A descendant of Merari, 1 Ch 24:29. (3) An officer under Jehoiakim, Je 36:26, employed to arrest Jeremiah and Baruch. **Ram.** Ru 4:19. Jb +32:2. Mt 1:3. Lk 3:33, Aram. **Chelubai.** i.e. *the bold, the valiant*, *S#3621h. ver. 18, 19, 24, 42, Caleb.

10. **Amminadab.** 1 Ch +15:11. Ru 4:19, 20. Mt 1:4. Lk 3:33, Aminadab. **Nahshon.** i.e. *a diviner*, *S#5177h. Ex 6:23. Nu 1:7. 2:3. 7:12, 17. 10:14. Nu 4:20, 20. 1 Ch 2:10, 11. Mt 1:4. Lk 3:32, Naasson.

11. **Salma.** i.e. *clothed, a garment; raiment,*

✻S#8007h. 1 Ch 2:11, 11, 51, 54. Ru 4:21. Mt 1:4, 5. Lk 3:32, Salmon. (1) One of the sons of Caleb, the son of Hur, 1 Ch 2:51, 54. (2) The father of Boaz, the husband of Ruth, Ru 4:20, 21; Mt 1:4, 5; Lk 3:32. He is supposed to be the same as Number 1. **Boaz.** Ru +2:1. Lk 3:32, Booz.

12. **Jesse.** i.e. *wealthy; firm; extant,* S#3448h. A shepherd of Bethlehem, father of king David. 1 Ch 10:14. 1 S 16:1. 17:58. 20:27, 30, 31. 22:7, 8. 2 S 20:1. Ru 4:22. 1 K 12:16. Is 11:1, 10. Mt 1:5. Lk 3:32. Ac 13:22. Ro 15:12.

13. **his firstborn.** 1 S 16:6, etc. 17:13, 28. **Eliab.** 1 Ch 27:18, Elihu. Nu +1:9. **Shimma.** i.e. *annunciation.* 1 Ch 20:7, Shimea. 1 S 16:9, Shammah. ✻S#8092h: 2 S 21:21. 1 Ch 2:13. 3:5. 6:30, 39. 20:7.

14. **Nethaneel.** Nu +1:8. **Raddai.** i.e. *subduing; trodden down,* ✻S#7288h.

15. **Ozem.** i.e. *strength; eagerness,* ✻S#684h. 1 Ch 2:15, 25. (1) The sixth son of Jesse and brother of David, 1 Ch 2:15. (2) One of the sons of Jerahmeel, 1 Ch 2:25. **David.** It appears from the parallel places of Samuel (1 S 16:10), that Jesse had *eight* sons, of whom David was the *eighth* and youngest; but one may have died before David came to the throne. 1 S 16:10, 11. 17:12-14.

16. **Zeruiah.** i.e. *pierce ye Jah; tribulation; cleft,* ✻S#6870h. 1 S 26:6. 2 S 2:13, 18. 3:39. 8:16. 14:1. 16:9, 10. 17:25. 18:2. 19:21, 22. 21:17. 23:18, 37. 1 K 1:7. 2:5, 22. 1 Ch 2:16, 16. 11:6, 39. 18:12, 15. 26:28. 27:24. A daughter of Jesse and mother of Joab. 1 S 26:6. 2 S 2:13. **Abigail.** 1 S +25:3. **the sons of.** 1 S 26:6. 2 S 2:18-23. 3:39. 16:9-11. 19:22. **Abishai.** 1 S +26:6. **Joab.** 1 S +26:6. **Asahel.** i.e. *God is doer; wrought of God, whom God created,* ✻S#6214h. 1 Ch 2:16. 11:26. 27:7. 2 S 2:18, 18, 19, 20, 21, 22, 23, 30, 32. 3:27, 30. 23:24. 2 Ch 17:8. 31:13. Ezr 10:15. (1) Son of Zeruiah, David's sister, 2 S 2:18-23. 1 Ch 2:16. (2) A Levite sent by Jehoshaphat to teach Judah, 2 Ch 17:8, 13, 31. (3) A Levite employed under Hezekiah, 2 Ch 31:13. (4) Father of Jonathan, employed in the matter of the strange wives, Ezr 10:15.

17. **Amasa.** 2 S +17:25. 19:13. 20:4-12. 1 K 2:5, 32. **Jether.** "Jether" is essentially the same with "Ithra," the latter only having the addition of an *aleph,* and it is probable, that he was an *Ishmaelite* by birth but an *Israelite* by religion. 2 S 17:25, Ithra an Israelite. **Ishmeelite.** S#3459, a descendant of Ishmael.

18. A.M. 2534, etc. B.C. 1470, etc. **Caleb.** "Caleb" is the same as "Chelubai," the latter simply having a *wav* inserted, and a *yood* affixed. This person must have lived some time before Israel left Egypt; for Bezaleel, the principal person employed in constructing the tabernacle, was his grandson. ver. 9, Chelubai, 42. **Hezron.** Ge +46:9. **Azubah.** 1 K +22:42. **Jerioth.** i.e. *breaking asunder,* ✻S#3408h. **Jesher.** i.e. *righteous,* ✻S#3475h. **Shobab.** i.e. *apostate; backsliding, rebellious,* ✻S#7727h. 1 Ch 2:18. 3:5. 14:4. 2 S 5:14. (1) A son of David and Bathsheba, 2 S 5:14; 1 Ch 3:5. (2) A son of Caleb, the son of Hezron, 1 Ch 2:18. **Ardon.** i.e. *fugitive,* ✻S#715h.

19. **Ephrath.** ver. 24, 50. 1 Ch 4:4. Ge +48:7. Mi +*5:2, Ephratah. **Hur.** Ex +17:10.

20. **Uri.** Ex +31:2. **Bezaleel.** Ex +31:2. 36:1, 2. 37:1. 38:22. 2 Ch 1:5.

21. **Hezron.** Ge +46:9. **Machir.** Ge +50:23. Nu 26:29. 27:1. 32:39, 40. Dt 3:15. **married.** Heb. took.

1 Ch 4:18. **Segub.** i.e. *elevated; exalted; made strong,* ✻S#7687h. 1 Ch 2:21, 22. 1 K 16:34. (1) The youngest son of Hiel the Bethelite, 1 K 16:34. (2) One of the sons of Hezron, the grandson of Judah, 1 Ch 2:21, 22.

22. **Jair.** Nu +32:41. Dt 3:14. Jsh 13:30.

23. **Geshur.** Jsh 13:13. 2 S +3:3. 13:38. **Kenath.** *Kenath* was situated in the tribe of Manasseh, east of Jordan. Eusebius says it was called in his time *Kanatha;* and was a town in the Trachonitis, near Bozra. Josephus (Bell. l. i. c. 14) places it in Caelo-syria; and Pliny (l. v. c. 18) reckons it among the cities of the Decapolis. It was also called *Nobah,* after Nobah an Israelite, who conquered it (Nu +32:42); which is placed by Eusebius, eight miles south of Heshbon: See Note on Jg 8:11.

24. **Caleb-ephratah.** i.e. *fruitfulness,* ✻S#3613h. ver. 9, 18, 19. 1 S 30:14. **Ashur.** i.e. *noble and happy; black,* S#804h. 1 Ch 4:5. **Tekoa.** i.e. *sound of the trumpet,* ✻S#8620h. 1 Ch 2:24. 4:5. 2 S 14:2. 2 Ch 11:6. 20:20. Je 6:1. Am 1:1.

25. **the sons of.** Of the persons mentioned in verses 25-33, nothing more is recorded or known. **Jerahmeel.** ver. 9. **firstborn.** Le 27:26. **Hezron.** Ge +46:9. **Ram.** Jb +32:2. **Bunah.** i.e. *understanding, discretion,* ✻S#946h. **Oren.** i.e. *a pine; tall and strong,* ✻S#767h. **Ozem.** 1 Ch +2:15. **Ahijah.** 1 K +14:6.

26. **another wife.** 1 Ch 4:5. Ge +4:19. **Atarah.** i.e. *a crown,* ✻S#5851h. **Onam.** Ge +36:23.

27. **Ram.** ver. 25. **Maaz.** i.e. *anger; closure,* ✻S#4619h. **Jamin.** Ge +46:10. **Eker.** i.e. *offshoot; eradication,* ✻S#6134h.

28. **Onam.** ver. 26. **Shammai.** i.e. *my desolations; destructive,* ✻S#8060h. 1 Ch 2:28, 28, 32, 44, 45. 4:17. Three descendants of Judah. **Jada.** i.e. *knowing,* ✻S#3047h. ver. 32. **Nadab.** Ex +6:23. **Abishur.** i.e. *uprightness,* ✻S#51h. ver. 29.

29. **Abihail.** Nu +3:35. **Ahban.** i.e. *brother of understanding,* ✻S#257h. **Molid.** i.e. *begetter,* ✻S#4140h.

30. **Nadab.** ver. 28. **Seled.** i.e. *exaltation; recoil,* ✻S#5540h. **Appaim.** i.e. *double-nosed,* ✻S#649h. ver. 31. **died without children.** ver. 32. Ge +*11:30. 15:2. Jg 13:2. 1 S 1:2. 2 S 6:23. 2 K 4:14. Lk 1:7. 20:29.

31. **Ishi.** i.e. *salutary,* ✻S#3469h. 1 Ch 2:31, 31. 4:20, 42. 5:24. (1, 2) Judites, 1 Ch 2:31; 4:20. (3) A man of Simeon, 1 Ch 4:42. (4) Head of a family in Manasseh, 1 Ch 5:24. **Sheshan.** i.e. *lily; fine linen,* ✻S#8348h. ver. 34, 35. **the children of Sheshan.** ver. 34, 35. **Ahlai.** ver. 35. 1 Ch +11:41.

32. **Jada.** ver. 28. **Jether.** i.e. *excellence, superiority,* ✻S#3500h. Ex 4:18. Jg 8:20. 1 K 2:5, 32. 1 Ch 2:17, 32, 32. 4:17. 7:38. (1) Father-in-law of Moses, Ex 3:1. 4:18. (2) Firstborn of Gideon, Jg 8:20. (3) Father of Amasa, slain by Joab, 1 K 2:5; called Ithra, 2 S 17:25. (4) A descendant of Jerameel, 1 Ch 2:32. (5) Son of Ezra, of Judah, 1 Ch 4:17. (6) A son of Asher, 1 Ch 7:38. **Jonathan.** 1 S +13:2. **died without children.** ver. +30.

33. **Peleth.** Nu +16:1. **Zaza.** i.e. *going back; brightness; fulness,* ✻S#2117h.

34. **no sons.** Nu 27:3, 4, 8. **but daughters.** Nu 36:2, 10, 11. **Jarha.** i.e. *increasing moon,* ✻S#3398h. ver. 35.

35. **Sheshan.** When the people of the East have no sons, they frequently marry their daughters to their

slaves, even when they have much property to bestow upon them. Hassan had been the slave of Kamel, his predecessor; but Kamel, according to the custom of the country, gave him one of his daughters in marriage, and left him at his death one part of his great riches which he had amassed in the course of a long and prosperous life (Maillet, Lett. xi. p. 118). **his daughter**. ver. 31. **Attai**. i.e. *opportune,* *S#6262h. ver. 36. 1 Ch 12:11. 2 Ch 11:20. (1) Son of Jarha, father of Nathan, 1 Ch 2:35, 36. (2) One who came to David to Ziklag, 1 Ch 12:11. (3). Son of Rehoboam by Maachah, 2 Ch 11:20.

36. **Zabad**. i.e. *gift; endowed,* *S#2066h. 1 Ch 2:36, 37. 7:21. 11:41. 2 Ch 24:26. Ezr 10:27, 33, 43. (1) A man of Judah, descendant of Sheshan, one of David's mighty men, 1 Ch 2:36, 37. (2) A grandson of Ephraim, 1 Ch 7:21. (3) A man of Ephraim, one of David's mighty men, 1 Ch 11:41. Perhaps the same as Number 1. (4) The son of Shimeath, who slew Joash, 2 Ch 24:26. Called Jozachar, 2 K 12:21. (5, 6, 7) Three Jews who took strange wives, Ezr 10:27, 33, 43.

37. **Ephlal**. i.e. *intercession,* *S#654h. **Obed**. Ru +4:17.

38. **Jehu**. 2 K +9:2. **Azariah**. 1 Ch +6:36. 2 Ch 23:1.

39. **Helez**. i.e. *strength,* *S#2503h. 2 S 23:26. (1) One of David's valiant men, 2 S 23:26; 1 Ch 11:27. (2) A descendant of Jerahmeel, 1 Ch 2:39. **Eleasah**. i.e. *God has wrought,* *S#501h. 1 Ch 2:39, 40. 8:37. 9:43. Ezr 10:22. Je 29:3. (1) Descended from Sheshan's daughter, 1 Ch 2:39. (2) One of the stock of Saul, 1 Ch 8:37; 9:43. (3) Rendered "Elasah," the bearer of Jeremiah's letter to the captives in Babylon, Je 29:3.

40. **Sisamai**. i.e. *distinguished one; swallow,* *S#5581h. **Shallum**. 2 K +15:10.

41. **Jekamiah**. i.e. *let Jah arise,* *S#3359h. 1 Ch 3:18. **Elishama**. Nu +1:10. 2 K 25:25.

42. **Caleb**. ver. 9, 18. This was not Caleb the son of Jephunneh, but Caleb the son of Hezron, and therefore called the brother of Jerahmeel: See the parallel texts. ver. 9, Chelubai, 18, 19, 24. **Mesha**. i.e. *safety,* *S#4338h, only here. Ge ❖+10:30. **his firstborn**. Ge 49:3. Ex 4:22, 23. Ro 8:29. He 12:23. **the father**. i.e. the founder, or, as the Targum renders, "the prince of the Ziphites;" for it was usual to call both the founder and the prince of a city its father. **Ziph**. 1 Ch 4:16. Jsh 15:+24, 55. 1 S 23:19. 26:1. **Mareshah**. 1 Ch 4:21. Jsh +15:44. **the father of**. ver. 23, 24, 45, 49, 52. 1 Ch 8:29. Ezr 2:21-35. Ne 7:25-38. **Hebron**. Ex +6:18. Jsh 15:54.

43. **Korah**. Ge +36:5. **Tappuah**. i.e. *bearing or fruitful in apples; thou wilt cause to breathe,* *S#8599h. (1) A city of Canaan, on the border of Ephraim and Manasseh, Jsh 12:17; 16:8; 17:7, 8. (2) A city of Judah, Jsh 15:34. (3) A son of Hebron, 1 Ch 2:43. **Rekem**. i.e. *flower garden; embroidery; variegation,* *S#7552h. Nu 31:8. Jsh 13:21. 1 Ch 2:43, 44. 7:16. (1) A king of the Midianites, Nu 31:8; Jsh 13:21. (2) A son of Hebron, son of Caleb, 1 Ch 2:43. (3) A chief man of Manasseh, called Rakem, 1 Ch 7:16. **Shema**. i.e. *rumor,* *S#8087h. ver. 44. 1 Ch 5:8. 8:13. Jsh ❖+15:26. Ne 8:4. (1) One of the descendants of Judah, 1 Ch 2:43, 44. (2) A descendant of Reuben, 1 Ch 5:8. (3) A descendant of Benjamin, 1 Ch 8:13. (4) One who stood with Ezra when he read the law to the people, Ne 8:4. (5) A town of Judah, Jsh 15:26.

44. **Raham**. i.e. *compassionate,* *S#7357h. **Jorkoam**. i.e. *paleness* or *spreading of the people,* *S#3421h.

45. **Beth-zur**. Jsh +15:58. Beth-zur was situated in the tribe of Judah, twenty miles south from Jerusalem, towards Hebron, according to Eusebius. It was fortified by Rehoboam (2 Ch 11:7), and was a fortress of great consequence, principally in the time of the Maccabees (1 Mac 4:28; 6:7, etc.).

46. **Ephah**. Ge +25:4. **Caleb**'s. ver. 18, 19, 48. **Haran**. i.e. *very dry,* *S#2771h. Ge 11:31, 32. 12:4, 5. 27:43. 28:10. 29:4. 2 K 19:12. 1 Ch 2:46, 47. Is 37:12. Ezk 27:23. Son of Caleb of Hezron, 1 Ch 2:46. **Moza**. 1 Ch +8:36. **Gazez**. i.e. *shearer,* *S#1495h.

47. **Jahdai**. i.e. *the Lord directs,* *S#3056h. **Regem**. i.e. *stoning; friend,* *S#7276h. **Gesham**. i.e. *large clod,* *S#1529h. **Pelet**. 1 Ch +12:3. Jsh 15:27. **Ephah**. Ge +25:4. **Shaaph**. i.e. *division; fleeing,* *S#8174h. ver. 49. (1) A son of Jahdai, 1 Ch 2:47. (2) A son of Caleb, the son of Hezron, 1 Ch 2:49.

48. **Maachah**. 1 K +2:39. **concubine**. ver. 46. Ge 16:2, 3. 21:10. 22:24. 25:5, 6. 29:24, 29. 35:22. 36:12. Ex 21:7-11. Le 19:20. Dt 21:10-14. Jg 8:31. 9:18. 2 S 3:7, 8. 5:13. 1 K 11:3. 2 Ch 11:21. 13:21. Mt 19:5. 1 C 7:2. **Sheber**. i.e. *hope; a breach,* *S#7669h. **Tirhanah**. i.e. *a camp-spy; inclination,* *S#8647h.

49. **the father of Madmannah**. See on ver. 42. *Madmannah* was a city situated in the southern part of Judah, and towards Gaza, according to Eusebius. Jsh +15:31. Is 10:31, Madmenah. **Sheva**. 2 S +20:25. **Macbenah**. i.e. *poverty of the son,* *S#4343h. **Gibea**. i.e. *a hill,* *S#1388h. It is probable that this was not Gibeah of Benjamin, and the royal residence of Saul, but Gibeah in the tribe of Judah, to which tribe all these other cities belonged. Jsh 15:57. 2 S 21:6, Gibeah. **Achsa**. i.e. *anklet,* *S#5915h. Not as Jsh 15:16, 17. Jg 1:12, 13. 1 Ch 2:49.

50. **Caleb**. This *Caleb* was the grandson of the preceding, and brother to Uri, the father of Bezalleel. **Ephratah**. i.e. *fruitfulness; land, region.* ver. 19, 20, Ephrath. *S#672h: 1 Ch 2:19, 50. 4:4. Also, *S#672h: Ge 35:16, 19. 48:7, 7. Ru 4:11. 1 Ch 2:24. Ps 132:6. Mi 5:2. (1) Wife of Caleb, son of Hezron, 1 Ch 2:19, 50; 4:4. (2) The ancient name of Bethlehem, Ge 35:16, 19; Ru 4:11. **Kirjath-jearim**. ver. 53. 1 Ch 13:5, 6. Jsh +9:17. 15:9, 60. 1 S 7:1.

51. **Salma**. ver. +11. 1 Ch 4:4. **Bethlehem**. Ge 35:19. Jsh +19:15. Ru 1:19. 2:4. 4:11. Mt 2:1, 6. Jn 7:42. **Hareph**. i.e. *reproachful,* *S#2780h. **Beth-gader**. i.e. *house of the wall,* *S#1013h.

52. **Shobal**. Ge +36:20. **Haroeh**. i.e. *vision; prophet,* *S#7204h. or, Reaiah, 1 Ch 4:2. As *Haroeh* and *Reaiah* have nearly the same signification, it is probable they were deemed perfectly interchangeable, and indifferently applied. **half of the Manahethites**. i.e. *midst of the resting places,* *S#2679h. or,* half of the Menuchites, *or,* Hatsiham-menuchoth.

53. **Ithrites**. 1 Ch 11:40. 2 S +23:38. **Puhites**. i.e. *a hinge; openness; simplicity,* *S#6336h. **Shumathites**. i.e. *the exalted; garlic,* *S#8126h. **Mishraites**. i.e. *a shepherd,* *S#4954h. **Zareathites**. i.e. *dwellers in Zareah or Zorah,* *S#6882h. 1 Ch 2:54 (Zorites). 4:2. Jsh 15:33. 19:41. Jg 13:2, 25. 16:31. **Eshtaulites**. i.e. *descendants of Eshtaol,* *S#848h.

54. **Salma**. ver. 51. **Bethlehem**. ver. 51. Ge 35:19. **Netophathites**. 1 Ch 11:30. 2 S 23:+28, 29. Ezr 2:22.

Ne 7:26. 12:28. **Ataroth.** *or,* Atarites, *or,* crowns of the house of Joab. Nu +32:3. Jsh 16:2. **Manahethites.** ver. 52. **Zorites.** i.e. *descendants of Zorah,* ✳S#6882h. Jsh 15:33.

55. **the scribes.** Ezr 7:6. Je 8:8. **Jabez.** 1 Ch 4:9, +10. **Tirathites.** i.e. *nourishers,* ✳S#8654h. **Shimeath-ites.** i.e. *descendants of Shimeah,* ✳S#8101h. **Suchath-ites.** i.e. *bushmen; hedges,* ✳S#7756h. **Kenites.** Nu +24:22. Jg 1:16. 4:11. 1 S 15:6. **Hemath.** i.e. *a wall,* ✳S#2575h. Jsh 19:35. **Rechab.** 2 S +4:2. 2 K 10:15. Je ✳35:2-8, 19.

1 CHRONICLES 3

The sons of David, 1-9. His line to Zedekiah, 10-16. The sons and successors of Jeconiah, 17-24.

1. A.M. 2951, etc. B.C. 1053, etc. **the sons of David.** 2 S 3:2-5. **Amnon.** 2 S +3:2. 13:1, 29. **Ahinoam.** 1 S +14:50. 25:42, 43. 27:3. **Jezreelitess.** Jsh 15:56. **Daniel.** It is probable this person had two names. The Targum-ist says he was "called *Chileab,* because he was in every respect like his father." 2 S 3:3. **of Abigail.** 1 S 25:39-42.

2. **Absalom.** 2 S 13:+1, 20-28, 38. 18:14, 18, 33. 19:4-10. **Geshur.** 1 Ch 2:23. Jsh 13:13. 2 S +3:3. 14:23, 32. 15:8. **Adonijah.** 2 S 3:4. 1 K +1:5. 2:24, 25.

3. **Eglah.** The Targumist, Jarchi, and others, main-tain that this was Michal; and though it is stated (2 S 6:23) that "she had no child to the day of her death," yet she might have had a child before, at that time living. 2 S +3:5.

4. **there he reigned.** 2 S 2:11. 5:4, 5. 1 K 2:11. **and in Jerusalem.** 2 S 5:4, 14, etc.

5. **Shimea.** i.e. *a report; fame,* ✳S#8092h. 1 Ch 14:4. 2 S 5:14, **Shammuah.** ✳S#8092h. 1 Ch 2:13. 3:5. 6:30, 39. 20:7. 2 S 21:21. **Nathan.** 2 S 7:2-4. 12:1-15. 2 Ch +9:29. Lk 3:31. **Solomon.** 1 Ch 28:5, 6. 2 S +5:14. 12:24, 25. **Bath-shua.** i.e. *daughter of the oath.* 2 S 11:3, Bath-sheba. Mt 1:6. ✳S#1340h. 1 Ch 2:3. 3:5. Ge 38:12. **Ammiel.** i.e. *my people are of God; one of the family of God,* ✳S#5988h. 1 Ch 3:5. 26:5. Nu 13:12. 2 S 9:4, 5. 17:27. (1) The man of Dan, chosen to search the land, Nu 13:12. (2) Father of Machir who hid Mephibosheth, 2 S 9:4; 5:17, 27. (3) Sixth son of Obed-edom, 1 Ch 26:5. (4) Father of Bathsheba, David's wife, 1 Ch 3:5; called Eliam, 2 S 11:3.

6. **Ibhar.** 2 S +5:15. **Elishama.** 1 Ch 14:5. Nu +1:10. 2 S 5:15, Elishua. **Eliphelet.** i.e. *God his deliverance; God of escape,* ✳S#467h. 1 Ch 3:6, 8. 8:39. 14:5, 7. 2 S 5:16. 23:34. Ezr 8:13. 10:33. Rendered also as Eliphalet, Elpalet. (1) One of David's mighty men, 2 S 23:34. Called Eliphal in 1 Ch 11:35. (2) A son of David, 1 Ch 3:6. Called Elpalet in 1 Ch 14:5. (3) A son of David, 1 Ch 3:8, called Eliphalet in 2 S 5:16; 1 Ch 14:7. (4) One of the stock of Saul, 1 Ch 8:39. (5) One who returned from Babylon with Ezra, Ezr 8:13. (6) An Israelite who took a foreign wife, Ezr 10:33.

7. **Nogah.** i.e. *brightness,* ✳S#5052h. 1 Ch 3:7h. 14:6h. 2 S 5:15, 16.

8. **Eliada.** 1 Ch 14:7, Beeliada. 1 K +11:23. **Eliphe-let.** ver. +6. 1 Ch 14:7. 2 S 5:14-16, Eliphalet.

9. **of the concubines.** 2 S 5:13. **Tamar.** Ge +38:6. 2 S 13:1-20.

10. **Rehoboam.** 1 K 11:43. 14:+21, 31. 15:6. Mt 1:7, Roboam. **Abia.** i.e. *whose father is Jah.* 1 K 15:1,

Abijam. 2 Ch 13:1, Abijah. ✳S#29h. 1 Ch 2:24. 3:10. 6:28. 7:8. 24:10. 2 Ch 11:20, 22. 14:1. 29:1. Ne 10:7. 12:4, 17. (1) Son of Samuel, 1 S 8:2. (2) Son of Becher, 1 Ch 7:8. (3) Mother of Ashur, 1 Ch 2:24. (4) Son of Roboam, and father of Asa, Mt 1:7. (5) A descendant of Aaron, 1 Ch 24:1, 6, 10. (6) A priest who signed the covenant in the days of Nehemiah, Ne 10:7. (7) A chief of the priests who returned with Zerubbabel from Babylon, Ne 12:4, 17. Lk 1:5. (8) The mother of Hezekiah, 2 Ch 29:1; 2 K 18:2, Abi. **Asa.** 1 Ch +9:16. 1 K 15:8. 2 Ch 14:1. **Jehoshaphat.** 2 S +8:16. 1 K 15:24. 2 Ch 17:1. Mt 1:8, Josaphat.

11. **Joram.** 1 Ch +26:25. 1 K 22:50. 2 Ch 21:1, Jehoram. **Ahaziah.** 1 K +22:40. 2 K 8:24. 2 Ch 21:17, Jehoahaz. 22:1-6, Azariah. **Joash.** 1 Ch ◗7:8. Jg +6:11. 2 K 11:21. 2 Ch 24:1.

12. **Amaziah.** 1 Ch +4:34. 2 K 14:1. 2 Ch 25:1. **Azariah.** 1 Ch +6:36. 2 K 14:21. 15:30. 2 Ch 26:1, Uzziah. Mt 1:8, 9, Ozias. **Jotham.** Jg +9:5. 2 K 15:5, 32. 2 Ch 27:1. Mt 1:9, Joatham.

13. **Ahaz.** 1 Ch +8:35. 2 K 16:1. 2 Ch 28:1-8. Mt 1:9, Achaz. **Hezekiah.** 2 K +16:20. 18:1. 2 Ch 29:1. Mt 1:9, Ezekias. **Manasseh.** Ge +41:51. 2 K 21:1. 2 Ch 33:1. Mt 1:10, Manasses.

14. **Amon.** 2 K 21:19. 2 Ch 33:20, 21. Ne +7:59. **Josiah.** 1 K +13:2. 2 K 22:1. 2 Ch 34:1. Mt 1:10, 11, Josias.

15. **Johanan.** *or,* Jehoahaz. 2 K +10:35. 23:30. +25:23. **Jehoiakim.** i.e. *Jehovah will raise.* 2 K 23:34, Eliakim. 2 Ch 36:5. Je 22:18. ✳S#3079h. 1 Ch 3:15, 16. 2 K 23:34, 35, 36. 24:1, 5, 6, 19. 2 Ch 36:4, 5, 8. Je 1:3. 22:18, 24. 24:1. 25:1. 26:1, 21, 22, 23. 27:1, 20. 28:4. 35:1. 36:1, 9, 28, 29, 30, 32. 37:1. 45:1. 46:2. 52:2. Da 1:1, 2. Son of Josiah, king of Judah, 611-600 B.C., previously called Eliakim. **Zedekiah.** 1 K +22:11. 2 K 24:17, 18, Mattaniah. 2 Ch 36:11. **Shallum.** i.e. *retribution.* 2 K +15:10. The Targumist says he was called *Shallum,* "because the kingdom departed from the house of David in his days." 2 K 23:30. 2 Ch 36:1, Jehoahaz. Je 22:11.

16. **Jeconiah.** 2 K 24:6, 8. 25:27. 2 Ch 36:9, Jehoia-chin. Je 22:24, 28, Coniah. +24:1. Mt 1:11, Jechonias. **Zedekiah.** ver. 15. 1 K +22:11. As the sons of Jeconiah are enumerated in the succeeding verse, and as Zede-kiah is no where else mentioned as the son of Jeconiah, but as the son of Josiah, it is highly probable that *son* here means *successor.* 2 K 24:17, being his uncle. Matthew Poole comments, "Not his natural son, for he was his uncle, 2 K 24:17; but his legal son, or his successor, upon whom the son's right was devolved by virtue of that law, Nu 27:8-10, and therefore it is not strange if he have the name of *son* with it." See 1 K +15:10n.

17. **Assir.** Ex +6:24. As Salathiel was not the son of *Assir,* but of Jeconiah, it is probable that the word *assir,* which signifies a *prisoner,* is an epithet applied to Jeconiah, who was a long time a *prisoner* at Babylon. **Salathiel.** i.e. *asked of God.* Ezr 3:2, 8. 5:2, Shealtiel. Mt 1:12. ✳S#7597h. 1 Ch 3:17. Ezr 3:2, 8. Ne 12:1. Hg 1:1. 2:23. See also ✳S#7597h: Hg 1:12, 14. 2:2.

18. **Malchiram.** i.e. *king of altitude,* ✳S#4443h. **Pedaiah.** 2 K +23:36. **Shenazar.** i.e. *light of splendor; tribulation,* ✳S#8137h. **Jecamiah.** i.e. *Jah will rise,* ✳S#3359h. 1 Ch 2:41, 41. 3:18. **Hoshama.** i.e. *Jehovah hears,* ✳S#1953h. **Nedabiah.** i.e. *Jah impels,* ✳S#5072h.

19. **the sons of Pedaiah**. As St. Matthew states that Zerubbabel was the son of Salathiel, Houbigant thinks these words should be omitted; and *Pedaiah* is wanting in the Arabic and Syriac. But since the same Zerubbabel is called "the son of Pedaiah" here, but the son of Salathiel, Mt 1:12, the term son in Matthew is put for grandson, as is elsewhere the case: 1 K 15:10n. **Zerubbabel**. Ezr 2:2. 3:2. Hg 1:+1, 12-14. 2:2, 4. Zc 4:6-9. Mt 1:12, Zorobabel. **Meshullam**. 1 Ch +9:12. **Hananiah**. 1 Ch +25:23. **Shelomith**. Le +24:11. **their sister**. Matthew Poole notes, "Sister to the two last named sons of Zerubbabel, to wit, by both parents; and therefore named before the other five, ver. 20, who were her brethren by the father, but not by the mother."

20. **Hashubah**. i.e. *esteemed*, *S#2807h. **Ohel**. i.e. *a tent*, *S#169h. **Berechiah**. Zc +1:7. **Hasadiah**. i.e. *love or mercy of the Lord*, *S#2619h. **Jushab-hesed**. i.e. *mercy restored*, *S#3142h.

21. **Hananiah**. 1 Ch +25:23. **Pelatiah**. i.e. *deliverance of the Lord*, *S#6410h. 1 Ch 3:21. 4:42. Ne 10:22. Ezk 11:1, 13. (1) One in the succession of Jeconiah, 1 Ch 3:21. (2) A Simeonite who smote the Amalekites, 1 Ch 4:42. (3) A prince who, opposing Ezekiel, dies, Ezk 11:1-13. (4) A chief of the people who with Nehemiah sealed the covenant, Ne 10:22; perhaps the same person as (1). **Jesaiah**. i.e. *Jah has saved*, *S#3470h. (1) Grandson of Zerubbabel, 1 Ch 3:21. (2) A son of Benjamin, dwelling at Jerusalem, of a family of exiles, Ne 11:7. **Rephaiah**. 1 Ch +9:43. **Arnan**. i.e. *lion of perpetuity*, *S#770h. **Obadiah**. Ob +1. **Shechaniah**. ver. +22.

22. **Shechaniah**. i.e. *intimate with Jehovah; dwelling of Jehovah*, *S#7935h. 1 Ch 3:21, 22. Ezr 8:3, 5. 10:2. Ne 3:29. 6:18. 12:3. Also *S#7935h: 1 Ch 24:11. 2 Ch 31:15. (1) Successor with his sons of Jeconiah, in David's line, 1 Ch 3:21. (2) One set over the tithes by Hezekiah, 2 Ch 31:15. (3) One whose sons returned from Babylon with Ezra, Ezr 8:3, 5. (4) He who urged Ezra to reform the strange marriages, Ezr 10:2. (5) Father of Shemaiah, who helped to build the wall, Ne 3:29. (6) Father-in-law of Tobiah, who tried to terrify Nehemiah, Ne 6:18. (7) One of the priests who came up with Zerubbabel from Babylon, Ne 12:3. Called Shebaniah, Ne 12:14. **Shemiah**. 1 Ch +9:16. **Hattush**. Ezr +8:2. **Igeal**. i.e. *he will redeem*, *S#3008h. Nu 13:7. 2 S 23:36. 1 Ch 3:22. (1) The man of Issachar chosen to search the land, Nu 13:7. (2) One of David's mighty men, 2 S 23:36. (3) A successor of Jeconiah, 1 Ch 3:22. **Bariah**. i.e. *fugitive*, *S#1282h. **Neariah**. i.e. *servant of Jah*, *S#5294h. ver. 23. 1 Ch 4:42. (1) Among the successors of Jeconiah, 1 Ch 3:22, 23. (2) A captain of Simeonites, who went against Amalek, 1 Ch 4:42. **Shaphat**. i.e. *judge*, *S#8202h. 1 Ch 3:22. 5:12. 27:29. Nu 13:5. 1 K 19:16, 19. 2 K 3:11. 6:31. (1) Sent to search the land for Simeon, Nu 13:5. (2) Of Abel-meholah, father of the prophet Elisha, 1 K 19:16. (3) Successor of Jeconiah, of David's line, 1 Ch 3:22. (4) A chief of Gad, 1 Ch 5:12. (5) Son of Adlai, set over the herds by David, 1 Ch 27:29. **six**. *Five* only are enumerated in the text, which Houbigant would substitute as the true reading; but probably the *father* is reckoned with his sons. Matthew Poole further comments, "But the Hebrew word *shisha*, which is rendered *six*, may be the proper name of one of the sons of Shemaiah, who may be so

called, because he was the sixth son."

23. **Elioenai**. 1 Ch +26:3. **Hezekiah**. Heb. Hiskijah. or, Hiskijahu. S#2396h, 1 K +16:20. **Azrikam**. i.e. *help against an enemy; my help has arisen*, *S#5840h. 1 Ch 3:23. 8:38. 9:14, 44. 2 Ch 28:7. Ne 11:15. (1) A descendant of Jeconiah, 1 Ch 3:23. (2) A chief man of Benjamin, of the stock of Saul, 1 Ch 8:38; 9:44. (3) Governor of the house, slain by Zichri, 2 Ch 28:7. (4) A Levite, descended from Merari, 1 Ch 9:14. Ne 11:15.

24. **Hodaiah**. i.e. *majesty of Jah*, *S#1939h. **Eliashib**. i.e. *God will restore*, *S#475h. 1 Ch 3:24. 24:12. Ezr 10:6, 24, 27, 36. Ne 3:1, 20, 21, 21. 12:10, 10, 22, 23. 13:4, 7, 28. (1) A successor of Jeconiah, 1 Ch 3:24. (2) Son of Aaron, to whom the eleventh lot fell, 1 Ch 24:12. (3) Father of Johanan, Ezr 10:6. (4) High priest during the building of the wall, Ne 3:1, 20; 12:10. (5-7) Three of those that took strange wives, Ezr 10:24, 27, 36. **Pelaiah**. Ne +8:7. **Akkub**. i.e. *lain in wait; insidious*, *S#6126h. 1 Ch 3:24. 9:17. Ezr 2:42, 45. Ne 7:45. 8:7. 11:19. 12:25. (1) A descendant of Jeconiah, 1 Ch 3:24. (2) A porter for the sanctuary, 1 Ch 9:17; Ne 11:19. (3) A name applied to a family of hereditary porters for the sanctuary, Ezr 2:42; Ne 7:45. (4) One with Ezra when he read the law, Ne 8:7. (5) One whose children came up from Babylon, head of a family of the Nethinims who returned to Jerusalem after the captivity, Ezr 2:45. **Johanan**. 2 K +25:23. **Dalaiah**. i.e. *drawn of Jah, delivered*, *S#1806h. 1 Ch 3:24. Ezr 2:60. Ne 6:10. 7:62. Also S#1806h, 1 Ch 24:18. Je 36:12, 25. Usually rendered "Delaiah," Je +36:12. (1) A son of Elioenai, a successor of Jeconiah, 1 Ch 3:24. **Anani**. i.e. *my cloud*, *S#6054h.

1 CHRONICLES 4

The posterity of Judah, in the line of Hezron, Carmi, and Hur, 1-4. The posterity of Ashur, Hezron's son, 5-8. Jabez, and his prayer, 9, 10. Other descendants of Judah by Pharez, 11-20. The posterity of Shelah, Judah's son, 21-23. The sons of Simeon and their cities, 24-38. They conquer Gedor and the Amalekites, 39-43.

1. A.M. 2283, etc. B.C. 1721, etc. **Pharez**. 1 Ch 2:5. Ge 38:29. +46:12. Nu 26:20, 21. Ru 4:18. Mt 1:3. Lk 3:33, Phares. **Hezron**. Ge +46:9. Lk 3:33, Esrom. **Carmi**. i.e. *my vineyard*, *S#3756h. Ge 46:9. Ex 6:14. Nu 26:6. Jsh 7:1, 18. 1 Ch 2:7. 4:1. 5:3. (1) A son of Reuben, Ge 46:9; Ex 6:14. (2) Father of Achan, Jsh 7:1. 1 Ch 2:6, 7. or, Chelubai, 1 Ch 2:9. 2:18, Caleb.

2. **Reaiah**. i.e. *whom Jehovah cares for; seen of Jah*. 1 Ch 2:52, Haroeh. *S#7211h. 1 Ch 4:2. 5:5. Ezr 2:47. Ne 7:50. (1) Son of Shobal, son of Judah, 1 Ch 4:2. Called Haroeh, 1 Ch 2:52. (2) A descendant of Reuben, 1 Ch 5:5. (3) One whose children returned from Babylon, Ezr 2:47; Ne 7:50. **Shobal**. Ge +36:20. **Jahath**. i.e. *he will carry away; comfort; union*, *S#3189h. 1 Ch 4:2, 2. 6:20, 43. 23:10, 11. 24:22. 2 Ch 34:12. (1) A man of Judah, of the Zorathites, 1 Ch 4:2. (2) A son of Libni, a Levite, family of Gershom, 1 Ch 6:20, ?43. (3) A Levite, family of Gershom and head of a subdivision of the house of Shimei, 1 Ch 23:10; ?6:43. (4) A Levite, family of Kohath, house of Izhar, 1 Ch 24:22. (5) A Merarite

Levite, an overseer of the workmen engaged in repairing the temple during Josiah's reign, 2 Ch 34:12. **Ahumai**. i.e. *dweller near waters*, ✱S#267h. **Lahad**. i.e. *oppressed; in triumph or joy; towards exultant shout*, ✱S#3855h. **Zorathites**. i.e. *inhabitants of Zorah*. 2 Ch 2:53, 54. Jsh 15:33. Jg 13:25. ✱S#6882h: 1 Ch 2:53, 54. 4:2. For Zorah, see Jsh +19:41.

3. **Etam**. Jg 15:11. 2 Ch 11:6. **Jezreel**. i.e. *God soweth*, ✱S#3157h. 1 Ch 4:3. Jsh 15:56. 17:16. 19:18. Jg 6:33. 1 S 25:43. 29:1, 11. 2 S 2:9. 4:4. 1 K 4:12. 18:45, 46. 21:1, 23. 2 K 8:29, 29. 9:10, 15, 15, 16, 17, 30, 36, 37. 10:1, 6, 7, 11. 2 Ch 22:6, 6. Ho 1:4, 4, 5, 11. 2:22. (1) A man of Judah, 1 Ch 4:3. (2) Son of Hosea, Ho 1:4. (3) A city of Issachar, in the plain of Esdraelon, or Valley of Jezreel, Jsh 17:16; 19:18; 1 K 21:1. (4) A city of Judah, Jsh 15:56. **Ishma**. i.e. *desolation*, ✱S#3457h. **Idbash**. i.e. *honeyed; fat one*, ✱S#3031h. **Hazelelponi**. i.e. *the shadow turned towards me*, ✱S#6753h.

4. **Penuel**. i.e. *the face of God*, ✱S#6439h. 1 Ch 4:4. 8:25. Also Ge 32:31, Peniel. Also Ge 32:30. Jg 8:8, 8, 9, 17. 1 K 12:25. (1) A descendant of Caleb of Judah, 1 Ch 4:4. (2) A chief man of Benjamin, 1 Ch 8:25. (3) A place east of Jordan, near the river Jabbok, Ge 32:30, 31. Jg 8:8. 1 K 12:25. **Gedor**. ver. 18, 39. Jsh 15:36, +58. **Ezer**. i.e. *help*, ✱S#5829h. 1 Ch 4:4. 12:9. Ne 3:19. 12:42. (1) A descendant of Judah through Caleb, the son of Hur, 1 Ch 4:4. Supposed to be the same as Ezra, 1 Ch 4:17, but uncertain. (2) A descendant of Ephraim, 1 Ch 7:21, S#5827h. (3) One of the valiant men of Gad, 1 Ch 12:9. (4) A Jew who repaired part of the wall of Jerusalem after the captivity, Ne 3:19. (5) A priest who officiated in purifying the rebuilt wall of Jerusalem, Ne 12:42. Compare Ge +36:21. **Hushah**. i.e. *haste*, ✱S#2364h. 1 Ch 2:19, 50. Ex +17:10. **firstborn**. Le +27:26. **Ephratah**. 1 Ch +2:50. **the father**. 1 Ch 2:19, 42n.

5. **Ashur**. See on 1 Ch +2:24. **Tekoa**. 1 Ch +2:24. **two wives**. Ge +4:19. **Helah**. i.e. *scum*, ✱S#2458h. ver. 7. **Naarah**. i.e. *a maiden*, ✱S#5292h. ver. 6. Also, Jsh 16:7.

6. **Ahuzam**. i.e. *their possession*, ✱S#275h. **Hepher**. Nu +26:32. **Temeni**. i.e. *ordained; my right hand*, ✱S#8488h. **Haahashtari**. i.e. *muleteer; courier; I will diligently observe the searching*, ✱S#326h.

7. **Helah**. ver. 5. **Zereth**. i.e. *splendor*, ✱S#6889h. **Jezoar**. i.e. *whiteness; he will shine*, ✱S#3328h. **Ethnan**. i.e. *hire*, ✱S#869h. ✱6312, Jsh +3:3. Supply by ellipsis from the succeeding clause, ver. 8, (and Coz).

8. **Coz**. i.e. *thorn; trouble*, ✱S#6976h. 1 Ch 4:8. 24:+10, Hakoz. Ezr 2:+61, Koz. Ne 3:4, 21. 7:63. (1) Father of Anub and Zobebah, 1 Ch 4:8. (2) The son of Aaron, to whom the seventh lot fell, 1 Ch 24:10. (3) One whose children returned from Babylon, Ne 7:63. (4) One whose son helped build the wall, Ne 3:4, 21. **Anub**. i.e. *clustered*, ✱S#6036h. **Zobebah**. i.e. *sluggish; an army*, ✱S#6637h. **Aharhel**. i.e. *behind the breastwork*, ✱S#316h. **Harum**. i.e. *high*, ✱S#2037h. Probably *Jabez* should be mentioned here; as otherwise he is as a *consequent* without an antecedent.

9. **more honorable**. Ge 34:19. Is 43:4. Ac *17:11. **Jabez**. i.e. *Sorrowful*. ver. +10. **I bare him**. 1 Ch 7:23. Ge *3:16. 35:18. 1 S 4:21. Is 53:3.

10. **Jabez**. i.e. *trouble; he will cause pain*, ✱S#3258h. 1 Ch 2:55. 4:9, 9, 10. (1) The head of a

family of Judah, 1 Ch 4:9, 10. (2) Apparently a place. It is mentioned only in 1 Ch 2:55, but its situation is not known. **called on**. 1 Ch 16:8. Ge 12:8. Jb 12:4. Ps 55:16. 99:6. 116:2-4. Je *33:3. Ro *10:12-14. 1 C 1:2. **the God**. Ge 32:28. 33:20. 1 S 1:17. Is 41:17. **Oh that**, etc. Heb. If thou wilt, etc. Lk 19:42. **bless me**. Ge 12:2. 32:26. Ps 72:17. Ac 3:26. Ep 1:3. **enlarge**. Jsh 17:14-18. Jg 1:27-36. Pr 10:22. **thine hand**. Ps 119:173. Is 41:10. Jn *10:28. **that thou**. Ge 48:16. Pr 30:8, 9. Mt *6:13. Ro 12:9. 16:19. 2 T 4:18. **keep me**. Heb. do *me*. **from evil**. Ps 121:7. Jn 17:15. **that it may**. Ps 32:3, 4. 51:8, 12. Mt 26:75. Jn 21:17. 2 C 2:1-7. Ep 4:30. Re 3:19. **grieve me**. ſ37A, Ex +32:32. **God granted**. 1 K 3:7-13. Jb 22:27, 28. Ps 21:4. 65:2. 66:19, 20. 116:1, 2. Mt *7:7-11. Ep 3:20.

11. **Chelub**. i.e. *binding together; basket; coop*, ✱S#3620h. 1 Ch 4:11. 27:26. (1) A descendant of Judah, 1 Ch 4:11. (2) An Israelite whose son Ezri superintended the tillers of the ground in David's time, 1 Ch 27:26. **Shuah**. Ge +25:2. **Mehir**. i.e. *price; ability*, ✱S#4243h. **Eshton**. i.e. *effeminate; womanly*, ✱S#850h. ver. 12.

12. **Bethrapha**. i.e. *house of the healer* or *giants* or *feeble*, ✱S#1051h. **Paseah**. i.e. *lame, limping*, ✱S#6454h. 1 Ch 4:12. Ezr 2:49. Ne 3:6. 7:51. (1) A son of Eshton, son of Mehir, 1 Ch 4:12. (2) One whose children returned from Babylon, Ezr 2:49; Ne 7:51. (3) Father of Jehoiada, who helped to build the wall, Ne 3:6. **Tehinnah**. i.e. *graciousness*, ✱S#8468h. **Irnahash**. or, the city of Nahash. i.e. *city of the serpent*, ✱S#5904h. **Rechah**. i.e. *tenderness*, ✱S#7397h.

13. **Kenaz**. Ge +36:11. Jsh 15:17. Jg 1:13. 3:9-11. **Othniel**. Jsh +15:17. **Seraiah**. 2 S +8:17. **Hathath**. i.e. *casting down*, ✱S#2867h. or, Hathath *and* Meonathai, *who* begat, etc.

14. **Meonothai**. i.e. *my dwellings*, ✱S#4587h. **Ophrah**. i.e. *dustiness; fawn-like*, ✱S#6084h. (1) A son of Meonothai, 1 Ch 4:14. (2) A town of Benjamin, Jsh 18:23; 1 S 13:17. (3) A town of Manasseh. It is called Ophrah of the Abi-ezrite in Jg 6:11, 24. **Seraiah**. 2 S +8:17. **Joab**. 1 S +26:6. **valley**. Ne 11:35. or, *inhabitants* of the valley. Ge 41:57. 1 K 10:24. 2 K 16:9. **Charashim**. i.e. *craftsmen*, ✱S#2798h. Ne 11:35. **for they were craftsmen**. 2 K 24:14. Ne 11:35.

15. **Caleb**. Nu 13:+6, 30. 14:6-10, 24, 30. Jsh 14:6-14. 15:13-20. Jg 1:12-14. **Jephunneh**. Nu +13:6. **Iru**. i.e. *city-wise*, ✱S#5900h. **Elah**. Ge +36:41. **Naam**. i.e. *pleasantness*, ✱S#5277h. **Kenaz**. Ge +36:11. or, Uknaz. S#7073h.

16. **Jehaleleel**. i.e. *he praises God*, ✱S#3094h. 2 Ch 29:12, Jehalelel. **Ziph**. 1 Ch 2:42. Jsh +15:24. **Ziphah**. i.e. *flowing; refinery*, ✱S#2129h. **Tiria**. i.e. *fear; beholding*, ✱S#8493h. **Asareel**. i.e. *right of God*, ✱S#840h.

17. **Ezra**. Ezr +7:12. Ezra seems to be the person before called *Asareel* in ver. 16. **Jether**. 1 Ch +2:32. **Mered**. i.e. *rebellion*, ✱S#4778h. ver. 18. **Epher**. Ge +25:4. **Jalon**. i.e. *lodging*, ✱S#3210h. **and she bare**. It is probable that the latter part of verse 18 should be transposed before this passage, which Michaelis thinks its right place; for otherwise we have the pronoun *she* without an antecedent, and children born without their father's being mentioned. **Miriam**. Ex +15:20. **Shammai**. 1 Ch +2:28. **Ishbah**. i.e. *he will praise*, ✱S#3431h. **Eshtemoa**. ver. 19. 1 Ch 6:57. Jsh 15:50, Eshtemoh. 21:14. 1 S +30:28.

18. **Jehudijah**. i.e. *Jewess*, *S#3057h. See ver. 19. **Jered**. 1 Ch +1:2. **the father of**. ver. 4, 39. 1 Ch 2:42n. Jsh 15:58. **Gedor**. Jsh +15:58. Gedor was a city in the tribe of Judah; and probably the same which Eusebius calls *Kedous*, And Jerome *Gedrus*, ten miles from Diospolis, or Lydda, towards Eleutheropolis. **Heber**. Ge +46:17. **Socho**. i.e. *inclosure; his branch*, *S#7755h. 1 Ch 4:18. 2 Ch 11:7, Shocho. 28:18. Also *S#7755h: Jsh 15:35, 48. 1 S 17:1, 1. 1 K 4:10. (1) A city of Judah, Jsh 15:35; 1 S 17:1; 1 K 4:10; 2 Ch 11:7. (2) Another city of Judah, Jsh 15:48. **Jekuthiel**. i.e. *the fear* or *veneration* or *preservation of God; God is almightiness*, *S#3354h. **Zanoah**. Jsh +15:34. **Bithiah**. i.e. *worshiper of Jah; daughter of Jah*, *S#1332h. **daughter of Pharaoh**. 1 K 3:1, 6. 7:8. 9:16, 24. 2 Ch 8:11. **Mered**. ver. 17.

19. **Hodiah**. i.e. *my glory is Jah*, *S#1940h. or, Jehudijah, mentioned before, ver. 18. **Naham**. i.e. *comforter*, *S#5163h. **Keilah**. Jsh +15:44. 1 S 23:1, etc. **Garmite**. i.e. *bony, strong*, *S#1636h. **Eshtemoa**. 1 S +30:28. **Maachathite**. 2 S 10:6. +23:34.

20. **Shimon**. i.e. *waste*, *S#7889h. Shimon is supposed to have been another son of Mered, by Jehudijah. As this latter name signifies a Jewess, it rather favors the opinion that Bithiah was not a Jewess, but an Egyptian. **Amnon**. 2 S +3:2. **Rinnah**. i.e. *a joyful shout*, *S#7441h. **Ben-hanan**. i.e. *son of the gracious giver; son graciously given*, *S#1135h. **Tilon**. i.e. *suspension; thou shalt abide*, *S#8436h. **Ishi**. Ho +2:16. **Zoheth**. i.e. *releasing; strong*, *S#2105h. **Ben-zoheth**. i.e. *son of releasing* or *violent removal*, *S#1132h.

21. **Shelah**. 1 Ch 2:3. 9:5. Ge 38:1, +5. 46:12. Nu 26:20. Ne 11:5, Shiloni. **Judah**. Ge +35:23. **Er**. Ge +38:3. **Lecah**. i.e. *journey*, *S#3922h. **Laadah**. i.e. *order, to put in order; adornment*, *S#3935h. **Mareshah**. 1 Ch 2:42. Jsh +15:44. **fine linen**. 1 Ch 15:27. 2 Ch 2:14. 3:14. 5:12. Est 1:6. 8:15. Ezk 27:16. **Ashbea**. i.e. *adjurer; I shall make to swear*, *S#791h.

22. **Jokim**. i.e. *Jah will rise*, *S#3137h. **Chozeba**. i.e. *falsehood*, *S#3578h. **Joash**. 1 Ch ❶+7:8. Jsh +6:11. **Saraph**. i.e. *fiery serpent*, *S#8315h. **Moab**. Ge +19:37. **Jashubi-lehem**. i.e. *restorer of bread*, *S#3433h. **things**. or, records.

23. **the potters**. ver. 14. Ps 81:6. **dwelt with**. Mk 3:14.

24. **The sons of Simeon**. This genealogy differs in many particulars from those in the parallel places; probably occasioned by the same person's having several names. **Simeon**. Ge +29:33. **Nemuel**. Nu +26:12. or, Jemuel. Ge 46:10. Ex 6:15. **Jamin**. Ge +46:10. **Jarib**. i.e. *an adversary*, *S#3402h. 1 Ch 4:24. Ezr 8:16. 10:18. (1) A son of Simeon, Ge 46:10, called Jachin. Called Jarib, 1 Ch 4:24. (2) A companion of Ezra, Ezr 8:16. (3) A priest who was induced to put away his foreign wife, Ezr 10:18. or, Jachin. Ge +46:10. Nu 26:12-14. **Zerah**. Ge +36:13. +46:10, Zohar.

25. **Shallum**. 2 K +15:10. **Mibsam**. ver +25:13. **Mishma**. Ge +25:14.

26. **Hamuel**. i.e. *God is sun; heat of God; they were heated of God*, *S#2536h. **Zacchur**. i.e. *remembered; mindful*, S#2139h. **Shimei**. 2 S +16:5.

27. **sixteen sons and six daughters**. Ps +*127:3. **like to**. Heb. unto. Nu 2:4, 13. 26:14, 22. **multiply**. ver. 38. Ge 49:7. Nu 2:4.

28. **they dwelt**. Jsh 19:2-8. **Beer-sheba**. Ge +21:31. Beer-sheba was situated twenty miles south of Hebron,

according to Eusebius and Jerome, in whose time it was occupied by a Roman garrison. Jsh 15:28, 29. 19:2, 3, 9. **Moladah**. Jsh +15:26. Probably the same as *Malatha*, so often mentioned by Eusebius; from whom it appears it was situated about twenty miles from Hebron. **Hazar-shual**. Jsh +15:28.

29. **Bilhah**. Ge +29:29. or, Balah, Jsh 19:3. **Ezem**. i.e. *bone*, *S#6107h. 1 Ch 4:29. Jsh 15:+29, Azem. 19:3. **Tolad**. i.e. *posterity*, *S#8434h. Jsh 19:4, Eltolad.

30. **Bethuel**. Ge +22:22. Jsh 19:4, Bethul. **Hormah**. Nu +14:45. 1 S 30:30. **Ziklag**. 1 Ch 12:1. Jsh +15:31. 19:5. 1 S 27:6. 30:1. Ne 11:28.

31. **Beth-marcaboth**. i.e. *the chariot-house*, *S#1024h. Jsh 19:5. **Hazar-susim**. i.e. *court of the horses*, *S#2702h. or, Hazar-susah, Jsh 19:5, 6. **Beth-birei**. i.e. *house of my creator, house created of the Lord; house of creation*, *S#1011h. Jsh 19:6, Bethlebaoth. **Shaaraim**. Jsh +15:36. 19:6, Sharuhen.

32. **Etam**. i.e. *ravenous creatures*, *S#5862h. 1 Ch 4:3, 32. Jg 15:8, 11. 2 Ch 11:6. (1) A city of Judah, 2 Ch 11:6. (2) A town of Simeon, probably the same as Ether, Jsh 15:42; 19:+7; 1 Ch 4:32. (3) A rock, Jg 15:8, 11. *Ether* or *Etham*, was situated near Malatha, according to Eusebius. **Ain**. Nu +34:11. Jsh 15:32. **Rimmon**. Jsh 19:7, Remmon. 2 K +5:18. **Tochen**. i.e. *measurement; portion cut out, task assigned*, *S#8507h. **Ashan**. Jsh +15:42. Eusebius says *Beth-ashan* was sixteen miles west of Jerusalem.

33. **Baal**. Jsh 19:8, Baalath-beer. Jg +6:25. **their genealogy**. or, as they divided themselves by nations among them.

34. **Meshobab**. i.e. *returned; restored; backsliding*, *S#4877h. **Jamlech**. i.e. *let him reign*, *S#3230h. **Joshah**. i.e. *aid; setting upright; Jah a gift; he will be prospered; let him subsist; he will be made wise*, *S#3144h. **Amaziah**. i.e. *whom Jehovah strengthened; strength of Jah*, *S#558h. 1 Ch 4:34. 6:45. 2 K 12:21. 13:12. 14:8. 15:1. Am 7:10, 12, 14. Also *S#558h: 1 Ch 3:12. 2 K 14:1, 9, 11, 11, 13, 15, 17, 18, 21, 23. 15:3. 2 Ch 24:27. 25:1, 5, 9, 10, 11, 13, 14, 15, 17, 18, 20, 21, 23, 25, 26, 27. 26:1, 4. (1) King of Judah from 838-811 B.C., 2 K 12:21; 14:1, etc.; 2 Ch 25:1, etc. (2) Father of Joshah, of Simeon, 1 Ch 4:34. (3) A descendant of Merari, 1 Ch 6:45. (4) A priest of Bethel, who tried to silence the prophet Amos, Am 7:10-17.

35. **Joel**. 1 S +8:2. **Jehu**. 2 K +9:2. **Josibiah**. i.e. *Jehovah will cause to dwell; will be made to sit down of the Lord*, *S#3143h. **Seraiah**. 2 S +8:17. **Asiel**. i.e. *wrought of God*, *S#6221h.

36. **Elioenai**. 1 Ch +26:3. **Jaakobah**. i.e. *supplanter, deceiver*, *S#3291h. **Jeshohaiah**. i.e. *Jah will empty; depression of the Lord*, *S#3439h. **Asaiah**. 2 Ch +34:20. **Adiel**. i.e. *witness of God; ornament of God*, *S#5717h. 1 Ch 4:36. 9:12. 27:25. (1) A Simeonite, 1 Ch 4:36. (2) Father of one of the priests who dwelt in Jerusalem, 1 Ch 9:12. (3) Father of one of David's officers, 1 Ch 27:25. **Jesimiel**. i.e. *naming of God; made of God; he will be placed of God*, *S#3450h. **Benaiah**. 1 Ch +15:24.

37. **Ziza**. i.e. *abundance*, *S#2124h. 1 Ch 4:37. 2 Ch 11:20. (1) A Simeonite, 1 Ch 4:37. (2) A son of Rehoboam, 2 Ch 11:20. **Shiphi**. i.e. *my abundance; bald, naked, eminent*, *S#8230h. **Allon**. i.e. *an oak; thick through*, *S#438h. 1 Ch 4:37. Also S#438h:

Jsh 19:33. See Ge 35:8. **Jedaiah**. Ne +3:10. **Shimri**. i.e. *watchful; vigilant*, *S#8113h. 1 Ch 4:37. 11:45. 26:+10, Simri. 2 Ch 29:13. (1) A Simeonite, son of Shemaiah, 1 Ch 4:37. (2) Father of one of David's mighty men, 1 Ch 11:45. (3) A Merarite Levite, a son of Hosah, 1 Ch 26:10. (4) A Levite, who lived in the reign of Hezekiah, a son of Elizaphan, 2 Ch 29:13. **Shemaiah**. 1 Ch +9:16.

38. **mentioned by their names**. Heb. coming by names. ver. 41. 1 Ch 5:24. Ge 6:4. Jb 3:6. **the house**. ver. 27. **increased greatly**. Ge 28:14.

39. **they went**. This expedition of the Simeonites took place in the days of Hezekiah, and, as Calmet conjectures, near the time of the captivity of the ten tribes, when the remnant of Simeon would feel themselves obliged to retire more southward into Arabia Petraea, for fear of the Jews, and to seek pasture for their flocks. **Gedor**. ver. 4, 18. Jsh 12:13, Geder. 15:58.

40. **fat pasture**. Nu 13:20. Ne 9:25, 35. **the land**. Jg 18:7-10. **wide**. Ps 104:25. **quiet**. Jg 18:7, 27. **peaceable**. 1 T *2:1, 2. **Ham**. Ge +5:32. These were probably either *Philistines* or *Egyptians*, who dwelt at Gedor. Ge 9:22, etc. 10:6. Ps 78:51. 105:23.

41. **these written**. ver. 33-38. **Hezekiah**. 2 K +16:20. 18:8, etc. Is 14:28-32. **the habitations**. Or, the *Meunnim*, or Maonites. Jg +10:12. 2 Ch 26:27. **destroyed them utterly**. 2 K 19:11. 2 Ch 20:23. **rooms**. 1 Ch 5:22. **pasture**. Nu 32:1-4.

42. **mount Seir**. Ge 36:8, 9. Dt 1:2.

43. **the rest**. That is, those who had escaped in the war which Saul, and afterwards David, made against them. Ex 17:14-16. Dt 25:17-19. 1 S 15:7, 8. 30:17. 2 S 8:12. **unto this day**. 1 Ch 5:26. 13:11. Ge +19:38. Dt +29:4. 34:6. Jsh +4:9. Jg 1:26. 2 K 8:22n. 2 Ch 5:9n. Je 44:6. Mt 27:8. 28:15.

1 CHRONICLES 5

Judah and Joseph preferred before Reuben, who forfeited his birthright, 1, 2. Reuben's descendants; some of whom vanquish the Hagarites, 3-10. The chief men of Gad, and their habitations, 11-17. Reuben, Gad, and half of Manasseh, obtain a victory over the Hagarites, 18-22. The habitations and chief men of that half of Manasseh, 23, 24. The captivity of the two tribes and half, for their sins, 25, 26.

1. A.M. 2294, etc. B.C. 1710, etc. **he was**. 1 Ch 2:1. Ge 29:32. 46:8. 49:3. Ex 6:14. Nu 1:5. 16:1. 26:5. **forasmuch**. Ge 35:22. 49:4. Le 18:8. 20:11. Dt 27:20. 1 C 5:1. **birthright**. 1 Ch 26:10. Ge 48:15-22. Dt 21:17. Col +√1:15. **and**. Ge 25:23. 1 S 16:6-11. **reckoned**. Jsh 14:6n.

2. **Judah**. Ge +35:23. +*49:8-10. Nu 2:3. 7:12. Jsh 14:6n. Jg 1:2. Ps ☉+60:7. 108:8. Mi +*5:2. Mt *2:6. He *7:14. Re *5:5. **the chief ruler**. *or*, the prince. By *the chief ruler* is meant first David, and after him the Messiah, agreeably to the celebrated prophecy of Jacob (Ge 49:10). The Syriac calls him "Christ the king," and the Arabic, "Messiah the king." 1 S 16:1, 10, 12. 2 S 8:15. Ps 78:68-71. Je *23:5, 6. Mi +*5:2. Mt 2:6. He 7:14. **birthright was**. Ge 49:26. Ro=8:29.

3. **sons**. Ge 46:9. Ex 6:14. Nu 26:5-9. **Hanoch**. Ge +25:4. **Pallu**. Ge 46:9, Phallu. Nu +26:5. **Hezron**. Ge +46:9. **Carmi**. 1 Ch +4:1.

4. **Joel**. 1 S +8:2. **Shemaiah**. 1 Ch +9:16. **Gog**. i.e. *to cover; surmount; top; roof; extension; mountain,*

*S#1463h. 1 Ch 5:4. Ezk 38:2, 3, 14, 16, 18. 39:1, 1, 11, 11, 11, 15. (1) A Reubenite, 1 Ch 5:4. (2) Prince of the land of Magog, Ezk 38:2, 3, 14, 16, 18; 39:1, 11. (3) Also of the Rossi, Moschi, and Tibareni, who is to come with great forces from the extreme north, Ezk 38:15; 39:2; after the exile, Ezk 38:8, 12, to invade the holy land, and to perish there. Gog and Magog, Re 20:8, belong to a different time to those spoken of in Ezekiel. **Shimei**. 2 S +16:5.

5. **Micah**. Mi +1:1. **Reaia**. i.e. *seen of Jah; whom Jehovah cares for*, *S#7211h. 1 Ch 4:2, Reaiah. 5:5. Ezr 2:47. Ne 7:50. (1) Son of Shobal, son of Judah, 1 Ch 4:2. Called Haroeh, 1 Ch 2:52. (2) A descendant of Reuben, 1 Ch 5:5. (3) One whose children returned from Babylon, Ezr 2:47; Ne 7:50. **Baal**. i.e. *master; possessor; owner; lord*, *S#1168h. (1) Son of Joel, a descendant of Reuben, 1 Ch 5:5. (2) A descendant of Benjamin, 1 Ch 8:30; 9:36. (3) A city of Simeon, 1 Ch 4:33. (4) An idol of the Phoenicians, especially of the Tyrians: also worshipped by the Hebrews, Jg 6:25; 2 K 10:18. +23:4. The chief male deity of the Phoenicians and Canaanites, as Ashtoreth was their principal female deity. The worship of Baal, together with that of Astarte, was common among the Hebrews. The Babylonians worshipped Baal under the name of Bel. Human sacrifices were offered to Baal by the Jews, Je 19:5.

6. **Beerah**. i.e. *a well*, *S#880h. After their separation from the house of David, the ten tribes continued to have princes of the tribes, till the time that Tiglath-pileser carried them captive; at which time *Beerah*, who according to the Targum was the same as Baruch, was their *prince*. **Tilgath-pilneser**. ver. 26. 2 K +15:29. 16:7, Tiglath-pileser. **Reubenites**. Nu +26:7.

7. **when the genealogy**. ver. 17. **Jeiel**. i.e. *swept away of God; treasure of God*, *S#3273h. 1 Ch 5:7. 9:35. 11:44. 15:18, 21. 16:5, 5. 2 Ch 20:14. 26:11. 29:13. 35:9. Ezr 8:13. 10:43. Also *S#3273h: 1 Ch +9:35, Jehiel. 11:44, Jehiel. 2 Ch 26:11. 29:13. Ezr 8:13. (1) A Reubenite, 1 Ch 5:7. (2) One of the porters appointed to bring up the ark from Obed-edom, 1 Ch 15:18. (3) Two of the singers, 1 Ch 15:20, 21. (4) Father of the inhabitants of Gibeon and ancestor of king Saul, 1 Ch 9:35, 36, 39. (5) A son of Hotham, an Aroerite, in the reign of David, 1 Ch 11:44. (6) A Levite musician, 1 Ch 16:5a. (7) A Levite of the second degree, a doorkeeper, and played the harp at the removal of the ark to Jerusalem, 1 Ch 15:18, 21; 16:5b. (8) A Levite of the sons of Asaph, 2 Ch 20:14. (9) A scribe who recorded the number of soldiers in Uzziah's army, 2 Ch 26:11. (10) A Levite, a descendant of Elizaphan, who took part in the reformation under Hezekiah, 2 Ch 29:13. (11) A contemporary of Ezra who with members of his family returned from Babylonia with the scribe, Ezr 8:13. **Zechariah**. Zc +1:1.

8. **Bela**. Ge +14:2. **Azaz**. i.e. *the strong one*, *S#5811h. **Shema**. Jsh +15:26. *or*, Shemaiah, ver. 4. **Aroer**. Nu +32:34. Dt 2:36. Jsh 13:15-21. Is 17:2. **Nebo**. Nu +32:3. The city of *Nebo* was doubtless situated on or near the celebrated mountain of the same name, east of Jordan. Nu 32:38. Dt 32:49. 34:1. Is 15:2. **Baal-meon**. Nu +32:38. Jsh 13:17. Ezk 25:9.

9. **unto the entering**. That is, unto the borders of Arabia Deserta, which extends to the Euphrates. **Euphrates**. 1 Ch 18:3. Ge +2:14. 2 K 24:7. **Gilead**. ver.

16. 1 Ch 26:31. Ge +31:23. Jsh 22:9. 1 K 17:1. **because.** Jsh 22:8, 9.

10. A.M. 2944. B.C. 1060. **the Hagarites.** i.e. *fugitives.* ver. 19, 20. Ge 21:9. 25:12. 2 S 24:6. Ps +83:6, Hagarenes. ❋S#1905h: 1 Ch 5:10, 19, 20. Ps 83:6. Also 1 Ch +11:38, Haggeri. +27:31. **throughout,** etc. Heb. upon all the face of the East.

11. **the children.** The Gadites and the half tribe of Manasseh are joined to the genealogy of Reuben, because they inhabited the same country, and formed a sort of separate colony east of Jordan. **Gad.** Ge +30:11. **in the land of Bashan.** Nu +21:33. 32:34-36. Dt 3:10-17. Jsh +12:4n. 13:11, 24-28. Ps 22:12. **Salcah.** Jsh +13:11.

12. **Joel.** 1 S +8:2. **Shapham.** i.e. *bald,* ❋S#8223h. **Jaanai.** i.e. *responsive,* ❋S#3285h. **Shaphat.** 1 Ch +3:22. **Bashan.** ver. 11. Nu +21:33.

13. This verse is wanting both in the Syriac and Arabic. **Michael.** Da +12:1. **Meshullam.** 1 Ch +9:12. **Sheba.** 1 K +10:1. **Jorai.** i.e. *rainy,* ❋S#3140h. **Jachan.** i.e. *afflicted,* ❋S#3275h. **Zia.** i.e. *trembling; smelling,* ❋S#2127h. **Heber.** Ge +46:17.

14. **Abihail.** Nu +3:35. **Huri.** i.e. *nobleman,* ❋S#2359h. **Jaroah.** i.e. *making a sweet odor,* ❋S#3386h. **Gilead.** Ge +31:23. **Michael.** Da +12:1. **Jeshishai.** i.e. *aged,* ❋S#3454h. **Jahdo.** i.e. *together,* ❋S#3163h. **Buz.** Ge +22:21.

15. **Ahi.** i.e. *brotherly,* ❋S#277h. 1 Ch 5:15. 7:34. (1) Son of Abdiel, 1 Ch 5:15. (2) Son of Shamer, 1 Ch 7:34. **Abdiel.** i.e. *servant of God,* ❋S#5661h. **Guni.** Ge +46:24.

16. **Gilead.** Ge +31:23. **Bashan.** ver. 11. **Sharon.** 1 Ch 27:29. SS 2:1. Is +35:2. **their borders.** Heb. goings forth.

17. **reckoned by genealogies.** ver. 7. **Jotham.** Jg +9:5. 2 K 15:5, 32. 2 Ch 27:1. **Jeroboam.** 1 K +11:26. 2 K 14:16, 23, 28.

18. **Reuben.** 1 Ch 12:37. Ge +29:32. 2 K 10:33. **Gadites.** Dt +3:12. **Manasseh.** Ge +41:51. **valiant men.** Heb. sons of valor. 1 S 18:17mg. 2 S +2:7mg. **to shoot.** 1 Ch 8:40. 2 Ch 14:8. Ps 7:13. **four and forty.** Jsh 4:12, 13. **that went.** Nu 1:3.

19. **made war.** See on ver. 10. **the Hagarites.** ver. +10. The *Hagarites,* and these other tribes, were descendants of *Hagar,* and dwelt, according to Strabo, in Arabia Deserta. **Jetur.** 1 Ch 1:31. Ge +25:15. **Nephish.** i.e. *pleasure; refreshment; respiration,* ❋S#5305h. 1 Ch 1:31. 5:19. Ge +25:15, Naphish. (1) A son of Ishmael, Ge 25:15. (2) A people or tribe descended from Ishmael, 1 Ch 5:19. **Nodab.** i.e. *nobility; liberal,* ❋S#5114h.

20. **And they.** ver. 22. Ex 17:11. Jsh 10:14, 42. 1 S 7:12. 19:5. Ps 46:1. 146:5, 6. **for they cried.** T#1178. 1 K 8:44, 45. 2 Ch 13:14, 15. 14:11-13. 18:31. 20:12. 32:20, 21. **in the battle.** T#1227. 1 K 22:32. 2 Ch 13:13, 14. 14:10, 11. 18:31. **because.** Ps √9:10. 20:7, 8. 22:4, 5. *84:11, 12. Je 17:7, 8. Na 1:7. Ep 1:12.

21. **took away.** Heb. led captive. **camels.** The *camel,* in Hebrew *gamal,* retained with little variation in all languages, is, according to the Linnaean system, a genus of quadrupeds of the order *pecora;* comprehending the camel, properly so called, with two prominences; the dromedary, with a single one; the lama, or Peruvian camel, with the back even and the breast gibbose, and the pacos, or camel without any gibbosity. The camel, properly so called, is about 6 1/2 feet in

height: its head is small; ears short; neck long, slender, and bending; legs long and slender, having four callosities on the fore legs and two on the hinder, on which it rests; feet soft, parted, but not thoroughly divided; bottom of the foot tough and pliant; tail about two feet in length, terminating in a tuft; and hair fine, soft, of considerable length, and of a dusky reddish color. Besides the same internal structure as other ruminating animals, it is furnished with an additional bag for containing a quantity of water till wanted. **men.** Heb. souls of men. Nu 31:35. Ezk 27:13. Re 18:13. souls, Heb. *nephesh,* Ge +12:5.

22. **the war was of God.** Ex 14:14. Jsh *23:10. Jg 3:2. 2 Ch *32:8. Ne 4:20. Ps 24:8. Pr +*22:3. Zc 14:3. Lk *14:31, 32. +*22:36. Ro *8:31. **they dwelt.** Nu 32:33. **steads.** 1 Ch 4:41. **until the captivity.** ver. 6, 26. 2 K 15:29. 17:6.

23. **Manasseh.** Ge +41:51. **Bashan.** Nu +21:33. Jsh 12:4n. 1 K +4:13. **Baal-hermon.** Jsh 13:29-31. Jg +3:3. **Senir.** i.e. *coat of mail; bear the lamp; pointed,* ❋S#8149h. 1 Ch 5:23. Ezk 27:5. Also Dt 3:9. SS 4:8, Shenir. (1) A mountain in the north of Canaan, near Hermon, 1 Ch 5:23; Ezk 27:5. Rendered *Shenir,* Dt 3:9; SS 4:8. (2) The Amorite name of Hermon, Dt 3:9; in SS 4:8, Senir and Hermon are distinguished, each probably being a distinct peak of the giant mountain. **mount Hermon.** Dt 3:+8, 9. 4:48. Jsh 13:11. Ps 133:3. SS 4:8.

24. **Epher.** Ge +25:4. **Ishi.** 1 Ch +2:31. **Eliel.** 1 Ch +8:20. **Azriel.** i.e. *help of God,* ❋S#5837h. (1) Chief of a family of Manasseh, 1 Ch 5:24. (2) Father of Jerimoth, 1 Ch 27:19. (3) Father of Seraiah, Je 36:26. **Jeremiah.** Je +1:1. **Hodaviah.** i.e. *majesty of God; praise ye Jehovah,* ❋S#1938h. 1 Ch 5:24. 9:7. Ezr 2:40. (1) A descendant of Jeconiah, 1 Ch 3:24, Hodaiah. (2) A chief of the half tribe of Manasseh, 1 Ch 5:24. (3) A descendant of Benjamin, 1 Ch 9:7. (4) A Levite whose children returned from Babylon, Ezr 2:40. Called Hodevah, Ne 7:43. **Jahdiel.** i.e. *he will be gladdened of God,* ❋S#3164h. **mighty men of valor.** ver. 18mg. Jg +6:12. **famous men.** Heb. men of names. 1 Ch 4:38. 12:30mg.

25. **and went.** Jg 2:17. 8:33. 2 K 17:7-18. Ho 1:2. 9:1. Re 17:5. **a whoring.** Ex 34:15. Jg 8:27. 2 K 17:7. 2 Ch 21:11, 13. **after the gods.** Jg 2:12. 2 Ch 25:14, 15. Ps 106:34-39.

26. **stirred up.** 2 S 24:1. 2 Ch 33:11. Ezr 1:5. Is 10:5, 6. 13:2-5. **the spirit.** Heb. *ruach,* Ge +41:8. ∫121A10, Ge +26:35. **Pul.** 2 K +15:19. **Tilgath-pilneser.** i.e. *that takes away captivity; lord of the Tigris; wine-press heap of the wonderful bond; winepress heap of the distinguished captive,* ❋S#8407h. 1 Ch 5:6, 26. 2 Ch 28:20. Also 2 K +15:29, Tiglath-pilneser. 16:7, 10. **Reubenites.** Nu +26:7. **Gadites.** ver. 18. **and brought them.** 2 K 17:6. 18:11. 19:12. Is 37:12. **Halah.** 2 K +17:6. **Habor.** 2 K +17:6. **Hara.** i.e. *mountainous,* ❋S#2024h. **Gozan.** 2 K +17:6. **unto this day.** 1 Ch +4:43.

1 CHRONICLES 6

The sons of Levi, by Aaron, to Eleazar, 1-3. The line of Eleazar to the captivity, 4-15. The families of Levi, 16-19. The sons of Gershom, 20, 21; of Kohath, 22-28; of Merari, 29, 30. The singers appointed by David, 31-48. The office of Aaron and his sons, 49.

Aaron's line to Ahimaaz, 50-53. The cities of the priests and Levites, 54-81.

1. A.M. 2304, etc. B.C. 1700, etc. **sons of Levi.** 1 Ch 23:6. Ge +29:34. 46:11. Ex 6:16. Nu 3:17. 26:57. **Gershon.** Ge +46:11. *or,* Gershom. ver. 16, 17, 20. Ex +2:22. **Kohath.** Ge +46:11. **Merari.** Ge +46:11.

2. **the sons of Kohath.** 1 Ch 23:12. Ex 6:18, 21-24. **Amram.** ver. 22, Amminadab. Ex +6:18. **Izhar.** ver. 22. Ex +6:18. **Hebron.** Ex +6:18. **Uzziel.** Ex +6:18.

3. **Aaron.** 1 Ch 23:13. Ex +4:14. 6:20. **Miriam.** Ex 2:4, 7. +15:20. Mi 6:4. **Nadab.** 1 Ch 24:1, 2. Ex +6:23. 24:1. 28:1. Le 10:1, 12, 16. **Abihu.** Ex +6:23. **Eleazar.** 1 Ch 24:3-6. Ex +6:23.

4. **Phinehas.** ver. 50. 1 Ch 9:20. Ex +6:25. Nu 25:6-11, 13. 31:6. Jsh 22:13, 30-32. 24:33. Jg 20:28. Ezr 8:2. Ps 106:30, 31. **Abishua.** i.e. *prosperous; father of welfare* or *help* or *riches* or *salvation* or *good fortune* or *success,* *S#50. 1 Ch 6:4, 5, 50. 8:4. Ezr 7:5. (1) The son of Phinehas the priest, 1 Ch 6:4, 5, 50. (2) Son of Bela, 1 Ch 8:4. (3) Ancestor of Ezra, Ezr 7:5.

5. **Bukki.** Nu +34:22. **Uzzi.** i.e. *my strength,* *S#5813h. 1 Ch 6:5, 6, 51. 7:2, 3, 7. 9:8. Ezr 7:4. Ne 11:22. 12:19, 42. (1) A Levite, son of Bukki, 1 Ch 6:5, 51. Ezr 7:4. (2) A son of Tola of Issachar, 1 Ch 7:2. (3) A son of Bela, of Benjamin, 1 Ch 7:7. (4) A son of Bani, and overseer of Levites at Jerusalem, Ne 11:22. (5) One of the high priests, who assisted at the dedication of the wall, Ne 12:19, 42. (6) A son of Michri, and father of Elah, 1 Ch 9:8.

6. **Zerahiah.** Ezr +7:4. **Meraioth.** Ne +12:15.

7. **Amariah.** Ezr +7:3. **Ahitub.** 1 S +14:3.

8. **Ahitub.** 2 S 8:17. **Zadok.** 2 S +8:17. 15:35. 17:15. 20:25. 1 K 1:8, 34, 44. 2:35. **Ahimaaz.** 1 S +14:50. 2 S 15:27, 36. 17:17, 20. 18:19, 22, 27-29.

9. **Azariah.** ver. +36. **Johanan.** 2 K +25:23.

10. A.M. 3244. B.C. 760. **Johanan.** *Johanan* is supposed to be the same as *Jehoiada,* as he would otherwise not be mentioned. **executed.** 2 Ch 26:17-20. **the temple.** Heb. the house. **Solomon built.** 1 K ch. 6, 7. 2 Ch 3:4.

11. **Azariah.** ver. 9, +36. **Amariah.** 2 Ch 19:11. Ezr +7:3. **Ahitub.** 1 S +14:3.

12. **Zadok.** 2 S +8:17. **Shallum.** 1 Ch 9:11. 2 K +15:10. Ne 11:11, Meshullam.

13. **Hilkiah.** 2 K +18:18. 22:4, 12-14. 2 Ch 34:14-20. 35:8. Ezr 7:1. **Azariah.** ver. +36. 2 Ch 31:10.

14. A.M. 3416. B.C. 588. **Seraiah.** 2 S +8:17. Seraiah was carried to Riblah, and there put to death by order of Nebuchadnezzar; so that with him ended the succession of high priests in the first temple. 2 K 25:18. Ezr 7:1. Ne 11:11. Je 3:24-27. Zc 6:11.

15. **Jehozadak.** i.e. *whom Jehovah has made just; Jehovah is the righteous one.* Ezr +3:2, Jozadak. 5:2. Hg 1:+1, 12, 14. 2:2, Josedech. *S#3087h. 1 Ch 6:14, 15. Hg 1:1, 12, 14. 2:2, 4. Zc 6:11. **when the Lord.** 2 K 25:18, 21. 2 Ch 36:17-21. Je 39:9. 52:12-15, 28. **by the hand.** T#247. Ezr 4:13. 2 S +7:14 (T#265). 2 K 14:27. 25:21. Ac 14:27. Ro 15:18.

16. A.M. 2304, etc. B.C. 1700, etc. **Gershom.** ver. 1. Ex 6:16, Gershon.

17. **the sons of Gershom.** 1 Ch 23:7. Nu 3:18, 21. **Libni.** ver. +29. 1 Ch 23:7. **Shimei.** Ex 6:17, Shimi. 2 S +16:5.

18. **sons of Kohath.** 1 Ch 23:12. Ge +46:11. **Amram.** ver. 2, 3. Ex +6:18.

19. **Merari.** Ge +46:11. **Mahli.** 1 Ch 9:19. 23:21. 24:26. Ex +6:19, Mahali. Nu +3:20. 26:28, 57, 58. **Mushi.** Ex +6:19.

20. **Libni.** ver. 17, +29. **Jahath.** 1 Ch +4:2. **Zimmah.** ver. 42. 2 Ch +29:12. **his son.** i.e. His grandson, by his son Shimei, as appears from ver. 42, 43, the names "father" and "son" being oft used in Scripture of more remote progenitors or successors (Matthew Poole). 1 Ch 3:19n. 1 K +15:10n.

21. **Joah.** 1 +36:3. *or,* Ethan, ver. 42. **Iddo.** Ezr +5:1. *or,* Adaiah, Ne +11:5. **Zerah.** ver. 41. Ge +38:30. **Jeaterai.** i.e. *stepping; he will abound of the Lord; my profits; my steps; my remainders; following the track of one,* *S#2979h. ver. 41, Ethni.

22. **Amminadab.** ver. 2, 18. 1 Ch +15:11. Ex 6:+18, 21, 24, Izhar. **Korah.** 1 Ch 9:19. Ge +36:5. **Assir.** Ex +6:24. Nu *26:11n.

23. **Elkanah.** Ex +6:24. **Ebiasaph.** i.e. *father of increase,* *S#43h. 1 Ch 6:23, 37. 9:19. Ex +6:24, Abiasaph. **Assir.** Ex +6:24.

24. **Tahath.** Nu 33:26. **Uriel.** 1 Ch +15:5. *or,* Zephaniah, ver. 36. **Uzziah.** 2 Ch +26:1. *or,* Azariah, ver. +36. **Shaul.** Ge +46:10. *or,* Joel, ver. 36.

25. A.M. 2904, etc. B.C. 1100, etc. **Elkanah.** ver. 35, 36. Ex +6:24. Elkanah, the son of that *Korah* mentioned above, ver. 22, as is manifest by ver. 35-37 (Matthew Poole). **Amasai.** 2 Ch +29:12. **Ahimoth.** i.e. *brother of death,* *S#287h.

26. **Elkanah.** This was another *Elkanah,* son or grandson of the former Elkanah, and either the son or brother of *Ahimoth,* last mentioned, or of *Amasai.* **Zophai.** i.e. *my honeycombs; my overflows; honey of the Lord,* *S#6689h. 1 Ch 6:26. Also 1 Ch 6:35, Zuph. 1 S 1:1, Zuph. Also 1 S 9:5, Zuph. **Nahath.** ver. 34, Toah. Ge +36:13. 1 S 1:1, Tohu.

27. **Eliab.** ver. 34, Eliel. Nu +1:9. 1 S 1:1, Elihu. **Jeroham.** 1 S +1:1. **Elkanah.** Ex +6:24. 1 S 1:1, 19, 20. Houbigant says that we may venture to add, "Samuel his son."

28. **firstborn.** 1 Ch +5:1. Le +27:26. *J*63A1, Ge +14:20. Here there is an ellipsis of the name of the firstborn, which the margin correctly supplies as Joel. The word *Vashni* when otherwise pointed means "second," so that the verse more properly reads "And the sons of Samuel; the firstborn (Joel) and the second Abiah." **Vashni.** i.e. *Jah is strong; wherefore, sleep thou; changed; my year; second; liberal gift of the Lord,* *S#2059h. It appears that *Joel* is here lost out of the text; and that *washni,* which signifies *"and the second,"* and which refers to *Abiah,* is made into a proper name. The Syriac and Arabic read as in Samuel. The marginal references contain the variation in the names given to the same persons, in different parts of sacred history, as far as it can be ascertained; and nearly the whole, that is at present known concerning them, may be learned by carefully consulting them. ver. 33. 1 S *8:2, Joel.

29. **Merari.** Ge +46:11. **Mahli.** ver. 19. 1 Ch 23:21. Nu 3:+20, 33. **Libni.** i.e. *my whiteness; white, transparent,* *S#3845h. 1 Ch 6:17, 20, 29. Ex 6:17. Nu 3:18. **Shimei.** ver. 17. **Uzza.** 2 K +21:18.

30. **Haggiah.** i.e. *festival of Jah,* *S#2293h. **Asaiah.** 2 Ch +34:20.

31. A.M. 2962. B.C. 1042. **whom David.** 1 Ch 15:16-22, 27. 25:1-31. **service.** *J*144A5, Ge +9:5. **after that.**

1 Ch 16:1. 2 S 6:17. Ps 132:8, 14. **had rest**. He=4:9. Re=14:13.

32. they ministered. 1 Ch 16:4-6, 37-42. Ps 68:24, 25. **with singing**. Ep 5:19. **until Solomon**. ver. 10. 1 K 8:6-13. **and then**. 1 Ch 9:33. 25:8-31. 2 Ch 29:25-30. 31:2. 35:15. Ezr 3:10, 11. 6:18. Ne 11:17-23. 12:27, 28, 45-47. Ps 134:1, 2. 135:1-3. **waited**. Heb. stood. ver. 33. 1 K 12:6, 8. **according to their order**. This order is specified below. 1 C=12:11.

33. waited. Heb. stood. ver. 32. Dt 10:8. Pr 8:34. Ep=6:13. **Heman**. 1 Ch +2:6. 15:17, 19. 16:41, 42. 25:1-5. 2 Ch 5:12. 29:14. Ps 88, title. **Joel**. ver. 28n, Vashni. 1 S +8:2. **Shemuel**. This variation, as well as some others, only exists in the translation; the Hebrew being uniformly *Shemuel*. ver. 28. 1 Ch 7:2. Nu +34:20. 1 S 1:20, 28, Samuel.

34. Elkanah. Ex +6:24. **Jeroham**. 1 S +1:1. **Eliel**. ver. 27, Eliab. 1 Ch +8:20. **Toah**. i.e. *depressing; inclination; sinking, prostration*, *S#8430h. ver. 26, Nahath.

35. Zuph. ver. +26, Zophai. 1 S +1:1. **Elkanah**. ver. 25.

36. Joel. ver. 24, Shaul, 28n. **Azariah**. i.e. *whom Jehovah aids; Jah has helped*, *S#5838h. 1 Ch 2:8, 38, 39. 3:12. 6:9, 9, 10, 11, 13, 14, 36. 9:11. 2 Ch 21:2. 23:1. Ezr 7:1, 3. Ne 3:23, 24. 7:7. 8:7. 10:2. 12:33. Je 43:2. Da 1:6, 7, 11, 19. Also *S#5838h: 1 K 4:2, 5. 2 K 15:6, 8. 2 Ch 15:1. 21:2. 22:6. 23:1. 26:17, 20. 28:12. 29:12, 12. 31:10, 13. (1) A man of Judah, family of Zerah, house of Ethan, 1 Ch 2:8. (2) A Levite, family of Kohath, line of Izhar, and an ancestor of Samuel the prophet and Heman the singer, 1 Ch 6:36; perhaps, 2 Ch 29:12. (3) One of Solomon's officials, son of the high priest Zadok, and brother of Ahimaaz, 1 K 4:2. (4) Grandson of Zadok and son of Ahimaaz, in the line of high-priestly succession, 1 Ch 6:9. (5) Son of Nathan, and hence probably Solomon's nephew (2 S 5:14), who was over Solomon's twelve tax-collectors, 1 K 4:5. (6) A prophet, son of Oded, who encouraged king Asa to persevere in national religious reformation, 2 Ch 15:1-8. (7) Two sons of king Jehoshaphat, 2 Ch 21:2. The recurrence of the same name in the family is surprising. It may be due to an early corruption of the text; or, if the text is correct, to a difference of mother, the two boys being half-brothers (Compare the Herods). It cannot be explained by the theory that the younger was named after a deceased elder brother, for the two seem to have been alive together and to have been put to death at the same time (Davis). (8) A man of Judah, family of Hezron, house of Jerahmeel, 1 Ch 2:38, 39. His grandfather was Obed (1 Ch 2:38); hence he was perhaps the captain Azariah, son of Obed, who assisted in overthrowing Athaliah and placing Joash on the throne, 2 Ch 23:1. (9). Another captain, son of Jeroham, who aided in overthrowing Athaliah, 2 Ch 23:1. (10) A prince of Ephraim, son of Johanan, who aided in persuading the soldiers of Pekah's army to release the captives of Judah, 2 Ch 28:12. (11) A king of Judah, called also Uzziah (B.C. 811-759). 2 K 14:21; 15:1 w 2 Ch 26:1; 2 Ch 22:6; 23:1. (12) A high priest, 1 Ch 6:10; probably he who rebuked Uzziah for encroaching on the priest's office, 2 Ch 26:17-20. (13) A high priest during Hezekiah's reign, possibly the same as (12), 2 Ch 31:10, 13. (14) A Levite, family of Merari, who assisted in purifying the temple in Hezekiah's reign,

2 Ch 29:12. (15) A high priest, son of Hilkiah and father of Seraiah, not long before the exile, 1 Ch 6:13, 14; perhaps 9:11. (16) A son of Hoshaiah and an opponent of the prophet Jeremiah, Je 43:2. (17) The Hebrew and original name of Abednego, Da 1:7. (18) Grandfather of Ezra, Ezr 7:1. (19) A prominent person, probably prince of Judah, who marched in the procession at the dedication of the wall of Jerusalem, Ne 12:32, 33. (20) A son of Maaseiah, who had a house at Jerusalem in Nehemiah's time, and repaired the wall in its immediate vicinity, Ne 3:23, 24. (21) A priest, doubtless head of a father's house, who in the days of Nehemiah sealed the covenant to keep separate from foreigners and observe the law of God, Ne 10:2. (22) A descendant of Hilkiah who was ruler of the house of God after the exile, 1 Ch 9:11; see, however, Seraiah, Ne 11:11. (23) A king of Israel (not Uzziah), called Azariah in 2 Ch 22:6, but this seems a copyist's error for Ahaziah, which is given in the next verse, 2 Ch 22:6, 7; compare 2 K 8:29 (adapted from Davis *Dictionary of the Bible*, pp. 66, 67). **Zephaniah**. Zp +1:1. While it is sufficiently evident that many of the variations of the names of persons have arisen from the carelessness of transcribers, or the inattention of translators, and others from a difference (probably dialectical) in the pronunciation (Jg 12:6n; 2 K +8:21n); it is also evident, that the same persons, as in these instances, must have had two or more totally distinct names. ver. 24, Shaul, Uzziah, Uriel.

37. Tahath. Nu +33:26. **Assir**. Ex +6:24. **Ebiasaph**. ver. +23. Ex 6:21-24, Abiasaph. **Korah**. Ge +36:5. Nu 16:1, etc. 26:10, 11. Ps ch. 42, 44, 45, 49, 84, 85, titles.

38. Izhar. Ex +6:18. Nu 3:19, Izehar. 16:1. **Kohath**. Ge +46:11. **Levi**. Ge +29:34. **Israel**. Ge +32:28.

39. his brother. Asaph is probably called his *brother*, because he was of the same tribe as Heman; or, perhaps, because he was his companion or associate. **Asaph**. 1 Ch 15:17-19. 16:7. 25:2. 26:1. 2 K +18:18. 2 Ch 5:12. 20:14. 29:13, 30. 35:15. Ezr 2:41. 3:10. Ne 7:44. 11:17, 22. 12:35, 46. Ps ch. 50, ch. 73-83, titles. **on his right hand**. ver. 31. 1 Ch 25:3. **Berachiah**. i.e. *blessed of Jehovah*, *S#1296h. 1 Ch 15:17. 2 Ch 28:12. Zc 1:7. Also *S#1296h: 1 Ch 3:20. 9:16. 15:23. Ne 3:4, 30. 6:18. Zc 1:1. (1) A son of Zerubbabel, 1 Ch 3:20. (2) A Levite, the father of Asaph, descended from Gershom, 1 Ch 6:39; 15:17. (3) A Levite, descended from Elkanah of Netopha, 1 Ch 9:16. (4) A Levite, one of the four doorkeepers for the ark in David's reign, 1 Ch 15:23, 24. (5) One of the chief men of Ephraim in the reign of Pekah. He took the part of the captives from Judah. He was a son of Meshillemoth, 2 Ch 28:12. (6) Father of one that builded the wall, Ne 3:4, 30. (7) Father of Zechariah the prophet, Zc 1:7. (8) A chief man of Ephraim, 2 Ch 28:12. **Shimea**. 1 Ch 3:5.

40. Michael. Da +12:1. **Baaseiah**. i.e. *pressing together; work of the Lord*, *S#1202h. **Malchiah**. Je +38:1.

41. Ethni. i.e. *Jehovah's reward; my hire*, *S#867h. ver. 21, Jeaterai. **Zerah**. ver. 21. **Adaiah**. ver. 21, Iddo. Ne +11:5.

42. Ethan. ver. 21, Joah. 1 Ch +2:6. **Zimmah**. ver. 20. **Shimei**. 2 S +16:5.

43. Jahath. ver. 20. **Gershom**. ver. 1, 16, 17, 20. 1 Ch 23:6. Ge 46:11. Ex +2:22. 6:16. Nu 3:17, Gershon.

44. **stood**. ver. 32, 39. **on the left hand**. Ge +48:13. Jg +20:16. **Ethan**. 1 Ch +2:6. 25:1, 3, 6, Jeduthun. Ps 89, title. **Kishi**. i.e. *sharing of the Lord*, *S#7029h. 1 Ch +15:17, Kushaiah. 2 Ch 29:12. **Abdi**. i.e. *servant of Jehovah; my servant*, *S#5660h. 1 Ch 6:44. 2 Ch 29:12. Ezr 10:26. (1) A Levite of the family of Merari; the son of Malluch, and father of Kishi, 1 Ch 6:44. (2) Son of Merari, 2 Ch 29:12. (3) Son of Elam, Ezr 10:26.

45. **Hashabiah**. 1 Ch +9:14. **Amaziah**. 1 Ch +4:34. Hilkiah. 2 K +18:18.

46. **Amzi**. Ne 11:12. **Bani**. Ezr +2:10. **Shamer**. i.e. *guardian; prison; the lees, or crust of wine*, *S#8106h. 1 Ch 6:46. 7:34. 8:12. (1) A Merarite Levite, the son of Mahli, 1 Ch 6:46. (2) An Asherite, 1 Ch 7:34; the same as the Shomer of ver. 32.

47. **Mahli**. 1 Ch 23:23. 24:30. Nu +3:20. **Mushi**. Nu +3:33. **Merari**. 1 Ch 23:21, 28. Ge +46:11. Ex 6:19. Nu 3:33. 4:29-36. 4:42. 7:8. 10:17. Jsh 21:7, 34-40. **Levi**. Ge +29:34.

48. **brethren**. 1 Ch 23:2, etc. ch. 25. 26. Nu ch. 3. 4. 8:5-26. 16:9, 10. ch. 18. **appointed**. 1 C=12:28.

49. A.M. 2513. B.C. 1491. **Aaron**. Ex *27:1-8. 30:1-7. Le 1:5, 7-9. ch. 8-10, 21, 22. Nu *16:16-50. ch. 17. Dt 18:1-8. He 7:11-14. **make an atonement**. Ex 29:33, 36, 37. *30:10-16. Le 4:20. Nu *15:25. *16:46. Jb 33:24mg. **Moses**. Dt *34:5. Jsh *1:1.

50. **these are**, etc. We have already had a list of these, though more extensive. **Eleazar**. ver. 3-9. 1 Ch 24:1. Ex 6:23. 28:1. Le 10:16. Nu 3:4, 32. 20:26-28. 27:22. Ezr 7:1-5. 8:33. **Phinehas**. See on ver. 4. 1 Ch 9:20.

51. **Bukki**. ver. 5.

52. **Meraioth**. ver. 6, 7.

53. **Zadok**. ver. 8. 1 Ch 12:28. 23:16. 24:3, 31. 1 S 2:35. 2 S 8:17. 15:24-27, 35, 36. 17:15-17. 20:25. 1 K 1:8, 26, 34. 2:35. 4:4. Ezk 44:15.

54. A.M. 2561. B.C. 1443. **these are**. Nu 35:1-8. Jsh 21:3-8. **castles**. Ge 25:16. Nu 31:10. Ps 69:25. Pr 18:10, 11. Ep=3:8. **of the families**. Jsh 21:4, 5. **for their's**. Jsh 21:4.

55. **Hebron**. Jsh 14:13. 15:13. 21:11-13. Jg 1:20.

56. **the fields**. Jsh 14:13. 15:13. **Caleb**. 1 Ch 4:15.

57. **they gave**. 1 S 22:10. 2 Ch 31:15. **the city of refuge**. Nu 35:13-15. Jsh +*20:7-9. **Libnah**. Jsh 10:29. 15:42. 21:13, 14. **Jattir**. Jsh on 1 Ch 4:17. Jsh 15:48.

58. **Hilen**. i.e. *fortress*, *S#2432h. or, Holon. Jsh 15:51. 21:15. This variation simply arises from the introduction of a *yood*, and a change of the vowel points. **Debir**. Jsh 10:+3, 38. 12:13. 15:49.

59. **Ashan**. It is probable that either *Ain*, in Joshua, is a mistake for *Ashan*, or that it was called by both names. 1 Ch 4:32. Jsh +15:42. 21:16, Ain. **Beth-shemesh**. Jsh 15:10. 21:16. 1 S 6:12-19. Je +43:13.

60. **Geba**. 1 Ch 8:6. Jsh 18:24. 21:17. 1 S +13:3. **Alemeth**. i.e. *covering; a hiding place*, *S#5954h. Jsh 21:18, Almon. (1) A Levitical city of Benjamin, 1 Ch 6:60, called also Almon, Jsh 21:18. (2) A descendant of Jonathan, son of Saul, 1 Ch 8:36; 9:42. (3) Compare Alameth, 1 Ch 7:8, son of Becher. *Almon* and *Alemeth* having the same signification, are perfectly interchangeable. **Anathoth**. 1 Ch +7:8. 1 K 2:26. Is 10:30. Je 1:1. 11:23. 37:12. **thirteen cities**. Here there are only *eleven* enumerated; but two more are added in the book of Joshua—*Juttah* and *Gibeon*—which make thirteen. Jsh +10:2. +15:55. √21:16, 17. 1 Ch +14:16.

None of the versions give the full number of names, though they all give the whole sum thirteen; and it is probable that these two cities had been destroyed and lay in ruins when this book was written, and hence were not enumerated.

61. **And unto**. ver. 1, 2, 18, 33. **left**. ver. 66. Jsh 21:4, 5, 20-26. **by lot**. Jsh 14:2n. **ten cities**. Jsh 21:26.

62. **Gershom**. ver. 71-76. Ex +2:22. Jsh 21:27-33.

63. **Merari**. ver. 77-81. Ge +46:11. Nu 3:20. Jsh 21:7, 34-40.

64. **the children**. Jsh 21:41, 42. **with their**. Nu 35:2-5.

65. **these cities**. ver. 57-60.

66. **the residue**. ver. 61. Jsh 21:20-26.

67. **Shechem**. Ge +33:18. 35:4. Jsh +*20:7n. 21:21. **Gezer**. Jsh 12:12. 16:3, 10. 21:21. 1 K +9:16.

68. **Jokmeam**. i.e. *gathered of the people; he will establish the people*, *S#3361h. 1 Ch 6:68. 1 K 4:12. Probably the same as Kibzaim, Jsh 21:22. **Beth-horon**. Jsh 10:+10, 11. 16:5. 1 S 13:18.

69. **Aijalon**. Jsh +10:12, Ajalon. +21:24. **Gath-rimmon**. Jsh 21:24, +25.

70. **Aner**. Aner is probably another name of *Tanach*, which was a city of the half tribe of Manasseh, west of Jordan; and Eusebius, Jerome, and Procopius of Gaza, say that it was in their time a considerable place, three miles from Legio. Jsh 21:25, Tanach, Gath-rimmon. **Bileam**. i.e. *devouring; foreigner*, *S#1109h. Compare the same Hebrew word, rendered Balaam, Nu +22:5. *Ibleam* is here called *Bileam*, by a transposition of letters common to all languages. It is evident, however, that many of these cities or their names have been changed since the time of Joshua; but as it has been well observed, Salop and Shrewsbury, Sarum and Salisbury, are as different names as any in these catalogs; yet those who live in their vicinity are not at all confused by them. Some cities also are here mentioned as belonging to Ephraim, which in Joshua are spoken of as cities of Dan; but various changes in such matters would occur in a course of ages. Jsh 17:11, Ibleam. Jg +1:27.

71. **Golan**. Dt +4:43. Jsh *20:8. 21:27. **Bashan**. Nu +21:33. Jsh 12:4n. 1 K +4:13. **Ashtaroth**. Dt 1:4. Jsh 9:10. 21:27, Beesh-terah. Jg +2:13.

72. **Kedesh**. Jsh +15:23. 19:37. 21:32. Jg 4:9. **Daberath**. Jsh +19:12. 21:28, 29, Kishon, Daberah, Jarmuth, En-gannim.

73. **Ramoth**. i.e. *heights; coral*, *S#7216h. Dt 4:43. Jsh *20:8. 1 Ch 6:73, 80. **Anem**. i.e. *double fountain; two eyes*, *S#6046h.

74. **Mashal**. i.e. *entreaty*, *S#4913h. Jsh 19:26. +21:30, Mishal.

75. **Hukok**. i.e. *a ditch; appointed portion; the engraving*, *S#2712h. 1 Ch 6:75. Jsh 19:34. Compare Jsh 19:+25, 26. 21:31, Helkath.

76. **Kedesh**. Jsh 12:22. 19:37. 20:7. 21:32. Jg 4:6, Kadesh-naphtali. **Hammon**. Jsh 19:35, 37. 21:32, Hammoth-dor, Kartan. **Kirjathaim**. Nu +32:37.

77. **Unto**. Jsh 21:34-39. **Rimmon**. Jsh 19:12, 13. 21:34, 35, Jokneam, Kartah, Dimnah, Nahalal. 2 K +5:18. **Tabor**. Jg +4:6. Probably the city on the summit of *Tabor*, mentioned by Polybius and Josephus, the remains of which still exist.

78. **Bezer**. Dt 4:41, 42, +43. Jsh +*20:8. 21:36. **Jahzah**. i.e. *threshing-floor*, *S#3096h. 1 Ch 6:78. Jsh +13:18. Je 48:21. Jsh 21:36, 37, Jahazah.

79. **Kedemoth**. Jsh +13:18. **Mephaath**. Jsh +13:18.
80. **Ramoth**. ver. +73. Jsh 21:38, 39. 1 K 22:3, etc. 2 K 9:1. **Mahanaim**. Ge +32:2. Jsh 21:38. 2 S 17:24, 27. 19:32.
81. **Heshbon**. Nu +21:25. 32:27. Dt 2:24. Jsh 13:26. Ne 9:22. SS 7:4. **Jazer**. Nu 32:+1, 3. Jsh 13:25. 21:39.

1 CHRONICLES 7

The sons of Issachar, 1-5; of Benjamin, 6-12; of Naphtali, 13; and of Manasseh, 14-19. The sons of Ephraim, of whom some were slain by the men of Gath, 20-22. His sons by Beriah, 23-27. Their habitations, 28, 29. The sons of Asher, 30-40.

1. **the sons of Issachar**. Ge +30:18. **Tola**. Ge +46:13. **Puah**. Ge +46:13, Phuvah. Ex +1:15. Nu 26:23, 24, Pua. **Jashub**. Ge 46:13, Job. Nu +26:24. **Shimrom**. i.e. *vigilant guardian*, *S#8110h. 1 Ch 7:1. Ge +46:13, Shimron. Nu 26:24. Also Jsh 11:1. 19:15.
2. **Uzzi**. 1 Ch +6:5. **Rephaiah**. 1 Ch +9:43. **Jeriel**. i.e. *founded of God*, *S#3400h. **Jahmai**. i.e. *guarded of the Lord*, *S#3181h. **Jibsam**. i.e. *pleasant*, *S#3005h. **Shemuel**. 1 Ch 6:33. Nu +34:20. **valiant men**. Jg +6:12. 2 S +2:7mg. **whose number**. This was probably the number returned by Joab and his assistants, when they made the census of the people with which God was so much displeased. We find that the effective men of Issachar amounted to 87,000 (ver. 5); 22,600 of whom descended from Tola his eldest son; but whether the 36,000 (ver. 4) were descendants of Tola by Uzzi, and the 22,600 his descendants by Tola's other sons; or whether another of Issachar's sons be intended, does not clearly appear; though the former seems the more obvious meaning. 1 Ch 21:1-5. 27:1, 23, 24. 2 S 24:1-9.
3. **Izrahiah**. i.e. *whom Jehovah brought to light; whom Jah brings forth*, *S#3156h. 1 Ch 7:3, 3. Ne 12:42. (1) Son of Uzzi, of Issachar, 1 Ch 7:3. (2) Overseer of singers at the dedication of the temple, written Jezrahiah, Ne 12:42. **Michael**. Da +12:1. **Obadiah**. Ob +1. **Joel**. 1 S +8:2. **Ishiah**. i.e. *whom Jehovah lends; gift of the Lord*, *S#3449h. 1 Ch 7:3. 23:20. 24:21, 25, 25. Ezr +10:31, Ishijah. (1) A chief man of Issachar, 1 Ch 7:3. (2) One of those who came to David at Ziklag, 1 Ch 12:6, Jesiah. (3) A Levite, descended from Moses, and head of the house of Rehabiah, 1 Ch 24:21; compare 23:14-17. (4) A Levite, family of Kohath, house of Uzziel, 1 Ch 23:20; 24:25. (5) Son of Harim, induced by Ezra to put away his foreign wife, Ezr 10:31, Ishijah.
4. **with them**. 1 Ch 12:32.
6. **of Benjamin**. In the parallel place of Genesis, *ten* sons of Benjamin are reckoned: Bela, Becher, Ashbel, Gera, Naaman, Ehi, Rosh, Muppim, Huppim, and Ard; and in Numbers, *five* only are mentioned: Bela, Ashbel, Ahiram, Shupham, and Hupham; and Ard and Naaman are said to be the sons of Bela, and consequently Benjamin's *grandsons*. In the beginning of the following chapter, also, *five* are only mentioned: Bela, Ashbel, Aharah, Nohah, and Rapha; and Addar, Gera, Abihud, Abishua, Naaman, Ahoha, another Gera, Shephuphan, and Huram, are all represented as *grandsons*, not *sons* of Benjamin: hence we see that in many cases, *grandsons* are called *sons*, and both are often confounded in the genealogical tables. It seems also, that the persons mentioned in the follow-

ing verses were neither *sons* nor *grandsons* of Bela and Becher, but distinguished persons among their *descendants*. See Note on 1 K +15:10n. 1 Ch 8:1, etc. Ge 46:21. Nu 26:38-41. **Jediael**. i.e. *known of God*, *S#3043h. 1 Ch 7:6, 10, 11. 11:45. 12:20. 26:2. (1) A son or descendant of Benjamin; was progenitor of the most powerful family of the tribe, 1 Ch 7:6, 10, 11. (2) One of David's valiant men, 1 Ch 11:45. (3) May be same as the chief of Manasseh who joined David, 1 Ch 12:20. (4) A Levite doorkeeper of the Temple in the time of David, 1 Ch 26:2.
7. **Bela**. Ge +14:2. **Ezbon**. Ge +46:16. **Uzzi**. 1 Ch +6:5. **Uzziel**. Ex +6:18. **Jerimoth**. i.e. *he who fears*, *S#3406h. 1 Ch 7:7. 12:5. 24:30. 25:4. 27:19. 2 Ch 11:18. 31:13. (1) A Benjamite, son of Bela, 1 Ch 7:7. (2) A son of Becher, the son of Benjamin, 1 Ch 7:8. (3) A Benjamite who joined David at Ziklag, 1 Ch 12:5. (4, 5) See Jeremoth, Numbers 2 and 3, Ezr 10:26. (6) Ruler of Naphtali in the time of David, 1 Ch 27:19. (7) A son of David, and father of Mahalath, a wife of Rehoboam, 2 Ch 11:18. (8) A Levite, an overseer in connection with the temple in Hezekiah's reign, 2 Ch 31:13. **Iri**. i.e. *urbane; my city*, *S#5901h. **mighty men**. Jg +6:12. 2 S +2:7mg. **were reckoned**. 1 Ch 21:1-5. 2 Ch 17:17, 18.
8. **Becher**. Ge +46:21. **Zemira**. i.e. *palm; causing singing; song, dance*; *S#2160h. **Joash**. i.e. *Jehovah has helped; Jehovah-fired*, *S#3135h. 1 Ch 7:8. 27:28. **Eliezer**. Ge +15:2. **Elioenai**. 1 Ch 26:3. **Omri**. 1 K +16:16. **Jerimoth**. Ezr +10:26, Jeremoth. **Abiah**. 1 S +8:2. **Anathoth**. i.e. *answers to prayers; affliction; answers*, *S#6068h. 1 Ch 7:8. Ne 10:19. Also Jsh 21:18. 1 K 2:26. 1 Ch 6:60. Ezr 2:23. Ne 7:27. 11:32. Is 10:30. Je 1:1. 11:21, 23. 32:7, 8, 9. (1) Head of a father's house of Benjamin, family of Becher, 1 Ch 7:8. (2) Head and representative of the men of Anathoth, who in their name sealed the covenant to worship Jehovah, Ne 10:19. (3) A city of Benjamin, the residence of the prophet Jeremiah, Jsh 21:18; Je 1:1; 29:27. **Alameth**. i.e. *concealment; covering*, *S#5964h. 1 Ch 7:8. 8:36. 9:42. Also 1 Ch +6:60, Alemeth. (1) A Benjamite, descended through Becher, 1 Ch 7:8. (2) A descendant of king Saul, 1 Ch 8:36; 9:42. (3) A city of Benjamin, Jsh 21:18, Almon; 1 Ch 6:60, Alemeth.
9. **mighty men**. ver. 7.
10. **Jediael**. ver. +6. **Bilhan**. Ge +36:27. **Jeush**. Ge +36:5. **Benjamin**. Ge +35:18. **Ehud**. 1 Ch +8:6. Jg 3:15, etc. **Chenaanah**. i.e. *submissive; humiliation; one who bends the knee or merchant; traffic; as if afflicted*, *S#3668h. 1 Ch 7:10. 1 K 22:11, 24. 2 Ch 18:10. (1) A man of Benjamin, 1 Ch 7:10. (2) Father of Zedekiah, the false prophet, 1 K 22:11; 2 Ch 18:10. **Zethan**. i.e. *olive tree*, *S#2133h. **Tharshish**. i.e. *a precious stone; will cause poverty; breaking*, *S#8659h. (1) A Benjamite, son of Bilhan, 1 Ch 7:10. (2) One of the seven highest princes of Persia, Est 1:14. (3) See also 1 K 10:22; 22:48; the people of Tarshish, descended from Javan (Ge 10:4), and their country, famous for ships. **Ahishahar**. i.e. *brother of the morning*, *S#300h.
11. **mighty men**. 2 Ch 17:13, etc.
12. **Shuppim**. i.e. *serpents*, *S#8206h. 1 Ch 7:12, 15. 26:16. (1) A son of Ir, of Benjamin, 1 Ch 7:12, 15. (2) He who had charge of the gate westward, under David, 1 Ch 26:16. Ge 46:21, Muppim, Huppim. Nu 26:39, Shupham, Hupham. **Huppim**. Ge +46:21. **Ir**.

i.e. *a city*, *S#5893. ver. 7, Iri. **Hushim**. Ge +46:23. **the sons**. ⌐171E13, Ge +46:7. Plural put for singular, for Hushim is mentioned as the only son of Dan, Ge 46:23, where the plural is likewise used. Poole notes that the term "another thing," the literal meaning of "Aher," is used by Hebrew writers to designate a detestable thing, which Dan was considered, because of its gross idolatry, Jg ch. 18; for which reason many interpreters conceive this tribe is omitted in the numbering of the sealed persons of Re 7. **Aher**. i.e. *another; coming slowly, following*, *S#313h. *Aher* signifies *another*, and it has been conjectured that these were Danites, "the sons of another *tribe*;" especially as Hushim is named as the only son of Dan, Ge 46:23. And they suppose that the name of Dan was not mentioned, because his descendants first established idolatry (Jg 18:30. 1 K 12:29, 30. 2 K 10:29. Am 8:14). But Zebulun, as well as Dan, is here omitted, perhaps because none of either of these tribes returned at first from Babylon. Though the Benjamites had been almost destroyed in the first days of the judges (Jg 20:35), they soon became numerous and powerful. 1 Ch 8:1, Aharah. Nu 26:38, Ahiram.

13. **Jahziel**. i.e. *allotted of God*, *S#3185h. Ge +46:24. Nu 26:48, Jahzeel. **Guni**. Ge +46:24. **Jezer**. Ge +46:24. **Shallum**. Ge +46:24. Nu 26:49, Shillem. 2 K +15:10. **the sons of**. Ge 30:3-8. 35:22. 46:25. i.e. the grandchildren; for Bilhah was Jacob's concubine, and mother both to Naphtali, the father of these last named persons, and to Dan (Matthew Poole). See 1 K +15:10n. **Bilhah**. Ge +29:29.

14. **The sons of**. Nu 26:29-33. i.e. grandchildren, as ver. 13. For both Ashriel and Zelophehad were the grandchildren of Machir son of Manasseh, Nu 26:29, etc.; 27:1. The text in these two verses seems to be strangely corrupted; and, as it stands, is scarcely intelligible. Probably it should be rendered "The sons of Manasseh were Ashriel, whom his Syrian concubine bore to him; and Machir the father of Gilead, whom (his wife) bore to him. Machir took for a wife Maachah, sister to Huppim and Shuppim." This is nearly the version of Dr. Geddes. **Ashriel**. i.e. *I shall be prince of God; vow of, or bound of God*, *S#844h. 1 Ch 7:14. Nu +26:31, Asriel. Jsh 17:2. **concubine**. 1 Ch +2:48. **Aramitess**. i.e. *highlandress; exalted of Jah*, *S#761h. Elsewhere rendered Syrian, Ge +25:20. **Machir**. 1 Ch 2:21-23. Ge +50:23. Nu 26:29-34. 27:1. 32:39-42. Dt 3:13-15. Jsh 13:31. 17:1-3. Jg 5:14. **Gilead**. Ge +31:23. A person so called, as is manifest from ver. 17; Nu 26:29.

15. **the sister**. ver. 16. **Huppim**. ver. 12. **Maachah**. 1 K +2:39. **and the name**. It is certain that Zelophehad was not a *son*, but a *descendant* of Manasseh's, three generations having intervened; for he was the son of Hepher, the son of Gilead, the son of Machir, the son of Manasseh. **the second**. Of the second son or grandson of Machir; for so Zelophehad was, Nu 26:29, etc. Or, Zelophehad is here called *the second*, because he was the younger brother of Ashriel, who was the eldest son of Hepher, the son of Gilead, the son of Machir. **and Zelophehad**. Nu +26:33. 27:1-11. 36:1-12. **had daughters**. 1 Ch 2:34.

16. **Peresh**. i.e. *excrement, dung*, *S#6570h. **Sheresh**. i.e. *a root*, *S#8329h. **Ulam**. i.e. *their strength; first of all, portico, vestibule*, *S#198h. 1 Ch 7:16, 17. 8:39, 40. (1) Grandson of Maachah, wife of Machir,

1 Ch 7:16. (2) A man of Benjamin, father of many valiant men, 1 Ch 8:39, 40. **Rakem**. i.e. *embroidery; versicolor*, *S#7552h. 1 Ch 2:+*43, 44. 7:16. Nu 31:8. Jsh 13:21.

17. **Bedan**. i.e. *son of judgment; servile; fat, robust*, *S#917h. 1 Ch 7:17. 1 S 12:11. (1) A judge of the Israelites whose name is not in the book of Judges, 1 S 12:11. It is probably a copyist's error for Barak. (2) A descendant of Machir, 1 Ch 7:17. **These**. That is, a reference to Ashriel and Zelophehad, named in ver. 14, 15; the relative pronoun here refers to the remoter antecedent, as is frequent in Hebrew (Matthew Poole).

18. **Hammoleketh**. i.e. *queen*, *S#4447h. **Ishod**. i.e. *man of renown*, *S#379h. **Abiezer**. Nu 26:30, Jeezer. Jsh +17:2. Jg 6:11, 24, 34. 8:2. **Mahalah**. i.e. *disease, infirmity, sickness*, *S#4244h. 1 Ch 7:18. Nu +26:33, Mahlah. 27:1. 36:11. Jsh 17:3. (1) A daughter of Zelophehad of Manasseh, who sued for an inheritance, Nu 26:33; 27:1; Jsh 17:3. (2) One of the children of Hammoleketh, a woman of Manasseh, 1 Ch 7:18.

19. **Shemidah**. i.e. *fame of wisdom; my name he knows*, *S#8061h. 1 Ch 7:19. Nu +26:32, Shemida. Jsh 17:2. **Ahian**. i.e. *brotherly; firmly bound*, *S#291h. **Shechem**. Ge +33:18. **Likhi**. i.e. *learned; my doctrine*, *S#3949h. **Aniam**. i.e. *lament of the people*, *S#593h.

20. **And the sons**. Nu 26:35, 36. **Ephraim**. Ge +41:52. **Shuthelah**. ver. +21. **Bered**. Ge +16:14. **Tahath**. Nu +33:26. **Eladah**. i.e. *God has adorned; God's ornament*, *S#497h.

21. **Zabad**. 1 Ch +2:36. **Shuthelah**. i.e. *noise of breaking; freshly appointed; resembling rejuvenation*, *S#7803h. 1 Ch 7:20, 21. Nu 26:35, 36. **Ezer**. S#5827h. 1 Ch ❶+4:4. Ge ❶+36:21. **Elead**. i.e. *God is witness*, *S#496h. **Gath**. Jsh +11:22. **because they came**. Or rather, "when (*kee*) they came down to take away their cattle;" for it does not appear that the sons of Ephraim were the aggressors, but the men of Gath, who appear to have been born in Egypt. This is the only place in the Sacred Writings where this piece of history is mentioned, and the transaction seems to have happened before the Israelites came out of Egypt; for it appears from the following verse, that Ephraim was alive when these children were slain.

22. **mourned**. Ge 37:34. **and his brethren**. 1 Ch +15:5. Jb 2:11. i.e. his kinsmen, as that word is frequently used (Matthew Poole).

23. **Beriah**. i.e. *in evil; gift, or calamity*, *S#1283h. 1 Ch 7:23, 30, 31. 8:13, 16. 23:10, 11. Ge 46:17, 17. Nu 26:44. (1) Fourth son of Asher, Ge 46:17; 1 Ch 7:30. (2) A son of Ephraim, 1 Ch 7:23. (3) A chief man of Benjamin, 1 Ch 8:13. (4) Son of Shimei, a Gershonite, 1 Ch 23:10. **because**. Many similar instances of the naming of children from passing circumstances, occur throughout the sacred volume. See those of a similar character with this verse: (1) Ge 35:18, where Rachel, while dying, names her new-born son Ben-oni, or, *the son of my sorrow*. (2) So in 1 S 4:21, the wife of Phinehas, on being apprised of the death of Eli and her husband, and that the ark was taken by the Philistines, while in the pains of travail, and dying, named her son Ichobod, or, *there is no glory*. (3) So also in the 4th chapter of this book, ver. 9, we read that Jabez, or, *sorrowful*, had that name given to him, because his mother "bare him with sorrow." 2 S 23:5.

24. **his daughter**. i.e. his grandchild, or great-grandchild, for such are often called *sons* or *daughters* in Scripture. 1 K +15:10n. 2 K 8:26. **Sherah**. i.e. *kinswoman; near kinship*, ✻S#7609h. **Beth-horon**. Jsh +10:10. 16:3, 5. 1 K 9:17. 2 Ch 8:5. **Uzzen-sherah**. i.e. *heard by near kinship; ear of Sherah*, ✻S#242h.

25. **Rephah**. i.e. *healing; to sustain; riches, wealth; healing* or enfeebling of the breath, ✻S#7506h. **Resheph**. i.e. *lightning; a flame*, ✻S#7566h. **Telah**. i.e. *making green; rejuvenator, invigorator*, ✻S#8520h. **Tahan**. i.e. *thou wilt encamp*, ✻S#8465h. 1 Ch 7:25. Nu 26:35.

26. **Laadan**. 1 Ch +23:7. **Ammihud**. 2 S +13:37. **Elishama**. Nu +1:10. 7:48.

27. **Non**. i.e. *perpetuity*, ✻S#5126h. Nu 13:8, 16, Nun. **Jehoshuah**. i.e. *Jehovah is salvation*, ✻S#3091h. Ex 17:9-14. 24:13. 32:17. Nu 11:28, Joshua. 13:8, 16, Oshea. 14:6. 27:18. Dt 31:23, Joshua. Ac 7:45. He 4:8, Jesus.

28. **Bethel**. Ge +12:8. 28:19. Jsh 16:2. Jg 1:22. **Naaran**. i.e. *juvenile; handmaid; damsel*, ✻S#5295h. *Naaran*, or *Naarath*, Eusebius says, was a town in his time called *Noorath*, five miles from Jericho. It appears to be the same as *Neara*, mentioned by Josephus, from whence, he says, they brought the water which watered the palm-trees of Jericho. Jsh 16:17, Naarath. **Gezer**. See on 1 Ch 6:66, 67. **Shechem**. Ge +33:18. **Gaza**. Ge +10:19. **towns**. Heb. daughters. ⨍155E5, Nu +21:25mg.

29. **Manasseh**. Jsh 17:7-11. **Beth-shean**. Jsh +17:11. 1 S 31:10, Bethshan. **Taanach**. Jsh +17:11. Jg 5:19. 1 K 4:12. **Megiddo**. Jsh +12:21. +*17:11. Jg 1:27. 1 K 9:15. 2 K 9:27. 23:29. 2 Ch 35:22. Zc 12:11. Ne 16:16. **towns**. Heb. daughters. ⨍155E5, Nu +21:25. **In these dwelt**. Jsh ch. 16, 17. Jg 1:22-29.

30. **Asher**. Ge +30:13. Dt +*33:24n. **Imnah**. i.e. *good fortune; dexterity; prosperity; right-handed; the right side; he will number; he allotteth*, ✻S#3232h. 1 Ch 7:30. 2 Ch 31:14. Ge 46:17. Nu 26:+44, Jimnah, +44, Jimnites. (1) Son of Asher and founder of a tribal family, 1 Ch 7:30; Ge 46:17; Nu 26:44. (2) A Levite, father of Kore, in Hezekiah's reign, 2 Ch 31:14. This variation only exists in the translation; the original being uniformly "Jimnah," or "Yimnah." **Isuah**. i.e. *likeness; even, level; he shall equalize*, ✻S#3438h. 1 Ch 7:30. Ge +46:17, Ishua. **Ishuai**. i.e. *Jah is self satisfying; he will justify me*, ✻S#3440h. 1 Ch 7:30. Ge +46:17, Isui. Nu +26:44, Jesui. 1 S +14:49, Ishui. This variation is also attributable to the translator; the Hebrew being in both places *Isui*, or rather, *Yishwi*. **Beriah**. ver. +23. **Serah**. Ge +46:17.

31. **Heber**. Ge +46:17. **Malchiel**. Ge +46:17. **Birzavith**. i.e. *in leanness; choice olive*, ✻S#1269h.

32. **Japhlet**. i.e. *God delivers; he will set free*, ✻S#3310h. ver. 33. **Shomer**. ver. 34, Shamer. 2 K +12:21. **Hotham**. i.e. *a seal; signet-ring*, ✻S#2369h. 1 Ch 7:32. 11:44. (1) A son of Heber, of Asher, 1 Ch 7:32. (2) The Aroerite, father of two of David's mighty men, 1 Ch 11:44. **Shua**. 1 Ch +2:3.

33. **Pasach**. i.e. *to divide; torn asunder*, ✻S#6457h. **Bimhal**. i.e. *in circumcision; son of mixture or corruption*, ✻S#1118h. **Ashvath**. i.e. *firmer, stronger; made; the joy of reward*, ✻S#6220h.

34. **Shamer**. ver. 32, Shomer. **Ahi**. 1 Ch +5:15. **Rohgah**. i.e. *agitation; copious rain*, ✻S#7303h. **Je-**

hubbah. i.e. *binding; he will be hidden*, ✻S#3160h. **Aram**. Ge +22:21.

35. **Helem**. i.e. *strength; smiter*, ✻S#1987h. 1 Ch 7:35. (For ✻S#2494h, Helem, see Zc 6:14). **Zophah**. i.e. *expanding; a vial*, ✻S#6690h. ver. 36. **Imna**. i.e. *he will restrain; he will keep back, or deny himself*, ✻S#3234h. **Shelesh**. i.e. *triplicate, triad, third, triplet; strength*, ✻S#8028h. **Amal**. i.e. *perverseness; wearisome labor, troublesome*, ✻S#6000h.

36. **Suah**. i.e. *offal; filth; sweepings*, ✻S#5477h. **Harnepher**. i.e. *roaring of breath; the frustrator burnt; snorting or panting*, ✻S#2774h. **Shual**. i.e. *a fox; a jackal; a burrower*, ✻S#7777h. 1 Ch 7:36. Also 1 S 13:17. (1) An Israelite of Asher, 1 Ch 7:36. (2) The land of Shual was probably near Bethel, 1 S 13:17. **Beri**. i.e. *my well; of the well; well of God*, ✻S#1275h. **Imrah**. i.e. *a rebel; he will extol himself*, ✻S#3236h.

37. **Bezer**. Dt +4:43. **Hod**. i.e. *glory, majesty; confession*, ✻S#1936h. **Shamma**. i.e. *destruction, desolation; astonishment*, ✻S#8037h. **Shilshah**. i.e. *triplication, triad, the third*, ✻S#8030h. **Ithran**. Ge +36:26. This name is essentially the same, the variation being caused by a parogogic *noon*; here it is written "Ithran," and in the following verse, "Jether." ver. 38, Jether. **Beera**. i.e. *a well*, ✻S#878h.

38. **Jether**. 1 Ch +2:32. **Jephunneh**. Nu +13:6. **Pispah**. i.e. *disappearance; dispersion*, ✻S#6462h. **Ara**. i.e. *I shall see; herd or assembly; a lion; cursing*, ✻S#690h.

39. **Ulla**. i.e. *burden; sacrifice killed on the altar; he was taken up; yoke*, ✻S#5925h. **Arah**. i.e. *a wayfarer; wandering, traveling*, ✻S#733h. 1 Ch 7:39. Ezr 2:5. Ne 6:18. 7:10. (1) Son of Ulla, 1 Ch 7:39. (2) His children returned from Babylon, Ezr 2:5; Ne 7:10. **Haniel**. i.e. *favor of God*, ✻S#2592h. 1 Ch 7:39. Nu 34:23. (1) Captain of the tribe of Manasseh, Nu 34:23. (2) A man of Asher, 1 Ch 7:39. **Rezia**. i.e. *delight, satisfaction; haste*, ✻S#7525h.

40. **the number**. 1 Ch 21:1-5. 2 S 24:1-9.

1 CHRONICLES 8

The sons and chief men of Benjamin, 1-32. The family of Saul and his descendants by Jonathan, 33-40.

1. **Bela**. 1 Ch 7:6-12. Ge +14:2. 46:21. **his firstborn**. Le +27:26. **Ashbel**. Ge +46:21. **the second**. ver. +39. 1 Ch 7:15. **Aharah**. i.e. *after his brother*, ✻S#315h. Nu 26:38, Ahiram.

2. **Nohah**. i.e. *quietude*, ✻S#5119h. **Rapha**. i.e. *he healed; the giant; the shrunken*, ✻S#7498h. 1 Ch 8:2. 20:4, 6, 8. Also 2 S 21:16, 18, 20, 22. 1 Ch 8:37. (1) One of the sons of Benjamin, 1 Ch 8:2. (2) A chief man of Benjamin, of the stock of Saul, 1 Ch 8:37. Called Rephaiah, 1 Ch +9:43. (3) An ancient giant, whose descendants were giants, 1 Ch 20:4.

3. **Addar**. i.e. *mighty one; honorable, great*, ✻S#146h. The variation in this name is occasioned simply by a transposition of *daleth* and *raish*, being in the parallel passage "Ard," and here, "Addar." Ge +46:21. Nu 26:40, Ard. **Gera**. Ge +46:21. **Abihud**. i.e. *father of majesty; father of praise*, ✻S#31h.

4. **Abishua**. 1 Ch +6:4. **Naaman**. Ge +46:21. Nu 26:40. **Ahoah**. i.e. *brotherly; brother of the Lord; brother of rest*, ✻S#265h. 2 S 23:28.

5. **Gera**. ver. 3. Ge +46:21. Jg 3:15. **Shephuphan**.

i.e. *serpent-like; their sinuosity; their bareness,* *S#8197h. 1 Ch 8:5. Also Nu 26:39. "Shuppim" seems to be merely a contracted form of "Shupham," or rather, "Shephupham," which, by the mutation of *mem* into *noon,* is here changed into "Shephuphan." 1 Ch 7:12, Shuppim. Nu 26:39, Shupham. **Huram.** i.e. *noble, ingenuous; their liberty; their whiteness,* *S#2361h. 1 Ch 8:5. 14:1. 2 Ch 2:3, 11, 12, 13. 4:11, 11, 16. 8:2, 18. 9:10, 21. (1) A Benjamite, perhaps a son of Bela, 1 Ch 8:5. (2) A king of Tyre, 2 Ch 2:3. (3) A Tyrian artificer, 2 Ch 4:11, 16. Huram appears to be an error for *Hupham,* in the parallel passage of Numbers +26:39, which, by contraction, is written *Huppim.*

6. **Ehud.** i.e. *strong; undivided; union; joining together,* *S#261. 1 Ch 7:10. Jg 3:20, etc. 4:1. (1) A son of Gera who slew Eglon and delivered the Israelites from the oppression of the Moabites. He was one of the judges in Israel, Jg 3:15, 16. (2) A grandson of Jediael, 1 Ch 7:10. (3) A descendant of Benjamin, 1 Ch 8:6. May be the same as Number 1. **Geba.** 1 Ch 6:60. Jsh 18:24. 1 S +13:3. **Manahath.** 1 Ch 2:52, 54. Ge +36:23.

7. **Naaman.** ver. 4. **Ahiah.** i.e. *brother, worshipper, or friend of Jehovah,* *S#281h. (1) Son of Ehud, descendant of Benjamin, 1 Ch 8:7. (2) A priest in the time of Saul, grandson of Phinehas, 1 S 14:3, 18. (3) A prince or scribe of Solomon's, 1 K 4:3. **Gera.** Ge +46:21. **Uzza.** 2 K +21:18. **Ahihud.** i.e. *my brother is united,* *S#284h.

8. **Shaharaim.** i.e. *double-dawn; two dawns or mornings; morning and evening twilight,* *S#7842h. **in the.** Ru 1:1. **Hushim.** Ge +46:23. **Baara.** i.e. *brutish; kindling of the moon; she hath kindled,* *S#1199h. **after he had sent them away.** Ge 25:6. Matthew Poole notes, Ehud or Gera last mentioned; others join these words with the former, and render the place thus, "after he had sent them (his sons) away, with Hushim and Baara his wives," i.e. as he also sent his wives away from him; which may be here mentioned as a brand upon him, to show that he was without natural affection to his wives and children. And it seems the more probable that he divorced them, because we find him married to another wife, ver. 9. Mt 19:3-9. 2 T 3:3. **wives.** 1 Ch 4:5. Ge +4:19.

9. **Hodesh.** i.e. *the new moon,* *S#2321h. In the preceding verse it is said that "*Hushim* and *Baara* were his wives;" and here it is said, "he begat of *Hodesh* his wife," etc.; and then in the eleventh verse, his children by *Hushim* are mentioned, but not a word of *Baara.* It is probable, therefore, that Hodesh was another name for *Baara;* and this is asserted by the Targumist: "And he begat of Baara, that is, Chodesh, his wife, so called because he espoused her anew." But it might be more probable to adopt Poole's view, given in the Note to verse 8, than to suppose Shaharaim divorced then remarried Baara after sending her away, accepting her back again, now giving her a new and more suitable name. **Jobab.** Ge +10:29. **Zibia.** i.e. *a gazelle; honorable chief,* *S#6644h. **Mesha.** i.e. *waters of devastation; making to forget; equalizing; existing; retreat, removal, deliverance,* *S#4331h, only here. (1) A king of Moab in the time of Ahab, 2 K 3:4. (2) A son of Caleb, 1 Ch 2:42. (3) A descendant of Benjamin, 1 Ch 8:9. **Malcham.** i.e. *most high king; their king,* *S#4445h.

10. **Jeuz.** i.e. *counselor; he will take counsel,*

*S#3263h. **Shachia.** i.e. *captivation; captive of the Lord; the return of Jah,* *S#7634h. **Mirma.** i.e. *deceit, guile, fraud,* *S#4821h.

11. **Hushim.** Ge +46:23. **Abitub.** i.e. *good; father of goodness,* *S#36h. **Elpaal.** i.e. *God the maker; God the reward,* *S#508h. ver. 12, 18.

12. **Eber.** Ge +10:24. **Misham.** i.e. *their cleansing or regarding,* *S#4936h. **Shamed.** i.e. *destruction; exterminator; persecution; guardian,* *S#8106h. A Benjamite, descended from Shaharaim through Elpaal; he was a rebuilder of Ono and Lod, with their dependent villages, 1 Ch 8:12. See on 1 Ch 6:46, Shamer, and 1 K 16:24, Shemer, for the other occurrences of S#8106h. **Ono.** *Ono* is stated by Reland to have been three miles from Lydda. Ezr +2:33. Ne 6:2. 7:37. 11:35. **Lod.** *Lod* or *Lydda,* was situated about four leagues from Joppa, and a day's journey, or about thirty-two miles, N.W. from Jerusalem; and, according to the Antoine Itinerary, twelve miles from Jamnia, eighteen from Eleutheropolis, and twenty-two from Bethar. Josephus says it was a village, not yielding to a city in greatness; and that it was one of three toparchies dismembered from Samaria, and given to the Jews. It was destroyed by Cestius in the Jewish war, and, when rebuilt, was called *Diospolis.* It is now called *Loudd,* and is a poor village, situated in a fine plain about a league to the E.N.E. of Ramla. Ezr 2:33. Ne 6:2. 7:37. 11:35. Ac 9:32, 35, 38.

13. **Beriah.** 1 Ch +7:23. **Shema.** ver. 21, Shimhi. Jsh +15:26. **the fathers.** 1 Ch 2:42n, 49, 50, 52. 4:4. **Aijalon.** Jsh 10:12. 19:42, Ajalon. +21:24. A place formerly belonging to the tribe of Dan, Jsh 19:42; but after the return from Babylon possessed by the Benjamites, because both Dan and the rest of the ten tribes were yet for the generality of them in captivity, and but few of them returned (Matthew Poole). 1 Ch 6:70n. **Gath.** Jsh +11:22. 1 S 17:4.

14. **Ahio.** 2 S +6:3. **Shashak.** i.e. *eagerness; vehement desire; the rusher; the longed-for,* *S#8349h. ver. 25. **Jeremoth.** Ezr +10:26.

15. **Zebadiah.** 1 Ch +26:2. **Arad.** i.e. *an ambush; wild ass; untamed,* *S#6166h. 1 Ch 8:15. Also Nu 21:1. 33:40. Jsh 12:14. Jg 1:16. (1) A chief Benjamite descended through Beriah, 1 Ch 8:15. (2) A royal city of the Canaanites, Nu 21:1; Jsh 12:14. **Ader.** i.e. *a flock; set in order; musterer, caretaker,* *S#5738h.

16. **Michael.** Da +12:1. **Ispah.** i.e. *he will scratch; he will lay bare; he will be visible or eminent; prominent,* *S#3472h. **Joha.** i.e. *whom Jehovah called back to life; who enlivens; haste; he will lead; lead thou, Jehovah,* *S#3109h. 1 Ch 8:16. 11:45. (1) A chief man of Benjamin, 1 Ch 8:16. (2) One of David's mighty men, 1 Ch 11:45. **Beriah.** ver. 13. 1 Ch +7:23.

17. **Zebadiah.** 1 Ch +26:2. **Meshullam.** 1 Ch +9:12. **Hezeki.** i.e. *my strong one; strength of the Lord,* *S#2395h. **Heber.** Ge +46:17.

18. **Ishmerai.** i.e. *preservative; will be kept of the Lord,* *S#3461h. **Jezliah.** i.e. *Jah preserves; he will be drawn out of the Lord; he shall pour out suitably; he will cause her to flow forth,* *S#3152h. **Jobab.** Ge +10:29. **Elpaal.** ver. +11.

19. **Jakim.** i.e. *God sets up,* *S#3356h. 1 Ch 8:19. 24:12. (1) A chief man of Benjamin, 1 Ch 8:19. (2) The son of Aaron, to whom the twelfth lot fell, 1 Ch 24:12. **Zichri.** 1 Ch +9:15. **Zabdi.** Jsh +7:1.

20. **Elienai.** i.e. *God of my eyes,* *S#462h. **Zilthai.**

i.e. *protection; shadow of the Lord; my shadows,* ✻S#6769h. 1 Ch 8:20. 12:20. (1) A man of Benjamin, 1 Ch 8:20. (2) A captain of Manasseh, 1 Ch 12:20. **Eliel.** i.e. *to whom God gives strength; strength of strength; God of might,* ✻S#447h. 1 Ch 5:24. 6:34. 8:20, 22. 11:46, 47. 12:11. 15:9, 11. 2 Ch 31:13. (1) A Levite, family of Kohath, ancestor of Samuel the prophet, 1 Ch 6:34. (2) A Mahavite, one of David's mighty men, 1 Ch 11:46. (3) Another of David's mighty men, 1 Ch 11:47. (4) One of the Gadites who came to David at Ziklag, 1 Ch 12:11. (5) A Levite, a son of Hebron, who lived in David's time, 1 Ch 15:9, 11. (6) A Benjamite, son of Shimhi, 1 Ch 8:20. (7) Another Benjamite, a son of Shashak, 1 Ch 8:22. (8) A chief man of the half-tribe of Manasseh east of the Jordan, 1 Ch 5:24. (9) An overseer of the tithes and offerings in the reign of Hezekiah, 2 Ch 31:13.

21. **Adaiah.** Ne +11:5. **Beraiah.** i.e. *created of Jah,* ✻S#1256h. **Shimrath.** i.e. *guardianship; ward,* ✻S#8119h. **Shimhi.** i.e. *renowned, famous, heard of,* S#8096h. For S#8096h rendered "Shimei," see on 2 S +16:5; rendered "Shimi," see on Ex +6:17. See ver. 13, Shema.

22. **Ishpan.** i.e. *strong one; he shall hide or cover; he will make them prominent,* ✻S#3473h. **Heber.** Ge +46:17. **Eliel.** ver. +20.

23. **Abdon.** Jg +12:13. **Zichri.** 1 Ch +9:15. **Hanan.** 1 Ch +9:44.

24. **Hananiah.** 1 Ch +25:23. **Elam.** Ge +10:22. **Antothijah.** i.e. *answer of the Lord; answers or afflictions of Jah,* ✻S#6070h.

25. **Iphedeiah.** i.e. *the Lord will redeem,* ✻S#3301h. **Penuel.** 1 Ch +4:4. **Shashak.** ver. +14.

26. **Shamsherai.** i.e. *sun-like; he desolated my observers; careful keeping of the Lord,* ✻S#8125h. **Shehariah.** i.e. *Jah has sought; sought of the Lord; sought early of Jah,* ✻S#7841h. **Athaliah.** i.e. *whom Jehovah remembered; due season for Jah; shaken, taken away, or afflicted of the Lord,* ✻S#6271h. 1 Ch 8:26. 2 K 11:1, 3, 13, 14. 2 Ch 22:12. Ezr 8:7. Also ✻S#6271h: 2 K 8:26. 11:2, 20. 2 Ch 22:2, 10, 11. 23:12, 13, 21. 24:7. (1) The wife of Jehoram, king of Judah, a daughter of Ahab by Jezebel, and granddaughter of Omri, 2 K 8:18, 26; 11:1-16; 2 Ch 21:6; 22:2. Slew all her grandchildren, 2 K 11:1, excepting Joash, 2 Ch 22:10, 11. (2) A Benjamite of the house of Jeroham, 1 Ch 8:26. (3) A man of the father's house of Elam, Ezr 8:7.

27. **Jaresiah.** i.e. *nourished of the Lord; honey which is of Jah,* ✻S#3298h. **Eliah.** i.e. *my God is Jah,* ✻S#452h. 1 Ch 8:27. 2 K 1:3, 4, 8, 12. Ezr 10:21, 26. Ml 4:5. (1) A Benjamite, a son of Jeroham, resident at Jerusalem, 1 Ch 8:27. (2) An Israelite induced by Ezra to put away his foreign wife, Ezr 10:26. For ✻S#452h rendered "Elijah," see on 1 K +17:1.

28. **dwelt.** Jsh 15:63. 18:28. Jg 1:21. Ne 11:1, 7-9. **Jerusalem.** *Jerusalem,* the ancient capital of Judea, is situated in long. 35 deg. 20 min. E., lat. 31 deg. 47 min. 47 sec. N.; and, according to the best authorities, 136 miles S.W. of Damascus, 34 miles S. of Shechem or Nablous, 45 miles E. of Jaffa, 27 miles N. of Hebron, and about 20 miles W. of Jericho. The city of Jerusalem was built on hills, and encompassed with mountains (Ps 125:2), in a stony and barren soil, and was about sixteen furlongs in length, says Strabo. The ancient city of *Jebus,* taken by David from the Jebusites, was not large, and stood on a mountain south of that on

which the temple was erected. Here David built a new city, called the city of David, wherein was the royal palace. Between these two mountains lay the valley of Millo, filled up by David and Solomon; and after the reign of Manasseh, another city is mentioned, called the *second.* The Maccabees considerably enlarged Jerusalem on the north, enclosing a third hill; and Josephus mentions a fourth hill, called *Bezetha,* which Agrippa joined to the former: this new city lay north of the temple, along the brook Kidron. See Note on 1 Ch 9:34.

29. **And.** 1 Ch 9:35-38. **Gibeon.** 1 Ch +14:16. Jsh 9:3. **the father.** 1 Ch 9:35, 36, Jehiel. **Maachah.** 1 K +2:39.

30. **Abdon.** 1 Ch 9:36, 37. Jg +12:13. **Zur.** Nu +25:15. **Kish.** 1 S +9:1. **Baal.** 1 Ch +5:5. **Nadab.** Ex +6:23.

31. **Gedor.** Jsh +15:58. **Ahio.** 2 S +6:3. **Zacher.** i.e. *memorial; remembrance,* ✻S#2144h. 1 Ch 9:37, Zechariah.

32. **Mikloth.** 1 Ch +27:4. **Shimeah.** ✻S#8039h, only here. 1 Ch 9:38, Shimeam. 2 S +21:21.

33. **And.** 1 Ch 9:39-44. **Ner.** 1 Ch 9:+36, 39. 1 S 9:1. 14:50, 51. **Kish.** 1 S +9:1. Ac 13:21, Cis. **Saul.** 1 S +9:2. 14:49. 31:2. **Jonathan.** 1 S +13:2. **Malchishua.** i.e. *king of aid; king of opulence, help, or riches; my king is salvation; the king (God) is salvation,* ✻S#4444h. 1 Ch 8:33. 9:39. 10:2. Also 1 S +14:49. 31:2, Melchishua. A son of king Saul, 1 S 14:49; 1 Ch 8:33; 9:39; he was killed at the battle of Gilboa, 1 S 31:2. **Abinadab.** 1 S 14:49, Ishui. +16:8. **Eshbaal.** i.e. *Baal's man; fire of Baal,* ✻S#792h. 1 Ch 8:33. 9:39. 2 S 2:8. 4:12, Ish-bosheth.

34. **Merib-baal.** 1 Ch +9:40. 2 S 4:4, Mephibosheth. 9:6, 10. 19:24-30. **Micah.** 2 S 9:12, Micha.

35. **Pithon.** i.e. *great enlargement; persuasion; mouth of a monster,* ✻S#6377h. 1 Ch 8:35. 9:41. A man of Benjamin, of the stock of Saul. **Melech.** i.e. *king; counselor,* ✻S#4429h. 1 Ch 8:35. 9:41. A chief man of Benjamin, of the stock of Saul and Jonathan. **Tarea.** i.e. *chamber of guile; chamber of a neighbor; mark out a neighbor; delaying cries,* ✻S#8390h. 1 Ch +9:41, Tahrea. **Ahaz.** i.e. *possessor; holder,* ✻S#271h. 1 Ch 3:13. 8:35, 36. 9:42. 2 K 15:38. 16:1, 2, 5, 7, 8, 10, 10, 11, 15, 16, 17, 19, 20. 17:1. 18:1. 20:11. 23:12. 2 Ch 27:9. 28:1, 16, 19, 21, 22, 24, 27. 29:19. Is 1:1. 7:1, 3, 10, 12. 14:28. 38:8. Ho 1:1. Mi 1:1. (1) King of Judah, contemporary with Isaiah, Hosea, and Micah, B.C. 744-728. 2 K 16:1; 2 Ch 28:16; Is 7:1; 38:8. (2) Son of Micah, descendant of Jonathan, 1 Ch 8:35, 36; 9:42.

36. **Jehoadah.** i.e. *Jehovah adorned; the Lord will adorn; Jehovah is adornment,* ✻S#3085h. 1 Ch 9:42, Jarah. **Alemeth.** 1 Ch +6:60. **Azmaveth.** 2 S +23:31. **Zimri.** 1 Ch +2:6. **Moza.** i.e. *origin, stock; going forth; fountain; the place from which one goes forth,* ✻S#4162h. 1 Ch 2:46. 8:36, 37. 9:42, 43. (1) A son of Ephah, Caleb's concubine, 1 Ch 2:46. (2) A chief man of Benjamin of the stock of Saul, 1 Ch 8:36; 9:42.

37. **Binea.** i.e. *a gushing forth; in wandering,* ✻S#1150h. **Rapha.** ver. +2. 1 Ch 9:43, Rephaiah. **Eleasah.** 1 Ch +2:39. **Azel.** i.e. *noble, separate; reserved,* ✻S#682h. 1 Ch 8:37, 38, 38. 9:43, 44, 44. (1) A descendant of Jonathan, Saul's son, 1 Ch 8:37, 38; 9:43, 44. (2) Probably a hamlet; and if so, it lay to

the east of Jerusalem, Zc +14:5; perhaps identical with Beth-ezel, Mi +1:11.

38. Azrikam. 1 Ch +3:23. **Bocheru.** i.e. *his first born; the first-born is he,* *S#1074h. 1 Ch 8:38. 9:44. Here is a case of a son being given a name which literally means "firstborn," but he was not born first, but second. This is another evidence that "firstborn" does not mean born first, but has primary reference to certain legal privileges pertaining to the birthright. The eldest son succeeded to his father's rank and position as head of the family or tribe, and as representative of its prerogatives. He also inherited a double portion of his father's property, a right guaranteed even when his mother was the less loved of two wives (Dt 21:17; 2 K 2:9). A birthright might be sold to a younger brother, as Esau sold his birthright to Jacob (Ge 25:29, 34; He 12:16). It might also be forfeited on account of misconduct (1 Ch +*5:1). 1 Ch +26:10. Ge +41:51. *48:18. Le +=23:10. 2 Ch 21:3. Jb *18:13. Ps *89:20, *27. Je +31:9. Col +√1:15n. **Ishmael.** Ge +16:11. **Sheariah.** i.e. *gate of Jah; Jah estimates; estimated of the Lord,* *S#8187h. 1 Ch 8:38. 9:44. **Obadiah.** Ob +1. **Hanan.** 1 Ch +9:44.

39. Eshek. i.e. *oppression,* *S#6232h. **Ulam.** 1 Ch +7:16. **Jehush.** i.e. *whom God hastens; a flock; hasty; he will gather together; he will succor; he will assemble (or hasten),* *S#3266h. 1 Ch 1:35. 7:10. 8:39. 23:10, 11. Ge 36:+5, Jeush, 14, 18. 2 Ch 11:19. (1) A son of Esau, Ge 36:5, 14, 18. 1 Ch 1:35. (2) A Benjamite, son of Bilhan, 1 Ch 7:10. (3) A Levite family of Gershon and a son of Shimei, 1 Ch 23:10, 11. (4) A descendant of Jonathan, 1 Ch 8:39. (5) A son of Rehoboam, 2 Ch 11:19. **the second.** 1 Ch 2:13. 3:1, 15. +7:12n, Aher, 15n. **Eliphelet.** 1 Ch +3:6.

40. archers. 1 Ch 12:2. 2 Ch 14:8. **many sons.** Ps *127:3-5. 128:3-6.

1 CHRONICLES 9

The original of the genealogies of Israel and Judah, 1. The first settlers in the land after the captivity, 2. The first who dwelt in Jerusalem, of the other tribes, 3-9; and of the priests and Levites, with their charge and service, 10-34. A repeated account of Saul's family, 35-44.

1. A.M. 2804, etc. **B.C.** 1200, etc. **all Israel.** Ezr 2:59, 62, 63. Ne 7:5, 64. Mt 1:1-16. Lk 3:28-38. **carried.** 2 Ch 33:11. 36:9, 10, 18-20. Je 39:9. 52:14, 15. Da 1:2. **transgression.** 1 Ch 5:25.

2. A.M. 3468. **B.C.** 536. **the first.** Ezr 2:70. Ne 7:73. 11:3. **the Nethinims.** i.e. *dedicated; given, offered; given ones,* *S#5411h. Jsh 9:21-27. Ezr 2:43, 58, 70. 7:7h, 24 (S*5412h). 8:17, 20, 20. Ne 3:26, 31. 7:46, 60, 73. 10:28. 11:3, 21, 21.

3. Jerusalem. Ne 11:1, 4-9. **of the children of Ephraim.** 2 Ch 11:16. 30:11, 18.

4. Uthai. i.e. *whom Jehovah succors; mine helper (by teaching); mine iniquity; in season or opportune of the Lord,* *S#5793h. 1 Ch 9:4. Ezr 8:14. (1) Descendant of Pharez, son of Judah, 1 Ch 9:4. (2) Son of Bigvai, and companion of Ezra, Ezr 8:14. **Ammihud.** 2 S +13:37. **Omri.** 1 K +16:16. **Imri.** i.e. *eloquent; promise of the lord; my saying,* *S#566h. 1 Ch 9:4. Ne 3:2. (1) One named in the genealogy of Israel, 1 Ch 9:4. (2) Father of Zaccur, who helped to build the wall, Ne 3:2. **Bani.** Ezr +2:10. Ne 8:7. 10:13.

Pharez. 1 Ch 2:5. 4:1. Ge +46:12. Nu 26:20. Ne 11:4, 6, Perez.

5. Shilonites. 1 Ch 4:21. Nu 26:20, Shelanites. Ne 11:5, Shiloni. 1 K +11:29. **Asaiah.** 2 Ch +34:20. **firstborn.** 1 Ch +*8:38n.

6. Zerah. 1 Ch 2:4, 6. Ge +36:13. 38:30, Zarah. Nu 26:20. **Jeuel.** i.e. *swept away of God; God has taken away,* *S#3262h.

7. Sallu. i.e. *elevation; have raised up; measured; lifted up,* *S#5543h. 1 Ch 9:7. Ne 11:7. (1) A man of Benjamin named in the genealogies, 1 Ch 9:7; Ne 11:7. (2) One of the chiefs of the priests who returned to Jerusalem with Zerubbabel, Ne 12:20, Sallai; 12:7, Sallu. Ne 8:4. 10:20. 11:7. **Meshullam.** ver. +12. **Hodaviah.** 1 Ch +5:24. **Hasenuah.** i.e. *the hated bristling; the thorny; the hated,* *S#5574h. 1 Ch 9:7. Ne 11:9.

8. Ibneiah. ✓66, Ge +9:3. i.e. *Jehovah will build; he will be built up of the Lord,* *S#2997h. **Jeroham.** 1 S +1:1. **Elah.** Ge +36:41. **Uzzi.** 1 Ch +6:5. **Michri.** i.e. *selling; bought of the Lord; my price,* *S#4381h. **Meshullam.** ver. +12. **Shephathiah.** i.e. *whom Jehovah defends; judgment of Jah; judge of the Lord; judged of Jehovah,* *S#8203h. 1 Ch 3:3. 9:8. 2 S +3:4, Shephatiah. Ezr 2:4, 57. 8:8. Ne 7:9, 59. 11:4. Je 38:1. Also 1 Ch 12:5. 27:16. 2 Ch 21:2. (1) A son of David, 2 S 3:4. (2) One who came to David to Ziklag, 1 Ch 12:5. (3) Ruler of the Simeonites under David, 1 Ch 27:16. (4) A son of Jehoshaphat, 2 Ch 21:2. (5, 6) Two whose children came up from Babylon, Ezr 2:4, 57; 8:8; Ne 7:9, 59; 11:4. (7) Son of Mattan, an opponent of the prophet Jeremiah, Je 38:1. **Reuel.** Ge +36:4. **Ibnijah.** i.e. *building of Jah; he will be built of Jah,* *S#2998h.

9. nine hundred and fifty-six. Ne 11:8. **in the house.** 2 Ch 35:4.

10. And of. 1 Ch 24:7, 17. Ne 11:10-14. **Jedaiah.** i.e. *for whom Jehovah cares; Jah has known; known of the Lord; know thou Jah; Jehovah has been kind,* *S#3048h. 1 Ch 9:10. 24:7. Ezr 2:36. Ne 7:39. 11:10. 12:6, 7, 19, 21. Zc 6:10, 14. (1) A descendant of Simeon, 1 Ch 4:37. (2) First in the genealogy of the priests officiating in Jerusalem, of the family of Jeshua, 1 Ch 9:10; Ezr 2:36; Ne 7:39; 11:10; (3) Another priestly family of the same name, Ne 12:6, 7, 19, 21. (4) Him of the sons of Aaron to whom the second lot fell, 1 Ch 24:7. (5) One of them that builded the wall, Ne +3:10 (S#3042h). (6) One to whom the crowns of Joshua were decreed, Zc 6:10, 14. **Jehoiarib.** 1 Ch +24:7. Ne 11:10, etc. 12:19, Joiarib. **Jachin.** Ge +46:10.

11. Azariah. 1 Ch 6:8-15, +36. Ne 10:2. 11:11, Seraiah. **Hilkiah.** 1 Ch 6:13. 2 K +18:18. **Meshullam.** ver. +12. **Zadok.** 2 S +8:17. **Meraioth.** Ne +12:15. **Ahitub.** 1 S +14:3. **the ruler.** 1 Ch 24:5. Nu 4:15, 16, 28, 33. 2 K 23:4. 25:18. Ne 11:11. Ac 4:1. 5:24, 26.

12. And. Ne 11:12. **Adaiah.** Ne +11:5. **Jeroham.** 1 S +1:1. **Pashur.** Je +20:1. **Malchijah.** i.e. *king of the Lord; my king is Jehovah,* *S#4441h. 1 Ch 9:12. 24:9. Ezr 10:25. Ne 3:11. 10:3. 12:42. (1) One named in the genealogies of the priests, 1 Ch 9:12. (2) The son of Aaron, to whom the fifth lot fell, 1 Ch 24:9. (3) One of them that took strange wives, Ezr 10:25. (4) One who helped to build the wall, Ne 3:11. (5) One who sealed the covenant, Ne 10:3. *S#4441 also rendered Malchiah: (1) Father of Baaseiah, 1 Ch 6:40. (2) A descendant of Parosh who took a strange wife, Ezr 10:25. (3) Another descendant of Parosh, Ne 11:12.

(4) A repairer of Jerusalem's wall, Ne 3:14. (5) Another repairer of Jerusalem's wall, Ne 3:31. (6) A priest who stood up with Ezra to read the law, Ne 8:4. (7) A priest who dedicated the wall, Je 38:1, 6. **Maasiai.** i.e. *work of the Lord; my works,* *S#4640h. **Adiel.** 1 Ch +4:36. **Jahzerah.** i.e. *protection; he will be made to return; he will lead to the crown; he will be narrow-eyed,* *S#3170h. **Meshullam.** i.e. *friend; recompensed; repaying; reconciled,* *S#4918h. 1 Ch 3:19. 5:13. 8:17. 9:7, 8, 11, 12. 2 K 22:3. 2 Ch 34:12. Ezr 8:16. 10:15, 29. Ne 3:4, 6, 30. 6:18. 8:4. 10:7, 20. 11:7, 11. 12:13, 16, 25, 33. (1) A Benjamite, descended from Shaharaim through Elpaal, 1 Ch 8:17. (2) A leading man among the Gadites in the reign of Jotham, 1 Ch 5:13. (3) An ancestor of Shaphan the scribe, 2 K 22:3. (4) A priest, son of Zadok, and father of the high priest Hilkiah who lived in Josiah's reign, 1 Ch 9:11; Ne 11:11. (5) A Kohathite Levite who with others helped faithfully to superintend the workmen who repaired the temple in Josiah's reign, 2 Ch 34:12. (6) A priest, son of Meshillemith of the house of Immer, 1 Ch 9:12. (7) A son of Zerubbabel, 1 Ch 3:19. (8) A Benjamite, father of Sallu, 1 Ch 9:7; Ne 9:7. (9) Another Benjamite, son of Shephatiah, 1 Ch 9:8. (10) A chief man among the companions of Ezra, Ezr 8:16. (10) One who helped to reform the strange marriages, Ezr 10:29. (11) One of those who busied themselves, probably adversely, in the matter of inducing the Jews who had married foreign wives to put them away, Ezr 10:15. (12) A son of Bani, induced by Ezra to put away his foreign wife, Ezr 10:29. (13) One who helped to build the wall, Ne 3:4. (14) Son of Besodeiah, who with another returned exile repaired the old gate of the wall of Jerusalem, Ne 3:6. (15) Father-in-law to Johanan, son of Tobiah, Ne 6:18. (16) One of those who stood on Ezra's left hand while he read and explained the law to the people, Ne 8:4. (17) A priest who sealed the covenant in behalf of a father's house, Ne 10:7. (18) A chief of the people who did so, Ne 10:20. (19) One of the princes of Judah who marched in the procession at the dedication of the wall of Jerusalem, Ne 12:33. (20) A priest in the days of Joiakim, the son of Jeshua, and representive of the house of Ezra, Ne 12:13. (21) Another priest at the same date, head of the father's house Ginnethon, Ne 12:16. (22) A porter who lived at the same date, Ne 12:25. **Meshillemith.** i.e. *reconciliation; those who repay,* *S#4921h. **Immer.** i.e. *talking; loquacious; promise; he hath said,* *S#564h. 1 Ch 9:12. 24:14. Ezr 2:37, 59. 10:20. Ne 3:29. 7:40, 61. 11:13. Je 20:1. (1) One who returned from Babylon, Ezr 2:59; Ne 7:61. (2) A descendant of Aaron of the sixteenth course of priests, 1 Ch 24:1, 6, 14. (3) Father of Pashur, who smote Jeremiah, Je 20:1.

13. **very able men.** Heb. mighty men of valor. 1 Ch 26:6, 30, 32. Jg +6:12. 2 S +2:7mg. Ne 11:14. Is +10:21 (*S#1368h).

14. **And.** Ne 11:15-19. **Shemiah.** ver. +16. Ne 11:15. **Hasshub.** i.e. *considerate; much esteemed,* *S#2815h. 1 Ch 9:14. Ne 3:+11, Hashub, 23. 10:23. 11:15. (1) A Levite, father of Shemaiah, 1 Ch 9:14; Ne 11:15. (2, 3) Two who helped to build the wall, Ne 3:11, 23. (4) One who sealed the covenant, Ne 10:23. **Azrikam.** 1 Ch +3:23. **Hashabiah.** i.e. *Jehovah regards; esteemed of the Lord,* *S#2811h. 1 Ch 6:45. 9:14. 25:19. 27:17. Ezr 8:19, 24. Ne 3:17. 10:11. 11:15, 22. 12:21, 24. (1) A Merarite Levite, descended through

Amaziah, and an ancestor of Jeduthun, 1 Ch 6:45. (2) A descendant of Bunni, ancestor of Shemaiah, 1 Ch 9:14; (3) A son of Jeduthun, and a singer, 1 Ch 25:3, 19. (4) An officer of David's, and ruler of the Levites, 1 Ch 26:30. (5) A Levite, son of Kemuel, prince of the tribe of Levi in David's reign, 1 Ch 27:17. (6) A chief of the Levites during the reign of Josiah, 2 Ch 35:9. (7) A chief of the Levites, Ne 12:24. (8) One who helped to build the wall, Ne 3:17. (9) One who sealed the covenant, Ne 10:11. (10) A Levite, descended from Asaph, Ne 11:22. (11) A priest, head of the father's house of Hilkiah, in the time of Joiakim the high priest, Ne 12:21. (12) One of a family of priests who returned from Babylon, Ezr 8:19. (13) Another priest, Ezr 8:24, of the same family as Number 12. (14) Another Levite, Ne 11:15, perhaps the same as Number 2. **of the sons.** See on 1 Ch 6:19, 29, 63. Nu 26:57. **Merari.** Ge +46:11.

15. **Bakbakkar.** i.e. *diligent; investigator; diligent searching; diligent investigator,* *S#1230h. **Heresh.** i.e. *an artificer; engrave, scratch; silence, dumb,* *S#2792h. **Galal.** i.e. *worthy; great; he has rolled away the reproach; a roller, as e.g. the rolling of one's way upon the Lord (Ps 37:5mg); because of,* *S#1559h. 1 Ch 9:15, 16. Ne 11:17. (1) A Levite who lived after the exile, who dwelt in the villages of the Netophathites and served at Jerusalem, 1 Ch 9:15. (2) Another Levite, the son of Jeduthun, 1 Ch 9:16; Ne 11:17. **Mattaniah.** 2 K +24:17. Ne 11:17, 22, Micha. 12:25. **Micah.** ✠S#4316h. Mi +1:1. **Zichri.** i.e. *memorable; remembered of the Lord; do thou remember; mindful, famous; celebrated,* *S#2147h. 1 Ch 8:19, 23, 27. 9:15. 26:25. 27:16. Ex 6:21. 2 Ch 17:16. 23:1. 28:7. Ne 11:9. 12:17. (1) Son of Uzziel of Levi, Ex 6:21. (2) Chief man of Benjamin, son of Shimei, 1 Ch 8:19. (3) A Benjamite, son of Shashak, 1 Ch 8:23. (4) A Benjamite, son of Jehoram, 1 Ch 8:27. (5) A Levite, son of Asaph, who dwelt in Jerusalem, 1 Ch 9:15. In all probability he is the person called Zaccur, a synonymous name, in 1 Ch 25:2, 10; Ne 10:12; 12:35, Zaccur; and also the person called Zabdi in Ne 11:17, Zabdi, in the latter instance the letters k, anglicized ch, and r having been misread as b and d (beth and daleth). (6) A Levite, descended from Moses' son, Eliezer, 1 Ch 26:25. (7) Father of Elishaphat, captain of Jehoiada, 2 Ch 23:1. (8) A man of Judah, and father of Amasiah, captain in the army of Jehoshaphat, 2 Ch 17:16. (9) A valiant Ephraimite in Pekah's army, who slew Maaseiah, a royal prince, and two of Ahaz' chief officers, 2 Ch 28:7. (10) A Reubenite, 1 Ch 27:16. (11) A Benjamite, father of Joel, overseer at Jerusalem, Ne 11:9. (12) A priest, head of the father's house of Abijah, who lived in the days of the high priest Joiakim, Ne 12:17. **Asaph.** 1 Ch 6:39. 2 K +18:18.

16. **Obadiah.** Ne 11:+17, Abda. Ob +1:1. **Shemaiah.** i.e. *whom Jehovah heard and answered; obeying Jah; heard of the Lord.* Ne 11:17, Shammua. *S#8098h: 1 Ch 3:22, 22. 4:37. 5:4. 9:14, 16. 15:8, 11. 24:6. 26:4, 6, 7. 2 Ch 12:5, 7, 15. 29:14. Ezr 8:13, 16. 10:21, 31. Ne 3:29. 6:10. 10:8. 11:15. 12:6, 18, 34, 35, 36, 42. Je 29:31, 31, 32. Also *S#8098h: 2 Ch 11:2. 17:8. 31:15. 35:9. Je 26:20. 29:24. 36:12. (1) A Simeonite, 1 Ch 4:37. (2) A son of Joel, of Reuben, 1 Ch 5:4. (3) A Levite, chief of the sons of Elizaphan, 1 Ch 15:8-11. (4) A Levite, a son of Nethanel, a scribe in the time of David who noted down the twenty-

four divisions then made of the priests, 1 Ch 24:6. (5) Eldest son of Obed-edom; father of various valiant sons who, with him, were doorkeepers of the tabernacle, 1 Ch 26:4. (6) A prophet in the time of Rehoboam, 1 K 12:22. (7) One of the Levites sent by Jehoshaphat to teach the people, 2 Ch 17:8. (8) A Levite, descendant of Jeduthun, who helped to cleanse the temple in Hezekiah's reign, 2 Ch 29:14, 15. (9) A Levite mentioned in 1 Ch 9:16, perhaps the same as Shammua in Ne 11:17. Possibly the same person as in (8). (10). A Levite in Hezekiah's reign, who distributed tithes, gifts, firstlings, to the Levites in the cities, 2 Ch 31:15. (11) A chief Levite in Josiah's reign, 2 Ch 35:9. (12) Father of Urijah, of Kirjath-jearim, who was put to death by king Jehoiakim for the true prophecies he had uttered, Je 26:20-23. (13) Father of Delaiah, the latter being a prince in the reign of Jehoiakim, Je 36:12. (14) A Nehlamite, a false prophet among the exiles in Babylonia, who contradicted Jeremiah's prophecy of a long captivity, Je 29:24-32. (15) A chief of the priests who returned from Babylon with Zerubbabel, Ne 12:6, 7. (16) A father's house bore this name, Ne 12:18. (17) A son of Adonikam, and one of the chief men who accompanied Ezra from the land of the captivity to Canaan, Ezr 8:13. (18) A chief man whom Ezra sent with others to Iddo to obtain Levites who were lacking in the party leaving the land of captivity for Canaan, Ezr 8:16. (19, 20) Two men, one descended from the priest Harim, and the other from the layman Harim, each of whom was induced by Ezra to put away his foreign wife, Ezr 10:21, 31. (21) A son of Shecaniah, 1 Ch 3:22. (22) A Levite, keeper of the east gate, who repaired part of the wall of Jerusalem in Nehemiah's time, Ne 3:29. (23) A Levite, descended from Bunni, Ne 11:15. (24) A false prophet, son of Delaiah, son of Mehetabel, Ne 6:10-13. (25) A priest who sealed the covenant in behalf of a father's house, Ne 10:8. (26) A prince of Judah who took part at the dedication of the wall of Jerusalem, Ne 12:34. (27) A Levite of the lineage of Asaph, Ne 12:35. (28) One of the company of Levite musicians at the dedication of the wall of Jerusalem, Ne 12:36. (29) A priest who blew a trumpet on the same occasion, Ne 12:42. **Galal.** ver. +15. **the son of.** 1 Ch 25:1, 3, 6. 2 Ch 35:15. **Jeduthun.** i.e. *praising, celebrating; let them give praise,* *S#3038h. 1 Ch 9:16. 16:41, 42, 42. 25:1, 3, 3, 3, 6. 2 Ch 5:12. 29:14. 35:15. Ne 11:17. Ps 39:t. 62:t. 77:t. Also *S#3038h: 1 Ch 16:38. Ne 11:17. Ps 30:t. 77:t. (1) A Levite, set by David as chief over a choir, 1 Ch 16:41, 42; 25:1, one of three chief musicians appointed by David, and founder of a musical family; known earlier as Ethan: 1 Ch 6:44, 47; 15:17, 19; 16:38-41; 25:1. His name, it appears, was changed to Jeduthun, "praising one," after his appointment to service in the tabernacle at Gibeon. (2) Father of Obed-edom the doorkeeper and apparently of the family of Korah, a division of the Kohathites, 1 Ch 16:38; 26:1,4, 8, 12, 15. Some interpreters regard him to be the same as (1). **Berechiah.** Zc +1:7. **Asa.** i.e. *healer; who will heal; physician,* *S#609h. 1 Ch 3:10. 9:16. 1 K 15:8, 9, 11, 13, 14, 16, 17, 18, 18, 20, 22, 22, 23, 24, 25, 28, 32, 33. 16:8, 10, 15, 23, 29. 22:41, 43, 46. 2 Ch 14:1, 2, 8, 10, 11, 12, 13. 15:2, 2, 8, 10, 16, 16, 17, 19. 16:1, 1, 2, 4, 6, 7, 10, 10, 11, 12, 13. 17:2. 20:32. 21:12. Je 41:9. (1) King of Judah, son of Abijah, B.C. 914, 1 K 15:9-24; 2 Ch ch. 14-16; Mt

1:7. (2) A Levite, 1 Ch 9:16. **Elkanah.** Ex +6:24. **Netophathites.** 1 Ch 2:54. 2 S +23:28. 2 K 25:23. Ne 7:26. 12:28-30.

17. **the porters.** 1 Ch +23:5. ch. 26. Ne 11:19. 12:45. **Shallum.** ver. 19. 1 Ch 26:1, 14. 2 K +15:10. Ezr 2:42. **Akkub.** 1 Ch +3:24. **Talmon.** i.e. *great or injurious oppression; captive; outcast,* *S#2929h. 1 Ch 9:17. Ezr 2:42. Ne 7:45. 11:19. 12:25. (1) A porter, and the family which he founded, 1 Ch 9:17. (2) Members of the family returned from exile with Zerubbabel, Ezr 2:42; Ne 7:45; and served as porters at the new temple, Ne 11:19; 12:25. **Ahiman.** i.e. *brother of a portion* or *gift; brother of whom?,* *S#289h. 1 Ch 9:17. Nu 13:22. Jsh 15:14. Jg 1:10. (1) One of the Anakim, Nu 13:22; Jsh 15:14; Jg 1:10. (2) A Levite, one of the porters of the house of God, 1 Ch 9:17.

18. **Who hitherto waited.** The original is *weudhennah,* which Houbigant and Dr. Geddes consider as a proper name, and render "And Adanah was over the eastern gate, called the king's;" i.e. the gate by which the kings of Judah went to the temple. The list is here nearly the same with those found in Ezra and Nehemiah, and contains those who returned to Jerusalem with Zerubbabel: but the list in Nehemiah is more ample, probably because it contains those who came *afterwards;* the object of the sacred writer here being to give the names of those who came *first,* ver. 2. These consisted of men belonging not only to the tribes of Judah and Benjamin, but to many of the other tribes of Israel, who took advantage of the proclamation of Cyrus to return to Jerusalem. Properly speaking, the divisions mentioned here constituted the *whole* of the Israelitish people, who were divided into priests, Levites, common Israelites, and Nethinims. **the king's.** 1 K 10:5. 2 K 11:19. 15:35. Ezk 44:2, 3. 46:1, 2. Ac 3:11. **they.** 1 Ch 26:12-19.

19. **Shallum.** ver. 17. **Kore.** i.e. *partridge; calling; happening,* *S#6981h. 1 Ch 9:19. 26:1. 2 Ch 31:14. (1) Son of Ebiasaph, and father of Shallum, one of the porters, 1 Ch 9:19. (2) Son of Imnah the Levite, the porter toward the east, 2 Ch 31:14. (3) The rebellious Levite, founder of a house, 1 Ch 26:19. **Ebiasaph.** 1 Ch 6:22, +23. 26:1. **Korah.** Ge +36:5. Nu 26:9-11. Ps 42:t. 44:t. 49:t. **Korahites.** i.e. *descendants of Korah.* *S#7145h. 1 Ch 9:19, 31. 12:6. 26:1, 19. Ex 6:24. Nu 26:58. 2 Ch 20:19. **keepers.** ver. 22. Mk=13:34. Lk 12:36-38. **gates.** Heb. thresholds. Jg +19:27. 1 K +14:17. 2 K 12:9mg. Ps 84:10mg. Is 6:5. **over the host.** 2 K 11:9, 15. 2 Ch 23:4-10. **keepers of the entry.** 1 Ch 26:7, 8, 13-19.

20. **Phinehas.** Ex +6:25. Nu 3:32. 4:16, 28, 33. 31:6. **Eleazar.** Ex +6:23. **the Lord.** Nu 25:11-13. 1 S 16:18. Ac 7:9, 10.

21. **Zechariah.** 1 Ch 26:14. Zc +1:1. **Meshelemiah.** i.e. *whom Jehovah treats amicably; the Lord my felicity; whom the Lord repays; bringing peace-offering of Jah,* *S#4920h. 1 Ch 9:21. Also 1 Ch 26:1, 2, 9. In 1 Ch 26:14, Shelemiah. Father of Zechariah, porter of the door of the tabernacle.

22. **chosen to be.** 1 Ch 7:40. **porters.** Mk=13:34. **gates.** ver. 19. **in their.** ver. 16, 25. Ne 11:25-30, 36. 12:28, 29, 44. **David.** 1 Ch ch. 23, 25, 26. 28:13, 21. **Samuel.** 1 S 9:9. **did ordain.** Heb. founded. Ps 8:2. **set office.** or, trust. ver. 26, 31. 2 Ch 31:15mg.

23. **the oversight.** 1 Ch 23:32. 2 Ch 23:19. Ne 12:45. Ezk 44:10, 11, 14.

24. **four**. 1 Ch 26:14-18. **quarters**. ↗121.O, Ge +28:22.

25. **in their villages**. ver. 16. **seven days**. 2 K 11:5, 7. 2 Ch 23:8. **time to time**. Ezk 4:10, 11.

26. **set office**. or, trust. ver. 22. 1 T =1:11. **chambers**. or, storehouses. ver. 33. 2 K 23:11. **treasuries**. 1 Ch 26:20-27. 2 Ch 31:5-12. Ne 10:38, 39. 13:5. Mt=13:52.

27. **round about**. Nu 1:50. Mt=18:20. Ac=11:23. Re=1:13. **the charge**. 1 Ch 23:32. Ro 12:7. **the opening**. Jg 3:25 (key). 1 S 3:15. Is 22:22 (key). Ml 1:10. Lk +=*11:52. 14:23. **morning**. 2 S 13:4mg.

28. **the charge**. 1 Ch 26:22-26. Nu 3:25-37. Ezr 8:25-30. Ne 12:44. 13:4, 5. **ministering vessels**. 2 T=2:20, 21. **bring them in and out**. Heb. bring them in by tale, and carry them out.

29. **oversee**. 1 Th=5:12, 13. He=13:17. **vessels**. 2 T=2:20, 21. **instruments**. or, vessels. Ge 49:5. **the oil**. Ex 27:20. **the frankincense**. Ex 30:23-38. **spices**. Ga=5:22, 23.

30. **of the sons**. Ex 30:25, 33, 35-38. 37:29. **ointment**. SS 1:*3, 12. 4:10. Mt 26:7. Jn=*16:23.

31. **Shallum**. ver. 17, 19. **set office**. or, trust. ver. 22, 26. **in the pans**. or, on flat plates, or slices. 1 Ch 23:29. Le 2:5, 7. 6:21. 7:9.

32. **the sons**. 1 Ch 6:33, etc. **showbread**. Heb. bread of ordering. 1 Ch 23:29. 28:16. Le 24:6 (row), 7 (row). 2 Ch 2:4. 13:11. 29:18. Ne 10:33. **to prepare**. Ex 25:30. Le 24:5-8.

33. **the singers**. See on 1 Ch 6:31-33. 15:16-22. 16:4-6. 25:1, etc. Ezr 7:24. **chambers**. SS 2:4. **were free**. Ne 11:17, 22, 23. Jn=8:36. Ro=6:22. **they**, etc. Heb. upon them. **employed**. A number of Levites were employed by rotation in singing the praises of Jehovah; and they seem to have continued the service day and night: see the References. Ps 134:1, 2. 135:1-3. Ac=20:18, 31. 1 C=15:58. Re=7:15.

34. **chief fathers**. ver. 13. Ne 11:1-15. **dwelt**. Jn=15:4. =16:33. **Jerusalem**. We have already seen the situation and extent of this ancient city (Note on 1 Ch 8:28); but the Jerusalem of sacred history is no more. After having been successively destroyed by the Babylonians and Romans, and taken by the Saracens, Crusaders, and Turks, in the possession of the latter of whom it still continues, not a vestige remains of the capital of David and Solomon—not a monument of Jewish times is standing. The very course of the walls is changed, and the boundaries of the ancient city are become doubtful. The monks pretend to show the sites of the sacred places; but they have not the slightest pretensions to even a probable identity with the real places. The Jerusalem that now is, however, called by the Arabs *El Kouds*, or "the holy city," is still a respectable, good-looking town, of an irregular shape: it is surrounded by high embattled walls, enclosing an area not exceeding two miles and a half, and occupying two small hills, having the valley of Jehoshaphat on the east, the valley of Siloam and Gehinnom on the south, and the valley of Rephaim on the west; and containing a population variously estimated at from 20,000 to 30,000 souls. Since the writing of the preceding Note in the early 19th century, how much has taken place! The nation of Israel was restored to its own land in 1948, and the entire city of Jerusalem is now in the possession of the Jews, a fulfillment of prophecy (Lk 21:24) which took place

during the "Six Day War" in 1967.

35. A.M. 2804, etc. B.C. 1200, etc. **in Gibeon**. 1 Ch 8:29-40. **the father**. 1 Ch 2:23, 24, 45, 50-52. **Jehiel**. i.e. *treasured; hidden of God; swept away of God*, ✣S#3273h. (1) Father of Gibeon, 1 Ch 9:35. (2) A mighty man of David, 1 Ch 11:44. See on 1 Ch +5:7 for Jeiel (✱S#3273h). **whose wife's**. Some editions read *achatho*, "his *sister*;" but in the parallel place, 1 Ch 8:29, it is *ishto*, "his *wife*," which is also the reading of the LXX., Vulgate, Arabic, and Syriac here, and is undoubtedly the true reading. This repetition of part of Benjamin's genealogy seems to have been intended merely as an introduction to the ensuing history.

36. **firstborn**. 1 Ch +8:38n. **Abdon**. Jg +12:13. **Zur**. Nu +25:15. **Kish**. ver. 39. See on 1 Ch 8:33. 1 S +9:1. **Baal**. 1 Ch +5:5. **Ner**. i.e. *a lamp; a light*, ✱S#5369h. 1 Ch 8:33. 9:36, 39. 26:28. 1 S 14:50, 51. 26:5, 14. 2 S 2:8, 12. 3:23, 25, 28, 37. 1 K 2:5, 32. (1) A Benjamite, son of Abiel and father of Abner, 1 S 14:51. He or Abner was Saul's uncle, 1 S 14:50. If Abner was Saul's uncle, Ner was Saul's grandfather and identical with the following. (2) A Benjamite, son of Jeiel and father or remoter ancestor of Saul's father, Kish, 1 Ch 8:33; 9:35, 36. **Nadab**. Ex +6:23.

37. **Gedor**. Jsh +15:58. **Ahio**. 2 S +6:3. **Zechariah**. 1 Ch +8:31, Zacher. *Zacher* is merely an abbreviation of Zechariah, by the omission of *Jah*, or *Yah*, one of the names of God. **Mikloth**. 1 Ch +27:4.

38. **Shimeam**. i.e. *their desolation; rumor; fame*, ✱S#8043h. Shimeam seems to be a mistake for *Shimeah*; the only difference being *mem final*, and *hay*; and the LXX. in both places read *Samaa*, "Samaa." 1 Ch 8:32, Shimeah.

39. **Ner**. ver. +36. 1 Ch 8:33. 1 S 14:50, 51. **Kish**. 1 S +9:1. **Saul**. 1 S +9:2. **and Saul**. 1 Ch 10:2. 1 S 13:22. 14:1, 49, Ishui. 31:2. **Esh-baal**. See on 1 Ch 8:33.

40. **Merib-baal**. i.e. *Baal is contentious*, ✱S#4807h. 1 Ch 8:34, 34. 9:40. **Merib-baal**. i.e. *rebellion of Baal; Baal is contentious*, ✱S#4807h. 1 Ch 8:34, 34. 9:40. **Merib-baal**. i.e. *rebellion of Baal; contender against Baal*, ✱S#4810h. See on 1 Ch 8:34-36. **Micah**. Mi +1:1.

41. **Pithon**. 1 Ch +8:35. **Melech**. 1 Ch +8:35. **Tahrea**. i.e. *cunning; delaying cries; separate the friend*, ✱S#8475h. **and Ahaz**. 1 Ch 8:35.

42. **Ahaz**. 1 Ch +8:35. **Jarah**. i.e. *honeycomb; honey-wood*, ✱S#3294h. 1 Ch 9:42, 42. Jarah seems also to be a mistake for *Jehoadah*, as the LXX. read uniformly *Iada*. 1 Ch 8:36, Jehoadah. **Alemeth**. 1 Ch +6:60. 8:36.

43. **Rephaiah**. i.e. *whom Jehovah healed; enfeebled of Jah; healed of the Lord*, ✱S#7509h. 1 Ch 3:21. 4:42. 7:2. 9:43. Ne 3:9. (1) One in the line of Jeconiah and David, 1 Ch 3:21. (2) One of the Simeonites who smote Amalek, 1 Ch 4:42. (3) A son of Tola, son of Issachar, 1 Ch 7:2. (4) One of the stock of Saul and Jonathan, 1 Ch 9:43; called Rapha, 1 Ch 8:2. (5) One of them that helped to build the wall, Ne 3:9. *Rapha* is merely a contracted form of *Rephaiah*. **Eleasah**. 1 Ch +2:39. **Azel**. 1 Ch +8:37.

44. **Azrikam**. 1 Ch 8:38. **Hanan**. i.e. *merciful; whom Jehovah gave; compassionate; a gracious giver*, ✱S#2605h. 1 Ch 8:23, 38. 9:44. 11:43. Ezr 2:46. Ne 7:49. 8:7. 10:10, 22, 26. 13:13. Je 35:4. (1) One of David's mighty men, 1 Ch 11:43. (2) A Benjamite,

son of Shashak, 1 Ch 8:23. (3) A son of Azel, a descendant of Jonathan, 1 Ch 8:38; 9:44. (4) A prophet, son of Igdaliah, whose sons had a chamber in the temple, Je 35:4. (5) Founder of a family of Nethinim, members of which returned from Babylon with Zerubbabel, Ezr 2:46; Ne 7:49. (6) A man, probably a Levite, whom Ezra employed with others to make the people understand the law, Ne 8:7; he seems to have sealed the covenant, Ne 10:10. (7, 8) Two chiefs of the people, who also sealed the covenant, Ne 10:22, 26. (9) A son of Zaccur, appointed assistant treasurer by Nehemiah, Ne 13:13.

1 CHRONICLES 10

Saul's defeat and death, 1-7. The Philistines abuse his dead body, 8-10. The men of Jabesh-gilead rescue it, with the bodies of his sons, 11, 12. Saul's sin; for which he died, and the kingdom was transferred to David, 13, 14.

1. A.M. 2948. B.C. 1056. **Now.** 1 S 31:1-13. **the Philistines fought.** 1 S 28:1. 29:1, 2. 31:1, 2, etc. **slain.** *or,* wounded. **mount Gilboa.** ver. 8. 1 S +28:4. 31:1. 2 S 1:6, 21. 21:12.

2. **Jonathan.** 1 Ch 8:33. 9:39. 1 S +13:2. 14:6, 39, 40. 2 K 23:29. Is 57:1, 2. **Abinadab.** 1 S 14:49, Ishui. +16:8. **the sons.** Ex *20:5. 2 K 25:7.

3. **went sore.** 1 S 31:3-6. 2 S 1:4-10. Am 2:14. **archers.** Heb. shooters with bows. 1 S 31:3. **hit.** Heb. found. **he was wounded.** Ge 49:23, 24.

4. **Draw.** Jg 9:54. **uncircumcised.** Jg 15:18. 1 S 14:6. 17:26, 36. 2 S 1:20. **abuse.** *or,* mock. Jg 16:21, 23-25. **he was.** 1 S 31:4. 2 S 1:14-16. **Saul took.** ver. 5. 2 S 1:9, 10. 17:23. 1 K 16:18. Mt 27:4, 5. Ac 1:18. 16:27.

6. **Saul.** 1 S 4:10, 11. 18. 12:25. Ec 9:1, 2. Ho 13:10, 11. **all his house.** *ſ171A, Ex +9:6. "All his men," in Samuel; that is, all who were present with him in the battle, namely, his three sons, as it is expressed in 1 S 31:6. For it is evident that Ishbosheth and Mephibosheth were not slain. But nothing is more common in Scripture and all authors, than to understand *all* of a great and most considerable part. ſ171A. Figure of speech Synecdoche of the Genus: all is put for the greater part, Ex +9:6. **house.** ſ121J4. Figure of speech Metonymy of the Subject: the container for the contents, the place for the thing placed in it; here, "house" is put for household, Ge +7:1. His family received such a blow, that it never recovered itself again. For though Ishbosheth reigned over a part of the country, yet it was not in any splendor. This history seems to be repeated here as an introduction to that of the kingdom of David.

7. **then they.** Le 26:31, 36. Dt 28:33, 43. Jg 6:2. 1 S 13:6. 31:7.

8. **to strip.** 1 S 31:8. 2 K 3:23. 2 Ch 20:25.

9. **took.** ver. 4. 1 S 31:9, 10. 2 S 1:20. Mt 14:11. **tidings.** Jg 16:23, 24. Da 5:2-4, 23.

10. **their gods.** 1 S 31:10, Ashtaroth. **in the temple.** 1 S 5:2-7. **Dagon.** i.e. *fish-god* (from its *fecundity*); *honored fish,* *S#1712h. 1 Ch 10:10. Jg 16:23. 1 S 5:2, 2, 3, 3, 4, 4, 4, 5, 5, 5, 7. Note *thirteen* occurrences of this word. Ge +14:4.

11. **when.** 1 S 11:1-11. 31:11-13. 2 S 2:4-7.

12. **the oak.** Ge 35:8. 2 S 21:12-14. 31:13. **fasted.** Ge 50:10. 2 S 3:35. That is, every day until evening, after the manner of the Jewish fasts (Matthew Poole).

13. **committed.** Heb. transgressed. 2 Ch 28:19. 36:14. **even against.** 1 S 13:13, 14. 15:3, *23, 28. **for asking.** 1 S 28:7-20. **a familiar spirit.** Ex 22:18. Le 19:31. 20:6. Dt +*18:10-14. 2 K +21:6. Is *8:19. Ac 8:9-11. 16:16-18.

14. **enquired not.** Jg 10:11-16. 1 S 28:6. Ps 106:13. Ezk 14:3-6. **he slew.** Ps 17:13. Is 10:7, 15. **turned.** 1 S 13:14. 15:28. 16:1, 11-13. 28:17. 2 S 3:9, 10. 5:3. **David.** 1 S +16:19. **Jesse.** Heb. Isai. 1 Ch +2:12.

1 CHRONICLES 11

David, by general consent, is made king over all Israel, at Hebron, 1-3. He takes Zion from the Jebusites; dwells there, and prospers, 4-9. The names and achievements of his principal warriors, 10-47.

1. A.M. 2956. B.C. 1048. An. Ex. Is. 443. **all Israel.** 1 Ch 12:23-40. 2 S *5:1, etc. **Hebron.** Ex +6:18. Nu 13:22. 2 S 2:1. 15:10. 1 K 2:11. **Behold.** Ge *29:14. Dt *17:15. Jg *9:2. 2 S *19:12, 13. Ep *5:30.

2. **in time past.** Heb. both yesterday and the third day. Ge +*31:2mg. Ex +4:10mg. Jsh 3:4mg. 2 K +13:5mg. **that leddest.** Nu 27:17. 1 S 18:13. Is 55:4. Jn +*10:4. **Thou shalt.** 1 S 16:1, 13. 2 S 7:7. Ps *78:71, 72. Is *40:11. Je *3:15. Mi *5:2, 4. Mt *2:6. **feed.** *or,* rule. Ezk 34:23. **ruler.** 2 S 5:2. 1 K *3:9. 14:7.

3. **elders.** 2 S *5:3. **David made.** 1 S 11:15. 2 K 11:17. 2 Ch 23:3. **before.** Jg 11:11. 1 S 23:18. **anointed.** 1 S 16:1, 12, *13. 2 S 2:4. 2 K 23:30. **according.** 1 S *15:28. 28:17. **by.** Heb. by the hand of. 1 K +16:12mg. 2 K 24:2. 2 Ch √34:14mg,n.

4. **David.** 2 S 5:6-10. **Jebus.** ver. 5. Jsh 15:63. 18:+16, 28, Jebusi. Jg 1:21. 19:+10, 11, 12. **Jebusites.** Ge +10:16. **the inhabitants.** Ge +10:16. 15:21. Ex 3:17.

5. **Thou shalt.** 1 S 17:9, 10, 26, 36. **the castle.** 1 K 8:1. 2 Ch 5:2. Ps 2:6. 9:11. 48:2, 12, 13. 78:68. 87:2, 5. 125:1, 2. 132:13. La 4:11, 12. Ro 9:33. He 12:22. Re 14:1. **the city.** ver. 7. 2 S 5:9. 6:10, 12. Ps 122:5.

6. **Whosoever.** Jsh 15:16, 17. 1 S 17:25. **chief.** Heb. head. ver. 10, 11, 20. 1 Ch 12:18, 23. **Joab.** 2 S 2:18. 3:27. 8:16. 20:23.

7. **David dwelt.** Ps 2:6. **the city of David.** that is, *Zion.* ver. 5. 2 S 5:7.

8. **Millo.** Jg 9:6, 20. 2 S +5:7. 1 K 9:15. 11:27. 2 K 12:20. **repaired.** Heb. revived. Ne 4:2.

9. **waxed greater and greater.** Heb. went in going and increasing. 2 S 3:1. 5:10. Est 9:4. Jb 17:9. Pr 4:18. Is *9:7. **for.** 1 Ch 9:20. Ps 46:7, 11. Is 8:9, 10. 41:10, 14. Ro *8:31.

10. A.M. 2949-89. B.C. 1055-1015. An. Ex. Is. 436-476. **the chief.** The valiant men who assisted David in his advancement, and helped to establish him in his authority, were those, in all likelihood, that had accompanied him during his persecution by Saul. 2 S 23:8. **strengthened themselves with.** *or,* held strongly with. Ge 48:2. 2 S 3:6. Da *10:21mg. **to make.** 1 Ch 12:38. 2 S 3:17, 18, 21. **according.** 1 S 16:1, 12-14.

11. **Jashobeam.** i.e. *to whom the people turn; the people will return; he will return among the people.* 2 S 23:8, The Tachmonite, Adino, the Eznite. *S#3434h: 1 Ch 11:11. 12:6. 27:2. (1) A chief of David's captains, 1 Ch 11:11; 27:2. Same as Adino in 2 S 23:8. (2) Another chief of David, 1 Ch 12:6. **an Hach-**

monite. i.e. *wise; very wise; of the wise one; I was wise*, *S#2453h. 1 Ch 11:11. 27:32. *or*, son of Hachmoni. ver. 38. 1 Ch 27:32. **the chief**. 1 Ch 12:18.

12. **Eleazar**. 1 Ch 27:+4, Dodai. Ex +6:23. 2 S 23:9. **Dodo**. 2 S +23:24. This variation arises from the mutations of *wav*, and *yood;* it being written here "Dodo," and in the parallel passage "Dodai." **Ahohite**. 1 Ch 8:4. 2 S +23:9. **the three**. ver. 19, 21. 2 S 23:17-19, 23.

13. **Pas-dammim**. i.e. *dell of bloodshed; vanishing of bloods; he spread out bloods*, *S#6450h. *Ephes-dammim* is here called *Pas-dammim*, by aphaeresis. 1 S +17:1, Ephes-dammim. *f*33. Figure of speech Aphaeresis; or, Front-cut: a figure of etymology which relates to the spelling of words, and is used of the cutting off of a letter or syllable from the beginning of a word. Examples in Scripture include Ephes-dammim being cut to Pas-dammim, and Jeconiah being cut to Coniah: compare 1 Ch 3:16, Jeconiah, with Je 22:24, Coniah. Also Je 37:1. 1 Ch 25:11n. The cutting off of the name corresponds with his being cut off from the throne, together with his sons, for not one of his seven sons (1 Ch 3:17, 18) sat upon his throne (see Je 22:30); only his grandson became governor after Coniah had died in Babylon, 2 K 25:29, 30. For other instances of this figure see 1 Ch 25:11n. 26:1n. Je 22:24. 37:1. **a parcel**. In Samuel it is, "a piece of ground full of *lentiles*," and there is probably a mistake of *seorim*, "barley," for *adashim*, "lentiles," or vice versa. Some, however, think there were both lentiles and barley in the field, which is not unlikely.

14. **set**. *or*, stood. 2 S 23:12. **and the Lord**. 1 S 14:23. 19:5. 2 S 23:10. 2 K 5:1. Ps 18:50. **deliverance**. *or*, salvation. 2 S 19:2. Ps 144:10. Pr 21:31.

15. **of the thirty captains**. *or*, captains over the thirty. 2 S 23:13, etc. **the cave**. Jsh 12:15. 1 S 22:1. Mi 1:15. **in the**. 1 Ch 14:9. 2 S 5:18, 22. Is 17:5. **Rephaim**. Jsh 15:8, the giants. +*17:15. 2 S +5:18.

16. **in the hold**. 1 S 22:1. 23:25. Ps 142:t. **the Philistines'**. 1 S 10:5. 13:4, 23.

17. **longed**. Nu 11:4, 5. 2 S 23:15, 16. Ps 143:6. **Oh**. *f*59, Ge +28:16. **of the water**. Ps 42:1, 2. 63:1. Is 12:3. Jn 4:10, 14. **well**. Heb. *bor*, Ge +37:20. **of Bethlehem**. 2 S 5:23n. 23:15n.

18. **brake**. 1 S 19:5. SS 8:6. Ac 20:24. 21:13. 2 C 5:14, 15. **well**. Heb. *bor*, Ge +37:20. **poured**. 1 S 7:6.

19. **My God**. 2 S 23:17. 1 K 21:3. Ro 6:1, 2. **forbid**. *f*63A1, Ge +14:20. Supply by ellipsis (absolute: of the nominative), "(God) be merciful to me (to keep me from doing) this thing." **shall I**. Le +*17:10. Jb 31:31. Ps 72:14. Mk 14:24. Jn 6:55. **that have put their lives**. Heb. with their lives. Ro 16:4. **lives**. Heb. *ne-phesh*, souls, Ge +44:30. **in jeopardy**. Jg 5:18. 9:17. 1 S 19:5. 1 C 15:30. **These**. See on ver. 12.

20. **Abishai**. 1 Ch 2:16. 1 S +26:6. 2 S 2:18. 3:30. 18:2. 20:6. 21:17. 23:18, 19, etc.

21. **howbeit**. Mt 13:8. 1 C 15:41. **honorable**. 2 S 23:19.

22. **Benaiah**. i.e. *built or son of Jah*. 1 Ch +15:24. 27:5, 6. 2 S 8:18. 20:23. 23:20-23. 1 K 1:8, 38. 2:30, 34, 35. **Jehoiada**. i.e. *Jah hath known*. 2 K +11:4. **Kabzeel**. Jsh +15:21. **who had done many acts**. Heb. great of deeds. **lion-like**. 1 Ch 12:8. 2 S 1:23. 23:20. **slew a**. Jg 14:5, 6. 1 S 17:34-36.

23. **a man of great stature**. Heb. a man of measure.

Nu 13:32. 2 S 21:20. 23:21. Is 45:14. **five cubits**. Dt 3:11. 1 S 17:4. That is, about seven and a half feet. **a spear**. 1 Ch 20:5. **like a weaver's beam**. 1 Ch 20:5. 1 S 17:7. 2 S 21:19. **slew him**. 1 S 17:51.

24. **the three**. 2 S 23:18.

25. **but attained**. ver. 21. **David**. 2 S 20:23.

26. **the valiant men**. 2 S 23:24. *or*, mighty ones. 1 Ch 9:13mg. **Asahel**. 1 Ch +2:16. 27:7. 2 S 2:18-23. 3:30. 23:24. **Elhanan**. i.e. *God has grace*. 2 S +21:19.

27. **Shammoth**. i.e. *desolations*, *S#8054h. Shammah, Shammoth, and as it is in 1 Ch 27:8, Shamhuth, having all the same signification, appear to have been deemed perfectly interchangeable, and accordingly used indifferently. 2 S 23:25, Shammah the Harodite. **Harorite**. i.e. *the mountaineer*, *S#2033h. The variation "Harorite" for "Harodite," arises from the mutation of *raish* and *daleth*. **Helez**. 1 Ch +2:39. **Pelonite**. i.e. *nameless; such an one; a certain unnamed one*, *S#6397h. 1 Ch 11:27, 36. 27:10. In 2 S 23:+26 he is called a Paltite. (1) A name applied to Helez, one of David's valiant men, 1 Ch 11:27; 27:10. Called Paltite in 2 S 23:26. (2) Ahijah, another of David's valiant men, is called the Pelonite in 1 Ch 11:36.

28. **Ira**. i.e. *a watcher*. 1 Ch 27:9. 2 S +20:26. **Ikkesh**. 2 S +23:26. **Tekoite**. 2 S +23:26. **Abi-ezer**. i.e. *father of help*. Jsh +17:2. **Antothite**. i.e. *a native of Anathoth* (i.e. *answers; songs*, 1 Ch +7:8), *S#6069h. 1 Ch 11:28. 12:3. 27:+12, Anetothite. 2 S 23:+27, Anethothite. Je 29:27. This variation springs simply from the points; the word being written "Anethothite" in Samuel, and here "Antothite."

29. **Sibbecai**. i.e. *thicket of Jah; my thickets*, *S#5444h. 1 Ch 11:29. 20:4. 27:11. 2 S 21:18. The reading of "Mebunnai," for "Sibbecai," seems to be occasioned by the mistake of a *samech* for a *mem*, and a *noon* for a *caph;* and a difference in the vowel points. 1 Ch 27:11. 2 S 23:+27, Mebunnai. **Ilai**. i.e. *supreme; most high; my elevations; my sucklings*, *S#5866h. 2 S 23:+28, Zalmon. **Ahohite**. ver. 12.

30. **Maharai**. i.e. *hasting*. 1 Ch 27:13. 2 S +23:28. **Netophathite**. 2 S +23:28. **Heled**. i.e. *the world is transient; the age* (see Heldai, i.e. *life, age, duration*, 1 Ch +27:15), *S#2466h. "Heleb" seems evidently a mistake for "Heled," which is essentially the same with "Heldai," the latter merely having a paragogic *yood*. 1 Ch 27:15, Heldai. 2 S 23:29, Heleb. **Baanah**. 2 S +4:5.

31. **Ithai**. i.e. *there is; my sign; with me*, *S#863h. *S#2833h. The variation of "Ithai" and "Ittai," simply arises from the elision of *yood*, which is compensated by the reduplication of the next letter. 2 S 23:29, Ittai (see on 2 S +15:19). **Ribai**. 2 S +23:29. **Gibeah**. Jg +19:12. **Benaiah**. i.e. *built* or son of Jah. 1 Ch +15:24. **Pirathonite**. Jg +12:15.

32. **Hurai**. i.e. *linen worker; of fine linen; my caves; my white (stuffs)*, *S#2360h. 2 S 23:+30, Hiddai. **Abiel**. 1 S +9:1. 2 S 23:31, Abi-albon. **Arbathite**. 2 S +23:31.

33. **Azmaveth**. 2 S +23:31. *or*, Armaveth. i.e. *strength of death*. **Baharumite**. i.e. *inhabitant of Bahurim* (i.e. *chosen, proved, or beloved; the young; choice youths*, 2 S +3:16), *S#978h. "Barhumhite" seems a mistake for "Baharumite," the letters *cheth* and *raish* being transposed. 2 S 23:+31, Barhumite. **Eliahba**. i.e. *God hides*. 2 S +23:32. **Shaalbonite**. 2 S +23:32.

34. Hashem. i.e. *dull, sleepy; to make desolate,* *S#2044h. 2 S 23:32, Jashen. **Gizonite.** i.e. *shearer; quarryman; stone-quarrier,* *S#1493h. **Jonathan.** i.e. *Jah hath given.* 1 S +13:2. **Shage.** i.e. *wandering, erring; touching softly,* *S#7681h. **Hararite.** 2 S +23:11.

35. Ahiam. i.e. *brother of a mother.* 2 S +23:33. **Sacar.** i.e. *recompense; wages; hire; a hireling,* *S#7940h. 1 Ch 11:35. 26:4. (1) Father of one of David's mighty men, 2 S 23:33, Sharar; 1 Ch 11:35. (2) The fourth son of Obed-edom, and one of the porters, 1 Ch 26:4. **Hararite.** ver. 34. **Eliphal.** i.e. *God is the judge; my God has judged,* *S#465h. 2 S 23:34, Eliphelet. **Ur.** 2 S 23:34, Ahasbai.

36. Hepher. i.e. *a pit.* Nu +26:32. **Mecherathite.** i.e. *inhabitant of Mecherah; he of the dugout; he of the digging tool; swordite (soldier); wicked counsels,* *S#4382h. 2 S 23:34. **Ahijah.** i.e. *brother of Jah.* 1 K +14:6. **Pelonite.** ver. +27. 1 Ch 27:10.

37. Hezro. i.e. *his court; bulwark of the Lord,* *S#2695h. 1 Ch 11:37. 2 S 23:35. Also 2 S 23:+35, Hezrai. The difference between "Hezrai" and "Hezro" appears to be the result of an ancient scribe's confusion of the Hebrew letters *yood* (English *i* and *j*) and *vaw* (English *f*). **Carmelite.** 1 S 30:5. **Naarai.** i.e. *child of the Lord; my boys; my shakings; my roarings,* *S#5293h. 2 S 23:35, Paarai the Arbite. **Ezbai.** i.e. *spoil; my humblings,* *S#229h.

38. Joel. i.e. *Jah is God.* 1 S +8:2. 2 S 23:36, Igal the son of Nathan. **Nathan.** 2 Ch +9:29. **Mibhar.** i.e. *choicest; most choice,* *S#4006h. One of David's valiant men. **Haggeri.** i.e. *wanderer; fugitive; ensnaring; the sojourner,* *S#1905h. 1 Ch 11:38. 27:+31, Hagerite. Also 1 Ch 5:+10, Hagarites, 19, 20. Ps 83:6, Hagarenes. *or,* the Haggerite.

39. Zelek. i.e. *a cleft.* 2 S +23:37. **Ammonite.** 1 S +11:11. **Naharai.** i.e. *snorer; snorter; neigher,* *S#5171h. 1 Ch 11:39. 2 S 23:37. **Berothite.** i.e. *inhabitant of Berothai* (i.e. *wells of the Lord,* 2 S +8:8); *my wells,* *S#1307h. **Joab.** 1 S +26:6. **Zeruiah.** 1 Ch +2:16.

40. Ira. i.e. *watcher.* ver. 28. **Ithrite.** 2 S +23:38. 2 S 20:26, Jairite. **Gareb.** i.e. *scurvy.* 2 S +23:38.

41. Uriah. i.e. *light of Jah.* 2 S 11:6, etc. 23:39. **Zabad.** i.e. *dowry.* This name and those following in ver. 42-47 are additional to the list in 2 S 23:8-39 (Young). 1 Ch 2:31, +36. **Ahlai.** i.e. *Jehovah is staying; wishful; would to God!; O, would that,* *S#304h. 1 Ch 2:31. 11:41. (1) A daughter of Shehan, 1 Ch 2:31. (2) Father of one of David's valiant men, 1 Ch 11:41.

42. Adina. i.e. *luxuriant; effeminate; soft, pliant, pleasant; voluptuous,* *S#5721h. **Shiza.** i.e. *raising up; who sprinkled; brightness,* *S#7877h.

43. Hanan. i.e. *gracious.* 1 Ch +9:44. **Maachah.** 1 K +2:39. **Joshaphat.** i.e. *Jehovah is judge,* *S#3146h. 1 Ch 11:43. 15:24. **Mithnite.** i.e. *slenderness; strength; an athlete (literally, he of loins); a giver,* *S#4981h.

44. Uzzia. i.e. *strength of God; power of God,* *S#5814h. **Ashterathite.** i.e. *a native of Ashtaroth* (i.e. *queen of heaven; thought searching).* Jsh 9:10. **Shama.** i.e. *a hearkener; hearing,* *S#8091h. **Jehiel.** i.e. *removed of God.* 1 Ch +9:35. **Hothan.** i.e. *signet-ring,* *S#2369h. 1 Ch 7:+32, Hotham. 11:44. Some regard "Hothan" to be an incorrect spelling of "Hotham." **Aroerite.** i.e. *gentilic of Aroer* (i.e. *destitute;*

naked; a naked tree, or heath, Nu 32:34); *a native or inhabitant of Aroer* (1 S 30:28), *S#6200h.

45. Jediael. 1 Ch +7:6. **the son of Shimri.** 1 Ch +4:37. *or,* the Shimrite. **Joha.** 1 Ch +8:16. **Tizite.** i.e. *going forth; thou shalt go forth,* *S#8491h.

46. Eliel. i.e. *my God is God.* 1 Ch +8:20. **Mahavite.** i.e. *assemblers; places of assembly; declarers; propagators; living ones,* *S#4233h. **Jeribai.** i.e. *my contender; defended; he will contend,* *S#3403h. **Joshaviah.** i.e. *Jehovah-set; set upright of the Lord; he will be prospered of Jah; may Jah sustain him,* *S#3145h. **Elnaam.** i.e. *God is delight; God of pleasantness,* *S#493h. **Ithmah.** i.e. *orphanage; bereavedness, loneliness; orphanhood,* *S#3495h. **Moabite.** Dt +23:3.

47. Eliel. ver. 46. **Obed.** i.e. *serving.* Ru +4:17. **Jasiel.** i.e. *made by God.* *S#3300h. 1 Ch 11:47. 27:21, Jaasiel. **Mesobaite.** i.e. *found of Jah; congregation of the Lord; the one set up of Jah,* *S#4677h.

1 CHRONICLES 12

The companies which came to David at Ziklag, 1-22. The armed troops that came to him at Hebron, 23-40.

1. these are. 1 S 27:2, 6. 2 S 1:1. 4:10. **while he yet,** etc. Heb. *being* yet shut up. Sometimes, in the East, when a successful prince endeavored to extirpate the preceding royal family, some of them escaped the slaughter, and secured themselves in an impregnable fortress, or in a place of great secrecy; while others have been known to seek an asylum in a foreign country, from whence they have occasioned, from time to time, great anxiety and great difficulties to the usurper of the crown. The expression *shut up,* so often applied to the extermination of eastern royal families (Dt 32:36. 1 K 14:10. 21:21. 2 K 9:8. 14:26), strictly speaking, refers to the two first of these cases; but the term may be used in a more extensive sense, for those who, by retiring into deserts, or foreign countries, preserve themselves from being slain by the men who usurp the dominions of their ancestors. Thus the term is here applied to David, though he did not shut himself up, strictly speaking, in Ziklag. It is described as a town in the country, and was probably an unwalled town; and it is certain that he did not confine himself to it, but, on the contrary, was continually making excursions from thence. **Saul.** 1 Ch 8:33. 9:39. **the mighty men.** 1 Ch 11:10, 19, 24, 25.

2. armed with bows. 2 Ch 17:17. Ps 78:9. **could use both.** Jg 3:15. 20:15, 16. Jb 36:32. **in hurling.** 1 S 17:49.

3. Ahiezer. i.e. *brother of help,* *S#295h. 1 Ch 12:3. Nu 1:12. 2:25. 7:66, 71. 10:25. (1) Danite captain, Nu 1:12; 2:25; 7:66. (2) Chief that came to David at Ziklag, 1 Ch 12:3. **Joash.** 1 Ch +7:8. **Shemaah.** i.e. *obeying; hearing, fame, report; the hearkener,* *S#8094h. *or,* Hasmaah. **Gibeathite.** i.e. *inhabitant of Gibeah* (i.e. *the hill,* Jg +19:12), *S#1395h. 1 S 11:4. 2 S 21:6. **Jeziel.** i.e. *sprinkled of God; assembly of God; let him be sprinkled of God,* *S#3149h. **Pelet.** i.e. *liberation; escape; deliverance,* *S#6404h. 1 Ch 2:47. 12:3. (1) A son of Jahdai, descendant of Caleb, 1 Ch 2:47. (2) One that came to David at Ziklag, 1 Ch 12:3. **Azmaveth.** i.e. *strength of death.* 1 Ch

11:33. 2 S +23:31. **Berachah**. i.e. *blessing; prosperity; benediction*, *S#1294h. **Jehu**. i.e. *he is*. 2 K +9:2. **Antothite**. 1 Ch +11:28. 27:12. Jsh 21:18.

4. **Ismaiah**. i.e. *whom Jehovah hears; Jah will hear; he will hear the Lord*, *S#3460h. 1 Ch 12:4. Also 1 Ch 27:19. (1) A mighty Gibeonite, who came to David to Ziklag, 1 Ch 12:4. (2) A prince of Zebulun, 1 Ch 27:19. **the Gibeonite**. Jsh 9:3, 17-23. **a mighty man**. 1 Ch 11:15. **Jeremiah**. Je +1:1. **Jahaziel**. i.e. *God sees*. 1 Ch +24:33. **Johanan**. i.e. *God has grace*. 2 K +25:23. **Josabad**. i.e. *God has endowed; Jehovah is bestower*, *S#3107h. 1 Ch 12:4, 20, 20. 2 Ch +31:13, Jozabad. 35:9. Ezr 8:33. 10:22, 23. Ne 8:7. 11:16. **Gederathite**. i.e. *inhabitant of Gederah* (i.e. *a wall or fence*, Jsh +15:36), *S#1452h. Jsh 15:36.

5. **Eluzai**. i.e. *God is my refuge* or *strength; God of my gathering; God is my praise; God is my gathering strength (for flight)*, *S#498h. **Jerimoth**. i.e. *high places*. 1 Ch +7:7. **Bealiah**. i.e. *mastered of Jah; possession of the Lord*, *S#1183h. **Shemariah**. i.e. *guarded of Jehovah; kept by Jah*, *S#8114h. (1) A soldier of David at Ziklag, 1 Ch 12:5. (2, 3) Two Jews who took foreign wives, Ezr 10:32, 41. **Shephatiah**. i.e. *judged by Jah*. 1 Ch +9:8, Shephathiah. 2 S +3:4. **Haruphite**. i.e. *descendants of Haruph or Hariph* (i.e. *maturity; time of fruit*, Ne +7:24); *matured*, *S#2741h.

6. **Elkanah**. i.e. *God has acquired*. Ex +6:24. **Jesiah**. i.e. *Jah will lend; he will be lent of Jehovah*, *S#3449h. (1) An Israelite who came to David in Ziklag, 1 Ch 12:6. (2) A Levite, 1 Ch 23:20, same as Jeshaiah in 1 Ch 26:25. **Azareel**. i.e. *whom God helps; helped by God*, *S#5832h. 1 Ch 12:6. 25:18. 27:22. Ezr 10:41. Ne 11:13. +12:36, Azarael. (1) One that came to David to Ziklag, 1 Ch 12:6. (2) A singer to whom the eleventh lot fell, 1 Ch 25:18. (3) A prince of Dan, 1 Ch 27:22. (4) Father of Amashai, Ne 11:13. (5) One engaged at the dedication of the walls, Ne 12:36. (6) One who took strange wives, Ezr 10:41. **Joezer**. i.e. *Jah is help; he that aids or assists; Lord of help*, *S#3134h. **Jashobeam**. i.e. *the people hath dwelt*. 1 Ch +11:11. **Korhites**. Ex +6:24.

7. **Joelah**. i.e. *Jah helps; removing of oaks; let him be profitable; he will sweep away the strong*, *S#3132h. **Zebadiah**. i.e. *endowed by Jah*. 1 Ch 26:2. **Jeroham**. i.e. *he has pity*. 1 S +1:1. **Gedor**. 1 Ch 4:18, 39. Jsh +15:58.

8. **into the hold**. ver. 16. 1 Ch 11:16. 1 S 23:14, 29. 24:22. **men of might**. lit. mighty men of valor. 1 Ch +9:13mg. Is +10:21 (*S#1308h). **of war**. Heb. of the host. **handle**. 2 Ch 25:5. Je 46:9. **whose faces**. 1 Ch 11:22. 2 S 1:23. 17:10. 23:20. Pr 28:1. **as swift as the roes upon the mountains**. Heb. as the roes upon the mountains to make haste. 2 S 2:18. Pr 6:5. SS 8:14.

9. **Ezer**. i.e. *help*. Ge +36:21. **Obadiah**. i.e. *servant of Jah*. Ob +1. **Eliab**. i.e. *my God is father*. Nu +1:9.

10. **Mishmannah**. i.e. *fatness; fattening*, *S#4925h. **Jeremiah**. ver. 4, 13.

11. **Attai**. i.e. *my time*. 1 Ch +2:35. **Eliel**. i.e. *my God is God*. 1 Ch +8:20.

12. **Johanan**. i.e. *God has grace*. 2 K +25:23. **Elzabad**. i.e. *God has endowed*. 1 Ch +26:7.

13. **Jeremiah**. ver. 4, 10. **Machbanai**. i.e. *bond of the Lord; he brought low my sons*, *S#4344h.

14. **one of the least**, etc. or, one that was least

could resist an hundred, and the greatest a thousand. Le 26:8. Dt 32:30.

15. **the first month**. Ex 12:2. Jsh 3:15. **it had overflown**. Heb. it had filled over. Jsh 3:15. 4:18. Je *12:5. 49:19.

16. **the children**. ver. 2. **the hold**. See on ver. 8.

17. **to meet them**. Heb. before them. **If ye be come**. 1 S 16:4. 2 S 3:20-25. 1 K 2:13. 2 K 9:22. Ps 12:1, 2. **heart**. 1 S 18:1, 3. 2 K 10:15. Ps 86:11. 2 C 13:11. Ph 1:27. **knit**. Heb. be one. Jg 20:1. 1 S 18:1. 2 Ch 5:13. Je 32:39. Ac 4:32. 1 C 1:10. **betray**. or, deceive. Ge 29:25. Jsh 9:22. 1 S 19:17. 28:12. 2 S 19:26. Pr *26:19. La 1:19. **wrong**. or, violence. Ge 16:5. Jb 16:17. *19:7mg. Is 53:9. **God**. Ge 31:42, 53. 1 S 24:11-17. 26:23, 24. Ps 7:6. 1 P 2:23. **rebuke it**. Ge 20:16. 21:25. 31:42. Zc 3:2. Ju 9.

18. **the spirit**. Heb. *ruach*, Ge +41:38. Jg 6:34. 13:25. Is 59:17. **came upon**. Heb. clothed. Jg *6:34mg. **Amasai**. 1 Ch 2:17. 2 S 17:+25. 19:13. 20:4, etc., Amasa. 2 Ch +29:12. **and on thy side**. Ru 1:16. 2 S 15:21. 2 K 9:32. Mt 12:30. **peace**. Ga 6:16. Ep 6:23, 24. **thy God**. 1 S 25:28, 29. 2 S 5:2. Zc 8:23. Jn 6:67, 68. **captains of the band**. 1 S 8:12. 22:7. 1 K 9:22.

19. **when he came**. 1 S 29:2-4. **to the jeopardy of our heads**. Heb. on our heads. 1 S 29:4.

20. **As he went**. These captains of Manasseh seem to have met with David as he was returning from the army of the Philistines to Ziklag. It is probable that they did not bring their companies with them; yet they both assured him of future assistance, and very seasonably helped him against the Amalekites who had spoiled Ziklag. 1 S 29:11. **Adnah**. i.e. *resting forever; time* or *pleasure*, *S#5734h. 1 Ch 12:20. Also 2 Ch 17:14. (1) One that came to David at Ziklag, 1 Ch 12:20. (2) One of Jehoshaphat's captains, 2 Ch 17:14. **Jozabad**. i.e. *Jah has endowed*. 2 Ch +31:13. **Jediael**. i.e. *God knows*. 1 Ch +7:6. **Michael**. i.e. *who is like God?* Da +12:1. **Elihu**. i.e. *my God is He*. 1 S +1:1. **Zilthai**. i.e. *my shadow*. 1 Ch +8:20. **captains of the thousands**. Ex +18:21. Dt 1:15. 33:17. Mi +*5:2.

21. **against the band**. or, with a band. 1 S 30:1-17. **mighty men**. ver. 20. 1 Ch 5:24. 9:13mg. 11:10, 21, 22. Jg +6:12. 2 S +2:7mg.

22. **day by day**. 2 S 2:2-4. 3:1. Jb 17:9. **like the host**. That is, says the Targumist, a very numerous army, like the army of the angel of God. Ge 32:2. Jsh 5:14. Ps 148:2. **of God**. Ge +*23:6mg. 1 S 14:15mg. Jb 1:16mg. *J*24L, Antimereia. Ge +*6:2.

23. A.M. 2956. B.C. 1048. An. Ex. Is. 433. **the numbers**. 1 Ch 11:1-3. 2 S 2:3, 4. 5:1-3. **bands**. or, captains, or men. Heb. heads. Jb 1:17. **came to David**. Some learned men understand this as relating to the time when David was made king over Judah, on his first coming to Hebron: but it seems wholly to refer to his being made king over all Israel, after the death of Ishbosheth; for there was no such union or assembly of the several tribes on the former occasion, as is here described. **to turn**. 1 Ch 10:14. **according**. 1 Ch 11:10. 1 S 16:1, 3, 12, 13. 2 S 3:18. Ps 2:6. 89:19, 20.

24. **spear**. 2 Ch 25:5. **armed**. or, prepared. Nu 31:5.

25. **children of Simeon**. 1 Ch 4:39-43. Ge 49:5. Nu 2:12. 10:19. 13:5. 34:20. Dt 27:12. Jsh 19:1. Jg 1:3. 2 Ch 15:9. 34:6.

26. **children of Levi**. ver. 6. Ge +29:34. Nu 1:47.

27. **Jehoiada**. i.e. *Jah hath known*. 2 K +11:4. **the leader**. 1 Ch 9:20. 2 K 11:4, 9. 25:18. **Aaronites**. i.e.

descendants of Aaron (i.e. *very high*, Ex +4:14), S#175h. 1 Ch 6:49-57. 27:17.

28. **Zadok.** 1 Ch 6:8, 53. 2 S +8:17. 1 K 1:8. 2:35. Ezk 44:15.

29. **kindred.** Heb. brethren. *171G*, Ge +13:8. ver. 2. Ge 31:23. **the greatest part of them.** Heb. a multitude of them. 2 S 2:8, 9. 2 Ch 30:18.

30. **famous.** Heb. men of names. 1 Ch 5:24mg. Ge 6:4.

31. **the half tribe.** Jsh ch. 17.

32. **had understanding.** 2 Ch 11:23. Jg ❍+9:37mg. Ezr 8:16. Ps ❍*74:9. Je ❍+8:7. Da *12:4, 9, 10. Mt +*24:45. Lk ❍+*11:52. Ac ❍*1:7. That is, as the following words indicate, intelligent men, who understood the signs of the times, well versed in political affairs, and knew what was proper to be done in all the exigencies of human life; and who now perceived that it was both the duty and political interest of Israel to advance David to the throne. Matthew Poole notes the possibility that this may be a reference to "Skill in the stars, and several seasons and changes of the air; which might be of good use in husbandry, to which this tribe was addicted, Ge 49:14; Dt 33:18." Lk +*3:14n. **the times.** Ge 49:14. Est *1:13. Is 22:12-14. 33:6. Mi 6:9. Mt 16:3. Lk *12:56, 57. *121P1. Figure of speech Metonymy of the Adjunct: the change of one noun for another related noun; here, "time" is put for the things done in it, or existing in it. Here, understanding of the times refers to those who understood statesmanship, and those who understood what was needful to be done in the times at hand. For other instances of this figure see Est *1:13. Jb 11:17. Ps *31:15. 2 T *3:1. **to know.** Pr 14:8. Ep 5:17. **all their.** Pr 24:5. Ec 7:19. 9:18.

33. **expert in war.** or, rangers of battle, or ranged in battle. ver. 35. **keep rank.** or, set the battle in array. **they were not of double heart.** Heb. they were without a heart and a heart. That is, they were all sincerely affected towards David, though so numerous. Ps 12:2. Jn 1:47.

34. **Naphtali.** Ge +30:8.

35. **Danites.** Jg +13:2.

36. **Asher.** Ge +30:13. Dt +*33:24n. **expert in war.** or, keeping their rank. ver. 33. Jl 2:7.

37. **the other side.** 1 Ch 5:1, etc. Nu 32:33-42. Dt 3:12-16. Jsh 13:7-32. 14:3. 22:1-10.

38. **came with.** Ps 12:3. 28:3. **with a perfect heart.** *121I1, Ge +3:7. "Heart" put for affections and desires. The meaning of this expression may be inferred from that of *a double heart* in ver. 33. If a double heart be expressive of insincerity or duplicity, a *perfect heart*, which seems to be put in opposition to it, must signify a sincere, faithful, and entire attachment. 1 K 8:61. 11:4. 2 K +*20:3. Ps 37:18n. 101:2. **all the rest.** ver. 17, 18. Ge *49:8-10. 2 Ch 30:12. Ps 110:3. Ezk 11:19. **one.** Heb. *yahad*. Dt ❍+*6:4. 2 S 19:14. 2 Ch 30:12. Ps 133:1. Ac 4:32. **heart.** Ps 12:2. 1 T 3:8. Ja 1:8.

39. **eating and drinking.** Ge 26:30. 31:54. 2 S 6:19. 19:42.

40. **brought.** The Septuagint reads *epheron autois*, "brought (to) *them*," which is probably correct; the Hebrew *lahem*, "to them," might be easily mistaken for *lechem*, "bread." The passage will then read "brought them on asses, on camels, and on mules, and on oxen, meat, meal, cakes of figs," etc. which renders the introduction of *and* unnecessary. From

the mention of *oil, figs*, and *raisins*, Mr. Harmer thinks that this assembly was held in autumn. 2 S 16:1. 17:27-29. **camels.** 1 S 27:9. 2 K 8:9. 2 Ch 9:1. **meat, meal.** or, victual of meal. or, fine flour. Ge 18:6. Nu 5:15. Jg 6:19. 1 S 1:24. 28:24. 2 S 17:28. 1 K 4:22. 17:12, 14, 16. **cakes of figs.** 1 S 25:18. 30:12. 2 K 20:7. Ne 13:15. Is 38:21. **bunches of raisins.** 1 S 25:18. 30:12. 2 S 16:1. Young translates "fig cakes, grape cakes." **wine.** Ge 9:21. 2 S 6:17-19. **oil.** Dt 12:17. 1 K 17:12. **sheep.** Dt 14:4. 23:14. **there was joy.** 1 K 1:40. 2 K 11:20. 2 Ch 30:22-26. Pr 11:10. 29:2. Je *23:5, 6. Lk 19:37, 38. Re 19:5-7.

1 CHRONICLES 13

David, with the princes and people, with great solemnity and zeal, fetches the ark from Kirjath-jearim, 1-8. Uzza is smitten, David is disconcerted, and the ark is left at the house of Obed-edom, 9-14.

1. **consulted.** 1 Ch 12:14, 20, 32. 2 S 6:1. 2 K 23:1. 2 Ch 29:20. 34:29, 30.

2. **If it seem.** 1 K 12:7. 2 K 9:15. Pr 15:22. Phm 8, 9. **and that it be.** Ex 18:23. 2 S 7:2-5. **send abroad.** Heb. break forth, *and* send. 1 Ch 4:38. Ge +28:14mg. 2 Ch 31:5mg. **left.** 1 Ch 10:7. 1 S 31:1. Is 37:4. **the priests.** 1 Ch 15:2-14. Nu 4:44, etc. 2 Ch 31:4, etc. **their cities and suburbs.** Heb. the cities of their suburbs. 1 Ch 6:54-81. Nu 35:2-9.

3. **bring again.** Heb. bring about. **the ark.** 1 S 7:1, 2. Ps 132:6. **we enquired.** 1 S 14:18, 36. 22:10, 15. 23:2, 9-12.

4. **the thing.** 1 S 18:20. 2 S 3:36. 2 Ch 30:4mg. Est 8:5.

5. **David.** 1 S 7:1. 2 S 6:1. **Shihor.** i.e. *turbid, very black, breaking forth.* Nu 34:5-8. Jsh 13:3-6, Sihor. 1 K 4:21. Je 2:18, Sihor. ✳S#7883h: 1 Ch 13:5. Jsh 13:3, Sihor. Is 23:3. Je 2:18, Sihor. **Hemath.** 1 Ch +2:55. Nu 34:8. Jsh 13:5. 1 K 8:65. 2 K 25:21, Hamath. **Kirjath-jearim.** ver. 6. Jsh +9:17. 1 S 6:21. 7:1.

6. **Baalah.** Jsh 15:+9, 60. 2 S 6:2, Baale. **that dwelleth.** Ex 25:22. Nu 7:89. 1 S 4:4. 2 K 19:15. Ps 80:1. 99:1. Is 37:16. **whose name.** Ex 20:24. 23:21. Nu 6:27. 1 K 8:16.

7. **carried the ark.** Heb. made the ark to ride. At Nu 3:10, and again at ver. 38, a particular caution is given that strangers must not touch, or even pry into, the most holy things connected with the tabernacle, *lest the offender die.* In giving the law, also, even a beast which touched Sinai's mount was, by the Almighty's fiat, to be stoned or thrust through with a dart. And again we read (Nu 4:15), after special orders to Aaron and his son about *covering* the sanctuary and all the vessels previously to a removal, that the Kohathites, who were to carry them, "shall not touch any holy thing, lest they die." These were positive commands. May the sin of Uzza in touching the ark, warn Christians to take heed of rashness and irreverence in dealing about holy things: see ver. 9, 10. Hab 2:20. **in a new cart.** 1 Ch 15:2, 13. Nu 4:15. 1 S 6:7. 2 S 6:3. **out of the house.** 1 S 7:1, 2.

8. **David.** 1 Ch 15:10-24. 1 S 10:5. 2 S 6:5, etc. 2 K 3:15. Ps 47:5. 68:25-27. 150:3-5. **singing.** Heb. songs. Ge 31:27. Jg 5:12. 1 K 4:32. **with harps.** The word *kinnor*, in Chaldee, *kinnora*, in Syriac *kainoro*, in Arabic, *kinnarat*, and in Greek *kinuros*, certainly denotes a *harp*, played on with the hand, according

to 1 S 16:23. The number of strings in the harp was at first three; but afterwards they were increased to four, and at last to seven. 1 Ch 15:28. 15:16, 21. 16:5, 42. 23:5. 25:1-6. Ge 4:21. 31:27. 1 S 10:5. 16:16, 23. 2 S 6:5. 1 K 10:12. Da 3:5-7. Am 5:23. 6:5. **psalteries.** *Naivel*, or *nablium*, in Greek *nabla*, and in Latin *nablium*, was an instrument of the harp kind; having twelve sounds. 1 S 10:5. **timbrels.** Ge 31:27. **cymbals.** 1 Ch 15:16, 19, 28. 16:5. √42. 25:1, 6. 2 Ch 5:12, 13. 29:25. Ezr 3:10. Ne 12:27. **trumpets.** Nu 10:2, 8, 9, 10. 2 K +11:14.

9. **threshingfloor.** Ge +50:10. Dt +*16:13mg. **Chidon.** i.e. *a spear, shield, dart; great destruction,* *S#3592h. 2 S 6:+6, Nachon. **stumbled.** *or*, shook it. *or*, were released. Ex 23:11. Dt 15:2, 3. 2 S *6:6. 2 K *9:33. Ps 141:6. Je 17:4.

10. **he put.** 1 Ch 15:13, 15. Nu 4:15. Jsh 6:6. **there he died.** Le 10:1-3. Nu 16:35. 1 S 6:19. 2 Ch 26:16-20. Ps *89:7. 1 C 11:30-32.

11. **displeased.** Ge 4:5. 2 S 6:7-9. Jon 4:4, 9. **breach.** 1 Ch 14:11mg. Ge 38:29. Jg 21:15. 2 S 5:20. 1 K 11:27. Ne 6:1. Jb 16:14. 30:14. **Perez-uzza.** *that is,* The breach of Uzza. i.e. *the breach was strengthened,* *S#6560h. 1 Ch 16:11. 2 S 6:8. **to this day.** 1 Ch +4:43. Ge 32:32. Dt +29:4. 34:6. Jsh +*4:9.

12. **afraid of God.** Nu 17:12, 13. 1 S 5:10, 11. 6:20. Ps 119:120. Is 6:5. Lk 5:8, 9. **How.** 1 K 8:27. Jb 25:5, 6. Mt 25:24.

13. **brought.** Heb. removed. 2 S 6:10. **Obed-edom.** i.e. *servant of Edom.* 1 Ch 15:18, 21, 24. 16:5. 26:4, 8. 2 S 6:+10, 11. **the Gittite.** 2 S 4:3. +6:10. Young suggests, "perhaps he was of Gath-Rimmon, a Levitical city, as in Jsh 21:24."

14. **the Lord blessed.** 1 Ch 26:5. Ge 30:27. 39:5. 2 Ch 25:24. Pr *3:9, 10. *10:22. Ml *3:10, 11.

1 CHRONICLES 14

Hiram sends timber and builders to build David a house, 1. He prospers in his kingdom, takes more wives, and has several children, 2, 3. The names of his sons, 4-7. He gains two signal victories over the Philistines, 8-17.

1. A.M. 2961. B.C. 1043. An. Ex. Is. 448. **Hiram.** 2 S 5:11, 12, etc. 1 K 5:1, 8-12. 2 Ch 2:11, 12, Huram. **and timber.** 1 Ch 22:2. 1 K 5:6, 9, 10, 18. 2 Ch 2:3, 8-10. Ezr 3:7. **to build him.** 1 Ch 17:1. 2 S 7:2. 1 K 7:1-12. Je 22:13-15.

2. **the Lord.** 1 Ch 17:17. 2 S 7:16. Ps 89:20-37. **his kingdom.** Nu 24:7. 2 S 7:8. **because.** 1 K 10:9. 2 Ch 2:11. Est 4:14. Is 1:25-27. Da 2:30.

3. **took.** 1 Ch 3:1-4. Dt 17:17. 2 S 5:13. 1 K 11:3. Pr 5:18, 19. Ec 7:26-29. 9:9. Ml 2:14, 15. Mt 19:4, 5, 8. **more.** Heb. yet. **wives.** Ge +4:19.

4. **Shammua.** i.e. *heard.* 1 Ch 3:5, etc., Shimea. Nu +13:4. 2 S 5:+14, Shammuah. **Shobab.** i.e. *bringer back.* 2 S 5:14. **Nathan.** i.e. *he gave.* 2 S 12:1. Lk 3:31. **Solomon.** i.e. *peace.* 1 Ch 22:9-12. 28:5, 6. 2 S 12:24, 25. 1 K 1:13, 17. 2:15. 3:3, 5-11. Mt 1:6.

5. **Ibhar.** i.e. *he chooses.* 2 S +5:15. **Elishua.** i.e. *my God saves.* 1 Ch 3:6, Elishama. 2 S +5:15. **Elpalet.** i.e. *God has escaped; God is escape,* *S#467h. 1 Ch +*3:6, Eliphelet. 2 S +5:16, Eliphalet.

6. **Nogah.** i.e. *shining, brightness.* 1 Ch +3:7. **Nepheg.** i.e. *a going forth.* 2 S +5:15. **Japhia.** i.e. *he breathes.* Jsh +10:3.

7. **Elishama.** i.e. *God hears.* Nu +1:10. **Beeliada.** i.e. *the Lord has known; lord of knowledge,* *S#1182h. Probably *Beeliada* is a mistake for *Eliada,* as the LXX., Syriac, and Arabic read here. 1 Ch 3:8. 2 S 5:16, Eliada. **and Eliphalet.** i.e. *God escapes.* 1 Ch 3:8, Eliphelet. 2 S 5:16. This variation merely arises from the change of vowel. Here we have 13 persons mentioned, but only 11 in Samuel; and it is probable that the duplicate *Elishama* and *Eliphelet* dying when young, were therefore omitted in the latter.

8. A.M. 2957. B.C. 1047. An. Ex. Is. 444. **And when.** 1 S 21:11. 2 S 5:17-25. **anointed.** 1 Ch 11:3. 2 S 5:3. **all the Philistines.** Ps 2:1-6. Re 11:15-18.

9. **the valley.** 1 Ch 11:15. 2 S 5:18. 23:13. Is 17:5.

10. **enquired.** T#1226. ver. 14, 15. 1 Ch 13:3. Jg 6:15, 16. 20:18, 23, 28. 1 S 7:8. 14:36, 37. 23:2-4, 9-12. 2 S 2:1. 5:19, 23, 24. 1 K 8:44, 45. 2 Ch 20:2-4. **Shall I go.** 1 S 30:8. Pr *3:6. **Go up.** Jg 4:6, 7. 1 K 22:6, 15-17.

11. **Baal-perazim.** i.e. *a place of breaches.* 2 S 5:20mg. Is 28:21. **God.** Ps 18:13-15. 44:3. 144:1, 10. **like the breaking.** Ex 14:28. Jb 30:14. Mt 7:27. **Baal-perazim.** *that is,* a place of breaches.

12. **were burned.** Ex 12:12. 32:20. Dt 7:5, 25. 1 S 5:2-6. 2 K 19:18.

13. **yet again.** ver. 9. 2 S 5:22-25. 1 K 20:22.

14. **enquired again.** ver. 10. Ps 27:4. **turn away.** Jsh 8:2-7. Jn 9:6, 7. **mulberry trees.** 2 S √5:23n. Ps 84:6mg. 2 K 18:17n.

15. **when thou shalt hear.** Some, taking the word *bechaim,* translated "mulberry trees," as a proper name, render, "when thou shalt hear a sound of going upon the summits of *Bechaim;*" others understanding *rosh,* "a top," in the sense of beginning or entrance, read, "when thou hearest a sound of footsteps at the entrance of the grove of mulberry trees;" and others think that a *rustling* among the leaves is intended. The Targumist reads, "When thou shalt hear the sound of the angels coming to thy assistance, then go out to battle; for an angel is sent from the presence of God, that he may render thy way prosperous." If there had not been an evident *supernatural* interference, David might have thought that the *ruse de guerre* (French, "strategem of war") which he had used, was the cause of his victory. Le 26:36. 2 K 7:6. 19:7. Ac 2:2. Taking the information from the note on 2 S 5:23n, where Robert Dick Wilson is cited to show that "baca" has reference, not to mulberry trees, but an underground acqueduct, and the hints given in the note above, very provisionally it might be suggested that the "sound of going in the mulberry trees" was either the sound of wind or rushing air flowing through the acqueduct, indicating either that it was now safe to enter and traverse, or that the top of it at some point had been opened which admitted fresh air, so making the sound, and indicating it was safe to enter. David's men then entered the acqueduct, crawled through it to the point where a well shaft went up into the city of Jebus inside the wall, ascended the shaft, and thus, gaining entrance to what had heretofore been an impregnable city, easy of defence, conquered it. Thus the references in the note above to "top," "summit," and "footsteps at the entrance," when taken in the light that what is referred to is an acqueduct, not a grove of mulberry trees, some semblance of an idea of David's actual strategem may be discerned. Perhaps hearing footsteps at the

entrance was a signal for David to know to pursue his attack, as such a sound would indicate his men had successfully traversed the acqueduct and associated shafts. **then thou.** Jg 4:14. 7:9, 15. 1 S 14:9-22. Ph 2:12, 13. **for God.** Is 13:4. 45:1, 2. Mi 2:12, 13.

16. **did as God.** Ge 6:22. Ex 39:42, 43. Jn *2:5. 13:17. 15:14. **Gibeon.** i.e. *hilly; high hill; little hill.* 2 S 5:25, Geba. *S#1391h: 1 Ch 8:29, 29. 9:35, 35. 14:16. 16:39. 21:29. Jsh 9:3, 17. 10:1, +2, 4, 5, 6, 10, 12, 41. 11:19. 18:25. 21:17. 2 S 2:12, 13, 16, 24. 3:30. 20:8. 1 K 3:4, 5. 9:2. 2 Ch 1:3, 13. Ne 3:7. 7:25. Is 28:21. Je 28:1. 41:12, 16. **Gazer.** 1 Ch 6:67. Jsh 16:10, Gezer. 2 S +5:25.

17. **fame of David.** Jsh 6:27. 2 Ch 26:8. Ps 18:44. **all lands.** *♫171A, Ex +9:6. **the fear of him.** Ex 15:14-16. Dt 2:25. 11:25. Jsh 2:9-11. 9:24. **all nations.** *♫171A, Ex +9:6.

1 CHRONICLES 15

David prepares a place for the ark, and gives orders to the priests and Levites, about bringing it from the house of Obed-edom, 1-24. He and all the chiefs of Israel attend its removal, with sacrifices and songs of praise, 25-28. Michal despises David for dancing before the ark, 29.

1. A.M. 2962. B.C. 1042. **And.** 1 S 6:12-23 abbreviates this and the following chapter. **houses.** 2 S 5:9. 13:7, 8. 14:24. **and prepared.** ver. 3. 1 Ch 16:1. 17:1-5. Ps 132:5. Ac 7:46.

2. **None ought to,** etc. Heb. *It is* not to carry the ark of God, but for the Levites. Jn=3:7. Ro=8:8. **them hath.** Nu 4:2-15, 19, 20. 7:9. Dt *10:8. 31:9. Jsh 3:3. 6:6. 2 Ch 35:3. **chosen.** Ac=9:15. **to minister.** Nu 8:13, 14, 24-26. 18:1-8. Is 66:21. Je 33:17-22. **for ever.** Ex +*12:24.

3. **gathered.** 1 Ch 13:5. 1 K 8:1. **to bring up.** ver. 1. 2 S 6:12.

4. **the children of Aaron.** 1 Ch 6:16-20, 49, 50. 12:26-28. Ex 6:16-22. Nu 3:4.

5. **Uriel.** i.e. *flame of God; light or fire of God; my light is God,* *S#222h. 1 Ch 6:24. 15:5, 11. 2 Ch 13:2. (1) A Levite, son of Kohath, 1 Ch 6:24; (2) Chief of the Kohathites, 1 Ch 15:5, 11. (3) Father of Michaiah, mother of king Abijah, 2 Ch 13:2. **brethren.** *or,* kinsmen. ver. 6-10, 12, 16-18. 1 Ch 7:22n. 16:7.

6. **Merari.** 1 Ch 6:29, 30. 23:6. Ge +46:11. Ex 6:16. Nu 26:57. **Asaiah.** i.e. *made by Jah.*

7. **Gershom.** Ex +2:22. The eldest son of Aaron. **Joel.** i.e. *Jah is God.* ver. 11. 1 Ch 23:8.

8. **Elizaphan.** i.e. *my God has hidden.* Ex 6:22, Elzaphan. **Shemaiah.** i.e. *heard by Jah.* ver. 11. 1 Ch +9:16.

9. **Hebron.** i.e. *companionship.* 1 Ch 6:2. 23:12, 19. 26:23, 30, 31. Ex +6:18. Nu 26:58. **Eliel.** i.e. *my God is God.* 1 Ch +8:20.

10. **Uzziel.** i.e. *my strength is God.* 1 Ch 6:18. 23:12. Ex 6:+18, 22. **Amminadab.** i.e. *my people is willing.* 1 Ch 6:22.

11. **Zadok.** 1 Ch 12:28. 18:16. 1 S 22:20-23. 2 S +8:17. 15:24-29, 35. 20:25. 1 K 2:35. **Abiathar.** 1 S 22:20. 1 K 2:26. **Uriel.** See on ver. 5-10. **Amminadab.** i.e. *kindred of the prince; my people is willing; people of the willing giver; people of liberality,* *S#5992h. 1 Ch 2:10, 10. 6:22. 15:10, 11. Ex 6:23. Nu 1:7. 2:3. 7:12, 17. 10:14. Ru 4:19, 20. (1) Father of Elisheba,

wife of Aaron, Ex 6:23. (2) Son of Ram, or Aram, father of Nahshon, or Naasson, Ru 4:19, 20; Mt 1:4. Lk 3:33. (3) A Levite, family of Kohath, house of Uzziel, in David's reign, 1 Ch 15:10, 11; compare Ex 6:18, 22. (4) A Levite, family of Kohath, 1 Ch 6:22. Davis notes that the genealogies of Kohath, however, regularly have the name Izhar in this place (1 Ch 6:37, 38; Ex 6:18, 21, 24), so that Amminadab is probably either another name of Izhar or a corruption of the genealogy.

12. **Ye are the chief.** 1 Ch 9:34. 24:31. **sanctify.** ver. 14. Ex 19:14, 15. 2 Ch 5:11. 29:4, 5. 30:15. 35:6. Ezk 48:11. Jn *17:17. Ro *12:1, 2. Re *5:9, 10.

13. **ye did it.** 1 Ch 13:7-9. 2 S 6:3. **the Lord.** 1 Ch 13:10, 11. 2 S 6:7, 8. **for that.** See on ver. 2. Nu 4:15. 7:9. Dt 31:9. 2 Ch *30:17-20. Pr *28:13. 1 J √1:8-10. **due order.** Ge 22:3. Dt +*16:16. Jsh 22:11, 16, 21n, 22-30. 1 C 11:2. √14:40.

14. **sanctified.** Le 10:3. 2 Ch 29:15, 34. Jl 2:16, 17.

15. **bare the ark.** Ex 25:12-15. 37:3-5. 40:20. Nu 4:6, 15. 7:9. 1 K 8:8. 2 Ch 5:9.

16. **And David.** 2 Ch 30:12. Ezr 7:24-28. Is 49:23. **chief.** ver. 12. Ac 14:23. 1 T 3:1-15. 2 T 2:2. T 1:5. **the singers.** ver. 27, 28. 1 Ch 6:31-38. 13:8. 16:42. 23:5. 25:1-6. 2 Ch 29:28-30. Ne 12:36, 46. Ps 87:7. 149:3. 150:3, 4. **instruments.** 1 Ch *16:42. **psalteries.** Ps *92:1-3. 144:9. **lifting up.** 2 Ch 5:13. Ezr 3:10, 11. Ne 12:43. Ps 81:1. 92:1-3. 95:1. 100:1. Je 33:11. **with joy.** Ep *5:19. Ph *4:4. Col *3:16.

17. **Heman.** i.e. *steadfast.* 1 Ch +2:6. 6:33. 25:1-5. 1 S 8:2. **Joel.** i.e. *Jah is God.* He was the son of Samuel, 1 Ch 6:33. 1 S +8:2. **Asaph.** i.e. *he gathers.* 1 Ch 6:39. 25:2. 2 K +18:18. Ps ch. 73-83, titles. **Berachiah.** i.e. *blessed of Jah.* 1 Ch +6:39. **Merari.** ver. 6. **Ethan.** i.e. *perennial.* ver. 19. 1 Ch +2:6. 6:44, son of Kishi. **Kushaiah.** i.e. *bow or snare of Jah; entrapped of Jah,* *S#6984h.

18. **the second degree.** 1 Ch 25:2-6, 9-31. **Zechariah.** i.e. *remembered by Jah.* 1 Ch 16:5, 6. Zc +1:1. **Ben.** i.e. *son; son, as a builder of the family name; building up,* *S#1122h. **Jaaziel.** i.e. *emboldened of God; comforted of God; it will be done of God,* *S#3268h. ver. 20, Aziel. **Shemiramoth.** i.e. *most high name or heaven; renown of high places; heights of heaven; most exalted name; name of heights,* *S#8070h. 1 Ch 15:18, 20. 16:5. 2 Ch 17:8. **Jehiel.** i.e. *God lives.* 1 Ch +9:35. **Unni.** i.e. *depressed; afflicted; afflicted song; afflicted of the Lord; he was afflicted,* *S#6042h. 1 Ch 15:18, 20. Ne 12:9. (1) One sent by David to bring up the ark from Obed-edom, 1 Ch 15:18, 20. (2) A Levite who came up with Zerubbabel, Ne 12:9. **Eliab.** i.e. *my God is father.* Nu +1:9. **Benaiah.** i.e. *son of Jah.* ver. +24. **Maaseiah.** i.e. *work of Jah.* Je +21:1. **Mattithiah.** i.e. *gift of Jah.* Ezr +10:43. **Elipheleh.** i.e. *who exalts God; God makes him wonderful; God distinguishes him; my God, set thou apart; God of his distinction,* *S#466h. **Mikneiah.** i.e. *possession of the Lord; acquisition of Jehovah,* *S#4737h. 1 Ch 15:18, 21. **Obed-edom.** i.e. *servant of Edom.* 1 Ch 13:14. 16:5, 38. 26:4, 8, 15. 2 S +6:10. **Jeiel.** 1 Ch +5:7. **porters.** or, gate keepers. 2 S 18:26. Ps *84:10.

19. **Heman.** ver. 17. **cymbals of brass.** ver. 16. 1 Ch 13:8. 16:5, 42. 25:1, 6. Ps 150:5.

20. **Aziel.** i.e. *strength of God; comforted of God,* *S#5815h. ver. 18, Jaaziel. **psalteries.** ver. 16. 1 S

+10:5. **Alamoth**. i.e. *hiding places; virgins* (as *covered, veiled, or private*); *girls,* i.e. *the soprano or female voice,* ✱S#5961h. 1 Ch 15:20. Ps 46:title. or, virgins. Virgins joined in the triumphal processions, Young notes, as Ex +15:20. Jg +21:21n. 2 K ✱4:23. For the related ✱S#5959h (*almah,* virgin), see Ge +✱24:43.

21. **Mattithiah**. ver. 18. 1 Ch 16:5. Ezr +10:43. **harps**. ver. 16. 1 Ch 25:6, 7. 1 S +10:5. Ps 33:2. 81:1, 2. 92:3. 150:3. **Sheminith**. i.e. *octave; eighth,* ✚S#8067h. Ps ch. 6, 12, titles. **to excell**. or, to oversee. 1 Ch 23:4. 2 Ch 34:12. Ezr 3:8, 9.

22. **Chenaniah**. i.e. *perfected* or *established of God; covered by Jah; as perpetuated of Jah,* ✱S#3663h. 1 Ch 15:22. 26:29. Also 1 Ch 15:27. **for,** etc. or, for the carriage: he instructed about the carriage. For "carriage," Young renders "burden," noting, "of the song." **song**. Heb. lifting up. ver. 16, 27. 1 Ch 6:32. 25:7. 2 Ch 23:13. **he instructed about**. 1 Ch ✱16:42. 25:7, 8. Ep ✱5:19. Col ✱3:16. **skillful**. or, intelligent. ✚S#995h (Hiphil, Participle). 1 Ch 25:7, ✱8 (teacher). 27:32. 28:9. 2 Ch 26:5. 34:12. 35:3. Ezr 8:16. Ne 8:2, 3, ✱7, 9. 10:28. Ps √119:130. Pr √8:9. 17:10, 24. 28:2, 7, 11. Is 57:1. Da 1:4. 8:5, 23, 27.

23. **Berechiah**. ver. 17. **Elkanah**. i.e. *God has got.* Ex +6:24. **doorkeepers**. 1 Ch 9:21-23. 2 K 22:4. 25:18. Ps ✱84:10.

24. **Shebaniah**. i.e. *Jehovah hath dealt tenderly; built of Jehovah; discerned of Jehovah; prospered; caused to grow up of the Lord,* ✱S#7645h. 1 Ch 15:24. Also Ne 9:4, 5. 10:4, 10, 12. 12:14. (1) One who blew the trumpet before the ark under David, 1 Ch 15:24. (2) A Levite who stood up and blessed the Lord in the time of Ezra, Ne 9:4, 5. (3, 4, 5) Three who sealed the covenant, Ne 10:4, 10, 12. (6) A Levite, who came up with Zerubbabel, Ne 12:14; called Shecaniah, 1 Ch 24:11; Ne 12:3. **Jehoshaphat**. i.e. *Jah has judged.* 2 S +8:16. **Nethaneel**. i.e. *gift of God.* Nu +1:8. **Amasai**. i.e. *borne by Jah.* 2 Ch +29:12. **Zechariah**. ver. 18. **Benaiah**. i.e. *built of Jehovah; built up of the Lord.* ver. 18. ✱S#1141h. 1 Ch 11:24. 15:18, 20, 24. 16:5, 6. 18:17. 27:5, 6, 34. 2 S 8:18. 23:20, 22, 30. 1 K 1:8, 10, 26, 32, 36, 38, 44. 2:25, 29, 30, 34, 35, 46. 4:4. 2 Ch 31:13. Ezk 11:1. (1) One who assisted in bringing up the ark from Obed-edom, and ministered, 1 Ch 15:18, 20; 16:5. (2) A priest who blew a trumpet in the company which escorted the ark to Jerusalem and afterwards in David's tabernacle, 1 Ch 15:24; 16:6. (3) One of Simeon, 1 Ch 4:36. (4) The Pirathonite, 2 S 23:30; 1 Ch 11:31; 27:14. (5) Son of Jehoiada, 2 S 8:18; 20:23. (6) Father of Jehoiada, 1 Ch 27:34. (7) One set by Hezekiah over the tithes, 2 Ch 31:13. (8) Grandfather of Jahaziel the prophet, 2 Ch 20:14; Ezk 11:1. (9-12) Four men, sons of Parosh, Pahath-moab, Bani, and Nebo, who had married strange wives, Ezr 10:25, 30, 35, 43. **Eliezer**. i.e. *my God is help.* Ge +15:2. **the priests**. 1 Ch 16:6. Nu 10:8. 2 Ch 5:12, 13. Ps 81:3. Jl 2:1, 15. **trumpets**. These were silver trumpets, as in Nu 10:5, 6 (Young). **Jehiah**. i.e. *Jah will live; he lives of the Lord; Jah shall save alive,* ✱S#3174h. **Obed-edom**. ver. 18, 23. **doorkeepers**. ver. 18. Ps ✱84:10.

25. **David**. 2 S 6:12, 13, etc. 1 K 8:1. **captains over thousands**. 1 Ch 12:20. Nu 31:14. Dt 1:15. 1 S 8:12. 10:19. 22:7. Mi +✱5:2. **Obed-edom**. 1 Ch 13:14. **with joy**. 1 Ch 13:11, 12. Dt 12:7, 18. 16:11, 15. 2 Ch

20:27, 28. Ezr 6:16. Ps 95:1, 2. 100:1, 2. Ph 3:3. 4:4.

26. **God helped**. 1 Ch 29:14. 1 S 7:12. Ac=26:22, 23. 2 C 2:16. 3:5. **they**. 2 S 6:13. Ps 66:13-15. **bullocks**. Nu 23:1, 2, 4, 29. 29:32. Jb 42:8. Ezk 43:23.

27. **a robe**. 1 S 2:18. 2 S 6:14. Mt 27:28. Jn 19:23. 1 J 3:2. Re 1:13. **Chenaniah**. ver. +22. **song**. or, carriage. ver. 22.

28. **brought up**. 2 S 6:15. Mt=21:1-11. Lk 19:29-38. Jn=12:12-15. **with shouting**. ver. 16. 1 Ch 13:8. 2 Ch 5:12, 13. Ezr 3:10, 11. Ps 47:1-5. 68:25. 98:4-6. 150:3-5. **the cornet**. Ex 19:16. Jerome on Ho 5:8, says this instrument is properly called in Greek *keratina,* from *keras,* a horn. The *trumpets* were, according to Josephus, made of metal, and about a cubit in length. See Note on Nu 10:2.

29. **as the ark**. 1 Ch 17:1. Nu 10:33. Dt 31:26. Jsh 4:7. Jg 20:27. 1 S 4:3. Je 3:16. He 9:4. **Lord**. 2 S 6:16. **Michal**. 1 S 18:27, 28. 19:11-17. 25:44. 2 S 3:13, 14. **window**. 2 S 6:16. **dancing**. Ex +✱15:20n. Ps 30:11. 149:3. 150:4. Ec 3:4. Je 30:19. 33:11. or, *skipping.* Jb 21:11. Ps 29:6. 114:4, 6. Ec 3:4. Is 13:21. Jl 2:5. Na 3:2. **playing**. 1 S 18:7. 2 S 6:5. **she despised**. 2 S 6:20-23. Ps 69:7-9. Ac 2:13. 1 C ✱2:14. 2 C 5:13.

1 CHRONICLES 16

The ark being placed in its tent, David offers sacrifices, and liberally feasts the people, 1-3. He appoints singers and musicians to praise the Lord, 4-6. The psalm of thanksgiving then used, 7-36. The priests, singers, and porters appointed to minister continually before the ark, 37-42. David dismisses the people, 43.

1. **they brought**. 2 S 6:17-19. 1 K 8:6. 2 Ch 5:7. **in the midst**. 1 Ch 15:1, 12. 2 Ch 1:4. Ps 132:8. **they offered**. 1 K 8:5. 2 Ch 5:6. Ezr 6:16-18. **burnt sacrifices**. Le +✱23:12. **peace offerings**. Le +✱23:19.

2. **the burnt offerings**. Le 1:3. +✱23:12. **peace offerings**. Le +✱23:19. **he blessed**. Ge 14:19. 20:7. 47:7, 10. Nu 6:23-27. Jsh 22:6. 2 S 6:18. 1 K 8:55, 56. 2 Ch 29:29. 30:18-20, 27. Lk 24:50, 51. He 7:7.

3. **to every one**. 2 Ch 30:24. 35:7, 8. Ne 8:10. Ezk 45:17. 1 P 4:9.

4. **he appointed**. 1 Ch 15:16. 23:2-6. 24:3. **minister**. ver. 37-42. 1 Ch 23:27-32. Nu 18:1-6. **to record**. ver. 8. Ps ch. 37-70, titles. 103:2. 105:5. Is 62:6, 7. Ac=14:27. Re=1:2. **the Lord God**. Ge 17:7. 32:28. 33:20mg. 1 K 8:15. Ps 72:18. 106:48.

5. **Asaph**. See on 1 Ch 6:39. 15:16-24. 25:1-6. **psalteries and with harps**. Heb. instruments of psalteries and harps. 1 Ch 15:20, 21. 2 Ch 29:25.

6. **with trumpets**. Nu ✱10:8. 2 Ch 5:12, 13. 13:12. 29:26-28.

7. **on that day**. 2 S 22:1. 23:1, 2. 2 Ch 29:30. Ne 12:24. **this psalm**. √63A2, 2 S +6:6. **into the hand**. Ps ch. 12-18, titles.

8. **Give thanks**. This beautiful hymn, to the 22nd verse, is nearly the same as Ps 105:1-15; from the 23rd to the 33rd it accords with Ps 96; and the conclusion agrees with Ps 106, with the addition of ver. 34-36. Ps ✱105:1-15. **call**. Is 12:4. Ac 9:14. 1 C 1:2. **make**. 1 K ✱8:43. 2 K 19:19. Ps 67:2-4. ✱78:3-6. 145:5, 6.

9. **Sing unto**. Ps 95:1, 2. 96:1, 2. 98:1-4. Ml ✱3:16. **psalms**. Mt 26:30. Ep ✱5:19. Col ✱3:16. Ja ✱5:13. **talk ye**. Ps ✱40:10. 71:17. 96:3. ✱145:4-6, 12.

10. **Glory**. Ps ✱34:2. Is 45:25. Je ✱9:23, 24. 1 C 1:30, 31, Gr. **let the heart**. 1 Ch ✱28:9. Pr 8:17. Is

45:19. *55:6, 7. Je √29:13. Mt *7:7, 8.

11. **Seek.** Am 5:6. Zp *2:2, 3. **his strength.** T#1537. 2 Ch 6:41. Ps 68:35. 78:61. +86:16 (T#1715). ƒ121M, Ex +8:23. i.e. the Ark of the Covenant, which was the sign and symbol of His Presence and strength. So Ps 105:4, according to Ps 132:8. **seek his.** Ps *4:6. *27:8, 9. 67:1. **continually.** T#1153. Ps 72:15. Is 62:6. Ho 12:6. Re 4:8.

12. **Remember.** ver. 8, 9. Ps *103:2. 111:4. **the judgments.** Ps *19:9. 119:13, *20, *75, 137. Ro *11:33. Re 16:7. 19:2.

13. **ye seed.** Ge 17:7. 28:13, 14. *35:10-12. **his chosen.** Ex 19:5, 6. Dt *7:6. Ps *135:4. 1 P *2:9.

14. **the Lord.** Ex 15:2. Ps 63:1. 95:7. 100:3. 118:28. **his judgments.** ver. 12. Ps 48:10, 11. 97:8, 9.

15. **ye mindful.** Ps 25:10. 44:17. 105:8. Ml 4:4. **always.** Heb. *olam,* Ge +*6:3. **a thousand generations.** Dt 7:9.

16. **which he made.** Ge 15:18. 17:2. 26:3. 28:13, 14. 35:11. Ex 3:15. Ne 9:8. Lk 1:72, 73. Ac 3:25. Ga 3:15-17. He 6:13-18.

17. **for a law.** Ps 78:10. **an everlasting.** Ge +9:16. 17:+*7, 8. Ex 3:17. Jsh 24:11-13. 2 S 23:5. Is 55:3. Je 11:2. He *13:20.

18. **Unto thee.** Ge 12:7. 13:15. 17:8. 28:13, 14. 35:11, 12. **lot.** Heb. cord. Dt +*32:9mg. 2 S 8:2. Mi 2:5. **inheritance.** Nu 26:53-56. Dt 32:8.

19. **but few.** Heb. but men of number. Ge 34:30. Is +10:19mg. **a few.** Ge 34:30. Dt 7:7. 26:5. Ac 7:5. He 11:13.

20. **they went.** Ge 12:10. 20:1. 46:3, 6. **one kingdom.** Ps 105:13.

21. **He suffered.** Ge 31:24, 29, 42. **he reproved.** Ge 12:17. 20:3. Ex 7:15-18. 9:13-18.

22. **Touch.** 1 K 19:16. Ps 105:15. 1 J *2:27. **prophets.** Ge 20:7. 27:39, 40. 48:19, 20. *49:8-10.

23. **Sing.** See on ver. 9. Ex 15:21. Ps 30:4. *96:1-13. Is 12:5. **show forth.** Ps 40:10. 71:15. Is 51:6-8.

24. **Declare.** 2 K 19:19. Ps 22:27. Is 12:2-6. Da 4:1-3.

25. **great.** Ps 89:7. 144:3-6. Is 40:12-17. Re *15:3, 4. **he also.** Ex 15:11. Ps 66:3-5. 76:7. Je 5:22. 10:6-10. Re 15:4.

26. **all the gods.** Le 19:4. Ps 115:4-8. Is 44:9, etc. Je 10:10-14. Ac 19:26. 1 C +*8:4. **the Lord.** Ps 102:25. Is 40:26. 42:5. 44:24. Je 10:11, 12. Re 14:7.

27. **Glory.** Ps 8:1. 16:11. 63:2, 3. Jn 17:24. **strength.** Ps 27:4-6. 28:7, 8. 43:2-4. **place.** Ps 96:6.

28. **Give.** Ps 29:1, 2. 68:34. **ye kindreds.** Ps 66:1, 2. 67:4, 7. 86:8-10. 98:4. 100:1, 2. Is 11:10. **glory.** 1 Ch 29:10-14. Ps 115:1, 2. 1 C 15:10. 2 C *12:9, 10. Ep 1:6, 17-19. Ph *4:13. 1 T +1:17.

29. **the glory.** Ps 89:5-8. 108:3-5. 148:13, 14. Is 6:3. Re 4:9-11. 5:12-14. 7:12. **bring.** 1 K 8:41-43. Ps 68:30, 31. 72:10, 15. Is 60:6, 7. **an offering.** T#1267. Dt *16:16. 26:1-3. Jg *20:26, 27. 1 S 7:9, 10. 2 S 24:18, 19, 25. 1 Ch 21:26, 27. 29:17. 2 Ch 15:11-14. Jb *42:8. Ps *20:1-4. Is 56:7. Mi 6:6, 7. **come.** Ps 95:2. 100:4. **the beauty.** 2 Ch 20:21. Ps 29:2. 50:2. 96:6, 9. 110:3. Ezk 7:20. 24:25.

30. **before him.** See on ver. 23, 25. Ps 96:9. Re 11:15. **stable.** Ps 33:9. 93:1. 104:5. 148:5, 6. Ec +*1:4. Is 49:8. Je 10:12. Col 1:17. He *1:3. 2 P ●3:10. **not moved.** Ps 104:5.

31. **Let the heavens.** Ps *19:1. 89:5. 148:1-4. Lk *2:13, 14. *15:10. **let the earth.** Ps 97:1. *98:4. Lk

*2:10. **The Lord.** Ps 93:1, 2. 96:10. *99:1. 145:1. Is 33:22. Mt *6:13. Re *19:6.

32. **the sea.** Ps 93:4. 98:7. **fields.** Ps 98:8. 148:9, 10. Is 44:23.

33. **the trees.** Ps *96:12, 13. Ezk 17:22-24. **because.** Ps *98:9. 2 Th *1:8, 10. 2 P *3:14. Re *11:17, 18.

34. **give thanks.** 2 Ch 5:13. 7:3. Ezr *3:11. Ps 106:1. 107:1. 118:1. 136:1, etc. Je *33:11. **for ever.** Heb. *olam,* Ex +12:24.

35. **Save us.** Ps 14:7. 53:6. *79:9, 10. 106:17, 48. **that we may give.** T#1143. 1 K 8:57, 58. Jb 13:21, 22. Ps 9:14. 35:27, 28. *51:13-15. 71:18. 79:13. 105:45. 119:8, 32, 43, 44, *145, 146. Is 43:21. Ep 1:12. 1 P *2:5, 9. **glory.** ver. 9, 10. Ps 44:8. Is *45:25. 1 C *1:31.

36. **Blessed.** 1 K 8:15, *56. Ps 72:18, 19. 106:48. Ep *1:3. 1 P *1:3. **for ever and ever.** Heb. *olam* doubled, Da +2:20. 1 Ch 29:10. Ne 9:5. Ps 41:13. **all the people said.** Dt 27:15-26. Ne 8:6. Je 28:6. 1 K 14:16. **Amen.** i.e. *so it is.* Nu 5:22. Dt 27:15-26. 1 K 1:36. Ne 5:13. 8:6. Ps 41:13. 72:19. Je 11:5mg. **praised.** ƒ24A, Ge +32:24.

37. **minister before.** Ep=6:7. Col=3:24. **the ark.** See on ver. 4-6. 1 Ch 15:17-24. 25:1-6. **as every day's.** 2 Ch 8:14. Ezr 3:4. Ac=2:46, 47.

38. **Obed-edom.** 1 Ch 13:14. 26:4-8. 2 S +6:10. **Jeduthun.** i.e. *confessing.* 1 Ch +9:16. 25:3. **Hosah.** i.e. *fleeing for refuge; place of refuge; trusting,* ✱S#2621h. 1 Ch 16:38. 26:10, 11, 16. Jsh 19:29. (1) Appointed porter with Obed-edom, 1 Ch 16:38; 26:10. (2) A village on the frontier of Asher, apparently south of Tyre, Jsh 19:29.

39. **Zadok.** See on 1 Ch 12:28. 2 S +8:17. **before.** 1 Ch *21:29. 2 Ch 1:3, 4, 13. **in the high.** 1 K 3:4.

40. **To offer.** Ex 29:38-42. Nu 28:3-8. 1 K 18:29. 2 Ch 2:4. 31:3. Ezr 3:3. Ezk 46:13-15. Da 9:21. Am 4:4. **morning and evening.** Heb. in the morning and in the evening.

41. **Heman.** ver. 37. 1 Ch +2:6. 6:39-47. 25:1-6. **chosen.** or, choice. 1 Ch 7:40. 9:22. Ne 5:18. Jb 33:3 (clearly). Is 49:2 (polished). Zp 3:9 (pure). Mk=7:13, 14. **expressed.** 1 Ch 12:31. Nu 1:17. Ezr 8:20. **by name.** Jn=10:3. **to give.** See on ver. 34. 2 Ch 5:13. 7:3. 20:21. Ezr 3:11. Ps 103:17. Je 33:11. Lk 1:50. **for ever.** Heb. *olam,* Ex +12:24.

42. **trumpets.** 2 Ch 29:25-28. Ps 150:3-6. **musical instruments.** 1 Ch *15:16, 22. 25:6. 2 Ch 5:13. Ps *84:10. 1 C 14:26. Ep *5:19n. Col *3:16. That musical instruments are to be used in the worship of God in the singing of hymns and psalms and spiritual songs cannot be denied on the basis of the silence of the New Testament as to this practice: the argument from silence is at best a very weak inference; and in the case of practices which are so common, so taken for granted, and therefore in need of no explanation or particular comment or additional instruction, such silence need not surprise us on a number of matters; such silence lends force to the argument that such practices continued unabated from the Old Testament era to the New Testament church, for had it been otherwise in each particular case, comment surely would have been made in the New Testament upon the matter (Jn 14:2. Ro 15:4. 2 T *3:16, 17). **of God.** ƒ24L. Antimereia, Ge +6:2. 1 Ch 12:22. 2 Ch 30:21mg. Jb +1:16mg. Ac *7:20mg. **porters.** Heb. for the gate. 1 Ch +23:5. Ne 11:19mg.

43. **all the people.** 2 S 6:19, +*20. 1 K 8:66. **to bless.** Ge *18:19. Jsh *24:15. Ps 101:2.

1 CHRONICLES 17

David, purposing to build a temple, is encouraged by Nathan, 1, 2. The Lord afterwards, by Nathan, prohibits it; but with many encouraging promises, 3-15. David's prayer and thanksgiving, 16-27.

1. **as David.** 2 S 7:1, 2, etc. 2 Ch 6:7-9. Da 4:4, 29, 30. **Nathan.** 1 Ch 29:29. 2 S 12:1, 25. 1 K 1:8, 23, 44. **I dwell.** 1 Ch 14:1. Je 22:15. Hg 1:4, 9. **the ark.** Ps 132:5. Ac 7:46. **under curtains.** ver. 5. 1 Ch 15:1. 16:1. Ex 40:19-21. 2 S 6:17. 2 Ch 1:4.

2. **Nathan said.** ver. ◐4. Dt ◐18:22. Pr 4:18. Jon 3:4, 10. 1 C 13:9. **Do all.** 1 Ch 22:7. 28:2. Jsh 9:14. 1 S 16:7. Ps 20:4. 1 C 13:9. **for God.** 1 S 10:7. 2 S 7:3. Zc 8:23. Lk 1:28.

3. **word.** Nu 12:6. 2 K 20:1-5. Is 30:21. Am 3:7.

4. **tell.** Is 55:8, 9. Ro 11:33, 34. **Thou shalt not.** 1 Ch 22:7, 8. 28:2, 3. 2 S 7:4, 5. 1 K 8:19. 2 Ch 6:8, 9.

5. **dwelt.** 2 S 7:6. 1 K 8:27. 2 Ch 2:6. 6:18. Is 66:1, 2. Ac 7:44-50. **gone.** Heb. been. **from tent to tent.** Ex 40:2, 3. 2 S 6:17. 1 K 8:4, 16.

6. **walked.** Le 33:14, 15. 40:35-38. Le 26:11, 12. Nu 10:33-36. Dt 23:14. 2 C 6:16. Re 2:1. **the judges.** Jg 2:16-18. 1 S 12:11. 2 S 7:7, tribes. Ac 13:20. **feed.** 1 Ch 11:2. Ps 78:71, 72. Je 23:4. Ezk 34:2. Mi 5:4. Mt 2:6mg.

7. **I took thee.** Ex 3:1-10. 1 S 16:11, 12. 17:15. 2 S 7:8. Ps 78:70, 71. Am 7:14, 15. Mt 4:18-22. Lk 5:10. **from following.** Heb. from after. **ruler.** 2 S 6:21. Mt 2:6.

8. **I have been.** ver. 2. Ge 28:15. 1 S 18:14, 28. 2 S 7:9. 8:6, 8, 14. Ps 46:7, 11. **have cut off.** 1 S 26:10. 31:1-6. 2 S 22:1, 38-41. Ps 18, title. **made thee.** ver. 17. 2 S 8:13. Ezr 4:20. Ps 71:21. 75:7. 113:7, 8. Lk 1:52.

9. **I will.** Je 31:3-12. Ezk 34:13. **plant.** Ps 44:2. 92:13. Is 61:3. Je 24:6. 32:41. **and shall be.** Ezk 28:4. 36:14, 15. 37:25. Am 9:15. Re 21:4. **the children of.** 2 S +3:34mg. 7:10. Ps 89:22. Ep 2:2, 3. 5:6. **waste.** Is 49:17. 60:18. **as at the.** Ex 1:13, 14. 2:23.

10. **And since.** Jg 2:14-18. 3:8. 4:3. 6:3-6. 1 S 13:5, 6, 19, 20. **Moreover.** Ps 18:40, etc. 21:8, 9. 89:23. 110:1. 1 C 15:25. **subdue.** Mi 7:19. **the Lord.** Ex 1:21. 2 S 7:11. Ps 127:1.

11. **when thy.** 1 Ch *29:15, 28. Ac 13:36. **go to be.** Ge *15:15. Dt *31:16. 1 K 1:21. 2:10. Ac 2:29. **I will raise.** 1 Ch 28:5. 2 S *7:12, 13. 12:24, 25. 1 K *8:20. Ps *132:11. Je *23:5, 6. Ro *1:3, 4.

12. **He shall.** 1 Ch *22:9, 10. *28:6-10. 1 K 5:5. 2 Ch ch. 3, 4. Ezr 5:11. Zc *6:12, 13. Jn *2:19-21. Ac 7:47, 48. Col *2:9. **I will.** Ps *89:4, 29, 36, 37. Is *9:7. Da *2:44. 1 C *15:25. Re *11:15. **for ever.** Heb. *olam*, Ex +12:24.

13. **I will be.** 2 S *7:14. Ps 89:26-28, etc. Is *55:3. 2 C ▶6:18. He *1:5. Re ▶21:7. **my son.** Ps *2:7, 12. Lk *9:35. Jn *3:35. **I will not.** 2 S *7:15, 16. 1 K *11:12, 13, 36. Is +55: 3. **as I took.** ver. 12. 1 Ch 10:14. 1 S *15:28.

14. **in mine.** In the parallel passage, it is "*thine house, and thy kingdom.*" Jehovah was Israel's king; and David and Solomon were merely his vicegerents, as well as types of the Messiah. Ps *2:6. *72:17. *89:36.

Lk *1:32, 33. He *3:6. **for ever.** Ex +12:24. **for evermore.** Ps +*18:50.

15. **According.** 2 S 7:17. Je √23:28. Ac *20:27.

16. **sat before.** T#1283. Jg +*20:26n, 27. 21:2. 2 S *7:18. 1 K 19:4. 2 K *19:14. Ne 1:4. Ezk 14:1-3. 20:1. **Who am I.** Ge *32:10. Ps 144:3. Ep *3:8. **what is.** Jg *6:15. 1 S 9:21. **that thou hast.** Ge *48:15, 16. 1 S *7:12. Ac *26:22. 2 C 1:10.

17. **a small thing.** ver. *7, 8. 2 S 7:19. 12:8. 2 K 3:18. Is *49:6. **thou hast.** ver. 11-15. Ep *3:20. **hast regarded.** ver. *8. 1 K *3:13. Ps *78:70-72. *89:19, etc. Ph *2:8-11.

18. **the honor.** 1 S 2:30. 2 S 7:20-24. **thou knowest.** √121C2A2, Ge +39:6. 1 S 16:7. Ps 139:1. Jn 21:17. Re 2:23.

19. **thy servants.** Is 37:35. 42:1. 49:3, 5, 6. Da 9:17. **according.** Mt 11:26. Ep 1:9-11. 3:11. **great things.** Heb. greatnesses. 1 Ch 29:11, 12. Ps 111:3, 6.

20. **none.** Ex 15:11. 18:11. Dt 3:24. 33:26. Ps 86:8. 89:6, 8. Is 40:18, 25. Je 10:6, 7. Ep 3:20. **beside thee.** Dt 4:35, 39. 1 S 2:2. Is 43:10. 44:6. 45:5, 22. **according.** Ps 44:1. 78:3, 4. Is 63:12.

21. **what one.** Dt 4:7, 32-34. 33:26-29. Ps 147:20. **redeem.** Ex 3:7, 8. 19:4-6. Dt 15:15. Ps 77:15. 107:2. 111:9. Is *63:9. T *2:14. **make thee.** Ne 9:10. Is 48:9. 63:12. Ezk 20:9, 10. **greatness.** Dt 4:34. Ps 65:5. 66:3-7. 114:3-8. Is 64:3. **by driving.** Dt 7:1, 2. Jsh 10:42. 21:43-45. 24:11, 12. Ps 44:2, 3.

22. **thy people.** Ge 17:7. Ex 19:5, 6. Dt 7:6-8. 26:18, 19. 1 S 12:22. Je *31:31-34. Zc *13:9. Ro 9:4-6, 25, 26. +√11:1, 2, etc. 1 P *2:9. **for ever.** Heb. *olam*, Ex +12:24. Jn *10:28. Ro +*11:1.

23. **let the thing.** Ge 32:12. 2 S 7:25-29. Ps 119:49. Je 11:5. Lk 1:38. **for ever.** Heb. *olam*, Ex +12:24.

24. **that thy name.** 2 Ch 6:33. Ps 21:13. 72:19. Mt 6:9, 13. Jn 12:28. 17:1. Ph 2:11. 1 P 4:11. **for ever.** Heb. *olam*, Ex +12:24. **a God.** Je 31:1. He 8:10. 11:16. Re 21:3. **and let.** Ps 90:17.

25. **told thy servant.** Heb. revealed the ear of thy servant. 1 S 9:15mg. 20:2mg. Ru +4:4mg. **that thou.** See on ver. 10. **found.** Ps 10:17. Ezk 36:37. 1 J *5:14, 15.

26. **thou art God.** Ex 34:6, 7. T *1:2. He *6:18.

27. **let it please.** *or,* it hath pleased. 2 S 7:29mg. 2 K 5:23. **blessest.** Ge 27:33. Ps 72:17. Ro *11:29. Ep *1:3. **for ever.** Heb. *olam*, Ex +12:24.

1 CHRONICLES 18

David subdues the Philistines, and makes the Moabites tributary, 1, 2. He smites Hadarezer and the Syrians, 3-8. Tou, king of Hamath, sends his son to David with presents, which he dedicates, with the spoil, unto God, 9-11. He puts garrisons into Edom, 12, 13. He reigns in equity, 14. His principal officers, 15-17.

1. A.M. 2964. B.C. 1040. An. Ex. Is. 451. **after this.** 2 S 8:1, 2, etc. **Gath.** 1 S 5:8. 27:4. 2 S 1:20. 8:1, Metheg-ammah. **towns.** √155E5, Nu +21:25.

2. **he smote.** Nu 24:17. Jg 3:29, 30. 2 S 8:2. Ps 60:8. Is 11:14. **brought gifts.** 1 S 10:27. 1 K 10:2, 25. 2 K 3:4, 5. Ps 68:29, 30. 72:8-10. Is 16:1.

3. **Hadarezer.** "Hadadezer" in the parallel passage, seems an evident mistake for "Hadarezer," for the LXX. and Vulgate there, as here, read "Adarezer." The difference arises from the mistake of a *raish* for a *daleth*, two letters very similar. 2 S 8:3, Hadadezer. **Zobah.**

1 S +14:47. 2 S 10:6. Ps 60, title. **by the river**. Ge 15:18. Ex 23:31.

4. **seven thousand**. 2 S 8:4, seven hundred. **David**. The words *wyakker Dawid eth col haraichev*, should be rendered "and David disjointed all the chariots;" which is nearly the rendering of the LXX., *kai paraluse Dauid panta to armata*. To have houghed the horses would have been both unreasonable and inhuman; for, as he had gained so complete a victory, there was no danger of their falling into the hands of the enemy; and if he did not choose to keep them, which indeed the law would not permit, he ought to have killed them outright. **houghed**. Dt 17:16. Jsh 11:6, 9. Ps 20:7. 33:16, 17. **an hundred chariots**. 1 K 4:26. 10:26.

5. **the Syrians**. 2 S 8:5, 6. 1 K 11:23, 24. **Damascus**. Heb. Darmesek. **to help**. Is 8:9, 10. **Zobah**. ver. 3. 1 S +14:47.

6. **Syria-damascus**. S#758h. A place where David put garrisons. **became David's**. See on ver. 2. Ps 18:43, 44. **Thus the Lord**. 1 Ch 17:8. Ps 121:8. Pr 21:31.

7. **shields**. 1 K 10:16, 17. 14:26-28. 2 Ch 9:15, 16. 12:9, 10.

8. **Tibhath**. i.e. *slaughter; confidence, security; the slaughter-place*, *S#2880h. 2 S 8:8, Betah, Berothai. **Chun**. i.e. *established; firm, choice; to stand upright*, *S#3560h. **wherewith**. 1 Ch 22:14. 1 K 7:15-47. 2 Ch 4:2-6, 12-18. Je 52:17-23.

9. **Tou**. i.e. *who wanders; error, going astray; do ye mock; do ye stray away*, *S#8583h. 1 Ch 18:9, 10. Also 2 S 8:9, 10, 10, Toi.

10. **Hadoram**. or, Joram. 2 S 8:10. *Joram*, in the parallel text, seems a mistake for "Hadoram," or "Idoram," for the LXX. have here *Ieddouram*. **enquire** or, salute him. 2 S 8:10. **congratulate him**. Heb. bless him. **had war**. Heb. was the man of wars. Is 41:12. **with him**. J63C, Ge +25:32. 2 S 8:10. **all manner**. 2 Ch 9:1, 23, 24. Is 39:1.

11. **dedicated**. 1 Ch 22:14. 26:20, 26, 27. 29:14. Ex 35:5, 21-24. Jsh 6:19. 2 S 8:11, 12. 1 K 7:51. 2 K 12:18. 2 Ch 5:1. Mi 4:13. **the children**. 1 Ch 20:1, 2. **Amalek**. 1 S 27:8, 9. 30:13, 20. Ps 83:6, 7.

12. **Moreover**. 1 Ch 2:16. 11:20. 1 S 26:6, 8. 2 S 3:30. 10:10, 14. 16:9-11. 19:21, 22. 20:6. 21:17. 23:18. **Abishai**. Heb. Abshai. 1 Ch 19:11mg. **slew of the Edomites**. 2 S 7:13. 8:13, 14. Ps 60:title, 8, 9. **the valley of Salt**. 2 K 14:7. 2 Ch 25:11.

13. **garrisons**. ver. 6. 1 S 10:5. 13:3. 14:1. 2 S 7:14, etc. 23:14. 2 C 11:32. **all the Edomites**. Ge 25:23. 27:29, 37, 40. Nu 24:18. **Thus the Lord**. ver. 6. Ps 18:48-50. 121:7. 144:10.

14. **David**. 1 Ch 12:38. **executed**. 2 S 8:15. Ps 78:71, 72. 89:14. Is 9:7. 32:1, 2. Je 22:15. 23:5, 6. 33:15.

15. **Joab**. 1 Ch 11:6. 1 S +26:6. 2 S 8:16. **Jehoshaphat**. 1 K 4:3. 2 S +8:16. **recorder**. or, remembrancer. 2 S +8:16mg.

16. **Abimelech**. 2 S 8:17, Ahimelech. **Abiathar**. 2 S 20:25. 1 K 2:35. **Shavsha**. i.e. *God's warrior; habitation; plain*, *S#7798h. 2 S 8:17, Seraiah. 20:25, Sheva. 1 K 4:3, Shisha.

17. **Benaiah**. 2 S 8:18. 15:18. 20:7, 23. 23:19-23. 1 K 1:38, 44. 2:34, 35. **Cherethites**. Zp 2:5. **about the king**. Heb. at the hand of the king. 1 Ch 23:28mg.

1 CHRONICLES 19

David sends ambassadors to comfort the king of Ammon, who abuses and insults them, 1-5. The Am-

monites and Syrians are vanquished by Joab and Abishai, 6-15. The king of Syria sends another army, which David conquers, slaying its commander, 16-18. The Syrians submit to David, 19.

1. **Nahash**. 1 S 11:1, 2. 12:12. 2 S 10:1-3.

2. **I will show**. 1 S 30:26. 2 S 9:1, 7. 2 K 4:13. Est 6:3. Ec 9:15. **the children**. Ge 19:37, 38. Dt 23:3-6. Ne 4:3, 7. 13:1.

3. **the princes**. 1 S 29:4, 9. 1 K 12:8-11. **Thinkest thou that David**. Heb. In thine eyes doth David. 1 C 13:5-7. **to search**. Ge 42:9-18. Jsh 2:1-3. Jg 1:23, 24. 18:2, 8-10.

4. **took David's**. Ps 35:12. 109:4, 5. **shaved them**. Le 19:27. Is 15:2. Je 41:5. 48:37. **and cut**. Is 20:4. 47:2, 3. **sent them**. 2 S 10:4, 5. 2 Ch 36:16. Mk 12:4. Lk 20:10, 11.

5. **and told David**. Mt 18:31. **at Jericho**. Jsh 6:24-26. 1 K 16:34. **your beards**. Jg 16:22.

6. **had made**. Lk 10:16. 1 Th 4:8. **odious**. Heb. to stink. Ge 34:30. Ex 5:21. 1 S 13:4. 27:12. Ps 14:3, margins. **a thousand**. 2 Ch 16:2, 3. 25:6. 27:5. Ps 46:9. **Syria-maachah**. S#758h. 2 S 10:6. **Zobah**. 1 Ch 18:3, 5, 9. 1 S +14:47. 2 S 8:3. 1 K 11:23, 24.

7. **hired**. 1 Ch 18:4. Ex 14:9. Jg 4:3. 1 S 13:5. 2 Ch 14:9. Ps 20:7-9. **thirty and two thousand chariots**. Thirty-two thousand soldiers, exclusive of the thousand sent by the king of Maachah, are mentioned in the parallel passage (2 S 10:6); but of *chariots* or cavalry there is no mention; and the number of chariots stated here is prodigious, and beyond all credibility. But as the word *raichev* denotes not only a *chariot*, but a *rider* (see Is 21:7), it ought most probably to be rendered here, in a collective sense, *cavalry*; and then the number of troops will exactly agree with the passage of Samuel. It is probable that they were a kind of auxiliary troops who were usually mounted on horses, or in chariots, but who occasionally served as foot-soldiers. **the king of Maachah**. This variation exists only in the translation, the original being the same in both places, *melech maachah*, "the king of Maachah." 2 S 10:6, king Maachah. **Medeba**. Nu 21:30. Jsh 13:9. Is 15:2.

8. **Joab**. 1 Ch 11:6, 10, etc. 2 S 23:8, etc.

9. **put the battle**. 1 S 17:2. 2 S 18:4. 2 Ch 13:3. 14:10. Is 28:6. Je 50:42. Jl 2:5. **the kings**. 2 S 10:8. 1 K 20:1, 24.

10. **when Joab**. 2 S 10:9-14. **battle**. Heb. face of the battle. **set against**. Jsh 8:22. Jg 20:42, 43. **choice**. or, young men. 1 S 8:16. 9:2.

11. **Abishai**. Heb. Abshai. ver. 15. 1 Ch 11:20. 18:12. 2 S 10:10. The variation of "Abishai" and "Abshai" is simply caused by the elision of *yood*, which is by no means uncommon. **and they set**. See on ver. 9.

12. **If the Syrians**. Ne 4:20. Ec 4:9-12. Ga 6:2. Ph 1:27, 28.

13. **of good**. Dt 31:6, 7. Jsh 1:7. 10:25. 1 S 4:9. 14:6-12. 17:32. 2 S 10:12. Ezr 10:4. Ne 4:14. Ps 27:14. 1 C 16:13. **let us behave**, etc. In Samuel, "let us play the men;" but the original is the same in both places, *nithchazzak*. **let the Lord**. Jg 10:15. 1 S 3:18. 2 S 15:26. 16:10, 11. Jb 1:22.

14. **they fled**. 1 K 20:13, 19-21, 28-30. 2 Ch 13:5-16. Je 46:15, 16.

15. **they likewise**. Le 26:7. Ro *8:31.

16. A.M. 2968. B.C. 1036. An. Ex. Is. 455. **and**

drew. Ps 2:1. Is 8:9. Mi 4:11, 12. Zc 14:1-3. **river.**
that is, Euphrates. ver. 6. 2 Ch +9:26. **Shophach.**
i.e. *poured forth; pouring out,* *S#7780h. 1 Ch 19:16,
18. This variation arises from the permutation of
baith and *pay;* being written in the parallel passage
"Shobach," and here, "Shophach." 2 S 10:16, Shobach.
17. **upon them.** Instead of *alaihem,* "upon them,"
it is in 2 S 10:17, *chelamah,* "to Helam:" the one seems
evidently to be a mistake for the other. **and set.** ver.
9. Is 22:6, 7.
18. **fled before Israel.** ver. 13, 14. Ps 18:32. 33:16.
46:11. **seven thousand.** In the parallel passage, *"the
men of* seven hundred chariots;" which difference probably arose from mistaking *noon final,* which stands
for 700, for *zayin,* with a dot above, which denotes
7000, or *vice versa:* the great similarity of these letters
might easily cause the one to be mistaken for the other.
footmen. If these troops were as we have supposed,
a kind of *dismounted cavalry,* the terms *footmen* and
horsemen might be indifferently applied to them. 2 S
10:18, horsemen.
19. **the servants.** Ge 14:4, 5. Jsh 9:9-11. 2 S 10:19.
1 K 20:1, 12. Ps 18:39, 44. Is 10:8. **would.** 1 Ch 14:17.
Ps 48:3-6.

1 CHRONICLES 20

*Rabbah is taken and spoiled, and the inhabitants
are treated with great severity, 1-3. Three giants are
slain by David's servants, in three battles against the
Philistines, 4-8.*

1. A.M. 2969. B.C. 1035. An. Ex. Is. 456. **And it
came.** 2 S 11:1. **after the year was expired.** Heb. at
the return of the year. 1 K 20:+22mg, 26. 2 K 13:20.
at the time. 2 S *11:1n. 1 K 20:22, 26. Jb 7:1mg. Ec
+*3:8. **wasted.** Is 6:11. 54:16. **Rabbah.** Dt 3:11. 2 S
12:26. 17:27. Je 49:2, 3. Ezk 21:20. 25:5. Am 1:14.
Joab smote. 2 S 11:16-25. 12:26-31.
2. **it.** Heb. the weight of it. **and he brought.** 1 Ch
18:11. 2 S 8:11, 12.
3. **And he.** 1 Ch 19:2-5. Ps 21:8, 9. **and cut.** Instead
of *wyyasar,* "and he cut," the parallel passage is *wyya-
sem,* "and he put them;" which is also the reading
here of seven MSS. collated by Dr. Kennicott. Sawing
asunder, etc. of human beings, have no more place
in the text, than they had in David's conduct toward
the Ammonites. **with saws.** Ex 1:14. Jsh 9:23. Jg 8:6,
7, 16, 17. 1 K 9:21.
4. A.M. 2986. B.C. 1018. An. Ex. Is. 473. **there
arose.** or, there continued. Heb. there stood. 2 S 21:15.
Gezer. or, Gob. Jsh 12:12. 16:3. 2 S 21:18, etc. **Sibbechai.** 1 Ch 11:29, Sibbecai. **Sippai.** i.e. *threshold; my
basins,* *S#5598h. 2 S 21:18, Saph. **the giant.** or,
Rapha. Dt +2:20. Jsh +17:15.
5. **Jair.** 2 S 21:19, Jaare-oregim. **Lahmi.** i.e. *my
bread; a warrior; an eater,* *S#3902h. **Goliath.** 1 S
17:4. 21:9. 22:10. 2 S 21:19. **weaver's beam.** 1 Ch
11:23. 1 S 17:7.
6. **of great stature.** Heb. a man of measure.
Nu 13:32mg. 2 S 21:20. **toes.** lit. fingers. 2 S 21:20.
the son of the giant. Heb. born to the giant, *or*
Rapha.
7. **defied.** or, reproached. 1 S 17:10, 26, 36. Is 27:33.
Shimea. 1 Ch 2:13, Shimma. 1 S 16:9, Shammah.
8. **they fell.** Jsh 14:12. Ec 9:11. Je 9:23. Ro *8:31.

1 CHRONICLES 21

*David, tempted by Satan, requires Joab to number
the people, 1-4. The number is returned to the king,
5, 6. God is displeased, and David owns his fault, 7,
8. The Lord, by Gad the prophet, proposes three judgments to David, who chooses three days' pestilence,
9-13. Seventy thousand are cut off and David, seeing
the destroying angel, intercedes for the people, 14-
17. Directed by Gad, he buys Ornan's threshingfloor;
and sacrifices: fire consumes the oblation, and the
plague is stayed, 18-27. He again sacrifices there, fearing to go to Gibeon by fear of the angel, 28-30.*

1. A.M. 2987. B.C. 1017. An. Ex. Is. 474. **Satan.**
T#16. Ge *3:13. 2 S 24:1. 1 K 22:20-22. Jb 1:6-12.
2:1, 4-6. Ps +5:9 (T#702). Zc 3:1. Mt 4:3. +7:15
(T#474). Lk 22:31. Jn 13:2. Ac 5:3. 2 C 11:3, *14.
2 Th 2:9. 1 T 4:1. 2 T 2:26. Ja 1:13. Re 12:10. 16:13,
14. **provoked David.** 1 Ch 11:53. Ga 5:26. He 10:24.
2. **Joab.** 2 S 24:2-4. **Beer-sheba.** Jg 20:1. 1 S 3:20.
2 S 3:10. 17:11. 24:15. 1 K 4:25. 2 Ch 30:5. **bring.**
1 Ch 27:23, 24. **that I may.** Dt 8:13-17. 2 Ch 32:25,
26. Pr 29:23. 2 C 12:7.
3. **The Lord.** 1 Ch 19:13. Ps 115:14. Pr 14:28. Is
26:15. 48:19. **why will.** Ge 20:9. Ex 32:21. Nu 32:9,
10. 1 S 2:24. 1 K 14:16.
4. **the king's.** Ec 8:4. **Wherefore.** Ex 1:17. Da 3:18.
Ac 5:29. **and went.** 2 S 24:3-8.
5. **number.** 1 S +11:8. **a thousand thousand and.**
The Syriac has 800,000, as in the parallel passage of
Samuel. 1 Ch 27:23. 2 S 24:9.
6. **Levi.** Nu 1:47-49. **Joab.** 2 S 3:27. 11:15-21. 20:9,
10.
7. **And God was displeased with this thing.** Heb.
And it was evil in the eyes of God concerning this
thing. 2 S 11:27. 1 K 15:5. **he smote.** ver. 14. Jsh
7:1, 5, 13. 22:16-26. 2 S 21:1, 14. 24:1.
8. **I have sinned.** 2 S 12:13. 24:10. Ps 25:11. *32:5.
Je 3:13. Lk *15:18, 19. 1 J √1:9. **do away.** Ps 51:1-3.
Ho 14:2. Jn 1:29. **I have done.** Ge 34:7. 1 S 13:13.
26:21. 2 S 13:13. 2 Ch 16:9.
9. **Gad.** 1 Ch 29:29. 1 S 9:9. 2 S 24:11.
10. **offer thee.** Heb. stretch out. Jb 9:8. 26:7. Ps
104:2. Is 40:22. 42:5. 44:24. 51:13. 66:12. Je 10:20.
Ezk 25:16. Zc 12:1. **choose.** Jsh *24:15. Pr *1:29-31.
that I may. Nu 20:12. 2 S 12:10-12. 1 K 13:21, 22.
Pr *3:12. Re 3:19.
11. **Choose thee.** Heb. Take to thee. Pr 19:20.
12. **three years' famine.** In 2 S 24:13, it is *seven
years;* but the Septuagint has there *three years,* as
here; which is, no doubt, the true reading; the letter
zayin, seven, being mistaken for the letter *gimmel,*
three. Le *26:26-29. 2 S 21:1. *24:13. 1 K 17:1. 2 K
8:1. La *4:9. Lk 4:25. **to be destroyed.** Le *26:17,
36, 37. Dt 28:15, 25, 51, 52. Je 42:16. **the sword.**
ver. 16. Is 66:16. Je 12:12. 47:6. **even the pestilence.**
Le 26:16, 25. Dt 28:22, 27, 35. Ps *91:6. Ezk *14:19-
21. **the angel.** ver. 15, 16. Ex *12:23. 2 K 19:35. Mt
*13:49, 50. Ac 12:23. Re 7:1-3. **Now therefore.** 2 S
24:13, 14.
13. **I am in.** 2 K 6:15. *7:4. Est 4:11, 16. Jn 12:27.
Ph *1:23. **let me fall.** David here acted nobly: had
he chosen *war,* his *personal safety* was in no danger,
as there was an ordinance preventing him from going
to battle; and in *famine,* his wealth would have secured
his and his family's support; but all were equally ex-

posed to the pestilence. He *10:31. **great.** *or,* many. Ex 34:6, 7. Ps 5:7. *51:1, 2. 69:13, 16. *86:5, 15. 103:8. 106:7. 130:7. Is *55:7. 63:7, 15. La *3:32. Jon 3:9. *4:2. Mi *7:18. Hab *3:2. **but let me.** 2 Ch *28:9. Pr 12:10. Is 46:7. 47:6.

14. **the Lord.** Nu 16:46-49. 2 S 24:15. **seventy.** Ex 12:30. Nu 25:9. 1 S 6:19. 2 K 19:35.

15. **unto Jerusalem.** 2 S 24:16. Je 7:12. 26:9, 18. Mt 23:37, 38. **repented him.** See on Ge 6:6. Ex 32:14. Jg 2:18. 10:16. Ps 78:38. Je 18:7-10. Jon 4:2. **It is enough.** Ex 9:28. 1 K 19:4. Ps 90:13. Mk 14:41. **Ornan.** i.e. *strong one; active; large pine, tall as a great pine; light was perpetuated; their fir tree.* 2 S 24:18, Araunah. ✱S#771h: 1 Ch 21:15, 18, 20, 20, 21, 21, 22, 23, 24, 25, 28. 2 Ch 3:1.

16. **lifted.** ℐ144A12, Ge +22:13. **and saw.** Ge +3:7. **the angel.** Ge 3:24. Ex 14:19, 20. Nu 22:31. Jsh 5:13, 14. 2 K 6:17. **clothed.** 1 K 21:27. 2 K 19:1. Ps 35:13, 14. Jon 3:6-8. **fell upon.** Nu 14:5. 16:22.

17. **Is it not I.** ℐ85B, Ge +13:9. ver. 8. 2 S 24:17. Ps 51:4. Ezk 16:63. **even I it is.** Gr. *ego eimi.* Is ◗+*41:4. Jn ◗+*8:28, 58n. **these sheep.** 1 K 22:17. Ps 44:11. **what have.** 2 S 24:1. **be on me.** T#1661. Ge 44:33. Ex 32:32, 33. Jn 10:11, 12. Ro 9:3. 1 J 3:16. **on my father's.** Ex 20:5. 2 S 12:10. Ps 51:14. Is 39:7, 8. **that they should.** Jsh 22:18.

18. **the angel.** ver. 11. Ac 8:26, etc. **that David.** ver. 15. 2 S 24:18. 2 Ch 3:1. **set up.** T#1220. 1 K 18:31, 32, 36, 37. **in the.** T#1210. Jg 6:11-16. 2 S 24:18, 19, 25.

19. **went up.** 2 K 5:10-14. Jn 2:5. Ac 9:6.

20. **And Ornan,** etc. *or,* When Ornan turned back and saw the angel, *then he,* and his four sons with him, hid themselves. Jg 6:11.

21. **bowed himself.** 1 S 25:23. 2 S 24:18-20.

22. **Grant.** Heb. Give. ℐ132D, Ge +19:25. 1 K 21:2. **thou shalt grant.** 2 S 24:21. **price.** ℐ121D5, Ge +23:9. **that the plague.** Nu 16:48. 25:8.

23. **Take it.** Ge 23:4-6. 2 S 24:22, 23. Je 32:8. **the oxen.** 1 S 6:14. 1 K 19:21. Is 28:27, 28. **burnt offerings.** Le +*23:12. **meat offering.** Le +*23:13.

24. **Nay.** Ge 14:23. 23:13. Dt 16:16, 17. Ml 1:12-14. Ro 12:17. **price.** ℐ121D5, Ge +23:9. **for I will not.** It is a maxim from heaven, "Honor the Lord with thy substance." He who has a religion that *costs him nothing*, has a religion that is *worth nothing*: nor will any man esteem the ordinances of God, if those ordinances cost him nothing. Had Araunah's noble offer been accepted, it would have been *Araunah's sacrifice*, not *David's*; nor would it have answered the end of turning away the displeasure of the Most High. It was David that sinned, not Araunah; therefore David must offer sacrifice. 2 S ‖24:24n. Pr 3:9. **burnt offerings.** Le +*23:12. **without cost.** Ge 29:15. Ex 23:15. Dt *16:16. 1 S *9:7, 8. 2 S ‖24:24n. Lk *21:4. 1 C +*16:2. Ph 3:8.

25. **David gave.** 2 S 24:24, 25.

26. **built there.** Ex 20:24, 25. 24:4, 5. **burnt offerings.** Le +*23:12. **peace offerings.** Le +*23:19. **and called.** 1 S 7:8, 9. Ps 51:15. 91:15. 99:6. Pr 15:8. Is 65:24. Je *33:3. **answered him.** T#1771. Nu 16:28-35. 1 K 18:36-38. **by fire.** Le 9:24. Jg 6:21. 13:20. 1 K 18:24, 38. 2 Ch 7:1.

27. **the Lord.** ver. 15, 16. 2 S 24:16. Ps 103:20. La *3:31-33. He *1:14. **he put.** ver. 12, 20. Je 47:6. Ezk 21:30. Mt 26:52. Jn 18:11.

28. **threshingfloor.** Ge +50:10. Dt +16:13mg.

29. **the tabernacle.** Ex ch. 40. **Gibeon.** 1 Ch 16:39. 1 K 3:4, etc. 2 Ch 1:3, 13.

30. **he was afraid.** ver. 16. 1 Ch 13:12. Dt 10:12. 2 S 6:9. Jb 13:21. 21:6. 23:15. Ps 90:11. 119:120. Je 5:22. 10:7. He 12:28, 29. Re 1:17. 15:4.

1 CHRONICLES 22

David makes large preparations for the temple, 1-5. He instructs Solomon, and charges him to build it, 6-16. He commands the elders of Israel to assist him, 17-19.

1. **This is the house.** David perhaps had some assurance that this was the *place* on which God designed that His house should be built; and perhaps it was this that induced him to buy not only the threshingfloor, but probably some adjacent ground also, as Calmet supposes, that there might be sufficient room for such a structure. 1 Ch 21:18-28. Ge 28:17. Dt 12:5-7, 11. 2 S 24:18. 2 Ch 3:1. 6:5, 6. Ps 78:60, 67-69. 132:13, 14. Jn 4:20-22. **and this is the altar.** 2 K 18:22. 2 Ch 32:12.

2. **the strangers.** Ge +*23:4 (S#1616h). Ex 12:48mg. Dt +26:11. Jsh +20:9. 1 K 9:20, 21. 2 Ch 2:17. 8:7, 8. Is 61:5, 6. Mt +25:35. Ep 2:12, 19-22. **masons.** 1 Ch 14:1. 2 S 5:11. 1 K 5:17, 18. 6:7. 7:9-12. 2 K 12:12. 22:6. Ezr 3:7.

3. **prepared iron.** 1 Ch 29:2, 7. **without weight.** ver. 14. 1 K 7:47. 2 Ch 4:18. Je 52:20.

4. **cedar trees.** 2 S 5:11. 1 K 5:6-10. 2 Ch 2:3. Ezr 3:7.

5. **Solomon.** 1 Ch 29:1. 1 K 3:7. 2 Ch 13:7. **exceeding.** 1 K 9:8. 2 Ch 2:5. 7:21. Ezr 3:12. Is 64:11. Ezr 7:20. Hg 2:3, 9. Lk 21:5. **fame and.** ℐ93A, Ge +1:26. By Hendiadys, "of glorious fame." **David prepared.** Dt 31:2-7. Ec 9:10. Jn 3:30. 4:37, 38. 9:4. 13:1. 2 P 1:13-15.

6. **charged him.** Nu 27:18, 19, 23. Dt 31:14, 23. Mt 28:18-20. Ac 1:2. 20:25-31. 1 T 5:21. 6:13-17. 2 T 4:1.

7. **it was in.** 1 Ch 17:1, etc. 28:2, etc. 29:3. 2 S 7:2. 1 K 8:17-19. 2 Ch 6:7-9. Ps 132:5. Ac 6:46. **unto the name.** Dt 12:5, 11, 21. 1 K 8:16, 20, 29. 9:3. 2 Ch 2:4. Ezr 6:12.

8. **Thou hast shed.** 1 Ch 28:3. Nu 31:20, 24. 1 K 5:3. **thou shalt not.** 1 Ch 17:4-10. 2 S 7:5-11.

9. **a son.** 1 Ch 17:11. 28:5-7. 2 S 7:12, 13. **man of rest.** Ge 5:29. **I will give.** 1 K 4:20, 25. 5:4. Ps 72:7. Is 9:6, 7. **Solomon.** that is, *Peaceable.* 2 S 12:24, 25. **I will give peace.** Jg 6:24mg. Jb 34:29. Is 26:12. 45:7. 57:19. 66:12. Hg 2:9.

10. **He shall build.** 1 Ch 17:12, 13. 28:6. 2 S 7:13. 1 K 5:5. 8:19, 20. Zc 6:12, 13. **he shall be.** Ps 89:26, 27. He 1:5. **I will establish.** 1 Ch 17:14. 28:7. Ps 89:36, 37. Is 9:7. **for ever.** Heb. *olam,* Ex +12:24.

11. **the Lord.** ver. 16. 1 Ch *28:20. Is 26:12. Mt *1:23. *28:20. Ro 15:33. 2 T 4:22.

12. **Only the.** 1 K *3:9-12. 2 Ch 1:10. Ps 72:1. Pr 2:6, 7. Lk *21:15. Ja *1:5. **give thee.** Jsh 1:5, 6. 2 Ch 19:11. **that thou mayest.** Dt *4:6. 1 K 11:1-10. Pr 14:8. Jn +*13:17. 1 J *2:3.

13. **Then shalt.** 1 Ch *28:7. Jsh *1:7, 8,mg. 1 K 2:3. 2 Ch *20:20. Ps 119:6. Je *22:3, 4. **to fulfill.** Mt 3:15. Ac 13:22. Ga *6:2. Ja *2:8. **be strong.** 1 Ch *28:10,

20. Dt 31:7, 8. Jsh 1:*6-9, 18. 1 C 16:13. Ep *6:10. 2 T 2:1.

14. **trouble**. *or,* poverty. 2 C *8:2. **hundred thousand talents**. 1 Ch 29:4-7. 1 K 10:14. **without weight**. As ver. 3. 2 K 25:16. Je 52:20.

15. **hewers and workers of stone and timber**. *that is,* masons and carpenters. See on ver. 2-4. **all manner**. Ex 28:6. 31:3-5. 35:32-35. 1 K 7:14.

16. **the gold**. See on ver. 3, 14. **Arise**. Jsh 1:2, 5, 9. 7:10. Jg 4:14. 18:9, 10. 2 Ch 20:17. 1 C *15:58. Ep 5:14. Ph *2:12, 13. *4:13. **be doing**. T#1. Ge 3:19. Ex 20:9. Nu +14:24. Jsh +*14:8. Jg 5:23. Pr 10:4, 5. 12:24. 13:4. 22:29. *27:23, 24. *28:19. Ec 5:12. 9:10. Is 52:1. Am *6:1. Lk +12:37 (T#738). *16:10. Jn +5:17 (T#63). Ro √12:11. 13:11. Ga +4:18 (T#749). Ep *4:28. 6:7. Col *3:23-25. 1 Th 4:11, 12. 1 T +5:13 (T#358). **and the Lord**. ver. 11. 1 S 17:37. 20:13.

17. **all the princes**. 1 Ch 28:21. 29:6. Ro 16:2, 3. Ph 4:3. 3 J 8.

18. **Is not**. Jg 6:12-14. Ro *8:31. **and hath**. See on ver. 9. 1 Ch 23:25. Dt 12:10, 11. Jsh 22:4. 23:1. 2 S 7:1. Ac 9:31. **before the Lord**. Dt 20:4. Jsh 10:42. 1 S 25:28. 2 S 5:19, 20. Ps 44:1-5.

19. **set your**. 1 Ch 16:11. 28:9. Dt 4:29. 32:46, 47. Ps 27:4. 2 Ch 20:3. Da 9:3. Hg 1:5mg. Ac *11:23. **soul**. Heb. *nephesh,* Ge +34:3. **arise**. See on ver. 16. Is 60:1. Ac *22:16. **to bring**. 1 K 8:6, 21. 2 Ch 5:7. 6:11. **to the name**. See on ver. 7. 1 K 5:3.

1 CHRONICLES 23

David makes Solomon king, 1. The Levites are numbered, and classed for different services, 2-6. The sons of Gershon, 7-11. Of Kohath, 12-20. Of Merari, 21-23. The several officers of the Levites, 24-32.

1. A.M. 2989. B.C. 1015. An. Ex. Is. 476. **old**. 1 Ch 29:28. Ge 25:8. 35:29. 1 K 1:1. Jb 5:26. **he made**. 1 Ch 28:5. 29:22-25. 1 K 1:33-39.

2. **he gathered**. 1 Ch 13:1. 28:1. Jsh 23:2. 24:1. 2 Ch 34:29, 30.

3. **the Levites**. Nu 4:2, 3, 23, 30, 35, 43, 47. **thirty and eight**. Nu 4:48.

4. **twenty**. ver. 28-32. 1 Ch 6:48. 9:28-32. 26:20-27. **set forward**. *or,* oversee. 1 Ch 15:21. 2 Ch 2:2, 18. 34:12. Ezr 3:8, 9. Ne 11:9, 22. Ac *20:28. **officers and judges**. 1 Ch 26:29-31. Dt 16:18. 17:8-10. 2 Ch 19:8. Ml 2:7.

5. **porters**. 1 Ch 9:17-27. 15:23, 24. 16:38, 42. 26:1-12. 2 S 18:26. 2 Ch 8:14. 35:15. Ezr 7:7. Ne 7:73. 11:19. 12:45. **praised**. 1 Ch 6:31-48. 9:33. 15:16-22. 16:41, 42. 25:1-7. 2 Ch 20:19-21. Ps 87:7. **the instruments**. 1 K 10:12. 2 Ch 29:25, 26. See on Am 6:5.

6. **divided**. 2 Ch 8:14. 29:25. 31:2. 35:10. Ezr 6:18. **courses**. Heb. divisions. 1 Ch 24:1. 26:1. **Gershon**. "Gershon" is called "Gershom" in the parallel passage, simply by the mutation of *noon* into *mem.* 1 Ch 6:1, 16, Gershom. Ex 6:16-24. Nu 26:57, 58.

7. **Gershonites**. 1 Ch 6:17-20. 15:7. 26:21. **Laadan**. i.e. *put in order; for their adornment,* *S#3936h. 1 Ch 7:26. 23:7, 8, 9. 26:21, 21, 21. (1) A man of Ephraim, 1 Ch 7:26. (2) One of the Gershonites under David who had three sons, 1 Ch 23:7, 8; 26:21. *Laadan* and *Libni* seem to have been two distinct names of this person; but the variation of *Shimi* and *Shimei* exists only in the translation, the original being uniform. Ex 6:17, Libni, Shimi.

8. **Jehiel**. i.e. *God lives.* 1 Ch 15:18, 20, 21. **Zetham**. i.e. *olive tree,* *S#2241h. 1 Ch 23:8. 26:22. **Joel**. i.e. *Jah is God.* 1 Ch 6:33, 34. 15:7, 11, 17.

9. **Shelomith**. i.e. *peaceful.* Le +24:11. **Haziel**. i.e. *seen of God; vision of God,* *S#2381h. **Haran**. i.e. *mountaineer.* Ge +11:26.

10. **Zina**. i.e. *nourishing; fruitful,* *S#2126h. *Zina* seems to be a mistake for *Zizah;* for both the LXX. and Vulgate read uniformly "Ziza." ver. 11, Ziza. **Jeush**. Ge 36:+5, 18. 2 Ch 11:18. **Beriah**. i.e. *a gift.* 1 Ch +8:21.

11. **Zizah**. i.e. *full breast; abundance; exuberance,* *S#2125h. ver. 10, Zina. **had not many sons**. Heb. did not multiply sons.

12. **sons of Kohath**. See on 1 Ch 6:2. Ex 6:18. Nu 3:27. 26:58. **Izhar**. i.e. *he shines* or *is bright.* Ex +6:18. **Hebron**. i.e. *companionship.* Ex +6:18. **Uzziel**. i.e. *strength of God.* Ex +6:18.

13. **The sons**. See on 1 Ch 6:3. Ex 6:20. Nu 3:27. 26:59. **Aaron**. i.e. *a mountaineer.* Ex +4:14. **Moses**. i.e. *a drawer out.* Ex +2:10. **separated**. Ex 28:1, etc. Nu 18:1. Ps 99:6. 106:16. Ac 13:2. Ro 1:1. Ga 1:15. He 5:4. **sanctify**. Ex 29:33-37, 44. 49:9-15. Le 10:10, 17, 18. 16:11-19, 32, 33. 17:2-6. Nu 18:3-8. **to burn incense**. Ex 30:6-10, 34-38. Le 10:1, 2. 16:12, 13. Nu 16:16-18, 35-40, 46, 47. 1 S 2:28. 2 Ch 26:18-21. Lk 1:9. Re 8:3. **to bless**. Le 9:22, 23. Nu √6:23-27. Dt 21:5.

14. **the man**. See on Dt 33:1. Ps 90, title. **his sons**. 1 Ch 26:23-25.

15. **Gershom**. Ex 2:22. 4:20. 18:3, 4.

16. **Shebuel**. i.e. *captive of God; abide ye with God,* *S#7619h. 1 Ch 23:16. 25:4. 26:24. Also 1 Ch 24:20, 20. 25:20, Shubael. (1) A son of Gershom, the son of Moses, 1 Ch 23:16; 26:24, called Shubael in 1 Ch 24:20. (2) A Levite singer, 1 Ch 25:4, called Shubael in 1 Ch 25:20.

17. **Rehabiah**. i.e. *breadth of Jah; Jah has enlarged; enlarging of the Lord,* *S#7345h. 1 Ch 24:21, 21. 26:25. **the chief**. *or,* the first. 1 Ch 26:25. **were very many**. Heb. were highly multiplied.

18. **Shelomith**. 1 Ch 24:22, Shelomoth. 26:26.

19. **Hebron**. ver. 12. 1 Ch 15:9. 24:23. **Jeriah**. i.e. *fear of the Lord; cast by God; Jehovah will teach,* *S#3404h. 1 Ch 23:19. 24:23. **Amariah**. i.e. *saying of Jah.* Ezr +7:3. **Jahaziel**. i.e. *Jah sees.* 1 Ch +24:23. **Jekameam**. i.e. *a people rises.* 1 Ch +24:23.

21. **Merari**. ver. 6. See on 1 Ch 6:29, 30. 24:26-30. **Mahli**. i.e. *sickly.* Ex 6:19, Mahali. **Mushi**. i.e. *touched of Jah.* Ex +6:19. **Eleazar**. i.e. *God has help.* Ex +6:23. **Kish**. i.e. *a snaring.* 1 Ch 24:29. 1 S +9:1.

22. **had no sons**. 1 Ch +2:34. 24:28. **but daughters**. 1 Ch +2:34. **brethren**. *or,* kinsmen. 1 Ch 7:22n. +15:5. **took them**. Nu 36:6-8.

23. **Eder**. i.e. *drove, order; a flock,* *S#5740h. 1 Ch 23:23. 24:30. Also Jsh 15:21. (1) Of the sons of Merari when David made Solomon king, 1 Ch 23:23; 24:30. (2) A town of Judah, Jsh 15:21. **Jeremoth**. 1 Ch 24:30, Jerimoth.

24. **the sons of Levi**. Nu 10:17, 21. **after the house**. Nu 1:4. 2:32. 3:15, 20. 4:34-49. **by their polls**. Nu 1:2, 18, 22. 3:47. **from the age**. At first David appointed Levites to serve from *thirty years* old and upwards; but considering, probably, that the temple which was about to be built, with its courts, chambers, etc., would require a more numerous ministry, he fixed this period,

by this subsequent regulation, at *twenty* years and upwards. In the time of Moses, the age was from *thirty* years to *fifty*: here this latter period is not mentioned, probably because the service was not so laborious now; for the ark being fixed, they had no longer any burdens to carry; and therefore even an old man might continue to serve. See the Note on Nu 8:24. **twenty.** ver. 3, 27. Nu 1:3. 4:3. 8:24. Ezr 3:8.

25. **The Lord.** See on 1 Ch 22:18. 2 S 7:1, 11. **given rest.** 1 T 2:1, 2. He=4:9. Re=14:13. **that they may dwell in Jerusalem.** *or,* and he dwelleth in Jerusalem. 1 K 8:13, 27. Ps 9:11. 68:16, 18. 132:13, 14. 135:21. Is 8:18. Jl 3:21. Zc 8:3. 2 C 6:16. Col 2:9. **for ever.** Ge +9:12. Ex +*12:24.

26. **no more carry.** Nu 4:5, 49. 7:9. 2 T=4:7, 8. Re=3:12. =7:15, 16. =14:13.

27. **by the last.** ver. 3, 24. 2 S 23:1. Ps 72:20. **numbered.** Heb. number.

28. **office was to wait,** etc. Heb. station *was* at the hand of Aaron. 1 Ch 18:17mg. Ne 11:24. Ps 123:2. 2 C=4:5. **for the service.** ver. 4. 1 Ch 28:13. Nu 3:6-9. 8:11-22, 26. 18:2-6. **in the chambers.** 1 Ch 9:26. 1 K 6:5. 2 Ch 31:11. Ezr 8:29. Ne 13:4, 5, 9. Je 35:4. Ezk 41:6-11, 26. 42:3, 13. **purifying.** 1 Ch 9:28, 29. 2 Ch 29:5, 18, 19. 35:3-6, 11-14.

29. **for the showbread.** It was the *priests'* office to place this bread before the Lord; and it was their privilege to feed on the old loaves when they were replaced by the *new.* 1 Ch 9:31, 32. Ex 25:30. Le 24:5-9. 1 K 7:48. 2 Ch 13:11. 29:18. Ne 10:33. Mt 12:4. He 9:2. **the fine flour.** 1 Ch 9:29, etc. Le 6:20-23. **meat offering.** Le +*23:13. **unleavened.** Le 2:4-7. 7:9. **pan.** *or,* flat plate. **for all manner of measure.** The *standards* of all weights and measures were in the sanctuary; and therefore the Levites had the inspection of weights and measures of every kind, that no fraud might in this way be committed. Honesty is inseparably connected with piety; and hence the Levites, being sufficiently numerous, were employed to superintend the former, as well as the latter. Le 19:35, 36. Nu 3:50.

30. **stand.** 1 Ch 6:31-33. 9:33. 16:37-42. 25:1-7. 2 Ch 29:25-28. 31:2. Ezr 3:10, 11. Ps 135:1-3, 19, 20. 137:2-4. Re 5:8-14. 14:3. **every morning.** Ex 29:39-42. 2 S 13:4mg. Ps +5:3. 92:1-3. 134:1, 2. **thank.** 1 Th 5:18. **at even.** Mt +14:23.

31. **in the sabbaths.** Le 23:24, 39. Nu 10:10. Ps 81:1-4. Is 1:13, 14. **set feasts.** Ge +*17:21. Le ch. *23. Nu ch. 28, 29. **the order.** T#1269. 1 Ch 15:11-13. Ne 11:17. **before.** Ep=1:4.

32. **keep.** 1 Ch 9:27. Nu 1:53. 1 K 8:4. **the charge of the sons.** Nu 3:6-8, 38.

1 CHRONICLES 24

The priests are divided by lot into twenty-four courses, 1-19. The rest of the Kohathites, and the Merarites, are divided in like manner, 20-31.

1. **the divisions.** 1 Ch 23:6mg. **The sons.** 1 Ch 6:3. Ex 6:23. 28:1. Le 10:1-6. Nu 3:2. 26:60.

2. **Nadab.** i.e. *a willing one.* Ex +6:23. 24:1, 9. **Abihu.** i.e. *my father is he.* Ex +6:23. **died.** Le 10:2. Nu 3:4. 16:39, 40. 18:7. 26:61. **Eleazar.** i.e. *God is help.* Ex +6:23. 29:9. Le 10:12. Nu 16:39, 40. 18:7. **Ithamar.** i.e. *land of palms* or *where is the palm?* Ex +6:23.

3. **Zadok.** i.e. *just.* ver. 6, 31. 1 Ch 6:4-8, 50-53. 12:27, 28. 15:11. 16:39. 2 S +8:17. 20:25. 1 K 2:35. **Ahimelech.** This was *Abiathar,* who appears to have had the name of *Ahimelech,* as well as his father. 1 S 21:1. 22:9, etc. 2 S 8:17. Mk 2:26.

4. **more.** 1 Ch 15:6-12, 16. **sons of Eleazar.** Nu 25:11-13. 1 S 2:30-38. **according.** See on 1 Ch 23:24.

5. **they divided by lot.** Jsh +14:2n. 18:10. Pr +16:33. Jon 1:7. Ac *1:26. **the governors.** 1 Ch 9:11. 2 Ch 35:8. Ne 11:11. Mt 26:3. 27:1. Ac 4:1, 6. 5:24.

6. **Shemaiah.** i.e. *heard of Jah.* 1 Ch +9:16. **Nethaneel.** i.e. *gift of Jah.* Nu +1:8. **the scribe.** 1 K 4:3. 2 Ch 34:13. Ezr 7:6. Ne 8:1. Mt 8:19. 13:52. 23:1, 2. **principal household.** Heb. house of the father. ver. 4. 1 Ch 23:24.

7. **Jehoiarib.** i.e. *Jehovah defended; the Lord will contend,* *S#3080h. 1 Ch 9:10. Ne 12:19, Joiarib. (1) The head of the first course of priests, 1 Ch 24:7. (2) A priest at Jerusalem, 1 Ch 9:10. **to Jedaiah.** i.e. *known of Jah.* 1 Ch +9:10. Ezr 2:36. Ne 7:39. 11:10.

8. **Harim.** i.e. *flat-nosed; compressed; bent upward,* *S#2766h. 1 Ch 24:8. Ezr 2:32, 39. 10:21, 31. Ne 3:11. 7:35, 42. 10:5, 27. 12:15. (1) One whose children returned from Babylon, Ezr 2:32. (2) One whose children married strange wives, Ezr 10:31. (3) Father of Malchijah, who helped to repair the wall, Ne 3:11. **Seorim.** i.e. *barley; bearded ones,* *S#8188h.

9. **Malchijah.** i.e. *king of Jah.* 1 Ch +9:12. **Mijamin.** i.e. *from the right hand,* *S#4326h. 1 Ch 24:9. Ezr 10:25. Ne 10:7. Ne 10:7. 12:5, Miamin, 17, Miniamin. (1) A priest in the time of David, 1 Ch 24:9. (2) One who sealed the covenant made by Nehemiah, Ne 10:7.

10. **Hakkoz.** i.e. *the thorn,* *S#6976h. **Abijah.** i.e. *my father is Jah.* 1 K +14:1. As the Evangelist Luke mentions *the course of Abia,* it is evident that these courses of the priests, established by David, no doubt under Divine direction, were continued, with some alteration, till the days of Christ: these records must therefore have been very useful after the Babylonian captivity. Ne 12:4, 17. Lk 1:5, Abia.

11. **Jeshuah.** i.e. *a savior; Jah will save; salvation of the Lord,* *S#3442h. 1 Ch 24:11. 2 Ch 31:15. Ezr 2:2, 6, *36, 40. 3:2, 8, 9. 4:3. 8:33. 10:18. Ne 3:19. 7:7, 11, *39, 43. 8:7, 17. 9:4, 5. 10:9. 11:26. 12:1, 7, 8, *10, 24, 26. (1) A sanctuary servant, Ezr 2:36; Ne 7:39. (2) A Levite in Hezekiah's time, 1 Ch 24:11; 2 Ch 31:15; Ezr 2:40; Ne 7:43. (3) A priest in exile, Ezr 2:2; 3:2, 8, 9; 4:3; 5:2; 10:18; Ne 7:7; 12:1, 7, 10, 26. (4) Father of Jozabad, Ezr 8:33. (5) A family of exiles, Ezr 2:6; Ne 7:11. (6) Father of Ezer, Ne 3:19. (7) A priest who assisted Ezra, Ne 8:7; 9:4, 5; 12:8, 24. (8) Same as Joshua, son of Nun, Ne 8:17. (9) A Levite who renewed the covenant, Ne 10:9. (10) A city in Benjamin, Ne 11:26. **Shecaniah.** i.e. *tabernacle of Jah; intimate with Jehovah; Jah has dwelt; habitation of the Lord,* *S#7935h. 1 Ch 3:21, 22. Ezr 8:3, 5. 10:2. Ne 3:29. 6:18. 12:3. (1) Successor with his sons of Jeconiah, in David's line, 1 Ch 3:21, +22, Shechaniah. (2) A priest in David's time, 1 Ch 24:11. (3) One set over the tithes by Hezekiah, 2 Ch 31:15. (4) One whose sons returned from Babylon with Ezra, Ezr 8:3, 5. (5) He who urged Ezra to reform the strange marriages, Ezr 10:2. (6) Father of Shemaiah, who helped to build the wall, Ne 3:29. (7) Father-in-law of Tobiah, who tried to terrify Nehemiah, Ne 6:18. (8) One of the priests who came

up with Zerubbabel from Babylon, Ne 12:3.

12. **Eliashib**. i.e. *God brings back.* 1 Ch +3:24. Ne 12:10. **Jakim**. i.e. *He raises up.* 1 Ch +8:19.

13. **Huppah**. i.e. *a covering; nuptial bed; chamber,* ✱S#2647h. **Jeshebeab**. i.e. *seat* or *habitation of his father; father's dwelling,* ✱S#3428h.

14. **Bilgah**. i.e. *brightness.* Ne +12:5. **Immer**. i.e. *a sayer.* 1 Ch +9:12. Ezr 2:37. 10:20. Ne 7:40.

15. **Hezir**. i.e. *protected; a sow; swine,* ✱S#2387h. 1 Ch 24:15. Ne 10:20. (1) The son of Aaron to whom the 17th lot fell, 1 Ch 24:15. (2) One who sealed the covenant, Ne 10:20. **Aphses**. i.e. *the shattering; dispersion,* ✱S#6483h.

16. **Pethahiah**. i.e. *opening of Jah.* Ne +11:24. **Jehezekel**. i.e. *God will strengthen; God is strong,* ✢S#3168h.

17. **Jachin**. i.e. *He prepares.* Ge +46:10. **Gamul**. i.e. *weaned; deed; recompensed,* ✱S#1577h.

18. **Delaiah**. i.e. *drawn up of Jah.* Je +36:12. **Maaziah**. i.e. *strengthened of Jehovah; consolation of the Lord,* ✱S#4590h. (1) A sanctuary servant, 1 Ch 24:18. (2) A priest who renewed the covenant, Ne 10:8.

19. **the orderings**. 1 Ch 9:25. 2 Ch 23:4, 8. 1 C +*14:40. **under Aaron**. ver. 1. Ne 7:11.

20. **Amram**. 1 Ch 6:18. 23:12-14. **Shubael**. i.e. *captive; the return of God,* ✱S#7619h. 1 Ch 23:16. 24:20. 25:4, 20. 26:24, Shebuel. **Jehdeiah**. i.e. *whom Jehovah makes joyful; he will be gladdened of Jehovah; unity of Jah,* ✱S#3165h. 1 Ch 24:20. 27:30. (1) The son of Shubael, a descendant of Levi, 1 Ch 24:20. (2) The overseer of the asses in the time of David, 1 Ch 27:30.

21. **Rehabiah**. i.e. *breadth of Jah.* 1 Ch 23:17. **Isshiah**. i.e. *whom Jehovah lends; forgotten of Jah,* ✢S#3449h. (1) A descendant of Moses, 1 Ch 24:21. (2) A Levite, 1 Ch 24:25. Probably **Isshiah** is a contracted form, or a corruption, of **Jeshaiah**. 1 Ch 26:25, Jeshaiah.

22. **Izharites**. i.e. *descendants of Izhar* (i.e. *anointed; oil,* Ex +6:18), ✱S#3325h. 1 Ch 24:22. 26:23, 29. Nu 3:27. The original is uniformly *Izharites.* 1 Ch 23:18. Ex 6:21. Nu 3:19, 27, Izeharites. **Shelomoth**. i.e. *peaceful; pacifications; retributions,* ✱S#8013h. 1 Ch 23:9. 24:22, 22. 26:25, 26. The variation of "Shelomith" and "Shelomoth" arises from the mutation of *wav* and *yood.* 1 Ch 23:18. 26:26, Shelomith. **Jahath**. i.e. *he affrights.* 1 Ch +4:2.

23. **Jeriah**. The following variations exist only in the translation, the original being uniformly "Jerijah," "Michah," and "Isshiah." 1 Ch +23:19. +26:31, Jerijah. **Jahaziel**. i.e. *beheld of God; God will cause to see,* ✢S#3166h. (1) A captain in David's army, 1 Ch 12:4. (2) A priest, 1 Ch 16:6. (3) A son of Hebron, 1 Ch 23:19; 24:23. (4) A Levite, 2 Ch 20:14. (5) A family of exiles, Ezr 8:5. **Jekameam**. i.e. *the people will rise; he will gather the people; let the people be established,* ✱S#3360h. 1 Ch 23:19. 24:23.

24. **Uzziel**. i.e. *strength of God.* Ex +6:18. **Michah**. i.e. *who is thus?; who is like Jehovah?; who is like unto the Lord?,* ✢S#4318h. ver. 25. 1 Ch 23:20, Micah. **Shamir**. i.e. *guarding; a thorn; a briar, diamond; a sharp point; a guard; keeping; observed,* ✱S#8053h. (1) A descendant of Uzziel, the grandson of Levi, 1 Ch 24:24. (2) A city of Judah, Jsh 15:48. (2) A place in Mount Ephraim, Jg 10:1, 2.

25. **Isshiah**. i.e. *forgotten of Jah.* 1 Ch 23:20, Jesiah. **Zechariah**. i.e. *remembered by Jah.* 1 Ch 15:18, 20.

26. **Jaaziah**. i.e. *comforted of the Lord; he will be strengthened of Jehovah,* ✱S#3269h. ver. 27. **Beno**. i.e. *son of him,* ✱S#1121h. ver. 27.

27. **sons**. 1 Ch 6:19. 23:21. Ex 6:19. Nu 3:20. **Shoham**. i.e. *an onyx stone; their equalizing; justifying them; precious as the onyx,* ✱S#7719h. **Zaccur**. i.e. *mindful.* 1 Ch +25:2. **Ibri**. i.e. *born beyond the river; one who has crossed; a passer over,* ✱S#5681h.

28. **who had no sons**. 1 Ch +2:34. 23:22.

29. **Jerahmeel**. i.e. *God is merciful.* 1 Ch +2:9.

30. **Mushri**. 1 Ch 6:47. 23:23. **Jerimoth**. i.e. *high places.* 1 Ch +7:7.

31. **lots**. ver. 5, 6. Nu 26:56. **even the principal**. The whole company being arranged according to their families, with the proper number of the divisions, the order of the courses was assigned them by lot, without respect to rank or seniority. 1 Ch 25:8. 26:13.

1 CHRONICLES 25

The names and offices of the principal singers and musicians, 1-7. They are divided by lot into twenty-four courses, 8-31.

1. **the captains**. That is, the chiefs of the several orders; not *military* captains. 1 Ch 12:28. 23:2. 24:5, 6. 2 Ch 23:1, 9. **Asaph**. See on 1 Ch 6:33, 39, 44. 15:16-19. **prophesy**. The word *prophesy,* here, seems to mean no more than praising God by singing inspired prophetical hymns. ver. 3. 1 S 10:5. 2 K 3:15. 1 C *14-24-26. **harps**. 1 Ch +13:8. 15:16-21. 16:4, 5, 42. 23:5-7. 2 Ch 23:13. 29:25, 26. 31:2. 34:12. Ezr 3:10, 11. Ne 12:24, 27, 43-46. Ps 81:2. 92:1-3. 150:3-5. Re 15:2-4. **psalteries**. 1 S +10:5. **cymbals**. 1 Ch +13:8.

2. **Asaph**. ver. 1. 1 Ch 6:39. 15:17. 16:5. Ps 73-83, titles. **Zaccur**. i.e. *remembered; mindful,* ✢S#2139h. (1) Father of Shammua, a Reubenite, Nu 13:4. (2) A sanctuary servant, 1 Ch 24:27. (3) A son of Asaph, 1 Ch 25:2, 10; Ne 12:35. (4) One that rebuilt Jerusalem's wall, Ne 3:2. (5) A Levite who sealed the covenant, Ne 10:12. (6) Father of Hanan, set over treasures, Ne 13:13. See also Zacchur, 1 Ch +4:26; Zabbud, Ezr +8:14. **Joseph**. i.e. *he is adding.* Ge +30:24. **Nethaniah**. i.e. *gift of Jah.* ver. +12. **Asarelah**. i.e. *upright toward God; an upright or straight oak; guided towards God,* ✱S#841h. "Otherwise called Jesharelah, ver. 14." **under the hands**. ver. 3, 6. Is 3:6. **according to the order of the king**. Heb. by the hands of the king. ⌐144A5, Ge +9:5. ver. 6mg. 1 Ch 11:3mg, 2 Ch 23:18mg. √34:14mg,n. 1 K +16:12mg. Ezr 3:10.

3. **Jeduthun**. 1 Ch 9:16. 16:41, 42. 2 Ch 29:14. **Gedaliah**. i.e. *whom Jehovah has made great; magnified of Jehovah; greatness of Jah,* ✱S#1436h. 1 Ch 25:3, 9. 2 K 25:22, 23, 23, 24, 25. Je 38:1. 39:14. 40:6, 7, 9, 11, 12, 13, 14, 15, 16. 41:1, 2, 3, 4, 6, 9, 10, 18. 43:6. Also Ezr 10:18. Je 40:5, 8. 41:16. Zp 1:1. (1) A governor of the Jews, appointed by Nebuchadnezzar, 2 K 25:22; Je 40:5; 41:1. (2) One of the singers, 1 Ch 25:3, 9. (3) One of the sons of the priests who had taken strange wives, Ezr 10:18. (4) One of those who afflicted Jeremiah, Je 38:1. (5) Grandfather of Zephaniah, Zp 1:1. **Zeri**. i.e. *distillation; balm; formation,* ✱S#6874h. ver. 11, Izri. **Jeshaiah**. i.e. *the salvation of Jehovah; Jah has saved; safety of Jah,* ✢S#3470h. (1) One of the singers, son of Jeduthun, 1 Ch 25:3, 15. (2) One of the Levites who had charge of the trea-

sure, 1 Ch 26:25. (3, 4) Two companions of Ezra, Ezr 8:7, 19. **Hashabiah**. i.e. *reckoning of Jah.* 1 Ch +9:14. **Mattithiah**. i.e. *gift of Jah.* ver. 21. 1 Ch 15:18, 21. Ezr +10:43. **six**. *"With Shimei, mentioned* ver. 17." or, "Shishah." i.e. "six." Perhaps the same as "Shimea" in ver. 17 (Young). *Shimei* is not only mentioned in the parallel passage, but is supplied here by the Arabic version. **to give thanks**. 1 Ch 23:30. Ps 92:1. Je 33:11.

4. **Heman**. 1 Ch 6:33. 15:17, 19. 16:41, 42. Ps 88, title. **Bukkiah**. i.e. *emptiness of Jah.* ver. +13. **Mattaniah**. i.e. *gift of Jah.* ver. 16. 2 K +24:17. **Uzziel**. i.e. *strength of God.* ver. 18, Azareel. 1 Ch 24:24. **Shebuel**. ver. 20. 1 Ch 24:20, Shubael. **Jerimoth**. ver. 22. 1 Ch 24:30. **Hananiah**. i.e. *grace of Jah.* ver. +23. **Hanani**. i.e. *favorable; gracious; graciously given of the Lord; my grace,* *S#2607h. 1 Ch 25:4, 25. 1 K 16:1, 7. 2 Ch 16:7. 19:2. 20:34. Ezr 10:20. Ne 1:2. 7:2. 12:36. (1) A prophet, father of Jehu, 1 K 16:1; 2 Ch 19:2; 20:34. (2) A son of Heman, 1 Ch 25:4, 25. (3) A seer who reproved Asa for seeking help from the king of Syria, 2 Ch 16:7. Perhaps the same as Number 1. (4) One of those who married a strange wife, Ezr 10:20. (5) Brother of Nehemiah, Ne 1:2; 7:2. (5) A Levite at the dedication of the wall, Ne 12:36. **Eliathah**. i.e. *to whom God comes; God of the coming one; my God hath come,* *S#448h. ver. 27. **Giddalti**. i.e. *I have made great; I have trained up; I have magnified,* *S#1437h. ver. 29. **Romamti-eser**. i.e. *exultation of help; I have exalted the helper; I have heightened help,* *S#7320h. ver. 31. **Joshbekashah**. i.e. *a hard or sharp seat; seat in a hard place; dwelling in hardness,* *S#3436h. ver. 24. **Mallothi**. i.e. *I have spoken; I speak; my fulness,* *S#4413h. ver. 26. **Hothir**. i.e. *he made abundant; a surplus; who remains, abounds, or is undaunted,* *S#1956h. ver. 28. **Mahazioth**. i.e. *visions; seeing a sign,* *S#4238h. ver. 30.

5. **the king's seer**. 1 Ch 21:9. 1 S 9:9. 2 S +24:11. **words**. *or,* matters. **to lift up**. This may denote that he presided over those who used wind instruments. **God gave**. 1 Ch 4:27. 28:5. Ge +29:31. 33:5. Ps +*127:3. Is 8:18.

6. **under the hands**. ver. 2, 3. **for song**. ver. 1-3. 1 Ch 15:22. 23:5. Ps 68:25. Ep *5:19. Col *3:16. **according to the king's order**. Heb. by the hands of the king. ꜰ144A5, Ge +9:5. ver. +2mg. **Asaph**. See on ver. 1-4.

7. **two hundred**. These two hundred and eighty-eight, being twenty-four courses of twelve each, were more skilful than the other Levites; and being placed under the twenty-four sons of the chief singers, they had the four thousand before mentioned divided among them, to officiate by courses, according to their instructions: 1 Ch 23:5. **instructed**. *or,* taught. SS 3:8. Is 29:13. Ho 10:11. **cunning**. *or,* intelligent. In music, etc. 1 Ch +*15:22.

8. **cast lots**. See on 1 Ch 24:5. Le 16:8. Jsh +14:2n. 1 S 14:41, 42. Pr *16:33. Ac *1:26. **ward against ward**. 1 Ch 24:31. 26:13, 16. Ne 12:24. **the teacher**. Even among the twenty-four leaders, some were more expert than others; some were *teachers,* and others were *scholars;* but every one was taken by the solemn casting of lots, without any regard to these distinctions. Thus all things were disposed for the preserving of order, and avoiding all disputes about precedence: there being no respect had, in this divine distribution, to birth,

but the younger in course preceded the elder. 1 Ch 15:22. 2 Ch 23:13.

9. **Joseph**. ver. 2. **the second**. Dr. Geddes, chiefly on the authority of the Arabic, adds, "who with his sons and brethren were twelve."

10. **Zaccur**. ver. 2.

11. **Izri**. i.e. *created; my imagination; my thought; my formation,* *S#3339h. "Izri" seems to be called "Zeri" by the aphaeresis of *yood.* ꜰ33, Aphaeresis. 1 Ch +11:13. ver. 3, Zeri.

12. **Nethaniah**. i.e. *gift of Jah; given of the Lord,* *S#5418h. 1 Ch 25:12. 2 Ch 17:8. Je 36:14. 40:8. 41:9. Also 1 Ch 25:2. 2 K 25:23, 25. Je 40:14, 15. 41:1, 2, 6, 7, 10, 11, 12, 15, 16, 18. (1) Father of Ishmael, one of the captains who came to Gedaliah, 2 K 25:23, 25; Je 40:8, 14. (2) A son of Asaph, 1 Ch 25:12. (3) A Levite sent by king Jehoshaphat to teach Judah, 2 Ch 17:8. (4) Father of Jehudi, who was sent to fetch Baruch's roll, Je 36:14.

13. **Bukkiah**. i.e. *emptied by Jah; emptied out by Jehovah; emptying of the Lord,* *S#1232h. ver. 4.

14. **Jesharelah**. i.e. *upright toward God; right towards God,* *S#3480h. This variation arises from the mutation of *aleph* and *yood;* the word being written in the parallel passage "Asarelah," and here, "Jesarelah." ver. 2, Asarelah.

15. **Jeshaiah**. i.e. *safety of Jah.* ver. +3.

16. **Mattaniah**. i.e. *gift of Jah.* ver. 4.

17. **Shimei**. i.e. *hearing.* 2 S +16:5.

18. **Azareel**. i.e. *help of God.* ver. 4. Probably this person was called by both names; or *Uzziel* may be a mistake for *Azareel.* In the Syriac and Arabic, the name is nearly the same in both places. ver. 4, Uzziel.

19. **Hashabiah**. i.e. *reckoning of Jah.* ver. 3.

20. **Shubael**. i.e. *return of God.* ver. 4, Shebuel. 1 Ch +24:20.

21. **Mattithiah**. i.e. *gift of Jah.* ver. 3.

22. **Jerimoth**. i.e. *high places.* ver. 4. 1 Ch 23:23. 24:30.

23. **Hananiah**. i.e. *whom Jehovah gave; the grace of Jah; graciously given of the Lord,* *S#2608h. 1 Ch 25:23. 2 Ch 26:11. Je 36:12. Also 1 Ch 3:19, 21. 8:24. 25:4. Ezr 10:28. Ne 3:8, 30. 7:2. 10:23. 12:12, 41. Je 28:1, 5, 10, 11, 12, 13, 15, 15, 17. 37:13. Da 1:6, 7, 11, 19. Also Da 2:17. (1) A Benjamite, son of Shashak, 1 Ch 8:24. (2) A son of Heman, singer for David's sanctuary, 1 Ch 25:4, 23. (3) One of king Uzziah's captains, 2 Ch 26:11. (4) Father of Jeremiah's contemporary, the prince of Zedekiah, Je 36:12. (5) A false prophet, contemporary with Jeremiah, the son of Azzur of Gibeon, Je 28:1. (6) Grandfather, or remoter ancestor, of Irijah, the captain of the watch who arrested Jeremiah on the charge of intending to desert to the Chaldeans, Je 37:13. (7) A companion of Daniel, afterwards called Shadrach, Da 1:6, 7. (8) A son of Zerubbabel, and father of Pelatiah and Jeshaiah, 1 Ch 3:19, 21; perhaps the ancestor of Christ called, by transposition of the constituent parts of the name, Joanan, Lk 3:27. (9) A son of Bebai, induced by Ezra to put away his strange wife, Ezr 10:28. (10) One who helped rebuild the wall of Jerusalem, Ne 3:8. (11) Another who helped rebuild the wall of Jerusalem, Ne 3:10. (12) A priest who blew a trumpet at the dedication of the wall, Ne 12:41. (13) One who sealed the covenant with Nehemiah, Ne 10:23. (14) The governor of the castle and joint ruler with Hanani, Nehemiah's brother, over

Jerusalem, Ne 7:2. (15) A priest, head of the father's house of Jeremiah, in the days of the high priest Joiakim, a generation after the exile, Ne 12:12.

25. **Hanani.** i.e. *my grace.* ver. 4.
26. **Mallothi.** i.e. *my fulness.* ver. 4.
27. **Eliathah.** i.e. *my God hath come.* ver. 4.
28. **Hothir.** i.e. *he has made abundant.* ver. 4.
29. **Giddalti.** i.e. *I have made great.* ver. 4.
30. **Mahazioth.** i.e. *vision of a sign.* ver. 4.
31. **Romamti-ezer.** i.e. *I have exalted help.* ver. 4.

1 CHRONICLES 26

The divisions of the porters, 1-12. The gates assigned to them by lot, 13-19. The Levites who had the charge of the treasures, 20-28. Those who were officers and judges, 29-32.

1. **the divisions.** There were four classes of these, each of which belonged to the four gates of the temple, which opened to the four cardinal points of heaven. The *eastern* gate fell to Shelemiah; the *northern* to Zechariah (ver. 15); the *southern* to Obed-edom (ver. 15); and the *western* to Shuppim and Hosah (ver. 16). These several persons were *captains* of these porter-bands, or doorkeepers, at the different gates. There were probably *a thousand men* under each of these captains; as we find, from 1 Ch 23:5, that their whole number was *four thousand.* **the porters.** 1 Ch 9:17-27. 15:18, 23, 24. 2 Ch 23:19. **Korhites.** Nu 26:9-11. Ps 44-49, titles. **Meshelemiah.** "Shelemiah" is merely an abbreviation of "Meshelemiah," by the aphaeresis of the letter *mem.* ♪33. Aphaeresis, 1 Ch +11:13. ver. 14, Shelemiah. **Kore.** i.e. *a partridge.* 1 Ch +9:19. **Asaph.** This variation arises from the rejection of *yood* into *aleph*; being written in the parallel passages "Ebiasaph," and here, "Asaph." 1 Ch 6:37. 9:19, Ebiasaph.

2. **Zechariah.** i.e. *remembered by Jah.* Zc +1:1. **Jediael.** i.e. *known of God.* 1 Ch +7:6. **Zebadiah.** i.e. *the gift of Jehovah; the Lord is my portion; given of the Lord; endowed of Jehovah,* ✳S#2069h. 1 Ch 26:2. 2 Ch 17:8. 19:11. Also 1 Ch 8:15, 17. 12:7. 27:7. Ezr 8:8. 10:20. (1) One of the porters, 1 Ch 26:2. (2) A Levite, sent by Jehoshaphat to teach Judah, 2 Ch 17:8; 19:11. (3, 4) Two chief men of Benjamin, 1 Ch 8:15, 17. (5) One that came to David to Ziklag, 1 Ch 12:7. (6) One of the twelve captains of David, 1 Ch 27:7. (7) One who returned with Ezra from Babylon, Ezr 8:8. (8) One of those who married strange wives, Ezr 10:20. **Jathniel.** i.e. *given of God; he will be hired of God; continued of God,* ✳S#3496h.

3. **Elam.** i.e. *hidden.* Ge +10:22. **Jehohanan.** i.e. *Jah has grace.* 2 Ch +17:15. **Elioenai.** i.e. *unto Jehovah my eyes are turned; mine eyes are toward God; God the Lord of my eyes; unto Jehovah mine eyes,* ✳S#454h. 1 Ch 26:3. Ezr 8:4, Elihoenai. Also 1 Ch 3:23, 24. 4:36. 7:8. Ezr 10:22, 27. Ne 12:41. (1) A successor of Jeconiah, 1 Ch 3:23. (2) A son of Simeon, 1 Ch 4:36. (3) A son of Becher, of Benjamin, 1 Ch 7:8. (4) One of the porters, 1 Ch 26:3. (5, 6) Two who took strange wives, Ezr 10:22, 27. (7) One who returned from Babylon with Ezra, Ezr 8:4. (8) A priest during Nehemiah's time, Ne 12:41.

4. **Obed-edom.** i.e. *a servant of Edom.* 1 Ch 15:18, 21, 24. 16:5, 38. 2 S +6:10. **Shemaiah.** i.e. *heard of Jah.* 1 Ch +9:16. **Jehozabad.** i.e. *whom Jehovah gave; Jehovah endowed; the Lord gave,* ✳S#3075h. 1 Ch 26:4. 2 K 12:21. 2 Ch 17:18. 24:26. (1) Servant of king Jehoash, who slew his master, 2 K 12:21; 2 Ch 24:26. (2) One of the porters, 1 Ch 26:4. (3) A Benjamite, one of Jehoshaphat's captains, 2 Ch 17:18. **Joah.** i.e. *Jah is brother.* Is +36:3. **Sacar.** i.e. *sweetness, hire, reward.* 1 Ch +11:35. **Nethaneel.** i.e. *given by God.* Nu +1:8.

5. **Ammiel.** i.e. *people of God.* 1 Ch +3:5. **Issachar.** i.e. *there is hire* or reward. **Peulthai.** i.e. *wages or work of the Lord; my works; my wages,* ✳S#6469h. him. "That is, *Obed-edom,* as 1 Ch 13:14." 1 Ch 15:24. 16:38. 2 S 6:11. Ps 128:1.

6. **mighty men of valor.** They were not only porters, or door-keepers, in the ordinary sense of the word, but they were a military *guard* to the gate, as Dr. Delaney suggests that the word *shoarim* should be rendered here: and perhaps in this sense alone are we to understand their office, which appears to have been of considerable dignity, and conferred only on men of the first rank. They were appointed to attend the temple, to guard all the outer gates, and attend at them, not only for state but for service. They were also required to direct and instruct those who were going to worship in the courts of the sanctuary in the conduct they were to observe, to encourage those who were timid, to send back the strangers and unclean, and to guard against thieves and others who were enemies to the house of God. ver. 8. 1 Ch 12:28. Jg +6:12. 2 S +2:7mg. 2 Ch 26:17. Ne 11:14. 1 T 6:12. 2 T 2:3.

7. **Othni.** i.e. *my lion; forcible; lion of the Lord; my seasonable speaking,* ✳S#6273h. **Rephael.** i.e. *healed of God; feebleness of God,* ✳S#7501h. **Obed.** i.e. *a servant.* Ru +4:17. **Elzabad.** i.e. *whom God gave; God is endower; God gave,* ✳S#443h. 1 Ch 12:12. 26:7. (1) One that came to David to Ziklag, 1 Ch 12:12. (2) One of the porters, 1 Ch 26:7. **strong men.** ver. 9. 2 K 2:16. **Elihu.** i.e. *my God is he.* 1 S +1:1. **Semachiah.** i.e. *Jah sustains; cleaving; sustained of the Lord,* ✳S#5565h.

8. **able men.** Ex +✳18:21, 25. Mt 25:15. 1 C 12:4-11. 2 C=3:6. 2 T 2:2. 1 P 4:11. **strength.** Ep=6:10.

9. **Meshelemiah.** ver. 1, 14.

10. **Hosah.** i.e. *taking refuge.* 1 Ch +16:38. **Simri.** i.e. *watchful,* S#8113h. **firstborn.** 1 Ch +5:1, 2. Ge *48:14, 19. Jsh 14:6n. 2 Ch 21:3. Je +*31:9. Col +√1:15n. **yet.** Ge +44:30. **his father.** See on 1 Ch 5:1, 2. **made him.** 2 Ch 11:22.

11. **Hilkiah.** i.e. *portion of Jah.* 2 K +18:18. **Tebaliah.** i.e. *goodness of God; dipped of Jehovah; whom Jehovah has purified,* ✳S#2882h. Strong in the lexicon to his exhaustive concordance gives the definition for this name: "Jah has dipped." John Ritchie in his *Scripture Proper Names* gives "Immersed of God, (purified)." The Hebrew word *tabal* (✳S#2881h, Ex 12:22) favors the definition "dip," often merely meaning to "moisten." **Zechariah.** i.e. *remembered of Jah.* Zc +1:1.

12. **wards.** That is, classes against each other. *Ward* formerly signified a class or division: we still apply the term to the different apartments in hospitals, and to the more extensive districts into which the city of London is divided. See on 1 Ch 25:8.

13. **as well the small as the great.** Heb. *or,* as well

for the small as for the great. 1 Ch 24:31. *25:8.

14. **Shelemiah**. i.e. *the peace-offering of Jehovah; repaid of the Lord*. ver. 1, Meshelemiah. *S#8018h: 1 Ch 26:14. Ezr 10:41. Je 36:14, 26. 38:1. Also Ezr 10:39. Ne 3:30. 13:13. Je 37:3, 13. (1) He who, by lot, had the eastern gate, 1 Ch 26:14. (2) Son of Cushi, Je 36:14. (3) Son of Abdeel, Je 36:26. (4) Son of Hananiah, Je 37:13. (5) Father of Jucal, Je 38:1. (6, 7) Two who under Ezra put away their strange wives, Ezr 10:39, 41. (8) Father of Hananiah, who helped build the wall, Ne 3:30. (9) A priest appointed by Nehemiah over the tithes and their distribution, Ne 13:13. **Zechariah**. ver. 2. **wise**. or, understanding. 1 Ch 22:12. 1 S 25:3. **counsellor**. 2 S 15:12.

15. **Asuppim**. Heb. gatherings. *S#624h. ver. 17h. 2 Ch 25:24. Ne 12:25h. Ec 12:11. *Or, collections*; probably the place where either the supplies of the porters, or the offerings made for the priests and Levites, were laid up. Obed-edom is said to have had the charge of the treasures, etc. in 2 Ch 25:24.

16. **Shupphim**. i.e. *adders, serpents*. 1 Ch +7:12. **Hosah**. ver. 10, 11. **Shallecheth**. i.e. *casting forth; casting down*, *S#7996h. That is, *ejection*; probably the gate through which all the filth, which from time to time might accumulate in the temple and its courts, was cast out. **causeway**. Nu 20:19. Jg 5:20mg. 1 K 10:5. 2 Ch 9:4. **going up**. 1 K 10:5. 2 Ch 9:4. Ne 3:31. **ward against ward**. That is, their stations were opposite to each other; as the north to the south, and the east to the west. ver. 12. 1 Ch 25:8. Ne 12:24.

17. **Eastward**. 1 Ch 9:24. 2 Ch 8:14. **Asuppim**. ver. 15.

18. **Parbar**. i.e. *the outside place; he annulled the corn; a quarter of Jerusalem* (Strong), *S#6503h. 1 Ch 26:18. Also 2 K 23:11. *Parbar* is most probably the same as *parwar*, which denotes *suburbs* (2 K 23:11), in which sense it is often used in the Chaldee Targums; and consequently this may be considered as leading to the suburbs.

19. **Kore**. *Kore*, or rather, *Korhi*, is essentially the same with *Korah*, merely having a paragogic *yood*. Nu 16:11, Korah.

20. **Ahijah**. i.e. *brother of Jah*. 1 K +14:4. **treasures**. ver. 22. 1 Ch 9:26-30. 22:3, 4, 14-16. 28:12-19. 29:2-8. 1 K 14:26. 15:18. Ml 3:10. **dedicated things**. Heb. holy things. ver. 26-28. 1 Ch 18:11. 1 K 7:51. 15:15. 2 Ch 31:11, 12.

21. **Laaden**. 1 Ch 6:17, Libni. 23:7. **Jehieli**. i.e. *my God lives; descendant of Jehiel*, *S#3172h. ver. 22n.

22. **Jehieli**. *Jehieli* is the same as "Jehiel," with the addition of *yood*. 1 Ch 23:8. 29:8, Jehiel. **over the treasures**. ver. 20. Ne 10:38.

23. **Amramites**. 1 Ch 23:12. Nu 3:19, 27.

24. **Shebuel**. i.e. *captive of God*. The difference between "Shubael" and "Shebuel" simply arises from the elision of *wav*, and a change of vowels. 1 Ch 23:15, +16. 24:20, Shubael. **Gershom**. i.e. *a sojourner there*. Ex +2:22. **Moses**. i.e. *a drawer out*. Ex +2:10.

25. **Eliezer**. i.e. *my God is help*. 1 Ch 23:15. Ex 18:4. **Rehabiah**. i.e. *breadth of Jah*. 1 Ch +23:17. **Jeshaiah**. i.e. *safety of Jah*. 1 Ch +25:3. **Joram**. i.e. *height; Jehovah has* or *is exalted*, *S#3141h. 1 Ch 3:11. 26:25. 2 S 8:10. 2 K 8:16, 21, 23, 24, 25, 28, 28, 29, 29. 9:14, 14, 16, 16, 29. 11:2. 2 Ch 22:5, 7. (1) Son of Toi, king of Hamath, 2 S 8:10, for which

1 Ch 18:10 is Hadoram. (2) Same as Jehoram, 2 K 8:21, 23, 24. (3) A son of Ahab, 2 K 8:16, 25, 28, 28, 29, 29. (4) A Levite, descendant of Eliezer, 1 Ch 26:25. **Zichri**. i.e. *mindful*. 1 Ch +9:15. **Shelomith**. i.e. *peaceful*. 1 Ch 23:18. Le +24:11.

26. **over all the treasures**. 1 Ch 18:11. 22:14. 29:2-9. Nu 31:30-52.

27. **Out**. Jsh 6:19. **spoils won in battles**. Heb. battles and spoils. **to maintain**. 2 K 12:14. Ne 10:32-34.

28. **Samuel**. 1 S 9:9. **Kish**. i.e. *a snare*. 1 S +9:1. **Abner**. 1 S 14:47-51. 17:55. **Ner**. i.e. *a light, lamp*. 1 Ch +9:36. **Joab**. 2 S 10:9-14. **Zeruiah**. i.e. *cleft of Jah*. 1 Ch +2:16. 1 S 26:6. 2 S 2:13.

29. **Izharites**. ver. 23. 1 Ch 23:12, 18. **Chenaniah**. i.e. *prepared by Jah*. 1 Ch +15:22. **the outward**. 2 Ch 34:13. Ne 11:16. **officers**. 1 Ch 23:4. 2 Ch 19:8-11.

30. **the Hebronites**. 1 Ch 23:12, 19. **Hashabiah**. i.e. *reckoning of Jah*. 1 Ch +9:14. **men of valor**. ver. +6n. **officers**. Heb. over the charge.

31. **Jerijah**. i.e. *shot by Jah; Jah will throw; teach thou Jah*, *S#3404h. 1 Ch 26:31. Also 1 Ch +23:19, Jeriah. 24:23. **fortieth**. 1 Ch 29:27. 1 K 2:11. **sought for**. Ge 42:22. Is 65:1. Ezk 14:3. 20:3, 31. 36:37. **Jazer**. Nu 21:+32, Jaazer. 32:+1, 3, 35. Jsh 21:39. Is 16:9.

32. **men of valor**. ver. 6n-9. **chief fathers**. 1 Ch 15:12. 23:24. 24:31. **Reubenites**. 1 Ch 12:37. **and affairs**. Heb. and thing. 1 Ch 27:1. 2 Ch 19:11. There were more Levites employed as judges with the two tribes and a half on the other side of Jordan, than with all the rest of the tribes—there were two thousand seven hundred, whereas on the west side of Jordan there were only one thousand seven hundred. Either those remote tribes were not so well furnished as the rest with judges of their own, or because they lay farthest from Jerusalem, on the borders of the neighboring nations, and were thus much in danger of being infected with idolatry, they most needed the help of Levites to prevent their running into the abominations of the idolaters.

1 CHRONICLES 27

David's twelve captains, one for each month, 1-15. The princes of the twelve tribes, 16-22. The numbering of the people was hindered, 23, 24. David's several officers and counsellors, 25-34.

1. **the chief fathers**. The patriarchs, chief generals, or generals of brigade. This enumeration is widely different from that of the preceding. In *that*, we have the order and courses of the *priests* and *Levites*, in their *ecclesiastical* ministrations: in *this*, we have the account of the order of the *civil* service, what related simply to the *political state* of the king and the kingdom. Twenty-four persons, chosen out of David's worthies, each of whom had a second, were placed over 24,000 men, who all served a month at a time, in turn; and this was the whole of their service during the year, after which they attended to their own affairs. Thus the king had always on foot a regular force of 24,000, who served without expense to him or the state, and were not oppressed by the service, which took up only a **twelfth** part of their time; and by this plan he could, at any time, bring into the field 12 times 24,000 or 288,000 fighting men, independently of the 12,000 officers, which made in the whole an effective force

of 300,000 soldiers; and all these men were prepared, disciplined, and ready at a call, without the smallest expense to the state or the king. These were, properly speaking, the *militia* of the Israelitish kingdom. **captains of thousands.** 1 Ch 12:20. 13:1. 15:25. Ex *18:25. Dt 1:15. 1 S 8:12. Mi +*5:2. **served.** 1 Ch 28:1. 2 Ch 17:12-19. 26:11-13. **any matter.** 1 K 5:14. **month.** 1 K 4:7, 27.

2. **first month.** called Nisan *or* Abib. **Jashobeam.** i.e. *sitting of the people.* 1 Ch +11:11. 2 S 23:8, Adino the Eznite. **Zabdiel.** i.e. *endowed of God.* Ne +11:14.

3. **Perez.** i.e. *rupture; breach; division,* *S#6557h. 1 Ch 2:4, 5. 4:1. 9:4. 27:3. Ge 38:29. 46:12, 12. Nu 26:20, Pharez, 21. Ru 4:12, 18, 18. Ne 11:4, 6. (1) A son of Judah by Tamar, Ge 38:29; 46:12; Nu 26:20; 1 Ch 2:4; Mt 1:3. (2) A son of Judah, same as Pharez, Ne 11:4, 6. (3) An ancestor of Jashobeam, 1 Ch 27:3. **the chief.** Ge *49:8-10. Nu 7:12. 10:14.

4. **second month.** called Ziv *or* Ijar. **Dodai.** i.e. *beloved of the Lord; amatory; my beloved,* *S#1737h. 1 Ch 11:12. 2 S 23:9, Dodo. **Mikloth.** i.e. *lots; sprouts; triflings; staves,* *S#4732h. 1 Ch 8:32. 9:37, 38. 27:4. (1) A chief man of Benjamin, 1 Ch 8:32; 9:37, 38. (2) Ruler over the course of the second month under David, 1 Ch 27:4.

5. **third month.** called Sivan. **Benaiah.** i.e. *built up by Jah.* 1 Ch +15:24. Or, "Benaiah, the son of Jehoiada the chief priest:" it was Jehoiada, and not Benaiah, who was a priest. 1 Ch 18:17. 1 K 4:4. **Jehoiada.** i.e. *Jah has known.* 2 K +11:4. **chief priest.** *or,* principal officer. Ge 41:45. 1 K 4:5.

6. **mighty.** 1 Ch 11:22-25. 2 S 22:20-23. 23:20-23. **Ammizabad.** i.e. *people of the endower* or *bountiful giver,* *S#5990h.

7. **fourth month.** called Tammuz. **Asahel.** i.e. *made by God.* 1 Ch +2:16. 11:26. 2 S 2:18-23. 23:24. **Zebadiah.** i.e. *endowed by Jah.* 1 Ch +26:2.

8. **fifth month.** called Ab. **Shamhuth.** i.e. *desolation, astonishment; exaltation; destruction,* *S#8049h. If this person was the same as *Shammoth the Hararite,* or *Shammah the Harodite,* it is probable that he took the denomination *Izrahite* from one of his progenitors of the name of *Izrah,* and derived the other from the place of his residence. 1 Ch 11:27, Shammoth the Hararite. 26:29. 2 S 23:25, Shammah the Harodite. **Izrahite.** i.e. *he will arise; he will be bright,* *S#3155h.

9. **sixth month.** called Elul. 1 Ch 11:28. **Ira.** i.e. *watchful.* 1 Ch 11:28. 2 S +20:26. 23:26. **Ikkesh.** i.e. *perverse.* 2 S +23:26.

10. **seventh month.** called Tizri. **Helez.** i.e. *armed, drawn out.* 1 Ch +2:39. 11:27. **Pelonite.** 2 S 23:26, Paltite.

11. **eighth month.** called Marchesvan *or* Bul. **Sibbecai.** i.e. *my thicket.* 1 Ch +11:29. 2 S 21:18. **Zarhites.** Nu 26:20.

12. **ninth month.** called Cisleu. **Abiezer.** i.e. *my father is help.* Jsh +17:2. **Anetothite.** i.e. *an inhabitant of Anathoth* (i.e. *answers, songs,* 1 Ch +7:8), S#6069h. 1 Ch +*11:28, Antothite. 2 S 23:27, Anethothite.

13. **tenth month.** called Tebet. **Maharai.** i.e. *hasting.* 1 Ch 11:30. 2 S +23:28. **Zarhites.** ver. 11.

14. **eleventh month.** called Shebet. **Benaiah.** i.e. *built up by Jah.* 1 Ch 11:31. +15:24. 2 S 23:30.

15. **twelfth month.** called Adar. **Heldai.** i.e. *worldly; vital; long-lived; life, age, duration; my times,* *S#2469h. 1 Ch 11:30, Heled. 27:15h. 2 S 23:29, He-

leb. Zc 6:10h. (1) One of the captivity, Zc 6:10; called Helem, ver. 14. (2) One of David's captains, 1 Ch 27:15. **Othniel.** i.e. *lion of God.* 1 Ch 4:13. Jsh +15:17. Jg 1:13. 3:9.

16. **Furthermore.** These persons, called "princes of the tribes," in ver. 22, and 1 Ch 28:1, appear to have been *civil* rulers over their several tribes, and honorary men, without pay, not unlike the lords lieutenants of our counties. In this enumeration there is no mention of the tribes of Gad and Asher, probably because they were joined to the neighboring tribes; or, perhaps, the account of these has been lost from the register. **Eliezar.** i.e. *my God is help.* Ge +15:2. **Shephatiah.** i.e. *judged of Jah.* 2 S +3:4.

17. **Hashabiah.** i.e. *reckoning of Jah.* 1 Ch +9:14. 26:30. **of the Aaronites.** 1 Ch 12:27, 28. 24:4, 31. **Zadok.** i.e. *just.* 2 S +8:17.

18. **Elihu.** i.e. *my God is he.* 1 S +1:1. If *Elihu* be not a mistake for *Eliab,* it is probable that he was called by both names. 1 S 16:6. 17:13, 29, Eliab. **Omri.** i.e. *my sheaf.* 1 K +16:16.

19. **Ishmaiah.** i.e. *Jehovah will hear; he will hear the Lord,* *S#3460h. **Jerimoth.** i.e. *high places.* 1 Ch +7:7.

20. **Azaziah.** i.e. *Jah has strengthened; strengthened of the Lord,* *S#5812h. 1 Ch 15:21. 27:20. 2 Ch 31:13. (1) One engaged in bringing up the ark from Obededom, 1 Ch 15:21. (2) Father of Hoshea, prince of Ephraim, 1 Ch 27:20. (3) Set over the tithes under Hezekiah, 2 Ch 31:13. **Pedaiah.** i.e. *redeemed of Jehovah.* 2 K +23:36.

21. **Iddo.** i.e. *timely; throwing, casting.* *S#3035h. 1 Ch 27:21. 1 K 4:14. Ezr 10:+43h, Jadau. (1) A prophet or seer who denounced the wrath of God against Jeroboam, the son of Nebat, 2 Ch 9:29; 12:15. (2) Grandfather of the prophet Zechariah, Zc 1:1, 7. (3) The father of Ahinadab, 1 K 4:14. (4) A descendant of Gershom, the son of Levi, 1 Ch 6:21. (5) i.e. *calamity.* A chief officer among the Jews of the captivity; a Nethinim. Ezr 8:17. (6) i.e. *favorite.* Prince of Manasseh, 1 Ch 27:21. (7) A priest who returned from Babylon with Zerubbabel, Ne 12:4, 16. **Jaasiel.** i.e. *made of God; it will be done of God,* *S#3300h. 1 Ch 11:+47, Jasiel. 27:21. **Abner.** 1 S 14:50, 51. 2 S 3:27, 37.

23. **David took not.** It seems probable, from this passage, that Joab began, by David's order, to number the children, as well as adults, but was prevented from finishing the account, probably because the plagues had begun. The numbering of the effective men might have been deemed a political expedient; but pride and ostentation alone could dictate the numbering of minors and infants, especially as God had pronounced the seed of Abraham, Isaac, and Jacob, innumerable. **from twenty.** Nu 1:18. **he would increase.** Ge 15:5. 22:17. He 11:12. **like.** ✓138B, Ge +13:16.

24. **began to number.** 1 Ch 21:1-17. 2 S 24:1-15. **finished not.** Levi and Benjamin being omitted. 1 Ch 21:6, 7. 2 S 24:15. **was the number put.** Heb. ascended the number. On the roll of the account prepared for the king (Young). **account.** Ge 34:30 (number). 41:49. **chronicles.** lit. "words *or* matters of the days," as in 1 K 14:19.

25. **the king's.** 2 K 18:15. 2 Ch 16:2. **Azmaveth.** i.e. *strength of death.* 2 S +23:31. **the storehouses.** Ge 41:48. Ex 1:11. 2 Ch 26:10. Je 41:8. **fields.** The cultivated land, as in Ge 27:27. **cities.** With or without

walls, as in Ge 41:35, 48. **villages**. lit. "coverings," as in Jsh 18:24. 1 S 6:18. Ne 6:2. SS 7:11. **castles**. or, towers. lit. "great places." ✴S#4026h. Ge 11:4, 5. 35:21. Jsh 15:37. 19:38. Jg 8:9, 17. 9:46, 47, 49, 51, 51, 52, 52. 2 K 9:17. 17:9. 18:8. 2 Ch 14:7. 26:9, 10, 15. 27:4. 32:5. Ne 3:1, 11, 25, 26, 27. 8:4mg. 12:38, 39. Ps 48:12. *61:3. Pr *18:10. SS 4:4. 5:13mg. 7:4. 8:10. Is 2:15. 5:2. 30:25. 33:18. Je 31:38. Ezk 26:4, 9. 27:11. Mi 4:8. Zc 14:10. **Jehonathan**. i.e. *Jehovah-given; Jehovah is giver,* ✚S#3083h. (1) A storehouse servant, 1 Ch 27:25. (2) A Levite sent by Jehoshaphat to teach in the cities of Judah, 2 Ch 17:8. (3) A priest, head of the father's house of Shemaiah in the days of the high priest Joiakim, Ne 12:18.

26. **Ezri**. i.e. *helpful; my help; help of the Lord,* ✴S#5836h.

27. **Shimei**. i.e. *hearing.* 2 S +16:5. **the increase of the vineyards**. Heb. that which *was* of the vineyards. **Ramathite**. i.e. *citizen of Ramath* (i.e. *lofty place,* Jsh +19:8), ✴S#7435h. **Shiphmite**. i.e. *native of Shepham* (i.e. *bare, bald,* Nu +34:10), ✴S#8225h.

28. **And over**. 1 K 4:7. **the sycamore trees**. The Hebrew *shikmim,* Syriac *shekmo,* and Arabic *jummeez,* is the *sukomoros,* or *sycomore,* of the Greeks, so called from *sukos,* a *fig tree,* and *muros,* a *mulberry tree,* because it resembles the latter in its leaves, and the former in its fruit. "The sycamore," says Mr. Norden (*Travels into Egypt and Nubia,* vol. i. p. 79), "is of the height of a beech, and bears its fruit in a manner quite different from other trees: it has them on the trunk itself, which shoots out little sprigs, in form of grape stalks, at the end of which grow the fruit close to one another, almost like a cluster of grapes. The tree is always green, and bears fruit several times in the year, without observing any certain seasons; for I have seen some sycamores that have given fruit two months after others. The fruit has the figure and smell of real figs, but is inferior to them in the taste, having a disgustful sweetness. Its color is a yellow, inclining to an ochre, shadowed by a flesh color. In the inside it resembles the common figs, excepting that it has a blackish coloring with yellow spots. This sort of tree is pretty common in Egypt; the people, for the greater part, live on its fruit, and think themselves well regaled when they have a piece of bread, a couple of sycamore figs, and a pitcher of water." 1 K 20:27. **Baal-hanan**. i.e. *master of grace* or *favor.* Ge +36:38. **Gederite**. i.e. *inhabitants of Geder or Gederah* (i.e. *a wall or fence,* Jsh +12:13; +15:36), ✴S#1451h. **Joash**. 1 Ch +7:8.

29. **Sharon**. 1 K 5:16. Is 65:10. **Shitrai**. i.e. *Jah is arbitrator; scribe of the Lord; my officers,* ✴S#7861h. **Sharonite**. i.e. *inhabitant of Sharon* (i.e. *a great plain,* Is +35:2), ✴S#8290h. **Adlai**. i.e. *my ornament; justice of the Lord; the prey is mine,* ✴S#5724h.

30. **the camels**. Jb 1:3. **Obil**. i.e. *mournful; overseer of camels,* ✴S#179h. **the Ishmaelite**. i.e. *descendant of Ishmael,* ✴S#3459h. 1 Ch +2:17, Ishmeelite. Ge 47:6. **the asses**. Ge 36:24. Nu 31:34. Ne 7:69. **Jehdeiah**. i.e. *unity of Jah.* 1 Ch +24:20. **Meronothite**. i.e. *the joyful shouter; inhabitant of Meronoth* (i.e. *sharp tempestuous sea),* ✴S#4824h. 1 Ch 27:30. Ne 3:7.

31. **Jaziz**. i.e. *gives life and motion; he will shine, or bring abundance; he will cause to abound,* ✴S#3151h. **Hagerite**. i.e. *fugitive,* ✴S#1905h. 1 Ch +11:38, Haggeri. 27:31.

32. **uncle**. 2 S 13:3. 21:21, nephew. **counsellor**. 1 Ch 26:14. 2 S 15:12. **wise**. or, understanding. Pr 28:2. **scribe**. *or,* secretary. Jg 5:14. **Jehiel**. i.e. *God lives.* Ezr +8:9. **son of Hachmoni**. i.e. *very wise,* ✴S#2453h. *or,* Hachmonite. 1 Ch 11:11h.

33. **Ahithophel**. i.e. *brother of folly* or *my brother is foolish.* 2 S +15:12. 16:23. 17:23. **Hushai**. i.e. *hasty, hasting.* 2 S 15:32, 37. 16:16. **Archite**. Jsh 16:2. **companion**. 2 S 15:37. 16:16, 17. Ps 55:13. Zc 13:7.

34. **Jehoiada**. i.e. *Jah has known.* 2 K +11:4. **Benaiah**. ver. 5. **Abiathar**. i.e. *father of abundance.* 1 S +22:20. 1 K 1:7. **the general**. 1 Ch 11:6. **Joab**. i.e. *Jah is father.* 1 Ch 11:6. 1 S +26:6. 2 S 2:32.

1 CHRONICLES 28

David assembles the chiefs of Israel; shows them how his purpose of building a temple had been disallowed, and relates the LORD'S special favor to him; and his promises to Solomon, 1-8. He charges Solomon to know and serve God, and to build the temple, 9, 10. He gives a pattern for the form of the several parts (as God had showed it to him), and gold and silver for the materials, 11-19. He encourages Solomon with the assurance of help, both from God, and from his people, 20, 21.

1. **assembled**. 1 Ch 23:2. Jsh 23:2. 24:1. **the princes**. 1 Ch 27:16-22. **the captains of the companies**. 1 Ch 27:1-15, 25. **the stewards**. 1 Ch 27:25-31. **substance**. or, cattle. **and of his sons**. or, and his sons. **officers**. or, eunuchs. 1 Ch 27:32-34. Ge +37:36mg. 2 K +8:6mg. **the mighty men**. 1 Ch 11:10.

2. **stood up**. Ge 48:2. 1 K 1:47. **my brethren**. 1 Ch 11:1-3. Dt 17:15, 20. Ps 22:22. He 2:11, 12. **I had in mine heart**. 1 Ch 17:1, 2. 2 S 7:1, 2. 1 K 8:17, 18. **rest**. 1 Ch 6:31. Ps 132:3-8, 14. **the footstool**. ♪22D3D1, Is +66:1. Ps 99:5. 132:7. Is 66:1. La 2:1. Ac 7:49. **had made ready**. 1 Ch 18:7-11. 22:2-5, 14.

3. **Thou shalt**. 1 Ch 17:4. 22:8. 2 S 7:5-13. 1 K 5:3. 2 Ch 6:8, 9. **blood**. Heb. bloods. ♪96F2, Ge +4:10. 2 K +*9:26mg.

4. **chose me**. 1 S 16:6-13. 2 S *7:7-16. Ps 78:68-72. 89:16-27. **for ever**. Heb. *olam,* Ex +12:24. 1 Ch √29:27. Ps +*24:9n. **chosen Judah**. 1 Ch 5:2. Ge *49:8-10. Ps 60:7. 78:67, 68. 108:8. He 7:14. **the house of Judah**. 1 S 16:1. **the house of my father**. 1 S 26:1. **among the sons**. 1 S 16:12, 13. Ps 18:19. 147:10, 11.

5. **all my sons**. 1 Ch 3:1-9. 14:4-7. **he hath chosen**. 1 Ch 22:9, 10. 23:1. 29:1. **to sit**. 1 Ch 17:14. 29:23. 2 Ch 1:8, 9. Ps 72, title, 1, etc. Is *9:6, 7.

6. **he shall**. 1 Ch 17:11-14. 22:9, 10. 2 S *7:13, 14. 2 Ch 1:9. Zc 6:12, 13. He 3:3, 6. **I have**. He 4:5.

7. **Moreover**. Ps 89:28-37. 132:12. Da 2:44. **if**. 1 Ch 22:13. 1 K 6:12, 13. 9:4, 5. 11:9-13. **for ever**. ver. 7, 8. 1 Ch 17:23, 27. Heb. *olam,* Ex +12:24. **constant**. Heb. strong. ver. 10. Jsh *1:6, 7. 1 K 2:2-4. **as at this day**. 1 K 8:61. 11:4.

8. **in the sight**. Dt 4:6. Mt 5:14-16. Ph 2:15, 16. He 12:1, 2. **in the audience**. Dt 4:26. 29:10, 15. Ac 10:33. **keep**. Ps 119:4, 10, 11, 27, 33, 34, 44. Pr 2:1-5. 3:1. Is *34:16. Ac √17:11. **that ye may**. Dt 4:1. 5:32, 33. 6:1-3. **leave it**. Ezr 9:12. Pr 13:22. **for ever**. Heb. *olam,* Ex +12:24.

9. **know thou**. Dt *4:35. 1 K *8:43. Ps √9:10. Je *9:24. *22:16. *24:7. *31:34. Ho *4:16. Jn *8:55. *17:3. Ac *17:23, 30. Ro *1:28. 1 C *15:34. 2 C *4:6. **the**

God. Ge 28:13. Ex 3:16. 15:2. 1 K *3:6. Ps *18:2. 89:26. **serve him**. 1 Ch *29:9, 17-19. 1 K *8:61. 2 K *20:3. *22:2. Jb *36:11, 12. Ps *101:2. Jn *1:47. √4:24. Ro *1:9. He *12:28. **a willing**. 2 C *8:12. *9:7. 1 P *5:2. **mind**. Heb. *nephesh*, Ge +23:8. **the Lord searcheth**. 1 Ch *29:17. 1 S *16:7. 1 K *8:39. Ps *7:9. *139:2. Pr *17:3. Je *11:20. √17:10. *20:12. Jn *2:25. *21:17. Ac *1:24. He *4:13. Re *2:23. **the imaginations**. Ge *6:5. *8:21. Dt 31:21. Ps *139:2. Ezk 38:10. **if thou seek him**. 2 Ch *15:2. Pr ◑1:28. *2:1-6. Is 45:19. *55:6, 7. Je *29:13. Mt *7:7, 8. He √11:6. Ja *4:8-11. **but if**. T#555. Ge +4:7. Pr 1:29-32. 8:36. 9:12. *11:19. Mt 5:25, 26. √7:13, 14. 25:1-13, 14-30, +*46 (T#567). Mk 16:16. Lk 19:12-27. Ro 2:5-10. Ga *6:7, 8. Re 22:19. **thou forsake him**. Dt 31:16, 17. 1 K 9:6-9. Ezr 8:22. Is *1:28. He *10:38, 39. **he will**. 2 S ◑7:15.

10. **Take heed now**. ver. 6. 1 Ch 22:16-19. 1 K 2:3, 4. 1 T *4:16.

11. **David**. He gave him an ichnograph of the building, with elevations, sections, and specifications of every part; and all this he himself received by inspiration from God himself (ver. 12, 19), just as Moses had received the plan of the tabernacle. **the pattern**. ver. 19. Ex 25:40. 26:30. 39:42, 43. 2 Ch 3:3. Ezk 43:10, 11. He 8:5. **the porch**. 1 K 6:3. 2 Ch 3:4. Ezk 40:8, 9, 15, 48, 49. **the houses**. 1 K 6:16-20. 2 Ch 3:5-10. Ezk 41:13, etc. He 9:2-8. **the treasuries**. *Ganzukkaiv*: the word *ganzach* is supposed to be not Hebrew, but Persian; in which language we have *ganj*, a granary, a hidden treasure, and *gunjoor*, and *gunjineh*, a treasure, treasury, or barn. It may, however, be a Chaldee form of the Hebrew *genez*, (from *genaz*, to treasure up); the *daleth* being merely formative, as in *dech*, *illaich*, and other Chaldee words. 1 Ch 9:26-29. 26:20-27. Lk 21:1. **upper chambers**. 2 S 18:33. 1 K 6:5, 6, 10. 2 Ch 3:9. Ne 10:38, 39. 13:5. Je 35:2. Ezk 41:6, etc. **the place**. Ex 25:17-22. 40:20, 21. 1 K 6:19. 2 Ch 5:7. He 9:5.

12. **the pattern**. Ex 31:2. Jn=13:15. Ep=4:11-13. **all**. "By the spirit of prophecy that was with him," says the Targumist. **that he had by**. Heb. that was with him by. **the spirit**. Heb. *ruach*, Ge +41:38. Ex 25:40. He 8:5. **the treasuries**. 1 Ch 26:20, 26-28. 1 K 14:26. 15:15, 18. 2 K 16:8. 18:15.

13. **the courses**. 1 Ch 24:1, etc. 25:1, etc. **the vessels**. 1 Ch 9:29. 1 K ch. 7. Ezr 8:25-30, 33.

14. **of gold**. The quantity of gold which was to be put in *each article*.

15. **the candlesticks**. Ex 25:31-39. 1 K 7:49. 2 Ch 4:7. Zc 4:2, 3, 11-14. Re 1:12, 13, 20. 2:1.

16. **tables of showbread**. Ex 25:23-30. 1 K 7:48. 2 Ch 4:8, 19.

17. **pure gold**. 1 S 2:13, 14. 2 Ch 4:20-22. **the bowls**. Nu 7:13, 14. 1 K 7:+*40, 48-50. 10:21.

18. **the altar**. Ex 30:1-10. 1 K 7:48. **the chariot**. Ex 25:18-22. 1 S 4:4. 1 K 6:23-30. 2 K 2:11, 12. Ps 18:10. +*68:17. 80:1. 99:1. Ezk 1:*4, 15-24. 10:2, etc. He 9:5.

19. **the Lord**. ver. 11, 12. Ex 25:40. 26:30. **understand in writing**. Is *8:20. Mk=12:24. **by his hand upon me**. Ezk 1:3. 3:14, 22. **pattern**. Ex 25:40. Jn=13:15. Ep=4:11-17.

20. **Be strong**. ver. 10. 1 Ch 22:13. Dt 31:6-8. Jsh *1:5-9. 1 C 16:13. **fear not**. Ps 27:1, 2. Is 41:10, 13. Ro *8:31. **he will not fail thee**. Jsh *1:5. He +*13:5.

21. **the courses**. 1 Ch ch. 24-26. **with thee…service**.

Mt=28:20. Mk 16:20. **all manner**. Ex 31:3. **willing**. Ex 35:25, 26, 35. 36:1-4. Ps 110:3. Ro 13:1. **also the princes**. 1 Ch 22:17, 18. T 3:1. **at thy**. Ne 11:23.

1 CHRONICLES 29

David shows the princes and people what treasures he had prepared for the building and service of the temple, 1-5. After his example, and at his exhortation, they offer liberally, 6-9. He adores and blesses God, and prays for the people and for Solomon, 10-19. The people worship, sacrifice, and feast with joy; and then make Solomon king the second time, 20-22. He reigns in majesty and prosperity, 23-25. David's long and prosperous reign, and happy death, 26-30.

1. **said unto**. 1 Ch 28:1, 8. **whom**. 1 Ch 28:5, 6. 1 K 8:19, 20. **young**. 1 Ch 22:5. 1 K 3:7. 2 Ch 13:7. Pr 4:3. Je 1:6, 7. **palace**. 1 Ch 28:10. 2 Ch 2:4, 5.

2. **I have prepared**. 1 Ch 22:3-5, 14-16. **with all**. 2 Ch 31:20, 21. Ec 9:10. 2 C 8:3. Col 3:23. 1 P 4:10, 11. **the gold**. √121D5, Ge +23:9. 1 Ch 28:14-18. **silver**. √121D5, Ge +23:9. **onyx stones**. *Avney shoham*, which was, probably, not the precious stone or gem called *onyx*, but a marble called in Greek *onychites*, which Pliny mentions as a stone of Caramania; for one would hardly think that gems of any kind were used externally in such a building as the temple. Antiquity gave both stones this name, because of their resemblance to the nail of the finger. Ge 2:12. Ex 28:17, 20. 39:6, 13. Jb 28:16. Is 54:11, 12. Re 21:18-21. **glistering stones**. *Avney phuch* seems to denote a kind of *black marble*, so called from its color resembling *stibium*: so Vulgate, *quasi stibinos*. **marble stones**. *Avney shayish* is rendered in the Targum *avney marmoraiyah*, "stones of marble," and by the LXX. and Vulgate, *Parion* or *Pari-non*, *marmor Parium*, "Parium marble," which was remarkable for its *bright white* color (Pindar, Nem. iv. v. 132. Horace l. I. Od. xix. v. 6). Josephus (Bell. l. v. c. 5, 2.) says that the temple was built of large blocks of white marble, beautifully polished, so as to produce a most splendid appearance.

3. **I have set**. Ps 26:8. 27:4. 84:1-10. 122:1-9. **I have**. 1 Ch 21:24. Pr *3:9, 10. **of mine own proper good**. i.e. "of mine own private property:" at present we only use the plural *goods* to designate property or personal effects. **over and above**. 1 Ch 22:4, 5, 14-16.

4. **gold of Ophir**. 1 K +9:28n. Jb 28:16.

5. **who then**. Ex 25:2-9. 35:5, etc. Nu 7:2, 3, 10-14, etc. Ezr 1:4-6. 2:68, 69. 7:15, 16. **consecrate his service**. Heb. to fill his hand. Ex +29:9mg.

6. **the chief**. 1 Ch 27:1, etc. Is 60:3-10. **the rulers**. 1 Ch 27:25, etc. 2 C 9:7.

7. **drams**. Ezr 2:69. 8:7. Ne 7:70-72.

8. **by the hand**. 1 Ch 25:2mg. **Jehiel the Gershonite** 1 Ch 23:8. 26:21, 22.

9. **they offered willingly**. Ex 25:2. Le +*23:38. Dt 16:10, 11. Jg 5:9. Ps 110:3. 2 C *8:3, 12. *9:7, 8. **perfect heart**. ver. 17. 1 Ch 12:38n. 1 K 8:61. 2 K +*20:3. **David**. Pr 23:15, 16. Lk 15:6. Jn 15:11. Ph 2:15-17. 4:1, 10. 1 Th 3:6-9.

10. **David blessed**. ver. 20. 2 Ch 20:26-28. Ps *103:1, 2. 138:1. 146:2. **Blessed be thou**. 1 K 8:15. 2 Ch 6:4. Ps *72:18, 19. 89:52. Ezk 3:12. Ep *1:3. 1 T 1:17. 1 P 1:3. Re *5:12. **Lord God**. Ge 32:28. 33:20.

our father. Is 63:16. Mt *6:9. Lk 11:2. Ro 1:7. 8:15. Ph 4:20. 2 Th 2:16. **for ever and ever.** Heb. *olam* doubled, Da +2:20.

11. **is the greatness.** T#214. Ne 9:6. Jb 11:7-9. 26:14. 36:26. 37:22, 23. Ps 29:4. 47:7. 93:1. 104:1-4. 145:3. Is 40:12-18. Da 2:37. 4:30, 34, 35. Na 1:3-6. Mt √6:13. 1 T *1:17. *6:15, 16. Ju 25. Re *4:10, 11. *5:12, 13. 7:9-12. 19:1. and. ✓148, Ge +8:22. **the victory.** 1 S 15:29. Jb +4:20 (❋S#5331h). Ps 98:1. **majesty.** Dt 10:17. Jb *37:22. Ps 29:4. 45:3, 4. *93:1. +*104:1. Is 2:10. +*57:15. Mi *5:4. He 1:3. **for all that.** Ge 1:1. 14:19, 22. Ps *115:15, 16. Is 42:5. 66:1. Je 10:10-12. 27:5. Da *4:32, 34, 35. Ro +14:8. **thine is the.** Ps 97:1. 99:1. 145:1, 12, 13. Da *4:3. Re *11:15. **exalted.** Ne *9:5. Ps 21:13. *46:10. 47:9. 57:5, 11. *97:9. Is *2:11. 12:4.

12. **riches.** Dt *8:18. 1 S *2:7, 8. Jb *42:10. Ps 75:6, 7. 113:7, 8. Pr 8:18. *10:22. Ec *5:19. Lk 1:51-53. Ro *11:35, 36. and. ✓148, Ge +8:22. **reignest over all.** Da *6:26. Ep +1:11. **power.** Jb 9:19. Ps *62:11. Is 43:13. *46:10. Da 5:18-21. Mt *28:18. Jn *19:11. Ep *3:20. Re 11:17. **to make great.** Ps +115:3. Da 2:37. **give strength.** 2 Ch *16:9. Ps 18:31, 32. 28:8. 29:1, 11. 68:28, 34, 35. 144:1, 2. Is *40:29. 45:24. Ep *3:16. Ph *4:13. Col 1:11.

13. **we thank.** Ps 105:1. 106:1. Da 2:23. 2 C 2:14. 8:16. 9:15. 1 Th √2:13. and. ✓148, Ge +8:22.

14. **who am I.** Ge 32:10. 2 S 7:18. Da 4:30. 1 C 15:9, 10. 2 C 3:5. 12:9-11. **that we should.** Ps 115:1. Re 4:10. **be able.** Heb. retain, *or* obtain strength. 2 Ch 2:6mg. 13:20. 14:11. 20:37. 22:9. Da 10:8, 16. 11:6. **willingly.** ver. 9. Ph *2:13. Ja 1:17. **all things.** Ge 28:22. Ps 50:10-12. Ro 11:36. 1 C 16:2. **of thine own.** Heb. of thine hand. ver. 16. Dt 26:10. **given thee.** Pr 23:26.

15. **For we.** Ge 47:9. Ps 39:12. 119:19. He 11:13-16. 1 P 2:11. **strangers.** Ge +*23:4 (❋S#1616h). Ex 12:48mg. Dt +26:11. Jsh +20:9. Mt +25:35. **sojourners.** Ge 23:4 (S#8453h). 1 K 17:1. Ps 39:12. He *11:13. **our days.** Jb *14:2. Ps 90:9. 102:11. 144:4. Ec 6:12. Is 40:6-8. Ja *4:14. **abiding.** Heb. expectation. or, "no hope" of continuance here (Young), as in Ezr ◉10:2. Je 14:8. *17:13. 50:7.

16. **all this store.** ver. 14. 2 Ch 31:10. Ps 24:1. Ho 2:8. Lk 19:16.

17. **triest the heart.** 2 Ch 28:9. Dt 8:2. 1 S *16:7. Ps 7:9. 51:6. Pr 16:2. 21:2. Je *17:10. He √4:12. Re 2:23. **hast pleasure.** Pr 11:20. 15:8, 9. Jn 1:47. **in uprightness.** T#873. 2 Ch *16:9. Jb 8:6. Ps 11:7. *15:1, 2. 18:25. 37:18. 125:4. 119:80. Pr 2:7, 21. 10:29. 11:3, 6, 20. 12:22. 13:6. *15:8. 21:18. 28:10, 18, 20. Mi *1:7. Ro *14:22. **in the uprightness.** Ac 24:16. 2 C 1:12. 1 Th 2:10. **with joy thy people.** ver. 9. Phm 7, 20. **present.** Heb. found. Jg +20:48mg.

18. **Lord God of.** Ex 3:6, 15. 4:5. Mt +√22:32. Ac 3:13. **keep.** Dt 30:6. Ps 51:10. 119:116, 117. Je 10:23. 32:39, 40. Ph *1:6, 9-11. 1 Th 3:11, 12. He *13:21. **for ever.** Heb. *olam,* Ex +*12:24. **in the imagination.**

1 Ch *28:9. Ge 6:5. Ps 119:113. Is 26:3mg. **prepare.** Heb. stablish. 1 Ch 17:12. Ps 10:17mg. 2 Th 2:16, 17. 1 P 5:10.

19. **And give.** 1 Ch *28:9. Ps 72:1. 119:80. Ja 1:17. **perfect heart.** T#1550. 2 K +*20:3. 1 Ch 12:38n. Ps +*37:18n. **the which.** ver. 2. 1 Ch 22:14.

20. **Now bless.** 1 Ch 16:36. 2 Ch 20:21. Ps 134:2. 135:19-21. ch. 145. 146:1, 2. 148:13, 14, etc. **bowed down.** T#1229. Ge 24:26, 48. Ex 4:31. 34:8, 9. 2 Ch 29:29, 30. Ne 8:6. Ps 29:1, 2. *95:6, 7. Mi 6:6. **worshipped.** Ex 14:31. 1 S 12:18. Pr 24:21. 1 P 2:17.

21. **sacrificed.** 1 K 8:62-65. 2 Ch 7:4-9. Ezr 6:17. **burnt offerings.** Le +*23:12. **drink offerings.** Le +*23:13. Nu 15:5, 7, 10.

22. **eat and drink.** Ex 24:11. Dt 12:7, 11, 12. 16:14-17. 2 Ch 7:10. Ne 8:12. Ec 2:24. 3:12, 13. 8:15. 9:7. 1 T 6:17, 18. **the second time.** 1 Ch 23:1. Ac 19:3, 5. **and anointed.** 1 K 1:31, 34-39. **Zadok.** 1 K 2:35.

23. **sat on the throne.** 1 Ch 17:11, 12. 28:5. Ps 132:11. Is *9:6, 7. **prospered.** 1 Ch 22:11. **all Israel.** Ec 8:2-5. Ro 13:1.

24. **all the princes.** 1 Ch 22:17. 28:21. **all the sons.** 1 Ch 3:39. 1 K 1:50-53. 2:24, 25. **submitted themselves unto.** Heb. gave the hand under. Ge +*24:2. 47:29. 2 K 10:15. 2 Ch 30:8mg. Ezr 10:19. Je 50:15. La 5:6. Ezk 17:18. 27:21mg. ✓121S3I. Metonymy of the Adjunct B607: to *give the hand* is put for voluntary submission, fellowship, or confederacy. For other instances of this figure see 2 Ch 30:8mg. Je 50:15. La 5:6. Ezk 17:18. Ga 2:9.

25. **magnified Solomon.** Jsh 3:7. 4:14. 2 Ch 1:1. Jb 7:17. Ac 19:17. **bestowed.** 1 K 3:13. 2 Ch 1:12. Ec 2:9. Da 5:18, 19. He 2:9.

26. **over all Israel.** 1 Ch 18:14. Ps 78:71, 72.

27. **forty years.** 1 Ch 3:4. 2 S 5:4, 5. 1 K 2:11.

28. **he died.** David at his death had every thing that his heart could wish: "he died in a good old age, full of days, riches, and honor," having gained more renown than any crowned head ever did. "David," says Dr. Delaney, "was a true believer, a zealous adorer of God, teacher of His law and worship, and inspirer of His praise; a glorious example, a perpetual and inexhaustible fountain of true piety; a consummate and unrivalled hero; a skilful and successful captain; a steady patriot; a wise ruler; a faithful, generous, and magnanimous friend; and what is yet rarer, a no less generous and magnanimous enemy; a true penitent, a divine musician, a sublime poet, and an inspired prophet. By birth a peasant, by merit a prince! In youth a hero, in manhood a monarch, and in age a saint." **a good old age.** Ge 15:15. +*25:8n. Jb 5:26. Pr 16:31. Ac 13:36. **full of days.** 1 Ch 23:1. Ge 35:29. Jb 5:26.

29. **the acts.** 1 K 11:41. 14:29. He 11:32, 33. **book.** *or,* history. Heb. words. **Samuel.** 1 S 9:9. **Nathan.** 2 S 7:2-4. 12:1-7. **Gad the seer.** 1 Ch 21:9-11. 2 S +24:11.

30. **his might.** 2 K 10:34. 14:28. **the times.** Da 2:21. 4:23, 25.

2 CHRONICLES

2 CHRONICLES 1

Solomon, established as king, calls on his nobles and people, to join in sacrificing at Gibeon, 1-6. The Lord appears to him there by night, and allows him to choose what blessing to ask: he asks wisdom, and is promised also riches and honor, 7-12. Solomon's forces, riches, and commerce, 13-17.

1. A.M. 2989. B.C. 1015. An. Ex. Is. 476. **was strengthened**. 1 K 2:12, 46. **the Lord**. Ge 21:22. 39:2, 21. Ex 3:12. 1 Ch 17:8. 22:11. Mt *28:20. **magnified**. 1 Ch 29:25. Ph 2:9-11.

2. **Then Solomon**. This seems to have taken place a short time after David's decease, and, according to some, in the *second* year of Solomon's reign; when being established in his kingdom, he convened his chief men, and spake to them concerning the solemn sacrifice which he purposed to offer to God. **to the captains**. 2 Ch 29:20. 30:2. 34:29, 30. 1 Ch 13:1. 15:3. 27:1. 28:1. 29:1. **the chief**. 1 Ch 15:12. 24:4, 31.

3. **Gibeon**. 1 K 3:4, etc. 1 Ch +14:16. 16:39. 21:29. **the tabernacle**. Ex 26:1, etc. 40:2, 34. Le 1:1. **the servant**. Dt 34:5.

4. **the ark**. The tabernacle and the brazen altar still remained at Gibeon; but David had brought away the ark out of the tabernacle, and placed it in a tent at Jerusalem. 2 S 6:2, 17. 1 Ch 13:5, 6. 15:1, 25-28. **for he had pitched**. 1 Ch 16:1. Ps 132:5, 6.

5. **the brasen**. Ex 27:1-8. 38:1-7. **Bezaleel**. Ex 31:2. 1 Ch 2:19, 20. **he put**. *or, was* there. ver. 3. **sought unto it**. went to seek the Lord there. 1 Ch 13:3.

6. **a thousand**. 1 K 3:4. 8:63. 1 Ch 29:21. Is 40:16.

7. **In that night**. This was the night following the sacrifice which Solomon had offered. 1 K 3:5-15. Pr *3:5, 6. **Ask**. Mt 7:7, 8. Mk 10:36. Lk *11:9. Jn *16:23. 1 J √5:14, 15.

8. **Thou hast showed**. 2 S 7:8, 9. 12:7, 8. 22:51. 23:1. Ps 86:13. 89:20-28, 49. Is 55:3. **to reign**. 1 Ch 28:5. 29:23.

9. **let thy promise**. T#1655. 2 Ch 6:16, 17. Ge *32:11, 12. 2 S 7:12-16, 25-29. 1 Ch 17:11-14, 23-27. 28:6, 7. Ne 1:8-10. Ps 89:35-37. 119:38, 41, 49, 58. *132:11, 12. **for thou hast**. 1 K 3:7, 8. **like the dust**. Heb. much as the dust. *102B, *138B, Ge +13:16. Ge 13:16. 22:17. Nu 23:10.

10. **Give me**. 1 K 3:9. Jb 28:28. Ps +32:8. 119:34, 73. Pr 2:2-6. 3:13-18. √4:7. 9:10. 23:12. Ho 6:3. Mt 7:7. Lk *11:9. Jn *17:3. Ja √1:5. **go out**. *171J3, Nu +27:17. Dt 31:2. 2 S 5:2. **for who can**. 2 C 2:16. 3:5.

11. **Because**. This does not occur in Kings: and it implies that the request of Solomon, as arising from a spiritual judgment and heart, was peculiarly acceptable to that God who searches, regards, and demands the heart. God promised Solomon all the things which he had not asked, except the life of his enemies; for he was to be a peaceable king, a type of the Prince of peace. **this was**. 1 S *16:7. 1 K 3:11-13. 8:18. 1 Ch 28:2. 29:17, 18. Pr *23:7. Ac 5:4. He *4:12. **the life**. Heb. *nephesh*, soul, Ge +44:30. **that thou mayest**. 1 K 3:28. Pr 14:8. Ja *3:13, 17.

12. **I will give**. Mt √6:33. Ep *3:20. **such as none**.

2 Ch *9:22. 1 Ch 29:25. Ec *2:9. Ja *1:5.

13. **at Gibeon**. ver. 3. **reigned**. 1 K 4:24, 25.

14. **Solomon**. 2 Ch 9:25. Dt 17:16. 1 K 4:26. 10:16, 26, etc. **the chariot cities**. Cities where the chariots, and horses belonging to them, were kept.

15. **the king**. He destroyed its value by making it so exceedingly plentiful. ver. 12. 2 Ch 9:27. 1 K 10:27, etc. Jb 22:24, 25. Is 60:17. **made**. Heb. gave. Ge 9:12. **as stones**. *102B, Ge +13:16. **sycamore trees**. 2 Ch 9:27. 1 Ch 27:28n. Is 9:10. Am 7:14.

16. **Solomon**. Heb. the going forth of the horses which *was* Solomon's. 2 Ch 9:28. 1 K 10:28, 29. **linen yarn**. Or, Keva, the name of a place in Egypt (Young).

17. **the kings**. 2 K 7:6. 10:29. **Hittites**. Ge +15:20. **means**. Heb. hand.

2 CHRONICLES 2

Solomon purposes to build the temple, and a palace, 1. His workmen, 2. He sends to Huram for skilful artificers, and for timber, 3-10. Huram's friendly answer, 11-16. Solomon employes strangers, as laborers and overseers, 17, 18.

1. **determined**. 1 K 5:5. **for the name**. Dt 12:5, 11. 28:58. 1 K 8:18, 20. 1 Ch 22:10. Mt *6:9, 10. **an house**. 1 K 7:1. 9:1.

2. **told out threescore**. ver. 18. 1 K 5:15, 16.

3. **Huram**. 1 K 5:1, Hiram. **As thou didst**. 2 S 5:11. 1 Ch 14:1. **even so**. *63D2, Ge +30:27.

4. **build**. ver. 1. 1 K 8:18. **to dedicate**. 1 K 8:63. **to burn**. Ex 30:7. **sweet incense**. Heb. incense of spices. Ex 25:6. 30:7. 39:38. **the continual**. Ex 25:30. Le 24:5-9. **the burnt**. Ex 29:38-42. Nu 28:3, 4, 9-11. **new moons**. Nu 10:10. 28:11-15. 1 S 20:5. 2 K *4:23. 1 Ch 23:31. 2 Ch +8:13. Ps 81:3. Is 1:13. 66:23. Ho 2:11. **the solemn feasts**. or, set feasts. Ge +*17:21. Le 23:2n. Nu ch. 28, 29. **for ever**. Heb. *olam*, Ex +12:24.

5. **great**. ver. 9. 1 K 9:8. 1 Ch 29:1. Ezk 7:20. **great is our God**. Ex 15:11. 1 Ch 16:25. Ps 86:8, 9. 135:5. *145:3. Je 10:6. 1 T *6:15.

6. **But who**. 2 Ch *6:18. 1 K 8:27. Is 66:1. Ac 7:48, 49. **is able**. Heb. hath retained, *or* obtained strength. 1 Ch +29:14mg. **who am I then**. 2 Ch 1:10. Ex *3:11. 2 S 7:18. 1 Ch *29:14. 2 C 2:16. Ep 3:8. **save only**. Dt 12:5, 6, *11, *14, *26.

7. **cunning**. Ex 31:3-5. 1 K 7:14. Is 28:26, 29. 60:10. **to grave**. Heb. to grave gravings. ver. 14. Ex 39:6. **whom David**. 1 Ch 22:15, 16.

8. **Send me also**. 1 K 5:6. **algum trees**. *or*, algum-mim. Called in the parallel passage, by a transposition of letters, *almuggim*, or "almug trees;" which is rendered by the Vulgate, *ligna thyina*, the *thya* or "lignum vitae" wood. Theophrastus (Hist. Plant. v. 5) says that "the *thyon* or *thya* tree grows near the temple of Jupiter Ammon (in Africa), and in the Cyrenaica; that it resembles the cypress in its boughs, leaves, stalk, and fruit; and that its wood (from its close texture) never rots." The LXX. render here *peukina;* and Josephus calls it *Xula peukina*, "torch" or "pine trees;" but cautions us against supposing that the wood was like what was known in his time by that name; for these "were to

the sight like the wood of the fig tree, but more white and shining." The Syriac version has *kaiso dekeesotho,* probably *cypress wood;* and Dr. Shaw supposes it denotes the *cypress.* Several critics understand it to mean *gummy wood;* and Celsius queries whether it may not be the *sandal tree,* as the Rabbins and Dr. Geddes suppose. 1 K 10:11, almug trees.

9. **wonderful great.** Heb. great and wonderful. ♪93A, Ge +1:26. ver. 5. 2 Ch 7:21. 1 K 9:8. Jl 2:26.

10. **I will give.** 1 K 5:11. Lk 10:7. Ro 13:7, 8. **measures.** 1 K +4:22mg. Ezr 7:22mg. **baths of wine.** 1 K 7:26, 38. Ezr 7:22.

11. **Because.** 2 Ch 9:8. Dt 7:7, 8. 1 K 10:9. Ps 72:17.

12. **Huram.** 1 K 5:7. 1 Ch 29:20. Ps 72:18, 19. Lk 1:68. 1 P 1:3. **that made heaven.** Ge ch. 1, 2. Ps 33:6. 102:25. 124:8. 136:5, 6. 146:5, 6. Je 10:10. Ac 4:24. 14:15. Col 1:16, 17. Re 4:11. 10:6. **endued,** etc. Heb. knowing prudence and understanding. 2 Ch 1:10-12. **an house.** ver. 1.

13. **of Huram.** 2 Ch 4:16.

14. **The son.** 1 K 7:13, 14. **skilful.** ver. 7. Ex 31:3, 4.

15. **which my lord.** ver. 10. 1 K 5:11.

16. **we will cut.** 1 K 5:8, 9. **as much as thou shalt need.** Heb. according to all thy need. **Joppa.** i.e. *lovely; fair to him,* *S#3305h. 2 Ch 2:16. Jsh 19:46. Ezr 3:7. Jon 1:3. Ac 9:36. 10:32.

17. **numbered.** ver. 2. 2 Ch 8:7, 8. 1 K 5:13-16. 9:20, 21. **the strangers.** Heb. the men the strangers. Ge 13:8mg. **after the numbering.** 1 Ch 22:2.

18. **threescore.** *"As it is* ver. 2."

2 CHRONICLES 3

The place of the temple, and the time when the building of it was begun, 1, 2. Its dimensions and ornaments, 3-7. Those of the most holy place, 8-10. The cherubim placed in it, 11-13. The veil, 14. The two pillars, 15-17.

1. A.M. 2993. B.C. 1011. An. Ex. Is. 480. **Solomon.** 1 K 6:1, etc. **in mount Moriah.** Ge *22:2, 14. **where the Lord appeared unto David.** *or,* which was seen of David. **Ornan.** 2 S 24:18-25, Araunah. 1 Ch 21:18. 22:1.

2. **in the second.** 1 K 6:1.

3. A.M. 2993-3000. B.C. 1011-1004. **Solomon.** 1 Ch 28:11-19. **instructed.** Heb. founded. ♪24A, Ge +32:24. Ezr 3:11. **The length.** 1 K 6:2, 3. **the first measure.** It is supposed, with much probability, that the *first measure* means the cubit used in the time of Moses, contradistinguished from that used in Babylon, and which the Israelites used after their return from captivity: and, as these Books were written after the captivity, it was necessary for the writer to make this remark, lest it should be thought that the measurement was by the Babylonish cubit, which was a *palm* or *one-sixth* shorter than the cubit of Moses; which may serve to reconcile some variations in the historical books, with respect to numbers when applied to measures.

4. **the porch.** Jn 10:23. Ac 3:11. 5:12. **an hundred and twenty.** As the height of the temple was only thirty cubits, 120 seems too great a height for the porch; but the Syriac, Arabic, and LXX. in the codex

Alexandrinus, have only *twenty,* probably reading, instead of *maiah weesrim,* "one hundred and twenty," *ammoth esrim,* "twenty cubits," which brings it within the proportion of the other measures.

5. **the greater.** 1 K 6:15-17, 21, 22.

6. **garnished.** Heb. covered. ver. 4, 10. **precious.** 1 Ch 29:2, 8. Is 54:11, 12. Re 21:18-21. **Parvaim.** i.e. *Oriental regions; he broke their hooks,* *S#6516h. *Parvaim* is supposed by Calmet to be the same as *Sepharvaim* in Armenia or Media; Bochart is of opinion that it is *Taprobanes,* now the island of *Ceylon,* which he derives from *taph,* a border, and *Parvan,* i.e. "the coast of Parvan;" but the late Editor of Calmet thinks it the same as the *Parvatoi* mountains of Ptolemy, at the head of the Indus.

7. **overlaid.** Ex 26:29. 1 K 6:20-22, 30. Ezk 7:20. **beams.** 2 K 6:2, 5. SS 1:17. **posts.** 1 K +14:17 (*S#5592h). Is 6:4. **graved cherubims.** Ex 26:1. 1 K 6:35.

8. **the most holy.** Ex 26:33. 1 K 6:19, 20. He 9:3, 9. 10:19.

9. **was.** ♪63B, Ge +2:10. **upper chambers.** 1 Ch 28:11.

10. **two cherubims.** 1 K 6:23-28. **image work.** *or, as some think,* of moveable work.

13. **inward.** *or,* toward the house. 2 Ch 4:4. Ex 25:20. 28:26. 39:19. 2 S 5:9. 1 K 7:25. Ezk 40:9.

14. **the vail.** Ex 26:31-35. Mt 27:51. He 9:3. 10:20. **blue.** Ex 26:31. 36:35. **purple.** Ex +25:4n. 26:31n. 36:35. **wrought.** Heb. caused to ascend.

15. **two pillars.** 1 K 7:15-24. Je 52:20-23. **thirty.** The Syriac and Arabic have, agreeably to the parallel passage, "eighteen cubits high;" but the Septuagint, Chaldee, and Vulgate have "thirty and five cubits high." See the Note on 1 K 7:15. **high.** Heb. long.

16. **chains.** ver. 5. Ex 28:14. 39:15. 1 K 6:21. 7:17. Ezk 7:23. **the oracle.** 2 Ch 4:20. 5:7, 9. 1 K 6:+5, 16n, 19, 20, 21, 22, 23, 31. 7:49. 8:6, 8. Ps 28:2. **an hundred.** 1 K 7:20.

17. **reared up.** 1 K 7:21. **Jachin.** *that is,* He shall establish. **Boaz.** *that is,* In it *is* strength.

2 CHRONICLES 4

The altar of brass, 1. The molten sea supported by twelve oxen, 2-5. The lavers, candlesticks, and tables, 6-8. The two courts of the temple, 9, 10. The vessels, furniture, and instruments of brass, 11-18. Those of gold, 19-22.

1. **an altar.** 2 Ch 1:5. Ex 27:1-8. 1 K 8:22, 64. 9:25. 2 K 16:14, 15. Ezk 43:13-17.

2. **a molten sea.** Ex 30:18-21. 1 K 7:23. Zc 13:1. T *3:5. Re 7:14. **brim to brim.** Heb. his brim to his brim. lit. lip. ver. 5. Jg +7:22mg. 1 K 9:26.

3. **And under.** 1 K 7:24-26. Ezk 1:10. 10:14. 1 C 9:9, 10. Re 4:7. **Oxen.** In the parallel passage of Kings, instead of *bekarim,* "oxen," we have *pekaim,* "knops," in the form of *colocynths* (See on 1 K 6:18, and 2 K 4:39); which last is supposed by able critics to be the reading which ought to be received here; *bekarim,* "oxen," being a mistake for *pekaim,* "knops." Houbigant, however, contends that the words in both places are right; but that *bakar* does not signify an *ox* here, but a large kind of *grape,* according to its meaning in Arabic. But Dr. A. Clarke states that *bakar,* or *bakarat,* has no such meaning in Arabic, though the phrase

aino lbikri, or "ox eye," signifies a species of black grape, very large, and of incredible sweetness; that consequently the criticism of this great man is not solid; and that the likeliest method of reconciling the two places is supposing a change in the letters as above. **round.** J84, Ge +6:17. Ezk 37:2. 40:5, 14, 16, 16, 17, 25, 29, 30, 33, 36, 43. 41:5, 6, 7, 8, 10, 11, 12, 16, 17, 19. 42:15, 20. 43:12.

4. **It stood.** Mt 16:18. Ep 2:20. Re 21:14. **three.** Mt *28:19, 20. Mk 16:15. Lk 24:46, 47. Ac 9:15.

5. **thickness.** 1 K 7:26. Je 52:21. **handbreadth.** J79, Ge +21:16. Ex 25:25. 37:12. 1 K 7:26. Ps 39:5. Ezk 40:5, 43. 43:13. **brim.** ver. 2. **cup.** Ge 40:11, 13, 21. 1 K 7:26. **with flowers.** ver. 21. Ex 25:31, 33, 34. 37:17, 19, 20. Nu 8:4. 17:8. 1 K 7:26, 49. Is 5:24. 18:5. Na 1:4. **of lilies.** SS 2:1, 2. Ho 14:5. *or*, like a lily flower. **three thousand baths.** In the parallel passage, it is said to hold only *two thousand baths*; which some think may be reconciled by supposing the quantity of water which was commonly in it was 2000 baths, but that, if filled up to the top, it would hold 3000. But, as we have already seen that the Babylonish cubit was *less* than that of the ancient Hebrews (2 Ch 3:4n), it might be the same with measures of capacity; so that 2000 of the *ancient* Jewish baths might have been equal to 3000 of those used *after the captivity*. The Targum cuts the knot: "It received 3000 baths of dry measure, and held 2000 of liquid measure." See 1 K 7:26n.

6. **ten lavers.** Ex 30:+*18, 19-21. 1 K 7:38, 40. Ps 51:2. 1 C 6:11. 1 J *1:7. **such things as they offered for the burnt offering.** Heb. the work of the burnt offering. Le 1:9, 13. Ezk 40:38. **but the sea.** ver. 2. Ex 29:4. He 9:14, 23. Re *1:5, 6. 7:14.

7. **ten candlesticks.** 1 K 7:49. 1 Ch 28:15. Zc 4:2, 3, 11-14. Mt *5:14-16. Jn *8:12. Re 1:20. **according to.** Ex 25:31-40. 1 Ch 28:12, 19. He 8:5.

8. **ten tables.** Ex 25:23-30. 37:10-16. 1 K 7:48. Is 25:6. Ezk 44:16. Ml 1:12. 1 C 10:21. **basons.** *or*, bowls. 1 K +*7:40. Ne 7:70. Je 52:18, 19. Zc 14:20.

9. **the court.** 1 K 6:36. 7:12.

10. **he set.** 1 K 7:39.

11. **the pots.** See 1 K 7:40, 45. **basons.** *or*, bowls. 1 K +7:40. **finished.** Heb. finished to make.

12. **To wit.** 2 Ch 3:15-17. **the pommels.** 1 K 7:41.

13. **four hundred.** Ex 28:33, 34. 1 K 7:20, 42. SS 4:13. Je 52:23. **pillars.** Heb. face of the pillars.

14. **made also.** Ga 4:25. **bases.** 1 K 7:27-43. **lavers.** *or*, caldrons. ver. 6.

15. **One sea.** ver. 2-5.

16. **pots also.** ver. 11. Ex 27:3. 38:3. Zc 14:20, 21. **flesh-hooks.** 1 S 2:13, 14. 1 Ch 28:17. **Huram.** 1 K 7:13, 14, 45, Hiram. **his father.** 2 Ch 2:13. **bright.** Heb. made bright, *or*, scoured. or, purified. Le 6:28. Je 46:4 (furbish).

17. **clay ground.** Heb. thicknesses of the ground. Ex 19:9h. Jg 5:4. 1 K *7:46n. **Zeredathah.** i.e. *puncture; scene of the adversary's rule; cooling,* *S#6868h. 1 K 7:46, Zarthan.

18. **the weight.** 1 K 7:47. 1 Ch 22:3, 14. Je 52:20.

19. **all the vessels.** 2 Ch 36:10, 18. 1 K 7:48-50. 2 K 24:13. 25:13-15. Ezr 1:7-11. Je 28:3. 52:18, 19. Da 5:2, 3, 23. **the golden.** 2 Ch 26:16-18. Ex 30:1-10. 37:25-29. Re 8:3. 9:13. **the tables.** Ex 25:23-30. Le 24:5-8. 1 Ch 28:16.

20. **the candlesticks.** ver. 7. Ex 25:31-37. **burn after.**

Ex 27:20, 21. **the oracle.** 1 K 6:+5, 16n, 17. 8:6. Ps 28:2.

21. **the flowers.** Probably each branch of the chandelier was made like a *plant in flower;* and the opening of the flower was either the *lamp*, or served to support it. ver. 5. Ex 25:31, etc. 37:20. 1 K 6:18, 29, 35. **perfect gold.** Heb. perfections of gold. That is, the purest and best gold.

22. **snuffers.** Ex 37:23. 1 K 7:50. 2 K 12:18. 25:14. Je 52:18. **basons.** *or*, bowls. ver. 8, 11. 1 K +7:40. **the entry.** Capellus and others suppose we should read, agreeably to 1 K 7:50, "The hinges also of the doors of the inner house," etc.; the word *pothoth*, "hinges," being mistaken for *paithach*, "an entry" or "doorway." 1 K 6:31, 32.

2 CHRONICLES 5

The temple is finished, and the dedicated treasures deposited in it, 1. The ark is brought into the most holy place, 2-10. While the Levites sing praises to God, a cloud fills the temple, 11-14.

1. A.M. 3000. B.C. 1004. **finished.** Ep=5:27. 2 Th=1:10. **brought in all.** 1 K 7:51. 1 Ch 22:14. 26:26-28.

2. **Then Solomon.** ver. 1, 12. 1 K 8:1-11. 1 Ch 28:1. **the chief.** 1 Ch 15:12. 24:6, 31. 26:26. **the ark.** Nu 10:33, 36. **out.** 2 Ch 1:4. 2 S 6:12. 1 Ch 16:1. **the city.** 2 S 5:7. **which is Zion.** Ps 2:6. 87:2. 132:13-17.

3. **Wherefore.** 1 K 8:2. **in the feast.** That is, as the Targumist observes, in the feast of tabernacles, which was held in the *seventh* month of the ecclesiastical year, which was called *Ethanim.* 2 Ch 7:8-10. Le 23:34-36. 1 K 8:2.

4. **the Levites.** Probably the Levites, of the family of Kohath, carried the ark into the courts of the temple; and then the priests conveyed it into its proper place. Nu 4:15. Jsh 3:6. 6:6. 1 K 8:3. 1 Ch 15:2, 12-14.

5. **the tabernacle.** 2 Ch 1:3. 1 K 8:4, 6.

6. **king Solomon.** 2 S 6:13. 1 K 8:5. 1 Ch 16:1, 2. 29:21.

7. **the priests.** Ps 132:8. **his place.** 2 Ch 35:3. He=1:3. Re=21:3. **to the oracle.** 2 Ch 4:20. Ex 37:6-9. 1 K 6:16n, 23-28. 8:6, 7. He 9:4, 5.

8. **the staves.** Ex 25:12-15. 37:3-5. Nu 4:6.

9. **they drew.** As the ark was no longer to be carried about, the staves were unnecessary. **the ends.** 1 K 8:8, 9. **there it is.** *or*, they are there: as 1 K 8:8. **unto this day.** That is, the day *when these events were recorded;* not the day when these extracts were made, after the captivity, and consequently, long after the destruction of the temple. 1 Ch +4:43.

10. **There was nothing.** In the parallel passage in the Epistle to the Hebrews, it is expressly stated that in the ark were "the golden pot that had manna, and Aaron's rod that budded, and the tables of the covenant;" but it is evident that the apostle speaks there of the tabernacle erected by Moses, and of the state and contents of that tabernacle in the time of Moses; and in the temple there were several things *added*, and several *left out.* **save.** 2 Ch 6:11. Ex 31:18. 32:15, 16, 19. 34:1. 40:20. Dt 10:2-5. He *9:4. **when.** *or*, where. **the Lord.** Ex 19:5. 24:7, 8. Dt 29:1, 10-14. Je 31:31-34. He 8:6-13.

11. **priests.** Re=5:9, 10. **present.** Heb. found. 2 Ch +29:29mg. Jg +20:48mg. 1 S 13:15mg, 16. **sancti-**

fied. 2 Ch 29:5, 15, 34. 30:15, 17-20. Ex 19:10, 14, 15. Jb 1:5. **by course**. 2 Ch 35:4. 1 Ch ch. 24.

12. **the Levites**. 2 Ch 29:25. 1 Ch 15:16-22. 16:4-6, 41, 42. 23:5, 30. 25:1-7. Ezr 3:10, 11. **singers**. ver. 13. 1 K 10:12. 1 Ch 9:33. 15:16, 19, 27. **Asaph**. 1 Ch 6:33, 39. 25:6. Ps 50, 62, 88, titles. **arrayed**. 1 Ch 15:27. Re 15:6. 19:8. **white linen**. 2 Ch 2:14. 3:14. 1 Ch 4:21. 15:27. Est 1:6. 8:15. Ezk 27:16. **cymbals**. 1 Ch +13:8. Ps 92:3. 149:3. 150:3-5. **psalteries**. 1 S +10:5. 2 S 6:5. **harps**. Ge 4:21. 31:27. 1 Ch +13:8n. Re=5:8. **stood**. Le=1:16. Ps=20:3mg. Ep =1:6. **an hundred**. Nu 10:1-5. Jsh 6:6-20. 1 Ch 15:24. 16:6. Ps 68:25. **trumpets**. 2 Ch 13:12, 14. 29:26. Nu 10:2n. 1 Ch 15:24. 16:6. Ezr 3:10. Ne 12:35, 41.

13. **as one**. Jg 20:11. 1 S 18:1. 1 Ch 12:17. Ps 95:1, 2. 100:1, 2. Is 52:8. Je 32:39. Ac 4:32. Ro *15:6. Re 5:8-14. **one sound**. Re=5:9. **praising**. 1 Ch 16:4, 36. 23:5, 30. 25:3. **thanking**. or, confessing. 1 Ch 16:4, 7, 35, 41. 23:30. 25:3. **lifted**. ƒ144A12, Ge +22:13. **with the trumpets**. ver. +12. Ps 68:25, 26. **instruments of music**. 1 Ch 16:42n. **he is good**. 2 Ch 7:3. 20:21. 1 Ch 16:34-41. Ezr 3:11. Ps ch. 136. Je 33:11. **for ever**. Heb. *olam*, Ex +12:24. **then the house**. Ex 40:34, 35. 1 K 8:10-12. **was filled**. Is 6:4. Re=15:8. **with a cloud**. The usual symbol of the Divine presence (Young). Ex +*13:21, 22. 14:19, *20, 24. 16:10. 19:9, 16. 24:15, 16, 18. +*40:35. Da *7:13. Zc +*2:5. Mt 17:5. +*24:30. 26:64. Mk *13:26. 14:62. Lk 21:27. Ac 1:9. 1 Th 4:17. Re *1:7. *14:14.

14. **the priests**. 2 Ch 7:2. 1 T 6:16. **the glory**. Ex 40:35. Is 6:1-4. Ezk 10:4. Hg 2:9. Re 15:8. **filled**. ver. 13. 2 Ch 7:1, 2. Ex 40:34, 35. 1 K 8:10, 11.

2 CHRONICLES 6

Solomon blesses the people, and praises God, 1-11. His prayer at the dedication of the temple, 12-39. He concludes by earnestly entreating the Lord's special presence and blessing, 40-42.

1. **The Lord**. Ex 20:21. 24:15-18. Le 16:2. Dt 4:11. 1 K 8:12, etc. Ps 18:8-11. 97:2. Na 1:3. He 12:18.

2. **I have built**. 2 Ch 2:4-6. 2 S 7:13. 1 K 8:13. 1 Ch 17:12. 22:10, 11. 28:6, 20. Ps 132:5, 13, 14. Jn 4:21-23. He 9:11, 12. Re 21:3. **for ever**. Heb. *olam*, plural, Ps +61:4.

3. **turned his face**. 1 K 8:14. **blessed**. 2 Ch 29:29. Nu *6:23-27. Jsh 22:6. 1 K 8:55-61. 1 Ch 16:2. Lk 24:50, 51. **all the congregation**. 1 K 8:14. Ne 8:5-7. Mt 13:2.

4. **Blessed**. 1 K 8:15. 1 Ch 29:10, 20. Ps 41:13. 68:4, 32-35. 72:18, 19. Lk 1:68, 69. Ep *1:3. **who hath with**. 1 Ch 17:12. Ps 138:1, 2. Mt 24:35. Lk 1:70.

5. **Since the day**. 2 S 7:6, 7. 1 K 8:16. **my name**. Ex 20:24. 23:21. Dt 12:5, 11. Da 9:19. **neither chose**. The judges and Saul were chosen by God, for a season, to be rulers of Israel; but not to establish a *permanent* and *hereditary* authority over that people, as was the case with David. This clause is wanting in the parallel passage in Kings; but it helps to clear the sense. 1 S 10:24. 13:13, 14. 15:23. 2 S 7:15, 16.

6. **But I have chosen Jerusalem**. This clause is also not found in Kings. Jerusalem was expressly marked out, by the building of the temple, to be the center of the worship of Israel; as Jehovah had before spoken by Moses: see the parallel passages. 2 Ch 12:13. Dt 12:5-7, 11. Ps 48:1. 78:68-70. 132:13. Is 14:32. **chosen**

David. 1 S 16:1. 1 Ch 28:4. Ps 89:19, 20.

7. **it was**. 2 S 7:2, 3. 1 K 5:3. 8:17. 1 Ch 17:1. 22:7. 28:2, etc.

8. **Forasmuch**. 1 S *30:24. **heart**. 1 S *16:7. **thou didst well**. 1 K 8:18-21. Mk 14:8. 2 C 8:12.

9. **thy son**. 2 S 7:12, 13. 1 Ch 17:4, 11, 12.

10. **performed his word**. See on ver. 4. **I am risen**. 2 Ch 1:1. 1 K 2:12. 3:6, 7. 1 Ch 29:15, 23. Ec 1:4. 2:18, 19. **as the Lord**. 1 Ch 17:11. 28:5.

11. **I put the ark**. 2 Ch 5:7, 10. Ex 40:20. 1 K 8:9, 21. He 9:4. **the covenant**. As "there was nothing in the ark but the two tables of stone," consequently they are called *the covenant*, i. e. a *sign* of the covenant. ƒ121S. Figure of speech Metonymy of the adjunct, where some circumstance pertaining to the subject is put for the subject itself; here, the sign is put for the thing signified. For other instances of this figure, see Ge +49:10.

12. **he stood**. 1 K 8:22, etc. 2 K 11:14. 23:3. Ps 29:1, 2. **spread forth**. Ex 9:33. Jb 11:13. Ps 28:2. 63:4. 68:31. 141:2. 143:6. Is 50:15. 1 T 2:8.

13. **scaffold**. Ne 8:4. **long**. Heb. the length thereof, etc. **the court**. 2 Ch 4:9. 1 K 6:36. 7:12. **kneeled down**. 1 K 8:54. Ezr 9:5. Ps 95:6. Da 6:10. Lk 22:41. Ac 20:36. 21:5.

14. **O Lord God**. Ge 33:20. 35:10. Ex *3:15. 1 K 8:23. 18:36. 1 Ch 29:10, 20. **no God**. Ex 15:11. Dt *4:39. 2 S *7:22. Ps 86:8. 89:6, 8. Je 10:6, 16. **keepest covenant**. Dt *7:9. Ne 1:5. Ps 89:28. Da 9:4. Mi *7:18-20. Lk 1:72. **mercy**. Ps 103:17, 18. Lk 1:50, 54, 55. **walk before**. Ge 5:24. *17:1. 1 K 3:6. 6:12. Lk *1:6. 1 Th *2:12.

15. **and spakest**. 2 S *7:12. 1 K 8:24. 1 Ch 22:9, 10. **hast fulfilled**. ver. 4. Jsh *21:45.

16. **keep**. Ezk 36:37. Jn *15:14, 15. **hast promised**. T#1125. ver. 17, 42. Ge 32:9, 12. Ex 32:13. 1 K 8:26. Ne 1:8-10. 9:32. Ps 105:42. 119:41, 49, 58, 76, 154, 169. Je 14:21. Lk 2:29. **saying**. 2 Ch *7:18. 2 S *7:12-16. 1 K 2:4. 6:12. Ps 132:12. **There shall not fail thee a man**. Heb. There shall not a man be cut off. 2 Ch 7:18. **to walk**. Ps 26:3. 119:1.

17. **O Lord**. ver. 4, 14. Ex 24:10. Is *41:17. *45:3. **let thy**. 2 S 7:25-29. Je 11:5. **verified**. T#1137. Ps 89:49. Je 15:15-18.

18. **But will**. Ex 29:45, 46. 1 K *8:27. Ps 68:18. 113:5, 6. Is *57:15. 66:1. Ac 7:48, 49. *17:24. **heaven**. *Hashamayim ooshemey hashamayim*, "the heavens and the heavens of heavens;" which words seem to imply that there are systems and systems of systems, each possessing its sun, its primary and secondary planets; all extending beyond each other in unlimited space, in the same regular and graduated order which we find to prevail in our solar system; which, probably, in its thousands of millions of miles in diameter, is, to some others, no more than the area of the lunar orbit to that of the Georgium Sidus. 2 Ch 2:6. Ps *139:7-10. Je 23:24. 2 C 12:2. **how much**. 2 Ch 32:15. Jb 4:19. 9:14. 25:4-6. Mt 7:11.

19. **Have respect**. 1 K 8:28. Ps 74:20. 130:2. Da 9:17-19. Lk *18:1-7. **to hearken**. Ps 4:1. 5:1, 2. 20:1-3. Jn 17:20.

20. **thine eyes**. 2 Ch 16:9. 1 K 8:29, 30. 2 K 19:16. Ne 1:6. Ps 34:15. 121:5. **put thy name**. ver. 6. Dt 26:2. Col 2:9. **toward this place**. or, in this place. 1 K 8:29, 30, 38. Ps 5:7. 28:2mg. 132:7. 138:2. Da *6:10. Jon 2:4.

21. **make**. Heb. pray. 1 K 8:29. **thy dwelling place**. ver. 39. 2 Ch 30:27. Jb 22:12-14. Ps 123:1. Ec 5:2. Is 57:15. Mt *6:9. **forgive**. Ps 85:2, 3. 130:3, 4. Is 43:25. Da 9:19. Mi *7:18. Mt 6:12.

22. **sin**. 1 K 8:31, 32. **and an oath**, etc. Heb. and he require an oath of him. Ex 22:11. Le 5:1. Pr 30:9. **the oath**. Nu 5:19-22. Mt 23:18.

23. **from heaven**. ver. 21. **and judge**. Ezk 33:20. **requiting**. Nu 5:27. 2 K 9:26. Ps 10:14. Pr 1:31. Is 3:11. Je 28:16, 17. 51:56. Ro 2:9. **justifying**. Dt 25:1. Pr 17:15. Is 3:10. Ezk 18:20. Ro 2:10.

24. **put to the worse**. *or,* be smitten. Le 26:17, 37. Dt 28:25, 48. Jsh 7:8. 1 K 8:33, 34. Ps 44:10. **because**. Jsh 7:11, 12. Jg 2:11, 14, 15. 2 K 17:7-18. **shall return**. Le 26:40-42. Dt 4:29-31. 30:1-6. Ne 1:8, 9. Pr *28:13. Je 3:12, 13. **pray**. Ezr 9:5, etc. Ne 9:1, etc. Is ch. 63, 64. Da 9:3, etc. **in**. *or,* toward. ver. 20.

25. **forgive the sin**. Ezr 1:1-6. Ps 106:40-47. Je 33:6-13. **which thou**. Ge 13:15. Ex 6:8. Jsh 21:43.

26. **the heaven**. Le 26:19. Dt 11:17. 28:23. 1 K ch. 17, 18. Lk 4:25. **there is no rain**. Is 5:6. 50:1, 2. Ezk 14:13. Am 4:4-9. Re 11:6. **if they pray**. Je 14:1-9. Jl 1:13-20. 2:15-17. **turn from**. Ps *28:13. Ezk 18:27-32. **thou dost**. 2 Ch 33:12, 13. Is 26:16. Ho 5:15. 6:1.

27. **when thou hast**. 1 K 8:35, 36. Ps 25:4, 5, 8, 12. 94:12. 119:33. Mi 4:2. Jn 6:45. **good way**. Is 30:21. Je 6:16. 42:3. **send rain**. 1 K 18:40-45. Jb 37:11-14. Ps 68:9. Je 5:24. 14:22. Ezk 34:26. Ho 2:21, 22. Jl 2:23. Zc 10:1. Ja *5:17, 18.

28. **if there be dearth**. "Persia," says Chardin, "is subject to have its harvest spoiled by hail, by drought, or by insects; either locusts, or small insects, which they call *sim*, which are small white lice;" probably the caterpillars of the text. 2 Ch 20:5-13. Le 26:16, 25, 26. Dt 28:21-61. Ru 1:1. 1 K 8:37-40. 2 K 6:25-29. 8:1. **locusts**. Ex 10:12-15. Jl 1:4-7, 11. 2:25. Re 9:3-11. **their enemies**. 2 Ch 12:2-5. 20:9-13. 32:1. Le 26:25. Dt 28:52-57. **cities of their land**. Heb. land of their gates. Ge +14:7. 2 Sm 19:8n. 1 K 8:37. 2 K 7:1n. **whatsoever**. 2 Ch 32:24. 1 K 8:37, 38. Ja 5:13.

29. **what prayer**. Ps 33:12, 13. 50:15. 91:15. **know**. Ps 32:2-6. 142:1, 2. Pr 14:10. **spread forth**. ver. 12, 13. Is 1:15. **in**. *or,* toward. ver. +20.

30. **render**. Ps 18:20-26. 62:12. Je *17:10. Ezk 18:30. Mt 16:27. **thou only**. 1 K 8:39. 1 Ch +√28:9. 29:17. Ps 11:4, 5. Jn +*2:25. He √4:13. Re 2:23.

31. **fear thee**. Ex 20:20. 1 S *12:24. Jb *28:28. Ps 128:1. 130:4. Ac 9:31. **so long**, etc. Heb. all the days which they live upon the face of the land.

32. **the stranger**. Ex +*12:48mg, 49. Ru 1:16. 2:11, 12. 1 K 8:41-43. 10:1, 2. Is 56:3-7. Mt 2:1. 8:10, 11. Jn 10:16. 12:20. Ac 8:27-39. 10:1-4. Ep 2:12, 13. **is come**. Ex 18:8-12. Jsh 2:9. 9:9. 2 K 5:3, 8, 15. Is 60:1-10. Zc 8:22. Mt 12:42. **thy mighty**. Ex 3:19, 20. 13:14. Ps 89:13. **if they come**. Is 66:20. Zc 14:16, 17. Ac 2:10.

33. **that all people**. 1 S 17:46. 2 K 19:19. Ps 22:27. 46:10. 67:2. 137:4, 5. Is *11:10. 49:6. 54:1-3. Re 11:15. **fear thee**. Je 10:7. **this house**, etc. Heb. thy name is called upon this house. Nu 6:27. 1 K 8:16.

34. **thy people**. 2 Ch 14:11, 12. 20:4. Dt 20:1-4. Jsh 1:2-5. 1 K 8:44, 45. **to war**. T#1739. Nu 21:1, 2. 1 Ch +5:20 (T#1178). +14:10 (T#1226). Ps 60:9, 10. **by the way**. Nu 31:2-6. Jsh 8:1-8. Jg 1:1, 2. 1 S 15:3, 18. **they pray**. 2 Ch 14:9-12. 18:31. 20:6-13. 32:20,

21. **toward**. ver. 6, +20. 1 K 8:13. Is 14:32. Da *6:10. 35. **hear thou**. Da 9:17-19. **maintain**. Is 37:21-36. **cause**. *or,* right. Ps 9:3, 4. Je 5:28. 36. **they sin**. 1 K 8:46, 50. **for there is no man**. ſ138C, Ge +22:14. Jb 15:14-16. Ps 130:3. *143:2. Pr *20:9. Ec √7:20. Is *53:6. *64:6. Ro √3:23. Ja 3:2, 8. 1 J √1:8-10. **thou be angry**. Le 26:34-44. Dt 4:26, 27. 28:36, 64-68. 29:24-28. 2 K 17:6, 18, 23. 15:21. Da 9:7-14. Lk *21:24. **they carry away captives**. Heb. they that take them captives carry them away. 1 K 8:46.

37. **Yet if**. Le *26:40-45. Dt *4:29, 30. *30:1-3. Lk *15:17. **bethink themselves**. Heb. bring back to their heart. **and pray**. T#1232. Ex +2:23 (T#1228). Dt 4:27-29. Ps +119:134 (T#1268). Je 29:12-14. 31:8, 9. La 5:1-8. Da 9:1-3. **We have sinned**. Ezr 9:6, 7. Ne 1:6. 9:26-30. Jb 33:27, 28. Ps 106:6. Is 64:6-12. Je 3:12-14. 31:18-20. Da *9:5-11. Lk 15:18, 19.

38. **return**. Dt 30:2-6. Je 29:12-14. Ho 14:1-4. Jl 2:12, 13. **soul**. Heb. *nephesh,* Ge +34:3. **pray toward**. ver. +20. 2 Ch 33:11-13. Da 9:3, 4. **the city**. ver. 34. Da *6:10.

39. **cause**. *or,* right. ver. 35. Zc 1:15, 16. **forgive**. Ps 25:18. Mi *7:18-20.

40. **my God**. Ps 7:3. 13:3. 22:1, 2. 88:1. **thine eyes**. 2 Ch 7:15. 16:9. 1 K 8:52. Ps 34:15. Is 37:17. Da 9:16-19. **thine ears**. Ps 17:1. 31:2. 116:2. **that is made in this place**. Heb. of this place. 2 Ch 7:15mg.

41. **arise**. Ps *132:8-10, 16. **thy resting**. 1 Ch 28:2. Is 66:1. **the ark**. Jsh 3:13. 6:4, 5. Ps 110:2. Ro *1:16. **thy priests**. T#1652. Is 59:16-18. 61:3, 6, 10. Ro *13:14. Ga 3:27. Ep *4:22-24. 1 Th +5:25 (T#1618). Re 19:8, 14. **thy saints**. Ne 9:25. Ps 65:4, 11. Is 65:18, 19. Zc 9:17. Ph 3:3. 4:4.

42. **turn not**. That is, "reject not thine anointed;" or, "repulse him not," agreeably to the interpretations of this phrase in the Syriac and Arabic versions. See 1 K 2:16. **thine anointed**. 1 K 1:34. Ps *2:2. Is 61:1. **remember**. Ps 132:1. Is 55:3. Ac 13:34. **the mercies**. Or, as Dr. Geddes renders, "the pious deeds of thy servant David." The Syriac has, "the good actions of thy servant."

2 CHRONICLES 7

God testifies his acceptance of Solomon's prayer by fire from heaven; the glory of the Lord fills the temple, and the people worship, 1-3. Solomon's numerous sacrifices at the dedication, 4-7. The congregation to keep the feast of tabernacles, and the feast of the dedication, fourteen days, 8, 9. He dismisses the people joyful, and is prospered, 10, 11. God again appears to Solomon, and makes a covenant with him, 12-22.

1. **when Solomon**. 1 K 8:54, etc. Is 65:24. Da 9:20. Ac 4:31. 16:25, 26. **the fire**. Ge 15:17. Ex 29:43. Le 9:24. Jg 6:21. 1 K 18:24, 38. 1 Ch 21:26. Ml 3:1, 2. **the glory**. 2 Ch 5:13, 14. Ex 40:34, 35. Le 9:23. 1 K 8:10, 11. Is 6:1-4. Ezk 10:3, 4. 43:5. 44:4. Hg 2:7-9. Re 21:23.

2. **the priests**. 2 Ch 5:14. Ex 24:17. Is 6:5. Re 15:8.

3. **they bowed**. Ex 4:31. Le 9:24. Nu 14:5. 16:22. 1 K 18:39. 1 Ch 29:20. Ps 95:6. **For he is**. 2 Ch 5:13. 20:21. 1 Ch 16:41. Ezr 3:11. Ps 103:17. 136:1, etc. Is 63:7. Je 33:11. Lk 1:50. He *7:24, 25. **for ever**. Heb. *olam,* Ex +12:24.

4. **Then the king**. They presented the victims to

the priests, and they and the Levites slew them, and sprinkled the blood; or, perhaps, the people themselves slew them, and having caught the blood, collected the fat, etc., presented them to the priests to be offered as the law required.

5. **a sacrifice.** 2 Ch 1:6. 5:6. 15:11. 29:32, 33. 30:24. 35:7-9. 1 K 8:62, 63. 1 Ch 29:21. Ezr 6:16, 17. Ezk 45:17. Mi 6:7. **twenty and two.** The number of sheep and oxen here mentioned has to some appeared incredibly large; but it must be considered that a prodigious number of persons was now at Jerusalem, and that this was the amount of all the victims that had been offered during the seven days of the feast of tabernacles, as well as the time the feast of the dedication lasted. **dedicated.** 2 Ch 2:4. Nu 7:10. 1 K 8:63. Ezr 6:16. Jn 10:22.

6. **the priests.** 1 Ch 16:39, 40. 24:1-3. **the Levites.** 2 Ch 29:25. 1 Ch 6:31, 32. 15:16-21. 16:4-6, 41, 42. 25:1-7. Ps 87:7. **which David.** Am 6:5. **because his mercy.** ver. 3. 1 Ch 16:34. Ps 106:1. 107:1. 118:1-4. 138:8. **for ever.** Heb. *olam,* Ex +12:24. **ministry.** Heb. hand. 2 Ch 8:18. Nu 15:23. Is 52:6. **the priests.** 2 Ch 5:12. Nu 10:1-10. Jsh 6:4. 1 Ch *13:8. 15:24. 16:6, 42.

7. **hallowed.** 2 Ch 36:14. Nu 16:37, 38. 1 K 8:64. He 13:10-12. **burnt offerings.** Le +*23:12. **peace offerings.** Le +*23:19. **the brazen.** 2 Ch 4:1. **meat offerings.** Le +*23:13.

8. **kept.** Le 23:34-43. Nu 29:12-38. Dt 16:13-15. 1 K 8:65. Ne 8:13-18. Zc 14:16-19. Jn 7:2, 37-39. **a very great.** 2 Ch 30:13. **from the entering.** That is, from one extremity of the land to another; *Hamath* being situated on the *north,* and the river of Egypt on the *south.* Ge 15:18. Nu 34:5-8. Jsh 13:3-5. 1 K 4:21-25. Am 6:14.

9. **solemn assembly.** Heb. restraint. Le 23:36. Dt 16:8. Ne 8:18. Jl 1:14. **seven days.** 2 Ch 30:23. 1 K 8:65.

10. **three and twentieth.** 1 K 8:66. **glad.** 2 Ch 29:36. 30:26. Dt 12:7, 12, 18. 16:11, 14. Ne 8:10. Ps 32:11. 33:1. 92:4. 100:2. 105:3. 106:5. Ac 2:46. 16:34. Ph 4:4. **goodness.** 2 Ch 6:41. Ex 18:1.

11. **Solomon.** 2 Ch 2:1. 1 K 9:1, etc. **all that came.** Ec 2:4, 10, 11.

12. **the Lord.** 2 Ch 1:7. Ge *17:1. 1 K 9:2. **I have heard.** 2 K 20:5. Ps 10:17. 66:19. Lk 1:13. Ac 10:31. 1 J √5:14, 15. **have chosen.** ver. 16. Dt 12:5, 11. Ps 78:68, 69. 132:13, 14. **an house of sacrifice.** 2 Ch 2:6. Dt 12:6.

13. **If I shut up heaven.** 2 Ch 6:26-28. Dt 11:17. Jb 11:10. 12:14. Ps 107:34. Lk 4:25. Re 3:7. 11:6. **I command.** Ex 10:4-6. Ps 105:34. Jl 1:4-7. 2:25. **devour.** 2 S 18:8mg. **I send.** Nu 14:12. 16:46, 47. 2 S 24:13-15. Ezk 14:19-21.

14. **If.** Ge +4:7. **my people.** Is 63:19. **which are called by my name.** Heb. upon whom my name is called. 2 Ch 6:33mg. Nu +*6:27. Is 63:19mg. Je *15:16mg. **humble.** T#1366. 2 Ch *6:37-39. 12:6, 7. *33:12, 13, 18, 19. Le 26:40, 41. Dt *4:29, 30. *30:1-6. Jg 20:26n. 1 K 21:27-29. 2 K 22:18, 19. 1 Ch *17:16. 29:14. Jb 7:7, 18. 40:3-5. 42:5, 6. Ps 9:12. 22:6. *25:9. 34:18. 35:13. 42:5. 51:17. Ec 5:2. Is 57:15. 66:2. Je 1:6. 45:3. La 3:20. Ezk *33:11. Da +√10:12. Jl 2:13. Mi +*6:8. Zc *12:10. Mt 8:8. Lk *18:13. 22:41, 42. 2 C *7:10. Ja *4:9, 10. **and pray.** T#1388. 2 Ch 20:9. Dt 4:29-31. 2 K 20:1-5. Ps 17:1. *145:18, 19. Is √26:8,

9. 58:9. Je √29:13. Ho 7:14. Mt 23:14. Mk *11:23, 24. Lk 22:44. Jn 11:33. Ac 9:11. 1 T √2:1-4. He *10:22. **seek my face.** √22A4, Ge +19:13. T#1386. 1 Ch √28:9. Jb 8:5, 6. Ps +√9:10. 27:4, 8. Pr 2:4-6. 8:17. Is *26:9. 45:19. √55:6, 7. *56:6, 7. Je *29:13. 50:4, 5. La 3:40, 41. Ho 5:6, 7, *15. Am 5:4-6. Mt 7:7, 8. Lk *11:9, 10. He *11:6. **turn from.** T#607. Ps 34:18. 51:17. 147:3. Pr *28:13. Is *55:6, 7. 59:20. *66:2. Ezk 18:27-30. Ho *6:1-3. Jl *2:12, 13. Zc 1:3. Mt 5:3, 4. Lk *15:21-23. Ja +4:10 (T#357). **then will I hear.** 2 Ch 6:27, 30, 39. Ps 91:15. Is *30:18. +*65:24. Je *33:3. Zc *13:9. Jn 15:7. Re *3:20. **forgive their sin.** Ex 34:7. Is *1:18. 43:25. 44:22. 59:1, 2. Je +*31:34. Ho 5:15. 6:1. Zp 3:15. Lk 24:47. Ac +√3:19-21. +*10:36, 43. Ja 5:15. 1 J √1:7, 9. **heal their land.** T#1640. 2 Ch 6:28-31. Nu 14:11-13, 19. 2 S 24:15-17. Ps 60:2. Is 11:6. 27:6. *35:1. Je 8:22. *33:6. 51:9. Am +*9:13-15. Mt +*19:28. Ac +√3:19. Ro +*8:19, 21. Re +*22:3.

15. **mine eyes.** 2 Ch 6:20, 40. Dt 11:12. Ne 1:6. Ps 65:2. 130:2. 1 P 3:12. **that is made in this place.** Heb. of this place. 2 Ch 6:40.

16. **have I chosen.** Dt 12:21. 16:11. 1 K 8:16, 44, 48. Ps 132:14. Zc 3:2. **my name.** See on 2 Ch 6:5, 6, 20. 33:4-7. 1 K 8:35. 9:3. 2 K 21:4, 7, 8. **for ever.** Heb. *olam,* Ex +12:24. **eyes.** See on ver. 15. Mt 3:17. Jn +*2:19-21. Col *2:9.

17. **if thou wilt.** Dt 28:1, etc. 1 K 2:3. 3:14. 8:25. 9:4, etc. 11:38. 1 Ch +√28:9. Zc 3:7. **observe.** Dt *4:40. Ps 105:45. Ezk 36:27. Jn *14:21. *15:10. 1 J √2:3.

18. **stablish.** 2 S 7:13-16. **as I have.** Ps 89:28-40. 132:11, 12. **shall not.** 1 K 9:5. Je +√33:20, 21, 25, 26. **fail thee.** Heb. be cut off to thee. 2 Ch 6:16mg. 1 K 8:25.

19. **if ye turn away.** Le 26:14, 33, etc. Dt 28:15, 36, 37, etc. 1 S 12:25. 1 Ch +√28:9. **shall go.** See on Dt 4:23-27. Jsh 23:15, 16. 1 K 9:6, 7. 11:4-8.

20. **I pluck.** 2 K 17:20. Ps 52:5. Je 12:17. 18:7. 31:28. 45:4. Ju 12. **a proverb.** Dt 28:37. 1 K 9:7. Ne 4:1-4. Ps 44:14. Je 24:9. La 2:15, 16.

21. **this house.** 1 K 9:8. **astonishment.** 2 Ch *29:8. Je 19:8. 49:17. 50:13. **Why.** Dt 29:24-28. 1 K 9:8, 9. Je 5:19. 13:22. 16:10-12. 22:8, 9, 28.

22. **Because they forsook.** Jg 2:12, 13. Je 1:16. La 2:16, 17. 4:13-15. Ezk 14:23. 36:17-20. **therefore.** 2 Ch 36:17. Da 9:12.

2 CHRONICLES 8

The cities built by Solomon, 1-6. The remnant of the devoted nations are subjected to tribute, and the Israelites employed in honorable services, 7-10. Pharaoh's daughter removes to her house, 11. Solomon's daily sacrifices, and those on festival days, 12, 13. He appoints the priests and Levites to their services in order, 14, 15. The work of the house of God is finished, 16. Solomon's navy brings gold from Ophir, 17, 18.

1. **at the end.** See on 1 K 9:10.

2. **the cities.** 1 K 9:11-13.

3. **Hamath-zobah.** i.e. *the swelling host's enclosure of wrath; fortress of Zobah* (i.e. *depression,* 1 S +14:47), ❋S#2578h. Nu 13:21. 34:8. 2 S 8:3. 1 K 11:23-25. 1 Ch 18:3. Am 6:2.

4. **he built.** 1 K 9:17-19. **Tadmor.** i.e. *thou wilt scatter myrrh; wonder, admiration; palm city,* ❋S#8412h. 2 Ch 8:4. 1 K 9:18. Tadmor, the *Palmyra*

of the Greeks, as we learn from Josephus (Ant. l. viii. c. 6), a celebrated city of Syria, situated in an *oasis*, or fertile spot of land, surrounded on all sides by a vast sandy desert, like an island in the midst of an ocean; according to Pliny (l. v. c. 25), 337 miles from Seleucia and Tigrim, 203 from the nearest part of the Mediterranean, and 176 from Damascus; according to Josephus, one day's journey west of the Euphrates, and six from Babylon; and according to Ptolemy, in lat. 34 degrees north, or that of Tripoli, and about 4 degrees more easterly; and it is described by Mr. Wood as "situated under a barren ridge of hills to the west, and open on the other sides to the desert;" "about six days' journey from Aleppo, and as much from Damascus, and about twenty leagues west of the Euphrates." Palmyra attained the height of its splendor when the royal city of Zenobia was conquered by the emperor Aurelian; became a Roman colony after the victories of Trajan; and was probably reduced to its present miserable state in the wars of the Saracens. Its magnificent ruins, however, scattered over an extent of several miles, sufficiently attest its former splendor and riches.

5. **Beth-horon.** The upper, of which there is no mention in 1 K 9:17 (Young). Jsh 16:3, 5. 1 Ch 7:24. **with walls.** 2 Ch 14:7. Dt 3:5. 1 S 23:7. 1 K 4:13.

6. **Baalath.** Jsh 19:44. 1 K 9:18. **the store cities.** ver. 4. 2 Ch 17:12. 1 K 9:19. **chariot cities.** 2 Ch 1:14. 1 K 10:26. **all that Solomon desired to build.** Heb. all the desire of Solomon which he desired to build. 1 K 9:19. Ec 2:4, 10, etc. **and in Lebanon.** 1 K 7:2. SS 4:8.

7. **As for all.** 1 K 9:20-22. **the Hittites.** Ge 15:19, +20, 21. Dt 7:1. **Amorites.** Ge +10:16. **Perizzites.** Ge +13:7. **Hivites.** Ge +10:17. **Jebusites.** Ge +10:16.

8. **whom the children.** Jg 1:21-36. Ps 106:34. **to pay.** 2 Ch 2:17, 18. Jsh 16:10. 17:13. 1 K 5:13, 14.

9. **But of the.** Ex 19:5, 6. Le 25:39-46. Ga 4:26, 31. **they were men.** 1 S 8:11, 12.

10. **two hundred.** 2 Ch 2:18. 1 K 5:16. 9:23.

11. **brought up.** 1 K 3:1. 7:8. 9:24. **holy.** Heb. holiness. Ex 3:5. 29:43. 35:2. Ezk 21:2. 2 P 1:18.

12. **on the altar.** 2 Ch 4:1. 1 Ch 28:11. Ezk 8:16. Jl 2:17. **before the porch.** Jn 10:23.

13. **every day.** Ex 29:38-42. Le ch. 23. Nu ch. 28, 29. Ezk 45:17. 46:3-15. **new moons.** 2 Ch +2:4. **three times.** Ex 23:14-17. Dt 16:16. 1 K 9:25. **unleavened.** Le *23:6. **weeks.** Le +*23:16. Dt *16:10. Ac 2:1. **booths.** Le *23:34. Dt 16:13.

14. **the courses.** 2 Ch 5:11. 23:4. 31:2. 1 Ch 24:1-19. Lk 1:5, 8. **the Levites.** 2 Ch 35:10. 1 Ch 6:31, 32, etc. 15:16-22. 16:4-6, 42. ch. 23. 24:20-31. ch. 25. Ezr 6:18. **the porters.** See on 1 Ch 9:17. +23:5. 26:1-19. **so had David the man of God commanded.** Heb. so *was* the commandment of David the man of God. Dt 33:1. 2 S 23:2. 1 K 13:1. 1 Ch 28:19. Ac 13:22, 36.

15. **they departed not.** See on 2 Ch 30:12. Ex 39:42, 43. **commandment of.** 2 Ch 29:25. Jn=14:21. =15:14. 1 C=12:18. 1 J=*2:3. **the treasures.** 1 K 7:51. 1 Ch 9:29. 26:20-26.

16. **all the work.** 1 K 5:18. 6:7.

17. **Ezion-geber.** 2 Ch 20:36. Nu 33:35. 1 K 9:26, 27. 22:48. **Eloth.** Dt 2:8. 2 K 14:22. 16:6, Elath.

18. **Huram.** 2 Ch 9:10, 13. See on 1 K 9:27, 28. 10:22, Hiram. **Ophir.** 2 Ch 9:10. Ge 10:29. 1 K +9:28n.

10:11. 1 Ch 1:23. 29:4. Jb 22:4. 28:16. Ps 45:9. Is 13:12. Conjectures respecting the location of *Ophir* are endless. Some have placed it in Hispaniola; and Postel and others think it was Peru. Bp. Huet says it was Zanguebar, on the eastern coast of Africa, the name *Ophir* being more particularly applied to the small country of Sophala on the same coast; which opinion Mr. Bruce has labored to support by many ingenious arguments. Grotius conjectures it to be a part of Arabia called Aphar by Arrian; while Bochart and others have placed it in the island of Ceylon, the Taprobanes of the ancients. Calmet supposes it to have been situated in Armenia; but his late learned Editor places it at the head of the Indus. Josephus (Ant. l. viii. c. 3) says that Ophir is the Indies, called the Gold country; by which he is supposed to mean Chersonesus Aurea, now Malacca, opposite Sumatra; and Le Poivre observes that the inhabitants of these places call their gold mines *ophirs*. More recently, Merrill F. Unger in his *Bible Dictionary* suggests Ophir was located in what is now Yemen in south-west Arabia. **took thence.** 1 K 9:28. Ec 2:8.

2 CHRONICLES 9

The queen of Sheba's visit to Solomon; her admiration of his wisdom and magnificence; her presents and return, 1-12. Solomon's annual revenue in gold, 13, 14. His golden shields and targets, 15, 16. His ivory throne, and rich vessels of gold, 17-21. The honor paid him by other kings, 22-24. His stalls, horses, and chariots, 25. He dies, and is succeeded by Rehoboam, 29-31.

1. A.M. 3014. B.C. 990. **And when.** See on 1 K 10:1, 2, etc. Mt 12:42. Lk 11:31. **Sheba.** Ge 10:7, 28. 25:3. **fame.** 2 Ch 1:1, 12. 1 K 4:31. **hard questions.** Nu +12:8. Jg 14:12-19. 1 K 10:1. Ps 49:4. 78:2. Pr 1:6. Mt 13:11, 35. **great.** 2 K 6:14mg. 7:6. **camels.** Ps 72:10, 15. Is 60:6. **spices.** ver. 9. Ex 25:6. 30:23. 35:8. Mt 2:11. **precious stones.** 2 S 12:30. **communed.** 1 S 1:15. Ps 142:2. Mt 12:34.

2. **all.** Pr 13:20. 18:4. Mk 4:11, 34. Jn 15:15. Ja *1:5. **there.** 1 K 3:12. 4:29. Col *2:3. He *4:12.

3. **seen the wisdom.** 1 K 10:3, 4. Ac *11:23. **the house.** 2 Ch ch. 3, 4. 1 K ch. 6, 7.

4. **the meat.** 1 K 4:22, 23. Pr 9:5. Jn 6:53-57. **the sitting.** Ge 10:30h (dwelling). 1 K 10:5. Lk 12:37. Re *3:20. **cupbearers.** *or*, butlers. Ge 40:1-23. 1 K 10:5. Ne 1:11. **ascent.** 2 Ch 23:13. 2 K 16:18. 1 Ch 9:18. Ezk 44:3. 46:2. **there was.** Ps 119:81. 143:7. SS 5:8. Da 10:17. Re 1:17. **spirit.** Heb. *ruach*, Ge +41:8.

5. **report.** Heb. word. See on 1 K 10:6. **acts.** *or*, sayings.

6. **I believed not.** Jn √20:25-29. **the one half.** See on 1 K *10:7. Ps *31:19. Zc *9:17. 1 C √2:9. 1 J √3:2. **for thou.** Jn 1:45-49. **exceedest.** ver. 5. 1 K 4:31, 34. SS *5:9-16. Jn *7:46.

7. **Happy are.** Dt *33:29. 1 K *10:8. Ps *27:4. √84:10-12. Pr 3:3, 14. *8:34. 10:21. 13:20. Mt *13:16, 17. Lk √10:39-42. √11:28.

8. **Blessed.** 1 Ch *29:10, 20. Ps *72:18, 19. 2 C 9:12-15. **which delighted.** 2 S *15:25, 26. See on 1 K *10:9. Ps *18:19. *22:8. Is *42:1. 62:4. **because thy God.** 2 Ch *2:11. Dt *7:8. 1 Ch 17:22. **establish them.** Ro +√11:1. **for ever.** Heb. *olam*, Ex +12:24. **to do judgment.** 2 S *8:15. *23:3. 1 K *3:28. Ps *72:2. 99:4.

Pr *21:3. Is *9:7. *11:1-5. *32:1, 2. Je √33:15, 16. He +√1:8, 9.

9. she gave. ver. 24. 1 K 9:14. 10:10. Ps 72:10, 15. **of spices.** ver. 1. Ge 43:11. Ex 30:34. **Sheba.** This queen is called *Balkis* by the Arabians, who say she came from the city of *Sheba*, also called *Mareb*, in Yemen or Arabia Felix; but the Ethiopians call her *Maqueda*, claim her as their sovereign, and say that her posterity reigned there for a long time. Mr. Bruce has given us the history of her and her descendants from Abyssinian records; and Josephus says that *Sheba* was the ancient name of the city of *Meroe* (south of Egypt, and sometimes comprehended in Ethiopia), and that this princess came from thence. Those who think the princess came from Arabia, rely chiefly on the fact that gold, silver, spices, and precious stones, which were the presents she made to Solomon, are the natural products of that country; and that it may well be placed at the uttermost part of the earth, as it borders on the southern ocean, and formerly they knew no land beyond it.

10. brought gold. See on 2 Ch 8:18. 1 K 9:27, 28. 10:22. **algum trees.** 2 Ch 2:8n. 1 K 10:11, almug trees.

11. terraces. or, stays. Heb. highways. Nu 20:19. 1 K 10:22. Ps 84:6. Pr 16:17. **harps.** 1 K 10:12. 1 Ch +13:8n. 23:5. 25:1. Ps 92:1-3. 150:3-5. Re 5:8.

12. all her desire. 1 K 10:13. Ps 20:4. Ep 3:20.

13. the weight. 1 K 10:14, 15. Ps 68:29. 72:10, 15.

14. chapmen. or, tourists. Nu 14:6 (spies). 1 K 10:15. **merchants.** Ge 23:16. 37:28. **Arabia.** i.e. *dusky; mixed; desert or sterile,* *S#6152h. 2 Ch 9:14. Is 21:13, 13. Je 25:24. Ezk 27:21. **governors.** or, captains. 1 K 10:15.

15. two. 2 Ch 12:9, 10. See on 1 K 10:16, 17.

16. in the house. 1 K 7:2.

17. a great throne. See on 1 K 10:18-20. Ps 45:8. Re *20:11. **pure.** S#2889h. 2 Ch 3:4. 9:17. 13:11. 30:17 (clean). Ge 7:2 (clean). Ex 25:11, 17, 24, 29, 31, 36, 38, 39, (pure). Le 4:12 (clean). 10:10 (clean). 1 S 20:26 (clean). 1 Ch 28:17 (pure). Ezr 6:20 (pure). Jb *14:4 (clean). 28:19 (pure). Ps *12:6 (pure). *19:9 (clean). *51:10 (clean). Pr 15:26 (pure). 22:11 (pureness). 30:12 (pure). Ec 9:2 (clean). Is 66:20. Ezk 22:26. *36:25. 44:23. Hab *1:13 (purer; lit. pure of eyes). Zc 3:5 (fair). Ml 1:11 (pure). ◐*S#5462h, ver. +20.

18. stays. Heb. hands. 1 K 7:35, 36. **two lions.** Ge *49:9, 10. Nu 23:24. 24:9. Re 5:5.

19. twelve lions. Mt *19:28. Re 21:12.

20. all. √102B, Ge +13:16. **drinking.** 1 K 10:21. Est 1:7. Da 5:2, 3. **pure.** Heb. shut up. or, refined. ✛S#5462h. 2 Ch 4:20, 22. 1 K 6:20, 21. 7:49, 50. 10:21. Jb 41:15 (shut up). Ezk 44:1, 2. 46:1. ◐S#2889h, ver. +17. **none were of silver.** or, there was no silver in them. **it was.** ver. 27. Is 2:22. Je 31:5. **not.** 1 K 10:21.

21. Tarshish. Bochart thinks this *Tarshish* was probably the promontory *Cory*, on the north of the island of Ceylon, which, according to him, was the land of *Ophir*. That it was the name of a place in the East Indies, seems probable from the articles brought thence, and also from the ships sent thither being built at Ezion-geber, on the Red sea; though Michaelis (Spicileg. Geog. Heb. Exter. p. 98, etc.) supposes that the fleet coasted along the shore of Africa, doubling the Cape of Good Hope, and came to *Tartessus*, in Spain, and thence back again the same way; that this accounts for their three years' voyage out and home;

and that Spain and the coasts of Africa furnish all the commodities which they brought back. More recently it has been determined that "ships of Tarshish" or "Tarshish ships" were in Solomon's time ore-bearing ships, a refining fleet; that Solomon exchanged the copper mined in the Arabah and smelted at Ezion-geber, where Solomon had a copper smeltery set up by Phoenician craftsmen, for gold, silver, ivory, apes, baboons (1 K 9:26, 28. 10:22). Ge +10:4. See on 1 K 10:22. 22:48, Tharshish. **ivory.** or elephant's teeth. **peacocks.** *Tukkeeyim* is rendered *taysin* in the Targum, *taonon* in the Alexandrian MS. of the LXX., and *pavos*, "peacocks," in the Vulgate; with which the Syriac, Arabic, and Rabbins agree. Jb 39:13.

22. passed all the kings. 2 Ch 1:12. 1 K 3:12, 13. 4:30, 31. 10:23, 24. Ps 89:27. Mt 12:42. Col 2:2, 3.

23. sought. ver. 6, 7. 1 K 4:34. Is 11:2, 10. **God.** 2 Ch 1:10-12. See on 1 K 3:28. Pr 2:6. Da 1:17. 2:21-23. 5:11. Lk 21:15. 1 C 1:30. 12:8. Ep 1:17. Ja 1:5, 16, 17. 3:17.

24. every man. ver. 9. 1 S 10:27. 1 K 9:14. 10:10, 25. Jb 42:11.

25. four thousand stalls. 2 Ch 1:14. Dt 17:16. 1 K 4:26. 10:26.

26. reigned over. Jsh √21:43n. 1 K 4:21n, 24. Ps 72:8-11. Da 7:14. Ac *7:5n. Re 19:16. **river.** "That is, Euphrates." Ge 2:14. 15:18. 31:21. Ex 23:31. Jsh 13:2-7. Jsh 24:2. 1 Ch 19:16. Ezr 4:20. 7:25. Ps 72:8. Is +*27:12.

27. the king. ver. 20. 2 Ch 1:15-17. 1 K 10:27, etc. Jb 22:24, 25. **made.** Heb. gave. 1 Ch 27:28n. Ps 78:47. Is 9:10. Am 7:14. Lk 19:4.

28. brought. "Moses," says Bp. Warburton (*Divine Legation*, vol. iii. p. 289), "had expressly prohibited the multiplying of *horses* (Dt 17:16); by which the future king was forbidden to establish a body of cavalry, because this could not be effected without sending into Egypt, with which people God had forbidden any communication, as this would be dangerous to religion. When Solomon had violated *this law*, and multiplied horses to excess (1 K 4:26), it was soon attended with those fatal consequences that the law foretold: for this wisest of kings having likewise, in violation of *another* law, married Pharaoh's daughter (the early fruits of this commerce), and then, by a repetition of the same crime, but a transgression of *another* law, had espoused more strange women (1 K 4:26. 11:1), they first, in defiance of a *fourth* law, persuaded him to build them idol temples for *their use*; and afterwards, against a *fifth* law, brought him to erect other temples for *his own*." ver. 25. 2 Ch 1:16. 1 K 10:28. Is 2:7, 8. 31:1.

29. the rest. 1 K 11:41-43. **book.** Heb. words. **Nathan.** i.e. *whom God gave; given, placed; a giver,* *S#5416h. 2 Ch 9:29. 29:25. 2 S 5:14. 7:2, 3, 4, 17. 12:1, 5, 7, 13, 13, 15, 25. 23:36. 1 K 1:8, 10, 11, 22, 23, 24, 32, 34, 38, 44, 45. 4:5, 5. 1 Ch 2:36, 36. 3:5. 11:38. 14:4. 17:1, 2, 3, 15. 29:29. Ezr 8:16. 10:39. Ps 51:t. Zc 12:12. (1) A son of David, 2 S 5:14. (2) A prophet in the time of David, 2 S 7:1-3; 12:1, 25; 1 K 1:8, 10, 11, 22-27, 32-38; 4:5; 1 Ch 17:2; 29:29. 2 Ch 29:25. (3) Father of Igal, one of David's mighty men, 2 S 23:36. (4) Father of Azariah and Zabad, two of Solomon's princes, 1 K 4:5. (5) One of Sheshan's posterity, 1 Ch 2:36. (6) One of the companions of Ezra from Babylon, Ezr 8:16. (7) One of them that married strange wives, Ezr 10:39. **Ahijah.** 1 K 11:29.

14:2. **Iddo**. 2 Ch 12:15, 25. 13:22.

30. **Solomon**. 1 K 11:42, 43.

31. A.M. 3029. B.C. 975. **slept with**. Ge +*25:8n. Dt 31:16n. See on 2 S 7:12. 1 K 1:21. 2:10. +*11:43. +14:20. 2 K ◐√24:6n.

2 CHRONICLES 10

The Israelites, at Shechem, make Rehoboam king; and with Jeroboam require him to lighten their yoke, 1-5. Rehoboam, rejecting the advice of his father's counselors, and consulting with the young men, answers very roughly, 6-15. The ten tribes revolt, kill Hadoram, and drive away Rehoboam, 16-19.

1. **Rehoboam**. 1 K 12:1. 1 Ch 3:10. Mt 1:7, Roboam. **Shechem**. Ge 12:6, Sichem. 37:12, 13. Jsh √20:7n. 24:1. Jg 9:1. **all**. 1 K 4:1. 1 Ch 12:38.

2. **Jeroboam**. 1 Ch 11:26, 28, 40. 12:2.

3. **they sent**. 1 K 12:3.

4. **Thy father**. 1 S 8:11-18. 1 K 12:4. Is 47:6. Mt *11:29, 30. 23:4. 1 J 5:3. **grievous**. Ex 1:13, 14. 2:23. 1 K 4:20, 25. 9:22. **ease thou**. Mt 11:28.

5. **Come again**. 1 K 12:5. Pr 3:28.

6. **took counsel**. Jb 12:12, 13. 32:7. Pr 12:15. 19:20. 27:10. Je 42:2-5, 20. **What counsel**. 2 S 16:20. 17:5, 6.

7. **If thou be kind**. 1 K ∥12:7. Pr *15:1. **speak good**. Ge 49:21. 2 S 15:2-6.

8. **he forsook**. 2 Ch 25:15, 16. 1 S +√25:17. 2 S 17:14. 1 K +*∥12:8. Pr 1:25. 9:9. 19:20. 25:12. Ec 10:2, 3, 16. Is 30:1. **the young men**. 2 Ch √13:7. It was a custom in different countries to educate with the heir to the throne, young noblemen of nearly the same age. This, as Calmet observes, answered two great and important ends: (1) It excited the prince to emulation; that he might, as far as possible, surpass in all manly exercises, and in all acts of prudence and virtue, those whom one day he was to surpass in the elevation and dignity of his station; (2) That he might acquire a correct knowledge of the disposition and views of those who were likely to be, under him, the highest officers of the state, and consequently know the better how to trust and employ them. To the preceding note the observation ought to be added that in this case, such an education, involving as it did the segregation of the young from the old, resulted in his exercise of very poor, even disastrous, judgment. A Biblical education does not practice age segregation, but lets the younger learn from the older (1 T 5:1, 2, 10, 14. T *2:1-5. 1 P 5:5).

9. **What advice**. ver. 6. 2 S 17:5, 6. 1 K 22:6-8. **Ease**. See on ver. 4. While Scripture says there is safety in the multitude of counselors (Pr 24:6), this does not give license to shop around until we find the counselors who give the advice with which we agree (2 T 4:3). Rather, wise counsel must be sought from those qualified by experience and spiritual character. 1 K 12:9n. 2 T 3:14.

10. **Thus shalt**. 2 S 17:7-13. Pr +*21:30. Is 19:11-13. **My little finger**. "My weakness," says the Targumist, "shall be stronger than the might of my father." 1 K *12:10, 11. Pr 10:14. *13:16. *14:16. 18:6, 7. *28:25. √29:23. **tents**. ♪182, Ge +18:22.

11. **my father**. See on ver. 4. **put**. Heb. laded. **I will put**. Ex 1:13, 14. 5:5-9, 18. 1 S 8:18. Is 47:6. 58:6. Je 28:13, 14. Mt *11:29. **scorpions**. ver. 14. Dt

8:15. Ezk 2:6. Lk 10:19. Re 9:3, 5, 10.

12. **Come**. ver. 5. 1 K 12:12-15.

13. **answered**. Ge 42:7, 30. Ex 10:28. 1 S 25:10, 11. 1 K 20:6-11. Pr √15:1. **forsook**. ver. 8. Pr *19:27.

14. **the advice**. 2 Ch 22:4, 5. Pr 12:5. Da 6:7. **My father**. See on ver. 10, 11. Pr *17:14. Ec *2:19. *7:8. 10:16. Ja *3:14-18. 4:1, 2.

15. **the king**. Is 30:12, 13. **the cause**. 2 Ch 25:16-20. Dt +*2:30. Jg 14:4. 1 S 2:25. 1 K 12:15, 24. 22:20. Is 19:14. Ac 2:23. 4:28. **that the Lord**. See on 1 K 11:29-39. Jn 12:37-39. 19:24, 32-36. **by the hand**. 1 K +16:12mg. **Ahijah**. See on 2 Ch 9:29. 1 K 11:31.

16. **What portion**. 2 S 20:1. 1 K 12:16, 17. **the son**. 1 S 20:27, 30, 31. 22:7, 9, 13. **David**. 2 S 7:15, 16. 1 K 11:13, 34-39. 1 Ch 17:14. Ps 2:1-6. 76:10. 89:29-37. 132:17. Is *9:6, 7. 11:1. Je +√33:20, 21, 25, 26. Ezk 37:24, 25. Am 9:11. Lk 1:32, 33. 19:14, 27. Ac 2:30. 1 C 15:25. Re 22:16. **So all Israel**. ver. 19. Jg 8:35. 2 S 15:13. 16:11. Jn 6:66. 7:53.

17. **But as for**. 2 Ch 11:1. 1 K 11:36. 12:17.

18. **Hadoram**. 1 K 4:6. 5:14, Adoniram. 12:18, Adoram. **stoned him**. 2 Ch 24:21. Ac 7:57, 58. **made speed**. Heb. strengthened himself. 2 Ch *13:7. Ru 1:18mg. 1 K 12:18mg. **chariot**. 1 K 12:18.

19. **Israel**. ver. 16. 2 Ch 13:5-7. 1 K 12:19, 20. 2 K 17:21-23. Ps 89:30. **unto this day**. 2 Ch +5:9n. Jsh +4:9. Ezr 9:7.

2 CHRONICLES 11

Rehoboam, preparing to reduce Israel, is forbidden by the prophet Shemaiah, 1-4. He builds and fortifies several cities, 5-12. The priests and Levites, being cast off by Jeroboam, resort to Jerusalem, attended by other pious Israelites, 13-17. Rehoboam's wives and children, 18-23.

1. **when Rehoboam**. See on 1 K 12:21. **an hundred and**. Ps 33:10, 16. Pr 21:30, 31.

2. **to Shemaiah**. 2 Ch 12:5, 7, 15. 1 K 12:22-24. **the man**. 2 Ch 8:14. Dt 33:1. 1 S 2:27. 1 T 6:11.

3. **to all Israel**. Ge 49:28. Ex 24:4. 2 K 17:34. Ph 3:5. Re 7:4-8.

4. **against**. Ge 13:8. 2 S 2:26. Ac 7:26. 1 C 6:5-8. He 13:1. 1 P 3:8. 1 J 3:11-13. **return**. 2 Ch 10:16. 1 K 22:36. **for this thing**. See on 2 Ch 10:15. Ge 50:20. 1 K 11:29-38. Ps 33:11. Ho 8:4. **they obeyed**. 2 Ch 25:7-10. 28:9-15.

5. A.M. 3029-3032. B.C. 975-972. **built**. 2 Ch 8:2-6. 14:6, 7. 16:6. 17:12. 26:6. 27:4. Is 22:8-11.

6. **Beth-lehem**. *Bethlehem*, called "Bethlehem Judah" (Jg 17:7), to distinguish it from another *Bethlehem* in Zebulun (Jsh 19:15), and also *Ephratah* (i.e. *fruitful*), and by the Arabs, *Bait-el-lahm*, is situated on a rising ground on the southern side of a deep and extensive valley, and reclining from E. to W., not quite six miles S. of Jerusalem. Ge 35:19. 1 S 17:12. Mt 2:5, 6. **Etam**. Jg 15:8. 1 Ch 4:32. **Tekoa**. 2 Ch 20:20. 2 S 14:2. Ne 3:5, 27. Je 6:1. Am 1:1.

7. **Beth-zur**. Jsh 15:58. **Shoco**. i.e. *his hedge* or *fence*, ✱S#7755h. 2 Ch 11:7. 28:18. Jsh 15:35, Socoh, 48. 1 S 17:1, 1. 1 K 4:10. **Adullam**. Jsh 12:15. 15:35. 1 S 22:1. 2 S 23:13. Mi 1:15.

8. **Gath**. 1 Ch 18:1. **Mareshah**. Jsh 15:44. **Ziph**. Jsh 15:24. 1 S 23:14, 19. Ps 54, title.

9. **Adoraim**. i.e. *double mound; double glory; two-*

fold habitation, ✱S#115h. **Lachish.** 2 Ch 32:9. Jsh 10:5, 11. 15:35, 39.

10. **Zorah.** Jsh 15:33, Zoreah. 19:41, 42, Ajalon. **Hebron.** Ge 23:2. Nu 13:22. Jsh 14:14. +✱20:7n. 2 S 2:11.

11. **he fortified.** Is 22:10, 11. **captains.** ver. 23. 2 Ch 17:19.

12. **he put shields.** 2 Ch 26:14, 15. 32:5. 2 S 13:19, 22. **having Judah.** See on ver. 1.

13. A.M. 3030. B.C. 974. **resorted to him.** Heb. presented themselves to him.

14. **suburbs.** Nu 35:2-5. Jsh 21:20-42. 1 Ch 6:66-81. **their possession.** Le 27:30-34. Nu 18:21-28. **Jeroboam.** 2 Ch 13:9. 1 K 12:28-33. 13:33.

15. **for the devils.** The word *seirim* literally signifies "hairy ones," or "goats." See Note on Le 17:7. Dt 32:17. 1 C ✱10:20, 21. 1 T 4:1. Re 16:14. **for the calves.** Ex 32:4-8, 31. 1 K 12:28. 14:9. Ps 106:19, 20. Ho 8:5, 6. 13:2.

16. **And after.** 2 Ch 15:9. 30:11, 18, 19. Jsh 22:19. Ps 84:5-7. **set.** Ex 9:21mg. Dt 32:46. 1 S 7:3, 4. 1 Ch 22:19. Jb 34:14. Ps 62:10. 108:1. Da 6:14. Ho 4:8. Hg 1:5mg. Ac ✱11:23. **to sacrifice.** Dt 12:5, 6, 11, 13, 14. 1 Ch 16:29. 22:1.

17. A.M. 3029-3032. B.C. 975-972. **strengthened.** 2 Ch 12:1. **three years.** 2 Ch 1:1-12. 7:17-19. 8:13-16. Ho 6:4. Mt 13:20, 21.

18. A.M. 3029-3046. B.C. 975-958. **Mahalath.** i.e. *sickness; harp, wind instrument; appeasing,* ✱S#4258h. 2 Ch 11:18. Ge 28:9. (1) A daughter of Ishmael, whom Esau married, Ge 28:9. (2) Wife of Rehoboam, 2 Ch 11:18. **daughter.** Eliab was David's eldest brother; and more than eighty years had elapsed since David, at the age of thirty, began to reign: *Abihail* must therefore have been grand-daughter to Eliab; and this shows the latitude in which the words *son* and *daughter* are used in Scripture. 1 K +15:10n. 2 K 8:26. 1 Ch 7:24n. **to wife.** Ge +4:19. **Eliab.** 1 S 16:6. 17:13, 28. 1 Ch 2:13. 27:18, Elihu.

19. **Jeush.** i.e. *he hastens.* Ge +36:5. **Shamariah.** i.e. *preserved* or *guarded of Jah,* ✱S#8114h. **Zaham.** i.e. *loathing, disgust; fat,* ✱S#2093h.

20. **Maachah.** ver. 21. 2 Ch 13:2, Michaiah the daughter of Uriel. **Absalom.** 1 K 15:2, Abishalom. **Abijah.** 2 Ch 12:16. 1 K 15:1, Abijam. Mt 1:7, Abia.

21. **eighteen wives.** ver. 23. Ge +4:19. Dt 17:17. Jg 8:30. 2 S 3:2-5. 5:13. 1 K 11:3. 1 Ch 3:1-9. SS 6:8, 9. **concubines.** 1 Ch +2:48.

22. **made Abijah.** Dt 21:15-17. 1 Ch +✱5:1, 2. ✱26:10. 29:1.

23. **he dealt.** 2 Ch 10:8-15. Lk √16:8. **wisely.** Young renders, "he hath understanding," commenting "of the times and seasons." 1 Ch +✱12:32n. **dispersed.** 2 Ch 21:3. Ge 25:6. 1 K 1:5, 6. **every fenced city.** ver. 11. **desired.** Dt 14:26. **many wives.** Heb. a multitude of wives. See on ver. 21.

2 CHRONICLES 12

Rehoboam forsakes God, and Shishak king of Egypt invades Judah, 1-4. Rehoboam and his princes, being warned by Shemaiah, humble themselves; and, though spoiled, are not destroyed, 5-12. Rehoboam's reign and death. Abijah succeeds him, 13-16.

1. A.M. 3032. B.C. 972. **when Rehoboam.** ver. 13. 2 Ch 11:17. **had strengthened.** Ps 118:8, 9. Is 30:2,

3. Je 17:5-8. **he forsook.** 2 Ch 26:13-16. Dt 6:10-12. 8:10-14. 32:15, 18. 1 K 9:9. Je 2:31. Ho 13:1, 6-8. **all Israel.** 2 Ch 11:3. 1 K 12:17. 14:22-24. 2 K 17:19. Ho 5:10, 11. Mi 6:16.

2. A.M. 3034. B.C. 970. **Shishak.** See on 1 K 11:40. 14:24-26. **because.** 2 Ch 7:19, 20. 36:14-19. Jg 2:13-15. 1 Ch +√28:9. Ne 9:26, 27. Ps 106:43, 44. Is 63:10. Je 2:19. 44:22, 23. La 5:15, 16. Ga ✱6:7.

3. **twelve hundred.** Jg 4:13. 1 S 13:5. 2 S 10:18. **without number.** 2 Ch 14:9. Jg 6:5. Re 9:16. **Lubims.** i.e. *inhabitants of the interior of Africa; dwellers in a thirsty land,* ✱S#3864h. 2 Ch 12:3. 16:8. Na 3:9. Also Da 11:43, Libyans. *Lubim,* apparently the same with *Lehabim* (Ge 10:13), were probably the ancient inhabitants of *Lybia* (called *Lubi* in the Syriac version, Ac 2:10), a district of Africa, adjoining to Egypt, and extending along the shore of the Mediterranean as far as the city of Cyrene. 2 Ch 16:8. Ezk 30:5. Na 3:9. **the Sukkims.** i.e. *dwelling in booths; thicket men,* ✱S#5525h. The *Sukkim,* (from *sachach,* "to cover"), are supposed to have been the *Troglodites,* as the LXX. and Vulgate render, a people of Egypt, on the west of the Red sea, so called because they dwelt *en troglais,* in caves. **Ethiopians.** These *Cushim* were probably the inhabitants of *Ethiopia,* south of Egypt. 2 Ch 14:12. 16:8. Is 43:3. Da 11:43. Na 3:9, Cushim. Heb. Ge 10:6-8.

4. **the fenced.** 2 Ch 11:5-12. Is 36:1. Je 5:10. **came.** 2 K 18:17. Is 8:8. 10:11.

5. **Shemaiah.** 2 Ch 11:2. 1 K 12:22. 1 Ch +9:16. **Ye have forsaken me.** See on ver. 1, 2. 2 Ch ✱15:2. Dt 28:15, etc. Jg 10:9-14. 1 Ch +√28:9. Je 2:19. 4:18. 5:19. 23:33. **left you.** 2 S 24:14. Ps 37:33.

6. **humbled.** 2 Ch 32:26. 33:12, 19, 23. Ex 10:3. Le 26:40, 41. 1 K 8:37-39. Ps 78:34, 35. Je 13:15, 18. 44:10. Da 5:22. Ho 5:15. Lk 18:14. Ja 4:6, 10. **The Lord.** Ex 9:27. Jg 1:7. Jb 33:27. Ps 129:4. La 1:18. Da 9:14. Ro 10:3.

7. **the Lord.** Jg 10:15, 16. 1 K ✱21:28, 29. Je 3:13. Lk 15:18-21. **humbled themselves.** 2 Ch +√7:14. 1 K 21:27. Ja ✱4:10. 1 P 5:6. **therefore.** Le 26:41, 42. **some deliverance.** or, a little while. T#1785. Ex 33:18-23. Nu 21:6-9. Dt 3:23-27. 2 K 13:4-7, 23. 1 Ch 16:19. Is 1:9. Je 21:1-9. Ezk 14:13-20. Am 7:6-8. Mk ✱10:35-40. Lk 22:41-43. **and my wrath.** 2 Ch 34:21, 25. Ps 79:6. Is 42:25. Je 7:20. Re 14:10. 16:2-17.

8. **Nevertheless.** Ne 9:36. Is 26:13. **his servants.** Ps 40:17. 44:4. Is 43:15. Ac 27:23. **that they may.** Dt √28:47, 48. Jg 3:1, 2. Je 10:24. Ho 8:10.

9. **Shishak.** 1 K 14:25, 26. **took away.** 1 K 15:18. 2 K 16:8. 18:15, 16. La 1:10. **the shields.** 2 Ch 9:15, 16. 1 K 10:16, 17.

10. **shields of brass.** 1 K 14:27. La 4:1. **the chief.** 2 S 8:18. 23:23. 1 Ch 11:25. SS 3:7, 8. **guard.** 2 K 10:25mg.

11. **chamber.** 1 K 14:28. Ezk 40:7, 10, 12, 13, 16, 21, 29, 33, 36.

12. **when.** See on ver. 6, 7. 2 Ch 19:3. 33:12, 13. Is 57:15. La 3:22, 33, 42. 1 P 5:6. **also in Judah things went well.** or, yet in Judah there were good things. 2 Ch 19:3. Ge 18:24. 1 K 14:13. Is 6:13.

13. A.M. 3029-3046. B.C. 975-958. **for Rehoboam.** 2 Ch 13:7. 1 K 14:21. **the city.** See on 2 Ch 6:6. Ps 48:1-3. 78:68, 69. **to put.** Ex 20:24. Dt 12:5, 11. Ezk 48:35. **an Ammonitess.** Dt 23:3. 1 K 11:1. Ne 13:1, 26.

14. **he did evil**. 2 Ch ●19:3. 1 K 14:22. **he prepared**. Heb. he fixed. ver. 1. 2 Ch 11:16. 19:3. 27:6. 30:19. 1 S 7:3. 1 K 15:14. 1 Ch 29:18. Ps 57:7mg. 78:8, 37. 112:7. 1 C √15:58. 16:13. **to seek**. Dt 5:29. Ps 105:3, 4. Is 45:19. √55:6, 7. Ezk 33:31. Mt *7:7. Lk *11:9.

15. **first and last**. 2 Ch 9:29. **book**. Heb. words. Shemaiah. ver. 5. 1 K 12:22. **Iddo**. 2 Ch 9:29. 13:22. Ezr +5:1. **wars**. 1 K 14:30.

16. **slept**. 1 K +*11:43. 14:+20, 29-31. **Abijah**. 2 Ch 13:1. 1 K 14:+1, 31, Abijam. 1 Ch 3:10. Mt 1:7, Abia.

2 CHRONICLES 13

Abijah reigns; he and Jeroboam, with vast preparations, engage in war, 1-3. Abijah shows the justice of his cause, 4-12. Judah, relying on God, gains a signal victory over Jeroboam, with immense slaughter of the Israelites, 13-19. Jeroboam dies, 20. Abijah's wives and children, 21, 22.

1. A.M. 3046-3049. B.C. 958-955. **in the eighteenth**. See on 2 Ch 12:16. 1 K 15:1, etc.

2. **Michaiah**. 2 Ch 11:20, Maachah the daughter of Absalom. 1 K 15:2, Abishalom. **Gibeah**. Jsh 18:28, Gibeath. Jg 19:14, 16. 1 S 10:26. A.M. 3047. B.C. 957. **And there was**. 1 K 15:6, 7.

3. **set**. Heb. bound together. 1 S 17:1-3. 1 K 18:44mg. 20:14mg. 2 K 9:21mg. **four hundred thousand**. 2 Ch 11:1. 14:8. 17:14-18. 26:12, 13. 1 Ch 21:5. **eight hundred thousand**. 2 Ch 14:9. **mighty men**. Jg +6:12.

4. **Zemaraim**. Zemaraim could not be, as some have supposed, the same as the hill of Samaria, so called from *Shemer*, in the days of Omri; but was probably a hill on the confines of Ephraim, near *Zemaraim*, a city of Benjamin, near Bethel. Ge 10:18. Jsh 18:22. **Hear me**. 2 Ch 15:2. Jg 9:7.

5. **Ought ye not**. Ne 5:9. Pr 1:29. Mk 12:24. 2 P 3:5. **the Lord**. Jg 11:21-24. Je 27:5-7. Da 4:25-32. 5:18. **to David**. 1 S 16:1, 12. 2 S 7:12-16. 1 K 8:20. 1 Ch 17:11, 14. 28:4, 5. Ps 89:19-37. Je +√33:21, 22, 25, 26. Lk 1:31-33. **for ever**. Heb. *olam*, Ex +12:24. **a covenant of salt**. Le 2:13. Nu *18:19. Ezk 43:24. Mk 9:49, 50.

6. **rebelled**. 2 Ch 10:19. 1 K 11:26. 12:20, 27.

7. **vain men**. or, "empty ones." Ge 37:24h. 41:27h. Jg 9:4. 11:3. 1 S 22:2. Jb 30:8. Ps 26:4. Pr +*12:11. *13:20. 28:19. Ac 17:5. T 1:10. **the children of Belial**. See on Dt 13:13. +15:9. Jg +19:22. 1 K 21:10, 13. **young**. 2 Ch 10:*8n, 14, 16. 12:13. Ec 10:16. Is 3:4. 1 C 14:20. He 5:12. **could not**. 2 Ch 10:1-4, 8n. 1 K +*12:7n, 10n. Ps +√119:63. Pr *1:10. +*19:27. 1 C √10:13. +*15:33.

8. **the kingdom**. 2 Ch 9:8. Ps 2:1-6. Is 7:6, 7. 9:6, 7. Lk 19:14, 27. **a great multitude**. 2 Ch 14:9-11. 20:6, 12. Ps 33:16. **with you golden**. 2 Ch 11:15. 1 K 12:28. 14:9. Ho 8:5, 6.

9. **cast out**. 2 Ch 11:14, 15. Lk=6:22, 23. =20:15. Jn=9:34, 35. **made you priests**. 1 K 12:31-33. 12:13. 13:33. **consecrate himself**. Heb. fill his hand. 2 Ch 29:31mg. Ex 29:9mg. 32:29mg. Le 16:32mg. 1 Ch 29:5mg. **young**. Ex 29:1, 35. Le 8:2. **no gods**. Dt 32:17. 2 K 19:18. Je 2:11. Ho 8:6. Ac 19:26. Ga 4:8.

10. **the Lord**. We have not abandoned the Lord; and we still serve Him according to His own law. But what Abijah urged concerning the state of religion in Judah was not strictly just; and, as spoken by him, it savored of ostentation. Abijah himself was but an indifferent character; and idolatry was evidently connived at in his days. Yet it was true, that the men of Judah had the priests, ordinances, and worship of Jehovah among them; that there were numbers of pious worshippers in the land; that theirs was the more righteous cause; that Jehovah was on their side as their Captain, while Israel fought against him; and that the presence of the priests with the sacred trumpets was a token of His presence and favor. 2 Ch 11:16, 17. Ex 19:5, 6. Zc 13:9. **the priests**. Ex 29:1, etc. Nu 16:40. 18:1-7. **business**. Nu 3:7. Ne 11:22. Ro=12:11. Col=3:24.

11. **they burn**. 2 Ch 2:4. Ex 29:38-42. **morning**. 2 S 13:4mg. **sweet incense**. Ex 30:1-10. Le 2:1-3. Nu 16:6, 7, 46, 47. Dt 33:10. Ps=141:2. Lk 1:9. 2 C=2:15. Re 5:8. =8:3, 4. **showbread**. Ex 25:30. Le 24:5-9. **the candlestick**. Ex 25:31-39. 27:20, 21. Le 24:2-4. **every evening**. Ex +30:8. **we keep**. Ge 26:5. Nu 9:19, 23. Ezk 44:8, 15. 48:11.

12. **God**. Nu 23:21. 1 S 4:5-7. Is 8:10. Zc 10:5. Ro *8:31. **with us**. 2 K *6:16. Ro *8:31. 1 J 4:4. **for our captain**. Dt 20:4. Jsh 5:13-15. Ps 20:7. He 2:10. **his priests**. Nu 10:8, 9. 31:6. Jsh 6:13-20. **fight ye**. Jb 15:25, 26. 40:9. Is 45:9. Je 50:24. Ac 5:39. 9:4, 5. **ye shall not**. 2 Ch 24:20. Nu 14:41. Dt 28:29. Jb 9:4. Is 54:17. Je 2:37. Ezk 17:9.

13. **an ambushment**. 2 Ch 20:22. Jsh 8:4. Pr 21:30. Je 4:22.

14. **looked back**. Ex 14:10. Jsh 8:20. Jg 20:33-43. 2 S 10:8-14. **cried**. T#1158. 2 Ch *14:10, 11. 18:31. Ps 50:15. 91:5. **the priests**. See on ver. 12.

15. **as the men**. 2 Ch 20:21. Jsh 6:16, 20. Jg 7:18-22. Ps 47:1-5. **God smote**. 2 Ch 14:12. Nu 32:4. Jsh 11:8. Jg 4:15. 2 K 5:1. Ps 118:4-7. Is 37:36.

16. **God delivered**. Ge 14:20. Dt 2:36. 3:3. Jsh 10:12. 21:44. Jg 1:4. 11:21. 1 S 23:7.

17. **five hundred thousand**. ver. 3, 12. 2 Ch 28:6. Is 10:16-19. 37:36. Na 1:5. 1 C 10:22.

18. **relied**. 2 Ch 16:8, 9. 20:20. 2 K 18:5. 1 Ch 5:20. Ps 22:4, 5. 146:5. Da 3:28. Na 1:7. Ep 1:12.

19. **took cities**. Jsh 10:19, 39. 11:12. 1 S 31:7. **Jeshanah**. i.e. *old, ancient,* *S#3466h. *Jeshanah*, according to the Talmud (Mishnah, Kiddushin, iv. 5), was not far from *Sephoris*. Perhaps it is the *Migdal-Senna* of Eusebius, eight miles north of Jericho. **Ephrain**. i.e. *the two fawns; doubly dust*, S#6085h. *Ephrain*, or *Ephron* (Ge +23:8), a city of Benjamin, is placed by Eusebius, eight miles north of Jerusalem, near Bethel. Josephus (Bell. l. v. c. 8) calls **Ephrain** and Bethel two little cities; and places the former in the tribe of Benjamin, near the wilderness of Judea, in the way to Jericho. 2 Ch 15:8. Jsh 15:9, Ephron. Jn 11:54. **towns**. lit. "daughters," as in Nu 21:25mg. Nu 21:25mg. Jsh 15:45.

20. **did**. Ps 18:37, 38. **the Lord struck**. 1 S 25:38. 26:10. Ezk 26:14. Ac 12:23. **he died**. 1 K 14:20. 15:9.

21. **waxed**. 2 S 5:12, 13. **fourteen wives**. See on 2 Ch 11:21. Ge +4:19. **begat**. Jg 8:30, 31. 9:5. 10:4.

22. **the rest**. 1 K 15:7. **story**. or, commentary. 2 Ch 24:27. **Iddo**. 2 Ch 9:29. 12:15.

2 CHRONICLES 14

Abijah dies, and Asa succeeds him, 1. He abolishes idolatry, 2-5. Enjoying peace, he fortifies his kingdom, and establishes a large army, 6-8. Being attacked by Zerah, with an immense army of Ethiopians, he calls on God, is victorious, and acquires much spoil, 9-15.

1. A.M. 3049. B.C. 955. **slept with his fathers.** 2 Ch 9:31. See on 1 K 2:10. +*11:43. 14:+20, 31. 2 K *24:6n. **Asa.** 1 K 15:8, etc. 1 Ch 3:10. Mt 1:7, 8.

2. A.M. 3063-3073. B.C. 941-931. **good and right.** 2 Ch 31:20. 1 K 15:11, 14. Lk 1:75.

3. **For he took.** Dt 7:5. 1 K 11:7, 8. 14:22-24. Pr *16:7. **strange.** 2 Ch 33:15. Ex 12:43 (*S#5236h). 2 S 22:45, 46. **the high places.** 2 Ch 15:17. Le 26:30. 1 K 15:12-14. 2 K +21:3. **brake.** 2 Ch 34:4. Ex 34:13. Dt 7:5, 25. **cut down.** Jg 6:25-28. 1 K 11:7. 2 K 18:4. 23:6, 14.

4. **commanded.** 2 Ch 29:21, 27, 30. 30:12. 33:16. 34:32, 33. Ge *18:19. Jsh *24:15. 1 S 3:13. Ezr 10:7-12. Ne 13:9, 19-22. Ps 101:2-8. **seek.** See on 2 Ch 11:16. 30:19. Is *55:6, 7. Am 5:4. **to do.** Ne 10:29-39. Ps 119:10. Jn *13:17. **law and.** 2 Ch +34:14n.

5. **images.** Heb. sun-images. 2 Ch 34:4mg, 7. Le +26:30. Is 17:8. 27:9. Ezk 6:4, 6.

6. **And he built.** 2 Ch 8:2-6. 11:5-12. **for the land.** Jg 3:11, 30. 5:31. 1 K 5:4. 1 Ch 22:9. **the Lord.** 2 Ch 15:15. Jsh 23:1. Jb 34:29. Ps 46:9.

7. **Therefore.** 2 Ch 32:5. Ac 9:31. **while the land.** Jn 9:4. 12:35, 36. He √3:13-15. **because we have sought.** T#1765. See on ver. 4. 2 Ch 15:2-4. 17:3-5. 20:21, 22. 26:1-5. 30:27. *31:21. Dt 4:7, *29-31. 1 Ch +*28:9. Ezr 8:22, 23. Ne 9:26-28. Jb 5:8, 9. *8:5-7. *22:23-30. *33:26-29. 34:28, 29. 38:41. *42:10. Ps 2:8. 30:1-5. 31:22. 34:10. *37:4, 5. *50:14. 55:16-18, *22. 65:2. 66:19, 20. 69:32, 33. 73:28. 81:7-10. 91:15, 16. *105:3, 4. 107:12, 13. 116:1-4. *138:3. *145:18, 19. Pr 2:3-5. 8:17. *15:8. 20:22. 28:5. Is 2:3. 19:19, 20. √30:18, 19. 40:27-31. *41:17, 18. *45:22-24. 50:10. 55:1, √6, 7. 64:3, 4. 65:10. Je 26:19. *29:12-14. La *3:25, 26, 54-58. Da 9:20-23. Jl 2:15-19, *32. Am 5:4-6, 8. 7:1-6. Jon 2:1-7. Mi *7:7, 8. Mt √6:33. *7:7-11. √18:19, 20. Lk √11:9-13. Ro *8:26, 27. √10:13. Ph *4:6, 7. Ja *5:13-15. 1 P 3:12. 1 J √5:14-16. Re *3:20. **and he hath given.** See on ver. 6. Jsh 23:1. Mt *11:28, 29. 1 T 2:1, 2.

8. **out of Judah.** 2 Ch 11:1. 13:3. 17:14-19. 25:5.

9. A.M. 3063. B.C. 941. **Zerah.** See on 2 Ch 12:2, 3. 16:8. 2 K 19:9. Is 8:9, 10. Ezk 30:5. Re 16:14. **Mareshah.** Jsh 15:44. Mi 1:15.

10. **Zephathah.** i.e. *that covers; place of watching; watch tower,* *S#6859h. Jsh 19:4. Jg 1:17, Zephath.

11. **cried unto.** 2 Ch 13:14. *18:31. *32:20. Ex 14:10. 1 Ch *5:20. Ps 18:6. 22:5. *34:6. *50:15. *91:15. 120:1. Ac *2:21. **nothing.** 2 Ch *16:8. Le 26:8. Dt 32:30. Jg 7:7. 1 S *14:6. 1 K 20:27-30. Am 5:9. 2 C *12:9, 10. **them that.** 2 Ch *20:12. Dt 32:36. 1 K 20:27. Is *40:29-31. **rest on thee.** T#1140. 2 Ch *32:8. 1 S 17:35, 36. Ps 7:1. 13:5. 16:1. 21:7. 22:4, 5. 25:2, 20. 26:1. 28:7. 31:1. 33:22. *37:5. 38:15. 39:7. 56:3, 4. 57:1. 71:1, 5. 86:2, 4. 119:41, 42. 141:8. 142:5. 143:1, 8. Pr *18:10. Is √26:3, 4. *41:10-14. Jn *14:1, 27. Ro *8:31. **in thy name.** 2 Ch 13:12, 18. 1 S *17:45, 46. Ps 20:5, 7. Is 26:13. Ac *3:16. **man.** *or,* mortal man. Ge 13:8mg. Dt 32:27. Jsh 7:8, 9. 1 S *2:9. Jb *4:17. Ps *9:19. 79:9, 10. Is *2:22. Je *1:19. Zc *2:8. Mt 16:18.

12. **the Lord smote.** 2 Ch 13:15. 20:22. Ex 14:25. Dt 28:7. 32:39. Jsh 10:10. Ps 60:12. 136:17, 18. 1 C 9:26. 15:57.

13. **Gerar.** ver. 14. Ge 10:1, 19. 20:1. 26:1. **de**

stroyed. Heb. broken. lit. "shivered." ver. 3. 2 Ch 20:37. Ex 22:10, 14. Le 6:28. 15:12. **before the Lord.** Jb 6:9. 9:4. 2 Th 1:9. **his host.** Jsh 5:14. 1 S 25:28. 1 Ch 12:22. Ps 108:11.

14. **the fear.** 2 Ch 17:10. 20:29. Ge 35:5. Dt 2:25. Jsh 2:9-11, 24. 5:1. 1 S 14:15. 2 K 7:6. Jb 15:21. Ps 48:5, 6. Is 31:9. **exceeding.** 2 Ch 20:25. Jg 14:19. 2 K 7:7, 8, 16. Ps 68:12. Is 33:23. Ro 8:37.

15. **the tents of cattle.** 1 Ch 4:41. **carried away.** Nu 31:9, 30-47. 1 S 30:20. 1 Ch 5:21.

2 CHRONICLES 15

The encouraging prophecy of Azariah before Asa, 1-7. Asa puts away idolatry, assembles the people, and enters into covenant with God, 8-15. He removes his mother from being queen, for her idolatry; yet the high places are not taken away, 16, 17. He brings the dedicated things into the temple, and enjoys a long peace, 18, 19.

1. **the Spirit.** Heb. *ruach,* Ge +41:38. 2 Ch 20:14. *24:20. Nu 24:2. Jg 3:10. 2 S 23:2. 2 P *1:21. **Azariah.** i.e. *help of Jah.* 1 Ch +6:36. **Oded.** i.e. *causing to stand; reiteration; restoration; surrounding; established, setting up,* *S#5752h. 2 Ch 15:1, 8. 28:9. (1) Father of Azariah the prophet, 2 Ch 15:1, 8. (2) The prophet who besought Israel for their brethren of Judah, their captives, 2 Ch 28:9.

2. **to meet Asa.** Heb. before Asa. **Hear ye me.** 2 Ch 13:4. *20:15, 20. Jg 9:7. Ps 49:1, 2. Is *7:13. Mt 13:9. Re 2:7, 11, 17, 29. 3:6, 13, 22. **The Lord.** 2 Ch 13:12. *32:8. Dt 20:1. Ja *4:8. **if.** Ge +4:7. **ye seek him.** ver. *4, *15. 2 Ch *33:12, 13. Is √55:6, 7. Je *29:12-14. Mt *7:7, 8. Lk *11:9. **if ye forsake.** 2 Ch 12:1-3. *24:20. 2 K 21:14. 1 Ch +√28:9. Lk +√8:13. Ro +*11:1, 2. 1 C *15:2. Col +*1:23. He 10:38. *12:25. 2 P *1:10.

3. **a long.** 1 K 12:28-33. Ho 3:4. **true God.** Je 10:10. Jn √17:3. 1 Th 1:9. 1 J 5:20. **a teaching priest.** 2 Ch ❍*17:8, 9. Le 10:11. Dt +17:11. 33:10. Ne 8:9. Je *23:22. Ezk 44:21-23. Am *8:11. Mi 3:11. Ml 2:7. Mt 2:4, 5. Ro 12:7. Ep *4:11. 1 T 3:2. 2 T 2:24. **without law.** Ro 2:12. 7:8, 9. 1 C 9:21.

4. **in their trouble.** Dt 4:29, 30. Jg 3:9, 10. 10:10-16. Ps 106:44. Ho 6:1. 14:1-3. **found of them.** ver. 15. Is *55:6. 65:1, 2. Ro 10:20.

5. **no peace.** Jg 5:6. 1 S 13:6. Ps 121:8. **great vexations.** Mt 24:6, 7. Lk 21:25.

6. **nation.** 2 Ch 12:15. 13:17. Mk 13:8. Lk 21:9, 10. **destroyed.** Heb. beaten in pieces. Jb 4:20mg. Is 30:14. **God.** 2 Ch 33:11. 36:17. Jg 2:14. Ps 106:41. Is 10:6. Am 3:6. Lk *21:22-24.

7. **ye strong.** Jsh 1:7, 9. 1 Ch 28:20. Ps 27:14. Is 35:3, 4. Da 10:19. 1 C 16:13. Ep *6:10. **your work.** Ge 15:1. Ru 2:12. Ps 19:11. 58:11. Mt 5:12, 46. 6:1, 4, 6, 18. 10:41, 42. Lk √6:35. Ro *4:4, 5. 1 C 3:8, 14. 9:17, 18. √15:58. Ga *6:9. Col 3:24. He *6:10. √10:35. 2 J 8.

8. **Oded.** ver. 1. **took courage.** 2 Ch 19:11mg. Is 44:14mg. Ac *28:15. **abominable idols.** Heb. abominations. Le 18:30. Dt 27:15. 1 K 11:5, 7. 2 K 23:13. Is 65:4. Je 16:18. Ezk 8:10. 1 P 4:3. Re 17:4, 5. **the cities.** 2 Ch 13:19. **the altar of the Lord.** 2 Ch 4:1. 8:12. 29:18. 2 K 16:14. 18:22.

9. **the strangers.** 2 Ch 11:16. 30:1-11, 25. **they fell.** 1 K 12:19. 1 Ch 12:19. **they saw.** Ge 39:3. 1 S 18:28.

1 K 3:28. Zc 8:21-23. Ac 7:9, 10. 9:31.

10. **the third month**. Est 8:9. That is, Sivan, about the time of pentecost, or feast of weeks; so Targum (Young).

11. **offered**. 2 Ch 14:13-15. Nu 31:28, 29, 50. 1 S 15:15, 21. 1 Ch 26:26, 27. **the same time**. Heb. in that day. **seven hundred**. 2 Ch 1:6. 7:5.

12. **they entered**. 2 Ch 23:16. 29:10. *34:31, 32. Dt 29:1, 12. 2 K 23:3. Ne 9:38. 10:29. Je 50:5. 2 C 8:5. **covenant**. T#1321. 2 K 11:14h. 23:3. Ezr 10:3. Ne 9:36-38. Je *50:4, 5. **seek**. See on ver. 4. 2 Ch *7:14. Dt 4:29. 10:12. 1 K 8:48. Je √29:12, 13. Ac 24:14. He √11:6. **with all their heart**. T#1306. 2 Ch 6:37, 38. 31:21. Dt *4:29. 2 K 23:3. 1 Ch 22:19. Ps 42:1. *119:10, 58, 145. Je √29:13. La 2:19. Ho 7:14. Jl 2:12. **soul**. Heb. *nephesh*, Ge +34:3.

13. **whosoever**. Ex *22:20. Dt 13:5-15. 17:2-5. 1 K 18:40. Jn *1:17. *3:18, 36. **whether small**. Ge 19:11. Ex 12:29. Dt 29:18. Jb 3:19. 34:19. Ps 115:13. Ac 26:22. Re 6:15. 20:12.

14. **sware**. Ne 5:13. 10:29. **trumpets**. Ps 81:1-4.

15. **rejoiced**. 2 Ch 23:16-21. 29:10, 36. Dt 26:11. Ne 8:9. Ps 32:11. 119:111. Pr 3:17. 2 C 1:12. **sworn**. Ps 119:106. **sought him**. See on ver. 2, 4, 12. Is 26:8. 45:19. Ph 1:23. **and he was**. See on ver. 4. Lk *11:9, 10. **the Lord gave**. See on ver. ●6. Jsh *23:1. Jb √34:29. 1 T *2:1, 2.

16. **Maachah**. 1 K +2:39. 15:13, etc. **the mother**. *that is*, grandmother. 1 K *15:2, +10n. **he removed**. 2 Ch 14:3-5. Ex 32:27, 28. Dt 13:6-8. 33:9. Zc 13:3. Mk 3:21, 31-35. 2 C 5:16. **idol**. Heb. horror. 1 K 15:13. **grove**. 2 K +17:10. 21:3n. 23:6. **cut down**. See on 2 Ch 14:3-5. 34:7. Ex 32:20. Le *26:30. Dt 7:5, 25, 26. 9:21. 1 K 15:14, etc. 2 K 23:6, 12, 15.

17. **the high places**. 2 Ch 14:3-5. Dt 12:13, 14. 1 K 3:2-4. 22:43. 2 K 12:3. 14:4. +21:3. **nevertheless**. Ჟ127. Palinodia, Re +2:6. **the heart of Asa**. 2 Ch 16:7-12. 1 K 11:4, +34. Jn +*17:6.

18. **brought**. 1 K *7:51. 15:14, 15. 1 Ch 26:20-26.

19. A.M. 3063-73. B.C. 941-931. **five and thirtieth**. 2 Ch 16:1. 1 K 15:16, 17, 32, 33.

2 CHRONICLES 16

Asa makes a league with Benhadad against Baasha, who is hindered from building Ramah; and Asa with the stones of it builds Geba and Mizpah, 1-6. Hanani the prophet reproves him for trusting in the Syrians, rather than in God, and is imprisoned by Asa, who at the same time oppressed some of his subjects, 7-10. When sick, Asa seeks to physicians, and not to God, 11, 12. His death and burial, 13, 14.

1. A.M. 3074. B.C. 930. **In the sixth and thirtieth year**. See Note on 1 K 15:32. "From the rending of the ten tribes from Judah, over which Asa was now king." See on 1 K 15:16-22 w 16:8. **of the reign**. or, kingdom. 2 Ch 15:19. Nu 24:7. 1 S 20:31. 1 K 2:12. 1 Ch 11:10. 14:2. 17:14. 22:10. 28:5. An interesting problem in chronology is manufactured when the "thirty-sixth year" of Asa's reign is not properly understood to be that of his kingdom (see references), for such an error of understanding leads to the problem that Baasha came up against Judah some 9 years after he was dead! 1 K √16:6, 8. The explanation is simple: the thirty-sixth year of Asa's kingdom, dating from Rehoboam, is therefore the sixteenth year of his reign.

to the intent. See on 2 Ch 11:13-17. 15:5, 9. 1 K 12:27.

2. **brought out**. 2 Ch 28:21. 2 K 12:18. 16:8. 18:15. **Damascus**. Heb. Darmesek. 1 Ch 18:5mg.

3. **a league**. 2 Ch 18:3. 19:2. Jg 2:2. Is 31:1-3. 2 C 6:16. **break**. Ge 20:9, 10. Ex 32:21. Jsh 9:19, 20. 2 S 21:2. Ps 15:4. Ezk 17:18, 19. Ro 1:31, 32. 2 T 3:3.

4. **hearkened**. 1 T 6:10. 2 P 2:15. **his armies**. Heb. armies which *were* his. 1 K 15:20. **Ijon**. 1 K +15:20. **Dan**. Ge 14:14. +30:6. Jg 18:28, 29. 20:1. **Abel-maim**. i.e. *mourning of the waters* or *meadow; place of waters*, ✻S#66h. *Abel-maim* is called *Abel-beth-maachah* in 1 K 15:20, and elsewhere, on account of its belonging to the district of *Beth-maachah*. **the store cities**. 2 Ch 8:6. 17:12. 1 K 9:19.

5. **that he left off**. See on ver. 1.

6. **they carried**. 1 K 15:22. **Geba**. Jsh 18:24-26, Gaba. 21:17. 1 Ch 6:60. Is 10:29. Zc 14:10. **Mizpah**. Jsh 15:38. 18:26. 1 S 7:6, 16. 10:17, Mizpeh.

7. **Hanani**. 2 Ch 19:2. 20:34. 1 K 16:1. **Because**. Ps 146:3-6. Is *31:1. 32:2. Je *17:5, 6. Ep 1:12, 13. **relied on**. 2 Ch 13:18. 32:7, 8. 2 K 18:5. 1 Ch 5:20. **the host**. See on ver. 3.

8. **the Ethiopians**. See on 2 Ch 12:3n. 14:9-12. **the Lubims**. 2 Ch 12:3n. **a huge host**. Heb. in abundance. **because**. See on ver. 7. Ps √9:9, 10. 37:39, 40.

9. **the eyes**. Ჟ22A7, Dt +11:12. 2 Ch *6:20. Jb *34:21. Ps *34:15. 113:6. Pr *5:21. *15:3. Je 16:17. *32:19. Zc *4:10. He √4:13. 1 P *3:12. ●5:8. **to show himself**, etc. *or*, strongly to hold with *them*, etc. **whose heart**. See on 2 Ch *15:17. 2 K +√20:3. Ps 37:37. **Herein**. 1 S *13:13. 2 S *12:7-12. 1 Ch *21:8. Jb 34:18, 19. Je *5:21. Mt *5:22. Lk *12:20. 1 C 15:36. Ga *3:1. **henceforth**. 1 K 15:32.

10. **wroth**. 2 Ch 25:16. 26:19. 2 S 12:13. 24:10-14. Ps 141:5. Pr 9:7-9. **put him**. 2 Ch 18:26. Je 20:2. 29:26. Mt 14:3, 4. Lk 3:20. Ac 16:23, 24. **oppressed**. Heb. crushed. Jg 10:8mg. Jb 20:19mg. Is 51:23. Je 51:34. La 3:34. **the same time**. 2 S 11:4. 12:31.

11. A.M. 3049-3090. B.C. 955-914. **the acts of Asa**. 2 Ch 9:29. 12:15. 20:34. 26:22. **in the book**. Nu 21:14. Jsh 10:13. 2 S 1:18. **Judah**. 2 Ch 25:26. 27:7. 32:32. 33:18. 35:27. 1 K 15:23.

12. A.M. 3088. B.C. 916. **diseased**. Mt 7:2. Lk 6:37, 38. Re 3:19. **in his disease**. See on ver. 9. 2 Ch 28:22. 1 Ch 10:14. Je √17:5. **physicians**. Ge 50:2. Jb 13:4. Je 8:22. Mt 9:12. Mk 2:17. 5:26. Col 4:14.

13. A.M. 3090. B.C. 914. **slept with**. 1 K +*11:43. 15:24. 2 K 24:6n.

14. **his own**. 2 Ch 35:24. Is 22:16. Jn 19:41, 42. **sepulchres**. Heb. *qeber*, Ge +23:4. **made**. Heb. digged. Ge 50:5. **sweet odors**. Ge 50:2. Mk 16:1. Jn 19:39, 40. **and**. Ჟ93A, Ge +1:26. By the figure Hendiadys, "sweet odors, yes—and of all manner of kinds." **the apothecaries' art**. Ex 30:25-37. Ec 10:1. **a very great burning**. 2 Ch 16:14. 21:19. ●34:5. Ge 11:3mg. Jsh ●+7:25. Je 34:5.

2 CHRONICLES 17

Jehoshaphat succeeds Asa, reigns well, and prospers, 1-6. He sends priests and Levites, accompanied by princes, to teach the law throughout Judah, 7-9. God overawes the minds of Jehoshaphat's neighbors, so that they submit to him, 10, 11. His greatness, and his army, with the captains, 12-19.

1. **Jehoshaphat**. i.e. *Jah has judged*. 2 S +8:16.
1 K 15:24. 22:41. 1 Ch 3:10. Mt 1:8, Josaphat. **and
strengthened**. 2 Ch 12:1. 26:8. 32:5. 1 S 23:16. Ezk
7:28. Ep *6:10.

2. **placed forces**. See on 2 Ch 11:11, 12. **in the
cities**. 2 Ch 11:5. 15:8.

3. **the Lord**. 2 Ch 15:2, 9. Ge 39:2, 3, 21. Ex 3:12.
4:12. Jsh *1:5, 9. Jg 2:18. 6:12. 2 S 5:10. 1 Ch 22:18.
Ps 46:7, 11. Is 8:10. 41:10. Mt 1:23. 18:20. 28:20.
2 T 4:22. **he walked**. 2 S 8:15. 1 K 11:6. 15:3, 4. 2 K
14:3. 16:2. 18:3. 22:2. Ps 132:1-5. **first ways**. As the
best, wherein he served God most faithfully (Young).
Re 2:4. **his father David**. *or*, his father, and of David.
2 Ch 14:2-5, 11. 15:8-13. **sought not**. Jg 2:11. 8:33.
Je 2:23. **Baalim**. 1 K 16:32.

4. **walked**. Lk 1:6. 1 Th 2:12. 4:1. **not after**. 1 K
12:28, 30, 33. 13:33, 34. 16:31-33. 2 K 8:18. 17:19.
Je 3:7, 8. Ho 4:15.

5. A.M. 3091. B.C. 913. **the Lord**. 2 S 7:25, 26.
1 K 9:4, 5. Ps 127:1. 132:12. 1 P 5:10. **brought**. Heb.
gave. **presents**. 2 Ch 32:23. 1 S 10:27. 1 K 4:21. 10:25.
Ps 68:29. 72:10. 76:11. Mt 2:11. **he had riches**. 2 Ch
1:15. 9:27. 18:1. 32:27-29. Ge 13:2. 26:13, 14. Dt 8:13,
14. 1 K 10:27. Jb 42:12. Mt *6:33.

6. **his heart**. Dt 28:47. Jb 22:26. **lifted up**. *that is*,
was encouraged. **in the ways**. 1 K 22:43. Ps 18:21,
22. 119:1. 138:5. Ho 14:9. Ac 13:10. **he took away**.
2 Ch 14:3. 15:17. 19:3. ◐20:33n. 31:1. 34:3-7. 1 K
◐22:43. Matthew Poole notes, "to wit, such only
wherein idols were worshipped, as appears by comparing this with 2 Ch 20:33." **high places**. 2 K +21:3.
groves. 2 Ch 19:3. 2 K +17:10. 21:3n. 23:6.

7. A.M. 3092. B.C. 912. **he sent**. In these verses
we have an account of a remarkable itinerant ministry
established by Jehoshaphat, in which *three* classes of
men were employed: (1) the Princes; (2) the Levites;
(3) the Priests. We may presume that the *Princes* instructed the people in the nature of the *civil law* and
constitution of the kingdom; that the *Levites* instructed
them in every thing that appertained to the *temple
service*, and *ritual law*; and that the *Priests* instructed
them in the *nature* and *design* of their religion. Thus
the nation became throughly instructed in their duty
to *God*, to the *king*, and to *each other*: they therefore
became as *one man*; and against a people thus united,
on *such principles*, no enemy could be successful. Dt
4:5. Ps 34:11. 51:13. Ec 1:12. 12:9, 10. Is 49:23. **Benhail**. i.e. *son of strength or valor, might or worth*,
*S#1134h. **Obadiah**. i.e. *servant of Jah*. Ob +1. **Zechariah**. i.e. *remembered of Jah*. Zc +1:1. **Nethaneel**.
i.e. *given of God*. Nu +1:8. **Michaiah**. i.e. *who is
like Jah?* 2 K +22:12. **to teach**. 2 Ch 15:3. 30:22.
35:3. Dt 33:10. Ne 8:7, 8, 13, 14. 9:3. Mt 4:23. Mk
4:2. Lk 4:43, 44. Ac 1:1.

8. **Shemaiah**. i.e. *heard of Jah*. 1 Ch 9:16. **Nethaniah**. i.e. *given of Jah*. 1 Ch +25:12. **Zebadiah**. i.e.
endowed of Jah. 1 Ch +26:2. **Asahel**. i.e. *made of
God*. 1 Ch +2:16. **Shemiramoth**. 1 Ch 15:+18, 20.
16:5. **Jehonathan**. i.e. *Jah has given*. 1 Ch +27:25.
Adonijah. i.e. *my lord is Jah*. 1 K +1:5. **Tobijah**. i.e.
goodness of Jehovah, *S#2900h. (1) One of the Levites
sent by Jehoshaphat to teach in the cities of Judah,
2 Ch 17:8. (2) A leader of the exiles from whom Zechariah obtained gold for the crown of Joshua the high
priest, Zc 6:10, 14. **Tob-adonijah**. i.e. *good is my
God; distinguished of my Lord Jehovah*, *S#2899h.

Elishama. i.e. *my God has heard*. Nu +1:10. **Jehoram**.
i.e. *Jah is high*. 2 K +1:17. **priests**. Ezr 7:1-6. Ml
2:7.

9. **they taught**. T#1072. 2 Ch ◐+*15:3. 35:3n. Jg
13:8. 2 K 4:23. Ne 8:7, 8. 1 T 5:17. **the book**. 2 Ch
+34:14n. Dt 6:6-9. 17:18. 31:9, 11-13. Jsh √1:7, 8. Is
√8:20. Mt 15:2-9. 28:19, 20. Lk 4:17-19. Jn √5:39, 46.
Ac 13:15. 15:21. 28:23. Ro 3:2. 2 C=5:19. Col *3:16.
1 Th=2:4. 1 P 4:11. **throughout**. Mt 10:23. 11:1. Ac
8:40.

10. **the fear**. See on 2 Ch 14:14. Ge 35:5. Ex 15:14-
16. Jsh 2:9-11. 1 S 11:7. **fell**. Heb. was. so that.
2 Ch 16:9. Ex 34:24. Pr *16:7.

11. **brought**. See on ver. 5. 2 Ch 9:14. 26:8. 2 S
8:2. 2 K 3:4.

12. A.M. 3092-3115. B.C. 912-889. **waxed great**.
2 Ch 18:1. 1 Ch 29:25. **in Judah**. 2 Ch 8:2-6. 11:5-
12. 14:6, 7. 26:6-9. 27:4. 32:5, 27-29. **castles**. *or*, palaces. 2 Ch 27:4. 1 Ch 29:1, 19. Ezr 6:2. **cities of store**.
2 Ch 8:4, 6. 16:4. 32:28. Ex 1:11. 1 K 9:19.

13. **much business**. 2 Ch 26:10-15. 1 Ch 27:25-31.
mighty men of valor. 2 Ch 13:3. Jg +6:12.

14. **the numbers**. Ge *12:2. 13:16. 15:5. **to the
house**. See on Nu 1:2, 18. **Adnah**. i.e. *pleasure*.
1 Ch +12:20. **three hundred**. 2 Ch 11:1. 13:3. 14:8.
26:13. **thousand**. or, chiefs. 1 S 6:19. +23:23. 1 K
*20:30n. Jb 33:23. SS 4:4. Is *60:22. Mi +*5:2.

15. **next to him**. Heb. at his hand. ver. 16, 18.
2 Ch 23:18mg. 29:27mg. 31:15mg. Jsh 15:46mg. 1 Ch
25:2mg, 6mg. Ne 3:2mg. 13:13mg. **Jehohanan**. i.e.
Jehovah is a gracious giver; the Lord gave in grace,
✛S#3076h. 2 Ch 17:15. 23:1. 1 Ch 26:3. Ezr 10:28.
Ne 12:13, 42. (1) One of Jehoshaphat's captains, 2 Ch
17:15. (2) Father of Ishmael, a captain under Jehoiada,
2 Ch 23:1. (3) A Korahite Levite, who had the sixth
course of the doorkeepers in David's reign, 1 Ch 26:3.
(4) a priest, head of the father's house of Amariah during
the exile, Ne 12:13. (5) A priest who dedicated the
wall, Ne 12:42. (6) A son of Bebai, who put away his
strange wife under Ezra, Ezr 10:28. **thousand**. or,
chiefs. ver. +14.

16. **Amasiah**. i.e. *lord of Jah; laden of Jah; lifted
up, or borne of the Lord*, *S#6007h. **Zichri**. i.e. *mindful*. 1 Ch +9:15. **willingly**. Jg 5:2, 9. 1 Ch 29:9, 14,
17. Ps 110:3. 2 C 8:3-5, 12. **thousand**. or, chiefs. ver.
+14. **mighty men**. ver. 13.

17. **Eliada**. i.e. *God has known*. 2 S +5:16. **mighty
man of**. Jg +6:12. **armed men**. 2 Ch 14:8. 2 S 1:21,
22. **thousand**. or, chiefs. ver. +14.

18. **Jehozabad**. i.e. *Jah has endowed*. 1 Ch +26:4.
thousand. or, chiefs. ver. +14.

19. **put in**. ver. 2, 12. 2 Ch 11:12, 23. **fenced cities**.
or, cities of fortress. Nu 13:19. 32:17, 36. Jsh 10:20.

2 CHRONICLES 18

*Jehoshaphat joins affinity with Ahab, and agrees
to go with him against Ramoth-gilead, 1-3. The false
prophets assure them of success, 4, 5. At Jehoshaphat's
request Micaiah is sent for, who foretells Ahab's death,
and shows that his prophets were instigated by a lying
spirit, 6-22. He is reviled and sent back to prison,
23-27. Ahab goes in disguise to the battle; where Jehoshaphat, in imminent danger, calls on God, and is
preserved, 28-32. Ahab is slain by an arrow shot at
a venture, 33, 34.*

1. A.M. 3107. B.C. 897. **riches.** 2 Ch 1:11-15. 17:5, 12. Mt *6:33. **joined affinity.** He took Athaliah, the daughter of Ahab, to be wife to his son Joram (2 K 8:18); which fatal connection was highly displeasing to God, and Jehoshaphat was severely reproved for it by Jehu the seer, 2 Ch 19:1-3. ver. 31. 2 Ch 19:2. 21:6. 22:2, 3. Dt 22:10. 1 K 16:31-33. 21:25. 2 K 8:18, 26, 27. 11:1. 2 C *6:14.

2. **after certain years.** Heb. at the end of years. 2 Ch 8:1. 1 K 17:7mg. Ne 13:6mg. **he went.** 2 Ch 19:2. 1 K 22:2, etc. **Ahab.** 1 K 1:9. Is 22:12, 13. Lk 17:27-29. **persuaded.** 1 K 22:4, 20-22. Pr 23:7. **Ramoth-gilead.** Dt 4:43. Jsh 20:8. 1 K 4:13. 2 K 9:1.

3. **I am as thou.** See on 1 K 22:4. 2 K 3:7. Ps 139:21. Am 3:3. Ep √5:11. 2 J √10, 11.

4. **Enquire.** 2 Ch 34:26. 1 S 23:2, 4, 9-12. 2 S 2:1. 5:19, 23. 1 K 22:5, 6. Ps 27:4. Je 21:2. Ezk 20:3.

5. **prophets.** 1 K 18:19. 2 K 3:13. 2 T 4:3. **Shall we go.** Je 38:14, etc. 42:2, 3, 20. **Go up.** ver. 14, 20, 21. Je 8:10, 11. 23:14, 17. 28:1, etc. Ezk 13:3-16, 22. Mi 2:11. 3:11. Re 19:20.

6. **Is there not.** See on 1 K 22:7-9. 2 K 3:11-13. **besides.** Heb. yet, or more. ver. 7.

7. **one man.** 1 K 18:4. 19:10. **I hate him.** 1 K 18:17. 20:42, 43. 21:20. Ps 34:21. 55:3. 69:14. Pr 9:8. 29:10. Je 18:18. Am 5:10. Mk 6:18, 19, 27. Lk 6:22. Jn 7:7. 15:18, 19, 24. Ga 4:16. **good.** Is 30:10. Je 38:4. **me.** ver. 13. 2 K 9:22. Ezk *3:17-19. Ac *20:26, 27. **Micaiah.** i.e. *like him; who is like Jah?*, ✠S#4319h, so rendered only here. ver. ◐14. 1 K 22:+8, 14. **Imla.** i.e. *he fills; he will fulfill,* ✱S#3229h. 2 Ch 18:7, 8. Also 1 K 22:8, 9. **Let not the.** Pr 25:12. Mi *2:7.

8. **officers.** or, eunuchs. Ge +37:36mg. 1 S 8:15mg. 1 Ch 28:1mg. Is 39:7. Da 1:3, 7, 8. **Fetch quickly.** Heb. Hasten. ver. 25, 26. Ge 18:6. 19:22. 45:9. Jg 9:48. 1 S 9:12. 23:27. 2 S 15:14. 1 K ‖22:9. Est 5:5. 6:10.

9. **sat either.** See on 1 K 22:10-12. Is 14:9. Ezk 26:16. Da 7:6. Mt 19:28. **clothed.** ver. 29. Mt 6:29. 11:8. **void place.** or, floor. i.e. threshingfloor. Ge +50:10. Dt +*16:13mg. Threshingfloors, among the ancient Jews, as we have before remarked, were only, as they are to this day in the East, round level plats of ground in the open air. Hence a floor might well be near the gate of Samaria, which was built on a hill, and afford no improper place for the kings of Judah and Israel to give audience to the prophets. **gate.** Where in the east justice is administrated (Young). Ge +14:7. 2 S 19:8n. 2 K 7:1n. **all the prophets.** Je 27:14-16.

10. **Zedekiah.** i.e. *the rightness of Jah.* 1 K +22:11. **Chenaanah.** i.e. *a Canaanitess.* 1 Ch +7:10. **horns of iron.** Mr. Bruce, in describing the head-dress of the governors of Abyssinia, says, "A large broad fillet was bound upon their forehead, and tied behind their head: in the middle of this was a *horn,* or conical piece of silver, gilt, about four inches long, much in the shape of our common candle extinguishers. This is called *kirn* ('keren), and is only worn in reviews, or parades after victory." Such, it may be supposed, were the *horns of iron* which Zedekiah (who appears to have acted the hero returning from a military triumph) made for himself, when he presumed, in the name of Jehovah, to flatter his prince with the promise of victory: "Thus saith the Lord, With these thou shalt push Syria, until they be consumed." Je 27:2. 28:10-

14. Zc 1:18-21. 2 T 3:8. **Thus.** Je 23:17, 21, 25, 31. 28:2, 3. 29:21. Ezk 13:7. 22:28. **they be consumed.** Heb. *thou* consume them. 1 K 22:11.

11. **all the prophets.** ver. 5, 12, 33, 34. Pr 24:24, 25. Mi 3:5. 2 P 2:1-3. Ju 16. Re 16:13, 14. 19:20.

12. **Behold.** Jb 22:13. Ps 10:11. Is 30:10. Ho 7:3. Am 7:12, 13. Mi 2:6, 11. 1 C *2:14-16. **assent.** Heb. mouth. Jsh 9:2mg. 1 K 22:13.

13. **even what my God.** Nu 22:18-20, 35. 23:12, 26. 24:13. 1 K 22:14. Je 23:28. 42:4. Ezk 2:7. Mi 2:6, 7. Ac *20:27. 1 C 11:23. 2 C 2:17. Ga *1:10. 1 Th *2:4.

14. **Micaiah.** ✠S#4318h, so rendered only here. **Go ye up.** 1 K 18:27. 22:15. Ec 11:1. La 4:21. Am 4:4, 5. Mt 26:45.

15. **shall I adjure.** 1 S 14:24. 1 K 22:16. Mt *26:63. Mk 5:7. Ac 19:13.

16. **he said.** Mt 26:64. **as sheep.** ver. 33, 34. 1 K 22:17, 34-36. Je 23:1, 2. Ezk 34:5, 6, 8. Zc 10:2. 13:7. Mt ⦁9:36. Mk ⦁6:34. **master.** 2 S 2:7. 5:2. 2 K 10:3.

17. **Did I not tell.** ver. 7. 1 K 22:18. Pr 29:1. Je 43:2, 3. **but evil.** *or,* but for evil.

18. **hear the word.** Is 1:10. 28:14. 39:5. Je 2:4. 19:3. 34:4. Am 7:16. **I saw.** 1 K 22:19-23. Is 6:1-5. Da 7:9, 10. Ac 7:55, 56. **all the host.** Ge 32:2. Ps 103:20, 21. Zc 1:10.

19. **Who shall entice.** 1 K 22:20. Jb 12:16. Is 6:9, 10. 54:16. Ezk 14:9. 2 Th √2:11, 12. Ja *1:13, 14. **go up.** 2 Ch 25:8, 19. Pr 11:5.

20. **there came.** Jb 1:6. 2:1. 2 C *11:3, 13-15. **spirit.** Heb. ruach, Jg +9:23.

21. **a lying.** ver. 22. Ge 3:4, 5. See on 1 K 22:21, 22. Jn *8:44. 1 J 4:6. Re 12:9. 13:14. 20:8. **spirit.** Heb. ruach, Jg +9:23. **Thou shalt.** See on ver. 19. Jg +9:23. Jb 1:12. 2:6. Ps 109:17.

22. **the Lord hath.** Ex 4:21. 1 S 18:10n. 2 S 12:11n. *24:1n. Jb 12:16. Is 19:14. Ezk 14:3-5, 9. Mt 24:24, 25. 2 C 11:11-13. 2 Th √2:9-11. 1 T *4:1, 2. **spirit.** Heb. ruach, Jg +9:23. **and the Lord.** See on ver. 7, 17. 2 Ch 25:18. Is 3:11. Je 18:11. Mi 2:3. Mt 26:24, 25. Mk 14:20, 21.

23. **Zedekiah.** See on ver. 10. 1 K 22:23-25. Is 50:5, 6. Je 20:2. La 3:30. Mi 5:1. Mt 26:67. Mk 14:65. Jn 18:22, 23. Ac 23:2, 3. **Which way.** Je 29:26, 27. Mt 26:67, 68. Jn 9:40, 41. **Spirit.** Is +48:16.

24. **Behold.** Is 26:11. Je 28:16, 17. 29:21, 22, 32. **into an inner chamber.** *or,* from chamber to chamber. Heb. into a chamber in a chamber. "In one of the halls of the seraglio at Constantinople," says De la Motraye (vol. ii. p. 170), "the eunuch made us pass by several little chambers, with doors shut, like the cells of monks or nuns, as far as I could judge by one that another eunuch opened." This exactly corresponds with the idea of a "chamber within a chamber;" and it would appear that Michaiah predicted, that Zedekiah should fly for shelter to a *Harem,* which we have seen was deemed *inviolate* (See on 1 S 19:16n). 1 K 20:30mg. 22:25mg. 2 K 9:2mg. Is 26:20.

25. **and carry him back.** ver. 8. Je 37:15-21. 38:6, 7. Ac 24:25-27.

26. **Put.** See on ver. 15. 2 Ch 16:10. 1 K 22:26-28. Je 20:2, 3. Mt 5:12. Lk 3:19, 20. Ac 5:18. 2 C 11:23. Re 11:10. **this fellow.** 1 S 25:21. Mt 12:24. Lk 23:2. Ac 22:22. **prison.** 1 K ‖22:27. 2 K 17:4. 25:27, 29. Is 42:7, 22. Je 37:15, 18. 52:33. **bread of affliction.** Ps 80:5. 102:9. Is 30:20. **until I return.** Dt 29:19.

Ps 10:5. Pr 14:16. 1 Th 5:2, 3.

27. **If.** Nu 16:29. Am 9:10. Ac 13:10, 11. **Hearken.** Mt 13:9. 15:10. Mk 7:14. Lk 20:45, 46.

28. **the king.** See on 1 K 22:29-33.

29. **I will disguise.** √96B, Ge +8:5. Ge +27:16. 1 S 28:8. 1 K 14:2-6. 20:38. 22:30. Jb 24:15. 30:18. Je 23:24. **put thou on thy robes.** Ps 12:2. Pr 26:25. **the king.** 2 Ch 35:22, 23.

30. **Fight ye.** 1 K 20:33, 34, 42. **small or great.** See on 2 Ch 15:13. Ge 19:11. Dt 1:17.

31. **but.** 2 Ch 20:37. **Jehoshaphat.** 2 Ch 13:14. 14:11. Ex 14:10. Ps 116:1, 2. 2 C 1:9, 10. **the Lord.** 2 Ch 26:7. Ps 34:7. 46:1, 11. 94:17. 118:13. **God moved them.** T#264. 1 Ch 5:26. Ezr 1:1. 6:22. 7:27. Ne 1:11. Pr *16:1, 7, 9. 21:1. Is 64:8. Zc 12:1. Ac 16:14.

32. **from pursuing him.** Heb. from after him. 1 K 22:33.

33. **a certain man.** See on 1 K 22:34. **at a venture.** Heb. in his simplicity. Ge 24:44n. 2 S 15:11. 1 K 9:4. 22:34. **between the,** etc. Heb. between the joints and between the breastplate. The *shiryon,* in Syriac, *sheryono,* seems to have covered both the back and breast of the warrior, and was consequently not properly a breastplate, but a coat of mail or corslet. The corslet was made of flax or of wool woven very thick, of ox-hide, of brass or of iron. The metalic corslet consisted not of one solid piece, but of scales, hooks, or rings, connected like the links of a chain, that the warrior might move with greater ease. It was between the joints of this harness that Ahab received his mortal wound. 1 K 22:34, 35. Is 41:7. **harness.** or, coat of mail. 2 Ch 26:14. 1 S 17:5. 1 K 22:34. Ne 4:16. Is 59:17. **wounded.** Heb. made sick. 2 Ch 35:23mg. 1 K 22:34mg. 2 K 8:25mg.

34. **he died.** See on ver. 16, 19, 27. Nu +*32:23. Pr 13:21. 28:17.

2 CHRONICLES 19

Jehoshaphat, on his return, is reproved by Jehu the prophet, for joining alliance with Ahab; but commended in other respects, 1-3. He visits and reforms his kingdom, 4; and gives a charge to the judges, priests, and Levites, in the cities of Judah, and at Jerusalem, 5-11.

1. A.M. 3108. B.C. 896. **in peace.** 2 Ch 18:31, 32.

2. **And Jehu.** 2 Ch 20:34. 1 K 16:1, 7, 12. **Hanani.** 2 Ch 16:7. **the seer.** See on 1 S 9:9. **help the ungodly.** 2 Ch 18:3, 28. 2 S √12:14. 1 K 21:25. Jb 8:20. Ps 15:4. *139:21, 22. Pr 1:10-19. Mk ◐+*1:25. Ro 1:32. 16:17. 2 C *6:14-17. Ep √5:11. 2 J √10, 11. Ju 3. **love them that.** T#112. Mt 10:11-14. 1 C 5:9-11. 10:20. Ep *5:11. 2 Th 3:6, 14, 15. 2 T 3:5. 2 J *9-11. **hate the Lord.** 2 Ch 18:7. Ex *20:5. Dt 5:9. 7:10. 32:41. 33:11. Ps 21:8. 68:1. 71:15. Pr 13:20. Jn 15:18, 23. Ro 1:30. 8:7. 1 C 15:33. Ja √4:4. **is wrath.** 2 Ch +24:18. 32:25. Ps 90:7, 8. Ro 1:18. 1 C 11:31, 32.

3. **Nevertheless.** √127. Palinodia, Re +2:6. **good things.** 2 Ch 12:12mg, ◐14. 17:3-6. 1 K 14:13. Ro 7:18. **taken away.** 2 Ch 17:4, 6. 20:33. **groves.** 2 K +17:10. 21:3n. 23:6. **prepared.** See on 2 Ch 12:14. 30:19. Ezr 7:10. Ps 57:7.

4. **went out again.** Heb. returned and went out. 1 S 7:15-17. **Beer-sheba.** Ge 21:33. Jg 20:1. **mount Ephraim.** Jsh 17:15. Jg 19:1. **brought them back.** See

on 2 Ch 15:8-13. *17:7-9. 29:10, 11. 1 S 7:3, 4. Ml 4:6. Lk 1:17.

5. **he set.** ver. 8. Dt 16:18-20. 1 Ch 26:29, 32. Ro 13:1-5. 1 P *2:13, 14. **fenced cities.** 2 Ch 17:2.

6. **Take.** Jsh 22:5. 1 Ch 28:10. Lk 12:15. 21:8. Ac 5:35. 22:26. **ye judge.** Dt 1:17. Ps 82:1-6. Ec 5:8. **not for.** Ex *18:17, 23. Ep *6:6, 7. Col *3:23. **judgment.** Heb. matter of judgment. Ec 5:8.

7. **let the.** Ge 42:18. Ex +*18:21, 22, 25, 26. Ne 5:15. Is 1:23-26. **no iniquity.** Ge +*18:25. Dt 32:4. Ps 92:15. Zp 3:5. Ml 2:6. Ro 3:5, 6. 9:14. **respect of persons.** Dt 10:17, 18. Jb 34:19. Mt 22:16. Ac 10:34. Ro 2:11. Ga 2:6. Ep 6:9. Col 3:25. 1 P 1:17. **taking of gifts.** Ex 23:8. Dt 16:18, 19. Is 1:23. 33:15. Mi 7:3.

8. **Levites.** 2 Ch 17:8. Dt 17:8-13. 1 Ch 23:4. 26:29. **the judgment.** Ex *18:19-26. Dt 21:5. 25:1. Ps *19:9. Is 58:2. Je 5:4, 5. +*8:7.

9. **in the fear.** See on ver. 7. Dt 1:16, 17. 2 S *23:3. Is 11:3-5. 32:1. **faithfully.** 2 Ch 34:12. Ex 17:12. Nu 12:7. Dt 32:4. Pr 25:13. Lk 16:10. 3 J 5. **perfect heart.** 1 K 8:61. 11:4. 15:3, 14. 2 K +*20:3. 1 Ch 12:38n.

10. **between blood.** Dt 17:8-13. **law and commandment.** Ex 24:12. **statutes and judgments.** Ex 15:25. Dt 4:1, 45. 12:1. Ps 147:19. **warn them.** Ezk *3:18-21. 33:6. Ac √20:20, 31. 1 Th 5:14. **wrath come.** Nu 16:46. Jsh 22:18-20.

11. **Amariah.** 1 Ch 6:11. **all matters.** ver. 8. 1 Ch 26:30. Ml 2:7. **officers.** Ex 5:6, 10, 14, 15, 19. Nu *11:16. Dt *1:15. *16:18. 20:5, 8, 9. 29:10. 31:28. Jsh 1:10. 3:2. 8:33. **Deal courageously.** Heb. Take courage and do. Jsh *1:6, 9. 1 Ch 22:11, 13, 16, 19. 28:10. Ezr 10:4. 1 C 16:13. 2 T 2:1. **the Lord.** ver. 6. 2 Ch 15:2. Ps 18:25, 26. Jn 14:23, 24. Ro 2:4-13. Ph *4:8, 9. **the good.** Ps 37:23. 112:5. Pr 2:20. Ec 2:26. Lk 23:50. Ac 11:24.

2 CHRONICLES 20

Jehoshaphat, alarmed by an invasion of the Moabites, Ammonites, and others, proclaims a fast, 1-4. His prayer, 5-13. Jahaziel, the prophet, assures him of a signal deliverance, 14-17. Jehoshaphat and his people receive the promise with adoring thankfulness, 18, 19. He exhorts them to believe, and appoints singers to praise the Lord, 20, 21. The invaders destroy one another, and the people of Judah gather immense spoils, 22-25. They bless God at Berachah, return in triumph, and enjoy peace, 26-30. Jehoshaphat's good reign and acts, 31-34. He joins with Ahaziah in sending ships to Tharshish, which are wrecked, according to the prediction of Eliezer, 35-37.

1. **after this also.** 2 Ch 19:5, 11. 32:1. **the children of Moab.** Ps 83:5-8. Is 7:1. 8:9, 10. 16:6. **came against.** 2 Ch 19:2. Je 10:24. Re 3:19.

2. **beyond the sea.** That is, the *Dead* or *Salt sea,* the western and northern boundary of *Edom,* which is the reading of one of Dr. Kennicott's MSS. (89), instead of *aram,* "Syria." The difference involves the change of only one letter in Hebrew. Ge 14:3. Nu 34:12. Jsh 3:16. **Hazazon-tamar.** i.e. *pruning of the palm; division of the palm,* *S#2688h. 2 Ch 20:2. Ge 14:7. **En-gedi.** Jsh 15:62. 1 S 23:29. SS 1:14.

3. **feared.** T#1336. Ge 28:20-22. 32:7-11, 24-28. Ex 14:10. Ne 2:2-4. Ps 27:12, 13. 31:22. +*34:4. *56:1-4. 69:14-18. 141:8, 9. Pr 30:7-9. Is 37:3-6. Je 26:19.

Jon 1:16. 3:5. Mt +*10:28. **himself**. Heb. his face. **seek the Lord**. See on 2 Ch 11:16. 19:3. Ps +*9:10. +*34:4. Is *55:6. **proclaimed**. Jg +*20:26n. 1 S 7:6. Ezr 8:21-23. Est 4:16. Je 36:9. Da 9:3. Jl 1:14. 2:12-18. Jon 3:5-9.

4. **gathered**. T#1244. 2 Ch 15:10-12. Jg 20:26n, 27. 1 S 7:5, 6. 2 K 23:1-3. Ezr 9:4, 5. Ne 9:1-3. Ps 42:4. 116:17-19. Is 2:3. Je 31:8, 9. 42:1, 2. Jl 1:14. 2:15-19. Jon 3:5-8. Zc 8:21, 22. Lk 1:10. Ac 4:31, 32. **ask help of the Lord**. Ps 34:5, 6. 50:15. 60:10-12. **the cities**. 2 Ch 19:5. Ps 69:35.

5. **Jehoshaphat**. See on 2 Ch 6:12, 13. 34:31. 1 K 8:22. 2 K 19:14-19. **in the house**. T#1196. 1 K 8:27-30. 2 K 19:14, 15. Ne 9:4-6. Ps 42:4. Is 2:3. 56:7. Jl 1:14. 2:16-18. Zc 7:1, 2. Mt 21:12, 13. Lk 1:9, 10. 2:27-29, 37. 18:10. Ac 3:1. 22:17.

6. **O Lord**. See on Ex 3:6, 15, 16. 1 Ch 29:18. **God in heaven**. Dt 4:39. Jsh 2:11. 1 K 8:23. Ps 115:3. Is 57:15, 16. 66:1. Mt *6:9. **rulest not**. 1 Ch 29:11, 12. Jb 25:2. Ps 47:2, 8. Je 27:5-8. Da 4:17, 25, 32-35. Mt 28:18. **in thine hand**. 1 Ch 29:11, 12. Ps 62:11. Mt 6:13. **none is able**. Ac 11:17.

7. **our God**. 2 Ch 14:11. Ge 15:7, 18. +*17:7. Ex 6:7. 19:5-7. 20:2. 1 Ch 17:21-24. **who**. Heb. thou. **drive out**. See on Ex 33:2. Ps 44:2. **thy people**. Dt +*32:43. Ps 83:3. **gavest**. Ge *12:7. 13:15. Jsh 24:3, 13. 1 K +*4:21n. Ne 9:8. **Abraham**. Ac +*7:5. Ro +*4:13. **thy friend**. Ge *18:19. Is *41:8. Jn 11:11. 15:15. Ja *2:23. **for ever**. Heb. *olam*, Ex +12:24. Is ` +√41:9. +*54:7-10. +*55:3. Je √32:40, 41. √33:20, 21, 25, 26. Mi 7:20. Ml 3:6.

8. **built thee**. See on 2 Ch 2:4. 6:10.

9. **If, when evil**. See on 2 Ch 6:28-30. Ex 32:12. Jsh 7:6, 9. 1 K 8:33, 37. **we stand**. 1 Ch ⦿+17:16. Lk +18:13. **and in thy presence**. Mt *18:20. **thy name**. See on 2 Ch 6:20. Ex 20:24. 23:21. **is in this house**. Several MSS., with the Syriac, Arabic, and Vulgate, read *nikra*, "is invoked;" "thy name is *invoked* in this house."

10. **whom thou**. Nu 20:17-21. Dt 2:4, 5, 9, 19. Jg 11:15-18.

11. **how they reward us**. Six of Dr. Kennicott's and De Rossi's MSS. add *ruah*, "evil:" "Behold they reward us *evil*:" which is also the reading of the Targum. Ge 44:4. Ex 32:12. Jsh 7:6, 9. Ps 7:4. 35:12. Pr 17:13. Je 18:20. **to cast us**. Jg 11:23, 24. Ps 83:3-12. **hast given**. Dt 6:23.

12. **wilt**. That is, thou wilt inflict deserved punishment upon them. This prayer of Jehoshaphat's is justly accounted one of the most sensible, pious, correct, and, as to its composition, one of the most elegant prayers offered under the Old Testament dispensation; and a careful examination of the parallel passages will afford a better illustration of it than the longest and most elaborate commentary. Dt 32:36. Jg 11:27. 1 S 3:13. Ps 7:6, 8. 9:19. 43:1. 83:11, 12. Is 2:4. 72:4. Jl 3:12. Re 19:11. **judge**. √121C2D2, Ge +15:14. **we have**. See on 2 Ch 14:11. 1 S 14:6. 2 C 1:8, 9. **neither**. 2 K 6:15. **our eyes**. Ps 25:15. 121:1, 2. 123:1, 2. 141:8. Jon 2:4.

13. **all Judah**. Dt 29:10, 11. Ezr 10:1. Jon 3:5. Ac 21:5. **stood**. Lk +18:13. **with their little ones**. Dt +29:11n. 1 C √7:14.

14. **Then upon**. Is 58:9. 65:24. Da 9:20, 21. Ac 10:4, 31. **came the Spirit**. Heb. *ruach*, Ge +41:38. 2 Ch 15:1. 24:20. Nu 11:25, 26. 24:2.

15. **Be not afraid**. 2 Ch 32:7, 8. Ex 14:13, 14. Dt 1:29, 30. 20:1, 4. 31:6, 8. Jsh 11:6. Ne 4:14. Ps 27:1, 2. Is 41:10-16. 43:1, 2. **the battle**. 2 Ch 32:8. 1 S 17:47. Ps *35:1.

16. **cliff**. Heb. ascent. 1 S 9:11. **Ziz**. i.e. *blossom, fringe; wing; flower, branch*, ✻S#6732h. The cliff of Ziz was probably near *Ziza*, which Ptolemy places in Arabia Petraea, long. 68 11/24 degrees, lat. 31 degrees. **brook**. *or*, valley. Ge 26:17, 19. 32:23. Nu +13:23mg. Jg +16:4mg. **the wilderness**. The wilderness of *Jeruel* seems, from ver. 20, to have been a part of the wilderness of *Tekoa*. **Jeruel**. i.e. *foundation of God; founded of God; fear ye God; taught of God*, ✻S#3385h.

17. **not need**. ver. 22, 23. Ex *14:13, 14, 25. **stand ye still**. Ps 46:10, 11. Is 30:7, 15. La 3:26. **for the Lord**. 2 Ch 15:2. *32:8. Nu *14:9. Ps 46:7, 11. Is 8:9, 10. 41:10. Am 5:14. Mt 1:23. 28:20. Ro *8:31. 2 T 4:22.

18. **bowed his head**. 2 Ch 7:3. Ge 24:26. Ex *4:31. **fell before**. Jb 1:20. Ps 95:6.

19. **Levites**. 1 Ch 15:16-22. 16:5, 42. 23:5. 25:1-7. **Korhites**. Ps ch. 44, 49, titles. **stood**. Lk +18:13. **a loud**. 2 Ch 5:13. Ezr 3:12, 13. Ne 12:42, 43. Ps 81:1. 95:1, 2.

20. **rose early**. Ge +21:14. **Tekoa**. 2 Ch 11:6. 2 S 14:2. 1 Ch 4:5. Je 6:1. **Hear me**. See on ver. 15. **Believe in the Lord**. Ps 106:12. Is *7:9mg. √26:3. +*50:10. Jn *11:40. *14:1. Ro 8:31. He 6:12. √11:6. or, remain stedfast in Jehovah. Ge 15:6. 45:26. **be established**. Col +*1:23. or, become stedfast. 2 Ch 1:9. 6:17. Ge 42:20. 2 S *7:16. 1 K 8:26. 1 Ch 17:23, 24. 1 C +√15:58. 2 P √1:3-10. **believe his prophets**. Ex 14:31. Lk +√16:31. *24:25. Jn √5:46, 47. 13:20. Ac *10:43. 13:27, 40. 15:15. *24:14. *26:22, 27. *28:23. Ro 1:2. **prosper**. 2 Ch *24:20. *26:3. Ps *1:3.

21. **consulted**. 1 Ch 13:1, 2. Pr 11:14. **appointed**. 2 Ch 29:25-30. 30:21. Ezr 3:10, 11. Ne 12:27. **that should praise**. Heb. praisers of. **the beauty**. 1 Ch 16:29. Ps 29:2. 50:2. 90:17. 96:9. **praise the Lord**. 2 Ch 5:13. 7:3, 6. 1 Ch 16:34, 41. Ezr 3:11. Ps 106:1. 107:1. ch. 136. Je 33:11. **for ever**. Heb. *olam*, Ex +12:24.

22. **when they**. Heb. in the time that they, etc. **to sing and to**. Heb. in singing and. **the Lord set ambushments**. Houbigant's version is, "the Lord set against the children of Ammon and Moab ambushments of those who came from mount Seir against Judah; and the children of Ammon and Moab were smitten: but they afterwards rose up against the inhabitants of mount Seir, and utterly destroyed them; who being destroyed, they rose up one against another, and mutually destroyed each other." Jg 7:22. 1 S 14:16, 20. 2 K 6:17. Ps 35:5, 6. Is 19:2. Ezk 38:21. **were smitten**. *or*, smote one another.

23. **mount Seir**. Ge 14:6. 36:8, 9. Dt 2:5. Jsh 24:4. Ezk 35:2, 3. **to destroy another**. Heb. for the destruction. Jg 7:22. 1 S 14:20.

24. **they were dead**. Ex 14:30. 1 Ch 5:22. Ps 110:6. Is 37:36. Je 33:5. **none escaped**. Heb. *there was* not an escaping. 2 Ch 12:7. Jg 21:17. Ezr 9:8, 14.

25. **they found**. Ex 12:35, 36. 1 S 30:19, 20. 2 K 7:9-16. Ps 68:12. Ro 8:37. **dead bodies**. Instead of *pegarim*, "dead bodies," eight MSS. and several ancient editions read *begadim*, "garments." None of the ancient versions, except the Chaldee, have *dead bodies*: *garments* would therefore appear to be the true reading; and the succeeding clause should be rendered, "which

they seized for themselves." **precious jewels.** Ex 3:22. Nu 31:51. Jg 8:24-26. Pr 3:15. **it was so much.** Ezk 39:8, 9.

26. **Berachah.** *that is,* Blessing. Having previously sought deliverance by fasting and prayer, and received the assurance of it with grateful joy, Jehoshaphat and his army returned immediate and fervent thanks and praise to the Lord, who had in so wonderful a manner performed his promise (Scott, who quotes the following from Bp. Patrick): "They did not return every man to his own home; but first went back to Jerusalem, to bless the Lord again for hearing their prayer and making good his promises." **blessed.** Ex 15:1-19. 2 S 22:1. Ps 103:1, 2. 107:21, 22. Lk 1:68. Re 19:1-6. **the name.** Ge 28:19. 32:30. Ex 17:15. 1 S 7:12. Is 62:4. Ac 1:19. **unto this day.** 2 Ch 5:9n. 10:19. Jsh +4:9. 1 Ch +4:43.

27. **forefront.** Heb. head. 2 S 6:14, 15. Mi 2:13. He 6:20. **the Lord.** 1 S 2:1. Ne *12:43. Ps 20:5. 30:1. Is 35:10. 51:11. Re 18:20.

28. **they came to.** Instead of celebrating his own heroism or the valor of his troops on this memorable occasion, this excellent prince sung with his whole army the praises of Jehovah, the God of hosts, who disposes of the victory according to his pleasure. This conduct was becoming the descendant and successor of David, the man after God's own heart, and of a religious people, the peculiar inheritance of Jehovah. **with.** 2 S 6:5. 1 Ch *13:8. 16:42n. 23:5. 25:6. Ps 57:8. 92:3. 149:3. 150:3-5. Re 14:2, 3. **psalteries.** 1 S +10:5. **harps.** 1 Ch +13:8n. **trumpets.** 2 Ch +5:12.

29. **the fear.** ♪24L, Ge +6:2. 2 Ch 17:10. Ge 35:5. Ex 23:27. Jsh 5:1. 2 K 7:6. **they had heard.** Ex 15:14-16. Jsh *2:9-11. *9:9-11.

30. **was quiet.** Jb *34:29. 1 T +*2:1, 2. **his God.** 2 Ch 14:6, 7. 15:15. Jsh 23:1. 2 S 7:1. Jb 34:29. Pr √16:7. Jn *14:27.

31. A.M. 3090-3115. B.C. 914-889. **Jehoshaphat reigned.** 1 K ‖22:41-44.

32. **he walked.** See on 2 Ch 17:3-6. **the way.** See on 2 Ch 14:2-4, 11-13. 1 K 15:11. **departed not.** 2 Ch 16:7-12. Ps 18:21. 36:3.

33. **the high places.** 2 Ch 14:3. ◑17:6. ◑19:3. 32:12n. 33:17. Matthew Poole notes, not fully nor universally; of which see on 2 Ch 17:6. The fault was not in Jehoshaphat, but in the people, who, though they did worship the true God, yet would not be confined to the temple, but for their own conveniency, or from their affection to their ancient custom, chose to worship him in the high places; which Jehoshaphat was forced to connive at, lest those people, being debarred from that dearly-beloved practice, should fall into a neglect of God and his worship. **had not.** See on 2 Ch 12:14. 19:3. 30:19. Dt 29:4. 1 S 7:3.

34. **the rest.** See on 2 Ch 12:15. 13:22. 16:11. **book.** Heb. words. **Jehu the son of Hanani.** 2 Ch 19:2. 1 K 16:1, 7. **is mentioned.** Heb. was made to ascend. 2 Ch 3:14. 1 Ch 27:24.

35. A.M. 3108. B.C. 896. **did Jehoshaphat join.** 1 K 22:48, 49. **who did very wickedly.** 2 K 1:2-16.

36. **And he joined.** "At first Jehoshaphat was unwilling, 1 K 22:48, 49." 2 Ch 18:1. Lk 15:15. **make ships.** 1 K 22:48, 49. **Tarshish.** "Tarsos in the great sea," says the Targumist, by which is meant a place in the Mediterranean, called the *Great Sea* by the Hebrews.

See on 1 K 10:22, Tharshish. **Ezion-gaber.** 1 K 9:26, Ezion-geber.

37. **Eliezer.** i.e. *my God is help.* Ge +15:2. **Dodavah.** i.e. *beloved of Jehovah; love of the Lord,* ✳S#1735h. **Mareshah.** 2 Ch 11:8. Jsh +15:44. **Because.** 2 Ch ◑18:31. See on 19:2. Jsh 7:11, 12. Pr 13:20. **the Lord.** 2 Ch 16:9. Pr 9:6. 13:20. He 12:6. Re 3:19. **And the ships.** 1 K 22:48. 1 Ch 29:14. **broken.** Ps 48:7. **to Tarshish.** 2 Ch 9:21.

2 CHRONICLES 21

Jehoshaphat dies; Jehoram succeeds, slays his brethren, and reigns wickedly, 1-7. Edom and Libnah revolt, 8-10. He establishes idolatry, 11. Elijah's written prophecy against him, 12-15. The Philistines and Arabians invade and plunder his kingdom, and carry all his family captive, except Jehoahaz, 16, 17. Elijah's prophecy fulfilled in Jehoram's incurable disease and death; and he is interred without honor, 18-20.

1. A.M. 3115. B.C. 889. **Jehoshaphat. was buried.** See on ver. 20. 2 Ch 9:31. 12:16. **Jehoram.** 2 K 8:16, 17. **reigned.** "Alone." 1 K 22:50.

2. **Israel.** Jehoshaphat was certainly not king of *Israel,* but of *Judah: Yisrael* must therefore be a mistake for *Yehoodah;* which is the reading of thirty-eight of Dr. Kennicott's and De Rossi's MSS., and of the Syriac, Arabic, Septuagint, and Vulgate. ver. 4. 2 Ch 12:6. 23:2. 24:5, 16. 28:19, 23, 27. 33:18. 35:18.

3. **gave them.** 2 Ch 11:23. Ge 25:6. Dt 21:15-17. **the kingdom.** He associated him with himself in the kingdom about *three* years before his death, and in the fifth year of Joram king of Israel; so that Jehoram reigned **three** years with his father, and *five* years alone—in all *eight* years. **Jehoram.** "Jehoram made partner of the kingdom with his father, 1 K 8:16." **firstborn.** 1 Ch +26:10.

4. **slew all.** ver. 17. 2 Ch 22:8, 10. Ge 4:8. Jg 9:5, 56, 57. 1 J 3:12.

5. A.M. 3112-3119. B.C. 892-885. **Jehoram.** "In consort, 2 K 8:16, 17."

6. **in the way.** 1 K 16:25-33. **he had.** 2 Ch 18:1. 22:2. 2 K 8:18. Ne 13:25, 26.

7. **Howbeit.** 2 Ch 22:11. Is 7:6, 7. **because.** 2 S 23:5. Ps 89:28-34, 39. Je 33:20-26. **as he promised.** 2 S 7:12-17. 1 K 11:13, 36. 2 K 8:19. Ps 132:11, 17, 18, etc. Lk 1:69, 79. **light.** Heb. lamp, *or* candle. 1 K *11:36mg. 15:4mg. 2 K 8:19mg.

8. A.M. 3115. B.C. 889. **the Edomites.** Ge 27:40. 2 K 8:20-22. **dominion.** Heb. hand. 2 K 8:20. **and made.** 1 K 22:47. 2 K 3:9.

9. **with his.** 2 K 8:21.

10. **unto this day.** 2 Ch 5:9n. 10:19. 20:26. **Libnah.** Nu +33:20. Jsh 21:13. 2 K 19:8. **because.** 2 Ch 13:10. 15:2. Dt 32:21. 1 K 11:31-33. Je 2:13.

11. **Moreover.** Dt 12:2-4. 1 K 11:7. Ps 78:58. Ezk 20:28. **caused.** 1 K 14:9, 16. 2 K 21:11. Hab 2:15. Re 2:20. **fornication.** ver. 13. Le 17:7. 20:5. 2 K 9:22. Ps 106:39. Ezk 16:15, etc. Re 2:20-22. 17:1-5. **compelled.** 2 Ch 33:9. 2 K *17:21. Da 3:5, 6, 15. Re 13:15-17. 17:5, 6.

12. A.M. 3116. B.C. 888. **there came.** T#977‡. 2 K 2:11, 12. **a writing.** "Which was writ before his assumption, 2 K 2:1." Je 36:2, 23, 28-32. Ezk 2:9, 10. Da 5:5, 25-29. **Elijah the prophet.** If the account of the translation of Elijah be given in the order in

which it happened, then it occurred in the reign of Jehoshaphat, the father of Jehoram. Hence it is probable that he wrote it before his assumption, and left it to be delivered by Elisha or one of the prophets. 2 K 2:11. **in the ways of Jehoshaphat**. 2 Ch 17:3, 4. 1 K 22:43. **nor in the ways of Asa**. 2 Ch 14:2-5. 1 K 15:11.

13. **in the way**. 1 K 16:25, 30-33. **a whoring**. ver. 11. Ex 34:12, 15. Dt 31:16. 2 K 9:22. Je 3:8, 9. **of Ahab**. 1 K 16:33. **hast slain**. ver. 4. Ge 4:10-12. 42:21, 22. Jg 9:56, 57. 1 K 2:31-33. Is 26:21. Hab 2:12. 1 J 3:12. **better than**. 1 K 2:32.

14. **plague**. Heb. stroke. Le 26:21. **thy people**. Many of the people had concurred in Jehoram's idolatry, and some of them must have been instruments in his base, unnatural murders; they were therefore joined in his punishment, and he suffered by the loss of his subjects. Ho 5:11. Mi 6:16. **thy children**. Ex 20:5.

15. **by disease**. This is supposed to have been a violent dysentery, a disease which is often attended with symptoms similar to those described in the text (Dr. Mead's *Medica Sacra*, cap. iv.); by the same death perished Antiochus Epiphanes, and Herod Agrippa. ver. 18, 19. Nu 5:27. Dt 28:61. Ac 12:23. **thy bowels fall**. Ps 109:18. Ac 1:18. **the sickness**. ver. 18. Dt 28:27, 35, 59, 67.

16. A.M. 3117. B.C. 887. **the Lord stirred**. 2 Ch 33:11. 1 S 26:19. 2 S 24:1. 1 K *11:11, 14, 23. Ezr 1:1, 5. Is 10:5, 6. 45:5-7. Am 3:6. **spirit**. Heb. *ruach*, Ge +41:8. ♪121A10, Ge +26:35. **Philistines**. 2 Ch 17:11.

17. **carried away**. Heb. carried captive. Jb 5:3, 4. **his sons also**. 2 Ch 22:1. 24:7. **Jehoahaz**. 2 Ch 22:1, Ahaziah. 22:6, Azariah. **youngest**. lit. the small one. ♪96E2, 1 S +17:14.

18. A.M. 3117-3119. B.C. 887-885. **And after all**. "His son Ahaziah Prorex, 2 K 9:29, soon after." **an incurable disease**. See on ver. 15. 2 Ch +36:16mg. 2 K 9:29. Ac 12:23.

19. **made no**. 2 Ch 16:14. Je 34:5.

20. A.M. 3119. B.C. 885. **Thirty and two**. ver. 5. **without being desired**. Heb. without desire. 1 S 9:20. Hg 2:7. That is, without being regretted: no one wished him to live any longer. He was hated while he lived, and neglected when he died. 2 Ch 23:21. Pr 10:7. Je 22:18, 28. **but not**. 2 Ch 24:25. 28:27. Je 22:18. **sepulchres**. Heb. *qeber*, Ge +23:4.

2 CHRONICLES 22

Ahaziah succeeds Jehoram, reigns wickedly, joins Jehoram king of Israel, and is slain by Jehu, 1-9. Athaliah murders the seed royal, and usurps the throne, 10. Joash is preserved by Jehoshabeath, 11, 12.

1. **the inhabitants**. 2 Ch 23:3. 26:1. 33:25. 36:1. **Ahaziah**. ver. 6, Azariah. 2 Ch 21:17, Jehoahaz. 2 K 8:24, etc. 1 Ch 3:11. **slain**. 2 Ch 21:16, 17.

2. A.M. 3119, 3120. B.C. 885, 884. **Forty and two**. In the parallel passage (on which see the Note, 2 K 8:26n) he is said to be only *twenty-two*; and this is doubtless the true reading, as it is supported here by several MSS. and Versions. 2 K 8:26. **Athaliah**. 2 Ch 21:6. 1 K 16:28.

3. **his mother**. Ge 6:4, 5. Dt 7:3, 4. 13:6-10. Jg 17:4, 5. Ne 13:23-27. Ml 2:15. Mt 14:8-11. **his counsel-**

ler. Ge 27:12, 13. Mt 10:37. Ac 4:19.

4. **they were his**. 2 Ch 24:17, 18. Pr *1:10. 12:5. 13:20. 19:27.

5. **He walked**. Ps 1:1. Mi 6:16. **went with**. 2 K 8:28, 29, etc. **Ramoth-gilead**. 2 Ch 18:3, 31. 19:2. 1 K 22:3, 4. Da 5:22.

6. **And he returned**. 2 K 9:15. **which were given him**. Heb. wherewith they wounded him. **Azariah**. "Ahaziah" and "Jehoahaz" are essentially the same both in letters and sense, the word *yeho* or *yah* being merely transposed; but *Azariah* seems to have been a distinct name by which he was known. ver. 1, 7, Ahaziah. 2 Ch 21:17, Jehoahaz. 1 Ch +6:36. **to see Jehoram**. 2 K 8:29. 10:13, 14.

7. **destruction**. Heb. treading down. Ml 4:3. **was of God**. 2 Ch 10:15. Dt 32:35. Jg 14:4. 1 K 12:15. 22:20. Ps 9:16. Is 46:10. Ho 14:9. **he went out**. 2 K 9:21. **the Lord had**. 1 K 19:16. 2 K 9:1-7.

8. **when Jehu**. 2 K 10:10-14.

9. **he sought Ahaziah**. The account in the parallel passage is somewhat different. "The current of the story at large is this," says Dr. Lightfoot (*Works*, vol. i. p. 88): "Jehu slayeth Joram in the field of Jezreel, as Ahaziah and Joram were together: Ahaziah seeing this, flies, and gets into Samaria, and hides himself there. Jehu marcheth to Jezreel, and makes Jezebel dog's meat: from thence sends to Samaria for the heads of Ahab's children and posterity; which are brought him by night, and showed to the people in the morning. Then he marcheth to Samaria, and, by the way, slayeth forty-two of Ahab's kinsmen, and findeth Jehonadab, the father of the Rechabites. Coming into Samaria, he maketh search for Ahaziah: they find him hid, bring him to Jehu, and he commands to carry him towards *Gur*, by *Ibleam*, and there to slay him. They do so: smite him in his chariot, and his charioteer driveth away to *Megiddo* before he dies." "2 K 9:27, at Megiddo, in the kingdom of Samaria." **in Samaria**. 1 K 13:32. **Because**. 1 K 14:13. 2 K 9:28, 34. **the son of Jehoshaphat**. 2 Ch 17:3, 4. 21:20. **the house**. ver. 1, 8. 2 Ch 21:4, 17.

10. **Athaliah**. ver. 2-4. 2 K 11:1.

11. **Jehoshabeath**. i.e. *Jehovah's oath*. *S#3090h. 2 K 11:2, Jehosheba. **bedchamber**. Ezk 40:45, 46. **Jehoiada**. 2 Ch 23:1. **she slew him not**. 2 Ch 21:7. 2 S 7:13. 1 K 15:4. Ps 33:10. 76:10. Pr 21:30. Is 65:8. Ac 4:28.

12. A.M. 3120-3126. B.C. 884-878. **hid in the house**. Ps 27:5. **Athaliah**. Ps 12:8. 73:14, 18, 19. Je 12:1. Hab 1:12.

2 CHRONICLES 23

Jehoiada takes proper measures, and makes Joash king, 1-11. Athaliah is slain, 12-15. Jehoiada subverts idolatry; restores the worship of God, and places Joash on the throne, to the great joy of the people, 16-21.

1. **seventh year**. 2 K 11:4, etc. **Elishaphat**. i.e. *God of judgment; God of defense*, *S#478h. **covenant with him**. 2 Ch 15:12. 1 S 18:3. Ne 9:38.

2. **went about**. Ps 112:5. Mt 10:16. Ep 5:15. **the chief of**. Houbigant omits the words *of Israel*. Bp. Patrick, however, is of opinion that Judah is here called by the general name of *Israel*: but it is probable, that these "chief of the fathers of Israel," were the descendants of those priests and Levites, and other pious persons of the ten tribes, who left their cities and

possessions, and joined themselves to Judah, in the days of Jeroboam. See the parallel passages. 2 Ch 11:13-17. 1 Ch 15:12. 24:6.

3. **made a covenant.** ver. 16. 2 S 5:3. 2 K 11:17. 1 Ch 11:3. **as the Lord.** 2 Ch 6:16. 7:18. 21:7. 2 S 7:12, 16. 1 K 2:4. 9:5. 1 Ch 9:9-27. Ps 89:29, 36.

4. **entering.** 1 Ch 23:3-6. 24:3-6. Lk 1:8, 9. **porters.** 1 Ch 26:13-16. **doors.** Heb. thresholds. 1 K +14:17. Is 6:4.

5. **the king's house.** 2 K 11:5, 6. Ezk 44:2, 3. 46:2, 3. **the gate.** Ac 3:2. **of the foundation.** 2 K 11:6n.

6. **they that minister.** 2 K 11:6, 7. 1 Ch 23:28-32.

7. **the Levites.** 2 K 11:8, 9. **whosoever.** Ex 19:12, 13. 21:14. Nu 3:10, 38.

8. **the Levites.** 2 K 11:9. **the courses.** 1 Ch ch. 24-26.

9. **spears.** 1 S 21:9. 2 S 8:7. **which were in the house.** When the soldier retired from the tumults of war to the bosom of his family, he frequently hung up his arms in the temple, as a grateful acknowledgment of the protection he had received, and of the victories he had won. It is highly probable, therefore, that the arms of David which Jehoiada delivered to the captains of hundreds, "which were in the house of God," were laid up in the tabernacle by David when he resigned the command of his armies to his generals; and there is reason to believe that his conduct, in this respect, was followed by many of his companions in arms.

10. **side of the temple.** Heb. shoulder of the house. Ex 27:14, 15. 38:14, 15. 1 K 6:8mg. 2 K 11:11. Ezk 25:9mg. **along by.** 2 Ch 6:12. Ex 40:6.

11. **they brought.** 2 Ch 22:11. 2 K 11:12. **put upon.** 2 S 1:10. Ps 21:3. 89:39. 132:18. He 2:9. Ja 1:12. 2:5. Re 4:4, 10. 5:10. 19:12. **gave him.** ƒ180A, Ge +4:20. **the testimony.** Ex 25:16. 31:18. Dt 17:18-20. Ps 2:10-12. 78:5. Is 8:16, 20. 49:23. **anointed him.** 1 S 10:1. 2 S 5:3. 1 K 1:39. Ps 89:20. Ac 4:26, 27. **God save the king.** Heb. Let the king live. 1 S 10:24. 2 S 16:16. 1 K 1:34. Mt 21:9.

12. **Now when.** 2 K 11:13-16. **she came.** 2 K 9:32-37.

13. **she looked.** Ps 14:5. **the king.** 2 Ch 34:31. 2 K 23:3. **his pillar.** 2 K 11:14n. **and the princes.** Nu 10:1-10. 1 Ch 15:24. **all the people.** 1 K 1:39, 40. 1 Ch 12:40. Pr 11:10. 29:2. **sounded.** Jg 7:8, 18-22. 2 K 9:13. **the singers.** 1 Ch 15:16-22, 27. 25:1-8. **instruments of music.** 1 Ch 16:42n. **taught to sing.** 1 Ch 6:32. *15:22. 25:7. Ep *5:19. Col *3:16. **Then Athaliah.** Ec 9:12. **Treason.** Heb. Conspiracy. 1 K 16:20. 18:17, 18. 2 K 9:23. 11:14. Ro 2:1, 2.

14. **captains.** 2 K 11:15. **Have her forth.** The Vulgate has here, and in the parallel place, *Educite illam extra septa templi,* "Take her out beyond the precincts of the temple." These were walls erected in parallel lines, and forming an extensive range of buildings around the sacred edifice. Ex 21:14. **whoso followeth her.** He who takes her part let him be instantly slain. 2 K 10:25. 11:8, 15. **Slay her not in.** Ezk 9:7.

15. **the horse gate.** This gate was in the *eastern* wall of the city, towards the brook Kidron (Je 31:40), at which the king's horses probably went out from the stables at Millo. It was near the temple; and some Rabbins suppose that, in order to go to the temple, a person might go on horseback to this place, but was then obliged to alight. Ne 3:28. **they slew her there.**

2 Ch 22:10. Jg 1:7. Ps 5:6. 55:23. Mt 7:2. Ja 2:13. Re 16:5-7.

16. **made a covenant.** 2 Ch 15:12, 14. 29:10. 34:31, 32. Dt 5:2, 3. 29:1-15. 2 K 11:17. Ezr 10:3. Ne 5:12, 13. 9:38. 10:29, etc. **that they should.** Dt 26:17-19. Jsh 24:21-25. Is 44:5.

17. **the house of Baal.** 2 Ch 34:4, 7. 2 K 10:25-28. 11:18. 18:4. **brake his altars.** Dt 12:3. Is 2:18. Zc 13:2, 3. **slew Mattan.** Dt 13:5, 9. 1 K 18:40. 2 K 11:18, 19.

18. **whom David.** 1 Ch ch. 23, 24. **as it is written.** Nu ch. 28. **by David.** Heb. by the hands of David. ƒ144A5, Ge +9:5. 2 Ch 29:25mg. √34:14mg,n. 1 K +16:12mg. 1 Ch 25:2mg, etc.

19. **porters.** 1 Ch 9:23, 24. ch. 26. **that none.** Is 52:1. Re 21:27. **unclean.** 2 C=6:16-18. Zc 14:21.

20. **the captains.** 2 K 11:9, 10, 19.

21. **all the people.** 2 K 11:20. Ps 58:10, 11. Pr 11:10. Re 18:20. 19:1-4.

2 CHRONICLES 24

Joash reigns well during Jehoiada's life, and zealously repairs the temple, 1-14. Jehoiada dies, and is honorably buried, 15, 16. Joash, seduced by his princes, turns aside to idolatry; and causes Zechariah, Jehoiada's son, to be stoned, for reproving him in the name of God, 17-21. Zechariah's dying prediction, 22. Joash is plundered by the Syrians, left sick, and then slain by his own servants, 23-26. Amaziah succeeds him, 27.

1. A.M. 3126-3165. B.C. 878-839. **Joash.** "Joash" is merely an abbreviation of "Jehoash," by the elision of *hay* and here also of *wav.* 2 K 11:21. 12:1, Jehoash. 1 Ch 3:11. **seven years old.** As Joash was hidden *six* years in the temple, and was but *seven* when he came to the throne, he could have been but *one year* old when secreted by his aunt.

2. A.M. 3126-3162. B.C. 878-842. **Joash.** 2 Ch 25:2. 26:4, 5. 2 K 12:2. Ps 78:36, 37. 106:12, 13. Mk 4:16, 17. **all the days of Jehoiada.** ver. 17-22. Is 29:13.

3. **took for him.** Not *for himself,* as the Jewish expositors suppose, but for *Joash;* for Jehoiada's advanced age renders it highly improbable that he should take them for himself. He was born in the reign of Solomon, and lived through six successive reigns; and must, on any computation, have been upwards of 100 years old when Joash began to reign. See ver. 15. Ge 21:21. 24:4. **two wives.** Ge +4:19. Mt 19:4-8.

4. A.M. 3148. B.C. 856. **repair.** Heb. renew. ver. 5-7, 12. Is 61:4.

5. **gather of all Israel.** 2 Ch 29:3. 34:8, 9. 2 K 12:4, 5. 1 C=16:1, 2. 2 C=8:19, 20, 23, 24. =9:7. **Howbeit.** 2 K 12:6, 7.

6. **Why hast thou.** 2 S 24:3. **the collection.** This was the poll tax fixed by Moses, of half a shekel, which was levied on every man of twenty years old and upwards, as "a ransom for their souls, that there might be no plague among them." Ex 30:12-16. **tabernacle.** Nu 1:50. 17:7, 8. 18:2. Ac 7:44.

7. **the sons of Athaliah.** As Jehoram's sons, Ahaziah excepted, whether by Athaliah or any other, were all slain before his death (2 Ch 22:1), this spoliation of the temple must have taken place in his lifetime. 2 Ch 21:17. **that wicked.** 2 Ch 28:22-24. Est 7:6. Pr *10:7. 2 Th *2:8. Re 2:20. **the dedicated.** 2 K 12:4.

did they bestow. Dt 32:15-17. Ezk 16:17-21. Da 5:2-4, 23. Ho 2:8, 9, 13.

8. **at the king's.** 2 K 12:8, 9. Mk 12:41.

9. **proclamation.** Heb. voice. Ezr 1:1. **collection.** ver. 6. Mt 17:24-27.

10. **rejoiced.** 1 Ch 29:9. Is .64:5. Ac 2:45-47. 2 C 8:2. 9:7.

11. **at what time.** 2 K 12:10-12. **the king's scribe.** 2 K 12:10. It was necessary to associate with the high priest some *civil authority* and activity, in order to get the neglected work performed. **Thus they did.** 1 C 16:2.

12. **gave it to such.** 2 Ch 34:9-11. **masons.** 1 K 5:15.

13. **the work was perfected by them.** Heb. the healing went up upon the work by their hand. Ne 4:7. Je +*8:22. **they set,** etc. That is, "they restored it to its former proper state." **in his state.** Ex +5:8. 1 Ch 22:5. Ezk 45:11h. Hg 2:3. Mk 13:1, 2.

14. **vessels of the house.** 2 K 12:13, 14. **vessels to minister.** 1 K 7:50. **to offer withal.** or, pestils. Le 16:12. Pr 27:22. **And they offered.** It appears from this, that the daily morning and evening sacrifices had been previously intermitted; and that they were again neglected after the death of Jehoiada. Ex 29:38-42. Nu 28:2, etc. **all the days.** ver. 2.

15. A.M. 3162. B.C. 842. **and was full of days.** *Wyyisba yammim,* "satiated with days;" which seems to be a metaphor taken from a guest regaled by a plentiful banquet, used to express the termination of life without reluctance. Ge *15:15. +*25:8n. 1 Ch 23:1. Jb 5:26. Ps *91:16mg. **an hundred and thirty.** Ge 47:9. Ps *90:10.

16. **in the city.** 1 S *2:30. 1 K 2:10. Ac 2:29. **because.** 2 Ch ch. 23. *31:20. Ne *13:14. He *6:10.

17. A.M. 3162-3165. B.C. 842-839. **Now after.** Dt 31:27. Ac 20:29, 30. 2 P *1:15. **the princes of Judah.** 2 Ch *10:8-10. 22:3, 4. Pr 7:21-23. *20:19. *26:8, 28. *29:5. Da *11:32. **Then the king.** Pr *29:12.

18. **And they left.** ver. 4. 2 Ch 21:13. *33:3-7. 1 K 11:4, 5. 14:9, *23. **wrath.** 2 Ch *19:2. *28:13. 29:8. 30:8. 32:25. *36:14-16. Jsh *22:20. Jg 5:8. 2 S *24:1. Ho 5:10, 11, 14. Zp *1:4-6. Ep *5:6.

19. **Yet he sent.** 2 Ch *36:15, 16. 2 K *17:13-15. Ne *9:26. Je *7:25, 26. *25:4, 5. 26:5. 44:4, 5. Lk *11:47-51. *16:31. *20:9-15. **but they would.** Ps 95:7, 8. Is 28:23. 42:23. 51:4. *55:3. Mt *13:9, 15, 16.

20. **And the Spirit.** Heb. *ruach,* Ge +41:38. 2 Ch 15:1. 20:14. **came upon.** Heb. clothed. Jg 6:34. 1 Ch 12:18. **the son.** 2 Ch 23:11. **transgress.** Nu 14:41. 1 S 13:13, 14. 2 S 12:9, 10. Zc 7:11-14. **cannot prosper.** 2 Ch 13:12. ◐*20:20. ◐26:3. Ge 24:21. Nu 14:41. Dt 28:29. Pr 28:13. Is *54:17. Je 2:37. 22:30. 32:5. Ezk 17:9. Da 11:27. **because.** 2 Ch 15:2. Dt 29:25, 26. 31:17. 1 Ch +*28:9. Je 2:19. 4:18. 5:19, 25.

21. **conspired.** Je 11:19. 18:18. 38:4-6. **stoned him.** Mt 21:35. 23:34-37. Ac 7:58, 59.

22. **remembered not.** Ps 109:4. Lk 17:15-18. Jn 10:32. **but slew his son.** Pr 17:13. **he said.** Lk ◐23:34. Ac ◐7:60. 2 T ◐4:16. **The Lord.** These words were *prophetic,* and not *imprecatory;* and should be rendered, as Houbigant proposes, in the *future* tense: "The Lord *will* look upon it, and avenge it." The event soon verified this prediction; for before the year was expired, the Syrians came up against Jerusalem, and destroyed all the princes of the people, and Joash himself was slain in his bed by his own servants. Many

circumstances served to aggravate this barbarous act. Zechariah was a high priest and a prophet, upright and unblameable in the discharge of his high offices; this murder was perpetrated within the very precincts of the courts of the Lord; and this truly good man was by blood the nearest relative of Joash, and the son of the man who had saved him from being murdered, and raised him to the throne! Ge 9:5. Je 11:20. 26:14, 15. Lk √11:51. 2 T 4:14, 16. Re *6:9-11. 18:20. 19:2. **and require it.** Ps 10:14. Je 51:56.

23. A.M. 3165. B.C. 839. **at the end,** etc. Heb. in the revolution of the year. 2 Ch 36:10mg. Ex 34:22mg. 1 S +1:20mg. 2 S 11:1mg. 1 K 20:22, 26. Ps 19:6. **the host.** Dt 32:35. 2 K 12:17, 18. **princes.** ver. 17, 18. Ps 2:10, 11. 58:10, 11. 82:6, 7. **Damascus.** Heb. Darmesek. 1 Ch 18:5mg.

24. **came.** Le 26:8, 37. Dt 32:30. Is 30:17. Je 37:10. **delivered.** 2 Ch 16:8, 9. 20:11, 12. Le 26:25. Dt 28:25, 48. **So.** 2 Ch 22:8. Is 10:5, 6. 13:5. Hab 1:12.

25. **great diseases.** 2 Ch 21:16, 18, 19. 22:6. **his own servants.** 2 K 12:20. 14:19, 20. **for the blood.** ver. 21, 22. Ps 10:14. Re 16:6. **the sons of Jehoiada.** √171E13, Ge +46:7. Houbigant reads, "the *son* of Jehoiada;" but perhaps Joash slew some other sons of Jehoiada. **not.** ver. 16. 2 Ch 21:20. 28:27. **sepulchres.** Heb. *qeber,* Ge +23:4.

26. **Zabad.** or, Jozachar. 2 K 12:21. **Shimrith.** i.e. *female guard; a guardian,* *S#8116h. or, Shomer. 2 K 12:21.

27. **burdens.** 2 K 12:18. **repairing.** Heb. founding. ver. 13. 2 Ch 23:5. **story.** or, commentary. 2 Ch 9:29. 13:22mg. 16:11. 20:34. **Amaziah.** 2 Ch 25:1. 2 K 12:21. 1 Ch 3:12.

2 CHRONICLES 25

Amaziah at first reigns well, and justly punishes his father's murderers, 1-4. He gathers a great army, and hires, for a hundred talents, a hundred thousand Israelites against Edom: but, having paid the money, he dismisses them at the word of a prophet; and they depart in great anger, 5-10. He smites the Edomites, and exercises great cruelty towards the captives, 11, 12. The Israelites, on their return, spoil the cities of Judah, 13. Amaziah serves the gods of Edom, and rejects the admonitions of a prophet, 14-16. He challenges Joash, who in vain warns him; he is vanquished, and Jerusalem spoiled, 17-24. The rest of his reign, 25, 26. He is slain by a conspiracy, 27, 28.

1. **twenty and five.** 2 K 14:1-3.

2. **but not.** ver. 14. 2 Ch 24:2. 26:4. 1 S *16:7. 2 K 14:4. Ps 78:37. Is *29:13. Ho 10:2. Ac *8:21. Ja 1:8. 4:8.

3. A.M. 3166. B.C. 838. **Now it came.** 2 K 14:5, etc. **established to him.** Heb. confirmed upon him. 2 K 14:5. 15:19. **he slew.** 2 Ch 24:25, 26. Ge *9:5, 6. Ex 21:14. Nu 35:31-33. No doubt those wicked men, Jozachar and Jehozabad, who murdered his father, had considerable power and influence; and therefore he found it dangerous to bring them to justice, till he was assured of the loyalty of his other officers: when this was clear, he called them to an account, and justly put them to death for treason and murder; for, if even these conspirators against Joash intended to avenge upon him the death of Zechariah, they acted without

commission from that God "to whom vengeance belongeth."

4. **as it is written.** 2 Ch 34:14n. Dt 24:16. 2 K 14:5, +6n. Je 31:29, 30. Ezk 18:4, 20. **of Moses.** Ex +*24:4.

5. A.M. 3177. B.C. 827. **captains over thousands.** Ex +*18:25. 1 S 8:12. 1 Ch 13:1. 27:1. **numbered.** 1 S +11:8. **from twenty.** Nu 1:3. **three.** 2 Ch 11:1. 14:8. 17:14-18.

6. **mighty men of valor.** 2 Ch 13:3. 17:13. Jg +6:12. **an hundred talents of silver.** Estimating the shekel at 2s. 6d., and the talent, being about 3000 shekels (see Ex 38:25, 26), at 375l., one hundred talents would amount to 37,500l.; which, divided among 100,000 men, quotes only 7s.6d.; hence we may suppose, that this was only an earnest of their pay, or that they expected to be enriched by the plunder of the Edomites.

7. **a man of God.** 2 S 12:1. 1 K 13:1. 1 T 6:11. 2 T 3:17. **for the Lord.** 2 Ch 13:12. 19:2. 1 K 12:28. Is 28:1-3. Ho 5:13-15. 9:13.

8. **be strong.** 2 Ch 18:14. Ec 11:9. Is 8:9, 10. Jl 3:9-14. Mt 26:45. **God hath power.** 2 Ch 14:11. 20:6. Jg 7:7. 1 S 14:6. Jb 5:18. 9:13. Ps 20:7. 33:16-20. 62:11. Ec 9:11. **cast down.** 2 Ch 28:23.

9. **army.** Heb. band. ver. 10, 13. 2 K 6:23. **The Lord.** 2 Ch 1:12. Ge 45:20. Dt *8:18. Ps 24:1. Pr *10:22. Hg *2:8. Lk *18:29, 30. Ep √3:20. Ph 3:8. √4:19.

10. **Amaziah.** 1 K 12:24. **home.** Heb. to their place. 1 S 2:20. **great anger.** 2 Ch 28:11, 13. 29:10. 30:8. Ex 11:8. 2 S 19:43. Pr 29:22.

11. **valley of salt.** 2 S 8:13. 2 K 14:7. Ps 60, title. **children of Seir.** ver. 14. 2 Ch 20:10.

12. **And other ten thousand.** No intimation is given on what account, or on what provocation, this most cruel conduct towards the prisoners of war was adopted. The enmity between Israel and Edom seems to have been reciprocal and deeply malignant. The victorious king and his army considered every individual of Edom as a traitor and rebel; and so adjudged them to death, and acted on this judgment. But their conduct was wholly inexcusable, and could only perpetuate rancor to future generations, and provoke the surviving Edomites to cruel retaliations, whenever they had it in their power. **the rock.** Heb. "Selah," as in 2 K 14:7n. The same with Petra (Young). **cast them.** 2 S 12:31. 1 Ch 20:3. **broken in pieces.** 2 Ch 20:10. 21:8-10. Ge 7:11.

13. **soldiers of the army.** Heb. sons of the band. ver. 9. **fell upon the cities.** These Israelites seem to have returned *home,* when discharged by Amaziah, whose powerful army deterred them from attempting revenge at that time; but when he was engaged in war with the Edomites, they marched from Samaria, and plundered all the cities till they came to Beth-horon, where they slew 3000 of the inhabitants. **Samaria.** 1 K 16:24, 29. **Beth-horon.** 2 Ch 8:5. Jsh +10:10. 1 K 9:17.

14. **he brought.** 2 Ch 28:23. Is 44:19. **his gods.** Ex *20:3-5. Dt 7:5, 25. 2 S 5:21.

15. **a prophet.** ver. 7. 2 Ch 16:7-9. 19:2. 20:37. 2 S 12:1-6. **Why hast thou sought.** 2 Ch 24:20. Jg 2:2. Je 2:5. **the gods.** 2 Ch 13:9. 32:19. Ps 96:5. **which could not.** ver. 11, 12. Ps 115:4-8. Is 44:9, 10. 46:1, 2. Je 10:7. 1 C *8:4. 10:20.

16. **Art thou made.** 2 Ch 16:10. 18:25. 24:21. Am 7:10-13. Mt *21:23. **forbear.** 2 Ch 35:21. Ex 14:12.

1 S +*25:17. Pr 9:7, 8. Is 30:10, 11. Je 29:26. 2 T *4:2, 3. Re 11:10. **why.** √85L, Ge +27:45. **determined.** Heb. counselled. 2 Ch 18:20, 21. Ex *9:16. Dt +*2:30 (T#267). 1 S 2:25. Is *19:17. 46:10. Ac 4:28. Ro *9:22. Ep 1:11. **hast not hearkened.** Dt ◑*28:1, 2, 15. 1 S +*25:17. Ps 81:11. *107:11. *119:24mg. Pr 1:25, 26, 30. Lk *7:30.

17. A.M. 3178. B.C. 826. **Amaziah.** ver. 13. 2 K 14:8-14. **let us see.** 2 S 2:14. Pr 20:3. **in the face.** ver. 21n. Ge 42:1. 2 K 14:8, 11.

18. **thistle.** *or,* furze-bush, *or* thorn. 2 Ch 33:11. Jg 9:8-15. 1 S 13:6. 1 K 4:33. 2 K ||14:9n. Jb 31:40. 41:2. Pr 26:9. SS 2:2. Is 34:13. Ho 9:6. **a wild beast.** Heb. a beast of the field. Le 26:22. 2 S 2:18. 2 K 4:39. Jb 39:15. Ps 80:13. Ho 13:8.

19. **heart.** 2 Ch 26:16. 32:25. Dt 8:14. Pr 13:10. 16:18. 28:25. Da 5:20-23. Hab 2:4. Ja 4:6. 1 P 5:5. **to boast.** Je 9:23. 1 C 1:29. **why shouldest.** 2 Ch 35:21. Pr 18:6. 20:3. 26:17. Lk 14:31.

20. **it came of God.** ver. 16. 2 Ch 22:7. 1 K 12:15. Ps 81:11, 12. Ac 28:25-27. 2 Th *2:9-11. 1 P 2:8. **sought after.** ver. 14, 15.

21. **they saw one another.** That is, "they fought against each other." To face an enemy, or to face one another, is still a common expression. The reason of this war was evidently the injury the army of Joash had done to the unoffending inhabitants of Judah. The ravages committed by them were totally unprovoked, base, and cowardly: they fell upon women, old men, and children, and butchered them in cold blood, when all the effective men were gone with their king against the Edomites. The quarrel of Amaziah was certainly *just,* yet he was put to the rout: he fell, and Judah with him, as Joash had said; and the reason was, because "it came of God, that he might deliver them into the hands *of their enemies,* because they sought after the gods of Edom." This was the reason why the Israelites triumphed. ver. 17. **Beth-shemesh.** Jsh 21:16. 1 S 6:9, 19, 20. Je +43:13.

22. **put to the worse.** Heb. smitten. 2 Ch 28:5, 6. **fled.** 1 S 4:10. 1 K 22:36.

23. **took Amaziah.** 2 Ch 33:11. 36:6, 10. Pr 16:18. 29:23. Da 4:37. Ob 3. Lk 14:11. **Jehoahaz.** 2 Ch 21:17. 22:1, Ahaziah. 22:6, Azariah. **gate of Ephraim.** Ne 8:16. 12:39. **corner gate.** Heb. the gate of it that looketh. 2 Ch 26:9. 2 K 14:13. Je 31:38.

24. **all the gold.** 2 Ch 12:9. 2 K 14:14. **the hostages also.** It is probable that these *hostages* were given in order that Amaziah might regain his liberty.

25. A.M. 3179-3194. B.C. 825-810. **Joash.** 2 K 14:17, etc., Jehoash.

26. **rest of the acts.** 2 Ch 20:34. 2 K 14:15.

27. A.M. 3194. B.C. 810. **after the time.** 2 Ch 15:2. **from following.** Heb. from after. 2 Ch 34:33. Ex 7:2. **made.** Heb. conspired a conspiracy. 2 Ch 24:25. 2 K 12:20. 14:+11, 19. 15:15, 30. **Lachish.** Jsh 10:+3, 31.

28. **the city of Judah.** that is, *the city of David, as it is,* 2 K 14:20.

2 CHRONICLES 26

Uzziah succeeds Amaziah, reigns well for a time, and is greatly prospered, 1-8. His buildings, husbandry, army, and engines of war, 9-15. Being lifted up in pride he attempts to burn incense in the temple, is opposed by the priests, and smitten with leprosy by

God, 16-21. He dies, and is succeeded by Jotham, 22, 23.

1. all the. 2 Ch 22:1. 33:25. **Uzziah.** i.e. *power of Jehovah; strength of God; my strength is Jehovah.* 2 K 14:21. 15:1, etc. 1 Ch 3:12, Azariah. Mt 1:8, 9, Ozias. *S#5818h: 2 Ch 26:1, 3, 8, 9, 11, 14, 18, 18, 19, 21, 22, 23. 27:2. 2 K 15:32, 34. 1 Ch 27:25. Is 1:1. 6:1. 7:1. Also 2 K 15:13, 20. 1 Ch 6:24. Ezr 10:21. Ne 11:4. Ho 1:1. Am 1:1. Zc 14:5. (1) King of Judah, from 811-759 B.C. 2 K 15:13, 30, 32, 34; Is 1:1; 6:1; 7:1; Ho 1:1; Am 1:1. Called Azariah, 2 K 14:21; 15:1, 6, 8, 23, 27. (2) Father of Jehonathan, set over the treasures by David, 1 Ch 27:25. (3) A son of Merari, 1 Ch 6:24. (4) One of those who took strange wives, Ezr 10:21. (5) Father of Athaiah, who dwelt in Jerusalem, Ne 11:4.

2. Eloth. 2 Ch 8:17. 2 K 14:22. 16:6, Elath. **restored.** 2 Ch 25:23, 28.

3. A.M. 3194-3246. B.C. 810-758. **Uzziah.** Is 1:1. 6:1. Ho 1:1. Am 1:1. Zc 14:5. **Jecoliah.** i.e. *able through Jehovah; made strong of the Lord; the prevailing of Jah,* *S#3203h. 2 Ch 26:3. Also 2 K 15:2.

4. he did. 2 T +*3:15. **in the sight.** Ac +*10:31. **according to all.** 2 Ch 25:2. **his father.** 2 Ch 17:3. 1 K 9:4. Ep +*6:4.

5. as long. Notice the explicit cause/effect relationship stated to exist between seeking God (the cause), and prosperity, the effect (Ps +√9:10). **he sought the Lord.** 2 Ch 24:2. Jg 2:7. Ho 6:4. Mk 4:16, 17. Ac 20:30. **had.** Ge 41:15, 38. Da 1:17. 2:19. 5:16. 10:1. **visions.** Heb. seeing. √142, Ge +20:16. **and as long.** 2 Ch 15:2. 25:8. 1 Ch 22:11, 13. **prosper.** Dt +*28:12, ◖44, ◖+*48n. 2 Ch *20:20. *24:20. Ps √1:3.

6. warred against. 2 Ch 21:16. Is 14:29. **the wall of Gath.** 2 S 8:1. 1 Ch 18:1. **Jabneh.** i.e. *God lets build; he will cause to build,* *S#2996h. Jabneh, or Jamnia, according to Josephus (Ant. l. v. c. 1), was given to the tribe of Dan; and was situated between Lydda and Azotus. It is now called *Yebna,* which Dr. Wittman describes as "a village about twelve miles distant from Jaffa (Joppa), in a fine open plain, surrounded by hills, and covered with herbage. Northeast of Yebna is a lofty hill, from which is an extensive and pleasing view of Ramnia, distant about five miles. On sloping hills of easy ascent, by which the plains were bordered, Yebna, Ekron, Ashdod, and Askalon were in sight." **about.** *or, in the country of.* 1 S 5:1, 6.

7. God helped. 2 Ch 14:11. 1 Ch 5:20. 12:18. Ps 18:29, 34, 35. Is 14:29. Ac 26:22. **the Arabians.** 2 Ch 17:11. 21:16. **Gur-baal.** i.e. *sojourn of Baal or the possessor,* *S#1485h. **Mehunims.** i.e. *dwellings, habitations,* *S#4586h. 2 Ch 26:7. Also Ezr 2:50. Ne 7:52. Compare *S#4584h, Maon, Maonites, Jsh +15:55; Jg +10:12.

8. the Ammonites. 2 Ch 20:1. Ge 19:38. Dt 2:19. Jg 11:15-18. 1 S 11:1. 2 S 8:2. **his name.** Ge 12:2. 2 S 8:13. 1 K 4:31. Mt 4:24. **spread.** Heb. went. ver. 15. Ne 14:6mg.

9. the corner gate. 2 Ch 25:23mg. 2 K 14:13. Je 31:38. Zc 14:10. **the valley gate.** Ne 2:13. 3:13, 19, 32. Je 31:40. **the turning.** Ne 3:20, 24. **fortified.** *or,* repaired.

10. digged many wells. *or,* cut out many cisterns. Heb. *bor,* Ge +37:20. Ge ◖21:30. 26:◖15, 18-21, ◖32. Ne 9:25. **he had much cattle.** 2 K 3:4. 1 Ch 27:26-

31. husbandmen. Jl 1:11. **Carmel.** *or,* fruitful fields. 2 K 19:23. Is 29:17. **husbandry.** Heb. ground. Ge 4:2. That is, he was given to agricultural pursuits.

11. went out. 2 K 5:2.

13. an army. Heb. the power of an army. **three hundred.** 2 Ch 11:1. 13:3. 14:8. 17:14-19.

14. slings to cast stones. Heb. stones of slings. Jg 20:16. 1 S 17:49. 2 K +3:25mg. Zc 9:15mg.

15. cunning men. 2 Ch 2:7, 14. Ex 31:4. **to shoot arrows.** These engines, it is probable, bore some resemblance to the *balistae* and *catapultae* of the Romans, which were employed for throwing stones and arrows, and were in reality the mortars and carcasses of antiquity. With respect to the towers which Uzziah built in the wilderness (ver. 10), Mr. Harmer appears to have given a truer view of the subject than commentators in general have done, who suppose that they were conveniences made only for sheltering the shepherds from bad weather, or to defend them from incursions of enemies; for they might rather be designed to keep the nations that pastured there in awe, and also to induce them quietly to pay the tribute to which the 8th verse seems to refer. William of Tyre describes a country not far from the Euphrates as inhabited by Syrian and Armenian Christians, who fed great flocks and herds there, but were kept in subjection to the Turks, in consequence of their living among them in strong places. **spread far.** Heb. went forth. Mt 4:24. **strong.** Dt 32:15. Jsh 17:13. 1 C *10:12.

16. when he was. 2 Ch 25:19. 32:25. Dt 8:14, 17. 33:13-15. Pr 16:18. Hab 2:4. Mk +4:19. 1 C *10:12. Col 2:18. **went into.** 2 K 16:12, 13. **to burn incense.** Nu 16:1, 7, 18, 35. 1 K 12:33. 13:1-4. **the altar of incense.** Ex 40:5.

17. Azariah. 1 Ch 6:10. **valiant men.** 2 Ch 28:6mg. 2 S +2:7mg. 1 Ch 12:28. 26:6.

18. withstood Uzziah. 2 Ch 16:7-9. 19:2. Je 13:18. Mt 10:18, 28. 14:4. 2 C 5:16. Ga *2:11. **not unto thee.** Nu *16:40, 46-48. 18:6, 7. **incense.** 2 Ch 13:10, 11. Ex +30:1. Jn=9:31. **but to the priests.** Ex 30:7, 8. Dt 33:10. 1 Ch 6:49. 9:30. 1 C +*14:40. He 5:4. **go out.** 1 C 5:5. **thou hast trespassed.** 1 Ch *15:13. **neither shall it be.** 1 S 2:30. Da 4:37. Jn *5:44. Ja 2:1.

19. while he was wroth. 2 Ch 16:10. 25:16. **the leprosy.** Nu 12:10. 2 K 5:27.

20. hasted also. Est 6:12. **the Lord.** Le 14:34. 28:22, 35.

21. A.M. 3239-3246. B.C. 765-758. **Uzziah.** 2 K 15:5. **dwelt.** Le *13:46. Nu 5:2, 3. 12:15. 2 K 7:3. **several.** Heb. free. 2 K 15:5. *or,* separate. Lk 17:12. **22. first.** 2 Ch 9:29. 12:15. 1 Ch 29:29. **Isaiah.** Is 1:1. 6:1.

23. A.M. 3246. B.C. 758. **slept with.** 2 Ch +*28:27n. 1 K +*11:43. +14:20. 2 K 15:6, *7. *24:6n. **they buried him.** ver. 18. 2 Ch 21:20. 28:27. 33:20. **the burial.** Heb. *qeburah,* Ge +35:20 (*S#6900h).

2 CHRONICLES 27

Jotham reigns well and prospers, 1, 2. His buildings, 3, 4. He subdues the Ammonites, 5, 6. He dies, and is succeeded by Ahaz, 7-9.

1. A.M. 3246-3262. B.C. 758-742. **twenty and five.** 2 K 15:32, 33, etc. 1 Ch 3:12. Is 1:1. Ho 1:1. Mi 1:1. Mt 1:9, Joatham. **Jerushah.** i.e. *possessed; possession,* *S#3388h.

2. **And he did**. 2 Ch 26:4. 2 K 15:34. **he entered not**. He copied his father's conduct as far as it was pious and constitutional; and avoided his transgression. 2 Ch 26:16-21. Ps 119:120. Ac 5:13. **the people**. 2 K 15:35.

3. **high gate**. 2 Ch 23:20. Je 20:2. **Ophel**. i.e. *a height; mound; hill; swelling; tumor; darkness,* *S#6077h. or, the tower. "The wall," says the Targum, "of the interior palace." *Ophel* appears to have been a tower, or fort, on the city wall, in which we read "the Nethinim dwelt." 2 Ch 33:14. 2 K +5:24mg. Ne 3:26, 27. 11:21. Young states Ophel is a hill on the east of Zion.

4. **he built cities**. 2 Ch 11:5-10. 14:7. 26:9, 10. **the mountains**. Jsh 14:12, 13. Lk 1:39. **castles and towers**. These castles and towers he doubtless built for the protection of the country people against marauders. lit. "great places." Ge 11:4, 5. 35:21. 1 Ch +*27:25 (*S#4026h).

5. **the king of the Ammonites**. We find here, that he brought the Ammonites under a heavy tribute for three years; but whether this was the effect of his prevailing against them, is not so evident. Some think that they paid this tribute for three years and then revolted; that, in consequence, he attacked them, and their utter subjection was the result. 2 Ch 20:1. Jg 11:4, etc. 2 S 10:1-14. Je 49:1-6. **ten thousand**. Rather, "ten thousand *cors (korim)* of wheat." The *cor* was the same as the *homer*, and contained about 32 pecks 1 pint. 1 K +4:22mg. **So much**. Heb. This.

6. **Jotham**. 2 Ch 26:5. **prepared**. *or*, established. 2 Ch 12:14mg. 19:3. 1 K 15:14. 1 Ch 17:11.

7. **Now the rest**. 2 Ch 20:34. 26:22, 23. 32:32, 33. A.M. 3262. B.C. 742. **they are written**. There is not so much found in the book of Kings, which we have now, as here: in both places we have abridged accounts; the larger histories having been lost.

8. **He was**. ver. 1. 2 K 15:33.

9. **Jotham**. 2 K 15:38.

2 CHRONICLES 28

Ahaz reigns very wickedly, 1-4. He is defeated with terrible slaughter of his army by the kings of Syria and Israel, 5-7. The Israelites lead to Samaria an immense number of captives, 8. The people are induced, by the remonstrance of a prophet, and the interference of the princes, to treat them kindly and send them home, 9-15. Ahaz, attacked by the Edomites and the Philistines, sends to the king of Assyria, but receives no benefit from his assistance, 16-21. In his distress he adds to his idolatries, 22-25. He dies, and is succeeded by Hezekiah, 26, 27.

1. A.M. 3262-3278. B.C. 742-726. **Ahaz**. 2 K 16:1, 2, etc. 1 Ch 3:13. Is 1:1. 7:1-12. Ho 1:1. Mi 1:1. Mt 1:9. **like David his father**. 2 Ch 17:3.

2. **For he walked**. 2 Ch 21:6. 22:3, 4. 1 K 16:31-33. 2 K 10:26-28. **molten images**. Ex 34:17. Le 19:4. **Baalim**. Jg 2:11-13. Ho 2:13, 17.

3. **burnt incense**. *or*, offered sacrifice. ver. 4, 25. 2 Ch 29:11. 2 K 16:13, 15. **the valley**. 2 K 23:10. Je 7:31, 32. 19:2-6, 13. **son of Hinnom**. Jsh +*15:8n. **burnt**. 2 Ch 33:6. Le *18:21. 2 K 16:3. Ps 106:37, 38. Je 2:34. 32:35. Ezk 16:20, 21. Mi 6:7. **after the abominations**. 2 Ch 33:2. Dt 12:31.

4. **He sacrificed**. Le 26:30. Dt 12:2, 3. 2 K 16:4.

high places. 2 K +21:3. **the hills**. 2 K 16:4n. +17:10. **green tree**. 2 K 16:4n. +17:10.

5. **his God**. 2 Ch 36:5. Ex *20:2, 3. **delivered him**. 2 Ch 24:24. 33:11. 36:17. Jg 2:14. 2 K 16:5, 6. Is 7:1, 6. **Damascus**. Heb. Darmesek. ver. 23. 1 Ch 18:5.

6. **Pekah**. 2 K 15:27, 37. Is 7:4, 5, 9. 9:21. **an hundred and twenty thousand**. 2 Ch 13:17. **valiant men**. Heb. sons of valor. 2 Ch 26:17. 2 S +2:7mg. **because**. 2 Ch 15:2. Dt 6:14, 15. 28:15, 25. 29:24-26. 31:16, 17. 32:30. Jsh 23:16. 24:20. Is 1:28. 24:5, 6. Je 2:19. 15:6.

7. **next to the king**. Heb. the second to the king. Ge 41:43. 43:12, 15. Est 10:3.

8. **carried**. Dt 28:25, 41. **brethren**. 2 Ch 11:4. Ac 7:26. 13:26.

9. **he went out**. 2 Ch 19:1, 2. 25:15, 16. 1 K 20:13, 22, 42. 2 K 20:14, 15. **Behold**. To this beautiful speech nothing can be added by the best comment: it is simple, humane, pious, and overwhelmingly convincing; and it is no wonder that it produced the effect here described. That there was much humanity, as well as firmness, in the heads of the children of Ephraim, who joined with the prophet of Jehovah on this occasion, their subsequent conduct, as detailed in the fifteenth verse, sufficiently proves. They did not barely dismiss these most unfortunate captives, but they took that very spoil which their victorious army had taken, and with it clothed, shod, fed, and anointed these distressed people, set the feeblest of them upon asses, and escorted them safely to Jericho! We can scarcely find a parallel to this in the universal history of wars which savage man has carried on against his fellows from the foundation of the world. The compliance also of the whole army, in leaving both the captives and spoil to the disposal of the princes, was really wonderful, and perhaps unparalleled in history. Both the princes and the army are worthy to be held up to the admiration and imitation of mankind. **because the Lord God**. ver. 5. Jg 3:8. Ps 69:26. Is 10:5-7. 47:6. Je 15:17, 18. Ezk 25:12-17. 26:2, 3. Ob 10-16. Zc 1:15. **reacheth**. ♪102, Ge +2:24. Ge 4:10. 11:4. Ezr 9:6. Re 18:5.

10. **keep under**. Le 25:39-46. or, subdue. Ge 1:28. Ne 5:5. Est 7:8. Je 34:11, 16. Mi 7:19. Zc 9:15. **not with**. Je 25:29. Mt 7:2-4. Ro 12:20, 21. 1 P 4:17, 18. **sins against**. 2 Ch 24:18. 33:23. Le 4:3. 6:5, 7. 22:16. 1 Ch 21:3. Ezr 9:6. Pr *20:9. Ec *7:20. **the Lord**. ver. 5.

11. **deliver**. Is 58:6. Je 34:14, 15. He 13:1-3. **the fierce wrath**. Ex 32:12. Nu 25:4. 32:14. Dt 13:17. Ezr 10:14. Mt 5:7. 7:2. Ja *2:13.

12. **the heads**. 1 Ch 28:1. **Azariah**. i.e. *help of Jah.* 1 Ch +6:36. **Johanan**. i.e. *Jah has grace.* 2 K +25:23. **Berechiah**. i.e. *blessed of Jah.* Zc +1:7. **Meshillemoth**. i.e. *recompenses; reconciliation; those who repay,* *S#4919h. 2 Ch 28:12. Ne 11:13. **Jehizkiah**. i.e. *strengthened by Jah,* ✛S#3169h. **Shallum**. i.e. *recompensed.* 2 K +15:10. **Amasa**. i.e. *a load.* 2 S +17:25. **Hadlai**. i.e. *ceasing; worldly; forsaken of the Lord; my forbearings,* *S#2311h. **stood up**. Je 26:6.

13. **offended**. ♪24L, Ge +6:2. **add more**. Nu 32:14. Jsh 22:17, 18. Mt 23:32, 35. Ro 2:5.

14. **the armed men**. 2 Ch 20:21. 1 Ch 12:23.

15. **expressed by name**. ver. 12. **clothed**. Jb 31:15-23. Is 58:7. Mt *25:35-45. Ac 9:39. 1 T 5:10. Ja 2:15, 16. 1 J *3:17, 18. **gave them**. 2 K 6:22. Pr 25:21, 22.

Lk √6:27. 8:27, 35. Ro *12:20, 21. **carried**. Ro 15:1. **the city**. Dt 34:3. Jg 1:16.

16. **did king**. 2 K 16:5-7. Is 7:1-9, 17. **the kings**. Instead of *malchey*, "kings," the Chaldee, Syriac, Arabic, and Vulgate, one MS. and the parallel place, have *mailech*, "king."

17. **the Edomites**. 2 Ch 25:11, 12. Le 26:18. Ob 10, 13, 14. **captives**. Heb. a captivity. ver. 11, 13, 14, 15. Is 49:25mg. Am +1:6mg.

18. **Philistines**. Ezk 16:27, 57. **Beth-shemesh**. Jsh 15:10. 1 S 6:9, 13. **Ajalon**. 2 Ch 11:10, Aijalon. **Gederoth**. Jsh 15:41. **Shocho**. i.e. *to entwine; hedge, fence; branch,* *S#7755h. 2 Ch 11:7. 28:18. Jsh 15:35, 48, Socoh. 1 S 17:1, 1. 1 K 4:10. 1 Ch 4:18. **Timnah**. Jg 14:1, Timnath. **Gimzo**. i.e. *producing sycamores,* *S#1579h. **villages**. Nu +21:25mg.

19. **the Lord**. Dt 28:43. 1 S 2:7. Jb 40:12. Ps 106:41-43. Pr 29:23. **because of Ahaz**. Ho 5:11. Mi 6:16. **Israel**. 2 Ch 21:2. **made Judah**. Ge 3:7, 11. Ex 32:25. Re 3:17, 18. 16:5.

20. A.M. 3264. B.C. 740. **Tilgath-pilneser**. 2 K 15:29. 16:7-10, Tiglath-pileser. 1 Ch 5:26. Ho 5:13. **distressed him**. 2 K 17:5. Is 7:20. 30:3, 16. Je 2:37.

21. **took away**. 2 Ch 12:9. 2 K 18:15, 16. Pr 20:25.

22. **in the**. 2 Ch 33:12. Ps 50:15. Is 1:5. Ezk 21:13. Ho 5:15. Re 16:9-11. **this is**. Est 7:6. Ps 52:7.

23. **For he sacrificed**. This passage, says Mr. Hallet, greatly surprised me; for the sacred historian himself is here represented as saying, "The gods of Damascus had smitten Ahaz." But it is impossible to suppose that an inspired author should say this; for the Scripture everywhere represents the heathen idols as *nothing* and *vanity*, and as incapable of doing either good or hurt. All difficulty is avoided if we follow the old Hebrew copies from which the Greek translation was made: "And king Ahaz said, I will seek to the gods of Damascus which have smitten me." 2 Ch 25:14. 2 K 16:12, 13. **Damascus**. Heb. Darmesek. ver. 5mg. **Because the gods**. Hab 1:1. **sacrifice to them**. Je 10:5. 44:15-18. **But they were**. Is 1:28. Je 44:20-28. Ho 13:9.

24. **cut in pieces**. 2 K 16:17, 18. 25:13, etc. **shut up**. 2 Ch 29:3, 7. **he made**. 2 Ch 33:3-5. Je 2:28. Ho 12:11. Ac 17:16, 23.

25. **burn**. *or*, offer. ver. 3mg.

26. **the rest**. 2 Ch 20:34. 27:7-9. 2 K 16:19, 20.

27. A.M. 3278. B.C. 726. **slept with**. 2 Ch 26:23. Ge +*25:8n. Dt 31:16n. 1 K +*11:43. 2 K *24:6n. **they brought**. 2 Ch 21:30. 24:25. 26:23. 33:20. 1 S 2:30. Pr 10:7. **sepulchres**. Heb. *qeber*, Ge +23:4. **the kings of Israel**. Or, "the kings of *Judah*;" the name *Israel* being sometimes applied, by the writer of this book, in a general way, to *Judah*. The Hebrews were accustomed to honor the memory of those kings who had reigned well, by depositing their remains in the royal cemetery. On the contrary, those who died under the disapprobation of the people, as a mark of posthumous disgrace, were denied interment with their predecessors, and were buried in some other place in Jerusalem. So it was with Ahaz, who, though brought into the city, was not buried in the sepulchres of the kings of Judah. It was doubtless with a design to make a suitable impression on the minds of their kings while living, that such distinctions were observed. They might thus restrain them from evil, or excite them to good, according as they were fearful of being execrated, or desirous of being honored, when dead.

2 CHRONICLES 29

Hezekiah reigns well, opens the doors of the temple, and exhorts the priests and Levites to prepare everything for the worship of God, 1-11. They sanctify themselves, and cleanse the temple and its vessels, 12-19. Hezekiah offers solemn sacrifices; and the Levites show more zeal than the priests, 20-36.

1. A.M. 3278-3306. B.C. 726-698. **Hezekiah**. i.e. *strength of the Lord*. 2 K +16:20. 18:1-3. 1 Ch 3:13. Is 1:1. Ho 1:1. Mi 1:1. Mt 1:9, 10, Ezekias. **Abijah**. i.e. *desire of the Lord; my father is Jah*. 1 K +14:1. **Zechariah**. i.e. *remembered of the Lord*. 2 Ch 26:5. Is 8:2. Zc +1:1.

2. **he did**. 2 Ch 28:1. 34:2. 2 K 18:3. Of several of Hezekiah's predecessors it had been said that they did that which was right, **but not like David**, that is, not with David's integrity and zeal.

3. A.M. 3278. B.C. 726. **He in the first**. 2 Ch 34:3. Ps 101:3. Ec 9:10. Mt *6:33. Ga 1:16. **opened**. ver. 7. 2 Ch ●28:24. 2 K 16:14-18.

4. **east street**. 2 Ch 32:6. Ne 3:29. Je 19:2.

5. **sanctify now**. 2 Ch 35:6. Ex 19:10, 15. 1 Ch 15:12. **sanctify the house**. ver. 16. 2 Ch 34:3-8. Ezk 36:25. Mt 21:12, 13. 1 C *3:16, 17. 2 C *6:16. *7:1. Ep *5:26, 27. **carry forth**. Ezk 8:3, 9, etc.

6. **For our fathers**. 2 Ch 28:2-4, 23-25. 34:21. Ezr 5:12. 9:7. Ne 9:16, 32. Je 16:19. 44:21. La 5:7. Da 9:8, 16. Mt *10:37. 23:30-32. **have forsaken him**. Je 2:13, 17. **turned away**. Je 2:27. Ezk 8:16. **turned their backs**. Heb. given the neck. Ex 23:27mg. Ps 18:40.

7. **they have shut**. ver. 3. 2 Ch 28:24. Le 24:2-8. 2 K 16:17, 18. Ml 1:10. Those, says Matthew Henry, who turn their backs upon God's ordinances, may truly be said to forsake God himself. The lamps were not lighted, and incense was not burnt: there are still such neglects as these, and they are no less culpable, if the Word be not duly read and opened, answering to the lighting of the lamps—and if prayers and praises be not duly offered up, which was signified by the burning of incense. Ps *119:105. Re 8:4. **nor offered**. Ne *13:10. Pr +*11:24. Is 43:23, 24. Ml 3:8. Ac 5:1, 2.

8. **Wherefore**. ver. 10. 2 Ch +*24:18. 34:24, 25. 36:14-16. Le 10:6. Nu 1:53. 16:46. 18:5. Dt 28:15-20. Jsh 7:1. 22:18, 20. 1 S 6:19. 2 S 24:1. 1 Ch 27:24. Ps 106:29. **he hath delivered**. It is probable Hezekiah refers to that dreadful defeat by the Israelites, in which one hundred and twenty thousand were slain, and two hundred thousand taken prisoners: see 2 Ch 28:6-8. **trouble**. Heb. commotion. Dt 28:25. Is 28:19. Je 15:4. 24:9. 29:18, 19. 34:17. **to astonishment**. Le 26:32. Dt 28:37, 59. 1 K 9:8. 2 K 22:19. Je 18:15, 16. 19:8. 25:9, 18. 29:18. 51:37. **hissing**. 1 K 9:8. Je 19:8. 25:9, 18. 29:18. 51:37. Mi 6:16.

9. **our fathers**. 2 Ch 28:5-8, 17. Le 26:17. La 5:7.

10. **Now it is**. 2 Ch 6:7, 8. **to make a covenant**. To renew that covenant under which the whole people were constantly considered, and of which circumcision was the sign, and the *spirit* of which was, "I will be your God—ye shall be my people." 2 Ch 15:12, 13. 23:16. 34:30-32. Ezr 10:3. Ne 9:38. 10:1, etc. Je 34:15, 18. 50:5. 2 C 8:5. **that his fierce**. ver. 8. 2 Ch 19:2, 10. +24:18. 2 K 23:3, 26. Ex 32:12. Nu 25:4.

11. **negligent**. *or*, deceived. 2 K 4:28. Ga *6:7, 8. **the Lord**. Nu 3:6-9. 8:6-14. 18:2-6. Dt 10:8. **chosen**.

Ep=1:4. **burn incense.** *or*, offer sacrifice. 2 Ch 28:3mg. Nu 16:35-40. 18:7.

12. **Mahath.** i.e. *taking hold; snatching; seizing, taking away*, *S#4287h. 2 Ch 29:12. 31:13. 1 Ch 6:35. (1) One of the Levites who sanctified themselves under Hezekiah, 2 Ch 29:12. (2) A Kohathite, son of Zuph, 1 Ch 6:35. (3) One set over the tithes by Hezekiah, 2 Ch 31:13. **Amasai.** i.e. *burdensome; my load; my burdens; burden of the Lord*, *S#6022h. 2 Ch 29:12. 1 Ch 6:25, 35. 12:18. 15:24. (1) Son of Elkanah, the Kohathite, 1 Ch 6:25. (2) One of the priests who went up with the ark, 1 Ch 15:24. (3) A captain in David's army, 1 Ch 12:18. (4) Father of Mahath, 2 Ch 29:12. **Joel.** i.e. *Jah is God.* 1 S +8:2. **Azariah.** i.e. *strength of Jah.* 1 Ch +6:36. **Kohathites.** Ex 6:16-25. Nu 4:2, etc. 1 Ch 6:16-18. 15:5. 23:12-20. **of the sons.** 1 Ch 6:19, 44. 15:6. 23:21-23. **Merari.** Ge +46:11. Nu 3:17, 20, 33, 35, 36. **Kish.** i.e. *snaring; bird-catching.* 1 S +9:1. **Abdi.** i.e. *my servant.* 1 Ch +6:44. **Jehalelel.** i.e. *he praises God; he will praise God*, *S#3094h. 2 Ch 29:12. 1 Ch 4:+16, Jehaleleel. (1) Father of Ziph, Ziphah, Tiria, and Asareel, 1 Ch 4:16. (2) Father of Azariah, who sanctified himself with king Hezekiah, 2 Ch 29:12. **of the Gershonites.** Nu 3:21, 23, 24. 1 Ch 6:17, 20, 21. 15:7. 23:7-11. **Joah.** i.e. *Jah is brother.* Is +36:3. **Zimmah.** i.e. *bad counsel; device; wickedness; wicked device; lewdness*, *S#2155h. 2 Ch 29:12. 1 Ch 6:20, 42. (1) A son of Jahath, 1 Ch 6:20. (2) A Gershonite, 1 Chr 6:42. (3) A Levite, under Hezekiah, whose son sanctified himself, 2 Ch 29:12. **Eden.** i.e. *delight.* Ge +2:8.

13. **Elizaphan.** Le 10:4, Elzaphan. Nu +3:30. 1 Ch 15:8. **Asaph.** 2 K +18:18. 1 Ch 6:39. 15:17. 25:2.

14. **Heman.** 1 Ch 6:33. 15:19. **Jeduthun.** 1 Ch 25:1, 3, 6.

15. **sanctified themselves.** ver. 5. **by the words of the Lord.** *or*, in the business of the Lord. ver. 30. 2 Ch 30:12. **to cleanse.** 1 Ch 23:28.

16. **the priests.** The priests and Levites cleansed first the courts both of the *priests* and of the *people.* On this labor they spent eight days. Then they cleansed the *interior* of the temple; but, as the Levites had no right to enter the temple, the priests carried all the dirt and rubbish to the *porch*, whence they were collected by the Levites, carried away, and cast into the brook Kidron: in this work, eight days more were occupied; and thus the temple was purified in sixteen days. **the inner part.** 2 Ch 3:8. 5:7. Ex 26:33, 34. 1 K 6:19, 20. He 9:2-8, 23, 24. **to cleanse.** 2 C=6:16-18. **all the uncleanness.** Ezk 36:29. Mt 21:12, 13. 23:27. **Kidron.** 2 Ch 15:16. 2 K 23:4-6. Jn 18:1, Cedron.

17. **the porch.** ver. 7. 2 Ch 3:4. 1 K 6:3. 1 Ch 28:11. **the sixteenth.** Ex 12:2-8.

18. **the altar.** 2 Ch 4:1, 7. **the showbread.** 2 Ch 4:8. 13:11.

19. **all the vessels.** 2 Ch *28:24. **did cast away.** Or, as the LXX., Vulgate, and Targum read, "did pollute," *hizneeach*, he rendered them so abominable that they were *rejected* with abhorrence.

20. **rose.** Ge 22:3. Ex 24:4. Jsh 6:12. Je 25:4.

21. **they brought.** The law only required *one bullock* for the sins of the *high priest*, another for the sins of the *people*, and *one he-goat* for the sins of the *prince*: but Hezekiah offered many more, and the reason appears sufficiently evident: the law only speaks of *sins of ignorance*, but here there were sins of every dye—

idolatry, apostasy from the Divine worship, profanation of the temple, etc. etc. The sin offerings, we are informed, were offered, *first*, for the kingdom—for the transgressions of the *king* and his family; *secondly*, for the sanctuary—which had been defiled and polluted; and for the *priests*, who had been profane, negligent, and unholy; and *finally*, for Judah—for the whole mass of the people, who had been led away into every kind of abomination by the above examples. **seven.** Nu 23:1, 14, 29. 1 Ch 15:26. Ezr 8:35. Jb 42:8. Ezk 45:23. **a sin offering.** Le 4:3-14. Nu 15:22-24. 2 C *5:21.

22. **sprinkled.** Le 1:5. 4:7, 18, 34. 8:14, 15, 19, 24. He *9:21, 22.

23. **forth.** Heb. near. ver. 31. **they laid.** Le 1:4. 4:15, 24.

24. **reconciliation.** Le 6:30. 8:15. Ezk 45:15, 17. Da 9:24. Ro 5:10, 11. 2 C *5:18-21. Col *1:20, 21. He 2:17. **to make.** Le 14:20. **the sin offering.** Le 4:13, etc.

25. **And he set.** 1 Ch 9:33. 15:16-22. 16:4, 5, 42. 25:1-7. **cymbals.** 1 Ch +13:8. **psalteries.** 1 S +10:5. **harps.** 1 Ch +13:8n. **according.** 2 Ch 8:14. 35:15. 1 Ch 23:5. 28:12, 19. **Gad.** 2 S 24:11. 1 Ch 21:9. 29:29. **Nathan.** 2 S 7:2-4. 12:1-7. **for so was.** 2 Ch 30:12. **of the Lord by his prophets.** Heb. by the hand of the Lord, by the hand of his prophets. 2 Ch 23:18mg. √34:14mg,n. 1 K +16:12mg.

26. **the instruments.** 1 Ch 23:5. Ps 87:7. 150:3-5. Is 38:20. Am 6:5. **the priests.** 2 Ch 5:12, 13. Nu 10:8, 10. Jsh 6:4-9. 1 Ch 15:24. 16:6. Ps 81:3. 98:5, 6. 150:3.

27. **when.** Heb. in the time. **the song of.** 2 Ch 7:3. 20:21. 23:18. 1 Ch 25:7. Ps 136:1. 137:3, 4. **the instruments.** Heb. hands of instruments. √144A5, Ge +9:5. 2 Ch 23:18mg.

28. **And all the congregation.** Ps 68:24-26. Re 5:8-14. **worshipped.** or, did obeisance. Ge 37:9. 2 K 19:37. Ne *9:3, 6. Est 3:2, 5. Is 37:38. Ezk 8:16. Zp 1:5. **the singers sang.** Heb. song. Ps 89:15.

29. **present.** Heb. found. 2 Ch 5:11. 30:21. 31:1. 34:32, 33. 35:7, 17, 18. Ge 19:15mg. Jg +20:48mg. Est +*1:5mg. **bowed themselves.** 2 Ch 20:18. 1 Ch 29:20. Ps 72:11. Ro 14:11. Ph 2:10, 11.

30. **with the words.** 2 S 23:1, 2. 1 Ch 16:7-36. **they sang.** Ps 32:11. 33:1. 95:1, 2, 6. 100:1, 2. 149:2. Ph 4:4. **with gladness.** 2 Ch 30:21. Ac 2:46, 47.

31. **consecrated yourselves.** *or*, filled your hand. 2 Ch 13:9mg. Ex 28:41mg. 29:9mg. 32:29mg. Le 8:33. 16:32mg. 21:10. Ezk 43:26mg. **sacrifices.** Le ch. 1, 3. **thank.** Le 7:12. **and as many**, etc. As the burnt offerings were wholly consumed on the altar, the offering of them evinced greater zeal and liberality than the oblation of peace offerings, the greater part of which was eaten by the offerer and his friends. Le 1:3. 23:38. Ezr 1:4.

32. **the number.** Comparing the sacrifices offered on this occasion with those of Solomon at the dedication of the temple, we may form some idea of the decrease of prosperity and riches of Judah, or of the decline of the general spirit of piety. 1 K 3:4. 8:63. 1 Ch 29:21. Ezr 6:17.

33. **the consecrated things.** It is probable that *the consecrated things* denote the peace offerings and thank offerings. ver. 31.

34. **the priests.** Peace offerings, and such like, the Levites might flay and dress; but the whole burnt offer-

ings could be touched only by the priests, except in a case of necessity, such as the present. ver. 5. 2 Ch 30:16, 17. **their brethren**. 2 Ch 35:11. Nu 8:15, 19. 18:3, 6, 7. **did help them**. Heb. strengthened them. Jb 8:20mg. Ro=16:3. **for the Levites**. 2 Ch *30:3. **upright**. 1 Ch 29:17. Ps 7:10. 26:6. 94:15. 1 C=5:8. Ph=1:10.

35. **the burnt offerings**. ver. 32. Le +*23:12. **the fat**. Ex 29:13. Le 3:15, 16. **peace offerings**. Le +*23:19. **the drink offerings**. Ge 35:14. Le +*23:13. Nu 15:5-10. **So the**. 1 Ch 16:37-42. Ezr 6:18. 1 C +*14:40.

36. **Hezekiah rejoiced**. Both Hezekiah and the people rejoiced, that God had prepared the hearts of the people to bring about so great and glorious a reformation in so short a time. This good king's example and influence were here, as in many other cases, under God, the grand spring of all those mighty movements. 1 Ch 29:9, 17. Ezr 6:22. 1 Th 3:8, 9. **and all**. Mt 3:5. **God**. 2 Ch 30:12. 1 Ch 29:18. Ps 10:17. Pr 16:1. Lk 1:17. **the thing**. Ac 2:41.

2 CHRONICLES 30

Hezekiah proclaims a solemn passover to be kept in the second month, and calls on both Judah and Israel to unite in celebrating it, 1-5. His message to the Israelites, and the reception with which it met, 6-12. A great multitude, having destroyed the altars for idolatry in Jerusalem, prepare to keep the feast, 13-16. Hezekiah prays for those who are not ceremonially clean, and is graciously answered, 17-20. They keep the feast fourteen days with great joy, 21-26. The priests bless the people, 27.

1. **Israel**. 2 Ch 11:13, 16. **Ephraim**. ver. 10, 11. 2 Ch 25:7. 35:6. Ho 5:4. 7:8, 9. 11:8. **to the house**. Dt 16:2-6. **to keep**. Ex 12:3-20. Le +*23:5. 1 C 5:7, 8.

2. **the king**. 1 Ch 13:1-3. Pr 11:14. 15:22. Ec 4:13. **in the second month**. In *Ijar*, as they could not celebrate it in *Nisan*, the fourteenth of which month was the proper time. But Hezekiah and his counselors justly concluded, that the regulation of the 14th day of the second month, which had been made for individuals who were hindered from eating the passover at the appointed season, might in their present circumstances, be extended to the people at large. Nu 9:10, 11.

3. **at that time**. Ex 12:6, 18. **because**. 2 Ch 29:34.

4. **pleased the king**. Heb. was right in the eyes of the king. Jsh +22:30mg. Ge 16:6mg. Jg +14:3mg. 2 S 17:4mg. 1 K 21:2mg. 1 Ch 13:4. Zc 11:12mg.

5. **established**. Ezr 6:8-12. Est 3:12-15. 8:8-10. 9:20, 21. Da 6:8. **to make proclamation**. 2 Ch 24:9. 36:22. Le +*23:2, 4. Da 4:1, etc. **from Beer-sheba**. Jg 20:1. 2 S 3:10. **for they**. 2 Ch 35:18. Dt 12:32. 1 C 11:2.

6. **the posts went**. *Ratzim*, "runners," or *couriers*, of the same kind as running footmen, who were formerly, before the establishment of posts, and still are in some places, trained, and kept on purpose to convey dispatches speedily by running. 1 S 22:17mg. Jb 9:25. Est 3:13, 15. 8:10, 14. Je 51:31. **the king**. Heb. the hand of the king. 2 Ch 31:13mg. **turn again**. Is *55:6, 7. Je 4:1. La 5:21. Ezk 33:11. Ho 14:1. Jl 2:12-14. Ja *4:8. **and he will**. Is 6:13. **escaped**. 2 Ch 28:20. 1 K 15:19, 29. 1 Ch 5:26. Is 1:9.

7. **like**. Ezk 20:13-18. Zc 1:3, 4. **as**. 2 Ch 29:8.

8. **be ye not stiffnecked**. Heb. harden not your necks. 2 Ch 36:13. Ex 32:9. 33:3, 5. 34:9. Dt 9:6, 13. 10:16. 31:27. 2 K 17:14. Ne 9:16, 17, 29. Je 7:26. 17:23. 19:15. Ro 10:21. **yield yourselves**. Heb. give the hand. ♪121S3I, 1 Ch +29:24. 1 Ch +29:24mg. Ge +24:2. Ezr 10:19. Ps 68:31. Ro *6:13-19. **enter into**. Ps 63:2. 68:24. 73:17. **which he hath**. Ps 132:13, 14. **for ever**. Heb. *olam*, Ex +*12:24. **serve**. Dt 6:13, 17. Jsh *24:15. Mt +*4:10. Jn 12:26. Ro 6:22. Col 3:22-24. Re 7:15. **the fierceness**. 2 Ch +24:18. 28:11, 13. 29:10. 2 K 23:26. Ps 78:49.

9. **if**. Ge +4:7. **ye turn**. 2 Ch +√7:14. Le 26:40-42. Dt 30:2-4. 1 K 8:50. Ps 106:46. **so that they shall**. Je 29:12-14. 31:27, 28. **the Lord**. Ex 34:6, 7. Ne 9:17, 31. Ps 86:5, 15. 111:4. 145:7, 8. Jon 4:2. Mi *7:18. **will not**. 2 Ch 15:2. Pr *28:13. Is *55:7. Ezk 18:30-32. **turn away**. Je 18:17.

10. **the posts**. ver. +6. Est 3:13, 15. 8:10, 14. Jb 9:25. **they laughed**. 2 Ch *36:16. Ge 19:14. Ne 2:19. Jb 12:4. Pr ◐+*1:26. Lk 8:53. 16:14. 22:63, 64. 23:35. Ac 17:32. He 11:36.

11. **divers of Asher**. It has been said, that Hezekiah had no right to invite Hoshea's subjects to repair to Jerusalem to his passover; but it may be presumed, that he was encouraged to do this by Hoshea himself, who was one of their best kings; besides which, both the golden calves having been taken away by the Assyrians, the apostate Israelites, being thus deprived of their idols, had begun to return to the Lord, and to go up to Jerusalem to worship, some time before Hezekiah gave them this invitation. ver. 18, 21. 2 Ch 11:16. Ac 17:34. **humbled themselves**. 2 Ch 12:6, 7, 12. 33:12, 19, 23. 34:27. Ex 10:3. Le 26:41. Da 5:22. Lk 14:11. 18:14. Ja *4:10. 1 P *5:6.

12. **the hand of God**. 2 Ch 29:36. 1 Ch 29:18, 19. Ezr 7:27. Ps 110:3. Je 24:7. 32:39. Ezk 36:26. Ph *2:13. 2 Th *2:13, 14. **the commandment**. Dt 4:2, 5, 6. 1 Th 4:2. **by the word**. 2 Ch 29:25. Ac 4:19.

13. **there assembled**. Ps 84:7. **feast of unleavened**. Le +*23:6. **the second month**. See on ver. 2.

14. **altars**. 2 Ch 28:24. 34:4, 7. 2 K 18:22. 23:12, 13. Is 2:18-20. **the brook**. 2 Ch 15:16. 29:16. 2 S 15:23. Jn 18:1, Cedron.

15. **passover**. Le +*23:5. **were ashamed**. 2 Ch 29:34. Ezk 16:61-63. 43:10, 11. **and sanctified**. ver. 24. 2 Ch 5:11. 29:15, 34. 31:18. Ex 19:10, 22.

16. **they stood**. 2 Ch 35:10, 15. **place**. Heb. standing. 2 Ch 34:31. 35:10, 15. 1 K 10:5. Ne 8:7. 9:3. 13:11. **after their manner**. 2 K 11:14. **Moses**. See on Dt 33:1. **the priests**. 2 Ch 35:10, 11. Le 1:5. He 11:28.

17. **the Levites**. 2 Ch 29:34. 35:3-6. **the killing**. Ex 12:6. **passovers**. ♪121P8, Ex +12:21.

18. **many of Ephraim**. See on ver. 11. **had not cleansed**. Nu *9:10, etc. 19:20. 1 C 11:28. **the passover**. Ex 12:43, etc. **prayed**. Ce 20:7, 17. Jb 42:8, 9. Ja *5:15, 16. 1 J *5:16. **The good**. 2 Ch 6:21. Ex 34:6-9. Nu 14:18-20. Ps 25:8. 36:5. 86:5. 119:68. Da 9:19.

19. **prepareth**. 2 Ch 19:3. 20:33. 1 S 7:3. 1 Ch 29:18. Ezr 7:10. Jb 11:13. Ps 10:17. Pr 23:26. **though he be not**. Le 12:4. 15:31-33. 21:17-23. 22:3-6. Nu 9:6. 19:13-20.

20. **healed**. Ex *15:26. Ps +*103:3. Ja *5:15, 16.

21. **present**. Heb. found. 2 Ch +29:29mg. Jg +20:48mg. **the feast**. Ex 12:15. 13:6. Le 23:6. Ru 1:22. Lk 15:23. 22:1, 7. 1 C 5:7, 8. **great gladness**. ver. 26. 2 Ch 7:10. 29:30. Dt 12:7, 12. 16:14. Ne 8:10. Ac

2:46, 47. Ph 4:4. **the priests**. See on 2 Ch 20:21. 29:25-27. **day by day**. Ac 2:46, 47. **loud instruments**. Heb. instruments of strength. 1 Ch 16:42n. Ps 68:33. 150:3-5.

22. **comfortably unto all**. Heb. to the heart of all. 2 Ch 32:6mg. Ge +34:3mg. Is 40:1, 2mg. Ho 2:14mg. **taught**. 2 Ch *15:3. √17:9. 35:3. Le 10:11. Dt 33:10. Ezr *7:10, 25. Ne *8:7, 8, 18. 9:3. Hg 2:11. Ml *2:7. Ga=6:6. 2 T *2:2. *4:2. **the good knowledge**. Pr 2:6, 7. 8:6. Je *23:28. Jn √17:3. 2 C=2:14. 4:6. Ph 3:8. **feast**. Ge +17:21. Le *23:2n. **peace offerings**. Le +*23:19. **and making**. Dt 26:3-11. Ezr 10:11. Ne 9:3. **confession**. 1 J √1:9.

23. **took counsel**. See on ver. 2. **to keep**. They did not observe other seven days of unleavened bread, but offered sacrifices with praise and thanksgiving, and feasting, other seven days; and, as the people in general, and especially those who came out of the kingdom of Israel, would be unprepared for this additional expense, both Hezekiah and his princes liberally supplied them with cattle for their sacrifices. 2 Ch 7:9. 1 K 8:65. **they kept**. 2 Ch 35:18. Ne 8:17.

24. **did give**. Heb. lifted up, or, offered. 2 Ch 35:7, 8. 1 Ch 29:3-9. Ezk 45:17. Ep 4:8. **a great**. 2 Ch 29:34.

25. **the strangers**. See on ver. 11, 18. Ge +*23:4 (*S#1616h). Ex *12:43-47, +*48mg, 49. Dt +26:11. **rejoiced**. 1 Ch 16:10, 11. Ps 92:4. 104:34.

26. **since the time**. 2 Ch 7:9, 10.

27. **the priests**. See on Nu √6:23-26. Dt 10:8. **their prayer**. See on 1 K 8:30, 39. Ac *10:4. 1 J *5:14, 15. **his holy dwelling place**. Heb. the habitation of his holiness. Dt +26:15. Ps 68:5. Is +*57:15. 63:15. 66:1. Je 25:30. Zc 2:13mg.

2 CHRONICLES 31

The people destroy the idols, and their temples and altars, through the cities of Judah and in Ephraim and Manasseh, 1. Hezekiah orders the courses of the priests and Levites, and provides for their maintenance, as well as for the stated sacrifices, 2-4. The people readily bring their firstfruits and tithes, 5-10. Hezekiah appoints officers to dispose of these oblations, 11-19. A high commendation of his zeal and integrity, 20, 21.

1. **Now when**. 2 Ch ch. 30. **all Israel**. 1 K 18:38-40. 2 K 23:2-20. **present**. Heb. found. 2 Ch +29:29mg. Ge 19:15. Jg +20:48mg. Est 4:16. **brake**. 2 Ch 14:3. 23:17. 32:12. 34:3-7. Ex 23:24. Dt 7:5. 2 K 18:4. **images**. Heb. statues. 2 Ch 30:14. 2 K +17:10. **groves**. 2 K +17:10. 21:3n. 23:6. **high places**. 2 K +21:3. **in Ephraim**. 2 Ch 30:1, 18. 34:6, 7. 2 K 17:2. 18:4. 23:15. **until**, etc. Heb. until to make an end. **possession**. Ge 17:8. 23:4.

2. **the courses**. 2 Ch 5:11. 8:14. 23:8. 1 Ch 16:37, 40. ch. 23-26. Ezr 6:18. Lk 1:5. **to give thanks**. 2 Ch 29:24-26. 1 Ch 16:4-6, 41. 23:30. 25:1-3. Ne 11:17. Ps 134:1-3. 135:1-3, 26. Je 33:11. **burnt offerings**. Le +*23:12. **peace offerings**. Le +*23:19. **in the gates of the tents of the Lord**. *Behaarey machanoth Yehowah,* "within the gates of the camps of Jehovah;" which comprehended the whole of the buildings that surrounded the temple in which the priests and Levites were stationed, and which resembled military encampments.

3. **the king's**. 2 Ch 30:24. 1 Ch 26:26. Ezk 45:17. 46:4-7, 12-18. **for the morning**. See on Ex 29:38-42. Nu 28:3-8. **the burnt**. See on Nu 28:9, 10. **for the new moons**. See on Nu 28:11-31. ch. 29. Dt 16:1-17. 2 K *4:23. 2 Ch +2:4. Ps 81:1-4. Col *2:16, 17. **the set feasts**. Ge +17:21. Le *23:2n.

4. **the portion**. ver. 16. Le 27:30-33. Nu 18:8-21, 26-28. Ml 3:8-10. **that they might**. 2 Ch 17:9. Ne 13:10-13. Ro 15:4. 1 C 9:9-14. Ga 6:6. **the law**. Ml *2:7.

5. **as soon**. 2 Ch 24:10, 11. Ex 22:29. 35:5, 20-29. 36:5, 6. 2 C 8:2-5. **came abroad**. Heb. brake forth. Ge 28:14mg. 1 Ch 4:38mg. 13:2mg. **the firstfruits**. Ex 22:29. 23:19. 34:22, 26. Nu 18:12. Ne 10:35-39. 12:44. 13:12, 31. Pr *3:9. 1 C=15:20. Ja *1:18. Re 14:4. **honey**. or, dates. The word *devash* generally denotes the *honey* produced by bees; but, as we have already observed (on Ge 43:11), the Jewish doctors are of opinion that it here signifies *dates*, or the fruit of the palm tree; which the Arabians call *daboos*, and the honey produced from them, *dibs*. "This liquor," says Dr. Shaw (*Travels*, p. 143), "which has a more luscious sweetness than honey, is of the consistence of a thin syrup, but quickly grows tart and ropy, acquiring an intoxicating quality, and giving by distillation an agreeable spirit, or *araky*, according to the general name of these people for all hot liquors extracted by the alembic." Though Jehovah forbad any *devash*, or honey, to be offered to him upon the altar, yet it appears it might be presented as firstfruits, or in the way of *tithes*, which were designed for the sustenance of the priests. **tithe of all**. Le 27:30. Ne 13:12. Mt 23:23. Lk 18:12.

6. **the children**. 2 Ch 11:16, 17. **the tithe**. Le 27:30. Dt 14:28. **by heaps**. Heb. heaps, heaps. Ex 8:14. 2 K 3:16. Ru 3:7. Ne 4:2. 13:15 (sheaves). SS 7:2. Je 50:26. Hg 2:16.

7. **the third month**. Le 23:16-24. That is, Sivan.

8. **blessed**. √162B. Syllepsis; or, Combination B296: Repetition of the sense without the repetition of the word. They blessed the Lord, that is they gave Him thanks and celebrated His praises; and they blessed His People Israel; but in a different way; they prayed for all spiritual and temporal blessings for them in the name of the Lord. Two meanings are thus given to the word, which is used only once. The sense is repeated, but not the word, and the sense is not the same in each case. For another instance of this figure see Jl 2:13. **the Lord**. Ge 14:20. Jg 5:9. 1 K 8:14, 15. 1 Ch 29:10-20. Ezr 7:27. 2 C 8:16. Ep 1:3. Ph 4:10, 19. 1 Th 3:9. 1 P *1:3. **and his people**. 2 Ch 6:3. Ge 14:19. 2 S 6:18. 1 K 8:55.

10. **Azariah**. 2 Ch 26:17. 1 K 2:35. 1 Ch 6:8, 14. Ezk 44:15. **Since**. Pr *3:9, 10. Hg 2:18, 19. Ml *3:10. 1 T +*4:8. **we have had**. 2 K 4:43, 44. Mt 15:37. Ph 4:18. **to eat**. √96B, Ge +8:5. **left plenty**. Ex +36:6. Le 7:10. Ml +3:10. Mt=14:20. Lk=15:17. Ph=4:18. **the Lord**. Ge 26:12. 30:27-30. 39:5, 23. Le 25:21. 26:4, 5. Dt 28:8. Pr 10:22. 2 C 9:8-11.

11. **chambers**. or, storehouses. 1 S 9:22. 2 K 23:11. 1 Ch 9:26, 33. 23:28. 28:12. Ezr 8:29. 10:6. Ne 10:37, 38, 39. 13:5, 12, 13.

12. **the offerings**. ver. 14. Ne 10:39. or, heave offering. Ex 29:27n. **the dedicated**. 2 K 12:15. **faithfully**. 2 K 12:15. 22:17. Lk *16:10. 1 C 4:2. 3 J 5. **over which**. 1 Ch 26:20-26. **Cononiah**. i.e. *prepared of Jah; established of Jehovah,* *S#3562h. 2 Ch 31:12, 13.

35:9. **Shimei.** i.e. *hearkening.* 2 S +16:5.

13. **Jehiel.** i.e. *God lives.* Ezr +8:9. **Azaziah.** i.e. *strength of Jah.* 1 Ch +27:20. **Nahath.** i.e. *quiescence, descent.* Ge +36:13. **Asahel.** i.e. *made of God.* 1 Ch +2:16. **Jerimoth.** i.e. *heights.* 1 Ch +7:7. **Jozabad.** i.e. *whom Jehovah bestows; Jah has endowed; the Lord gave,* *S#3107h. 2 Ch 31:13. 35:9. 1 Ch 12:4, 20, 20. Ezr 8:33. 10:22, 23. Ne 8:7. 11:16. (1) An inhabitant of Gederah who joined David in Ziklag, 1 Ch 12:4. (2) A warrior in David's army, a man of Manasseh who came to David in Ziklag, 1 Ch 12:20. (3) A Levite set over tithes who aided Hezekiah in reforms, 2 Ch 31:13. (4) A Levite chief in the time of Josiah, 2 Ch 35:9. (5) A Levite who weighed the gold and silver vessels in the Temple, Ezr 8:33. (6) A priest who took a foreign wife, Ezr 10:22. (7) A Levite who took a foreign wife, Ezr 10:23. (8) A chief Levite in exile who notably helped Ezra explain the law, Ne 8:7. (9) Another chief Levite in exile, Ne 11:16. Perhaps the same as Number 8. **Eliel.** i.e. *my God is God.* 1 Ch +8:20. **Ismachiah.** i.e. *whom Jehovah upholds; supported of Jah,* *S#3253h. **Mahath.** i.e. *laying hold of.* 2 Ch +29:12. **Benaiah.** i.e. *built up of Jah.* 1 Ch +15:24. **under,** etc. Heb. at the hand. ver. 15. 2 Ch 30:6mg. **at the commandment.** ver. 4, 11. See on 2 Ch 30:12. **Azariah.** See on ver. 10. 1 Ch 9:11. 24:5. Ne 11:11.

14. **the porter.** 1 Ch 26:12, 14, 17. **the freewill offerings.** Le 22:18. +*23:38. Nu 29:39. Dt 12:6, 17. 16:10. Ezr 1:4. 3:5. 7:16. Ps 119:108. **to distribute.** Ne 13:13. Lk=12:42. **the most.** Le 2:10. 6:16, 17. 7:1-6. 10:12, 13. 27:28.

15. **next him.** Heb. at his hand. ver. 13mg. 2 Ch +17:15mg. **Miniamin.** Instead of *Miniamin, Benjamin* is the reading of three MSS., and of the Syriac, Arabic, LXX., and Vulgate. **the cities.** Jsh 21:9-19. 1 Ch 6:54-60. **set office.** or, trust. 1 Ch 9:22mg. **as well.** 1 Ch 25:8.

16. **his daily.** Ex 5:13mg. 16:4mg. Le 21:22, 23. 23:37. 1 K 8:59mg. 2 K 25:30. Ezr 3:4mg. Je 52:34. Lk=12:42.

17. **genealogy.** Nu 3:15, 20. 4:38, 42, 46. 17:2, 3. Ezr 2:59. **twenty.** Nu 4:3. 8:24. 1 Ch 23:24, 27. **by their courses.** See on ver. 2. 1 Ch 24:20-31. ch. 25, 26.

18. **set office.** or, trust. ver. 15mg. 1 Ch 9:22mg. **they sanctified.** Is 5:16. Ro 15:16. **holiness.** 2 C=7:1. He *12:14.

19. **the fields.** ver. 15. Le 25:34. Nu 35:2-5. 1 Ch 6:54, 60. **the men.** ver. 12-15. 2 Ch 28:15.

20. **wrought.** 1 K 15:5. 2 K 20:3. 22:2. Jn 1:47. Ac 24:16. 1 Th 2:10. 3 J 5.

21. **work.** Ec *9:10. Col *3:23. **in the law.** Ps *1:2, 3. **he did it.** Dt 6:5. 10:12. 1 K 2:4. 1 Ch 22:19. Ec *9:10. Je √29:13. **prospered.** 2 Ch 14:7. √20:20. √26:5. Dt +29:9. Jsh √1:7, 8. 1 Ch 22:13. Ps *1:3. Mt *6:33. 7:24-27.

2 CHRONICLES 32

Sennacherib invades Judah; and Hezekiah fortifies Jerusalem, and encourages the people, 1-8. Sennacherib's blasphemous messages and letters, 9-19. Hezekiah and Isaiah pray for deliverance: an angel destroys the Assyrian army; and their king, when returned to Nine-

veh, is slain by his sons when worshipping his idol, 20, 21. Hezekiah prospers and is renowned, 22, 23. In his sickness he prays, and is miraculously recovered: his heart is lifted up, but he afterwards humbles himself, 24-26. His riches and works, 27-30. His misconduct in respect of the ambassadors from the king of Babylon, 31. He dies, his memory is honored; and Manasseh succeeds him, 32, 33.

1. **these things.** 2 Ch 20:1, 2. 2 K 18:13, etc. Is 36:1, etc. **king of Assyria.** 2 K 15:19. 17:6. 18:11, 19, 20. Is 7:17, 18. 8:6-8. 10:5, 6. Ho 11:5. **win them.** Heb. break them up. √63H, Ge +12:15. Is 10:7-11. 37:24, 25. Mi 2:13.

2. **he was purposed to fight.** Heb. his face *was* to war. 2 K 12:17. Lk 9:51, 52.

3. **took counsel.** 2 Ch 30:2. 2 K 18:20. Pr 15:22. 20:18. *24:6. Is 40:13. Ro 11:34. **to stop.** Ge 26:15, 18. 2 K 20:20. Is 22:8-11.

4. **who stopped.** This was prudently done; for, without water, how could an immense army subsist in an arid country? No doubt the Assyrian army suffered much through this; as a Christian army did, through the same cause, 1800 years afterwards (See Harmer, ch. viii. Ob. 52). **fountains.** Heb. *mayan,* Ge +7:11 (*S#4599h). **the brook.** ver. 30. 2 Ch 30:14. **ran through the midst of.** Heb. overflowed. Jb 14:19. Is 10:22. 28:2. **kings.** The Septuagint, Syriac, and Arabic read *king,* in the singular number. See on ver. 1. 2 K 18:9, 13. 19:17. Is 10:8. 2 K 3:9, 16, 17. 19:21.

5. **he strengthened.** 2 Ch 12:1. 14:5-7. 17:1, 2. 23:1. 26:8. Is 22:9, 10. **that was broken.** 2 Ch 25:23. **another wall.** 2 K 25:4. Je 39:4. **Millo.** Jg 9:6. 2 S 5:9. 1 K 9:24. 11:27. 2 K 12:20. **darts.** or, swords, *or* weapons. 2 Ch 23:10. 26:14, 15. Ne 4:17. Jl 2:8mg.

6. **he set captains.** 2 Ch 17:14-19. 1 Ch 27:3, 4, etc. **in the street.** Ezr 10:9. Ne 8:1-3, 16. **gate.** √171S7B, Ge +14:7. **comfortably to them.** Heb. to their heart. 2 Ch 30:22mg. Ge +34:3mg. 2 S 19:7mg. Is 40:2mg. Ho 2:14mg.

7. **strong.** Dt 31:6, 7, 23. Jsh 1:6-9. 1 Ch 28:10, 20. Is 35:4. Da 10:19. Zc 8:9, 23. Ep *6:10. 2 T 2:1. **be not afraid.** 2 Ch 20:15. 2 K 18:30. 19:6, 7. **for there.** 2 K 6:16. Ro *8:31. 1 J *4:4. **with us.** √25, Ge +4:4. √132G, Ge +3:19.

8. **an arm.** Jb 26:2. 40:9. Je 17:5. 1 C 1:29. 1 J *4:4. **with us.** 2 Ch 13:12. 14:11. 1 S ●8:20. 17:45. Ps 20:7. 44:6. 46:7, 11. 125:1. Is 8:10. 41:10. Ac 18:10. 2 T 4:17, 22. **to fight.** 2 Ch 20:15. Dt 20:1, 4. Jsh 10:42. **rested.** Heb. leaned. ver. 15. 2 Ch *20:20. Ps 71:6. SS 8:5. Is 36:18. 48:2. **upon the words.** Pr 12:25. Jn 4:50.

9. A.M. 3294. B.C. 710. **Sennacherib.** See on 2 K 18:17. Is 36:2. **Lachish.** Jsh 10:31. 12:11. 15:39. Is 36:2. 37:8. Mi 1:13. **power.** Heb. dominion. 1 K 9:19. 2 K 20:13.

10. **Thus saith.** See on 2 K 18:19. Is 36:4. **siege.** Heb. stronghold. 2 Ch 8:5. 11:5. Dt 20:19, 20. 2 K 19:24mg. 24:10mg. Ps 31:21mg. Hab 2:1.

11. **to give over.** See on 2 K 18:27. Is 36:12, 18. **The Lord our God.** ver. 15. 2 K 18:30. 19:10. Ps 3:2. 11:1-3. 22:8. 42:10. 71:11. Mt 27:43.

12. **Hath not.** 2 Ch 31:1. 2 K 18:4, 22. Is 36:7. **taken away.** This was artfully malicious: many of the people had sacrificed to Jehovah on *high places* (2 Ch *20:33n. 31:1); and Hezekiah had removed them, as

incentives to idolatry. Hence Rabshakeh insinuates that by so doing he had offended Jehovah, deprived the people of their religious rights, and that, consequently, he could neither expect the blessing of God nor the cooperation of the people. **Ye shall worship.** See on Dt 12:13, 14, 26, 27. **one altar.** 2 Ch 4:1. Ex 27:1-8. 30:1-6. 40:26-29. 1 K 7:48.

13. **I and my.** 2 K 15:29. 17:5, 6. 19:11-13, 17, 18. Is 10:9, 10, 14. 37:12, 13, 18-20. Da 4:30, 37. 5:19. **were the gods.** See on ver. 19. 2 K 18:33-35. 19:18, 19. 20:23n. Ps 115:3-8. Is 44:8-10. Je 10:11, 12, 16. Ac 19:26. 1 C *8:4.

14. **among.** See on Is 10:11, 12. **your God.** Ex 14:3. 15:9-11. Is 42:8.

15. **deceive.** See on 2 K 18:29. 19:10. **persuade.** ver. 11. Dt 13:6. Jsh 15:18. 1 K 22:22. Is 36:18. Ac 19:26. Ga 1:10. **much less.** Ex 5:2. Da 3:15. Jn 19:10, 11.

16. **yet.** Jb 15:25, 26. Ps 73:9. **against.** Jn 15:21.

17. **He wrote.** See on 2 K 19:9, 14. Ne 6:5. Is 37:14. **to rail.** 2 K 19:22, 28. Is 10:15. 37:23, 24, 28, 29. Re 13:6. **As the gods.** 2 K 19:12.

18. **they cried.** 2 K +*||18:26-28. Is 36:13. **to affright.** 1 S 17:10, 26. Ne 6:9.

19. **spake.** See on ver. 13-17. 1 S 17:36. Jb 15:25, 26. Ps 10:13, 14. 73:8-11. 139:19, 20. **the God.** 2 Ch 6:6. Ps 76:1, 2. 78:68. 87:1-3. 132:13, 14. Is 14:32. He 12:22. **the gods of.** ver. 13. Jg 11:24n. 1 K 20:23n. 2 K 17:26. 18:33. **the work.** Dt 4:28. 27:15. 2 K 19:18. Ps 135:15-18. Is 2:8. 37:19. 44:16-20. Je 1:16. *10:3, 9. 32:30. Ho 8:5, 6.

20. **Hezekiah.** See on 2 K 19:14-19. Is 37:1, 14-20. **the prophet.** 2 K 19:2-4. Is 37:2-4. **prayed.** 2 Ch 14:11. 20:6-12. Ps *50:15. +√91:14, 15. **to heaven.** ʄ121J20, Ps +73:9.

21. **the Lord.** See on 2 K 19:20, 35, etc. Is 10:16-18. 37:21, 36, 37. 42:8. **angel.** 2 S 24:16. Ps 18:50. Da 3:28. 6:22. Mt 13:49, 50. Ac 12:23. **cut off all.** Ex 12:29. Jb 9:4. Ps 76:5, 7, 12. **mighty men of.** 2 Ch 13:3. 17:13. 25:6. Jg +6:12. **the leaders.** Is 10:8, 16-19, 34. 17:12-14. 29:5-8. 30:30-33. 33:10-12. 36:9. Re 6:15, 16. 19:17, 18. **with shame.** Ps 132:18. Pr 11:2. 16:18. **he was come.** See on 2 K 19:36, 37. Is 37:37, 38. **that.** ʄ142, Ge +20:16. **slew him.** Heb. made him fall. 2 K 19:7.

22. **Lord.** Ps 18:48-50. *37:39, 40. 144:10. Is 10:24, 25. 31:4, 5. 31:4, 5. 33:22. Ho 1:7. **guided.** 2 Ch 28:15. Ge 47:17. Ex 15:13. Ps 48:14. 71:20, 21. 73:24. Is *58:11. Jn *16:13. 2 Th *3:5.

23. **gifts.** 2 S 8:10, 11. Ezr 7:15-22, 27. Ps 68:29. 72:10. Is 60:7-9. Mt 2:11. **presents.** Heb. precious things. 2 Ch 9:9, 10, 24. 17:5, 11. 1 K 4:21. 10:10, 25. **he was magnified.** 2 Ch 1:1. 1 Ch 29:25.

24. **Hezekiah.** See on 2 K +*||20:1-3. Is 38:1-3. **gave him a sign.** or, wrought a miracle for him. See on 2 K *20:4-11. Is 38:4-8, 21, 22.

25. **rendered not again.** Dt 32:6. Ps 116:12, 13. Ho 14:2. Lk *17:17, 18. **his heart.** ver. 31. 2 Ch 25:19. 26:16. Dt 8:12-14, 17. 2 K 14:10. 20:13. Ezk 28:2, 5, 17. Da 5:20, 23. Hab 2:4. 2 C *12:7. 1 T 3:6. 1 P 5:5, 6. **therefore.** 2 Ch 24:18. See on 2 S 24:1, 10-17. 1 Ch 21:1, 12-17. Ps +9:10. 115:1. **wrath upon.** 2 Ch +24:18.

26. **Hezekiah.** 2 Ch 33:12, 19, 23. 34:27. Le 26:40, 41. 2 K 20:19. Je 26:18, 19. Ja *4:10. **pride.** Heb. lifting up. Ps 10:4. **so.** 1 K 21:19. **came not.** Ps 115:1.

days. 2 Ch 34:27, 28. 1 K 21:29. See on 2 K 20:16-19. Is 39:6-8.

27. A.M. 3278-3306. B.C. 726-698. **exceeding much.** 2 Ch 1:12. 9:27. 17:5. Pr *10:22. **treasuries.** 1 Ch 27:25, etc. **precious stones.** 2 S 12:30. 1 K 5:17. **pleasant jewels.** Heb. instruments of desire. 2 Ch 20:25. 36:10mg, 19. Ge 27:15mg. 2 K 20:13. Is 32:12mg. Je +25:34mg. Ezk +26:12mg.

28. **Storehouses.** 2 Ch 26:10. **stalls.** 1 K 4:26. **cotes.** 2 S 7:8.

29. **possessions.** 2 Ch 26:10. Ge 13:2-6. 1 Ch 27:29-31. Jb 1:3, 9. 42:12. **God.** 2 Ch 25:9. Dt 8:18. 1 S 2:7. 1 Ch 29:12. Pr *10:22. 1 T *6:17, 18.

30. **Hezekiah.** Or, "Hezekiah stopped the upper going out (motza, i.e. the egress into the open air) of the waters of Gihon, and brought them underneath (lemattah, by a subterraneous course) to the west of the city of David:" see Note on 1 K 1:45. 2 S 5:23n. 2 K 18:17n. 20:20. **stopped.** See on ver. 4. Is 22:9-11. **Gihon.** 1 K 1:33, 38, 45n. **And Hezekiah.** 2 Ch *20:20. Jsh *1:7, 8. Ps *1:1-3.

31. A.M. 3292. B.C. 712. **in the business.** 2 K 20:12, 13. Is 39:1, 2, etc. **ambassadors.** Heb. interpreters. Ge 42:23. Jb 16:20 (scorn). 33:23. Is 43:27mg. **the wonder.** ver. 24. 2 K 20:8-11. Is 38:8. **God left him.** Jg 16:20. Ps 27:9. 51:11, 12. 119:116, 117. Jn 15:5. **to try him.** Ge 22:1. Ex 15:25. Dt 8:2, 16. Jb 1:11, 12. 2:3-6. Ps 139:1, 2, 23, 24. Pr 17:3. Da 11:35. Zc 13:9. Mt 3:2, 3. Ja √1:13. 1 P 1:7. **that he might.** Dt 8:2. 13:3.

32. A.M. 3278-3306. B.C. 726-698. **goodness.** Heb. kindnesses. ʄ121C1B, Ge +20:13. 2 Ch 31:20, 21. 35:26. Ne 13:14. **in the vision.** Is ch. 36-39. **in the book.** 2 K ch. 18-20.

33. **slept.** See on 1 K 1:21. 2:10. +*11:43. +14:20. 2 K 24:6n. 2 Ch 28:27n. **chiefest.** or, highest. 2 S 15:30. **sepulchres.** Heb. qeber, Ge +23:4. **did him.** 2 Ch 16:14. Ge 50:10, 11. Nu 20:29. Dt 34:8. 1 S 2:30. 25:1. Pr 10:7. **And Manasseh.** See on 2 Ch 33:1, etc.

2 CHRONICLES 33

Manasseh reigns long, is very wicked, and multiplies idolatries, corrupts the people, and rejects the admonitions of God, 1-10. He is carried captive to Babylon; he humbles himself greatly before God, with earnest and fervent prayer; and is restored to his kingdom, 11-13. He fortifies his dominions, and restores the worship of God, 14-17. His acts and prayers, 18, 19. He dies, and Amon succeeds, who reigns wickedly, and is murdered, 20-24. The people slay the murderers, and make Josiah king, 25.

1. A.M. 3306-3361. B.C. 698-643. **Manasseh.** 2 Ch 32:33. 2 K 21:1, etc. 1 Ch 3:13. Mt 1:10, Manasses. **twelve.** 2 Ch 34:1, 2. Ec 10:16. Is 3:4, 12.

2. **like unto.** 2 Ch 28:3. 36:14. Le 18:24-30. 20:22, 23. Dt 12:31. 18:9-14. 2 K 17:11, 15. 21:2, 9. Ezr 9:14. Ps 106:35-40. Ezk 11:12.

3. **he built again.** Heb. he returned and built. 2 Ch 19:4. Ec 2:19. 9:18. **which Hezekiah.** 2 Ch 30:14. 31:1. 32:12. 2 K 18:4. 21:3. **he reared.** 2 Ch 28:2-4. Jg 2:11-13. **made groves.** Dt 16:21. 1 K 14:23. 2 K +17:10. 21:3n. Je 17:2. **the host.** Dt 4:19. 17:3. 2 K +21:3. 23:5, 6, 11. Je 8:2. 19:13. Zp 1:5. Ac 7:42.

4. **he built.** ver. 15. 2 Ch 34:3, 4. 2 K 21:4, 5. Je

7:30. **In Jerusalem.** 2 Ch 6:6. 7:16. 32:19. Dt 12:11.
1 K 8:29. 9:3. **for ever.** Heb. *olam*, Ex +*12:24.

5. **in the two.** 2 Ch 4:9. Je 32:34, 35. Ezk 8:7-18.
6. **caused.** 2 Ch 28:3. Le *18:21. 20:2. Dt 12:31.
+*18:10. 2 K 21:6. 23:10. Je 7:31, 32. Ezk 23:37, 39.
he observed times. Le 19:26. 20:6. Dt *18:10-14. 1 S
15:23. 2 K 17:17. +*21:6. Is 47:9-12. Ga 5:20. **enchantments.** Ge 30:27. 2 K +21:6. **witchcraft.** 2 K 9:22. Is
47:9, 12. Mi 5:12. Na 3:4. **dealt with.** 2 K 21:6. 23:24.
1 Ch 10:13. Is 8:19. 19:3. **familiar spirit.** Dt +*18:11.
2 K +21:6. **wizards.** Dt +*18:11. 2 K +21:6. **anger.**
Dt 4:25. 9:18. 31:29. 32:16, 21.

7. **he set a carved image.** The Targumist says, "He
set up an image, the likeness of himself, in the house
of the sanctuary." In the parallel passage it is, "a graven
image of the grove," or rather, *Asherah* or *Astarte*.
Manasseh, as Bp. Patrick observes, seems to have studied to find out what God had forbidden in his law
that he might practice it: a most prodigious change
from the height of piety in his father's time, into the
sink of impiety in this! **in the house.** 2 K 21:7, 8.
23:6. **God had said.** See on ver. 4. 1 K 8:29. Ps 132:13,
14. **which I have.** 2 Ch 6:6. 1 K 8:44, 48. 11:13, 32.
Ps 78:68. **for ever.** Heb. *olam*, Ex +*12:24.

8. **will I.** See on 2 S 7:10. 1 Ch 17:9. **so that they.**
See on 2 Ch 7:17-22. Dt 28:1-14. 30:15-20. Is 1:19,
20. Ezk 33:25, 26. **to do all.** Dt 4:40. 5:1, 31-33. 6:1.
8:1. 27:26. Lk 1:6. Ga 3:10-13. **by the hand.** 2 Ch
√34:14mg,n. Le 8:36. 10:11.

9. **made Judah.** 1 K 14:16. 15:26. 2 K 21:16. 23:26.
24:3, 4. Pr 29:12. Mi 6:16. **to err.** Ge 20:13. 2 K 21:9.
Jb 12:24, 25. Ps 95:10. 119:21, 118. Pr 19:27. Is 3:12.
9:16. 28:7. 30:28. 35:8. 63:17. Je 23:13, 32. Ho 4:12.
Am 2:4. Mi 3:5. Mt 22:29. Mk *12:24, 27. He 3:10.
Ja 1:16. 5:19. **to do worse.** See on ver. 2. 2 K 21:9-
11. Ezk 16:45-47. Ps 86:13. Mt *11:22. Lk +*12:48.
Ro +2:12. **the heathen.** Le 18:24. Dt 2:21. Jsh 24:8.
2 K 17:8-11.

10. **the Lord spake.** 2 Ch 36:15, 16. Ne 9:29, 30.
Je 25:4-7. 44:4, 5. Zc 1:4. Ac 7:51, 52.

11. A.M. 3327. B.C. 677. **the Lord.** Dt 28:36. Jb
36:8. **the captains.** Is 10:8. 36:9. **of the king.** Heb.
which were the king's. 1 S 24:4. 2 K 16:13. Ne 9:32,
37. Is 5:26-30. 7:18-20. **among the thorns.** Young renders, "thickets," noting, where he had fled for safety.
The word *bachochim* may possibly here signify with
fetters or chains, as the kindred word *chachim* denotes,
Ezk 19:4, 6. The Syriac and Arabic have *alive*, probably
reading *bechayim*. 1 S 13:6. La 3:7. **bound him.** 2 K
23:33. 25:6. Jb 36:8-11. Ps *107:10-14. **fetters.** *or*,
chains. 2 Ch 36:6. Jg 16:21. 2 S 3:34. 2 K 25:7. Je
39:7. 52:11.

12. **And when.** 2 Ch 28:22. Le 26:39-42. Dt 4:30,
31. Je 31:18-20. Ho 5:15. Mi 6:9. Lk 15:16-18. **affliction.**
Ps 106:43, 44. **he besought.** ver. 18, 19. Ps *50:15.
Ac 9:11. **the Lord.** See on 2 Ch 28:5. **humbled.** ver.
19, 23. 2 Ch 32:26. Ex 10:3. Lk 18:14, 15. Ja *4:10.
1 P *5:5, 6.

13. **he was intreated.** 1 Ch 5:20. Ezr 8:23. Jb 22:23,
27. 33:16-30. 36:8-10. Ps 32:3-5. 86:5. Is *55:6-9. Je
*29:12, 13. Mt *7:7, 8. Lk 23:42, 43. Jn 4:10. **brought
him.** Ezr 7:27. Pr *16:7. 21:1. Mt *6:33. **knew.** Dt
29:6. Ps 9:16. 46:10. Je 24:7. Da 4:25, 34, 35. Jn √17:3.
He 8:11.

14. A.M. 3327-3361. B.C. 677-643. **he built.** 2 Ch
32:5. **Gihon.** 2 Ch 32:30. 1 K 1:33, 45. **fish gate.** Ne

3:3. 12:39. Zp 1:10. **Ophel.** *or*, the tower. 2 Ch 27:3.
2 K +5:24mg. Ne 3:26, 27. **put.** 2 Ch 11:11, 12. 17:19.

15. **he took.** See on ver. 3-7. 2 K 21:7. Is 2:17-21.
Ezk 18:20-22. Ho 14:1-3. Mt 3:8. **strange.** 2 Ch 14:3.
Ex 12:43 (*S#5236h). Ne 9:2.

16. **repaired.** 2 Ch 29:18. 1 K 18:30. **peace.** Le
3:1, etc. **thank.** Le 7:12-18. **commanded.** ver. 9.
2 Ch 14:4. See on 2 Ch 30:12. Ge *18:19. Lk 22:32.

17. **people.** 2 Ch 15:17. 20:33n. 32:12n. 1 K 22:43.
2 K 15:4.

18. A.M. 3306-3361. B.C. 698-643. **the rest.** 2 Ch
20:34. 32:32. See on 1 K 11:41. **his prayer.** See on
ver. 12, 13, 19. **the seers.** ver. 10. 1 S 9:9. 2 K 17:13.
Is 29:10. 30:10. Am 7:12. Mi 3:7. **in the book.** 1 K
14:19. 15:31.

19. **his prayer also.** ver. 11, 12, 19. Pr 15:8. Ac
9:11. 1 J √1:9. **all his sins.** ver. 1-10. Ro 5:16. **before
he.** See on ver. 12. 2 Ch 30:11. 36:12. Ps 119:67, 71,
75. Je 44:10. Da 5:22. **the seers.** *or*, Hosai. So the
Targum and Vulgate: the Syriac has "Hanun the
prophet;" and the Arabic, "Saphan the prophet." This
record is totally lost; for the captivity and repentance
of Manasseh are related no where else; and the prayer
of Manasseh in the Aprocrypha was probably composed
long afterwards: it is not acknowledged as canonical
even by the Romish church, though it was anciently
used as a form of confession, and as such still received
by the Greek church.

20. **Manasseh.** See on 2 Ch +32:33. 2 K 21:18.
Amon. 2 K 21:19-25. 1 Ch 3:14. Mt 1:10.

21. A.M. 3361-3363. B.C. 643-641. **two years.** ver.
1. Lk 12:19, 20. Ja 4:13-15.

22. **as did Manasseh.** See on ver. 1-10. 2 K 21:1-
11, 20. Ezk 20:18. **for Amon sacrificed.** Amon's conduct
is recorded as like his father Manasseh, in sacrificing
to graven images; by which some think it is an evidence
that Manasseh did not truly repent, but they forget
how many good kings had wicked sons. In *one* point
of view Manasseh was defective, although it cannot
be supposed that it affected his eternal state; for when
he *cast out the images*, he did not utterly deface and
destroy them, according to the law in Dt 7:5, which
required, moreover, that the graven images should
be burnt with fire. How necessary that law was, this
instance shows; for the *carved images* being only
thrown aside, and not burnt, Amon knew where to
find them, soon set them up, and sacrificed to them.
Is 44:13, etc. Ac 19:19.

23. **humbled not.** See on ver. 1, 12, 19. Je 8:12.
trespassed more and more. Heb. multiplied trespass.
ver. 6. 2 Ch 28:22. 36:14. Ex 36:5. Le 11:42. Je 7:26.
2 T 3:13.

24. A.M. 3363. B.C. 641. 2 Ch 24:25, 26. 25:27,
28. 2 S 4:5-12. 2 K 21:23-26. Ps 55:23. Ro 11:22.

25. **slew.** Ge 9:5, 6. Nu 35:31, 33. **the people.**
2 Ch 26:1. 36:1. **Josiah.** See on 2 Ch 34:1.

2 CHRONICLES 34

*Josiah reigns well, and destroys idolatry both in
Judah and Israel, 1-7. He provides for the repair of
the temple, 8-13. Hilkiah finds the book of the law,
and reads it before the king; who is greatly alarmed,
and sends to inquire of God by the prophetess Huldah,
14-22. Huldah predicts the destruction of Jerusalem,
but not till after Josiah's death, 23-28. He causes the*

law to be read in solemn assembly, and renews the covenant between God and the people, 29-33.

1. A.M. 3363-3394. B.C. 641-610. **Josiah.** 2 Ch 33:25. 1 K *13:2. 2 K 22:1, etc. 1 Ch 3:14, 15. Je 1:2. Zp 1:1. Mt 1:10, 11, Josias. **eight years.** 2 Ch 24:1. 26:1. 33:1. 1 S 2:18, 26. 1 K 3:7-9. Ec *4:13.

2. **right in the sight.** 2 Ch 14:2. *17:3. 29:2. 1 K *14:8. *15:5. 2 K 22:2. **declined.** Dt *5:32. 17:11, 20. 28:14. Jsh 1:7. 23:6. Pr *4:27.

3. A.M. 3370. B.C. 634. **while he.** 1 Ch 22:5. 29:1. Ps *119:9. Ec *12:1. 2 T *3:15. **to seek.** See on 2 Ch *15:2. 1 Ch √28:9. Pr *8:17. Mt *6:33. **purge.** See on 2 Ch 33:17, 22. Le 26:30. 2 K *23:4, 14. **the high places.** 2 Ch 30:14. See on 2 K *18:4. +21:3. **the groves.** 2 K +17:10. 21:3n. Heb. Asherim. or, Asherah poles. 2 Ch 14:3. Ex 34:13. **carved images.** ver. 4, 7. 2 Ch 33:19, 22n. Dt 7:5, 25. 12:3. Jg 3:19, 26. 2 K 17:41. **molten images.** Ex 32:4, 8. 34:17. Le 19:4. Nu 33:52. Dt 9:12, 16. 27:15.

4. **brake down.** 2 Ch *33:3. Ex *23:24. Le *26:30. Dt *7:5, 25. **images.** or, sun images. 2 Ch 14:5. Le +26:30. 2 K 23:4, 5, 11. Is 17:8mg. **made dust.** ver. 7. ○33:22n. Ex 32:20. Dt 9:21. 2 K *23:12. Ps 18:42. Is 27:9. **graves.** Heb. face of the graves. 2 K 10:26, 27. 23:4, 6. Heb. *qeber*, Ge +*23:4.

5. **he burnt the bones.** 1 K *13:2n. 2 K +*‖23:16n. Note in the parallel passage that by this means Josiah "polluted" the heathen altars and worship places (groves); no one familiar with the position the Old Testament takes toward ceremonial uncleanness associated with even the touching of a bone would countenance the practice of some today of honoring the relics of dead "saints," placing such in their altars! These events show that the honoring of relics and the veneration of saints are abhorrent to the God of Scripture. Such practices are considered idolatry (Is 65:4). Ezk *24:10, 12n. **cleansed.** ver. 7. Nu 35:33. Je 3:10. 4:14. Ezk 22:24.

6. in. 2 Ch 30:1, 10, 11. 31:1. 2 K 23:15-20. **mattocks.** or, mauls. 1 S 13:20, 21. Pr 25:18. Is 7:25.

7. **beaten.** See on ver. 1. Dt 9:21. **into powder.** Heb. to make powder. ver. 4. **he returned.** 2 Ch 31:1.

8. A.M. 3380. B.C. 624. **the eighteenth.** Je 1:2, 3. **sent Shaphan.** i.e. *a rabbit* or *coney*. Nu +32:35. 2 K 22:3, 12, 14. Je 26:24. 29:3. 36:10. 39:14. 40:11. Ezk 8:11. **Azaliah.** i.e. *kept back by Jah; Jah has reserved,* ✳S#683h. 2 Ch 34:8. 2 K 22:3. **Maaseiah.** i.e. *work of Jah.* Je +21:1. 29:21, 25. 37:3. **governor.** 2 Ch 18:25. **Joah.** i.e. *Jah is brother.* Is +36:3. **Joahaz.** i.e. *Jah has laid hold; Jehovah-seized; whom the Lord holds fast,* ✳S#3099h. 2 Ch 34:8. 36:2, 4. 2 K 14:1. **recorder.** 2 S +8:16mg. 20:24. 1 Ch 18:15.

9. **Hilkiah.** ver. 14, 15, 18, 20, 22. 2 K 22:4. 23:4. **they delivered.** 2 Ch 24:11-14. 2 K 22:5-7. Ph 4:8. **doors.** 1 K +14:17. 2 K 12:9mg. **Manasseh.** 2 Ch 30:10, 18. 31:1. **and they returned.** Instead of *wyyashuvoo,* "and they returned," as the *Keri* has, we should, with the *Kethiv,* read *weyoshevey,* "and the inhabitants of;" a reading which is supported by many MSS., printed editions, and all the versions, as well as necessity and common sense. ver. 7.

10. **in the hand.** 2 K 12:11, 12, 14. 22:5, 6. Ezr 3:7.

11. **floor.** or, rafter. Ne 2:8. 3:3, 6. **the kings.** 2 Ch 33:4-7, 22.

12. **faithfully.** 2 Ch 19:9. 31:12. Nu 12:7. 2 K 12:15.

22:7. Ne 7:2. Pr *25:13. *28:20. 1 C *4:2. 3 J 5. **overseers.** 1 Ch 9:29. 1 Th=5:12, 13. He=13:17. **all.** 1 Ch 6:31, etc. 15:16-22. 16:4, 5, 41, 42. 23:5. 25:1, etc. **skill.** The verb *skill* is now obsolete: the meaning is, "every one who is skillful, *maiveen,* on instruments of music."

13. **over.** 1 Th=5:12, 13. He=13:17. **the bearers.** 2 Ch 2:10, 18. Ne 4:10. Ga 6:2, 5. **overseers.** 1 Ch 9:28, 29. 1 Th=5:12, 13. He =13:17. **and of the Levites.** 1 Ch 23:4, 5. **scribes.** Ezr 7:6. Je 8:8. Mt 26:3. 2 C=3:2, 3. **officers.** 2 Ch 19:11. 1 Ch 23:4. 26:29, 30. **porters.** 2 Ch 8:14. 1 Ch 9:17. 15:18. 16:38, 42. 26:1, etc. Ezr 7:7.

14. **Hilkiah.** See on 2 K 22:8, etc. Dt 31:24-26. **found.** That the book was extant and well known may be seen by such references as 1 K 14:6; 2 K 11:12; 2 Ch 14:4; 17:9; 25:4. "These scriptures suffice to refute the assertion of some in our time that the book which Hilkiah found in the temple was of comparatively recent compilation, with the name of Moses attached to it to give it authority in the eyes of the king and his people. The assertion is as absurd as it is wicked. That which was brought to light once more was God's own revelation to His people, against which, unhappily they so frequently transgressed. In the stirring times of Josiah, when the Spirit of God was working to give Jehovah's poor fickle people one more opportunity, the rediscovery of the book of the law had tremendous effect upon the heart and conscience of the king; and, we may hope, upon the hearts and consciences of many of his subjects (W. W. Fereday, *Josiah and Revival,* p. 35). 2 K 14:6n. 22:8n. **a book.** Literally, "a book of the law of the Lord, *by the hand* of Moses;" i.e. as Dr. Kennicott understands it, "in the handwriting of Moses;" for, says he, though there are fifteen places in the Old Testament which mention "the law of Moses," and "book of Moses," yet this one place only mentions "the book of the law in, or by, the hand of Moses." **the law.** 2 Ch 12:1. 31:4. 35:26. Dt 17:18, 19. Jsh *1:8. Ezr *7:10. Ps *1:2. Is 5:24. 30:9. Je 8:8. Lk 2:39. **by Moses.** Heb. by the hand of Moses. 2 Ch 35:6. Ex +*24:4. Le 8:36. 10:11. 26:46. 1 K +16:12mg. 2 K 14:6n. 22:8n.

15. **answered.** Jg 18:14. 1 S 9:17. **Shaphan.** 2 K 22:10. **the book.** 2 K 22:8. Ezr 7:6. Ne 8:1.

16. **Shaphan.** See on 2 K 22:9, 10. Je 36:20, 21. **thy servants.** Heb. the hand of thy servants. **they do.** 2 S 15:15. Jn 2:5.

17. **And they.** See on ver. 8-10. **gathered together.** Heb. poured out, or melted. ver. 21, 25. 2 K 22:9. Jb 10:10.

18. **And Shaphan read.** Dt *17:19. Jsh *1:8. Ps 119:46, *97-99. Je 36:20, 21. Re 1:3. Aloud, as orientals generally do, even when alone (Young). **it.** Heb. in it. 2 K ○22:10.

19. **the words.** Ro *3:20. 7:7-11. Ga 2:19. 3:10-13. **that he rent.** 2 K 19:1. 22:11, 19. Je ○*36:22-24. Jl *2:13. Lk 14:11.

20. **Ahikam.** i.e. *brother of a withstander.* 2 K +22:12. 25:22. Je 26:24. 40:6, 9, 14. **Abdon.** i.e. *servile.* Jg +12:13. This person seems to have borne both the name of *Achbor* and *Abdon.* 2 K 22:12, Achbor. Je 26:22. **Micah.** i.e. *who is like Jah.* Mi +1:1. "Michaiah," as he is named in the parallel passage, is here called "Michah," merely by the omission of *yah,* one of the Divine names. **Asaiah.** i.e. *doing of Jah; the Lord has*

wrought; made of Jehovah, *S#6222h. 2 Ch 34:20. 2 K 22:12, 14. 1 Ch 4:36. 6:30. 9:5. 15:6, 11. (1) A man of Simeon, 1 Ch 4:36. (2) A son of Merari, of Levi, 1 Ch 6:30; 15:6, 11. (3) A Shilonite, one of the first who dwelt in their possessions, 1 Ch 9:5. (4) A servant sent by king Josiah to enquire about the book found, 2 Ch 34:21; 2 K 22:12, 14. This variation only exists in the translation; the original being uniformly *Asaiah,* or rather, "Asayah." 2 K 22:12, +14, Asahiah.

21. **enquire**. Ex 18:15. 1 S 9:9. 1 K 22:5-7. Je 21:2. Ezk 14:1, etc. 20:1-7. **that are left**. 2 Ch 28:6. 33:11. 2 K 17:6, 7. 22:13. Is 37:2-4. Je 42:2. **great**. Le 26:14, etc. Dt *28:15. 29:18-28. 30:17-19. 31:16-22. 32:15-25. Ro 1:18. *2:8-12. 4:15.

22. **the prophetess**. Ex +15:20. Jg 4:4. 2 K 22:14. Ne 6:14. Is 8:3. Lk 1:41-45. 2:36. Ac 21:9. **Tikvath**. i.e. *expectation; shall be gathered; hope,* *S#8616h. 2 Ch 34:22. Also 2 K 22:+14. Ezr 10:15, Tikvah. **Hasrah**. i.e. *extreme poverty; she was lacking,* *S#2641h. "Hasrah" is most probably a mistake for "Harhas;" as the Septuagint reads, both here and in the parallel place, *Aras*. See on 2 K 22:14, Harhas. **wardrobe**. Heb. garments. Of the priests, most probably (Young). **college**. or, school, or second part. It is probable that "Mishneh" was either the name of a street, or a particular part of the city of Jerusalem. 2 K 22:14mg. Ne 11:9. Zp 1:10.

23. **Tell ye the man**. See on 2 K 22:15-20. Je 21:3-7. 37:7-10.

24. **I will bring**. 2 Ch 36:14-20. Jsh 23:16. 2 K 21:12. 23:26, 27. Is 5:4-6. Je 6:19. 19:3, 15. 35:17. 36:31. **all the curses**. See on ver. 21.

25. **Because**. See on 2 Ch 12:2. 15:2. 33:3-9. 2 K 24:3, 4. Is 2:8, 9. Je 15:1-4. **my wrath**. Is 42:25. Je 7:20. La 2:4. 4:11. Na 1:6. Re 14:10, 11. **shall not**. 2 K 22:17. See on Je 4:4. 7:20. Ezk 20:48. Mk 9:43-48.

26. **as for**. ver. 21, 23.

27. **Because**. "Because," says the Targumist, "thy heart was melted, and thou hast humbled thyself in the sight of the *word* of the Lord, *meymra dyya*, when thou didst hear His *words, yath pithgamoi*, against this place." Here *meymra*, the *personal word*, is plainly distinguished from *pithgam*, a *word spoken*. *Meymra,* *S#3982h. Est 1:15 (commandment); 2:20; 9:32 (decree). Also *S#3983h: Ezr 6:9 (appointment). Da 4:17 (word). *Pithgam,* *S#6599h: Est 1:20 (decree); Ec 8:11 (sentence). Also *S#6600h: Ezr 4:17 (answer); 5:7 (letter); 11; 6:11 (word); Da 3:16 (matter); 4:17. **thine heart**. See on 2 Ch 32:12, 13. 2 K 22:18, 19. Ps 34:18. 51:17. Is 57:15. 66:2. Ezk *9:4. 36:26. **humble**. See on 2 Ch 32:26. 33:12, 19. Ja *4:6-10. **didst rend**. See on ver. 19. Je ◐*36:23, 24. **I have even**. 2 Ch +*7:14. Ps 10:17. Is 65:24.

28. **I will gather**. 2 Ch 35:24. See on 2 K 22:20. Is 57:1, 2. Je 15:1. Ezk 14:14-21. **grave**. Heb. *qeber,* Ge +23:4. **in peace**. Ps 37:37. **neither**. 1 K 21:29. 2 K 20:19. Is 39:8.

29. **the king**. 1 S 12:23. 1 Ch 29:2, etc. Mk 14:8. **gathered**. 2 Ch 30:2. 2 K ‖23:1-3.

30. **great and small**. Heb. from great even to small. 2 Ch 15:12, 13. 18:30. Dt 1:17. Jb 3:19. **he read**. 2 Ch 6:1, etc. 17:7-9. Dt *17:18-20. Ne *8:2-5. Ec 1:12. 12:9, 10. **their ears**. Jn=8:47. Ja=1:19-22. **the book**. ver. 15, 18, 19, 24. Ex 24:7. 2 K 23:2, 21. Je 31:31, 32.

31. **in his place**. Instead of *al omdo,* "in his place," the parallel passage, 2 K 23:3, has *al haammood,* "by the pillar;" which is probably the true reading, as the LXX. in both places read *ton stulon,* "the pillar." 2 Ch 6:13. 2 K *11:14. *23:3. Ezk 46:2. **made a covenant**. This was expressed, (1) In general, To walk after Jehovah; to have no gods beside him. (2) To take his law for the regulation of their conduct. (3) In particular, To bend their whole heart and soul to the performance of it; so that they might not only have *religion* without, but *piety* within. 2 Ch 23:16. 29:10. Ex *24:6-8. Dt 29:1, 10-15. Jsh 24:25. Ne 9:38. 10:29. Je *50:5. He 8:6-13. **and his testimonies**. Ps 119:111, 112. **with all his heart**. 2 Ch 15:12, 15. See on 2 Ch *31:21. Dt *6:5. Lk *10:27-29. **soul**. Heb. *nephesh,* Ge +34:3. **to perform**. Ps 119:106.

32. **caused**. 2 Ch 14:4. 30:12. 33:16. Ge *18:19. Ec 8:2. **present**. Heb. found. 2 Ch +29:29mg. Jg +20:48mg. **did**. Je 3:10.

33. **took away**. See on ver. 3-7. 2 K 23:4-20. **the abominations**. Ge 43:32. 46:34. Ex 8:26. 1 K 11:5-7. **all his days**. Jsh 24:31. Je 3:10. Ho 6:4. **from following**. Heb. from after. 2 Ch 25:27mg.

2 CHRONICLES 35

Josiah causes a solemn passover to be celebrated, 1-19. He is slain in battle against Pharaoh-necho, 20-24. Great lamentations are made for him, 25. His acts and goodness, 26, 27.

1. **Josiah**. The whole solemnity was performed with great exactness according to the law, and upon that account there was none like it since Samuel's time; for even in Hezekiah's passover there were several irregularities. Bp. Patrick observes, that in this also it exceeded the other passovers which preceding kings had kept, that though Josiah was by no means so rich as David, or Solomon, or Jehoshaphat, yet he furnished the whole congregation with beasts for sacrifice, both paschal and eucharistical, at his own proper cost and charge, which was more than any king ever did before. 2 Ch ch. 30. 2 K 23:21-23. **the fourteenth**. Ex 12:6. Nu 9:3. Dt 16:1-8. Ezr 6:19. Ezk 45:21. Josiah's solemnization of the passover, which is merely alluded to at 2 K 23:21, is very particularly related here—while the destruction of idolatry is largely related in the Kings, and here only touched upon. The feasts of the Lord God, appointed by the ceremonial law, were very numerous; but the passover was the chief. It was *the first* which was solemnized in the night wherein Israel came out of Egypt, and ushered in those which were afterwards instituted: and it was *the last* great feast which was held in the night wherein Christ was betrayed, before the vail of the temple was rent in twain. By means of this feast, both Josiah and Hezekiah revived religion in their day.

2. **charges**. 2 Ch 23:8, 18. 31:2. Nu 18:5-7. 1 Ch ch. 24. Ezr 6:18. **encouraged**. 2 Ch 29:5-11. 31:2. 1 Ch 22:19. 1 C=15:58.

3. **the Levites that taught**. The Levites, by courses, served the priests at the sanctuary, as their primary employment: but when at home in their several cities, they were the stated teachers of the people in their several districts (Scott). 2 Ch +*15:3. 17:8, *9. *30:22. Le 10:11. 23:3n. Dt 17:9. 33:10. 2 K +*4:22, 23. 1 Ch 25:7n, 8n. 26:32n. Ezr *7:10, 25. Ne √8:7, 8.

Ml *2:7. Mt 23:2, 3. 2 1 C 14:34n. T 2:2. **Put.** 2 Ch 5:7. 8:11. 34:14. He=1:3. Re=21:3. **in the house.** See on 2 Ch 5:7. **not be.** Nu 4:15-49. 1 Ch 23:26. He=4:9. Re=7:15, 16. =*14:13. **serve now.** Nu 8:19. 16:9, 10. 2 C 4:5. Re=7:15.

4. **the houses.** 1 Ch 9:10-34. Ne 11:10-20. **after your courses.** The regulations formed by David, and established by Solomon, concerning the courses of the priests and Levites, were committed to writing, and preserved, for them to refer to continually. Josiah, as well as Hezekiah, required the priests and Levites to attend to their several duties, and encouraged them therein, but he neither added, altered, nor retrenched any thing: he merely enforced what had been established in the law, and in the regulations made by David and the contemporary prophets: "the commandment of the king...was by the word of the Lord." 1 Ch ch. 23-26. **and according.** 2 Ch 8:14.

5. **And stand.** Ps 134:1. 135:2. **divisions.** Ezr 6:18. **families of the fathers.** Heb. house of the fathers. **the people.** Heb. the sons of the people. ver. 7, 12. Ex 12:3.

6. **So kill.** 2 Ch 30:15-17. Ex 12:6, 21, 22. Ezr 6:20, 21. **sanctify.** 2 Ch 29:5, 15, 34. 30:◐3, 15-19. Ge 35:2. Ex 19:10, 15. Nu 19:11-20. Jb 1:5. Ps 51:7. Jl 2:16. He 9:13, 14.

7. **Josiah.** 2 Ch 7:8-10. *30:24. Is 32:8. Ezk 45:17. **gave.** Heb. offered. ver. 8mg, 9mg. 2 Ch 30:24mg. 1 K 8:63. **passover offerings.** 2 Ch 30:17. **present.** 2 Ch +29:29mg. Jg +20:48mg. **thirty thousand.** According to the calculation, that not fewer than ten, nor more than twenty persons, were to join for one kid or lamb, the numbers given on this occasion would suffice for above 400,000 persons. **the king's substance.** 1 K 8:63. 1 Ch 29:3.

8. **his princes.** 2 Ch 29:31-33. 1 Ch 29:6-9, 17. Ezr 1:6. 2:68, 69. 7:16. 8:25-35. Ne 7:70-72. Ps 45:12. Ac 2:44, 45. 4:34, 35. **gave.** Heb. offered. ver. +7mg. **willingly.** Le +*23:38. 2 C *8:12. *9:7. **Hilkiah.** 2 Ch 34:14-20. **rulers.** 1 Ch 9:20. 24:4, 5. Je 29:25, 26. Ac 4:1. 5:26.

9. **Conaniah.** i.e. *prepared of Jah; established of Jehovah,* ✱S#3562h. 2 Ch 31:12, 13. 35:9. **gave.** Heb. offered. ver. +7mg. Is 1:10-15. Je 3:10. 7:21-28. Mi 6:6-8.

10. **the priests.** ver. 4, 5. 2 Ch 30:16. Ezr 6:18. **king's.** 1 C=12:18. **commandment.** Jn=14:21. =15:14.

11. **passover.** 1 C=5:7, 8. **the priests.** 2 Ch 29:22-24. 30:16. Le 1:5, 6. Nu 18:3, 7. He 9:21, 22. **flayed them.** 2 Ch 29:34.

12. **as it is written.** Le 3:3, 5, 9-11, 14-16.

13. **roasted.** Ex *12:8, 9. Dt 16:7. Ps 22:14. La 1:12, 13. **sod.** Le 6:28. Nu 6:19. 1 S 2:13-15. Ezk 46:20-24. **pots.** Ex 16:3. 27:3. 38:3. 1 K 7:45. **caldrons.** 1 S 2:14. 2 K 10:7. Jb 41:20. Ps 81:6. Je 24:2. **pans.** 2 K 2:20 (cruse). 21:13 (dish). Pr 19:24 (bosom). 26:15 (bosom). (✱S#6745h; 6746h; 6747h). **divided them speedily.** Heb. made *them* run. 2 K 23:12. Ro *12:11.

14. **because the priests.** Ac 6:2-4. **busied.** 2 Ch 13:10. Ne 11:22. Ro=12:11.

15. **singers.** ✚S#7891h (Polel, Participle): 2 Ch 5:12, 13. 20:21. 23:13. 29:28. 1 Ch 6:33. 9:33. 15:16, 19, 27. Ezr 2:41, 65, 70. 7:7. 10:24. Ne 7:1, 44, 67, 73. 10:28, 39. 11:22, 23. 12:28, 29, 42, 45, 46, 47. 13:5, 10. **place.** Heb. station. ver. 10. 1 Ch 23:28. **according.** 2 Ch 29:25, 26. 1 Ch 16:41, 42. 23:5. 25:1-7. Ps ch.

77-79, titles. **the porters.** 1 Ch 9:17-19. +23:5. 26:14-19. **not depart.** Mt=24:46.

17. **present.** Heb. found. 2 Ch +29:29mg. Jg +20:48mg. **passover.** Le +*23:5. **the feast.** 2 Ch 30:21-23. Ex 12:15-20. 13:6, 7. 23:15. 34:18. Le 23:5-8. Nu 28:16-25. Dt 16:3, 4, 8. 1 C 5:7, 8. **unleavened.** Le +*23:6.

18. **there was no passover.** Not one on *purer* principles, more *heartily* joined in by the people present, more *literally* or *exactly consecrated*, according to the law, or more *religiously* observed. The words do not refer to the number present, but to the manner and spirit. 2 Ch 30:5, 23. 2 K 23:21-23. Ne 8:17. **neither did.** 2 Ch 30:26, 27. **present.** Heb. found. 2 Ch +29:29mg. Jg +20:48mg.

20. A.M. 3394. B.C. 610. **After.** 2 K 23:29. **temple.** Heb. house. 2 Ch 34:8, 10. **Necho.** i.e. *the smitten* or *lame,* ✱S#5224h. 2 Ch 35:20, 22. 36:4. *Pharaoh the lame,* says the Targumist. 2 K 23:29, etc., Pharaohnechoh. Je 46:2, etc. **Charchemish.** i.e. *fortified city; fortress of refuge; fortress of Chemosh,* ✱S#3751h. 2 Ch 35:20. Is 10:9. Je 46:2.

21. **What have I.** ✓85H, Jg +*11:12. 2 S 16:10. Mt 8:29. Jn +*2:4. **to do.** Mt 27:19. **house wherewith I have war.** Heb. house of my war. **God.** 2 K 18:25. Is 36:10. **forbear thee.** 2 K 25:19.

22. **Nevertheless.** Josiah's conduct in this affair has been treated with great severity; and he has been charged with engaging rashly in an *unjust* war, and *disregarding the express command of God.* But Scripture no where condemns him; and Pharaoh, in marching through Josiah's territories, against his will, certainly committed an act of hostility. It is evident that Josiah was in possession of the whole land of Israel (2 Ch 26:6); and probably he held the northern parts of it as a grant from the king of Babylon; and was not only in alliance with him, but bound to guard his frontiers against hostile invaders. He may, therefore, be fairly justified from the charge of *unjustly* meddling in a war that did not belong to him. It is true the ambassadors assured Josiah, that "God had commanded Pharaoh to make haste;" and he is therefore said not to have "hearkened to the words of Necho, from the mouth of God." But Necho produced no proof that he was a prophet of Jehovah; and the word he employed, *elohim,* may denote gods or idols (Ex 12:12; 20:23; 1 S 5:7; 1 K 11:5; Ps *96:5; *97:7); and critics have noticed that the expression, "from the mouth of God," is not used when the true God is meant. **but disguised.** 2 Ch 18:29. Ge +27:16. 1 K 14:2. 22:30, 34. **the mouth.** ver. 21. 2 Ch 18:4-6. Jsh 9:14. **Megiddo.** Jsh +17:11. Jg 5:19. 2 K 9:27. 23:30. Zc 12:11, Megiddon. Re 16:16, Armageddon.

23. **the archers.** 2 Ch 18:33. Ge 49:23. 2 K 9:24. La 3:13. **wounded.** Heb. made sick. 2 Ch 18:33mg. 1 K 22:34mg. 2 K 8:29.

24. **the second.** Ge 41:43. **they.** 2 K 22:30. **died.** Ps 36:6. Ec 8:14. 9:1, 2. **in one of the.** or, among the. 2 Ch 34:28. **sepulchres.** Heb. qeber, Ge +23:4. **Judah.** Zc 12:11.

25. **Jeremiah.** Je 22:10. La 4:20. **lamented.** 2 S 1:17. 3:33. Je 9:17. Ezk 27:32. 32:16. Am 5:16. Mt 9:23. **all the singing.** Jb 3:8. Ec 12:5. Je 9:17-21. Mt 9:23. **singing women.** 2 S 19:35. Ec 2:8. Ezr 2:65. Ne 7:67. **and made them.** Je 22:20. **an ordinance.** Jg 11:39mg. Je 10:3mg.

26. **goodness.** Heb. kindnesses. *121C1B, Ge +20:13. 2 Ch 31:20. 32:32. Ne 13:14.

27. **deeds.** 2 Ch 20:34. 24:27. 25:26. 26:22. 32:32. 33:19. 2 K 10:34. 16:19. 20:20. 21:25.

2 CHRONICLES 36

Jehoahaz succeeds Josiah, but Necho carries him into Egypt; and makes Jehoiakim king, 1-4. He reigns wickedly and is put in chains by Nebuchadnezzar, who carries some of the sacred vessels to Babylon, 5-7. Jehoiachin is made king, who in a short time is carried captive to Babylon, with other of the sacred vessels; and Zedekiah succeeds, 8-10. He reigns very wickedly, despises the warnings of Jeremiah, and rebels against Nebuchadnezzar, 11-13. The sins of the priests and people cause the utter destruction of Jerusalem and the desolation of the land, for seventy years, 14-21. Cyrus's proclamation for rebuilding the temple, 22, 23.

1. **the people.** 2 Ch 26:1. 33:25. 2 K 23:30, etc. **Jehoahaz.** 2 K 23:31-34. 1 Ch 3:15. Je 22:11.

3. **put him down.** Heb. removed him. 2 K 23:33. **condemned.** Heb. mulcted. or, fineth. Ex 21:22. Pr 19:19.

4. **made Eliakim.** 2 K 23:34, 35. 1 Ch 3:15. **Necho.** Je 22:10-12. Ezk 19:3, 4.

5. **Jehoiakim.** 2 K 23:36, 37. Je 22:13-19. 26:21-23. 36:1, 27-32.

6. A.M. 3397. B.C. 607. **came up.** 2 K 24:1, 2, 5, 6, 13, etc. Ezk 19:5-9. Da 1:1, 2. Hab 1:5-10. **fetters.** *or,* chains. Jg 16:21. 2 S 3:34. **carry him to.** 2 K 24:6.

7. A.M. 3398. B.C. 606. **the vessels.** 2 K 24:13. Ezr 1:7-11. Je 27:16-18. 28:3. Da 5:2-4.

8. A.M. 3394-3405. B.C. 610-599. **written.** 2 K 24:5, 6. **Jehoiachin.** 1 Ch 3:16, 17, Jeconiah. Je 22:24, 28, Coniah. Mt 1:11, 12, Jeconias.

9. A.M. 3405. B.C. 599. **eight years old.** The Syriac, Arabic, and the parallel place (2 K 24:8, on which see the Note), have "eighteen years;" which, as Scaliger observes, is no doubt the genuine reading. 2 K 24:8, 9.

10. **when the year was expired.** Heb. at the return of the year. 1 K +20:22. **king Nebuchadnezzar.** 2 K 24:10-17. 25:27-30. Je 29:2. Ezk 1:2. **goodly vessels.** Heb. vessels of desire. *121R5, Ge +27:15. ver. 7. Je +25:34mg. 27:18-22. Da 1:1, 2. 5:2, 23. +10:3mg. +11:8mg. **Zedekiah.** 2 K 24:17, Mattaniah his father's brother. 1 Ch 3:15, 16. Je 37:1.

11. A.M. 3405-3416. B.C. 599-588. **one and twenty.** 2 K 24:18-20. Je 52:1-3.

12. **humbled.** 2 Ch 32:26. 33:12, 19, 23. Ex 10:3. Da 5:22, 23. Ja *4:10. 1 P *5:6. **before Jeremiah.** Je 21:1, etc. 27:12, etc. 28:1, etc. 34:2, etc. 37:2, etc. 38:14, etc. **the mouth.** 2 Ch 35:22.

13. **rebelled.** 2 K 24:20. Je 52:2, 3. Ezk 17:11-20. **who had.** Jsh 9:15, 19, 20. 2 S 21:2. **stiffened.** 2 K 17:14. Ne 9:16, 17. Is 48:4. **hardened.** Ex 8:15, 32. 9:17. Ne 9:29. Ro 2:4, 5. He 3:8, 13.

14. **all the chief.** 2 K 16:10-16. Ezr 9:7. Je 5:5. 37:13-15. 38:4. Ezk 22:6, 26-28. Da 9:6, 8. Mi 3:1-4, 9-11. 7:2. Zp 3:3, 4. **very much.** 2 Ch 28:3. 33:9. **polluted.** 2 Ch 33:4-7. Ezk 8:5-16.

15. **the Lord.** 2 Ch 24:18-21. 33:10. 2 K 17:13. Je 25:3, 4. 26:5. 35:15. 44:4, 5. **by his messengers.** Heb. by the hand of his messengers. **betimes.** i.e. continually and carefully. **because.** Jg 10:16. 2 K 13:23. Ho 11:8. Lk *19:41-44.

16. **mocked.** 2 Ch 30:10. Ps 35:16. Is 28:22. Je 5:12, 13. 20:7. Lk 18:32. 22:63, 64. 23:11, 36. Ac 2:13. 17:32. He 11:36. **despised.** Pr *1:24-30. Lk 16:14. Ac 13:41. 1 Th 4:8. **misused.** Je 32:3. 38:6. Mt *5:12. 21:33-41. 23:34-47. Ac 7:52. **the wrath.** Ps 74:1. 79:1-5. **till.** Pr 6:15. 29:1. **remedy.** Heb. healing. 2 Ch 21:18. Pr 4:22. 6:15. 12:18. 13:17. 16:24. 29:1. Je 8:15. 14:19. 33:6. Ml 4:2.

17. **he brought.** 2 Ch 33:11. Dt 28:49. 2 K 24:2, 3. Ezr 9:7. Je 15:8. 32:42. 40:3. Da 9:14. **the king.** 2 K 25:1, etc. Je 39:1, etc. 52:1, etc. **who slew.** Le 26:14, etc. Dt 28:15, etc. 29:18-28. 30:18. 31:16-18. 32:15-28. Ps 74:20. 79:2, 3. Je +*11:22. 15:9. 18:21. La 2:21, 22. **in the house.** 2 Ch 24:21. La 2:20. Ezk 9:5-7. Lk 13:1, 2. **no compassion.** Dt 28:50. Ps 74:20. **or maiden.** or, virgin. Ge +24:16 (*S#1330h). Ex 22:16, 17.

18. A.M. 3416. B.C. 588. **all the vessels.** ver. 7, 10. 2 K 25:13-17. Je 27:18-22. 52:17-23. Da 5:3. **treasures.** 2 K 20:13-17. Is 39:6. Zc 1:6.

19. **they burnt.** 2 K 25:9. Ps 74:4-8. 79:1, 7. Is 64:10, 11. Je 7:4, 14. 52:13. La 4:1. Mi 3:12. Lk 21:6. **brake down.** 2 K 25:10, 11. Je 52:14, 15.

20. A.M. 3416-3468. B.C. 588-536. **And them that had escaped from.** Heb. And the remainder from. 2 K 25:11. **they were servants.** Dt 28:47, 48. Je 27:7. **until the reign.** ver. 22. Ezr 1:1, etc.

21. **To fulfil.** Je 25:9, 12. 26:6, 7. 27:12, 13. 29:10. Da 9:2. Zc 1:4-6. **until the land.** Le 25:4-6. 26:34, 35, 43. Zc 1:12.

22. A.M. 3468. B.C. 536. This verse and the next have a double aspect. They look back to the prophecy of Jeremiah, and show how that was accomplished; and they look forward to the history of Ezra, which begins with a repetition of these two last verses. **in the first.** Ezr 1:1-3. **Cyrus.** i.e. *supreme power; the sun; possess thou the furnace.* Is +45:1. 44:28. Da 10:1. **Persia.** i.e. *he divided,* *S#6539h. 2 Ch 36:20, 22, 22, 23. Ezr 1:1, 1, 2, 8. 3:7. 4:3, 5, 5, 7. 7:1. 9:9. Est 1:3, 14, 18, 19. 10:2. Ezk 27:10. 38:5. Da 8:20. 10:1, 13, 13, 20. 11:2. **that the word.** ver. 21. Je 25:12, 14. 29:10. 32:42-44. 33:10-14. He 10:23. **the Lord stirred.** 2 Ch 21:16. 1 S 26:19. 1 K 11:14, 23. 1 Ch 5:26. Ezr 1:5. Is 13:3-5, 17, 18. 44:28. 45:1-5. Hg 1:14. **spirit.** Heb. *ruach,* Ge +41:8. *121A10, Ge +26:35. **a proclamation.** 2 Ch 24:9. 30:5.

23. **All the kingdoms.** Ps 75:5-7. Da 2:21, 37. 4:35. 5:18, 23. **he hath charged.** Is 44:26-28. **Who is there.** 1 Ch 22:16. 29:5. Ezr 7:13. Zc 2:6, 7. Ro *8:31.

EZRA

Cyrus issues a proclamation, allowing the Jews to go up to Jerusalem and build the temple; and exhorting those who stayed behind to assist them, 1-4. Many prepare to return, and others contribute to the expense, 5, 6. Cyrus restores the vessels of the temple to Shesh-bazzar, 7-11.

1. A.M. 3468. B.C. 536. **Now in the.** 2 Ch *36:22, 23. **Cyrus.** *Cyrus* is said to have been the son of *Cambyses*, king of Persia, and *Mandane*, daughter of Astyages, king of Media: he was born about 600 years before Christ, and died at the age of 70, after a reign of 30 years. He was mentioned by name, and his conquests foretold, by the prophet Isaiah, above a century before his birth. Josephus (Ant. l. ii. c. 2) accounts for the partiality he evinced towards the Jews, from the circumstance of these prophecies being shown him, probably by Daniel. **by the mouth.** Je *25:12-14. *29:10. 33:7-13. Da 9:2. **the Lord.** Ezr 5:13-15. 6:22. 7:27. Ps *106:46. Pr *21:1. Da 2:1. **stirred up.** 2 Ch 36:21. Je 51:11. Hg 1:14. **spirit.** Heb. *ruach*, Ge +41:8. ʃ121A10, Ge +26:35. **made a proclamation.** Heb. caused a voice to pass. Ezr 10:7. Ex 36:6. Le 25:9. 2 Ch 30:5. Ne 8:15. Da 9:25. Mt 3:1-3. Jn 1:23.

2. **Lord God.** 1 K 8:27. 2 Ch 2:12. Is 66:1. Je *10:11. Da *2:21, 28. *5:23. **hath given.** 2 Ch 36:23. Je 27:6, 7. Da 2:37, 38. *4:25, 32. 5:19-21. 7:5, 15. **all the kingdoms.** According to the testimony of ancient writers, Cyrus, at this time, reigned over the Medes, Persians, Hyrcanians, Syrians, Assyrians, Indians, etc. and all lesser Asia. **he hath charged.** Is *44:26-28. *45:1, 12, 13.

3. **all his people.** 2 Ch 36:23. 1 K 18:39. **his God.** Jsh *1:9. 1 Ch *28:20. Mt *28:20. **he is the God.** Dt *32:31. Ps *83:18. Is *45:5. Je *10:10. Da 2:47. *6:26. Ac *10:36.

4. **let the men.** Ezr 7:16-18. Ac 24:17. 3 J 6-8. **help him.** Heb. lift him up. Ezr 8:36. 1 K 9:11. Est 9:3. Ps 28:9. Ec *4:9, 10. Ga *6:2. **the freewill.** Le +*23:38. Ezr 2:68-70. 1 Ch 29:3, 9, 17.

5. **with all whose.** ver. 1. 2 Ch 36:22. Ne 2:12. Pr 16:1. 2 C 8:16. Ph *2:13. Ja 1:16, 17. 3 J 11. **spirit.** Heb. *ruach*, Ge +41:8. Ps 78:8. Da 5:12. 2 C +*12:8.

6. **about.** ʃ121J1, Nu +22:4. **strengthened their hands.** *that is*, helped them. Ezr 4:4. 7:15, 16. 8:25-28, 33. Je 38:4. **willingly offered.** ver. 4. Ps 110:3. 2 C *9:7.

7. **Also Cyrus.** Ezr 5:14. 6:5. **brought forth the vessels.** Some of the vessels of the temple had been cut in pieces by the victors (2 K 24:13), but the most valuable had been providentially preserved through all the succeeding revolutions, and were now ordered by Cyrus to be restored to Sheshbazzar; and so were at last brought back to Jerusalem, and again employed in the service of the sanctuary. It is generally agreed that the ark was lost or destroyed (Je 3:16n) when the temple was burnt: and it is likely, that by the absence of it, and the visible glory, that "God would signify, he was withdrawing his presence from that house of stone, to dwell in the temple of Christ's body,

who offered himself to God, and thereby put an end to these figurative sacrifices" (Bp. Patrick, cited by Scott). Je +*3:16n. **Nebuchadnezzar.** 2 K 24:13. 25:13-16. 2 Ch 36:7, 10, 18. Je 27:21, 22. 28:3-6. Da 1:2. 5:2, 3, 23.

8. **Mithredath.** i.e. *given by Mithras; searching out of law; given by the genius of the sun*, *S#4990h. Ezr 1:8. 4:7. (1) The treasurer of Cyrus, king of Persia, Ezr 1:8. (2) A Persian who opposed the Jews in the time of Artaxerxes, king of Persia, Ezr 4:7. **Sheshbazzar.** i.e. *joy in tribulation; worshipper of fire; deliverance of brightness; fine linen in the tribulation*, *S#8339h. ver. 11h. Ezr 5:14, 16. Hg 1:1, 14. 2:2-4. Zc 4:6-10.

9. **chargers of gold.** Nu 7:13, 19, etc. 1 K 7:50. 2 Ch 4:8, 11, 21, 22. 24:14. Mt 14:8. **nine.** Mt 10:29-31.

11. **the vessels.** 2 K 25:15. Ro 9:23. 2 T 2:19-21. Instead of 5400, the enumeration of the articles in ver. 9, 10, only amounts to 2499; but in the account, Esdras 2:13, 14, the amount is 5469, as will be apparent from the following statements: IN EZRA: (1) gold chargers, 30; (2) silver chargers, 1000; (3) knives, 29; (4) gold basons, 30; (5) silver basons, 410; (6) other vessels, 1000; said to be 5400, but only 2499; deficiency, 2901. IN ESDRAS: (1) gold cups, 1000; (2) silver cups, 1000; (3) silver censers, 29; (4) gold vials, 30; (5) silver vials, 2410; other vessels, 1000; total, 5469; surplus, 69. It is supposed that they actually amounted to 5400, but that only the *chief* of them were specified, the spoons, etc., being omitted. Young suggests that this number (5400) probably included those given in presents, ver. 6 above. **captivity.** Heb. transportation. Ezr 4:1mg. Mt 1:11, 12.

The principal persons who returned from Babylon, 1, 2. The number of the several families which accompanied them, 3-35. The priests, 36-39. The Levites, 40-42. The Nethinims, 43-54. The children of Solomon's servants, 55-60. The priests who could not show their pedigree, 61-63. The sum total, with their retinue, 64-67. Their oblations towards the temple and its service, 68-70.

1. **the children.** Ezr 5:8. 6:2. Ne 7:6, etc. Est 1:1. 3:8, 11. 8:9. Ac 23:34. **whom Nebuchadnezzar.** 2 K 24:14-16. 25:11. 2 Ch ch. 36. Je 39:52. La 1:3, 5. 4:22. Zp 2:7.

2. **Zerubbabel.** i.e. *scattered* or *born at Babylon*. Ezr 1:11, Sheshbazzar. Ne 7:7. Hg +1:1, 12, 14. 2:2, 4, 21. Zc 4:6-10. Mt 1:12, 13, Zorobabel. **Jeshua.** i.e. *saviour*. Ezr 3:8, 9. 4:3. 5:2. Hg 1:12, 14. 2:4. Zc 3:1, 3, 8, 9, Joshua. **Nehemiah.** i.e. *comforted of Jah.* Ne +1:1. **Seraiah.** i.e. *head of Jah.* 2 S +8:17. Ne 7:7, Azariah, Raamiah, Nahamani, Mispereth, Nehum. **Reelaiah.** i.e. *a reeling of Jah; shaken of Jah; trembling of the Lord*, *S#7480h. **Mordecai.** i.e. *a little man or worshipper of Mars*. Est +2:5. **Bilshan.** i.e. *son of the tongue, i.e. loquacious or eloquent*, *S#1114h. Ne 7:7. **Mizpar.** i.e. *number*, *S#4558h. **Bigvai.** i.e.

happy; a gardner; in my bodies, ✱S#902h. Ezr 2:2, 14. 8:14. Ne 7:7, 19. 10:16. **Rehum**. i.e. *merciful.* Ezr 4:8. Ne +12:3.

3. **children**. The word *children*, in this table, when prefixed to the name of a *man*, signifies the *descendants* of that person, as from ver. 3-21; and when prefixed to the name of a *town, place,* etc., it signifies the *inhabitants* of that place, as from ver. 21-25. **Parosh**. i.e. *dancing; a flea,* ✱S#6551h. Ezr 2:3. 8:3, Pharosh. 10:25. Ne 3:25. 7:8. 10:14. (1) One whose children came up from Babylon, Ezr 2:3. (2) One whose sons married strange wives, Ezr 10:25. (3) Father of Pedaiah, who helped to build the wall, Ne 3:25.

4. **Shephatiah**. i.e. *judged of Jah.* Ezr 8:8. 2 S +3:4. Ne 7:9.

5. **Arah**. i.e. *a path.* 1 Ch +7:39. Ne 6:18. 7:10: 652.

6. **Pahath-moab**. i.e. *pit, snare,* or *governor of Moab,* ✱S#6355h. Ezr 2:6. 8:4. 10:30. Ne 3:11. 7:11: 2818. 10:14. **Joab**. i.e. *Jah is father.* Ezr 8:9. 1 S +26:6.

7. **Elam**. i.e. *concealed.* ver. 31. Ezr 8:7. 10:26. Ge +10:22. Ne 7:12.

8. **Zattu**. i.e. *brightness; branch; ornament; beauty,* ✱S#2240h. Ezr 2:8. 10:27. Ne 7:13: 845. 10:14.

9. **Zaccai**. i.e. *pure.* Ne +7:14.

10. **Bani**. i.e. *built up,* ✱S#1137h. Ezr 2:10. 10:29, 34, 38. 2 S 23:36. 1 Ch 6:46. 9:4. Ne 3:17. 8:7. 9:4, 4, 5. 10:13, 14. 11:22. The variation of *Bani* and *Binnui* arises from the elision of *wav;* but the LXX. have here *Banoui,* as in the parallel place. Ezr 10:34. Ne 7:15, Binnui, 648. (1) One of David's heroes, 2 S 23:36. (2) A son of Merari, 1 Ch 6:46. (3) A dweller in Jerusalem, 1 Ch 9:4. (4) A Levite; Rehum his son built the wall, Ne 3:17; 9:4, 5. (5) A Levite who lived before the return from the exile, of the sons of Asaph, family of Gershom, Ne 11:22. (6) Founder of a house or family, Ezr 10:34. (7) A Jewish descendant of a strange wife, Ezr 10:38. (8) A priest who assisted Ezra, Ne 10:13, some consider same as (4). (9) A family of exiles, Ezr 2:10; 10:29. (10) One who renewed the covenant under Nehemiah, Ne 10:14, some consider same as (4).

11. **Bebai**. i.e. *fatherly; with the desire of the Lord, i.e. with supreme desire; my cavities,* ✱S#893h. Ezr 2:11. 8:11, 11. 10:28. Ne 7:16: 628. 10:15.

12. **Azgad**. i.e. *stern troop; strength of a troop; strong of fortune; the god Gad is strong,* ✱S#5803h. Ezr 2:12. 8:12. Ne 7:17: 2322. 10:15.

13. **Adonikim**. i.e. *my lord has risen.* Ezr 8:13. Ne +7:18: 667.

14. **Bigvai**. ver. +2. Ezr 8:14. Ne 7:19: 2067.

15. **Adin**. i.e. *ornament; dainty; soft, pliant, pleasant; luxuriant,* ✱S#5720h. Ezr 2:15. 8:6. Ne 7:20: 655. 10:16. (1) An Israelite whose descendants returned from Babylon with Zerubbabel, Ezr 2:15; Ne 7:20. (2) One whose posterity came up with Ezra, Ezr 8:6. (3) Probably the same as Number 1. The name of a family who, with Nehemiah and the people, sealed the covenant, Ne 10:16.

16. **Ater**. i.e. *lame; binder; left handed (i.e. shut as to the right hand); shut, stopped; bound, dumb,* ✱S#333h. Ne 7:21. (1) An Israelite whose descendants returned to Jerusalem after the captivity, Ezr 2:16; Ne 7:21. (2) Head of a family whose descendants returned after the captivity, Ezr 2:42; Ne 7:45.

17. **Bezai**. i.e. *miry.* Ne +7:23: 324.

18. **Jorah**. i.e. *casting, shooting, sprinkling; autumnal rain,* ✱S#3139h. Ne 7:24, Hariph.

19. **Hashum**. i.e. *rich, wealthy; the desolate hasted; enriched,* ✱S#2828h. Ezr 2:19. 10:33. Ne 7:22: 328. 8:4. 10:18. (1) One whose children returned from Babylon, Ezr 2:19; Ne 7:22. (2) One whose sons took strange wives, Ezr 10:33. (3) One who stood up with Ezra to read the law, Ne 8:4. (4) One who sealed the covenant, Ne 10:18.

20. **Gibbar**. i.e. *mighty; the valiant; a mighty one, a hero,* ✱S#1402h. Ne 7:25, Gibeon.

21. **Beth-lehem**. 1 Ch 2:50-52.

22. **Netophah**. i.e. *dropping; distillation; prophesy; falling in drops,* ✱S#5199h. 2 S 23:28. 1 Ch 2:54. Ne 7:26h: 188. Je 40:8.

23. **Anathoth**. i.e. *responses, echoes.* Jsh 21:18. 1 Ch +7:8. Ne 7:27. Is 10:30. Je 1:1. 11:21.

24. **Azmaveth**. i.e. *strength of death.* 2 S +23:31. Ne 7:28, Beth-azmaveth.

25. **Kirjath-arim**. i.e. *city of forests* or *enemies* or *cities,* ✱S#7157h. Ezr 2:25. Jsh 18:28. Also Jsh 9:17. 15:9, 60. 18:14, 15. Jg 18:12, 12. 1 S 6:21. 7:1, 2. 1 Ch 2:50, 52, 53. 13:5, 6. 2 Ch 1:4. Ne 7:29, Kirjath-jearim. Je 26:20. **Chephirah**. i.e. *a village.* Jsh +9:17. 18:26. Ne 7:29. **Beeroth**. i.e. *wells.* Dt +10:6. Jsh 9:17. Ne 7:29.

26. **Ramah**. i.e. *high place.* Jsh 18:24, 25. Ne 7:30. Je +31:15. **Gaba**. i.e. *a height, hill.* Jsh +18:24.

27. **Michmas**. i.e. *laid up; a treasure; something hidden; treasury; poverty was melted; poverty of servile work,* ✱S#4363h. Ezr 2:27. 1 S 13:+2, Michmash, 5, 11, 16, 23. 14:5, 31. Ne 7:31h. 11:31. Is 10:28, Michmash.

28. **Bethel**. i.e. *house of God.* Ge +12:8. **Ai**. i.e. *heap.* Ge 12:8, Hai. Jsh +7:2. 8:9, 17. Ne 7:32: 123.

29. **Nebo**. i.e. *prophet.* This *Nebo* was probably the *Nabau* which Eusebius and Jerome place eight miles south from Hebron. Nu +32:3. Dt 32:49. Ne 7:33. Is 15:2. Je 48:1, 22.

30. **Magbish**. i.e. *congregating; crystallizing,* ✱S#4019h. The children of Magbish are not named in our present copies of Nehemiah; but the Alexandrian MS. of the LXX. has the same reading as here.

31. **Elam**. i.e. *hidden, concealed.* ver. 7. Ge +10:22. Ne 7:34.

32. **Harim**. i.e. *flat nosed.* Ezr 10:31. 1 Ch +24:8. Ne 3:11. 7:35.

33. **Lod**. i.e. *contention, strife.* 1 Ch 8:12. Ne 6:2. +7:37. 11:34, 35. **Hadid**. *or,* Hadrid, as in some copies. i.e. *sharp; making sharp,* ✱S#2307h. Ezr 2:33. Ne 7:37. 11:34. *Hadid* is probably the *Adida* of Josephus, and the Maccabees (1 Mac 12:38. 13:13), a city situated on a hill in the plain country of Judah, and the *Aditha* of Eusebius, which he places near Diospolis, *Lydda,* or *Lod.* **Ono**. i.e. *strong; gain-bringing; strength, power; his vigor, his iniquity,* ✱S#207h. Ezr 2:33. 1 Ch 8:12. Ne 6:2. 7:37. 11:35.

34. **Jericho**. 1 K 16:34. Ne 7:36.

35. **Senaah**. i.e. *thorny, bushy; an enemy; lifted up, high; hatred,* ✱S#5570h. Ezr 2:35. Ne 3:3. 7:38: 3930.

36. **Jedaiah**. i.e. *known of Jah.* 1 Ch +9:10. 24:7. **Jeshua**. i.e. *a savior.* Ezr 3:9. Ne 7:39. +8:17.

37. **Immer**. i.e. *lamb; talkative.* Ezr 10:20. 1 Ch +9:12. 24:14. Ne 7:40.

38. **Pashur**. i.e. *prosperity everywhere.* Ezr 10:22. 1 Ch 9:12. Ne 7:41. Je +20:1.

39. **Harim**. i.e. *flat nosed*. ver. 32. Ezr 10:21. 1 Ch 24:8. Ne 7:42.

40. **Kadmiel**. i.e. *he who is before God, i.e. servant of God; going before God*, *S#6934h. Ezr 2:40. 3:9. Ne 7:43. 9:4, 5. 10:9. 12:8, 24. (1) A Levite whose children returned from Babylon, Ezr 2:40; Ne 7:43. (2) A Levite who forwarded the foundations of the temple, Ezr 3:9, and the solemn fast, Ne 9:4, and sealed the covenant, Ne 10:9, and went up with Zerubbabel, Ne 12:8. **Hodaviah**. i.e. *praise Jah*. Ezr 3:9, Judah. 1 Ch +5:24. Ne 7:43, Hodevah.

41. **singers**. Those who conducted the temple psalmody, 2 Ch 35:15. **Asaph**. i.e. *he gathers*. 2 K +18:18. 1 Ch 6:39. 15:17. 25:1, 2. Ne 7:44: 148.

42. **the porters**. 1 Ch 26:1, etc. Ne 7:45: 138. **Shallum**. i.e. *recompensed*. 2 K +15:10. **Ater**. i.e. *bound, shut*. ver. +16. **Talmon**. i.e. *oppressed*. 1 Ch +9:17. **Akkub**. i.e. *taken by the heel*. 1 Ch +3:24. **Hatita**. i.e. *digging, exploring; a digging; my sin removed*, *S#2410h. Ezr 2:42. Ne 7:45. **Shobai**. i.e. *a captor; sitting; my backslidings; return, restoration, or recompense of the Lord*, *S#7630h. Ezr 2:42. Ne 7:45.

43. **Nethinims**. ver. 58. 1 Ch 9:2. Ne 7:46-56. 10:28. **Ziha**. i.e. *dryness; drought; parching*, *S#6727h. Ezr 2:43. Ne 7:46. 11:21. (1) A Nethinim whose descendants returned from Babylon, Ezr 2:43; Ne 11:21. (2) A ruler of the Nethinim, Ne 11:21. **Hasupha**. i.e. *made naked; stripped; exhausted; made bare*, *S#2817h. Ezr 2:43. Ne 7:46. This variation only exists in the translation, the original being written here *Husupha*, and in the parallel place defectively, *Hasupha*. Ne 7:46, Hashupha. **Tabbaoth**. i.e. *signets*. Ne +7:46.

44. **Keros**. i.e. *a weaver's comb; a tach or hook; stooping*, *S#7026h. Ezr 2:44. Ne 7:47. **Siaha**. i.e. *council, congregation; multitudes; departing*, *S#5517h. Ezr 2:44. Ne 7:47. "Sia" is merely a contraction of "Siaha," by the elision of *hay*. Ne 7:47, Sia. **Padon**. i.e. *liberation, redemption; ransom*, *S#6303h. Ezr 2:44. Ne 7:47.

45. **Lebanah**. i.e. *white, the moon*, *S#3838h. Ezr 2:45. Ne 7:48. These variations merely arise from the mutation of *hay* into *aleph*, according to the Chaldee dialect; the original being respectively "Lebanah" and "Lebana;" "Hagabah" and "Hagaba." Ne 7:48, Lebana, Hagaba. **Hagabah**. i.e. *a locust; grasshopper, leaper*, *S#2286h. Ezr 2:45. Ne 7:48. **Akkub**. i.e. *taken by the heel*. 1 Ch +3:24.

46. **Hagab**. i.e. *a locust; grasshopper*, *S#2285h. **Shalmai**. or, Shamlai. i.e. *peaceable; my peace-offerings; my garment; peace offerings of the Lord*, *S#8073h. Shamlai, of the Kethiv, is evidently a mistake for *Shalmai*, as the *Keri* and LXX. have. **Hanan**. i.e. *he has grace*. 1 Ch +4:24.

47. **Giddel**. i.e. *too great; he has magnified; he has become great*, *S#1435h. Ezr 2:47, 56. Ne 7:49, 58. **Gahar**. i.e. *hiding place; lurking place; the valley burned*, *S#1515h. Ezr 2:47. Ne +7:49. **Reaiah**. i.e. *seen of Jah*. 1 Ch +4:2.

48. **Rezin**. i.e. *firm, stable, prince*. 2 K +15:37. **Nekoda**. i.e. *speckled, spotted; shepherd; distinguished*, *S#5353h. Ezr 2:48, 60. Ne 7:50, 62. **Gazzam**. i.e. *palmer-worm; violently torn off*, *S#1502h. Ezr 2:48. Ne 7:51.

49. **Uzza**. i.e. *strength*. 2 K +21:18. **Paseah**. i.e. *lame*. 1 Ch +4:12. Ne 7:51, Phaseah. **Besai**. i.e. *a sword; domineering; victory; trodden down of the*

Lord, *S#1153h. Ezr 2:49. Ne 7:52.

50. **Asnah**. i.e. *storehouse; bramble; to be sharp*, *S#619h. **Mehunim**. i.e. *dwellings, habitations*, *S#4586h. Ne 7:52, Meunim, Nephisheshim. **Nephusim**. i.e. *expansions; torn in pieces; scatter spices*, *S#5304h. Ezr 2:50. Also Ne 7:52.

51. **Bakbuk**. i.e. *a bottle; emptied*, *S#1227h. Ezr 2:51. Ne 7:53. **Hakupha**. i.e. *bent, bowed; decree of the month*, *S#2709h. Ezr 2:51. Ne 7:53. **Harhur**. i.e. *inflammation; burning fever; extreme burning*, *S#2744h. Ezr 2:51. Ne 7:53.

52. **Bazluth**. i.e. *a making naked; stripping*, *S#1213h. Ne 7:54, Bazlith. **Mehida**. i.e. *a joining together; junction; noble; allegorist*, *S#4240h. Ezr 2:52. Ne 7:54. **Harsha**. i.e. *enchanter, magician; hidden; secret work*, *S#2797h. Ezr 2:52. Ne 7:54.

53. **Barkos**. i.e. *a painter; a son like his father; the son cut off; son who observes his father's ways*, *S#1302h. Ezr 2:53. Ne 7:55. **Sisera**. i.e. *a field of battle*. Jg +4:2. **Thamah**. i.e. *laughter; suppresses; will be fat*, *S#8547h. Ezr 2:53. Ne 7:55, Tamah.

54. **Neziah**. i.e. *pure, sincere; illustrious; overseer; victorious*, *S#5335h. Ezr 2:54. Ne 7:56. **Hatipha**. i.e. *seized, caught; captive; captivated*, *S#2412h. Ezr 2:54. Ne 7:56.

55. **Solomon's**. 1 K 9:21. **Sotai**. i.e. *drawing back; drawn back of the Lord; my swervings*, *S#5479h. Ezr 2:55. Ne 7:57. **Sophereth**. i.e. *scribe*. Ne +7:57. **Peruda**. i.e. *grain, kernel; separation; dispersion; separate, eminent*, *S#6514h. Ezr 2:55. Ne 7:57, Perida.

56. **Jaalah**. i.e. *female ibex, chamois; a wild goat; climber*, *S#3279h. Ezr 2:56. Ne 7:58, Jaala. **Darkon**. i.e. *scatterer; bearer; thrusting through; the dwelling of lamentation*, *S#1874h. Ezr 2:56. Ne 7:58. **Giddel**. i.e. *too great; giant*. ver. +47.

57. **Shephatiah**. i.e. *judged of Jah*. 2 S +3:4. **Hattil**. i.e. *waving; fluctuating; sin cast out; inquietude*, *S#2411h. Ezr 2:57. Ne 7:59. **Pochereth**. i.e. *a snaring; beguiling; detaining the glory*, *S#6380h. Ezr 2:57. Ne 7:59. **Zebaim**. i.e. *gazelles*, *S#6380h. **Ami**. i.e. *increased; a workman; bond-servant*, *S#532h. Ne 7:59, Amon.

58. **Nethinims**. Ezr 7:7. Jsh 9:21, 23, 27. 1 Ch 9:2. Ne 3:26. 7:60. **Solomon's**. 1 K 9:21.

59. **Tel-harsa**. i.e. *hill or heap of salt*, *S#8528h. Ezr 2:59. Ne 7:61, Tel-haresha, Addon. **Tel-harsa**. i.e. *mound of workmanship; hill of a wood; hill of plowing*, *S#8521h. Ezr 2:59. Ne 7:61. **Cherub**. i.e. *celestial; guard; as if contending*, *S#3743h. Ezr 2:59. Ne 7:61. **Addan**. i.e. *lord, judge; strong; their hap; grievous calamity*, *S#135h. **Immer**. i.e. *talkative, loquacious*. 1 Ch +9:12. **seed**. or, pedigree.

60. **of Delaiah**. i.e. *drawn up by Jah*. Ne 7:62: 642. Je +36:12. **Tobiah**. i.e. *pleasing to Jehovah; goodness of Jehovah; distinguished of the Lord*, *S#2900h. Ezr 2:60. Ne 2:10, 19. 4:3, 7. 6:1, 12, 14, 17, 17, 19. 7:62. 13:4, 7, 8. Zc 6:14. Also 2 Ch 17:8. Zc 6:10, Tobijah. (1) One who came with his children from Babylon, Ezr 2:60. Ne 7:62; Zc 6:10. (2) An Ammonite who resisted Nehemiah, Ne 2:10; 4:3; 6:17; 13:4.

61. **the children**. Ne 7:63, 64. **Habaiah**. i.e. *hidden of Jah*, *S#2252h. Ezr 2:61. Ne 7:63. **Koz**. i.e. *the thorn; a trouble*, *S#6976h. Ezr 2:61. 1 Ch 4:+8, Coz. 24:+10, Hakkoz. Ne 3:4, 21. 7:63. **Barzillai**. i.e. *of iron; iron of the Lord*. 2 S 17:27. 19:31-39. +21:8. 1 K 2:7.

62. **therefore**. Le 21:21-23. Nu 3:10. 16:40. 18:7. **not found**. Lk ☽=10:20. 2 T ☽=2:19. **were they, as polluted, put from the priesthood**. Heb. they were polluted from the priesthood. Ezk 44:10-14. **put**. ☾63H, Ge +12:15. A more correct translation of the figure Ellipsis (Relative: of a combined word) would be: "Therefore they were polluted (and put) from the priesthood."

63. **Tirshatha**. *or*, governor. i.e. *severity, severe; governor; that overturns; thou shalt possess there*, ✽S#8660h. Ezr 2:63. Ne 7:65, 70. 8:9. 10:1. The person who held this office at this time was probably Zerubbabel. The word "Tirshatha" is supposed to be Persian; and if, as Castel supposes, it signifies *austerity*, or that *fear* which is impressed by the authority of a governor, it may be derived from *tars*, "ear," or *tursh*, "acid, austere." Ne 7:65. 8:9. 10:1. **should not**. Le 2:3, 10. 6:17, 29. 7:16. 10:17, 18. 22:2, 3, 10, 14-16. Nu 18:9-11, 19, 32. **Urim**. Le 8:8. Nu 27:21. Dt 33:8. 1 S 28:6.

64. **forty and two thousand three**. Though the sum total, both here and in Nehemiah, is equal, namely, 42,360, yet the particulars reckoned up only make 29,818 in Ezra, and 31,089 in Nehemiah; and we find that Nehemiah mentions 1765 persons who are not in Ezra, and Ezra has 494 not mentioned in Nehemiah. This last circumstance, which seems to render all hope of reconciling them impossible, Mr Alting thinks is the very point by which they can be reconciled; for, if we add Ezra's *surplus* to the *sum* in Nehemiah, and Nehemiah's *surplus* to the *number* in Ezra, they will both amount to 31,583; which subtracted from 42,360, leaves a deficiency of 10,777, which are not named because they did not belong to the tribes of Judah and Benjamin, or to the priests, but to the other Israelitish tribes. Ezr 9:8. Ne 7:66-69. Is 10:20-22. Je 23:3.

65. **servants**. Is 14:1, 2. **two hundred**. Ex 15:20, 21. 2 S 19:35. 2 Ch +35:25. Ne 7:67. Ps 68:25. 148:12, 13. Ec 2:8. Je 9:17, 18. Mt 9:23.

68. **offered freely**. Ex 25:2. 35:5, etc., 29. 36:3. Le +*23:38. Nu 7:3, etc. 1 Ch 29:5-17. Ne 7:70, etc. Ps 110:3. Lk 21:1-4. 2 C *8:3, 12. *9:7. **in his place**. Ezr 3:3. 1 Ch 21:18. 22:1. 2 Ch 3:1.

69. **the treasure**. Ezr 8:25-34. 1 K 7:51. 1 Ch 22:14. 26:20-28. Ne 7:71, 72.

70. **the priests**. Ezr 6:16, 17. 1 Ch 11:2. Ne 7:73. 11:3.

EZRA 3

The Jews re-assemble at Jerusalem, build an altar, offer sacrifices, keep the feast of tabernacles, and prepare to re-build the temple, 1-7. Under the direction of Zerubbabel and Jeshua the foundation is laid, amidst the rejoicing of some, and the weeping of others, 8-13.

1. **the seventh month**. That is, *Tisri*. Ex 23:14-17. Le 16:29. 23:24, 27, etc. Nu 29:1, etc. Dt 16:16. Ne 8:2, 14. **as one**. Jg 20:1. Ne 8:1. Zp 3:9. Ac 2:46. 4:32. 1 C 1:10.

2. **Jeshua**. Hg 1:1, 12, 14. 2:2-4. Zc 3:1, 8. 6:11, Joshua the son of Josedech. **Jozadak**. i.e. *Jah is just; Jehovah is the righteous one*, ✽S#3136h. Ezr 3:2, 8. 5:2. 10:18. Ne 12:26. **Zerubbabel**. Ezr 2:2. 1 Ch 3:17, 19. Hg 2:21, 23. Zc 4:6-10. Mt 1:12, 13. Lk 3:27,

Zorobabel, Salathiel. **as it is written**. Ex 20:24, 25. Nu 28:3, etc. Dt 12:5-7, *11. 2 Ch 6:6. Ps 78:68. Bp. Patrick observes, that before the temple was built, there seems to have been a tabernacle pitched for Divine service, as was in David's time, not on mount Moriah, but mount Sion, to be used while the temple was building. Let us learn hence to begin with God, and to do what we can in the worship of God, when we cannot do what we would. They could not immediately have a temple, but they would not be without an altar. Wherever a Christian goes, if he carry not with him the sacrifices of prayer and praise, he is wanting in his duty; for he has an altar ever ready that sanctifies both the gift and the giver.

3. **the altar**. 2 Ch 4:1. **for fear**. Ezr 4:11-16. 8:21, 22. Ps 27:1, 2. 56:2-4. **even burnt**. Ex 29:38-42. Nu 28:2-8.

4. **the feast**. Ex 23:16. Le 23:34-36. Ne 8:14-17. Zc 14:16-19. Jn 7:2, 37. **the daily**. Nu 29:12-38. **as the duty of every day required**. Heb. the matter of the day in his day. Ex 5:13mg. 16:4mg. 29:38. Le 23:37. 1 K 8:59mg. 2 Ch 31:16. Je 52:34mg.

5. **the continual**. Ex 29:38-42. Nu 28:3-10, 11, 19, 27. 29:2, 8, 13. **burnt offering**. Le +*23:12. **new moons**. 2 Ch +2:4. **set feasts**. Ge +17:21. Le *23:2n. 1 Ch 23:31. **willingly**. Le 1:3. Dt 12:6, 17. 2 Ch 29:31, 32. **freewill offering**. Le +*23:38.

6. **first day of**. Le 23:23-25. Ne 8:18. **burnt offerings**. Le +*23:12. **the foundation of the temple of the Lord was not yet laid**. Heb. the temple of the Lord was not *yet* founded.

7. **gave money**. 2 K 12:11, 12. 22:5, 6. 2 Ch 24:12, 13. **masons**. 1 K 5:15. 2 K 12:12. **carpenters**. *or*, workmen. Ex 28:11. 35:35. **meat**. 1 K 5:6, 9-11. 2 Ch 2:10-15. Ezk 27:17. Ac 12:20. **Joppa**. *Joppa*, now *Jaffa* or *Yaffa*, one of the most ancient sea-ports in the world, is situated in a fine plain on the shore of the Mediterranean, between Jamnia south and Caesarea of Palestine north, 150 stadia from Antipatris, according to Josephus, 30 miles south of Caesarea, 12 miles north of Ashdod, 9 miles west of Ramla, and 40 miles west of Jerusalem, according to modern authorities; and in lat. 32 degrees 50 min., long. 65 degrees 40 min. according to Ptolemy. It is still a considerable town, containing about 4000 or 5000 souls, and occupying a circular eminence close to the seaside, with a citadel on the summit; the bottom of the hill being surrounded by a wall 12 or 14 feet high, and two or three feet thick. The environs are occupied by extensive gardens. 2 Ch 2:16. Jon 1:3. Ac 9:36. 10:5, 6. **according**. Ezr 6:3-5.

8. **Zerubbabel**. See on ver. 2. **twenty years old**. Nu 4:3. 1 Ch 23:24-32.

9. **Jeshua**. Not *Jeshua* the high priest, before mentioned, but another *Jeshua*, a Levite, mentioned in the parallel passage. Ezr 2:40. **Judah**. *Hodaviah* is called *Hodevah* by the elision of *yood*, and was probably named *Judah*, from the word having the same signification. Ezr 2:40, Hodaviah. Ne 7:43, Hodevah. **together**. Heb. as one. Ezr 2:64. 6:20. 2 Ch 5:13. **Henadad**. i.e. *grace* or *favor of Hadad* (i.e. *chief, most high*, Ge +36:35), ✽S#2582h. Ezr 3:9. Ne 3:18, 24. 10:9. (1) One who helped to lay the foundations of the temple, Ezr 3:9. (2) One whose sons helped rebuild the wall of Jerusalem, Ne 3:18. (3) One whose descendants sealed the covenant under Nehemiah, Ne 10:9.

10. **when the builders.** Zc 4:10. **they set.** Ex 28:40-42. 1 S 22:18. 1 Ch 15:27. Ne 12:24, etc. **trumpets.** Nu 10:1-10. 1 Ch 15:24. 16:5, 6, 42. **the sons of Asaph.** 1 Ch 6:39. 16:37. 25:1-7. 2 Ch 35:15. **after the ordinance.** 1 Ch 6:31, etc. 16:4-7. 23:5. 2 Ch 29:25, 26.

11. **they sang.** Ex 15:21. Ne 12:24, 40. Ps 24:7-10. Is 6:3. **because.** 1 Ch 16:34, 41. 2 Ch 7:3. Ps 103:17. 106:1. 107:1. 118:1-4. 135:3. ch. 136. 145:1-11. Je 33:10, 11. Lk 1:50. **for ever.** Heb. *olam*, Ex +*12:24. **shouted.** Jsh 6:5, 10, 16. Ps 47:1, 5. Is 12:6. 44:23. Zc 9:9. **because.** Ps 102:13, 14. Re 21:10-14.

12. **many.** Hg *2:3. **had seen.** 2 K 25:2, 9. **when the foundation.** Jb *8:7. 38:4, 6, 7. Is 41:14. 60:22. Da 2:34, 35. Zc 4:10. Mt 13:31, 32. **wept.** Ps *126:6. Je 31:8, 9.

13. **So that.** This sight must have been very affecting; a whole people, one part *weeping* aloud with *sorrow*, the other *shouting* aloud for *joy*; and on the same occasion too, in which both sides felt an equal interest. The prophet Haggai (Hg 2:1-9) comforted them on this occasion, by assuring them that the glory of this latter house should exceed that of the former, because the Lord would come to this temple, and fill it with his glory. **the noise.** Jg 2:5. **shouted.** Ne 12:43. Ps 5:11. Je 33:11. Zc 4:7. Lk 19:37-40. **and the noise.** Ex 32:17, 18. 1 S 4:5. 1 K 1:40, 45. Ps 100:1, 2.

EZRA 4

The adversaries of the Jews offer to join in building the temple; and, being rejected, they endeavor to hinder the work, 1-6. They write to Artaxerxes, king of Persia, 7-10. A copy of their letter, 11-16. The answer of Artaxerxes, who decrees that the work shall be stopped, 17-22. The Jews are compelled to cease from building, 23, 24.

1. **the adversaries.** These were the Samaritans, the descendants of the various nations with which the kings of Assyria had peopled Israel, when they had carried the original inhabitants captive. ver. 7-9. 1 K 5:4, 5. 1 Ch 22:9, 10. Ne 4:1-11. Da 9:25. 1 C 16:9. **children of the captivity.** Heb. sons of the transportation. Ezr 1:11mg. 6:16, 19, 20. 10:7, 16. Da 5:13.

2. **Zerubbabel.** Ezr 1:5. 2:2. 3:2, 12. **Let us.** Pr 26:23-26. 2 C √11:13-15. Ga *2:4. 2 T *3:8. 2 P 2:1, 2. **we seek.** Dt 27:4n. Jn 4:20. **we do.** 2 K 17:24, 27-33, 41. **Esar-haddon.** ver. 10, Asnapper. 2 K 19:37. **Assur.** i.e. *a step, going; success,* ✛S#804h. Ge 10:11. Ps 73:8. 83:3h. Is 37:37, Assyria. Ho 14:3, Asshur.

3. **Ye have nothing.** Ne 2:20. Jn 4:22, 23. Ac *8:21. Ro 9:4, 5. 2 C *6:14-16. 3 J 9, 10. **king Cyrus.** Ezr 1:1-3. 6:3-5. 2 Ch 36:22, 23. Is 44:28. 45:1, 4. Mt 10:16.

4. **weakened.** Ezr 3:3. Ne 6:9. Is 35:3, 4. Je 38:4. **troubled.** Ne 4:7, 8, 11.

5. **hired.** Ps 2:1, 2. Na 1:11. Ac 24:1, etc. **Darius.** i.e. *conservator; a restrainer; investigation; the dwelling will be full of heaviness.* ver. 24. Ezr 5:5, etc. 6:1, etc. *S#1867h; Ezr 4:5. Ne 12:22. Da 9:1. 11:1. Hg 1:1, 15. 2:10. Zc 1:1, 7. 7:1. *Darius* is a common name among the kings of Media and Persia. Those mentioned in the Bible are: (1) *Darius the Median,* Da 5:31, was the son of Ahasuerus. He took Babylon from Belshazzar the Chaldean. Only one year of his reign is spoken of, Da 9:1; 11:1; during which Daniel rose to the highest dignity. (2) *Darius Hystaspes,* B.C.

521-486, confirmed the decree of Cyrus concerning the building of the Temple, Ezr 4:5; Hg 1:1; Zc 1:1; 7:1. (3) *Darius Cadomannus,* Ne 12:22, the last king of the ancient Persian monarchy, was conquered by Alexander the Great, B.C. 330, and thus the prophecy in Daniel, chapter 8, was fulfilled. **to frustrate.** ver. 24.

6. A.M. 3475. B.C. 529. **Ahasuerus.** Heb. Ahashverosh. Est 1:1. Da 9:1. This was *Cambyses,* son of Cyrus, who succeeded his father, A.M. 3475, and reigned seven years and five months. **wrote.** Mt 27:37. Ac 24:5-9, 13. 25:7. Re 12:10.

7. A.M. 3482. B.C. 522. **Artaxerxes.** i.e. *silence of light; great king or warrior; I will make the spoiled to boil; I will stir myself in winter; I will make the sixth to boil; I will stir myself with drink,* *S#783h. Ezr 4:7, 7, 8, 11, 23. 6:14. 7:1, 7, 11, 12, 21. 8:1. Ne 2:1. 5:14. 13:6. (1) A king of Persia, Ezr 4:7-24, in whose time the governor of Samaria obtained an order to stop the rebuilding of Jerusalem by Zerubbabel. He is supposed to have been Smerdis the Magian. This *Artaxerxes* was one of the Magi, who usurped the throne after the death of Cambyses, for seven months, feigning himself to be *Smerdis,* brother of Cambyses: he is called "Oropaestus" by Justin, "Smerdis" by Herodotus, "Mardus" by Aeschylus, and "Sphendatates" by Ctesias. (2) A king of Persia, in the seventh year of whose reign Ezra went up from Babylon to Jerusalem with some of his countrymen, fourteen years afterward Nehemiah was allowed by Artaxerxes to return and rebuild Jerusalem, Ezr 7:7; Ne 2:1. He is supposed to be the same as Artaxerxes Longimanus, son of Xerxes, who reigned B.C. 464-425. **Bishlam.** or, in peace. ver. 17. i.e. *in peace; son of peace,* *S#1312h. **Mithredath.** Ezr +1:8. **Tabeel.** i.e. *God is good; goodness of God,* *S#2870h. Ezr 4:7. Also Is 7:6, Tabeal. **companions.** Heb. societies. ver. 9, 17. Ezr 5:6. **the Syrian tongue.** That is, probably, both the *language* and *character* were Syrian or Chaldaic; and therefore, from the 8th verse of this chapter, to Ezr 7:27, the original is not Hebrew, but Chaldee, in those parts which consist of letters, decrees, etc. originally written in that language. 2 K 18:26. Is 36:11. Da 2:4.

8. **Rehum.** i.e. *merciful.* Ne +12:3. **chancellor.** or, counsellor. lit. "master of taste," that is, discretion, counsel. **Shimshai.** i.e. *my minister; sunny; sun of the Lord,* *S#8124h. Ezr 4:8, 9, 17, 23. **scribe.** or, secretary. ver. 9. 2 S 8:17. 20:25. 1 K 4:3. 2 K 18:18.

9. **companions.** Chal. societies. ver. 17, 23. Ezr 5:3, 6. 6:6, 13. **the Dinaites.** i.e. *a cause; judgment,* *S#1784h. 2 K 17:24, 30, 31. **Apharsathchites.** i.e. *I will divide the deceivers; causers of division,* *S#671h. Ezr 5:6. 6:6, Apharsachites. **Tarpelites.** i.e. *hill of wonder; gate or passage of bulls; they of the fallen* or *wondrous mountain,* *S#2967h. **Apharsites.** i.e. *causers of division,* *S#670h. **Archevites.** i.e. *length,* *S#756h. **Babylonians.** i.e. *inhabitants of Babylon* (i.e. *confusion, mixture,* Da +1:1), *S#896h. **Susanchites.** i.e. *inhabitants of Susa* (Shushan, i.e. *lily,* Da +8:2) or *Susi* (i.e. *horseman,* Nu +13:11), *S#7801h. Est 1:2. 2:3. Da 8:2. **Dehavites.** i.e. *villagers; the sickly,* *S#1723h. **Elamites.** i.e. *original inhabitants of the country of Elam* (i.e. *hidden time; eternity; their heaps; suckling them,* Ge +10:22), *S#5962h. Ge 10:22. Is 21:2. Je 25:25. 49:34. Ezk 32:24. Ac 2:9.

10. **And the rest**. ver. 1. 2 K *17:24, etc. **noble Asnapper**. i.e. *the swift; horned bull; thorn abolished,* *S#620h. Ro 13:7. **at such a time**. Chal. *Cheeneth*. ver. 11, 17. Ezr 7:12.

11. **at such a time**. ver. 15, 19. 2 K 18:20. 24:1. 2 Ch 36:13. Je 52:3. Ezk 17:12-21. Lk 23:2-5. Ac 24:5. 1 Th 5:22. 1 P 2:13-15. **Artaxerxes**. ver. 17. Ezr 7:12.

12. **rebellious**. ver. 15, 19. 2 K 18:20. 24:1. 2 Ch 36:13. Je 52:3. Ezk 17:12-21. Lk 23:2-5. Ac 24:5. 1 Th 5:22. 1 P 2:13-15. **bad city**. Ps 48:1, 2. Is 1:21-23. Lk 13:34. **set up**. *or,* finished. ver. 13, 16. Ezr 5:3, 9, 16. 6:14. Ne 1:3. Da 9:25. **joined**. Chal. sewed together.

13. **if this city**. Ne 5:4. Ps 52:2. 119:69. **pay**. Chal. give. ver. 20. **not pay toll**. Ezr *7:24. Mt 9:9. 17:25. Ro 13:6, 7. **revenue**. *or,* strength.

14. **have maintenance**, etc. Chal. are salted with the salt of the palace. *Salt* is reckoned among the principal necessaries of life (Ecclus 39:26 or 31); hence, by a very natural figure, *salt* is used for *food* or *maintenance* in general. I am well informed, says Mr. Parkhurst, that it is a common expression of the natives in the East Indies, "I eat such a one's *salt*," meaning, I am *fed* by him. *Salt* was also, as it still is, among eastern nations, a symbol of *friendship* and *hospitality;* and hence, to eat a man's *salt*, is to be bound to him by the ties of friendship. **and it was**. Ezk 33:31. Jn 12:5, 6. 19:12-15.

15. **this city**. ver. 12. Ne 2:19. 6:6. Est 3:5-8. Da 6:4-13. Ac 17:6, 7. **moved**. Chal. made. ver. 19. **within the same**. Chal. in the midst thereof. Ezr 5:7. 6:2. **old time**. Heb. *olam*, Jb +*22:15. **for which**. 2 K 24:20. 25:1, 4. 2 Ch 36:13, 19. Je 52:3, etc.

16. **thou shalt have**. ver. 20. 2 S 8:3. 1 K 4:24.

17. **companions**. Chal. societies. ver. 7, 9. **Peace**. Ezr 5:7. 7:12. Lk 10:5. Ac 23:26. Ro 1:7. **at such a time**. ver. 10, 11.

18. **plainly read**. Le 24:12mg. Nu 15:34. Ne 8:8.

19. **I commanded**. Chal. by me a decree is set. ver. 21. Ezr 5:3, 9, 13, 17. **search**. ver. 15. Ezr 5:17. 6:1, 2. Dt 13:14. Pr 25:2. **and it is found**. 2 K 18:7. 24:20. Ezk 17:13-19. **made insurrection**. Chal. lifted up itself. Nu 16:3.

20. **mighty kings**. 1 K 4:21, 24. 1 Ch 18:3. Ps 72:8. **beyond**. ver. 16. Ge 15:18. Jsh 1:3, 4. 1 K 4:21. 1 Ch 19:16. 2 Ch +9:26. Ps 72:8. **toll**. 1 Ch 18:6, 13. 19:19. 2 Ch 9:14, 23, 24. 17:10, 11. 26:7, 8.

21. **Give ye**, etc. Chal. Make a decree. ver. 19.

22. **why should**. ver. 13. Est 3:8, 9. 7:3, 4.

23. **Rehum**. ver. 8, 9, 17. **they went up**. Pr 4:16. Mi 2:1. Ro 3:15. **force**. Chal. arm.

24. **So**. Ne 6:3, 9. Jb 20:5. Ps 44:23-26. 1 Th 2:18. **Darius**. This was *Darius Hystaspes*, one of the seven princes who slew the usurper Smerdis: he ascended the throne of Persia, A.M. 3483, B.C. 521, and reigned 36 years. Ezr 5:5. 6:1. Hg 1:15.

EZRA 5

Zerubbabel and Jeshua, excited by Haggai and Zechariah, begin again to build the temple, 1, 2. Tatnai and Shetharboznai are not able to hinder them, 3-5. A copy of their letter to Darius, 6-17.

1. A.M. 3484. B.C. 520. **Haggai**. These are the same *Haggai* and *Zechariah*, whose writings we have among the twelve minor prophets; and, as a great part

of them refer to the events here recorded, the reader will find it very profitable to compare them with the history. Hg 1:1, etc. **Zechariah**. Zc 1:1, etc. **the son of Iddo**. That is, "the *grandson* of Iddo;" for Zechariah was the son of Berechiah, the son of Iddo. 1 K +15:10n. 1 Ch 6:20n. 7:6n. **Iddo**. i.e. *timely; favorite; due time; appointed; adorn him,* *S#5714h. Ezr 5:1. 6:14. Ne 12:16. Also 1 K 4:14. Ne 12:4, 16. Zc 1:7. Also 1 Ch 6:21. 2 Ch 12:15. 13:22. Zc 1:1. (1) A Levite, a descendant of Gershom, 1 Ch 6:21. (2) Father of Ahinadab, 1 K 4:14. (3) A prophet and writer, 2 Ch 12:15; 13:22. (4) Grandfather of Zechariah the prophet, Zc 1:1, 7; Ezr 5:1; 6:14; Ne 12:4, 16. **in the name**. Mi 5:4. Hg 1:2-8. Zc 1:3, 4. 4:6-10.

2. **rose up**. Ezr 3:2. Hg 1:12-15. **Jeshua**. Zc 6:11, Joshua, Josedech. **the prophets**. Ezr 6:14. Hg 2:4-9, 20-23. Zc ch. 3, 4. 2 C 1:24.

3. **Tatnai**. i.e. *a gift; liberal; a rewarder,* *S#8674h. Ezr 5:3, 6. 6:6, 13. *Tatnai* was governor of the provinces which belonged to the Persian empire west of the Euphrates, comprehending Syria, Arabia Desert, Phoenicia, and Samaria. He seems to have been a mild and judicious man, and to have acted with great prudence and caution, and without any passion or prejudice. ver. 6. Ezr 6:6, 13. 7:21. Ne 2:7-9. **Shetharboznai**. i.e. *star of splendor; one that despiseth; who searched my despisers,* *S#8370h. Ezr 5:3, 6. 6:6, 13. **Who hath commanded you**. ver. 9. Ezr 1:3. Mt 21:23. Ac 4:7.

4. **What are**. ver. 10. **make this building**. Chal. build this building.

5. **But the eye**. Ezr 7:6, 28. 8:22. 2 Ch 16:9. Ps 32:8. 33:18, 19. 34:15. 76:10. Ph 1:28. 1 P 3:12. **that they**. Ps 129:2-5. **then they returned**. Ezr 6:6-12.

6. A.M. 3485. B.C. 519. **copy**. Ezr 4:11, 23. **Apharsachites**. Ezr 4:9, Apharsathchites. 6:6.

7. **wherein**. Chal. in the midst whereof. **all peace**. Ezr 4:17. Da 3:9. 4:1. 6:21. Jn 14:27. 2 Th 3:16.

8. **the province**. Ezr 2:1. Ne 7:6. 11:3. Est 1:1, 22. **Judea**. i.e. *confession; praised,* *S#3061h. Ezr 5:1, 8. 7:14. Da 2:25. 5:13, 13. 6:13. **the great God**. *f*22I2, Ex +15:16. Ezr 1:2, 3. 6:10. 7:23. Dt 10:17. 32:31. Ps 145:3. Da 2:47. 3:26. 4:2, 34-37. 6:26. **great stones**. Chal. stones of rolling. Ezr 6:4. Mk 13:1, 2.

9. **Who commanded**. ver. 3, 4. 2 Ch 36:23.

10. **asked**. ver. 4.

11. **We are**. Jsh 24:15. Ps 119:46. Da 3:26. Jon 1:9. Mt 10:32. Lk 12:8. Ac 27:23. Ro *1:16. 6:16. Ga 6:14. **which a great**. 1 K ch. 6, 7. 2 Ch ch. 3-5.

12. A.M. 3408. B.C. 536. **But after**. 2 K 21:12-15. 2 Ch 34:24, 25. 36:16, 17. Ne 9:26, 27. Is 59:1, 2. Je 5:29. Da 9:5. **he gave**. Dt 28:15, etc. 29:24-28. 31:17. 32:30. Jg 2:14. 4:2. 6:1. 1 K 9:6-9. 2 Ch 7:19-22. Ps 106:40. **into the hand**. 2 K 24:2, 10, etc. 25:1, 8-11, etc. 2 Ch 36:6, etc. Je 39:1, etc. 52:1, etc. Da 1:1, 2. **Babylon**. *S#895h. ver. 12, 13, 14, 14, 17. Ezr 6:1, 5. 7:16. Da 2:12, 14, 18, 24, 24, 48, 48, 49. 3:1, 12, 30. 4:6, 29, 30. 5:7. 7:1.

13. **in the first year**. Ezr 1:1-8. 6:3-5. Is 44:28. 45:1.

14. **the vessels**. Ezr 1:7-10. 6:5. 2 Ch 36:7, 18. Je 52:19. Da 5:2, 3. **the king**. Ezr 7:27. Pr 21:1. **Sheshbazzar**. ver. 16. Ezr 1:11. **whom**. Hg 1:1, 14. 2:2, 21. **governor**. *or,* deputy. Ac 13:7, 8, 12.

15. **let the house**. Ezr 1:2. 3:3. 6:3.

16. **Sheshbazzar**. ver. 14. **laid**. ver. 2. Ezr 3:8, 10. Hg 1:12-14. 2:18. Zc 4:10. A.M. 3468-3485. B.C. 536-

519. **it is not finished.** Ezr 6:15.

17. A.M. 3485. B.C. 519. **let there be.** Ezr 4:15, 19. 6:1, 2. Pr 25:2. **a decree.** Ezr 6:3-5.

EZRA 6

Darius finds the decree of Cyrus, confirms it, allows out of his revenues the expenses of building the temple, and denounces penalties on all opposers, 1-12. The temple is finished and dedicated, and the passover is celebrated with great joy, 13-22.

1. **and search.** Ezr 4:15, 19. 5:17. Jb 29:16. Pr 25:2. **rolls.** Chal. *books.* Ps 40:7. Je 36:2-4, 20-23, 29, 32. Ezk 2:9. 3:1. Re 5:1. **laid up.** Chal. *made to descend.*

2. **at Achmetha.** *or,* Ecbatana, *or,* in a coffer. i.e. *place of assemblage; brother of death; citadel, or summer house,* ✻S#307h. Probably from the Persian *kham,* "a house for a summer residence," with a prefix *aleph,* and the Chaldee termination *tha,* most likely denotes *Ecbatana,* as the Vulgate and Josephus (Ant. l. xi. c. 4. sec. 6) read, the *summer residence* of the Persian monarchs (Xenophon, Cyrop. l. viii. c. 6, sec. 1). It was situated in a mountainous region at the foot of mount Orontes (Diodorus, l. ii. c. 1; Polybius, l. x.), or Jasonius, according to Ammianus (l. xxiii. c. 28), on the southern confines of Media and Persia, and according to Pliny (l. vi. c. 1. 13, 27), 750 miles from Seleucia the Great, 20 miles from the Caspian passes, 450 miles from Susa, and the same from Gazae Atropatene, and in lat. 37 deg. 45 min., long. 88 deg., according to Ptolemy. The building of the city is ascribed to Semiramis by Diodorus, but to Deioces by Eusebius (in Chron. l.1), and Herodotus (l. i. c. 98), who states that it was surrounded by seven walls, strong and ample, built in circles one within another, rising each above each by the height of their respective battlements; each being distinguished by a different color,— the first white, the second black, the third purple, the fourth blue, the fifth orange, the sixth plated with silver, and the seventh with gold. The largest of these was nearly the extent of Athens, i.e. 200 furlongs, according to Dion Chrysostom (Orat. vi.); but Diodorus Siculus states the circumference of Ecbatana to be 250 furlongs.—Within the inner circle stood the king's palace and the royal treasury, so much celebrated for its splendor and riches by Polybius. It is highly probable, as D'Anville and Major Rennel suppose, that the present *Hamadan,* whose ruins attest its former splendor, occupies the sight of *Ecbatana.* It is situated in Al Gebal, at the foot of the lofty mountain Alwend, about 80 leagues from Ispahan, and also from Bagdad. **Medes.** i.e. *measure; abounding; garment; extended of the Lord,* ✻S#4075h. Ezr 6:2. Da 5:28. 6:8, 12, 15.

3. **the first year.** Young indicates B.C. 536. Ezr 1:1-4. 5:13-15. 2 Ch 36:22, 23. Is 44:28. **the place.** Dt 12:5, 6, 11-14. 2 Ch 2:6. Ps 122:4. **the height.** 1 K 6:2, 3. 2 Ch 3:3, 4. Ezk 41:13-15. Re 21:16.

4. **three rows.** 1 K 6:36. **great stones.** Ezr 5:8mg. **the expenses.** Ezr 7:20-23. Ps 68:29. 72:10. Is 49:23. 60:6-10. Re 12:16.

5. **the golden.** Ezr 1:7, 8. 5:14. Je 27:16, 18-22. Da 1:2. 5:2. **which Nebuchadnezzar.** 2 K 24:13. 25:14, 15. 2 Ch 36:6, 7, 10, 18. Je 52:19. **brought.** Chal. *go.* Ezr 5:5. 7:13.

6. **Tatnai.** Ezr 5:3. **your companions.** Chal. *their societies.* ver. 13. Ezr 4:9mg. 5:6. **Apharsachites.** i.e.

causers of division; I will divide the deceivers, ✻S#671h. Ezr 4:9. 5:6. 6:6. **be ye far.** Ge 32:28. 43:14. Ne 1:11. Ps 76:10. Pr 21:1, 30. Is 27:8. Ac 4:26-28. Ro ✻8:31.

7. **Let the work.** Ac 5:38, 39.

8. **I make a decree.** Chal. *by me a decree is made.* ver. 11, 12, 14. Ezr 7:13, 21, 23. **the king's.** ver. 4. Ezr 4:16, 20. 7:15-22. Ps 68:29-31. Hg 2:8. **hindered.** Chal. *made to cease.* Ezr 4:21, 23. 5:5.

9. **young bullocks.** Le 1:3-5, 10. 9:2. Ps 50:9-13. **lambs.** Ex 29:38-42. Nu ch. 28, 29. **wheat.** Le 2:1, etc. Nu 15:4, etc. 1 Ch 9:29. **salt.** Le 2:13. Mk 9:49. **let it be given.** Is 49:23.

10. **sweet savors.** Chal. *rest.* Ge 8:21. Le 1:9, 13, 17. Ep 5:2. **pray.** Ezr 7:23. Je ✻29:7. 1 T +✻2:1, 2.

11. **whosoever.** Ezr 7:26. **timber.** Est 5:14. 7:10. **hanged.** Chal. *destroyed.* **his house.** 2 K 9:37. 10:27. Da 2:5. 3:29.

12. **caused.** Ex 20:24. Dt 12:5, 11. 16:2. 1 K ✻9:3. 2 Ch 7:16. Ps 132:13, 14. **destroy.** Ps 5:10. 21:8-10. 137:8, 9. Is 60:12. Ob 10. Zc 12:2-4. Ac 5:38, 39. 9:5. Re 19:14-21. **I Darius.** Est 3:14, 15. 8:14. **speed.** ver. 13. Ec 9:10.

13. **Tatnai.** Ezr 4:9, 23. 5:6. **so they did.** Est 6:11. Jb 5:12, 13. Pr 29:26.

14. **And the elders.** Ezr 3:8. 4:3. **prospered.** 2 Ch +✻20:20. **through.** Ezr 5:1, 2. Hg 1:12-14. 2:2, etc. Zc ch. 2-4, 6. **finished it.** Zc 4:9. **according.** Is 44:28. Hg 1:8. **commandment.** Chal. *decree.* ver. 8. Ezr 4:19. **Cyrus.** ver. 3. Ezr 1:1-4. 4:24. 5:13. **Artaxerxes.** This was *Artaxerxes,* the third son and successor of Xerxes, surnamed "Makroxeir," or *Longimanus,* or in Persian, *Ardsheer deeraz dest,* "Ardheer the long-handed;" so called, according to the Greeks, from the extraordinary length of his hands, but according to the Easterns, from the extent of his dominions. He ascended the Persian throne, A.M. 3540, B.C. 464, and reigned forty-one years. He is said to have been the most handsome person of his age, and to have been a prince of a very mild and generous disposition. Ez 7:1.

15. A.M. 3489. B.C. 515. **Adar.** Est 3:7, 13. 8:12. 9:1, 15, 17, 19, 21.

16. **the children.** 1 Ch 9:2. Ne 7:73. **children of the captivity.** Chal. *sons of the transportation.* See on Ezr 4:1mg. **the dedication.** 1 K 8:63. 2 Ch 7:5, 9. Jn 10:22. **with joy.** ver. 22. Ezr 3:11, 12. Dt 12:7. 1 Ch 15:28. 2 Ch 7:10. 30:23, 26. Ne 8:10. 12:43. Ps 122:1. Ph 4:4. Having set up the worship of God in this dedication, they took care to keep it up, and made the *book of Moses* their rule, to which they had an eye in this establishment. Though the temple service could not now be performed with so much pomp and plenty as formerly, because of their poverty, yet no doubt it was performed with as much purity and close adherence to the Divine institutions as ever. No beauty is like the beauty of holiness.

17. **offered.** Ezr 8:35. Nu 7:2, etc. 1 K 8:63, 64. 1 Ch 16:1-3. 2 Ch 7:5. 29:31-35. **a sin offering.** Le 4:3, 13, 14, 22, 23, 28. 2 Ch 29:21-23. **according to.** Though the tribes of Benjamin and Judah, with the priests and Levites, formed the bulk of the people, yet many from other tribes had returned with them from captivity. 1 K 18:31. Lk 22:30. Re 7:4-8. 21:12.

18. **the priests.** 1 Ch ch. 23-26. 2 Ch 35:4, 5. **as it is written.** Chal. *according to the writing.* Nu 3:6. 8:9, etc.

19. **the children**. ver. 16. **kept**. Ex 12:6, etc. Jsh 5:10. 2 Ch ch. 30-35. **passover**. Le +*23:5.

20. **purified together**. 2 Ch 29:34. 30:15-17. **killed**. Ex 12:21. 2 Ch 35:11. He 7:27.

21. **all such**. Ezr 9:11. Nu 9:6, 7, 10-14. 1 Ch 16:10, 11. 2 Ch 30:17. Is 52:11. Ezk 36:25. 2 C 6:17. 7:1. **did eat**. Ex 12:47-49. Ps 93:5.

22. **the feast**. Ex 12:15-20. 13:6, 7. 2 Ch 30:21. 35:17. Mt 26:17. 1 C 5:7, 8. **unleavened**. Le +*23:6. **with joy**. Ga 5:22. Ph 4:4. **turned**. Ezr 7:27. Pr *16:7. 21:1. Jn 19:11. **the king**. Darius, as reigning over the country of Assyria, is here called "the king of Assyria." ver. 6, etc. Ezr 1:1. 2 K 23:29. 2 Ch 33:11. Zc 10:10, 11.

EZRA 7

Ezra's genealogy from Aaron, 1-5 He goes up to Jerusalem, 6-10. A copy of Artaxerxes's favorable commission to him, 11-26. He blesses God for putting this into the king's heart, 27, 28.

1. A.M. 3547. B.C. 457. **Artaxerxes**. ver. 12, 21. Ezr 6:14. Ne 2:1. **Ezra**. i.e. *help*. ver. *10, +12. Ezr ch. 8-10. Ne *8:2-9. **the son**. i.e. *his grandson*; here are divers persons omitted for brevity sake, which may be supplied out of 1 Ch ch. 6-9 (Matthew Poole). Ezr 5:1n. 1 K +15:10n. 1 Ch 3:19n. 6:20n. 7:6n. **Seraiah**. i.e. *prince, leader, or soldier of the Lord*. The high priest slain by Nebuchadnezzar. 2 K 25:18. 1 Ch 6:4-14. 9:11. Ne 11:11. Je 52:24-27. **Azariah**. i.e. *help of Jah*. 1 Ch +6:36. **Hilkiah**. i.e. *portion of Jah*. 2 K +18:18. 22:4, 8. 2 Ch 34:9, 15.

2. **Shallum**. i.e. *recompense*. 2 K +15:10. **Zadok**. i.e. *right, just*. 2 S +8:17. 1 K 2:35. **Ahitub**. i.e. *brother of goodness*. 1 S +14:3.

3. **Amariah**. i.e. *whom Jehovah spoke of; the saying of Jehovah*, *S#568h. Ezr 7:3. 10:42. 1 Ch 6:7, 7, 11, 11, 52. 23:19. Ne 10:3. 11:4. 12:2, 13. Zp 1:1. (1) Son of Meraioth, and father of Ahitub, 1 Ch 6:7. (2) Son of Azariah, father of Ahitub, 1 Ch 6:11. (3) Second son of Hebron, of Levi, 1 Ch 23:19; 24:23. (4) Chief priest, time of Jehoshaphat, 2 Ch 19:11. (5) Set over tithes and offerings by Hezekiah, 2 Ch 31:15. (6) Great grandfather of prophet Zephaniah, Zp 1:1. (7) One of those who had married strange wives, Ezr 10:42. (8) One that sealed the covenant, Ne 10:3. (9) Son of Shephatiah, and grandfather of Uzziah, Ne 11:4. (10) A priest who went up with Zerubbabel, Ne 12:2. **Azariah**. i.e. *help of Jah*. ver. +1. Six generations are omitted between him and Meraioth, see 1 Ch 6:7-10. **Meraioth**. i.e. *high places*. Ne +12:15.

4. **Zerahiah**. i.e. *whom Jehovah caused to rise; rising of Jah; rising of light of the Lord*, *S#2228h. Ezr 7:4. 8:4. 1 Ch 6:6, 6, 51. (1) A Levite, 1 Ch 6:6. (2) A progenitor of Ezra, Ezr 7:4. Called Izrahiah, 1 Ch 7:3. (3) One who returned from Babylon with Ezra, Ezr 8:4. **Uzzi**. i.e. *my strength*. 1 Ch +6:5. **Bukki**. i.e. *cast off by Jah*. Nu +34:22.

5. **Abishua**. i.e. *father of riches*. 1 Ch 6:4. **Phinehas**. i.e. *mouth of brass*. Ex +6:25. Nu 25:7-13. 31:6. Jsh 22:13, 31. Jg 20:28. 1 Ch 6:4, 50-52. Ps 106:30, 31. **Eleazar**. i.e. *God is help*. Ex +6:23. Le 10:6, 12, 16. Nu 3:32. 20:25-28. 27:2. 31:31, 54. Jsh 14:1. 24:33. 1 Ch 24:1-6. **Aaron**. i.e. *a mountaineer*. Ex +4:14. **chief priest**. 2 Ch 19:11. 26:20. He 5:4.

6. **a ready**. i.e. a learned and expert doctor (Mat-

thew Poole). *Sopher mahir* does not merely signify a *speedy writer*, or an *excellent penman*, but one eminently skillful in *expounding the law, sophro chochmo*, "a wise scribe," as the Syriac renders. ver. 11, 12, 21. Ps 45:1. Pr 22:29. Is 16:5. Mt 13:52. **scribe**. Ne *8:4, 9, 13. 12:26, 36. Je 8:8. Mt 7:29. 17:10. 22:35, 36. 23:2, 13. Mk 12:28. 1 C 1:20. **the law**. Dt 4:5. 28:1. Mt 28:20. 1 C 15:1. 1 Th 4:1, 2. **granted him**. ver. 11-26. **according to**. ver. 9, 28. Ezr 6:22. 8:18, 22, 31. Ge *32:28. Ne 1:10, 11. 2:8, 12, 18. 4:15. Pr *3:6. Is 50:2. 59:1. **the hand**. ⨍22A14.5, Ne +2:8.

7. **the children**. Ezr 8:1-14. **the Levites**. Ezr 2:40, 41. 8:15-20. **singers**. 1 Ch 6:31, etc. 25:1-8. 2 Ch +35:15. **porters**. Ezr 2:42. 1 Ch 9:17, etc. +23:5. Ne 7:45. **Nethinims**. ver. 24. Ezr 2:43, etc. 8:20. Ne 7:46, etc. 10:28. **Artaxerxes**. ver. 11, 12. Ezr 6:14n. 8:1. Ne 2:1.

9. **began he to go up**. Heb. *was the foundation* of the going up. **according to**. ver. 6. Ne 2:8, 18. **hand**. ⨍22A14.5, Ne +2:8.

10. **prepared**. or, directed. He had set his mind and affections upon it, and made it his chief design and business. 1 S 7:3. 1 Ch 29:18. 2 Ch *12:14. *19:3. Jb 11:13. Ps *10:17. 57:7. Pr 16:1. **to seek the law**. i.e. *to search and find out the true sense and meaning of it, and thence to learn what sins or errors were to be reformed, and what duties were to be performed*. ver. 6. Ps *1:2. *19:7. *119:45, 96-100. Jn +√5:39. Ac +*17:2, 3, 11. **to do it**. Dt 16:12. +*26:16, 18. Mt *5:19. *7:24. Lk √6:46. *11:28. Jn +*13:17. Re *22:14. **and to teach**. The order of things in this verse is very observable; first he endeavors to understand God's law and word, and that not for curiosity or ostentation, but in order to practice; next he conscientiously practiseth what he did understand, which made his doctrine much more effectual; and then he earnestly desires and labors to instruct and edify others, that they also might know and do it (Matthew Poole). ver. *25. Dt 33:10. 2 Ch *17:8, 9. +*20:20. 30:22. 35:3n. Ne *8:1-9. Ml *2:7. Ac 1:1. 1 T 3:2. 2 T +√2:2. *4:2. T *2:1, 15.

11. **the copy**. Ezr 4:11. 5:6. **a scribe**. ver. 6. Mt 23:2, 13. Mk 7:1-13.

12. **Artaxerxes**. The title of the king would, in Persian, run thus: *Ardsheer shahinshah*, or *padshah*, "Ardsheer, king of kings," i.e. *great or supreme king or emperor*. 1 K 4:24. 20:1. Is 10:8. Ezk 26:7. Da 2:37, 47. 1 T 6:15. Re 17:14. 19:16. **unto Ezra**, etc. or, to Ezra the priest, a perfect scribe of the law of the God of heaven, *peace*, etc. **Ezra**. i.e. *help*, *S#5830h. Ezr 7:1, 6, 10, 11. 10:1, 2, 5, 6, 10, 16. Ne 8:1, 2, 4, 5, 6, 9, 13. 12:1, 13, 26, 33, 36. Also *S#5831h. Ezr 7:12, 21, 25. (1) The priest who (458 B.C.) led a colony of Jews from Babylon to Jerusalem, Ezr ch. 7-10. Ne ch. 8. (2) A contemporary of Zerubbabel, Ne 12:1. **and at such a time**. Ezr 4:10, 11, 17. 1 Ch 12:32n.

13. **I make**. Ezr 5:13. 6:1. 2 Ch 30:5. Est 3:15. 9:14. Ps 148:6. **minded**. Ezr 1:3. Ps 110:3. Ph *2:13. Re 22:17.

14. **of the king**. Chal. from before the king. **seven counselors**. *Seven* princes of Persia having conspired against and slain the usurper Smerdis, and thus made way for the family of Darius, which afterwards filled the throne, the Persian kings of this race had always *seven* chief princes as their counselors, who possessed

peculiar privileges, were his chief assistants in public affairs of the government, and by whose advice all the public affairs of the empire were transacted. The names of these counselors are given in the parallel place of the book of Esther. Est 1:14. **according.** ver. *25, 26. Dt 17:18, 19. Is √8:20. **thy God.** Ezr 1:3. 5:8. 6:12. Da 2:47. 6:20, 26.

15. **the silver.** Ezr 6:4, 8-10. Ps 68:29, 30. 72:10. 76:11. Is 60:6-9. Re 21:24-26. **whose habitation.** Ezr 6:12. 2 Ch 2:6. 6:1, 2, 6. Ps 9:11. 26:8. 76:2. 132:13, 14. 135:21.

16. **all the silver.** Ezr 8:25-28. **offering.** Ezr 1:4, 6. 1 Ch 29:6, 9, 17. 2 C *8:12. *9:7.

17. **buy speedily.** See on Ezr 6:9, 10. Dt 14:24-26. Mt 21:12, 13. Jn 2:14. **their meat offerings.** Le +*23:13. Nu 15:4-13. **drink offerings.** Le +*23:13. **offer them.** Dt 12:5-11.

18. **whatsoever.** 2 K 12:15. 22:7. **that do.** ver. 23. Ep 5:17. **after the will.** He gave them the fullest liberty to order every thing according to their own institutions; binding them to no form or mode of worship.

19. **The vessels.** Ezr 8:27-30, 33, 34. **the God of Jerusalem.** 2 Ch 32:19. Je 3:17.

20. **bestow it.** Ezr 6:4, 8, etc.

21. **Artaxerxes.** ver. 12, 13. **beyond the river.** Ezr 4:16, 20. 6:6. **Ezra the priest.** ver. 6, 10, 11.

22. **measures.** Chal. cors. 1 K +4:22mg. Lk 16:6mg. **baths of wine.** Ezk 45:14. Lk 16:6mg. **salt.** Le 2:13. **without prescribing.** Jn=3:34.

23. **Whatsoever is commanded.** Chal. Whatsoever is of the decree. ver. 13, 18. **let it be.** Dt 6:17. 11:22. Ps *119:4. Ec 9:10. **why should there be wrath.** As Artaxerxes believed he was appointed by the Almighty to do this work, he therefore wished to do it heartily; knowing that if he did not, God would be displeased, and that the kingdom would be cut off from him or his posterity. Ezr 6:10-12. 2 Ch +24:18. 30:8. Zc 12:3.

24. **touching any.** ver. 7. Ezr 2:36-55.

25. **the wisdom.** ver. 14. 1 K 3:28. 1 Ch 22:12. Ps *19:7. *119:98-100. Pr 2:6. 6:23. Ja *1:5. 3:17, 18. **set magistrates.** Ex +*18:14-25. Dt 16:18. 1 Ch 23:4. 2 Ch 19:8-10. **beyond.** That is, "west of the Euphrates," which was *beyond* with regard to the king of Persia, who was on the east. Ezr 6:6. **the river.** Ezr 4:20. 1 Ch 19:16. 2 Ch +9:26. **teach ye.** ver. +*10. 2 Ch +*17:7-9. Ne *8:1-3, 7, 8. 9:3. 13:1-3. Ml *2:7. Mt 13:52. 23:2, 3. 28:19. Mk 6:34. Ro 10:14-17. Ep 4:11. 1 T *4:11-16. 2 T √2:2.

26. **whosoever.** Ezr 6:11. Da 3:28, 29. 6:26. **the law of thy God.** 2 Ch 30:12. **whether it be.** Ex ch. 21, 22. Le ch. 20. Dt ch. 13. **banishment.** Chal. rooting out. Ps 52:5. **confiscation.** 2 K 23:33. Pr 19:19. He 11:37. **imprisonment.** Da 4:15, 23.

27. **Blessed.** There is a most amiable spirit of piety in these reflections. Instead of expatiating on the praises of his munificent patron, or boasting of his own services, he blesses God for "putting such a thing in the king's heart;" and for all the assistance and favor shown him by the king and his counselors. Ezr 6:22. 1 Ch 29:10, etc. Ph 4:10. **put such.** Ezr 6:22. Ne 2:12. 7:5. 2 C 8:16. He 8:10. 10:16. Ja 1:17. Re 17:17. **in the king's heart.** Ne 2:8. Pr *21:1. **to beautify.** Is 60:13.

28. **extended.** Ezr 9:9. Ge 32:28. 43:14. Ne 1:11. **his counsellors.** ver. 14. Jon 3:7. **And I was strengthened.** In what the king decreed he saw the hand of God: he therefore gave him the praise, and took cour-

age. **as the hand.** √22A14.5, Ne +2:8. ver. 6, 9. Ezr 5:5. 8:18. Ne 2:8. 2 T 4:17, 18.

EZRA 8

The names of those who joined Ezra, when he was about to go up to Jerusalem, 1-14. Finding no Levites, he sends to Iddo, at Casiphia, and obtains some, 15-20. They observe a solemn fast, to seek of God a prosperous journey, 21-23. Ezra entrusts the sacred treasures to the priests, 24-30. They arrive in safety at Jerusalem, 31, 32. The treasures, by weight, are delivered up; and sacrifices offered, 33-35. The king's commission is produced, 36.

1. **the chief.** Ezr 1:5. 1 Ch 9:34. 24:31. 26:32. 2 Ch 26:12. Ne 7:70, 71. **genealogy.** Ezr 2:62. 1 Ch 4:33. 9:1. **them that went up.** Ezr 7:7, 13.

2. **Phinehas.** 1 Ch 6:3, 4, etc. 24:1-6. **Gershom.** i.e. *a stranger there.* Ex +2:22. **Ithamar.** i.e. *land of palms; he is bitter.* Ex +6:23. **Daniel.** i.e. *judge of God.* Da +1:8. **David.** 1 Ch 3:1, 22. **Hattush.** i.e. *assembled; sin was hasted,* *S#2407h. Ezr 8:2. 1 Ch 3:22. Ne 3:10. 10:4. 12:2. (1) A successor of Jeconiah, 1 Ch 3:22. (2) One who returned with Ezra from Babylon, Ezr 8:2. (3) One who helped to build the wall, Ne 3:10. (4) One who sealed the covenant, Ne 10:4; 12:2.

3. **Shechaniah.** i.e. *neighbor with Jah.* 1 Ch +3:22. **Pharosh.** i.e. *flea; a weak, cowardly man; dancing,* *S#6551h. Ezr +*2:3, Parosh. 8:3. 10:25. Ne 3:25. 7:8. 10:14. This variation is attributable to the translators; the original being uniformly *Parosh.* Ezr 2:3. Ne 7:8. 10:14, Parosh. **Zechariah.** i.e. *remembered of Jah.* Zc +1:1.

4. **Pahath-moab.** i.e. *pit, snare,* or *governor of Moab.* Ezr +2:6. Ne 7:11. 10:14. **Elihoenai.** i.e. *God the Lord of my eyes; unto Jehovah mine eyes,* *S#454h. 1 Ch 26:3, Elioenai. **Zerahiah.** i.e. *rising of Jah.* Ezr +7:4.

5. **Shechaniah.** ver. 3. **Jahaziel.** i.e. *seen of God.* 1 Ch +24:23.

6. **Adin.** i.e. *luxuriant.* Ezr +2:15. Ne 7:20. 10:16. **Ebed.** i.e. *servant of God; servant; toiler,* *S#5651h. Ezr 8:6. Jg 9:26, 28, 30, 31, 35. (1) Father of Gaal, who conspired against Abimelech, Jg 9:26, 28. (2) A companion of Ezra from Babylon, Ezr 8:6. **Jonathan.** i.e. *Jah has given.* 1 S +13:2.

7. **Elam.** Ezr 2:7, 31. Ge +10:22. Ne 7:12, 34. **Jeshaiah.** i.e. *safety of Jah.* 1 Ch +25:3. **Athaliah.** i.e. *afflicted of Jah.* 1 Ch +8:26.

8. **Shephatiah.** i.e. *judged of Jah.* Ezr 2:4. 2 S +3:4. Ne 7:9. 11:4. **Zebadiah.** i.e. *endowed of Jah.* 1 Ch +26:2. **Michael.** i.e. *who is like God?* Da +12:1.

9. **Joab.** i.e. *Jah is father.* Ezr 2:6. 1 S +26:6. Ne 7:11. **Obadiah.** i.e. *servant of Jah.* Ob +1. **Jehiel.** i.e. *whom God preserves alive; God lives; he lives of God,* *S#3171h. Ezr 8:9. 10:2, 21, 26. 1 Ch 15:18, 20. 16:5. 23:8. 27:32. 29:8. 2 Ch 21:2. 29:14. 31:13. 35:8. (1) A son of Jehoshaphat, 2 Ch 21:2. (2) A son of Laadan, of the Gershonites, 1 Ch 23:8. (3) The Gershonite through whom precious stones were given to the house of the Lord, 1 Ch 29:8. (4) A son of Hachmoni in David's reign, 1 Ch 27:32. (5) A Levite, family of Kohath and house of Heman the singer, 2 Ch 29:14. (6) Assistant overseer of the temple revenues, 2 Ch 31:13. (7) A ruler of the temple at the time of Josiah's

religious reformation, 2 Ch 35:8. (8) Father of Ezra's contemporary Obadiah, Ezr 8:9. (9) A son of Elam and father of Ezra's contemporary Shechaniah, Ezr 10:2. (10) One who put away his strange wife, Ezr 10:26. (11) A priest, of the course of Harim, induced by Ezra to put away his strange wife, Ezr 10:21. See on 1 Ch +9:35, Jehiel (*S#3273h).

10. **Shelomith.** i.e. *peaceful.* Le +24:11. **Josiphiah.** i.e. *added to by Jah; Jah will increase,* *S#3131h.

11. **Bebai.** i.e. *with the desire of the Lord; with supreme desire.* Ezr +2:11. 10:28. Ne 7:16.

12. **Azgad.** i.e. *strength of a troop.* Ezr +2:12. Ne 7:17. **Johanan.** i.e. *Jah has grace.* 2 K +25:23. **the son of Hakkatan.** *or,* the youngest son. **Hakkatan.** i.e. *small; son of the little one,* *S#6997h.

13. **Adonikam.** i.e. *my lord has risen.* Ezr 2:13. Ne +7:18. **Eliphelet.** i.e. *God delivers.* 1 Ch +3:6. **Jeiel.** i.e. *removed of God.* 1 Ch +5:7. **Shemaiah.** i.e. *heard of Jah.* 1 Ch +9:16.

14. **Bigvai.** Ezr 2:+2, 14. Ne 7:19. **Uthai.** i.e. *aided by God.* 1 Ch +9:4. **Zabbud.** *or,* Zaccur, *as some read.* i.e. *endowed; given,* *S#2072h. Ne 10:12.

15. **the river that runneth. Ahava.** i.e. *continual flowing; water; I shall subsist,* *S#163h. Ezr 8:15, 21, 31. *Ahava* is supposed to be the river *Adiava,* which, with the *Diava,* is said by Ammianus to have given name to *Adiabene,* a province of Assyria, through which they flowed into the Tigris. These rivers were also called respectively, *Anzabas* and *Zabas,* the *Caprus* and *Lycus* of Ptolemy; the former of which he places, at its source, in long. 79 degrees, lat. 39 1/2 degrees, and at its junction with the Tigris, in long. 79 1/2 degrees, lat. 36 degrees, 6 minutes; and the latter, at its source, in long. 78 degrees, lat. 39 degrees; and where it falls into the Tigris, in long. 79 degrees, lat. 36 1/2 degrees. They are now called the *Great and Little Zab,* or the *Zabein,* i.e. the *two Zabs,* which, says Ibn Haukal, "are considerable streams, each about half as large as the Dejleh (or Tigris). They rise among the mountains of Azerbaijan: of these, the larger is that which runs towards *Haditheh.* These streams form part of the Tigris, and water the district of *Semerah.*" Ps 137:1. Ezk 1:1. 3:15. Ac 16:13. **Ahava.** ver. 21, 31. **abode.** Heb. pitched. Nu 9:20, 22. 31:19. **and found.** ver. 2. Ezr 7:7, 24.

16. **Eliezer.** i.e. *my God is help.* Ge +15:2. **Ariel.** i.e. *lion of God.* Is +29:1. **Shemaiah.** ver. 13. Ezr 10:21. **Elnathan.** i.e. *God hath given.* 2 K +24:8. **Jarib.** i.e. *he strives, contends.* 1 Ch +4:24. **Nathan.** i.e. *he gave.* Ezr 10:39. 2 Ch +9:29. **Zechariah.** ver. 11. **Meshullam.** i.e. *recompensed.* 1 Ch +9:12. **chief men.** ver. 1. **Joiarib.** i.e. *Jah will contend,* *S#3114h. Ezr 8:16. Ne 11:5, 10. 12:6, 19. (1) A man of understanding who returned from Babylon with Ezra, Ezr 8:16. (2) A man of Judah, descended from a certain Zechariah, Ne 11:5. (3) A chief of the priests who returned from Babylon with Zerubbabel, Ne 12:6, 7. **men of understanding.** ver. 18. 1 K 3:11. 1 Ch +*12:32n. 26:14. 2 Ch 2:12. Pr 2:6. 20:5. 28:2. Da 2:21. 2 T 2:7. 1 J 5:20.

17. **Iddo.** i.e. *great calamity; I will praise him,* *S#112h. **Casiphia.** i.e. *silver of the Lord; longing of Jah,* *S#3703h. *Casiphia* is supposed to denote the *Caspian mountains,* between Media and Hyrcania, near the *Caspian* sea. It is evident, from a comparison of Ezr 7:9 with ver. 31, that *Casiphia* could not be

far from Ahava. **I told them.** Heb. I put words in their mouth. Ex 4:15. Dt 18:18. 2 S 14:3, 19. Je 1:9. 15:19. **the Nethinims.** Ezr 2:43, 58. 7:7. **ministers.** Nu 8:22-26. 18:6. 1 Ch 23:3-6, 26-32. T 1:5.

18. **by the good hand.** ✓22A14.5, Ne +2:8. ver. 22. Ezr 7:28. Ne 2:8. Pr *3:6. **a man of understanding.** See on ver. +*16. 1 S 25:3. 1 Ch 22:12. Pr 24:3. Je 3:15. Da 1:20. 1 C 14:20. **Mahli.** i.e. *sick.* Nu +3:20. 1 Ch 6:19. **Sherebiah.** i.e. *heat of Jah; set free of Jah; deliverance of the Lord,* *S#8274h. ver. 24. Ne 8:7. 9:4, 5. 10:12. 12:8, 24.

19. **Hashabiah.** i.e. *reckoning of Jah.* 1 Ch +9:14. Ne 3:17. 10:11. **Jeshaiah.** i.e. *safety of Jah.* 1 Ch +25:3. **Merari.** i.e. *bitter.* Ge +46:11. 1 Ch 6:1, 16, 19.

20. **Nethinims.** ver. 17. Ezr 2:43. 7:7. 1 Ch 9:2. **all of them.** Ph 4:3.

21. **I proclaimed.** Jg *20:26n. 1 S 7:6. 2 Ch *20:3. Jl 1:14. *2:12-18. Jon 3:5. **afflict ourselves.** Le 16:29, 31. 23:29. Is *58:3, 5. Je 31:8, 9. 50:4, 5. **to seek.** 2 Ch +*7:14. **a right way.** Ps 5:8. 107:2-8. 143:8-10. Pr *3:6. Is *30:21. *35:8. *42:16. 49:10. Je 10:23. **for our little ones.** Nu 14:3, 31. Dt +29:11. Ps *8:2. Mk *10:13-16. Ac *2:39.

22. **I was ashamed.** 1 C 9:15. 2 C 7:14. **The hand.** Ezr 7:*6, 9, 28. 1 Ch +*28:9. 2 Ch *16:9. Ps *33:18, 19. *34:15, 22. Is *33:10, 11. Je *17:5, 7. La *3:25. Ro *8:28. 2 C 10:3, 4. 1 P *3:12. **his power and his wrath.** Jsh 23:16. 2 Ch *15:2. Ps 21:8, 9. *34:16. 90:11. Zp 1:2-6. He *10:38. 1 P *3:12. **against.** T#27. Ex 32:9, 10. 1 S +15:11 (T#19). 2 Ch 15:2. Pr 14:14. Is 1:28. Je 2:19. Ho 6:4, 5. Zp 1:4, 6. He *10:38.

23. **we fasted.** Ne 9:1. Est *4:16. Da *9:3. Lk *2:37. Ac 10:30. **besought.** Je *29:12, 13. *33:3. 50:4, 5. **and he was intreated.** ver. 31. Dt *4:29. 1 Ch 5:20. 2 Ch 33:12, 13. Ps *66:18-20. Is 19:22. Je *29:12, 13. Mt *7:7, 8.

24. **Sherebiah.** ver. 18, 19.

25. **weighed.** ver. 33, 34. Ezr 1:8. 2 C ✓8:20, 21. Ph *4:8. **the silver.** Ezr 7:15, 16. **offering.** or, heave-offering. Ex 25:2, 3. 29:27n. 2 S 1:21.

27. **fine copper.** *or,* yellow *or* shining brass. The Syriac renders, *nechosh korintyo tovo,* "good Corinthian brass;" so called from the brass found after the burning of Corinth by Lucius Mummius, which was, as is generally supposed, brass, copper, silver, and gold, melted together. Sir J. Chardin, however, in a MS. note, cited by Harmer (ch. xi. Ob. 87), mentioned a factitious metal used in the East, and highly esteemed there, which might probably be of an origin as ancient as Ezra. He says, "I have heard some Dutch gentlemen speak of a metal in the island of Sumatra, and among the Macassars, much more esteemed than gold, which royal personages alone are privileged to wear. It is a mixture, if I remember right, of gold and steel, or copper and steel." He afterwards added, "calmbac is the name of this metal, which is composed of gold and copper." **precious.** Heb. desirable. 2 Ch 20:25. La 4:2. Da 11:8.

28. **Ye are holy.** Le 21:6-8. Dt 33:8. Is 52:11. **the vessels.** Ezr 1:7-11. Le 22:2, 3. Nu 4:4-15, 19, 20. 7:13, 84-88. 1 K 7:48-51. 1 Ch 23:28. 2 Ch 24:14. **freewill offering.** Le +*23:38.

29. **Watch ye.** 1 Ch 26:20-26. Mk 13:34, 35. Ac 20:31. 2 T 4:5. **until ye weigh them before.** ver. 33, 34. **in the chambers.** Ezr 10:6. 2 K 23:11.

30. **the house of our God.** ver. 22. 1 Ch 29:2, 3. Ps 122:9. Is 60:13.

31. **the river of Ahava.** ver. 15n, 21. **the hand.** ver. 22. Ezr 7:9, 28. Jb 5:19-24. Ps 91:9-14. Is 41:10-14. Ac 25:3. 26:22. **and he delivered.** Ezra and his company had now entered upon a journey of several hundred miles through the desert, which they were nearly four months in completing, encumbered with families and possessions, and carrying large treasures with them, which would invite the attempts of the Arabian hordes, and others, that infested that neighborhood; yet, having declared to the king, "that the hand of God was upon all them for good that seek him, and that his power and wrath were against all them that forsook him" (ver. 22), he determined to travel without a guard, except that of the Almighty, being ashamed to ask any other, after his former avowed confidence in Him! Having, therefore, humbled themselves before the Lord, and besought his guidance and protection, he was entreated by them, their enemies were restrained or disabled, and they arrived unmolested at Jerusalem. **lay in wait.** Jsh 8:2, 4, 7, 12, 14, 19, 21. Jg 16:9, 12. 20:29, 33, 36, 37, 38. 1 S 22:8, 13. Je 51:12. La 3:10.

32. **we came.** Ezr 7:8, 9. Ne 2:11.

33. **weighed.** ver. 26, 30. 1 Ch 28:14-18. 2 C √8:20, 21. **Meremoth.** i.e. *heights; elevations,* ＊S#4822h. Ezr 8:33. 10:36. Ne 3:4, 21. 10:5. 12:3. (1) A son of Uriah, the priest. He weighed and registered the gold and silver vessels of the Temple in the time of Ezra, and aided in repairing the walls of Jerusalem, Ezr 8:33; Ne 3:4. (2) A Jew who took a foreign wife, Ezr 10:36. (3) A priest who sealed the covenant, Ne 10:5. See Meraioth, Ne +12:15. **Uriah.** i.e. *light of Jah.* 2 S +11:3. Ne 3:4, Urijah. **Jozabad.** i.e. *Jah has endowed.* 2 Ch +31:13. Ne 8:7. **Jeshua.** i.e. *a savior.* Ne +8:17. **Binnui.** i.e. *built up.* Ezr +10:30. Ne 10:9.

35. **children of,** etc. or, sons of the removal. Ezr 4:1. 6:19, 20. **offered burnt offerings.** Le ch. 1, etc. +*23:12. 2 Ch 29:31, 32. Ps 66:10-15. 116:12-19. Lk 1:74, 75. **twelve bullocks.** Ezr 6:17. Nu 7:27. **sin offering.** Le +*23:19.

36. **the king's commissions.** Ezr 7:21-24. **lieutenants.** Ezr 4:7, etc. 5:6, etc. **they furthered.** Ezr 6:13. Is 56:6, 7. Ac 18:27. Re 12:16.

EZRA 9

Ezra, learning that many of the priests and people had married heathen wives, expresses great sorrow and consternation, 1-4 He prays, and makes confession of sin unto God, 5-15.

1. **the princes.** Ezr 10:8. Je 26:10, 16. **have not separated.** Ezr 6:21, 22. 10:10, 11. Ex 33:16. Nu 23:9. Ne 9:2. 13:3. Is 52:11. 2 C √6:14-18. **doing according.** Le 18:3, 24-30. Dt *12:30, 31. *18:9. 2 K 21:2. 2 Ch 33:2. Ps 106:35. Je √10:2. Ro 2:17-25. **of the Canaanites.** Ge +10:18. 15:16, 19-21. Ex 23:23. Dt 20:17, 18. **Hittites.** Ge +15:20. **Perizzites.** Ge +13:7. **Jebusites.** Ge +10:16. **Ammonites.** Dt 23:3-5. 1 S 11:1. 1 K 11:1, 5-7. Ne 4:3, 7. 13:1-3. **Moabites.** Nu 25:1-3. **Amorites.** Ge +10:16.

2. **taken of their.** Ezr 10:18-44. Ge 6:2, 9. Ex 34:16. Dt 7:1-4. Ne 13:23, 24. Ml 2:11. **the holy seed.** Ex 19:6. 22:31. Dt 7:6. 14:2. Is 6:13. Ml 2:15. 1 C 7:14. **mingled.** Ge 6:2. Ne 13:3, 23, 24. 2 C *6:14. **the hand.**

Ezr 10:18-44. Ne 13:4, 17, 28.

3. **rent.** ver. +5. Jsh 7:6. 2 K 18:37. 19:1. Jb *1:20. Je 36:24. **off.** Le 21:5. Ne 13:25. Is 15:2. Je 7:29. 48:37, 38. Ezk 7:18. Mi 1:16. **sat.** Ne 1:4. Jb 2:12, 13. Ps 66:3. 119:53. 143:4. Je 8:21. Ezk 3:15. Da 4:19. 8:27.

4. **trembled.** Ezr *10:3. 2 Ch 34:27. Ps 119:136. Pr 28:14. Is +*66:2. Ezk +*9:4. Ml *3:16. He 12:28, 29. **until.** Ex 29:39. Da 9:21. Ac 3:1.

5. **evening sacrifice.** Mt +14:23. **heaviness.** *or,* affliction. **rent my garment.** T#1273. ver. 3. Jsh 7:6. 1 K 21:27. 2 K 19:1. 22:11, 19. Jb 1:20. **I fell.** 2 Ch *6:13. Ps 95:6. Lk 22:41. Ac 21:5. Ep *3:14. **spread.** Ex 9:29, 33. 1 K 8:22, 38, 54. Ps *141:2. 143:6. Is 1:15. 1 T 2:8.

6. **I am ashamed.** T#1310. Jb 40:4. 42:6. Ps 38:4. Je 3:3, 24, 25. 6:15. 8:12. 31:19. Ezk 16:63. Da 9:7-9. Ro 6:21. **our iniquities.** Ge 13:13. Ps 38:4. Is 1:18. 59:12. **trespass.** *or,* guiltiness. 2 Ch 24:18. **grown up.** √102, Ge +2:24. 2 Ch 28:9. Lk 15:21. Re 18:5.

7. **Since the days.** Nu 32:14. 2 Ch 29:6. 30:7. Ne 9:32-34. Ps 106:6, 7. La 5:7. Da 9:5-8. Zc 1:4, 5. Mt 23:30-33. Ac 7:51, 52. **for our iniquities.** Le 26:14, etc. Dt 4:25-28. 28:15, etc. 29:22-28. 30:17-19. 31:20-22. 32:15-28. 1 S 12:15. 1 K 9:6-9. Ne 9:30. **into the hand.** 2 K 17:5-8. 18:9-12. 24:1-4. 2 Ch 36:16-19. Ne 9:36, 37. Da 9:11-14. **to confusion.** Da 9:7, 8. **as it is this day.** 1 K 8:24. Ne 9:32. Je 25:18. 44:22.

8. **little space.** Heb. moment. √111, Ge +18:27. Nu 16:21. Is 26:20. **grace hath.** ver. 9. Ne 1:11. 9:31. Hab 3:2. **a remnant.** ver. 14. 2 K 19:4, 30, 31. Is *1:9. *10:20-22. Je 42:2. 44:14. Ezk 6:8, 9. 14:22. Zc 8:6, 12. Ro 9:27. 11:5, 6. **a nail.** *or,* a pin. i.e. *a constant and sure abode.* Ec 12:11. Is *22:23-25. Zc 10:4. **in his holy place.** Is 56:5. Re 3:12. **lighten.** 1 S 14:27, 29. Jb 33:30. Ps 13:3. 34:5. **reviving.** Ps 85:6. 138:7. Is 57:15. Ezk 37:11-14. Ho 6:2.

9. **we were bondmen.** Ne 9:36, 37. **yet our God.** Ps 106:45, 46. 136:23, 24. Ezk 11:16. **in the sight.** Ezr 1:1-4, 7-11. 6:1-12. 7:6, 8, 11-28. **to set up.** Ezr 6:14, 15. Hg 1:9. Zc 4:6-10. **repair.** Heb. set up. 2 S 22:34. **a wall.** Or rather, a *hedge* or *fence, gader,* such as were made for sheep-folds. Is 5:2, 5. La 2:8, 9, 18. Da 9:25. Zc 2:5.

10. **what shall we say.** Ge 44:16. Jsh 7:8. La 3:22. Da 9:4-16. Ro 3:19.

11. **by thy servants.** Heb. by the hand of thy servants. 1 K +16:12mg. √121BB. Metonymy of the Cause B547: the *hand* is put for instrumentality or agency, especially in connection with *inspiration.* For other instances of this figure see Ne 9:30. Zc *7:12. **The land.** ver. 1. Le 18:24-30. Dt 12:31. 18:12. 2 Ch 33:2. **the filthiness.** Ezr 6:21. Ezk 36:25-27. 2 C *7:1. **one end to another.** Heb. mouth to mouth. 2 K 10:21mg. 21:16mg.

12. **give not.** Ex 23:32. 34:16. Dt *7:3. Jsh 23:12, 13. **nor seek their peace.** Dt 23:6. 2 Ch 19:2. 2 J √10, 11. **for ever.** Heb. *olam,* Ex +*12:24. **that ye may.** Dt 6:1, 2. 28:4. Jsh *1:6-9. **and eat.** Is 1:19. **and leave it.** Ge *18:18, 19. Ps 112:1, 2. Pr *13:22. *20:7. **for ever.** Heb. *olam,* Ex +*12:24.

13. **after all.** Ne 9:32. Ezk 24:13, 14. Ga 3:4. **hast punished,** etc. Heb. hast withheld beneath our iniquities. **less.** Ps *103:10-14. La 3:22, 39, 40. Hab 3:2. **hast given us.** Ps 106:45, 46.

14. **we again.** Jn *5:14. Ro 6:1. 2 P *2:20, 21. **join in.** ver. 2. Ex 23:32. Jg 2:2. Ne 13:23-27. **wouldst not**

thou. Ex 32:10. Nu 16:21, 45. Dt 9:8, 14. **no remnant.** ver. 8. Dt 32:26, 27. Is 1:9. Je 46:28. Ezk 6:8.

15. **thou art righteous.** Ne 9:33, 34. Da 9:7-11, 14. Ro 10:3. **for we remain.** La 3:22, 23. **in our trespasses.** Is √64:6, 7. Ezk 33:10. Zc 3:3, 4. Jn *8:21, 24. 1 C 15:17. **we cannot.** Jb 9:2, 3. Ps 130:3, 4. 143:2. Ro 3:19.

EZRA 10

The people weep with Ezra, 1. Shechaniah proposes that the people should divorce their heathen wives, and encourages Ezra to attempt this; who requires the priests, and others, to engage by oath so to do, 2-5. By proclamation he assembles the people, who promise to comply, 6-14. The measure is regularly carried into execution, 15-17. The names of those who put away their strange wives, 18-44.

1. **when Ezra.** Da *9:3, 4, 20. Ac 10:30. **when he had.** Le 26:40, 41. Ps *32:5. Ho *14:2. 1 J √1:8-10. **weeping.** Ps *119:136. Je 9:1. 13:17. Zc *12:10. Lk *19:41. Ro 9:2. **before the house.** 1 K *8:30. 9:3. 2 Ch 7:12. *20:9. **a very great.** Dt *31:12. 2 Ch 20:13. Ne 10:28. Jl *2:16-18. Ac 21:5. **very sore.** Heb. wept a great weeping. Jg 2:4, 5. Ne *8:9.

2. **Shechaniah.** ver. 26. Ne 3:29. **Elam.** Ezr 2:7, 31. Ne 7:12-34. **We have trespassed.** Shechaniah here speaks in the name of the *people*, not acknowledging himself culpable; for he is not in the following list. Compare Ja 2:9. Ex *34:12. Ne 13:27. **yet now there is hope.** Ex 34:6, 7. Is *55:6, 7. Je *3:12, 13. 1 J √1:7-9.

3. **let us make.** *Nichrath berith,* "let us cut a covenant:" see on Dt +*29:12n. Jsh 9:6. 2 K 11:17. 2 Ch 29:10. *34:31, 32. Ne 9:38. *10:29, etc. **put away.** Heb. bring forth. ver. 19. Ne 9:2. 13:30. **according to the counsel.** 2 Ch 30:12. **of those that.** Ezr *9:4. 2 Ch 34:21, 27. Ps 119:59, 120. Is 66:2. Ezk +*9:4. **at the commandment.** Dt *7:2, 3. Jsh *23:12, 13. **let it.** Ne *8:14. *13:1-3. Is √8:20. Shecaniah's counsel, which he was then so clear in, will not hold now: such marriages, it is certain, are contrary to the will of God, and ought not to be made; but they are not null. Our rule under the gospel is, *Quod fieri non debuit, factum valet,* "That which ought not to have been done must, when done, abide." Nevertheless the principle is clear: believers are not to marry unbelievers (1 C 7:39. 2 C √6:14.) See 1 C 7:12, 13.

4. **Arise.** Jsh 7:10, etc. 1 Ch 22:16, 19. Ec *9:10. **for this matter.** By the decree of Artaxerxes, Ezra was authorized to do everything that the law of God required. Ezr *7:23-28. Mk 13:34. **we also will.** Jsh 1:16-18. 1 Ch 28:10, 21. **be of good.** Jsh 1:7. 1 Ch 19:13. *22:13. Is 35:3, 4. He *10:24. 12:12, 13.

5. **arose.** Pr *1:5. *9:9. 15:23. 25:11, 12. 27:9. **made.** ver. 3. Ne 5:12. 10:29. *13:25. Mt 26:63.

6. **the chamber.** Ezr 8:29. 1 S 9:22. 2 K 23:11. 1 Ch 9:26. Ne 13:5. **Johanan.** Ne 3:1, 20. 12:10, 22. 13:28. **he did eat.** Dt 9:18. Jb √23:12. Jn 4:31-34. **he mourned.** Ezr 9:4. Is 22:12. Da 9:3.

7. **they made.** Ezr 1:1. 2 Ch 30:5.

8. **And that whatsoever.** Ezr 7:26. Jg 21:5. 1 S 11:7. **forfeited.** Heb. devoted. Ex 22:20. Le 27:+28, 29n. Jsh 6:19. **himself separated.** Ne 13:3. Mt 18:17. Jn 9:22, 34. 16:2. 1 C 5:13.

9. **the ninth month.** That is, *Chisleu*, five months

after Ezra came to Jerusalem (Young). That is, some time in *December*, which is the coldest and most rainy time of the year in Palestine. Dr Russel (*Description of Aleppo*, p. 63, etc.), in his account of the weather at Aleppo, which very much resembles that in Judea, says, that the natives reckon the severity of the winter, which they call *marbania*, to last but forty days, beginning from the 12th of December, and ending the 20th of January, and that this computation comes in fact very near the truth: and that the air during this time is excessively piercing, even to those that are just come from a cold climate. Ezr 7:8, 9. Est 2:16. **trembling.** 1 S 12:17, 18. Je *10:10, 13. **great rain.** Heb. showers. ver. 13.

10. **taken.** Heb. caused to dwell, *or,* brought back. **to increase.** Ezr 9:6. Nu 32:14. Jsh 22:17, 18. 2 Ch 28:13. Mt 23:32.

11. **make confession.** Le 26:40-42. Jsh 7:19. Ps *32:5. Pr √28:13. Je 3:13. 1 J √1:7-9. **do his.** Is *1:16-18. 56:4. Ro *12:2. Col +√1:10. He *13:21. **separate.** Ezr 9:1. Ne 13:3. 2 C *6:17. **and from the.** Dt 7:3, 4. 1 C 2:12-14.

12. **As thou hast said.** They all resolved to do what Ezra had commanded; and they did put away their wives, even those by whom they had children (ver. 44), each of whom doubtless received a portion according to the circumstances of her husband, and was not turned away desolate. *Humanity* must have dictated this, and no law of God is contrary to humanity (Ge 18:25. Lk 6:35). **so must we do.** ver. 3, 4. 2 Ch 30:8. Ne 13:23. Ps 78:37, 57.

13. **the people.** ver. 18-44. Mt √7:13, 14. **time of.** lit. the season (is) showers. ℐ119, Ge +49:9. **we are many that have transgressed in this thing.** *or,* we have greatly offended in this thing.

14. **our rulers.** Dt *17:9, 18, 19. 2 Ch 19:5-7. Ac 5:21. 6:12. 23:1. **the fierce wrath.** Ex 32:12. Nu 25:4. 32:14. Dt 13:17. Jsh 7:26. 2 Ch +24:18. 29:10. 30:8. Ps 78:38. Is 12:1. **for this matter be turned from us.** *or,* be turned from us, till this matter *be dispatched.* ℐ63B, Ge +25:28.

15. **Jonathan.** i.e. *Jah hath given.* 1 S +13:2. **Asahel.** i.e. *made* or *done by God.* 1 Ch +2:16. **Jahaziah.** i.e. *seen of Jah; Jah beholds; he will see the Lord,* ✱S#3167h. **Tikvah.** i.e. *hope, expectation.* 2 K +22:14. **were employed.** Heb. stood. or, against. Young notes, not "employed about;" so Jarchi and Lightfoot. **Meshullam.** i.e. *recompensed.* 1 Ch +9:12. Ne 3:6. 10:20. 12:33. **Shabbethai.** i.e. *sabbatic; my sabbaths; restful; rest of the Lord,* i.e. *born on the Sabbath,* ✱S#7678h. Ezr 10:15. Ne 8:7. 11:16.

16. **to examine the matter.** Dt 13:14. Jb 29:16. Jn 7:51.

17. A.M. 3548. B.C. 456. **the first day.** The cases brought before the council were either so many, or so complicated, that though they separated themselves from other employments, yet they were *three whole months* in examining into their affairs, and making the necessary separations required by law.

18. **the sons.** Ezr 9:1. Le 21:7, 13-15. 1 S 2:22-24. Ne 13:28. Je 23:11, 14. Ezk 44:22. Ml 2:8, 9. 1 T 3:11. **Jeshua.** See on Ezr 2:2. 3:2. 5:2. 1 Ch 6:14, 15. Ne 12:10. Hg 1:1. Zc 3:1, Joshua. **Maaseiah.** Ne 8:4, 7.

19. **gave their hands.** They bound themselves in the most solemn manner to do as the rest of the delin-

quents had done, and make an acknowledgment to God of their iniquity, by offering each a *ram* for a trespass offering. Le 5:17-19. 2 K 10:15. 1 Ch +*29:24mg. 2 Ch 30:8mg. La 5:6. Ezk 17:18. Ga 2:9. **offered.** ✗63B, Ge +25:28. **a ram.** Le 5:15, 16. 6:4, 6. **trespass.** Le +*5:6.

20. **Immer.** i.e. *talkative; loquacious.* Ezr 2:37. 1 Ch +9:12. 24:14. Ne 7:40. **Hanani.** i.e. *my grace.* 1 Ch +25:4. **Zebadiah.** i.e. *endowed by Jah.* 1 Ch +26:2.

21. **Harim.** i.e. *flat-nosed,* or *devoted.* Ezr 2:39. 1 Ch +24:8. Ne 7:42. **Maaseiah.** i.e. *work of Jah.* Je +21:1. **Elijah.** i.e. *God is Jah.* 1 K +17:1. **Shemaiah.** i.e. *heard of Jah.* 1 Ch +9:16. **Jehiel.** i.e. *God lives.* Ezr +8:9. **Uzziah.** i.e. *strength of Jah.* 2 Ch +26:1.

22. **Pashur.** i.e. *prosperity everywhere.* Ezr 2:38. 1 Ch 9:12. Ne 7:41. Je +20:1. **Elioenai.** i.e. *unto Jah are my eyes.* 1 Ch +26:3. **Maaseiah.** i.e. *work of Jah.* ver. 18. Ne 8:4. Je +21:1. **Ishmael.** i.e. *God hears.* Ge +16:11. **Nethaneel.** i.e. *gift of God.* Nu +1:8. **Jozabad.** i.e. *Jah has endowed.* 2 Ch +31:13. **Elasah.** i.e. *God has made; God has wrought; whom God made,* ✱S#501h. Ezr 10:22. 1 Ch 2:+39, 40. 8:37. 9:43, Eleasah. Je 29:3. (1) One who put away his strange wife under Ezra, Ezr 10:22. (2) The bearer of Jeremiah's letter to captives in Babylon, Je 29:3.

23. **Jozabad.** i.e. *Jah has endowed.* Ezr 8:33. 2 Ch +31:13. Ne 11:16. **Shimei.** i.e. *hearkening.* 2 S +16:5. **Kelaiah.** i.e. *light* or *swift one of Jah; voice of Jah; lightly esteemed of Jah; congregation of the Lord,* ✱S#7041h. **Kelita.** i.e. *congregation of the Lord; contracted, lacking, stunted,* ✱S#7042h. Ezr 10:23. Ne 8:7. 10:10. **Pethahiah.** i.e. *opening of Jah.* Ne +11:24. **Judah.** i.e. *confessed, praised.* Ge +35:23. **Eliezer.** i.e. *my God is help.* Ge +15:2.

24. **singers.** 2 Ch +35:15. **Eliashib.** i.e. *God brings back.* 1 Ch +3:24. **porters.** 1 Ch 16:42mg. 23:5. 2 Ch 35:15. **Shallum.** i.e. *recompensed.* 2 K +15:10. **Telem.** i.e. *oppression; covering them, casting them out,* ✱S#2928h. Ezr 10:24. Also Jsh 15:24. (1) One of them that took strange wives, Ezr 10:24. (2) A city of Judah, Jsh 15:24; the same as Telaim, 1 S 15:4.

25. **Moreover of Israel.** That is, as Calmet observes, *simple Israelites*; thus distinguished from the *priests, Levites,* and *singers,* mentioned in ver. 18, 23, 24. **sons of Parosh.** i.e. *a flea.* Ezr +2:3. Ne 7:8. **Ramiah.** i.e. *exaltation of Jah; Jah has exalted; placed of the Lord,* ✱S#7422h. **Jeziah.** i.e. *sprinkled of Jah; he will be sprinkled of the Lord,* ✱S#3150h. **Malchiah.** i.e. *king of the Lord.* Je +38:1. **Miamin.** i.e. *southward, on the right hand; from the right hand.* Ne +12:5. **Eleazar.** i.e. *God is help.* Ex +6:23. **Malchijah.** i.e. *my king is Jehovah.* 1 Ch +9:12. **Benaiah.** i.e. *built up of Jah.* 1 Ch +15:24.

26. **Elam.** ver. 2. Ezr 2:7, 31. 8:7. Ne 7:12, 34. **Mattaniah.** i.e. *gift of Jah.* 2 K +24:17. **Zechariah.** i.e. *remembered of Jah.* Zc +1:1. **Jehiel.** i.e. *God lives.* ver. 2. Ezr +8:9. **Abdi.** i.e. *my servant.* 1 Ch +6:44. **Jeremoth.** i.e. *heights; high places; liftings up; there shall be elevations,* ✱S#3406h. Ezr 10:26, 27. 1 Ch 7:8. 8:14. 23:23. 25:22. See also 1 Ch +7:7, Jerimoth. (1, 2) Two chief men of Benjamin, 1 Ch 7:8; 8:14. (3) A son of Mushi, of Merari, 1 Ch 23:23; 24:30. (4) He who obtained the fifteenth lot of the singers, 1 Ch 25:22. (5, 6, 7) Three of those who married strange wives, Ezr 10:26, 27, 33.

27. **Zattu.** Ezr +2:8. Ne 7:13. **Aziza.** i.e. *strong; mightiness; fortified,* ✱S#5819h.

28. **Bebai.** Ezr 2:11. 8:11. Ne 7:16. **Zabbai.** i.e. *pure; portion of God; my wanderings; clemency of the Lord,* ✱S#2079h. Ezr 10:28. Ne 3:20. (1) A Jew who took a foreign wife, Ezr 10:28. (2) Father of Baruch, Ne 3:20. **Athlai.** i.e. *my due times,* ✱S#6270h.

29. **Bani.** i.e. *built up.* Ezr +2:10. Ne 7:15, Binnui. **Malluch.** i.e. *reigning* or *counselor.* Ne +10:4. **Adaiah.** i.e. *adorned of Jah.* Ne +11:5. **Jashub.** i.e. *he turns back.* Nu +26:24. **Sheal.** i.e. *he asked; prayer; petition,* ✱S#7594h. **Ramoth.** i.e. *heights.* 1 Ch +6:73.

30. **Pahath-moab.** Ezr +2:6. 8:4. Ne 7:11. **Adna.** i.e. *pleasure,* ✱S#5733h. Ezr 10:30. Ne 12:15. (1) One of the family of Pahath-moab, who had taken a foreign wife during or after the captivity, Ezr 10:30. (2) A priest in the time of Joiakim, Ne 12:15. **Chelal.** i.e. *completion, perfection; finished,* ✱S#3636h. **Benaiah.** i.e. *built up of Jah.* 1 Ch +15:24. **Maaseiah.** i.e. *work of Jah.* Je +21:1. **Mattaniah.** i.e. *gift of Jah.* 2 K +24:17. **Bezaleel.** i.e. *in the shadow of God.* Ex +31:2. **Binnui.** i.e. *built up; building,* ✱S#1131h. Ezr 8:33. 10:30, 38. Ne 3:24. 7:15. 10:9. 12:8. (1) One whose children returned from Babylon, Ezr 2:10; Ne 7:15. (2) One of those who had married strange wives, Ezr 10:30, 38. (3) Father of Noadiah, who assisted to weigh the vessels, Ezr 8:33. (4) One who helped to build the wall, Ne 3:24. (5) One who sealed the covenant, Ne 10:9. (6) One who went up with Zerubbabel, Ne 12:8. **Manasseh.** i.e. *causing to forget.* Ge +41:51.

31. **Harim.** Ezr 2:32. Ne 7:35. **Ishijah.** i.e. *Jah will lend; gift of the Lord; forgotten of Jah,* S#3449h. 1 Ch +*7:3, Ishiah. +12:6, Jesaiah. **Malchiah.** i.e. *my king is Jah.* This variation only exists in the translation, the original being uniformly *Malchijah,* or rather, "*Malkeeyah.*" Ne 3:11, Malchijah. Je +38:1. **Shemaiah.** i.e. *heard of Jah.* 1 Ch +9:16. **Shimeon.** i.e. *hearkening; a hearkener,* ✚S#8095h. For ✱S#8095h, Simeon, see Ge +29:33.

33. **Hashum.** i.e. *rich, wealthy.* Ezr +2:19. Ne 7:22. **Mattenai.** i.e. *gift of Jah; gift of the Lord.* Ne +12:19. **Mattathah.** i.e. *gift of Jah; gift of the Lord; givingness,* ✱S#4992h. **Zabad.** i.e. *he endowed.* 1 Ch +2:36. **Eliphelet.** i.e. *God causes to escape.* 1 Ch +3:6. **Jeremai.** i.e. *dweller on high; elevated; he will be exalted of the Lord; let me have promotions,* ✱S#3413h.

34. **Bani.** ver. 29. **Maadai.** i.e. *ornament; pleasant; ornament of the Lord; my unclothings, my slidings,* ✱S#4572h. **Amram.** i.e. *exalted people.* Ex +6:18. **Uel.** i.e. *desire of God; wish or will of God,* ✱S#177h.

35. **Benaiah.** i.e. *built up of Jah.* 1 Ch +15:24. **Bedeiah.** i.e. *servant of Jehovah; separated of the Lord; in the strength, defense, or covering of the Lord; isolated of Jah,* ✱S#912h. **Chelluh.** i.e. *completion of Jah; completed; consumed of the Lord; determine ye him,* ✱S#3622h.

36. **Vaniah.** i.e. *oppression; Jah is praised; torpid; weak; and we were oppressed,* ✱S#2057h. **Meremoth.** i.e. *heights.* Ezr +8:33. **Eliashib.** i.e. *God brings back.* 1 Ch +3:24.

37. **Mattaniah.** ver. 30. **Mattenai.** ver. 33. **Jaasau.** i.e. *made by Jah; whom Jehovah has made; made of the Lord; they will make of him; they will perform,* ✱S#3299h.

40. **Machnadebai.** or, Mabnadebai, *according to some copies.* i.e. *a bond; what is like the liberality of*

the Lord; he brought low my willing ones, *S#4367h. **Shashai**. i.e. whitish, or sixth; habitation of the Lord; my linens, *S#8343h. **Sharai**. i.e. beginning; liberated of the Lord; my settings free; my observers, *S#8298h.

41. **Azareel**. i.e. help of God. 1 Ch +12:6. **Shelemiah**. i.e. peace of Jah. 1 Ch +26:14. **Shemariah**. i.e. kept of Jah. 1 Ch +12:5.

43. **Nebo**. i.e. a prophet. Ezr 2:29. Nu +32:3. Ne 7:33. **Jeiel**. i.e. heaps of God. 1 Ch +5:7. **Mattithiah**. i.e. gift of Jah; gift of Jehovah, *S#4993h. Ezr 10:43. 1 Ch 9:31. 16:5. Ne 8:4. Also 1 Ch 15:18, 21. 25:3, 21. (1) A Levite set over the things made in the pans, 1 Ch 9:31. (2) One who helped to bring up the ark from Obed-edom, 1 Ch 15:18, 21; 16:5. (3, 4) Two of those that married strange wives, Ezr 10:33, 43. (5) One who stood up with Ezra to read the law, Ne 8:4. (6) A Levite, son of the singer Jeduthun, 1 Ch 25:3. **Zabad**. ver. 33. **Zebina**. i.e. bought; a precious possession; we are bought, *S#2081h. **Jadau**. i.e. loving or judging; praised; beloved of the Lord, *S#3035h. Ezr 10:43. Also 1 Ch +27:21, Iddo.

44. **strange wives**. Pr 2:16. 5:3, 20. **and some of them**. This observation was probably intended to show that only a few of them had children, and also how rigorously the law was kept in execution. According to a passage in Justin Martyr's Dialogue with Trypho, a Jew (sec. 72), Ezra offered a paschal lamb on this occasion, and addressed the people thus: "And Ezra said to the people, This passover is our Savior and our Refuge; and if ye will be persuaded of it, and let it enter into your hearts, that we are to be humble to Him in a sign, and afterwards shall believe in Him, this place shall not be destroyed for ever, saith the Lord of hosts; but, if ye will not believe in Him, nor hearken to his preaching, ye shall be a laughing-stock to the Gentiles." This was probably a marginal note added by some early Christian.

NEHEMIAH

NEHEMIAH 1

Nehemiah, being informed of the afflicted state of the Jews, mourns, fasts, and prays, 1-4 His prayer, 5-11.

1. **Nehemiah**. i.e. whom Jehovah comforts; comforted of Jah; comfort of the Lord, *S#5166h. Ne 1:1. 3:16. 7:7. 8:9. *10:1h, 8. 12:26, 47. Ezr 2:2. (1) Son of Hachaliah, the governor of Judea, in the reign of Artaxerxes Longimanus, Ne 1:1; 8:9; 10:1. (2) One who helped to build the wall, Ne 3:16. (3) One who came up with Zerubbabel, Ezr 2:2; Ne 7:7. **Hachaliah**. i.e. reddened or dimmed by Jah; whose eyes Jehovah enlivens; dark flashing of the Lord; the waiting on Jah, *S#2446h. Ne 1:1. 10:1. **in the month**. Ezr 10:9. Zc 7:1. **in the twentieth**. Ezr 7:7. **Shushan**. Shushan, or Susa, was the capital of Susiana, a province of Persia, and the winter residence of the Persian monarchs; situated about 252 miles east of Babylon, and the same distance south south-east of Ecbatana, in lat. 32 degrees, long. 49 degrees. The circumference of its walls was above 120 stadia. Shouster is supposed to occupy its site. Est 1:2. 3:15. Da 8:2.

2. **Hanani**. Ne 7:2. **I asked**. Ps 122:6-9. 137:5, 6. **that had escaped**. Ezr 9:8, 9, 14. Je 44:14. Ezk 6:9. 7:16. 24:26, 27.

3. **the province**. Ne 7:6. 11:3. Ezr 2:1. 5:8. Est 1:1. **in great**. Ne 9:36, 37. Ps 44:11-14. 137:1-3. Is 32:9-14. La 1:7. 3:61. 5:1. **reproach**. 1 K 9:7. Ps 79:4. Is 43:28. Je 24:9. 29:18. 42:18. 44:8-12. **the wall**. Ne 2:17. 2 K 25:10. Is 5:5. 64:10, 11. Je 5:10. 39:8. 52:14.

4. **I sat down**. Jg +20:26n. 1 S 4:17-22. Ezr 10:1. Ps 69:9, 10. 102:13, 14. 137:1. Da 9:3. Zp 3:18. Ro 12:15. **certain days**. T#1760. **and prayed**. 1 K 8:44, 48. Da 6:10. **the God**. Ne 2:4. Ezr 5:11, 12. Da 2:18. Jon 1:9.

5. **beseech**. T#1313. Ex 32:11. 33:18. Nu 12:13. Ps 80:14. 116:4. 118:25. 119:108. Am 7:2. Jon 1:14. 4:3. Ml 1:9. Mt 8:5. Mk 1:40. Lk 8:28. 9:38. **the great**. Ne 4:14. Dt 7:21. 1 Ch 17:21. Ps 47:2. Da *9:4, etc. **keepeth**. Ex 20:6. Dt *7:9. Jg 2:1. 1 K 8:23. Ps 111:5, 9. He *6:13-18. **and mercy**. ♪174, Ge +18:27.

6. **thine ear**. 1 K *8:28, 29. 2 Ch 6:40. Ps *34:15. 130:2. Da *9:17, 18. **eyes open**. 1 K 8:29. Zc 12:4. Lk 22:61. **day and night**. 1 S 15:11. Ps *55:17. 88:1. Lk 2:37. *18:7. 1 T 5:5. 2 T *1:3. **confess**. Ezr 9:6, 7. 10:11. Ps *32:5. Is *64:6, 7. La 3:39-42. Da 9:4, 20. 1 J ✓1:9. **both I**. 2 Ch 28:10. 29:6. Ps *106:6. Is *6:5. La *5:7. Ep *2:3.

7. **dealt**. Ne 9:29-35. Ps 78:56, 57. 106:6. Da *9:5, 6. **corruptly**. 2 Ch 27:2. Ho 9:9. Zp *3:7. Re 19:2. **the commandments**. Le 27:34. Dt 4:1. *5:1. 6:1. *28:15. 1 K *2:3. Ps *19:8, 9. 119:5-8. **which thou**. Dt 4:5. 2 Ch *25:4. Ezr *7:6. Da *9:11, 13. Ml 4:4.

8. **Remember**. Ps 119:49. Lk *1:72. **If**. Ge +4:7. **ye transgress**. Le *26:33, etc. Dt *4:25-27. *28:64. 32:26-28. 1 K 9:6, 7.

9. **if ye turn**. Le 26:39-42. Dt *4:29-31. 30:2-5. Je *29:11-14. **heaven**. 121Q3, 2 S +22:8. **yet will I**. 1 Ch 16:35. Ps 106:47. 147:2. Is 11:12. *56:8. Je 12:15. *31:10. *32:37. *50:19, 20. Mt *24:31. **will bring**. Je *3:14. Ezk *36:24. **the place**. Dt *12:5, 21. + *16:16. 1 K 9:3. Ezr 6:12.

10. **Now these**. Ex *32:11. Dt 9:29. Is 63:16-19. 64:9. Da 9:15, etc. **whom**. Ex 15:13. Dt 15:15. Ps 74:2. **thy strong**. Ex 6:1. 13:9. Ps 136:12. Da *9:15.

11. **let now**. See on ver. 6. Ps 86:6. *130:2. **who desire**. Pr 1:29. Is *26:8, 9. He 13:18. **grant**. Ne 2:8. Ge 32:11, 28. 43:14. Ezr 1:1. *7:6, 27, 28. Pr 21:1. **For I was**. The office of cup-bearer was one of great trust, honor, and emolument, in the Persian court. To be in such a place of trust he must have been in the king's confidence; for no eastern potentate would have a cup-bearer to whom he could not trust his life, poison being often administered in that way. It was an office much desired, because it gave access to the king in those seasons of hilarity when men are most disposed to grant favors. Ne 2:1. Ge 40:2, 9-13, 21, 23. 41:9.

NEHEMIAH 2

Artaxerxes, observing Nehemiah sad before him, asks the cause, 1, 2. Nehemiah is afraid, assigns the reason, prays, petitions the king, and obtains authority *to rebuild the wall of Jerusalem, 3-8. He delivers the king's letters to the governors beyond the river; the enemies of the Jews are much grieved; and he arrives at Jerusalem, 9-11. He examines the state of the walls secretly by night, 12-16. He encourages the Jews to build, 17, 18. The scorn and menaces of their enemies, and his answer, 19, 20.*

1. **Nisan.** i.e. *their flight; standard; proving,* *S#5212h. Ne 2:1. Est 3:7. **the twentieth.** Ne 1:1. Ezr 7:1, 7. **I took up.** Ne 1:11. Ge 40:11, 21.

2. **Why is thy.** Ge 40:7. **sorrow.** Pr *15:13. **Then I.** Probably the king spoke as if he had some suspicion that Nehemiah harbored some bad design, and that his face indicated some conceived treachery, or remorse; and, indeed, the words rendered *sad,* and *sorrow of heart,* might be rendered *evil,* and *wickedness of heart.*

3. **Let the king.** Far from wishing ill to my master, I wish him to live for ever. 1 K 1:31. Da 2:4. 3:9. 5:10. 6:6, 21. **for ever.** Heb. *olam,* Ex +*12:24. **the city.** Ne 1:3. Ps 102:14. *137:6. La *2:9. **the place.** 2 Ch 21:20. 28:27. *32:33. **sepulchres.** Heb. *qeber,* Ge +23:4.

4. **For what.** 1 K *3:5. Est *5:3, 6. 7:2. Mk *10:51. **So I prayed.** T#1201. Ne 1:4, 11. 2 S 12:13-17. *15:31. Pr *3:6. Jon 3:6-9. Ph *4:6. 1 Th 5:17. 1 T 2:8.

5. **And I said.** Nehemiah both prayed to God, and asked the king's assistance, just as Jesus when on earth, though he was the creator of the worlds, asked assistance when he wanted a drink of water (Jn 4:7). So in the work of God, contrary to the opinion of some, it is not unspiritual or unscriptural to make needs, financial and otherwise, known to others, to obtain assistance for the work of God. **If it please.** Ezr 5:17. Est 1:19. 5:8. 7:3. *8:5. **and if thy.** Ru *2:13. 2 S 14:22. Pr *3:4. **sepulchres.** Heb. *qeber,* Ge +23:4.

6. **the queen.** Heb. the wife. Ps 45:9. It was probably Esther who was present at this time, and who seconded Nehemiah's request. **So it pleased.** ver. 4. Ne 1:11. Is *58:12. 61:4. *65:24. **I set him a time.** It is probable that this time was no more than six months, or a year; after which he either returned, or had his leave extended, as we find he was twelve years governor of the Jews. Ne 5:14. 13:6.

7. **let letters.** ver. 9. Ezr 6:6. 7:21. **that they may.** Ezr 8:22.

8. **forest.** Ec 2:5. SS 4:13. **palace.** Ne 7:2. 1 Ch 29:1. **the wall.** ver. 17. Ne 3:1, etc. **the house.** Ne 3:7. 7:2. **the king.** ver. 18. Ge 32:28. Ezr 5:5. 6:22. 7:6, 9, 27, 28. Pr *21:1. Is 66:14. Da 1:9. Ac 7:10. 26:22. 2 C 8:16. **hand.** Ru ◐+*1:13. ♪22A14.5. Anthropopatheia, or Anthropomorphism B878. A hand is attributed to God indicative of *prospering.* For other instances of this figure see Ezr 7:6, 9, 28. 8:18. Ne 2:18.

9. **to the governors.** ver. 7. **Now the.** Ezr 8:22.

10. **Sanballat.** i.e. *hated in secret; hate in disguise; hatred (or thorn) in secret,* *S#5571h. ver. 19. Ne 4:1h-3, 7. 6:1, 2, 5, 12, 14. 13:28. **Horonite.** i.e. *one from Horonaim* (i.e. *two caverns,* Is +15:5), *S#2772h. Ne 2:10, 19h. 13:28h. Is 15:5. Je 48:5, 34. **the servant.** Pr 30:22. Ec 10:7. **the Ammonite.** Ne 13:1. Dt *23:3, 4. **it grieved.** Nu 22:3, 4. Ps 112:10. 122:6-9. Pr 27:4. Ezk 25:6-8. Mi 7:9, 10, 16, 17. Ac 4:2. 5:24. 19:26, 27. **there was come.** Ezr 4:4, etc.

11. **I came.** Ezr 8:32.

12. **I arose.** Ge 32:22-24. Jsh 10:9. Jg 6:27. 9:32. Mt 2:14. Mk *1:35. **some few.** ♪24E, Ge +30:33. **neither.** Ec 3:7. Am 5:13. Mi 7:5. Mt 10:16. **my God.** This pious and noble-minded man attributes every thing to God. If he *purposed* any good, it was because *God put it into his heart;* if he *did or received* any good, it was because *the good hand of his God was upon him;* if he *expected* any good, it was because he earnestly *prayed God to remember him for good.* Ezr 7:27. Ps *51:18. +√122:6. Je 31:33. 32:40. 2 C 8:16. Ja 1:16, 17. Re 17:17.

13. **the gate.** ver. 15. Ne 3:13. 2 Ch 26:9. **well.** Heb. *ayin,* Ge +24:13. **the dung port.** This was the gate on the eastern side of the city, through which the filth was carried to the brook Kidron and valley of Hinnom (Jsh +*15:8n). Ne 3:13, 14. 12:31. **the walls.** ver. 3, 17. Ne 1:3. Je 5:10.

14. **the gate of the fountain.** The gate leading either to the fountain of *Siloam,* on the east of the city, or to that of *Gihon,* on the west. Ne 3:15. 2 K 18:17n. 20:20. 2 Ch 32:30n. **the king's pool.** Probably the *aqueduct* made by Hezekiah to bring the waters of Gihon to the city of David. 2 S 5:23n. 1 K 1:45n.

15. **the brook.** The brook *Kidron.* 2 S 15:23. Je 31:38-40. Jn 18:1. **the gate.** The gate leading to the valley of Jehoshaphat, east of the city, through which the brook Kidron flows. It was by this gate he went out; so that he went around the whole of the city, and entered by the same gate. ver. 13.

16. **the rulers.** ver. 12.

17. **Ye see.** La 2:2, 8, 9. 3:51. **come.** Ezr 5:1, 2. 10:2-4. Is 35:3, 4. **build.** Ps 127:1. **a reproach.** Ne 1:3. 1 S 11:2. Ps 44:13. 79:4, 12. 89:50, 51. Je 24:9. La 3:45, 46. Ezk 5:14, 15. 22:4, 5.

18. **I told.** 1 J 1:3. **the hand.** ♪22A14.5, See on ver. +8. **So they strengthened.** 2 S 2:7. 1 Ch 11:10. 19:13. 2 Ch 32:5. Ezr 6:22. Hg 1:13, 14. Ep *6:10. Ph *2:13. He 12:12.

19. **Sanballat.** ver. 10. Ne 6:1, 2. **Geshem.** Ne 6:6, Gashmu. **they.** Jb 30:1. Ps 44:13, 14. 79:4. 80:6. Je 20:8. Mk 5:40. He 11:36. **will ye rebel.** Ne 6:6. Ezr 4:15, 16. Lk 23:2. Jn 19:12. Ac 24:5.

20. **The God.** ver. 4. 2 Ch 26:5. Ps 20:5. 35:27. 102:13, 14. 122:6. Ec 7:18. **ye have no.** Ezr 4:3. Ac 8:21. **memorial.** Ex 28:29. Le 2:2. 24:7. Nu 10:10. Is 56:5. Zc 6:14. Ac 10:4, 31. When Nehemiah had prayed for the relief of his countrymen, and perhaps in David's words, Ps 51:18, he did not sit still and say, "Let God now do his own work, for I have no more to do;" but set himself to do what he could towards it; and here we find that the people were of one heart with Nehemiah. Our prayers must be seconded with our serious endeavors, or else we mock God. Nearly four months had passed, namely, from *Chisleu* to *Nisan* (November to March), before Nehemiah made his application to the king for leave to go to Jerusalem; either because the winter was not a proper time for such a journey, and he would not make a motion till he could pursue it, or because it was so long before his month of waiting upon the king came, and there was no coming into his presence until called for. Est 4:11. We are not thus limited to certain moments in our addresses to the King of kings, but have liberty of access to him at all times—to the throne of grace we never come unseasonably.

NEHEMIAH 3

The names and order of those who built the walls of Jerusalem, 1-32.

1. Eliashib. Ne 12:10. 13:28. **the sheep gate.** This gate is supposed to have immediately communicated with the temple, and to have been called *the sheep gate*, because the sheep intended for sacrifice passed through it. But, after all which learned men have written on this subject, which is but of little interest, we scarcely know any thing about these gates—what they were—why called by these names—or in what part of the wall they were situated, beyond what may be learned from the parallel passages. Ne 12:39. Jn 5:2. **sanctified it.** Ne 12:30. Dt 20:5. Ps ch. 30, title. Pr 3:6, 9. **the tower.** Ne 12:39. Je 31:38. Zc 14:10. **Meah.** i.e. *an hundred*, *S#3968h. Ne 3:1. 12:39.

2. next unto him. Heb. at his hand. 2 Ch +17:15mg. **the men.** Ne 7:36. Ezr 2:34. **Zaccur.** Ne 10:12.

3. the fish gate. Ne 12:39. 2 Ch 33:14. Zep 1:10. **Hassenaah.** i.e. *thorny place; thorn-bush*, *S#5570h. Ne 3:3. 7:38. Ezr 2:35. **the beams.** ver. 6. Ne 2:8. **the doors.** Ne 6:1. 7:1. **locks.** ver. 6, 13, 14, 15. SS 5:5. **bars.** ver. 6, 13, 14, 15. Ex 26:26. Dt 3:5. Jg 16:3.

4. Meremoth. i.e. *high places.* ver. 21. Ne 10:5. Ezr +8:33. **Urijah.** i.e. *light of Jah.* Ezr 8:33, Uriah. Je +26:20. **Koz.** i.e. *the thorn.* Ezr +2:61. **Meshullam.** i.e. *recompensed.* Ne 10:7. 1 Ch +9:12. **Berechiah.** i.e. *blessed of Jah.* Zc +1:7. **Meshezabeel.** i.e. *delivered of God; the salvation of God; set free of God*, *S#4898h. Ne 3:4. 10:21. 11:24. (1) A Jew whose descendant Meshullam repaired part of the wall of Jerusalem, Ne 3:4. (2) A Jew who sealed the covenant made by Nehemiah, Ne 10:21. (3) A descendant of Zerah, Ne 11:24. **Zadok.** i.e. *right, just.* 2 S +8:17. **Baana.** i.e. *son of affliction.* 1 K +4:12.

5. the Tekoites. ver. 27. 2 S 14:2. Am 1:1. **their nobles.** Jg 5:23. Je 5:4, 5. 1 C 1:26. 1 T 6:17, 18. **put not.** Je 27:2, 8, 12. 30:8, 9. Mt 11:29. Ac 15:10.

6. the old gate. Ne 12:39. **Jehoiada.** i.e. *Jah has known*, *S#3111h. Ne +12:10, Joiada. For *S#3077h, see 2 K +11:4, Jehoiada. **Paseah.** i.e. *passing over, lame.* 1 Ch +4:12. **Meshullam.** ver. 4. **Besodeiah.** i.e. *in the counsel of Jah; counsel of Jehovah; in Jah's secret*, *S#1152h.

7. Melatiah. i.e. *escaped of Jah; Jah's escape; delivered of the Lord; Jah's (way of) escape*, *S#4424h. **the Gibeonite.** Jsh 9:3, etc. 2 S 21:2. **Jadon.** i.e. *he judges; he will judge; God will judge; he will strive*, *S#3036h. **Mizpah.** ver. 19. 2 Ch 16:6. **Meronothite.** 1 Ch 27:30. **the throne.** Ge +*41:40. Ex 11:5. 12:29. Dt 17:18. Jg 3:20. 1 S 1:9. 2:8. 4:13, 18. 2 S 3:10. That is, probably, the *palace* of the Persian governor, west of the Euphrates; the term *throne* being used to signify any royal abode (*121L11. Figure of speech Metonymy of the subject, where the object is put for that which pertains or relates to it: here, throne is put for any royal abode. For other instances of this figure see Ge +4:7; Jsh 13:23; 1 K 8:21; Ro 9:8; 2 C 11:4.): for Sir J. Chardin, describing a splendid tent erected by the king of Persia (Tom. i. p. 203), says "that there was an inscription wrought upon the cornice of the anti-chamber, which gave it the appellation of the *throne* of the second Solomon." Sitting upon a *throne* has, however, sometimes been granted to gover-

nors (See D'Herbelot, art. Bab al Abuab, and Harmer, ch. vi. Ob. 63). Ne 2:8.

8. Uzziel. i.e. *strength of God.* Ex +6:18. **Harhaiah.** i.e. *dried up; kindled of Jah; Jah is protecting; burning or anger of the Lord*, *S#2736h. **the goldsmiths.** or, refiners. ✓96F3, Ge +8:4. ver. 31, 32n. Jg 17:4. Pr 25:4. Is 40:19. 46:6. **Hananiah.** i.e. *grace of Jah.* 1 Ch +25:23. **of the apothecaries.** or, compounders. Ge 50:2. Ex 30:25, 35. 37:29. Ec 10:1. **fortified.** or, left. **the broad wall.** Ne 12:38. 2 Ch 25:23. 26:9.

9. Rephaiah. i.e. *healed of Jah.* 1 Ch +9:43. **Hur.** i.e. *a hole; whiteness.* Ex +17:10. **the ruler.** ver. 12, 17.

10. Jedaiah. i.e. *he confesses Jah; praised of Jah; praise of the Lord; praise thou Jah*, *S#3042h. Ne 3:10h. 1 Ch 4:37h. Zc 6:10, 14. (1) A descendant of Simeon, 1 Ch 4:37. (2) First in the genealogy of the priests, 1 Ch +9:10 (*S#3048h). (3) Him of the sons of Aaron to whom the second lot fell, 1 Ch 24:7. (4) One of them that built the wall, Ne 3:10. (5) One to whom the crowns of Joshua were decreed, Zc 6:10, 14. **Harumaph.** i.e. *flattened in the nose; snub-nosed; banned of nose*, *S#2739h. **even.** ver. 23, 28-30. **Hattush.** i.e. *assembled.* Ne 9:38. 10:1, 4. Ezr +8:2. **Hashabniah.** i.e. *reckoning of Jah; the devising of Jah; esteemed of the Lord*, *S#2813h. Ne 3:10. 9:5.

11. Malchijah. i.e. *king of Jah.* 1 Ch +9:12. Ezr 10:31. **Harim.** i.e. *flat-nosed, devoted.* Ne 10:5. 1 Ch +24:8. Ezr 2:6, 39. **Hashub.** i.e. *imputed; considerate; much esteemed*, *S#2815h. Ne 3:11, 23. 10:23. 11:15. 1 Ch 9:14. (1) A Levite, father of Shemaiah, 1 Ch 9:14; Ne 11:15. (2, 3) Two who helped to build the wall, Ne 3:11, 23. (4) One who sealed the covenant, Ne 10:23. **Pahath-moab.** i.e. *fear or governor of Moab.* Ne 7:11. 10:14. Ezr +2:6. 8:4. **furnaces.** Ne 12:38. Ge 15:17. **other piece.** Heb. second measure. **the tower.** Ne 12:38.

12. Shallum. i.e. *recompensed.* 2 K +15:10. **Halohesh.** i.e. *the whisperer, charmer; enchanter*, *S#3873h. Ne 3:12h. 9:38. 10:1, 24h. **the ruler.** ver. 9, 14-18. **he and his daughters.** Ex 35:25. Ac 21:8, 9. Ph 4:3. Young notes, having probably no sons. 1 Ch +2:34.

13. The valley gate. Ne 2:13. **Hanun.** Ne 3:30. **Zanoah.** There were two towns of the name of *Zanoah* in the tribe of Judah: see the parallel passages. Ne 11:30. Jsh 15:34, 56. 1 Ch 4:18.

14. the dung gate. Ne 2:13n. 12:31. **Rechab.** i.e. *a rider, chariot.* 2 S +4:2. 1 Ch 2:55. Je 35:19. **the ruler.** ver. 9, 12, 15-18. **Beth-haccerem.** i.e. *house of the vineyard.* Je +6:1. *Beth-haccerem* was a town of Judah, situated on a mountain, between Jerusalem and Tekoa, according to Jerome on Je ch. 6. Dr. Pococke conjectures that the *Mountains of the Franks*, called also the *Mount of Bethulia*, from a village of that name near it, west-north-west of Tekoa, is the ancient *Beth-haccerem*; the position of which seems to agree with the citadel of Herodium, built by Herod, on a moderate-sized hill, sixty furlongs from Jerusalem (Josephus, Ant. l. xiv. c. 13, sec. 9. l. xv. c. 9. sec. 4). Je 6:1.

15. the gate. Ne 2:14. 12:37. 2 Ch 32:30. **Shallun.** i.e. *revenge; retribution; recompensed*, *S#7968h. **Col-hozeh.** i.e. *every seer; all-seer*, *S#3626h. Ne 3:15. 11:5. **the ruler.** ver. 9, 12, 14. **Mizpah.** ver. 7. Jsh 15:38. Jg 20:1, 3, Mizpeh. Je 40:6. **Siloah.** i.e.

sent; a missile; branch; dart, shoot, sent forth,
*S#7975h. Ne 3:15. Also Is 8:6, Shiloah. *Siloah* was
situated under the eastern wall of Jerusalem, between
that city and the brook Kedron, and is described by
Chateaubriand as lying at the foot of Mount Zion. Dr.
Richardson (*Travels*, vol. ii. pp. 357, 358) represents
the pool of Siloam as occurring higher up the valley
of Jehoshaphat, towards the north, than the well of
Nehemiah, a little beyond the village of Siloa, and
nearly opposite the tombs of Jehoshaphat and Zechariah. Is 8:6, Shiloah. Lk 13:4. Jn 9:7, Siloam. **king's
garden**. 2 K 25:4. **the stairs**. Ne 12:37. Ex 20:26. 2 S
5:6, 7.

16. **Nehemiah**. i.e. *comforted of Jah*. Ne +1:1. **Azbuk**. i.e. *wholly forsaken; strong emptier; the strong
emptied; stern depopulator*, *S#5802h. **the ruler**. ver.
9, 12, 14. **Beth-zur**. Jsh 15:58. 1 Ch 2:45. 2 Ch 11:7.
the sepulchres. Heb. *qeber*, Ge +23:4. **of David**.
2 Ch 16:14. Ac 2:29. **the pool**. 2 K 18:17n. 20:20. Is
7:3. 22:11. **the house**. 1 K 14:27, 28. 2 Ch 12:10, 11.
SS 3:7.

17. **repaired**. 1 C=3:10-13. **the ruler**. ver. 16.
1 Ch 23:4. **Keilah**. Jsh 15:44. 1 S 23:1, 2, etc.

18. **Bavai**. i.e. *with the desire of God; my goings;
by the mercy of the Lord*, *S#942h. **Henadad**. i.e.
grace of Hadad. Ezr +3:9.

19. **Ezer**. Ne 12:42. **Jeshua**. Ne 10:9. 12:8. **Mizpah**.
ver. 15. **another piece**. or, a second measure. Ex 26:2,
8. 36:9, 15. **the turning**. ver. 20, 24, 25. Ex 26:24.
36:29. 2 Ch *26:9. Ezk 41:21, 22.

20. **Zabbai**. or, Zaccai. **earnestly**. Ec *9:10. Ro
+*12:11. **Eliashib**. ver. 1, 21. Ne 12:22, 23. 13:4, 28.

21. **Meremoth**. ver. 4. **Koz**. Ne 7:63. Ezr 2:61.

22. **repaired**. 1 C=3:10-13. **the men of the plain**.
Ne 6:2. 12:28.

23. **over against**. ver. 10, 29, 30. **Azariah**. Ne 10:2.
Maaseiah. Ne 8:4, 7. **Ananiah**. i.e. *Jah's cloud; cloud
of the Lord*, *S#6055h. Ne 3:23. 11:32. (1) Father of
Maaseiah, Ne 3:23. (2) A town of Benjamin, Ne 11:32.

24. **Binnui**. Ne 10:9. **another piece**. That which had
been left by Azariah, after he had repaired the wall
by his own house. It is probable that some of the
principal people were either obliged, or voluntarily
offered, to repair those parts of the wall which were
opposite, or adjacent, to their own houses. The names
of those who repaired the walls are commemorated,
because it was an undertaking of piety, virtue, and
courage, to restore the holy city. ver. 11, 19, 27. **the
turning**. ver. 20.

25. **Palal**. i.e. *he judged; judge; mediator*,
*S#6420h. **Uzai**. i.e. *robust; strong; swiftness of the
Lord; I shall have my sprinklings*, *S#186h. **the king's**.
Je 22:14. 39:8. **by the court**. Ne 12:39. Je 32:2. 33:1.
37:21. 39:15. **Pedaiah**. Ne 8:4. **Parosh**. Ne 7:8. Ezr
2:3.

26. **Nethinims**. Ne 7:46-56. 10:28. 1 Ch 9:2. Ezr
2:43-58. **dwelt**, etc. or, *which* dwelt in Ophel, *repaired*
unto. **Ophel**. or, the tower. ver. 27. Ne 11:21. 2 K
+5:24mg. 2 Ch 27:3. 33:14. **the water gate**. The water
gate is supposed to have been that by which the Nethinim brought in water for the use of the temple. Ne
8:1, 3. 12:37.

27. **the Tekoites**. ver. 5. **the wall**. ver. 26. **Ophel**.
2 K +5:24mg.

28. **the horse**. 2 K 11:16. 2 Ch 23:15. Je 31:40.
every one. ver. 10, 23.

29. **Zadok**. Ne 13:13. **the son**. Ne 7:40. Ezr 2:37.
Shemaiah. Ezr 8:16. **Shechaniah**. Ezr 10:2. **the east
gate**. Je 19:2.

30. **Zalaph**. i.e. *fracture, wound; a shadow; fracture, break; the shadow beautified*, *S#6764h. **another
piece**. ver. 21. **Meshullam**. ver. 4. Ezr 8:16.

31. **the goldsmith's**. ver. 8, 32. **Nethinims**. i.e. *given
ones*. ver. 26. 1 Ch +9:2. **merchants**. ver. 32. Ne
13:20. 1 K 10:15. SS 3:6. Ezk 17:4. 27:3, 13, 15, 17,
20, 22, 23, 24. Na 3:16. **Miphkad**. i.e. *assignment;
inspection; review; muster; apportionment*, *S#4663h.
going up of the corner. or, corner-chamber. 1 K 10:5.
1 Ch 26:16mg. 2 Ch 9:4.

32. **the sheep gate**. Thus the whole city was surrounded with a wall; for Eliashib began at the sheep
gate. ver. 1. Ne 12:39. Jn 5:2. **the goldsmiths**. The
word *tzeraphim* may denote *smiths*, or *refiners*, or
persons that worked in *metals* of any kind; but it is
generally understood of those who worked in *gold*.
From the remotest period of the history of the Jews,
they had artists in all the elegant and ornamental trades;
and it appears that goldsmiths, apothecaries, and merchants were formed into *companies* in the time of Nehemiah. ver. 8, 31.

NEHEMIAH 4

*Sanballat and his company are very wroth, and mock
the Jews: but Nehemiah prays, and builds the wall,
1-6. He discovers that they secretly are plotting against
him, and sets a watch, 7-12. He arms the builders,
and gives them suitable orders and directions, 13-23.*

1. **Sanballat**. Ne 2:10, 19. Ezr 4:1-5. Ac 5:17.
mocked. Ps 35:15, 16. 44:13, 14. Mt 27:29. He 11:36.

2. **the army**. Ezr 4:9, 10. **What do**. 1 S 17:42. Ps
123:4. **feeble**. 1 S 14:11, 12. 17:43, 44. Zc 12:8. 1 C
1:27. **fortify themselves**. Heb. *leave to themselves*.
Ne 3:8. **sacrifice**. Ne 12:27, 43. **revive**. ver. 10. Ezk
37:3-13. Hab 3:2.

3. **Tobiah**. Ne 2:10, 19. 6:1. 1 K 20:10, 18. 2 K
18:23.

4. **Hear**. Ps 123:3, 4. *₰*38A. Apostrophe B901: Turning aside from the direct subject matter to address
others; here, God. For other instances of this figure
see Ne 6:9. Ps 33:22. 82:8. 104:24. 109:21. **despised**.
Heb. despite. **turn**. 1 S 17:26. Ps *79:12. Pr *3:34.
Ho 12:14.

5. **cover not**. Ps 59:5-13. *69:27, 28. 109:14, 15.
Je *18:23. 2 T *4:14. **their sin**. Ps 51:1, 9. Is *43:25.
44:22. **before the builders**. Is 36:11, 12.

6. **we built**. Da *9:25. **and all the wall**. That is,
the whole circuit of the wall was completed unto *half*
the intended height. **for the people**. The original is
very emphatic, *wyhee laiv leam laasoth*, "for the people
had a *heart* to work." Their heart was engaged in it,
and they went about it cheerfully and vigorously. **had
a mind**. Ne 6:15. 1 Ch 29:3, 14, 17, 18. 2 Ch 29:36.
Ps *110:3. 2 C 8:16, 17. Ph *2:13. He *13:21.

7. **Sanballat**. ver. 1. Ne 2:10, 19. **the Ammonites**.
Jg 10:7, etc. 11:12, etc. 1 S 11:2. 2 S 10:1-5. 2 K
24:2. 2 Ch 20:1. Ezk 25:3-7. Am 1:13. **Ashdodites**.
i.e. *inhabitants of Ashdod* (i.e. *strong to oppress or
spoil*, Jsh +11:22), *S#796h. Ne 4:7h. 13:23h, 24.
Jsh 13:3h. 1 S 5:1, 2, 3h, 6h. 2 Ch 26:6-8. Je 25:20.
Am 1:8. 3:9. Zc 9:5, 6. **heard**. Ezr 4:4-16. 5:8. **were
made up**. Heb. ascended. lit. healing went up to the

walls. 2 Ch 24:13mg. Je +*8:22. **then.** Ge *3:15. Ac 4:17, 18. 5:33. Re 12:12, 13, 17.

8. **all.** Ps 2:1-3. 83:3-11. Is 8:9, 10. Ac 23:12, 13. **hinder it.** Heb. make an error to it. Je 20:10. Lk 11:52. 1 Th 2:18.

9. **Nevertheless.** Ne 1:11. Ge 32:9-12, 28. 2 K 19:14-19. Ps *50:15. 55:16-22. Lk 6:11, 12. Ac 4:24-30. **set a watch.** T#1296. Mt 26:41. Mk 13:33. 14:38. Lk +√21:36. Col *4:2. 1 P *5:8.

10. **The strength.** Nu 13:31. 32:9. Ps 11:1, 2. Hg 1:2. **bearers.** 2 Ch 2:18. Ezk 29:18.

11. **They shall not.** Jg 20:29, etc. 2 S 17:2. Ps 56:6. Is 47:11. Ac 23:12, 21. 1 Th 5:2.

12. **ten times.** Ge 31:7, 41. Nu 14:22. 1 S +1:8n. Jb 19:3. Young notes, that is, many times. **From all places**, etc. *or*, That from all places ye must return to us. **ye shall return.** Houbigant, Michaelis, and Dathe contend, that instead of *tashoovoo*, "ye shall return," we should read *chashevoo*, "they designed." **they.** 63K, Ge +37:13. EWB suggests that this is not a case in which the *apodosis* is to be supplied, but it may be taken literally, and so read "They said unto us ten times, From all places ye shall return to us" (B117).

13. **Therefore.** Ge 32:13-20. 2 Ch 32:2-8. Ps *112:5. Mt *10:16. 1 C *14:20. **in the lower places.** Heb. from the lower parts of the place, etc. **their swords.** ver. 17, 18. Jg 3:2. 1 Ch +5:22. SS *3:7, 8. Lk +*22:36. Ep *6:11-20.

14. **Be not ye afraid.** Nu 14:9. Dt 1:21, 29, 30. 20:3, 4. Jsh 1:9. 2 Ch 20:15-17. 32:7. Ps 27:1. 46:11. Is 41:10-14. Mt +*10:28. He +*13:6. **remember.** Ps 20:7. 77:10-20. 143:5. Is 51:12, 13. 63:11-13. **great.** Ne 1:5. Dt 10:17. Jb 37:22. Ps 65:5. 66:3, 5. Is 64:1-3. Na 1:2-7. He 12:20, 21, 28, 29. **fight.** Dt 10:18. 2 S 10:12.

15. **God.** 2 S 15:31. 17:14. Jb *5:12, 13. Ps 33:10, 11. Pr √21:30. Is *8:10. *44:25. La *3:37, 38. 1 C *3:19, 20. **every one.** Mk 13:34. Ro +√12:11. 1 Th *4:11.

16. **my servants.** ver. 23. Ne 5:15, 16. Ps 101:6. **and the other half.** This is no unusual thing in Palestine, even at the present day; people sowing their seed are often attended by armed men, to prevent the Arabs from robbing them of it. **habergeons.** *Habergeon*, from the Teutonic *hals*, the *neck*, and *bergen*, to *cover*, *defend*, may be considered as signifying a *breast-plate*, though the Franco-Gallic *hautbergon* signifies a *coat of mail*; the original *shiryon*, we have already seen, denotes a *corslet*. ❋S#8302h. 1 S 17:5, 38. 1 K 22:34. 2 Ch *18:33n. 26:14. Is 59:17.

17. **builded.** 1 C=3:10-13. **bare burdens.** ver. 10. **every one.** That is, he had his *arms* at hand; and was as fully prepared to *fight* as to *work*. The builders could not possibly have made any progress, if they had *literally* held a weapon in one of their hands; but the expression is evidently figurative, implying that every man was as much a soldier as a builder. Matthew Poole notes that this is proverbial speech, such as is frequent amongst the Latins, as when they say of a man pretending kindness with evil design, "He carries bread in one hand, and a stone in another." The next verse tells us the sword was not in their hands, but by their sides. **with one.** Da 9:25. 1 C 9:26. 16:9, 13. 2 C 6:7. Ep 6:11, etc. Ph 1:28. 2 T 2:3. 4:7.

18. **builders.** 1 C=3:10-13. **by his side.** Heb. on

his loins. Ezk 9:2, 3, 11. **he that sounded.** Nu 10:9. 2 Ch 13:12-17. 1 C 14:8.

19. **I said.** ver. 14. Ne 5:7. 7:5.

20. **our God.** Ex 14:14, 25. Dt 1:30. 3:22. 20:4. Jsh *23:10. Zc 14:3. Ro *8:31.

21. **So we.** 1 C *15:10, √58. Ga *6:9. Col 1:29.

22. **every one.** Ne 11:1, 2.

23. **So neither I.** Ne 5:16. 7:2. Jg 9:48. 1 C *15:10. **saving that**, etc. ♪88, Ge +15:15. *or*, every one *went* with his weapon *for* water, Jg 5:11. The original of this obscure clause is *ish shilcho hammayim*, which is rendered by Montanus, *vir missile suum aquas*, "a man and his dart to the waters," of which it is difficult to make sense. It is wholly omitted by the LXX.; and one of Dr. Rossi's MSS. reads, *meshallachah al hammayim*, "in order to send them to the water."

NEHEMIAH 5

The poor Jews complain of the debts which they had unavoidably contracted, and which compelled them to mortgage their lands, and even sell their children, 1-5. Nehemiah rebukes the rich usurers, who oppress their brethren; and obliges them to engage by oath to make full restitution, 6-13. He refuses the governor's customary allowances, and maintains great hospitality at his own charge, 14-19.

1. **a great cry.** Ex 3:7. *22:25-27. Jb 31:38, 39. 34:28. Is 5:7. Lk 18:7. Ja +*5:4. **their brethren.** Le 25:35-37. Dt *15:7-11. Ac 7:26. 1 C 6:6-8.

2. **We, our sons.** Ps 127:3-5. 128:2-4. Ml 2:2. **many.** ♪63I2, Jsh +3:3. Supply ellipsis from succeeding clause, "our daughters, (being) many, (are mortgaged)." **we take up corn.** Ge 41:57. 42:2. 43:8.

3. **mortgaged.** Ge 47:15-25. Le 25:35-39. Dt 15:7. **because.** Ml 3:8-11.

4. **the king's tribute.** Ne 9:37. Dt 28:47, 48. Jsh 16:10. 1 K 9:21. Ezr 4:13, 20.

5. **our flesh.** Ge 37:27. Pr 11:17. Is *58:6, 7. Ja 2:5, 6. **we.** Ex 21:1-11. Le 25:39-43. 2 K 4:1. Mt 18:25.

6. **I was very.** Ne 13:8, 25. Ex 11:8. Nu 16:15. Mk 3:5. Ep 4:26.

7. **I consulted with myself.** Heb. my heart consulted in me. Ps 4:4. 27:8. **I rebuked.** Le *19:15, 17. 2 Ch 19:6, 7. Ps 82:1-4. Pr 27:5. 2 C 5:16. Ga 2:11. 1 T 5:20. T 2:15. **Ye exact usury.** Ex 22:25. Le 25:36. Dt 15:2, 3. *23:19, 20. 24:10-13. Ps 15:1, 5. Pr 28:8. Is +*24:2. Ezk 22:12. 45:9. **I set a great assembly.** 2 Ch 28:9-13. Mt *18:17.

8. **We after.** Mt 25:15, 29. 2 C 8:12. Ga *6:10. **redeemed.** Le 25:47-49. **sell your.** Ex 21:16. Dt 24:7. **shall they.** Ro 14:15. 1 C 8:11. **held.** Jb 29:10. 32:15. Mt 22:12. Ro 3:19.

9. **It is not.** 1 S 2:24. Pr 16:29. 17:26. 18:5. 19:2. 24:23. **ought ye.** Da 6:4, 5. T 2:8. 1 P 2:15. **walk.** ver. 15. Ge 20:11. 42:18. Le 25:36. Ac 9:31. **reproach.** ♪121N1, Ge +31:54. Ge 13:7, 8. 2 S *12:14. Ezk 36:20. Ro 2:24. 1 T 5:14. T 2:5. 1 P 2:11, 12.

10. **I likewise.** Mi 2:1. Lk 3:13, 14. 1 C 9:12-18. **I pray you.** 2 C 5:11, 20. 6:1. Phm 8, 9. **leave.** ver. 7. Ex 22:25-27. Ps 15:5. Ezk 18:8, 13.

11. **Restore.** Ex 22:1. Le 6:4, 5. Nu 5:7. 1 S 12:3. 2 S 12:6. Is 58:6. Lk 3:8. *19:8. **their lands.** ver. 3, 4. **the hundredth.** This was probably the rate of interest which they obliged their poor debtors to pay each month, which would amount to about 12●. Another

author (Volney, *Travels*, vol. ii. p. 410) states that this is the lowest rate of interest in Syria: the usual rate is 20◑; and it is sometimes as high as 30◑. Is +24:2.

12. **We will restore.** 2 Ch 28:14, 15. Ezr 10:12. Mt 19:21, 22. Lk +*19:8. **I called.** Ne 10:29. 13:25. 2 K 23:2, 3. 2 Ch 6:22, 23. 15:13, 14. Ezr 10:5. Je *34:8-10. Mt 26:63.

13. **I shook.** Ex 14:27mg. Jg 16:20. **my lap.** Ps 129:7. Is 49:22mg. So "when the Roman ambassadors entered the senate of Carthage, they had their toga gathered up in their bosom, and said, We carry here peace and war; you may have which you will. The senate answered, You may give which you please. They then *shook their toga*, and said, We bring you war," Livy (l. xxi. c. 18). Mt 10:14. Ac 13:51. 18:6. **So God.** 1 S 15:28. 1 K 11:29-31. Zc 5:3, 4. **emptied.** Heb. *empty, or void.* *S#7386h. Ge 37:24. 41:27. Dt *32:47. Jg 7:16. *9:4. 11:3. 2 S 6:20. 2 K 4:3. 2 Ch 13:7. Pr *12:11. 28:19. Is 29:8. Ezk 24:11. **Amen.** Nu 5:22. Dt 27:14-26. **praised.** Ge 12:15. Jg 16:24. 1 Ch 16:36. **the people.** 2 K 23:3. Ps 50:14. 76:11. 119:106. Ec 5:5.

14. **from the twentieth.** Ne 2:1. 13:6. **I and my.** 1 C 9:4-15, 18. 2 Th 3:8, 9. **the bread.** Ezr 4:13, 14. Ro 13:6, 7.

15. **governors.** 1 K 10:15. **bread.** ʃ171I8, Ge +3:19. **and wine.** ʃ174, Ge +18:27. ʃ121D13, Ge +27:28. **even their.** 1 S 2:15-17. 8:15. Pr 29:12. **so did.** Mt 5:47. 2 C 11:9. 12:13. **because.** ver. 9. Jb 31:23. Ps 112:1. 147:11. Pr 16:6. Ec 12:13, 14. Is 50:10. Lk 18:2-4.

16. **I continued.** Lk 8:15. Ro 2:7. 1 C √15:58. Ga *6:9. **neither bought.** Nu 16:15. Ac 20:33-35. 1 Th 2:5, 6. **all my.** 2 C 12:16-18. Ph 2:20, 21.

17. **Moreover.** He kept open house, and entertained all comers; besides having 150 Jews, who had their food constantly at his table, and at his expense. **at my table.** 2 S 9:7, 13. 1 K 18:19. **an hundred and fifty.** Is 32:8. Ro 12:13. 1 P 4:9, 10.

18. **Now that.** 1 K 4:22, 23. **one ox.** This was food sufficient for more than two hundred men. Bp. Pococke says that the bey of Tunis had daily twelve sheep, with fish and fowls, soups, oranges, eggs, onions, boiled rice, etc. His nobles dined with him; after they had done, the servants sat down; and when they had finished, the poor took what was left. Here the bey's twelve sheep are equal to Nehemiah's one ox and six choice sheep; and probably the mode of living between the two was nearly alike. It is still the practice in the East to calculate the expenses of the table, not by the money paid, but by the provisions consumed by the guests. **required.** ver. 14, 15. **because the bondage.** Ps 37:21, 26.

19. **Think.** T#1520. Ne 13:14, 22, 31. Ge 40:14. Ps 25:6, 7. +*40:17. 106:4. Je 29:11. Jon *1:6. **according to.** Ps 18:23-25. Mt 10:42. 25:34-40. Mk 9:41. **have done.** T#1141. Ne 13:14. Ge 20:5. Dt 26:13-15. 2 K 4:1. *20:3. Ps 7:8, 9. 25:21. 26:1, 3. 40:9, 10. 69:8-10. 119:29, 30, 77, 94, 121, 132, 173.

NEHEMIAH 6

Sanballat and his party practice against Nehemiah, by insidious attempts, false rumors, and the hired counsel of false prophets, 1-14. The wall is finished, and

the enemies are disheartened, 15, 16. The nobles of Judah traitorously correspond with Tobiah, 17-19.

1. **when Sanballat.** Ne 2:10, 19. 4:1, 7. **Geshem.** i.e. *shower,* *S#1654h. Ne 2:19. 6:1, 2. Also ver. 6, Gashmu. **no breach.** Ne 4:6, 7. Da *9:25. **at that time.** Ne 3:1, 3, 6.

2. **Come.** They wished to get him out of Jerusalem, from his friends, that they might either carry him off or murder him. 2 S *3:27. 20:9. Ps *37:12. Pr 26:24-26. Ec 4:4. **Ono.** Ne 11:35. 1 Ch 8:12. **they thought.** Ps 12:2. *37:12, 32. Je 41:2. Ezk √33:31. Mi 7:4, 5. Lk 20:19-21.

3. **And I sent.** Pr *14:15. Mt *10:16. **I am doing.** Ec *9:10. Lk 14:30. Jn *9:4. 1 T √4:15, 16.

4. **four times.** Jg 16:6, 10, 15-20. Pr 7:21. Lk 18:5. 1 C *15:58. Ga 2:5. **and I answered.** Pr *14:15.

5. **with an open letter.** This was a gross insult to a person of Nehemiah's quality; as the letters sent to chiefs and governors in the East are always carefully folded up, put in silk bags, and then sealed. 2 K 18:26-28. 2 C 2:11. 11:13-15. Ep 6:11. 2 Th 2:10.

6. **It is reported.** Je 9:3-6. 20:10. Mt 5:11. Ro 3:8. 2 C 6:8. 1 P 2:12, 13. 3:16. **Gashmu.** i.e. *a shower,* *S#1654h. ver. +1, 2, Geshem. **that thou and.** Ne 2:19. Ezr 4:12, 15. **that thou mayest.** Lk 23:2. Jn 19:13.

7. **appointed.** ver. 12, 13. **a king.** 2 S 15:10-12. 1 K 1:7, 18, 25, 34. Ac 17:7. **Come now.** Pr 26:24-26. Ac 23:15.

8. **There are.** Ac 24:12, 13. 25:7, 10. **thou feignest.** Jb 13:4. Ps 36:3. 38:12. 52:2. Is 59:4. Da 11:27. Mt 12:34. Jn *8:44. **own heart.** Nu +16:28.

9. **For they.** ver. 14. Ne 4:10-14. 2 Ch 32:18. **Their hands.** 2 Ch 15:7. Ezr 4:1-24. Is 35:3, 4. Je 38:4. He 12:12. **Now therefore.** 1 S 30:6. Ps 56:3. 68:35. 71:1. 138:3. Is 41:10. Zc 10:12. 2 C 12:9. Ep 3:16. 6:10. Ph *4:13. 1 P 5:10. **O God.** ʃ38A, Ne +4:4. ver. 14. Ne 5:19.

10. **Shemaiah.** i.e. *heard of Jah.* ver. *12. 1 Ch +9:16. Ezr *8:16. 10:31. Pr *11:9. Mt *7:15. **Delaiah.** i.e. *drawn up of Jah.* 1 Ch 24:5, 18. Je +36:12. **Mehetabeel.** i.e. *done good to by God; God's best; benefited of God,* *S#4105h. Ne 6:10. Ge +36:39, Mehetabel. 1 Ch 1:50. (1) Wife of Hadar, last of the kings of Edom, Ge 36:39; 1 Ch 1:50. (2) The grandfather of Shemaiah, who tried to terrify Nehemiah, Ne 6:10. **shut up.** 2 K 9:8. Je 36:5. Ezk 3:24. **Let us meet.** Ps *12:2. 37:12. 120:2, 3. **the house.** 1 K 6:5. 2 K *11:3. **let us shut.** 2 Ch 28:24. 29:3, 7. Ml 1:10. Ac *21:30. **in the night.** Jb *24:13-17. Jn *3:20.

11. **Should such.** ver. *3. 1 S 19:5. Jb *4:3-6. Ps 11:1, 2. 112:6, 8. Pr *28:1. Is 10:18. Lk *13:31-33. Ac *8:1. *20:24. *21:13. He 11:27. **would go.** ver. 9. Nu 32:7-9. Ps 56:2, 3. Ec *10:1. Ph 2:17, 30.

12. **I perceived.** Ezk 13:22. 1 C 2:15. 12:10. **God had.** Je 14:14. 23:16, 25. 28:15. Ezk 13:7. 1 J 4:1. **hired him.** Is 56:11. Ezk 13:19. Mi 3:11. Ac 20:33. 1 T 3:3. T 1:7. 1 P 5:2. 2 P 2:3. Re 18:13.

13. **that I should.** Pr 29:5. Is 51:7, 12, 13. 57:11. Je 1:17. Ezk 2:6. 13:17, etc. Mt *10:28. 2 T 1:7. Re *21:8. **and sin.** Ja *4:17. **and that they.** ver. 6. Pr 22:1. Ec 7:1. **report, that.** Je 18:18. 20:10. Da 6:4, 5. Mt 22:15. 26:59. Ac 6:13. 2 C 11:12. 1 T 5:14. T 2:8. **reproach me.** Ne 4:4.

14. **My God.** ver. 19. Ps 22:1. 63:1. **think thou.** Ne 4:4, 5. 13:29. Ps 36:11, 12. 140:5-11. Je 11:20-23. 18:20-23. 2 T 4:14, 15. 1 J 5:16. **on the prophetess.**

Ex 15:20n. 1 K 22:22-24. Is 9:14, 15. Je 14:15, 18. 28:1, 10, 15. Ezk *13:16, 17. Mt 7:15. 24:11, 24. 2 T 3:8. Re 19:20. **Noadiah.** i.e. *convened of Jah; met by Jah,* ✳S#5129h. Ne 6:14. Ezr 8:33. (1) One of the Levites, Ezr 8:33. (2) A prophetess who attempted to hinder Nehemiah in his work of reconstruction, Ne 6:14. **put me.** Ps 62:4. 2 T 4:14.

15. **wall.** Ezr 6:15. Ps *1:3. Da *9:25. **Elul.** i.e. *outcry; nothingness,* ✳S#435h. The sixth month of the Hebrew year, part of August and September. **fifty.** Ne 4:1, 2.

16. **when all our enemies.** Ne 2:10. *4:1, 7. 6:1, 2. **for they perceived.** Ex *14:25. Nu *23:23. Jsh 5:1. Ps 14:5. *126:2, 3. Ac *5:38.

17. **the nobles.** Ne 3:5. 5:7. 13:28. Mi 7:1-6. Mt 24:10-12. **sent many letters unto Tobiah.** Heb. multiplied their letters passing to Tobiah.

18. **Arah.** Ne 7:10. Ezr 2:5. **Meshullam.** Ne 3:4, 30.

19. **they reported.** Le 19:16. Pr 20:19. 26:20. 28:4. Jn 7:7. 15:19. 1 J 4:5. **words.** or, matters. **letters.** ver. 5, 17. Ne 2:7, 8, 9. 2 Ch 30:1, 6. Est 9:26, 29. **to put.** ver. 9, 13. Is 37:10-14. Ac 4:18-21.

NEHEMIAH 7

Nehemiah, having finished the wall, and regulated the attendance of the Levites, commits the charge of the city to Hanani and Hananiah, 1-4 He finds a register of those who first came from Babylon, 5-7. The register is inserted; of the people, 9-38; of the priests, 39-42; of the Levites, 43-45; of the Nethinims, 46-56; of Solomon's servants, 57-62; and of the priests which could not find their pedigree, 63-65. The whole number of them, 66, 67. Their substance, 68, 69. The oblations made to the temple, 70-73.

1. **the wall.** Ne 3:1, etc. 6:15. **I had set up.** Ne 3:3. 6:1. **the porters.** Ne 10:39. 11:3. 12:24. 1 Ch ch. 23, 25, 26. 2 Ch 31:2. Ezr 3:8.

2. **my brother.** Ne 1:2. **Hananiah.** Ne 10:23. **the ruler.** Ne 2:8. **was.** ✔160B, Ge +25:31. **a faithful man.** Nu 12:7. Ps 101:6. Da 6:4. Mt 24:45. 25:21. Lk *16:10-12. 1 C 4:2. 2 T 2:2. **feared God.** Ne 5:15. Ge 42:18. Ex +*18:21. 2 S 23:3. 1 K 18:3, 12. Jb 1:1. Is 33:5, 6.

3. **Let not the gates.** That is, the gates were not to be opened till *sunrise*, and to be shut at *sunset*; which is still the custom in many cities of the East. If a traveler arrives after sunset, he finds the gates shut, and on no consideration will they open them till the morning. Ne 13:19. Ps 127:1. Mt 10:16. **every one to be.** Ne 3:23, 28-30.

4. **large and great.** Heb. broad in spaces. Jg 18:10. Ps 119:45mg. Is 22:18mg. **the houses.** Is 58:12. Hg 1:4-6. Mt *6:33.

5. **my God.** Ne 5:19. 6:14. **put into mine.** Ezr 7:27. 1 C 15:10. 2 C 3:5. 8:16. Ph *2:12, 13. Col 1:29. Ja 1:16. Whatever good motion is in our minds, whether prudent or pious, we must acknowledge it to come from God; for every good gift and every good work are from above; he gives knowledge, he gives grace. What is commonly called human prudence, ought to be ascribed to the direction of Divine Providence. He who teaches the husbandman discretion, Is 28:26, as certainly overrules the deliberations of senators. **that.** ver. 64. 1 Ch 9:1, etc. Ezr 2:62.

6. **the children.** Ezr ch. 2. 5:8. 6:2. **whom Nebuchadnezzar.** 2 K 24:14-16. 25:11. 2 Ch ch. 36. Je ch. 39, 52.

7. **Zerubbabel.** i.e. *scattered to Babel.* Ne 12:1, 7, 10. Ezr 1:11; Sheshbazzar. 2:2. Hg +1:1. Mt 1:12, 13, Zorobabel. **Jeshua.** Ezr 3:8, 9. 5:2. Zc 3:1-3, Joshua. **Azariah.** One of Dr. Kennicott's codices has *Seraiah,* as in the parallel passage. Ezr 2:2, Seraiah, Reelaiah. **Raamiah.** i.e. *thunder of Jah,* ✳S#7485h. **Nahamani.** i.e. *comforting; repenting; he comforted me,* ✳S#5167h. **Mispereth.** i.e. *enumerator; number, a few,* ✳S#4559h. Ezr 2:2, Mizpar. **Nehum.** i.e. *penitent; merciful; comfort,* ✳S#5149h. Three MSS. in the parallel place have *Nehum,* and four have here *Rehum.* Ne 12:3. Ezr 2:2, Rehum.

8. **Parosh.** Ne 10:14. Ezr 2:3, 8:3, Pharosh. 10:25.

9. **Shephatiah.** Ezr 2:4. 8:8.

10. **Arah.** Ne 6:18. Ezr 2:5: 775.

11. **Pahath-moab.** Ne 10:14. Ezr 2:6: 2812. 8:4.

12. **Elam.** Ezr 2:7. 8:7. 10:26.

13. **Zattu.** Ezr 2:8: 945.

14. **Zaccai.** i.e. *pure; just; pure of the Lord,* ✳S#2140h. Ne 7:14. Ezr 2:9. +10:28, Zabbai.

15. **Binnui.** Ezr 2:10, Bani. 642.

16. **Bebai.** Ezr 2:11, 623.

17. **Azgad.** Ezr 2:12: 1222.

18. **Adonikam.** i.e. *my lord has arisen; the Lord has risen up,* ✳S#140h. Ne 7:18. Ezr 2:13: 666. 8:13.

19. **Bigvai.** Ezr 2:14: 2056. **two thousand three score and seven.** One MS. of Dr. Kennicott's reads "two thousand sixty and six;" but no doubt "two thousand and fifty-six," is the true reading, as in the parallel passage.

20. **Adin.** Ezr 2:15: 454. **six hundred fifty five.** One of Dr. Kennicott's codices has "six hundred fifty and four."

21. **Ater.** Ezr 2:16.

22. **Hashum.** Ezr 2:19: 223.

23. **Bezai.** i.e. *shining; conqueror; in the labor or hastening of the Lord; my fine linen garments,* ✳S#1209h. Ne 7:23. 10:18. Ezr 2:17: 323. (1) An Israelite whose descendants returned with Zerubbabel from Babylon, Ezr 2:17; Ne 7:23. (2) A family who sealed the covenant made by Nehemiah, Ne 10:18.

24. **Hariph.** i.e. *plucking off; autumnal; winter; autumn rains; reproach,* ✳S#2756h. Ne 7:24. 10:19. (1) A Jew some of whose posterity went up from Babylon, Ne 7:24. (2) The head of a family of Jews, who sealed the covenant made by Nehemiah, Ne 10:19. *Hariph* and *Jorah* were probably two distinct names of this person: Ezr 2:18, Jorah. 2 Ch 34:20n.

25. **Gibeon.** *Gibeon* is probably a mistake for *Gibbar,* or the contrary; though this person may have been called by both names. Ezr 2:20, Gibbar.

26. **The men.** The Septuagint reads here the same as in the parallel place, "The children of Bethlehem, one hundred twenty and three; the children of Netopha, fifty and six." Though this reading is not found in any Hebrew MS. yet collated, it is doubtless the true one. **Bethlehem.** Ezr 2:21, 22: 179.

27. **Anathoth.** Ezr 2:23. Is 10:30. Je 1:1. 11:21.

28. **Beth-azmaveth.** i.e. *house of death's power; house strong with death,* ✳S#1041h. Ezr 2:24, Azmaveth.

29. **Kirjath-jearim.** Instead of *Kirjath-arim,* in the parallel place of Ezra, many MSS. read *Kirjath-jearim,*

as here. Jsh 9:17. 18:25. Jg 18:12. Ezr 2:25, Kirjath-arim.

30. **Ramah**. Jsh 18:24, 25. Ezr 2:26.

31. **Michmas**. The variation between "Michmash" and "Michmas" arises from the mutation of *sheen* and *samech;* though several MSS. have the former reading here also. 1 S 13:5, 23. Ezr 2:27. Is 10:28, Michmash.

32. **Bethel**. Jsh 8:9, 17. Ezr 2:28: 223.

33. **Nebo**. Ezr 2:29. **fifty and two**. The Alexandrian MS. of the Septuagint adds "The children of Magbish an hundred and fifty and six," as in Ezr 2:30.

34. **the other Elam**. ver. 12. Ezr 2:31.

35. **Harim**. Ezr 2:32. 10:31.

36. **Jericho**. Ezr 2:34.

37. **Lod**. i.e. *strife; division; contention; travail; to bear*, *S#3850h. Ne 6:2. 7:37h. 11:34, 35h. 1 Ch 8:12h. Ezr 2:33h, 725.

38. **Senaah**. Ezr 2:35: 3630.

39. **Jedaiah**. 1 Ch 24:7, etc. Ezr 2:36.

40. **Immer**. 1 Ch 24:14. Ezr 2:37.

41. **Pashur**. 1 Ch 9:12. 24:9. Ezr 9:38. 10:22.

42. **Harim**. 1 Ch 24:8. Ezr 2:39. 10:31.

43. **Hodevah**. i.e. *honor of Jah; glory of Jah*, *S#1937h. Ezr 2:40, Hodaviah. 3:9, Judah.

44. **The singers**. 1 Ch 25:2. Ezr 2:41: 128. **an hundred forty and eight**. One of Dr. Kennicott's MSS. reads in the parallel place of *Ezra*, "an hundred and forty and eight," as here.

45. **The porters**. 1 Ch +23:5. ch. 26. Ezr 2:42: 130.

46. **Nethinims**. Le 27:2-8. Jsh 9:23-27. 1 Ch 9:2. **Hashupha**. i.e. *stripped; exhausted; made bare*, *S#2817h. Ne 7:46. Ezr 2:43, Hasupha. **Tabbaoth**. i.e. *signets; rings; good hour*, *S#2884h. Ne 7:46. Ezr 2:43.

47. **Sia**. i.e. *congregation; departing; council*, *S#5517h. Ne 7:47. Also Ezr 2:44, Siaha.

48. **Lebana**. i.e. *whiteness; brick; the moon*, *S#3838h. Ne 7:48. Ezr 2:45. **Hagaba**. i.e. *locust; grasshopper; leaper*, *S#2286h. Ne 7:48h. Ezr 2:45h, 46, Hagabah, *or* Hagab. The Alexandrian MS. of the Septuagint inserts here, "the children of Akoud, the children of Outa, the children of Ketar, the children of Agab," *or* Hagab: see the parallel passages. **Shalmai**. i.e. *clothed; my garments; peace offering of the Lord*, *S#8014h. In the parallel passage not only the *Keri* and Septuagint, but many of Dr. Kennicott's MSS. read *Shalmai*, as here. A more extensive collation of MSS. would doubtless tend still more to harmonize both the names and numbers. Ezr 2:46, Shamlai.

51. **Phaseah**. i.e. *limping; lame; halting; vacillating*, *S#6454h. Ne 3:6. 7:51. 1 Ch +4:12, Paseah. Ezr 2:49. This variation only exists in the translation; the original being uniformly *Paseah*. Ezr 2:49, Paseah.

52. **Meunim**. i.e. *a residence; habitations*, *S#4586h. Ne 7:52. Ezr 2:50. The first of these variations is attributable to the translation, the original being uniformly "Meunim;" and the latter arises from the mutation of *wav* and *yood*, and insertion of *sheen*, though in the parallel passage the *Kethiv* is "Nephisim;" and here the *Keri* and many MSS. have "Nephishesim." Ezr 2:50, Mehunim, Nephusim. **Nephishesim**. i.e. *expansions; we shall shake the spoilers; refreshed of spices*, *S#5300h. Ne 7:52. Ezr 2:50.

54. **Bazlith**. i.e. *stripping; making naked*, *S#1213h. Ne 7:54. Ezr 2:52. Instead of *Bazlith*, many MSS. and the LXX. have *Bazluth*, as in the parallel place. Ezr 2:52, Bazluth.

55. **Tamah**. i.e. *laughter; thou wilt be fat*, *S#8547h. Ne 7:55. Ezr 2:53. Here there is no variation in the original; it being uniformly *Tamah*. Ezr 2:53, Thamah.

57. **Solomon's**. Ne 11:3. **Sophereth**. i.e. *female scribe; registrar*, *S#5618h. Ne 7:57. Ezr 2:55. **Perida**. i.e. *separation; grain, kernel; eminent*, *S#6514h. Ne 7:57. Ezr 2:55. Three MSS. have *Peruda*, instead of *Perida*, as in *Ezra*. Ezr 2:55, Peruda.

58. **Jaala**. i.e. *a wild goat*, *S#3279h. Ne 7:58. Ezr 2:56. The variation of "Jaalah" and "Jaala" merely arises from the mutation of *hay* into *aleph*, according to the Chaldee dialect. Ezr 2:56, Jaalah.

59. **Amon**. i.e. *architect; workman; artificer; to nourish; a multitude; to be faithful*, *S#526h. Ne 7:59. 1 K 22:26. 2 K 21:18, 19, 23, 24, 25. 1 Ch 3:14. 2 Ch 18:25. 33:20, 21, 22, 23, 25. Je 1:2. 25:3. (1) A son of Manasseh, king of Judah, 644-642 B.C. 2 K 21:18-26; 2 Ch 33:20. (2) Governor of Ramoth Gilead, 1 K 22:26. (3) A servant of Solomon, Ezr 2:57; Ne 7:59. Instead of *Amon*, two of De Rossi's MSS. have *Amin*, and the LXX. have "Emim;" which nearly approaches the *Ami* of Ezra. Ezr 2:57, Ami.

60. **the Nethinims**. Ezr 2:58.

61. **Tel-haresha**. i.e. *hill of the magus; heap of the artificer; height of an enchanter; hill of plowing*, *S#8521h. Ne 7:61. Ezr 2:59. The first of these variations only exists in the translation; the original being uniformly "Tel-harsha:" the latter simply arises from the insertion of a *wav;* being written *Addan*, in the parallel passage, and "Addon" here. Ezr 2:59, Tel-harsha, Addan. **Addon**. i.e. *foundation; depression; calamity*, *S#114h. seed. or*, pedigree.

62. **six hundred**. Ezr 2:60: 652.

63. **of the priests**. Ezr 2:61-63. **Barzillai**. 2 S 17:27. 19:31-33. 1 K 2:7.

64. **These sought**. Mt 22:11-13. **those that were**. ver. 5. 1 Ch 9:1. **but it was**. Mt 25:11, 12. **as polluted**. Ne 13:29. Le 4:3.

65. **the Tirshatha**. *or*, the governor. Ne 8:9. 10:1. Ezr 2:63. **that they should**. Le 2:3, 10. 6:17. 7:19, 20. 10:17, 18. 21:21-23. **till there**. Ex 28:30. Nu 27:21. Dt 33:8.

66. **whole congregation**. Ezr 2:64.

67. **their manservants**. Is 45:1, 2. Je 27:7. **two hundred**. Ezr 2:65: 200.

68. **Their horses**. Ezr 2:66, 67.

69. Here Jerome adds, in the Vulgate, "Thus far do the words extend which were written in the register; what follows belongs to the history of Nehemiah." This addition is not found in the Hebrew, or any ancient version: it is also wanting in the Paris and Complutensian Polyglotts; but is found in the Editio Prima of the Vulgate. What follows, however, seems to relate to a distinct oblation from that recorded in Ezra; and was probably made after the people were registered by Nehemiah, who was the Tirshatha, or governor, at this time, as Zerubbabel had been at the first return of the Jews from captivity. Blessed be God that our faith and hope are not in names and numbers, genealogy and chronology, but on the great things of the law and gospel. Whatever is given to the work of God and his cause will surely be remembered by him (He 6:10).

70. **some.** Heb. part. Ezr 2:68-70. Da 1:2. **the chief.** Nu 7:2-86. 1 Ch 29:3-9. **gave.** Le +*23:38. **The Tirshatha.** Ne 8:9. 10:1. **drams.** *Darkemonim,* or *darics;* a Persian gold coin. **basons.** Ex 12:22. 24:6. 1 K 7:+40, 45. 1 Ch 28:17. 2 Ch 4:8, 11. Je 52:19.

71. **chief.** Jb 34:19. Lk 21:1-4. 2 C 8:12. **pound.** *Manim,* manehs or minas. As a weight, the maneh was equal to 100 shekels; but as a coin, equal to 60 shekels.

73. **all Israel.** It was for the purpose of ascertaining the different *families,* and consequently the different cities, villages, etc. which belonged to them, according to the ancient division of the land, that the public registers were examined. **when the seventh.** Ezr 2:70. 3:1.

NEHEMIAH 8

The people being assembled, Ezra, with solemn worship, reads and expounds the law, 1-8. The people are greatly affected; but Nehemiah, Ezra, and the Levites, exhort them to joy in God, to cheerful feasting, and to liberality towards the poor, 9-12. The eagerness of the people to hear and to be instructed in the law, 13-15. Being instructed from the law concerning the feast of tabernacles, they keep it with great solemnity, 16-18.

1. A.M. 3559. B.C. 445. **all the people.** Ezr 3:1, etc. **as one man.** Jg 20:1, 8. **before.** ver. 16. Ne 3:26. 12:37. **gate.** ſ171S7B, Ge +14:7. **they spake.** T#1077. **Ezra.** ver. 4-9. Ezr *7:6, 11. Je 8:8, 9. Mt 13:52. 23:2, 13, 34. **bring.** Dt 31:11. 2 Ch 34:15. Is √8:20. Ml 4:4.

2. **priest.** Dt *17:18. 31:9, 10. Ml *2:7. **congregation.** Dt *31:11-13. 2 Ch *17:7-9. Ac 15:21. **could hear with understanding.** Heb. understood in hearing. Is √28:9. **the first.** Le +*23:24. Nu 29:1. 1 K 8:2.

3. **he read.** T#1064. ver. *8. Dt 31:11-13. Je 36:6. Lk *4:16-20. Ac 13:15, 27. 15:21. **gate.** ſ171S7B, Ge +14:7. **morning.** Heb. light. Ac *20:7, 11. *28:23. **could understand.** ver. *2. Is *28:9. **ears.** Mt 7:28, 29. Mk *12:37. Lk *8:18. 19:48. Ac 16:14. √17:11. 1 Th *2:13. He *2:1-3. Re 2:29. 3:22.

4. **pulpit.** Heb. tower. ſ102, Ge +2:24. **Anaiah.** i.e. *answer of the Lord; afflicted of Jah,* *S#6043h. Ne 8:4. 10:22. (1) A priest who was at the right hand of Ezra while he read the book of the law to the people, Ne 8:4. (2) A Jew who, with Nehemiah, sealed the covenant, Ne 10:22. **Maaseiah.** Ne 10:25. 11:5. **Malchiah.** Ne 10:3. **Hashum.** Ne 10:18. Ezr 10:33. **Hashbadana.** i.e. *esteemed in judging; considerate in judging,* *S#2806h. **Meshullam.** Ne 10:7, 20. 11:7. 12:13. Ezr 10:29.

5. **opened.** Lk 4:16, 17. **sight.** Heb. eyes. Ge 18:3. **stood up.** Ex 15:20n. Jg 3:20. ◐20:26n. 1 K 8:14. 2 Ch 7:6.

6. **blessed.** 1 Ch 29:20. 2 Ch 6:4. Ps 41:13. 72:18, 19. Ep *1:3. 1 P *1:3. **Amen.** Ne 5:13. Je 28:6. Mt 6:13. 1 C 14:16. **with lifting.** Ge 14:22. Ps 28:2. 63:4. 134:2. 141:2. La 3:41. 1 T 2:8. **bowed.** Ge 24:26. Ex 4:31. 12:27. 2 Ch 20:18. 29:30. **with their faces.** Le 9:24. Mt 26:39. Re 7:11.

7. **Jeshua.** Ne 3:19. 9:4. 10:9. 12:24. **Bani.** Ne 3:17. 9:4. 10:13. **Sherebiah.** Ne 9:4. 10:12. 12:24. Ezr 8:18. **Akkub.** Ne 11:16, 19. 12:25. **Hodijah.** i.e. *majesty of God; my glory is Jah; praise of the Lord,* *S#1941h. Ne 8:7. 9:5. 10:10, 13, 18. 1 Ch 4:19. (1) A man reckoned

of the tribe of Judah, married to the sister of Naham, 1 Ch 4:19. (2) A Levite, who with Ezra, explained the law to the people, Ne 8:7; 9:5. (3, 4) Two who sealed the covenant, Ne 10:10, 13. **Maaseiah.** ver. 4. Ne 3:23. 12:41, 42. Ezr 10:22. **Kelita.** Ne 10:10. Ezr 10:23. **Azariah.** Ne 3:23. 10:2. 12:33. **Jozabad.** Ezr 10:22, 23. **Hanan.** Ne 10:10. **Pelaiah.** i.e. *Jah has distinguished; distinguished of the Lord,* *S#6411h. Ne 8:7. 10:10. 1 Ch 3:24. (1) One in the succession of Jeconiah, 1 Ch 3:24. (2) One who, with Ezra, caused the people to understand the law, Ne 8:7. (3) One who sealed the covenant, Ne 10:10. **caused.** Le 10:11. Dt 33:10. 2 Ch 17:7-9. 30:22. Ml *2:7.

8. **they read.** Is *34:16. Jn +√5:39. 1 T *4:13. 2 T +√3:15. Re *1:3. **distinctly.** or, explaining. lit. "spread out," as in Le 24:12mg. Nu 15:34. Ezr 4:18. Ezk 34:12. Lk √24:32. Ac +*17:2, 3. **and gave the sense.** 1 S 25:3. 1 Ch 22:12. Hab *2:2. Mt *5:21, 22, 27, 28. Lk *24:27, 32, 45. Ac*8:30-35. +*17:2, 3. *28:23. **reading.** ſ121R7, Ge +43:11.

9. **Nehemiah.** Ne 7:65, 70. 10:1. Ezr 2:63. **Tirshatha.** or, governor. Ne 7:65, 70. 10:1. 12:26. Ezr 2:63. **Ezra.** Ezr 7:11. **the Levites.** ver. 7, 8. 2 Ch *15:3. *30:22. 35:3n. Ho 4:6. **This day.** ver. 2. Le 23:24. Nu 29:1-6. **mourn not.** Dt 12:7, 12. 16:11, 14, 15. 26:14. Ec 3:4. Is 61:3. Ml 2:13. **all the people.** 2 K 22:11, 19. 2 Ch 34:19, 21. Ro 3:20. 7:9. 2 C 7:9-11.

10. **Go your way.** Ec 2:24. 3:13. 5:18. 9:7. 1 T 6:17, 18. **eat.** SS 5:1. **send.** Dt 26:11-13. Est 9:19, 22. Jb 31:16-18. Ec 11:2. Lk 11:41. Re 11:10. **neither.** Dt 28:47. Ps 100:2. Lk 1:74. **the joy.** T#52. Ps 5:11. 21:1. 28:7, 8. 119:80. 149:2. Pr 14:30. 15:13, 15. *17:22. Ec 3:22 (T#634). Is 6:7, 8. 12:1-3. 35:1-4. 61:10. Jl 2:23. Jn 16:33. Ro 14:17. 2 C 8:2. 12:8, 9. Ph 3:4. 1 Th 5:16 (T#296).

11. **stilled.** Nu 13:30.

12. **to send.** ver. 10. **to make.** Ps 126:1-3. **because.** ver. 7, 8. Jb √23:12. Ps *19:8-11. 119:14, 16, 72, 97, 103, 104, 111, 127, 128, 130, 171, 174. Pr 2:10, 11. 24:13, 14. Je √15:16. Lk 24:32. Ro 7:18.

13. **the second.** 2 Ch 30:23. Pr 2:1-6. 8:33, 34. 12:1. Mk 6:33, 34. Lk 19:47, 48. Ac 4:1. 13:42. **to understand the words of the law.** or, that they might instruct in the words of the law. ver. 7, 8. Lk 24:32. 2 T 2:24, 25.

14. **by.** Heb. by the hand of. Ne 9:14, 30. 10:29. 1 K 16:12mg. 2 Ch √34:14mg,n. Ezr 9:11mg. **dwell.** Le 23:34, 40-43. Dt 16:13-15. Zc 14:16-19. Jn 7:2. **booths.** Ge 33:17. Mt 17:4. **the feast.** That is, the *feast of tabernacles,* which was held in the month *Tisri,* the seventh of the ecclesiastical year, in commemoration of the sojourning of the Israelites in the wilderness, after they had been delivered from Egyptian bondage. For other particulars see the parallel passages. Le 23:34, 42. Dt 16:13.

15. **And that.** Ex 23:14, 17. Le 23:4. Nu 10:10. Ps 81:3. **in Jerusalem.** Dt 16:16. **the mount.** Jg 9:48, 49. Mt 21:1. **fetch.** Le +*23:40. **olive.** Ge 8:11. Jg 9:8, 9. 1 K 6:23. Je 11:16. Zc 4:11-14. Ro 11:16-25. He 4:16. Re 11:4. **pine.** Mi 4:2. **myrtle.** Is 35:10. 55:13. **palm.** Jn 12:13. Re 7:9.

16. **the roof.** Dt 22:8. 2 S 11:2. Je 19:13. 32:29. **the courts.** 2 Ch 20:5. 33:5. **the street of the water gate.** ver. 3. Ne 3:26. 12:37. **gate of Ephraim.** Ne 12:37, 39. 2 K 14:13.

17. **sat under.** Jn 1:14. He 11:9, 13. **Jeshua.** i.e.

salvation of the Lord. Jsh 1:1, Joshua. He 4:8, Jesus.
❋S#3442h: Ne 3:19. 7:7, 11, 39, 43. 8:7, 17. 9:4, 5.
10:9. 11:26. 12:1, 7, 8, 10, 24, 26. 1 Ch 24:11. 2 Ch
31:15. Ezr 2:2, 6, 36, 50. 3:2, 8, 9. 4:3. 8:33. 10:18.
Also Ezr 5:2. (1) The leader of the Israelites, Ne 8:17.
(2) A descendant of Aaron, of the ninth of twenty-four
courses into which David divided the priests, 1 Ch
24:1, 6, 11. (3) A Levite under Hezekiah who assisted
with the collection and distribution of the freewill offerings, 2 Ch 31:15. (4) A high priest who returned with
Zerubbabel from Babylon, Ezr 2:2; Ne 7:7. (5) A man
of the house of Pahath-moab, some of whose children
returned with Zerubbabel and others from captivity,
Ezr 2:6; Ne 7:11. (6) A Levite who returned from captivity with Zerubbabel, Ezr 2:40; Ne 7:43; 12:8. (7) One
who sealed the covenant, Ne 10:9. (8) Father of Ezer,
ruler of Mizpah, who helped repair the wall, Ne 3:19.
(9) A Levite who aided Ezra in explaining the law,
Ne 8:7; 9:4, 5. (10) A village of southern Judah, Ne
11:26. **for since.** 2 K 23:22, 23. 2 Ch 30:23. 35:18.
had not. 2 Ch 7:8-10. 8:13. Ezr 3:4. **done so.** 2 Ch
30:26. 35:18. **there was.** 1 Ch 29:22. 2 Ch 7:10. 30:21-
23.

18. **day by day.** Dt 31:10-13. **a solemn assembly.**
Heb. a restraint. Le 23:36. **according.** Le 23:36. Nu
29:35. Jn 7:37.

NEHEMIAH 9

*A solemn fast is observed, 1-3. The Levites, as leading
the worship of the people, piously acknowledge the
manifold goodness of God to Israel, and humbly confess
the sins of the nation, as the cause of their miseries,
4-8; in Egypt, 9, 10; in their journey out of it, 11,
12; upon Mount Sinai, 13, 14; in their journey towards
Canaan, 15-18; in the wilderness, 19-21; in driving
out the nations before them, 22-26; in hearing their
prayer when in trouble, and saving them, 27-31; they
confess their sins, 32-37; and seal a covenant, 38.*

1. **Now.** On the *first* of this month was the *feast
of trumpets;* on the *tenth,* the *day of atonement;* on
the *fourteenth* began the *feast of tabernacles,* which
lasted seven days, ending on the *twenty-second;* on
the *twenty-third,* they separated themselves from their
illegitimate wives; and on the *twenty-fourth,* they held
a solemn day of fasting and confession of sin, and reading the law; the whole of which they closed by renewing
their covenants. **twenty.** Le 23:34, 39. 2 Ch 7:10. **of
this month.** Ne 8:2. **children.** Jg 20:26. 2 Ch 20:3.
Ezr 8:23. Est 4:3, 16. Is 22:12. Jl 1:13, 14. 2:15-17.
Jon 3:5-8. Ac 13:2, 3. **sackclothes.** Da +9:3. Jon 3:6.
earth. T#1239. Jsh 7:6. 1 S 4:12. 2 S 1:2. Jb 2:12.

2. **the seed.** Ne 13:3, 30. Ezr 9:2. 10:11. 2 C 6:17.
strangers. Heb. strange children. Ne 13:30. Ex 12:43
(❋S#5236h). 2 Ch 33:15. Ps 144:7, 11. Is 2:6. Ho 5:7.
confessed. Ne 1:6. Le 26:39, 40. Ezr 9:6, 7, 15. Ps
106:6, 7. Da 9:3-10, 20. 1 J √1:7-9.

3. **they stood.** Ne 8:4, 7, *8.* **one fourth.** Ne 8:3.

4. **stood.** Lk +18:13. **stairs.** *or,* scaffold. Ne 3:15.
Ex 20:26. **Jeshua.** ver. 5. See on Ne 8:7. 10:9-13. 12:8.
Kadmiel. i.e. *before God.* Ezr +2:40. **Shebaniah.** Ne
10:10, 12. 12:3, 14. 1 Ch +15:24. **Bunni.** i.e. *built,*
❋S#1138h. Ne 9:4. 10:15. 11:15. (1) A Levite who
lived before the exile, Ne 11:15. (2) A Levite, contemporary with Nehemiah, Ne 9:4. (3) A Levite who sealed
the covenant, Ne 10:15. **Sherebiah.** i.e. *heat of Jah.*

Ezr +8:18. **Bani.** i.e. *built up.* Ne 8:7. Ezr +2:10.
Chenani. i.e. *perpetuator; perfector, protector,*
❋S#3662h. **cried.** 2 Ch 20:19. Ps 3:4. 77:1. 130:1. La
3:8. Jn 11:43. Ac 7:60.

5. **Hashabniah.** i.e. *reckoning of Jah.* Ne +3:10.
Hodijah. i.e. *honor of Jah.* Ne +8:7. **Pethahiah.** Ne
+11:24. Ezr 10:23. **Stand up.** 1 K 8:14, 22. 1 Ch
◑+17:16. 2 Ch 20:13, 19. Ps ch. 134. 135:1-3. Lk
+18:13. **bless.** 1 Ch 29:20. Ezr 3:11. Ps 103:1, 2. ch.
117. 145:2. 146:2. Je 33:10, 11. Mt 11:25. Ep 3:20,
21. 1 P 1:3. **for ever and.** Heb. *olam.* doubled, Da
+2:20. **thy glorious.** Ex 15:6, 11. Dt 28:58. 1 Ch 29:13.
Ps 72:18, 19. 145:5, 11, 12. 2 C 4:6. **exalted.** 2 S 7:26.
1 K 8:27. 1 Ch 29:11. Ps 16:2. 106:2.

6. **even thou.** Dt 6:4. 2 K 19:15, 19. Ps 86:10. Is
37:16, 20. 43:10. 44:6, 8. Mk 12:29, 30. Jn *10:30.
Lord alone. Ps 24:7, 10. 97:9. 102:24-27. Pr 16:4. Ec
12:14. Is 6:1-3. 40:+*3, 10, 11, 28. 44:6. Je 23:5, 6.
Ho 1:7. Zc 13:7. Ml 3:1. Jn √8:24. 1 C √12:3. Col
1:17. He 1:3. **thou hast.** Ge 1:1. 2:1. Ex 20:11. Ps
33:6. 136:5-9. 146:6. Je 10:11, 12. Col +*1:15, 16.
Re 4:11. 14:7. **the heaven.** Dt 10:14. 1 K 8:27. **preservest.** Ps +36:6. Col *1:17. He *1:3. **the host.** Ge
2:1. 32:2. 1 K 22:19. Ps 103:21. 148:2-4. Is 6:2, 3.
He √1:6. Re *5:11-13. **worshippeth.** He √1:6. Re
+*5:12.

7. **choose.** Ge 12:1, 2. Dt 10:15. Jsh 24:2, 3. Is
41:8, 9. 51:2. Ac 13:17. **Ur.** Ge 11:31. 15:7. Ac 7:2-4.
gavest. Ge 17:5.

8. **foundest.** Ge 12:1-3. *15:6, 18. 22:12. Ac 13:22.
1 T 1:12, 13. He 11:8, 17. Ja 2:21-23. **madest.** Ge
12:7. 15:18. 17:7, 8. 22:16-18. Dt 7:8, 9. 9:5. Ps 105:8,
9. Lk 1:72, 73. **the Canaanites.** Ge +10:18. 15:18-
21. Ex 3:8, 17. Dt 7:1. Jsh 9:1. 11:3. **Hittites.** Ge
+15:20. **Amorites.** Ge +10:16. **Perizzites.** Ge +13:7.
Jebusites. Ge +10:16. **hast performed.** Dt 26:3. Jsh
11:23. 21:43-45. 23:14. Ps 105:43, 44. **righteous.** Nu
23:19. Ps 92:14, 15. T *1:2. He *6:18. 1 J √1:9.

9. **didst see.** Ex 2:25. 3:7, 8, 9, 16. Ac 7:34. **heardest.**
Ex 14:10-12.

10. **showedst.** Ex ch. 7—10. 12:29, 30. 14:15-31.
Dt 4:34. 11:3, 4. Ps 78:12, 13, 43-53. 105:27-37. 106:7-
11. 135:8, 9. 136:10-15. Ac 7:36. **they.** Ex 5:2, 7, 8.
9:17. 10:3. 18:11. Jb 40:11, 12. Da 4:37. 5:23. 1 P
5:5. **didst.** Ex 9:16. Jsh 2:10, 11. Ps 83:18. Is 63:12,
14. Je 32:20. Ezk 20:9. Da 9:15. Ro 9:17.

11. **divide.** Ex 14:21, 22, 27, 28. Ps 66:6. 74:13.
78:13. 114:3-5. 136:13-15. Is 63:11-13. **their persecutors.** Ex 15:1-21. Ps 106:9-11. He 11:29. **as a stone.**
Ex 15:5, 10. Re 18:21.

12. **thou leddest.** ver. 19. Ex 13:21, 22. 14:19, 20.
40:38. Ps 78:14. 105:39. **in the way.** Ps 107:7. 143:8.

13. **camest.** Ex 19:11, 16-20. Dt 33:2. Is 64:1, 3.
Hab 3:3. **spakest.** Ex 20:1, 22. Dt 4:10-13, 33. 5:4,
22-26. He 12:18-26. **gavest.** Dt 4:8. 10:12, 13. Ps *19:7-
11. 119:127, 128. Ezk 20:11-13. Ro 7:12-14, 16. **true
laws.** Heb. laws of truth. Ps 119:160.

14. **madest.** Ge 2:3. Ex 16:29. 20:8-11. Ezk 20:12,
20. **commandest.** Ex ch. 21-23. Le 27:34. Dt 4:5, 45.
5:31. **Moses.** Ne 1:8. Jn 1:17.

15. **gavest.** Ex 16:4, 14, 15. Dt 8:3, 16. Ps 78:24,
25. 105:40. Jn 6:31-35. 1 C 10:3. **broughtest.** ver. 20.
Ex 17:6. Nu 20:7-11. Dt 8:15. Ps 78:15-20. 105:41.
114:8. 1 C 10:4. **go.** Dt 1:8. Jsh 1:2-4. **sworn.** Heb.
lift up thine hand. Ge 14:22. Nu 14:30mg. Ezk 20:15.

16. **dealt.** See on ver. 10, 29. Ex 32:9. Dt 9:6, 13,

23, 24, 27. 32:15. Ps 78:8, etc. 106:6. Is 63:10. Je 2:31. Ac 7:51. **hardened.** Dt 31:27. 2 K 17:14. 2 Ch 30:8. 36:13. Ps 95:8-10. Pr *29:1. Is 48:4. Je 19:15. Ro 2:5. He *3:13, 15. **hearkened not.** Ex 15:26. Dt 5:29. Ps 81:8, 11-14. Is 48:18. There were two things to which the Israelites did not duly give heed, else they had not done as they did. The word of God they heard, but they gave no heed to God's commandments: and the works of God they saw, but were not mindful of his wonders. Had they really considered them as miracles, they would have obeyed from a principle of faith and holy fear: had they duly considered them as mercies, they would have obeyed from a principle of gratitude and holy love.

17. **refused.** Nu 14:3, 4, 11, 41. 16:14. Ps 106:24, 25. Pr 1:24. He 12:25. **mindful.** Ps 78:11, 42, 43. 86:5, 15. 106:7, 13. Mt 16:9-11. 2 P 1:12-15. **in their rebellion.** Instead of *bemiryam*, "in their rebellion," seven MSS., one edition, and the LXX. have *bemitzrayim*, "in Egypt:" "appointed a captain to return to their bondage in Egypt." **appointed.** Nu 14:4. Ac 7:39. **a God.** Nu 14:18, 19. Ps 86:5, 15. 130:4. Mi *7:18, 19. **ready to pardon.** Heb. of pardons. Ps 130:4. Da 9:9. **gracious.** Ex 34:6, 7. Ps 78:38. 103:8-18. 145:8, 9. Is *55:7-9. Jl 2:13. Jon 4:2. Ro 9:15. Ep 1:6, 7. **forsookest.** 1 K 6:13. 8:57. Ps 106:43-46.

18. **when they made.** Ex 32:4-8, 31, 32. Dt 9:12-16. Ps 106:19-23. Ezk 20:7, etc.

19. **in thy.** ver. 27. 1 S 12:22. Ps 78:38. 99:8. 106:7, 8, 45. Is 44:21. La 3:22. Ezk 20:14, 22. Da 9:9, 18. Ml 3:6. **the pillar.** See on ver. 12. Ex 13:21, 22. 40:38. Nu 9:15-22. 14:14. Is 4:5, 6. 1 C *10:1, 2.

20. **gavest.** ver. 30. Nu 11:17, 25-29. Is 63:11-14. **good.** Ps 143:10. Ro 15:30. Ga √5:22, 23. Ep 5:9. 2 P 1:21. **spirit.** Is +48:16. 63:10. Hg 2:4, 5. **withheldest.** Ex 16:15, 35. Jsh 5:12. **gavest.** Ex 17:6. Ps 105:41. Is 41:17, 18. 48:21. 49:10. Jn 4:10, 14. 7:37-39. 1 C 10:4.

21. **forty.** Ex 16:35. Nu 14:33, 34. Dt 2:7. 8:2. Am 5:25. Ac 13:18. **clothes waxed not old.** Dt 8:4. 29:5. **lacked nothing.** 1 K 4:27. Lk 22:35. **their.** Dt 8:4. 29:5. Ps 34:10.

22. **thou.** Jsh 10:11. Ps 78:65. 105:44. **divide.** Dt 32:26. Jsh 11:23. **Sihon.** Nu 21:21-35. Dt 2:26-36. 3:1-17. Ps 135:10-12. 136:17-22. **Bashan.** Nu +21:33. Jsh 12:4n. 1 K 4:13. Ps 22:12.

23. **multipliedst.** Ge 15:5. 22:17. 1 Ch 27:23. **as the stars.** ♪102B, ♪138B, Ge +13:16. **broughtest.** Jsh ch. 1, 3, etc. **which thou.** Ge 12:7. 13:15-17. 15:18. 17:8. 26:3.

24. **So the.** Nu 14:31. Jsh 21:43, 45. 23:4. 24:11, 12. **thou subduest.** Jsh 18:1. 1 Ch 22:18. Ps 44:2, 3. **as they would.** Heb. according to their will. 2 T 2:26.

25. **strong.** Nu 13:27, 28. Dt 3:5. 6:10-12. 9:1-3. **a fat land.** ver. 35. Dt 6:11. 8:7-10. 32:13. Jsh 24:13. Ps 105:44. Ezk 20:6. **wells.** *or*, cisterns. Heb. *bor*, Ge +37:20. **fruit trees.** Heb. trees of food. **did eat.** Dt 32:15. Ps 65:11. Is 6:10. Je 5:27, 28. Ho 13:6. **and became fat.** They became effeminate, fell under the power of *luxury*, got totally corrupted in their manners, sinned against all the mercies of God, and then were destroyed by his judgments. Dt 32:15. Is 6:10. **delighted.** 1 K 8:66. Je 31:14. Ho 3:5. Ro 2:4.

26. **they were.** Jg 2:11, 12. 3:6, 7. 10:6, 13, 14. Ps 78:56, 57. 106:34-40. Ezk 16:15, etc. 20:21. 23:4, etc. **cast thy law.** 1 K 14:9. Ps 50:17. Ezk 33:3-5. **slew.** 1 K 18:4, 13. 19:10, 14. 2 Ch 24:20, 21. 36:16. Je 26:20-

23. Mt 21:35. 23:34-37. Ac 7:52. 1 Th 2:15. **wrought.** ver. 18. 2 K 21:11. Ezk 22:25-31.

27. **thou deliveredst.** Dt 31:16-18. Jg 2:14, 15. 3:8, etc. 2 Ch 36:17. Ps 106:41, 42. Da 9:10-14. **in the time.** Dt 4:29-31. Jg 3:15. 6:6-10. 10:15, 16. Ps 106:43-45. **manifold.** Am ◐5:12. **saviors.** Jg 2:18. 3:9-15. 1 S 12:10, 11. 2 K 13:5. 14:27. Ob 21.

28. **did evil again.** Heb. returned to do evil. Jg 3:11, 12, 30. 4:1. 5:31. 6:1. Ps 78:34, 36. **heardest.** 1 K 8:33, 34, 39. Is 63:15. **many times.** Ps 106:43-45.

29. **testifiedst.** ver. 26. Dt 4:26. 31:21. 2 K 17:13. 2 Ch 24:19. 36:15. Je 25:3-7. Ho 6:5. **yet they.** ver. 10, 16. Ex 10:3. Je 13:15-17. 43:2. 44:10, 16, 17. Da 5:20. Ja 4:6-10. **which.** Le 18:5. Ezk 20:11. Lk 10:28. Ro 10:5. Ga 3:12. **withdrew the shoulder.** Heb. gave a withdrawing shoulder. Zc 7:11, 12. **and hardened.** See on Je 7:26. 17:23. 19:15.

30. **many years.** Ps 86:15. Ro 2:4. 2 P 3:9. **forbear them.** Heb. protract over them. **testifiedst.** 2 K 17:13. 2 Ch 36:15. Je 7:25. 25:4. **by thy spirit.** ver. 20. Is +48:16. 63:10. Ac 7:51. 28:25. 1 P 1:11. 2 P *1:21. **thy prophets.** Heb. the hand of thy prophets. ♪121BB, Ezr +9:11. 2 Ch 32:15mg. Ho 6:5. **therefore.** Is 5:5, 6. 42:24. Je 40:2, 3. 44:22. La 2:17. Zc 7:13.

31. **for thy great.** Je 4:27. 5:10, 18. La 3:22. Ezk 14:22, 23. Da 9:9. **didst not.** Is 1:9. *57:16. Je 5:18. **gracious.** See on ver. 17. Ex 34:6, 7. 2 K 13:23. 2 Ch 30:9. Ps 103:8, 9. 145:8, 9.

32. **our God.** Ne 1:5. Dt 7:21. Ps 47:2. 66:3, 5. **keepest.** Dt 7:9. 1 K 8:23. Da 9:4. Mi *7:18-20. **and mercy.** ♪174, Ge +18:27. **trouble.** Heb. weariness. or, travail. Ex 18:8. Nu 20:14. La 3:5. **little before thee.** Le 26:18, 21, 24, 28. Ezr 9:13. **come upon us.** Heb. found us. Ge +44:34mg. 2 K +9:21mg. **on our kings.** 2 K 23:29, 33, 34. 25:7, 18-21, 25, 26. 2 Ch ch. 36. Je 8:1-3. 22:18, 19. 34:19-22. ch. 39, 52. Da 9:6, 8. **since the time.** 2 K 15:19, 29. 17:3. Is 7:17, 18. 8:7, 8. 10:5-7. ch. 36, 37. **unto this day.** Jsh +4:9. 1 K 8:24. Je +25:18. 44:22.

33. **Howbeit.** Ge *18:25. Jb 34:23. Ps 119:137. 145:17. Je 12:1. La 1:18. Da 9:5-14. **just.** Ps *145:17. Da 9:7. **but we.** Le 26:40, 41. Jb 33:27. Ps 106:6. Da 9:5-10.

34. **Neither.** Da 9:7. **nor hearkened.** Je 29:19. **thy testimonies.** ver. 30. 2 K 17:15. **thou didst.** Dt 31:21. 2 K 17:13.

35. **For they.** Dt 28:47. Je 5:19. Ro 3:4, 5. **in their kingdom.** Instead of *bemalkuthom*, "in *their* kingdom," *bemaluthecha*, "in *thy* kingdom," is the reading of two of Dr. Kennicott's MSS., LXX., Syriac, and Arabic. **thy great.** ver. 25. **fat land.** Dt 8:7-10. 31:21. 32:12-15.

36. **we are.** Dt *28:48. 2 Ch 12:8. Ezr 9:9.

37. **it yieldeth.** Dt 28:33, 39, 51. Ezr 4:13. 6:8. 7:24. **dominion.** Ne 5:8. Le 26:17. Dt 28:48. Jn 8:33. **distress.** T#1237. Ge 32:9-11. 35:2, 3. 1 S *30:6. 2 S *22:7. 2 Ch 20:12, 13. Ps 4:1. 18:6. 25:17. 107:6. 118:5. 120:1. La 1:20. 3:52-58. 5:1-6.

38. **we make.** Ne 10:29. 2 K 23:3. 2 Ch 15:12, 13. 23:16. 29:10. 34:31. Ezr 10:3. **seal unto it.** Heb. *are* at the sealing, *or* sealed. Ne 10:1. Jn=3:33.

NEHEMIAH 10

The names of those who sealed the covenant, 1-27. The rest of the people bind themselves to observe it,

28, 29. Some particulars to which they bound themselves, 30-39.

1. **those that sealed.** Heb. at the sealings. Ne 9:38. **Nehemiah.** i.e. *comforted of Jah.* Ne +1:1. 8:9. **Tirshatha.** *or,* governor. Ne 7:70. Ezr 2:63. **son of Hachaliah.** Ne 1:1. **Zidkijah.** i.e. *right of Jah; righteousness of Jehovah; justice of the Lord,* ✛S#6667h. See 1 K +22:11, Zedekiah.

2. **Seraiah.** i.e. *head of Jah.* Ne 3:23. 11:11. 12:1, 33, 34. 2 S +8:17.

3. **Pashur.** i.e. *prosperity everywhere.* Ne 11:12. Je +20:1. **Amariah.** Ne 12:2, 13. **Malchijah.** The original is uniformly *Malchijah,* or rather, "Malkeeyah." Ne 3:11. 8:4, Malchiah.

4. **Hattush.** i.e. *assembled.* Ne 3:10. Ezr +8:2. **Shebaniah.** Ne 12:14. **Malluch.** i.e. *reigning; counselor; kingly,* ✳S#4409h. Ne 10:4, 27. 12:2. 1 Ch 6:44. Ezr 10:29, 32. (1) A Levite, family of Merari, house of Mushi, 1 Ch 6:44. (2) One of them that married strange wives, Ezr 10:29. (3, 4) Two that sealed the covenant, Ne 10:4, 27. (5) One of the priests that went up with Zerubbabel; also named in the succession of high priests, Ne 12:2, +14, Melicu.

5. **Harim.** Ne 3:11. **Meremoth.** Ne 3:4, 21. 12:3.

6. **Ginnethon.** i.e. *gardener; protection,* ✳S#1599h. Ne 10:6. 12:4, Ginnetho, 16. **Baruch.** Ne 3:20.

7. **Meshullam.** Ne 3:6. 8:4. 11:11. 12:13, 25-33. **Abijah.** Ne 12:4. **Mijamin.** *Mijamin* and *Miamin* are the same in the original, which is a defective form of *Miniamin.* Ne 12:5, Miamin, 17, 41, Miniamin.

8. **Bilgai.** i.e. *consolation of the Lord; my comforts; desistant,* ✳S#1084h. Ne 12:5, Bilgah. **Shemaiah.** Ne 3:29. 12:6, 18, 42. Ezr 10:21.

9. **Jeshua.** Ne 3:19. 7:43. 8:7. 9:4. **Azaniah.** i.e. *heard of Jah,* ✳S#245h. **Henadad.** Ne 3:18, 24. 12:8, 24.

10. **Shebaniah.** Ne 8:7. 9:4, 5. Ezr 10:23.

11. **Hashabiah.** Ne 11:15, 22. 12:24. Ezr 8:19, 24.

12. **Sherebiah.** Ne 8:7. 9:4. 12:8.

13. **Beninu.** i.e. *our son; our edification,* ✳S#1148h.

14. **Parosh.** Ne 3:11. 7:8, 11-12. **Zatthu.** i.e. *an ornament; sprout,* S#2240h. Ne 7:13, Zattu. Ezr +2:8, etc. The original is uniformly **Zattu.** (1) One whose children went up from Babylon, Ezr 2:8; Ne 7:13. (2) One whose children took strange wives, Ezr 10:27. (3) One who sealed the covenant, Ne 10:14. **Bani.** Ne 7:15, Binnui. Ezr 2:10.

15. **Azgad.** Ne 7:16, 17. Ezr 2:11, 12. 8:11, 12. 10:28.

16. **Bigvai.** Ne 7:19-21. Ezr 2:14-16. 8:14.

17. **Ater.** i.e. *bound, shut.* Ezr +2:16. **Hizkijah.** i.e. *the strength of God; strengthened of Jehovah; strength of the Lord,* S#2396h. See on 2 K +16:20, Hezekiah. **Azzur.** i.e. *helped; helpful,* ✳S#5809h. Ne 10:17. Je +28:1, Azur. Ezk 11:1. (1) Father of Hananiah the false prophet, Je 28:1. (2) Father of Jaazaniah, Ezk 11:1. (3) One of those who sealed the covenant with Nehemiah, Ne 10:17.

18. **Hashum.** Ne 7:22, etc. Ezr 2:17, etc.

19. **Hariph.** i.e. *autumnal showers.* Ne +7:24. **Anathoth.** i.e. *answers; songs.* 1 Ch +7:8. **Nebai.** i.e. *fruitful; fruit of the Lord,* ✳S#5109h.

20. **Magpiash.** i.e. *killer of moths; collector; plague of the moth; the plague is consumed,* ✳S#4047h.

21. **Meshezabeel.** i.e. *freed by God.* Ne +3:4.

22. **Pelatiah.** i.e. *escaped of Jah.* 1 Ch +3:21.

23. **Hoshea.** i.e. *he gave safety.* 2 K +15:30.

24. **Hallohesh.** i.e. *the whisperer; enchanter; the charmer,* ✳S#3873h. Ne 3:12. 10:24. **Pileha.** i.e. *cleavage; a slice; servitude,* ✳S#6401h. **Shobek.** i.e. *forsaking,* ✳S#7733h.

25. **Rehum.** i.e. *merciful.* Ne 3:17, etc. +12:3. **Hashabnah.** i.e. *inventiveness; esteemed of the Lord; the device was lamented,* ✳S#2812h.

26. **Ahijah.** i.e. *brother of Jah.* 1 K +14:6. **Hanan.** i.e. *compassionate.* 1 Ch +9:44. **Anan.** i.e. *a cloud; covering,* ✳S#6052h.

28. **the rest.** Ne 7:72, 73. Ezr 2:36-43, 70. **all they.** Ne 9:2. 13:3. Le 20:24. Ezr 9:1, 2. 10:11-19. 2 C *6:14-17. **unto the law.** Ro 1:1. **every one.** Ne 8:2. Ps 47:7. Ec 5:2. Je 4:2.

29. **clave.** Is 14:1. Ac √11:23. 17:34. Ro 12:9. **entered into.** T#502. Ne 5:12, 13. 13:25. Ex 24:7. Dt 27:15, etc. *29:10-14. 2 K 11:17. 2 Ch 15:13, 14. *34:31, 32. Ps 76:11. 119:106. Is 56:4. Je 50:5. Ezk 20:37. Ac 23:12-15, 21. Ro +2:29 (T#118). **curse.** or, execration. ✳S#423h. Ge 24:41. 26:28. Le 5:1. Nu 5:21, 21, 23, 27. Dt 29:12, 14, 19, 20, 21. 30:7. 1 K 8:31, 31. 2 Ch 6:22, 22. 34:24. Jb 31:30. Ps 10:7. 59:12. Pr 29:24. Is 24:6. Je 23:10. 29:18. 42:18. 44:12. Ezk 16:59. 17:13, 16, 18, 19. Da 9:11. Zc 5:3. **oath.** ✳S#7621h. Ge 24:8. 26:3. Ex 21:23. 22:11. Le 5:4. Nu 5:21, 21. 30:2, 10, 13. Dt 7:8. Jsh 2:17, 20. 9:20. Jg 21:5. 1 S 14:26. 2 S 21:7. 1 K 2:43. 1 Ch 16:16. 2 Ch 15:15. Ne 6:18 (sworn; lit. were *oath* masters). 10:29. Ps 105:9. Ec 8:2. 9:2. Is 65:15 (curse). Je 11:5. Da 9:11. Hab 3:9. Zc 8:17. **to walk.** 2 K 10:31. 23:3. 2 Ch 6:16. 34:31. Je 26:4. Col √1:10. 1 Th 4:1, 2. **given.** Dt 33:4. Ml 4:4. Jn 1:17. 7:19. **by.** Heb. by the hand of. Ne 8:14mg. 1 K +16:12mg. 2 Ch √34:14mg,n. **to observe and do.** Dt 5:1, 32. *26:16, 18. Ezr +*7:10. Ps 105:45. Ezk 36:27. Jn √13:17. 15:14. T *2:11-14. **the Lord.** Ps 8:1, 9.

30. **not give.** Ex *34:16. Dt *7:3. Ezr 9:1-3, 12-14. 10:10-12. 2 C √6:14. **nor take.** ♪15G, Ge 35:3. Anacoluthon; or, Non-sequence: a breaking off the sequence of thought. Here, an instance of two equivalent constructions united in the same proposition B724.

31. **the people.** Ne 13:15-22. Ex 20:10. Le 23:3. Dt 5:12-14. Is 58:13, 14. Je 17:21, 22. **on the holy day.** Ex 12:16. Le 16:29. 23:21, 35, 36. Col 2:16. **and that we.** Ex 23:10, 11. Le 25:4-7. 2 Ch 36:21. **the exaction.** Ne 5:1-13. Dt *15:1-3, 7-9. Mt +*6:12. 18:27-35. Ja 2:13. **debt.** Heb. band. Is 58:6. *or,* hand. Dt 15:2mg.

32. **to charge.** Ge 28:22. Pr 3:9. Mt 5:17. 17:24-27. **the third part.** According to the law, every one above twenty years of age was to give half a shekel to the sanctuary for a ransom of their souls. But, on account of the general poverty of the people, occasioned by their wars, and captivity, and by heavy tributes, etc., in the land of their captivity, this sum was reduced to the third part of a shekel. Ex 30:11-16. Mt 17:24-27. 2 C √8:12.

33. **the showbread.** Le 24:5. 2 Ch 2:4. **meat offering.** Le +*23:13. **the continual burnt offering.** Le +*23:12. Nu ch. 28, 29. Ne 10:11. **sabbaths.** Ex 31:13. Le 19:3. **new moons.** 1 S 20:5, 18, 24. 2 Ch +2:4. Ezr 3:5. **set feasts.** Ge +17:21h. Le *23:2n. **holy things.** Le 5:15. 22:14. **sin offerings.** Le +*23:19. **all the work.** 2 Ch 24:5-14.

34. **cast.** 1 Ch 24:5, 7. 25:8, 9. Pr 18:18. **the wood offering.** ♪100, Ge +10:9. It was the business of the

Nethinim to procure the *wood* for the fires of the temple: but it is probable few of them returned to their former masters after the captivity; and therefore they found it necessary to cast lots among the priests, Levites, and people, who should furnish the wood at appointed times. This bringing of the wood to the temple at last became a great day; and was constituted into a *feast*, called by Josephus, "the carrying of the wood" (Bell. l. ii. c. 17. sec. 6). Ne 13:31. Le 6:12. Jsh 9:27. Is 40:16. **at times.** He 10:3-7. **as it is written.** Le 6:12, 13.

35. **the firstfruits.** Ex 23:19. 34:26. Le 19:23-26. Nu 18:2, 12. Dt 26:2. 2 Ch 31:3-10. Pr *3:9, 10. Ml *3:8-12.

36. **the firstborn.** Ex 13:2, 12-15. 34:19. Le 27:26, 27. Nu 18:15, 16. Dt 12:6. **unto.** Nu 18:9-19. 1 C 9:6-14. Ga 6:6.

37. **should bring.** Ml 3:8-10. 1 C 9:13. **the firstfruits.** Le 23:17. Nu *15:19-21. 18:12, 13. Dt 18:4. 26:2. **offerings.** or, heave-offerings. Ex 25:2, 3. 29:27n. Nu 15:21. 2 S 1:21. Ezr 8:25. **to the chambers.** Ne 13:5, 9. 1 K 6:5-10. 2 Ch 31:11, 12. **and the tithes.** Le 27:30-33. Nu 18:21, 24-32. 2 Ch 31:6, 11, 12. Ml *3:8, 10.

38. **when the Levites.** Nu 18:26-28. **the tithe.** The tithes of all the produce of the fields were brought to the Levites; and out of these a *tenth* part was given to the priests, which is here called *the tithe of the tithes*: see the parallel passages. **the chambers.** 1 S 9:22. 2 K 23:11. **the treasure house.** Ne 13:12, 13. 1 Ch 9:26. 2 Ch 31:11, 12. Da 1:2. 1 C 16:1, 2. 2 C *9:7. Ph *4:17, 18.

39. **For the children.** Dt 12:6-11, 17. 14:23-27. 2 Ch 31:12. **the children.** Nu 18:30. **we will not.** Ne 13:10, 11. Ps 122:9. He √10:25.

NEHEMIAH 11

The rulers, with every tenth man taken by lot, and those who offered voluntarily, dwell at Jerusalem, 1, 2. Their names, 3-19. The rest dwell in other cities, 20-36.

1. **the rulers.** Ne 7:4, 5. Dt 17:8, 9. Ps 122:5. **cast lots.** Jerusalem certainly had many inhabitants at this time, but not sufficient to preserve the city, which was now encompassed with a wall, the building of which was going on fast. Nehemiah, therefore, obliged *one tenth* of the country people to come and dwell in it, that the population might be sufficient for the defense of the city. Some *volunteered* their services, which was at that time considered a sacrifice to patriotism; as Jerusalem then afforded very few advantages, and was a place of considerable danger: hence "the people blessed them that willingly offered themselves." Ne 10:34. Ge 24:44n. Jsh 14:2n. 18:10. 20:22n. 1 Ch 26:13. Pr *16:33. Ac 1:24. **one of ten.** Jg 20:9, 10. **the holy.** ver. 18. Is 48:2. 52:1. Mt 4:5. 27:53. **parts.** 2 K 11:7mg.

2. **blessed.** Dt 24:13. Jb 29:13. 31:20. **willingly.** Jg 5:9. 2 C 8:5, 16, 17.

3. **Now.** There is a good deal of difference between this enumeration and that in *Chronicles*; as this comprehends not only those who came *first* with Zerubbabel, but also those who came with Ezra and Nehemiah: see on 1 Ch 9:18. **the chief.** Ne 7:6. Ezr 2:1. **Israel.** Ne 7:73. 1 Ch 9:1-3. Ezr 2:70. **Nethinims.** Ezr 2:43, 55. **the children.** Ne 7:57-60. Ezr 2:55-58.

4. **dwelt.** 1 Ch 9:3, 4, etc. **Athaiah.** i.e. *Jah's due season; made opportunely of the Lord*, *S#6265h. **Perez.** The variation of *Pharez* and *Perez* is only found in the translation. Ge 38:29. Ru 4:18, Pharez. Mt 1:3. Lk 3:33, Phares.

5. **Col-hozeh.** Ne 3:15. **Hazaiah.** i.e. *Jah has seen; seen of the Lord*, *S#2382h. **Adaiah.** i.e. *witness of Jehovah; ornament of the Lord; adorned of Jah*, *S#5718h. Ne 11:5, 12. 2 K 22:1. 1 Ch 6:41. 8:21. 9:12. Ezr 10:29, 39. Also 2 Ch 23:1. (1) Grandfather of king Josiah, 2 K 22:1. (2) One of the priests which dwelt in Jerusalem, Ne 9:12; Ne 11:12. (3) A man of Benjamin, 1 Ch 8:21. (4) A Levite descended from Gershom, 1 Ch 6:41, 42. (5, 6) Two who put away their strange wives, Ezr 10:29, 39. (7) A son of Joiarib, Ne 11:5. (8) Father of Maaseiah, 2 Ch 23:1. **Shiloni.** i.e. *descendants of Shelah* (i.e. *quietness, request; prayer, petition*, Ge +38:5), *S#8023h. See *S#7888h, Shilonite, 1 K +11:29. Some suppose *Shiloni* to be the name of a man; others derive it from *Shiloh*, the city so called; and others derive it from *Shelah*, son of Judah. Ge 38:5, Shelah. Nu 26:20, Shelanites. 1 Ch 4:21. 9:5.

7. **the sons.** 1 Ch 9:7-9. **Joed.** i.e. *witness of Jehovah; Lord of witness; Jehovah is witness*, *S#3133h. It is probable that *Joed* was also called *Hodaviah*, and that *Pedaiah* had also the name of *Hasenuah*. **Kolaiah.** i.e. *the voice of Jehovah*, *S#6964h. Ne 11:7. Je 29:21. (1) A son of Benjamin, who dwelt at Jerusalem after the captivity, Ne 11:7. (2) Father of Ahab, one of the lying prophets, Je 29:21.

8. **Gabbai.** i.e. *exactor of tribute; collective*, *S#1373h. **Sallai.** i.e. *lifted up of the Lord.* Ne +12:20.

9. **Judah.** 1 Ch 9:7, Hodaviah, Hasenuah. **Senuah.** i.e. *the hatred; pointed; light*, *S#5574h. Ne 11:9. 1 Ch 9:7. (1) A Benjamite, father of Hodaviah, 1 Ch 9:7. (2) A man of Benjamin, whose son was second over the city of Jerusalem, Ne 11:9. **second.** 2 K 22:14mg. 2 Ch 34:22mg,n. Zp 1:10.

10. **Jedaiah.** One of Dr. Kennicott's MSS. omits *ben*, "son of," and reads "Jedaiah, Joiarib, Jachin;" which is nearly that of the parallel place. *Joiarib* is merely a contracted form of *Jehoiarib*, by the elision of *hay*. Ne 7:39. 12:19. 1 Ch 9:10, and Jehoiarib. Ezr 2:36. 8:16. **Joiarib.** Ne 12:6.

11. **Seraiah.** *Seraiah* probably had also the name of *Azariah*. 1 Ch 6:7-14. 9:11, Azariah. Ezr 7:1-5. **the ruler.** He had the command over all *secular* matters; as the high priest had over all those which were *spiritual*. Nu 3:32. 1 Ch 9:1. 2 Ch 19:11. 31:13. Ac 5:24.

12. **Adaiah.** i.e. *adorned of Jah.* ver. +5. 1 Ch 9:12, 13. **Pelaliah.** i.e. *Jah has judged; judge of the Lord; intervention of Jah*, *S#6421h. **Amzi.** i.e. *my strength; strong; strength of God*, *S#557h. Ne 11:12. 1 Ch 6:46. (1) One that waited, 1 Ch 6:46. (2) One that willingly dwelt in Jerusalem, Ne 11:12.

13. **Amashai.** i.e. *burdensome; burden borne of the Lord; people of my spoilers; gift of the people*, *S#6023h. **Ahasai.** i.e. *possessor of God; protector; my possessions*, *S#273h.

14. **mighty men.** Jg +6:12. **Zabdiel.** i.e. *endowed of God; portion of God; gift of God*, *S#2068h. Ne 11:14. 1 Ch 27:2. (1) Father of Jashobeam, 1 Ch 27:2. (2) Overseer of mighty men of valor, Ne 11:14. **of one of the great men.** or, of Haggedolim.

15. **Shemaiah.** 1 Ch 9:14, 19.

16. **Shabbethai**. Ne 8:7. **had the oversight of**. Heb. *were* over. 1 Ch 9:28, 29. 26:20. 2 Ch 34:12, 13. 1 Th=5:12, 13. 2 T=2:20, 21. He=13:17. **outward**. Calmet supposes they provided the victuals for the priests, the victims for the sacrifices, the sacerdotal vestments, the sacred vessels, and other necessaries for the service of the temple. Ac 6:2, 3.

17. **Zabdi**. In the parallel passage, instead of *Zichri*, many manuscripts have *Zabdi*, as here: he is also called *Zaccur*, Ne 10:12. 1 Ch 9:15, Zichri. **to begin**. Ne 12:8, 31. 1 Ch 16:4, 41. 25:1-6. **thanksgiving in prayer**. Ph *4:6. 1 Th 5:17, 18. **Bakbukiah**. i.e. *emptying by God; emptied of the Lord; Jah's bottle*, *S#1229h. Ne 11:17. 12:9, 25. **Abda**. i.e. *servant of God; service; servant, worshipper*, *S#5653h. Ne 11:17. 1 K 4:6. (1) Father of Adoniram, 1 K 4:6. (2) Son of Shammua, Ne 11:17.

18. **the holy**. ver. 1. 1 K 11:13. Da 9:24. Mt 24:15. 27:53. Re 11:2. 21:2.

19. **Akkub**. Ne 7:45. 12:25. 1 Ch 9:17-22. **that kept**. Ps 84:10. **the gates**. Heb. at the gates. 1 Ch 16:42mg.

21. **the Nethinims**. *66, Ge +9:3. Ne 3:26, 31. 2 Ch 27:3. **Ophel**. or, the tower. Ne 3:26mg. 2 K +5:24mg. 2 Ch 27:3mg. **Gispa**. i.e. *soothing; caress; touching gently; the clod breathed*, *S#1658h.

22. **overseer**. ver. 9, 14. Ne 12:42. Ac *20:28. **Uzzi**. Ne 12:42. **Bani**. Ne 3:17. 8:7. 9:4, 5. 10:13. **Hashabiah**. Ne 10:11. 12:24. Ezr 8:19. **Mattaniah**. ver. 17. Ne 12:25, 35. 13:13. 1 Ch 9:15. **Of the sons**. ver. 17. Ne 12:46. 1 Ch 25:1-6. **were over**. ver. 11, 16. 1 Ch 9:16-32. **business**. Nu 3:7. 2 Ch 13:10. Ro=12:11. Col=3:24.

23. **the king's commandment**. 1 Ch 9:33. 16:4, 37. 25:6. 28:21. Ezr 6:8, 9. 7:20-24. **a certain portion**. or, a sure ordinance. Ne 9:38. 1 K 8:59. Je 52:34. Da 1:5. **for every day**. Ne 12:47. Ex 5:13mg, 19. 2 K +25:30. 2 Ch 31:16. Lk=11:3. 2 C=4:16.

24. **Pethahiah**. i.e. *whom Jehovah has set free; opening of Jah; Jah sets free; loosed of the Lord*, *S#6611h. Ne 9:5. 11:24. 1 Ch 24:16. Ezr 10:23. (1) The son of Aaron to whom the nineteenth lot fell, 1 Ch 24:16. (2) One of the Levites who took strange wives, Ezr 10:23. (3) A Levite who urged the people to repentance, Ne 9:5. (4) One at the king's hand in all matters concerning the people, Ne 11:24. **Meshezabeel**. Ne 10:21. **Zerah**. Ge 38:30, Zarah. Nu 26:20. Mt 1:3, Zara. **at the king's**. 1 Ch 18:17mg. 23:28mg.

25. **Kirjath-arba**. Jsh 14:15. **Dibon**. Jsh 15:22, Dimonah. **Jekabzeel**. i.e. *God will gather together; he will be gathered of God*, *S#3343h. Jsh 15:21, Kabzeel. **villages thereof**. lit. daughters. Nu +21:25mg.

26. **Moladah**. Jsh 15:26. 19:2. **Beth-phelet**. i.e. *house of escape; place of escape*, *S#1046h. Ne 11:26. Jsh 15:27, Beth-palet.

27. **Hazar-shua**. Jsh 15:28. 19:3. **Beer-sheba**. Ge 21:31. 26:33. Jg 20:1.

28. **Ziklag**. Jsh 15:31. 1 S 27:6. **Mekonah**. i.e. *basis; provision; base, foundation; a settlement*, *S#4368h. Probably the *Mechanam* which Jerome (in *Beth-macha*) places eight miles from Eleutheropolis, towards Jerusalem.

29. **En-rimmon**. i.e. *fountain of the pomegranate*, *S#5884h. *Rimmon* is placed by Eusebius in the south of Judah, 16 miles south of Eleutheropolis. Jsh 15:32, Rimmon. **Zareah**. i.e. *nest of hornets; a hornet; leprosy; smitten with leprosy*, *S#6881h. Ne 11:29. Jsh 15:33. 19:41. Jg 13:2, 25. 16:31. 18:2, 8, 11. 2 Ch

11:10. These variations are only chargeable to the translator; the original being uniformly *Zorah*. Jsh +15:33, Zoreah. +19:41, Zorah. Jg 13:25, Zorah. **Jarmuth**. Jsh 12:11. 15:35.

30. **Zanoah**. Ne 3:13. Jsh 15:34. **Adullam**. Jsh 12:15. Mi 1:15. **Lachish**. Jsh 10:3. 15:39. Is 37:8. **Azekah**. Jsh 15:35. **the valley of Hinnom**. Ne 2:13n. Jsh +*15:8n. 18:16. 2 K 23:10. Je 7:31, 32. 19:2, 6. 32:35.

31. **from Geba**. or, of Geba. Ne 7:30, Gaba. Jsh 18:24. **at Michmash**. or, to Michmash. Ne 7:31, Michmas. 1 S 13:11, 23. Is 10:28. **Aija**. i.e. *heap of ruins*, +S#5857h. Ne 7:32, Ai. Ge +12:8, Hai. Jsh +7:2, Ai. 8:9. Is +10:28, Aiath. **Beth-el**. Ge 28:19. Jsh 18:13.

32. **Anathoth**. i.e. *answers; songs*. Ne 7:27. Jsh 21:18. 1 Ch +7:8. Is 10:30. Je 1:1. **Nob**. 1 S 21:1. 22:19. Is 10:32.

33. **Ramah**. Jsh 18:25. 1 S 7:17. Mt 2:18, Rama. **Gittaim**. 2 S 4:3.

34. **Zeboim**. 1 S 13:18. **Neballot**. i.e. *secret folly*, *S#5041h.

35. **Lod**. Ne 7:37. 1 Ch 8:12. **the valley**. 1 Ch 4:14.

36. **And of**. Jsh ch. 21. 1 Ch 6:54-81. **divisions**. Ge 49:7.

NEHEMIAH 12

The priests and Levites who came up with Zerubbabel, 1-9. The succession of high priests after the captivity, 10, 11. The names of some chief priests, 12-21; and of some eminent Levites, 22-26. The solemnity of dedicating the wall, 27-43. The offices and portions of the priests and Levites, 44-47.

1. We have in this chapter a record of little more than the names of a great many priests and Levites, that were eminent in their day among the returned Jews. It is good to know what our godly ancestors and predecessors were, that we may learn thereby what we should be. **the priests**. Ne 7:7. Ezr 2:1, 2. **Zerubbabel**. 1 Ch 3:17-19. Ezr 3:8. 4:2. 5:2. Hg 1:1, 12, 14. 2:2, 21-23. Zc 4:6-10. Mt 1:12, 13, Zorobabel, Salathiel. **Jeshua**. ver. 10. Zc 3:1-9. 6:11, Joshua. **Seraiah**. ver. 12-21. Ne 10:2-8. Ezr 2:2.

2. **Amariah**. i.e. *saying of Jah*. Ezr +7:3. **Malluch**. ver. +14, Melicu. Ne +10:4.

3. **Shechaniah**. i.e. *neighbor of Jah*. ver. 14, Shebaniah. 1 Ch +3:22. **Rehum**. i.e. *compassionate; merciful*. ver. 15, Harim. *S#7348h: Ne 3:17. 10:25. 12:3. Ezr 2:2. Also Ezr 4:8, 9, 17, 23. (1) One who returned with Zerubbabel, Ezr 2:2. Called Nehum, Ne 7:7. (2) A Persian governor in Samaria, Ezr 4:8. (3) A Levite who helped build the wall, Ne 3:17. (4) One who sealed the covenant, Ne 10:25. (5) One of the priests who returned with Zerubbabel, Ne 12:3. Perhaps the same as Number 1. **Meremoth**. ver. 15, Meraioth.

4. **Iddo**. i.e. *timely*. Ezr +5:1. **Ginnetho**. i.e. *gardener; his protection*, *S#1599h. Instead of *Ginnetho*, many MSS. and Vulgate have *Ginnethon*. ver. 16, Ginnethon. **Abijah**. Lk 1:5, Abia.

5. **Miamin**. i.e. *on the right hand; from the right hand*. ver. 17, Miniamin. *S#4326h: Ne 10:7. 12:5. 1 Ch 24:+9, Mijamin. Ezr 10:25. (1) The son of Aaron, to whom the sixth lot fell, 1 Ch 24:9. (2) One of those who took strange wives, Ezr 10:25. (3) One who sealed the covenant, Ne 10:7. (4) A priest who came up with Zerubbabel, Ne 12:5. Called also Melicu, Ne 12:14; and Miniamin, Ne 12:17, 41. **Maadiah**. i.e. *pleasant-*

ness; ornament of the Lord; adorned of Jah; shaken of Jah, *S#4573h. The variation between *Modiah* and *Maadiah* merely arises from the elision of *wav;* the LXX. however, in ver. 17, have "Moadai." ver. 17, Moadiah. **Bilgah.** i.e. *cheerfulness; desistance; consolation, reviving,* *S#1083h. Ne 12:5, 18. 1 Ch 24:14. (1) A descendant of Aaron, 1 Ch 24:14. (2) A chief of the priests who returned from Babylon with Zerubbabel, Ne 12:5, 7. Compare Bilgai, Ne +10:8.

6. **Shemaiah.** i.e. *heard of Jah.* 1 Ch 9:16. **Joiarib.** Ne 11:10. 1 Ch 9:10, Jehoiarib. Ezr +8:16.

7. **Sallu.** i.e. *elevation.* 1 Ch +9:7. The variation of "Sallu" and "Sallai" is simply caused by the mutation of *wav* and *yood.* ver. 20, Sallai. **Amok.** i.e. *to be deep; deep, unsearchable,* *S#5987h. Ne 12:7, 20. **the chief.** "The chief of the priests" seem to have been the heads of the courses established by David, 1 Ch 24:18. **of Jeshua.** ver. 1. Ezr 3:2. Hg 1:1. Zc 3:1.

8. **Jeshua.** Ne 7:43. 9:4. 10:9-13. **Mattaniah.** Ne 11:17, 22. **the thanksgiving.** That is, *The psalms of thanksgiving.* or, confession. ver. 24. 1 Ch 9:33.

9. **over against.** Ps 134:1-3. **watches.** or, charges. Young notes, of which there were 24; see 1 Ch 23:6; 26:12.

10. **Jeshua.** i.e. *a savior.* ver. 26. 1 Ch 6:3-15. The high-priest. **Joiakim.** i.e. *whom Jehovah sets up; Jehovah will establish,* *S#3113h. Ne 12:10, 10, 12, 26. **Joiada.** i.e. *whom Jehovah cares for; Jehovah-known,* *S#3111h. Ne 3:6, Jehoiada. 12:10, 11, 22. 13:28. (1) A son of Paseah, who repaired a gate of Jerusalem, Ne 3:6, Jehoiada. (2) A high priest, great grandson of Jeshua, Ne 12:10. **Eliashib.** Ne 3:1. 13:4, 7, 28.

11. **Jonathan.** i.e. *Jah hath given.* 1 S +13:2. **Jaddua.** i.e. *known; celebrated,* *S#3037h. Ne 10:21. 12:11, 22. (1) One who sealed the covenant, Ne 10:21. (2) One of the high priests, Ne 12:11, 22. *Jaddua* is supposed to be *Jaddus* the high priest, who went in his pontifical robes to meet Alexander the Great, when advancing to destroy Jerusalem; who was so struck with his appearance, that he forbore all hostilities, and granted many privileges to the Jews (332 B.C.). According to Eusebius, he was high priest from A.M. 3665 to 3982. Died about the same time as Alexander, 323 B.C. (Josephus, Antiq. xi. viii. 4, 5, 7). It is evident that he was high priest long after the events which are mentioned at the close of this book, for Joiada then filled that office, Ne 13:28; and as "Darius the Persian" (ver. 22) is supposed to mean the last king of Persia, who was subdued by Alexander, about a hundred years after the principal transactions recorded in this book, this verse, and the twenty-second, must have been added by another hand after the death of Nehemiah (ver. 26).

12. **the chief.** ver. 22. 1 Ch 9:33, 34. 15:12. 24:6-31. **Seraiah.** i.e. *head of Jah.* ver. 1. 2 S +8:17. **Meraiah.** i.e. *rebellion against Jah; lifted up of the Lord,* *S#4811h.

14. **Melicu.** i.e. *my reign* or *counsel; my royalty,* *S#4409h. ver. 2, Malluch. In this passage the form "Malluchi," in itself an unessential variation, is probably due to dittography. The final letter of "Malluchi" is the initial letter of the following word, and moreover is not found in the Septuagint. The consonants of "Malluchi" are written in the Hebrew text, but were read "Melicu" (*Davis Bible Dictionary*). **Shebaniah.** Two MSS. and Vulgate in ver. 3, have *Shebaniah;* and here

many MSS. have *Shechaniah.* ver. 3, Shechaniah.

15. **Harim.** ver. 3, Rehum. **Meraioth.** i.e. *rebellious; rebellions.* ver. 3, Meremoth. *S#4812h. Ne 11:11. 12:15. 1 Ch 6:6, 7, 52. 9:11. Ezr 7:3. (1) One in the line of priests before the captivity, 1 Ch 6:6, 7, 52; and a progenitor of Ezra, Ezr 7:3. (2) A priest of the line of Azariah, or Seraiah, 1 Ch 9:11; Ne 11:11. (3) One in the succession of high priests, Ne 12:15. **Helkai.** i.e. *apportioned; portion of the Lord,* *S#2517h.

16. **Iddo.** ver. 4. **Ginnethon.** ver. 4, Ginnetho.

17. **Miniamin.** i.e. *from* or *on the right hand,* *S#4509h. Ne 12:17, 41. 2 Ch 31:15. (1) One of those in charge of receiving and distributing the freewill offerings in the temple in the time of Hezekiah, 2 Ch 31:15. (2) A father's house in the days of the high priest Joiakim, Ne 12:17. (3) A priest who blew a trumpet at the dedication of the wall of Jerusalem, Ne 12:41. The LXX. and Vulgate have here *Miamin.* ver. 5, Miamin. **Moadiah.** i.e. *set time of Jah; assembly or festival of Jah,* *S#4153h. ver. 5, Maadiah. **Piltai.** i.e. *flight; deliverance of the Lord; my escapes,* *S#6408h.

18. **Bilgah.** i.e. *cheerfulness.* ver. +5. **Shemaiah.** ver. 6.

19. **Joiarib.** i.e. *Jah contends.* Ezr +8:16. **Mattenai.** i.e. *liberal; my gifts; gift of the Lord,* *S#4982h. Ne 12:19. Ezr 10:33, 37. (1) A priest, head of the father's house Joiarib in the time of Joiakim, Ne 12:19. (2, 3) Two who put away his strange wife, Ezr 10:33, 37.

20. **Sallai.** i.e. *lifted up* or *basket weaver; lifted up of the Lord; my baskets; my castings up.* ver. 7, Sallu. *S#5543h. Ne 11:8. 12:20. See also for S#5543h: Ne 12:7, Sallu. Also Nu 25:14, Salu. Also 1 Ch +9:7. Ne 11:7, Sallu. **Kallai.** i.e. *swift messenger of Jehovah; lightly esteemed of the Lord; my swiftnesses (or light ones),* *S#7040h.

22. **Eliashib.** ver. 10, 11. **recorded.** ver. 12, 13.

23. **the book.** 1 Ch 9:14, etc.

24. **Hashabiah.** i.e. *reckoning of Jah.* ver. 8. Ne 8:7. 9:4. 10:9-13. 1 Ch +9:14. **over against.** ver. 9. **to praise.** 2 S 14:25h. 2 Ch 5:13. **to give thanks.** ver. 8, 27, 31, 38, 40. Ne 11:17. 1 Ch 16:4, 7, 35. **according.** 1 Ch ch. 23, 25, 26. **the man of God.** ver. 36. Dt 33:1. Jsh 14:6. 1 K 17:24. 2 Ch 8:14. 1 T 6:11. 2 T 3:17. **ward.** ver. 9. 1 Ch 25:8. 26:16. Ezr 3:10, 11.

25. **Mattaniah.** ver. 8, 9. Ne 11:17-19. 1 Ch 9:14-17. **keeping.** 1 Ch 23:32. 26:12. Is 21:8. **thresholds.** or, treasuries, or assemblies. 1 Ch 26:15mg, 17.

26. **Joiakim.** ver. 10. **Nehemiah.** Ne 8:9. Ezr 7:6, 11.

27. A.M. 3559. B.C. 445. **the dedication.** Jerusalem was the holy city, and the wall was built under the immediate superintendence and blessing of Jehovah: it was therefore proper that it should be dedicated to that God who was there worshipped by solemn praises, prayers, and sacrifices. The dedication seems to have consisted in processions of the most eminent persons around the walls, with thanksgivings to God, who had enabled them to bring the work to so happy a conclusion; and, no doubt, to all this were added a particular *consecration* of the city to God, and the most earnest *invocation* that he would take it under his guardianship, and defend it and its inhabitants against their enemies. Dt 20:5. Ps 30, title. **out.** Ne 11:20. 1 Ch 15:4, 12, 13. 25:6. 26:31, 32. 2 Ch 5:13. 29:4-11, 30. Ezr 8:15-20. **gladness.** Ne 8:17. Dt 16:11. 2 S 6:12.

2 Ch 29:22. Ezr 6:16. Ps 98:4-6. 100:1, 2. Ph 4:4. **thanksgivings.** 1 Ch 13:8. 15:16, 28. 16:5, 42. 23:5. 25:1-6. 2 Ch 5:13. 7:6. Ezr 3:10, 11. Ps 81:1-4. 92:1-3. 149:3. 150:2-5. Re 5:8.

28. **plain.** Ne 6:2. **Netophathi.** i.e. *distillation; a dropping, prophesy,* ✛S#5200h. 2 S +23:28, Netophathite. 1 Ch 2:54. 9:16.

29. **the house.** Or, *Beth-Gilgal,* a village erected where the Israelites encamped after they had crossed the Jordan. Dt 11:30. Jsh 5:9. 10:43. **Geba.** Ne 11:31. Jsh 21:17. 1 Ch 6:60. **Azmaveth.** Ezr 2:24.

30. **themselves.** Ge 35:2. Ex 19:10, 15. Nu 19:2-20. 2 Ch 29:5, 34. Ezr 6:21. Jb 1:5. He 5:1, 3. **purified.** He 9:22, 23.

31. **the princes.** 1 Ch 13:1. 28:1. 2 Ch 5:2. **two great.** ver. 38, 40. **thanks.** ∫121E1, Ge +25:23. Heb. celebrations; "celebrations," or thanksgivings, put for the choirs who rendered them, by the figure Metonymy of Effect. **dung gate.** Ne 2:13. 3:13, 14.

32. **Hoshaiah.** i.e. *saved by Jah; Jah has saved; set free of the Lord,* ✶S#1955h. Ne 12:32. Je 42:1. 43:2. (1) One who assisted at the dedication of the wall, Ne 12:32. (2) Father of Jezaniah, captain of the forces, Je 42:1. (3) Father of Azariah, Je 43:2.

33. **Azariah.** Ne 10:2-7.

35. **with trumpets.** Nu 10:2-10. Jsh 6:4. 2 Ch 5:12. 13:12. **Zechariah.** Ne 11:17. 1 Ch 6:39-43. 25:2. 26:10, 11.

36. **Azarael.** i.e. *God helped,* ✛S#5832h. See on 1 Ch +12:6, Azareel. **Milalai.** i.e. *eloquent; my utterances; talkative,* ✶S#4450h. **Gilalai.** i.e. *rolled off of the Lord; my rolls; my dung; weighty,* ✶S#1562h. **Maai.** i.e. *compassionate; compassion; my bowels; sympathetic,* ✶S#4597h. **musical instruments.** 1 Ch 16:42n. 23:5. 2 Ch 8:14. Am 6:5. **the man of God.** ver. 24. **Ezra.** Ezr 7:1. 8:1.

37. **the fountain gate.** Ne 2:14. 3:15, etc. **the stairs.** Jerusalem was built on very uneven ground, some hills being enclosed within the walls; there was a necessity, therefore, for *steps,* by which to ascend and descend; probably similar to what is seen in the city of Bristol. Ne 3:15. 2 S 5:7-9. **water gate.** Ne 3:26. 8:1, 3, 16.

38. **other.** ver. 31. **thanks.** ∫121E1, Ge +25:33. See on ver. 31. **tower.** Ne 3:11. **broad.** Ne 3:8.

39. **the gate of Ephraim.** Ne 8:16. 2 K 14:13. **the old gate.** Ne 3:6. **the fish gate.** Ne 3:3. Zp 1:10. **the tower.** Ne 3:1. Je 31:38. **the sheep gate.** Ne 3:32. Jn 5:2. **the prison gate.** Ne 3:25, 31h. Je 20:1, 2. *32:2. 40. **two companies.** ver. 31, 32. Ps 42:4. 47:6-9. ch. 134. **thanks.** ∫121E1, Ge +25:33. ver. 31n. **rulers.** ✶S#5461h. Ne 2:16, 16. 4:14, 19. 5:7, 17. 7:5. 13:11. Ezr 9:2. Is 41:25. Je 51:23, 28, 57. Ezk 23:6, 12, 23.

41. **with trumpets.** ver. 35. 2 Ch +5:12.

42. **sang loud.** Heb. made *their voice* to be heard. Ps 81:1. 95:1. 98:4-9. 100:1, 2. Is 12:5, 6. **Jezrahiah.** i.e. *God is risen; brought to the light of the Lord,* ✶S#3156h. Ne 12:42. 1 Ch +*7:3, 3, Izrahiah. **overseer.** or, inspector. Ne 11:9, 14, 22. Ge 41:34mg.

43. **offered.** Nu 10:10. Dt 12:11, 12. 1 Ch 29:21, 22. 2 Ch 7:5-7, 10. 29:35, 36. Ps 27:6. **God.** 2 Ch 20:27. Jb 34:29. Ps 28:7. 30:11, 12. 92:4. Is 61:3. 66:10-14. Je 33:11. Jn 16:22. **the wives also.** Ne 8:2. Ex 15:+20n, 21. Jg +21:21n. 1 S 18:6. 2 S ◑1:20. 1 K *4:23. 1 Ch 15:20n. 2 Ch 20:13. Ps 148:11-13. Je 31:13. Mt 21:9, 15. Ep 5:19. Ja 5:13. **the children.** Dt +29:11. 2 Ch 20:13. Ps 148:12. Jl *2:16. Mt 14:21. 15:38. 19:13-

15. 21:15. Mk 9:36, 37. Lk +18:15. 2 T +*3:15. **the joy.** 1 S 4:5. Ezr 3:13.

44. **some.** Ne 10:37-39. 13:5, 12, 13. 2 Ch 13:11, 12. 31:11-13. **chambers.** 1 Ch 9:26. 26:21-26. **treasures.** Ne 7:70, 71. 10:38. 13:12mg. **offerings.** Young renders, heave offerings. Ne 10:+37, 39. 13:5. **firstfruits.** Le +*23:10. **fields of the cities.** Jsh 21:12. 1 Ch 6:56. **of the law.** that is, *appointed by the law.* **Judah rejoiced.** Heb. the joy of Judah. **Levites.** Nu 3:10. 8:24, 25. 1 Ch 23:28. 2 Ch 5:11, 12. Pr 8:34. Is 40:31. Ro 12:7. **waited.** Heb. stood.

45. **the singers.** 1 Ch ch. 25, 26. 2 Ch +35:15. **porters.** 1 Ch +23:5. **ward of the purification.** That is, *they suffered no unclean person to enter the temple.* Le 12:*4, 5. 13:8, 35. 15:31n. 1 Ch 23:28. 2 Ch 23:6. Is 35:8. Ac 16:3. Ga 2:3. **commandment of.** 1 Ch 25:1. 26:1. 2 Ch 8:14.

46. **and Asaph.** 1 Ch 25:1, etc. 2 Ch 29:30. Ps 73, 83, titles. **of old.** Heb. *kedem,* Mi +5:2.

47. **Zerubbabel.** ver. 1, 12, 26. **gave.** Ne 10:35-39. 13:10-12. 2 Ch 31:5, 6. Ml *3:8-10. Ga 6:6. **and they.** That is, the people separated, or set apart, the *tenth* of the produce of their lands for the use of the Levites; and the Levites separated the *tenth* of their tithes for the priests. Nu 18:21-29. **every day.** Ne 11:23. Ge 39:10. Ex +5:13mg. 2 K +25:30. 2 Ch 31:16. **sanctified.** that is, *set apart.* Ne 3:1.

NEHEMIAH 13

On reading the law, Israel separates from the mixed multitude, 1-3. Eliashib, having, during Nehemiah's absence, prepared a chamber at the temple for Tobiah, Nehemiah on his return, being grieved and indignant, causes the chambers to be cleansed, 4-9. He reforms abuses concerning tithes and offerings, 10-14. He prevents the profanation of the sabbath, 15-18. He shuts the gates, and sets a watch at them, 19-22. He opposes those who had married strange wives, and drives away the grandson of Eliashib, 23-28. His other services and prayers, 29-31.

1. **that day.** Some suppose that the events recorded in these verses took place several years after those related in the preceding chapter, while Nehemiah was absent at the Persian court; but the introductory language, *on that day,* seems rather to imply that they occurred immediately, or at least *about that time.* **they read.** Heb. there was read. Ne 8:3-8. 9:3. Dt 3:11, 12. 2 K 23:2. Is *34:16. Lk 4:16-19. 10:26. Ac 13:15. 15:21. **audience.** Heb. ears. **the Ammonite.** ver. 23. Dt *23:3-5. Is ch. 15, 16. Je ch. 48. Ezk 25:1-11. Am 2:1-3. **Moabite.** Ne 2:10, 19. 4:3. Ps 83:7-9. Je 49:1-6. Am 1:13-15. **for ever.** Heb. *olam,* Ex +*12:24.

2. **Because.** Dt *23:4. Mt 25:40. **hired Balaam.** Nu 22:3-6. Jsh 24:9, 10. **our God.** Nu 23:8-11, 18. 24:5-10. Dt *23:5. Ps 109:28. Mi 6:5.

3. **when they.** Ps 19:7-11. 119:9, 11. Pr 6:23. Ro 3:20. **that they separated.** Ne 9:2. 10:28. Ge 12:4. Ex 12:38. Ezr 10:11. Is 51:2. Mt 10:37. Ja 1:27. **the mixed.** Ex 12:38. Nu 11:4.

4. **Eliashib.** ver. 7. Ne 12:10. **having the oversight of.** Heb. being set over. Ne 12:44. **the chamber.** i.e. of the chambers, as appears from the following verse, and from ver. 9, where it is called *chambers,* and from the nature of the thing, the high priest having the chief power over the house of God, and all the chambers

belonging to it. The singular number for the plural (Matthew Poole). ✗96F1. Figure of speech Heterosis of Number, the Singular for the Plural, Ge +3:8. **allied.** ver. 28. Ne 6:17, 18.

5. **a great.** Ne 10:38. 12:44. 2 Ch 34:11. **meat offering.** Le +*23:13. **which was commanded to be given to the.** Heb. the commandment of the. Nu 18:21-24.

6. **But.** Ex 32:1. 2 Ch 24:17, 18. Mt 13:25. **was.** Nehemiah came to Jerusalem in the twentieth year of Artaxerxes, and remained there till the thirty-second, being twelve years; then returned to Babylon; and probably, after about a year, got leave to revisit his brethren, and found matters as here stated. **the two.** Ne 2:1. 5:14. **after certain days.** Heb. at the end of days. Ne 2:5, 6. Ge +4:3mg. +*24:55mg. Le 25:29. 1 K 17:7mg. **obtained I.** *or,* I earnestly requested. 1 S 20:6, 28.

7. **understood.** Ezr 9:1. 1 C 1:11. **Tobiah.** Ne 4:3. **in preparing.** ver. 1, 5. La 1:10. Mt 21:12, 13. Ac 21:28, 29.

8. **it grieved.** Ezr 9:3, 4. 10:1. Ps 69:9. **I cast.** Mk 11:15-17. Jn *2:13-17.

9. **they cleansed.** Ne 12:45. 2 Ch 29:5, 15-19. **meat offering.** Le +*23:13.

10. **the portions.** Ne 10:37. 12:47. Ml 1:6-14. *3:8. 1 T *5:17, 18. **to his field.** Nu 35:2.

11. **contended.** ver. 17, 25. Ne 5:6-13. Jb *31:34. Pr √28:4. Ep *5:11. Ju √3. **Why is the house.** Ne 10:39. 1 S 2:17. Ml 3:8-11. **place.** Heb. standing. 2 Ch 30:16mg.

12. **brought.** Ne 10:37-39. 12:44. Le 27:30. Nu 18:20-26. Dt 14:22. **treasuries.** *or,* storehouses. Ml *3:10.

13. **I made.** Ne 12:44. 2 Ch 31:12-15. **Shelemiah.** Ne 3:30. **Pedaiah.** Ne 8:4. **next to them.** Heb. at their hand. Ne 3:2mg. 2 Ch +17:15mg. **Zaccur.** Ne 10:12. **Mattaniah.** Ne 11:22. 12:35. **counted faithful.** Ne 7:2. 2 K 12:15. 22:7. Lk +*12:42. √16:10-12. Ac 6:3. 1 C=4:1, 2. 1 T 1:12. 3:10. 3 J 5. **their office.** Heb. *it was* upon them. **to distribute.** 2 Ch 31:14-16. Lk=*12:42, 43. Ac 4:35. 6:1.

14. **Remember me.** ver. 22, 31. Ne 5:19. Ps 122:6-9. He √6:10. Re *3:5. **wipe not.** If thou wert strict to mark what is done amiss, even *my good deeds* must be *wiped out:* but, Lord, remember me in thy mercy, and let my upright conduct be acceptable to Thee! By some, Nehemiah has been thought to deal too much with God on the principle of *merit.* That he wished God to *remember him for good* is sufficiently evident—and who does not wish the same?—but that he *expected heaven for his good deeds* does not appear; for it is perfectly clear that he expected nothing from God but through the *greatness of his mercy.* ver. 22. **good deeds.** Heb. kindnesses. ✗121C1B, Ge +20:13. 2 Ch 32:32mg. **house.** 1 Ch 29:3. 2 Ch 24:16. 31:20, 21. Ezr 7:20, 24, 27. Ps 122:6-9. **offices.** *or,* observations. 2 Ch 7:6. or, charges. Ne 4:9, 22, 23. 7:3.

15. **treading wine.** Ex *20:8-11. 34:21. 35:2. Ne *58:13. Ezk 20:13. **burdens.** Ne 10:31. Nu 15:32-36. Je 17:21, 22, 24, 27. **I testified.** ver. 21. Ne 9:29. Dt 8:19. 2 Ch 24:19. Ps 50:7. Je 42:19. Mi 6:3. Ac 2:40.

20:21. Ga 5:3. Ep 4:17. 1 Th 4:6. Re 22:18, 19.

16. **men of Tyre.** Ex 23:12. Dt 5:14. Ezk 27:3.

17. **I contended.** ver. 11, 25. Ne 5:7. Ps 82:1, 2. Pr √28:4. Is 1:10. Je 5:5. 13:18. 22:2, etc. Mi 3:1, 9. Ju √3. **profane the sabbath day.** Ezk 20:12. 22:26, 31. 23:38.

18. **Did not your.** Ezr 9:13-15. Je 17:21-23, 27. 44:9, 22. Ezk 23:8, 26. Zc 1:4-6. **ye bring more.** Le 26:18, 28. Nu 32:14. Jsh 22:17, 18.

19. **began to be.** Le 23:32. **I commanded.** Ne 7:3. Ex 31:14-17. Je 17:19-22.

21. **I testified.** See on ver. 15. **about the wall.** Heb. before the wall. **I will lay.** Ezr 7:26. Ro 13:3, 4. 1 P 2:14.

22. **I commanded.** Ne 7:64, 65. 12:30. 2 K 23:4. 1 Ch 15:12-14. 2 Ch 29:4, 5, 24, 27, 30. Is 49:23. **cleanse.** Ne 12:10. **sanctify.** Dt 5:12. **Remember.** ver. 14, 31. Ne 5:19. Ps 132:1-5. Is 38:3. 2 C 1:12. 2 T 4:7, 8. **spare me.** Ps 25:6, 7. 51:1. 130:3, 4, 7. 143:1, 2. **greatness.** *or,* multitude. Ps 5:7. Is 55:7. **thy mercy.** T#1127. Ge 19:19, 20. Nu 14:19. Dt 4:31. 1 K 3:6, 7. Ps 25:6. 31:16. 44:26. 51:1. 69:13, 16. 86:4, 5, 14, 15. 106:44, 45. 109:21, 26. Is 63:15. La *3:22, 23. Da 9:18. Jl 2:13.

23. **married.** Heb. made to dwell *with them.* Ne 10:30. Ezr 9:2, 11, 12. 10:10, 44. 2 C 6:14. **Ashdod.** Ne 4:7. Jsh 13:3. 1 S 5:1, 3, 6. Zp 2:7. Zc 9:6. **Ammon.** See on ver. 1-3. Ge 19:38.

24. **could not speak.** Heb. they discerned not to speak. **each people.** Heb. people and people. Zp *3:9.

25. **I contended.** ver. 11, 17. Pr √28:4. Je *9:3. Ju +√3. **cursed.** *or,* reviled. ver. 2h. Ne 5:13. ☾+10:29. Dt 27:14-26. Ps 15:4. Lk 11:45, 46. ✠S#7043h: Ge 8:21. Dt 23:4. Jsh 24:9. 2 S 16:7. **smote.** Dt 25:2, 3. Ezr 7:26. **plucked.** Is 50:6. **made them.** Ne 10:+29, 30. Dt 6:13. 2 Ch 15:12-15. Ezr 10:5. **Ye shall not.** Ex *34:16. Dt *7:3. 2 C √6:14.

26. **Did not Solomon.** 1 K *11:1-8. Ec *7:26. **yet among.** 2 S 12:24, 25. 1 K *3:13. 2 Ch *1:12. *9:22. **who was beloved.** 2 S *12:24.

27. **Shall we then.** 1 S 30:24. **to transgress.** Ezr 10:2.

28. **And one.** Josephus relates, that this young man was named *Manasseh*; and that at his request, Sanballat and the Samaritans built their temple upon mount Gerizim, in opposition to that at Jerusalem, at which he officiated, in some measure, according to the Mosaic ritual. Dt 27:4n. Jn 4:20. **Joiada.** Ne 12:10, 22. **Eliashib.** Ne 3:1. **son in law.** ver. 4, 5. Ne 6:17-19. **Sanballat.** Ne 2:19. **I chased.** ver. 25. Ps 101:8. Pr 20:8, 26. Ro 13:3, 4.

29. **Remember.** Ne 6:14. Ps 59:5-13. 2 T 4:14. **because they have defiled.** Heb. for the defilings of. Le 21:1-7. **the covenant.** Nu 16:9, 10. 25:12, 13. 1 S *2:30. Ml 2:4-8, 10-12.

30. **cleansed.** Ne 10:30. **strangers.** Ne 9:2. Ex 12:43 (✱S#5236h). Ps 18:44, 45. **appointed.** Ne 12:1-26. 1 Ch ch. 23-26.

31. **the wood.** Ne 10:34n. **at times appointed.** Ezr 10:14. **Remember.** ver. 14, 22. Ps 25:7. 26:8, 9. 106:4. Lk *23:42.

ESTHER

ESTHER 1

*Ahasuerus, king of Persia, makes a royal feast, 1-
9. He sends for Vashti, his queen, who refuses to come,
10-12. By the advice of his counselors, he divorces
her, and asserts, by a public decree, the authority of
men over their wives, 13-22.*

1. A.M. 3540. B.C. 464. **Ahasuerus.** i.e. *lion king;
a prince clothed with majesty; I will be silent and poor,*
✻S#325h. Est 1:1, 1, 2, 9, 10, 15, 16, 17, 19. 2:1,
12, 16, 21. 3:1, 6, 7, 8, 12. 6:2. 7:5. 8:1, 7, 10, 12.
9:2, 20, 30. 10:1, 3. Ezr 4:6. Da 9:1. (1) A king of
Persia, B.C. 529-521, who succeeded Cyrus and preceded Darius, in whose time the rebuilding of the
temple at Jerusalem was interrupted, Ezr 4:6. He was
probably the Cambyses of profane history. (2) A king
of the Medes, B.C. 594; was the one called Astyages
in profane history, Da 9:1. (3) A king of Persia, B.C.
485, who seems to have been subsequent to Darius,
and is undoubtedly the Xerxes of profane history, Est
1:1; 8:1, 7. Prideaux (*Connection,* v. i. pp. 361-364,
1749 ed.) has shown satisfactorily that *Ahasuerus* was
the *Artaxerxes Longimanus* of the Greeks, agreeably
to the Septuagint and Josephus. See Note on Ezr 6:14n.
Ezr 4:6. Da 9:1. **from India.** i.e. *praise; murmuring
or roaring of the sea; flee ye away; give ye thanks,*
✻S#1912h. Est 1:1. 8:9h. Is 18:1. 37:9. **an hundred
and.** Da 6:1.

2. **sat.** 2 S 7:1. 1 K 1:46. Da 4:4. **Shushan.** Est
2:3. 3:15. 4:16. 9:12-15. Ne 1:1. Da 8:2.

3. A.M. 3542. B.C. 462. **he made.** Est 2:18. Ge
40:20. 1 K 3:15. Da 5:1. Mk 6:21. **of Persia.** ver. 14.
Ezr 1:2. Is 21:2. Je 51:11. Da 5:28. 8:20. **Media.** i.e.
a garment; extended of the Lord; measured, ✛S#4074h.
Est 1:3, 14, 18. 10:2. Is 21:2. Da 8:20. For other renderings of S#4074h, see Madai, Ge +10:2; Medes, Ezr
+6:2. A country of Asia, the modern Iraq. **the nobles.**
Da 3:2, 3. 6:1, 6, 7.

4. **When he.** Is 39:2. Ezk 28:5. Da 4:30. **the riches.**
Ps 76:1-4. 145:5, 12, 13. Da 2:37-44. 7:9-14. Mt 4:8.
6:13. Ro 9:23. Ep 1:18. Col 1:27. Re 4:11. **excellent.**
1 Ch 29:11, 12, 25. Jb 40:10. Ps 21:5. 45:3. 93:1. Da
4:36. 5:18. 2 P 1:16, 17.

5. **present.** Heb. found. Est 4:16mg. Ge 19:15mg.
Jg +20:48mg. 1 S 13:15mg. 21:3mg. 2 K 19:4mg.
2 Ch 5:11mg. +29:29mg. 30:21mg. 31:1mg. 34:32mg,
33mg. 35:17mg. Is 37:4mg. Zc 11:6mg. **seven days.**
2 Ch 7:8, 9. 30:21-25.

6. **white.** Ex 26:1, 31, 32, 36, 37. **blue.** *or,* violet.
Est 8:15. Ex 25:4n. **fastened.** 1 Ch 24:6 (taken). Ec
9:12 (caught). SS 3:8 (hold). **cords.** Jsh 2:15. 2 S 8:2.
fine linen. Est 8:15. 1 Ch 4:21. 15:27. **purple.** Est
8:15. Ex 25:4. **rings.** SS 5:14. **pillars.** Ex 13:21, 22.
14:19. **marble.** SS 5:15. **the beds.** These were *couches,*
covered with gold and silver cloth, on which the guests
reclined; for the Orientals do not sit, but *recline* at
their meals. Est 7:8. Ge 47:31. 48:2. SS 3:7-10. Is
57:1. Ezk 23:41. Am 2:8. *6:4. **pavement.** 2 Ch 7:3.
Ezk 40:17, 18. 42:3. **red,** etc. *or,* of porphyre, and
marble, and alabaster, and stone of blue color.

7. **vessels of gold.** 1 K 10:21. 2 Ch 9:20. Da 5:2-4.

royal wine. Heb. wine of the kingdom. **state of the
king.** Heb. hand of the king. 2 Ch 9:3, 4.

8. **none did compel.** Every person drank what he
pleased. Among the Greeks, however, each guest was
obliged to *keep the round,* or leave the company: hence
the proverb, "Drink, or begone." Mr. Herbert, in his
poem "The Church Porch," has severely reprobated
this vile custom. Je *35:8. 51:7. Hab √2:15, 16. **the
officers.** Jn 2:8.

9. **the queen.** Est 5:4, 8.

10. **the heart.** Ge 43:34. Jg 16:25. 1 S 25:36, 37.
2 S 13:28. Pr *20:1. Ec 7:2-4. 10:19. Ep √5:18, 19. **Mehuman.** i.e. *steadfast; faithful; their discomfiture,*
✻S#4104h. **Biztha.** i.e. *a eunuch; despite; unfruitful,
gelding; booty,* ✻S#968h. **Harbona.** i.e. *an ass-driver;
warlike; martial,* ✻S#2726h. Est 7:9, Harbonah. **Bigtha.** i.e. *a gardener; given by fortune,* i.e. *the sun;
in the wine-press,* ✻S#903h. **Abagtha.** i.e. *gardener;
father of the wine press; fortune, by fortune,* ✻S#5h.
Zethar. i.e. *a star; very great; stair; searcher,*
✻S#2242h. **Carcas.** i.e. *an eagle; covering of a lamb;
severe,* ✻S#3752h. **chamberlains.** *or,* eunuchs. Est
2:15, 21. Ge +*37:36mg. 2 K +9:32mg. Da 1:3-5,
18, 19.

11. **To bring.** Pr *16:9. √23:29-33. Mk 6:21, 22.
1 C *5:11. **Vashti.** i.e. *beautiful woman; drinking; doubling; wherefore waste thou away; wherefore banquet
thou,* ✻S#2060h. Est 1:9, 11, 12, 15, 16, 17, 19. 2:1,
4, 17. **beauty.** Ps 45:11. 50:2. Pr 6:25. Is +*33:17.
fair to look on. Heb. good of countenance. Ge
*24:16mg. +29:17. 1 S 25:3. 2 S 14:25. Pr *31:30.

12. **the queen.** This refusal of Vashti's, to expose
herself to the view of such a group of drunken Bacchana-
lians was highly praiseworthy, and became the dignity
of her rank and the modesty of her sex. **refused.** Ge
3:16. 37:35. √39:8. Ps +*101:4. +*119:63. Pr *1:10.
Da *1:8. 11:17. Ep 5:22, 24. He *11:24-26. 1 P 3:1.
*4:3, 4. **by his chamberlains.** Heb. which *was* by the
hand of *his* eunuchs. 1 K +16:12mg. **was the king.**
Pr 19:12. 20:2. Da 2:12. 3:13, 19. Na 1:6. Re 6:16,
17. **burned.** Ex 32:19. Dt 29:20. Ps 74:1. 79:5.

13. **the wise.** Je 10:7. Da 2:2, 12, 27. 4:6, 7. 5:7.
Mt 2:1. **knew.** 1 Ch +√12:32n. Mt 16:3. **the times.**
√121P1, 1 Ch +12:32.

14. **Carshena.** i.e. *spoiling of war,* or *black; distinguished; illustrious; change thou the lamb (or head,
or pasture),* ✻S#3771h. **Shethar.** i.e. *a star; appointed
searcher; a remnant,* ✻S#8369h. **Admatha.** i.e. *human;
having a dark complexion; her earthiness; man's chamber,* ✻S#133h. **Tarshish.** i.e. *breaking, subjection.* Ge
+10:4. **Meres.** i.e. *lofty, worthy; elevated; moisture;
fractured,* ✻S#4825h. **Marsena.** i.e. *lofty, worthy;
high; bitter is the thorn bush,* ✻S#4826h. **Memucan.**
i.e. *established, prepared; strong in authority; their
poverty,* ✻S#4462h. Est 1:14, 16, 21. **the seven.** Ezr
7:14. **saw.** Ge +43:3. 2 K 25:19. Mt 18:10. Re 22:4.
face. √22A4, Ge +19:13.

15. **What shall we do.** Heb. What to do. Est 6:6.

16. **Vashti.** This reasoning was inconsequent and
false. Vashti had not *generally* disobeyed the king,
therefore she could be no *precedent* for the *general*

conduct of the Persian women. She disobeyed only in *one particular*; and this, to serve a purpose, Memucan draws into a *general consequence*: and the rest came into the conclusion, being either too intoxicated to be able to discern right from wrong, or too intent on reducing women to a state of vassalage, to neglect the present favorable opportunity. **done wrong**. Ac 18:14. 25:10. 1 C 6:7, 8.

17. **women**. Nu 30:3-13. 1 C +14:34. **despise**. 2 S 6:16. Ep 5:33.

18. **the ladies**. *Saroth*, the *princesses*: but the meaning is well expressed by our term *ladies*. Jg *5:29. 1 K 11:3.

19. **it please the king**. Heb. it be good with the king. ver. 21mg. Est 3:9. 8:5. Dt 23:16mg. Ne 2:5, 7. **from him**. Heb. from before him. **Persians**. i.e. *inhabitants of Persia* (2 Ch +36:22), ✣S#6539h. **it be not altered**. Heb. it pass not away. Est 8:8. Da 6:8-15, 17. Let it be inserted among the permanent laws, and be made a part of the constitution of the empire. The Persians seem to have affected such a degree of wisdom in the construction of their laws, that they could never be amended, and should never be repealed; and this formed the ground of the saying, "The laws of the Medes and Persians that change not." **another**. Heb. her companion. Ex 11:2. Is 34:15, 16. Je 9:20. Zc 11:9mg. **that is better**. 1 S 15:28. 1 K 3:32.

20. **throughout**. Dt 17:13. 21:21. **all the wives**. Ep 5:33. Col 3:18. 1 P 3:1-7.

21. **pleased the king**. Heb. was good in the eyes of the king. ver. 19mg. Est 2:4. Ge 41:37. Nu 24:1. Jsh +22:30mg. 2 S 17:4mg.

22. **into every province**. Est 3:12. 8:9. Da 3:29. 4:1. **that every man**. Both the law of God and common sense taught this from the foundation of the world; and this parade of enactment was only to deprive Vashti of her crown. Ge +*18:19. Ep *5:22-24. 1 T 2:12. √3:3-5. T *2:4, 5. **it should**, etc. Heb. one should publish *it* according to the language of his country. Est 3:12. **according**. Lk 16:8. Ac *2:5-11. 1 C 14:19, 20.

ESTHER 2

By advice of his servants, Ahaseurus causes fair virgins to be sought out in every province of his kingdom, that he may choose a queen, 1-4. Esther had been brought up by Mordecai, 5-7. She obtains favor with the keeper of the women, pleases the king; and is made queen, having observed Mordecai's directions, 8-20. Mordecai discovers a plot against the king; the criminals are punished; and his service is registered in the chronicles of the kingdom, 21-23.

1. A.M. 3543. B.C. 461. **he remembered**. Da 6:14-18. **what was decreed**. Est 1:12-21.

2. **king's servants**. Est 1:10, 14. 6:14. **Let there be**. Ge 12:14. 1 K *1:2. **virgins**. ver. 3, 17, 19. Ge +*24:16.

3. **in all the provinces**. Est 1:1, 2. **that they may gather**. This was the usual way in which the *harem*, or *seraglio*, was furnished: the finest women in the land, whether of high or low birth, were sought out and brought to the harem. They all became the king's concubines; but *one* was raised as *chief wife*, or *sultana*, to the throne; and her issue was especially entitled to inherit. **the custody**. Heb. the hand. ver. 8, 14. **Hege**. i.e. *eunuch; brier; venerable; meditation,*

✱S#1896h. ver. 8, Hegai. **the king's chamberlain**. *Saris hammelech*, "the king's eunuch:" so the LXX., Vulgate, Targum, and Syriac. **their things**. ver. 12-14. Pr 20:30. Is 3:18-23.

4. **let the maiden**. Mt *20:16. 22:14. **the thing**. Est 1:21. 3:9, 10. 2 S 13:4-6. 16:21-23. 17:4. Mt 14:6.

5. **Shushan**. ver. 3. Est 1:2. 5:1. **a certain**. Est 3:2-6. 10:3. **Jew**. i.e. *celebrated; praised*, ✣S#3064h. Est 2:5. 3:4. 5:13. 6:10. 8:7. 9:29, 31. 10:3. Je 34:9. Zc 8:23. **Mordecai**. i.e. *a little man; worshipper of Mars; bitterness of my oppressed*, ✱S#4782h. Est 2:5, 7, 10, 11, 15, 19, 20, 20, 21, 22, 22. 3:2, 3, 4, 5, 6, 6, 6. 4:1, 1, 4, 5, 6, 7, 9, 10, 12, 13, 15, 17. 5:9, 9, 13, 14. 6:2, 3, 4, 10, 11, 12, 13. 7:9, 10. 8:1, 2, 2, 7, 9, 15. 9:3, 4, 4, 20, 23, 29, 31. 10:2, 3. Ezr 2:2. Ne 7:7. (1) A Benjamite, by whom Esther was brought up, afterwards chief minister of the king, Est 2:5; 10:3. (2) One who returned with Zerubbabel, Ezr 2:2; Ne 7:7. **the son of Shimei**. 1 S 9:1. 2 S *16:5. **Kish**. 1 S 9:1, 2.

6. **Jeconiah**. 2 K 24:6, 14, 15. 1 Ch 3:16. 2 Ch 36:9, 10, 20, Jehoiachin. Je 22:24, 28, Coniah. 24:1.

7. **brought up**. Heb. nourished. ver. 20. Nu 11:12. 2 K 10:1mg, 5. Ep *6:4. **Hadassah**. i.e. *a myrtle*, ✱S#1919h. Da 1:6, 7. **his uncle's**. ver. 15. Je 32:7-12. **neither father nor mother**. Ge +11:28. **fair and beautiful**. Heb. fair of form and good of countenance. Est 1:11mg. Ge 12:11. 29:17. 39:6. **took**. Ge 48:5. 2 C *6:18. 1 J *3:1.

8. **were gathered**. ver. 3. **Hegai**. i.e. *grooming; venerable; an eunuch; my meditations*, ✱S#1896h. Est 2:8, 8, 15. One of Dr. Kennicott's MSS. instead of *Hegai* has *Hege*, as in ver. 3. **Esther**. i.e. *star; happiness; I will be hidden*, ✱S#635h. Est 2:7, 8, 10, 11, 15, 15, 16, 17, 18, 20, 20, 22, 22. 4:4, 5, 8, 9, 10, 12, 13, 15, 17. 5:1, 2, 2, 2, 3, 4, 5, 5, 6, 7, 12. 6:14. 7:1, 2, 2, 3, 5, 6, 7, 8. 8:1, 1, 2, 3, 4, 4, 7, 7. 9:12, 13, 29, 31, 32.

9. **she obtained kindness**. ver. 15, 17. Est 5:2. Ge *39:21. 1 K 8:50. Ezr 7:6. Ne 2:8. Ps 106:46. Pr *16:7. Da 1:9. Ac 7:10. **gave her her things**. ver. 3, 12. **such things**. Heb. her portions. Est 9:19, 22. Ex 29:26. **preferred her**. Heb. changed her. 1 S 21:13. Ps ch. 34, title.

10. **had not showed**. Est 3:8. 4:13, 14. 7:4. Mt *10:16. **for Mordecai**. ver. *7, *20. Ep *6:1.

11. **Mordecai**. The apartments of the women are accounted so inviolable, that it is even a crime to inquire what passes within their walls. A man, says Chardin, may walk a hundred days, one after the other, by the house where the women are, and yet know no more what is done there than at the farther end of Tartary. This sufficiently explains the conduct of Mordecai. **walked**. ver. 13, 14. **how Esther did**. Heb. the peace of Esther. Ge +37:14mg. 43:27mg. Jg +18:15mg. 1 S 17:18, 22mg. Ac *15:36.

12. A.M. 3546. B.C. 458. **to go in**. 1 Th 4:4, 5. **six months**. Pr 7:17. SS 3:6. Is 57:9. Lk 7:37, 38.

14. **Shaashgaz**. i.e. *servant of the beautiful; who succored the cut off*, ✱S#8190h. **concubines**. 1 Ch +2:48. **delighted**. Est 4:11. Ge 34:19. Dt 21:14. Is 62:4, 5. **she were called**. Ex 33:17. Is 43:1. 45:4.

15. **who had taken**. ver. *7. **chamberlain**. Est 1:10mg. Ge +*37:36mg. **Esther**. SS *6:9. 8:10. Ac 7:10.

16. **the tenth month**. Est 8:9. Tebeth. i.e. *goodness,*

✻S#2887h. Tenth month of the Hebrew sacred year, fourth month of the civil year; part of our December and January. **the seventh year.** ver. 1, 3. Ezr 7:8.

17. **favor.** *or*, kindness. ver. 9. **in his sight.** Heb. before him. ver. 9. Est 1:19. **so that he set.** Est *4:14. 1 S *2:8. Ps 45:14, 15. *75:6, 7. 113:7, 8. Ezk 17:24. Lk *1:48-52. Bishop Patrick observes, that those who suggest that Esther committed a great sin to come at the dignity of queen of Persia, do not consider the custom of those times and countries. Every one that the king took to his bed was married to him, and was his wife of a lower rank, as Hagar was to Abraham.

18. A.M. 3547. B.C. 457. **made a great.** Est 1:3-5. Ge 29:22. Jg 14:10-17. SS 3:11. 5:1. Mt 22:2. Lk 14:8. Re 9:19. **he made.** We learn from Herodotus and Athenaeus, that the Persian monarchs were accustomed to give their wives distinct cities and provinces for the purpose of supplying them with different articles of dress: one was assigned for ornamenting the head and neck; another provided robes, zones, etc.; and the city of Anthilla was given to a Persian queen, we read, to supply her with shoes and sandals. It is probable, therefore, that, at the desire of Esther, Ahasuerus relieved those cities and provinces that had before paid it, from this expense. **release.** Heb. rest. **gave gifts.** Est 9:22. Ge 43:34. Jg 20:38 (flame), 40. 1 S 25:8. 2 S 11:8h. Ne 8:11. Re 11:10.

19. **the virgins.** ver. 3, 4. **sat in the king's gate.** ſ171S7B, Ge +14:7. ver. 21. Est 3:2, 3. 5:13.

20. **had not yet showed.** ver. 10. **for Esther.** Ep 6:1-3. **brought up.** ver. 7.

21. **gate.** ſ171S7B, Ge +14:7. **chamberlains.** ver. 15. Est 1:10mg. Ge +*37:36mg. **Bigthan.** i.e. *a gift; garden; given of fortune,* i.e. *the sun; in their wine-press,* ✻S#904h. Est 6:2, Bigthana. **Teresh.** i.e. *severe; austere; rude; possession,* ✻S#8657h. Est 2:21. 6:2. **door.** Heb. threshold. 1 K +14:17. 2 K 12:9mg. Is 6:4. **and sought.** 2 S 4:5, 6. 16:11. 1 K 15:25-27. 16:9. 2 K 9:22-24. 12:20. 21:23. Ps 144:10. **lay hand.** 1 S 24:6. Ro 13:1, 2.

22. **the king.** Ec 10:20. Ac 23:12-22. **and Esther certified.** Est 6:1, 2. Ro 11:33. **Mordecai's name.** Ph 2:4.

23. **hanged.** Est 5:14. 7:10. Ge 40:19, 22. Dt 21:22, 23. Jsh 8:29. **the book.** Est 6:1, 2. Ml *3:16.

ESTHER 3

Haman is advanced by the king, who commands his servants to bow down to him; but Mordecai refuses to do it, 1, 2. Haman, being informed, in revenge, purposes to destroy the whole Jewish nation, 3-6. He chooses a day, by casting lots, for executing his purpose, 7. By calumniating the Jews, he obtains a decree from the king to extirpate the nation, and publishes it through all the provinces, 8-15.

1. A.M. 3551. B.C. 453. **promote.** Est 7:6. Ps 12:8. Pr 29:2. **Haman.** i.e. *magnificent, Mercury; solitary; the rager; their tumult,* ✻S#2001h. Est 3:1, 2, 4, 5, 5, 6, 7, 8, 10, 11, 12, 15. 4:7. 5:4, 5, 5, 8, 9, 9, 9, 10, 11, 12, 14. 6:4, 5, 6, 6, 7, 10, 11, 12, 13, 14. 7:1, 6, 6, 7, 8, 9, 9, 10. 8:1, 2, 2, 3, 5, 7. 9:10, 12, 13, 14, 24. **Hammedatha.** i.e. *a twin; measurement; given by the god Hom,* ✻S#4099h. Est 3:1, 10. 8:5. 9:10, 24. **Agagite.** i.e. *of the royal seed of Agag* (i.e. *blazing, sublime,* Nu +24:7), ✻S#91h. Est 3:1, 10. 8:3, 5. 9:24.

For ✻S#90h, see on Nu +24:7, Agag. 1 S 15:8, 33. **above all princes.** Est 1:14. Ge 41:40, 55. Ezr 7:14. Da 6:2.

2. **the king's servants.** Dr. Shaw, speaking of the cities in the East, says, "If we quit the streets, and enter into any of the principal houses, we shall first pass through a porch, or gate-way, with benches on each side, where the master of the family receives visits, and dispatches business; few persons, not even the nearest relations, having admission any farther, except on extraordinary occasions." These *servants* were probably *officers* who here waited the king's call; and it is likely that Mordecai was one of them. Est 2:19, 21. **gate.** ſ171S7B, Ge +14:7. **bowed.** Ge 41:43. Ph *2:10. **bowed not.** *Yichra welo yishtachaweh,* "bowed not down, nor prostrated himself," or *worshipped* him. Had this meant only *civil reverence* the king would not have needed to *command* it: there was, therefore, some kind of divine honor intended, such as was paid to the Persian kings, and which even the Greeks refused, as express adoration. ver. 1, 5. Ex *17:14, 16. Dt 25:19. 1 S 15:3. Ps *15:4. 139:21, 22. Re +*22:8, 9.

3. **Why.** ver. 2. Ex 1:17. Mt 15:2, 3.

4. **when they spake.** Ge 39:10. **hearkened not.** Ac *4:19. *5:29. **that they told.** Da 3:8, 9. 6:13. **he had told.** Ezr 1:3. Da 3:12, 16-18, 23-30. 6:20-28. Jon 1:9.

5. **that Mordecai.** ver. 2. Est 5:9. **full of wrath.** Est 1:12. Ge 4:5, 6. Jb 5:2. Pr 12:16. 19:19. 21:24. 27:3, 4. Da 3:19.

6. **sought.** Ps 10:2. 83:4. Re 12:12.

7. **the first month.** Ne 2:1. **Nisan.** Part of February and March. Ex 12:2. 13:4. **in the twelfth.** Est 1:3. 2:16. **they cast Pur.** i.e. *a part, a portion; lot; frustration,* ✻S#6332h. Est 3:7. 9:24, 26, 28, 29, 31, 32. **lot.** Est 9:24-26. Ge +24:44n. Pr *16:33. Ezk 21:21, 22. Mt 27:35. **from day to day.** To obtain a lucky day. **month to month.** Throughout a year. Matthew Poole notes that the diviners cast lots, according to the custom of those ancient and eastern people, what day and what month would be most lucky, for the most effectual and universal extirpation of the Jews; wherein appears both his implacable malice and unwearied diligence in seeking vengeance, and God's singular providence in disposing the lot to that time, that so the Jews might have sufficient space of time to get the decree reversed, as they did. Scott notes that the event showed the vanity of his oracles or auguries; and illustrates the doctrine of a particular providence over all the affairs of men, and the care of God over his church. **Adar.** i.e. *glorious; power; fire,* ✻S#143h. Est 3:7, 13. 8:12. 9:1, 15, 17, 19, 21. Twelfth month of the Jewish sacred year. Part of January and February. Est 9:1, 5, 17-19, 21. Ezr 6:15.

8. **scattered abroad.** Le *26:33. Dt *4:27. 30:3. 32:36. Ne 1:8. Je 50:17. Ezk 6:8. 11:16. Zc 7:14. Jn 7:35. Ja 1:1. 1 P 1:1. **their laws.** Ezr 4:12-15. Ac *16:20, 21. *17:6, 7. 24:5. 28:22. **for the king's profit to.** Heb. meet, *or* equal for the king to, etc.

9. **that they may be destroyed.** Heb. to destroy them. Ps 37:12-15. **and I will pay.** Heb. and I will weigh. Est 4:7. Ge 23:16. 1 K 20:39. Here Haman is obliged to acknowledge that there would be a *loss* to the revenue, which he was willing to make up out of his own property. Ten thousand talents of silver, counted by the Babylonish talent, amount to 2,119,000l.;

but reckoned by the Jewish talent, they amount to double that sum. In those days, silver and gold were more plentiful than at present; and we have many instances of individuals possessing almost incredible riches. Herodotus (l. vii.) relates, that when Xerxes went into Greece, Pythius the Lydian had 2000 talents of silver, and 4,000,000 of gold darics, which unitedly amount to nearly 5,500,000l. Plutarch tells us, that after Crassus had dedicated the *tenth* of all he had to Hercules, he entertained the Roman people at 10,000 tables, and distributed to every citizen as much corn as was sufficient for three months; and, after all these expenses, he had 7100 Roman talents left, which amount to more than 1,500,000l. Lentulus the augur is said to have possessed no less than 3,333,333l. 6s. 8d. Apicus was worth more than 916,671l. 13s. 4d.; and, after having spent in his kitchen 833,333l. 6s. 8d. he considered the remainder too little for his support, and poisoned himself! **ten thousand.** Mt 18:24.

10. **took.** Est 8:2, 8. Ge 41:42. **enemy.** *or,* oppressor. Est 7:6. 8:1. 9:10, 24. Ps 6:7.

11. **to do.** Ps 73:7. Je 26:14. 40:4. Lk 23:25.

12. **then were.** Est 8:9, etc. **scribes.** *or,* secretaries. Jg 5:14. 1 K 4:3mg. **according.** Est 1:22. 8:9. 9:27. **in the name.** 1 K 21:8. Da 6:8, 12, 15. **sealed.** Est 8:2, 8, 10.

13. **by posts.** Est 8:10, 14. 2 Ch 30:6n. Jb 9:25. Je 51:31. Ro 3:15. **both young.** Ge 19:4. Ex 10:9. 1 S 15:3. 22:19. **and old.** ✠174, Ge +18:27. **in one day.** Est 8:12-14. Ja 2:13. **the spoil.** Est 8:11. 9:10. Is 10:6.

14. **The copy.** Est 8:13, 14. **published.** or, revealed. Est 8:13. Nu 24:4, 6. Je 32:11, 14.

15. **The posts.** ver. 13. **hastened.** Est 6:12. 8:14. 2 Ch 26:20. Pr 1:16. 4:16. **sat down.** Ge 37:24, 25. Pr 10:23. Ho 7:5. Am 6:6. Jn 16:20. Re 11:10. **drink.** Ex 32:6. 2 S 11:11. **the city.** Est 4:16. 8:15. Pr 29:2. **perplexed.** Ex 14:3. Pr 29:2. Jl 1:18.

ESTHER 4

Mordecai and the Jews fast, and mourn exceedingly, 1-3. Esther, sending to inquire of Mordecai the reason, is informed of the decree, and required to petition the king for her people, 4-9. She excuses herself by alleging the peril of the attempt; but being shown the consequences, she appoints a fast of three days, and consents to approach the king, though at the hazard of her life, 10-17.

1. **all that.** Est 3:8-13. **rent.** 2 S 1:11. 1 K 21:27. Jb 1:20. Jon 3:4-9. Ac 14:14. **sackcloth.** Da +9:3. Am 8:10. **with ashes.** ver. 3. Jsh 7:6. 2 S 13:19. Jb 2:8. 42:6. Is 58:5. Ezk 27:30, 31. Da 9:3. Jon 3:6. Mt 11:21. **and cried.** Mordecai gave every demonstration of the most poignant grief. Nor did he hide this from the city; and the Greek says that he uttered these words aloud: *Airetai ethnos maden adikakos,* "A people is going to be destroyed who have done no evil." Ge 27:34. Is 15:4. 22:4. Ezk 21:6. 27:31. Mi 1:8. Zp 1:14. Re 18:17-19.

3. **in every province.** Est 1:1. 3:12. **great mourning.** It cannot reasonably be doubted, that the mournings, fastings, and weepings of the Jews were attended by constant prayers and supplications; though all mention of them, and of the glorious God whom they worshipped, seems to have been studiously avoided. 1 S 4:13, 14. 11:4. Is 22:4, 12. 37:1-3. **weeping.** Mt 13:42.

22:13. 25:30. **many lay in sackcloth and ashes.** Heb. sackcloth and ashes were laid under many. Is 58:5. Da 9:3.

4. **chamberlains.** Heb. eunuchs. Est 1:12. 1 S 8:15mg. 2 K 9:32. Is 56:3. Ac 8:27. **sent raiment.** Is 52:1, 2. Is 61:3. **but he received it not.** Ge 37:35. Ps 77:2. Je 31:15.

5. **Hatach.** i.e. *gift; truth; he that strikes,* ✱S#2047h. Est 4:5, 6, 9, 10. **appointed to attend upon her.** Heb. set before her. Est 1:10, 12. **to know.** Ro 12:15. 1 C 12:26. Ph 2:4. He 4:15.

7. **all that had.** Est 3:2-15.

8. **the copy.** Est 3:14, 15. **to charge.** Est 2:20. 1 T 6:13, 17. **to make supplication.** Jb 9:15. Pr 16:14, 15. Ec 10:4. Ac 12:20. **request.** Est 7:3, 4. 8:6. Ne 2:3-5. Pr *21:1.

11. **shall come.** Herodotus informs us, that ever since the reign of Deioces, king of Media, for the security of the king's person, it was enacted that no one should be admitted into his presence; but that if any one had business with him, he should transact it through the medium of his ministers. **the inner court.** Est 5:1. **one law.** Da 2:9. **the king shall.** Est 5:2. 8:4. **the golden sceptre.** That the kings of Persia carried a golden sceptre, we have the following proof in Xenophon: *Oti ou tode to xrusoun skaptron to man basileian diasozon estin, all' oi postoi philoi skaptron basileusin alathestaton kai asphalestaton.* "It is not (said Cyrus to his son Cambyses) the *golden* sceptre that saves the kingdom; but faithful friends are the truest and best sceptre of the kingdom." **but I.** Est 1:19. 2:14. 1 P 3:7.

13. **Think not.** Pr *24:10-12. Mt *16:24, 25. Jn *12:25. Ph 2:30. He *12:3. **thyself.** Heb. *nephesh,* soul, Ex +15:9.

14. **holdest thy peace.** Pr ◐*31:8, 9. **then shall.** Ge 22:14. Nu *23:22-24. Dt 32:26, 27, 36. 1 S 12:22. Is *54:17. Je 30:11. *33:24-26. 46:28. Am 9:8, 9. Mt 16:18. *24:22. **enlargement.** Heb. respiration. Ex 8:15. Ezr 9:9. Jb 9:18. **but thou.** Est 2:7, 15. Jg 14:15-18. 15:6. **whether.** Ge *45:4-8. Is *45:1-5. 49:23. Ac 7:20-25. **for such a time.** 1 S 17:29. 2 K 19:3. Ne 6:11. The fact related in this verse was unquestionably the reason why Esther was raised to regal honors, by the overruling providence of God:—she was therefore bound in gratitude to do this service for God, else she would not have answered the end of her elevation: and she need not fear the miscarriage of the enterprise, for if God designed her for it, he would surely bear her through and give success. It appeared by the event that Mordecai spoke prophetically, when he modestly *conjectured* that Esther came to the kingdom that she might be the instrument of the Jew's deliverance. Mordecai thoroughly believed that it was a cause which one way or other would certainly be carried, and which, therefore, she might safely venture upon. Instruments might fail, but God's covenant cannot. There is a wise design in all the providences of God, which is unknown to us till it is accomplished; but it will prove in the issue that all is intended for and center in the good of those who trust in him.

16. **present.** Heb. found. Est 1:5mg. **fast.** 2 Ch 20:3. Is 22:12. Jl 1:14, 15. 2:12-17. Jon 3:4-9. **eat nor drink.** Ac 9:9. 27:33. **three days.** ✠108H12, 1 S +30:12. Est 5:1. Jsh 5:11n. 1 S *30:12n. Mt +*12:40. Young notes, one whole day and part of two others. **I also.** Ge *18:19.

Jsh *24:15. Ac 10:7. **if I perish.** If I lose my life in the attempt to save my people, I shall lose it cheerfully. I see it is my duty to make the attempt; and, come what will, I am resolved to do it. Ge 43:14. 1 S 19:5. 2 S 10:12. 2 K *7:4. Lk 9:24. Ac 20:24. 21:13. Ro 16:4. Ph 2:30.

17. **went.** Heb. passed. Ex 17:5. 32:27. 38:26. 1 K 22:24.

ESTHER 5

ESTHER, venturing uncalled before the king, is graciously received; and, being encouraged to make her request, she invites the king and Haman to a banquet, 1-5 Being again asked what was her request, she invites them to another banquet the next day, 6-8. Haman, proud of this distinction, and elated by prosperity, is yet disquieted by Mordecai's neglect, and amidst his vain-glorying complains of it to his friends and his wife, 9-13. By their advice he erects a gallows for Mordecai's execution the next morning, 14.

1. **on the third day.** Est 4:16. Mt 27:64. **royal.** Est 1:11. 8:15. Mt 10:16. 11:8. 1 P 3:3-5. **inner.** Est 4:11. 6:4. **sat.** 1 K 10:18-20. Lk 22:30. Re 3:21.

2. **she.** Ge 32:28. Ne 1:11. Ps 116:1. Pr *21:1. Ac 7:10. *10:4. **golden sceptre.** Est *4:11. 8:4.

3. **What.** ver. 6. 7:2. 9:12. 1 K 2:20. *3:5. Mt 20:20-22. Lk *18:41. **to.** ver. *6. Mk *6:23.

4. **If it seem.** ver. 8. Pr *29:11. **the banquet.** *Mishteh,* from *shathah,* "to drink," a *compotation, feast,* or *banquet* accompanied with *drinking;* the drinking in the East being at the *beginning,* and not at the end of the entertainment. Olearius (p. 709 et seq.), describing an entertainment at the Persian court, says, "The floor of the hall was covered with cotton cloth, which was covered with all sorts of fruits and sweetmeats in basons of gold. With them was served up excellent Shiraz wine. After an hour's time, the sweetmeats were removed, to make way for the more substantial part of the entertainment, such as rice, boiled and roast mutton, etc. When the company had been at table an hour and a half, warm water was brought, in a ewer of gold, for washing, and grace being said, they began to retire without speaking a word, according to the custom of the country." ver. 8. Est 3:15. Ge 27:25. 32:20. Ps 112:5. 1 C 14:20.

5. **Cause Haman.** Est 6:14.

6. **the king said.** ver. 3. Est 7:2. 9:12.

7. **petition.** ver. 6, 8. Est 7:2, 3. 9:12. **request.** ver. 3, 8. Est 7:2, 3. 9:12.

8. **perform.** Heb. do. **let the king.** Esther probably wished another interview, that she might ingratiate herself more fully into the king's favor, and thus secure the success of her design. But Providence disposed of things thus, to give time for the important event mentioned in the following chapter. **tomorrow.** Est 6:1, etc. Pr *16:9.

9. **joyful.** Jb *20:5. Am 6:12, 13. Lk *6:25. Jn 16:20. Ja 4:9. **he stood not up.** Est 3:2. Ps *15:4. Mt *10:28. **he was full.** Est 3:5. 1 K *21:4. Jb 31:31. Ps *27:3. Da 3:13, 16-19. Mt *2:16. Ac 7:54.

10. **refrained.** Ge 43:30, 31. 45:1. 2 S 13:22, 23. Ps 55:21. Ec 7:9. **called for his friends.** Heb. caused his friends to come. **Zeresh.** i.e. *golden; star of adoration; a stranger in want; misery,* *S#2238h. Est 5:10, 14. 6:13, 13.

11. **the glory.** Est 1:4. Ge 31:1. Jb 31:24, 25. Ps 49:6, 16, 17. Is 10:8. Je 9:23, 24. Da 4:30. Mk 10:24. Lk 12:19, 20. 1 T 6:17. **the multitude.** Est 9:7-10, 12, 13. Jb 27:14, 15. Ps 17:14. Ho 9:13, 14. **and how he had.** Est 3:1.

12. **Yea, Esther.** Plutarch, in his life of Artaxerxes, informs us, that none but the king's mother, and his real wife, were permitted to sit at his table; and therefore he mentions it as a condescension in that prince, that he sometimes invited his brothers. Haman, therefore, had some reason to be proud of this favor. **tomorrow.** Jb 8:12, 13. 20:5-8. Ps 37:35, 36. Pr 7:22, 23. 27:1. Lk 21:34, 35. 1 Th 5:3.

13. **Yet all this.** *Pride* will ever render its possessor unhappy. Haman, though possessed of immense riches, glory, and honor, and the prime favorite of the king, is wretched, because he could not have the *homage* of that man whom his heart even despised! Oh, how distressing are the inquietudes of pride and vanity! 1 K 21:4-6. Jb 15:20. 18:4. Pr *10:2. Ec 1:2, 14. Ph 4:11, 12.

14. **said Zeresh.** 2 S 13:3-5. 1 K 21:7, 25. 2 Ch 22:3, 4. Mk 6:19-24. **Let a gallows.** Heb. Let a tree. Est 7:9. **speak thou.** Est 3:8, etc. 6:4. **go thou in.** Est 3:15. 1 K 21:7. Am 6:4-6. Re 11:10. **the thing.** 2 S 16:21-23. 17:1-4. Mk 14:10, 11. Ac 23:14, 15. Ro 1:32. **he caused.** Est 7:10. Ps 7:13-16. 9:15. 37:14, 32. Pr 1:18. 4:16. Ro 3:15.

ESTHER 6

The king, unable to sleep, orders the records of the kingdom to be read, 1; and discovering that Mordecai's service had not been rewarded, he considers how to honor him, 2, 3. Haman, coming early to request that Mordecai might be hanged, is himself appointed to confer the highest honors upon him, 4-11. He is extremely cast down, and distressed; his friends and wife predict his ruin; and in this state of mind he is called to attend Esther's banquet, 12-14.

1. **that night.** Est 5:8. Ge 22:14. 1 S 23:26, 27. Is 41:17. Ro *11:33. **could not the king sleep.** Heb. the king's sleep fled away. Ge 28:16. 31:40. Jg 16:14. Ps 31:11h. Da 2:1. 6:18. **the book of records.** As *chronicles* were composed among the Persians, a more instructive and interesting work could not be brought before the king; because they were all written in verse, and were generally the work of the most eminent poets of the empire. Est 2:23. Ml *3:16.

2. **Bigthana.** i.e. *given of fortune,* i.e. *of the sun; gardener; in their winepress,* *S#904h. Est 2:21, Bigthan. **door.** Heb. threshold. Est 2:21mg. 1 K +14:17. 2 K 12:9mg.

3. **What honor.** Jg 1:12, 13. 1 S 17:25, 26. 1 Ch 11:6. Da 5:7, 16, 29. Ac 28:8-10. **There is nothing.** Ge 40:23. Ps 118:8, 9. Ec 9:15.

4. **Who is in the court.** Pr 3:27, 28. Ec 9:10. **the outward.** Est 4:11. 5:1. **to speak.** Est 3:8-11. 5:14. 7:9. Jb 5:13. Ps 2:4. 33:19.

5. **came in.** ⌐16, Ge +1:27. **whom the king,** etc. Heb. in whose honor the king delighteth. Ps 35:27. Is 42:1. 62:4, 5. Je 32:41. Mt 3:17. Jn √5:23. **To whom.** Est 3:2, 3. 5:11. Ps +*119:21. Pr*1:32. *16:18. *18:12. 30:13. Ob *3. 1 C *10:12. Ph +*2:3.

7. **whom the king,** etc. Heb. in whose honor the king delighteth. ver. 9, 11.

8. **Let the royal apparel**. lit. the clothing of the kingdom. Heb. Let them bring the royal apparel, wherewith the king clotheth *himself*. 1 S 18:4. Lk 15:22. **the horse**. Herodotus relates, that the kings of Persia had horses peculiar to themselves, which were brought from Armenia, and were remarkable for their beauty; and if the same law prevailed in Persia as in Judea, no man, under the penalty of death, might ride on the king's horse, any more than sit on his throne, wear his crown, or hold his sceptre. 1 K 1:33n.

9. **bring him**. Heb. cause him to ride. **proclaim**. Ge 41:43. 1 K 1:33, 34. Zc 9:9. **honor**. Est 8:15. 1 S *2:30.

10. **Make haste**. Da 4:37. Lk 14:11. Re 18:7. **let nothing fail**. Heb. suffer not a whit to fall. 1 S 3:19. 2 K 10:10.

11. **took Haman**. Ezr 6:13. Is 60:14. Lk 1:52. Re 3:9. **and arrayed**. Est 8:15. 9:3. Ps 30:11. Is 61:3. **the street**. Pitts (pp. 198, 199) gives a similar account of the mode of honoring a person who turns a Mohammedan, at Algiers: "The apostate is to get on a stately steed, with a rich saddle and fine trappings: he is also richly habited, and has a turban on his head, but nothing of this is to be called his own; only there are given him about two or three yards of broad cloth, which is laid before him on the saddle. The horse, with him on his back, is led all around the city, which he is several hours in doing. The apostate is attended with drums and other music, and twenty or thirty serjeants. They march in order on each side of the horse, with naked swords in their hands. The crier goes before, with a loud voice giving thanks to God for the proselyte that is made."

12. **came again**. Est 2:19. 1 S 3:15. Ps 131:1, 2. **hasted to his house**. 2 S 17:23. 1 K 20:43. 21:4. 2 Ch 26:20. Jb 20:5. **having**. Est 7:8. 2 S 15:30. Jb 9:24. Je 14:3, 4.

13. **Zeresh**. Est 5:10-14. **said his wise**. Ge 41:8. Da 2:12. **If Mordecai**. Ge 40:19. 1 S 28:19, 20. Jb 15:24. Da 5:26-28. Zc 12:2, 3. **but shalt surely**. Jg 7:14. Jb 16:2. Pr 28:18. Ho 14:9.

14. **hasted to bring**. Est 5:8, 14. Dt 32:35, 36.

ESTHER 7

ESTHER, at the banquet, petitions the king for her own life, and the lives of her people, and accuses Haman as their enemy, 1-6 The king, in wrath and jealousy, condemns Haman, who is hanged on the gallows prepared for Mordecai, 7-10.

1. **banquet**. Heb. drink. Est 3:15. 5:4n, 8. Ge 24:19.

2. **the king said**. See on Est 5:6. Jn *16:24.

3. **let my**. ver. 7. 1 K *20:31. 2 K 1:13. Jb 2:4. Je 38:26. **life**. Heb. *nephesh*, soul, Ge +44:30. **my people**. Est 4:8. Ps *122:6-9.

4. **we are sold**. Est 3:9. 4:7, 8. Dt 28:68. 1 S *22:23. **to be destroyed**, etc. Heb. that they should destroy, and kill, and cause to perish. Est 3:13. 8:11. Ps *44:22, 23. Pr 14:28. **But if we**. Ge *37:26-28. Dt 28:68. Jsh *9:23. Ne 5:5. Jl 3:6. Am 2:6. **the enemy**. ver. 6. Est 3:9.

5. **Who is he**. Ge 27:33. Jb 9:24. **that durst**, etc. Heb. whose heart hath filled him. Ac *5:3.

6. **The adversary**. Heb. The man adversary. lit. "distresser, straitener." Est 3:10. **enemy**. Est 8:13. 9:1, 5, 16, 22. **this wicked**. 1 S *24:13. Ps 27:2. *139:19-

22. Pr *24:24, 25. Ec *5:8. 1 C *5:13. 2 Th *2:8. **was afraid**. Ne *6:16. Jb 15:21, 22. *18:5-12. Ps 73:5-9, *17-20. Pr 16:14. Is 21:4. Da *5:5, 6. **before**. *or*, at the presence of. Est 1:19.

7. **king**. *66, Ge +9:3. **in his wrath**. Est 1:12. **Haman**. Pr 14:19. Is 60:14. Re 3:9. **life**. Heb. *nephesh*, soul, Ge +44:30. **for he saw**. 1 S 20:7, 9. 25:17. Ps 112:10. Pr 19:12. Da 3:19.

8. **the king**. *16, Ge +1:27. **the bed**. Est 1:6. Is 49:23. **before me**. Heb. with me. **they covered Haman's**. *121S3F2, 2 S +15:30. When a criminal was condemned by a Roman judge, he was delivered to the sergeant with these words: *I lictor, caput obnubito, arbori infelici suspendito*, "Go, sergeant, cover his head, and hang him on the accursed tree." Est 6:12. Jb *9:24. Is 22:17.

9. **Harbonah**. i.e. *very warlike; martial; droughtiness; his sword*, *S#2726h. Est 1:10, Harbona. **one of the chamberlains**. Est 6:14. 2 K 9:32, 33. **Behold**. Est 5:14. Jb 27:20-23. Ps *7:15, 16. 35:8. 141:10. Pr 14:5, 6. **gallows**. Heb. tree. *121D8, Ge +40:19. Est 5:14. **had made**. Pr *26:27. **who had spoken**. Est 2:21-23. 6:2. **Hang him thereon**. Est 9:25. 1 S 17:51. Ps *7:15, 16. *9:15, 16. *35:8. *37:35, 36. 73:19. Pr *11:5, 6. Da *6:7, 24.

10. **gallows**. lit. tree. *121D8, Ge +40:19. **Then was the king's**. Jg 15:7. Ezk 5:13. Zc 6:8.

ESTHER 8

Haman's estate is given to Esther, and Mordecai, as her near relation, is preferred in Haman's stead, 1, 2. Esther, with tears, entreats the king to reverse the decree against the Jews, 3-6. The king authorizes the Jews to defend themselves, and sends letters to that effect, throughout the provinces, 7-14. The honors conferred on Mordecai, and the joy of the Jews, 15-17.

1. **give the house**. Jb 27:16, 17. Ps 39:6. *49:6-13. Pr *13:22. 28:8. Ec *2:18, 19. Lk *12:20. **came before**. Est 1:14. 2:7, 15.

2. **his ring**. Est 3:10. Ge *41:42. Is 22:19-22. Lk *15:22. **Esther set**. 2 S 9:7-10. Ps *37:34. Ec 2:18-26. 5:13, 14. Da 2:48.

3. **fell**. 1 S 25:24. 2 K 4:27. **besought him with tears**. Heb. she wept and besought him. Is 38:3. Ho 12:4. He *5:7. **mischief**. Est 3:8-15. 7:4.

4. **held out**. Est 4:11. 5:2.

5. **king**. *132D, Ge +19:25. **and if I**. Est 7:3. Ex 33:13, 16. 1 S 20:29. **I be pleasing**. Est 2:4, 17. **letters**. Heb. device. Est 3:12, 13. **which he wrote**. *or*, who wrote.

6. **For how**. Ge 44:34. Je 4:19. 9:1. Lk 19:41, 42. Ro 9:2, 3. 10:1. **endure to see**. Heb. be able that I may see. **the evil**. Est 7:4. Ne *2:3.

7. **Behold**. ver. 1. Pr 13:22. **him they have hanged**. Est 7:10. Ga 3:13.

8. **as it liketh**. Dt 23:16. Is *45:11. Jn *15:7. **in the king's name**. Est 3:12. 1 K 21:8. **may no man reverse**. No, not the king himself; and this was the reason that the king was forced, not to reverse, but to give a contradictory decree; that if the Jews, pursuant to the first decree, were assaulted, they might legitimately, by virtue of the second, defend themselves, slay their enemies, and even take the spoil. ver. 5. Est 1:19. Da 6:8, 12-15. 2 T *2:19. He *6:17, 18.

9. **the king's.** Est 3:12. **Sivan.** i.e. *their covering,* ✱S#5510h. The third month of the Jewish sacred year. Part of May and June. **and to the lieutenants.** Est 1:1, 22. 3:12, 13. Da 6:1. **India.** The Hebrew word *Hoddo,* in Syriac, *Hendoo,* and in Arabic, *Hind,* is rendered *India* by all the versions. *India,* or *Hindostan,* is a large country of the south of Asia, extending from north to south about 2400 miles, and from east to west 1800, between 8 degrees and 35 degrees N. lat. and 68 degrees and 92 degrees E. long.; being bounded on the west by the Indus, east by the Birman empire and Thibet, north by the Indian Caucasus, and south by the Indian ocean. It is probable, however, that all the country east of the Indus was anciently called *India.* **and according.** Est 1:22. 3:12. 2 K 18:26. Da 4:1. 1 C 14:9-11.

10. **in the king.** 1 K 21:8. Ec 8:4. Da 4:1. **by posts.** Est 3:13, 15. 2 Ch 30:6n. Jb 9:25. Je 51:21. **mules.** *Rechesh,* in Syriac, *rechesha,* probably denotes a swift horse. **camels.** *Achashteranim,* from the Persian *akhash,* large, and *aster,* a mule, probably, as Bochart supposes, denotes a *large mule.* **young dromedaries.** *Beney harammachim,* "the sons of mares," as the word *ramakat* denotes in Arabic; probably an expletive of the preceding word. Is 60:6. 66:20. Je 2:23.

11. **to gather.** Est 9:2-16. **life.** Heb. *nephesh,* soul, Ge +44:30. ♪121A7, Ge +9:5. Le 17:11. 2 S 14:7. Mt +*2:20. Lk 12:22. **to destroy.** Ps 37:14, 15. 68:23. 137:8. *146:6-9. Ezk *39:10. **and to take the spoil.** Est 3:13. *9:10, 15, 16. Is 10:6.

12. **one day.** Est 9:1. Ex 15:9, 10. Jg 1:6, 7. **upon the thirteenth.** Est 3:13-15.

13. **publish.** Heb. revealed. Est 3:14mg. **avenge themselves.** Jg 16:28. Ps 37:14, 15. 68:23. 92:10, 11. +*149:6-9. Lk *18:7. Re *6:10. *19:2.

14. **being hastened.** 1 S 21:8. Ec 9:10. **Shushan.** Est 1:2. 2:3. 3:15. Ne 1:1. Da 8:2.

15. **the presence.** Est 6:9, 10. 1 S *2:30. **royal apparel.** Est 5:1. 6:8, 11. Ge 41:42. Mt 6:29. 11:8. Lk 16:19. **blue.** *or,* violet. Est 1:6mg. **and with a great crown.** Mordecai was now made the chief minister, or *vizier,* instead of Haman; and was accordingly invested with the "royal apparel," in conformity to the custom of the East. So we are informed, in the History of the Revolt of Ali Bey (p. 43), that on the election of a new *sheikh bellet,* or chief of the country, in Egypt, the pasha who approves of him invests him with a robe of valuable fur. Perhaps the *crown* was one of the *insignia* of the office of vizier. Concerning the *blue, fine linen,* and *purple,* see the Notes on Ex 25:4n. 39:27n. **the city.** Haman was too *proud* to be *popular:* few lamented his fall. Est 3:15. Pr *29:2.

16. **Jews.** Est 4:1-3, 16. Ps 30:5-11. **had light.** That is, *prosperity* and *hope.* The dark cloud which had so long time hung over them was dispelled; and again the sunshine of prosperity beamed upon them. Est 9:17. Ps 18:28. *97:11. Pr *4:18, 19. 11:10. Is 30:29, 39. 35:10.

17. **a feast.** Est 9:17, 19, 22. 1 S 25:8. Ne *8:10. **many of the people.** Ps *18:43. Zc *8:20-23. **for the fear.** Est 9:2. Ge *35:5. Ex 15:16. Dt *2:25. 11:25.

ESTHER 9

On the day appointed, the Jews, aided by the rulers, slay their enemies; and among the rest are five hundred

men in Shushan, and Haman's ten sons, 1-10. The king hearing this, at Esther's request, allows the Jews in Shushan to stand against their enemies on the day following, when three hundred more are slain; and he causes Haman's sons to be hanged on the gallows erected by Haman, 11-15. The Jews throughout the provinces slay seventy-five thousand men, 16. They rejoice with feasting on the two following days, 17-19. These days are appointed by Esther and Mordecai as an annual festival, in commemoration of this deliverance, and called the feast of Purim, 20-32.

1. **A.M.** 3552. **B.C.** 452. **in the twelfth.** Est 3:7, 13. 8:12. **hoped.** Ac 12:11. **though it was turned.** Dt 32:36. 2 S *22:41. Ps 30:11. Is 14:1, 2. 60:14-16. Re 11:18.

2. **gathered.** ver. 10, 16. Est 8:11. **as sought.** Dt +*2:30. Jsh 11:20. Ps *71:13, 24. Is 8:9. **the fear.** Est 8:17. Ge 35:5. Ex 23:27. Jsh 2:9.

3. **the rulers.** Est 3:12. 8:9. Ezr 8:36. Da 3:2. 6:1, 2. **officers of the king.** Heb. those which did the business that *belonged* to the king. **the fear.** Est 3:2-6. 8:5.

4. **was great.** Ps 18:43. **his fame.** Jsh 6:27. 1 S *2:30. 1 Ch 14:17. Zp 3:19. Mt 4:24. **waxed.** 2 S 3:1. 1 Ch 11:9. Jb *17:9. Ps *1:3. *84:7. Pr *4:18. Is *9:7.

5. **smote.** Ps 18:34-40, 47, 48. 20:7, 8. *149:6-9. 2 Th 1:6. **the stroke.** Je 18:21. **what they would.** Heb. according to their will. Ne 9:24. The Chaldee paraphrast says that none appeared against the Jews but Amalekites only, who were infatuated, and had their hearts hardened, as Pharaoh's heart against Israel, to take up arms to their own destruction. Some had such an inveterate, implacable malice against the Jews, that Haman's fall and Mordecai's advancement, instead of convincing, seemed only to exasperate them the more. How have the most dreadful scourges ravaged a country, and yet the inhabitants are unmindful of the Almighty Disposer of events, and that the cause of his righteous displeasure is their continual provocation! Forty years long was he grieved with one generation, who learned not his ways, though daily fed and clothed by a miracle.

6. **Shushan.** See on Est 3:15.

7. **Parshandatha.** i.e. *given forth to light; revelation of corporeal; of noble birth; he repeatedly broke the decree,* ✱S#6577h. **Dalphon.** i.e. *a dropping; strenuous dripping,* ✱S#1813h. **Aspatha.** i.e. *given by the horse; the enticed gathered,* ✱S#630h.

8. **Poratha.** i.e. *ornament; fruitful; favored; frustration,* ✱S#6334h. **Adalia.** i.e. *fire-god; strong hearted; I shall be drawn up of Jah,* ✱S#118h. **Aridatha.** i.e. *strong; the lion of the decree; great (noble) birth,* ✱S#743h.

9. **Parmashta.** i.e. *strong fisted; superior; spoiled is the banquet,* ✱S#6534h. **Arisai.** i.e. *lion-like; lion of my banners,* ✱S#747h. **Aridai.** i.e. *strong; the lion is enough; great, brilliant,* ✱S#742h. **Vajezatha.** i.e. *pure; white; he sprinkled there; olive trees; sincere,* ✱S#2055h.

10. **ten sons.** Est 5:11. Ex *20:5. Jb *18:18, 19. 27:13-15. Ps 21:10. 69:25. 109:12, 13. **enemy.** Est 3:1. 7:4, 6. Ex 17:16. **but on the spoil.** It does not appear that the Jews slew any person who did not rise up to destroy them: they stood for their lives; and gave full proof that they sought their own personal safety, and not the *property* of their enemies: though the decree

in their favor gave them authority to take the property of all their adversaries. ver. 15, 16. Est 8:11. Ge 14:23. Ro *12:17. Ph *4:8.

11. **was brought.** Heb. came.

12. **what is thy petition.** Est 5:6. 7:2.

13. **If it please the king.** Esther had probably been informed by Mordecai, that there were still many enemies of the Jews who sought their destruction, who had escaped the preceding day; and therefore begged that the second day might be added to the former permission; and that the sons of Haman, who had already been slain, might be suspended on gibbets, as a terror to those who sought the destruction of the Jews. **according unto.** Est 8:11. **let Haman's ten sons be hanged.** Heb. let men hang Haman's ten sons. Dt 21:23. 2 S 21:6, 9. Ga 3:13.

15. **gathered themselves.** ver. 2, 13. Est 8:11. Ps 118:7-12. **but on the prey.** ver. 10, 16. 1 Th 5:22. He 13:5.

16. **gathered themselves.** ver. 2. Est 8:11. **stood.** Est 8:11. Le 26:7, 8. **lives.** Heb. *nephesh*, souls, Ge +44:30.

17. **of the same.** Heb. in it. ver. 1, 18, 21. Est 3:12. 8:9.

18. **on the thirteenth.** ver. 1, 11, 13, 15.

19. **gladness.** ver. 22. Est 8:17. Dt *16:11, 14. Ne *8:10-12. Ps 118:11-16. Lk 11:41. Re 11:10. **sending portions.** The eastern princes and people not only invite their friends to feasts, but it is their custom to send a portion of the banquet to those that cannot well attend, especially their relations, and those in a state of mourning. Thus, when the Grand Emir found that it incommoded M. D'Arvieux to eat with him, he desired him to take his own time for eating, and sent him from his kitchen what he liked best (*Voy. dans la Palest.* p. 20. Harmer, ch. iv. Ob. 56).

20. **Mordecai.** That is, as the words imply, the history contained in this book; and not merely the letters afterwards mentioned, as some understand it. **wrote these.** Ex *17:14. +24:4. Dt 31:19-22. 1 Ch 16:12. Ps 124:1-3. 145:4-12. 2 C 1:10, 11. **in all the provinces.** Est 1:1, 22. 3:12. 8:9.

22. **the days.** Est 3:12, 13. Ex 13:3-8. Ps *103:2. Is 12:1, 2. 14:3. **from sorrow.** Ps 30:11. Is 61:3. Je 31:13. Mt *5:4. Jn *16:20-22. **sending portions.** ver. 19. Ne *8:10-12. Lk 11:41. Ac *2:44-46. Ga 2:10.

24. **the enemy.** or, adversary. ver. 10. Est 3:5-13. 7:6. **Pur.** The word *pur* seems to be derived either from the Persian *bahr* and *bar*, a part, portion, lot, or *pari*, any thing which happens *fortuitously* or *fortunately*; whence the annual festival in commemoration of the wonderful deliverance of the Jews was called *Purim*, or in Arabic and Persian, *Fuhr*, or *Lots*; which has been observed by them, in all places of their dispersion, from that day to the present time, without any interruption. Est 3:7. Ge ◐24:44n. **consume.** Heb. crush. Ex 14:24 (troubled). 23:27 (destroy). Dt 2:15. Je 51:34.

25. **when Esther came.** Heb. when she came. ver. 13, 14. Est 7:5-10. 8:1-14. **return upon.** Nu +*32:23. Jg 1:7. Ps *7:16. *9:15, 16. 109:17, 18. 140:9. 141:10. Ec *10:8. Da 6:24. Mt 21:44.

26. **they called.** Nu 16:40. Ezk *39:11. **Purim.** i.e. *lot; frustration*, ✛S#6332h. Est 9:26, 28, 29, 31, 32. **Pur.** that is, Lot. ver. 24. Est 3:7. **letter.** ver. 20.

27. **and upon their seed.** Dt 5:3. 29:14, 15. Jsh 9:15. 1 S 30:25. 2 S 21:1, 2. **all such.** Est 8:17. Is *56:3, 6. Zc *2:11. 8:23. **fail.** Heb. pass. ver. 28.

28. **remembered.** Ex 12:17. Ps 78:5-7. 103:2. **fail.** Heb. pass. ver. 27. **the memorial.** Ex 13:8, 9. Jsh 4:7. Zc 6:14. **perish from their seed.** Heb. be ended from their seed. Is 66:17.

29. **the daughter of Abihail.** Est 2:15. **authority.** Heb. strength. Est 10:2. Da 2:37. 11:17. **confirm.** ver. 20. Est 8:10.

30. **the hundred twenty and.** Est 1:1. 8:9. **words of peace.** Is 39:8. Zc 8:19.

31. **themselves.** Heb. their souls. Heb. *nephesh*, Ge +*27:31. Le 11:43. Jb 18:4. Ps 131:2. Is 46:2. Je 37:9. **and for their seed.** ver. 27. **the fastings.** Est 4:3, 16. 2 S 12:16. Jon 3:2-9. **their cry.** Ps *145:18, 19.

32. **decree.** or, saying. Est 1:15. 2:20. 2 Ch +*34:27n. **was written.** Ex 17:14.

ESTHER 10

The greatness of Ahasuerus, and the advancement and usefulness of Mordecai, 1-3.

1. **laid a tribute.** Est 1:1. 8:9. Lk 2:1. **the isles.** Ge 10:5. Ps 72:10. Is 24:15. Da 11:18.

2. **all the acts.** 1 K 11:41. 22:30. **advanced him.** Heb. made him great. Est 8:15. 9:4. Ps 18:35. Da 2:48. **in the book.** Est 2:23. 6:1. 1 K 14:19. **Media.** *Media*, which comprehended the modern *Azerbijan* and part of *Iraq*, was a celebrated country of Asia, bounded on the north by the Caspian sea and Armenia, west by Assyria, south by Susiana and Persia, and east by Hyrcania and Parthia, extending from 30 degrees to 37 degrees N. lat. and 45 degrees to 53 degrees E. long. **Persia.** *Persia* Proper, now *Fars*, was but a small province, being bounded on the north by Media, west by Susiana, south by the Persian gulf, and east by Caramania, extending from about 27 degrees to 33 degrees N. lat. and 50 degrees to 55 degrees E. long. But the Persian empire in its ancient state extended from the Hellespont to the Indus, above 2800 miles, and from Pontus to the shores of Arabia, above 2000 miles; comprehending a multitude of various nations.

3. **Jew.** Est 2:5. 5:13. 6:10. **next unto the king.** Ge 41:+*40, 44. 1 S 23:17. 2 Ch 28:7. Da 5:16, 29. **accepted.** Est 3:2. Dt 33:24. Ro 14:18. **seeking.** Dt 11:12. Ne 2:10. Ps 122:6-9. Ro 9:2, 3. 10:1. **speaking peace.** Ps 28:3. 37:37, 38.

JOB

JOB 1

The uprightness, piety, prosperity, and numerous family of Job, and his religious concern for his children, 1-5. Satan appearing before God, accuses Job, and obtains leave to try him, 6-12. Job, receiving successive accounts of calamities, which deprived him of all his substance, and all his children, mourns with humble resignation, and worships God, 13-22.

1. **Uz.** Ge 10:23. 22:20, 21, Huz. 36:28. 1 Ch 1:17, 42. Je 25:20. La 4:21. Some suppose "the land of Uz" took its name from Uz, the grandson of Seir the Horite, and that it was a part of Idumaea; but others, with Bochart and Michaelis, think it was *El Gouta*, or the valley of Damascus, of which city Uz, the grandson of Shem, is said to have been the founder (Josephus, Ant. l. i. c. 7). **Job.** i.e. *hated, at enmity with; the persecuted; the cry of woe; I will exclaim,* *S#347h. Jb 1:1, 5, 5, 5, 8, 9, 14, 20, 22. 2:3, 7, 10. 3:1, 2. 6:1. 9:1. 12:1. 16:1. 19:1. 21:1. 23:1. 26:1. 27:1. 29:1. 31:40. 32:1, 2, 3, 4, 12. 33:1, 31. 34:5, 7, 35, 36. 35:16. 37:14. 38:1. 40:1, 3, 6. 42:1, 7, 7, 8, 8, 8, 9, 10, 10, 12, 15, 16, 17. Ezk *14:14, 20. Ja *5:11. **perfect.** ver. 8. Jb 2:3. 23:11, 12. 31:1, etc. Ge 6:9. *17:1. 2 K +*20:3. 2 Ch 31:20, 21. Ps *37:37. 64:4. Pr 29:10h. SS 5:2h. 6:9h. Lk 1:6. Jn 1:47. +*17:6. Ro ◐*3:23. **upright.** ver. 8. Jb 2:3. 4:7. 8:6. 17:8. 23:7. *33:27. Ex 15:26. **feared God.** Ge 22:12. 42:18. Ex +*18:21. Ne 5:15. Pr *1:7. 8:13. 16:6. Da 6:20. **eschewed evil.** ver. 8. Jb *28:28. Ps 34:14. Pr 11:22mg. *14:16. 1 P 3:11.

2. **seven.** Ru 4:15n. 1 S 2:5. Je 15:9. **sons.** Jb 13:13. Est 5:11. Ps 107:38. +*127:3-5. 128:3, 4. **three daughters.** Jb 42:13.

3. **substance.** *or,* cattle. Ge 12:5. 13:6. 34:23. 2 Ch 32:29. **seven thousand.** Jb 42:12. Ge 12:16. 26:14. Nu 31:32-34. Jg 6:5. 1 S 25:2. 2 K 3:4. Pr *10:22. **household.** *or,* husbandry. Ge 26:14. 2 Ch 26:10. **greatest.** Jb 29:9, 10, 25. 31:37. **men.** Heb. sons. Jg 6:3. 7:12. 8:10. 1 K 4:30. **of the east.** Ge 25:6. 29:1. Nu 23:7. Jg 6:3.

4. **feasted.** lit. "drinking." ver. 5. Ge 19:3. Est 5:4n. **sent and called.** Est 5:12. Ps 133:1. He 13:1.

5. **gone about.** or, gone round. Jb 19:6. Le 19:27. **sanctified.** Jb 41:25. Ge 35:2, 3. Ex *19:10, 14. 1 S 16:5. Ne 12:30. Jn 11:55. **rose up.** Ge +*22:3. Ps *5:3. Ec 9:10. **offered.** Jb 42:8. Ge *8:20. Ex 18:12. 24:5. Le 1:3-6. **according.** 1 K 18:31. Ac 21:26. **Job said.** Ge *18:19. Dt +6:20. 1 S *12:23. 2 S +6:20. Ep *6:18. 1 Th *5:17. Ja √5:16. **It may be.** Ge 8:21. Ezk 18:31. 36:26. 2 C 11:2. **cursed.** ver. 11. Jb 2:9. Ex 21:17 w Dt 27:16. Le 24:10-16. 1 K 21:10, 13. Ezk 22:7. 2 P 2:10. Ju 9. or, blessed. Young notes, so Vulgate, Lee, Hengstenberg, and others. The original word occurs 320 times in the Old Testament, and in all passages with the exception of 1 K 21:10, 13; Jb 1:5, 11; 2:5, 9, it is universally admitted as meaning "to bless," as in ver. 10, 21 of this very chapter; forsaken—renounced—cursed, are equally false and worthless; the simple meaning here is, "they blessed God in their self-satisfaction, as if He had not seen or known or cared for sin." Lk 12:15-21. **in their hearts.** Ge 6:5. Je 4:14. *17:9, 10. Mk √7:21-23. Ac 8:22. 1 C 4:5. **Thus.** Jb 27:10. **continually.** Heb. all the days. Jb 15:20. Ge 6:5mg. 1 S 18:29. Lk 1:75. 18:7. Ep *6:18.

6. **Now.** Jb 2:1. **the sons.** ♪108H11, Ge +6:2. **of God.** ♪24L, Jb 38:7. Ge +6:2. +*6:2. Ps 89:6. Da 3:25. Lk 3:38. **came to.** Ps 103:20. Mt 18:10. or, station themselves. Jb 2:1. Ex 8:20. Zc 4:14. **Satan.** Heb. the adversary. i.e. *adversary, opposer,* *S#7854h. ver. 7, 8, 9, 12. 2:1, 2, 3, 4, 6, 7. Nu 22:22, 32mg. 1 S 29:4. 2 S 19:22. 1 K 5:4. 11:14, 23, 25h. *22:19. 1 Ch *21:1. Ps *109:6. Zc *3:1, 2, 2. 2 C *11:14. Re *12:9, 10. **came also.** 1 K *22:19, 21. Jn 6:70. **among them.** Heb. in the midst of them. Jb 2:1, 8. 15:19. 20:13 (within). 42:15. Ge 1:6 (in the midst). 18:24 (within). Ps 22:14, 22. 40:8mg, 10. Pr 1:14. 4:21. Je 44:7mg. Ezk *14:16mg. Zc 2:10.

7. **Satan.** T#15. Mt 13:19, 38, 39. Lk 4:5. 8:12. 22:31. Jn *8:44. 13:2. Ac 5:3. 2 C 2:11. *4:4. Ep 2:2. 6:12. 2 T 2:26. 1 P *5:8. Re 2:24. 12:9, 10, 12. 20:7, 8. **Whence.** Jb 2:2. 2 K 5:25. **From going.** Is 57:20. Zc 1:10, 11. 6:7. Mt 12:43. 1 P *5:8. Re 12:9, 12-17. 20:8.

8. **considered.** Heb. set thy heart on. Jb 2:3. 34:14. Ex +9:21mg. Ps +78:43mg. Ezk 40:4. Lk *22:31, 32. **my servant.** Nu 12:7, 8. Ps 89:20. Is 42:1. **none.** Nu 12:3. 1 K 4:30, 31. 2 K 23:25. Na 1:7. 2 T *2:19. **a perfect.** ver. 1. Jb 8:20. 9:22, 23. Ps 18:23. Jn 1:47. **upright.** Jb 12:4. 17:8, 9. 23:11, 12. Ps *84:11. **one that feareth.** Ne 5:15. Ps 36:1. Pr 8:13. Lk 23:39, 40. **escheweth.** ver. 1. Ps 34:14. 37:27. Is 1:16.

9. **Then Satan.** Zc 3:1. **Doth Job.** ver. 21. Jb 2:10. 21:14, 15. Ml 1:10. Mt 16:26. 1 T 4:8. 6:6.

10. **an hedge.** Ge 15:1. Dt 33:27-29. 1 S 25:16. Ps 5:12. *34:7. 80:12. Is *5:1, 2, 5. Zc *2:5, 8. 1 P 1:5. **about.** Ge 39:5. Dt 28:2-6. Ps 71:21. 128:1-4. **thou hast blessed.** Jb 42:12. Ge 26:12. 30:30. 49:25. Dt 7:13. 33:11. Ps 90:17. 107:38. Pr +*10:22. **substance.** *or,* cattle. Ge 30:43.

11. **But.** ver. 12. Jb 2:5. 19:21. Is 5:25. Ezk 25:7, 13, 16. **put forth.** ♪22A14.8B. Anthropomorphism B879: in idiomatic expressions. "To put forth the hand," to inflict punishment. For another instance of this figure see Jb 2:5. **thine hand.** Ru ◐+*1:13. **touch.** ♪108B, Jb 4:5. 19:21. Ge 26:11. +26:29. Ru 2:9. Ps 105:15. Zc 2:8. Lk *22:31. Jn *19:11. **and he will curse thee.** Heb. if he curse thee not. ver. 5, 21. See on Jb 2:9. Is *8:21. Ml 3:13, 14. Re 16:9, 11, 21.

12. **Behold.** 1 K 22:22, 23. Lk 8:32. 22:31, 32. Jn *19:11. 2 C *12:7. **power.** Heb. hand. Ge 16:6. Dt 32:36mg. Je 38:5. Jn 3:35, 36. **only.** Jb 2:4-6. Ps *76:10. Is 27:8. 1 C √10:13. **So Satan.** Jb 2:7. Lk 8:33. **from the presence.** Ge 4:16. Ps *5:4.

13. **there was.** ver. 13. 1 S 1:4. 2 K 4:8. Lk 16:19. **a day.** ver. 6. Jb 2:1. **when.** ver. 4. Pr 27:1. Ec 9:12. Lk 12:19, 20. 17:27-29. 21:34. **eldest brother's.** or, the first-born. ver. 18. Jb +*18:13.

14. **messenger.** 1 S 4:17. 2 S 15:13. Je 51:31. **plowing.** Jb 4:8. 1 K 19:19.

15. **Sabeans.** lit. Sheba. ♪121J14, Ge +47:15. i.e. *he who is coming; eminent,* ✛S#7614h. Ge 10:7, 28.

25:3. Ps 72:10. Is 45:14. Ezk 23:42. Jl 3:8. **edge**. Ge 34:26mg. Ex 17:13. **and I only**. ver. 16, 17, 19. 1 S 22:20, 21.

16. **there came**. Ge 19:24. Le 9:24. 1 K 18:38. 2 K 1:10, 12, 14. Am 7:4. Re 13:13. **The fire of God**. *or*, A great fire. Ge 19:24. +*23:6mg. Ex 9:28. Nu 11:1, 3. 1 S 14:15mg. 26:12. 1 K 18:38. 2 K 1:12. 1 Ch 12:22. +*16:42. SS 8:6. Ho 13:5. Jon 3:3mg.

17. **The Chaldeans**. Ge 11:28. Is 23:13. Hab 1:6. **fell**. Heb. rushed. Jg 9:33, 44. 20:37. **I only am**. ver. 15. 2 S 1:3.

18. **there came**. Jb 6:2, 3. 16:14. 19:9, 10. 23:2. Is 28:19. Je 51:31. La 1:12. Am 4:6-11. **Thy sons**. ver. 4, 13. Jb 8:4. 27:14. Ps 34:19. Ec 9:2. **eating**. 2 S 13:28.

19. **a great**. Je 4:11, 12. Ep 2:2. **from**. Heb. from aside, etc. **it fell**. Jg 16:30. 1 K 20:30. Mt 7:27. Lk 13:1-5. Ac 28:4. **they are dead**. Ge 37:32, 33. 42:36. 2 S 18:33. **to tell thee**. Ps 34:19. 36:6. Ec 9:2. Is 21:4. Lk 13:1-5.

20. **rent**. Ge 37:29, 34. Jsh 7:6. Ezr 9:3. **mantle**. *or*, robe. Jb 2:12. 29:14. Ex 28:4n. **shaved**. T#1279. Ge 41:14. Le 21:5. Ezr 9:3. Is 15:2. Je 7:29. 16:6. 48:37. Ezk 7:18. Mi 1:16. **fell**. Dt 9:18. 2 S *12:16-20. 2 Ch *7:3. Mt *26:39. 1 P *5:6. **and worshipped**. Ps 101:1. Is 24:15. Hab *3:17, 18. 21. **Naked**. Jb 22:6. 24:7, 10. 26:6. Ge 2:25. **came I**. Ge *3:19. Ps *49:17. Ec *5:15. *12:7. 1 T *6:7. **the Lord gave**. Jb *2:10. Ge 30:2. Ps +*39:9. Ec 5:19. La +√3:38. Ac +21:14. Ja *1:17. **the Lord**. 1 S +3:18. 2 K 20:19. Ps 89:52. **taken away**. Ge 45:5. 2 S 16:12. 1 K *12:15. Ps 39:9. Is 42:24. +√45:7. Am +√3:7. Mt *20:15. Ac 4:28. **blessed**. ver. 11. 1 S *3:18. 2 K 20:19. Mt *34:1. 89:38-52. Is 24:15. Ep *5:20. 1 Th *5:18.

22. **In all this**. Jb *2:10. Ja *1:4, 12. 5:11. 1 P *1:7. **charged God foolishly**. *or*, attributed folly to God. Jb +*2:10. 24:12. 33:13. *34:10, 18, 19. *40:4-8. Ru +*1:13. Ps 74:22. +*77:3. Pr +√19:3. Is +√29:24. Je 23:13mg. Ezk +*18:25. Ro *9:20.

JOB 2

Satan again appears before God, and obtains permission still further to try Job, 1-6. He smites him with sore boils from head to foot, 7, 8. His wife moves him to curse God and die; but he rebukes her, 9, 10. Three of his friends visit him; and, overwhelmed with surprise and grief, they keep silence seven days, 11-13.

1. **Again**. See on Jb 1:6. Is 6:1, 2. Lk 1:19. He 1:14. **sons**. ƒ108H11, Ge +6:2. **of God**. ƒ24L, Ge +6:2.

2. **From whence**. Ge 16:8. **From going**. Jb 1:7. Jn 14:30. 2 C *4:4. 1 P *5:8.

3. **Hast thou**. See on Jb 1:1, 8. 9:20. Ge 6:9. Ps *37:37. Lk *12:8. Ph 3:12. 1 P 5:10. **none like**. T#645. Ge 7:1. Ps 1:2, 4. Je 15:19. Ezk 44:23. Jn 15:19. Ac 8:21. 2 C +*5:17 (T#591). T *2:14. 1 P 2:9. 1 J 5:19. **an upright**. Pr 11:3. 13:6. 14:2. 15:8. 16:17. Ro 12:12. **holdeth**. Jb 1:21, 22. 13:15. 27:5, 6. Ps 26:1. 41:12. Ro 12:12. 2 C 4:9. 1 Th 3:3. Ja 1:12. 1 P 1:7. **thou movedst**. Jb 1:11. **destroy him**. Heb. swallow him up. Jb 5:5. 7:19. 8:18. 10:8. 20:15, 18. Ge 41:7. 2 S 20:20. **without**. Jb 9:17. Jn √9:3.

4. **all that**. Est 7:3, 4. Is 2:20, 21. Je 41:8. Mt *6:25. *16:26. Ac 27:18, 19. Ph 3:8-10. **Skin for skin**. In the rude and early ages skins were considered the most

valuable property. The term *skin* is also used to denote the person of a man generally (Jb 18:13), and hence the proverb "skin for skin" is, in plain English, "property for person." **life**. Heb. *nephesh*, soul, Ge +44:30.

5. **put forth**. ƒ22A14.8B, Jb +1:11. Jb 1:11. 19:20, 21. 1 Ch 21:17. Ps 32:3, 4. 38:2-7. 39:10. Mt *10:29-31. Re *12:9, 10. **touch**. ƒ108B, Ge +26:29. Ps 6:2. 32:3. 51:8. **bone and**. Jb 19:20. Lk +*24:39. **he will curse**. ver. 9. Jb 1:5, 11. Le 24:15. Is 8:21.

6. **Behold**. See on Jb 1:12. **but**. *or*, only. **save**. Jb 38:10, 11. Ps 65:7. 72:13. 118:18. *121:3. Lk 8:29-33. 22:31, 32. 1 C √10:13. Re 2:10. 20:1, 2, 7. **his life**. Heb. *nephesh*, soul, Ge +44:30. By *naphsho*, "his soul," Maimonides understands the mind, or intellectual powers.

7. **So went**. 1 K 22:22. **sore boils**. *Shechin ra*, supposed to be the *judham*, or black leprosy, of the Arabs, termed *elephantiasis* by the Greeks, from its rendering the skin, like that of the elephant, scabrous, dark colored, and furrowed all over with tubercles. This loathsome and most afflictive disease is accompanied with most intolerable itching. Jb 30:17-19, 30. Ex 9:9-11. Dt 28:27, 35. Ps 38:7. Lk 16:20. 1 P 4:12. Re 16:11. **from the sole**. Dt 28:35. 2 S 14:25. Is *1:6. 3:17.

8. **took him**. Jb 19:14-17. Ps 38:5, 7. Lk 16:20, 21. **he sat**. Jb 42:6. 2 S 13:19. Is 61:3. La 4:5. Ezk 27:30. Jon 3:6. Mt 11:21.

9. **his wife**. Ge 3:6, 12. 1 K 11:4. **retain**. ver. 3. Jb 21:14, 15. 2 K 6:33. Ml 3:14. **curse God**. ver. 5. Jb √1:11n. Young notes, Bless God for this comfort and grace; so Targum, etc. Others take the use of *barak*, to bless, as a euphemism for "to curse." This is one of eighteen or so emendations of the Sopherim, by which the primitive Hebrew text was changed from *kalal*, "to curse," to *barak*, "to bless," out of reverence for the name of God. This change was made at Jb 1:5, 11; 2:5, 9. See 2 S 12:14; 1 K 21:10, 13; and Ps 10:3, where similar changes were made. For a list of other passages where the Sopherim made changes, often for the sake of euphemy, see Ge +18:22.

10. **Thou speakest**. Ge *3:17. 2 S 19:22. Mt *16:23. **as one**. 2 S 6:20, 21. *13:13. *24:10. 2 Ch *16:9. Pr *9:6, 13. Mt *25:2. **the foolish**. Jb 30:8. Dt 32:6. Pr +√19:3. **women speaketh**. 2 S ◑+*20:16. 1 T 5:13-15. 2 T 3:6-8. **receive good**. Jb *1:1-3, 10, 21. 2 S 19:28. Ps +*37:24. *104:28. +*145:9. Je +√29:11. La +*3:38-41. Mt +*5:45. Lk +*6:35. Jn *18:11. Ro *12:12. He *12:9-11. Ja +*1:17. *5:10, 11. **not receive**. He seems persuaded his troubles came from the Adversary, not from God (Young), see Jb 9:24. **evil**. Ru +√1:13. 2 K +*6:23. Am +√3:6. **In all this**. Jb *1:22. Ps *39:1. *59:12. Mt *12:34-37. Ja *3:2. 5:10.

11. **friends**. Jb 6:14. 16:20. 19:19, 21. 42:7. Pr 17:17. 18:24. 27:10. **Eliphaz**. i.e. *my God is strong*. Ge +36:4. **Temanite**. *S#8489h. Jb 2:11. 4:1. 15:1. 22:1. 42:7, 9. Ge 36:34. 1 Ch 1:45. From Teman (i.e. *the southern country; southward*, Ge +36:11), in Edom. Jb 6:19. 15:1. Ge 36:11, 15. Je 49:7. **Bildad**. i.e. *son of contention; confusing (by mingling) love*, *S#1085h. Jb 2:11. 8:1. 18:1. 25:1. 42:9. **Shuhite**. *S#7747h. Jb 2:11. 8:1. 18:1. 25:1. 42:9. Descendant of Shuah (i.e. *depression; prostration*, Ge +25:2), in Arabia Petraea. Jb 8:1. 18:1. Ge 25:2. 1 Ch 1:32. **Zophar**. i.e. *chirper; departing early; insolence; a climber; crown*, *S#6691h. Jb 2:11. 11:1. 20:1. 42:9. **Naamathite**. i.e. *inhabitant of Naamah* (i.e. *pleasantness*, Ge +4:22), in Edom. *S#5284h.

Jb 2:11. 11:1. 20:1. 42:9. **appointment.** Ex 25:22. 29:42, 43. 30:6, 36. **to come.** Jb 42:11. Ge 37:35. Is 51:19. Jn 11:19. Ro 12:15. 1 C 12:26. He 13:3. **to mourn.** Pr 17:17. Ec 7:4. Ro 12:15. lit. "nod to him." Jb 42:11. **to comfort.** Jb 13:4. 16:2.

12. **lifted.** ℐ144A12, Ge +22:13. **knew him.** Jb 19:14. Ru 1:19-21. La 4:7, 8. **their voice.** Ge 27:34. Jg 2:4. 1 S 11:4. 30:4. 2 S 13:36. Est 4:1. **they rent.** Jb +1:20. **sprinkled.** Ex 9:8, 10. 24:6, 8. 29:16, 20. **dust upon.** Jsh 7:6. Ne 9:1. La 2:10. Ezk 27:30. Re 18:19.

13. **they sat.** ℐ121S3Y, La +2:10. Ezr 9:3. Ne 1:4. Is 3:26. 47:1. **seven days and.** Ge 1:5, 8. 50:10. Ezk 3:15. **none spake.** Jb 4:2. Ps 77:4. Ec 3:7. **grief.** or, pain. Jb 5:18. 14:22. 16:6. Ps 39:2. Is 17:11. 65:14. Je 15:18. La 1:12.

JOB 3

Job vehemently curses the day of his birth, 1-10. He complains, because he died not from the womb; and expatiates on the quietness of the grave, 11-19. He longs for present death, and bemoans his misery, 20-26.

1. Here the style of the book is changed to poetry, which is adorned by bold figures, according to the genius of the East. **After.** Jb 1:22. 2:10. **opened.** ℐ171J11. Synecdoche of the Species B632: to answer, or open the mouth, is put for *speaking.* For other instances of this figure see Ps 119:172. Mt 11:25. Mk 11:14. **his mouth.** Jb 35:16. Ps 39:2, 3. 106:33. **cursed.** ver. 3. Jb 1:11. 2:5, 9. Je 20:14, 15. La 4:1. Ja 3:8. **his day.** That is, the day of his birth.

2. **spake.** Heb. answered. Jg 18:14.

3. **Let the day.** That is, as we say, "Let it be blotted out of the calendar." Jb 10:18, 19. Je 15:10. *20:14, 15.

4. **darkness.** Ex 10:22, 23. Jl 2:2. Am 5:18. Mt 27:45. Ac 27:20. Re 16:10. **God regard.** Dt 11:12.

5. **the shadow.** Jb 10:21, 22. 16:16. 24:17. 28:3. 38:17. Ps *23:4. 44:19. 107:10, 14. Is 9:2. Je 2:6. 13:16. Am 5:8. Mt 4:16. Lk 1:79. **stain it.** or, challenge it. Nu 35:19. or, redeem. Jb 19:25. Ge 48:16. Ex 6:6. **let a cloud.** Dt 4:11. Ezk 30:3. 34:12. Jl 2:2. He 12:18. **let the blackness.** or, let them terrify it, as those *who have* a bitter day. Jg +18:25mg. Je 4:28. Am 8:10.

6. **let it not be joined unto the days.** or, let it not rejoice among the days. Is 14:20. **joined.** Ge 49:6. Ps *86:11. Is 14:20. **months.** Jb 7:3. 29:2. 39:2. Ex 2:2.

7. **solitary.** Is 13:20-22. 24:8. Je 7:34. Re 18:22, 23.

8. **Let them curse.** That is, probably, "Let them curse my birthday who hate daylight, such as thieves, murderers, etc.; and let them curse it who, like me, being weary of life, are so desperate as to provoke the leviathan." **who are ready.** 2 Ch 35:25. Je 9:17, 18. Am 5:16. Mt 11:17. Mk 5:38. **their mourning.** or, a leviathan. Jb 41:1, 10. Ps 74:14.

9. **look.** ℐ155D, Ge +4:10. **for light.** Jb 30:26. Je 8:15. 13:16. **the dawning of the day.** Heb. the eyelids of the morning. ℐ155D, Ge +4:10. Jb 41:18.

10. **it shut not.** Jb 10:18, 19. Ge 20:18. 29:31, 32. 1 S 1:5. Ec 6:3-5. Je 20:17, 18. **hid.** Jb 6:2, 3. 10:1. 23:2. Ec 11:10.

11. **died I.** Ps 58:8. Je 15:10. Ho 9:14. **ghost.** Heb. *gava,* Ge +49:33 (*S#1478h). **when I came.** Ps 22:9, 10. 71:6. 139:13-16. Is 46:3.

12. **the knees.** Ge 30:3. 50:23. Ps 71:6. Is 66:12. Ezk 16:4, 5.

13. **then had I been at rest.** Ec 6:3-5. 9:10.

14. **kings.** Jb 30:23. 1 K 2:10. 11:43. Ps 49:6-10, 14. 89:48. Ec 8:8. Is 14:10-16. Ezk 27:18-32. **which built.** Who erect splendid mausoleums, funeral monuments, etc. to keep their names from perishing, while their bodies are turned to corruption. Jb 15:28. Is 5:8. Ezk 26:20.

15. **who filled their houses.** That is, "the *covetous,* whom nothing can satisfy," as the poet Saady has observed, "but the dust that fills his mouth, when laid in the grave." Jb 22:25. 27:16. Nu 22:18. 1 K 10:27. Is 2:7. Zp 1:18. Zc 9:3.

16. **an hidden.** Ps *58:8. 1 C *15:8. **untimely birth.** or, abortion. Ec 4:3. *6:3. Lk +√1:44n. **infants.** 1 S 15:3. 22:19.

17. **the wicked.** Jb *14:13. Ps *55:5-8. Mt +√10:28. Lk *12:4. 2 Th *1:6, 7. 2 P 2:8. **the weary.** Heb. the wearied in strength. Dt 25:18. 2 S 17:2. Ec 1:8. **at rest.** Is *57:1, 2. Mt 11:28. He *4:9, 11. Re +*14:13.

18. **they.** Jb 39:7. Ex *5:6-8, 15-19. Jg *4:3. Is *14:3, 4.

19. **The small.** Jb *30:23. Ps *49:2, 6-10. Ec *8:8. *12:5, 7. Lk *16:22, 23. He +√9:27. **and the servant.** Ps *49:14-20.

20. **Wherefore.** Jb 6:9. 7:15, 16. Je 20:18. **is.** ℐ96C9, Ge +2:10. **light.** ver. 16. Jb 33:28, 30. **the bitter.** Jb 7:15, 16. 1 S 1:10. 2 K +4:27mg. Pr 31:6. **soul.** Heb. *nephesh,* Ge +34:3.

21. **long.** Heb. wait. Nu *11:15. 1 K 19:4. Jon 4:3, 8. Re 9:6. **cometh.** ℐ63B, Ge +25:28. **dig.** Pr 2:4.

22. **rejoice exceedingly.** Ps 43:4. 45:15. 65:12. Pr 23:24. Is 16:10. Je 48:33. Da 1:10. Ho 9:1. Jl 1:16. **grave.** Heb. *qeber,* Ge +23:4. Jb 5:26. 10:19. 17:1. 21:32.

23. **Why.** ℐ63I1D, Nu +26:4. **whose way.** Is 40:27. **hedged in.** Jb 12:14. 19:8. Ps 31:8. La 3:7, 9. Ho 2:6.

24. **my sighing.** Jb 7:19. Ps 80:5. 102:9. **I eat.** Heb. my meat. **my roarings.** Ps 22:1, 2. 32:3. 38:8. Is 59:11. La 3:8.

25. **the thing,** etc. Heb. I feared a fear and it came upon me. Jb 15:21mg. Ps ◐+*34:4. Pr +*10:24. Ec 9:12. Is +*8:12. Je +*10:5. 15:17, 18. Jon 4:2. **come upon.** Jb 4:5. **that which.** Jb 1:5. 31:23. Pr +*10:24.

26. **yet trouble came.** Jb 27:9. Ps 143:11.

JOB 4

Eliphaz reproves Job for impatience, and want of confidence in God, 1-6. He states that divine judgments come not on the righteous, but on the wicked, 7-11. He relates his vision, confirming this doctrine, 12-21.

1. **Eliphaz.** Jb 2:11. 15:1. 22:1. 42:9. **answered.** Jb 3:1, 2. 6:1. 8:1.

2. **to commune.** Heb. a word. **wilt thou.** 2 C 2:4-6. √7:8-10. **withhold himself from speaking.** Heb. refrain from words. Jb 32:18-20. Je 6:11. *20:9. Ac *4:20.

3. **Behold.** Ge *18:19. Pr *10:21. *15:7. 16:21. Is *50:4. Ep *4:29. Col *4:6. **and thou hast strengthened.** Jb *16:5. Dt *3:28. Ezr 6:22. Is *35:3. Ezk 13:22. Lk *22:32, 43. He *10:24.

4. **Thy words.** Ep *4:29. Col *4:6. **upholden.** 1 S *23:16. Ps *145:14. Pr *12:18. *16:23, 24. 2 C *1:4. *2:7. *7:6. 1 Th *5:14. He 12:12, 13. **strengthened.** 1 S *23:16. 2 C *1:4. He *10:24. **feeble knees.** Heb.

bowing knees. Is *35:3, 4. Da 5:6. He *12:12.

5. **it is come.** Jb 3:25, 26. **thou faintest.** Pr *24:10. Je *12:5. 2 C 4:1, 16. He 12:3, 5. **it toucheth.** Jb 1:11. 2:5. 19:21.

6. **Is this.** ƒ63B, Ge +25:28. **thy fear.** Jb 1:1, 9, 10. 2 K 20:3. **thy confidence.** Jb 13:15. Pr 3:26. 14:26. **thy hope.** Jb 17:15. 1 P 1:13, 17. **the uprightness.** Jb 1:8. 16:17. 23:11, 12. 27:5, 6. 29:12-17. 31:1, etc.

7. **who ever.** Jb 8:20. 9:22, 23. 36:6, 7. Ge ◐+19:30. Ps *37:25. Ec 7:15. 9:1, 2. Ac 28:4. 2 P 2:9.

8. **they that plow.** Ps 7:14-16. Pr 22:8. Je 4:18. Ho 8:7. 10:12, 13. 2 C 9:6. Ga *6:7, 8. **reap the same.** Jb 5:13. 34:11. Ge +6:13 (T#566). Nu +*32:23. Ps 5:10. 7:16. Pr 1:31. 5:22. 11:5, 6. 12:13, 14. 26:27. Is 3:10, 11. Je *2:19. 6:19. Ezk 22:31.

9. **the blast.** ƒ24L, Ge +6:2. Ex 15:8, 10. 2 K 19:7. Ps 18:15. **by the breath.** Heb. *ruach*, Ge +2:7. Ex 15:8. ƒ22K3. Anthropomorphism B896. Breath is attributed to God. For other instances of this figure see Ps 18:15. Is *30:33. **of his nostrils.** that is, *by his anger*. ƒ22A9, Ex +15:8. Jb 1:19. 15:30. Is 11:4. 30:33. 2 Th 2:8. Re 2:16.

10. **the teeth.** Jb 29:17. Ps 3:7. 57:4. 58:6. Pr 30:14.

11. **old lion.** Jb 38:39. Ge 49:9. Nu 23:24. 24:9. Ps 7:2. Je 4:7. Ho 11:10. 2 T 4:17. **perisheth.** Ps 34:10. **the stout.** Jb 1:19. 8:3, 4. 27:14, 15.

12. **a thing.** Jb 62:11. **secretly.** Heb. by stealth. ƒ46A, Le +26:30. Ge 40:15. **a little.** 1 C 13:12.

13. **thoughts.** Jb 33:14-16. Ge 20:3. 28:12. 31:24. 46:2. Nu 12:6. 22:19, 20. Da 2:19, 28, 29. 4:5. **deep sleep.** Ge 2:21. 15:12. Da 8:18. 10:9.

14. **Fear.** Jb 7:14. Ps 119:120. Is 6:5. Da 10:11. Hab 3:16. Lk 1:12, 29. Re 1:17. **came upon.** Heb. met. Jb 39:21. Ge 42:38. **all my bones.** Heb. the multitude of my bones. Jb 33:19.

15. **a spirit.** Heb. *ruach*, Ps +104:4. Mt 14:26. Lk 24:37-39. He 1:7, 14. **the hair.** Is 13:8. 21:3, 4. Da 5:6.

16. **there**, etc. *or,* I heard a still voice. 1 K 19:12. Ps 107:29.

17. **Shall mortal.** Jb 8:3. 9:2. 35:2. 40:8. Ge *18:25. Ps 143:2. 145:17. Ec *7:20. Je 12:1. Ro 2:5. 3:4-7. 9:20. *11:33. ƒ85R. Erotesis B956: In absurdities and impossibilities. For other instances of this figure see Jb 14:4. Je 13:23. Jn 3:4. 6:52. 7:48. 12:34. **shall a man.** Jb 9:30, 31. 14:4. 15:14. 25:4. Je *17:9. Mt *19:17. Mk √7:20-23. Re 4:8. ƒ85S. Erotesis B956: Double Questions. For other instances of this figure see Jb 6:5. 8:3. 10:4. 11:2, 7. 22:3. Is 10:15. Je 5:9, 29.

18. **he put.** Jb 15:15, 16. 25:5, 6. Ps 103:20, 21. 104:4. Is 6:2, 3. **and his angels he charged with folly.** *or,* nor in his angels *in whom* he put light. 2 P 2:4. Ju 6.

19. **How much less.** Jb 15:16. **dwell.** Jb 10:9. 13:12. 33:6. Ge +*2:7. +*3:19. 18:27. Ec +*12:7. 2 C 4:7. 5:1. **crushed.** Jb 13:28. 14:2. Ps 39:4, 5, 11. 90:5-7. 103:15, 16. +*146:4. 1 P 1:24.

20. **destroyed.** Heb. beaten in pieces. 2 Ch 15:6mg. Is 24:12. Je 46:5mg. Mi 1:7. **from morning.** Is 38:12, 13. **they perish.** Jb 14:14. 16:22. Ps 39:13. 90:5, 6. 92:7. **for ever.** ✽S#5331h. Jb 4:20. 14:20. 20:7. 23:7. 34:36 (the end). 36:7. 1 S 15:29 (strength, mg; or eternity, or victory). 2 S 2:26. 1 Ch 29:11 (victory). Ps 9:6 (perpetual end; lit. completed forever), 18 (alway). 10:11 (lit. not forever). 13:1. *16:11 (evermore). 44:23. 49:9, 19. 52:5. 68:16. 74:1, 3 (perpetual), 10, 19. 77:8.

79:5. 89:46. 103:9 (always). Pr 21:28 (constantly). Is 13:20. *25:8 (victory). 28:28. 33:20. 34:10 (forever and ever). 57:16 (always). Je 3:5 (the end). 15:18 (perpetual). 50:39. La 3:18 (strength). 5:20. Am 1:11. 8:7. Hab 1:4 (never). **without.** Jb 18:17. 20:7. 2 Ch 21:20. Ps 37:36. Pr 10:7.

21. **excellency.** Ps *39:5, 11. *49:14. *146:3, 4. Is *14:16. Lk *16:22, 23. Ja *1:11. **die.** Jb *36:12. Ps *49:20. Is *2:22. Lk *12:20. **without wisdom.** Pr *5:23. Ho *4:6. Lk +*11:52.

JOB 5

Eliphaz proceeds to show the close connection between wickedness and misery, and that man is born to trouble, 1-7. He recommends seeking to God in affliction, by declaring his power and wonderful works, 8-16. He speaks of the benefit of correction, and the privileges of those who duly improve it, 17-27.

1. **and to which.** Jb 15:8-10, 15. Is 41:1, 21-23. He *12:1. **the saints.** Jb 4:18. 15:15. Dt 33:2, 3. Ps 16:3. 106:16. Ep 1:1. **turn.** *or,* look. Jb 6:28. 21:5mg. 24:18. 36:21.

2. **wrath.** T#735. Jb 18:4. Ps 37:8. Pr 11:17. 14:16. 17, 29. 15:18. 16:32. 19:19. 22:24. 24:17, 18. 25:28. 26:21. 27:4. 29:22. Ec 7:9. Jon 4:9. Ep 4:31. **the foolish.** Ps *14:1. 75:4. 92:6. 94:8. 107:17. Pr *1:22, 23. 8:5. Ec 7:9. **envy.** *or,* indignation. Ge 30:1. 1 S 18:8, 9. Ro 2:8. **one.** Ho 7:11. 2 T 3:6.

3. **taking.** Jb 27:8. Ps 37:35, 36. 73:3-9, 18-20. 92:7. Je 12:1-3. **cursed.** Dt 27:15, etc. Ps 69:25. Ac 1:20.

4. **children.** Jb 4:10, 11. 8:4. 18:16-19. 27:14. Ex *20:5. Ps 109:9-15. 119:155. 127:5. **they are crushed.** Jb 1:19. Lk 13:4, 5. **neither.** Jb 10:7. Ps 7:2. 50:22.

5. **harvest.** Dt 28:33, 51. Jg 6:3-6. Is 62:8. **the thorns.** Jg 6:11. 2 Ch 33:11. **the robber.** Jb 1:15, 17. 12:6. 18:9. Ho 8:7. **swalloweth.** Jb 2:3mg. 20:15. Je 51:34, 44. La 2:5, 16.

6. **affliction.** *or,* iniquity. Jb 4:8. Pr 14:22. *22:8. **trouble.** Jb 34:29. Dt 32:27. 1 S 6:9. Ps 90:7, 8. Is 45:7. La 3:38, 39. Am +*3:6. **spring out.** Ho 10:4. He *12:15.

7. **man.** T#2. Jb 7:17, 18. 14:1. Ge *3:17-19. Ps *90:8, 9. 1 C √10:13. **born.** Ge 4:26. 6:1. 10:21. **trouble.** *or,* labor. Jb 14:1. Ec 1:8. 2:22. 5:15-17. **sparks fly upward.** Heb. sons of the burning coal lift up to fly. Jb 39:27. Pr 26:2. Ob 4.

8. **seek.** Jb 8:5. 22:21, 27. Ge 32:7-12. 2 Ch 33:12, 13. Ps +*50:15. 77:1, 2. 116:3, 4. Jon 2:1-7. **unto God.** Ps *37:5. 2 T *1:12. 1 P 2:23. 4:19.

9. **doeth.** Jb 9:10. 11:7-9. 37:5. Ex 15:11. Ps 40:5. 72:18. 86:10. 136:4. 145:3. Da +4:3. Ro *11:33. **unsearchable.** Heb. there is no search. Is 40:28. Ro 11:33. Ep 3:8. **marvellous.** Jb 26:5-14. **without number.** Heb. till *there be* no number. Ps 40:5. 139:18.

10. **giveth.** Jb 28:26. Ps 65:9-11. 104:13. 147:8. Je 5:24. 10:13. 14:22. 51:16. Am 4:7. Mt *5:45. Ac 14:17. **fields.** Heb. outplaces. Jb 18:17. 31:32. 38:26-28. Am +5:16n (✚S#2351h, highways).

11. **set up.** 1 S 2:7, 8. Ps 91:14. 107:41. 113:7, 8. Ezk 17:24. Lk 1:52, 53. **low.** ƒ138B, Ge +13:16. **those.** Lk 6:21. Ja 1:9. 4:6-10. 1 P 5:10. **exalted.** ƒ138B, Ge +13:16. Dt 33:27-29. 1 P 1:3.

12. **disappointeth.** Jb 12:16, 17. Ne 4:15. Ps 33:10, 11. 37:17. Pr +*21:30. Is *8:10. 19:3, 11-14. **their hands.** Ps 21:11. 76:5. Is 37:36. Ac 12:11. 23:12, etc.

their enterprise. *or*, any thing.

13. **taketh.** 2 S 15:31, 34. 17:23. Est 6:4-11. 7:10. *9:25. Ps *7:15, 16. 9:15, 16. 35:7, 8. 141:10. Pr 5:22. Da 6:24. Lk 1:51. 1 C ⟩1:19, 20, 27. ⟩3:19, 20. **of the froward.** Ps 18:26. Pr 3:32. 8:13.

14. **meet with.** *or*, run into. Ge 32:17. 33:8. Ex 4:24. **darkness.** Jb 12:25. Dt *28:29. Pr *4:19. Is 59:10. Am 8:9. **grope.** Jb *12:25. Ge 27:12, 22. 31:34mg, 37mg. Ex 10:21.

15. **he saveth.** Ps 10:14, 17, 18. 35:10. 72:4, 12, 13. 107:41. 109:31. 140:12.

16. **the poor.** 1 S 2:8, 9. Ps 9:18. Is 14:32. Zc 9:12. Lk +*4:18. **and iniquity.** ⌐121N1, Ge +31:54. Ex 11:7. Ps 63:11. 107:42. Ro 3:19.

17. **happy.** Jb 34:31, 32. Ps *94:12. *119:75. Pr *3:11, 12. Je 31:18-20. He *12:5-11. Ja *1:12. *5:11. Re *3:19. **despise not.** Pr 24:10. He 12:5. **chastening.** Jb 34:31, 32. **Almighty.** ✚S#7706h. Ex +6:3. Jb 6:4, 14. 8:3, 5. 11:7. 13:3. 15:25. 21:15, 20. 22:3, 17, 23, 25, 26. 23:16. 24:1. 27:2, 10, 11, 13. 29:5. 31:2, 35. 32:8. 33:4. 34:10, 12. 35:13. 37:23. 40:2.

18. **he maketh sore.** Dt +*32:39. 1 S 2:6, 7. Ps *147:3. Is 30:26. **bindeth up.** Ex *15:26. Is 30:26. 61:1. Ho 6:1. ⌐22C29. Anthropomorphism B889. Human actions are attributed to God: binding up. For other instances of this figure see Ps 147:3. Is 61:1. Ho 6:1. **make whole.** Ps +*103:2, 3. Is 12:3. Lk 4:18, 40.

19. **deliver thee.** Ps *34:19. *91:3-7. Pr *24:16. 1 C √10:13. 2 C 1:8-10. 2 P *2:9. **in seven.** Young notes, that is, any indefinite number. In Jb 2:13 Young suggests seven is a "round, sacred number." Pr 24:16. Is 4:1. **no evil.** Ps 91:7-10.

20. **famine.** Ge 45:7-11. 1 K 17:6, 9, 14, 15. Ps 33:19. 34:9, 10. 37:19. Pr 10:3. Is 33:16. Hab *3:17, 18. **redeem.** Ps *49:7, 15. 103:4. Ho *13:14. **in war.** T#774. Dt 20:4. 23:14. 2 Ch 13:12. Ps 27:3. 60:12. 91:5. 144:10. Pr 3:25, 26. Is *41:11, 12. Je *39:17, 18. Mt 24:6. **power.** Heb. hands. Ps 63:10mg. **the sword.** Le 26:6.

21. **be hid.** T#777. Jb 11:15. Ps *31:20. 37:6. 55:21. 57:3, 4. Pr 12:18. Is *54:17. Je 18:18. Ja 3:5-8. **from the scourge.** *or*, when the tongue scourgeth. ⌐121S1, Ge 49:10. "Scourge" is put for the power of the tongue, the sign put for the thing signified. Jb 9:23. Ps *31:20. **neither.** Ps 91:5-7.

22. **famine.** Ge 45:7. 1 K 17:6, 15, 16. Ps 33:18, 19. **laugh.** ⌐121S2, Ge +21:6. 2 K 19:21. **afraid.** Ps 91:5-7. Is 11:9. 35:9. 65:25. Ezk 34:25. Da 6:22.

23. **thou.** Ps 91:12, 13. Ho *2:18. Ro *8:38, 39. **stones.** ⌐171I4. Synecdoche of the Species B626. Stones are put for whatever is hurtful to the soil. **beasts.** Le 26:6. Is 11:9. Ezk 14:15, 16. Da 6:22.

24. **thou shalt know.** Jb *18:6, 15, 21. *21:7-9. 1 S 30:3. Is *4:5, 6. **thy tabernacle**, etc. *or*, peace is thy tabernacle. Ps *25:13mg. **thou shalt visit.** Dt *28:6. Ps *91:10. *121:7, 8. or, inspect. Jb 7:18. 31:14. **sin.** *or*, err. Young notes, in the examination. Ps 107:4, 40. +130:8. Is +60:21. Je *32:40. 31:31-34. Ezk *36:27. Zp 3:13. 1 C 15:24-28. Re 21:3-7. 22:3.

25. **thy seed.** Jb 42:13-16. Ge 15:5. Le 26:9. Dt 28:4. Ps 112:2. 127:3-5. 128:3-6. **great.** *or*, much. or, numerous. **as the grass.** Ps 72:16. Is 44:3, 4.

26. **grave.** Heb. *qeber*, Ge +23:4. **in a full age.** Jb *42:16, 17. Ge *15:15. +*25:8n. Ex +23:26. Ps *91:16. Pr 9:11. +*10:27. **cometh.** Heb. ascendeth. Jb 36:20h. Ge 32:24mg.

27. **we have searched.** Jb 8:8-10. 12:2. 13:2. 15:9, 10, 17. 32:11, 12. Ps 111:2. Pr 2:3-5. **for thy good.** Heb. for thyself. Jb 22:2. Dt 10:13. Pr 9:12.

JOB 6

Job shows that his sufferings were very great, and his complaint natural, 1-7. He prays for death, as the only comfort which he could hope for, 8-13. He reproves his friends, as unkind and unfaithful, 14-30.

1. **answered.** Jb 4:1.

2. **throughly.** Jb 4:5. 23:2. 31:6. **laid.** Heb. lifted up. Is 40:15.

3. **heavier.** Pr 27:3. Mt 11:28. **than.** ⌐102B, Ge +13:16. **my words are swallowed up.** that is, I want words to express my grief. Jb 37:19, 20. Ps 40:5. 77:4.

4. **the arrows.** ⌐22D5B, Dt +32:23. Jb 16:12-14. Dt 32:23, 42. Ps 7:13. 18:14. 21:12. 38:2. 45:5. La 3:12, 13. **drinketh up.** Dt 32:24. Ps 143:7. Pr 18:14. Mk 14:33, 34. 15:34. **spirit.** Heb. *ruach*, Ge +41:8. **the terrors.** Jb 9:17. 30:15. 31:23. Ps 88:15, 16. 2 C *5:11.

5. **Doth.** ⌐138C, Ge +22:14. **when he hath grass.** Heb. at grass. Ps 104:14. **or.** ⌐85S, Jb +4:17. **loweth.** Ps 42:1. Je 14:6. Jl 1:18-20.

6. **that which.** ver. *25. Jb *16:2. Le *2:13. Ps 107:18. Lk *14:34. Col *4:6. **without salt.** Mt *5:13. Mk *9:50. **taste.** ver. 30. Jb *12:11. *34:3. Ps *119:103. He 6:4, 5.

7. **soul.** Heb. *nephesh*, Nu +11:6. **as my sorrowful meat.** ⌐171I8, Ge +3:19. 1 K 17:12. 22:27. Ps 102:9. Ezk 4:14, 16. 12:18, 19. Da 10:3.

8. **O that.** Jb 14:13. **might have.** Ps +*27:7 (T#1434). *37:4. **the thing that I long for.** Heb. my expectation. ⌐121R7, Ge +43:11. ver. 11-13. Jb 17:14-16. Ps *119:81.

9. **that it would.** Jb *3:20-22. *7:15, 16. *14:13. Nu 11:14, 15. 1 K *19:4. Jon 4:3, 8. Re *9:6. **that he would.** Jb 19:21. Ps *32:4. Is *38:10-13.

10. **Then.** Jb 3:22. 21:33. **I would.** Jb 9:4. **let him not.** Dt 29:20. Ro *8:32. 2 P 2:4, 5. **have not concealed.** Jb *23:12. Ps 37:30. 40:9, 10. 71:17, 18. 119:13. Ac *20:20, 27. **the Holy One.** Le 19:2. 1 S 2:2. Is 30:11, 12. +*57:15. Ho 11:9. Hab 1:12. 3:3. Re 3:7. 4:8.

11. **What.** Jb 7:5-7. 10:20. 13:25, 28. 17:1, 14-16. Ps 39:5. 90:5-10. 102:23. 103:14-16. **life.** Heb. *nephesh*, soul, Ge +44:30.

12. **of brass.** Heb. brazen. Jb 40:18. 41:24.

13. **Is not my.** Jb 19:28. 2 C 1:12. Ga 6:4. **and is wisdom.** Jb 12:2, 3. 13:2.

14. **To him.** Jb 4:3, 4. 16:5. 19:21. Le +25:35 (T#526). 2 S 16:17. Ps 35:14, 15. Pr 17:17. Ro *12:15. 1 C 12:26. 2 C 11:29. Ga *6:2. Ph 4:14. He 13:3. **is afflicted.** Heb. melteth. Dt 20:8. **he forsaketh.** Ge 20:11. Ps 36:1-3. Lk 23:40. He +*3:12, 13.

15. **My brethren.** Jb 19:19. Ps 38:11. 41:9. 55:12-14. 88:18. Je 9:4, 5. 30:14. Mi 7:5, 6. Jn 13:18. 16:32. **as the stream.** Je 15:18. Ju 12.

16. **blackish.** Jb 5:15 (mourn). 30:28. Ps 35:14 (heavily). **ice.** Jb 37:10. 38:29. Ge 31:40. Ps 147:17. Je 36:30. Ezk 1:22. **snow.** Jb 37:6. 1 Ch 11:22. Ps 147:18. **is hid.** Dt 22:1, 3. Ps 55:1. Is 58:2.

17. **vanish.** Heb. are cut off. Jb 23:17. **when it is hot they are consumed.** Heb. in the heat thereof they are extinguished. Jb 24:19. 1 K 17:1, 7.

18. **The paths.** Is 3:12. **are turned.** Jg 16:29. Ru

3:8mg. **nothing.** Jb 12:24. 26:7. Ge 1:2. Is 40:23. **perish.** Jb 3:3. 4:7, 9, 11, 20. 8:13.

19. **troops.** Jb 31:32. **Tema.** i.e. *untilled.* ✗121J14, Ge +47:15. Ge 25:15. Is 21:14. Je 25:23. **looked.** Jb 28:24. 35:5. *36:25. 39:29. **companies.** lit. goings. Jb 29:6. Ps 68:24. Pr 31:27. Na 2:5. Hab 3:6. **Sheba.** ✗121J14, Ge +47:15. Jb 1:15. Ge 10:7. 25:3. 1 K 10:1. Ps 72:10. Ezk 27:22, 23. **waited.** or, hoped. Jb 3:9. 7:2. 17:13. 30:26.

20. **confounded.** Je 14:3, 4. 17:13. Ro 5:5. 9:33. **ashamed.** Ps ◑34:5.

21. **ye are nothing.** *or,* ye are like to them. Heb. to it. ver. 15. Jb 13:4. Ps 62:9. Is 2:22. Je 17:5, 6. **nothing.** Heb. not. Da 4:35. Ga 2:6. **ye see.** Jb 2:11-13. Ps 38:11. Pr 19:7. Je 51:9. Mt 26:31, 56. 2 T 4:16. Re 18:9, 10, 17, 18.

22. **Bring unto me.** Jb 42:11. 1 S 12:3. Ac 20:33. **reward.** ✗121N2, Ge +34:29.

23. **Redeem.** Jb 5:20. Le 25:48. Ne 5:8. Ps 49:7, 8, *15. 107:2. Je 15:21.

24. **Teach me.** Jb 5:27. 32:11, 15, 16. 33:1, 31-33. 34:32. Ps +*25:9. ✓32:8. ✓39:1. Pr 9:9. *25:12. Ja 1:19. **I will.** Jb 2:10. 33:3. Ps +*39:1, 2. *141:3. Pr *10:19. 11:12. *17:27, 28. Ec +*5:2. Mt *6:7. Ja *3:2. **cause me.** Jb 10:2. Ps *19:7, 12. *119:11, 99, 104, 105, 130. Pr +*8:8, 9. Mk ✓12:24. **erred.** Jb 19:4. Le 4:13. Is +*29:24.

25. **forcible.** Jb *4:4. 16:5. Pr *12:18. 16:21-24. *18:21. *25:11. Ec 12:10, 11. **what doth.** Jb 13:5. 16:3, 4. *21:34. 24:25. *32:3.

26. **reprove.** Jb 2:10. 3:3, etc. 4:3, 4. 34:3-9. 38:2. 40:5, 8. 42:3, 7. Mt 12:37. **one that.** ver. 4, 9. Jb 10:1. **as wind.** Jb 8:2. Ho 12:1. Ep *4:14.

27. **overwhelm.** Heb. cause to fall upon. Ge 2:21. 1 Ch 24:31. Est 6:10mg. Ps 22:18. Ezk 47:22. 48:29. Jon 1:7. **the fatherless.** Jb 22:9. 24:3, 9. 29:12. 31:17, 21. Ge +11:28. Ex +*22:22-24. Dt +10:18. Ps 82:3. Pr 23:10, 11. Ezk 22:7. Ml +*3:5. Ja 1:27. **ye dig.** Ps 7:15. 57:6. Je 18:20, 22.

28. **evident unto you.** Heb. before your face. **if I lie.** Jb 11:3. 13:4. 34:6. Nu 23:19.

29. **Return.** Jb 17:10. Ml 3:18. **my righteousness.** Jb 27:4-6. **in it.** that is, *in this matter.* Jb 13:18. 23:10. 34:5.

30. **iniquity.** Jb 33:8-12. 42:3-6. **cannot.** ver. 6. Jb 12:11. 34:3. He 5:14. **taste.** Heb. palate. Jb 12:11mg. 20:13mg. 29:10. 31:30mg. 33:2mg. 34:3mg. Ps 119:103mg. **discern.** Ml *3:18. **perverse things.** Ps 5:9. La ◑1:7mg.

JOB 7

Job excuses his desire of death, by representing the vanity, misery, and uselessness of his life, 1-6. He expostulates with God, in a mixture of complaints and petitions, that his life is as wind, and he was consumed out of this world and should appear in it no more, 7-10; therefore he will speak to God, 11, 12; he is tired out and weary of life, 12-16; man is unworthy of God's notice, 17-19; and concludes with confessing that he had sinned, and asking forgiveness before his death, 20, 21.

1. **Is there.** ✗85B, Ge +13:9. Jb 14:5, 13, 14. 2 K 8:9, 10. *20:6. Ps *39:4. Is *38:5. Jn 11:9, 10. **an appointed time.** *or,* a warfare. T#146. Jb 10:17. *14:1, 3, 5, 6, 14. 2 S 11:1n. 1 K 20:22, 26. 1 Ch *20:1. Ec

3:2, +*8. ✓8:8. Is 40:2mg. He *9:27. **like the days.** Jb 14:6. Le 25:50. Dt 15:18. Is 21:16. Mt 20:1-15.

2. **earnestly desireth.** Heb. gapeth after. Ps 119:131. 143:6. Ec +*2:23. Is +*42:14mg. Am 2:7. **the shadow.** Je 6:4. **as an hireling.** Le +*19:13. Dt +*24:15. Ml +*3:5. Ja +*5:4.

3. **months of.** Jb 29:2. Ps *6:6. 39:5. Ec 1:14. **wearisome.** Jb 30:17. Dt 28:67. Ps 42:3. Ec +*2:23. La 1:2, 16.

4. **When.** ver. 13, 14. Jb 17:12. 30:17. Dt *28:67. Ps 6:6. 77:4. 130:6. **night,** etc. Heb. evening be measured. Jb 4:12. 28:25. Ro 13:12. **tossings.** Jb 15:23h. Ps 109:23. Is 54:11.

5. **flesh.** Jb 2:7, 8. 17:14. +*19:26. 24:20. 30:18, 19. Ps 38:5-7. Is 1:6. 14:11. Ac 12:23. **loathsome.** Jb 9:31. Is +*66:24. Ezk 20:43.

6. **swifter.** Jb *9:25. 10:20. *16:22. *17:11. Ps *90:5, 6. *102:11. *103:15, 16. *144:4. Is *38:11-13. *40:6, 7. Ja *1:11. ✓4:14. 1 P *1:24. **without hope.** Jb *6:11. *17:15. Pr *14:32. Is 38:11. Je 2:25. Ep *2:12. 1 Th *4:13. 1 P *1:13.

7. **remember.** Jb *10:9. Ge 42:36. Ne 1:8. Ps 74:18, 22. 89:*47, 50. Je 15:15. **my life.** Ps *78:39. Ja *4:14. **no more see.** Heb. not return to see, that is, *to enjoy.* Jb +✓10:21, 22. Ps 39:13.

8. **The eye.** Jb 20:9. Ps 37:36. **thine eyes.** Jb 13:27. 14:3. Ps 39:11. 90:8, 9. **I am not.** that is, *I can live no longer.* ver. +*9, 21.

9. **the cloud.** Jb 37:11. **vanisheth.** Ja *4:14. **he that.** Jb ✓10:21. 14:10-14. 16:22. 2 S *12:23. 14:14. Ps 39:13. Is 38:11. **goeth down.** Ge 37:35. **grave.** Heb. *sheol,* Ge +37:35. **come up no more.** ver. 8, 10. ✓10:21. +*16:22. Ps *39:13. He +✓9:27 (T#150).

10. **shall return.** ver. 8, +*9. Jb 8:18. 20:9. Ps *103:16. **know.** ✗155D, Ge +4:10.

11. **I will not.** Jb 6:26. 10:1. 13:13. 16:6. 21:3. Ps 39:3. 40:9. **the anguish.** T#1309. Ge 42:21. 2 K 4:27, 28. Mt 26:37, 38. Lk 22:44. 2 C 2:4. **spirit.** Heb. *ruach,* Ge +41:8. **the bitterness.** T#1397. Jb 10:1, 15. 21:25. 1 S +1:10mg. 2 K +4:27mg. Is 38:15, 17. **soul.** Heb. *nephesh,* Ge +34:3.

12. **Am I a sea.** ver. 17. Jb 38:6-11. La *3:7. **a whale.** Jb 41:1, etc.

13. **My bed.** ver. 3, 4. Jb 9:27, 28. Ps 6:6. 77:4.

14. **thou scarest.** Ge 40:5-7. 41:8. Jg 7:13, 14. Ec +*2:23. Da 2:1. Mt *27:19.

15. **soul.** Heb. *nephesh,* Ge +12:13. **chooseth.** 2 S 17:23. Na 2:12. Mt 27:5. **death.** 1 K 19:4. **life.** Heb. bones. Jb 19:20.

16. **I loathe it.** Jb 3:20-22. 6:9. 10:1. Ge *27:46. 1 K 19:4. Jon 4:3, 8. **alway.** Heb. *olam,* Ge +*6:3. **let me alone.** Jb 10:20. 14:6. Ps 39:10, 13. **my days.** Ps 62:9. *78:33. *144:4. Ec 6:11, 12.

17. **What is man.** ✗85F, Ps +*8:4. 144:3. He 2:6. **magnify.** ver. 12. 1 S 24:14. **set thine.** Jb 34:14, 15.

18. **visit.** Ex *20:5. 32:34. Is 26:14. 27:3. 38:12, 13. **every morning.** Is 33:2. La 3:23. ✗171T4. Synecdoche of the Part B655. *Morning is put for a more lengthened period or continuous time. For other instances of this figure see* Ps 73:14. 101:8. Ec 11:6. Is 33:2. La 3:23. **try.** Ge 22:1. Dt 8:16. Je 9:7. Da 12:10. Zc 13:9. 1 P 1:7.

19. **How long.** Jb 9:18. Ps 6:3. 13:1-3. 80:4. 94:3. Re 6:10.

20. **I have sinned.** Jb 9:29-31. 13:26. 14:16, 17. 22:5. 31:33. 33:9, 27. Ps 80:4. **O thou preserver.** Ne *9:6.

Ps +36:6. **why hast.** ver. 12. Jb 6:4. 16:12-14. Ps 21:12. La 3:12. **I am.** ver. 11. Jb 3:24. **myself.** ⌐182, Ge +18:22.

21. **why dost.** Jb 9:28. 10:14. 13:23, 24. Is 64:9. La 3:42-44. 5:20-22. **take away.** 2 S *24:10. Ho 14:2. Mi *7:18, 19. Jn *1:29. T *2:14. 1 J √1:9. *3:5. **sleep.** Jb 3:13. 10:9. 17:14. 20:11. 21:26, 32, 33. Ps 104:29. Ec +*12:7. Is +*26:19n. Da +√12:2n. **seek me.** Jb 8:5h. 24:5h. Pr 1:28. **in the morning.** ver. 18. **but I shall not be.** ver. 8, +*9. Ps 37:36. *103:15.

JOB 8

Bildad blames Job for reflecting on the justice of God, 1-3. He intimates that his children had been cast off for their sins; yet encourages Job to seek unto God, 4-7. He appeals to the ancients, to prove the certain doom of hypocrites, 8-19. He applies the argument to the case of Job, 20-22.

1. **Bildad.** Jb +2:11.

2. **How long.** Jb 11:2, 3. 16:3. 18:2. 19:2, 3. Ex 10:3, 7. Pr 1:22. **the words.** Jb 6:9, 26. 7:11. 15:2. 1 K 19:11.

3. **God.** Jb 4:17. 9:2. 10:3. 19:7. 34:5, 12, 17-19. 40:8. Ge +*18:25. Dt *32:4. 2 Ch *19:7. Ps 89:14. Ezk +*18:25. 33:17, 20. Da 9:14. Ro 2:5. 3:4-6. **or doth.** ⌐85S, Jb +4:17. **Almighty.** Jb 21:15, 20. 34:10-12. 35:13. 40:2. Ps 99:4. Re 15:3. 16:7.

4. **he have cast.** Jb 1:5, 18, 19. 5:4. 18:16-19. Ge 13:13. 19:13-25. **for their transgression.** Heb. in the hand of their transgression. Is 64:7mg.

5. **thou wouldest.** Jb 5:8. 11:13. 22:21-23, etc. 2 Ch 33:12, 13. Is *55:6, 7. Mt *7:7, 8. He 3:7, 8. Ja *4:7-10. **betimes.** T#1152. *S#7836h. Jb 7:21 (seek). 24:5 (rising betimes). Ps 63:1 (early will I seek). 78:34 (enquired early). Pr 1:28. 7:15. 8:17. 11:27 (diligently seeketh). 13:24. Is *26:9. Ho 5:15. **supplication.** Jb 9:15. 19:16. Ge 42:21.

6. **thou wert.** Jb 1:8. 4:6, 7. 21:14, 15. 16:17. Ps 26:5, 6. Pr *15:8. Is *1:15-19. 1 T *2:8. 1 J *3:19-22. **he would.** Ps 44:23. 59:4, 5. Is 51:9. **make.** Jb 22:23-30. Is 3:10.

7. **thy beginning.** Jb 42:12, 13. Pr +*4:18. Zc *4:10. Mt 13:12, 31, 32. **thy latter.** Dt 8:16. Pr 19:20. Zc 14:7. 2 P *2:20.

8. **enquire.** Jb 12:12. 15:10, 18. 32:6, 7. Dt 4:32. 32:7. Ps 44:1. 78:3, 4. Is 38:19. Ro √15:4. 1 C 10:11.

9. **we are but.** or, "we (are) yesterday." ⌐119, Jb 7:6. Ge 47:9. +49.9. 1 Ch 29:15. Ps *39:5. 90:4. 102:11. 144:4. **nothing.** Heb. not. **a shadow.** Jb 14:2.

10. **Shall not.** Jb 12:7, 8. 32:7. Dt 6:7. 11:19. Ps *145:4. Is 38:19. He 11:4. *12:1. **utter words.** Pr *16:23. 18:15. Mt *12:35. **their heart.** Nu +16:28.

11. **the rush.** Ex 2:3. Is 19:5-7.

12. **yet in.** Ps 129:6, 7. Je 17:6. Mt 13:20. Ja 1:10, 11. 1 P 1:24.

13. **that forget God.** Dt *6:12. *8:11, 14, 19. Ps *9:17. *10:4. 50:22. Is 51:13. **the hypocrite's hope.** T#573-1. Jb 11:20. *13:16. *15:34. *18:14. *20:5. *27:8-10. *36:13. Pr *10:28. *11:7. 12:7. Is *33:14. +*38:18. La 3:18, 64, 65. Ezk 22:14. Mt *24:51. +25:46 (T#567). Lk 12:1, 2. +16:26 (T#390). **shall perish.** Jb +36:18. Ps 36:12. 112:10. Pr +10:28. He +*9:27.

14. **web.** Heb. house. Is 59:5, 6.

15. **it shall not stand.** Jb 18:14. 27:18. Ps 52:5-7. 112:10. Pr 10:28. Mt *7:24-27. Lk 6:47-49.

16. **green.** Jb 21:7-15. Ps *37:35, 36. 73:3-12. **his branch.** Jb 5:3.

17. **roots.** Jb 18:16. 29:19. Is 5:24. 40:24. Je 12:1, 2. Mk 11:20. Ju 12.

18. **he.** Jb 7:10. 20:9. Ps *37:10, 36. *73:18, 19. *92:7. **from his place.** Jb 7:8. 27:21. **deny.** ⌐155D, Ge +4:10. **saying.** ⌐63BA, Jb 15:23. 32:17. Ge +26:7. Ex 16:4.

19. **this is the joy.** Jb 20:5. Mt 13:20, 21. **out of the earth.** 1 S 2:8. Ps 75:7. 113:7. Ezk 17:24. Mt 3:9.

20. **God.** Jb 4:7. 9:22. Ps *37:24, 37. 94:14. **help the evil doers.** Heb. take the ungodly by the hand. 2 Ch +19:2. Is 45:1. 51:18.

21. **he fill.** Ge 21:6. Ps 126:2, 6. Lk 6:21. **laughing.** ⌐121S2, Ge +21:6. **rejoicing.** Heb. shouting for joy. Ezr 3:11-13. Ne 12:43. Ps 32:11. 98:4. 100:1. Is 65:13, 14.

22. **clothed.** Ps 35:26. 109:29. 132:18. 1 P 5:5. **dwelling place.** Jb 5:24. 11:14. 12:6. 15:34. 18:14. 21:28. **come to nought.** Heb. not be. ver. 18. Jb 7:21. 24:24mg.

JOB 9

Job acknowledges and celebrates God's justice, wisdom, power, and wonderful works, 1-13. He disclaims all attempts to justify himself, 14-21; but insists that a man's innocency should not be judged of by what befalls him in this world, 22-24. He alleges his sufferings, but will not presume to dispute with the author of them, 25-35.

2. **it is so.** Jb 8:20. **of a truth.** Jb 12:2. **how should.** Jb 4:17. 14:3, 4. 25:4. 32:2. 33:9. 34:5. 1 K *8:46. Ps 40:12. 130:3. *143:2. Ro *3:20. √5:1. 1 J *1:8. **with.** or, before. **God.** Heb. *El*, Ex +15:2.

3. **he will contend.** ver. 20, 32, 33. Jb 10:2. 23:3-7. 31:35-37. 33:13. 34:14, 15. 40:2. Is 57:15, 16. Ro 9:20. **he cannot.** Ps *19:12. 40:12. 1 J *1:8. *3:20. **thousand.** Jb *33:23.

4. **wise in heart.** ver. 19. Jb 36:5. 2 S 22:28. Ps 104:24. 136:5. Pr 16:18. Da 2:20. 4:34-37. 5:20. Ro *11:33. Ep 1:8, 19. 3:10, 20. Ju *24, 25. **who hath hardened.** Jb 6:10. 15:23-27. 40:9. Ex 9:14-17. 14:17, 18. Pr *28:14. *29:1. Da 5:20-30. 1 C 10:22. *He 3:7, 12, 13.

5. **removeth.** Jb 28:9. 46:2. 68:8. 114:6. Is 40:12. Hab 3:6, 10. Zc 4:7. Mt √21:21. 1 C *13:2. Re 6:14. 11:13. **mountains.** ⌐171K1, Dt +19:5. **which overturneth.** Na 1:5, 6. Zc 14:4, 5. Mt 27:51. Lk 21:11. Re 16:18-20.

6. **shaketh.** Is 2:19, 21. 13:13, 14. 24:1, 19, 20. Hg 2:6, 21. He 12:26. Re 20:11. **the pillars.** Jb 26:11. 38:4-7. 1 S 2:8. Ps 75:3. 114:7. Je 4:24. Jl 2:10.

7. **commandeth.** Ex 10:21, 22. Jsh 10:12-14. Da 4:35. Am 4:13. 8:9. Mt 24:29. **sealeth.** Jb 37:7. 38:12-15, 19, 20. Is 13:10. Ezk 32:7. Lk 21:25, 26.

8. **Which.** Jb 37:18. Ge 1:6, 7. Ps *33:6. 104:2, 3. Is *40:22. *42:5. *44:24. Je 10:11. Zc 12:1. **treadeth.** Jb 38:11. Ps 77:19. 93:3, 4. Mt *14:25-30. Jn 6:19. **waves.** Heb. heights. Le 26:30. Nu 21:28. Is 14:14.

9. **maketh.** Jb 38:31, 32, etc. Ge 1:16. Ps 147:4. Am 5:8. **Arcturus.** Heb. *Ash. lit.* moth. i.e. *consuming; gathering*, *S#5906h. Jb 9:9. 38:32. **Orion.** Heb. *Cesil. lit.* fool; burly one, *S#3685h. Jb 9:9. 38:31. Is 13:10 (constellations). Am 5:8. **Pleiades.** Heb. *Cimah.* i.e. *to sail; for what,* *S#3598h. Jb 9:9. 38:31. Am 5:8

(seven stars). **chambers of**. Jb 37:9mg. Ps 104:3, 13. Ac 28:13.

10. **great things**. Jb 5:9. 26:12-14. 37:23. Ps 71:15. 72:18. Ec 3:11. Is 40:26-28. Je *33:3. Ro *11:33. Ep 3:20. **wonders**. Ex 15:11. Ps 136:4. Da 4:2, 3. **without number**. Jb 1:5. 3:6. *5:9. 14:5.

11. **he goeth**. Jb 23:8, 9. 35:14. Ps 77:19. 1 T 6:16.

12. **he taketh**. Jb 23:13. 34:29. Da 4:35. Ep 1:11. **hinder him**. Heb. turn him away. Jb 11:10. **What**. Jb 33:13. Is 45:9. Je 18:6. Da 4:35. Mt 11:26. 20:15. Ro 9:18-20. 11:34. Ep +*1:11.

13. **the proud helpers**. Heb. the helpers of pride, *or* strength. Jb 26:12. 40:9-11. Ps 89:10mg. Is 30:7. 31:2, 3. 51:9. Ja 4:6, 7.

14. **How much**. Jb 4:19. 25:6. 1 K 8:27. **shall I**. Jb 11:4, 5. **choose**. Jb 7:15. 15:5. 23:4, 7. 29:25. 33:5.

15. **though**. Jb 10:15. 1 C 4:4. **I would**. Jb 5:8. 8:5. 10:2. 22:27. 34:31, 32. 1 K 8:38, 39. 2 Ch 33:13. Je 31:9. Da 9:3, 18. **my judge**. Jb 23:7. 1 P *2:23.

16. **If I had**. Ps 18:6. *66:18-20. 116:1, 2. **would I**. Jb 29:24. Ex 6:9. Jg 6:13. Ps 126:1. Lk 24:41. Ac 12:14-16.

17. **For he**. Jb 16:14. Ps 29:5. 42:7. 83:15. Is 28:17. Je 23:19. Ezk 13:13. Mt 7:27. 12:20. **multiplieth**. Jb 1:14-19. 2:7, 13. **without cause**. Jb 2:3. 16:17. 34:6. Ps 25:3. Jn √9:3. 15:25.

18. **will not**. Jb 7:19. Ps 39:13. 88:7, 15-18. La 3:3, 18. **to take**. Est 4:14. **breath**. Ge +*6:17. **filleth me**. Jb 3:20. La 3:15, 19. He *12:11. **bitterness**. 1 S +1:10mg.

19. **he is strong**. See on ver. 4. Jb 36:17-19. 40:9, 10. Ps 62:11. Mt 6:13. 1 C 1:25. *10:22. **who shall**. ver. 32, 33. Jb 31:35. 33:5-7.

20. **justify**. ver. *2. Jb 4:17. 32:1, 2. Ps 130:3. 143:2. Lk 10:29. 16:15. *18:14. **mine**. Lk 15:5, 6. 34:35. 35:16. Pr 10:19. Is 6:5. Mt 12:36, 37. Ja 3:2. **I am perfect**. Jb 1:1. Ph 3:12-15. 1 J √1:8, 10. **it shall**. Jb 33:8-13. Pr 17:20. 1 T 6:5.

21. **yet would**. Ps √139:23, 24. Pr 28:26. Je *17:9, 10. 1 C 4:4. 1 J *3:20. **soul**. Heb. *nephesh*, Ge +34:3. **I would**. Jb 7:15, 16, 21.

22. **I said**. Jb 38:2. 40:2. *42:3. **He destroyeth**. Jb 10:8. Ge 18:23, √25. Le 26:16. Je 14:12. Mi 1:4. Na 1:5. Zc 14:4. Re 6:14. 16:20. **the perfect**. Is ◑√57:1, 2. Ezk ◑18:9, 19. **and**. Jb 3:19. Ps ◑73:2. Ec *9:1-3. Je ◑12:1. Ezk *21:3, 4. Am +√3:6. Mt *5:45. Lk *13:2-4. **the wicked**. Ezk ◑33:19. Here Job lays down the precise subject, upon which he was at issue with his friends, and on which the Lord at length decided in his favor (Jb 42:7-9). He maintained against them, that the dispensations of Providence, in this world, make no exact discrimination between the righteous and the wicked; that when God scourges guilty nations, by war, famine, or pestilence, those who are comparatively innocent and truly pious are often involved in the common calamity; and that in these sudden desolations the Lord does not wait, so to speak, to try their causes (Scott). Lk 13:3n. Jn *9:3.

23. **If the**. Jb 1:13-19. 2:7. **he will**. Jb 4:7. 8:20. 2 S 24:15, 17. Ps 44:22. Ezk 14:19-21. 21:13. He 11:36, 37.

24. **earth**. Jb 12:6-10. 21:7-15. Ps 17:14. 73:3-7. Je 12:1, 2. Dt 4:17. 5:18-21. 7:7, etc. Hab 1:14-17. **is given**. Da 4:17. **he covereth**. *121S3F2, 2 S +15:30. 19:4. Est 6:12. 7:8. Je 14:4. **if not**. Jb 24:25. 32:2.

25. **swifter**. Jb *7:6, 7. **a post**. *Rotz*, a runner or

courier; some of whom are said to go 150 miles in less than 24 hours. 1 S 20:36. 22:17mg. 2 Ch 30:6n. Est 8:14. **they flee away**. Ps *39:5, 11. *89:47. *90:9, 10. Ja *4:14.

26. **swift ships**. Heb. ships of desire, *or*, ships of Ebeh. or, reed *or* enmity. Ex 2:3. Is 18:2. **as the eagle**. Jb 39:27-30. 2 S *1:23. Pr *23:5. Je 4:13. La 4:19. Hab 1:8.

27. **If I say**. Jb 7:13. **my complaint**. Jb 7:11. 10:1. 21:4. 23:2. 1 S 1:10. Ps 77:2, 3. **comfort**. Jb 10:20. Ps 39:13. Je 8:18. Am 5:9.

28. **afraid**. Jb 21:6. Ps 88:15, 16. 119:120. Je 8:18. **I know**. ver. 2, 20, 21. Jb 14:16, 17. Ex 20:7. Ps *130:3.

29. **be wicked**. ver. +*22. Jb 10:7, 14-17. 21:16, 17, 27. 22:5, etc. Ge ◑*15:6. Ps 73:13. Je 2:35. **in vain**. Jb 7:16. 21:34. 27:12. 35:16. He ◑*6:10.

30. **wash**. S#7364h, +*Ex 29:4. Jb 14:4. 1 K 8:36. Ps 26:6. 51:7. Pr 20:9. *28:13. Is *1:16-18. √64:6. Je *2:22. 4:14. Ro 10:3. 1 J √1:8.

31. **shalt**. ver. 20. Jb 15:6. **plunge**. or, dip. Heb. *tabal*, ✣S#2881h. Ge 37:31. Ex +*12:22 (*S#2881h). Le 9:9. 1 S 14:27. 2 K *5:14. 8:15. **ditch**. *S#7845h. *shachath*, "pit," "ditch," "corruption," "grave." Jb 9:31. 17:14 (corruption). 33:18 (pit), 22 (grave), 24, 28, 30. Ps 7:15 (ditch). 9:15. √16:10 (corruption). 30:9. 35:7. 49:9. 55:23 (destruction). 94:13. 103:4. Pr 26:27. Is 38:17 (pit). 51:14. Ezk 19:4, 8. 28:8. Jon 2:6 (corruption; mg, pit). For *S#6900h, *qeburah*, grave, see Ge +35:20. For *S#6913h, *qeber*, "grave," "burying place," see Ge +23:4. For *S#7585h, *sheol*, see Ge +37:35. **mine**. Is 59:6. √64:6. Ph 3:8, 9. **abhor me**. *or*, make me to be abhorred. Jb 19:19. 30:10. Dt 7:26.

32. **not a man**. Jb 33:12. 35:5-7. Nu 23:19. 1 S √16:7. Ec *6:10. Is 45:9. Je *49:19. Ro 9:20. 1 J 3:20. **we should**. Jb 13:18-23. 23:3-7. Ps 143:2.

33. **is there**. ver. 19. 1 S *2:25. Ps *106:23. 1 J √2:1, 2. **daysman**. Heb. one that should argue, *or*, umpire. lit. a reasoner. Jb 32:12. 40:2. 1 S 2:25. Is *1:18. +*S#3198h: Jb 9:33. 32:12 (convinced). 40:2 (reproveth). Pr 9:7 (rebuketh). 24:25. 25:12 (reprover). 28:23. Is 29:21. Ezk 3:26. Am 5:10. **that might**. 1 K 3:16, etc. **lay**. Ps 139:5. **his hand**. Jb 13:21.

34. **take his rod**. T#1673. La 3:1-8. **let not**. Jb 13:11, 20-22. 23:15. 31:23. 33:7. 37:1. Ps 39:10. *90:11.

35. **Then would**. Jb 13:22. **but it is not so with me**. Heb. but I am not so with myself. Jb 29:2, etc.

JOB 10

Job entreats God to show on what account he contended with him; and pleads for compassion as from his Creator, 1-13. He states that his sins were strictly marked and rigorously punished, 14-17. He repines, that he had never been born, or had not died immediately after; and craves respite from pain to prepare for death, 18-22.

1. **My soul**. Heb. *nephesh*, Ge +34:3. Jb 3:20-23. 6:8, 9. 7:15, 16, 20. 9:21. 14:13. Nu 11:15. 1 K 19:4. Jon 4:3, 8. **is weary of my life**. *or*, cut off while I live. Jb 8:14. Ps 95:10. **I will leave**. Jb 7:11. 19:4. 21:2-4. **upon myself**. Jb 30:16. **I will speak**. ver. 15, 16. Jb 6:2-4, 26. 7:11. 16:6-16. Ps 32:3-5. Is 38:15, 17. **bitterness**. Jb 7:11. 1 S +1:10mg. 2 K +4:27mg. **soul**. Heb. *nephesh*, Ge +34:3.

2. **Do not**. Ps 6:1-4. 25:7. 38:1-8. 109:21. 143:2. Ro √8:1. **show me**. Jb 8:5, 6. 34:31, 32. Ps 139:23,

24. La 3:40-42. 5:16, 17. 1 C 11:31, 32.

3. **Is it good.** Jb 34:5-7, 18, 19. 36:7-9, 17, 18. 40:2, 8. La 3:2-18. **oppress.** ♪108J, Ge +43:18. **despise.** Ps 69:33. **the work.** Heb. the labor. Jb 14:15. 34:19. Ps 138:8. Is 64:8. 1 P 4:19. **shine upon.** Jb 8:20. Je 12:1-3.

4. **seest thou.** ♪85S, Jb +4:17. 9:32. 1 S *16:7. Lk *16:15. Re 1:14.

5. **thy days as.** Ps *90:2-4. 102:12, 24-27. He 1:12. 2 P *3:8.

6. **thou inquirest.** ver. 14-17. Ps 10:15. 44:21. Je 2:34. Zp 1:12. Jn +*2:24, 25. 1 C 4:5.

7. **thou knowest.** Heb. *It is* upon thy knowledge. Jb 23:10. 31:6, 14, 35. 42:7. Ps *1:6. 7:3, *8, 9. 17:3. 26:1-5. *139:1, 2, 21-24. Jn 21:17. 2 C 1:12. 1 Th 2:10. **and there.** Jb 23:13, 14. Dt +*32:39. Ps 50:22. Da 3:15. Ho 2:10. Jn +√10:27-30.

8. **hands.** ♪22A14.1, Nu +11:23. Ps 119:73. Is 43:7. **have made me.** Heb. took pains about me. or, grieved me. Ps 56:5. Is *63:10. **yet thou.** ver. 3. Ge 6:6, 7. Je 18:3-10.

9. **Remember.** Jb 7:7. Ps 25:6, 7, 18. 89:47. 106:4. **thou hast.** Ge +*2:7. +*3:19. Is 45:9. *64:8. Je 18:6. **into dust again.** Jb 17:14. Ps 22:15. 90:3. Ec *12:7. Ro 9:21.

10. **poured.** Jb 3:24. 2 K 22:9. Ps *139:14-16.

11. **clothed.** 2 C 5:2, 3. **fenced.** Heb. hedged. Jb 1:10. 40:17, 18. Ezk 37:4-8. Ho 2:6. Ep 4:16.

12. **life and favor.** Ge 19:19. Mt 6:25. Ac 17:25, *28. **spirit.** Heb. *ruach*, Ge +41:8.

13. **hid.** Jb 23:9. Ec 8:6, 7. Is 45:15. Ro *11:33. **I know.** Jb 23:13. Dt +*32:39. Is 45:7. 46:9-11. La 3:37. Ep 3:11.

14. **then.** Jb 13:26, 27. 14:16, 17. Ps 130:3. 139:1. **thou wilt.** Jb 7:21. Ex *34:6, 7. Nu 14:18.

15. **If I be wicked.** ver. 7. Jb 9:29. 27:7. Ps 9:17. Is *3:11. 6:5. Ml 3:18. Ro *2:8, 9. **righteous.** Jb 9:12, 15, 20, 21. Is *64:5, 6. Lk √17:10. **I am full.** Jb 21:6. 23:15. **see.** Ex *3:7, 8. Ps 25:18. 119:153. La 1:20. 5:1, etc.

16. **Thou huntest.** Is 38:13. La 3:10. Ho 13:7, 8. Am 3:8. **marvelous.** Nu 16:29, 30. Dt 28:59.

17. **witnesses.** that is, *plagues.* Jb 16:8. Ge 31:44. Ru 1:21. Ml +*3:5. **changes.** I am as if attacked by successive troops; if one company be wearied, another succeeds to the attack. Jb √14:14. Ge 45:22. Jg 14:12. 2 K 5:22. Ps 55:19. Je 48:11. Zp 1:12. **and.** ♪93A, Ge +1:26. By Hendiadys, read "changes, yes—and warlike ones too—are against me": i.e. *successive changes of attack.* Or it may be read: "changes, aye—a host of them." **war.** Jb +*7:1. 14:14. 16:11-16. 19:6-11.

18. **hast thou.** Jb 3:10, 11. Je 15:10. 20:14-18. Mt 26:24. **given up.** Jb 11:20. 14:10. **ghost.** Ge +49:33 (✱S#1478h).

19. **as though.** Ps 58:8. **not been.** Ob 16. **womb.** Jb 1:21. 3:10, 11. 15:2 (belly), 35. **grave.** Heb. *qeber,* Jb 3:3. Ge +23:4. Je 15:10.

20. **my days few.** Jb *7:6, 7, 16. *8:9. *9:25, 26. *14:1. Ps *39:5. *103:15, 16. **cease.** Jb *7:17-21. 13:21. Ps *39:13.

21. **I go whence.** ♪88, Jb +√7:8-10. *14:10-14. Ge +15:15. 2 S *12:23. *14:14. Is *38:11. **not return.** Jb +*16:22. 2 S *12:23. √14:14. **the land.** ♪88, Jb 3:5. Ge +15:15. Ps *88:6, 11, 12. Is 9:2. Mt 4:16. **and.** ♪93A, Ge +1:26. By Hendiadys, "the land of darkness, yes—and the darkness of death's shadow too." **the**

shadow. See on Jb 3:5. Ps +*23:4. Je 2:6.

22. **darkness.** or, obscurity. Jb 3:5. Ps 88:6, 11, 12. Pr 1:12. 15:24. Is 14:9. Am 4:13. Lk 16:23. **as darkness.** or, thick darkness. Jb 3:6. 23:17. 28:3. **the shadow of death.** ♪88, Ge +15:15. Where death projects his shadow, intercepting the light of life: without any order, having no distinction of inhabitants; the poor and the rich are there, the king and the beggar, their bodies in equal corruption and disgrace: where the light is as darkness, a palpable, obscure, space and place, with only such a light or capability of distinction, as renders darkness visible. Jb 3:5. 34:22. 38:17. Ps *23:4. 44:19. 88:12. Je 2:6. 13:16. Lk 16:26. **without any order.** ✱S#5468h, only here, arrangement; order; disorder, confusion, of the dark underworld (Gesenius). Ge 1:2 Is ❍45:18. Lk 16:23, 24. 1 C ❍14:33, 40. **where light is as.** Ps 91:6. Mt *6:23. Lk *11:35. 16:27-31.

JOB 11

Zophar sharply rebukes Job for justifying himself and earnestly desires that God would answer him, 1-6. He shows that God is unsearchable, and man ignorant and presumptuous, 7-12. He reminds Job that repentance is the only way of recovering comfort and prosperity, 13-20.

1. **Zophar.** See on Jb +2:11. 20:1.

2. **the multitude.** Jb 16:3. 18:2. Ps 140:11. Pr *10:19. Ac 17:18. Ja *1:19. **and should.** ♪85S, Jb +4:17. **full of talk.** Heb. of lips. Jg +7:22mg. Pr 10:8, 10.

3. **thy lies.** *or,* thy devices. Jb 13:4. 15:2, 3. 24:25. **mockest.** Jb 12:4. 13:9. 17:2. 34:7. Ps 35:16. Je 15:17. Ju 18. **make thee.** Ps 83:16. 2 Th 3:14. T 2:8.

4. **For thou.** Jb 6:10. 10:7. 1 P √3:15. **my doctrine.** Dt 32:2. Pr 1:5. Is 29:24. **pure.** Jb 8:6. 16:17. 33:9. **I am clean.** Jb 6:29, 30. 7:20. 9:2, 3. 10:7. 14:4. 34:5, 6. 35:2. Ps *19:9. 24:4. 73:1.

5. **oh that God.** Jb 23:3-7. 31:35. 33:6-18. 38:1, 2. 40:1-5, 8. 42:7. **lips.** ♪22A10, Nu +12:8.

6. **show thee.** Jb 15:8, 11. 28:28. Dt 29:29. Ps *25:14. Da 2:28, 47. Mt *13:35. Ro *16:25, 26. 1 C 2:9-11. Ep *3:5. **double.** ♪121L9, Ge +43:12. **God exacteth.** ♪22C4, Ps +13:1. The A.V. and R.V. rendering requires "less" and "deserveth" to be supplied, through not seeing the figure, which denotes that "God causeth the punishment of thine iniquity to be deferred." The Hebrew is, "He constantly lendeth to thee": i.e. *crediteth thee like a lenient creditor.* The verse may be read, "Know therefore that God causeth to be forgotten for thee of thine iniquity." Ezr *9:13. Ps *103:10. 106:43-46. La *3:22.

7. **Canst.** ♪85S, Jb +4:17. 5:9. 26:14. 37:23. Ps *77:19. 139:6-10. 145:3. Ec 3:11. Is 40:28. Mt 11:27. Ro *11:33. 1 C 2:10, 16. Ep 3:8, 19. He *11:6.

8. **It is as high as heaven.** Heb. the heights of heaven. ♪22I1. Anthropomorphism B895. Inanimate things are sometimes used as figures of God: universals. The heights of heaven. For another instance of this figure see Jb 22:12. 35:5. 2 Ch 6:18. Ps 103:11. 148:13. Pr 25:2, 3. Is √55:9. Ep 3:18. **deeper.** Jb 26:6. Ps 139:6-8. Am +*9:2. Ep 3:18, 19. **hell.** Heb. *sheol,* Ge +37:35. **what canst.** Ep 3:18, 19.

9. **longer.** Jb 28:24, 25. Ps 65:5-8. 139:9, 10.

10. **If he cut off.** *or,* If he make a change. Jb 5:18. 9:4, 12, 13. 12:14. 34:29. Is *14:27. Da *4:35. **shut up.** Jb 38:8. Dt 32:30. Ps 31:8. Re *3:7. **hinder him.**

Heb. turn him away. Jb 9:12. Is 43:13.

11. **he knoweth**. Ps 94:11. Je √17:9, 10. Jn +*2:24, 25. He *4:13. Re 2:23. **vain men**. Ps 26:4. **he seeth**. Jb 22:13, 14. Ps 10:11, *14. 35:22. Ec 5:8. Ho 7:2. Hab 1:13. He *4:13.

12. **For vain**. Heb. For empty. Ex 27:8. 38:7. Ps 62:9, 10. 73:22. 92:6. Ec 3:18. Je 52:31. Ro 1:22. Ja 2:20. **would**. Jb 5:13. 12:2, 3. 28:28. Pr 30:2-4. Ro 12:16. 1 C 3:18-20. Ja 3:13-17. **man be**. Jb 15:14. Ps 51:5. Ep 2:3. **a wild**. Jb 6:5. 39:5-8. Je 2:24.

13. **prepare**. T#1354. Jb 5:8. 8:5, 6. 22:21, 22. 1 S 7:3. 2 Ch ◐12:14. *19:3. Ps 78:8. Pr *16:1. Lk +√12:47. **stretch**. Ps 68:31. 88:9. 143:6. La *3:41. 1 T 2:8.

14. **iniquity**. Jb 4:7, 8. 22:5. Is *1:15. **put it far**. Jb 22:23. 34:32. Is *1:16. Ezk *18:30, 31. Ja 4:8. **let not**. Ps 101:2. Zc 5:3, 4.

15. **lift up**. Jb 10:15. 22:26. Ge 4:5, 6. Ps *119:6, 7. 2 C 1:12. 1 T *2:8. 1 J √2:28. *3:19-22. **thou shalt be**. Ps 27:1, 2. 46:1, 2. 112:6-8. Pr *14:26. 28:1.

16. **Because**. Ge 41:51. Pr 31:7. Ec 5:20. Is *54:4. *65:16. Jn 16:21. Re 7:14-17. **as waters**. Jb 6:15. Ge 9:11. Is 12:1, 2. +√54:9.

17. **age**. √121P1, Jb 42:11-17. 1 Ch +12:32. Ps 37:6. 92:14. 112:4. Pr *4:18. Is 58:8-10. Mi 7:8, 9. Zc 14:6, 7. Ml *4:2. Lk 2:26-32. **be clearer than**. Heb. arise above, etc. or, fliest. Jb 5:7. 20:8. Dt 4:17. **thou shalt**. 1 Ch 29:10. Ho 6:3.

18. **secure**. Ge ◐19:30. Ps 91:5. 112:7. 125:1. Pr *1:33. *3:24. Is 33:16. *43:2. He *13:6. **because**. Jb 6:11. 7:6. 22:27-29. Ps 43:5. Pr 14:32. Ro 5:3-5. Col 1:27. **thou shalt take**. Le 26:5, 6. Ps *3:5. 4:8. Pr √3:24-26.

19. **many**. Jb 42:8, 9. Ge 26:26-31. Ps 45:12. Pr 19:6. Is 60:14. Re 3:9. **make suit unto thee**. Heb. intreat thy face. √171Q, Ge +3:19. Ex 32:11mg. 1 S +13:12mg. 1 K 13:6mg. Ps 45:12mg. 119:58mg. Pr 19:6. Je +26:19mg.

20. **the eyes**. Jb 31:16. Le 26:16. Dt 28:65. Ps 69:3. La 4:17. **they shall not escape**. Heb. flight shall perish from them. Am 2:14. 5:19, 20. 9:1-3. He √2:3. or, refuge shall, etc. 2 S 22:3. Ps 59:16. **their hope**. Jb 8:13, 14. 18:14. 27:8. Pr 10:24. *11:7. 20:20. Is +*38:18. Lk 16:23-26. **the giving up of the ghost**. or, a puff of breath. Heb. nephesh, soul, Nu +23:10. Je 15:9.

JOB 12

Job maintains himself against his friends that reprove him, censures their pretensions to superior knowledge, and complains of their wickedness, 1-4. The miserable always despised, though upright, 5. He shows that God often permits the wicked to prosper in this world, 6. God's power and providence is seen in his works, 7-11. With the ancient is wisdom, but especially in God, and power; judges are fools, princes weak and mean, darkness light, before him, 12-22; and whole nations are overruled by him, 23-25.

2. **No doubt**. or, truly. √60B, Jb 9:2. 19:4, 5. 34:12. Ge +20:16. **ye are the people**. Jb 6:24, 25. 8:8-10. 11:2, 3, 6, 12. 15:2, 10. 17:4. 20:3. 32:7-13. Pr 28:11. Is 5:21. 1 C 4:10. 6:5. **wisdom shall die**. Jb 15:8. 17:10. Is 5:21. Je 7:4. 1 C *6:5. 13:8. He 8:11.

3. **But I have**. Jb 13:2-5. Pr 26:4. 2 C 11:5, 6, 21-23. **understanding**. Heb. an heart. Jb 1:5. 9:4. 10:13. 17:11. √121J23. Figure of speech Metonymy of the

Subject: the container (heart) put for the contents (understanding); here, the heart is put for understanding. For other instances of this figure see Jb 34:34. Je 5:21. Ac 8:22. **I am not inferior to you**. Heb. I fall not lower than you. Jb *13:2. 14:18. **who knoweth not such things as these**. Heb. with whom *are* not such as these. Jb 6:6, 7. *15:9. 26:2, 3. Ac 17:28. Ro *1:19. 1 C 10:13.

4. **one mocked**. Jb 11:3. 16:10, 20. 17:2, 6. 21:3. 30:1. Ps *22:7, 8. 35:16. Mt *27:29, 30, 41, 42. He *11:36. **calleth**. Jb 16:20. Ps 91:15. Je *33:3. Mi 7:7. **the just**. Pr 14:2. Mk 5:40. Lk 16:14. Ac 17:32.

5. **ready**. Dt 32:35. Ps 17:5. 94:18. Je 13:16. **a lamp**. Jb 18:5. Pr 13:9. 20:20. Mt 25:8. **of him**. Jb 6:5. 16:4. Ps 123:3, 4. Am 6:1-6. Lk 12:19. 16:19, 20.

6. **tabernacles**. Jb 9:24. 21:7-15. Ps 17:14. *37:1, 35. *73:11, 12. 92:7. Je 5:27, 28. Ml *3:15.

7. **But ask**. Jb 21:29, 30. Pr 6:6. Is 1:3. Je +*8:7. Ro 8:20-22. **teach**. √155B, Ge +9:5. **tell**. √155B, Ge +9:5.

8. **speak**. Jb 7:11. Jg 5:10. 1 Ch 16:9. **teach**. √155B, ver. 7. Jb 8:10. Ge +9:5. Is 28:9. **fishes**. Ge 9:2. **declare**. √155B, Jb 15:17. 28:27. 38:37mg. Ge +9:5.

9. **Who**. ver. 3. Ac 19:35. **the hand**. √22A14.1, Jb 22:18. Nu +11:23. Dt 8:17, 18. 1 S *2:7. Je 27:5, 6. Da 4:17. 5:18. Ro 11:36. Ja 2:5-7.

10. **whose hand**. √22A14.1, Nu +11:23. Nu *16:22. Ps *22:29. Da *5:23. Ac *17:25, 28. 2 C +3:5. **soul**. or, life. Heb. *nephesh*, Jb 2:4, 6. 3:20. Ge +√2:19. T#988‡; Jsh 11:11 (T#989‡). 1 Th *5:23. He *4:12. **living thing**. Jb 3:20. 5:22, 23. 7:7. 28:21. **the breath**. Heb. *ruach*, Jb 27:3. *34:14, 15. Ge *2:7. +*6:17. Nu +*27:16n. Ps *104:29. 146:3, +*4. Ec +*12:7. Zc +*12:1n. **mankind**. Heb. flesh of man. Heb. *ish*. Ge 2:23. 3:22, 24. 4:1. Ps 49:2. 62:9. Is 2:9. 5:15. 31:8. Jn *3:6. Ac 17:26, 31. 1 C 15:39.

11. **Doth**. Jb 34:3. 1 C 10:15. Ph *1:10mg. He *5:14. 1 P 2:3. **mouth**. Heb. palate. Jb +6:30mg.

12. **the ancient**. Jb 8:8. 15:10. 29:8. 32:7. 2 Ch 36:17. **length of days**. Dt 30:20. Ps 21:4. **understanding**. ver. 13. Jb 26:12. 32:11mg. Pr *16:31.

13. **him**. *that is*, God. Jb 32:6-9. **wisdom**. ver. 16. Jb 9:4. 28:20-28. 36:5. Ps 104:24. 147:5. Pr 2:6, 7. 3:19. Je 10:12. Da 2:20. Mt +*28:19n. Lk 21:15. Ro 11:33. +*16:27. 1 C 1:24. 2:7. Ep 1:8. 3:10. Col *2:3. 1 T *1:17. Ja *1:5. **counsel**. Pr *8:14. Is 40:13, 14. 46:10. Ro 11:34. Ep 1:8, 11.

14. **he breaketh**. Jb 9:12, 13. 11:10. Is 14:23. Je 51:58, 64. Ml *1:4. **he shutteth**. Jb 16:11. 1 S 17:46. 24:18. 26:8mg. Is 22:22. Ro 11:32mg. Re 3:7. √121S3B. Metonymy of the Adjunct B606. To open and shut is put for the power of administration. For other instances of this figure see Is 22:22. Re 3:7. **up**. Heb. upon.

15. **Behold**. ver. 10. Ge 8:1, 2. Dt 11:17. 1 K 8:35, 36. 17:1. Je *14:22. Na 1:4. Lk 4:25. Ja 5:17, 18. Re 11:6. **he sendeth**. Ge 6:13, 17. 7:11, 23. Ps 104:7-9. Am 5:8.

16. **With**. ver. 13. Mt 6:13. **the deceived**. Nu 15:28. 1 K *22:22, 23. Ps 119:67. Ezk *14:9. Ga 3:1. Ep 4:14. **the deceiver**. Dt *27:18. Pr *28:10. Mt 23:13. Mk 9:42. Lk +11:52. 2 T 3:13.

17. **He leadeth**. 2 S 15:31. *17:14, 23. Is 19:12-14. 29:14. 1 C 1:19, 20.

18. **He looseth**. 2 Ch 33:11-14. Je 52:31-34. Da *2:21. Re 19:16.

19. **leadeth princes**. Jsh 10:24, 42. 1 S 17:45, 46.

Is 37:36-38. 45:1. Re 17:14. 19:19-21.

20. **the speech of the trusty.** Heb. the lip of the faithful. Pr 10:21. 12:19, 22. **taketh.** ver. 24. Jb 17:4. 32:9. 39:17. Is 3:1-3.

21. **poureth.** Ex 8:2, 16, 24. 1 K 21:23, 24. 2 K 9:26, 34-37. Ps 107:40. Is 23:9. 24:21, 22. 37:38. Da 2:21, 22. 4:32, 33. Mt 2:12, 13. Ac 12:23. **weakeneth the strength of the mighty.** or, looseth the girdle of the strong. ♪22C39, Ps 18:32n. Is 5:27. 11:5. 22:21. Is +45:1. 45:5. Je +1:17. Ep 6:10, 14.

22. **discovereth.** Jb 11:6. 28:20-23. 2 K 6:12. Ps 44:21. 139:12. Da 2:22. Mt 10:26. 1 C 2:10. 4:5. **bringeth.** Jb 3:5. 24:17. 34:22. Am 5:8. Lk 1:79.

23. **increaseth.** Ex 1:7, 20. Ps 107:38. Is 9:3. 26:15. 27:6. 51:2. 60:22. Je 30:19. 33:22. Zc 10:8. **straiteneth them again.** Heb. leadeth in. Is 3:1-3.

24. **He taketh.** ver. 20. Jb 17:4. Ex 8:2, 6, 16, 24. Is 6:9, 10. 19:1. 23:9. Da 4:16, 33. Ho 7:11. Ac 12:23. **and causeth.** Ps *107:4, 40. **wander.** ver. 25. Ge 20:13. 2 K 21:9. 2 Ch 33:9. Ps 107:40. Pr 12:26. Is 63:17. Je 23:13, 32. Am 2:4. **in a wilderness.** Bethohoo, "in chaos," i.e. in a state of utter confusion; it is the same word which is employed in Ge 1:2, to describe the chaotic state of the earth at the creation. Jb 6:18. *26:7. Dt 32:10.

25. **grope.** Jb 5:14. Ge 19:11. Dt 28:29. Is 59:10. Ac *13:11. 1 J 2:11. **maketh.** Ps 107:27. Is 19:14. 24:20. **stagger.** Heb. wander. ver. +24. **like a.** Ps 107:27. **drunken.** 1 S 1:13. 25:36.

JOB 13

Job, confident of his knowledge, appeals to God; disdainfully and peevishly reproves his friends for pleading against him with false reasonings and partiality; and warns them to fear the judgment of God, 1-12. In extreme suffering and expectation of death, he professes confidence that God would justify him, 13-19. He craves respite and desires to know his sins and God's purpose in afflicting him, since God does not delight in our misery, 20-28.

1. **Lo.** Jb 5:9-16. 12:9, etc. 42:3-6. **ear.** Jb 4:12. 5:27. 8:8-10. 15:17, 18. Ps 78:3, 4. 1 J 1:3.

2. **ye know.** Jb 12:3. 15:8, 9. 34:35. 35:16. 37:2. 40:4, 5. 42:7. 1 C 8:1, 2. 2 C 11:4, 5, 16-18. 12:11.

3. **Surely.** ver. 22. Jb 9:34, 35. 11:5. 23:3-7. 31:35. **I desire.** Jb 9:3, 14, 15. Is *1:18-20. 41:21. Je 12:1mg, 2. Mi 6:2. **reason.** ver. +15mg. Ps ch. 73. Is *1:18-20. **God.** Heb. El, Ex +15:2.

4. **ye are forgers.** Jb 4:7-11. 5:1-5. 8:3, 4. 18:5, etc. 21:27-34. 22:6, etc. Ex 20:16. Ps *119:69. **physicians.** ♪24B, Jb 6:21. 16:2. Ge +23:16. Je *6:14. 8:11, 22. 30:13. *46:11. Ezk 34:4. Ho 5:13. Mk 2:17. *5:26.

5. **Oh that ye.** ver. 13. Jb 11:3. 16:3. 18:2. 19:2. 21:2, 3. 32:1. **and it.** Pr *17:28. Ec 5:3. Am *5:13. Ja 1:19.

6. **Hear now.** Jb 21:2, 3. 33:1-3. 34:2. Jg 9:7. Pr 8:6, 7.

7. **speak wickedly for.** Jb 4:7. 11:2-4. 17:5. 32:21, 22. 36:4. Jn 16:2. Ro 3:5-8. 2 C *4:2.

8. **accept.** Jb 32:21. 34:19. Ex 23:2, 3. Pr 24:23. Ml 2:9mg.

9. **search.** Jb 34:36. Ps 44:21. 139:23. Je *17:10. **as one.** Jb 17:2. Is 28:22. Ga *6:7, 8.

10. **reprove.** Jb 42:7, 8. Ps 50:21, 22. 82:2. Pr 24:23. Ja 2:9.

11. **Shall.** Ps 119:120. Je 5:22. 10:10. Mt +*10:28. Re 15:3, 4. **his dread.** ver. 21. Ex 15:16. Is 8:13.

12. **remembrances.** Jb 18:17. Ex 17:14. Ps *34:16. 102:12. 109:15. Pr 10:7. Is 26:14. **like.** or, similes of. Jb 27:1. 29:1. Nu +*21:27. +23:7n. **ashes.** Ge 18:27. Is 44:20. **to bodies.** Jb 4:19. Ge +*2:7. 2 C *5:1.

13. **Hold your peace.** Heb. Be silent from me. Jb 33:31, 33. 1 S 7:8mg. Is 41:1. **let me.** See on ver. 5. Jb 7:11. 10:1. 21:3. **and let come.** Jb 6:9, 10. 7:15, 16.

14. **I take.** Jb 18:4. Ec 4:5. Is 9:20. 49:26. **and put.** Jg 12:3. 1 S 19:5. 28:21. Ps 119:109. **life.** Heb. nephesh, soul, Ge +44:30. 1 C 15:30, 31.

15. **slay me.** ver. 18. Jb +*19:25-27. *23:10. 24:14. Ru +*1:13. Ps *23:4. ●139:19. Pr *14:32. +*19:3. Ro *8:38, 39. **yet will.** Hab +*3:17, 18. **trust.** T#294. 1 S 17:37. 2 K 18:5-7. Ps 7:1. +*9:10. 56:4. 71:5. Is *50:10. Da 3:16-18. Mi 7:8. 1 J 3:21. **but I will.** Jb *10:7. 16:17, 21. *23:4-7. 27:5. 31:31-37. 40:2, 4, 5, 8. 1 J *3:20. **maintain.** Heb. prove, or argue. ver. 3. Jb 15:3. Is *1:18.

16. **my salvation.** Ex 15:2. Ps 27:1. 62:6, 7. 118:14, 21. Is *12:2. Je 3:23. Ac √4:12. 13:47. **for an hypocrite.** Jb 8:13. 27:8-10. 36:13. Is 33:14.

17. **diligently.** ver. 6. Jb 33:1.

18. **I have ordered.** Jb 16:21. 23:4. 40:7. **I know.** Jb 9:2, 3, 20. 40:7, 8. *42:9. Ps 37:6. Is 43:26. Ro 8:33, 34. 2 C 1:12.

19. **that will plead.** Jb 19:5. 33:5-7, 32. Is 50:7, 8. Ro 8:33. **if I hold.** ver. 13. Jb 7:11. Je 20:9. **ghost.** Ge +49:33 (S#1478h).

20. **do not two.** Jb 9:34, 35. **hide myself.** Ge 3:8-10. Ps 139:12. Re 6:15, 16.

21. **Withdraw.** Jb 10:20. 22:15-17. Ps 39:10. **let not.** ver. 11. See on Jb 33:7. Ps 119:120.

22. **call.** Jb 9:32. *38:3. *40:4, 5. *42:3-6.

23. **many.** Jb *22:5. Ps 44:20, 21. **and sins.** ♪174, Ge +18:27. **make me.** T#1698, 1701. Jb 36:8, 9. Ps *139:23, 24. **to know.** Ps 25:8, 9. Pr 20:12. Jn 9:36. Ac 8:31.

24. **hidest thou.** Jb 10:2. 29:2, 3. Dt 32:20. Ps 10:1. 13:1. 44:24. 77:6-9. 88:14. Is 8:17. **holdest me.** Jb 16:9. 19:11. 30:21. 31:35. 33:10. 1 S 28:16. La 2:5. 2 Th 3:15.

25. **break.** Jb 14:3. 1 S 24:14. 17:13. Is *42:3. Mt 12:20.

26. **writest.** Jb 3:20. Ru 1:20. Ps 88:3, etc. **makest.** Jb 20:11. Ps 25:7. Pr 5:11-13. Je 31:19. Jn 5:5, 14.

27. **puttest.** Jb 33:11. 2 Ch 16:10-12. Pr 7:22. Ac 16:24. **and lookest.** Heb. and observest. Jb 10:6, 14. 14:16, 17. 16:9. **settest.** Jb 2:7. **print.** ❋S#2707h. 1 K 6:35 (carved work). Ezk 8:10 (portrayed). 23:14. **heels.** Heb. roots. Jb 8:17. 14:8. 18:16. 19:28. 36:30mg.

28. **And he.** Jb 30:17-19, 29, 30. Nu 12:12. **as a garment.** Jb 4:19. Ps 39:11. Ho 5:12.

JOB 14

Job pleads with God for relief, because of the shortness and misery of life and the sinfulness of human nature, 1-6. Viewing death as destructive to all earthly hopes, he yet desires to be hid in the grave and determines to wait the time appointed for his change, 7-15. He complains that God dealt severely with him; and shows that all things on earth, men especially, are subject to corruption, 16-22.

1. **born.** ⨍142, Jb 15:14. 25:4. Ge +20:16. Ps 51:5. Mt 11:11. **of few days.** Heb. short of days. Jb 7:1, 6. 9:25. Ge 47:9. Ps 39:5. **full.** ver. 5, 7. See on Ec 2:17, *23. Jn ●15:11. He 12:11. **trouble.** Jb 5:7.

2. **like.** Ps 90:5-9. 92:7, 12. 103:15, 16. Is 40:6-8. Ja 1:10, 11. 4:14. 1 P 1:24. **fleeth.** Jb 8:9. 9:25, 26. 1 Ch 29:15. Ps 102:11. 144:4. Ec 8:13.

3. **And dost.** Jb 7:17, 18. 13:25. Ps 144:3. **bringest.** Jb 9:19, 20, 32. 13:27. Ps *143:2. Ro 3:19.

4. **Who can bring.** Heb. Who will give. ⨍85R, Jb +4:17. 15:14-16. 25:4-6. Ge 5:3. Ps 14:7. 51:5. 90:5. Je *13:23. Mt 7:16-18. 12:33. Jn *3:6. 6:44, 65. Ro *5:12. 8:8, 9. Ep 2:3. **a clean.** Lk +*1:35. **not one.** Ps 14:3.

5. **his days.** ver. 14. Ps 39:4. 139:16mg. Pr 7:1. 12:10. Da 5:26, 30. 9:24. 11:36. Lk *12:20. Ac *17:26. He +√9:27. **determined.** T#251. Ex +26:36. Is 14:26. Ac 17:26. Ep +*1:11. **the number.** Jb 21:21. Ps 55:23. 90:10, *12. Ec +*7:17. Is +*38:10. **thou hast.** Jb 23:13, 14. Ps 104:9, 29. Da 4:35. Re 1:18. 3:7. **bounds.** ver. 13. Jb 23:12, 14. 26:10. **cannot pass.** Jb 19:8.

6. **Turn.** Jb 7:16, 19. 10:20. Ps 39:13. **rest.** Heb. cease. ver. 7. Jb 3:17. 7:16. 10:20. 16:6. **accomplish.** or, enjoy. Jb 33:26. 34:9. Le 26:43. 2 Ch 36:21. **as an hireling.** Jb 7:1, 2. Mt 20:1-8.

7. **that it will sprout.** ver. 14. Jb 19:10. Is 11:1. 27:6. Da 4:15, 23-25.

8. **die in the ground.** Is +*26:19n. Jn *12:24. 1 C *15:36.

9. **and bring.** Ezk 17:3-10, 22-24. 19:10, 11. Ro 11:17-24.

10. **wasteth away.** Heb. is weakened, or, cut off. Ex 17:13 (discomfited). Ps 90:10. Is 14:12. Jl 3:10. **man.** Jb 3:11. 10:18. 11:20. 17:13-16. Ge 49:33. Mt 27:50. Ac 5:10. **ghost.** Jb 3:11. 10:18. 13:19. Ps +146:4. **where is he.** ver. 12. Jb 7:7-10. 19:26. Pr 14:32. Lk √16:22, 23.

11. **the flood.** Jb 6:15-18. Je 15:18.

12. **So man.** Jb 10:21, 22. 30:23. Ec 3:19-21. 12:5. **till the heavens.** Jb *19:25-27. Ps 102:26. Is 51:6. 65:17. 66:22. Mt *24:35. Ac 3:21. Ro *8:20. 2 P *3:7, 10-13. Re *20:11. 21:1. **awake.** Jb 3:13. 7:21. Is +*26:19n. Da +*12:2. Jn 11:11-13, 25. Ep 5:14. 1 Th 4:14-16.

13. **hide me.** Jb 3:17-19. Ps *16:10. 30:3. 139:8. Is 38:10. 57:1, 2. **grave.** Heb. sheol, Ge +37:35. T#999X, 1000X: Ps 6:5. 16:10. Ec *9:10. Is 38:18, 19. **until.** Is 12:1. 26:20, 21. **appoint me.** Mk 13:32. Ac *1:7. √17:31. **remember.** Ge 8:1. Ps 106:4. Lk 23:42.

14. **shall he live.** T#1594. Jb *19:25, 26. 1 S +*2:6. Ps *89:48. Is +*26:19n. Ezk *37:1-14. Mt *22:29-32. Jn *5:28, 29. Ac *26:8. 1 C *15:42-44. 1 Th *4:14-16. Re *20:12, 13. **all the days.** ver. *5. Jb *7:1. 42:16. Ge 47:8mg. 2 S 19:34mg. Ps *27:14. *40:1, 2. La *3:25, 26. Ja *5:7, 8. **will I wait.** T#154. Jb *13:15. La 3:26. 1 C *15:51, 52. Ph 1:23-25. *3:21. Ju 21. **change.** Jb 10:17. Ge 45:22. Jg 14:12. 2 K 5:22. 1 C √15:51, 52. Ph *3:21. ⨍171E7. Synecdoche of the Genus B621. *Change* is put for *death*. For another instance of this figure see Pr 31:8.

15. **shall call.** Jb 13:22. Ps 50:4, 5. 1 Th √4:16, 17. 1 J 2:28. **thou wilt have.** Jb 7:21. 10:3, 8. Ps *138:8. Ph *1:6. 1 P 4:19.

16. **thou numberest.** Jb 10:6, 14. 13:27. 31:4. 33:11. 34:21. Ps 56:6. 139:1-4. Pr 5:21. Je 32:19. Mt 10:30. **watch.** Pr 5:21. Je 16:17.

17. **sealed up.** Jb 21:19. 37:7. Dt 32:34. Ne 9:38. Ho 13:12. **bag.** or, bundle. Ge 42:35. **iniquity.** Je 2:22.

18. **the mountain.** Ps 102:25, 26. Is 40:12. 41:15, 16. 54:10. 64:1. Je 4:24. Re 6:14. 8:8. 20:11. **cometh to nought.** Heb. fadeth. **the rock.** Jb 18:4. Mt 27:51.

19. **The waters.** ⨍138C, Ge +22:14. Hence the proverb, "Constant droppings make a hole in a stone." **washest.** Heb. overflowest. Ge 6:17. 7:21-23. Le 15:11. 1 K 22:38. 2 Ch 32:4mg. **destroyest.** Jb 19:10. 27:8. Ps 30:6, 7. Ezk 37:11. Lk 12:19, 20.

20. **prevailest.** Jb 15:24. Ec 4:12. *8:8. **for ever.** Heb. *netsach*, Jb +4:20 (❋S#5331h). **he passeth.** i.e. *he dieth*, or is about to die. Man's death is often called a *passage*, or *a going*, to intimate that it is not an annihilation but only a translation of him into another place and state (Matthew Poole). Ge *25:32mg. 2 S √12:23. 1 K *2:2. Ps 1:1 (walketh). *78:39. 109:23. Pr 4:18 (more and more; lit. going and shineth). Ec *1:4. 3:20 (go). 6:6 (go). *9:10 (goest). *12:5 (goeth). Ho 13:3. ✛S#1980h: Jb 16:6 (eased; mg, goeth), √22 (go). 20:25 (cometh). 23:8 (go). 41:19 (go). Ex 9:23 (ran along). Ps 58:8 (pass away). 73:9 (walketh). 91:6. Je 9:4. **changest.** ver. 14. Jb 2:12. La 4:8.

21. **he knoweth it not.** 1 S 4:20. Ps *39:6. Ec 2:18, 19. 9:5. Is 39:7, 8. 63:16. **not.** Ps +146:4.

22. **his flesh.** Jb 19:20, 22, 26. 33:19-21. Da +*7:15. **pain.** Jb 5:18. Ge 34:25. **his soul.** Heb. *nephesh*, Ge +34:3. Pr 14:32. Is 10:18. Lk 16:23, 24. **within him.** Jb 33:18, 22. Ge 25:+*8n, 9, 17. *35:18. Nu 27:16n. 1 K √17:22. 2 K 4:27. Ps 42:6. 43:5. 63:1. 88:3. Ec +*3:21. Ezk +*18:20n. Da +*7:15. Zc +*12:1n. Mt +√10:28. 1 Th 5:23. **mourn.** Is 3:26. 19:8. 24:4.

JOB 15

Eliphaz sharply reproves Job as arrogant and impious; his own mouth uttered his iniquity and should condemn him, 1-6. Job not the wisest of men, 7, 8; nor wiser than they who were elder than he, 9, 10. He despised the consolations of God and turned away his spirit against him, 11-13. He declares God's holiness and man's sinfulness: the angels not clean in God's sight, much less man, 14-16. He appeals to observation and tradition in proof that the wicked are miserable in this world, 17-35.

1. **Eliphaz.** Jb +2:11. 4:1. 22:1. 42:7, 9.

2. **a wise man.** Jb 11:2, 3. 13:2. Ja 3:13. **vain knowledge.** Heb. knowledge of wind. Jb 6:26. 8:2. 16:3. **fill.** Ho 12:1. **east wind.** Jb 27:21. 38:24.

3. **he reason.** Jb 13:4, 5. 16:2, 3. 26:1-3. Ml 3:13-15. Mt √12:36, 37. Col *4:6. 1 T *6:4, 5.

4. **castest off.** Heb. makest void. Jb 4:5, 6. 5:12. 6:14. 40:8. Nu 30:12. Ps 36:1-3. 119:126. Zp 1:6. Ro 3:31. Ga 2:21. **restrainest.** Jb 5:8. 27:10. 1 Ch 10:13, 14. Ho 7:14. Am 6:10. Lk *18:1. Ja 4:2. **prayer.** or, speech. or, meditation. Ps 64:1, 119:97, 99.

5. **uttereth.** Heb. teacheth. Jb 9:22-24. 12:6. 33:33. 35:11. Pr 22:25. Mk 7:21, 22. Lk *6:45. Ja 1:26. **thou choosest.** Ps 50:19, 20. 52:2-4. 64:3. 120:2, 3. Je 9:3-5, 8. Ja 3:5-8.

6. **own mouth.** Jb 9:20. Ps 64:8. Mt 12:37. 26:65. Lk 19:22. **thine own.** Jb 33:8-12. 34:5-9. 35:2, 3. 40:8. 42:3.

7. **the first.** ver. 10. Jb 12:12. Ge 4:1. **or wast thou.** Jb 38:4, etc. Ps 90:2. Pr 8:22-25.

8. **the secret.** Jb 11:6. Dt *29:29. Ps 25:14. Pr *3:32.

Je 23:18. Am 3:7. Mt 11:25. 13:11, 35. Jn 15:15. Ro 11:34. *16:25, 26. 1 C 2:9-11, 16. **thou restrain.** Jb 12:2. 13:5, 6.

9. **knowest.** Jb 13:2. 26:3, 4. 2 C 10:7. 11:5, 21-30.

10. **the gray-headed.** Jb 8:8-10. 12:20. 32:6, 7. Dt 32:7. Pr 16:31.

11. **the consolations.** Jb 5:8-26. 11:13-19. 2 C *1:3-5. 7:6. **is there.** ver. 8. Jb 13:2. 1 K 22:24.

12. **thine heart.** Ec 11:9. Mk 7:21, 22. Ac *5:3, 4. 8:22. Ja 1:14, 15. **thy eyes.** Jb 17:2. Ps 35:19. Pr 6:13. *10:10.

13. **turnest.** ver. 25-27. Jb 9:4. Ro 8:7, 8. **spirit.** Heb. *ruach*, Ge +41:8. **and lettest.** Jb 10:3. 12:6. Ps 34:13. Ml 3:13. Ja 1:26. 3:2-6.

14. **is man.** Jb 9:2. 14:4. 25:4-6. 1 K 8:46. 2 Ch 6:36. Ps 14:3. 51:5. 130:3. 143:2. Pr *20:9. Ec 7:√20, 29. Is *53:6. *64:6. Jn *3:6. Ro 3:8-12. 7:18. Ga 3:22. Ep *2:2, 3. Ja 3:2, 8. 1 J √1:8-10. **born of.** ♪142, Jb 25:4. Ge +20:16.

15. **he putteth.** See on Jb 4:18. 25:5. Is 6:2-5.

16. **How much.** Rather, "How much less (*aph kee*), abominable and filthy man," who, under the influence of sinful propensities, commits sin as greedily as a thirsty man or camel drinks down water. **abominable.** Jb 4:19. 42:6. Ps 14:1-3. 53:3. Ro *1:28-30. *3:9-19. T 3:3. **drinketh.** Jb 20:12. 34:7. Pr 19:28.

17. **hear me.** Jb 5:27. 13:5, 6. 33:1. 34:2. 36:2.

18. **from their.** ver. 10. Jb 8:8. Ps 71:18. 78:3-6. Is 38:19.

19. **Unto whom.** Ge 10:25, 32. Dt 32:8. Jl 3:17.

20. **travaileth.** Ec 9:3. Ro *8:22. **the number.** Ps 90:3, 4, *12. Lk 12:19-21. Ja 5:1-6.

21. **dreadful sound.** Heb. sound of fears. Jb 18:11. Ge 3:9, 10. Le 26:36. 2 K 7:6. Pr 1:26, 27. **in prosperity.** Jb 1:13-19. 20:5-7, 22-24. Le 26:36. 1 S 25:36-38. Ps 73:18-20. 92:7. Ac 12:21-23. 1 Th 5:3. **the destroyer.** 1 C 10:10. Re 9:11.

22. **He believeth not.** Jb 6:11. 9:16. 2 K 6:33. Is 8:21, 22. Mt 27:5. **and he is.** Jb 20:24, 25.

23. **wandereth.** Jb 30:3, 4. Ge 4:12. Ps 59:15. 109:10. La 5:6, 9. He 11:37, 38. **the day.** Jb 18:5, 6, 12, 18. Ec 11:8. Jl 2:2. Am 5:20. Zp 1:15. He 10:27.

24. **anguish.** Jb 6:2-4. Ps 119:143. Pr *1:27. Is 13:3. Mt 26:37, 38. Ro 2:9. **as a king.** Pr 6:11. 24:34.

25. **he stretcheth.** Le 26:23. Ps 73:9, 11. Is 27:4. Da 5:23. Ml *3:13. Ac *9:5. 12:1, 23. **strengtheneth.** Jb 9:4. 40:9-11. Ex 5:2, 3. 9:17. 1 S 4:7-9. 6:6. Ps 52:7. Is 8:9, 10. 10:12-14. 41:4-7.

26. **runneth.** 2 Ch 28:22. 32:13-17. **even on.** Jb 16:12. Ge 49:8. Ps 18:40.

27. **he covereth.** Jb 17:10. Dt *32:15. Ps 17:10. 73:7. 78:31. Is 6:10. Je 5:28.

28. **desolate.** Jb 3:14. 18:15. Is 5:8-10. Mi *7:13. **which are ready.** Je 9:11. 26:18. 51:37. Mi 3:12.

29. **neither shall.** Jb 20:22-28. 22:15-20. 27:16, 17. Ps 49:16, 17. Lk 12:19-21. 16:2, 19-22. Ja 1:11. 5:1-3.

30. **depart.** ver. 22. Jb 10:21, 22. 18:5, 6, 18. Mt 8:12. 22:13. 2 P 2:17. Ju *13. **the flame.** Jb 20:26. Is 30:33. Ezk 15:4-7. 20:47, 48. Mt 25:41. Mk 9:43-49. 2 Th 1:7-9. **by the breath.** Jb 4:9. Is 11:4. Re 19:15.

31. **not him.** Jb 12:16. Is 44:20. Ga *6:3, 7, 8. Ep 5:6. **trust.** Ps 62:10. Is 59:4. Jon 2:8. **for vanity.** Jb 4:8. Pr 22:8. Is 17:10, 11. Ho 8:7. Ga *6:8.

32. **accomplished.** *or*, cut off. Jb 22:16. Ps 55:23. Ec 7:17. **before his time.** Jb 14:5. 22:16. Ps 55:23.

102:24. Pr *10:27. Ec +*7:17. Is +*38:10. **and his branch.** Jb 8:16-19. 14:7-9. 18:16, 17. Ps 52:5-8. Is 27:11. Ezk 17:8-10. Ho 9:16. 14:5-7. Jn 15:6.

33. **shake off.** Is 33:9. Re 6:13. **and.** Dt 28:39, 40.

34. **the congregation.** Jb 8:13. 20:5. 27:8. 36:13. Is 33:14, 15. Mt 24:51. **the tabernacles.** Jb 11:14. 12:6. 22:5-9. 29:12-17. 1 S 8:3. 12:3. Mi 7:3. Am 5:11, 12.

35. **conceive.** Ps 7:14. Is 59:4, 5. Ho 10:13. Ga 6:7, 8. Ja 1:15. **vanity.** *or*, iniquity. Jb 31:5. Ge 27:35. **belly.** ♪121J22. Metonymy of the Subject B582. *Belly* is put for heart or thoughts. For other instances of this figure see Pr 18:8. 20:27. 26:22. Jn 7:38.

JOB 16

Job reproves his friends for their conduct towards him; and shows how he would have acted, if they had been afflicted as he was, 1-5. He pathetically describes his heavy and varied sorrows: his grief and weariness, 6-8; his insulting enemies, 9-11; God's power against him, 12-16. As a dying man, he appeals to God to attest to his integrity, 17-22.

2. **heard.** Jb 6:6, 25. 11:2, 3. 13:5. 19:2, 3. 26:2, 3. Ja 1:19. **miserable.** *or*, troublesome. Jb 13:4. Ps 69:26. Ph 1:16.

3. **vain words.** Heb. words of wind. Jb 6:26. 8:2. 15:2. **what emboldeneth.** Jb 20:3. 32:3-6. Mt 22:46. T 1:11. 2:8.

4. **if your soul.** Heb. *nephesh*, Jb 6:2-5, 14. Ge +27:31. Mt 7:12. Ro 12:15. 1 C 12:26. **soul's.** Heb. *nephesh*, Ge +27:31. **up words.** Jb 11:2. 35:16. Pr 10:19. Ec 10:14. **shake mine.** Nu 32:13 (wander). 2 S 15:20. 2 K 19:21. Ps *22:7. 44:14. 59:15. 109:25. Je 18:16. La 2:15. Zp 2:15. Mt 27:39, 40.

5. **But I would.** Jb 4:3, 4. 6:14. 29:25. Ps 27:14. Pr 27:9, 17. Is 35:3, 4. Ga 6:1.

6. **my grief.** Jb 10:1. Ps 77:1-9. 88:15-18. **what am I eased.** Heb. what goeth from me. Jb +14:20n.

7. **he hath.** Jb 3:17. 7:3, 16. 10:1. Ps 6:6, 7. Pr 3:11, 12. Is 50:4. Mi 6:13. **hast made.** Jb 1:15-19. 29:5, etc.

8. **And thou hast,** etc. Some render, "thou hast fettered me," as *kamat* signifies in Arabic; but as it signifies in Syriac to be *wrinkled*, the common version seems from the connection to be more correct; and if Job's disease were the elephantiasis, these words would apply most forcibly to the wrinkled state of the skin of that disorder. **is a witness.** Jb 10:17. Ru *1:21. Ep 5:27. **my leanness.** ♪155F, Ge +4:7. Ps 106:15. Is 10:16. 24:16.

9. **teareth me.** Jb 10:16, 17. 18:4. Ps 50:22. La *3:10, 11. Ho *5:14. **he gnasheth.** Ps 35:16. 37:12. La 2:16. **mine.** Jb 13:24, 27. 19:11. Mi 7:8.

10. **gaped.** Ps 22:*13, 16, 17. *35:21. 69:20. Mt ✱26:67. Lk 23:35, 36. **they have smitten.** 1 K 22:24. 2 Ch 18:23. Is *50:6. La 3:30. Mi 5:1. Mt *26:67. Jn 18:22. Ac 23:2. 2 C 11:20. **gathered.** Ps *35:15. 94:21. Ac 4:27.

11. **delivered me.** Heb. shut me up. 1 S 23:12mg. 24:18mg. Ps *27:12. 31:8. Ro 11:32mg. **to the ungodly.** Jb 1:13-19. 2:7. Ps 7:14. Jn 19:16. 2 C 12:7. **turned.** Ps 27:12.

12. **at ease.** Jb 1:2, 3. 3:26. 29:3, 18, 19. **broken me.** Jb 4:10. Ps 44:19. La 3:4. Mt 21:44. **by my neck.** Jb 15:26. Ro 16:4. **shaken.** La 3:11. Ezk 29:7. **set me up.** Jb 7:12, 20. La 3:12.

13. **archers**. Jb 6:4. Ge 49:23. Ps 7:12, 13. **he cleaveth**. Jb 19:27. La 3:13. **doth**. Jb 6:10. Dt 29:20. Ezk 5:11. Ro 8:32. 2 P 2:5. **poureth**. Jb 20:25. La 2:11.

14. **breaketh**. La 2:11. 3:3-5, 11. **runneth**. Jg 15:8. Ps 42:7.

15. **sewed**. 1 K 21:27. Is 22:12. **sackcloth**. ✗121S3U. Metonymy of the Adjunct B607. The clothing in sackcloth is put for sorrowing. For other instances of this figure see Ps 35:13. 69:11. La 2:10. Jl 1:13. Am 8:10. **defiled my horn**. Jb 30:19. 1 S 2:10. Ps 7:5. 75:5, 10.

16. **face**. Ps 6:6, 7. 31:9. 32:3. 69:3. 102:3-5, 9. Is 52:14. La 1:16. **on my eyelids**. Jb 17:7. Ps 116:3. Jon ch. 2. Mk 14:34.

17. **Not for**. Jb 11:14. 15:20, 34. 21:27, 28. 22:5-9. 27:6, 7. 29:12-17. 31:1, etc. Ps 7:3-5. 44:17-21. **my prayer is pure**. T#1379. Jb 8:5, 6. 11:13-15. Ps *66:18, 19. Pr *15:8, 29. 1 T *2:8. 2 T 2:22. Ja *4:8.

18. **O earth**. Je 22:29. **cover not**. Ge 4:11. Ne 4:5. Is 26:21. Ezk 24:7. **let my cry**. Jb 27:9. Ps *66:18, 19. Is *1:15. 58:9, 10. Ja 4:3, 4.

19. **my witness**. 1 S 12:5. Ro *1:9. 9:1. 2 C 1:23. 11:31. 1 Th 2:10. **on high**. Heb. in the high places. Jb 5:11. 25:2. 31:2. Ps 113:5.

20. **scorn me**. Heb. *are* my scorners. ver. 4. Jb 12:4, 5. 17:2. **poureth**. Ps 109:4. 142:2. Ho 12:4, 5. Lk 6:11, 12. He *5:7. Heb. *dalaph*, *S#1811h: Kal, Preterite: Jb 16:20. Ps 119:28 (melteth. mg, droppeth). Kal, Future: Ec 10:18.

21. **plead**. T#1376. Jb 9:34, 35. 13:3, 22. 23:3-7. 31:35. 40:1-5. Ec 6:10. Is 43:26. 45:9. Je 2:29. Ro 9:20. **neighbor**. *or*, friend.

22. **a few years**. Heb. years of number. Jb 14:5, 14. Is +10:19mg. **the way**. ✗88, Ge +15:15. **not return**. Jb +*7:9, 10. 10:21. 14:10. +36:18. 2 S *12:23. Ec 12:5. He +√9:27.

JOB 17

Job continues his complaints, and shows that his sufferings would astonish the righteous but not discourage them, 1-10. His hope is not in life but in death, 11-16.

1. **breath is corrupt**. *or*, spirit is spent. Jb 19:17. Ge +6:17. Ps +146:4. **my days**. Jb 6:11. 42:16. Is 57:16. **the graves**. Heb. *qeber*, ver. 13, 14. Ge +23:4. Ps 88:3-5. Is *38:10-14.

2. **mockers**. Jb 12:4. 13:9. 16:20. 21:3. Ps 35:14-16. Mt 27:39-44. **continue**. Heb. lodge. Jb 19:4. 29:19. *31:32. Ps 25:13mg. 91:1mg. **provocation**. 1 S 1:6, 7.

3. **put me**. Jb 9:33. Ge 43:9. 44:32. Pr 11:15. 20:16. He *7:22. **strike**. ✗121S3L. Metonymy of the Adjunct B607. "To strike hands" is put for making a promise or bargain. Pr 6:1. 11:15mg. 17:18. 22:26.

4. **thou hast**. 2 S 15:31. 17:14. 2 Ch 25:16. Is 19:14. Mt *11:25. 13:11. Ro 11:8. 1 C 1:20.

5. **He that**. Jb *32:21, 22. Ps *12:2, 3. Pr 19:22. *20:19. *29:5. 1 Th *2:5. **the eyes**. Ex *20:5. Dt *28:65. 1 K 11:12. La *4:17.

6. **a by-word**. *or*, proverb. Jb +13:12. 27:1. 29:1. 30:9. 1 K *9:7. Ps *44:14. **aforetime**. *or*, before them. **as a tabret**. Ge 31:27. Is 5:12.

7. **Mine eye**. Jb 16:16. Ps 6:7. 31:9, 10. La 5:17. **members**. *or*, thoughts. ver. 11. **shadow**. Ps 109:23, 24. Ec 6:12.

8. **astonied**. Le 26:32. 1 K 9:8. Ps 73:12-15. Ec *5:8. Hab 1:13. Ro *11:33. **stir up**. Jb 29:31. 34:30. Ac 13:46.

9. **hold on**. Jb 16:12. 18:9, 20mg. Ps *84:7, 11. Pr *4:18. 14:16. Is *35:8-10. 1 P *1:5. 1 J *2:19. **clean**. Ge 20:5. Ex=30:18. Ps *24:4. 26:6. 73:13. Is *1:15, 16. Mk 7:2. **hands**. 2 S 22:21, 25. Ps 24:3, 4. 26:6. Ja 4:8. **be stronger and stronger**. Heb. add strength. 2 S 3:1. Ec 1:18. Is *40:29-31. 2 C *12:9, 10.

10. **do ye return**. Jb 6:29. Ml 3:18. **for I**. ver. 4. Jb 15:9. 32:9. 42:7. 1 C 1:20. *6:5.

11. **My days**. Jb 7:6. 9:25, 26. Is 38:10. **purposes**. Pr 16:9. 19:21. Ec 9:10. Is 8:10. La 3:37. Ro *1:13. 2 C 1:15-17. Ja 4:13-15. **thoughts**. Heb. possessions. Ps +√146:4. Is 14:23. Ob 17.

12. **change**. Jb 7:3, 4, 13, 14. 24:14-16. Dt 28:67. **short**. Heb. near. Jb 19:14. 20:5mg.

13. **If I wait**. Jb 14:14. Ps 27:14. La 3:25, 26. **the grave**. Heb. *sheol*, Ge +37:25. See on ver. ●1, 16. Jb 7:9. 10:21, 22. 11:8. 14:13. 30:23. **I have made**. Jb 41:30 (spreadeth). Ps 139:8. SS 2:5 (comfort; mg. straw). Is 57:2. **bed**. *or*, couch. Ge 49:4. 1 K 6:5 (chambers; mg, floors), 6, 10.

14. **said**. Heb. cried, *or* called. **corruption**. Jb 9:31. 21:32, 33. 33:18, 22, 24. Ps *16:10. 49:9. Ac 2:27-31. 13:34-37. 1 C *15:42, 53, 54. **to the worm**. Jb 7:5. 19:26. 21:26. 24:20. 25:6. Is 14:11.

15. **my hope**. Jb 4:6. 5:16. 6:8, 11. 7:6. 8:13. 13:15. 19:10.

16. **the bars of the**. Jb 18:13mg, 14. 33:18-28. Ps 88:4-8. *143:7. Is 38:17, 18. Jon *2:6. **pit**. Heb. *sheol*, Ge +37:35. **rest**. Jb 3:17-19. Ezk 37:11. 2 C 1:9.

JOB 18

Bildad sharply reproves Job for presumption and impatience, 1-4. He enlarges on the miseries of the wicked, 5-21.

1. **Bildad**. Jb +2:11. 8:1. 25:1. 42:7-9.

2. **How long**. Jb 8:2. 11:2. 13:5, 6. 16:2, 3. **mark**. Jb 13:5, 6, 17. 21:2. 33:1. or, set an end. Jb 16:3. 28:3. **afterwards**. Pr *18:13. Ja 1:19. **we**. ✗96D4, Ge +29:27.

3. **Wherefore**. Jb 12:7, 8. 17:4, 10. Ps 73:22. Ec 3:18. Ro 12:10.

4. **teareth**. Jb 5:2. 13:14. 16:9. Jon 4:9. Mk 9:18. Lk 9:39. **himself**. Heb. his soul. Heb. *nephesh*, Ge +27:31. **shall the**. Jb 40:8. Ezk 9:9. **the rock**. Jb 14:18. Is 54:10. Mt 24:35.

5. **the light**. Jb 20:5. Ps ●112:4. Pr 4:19. 13:9. 20:20. 24:20. **spark**. Is 50:11.

6. **candle**. *or*, lamp. Jb 21:17mg. Ps 18:28. Re 18:23. **put out**. Pr *20:20. *24:20.

7. **steps**. Jb 20:22. 36:16. Ps 18:36. Pr 4:12. **his own**. Jb 5:12, 13. 2 S 15:31. 17:14. Ps 33:10. Pr *1:30-32. Ho 10:6. 1 C 3:19.

8. **he is cast**. Jb 22:10. Est 3:9. 6:13. 7:5, 10. Ps 9:15. 35:8. Pr 5:22. 29:6. Ezk 32:3. 1 T 3:7. 6:9. 2 T 2:26.

9. **The gin**. Is 8:14, 15. **robber**. Jb 1:15, 17. 5:5. 10. **snare**. Ps *9:15. 11:6. Ezk 12:13. Ro 11:9. **laid**. Heb. hidden. Jb 3:16. 20:26. 40:13.

11. **Terrors**. Jb 6:4. 15:21. 20:25. Ps 73:19. 91:5. Je 6:25. 20:3, 4. 46:5. 49:29. 2 C 5:11. Re 6:15, 16. **drive him**. Heb. scatter him. Jb 37:11. 38:24. Ge 11:8. **to his feet**. Le 26:36. 2 K 7:6, 7. Ps 53:5. Pr 28:1.

12. **hunger-bitten**. Jb 15:23, 24. 1 S 2:5, 36. 34:10. 109:10. **destruction**. Ps 7:12-14. 1 Th *5:3. 2 P 2:3.

13. **strength**. Heb. bars. Jb 17:16. Jon 2:6. **the first-born**. or, chief, worst, or cruelest of death. ⨍88, Ge +15:15. Ge +41:51. 49:3. Is 14:30. Col +√1:15n. Re 6:8.

14. **confidence**. Jb 8:14. 11:20. Ps *112:10. Pr *10:28. Mt 7:26, 27. **the king of terrors**. ⨍88, Jb 24:17. 41:34. Ge +15:15. Ps 55:4. Pr 14:32. 1 C 15:55, 56. He 2:15.

15. **dwell**. ver. 12, 13. Zc 5:4. **because**. Jb 20:18-21. 31:38, 39. Je 22:13. Hab 2:6-11. **brimstone**. Ge 19:24. Dt 29:23. Ps 11:6. Is 34:9, 10. Re 19:20. *21:8.

16. **roots**. Jb 29:19. Is 5:24. Ho 9:16. Am 2:9. Ml *4:1. **shall his branch**. Jb 5:3, 4. 15:30.

17. **remembrance**. Jb 13:12. Ps *34:16. 83:4. 109:13. Pr 2:22. 10:7.

18. **He shall be driven**. Heb. They shall drive him. Jb 3:20. 10:22. 11:14. Pr 2:22. Is 8:21, 22. Ju 13. **chased**. Jb 20:8. Pr 14:32. Is 17:13, 14. Da 4:33. 5:21.

19. **neither**. Jb 1:19. 8:4. 42:13-16. Ps 109:13. Is 14:21, 22. Je *22:30. **nor any**. Jb 20:26-28. Is 5:8, 9.

20. **come after**. lit. those behind. or, western. Zc 14:8. **astonied**. Dt 29:23, 24. 1 K 9:8. Je 18:16. **his day**. ⨍121P4, Dt +4:32. i.e. *his fate*. By Metonymy of the Adjunct, "day" is put for what transpires within it. Ps 37:13. 137:7. Ezk 21:25. Ob 11-15. Lk 19:42, 44. **went before**. or, lived with him. or, easterns. Jl 2:10. Zc *14:8mg. **were affrighted**. Heb. laid hold on horror. Jb 2:12, 13. 19:13-19. Ezk 27:35. 32:10.

21. **such are**. ver. 14-16. Ex 12:30. **knoweth**. Jb 21:14. Ex *5:2. Jg 2:10. 1 S 2:12. 1 Ch +*28:9. Ps 79:6. Je 9:3. 10:25. Ro 1:28. 1 Th 4:5. 2 Th √1:8. T 1:16.

JOB 19

Job complains of the persevering cruelty, with which his friends distressed him, 1-3; and shows the greatness and variety of his sufferings, 1-20. He entreats their pity, 21, 22. He wishes his words might be recorded, 23, 24. He professes his faith in a divine Redeemer, and a future resurrection, 25-27. He warns his friends not to persecute him, for fear of like judgment, 28, 29.

2. **How long**. Jb 8:2. 18:2. Ps 13:1. Re 6:10. **vex**. Jb 27:2. Jg 16:16. Ps 6:2, 3. 42:10. 2 P 2:7, 8. **soul**. Heb. *nephesh*, Ge +34:3. **break me**. Ps 55:21. 59:7. 64:3. Pr *12:18. *18:21. Ja 3:6-8.

3. **ten times**. Ge 31:7. Le 26:26. Nu *14:22. 1 S 1:8n. Ne *4:12n. Da 1:20. **ye reproached**. Jb 4:6-11. 5:3, 4. 8:4-6. 11:3, 14. 15:4-6, 11, 12. 18:4, etc. **make yourselves strange to me**. or, harden yourselves against me. ver. 17. Ge 42:7. Ps +*69:8.

4. **I have erred**. Jb 11:3-6. **mine**. 2 S 24:17. Pr 9:12. Ezk *18:4. 2 C *5:10. Ga *6:5.

5. **magnify**. Ps 35:26. 38:16. 41:11. 55:12. Mi 7:8. Zp *2:10. Zc 12:7. **plead**. 1 S 1:6. Ne 1:3. Is 4:1. Lk 1:25. 13:2-4. Jn 9:2, 34.

6. **God**. Jb 7:20. 16:11-14. Ps 44:9-14. 66:10-12. **compassed**. Jb 18:8-10. La 1:12, 13. Ezk 12:13. 32:3. Ho 7:12. Mt 13:47.

7. **I cry**. Jb 10:3, 15-17. 16:17-19. 21:27. Ps 22:2. Je 20:8. La 3:8. Hab *1:2, 3. **wrong**. or, violence. Jb 16:17. Ge 6:11, 13. 1 Ch 12:17mg. **no judgment**. Jb 9:32. 13:15-23. 16:21. 23:3-7. 31:35, 36. 34:5. 40:8.

8. **fenced**. Jb 3:23. Ps 88:8. La 3:7, 9. Ho 2:6. **set**. Jsh 24:7. Pr 4:19. Is 50:10. Je 13:16. 23:12. Jn *8:12.

9. **stripped**. Jb 29:7-14, 20, 21. 30:1. Ps 49:16, 17. *89:44. Is 61:6. Ho 9:11, 12.

10. **destroyed**. Jb 1:13-19. 2:7. Ps 88:13-18. La 2:5, 6. 2 C 4:8, 9. **I am gone**. Jb 17:11. Ps 102:11. **mine hope**. Jb 6:11. 8:13-18. 17:15. 24:20. Ps 37:35, 36.

11. **kindled**. Dt 32:22. Ps 89:46. 90:7. **he counteth**. Jb 13:24. 16:9. 33:10. La *2:5.

12. **His**. Jb 16:11. Is 10:5, 6. 51:23. **raise**. Jb 30:12.

13. **put my brethren**. Ps 31:11. 38:11. 69:+*8, 20. *88:8, 18. Mt *26:56. 2 T 4:16. **estranged**. Jb 6:21-23.

14. **kinsfolk**. 2 K 10:11mg. Ps 38:11. Pr 18:24. Mi 7:5, 6. Mt *10:21. **familiar**. 2 S 16:23. Ps *55:12-14. Je 20:10. Jn *13:18.

15. **dwell**. ver. 16-19. **count me**. Jb 31:31, 32. Ps 123:3, 4.

16. **my servant**. Jb 1:15, 16, 17, 19.

17. **breath**. Heb. *ruach*, spirit, put for manner, Jb 1:19. 2:9, 10. 4:9, 15. 6:4, 26. Ge +26:35. 17:1. **body**. Heb. belly. Dt +28:11mg. Ps 132:11mg. Mi 6:7mg.

18. **Yea**. Jb 30:1, 12. 2 K 2:23. Is *3:5. **young children**. or, the wicked. Jb 16:11. 21:11. 2 K +*2:23. **despised**. Jb 5:17. 7:16. 8:20. 9:21.

19. **my inward friends**. Heb. the men of my secret. Ps *41:9mg. 55:12-14, 20. **they whom**. Jb 6:14, 15. Ps *109:4, 5. Lk 22:48.

20. **bone**. Jb 30:30. 33:19-22. Ps 22:14-17. 32:3, 4. *38:2. 102:3, 5. La 4:8. **and to**. or, as. **and I am**. Jb 2:4-6. 7:5. La 3:4. 5:10.

21. **have pity**. Jb 6:14. Ro *12:15. 1 C 12:26. He *13:3. **the hand**. ⨍108B, Jb 1:11. 2:5, 10. 6:4. Ge +26:29. Ps 38:2. **touched**. ⨍108B, Ge +26:29.

22. **persecute**. Jb 10:16. 16:13, 14. Ps *69:26. **and are not**. Jb 2:5. 31:31. Is 51:23. Mi 3:3.

23. **Oh**. Heb. Who will give, etc. **my words**. Jb 31:35. Is 8:1. 30:8. **oh that they were**. Rather, "Oh that they were *described* (*yuchakoo*) in a book, with an iron stile and lead! Were graven on a rock for ever!" Pliny (l. xiii. c. 11) observes, "At first men wrote on palm leaves, and afterwards on the bark or rind of other trees. In the process of time, public monuments were written on rolls of lead (*plumbeis voluminibus*); and those of a private nature on linen books, or tables covered with wax."

24. **graven**. Ex 28:11, 12, 21. 32:16. Dt 27:2, 3, 8. Je 17:1. 2 C 3:1-6.

25. **I know**. T#353. Jb *33:23, 24. Ps *19:14. Is *54:5. *59:20, 21. Ro 8:35, 37. Ep *1:7. 2 T 4:6-8. He 6:11, 12, 17-20. 1 J 3:18, 19. ⨍121C2A1. Metonymy of the Cause B552. Verbs of knowing are used of the effect of knowing: understanding, caring for, approving, believing with saving faith. Here Job knows, believes, and has a saving knowledge of the fact. For other instances of this figure see Dt 1:17mg. Ps 1:6. +√9:10n. 35:11. 90:11. Pr 24:23. Is 1:3. Je 9:24. 31:34. Jn 8:43. *10:27. *17:3. Ac 10:34. Ro 7:15mg. 1 C 8:3. Re 2:24. **he shall**. Ge +√3:15. *22:18. Jn *5:22-29. Ju *14, 15.

26. **And though**, etc. or, After I shall awake, though this *body* be destroyed, yet out of my flesh shall I see God. Ps *17:15. **after**. Is +*26:19n. Da *12:2. Ph *3:21. **destroy**. ❋S#5362h. Young renders, "compassed," and notes "It never means *destroy*." ver. *6. Jb 1:5. Le 19:27. Jsh 6:3, 11. 1 K 7:24. 2 K *6:14. 11:8. 2 Ch 4:3. 23:7. Ps 17:9. 22:16. 48:12. 88:17. Is 10:34mg. 15:8. 29:1. La *3:5. **in my flesh**. Ps *16:9, 11. Mt *5:8. Jn +*5:29. 1 C *13:12. *15:53. Ph *3:21.

1 J *3:2. Re *1:7. **see God**. Ps 45:6. Is 25:9. 52:7. Jn 1:1. √20:28. Ac *20:28. Ro 9:5. 2 C 5:19. Col 2:8, 9. 1 T 3:16. T *2:13. He *1:8. 2 P *1:1mg. Ju 4. Re √1:6, 7.

27. **I shall**. Nu *24:17. Is +*26:19n. **mine eyes**. Is 33:17. **shall behold**. lit. have beheld. √96C2, Ge +45:9. **another**. Heb. a stranger. **though my reins**, etc. *or*, my reins within me are consumed with earnest desire (for that day). Ps 119:81. Ph *1:23. **within me**. Heb. in my bosom. Ge 16:5. Ex 4:6, 7. Pr 22:18mg.

28. **Why**. ver. 22. Ps 69:26. **seeing**, etc. *or*, and *what* root of matter is found in me? **the root**. 1 K 14:13. **in me**. Instead of *bee*, "in me," *bo*, "in him," is the reading of more than one hundred MSS.

29. **ye afraid**. Jb 13:7-11. Ro *13:1-4. **that ye may**. Ps 58:10, 11. Ec 11:9. Mt *7:1, 2. Ja 4:11, 12.

JOB 20

Zophar, with eagerness and warmth, enlarges on the certain ruin and manifold calamities of the wicked, notwithstanding for a time he may prosper and flourish, 1-29.

1. **Zophar**. Jb +2:11. 11:1. 42:9.

2. **my thoughts**. ver. 3. Jb 4:2. 13:19. 32:13-20. Ps 39:2, 3. Je 20:9. Ro *10:2. **and for**. Ps 31:22. 116:11. Pr 14:29. 29:20. Ec 7:9. Mk 6:25. Ja *1:19, 20. **I make haste**. Heb. my haste *is* in me.

3. **the check**. Jb 19:29. **the spirit**. Heb. 'ruach,' Ge +41:8. ver. 2. Jb 27:11. 33:3. Ps 49:3. 78:2-5.

4. **thou not**. Jb 8:8, 9. 15:10. 32:7. **man**. Ge 1:28. 9:1-3. Ps 115:16.

5. **the triumphing**. Jb 5:3. 15:29-34. 18:5, 6. 27:13-23. Ex 15:9, 10. Jg 16:21-30. Est 5:11, 12. *7:10. Ps *37:35, 36. 73:18-20. 94:3. Ac 12:22, 23. **short**. Heb. from near. Jb 17:12mg. 1 K 16:15. Ezk 7:8. **the joy**. Jb 8:19. 27:8. Mt 7:21. 13:20, 21. Ga 6:4. Ja 4:16.

6. **his excellency**. Ge 11:4. Is 14:13, 14. Da 4:11, 22. Am *9:2. Ob 3, 4. Mt *11:23. **clouds**. Heb. cloud. Ge 9:13.

7. **perish**. 1 K 14:10. 2 K 9:37. Ps 83:10. Je 8:2. **for ever**. Heb. 'netsach,' Jb +4:20. **shall say**. Jb 14:10.

8. **fly away**. Ps *73:20. 83:10. *90:5. Is 29:7, 8.

9. **The eye**. ver. 7. Jb 7:8, 10. 8:18. 27:23. Ps 37:10, *36. 103:15, 16.

10. **His children**, etc. *or*, The poor shall oppress his children. Jb 5:4. 27:14. Pr *28:3. Mt 18:28. **seek**. Ps 109:10. **his hands**. ver. 15, *18, 20. Ex 12:36. 22:1, 3, 9. 2 S 12:6. Pr *6:31. Lk +*19:8.

11. **bones**. Jb 13:26. 19:20. Ps *25:7. Pr 5:11-13, 22, 23. Ezk 32:27. **which shall lie**. Jb 21:26. Pr 14:32. Ezk 24:13. Jn 8:21, 24. Ac 1:25.

12. **wickedness**. Jb 15:16. Ec 3:6. Pr *9:16-18. 20:17. Ec 11:9. **he hide**. Ps *10:7. 109:17, 18.

13. **spare it**. Mt *5:29, 30. Mk 9:43-49. Ro 8:13. **within his mouth**. Heb. in the midst of his palate. Jb 6:30mg. 12:11. 29:10. 34:3mg.

14. **his meat**. √17I18, Ge +3:19. 2 S 11:2-5. 12:10, 11. Ps 32:3, 4. 38:1-8. 51:8, 9. Pr *1:31. 23:20, 21, 29-35. Je √2:19. Ml 2:2. **the gall**. ver. 16. Dt 32:24. Ro 3:13.

15. **swallowed**. Pr *23:8. Mt 27:3, 4. **vomit**. Pr 26:11. 2 P 2:22.

16. **the poison**. Ro 3:13. **the viper's**. Is 30:6. Mt 3:7. Ac 28:3-6.

17. **shall not see**. Nu 14:23. 2 K 7:2. Je 17:6-8. Lk

16:24. **the rivers**. Jb 29:6. Ps *1:3. 36:8, 9. 46:4. Is 41:17. Je 17:6. Re 22:1. √63I2, Jsh +3:3. Supply the ellipsis from the succeeding clause so as to read "He shall not see the (flowing) rivers, the flowing brooks of honey and butter." **floods**. *or*, streaming brooks. or, flowing. Jb 14:11. 22:16. 28:11. **brooks**. √102, Ge +2:24. Jb 6:15. 21:33. 22:24. Ps 36:8. **of honey**. √17I17, Ex +3:8. Dt 32:13, 14. 2 S 17:29. Ps *81:13, 16. Is 7:15, 22. *58:9-11. Jn 7:37.

18. **shall he restore**. See on ver. 10, 15. **swallow**. ver. 5. Pr 1:12. Je 51:34, *44. La 2:16. Ho 8:7, 8. Am 8:4. Mt 23:14, 24. **his substance**. Heb. the substance of his exchange. Jb 15:31 (recompence). 28:17. Le 27:10, 33. Ru 4:7. **and he shall**. Jb 31:25, 29. Is 24:7-11. Je 11:15, 16. 22:13, 17. Ezk 7:12. Ho 9:1. Ja 4:8, 9.

19. **Because**. Jb 21:27, 28. 22:6. 24:2-12. 31:13-22, 38, 39. 35:9. 1 S 12:3, 4. Ps 10:18. 12:5. Pr 14:31. 22:22, 23. Ec 4:1. 5:8. Ezk 22:29. Am 4:1-3. Ja 2:6, 13. +*5:4. **oppressed**. Heb. crushed. Dt 28:33. La 3:34. Am +*4:1. **he hath violently**. Jb 18:15. 24:2. 1 K *21:19. Is 5:7, 8. Mi 2:2, 9.

20. **Surely**. Ec 5:13, 14. Is *57:20, 21. **feel**. Heb. know. Pr 23:35mg. Ec 8:5mg. Is 59:8. **that which**. Ps 39:11. 1 K *21:19. Is 44:9.

21. **none of his meat be left**. *or*, *be* none left for his meat. Jb 18:19. Pr *22:22, 23. Ec 5:13, 14. Je *17:11. Am 4:1, 2. Lk 16:24, 25.

22. **the fulness**. Jb 15:29. 18:7. Ps 39:5. Ec 2:18-20. Re 18:7. **every hand**. Jb 1:15, 17. 16:11. 2 K 24:2. Is 10:6. **wicked**. *or*, troublesome. Jb 3:17.

23. **he is about**. Nu *11:33. Ps 78:30, 31. Ml *2:2. Lk *12:17-20. **rain it**. Ge 19:24. Ex 9:23. Ps 11:6. *78:30, 31. Is 21:4.

24. **flee from**. 1 K 20:30. Is *24:18. Je 48:43, 44. Am *5:19. 9:1-3. **the bow**. 2 S 22:35. **strike him**. Pr 7:23.

25. **drawn**. Jb 16:13. Dt 32:41. 2 S 18:14. Ps 7:12, 13. **terrors**. Jb 6:4. 15:21. 18:11. 27:20. Ps 73:19. 88:15. Je 20:3, 4. 2 C *5:11.

26. **darkness**. Jb 18:5, 6. Is 8:22. Mt 8:12. Ju 13. **a fire**. Ps *21:9. 120:4. Is +*30:33. Mt 3:12. **it shall go**. Jb 18:19. Ps 109:9-15. Is 14:20-22.

27. **heaven**. Ps 44:20, 21. Je 29:23. Ml +*3:5. Lk *12:2, 3. Ro 2:16. 1 C *4:5. **earth**. Jb 16:18. 18:18. Is *26:21.

28. **increase**. ver. 10, 18-22. Jb 5:5. 27:14-19. 2 K 20:17. Re *18:17. **and his goods**. Pr +*11:4. Zp *1:18. Mt *16:26. Ja 5:1-3. **day of his wrath**. Jb +*21:30. Pr +*11:4. Zp +*1:18. Ro +*2:5.

29. **the portion**. Jb 18:21. 27:13. 31:2, 3. Dt 29:20-28. Ps *11:5, 6. 17:14. Ec 8:13. Is 3:11. 54:17. Mt √24:51. **heritage**. Ps 16:6. **appointed unto him by God**. Heb. of his decree from God. Jb 2:10. La *3:38. Is *45:7. Da 4:24. Am +*3:6.

JOB 21

Job entreats a patient hearing because of his singular calamities, 1-6. He shows that wicked men sometimes so prosper as to grow bold in presumption, 7-16. Yet that they at length fall into destruction, 17-22. The dealings of God with them in life and death are greatly varied, as their judgment is deferred to the day of wrath, 23-34.

2. **Hear.** Jb 13:3, 4. 18:2. 33:1, 31-33. 34:2. Jg 9:7. Is 55:2. He *2:1. **let this be.** Jb 15:11. 16:2.

3. **that I may.** Jb 13:13. 33:31-33. **mock on.** Jb 12:4, 5. 13:9. 16:10, 20. 17:2.

4. **is my complaint.** Jb 7:11-21. 10:1, 2. 1 S 1:16. Ps 22:1-3. 77:3-9. 102, title. 142:2, 3. Mt 26:38, 39. **if it were.** 2 K 6:26, 27. Ps 42:11. **spirit.** Heb. *ruach*, Ge +41:8. **troubled.** Heb. shortened. Ex 6:9mg. Nu 21:4mg. Jg +10:16mg. 16:16mg. Pr 14:29mg. Mi 2:7mg.

5. **Mark me.** Heb. Look unto me. Jb +5:1mg. **be astonished.** Jb 2:12. 17:8. 19:20, 21. **lay your.** ſ121S3N, Jb 29:9. 40:4. Jg +18:19. Ps *39:9. Pr *30:32. Am 5:13. Mi 7:16. Ro 11:33.

6. **Even when.** Ps *77:3. 88:15. 119:120. La 3:19, 20. Hab 3:16.

7. **Wherefore.** Jb 12:6. Ps 17:10. 73:3-12. Je 12:1-3. Hab 1:15, 16. **mighty.** Ps 37:35. Da 4:17. Re 13:2-7. 17:2-4.

8. **Their seed.** Jb 5:3, 4. 18:19. 20:10, 28. Pr 17:6.

9. **safe from fear.** Heb. peace from fear. Jb 3:25. 4:14. 13:11. 15:21mg. 18:11. Ps 73:19. Is 57:19-21. **the rod.** Jb 9:34. 37:13mg. Ge 49:10. Ps 73:5. 89:32.

10. **their cow.** Ex 23:26. Dt 7:13, 14. 28:11. Ps 144:13, 14. Ec 9:1, 2. Lk 12:16-21. 16:19.

11. **send forth.** Ps *17:14. 107:41. 127:3-5. **dance.** 1 Ch 15:29. Mt 11:16, 17.

12. **They take.** Ge 4:21. 31:27. Is *5:12. 22:13. Am 6:4-6. **timbrel.** Ge 31:27. Ex 15:20. **harp.** Jb 30:31. Ge 4:21. 31:27. 1 Ch +13:8n. **organ.** Jb 30:31. Ge 4:21. Ps 150:4.

13. **They spend.** Jb *36:11. Ps 73:4. Mt *24:38, 39. Lk *12:19, 20. 16:19, 22. *17:28, 29. or, wear out. Jb 13:28. Ge 18:12. **wealth.** or, mirth. 2 S 13:28. Pr 14:13. Lk 16:25. **moment.** Jb 7:18. 20:5. 34:20. Lk 16:19, 22. Mt *8:29. **grave.** Heb. *sheol*, Jb 7:9. 11:8. 14:13. 17:13. Ge +37:35.

14. **they say.** Jb *22:17. Ps *10:4, 11. Hab 1:15. Mt *8:29. Lk *8:28, 37. Jn *15-23, 24. Ro *8:7. **for we.** Ps 54:3. Pr 1:7, 22, 29. Je *44:16, 17. Lk *19:14, 27. Jn *3:19, 20. *8:45-47. Ro *1:28. 8:7. 2 Th *2:10-12. 2 T *4:3, 4. **knowledge.** T#363. Ps 32:9. Pr 13:18. 15:32. 19:2. Is 5:13. Je +44:17 (T#699). Ezk +39:23 (T#486). Ho *4:1, 6. Jn 16:2, 3. *17:3. 1 C 2:7, 8. 14:20. 2 Th *1:7, 8.

15. **What is.** Ex *5:2. Ps 12:4. Pr *30:9. Ho 13:6. **and what profit.** T#689. Jb *34:9. *35:3. Nu +32:23 (T#733). Ps ◑+*37:9 (T#1819). +106:13 (T#411). Pr +28:16 (T#137). Is 30:11. 56:11. Je *6:13. *22:17. Ezk 22:12. 33:31. Ho 10:1. Ml 1:13, 14. 3:14. Mt 5:46, 47. Lk 6:32-34. +18:12 (T#194). 2 C +7:10 (T#609). Ga +4:17 (T#623). Ph *2:21. 1 Th +4:6 (T#732). 1 T *6:5. 2 T 3:2, +5 (T#191). Ja +3:6 (T#728). **if we.** Is *45:19. Mt *7:7. Jn *16:24. Ja 4:2.

16. **Lo.** Jb 1:21. 12:9, 10. Ps *49:6, 7. 52:5-7. Ec 8:8. Lk 16:2, 25. **the counsel.** Jb 22:18. Ge 49:6. Ps *1:1. Pr √1:10. 5:8.

17. **How oft.** Jb 18:5, 6, 18. Pr 13:9. 20:20. 24:20. Mt *25:8. **candle.** or, lamp. Jb 18:6mg. 29:3. 2 S 21:17mg. **how oft.** ſ63I1C2B. Ellipsis (Repetition: particles from preceding clause), interrogatives B94. For other instances of this figure see Ps 4:2. 73:19. 89:46. 94:3, 4. La 1:1, 2. Jl 1:18. **cometh.** Ro 1:27. **distributeth.** Ps 32:10. 90:7-9. Lk 12:46. Ro *2:8, 9.

18. **as stubble.** Jb 13:25. Ex 15:7. Ps *1:4. 35:5. 83:13. Is *5:24. 17:13. 29:5. 40:24. 41:15, 16. Je 13:24.

Ho 13:3. Na 1:10. Mt *3:12. **carrieth.** Heb. stealeth. Jb 27:20.

19. **layeth.** Jb 22:24. Dt 32:34. Mt 6:19, 20. Ro 2:5. **iniquity.** *that is*, the punishment of his iniquity. Ge 4:7. Is *53:4-6. 2 C √5:21. **for his children.** Ex *20:5. Ps 109:9, etc. Is *14:21. Ezk 18:14, 19, 20. Mt 23:31-35. **he rewardeth.** Dt 32:41. 2 S 3:39. Ps 54:5. Mt 16:27. 2 T 4:14. Re 18:6. **he shall.** Ml 3:18.

20. **see.** Jb 27:19. Lk 16:23. **drink.** Ps *75:8. Is 51:17. Je *25:15, 16. 51:7. Re *14:10. 19:15.

21. **For what.** Jb 14:21. Ec 2:18, 19. Lk 16:27, 28. **the number.** Jb 14:5. Ps 55:23. *102:24.

22. **teach.** Jb 40:2. Is *40:13, 14. 45:9. Ro *11:34. 1 C *2:16. **he judgeth.** Jb 34:17-19. Ps 113:5, 6. Ec 5:8. Is 40:22, 23. 1 C 6:3. 2 P *2:4. Ju 6. Re 20:1-3, 12-15.

23. **in his full strength.** Heb. in his very perfection, *or*, the strength of his perfection. Jb 20:22, 23. Ps 49:17. 73:4, 5. Lk 12:19-21.

24. **His breasts.** *or*, His milk pails. Jb 15:27. Ps *17:10. **moistened.** Pr 3:8.

25. **in the bitterness.** Jb 3:20. 7:11. 9:18. 10:1. 2 S 17:8mg. Pr 14:10. Is 38:15-17. **soul.** Heb. *nephesh*, Ge +34:3. **never.** Jb 20:23. 1 K 17:12. Ec *6:2. Ezk 4:16, 17. 12:18.

26. **alike.** Jb 3:18, 19. 20:11. Ec *9:2. **the worms.** Jb 17:14. 19:26. Ps *49:14. Is 14:11.

27. **I know.** Jb 4:8-11. 5:3-5. 8:3-6. 15:20, etc. 20:5, 29. Lk 5:22. **ye wrongfully.** Jb 32:3. 42:7. Ps 59:4. 119:86. 1 P *2:19.

28. **Where.** Jb 20:7. Ps 37:36. 52:5, 6. Hab 2:9-11. Zc 5:4. **dwelling places.** Heb. tent of the tabernacles. Jb 8:22. 15:34. 18:14, 21. Nu 16:26-34.

29. **go by.** Ps 129:8. **tokens.** Ge 1:14. 4:15. 9:12, 13, 17.

30. **the wicked.** Pr *16:4. Na *1:2. Mt *8:29. 2 P *2:9, 17. *3:7. Ju *13. **reserved.** Jb 33:18. Ju 6. **day.** Jb 20:28. Ps *110:5. Pr *11:4. Is +2:11. Zp *1:15. Ro *2:5. Re *6:17. **brought forth.** ver. 32. Jb 10:19. Ps 45:14. **wrath.** Heb. wraths. Jb 20:28. ◑24:1. Ps 7:6. 110:5. Pr +*11:4. La 1:12. 2:1. Is 13:13. Je +*30:7. Ezk +*7:19. Zp +*1:18. Lk +*21:34-36. Ro +*2:5. *5:9. Ep 2:6. 5:6. 1 Th *1:10. *5:9.

31. **declare.** 2 S *12:7-12. 1 K *21:19-24. Ps *50:21. Is *58:1. Je 2:33-35. Mk *6:18. Lk *16:28. Ac *24:25. Ga *2:11. Ep *5:11. **repay.** ver. *19. Jb 41:11. Dt *7:10. Is *59:18. Ro *12:19. Ja *2:13.

32. **he be.** Ps 49:14. Ezk 32:21-32. Lk 16:22. **grave.** Heb. graves. *qeber*, Ge +23:4. ſ96F3, Ge +8:4. Jb 3:12. 5:26. 10:19. **remain in the tomb.** Heb. watch in the heap. *S#1430h. Jb 5:26 (shock). Ex 22:6 (stacks). Jg 15:5 (shocks).

33. **sweet.** Jb 3:17, 18. **every man.** Jb 30:23. Ge 3:19. Ec 1:4. *8:8. *12:7. He +√9:27.

34. **comfort.** Jb 16:2. **seeing.** Jb 13:4. 32:3. 42:7. **falsehood.** Heb. transgression. Le 5:15. 6:2. 26:40.

JOB 22

Eliphaz shows that man's goodness cannot profit God, 1-4. He accuses Job of various crimes, which he supposes had brought on him his calamities, 5-14. He contrasts the doom of sinners visited by divine judgments with the security of the righteous, 15-20. He exhorts Job to repent and encourages him to hope for mercy, 21-30.

2. **a man**. Jb 35:6-8. Ps 16:2. Lk 17:10. **as he that,** etc. *or,* if he may be profitable, *doth his* good success depend thereon? Jb 21:15. Dt 10:13. Pr 3:13-18. 4:7-9. 9:12. Ec 7:11, 12. Mt 5:29. Ga 6:7, 8.

3. **any pleasure**. 1 Ch 29:17. Ps 16:2. 147:10, 11. Pr 11:1, 20. 12:22. 15:8. Ml 2:17. Ph 4:18. **or.** √85S, Jb +4:17. **thou makest**. Jb 23:10-12. Ps 39:1. 119:3-6, 59. Lk √17:10. Ac 24:16. 2 C *7:1.

4. **reprove**. Ps 39:11. 76:6. 80:16. Re 3:19. **for fear.** Jb 7:12. **will he enter**. Jb 9:19, 32. 14:3. 16:21. 23:6, 7. 34:23. Ps 130:3, 4. *143:2. Ec 12:14. Is 3:14, 15.

5. **not thy**. Jb 4:7-11. 11:14. 15:5, 6, 31-34. 21:27. 32:3. **thine**. Ps 19:12. 40:12.

6. **For thou**. Jb 24:3, 9, 10. Ex +√22:26, 27. Dt 24:10-18. Ezk 18:7, 12, 16. Am 2:8. **stripped**, etc. Heb. stripped the clothes of the naked. **stripped**. √125. Oxymoron; or, Wise Folly B816: a wise saying that seems foolish. For other instances of this figure see Is 58:10. Je 22:19. Mt √6:23. *16:25. Ac 5:41. 1 C 1:25, 27-29. 9:17. 2 C 6:4, 8-10. *8:2. 12:10, 11. Ep 3:8. 1 T 5:6. **naked**. √171N, Ge +8:13. By the figure Synecdoche of the Whole, where the whole is put for one of its parts, "naked" is put for being scantily clothed, or poorly clad. Jb 19:9. +*24:10. 31:19, 20. Ge 37:23. Jn *21:7n.

7. **not given**. Jb 31:17. Dt *15:7-11. Ps 112:9. Pr 11:24, 25. *19:17. Is 58:7, 10. Ezk 18:7, 16. Mt *25:42. Ro 12:20. Ja 2:15, 16.

8. **But as**. Jb 29:7-17. 31:34. 1 K 21:11-15. Ps 12:8. Mi 7:3. **mighty man**. Heb. man of arm. **honorable.** Heb. eminent, *or,* accepted for countenance. Jb 13:8. 2 K +5:1mg.

9. **widows**. Jb 24:3, 21. 29:12, 13. 31:16-18, 21. Ex *22:21-24. Dt √27:19. Ps *94:6. Is 1:17, 23. 10:2. Ezk 22:7. Ml +*3:5. Lk 18:3-5. **arms**. Ps 10:15. 37:17. Ezk 30:22. **fatherless**. Ge +11:28. Dt +*10:18.

10. **snares**. Jb 18:8-10. 19:6. Ps 11:6. **sudden**. Jb 6:4. 13:21. Pr 1:27. 3:25, 26. 1 Th 5:3.

11. **darkness**. Jb 18:6, 18. 19:8. Pr 4:19. Is 8:22. La 3:2. Jl 2:2, 3. Mt 8:12. **abundance**. Ps 42:7. 69:1, 2. 124:4. La *3:54. Jon 2:3.

12. **not God**. Ps 115:3, 16. Ec 5:2. Is +*57:15. 66:1. **height**. Heb. head. Jb 1:20. 12:24 (chief). Ge 2:10. **stars**. Jb 3:9. 9:7. 25:5. 38:7. Ps +*8:3n, 4.

13. **How**. *or,* What. **doth God know**. Ps 10:11. 59:7. 73:11. 94:7-9. *139:11, 12. Ezk 8:12. 9:9. Zp 1:12.

14. **Thick clouds**. Jb 20:6. 26:8. 30:15. 34:22. Ge +9:13. Ps 33:14. 97:2. 139:1, 2, 11, 12. Je 23:24. Lk 12:2, 3. **covering**. or, secret place. Jb 13:10. 24:15. 31:27. **circuit**. Pr 8:14. Is *40:22.

15. **the old**. Heb. *olam.* ✤S#5769h. Ezr 4:15, 19. Pr 22:28. 23:10. Is 44:7. 58:12. 61:4. Je 5:15. 6:16. 18:15. Ezk 25:15. 36:2. **way**. Ge 6:5, 11-13. Lk 17:26, 27.

16. **cut down**. Jb 15:32. Ps 55:23. 102:24. Ec 7:17. **out of time**. Ec +*7:17. Is +*38:10. **whose foundation was overflown with a flood**. Heb. a flood was poured upon their foundation. Ge 7:11, 17-24. Mt 24:37-39. 1 P 3:19, 20. 2 P 2:5.

17. **Depart**. Jb 21:10, +*14, 15. Is 30:11. Mt 8:29, 34. Ro 1:28. **and what**. Ps 4:6. Ml 3:14. **for them.** *or,* to them.

18. **he filled**. Jb 12:6. 1 S 2:7. Ps 17:14. Je 12:2. Ac *14:17. 15:16. **the counsel**. Jb 21:16. Ps *1:1.

19. **righteous**. Ps 48:11. 58:10. 97:8. 107:42. Pr *11:10. Re 18:20. 19:1-3. **innocent**. Jb 9:23. Ps 52:6.

20. **our substance**. *or,* our estate. Jb 4:7. 8:3, 4. 15:5, 6. 20:18, 19. 21:27, 28. Lk *13:1-5. **the remnant.** *or,* their excellency. Jb 4:21. Ge 49:3. Ps 17:14. **the fire**. Jb 1:16. 20:26. Ge *19:24. Lk 17:29, 30. 2 P *2:6, 7.

21. **Acquaint**. Jb 27:8-10. 1 Ch +*28:9. Ho *6:6. Jn *17:3. 2 C *4:6. 2 P *1:2. **him**. that is, *God*. **be at peace**. Is 27:5. *57:19-21. Mt 5:25. Ac 10:36. 2 C *5:20. Ep *2:14-17. Ph *4:7.

22. **receive**. Dt *4:1, 2. Pr *2:1-9. 1 Th *4:1, 2. **lay up**. Jb *23:12. Dt *6:6-9. Ps √119:11. Pr *4:4, 21. Je √15:16. Mt *12:35. *13:52. Lk 2:19, 51. Col *3:16. Re 22:18, 19.

23. **return**. Jb *8:5, 6. *11:13, 14. Is *55:6, 7. Ho *14:1, 2. Zc *1:3. Ac *26:20. **built up**. Jb 12:14. Je 31:4. Col *2:7. Ju *20. **thou shalt**. Jb *11:14. 18:15. Jsh *7:13-16. Is *33:15. Zc 5:3, 4. **put**. 2 T *2:19.

24. **lay up**. 1 K 10:21. 2 Ch 1:15. 9:10, 27. **as dust**. *or,* on the dust. √138B, √102B, Ge +13:16. **Ophir.** √121J12. Metonymy of the Subject B577. *Ophir* is put for the gold of Ophir. Ge 10:29. 1 K 9:28n. 22:48. 2 Ch 8:18n. Ps 45:9. Is 13:12.

25. **the Almighty**. Ge 15:1. Ps 18:2. *84:11. Is 41:10. Ro *8:31. **defence**. *or,* gold. Ps 16:5, 6. Is 33:6. 2 C 6:10. Ja 2:5. **plenty of silver**. Heb. silver of strength. Nu 23:22. 24:8. Ps 95:4. Ec 7:12.

26. **shalt thou**. Jb 27:10. 34:9. Ps *37:4. SS 2:3. Is *58:14. Ro 7:22. **lift up**. Jb 11:15. Ps 25:1. 86:4. 143:8. 1 J *3:20, 21.

27. **make thy**. Ps *50:14, 15. √66:17-20. 91:15. 116:1. Is 58:9. 1 J √5:14, 15. **pay thy**. Ps 56:12, 13. 66:13, 14. 116:14. Ec *5:4, 5. Jon 2:9. **vows**. Le +*23:38.

28. **decree**. Ps 20:4. 90:17. Is +*45:11n. La 3:37. Mt 21:22. Ja 4:15. **the light**. Jb 29:3. Ps 97:11. 112:4. Pr +*4:18. Is *30:21. Ml 4:2. Jn *8:12.

29. **men**. Jb 5:19, etc. Ps 9:2, 3. 91:14-16. 92:9-11. **cast down**. Ps 147:6. **he shall**. Pr 29:23. Is √57:15. Lk *14:11. 18:9-14. Ja *4:6. 1 P 5:5. **the humble person.** Heb. him that hath low eyes. √138B, Ge +13:16. Ps *138:6. Is *66:2. Ezk *21:26, 27. Lk 1:52. 18:13, 14.

30. **He shall deliver the island of the innocent**. *or,* The innocent shall deliver the island. Jb 42:8. Ge *18:26-32. Is 58:12. Je 5:1. Ac *27:24. **pureness**. Is *1:15. Ml 1:9. Mt 17:19, 20. Ac 19:15, 16. 1 T *2:8. Ja 5:15, 16.

JOB 23

Job longs to plead his cause before God, being assured of a favorable event, 1-7. He laments that he cannot perceive the presence of God, but is confident that God knows his way, and will bring him forth as gold, 8-10. He attests his own integrity, 11, 12; but is troubled by the immutable counsel of God, 13-17.

2. **my complaint**. Jb 6:2. 10:1. La 3:19, 20. Ps 77:2-9. **stroke**. Heb. hand. Ps 22:20mg. **heavier**. Jb 11:6.

3. **Oh that**. Jb 13:3. 16:21. 40:1-5. Is 26:8, 13. 14:7. **where**. Is *55:6, 7. 2 C 5:19, 20. He *4:16. **that I might**. Jb 31:35-37. Re *3:20.

4. **order**. Jb 13:18. 37:19. Ps 43:1. Is *43:26. **fill my mouth**. Ge *18:25-32. 32:12. Ex 32:12, 13. Nu 14:13-19. Jsh 7:8, 9. Ps 25:11. Da 9:18, 19.

5. **know**. Jb 10:2. 13:22, 23. 42:2-6. 1 C 4:3, 4.

6. **plead**. Jb 9:19, 33, 34. 13:21. Ps 78:38. Is 27:4, 8. *57:16. Mi 2:1. **power**. Mt 28:18. **but he would**. Ps 138:3. 2 C 12:9, 10. 2 T *4:17.

7. **There**. Is *1:18. Je 3:5. 12:1. **so should**. Jb 9:15. Ro 3:19-22. 8:1, 33, 34. **for ever**. Heb. *netsach,* Jb +4:20.

8. **I go**. Jb 9:11. Ps 10:1. 13:1-3. Is 45:15. 1 T *6:16.

9. **he hideth himself**. Ps 89:46. Is 8:17.

10. **he knoweth**. Ge *18:19. 2 K *20:3. Ps *1:6. +40:17. 103:14. 139:1-3. Jn 21:17. 2 T *2:19. **the way that I take**. Heb. the way that is with me. **he hath**. Jb 1:11, 12. 2:5, 6. Dt 8:2. Ps 17:3. 66:10. Pr *17:3. Zc 13:9. Ml 3:2, 3. He 11:17. Ja 1:2-4, *12. 1 P 1:7. **I shall**. Jb 42:5-8.

11. **My foot**. 1 S 12:2-5. Ps 18:20-24. *44:18. Ac 20:18, 19, 33, 34. 2 C 1:12. 1 Th 2:10. **his way**. Jb 17:9. Ps 36:3. 125:5. Zp 1:6. Lk 8:13-15. Ro 2:7. 2 P 2:20-22.

12. **Neither**. Jn *6:66-69. *8:31. Ac *14:22. He *10:38, 39. 1 J *2:19. **I have esteemed**. Heb. hid, *or,* laid up. T#1083. Jb *22:22. Ps *19:9, 10. *119:11, 103, 127. Je √15:16. Jn 4:32, 34. 1 P √2:2. **necessary food**. or, appointed portion. √171E9, Ge +47:22. ver. 14. Jb 14:5, 13. Ezr 10:6. Lk *12:+42, 46.

13. **who can**. Jb 9:12, 13. 11:10. 12:14. 34:29. Nu 23:19, 20. Ec 1:15. 3:14. Ro 9:19. Ja 1:17. **and what**. Ps *115:3. 135:6. Pr 19:21. Is *14:24-27. 46:10. Da 4:35. Ro +9:18. Ep 1:9-11. **soul**. Heb. *nephesh,* Ge +34:3. Le +26:11.

14. **performeth**. Ps 57:2. **appointed**. Jb 7:3. Mi 6:9. 1 Th *3:3. 5:9. 1 P 2:8. **many such**. Ps 77:19. 97:2. Is 40:27, 28. Ro 11:33.

15. **am I troubled**. ver. 3. Jb 10:15. 31:23. Ps 77:3. 119:120. Hab *3:16. **presence**. √22A4, Ge +19:13.

16. **For God**. Ps *22:14. Is 6:5. 57:16. **Almighty**. Jb 27:2. Ru 1:20. Ps 88:16. Jl 1:15.

17. **cut off**. Jb 6:9. 2 K 22:20. Is 57:1. **the darkness from**. Jb 15:22. 18:6, 18. 19:8. 22:11.

JOB 24

Job inquires why the judgments of God on the wicked are not evident to his people, 1. He shows that the most atrocious offenders often go unpunished in this life and die as all other men, 2-24. He challenges any man to confute him, 25.

1. **Why**. Ge 26:27. **seeing**. Ps 31:15. Ec 3:17. 8:6, 7. 9:11, 12. Is 60:22. Da 2:21. Lk 21:22-24. Ac *1:7. *17:26. 1 Th 5:1. 1 T 4:1. 6:15. 2 P 2:3. 3:7, 8. **times**. Ge 24:11. Ps 31:15. 119:126. Ac +*1:6n, 7n. **hidden**. Jb 15:20. Je 16:17. **they that know**. Ps +√9:10. 36:10. 91:14. Jn *17:3. **not see**. Ge 7:4. 18:17, 20, 21. Ps 73:16-19. Je 12:1-3. Mt 24:38. Ro +*2:5. **his days**. √121P4, Dt +4:32. Jb +20:28. Pr 6:34. Is +*2:12. +*13:6, 9. Je 46:10. Jl 1:15. 2:1. Ob 15. Zp 1:7. Ac 2:20. 1 C +*3:13. 4:3.

2. **landmarks**. Dt *19:14. 27:17. Pr 22:28. 23:10. Ho *5:10. **violently**. Jb 1:15, 17. 5:5. **feed thereof**. *or,* feed them. or, do evil. ver. 9, 19. Jb 20:19. Ge 21:25.

3. **drive**. Jb 22:6-9. 31:16, 17. Dt 24:6, 10-13, 17-21. 1 S 12:3.

4. **turn**. ver. 14. Jb 31:16. Ps 109:16. Pr 22:16. 30:14. Is 10:2. Ezk 18:12, 18. 22:29. Am *2:7. 8:4-6. Mi 2:1, 2. **hide**. Pr 28:12, 28. Ja 5:4-6.

5. **wild asses**. Jb 39:5-7. Je 2:24. Ho 8:9. **rising**. ver. 14. Pr *4:16. Ho 7:6. Mi *2:1. Zp 3:3. Jn *18:28. Ac 23:12. **the wilderness**. Jb 5:5. 12:6. Ge 16:12. 27:40.

6. **They reap**. Dt 28:33, 51. Jg 6:3-6. Mi 6:15. **every**

one. √63A2, 2 S +6:6. By supplying the ellipsis of the accusative, taking the word rendered "his corn" as two words meaning "not their own," the verse will read "They reap (their corn) in a field not their own: they glean the vintage of the wicked" (EWB, B8, 9). **corn**. Heb. mingled corn, *or* dredge. **they gather**, etc. Heb. the wicked gather the vintage. Am 8:4-6.

7. **the naked**. √171N, Ge +8:13. ver. 10. Jb 22:6. 31:19, 20. Ex *22:26, 27. Dt 24:11-13. Is 58:7. Ac 9:39. **no covering**. Ge 31:40. Pr 31:21mg.

8. **are wet**. Jb 8:16. SS 5:2. **showers**. or, inundation. Is 4:6. 25:4. 28:2. 30:30. 32:2. Hab 3:10. **embrace**. Ge 29:13. 48:10. La 4:5. He 11:38. **shelter**. or, refuge. Ps 14:6. 46:1. 61:3. 62:7, 8. 71:7. 73:28. 91:2, 9. 94:22. 104:18. 142:5.

9. **They pluck**. 2 K 4:1. Ne 5:5.

10. **naked**. √171N, Ge +8:13. Ex 32:25n. 2 S 6:20n. Mt 25:43. Jn 21:7n. **without clothing**. Jb 22:6. Ex *22:26, 27. Dt 24:12, 13. Jn 21:7n. **they take away**. Dt 24:19. Am 2:7, 8. 5:11, 12.

11. **make oil**. Dt *25:4. Je +*22:13. Ja +*5:4.

12. **groan**. Ex 1:13, 14. 2:23, 24. 22:27. Jg 10:16. Ps +*12:5. Ec 4:1. Is *52:5. **soul**. Heb. *nephesh,* Ge +34:3. **wounded**. Ps 69:26. 109:22. **yet God**. Ps *50:21. Ec √8:11, 12. Ml 2:17. *3:15. Ro 2:4, 5. 2 P 3:15.

13. **rebel**. Lk √12:47, 48. Jn √3:19, 20. 9:39-41. 15:22-24. Ro 1:32. 2:17-24. Ja √4:17. **they know not**. Pr *4:19. Jn 12:35, 40. Ro 3:11-17. 2 Th √2:10-12. **nor abide**. Jb 23:11, 12. Jn 8:√31, 44. *15:6. 2 P √2:20-22. 1 J √2:19. Ju 6.

14. **murderer**. 2 S 11:14-17. Ps *10:8-10. Mi 2:1, 2. Ep 5:7-11. **in the night**. Lk 12:39. 1 Th 5:2. Re 3:3.

15. **eye**. Ex 20:14. 2 S 11:4-13. 12:12. Ps 50:18. Pr 6:32-35. 7:9, 10. **No eye**. Jb 22:13, 14. Ps 10:11. *73:11. *94:7. Ezk 8:12. 9:9. **disguiseth his face**. Heb. setteth his face in secret. Or, "putteth a covering on his face;" probably the hood of the burnoose, or cloak, which the Arabs sometimes throw over their other garments. Ge +27:16. 38:14, 15.

16. **In the dark**. Ex 22:2, 3. Ezk 12:5-7, 12. Mt 24:43. **they know not**. ver. 13. Jb 38:12, 13. Ps *119:105, 130. Is √8:20. Mk *12:24. Jn *3:19-21. *8:12. 2 C *4:3-6. Ep 5:11-13.

17. **in the terrors**. See on Jb 3:5. Ps 73:18, 19. Je *2:26. 2 C 5:10, 11. Re 6:16, 17.

18. **swift**. Ps 58:7. 73:18-20. Is 23:10. **their portion**. Dt 28:16-20. Ps 69:22. Pr 3:33. Ml 2:2.

19. **Drought**. Jb 6:15-17. 30:3. Ps 63:1. 78:17. **consume**. Heb. violently take. **snow waters**. Jb 9:30. **so doth**. Jb 21:23, 32-34. Ps 49:14. 58:8, 9. 68:2. Pr *14:32. Ec 9:4-6. Lk 12:20. 16:22.

20. **the worm**. Jb 17:14. 19:26. **he shall be**. Pr *10:7. Ec *8:10. Is *26:14. **wickedness**. Jb 14:7-10. 18:16, 17. Da 4:14. Mt *3:10.

21. **evil entreateth**. Ge 30:23. 1 S 1:6, 7. Is 4:1. Lk 1:25. or, devoureth. Jb 1:14. Mt 23:14. **the barren**. Ge +11:30. **doeth not**. ver. 3. Jb 29:13. 31:16-18. **widow**. Jb 22:9. Ex 22:22. Ps 10:14. Zc 7:10.

22. **draweth**. Est 3:8-10. Da 6:4-9. Jn 19:12-16. Re 16:13, 14. 17:2. **no man is sure of life**. *or,* he trusteth not his own life. Jb 29:24. Dt 28:66. Mt 6:27. Ja 4:14.

23. **it be given**. Ps 73:3-12. Je 12:1-3. **whereon**. Ec 8:11. Is 10:8-11. 56:12. Lk 12:16-20, 45. 1 Th 5:3. **yet his eyes**. Ps *10:13, 14. 11:4, 5. Pr 5:21. 15:3.

25:21-23. Ec 5:8. Je *16:17. *32:19. Am 8:7. 9:2. Hab 1:13. Re 2:1, 2, 23.

24. **are exalted**. Jb 20:5. Ps 37:10, 35, 36. 73:19. 92:7. Ja 1:11. 5:1-3. **gone**. Heb. not. Jb 8:22mg. 27:19. **brought low**. Ps 106:43. Ec 10:18. **taken out**. Heb. closed up. Jb 5:16. Dt 15:7. **cut off**. Jb 14:2. 18:16. Ge 17:11. Ps 37:2. **the ears of corn**. Is 17:5, 6. Re 14:14-20.

25. **who will make**. Jb 9:24. 11:2, 3. 15:2.

JOB 25

Bildad asserts the dominion and power of God, before whom man cannot be justified, 1-6.

1. **Bildad**. Jb +2:11.

2. **dominion**. Jb 9:2-10. 26:5-14. 40:9-14. 1 Ch 29:11, 12. 2 Ch 20:6. Ps *99:1-3. Je *10:6, 7. Da 4:34-37. Mt *6:13. *28:18. Ep *1:20, 21. Ju 25. Re 6:16. **he maketh**. Is 57:15, *19. Mt *5:9. 2 C 5:18-21. Ep 2:16, *17. Col *1:20.

3. **there**. Ps 103:20, 21. 148:2-4. Is *40:26. Je *31:35. Da *7:10. Mt *26:53. Re *5:11. **upon whom**. Jb 38:12, 13. Ge 1:3-5, 14-16. Ps *19:4-6. Mt √5:45. Jn 1:4, *9. Ja 1:17.

4. **How then**. Jb *4:17-19. *9:2. *15:14-16. Ps *130:3. *143:2. Ac 13:39. Ro *3:19, 20, 26. √5:1. T √3:5. **how can**. Jb *14:3, 4. Ps *51:5. Zc *13:1. 1 C *6:11. Ep *2:3. 1 J √1:9. Re *1:5. **born**. ♪142, Ge +20:16. Jb 14:1.

5. **even to**. Is 24:23. 60:19, 20. 2 C 3:10.

6. **How much less**, etc. The original is degradingly expressive: "How much less *enosh*, miserable man, who is a worm; and the son of Adam, who is *toleah*, a maggot." Jb 4:19. 17:14. Ge 18:27. Dt 28:39. Ps *22:6. Is 14:11. *41:14. Da 3:1n. **worm**. ♪111, Ge +18:27. **son of man**. Jb 35:8. **worm**. Ps 22:6.

JOB 26

Job derides Bildad's speech as little to the purpose, 1-4. He shows the works and perfections of God to be unsearchable, 5-14.

2. **How hast thou**. ♪60B, Ge +20:16. ♪91, 2 S +6:20. Bildad had produced no argument to refute Job's doctrine, and therefore Job ironically admires the assistance which Bildad had given to his friends in their extremity and the instruction he had afforded him in his perplexity. Jb 12:2. 1 K 18:27. **helped**. Jb 4:3, 4. 6:25. 16:4, 5. 2 Ch 32:8. Is 35:3, 4. 40:14. 41:5-7. **without**. Is 40:29. **no strength**. Is 41:1. Ro 5:6.

3. **counselled**. Jb 6:13. 12:3. 13:5. 15:8-10. 17:10. 32:11-13. **plentifully**. Jb 33:3, 33. 38:2. Ps 49:1-4. 71:15-18. Pr 8:6-9. Ac 20:20, 27.

4. **and whose**. Jb 20:3. 32:18. 1 K 22:23, 24. Ec 12:7. Lk 9:55. Jn 3:6. 1 C 12:3. 1 J 4:1-3. Re 16:13, 14. **spirit**. Heb. *neshamah*, breath. Jb 4:9. 27:3. 32:8. 33:4. Ge +2:7.

5. **Dead things**. Or, "The giants (*rephaim*) are in anguish under the waters and their inhabitants;" probably in allusion to the destruction of the earth by the deluge. Jb 41:1, etc. Ge 6:4. Ps 104:25, 26. Ezk 29:3-5. or, Rephaim. Ps 88:10. Pr 2:18. **formed**. ver. 13. Jb 15:7. 35:14. 39:1. **waters**. ver. 8, 10. 3:24. 5:10. 8:11. **and**. *or*, **with**. **inhabitants**. Jb 4:19. Ge 14:13.

6. **Hell**. Heb. *sheol*, Jb 7:9. 11:8. 14:13. 17:13. 31:12. Ge +37:35. Dt +32:22. Ps *9:17. 139:8, 11. Pr 15:11.

Is 14:9. Am 9:2. He *4:13. **naked**. Jb 1:21. 22:6. 24:7, +10. **destruction**. Heb. *abaddon*, ✱S#11h: Jb 26:6. 28:22. 31:12. Ps 88:11. Pr *15:11. *27:20. **no covering**. Jb 24:7. 31:19. Ge 20:16. Is +66:24.

7. **stretcheth**. Jb 9:8. Ge 1:1, 2. 1 Ch 21:10. Ps 24:2. 104:2-5. Pr 8:23-27. Is *40:22, 26. 42:5. **the north**. Jb 37:22. Ge 13:14. 28:14. Ps 89:12. **hangeth**. Ge 40:19, 22. 41:13. **nothing**. Jb 38:6. Ps 104:5. Pr 3:19, 20. 8:27. Is 40:22. ✱S#1099h, only here.

8. **bindeth up**. Jb 36:29. 38:9, 37. Ge 1:6, 7. Ps *135:7. Pr 30:4. Je *10:13. **thick clouds**. Jb 37:11-16. Ge +9:13. Ps 18:10, 11. **and the cloud**. Is 5:6.

9. **holdeth back**. Ex 20:21. *33:20-23. 34:3. 1 K 8:12. Ps *97:2. Hab 3:3-5. 1 T 6:16.

10. **compassed**. Jb 38:8-11. Ps 33:7. 104:6-9. Pr *8:29. Je 5:22. **bounds**. Ge 1:9. Ps 104:9. **until**. Ge 8:22. Is +*54:9, 10. **day and night come to an end**. Heb. end of light with darkness.

11. **pillars**. ♪121Q3, 2 S +22:8. 1 S 2:8. Ps 18:7. Hg 2:21. He 12:26, 27. 2 P 3:10. Re *20:11. **are astonished**. Jb 15:15.

12. **divideth**. Ex *14:21, etc. Ps 29:10. *74:13. 93:3, 4. 114:2-7. Is 51:15. Je 31:35. **he smiteth**. Jb 40:11, 12. Is *2:12. Da *4:37. Ja *4:6. **the proud**. Heb. pride. Ps 89:9, 10. Is 51:9.

13. **his spirit**. Heb. *ruach*, Ge *1:2. Ps *33:6, 7. 51:11. 104:30. 139:7. Is 11:1, 2. +48:16. 57:15. Jn 1:3. **hand**. Ps 102:24, 25. Is 64:8. **formed**. Ge 1:24, 25. **the crooked serpent**. Ge 3:1. Ps 74:13, 14. Is *27:1. 51:9. Re 12:9.

14. **how little**. Jb 11:7-9. Ps 139:6. *145:3. Is 40:26-29. Ro *11:33. 1 C *13:9-12. **the thunder**. Jb 40:9. 1 S 2:10. Ps 29:3.

JOB 27

Job solemnly attests his integrity and resolves to vindicate it as long as he lives, 1-6. He declares the character and doom of the hypocrite, 7-10. He shows that the prosperity of the wicked is soon changed into hopeless misery, 11-23.

1. **Job**. Nu 23:7. 24:3, 15. Ps 49:4. 78:2. Pr 26:7. **continued**. Heb. added to take up. Jb 29:1. Nu 23:7. **parable**. Jb 13:12. 29:1. Nu +23:7n.

2. **God liveth**. Nu 14:21. Ru 3:13. 1 S 14:39, 45. 20:21. 25:26, 34. 2 S 2:27. 1 K 17:1. 18:15. Je *4:2. 5:2. *12:16. Ezk 33:11. **taken**. Jb 10:3. 34:5. Is 40:27. **vexed my soul**. Heb. made my soul bitter. Jg +18:25mg. Ru 1:20, 21. 1 S 30:6. 2 K 4:27. **soul**. Heb. *nephesh*, Ge +34:3.

3. **breath**. Heb. *neshamah*, Ge +*2:7. Jb +14:22. 32:8. 33:4. Ps +146:4. Ec 3:21. 12:7. **the spirit of God**. that is, *the breath which God gave him*. Heb. *ruach*, Nu +16:22. Ge +*2:7n. Is 2:22. Ac 17:25.

4. **My lips**. Jb 13:7. 34:6. Jn 8:55. 2 C 11:10.

5. **justify**. Jb 32:3. 42:7. Dt 25:1. Pr *17:15. Ga 2:11. **die**. Ge +49:33 (✱S#1478h). **I will not**. Jb 2:9. 13:15. 29:14. 2 C 1:12.

6. **righteousness**. Mt 5:20. Ph 3:9. **I hold fast**. Jb 2:3. Ps 18:20-23. Pr 4:13. **my heart**. Ac *24:16. 2 C 12:11. 1 J *3:20, 21. **so long as I live**. Heb. from my days.

7. **mine enemy**. 1 S 25:26. 2 S 18:32. Da 4:19.

8. **what is**. Jb 11:20. 13:16. 15:34. 20:5. 22:21-27. 31:3. Is 33:14, 15. Mt 16:26. *23:14. Mk 8:36, 37. Lk 9:25. *12:20, 21. 1 T 6:9, 10. Ja 5:1-3. **when**. T#572.

1 Ch +*28:9 (T#555). Pr 1:24-32. Is +27:11 (T#559). Mt +25:46 (T#567). Lk +9:24 (T#554). 13:25. *16:24-25, +26 (T#390). 2 C +6:2 (T#553). **soul.** Heb. *nephesh,* Ge +12:13.

9. **Will God.** Jb 35:12, 13. Ps 18:41. *66:18. 109:7. Pr 1:28. *28:9. Is *1:15. Je *11:11. *14:12. Ezk *8:18. Mi 3:4. Zc *7:13. Jn +*9:31. Ja *4:3. 1 J ◐5:14. **his cry.** Ho 7:14. Lk 13:25.

10. **delight.** Jb 22:26, 27. Ps *37:4. 43:4. Hab 3:18. **will he always call upon.** T#547. Ps +14:1 (T#22). *78:34-36. Je +*10:25 (T#548). Mt √13:21. Lk *18:1. Ac 10:2. Ep *6:18. 1 Th *5:17.

11. **teach.** Jb 4:3, 4. 6:10. Is 8:11. **by the hand.** *or, being* in the hand. Ps 25:8, 12. 32:8. Pr 4:11. **that which.** Jb 32:8-10. Dt 4:5. Ps *71:17, 18. Ac *20:20, 27. **not conceal.** Jb 6:10. 15:18.

12. **ye yourselves.** Jb 21:28-30. Ec 8:14. 9:1-3. **altogether.** Jb 6:25-29. 13:4-9. 16:3. 17:2. 19:2, 3. 21:3. 26:2-4.

13. **the portion.** Jb 20:29. 31:3. Ps 11:6. Ec 8:13. Is *3:11. 2 P 2:9. **the heritage of oppressors.** T#490. Jb 15:20, etc. 20:19, etc. Ex 3:7, 9. Ps +*12:5. *72:4. Pr 14:31. 22:22, 23. Ec 5:8. Is 61:8. Je 5:27-29. Ezk 18:10, 12, 13. 22:12-14, 29, 31. Ml +*3:5. Ja 2:13. +√5:4-6.

14. **children.** Jb 21:11, 12. Dt *28:32, 41. 2 K 9:7, 8. *10:6-10. Est 5:11. 9:5-10. Ps 109:13. Ho 9:13, 14. Lk 23:29. **his offspring.** 1 S 2:5.

15. **Those.** 1 K 14:10, 11. 16:3, 4. 21:21-24. **his widows.** Ps *78:64. Je *22:18.

16. **heap up.** Jb 22:24, 25. 1 K 10:27. Hab 2:6. Zc 9:3. **as the dust.** ∫102B, ∫138B, Ge +13:16. **prepare raiment.** D'Herbelot (p. 208) tells us, that Bokhten, an illustrious poet of Cufah, in the 9th century, had so many presents made him, that at his death he was found possessed of 100 suits of clothes, 200 shirts, and 500 turbans. Mt 6:19. Ja 5:2.

17. **but the just.** Pr *13:22. 28:8. Ec 2:26.

18. **as a moth.** Jb 8:14, 15. Is 51:8. **as a booth.** Is 1:8. 38:12. La 2:6.

19. **shall lie.** Jb 14:13-15. 21:23-26, 30. 30:23. **gathered.** Ge *49:10. Je *8:2. Mt 3:12. 23:37. **he openeth.** Jb 20:7-9. Ps 58:9. 73:19, 20. **he is not.** Jb 8:22. 14:10, 12. 24:24mg.

20. **Terrors.** Jb 15:21. 18:11. 22:16. Ps 18:4. 42:7. 69:14, 15. Jon 2:3. **a tempest.** Jb 20:23. 21:18. Ex 12:29. 2 K *19:35. Da 5:30.

21. **east wind.** Je *18:17. Ho 13:15. **a storm.** Ex 9:23-25. Ps 11:6. 58:9. 83:15. Na 1:3-8. Mt *7:26, 27.

22. **For God.** Ex 9:14. Dt 32:23. Jsh 10:11. **not spare.** Dt 29:20. Ezk 9:5, 6. Ro 8:32. 2 P 2:4, 5. **he would fain flee.** Heb. in fleeing he would flee. Jb 20:24. Ex 14:25-28. Jg 4:17-21. Is 10:3. Am 2:14. 9:1-3.

23. **clap.** Est 9:22-25. Pr 11:10. La 2:15. Na 3:19. Re 18:20. **hiss him.** 1 K 9:8. Je 19:8. Mi 6:16. Zp 2:15.

JOB 28

Job shows that man is industrious and ingenious in searching out the treasures hidden in the earth, 1-11. But the more valuable treasure of the knowledge of God lies beyond his reach, 12-22. God alone comprehends it; and man's wisdom is to fear God and to depart from evil, 23-28.

1. **vein.** *or,* mine. Jb 38:27. Nu 30:12. 1 K 10:28. **the silver.** Ge 2:11, 12. 23:15. 24:22. 1 K 7:48-50. 10:21. 1 Ch 29:2-5. **where they fine it.** Ps 12:6. Pr *17:3. 27:21. Is 48:10. Zc 13:9. Ml 3:2, 3. 1 P 1:7.

2. **Iron.** Ge 4:22. Nu 31:22. Dt *8:9. 1 Ch 22:14. **earth.** *or,* dust. ver. 6. Jb 2:12. 4:19. 5:6. 7:5, 21. 27:16.

3. **searcheth.** Pr 2:4. Ec 1:13. Hab 2:13. Mt *6:33. Lk 16:8. **the stones.** Jb 10:21, 22. 12:22. 38:16, 17.

4. **flood.** or, stream *or* valley. That is, *a mine.* **sojourner.** Jb 19:15. Ex 3:22. +12:49. **forgotten of the foot.** That is, *unvisited.* **dried up.** or, low. Ps 79:8. 116:6. 142:6. **gone away.** or, wandered, or moved. Ex 20:18.

5. **out of it.** Ge 1:11, 12, 29. Ps 104:14, 15. Is 28:25-29. **fire.** Ezk 28:13, 14.

6. **sapphires.** ver. 16. Ex *24:10. SS 5:14. Is *54:11. Re *21:19. **dust of gold.** *or,* gold ore.

7. **a path.** ver. 21-23. Jb 11:6. 38:19, 24. Ro 11:33. **the vulture's eye.** *Ayah,* rendered the *kite* in Le 11:14 and *vulture* in Dt 14:13, is supposed by Bochart (vol. iii. p. 192) to be the bird called by the Arabians *juju,* from its note, and which the ancients named *aesalon,* i.e. *the merlin,* a bird celebrated for its sharp-sightedness.

8. **trodden.** Jg 20:43. Ps 25:5, 9. **lion's whelps.** or, sons of pride. Jb 41:34. **fierce lion.** Jb 4:10. 10:16. Ps 91:13.

9. **rock.** *or,* flint. Dt 8:15. *32:13. Ps *114:8. Is *50:7. **he overturneth.** Na 1:4-6.

10. **cutteth.** Jb 26:8. Ge 22:3. **rivers.** or, brooks. Ge 41:1, 2, 3, 17, 18. **every precious thing.** Pr 14:23. 24:4. Is 43:4. Hab 3:9.

11. **bindeth.** Jb 26:8. Is 37:25. *43:2. 44:27. **overflowing.** Heb. weeping. Jb 16:16. Ge 45:2mg. 2 S 13:36mg. **and the thing.** Is 45:2, 3. 1 C *4:5.

12. **where shall wisdom.** ver. 20, 28. 1 K 3:9. Ps *51:6. Pr 2:4-6. 18:1. Ec 7:23-25. 1 C 1:19, 20, *30. Col *2:3. Ja *1:5, 17.

13. **knoweth.** ver. 15-19. Ps 19:10. 119:72. Pr 3:14, 15. 8:11, 18, 19. 16:16. 23:23. Ec 8:16, 17. **in the land.** ver. 21, 22. Ps 52:5. Is 38:11. 53:8.

14. **depth.** Jb 38:16, 30. Ge 1:2. 7:11. Ro 11:33, 34. **the sea.** Jb 6:3. 7:12. 9:8. 11:9. 12:8.

15. **It cannot be gotten for gold.** Heb. Fine gold shall not be given for it. ver. 18. Pr 3:13-15. 8:10, 17, 19. 16:16. 23:23. Ac 8:18.

16. **the gold.** 1 Ch 29:4. Ps 45:9. Is 13:12. **Ophir.** Jb 22:24. Ge 10:29. 1 K +9:28n. 2 Ch +8:18n. **onyx.** Ex 28:20. Ezk 28:13.

17. **crystal.** Ezk 1:22. Re 4:6. 21:11. 22:1. **jewels.** or, vessels. 2 Ch 9:20, 24. Est 1:7. Is 39:2mg.

18. **coral.** *or,* Ramoth. Ezk 27:16. **pearls.** Mt 7:6. 13:45, 46. 1 T 2:9. Re 17:4. 18:12. 21:21. **for.** ∫138C, Ge +22:14. **price of wisdom.** Pr *4:7. *17:16. 18:1. **rubies.** Pr *3:13-15. 8:11. 31:10. La 4:7.

19. **topaz.** Ex 28:17. 39:10. Ezk 28:13. Re 21:20.

20. **Whence then.** See on ver. 12. Pr *2:6. Ec 7:23, 24. Is 53:8. 1 C 2:6-15. Ja *1:5, 17.

21. **hid.** Ps 49:3, 4. Mt 11:25. 13:17, 35. 1 C *2:7-10. Col *2:3. **from the fowls.** ver. 7. **air.** *or,* heaven. Jb 2:12. 12:7. Ge 1:1, 26, 28.

22. **Destruction.** Heb. *abaddon,* Jb +26:6. ver. 14. Jb 31:12. Ps 83:10-12. **death.** Jb 3:21. 5:20. 7:15. 18:13. **say.** ∫155D, Ge +4:10. **heard.** ∫155D, Ge +4:10.

23. **God understandeth.** Ps *19:7. *147:5. Pr 2:6. 8:14. Mt 11:27. Lk *10:21, 22. Ac 15:18. Ro 11:33.

1 C *1:30. Ju 25. **knoweth the place.** Pr 15:3.

24. **he looketh.** 2 Ch 16:9. Pr 15:3. Zc 4:10. Re 5:6.

25. **To make the weight,** etc. God has given an atmosphere to the earth which, possessing a certain degree of gravity perfectly suited to the necessities of all animals, vegetables, and fluids, should be the cause, in his hands, of preserving animal and vegetable life; for by it the blood circulates in the veins of animals and the juices in the tubes of vegetables. Without this atmospheric pressure there could be no respiration; and the elasticity of the particles of air in animal and vegetable bodies would rupture the vessels in which they are contained and destroy both kinds of life. Ps 135:7. Is *40:12. **he weigheth.** He has exactly proportioned the aqueous surface of the earth to the terrene parts, for the purpose of evaporation. Is 40:15.

26. **he made.** Jb 36:26, 32. 38:25. Ps 148:8. Je 14:22. Am 4:7. Zc 10:1. **a way.** Jb 37:3-5. Ps 29:3-10.

27. **declare it.** or, number it. Jb 12:8. 15:17. *38:37. **he prepared it.** Ps 19:1. Pr 8:22-29.

28. **unto man.** Dt *29:29. Pr *8:4, 5, 32-36. **said.** ſ138C, Ge +22:14. **fear.** T#291. Dt *4:6. Ps *25:12-14. *31:19, 20. *33:18, 19. *34:7-9. *103:11-13. *111:5, 10. *145:19. 147:11. Pr *1:7. 8:13. *9:10. 14:26, 27. Ec 8:12. *12:13. Ml *3:16, 17. 4:2. Lk 1:50. Ja *3:13-17. **to depart.** Ps *34:14. Pr *3:7. 5:7. *13:14. *16:6, 17. Is *1:16. 2 T *2:19. 1 P *3:11.

JOB 29

Job regrets the loss of his comforts and of the respect which had been shown him, 1-11. He declares the good use which he had made of his authority, 12-17; and the grounds on which he had hoped for abiding prosperity, 18-25.

1. **continued.** Heb. added to take up. Jb 27:1mg. **parable.** Jb 13:12. 27:1. Nu +23:7n.

2. **as in months.** Jb 1:1-5. 7:3. **past.** Heb. *kedem,* Mi +5:2. **God.** Jb 1:10. Ps 37:28. Ju 1.

3. **candle.** or, lamp. Jb 18:6. 21:17. Ps +*18:28mg. Pr 13:9. 20:20. 24:20. **by his light.** Jb 22:28. Ps 4:6. 23:4. *27:1. *84:11. Is 2:4. Jn *8:12. 12:46. Ep 5:*8, 14.

4. **the secret.** Jb 1:10. 15:8. Ps *25:14. 27:5. 91:1. Pr *3:32. Col 3:3.

5. **the Almighty.** Jb 23:3, 8-10. Dt 33:27-29. Jsh 1:9. Jg 6:12, 13. Ps 30:7. 43:2. 44:8, 9. SS 2:4. 3:1, 2. Je 14:8. Mt 9:15. **my children.** Jb 1:2-5. 42:13-16. Ps 127:3-5. 128:3. Pr 17:6.

6. **I washed.** Jb 9:30. 20:17. Ge 49:11. Dt 32:13. *33:24n. **rock.** Ps 81:16. Ac 2:33. **poured.** ſ102, Jb 28:2. Ge +2:24. **me out.** Heb. with me. **rivers.** Ps 1:3. 46:4. 65:9. 119:136. **oil.** Ge 28:18. 35:14. Ex 25:6. Dt +*33:24n.

7. **to the gate.** ſ171S7B, Ge +14:7. Dt 16:18. 21:19. Ru 4:1, 2, 11. Zc 8:16.

8. **young men.** Le 19:32. Pr 16:31. 20:8. Ro 13:3, 4. T 3:1. 1 P 5:5. **the aged.** Ro 13:7. 1 P 2:17.

9. **refrained.** Jb 4:2. 7:11. Pr 10:19. Ja 1:19. **laid.** ſ121S3N, Jb 21:5. 40:4. Jg 18:19. Pr 30:32.

10. **nobles held their peace.** Heb. voice of the nobles was hid. **their tongue.** Ps 137:6. Ezk 3:26.

11. **the ear.** Jb 31:20. Pr *29:2. Lk *4:22. 11:27. **blessed.** ſ155A, Ge +31:35. **gave witness.** ſ155A, Ge +31:35.

12. **I delivered.** Jb 22:5-9. Ne 5:2-13. Ps 72:12. 82:2-4. Pr 21:13. 24:11, 12. Je 22:16. **the fatherless.** Ex 22:22-24. Dt 10:18. Ps 68:5. Ja 1:27.

13. **The blessing.** Dt 24:13. Ac 9:39-41. 2 C 9:12-14. 2 T 1:16-18. **ready.** Jb 31:19. Dt 26:5. Pr 31:6-9. Is 27:13. **I caused.** Dt 16:11. Ne 8:10-12. Phm 7. **the widow's.** Ja 1:27. **sing.** Ps 67:4. Is 65:14.

14. **I put.** Dt 24:13. Ps 132:9. Is 59:17. 61:10. Ro *13:14. 2 C 6:7. Ep 6:14. 1 Th 5:8. Re 19:8. **a diadem.** Is 28:5. 62:3.

15. **eyes.** Nu *10:31. Mt *11:5. 1 C 12:12, etc.

16. **a father.** Jb 31:18. Est *2:7. Ps *68:5. Ep *5:1. Ja *1:27. **the cause.** Ex 18:26. Dt *13:14. 17:8-10. 1 K *3:16-28. Pr 25:2. *29:7.

17. **I brake.** Ps 3:7. 58:8. Pr *30:14. **jaws.** Heb. jaw teeth, *or,* grinders. Pr 30:14. Jl 1:6. **and plucked.** Heb. and cast. 1 S 17:35. Ps 124:3, *6.

18. **I shall die.** Ge +49:33 (*S#1478h). Jb 3:11. 10:18. 13:19. 14:10. Ps 30:6, 7. Je 22:23. 49:16. Ob 4. Hab 2:9. **multiply.** Jb 5:26. 42:16, 17. Ps 91:16. **as the sand.** ſ102B, ſ138B, Jb 6:3. Ge +13:16. 22:17. 32:12. 41:49.

19. **root.** Jb 18:16. Ps *1:3. Je *17:8. Ho 14:5-7. **spread out.** Heb. opened. Nu 19:15. Jsh 8:17. 1 K 8:29. **dew.** Jb 38:28. Ge 27:28, 39. **branch.** Jb 5:5. 14:9.

20. **glory.** ver. 14. Jb 19:9. Ge 45:13. Ps 3:3. **fresh.** Heb. new. Is 43:19. **my bow.** Ge 49:24. **renewed.** Heb. changed. Ps 103:5. Is 40:31. 2 C 4:16.

21. **gave ear.** ver. 9, 10. Jb 32:11, 12.

22. **After my.** Jb 32:15, 16. 33:31-33. Is 52:15. Mt *22:46. **speech.** Dt 32:2. SS 4:11. Ezk 20:46. Am 7:16. Mi 2:6mg.

23. **as for the rain.** Ps 72:6. **the latter rain.** Dt +11:14. Ho 6:3. Zc 10:1.

24. **they believed.** Ge 45:26. Ps 126:1. Lk 24:41. **the light.** Ps *4:6. *89:15.

25. **chose out.** Ge 41:40. Jg 11:8. 2 S 5:2. 1 Ch 13:1-4. **dwelt.** Ge 14:14-17. Dt 33:5. **one that.** Jb 4:3, 4. Is 35:3, 4. *61:1-3. 2 C *1:3, 4. 7:5-7. 1 Th 3:2, 3.

JOB 30

Job complains that he is sunk into extreme contempt, 1-14; that he suffers great anguish of soul and body, 15-19; that God deals rigorously with him, 20-24; that he, who had comforted others, now suffers without a comforter, 25-31.

1. **they that are.** Jb 19:13-19. 29:8-10. 2 K +*2:23. Is *3:5. **younger than I.** Heb. of fewer days than I. Jb 32:6mg. **whose.** Ps 35:15, 16. 69:12. Mk 14:65. 15:17-20. Lk 23:14, 18, 35, 36, 39. Ac 17:5. T 1:12.

2. **strength of.** Is 10:13. **old age.** Jb 5:26.

3. **solitary.** or, dark as the night. Jb 24:13-16. Is 49:21. **fleeing into.** Jb 24:5. He 11:38. **in former time.** Heb. yesternight. Ge 19:34.

4. **mallows.** The Hebrew *malluach,* in Arabic, *malluch,* and in Syriac, *mallucho,* is probably the *alima* or *alimos* of the Greeks and the *halimus* of the Romans which Dioscorides describes as a kind of bramble without thorns, the leaves of which are boiled and eaten. **juniper roots.** The Hebrew *rothem,* in Arabic, *ratim,* and in Spanish, *ratama,* most probably signifies the *genista* or *broom,* which is very abundant in the deserts of Arabia. 1 K 19:4, 5. Ps 120:4. **for their meat.** 2 K 4:38, 39. Am 7:14. Lk *15:16.

5. **driven.** Ge 4:12-14. Ps 109:10. Da 4:25, 32, 33.
6. **dwell.** Jg *6:2. 1 S 22:1, 2. Is 2:19. Re 6:15. **caves.** Heb. holes. 1 S 14:11. 2 K 12:9. **the rocks.** Je 4:29.
7. **brayed.** Jb 6:5. 11:12. Ge 16:12. **the nettles.** *Charul* probably denotes some kind of briar or bramble; Vulgate renders it by *spina* or *sentis* (Pr 24:31; Zp 2:9). Celsius and Scheuchzer are inclined to think it the *paliurus*, a shrub growing sometimes to a considerable height in desert places. "One of the inconveniences of the vegetable thickets of Egypt is," says Denon, "that it is difficult to remain in them, as ninetenths of the trees and plants are armed with inexorable thorns, which suffer an unquiet enjoyment of the shadow which is so constantly desirable."
8. **children.** 2 K 8:18, 27. 2 Ch 22:3. Ps *49:10-13. Je 7:18. Mk 6:24. **fools.** Pr 1:7, 22. 16:22. **base men.** Heb. men of no name. Jb 18:17. 1 Ch 11:27n. **viler.** Jb 40:4. Ps 15:4. Is 32:6.
9. **am I.** Jb 17:6. Ps 35:15, 16. 44:14. 69:12. La *3:14, 63.
10. **abhor me.** Jb 19:19. 42:6. Ps 88:8. Zc 11:8. **flee far.** Jb 19:13, 14. Ps 88:8. Pr 19:7. Mt 26:56. **spare not to spit in my face.** Heb. withhold not spittle from my face. Nu 12:14. Dt 25:9. Is *50:6. Mt *26:67. *27:30.
11. **loosed.** Jb 12:18, 21. 2 S *16:5-8. **let loose.** Ps 35:21. Mt 26:67, 68. 27:39-44. Ja 1:26.
12. **rise.** Jb 19:18. Is 3:5. **they raise up.** Jb 19:12.
13. **they set forward.** Ps *69:26. Zc *1:15.
14. **as a wide.** Jb 22:16. Ps *18:4. 69:14, 15. Is 8:7, 8.
15. **Terrors.** Jb 6:4. 7:14. 9:27, 28. 10:16. Ps 88:15. **soul.** Heb. principal one. Ps 51:12. **as a cloud.** Is 44:22. Ho 6:4. 13:3.
16. **my soul.** Heb. *nephesh,* Ge +34:3. Ps *22:14. 42:4. Is *53:12. **have taken hold.** Ps 40:12.
17. **My bones.** Jb 33:19-21. Ps 6:2-6. 38:2-8. **in the night season.** Jb 7:4. Ps 22:2. Is 38:13.
18. **By the great.** Jb 2:7. 7:5. 19:20. Ps 38:5. Is 1:5, 6.
19. **cast me.** Jb 9:31. Ps 40:2. *69:1, 2. Je 38:6. **become like.** Nu 21:27. **dust.** Jb 2:8. 42:6. Ge 18:27.
20. **I cry.** Jb 19:7. 27:9. Ps 22:2. *80:4, 5. La *3:8, 44. Mt 15:23. **dost not hear.** Jb +*35:12.
21. **become cruel.** Heb. turned to be cruel. Jb 7:20, 21. 10:14-17. 13:25-28. 16:9-14. 19:6-9. Ps 77:7-9. Le *30:14. **thy strong hand.** Heb. the strength of thy hand. Jb 6:9. 23:6. Ps 89:13. 1 P 5:6. **against me.** Ru +√1:13.
22. **liftest me.** Jb 21:18. Ps 1:4. Is 17:13. Je 4:11, 12. Ezk 5:2. Ho 4:19. 13:3. **to ride.** Ps 18:10. 104:3. **substance.** or, wisdom. Jb 6:13. 12:16. Pr 2:7.
23. **the house.** Jb *14:5. 21:33. Ge 3:19. 1 S 13:11. 2 S *14:14. Ec *8:8. 9:5. 12:5-7. He +√9:27. **appointed.** Ge +17:21h.
24. **grave.** Heb. heap. *S#1164h, only here. Ps 79:1. Je 26:18. Mi 1:6. 3:12. **they cry.** Jg 5:31. Ps 35:25. Mt 27:39-44.
25. **Did not I.** Ps 35:13, 14. Je 13:17. 18:20. Lk 19:41. Jn 11:35. Ro *12:15. **in trouble.** Heb. hard of day. Ge 42:7mg, 30. Ex 1:14. 6:9. **was.** Jb 31:16-21. Ps 12:1. Pr 14:21, 31. 17:5. 19:17. 28:8. Is 58:7, 8. Da 4:27. 2 C 9:9. **soul.** Heb. *nephesh,* Ge +34:3.
26. **When I looked.** Jb 3:25, 26. 29:18. Je *8:15. 14:19. 15:18. Mi 1:12. **light.** Jb 18:6, 18. 23:17. Ps 97:11. Is 50:10.

27. **My bowels.** Ps 22:4. Je 4:19. 31:20. La 1:20. 2:11.
28. **I went.** Ps 38:6. 42:9. 43:2. Is 53:3, 4. La 3:1-3.
29. **a brother.** Jb 17:14. Ps 102:6. Is 13:21, 22. 38:14. Mi 1:8. Ml 1:3. **owls.** *or,* ostriches. *Benoth yaanah,* in Arabic, *bintu naamatin,* not "owls," but "ostriches," so called from their doleful and hideous noises. "I have often," says Dr. Shaw, "heard them groan as if they were in the greatest agonies." *S#3284h; Le 11:16. Dt 14:15. Is 13:21. 34:13. 43:20. Je 50:39. Mi 1:8. See also *S#3283h, La 4:3.
30. **my skin.** Ps 119:83. La 3:4. 4:8. 5:10. **black.** Le 13:31., 37. SS 1:5. **my bones.** Ps 102:3.
31. **My harp.** Jb 21:12. Ge 4:21. 31:27. 1 Ch +13:8n. **mourning.** Ge 27:41. 50:10, 11. Ps 137:1-4. Ec 3:4. Is 21:4. 22:12. 24:7-9. La 5:15. Da 6:18. **organ.** Jb 21:12. Ge 4:21. Ps 150:4. **weep.** Ex 2:6.

JOB 31

Job solemnly before God protests that he was not guilty of unchastity or dishonesty, 1-12; of unkindness to his servants or to the poor, 13-22; of trusting in riches; of idolatry, revenge, neglect of hospitality, hypocrisy, or fear of man, 23-34. He appeals to God and challenges his accusers to prove their allegations, 35-40.

1. **a covenant.** Ge *6:2. 2 S *11:2-4. Ps +*101:3. *119:37. Pr *4:25. 23:31-33. Mt *5:28, 29. 2 P *2:14. 1 J *2:16. **think.** Pr *6:25. Ja *1:14, 15.
2. **what portion.** Jb 20:29. 27:13. He 13:4.
3. **destruction.** Jb 21:30. Ps *1:6. 37:20. 55:23. 73:18. 145:20. Pr 1:27. *10:29. 21:15. Mt ++*7:13. Ro 9:22. 1 Th *5:3. 2 Th √1:9. 2 P *2:1. **a strange.** Is 28:21. Ju 7.
4. **Doth not he see.** Jb *14:16. *34:21. Ge 16:13. 2 Ch *16:9. Ps *44:21. *139:1-3. Pr *5:21. *15:3. Je *16:17. *32:19. Jn *1:48. He *4:13. **count.** Mt 6:8, 26. *10:29-31.
5. **If.** Ps 7:3-5. **walked.** Ps 4:2. 12:2. 44:20, 21. Pr 12:11. Je 2:5. Ezk 13:8.
6. **Let me be weighed in an even balance.** Heb. Let him weigh me in balances of justice. 1 S *2:3. Ps 7:8, 9. 17:2, 3. 26:1. Pr 16:11. Is *26:7. Da *5:27. Mi 6:11. **know.** Jsh 22:22. Ps *1:6. 139:23. Mt 7:23. 2 T *2:19.
7. **If my.** Ps 44:20, 21. **mine heart.** Nu *15:39. Ec *11:9. Ezk 6:9. 14:3, 7. Mt 5:29. 1 J √2:16. **walked.** ♪155A, Ge +31:35. **cleaved.** Ps 101:3. Is 33:15.
8. **let me.** Jb 5:5. 24:6. Le 26:16. Dt 28:30-33, 38, 51. Jg 6:3-6. Mi 6:15. **let my.** Jb 5:4. 15:30. 18:19. Ps 109:13.
9. **If mine.** Jg 16:5. 1 K 11:4. Ne 13:26. Pr 2:16-19. 5:3, etc. 6:25. 7:21. 22:14. Ec *7:26. **if I.** Jb 24:15, 16. Je 5:8. Ho 7:4.
10. **grind.** Ex 11:5. Dt 28:30. Is 47:2. Mt 24:41. **and let.** 2 S 12:11. Je 8:10. Ho 4:13, 14.
11. **For this.** Le 20:10. 1 C 7:9. Col 3:5, 6. He 13:4. Re 22:15. **an heinous.** Ge 20:9. 26:10. *39:9. Ex 20:14. Pr 6:29-33. **an iniquity.** ver. 28. Ge 38:24. Le *20:10. Dt 22:22-24. Ezk *16:38.
12. **a fire.** Pr 3:33. *6:27-29, 32. Je 5:7-9. Ml +*3:5. He 13:4. **destruction.** Heb. *abaddon,* Jb +26:6. 28:22. Ps 88:1.
13. **the cause.** T#676. Ge 14:14. 17:12. 24:2-4, 10.

Ex 21:20, 21, 26, 27. Le *25:43, 46. Dt 15:12-15. Je 34:14-17. Ep 6:9. Col *4:1. **when**. In ancient times slaves had no action at law against their owners, but Job permitted them to all civil rights and permitted them to complain even against himself. 1 S ⦿+*25:17. 2 K 5:13, 16.

14. **What then**. Jb 9:32. 10:2. Ps 7:6. 9:12, 19. 10:12-15. 44:21. 76:9. 143:2. Is 10:3. Zc 2:13. **when he**. Ho 9:7. Mi 7:4. Mt 7:2. Ja *2:13. **what shall**. Ro 3:19.

15. **Did not he**. Jb 34:19. Ne 5:5. Pr *14:31. *22:2. Is 58:7. Ml 2:10. **did not one fashion us in the womb?** or, did not he fashion us in one womb? Jb 10:8-12. Ge 3:20. Ps 139:14-16. Ml 2:10. Ac 17:26.

16. **withheld**. Jb 22:7-9. Dt 15:7-10. Ps 112:9. Lk 16:21. Ac 11:29. Ga *2:10. **the eyes**. Dt 28:32. Ps 69:3. 119:82, 123. Is 38:14. La 4:17.

17. **eaten my morsel**. Dt 15:11, 14. Ne 8:10. Is *58:6, 7. Ezk +*18:7. Lk *11:41. *14:13, 14. Jn 13:29. Ac 4:32. **the fatherless**. Jb 29:13-16. Ge +11:28. Dt +10:18. Ezk 18:7, 16. Ro *12:13. Ja *1:27. 2:15, 16. 1 J *3:17.

18. **youth**. Jb 13:26. Ge 8:21. **guided**. Jb 12:23mg. 38:32. Ge 24:48. **her**. that is, *the widow*. ver. 16.

19. **perish**. Jb 22:6. 2 Ch 28:15. Is +*58:7. Ezk +*18:7. Mt 25:36, 43. Lk 3:11. Ac 9:39. Ja 2:16. 1 J 3:18.

20. **his loins**. Jb 29:11. 38:3. 40:7. Ge 35:11. Dt 24:13.

21. **lifted**. 2 K 5:11mg. **against**. Jb 6:27. *22:9. 24:9. *29:12. Pr *23:10, 11. Je *5:28. Ezk 22:7. **when**. Mi 2:1, 2. 7:3. **help**. ʃ121N1, Ge +31:54. "Help" is put, by Metonymy of the Adjunct, for those who helped or would be on his side in the gate. **gate**. ʃ171S7B, Ge +14:7.

22. **let**. ver. 10, 40. Jsh 22:22, 23. Ps 7:4, 5. 137:5. **arm**. Je 32:21. **shoulder**. Ex 28:7. **blade**. ver. 36. Ge 9:23. 21:14. **bone**. or, channel bone. Jb 40:21 (reed). Ge 41:5 (stalk). Is 42:3 (reed).

23. **destruction**. Jb 20:23. 21:20. Ge 39:9. Ps *119:120. Is 13:6. Jl *1:15. 2 C 5:11. **by**. Jb 13:11. 40:9. 42:5, 6. Ps *76:7.

24. **made gold my hope**. Ge 31:1. Dt 8:12-14. Ps 49:6, 7, 17. 52:7. *62:10. Pr 10:15. *11:28. 30:9. Mk *10:24, 25. Lk +*12:15. Col *3:5. 1 T √6:9, 10, 17.

25. **rejoiced**. Est 5:11. Pr *23:5. Je *9:23. Ezk 28:5. Da 4:30. Lk 12:19. 16:19, 25. **because**. Dt 8:17, 18. Is 10:13, 14. Da 4:30. Ho *12:8. Hab 1:16. **gotten much**. Heb. found much. ver. +29. Jb 11:7. 17:10.

26. **beheld**. Ge 1:16-18. Dt *4:19. 11:16. *17:3. 2 K *23:5, 11. Je *8:2. Ezk *8:16. Ro 1:20. **sun**. Heb. light. ʃ121N2, Ge +34:29. By Metonymy of the Adjunct "light" is put for sun. Jb 3:9, 16, 20. 12:22, 25. **the moon**. Ps 8:3, 4. Je 44:17. **in brightness**. Heb. bright.

27. **my heart**. Dt 11:16. 13:6. Is 44:20. Ro 1:21, 28. **my mouth hath kissed my hand**. Heb. my hand hath kissed my mouth. 1 K 19:18. Ps 2:12. Ho 13:2. **hand**. ʃ100, Ge +10:9. **kissed**. ʃ121S2, Ge +21:6.

28. **an iniquity**. ver. 11. Jb 9:15. 23:7. Ge *18:25. Dt 17:2-7, 9. Jg 11:27. Ps 50:6. He 12:23. **for**. Jsh 24:23, 27. Pr 30:9. T 1:16. 2 P 2:1. 1 J 2:23. Ju 4.

29. **I rejoiced**. 2 S *1:12. *4:10, 11. *16:5-8. Ps *35:13, 14, 25, 26. Pr *17:5. *24:17, 18. **found**. ʃ155F, Ge +4:7. 44:34mg.

30. **have**. Ex *23:4, 5. Mt *5:43, 44. Ro *12:14. 1 P *2:22, 23. *3:9. **mouth**. Heb. palate. Jb 6:30mg.

12:11mg. 20:13mg. 34:3mg. Ps 119:103mg. Pr 5:3mg. 24:13mg. Ec *5:2, 6. SS 2:3mg. 5:16mg. Ho 8:1mg. Mt *5:22. *12:36. Ja *3:6, 9, 10. **soul**. Heb. *nephesh*, Ge +27:31.

31. **the men**. 1 S 24:4, 10. 26:8. 2 S 16:9, 10. 19:21, 22. Je 40:15, 16. Lk 9:54, 55. 22:50, 51. **Oh**. Jb 19:22. Ps 27:2. 35:25. Pr 1:11, 12, 18. Mi 3:2, 3.

32. **The stranger**. ver. 17, 18. Ge 19:2, 3. 23:4 (❋S#1616h). Ex 12:48. Dt +26:11. Jsh +20:9. Jg 19:15, 20, 21. Is 58:7. Mt 25:+*35, 40, 44, 45. Ro 12:13. 1 T 5:10. He 13:2. 1 P 4:9. **in the street**. lit. outplace. Jb 5:10mg. 18:17(street). Am +5:16n(✛S#2351h, high-ways). **opened**. T#355. Ge 18:2-7. 19:1-3. Ac 28:7. 3 J 5, 6. **traveller**. or, way. Jb 6:18, 19. Is 3:12.

33. **covered**. Ge *3:7, 8, 12. Jsh 7:11. Pr *28:13. Ho *6:7. Ac 5:8. 1 J √1:8-10. **as Adam**. or, after the manner of men. Ps 82:7. Ho 6:7mg.

34. **Did I**. Ex √23:2. Pr 29:25. Je 38:4, 5, 16, 19. Mt *27:20-26. Ac *24:27. **the contempt**. Jb 22:8. 34:19. Ex 32:27. Nu 25:14, 15. Ne 5:7. 13:4-8, 28. 2 C 5:16. **that I**. Est 4:11, 14. Pr 24:11, 12. Am 5:11-13. Mi 7:3.

35. **Oh**. Jb 13:3. 17:3. 23:3-7. *33:6. 38:1-3. 40:4, 5. **my desire is, that the Almighty would answer me**. or, my sign is that the Almighty will answer me. Jb 13:21, 22. 38:1. Ps 26:1. **mine**. Jb 13:24. 19:11, 23, 24. 33:10, 11. Mt 5:25.

36. **I would**. Ex 28:12. Is 22:22. **a crown**. Jb 29:14. Is 62:3. Ph 4:1.

37. **declare**. Jb 9:3. 13:15. 14:16. 42:3-6. Ps 19:12. **as a prince**. Ge *32:28. Ep *3:12. He √4:15, 16. 1 J 3:19-21.

38. **cry**. ʃ155D. Jb 20:27. Ge +4:10. Hab 2:11. Ja +*5:4. **complain**. Heb. weep. ʃ155D, Ge +4:10. Ps 65:13.

39. **fruits**. Heb. strength. Ge 4:12. **without money**. Le +*19:13. Dt √24:14, 15. Je *22:13. Ml +*3:5. Ja +*5:4. **caused the owners thereof to lose their life**. Heb. caused the soul of the owners thereof to expire, or breathe out. 1 K 21:13-16, 19. Pr *1:19. Is 26:21. Ezk 22:6, 12, 13. Ml 1:13. **life**. Heb. *nephesh*, soul, Ge +44:30.

40. **thistles**. *Choach*, probably the black thorn (see on 2 K 14:9). Ge 3:17, 18. Is 7:23. Zp 2:9. Ml 1:3. **cockle**. or, noisome weeds. **The words**. Ps 72:20.

JOB 32

Job's three friends being silenced, Elihu speaks and is angry with Job and them both, 1-5. Though young, he excuses his interference, because great and aged men are not always wise, 6-10. He complains that the reasonings of the disputants were not suited to produce conviction, 11-14. He shows that he is earnestly desirous of speaking and declares that he will be impartial, 15-22.

1. **to answer**. Heb. from answering. **righteous**. Jb 6:29. 10:2, 7. 13:15. 23:7. 27:4-6. 29:11-17. 31:1, etc. 33:9.

2. **kindled**. Ps 69:9. Mk 3:5. Ep *4:26. **Elihu**. i.e. *my God is He*. ver. 5, 6. Jb 34:1. 36:1. 1 S +1:1. **Barachel**. i.e. *blessed of God*, ❋S#1292h. ver. 6. **Busite**. i.e. *despised one*, ❋S#940h. ver. 6. Ge 22:21. Je 25:23. **kindred**. Jb 31:34. Ge 8:19mg. 10:5, 18. **Ram**. i.e. *high one; elevated*, ❋S#7410h. Jb 32:2. Ru 4:19, 19. 1 Ch 2:9, 10, 25, 27. (1) A Buzite, Jb 32:2. (2)

The second in the generation of Pharez to David, Ru 4:19; 1 Ch 2:9; called Aram, Mt 1:3; Lk 3:33. (3) The firstborn of Jerahmeel, 1 Ch 2:25, 27. **because**. Jb 10:3. 27:2. 34:5, 6, 17, 18. 35:2. 40:8. Lk 10:29. **himself**. Heb. his soul, *nephesh*, Ge +27:31. Ex 30:12. 1 P +*4:19.

3. **because**. ver. 1. Jb 24:25. 25:2-6. 26:2-4. **and yet**. Jb 8:6. 15:34. 22:5, etc. Ac 24:5, *13. **Job**. ◊182, Ge +18:22.

4. **waited till Job had spoken**. Heb. expected Job in words. ver. 11, 12. Pr 18:13. **Job**. ◊171R, Ex +12:40. By Synecdoche of the Part, Job is named but the others are included, as the following words show: "because they." **elder**. Heb. elder for days.

5. **his wrath**. ver. 2. Ex 32:19.

6. **I am**. Le *19:32. Ro *13:7. 1 T *5:1. T 2:6. 1 P *5:5. **young**. Heb. few of days. Jb 30:1mg. **ye are**. Jb 15:10. **durst not**. Heb. feared. Jb 15:7. 1 S 17:28-30.

7. **Days**. ◊121N1, Ge +31:54. By Metonymy of the Adjunct, "days" is put for men of full age. **should speak**. Jb 8:8-10. 12:12. 1 K 12:6-8. Ps 34:11, 12. Pr 1:1-4. 16:31. He 5:12. **years**. ◊121N1, Ge +31:54. "Years" is put for aged men.

8. **spirit**. Heb. *ruach*, Jb +14:22. Ge +41:8. Ec +3:21. 12:7. Zc 12:1. **the inspiration**. Heb. *neshamah*, Jb 4:12-21. 33:16. 35:11. 38:36. Ge +2:7. 41:39. 1 K *3:12, 28. 4:29. Pr *2:6. Ec 2:26. Da 1:17. 2:21. Mt 11:25. 1 C *2:10-12. *12:8. 2 T √3:16. Ja *1:5. **giveth them**. Ps 32:8. 119:99.

9. **Great**. Je 5:5. Mt 11:25. Jn *7:48. 1 C 1:26, 27. *2:7, 8. Ja 2:6, 7. **neither**. Jb 12:20. Ec *4:13. **the aged**. Jb ◊12:12. Ps *119:100.

10. **Hearken**. ◊96B, Ex +20:8. Ec 3:7. 1 C 7:25, 40.

11. **I waited for**. ver. 4, 16. Jb 29:21, 23. 1 S 10:8. 13:8. Pr *18:13. **reasons**. Heb. understandings. Jb 12:12, 13. 26:12. Ex 31:3. Instead of *tevoonotheychem*, nine MSS. read *techoonotheychem*, "your arguments;" but the sense is nearly the same. **whilst**. *Ad tachkeroon millin*, "whilst ye were searching for words;" a fine irony, which they must have felt. Jb 5:27. 13:9. 28:27. Pr 18:17. 28:11. Ec 12:9, 10. ◊60B. Irony, Ge +20:16. **what to say**. Heb. words. Jb 33:1.

12. **unto you**. *Weadeychem* is rendered "and your testimonies," by the Syriac, Arabic, and LXX., and one of De Rossi's MSS. (874) is so pointed as to require this reading. **behold**. ver. 3. 1 T 1:7.

13. **Lest**. Ge 14:23. Jg 7:2. Is 48:5, 7. Zc 12:7. **We**. Jb 12:2. 15:8-10. Is *5:21. Je *9:23. Ezk 28:3. 1 C 1:19-21, 27-29. *3:18, 19. **God**. Jb 1:21. 2:10. 4:9. 6:4. 19:6, 21. Jn 19:11.

14. **directed**. Heb. ordered. or, set in array. Jb 6:4. 13:18. 23:4. 33:5. **speeches**. or, sayings. ver. 12. Jb 6:10, 25, 26. 8:2.

15. **amazed**. Jb 6:24, 25. 29:22. 2 K 19:26h. Mt 7:28. 22:22, 26, 34, 46. **left off speaking**. Heb. removed speeches from themselves. Jb 9:5. Ge 12:8. 26:22.

16. **for they**. Jb 13:5. Pr 17:28. Am 5:13. Ja 1:19.

17. **I said**. ◊63BA, Ge +26:7. **I will answer**. ver. 10. Jb 33:12. 35:3, 4. **opinion**. ver. 6, 10. Jb 36:3. 37:16.

18. **matter**. Heb. words. Jb 4:2mg. 16:4. **the spirit**. Heb. *ruach*, Ge +41:8. Ps *39:3. Je *6:11. *20:9. Ezk 3:14, etc. Ac *4:20. 2 C 5:13, 14. **within me**. Heb. of my belly. Jb 19:27. Pr 22:18mg. **constraineth**. or, distressed. Dt 28:53, 55, 57.

19. **hath no vent**. Heb. is not opened. Jb 12:14. Ge 7:11. **burst**. Jb 26:8. Ge 7:11. **new**. Mt 9:17. **bottles**. Everywhere else the original word signifies a familiar spirit, as in Le +19:31 (Young). 2 K +21:6 (S#178h).

20. **I will speak**. Jb 13:13, 19. 20:2. 21:3. **be refreshed**. Heb. breathe. 1 S 16:23. **I will open**. Pr 8:6, 7.

21. **accept**. Jb 13:8. 34:19. Le *19:15. Dt 1:17. 16:19. Pr *24:23. Mt 22:16. **flattering**. 2 S 14:17, 20. Ac 12:22, 23. 24:2, 3.

22. **I know not**. That is, *I cannot*. Jb 5:24, 25. 9:2. 5. **flattering titles**. Jb 17:5. Ps 12:2, +3. Pr 29:5. Mt 23:9. Ga 1:10. 1 Th 2:5. **maker**. Jb 4:17. 31:15. 35:10. 40:19. **take me away**. Jb 21:21. Ps 12:3. 102:23, 24. Is 38:10. 64:6. Ac 12:23. 1 C 11:30. Ja 5:20. 1 J 5:16.

JOB 33

Elihu requires Job's attention while he pleads with him, in God's stead and without terrifying him, 1-7. He blames him for being too earnest in vindicating himself and for irreverently complaining to God, 8-13. He shows how God instructs men by dreams, afflictions, and messengers; that repenting they may find mercy, 14-30. He calls on Job to answer or patiently to attend to his discourse, 31-33.

1. **hear**. Jb 13:6. 34:2. Ps 49:1-3. Mk 4:9.

2. **I have**. Jb 3:1. Ps 78:2. Mt 5:2. **opened**. ◊108H6A, Jg +11:35. **mouth**. Heb. palate. Jb +31:30mg.

3. **the uprightness**. Jb 27:4. Pr 8:7, 8. 1 Th *2:3, 4. **my lips**. Jb 15:2. 36:3, 4. 38:2. Ps 37:30, 31. Pr 15:2, 7. 20:15. 22:17, 18.

4. **The Spirit**. Heb. *ruach*, Jb 10:12. 26:13. 27:3. 32:8. Ge 2:7. Ps 33:6. Is +48:16. Ac 5:3, 4. Ro 8:2. 1 C 15:45. **God**. Heb. *El*, Ex +15:2. **made**. Jb 10:9. 12:9. 31:15. 40:15. Lk 1:35. **breath**. Heb. *neshamah*, Ge +2:7. **the Almighty**. Ge 17:1. 2 C 6:18.

5. **If**. ver. 32, 33. Jb 32:1, 12. **set**. Jb 23:4, 5. 32:14. Ps 50:21. **stand**. Ac 10:26.

6. **I am**. Jb 9:32-35. 13:3, 20-22. 23:3, 4. 31:35. **wish**. Heb. mouth. Zc 1:21. **in**. Ge 30:2. Ex 4:16. 2 C *5:20. He 2:14. **I also**. Jb 4:19. 10:9. 13:12. Ge *2:7. *3:19. 2 C 5:1. **formed**. Heb. cut. lit. nipped. Ps 35:19. Is 51:1. 2 C 4:7.

7. **my terror**. Jb 9:34. 13:21. Ps 88:16. **my hand**. Ps 32:4. *103:14. He *4:15.

8. **hearing**. Heb. ears. Jb 4:12. 12:11. 13:1, 17. Ex 17:14. Dt 13:14. Je 29:23.

9. **clean**. Jb 9:17. 10:7. 11:4. 16:17. 23:11, 12. 27:5, 6. 29:14. **innocent**. Jb 9:23, 28. 17:8. Je 2:35.

10. **he findeth**. Jb 9:30, 31. 10:15-17. 13:25, 26. 14:16, 17. 34:5, 6. **he counteth**. Jb 6:26. 13:24. 16:9. 19:11. 30:21, 22. 31:35.

11. **putteth**. Jb 13:27. Ps 105:18. Je 20:2. Ac 16:24. **marketh**. Jb 31:4. Da 4:35.

12. **thou**. Jb 1:22. 34:10-12, 17-19, 23. 35:2. 36:22, 23. Je *2:35. Ezk 18:25. Ro 9:19-21. **I will**. Jb 32:17. 35:4. **God**. Jb 9:4. 26:14. 36:5. 40:2, 8, 9. Je 18:6.

13. **strive**. Jb 9:14. 15:25, 26. Is *45:9. Je 50:24. Ezk 22:14. Ac 5:39. 9:4, 5. 1 C 10:22. **giveth not account**. Heb. answereth not. Jb 40:2. Dt *29:29. Ps 62:11. 115:3. Is 44:10. 46:10. Da 4:35. Mt 20:15. Ac *1:7. Ro 11:34.

14. **God**. Jb 40:5. Ps *62:11. **perceiveth**. 2 Ch *33:10. Pr *1:24, 29. Is 6:9. Mt 13:14. Mk 8:17, 18. Lk 24:25. Jn *3:19.

15. **a dream**. Jb 4:13. Ge *20:3. 31:24. Nu *12:6. Je √23:28. Da 4:5. Mt *27:19. 2 C 3:14-17. He 1:1. 2 P 1:19-21. **deep**. Ge *15:12. Da *8:18, 19. 10:9.
16. **openeth**. Heb. revealeth, *or*, uncovereth. Jb 36:10, 15. 2 S 7:27. Ps 40:6. Is 6:10. 48:8. 50:5. Lk 24:45. Ac 16:14. **sealeth**. Jb 37:7. Ne 9:38. Ro 15:28.
17. **withdraw**. Jb 17:11. Ge 20:6. Is 23:9. Ho 2:6. Mt 27:19. Ac 9:2-6. 26:10-13. **purpose**. Heb. work. Jb 1:10. 14:15. 34:19. 37:7. Ge 5:29. **hide**. Dt 8:16. 2 Ch 32:25, 26. Is 2:11. Da 4:30-37. 2 C 12:7. Ja 4:10.
18. **keepeth**. Ac 16:27-33. Ro 2:4. 2 P 3:9, 15. **soul**. Heb. *nephesh*, Ps +30:3. Jb +*14:22. Ge 25:8n, 9, 17. 35:18. 1 K 17:22. Ps 88:3. Mt +*10:28. **pit**. Heb. *shachath*, Jb +9:31 (✱S#7845h). *Shachath* occurs in connection with *nephesh* here and Jb 33:22, 28, 30. Ps 35:7. Is 38:17. **perishing**. Heb. passing. ver. 28. 2 K 4:8. 6:9. Pr 10:25. 19:11. La 3:44. Ac 16:27, 28.
19. **chastened**. Jb 5:17, 18. Dt *8:5. Ps *94:12, 13. *119:67, 71. Is 27:9. 1 C *11:32. He *12:5-11. Re 3:19. **pain**. Jb 7:4. 20:11. 30:17, 18, 30. 2 Ch 16:10, 12. Ps 38:1-8. Is 38:12, 13.
20. **his life**. Ps 107:17, 18. **soul**. Heb. *nephesh*, Nu +11:6. **dainty meat**. Heb. meat of desire. Ge *3:6. 49:26. Nu 11:4. Pr 23:3. Je 3:19. Ezk +26:12mg. Am +5:11mg.
21. **His flesh**. Jb 7:5. 13:28. 14:20, 22. 19:20. Ps 32:3, 4. 39:11. 102:3-5. Pr 5:11. **his bones**. Ps 22:15-17.
22. **his soul**. Heb. *nephesh*, Ps +30:3. Jb 7:7. +14:22. 17:1, 13-16. 1 S 2:6. Ps 30:3. 88:3-5. Is 38:10. Mt +*10:28. **draweth near**. Ge 27:41. 47:29. Dt 31:14. **grave**. Heb. *shachath*, ver. 18. Jb +9:31. **his life**. Jb 15:21. Ex 12:23. 2 S 24:16. Ps 17:4. Ac 12:23. 1 C 10:10. Re 9:11. **the destroyers**. 1 S 2:6. 2 K 17:26. Je 26:15. Mt +*10:28.
23. **a messenger**. Jg 2:1mg. 2 Ch *36:15, 16. Is 63:9. Hg 1:13. Ml *2:7. *3:1. Ac 10:43. 2 C *5:20. **an interpreter**. Jb *34:32. Ge 40:8. Ps *94:12. Is *61:1-3. Ac *8:30, 31. 1 C 11:30-32. Ga 3:19. 1 T *2:5. He 8:6. 9:15. 12:5-12. lit. "sweetener," as in Jb 16:20. 2 Ch 32:31. Ps 119:103. Is 43:27. **one among**. Jb *9:3. Ps 12:1. 89:19. Ro 11:13. **a thousand**. Dt 33:2. Ec 7:28. SS 5:10. Mi +*5:2. **to show**. Jb *11:6. *34:10, 12. *35:14. *36:3, 8-13. *37:23. Ne *9:33. Ps *119:75. La *3:22, 23, 32, 39-41. Ezk *18:25-28. Da *9:14. **his uprightness**. ver. 3. Jb 6:25. Dt 9:5. Pr 14:2.
24. **Then**. ver. *18. Jb *22:21. Ex 33:19. 34:6, 7. Ps *86:5, 15. Ho 14:2, 4. Mi *7:18-20. Ro *5:20, 21. **Deliver**. Jb *36:10, 11. Ex *15:26. Ps *30:9-12. *40:2. *71:3. 86:13. Is *38:17-19. Je 31:20. Zc *9:11. **soul**. Heb. *nephesh*, Ps +30:3. **pit**. *or*, corruption. ver. +18, 22. **I have found**. Jb *36:18. Ps *49:7, 8. 89:19. Mt *20:28. Jn 1:17. Ro *3:24-26. 1 T *2:5, 6. He 9:12. 1 P *1:18, 19. **a ransom**. *or*, an atonement. Jb 36:18. 1 S +12:3 (✱S#3724h). Is *53:10, 11. Mt 20:28.
25. **His flesh**. 2 K *5:14. **a child's**. Heb. childhood. Jb 36:14. Ps 88:15. Pr 29:21. **return**. Jb 42:16. Dt 34:7. Jsh 14:10, 11. Ps *103:5. Is 40:31. Ho 2:15.
26. **pray**. 2 K 20:2-5. 2 Ch *7:14. 33:12, 13, 19. Ps 6:1-9. 28:1, 2, 6. 30:7-11. 41:8-11. *50:15. 91:15. 116:1-6. Is 30:19. Je *33:3. Jon 2:2-7. Mt *7:7, 8. Ac 9:11. **and he shall**. Jb 42:8, 9. Nu 6:25, 26. Ps 4:6, 7. 16:11. 30:5. 67:1. Ac 2:28. Ju 24. **he will**. Jb 34:11. 1 S 26:23. Ps 18:20. 62:12. Pr 24:12. Mt 10:41, 42. He 11:26.
27. **looketh**, etc. *or*, shall look upon men, and say,

I have sinned, etc. Ge 16:13. 2 Ch 16:9. Ps 11:4. 14:2. 53:2. 139:1-4. Pr 5:21. 15:3. Je 23:24. **I have sinned**. Jb 7:20. Nu 12:11. 2 S *12:13. Pr *28:13. Je 3:13. 31:18, 19. Lk *15:18-22. *18:13. 1 J √1:8-10. **perverted**. Ec 5:8. **right**. Ps 19:7, 8. 119:128. Ro 7:12-14, 16, 22. **it profited**. Jb 34:9. Je 2:8. Mt 16:26. Ro 6:21.
28. **will deliver**, etc. *or*, hath delivered my soul, etc. T#785. ver. 18, 24. Jb 17:16. Dt +32:39. 1 S 2:6. Ps 9:13. 40:2. 55:23. 66:8, 9. 68:20. 69:15. *91:7. 102:19, 20. 107:18, 19. *116:15. Is *38:17, 18. Re 20:1-3. **soul**. Heb. *nephesh*, Ps +30:3. **pit**. Heb. *shachath*, ver. +18. **shall see**. ver. 20, 22. Jb 3:9, 16, 20. Ps 49:19. Is 9:2. Jn 11:9.
29. **all**. ver. 14-17. 1 C *12:6. 2 C 5:5. Ep +*1:11. Ph *2:13. Col 1:29. He *13:21. **worketh**. Jb 7:20. 11:8. 22:17. 34:32. **oftentimes**. Heb. twice and thrice. ver. 14. Jb 40:5. 2 K 6:10. 2 C 12:8.
30. **To bring**. ver. 24, 28. Ps 40:1, 2. 118:17, 18. Is 51:1. **soul**. Heb. *nephesh*, Ps +30:3. **pit**. Heb. *shachath*, ver. +18. **enlightened**. Ps *56:13. Is 2:5. 38:17. Jn *8:12. Ac 26:18.
31. **Mark well**. Jb 13:6. 18:2. 21:2. 32:11.
32. **I desire**. Jb 9:3. 13:3. 15:4, 5. 21:27. 22:5-9. 27:5. **justify**. Jb 32:2. Ezk 16:52. Ro *3:26. *8:33.
33. **hearken**. Ps 34:11. Pr 4:1, 2. 5:1, 2. **I shall teach**. ver. 3. Ps 49:3. Pr 8:5. **wisdom**. Jb 4:21. 11:6. 12:2. 1 C *1:30.

JOB 34

Elihu calls on the wise to judge in the cause and charges Job with arraigning the divine justice, 1-9. He affirms that the all-powerful and all-perfect God cannot do iniquity and vindicates his dealings with men, 10-30. He shows Job that he ought to humble himself before God and sharply reproves his words, 31-37.

1. **answered**. Jg 18:14.
2. **wise men**. ver. 34. Jb 5:13. Pr 1:5. 1 C *10:15. 14:20. **have knowledge**. Jb 19:13. 24:1. 42:11.
3. **the ear**. Jb 6:30. 12:11. 1 C 2:15. He *5:14. **mouth**. Heb. palate. Jb 20:13mg. +31:30mg. 33:2mg.
4. **choose**. ver. 36. Jg 19:30. 20:7. 1 C *6:2-5. Ga 2:11-14. 1 Th 5:21. **know**. Is 11:2-5. Jn *7:24. Ro *12:2.
5. **I am righteous**. Jb 10:7. 11:4. 16:17. 29:14. 32:1. 33:9. **God**. Jb 9:17. 27:2.
6. **I lie**. Jb 6:28. 27:4-6. **wound**. Heb. arrow. Jb 6:4. 16:13. Ge 49:23. Nu 24:8. **incurable**. ✱S#605h. 2 S 12:15 (very sick). Is 17:11 (desperate). Je 15:18. √17:9, 16 (woeful). 30:12, 15. Mi 1:9. **without transgression**. ver. 37. Jb 7:21. 8:4. *33:9.
7. **drinketh**. Jb 15:16. Dt 29:19. Pr 1:22. 4:17.
8. **Which goeth**. Jb 22:10. 11:3. 15:5. Ps *1:1. 26:4. 50:18. 73:12-15. Pr 1:15. 2:12. 4:14. *13:20. 1 C 15:33.
9. **It profiteth**. Jb 9:22, 23, *29-31. 21:14-16, 30. 22:17. 35:3. Ml *3:14. **delight**. Jb 27:10. Ps *37:4.
10. **understanding**. Heb. heart. ver. 2, 3, *34. Jb +12:3. Pr 6:32. 15:32mg. Je 5:21. Ac 8:22. √121J23. Metonymy of the Subject, "heart" put for understanding, Jb +12:3. Jb 8:3. 36:23. Ge √18:25. Dt *32:4. 2 Ch *19:7. Ps *92:15. Je 12:1. Ro 3:4, 5. 9:14. Ja *1:13.
11. **the work**. Jb 33:26. Ps *62:12. Pr 24:12. Je *32:19. Ezk 33:17-20. Mt +16:27. Ro 2:6. 1 C 3:13. 2 C *5:10. 1 P 1:17. Re *22:12. **cause**. Pr 1:31. Ga *6:7, 8.

12. **surely**. Ps 11:7. 145:17. Hab 1:12, 13. **do wickedly**. ver. 17, 29. Jb 9:20. **pervert**. Jb 8:3. 19:6. Ps 119:78.

13. **Who hath given**. Jb 36:23. 38:4, etc. 40:8-11. 1 Ch *29:11. Pr 8:23-30. Is *40:13, 14. Da 4:35. Ro 11:34-36. **the whole world**. Heb. the world, all of it. Jb 18:18. 37:12.

14. **set**. ver. 23. Jb 7:17. 9:4. **upon man**. Heb. upon him. **he gather**. Jb 39:12. Ps ◐+36:6. 104:29. Is 24:22. **spirit**. Heb. *ruach*, Nu +16:22. Ps 104:29. **and**. ♪93A. Hendiadys: two words used, but one thing meant, Ge +1:26. **breath**. Heb. *neshamah*, Ge +2:7. Jb 4:9. 26:4. 27:3. 32:8.

15. **All flesh**. Jb 30:23. Ge 3:19. +*6:3. Ps *90:3-10. Ec 12:7. Is 27:4. 57:16. **perish**. Jb 3:11. 10:18. 13:19. 14:10. Ge +49:33 (*S#1478h). **turn again**. Jb 10:9, 21. Ge *3:19. Ps *104:29. +*146:4. Ec 3:20. 12:7.

16. **thou hast**. Jb 12:3. 13:2-6. **understanding**. Jb 20:3. 28:12.

17. **even**. Ge √18:25. 2 S *23:3. Ro 3:5-7. **govern**. Heb. bind. Jb 5:18. Jg 18:7. **wilt**. Jb 1:22. 40:8. 2 S 19:21. Ro *9:14.

18. **to say**. Ex *22:28. Pr 17:26. Ac 23:3, 5. Ro 13:7. 1 P *2:17. 2 P 2:10. Ju *8. **ungodly**. 1 S +30:22. Ps 18:4mg.

19. **accepteth**. Jb 13:8. Dt 10:17. 2 Ch 19:7. Ac 10:34. Ro *2:11. Ga 2:6. Ep 6:9. Col 3:25. He 12:28. 1 P *1:17. **princes**. Jb 12:19, 21. Ps 2:2-4. Ec 5:8. Is 3:14. **regardeth**. Le +*19:15. Jb 36:19. Ps 49:6, 7. Ja +*2:5. **they**. Jb 31:15. Pr 14:31. 22:2.

20. **a moment**. Ps 73:19. Is 30:13. 37:38. Da 5:30. Lk 12:20. Ac 12:23. 1 Th *5:2. 2 P 2:3. **troubled**. Ex *12:29, 30. Is 37:36. Mt 25:6. Lk 17:26-29. **the mighty shall be taken away**. Heb. they shall take away the mighty. Jb 18:18. **without**. 1 S *25:37-39. 26:10. Is 10:16-19. 30:30-33. Da *2:34, 44, 45. Zc *4:6.

21. **his eyes**. ♪22A6, Ps +11:4. Jb 31:4. Ge 16:13. 2 Ch *16:9. Ps 34:15. 139:23. Pr 5:21. 15:3. Je 16:17. 17:10. 32:19. Am 9:8.

22. **no darkness**. Ps 139:11, 12. Is 29:15. Je *23:24. Am *9:2, 3. 1 C 4:5. He *4:13. Re 6:15, 16. **nor shadow**. Jb 3:5. 24:17. Is 9:2. **the workers**. Jb 31:3. Ps 5:5. Pr 10:29. Mt 7:23. Lk 13:27.

23. **he will**. ver. 10-12. Jb 11:6. Ezr *9:13. Ps 119:137. Is 42:3. Da 9:7-9. **that he**. Jb 9:32, 33. 16:21. 23:7. Je 2:5. Ro 9:20. **enter**. Heb. go. Jb 14:3.

24. **break**. Jb 19:2. Ps *2:9. 72:4. 94:5. Je 51:20-23. Da 2:21, 34, 35, *44, 45. Lk 1:52. **number**. Heb. searching out. Jb 5:9. 8:8. 9:10. 11:7. 36:26. **set**. 1 S 2:30-36. 15:28. 1 K 14:7, 8, 14. Ps 113:7, 8. Da 5:28-31.

25. **he knoweth**. Ps 33:15. Is *66:18. Ho 7:2. Am 8:7. Re 20:12. **in the night**. ver. 20. SS 3:8. Is 15:1. 1 Th 5:2. **destroyed**. Heb. crushed. Jb 5:4.

26. **in the**. Ex 14:30. Dt 13:9-11. 21:21. 2 S *12:11, 12. Ps 58:10, 11. Is *66:24. 1 T *5:20, 24. Re 18:9, 10, 20. **open sight of others**. Heb. place of beholders. Lk 12:2, 3. 2 T 3:9.

27. **turned**. 1 S 15:11. Ps *125:5. Zp 1:6. Lk 17:31, 32. Ac 15:38. 2 T 4:10. He 10:39. **from him**. Heb. from after him. **would**. Ps 28:5. 107:43. Pr 1:29, 30. Is 1:3. 5:12. Hg 2:15-19.

28. **cry of the poor**. Jb 22:9, 10. 24:12. 29:12, 13. 31:19, 20. 35:9. Ex 2:23, 24. 3:7, 9. Ps +*12:5. Is *5:7. Ja +*5:4. **and he heareth**. Ex +√22:23-27.

29. **When he giveth**. Jb 29:1-3. 2 S 7:1. Is 14:3-8. √26:3. 30:15. 32:17. Jn *14:27. Ro *8:31-34. Ph *4:7. **when he hideth**. Jb 23:8, 9. Ps 13:1. 27:9. 30:7. 143:7. **who then can behold**. Jb 12:14. 23:13. Pr 16:7. **whether**. 2 K 18:9-12. 2 Ch 36:14-17. Je 27:8.

30. **That the**. ver. 21. 1 K 12:28-30. 2 K 21:9. Ps 12:8. Ec 9:18. Ho 5:11. 13:11. Mi 6:16. 2 Th 2:4-11. Re 13:3, 4, 11-14.

31. **it is meet**. Jb *33:27. 40:3-5. *42:6. Le *26:41. Ezr 9:13, 14. Ne *9:33-38. Je 31:18, 19. Da *9:7-14. Mi *7:9.

32. **which**. Jb 10:2. Ps *19:12. *25:4, 5. *32:8. *119:18. *139:23, 24. *143:8-10. **teach**. T#1593. 2 Ch 1:7-10. Ps *25:9. *119:66. Pr *2:3-6. Is 45:11, 12. Da 2:17-21. Ph 1:9. **if**. Pr *28:13. Lk *3:8-14. Ep *4:22, 25-28. 1 P 4:3.

33. **Should**. Jb 9:12. 18:4. Is 45:9. Ro 9:20. 11:35. **according to thy mind**. Heb. from with thee. Jb 23:10. **he will**. ver. 11. Jb 15:31. Ps 89:30-32. Pr *11:31. 2 Th *1:6, 7. He 2:2. 11:26. **whether thou refuse**. Ps 135:6. Mt 20:12-15. **what**. Jb 33:5, 32.

34. **understanding**. Heb. heart. ver. 2, 4, +*10, 16. 1 C 10:15.

35. **hath spoken**. Jb 13:2. 15:2. 35:16. 38:2. 42:3.

36. **My desire is that Job may be tried**. or, My father, let Job be tried. Jb 23:16. Ps 17:3. 26:2. Ja 5:11. **the end**. Heb. *netsach*, Jb +4:20. **his answers**. ver. 8, 9. Jb 12:6. 21:7. 24:1.

37. **rebellion**. 1 S √15:23. Is *1:19, 20. **he clappeth**. Jb 27:23. **multiplieth**. Jb 8:2, 3. 11:2, 3. 35:2, 3, 16. 42:7.

JOB 35

Elihu further reproves Job's words in justifying himself and shows that the effects of man's conduct extend to man alone, and not to God, 1-8. He observes that if God hear not the cry of the oppressed, it is because they do not address him aright, 9-13. He exhorts Job to patience and trust in God, 11-16.

2. **Thinkest**. Mt 12:36, 37. Lk 19:22. **My**. Jb 9:17. 10:7. 16:17. 19:6, 7. 27:2-6. 34:5. 40:8.

3. **What advantage**. Jb 9:21, 22. 10:15. 21:15. 31:2. 34:9. Ps 73:13. Ml 3:14. **if I be cleansed from my sin**. or, by it more than my sin.

4. **answer thee**. Heb. return to thee words. **thy**. Jb 34:8. Pr 13:20.

5. **Look**. Jb 22:12. 25:5, 6. 36:26-33. 37:1-5, 22, 23. 1 K 8:27. Ps *8:3, 4. Is 40:22, 23. 55:9. **the clouds**. Jb 36:29. 37:16. Na 1:3. *Shechakim*, the *aethers*, or conflicting air; the strong agitation of which produces both light and heat: so Vulgate, *aethera*.

6. **what doest**. Pr 8:36. *9:12. Je *7:19.

7. **what givest**. Jb 22:2, 3. 1 Ch *29:14. Ps *16:2, 3. Pr *8:36. Ro *11:35.

8. **may hurt**. Jsh 7:1-5, 24, 25. *22:20. Ec 9:18. Jon *1:12. **may profit**. Jb 42:8. Ge *12:2. 18:24, etc. *19:29. Ps 106:23, 30. Ezk *22:30, 31. Ac *27:24. He 11:7.

9. **oppressions**. ♪108J, Ge +43:18. **they make**. Jb 24:12. 34:28. Ex *2:23. 3:7, 9. Ne 5:1-5. Ps +*12:5. 43:2. 55:2, 3. 56:1, 2. Lk 18:3-7. **the arm**. Jb 40:9. Ps 10:15.

10. **none**. Jb 36:13. 2 K *1:2, 3. 1 Ch 10:13, 14. 2 Ch 28:22, 23. Is 8:21. **Where**. Ec 12:1. Is 51:13. 1 P 4:19. **my**. Jb 32:22. 36:3. Is 54:5. **maker**. Heb. mak-

ers. Plural number, as in Ec 12:1 and Is 54:5, and that without any necessity, when it might as well have been put in the singular number, plainly implies a plurality of persons in the divine essence, of which see on Ge 1:26 (Matthew Poole). who. Ps *42:8. 77:6. 119:62. *149:5. Ac *16:25.

11. **Who teacheth.** Jb *32:8. Ge +√1:26. +√2:7. Ps *8:5, 6. *94:12.

12. **they cry.** Ps 18:41. Pr 1:28. **none giveth answer.** or, he answereth not. Jb 19:7. *30:20. Ps 22:2. La 3:8. Hab 1:2. Jn +*9:31. Ja 4:2, 3. **because.** Ps +*9:10n. **pride.** T#1808. Ps 73:6-8. +*119:21. 123:3, 4. Is 14:14-17.

13. **God.** Jb 22:22-27. 27:8, 9. Pr *15:8, 29. 28:9. Ec 5:1-3. Is *1:15. Je 11:11. Ho 7:14. 8:2, 3. Mt 6:7. 20:21, 22. Ja *4:3. **not hear.** T#1811. Ps *18:41. Jn +*9:31. **regard.** Jb *30:20. Ps ☾*102:17. Am 5:22.

14. **thou sayest.** Jb 9:11. 23:3, 8-10. **yet.** Jb 9:19. 19:7. Ps 77:5-10. 97:2. Is 30:18. 54:17. Mi 7:7-9. **trust.** Ps 27:12-14. *37:5, 6. *62:5, 8. Is *50:10. Ro *8:33, 34.

15. **because.** Jb 9:14. 13:15. Nu 20:12. Lk 1:20. **he.** that is, *God.* **visited.** Ps *89:32. Re 3:19. **he.** that is, *Job.* **in great.** Jb 4:5. 30:15, etc. Ps 88:11-16. Ho 11:8, 9. He 12:11, 12.

16. **open.** Jb 3:1. 33:2, 8-12. 34:35-37. 38:2. 42:3.

JOB 36

Elihu requires attention as with truth and knowledge he shows the justice of God in all his judgments, the designs of his chastisements, and the profit of making a right use of them: God is just in all his ways towards the wicked, 1-6; the godly, 7-11; the hypocrite, 12-14; the poor, 15. He reproves, warns, and counsels Job as to how his sins hinder God's blessings, 16-21. He reminds him that the power of God is uncontrollable and that his works and dispensations should be magnified, but cannot be comprehended, 22-33.

2. **Suffer.** Jb 21:3. 33:31-33. He *13:22. **I have yet to speak,** etc. Heb. there are yet words for God. Jb 13:7, 8. 33:6. Ex 4:16. Je 15:19. Ezk *2:7. 2 C 5:20.

3. **fetch.** Jb 28:12, 13, 20-24. 32:8. Pr 2:4, 5. Mt 2:1, 2. 12:42. Ac 8:27, etc. Ro 10:6-8. Ja 1:5, 17. 3:17. **ascribe.** Jb 32:2. 34:5, 10-12. Dt 32:4. Ps 11:7. *99:4. 145:17. Je 12:1. Da 9:7, 14. Ro 3:25, 26. 9:14. Re 15:3.

4. **my.** Jb 13:4, 7. 21:27, 34. 22:6, etc. Pr 8:7, 8. 2 C *2:17. 2 P √1:16. **perfect.** Jb 37:16. Lk 1:3. Ac 24:22. 1 C 14:20mg. Col 4:12. 2 T √3:16, 17. **in knowledge.** Ps 49:3. Pr 22:20, 21.

5. **despiseth.** Jb 10:3. 31:13. Ps 22:24. 138:6. **mighty.** Jb 9:4, 19. 12:13-16. 26:12-14. 37:23. Ps 99:4. 147:5. Je 10:12. 32:19. 1 C 1:24-28. **wisdom.** Heb. heart. Jb 34:10.

6. **preserveth.** Jb 21:7-9, 30. Ps 55:23. Je 12:1, 2. 2 P 2:9. **giveth right.** T#631. Jb 29:12-17. Ps 9:12. 10:14, 15. 72:4, 12-14. 82:1-4. Pr *22:22, 23. Is 10:1, 2. 11:4. La 3:35, 36. Am 5:12. Ga 5:13. 1 T +1:10 (T#682). **poor.** or, afflicted. Ex 22:22-24. Ps 140:12.

7. **withdraweth not.** T#585. Dt 7:9. 32:9-12. 2 Ch 16:9. Ne 9:17-21. Ps *33:18. 34:15. 105:12-15. Is *40:1. 49:13-16. 54:8, 10, 17. *63:9. Ho 2:19. Zp 3:17. Zc 2:8. Mt 28:20. Jn 14:16-18. 1 P 3:12. Re 1:5, 6. **with.** Jb 1:3. 42:12. Ge 23:6. 41:40. 1 S *2:8. Est 10:3. Ps 78:70-72. *113:7, 8. **he doth.** 2 S 7:13-16. Ps 112:7-

10. 2 Th 3:3. **for ever.** Heb. *netsach,* Jb +4:20.

8. **if.** Jb 13:27. 19:6. 33:18, 19. Ps 18:5. 107:10. 116:3. La 3:9. **cords.** Pr 5:22.

9. **he showeth.** T#347. Jb 10:2. Ge +6:3. Dt 4:21, 22. 2 Ch *33:11-13. Ps *94:12. *119:67, 71. La 3:39, 40. Lk 15:17-19. Jn 16:7, 8. 1 C 11:32. **their.** Ps 5:10. Is 59:12. Ezk 18:28-31. Ro 5:20. 1 T 1:15.

10. **openeth.** ver. 15. Jb 33:16-23. Ps 40:6. Is *48:8, 17. 50:5. Ac 16:14. **commandeth.** Dt *4:30, 31. Pr 1:22, 23. 8:4, 5. 9:4-6. Is *1:16-20. √55:6, 7. Je 4:3, 4. 7:3-7. Ezk 18:30, 31. Ho 14:1. Mt 3:8. Ac 3:19. 17:30. Ja 4:8.

11. **If they obey.** Jb *22:21. Dt 4:30, 31, +*40. Is *1:19, 20. Je *7:23. *26:13. Jn +*13:17. Ro *6:17. He *5:7, 9. *11:8. **spend.** Jb *11:13-19. *21:11-13. *22:23-25. *42:12. Ec 9:2, 3. Ja *5:5. Re 18:7. **prosperity.** 2 Ch *20:20. Ps 122:6. **pleasures.** or, pleasantness. or, pleasant places. Ps +*16:6, 11.

12. **if.** Dt *18:15, etc. 29:15-20. Is *1:19, 20. *3:11. Ro *2:8, 9. **perish.** Heb. pass away. Jb 6:15. 14:5. 19:8. 34:20. Ps 37:36. **sword.** Jb 33:18. 2 Ch 23:10. 32:5mg. **die.** Jb 4:21. Ge +49:33 (☀S#1478h). **without knowledge.** Ps +49:20. Jn *8:21-24.

13. **heap.** Nu 32:14. 2 Ch *28:13, 22. Ro *2:5. **they.** Jb 15:4. 27:8-10. 35:9, 10. Mt 22:12, 13. **bindeth.** ver. 8. Ps 107:10.

14. **They.** or, Their soul. Heb. *nephesh,* Nu +23:10. √171Q2, Nu +23:10. **die.** Jb 15:32. 21:23-25. 22:16. Ge 38:7-10. Le 10:1, 2. Ps *55:23. **unclean.** or, sodomites. Ge 19:5, 24, 25. Dt 23:17mg. 2 K 23:7.

15. **delivereth.** ver. 6. **poor.** or, afflicted. ver. 6. Jb 34:28. Ps 102:17. **openeth.** ver. 10. 2 Ch 12:8.

16. **broad place.** Jb 19:8. 38:18. 42:10-17. Ps 18:19. *31:7, 8. 40:1-3. *118:5. **that which should be set on thy table.** Heb. the rest of thy table. Jb 17:16. Pr 29:9. **full.** Ps *23:5. 36:8. 63:5. Is 25:6. 55:2.

17. **fulfilled.** Jb 15:5. 34:8, 36. Ps *9:4, 5, 7, 8. Ro 1:32. Re 18:4. **take hold on thee.** or, should uphold thee. Ge *48:17. Ex *17:12.

18. **Because.** Ps *2:5, 12. *110:5. Is √55:6. Mt *3:7. Lk 16:26. Ro *1:18. *2:5. Ep *5:6. He *2:3. *9:27. **wrath.** Is 66:16, 24. Jn +*3:36. **take thee away.** Jb 16:22. Ps 102:24. Ec +*7:17. Is +*38:10. **his.** Ps 39:10. Is *14:6. Ezk *24:16. **then.** Jb *33:24. Ps *49:7. 1 T *2:6. He *2:3. 10:26. **cannot.** Jb +*8:13. Is +*38:18. He +*9:27. **deliver thee.** Heb. turn thee aside. Jb 23:11 (declined). 24:4. Pr +10:28. 21:1.

19. **Will.** Pr 10:2. 11:4. Is 2:20. Zp 1:18. Ja +*5:3, 4. **nor all.** Jb 9:13. 34:20. Ps 33:16, 17. Pr *11:21. Is *37:36. **forces.** Is 60:5.

20. **Desire not.** Jb 3:20, 21. 6:9. 7:15. +*14:13. *34:20. Je *17:16. Am *5:18. **the night.** Jb +*10:21. 17:13, 14. 27:20. Jn *9:4. **cut off.** Ex 12:29. 2 K 19:35. Pr +*14:32. Ec 11:3. Da 5:30. Lk *12:20. Ac 1:25. 1 Th *5:2, 3.

21. **regard not iniquity.** Ps √66:18. Ezk 14:4. Mt 5:29, 30. **hast thou chosen.** Is ☾+*66:4. **affliction.** Jb 34:7-9. 35:3. Da 3:16-18. 6:10. Mt 13:21. 16:24. Ac 5:40, 41. He *11:25. 1 P 3:17. 4:15, 16.

22. **God.** 1 S 2:7, 8. Ps 75:7. Is 14:5. Je 27:5-8. Da 4:25, 32. 5:18. Lk 1:52. Ro 13:1. **who teacheth.** Jb 32:8, 9. Ps *32:8. 94:10, 12. Pr 4:11. Is 48:17. 54:13. Je 31:33. Jn *6:45.

23. **Who hath.** Jb 34:13-33. Is 40:13, 14. Ro 11:34. 1 C 2:16. Ep +*1:11. **Thou.** Jb 8:3. 34:10. 40:8. Ro 2:5. 3:5. 9:14.

24. **magnify.** Jb 12:13, etc. 26:5-14. Ps 28:5. *34:3. 72:18. 86:8-10. 92:4, 5. 104:24. 107:8, 15. 111:2-4, 8. 139:5, 6, 14. 145:10-12. Je 10:12, 13. Da 4:3, 37. Lk 1:46-55. 1 T +1:17. Re 15:3-5. **which.** Dt 4:19. Ps *19:1-4. Ac 14:17. Ro 1:19-21.

25. **may behold.** Jb 6:19. 28:24. 35:5. 39:29.

26. **God.** Jb 37:5. Ps 145:3. 147:5. **we.** Jb 11:7-9. 26:14. 37:5, 23. 1 K 8:27. Mt +*11:27. Jn 17:25, 26. 1 C 13:12. **neither.** Ps *90:2. *102:24-27. He 1:12. 2 P 3:8. **his years.** ♪22D4A. Anthropomorphism B893. Circumstances as to time are attributed to God; here, years are attributed to God. For other instances of this figure see Ps 102:24, 27.

27. **he.** Jb 5:9, 10. 38:25-28, 34. Ge 2:5, 6. Ps 65:9-13. 147:8. Is 5:6. Je 14:22. **pour.** Heb. *zaqaq*, ✱S#2212h. Kal, Future: Jb 28:1 (fine). 36:27. Piel, Preterite: Ml 3:3 (purge). Pual, Participle: 1 Ch 28:18 (refined). 29:4. Ps 12:6 (purified). Is 25:6 (well refined). **the vapor.** ver. 33. Ps 148:8.

28. **the clouds.** Jb 37:11-13. Ge 7:11, 12. Pr *3:20.

29. **the spreadings.** Jb 37:16. 38:9, 37. 1 K 18:44, 45. Ps 104:3. **the noise.** Jb 37:2-5. Ps 18:13. 29:3-10. 77:16-19. 104:7. Na 1:3. Hab 3:10.

30. **he.** Jb 38:25, 34, 35. Lk 17:24. **and.** Jb 38:8-11. Ge 1:9. Ex 14:22, 28. 15:4, 5. Ps 18:11-16. 104:5-9. **bottom.** Heb. roots. Jb 8:17. 9:8. 13:27mg. 14:8. 18:16. Ge 1:9.

31. **by them.** Jb 37:13. 38:22, 23. Ge *6:17. 7:17-24. 19:24. Ex *9:23-25. *14:26, 27. Dt 8:2, 15. Jsh *10:11. 1 S 2:10. 7:10. 12:18. **he giveth.** Jb 38:26, 27. Ps 65:9-13. 104:13-15, *27, 28. 136:25. Pr 31:15. Mt +24:45. Ac *14:17.

32. **With clouds.** Perhaps these difficult verses should be rendered, "He covereth the concave with lightning, and chargeth it what it shall strike. Its noise declareth concerning him; a magazine of wrath against iniquity." Jb 26:9. Ex 10:21-23. Ps 18:11. 135:7. 147:8, 9. 148:8. Ac 27:20. For "clouds," Young renders "two palms." Jb 2:7 (sole). 1 K 18:44. 1 Ch *12:2. **covered.** ver. 30. Jb 9:24. 15:27. 16:18. 21:26. **the light.** Jb 31:26. *37:3. Ps 136:7. **commandeth.** Jb 37:12. 38:12. **cometh betwixt.** lit. striking against. Jb 37:11, 12, 15. Ps *18:14. 29:7. Is 59:16h (intercessor).

33. **noise.** ver. 29. Jb 37:2. 2 S 22:14. 1 K *18:41-45. **the cattle.** Je 14:4-6. Jl 1:18. 2:22. **the vapor.** Heb. that which goeth up. ver. 27.

JOB 37

Elihu extols the power of God shown in thunder and lightning, snow, rain, whirlwinds, and frost, 1-13. His works in these things are inexplicable, 14-22. His perfections should impress men with lowly fear, 23, 24.

1. **my heart.** Jb 4:14. 21:6. 38:1. Ex 19:16. Ps *89:7. 119:120. Je *5:22. Da 10:7, 8. Hab 3:16. Mt 28:2-4. Ac 16:26, 29.

2. **Hear attentively.** Heb. Hear in hearing. ♪147B, Ge +2:16. Jb 32:10. Dt √28:1, 2, ◑15. Mt 11:15. 13:9. Mk +*4:24. Lk +*8:18. +√11:28. √16:31. **the noise.** ver. 5. Jb 36:29, 33. 38:1. Ex 19:16-19. Ps 29:3. 104:7.

3. **He.** Ps 77:13. 97:4. Mt 24:27. Re 11:19. **lightning.** Heb. light. Jb 36:32. **ends.** Heb. wings. Jb 38:13mg. Is 11:12mg. +24:16mg.

4. **a voice.** Ps 29:3-9. 68:33. **the voice.** Ex 15:7, 8. Dt 33:26. **he will.** Jb 36:27-33.

5. **thundereth.** 2 S 22:14, 15. Ps *68:32, 33. **great.**

Jb 5:9. 9:10. 11:7. 26:14. 36:26. Ec 3:11. Is 40:21, 22, 28. Ro 11:33. Re 15:3.

6. **he saith.** Jb 38:22. Ps *147:16-18. 148:8. **likewise to the small,** etc. Heb. and to the shower of rain, and to the showers of rain of his strength. Jb 36:27. **great rain.** Ge 7:10-12. Ezr 10:9, 13. Pr 28:3. Ezk 13:11, 13. Am 9:6. Mt 7:25-27.

7. **He sealeth.** Jb 5:12. 9:7. 33:16, 17. **that.** Jb 36:24. Ps 46:8. 64:9. 92:4. *109:26, 27. *111:2. Ec 8:17. Is 5:12. 26:11.

8. **the beasts.** Ps *104:22.

9. **south.** Heb. chamber. Jb 9:9. Ge 43:30. Ps 104:3. **the whirlwind.** Jb 38:1. Is *21:1. Zc 9:14. **north.** Heb. scattering *winds*. Jb 38:32. Ps 18:15. 147:17, 18.

10. **breath.** Heb. *neshamah*, Jb 4:9. 32:8. 33:4. Ge +2:7. **frost.** Jb 6:16. 38:29, 30. Ge 31:40. Ps 78:47. 147:16-18. **breadth.** Ge 6:15. 13:17. Ex 25:10.

11. **he wearieth.** Jb 36:27, 28. **he scattereth.** Jb 36:30, 32. Is 18:4. Mt 17:5. **his bright cloud.** Heb. the cloud of his light. Jb 36:32.

12. **it is turned.** Ps 65:9, 10. 104:24. Je 14:22. Jl 2:23. Am 4:7. **that.** Ps *148:8. Ja 5:17, 18. Re 11:6. **face.** Ge +1:2.

13. **whether.** ver. 6. Jb 36:31. 38:37, 38. Ex *9:18-25. 1 S *12:18, 19. Ezr 10:9. **correction.** Heb. a rod. Jb 9:34. 21:9. Ge 49:10. **for his land.** Jb 38:26, 27. **for mercy.** 2 S 21:10, 14. 1 K 18:45. Jl *2:23.

14. **stand.** Ex 14:13. Ps *46:10. Hab *2:20. **consider.** Jb 26:6-14. 36:24. Ps 111:2. 145:5, 6, 10-12.

15. **Dost.** Jb 28:24-27. 34:14. 38:4, etc. Ps 119:90, 91. Is 40:26. **the light.** ver. 11. Jb 36:30-32. 38:24, 25.

16. **the balancings.** Jb 26:8. 36:29. Ps 104:2, 3. Is 40:22. Je 10:13. **clouds.** Ge +9:13. **perfect.** Jb 36:4. 1 S *2:3. Ps 104:24. 147:5. Pr *3:19, 20. Je *10:12, 13.

17. **he quieteth.** Jb 6:17. 38:31. Ps 94:13. 147:18. Is 30:15. Lk 12:55. **south.** Dt 33:23. Ec 1:6. 11:3.

18. **spread.** Jb 9:8, 9. Ge 1:6-8. Ps 104:2. 148:4-6. 150:1. Pr 8:27. Is 40:12, 22. *44:24. **as.** Ex 38:8.

19. **Teach.** Jb 12:3. 13:3, 6. Lk *11:1. **we.** Jb 26:14. 28:20, 21. 38:2. 42:3. Ps 73:16, 17, 22. 139:6. Pr 30:2-4. Ro *8:26. 1 C *13:12. 1 J 3:2.

20. **Shall it.** Ps 139:4. Mt 12:36, 37. **surely.** Jb 6:3. 11:7, 8. Ec *5:2.

21. **see not.** Jb 26:9. 36:32. 38:25. **light.** ♪121N2, Ge +34:29.

22. **Fair.** Heb. Gold. Jb 28:1-6. **weather.** Ge +9:14. Pr 25:23. **with God.** Jb 40:10. 1 Ch 29:11. Ps 29:4. 66:5. 68:7, 8. 76:12. 93:1. 104:1. 145:5. Is *2:10, 19. Mi 5:4. Na 1:3. Hab 3:3, etc. He *1:3. *12:29. Ju 25.

23. **we cannot.** ver. 19. Jb 11:7. 23:3. 26:14. 36:26. Pr *30:3, 4. Ec *3:11. Is √10:22. Ro 11:33. 1 C *2:11. 1 T *6:16. **excellent.** Jb 9:4, 19. 12:13. 36:5. Ps 62:11. 65:6. 66:3. 93:1. 99:4. 146:6, 7. Is 28:29. 45:21. Mt *6:13. **in judgment.** Ps 36:5-7. **he will.** Jb 16:7-17. Ps 30:5. ◐+*90:15. ◐+√119:75. La *3:32, 33. He *12:10.

24. **fear.** Ps *130:4. Je 32:39. 33:9. Ho 3:5. Mt +*10:28. Lk 12:4, 5. Ro 2:4. 11:20-22. **he respecteth.** Jb 5:13. Ec 9:11. Is 5:21. Mt *11:25, 26. Lk *10:21. 1 C *1:26. 3:19.

JOB 38

The Lord, out of the whirlwind, challenges Job to answer him, 1-3. By enumerating several of his mighty works in creation and providence, he convinces Job of ignorance: the foundation and measures of the earth, 4-6; the stars; the sea, and its bounds, 7-11; the morning, and its light, 12-15; the depth of the sea; the gates and shadow of death; the breadth of the earth, 16-18; the place of light and darkness; the treasures of snow and hail for battle, 19-23; the east wind, springs, and rain for the earth, 24-30; the planets, ordinances of heaven, and their dominion on the earth; clouds and lightning, 31-35. Wisdom and understanding in the heart of man, and in his works more than we can understand; he feedeth the lion and the raven; thus God convinces Job of weakness, 36-41.

1. **the Lord.** or, Jehovah. Jb 1:6. 2:1. **out of.** Jb 37:1, 2, 9, 14. 40:6. Ex 19:16-19. Dt 4:11, 12. 5:22-24. 1 K 19:11. 2 K 2:1, 11. Ezk 1:4. Na 1:3. He 12:18.

2. **darkeneth counsel.** Jb 5:13. 12:3, 13. 23:4, 5. 24:25. 26:3. 27:11. 34:35. 35:16. 42:3. Ro 1:22. 1 T *1:7.

3. **Gird.** Jb 40:7. Ex 12:11. 1 K 18:46. Je 1:17. 1 P 1:13. **for.** Jb 13:15, 22. 23:3-7. 31:35-37. **answer thou me.** Heb. make me know. Jb 40:7. 42:4.

4. **Where.** *60A, Ge +3:22. Pr 8:22, 29, 30. 30:4. **when I laid.** Ge *1:1. 2:4. Ps *102:25. 104:5. He *1:2, 10. **hast.** Heb. knowest.

5. **laid.** Jb 11:9. *28:25. Pr 8:27. Is *40:12, 22. **who hath stretched.** Ps *19:4. 78:55. Is 34:11. Zc 2:1, 2. 2 C *10:16.

6. **Whereupon.** Jb √26:7. 1 S *2:8. Ps 24:2. *93:1. *104:5. Zc 12:1. 2 P 3:5. **foundations.** Heb. sockets. Ex 26:18-25. **fastened.** Heb. made to sink. Pr 8:25. Je 38:22. **or who laid.** Ps *118:22. 144:12. Is *28:16. Ep *2:20, 21.

7. **the morning stars.** Jb 3:9. 9:7. 22:12. 25:5. Re *2:28. *22:16. **sang.** *155D, Ge +4:10. Le 9:24. Ps 35:27. **the sons.** *108H11, Ge +6:2. **of God.** *24L, Jb *1:6. 2:1. Ge +6:2. 6:4. Ps *104:4. Re 5:11. **shouted.** Jb 30:5. Ezr 3:11, 12. Zc 4:7.

8. **who.** ver. 10. Ge 1:9. Ps 33:7. 104:9. Pr 8:29. Je *5:22. **out.** ver. 29.

9. **thick.** Ge 1:2. **thick.** Jb 22:13. Ex 20:21. **darkness.** Ge 1:2, 5, 18. 15:12, 17. Ex 20:21. 2 S 22:10, 12. 1 K 8:12. Ps 18:9, 11. 97:2. *104:20. Is 45:7. Jn 12:35. **swaddlingband.** Ezk 16:4.

10. **brake up for it my decreed place.** *or*, established my decree upon it. Jb 26:10. Ge 1:9, 10. 9:15. Ps 104:9. Je 5:22.

11. **Hitherto,** etc. or, Thus far shall thy flux and reflux extend. The tides are marvellously limited and regulated, not only by the lunar and solar attraction, but by the quantum of time required to remove any part of the earth's surface by its rotation round its axis, from under the immediate attractive influence of the sun and moon. Hence the attraction of the sun and moon and the gravitation of the sea to its own center, which prevent too great a flux on the one hand and too great reflux on the other, are some of those bars and doors by which "its proud waves are stayed," and prevented from coming farther. Ps 65:6, 7. 93:3, 4. Pr 8:29. Mk *4:39-41. **but.** Jb 1:12. 2:6. Ps 76:10. *89:9. Is 27:8. Lk 8:32, 33. Re 20:2, 3, 7, 8. **thy proud waves.** Heb. the pride of thy waves. Jb 35:12. Ps 42:7. Pr 21:24mg.

12. **commanded.** Ge 1:5. Ps *74:16. 136:7, 8. 148:3-5. **since.** ver. 4, 21. Jb 8:9. 15:7. **the dayspring.** Jb 3:9. 41:18. Ge 19:15. Ps 74:16. Am 5:8. Lk *1:78. 2 P *1:19.

13. **take.** Ps 19:4-6. 139:9-12. **ends.** Heb. wings. Jb 37:3mg. 39:13. **the wicked.** Jb 24:13-17. Ex 14:27. Ps *104:21, 22, 35.

14. **turned.** Jb 37:12. **clay.** Jb 4:19. 10:9. 13:12. 27:16. **seal.** Jb 41:15. Ge 38:18. Ex 28:11. **they stand.** Jb 1:6. 2:1. **as a garment.** Ps 104:2, 6.

15. **from.** Jb 5:14. 18:5, 18. Ex 10:21-23. 2 K 6:18. Pr 4:19. *13:9. Is 8:21, 22. Je *13:16. Ac 13:10, 11. **the high.** Ps 10:15. 37:17. Ezk *30:22.

16. **the springs.** Ps *77:19. Pr 8:24. Je 51:36. **walked.** Jb 26:5, 6.

17. **the gates.** *171S7B, Ge +14:7. Ps 9:13. 107:18. 116:3. Is 38:10. Mt *16:18. **opened.** Ge 35:7. 1 S 2:27. Re *1:18. **the shadow of death.** Jb 3:5. 10:21, 22. 12:22. 16:16. 28:3. Ps *23:4. 44:19. 107:10, 14. Je 13:16. Am 5:8. Mt 4:16. Lk 1:79.

18. **the breadth.** Ps 74:17. 89:11, 12. Is 40:28. Je 31:37. Re 20:9.

19. **the way.** ver. 12, 13. Ge 1:3, 4, 14-18. Dt 4:19. Is *45:7. Jn 1:9. *8:12. **where.** *63I2, Jsh +3:3. Supply ellipsis (of repetition: from succeeding clause B105), "Where (is) the way (to the place where) light dwelleth? and (as for) darkness, where (is) the place thereof?" **light.** Da 2:22. **darkness.** Ps 18:11. 104:20. 105:28. Je 13:16. Ezk 32:8. Am 4:13. Mt 27:45.

20. **it to.** *or*, it at. **the bound.** Ge 10:19. 23:17.

21. **because thou.** ver. 4, 12. Jb 11:12. 15:7.

22. **the treasures.** *121.O, Ge +28:22. Dt 28:12. 32:34. Jsh 6:19. 1 K 7:51. 14:26. 15:18. Ne 13:12mg. Ps 33:7. 135:7. Je 10:13. Ml 3:10. **snow.** Jb 6:16. 9:30. 24:19. 37:6. Ps 33:7. 135:7. **treasures.** *121.O, Ge +28:22. **hail.** Ex *9:18, 19, 22, 23, 24, 25. Jsh *10:11. Ps 18:13. 77:17. 78:47mg. 105:32. 148:8. Is 28:2. *30:30. 32:19. Ezk 13:11. 38:22. Re 8:7. 11:19. 16:21.

23. **Which I.** Jb 36:31. 37:13. Ex 9:18, 24. Jsh 10:11. Is 30:30. Ezk 13:11-13. Mt 7:27. Re 16:21. **reserved.** Jb 7:11. 16:5, 6. **the time.** 2 S +*11:1n. 1 Ch +*12:32. *20:1. Ec +*3:8. **of trouble.** or, distress. Jb 6:23. 7:11. 15:24. 16:9. Je *30:7. **battle.** 2 S 17:11. Ps 55:18. **war.** Jb 5:20. 39:25. 41:8.

24. **the light.** ver. 12, 13. Jon 4:8. Mt 24:27.

25. **divided.** Jb 28:26. 36:27, 28. 37:3-6. Ps 29:3-10. 55:9. **watercourse.** or, conduit. *S#8585h. 1 K 18:32, 35, 38. 2 K 18:17n. 20:20. Is 7:3. 36:2. Je 30:13 (healing). 46:11 (cured). Ezk 31:4mg. **overflowing.** Ps 32:6. Pr 27:4mg. **lightning.** *S#2385h. Jb 28:26. Zc 10:1mg. For *S#1300h, see on ver. +35. For *S#3940h, see Jb +41:19.

26. **To cause.** It is well known that rain falls copiously in thunderstorms. The flash is first seen, the clap is next heard, and last the rain descends; though in fact they all take place at the same time. The lightning traverses all space in no perceivable succession of time. Sound is propagated at the rate of 1142 feet in a second. Rain travels still more slowly, and will be seen sooner or later according to the weight of the drops, and the distance of the cloud. Now as water is composed of two elastic airs or gases, called oxygen and hydrogen, in the proportion of 88 1/4 of the former and 11 3/4 of the latter in 100 parts, the electric spark, or matter of lightning, passing through the atmosphere, ignites and decomposes those gases, which explode; and the water falls down in the form of rain. This explosion, as well as the rushing in of the circumambient air to restore the equilibrium, will account for the clap and peal; and thus by the lightning of thunder God causes

it to rain on the earth. **on the wilderness.** Ps 104:10-14. *107:35. 147:8, 9. Is 35:1, 2. 41:18, 19. *43:19, 20. Je 14:22. He 6:7, 8.

28. **Hath the.** ver. 8. Jb 5:9, 10. 1 S 12:17, 18. Ps 65:9, 10. *147:7, 8. Je 5:24. 10:13. 14:22. Jl 2:23. Am 4:7. Mt *5:45. **dew.** Jb 29:19. Ge 27:28, 39. Ex 16:13. Dt 33:13, 28. 2 S 1:21. 1 K 17:1. Pr 3:20. Ho 14:5.

29. **Out of.** ver. 8. Jb 6:16. 37:10. Ge 31:40. Ps *147:16, 17. **hoary frost.** Ex 16:14. 1 Ch 28:17 (bason). Ps 147:16.

30. **the face.** Jb 37:10. **frozen.** Heb. taken. Jb 41:17.

31. **bind.** Jb 39:10. 41:5. Ge 38:28. **sweet influences.** Ge 49:20. 1 S 15:32. Pr 29:17. La 4:5. **Pleiades.** or, the seven stars. Heb. Cimah. Jb +9:9mg. Am 5:8. **loose.** or, open. Jb 12:18. 30:11. 39:5. 41:14. **Orion.** or, Cesil. Jb +9:9. Am *5:8.

32. **Mazzaroth.** or, the twelve signs. Jb 37:9. i.e. *Great Bear; scatterings,* *S#4216h. Probably the same as *mazzaloth,* 2 K 23:5mg. **season.** ver. +23h. **guide Arcturus.** Heb. guide them. Jb +9:9.

33. **the ordinances.** T#240. Ge 1:16. 8:22. 26:5. Ex 12:14. Ps *119:90, 91. Pr 3:19. Je +*31:35, 36. *33:25, 26. **canst.** ver. 12, 13.

34. **Canst thou.** 1 S *12:18. Am 5:8. Zc *10:1. Ja *5:18. **clouds.** Jb 20:6. 22:14. Ge +9:13. **abundance.** Jb 22:11. 2 K 9:17. Is 60:6. Ezk 26:10. **cover.** Jb 9:24. 16:18. 21:26. 22:11. Ps 69:1, 2. 124:4. La 3:54.

35. **Canst.** Ex 9:23-25, 29. Le 10:2. Nu 11:1. 16:35. 2 K 1:10, 14. Re 11:5, 6. **lightnings.** *S#1300h. Jb 20:25. Ex 19:16. Dt 32:41 (glittering; lit. the lightning). 2 S 22:15. Ps 18:14. 77:18. 97:4. 135:7. 144:6. Je 10:13. 51:16. Ezk 1:13. 21:10 (glitter), 15, 28. Da 10:6. Na 2:4. 3:3mg. Hab 3:11. Zc 9:14. For *S#2385h, see on ver. +25. **Here we are.** Heb. Behold us. Jb 22:1mg. 1 S 22:12. Is 6:8mg. 65:1.

36. **Who hath put.** Jb 32:8. Ps 51:6. Pr *2:6. Ec *2:26. Ja *1:5, 17. **inward parts.** Ps 51:6. **who hath given.** Ex 31:3. 36:1, 2. Is *28:26.

37. **number.** Jb 12:8. 14:16. 15:17. Ge 15:5. Ps *147:4. **clouds.** Ge +9:13. **or who.** Ge *8:1, 2. 9:15. **stay.** Heb. cause to lie down. 2 S 8:2. 1 K 3:20. **bottles.** 1 S 1:24. 10:3. 25:18n. Je +*13:12n.

38. **groweth into hardness.** or, is turned into mire. Heb. is poured. Jb 22:16. 1 K 22:35. 2 K *3:11. 4:40. 9:6. Is 44:3. **clods.** Jb 21:33. **cleave.** Jb 41:17.

39. **Wilt thou.** Jb 4:10, 11. Ps 34:10. *104:21. *145:15, 16. **appetite.** Heb. life. or, desire. Jb 3:20. 7:7. 33:20.

40. **they couch.** Jb 9:3. Ge 49:9. Nu 23:24. 24:9. Ps 10:10. **dens.** Jb 37:8. Dt 33:27. Ps 76:2. **covert.** or, thicket. Jb 27:18. 36:29. Ge 33:17.

41. **Who provideth.** Jb 11:13. Ps *104:27, 28. *147:9. Mt *6:26. Lk *12:24. **raven.** Ge 8:7. Le 11:15. Lk *12:24. **his food.** or, provision. lit. "hunting," as in Ge 10:9. **young ones.** Jb 21:11. 39:3. Ge 4:23. **cry.** Jb 19:7. 24:12. 30:20, 28. **wander.** Ge 21:14. 37:15. Ex 23:4.

JOB 39

God shows his own power and man's weakness and ignorance by drawing examples from among the animals: the wild goats and hinds, 1-4; the wild ass, 5-8; the unicorn, 9-12; the peacock, stork and ostrich, 13-18; the war horse, 19-25; the hawk, 26; and eagle, 27-30. These creatures, neither fully known to Job nor

governed by him, are sufficient to convince him that he is no fit judge of the counsels of God.

1. **the wild goats.** 1 S 24:2. Ps 104:18. **when the hinds.** Ps *29:9. Je 14:5.

2. **number the months.** Je 2:24.

3. **bow.** Jb 31:10. Ge 49:9. **young ones.** Jb 21:11. 38:41. Ge 4:23. **bring forth.** lit. "cleave." Jb 16:13. 2 K 4:39. **cast out.** Jb 8:4. 12:15. 14:20. **sorrows.** or, pangs. Jb 18:10 (snare). 21:17. 36:8 (cords). 41:1 (cord). 2 S 22:6. 1 Ch 16:18mg. Ps 16:6 (lines).

5. **the wild ass.** Jb 6:5. 11:12. 24:5. Ge 16:12. Ps 104:11. Is 32:14. Je *2:23, 24. 14:6. Da 5:21. Ho *8:9. The *paire,* Arabic *fara,* Gr. *onos angros,* onager, or wild ass, is a taller and much more dignified animal than the common ass; its legs are more elegantly shaped; bears its head higher; is distinguished by a dusky, woolly mane; long erect ears; forehead highly arched; hair generally silvery white; upper part of the face, sides of the neck, and upper part of the thighs flaxen; fore-part of the body divided from the flank by a white line extending round the rump to the tail; a stripe of waved, coffee colored, bushy hair along the top of the back; another stripe of the same crossing the former at the shoulders; and two beautiful white lines, which bound the dorsal band and mane. They are found in various parts of the East and run so swiftly that they cannot be taken except by successive relays. **who hath loosed.** Ge 49:14.

6. **barren land.** Heb. salt places. Dt 29:23. Ps 107:34mg. Je 17:6. Ezk 47:11.

7. **scorneth.** ver. 18. Jb 3:18. Is 31:4. **driver.** Heb. exactor. Ex 5:13-16, 18. Is 58:3.

8. **The range.** Jb 40:15, 20-22. Ge 1:29, 30. Ps 104:27, 28. 145:15, 16.

9. **the unicorn.** Hebrew *reem,* the wild ox now extinct, distinguished from the common ox, by having a flatter forehead and large horns with double curvature. Nu 23:22. Dt 33:17. Ps *22:21. 92:10. **or abide.** Is 1:3.

10. **bind.** ver. 5, 7. Jb 1:14. 41:5. Ps 129:3. Ho 10:10, 11. Mi 1:13.

11. **trust.** Ps *20:7. 33:16, 17. 147:10. Is 30:16. 31:1-3. **leave.** Ge 1:26, 28. 9:2. 42:26. Ps 144:14. Pr 14:4. Is 30:6. 46:1.

12. **that he.** Ne 13:15. Am 2:13. **gather.** Pr 3:10. Hg 2:19. Mt 3:2. 13:30.

13. **Gavest.** √63B, Ge +25:28. **peacocks.** 1 K 10:22. 2 Ch 9:21. **wings and feathers unto the.** or, the feathers of the stork and. Jb 30:29mg. Le 11:19. Ps 104:17. Je 8:7. Zc 5:9.

14. **eggs.** Dt 22:6. Is 10:14. 59:5. **in dust.** Jb 20:11.

15. **crush.** Is 59:5. **break them.** Da 7:23.

16. **hardened.** La *4:3. **as though.** Dt 28:56, 57. 1 K 3:26, 27. 2 K 6:28, 29. La 2:20. Ro 1:31. **her labor.** Ec 10:15. Hab 2:13.

17. **deprived.** Jb 17:4. 35:11. Dt 2:30. 2 Ch 32:31. Is 19:11-14. 57:17. Je +*8:7. Ja 1:17.

18. **she scorneth.** ver. 7, 22. Jb 5:22. 41:29. 2 K 19:21.

19. **the horse.** Ex 15:1, 21. Ps 147:10. Pr 21:31. **clothed.** Ps 93:1. 104:1. **thunder.** √102, ver. 25. Ge +2:24. ver. 25. Mk 3:17.

20. **the glory.** Jb 41:20, 21. Je 8:16. **terrible.** Heb. terrors. Jb 9:34. 13:21. 18:11. 20:25.

21. **He paweth.** or, His feet dig. Jg 5:22. **and rejoiceth.** 1 S 17:4-10, 42. Ps 19:5. Je 9:23. **he goeth.**

Pr 21:31. Je 8:6. **armed men.** Heb. armor. Jb 20:24. 1 K 10:25.

22. **mocketh.** ver. 16, 18. Jb 41:33. Je *8:6.

23. **The quiver.** Jb 41:26-29. Ps 127:5. Is 22:6. 49:2. Je 5:16. La 3:13.

24. **He swalloweth.** Jb 37:20. Hab 1:8, 9. **neither.** Jb 9:16. 29:24. Lk 24:41.

25. **Ha, ha.** Ps 35:21, 25. 40:15. 70:3. Is 44:16. Ezk 25:3. 26:2. 36:2.

26. **the hawk.** *Netz,* Arabic *naz,* Latin *nisus,* the hawk, so called from *natzah,* to "shoot away, fly," because of the rapidity of its flight; whence Homer (*Iliad.* l. xv. v. 238) calls it "the swiftest of birds." It probably comprehends various species of the falcon family, as the ger-falcon, goshhawk, and sparrowhawk. Le 11:16. Dt 14:15. **stretch.** Is it through thy teaching that the falcon, or any other bird of passage, knows the precise time for taking flight, and the direction in which she is to go to arrive at a warmer climate? SS 2:12. Je 8:7. **south.** Jb 9:9. Ex 26:18, 35. 27:9.

27. **the eagle.** Jb 9:26. Ex 19:4. Le 11:13n. Ps 103:5n. Pr 23:5. Is 40:31. La 4:19n. Ho 8:1. **at thy command.** Heb. by thy mouth. Ge 45:21. **make.** Je *49:16. Ob 4. Hab 2:9. **nest.** Jb 29:18. Ge 6:14mg. Nu 24:21. **on high.** Jb 38:34. Ge 14:22. 31:45.

28. **dwell.** Jb 3:5. 4:19. **abideth.** Ps 91:1, 2. **rock.** ver. 1. **upon.** 1 S 14:4. **crag.** or, tooth. Jb 4:10. 13:14. 16:9. 19:20. 1 S 14:5mg. **strong place.** 1 S 22:4, 5. 24:22.

29. **she seeketh.** Jb 9:26. **her eyes.** The *eagle* is proverbial for her strong and clear sight. Hence Homer (*Iliad.* xvii. 676) calls her "the most quick-sighted of birds under heaven." **eyes behold.** Jb 6:19. 28:24.

30. **young ones.** or, brood. Dt 22:6. Ps 84:3. **where the slain.** Jb 24:12. Ge 34:27. Le 21:7 (profane). Ezk +*39:17-19. Mt *24:28. Lk *17:37.

JOB 40

God calls on Job to answer, 1, 2. Job humbles himself, and will proceed no further, 3-5. God requires him to show by acts of power that he is able to save himself, 6-14. The power of the Lord is shown in behemoth, 15-24.

1. **the Lord answered.** ver. 6. Jb 38:1.

2. **Shall.** ꟼ85C, Jb 9:3. 33:13. Ge +18:14. Ec 6:10. Is *45:9-11. 50:8. 1 C *10:22. **instruct.** Is 40:14. 1 C 2:16. **he that reproveth.** Jb 3:11, 12, 20, 23. 7:12, 19-21. 9:17, 18, 32-35. 10:3-7, 14-17. 13:21-27. 14:16, 17. 16:11-21. 19:6-11. 27:2. 30:21-23. Ezk 18:2, 25. Mt 20:11-15. Ro 9:19-23. *11:34-36.

4. **Behold.** Jb *42:6. Ge 18:27. *32:10. 2 S *24:10. 1 K 19:4. Ezr 9:*6, 15. Ne 9:33. Ps *51:4, 5. Is *6:5. √53:6. √64:6. Da 9:*5, 7. Lk *5:8. *15:18, 19, 21. *18:13. 1 T *1:15. **I am vile.** SS ◐1:15. ◐4:7. **what.** ꟼ85C, Ge +18:14. Jb 9:31-35. 16:21. *23:4-7. 31:37. **I will.** T#30. Jb 21:5. 29:9. Jg 10:15 (T#356). 18:19. Ps 39:9. 102:3-7. Pr 28:13 (T#124). *30:32. Mi 7:16. Hab √2:20. Zc 2:13. 2 C 7:10 (T#603). **lay.** ꟻ121S3N, Jg +18:19.

5. **once.** Jb 5:19. *33:14, 29. Ps *62:11. Pr 6:16. 30:15, 18, 21, 29. Ec 11:2. Am 1:3, 6, 9, 11, 13. 2:1, 4, 6. Mi 5:5. This use of numbers often signifies not the literal number, but is a figurative way of saying "many." Jb 19:3. 1 S 1:8n. Ne 4:12. **but I will not.**

Jb *34:31, 32. Ro *3:19. **twice.** Jb 33:14. 2 K 6:10. Ps *62:11. **but I will proceed.** Je 31:18, 19.

6. **out of the whirlwind.** Jb 38:1. Ps 50:3, 4. He 12:18-20. 2 P 3:10-12.

7. **Gird.** Jb 13:22. 23:3, 4. 38:3. Ps 18:32n. **I will.** Jb 42:4.

8. **Wilt.** Ps 51:4. Ro *3:4. **disannul.** Is *14:27. 28:18. Ga 3:15, 17. He 7:18. **wilt thou condemn.** Jb 10:3. 27:2-6. 32:2. 34:5, 6. 35:2, 3.

9. **Hast.** Jb 9:4. 23:6. 33:12, 13. Ex 15:6. Ps 89:10, 13. Is 45:9. 1 C 10:22. **arm.** ꟻ22A12, Ex +15:16. **canst.** Jb 37:4, 5. Ps 39:3-9.

10. **Deck.** Jb 39:19. Ps 93:1. 104:1, 2. Is 59:17. **majesty.** 1 Ch *29:11. Ps 21:5. 45:3, 4. Mt +*6:13. 2 P 1:16, 17. Ju 24, 25. **glory.** Ex 28:2. Ps 50:2. 90:16, 17. 149:4. Is 4:2mg. 1 C 15:54.

11. **Cast.** Jb 20:23. 27:22. Dt 32:22. Ps 78:49, 50. 144:6. Ro 2:8, 9. **behold.** Ex 9:16, 17. 15:6-12. *18:11. Is *2:11, 12, 17. 10:12-19. Ezk 28:2-9. Da 4:37. 5:20-23. Ob 3, 4. Ml 4:1. Lk 18:14. Ac 12:22, 23. Ja 4:6. 1 P 5:5, 6.

12. **tread.** Ps *60:12. Pr 15:25. Is 10:6. Zc 10:5. Ml 4:3. Ro 16:20mg. **in.** Jb 36:20. Ec 11:3. Ac 1:25.

13. **Hide.** Jb 14:13. Ps 49:14. Is 2:10. **bind.** Jb 36:13. Est 7:8. Jn 11:44.

14. **that.** Ps 44:3, 6. Is 40:29. Ro 5:6. Ep 2:4-9.

15. **behemoth.** *or,* the elephant, as some think. "Behemoth" is probably the same as the Egyptian *Pehemou, Pehemout,* (from P, the article, *ehe,* a bull, and *mout,* water: see Jablonsky, Opus i. 52. and Bochart), the hippopotamus or river horse. It is nearly as large as the elephant; its head is enormously large, its mouth very wide, the jaws extending upwards of two feet, armed with four cutting teeth, each twelve inches long. Its hide is so tough and so thick as to resist the strokes of a sabre and is thinly covered with hair of a lightish color; its legs are three feet long; though amphibious, its hoofs, which are quadrified, are unconnected; and its tail is naked, about a foot in length but exceedingly thick and strong. It inhabits the rivers of Africa, feeds on grass and other vegetables, moves slowly and heavily, swims dexterously, sleeps in reedy places, has a tremendous voice between the lowing of the ox, and the roar of the elephant, and when irritated will attack boats and men with fury. **which.** Ge 1:24-26. **he.** ver. 20. Jb 39:8. Ps 104:14.

17. **moveth.** *or,* setteth up. lit. delighteth, desireth. Jb 9:3. **tail.** Ex 4:4. Dt 28:13, 44. **cedar.** Le 14:4, 6, 49, 51, 52. **sinews.** Jb 10:11. 41:23. Ge 32:32. Is 48:4. Ezk 37:6, 8. **stones.** or, thighs. lit. fearful things. Jb 3:25. Ge ◐+24:2. Dt 23:1. **wrapped together.** La 1:14.

18. **his bones.** Jb 7:12. Is 48:4. Mi 4:13. **strong.** ꟻ102, Ge +2:24.

19. **the chief.** Jb 26:13, 14. Ps 104:24. **he that.** Ps 7:12. Is 27:1. 34:6. Lk 2:35.

20. **the mountains.** ver. 15. Ps 147:8, 9. **where.** Ps 104:14, 26.

21. **the reed.** Is 19:6, 7. *35:7.

22. **the willows.** Le 23:40. Is 15:7. Ezk 17:5.

23. **drinketh.** Heb. oppresseth. Jb 10:3. Le 6:2, 4. Is 37:25mg. **hasteth not.** Ps 55:8. Is 28:16. **Jordan.** Ge 13:10, 11. 32:10. Jsh *3:15.

24. **He taketh.** *or,* Will any take him in his sight, or bore his nose with a gin? Jb 41:1, 2. **pierceth.** Jb 3:8. 5:3. **snares.** Jb 34:30. Ex 10:7. 23:33.

JOB 41

God's kingly power and authority above all the children of pride shown in the huge and terrible leviathan, 1-34.

1. **draw**. Jb 21:33. 24:22. Ex 12:21. **leviathan**. that is, *a whale, or* a whirlpool. Jb 3:8mg. Ps *74:14. 104:26. Is *27:1. **hook**. Is 19:8. Hab 1:15. **cord**. Jb 18:10 (snare). 21:17 (sorrows). 36:8. **lettest down**. Heb. drownest. Ezk 32:14.

2. **put**. Is 30:28. *37:29. Ezk 29:4, 5.

3. **will he**. Ps *55:21. Pr *15:1. 18:23. 25:15. Is 30:10.

4. **Will he make**. 1 K 20:31-34. **wilt thou**. Ge 1:28. 2:19. Ps 8:5, 6. **a servant**. Jb 3:19. Ex 21:6. Dt 15:17. **for ever**. Heb. *olam*, Ex +*12:24.

5. **play**. Jg 16:25-30. **bird**. Ge 7:14. 15:10. Le 14:6, 7. **bind**. Jb 28:11. 38:31. 39:10. Ge 38:28. **maidens**. Ge 24:14, 16, 28, 55.

6. **thy companions**. Jb 34:8. Jg 14:11. 20:11. **make a banquet**. 2 K 6:23. **part him**. Ge 32:7. 33:1. Ex 21:35. Jg 7:16. **merchants**. Jg 1:31, 32. Pr 31:24. Is 23:11. Ho 12:7. Zp 1:11. Zc 14:21.

7. **Canst**. The leviathan, described here, has been solidly proved by Bochart to denote the crocodile, and the description suits no other species of amphibious animals. It is a species of lizard with a two-edged tail, large oblong head, small but vivacious eyes, short legs, and triangular feet, the fore ones having four, and the hinder ones five toes, armed with strong, sharp claws. Its length is usually about twenty feet, and its circumference about five feet; it has, in proportion to its size, the largest mouth of all monsters; moves both its jaws equally, the upper of which is armed with not less than forty, and the under with thirty-eight sharp, strong, and massy teeth; its voice is a loud, hollow growling, of the most terrific description; and is furnished with a coat of mail, so scaly and callous as to resist the force of a musket ball in every part, except under the belly. It is a natural inhabitant of the Nile and other African and Asiatic rivers; is of enormous voracity and strength as well as fleetness in swimming; attacks mankind and the largest animals with the most daring impetuosity; and when taken by means of a powerful net, will often overturn the boats that surround it. Nothing that it once seizes can escape, and shaking its prey to pieces, it swallows without mastication. **fish**. ver. 26-29.

8. **Lay thine**. 1 K 20:11. 2 K 10:4. Lk 14:31, 32.

9. **shall**. Dt 28:34. 1 S 3:11. Is 28:19. Lk 21:11.

10. **dare**. Ge 49:9. Nu 24:9. Ps 2:11, 12. Ezk 8:17, 18. **who**. Jb 9:4. 40:9. Je √12:5. 1 C 10:22.

11. **Who**. ſ85C, Ge +18:14. Jb 22:2, 3. 35:7. Ps 21:3. Ro *11:34, 35. **whatsoever**. Ex 19:5. Dt *10:14. 1 Ch *29:11-14. Ps 24:1. 50:12. 115:16. 1 C 10:26, 28.

12. **conceal**. Jb 6:24. 11:3. 13:5. **parts**. Jb 11:3. 18:13. **power**. Jb 12:13. 26:14. 39:19. **comely**. Ge 1:25. or, grace. Ge 6:8. 18:3. 19:19. 30:27. Pr 11:16. lit. the grace of his structure. **proportion**. or, arrangement. Jb 28:13. Ex 40:4.

13. **with**. *or*, within. **double**. ſ121L9, Ge +43:12. By Metonymy of the Subject, "double" is put for *strong*. 2 K 19:28. Ps 32:9. Ja 3:3.

14. **the doors**. Jb 38:10. Ec 12:4. **his teeth**. Ps 57:4. 58:6. Pr *30:14. Da *7:7.

15. **scales**. Heb. strong pieces of shields. Jb 15:26.

Ge 15:1. Dt 33:29. **pride**. Je 9:23. **a close**. Ezk 44:1, 2. 46:1. Re 5:2, 3, 5. **seal**. Jb 38:14. Ge 38:18. Ex 28:11.

16. **near**. Ge 18:23. 19:9. **air**. or, wind. Jb 1:19. 4:9, 15. 6:4.

17. **joined**. ver. 23. Jb 19:20. 29:10. 31:7.

18. **like**. ſ102B, Ge +13:16. **the eyelids**. ſ155D, Jb 3:9mg. Ge +4:10. Re 1:14.

19. **Out of his**. Ps 18:8. **lamps**. *S#3940h. Jb 12:5. 41:19. Ge 15:17. Ex 20:18 (lightnings). Jg 7:16, 20. 15:4, 5. Is 62:1. Ezk 1:13. Da 10:6. Na 2:4. Zc 12:6. For *S#1300h, see Jb +38:35. For *S#2385h, see Jb +38:25.

20. **smoke**. Ge 15:17. Ex 19:18. **seething**. or, blown. Jb 20:26. Je 1:13, 14. **pot**. 1 S 2:14. 2 K 10:7. **cauldron**. or, reeds. ver. 2, hook. Is 9:14. 19:15. 58:5.

21. **breath**. Heb. *nephesh*, soul, Ge +√2:19. **kindleth**. Dt 32:22. 2 S 22:13. Ps 18:8, 12. 57:4. Is 30:33. Hab 3:5. **flame**. *S#3851h. Jb 39:23 (glittering). Jg 3:22 (blade). 13:20. Is 13:8. 29:6. 30:30. 66:15. Jl 2:5. Na 3:3mg.

22. **In his neck**. Jb 39:19. 40:16. **is turned into joy**. Heb. rejoiceth. Ho 13:14. 1 C 15:55-57.

23. **flakes**. Heb. fallings. Am 8:6. **are joined**. ver. 17. **firm**. ver. 24. Jb 28:2. **moved**. 1 Ch 16:30. Ps 10:6. 13:4.

24. **as hard**. Is 48:4. Je 5:3. Zc 7:12.

25. **by reason**. Ps 107:28. Jon 1:4-6.

26. **The sword**. Jb 39:21-24. 1 S 13:19, 22. 17:7. **habergeon**. *or*, breastplate. 2 Ch 26:14.

27. **esteemeth**. Jb 6:26. 13:24. 19:11. **iron**. Jb 19:24. 20:24. 28:2. 40:18. **straw**. Jb 21:18. Ge 24:25, 32. **brass**. Jb 20:24h. 28:2. 40:18. **rotten wood**. Jb 13:28. Pr 10:7.

28. **slingstones**. 2 Ch 26:14. Zc 9:15.

29. **he laugheth**. ſ155B, Jb 39:7. Ge +9:5. Hab 1:10. **shaking**. Jb 39:24 (fierceness). 1 K 19:11, 12. Ezk 37:7. 38:19. Na 3:2 (rattling). **spear**. Jb 39:23. Jsh 8:18, 26.

30. **Sharp stones**. Heb. Sharp pieces of potsherd. **he**. So hard and impenetrable are his scales that splinters of flint are the same to him as the softest reeds. **spreadeth**. Jb 17:13. **sharp pointed things**. or, gold. Ps 68:13. Pr 3:14. 8:10. **mire**. 2 S 22:43. Ps 18:42.

31. **He maketh**. When a large crocodile dives to the bottom, the violent agitation of the water may justly be compared to liquor boiling in a caldron; and his body being strongly impregnated with the scent of musk, the water is affected by it to a considerable distance. In the original style, great rivers and lakes are called *seas*. ver. 20. **to boil**. Jb 30:27. Ezk 24:5. **pot**. Ex 16:3. 27:3. 38:3. 1 K 7:45. 2 K 4:38, 39, 40, 41. 2 Ch 4:16. Ps 58:9. Ec 7:6. **deep**. Ps 68:22. 69:2, 15. 107:24. **ointment**. Ezk 24:10.

32. **He maketh**. By his rapid passage through the water he makes it white with foam; and by his tail he causes the waves behind him to sparkle like a trail of light. **to shine**. Ge 1:15. **deep**. Jb 28:14. 38:16, 30. Ge 1:2. **hoary**. Ge 15:15 (old age). 25:8. 42:38. Pr 16:31. 20:29.

33. **Upon earth**. There is no creature among terrestrial animals so thoroughly dangerous, so exceedingly strong, and so difficult to be wounded or slain; and perhaps there is no creature so totally destitute of fear as the crocodile. Jb 40:19. **is made**. Heb. behave themselves. ver. 24. **without fear**. or, terror. *S#2844h. Ge 9:2 (dread). 1 S 2:4 (broken). Je 46:5 (dismayed).

34. **high things**. Ge 7:19. Dt 3:5. **he is**. Jb 26:12. Ex 5:2. Ps 74:13, 14. Is 27:1. Ezk *29:3. Re 12:1-3. 13:2. *20:2, 3. **children of pride**. Jb 28:8.

JOB 42

Job, in deep humility, submits to God, 1-6. God decides in Job's favor and requires his three friends to present burnt offerings for their sins and submissively to engage Job to pray for them, 7, 8. They obey, and God accepts Job, 9. His prosperity is restored and doubled, 10-12. His children, 13-15. His age and death, 16, 17.

2. **thou canst do every thing**. Ge *18:14. Ps +115:3. 135:6. Is 43:13. Je *32:17. Hab 3:6. Mt *19:26. Mk *10:27. *14:36. Lk 1:37. 18:27. Re *19:6. **no thought**. Ps *44:21. *139:2. Je *17:10. Ezk 38:10. Jn +*2:24, 25. 21:17. He √4:12, 13. **can be withholden from thee**. *or*, of thine can be hindered. Jb *23:13. Pr +*19:21. +*21:30. Ec *3:14. Is 8:10. *14:27. *46:10. Da *4:35. Ep +*1:11.

3. **Who**. Jb *38:2. **things**. Ps *40:5. 131:1. 139:6. Pr 30:2-4.

4. **Hear**. Ge 18:27, 30-32. **I will**. Jb *38:3. 40:7.

5. **heard**. Jb 4:12. 28:22. 33:16. Ro √10:17. **mine**. Jb 23:8, 9. Nu 12:6-8. Is 6:1. Jn *1:18. *12:41, 45. Ac 7:55, 56.

6. **I abhor**. Jb 9:31. *40:3, 4. Ezr 9:6. Ps *51:17. Is *6:5. Je *31:19. Ezk 16:63. *20:43. 36:31. Lk *15:18, 19. 1 C 15:8, 9. 1 T 1:13-16. Ja *4:7-10. **repent**. Jb 2:8. 30:19. 1 K 21:27. Est 4:1-3. Is 58:5. Da *9:3. Jon *3:6-10. Mt *11:21. Lk *10:13. **ashes**. Je 6:26. La 3:16. Ezk 28:18. Da 9:3.

7. **Eliphaz**. Jb +*2:11. 4:1. 8:1. 11:1. **My wrath**. Jb *32:2, 3, 5. **ye have**. Jb *11:5, 6. Ps *51:4.

8. **Therefore**. From this it appears that Job was considered as a *priest*, not only to his own family but also to others. For his children he offered burnt offerings (Jb 1:5), and now he is to make the same kind of offerings, accompanied with intercession, in behalf of his three friends. This is a full proof of the innocence and integrity of Job. **seven bullocks**. Nu 23:1, 14, 29. 1 Ch 15:26. 2 Ch 29:21. Ezk 45:23. He 10:4, 10-14.

go to. Mt 5:23, 24. **offer**. Jb 1:5. Ex 18:12. **my servant Job shall**. Ge 20:17. Is 60:14. Je 14:11. 15:1. Ezk 14:14. He √7:25. Ja *5:14-18. 1 J 5:6. Re 3:9. **him**. Heb. his face, *or* person. ver. 9. 1 S 25:35. Ml 1:8, 9. Mt *3:17. Ep 1:6. **lest**. Ps 103:10. 2 T 4:14. **folly**. Jsh +7:15.

9. **did**. Jb 34:31, 32. Is 60:14. Mt 7:24. Jn 2:5. Ac 9:6. 10:33. He 11:8. **Job**. Heb. the face of Job. ver. 8. Jb 22:27. Pr 3:11, 12. Ec 9:7. Zc 8:23.

10. **turned**. Jb 5:18-20. Dt 30:3. Ps *14:7. 53:6. 126:1, 4. **when**. Ge 20:17. Ex 17:3, 4. Nu 12:2, 13. 14:1-4, 10, 13-20. 16:21, 22, 46-48. Dt 9:20. Pr 11:25. Lk 14:14. 23:34. Ac 7:50, 60. **the Lord**. Jb 8:6, 7. 22:24, 25. Dt 8:18. 1 S *2:7. 2 Ch 25:9. Pr *22:4. Hg 2:8. **gave Job twice as much as he had before**. Heb. added all that had been to Job unto the double. Ge 41:43. 43:12, 15. Is *40:2. *61:7.

11. **all his brethren**. Jb 19:13, 14. Pr 14:20. *16:7. **bread**. ♪108H4, Is +58:7. **they bemoaned**. Jb 2:11. 4:4. 16:5. Ge 37:35. Is 35:3, 4. Jn 11:19. Ro *12:15. 1 C *12:26. He 12:12. 13:3. **every man**. Jb 6:22, 23. Ge 24:22, 53. 1 S ◐*10:27.

12. **So**. Jb 8:7. Dt *8:16. Pr *10:22. Ec *7:8. 1 T *6:17. Ja *5:11. **he had**. Jb 1:3. Ge 24:35. 26:12-14. Ps 107:38. 144:13-15.

13. **seven sons**. Jb 1:2. Ps *107:41. +*127:3. Is 49:20.

14. **Jemima**. i.e. *a dove; affectionate*, ✱S#3224h. **Kezia**. i.e. *cassia; scraped off*, ✱S#7103h. Ps 45:9. **Keren-happuch**. i.e. *horn of painting; flashes or splendor of color; horn of beauty*, ✱S#7163h.

15. **no women**. Ps *144:12. Ac 7:20. **fair**. Ge 12:11, 14. *29:17. 39:6. **gave**. Nu 27:7. Jsh 15:18, 19. 18:4. **inheritance**. Jb 20:29. 27:13. 31:2. **among**. Ge 24:3, 4.

16. **After**. How long he had lived before his afflictions we cannot tell: if we could rely upon the LXX. all would be plain, which adds here, "And all the years he lived were two hundred and forty." **an hundred and forty**. Ge 11:32. 25:7. 35:28. 47:28. 50:26. Dt 34:7. Jsh 24:29. Ps 90:10. **and saw**. Ge 50:23. Ps *128:6. Pr *17:6.

17. **full of days**. Jb 5:26. Ge 15:15. 25:8. Dt 6:2. Ps *91:16. Pr *3:16. Jn *11:25. He +*9:27.

PSALMS

PSALM 1

The character and happiness of the righteous, 1-3. The misery and ruin of the ungodly, 4-6.

1. A.M. 3560. B.C. 444. **Blessed**. ♪43, Dt *28:2. +28:3. *33:29. Ps *2:12. *32:1, 2. 33:12. *34:8. 40:4. 41:1. 65:4. 84:4, 5, 12. 89:15. 94:12. *106:3. 112:1. 115:12-15. *119:1, 2. 127:5. 128:1, 2. 137:8, 9. *144:15. 146:5. Je *17:7. Mt 16:17. Lk *11:28. Jn *13:17. *20:29. Re *1:3. *14:13. 16:15. 19:9. 20:6. 22:7, *14. **the man**. ♪29, Ex +19:6. ♪171G1, Ps 32:2. **that walketh**. ♪96C1, Ge +4:1. ♪132A, Ge +4:23. **not in**. T#900. Ps *81:12. +√119:63. Ge *5:24. Le *26:27, 28. 1 K 16:31. Jb 31:5. Pr *1:15. *4:14, 15. *13:20. Ezk 20:18. Mt +*7:13. 2 C *6:17. 1 P *4:3. ♪64. Enantiosis; or, Contraries B719: Affirmation or negation by contraries. For other instances of this figure see Is 45:22. Lk 7:44-46. Ro 8:15. Ph 3:9. **counsel**. Ps *64:2. Ge 49:6.

2 Ch *22:3-5. Jb 10:3. *21:16. Lk *23:51. **ungodly**. *or*, wicked. lit. One in a wrong state toward God or man (Young). ver. 4, 5, 6. Ge 18:23, *25. Ex 2:13. 9:27. ♪12. Anabasis; or, Gradual Ascent B429. An increase of sense in successive clauses or sentences. For other instances of this figure see Ps 7:5. 18:37, 38. Is 1:4. *19:8. Ezk 2:6. Da *9:5. Hab *1:5. Zc *7:11. 8:12. 1 C 4:8. 1 J 1:1. **standeth**. Ps 26:12. Ro *5:2. Ep *6:13, 14. **way**. ver. 6. Ps *36:4. 146:9. Pr *2:12. *4:19. *13:15. Mt *7:13, 14. Jn 18:18. **sitteth**. Ps *26:4, 5. *119:115. Je *15:17. Lk 22:55. **seat**. Ex +*12:20 (✱S#4186h). **scornful**. Pr *1:22. *3:34. 9:12. *19:29. 2 P 3:3.

2. **But his delight**. T#1081. Ps *40:8. *112:1. 119:*11, *35, *47, 48, 70, 72, *92. Jb √23:12. Je √15:16. Ro 7:22. Col 3:16. 1 J *5:3. **doth**. ♪96C9, Ge +2:10. **meditate**. T#665, 1090. Ps 16:8. 63:5. 77:11, 12. *104:34. 119:*11, 15, 23, 24, *87-99, 148. 143:5, 6.

Dt *17:18, 19. Jsh √1:8. Da 6:10. Mt +14:23 (T#64, 531). 1 T *4:15. **day.** Ps *88:1. *119:97. Dt 6:6, 7. Lk *2:37. *18:7. 1 Th *2:9. 2 T *1:3. **night.** Ps 119:148.

3. **like.** ∫160A. Simile; or, Resemblance B727: A declaration that one thing resembles another; or, comparison by resemblance. For other instances of this figure see Ps 1:4. 5:12. 17:8. 131:2. Mt 7:24-27. 9:36. 1 P 2:25. **tree.** Jb 14:9. Is 44:4. Je *17:8. Ezk 17:8. 19:10. *47:12. Re *22:2. **planted.** Mt 15:13. **rivers.** Ps 46:4. 65:9. 119:136. Jb 29:6. Pr 5:16. *21:1. Is 30:25. 32:2. 44:4. La 3:48. **bringeth forth.** Ps *92:14. Is 3:10. Mt 21:34, 41. Col 1:6. **shall not.** Is *27:11. Mt *13:6. *21:19. Jn √15:6. Ju *12. **wither.** Heb. fade. Ps 5:12. 18:45. 32:7, 10. 37:2. 92:12. Ex 18:18. **whatsoever.** Ps 128:2. 129:8. Ge *39:3, 23. Jsh *1:7, 8. 1 Ch 22:11. 2 Ch *31:21. 32:23. Is 3:10. **prosper.** T#761. Ps *37:5. 57:2. 128:2. Ge 24:56. 39:23. Dt +29:9. Jsh √1:8. 2 Ch +*20:20. Jb *11:15, 17. *22:28. Is 65:21-23. Ro √8:28. 1 T +*4:8.

4. **are.** ∫63K, Ge +37:13. **not so.** Mt 13:41, 49. **like.** ∫160A, ver. 3. Ps *35:5. Jb *21:18. Pr *14:32. Is *17:13. 29:5. Je √23:28. Ho *13:3. Mt *3:12. 1 J *2:17.

5. **shall.** Ps *5:5. 24:3. Ec 12:14. Ml 3:2. Lk *21:36. Ju *21, 24. **sinners.** Ps *26:9. Nu 16:33. Ml *3:18. Mt *13:49. *25:32, 41, 46. Lk *13:28. Ep 6:13.

6. **knoweth.** ∫121C2A1, Jb +19:25. Ps 34:15. *37:18-24. *139:1, 2, 24. *142:3. Jb *23:10. Pr 2:8. Na *1:7. Jn *10:14, 27. 2 T *2:19. **way.** Ps 73:20. *112:10. 146:9. Pr *14:12. *15:9. Mt *7:13. 2 P *2:12. **righteous.** ∫63J2. Ellipsis (of Repetition: Complex) B111, where sentences are involved. In the former sentence we have the *cause*, in the latter the *effect*. But both effect and cause are latent in each statement: "The Lord knoweth the way of the righteous (and it shall not perish), but (the Lord knoweth) the way of the ungodly (and it) shall perish." The passages EWB gives for this figure follow, but are not noticed in their location, being too complex and conjectural. For other possible instances of this figure see Ps 42:8. Is 32:3. Jn 5:21. 8:28. 14:10. 17:26. Ro 6:4. He 12:20. **ungodly.** Ps 37:20. 145:20. Jb 31:3. **perish.** Lk 12:20.

PSALM 2

The throne of Christ established in contempt of all opposers, 1-6. Christ declares the Father's decree concerning his kingdom, 7-9. Kings and rulers are warned to submit to him, 10-12.

1. A.M. 2962. B.C. 1042. **Why.** ∫85Q. Erotesis B956: in indignation. For another instance of this figure see Mt 17:17. **do the heathen.** ∫12, Ps +1:1. Ps 18:43. *46:6. 83:4-8. Is 8:9, 10. Lk 18:32. Ac ▶4:25, 26. **rage.** *or*, tumultuously assemble. Lk 22:1, 2, 5, 22, 23. Ac 16:22. 17:5, 6. 19:28-32. Re +*11:18. 19:19. **people.** Mt 21:38. Jn 11:49, 50. Ac 5:39. Re 17:14. **imagine.** Heb. meditate. Ps 1:2. **a vain.** Ps 4:2. 73:13. Le 26:16. Pr √21:30.

2. **kings.** ver. 10. Ps 48:4. 110:5. Mt *2:16. Lk 13:31. 23:11, 12. Ac 12:1-6. Re 17:12-14. **rulers.** T#1933. Mt 26:3, ✶57, *59. 27:1. Ac 4:5-8, ✶26, ✶28. **take counsel.** T#1932. Mt ✶27:1, 2. **Lord.** Ex 16:7. Pr +*21:30. Jn 15:23. Ac 9:4. **against his.** T#68. Is 53:2-4. Mt 10:24, 25. 13:55-57. 26:66-68. 27:29-31, 34. Mk 15:27-32. Lk 4:2, 29. 16:14. Jn 10:20, 31. *15:24. 19:5, 6. **anointed.** ∫22D5L, Ps +45:7. *45:7. 89:20. 2 S

+23:1. Is *61:1. Lk +23:2. Jn *1:41. 3:34. Ac √10:38. He 1:9. **saying.** ∫63BA, Ge +26:7. ∫108F, Ps +109:5.

3. **Let us break.** ∫121S3T. Metonymy of the Adjunct B607. The *breaking of bands* is put for liberating from servitude. Je 5:5. Mt *11:29, 30. Lk √19:14, 27. Ro 6:18. 1 P 2:7, 8.

4. **He that.** Ps *11:4. 68:33. 115:3. Is 40:22. +*57:15. 66:1. **sitteth.** ∫22C12, Ml +3:3. **heavens.** ∫22D3A, 1 K +8:39. **shall laugh.** ∫22C8. Anthropomorphism B887. Human actions are attributed to God: laughing. For other instances of this figure see Ps *37:13. 53:5. 59:8. 2 K 19:21. Pr *1:26. **in derision.** ∫48. Chleuasmos; or, Mocking B942: An expression of feeling by mocking and jeering. For other instances of this figure see Pr 1:24-33. Is 14:4, 12. Mi 2:4.

5. **Then.** Ps *50:16-22. Is *11:4. 66:6. Mt 22:7. *23:33-36. Lk *19:27, 43, 44. Re 1:16. *19:15. **vex.** *or*, trouble. Ps 83:15. Jb 22:10. Is *29:6. 31:8. **sore.** Ps 110:5, 6. Zc *1:15.

6. **Yet.** Ps 45:6. 89:27, 36, 37. *110:1, 2. Is *9:6, 7. Da 7:13, 14. Mt *28:18. Ac *2:34-36. *5:30, 31. Ep 1:22. Ph *2:9-11. **set.** Heb. anointed. lit. "poured out." 2 K 9:6. Is 29:10. Zc *14:4, 5, 8, 9. **my king.** T#83. Ps 45:6, 7. Is +*9:6. Je +*23:5, 6. *30:9. Ho √3:5. Mi +*5:2. Zc 9:9. Mt 27:11. Lk +*1:32, 33. Jn +*1:49. Ac 17:7. Re *1:5. my, etc. Heb. Zion, the hill of my holiness. Ps 48:1, 2. 50:2. 78:68. +*132:13, 14. 2 S 5:7. Is +*24:23. 51:11. 52:8. Mi +*4:7. He 12:22. Re 14:1.

7. **the decree.** *or*, for a decree. Ps *89:3, 4. 148:6. Jb *23:13. Is 46:10. Ro *1:4. **Thou art.** Mt 3:17. 8:29. 16:16. *17:5. Ac 8:37. ▶*13:33. Ro *1:3, 4. He ▶*1:5. *3:6. *5:▶5, 8. **my Son.** T#1913. Ps 72:1. 110:5-7. Ge 16:7, 13. 2 S *7:14. 1 Ch 17:13. Pr 30:4. Is *7:14. +*9:6. 11:1-5. Da +*3:25. Mi +*5:2. Mt 3:17. 17:5. Mk 1:1. Lk +*1:35. 22:70. Jn 1:34-50. *3:16-18. 5:25. √20:31. Ac 9:20. Ro +*1:4. He √1:1-5. 1 J 4:14. Re +*1:5, 6. **this.** Ps *89:26, 27. Jn 1:14, 18. √3:16n. He *1:6. Re ❍+3:14. **begotten.** Is *14:14. Ac Jd 1:33. Ro 1:4. Col √1:18. He 1:6. 5:5. ∫22C23. Anthropomorphism B889. Human actions are attributed to God: begetting. For other instances of this figure see Ps 22:31. 87:4-6. He 1:5. 1 J 2:29. 3:9.

8. **Ask.** Jn *17:4, 5. **and I.** Ps 22:27. 72:8. Da +*7:13, 14. **shall give.** T#939. Ps 22:27, 28. 67:2, 7. 68:31. *72:8, 11, 17, 19. 86:9. *102:15, 16. 110:3. Is 2:2, 3. 11:10. 19:21, 24, 25. 23:18. 27:6. 40:3-5. 42:1, 4, 6, 7. 45:14, 23, 24. 49:6, 12, 18, 20. 51:4, 5, 16. 52:10. 54:1-3. *55:4, 5. *59:19, 20. 60:3, 4, 8-10. 66:8, 9, 18-20, 23. Da *2:44. *7:13, 14, 27. Am 9:11, 12. Mi 4:2. Zc *2:10, 11. *14:9. 6:15. *8:21-23. Ml *1:11. Mt 8:+*11, 18, 19. Jn *12:32. Re 7:9, 10. *11:15. 12:10. **the heathen.** T#1552. Ps 67:2-5. 74:20. Is *22:26. Mt *9:38. **thine inheritance.** Ps +*82:8. **uttermost parts.** Ps 22:27. 67:7. +*72:8. Zc 14:9. Mt +*5:5. *28:18, 19. **thy possession.** Ge 17:8. Dt 32:49.

9. **break.** ∫22C32. Anthropomorphism B889. Human actions are attributed to God: breaking. For other instances of this figure see Ps 3:7. Is 38:13. 45:2. **them with.** Ps 21:8, 9. 89:23. 110:5, 6. Is 30:14. 60:12. Je 19:11. Da *2:44. Mt 21:44. Re *2:26, ▶27. +*12:5. *19:15. **a rod.** ∫22D5R. Anthropomorphism B894. A rod, staff, or sceptre is attributed to God or Christ, and by *Metonymy* (∫121S1, Ge +49:10), is put for his power and authority. For other instances of this figure see Ps 23:4. 45:6. 110:2. He 1:8.

10. **Be wise.** Je 6:8. Ho 14:9. **O ye kings.** ſ38B, 2 S +1:24. Ps 45:12. 72:10, 11. Is 49:23. 52:15. 60:*3, 10, 11. **be instructed.** Ps 82:1-8.

11. **Serve.** Ps 89:7. Ph *2:12. He *4:1, 2. *12:25, 28, 29. **rejoice.** Ps 95:1-8. 97:1. 99:1. 119:120. 1 C *7:29-31. Ph 2:12. He 4:1, 2. 12:25.

12. **Kiss.** ſ121S2, Ge +21:6. Ge *41:40, 43, 44. 1 S 10:1. 1 K *19:18. Jb 31:27. Ho *13:2. Jn √5:23. **Son.** ver. *7. Is 7:14. +*9:6. **and,** etc. Or, "and ye lose the way," or, "and ye perish in the way." The LXX. and Vulgate have, "and ye perish from the righteous way;" and the Syriac, "and ye perish from his way." **ye perish.** Ps *1:6. Is 24:6. 66:24. Ezk 20:38. Zc 14:3, 12, 13. Ml 4:1, 3. Jn *14:6. Re *6:16, 17. **from.** ſ63K, Ge +37:13. **the way.** Ex 33:3. **when.** ver. *5. 2 Th *1:8, 9. Re *6:16, 17. *14:9-11. **wrath is kindled.** Ex 33:5. Is 26:20. **Blessed.** ſ43, Dt +28:3. ſ74, Jg +5:31. Ps *34:8. *40:4. *84:12. *146:3-5. Pr *16:20. Is *26:3, 4. √30:18. Je *17:7. Jn *6:47. √14:6. Ro *9:33. *10:11. Ep 1:12. 1 P *1:21. *2:6. **their trust.** Ps +*9:10. 16:1. 17:7. 18:2. 31:19. *37:40. 46:1. 57:1. 91:9, 10. Dt 32:37. Ru 2:12. Je *17:5. Jn *6:27. He 6:18.

PSALM 3

David, amidst numerous insulting foes, firmly relies on the divine protection, 1-6. He prays for deliverance and ascribes salvation to the Lord, 7, 8.

(*Title.*) A.M. 2983. B.C. 1021. **Psalm.** *Mizmor,* from the verb *to cut, prune, sing:* a poem *cut* into short sentences, divided into syllables, *pruned* from every redundancy, and thus adapted for *singing.* **when.** 2 S ch. 15-18.

1. **how.** ſ85P, Ge +27:46. 2 S 15:12. 16:15. 17:11-13. Mt 27:25. **many.** Ps 17:7. Mt 10:21.

2. **Many.** ſ18, Dt +28:4. **my soul.** Heb. *nephesh,* Ge +12:13. ſ171Q2, Nu +23:10. **no.** Ps 22:7, 8. 42:3, 10. 71:11. 2 S 16:7, 8. Mt *27:42, 43. **Selah.** ver. 4, 8. Ps 4:2, 4. Hab 3:3, 9, 13.

3. **a shield.** ſ22D5F, Ge +15:1. Ps *18:2. 28:7. *84:11. *119:114. Ge *15:1. Dt 33:29. **for.** *or,* about. **my.** Ps 4:2. 62:7. Is 45:25. 60:19. Lk 2:32. Re 21:11, 23. **the lifter.** Ps *27:6. 110:7. Ge 40:13. 2 K 25:27. **head.** ſ171Q12, Jg +5:30.

4. **I cried.** T#1236. Ps 22:2-5. 28:1. 30:2. 31:22. 34:*4, 6, 17. 39:12. *50:15. 56:9. 57:2. 61:1, 2. 66:17-19. *69:3. 72:12. 77:1. 84:2. 86:3, 4. 88:1. 91:15. 102:1. *107:6. 116:1-4. 130:1, 2. 138:3. 142:1-3, 5, 6. Ex 2:23. 3:7. 8:12. 14:10. 17:4. Jsh 24:7. Jg 3:9, 15. 6:6. 1 S 7:8, 9. 15:11. 2 K 20:11. 2 Ch 13:13, 14. Is 65:24. Je 29:12, 13. Ezk 8:18. 9:8. 11:13. Ho 8:2. Jl 1:14, 19. 2:1. Mt *7:7. 15:22. 20:30, 31. 27:46, 50. Mk 10:46-48. He *5:7. Ja *5:13. Re 6:10. 7:9, 10. **he heard.** Ps 34:4. **his.** Ps *2:6. 43:3. 99:9. 132:13, 14.

5. **I laid.** Ps *4:8. 121:4-7. *127:2. Le 26:6. Jb 11:18, 19. Pr *3:24. 6:22. Ac 12:6. **slept.** ſ121S2, Ge +21:6. **the Lord.** Ps *4:8. 66:9. Pr *14:26. 18:10. Is √26:3.

6. **I will.** Ps *27:1-3. 46:2, 7. 118:10-12. 2 K 6:15-17. Ro *8:31. **ten thousands.** 2 S 18:7. **set.** Ps 2:2.

7. **Arise.** Ps 7:6. 9:19. 10:12. 12:5. 35:23. 44:23. 59:5. 74:11. 76:9. Is 51:9. Hab 2:19. **smitten.** Jb 16:10. **broken.** ſ22C32, Ps +2:9. Ps 58:6. Jb 29:17. La 3:30.

8. **Salvation.** ſ74, Jg +5:31. Ps 37:39, 40. 60:11. Pr 21:31. Is *43:11. *45:21, 22. Je *3:23. Ho 13:4.

Jon *2:9. Ac √4:12. Re *7:10. 19:1. **thy blessing.** Ps 29:11. 72:17. Ac 3:26. Ep *1:3. He 6:14. 1 P 3:9.

PSALM 4

David calls on God to hear him, 1. He reproves, warns, and counsels his enemies, 2-5. He shows his comfort and confidence in God, 6-8.

(*Title.*) **chief Musician.** *or,* overseer. Ps 22, 42, 45, titles. 1 Ch 25:1-6. **Neginoth.** i.e. *harp songs,* *S#5058h. Ps 4, 6, 54, 55, 61, 67, titles. 69:12. 76, title. 77:6. Is 38:20. La 3:14. 5:14. Hab 3:19mg.

1. **Hear me.** T#1646. Ps 5:1-3. 13:3. 17:1. 20:1, 2. 22:1, 2. 27:7. 28:1, 2. 30:10. 31:2. 39:12. 54:2. 55:1, 2. 64:1. 69:16, 17. 84:8. 86:1, 6. 88:1, 2. 102:1, 2. 119:169, 170. 130:1, 2. Da 9:18, 19. **O God.** Ps 11:7. 24:5. 41:12. Is 45:24. Je 23:6. 1 C *1:30. 2 C 5:20, 21. **of.** ſ181E, Ge +3:24. ſ24L, Ex +34:7. **thou.** Ps 18:18, 19. 31:8. 40:1-3. 116:6, 16. 1 S 17:37. 19:11, 12. 23:26-28. Jb 36:16. 2 C 1:8, 10. **enlarged.** ſ22C36, Ge +26:22. **have mercy upon me.** *or,* be gracious unto me. T#1617. Ps 6:2. 9:13, 14. *25:10, 16, 17. 26:11. 27:7. 31:9. 33:22. 40:11, 12. 41:4, 10. 51:1. 56:1. 57:1. 61:7. 66:20. 67:1. 77:7-9. 85:7. 86:3-5, 16. 90:14. 119:41, 58, 75-77, 132. 123:3. 143:2. Ex 34:6, 7. Zc 1:12. Mt 9:27. 17:14-16. 20:30, 31. Mk 10:47, 48. Lk 16:24. 17:12, 13. *18:13. 1 T 1:2. 2 T 1:2, 16-18. T 1:4. He √4:16. 2 J 1:3.

2. **ye sons.** Ps 57:4. 58:1. Ec 8:11. 9:3. **how.** Ps 82:2. Ex 10:3. Nu 14:11. Pr 1:22. **will ye.** ſ63B, Ge +25:28. **my glory.** Ps 3:3. 14:6. 106:20. Is 20:5. 45:17. Je 2:11. Ho 4:7. 1 C 1:31. **how long.** ſ63I1C2B, Jb +21:17. **love.** Ps 2:1. 1 S 12:21. Is 59:4. Je 2:5. Jon 2:8. **leasing.** Ps 5:6. 58:3. 63:11. Je 9:3. Ep *4:25. Re 21:8.

3. **that the.** Ex *33:16. Ep *2:10. 2 Th *2:13, 14. 2 T *2:19. 1 P *2:9. 2 P 2:9. **the Lord.** Ps *34:15. *55:16, 17. 56:9. *91:14, 15. Jn *15:16. **set apart.** 2 C *6:17. 2 Th *2:13. T *2:14. **godly.** T#646. Ps 1:1, 4, 5. **for.** Ps 56:9. T *2:14. **will hear.** ſ22C14, Ge +16:11. T#1149. Ps 3:4. 18:6. 28:6. *34:15. *55:16, 17. 56:9. 66:19, 20. 77:1. *91:14, 15. 99:6-8. 107:19. *145:18, 19. Nu 20:15, 16. Dt *4:7, 29. 5:28. Jsh 10:14. 2 K *20:5. 2 Ch *15:2. Jb *22:27. 33:26. Is *45:11, 19. *55:6, 7. 58:9. 65:1, √24. Je *29:12. √33:3. La 3:57, 58. Da *9:20, 21. *10:12. Ho 14:1, 2. Mi 7:7. Zc 13:9. Mt *6:6. *7:7, 8. √18:19, 20. Lk √11:9. 15:20. Jn *15:16. Ac 10:30, 31. Ro *10:12, 13, 20. Ph *4:6. Ja 4:8. *5:4. 1 P *3:12. Re √3:20. 5:8. 8:3, 4.

4. **Stand.** ſ96B, Nu +24:21. i.e. if ye stand in awe ye will not sin. Ps 2:11. 33:8. *119:161. Pr 16:6. Je 5:22. **sin.** Jb 28:28. Pr *3:7. 16:6, 17. Ep ᴹ4:26. **commune.** Ps 63:6. *77:6. 2 C *13:5. upon. Mi 2:1. **bed.** T#1179. 2 K 20:1, 2. Ps 63:5, 6. SS 3:1. **be still.** Ps 46:10. Jsh +10:13n. Hab *2:20. **Selah.** Ps 3:2, 4.

5. **Offer.** Ps 50:14. *51:17, 19. Dt 33:19. 2 S 15:12. Is *1:11-18. 61:8. Ml 1:8, 11-14. Mt 5:23, 24. He 13:15, 16. **put.** Ps 2:12. 26:1. *37:3. *62:8. *84:11, 12. Pr *3:5. Is *26:3, 4. 50:10. 1 P *4:19.

6. **many.** Ps 39:6. 49:16-20. Ec 2:3, etc. Is 55:2. Lk 12:19. 16:19. Ja 4:13. 5:1-5. **lift.** T#1604. Ps 21:6. 42:5. 44:3. 67:1. 80:1-3, 7, 19. 89:15. *119:135. Nu *6:26. 2 C *4:6. **countenance.** ſ22A4, Ge +19:13.

7. **put gladness.** Ps *37:4. 40:3. 43:4. 63:2-5. 92:4. Jb 8:21. Pr 17:22. SS *1:4. Jn *14:7. 1 P *1:8. **the time.** Jg *9:27. Pr *14:13. Is 9:3. Je 48:33. **their.** ſ142,

Ge +20:16. **corn.** ⨍121D4, Ge +27:28. **and.** ⨍174, Ge +18:27. **wine.** ⨍121D13, Ge +27:28.

8. **I will.** Ps *3:5. 16:8. +*34:4, 7. 112:7. 121:4-7. Le 26:6. Jb 11:18, 19. Pr *3:24. 6:22. Is 41:10. 1 Th *4:13, 14. 5:10. 2 T 1:7. Re *14:13. **sleep.** 121S2, Ge +21:6. By Metonymy of the Adjunct, whereby the sign is put for the thing signified, sleep is put for perfect security. Ps +*127:2. **for.** Ps *34:7. Le 25:18, 19. 26:5. Dt 12:10. 33:27-29. Jg 9:51. 2 K 20:19. Jb *11:18, 19. Pr 22:3. Ezk 34:25. Ho 2:18. Ro 8:35-39. 1 T 2:2. **dwell.** Ps 23:4. Dt *33:12. **safety.** T#1683. Ps 119:117. Ge ◐19:30. 1 S *30:6.

PSALM 5

David prays and purposes to persist in prayer, 1-3. He shows that God abhors the wicked, 4-6. He professes hope in God's mercy and entreats his guidance, because of the malice of his enemies, 7-9. He predicts that the wicked will be destroyed and the righteous made prosperous and joyful, 10-12.

(*Title.*) **Nehiloth.** i.e. *we shall divide the inheritance*, ✳S#5155h.

1. **Give.** Ps 17:1. 54:2. 55:1, 2. 64:1. 80:1. 86:1. 1 P *3:12. 1 J √5:14, 15. **ear.** ⨍22C14, Ge +16:11. **consider my.** ⨍173, Ge +27:44. Ps *19:14. 37:4. 145:19. 1 S 1:13, 16, mg. Ml *3:16. Ro 8:26.

2. **Hearken.** ⨍22C14, Ge +16:11. **unto the.** Ps 3:4. **my King.** Ps 10:16. 24:7, 8. 44:4. 47:6, 7. 74:12. 99:1-4. 145:1. Is 33:22. **unto thee.** Ps 65:2.

3. **My voice.** Ps 22:2. 55:17. 59:16. *88:13. 119:147. 130:6. Ge 19:27. Is *26:9. Mi 7:7. Hab 2:1. Mk *1:35. Col *4:2. **hear.** ⨍22C14, Ge +16:11. **morning.** T#1163. Ps *55:17. 88:13. 119:147. 1 Ch 23:30. Mk +*1:35.

4. **For thou.** He *12:14. **God.** Heb. *El*, Ex +15:2. ⨍171E12, Ge +14:22. Ps 50:21. 1 Ch 29:17. Hab √1:13. Ml 2:17. **evil.** Ps 94:20. 101:7. 140:13. Hab 1:13. Jn 14:23. He *12:14. 2 P 3:13. Re *21:23, 27.

5. **The foolish.** Ps *14:1. 73:3. 92:6. 94:8. Pr 1:7, 22. 8:5. Ec 5:4. Hab 1:13. **stand.** Ps *1:5. 130:3. in **thy sight.** Heb. before thine eyes. Ps 18:24mg. **thou hatest.** ⨍22B, Ex +15:7. Ps 10:3. Le 20:23. Pr 6:16-19. Ho 9:15. Zc 11:8. Mt √7:23. 25:41.

6. **destroy.** Ps 4:2. Re *21:8. 22:15. **the bloody**, etc. Heb. man of bloods and deceit. Ps 26:8-10. 43:1. *55:23. Ge 34:14, 25, 26, 28. 2 S +16:7mg, 8. 20:1. 2 K +9:26mg. 16:24. Pr 1:29. Ro 1:29.

7. **But.** Ps 55:16. Jsh 24:15. Lk 6:11, 12. **in the.** Ps 51:1. 52:8. 69:13, 16. Is *55:7. Ro *5:20, 21. **in thy fear.** T#1334. Ps 25:12-15. 34:9, 10. 130:4. 145:19. Is 50:10. Je 10:6, 7. 26:19. Ho 3:5. Jon 1:16. Hab 3:2. Ac 9:31. 10:2. He *5:7. *12:28, 29. 1 P 1:17-19. Re 15:4. **I worship.** Ps 28:2. 132:7. *138:2. 1 K 8:29, 30, 35, 38. Da +*6:10. Jon *2:4. He √4:16. **thy holy temple.** Heb. the temple of thy holiness. Ps 27:4. 29:9. 1 S 1:9n. Is 64:11.

8. **Lead.** Ps 23:3. *25:4, 5. *32:8. 86:11. 119:10, 64. 143:8-10. Pr √3:5, 6. 8:20. **righteousness.** T#1681. Ps 36:10. 118:19. 119:40. 132:9. Ho *10:12. Zp *2:3. Mt √6:33. 2 C 9:10. Ph 1:9-11. **mine.** Heb. those which observe me. Ps 27:11mg. 54:5mg. 59:10mg. 71:10mg. 2 S 12:14. **make.** Ps 25:4. *27:11. Pr 4:25. Mt 3:3. He 12:13. **straight.** ⨍22C37. Anthropomorphism B890. Human actions are attributed to God: making a straight way. For other instances of this figure see Is 45:2, 13mg.

9. **For.** Ps 36:1-4. 52:2. 58:3. 62:4, 9. 111:1-3. Je 9:3-6. Mi 6:12. Ro 1:29-31. 3:13. **no.** T#165. Ps +50:16 (T#589). +66:18 (T#546). Ge 6:5. Pr 21:4. Ec 8:11. 9:3. 2 Ch 5:14. Jb +21:15 (T#689). Mt +13:38 (T#690). Ro +7:18 (T#688). Ep 2:1-3, 12. Col 2:13. **faithfulness.** *or*, steadfastness. Ps 51:10mg. Jb 42:7, 8. **their mouth.** Heb. his mouth, *that is, the mouth of any of them*. **inward part.** T#702. 2 S 15:5, 6. 2 Ch 24:17, 18. Ps 10:7. 12:2, +3 (T#198). 28:3. 38:12. 51:6. 52:2. 58:2. 62:4mg. 64:5, 6. 106:13 (T#411). 140:5. 141:9, 10. Pr 7:21. 11:18. 12:5. 20:14. Is 29:20, 21. 66:5. Je 3:10. 4:14. 8:5. 9:2-8. *17:9. Ezk 33:30, 31. Da 11:21, 32. Ho 11:12. Mi 3:10, 11. Mt +7:15 (T#474). 26:48, 49. Mk *7:21, 22. Lk 11:39. +18:12 (T#194). Jn +8:44 (T#416). Ro 1:29, 30. 16:18. 2 Th 2:9, 10. 2 T +3:5 (T#191). He *3:13. Ja +3:6 (T#728). Re 18:23. **very wickedness.** Heb. wickednesses. Ps 38:12. 52:2, 7. 55:11. **throat.** Lk 11:44. Ro ⋊3:13. ⨍121BF1. Metonymy of the Cause B546. The throat is put for the words spoken. For another instance of this figure see Ro 3:13. **sepulchre.** Heb. *qeber*, Ge +23:4. Lk 11:44. **they flatter.** Ps *12:2, 3. Jb 32:21, 22. Pr 29:5. 1 Th 2:5. **tongue.** ⨍121BB. Metonymy of the Cause B546. The tongue is put for what is spoken by it. For other instances of this figure see Pr 10:20. 25:15. Je 18:18.

10. **Destroy.** *or*, Make them guilty. T#1474. Ps 34:21, 22. 35:26. 55:9, 15. 69:22-24. 71:13. 83:9-11. 137:7. *143:12. 144:6-8. Ge 27:29. Nu 21:1, 2. Jg 5:31. 2 S *15:31. 2 Ch *20:10-13. Ne 4:3-5. 6:14. Is *24:6mg. Je +√10:25. *17:18. La 1:21, 22. 3:63-66. Ezk 25:12. Ro 3:19, 20. **let.** Ps 7:9-15. *9:15, 16. 10:15. 17:13. 21:8-10. 28:3, 4. 31:18. 35:1-8, 26. 55:15. 59:12, 13. 64:6-8. 66:7. 68:1, 2. 69:22-25. 71:13. 79:12. 83:9-18. 109:6-20. 137:7-9. 140:9, 10. 144:6, 7. Dt +*2:30. 1 S 25:29, 39. 2 S *15:31. *17:14, 23. 2 Ch 25:16. Est 7:10. Jb 5:12-14. 1 C 3:19. 2 T +*4:14. **by.** *or*, from. **the multitude.** La 1:5. Ho 9:7. **they.** Is 1:2, 20. +*63:10. Da 9:5, 9.

11. **But.** Ps 35:27. 40:16. 58:10. 68:3. 70:1-4. Jg 5:31. Is *65:13-16. Re 18:20. 19:1-7. **rejoice.** ⨍121G2, Ps +25:2. 1 Th +5:16. **ever.** Heb. *olam*, ✛S#5769h: Ps 111:5. 119:98. Jl 2:2. **shout.** Ps 47:1-5. 65:13. Jb 38:7. Zc 9:9. **defendest.** Heb. coverest over, *or*, protectest. Ps 91:4. Ex 40:21. Jg 3:24. **love.** Ps 69:36. Ro √8:28. 1 C 2:9. Ja 1:12. 2:5.

12. **bless.** Ps *1:1-3. 3:8. *29:11. 32:7, 10. *112:1. *115:13. Dt 33:23. Is 3:10. **wilt.** Ps *32:10. **compass.** Heb. crown. Ps 8:5. 65:11. 103:4. **as.** ⨍160A, Ps +1:3. **shield.** Ps 3:3. *84:11.

PSALM 6

David, being sick, deprecates wrath and entreats mercy, with mournful complaints and earnest pleadings, 1-7. Confiding in God, he triumphs over his enemies, 8-10.

(*Title.*) A.M. 2970. B.C. 1034. **Neginoth.** Ps +4, title. **Sheminith.** *or*, the eighth. Ps 12, title. 1 Ch 15:21mg.

1. **rebuke.** Ps 2:5. 38:1. Is 54:9. *57:16. Je *10:24. *46:28. 1 C 11:31, 32. **neither chasten.** T#1444. Ps 74:1. Ex 32:11. Is 64:9.

2. **for I.** T#1297. Ps 38:7, 8. 41:3. 102:23, 24. *103:13-17. 109:22-24. **O Lord, heal.** T#954. Ps 22:11. 23:4. 27:1. *30:2. 41:4. 46:1. 61:2. 119:151. Ge 20:17. Ex *15:26. Nu 12:13. Dt +*32:39. 33:27. Jb *5:17,

18. Is 38:14. 40:29. Je 17:14. La 3:56, 57. Ho *6:1. Mt 4:24. 12:20. 2 Th 2:16, 17. **my.** Ps 32:3. 38:3. 51:8. Jb 19:20. 33:19-21.

3. **My.** Ps 22:14. 31:9, 10. 38:8. 42:5, 11. 77:2, 3. Pr 18:14. Mt *26:38. **soul.** Heb. *nephesh,* Ge +34:3. **how.** Ps 13:1, 2. 77:7. 90:13. Pr *13:12. Lk +*18:7. Re *6:10. **long.** ⸮37C, Ge +25:22.

4. **Return.** T#1515. Ps 60:1. 69:16, 17. 80:14, 15. 90:13, 14. Is 63:17. Ml 3:7. **deliver.** Ps 17:13. 22:20. 86:13. 116:4, 8. 120:2. 121:7. Is 38:17. **soul.** Heb. *nephesh,* Ge +12:13. **for.** Ps *25:7. 69:13. 79:8, 9. Da *9:18. Ep 1:6. 2:7, 8.

5. **For.** Ps *30:9. *88:10-12. +*115:17. *118:17. Is *38:18, 19. **no remembrance.** Ps +13:3. +*146:4. Ec +9:5. **in the.** Ec *9:10. Jn *9:4. **grave.** Heb. *sheol,* Ge +37:35. **give thee thanks.** He *13:15.

6. **I am.** Ps 38:8, 9. *69:3. 77:2-9. 88:9. 102:3-5. 143:4-7. Jb 7:3. 10:1. 23:2. **all the.** *or,* every. **I water.** Ps 39:12. *42:3. Jb 16:20. Je 14:17. La 1:2, 16. 2:11, 18, 19. 3:48-50. Lk 7:38.

7. **Mine.** Ps 31:9, 10. *38:10. *88:9. Jb *17:7. La *5:17. **it waxeth.** Ps 32:3.

8. **Depart.** ⸮38B, 2 S +1:24. Ps *119:115. 139:19. Mt √7:23. *25:41. Lk 13:27. **for.** Ps *3:4. 56:8. 116:8. 145:18. Is *30:18, 19. *38:3, 5. He *5:7. **heard.** ⸮173, Ge +27:44.

9. **hath heard.** Ps 3:4. *31:22. 40:1, 2. 66:19, 20. 118:5. 120:1. 138:3. Jon 2:2, 7. Mt *7:7. 2 C 12:8-10. 1 J √5:14, 15. **will receive.** Ps *116:1, 2. *145:18. 2 C 1:10, 11.

10. **Let all.** Ps 5:10. 7:6. 25:3. 35:26. 40:14, 15. 71:13. 83:16, 17. 86:17. 109:28, 29. 112:10. 132:18. Jb 6:20. Is 26:11. Je 20:11. **sore.** Ps 2:5. 21:8, 9. **return.** Ps *59:14. Jb 6:29. +*21:30. Is +*24:22. Ml 3:18. Re √20:5. **and be ashamed.** Ps √109:28. Pr *29:1. Je 48:1, 20. Hab 1:12. 1 Th *5:3.

PSALM 7

David, protesting his innocence of the crimes charged on him, entreats God to protect him from his enemies and to plead his cause for the sake of the people, 1-9. He expresses his confidence in God, predicts the destruction of persecutors, and determines to praise the Lord, 10-17.

(Title.) A.M. 2983. B.C. 1021. **Shiggaion.** i.e. *varieties in song; erratic,* *S#7692h. Hab 3:1. **Shiggaion** probably denotes a *mournful song,* or *elegy,* from the Arabic *shaga,* to be anxious, sorrowful. Hab 3:1. **words.** *or,* business. 2 S ch. 16. **Cush.** *Cush* signifies black, an epithet in all languages when applied to the mind, expressive of moral turpitude; and therefore probably here applied to *Shimei,* denoting that he was a calumniator and villain.

1. **O Lord.** Ps 13:3, 5. 18:28. 30:2, 12. 43:4. 89:26. Jsh 14:8. Je 31:18. Da 9:4, 19, 20. Zc 14:5. **in thee.** Ps *11:1. 18:2. 25:2. 26:1. 31:1. 32:10. *146:3-6. Pr *3:5. Is 50:10. 1 P 1:21. **save.** Ps 3:7. 17:7-9. 31:15. 35:1-3. Je 15:15. 20:11. 1 P *4:19. **persecute.** T#1638. Ps *31:15. 35:2-4. 119:84-86. 142:6. 143:3, 4. Je 15:15. 17:18.

2. **Lest.** Ps 35:15. Is 38:13. **soul.** Heb. *nephesh,* Ge +12:13. **like.** Ps 10:9. 17:12. 22:13. Dt 33:20. Pr 19:12. 2 T 4:17. 1 P 5:8. **rending.** Ps 50:22. Ho 13:7, 8. **while.** Jg 18:28. 2 S 14:6mg. Jb 10:7. **none to deliver.** Heb. not a deliverer.

3. **if I.** Ps 59:3. Jsh 22:22. 1 S 20:8. 22:8, 13. 24:9. 26:18, 19. 2 S 16:7, 8. Jb 16:17-19. **if there.** Ps √66:18. 1 S 24:11. Jb 11:14. 2 C 1:12. 1 J 3:21. **hands.** ⸮144A5, Ge +9:5. ⸮121BA, Dt +32:36.

4. **If I.** Ps 55:20. 109:5. Ge 44:4. Pr 17:13. Je 18:20, 21. **I have delivered.** 1 S 24:*7, 10, *11. 26:9-17, 24. **without.** 1 S 19:4, 5. 20:1. 22:14. 24:11-15, 17-19. 25:28, 29. 26:21.

5. **Let.** Jb 31:5-10, 38-40. **persecute.** ⸮12, Ps +1:1. **soul.** Heb. *nephesh,* Ge +12:13. **tread.** Ps 44:5. 60:12. Jb 40:12. Is 10:6. 63:3. Zc 10:5. Ml 4:3. **lay mine.** Ps 49:12. Jb 16:15. 40:13. Je 17:13. **honor.** ⸮121F, Ge +49:6. i.e. myself who gives honor. **Selah.** Ps 3:2. Hab 3:13.

6. **Arise.** Ps 3:7. 9:19. 10:12. 12:5. 35:1, 23. 44:26. 68:1, 2. ◑80:1, 17. ◑*110:1. Is 3:13. **lift up.** Ps 74:3. 94:1, 2. Is *33:10. 37:20. **rage of mine enemies.** 2 S 16:7, 8. **awake.** Ps 44:23. 59:5. 73:20. 78:65. Is 51:9. **to the judgment.** Ps 76:8, 9. *103:6. 2 S 17:14mg. Jb +*21:30. Na *1:2. 1 Th *1:10. *5:9.

7. **So.** Ps 48:11. 58:10, 11. Re 11:17, 18. 16:5-7. 18:20. 19:2. **congregation.** Ac 15:14. **compass thee.** Is 57:1. Jl 2:32. Zp +*2:3. Ro *5:9. 1 Th √1:10. *4:17. √5:9, 10. **for their sakes.** T#1138. Nu 27:17. Dt 9:29. 1 K 8:51. Ne 1:10. 9:32. Is 63:17-19. 64:8-11. **return.** Ps 93:4. 113:5, 6. 138:6. Ec +*5:8. Is +*57:15. 1 Th *4:17.

8. **The Lord.** Ps 9:8. 11:4. 82:1. 96:13. 98:9. Ge *18:25. Ac *17:31. Ro 14:10-12. 1 C 4:4, 5. **judge me.** T#1588. Ps *26:1, 2. *35:23, 24. 43:1. 54:1. 119:84. *130:3. 143:2. Ge 31:53. 2 Ch 6:22, 23. 20:12. La 3:59. 1 C 4:3-5. 1 J 3:21. Re 6:10, 11. **according.** Ps 17:2, 3. *18:20-24. 35:24-27. 2 C 1:12. **to mine.** Ps 25:21. 26:11. 41:12. 78:72. Pr 19:1. 1 Th 2:10.

9. **Oh.** Ps 9:5, 6. 10:15, 18. 58:6. 74:10, 11, 22, 23. Is 37:36-38. Da 11:45. Ac 12:23. **but establish.** T#1590. Ps 37:23mg. 40:2. 1 S 2:9. 2 Ch 6:22, 23. Ro 16:25. 1 Th 3:13. 1 P 5:10. Ju 1. **for.** Ps 17:3. 44:21. *139:1. 1 S √16:7. 1 Ch +*28:9. Je 11:20. *17:10. *20:12. Re *2:23. **trieth.** ⸮22C2, Ge +3:9. **the hearts.** ⸮121II, Ge +3:7. Ps 51:6. √66:18. 73:11. 1 K 15:14. 1 Ch +*28:9. Je √17:10.

10. **My,** etc. Heb. My buckler *is* upon God. Ps 3:3. 18:1, 2. 62:7. *84:11. 89:18. Ge *15:1. **which.** Ps 112:2. 125:4. Jb 8:6. Pr 2:21. 11:20. 28:18.

11. **God judgeth,** etc. *or,* God *is* a righteous judge. ver. 8. Ps 94:15. 140:12, 13. Ge +*18:25. **God.** Heb. *El,* Ex +15:2. **is angry.** T#208. Ps 103:13. 147:11. Ge *6:6. Ho 11:8. Zp 3:17. Mt 3:17. 1 J 4:8. **with.** ⸮63F, Ge +33:10.

12. **If.** Ps 85:4. Is √55:6, 7. Je 31:18, 19. Ezk *18:30. 33:11. Mt *3:10. 18:3. Ac 3:19. **he will.** Dt *32:41. Is 27:1. 34:5. Ezk 21:9-11, 23.

13. **He hath.** ⸮95. Hermeneia; or, Interpretation B402. Repetition for the purpose of interpreting what has been already said. Here, ver. 13 explains ver. 12. For other instances of this figure see Ps 77:19. Is 1:23. 34:6. 44:3. Is 51:1, 2. Ho 7:8, 9. Am 3:8. Mt 1:23. *6:24. Mk 5:41. 15:22, 34. Lk 16:13. Jn 1:38, 41, 42. 7:39. 9:7. Ac 4:36. 9:36. 13:8. 2 T 4:6. He 7:2. **prepared.** Is 33:11. **ordaineth.** Ps 11:2. 45:5. 64:3, 7. 144:6. Dt 32:23, 42. Jb 6:4. La 3:12, 13. Hab 3:11, 13. **persecutors.** Ac 9:4, 5. 2 Th 1:6. Re 6:10. 16:6.

14. **he travaileth.** ⸮173, Ge +27:44. ⸮132A, Ge +4:23. Jb 15:20, 35. Is 33:11. 59:4, 5. Ja *1:15.

15. **made.** Heb. hath digged. Ps 35:7. 119:85. Jb

6:27. Je 18:20. **pit**. Heb. *bor*, Ge +37:20. ♪173, Ge +27:44. **and is**. Ps 9:15, 16. *10:2. 35:8. 94:13. 140:9, 10. 141:10. Est *7:10. Jb 4:8. Pr 5:22. 26:27. Ec 10:8, 9.

16. **His mischief**. Ps 36:4, 12. 37:12, 13. 1 S 23:9. 24:12, 13. 26:10. 28:19. 31:3, 4. 1 K 2:32. Est 9:25. Mt 27:3-5. **shall return**. Jg 1:7. Est *9:25. Jb *4:8. Pr *5:22. *26:27. Da 6:24. **own pate**. ♪171Q12, Jg +5:30.

17. **according**. Ps 35:28. 51:14. *71:15, 16. 98:2. 111:3. 145:7. **Lord most high**. Ps 9:2. 21:7. *46:4. 47:2. *50:14. *57:2. 73:11. 77:10. *78:17, 35, 56. 82:6. *83:18. *91:1, 9. 92:1, 8. *107:11. Ge +14:18. Da 4:17, 25, 34. Mk +5:7. Lk 8:28. Ac 7:48. 16:17. He 7:1.

PSALM 8

The glory of God displayed in the works of creation, 1-3; and in his condescending love to man, 4-9. (Title.) **Gittith**. i.e. *a wine-press*, ❋S#1665h. Ps 81, 84, titles.

1. **our Lord**. ver. 9. Ps 63:1. 145:1. Is *26:13. Mt 22:45. Jn +√20:28. Ph *2:9-11. 3:8. Re 19:16. **how excellent**. Ps *72:17-19. 113:2-4. 148:13. Ex 15:11. *34:5-7. Dt *28:58. SS 5:16. **thy name**. SS 1:3. **set**. ♪96B, Ge +8:5. **thy glory**. Ps 36:5. 57:10, 11. 68:4. 108:4, 5. 1 K 8:27. Hab +*3:3. Ep 4:10. Ph *2:9, 10. He 7:26.

2. **Out**. Mt *11:25. ▶*21:16. Lk *10:21. 1 C *1:27. *12:9. **and**. ♪174, Ge +18:27. **ordained**. Heb. founded. Ps 24:2. 78:69mg. 89:11. 102:25. 1 Ch 9:22. Hab 1:12mg. **strength**. Ps *84:5-7. Is *40:31. Am 5:9. 2 C *12:9, 10. ♪121L3. Metonymy of the Subject B584. Attributes are put for the praise and celebration of them. Here, strength is put for the praise for the manifestation and putting forth of God's strength, as is clear from Mt *▶21:16, where it is rendered "Out of the mouth of babes and sucklings thou hast perfected praise." Thus in the New Testament quotation of this passage the figure is interpreted, not just translated (See related note, Ps +*16:9n). For other instances of this figure see Ps 29:1. 96:7. **still**. Ps *4:4. *46:10. Ex 11:7. 15:16. Jsh *2:9-11. 1 S *2:9. Is 37:20-29, *36-38. Hab *2:20. **the enemy**. Ps 44:16.

3. **When**. Ps *19:1. *111:2. Jb 22:12. 36:24. Ro 1:20. **work**. Ps 33:6. Ge 1:1. Ex 8:19. 31:18. Lk *11:20. **thy fingers**. ♪22A16, Ex +8:19. **moon**. Ps 104:19. 136:7-9. 148:3. Ge 1:16-18. Dt 4:19. Jb 25:3, 5. Is *40:26.

4. **What**. ♪85F. Erotesis B952: In rapture or exultation. For other instances of this figure see Ps 31:19. 139:17. 144:3. 2 S 7:18, 19. Jb 7:17. He 2:6. **is man**. Ps *144:3. 2 Ch 6:18. Jb *7:17. 25:6. Is 40:17. He ▶2:6-9. **mindful**. ♪173, Ge +27:44. **son of man**. Ps 4:2. 80:17. 146:3. Is 51:12. Ezk 8:15. Da +*7:13. 8:17. Mt 8:20. **visitest**. Ps 106:4. Ge 21:1. Ex 4:31. Lk 1:68. 7:16. 19:44. Ac 15:14. 1 P 2:12.

5. **For thou**. Ps 103:20. Ge *1:26, 27. +*2:7. 2 S 14:20. Jb 4:18-20. Ph *2:7, 8. He 2:7, 9, *16. **a little lower**. Lk ◐√20:36. **than the angels**. or, than God. Heb. *Elohim*. Ge 1:26. This rendering, favored by Young and found in several versions, is not acceptable from a doctrinal standpoint, for it is out of harmony with what the Old Testament and the Bible as a whole teaches about the transcendence (Ps *71:19n. √139:7n. Jb 36:26. Is 28:29. 40:12-26. +*57:15. Ezk +*28:9.

Ro 9:5. 1 T 6:16) of God—that there is an infinite gulf between man the creature and God the creator. Compare Jn 1:18mg. *Elohim* here is used in the sense of angels, as at Jb 1:6; 2:1; Ps 29:1mg; 89:6; 97:7; 138:1. **hast crowned**. Ps 21:3-5. 45:1-3, 6. Jn 13:31, 32. Ep 1:21. Ph 2:9-11. He 2:9. 1 P 1:20, 21. **glory**. Ps +*30:12mg.

6. **madest**. Ge +*1:26, 28. 9:2. 24:36. Mt *28:18. He +*1:2. **hands**. ♪22A14.1, Nu +11:23. **thou hast**. 1 C ▶15:27. **put**. Ps 110:1. Is 9:6. 1 C *15:24-27. Ep 1:22. He *2:8, 9. 1 P *3:22. **under**. ♪22D3D2, Ps +110:1.

7. **All sheep**, etc. Heb. Flocks and oxen, all of them. Ps 50:10. Ge 2:20. Nu 32:24. Dt 7:13. 28:4, 18, 51. **beasts of**. Ps 50:11. 80:13.

8. **The fowl**. Ps 148:10. Ge 1:20-25. Jb 38:39-41. 39:1, etc. 40:15-24. 41:1, etc.

9. **how excellent**. ver. 1. Ps 104:24. Dt 33:26. Jb 11:7.

PSALM 9

David praises God for punishing his enemies and maintaining his cause, 1-6. He shows that God will preserve his servants and calls on them to praise his name, 7-12. He prays for deliverance from present trials, that he may still praise the Lord, and predicts the ruin of the wicked, 13-20.

(Title.) A.M. 2941. B.C. 1063. **Muthlabben**. i.e. *death of the son*, ❋S#4192h. Ps 48:14. Probably "the death of the champion:" so the Chaldee has, "A Psalm of David, to be sung concerning the death of the man who went out between *(mibbeyney)* the camps;" evidently considering *labben*, of the same import as *bainayim*, "a middle-man or champion," as Goliath is termed 1 S 17:4, concerning whose defeat this psalm is generally supposed to have been composed.

1. **praise**. Ps 7:17. 34:1-4. 103:1, 2. *145:1-3. 146:1, 2. 1 Ch 29:10-13. Is 12:1. He *13:15. Re 5:9-14. **with my**. Ps 86:12. 111:1. 138:1. Lk 10:27. **show**. ver. 14. Ps 51:15. 106:2. 1 Ch 16:12, 24. Is 43:21. 60:6. Re *15:3.

2. **I will be glad**. Ps *4:7. *5:11. 27:6. 28:7. *32:11. 43:4. 92:4. *97:11, 12. *104:34. Hab √3:17, 18. Ph *4:4. **and rejoice**. Ps *33:21. *43:4. 1 S 2:1. Is 61:1-3, 10. Jl 2:21, 23. Lk 1:46, 47. Jn *15:11. 16:22. Ac 2:46, 47. 13:52. Ro *5:2, 11. *14:17. 15:13. Ga 5:22. Ph 3:3. Col 1:11. 1 Th 1:6. 1 P *1:8. **O thou**. Ps 7:17. 56:2, 3. 83:18. 97:9. Da 5:18.

3. **they shall**. Ps 68:1, 2. 76:7. 80:16. Is 64:3. 2 Th *1:9. Re *6:12-17. 20:11. **presence**. ♪22A4, Ge +19:13.

4. **For**. Ps 16:5. 140:12. **maintained**, etc. Heb. made my judgment. Ps *140:12. 2 S 18:19mg. **right**. Heb. in righteousness. Ps 45:6, 7. 47:8. 89:14. 96:13. 98:9. Is 11:4. 1 P 2:23.

5. **rebuked**. Ps 2:1, 8, 9. 78:55. 79:10. 149:7. 1 S 17:45-51. 2 S 5:6, etc. 8:1-15. 10:6-9. 21:15-22. 22:44-46. Re 19:15. **destroyed**. Ps 5:6. 1 S *25:39. 31:4. 2 S 17:23. Ml 4:3. **the wicked**. ver. 17. Ps 10:2-4, 13, 15. Hab 1:10, 11, *13. 2 Th 2:8. **put out**. Ps 109:13. Dt 9:14. 29:20. Jb *20:28. Pr *10:7. 13:9. Ec +*9:5. Is 14:22. **for ever**. Heb. *olam*, Ps +21:4.

6. **O thou**, etc. *or*, The destructions of the enemy are come to a perpetual end, and their cities hast thou destroyed, etc. Ps 7:5. 8:2. Ex 15:6. Mi 7:8, 10. **perpetual end**. Jb +4:20 (❋S#5331h). **destructions**. Ps 46:9.

Ex 14:13. Is 10:24, 25. 14:6-8. *51:12, 13. Na 1:9-13. 1 C 15:26, 54-57. Re 20:2. **thou hast.** 1 S 30:1. 31:7. Is 10:6, 7, 13, 14. 14:17. 37:26. Je 51:25. **memorial.** 2 K 19:25. Is *14:22, 23. Je 51:62-64.

7. **But.** Ps *90:2. 102:12, *24-27. He 1:11, 12. 13:8. 2 P 3:8. **for ever.** Heb. *olam,* Ex +*12:24. **he hath.** Ps 50:3-5. 103:19. Re *20:11-13.

8. **he shall judge.** Ps 50:6. 94:15. 96:13. *98:9. 99:4. Ge √18:25. Is 11:4, 5. Ac *17:31. Ro 2:5, 6, 16. Re 20:12, 13. **world.** ∫121J17, Ge +6:11.

9. **The Lord.** Ps *18:2. *32:7. *37:39. *46:1. 48:3. *62:8. *91:1, 2. 142:4, 5. Dt *33:27. Pr 18:10. Is 4:5, 6. 8:14. 32:2. Na *1:7. Lk *13:34. He *6:18. **be a refuge.** Heb. be a high place. Ps 18:2. 20:1mg. 46:7mg. 59:9mg. 62:2mg. 91:2. 2 S 22:3. **in times.** T#769. Ps 18:2. 22:24. 27:10, 14. *31:7. 37:24, 39. 41:1. *46:1-3. *50:15. *55:22. 71:3. 73:26. 77:1, 2. *108:12. *112:4. 136:23. 138:7. 145:14. Jb *34:23. Is *25:4. 27:8. 50:10. Je 16:19. 30:11. La *3:31-33. Mi 7:8, 9. Na 1:7. Mt *11:28. Jn 16:33. 2 C 1:5. 2 C *4:8, 9.

10. This verse furnishes an excellent, instructive illustration of two useful methods of practical Bible study and meditation. It is helpful, when meditating upon a passage of Scripture, to note what it states about "my responsibility," and what it states about "God's responsibility." The clauses of this verse are marked in the notes below to reflect this analysis. Since nearly every passage of Scripture opens up under this analysis, it is not necessary to furnish further examples, except to mention one additional particularly effective illustration for this method, Pr 3:5, 6.

It is also helpful to notice expressed or implied cause/effect relationships. The cause/effect relationships are noted below for each clause in this verse. The practical value of observing these relationships in study, teaching, and exhortation is discussed in the related note on exhortation (Ro 12:8n). Since texts of Scripture which display expressed or implied cause/effect relationships are not easy to find, the following list will furnish a number of such passages for further study. For other cause/effect relationships see Ps 33:21. 37:40. 67:5-7. 78:5-8 (correcting stubbornness and rebellion in children). 89:31, 32 (if/then). 106:12 (believed his word/sang his praises). *119:67, 71, 155, 171. Ge 22:18. Dt +*28:3 (most verses which contain the word "blessed" suggest cause/effect relationships). *28:15 (failure to listen to and obey God's word brings a curse). 1 Ch √5:20. +*28:9. 2 Ch +√7:14. 13:18. *20:20. *26:5 (seeking God/prosperity). Many cause/effect relationships pertaining to poverty may be found stated in the references given for the note on the "poverty curse," Dt +*28:48n. 2 Ch 33:12. Jb 35:12. 36:12. Pr +*3:33. 28:5. 29:15. 30:8, 9. Is 26:3 w Ph 4:6-8. Is 26:9. +√29:24n (erred in spirit/come to understanding; murmured/learn doctrine). 58:7, 8, 9-11, 13, 14. 66:4. Je 5:25. *6:19. 10:21. 23:22. Ezk 12:2 (rebellion blinds and deafens). 16:49. √33:31 (covetousness hinders response and obedience to God's word). Other cause/effect relationships pertaining to covetousness are stated or implied in the following references: Jsh 7:21 (theft); 1 S 15:9 (disobedience); 1 K 20:6 (robbery); 21:2 (meanness); 2 K 5:20 (unscrupulousness); Pr 21:25, 26 (laziness); Lk 16:14 (scoffing or derision). Da 6:23. *9:11, 13. Ho +*4:12 (*err,* *S#8582h. The context of nearly every occurrence of this Hebrew word contains a cause/effect relationship). 13:6. Am *2:4. 3:10.

Hab 1:4. Zp 1:17. Zc +*5:3, 4. *7:12. Ml 2:13, 14. 3:5, 9-12. Mt 13:22. Lk √7:47n. Jn 5:44. 16:27. 1 C *12:25 (lack of care/schism). Ep *6:1-3. 2 T 2:7. 2 P 3:16 (unlearned/unstable) w Col 1:23 (grounded/settled). 1 J 2:14. **they that know.** ∫68, Ge +10:1. ∫121C2A1, Jb +19:25. This clause represents "my responsibility." It also reflects the "cause." Ps *91:14. Ex *34:5-7. 1 Ch +*28:9. Pr *18:10. Is 52:6. Jn *17:3. 2 C 4:6. 2 T *1:12. 1 J 2:3, 4. 5:20. **thy name.** Ps 20:7. 89:24. Ex 3:13. +15:2. 34:5. Le +22:32. Nu +*6:27. 1 K 18:24. Am 9:12. Mt +*6:9. 10:41. Jn *17:6. Ac 15:14. **will put their trust.** This clause represents "my responsibility." It reflects the "result" or "effect" of knowing God's name, that is, His character. Ps 5:11. +*11:1. 57:1. 146:5, 6. Jb +*13:15. Is √26:3, 4. 50:10 (T#1419). **hast not forsaken.** This clause represents God's responsibility. It reflects the "result" or "effect" of seeking Him. Ps *37:24, 25, 28. 105:3, 4. 1 S *12:22. Is *41:17. 45:19. *46:3, 4. *55:6, 7. Je *29:13. Jn *6:37. 2 C 1:9, 10. 2 C 4:9. He +*13:5. Ju *24. **that seek.** This clause represents "my responsibility." It reflects the cause which effects the result described in the preceding clause, namely, seeking God results in reaping the benefit of his provision for our security. Ps +*34:4. Dt 4:29. 1 Ch +*28:9. 2 Ch +√7:14. √26:5. Pr 8:17. Je √29:13. Lk 11:9. He +*11:6.

11. **Sing.** Ps 33:1-3. 47:6, 7. 96:1, 2. 148:1-5, 13, 14. He *13:15. **which.** Ps 78:68. 132:13, 14. Is 12:6. 14:32. He 12:22. Re 14:1. **declare.** Ps 66:2, 5. 96:10. 105:1, 2. 107:22. 118:17. Is 12:4-6. Jn 17:26.

12. **When.** Ge *9:5. 2 K 24:4. Is 26:21. Mt 23:35. Lk 11:50, 51. *18:7, 8. Re 6:9, 10. 16:6. **blood.** ∫171I111, Dt +19:12. **he forgetteth.** Ps 10:14, 17. 22:24. 34:6. 102:17. Ex 3:7, 9. Lk 18:7, 8. **humble.** *or,* afflicted. Ps 10:12mg. Jg 10:16. Mt *18:4. Lk +18:14.

13. **Have.** Ps 51:1. 119:132. **consider.** Ps 13:3. 25:19. 119:153. 142:6. Ne 9:32. La 1:9, 11. **thou.** Ps 30:3. 56:13. 86:13. 107:18. 116:3, 4. Is 38:10. Jon 2:6. **the gates.** ∫171S7B, Ge +14:7. Ps *68:20. 107:18. Jb +*38:17.

14. **That.** Ps 51:15. 79:13. *106:2. 138:1. **show forth.** 1 P 2:9. **in the gates.** Ps 22:22, 25. 35:18. 42:4. 109:30, 31. 116:18, 19. 118:19, 20. 149:1, 2. **daughter.** Is 37:22. 62:11. Mi 4:13. Mt 21:5. **I will.** Ps *13:5. 20:5. 21:1. *35:9. 51:12. 1 S 2:1. Is 12:3. Hab 3:18. Lk 1:47.

15. **The heathen.** Ps 7:15, 16. 35:8. 37:15. 57:6. 94:23. Pr *5:22. *22:8. *26:27.

16. **known.** Ps 48:11. *58:10, 11. 83:17, 18. Ex 7:5. 14:4, 10, 31. Dt 29:22-28. Jsh 2:10, 11. Jg 1:7. 1 S 6:19, 20. 17:46. 2 K 19:19, 34, 35. **wicked.** Ps 11:6. 140:9. Pr *1:32. 6:2. 12:13. Is 8:15. 28:13. **Higgaion.** *that is,* Meditation. *S#1902h. Ps 5:1. 19:14. 92:3mg. **Selah.** i.e. *make clear; prominent,* *S#5542h. Ps 3:2, 4, 8. 4:2, 4. 7:5. 9:16, 20. 20:3. 21:2. 24:6, 10. 32:4, 5, 7. 39:5, 11. 44:8. 46:3, 7, 11. 47:4. 48:8. 49:13, 15. 50:6. 52:3, 5. 54:3. 55:7, 19. 57:3, 6. 59:5, 13. 60:4. 61:4. 62:4, 8. 66:4, 7, 15. 67:1, 4. 68:7, 19, 32. 75:3. 76:3, 9. 77:3, 9, 15. 81:7. 82:2. 83:8. 84:4, 8. 85:2. 87:3, 6. 88:7, 10. 89:4, 37, 45. 89:48. 140:3, 5, 8. 143:6. Hab 3:3, 9, 13.

17. **The wicked.** Pr 14:32. Is 3:11. 5:14. Mt *25:41-46. Ro *2:8, 9. 2 Th *1:7-9. Re *20:15. *21:8. **turned.** Ge 37:5. **hell.** Heb. *sheol,* Ge +37:35. T#561. Ps 1:5. 11:6. +*16:10. 18:5. *55:15. 139:8. Dt 32:+*22, +43 (T#237). Jb 21:20. 26:6. 31:3. 36:13. Pr 15:24. 27:20. Is 5:14. √33:14. +*66:24. Ho 13:9, 14. Ml *4:1. Mt

3:7, *10-12. 7:19, 27. 8:11, 12. 11:23, 24. *13:40-42, 47-50. 23:33. √25:+32 (T#387), 41. Mk 9:43, 44. Lk *16:22, 23, +24 (T#343). Jn 5:28, 29. 15:6. 17:12. Ro +11:22 (T#236). 1 C 16:22. Ph 3:18, 19. 2 Th 1:6-9. *2:3, 9-12. He 10:26, 27. Ja +1:15 (T#287). 2 P 2:4, 9, 10, 17. 3:7. Ju 7. Re 19:20. *20:15. +*21:8. **forget.** T#692. Ps +14:1 (T#22). 44:17, 20. *50:22. 106:13, 21. Dt 32:18. Jg 3:7. 1 S 12:9. Jb *8:13. Je 2:32. 3:21. *13:25. 18:15. 23:27. Ezk 22:12. Ho 2:13.

18. For the needy. ver. 12. Ps *12:5. 72:4, 12-14. 102:17, 20. 109:31. Is *41:17. Lk 1:53. 6:20. Ja 2:5. **alway.** Jb +4:20 (*S#5331h). **forgotten.** √22C4, Ps +13:1. **expectation.** Pr 23:17, 18. 24:14. Ph 1:20. **the poor.** Ps 10:17. *74:19. **not.** √63I1C1, Ge +2:6. **for ever.** *S#5703h. Heb. *ad.* Ps 9:5, 18. 10:16. 19:9. 21:4, 6. 22:26. 37:29. 45:6, 17. 48:14. 52:8. 61:8. 83:17. 89:29. 92:7. 104:5. 111:3, 8, 10. 112:3, 9. 119:44. 132:12 (for evermore), 14. 145:1, 2, 21. 148:6. Ex 15:18. Nu 24:20, 24. 1 Ch 28:9. Jb 19:24. 20:4 (of old). Pr 12:19. 29:14. Is 9:6 (everlasting). 26:4. 30:8. 45:17 (without end). 57:15 (eternity). 64:9. 65:18. Da 12:3. Am 1:11 (perpetually). Mi 4:5. 7:18. Hab 3:6 (everlasting).

19. Arise. Ps 3:7. 7:6. 10:12. 12:5. 44:23, 26. 68:1, 2. 74:22, 23. 76:8, 9. 80:2. Is 42:13, 14. 51:9. Zp 3:8. **let not.** Ge 32:28. 1 S *2:8-10. 2 Ch 14:11. Is 42:13. **let the.** Ps 2:1-3. 79:6. 149:7. Je 10:25. Jl 3:12. Mi 5:15. Zc 14:18. Re 19:15. **judged.** √121C2D2, Ge +15:14.

20. Put. Ps 76:12. Ex 15:16. 23:27. Dt 2:25. Je 32:40. Ezk 30:13. **the nations.** T#1624. Ps 67:1-4. 86:8, 9. Is 64:1, 2. **may.** Ps 82:6, 7. Is 31:3. Ezk 28:2, 9. Ac *12:22, 23.

PSALM 10

The psalmist complains that the Lord hid his face amidst the outrages of wicked persecutors, 1-11. He prays for redress and professes his confidence in God, 12-18.

1. A.M. 3463. **B.C.** 541. **standest.** Ps *22:1. *46:1. 109:31. Je *14:8. Mt 27:46. **afar off.** √22D3E. Anthropomorphism B892. God is spoken of in circumstances which have to do with place, as men are: standing afar off. **hidest.** Ps *13:1-3. *27:9. 30:7. 44:24. 88:14. Jb 13:24. 23:9. 34:29.

2. The wicked, etc. Heb. In the pride of the wicked he doth, etc. **pride.** T#549. Ps 31:18. 36:11. 59:12. 73:6-9. 119:+*21, 51, 69, 85, 122. 123:4. 140:5. Ge 11:4. Ex 9:17. 18:11. Is 10:12, 13. 14:13, 16. Je 43:2. Ezk +*16:49, 50. **let.** Ps 7:16. 9:15, 16. Pr 5:22.

3. boasteth. Ps 35:21. 49:6. 52:1. 73:8, 9. 94:4. Ex 15:9. Is 10:7-11. 37:23, 24. Ja 4:13, 16. **heart's.** Heb. soul's, *nephesh,* Ex +23:9. **and blesseth,** etc. *or,* the covetous blesseth *himself,* he abhorreth the Lord. Ps 49:11-13, 18. *52:1. Dt 29:19. 1 S 23:21. Jb 31:24, 25. Pr *28:4. Ho 12:7, 8. Zc 11:5-8. Lk 12:19. Ro *1:29, 30, 32. 2 T *3:2-4. 1 J +*2:15, 16. **blesseth.** √182, Ge +18:22. **covetous.** Ps 112:10. *119:36. Ex +*20:17. Pr 28:16. Lk *12:15, 20. 1 C 5:11. Ep 5:3, 5. He *13:5. **whom.** √63K, Ge +37:13. Ps +*34:16. Jsh 7:20, 21, 25, 26. Is *57:17. Je 22:17. Mi 6:10-12. Hab 2:9. Mt 26:15, 16. Lk *12:15. 16:14, 15. 1 C +*6:10. Ep 5:5. Col *3:5, 6. 1 T √6:9, 10. 2 P 2:3, 14, 15. **abhorreth.** Ps 5:6. Le 26:30. Dt 32:19. Ph *3:19.

4. the pride. T#696. Ps 18:27. 101:5. Pr 6:17. *21:4.

30:13. Is *2:11. *3:9. 10:12. Mt 20:10-15. Lk 15:28-30. Ro *10:3. 1 C 1:18, 23. **will not seek.** T#693. Ps *14:2. *27:8. 50:21. 94:8. Ex 5:2. Dt 8:14. Jb 22:17. Pr 6:+6 (T#132), 9. 30:9. Is 5:12. Je 2:31. 4:22. 8:7. Ho 7:11. Da *5:22, 23. Zp 2:3. Jn +17:25 (T#739). 2 P +3:5 (T#707). **God,** etc. *or,* all his thoughts *are, There is* no God. Ps *14:1. 53:1. Is *26:11. 2 C √2:14. Ep *2:12. **thoughts.** Ge *6:5. Is 59:7. *65:2. Je *4:14. Mk *7:21. Ac *8:22. Ro *1:21, 28.

5. His. Ge 6:12. Pr 1:19. 2:13-15. Is 10:1. Ho 9:9. Ro 3:16. **thy judgments.** Ps 92:5, 6. Pr 15:24. 24:1. Is 5:12. 26:11. 28:15. 42:25. Ho 14:9. **he puffeth.** √121S2, Ge +21:6. By Metonymy of the Adjunct, whereby the sign is put for the thing signified, "puffeth at them" signifies "despiseth them." Ps 12:5. Jg 9:27, 28, 38. 2 S 5:6. 1 K 20:10, 11, 13. 2 Ch 32:15-19.

6. said. Ps 11:1. 14:1. Mt 24:48. **not.** Ps 15:5. 30:6. Ec √8:11. Is √28:15, 16. 47:7. *56:12. Na 1:10. Mt 24:48-51. 1 Th *5:3. Re 18:7. **never.** Heb. unto generation and generation. Ps +*33:11mg. 45:17. 49:11mg. 61:6mg. 79:13mg. Dt 32:7mg. Jl 2:2mg.

7. full. Ps 59:12. 62:4. 109:17, 18. Ro 3:14. **and deceit.** Heb. deceits. Ps 5:9. 7:14. 36:3. 52:4. 55:21. 58:3. 64:3. Is 59:4. Je 9:3, 6. Ro 3:13. **under.** Jb 20:12. **mischief.** Ps 7:14. 140:9. Jb 15:35. Mt 12:34. Ja 3:6-8. **vanity.** *or,* iniquity. Ps 12:2. 41:6. 144:8, 11. Pr 21:6. 30:8. 2 P 2:18.

8. sitteth. 1 S 22:18, 19. 23:23. 1 K 21:20. 2 K 21:16. Pr 1:11, 12, *18. Hab 3:14. Lk 8:1. 10:1. **his eyes.** Ps 17:11. Pr 6:12, 13. Je 22:17. **are privily set.** Heb. hide themselves. Ps 27:5. 31:19, 20. 56:6.

9. He lieth. Ps 17:12. 59:3. Mi 7:2. Ac 23:21. **secretly.** Heb. in the secret places. La 3:10. Am 3:4. Na 2:11, 12. Zc 11:3. **to catch.** Je 5:26. Ezk 19:3-6. Hab 1:15. Jn 10:12. **poor, when.** Ps +*12:5. 14:6. 35:10. 37:14. 109:31. Jb 5:15, 16. 20:19. 24:14. Pr *14:31. 22:16. 28:15. Is 3:15. 32:7. Ezk 22:29. Am 2:6, 7. 4:1. 5:11, 12. 8:4, 6. Hab 3:14.

10. croucheth. Heb. breaketh himself. *S#1794h. Ps 38:8. 44:19. 51:8, 17 (contrite). Dt +23:1 (*S#1795h). 1 S 2:36. **humbleth.** 1 S 18:21-26. 23:21, 22. 2 S 15:5. **by his strong ones.** Heb. *or,* into his strong parts.

11. said. ver. 6. Mk 2:6. Lk 7:39. **God.** Ps 64:5. *73:11. *94:7. Jb *22:13, 14. Pr √15:3. Ec *8:11. Ezk 8:12. 9:9. **never.** Jb +4:20 (*S#5331h).

12. Arise. Ps 3:7. 7:6. 9:19. 12:5. **lift.** Ps 94:2. Is 26:11. 33:10. Mi 5:9. **forget.** Ps 9:12. 13:1. 44:24. 74:19. 77:9. **humble.** *or,* afflicted. T#1565. ver. 2, 9, 17. Ps 9:12mg, 18.

13. contemn. Ps 74:10, 18. Nu 11:20. 2 S 12:9, 10. Lk 10:16. 1 Th 4:8. **Thou.** Ge 9:5. 42:22. 2 Ch 24:22. Lk 11:50, 51.

14. Thou hast. Ps 35:22. Pr 15:3. Je 16:17. 23:24. He *4:13. **for thou.** Hab 1:13. **to requite.** Jg 1:7. 2 K 9:26. 2 Ch 6:23. Je 51:56. Jl 3:4. **thy hand.** 2 S 18:19mg. **the poor.** Ps 55:22. 2 T *1:12. 1 P *4:19. 5:7. **committeth.** Heb. leaveth. Ps *37:4. Is 10:3. Je 49:11. 1 P *2:23. **helper.** Ps 12:5. 68:5. 146:9. Dt 10:18. Ho 14:3. **fatherless.** ver. +18. Ps 68:5. Je *49:11. Ho 14:3.

15. Break. Ps 3:7. *37:17. Jb *38:15. Ezk 30:21, 22. Zc 11:17. **seek.** Ps 7:9. 2 K 21:12-15. Jb 10:6. 20:27. Je 2:34. Ezk 23:48. Zp 1:12.

16. The Lord. Ps 29:10. 93:1. *145:13. 146:10. Is 33:22. Je *10:10. La *5:19. Da 4:34. 6:26. 1 T *1:17. 6:15, 16. **for ever.** Heb. *olam,* Ps +21:4. **and ever.**

Ps +9:18 (✻S#5703h). **heathen.** Ps 9:5, 15. 18:43-45. 44:2, 3. 78:55. 80:8.

17. **Lord.** Ps 9:12, 18. 37:4. 145:19. Pr 10:24. **heard.** ⌐173, Ge +27:44. **humble.** 2 Ch 33:12, 13. 34:27. Pr 15:8. Mt +✻5:3. 18:4. Lk ✻18:13, 14. Ja ✻4:6, 10. 1 P 5:5. **thou wilt prepare.** *or,* establish. T#1149. Ps ✻65:4. 89:2, 4. 112:7, 8. Ex 4:11, 12. 1 Ch 29:18. 2 Ch 29:36. 30:12. Pr ✻16:1. Is 57:19. 65:1. Je 1:6-9. 24:7. 30:21. Am ✻4:12. Zp 3:9. Zc 12:10. 13:9. Jn ✻6:44, 65. Ro ✻8:26, 27. Ep 2:18. 3:12. 2 Th ✻3:5. Ja 1:16, 17. **cause.** Ps +✻34:15. 102:17. Is +✻65:24. Ac 4:24-31. 12:5, etc. Ja ✻4:3. 1 P 3:12. **thine ear.** ⌐22A8. Anthropomorphism B875: ears are attributed to God. For other instances of this figure see Ps 31:2. 40:6. 55:1. 71:2. 130:2. Is 50:4, 5. Ezk 8:18. Ja +✻5:4. **to hear.** ⌐22C14, Ge +16:11.

18. **judge.** ver. 14. Ps 72:4. 82:3. 94:1-6. Is ✻11:4. Lk 18:7, 8. **fatherless.** T#1490. ver. +14. Ps 82:3. Ge +11:28. Dt +10:18. Ml +✻3:5. **oppressed.** *or,* bruised. T#1630. Ps 9:9. 74:19-21. Pr 26:28. **the man.** Ps 17:14. Lk 16:25. 1 C 15:47, 48. Ph 3:18, 19. **oppress.** *or,* terrify. Dt 1:29 (dread). 7:21. 20:3. 31:6. Jsh 1:9 (afraid). Is 2:19, 21 (shake terribly).

PSALM 11

David, when advised to flee from his enemies, professes confidence in God, 1-3. He shows the Lord's abhorrence of the wicked and his care of the righteous, 4-7.

1. A.M. 2942. B.C. 1062. **In the.** Ps 7:1. +√9:10. 16:1. 25:2. 31:14. ✻56:11. 2 Ch 14:11. 16:8. Is ✻26:3, 4. **my trust.** Ps 2:12. 18:30. 20:7. 22:4. 28:7. ✻31:19. ✻32:10. 37:5, 40. 40:4. ✻56:3. 57:1. 112:7. 118:8, 9. 125:1. 1 S 30:6. 2 Ch 13:18. Jb 13:15. Pr √3:5, 6. 16:20. 18:10. 29:25. Is 12:2. √26:3, 4. ✻50:10. 57:13. Je 17:7. 39:18. Da 3:28. ✻6:23. Na 1:7. 2 C 1:9, 10. 1 T 4:10. 6:17. 1 P ✻5:7. **how.** ⌐85K, Ge +3:9. 1 S 19:11. 20:38. 21:10-12. 22:3. 23:14. 26:19, 20. 27:1. **soul.** Heb. *nephesh,* Ge +12:13. **Flee.** Ps 55:6, 7. Pr 6:5. Lk 13:31.

2. **For, lo.** Ps 10:2. 37:14. ✻64:3, 4. Je 9:3. **make.** Ps 21:12. **that.** Ps 10:8, 9. 64:5. 142:3. 1 S 18:21. 23:9. Mt 26:4. Ac 23:12-15. **privily.** Heb. in darkness. Ps 91:6. Jb 3:6. **the upright.** Ps 7:10. 32:11. 64:10. 94:15. 97:11. 125:4.

3. **If the foundations.** Ps 75:3. 82:5. Is 58:12. 2 T 1:13. ◐✻2:19. T 1:13. **what.** 1 K 19:13-18. 22:12-14. 2 Ch 32:13-15. Ne 6:10-12. Je 26:11-15. Da 3:15-18. 6:10, etc. Jn 11:8-10. Ac 4:5-12, 24-33.

4. **The Lord.** Ps 9:11. 18:6. Ex 40:34, 35. 1 Ch 17:5. Hab √2:20. Zc 2:13. 2 Th 2:4. **the Lord's.** Ps 2:4. 103:19. Is ✻66:1. Mt ✻5:34. 23:21, 22. Ac 7:49. Re 4:2. **throne.** ⌐22D3C1. Anthropomorphism B892: As to place, God is said to sit on a throne. For other instances of this figure see Ps 47:8. 103:19. Is 66:1. Je 14:21. Mt 5:34. **his eyes.** Ps 33:13. ✻34:15, 16. 44:21. ✻66:7. Ge 3:8. 2 Ch 16:9. Pr 15:3. Je ✻17:10. 23:24. He ✻4:13. ⌐22A6. Anthropomorphism B875: *eyes* are used for God's observation. For other instances of this figure see Jb 34:21. Is 1:16. 65:16. Ho 13:14. Am 9:3. He ✻4:13. **behold.** ⌐22C13, Ge +16:13.

5. **trieth.** Ps 7:9. ✻17:3. 26:2. 66:10. √139:1, 23, 24. Ge ✻22:1. Jb ✻23:10. Zc ✻13:9. Ml 3:3. Ja ✻1:12. 1 P ✻1:7. 4:12. **wicked.** Ps 5:4, 5. 10:3. 21:8. Pr 6:16-19. Je 12:8. Zc 11:8. **loveth.** ⌐121C2C1. Metonymy of the

Cause B555. Verbs of loving and hating are put for the actions consequent upon them. "To love" is put for to expect, desire, take, or practice. Here, "he that loveth violence" is put for he that practices it. For other instances of this figure see Pr 21:17. Mt 6:5. Lk 11:43. Jn 3:19. 2 T 4:8, 10. **his soul.** Heb. *nephesh,* Ge +34:3. Le +26:11. ⌐22A1, Le +26:11.

6. **Upon the wicked.** Ps 105:32. Ge 19:24. Ex 9:23, 24. Jb 18:15. 20:23. Is 24:17, 18. Ezk 13:13. 38:22. Lk 17:29. 2 P ✻3:7. **snares.** *or,* quick burning coals. Ps 69:22. 91:3. 119:110. Hab +✻3:5. The original word never means "lightning," as some suppose (Young). **fire.** Ps 18:8, 12, 13. 21:9. 2 P +✻3:7. **brimstone.** Ge 19:24. Dt 29:23. Ezk 38:22. Re 19:20. **horrible tempest.** *or,* a burning tempest. Ps 119:53. La 5:10mg. **portion.** Ps ●16:5. ✻17:14. Ge 43:34. 1 S 1:4. 9:23. Jb 20:29. 27:13, etc. **their cup.** Ps ●16:5. ✻75:8. Is 51:17, 22. Je 25:15-17. Hab 2:16. Jn 18:11.

7. **For.** Ps 45:7. 99:4. 146:8. Is 61:8. **his.** Ps 5:12. 21:6. 33:18. 34:15. 42:5. Jb ✻36:7. 1 P ✻3:12.

PSALM 12

David, lamenting the decay of godliness and the prevalence of deceit, craves help from God, 1, 2. He predicts the destruction of flatterers, proud boasters, and oppressors, 3-5. He comforts himself in assurance of divine protection, grounded on the faithful promises of God, notwithstanding the triumph of the wicked, 6-8.

(Title.) **chief.** *or,* overseer. Ps 4, 5, 6, 8, 9, titles. **Sheminith.** *or,* The eighth. *or,* octave. Ps 6, title. 1 Ch 15:21.

1. **Help.** *or,* Save. Ps 3:7. 6:4. 54:1. Mt 8:25. 14:30. **godly.** Ge 6:12. Is 1:9, 21, 22. ✻57:1. 63:5. Je 5:1. Mi ✻7:1, 2. Mt 24:12. 2 C ✻5:8. **faithful.** ⌐121N1, Ge +31:54. i.e. faithful men fail. Pr ✻20:6. Is 59:4, 13-15. Lk ✻18:8.

2. **speak vanity.** Ps 10:7. 36:3, 4. 38:12. 41:6. 52:1-4. 59:12. 144:8, 11. Is 58:9. Je 9:2-6, 8. Ezk 12:24. Ro 16:18. 1 Th 2:5. **a double heart.** Heb. an heart and an heart. T#330. Ps ✻28:3. 86:11. 1 Ch 12:33mg. Ho 10:2. 2 T 3:8. Ja ✻1:8.

3. **cut.** Ps 64:8. Jb 32:22. Pr 6:17. ✻10:31. 18:21. Ec 10:12. Ho 7:16. **flattering.** T#198. Ps 78:36. Jb 17:5. 32:21, 22. Pr 2:16. 6:24. 7:5, 21. 20:19. 24:24. 26:28. ✻28:23. 29:5. 1 Th ✻2:5. **tongue.** Pr 17:10. 73:8, 9. Ex 15:9. 1 S ✻2:3. 17:43, 44. 2 K 19:23, 24. Is 10:10. Ezk 28:2, 9. 29:3. Da 4:30, 31. 7:8, 25. Ml 3:13. 2 P 2:18. Ju 16. Re 13:5. **proud.** Heb. great. Ps 52:2. Pr 18:21.

4. **With.** Je ✻18:18. Ja ✻3:5, 6. **our own.** Heb. with us. 1 C ◐✻6:19. **who is.** T#705. Ps 2:2, 3. Ps +14:1 (T#22). Ge 3:5. Ex ✻5:2. Jg 21:25. Jb ✻21:14, 15. Je 2:31. 44:16, 17. Da 3:15. 11:36. Mt 25:24, 25. Lk +✻19:14 (T#695), 27. 2 Th ✻2:4. **lord.** Ps 8:1, 9. 45:11. 97:5.

5. **oppression.** T#523. Ps 10:12. 72:4. 74:21, 22. 79:10, 11. 146:7, 8. Ex 2:23, 24. ✻3:7-9. ✻22:21, 22. Dt +✻24:14. Jg 10:16. Pr ✻14:31. ✻21:13. ✻22:16, 22, 23. 23:10. Ec 4:1. 5:8. Is 3:15. √10:1-3. 19:20. Ezk +✻16:49. 18:12, 13, 18. Am 8:4-7. Ml +✻3:5. Ja +✻5:4. **poor.** Ps 9:12mg, 18. 10:2, 9, 12mg, 14. 35:10. **sighing.** T#1281. Ps 79:11. Ex 2:23. +✻22:23. Je 45:3. La 1:22. Ezk 9:4. Mk 7:34. **now.** Is 33:10. Mi 7:8, 9. **arise.**

ſ22C21, Nu +10:35. Ps 3:7. 7:6. 9:19. 10:12. Zp +*3:3.
puffeth at. *or,* would ensnare. ſ121S2, Ge +21:6. The
poor and needy being set in safety by Jehovah, despise
the oppression of the enemy. Ps 10:5. Jb 5:15, 21.

6. **words.** Ps 18:30. *19:8. *119:140. 2 S 22:31. Pr
*30:5. **as silver.** Ps 66:10. **tried.** ſ24C, 2 K +18:21.
of earth. By ellipsis (of repetition: noun from preceding
clause), supply to read: "The words of Jehovah are
pure words. (As) silver tried in a furnace: (Words) pertaining to the earth. Purified seven times." The first
and third member of the structure pertain to the words
(The words of Jehovah are pure words/Words pertaining to the earth); the second and fourth member pertain
to the purifying of silver (As silver tried in a furnace/
Purified seven times). ſ63I1A, Ex +12:4. See B74.

7. **thou shalt keep.** Ps 16:1. 37:28, 40. 121:8.
*145:20. Dt 33:3. 1 S 2:9. Is √26:3. 27:3. Jn *17:11.
1 P *1:5. Ju 1. Re *3:10. **them,** etc. Heb. him, i.e.
every one of them. Ps 17:12. 141:10. **this.** Ps 10:18.
Mt 3:7. **for ever.** Heb. *olam,* Ex +*12:24.

8. **wicked.** Pr 29:12. Ho 5:11. Mi 6:16. **when.** Jg
9:18, etc. 1 S 18:17, 18. Est 3:6, etc. Is 32:4-6. Mk
14:63-65. **men.** Heb. of the sons of men. ver. 1. Ps
8:4. Jb 30:8. Da 11:21.

PSALM 13

*David mournfully complains that God delays to com-
fort and deliver him, and prays for help, that his enemy
might not insult over him, 1-4. Trusting in the mercy
of God, he expects to rejoice and to sing his praises,
5, 6.*

(*Title.*) A.M. 3464. B.C. 510. **chief.** *or,* overseer.
Ps 12, title.

1. **How long.** T#1784. Ps 6:3. 10:1. 22:1, 2. 31:9-
14. 35:17. 37:7. 42:1-5. 69:1-3. 74:1, 10, 11. 77:7-10.
80:4-7. 85:5. 88:9-14. 89:46. 90:13, 14. 94:3, 4. 119:81-
84, 123. Is 64:9-12. Je 14:8, 9, 19-22. 15:18. La 1:10,
11. 3:7, *8. 5:13-22. Da √10:3, 12, 13. Hab *1:2. Mt
*15:22-28. Lk 18:7, 8. Re 6:10, 11. **forget.** T#1499.
Ps 10:12. 42:9. 44:23, 24. 74:19. *77:7-9. La 5:20, 21.
ſ22C4. Anthropomorphism B886. Forgetting and not
forgetting are attributed to God. For other instances
of this figure see Ps 9:18. 42:9. 74:23. Jb 11:6. Is 49:15.
Je 23:39. Ho 4:6. Am 8:7. Lk 12:6. **for ever.** Jb 4:20
(❋S#5331h). **wilt thou hide.** Ps 22:1, 2. 44:23, 24. 88:14.
Dt 31:17. Jb *13:24. Is √54:7, 8. *59:2. **face.** ſ22A4,
Ge +19:13.

2. **take.** Ps 77:2-12. *94:18, 19. 142:4-7. Jb 7:12-
15. 9:19-21, 27, 28. 10:15. 23:8-10. Je 15:18. **soul.** Heb.
nephesh, Ge +34:3. **sorrow.** Ps 38:17. 116:3. Ne 2:2.
Pr 15:13. Ec 5:17. Je 8:18. 45:3. Mt 26:38. Jn 16:6.
Ro 9:2. Ph 2:27. **enemy.** Ps 7:2, 4, 5. 8:2. 9:6. 10:18.
17:9. 74:10, 18. 1 S 18:29. 24:19. Est 7:6. La 1:9. Mi
7:8-10. **exalted.** Ps 22:7, 8. 31:18. 42:10. 44:14-16.
123:3, 4. 143:3, 4. La 1:5. Lk 22:53.

3. **Consider.** Ps 9:13. 25:19. 31:7. 119:153. La 5:1.
lighten. Ps 18:28. 1 S 14:27, 29. Ezr 9:8. Lk 2:32. Re
21:23. **lest.** Je 51:39, 57. Ep 5:14. **I sleep.** ſ147D,
Ge +1:29. Ps 6:5. 115:17. 146:3, +*4. Pr ◐10:7. Ec
3:19, 20. 9:5, 6, 10. Da +√12:2. 1 Th +*4:13n. **the
sleep of.** ſ63E1, Le ·+4:2.

4. **Lest mine enemy.** T#1143. Ps 10:11. 13:2. 22:6-
8. 25:2. 35:19, 25. 38:16. 86:17. 102:7, 8. 115:2. Ex
32:12. Nu 14:13-16. Dt 9:28. 32:27. Jsh 7:8, 9. La
1:21. Ezk 35:12-15. **I have.** Ps 9:19. Je 1:19. La 1:16.

when. Ps 55:22. 62:2, 6. 112:6. 121:1-3. Pr 12:3.

5. **But.** Ps 32:10. 33:18, 21, 22. 36:7. 52:8. 147:11.
Is 12:2. Ju 21. **my heart.** Ps 9:14. 20:5. 35:9. 43:4, 5.
51:12. 119:81. 1 S 2:1. Hab 3:18. Lk 1:47. *2:20, 29,
30.

6. **I.** Ps 21:13. 57:9-11. 59:16. **he.** Ps 116:7. 119:17.
dealt bountifully. 1 S +1:22n (❖S#1580h).

PSALM 14

*David describes the universal depravity of mankind,
and the enmity of the wicked against the people of
God, 1-6. He longs and prays for the salvation of Israel,
7.*

1. **fool.** T#200-1. Ps 73:3. 92:6. 94:6-8. 107:17. 1
S 25:25. Pr 1:7, 22. 13:19. 27:22. Je *4:22. Zc 11:15.
Lk 12:20. **said.** ſ96C1, Ge +4:1. **no God.** T#22. Ps
+9:17 (T#692). 10:4mg. +12:4 (T#705). 52:1-6. 59:7.
Jb 21:14, 15. 22:13. Ex 5:2. Is 22:13. Ezk 8:12. +13:22
(T#568). Lk +19:14 (T#695). Ro *1:28. 3:18. Ep *2:12.
He +3:12 (T#708). 2 P 3:3, 4. **They.** ſ96F4, Ex +10:2.
are corrupt. Ps 36:1-4. *51:5. 73:8, 9, 11, 12. 94:4-8.
Ge *6:5, 11, 12. Is 1:4. *48:8. Jn 3:6. 8:44. Ro *7:23.
Ep *4:22. **abominable.** Jb *15:14-16. Mt 12:34. 15:19.
Jn √3:19, 20. Ro *1:21, etc. Ep *2:1-3. T 1:16. 3:3.
1 P 4:3. Re *21:8. **there is none.** Pr *20:9. Ec 7:29.
9:3. Je 17:9. Ro ▶3:10-12. 5:19. 8:7, 8. Ep 2:1-3.

2. **The Lord.** Ps *33:13, 14. 102:19, 20. Ge *6:12.
*11:5. *18:21. Is 63:15. 64:1. La *3:50. **see.** ſ22C1,
Ge +18:21. **any.** Ps *82:5. *107:43. Pr *2:9. *8:5. 9:4,
16. Is *27:11. Je *4:22. Da *12:10. Mt *13:15. Ro
*3:11. **seek God.** Ps *69:32. 2 Ch *19:3. 30:19. Is *8:19.
√55:6. Ac 2:21. 17:27. He √11:6.

3. **all gone.** Ps 119:176. Ec 7:29. Is √53:6. 59:7, 8,
13-15. Je 2:13. Ro 3:10-12, 23. Ep 2:3. 2 P 2:13-15.
filthy. Heb. stinking. Ps 38:5. 53:3. Jb 15:16. Is √64:6.
Ezk 36:25. 2 C *7:1. **there.** ver. 1. Ex 8:31. 12:30.
Dt 1:35. Jb 14:4. Ro 3:10. 1 C 6:5.

4. **Have.** Ps 94:8, 9. Pr *1:29. Is 5:13. 27:11. 29:14.
44:19, 20. 45:20. Ho *4:6. Ro 1:21, 22, 28. 2 C 4:3,
4. Ep *4:17, 18. **eat up.** Je 10:25. Am *8:4. Mi 3:2,
3. 2 C 11:20. Ga 5:15. **and call not.** Ps *79:6. Jb 21:15.
27:10. Is *64:7.

5. **were,** etc. Heb. they feared a fear. ſ147D, Ge
+1:29. Ps 53:5mg. Ex 15:16. Est 8:17. Jb 3:25. Pr
1:26-28. 28:1. Is 7:2. +*8:12. **God.** Ps 46:5, 7, 11. Is
8:10. 12:6. 41:10. 43:1, 2. Mt 1:23. **the generation.**
Ps 22:30. 24:6. 73:15. 112:2. 1 P 2:9.

6. **Ye.** Ps 3:2. 4:2. *22:7, 8. 42:10. Ne 4:2-4. Is
37:10, 11. Ezk 35:10. Da 3:15. Mt *27:40-43. **Lord.**
Ps *9:9. *142:4, 5. He 6:18.

7. **Oh,** etc. Heb. Who will give, etc. ſ74, Jg +5:31.
Ps 25:22. See on Ps 53:6. 106:47. 1 Ch 16:35. **the
salvation.** Ps 25:22. 51:18. Is 14:32. +*25:9. 45:17.
46:13. 59:20. 62:11. Zc +*9:9. Lk 2:10, 11. Ro *11:26.
2 T 2:26. He +*9:28n. **Israel.** ſ121A5, ſ121T3, Ge
+9:27. **out of Zion.** Is +*51:11. Ro +*11:26. **bringeth
back.** Ps 126:1, 2, 4. Jb 42:20. Je 30:18. 31:23. Ezk
39:25. Jl 3:1. Am +*9:14. **Jacob.** ſ121A5, ſ121T3,
Ge +9:27. **shall rejoice.** Ps 48:11. *85:6. *149:2. Ne
12:43. Je 33:10, 11. Re 18:20. 19:7.

PSALM 15

*The inhabitant of Zion, or character of the heirs
of heaven, 1-5.*

1. **Lord.** Ps 1:1-4. 23:6. *24:3-5. 27:4. 61:4. 84:4. 92:13. Mt *5:8. Jn √3:3-5. 14:3. 17:24. Re 7:14-17. 14:4. 21:3, 4, 23, 24. **abide.** Heb. sojourn. ƒ180D, Ex +20:18. Ps *5:4. 61:4. 105:12, 23. **holy.** Ps *2:6. 3:4. *43:3, 4. 87:1-3. He 12:22. Re 14:1.

2. **He.** Ps *84:11, 12. Pr 2:7, 8. 28:18. Is *33:15-17. Mi 2:7. Lk 1:6. 1 C 13:5. Ga 2:14. 1 J *2:6. **worketh.** Ac 10:35. Ro 2:10. Ga √5:5, 6. Ep √2:10. He 11:*6, 33. 1 J 2:29. 3:7. Re 22:14, 15. **speaketh the truth.** Ps 34:12, 13. +*51:6. Ge ◐+*27:19. Le +*19:11. Jsh 24:14. Pr 12:19, 22. Is 63:8. Zc *8:16, 17. Jn 3:21. 4:23. 1 C 5:8. Ep *4:15, 25. 6:14. Ph +*4:8. Col 3:9. He 10:23. 1 J 1:6. 3:18. 2 J 1. Re *21:8.

3. **backbiteth not.** Ps *34:13. *101:5-8. Ex +*20:16. *23:1. Le *19:16. Je 9:4-9. Ro 1:30. T 3:2. Ja 4:11. 1 P 2:1, 2. **doeth.** 1 S 24:11. Is 56:2. Mt 7:12. Ro 12:17. 13:10. 3 J 11. **taketh up.** or, receiveth or, endureth. Ex *23:1mg. Pr 22:10. 25:23. Ep 5:11. 1 T +*5:19n.

4. **a vile.** Ps *101:4. 2 K 3:13, 14. Est *3:2. Jb 32:21, 22. Is 32:5, 6. Da 5:17, etc. Ac 24:2, 3, 25. Ja 2:1-9. **but he honoreth.** T#914. Ps *16:3. 101:6. √119:63. *122:6. Nu 24:9. Mt *12:49, 50. He *6:10. 1 J 3:14, 18, 19. *4:12. **sweareth.** T#901. Ps 24:4, 5. Le 5:4. 6:2. Nu +*30:2n. Jsh 9:18-20. Jg 11:+*31n, 35. 21:5. 1 S 20:16. 2 S 21:1, 2. Je 7:9. Ezk *17:12-19. Ho 4:2. 10:4. Am 1:9. Zc 5:4. 8:17. Ml 1:14. +*3:5. Mt 5:33-37. 23:16-22. Ro 1:31. Ga 3:15. 1 T 1:10. **changeth not.** Jsh +9:19. Jg √11:30, 35. Jn 13:1. He 12:2.

5. **putteth.** Ex *22:25. Le 25:35-37. Dt 23:19, 20. Ne 5:2-5, 7-13. Is +*24:2. Ezk 18:8, 17. 22:12. **nor taketh.** Ex 23:7, 8. Dt *16:19. Is 33:15. Mi 7:3. Mt 26:15. 27:3-5. **He that doeth.** Ps 16:8. 55:22. 106:3. 112:6. Pr *12:3. Ezk 18:27. Mi +√6:8. Mt *7:21-25. Jn +√13:17. Ja *1:22-25. 2 P +√1:10, 11.

PSALM 16

David seeks protection from God, disclaims all merit, and avows his love to the saints and his hatred of idolatry, 1-4. He rejoices in God as his portion and thanks him for giving him counsel, 5-7. He speaks prophetically of the resurrection and glory of Christ and of the happiness of his people, 8-11.

(Title.) A.M. 2962. B.C. 1042. **Michtam.** i.e. *secret treasure; golden; a song graven upon stone; the poverty of the perfect; (blood) staining* (i.e. *deep dyeing*), ✸S#4387h. Ps 56, 57, 58, 60, titles. or, A golden Psalm of David.

1. **Preserve.** Ps 17:5, 8. 31:23. 37:28. 97:10. 116:6. Pr 2:8. **God.** Heb. *El*, Ex +15:2. **for.** Ps +*9:10. +*11:1. 22:8. 25:20. 84:12. 125:1. 146:5. Is 26:3, 4. Je 17:7, 8. 2 C 1:9. 2 T *1:12.

2. **thou hast.** Ps 8:1. 27:8. 31:14. 89:26. 91:2. Is 26:13. 44:5. Zc 13:9. Jn +√20:28. **my goodness.** Ps 50:9, 10. Jb 22:2, 3. 35:7, 8. Lk √17:10. Ro 11:35.

3. **But.** Ga *6:10. T 3:8. He *6:10. **the saints.** Is 30:4. 116:15. 2 Ch 6:41. Mt *25:40. Ac 9:13. Ep 1:1. **the excellent.** Pr 12:26. SS 4:1, etc. 6:1, etc. 7:1, etc. Ml 3:17. **in whom.** Ps √119:63. Pr 8:31. 13:20. SS 7:10. Is 62:4. Ep 5:25-27. 1 J 3:14-17.

4. **Their.** Ps 32:10. 97:7. Jon *2:8. Re 14:9-11. 18:4, 5. **hasten.** etc. or, give gifts to another. **drink offerings.** Ge 35:14. Le +*23:13. Is 57:6. 65:11. 66:3. Je 7:18. **nor take.** Ex *23:13. Jsh 23:7. Je +*10:2. Ho 2:16, 17.

5. **The Lord is the portion.** T#823. Ps ◐11:6. 73:26. 119:57. 142:5. Ge 15:1. Nu 18:20. Dt 10:9. 18:1, 2. 32:9. Jsh 13:33. Je 10:16. La *3:24. **mine inheritance.** Heb. my part. Ps 17:14. 47:4. 50:18. 73:26. Jsh 13:33. **of my cup.** Ps 11:6. *23:5. 116:13. Ep *5:18. **thou maintainest.** Ps 2:6. 9:4. 21:7-12. 61:6, 7. 89:4, 20-37. 110:1, 2. 132:11, 17, 18. Jsh 13:1. Is 42:1. 53:12. Ac 2:32. 5:31. 1 C 15:25. 2 T *1:12. 1 P *1:5. **my lot.** Dt 32:9. Jsh 14:2n. 21:45. Da *12:13. Col *1:12.

6. **The lines.** ƒ121B, Jsh +17:4. Ps 78:55. Jsh 18:9n. Am 7:17. **fallen.** Jsh 18:11n. **in pleasant.** Ps 21:1-3. Jsh 15:8n. Jb 36:11mg. He 12:2. **places.** Consider the literal meanings of the sites in Jsh 15:15, 34, 41 (Naamah, i.e. *pleasantness*.), 49, 51, 55, 60. 19:8, 12, 13, 21, 37, 38. *20:7n. Jn *14:2. **I have.** Ps 73:24. Je 3:19. Jn 20:17. Ac 26:18. Ro *8:17. 1 C *3:21-23. Ep 1:18. Ph 2:9-11. 2 T 2:12. Re 3:21. **heritage.** Dt 32:9. Is *54:17. Ep *1:11. Col *1:12.

7. **who hath.** Ps 73:24. 119:7. Pr 8:14. Is 11:2-4. 48:17. 50:4. **my reins.** ƒ121ll, Ge +3:7. i.e. my thoughts. Ps 73:21. Je 12:2. *17:10. Re *2:23. **in the night.** Ps 17:3. 22:2. 42:8. 63:6. 77:2, *6. 119:55, 148. Jb 33:15, 16. Is *26:9. Lk 6:12.

8. **I have.** Ps 139:18. Ac 2:25-28. He 11:27. **he is.** Ps 73:*23, 26. 109:31. 110:5. *121:5. **always.** Is +*58:11. **right hand.** ƒ22D3F. Anthropomorphism B892. God is spoken of as standing at the right hand of His people. For another instance of this figure see Ac 2:25. **I shall.** Ps 15:5. 62:6. **not.** Ge ◐19:30.

9. **my heart.** Lk *10:21, 22. **my glory.** ƒ121F, Ge +49:6. By the figure Metonymy of the Effect, "my glory" is put for "my tongue," as is confirmed by the New Testament citation (Ac ❱2:26) which interprets the figure, rather than literally translates it. Other instances of New Testament quotations which interpret a figure rather than literally translate it include Ps 8:2 w Mt 21:16; Ps 40:6 w He 10:5; Is 6:10 w Mt 13:15, compare Jn ◐12:40; Is 65:1 w Ro 10:20; Ho 14:2n w He 13:15. Ps 7:5. +*30:12mg,n. 57:8. +*108:1. Ge 49:6. Ac *❱2:26. Ja *3:5-9. **my flesh.** ƒ171Q5, Ge +17:13. Ps 63:1. 84:2. Jb *14:14, 15, +*22. +*19:26, 27. Pr *14:32. Is +*26:19n. Mt 26:41. Mk 14:38. Lk +*24:39. Jn +*5:29. Ro 2:28. 1 C √5:5. 7:28. 2 C *4:11. 7:5. 12:7. 1 Th *4:13, 14. **shall rest.** Heb. dwell confidently. Jb +*19:26. Ezk +*38:8h, 11mg. Ph *1:21. He +*14:13. **in hope.** Jb 14:14, 15. √19:26, 27. Pr +*14:32. Is +*26:19n. Jn +*5:29. Ro 8:24, 25. 12:12. +*15:4. 1 C 15:19. Ga 5:5. Ep 1:18. 4:4. Ph 1:20. Col *1:5, 23, 27. 1 Th *4:13. T 1:2. √2:13. He 3:6. *6:11, 18, 19. 1 P 1:3, 13, 21. *3:15. 1 J *3:3.

10. **not leave my.** Ps +*9:17. *49:15mg. 71:20. *86:13. 139:8. Le 19:28. Nu 6:6. Dt *32:22. Jb 11:8. Pr *15:11. *27:20. Is *5:14. *14:9. Am *9:2. Lk *16:23. Jn *2:21, 22. Ac 2:24, ❱31. 3:15. 7:59. 1 C *15:55mg. Re *1:18. 20:13, 14. **soul.** Heb. *nephesh*, Ps +30:3. ƒ121A8. Metonymy of the Cause B545. "Soul" is put for the person, as when a city contains so many thousand souls. For other instances of this figure see Ps 49:15. 103:1. Lk 1:46. Ac 2:27, 31. Re +*6:9n. 20:4n. Probably the theological presuppositions of E. W. Bullinger have influenced his categorization of "soul" here, for he was a materialist who did not believe that the soul was a separate, conscious entity in man, and therefore he denied the conscious existence of man after death. Other more appropriate categorizations of "soul" here, equally if not more defensible than that assigned by

Bullinger, would be √ʃ171Q1, Ge +12:5, or ʃ171Q2, Nu +23:10. Other examples which should be carefully noted where the theology of the interpreter greatly influences the figure of speech categories assigned are discussed in the related notes (Ge 24:10n. Je 33:18n. Ph √1:23n). This materialist bias in the works of Bullinger necessitated considerable reorganization of the New Testament categories for "soul" (Mt +*2:20n) and "spirit" (Mt +*8:16n) presented in this edition of the *Treasury*, compared with Bullinger's original scheme presented in the otherwise helpful volume *The Giver and His Gifts*, Appendix I, "Classified List of Usages of *Pneuma*." **hell**. Heb. *sheol*, Ge +37:35. Ps +30:3. The word *hell*, from the Saxon *hillan* or *helan*, "to hide," or from *holl*, "a cavern," though now used only for the place of torment, anciently denoted the concealed or unseen place of the dead in general; corresponding to the Greek *adas*, hades, i.e. *o aidas topos*, the invisible place, and the Hebrew *sheol*, from *shaal*, "to ask," seek, the place and state of those who are out of the way, and to be sought for. Ps 139:8. Is 14:9. Am 9:2. Mt +*10:28. **neither**. T#44. Ps *49:15. 71:20. Ge +*3:15. +*49:10. Is +*7:14. 35:3-6. ch. √53. Zc 11:12, 13. Ac *2:27-31. *❯13:35-38. 1 C *15:42, 50-54. **suffer**. √ʃ108A4, Ge +31:7. **Holy One**. or, saint. T#1915. Ps 89:19. Dt 33:8. Is 10:17. 29:23. 49:7. Da *9:24. Ho 11:9. Hab 1:12. 3:3. Mk ♣1:24. Lk +*♣1:35. *4:34. Ac *3:14. 1 J 2:20. **corruption**. Heb. *shachath*, Jb +9:31 (✸S#7845h). Ps +30:3.

11. **show me**. Ex 33:13, 18. **path**. Ps 21:4. Pr 2:19. *4:18. 5:6. *12:28. Is *2:3. Mt *7:14. Ro 8:11. 1 P 1:21. **of life**. Jn √3:16. *10:10. **in thy presence**. ʃ22A4, Ge +19:13. Ps *17:15. 21:5, 6. Ex 33:15. Mt *5:8. Jn *16:24. Ac ❯*2:28. 1 C *13:12. 2 C *4:17. Ep *3:19. 1 J *3:2. Ju *24. Re *7:15-17. *22:5. **at thy**. Mk *16:19. Ac *7:56. He 12:2. 1 P *3:22. **pleasures**. Ps *36:8. Jb *36:11. Mt *25:33, 46. **evermore**. Jb +4:20 (✸S#5331h).

PSALM 17

David appeals to God for his integrity, 1-4. He prays to be upheld, and saved from his proud, malicious, and prosperous enemies, 5-14. He chooses the path of righteousness, and expects complete satisfaction when he shall awake in the likeness of God, 15.

(Title.) A.M. 2942. B.C. 1062. Ps 86, 142, titles.

1. **Hear**. Ps 7:8. 18:20. 43:1. *140:12. *145:18. 1 J 3:21. **the right**. Heb. justice. Ps 9:4. 119:75. Dt 16:20mg. Jb 8:3. **attend**. Ps 5:2. 55:2, 3. 61:1. 66:19. 142:6. 2 Ch 7:15. Ne 1:6. Da 9:18, 19. **give ear**. ʃ90. Exergasia; or, Working Out B399. A repetition so as to work out or illustrate what has already been said. In this figure the same thought, idea, or subject is repeated in other words, and thus worked out and developed. This figure differs from synonymia in that not merely synonymous words are repeated but also synonymous expressions or sense. This figure necessarily implies that the separate repetitions must be placed in parallel lines. Here, "Hear the right, O Lord,/Attend unto my cry,/Give ear unto my prayer." For other instances of this figure see Ps 18:1, 2. 35:1-3. 35:4. Jon 2:2. 2:3. Zc 6:12, 13. **not out of feigned lips**. Heb. without lips of deceit. Ps 18:44mg. 145:18. Je 3:10. Mt 15:8. Jn 1:47.

2. **Let my**. Ps 37:6, 33. 2 Th 1:6-9. Ju *24. **things**. Ezk 18:25, 29. 33:17, 20.

3. **proved**. ʃ22C31. Anthropomorphism B889. Human actions are attributed to God: proving and trying. For other instances of this figure see the following reference passages. Ps 11:5. *26:2. 66:10. 139:1-4. Jb *23:10. Zc 13:9. Ml 3:2, 3. 1 C 4:4. 1 P 1:7. **thou hast tried**. Ps 16:7. 24:14. Jb 24:15. Ho 7:6. Mi 2:1. Ac 16:9. 18:9, 10. **shalt**. Ps 7:4. 44:17-21. 1 S 24:10, 12. 26:11, 23. 2 C 1:12. **I am**. Ps *39:1. 119:106. Pr 13:3. Ac 11:23. Ja *3:2.

4. **works**. Ps 14:1-3. Ge 6:5, 11. Jb 15:16. 31:33. 1 C 3:3, 15. 1 P 4:2, 3, 18. **by the**. Ps *119:9-11, 105. Mt 4:4, 6, 7, 10. **word**. T#1046. Ps *119:9-11. Pr *2:10-15. Mt 4:4, 7, 10. Jn *17:17. Ep 6:17. Ja 1:18. Re *12:11. **destroyer**. 1 P 5:8. Re 9:11mg.

5. **Hold up**. ʃ96B, Ex +20:8. T#596, 1553. Ps 51:11, 12. 63:8. 68:35. 119:32, 116, *117, 133. *121:3, 7. 1 S *2:9. SS 1:4. Je *10:23. Jn 15:5. 1 C 15:10. 1 P 1:5. **that my footsteps**. Ps 18:36. 38:16. 94:18. **slip not**. Heb. be not moved. Ps 10:6. 13:4. 15:5. 16:8.

6. **I have**. Ps 55:16. 66:19, 20. *116:2. **God**. Heb. *El*, Ex +15:2. **incline**. Ps 13:3, 4. Is 37:17, 20. Da 9:17-19.

7. **Show**. Ps 31:21. 78:12. Ro 5:20, 21. Re 15:3. **lovingkindness**. T#1533. Ps *36:7, 10. 40:11. 89:49. *143:8. **savest**, etc. *or*, savest them which trust in thee, from those that rise up against thy right hand. Ps 5:11, 12. 10:12-16. 1 S 17:45-47. 25:28, 29. 2 K 19:22, 34. 2 Ch 16:9. **by thy**. Ps 20:6. 44:3. 60:5. Ex 15:6. Is 41:10. Ac 2:33.

8. **Keep me**. T#1511. Ps 33:18, 19. 140:4. Nu *6:24. Jn 17:11-15. **as**. ʃ160A, Ps +1:3. **apple**. Dt *32:10. 1 S 26:24. Pr 7:2. Zc *2:8. **hide**. Ps 32:7, 8. 36:7. *57:1. 61:4. 63:7. 91:1, 4. Ru 2:12. Mt *23:37. Lk 13:34. **shadow**. Ps 91:1. **wings**. ʃ22G2. Ps 91:4.

9. **oppress**. Heb. waste. Ps 137:8mg. 1 Ch 17:9. Pr 11:3 (destroy). Ezk 32:12 (spoil). **deadly enemies**. Heb. enemies against the soul. Heb. *nephesh*, Nu +23:10. Ps 7:5. 35:4, 7, 12. 1 S 24:11.

10. **They are**. Ps 73:7-9. 119:70. Dt 32:15. Jb 15:27. Is 6:10. Mt 13:15. Ac 28:27. **with**. Ps *12:3, 4. 31:18. 123:4. Ex 5:2. 15:9. 1 S 2:3. 2 P 2:18. Re 13:5, 6.

11. **compassed**. 1 S 23:26. 24:2, 3. 26:2, 3. **set**. Ps 10:8-10. Pr 6:13, 14.

12. **Like**, etc. Heb. The likeness of him, (that is, of every one of them), is as a lion that desireth to ravin. Ps 7:2. 22:13. 2 T 4:17. 1 P 5:8. **lurking**. Heb. sitting. Ps 2:4. 9:11 (dwelleth). 107:10, 34.

13. **Arise**. Ps 3:7. 7:6. 44:23, 26. 119:126. Is 51:9. **disappoint him**. Heb. prevent his face. Ps 95:2mg. **soul**. Heb. *nephesh*, Ge +12:13. **which is**. *or*, by. Ps 7:11-13. **thy**. Is *10:5, 15. *13:5. 37:26. *54:16. Hab 1:12. Ac 4:27, 28. **sword**. ʃ22D5D, Dt +32:41.

14. **which are**. *or*, by. ver. +13. **thy hand**. ʃ22A14.7, Ex +9:3. **men of**. Lk 16:8. Jn 8:23. 15:19. 17:14. 1 J 4:4, 5. **portion**. Ps 11:6. 49:17-19. *73:12, 17, 18. Jb 20:29. Mt *6:2, 5. Lk *12:19-21. *16:25. Ja 5:5. **belly**. Jb 12:6, 9. 21:7-15. 22:18. **hid**. ʃ24B, Ge +23:16. Pr 2:4. 13:22. Mt 13:44. **they are full**, etc. *or*, their children are full. Is 2:7. 57:17. **leave**. Ps 39:6. Jb 21:21. 27:14-17. Lk 16:27, 28.

15. **As**. Ps 5:7. Jsh 24:15. **I will**. Ps 4:6. 119:111. Jb *19:26, 27. Is 33:15. Mt *5:8. Ac 2:28. 1 C *13:12. 2 C *3:18. He 12:2. Re ◖6:16. **thy face**. ʃ22A4, +19:13. Ps 11:7. 16:11. 140:13. Ge +43:3. Re 22:4. **in righteous-**

ness. T#336. Ge 17:1. Is *61:10. Mt 5:8. Lk 1:6. Ep 5:25-27. 1 J *3:2. Re *21:27. **I shall be.** Ps *16:11. 36:8, 9. 65:4. Is *53:11. Mt *5:6. Re 7:16, 17. 21:3, 4, 23. **I awake.** Ps 49:14. Jb 14:12. Is +√26:19n. Mt 27:52, 53. **with thy.** Ge +*1:26, 27. Ph *3:21. 1 J *3:2, 3.

PSALM 18

David's psalm of thanksgiving for his manifold deliverances and singular prosperity: David professes his love to God, 1; and his confidence in his attributes, 2. He praises God for deliverance out of trouble, 3-5. His experience of God's hearing him in an awful manner, 6-31. He acknowledges God's help against his enemies, 32-50.

(Title.) A.M. 2986. B.C. 1018. **the servant.** Ps 36, title. 116:16. Ac 13:36. He 3:5. **this song.** 2 S ‖22:1-51. **in the day.** Ps 34:19. Ex 15:1, etc. Jg 5:1, etc. 1 S 2:1-10. Is 12:1-6.

1. **I will love.** Ps 31:23. *116:1-6. 144:1, 2. Ex *20:6. Dt *6:5. Jsh 23:11. Mt *10:37. *22:37, 38. Lk *7:47. Jn √14:21. 21:17. Ro 5:5. 1 C 13:13. 16:22. Ga 5:22. 2 Th 3:5. He *6:10. 1 P 1:8. 1 J *4:19. **my strength.** ♪121E1, Ge +25:23. ver. 32. Ps 19:14. 28:7, 8. 71:3, 16. 84:5. 118:14. Is 12:2. 26:4. 27:5. *40:31. *45:24. Je 16:19. 2 C *12:9. Ep 6:10. Ph *4:13. Col *1:11. 2 T 4:17.

2. **Lord.** Ps 28:1. 62:2, 7. Is *32:2. **rock.** ♪22L3, Dt +32:31. **fortress.** Ps *91:2. 144:2. Je *16:19. **deliverer.** Ps 34:√4, 7, 17. 54:7. *91:14. Pr 11:8. Da 3:17. 6:16. Mt +*6:13. 2 C 1:10. 2 T 3:11. 4:18. 2 P *2:9. **God.** Heb. *El*, Ex +15:2. **strength.** Heb. rock. ♪90, Ps +17:1. **whom.** Ps 22:4. Ro 11:29. He 2:13. **buckler.** ♪22D5F, Ps *91:4. Ge +15:1. Pr *2:7. **horn.** Ps 132:17. 2 S *22:3. **high.** Pr *18:10.

3. **I will.** Ps *5:2, 3. 28:1, 2. 55:16. *62:8. 2 S 22:4. Ph *4:6, 7. **who.** Ps *65:1, 2. 76:4. Ne 9:5. Re *4:11. *5:12-14. **praised.** ♪24C, 2 K +18:21. **so shall.** Ps *50:15. *91:15. Lk *1:71. Ac 2:21. Ro *8:31-39. **enemies.** T#1333. Ps 3:1-3. 7:6. 143:3, 4, 9. Ex 14:10. 1 S 7:7, 8. 24:15. 1 K 8:33, 34. 2 K 19:16-19. 2 Ch 14:9-11. Ne 4:7-9. 9:28. Lk 1:74.

4. **sorrows.** Ps 116:3. 2 S 22:5, 6. Is 13:8. *53:3, 4. Mt *26:38, 39. Mk 14:33, 34. 2 C 1:9. **floods.** Ps 22:12, 13, 16. Jon 2:2-7. Mt 26:47, 55. 27:24, 25, 39-44. Ac 21:30. **ungodly men.** Heb. Belial. Dt +15:9. Jg +19:22. 1 S +30:22. 2 S 22:5mg. Jb 34:18.

5. **The sorrows.** *or,* cords. Ps 86:13. 88:3-8, 15-17. Ac 2:24. **hell.** Heb. *sheol*, Ge +37:35. **snares.** Pr 13:14. Ec 9:12.

6. **distress.** ver. 3, 4. Ps 50:15. 130:1, 2. Mk 14:36. Ac 12:5. **heard.** Ps 5:7. 11:4. 27:4, 5. 2 S 22:7. Hab *2:10. Re 11:19. **my cry.** Ex 2:23. 1 K 8:27-30. 2 Ch *30:27.

7. **earth.** Ps 114:4-7. Mt 27:51. 28:2. Ac 4:31. 16:25, 26. **foundations.** Ps 46:2. Dt 32:22. Je 4:24. Ezk 38:19, 20. Hab 3:6, 10. Zc √14:4. 1 C *13:2.

8. **went.** Ps *11:6. 21:9. 74:1. 104:32. 144:5, 6. Ge 19:28. Ex 20:18. Le 10:2. Nu 11:1. 16:35. Dt 29:20, 23, 24. 2 Th *1:8. **out of his.** Heb. by his. **fire.** Is 30:27. Da 7:10. Am 4:11. Na *1:5, 6. Re *11:5.

9. **He bowed.** Jehovah is here represented as a mighty warrior going forth to fight the battles of David. When he descended to the engagement, the very heavens bowed to render his descent more awful: his mili-

tary tent was substantial darkness; the voice of his thunder was the warlike alarm which sounded to the battle; the chariot in which he rode was the thick clouds of heaven conducted by cherubs and carried on by the irresistible force and rapid wings of an impetuous tempest; and the darts and weapons he employed were thunderbolts, lightnings, fiery hail, deluging rains, and stormy winds! No wonder that when God arose all his enemies were scattered, and those that hated him fled before him. Ps 68:4. 144:5, etc. Dt 33:26. 2 S 22:10. Is 51:6. Jl +*3:16. Mt *24:29. He +*12:26. 2 P +*3:10. Re *20:11. **darkness.** Ex 20:21. Dt 5:22, 23. 2 S 22:10. Jb +*38:9. Mk *15:33. Jn 13:7.

10. **rode.** ♪22C18, Dt +33:26. Ps 99:1. 2 S 22:11, 12. Ezk 1:5-14. 10:20-22. He 1:7. **he did fly.** ♪22F3, 2 S +22:11. Ps 104:3. **wind.** ♪22D5H, Ps +104:3.

11. **darkness.** Ex 20:21. 2 S 22:10. Jb 38:9. **secret.** Ps 27:5. 81:7. 91:1. **thick.** Ps *97:2. Dt 4:11. Jl 2:2. **clouds.** ♪22D5H, Ps +104:3. Ge +9:13.

12. **At the.** Ps 97:3, 4. Hab 3:4, 5. Mt 17:2, 5. **clouds.** Ge +9:13. **hail.** Ex 9:23, 24. Jsh 10:11. 2 S 22:13-15. Re 16:21.

13. **thundered.** Ps 78:48. 104:7. Ex 20:18. 1 S 7:10. Jb 40:9. Jn 12:29. Re 4:5. 8:5. 19:6. **Highest.** Ps 29:3, 4. Ezk 10:5. **hail.** Jsh 10:11. Is 30:30. **coals.** Ps 120:3, 4. 140:10. Dt +*32:24mg. Hab 3:5.

14. **Yea.** Ps 21:12. 77:17. Nu 24:8. Dt 32:23, 42. Jsh 10:10. Jb 6:4. Is 30:30. Hab 3:11. **his arrows.** ♪22D5C. Anthropomorphism B893. Arrows are attributed to God. For other instances of this figure see Ps 144:6. Hab 3:11. **he shot.** Ps 144:6. Jb +38:35. 40:9-12. Zc 9:14, 15.

15. **channels.** Ps 74:15. *106:9. Ex 15:8. Jsh 3:13-16. 2 S 22:16. **foundations.** Ps 104:5. Jb 38:4-6. Je 31:37. Jon 2:6. Mi 6:2. **O Lord.** 2 K 19:7. Jb 4:9. Is 11:4. 30:27, 28, *33. **breath.** Heb. *ruach*, Ge +2:7. ♪22K3, Jb +4:9. Ex +15:8. **nostrils.** ♪22A9, Ex +15:8.

16. **He sent.** Ps 57:3. 144:7. **drew.** ver. 43. Ps 40:1-3. Ex 2:10. 2 S 22:17. **many waters.** *or,* great waters. Ps 29:3. Is *43:2. Jon 2:5, 6. Re 17:15.

17. **strong.** Ps 38:19. 2 S 22:1, 18. He *2:14, 15. **them.** ver. 40, 41. Ps 9:13. 25:19. 69:4-14. 118:7. Jb 16:9. Lk 19:14. **they were.** Ps 35:10. Ep *6:10-12.

18. **prevented me.** ver. 5. Ps 17:13. Mt 17:25. **in the day.** ♪171T2, Ge +2:17. i.e. *when I was in trouble.* Dt 32:35. 2 S 22:19. 23:12. Je 18:17. Ob 10-14. Zc 1:15. **but.** Ps 46:1, 2, 11. 1 S 30:6.

19. **brought.** ver. 36. Ps 31:8. 40:2. *118:5. Jb 36:16. **because.** Ps 37:23. 2 S 22:18-27. 1 K 10:9.

20. **rewarded.** Ps *58:11. 1 S 24:17, 20. Pr 11:18. Is 49:4. 62:11. Mt 6:4. Ro *2:6, 7. 1 C 3:8. **cleanness.** ver. 24. Ps 7:3. 24:4. 26:6. 1 S 24:11-13. Ac *24:16. He *7:26.

21. **For I.** Ps 17:4. 26:1. √119:10, 11. Mt 5:29. Ac 24:16. 1 Th 2:10. He *12:1. **have not.** Ps 119:102. 1 S 15:11. 1 J *2:19.

22. **For all.** Ps 119:13, 128. Jn 5:14. **I did.** Ps 119:112, 117.

23. **upright.** Ps 7:8. 11:7. 17:3. 37:27. 1 S 26:23. 1 Ch 29:17. **before.** Heb. with. **I kept.** Mt 5:29, 30. *18:8, 9.

24. **the Lord recompensed me.** 1 S 26:23. Ru 2:12. Mt 10:41, 42. 2 Th 1:6, 7. He *6:10. **in his eyesight.** Heb. before his eyes. Ps 5:5mg.

25. **With the merciful.** Ps *41:1-4. 112:4-6. 1 K *8:32. Is 57:1, 2. 58:7, 8. Mt 18:33-35. Lk 6:35-38.

thou wilt. Is 26:7. Ezk 18:25-30. Ro 9:14.

26. pure. 2 S 22:27. Is 52:11. froward. Ps 109:17-19. Le *26:23, 24, 27, 28. Pr *3:34. Ro 2:4-6, 9. Ja 2:13. and with. Lk *19:21, 22. show thyself froward. or, wrestle. *S#6617h. Ge 30:8. 2 S ||22:27mg. Jb 5:13. Pr 8:8.

27. save. ◊138B, Ge +13:16. Ps 9:18. *34:6, 18, 19. 40:17. 2 S 22:28. Is 57:15. 66:2. Lk 1:52, 53. 2 C 8:9. Ja 2:5. afflicted people. Je +*30:7. Da +*12:1. bring down. Ps 10:4. 17:10, 13. *101:5. Pr *6:16, 17. 30:12. Is 2:11. 3:9. 10:12. *57:15. Lk *18:14. high looks. Heb. soaring eyes. ◊171Q16. Synecdoche of the Part B647. The eye lifted up is put for a proud man and his high looks. Here, "high looks" signify proud people. For another instance of this figure see Pr 6:17mg.

28. thou wilt. Ps *112:4. Jb *18:6. *29:3. Pr 13:9. candle. or, lamp. ◊22K2, 2 S +22:29. Ps 119:105mg. 132:17mg. 2 S 21:17mg. 22:29mg. 1 K 11:36. Jb 18:6mg. 29:3mg. Pr 6:23mg. 20:27mg. Is 62:1. my God. Is 42:16. Mt 4:16. Lk 1:79. 1 P 2:9.

29. by thee. Ps 44:6, 7. 144:1, 10. 1 S 17:49. 23:2. 30:8. 2 S 5:19, 20, 25. Ep 6:10-13. Col 2:15. Re 3:21. run. or, broken. 2 K 23:12mg. by my God. 2 S 22:30. 1 C 15:10. 2 C 12:9, 10.

30. God. Heb. El, Ex +15:2. his way. Ps *19:7. *25:10. Dt *32:4. 2 S 22:31. Da *4:37. Ro *12:2. Re *15:3. tried. or, refined. Ps *12:6. *19:8-10. 119:140. Pr *30:5. a buckler. ver. 2. Ps 17:7. *84:11, 12. Pr 2:7.

31. For who. Ps *86:8. Dt 32:15, 31, 39. 1 S 2:2. 2 S 22:32. Is 45:5, 21, 22. a rock. Ps 62:6, 7. Is 26:4mg.

32. God. Heb. El, Ex +15:2. girdeth. ◊22C27. Anthropomorphism B889. Human actions are attributed to God: girding. For other instances of this figure see Ps 30:11. 45:3. The girdle was a necessary part of the eastern dress: it strengthened and supported the loins; served to confine the garments close to the body; and to tuck them in when journeying. The strength of God was to his soul what the girdle was to the body. Ps 28:7. 91:1. 93:1. Pr 31:17. Is 45:5. Je +*1:17. 2 C 3:5. maketh. Ps 37:37. 2 S 22:33. Jn 15:5. 1 C 15:10.

33. maketh. 2 S 2:18. high. Ps 81:16. Dt 32:13. *33:29. 2 S 22:34. Hab 3:19. Ep 2:6.

34. teacheth. Ps *144:1. 2 S 22:35. Is 28:6. 45:1. Lk +*22:36. so that. Ps 46:9. Je 49:35. Ho 1:5.

35. shield. Ps 5:12. 28:7. Dt 33:29. 2 S 22:36. right hand. Ps 17:7. 44:3. ◊22A15B. Anthropomorphism B880. A right hand is attributed to God, denoting His grace and mercy in delivering and saving his people. For other instances of this figure see Ps 20:6. 44:3. 63:8. 80:15, 17. gentleness. or, with thy meekness thou hast multiplied me. Ps 45:4. Is 40:11. 42:3. 2 C 10:1. Ga 5:22, 23. He 12:7-10. Ja 3:17, 18.

36. enlarged. Ps 4:1. *37:23. Jb 18:7. 36:16. Lk 12:50. 24:46-48. feet. Heb. ankles. 2 S 22:37. Pr *4:12. not slip. Ps 17:5.

37. pursued. ◊12, Ps +1:1. 3:7. 9:3. 35:2-5. 118:11, 12. Nu 24:17-19. Is 53:10-12. 62:1-6. Re 6:2. 19:19, 20.

38. wounded. 1 S 17:49-51. 23:5. 30:17. 2 S ch. 5, 8, 10. 18:7, 8. 21:15-22. 22:39. under my feet. 1 C 15:25.

39. For thou. ver. 32. girded. ver. 32. Ps 30:11. Ezk 30:24, 25. subdued. Heb. caused to bow. Ps 34:21. 66:3. 2 S 22:40. 1 Ch 22:18. Is 45:14. 1 C 15:25-28. Ep 1:22. Ph 3:21. under me. Ro *16:20.

40. necks. Jsh 10:24. La 5:5. that. Ps 34:21. 2 S 22:41. Pr 8:36. Jn 15:23.

41. but there. 2 S 22:42, 43. Jb 35:12, 13. Pr 1:28. Is *1:15. *59:1, 2. Je *11:11. 14:12. Ezk 8:18. Ho 7:14. Mi *3:4. Zc 7:13. Lk 13:25. answered them not. Ps √66:18. ●145:18. Pr *15:29. Jn +9:31. Ja 1:6-8.

42. beat. Ps 50:22. 2 K 13:7. Is 41:2, 15, 16. cast. Is 10:6. 25:10. Zc 10:5. Ml 4:3.

43. from. 1 S 2:9, 10. 2 S 3:1. 5:1-7. Ac 5:31. made me. Ps 22:27, 28. 108:9. Dt 28:13. 2 S ch. 5, 8, 10. 22:44-46. Is √49:6, 22, 23. 52:15. Zc +*14:9. Ro 15:12, 18. Ep 1:22. head of the heathen. Ps 110:2. Ge +*22:17. Dt +*28:13. Je 3:17. Mi 4:7. Zp 3:15. Zc *14:9. Ro +*11:25n. a people. Is 52:15. *55:5. Ho 1:10. Ac 13:46, 47. 28:28. Ro 16:26. 1 P *2:10. Re *11:15.

44. As soon, etc. Heb. at the hearing of the ear. Ps 150:5 (loud). Ge 29:13mg. Jb 42:5. Hab 3:2mg. Ro 10:16, 17. Ep 2:12. strangers. Heb. sons of the stranger. ver. 45. Ps 66:3. 81:9h, 15. 137:4. 144:7, 11. Ex 12:43 (*S#5236h). Dt 33:29. 2 S 1:13. Ne 13:30. Is 62:8. Ezk 44:7mg. shall submit. or, yield feigned obedience. Heb. lie. Ps 17:1mg. +66:3mg. 68:30. 81:15mg. 2 S 22:44-46. Je 3:10mg.

45. strangers. ver. +45. Ex 12:43 (*S#5236h). Is 24:4. Mi 7:17. Ja 1:11. afraid. Jsh 2:9. Re 6:16.

46. Lord. 2 S 22:47. Je *10:10. Jn 14:19. Re 1:18. blessed. ver. 2. Ps 42:9. the God. Ps 25:5. 68:20. 79:9. Ex 15:2. Is 12:2. Lk 1:47. exalted. Ps 21:13. 57:5, 11. 99:9.

47. God. Heb. El, Ex +15:2. avengeth. Heb. giveth avengements for me. Dt 32:35. 2 S 22:48. Na 1:2. Ro 12:19. subdueth. or, destroyeth. Ps 47:3.

48. liftest. Ps 22:27-30. 59:1, 2. 89:13. Ph *2:9. violent man. Heb. man of violence. Ps 7:16. 25:19mg. 86:14. 140:1, 4, 11.

49. Therefore. 2 S ||22:50. Ro ▸15:9. will I give thanks. or, confess. Ps 14:7. 30:12. 72:18, 19. 138:4. 2 S 22:50, 51. Ro 15:9. 1 T 6:13. sing. Ps 108:3. Mt 26:30. Ro 15:9.

50. Great. Ps 2:6. 78:71, 72. 89:3, 4. 144:10. 1 S 2:10. 16:1. Ac *2:34-36. Ph *2:9-11. to his king. Ps 89:20-38. 132:10. 1 S 2:10. 2 S 7:13. 1 Ch 17:11-14, 27. Is 9:6, 7. Lk 1:31-33, 69. Ro 1:3. 11:29. Ga 3:16. for evermore. Heb. olam, ✢S#5769h. Ps 37:27. 86:12. 89:28, 52. 92:8. 106:31. 113:2. 115:18. 121:8. 133:3. 2 S 22:51. 1 Ch 17:14. Ezk 37:26, 28.

PSALM 19

The heavens, and especially the sun, proclaim the Creator's glory to all lands, 1-6. The manifold excellence and usefulness of the word of God, 7-11. David prays to be delivered from his sins and accepted in his services, 12-14.

(*Title.*) A Psalm. It is uncertain when this highly finished and beautiful ode was composed, though some think it was written by David in the wilderness when persecuted by Saul.

1. The heavens. Ps 8:3. 33:6. 115:16. 148:3, 4. Is 40:22-26. Je 10:11, 12. Ro *1:19, 20. +2:12-16. declare. ◊155D, Ge +4:10. Ps 71:15. 78:4 (showing). Ge 24:66. Jg 7:13 (told). 2 K 8:5 (telling). God. Heb. El, Ex +15:2. the firmament. rakeea, from raka, to stretch out, the expanse; not only containing the celestial bodies, but also the air, light, rain, dews, all of which

display the infinite power and wisdom of their almighty Creator. Ps 150:1, 2. Ge 1:6-8, 14, 15. Da 12:3. **show-eth**. Ps 147:19. Ge 41:24. Jg 14:19 (expounded). 2 S 1:5, 6, 13 (told). Est *2:20. Is 41:26. 42:9. 45:19. 46:10. Je 4:15. Am 4:13. **handywork**. Ps 8:6. 28:4, 5.

2. **Day unto**. Ps 24:7-10. 78:3-6. 134:1-3. 148:12. Ex 15:20, 21. Is 38:19. **night unto**. Ps 74:16. 136:8, 9. Ge 1:17, 18. +*8:22.

3. **There**. *or*, "They have no speech, nor words, nor is their voice heard; yet into all the earth hath gone out their sound, and to the extremity of the world their words." The Hebrew *kav*, rendered *line*, like the Greek *phthongos*, by which the LXX. (who are followed by St. Paul), render it, no doubt signifies the *sound* as well as the *cord* which emits it. The Vulgate, Jerome, and Symmachus, render it to the same purpose. Dt 4:19. **where**. *or*, without *these* their voice is heard. Heb. without their voice heard. ✓63K, Ge +37:13.

4. **Their**. Ps 98:3. Is 49:6. Ro 10:18. 2 C 10:13-16. **line**. *or*, rule, *or*, direction. ✓121B, Jsh +17:14. Ro ▶10:18. **In them**. Ge 1:14-18. Ml *4:2. Jn 8:12.

5. **bridegroom**. Is 61:10. 62:5. Jn 3:29. **rejoiceth**. Ec 1:5. 1 C 9:24-26. Ph 3:13, 14. He 12:1, 2.

6. **His going**. Ps 139:9. Jb 25:3. Ec *1:5. Col *1:23. **circuit**. Jb 22:14.

7. **law**. *or*, doctrine. Ps 78:1-7. *119:72, 96-100, 105, 127, 128. 147:19, 20. Dt *6:6-9. *17:18-20. Jsh *1:8. Jb ✓23:12. Ro 3:2. ✓15:4. Ep 6:17. **perfect**. T#45.2; 1027. ver. 8, 9. Ps *18:30. 111:7. Dt 32:4. Pr 30:5. Mt +5:48 (T#548). Ro *12:2. Ja 1:17. **convert-ing**. *or*, restoring. T#47. Ps *23:3. *119:9, 93, *150. +126:5 (T#431). Mk +4:14 (T#428). Jn 5:39. 15:3. 17:17, 19. Ac +27:31 (T#429). Ro 1:16. ✓10:17. 1 C +1:17 (T#430). +4:15 (T#432). Ep 6:17. 1 Th ✓2:13. 2 T ✓3:15. Ja *1:18, 21-25. 1 P *1:23. **soul**. Heb. *ne-phesh*, Ge +34:3. **testimony**. ✓132C. Parallelism, Simple: Synthetic, or Constructive B351. This is where the parallelism consists only in the similar form of construction. There is neither gradation nor opposition of words in the several lines, which are independent and depend for their parallelism on their construction. Here in Ps 19:7-9, the lines are simply parallel and are chiefly in pairs. See the terms law/testimony, statutes/commandment, fear/judgments. Ps *93:5. 119:14, 24, 111, 152. Is 8:16, ✓20. Jn 3:32, 33. ✓5:39. Ac *10:43. 2 T 1:8. 1 J *5:9-12. Re *19:10. **sure**. Ps *111:7. 2 S 23:5. 2 T *2:19. He *6:18, 19. **making wise**. T#1039. Ps *119:98-100, 130. Pr *1:4, 5, 22, 23. 8:9. Is *8:20. Lk 10:21. Ro ✓15:4. Col *3:16. 2 T ✓3:15-17. 1 P *2:2. **simple**. ✓108K54, Pr +1:4.

8. **statutes**. Ps 105:45. *119:12, 16, 80, 171. Ge 26:5. Ex 18:16. Dt *4:5, 6. Ezk 36:27. **right**. Ps *119:128. Ne 9:13. **rejoicing the heart**. T#1052. Ps *1:2. *40:8. 119:14, 24, 54, 92, *111, 121, 143. Dt 12:11, 12. 16:11, 14. Ne *8:12. Is 64:5. Je ✓15:16. Ro 7:22. **is pure**. Ps *12:6. 119:140. Pr *30:5. Da *10:21. Ro 7:12-14. Ph ✓4:8. **enlightening**. Ps 13:3. *119:98-100, 105, 130. Pr 2:6. *6:23. *8:9. Is ✓8:20. Ro 2:17-20. *3:20. 7:7. Ga 2:19. *3:10-13, 21.

9. **The fear**. Ps *34:11-14. *36:1. *115:13. Ge *22:12. 42:18. 1 S *12:24. 1 K 18:3, 4, 12. Ne 5:15. Pr *8:13. Ac *10:22. Ro *3:10-18. **is clean**. Ps *119:9. Jn *17:17. **enduring**. Ps *111:10. *112:1-6. 119:160. Mt *5:17, 18. **for ever**. Ps +9:18 (❋S#5703h). **judg-ments**. Ps 10:5. *36:6. 72:1, 2. 119:*7, 39, *62, *75,

*106, 137, *138, 142, 160, *164. 147:19. Ex 21:1. Dt *4:8. Is *26:8. Ro *2:2. *11:22. Re *15:3. 16:7. 19:2. **true**. Heb. truth. Ps 15:2. 25:5. Da 10:21.

10. **desired**. T#1028. Jb *23:12. **than gold**. Ps 119:72, 127. Jb 28:15-17. Pr 3:13-15. *8:10, 11, 19. 16:16. **sweeter**. Ps 63:5. *119:103. Jb ✓23:12. Pr 24:13, 14. **honeycomb**. Heb. the dropping of honeycombs. 1 S 14:26-29.

11. **Moreover**. Ps ✓119:11. 2 Ch 19:10. Pr 6:22, 23. Ezk 3:17-21. 33:3-9. Mt 3:7. Ac 20:31. 1 C 4:14. *10:11. 1 Th 5:14. He 11:7. **keeping**. Pr *3:16-18. *11:18. *29:18. Is 3:10, 11. Mt 6:4, 6, 18. Lk +*11:28. He 11:6, 26. Ja *1:25. 2 J 8. Re 14:13. 22:7. **great reward**. T#302. Ps 25:10. 103:17, 18. Ex 20:6. Le 18:5. Dt 32:46, 47. Ne 9:29. Pr 3:1, 2. Is 1:19, 20. Ezk 18:5, 9. 20:13. Mt *7:21, 24, 25. 19:17. Lk 10:27, 28. Jn 12:26. Ro 10:5. 1 T +*4:8. Re 22:14.

12. **Who can**. T#45.1 Ps *40:12. 49:11. Le 4:2, 3. Jb *6:24. 34:32. Pr 16:4. Is 40:17. ✓64:6. Je ✓17:9. 1 C *4:4. 15:35, 44. 2 T 1:10. He 9:7. 2 P 3:10. 1 J 4:8. 5:7. Re 20:11. 22:16. **cleanse**. T#1453. Ps *51:2, +7 (T#1742), +10 (T#1669). 65:3. *119:9. Mt 8:2, 3. 1 J *1:7. **from secret**. T#1692. Ps *90:8. *139:2, 23, 24. Le *4:2, etc. Jb *34:32. Je *17:9.

13. **Keep back**. T#1651, 1700. Ps 119:10, 29, 37, *133. *141:3, 4. Ge *20:6. 1 S *25:32-34, 39. Pr 30:7-9. 2 C 13:7. Ph *1:9, 10. 1 Th *5:23. **presumptuous**. ✓100, Ge +10:9. Ex 21:14. Nu 15:30, 31. Dt 17:12, 13. He ✓10:26. 2 P 2:10. **let**. Ps 119:133. Ro 6:12-14, 16-22. **upright**. Ps 7:10. 11:7. *84:11. Ac 24:16. **I shall**. Ps 18:23. 1 Ch 10:13, 14. **great**. Heb. much. ver. 11. Ps *25:11. 29:3mg. **transgression**. Ps 5:10. 25:7. 32:1. Mt *12:31, 32. Ja *5:20. 1 J +5:16.

14. **Let**. Ps 5:1, 2. *51:15. ✓66:18-20. *119:108. Ge 4:4, 5. Pr *15:8. Ro 15:16. He 11:4. *13:15. 1 P 2:5. **meditation**. Ps 5:1. 37:4. 145:19. Ge 24:63. Ml *3:16. **strength**. Heb. rock. Ps *18:1, 2. 73:26mg. **redeemer**. Jb *19:25. Is 43:14. *44:6. 47:4. 54:5. 1 Th *1:10. T *2:14. 1 P *1:18, 19. Re 5:9.

PSALM 20

Israel prays that her king may be defended, ac-cepted, and prospered, 1-4: and rejoices in confidence of being answered and succeeded, 5-9.

1. A.M. 2968. B.C. 1036. **hear**. Ps 41:1. *46:1. 50:5. 60:11. *91:15. *138:7. Je 30:7. Mt 26:38, 39. He *5:7. **day of**. Ps *37:39, 40. +50:15. 2 C 1:3, 4. **name**. ✓121T1, Dt +28:58. ✓144A4A, Is +30:27. i.e. *Jacob's God himself*. Ps +✓9:10. +*83:18. Ex 20:24. 34:5-7. Dt 28:28. Pr 18:10. Is *50:10. **God of Jacob**. Ps 46:7, 11. +*84:8. Ge *32:27-29. 48:15, 16. Ex 3:13-15. **de-fend**. Heb. set thee on an high place. Ps +9:9mg. 18:2. 59:9mg. 91:14. 144:2.

2. **thee help**. Heb. thy help. **from**. Ps 73:17. 1 K 6:16. *8:44, 45. 1 Ch 21:26. 2 Ch 20:8, 9. **strengthen**. Heb. support thee. **out**. 2 S 5:7. 6:17. Is 12:6. 14:32. 37:34, 35.

3. **Remember**. Ge 4:4. Is 60:7. Ep *5:2. 1 P 2:5. **accept**. Heb. turn to ashes, *or*, make fat. ✓108H1D. Idiom B843. "Turn to ashes" was the Hebrew idiom for God's acceptance of offerings by fire. He accepted them by causing fire to fall from heaven and consume the sacrifice. No fire having its origin in this world ever consumed the sacrifices which God accepted. For another instance of this idiom see Le 9:24. Le +=1:16.

9:24. Jg 6:21. 13:15-23. 1 K 18:38. 1 Ch 21:26. 2 Ch=5:12. 7:1. Ep=*1:6.

4. **Grant.** Ps 2:8. 21:2. *37:4. 145:19. Pr *11:23. Is 49:8. 53:11. Mt *21:22. Jn 11:42. 16:23. Ro 8:27, 28. He *7:25. 1 J √5:14, 15.

5. **rejoice.** Ps 13:5. 19:4. 21:1. 35:9. *118:15. Is 12:1-3. 25:9. 61:10. Hab 3:18. Lk 1:47. **and in.** Ps *60:4. Ex +*17:15mg. Nu 10:35, 36. 1 S 17:45. Is 11:10. Mi 4:5.

6. **Now.** Ps 2:2. *18:50. 28:8. 89:20-23. Ac *2:36. 4:10. **he will.** 1 K 8:30, 43. Mt 6:9. **his holy heaven.** Heb. the heaven of his holiness. Is 57:15. 63:15. **with,** etc. Heb. by the strength of the salvation of his right hand. *22A15B, Ps +18:35. Ps 17:7. 18:35. Ac 2:33. 5:31.

7. **Some trust.** Ps *33:16, 17. 44:6. 125:1. 1 S 13:5. 17:39, 45. 2 S 8:4. 10:18. Pr *21:31. Is 30:16. *31:1. Je 17:5. **but we.** Ps 45:17. 2 Ch 13:10-12, 16. 14:11. 20:12, 20. *32:8. **the name.** Ps +√9:10.

8. **They.** Ps 34:21, 22. Jg 5:31. **but we.** Ps 125:1. *146:5-9. Je 17:7, 8. La 4:22.

9. **Save,** etc. or, "O Jehovah, save the king; answer us when we call upon thee." Ps 118:25, 26. Mt 21:9, 15. **let.** Ps 2:6-10. 5:2. 24:7. 44:4. 74:12.

PSALM 21

The king and people rejoice in God and bless him for fully answering their largest prayers, 1-6; expressing the strongest assurance of future success with the ruin of all enemies, 7-12; and calling upon God to exalt himself, that they might more and more sing his praises, 13.

(Title.) **A Psalm.** This is the people's song of triumph, after the victory for which they prayed in the former psalm.

1. **the king.** Ps 2:6. 20:6, 9. 63:11. 72:1, 2. Is *9:6, 7. Mt 2:2. **joy.** Ps 28:7. *62:7. *95:1. 99:4. Ne 8:10. **in thy.** Ps 20:5. 71:17-24. 118:14, 15. He *12:2.

2. **his heart's.** Ps 2:8, 9. *20:4, 5. 92:11. Is 49:6-12. He 7:25. **not withholden.** Jn *11:42. He +*5:7.

3. **preventest.** Ps 18:18. 1 S 16:13. 2 S 2:4. 5:3. Jb 41:11. Is *65:24. Ro 11:35. **blessings.** Ps 31:19. 2 Ch 6:41. Ro 2:4. Ep 1:3. **settest.** 2 S 12:30. 1 Ch 20:2. He *2:9. Re 19:12.

4. **asked life.** T#1601. Ps 13:3. 16:10, 11. 30:2, 3. 39:13. 41:10. 61:5, 6. 69:32, 33. 102:24. 107:18, 19. 119:17, 77, 175. 2 S 7:12, 13. Is 9:7. *38:1-3. Je 15:15. Da 2:17, 18. Jon 1:13, 14. Mt 8:24, 25. 14:30, 31. Jn 14:19. Ro 6:*9, √23. He *7:25. 1 J *5:16. **length of days.** T#1602. Ps 72:17. 89:29, 36, 37. 91:16. Re 1:18. **for ever.** ✜S#5769h, *olam* in conjunction with *ad.* Ps 9:5. 10:16. 45:6, 17. 48:14. 52:8. 111:8. 119:44. 145:1, 2, 21. 148:6. Ex 15:18. Is 30:8. Da 12:3. Mi 4:5. **and ever.** Heb. *ad,* Ps +9:18 (✱S#5703h).

5. **glory.** Ps 3:3. 62:7. 2 S 7:8, 9, 19. Is 49:5-7. 63:1. Jn 13:31, 32. 17:1, *5, 22. Ph *2:9-11. He 8:1. 2 P *1:17. Re 5:8-13. **honor.** Ps 110:1. 1 Ch 17:11-15, 27. Mt 28:18. Ep 1:20-22. 1 P 3:22.

6. **made.** Heb. set him to be blessings. Ps *72:17-19. Ge *12:2. Lk 2:10, 11, 30-32. Ac 3:26. Ga 3:9, 14. Ep *1:3. **for ever.** Ps +9:18 (✱S#5703h). **made him exceeding glad.** Heb. gladded him with joy. Ps 4:6, 7. *16:11. 45:7. 63:2-5. Ac *2:25, 28. **thy countenance.** Nu 6:26.

7. **For the.** Ps 13:5. *18:2. 20:7, 8. 26:1. 61:4, 6,

7. 91:2, 9, 10. 1 S *30:6. Mt 27:43. He 2:13. **most.** Ps 9:2. Dt 32:8, 9. **he shall.** Ps *16:8. Da 7:14.

8. **Thine hand.** *22A14.7, Ex +9:3. Ps 2:9. 18, title. 72:9. 89:22, 23. *110:1, 2. 1 S 25:29. 31:3. 2 S 7:1. Am 9:2, 3. Lk *19:14, 27. 1 C *15:25. He 10:28, 29. Re 19:15.

9. **Thou.** Ge 19:28. Da 3:20-22. Ml 4:1. Mt 13:42, 50. √25:41, 46. 2 Th *1:8. Re √20:14. **anger.** *22A4, Ge +19:13. **the Lord.** Ps 56:1, 2. 106:17. Jb 6:3. La 2:2. **in his.** Ps 2:5, 12. Mt 22:7. 1 Th 2:16. Re 6:16, 17. 19:15. **the fire shall.** T#1001‡. Ps 18:8. +*50:2, 3. Dt 9:3. *32:22. Is +√24:6. *26:11. Na 1:6. Ml +√4:1. Mt *3:10, 12. +*13:30. *25:41, 46. Lk +*16:24. He *10:26, 27. 12:29. 2 P +*3:7, 13n. Re 20:10, 14, 15.

10. **Their fruit.** Ps *37:28. 109:13. 1 K 13:34. Jb 18:16-19. 20:28. Is 14:20. Ml 4:1. **their seed.** Ex +*20:5.

11. **intended evil.** Mt 2:13. **against thee.** Pr *21:30. **imagined.** Ps *2:1. 10:2. 31:13. 35:20. Je 11:18, 19. Ezk 11:2. Mt 21:46. 26:4, 5. Ac 5:27, 28. **are not.** Ps 83:4. Is 7:6, 7. 8:9, 10. Mt 2:8, 16. *27:63, 64. 28:2-6. Ac 4:17, 18. **to perform.** *63BA. Ellipsis (Absolute: of the infinitive), after "able." For other instances of this figure see Ps 101:5. 139:6. Is 1:13. Ho 8:5. 1 C *3:2.

12. **Therefore.** Ps 9:3. 44:10. 56:9. **make,** etc. or, set them as a butt. Jb 7:20. 16:12, 13. La 3:12. **back.** Heb. shoulder. 1 S 10:9mg. **thou shalt.** Ps 7:13. 18:14. 64:7. **thine.** *63A2, 2 S +6:6. **arrows.** *22D5B, Dt +32:23.

13. **Be thou.** Ps 18:46. 46:10. 57:5, 11. 72:18, 19. 113:5mg. 1 Ch 29:11. Jb 9:19. Mt 6:10, 13. Re *11:16, 17. **so will.** Ps 58:10, 11. Re 15:3, 4. 16:5-7. 18:20. 19:1-6.

PSALM 22

David, prophetically speaking in the person of Christ, complains grievously that he was forsaken by his God and left to the insulting cruelty of his enemies; and he predicts many circumstances of the Messiah's sufferings, 1-21. He proclaims the name and praise of the Lord, calling on the people to trust and glorify him; and foretells the permanent success of the gospel, 22-31.

(Title.) A.M. 2962. B.C. 1042. **Aijeleth.** or, the hind of the morning. ✱S#365h. ver. 16. Ps 42:1, 2. Pr 5:19h. Je 14:5h.

1. **My.** *59, Ge +28:16. **God.** Heb. *El,* Ex +15:2. *171E12, Ge +14:22. T#1968. Ps 31:14-16. 43:1-5. Mt ✱▶27:46. Mk ▶15:34. Lk 24:44. **my God.** *84, Ge +6:17. 22:11. **why hast.** *85P, Ge +27:46. Ps 26:9. 37:28. 71:11. 1 S 12:22. He +*13:5. 1 P *1:11. **far.** ver. 11. Ps 46:1. **helping.** Heb. my salvation. Is 46:13. **words.** Ps 32:3, 4. 38:8. Jb 3:24. 4:10. Is 5:29. 59:11. Ezk 19:7. Zc 11:3. Lk 22:44. He √5:7. **roaring.** *22F2, Ps +29:3.

2. **I cry.** or, call. Ps *18:3, 6. 42:3. 55:16, 17. 80:18. *86:3, 7. 91:15. 102:2. Jb *14:15. 27:10. **daytime.** T#1157. Ps 42:3. *55:17. 88:1. Lk *18:7. 1 Th 3:10. 2 T 1:3. **but.** Ps 80:4. La 3:8, 44. **in the night.** Ps +119:55. Lk 6:12. *18:7, 8. 22:41-46. **am not silent.** Heb. there is no silence to me. Ps 39:2. 62:1mg. 65:1mg. Mt 26:44.

3. **But.** Ps *145:17-19. Jb *13:15. Is 6:3. Re 4:8. **that.** Ps 50:23. 65:1. Dt 10:21. **praises.** *96F2, Ge +4:10. *121N2, Ge +34:29. "Praises" are put by

Metonymy of Adjunct for the sanctuary where they are offered.

4. **Our fathers.** ♪171G, Ge +13:8. Ps *44:1-7. Ge √15:6. 32:9-12, 28. Ex 14:13, 14, 31. 1 S 7:9-12. Ro *4:18-22. He *11:8-32.

5. **cried.** Ps 99:6, 7. 106:44. Jg 4:3. 6:6. 10:10-16. **and were.** Ps 25:2, 3. 31:1. 69:6, 7. 71:1. Is 45:17. 49:23. Ro 9:33. 10:11. 1 P 2:6.

6. **I am.** Jb 25:6. Is 41:14. **worm.** ♪111, Ge +18:27. **a reproach.** Ps 31:11. 69:7-12, 19, 20. 88:8. Is 49:7. √53:3. Zc 11:8. Mt 11:19. 12:24. 27:20-23. Jn 7:15, 20, 47-49. 8:48. Ro 15:3. He 13:13. **despised of.** T#1954. Is 49:7. Mt ✱26:67, 68.

7. **All.** *♪171A, Ex +9:6. **laugh.** T#1959. Ps 35:15, 16. Mt *9:24. 27:29, 39. Mk 15:20, 29. Lk 16:14. 23:11, ✱35-39. **shoot out.** Heb. open. Ps 31:18. Jb 16:4, 10. 30:9-11. Is 57:4. Mt 26:66-68. **shake.** T#1956. Ps 44:14. *109:25. Is 37:22, 23. Mt *✱27:39, 40. Mk 15:29-32.

8. **He trusted.** Heb. rolled himself on. ♪96B, Ge +20:7. ♪60D, Ps *37:5. 55:22. Ge +37:19. Pr *16:3mg. Mt 27:42, ▶43. **let him.** ♪96B, Ex +20:8. T#1958. Ps 3:1, 2. 42:10. 71:11. *91:14. Mt ✱27:41-43. Mk 15:30-32. **seeing,** etc. *or,* if he delight. Ps *18:19. Is 42:1. Mt *3:17. 12:18. 17:5. Lk 23:35.

9. **that took.** Ps *71:6. 139:15, 16. Is 49:1, 2. **thou didst.** Ps 71:17. Is *7:14, 15. *9:6. **make me hope.** *or,* keep me in safety. or, trust, or, lean. 2 K 18:30. Is 36:15. Je 28:15. 29:31. Mt *2:13-15. Re 12:4, 5.

10. **cast.** Is 46:3, 4. 49:1. Lk *2:40, 52. **thou.** Jn 20:17. **from.** Je 1:5. Ga *1:15, 16.

11. **Be not far.** T#1625. Ps *10:1. 13:1-3. 35:22. 38:21. +51:11 (T#1536). 69:1, 2, 18. 71:12. Je 14:7, 8. Mk 5:18. Lk 24:29. Jn 4:40. 16:32. 17:21. Ep *3:17. 2 T 4:22. He *5:7. Re √3:20. **none to help.** Heb. not a helper. Ps 72:12. 142:4-6. Dt 32:36. Mt *26:56, 72-74.

12. **Many.** Ps 68:30. Je 50:11. **strong.** Dt 32:14, 15. Is 34:7. Ezk *39:18. Am 4:1-3. Mt 27:1. Ac *4:27. **of Bashan.** Ps 68:15, 22. 135:11. Nu +21:33. Jsh 12:4n. 1 K 4:13.

13. **gaped,** etc. Heb. opened their mouths against me. ver. 7. Ps 35:21. 66:14mg. Jb 16:10. La 2:16. 3:46. Mt 26:3, 4, 59-65. **as a ravening.** ver. 21. Ps 7:2. 17:12. 35:17. Ezk 22:27, 28. 1 P 5:8.

14. **I am.** Jsh 7:5. Mt 26:38. Lk 22:44. Jn 12:27. **poured out.** Dt 12:27. 1 S 7:6. 2 S 14:14. **all my bones.** ver. 17. Ps 6:2. 31:10. 32:3. Da 5:6. **out of joint.** *or,* sundered. Ps 92:9. Jb 4:11. 41:17. **my heart.** T#1972. Ps 68:2. Jsh 7:5. Jb 23:16. Mk 14:33, 34. Jn *19:34. **midst.** ♪144A6, Ge +45:6.

15. **strength.** Ps 32:3, 4. Pr 17:22. **tongue.** Ps 69:3, 21. Jb 29:10. La 4:4. Jn *19:28. **into the dust.** Ps 30:9. 104:29. Ge +*3:19. 18:27. Jb *7:21. 10:9. 34:15. Is 53:12. Da *12:2. Mt 27:50. 1 C +*15:3.

16. **dogs.** ♪103, Ge +3:13. Ps 22, title. ver. 20. Ps 59:6, 14. Mt +*7:6. Ph *3:2. Re *22:15. **compassed.** Je 12:6. Lk 11:53, 54. **assembly.** Ps *86:14. Je *12:6. Mt 26:57. Mk *15:16-20. Lk 22:63-71. 23:4, 5, 10, 11, 23, *35. **they pierced.** ♪63B, Ge +25:28. EWB in the margin of the CB notes "It is better to translate the Hebrew text literally, and supply the *Ellipsis* of the verb from Is 38:13, 'they break up.' The meaning is the same, and agrees with John 19:37." The textual reading is *kaari,* "*as a lion* my hands and my feet;" but several MSS. read *karoo* and others have *karoo* in the margin, which affords the reading adopted by

our translators. So the LXX., so also the Vulgate, Syriac, Arabic, and Ethiopic; and as all the Evangelists so quote the passage and apply it to the crucifixion of Christ, there seems scarcely the shadow of a doubt that this is the genuine reading, especially when it is considered that the other contains no clear sense at all. The whole difference lies between *wav* and *yood,* Hebrew letters which might easily be mistaken for each other. T#1951. Ps =105:18, 19. Zc *12:10. *13:6. Mt *27:35. Mk 15:24. Lk ✱23:33. √24:39. Jn 19:23, ▶37. *✱20:25, 27.

17. **I may.** Ps 102:3-5. Jb 33:21. Is 52:14. **look.** Mt 27:36, 39-41. Mk 15:29-32. Lk 23:27, 35. **stare upon.** T#1957. Lk ✱23:35.

18. **they part.** T#1961A. Ps 60:6 (divide). 68:12. 108:7. Jsh 18:10. Is 53:12. Mt 27:35. Mk 15:24. Lk 23:34. Jn ✱19:23, ▶24. **cast lots.** T#1961B. Jsh +14:2n. Jn ✱19:24.

19. **But.** ver. 11. Ps 10:1. **O my.** Ps 18:1. 21:1. **strength.** ♪121E1, Ge +25:23. **haste.** T#1545. Ps 38:22. *40:13, 17. 49:17. *69:13-18. 70:1-5. 71:12. 102:1, 2. 118:25. 141:1. 143:7. Is *65:24.

20. **soul.** Heb. *nephesh,* Ps 17:13. Ge +12:13. Zc 13:7. **my darling.** Heb. my only one. ✱S#3173h. Ps 25:16. *35:17mg. 68:6. Ge 22:*2, 12, 16. Jg 11:34. Pr 4:3. Je 6:26. Am 8:10. Zc *12:10. LXX. renders "only begotten." Jn 3:16. **from the power.** Heb. from the hand. ♪144A5, Ge +9:5. Ac 4:27. 1 P 5:8. **dog.** ver. 16.

21. **Save me from.** Lk 4:13. Ac 5:31. 2 T 4:17. **heard.** ♪63H, Ps 118:5. Ge +12:15. He *5:7. **me from.** Lk 22:53. Jn 14:30. 2 T 4:17. 1 P 5:8. **horns.** Nu 23:22. Dt 33:17. Jb 39:9, 10. Is 34:7. Jn 8:59. Ac 4:27. 5:30-32.

22. **I will declare.** Ps *40:9. 71:18, 19. Lk 15:6. Jn 7:25, 26. He 2:11, ▶12. Ju 24. **my brethren.** Mt 12:48, 49. 25:40. 28:10. Jn 20:17. Ro 8:29. **in the midst.** ♪144A6, ver. 25. Ps 40:9, 10. Ge +45:6.

23. **Ye that.** Ps 115:11, 13. 135:19, 20. 145:19. 1 Ch 16:8-13. Lk 1:50. **all ye.** Ps 105:3-7. 106:5. 107:1, 2. 135:19, 20. **glorify.** Ps *50:23. Is 25:3. Mt *5:16. Lk 2:20. Jn *17:4. 1 C *6:19, 20. √10:31. Ph 1:11. 1 P *4:11. Re 15:4. **all ye the.** ver. 30. 1 Ch 16:13. **seed of Israel.** Ga 6:16.

24. **For.** ver. 6. Ps 35:10. 69:29-34. Is 50:6-9. **neither.** Lk 23:46. **but.** ver. 2. Ps 34:6. 116:3-6. 118:5. He *5:7.

25. **My praise.** ver. 22. Ps 35:18. *40:9, 10. 111:1. **I will.** Ps 56:12. 65:1. *66:13, 16. *116:14-19. 118:19, 20. Ec *5:4, 5. **vows.** Le +23:38.

26. **The meek.** T#818. Ps 37:11. *69:32. 147:6. 149:4. Le 7:11-17. Is 11:4, 6-9. 25:6. *29:19. 65:13. Mt +5:5. Jn *6:48-58. **shall eat.** ver. 29. 1s 55:1, 2. Jn 6:51. **they.** Ps 105:3, 4. **your heart.** Ps *69:32. Pr 23:7. Mt 13:15. Jn *4:14. *6:51. Ro *10:10. **live.** ♪108B, 1 S +10:24. **for ever.** Ps +9:18 (✱S#5703h).

27. **All the ends.** Ps 2:8. 59:13. 67:7. 72:8, 11. 86:9. 98:3. Is +*43:6. *45:22. 46:8, 9. 49:6, 12. Je +31:8. **world.** ♪121J17, Ge +6:11. **turn.** Hg 1:5. Lk *15:17, 18. Ac 11:18. 14:15. 20:21. 26:18-20. Ro 16:26. 1 Th 1:9. **and all.** Ps *2:8. *72:11. 86:9. 96:7. 98:3. 102:15, 22. 117:1. Is 2:2. *11:9. *49:6. Re 7:9-12. 15:4.

28. **the kingdom.** Ps 47:7, 8. Da *7:14. Ob 21. Zc *14:9. Mt *6:13. Re *11:15. **governor.** T#280. Ps 47:2, 7, 8. 89:18. 99:1. *103:19. 146:10. Is *33:22. Da 4:34. Re *19:6, 16.

29. **that be.** Ps 73:7. 78:31. Is 10:16. **fat.** Ps 92:14. Is 30:23. **shall eat and worship.** Ps *113:7. Is *26:19. 29:4. Ph *2:10. Re 20:12-15. **bow.** Ps 45:12. 72:11. Is 45:23. 60:3. Ro *14:10-12. Ph *2:10. Re *5:13. **and none.** Ps *49:6-9. Jb *12:10. Ho *13:9. Jn √3:36. *11:25, 26. 2 C +3:5. **soul.** Heb. *nephesh*, Ge +12:13.

30. **A seed.** Is 53:10. He 2:13. **it shall.** Ps 14:5. 24:6. 73:15. 87:6. Mt 3:9. 24:34. Ga 3:26-29. 1 P *2:9.

31. **They.** Ps 78:6. 86:9. 102:18. 145:4-7. Is 44:3-5. 49:21-23. 54:1. 60:4. 66:7-9. **his righteousness.** Ro 1:17. 3:21-25. *5:19-21. 2 C √5:21. **unto.** Ps 78:6. Jn 20:29. Ro 3:21, 22. **people.** Is 28:11. Ho *2:23. Ro 9:24. **born.** √22C23, Ps +2:7. **he hath done.** Heb. it is finished. T#1969. Jn ✲19:30.

PSALM 23

David rejoices in the compassionate care of the Lord his shepherd, 1-3. He exults in the assurance of being supported by him through life and death and of spending eternity in his presence, 4-6.

1. **The Lord.** Ge 22:14, *Jehovah-roi*. Ex +15:26. **is.** √119, Ge +49:9. Here we have a metaphor, and in it a great and blessed truth is set forth by the representation of Jehovah as a shepherd. It is he who tends his people and does more for them than any earthly shepherd does for his sheep. All his titles and attributes are so bound up with this care that in this psalm we have the illustration of many of the Jehovah-titles (B737). **my shepherd.** √22D2F. Anthropomorphism B891. Ps 78:52, 72. *79:13. 80:1. 95:7. Ge 49:24. Is *40:11. Je 23:3, 4. 31:10. Ezk *34:11, 12, 23, 24. 37:24. Mi 5:+2, 4. Zc 13:7. Mt 26:31. Jn *10:11, 14, 16, 27-30. He 13:20. 1 P 2:25. *5:4. Re *7:17. **I shall not want.** Because He is *Jehovah-jireh* (Ge 22:14) and will provide. Ps 33:18, 19. *34:9, 10, 22. 37:18, 19. *84:11. Ge=47:12. 48:15. Mt √6:33. 17:20. *21:22. Mk 9:23. √11:22-24. Lk *11:9-13. 12:30-32. Jn *10:27, 28. 15:7, 16. 16:23-26. Ro *8:32. Ph *4:19. He 13:+*5, 6. Ja *1:5-8. 1 J *3:20-22. √5:13-15. 3 J 2.

2. **He maketh.** Is 30:23. *40:11. Je 31:2. Ezk 34:13-15. Mt 24:45. Jn *6:27. **lie down.** Ps *4:8. Pr *3:24. Ezk 34:15. Mt *11:28. **green pastures.** Heb. pastures of tender grass. Ps 37:2. 65:11-13. Ge 1:11, 12. Is 35:1, 2. Ezk *34:13-15. Lk 7:11. Jn 7:37. 10:9. Re *7:17. 22:17. Heb. ✲S#4999h. Ps 23:2 (pastures). 65:12. 74:20 (habitations). 83:12 (houses). Je 9:10 (habitations. mg, pastures). 23:10 (pleasant places). 25:37 (habitations). La 2:2. Jl 1:19, 20. 2:22. Am 1:2. **he leadeth.** ver. 3. Ps 5:8. 48:14. Is 40:10, 11. *42:16. *48:17. 49:9, 10. Re *7:17. **still waters.** Heb. waters of quietness. Because He is *Jehovah-shalom* (Jg 6:24) and will give peace. Ps 46:4. Jb 34:29. Is 8:6. 35:7. 41:18. 1 T +2:2. Re 21:6. 22:1, 17.

3. **He restoreth.** For He is *Jehovah-rophecha* (Ex 15:26) and will graciously heal. Ps +*16:10. *19:7mg. *49:15. *51:10-12. 85:4-7. 89:4. *116:3-8. *119:176. Ru 4:15. Jb 33:30. Is 58:12. Je *32:37-42. Ho 14:4-9. Mi *7:8, 9, 18, 19. Lk 22:31, 32. Jn 4:14. 21:15-19. 1 J *2:1. Re *3:19. **soul.** Heb. *nephesh*, Ge +12:13. **he leadeth.** T#806. ver. 2. Ps 5:8. *25:4, 5, 9,10. 27:11. *31:3. 33:18. 43:3. 48:14. 61:2. 73:24. 119:133. 139:9, 10, 23, 24. *143:8-10. Ge 12:1. Ex 13:21. 15:13. 33:13-15. Dt 32:10-12. Jg 4:14. 2 S 5:24. 22:29. 1 K +*13:9n. 2 Ch 32:22. Pr √3:5, 6. *8:20. Is 30:21. 40:10, 11. *42:16. 48:17. 49:9, 10. 55:4. 57:18. 58:11. 61:8.

Je 3:4. 6:16. 31:8-10. 42:2, 3. Mi 7:7, 8. Lk 1:79. Jn 10:*4, 13. 16:13. Ph 1:10. Col 1:9, 10. 1 Th 3:10, 11. Re 7:17. **paths.** Ps *16:11. 85:13. Pr 4:11. *8:20. Is 42:16. **righteousness.** For He is *Jehovah-tzidkenu* (Je 23:6) and is himself my righteousness, and I am righteous in him (Je 33:16). **for his.** Ps 25:11. 72:17-19. 79:9. 106:8. 1 S 12:22. Ezk 20:14. Ep *1:6. 1 J 2:12. **name's.** Ps +√9:10. 25:11. 143:11. 1 K 8:41. Is 48:9. Je 14:7. Ezk 36:22.

4. **though.** Jsh 3:11. **I walk through.** Ps *138:7. Jsh 3:11. **the valley.** Jl 3:2, 11. **shadow of death.** Heb. *tzalmaveth*, ✲S#6757h. Ps 44:19. 107:10, 14. Jb 3:5. *10:21, 22. *12:22. *16:16. *24:17. 28:3. 34:22. +*38:17. Is *9:2. Je 2:6. *13:16. Am 5:8. Lk *1:79. **I will fear no.** Ps *3:5, 6. *27:1-4. +*34:4. *46:1-3. *118:6. 138:7. Is *41:10. *43:2. Zp 3:16. Lk 12:32. 1 C 15:+*55-57. 2 T *1:7. **for thou.** T#6. Ps 14:5. 16:8. 31:7, 8. 46:1, 11. 1 S +2:1 (T#657). Jb 29:5. Is 8:9, 10. 25:4. *41:10. *43:1, 2. 49:13. Je 16:19. Zc 8:23. Mt 1:23. *28:20. Ac 18:9, 10. 27:20-25. Ro *8:31. 1 C +10:13 (T#725). 2 C 1:3, 4. 2 T 4:22. **art with me.** For thou art *Jehovah-shammah* (Ezk 48:35), and the Lord is there. Ps *40:17. 118:7, 10, 13, 18. Is *43:2. Mi 2:12, 13. Zp 3:17. Zc 9:14-16. **thy rod.** √22D5R, Ps +2:9. √121S1, Ge +49:10. The rod and staff signify, by the figure Metonymy of the Adjunct, whereby the sign is put for the thing signified, God's care and defense. The shepherd carried two implements: the "rod," to help the sheep, and the "club," to destroy the sheep's enemies. Ps 74:2. *110:2. Ge +*49:10. Ex 17:5, 6, 9. 4:17, 20. Ps *110:2. Is 9:4. Je 10:16. Mi *7:14. Zc 11:10, 14. Re 12:10. **thy staff.** Ex 21:19. Nu 21:18. Jg *6:21. 2 K *4:29, 31. ◐*18:21. Is 14:4, 5. 36:6. Ezk 29:6. Zc 8:4. **comfort.** Ps *119:50. Jn *14:16-18. Ro √15:4. 2 C *1:3, 4. 2 Th 2:16, 17. 2 T 4:16, 17.

5. **preparest.** Ps *22:26, 29. *31:19, 20. 78:25-28. 104:15. Ge 12:6. Jb 36:16. Is 25:6. Jn 6:53-56. *10:9, 10. 16:22. **a table.** Ps 69:22. ◐78:19. 128:3. Jb 36:16. Is *25:6. Ezk *39:17-22. Lk +*22:29, 30. 1 C 10:21. Re 7:17. *19:17, 18. √121J6. Metonymy of the Subject B574. "Table" is put for the things on it. For other instances of this figure see Ps *78:19. Ho 14:2. He 13:10. **presence.** or, over against. Ps 31:22. 38:11. Ge 12:6. Dt *8:2. Zc 14:1-5. Ph 1:12-18. Ep *6:13. 1 P *1:7. Re 19:9, 13-21. **enemies.** For thou art *Jehovah-nissi* (Ex 17:15), my banner, and will fight for me while I feast. Ps 6:7. 7:4. **anointest.** Heb. makest fat. √96C2, Ge +45:9. For thou art *Jehovah-mekaddeschem* (Ex 31:13), the Lord that sanctifieth me. Ps 28:8. *45:7. 89:20. 92:10. 104:15. 2 S 12:20. Pr 15:30. Am 6:6. Mt 6:17. 26:6, 7. Mk 14:8. Lk 7:45-50. 2 C 1:21. He +*1:9. 1 J *2:20, 27. √22C47. Anthropomorphism B891. Human actions are attributed to God: anointing. For other instances of this figure see Ps 92:10. 2 C 1:21. **with oil.** Ps 45:7. 55:21. 89:20. Ja 5:14. **my cup.** Ps *16:5. 31:19. 34:6, 8. 45:13-15. 73:10. 89:1. 97:10-12. 103:1-5. 116:13. Jn 1:16. 1 C 10:16. Ep 3:17-20. **runneth over.** or, is full. Ps 66:12mg (moist).

6. **Surely.** All these blessings are mine for time and eternity, for he is *Jehovah-rohi* (Ps 23:1), Jehovah my shepherd, pledged to raise me up from the dead and to preserve and bring me "through" the valley of death into His glorious kingdom (Jn 6:39). **goodness.** Ps 21:3. *25:7, 10. *30:11, 12. *36:7-10. *84:11. 100:5. 106:1. 107:1. 1 Ch 16:34. La 3:22, 23. 2 C 1:10. 2 T *4:18.

and. ♪174, Ge +18:27. **mercy**. Ps 103:17. **follow**. He 13:6. **and I**. Ps 15:1. *16:11. *17:15. *27:4-6. *73:24-26. *84:10. 116:16-19. Is 2:2. Jn √14:2, 3. 2 C *5:1. Ph *1:23. 2 T *4:18. He 11:10-16. 13:14. Re 7:15. 21:3. **dwell in**. or, return to. Is *35:10. +*51:11. **the house**. Ac +*15:16, 17. He *3:6. **for ever**. Heb. to length of days. S#3117h, 753h. Ps 21:4. +*91:16mg. 93:5mg. Pr 3:2mg, 16. La 5:20mg. Re 3:12.

PSALM 24

The Creator's dominion over the whole earth, 1, 2. The subjects of the Redeemer's kingdom, 3-6. Entrance demanded for the king of glory into his temple, 7-10.

1. A.M. 2962. B.C. 1042. **earth**. Ps 50:12. Ex 9:29. 19:5. Dt *10:14. 1 Ch 29:11. Jb 41:11. Da 4:25. Ro +14:8. 1 C ▶10:26, 28. **is the**. ♪52A3B. Repeated Alternation: three or more members in a series B373. Here we have an alternation of three members repeated in three series: (A) 1, 2. Right to the earth. (B) 3. Questions. (C) 4-6. Answer. (A) 7. Right to heaven. (B) 8-. Question. (C) -8. Answer. (A) 9. Right to heaven. (B) 10-. Question. (C) -10. Answer. EWB gives Ps 147 as another instance of this figure. **world**. Ps 89:11. 98:7. Na 1:5.

2. **For**. Ps 33:6, 7. 95:4, 5. 104:5, 6. 136:6. Ge 1:9, 10. Jb 38:4. Je 10:11-16. 2 P 3:5-7. **and**. Ps 93:1. 96:10. Ge 8:22. Jb 38:8-11. Je 5:22.

3. **Who**. Ps *15:1-5. *68:18. Ml *3:2. Jn *13:36. *20:17. Ep *4:8-10. Re *22:14. **the hill**. ♪22D3A, 1 K +8:39. Ps 68:15, 16. 78:68, 69. 132:13, 14. 2 S 6:12-17. 1 Ch 15:1, 25-28. He *12:22-24. **stand**. Le 10:3. Ml *3:1, 2. He 12:28, 29.

4. **He that**, etc. Heb. the clean of hands. Ps *18:20. *26:6. Ex=30:18. 2 S 22:21, 25. Jb 9:30. *17:9. Is *1:15, 16. *33:15, 16. 1 T *2:8. Ja *4:8. **pure**. Ps ◐37:18n. *51:10. 73:1. Ge *6:5. Pr √20:9. Je *4:14. Mt +*5:8. Ac *15:9. 2 C *7:1. He √12:14. Re 21:1-4, *27. 22:*14, 15. **heart**. ♪121J21. Metonymy of the Subject B582. "Heart" is put for nature and character. For other instances of this figure see Ps 84:2. 1 P 3:4. **lifted**. Ps 25:1. *143:8. Dt *4:19. Ezk 18:*6, 15. Ac *14:15. **his**. or, my (LXX.). **soul**. Heb. *nephesh*, Ge +34:3. Le +26:11. **sworn**. Ps *15:4. Je 5:2. 7:9, 10. Zc +*5:3, 4. Ml +*3:5. 1 T 1:10.

5. **receive**. Ps *50:23. 67:6, 7. 72:17. 115:12, 13. 128:1-5. Nu 6:24-27. Is 33:15, 17. Mt *5:3-12. Jn √7:17. Ro 4:6-9. Ga 3:9, 14. Ep 1:3. 1 P 3:9. **righteousness**. Is 46:13. 51:5, 6, 8. 54:17. 61:10. Ro *3:21, 22. 5:17, 18. 1 C *1:30. 2 C √5:21. Ga 5:5. Ph 3:9. 2 T *4:8. **God**. Ps 68:19, 20. 88:1. Is 12:2. 45:17. T *2:10-14. *3:4-6.

6. **This is**. Ps 22:30. 73:15. Is 53:10. Mt 24:34. Ro 4:16. 1 P 2:9. **that seek**. Ps 27:8. 105:4. Jn *1:47-49. **O Jacob**. or, O God of Jacob.

7. **Lift**. Ps 118:19, 20. Is 26:2. **everlasting**. Heb. *olam*, Ge +*17:7. **ver**. +9n. **King**. Ps 21:1, 5. 97:6. Je 23:5, 6. Hg *2:7, 9. Ml *3:1. 1 C *2:8. Ja *2:1. 2 P *3:18. Re *4:11. **shall**. Ps *68:16-18. 132:8. Nu 10:35, 36. 2 S 6:17. 1 K *8:6, 11. 2 Ch 6:41. Mk *16:19. 2 C *6:16. Ep *4:8-10. He 6:20. 1 P *3:22. Re *3:20.

8. **Who is**. Jb *22:21. Is *63:1-3. Je 23:6. 1 C 15:57. **The Lord strong**. Ps 45:3-6. 50:1. 93:1. Is *9:6. 49:24-26. 63:1-6. Col 2:15. Re 6:2. 19:11-21.

9. **Lift up**. ver. 7. **gates**. Ps 122:2. **everlasting**. Heb.

olam, Ge +*17:7. The word "everlasting" is sometimes used to express very long duration, either past or future. See the References. See related note (Jn +√6:54n). Ge 49:26. Ex +*21:6. Le 16:34. 1 K 8:13. 1 Ch *28:4. Ec ?*1:4. Is *32:14. Jn +*6:54n. **come in**. Ps 68:16.

10. **King**. ♪76, Ge +13:6. **of glory**. 1 C √2:8. Ja *2:8. **The Lord**. Ps +62:12. +102:24. Ne +9:6. Ec +12:14. Is 6:3-5. 54:5. Ho 12:3-5. Zc 2:8-11. Jn 12:40, 41. 14:9. **of hosts**. Ps 103:21. 148:2. Ex 12:41. 15:26n. Dt 4:19. 17:3. 1 S 1:3. 1 K 22:19. 2 K 17:16. Is 44:6. **he is**. Ps 2:6-12. Mt *25:31, 34. Lk 9:26. T *2:13.

PSALM 25

David, trusting in God and waiting on him, prays for protection and guidance, 1-5. Pleading the mercy of God and the honor of his name, he entreats forgiveness and shows the Lord's readiness to teach the meek and upright, 6-11. He states the privileges of the godly and blends his complaints with earnest prayers for himself and for Israel, 12-22.

1. A.M. cir. 3463. B.C. cir. 541. **do I**. Ps 24:4. 86:4. 143:8. 1 S 1:15. La *3:41. **soul**. Heb. *nephesh*, Ge +34:3.

2. **O my God**. Ps 7:1. 18:2. 22:1, *5, 8. 31:1. *34:8. 37:40. 71:1. Is 26:3, 4. 28:16. 41:16, 17. 49:23. Ro 5:5. *10:11. 1 P 2:6. **trust**. ♪96C1, Ps 22:4, 5. Ge +4:1. **let me not**. ver. 20. Ps 31:1. **be ashamed**. ♪121G2. Metonymy of the Effect B566. The effect put for the thing or action causing or producing it, in verbs. Here, enemies triumphing would be a cause of being put to shame. For other instances of this figure see ver. 20. Ps 5:11. 31:1. 70:4. 119:116. Is 28:16. Ro 9:33. 10:11. 1 P 2:6. **let not**. Ps 13:2-4. 35:19-25. 41:11. 56:1. 94:3, 4. 142:6. Is 36:14-20. 37:10, 20, 35.

3. **wait**. Ps *27:14. 33:20. 37:*7, 9, 34. 40:1-3. *59:9. *62:1, 5. 123:2. Ge 49:18. Is *25:9. 26:8. √30:18. 33:2. *40:31. *64:4. La *3:25, 26. Ho 12:6. Mi 7:7. Hab *2:3. Zp 3:8. Ro 8:25. **be ashamed**. Ps 69:6. Pr *3:35. Is 65:13. Da *12:2. **let**. Ps 6:10. 31:17. 35:26. 40:14, 15. 70:2, 3. 71:13. 132:18. Je 20:11. **without**. Ps 7:4, 5. 59:2-5. 69:4. 109:3, 5. 119:78. Jn 15:25.

4. **Show me**. T#1595. Ps *5:1, 8. *27:11. 67:2. *86:11. *119:17, 18, 27, 135. *143:8, 10. Ex *33:13. 1 K 18:37. Jb 23:3. *34:32. Pr 2:3-6. *8:20. Is 2:3. Je *6:16. 50:5. Jn 6:28. *17:3. Ep 1:17, 18. *3:17-19. Col *1:9. **thy ways**. Ps *86:11. 119:27. Is *53:6. Mt √7:14. Jn √14:6. **teach me**. Ps *32:8. *143:8, 10. Jb 36:22. Is 2:3. *48:17. Jn *14:26. 1 J *2:27. **thy paths**. Ps *16:11. 23:3. Is 2:3.

5. **Lead me**. T#1469. ver. 8, 10. Ps *43:3, 4. 107:7. *119:133. Ex 4:1, 10. 33:12, 13. Jsh 7:8. 1 S 28:5, 6. 30:7, 8. 2 S 2:1. Is *30:21. 35:8. 42:16. 49:10. Je 4:16. 31:9. Jn √8:31, 32. *14:26. *16:13. Ac 9:6. Ro 8:14. Ep 4:21. 1 Th 3:11. 1 J *2:27. Re 7:17. **in thy truth**. Ps *119:30. Jn 16:13. **teach**. Ps 119:26, 33, 66. Ne 9:20. Jb 36:22. Is *54:13. Je 31:33, 34. 50:5. Jn 6:45. Ep 4:20, 21. **God**. Ps 24:5. 68:20. 79:9. 88:1. **on thee**. Ps 22:2. 86:3. 88:1. 119:97. Pr 8:34. 23:17. Is *30:18. Lk 18:7. **all the day**. T#1758. Ps 32:3. 35:28. 38:6.

6. **Remember**. ♪22C3, Ge +8:1. Ps 98:3. 106:45. 136:23. 2 Ch 6:42. Lk 1:54, 71, 72. **thy**. Ps 40:11. 69:13, 16. 103:4. 119:77, 156. Is *55:7. 2 C 1:3. **tender mercies**. Heb. bowels. Ps 40:11. 77:9. 79:8. 103:4, 17. 119:77, 156. √145:9. Ex +*34:6. Ne 9:27. Is 63:15.

Je 16:5. 31:20. Lk 1:78mg. 2 C 1:3. Ph 1:8. 2:1. Col 3:12. 1 J 3:17. **lovingkindnesses.** T#1136. Ps 5:7h. 6:4h. 26:3. 36:7. 40:11. *42:8. 48:9. 51:1. 69:16. 88:11. 89:49. 119:88. **for they.** Ps 77:7-12. 103:17. 106:1. 107:1. 136:11, etc. Ge 24:27. 32:9, 10. Ex 15:13. 34:6, 7. Ne 9:19, 27, 28. Je 33:11. Mi 7:18-20. Lk 1:50. **ever of old.** Heb. *olam*, Ge +*6:4.

7. **Remember.** ♪22C3, Ps 79:8. 109:14, 16. Ge +8:1. Is 38:17. *43:25. 64:9. Mt 6:12. He 8:12. 10:16-18. **the sins.** Jb *13:26. *20:11. Pr 5:7-14. Je 3:25. Jn 5:5, 14. **according.** Ps 51:1. 109:26. 119:124. **for thy.** Ps 6:4. 31:16. Ep 1:6, 7. 2:4-8. **goodness' sake.** T#1135. Ps 27:13. 31:19. 86:4, 5.

8. **Good.** Ps 119:68. **upright.** Ps 92:15. Is 26:7. **teach.** Pr 1:20-23. 2:1-6. 9:4-6. Mi 4:2. Mt 9:13. 11:29, 30. Lk 11:13. Jn 6:44, 45. 2 C 4:6. Ep 1:17, 18. Ja *1:5.

9. **meek.** Ps *22:26. *37:11. 76:9. *147:6. *149:4. Is 11:4. *61:1. Zp *2:3. Mt +*5:5. Ga *5:23. Ep 4:1, 2. Col *3:12. Ja *1:21. 1 P *3:4, 15. **guide.** Ps 23:3. *32:8, 9. *73:24. *119:66. 143:10. Pr √3:5, 6. 8:20. Is 42:1-3. Ezk 11:19, 20. *36:27. **teach.** ver. 4. Ps 34:11. 119:12, 26, 64, 68. Jb 34:32. **his way.** Ps *119:35. Jn √14:6. Ac 9:2. 13:10. He 10:20.

10. **the paths.** Ps 18:25, 26. 23:4-6. 37:23, 24. 91:14. *119:75, 76. 138:7. Ge 5:24. 17:1. 48:15, 16. Is 43:2. Ho 14:9. Ro √8:28. **mercy.** Ps 33:4. 57:3. 85:10. 89:14. 98:3. Ge 24:27. 2 S 15:20. Is 25:1. Jn 1:14, 17. Ja 5:11. **and truth.** ♪174, Ge +18:27. **keep.** Ps 24:4, 5. 50:23. *103:17, 18. Is 56:1-6. Ho 14:9. Zp 2:3. Ac 10:35. Ro 2:13. He 8:8-12. 12:14. 13:20, 21.

11. **thy name's.** T#1124. Ps 31:3. 63:4. *79:9. 83:18. 102:15. 106:8. 109:21. 143:11. Jsh 7:8, 9. 1 Ch 16:35. Is 43:25. 48:9. 63:19. Je 14:7, 9, 21. Ezk 20:9. *36:22, 23, 31, 32. Da 9:19. 1 J *2:12. **for it.** Nu 14:17-19. Ro 5:15, *20, 21.

12. **What.** ♪85D. Erotesis B951: In demonstration, to make an affirmation as to a certain subject, demonstrating a fact or proving a truth. For other instances of this figure see Ps 34:12, 13. Pr 22:29. 29:10. Je 9:12. Ezk 8:6. Ho 14:9. Mt 11:7, 8, 9. **that feareth.** Ps 111:10. Pr *1:7, 23. 2:5. 14:26. 15:33. 16:6. Ec 12:13. Is 50:10. Ac 10:2, 22. *13:26. **him.** Ps *32:8. *37:23. Is 35:8. Jn 3:20, 21. *7:17. √8:31, 32. Ac 11:14. 2 Th 2:10-12. 1 J *2:27.

13. **His soul.** Heb. *nephesh*, Ge +34:3. ♪171Q2, Nu +23:10. Dt 33:12, 26-29. Pr 1:33. 19:23. 29:25. Ezk 34:25-28. Mt *11:28, 29. **dwell at ease.** Heb. lodge in goodness. Ps 31:19. 36:8. 63:5. Jb 17:2mg. Is 66:10-14. Je 31:12-14. Zp 3:17. Zc 9:17. Ph *4:19. **his seed.** Ps 37:26. 69:36. 102:28. *112:2. Ge 17:7-10. 2 K *2:4. Pr 11:21. *20:7. Is 44:3. 59:21. 65:23. Je 32:39. Ac +*2:39. **inherit.** Ps *37:9, 11, 22, 29. Ezk 33:24-26. Mt +*5:5. 1 P 3:10. Re √3:13n.

14. **secret.** Ps √119:18. Ge *18:17-19. Ex *33:13. Nu 12:7, 8. Jg 13:18. Dt +*29:29. Jb 15:8. 29:4. Ps *103:7. Pr *3:32. Je 23:18mg. Am +*3:7. Mt 13:*11, 12. Jn √7:17. 14:*17, 21-23. √15:15. *17:6. 1 C 2:10, √14. Ep *1:9, 18. Col 3:3. Re *2:17. **and he.** Jn *7:17. +*15:15. 17:26. **will,** etc. *or,* his covenant to make them know *it.* Ge 17:13. Dt 4:13. 2 Ch +*20:7. Ps 89:34. Is *54:7-10. +*55:3. Je *31:31-34. √32:36-42. Ac 3:19-21. Ro *11:26, 27, 29. *15:8.

15. **Mine eyes.** Ps ◑34:15. 121:1, 2. *123:1, 2. 141:8. **are.** ♪63B, Ge +25:28. **pluck.** Heb. bring forth. Ps 31:4. Ex 4:7. **my feet.** Pr 3:26. **out.** Ps 31:4. 124:7, 8. Je 5:26. 2 T 2:25, 26.

16. **Turn.** Ps 60:1. 69:16. 86:16. Mi *7:19. **for I.** Ps 69:14-20. 88:15-18. 143:4. Da 9:17. Mk 15:33-35.

17. **The troubles.** Ps *34:19. 38:1-8. 42:7. 77:2-4. Hab *3:17-19. 1 C 4:11-13. 2 C 1:9, 10. 4:8, 9. **bring.** T#1470. Ps 40:1, 2. 107:4-6. 116:3-6. 118:4, 5. 120:1, 2. Ge 35:2, 3. La 1:20.

18. **Look upon.** T#1513. Ps 80:14, 15. 119:132, 153. 1 S 1:11. 2 S *16:12. 2 Ch 24:22. La 5:1. Lk 1:25. **forgive.** Ps *32:1-5. *51:8, 9. Mt 9:2.

19. **Consider.** Ps 3:1, 2. 27:2, 12. 38:19. 56:2. 57:4. 138:7. 143:3. 2 S 16:11. 17:2-4. Lk 22:2. 23:5, 21-23. **cruel hatred.** Heb. hatred of violence. Ps 11:5. 18:48mg. 52:2. 74:20. 86:14. 140:1, 4, 11.

20. **O keep.** Ps 17:8. 22:20, 21. *121:7. Lk 23:46. Ac *7:59. **soul.** Heb. *nephesh*, Ge +12:5, 13. **let.** Ps 25:2. 71:1, 2. Jl 2:26, *27. **ashamed.** ♪121G2, ver. 2. **for.** Ps *16:1.

21. **Let integrity.** Ps 7:8. *18:20-24. 26:1, 11. 41:12. 1 S 24:11-13. 26:23. Pr *11:3. 20:7. Da 6:22. Ac +*6:3. *24:16. 25:10, 11.

22. **Redeem.** Ps 14:7. 51:18, 19. +*122:6. +*130:8. 137:5, 6.

PSALM 26

David professes his integrity and his delight in the people and ordinances of God with a solemn appeal to him, 1-8. He deprecates the doom of the wicked and unites earnest prayers with pious purposes and believing confidence in God, 9-12.

1. **Judge.** Ps 7:8. 35:24. 43:1. 54:1. 1 S 24:15mg. 1 C *4:3-6. ♪52A3A. Correspondence (Repeated Alternation) B372. This verse contains a prayer and profession. Throughout this psalm prayer and profession alternate, concluding with profession in verse 12. Repeated alternation with two members in each series is found frequently and may be seen graphically displayed in the *Companion Bible* margins and in B372, 373. For other instances of this figure involving alternation with two members in a series see Ps ch. 80, 145. For more than two members in a series see Ps ch. 24, 147. **for.** ver. 11. Ps 15:2. 25:21. 2 K *20:3. Pr 20:7. Ac 23:1. *24:16. 2 C *1:12. 1 Th *2:10. 1 J 3:21. **trusted.** Ps 4:5. 25:2. *28:7. 31:14. Pr *29:25. **I shall.** Ps 21:7. 37:31. 62:2, 6. 94:18. 121:3, 7, 8. 1 S *2:9. 1 T 1:19. 1 P 1:5. 2 P *1:10.

2. **Examine.** Ps 7:9. *17:3. 66:10. *139:23, 24. Jb 13:23. 31:4-6. Je 20:12. Zc 13:9. **prove me.** T#1660. Ge 22:1 (tempt). Da 1:12. **reins.** ♪12I1I, Ge +3:7.

3. **For.** Ps 52:1. 85:10-13. Mt 5:44-48. Lk 6:36. 2 C 3:18. √5:14, 15. 8:9. Ep √4:32. 5:1, 2. Col 3:12, 13. 1 J 4:7-12, 19-21. 3 J 11. **and.** Ps 25:5. 101:2. 119:142. 2 K 20:3. Is 2:5. √8:20. Jn √14:6. Ep 4:20-25. 1 J *1:7. 2 J 4. 3 J 3, 4.

4. **not sat.** T#122. ver. 5. Ps *1:1. 101:7. 119:+√63, 115. 139:19. Pr *1:10-16, 18. 4:14-17. 7:24-27. 9:6. 12:11. *13:20. *14:7. *22:24, 25. 24:1, 2, 21. 28:7, 19. 29:3. Je 15:17. 1 C *15:33. 2 C √6:17. **neither will.** Ps 141:4.

5. **hated.** Ps 5:5. 15:4. 31:6. 101:3-8. *139:21, 22. **will.** Ps *1:1. Mt 9:11, 12. 1 C 5:9-11.

6. **wash.** T#1294. Ps 24:4. 73:13. Ex =*30:18, 19, 20. Is *1:16-18. Ac 22:16. T *3:5. He *10:19-22. **hands.** Ps 24:4. 2 S 22:21, 25. Jb 17:9. Ja 4:8. **so will.** Ps 43:4. Ml 2:11-13. Mt *5:23, 24. 1 C *11:28, 29. 1 T *2:8.

7. **That**. Ps 9:14. 66:13-15. 95:2. 100:4, 5. *116:12-14, 18, 19. 118:19, 27. 134:2. Dt 26:2-10. 1 S 1:24, 27. 2 Ch 20:26-29. **tell**. Ps 71:17-19. 72:18. 105:2. 119:27. 136:4, 5. 145:5. Lk 19:37-40.

8. **Lord**. T#1371. Ps *27:4-6. 42:4. *84:1, 2, 10. *122:1-4, 9. 2 S 15:25. 1 Ch 29:3. Is 38:20, 22. Lk 2:37, 46, 49. 19:45-47. Jn 2:14-17. **where**, etc. Heb. of the tabernacle of thine honor. Ps 63:2, 3. Ex 25:21, 22. 40:34, 35. 2 Ch 5:14. 6:1, 2.

9. **Gather not**. *or*, Take not away. Ps 28:1-3. 1 S *25:29. Ml 3:18. Mt *13:30. *24:51. *25:32, 41, 46. Re 22:14, 15. **soul**. Heb. *nephesh*, Ge +12:13. **bloody men**. Heb. men of blood. Ps 51:14. 55:23. 139:19. 1 S 22:18, 19. 2 S +16:7mg. 21:1.

10. **In**. Ps 10:14. 11:2. 36:4. 52:2. 55:9-11. Pr 1:16. 4:16. Mi 2:1-3. Mt 26:3, 4. Ac 23:12. **full of**. Heb. filled with. **bribes**. Ex 23:8. Dt *16:19. 1 S 8:3. Is 33:15. Ezk 22:12, 13. Am 5:12. Mi 7:3.

11. **I will**. ver. 1. 1 S 12:2-5. 2 Ch 31:20, 21. Ne 5:15. Jb 1:1. Is 38:3. Lk 1:6. 1 Th 2:10. **redeem**. T#1667. Ps 44:26. 49:7, 15. 69:18. 130:7, 8. Mt *20:28. T *2:14. 1 P 1:18, 19. **and**. Ps 130:3, 4, 7, 8. Ne 13:14, 22, 31.

12. **My**. Ps 27:11. *40:2. 1 S 2:9. Pr *10:9. **in the**. ver. 7. Ps 22:22-25. 107:32. *111:1. 122:4. He 2:12.

PSALM 27

David by strong faith rises above the fear of his enemies, 1-3. He chooses the courts and service of God as his felicity, 4-6. He prays for guidance and assistance and encourages his brethren, 7-14.

1. **light**. Ps *18:28. *84:11. Jb 29:3. Is 2:5. 60:1-3, *19, *20. Mi *7:7, 8. Ml *4:2. Jn *1:1-5, 9. *8:12. Re *21:23. *22:5. *121E1, Ge +25:23. This is not a metaphor but a metonymy: Jehovah is the source of my light and the author of my salvation. Compare He 5:9. *22J. Anthropomorphism A896. Inanimate things are sometimes used as figures of God: here, light. For other instances of this figure see Nu 6:25. Ps 36:9. 43:3. Ja 1:17. **salvation**. Ps 3:8. *18:2. 62:2, 6. *68:19, 20. *118:14, 15, 21. Ex *15:2. Is *12:2. *51:6-8. *61:10. Lk 2:30. 3:6. Ep 6:17. Re 7:10. **fear**. Ge ●19:30. **strength**. Ps *18:1, 2, 46. *19:14. *28:7, 8. 43:2. Is *45:24. Hab 3:19. 2 C *12:9. Ph *4:13. **of whom**. Ps *11:1. 46:1, 2. *56:2-4. *118:6. Mt *8:26. Ro *8:31. He *13:6.

2. **wicked**. Ps 3:7. 18:4. 22:16. 62:3, 4. **came upon**. Heb. approached against. **to eat**. Ps 14:4. 53:4. Jb 19:22. 31:31. **they**. Ps 18:38-42. 118:12. Is 8:9, 15. Jn *18:3-6.

3. **host**. Ps *3:6. 52:6. 2 K *6:15-17. 2 Ch *20:15. Ph 1:28. 1 P 3:14. **war**. 1 S 28:15, 16. Is 41:11, 12. 54:16, 17. Ro 8:35-37. Re 2:10. 12:7-11. **in**. 2 C 5:6-8.

4. **One thing**. Ps 26:8. Ec 3:19. Mk 10:21. Lk *10:42. Jn 9:25. Ph 3:13. 2 P 3:8. **seek**. ver. 8. Je 29:13. Da 9:3. Mt √6:33. *7:7, 8. Lk *11:9, 10. 13:24. 18:1. He √11:6. **dwell**. T#106, 1530. Ps *23:6. 26:6. 36:8. *63:1, 2. *65:4. 84:1-4, 10. 87:5, 6. 92:13, 14. 1 S 1:11. Lk *2:37. 1 T 5:5. **behold**. Ps 50:2. 63:2. 90:17. Zc 9:17. 2 C 3:18. 4:6. **beauty**. Ps 45:11. Zc 9:17. *or*, delight. Ps 63:2-5. *S#5278h. Ps 90:17. Pr 3:17 (pleasantness). 15:26. 16:24. Zc 11:7, 10. **enquire**. 1 S 22:10. 30:8. 2 S 21:1. 1 Ch 10:13, 14. **temple**. Ps 5:7. 29:9. 1 S 1:9n.

5. **For in**. Ps 10:1. 32:6, 7. 46:1. 50:15. 77:2. 91:15. 138:7. Pr 1:24-28. Is 26:16. Je 2:27, 28. **hide me**. *121S2, Ge +21:6. Ps *31:20. 57:1. *83:3. *119:114. Pr 18:10. Is 4:5, 6. 26:20. 32:2. Mt 23:37. Col *3:3. **secret**. Ps 31:20. 91:1. 2 Ch 22:12. Ne 6:10, 11. **set me**. Ps 18:33. *40:2. 61:2. Hab 3:18, 19. Mt 7:24, 25. 16:16-18.

6. **And now**. Ps 3:3. 110:7. Ge 40:13, 20. 2 K 25:27. **above**. 2 S 7:9. 22:1, 49. 1 Ch 22:18. **therefore**. Ps 22:22-25. 26:6, 7. 43:3, 4. 66:13-16. 107:22. 116:17-19. 2 Ch 30:21-26. Je 33:11. He *13:15. 1 P 2:5. **joy**. Heb. shouting. Ps 47:1. Ezr 3:11-13. Is 12:6. Je 31:7. Zp 3:14, 15. Zc 9:9. Lk 19:37, 38. **I will**. Ps 21:1, 13. 81:1. 95:1. 100:1, 2. 138:5. Ep *5:19, 20. Re 5:9. 15:3.

7. **Hear**. Ps 4:1. 5:2. 130:2-4. 143:1, 2. **and answer**. T#1434. Ps *3:4. 6:8, 9. 18:6. 20:1-4. 21:2, 4. *22:4, 5, 24. 28:6. 30:2, 3. 31:22. +*34:4-6. 38:1. 40:1. 66:19, 20. 77:1, 2. 81:7. 86:6, 7. 91:14, 15. +*99:6. *102:1, 2. 106:44. 107:6. 108:6. 116:1, 2. 118:5, 21. 119:26. 120:1. *138:3. 143:1. 1 K 8:28-30. Jb 6:8. 13:20-22. La 3:57, 58. Ho *12:3, 4. Jon 2:2, 7. Lk 23:42, 43. Ac 4:31. 2 C *12:8, 9. Ja *5:16-18.

8. **When**, etc. *or*, My heart said unto thee, Let my face seek thy face, etc. **Seek**. Ps 24:6. 44:2. *105:4. Is 45:19. √55:6, 7. Ho +*5:15. **face**. *22A4, Ge +19:13. **Thy**. Ps 63:1, 2. 119:58mg. Je √29:12, 13. **face**. *22A4, Ge +19:13.

9. **Hide not**. T#1560. Ps 13:1. 44:24. 69:17. 88:14. 102:2. 143:7. Is *59:1, 2. **face**. *22A4, Ge +19:13. **put**. Ps 30:5. *51:11. Is 50:1. **thou**. Ps 71:5, 6, 17, 18. 1 S 7:12. Is 46:3, 4. 2 C 1:9, 10. 2 T 4:17, 18. **leave me not**. T#1512. Ps 38:21. 119:121. 141:8. 1 K 8:57, 58. 1 Ch +*28:9. Je 14:7-9. 32:40. He +*13:5. **neither forsake**. T#1500. Ps +√9:10. 43:2. 44:23, 24. +51:11 (T#1443). 71:9, 12, 18. 74:1. 77:7. 88:14. *119:8. La 5:20. Mt 27:46. He ●+*13:5. **O God**. Ps 24:5. 38:21, 22. 88:1.

10. **When**. Ps *10:14. *69:8. 2 S 16:11. Is *49:15. Je *49:11. Ho *14:3. Mt *10:21, 22, 36. **the Lord**. Jn *9:35. 16:32. 2 T 4:16, 17. **take me up**. Heb. gather me. Ps 26:9. 39:6. 50:5. 85:3. 104:29. Ge 42:17mg. Jb 34:14. 39:12. Is *40:11. 58:8mg.

11. **Teach me**. T#1540. Ps 5:8. 25:*4, 5, *9, 12. *32:8. *86:11. 119:10, 33. *143:8-10. Pr *2:6-9. Is 30:20, 21. Je *6:16. 42:3. 50:4, 5. **a plain path**. Heb. a way of plainness. Ps 26:12. Pr *8:9. *15:19. Is *35:8. Lk *3:4-6. **because of**. Ps 69:18. **mine enemies**. Heb. those which observe me. Ps *5:8mg. 54:5mg. 56:5, 6. 59:10mg. 64:6. Je 20:10. Da *6:4, 5. Lk *20:20.

12. **will**. Heb. *nephesh*, Ex +15:9. Ps 31:8. 35:25. 38:16. 41:11. 140:8. **false**. Ps 35:11. Ex *20:16. 1 S *22:9, 10. 26:19. 2 S *16:7, 8. Mt *26:59, 60. Ac 6:11-13. **breathe**. Ps 25:19. Ac 9:1. 26:11.

13. **I had**. *63K, Ge +37:13. **fainted**. Ps *42:5. *56:3. 116:9-11. *119:92. 2 C 4:1, 8-14, *16. Ep *2:8. **in the land**. Ps 52:5. *56:13. 142:5. Jb 33:30. Is *38:11, 19. Je 11:19. +*31:17. Ezk 26:20. **of the living**. Peters shows that this expression refers to living in resurrection in the promised land in the future kingdom to be ruled by Christ (*Theocratic Kingdom*, vol. 2, p. 254). Ps 116:3, 7-9, 15, 16. Je +*31:17.

14. **Wait**. *66, Ge +9:3. Ps 25:3, 21. *31:24. 33:20. 37:34. 62:1, 5. *130:5. Ge 49:18. Is 8:17. *25:9. 26:8. √30:18. La *3:26. Hab *2:3. Lk *2:25, 38. Ro 8:25. *38D. Apostrophe B903: to some second person or persons indefinite (put, by synecdoche, for anyone).

After prayer to God for himself, David turns and addresses anyone who is in like circumstances and exhorts him. For other instances of this figure see Ps 34:13. Ro 2:17. 9:19. 9:20. 12:20. 13:3. 14:4. 14:10. 1 C 7:16, 16. Ga 4:7. 6:1. **be of good courage.** T#1320. Ps *31:24. Da 6:10. Ac 28:15. 1 C 16:13. 2 T *4:5-8. **and.** Ps *138:3. Is *40:31. 2 C *12:9, 10. Ep *3:16. *6:10. Ph *4:13. Col 1:11.

PSALM 28

David earnestly prays for deliverance and denounces the righteous doom of the wicked, 1-5. He exults in God and prays for his people, 6-9.

1. **Unto.** Ps 3:4. 5:2. 22:2. 77:1. *138:3. 142:1. **O.** Ps 18:2. 42:9. Dt *32:4. Is 26:4mg. 40:31. **be.** Ps 35:22. 83:1. **to.** Heb. from. **I become like.** Ps 30:9. 69:15. 88:4-6. 143:7. +146:4. Nu +21:27. Jb 33:28. Pr 1:12. Is 38:18. Re 20:3. **pit.** Heb. *bor,* Ge +37:20.

2. **supplications.** Ps 5:7. 1 K 8:28, 29. **when.** Ps 63:4. 125:5. 134:2. 141:2. 143:6. 2 Ch 6:13. 1 T *2:8. **lift.** ſ121S3, Ge +14:22. By Metonymy of the Adjunct, whereby the sign is put for the thing signified, "lift up my hands" is put for praying, as in Ps 68:31; 2 T 2:8. **toward.** Ps 5:7. *138:2. Da +6:10. **thy holy oracle.** *or,* the oracle of thy sanctuary. Ps 5:7. 138:2. 1 K *6:19, 22, 23. 8:6-8, 28-30, 38. Da 6:10.

3. **Draw me not.** T#1750. Ps 26:9. Nu 16:26. Mt √7:23. 25:41, 46. 2 C *6:17. Re 18:4. **speak.** Ps 12:2, 3. 55:21. 62:4. Je 9:8, 9. Mi 3:5. Mt 22:15-18. **mischief.** Ps 7:14. 10:7, 14. 36:4. 52:1. 1 Ch 12:33. Pr 26:23-26.

4. **Give.** Ps 5:10. 59:12, 13. 69:22-24. Je 18:21-23. 2 T *4:14. Re *18:6. **and.** Ps 2:1-5. 21:10, 11. Ezk 38:10. **the work.** Ps 62:12. 103:10. 109:17-21. *130:3, 4. Ro *2:6-8. 11:22. Ja 2:13. **render.** Ezr *9:13. Jb 11:6.

5. **Because.** Ps 10:5. 92:4-6. *104:24. 107:31. *111:2-4. Jb *34:26, 27. Is 5:12. 22:11. 26:9-11. Ho *14:9. Jn 10:25. 12:37. Ro 1:20, 28. **operation.** Ps *8:3, 4. *19:1, 2. Nu *23:23. Is 5:12. 40:26. 45:8, 12, 18. Je 10:12, 13. Ep 1:19-21. **destroy them.** Ps *92:5-7. **not build.** Ps *64:7, 9. 2 S 7:13, 27. 1 K 11:38. Pr 21:12. Is *5:14. Je 31:4. 33:20, 21.

6. **Blessed.** Ps 31:21, 22. 66:19, 20. 69:33, 34. *107:19-22. 116:1, 2. 118:5.

7. **strength.** ver. 8. Ps 18:1, 2. 19:14. 46:1. Is 12:2. 45:24. Ep *6:10. **shield.** ſ22D5F, Ps *84:11. 91:4. Ge +15:1. **heart.** Ps 13:5. *22:4. 56:3, 4. 118:6-9, 13-15. **therefore.** Ps 16:9-11. 21:1. 30:11, 12. 33:21. 68:3, 4. Is 61:10. **with.** Ps 96:1-3. Ex 15:1, etc. Jg 5:1, etc. 1 S 2:1, etc. 2 S 22:1, etc. Re 5:9. 15:3.

8. **their.** *or,* his. **strength.** Is *49:5. Ep *6:10. 2 T 4:17. He 11:34. **saving strength.** Heb. strength of salvation. ſ96F2, Ge +4:10. Ps 3:2, 8. 9:14. 13:5. 27:1. 31:2, 4. 37:39. Is 33:6mg. **his.** Ps 2:2. *20:6. 1 S 16:13. Is 61:1.

9. **Save.** Ps 14:7. 25:22. 80:14-19. Je 31:7. **thy people.** T#1635. Ge +20:4 (T#1622). Ex 32:11, 31, 32. Nu 14:19. 21:7. Dt 9:26. 26:15. 2 S 24:17. 1 K +8:34 (T#1623). 1 Ch 21:17. 2 Ch 30:18, 19. Ne 1:8-10. **bless.** Dt *9:29. 2 S 21:3. 1 K *8:51, 53. Je 10:16. Ep 1:18. **feed.** *or,* rule. Ps 78:71, *72. 2 S 7:7. Is 40:11. Ezk *34:23, 24. Mi *5:2, 4. 7:14. Mt 2:6mg. **lift.** Ezr 1:4mg. 1 C 6:14. **for ever.** Heb. *olam,* Ex +*12:24. 1 P *5:4.

PSALM 29

David calls on the mighty to give glory to God, 1, 2. He shows the majesty and power of his voice, 3-9; and that, as the eternal King, he will strengthen and bless his people, 10, 11.

1. **Give.** Ps 2:10-12. 68:31-34. 96:7-9. Is 60:12. Je 13:16-18. Re *5:11-14. **mighty.** Heb. sons of the mighty. **sons.** ſ108H11, Ge +6:2. Ps 89:6. **mighty.** ſ24L, Ge +6:2. **glory.** ſ173, Ge +27:44. **strength.** Ps 68:34. ſ121L3, Ps +8:2. Metonymy of the Subject, whereby attributes are put for the praise and celebration of them. How can we give glory or strength to God? We can praise him for these, but we cannot give them. They are thus put, by metonymy, for the praise given him for his glory and strength.

2. **Give.** 1 Ch *16:28, 29. **glory,** etc. Heb. honor of his name. Ps 96:6, 8. 97:9. 113:3-6. 145:3-7. **worship.** Ps 27:4. 96:9. 2 Ch *20:21. **the beauty of holiness.** *or,* his glorious sanctuary. Ps 90:17. 1 Ch 16:29.

3. **The voice.** ſ70, Ex +16:35. ſ22A11, Is +30:30. Ps 18:13-15. 68:33. 77:16-19. SS 2:14. 8:13. Mt 8:26, 27. Jn *10:3. Re 17:14, 15. **God.** Heb. *El,* Ex +15:2. Ps 24:7-10. Ac 7:2. **thundereth.** ſ22F2. Anthropomorphism B894: thunder is called the voice of the Lord (Ps 38:8); the cry of Christ is called roaring (Ps 22:1). Ex 9:28, 33. 19:16. 1 S 7:10. Jb 37:2-5. Jn 12:29. Re 4:5. 8:5. 11:19. 16:18. 19:6. **many waters.** *or,* great waters. Ps 93:3, 4. 104:3.

4. **The voice.** ſ70, Ex +16:35. **powerful.** Heb. in power. Ps 33:9. Jb 26:11-14. Je 51:15, 16. Lk 4:36. 8:25. **the voice.** ſ70, Ex +16:35. **full of.** Heb. in. Jb *40:9-12. Is 66:6. Ezk *10:5.

5. **The voice.** ſ70, Ex +16:35. **breaketh.** Is 2:13.

6. **skip.** Ps 114:4-7. **Lebanon.** Je 4:23-25. Hab 3:6-11. Re 20:11. **Sirion.** Dt 3:9. **unicorn.** Ps 92:10. Nu 23:22.

7. **The voice.** ſ70, Ex +16:35. Jb 37:2-5. **divideth.** Heb. cutteth out. 1 K 5:15. **flames.** Ps 77:18. 144:5, 6. Ex 9:23. Le 10:2. Nu 16:35. 2 K 1:10-12. Jb 37:3. 38:35.

8. **The voice.** ſ70, Ex +16:35. **shaketh.** Ps 18:7. 46:3. Jb 9:6. *37:2-5. Is 13:13. Jl 3:16. Hg 2:6, 21. He *12:26. **wilderness.** ſ121J3. Metonymy of the Subject B573: wilderness is put for the wild beasts in it. Dt 8:15. **Kadesh.** Nu 13:26.

9. **voice.** ſ70, Ex +16:35. ver. +3. Ps 68:33. **maketh.** *Or,* as Bp. Lowth and others, "maketh the oaks to tremble, and maketh bare the forests;" understanding *ayyaloth,* as denoting here, not hinds but oaks, as it signifies in Syriac. Jb 39:1-3. **calve.** *or,* be in pain. Ps 90:2. A fact confirmed to me by those who have spent a lifetime in dairy farming: calves are often born just before or during a storm. **discovereth.** Ps 63:2. Is 9:18. 10:18, 19. Ezk 20:46-48. **in his temple.** Ps 5:7. 27:4. 46:2-5. 48:9. 134:1, 2. 135:1, 2. 1 S 1:9n. **doth,** etc. *or,* every whit of it uttereth.

10. **sitteth.** ſ22D3G. Anthropomorphism B892. God is spoken of in reference to place, as sitting upon the flood. ver. 3. Ps *65:7. 104:6-9. Ge *6:17. 8:1, 2. Jb 38:8-11, 25. Mk 4:41. **King.** Ps 2:6-9. 10:16. 93:1. 99:1. Da 2:44. Mt *6:13. 1 T 1:17. **for ever.** Heb. *olam,* Ex +*12:24.

11. **give.** Ps 28:8, 9. 68:35. *84:7. 85:8, 10. 138:3. Is 40:29, 31. 41:10. Zc 10:6, 12. Ep 3:16. 2 T 4:17. **bless.** Ps 72:3, 7. Nu *6:24-27. Is *9:6, 7. Jn *14:27.

16:33. 20:19. Ro *14:17. 1 C 1:3. Ep 2:17. Ph *4:7. 2 Th 3:16. Re 1:4.

PSALM 30

David praises God for deliverance and calls on the saints to join him, 1-5. He shows that undue confidence had preceded his troubles, and fervent prayers his deliverance, 6-10. He renews his animated praises, 11, 12.

(*Title.*) A.M. 2987. B.C. 1017. **A Psalm.** *Or*, "A psalm or song of David at the dedication of the house;" by which is supposed to be meant the place he built on the threshing floor of Araunah, after the grievous plague which had nearly desolated the kingdom. 2 S 24:25, etc. 1 Ch 21:6. **at the.** Dt 20:5. 2 S 5:11. 6:20. 7:2. 20:3.

1. **extol.** Ps 34:3, 4. 66:17. 145:1. Da 4:37. **for.** Ps 27:6. 28:9. **hast not.** Ps 13:4. *25:2. 35:19, 24, 25. 41:11. 79:4, 10. 89:41-46. 140:8. La 2:15.

2. **hast healed.** T#1695. Ps 6:1, 2. 13:3. 39:10-13. 41:10. 51:8. 77:2. 88:2, 3. 103:+*3, 4. 107:17-22. 118:18. 147:3. Ge 20:17. Ex *15:26. 2 S 12:15, 16. 2 K 8:7, 8. *20:1-6. 2 Ch 6:28-31. Je +17:14 (T#1546). Mt 8:5-7. 14:35, 36. Mk 5:22, 23. Lk 4:38. Jn 4:46, 47. 11:1-3. Ac 28:8. Ja *5:14, 15.

3. **brought.** Ps +*16:10. 40:1, 2. 56:13. 71:20. 86:13mg. 116:8. 139:8. Jb 14:13. 33:19-22, 28. Is 38:10, 17, 18. Jon 2:4-6. **soul.** Heb. *nephesh.* The soul is spoken of as going to *sheol* in Ps +*16:10. 86:13. 89:48. Pr 23:14. The following references speak of the soul going to *shachath,* *S#7845h (Jb +9:31), a pit for taking wild beasts: Ps 35:7. Jb 33:18, 22, 28, 30. Is 38:17. The soul is spoken of as going to *shuchah,* Je 18:20. The soul is spoken of as going to silence, Hebrew *dumah,* in Ps 94:17. For the other uses of *nephesh* see Ge +2:7. **grave.** Heb. *sheol,* Ge +37:35. Ps 6:5. 9:17. **down.** Ps 28:1. **pit.** Heb. *bor,* Ge +37:20 (*S#953h). Ps 7:15. 28:1. *40:2. 88:4, 6.

4. **Sing.** Ps 32:11. 33:1-3. *71:22. 97:12. 103:20-22. 132:9. 135:19-21. 148:14. 149:1. 1 Ch 16:4. Re 19:5, 6. **at the remembrance.** *or*, to the memorial. Ps 97:12mg. **holiness.** Ps *5:4, 5. 89:18, 35. *145:17. Ex 15:11. Le 11:44. Jsh 24:19. 1 S *2:2. 6:20. Is 6:3. 43:3, 15. 47:4. Ezk 39:7. Hab *1:13. Jn 17:11. 1 P *1:15. Re *4:8. *15:4.

5. **For.** Ps *103:9, 17. Is *12:1. *26:20. *54:7, 8. *57:15, 16. Je 3:5. 2 C √4:17. **his anger,** etc. Heb. there is but a moment in his anger. **in his favor.** Ps *16:11. 36:7-9. 63:3. Re *22:1, 17. **weeping.** Ps 6:6-9. *56:8 (T#1298)-11. √126:5, 6. Is 38:3-5. Je *31:15-17. Mt *2:18. +*5:4. Jn *16:20-22. 2 C *7:9, 10. for **a night.** Heb. in the evening. Ps 55:17. 59:6. **joy.** Heb. singing. Ps 17:1 (cry). 107:22mg. 126:2, 5mg, 6. Is 14:7. +*51:11. Zp 3:17. **cometh.** Ps 4:6. 36:9. **in the morning.** Ps *5:3. +*46:5mg. *59:16. *143:8. Ge +*32:24mg. Ho *6:3. Re +*2:28.

6. **And.** Jb *29:18-20. Is 47:7. 56:12. Da 4:30. Mk +4:19. Lk √12:19, 20. 2 C 12:7. **I shall.** Ps 15:5. 16:8. 119:117.

7. **by thy.** ver. 5. Ps 5:12. 18:35, 36. 44:3. 89:17. Jb 10:12. **made,** etc. Heb. settled strength for my mountain. Ps 40:2. 1 Ch 17:26, 27. **thou.** Ps 10:1. 13:1, 2. 102:10. 104:29. 143:7. Jb 30:26-31. Is 38:17. Mt 27:46. **face.** *22A4, Ge +19:13.

8. **unto.** Ps 34:6. 77:1, 2. 130:1, 2. 1 C 12:8, 9. Ph *4:6, 7.

9. **What.** Ps *6:5. *88:10-12. 115:17, 18. 118:17. Ec 9:10. Is √38:18. **Shall the dust.** Ps +*146:4.

10. **Hear.** Ps 51:1, 2. 143:1, 7-9. **be thou.** Ps *28:7. 54:4.

11. **turned.** ver. 5. Ps 126:1, 2. Ge 37:35. 45:28. 2 Ch *20:3, 9, 12, +20, 27, 28. Est 9:22. Is 25:8. 66:10, 11. Jn 16:20. Re 7:14-17. 21:4. **dancing.** Ps 149:3. 150:4. Ex +15:20n. 2 S 6:14. Ec 3:4. Je 31:4, 13, 14. La 5:15. **girded.** *22C27, Ps +18:32. Ps 18:39. Ne 8:10. Is 61:*3, 10. Lk 15:22. **gladness.** T#1340. Ps 31:7. 40:16. *118:24-26. 122:1. Ep *5:19, 20.

12. **my glory.** that is, *my tongue,* or, *my soul.* Ps 3:3. 4:2. 7:5. *8:5. *16:9. *57:8. 106:◑20n. *108:1, 2. 149:5. Ge +49:6. Ja *3:2-10. Matthew Poole notes on Ps 16:9 that *glory* is frequently a reference to man's tongue, as being man's glory and privilege above all other living creatures, and the instrument of glorifying both God and man, and so this very word is translated in Ac 2:26. *121F. Metonymy of the Effect: when the effect is put for the cause producing it; here, the thing for the organic cause of it, glory put for the tongue which gives it. For other instances of this figure, see Ge +49:6. John Laidlaw (*Biblical Doctrine of Man,* p. 71) cites or paraphrases Franz Delitzsch (*A System of Biblical Psychology,* p. 119), "In the Old Testament the soul is also called simply 'the glory' (Heb. *Chavod,* S#3519h), for the spirit is the image of the triune Godhead, but the soul is the copy of this image, and relates itself to the spirit as the 'seven spirits' (Re 4:5) are related to the Spirit of God." EWB (B563), while admitting "glory" may be put for the tongue which gives it, suggests an alternative: Since this verse corresponds, in the structure, with verse 4, "Sing to Jehovah, O ye saints of His," then "glory" in this verse may be understood to be put for the saints who give the glory. **and not.** Lk 19:40. Ac 4:20. **I will.** Ps 9:1, 2. 13:6. 71:14, 23. *100:4. 145:2. 146:1, 2. Lk +6:35. Ro 1:21, 28. Ep *5:19, 20. Ph *4:6. Col *2:7. 3:15. *4:2. He *13:15. Re 4:8, 9. *7:12. **for ever.** Heb. *olam,* Ex +*12:24.

PSALM 31

David avows his confidence in God, craves his help, and rejoices in his mercy, 1-8. He states his various trials and blends his complaints with prayers, 9-18. He admires the goodness of God to those who fear him and excites the saints to love and trust him, 19-24.

1. A.M. 2943. B.C. 1061. **In thee.** Ps *22:4, 5. *25:2. 71:1, 2. Is *49:23. Ro 5:5. 10:11. do. √96C1, Ge +4:1. **ashamed.** *121G2, Ps +25:2. **deliver.** Ps 7:8, 9. 43:1. 143:1, 11, 12. Da 9:16.

2. **Bow.** Ps 71:2. 86:1. 130:2. Pr 22:17. **thine ear.** *22A8, Ps +10:17. **deliver.** Ps 40:17. 69:17. 70:1. 102:2. 143:7. Jb 7:21. Lk 18:8. **my strong rock.** Heb. to me for a rock of strength. *22L3, Ps *18:1, 2, 31. 62:7. 94:22. Dt 32:31. +32.31. 2 S *22:3. 23:3. **an house.** Ps *71:3. *90:1. 91:9. Is 33:16. Jn 6:56. 1 J 4:12, 15, 16.

3. **rock.** *22L3, Dt +32:31. **fortress.** *22L5. Anthropomorphism B897. God is spoken of as a fortress. For other instances of this figure see Ps 71:3. 91:2. 144:2. Je 16:19. **for thy.** Ps *23:2, 3. 25:11. 79:9. Jsh

*7:9. Je 14:7. Ezk 36:21, 22. Ep 1:12. **lead.** Ps *23:3. *25:5, 9. 43:3. 139:24. 143:10, 11. Ne 9:12, 19. Is *49:10. Lk 1:79. Jn *16:13.

4. **Pull.** Ps *25:15. 35:7. 57:6. 124:7. 140:5. Pr 29:5. 2 T 2:26. **my strength.** Ps 19:14. 2 C 12:9.

5. **Into.** Ps *17:15. Mt 27:50. Mk 15:37. Lk ⟩*23:46. Jn 19:30. Ac *7:59. 2 C *5:1. 2 T *1:12. **thine hand.** ⌐22A14.3. Anthropomorphism B878. A hand is attributed to God, indicating His protection, gracious deliverance, and security. For other instances of this figure see Ps 144:7. Jn √10:28, 29. Ac 4:30. **I commit.** T#1970. Ps *4:8. 22:30. *23:4. 73:26. 2 S *23:5. Is 26:3. Mt ✱27:43. Lk ✱23:46. Ro 8:38, 39. 2 T *1:12. 1 J *3:2. √5:13. **spirit.** Heb. *ruach*, Nu +16:22. Ge ◐+35:18. Lk 23:46. Ac 7:59. **thou hast redeemed.** ⌐96C1, Ge +4:1. Ps 71:23. 130:8. Ge 48:16. Le 25:48. Jb +*19:25. SS 2:16. Is 50:2. T *2:14. 1 P 1:18, 19. Re 5:9. **God.** Heb. *El*, Ex +15:2. **of truth.** Dt 32:4. 2 T 2:13. T *1:2. He *6:18.

6. **hated.** T#1424. Ps 5:5. 11:5. 24:3, 4. 25:19. *26:3-5. 119:113. 139:21. Ju 23. **regard.** or, observe. Ps 34:20. 71:10mg. 97:10 (preserveth). Jsh ◐*1:8. **lying vanities.** "Lying vanities" is a reference to practicing idolatry; see the References. Ps 24:4. 96:7-9. Dt 32:21. 1 S 12:21. 1 K 16:13. 2 K 17:15. 1 Ch 16:28, 29. Is 41:24, 29. Je 10:8, 15. Jon *2:8. Ro 1:21. 1 C *8:4. *10:19, 20.

7. **I will.** Ps 13:5. Is 49:13. Je 33:11. **for.** Ps 9:13. 25:18. 71:20. 119:153. Ne 9:32. Jb 10:9. La 3:50. 5:1. **known.** Ps *1:6. *142:3. Jb *23:10. Is *43:2. 63:9, 16. Jn √10:27-30. 1 C 8:3. Ga 4:9. 2 T *2:19. **soul.** Heb. *nephesh*, Ge +34:3.

8. **shut me.** Ps 88:8. Dt 32:30. 1 S 17:46. 24:18. 26:8. 2 S 18:28mg. Jb 16:11. Is 19:4mg. **set.** Ps 4:1. *18:19. Jb 36:16.

9. **mine.** Ps 6:7. 88:9. Jb 17:7. La 4:17. 5:17. **my soul.** Heb. *nephesh*, Ge +34:3. Ps 6:1, 2. 22:14, 15. 38:1-10. 44:25. 73:14, 26. 88:3-5. 102:3-5. 107:10. Jb 33:19-22.

10. **my life.** Ps 78:33. 88:15. 102:3, etc. Jb 3:24. Ro 9:2. **strength.** Ps 71:9. **bones.** Ps 32:3, 4. 102:3-5.

11. **I was.** Ps 22:6. 69:19, 20. 89:50, 51. Is 49:7. *53:4, 5. Mt 27:39-44. Ro 15:3. 1 C *4:13. He 11:36. 13:13. 1 P 4:14. **especially.** Ps *38:11. 41:8, 9. 88:8, 18. Jb 19:13, 14. Je 12:6. Mi 7:6. Mt 10:21, 22. **a fear.** T#1931. Ps 64:8. Jb 6:21-23. Mt ✱26:69-75. 2 T 4:16. **acquaintance.** 2 K 10:11mg. Jb 19:13. **fled.** Mt 26:56, 74.

12. **forgotten.** Ps 88:4, 5. Jg 8:33. Ec 9:5. Is 38:11, 12. **a broken vessel.** Heb. a vessel that perisheth. Ps 2:9. 119:83. Is 30:14. Ro 9:21, 22. Re 2:27.

13. **I have.** Ps 55:10. 101:5. 1 S 22:8-10. 24:9. Je 20:10. Lk 23:1, 2, 5. **fear.** Ps 56:1-3. 57:4. Je 6:25. 20:3mg, 4, 10. La 2:22. **while.** 1 S 19:10-17. 20:33. 23:19, 20. 2 S 17:1-4. Je 11:19. Mt 26:3, 4, 59. 27:1. **life.** Heb. *nephesh*, soul, Ge +44:30.

14. **But I trusted.** Jb *13:15. **Thou.** Ps 16:1, 2. 18:2. 22:1, 2. 43:5. 56:3, 4. 63:1. 71:12, 22. Mt 26:39, 42. 27:46. Jn 20:17.

15. **My times.** ⌐121P1, Ps +*90:12. +*91:16. 116:15. 1 S 26:10. 2 S 7:12. 1 Ch +12:32. Jb 24:1. Ec 3:1-8. Is ◐+*38:10. Lk 9:51. Jn *7:6, 30. 12:27. 13:1. 17:1. Ac *1:7. 23:11. 27:24. 2 T 4:6. 2 P 1:14. **deliver.** Ps 17:8, 9, 13. 71:10-12. 142:6. 143:3, 12. Je 15:20, 21.

16. **Make thy face to shine.** ⌐22A4, Ge +19:13.

T#1524. Ps *4:6. 30:7. *67:1. 80:3, 7, 19. 119:135. Nu *6:25, 26. Da 9:17. **save me.** T#1685. Ps 2:8. 6:4. 20:9. 28:9. 35:3. 43:3. 51:1, *12. 60:5. *69:29. 85:7. 86:2, 16. 106:45. 119:41, 81, +94 (T#1688), 123, 174. Is 33:2. Je 3:22, 23. 17:14. Da 9:9, 18. Ac 2:21. Ro 9:15, 23. 10:1, √13. Ep 1:6, 7. 2:4-7. Ph 1:19.

17. **Let me.** ver. 1. Ps 25:2, 3. 34:5. *37:19, 20. 69:6, 7. Is 49:23. *50:6, 7. Jl 2:26, 27. Ph *1:20. **wicked.** Ps 6:10. 35:4, 26. 40:14, 15. 70:2, 3. 71:24. 83:16, 17. Is 41:11, 12. 45:16, 17. 65:13, 14. Je 20:11. Da *12:2. **them.** Ps 115:17. 1 S *2:9. Mt 22:12, 13. **silent in the grave.** or, cut off for the grave. **silent.** Ps 4:4. 30:12. 35:15. Re +*20:5. **the grave.** Heb. *sheol*, Ge +37:35.

18. **the lying.** Ps *12:3. 59:12. 63:11. 140:9-11. 1 S *2:3. Pr 12:19. Is 54:17. Jn √8:44. Re +√21:8. 22:15. **speak.** Ps 64:3, 4. 123:3, 4. 1 S 2:3. 2 Ch 32:16. Is 37:22-24. Mt 10:25. 12:24. Jn 8:48. Ac 25:7. **grievous things.** Heb. a hard thing. Ps *94:4. Mt 10:25. Ac 9:5. Ju *14, 15. or, ancient sayings. Ps 75:5. 94:4. 1 S 2:3. **proudly.** Ps 10:2. *17:10. 36:11. 46:3h. **contemptuously.** Ps 107:40. 119:22. 123:3, 4.

19. **how great.** ⌐85F, Ps +*8:4. T#952. Ps 36:7-10. 73:1, 24-26. 91:1. 145:7-9. Dt 11:11, 12. Jsh 1:3, 5, 9. Is 64:4. La 3:23-25. 1 C 2:9. 3:9. Ep 2:10. 1 J *3:1, 2. **laid up.** Ps *16:11. Is 35:10. Col 3:2-4. He 10:34. Ja 2:5. 1 P *1:4, 5. **wrought for.** Ps +68:28. 126:2, 3. Nu 23:23. Is *26:12. *64:4. Jn *3:21. Ac 15:12. 1 C *2:9. 2 C 5:5. 1 T 4:8. **before the sons.** Ps 36:7-9. Is 35:10. Mt 5:16. 1 P *2:15.

20. **hide.** ⌐121S2, Ge +21:6. By Metonymy of the Adjunct, whereby the sign is put for the thing signified, "hide" is put for "protect." Ps *27:5. *32:7. 64:2. 91:1-4. Je 36:26. ⌐22C25. Anthropomorphism B889. Human actions are attributed to God: *hiding* for protection and defense. For other instances of this figure see Ps *64:2. 91:1. **from.** Ps 10:2. 36:11. 40:4. 86:14. 124:5. 140:5. Ex 18:11. Ja 4:6. **the strife.** Ps 64:2-4. 140:3. Jb *5:21. Ro 13:13. 2 C 12:20. Ga 5:20. 1 T 6:4. Ja *3:5, 6, 14-16.

21. **Blessed.** Ps *103:2. **marvelous.** Ps *17:7. 98:1. 118:23. 1 P 2:9. **strong city.** or, fenced city. Ps 60:9mg. 1 S *23:7-13. 2 Ch 8:5. 11:5. Is +37:25mg. Je 1:18.

22. **I said.** Ps *116:11. 1 S 23:26. 27:1. **I am.** ver. 17mg. Ps 88:16. Jb 35:14. Is 6:5mg. 38:10-12. 49:14. La 3:54, 55. Ezk 37:11. Jon *2:4. **thine eyes.** ⌐22A7, Dt +11:12. **nevertheless.** Ps 6:9. 42:5. 2 Ch 33:11-13. La 3:56, 57. Jon 2:7-9. He *5:7.

23. **O love.** Ps *34:9. 97:10. Dt 10:12. 30:16. Is 56:6. Mk 12:33. 1 Th 4:1. **saints.** Ps 30:4. 89:7. 97:10. 145:10. Re 19:5, 6. **for the.** Dt 33:3. 1 S 2:9. Mt 24:13. Jn √10:27-30. Ju 1. **faithful.** ⌐121N1, Ge +31:54. Ps 12:1. 2 S 20:19. Mt +*24:45. Lk 19:17. 1 C +*15:58. He *6:10-12. Re 2:10. **plentifully rewardeth.** Ps 54:5. 94:2. Ge +*6:13 (T#566). Ro *12:19. Re 18:6. **proud doer.** Ps 10:4. 18:27. 101:5. *119:21. 138:6. 1 S *2:3. Est 3:5. *7:10. Pr 6:16-19. 8:13. 11:2. 13:10. 16:18. 28:25. Is *2:12. 16:6, 7. Ro *12:3, 16. Ja 4:6. 1 J √2:16.

24. **Be of.** Ps *27:14. Jsh *1:6. Is *35:3, 4. Lk 22:31, 32. He 12:12, 13. Ja 5:10, 11. **shall strengthen.** Ps *29:11. *138:3. Lk *22:32. Col *1:11. **all ye.** Ps *146:5. Ro *15:12, 13. 1 P 1:21. **that hope.** T#851. Ps 42:11. 71:5. 94:19. Col 1:5, 23, 27. He *6:18, 19. 1 P *1:3, 13, 21. 1 J *3:3.

PSALM 32

David shows the happiness of a pardoned sinner, 1, 2; and that penitent confessions alone can relieve the misery of the guilty conscience and make way for comfort, 3-7. He instructs and warns sinners to repent and believers to rejoice in God, 8-11.

(*Title.*) A.M. 2970. B.C. 1034. **A psalm.** *or,* a psalm of David giving instruction. **Maschil.** i.e. *with understanding,* ✛S#7919h. Ps 32, 41, 42, 44, 45, 52, 53, 54, 74, 88, 89, 142, titles. Ge 3:6 (wise). 1 S 18:14mg, 15. 2 Ch 30:22. Ne 8:13mg. Jb 22:2. Ps 14:2 (understand). 47:7. Pr 10:5.

1. **Blessed.** ♪43, Dt +28:3. Ps *1:1, 2. *40:4. 84:12. 89:15. *106:3. *119:1, 2. *128:1. Je *17:7, 8. Mt *5:3-12. 16:17. Lk *11:28. Ro ▶4:7, 8. Re *22:14. **transgression.** ♪173, Ge +27:44. Is *1:18. *43:25. *44:22. Mi *7:18, 19. Ac *13:38, 39. Ro *4:6-8. **forgiven.** Ge 3:7, 21. Pr *28:13. Je 31:34. 50:20. Mi *7:19. **covered.** Ps *85:2. Ex 34:7. Ne *4:5. Is *61:10. Je 23:6. Mi 7:18. Jn *1:29. Ro 4:9, 23-25. *5:1, 2. Re 3:18. 7:13-17.

2. **Blessed.** ♪43, Dt +28:3. **the man.** ♪171G1. Synecdoche of the Species B624. Words of a limited and special sense are used with a wider and more universal meaning. "Man" is used for both sexes, men and women. This is such a common phenomenon that the following instances suffice to illustrate this figure: Ps 1:1. 112:1. Je 17:5, 7. **the Lord.** Le 17:4. Ro *5:13. 8:33. 2 C *5:19-21. 1 P 2:24. **whose.** Jn *1:47. 2 C 1:12. 1 T 1:5. 1 P *2:1, 2, 22. Re *14:5. **spirit.** Heb. *ruach,* Ge +41:8.

3. **When.** Ps 39:3. *107:2. Ge 3:8-19. Ex 3:13. 1 S 31:13. 2 S 11:27. 12:1-12. 21:12-14. Pr *28:13. Is 57:17. Je *20:9. 31:18, 19. Lk *15:15, 16. **bones.** "Bones," by no unusual synecdoche, being used for the whole body; see 1 S 31:13; 2 S 21:12-14. Ps 6:2. 31:9, 10. 38:3. 51:8. 102:3-5. Jb 30:17, 30. La 1:13. 3:4. **roaring.** "Roaring" is here used metonymically for the pains or pangs which occasion it, as otherwise it would be a contradiction to the silence he maintained. Ps 22:1. 38:8. Jb 3:24. Is 51:20. 59:11. La 3:8. Ho 7:14.

4. **hand.** ♪22A14.8D. Anthropomorphism B879. A hand is attributed to God in the idiomatic expression "to make the hand heavy," meaning to make the chastisement severe. Ps *38:2-8. 39:10, 11. Ru +*1:13. 1 S 5:6, 7, 9, 11. 6:9. Jb 19:21. 33:7. **moisture.** Ps 22:15. 90:6, 7. 102:3, 4. Jb 30:30. La 4:8. 5:10.

5. **acknowledged.** Ps *38:18. *51:3-5. 86:5. Le 26:39, 40. Jsh 7:19. 2 S *12:13. *24:10. Jb 33:27, 28. Pr √28:13. Je *3:13. Lk 15:21-24. 1 J √1:8-10. **have.** Jb 31:33. Pr 30:20. Je 2:23, 35. Lk *16:15. **I said.** Is *65:24. Ho 6:1. Lk *15:17-19, 21. **confess.** T#1317. Ps 41:4. *51:3, 4. 106:6, 7. 119:176. Is 64:5. Je 3:25. *14:20. La 1:20. 3:41. Da 9:4-13. Lk 15:18, 19. Ja *5:16. **forgavest.** Ps *30:5. 86:5, 15. +*103:3. Ex *34:7. 2 S *12:13. Is *65:24. Je 31:20. Lk *7:47. *15:20-23. Jn *1:29. Ep √4:32. **iniquity.** Ps *51:4. 2 S *12:9, 13. Ml 3:8.

6. **For this.** Ps 34:2-5. 40:3. 51:12, 13. Is 26:20, 21. 2 C 1:4. 1 T 1:16. **godly.** Ps 4:3. 2 C *7:9, 10. T *2:12. **pray.** Pr *1:28. Is 49:8. √55:6. Lk *19:42-44. Jn *7:34. 2 C *6:2. Ja 4:3. **a time,** etc. Heb. a time of finding. Is *55:6. 1 T 1:16. He *4:16. **in the floods.** Ps 42:7. 69:1, 2, 13-15. 124:4, 5. Ge 7:17-22. Is *43:2.

Mt *7:24-27. Ac 20:23, 24. Re 12:15, 16.

7. **my hiding place.** Ps 9:9. 17:8. 27:5. *31:20. *119:114. 143:9. Ge ◐3:8. Dt 32:10. Is 32:2. Je 36:26. Col 3:3. ♪22L4. Anthropomorphism B897. God is spoken of as a *hiding place.* For other instances of this figure see Ps 119:114. Is 4:6. **preserve.** T#1730. Ps 12:7. 25:21. 40:11. 71:1, 2. **compass.** ver. 10. Ps 1:3. 5:12. 18:5. 109:3. La 3:5. **songs.** Ps 40:3. 98:1. Ex 15:1-3. Jg 5:1. 2 S *22:1. Re 7:10. 15:2, 3.

8. **instruct.** T#805. Ps *25:8, 12. *34:11. 51:13. 66:16. 94:8. 101:2. Dt +29:9 (S#7919h). Pr 3:1. *4:1-13. 8:10, 11. Mt *11:29. Lk 22:32. Jn *7:17. **teach.** Jn *14:26. Ja *1:5. **the way.** Ps 143:8. Ex 33:14. 1 K 3:7. 2 Ch 20:12. Pr *3:5-7. **I will guide,** etc. Heb. I will counsel thee, mine eye shall be upon thee. T#1543. Ps 5:8. *25:+4 (T#1469), 5, 9, 10. 27:11. 31:3-5. 33:18. 43:3. 48:14. 61:2. *73:24. 78:72. 107:4-7. *119:133. *139:23, 24. 143:8. 1 K 3:9. Pr √3:5, 6. Is 30:21. *49:10. Je 3:4. 6:16. 42:2, 3. Mi 7:7, 8. Jn 6:68. Ac 1:24. 9:6. 1 Th 3:10, 11. 2 Th 3:5. **mine eye.** ♪22A7, Dt +11:12. Ps 33:18. 123:2.

9. **Be ye.** Pr *26:3. Je *31:18. Ja *3:3. *4:7-10. **no understanding.** ♪96B, Ge +8:5. Jb *35:11. Je *4:22. *8:6, +7.

10. **Many.** Ps 16:4. *34:19-21. 140:11. Pr *13:21. Ec 8:12, 13. Is *3:11. *57:21. Ro *2:8, 9. 1 T 6:10. **but.** Ps 2:12. 5:12. 34:8. 40:4. 84:12. 146:5. 147:11. Pr 16:20. Is 12:2, 3. Je *17:7, 8. **compass.** Ps 1:3. 5:12. La 3:5.

11. **Be glad.** Ps 33:1. *64:10. 68:3. 97:12. Dt 12:12. 1 S 2:1. Ro 5:11. Ph 3:1, 3. *4:4. **shout.** Ps 5:11. 97:1. 98:4. Ezr 3:11-13. Zc 4:7. **upright.** ver. 2. Ps 125:4.

PSALM 33

The righteous are called on to rejoice in God and to praise his perfections as displayed in his word and works; and all men to fear the great Creator and Governor of the world, 1-12. His providential kindness to his chosen people in ordering all things for their good, 13-19. Their confidence and prayer, 20-22.

1. **Rejoice.** Ps 32:11. *97:12. 1 C 1:30, 31. Ph *4:4. 1 Th +5:16. **ye righteous.** Ps 118:15. Ro 3:10. 5:19. **praise.** Ps √50:14-16. 78:36, 37. 135:3. *147:1. Pr *15:8.

2. **Praise.** Ps 81:2, 3. 92:3. 98:4, 5. 144:9. 149:3. 150:3-6. Ex 15:20. 2 S 6:5. 1 Ch 15:16, 28. 25:3, 6. Re 5:8. 14:2. **with the psaltery.** *Benaivel asor,* rather, "with the ten-stringed *nabla*;" see on 1 Ch 13:8.

3. **a new.** Ps *40:3. 96:1. 98:1. 144:9. 149:1. Is *42:10. Ep *5:19. Col *3:16. Re *5:9. *14:3. **play.** 1 Ch 13:8. 15:22. 25:7. 2 Ch 34:12.

4. **the word.** Ps *42:10. *19:7, 8. *119:75, 128. Pr *30:5. Mi *2:7. Ro *7:12. **is.** ♪63B, Ge +2:10. **all his.** Ps *25:10. 36:5, 6. 85:10, 11. 96:13. Ge *24:27. Dt *32:4. Da *4:37. Jn √14:6. Ro 15:8, 9. T *1:2.

5. **He.** Ps *11:7. *45:7. 99:4. He *1:9. Re 15:3, 4. **judgment.** T#232. Ps 1:5. 7:6. 9:4mg, 7, 16. 48:10. 92:15. *97:2. 111:3. 119:137, 138, 142. 145:17. Ge +*18:25. 2 Ch *19:7. Jb 8:3. *34:12. 37:23. Je 9:24. Re 15:3, 4. **earth.** Ps 36:6. 104:24. 119:64. 145:15, 16. Mt +*5:45. Ac 14:17. **goodness.** *or,* mercy. ver. 18, 22. Ps 5:7. 6:4.

6. **By the.** ver. *9. Ps 148:1-5. Ge *1:1, 6, 7. Jn *1:1-3, 10. Col *1:16, 17. He *1:2, 10, 11. *11:3. 2 P *3:5. Re *19:13. **the host.** Ps 148:2, 3. Ge *2:1. Dt

*4:19. Je 8:2. Ro *1:25. **breath**. Heb. *ruach*, Ex +15:8. Ps *104:30. Ge *2:7. Jb 26:13. *33:4. Jn 20:22.

7. **He gathereth**. Ps 104:6-9. Ge *1:9, 10. Jb 26:10. 38:8-11. Pr 8:29. Je 5:22. **heap**. Ex 15:8. Jsh 3:13, 16. Hab 3:15.

8. **the earth**. Ps 22:27. 96:9, 10. Je *5:22. 10:7-12. Da 6:25, 26. Re *4:11. 14:6, 7. 15:4. **stand**. Ps 76:7. He 12:29.

9. **For**. ver. 6. Ps 148:5, 6. Ge 1:3. He +*11:3. **and it stood**. Ps 93:5. 119:90, 91. Col *1:16, 17. He *1:3. Re *4:11.

10. **The Lord**. Ps 2:1-4. 9:15. *76:10. Ex 1:10-12. 2 S 15:31, 34. 17:14, 23. Ge *50:20. Ex 1:12. 2 S 17:14. Jb 5:12, 13. Pr *21:30. Is 7:5-7. 8:9, 10. *19:3, 11-14. 44:23. Mt 2:16. Ac 2:36. 8:4. Ph 1:12, 13. 1 C *3:19. **bringeth**. Heb. maketh frustrate. Is 44:25. or, maketh void. Ps 89:33mg. Ezk 17:19. **to nought**. Ps +*146:4. **he maketh**. Ps 21:11. 140:8. +*146:4.

11. **The counsel**. T#250. Jb 23:13. Pr *19:21. Is *8:10. *14:24, 27. *46:9, 10. La *3:37. Ezk 38:10, etc. Da 4:37. Ac 4:27, 28. Ep +*1:11. 3:11. **for ever**. Heb. *olam*, Ex +*12:24. **thoughts**. Ps 92:5. Is √55:8, 9. Je 29:11. Mi 4:12. **all generations**. Heb. generation and generation. Ps +10:6mg. 49:11mg. 77:8mg. +79:13mg. 89:1mg. 100:5mg. 119:90mg. 135:13mg. Dt 32:7mg. Pr +*27:24mg. Jl 2:2mg. Ac 15:18.

12. **Blessed**. ſ43, Dt +28:3. Ps *144:15. 147:19, 20. Ex 19:5, 6. Dt 33:29. **chosen**. T#253. Ps 65:4. 106:5. 135:4. Dt 4:20. *7:6-8. +10:15. 32:9, 10. Is 45:4. Jn *15:16. Ro 3:1, 2. 9:4. Ga *3:29. Ep *1:3, 4. 1 P 2:9. **his own inheritance**. Ps *16:5. 28:9. Jsh 13:33. Je 10:16. T *2:14.

13. **looketh**. Ps 11:4. *14:2. *94:7, 9. 102:19. Ge 6:12. 2 Ch *16:9. Jb 28:24. Pr *15:3. La 3:50. **beholdeth**. Ps 53:2. Je 23:23, 24. He *4:13.

14. **the place**. Ps 123:1. 1 K 8:27, 30. Is 57:15. 66:1. Lk 11:2. 1 T 6:16.

15. **fashioneth**. Pr 21:1, 2. *22:2. 27:19. Ec 7:29. Is 64:8. Ac *17:26. 2 T +2:25. **considereth**. Ps 44:21. 94:11. Jb 11:11. *34:21, 22. Pr *5:21. 24:12. Je *32:19. Ho 7:2. 1 C 4:5.

16. **no king**. Ps *20:7, 8. *44:3, 6, 7. Ex 14:17, 18, 28. Jsh 11:4-8. Jg 7:2, 12, etc. 1 S 14:8-16. 1 K 20:10, 27-29. 2 Ch 14:9-13. *20:12, 15, 23. 32:8, 9, 21. **mighty**. Jsh 14:12. 1 S 17:4, 45-49. 2 S 21:16-22. Je 9:23.

17. **An horse**. Ps 20:7. Jg 4:15. 2 K 7:6, 7. Pr *21:31. Ec 9:11. Is 30:16. Ho 14:3. **his great**. Ps 147:10. Jb 39:19-25.

18. **the eye**. Ps 17:8. *32:8. *34:15-20. 123:2. 1 S 26:24. Jb *36:7. 1 P *3:12. **hope**. Ps 13:5. 52:8. *147:11. Ro *4:4-8. He *6:18, 19.

19. **To deliver**. Ps 91:3-7, 10. Jn √5:24. √10:28-30. **soul**. Heb. *nephesh*, Ge +12:13. ſ121A7, Ge +9:5. **in famine**. Ps *37:3, 19. 107:9. 146:7. Jb *5:19-22. Pr 10:3. Is 33:16. 41:17. Ezk 36:29, 30. Hab *3:17, 18. Zc *10:1. Mt *4:4. *6:31-33.

20. **soul**. Heb. *nephesh*, Ge +34:3. **waiteth**. Ps 27:14. *62:1, 2, 5, 6. 123:2. *130:5, 6. Pr *27:18. Is 40:31. **he is**. Ps *115:9-12. 144:1, 2. 1 Ch 5:20.

21. **For**. Ps *13:5. 28:7. 30:10-12. 32:10, 11. Is 25:9. Zc 10:7. Jn *16:22. his. 1 Ch 16:10, 35. Lk 1:47-50. Re 4:8.

22. **Let thy**. ſ38A, Ps 5:11, 12. 13:5. 32:10. 119:49, 76. Ne +4:4. **according**. Mt *9:29.

PSALM 34

David praises God and exhorts others from his own experience to bless and trust in God, 1-10. He teaches the fear of God and contrasts the privileges of the righteous with the miseries of the wicked, 11-22.

(*Title*.) A.M. 2942. B.C. 1062. **Abimelech**. *or,* Achish. Achish, king of Gath, is probably here called *Abimelech* because that was a common name of the Philistine kings (see the parallel texts). This is the second of the alphabetical psalms (the first being Ps 25), each verse beginning consecutively with a letter of the Hebrew alphabet. The verse, however, which begins with *wav*, and which should come in between the fifth and sixth, is totally wanting; but as the 22nd, which now begins with *pay, podeh,* "redeemeth," is entirely out of the series, it is not improbable that it was originally written *oophodeh,* "*and* redeemeth," and occupied that situation, in which connection it reads admirably. Ge 20:2. 26:1, 26n. 1 S 21:13-15. Pr 29:25.

1. **bless**. Ps *71:8, 14, 15. 145:1, 2. Is 24:15, 16. Ac *5:41. *16:25. Ep *5:20. Col *3:17. 1 Th √5:18. 2 Th 1:3. *2:13. He *13:15. **his praise**. Ps *67:5-7. 92:1, 2. 100:4, 5. *119:164. 147:1. Re 4:8.

2. **soul**. Heb. *nephesh*, Ge +34:3. **make**. Ps 44:8. 105:3. Is 45:25. Je *9:24. 1 C 1:31. 2 C 10:17. **the humble**. Ps 22:22-24. 32:5, 6. *66:16. *119:74. 142:7. Mt 5:16. 1 T 1:15, 16.

3. **magnify**. Ps 35:27. 40:16. 69:30. Lk 1:46. Ac 19:17. Ph 1:20. **let us**. Ps 33:1, 2. 66:8. 103:20-22. 148:1, etc. 1 Ch 29:20. 2 Ch 29:30. Re 14:7. 19:5, 6.

4. **sought**. Ps +*9:10. 18:6. *22:24. 31:22. *77:1, 2. 116:1-6. 2 Ch *20:3. Jon 2:2. Mt *7:7. Lk *11:9. 2 C *12:8, 9. He *5:7. **he heard**. Ps +*27:7 (T#1434). +*99:6. He *5:7. **delivered**. Ps *103:14. 1 C +*10:13. **from**. Ps 27:1, 2. 46:2. *56:3. Ge ◐+19:30. 1 S 27:1. 2 Ch +20:3 (T#1336). Jb +*3:25. Pr +*22:3. Is +*8:12. +*12:2 (T#814). Je +*10:5. 2 C *7:5, 6. 2 T √1:7.

5. **They looked**. Ps 67:1. 123:1, 2. Jb 6:19, 20. Is *45:22. Jn 1:29. He √12:2. 1 P *5:7. **and were**. Ps 13:3. 18:28. 97:11. 1 S 1:18. Est 8:16. Jb 33:30. Mi 7:8, 9. Jn *8:12. **lightened**. *or,* flowed unto him. Ps 83:16. 2 S 19:5. Jn *8:12. Ro *5:1.

6. **This**. Ps 3:4. 10:17. √40:17. 66:16-20. 102:17. **saved**. ver. 17-19. Ge 48:16. 2 S 22:1. Re 7:14-17.

7. **The angel**. Ps *91:11, 12. 2 K *6:17. 19:35. Da *6:22. Mt *18:10. Lk *16:22. He *1:14. **encampeth**. Ge *32:1, 2. Zc 9:8. **delivereth**. Ps 7:4. 18:19. 50:15. 81:7. 91:15. 2 S 22:20. Jb 36:15. Is *63:9. Ac *12:7. or, armeth. Jsh 4:13mg. 6:7, 9, 13. 1 Ch 12:23, 24mg.

8. **taste**. Ps 63:5. *119:103. SS *2:3. 5:1. He 5:13, 14. *6:4, 5. 1 P *2:2, ℣3. 1 J *1:1-3. **see**. ſ171J15, Ge +42:1. Verbs expressing the operation of one sense are in Hebrew often put for those of another: here, taste and see. **Lord**. Ps 36:7, 10. 52:1. Je *31:14. Zc *9:17. Lk +6:35. 1 J *4:7-10. **blessed**. ſ43, Dt +28:3. Ps *2:12. *84:12.

9. **fear**. Ps 22:23. *31:23. 89:7. Ge 22:12. Is 8:13, 14. Ho 3:5. He *12:28, 29. Re 15:3, 4. **no want**. T#752. Ps *23:1, 5. Mt √6:33. Lk 12:30-32. Ro *8:32. 1 C 3:22, 23. Ph *4:19. 1 T 6:6, 17.

10. **lions**. Ps 104:21. Jb 4:10, 11. Lk 1:51-53. **but**. Ps *84:11. Jsh 21:45. Mt *6:32, 33. Lk *12:31. Ph *4:11, 18, 19.

11. **Come.** Pr 1:8. 4:1. 7:24. *8:17, 32. √22:6. Ec *11:9, 10. *12:1. Is *28:9. Mt 18:2-4. Mk *10:14-16. Jn 13:33. 2 T *3:15. **hearken.** ver. 5. **I will teach.** T#1288. Ps *32:8. 66:16-20. *111:10. Pr 1:7. *2:1-9. Ec *12:13. Is *28:9, 26.

12. **What.** √85D, Ps +25:12. Ps *21:4. *91:16. Dt *6:2. *30:20. 1 P *〉3:10, 11. Re *22:14. **life.** √108B, 1 S +10:24. **that he.** Ps *4:6. Jb 7:7. Ec 2:3. *12:13. 1 T *4:8. Re *21:4.

13. **Keep.** √38D, Ps *12:3, 4. +27:14. √39:1. 120:3, 4. √141:3. Pr 12:14. *18:21. Mt √12:35-37. Ep √4:29. Ja *1:19, 26. *3:2, 5-10. **speaking.** Ps 55:11. Pr 12:17, 19, 22. 19:9. Is 63:8. Col 3:9. 1 P 2:1, *22. Re 14:4, 5.

14. **Depart from evil.** Ps *37:27. Jb 28:28. Pr *3:7. 4:27. 8:13. 13:14. 16:6, 17. *28:13. Is *1:16, 17. Ro *12:9. 2 T *2:19. He 12:1. 1 P 〉3:11. **do good.** Mi +*6:8. Lk +*6:9, 35. Ac *10:38. Ga +*6:10. T *2:14. He +*13:16. Ja +*4:17. 3 J *11. **seek peace.** Ps 120:7. Mt *5:9. Ro 12:18. 14:17, 19. 2 C 13:11. 1 Th 4:11. He √12:14. Ja *3:17, 18.

15. **The eyes.** Ps 1:6. ◐25:15. *33:18. Jb +*36:7. Pr +*15:3. 1 P +*〉3:12. **ears are open.** ver. *6, *17. Ps 10:17. 130:2. *145:18, 19. 2 Ch 6:40. Pr +*15:8, 29. Is *37:14-21. Da *9:17-23. Ja +*5:4, 16. **their cry.** ver. +*17.

16. **face.** √22A4, Ge +19:13. Le 17:10. 26:17. Je 44:11. Ezk 14:7, 8. Am 9:4. 1 P 〉3:12. **against them.** T#303. Ps 37:35, 36. Ge +6:13 (T#566). Is 1:20. Ml +*3:5. Ro 2:7-10. 1 C +√6:9, 10. **to cut.** Ps 10:16. √37:9, 10, 20, 36, 38. Jb 18:17. Pr *10:7. *11:7. ◑*14:32. Ec 8:10. Je 17:13. 1 C +*6:9, 10. Ep +*5:5, 6.

17. **The righteous.** √63A1, Ge +14:20. There is no word for "the righteous" in the present Hebrew text, but it is preserved in all the versions; it was probably lost from its similitude to *tzaakoo*, "they cry:" *tzaakoo tzaddeekim*, "the righteous cry." **cry.** ver. 6, 15, 19. Ps 91:15. *145:18-20. Ex +*22:23, 24. Dt +*24:15. 2 Ch 32:20, 21, 24. Is *65:24. Ac 12:5-11. **delivereth.** T#1729. Ps 20:1-4. 22:11. 25:22. *31:9, 10. 39:10. 40:1, 2. 50:14, 15. 54:6, 7. 71:20. 77:2. 107:4-6, 11-13, 25-28. 116:3, 4. Is 33:2. Jon 3:5-9. Jn 12:27, 28.

18. **is nigh.** Ps 75:1. 85:9. 119:151. *145:18. Is √55:6. **unto them,** etc. Heb. to the broken of heart. T#1342. Ps *51:15-17. 69:19, 20. *147:3. Is *61:1. Lk *4:18. **such as,** etc. Heb. the contrite of spirit. Heb. *ruach*, Ge +41:8. 2 K 22:19. Is √57:15. *66:2. Ezk *36:26, 31.

19. **Many.** Ps 71:20. +*119:75. Jb *5:19. 30:9, etc. *42:12. Pr *24:16. Jn *16:33. Ac +*14:22. 2 C 4:7-12, *17. 11:23-27. 1 Th 3:3, 4. 2 T 3:11, *12. He 11:33-38. Ja 1:2. 5:10, 11. 1 P *4:12, 13. Re 7:14-17. **but.** T#768. ver. *6, 17. Ps 25:17. *30:5. 42:11. 68:13. 71:20. 18:27, 28. 107:19. *126:5, 6. 146:8. Jb *8:20, 21. *11:16. 36:16. Pr 11:8. *12:13. 24:16. Je 29:11. *31:12, 13. Ho 6:1. 2 T 3:11.

20. **He keepeth.** Ps 35:10. 91:12. Da 6:22-24. **broken.** T#1971. Ps 22:14-17. Ex 12:46. Nu 9:12. Jn ✲*〉19:36.

21. **Evil.** Ps 37:30-40. *94:23. *145:20. Is 3:11. **they.** Ps 37:12-15. 40:15. 89:23. 1 S 19:4, 5. 31:4. 1 K 22:8, 37. Lk 19:14, 27, 41-44. Jn 7:7. *15:18-23. 1 Th 2:15, 16. 2 Th 1:6-9. **desolate.** *or,* guilty. Ex 20:7.

22. **redeemeth.** Ps 31:5. 71:23. 103:4. 130:8. Ge 48:16. 2 S *4:9. 1 K 1:29. La 3:58. 1 P 1:18, 19. Re

---

5:9. **soul.** Heb. *nephesh*, Ps *49:15. Ge +12:13. **none.** Ps 9:9, +*10. *84:11, 12. Jn √10:27-29. Ro *8:31-39. 1 P *1:5.

PSALM 35

David prays that God would fight against his enemies and anticipates their confusion and his triumph over them, 1-10. He complains of their calumny, malice, and ingratitude; blending supplications and appeals to God, 11-22. He renews his prayers and predictions, 23-28.

1. A.M. 2942. B.C. 1062. **Plead.** T#1514. Ps 43:1. 119:154. 1 S 24:15. *25:38, 39. Pr 22:23. 23:11. Je 51:36. La *3:58. Mi *7:8, 9. **fight.** Ex 14:25. Jsh 10:42. 2 Ch 20:15. Ne 4:20. Ac 5:39. 23:9.

2. **Take hold.** Ps 7:12, 13. Ex 15:3. Dt 32:41, 42. Is 13:5. 42:13. **shield.** √22D5A. Anthropomorphism B893. Arms or weapons of war are attributed to God. For other instances of this figure see Is 59:17, 18. Je 50:25. 51:20.

3. **Draw out.** √90, Ps 17:1. **stop.** Ps 27:2. 76:10. 1 S 23:26, 27. Jb 1:10. Is 8:9, 10. 10:12. Ac 4:28. **say.** Ps 51:12. 62:7. 85:8, 9. 91:16. Ge 49:18. Is 12:2. Lk 2:30. **soul.** Heb. *nephesh*, Ge +12:13.

4. **confounded.** ver. 26. Ps 31:17, 18. 40:14, 15. 70:2, 3. 71:24. **that seek.** Ps 38:12. 1 S 23:23. 1 K 19:10. Ezk 13:19. Mt 27:1. **soul.** Heb. *nephesh*, Ge +12:13. **let them.** √90, Ps +17:1. **turned.** Ps 129:5. Is 37:29. Je 46:5. Jn 18:6.

5. **as chaff.** Ps *1:4. 83:13-17. Jb 21:18. Is 17:13. 29:5. Ho *13:3. Mt 3:12. Lk 3:17. **and let.** ver. 6. Ex 14:19. Is 37:36. Ac 12:23. He 11:28.

6. **their.** Ps *73:18. Pr *4:19. Je 13:16. *23:12. **dark and slippery.** Heb. darkness and slipperiness. **and let.** ver. 5. 2 K 19:35. Ec +*5:6. Ezk 9:1-6. Mt *13:30, 39-43.

7. **without.** Ps 7:3-5. 25:3. 64:4. Jn *15:25. **hid.** Ps 9:15. 119:85. 140:5. Jb 18:8. **pit.** Heb. *shachath*, Jb +9:31 (✱S#7845h). 33:18. **soul.** Heb. *nephesh*, Ps +30:3.

8. **Let destruction.** All the verbs in these verses (ver. 4-8), in the original, are in the future tense, as a prediction, and should probably be so rendered; though as that tense is frequently used in Hebrew for the imperative, most translators, both ancient and modern, have considered them as an imprecation. Ps 40:14n. 64:7. +71:13n. 73:18-20. 106:9n. Pr *29:1. Je ◑+*10:25. Lk 21:34. 1 Th *5:3. **at unawares.** Heb. *which* he knoweth not of. ver. 15. Ps 73:22mg. **net.** Ps 7:15, 16. *57:6. 141:9, 10. Pr 5:22. **into.** 1 S 18:17. 31:2-4. 2 S 17:2-4, 23. 18:14, 15. Est *7:10. Mt *27:3-5.

9. **soul.** Heb. *nephesh*, Ge +34:3. **be joyful.** Ps 13:5. 21:1. 33:21. 48:11. 58:10, 11. 68:1-3. 1 S 2:1. Is 61:10. Hab 3:18. Lk 1:46, 47. Ga 5:22. Ph 3:1-3.

10. **All.** Ps 22:14. 32:3. 34:20. 38:3. 51:8. 102:3. Jb 33:19-25. **say.** √155A, Ge +31:35. **who.** √85C, +18:14. Ps 71:19. 86:8. 89:6-8. Ex 15:11. Is 40:18, 25. Je 10:7. **which deliverest** Ps 10:14. 12:5. 22:24. 34:6. 69:33. 79:11. 102:17-20. 109:31. 140:12. Jb 5:15, 16. Pr *22:22, 23. **too strong.** Ps 18:17.

11. **False witnesses.** Heb. Witnesses of wrong. T#1935. Ps 27:12. 1 S 24:9. 25:10. 1 K *21:13. Mt *✲26:59, 60. Ac 6:13. 24:5, 6, 12, 13. **laid.** Heb. asked me. **to my charge.** T#1936. Is 53:8. Mt 26:63-66.

✱27:23-26. Mk ✱15:55-59. **knew.** ⨍121C2A1, Jb +19:25.

12. **They.** Ps 38:20. *109:3-5. 1 S 19:4, 5, 15. 22:13, 14. Pr *17:13. Je 18:20. Jn *10:32. **spoiling.** Heb. depriving. 1 S 20:31-33. Is 47:8, 9. Lk 23:21-23. **my soul.** Or, "my life," as the word *nephesh* frequently denotes, Ge +12:13.

13. **when.** Ps 69:10, 11. Jb *30:25. Mt *5:44. Ro 12:14, 15. **sackcloth.** ⨍121S3U, Jb +16:15. Da +9:3. **humbled.** or, afflicted. Le 16:29, 31. 1 K 21:27-29. Is 58:3, 5. Mt 9:14, 15. **soul.** Heb. *nephesh*, Ge +27:31. ⨍171Q2, Nu +23:10. **my prayer.** Mt *10:13. Lk 10:6.

14. **I behaved,** etc. Heb. I walked as a friend, as a brother to me. **I bowed.** 2 S 1:11, 12, 17, etc. Lk *19:41, 42. Jn 11:35. **as one.** Or, "as a mourning mother," *kaavel aim*, Ge 24:67.

15. **in mine.** ver. 25, 26. Ps 41:8. 71:10, 11. Jb 31:29. Pr *17:5. *24:17, 18. **adversity.** Heb. halting. Ps 38:17mg. Je 20:10. 1 C 13:6. **the abjects.** Ps 22:16. 69:12. Jb 30:1-12. Mt 27:27-30, 39-44. Mk 14:65. Ac 17:5. **I knew.** ver. 8mg. **they.** Ps 7:2. 57:4. Jb 16:9.

16. **hypocritical.** ⨍63I2, Jsh +3:3. By ellipsis of repetition from the succeeding clause, "With hypocrites (at feasts), mocking at the feast," i.e. *like parasites who, for the sake of their belly, flatter others.* 1 S 20:24, etc. Is *1:14, 15. Jn *18:28. 1 C *5:8. **mockers.** T#1955. Mt ✱27:27-30. **gnashed.** Ps 37:12. Jb 16:9. La 2:16. Ac *7:54.

17. **how.** Ps 6:3. 13:1, 2. 74:9, 10. 89:46. 94:3, 4. **look.** Ps *10:14. Hab √1:13. **rescue.** Ps 22:20, 21. 57:4. 69:14, 15. 142:6, 7. **soul.** Heb. *nephesh*, Ge +12:13. **darling.** Heb. only one. Ps +22:20mg.

18. **give.** Ps 22:22-25, 31. *40:9, 10. 69:30-34. 111:1. 116:14, 18. He 2:12. **praise.** Ps 67:1-4. ch. 117. 138:4, 5. Ro 15:9. **much.** Heb. strong. Is 25:3.

19. **Let.** ver. 15. Ps 13:4. 25:2. 38:16. *59:10. Jn 16:20-22. Re 11:7-10. **wrongfully.** Heb. falsely. T#1934A. Ps 7:14. 38:19. *109:2, 3. Jb *20:5. Mk ✱✱14:55, 56, 59. **wink.** Jb *15:12. Pr 6:13. 10:10. **that hate.** Ps 69:4. 109:3. 119:161. 1 S 24:11, 12. La *3:52. Jn ❭15:25. **without a cause.** T#1934B. Ps *69:4. Mk ✱15:9, 10.

20. **For.** Ps 120:5-7. 140:2. Pr 15:18. 17:19. 18:6. 26:21. Hab 1:3. **but.** Ps 31:13. 36:3, 4. 38:12. 52:2. 64:4-6. 140:2-5. Je 11:19. Da 6:5. Mt 12:24. 26:4. Ac 23:15. 25:3. **devise.** Ps 10:2. 21:11. 32:2. 36:4. 40:17h. **deceitful matters.** Ps 36:4. 37:7. 38:12. 55:21. Pr 6:14. 14:22. 16:30. 24:8. Is 32:7. Je 9:8. 18:12. Ezk 11:2. Mi 2:1. 6:12. ⨍144A8. Pleonasm; or, Redundancy B412. lit. words of frauds. Here, "words" is an instance of pleonasm. For other instances of this figure see Ps 65:3mg. 105:27mg. 145:5mg. **quiet.** lit. "shrivelled," i.e. timid. ✱S#7282h, only here. From S#7280h: compare Is 34:14 (rest); Je 47:6 (rest); 50:34h. Mt *12:19. Ph 2:15. 1 Th 4:11. 1 T 2:2. 1 P 2:22, 23.

21. **Yea.** Ps *22:13. Is 9:12. Lk 11:53, 54. **Aha.** Ps *40:15. 54:7. 70:3.

22. **This.** Ex *3:7. Ac 7:34. **keep.** Ps 28:1. 39:12. 50:21. 83:1. **be.** Ps 10:1. 22:11, 19. 38:21. 71:12. Is 65:6.

23. **Stir.** Ps 7:6. 44:23. 80:2. Is 51:9. **my God.** Ps 89:26. 142:5. Jn +√20:28.

24. **Judge.** ⨍121C2D3. Metonymy of the Cause B557. To judge is used in the sense of acquit, an effect of judging. Ps 7:8. 18:20-24. 26:1. 43:1. *59:10. 2 Th *1:6. 1 P 2:22. **and let.** ver. 19. Jb 20:5.

25. **say.** Ps 27:12. 28:3. 70:3. 74:8. Jb 1:5. Mk 2:6, 8. **Ah.** Heb. Ah, ah, our soul. Heb. *nephesh*, Ex +15:9. **so would.** Ps 140:8. Ex 15:9. Mt 27:43. **We have.** Ps 56:1, 2. 57:3. 124:3. 2 S 20:19. La *2:16. 1 C 15:54.

26. **ashamed.** ver. 4. Ps 40:14, 15. 71:13. 129:5. *132:18. Is 41:11. 65:13-15. **clothed.** Ps 109:28, 29. 132:18. Jb *8:22. 1 P 5:5. **magnify.** Ps 38:16. 55:12. Jb 19:5. Je 48:26. Da 11:36.

27. **Let them.** T#1502. Jb *42:7-10. **shout.** Ps 40:16. 68:3. 132:9, 16. 142:7. Is 66:10, 11. Jn 16:22. Ro *12:15. 1 C 12:26. **righteous cause.** Heb. righteousness. Pr 8:18. **say.** Ps 70:4. **which.** Ps *149:4. Je 32:40, 41. Zp 3:14, 17. **prosperity.** T#1657. Ps 2:8. 18:18, 19. *25:12-14. 30:7, 8. *37:9, 34. 61:5. 71:20, 21. 90:17. 91:15, 16. 106:4, 5. *118:25. 144:12-15. Ge 27:26-29. *28:20-22. 48:14-16. Dt 33:1-29. Ru 1:8, 9. 4:11, 12. 1 Ch 4:10. 2 Ch 26:5. 31:21. Ne 1:11. 13:30, 31. Jb *8:5-7. *22:23-28. Pr 30:7-9. Is 65:10. Jl 2:17-19. Mt 20:20, 21. Ro 1:10. 1 T 2:1, 2.

28. **my tongue.** Ps 34:1. *50:15. 51:14, 15. 71:24. 104:33, 34. 145:1, 2, 5, 21.

PSALM 36

The corrupt principles and practices of wicked men, 1-4. An admiring view of the mercy and justice of God and of the felicity of his people, 5-9. David prays for his brethren and himself; and in faith triumphs over the workers of iniquity, 10-12.

(Title.) A.M. cir. 3463. B.C. cir. 541. **A Psalm.** This psalm is supposed by some to have been composed by David at the beginning of Saul's persecution; but Calmet and others, on good grounds, are of the opinion that it was written during the Babylonian captivity. **servant.** Ps 18, 90, titles. Ps 143:12. Dt 34:5. 2 T 2:24. T 1:1. Ja 1:1. 2 P 1:1. Ju 1. Re 1:1.

1. **The transgression.** Or, rather, "The speech of transgression to the wicked is within his heart: there is no fear of God before his eyes;" for instead of *libbi*, "my heart," four MSS. have *libbo*, "his heart," which is also the reading of the LXX., Vulgate, Syriac, Arabic, Ethiopic, and Anglo-Saxon. 1 S 15:13, 14. Pr 20:11. Mt 7:16-20. 12:33, 34. T 1:16. **no.** Ps 112:1. Ge 20:11. Pr *8:13. 16:6. Ec 12:13. Ro ❭3:18.

2. **For he.** Ps 10:3. 49:18. Dt 29:19. Je 2:23, 34, 35. 17:9. Ho 12:7, 8. Lk 10:29. *16:14, 15. Ro 7:9. 10:3. **until,** etc. Heb. to find his iniquity to hate. 1 S 15:18-24. 1 Ch 10:13, 14. Ro 3:9. He √3:13.

3. **The words.** Ps 5:9. 12:2, 3. 55:21. 58:3. 140:3. 1 S 18:21. 19:6, 7. 26:21. Mt 22:15-18, 35. **he hath.** Ps 125:5. 1 S 11:6-13. 13:13, 14. 15:26. 16:14. Je 4:32. Zp 1:6. He *10:38, 39. 1 J 2:19.

4. **deviseth.** Ps 38:12. 1 S 19:11. Est 5:14. 6:4. Pr *4:16. Ho 7:6, 7. Mi *2:1. Mt 27:1. Ac 23:12. **mischief.** or, vanity. ver. 3 (iniquity), 12. Ps 5:5. 6:8. 7:14. *10:7. **setteth.** Pr 24:23. Is *65:2. Je 6:16. 8:6. 9:2-9. Mi 6:8. **abhorreth.** Ps *97:10. Jb 15:16. Am 5:15. Ro 1:32. 12:9. Re 2:*2, 6.

5. **mercy.** Ps 52:1. *57:10. *103:11. 108:4. Ex 34:6. Is √55:7-9. **faithfulness.** Ps *89:2, 34. 92:2. *100:5. 111:5. *119:75, 89, 90. Dt 7:9. Nu *23:19. Jsh *23:14. Is 25:1. 49:7. La 3:23. Ho 2:19, 20. Mt *24:35. +*28:19n. 1 C 1:9. √10:13. 1 Th 5:24. 2 Th 3:3. 2 T 2:13. T *1:2. He ◗+*2:17. *6:18-20. *10:23. 1 P *4:19. 1 J √1:9. **clouds.** Ps 57:10. 68:34mg. 108:4mg.

6. **righteousness.** Ps 71:19. 97:2. 145:17. Ge *18:25.

Dt 32:4. Is 45:19, 21-24. Ro 3:25. **great mountains**. Heb. mountains of God. ſ24L, Ge +6:2. ſ108C4, 1 S +14:15. Ps 80:10mg. Ge +*23:6mg. Ex 9:28mg. 1 S 14:15mg. Jon 3:3mg. **judgments**. Ps *77:19. 92:5. Jb *11:7-9. 37:23. Is 40:28. Je 12:1. Mt 11:25, 26. Ro +11:33. Re *15:3. **thou preservest**. T#263. Ps 63:8. 66:8, 9. 104:14, etc. *121:7. *145:9. 147:9. Ne *9:6. Jb *7:20. 10:12. *34:14, 15. Pr 24:12. Jon 4:11. Mt *10:29, 30. 1 T *4:10. He 1:3.

7. **How**. Ps *31:19. 86:5, 15. *103:4. 145:7, 8. Ex 34:6. Is 63:7. Je *9:24. Jn √3:16. 1 J 3:1. *4:9, 10. **excellent**. Heb. precious. Ps +37:20mg. 139:17. 1 P 2:6, 7. 2 P 1:4. **children**. ſ144A3, Ge +11:5. **put their**. Ps *17:8. 57:1. 63:7. *91:4. Ru *2:12. Lk 13:34. **under**. Ge 45:11. Mt 23:37. **wings**. ſ22G2, Ps +91:4.

8. **abundantly**. Ps *16:11. *17:15. 63:5. 65:4. 81:16. 90:14. *107:9. SS 5:1. Is 25:6. 55:1, 2. Je *31:12-14. Zc 9:17. Mt 5:6. Jn *7:37. **satisfied**. Heb. watered. Yirweyun, "they shall be saturated," as a thirsty field by showers from heaven. Ps 65:10. Pr 7:18. Is 58:11. **and thou**. Ps *16:11. 46:4. 116:13. Jb 20:17. Is 43:20. 48:21. Re 22:1-17. **river**. ſ22K4, Je +2:13. **thy pleasures**. Or, adanecha, "thy pleasure," as four MSS. read; in which there is probably a reference to the garden of Eden, and the river that ran through, and watered it.

9. **For**. Is 12:3. Je *2:13. Jn *4:10, 14. 7:37-39. Ro √6:23. Re 21:6. 22:17. **fountain**. ſ22K4, Je +2:13. **in thy light**. ſ22J, Ps +27:1. T#279. Ps 27:1. Dt 32:2. Jb 29:3. Pr 4:18. Is 2:5. 60:1, 2, 19. Ml 4:2. Jn 1:8, 9. *8:12. 17:25, 26. 2 C 3:18. *4:6. Ja *1:17. 1 P *2:9. 1 J *1:7. Re 21:23. **see light**. T#335. Jb *29:3. Is 2:5. Re 21:23. 22:5.

10. **continue**. Heb. draw out at length. Ps *103:17, 18. Ex 12:21. SS 1:4. Je 31:3. Ezk 32:20. Jn √15:9, 10. 1 P *1:5. **that know**. Ps +√9:10. Je 22:16. 24:7. Jn *17:3. He *8:11. **and thy**. Ps *7:8-10. 18:24, 25. 94:14, 15. *97:10, 11. 143:1, 2. Is 51:6-8. 2 T 4:7, 8.

11. **foot**. Ps 10:2. 12:3-5. 119:51, 69, 85, 122. 123:3, 4. Jb 40:11, 12. Is 51:23. Da 4:37. **hand**. Ps 16:8. 17:8-14. 21:7, 8. 62:6. *125:1-3. Ro 8:35-39.

12. **There**. Ps 9:16. 55:23. 58:10, 11. 64:7-9. Jg 5:31. 2 Th 1:8, 9. Re 15:4. 19:1-6. **shall not**. Ps *1:5. 18:38. 112:10. Jb +*8:13. Is +*38:18. Je 51:64. He +*9:27.

PSALM 37

The psalmist persuades to patience and confidence in God and cautions against envy, anger, and discontent, 1-8; the different estate of the righteous and wicked in all their dealings; exhortations to faith, hope, patience, and obedience; and promises to believers under the trials of this evil world, 9-40.

(Title.) This is the third alphabetical psalm. It seems to have been intended as an instructive and consoling ode for the captives in Babylon, who might feel themselves severely tempted when they saw those idolaters in prosperity and themselves in adversity.

1. **Fret**. ver. 7. 1 S 1:6-8. Pr 19:3. 24:1, 19, 20. **envious**. T#174. Ps *73:3. 106:16. Ge 30:1. Jb 5:2. Pr 3:31. 14:30. *23:17. 24:1, 2, 19, 20. 27:4. +28:16 (T#137). Ec 4:4. Mt 16:26. 27:17, 18. Ac 7:9. 13:45. 17:5. Ro 13:13. Ga 5:21. T 3:3. Ja 3:14-16. 4:5, 6. 1 P 2:1, 2.

2. **they shall**. ver. 35, 36. Ps 73:17-20. 90:5, 6. 92:7. 129:5-7. Jb *20:5-9. Lk *12:20. Ja 1:10, 11. 1 P 1:24.

3. **Trust**. Ps 4:5. 26:1. Is *1:16-19. 50:10. Je 17:7, 8. 1 C √15:57, 58. He *6:10-12. **so shalt**. Ge 26:2. 1 S 26:19. He 11:13-16. **dwell**. ver. 27, 29. 2 S *7:10. **land**. Dt 30:20. **verily**. Heb. in truth, or, stableness. Ps 33:4. 36:5. Is 33:6. **be fed**. T#753. Ps 33:19. 34:9, 10. 111:5. 132:15. 147:14. Pr 13:25. Is 33:16. 65:13. Jl 2:26. Mt *6:31-33. Lk +6:38. 22:35. Ph *4:19.

4. **Delight**. T#1323. Ps *43:4. *104:34. Jb 22:26. 27:10. 34:9. SS 2:3. Is 58:2, *14. Ph *4:6, 7. 1 P *1:8. **and**. Ps 21:1, 2. *145:19. Dt 7:8. 10:15. Jn *15:7, 16. 1 J √5:14, 15. **desires**. Ps 5:1. 19:14. *145:19. 1 K 10:13. Jb *6:8. Ml *3:10. Ep *3:20.

5. **Commit**. Heb. Roll thy way upon. T#1428. Ps 10:14. 22:8mg. *55:22. Pr *16:3mg. Mt *6:25. Lk 12:22, 29, *30. Ph *4:6, 7. 1 P 2:23. √5:7. **and**. Ps *22:31. 119:126. Jb 22:28. Ec 9:1. La *3:37. Ja *4:15. **bring**. ſ108B. Idiom B828. The Hebrew idiom "to do" is used for to bring to pass, do a very great deal, do all. For another instance of this idiom see Da 9:19.

6. **he shall**. Ps 31:20. Is 54:17. Mi 7:8, 9. Mt *13:43. 1 C *4:5. **light**. Jb 11:17. Ml 3:18. Mt 13:43.

7. **Rest in**. Heb. Be silent to. William Kay notes "The *silence* is that of tranquil faith which abstains from fretfulness or self-vindication; not, of course, a ceasing from prayer; for prayer is *the* means by which this calmness of spirit is maintained. Compare the expression in Ps 143:9, 'unto Thee have I hidden;'—hidden all from man self-restrainingly, by revealing all to Thee" (*Psalms with Notes*, p. 119). Ps 38:13-15. 46:10. 62:1mg, 5. 65:1mg. 143:9mg. Ex 14:13, 14. Jsh 10:12mg. 2 Ch 20:17. Is *53:7. La *3:26. Ezk 24:17mg. Jon *1:11mg. Hab √2:20mg. **wait patiently**. T#536. Ps *27:14. +39:9 (‖278). 40:1mg. 62:1, 5. Pr *20:22. Is 8:17. *30:15, 18. 41:1. La *3:25, 26. Hab *2:3. Mt 6:9, *10. *26:39. Lk 22:41, 42. Ac 21:14. Ga √6:9. He 10:*36, 37. Ja +4:7 (T#298). *5:7-11. **fret not**. T#1339. ver. 1, 8. Ps 73:3-14. Je *12:1. **the man**. Jb 21:7, 17. Ec *5:8. Is 10:13, 14. Da *11:36. Re *13:3-10.

8. **Cease**. Jb 5:2. 18:4. Pr 4:24. *14:29. *15:1, 18. *16:32. 19:11. *22:24. 25:28. 27:3, 4. *29:8, 22. 30:33. Ec *7:9. Mt 5:22. Ro 12:19. Ga 5:19, 20. Ep *4:26, 31. Col 3:8. 1 T 2:8. Ja *1:19, 20. *3:14-18. **fret**. Ps 31:22. 73:15. 116:11. 1 S *25:21, 22, 33. Je 20:14, 15. Jon *4:1, 9. Lk *9:54, 55.

9. **evildoers**. ver. *35, *36. Ps +*34:16. *55:23. *104:35. Jb *20:23-29. *27:13, 14, etc. **cut off**. T#87. ver. 22, 23, 34, 38. Ps 2:8, 9. 12:3. +*34:16. 82:8. +*101:8. Ge 9:11. Jsh 11:21. 23:4. 1 S 2:10. 1 K 9:7. Pr √2:21, 22. Is 1:27, 28. 2:12. 11:1-6. *13:9. *17:14. 24:1, 3-6, 17-20, 23. 26:20, 21. 28:21, 22. 29:7, 8. Je *25:31-33. Ezk 38:21, 22. 39:1-10, 12, 17. Da 12:1. Jl 3:9, 13, 14, 15-17. Zp 1:2, 3, 17, 18. 3:8, 9, 12, 13. Ml 4:1-3. Re 16:17-21. 19:19, 21. 20:1, 2. **but those that wait**. T#1819. Ps 2:8. *45:22. 91:13-16. √122:6. Jb ☿*21:15. 2 Ch 14:7. *15:12-15. 17:3-5. *26:1, 5. *31:21. Jb 8:5-7. *22:23-28. *42:10-13. Is 19:19, 20. *41:17, 18. 65:10. Je 14:22. 29:7. Jl 2:17-19. Mt √6:33, 34. 1 T *2:1, 2. **inherit**. ver. *11, *22, 29, 34. Ps *25:13. Pr 2:21. Is 26:6. *57:13. 58:14. +*60:21. Da 7:18. Mt +*5:5. Ro +*4:13. He *11:16. Re +*5:10. **the earth**. Or, "the land," airetz, probably the land of Judea, given by God himself as an inheritance to their fathers and their posterity forever: and this verse seems to contain a promise of their return thither. William Kay remarks "There is a notable ambiguity

in the word *eretz*;—which may be rendered 'the *land*' (Canaan, the type); or 'the earth' (the full inheritance)" (*Psalms with Notes*, p. 119). Dt *30:4, 5. Ps 2:8. 27:13. *115:16-18. 116:8, 9. Pr 10:30. 11:31. 12:7. Ec +*1:4. Da *7:27. Mt +*5:5.

10. **yet.** Ps 73:18-20. Jb 24:24. Is 10:25. 29:17. He 10:36, 37. 1 P 4:7. Re 6:10, 11. **wicked.** ver. 35, 36. Ps 49:10. 103:16. Jb 7:10, 21. 14:10. *20:8, 9. Lk 12:20, 21. 16:27, 28. **thou.** Ps 52:5-7. 58:10, 11. 107:42, 43. 1 S 25:38, 39. 2 K 9:25, 34-37. Est 7:10. 8:1. Is 14:16-19.

11. **the meek.** Mt +*5:5. Ga *5:22, 23. 1 T 6:11. Ja 1:21. 3:13. **inherit.** ver. +*9. Ps 2:8. Mt +*5:5. 2 P *3:13. **delight.** Ps 36:8. 72:7. 119:165. Is *26:3. 48:18. 57:18-21. Jn *14:27. Ph *4:7. **abundance.** Is 55:7. **peace.** T#442. Ps 72:3, 7. Is 2:4. 52:8. ❂57:21. 60:17, 18. 66:12. Mi *4:3, 4.

12. **The wicked.** ver. 32. 1 S 18:21. 23:7-9. 2 S 15:10-12. Est 3:6. Mt 26:4, 16. **plotteth.** *or*, practiseth. Da 8:12, 24. Mi 2:1. **gnasheth.** ❋S#2786h. Ps 35:16. 112:10. Jb 16:9. La 2:16.

13. **laugh.** ✸22C8, Ps +*2:4. Ps *2:4. Pr *1:26. **his day.** ✸121P3, Dt +4:32. 1 S *26:10. Je 50:27. Ezk 21:25, 29. Da 5:26.

14. **wicked.** Ps 64:2-6. Ac 12:2, 3, 11, 23. **slay.** 1 S 24:11, 17. Pr 29:10, 27. Hab 1:13. Mt 23:30-34. Ac 7:52. 1 J *3:12, 13. **such as,** etc. Heb. the upright of way. Ps 7:10. 125:4.

15. **sword.** Ps 7:14, 15. 35:8. 1 S 31:4. 2 S 17:23. Est 7:9, 10. Is 37:38. Mi 5:6. Mt 27:4, 5. **bows.** Ps 46:9. 76:3-6. Je 51:56. Ho 1:5. 2:18.

16. **A little.** Pr 3:33. *10:22. 13:25. *15:16, 17. *16:8. *30:8, 9. Ec 2:26. 4:6. Mt *6:11. 1 T *6:6, 8-10. **the riches.** Heb. *hamon*, crowding, noise, disquiet, tur-moil. Is 60:5. William Kay notes "Aben Ezra takes *mamon* to be a variation of this word. It probably meant *originally* the hubbub caused by the pursuit after wealth; then the bustle of wealth itself. Compare the use of *hamah* in Ps 39:6" (*Psalms with Notes*, p. 120).

17. **arms.** Ps *10:15. Jb 38:15. Ezk 30:21-25. **Lord.** ver. 24. Ps *41:12. *51:12. 63:8. 119:116, 117. 145:14. 1 S 2:9. Is ✸41:10, 11. 42:1. Ro *8:31. Ju *24.

18. **knoweth.** ✸121C2A2, Ge +39:6. That is, takes loving note of (W. Kay). Ps *1:6. 31:7. Nu *16:5. Na 1:7. Mt 6:32. 2 T *2:19. **the days.** ver. 13. Ps 31:15. 49:5. Dt 33:25. Mt 24:21-24. 2 T 3:1-5. 4:2-4. Re 11:3-5. **upright.** Heb. *Temimim*, "perfect," who are wholly bent on following God, unreserved in their obedience to Him;—thorough-hearted (W. Kay). Ps 101:2. 119:1, 80. Ge 17:1. Jsh +*14:8. 2 K +*20:3. 1 Ch 12:38n. **their.** Ps *16:11. 21:4. 73:24. 103:17. Is +*60:21. Ro 5:21. ✸6:23. 1 P *1:4, 5. 1 J 2:25. **for ever.** Ex +*12:24.

19. **in the evil.** Ec 9:12. Am 5:13. Mi 2:3. Ep 5:16. **days.** Ps *33:18, 19. Jb 5:20-22. 15:20. Pr 10:3. Is 33:16.

20. **But the wicked.** Ps 1:6. 34:16. 68:2. 92:9. Jg 5:31. Lk *13:3, 5. 2 P 2:12. **shall perish.** ver. 22, 28, 34. Ps 52:5. 1 S 2:9. Pr 21:16. Re ✸20:5. **as the fat of lambs.** Heb. preciousness. Ps 36:7mg. 45:9 (honor-able). 72:14. 116:15. 1 S +*3:1. Zc 14:6mg. That is, as the fat was wholly consumed in sacrifices by the fire on the altar, so the wicked shall consume away in the fire of God's anger. Dt 33:14-16. **smoke.** Ps 18:8. 68:2. 102:3. Ge 19:28. Le 3:3-11, 16. Dt 29:20. He *12:29.

21. **borroweth.** Dt 15:6. ✸28:12, 43, 44. 2 K 4:1-5.

Ne 5:1-5. Pr 11:15. 17:18. ✸22:7, 26. Ro ✸13:8. 1 C 5:11. **payeth not again.** T#1827. He borrows what he has no means of repaying, for God's curse rests on him (William Kay). Ps *112:5. Le +*19:13. 2 K ❂*4:7. Ezk 18:7-9. Ml +*3:5. Lk *16:10. 1 C *10:32. **righteous.** Ps 112:5, 9. Dt 15:9-11. Jb 31:16-20. Is 32:8. 58:7-10. Lk 6:30, 34. Ac 11:29. *20:35. 2 C 8:9. 9:6, etc. He *6:10. 13:16. **showeth mercy.** Mi +*6:8. Mt +*23:23. **and giveth.** Pr *11:24-26. Lk +*6:35, 38. Ac +*20:35.

22. **blessed.** ver. 11, 18. Ps 32:1. 115:15. 128:1. Pr *3:33. **cursed.** Ps 119:21. Mt 25:41. 1 C 16:22. Ga 3:10, 13. **cut off.** ver. 9, 28. Zc +*5:3, 4.

23. **steps.** Ps 17:5. 85:13. *119:133. *121:3, 8. 1 S *2:9. Jb *23:11, 12. Pr *16:9. 20:24. Is 30:21. Je 10:23. **ordered.** *or*, established. Ps 7:9. *40:2. Pr *4:26. **delighteth.** Ps 147:10, 11. Pr 11:1, *20. Je *9:24. He *13:16.

24. **Though.** Ps 34:19, 20. 40:2. *91:12. 94:18. *145:14. Pr *24:16. Mi *7:7, 8. Lk 2:34. 22:*31, *32, 60-62. 2 C 4:9. **shall not.** Pr *24:16. 2 P +*1:10. Ju ✸24. **for.** ver. *17. Ps *145:14. Jn ✸10:27-30. **his hand.** Ps ✸104:28. Ru ❂+*1:13. 2 Ch 30:12. Ezr 7:9. 8:18. Ne *2:18. Jn +*10:28. Ja +*1:13, 17.

25. **I have.** ver. *71:9, 18. Jb *32:6, 7. Ac 21:16. Phm 8, 9. **yet.** ver. *28. Ps *94:14. Jsh *1:5. 1 S 12:22. Is *33:16. 2 C *4:9. He *12:5, 6. +*13:5. **nor his seed.** Ps 25:13. 59:15. 109:10. *112:2. Ge 17:7. Jb *15:23. Pr *13:22. Lk *1:53-55. **begging bread.** Ps *34:10. Ge 41:54.

26. **ever.** Heb. all the day. **merciful.** ver. 21. Ps 112:5, 9. Dt *15:8-10. Mt 5:7. Lk *6:35-38. **lendeth.** Lk +6:38. **his seed.** Pr *20:7. Je 32:39.

27. **Depart.** Ps 34:14. Jb 28:28. Pr 16:6, 17. Is *1:16, 17. 2 T 2:19. T *2:11-14. **do good.** ver. 3. 1 Th 5:15. T ✸3:8, 14. He 13:16, 21. 1 J *2:16, 17. **dwell.** ✸96B, Ge +20:7. Ps 102:28. **for evermore.** Ps +*18:50.

28. **loveth.** Ps *11:7. *45:6, 7. 99:4. Is *30:18. *61:8. Je *9:24. **judgment.** Heb. *mishpat*, justice, equity. ver. 6, 30. **forsaketh not.** ver. *25, *40. Ps *92:13-15. Is *59:21. Je *32:40, 41. Jn ✸5:24. *6:39, 40. ✸10:28-30. 15:9. He +*13:5. 1 J *2:19. 1 P *1:5. Ju *1. **for ever.** Heb. *olam*, Ex +*12:24. **but.** Ps *21:10. Ex +20:5. Jb 18:19. 27:14. Pr *2:22. Is *14:20, 21.

29. **The righteous.** ver. 9, 11, 18, 27. Dt 30:20. Pr *2:21. 2 P *3:13. Re 21:3, 4, *7. **for ever.** Ps +9:18 (❋S#5703h).

30. **The mouth.** Ps *71:15, 24. Dt *6:7-9. Jb 6:25. Pr *10:21, 31. 12:18. 15:2, *7, 23, 28. *25:11-13. 26:4, 5. 27:9. 29:11, 20. Ec 3:7. *10:12. Mt *12:35. Ep *4:29. Col *4:6. **his tongue.** Ps 17:3. 71:15. 119:43, 46, 172. Is 50:4. Ml ✸3:16. Lk 4:22. Ep *5:19. 1 Th 5:11.

31. **law.** Ps *1:2. 40:3, 8. *119:11, 98. Dt *6:6. *11:18-20. Pr 4:4. Is *51:7. Je *31:33. He 8:10. **none.** ver. *23. Ps *121:3. **steps.** *or*, goings. Ps 17:5. *40:2. 44:18mg. 73:2. Jb *23:11. Pr *14:15. Ezk 27:6mg.

32. **watcheth.** ver. 12. Ps 10:8-10. 1 S 19:11. Je 20:10. Da *6:4. Mk 6:20. Lk *6:7. 11:54. 14:1. 19:47, 48. 20:20. Ac 9:24.

33. **will not.** Ps 31:7, 8. 124:6, 7. 1 S 23:26-28. 2 T 4:17. 2 P *2:9. **condemn.** Ps 109:31. Ro *8:1, 33, 34.

34. **Wait.** *Kawah*, to wait, implies the extension of a right line from one point to another. The first point is the human heart; the line is its intense desire; and the last point is God, to whom the heart extends this

straight line of earnest desire. He who, while he waits on God, keeps his way, is sure to have the further blessings of which he is in pursuit. William Wilson defines this word (S#6960h) "to hope strongly, to trust, implying firmness and constancy of mind, to hope for, to wait for, to expect anything; to hope that a thing will be effected, and to wait steadily and patiently till it is effected" (*Old Testament Word Studies*, p. 470). Compare S#3176h, Ps 69:3; S#2442h, Is 30:18. T#1426. ver. 3, 7, 9h. Ps 25:3, 5, 21h. *27:14h. 33:20. 59:9. 62:1-5. 69:6h. 123:1, 2. *130:5h, 6. 145:15. Ge 49:18h. Pr *20:22h. Is 8:17. *25:9h. 26:8h. √30:18, 19. 33:2h. *40:30, 31h. 49:23h. Je 14:22h. La *3:25h. Ho *12:6h. Mi 7:7. **keep**. Ps *18:21. Jb *17:9. *23:10-12. Pr *4:25-27. *16:17. Mt *24:13. **exalt**. Ps 92:10. 112:9. Lk *14:11. He *10:36. 1 P 1:7. *5:6. **when**. Ps *52:5, 6. *91:8. *92:11. **thou shalt see**. Ex 14:30. Is +*66:24.

35. **I have**. Ps 73:3-11. Est 5:11. Jb 5:3. 21:7-17. Is 14:14-19. **spreading**. Col ◐2:7. **like**. ſ105, Ml +4:2. **a green bay tree**. *or*, a green tree that groweth in his own soil. Jb 8:13-19. Ezk 31:6-10, 18. Da 4:20, etc.

36. **he passed away**. See on ver. 10. Ex 15:9, 10, 19. 1 S 31:6. 2 S 17:23. Jb *20:5-9. Is 10:16-19, 33, 34. Da 4:25. Ac 12:22, 23. or, But one passed by. Pr 24:30.

37. **Mark**. ver. 34h. **the perfect**. Jb 1:1. 42:12-17. Pr *14:32. Is *32:17. 57:2. Lk 2:25-29. Ac 7:59, 60. 2 T 4:6-8. 2 P 1:14. **the end**. Heb. *Acharith*, sequel, after-life, after-history, issue, progeny. ver. 38. Ps 73:17. 109:13. Nu 23:10. Dt 8:16. 32:29. Pr *23:17, 18. *24:14, 20. 1 C +*15:55. **peace**. Mt +*5:9.

38. **the transgressors**. Ps 1:4-6. *9:17. 52:5. *104:35. Pr 14:32. Is +*24:22. Mt *13:30, 49, 50. 25:46. Ro *6:23. 2 Th 1:8, 9. **the end**. ver. +37. Nu 24:20. Pr *3:25.

39. **salvation**. Ps 3:8. +*42:5mg. 98:2. Is *12:2, 3. 45:17. 61:10. 63:5. Jon *2:9. Ep √2:8. He +*9:28n. **strength**. Ps *9:9. 46:1. *91:15. Is 33:2. Col *1:11. 2 T *4:17.

40. **the Lord**. Is 31:5. 46:4. Da *3:17, 28. *6:23. **from**. Ps 17:13. 27:2. 1 J 2:13, 14. 5:18. **and save**. Ps 32:6, 7. Pr 3:26. **because**. Ps 22:4, 5. 36:7. 1 Ch *5:20.

PSALM 38

The psalmist deprecates the wrath of God and describes the sufferings to which his sins had exposed him, 1-10. He complains that his friends deserted him while he was persecuted by his foes, 11, 12. He resigns himself to God and hopes in him while he confesses his sins, shows the character of his enemies, and pleads for deliverance, 13-22.

(*Title*). This deeply penitential psalm is supposed to have been composed by David under some grievous affliction, either bodily or mental, or both, after his illicit intercourse with Bath-sheba. **to bring**. Ps 70, title.

1. **rebuke**. Ps 6:1. 88:7, 15, 16. Is 27:8. 54:8. Je *10:24. *30:11. Hab 3:2. He *12:5-11. **neither**. ſ63I1C1, Ge +2:6. **hot**. Dt 9:19.

2. **thine**. Ps 21:12. *64:7. Jb 6:4. La 3:12. **arrows**. ſ22D5B, Dt +32:23. **thy hand**. ſ22A14.7, Ex +9:3. Ps *32:4. 39:10, 11. Dt 2:15. Ru +√1:13. 1 S 5:6, 11. 6:9.

3. **soundness**. Ps 31:9. 2 Ch 26:19. Jb 2:7, 8. 33:19-22. Is 1:5, 6. **neither**. Ps *6:2. 51:8. 102:3, 5. **rest**. Heb. peace, *or*, health. Ge 15:15 (peace). 29:6 (well). 43:27 (well, mg. peace), 28 (good health). **because**. Ps 51:8. 90:7, 8. La 3:40-42.

4. **mine**. Ps *40:12. Ezr *9:6. Ro 7:24. **gone over**. Ps 42:7. **as an**. Le 7:18. Is 53:11. La 1:14. Mt *11:28. He *12-1. 1 P 2:24.

5. **My wounds**. The soul being invisible, its distempers are also so; therefore the sacred writers describe them by the distempers of the body (see the parallel texts on these verses). On reading these and similar passages, says Bp. Lowth, some, who were but little acquainted with the genius of the Hebrew poetry, have pretended to inquire into the nature of the disease with which the poet was afflicted; no less absurdly, in my opinion, than if they had perplexed themselves to discover in what river he was plunged when he complains that "the deep waters had gone over his soul." ver. 7. Ps 32:3. Is 1:5, 6. Je *8:22.

6. **troubled**. Heb. wearied. Is 21:3. **bowed**. Ps 35:14. 42:5mg. 57:6. *145:14. **mourning**. Ps 6:6. 31:10. 42:9. 43:2. 88:9. Jb 30:28. Is *38:14.

7. **my loins**. Ps 41:8. 2 Ch 21:18, 19. Jb 7:5. 30:18. Ac 12:23. **no soundness**. ver. 3. Is 1:6. Lk 16:20.

8. **roared**. ſ22F2, Ps +29:3. Ps 22:1, 2. 32:3. Jb 3:24. 30:28. Is 59:11. **heart**. ſ121I1, Ge +3:7.

9. **Lord**. Instead of *adonay*, "Lord," several MSS. read *yehowah*, "Jehovah." **groaning**. Ps 102:5, 20. Jn *1:48. Ro *8:22, 23, 26, 27. 2 C 5:2.

10. **heart panteth**. T#1352. Ps 42:1. 119:81-83. 143:4-7. Is 21:4. **the light**. Ps 6:7. 69:3. 88:9. 119:123. 1 S 14:27-29. La 2:11. *5:16, 17. **gone from**. Heb. not with.

11. **lovers**. Ps 31:11. Jb 6:21-23. 19:13-17. Mt *26:56. Lk 23:49. Jn *16:32. **friends**. T#205. Ps 55:12-14. Jb 19:14, 19. Mt 26:56. 2 T 4:16. **stand aloof**. T#1963. Ps 88:8. Is 63:3. Lk 10:31, 32. ✦23:49. **sore**. Heb. stroke. or, plague. Ps 39:10. 89:32. 91:10. **kinsmen**. *or*, neighbors. Ps 15:3. Ge 19:20 (near). Ex 32:37. Dt 4:7 (nigh). Jsh 9:16. Jb 19:14. **afar off**. Lk 22:54. 23:49.

12. **life**. Heb. *nephesh*, soul, Ge +44:30. ſ121A7, Ge +9:5. **lay snares**. Ps 10:9. 64:2-5. *119:110. 140:5. 141:9. 2 S 17:1-3. Lk *20:19, 20. **speak**. Ps 35:20. 62:3, 4. 2 S 16:7, 8. Lk 20:21, 22.

13. **But I**. Ps 39:2, *9. 2 S 16:10-12. Is 53:7. 1 P 2:23. **openeth not**. Ps 39:1. 2 K 18:36. Ec 3:7. Is *53:7. Mt +✦26:63. ſ108H6B. Idiom B842. "Not to open the mouth" is a Hebraism for silence. Contrast ſ108H6A, Jg +11:35, where to "open the mouth" is a Hebraism for speaking at length. For other instances of this figure see Ps 39:9. Pr 24:7. Is 53:7. Ac 8:32.

14. **that heareth**. Am 5:13. Mi 7:5. Mk 15:3-5. Jn 8:6. **in whose mouth**. Is 53:7. Mt +✦26:63. 1 P 2:23.

15. **in thee**, etc. *or*, thee do I wait for. **do**. Ps 39:7. 123:1-3. 2 S 16:12. **hear**. *or*, answer. Ps 91:15. 138:3. Is 30:19. *65:24. **Lord**. Here also, instead of *adonay*, one hundred two MSS. read *yehowah*, "Jehovah."

16. **For I said**. Ps 13:3, 4. 35:24-26. **rejoice over**. Dt 32:35. Pr *24:17, 18. **foot**. Ps 94:18. Dt 32:35. **magnify**. Ps 35:26.

17. **to halt**. Heb. for halting. Ps 35:15mg. Je 20:10. Mi 4:6, 7. **sorrow**. ver. 6. Ps 6:6. 77:2, 3. Is *53:3-5.

18. **For**. Ps √32:5. *51:3. Jb 31:33. 33:27. Pr *28:13. **sorry**. T#1391. Ps 119:136. 1 S +9:5 (✦S#1672h). Ezr

10:1. Jb 42:6. Ezk 9:4. Da 9:3. Jl 2:12. Mt 26:75. Lk 15:18, 19. 18:13. 2 C *7:7-11.

19. **But.** Ps 3:1. 25:19. 56:1, 2. 59:1-3. **are lively,** etc. Heb. *being* living are strong. Instead of *chayim,* "lively," Bp. Lowth would read *chinnom,* "without cause:" "But mine enemies without cause have strengthened themselves." As this emendation renders this member of the sentence parallel to the other, it is by no means improbable: see Ps 35:19. 79:5. **they that.** Ps 35:19. 69:4. Mt 10:22. Jn *15:18-25. Ac 4:25-28.

20. **render.** Ps 7:4. 35:12. 109:3-5. 1 S 19:4-6. 23:5, 12. 25:16, 21. Je 18:20. **because.** Mt *5:10. Jn *10:31, 32. 1 P *3:13, 17, 18. *4:14-16. 1 J 3:12.

21. **Forsake.** He +*13:5. **O my God.** Ps 22:1, 11, 19, 24. 35:21, 22.

22. **Make.** Ps 40:13, 17. 70:1, 5. 71:12. 141:1. **to help me.** Heb. for my help. Ps *22:19. 27:9. 35:2. 40:13. 70:1mg. 146:5. **O Lord.** Ps *27:1. 62:2, 6. Is *12:2.

PSALM 39

David purposes not to offend with his tongue and describes his inward commotion, 1-3. His prayers and meditations on the shortness of life and the vanity of human pursuits, 4-6. His hope in God, with prayer for pardon and comfort before his death, 7-13.

(*Title.*) A.M. 2970. B.C. 1034. **Jeduthun.** Jeduthun, probably the same as *Ethan,* 1 Ch 6:44, was one of the sons of Merari, and is supposed to have been one of the four masters of music, or leaders of bands, belonging to the temple service. It is therefore probable that David, having composed this psalm, gave it to Jeduthun and his company to sing; and it is very likely that it was written on the same occasion as the preceding. Ps 62, 77, titles. 1 Ch 16:41. 25:1-6.

1. **I said.** Ps *119:9. 1 K 2:4. 2 K 10:31. Pr 4:26, 27. He *2:1. **that I.** Ps 12:4. *73:8, 9. *141:3. Pr 18:21. *21:23. **will keep.** Ps 38:13, 14. 2 K *18:36. Jb +*6:24. Pr *13:3. Ec 3:7. +*5:2. Mt 27:12. **my mouth,** etc. Heb. a bridle, *or,* muzzle, for my mouth. Ja *1:26. *3:2-8. **while.** 2 S *12:14. Pr +*25:26. Am 5:13. Mi *7:5, 6. Mt +*7:6. Col *4:5.

2. **I was.** Ps 38:13, 14. Is 53:7. Mt 27:12-14. **silence.** Ps 32:3. Je 20:9. **even.** Mt +*7:6. **my sorrow.** Jb 32:19, 20. Ac 4:20. **stirred.** Heb. troubled. Ge 34:30. Pr 15:6.

3. **My heart.** Je *20:9. Ezk 3:14. Lk 24:32. Ac *4:20. **fire.** T#1348. Ps 11:6. 18:8, 12. 21:9. 29:7.

4. **make me.** T#1466. Ps *90:12. 119:84. Nu 23:10. Jb 14:13. **how frail I am.** *or,* what time I have here. Ps 78:39. 89:47. 90:9. 102:11. 103:14-16. 144:4. Jb 14:1. Ec 6:12. Is 53:3. Ezk 3:27. Ja 4:14.

5. **Behold.** Ps 90:*4, 5, 9, 10. Ge 47:9. 2 S 19:34. Jb 7:6. 9:25, 26. *14:1, 2. Ja *4:14. **handbreadth.** ⌐79, Ge +21:16. 1 K 7:26. 2 Ch 4:5. **mine age.** ✳S#2465h. Ps 17:14 (world). 49:1 (world). 89:47 (short time; lit. transitory). Jb *11:17. **as nothing.** Ps 89:47. 2 C 4:18. 2 P 3:8. **verily.** ver. 11. Ps 62:9. *144:4. Ec 1:2. 2:11. Is 40:17. **at his best state.** Heb. settled. Ps 82:1. 119:89. Selah. ver. 11. Ps 3:2, 4, 8. 4:2, 4.

6. **vain show.** Heb. an image. Ps 73:20. There is but the semblance of being: he appeareth for a little, and then vanisheth away. 1 C *7:31. Ja *4:14. **surely.** Ec 1:14. 2:17, 18, 20, 21. 4:7, 8. 6:11, 12. 12:8, 13. Is *55:2. Lk *10:40-42. 12:20, 21, 29. 1 P 5:7. **he heap-**

eth. Ps 49:10, 11. Jb 27:16, 17. Pr *13:22. 23:5. 27:24. Ec 2:8, 18-21, *26. 5:14. Lk *12:20, 21. Ja 5:3.

7. **what wait.** Ps 33:18-20. *130:5-7. Ge 49:18. Lk 2:25. **hope.** Ps 38:15. *42:11. 71:14. 119:81, 166. +*146:5. 147:11. Jb *13:15. Je 3:23. *17:7. La *3:26. Ro *8:24, 25. *15:13. He *11:13, 16. 1 P 1:13.

8. **Deliver.** T#1699. Ps 25:11, 18. 40:12, 13. 41:14. 51:7-10, 14. 56:13. 65:3. *119:133. 130:8. Mi 7:19. Mt 1:21. +*6:13 (T#1478). Ro 6:14. 7:24. 2 T 4:18. T *2:14. **make.** Ps 35:21. 44:13. 57:3. 79:4. 119:39. 2 S 12:13, 14. 16:7, 8. *12:17, 19. Ro 2:23, 24.

9. **dumb.** Ps 38:13. 46:10. Le *10:3. 1 S 3:18. Jb 40:4, 5. Mi 7:9. **opened not.** ⌐108H6B, Ps +*38:13. Ps 38:13. 49:4. 51:15. **because thou didst it.** T#278. Ps 97:1. +*119:75. 1 S 3:18. 2 S 15:26. 16:10, 11. Ne 9:33. Jb 1:15, *21. *2:10. *34:31, 32. Is 38:15. 52:7. Ezk *14:23. Da *4:35. Am ⊙+*3:6. Mt 6:10. Mk *7:37. Jn 12:17, 28. *13:7. 18:11. Ac +21:14. He 12:9. Ja 4:7. 1 P *4:19.

10. **Remove.** T#1674. Ps 25:16, 17. 1 S 6:5. Jb *9:34. 13:21. Mt *26:39. **I am consumed.** Ps 38:3, 4. **blow.** Heb. conflict. Jb 40:8.

11. **When.** Ps 38:1-8. 90:7-10. 1 C 5:5. √11:30-32. He 12:6. Re *3:19. **his beauty,** etc. Heb. that which is to be desired in him to melt away. Ps 102:10, 11. Jb 4:19. 13:28. 30:30. Is 50:9. Ho 5:12. **surely.** ver. 5. Ps 144:4.

12. **hold.** Ps 116:3. **tears.** Ps 56:8. 2 S 16:12mg. 2 K 20:5. Jb 16:20. He *5:7. **for I am.** Ps 119:19, 54. Le 25:23. 1 Ch 29:15. 2 C 5:6. He 11:13. 1 P 1:17. 2:11. **stranger.** Ps 94:6. 119:19. 146:9. Ge +23:4 (✳S#1616h). Ex 12:48mg. Le 25:23. He *11:13. **sojourner.** Ge +23:4 (✳S#8453h). Ex 12:45. 1 Ch 29:15. 2 C 5:6. 1 P *1:17. 2:11. **as all.** Ge 47:9. 1 Ch 29:15.

13. **spare.** 1 Ch 29:28. Jb 10:20, 21. 14:5, 6. **be no.** Ps ◑*71:20. Ge 5:24. 42:36. Jb *14:10-12. √16:22. 17:13. 1 C *15:55.

PSALM 40

David praises God for deliverance out of deep distress and shows the benefit which would thence be derived to numbers, and the happiness of those who trust in God, 1-5. As a type of Christ (or, Christ speaking by him), he states the inefficacy of legal sacrifices and the efficacy of the Redeemer's obedience, 6-8. He declares that he had published God's righteousness and salvation and pleads for deliverance from urgent troubles and for the confusion of his enemies, with the triumphing of the righteous, 9-17.

(*Title.*) A.M. 2970. B.C. 1034. This psalm is supposed to have been composed by David about the same time and on the same occasion as the two preceding; with this difference, that here he magnifies God for having obtained the mercy which he sought there. It also contains a remarkable prophecy of the incarnation and sacrifice of Jesus Christ.

1. **I waited.** Heb. In waiting I waited. Ps *27:13, 14. *37:7. 123:2. Is *40:31. Mt 21:28. Lk 12:37. Ja *5:7-11. **inclined.** Ps *116:2. 130:2. Da *9:18.

2. **brought.** Ps 18:16, 17. 71:20. +*86:13. 116:3. *142:6, 7. 143:3. Jb 33:28mg. SS 2:4. Is +*24:22. 38:17. Je *38:6. Jon 2:5, 6. Zc 9:11. Ac 2:24, 27-31. **horrible.** Ps 65:7. 74:23. **pit.** Heb. pit of noise. Heb. *bor,* Ge +37:20. Ps 7:15. 28:1. 30:3. 88:4. Ge=37:24. Zc 9:11. Mt *13:50. **the miry.** Ps 69:2, 14, 15. Je *38:6-12. La

3:53-55. **set**. Ps *27:5. 61:2. Mt 7:24, 25. **established**. Ps 17:5. 18:36. *37:23. 119:133. Ac 5:30, 31.

3. **And he**. Ps 4:7. 33:3. 144:9. Re *5:9, 10. 14:3. **praise**. Ps 103:1-5. Is 12:1-4. **many**. Ps 34:1-6. 35:27. 52:6. 64:9, 10. 142:7. Ho 3:5. Ac 2:31-41. 4:4. **and fear**. T#593. Ac 2:41-43.

4. **Blessed**. ʃ43, Dt +28:3. T#326. Ps 2:12. 34:8. *84:11, 12. 118:8, 9. Je *17:7, 8. Ro 15:12, 13. **respecteth**. Ps 15:4. *101:3-7. 119:21. Ja 2:1-4. **as turn**. Ps 125:5. Is 44:18-20. Je 10:14, 15. Jon *2:8. 2 Th 2:9-11.

5. **Many**. Ps 136:4. Ex 11:15. 15:11. Jb 5:9. 9:10. 26:14. **thoughts**. ʃ22C5, Ge +50:20. Ps 71:15. 92:5. 139:6, 17, 18. Is √55:8, 9. Je 29:11. **they cannot**, etc. *or*, none can order them unto thee. Jb 5:8, 9. 37:19, 20.

6. **Sacrifice**. Ps 50:8. *51:16. 1 S √15:22. Is *1:11. 66:3. Je 7:21-23. Ho *6:6. Mt *9:13. 12:7. He 10:5-7, 8-12. **mine ears**. ʃ22A8, Ps +10:17. ʃ171N, Ge +8:13. By Synecdoche of the Whole, the writer of Hebrews interprets "ear" to represent the whole body of the listening and obedient servant of Jehovah in the citation of this passage at He ▶10:5. See related note (Ps +*16:9n). Ex *21:6. Jb 33:16. *36:10. Is *50:4, 5. **opened**. Heb. digged. or, prepared. Ps 7:15. 22:16. 57:6. 119:85. Dt √15:17. 2 K 6:23. Jb 41:6. **burnt offering**. Ps 20:3. 50:8. Le +*23:12. **sin offering**. Ge 4:7. Ex 29:14. Le +*23:19.

7. **Lo**. He ▶10:7-9. **I come**. Ge=37:13. **in the**. Ge +*3:15. Lk *24:27, 44. Jn +√5:39. Ac 10:43. 1 C +*15:3, 4. 1 P 1:10, 11. Re 19:10. **volume**. ʃ144B, Dt +33:19. Je 36:2. **written of me**. Lk +*24:44.

8. **I delight**. T#1924. Ps *22:29. *112:1. 119:16, *24, 47, 92. Jb √23:12. Is 53:12. Je √15:16. Jn=*4:34. =5:30. =6:38. √*10:11-18. Ro *7:22. 8:29. Ga √2:20. Ph *2:8. He 9:25, 26. 10:5-10. √12:2. **yea**. Ps *37:30, 31. Pr 3:1. Je *31:33. 2 C 3:3. **within my heart**. Heb. in the midst of my bowels. Ex ◑=32:19. Dt ◑=9:17. **midst**. ʃ144A6, Ge +45:6. Pr 4:21. **my bowels**. ʃ171E10. Synecdoche of the Species B622. The bowels are put for the heart.

9. **preached**. Ps 22:22, 25. 35:18. 71:15-18. Mk 16:15, 16. Lk *4:16-22. He 2:12. **righteousness**. Ro 3:21, 22. **congregation**. Ps 22:22. **not**. Ps 119:*13, 171, 172. He 2:3. **thou knowest**. Ps 139:2. Jn 21:17.

10. **not hid**. Ezk 2:7. 3:17, 18. Ac *20:20, 21, 26, 27. Ro *10:9, 10. 1 Th 1:8. Re 22:17. **righteousness**. Ro *1:16, 17. 3:22-26. *10:3. Ph 3:9. **within**. lit. in the midst. ʃ144A6, Ge +45:6. **faithfulness**. Ac 13:32, 33. Ro 15:8, 9. 2 Th *3:3. **salvation**. Is 49:6. Lk 2:30-32. 3:6. 1 T 1:15. **lovingkindness**. Ps 25:10. 34:6. Mi 7:20. Jn 1:17. √3:16, 17.

11. **Withhold**. From this verse to the end, we have quite a new subject; for the former contains a thanksgiving, and this contains a supplication. It is nearly the same as the seventieth and probably formed a distinct psalm. Ps 69:13, 16. **let thy**. Ps *23:6. 43:3. 57:3. 61:7. 85:10. He *5:7. **continually**. Is +*58:11.

12. **innumerable**. Ps 22:11-19. He *4:15. **mine iniquities**. Ps *38:4. Le +=*5:6. Is *53:6. Lk 18:13, 14. 1 P *3:18. **look up**. Lk +*18:13. **they are**. Ps 19:12. 69:4. **heart**. Ps *73:26. Ge 42:28. Lk 21:26. **faileth**. Heb. forsaketh. Ps 9:10. 22:1. 38:10. Is ◑42:4.

13. **Be pleased**. Ps 25:17, 18. Mt 26:36-44. **make**. ver. 17. Ps *38:22. 70:1, etc.

14. **Let them be ashamed**. The verbs in the preced-

ing verse, in which the psalmist simply prays for deliverance, are in the *imperative*; but here and in the following verses, they are in the *future* tense and naturally express the language of lively faith and hope, rather than that of wishing the destruction foreseen and predicted. Ps 31:17, 18. 35:4, 8n, 26. 70:2, 3. +*71:13n. Is 41:11. 45:24. **that**. Mt 21:38-41. **soul**. Heb. *nephesh*, Ge +12:13. **driven**. Ps 9:3. Jn 18:6. Ac 9:4-6. 12:23, 24.

15. **desolate**. Ps 69:24, 25. 70:3. *73:19. 109:6-20. Lk *19:43, 44. 21:23, 24. **say**. Ps 35:21, 25. 70:3, 4.

16. **all**. Ps 22:26. 35:27. 68:3. 105:3. Is 65:13, 14. **rejoice**. T31381. Ps 21:1, 2. 28:7. *31:7. *33:20, 21. 35:9. 63:5. 1 Ch 16:10. 2 Ch 30:26, 27. Is 12:3. *56:7. Hab *3:17, 18. Mt *13:44. Ac 16:25. 1 Th 5:16, 17. **love**. Ps 119:81, 111, 123, 166, 167. Mt 13:45, 46. Ph 3:7-9. **say**. Ps 35:27. Lk 1:46, 47. Ac 19:17.

17. **I am poor**. ver. 5. Ps *34:6. *69:33. *70:5. +*102:17. Is *41:17. Mt *8:20. 2 C *8:9. Ja +*2:5. **needy**. T#1626. Ps 9:18. +*12:5. *35:10. 37:14. +72:12 (T#1265). 86:1. 109:21, 22. Is *41:17. **the Lord**. 1 P 2:23. *5:7. **thinketh**. Ps 32:8mg. +35:20h (devise). 92:5. ◑104:34. Ne *5:19 (T#1520). **upon me**. Ps +*1:6. *139:1, 2. Ex +*33:12, 17. 1 Ch =16:41. 2 Ch +12:8. Je +*29:11. Na *1:7. Ml *3:16. Mt 6:26, 32. *10:29-31. Jn 10:3, 14. Ac 27:23. 1 C +*8:3. Ga 4:9. 2 T *2:19. **my help**. ver. 13. Ps *54:4. Is *50:7-9. He +*13:6. **my deliverer**. Ps 18:2, 48. +*34:17, 19. 70:5. 144:2. **make**. ver. 13. Ps 22:19. 38:22. 69:17mg. 70:5. 141:1. *143:7, 8. Ge 24:56. Is 30:19. *62:6, 7. +*65:24. Da *10:12, 13. Mt 6:8. Lk +*11:9. Re *22:20.

PSALM 41

David shows the blessedness of those who consider the poor, 1-3. He prays for mercy and complains of the treachery and malice of his enemies and the ingratitude of one who had been his friend, 4-10. He expresses confidence in God and praises him, 11-13.

(Title.) This psalm is supposed to have been written on the same occasion as the three former; to relate to David's affliction and the evil treatment he received from his enemies during its continuance.

1. **Blessed**. ʃ43, Dt +28:3. Ps 112:9. Dt *15:7-11. Jb 29:12-16. 31:16-20. Pr *14:21. *19:17. 28:27. Ec 11:1, 2. Is *58:7-11. Mt *25:40. Mk *14:7. Lk *14:13, 14. 2 C *8:9. *9:8-14. Ga 2:10. **the poor**. *or*, the weak, *or* sick. Ps 72:13. 82:3, 4. 113:7. Ex 23:3. 2 S 3:1 (weaker). Mt *25:34-39. Ac *20:35. 1 Th 5:14. **Lord**. Ps *34:19. 37:26, 39, 40. He *6:10. Ja *2:13. **time of trouble**. Heb. the day of evil. Ps *37:19. Pr *16:4. Ec *12:1. Re *3:10.

2. **preserve**. Ps *33:19. *91:3-7. Je 45:4, 5. **blessed**. Ps *128:1-6. 1 T *4:8. **thou wilt not**. *or*, do not thou. Ps *27:12. 37:32, 33. 140:8, 9. **the will**. Heb. *nephesh*, Ex +15:9.

3. **strengthen**. T#771. Ps *73:26. 116:6. Ge 49:25. Dt 7:13. 2 K *1:6, 16. *20:5, 6. 2 C *4:16, 17. Ph *2:26, 27. 1 T 2:15. **the bed**. or, couch. Ps 6:6. 132:3. **make**. Heb. turn. Ps 30:11. 66:6. 78:9. **his bed**. Ps 4:4. 36:4. 149:5. **sickness**. Dt 7:15. 28:59, 61.

4. **Lord**. Ps *32:5. *51:1-3. **be merciful**. Lk 18:13. **heal**. T#1706. Ps 6:2-4. +*103:3. 147:3. 2 Ch 30:18-20. Ho 6:1. Ja *5:15, 16. **soul**. Heb. *nephesh*, Ge +12:13.

5. **Mine.** Ps 22:6-8. 102:8. **his name.** Jb 18:17. 20:7. Pr *10:7.

6. **speaketh.** Ps 12:2. 26:24, 25. Ne 6:1-14. Pr 26:24-26. Da 11:27. Mi 7:5-7. Lk *11:53, 54. 20:20-23. 2 C 11:26. **when.** Je 20:10.

7. **whisper.** 2 S 12:19. Pr 16:28. 26:20mg. Ro 1:29. 2 C 12:20. **against.** Ps 31:13. 56:5, 6. Mt 22:15. 26:3, 4. **my hurt.** Heb. evil to me. ver. 1mg.

8. **An evil disease.** Heb. A thing of Belial. Ps 38:3-7. Dt +15:9mg. Jg +19:22. 1 S +30:22. Jb 2:7, 8. Lk 13:16. Ac *10:38. **and now.** Ps 3:2. 71:11. Mt 27:41-43, 63, 64.

9. **Yea.** Ps *55:12-14, 20-22. 2 S *15:12. Jb 19:19. Je 20:10. **mine own familiar friend.** Heb. the man of my peace. Je 20:10mg. 38:22mg. Ob 7. Lk 22:3. **which did eat.** T#1926. Dt 32:15. Ob 7. Mt *26:20-23. Jn 13:18, 26, 27. **bread.** ∫171I8, Ge +3:19. **lifted up.** Heb. magnified. Ps 35:26. 38:16. 55:12. +126:2mg. Jl 2:20mg. **heel.** Ps 49:5. 56:6. 77:19. 89:51. **against.** Lk 22:48.

10. **be merciful.** Ps 57:1. 109:21. **that.** Ps 18:37-42. 21:8-10. 69:22-28. 109:6-20. Lk 19:27.

11. **because.** Ps 13:4. 31:8. 35:25. 86:17. 124:6. Je 20:13. Col 2:15.

12. **thou.** Ps 25:21. 42:5. 94:18. **settest.** Ps *16:11. 17:15. 34:15. 73:23, 24. Jb 36:7. Jn 17:24. 2 T *4:18. **for ever.** Heb. olam, Ex +*12:24.

13. **Blessed.** Ps 72:18, 19. 89:52. *106:48. 1 Ch 29:10. Ep 1:3. Re 4:8. 5:9-14. *7:12. 11:17. **everlasting, and to everlasting.** Heb. olam doubled, Da +2:20 (✛S#5769h). Ps 90:2. 103:17. 106:48. **Amen.** With this psalm ends the first of the five books into which the Hebrews divided the Psalms. Nu 5:22. Dt 27:15, etc. 1 K *1:36. 1 Ch 16:36. Je *28:6. Mt *6:13. 1 C 14:16. Re 22:20.

PSALM 42

The psalmist thirsts after God, mourns his absence from the sanctuary while amid insulting foes, and recollects with regret former seasons of comfort, 1-4. He struggles against unbelief and despondency, complains unto God, and stays his dejected soul on him, 5-11.

(*Title.*) A.M. 2983. B.C. 1021. **Maschil.** *or, a psalm giving instruction of the sons, etc.* Or, "An instructive psalm," or didactic ode, "for the sons of Korah." It is generally supposed to have been written by David when driven from Jerusalem and beyond Jordan by Absalom's rebellion. **the sons.** Ps 44-49, 84, 85, titles. Nu 16:1, 32. 26:11. 1 Ch 6:33-37. 25:1-5.

1. **panteth.** Heb. brayeth. Jl 1:20. **so panteth.** Ps 63:1, 2. 84:2. 119:131. 143:6, 7. 2 S 15:14, 29, 30. SS 5:5. Is *26:8, 9. **soul.** Heb. nephesh, Ge +34:3.

2. **soul.** Heb. nephesh, Ge +34:3. **thirsteth.** T#1394. Ps 27:8. 36:8, 9. *63:1, 2. 143:5, 6. Is 44:3. 63:1. Jn *7:37. Re 22:1. **living.** Jb 23:3. Je 2:13. 10:10. Jn 5:26. 1 Th 1:9. **God.** Heb. El, Ex +15:2. **when shall.** ∫109. Interjection B478: parenthetic addition by way of feeling. For another instance of this figure see Ezk 16:23, 24. Ps 27:4. *84:4, 10. Jb 23:3.

3. **tears.** Ps 39:12. *80:5. 102:9. 2 S 16:12mg. **while.** ver. 10. Ps 3:2. 22:8. 79:10, 12. *115:2.

4. **When.** Ru 1:21. Jb 29:2, etc. 30:1, etc. La 4:1. Lk 16:25. **I pour out.** T#1406. Ps *62:8. 1 S 1:15, 16. Jb 30:16. **soul.** Heb. nephesh, Ge +34:3. **for I.**

1 Ch 15:15-28. ch. 16. **with the voice.** Ps 81:1-3. 122:1. Dt 16:11, 14, 15. 2 Ch 7:10. 30:23-26. Is *30:29. Na 1:15. **kept holyday.** Ps 84:7. 122:1. Ex 23:14. Dt 16:13.

5. **Why art thou cast down.** Heb. Why art thou bowed down. ∫53, 2 S 1:19. ver. 11. Ps 35:14. 38:6mg. 41:12. 43:5. 55:4, 5. 61:2. 142:2, 3. 143:3, 4. 1 S *30:6. Mt ⸙26:38. Mk 14:33, 34. **O my.** ∫38C. Apostrophe B903: to one's own self. For other instances of this figure see Ps 103:1, 22. 104:1. 146:1. **soul.** Heb. nephesh, Ge +34:3. **hope.** Ps 27:13, 14. 37:7. *56:3, 11. 71:14. Jb 13:15. Is *50:10. La *3:24-26. Ro 4:18-20. 5:3-5. 1 Th 1:3. He 10:36, 37. **praise him.** or, give thanks. Ps 18:49. **yet praise.** Jb 13:15. **for the help,** etc. **help.** ∫96F2, Ge +4:10. or, his presence is salvation. Ps 14:7. 44:3. 91:15, 16. +*102:16. Nu *6:26. Is +*25:9. +*59:19, 20. Mt 1:23. 28:20. He +*9:28n. Re 11:17n. **countenance.** ∫171Q, Ge +3:19. The face is put for the whole man, especially marking and emphasizing his presence. Here, "I shall yet praise him for the salvations (Heterosis of Number, Ge +4:10, the plural for the singular, to denote great excellence or magnitude: i.e. *the great salvation*) of his countenance": which he (his presence) shall give me.

6. **my God.** Ps 22:1. 43:4. 88:1-3. Mt 26:39. 27:46. **soul.** Heb. nephesh, Ge +34:3. **within me.** Ps 43:5. 88:3. Jb +*14:22. **therefore.** Ps *77:6-11. Jon *2:7. **from the.** Ps 61:2. 2 S 17:22, 27. **Hermonites.** i.e. *devoted, banned; nose, strong fortress,* ✻S#2769h, only here. Dt 3:8, 9. 4:47, 48. **the hill Mizar.** or, the little hill. ✻S#4706h. Ps 133:3.

7. **Deep calleth.** Ge +1:2. Jb 1:14-19. 10:17. Je 4:20. Ezk *7:26. **waterspouts.** A waterspout is a large tube formed of clouds by means of the electric fluid, the base being uppermost and the point let down perpendicularly from the clouds. It has a particular kind of circular motion at the point, and, being hollow within, attracts vast quantities of water, which it frequently pours down in torrents upon the earth. These spouts are frequent on the coast of Syria; no doubt the psalmist had often seen them and the ravages which they made. 2 S 5:8 (the gutter). **all thy.** Ps 69:14, 15. 88:*7, 15-17. La 3:53-55. Jon *2:3.

8. **command.** Ps 44:4. *133:3. Le 25:21. Dt *28:8. Mt 8:8. **in the night.** Ps *32:7. *63:5, 6. +119:55. *149:5. Jb *35:10. Is *30:29. Ac *16:25. **the God.** Heb. El, Ex +15:2. Ps *27:1. Ac 17:28. Col *3:3.

9. **God.** Ps 18:2. 28:1. 62:2, 6, 7. 78:35. **rock.** ∫22L3, Dt +32:31. **Why hast.** Ps 13:1. 22:1, 2. 44:23, 24. 77:9. Is *40:27. 49:14, 15. **forgotten.** ∫22C4, Ps +13:1. **why go.** Ps 38:6. 43:2. 88:9. Jb 30:26-31. **because.** Ps 55:3. Ec 4:1. La 5:1-16.

10. **As with.** ver. 3. Pr 12:18. Lk 2:35. **sword.** or, killing. Ezk 21:22. **bones.** Pr 16:24. **reproach.** T#511. Ps 14:4. 22:6-8. 31:11, 13. *35:15. 44:22. 64:2-4. 69:4, 7-10, 19, 20. 79:4. 89:50, 51. 102:8. Ne 4:4. Jb 16:10. Da 7:25. Jn 10:20. He 11:36-38. Re 7:14. **while.** ver. 3. Jl *2:17. Mi 7:10.

11. **Why art.** Mt ⸙26:38. Mk 14:34. **cast down.** ver. 5. Ps 43:5. **O my.** ∫38C, ver. +5. **soul.** Heb. nephesh, Ge +34:3. **hope.** T#1365. Ps 31:24. 33:22. 38:15. 39:7. 71:5, 14. 119:49, 74, 81, 114. 130:7. 131:3. Je 17:7. La 3:21, 24, 26. He *6:18, 19. **the health.** ∫96F2, Ge +4:10. Je *30:17. *33:6. Mt *9:12. **countenance.** ∫171Q, Ge +3:19. ver. 5n.

PSALM 43

*The psalmist prays that God would judge his cause
and restore him to his sanctuary, 1-3. He anticipates
his joy and praise which should then take place and
encourages himself to hope in God, 4, 5.*

(Title.) A.M. 2983. B.C. 1021. This psalm is evidently a continuation of the preceding with the same
author; they are written as one in forty-six MSS. The
sameness of subject, similarity of composition, and return of the same burden in both are sufficient evidence
of this opinion.

1. **Judge.** Ps 7:8. 26:1. *35:24. 75:7. 1 C 4:4. 1 P
*2:23. **plead.** Ps 35:1. 1 S 24:15. Pr 22:23. 23:11. Mi
7:9. **ungodly.** *or,* unmerciful. ✓175B, Ge +21:16. Ps
4:3. 18:25. 145:17mg. Mi 7:2mg. **the deceitful.** Heb.
a man of deceit and iniquity. Ps 71:4. 2 S 15:31. 16:20-
23. 17:1-4.

2. **the God.** Ps *28:7. 140:7. Ex 15:2. Is 40:31. 45:24.
Zc 10:12. Ep *6:10. Ph *4:13. **why dost.** Ps 71:9. 77:7.
+*94:14. 1 Ch +*28:9. **why go.** Ps 42:9.

3. **send.** T#1731. Ps *40:11. 57:3. *97:11. *119:105.
2 S 15:20. Mi 7:8, 20. Jn 1:4, 17. **light.** ✓22J, Ps +27:1.
truth. Jn 15:3. *17:17. **lead.** Ps 25:4, 5. *32:8. 119:9,
11, 105. 143:10. Pr ✓3:5, 6. **thy holy.** Ps 2:6. *3:4.
*23:3, 6. 68:15, 16. 78:68. 132:13, 14. **tabernacles.**
1 Ch 16:1, 39. 21:29.

4. **Then.** Ps 66:13-15. 116:12-19. Is *38:22. **I go
unto.** Ju 24. **my exceeding joy.** Heb. the gladness of
my joy. Ps 71:23. Is *61:10. Hab *3:17, 18. Ro 5:11.
upon. Ps 57:8. 71:22. 81:2. 2 S 6:5. Re 5:8. **O God.**
Ps 42:6.

5. **Why.** ✓53, 2 S +1:19. Mt 26:38. Mk ▶14:34. **cast
down.** Ps 42:5, 11. **soul.** Heb. *nephesh*, Ge +34:3.
Ps 63:1. 88:3. **within me.** Jb +*14:22. Ps *42:6. **health.**
✓96F2, Ge +4:10. *Yeshuoth,* "salvations," or deliverances: see Ps 44:4. Ps 3:2, 8. 42:5n. **countenance.**
✓171Q, Ge +3:19. Ps *42:5n.

PSALM 44

*The psalmist acknowledges the former mercies of
God and resolves to trust in him, 1-8; complains of
being left under grievous distresses and persecutions,
9-16; professes integrity under sufferings, 17-22; and
earnestly prays for speedy deliverance, 23-26.*

(Title.) A.M. 3294. B.C. 710. **for the sons.** Ps 42,
title.

1. **have heard.** Ps 22:31. 71:18. *78:3-7. 105:1, 2.
*145:4. Ex *12:24-27. 13:14, 15. Is ✓38:19. Jl 1:3. **in
the times.** Nu 21:14-16, 27-30. Jb 8:8, 9. 15:17-19. **of
old.** Mi +5:2 (✚S#6924h).

2. **drive out.** Ps *78:55. 80:8. 105:44. 135:10-12.
136:17-22. Ex 15:17, 19. 34:11. Dt *7:1. Jsh 10:42.
11:23. 21:43. Ne 9:22-27. **how thou didst afflict,** etc.
Or, rather, "how thou didst afflict the peoples (of Canaan), and madest them (the Hebrews) to shoot forth;"
shalach is to send forth in any manner and is applied
to a vine spreading its roots, etc. Ps 89:9. Je 17:8.
Ezk 17:6; and this sense is parallel with *plantest* in
the former line. Ex 23:28. Nu 13:32. Jsh 10:11. 24:12.
1 S 5:6, 7.

3. **For.** Dt *4:37, 38. *8:11, 12, 14, 17, 18. 9:5, 6.
Jsh *24:12. Zc 4:6. 2 C 4:7. **thy right hand.** ✓22A15B,
Ps +18:35. Ps 17:7. 20:6. 74:11. Ex 15:6. Is 63:12.

light. Ps 42:5, 11. 80:16. **because.** Nu 14:8. Dt *7:7,
8. 1 S 12:22. Ml 1:2, 3. Ro 9:10-15.

4. **my King.** Ps *74:12. 89:18. 149:2. 2 Ch 12:8. Is
*33:22. 43:15. Ac 27:23. **command.** Ps 42:8. Mk 1:25,
26, 31, 41. 9:25. **deliverances.** Ps 3:2, 8. 9:14. 13:5.
*43:5.

5. **Through thee.** Ps 18:39-42. 118:10-13. Is 41:14-
16. Ph *4:13. **push.** Dt *33:17. 1 K 22:11. Da 8:4.
tread. Ps 60:12. 91:13. 108:13. Is 41:14, 15. Zc 10:5.
Ro 16:20mg.

6. **not trust.** Ps *20:7. *33:16, 17. 125:1. 1 S 17:39,
45. 2 Ch 32:8. Ho *1:7. **bow.** ✓121S1, Ge +49:10.
By Metonymy of the Adjunct, whereby the sign is
put for the thing signified, bow is put for military science, of which the bow and sword were the signs.
sword. ✓171I1. Synecdoche of the Species B625. A
species of a thing is put for the whole genus; a bow
or spear are put for all kinds of arms. For other instances
of this figure see Ps 46:9. Zc 10:4.

7. **But.** Ps 140:7. 144:10. Jsh 1:5. 10:8-10, 42. 11:6.
*23:9, 10. Jg 2:18. 7:4-7. 1 S 7:8-12. 14:6-10. 17:47.
2 S 7:10. **put them.** Ps *40:14. 83:1-18. 132:18.

8. **In God.** Ps *34:2. Is 45:25. Je *9:24. Ro 2:17.
15:17. 1 C 1:29-31. **praise.** Ps 115:1, 18. **for ever.**
Heb. *olam,* Ex +*12:24.

9. **thou hast.** Ps 43:2. 60:1, 10. 74:1. 80:12, 13. 88:14.
89:38-45. ◐*94:14. 108:11. Je 33:24-26. La *3:31, 32.
Ro +*11:1-6. **goest not.** Nu 14:42.

10. **Thou.** Ps 78:9. Le *26:14, 17, 36, 37. Dt 28:25.
Jsh 7:8, *12. 1 S 4:17. 31:1-7. **spoil.** ✓63A2, 2 S +6:6.
Supply ellipsis (our goods). Ps 89:41. Is 10:6, 14. Je
15:13. 20:8.

11. **given.** Je 12:3. Ro *8:36. **like sheep appointed
for meat.** Heb. as sheep of meat. Ps 14:4. **scattered.**
Ps 60:1. Dt *4:27. 28:64. 2 K 17:6. Is 11:11, 12. Je
32:37. Ezk 34:12. Lk *21:24.

12. **sellest.** Dt 32:30. Is *50:1. 52:3, 4. Je *15:13.
for nought. Heb. without riches. Ps 112:3. 119:14.
increase. Ne 5:8-12. Re 18:13. **thy wealth.** ✓63A2,
2 S +6:6.

13. **makest.** Ps 79:4. 80:6. 89:51. Je 24:9. Ezk 36:19-
23. **scorn.** Ps 123:3, 4. Je 48:27.

14. **byword.** Dt *28:37. 1 K 9:7. 2 Ch 7:20. Je *24:9.
shaking. Ps 22:7. 2 K 19:21. Jb 16:4. Is 37:22. La
2:15-17.

15. **confusion.** Jsh 7:7-9. Ezr 9:6. Je 3:25. **covered.**
Ps 69:7. 71:13. 89:45. Je 51:51.

16. **For the.** Ps 74:18, 22, 23. 79:12. Is 37:3, 4,
17, 23, 24. **reproacheth.** Ps 69:9. 119:42. 1 S 11:2.
Pr 27:11. **blasphemeth.** Nu 15:30. **enemy.** Ps 8:2.
avenger. Ps 8:2. Je 5:9, 29.

17. **All this.** Da *9:13. **yet.** ver. 20. Ps 9:17. Dt
6:12. 8:14. Is 17:10. Je ◐*2:32. **dealt.** Je ◐*31:32.
Ezk 16:59. 20:37. Ac *24:16.

18. **heart.** Ps *119:2. Pr +*4:23. **turned back.** Ps
78:57. 125:5. 1 K *15:5. Jb *34:27. Je *11:10. Zp *1:6.
Lk +*8:13. 17:32. He *10:39. **steps.** *or,* goings. Ps
+37:31mg. 119:3. **declined.** Ps 119:51, 157. Jb *23:11,
12. Pr *4:23. 1 C ✓15:58. 1 Th 2:10.

19. **Though.** Ps 38:8. 60:1-3. Je 14:17. **in the.** Ps
74:13, 14. Is 27:1. 34:13, 14. 35:7. Ezk 29:3. Re 12:9.
13:2, 11-13. 16:10. **shadow of death.** Ps *23:4. Jb *3:5.
*10:21, 22. Mt *4:16.

20. **If we.** ver. 17. Ps 7:3-5. Jb 31:5, etc. **stretched.**
Ps 68:31. Ex 9:29. 1 K 8:22. Jb 11:13.

21. **Shall.** Ps *139:1, etc. Jb *31:4, 14. 34:21, 22.

Je *17:10. 23:24. **knoweth.** Ps *90:8. Jsh 22:22, 23.
1 S 2:3. 1 K 8:39. Pr 5:21. *15:11. Ec 12:14. Ezk
*11:5. Jn 21:17. Ro 2:16. 1 C *4:5. He *4:12, 13. Re
2:23.

22. **Yea.** Ro ▶8:36. **killed.** ver. 11. Ps 79:2, 3. 1 S
22:17-19. 1 K 19:10. Mt *5:10-12. Jn 15:21. 16:2, 3.
Ro 8:35, 37. 1 C 4:9. 15:30, 31. 1 P 4:14. Re 11:3-9.
17:6. **for.** ƒ181E, Ge +3:24.

23. **Awake.** Ps 7:6. 12:5. 35:23. 59:4, 5. 78:65.
◗*121:3, 4. Is ◗*40:27, 28. 51:9. Mk 4:38. 8:24-26.
cast. ver. 9. Ps 74:1. 88:14. **for ever.** Jb +4:20
(✻S#5331h).

24. **Wherefore.** Ps 10:1, 11. 13:1. 43:1-4. Dt 32:20.
Jb 13:24. **forgettest.** Ps 74:19, 23. Ex 2:23, 24. Is 40:27,
28. 49:14-16. Re *6:9, 10. **affliction.** Ps 9:13. 25:8.
31:17. Ex 3:7. **oppression.** T#1631. Ps 17:8, 9. 42:9.
119:121, 122, +134. Ex 3:9. Dt 26:7. Is 19:19, 20.
38:14.

25. **For our.** Ps 66:11, 12. La 4:5. **soul.** Heb. *ne-phesh*, Ge +34:3. **bowed down.** T#1395. Pr 2:8. Is
51:23. La 3:20mg. **to the dust.** Ps 7:5. 18:42. 22:15,
29. *119:25.

26. **Arise.** ƒ22C21, Nu +10:35. **for our help.** Heb.
a help for us. Ps 63:7. **redeem.** Ps *26:11. *130:7, 8.

PSALM 45

*The excellency, dignity, and deity of the Messiah,
with his victories and dominion, 1-8. The bride is invited to forsake her father's house, that Christ might
delight in her, 10-12. Her glory and excellency by his
graces, which shall be remembered and praised forever, 13-17.*

(*Title.*) **To the chief.** Or, rather, "To the chief musician upon the hexachords, a didactic ode for the sons
of Korah, and a song of loves." *Shoshannim* most probably denotes hexachords, or six-stringed instruments,
from *shesh*, "six;" hence the Persian *shashta*, a six-
stringed lute. This Psalm is supposed by some to be
an epithalamium, or nuptial song, on the marriage of
Solomon with Pharaoh's daughter; but with what propriety could Solomon be described as "fairer than the
children of men, a mighty warrior, a victorious conqueror," and a prince whose "throne is for ever and
ever"? One greater than Solomon is here; and the
person described is none other than the Messiah, as
is acknowledged by many Jewish writers. The Targum
on ver. 3 says, "Thy beauty, *malka mesheecha*, O King
Messiah, is greater than the children of men;" and
the apostle expressly quotes it as such, He 1:8, 9. It
was probably written by David after Nathan's prophetic
address, 1 Ch 17:27. **Shoshanim.** Ps 69, 80, titles.
Maschil. *or*, of instruction. **A Song.** SS 1:1, 2, etc. Is
5:1. Ep 5:32.

1. **is inditing.** Heb. **boileth**, *or*, bubbleth up. Jb
32:18-20. Pr 16:23. Mt √12:35. **a good.** Ps 49:3. Jb
33:3. 34:4. Pr 8:6-9. **touching.** Ps 2:6. 24:7-10. 110:1,
2. SS 1:12. Is 32:1, 2. Mt 25:34. 27:37. **tongue.** 2 S
*23:2. 2 P √1:21.

2. **Thou art.** ƒ105, Ml +4:2. **fairer.** 1 S 16:12. SS
2:3. *5:10-16. Is *33:17. Da 1:15. Zc 9:17. Mt 17:2.
Jn *1:14. Col 1:15-18. He *1:3, 4. 7:26. Re 1:13-18.
grace. Pr 22:11. Is *50:4. Lk *4:22. Jn 1:16. *7:46.
He 12:27, 28. **thy lips.** Jn 7:46. **God.** Ps 21:6. 72:17-
19. Ph 2:9-11. **for ever.** Heb. *olam*, Ex +*12:24.

3. **Gird.** ƒ22C27, Ps +18:32. Is *49:2. 63:1-6. He

*4:12. Re 1:16. 19:15, 21. **O most mighty.** ƒ22D2C,
Ex +15:2. Is *9:+6, 7. Ac +*10:36. Ro 14:9. **glory.**
Ps 21:5. 96:6. 104:1. 145:5, 12. He *1:3. 8:1. Ju *25.

4. **ride,** etc. Heb. prosper thou, ride thou. Re 6:2.
19:11. **prosperously.** Ps *110:2, 3. Is *53:10. 1 Th 1:5.
2:13. 2 Th 3:1. **because.** Ps 60:4. Jn *1:17. √14:6. **meekness.** Zp +*2:3. Zc √9:9. Mt √11:29. 12:19, 20. 2 C
10:1. **right.** Ps 2:9. 21:8, 9. 65:5. 110:5, 6. Is 59:17,
18. √63:1-6. Lk 19:27. 2 Th √1:8, 9. Re 6:16, 17.
+*11:18. *19:17-21. *20:15.

5. **Thine.** Ps 21:12. 38:2. Nu 24:8. Zc 9:13, 14. **sharp.**
Ps 2:1-9. Is 49:2. Lk 19:42-44. 20:18, 19. Ac *2:37,
41. 5:33. 7:54. **people.** Ps 22:27. 66:3, 4. Lk *19:27.
Ac 4:4. 5:14. 6:7. Ro 15:18, 19. 2 C *10:4.

6. **throne.** Ps 47:8. +*89:29, 36, 37. *93:2. *145:13.
Da √2:44. Lk *1:32, 33. He +√J1:8. ƒ22D3C2. Anthropomorphism B892. Christ is spoken of as having a
throne. For other instances of this figure see Is *16:5.
Mt +*19:28. He √1:8. *4:16. 8:1. Re *3:21. **O God.**
Heb. *Elohim*, S#430h. ver. 2, 7. Ge 1:1. 6:13, *18.
17:1-8. +19:29. 50:24. Ex +2:24. Nu *23:19. 2 S √23:1-
5. Jb +19:26. Is *9:6, 7. *40:9, 10. *45:22, 23. Je
√23:5, 6. Jn √1:1. 1 T *3:16. He √6:17, 18. **for ever.**
Heb. *olam*, Ps +21:4. Ps 10:16. +*72:5. *89:4. 110:4.
2 S 7:13. Is *9:7. Lk √1:33. Re √11:15. **and ever.** Ps
+9:18 (✻S#5703h). **the sceptre.** ƒ22D5R, Ps +2:9.
Ps 72:1, etc. 2 S √23:3-5. Je *33:15, 16. Re 19:11.
kingdom. Ps *47:7. 1 C √15:24n, 25n. Re *19:16.

7. **Thou.** Ps *33:5. 99:4. Mt 3:15. Lk 23:47. 2 C
√5:21. He 1:9. 7:26. 1 J 3:5. **hatest.** Ps *5:4. 101:3,
4, 8. Mt √7:23. Lk *13:27. Re *21:27. **God.** *or*, O
God. Heb. *Elohim*, S#430h. ver. 6. Ps 89:26. Is 61:1. Jn *20:17.
Ep 1:3. **hath.** Ps 89:20. Ge=49:25, 26. Le 8:12. 1 S
16:13. 1 K 1:39, 40. 19:16. Is *61:1-3. Lk 3:22. 4:18-
21. Jn *3:34. 1 J *2:20, 27. **anointed.** ƒ22D5L. Anthropomorphism B894. Oil or anointing is attributed to
God. For other instances of this figure see Ps 2:2. Is
61:1. Da 9:25, 26. Jn 1:41mg. 4:25. Ac 10:38. He 1:9.
1 J 2:27. **oil.** Ps *21:6. 23:5. 89:20. 92:10. Le 8:12.
1 K 1:39, 40. Ac 2:28. **gladness.** Ps *21:6. Is *53:10,
11. Lk *15:10. **above.** Jn 1:16. Ro *8:29. Ep 4:7. Ph
*2:9. Col *1:18, 19. He 2:14.

8. **All.** Pr 27:9. SS 1:*3, 13. 3:6. 4:6, 13, 14. 5:1,
5, 13. Mt 2:11. Jn 19:39. 2 C 2:14-16. **garments.** Ps
133:1, 2. SS 4:16. **smell of.** *or*, are. ƒ119, Ge +49:9.
myrrh. Jn *19:39. **cassia.** Ex 30:23, 24. **ivory.** ver.
15. 1 K 22:39. Am 3:15. Jn 14:2. **whereby.** Ps *16:11.
He *12:2.

9. **Kings.** ver. 13. Ps 72:10. SS *6:8, 9. 7:1. Is 49:23.
60:10, 11. 2 C 6:18. Re 21:24. **upon.** 1 K 2:9, 19.
queen. SS 4:8-11. Jn 3:29. Ep *5:26, 27. Re *19:7,
8. 21:2, 9. **gold.** 1 K 10:11. Jb 22:24. **of Ophir.** 1 K
+9:28n. Jb +8:18n.

10. **Hearken.** SS 2:10-13. Is 55:1-3. 2 C 6:17, 18.
7:1. **forget.** Ge 2:24. 12:1. Dt 21:13. 33:9. Mt *10:37.
19:29. Lk 14:26. 2 C 5:16. 6:17.

11. **So shall.** SS 1:8, 12-16. 2:2, 14. 4:1-5, 7, 9,
10. 6:4. 7:1-10. Is 62:4, 5. Zp *3:17. Ep 5:26, 27.
desire. Ps 27:4. 73:25. SS *7:10. Is 62:5. 1 P 1:8. **Lord.**
ver. 6. Is 54:5. Je *23:5, 6. Jn +√20:28. Ac 10:36. Ro
14:9. Ph *2:10, 11. 3:8. **worship.** Ps *2:12. *95:6. Is
*54:5. Lk *24:52. Jn *4:21, 22. √5:23. Re *5:8-14.

12. **And the.** Is 23:17, 18. Ac 21:3-6. **daughter.**
ƒ155E5, Nu +21:25. **with.** Ps *72:10. Is 60:6, 7. Mt
2:11. **rich.** Ps 22:29. Is 49:23. 60:3, 10, 11. **favor.** Heb.

face. ℐ171Q, Ge +3:19. Ps 119:58mg. Jb +11:19mg.

13. king's. ver. 9, 10. SS *7:1. Is *61:10. 1 P 2:9. Re *19:7, 8. all glorious. 1 S *16:7. Lk 11:40. Ro 2:29. 2 C 5:17. 1 P *3:3, 4. within. Le 10:18. Young notes "in the inside of the palace, not 'inwardly,' in her mind, as most critics suppose, but which the original text cannot possibly mean." Mt ◑23:26-28. Lk 11:40. Ro *2:29. her clothing. ver. 9. Pr 31:22. Mt 5:16. 22:11, 12. Ro *3:22. √13:14. Re 3:18.

14. She. SS *1:4. Jn *17:24. 2 C 11:2. be brought. Ps 43:4. SS 3:11. Ju 24. raiment. Ex 28:39. Jg 5:30. Mt *22:11. virgins. Ge 24:16 (✻S#1330h). SS 1:3, 5. 2:7. 5:8, 9. 6:1, 8, 13. 8:13. Re *14:1-4.

15. With gladness. ℐ96F2, Ge +4:10. Is +*35:10. +*51:11. +*55:12, 13. +*60:19, 20. 61:10. Lk *15:32. Ju √24. Re 7:15-17. they shall. Is 56:5. Jn +*14:3. Re 3:12, 21.

16. Instead. Ps *22:30. Mt +*19:29. Mk +*10:29, 30. Ph *3:7, 8. children. Is *49:21, 22. +*54:1-5. √60:1-5. Ro 11:19. Ga 4:26, 27. princes. 1 P *2:9. Re *1:6. +*5:10. √20:6. in all the earth. Mt +*5:5.

17. I will. Ps 22:30, 31. √72:17-19. 145:4-7. Is *59:21. Ml *1:11. Mt 26:13. 1 C 11:26. generations. Ge +9:12. therefore. Ps *72:17. SS 6:9. Is √61:9. √62:1-3. the people. Is √41:9. Zc √10:6. Ro +*11:1, 2. for ever. Heb. olam, Ps +21:4. and ever. Ps +9:18 (✻S#5707h).

PSALM 46

The psalmist exults in the assurance of protection and consolation from God, 1-5; recounts his wondrous works in Israel's behalf, 6-9; and while God demands submission from all the earth, Israel declares her confidence in him, 10, 11.

(Title.) A.M. 3108. B.C. 896. for. or, of. the sons. Ps 84, 85, 87, titles. Alamoth. or, virgins. 1 Ch 15:20. It has been argued ably and shown conclusively that the psalm titles are generally misplaced: this title should be a subscription for the preceding Psalm 45, as the reference to "virgins" would indicate, such being in harmony with the theme of the preceding psalm. In the two independent psalms found in Scripture, Is 38:9-20, and Hab ch. 3, the pattern (1) superscription, or title proper; (2) the body of the psalm itself; (3) the subscription is clearly displayed. The phrase "To the chief musician" is the subscription of the preceding psalm, not the first line of a psalm. These matters were first discovered by Dr. James W. Thirtle and set forth in his *The Titles of the Psalms.*

1. refuge. ver. 7, 11. Ps *62:7, 8. 91:1-9. *142:5. Dt *33:27. Pr *14:26. *18:10. Lk 13:34. He *6:18. a very. Ps *145:18. Ge 22:14. Dt *4:7. 2 S 22:17-20. in trouble. Ps 60:11.

2. will. Ps *23:4. *27:3. Mt *7:24, 25. *8:24-26. Ro *8:31. He *13:6. though. Ge 7:11, 12. Lk *21:9-11, 25-28, 33. 2 P *3:10-14. mountains. Mt *21:21. midst of the sea. Heb. heart of the seas. ℐ144A7, Ex +15:8. Ex 15:8. Ezk 27:4mg.

3. the waters. Ps *18:4. 65:7. *93:3, 4. Jb 38:11. Is 5:30. *17:12, 13. Je 5:22. Mt *7:25. Re *17:15. mountains. Ps 114:4-7. Jg 5:4, 5. 1 K 19:11. Jb 9:5, 6. Je 4:24. Mi *1:4. Na 1:5. Re 16:20.

4. a river. Ps *23:2. *36:8, 9. Is 8:6, 7. 48:18. Ezk 47:1-12. Jn 7:37-39. Re *22:1-3. city. Ps 48:1, 8. 87:3. 2 Ch *6:6. Is 37:35, 36. 60:14. He *12:22. Re *21:2,

3, 10. holy. Dt 12:11, 12. most. Ps *91;1. 92:1, 8. Ec 5:8. Mi 6:6.

5. God is. Ps *68:18. Dt 23:14. Is *12:6. Ezk 43:7, 9. Ho 11:9. Jl 2:27. Zp 3:15. Zc 2:5, 10, 11. 8:3. Mt √18:20. Re *2:1. she. Ps 62:2, 6. 112:6. 125:1. Mt 16:16, 18. God shall help. Zc +*12:8. +*14:3. and that, etc. Heb. when the morning appeareth. Ps *30:5. +*49:14, 15. +*59:16. 88:13. +*101:8. 110:3. 143:8. Ex 14:24, 27. 2 S 23:4. Jb 7:21. Is 8:20mg. +*17:14. 21:11, 12. +*26:19n. Ho 5:15. *6:3. Zp 3:5. Lk *18:8. Ro 13:12. 2 P 1:19. Re +*2:28. 22:16.

6. heathen. Ps 2:1-4. 76:3. 83:2-8. 2 Ch 14:9-13. 20:1, 20-24. Is 8:9, 10. 10:26-34. 37:21-36. kingdoms. Is 14:12-16. earth. Ps 68:8. 97:5. Jsh *2:9, 11, 24. Is 64:1, 2. Am 9:5, 13. Na 1:5. Hab 3:5, 6, 10, 11. 2 P 3:10-12. Re 6:13, 14. 14:6-8. 20:11.

7. Lord. ℐ53, 2 S 1:19. ver. 11. Ex 33:14, 15. Nu 14:9. 2 Ch *13:12. Is 8:10. *43:2. Mt 1:23. *28:20. Ro *8:31. 2 T 4:22. Jacob. Ge 32:28. our refuge. Heb. an high place for us. Ps +9:9mg. 59:9mg.

8. Come. Ps 66:5. 92:4-6. 111:2, 3. Nu 23:23. desolations. Ps 66:3. Ex 10:7. 12:30. 14:30, 31. Jsh 11:20. 2 Ch 20:23, 24. Is 24:1. 34:2, etc. 45:7. Am +*3:6. Na 1:4, 5, 8.

9. maketh. Is *2:4. 11:9. 60:18. Mi 4:3, 4. breaketh. ℐ22D2C, Ex +15:3. Ps *76:3-6. Ezk *39:3, 9, 10. bow. ℐ17I1I, Ps +44:6. burneth. Jsh 11:6, 9. Mi 5:10.

10. Be still. Ps 37:7mg. Ex 14:13. Is *30:7, 15. 41:1. Hab √2:20. Zc 2:13. know. Ps *83:18. 100:3. Ex 18:11. 1 S 17:46. 1 K 18:36. 2 K 19:19. I will be. T#277. Ps 21:13. 57:5. 86:9. 104:31. 145:10-12. Nu 14:20, 21. 1 Ch *29:11. Is 2:11, *17. 5:16. Ezk 38:23. Lk 10:18. Jn 11:40. 1 J 3:8. Re *15:3, 4.

11. with us. 1 S 17:47. the God. ver. 1, 7. Ps 48:3. Dt 33:27. Je 16:19.

PSALM 47

The people are excited to rejoice in God, the universal sovereign, who has given Israel victory and inheritance, 1-4. The ascension and kingdom of Christ are celebrated with fervent praises and the conversion of the nations and their princes predicted, 5-9.

(Title.) A psalm. This psalm is supposed to have been composed by Solomon on the removal of the ark into the temple, 2 Ch ch. 7. for. or, of. Ps 46, title.

1. clap. Ps 98:8. 2 K 11:12. Is *55:12. shout. ver. 5. Ps 98:4. 1 S 10:24. 2 S 6:15. 2 Ch 13:15. Ezr 3:11-13. Je 31:7. Zp 3:14. Zc 4:7. 9:9. Lk 19:37-40. Re 19:1, 2.

2. Lord most high. Ex 15:26. is terrible. Ps 65:5. 66:3-5. 68:35. 76:12. *99:3. 145:6. Dt *7:21. 28:58. Ne 1:5. Na 1:6, 7. Re 6:16, 17. a great King. ℐ22I2, Ex +15:16. ver. 7. Ps 22:27-29. 95:3. 102:16. Ne +*9:6. Is *40:3. Je √23:5, 6. Da √7:13, 14. Zc 2:10. 12:10. √14:9. Ml *1:14. Mt 28:18. Ph *2:9-11.

3. subdue. Ps 18:47. 81:14. Dt +33:29mg. Jsh 21:44. Je +20:11. Ph 3:21. 1 P 2:25. our feet. Ps 110:1-3. Jsh 10:24, 25. Is 49:23. 1 C *15:25. Re 2:27.

4. choose. Dt 11:12. Je 3:19. Ezk 20:6. Mt 25:34. 1 C 3:22, 23. inheritance. Ps +*16:5, 6. Dt 32:9. Jsh 13:33. Ep *1:18. 1 P *1:4. excellency. Ps 16:3. Is *60:15. Am 6:8. 8:7. Na 2:2. whom. Dt 7:6-8. 33:3. Ho 14:4. Ml 1:2. Ep *2:4, 5. 1 J 4:9, 10.

5. God. Ps 24:7-10. 68:17-19, 24, 25, 33. Lk *24:51-

53. Ac *1:5-11. Ep 4:8-10. 1 T 3:16. He *9:24. **gone up.** 1 Th 4:16. **with a shout.** Ps 78:65. Nu 23:21. 2 S *6:15. 1 Ch 15:28. **sound.** Ps 81:3. 150:3. Nu 10:1-10. Jsh 6:5. 1 Ch 15:24. 16:42. 1 C 15:52. 1 Th *4:16. Re 8:6, etc. 11:15.

6. **praises.** ♪96F2, Ge +4:10. **to God.** Ps 96:1, 2. ch. 117. *149:1-3. Ex 15:21. 1 Ch 16:9. 29:20. Is 12:4-6. Ep *5:18-20. **our King.** Ps 145:1. Is 33:22. Zc 9:9. Mt 25:34. 27:37. **sing praises.** ♪72, Ex +32:16.

7. **King.** ver. 2, 8. Zc *14:9. Re √11:15. **sing.** 1 C *14:14, 15. Col *3:16. **with understanding.** or, every one that hath understanding. Ps 107:43. Dt 32:29. Lk 19:42.

8. **reigneth.** Ps 22:27-29. 93:1. *96:10. 97:1. 99:1. 110:6. 1 Ch 16:31. Is 40:9, 10. 1 C +*15:24n, 25n. Re √11:15. *19:6. **God sitteth.** ♪22D3C1, Ps +11:4. Ps +*45:6. He +√1:8. **throne.** Ps 9:4. +*45:6, 7. 48:1. 89:14. 94:20. He *4:16. Re 20:11.

9. **The princes,** etc. or, The voluntary of the people are gathered unto the people of, etc. Ps 72:7-9. *110:2, 3. Ge +√49:10. Is 11:10. 60:4, 5. 66:19, 20. Ro 11:25. **the God.** Ge 17:7, 8. Ex *3:6, 15. Is 41:8-10. Mt 22:32. Ro 4:11, 12. Ga *3:29. **shields.** Ps 89:18mg. Pr 30:5. **he is.** Ps 46:10. Re 21:24.

PSALM 48

The praises of God are celebrated in connection with the beauty and security of Zion and the deliverances wrought for her, 1-8. Israel praises God and rejoices in him and in her privileges, 9-14.

(Title.) A.M. 3489. B.C. 515. **Song.** This psalm is supposed to have been sung at the dedication of the second temple; though some think it was composed on the victory obtained by Jehoshaphat, 2 Ch ch. 20. Ps 30, title. **for.** or, of. Ps 46, title.

1. **Great.** ♪22I2, Ex +15:16. Ps 86:10. 87:3. 99:3, 4. *145:3. 147:5. **greatly.** Ps 89:1-7. Ne *9:5. He 2:12. Re *15:3, 4. 19:5. **city.** Ps 46:4. 65:1. 78:68. *87:3. √102:13, 16. Zc *14:8, 9, 11. He *12:22. Re *21:2, 10-22. **mountain.** Ps 47:8. 99:9. Is *2:2, 3. 27:13. Je *31:23. Ob 17. Mi 4:1. Zc √8:3. Mt 24:15.

2. **Beautiful.** Ps *50:2. Je 3:19. La 2:15. Da 8:9. 11:16. **joy.** Is 60:15-20. 66:10. Ezk 20:6. Ml 3:12. He 12:22. **on the sides.** Is 14:13. **the city.** Ps 47:7, 8. Ml 1:14. Mt *5:35.

3. **God is known.** Ps 76:1-5. 125:1. 2 Ch 12:7. 14:9-15. 20:1, etc. Is 4:5, 6. 37:33-36. Zc 2:4, 5.

4. **lo.** Ps 83:2-8. 2 S 10:6, 14, 16-19. Is 7:1. 8:8-10. 10:8. 29:5-8. Re 17:12-14. 19:19, 20. 20:8, 9. **they passed.** Re *21:24.

5. **were.** Ex 14:25. 2 K 7:6, 7. 19:35-37.

6. **Fear.** Ex 15:15, 16. Is 13:6-8. Da 5:6. **pain.** Is 21:3. Je 30:6, 7. Ho 13:13. **travail.** Ge 16:11. Mt +√24:8.

7. **breakest.** Ezk *27:25, 26. **ships.** 1 K 22:48. 2 Ch 20:36. Is 2:16. **Tarshish.** Ge +10:4. **east.** Ps 78:26. Ge 41:6, 23, 27. Je *18:17.

8. **As we.** Ps 44:1, 2. 78:3-6. Is 38:19. **city of the Lord.** See on ver. 1, 2. Ps +*101:8. Is 60:21. Zc *2:12. **God.** Ps 46:5. *87:5. Is 2:2. *14:32. Mi 4:1. Mt 16:18. **for ever.** Heb. olam, Ex +*12:24.

9. **thought.** Ps *26:3. 77:10, 11. 104:34. 105:5, 6. **lovingkindness.** Ps *40:10. 63:3. SS 1:4. Lk *22:19, 20. **in the midst.** ♪144A6, Ge +45:6. Ps 63:2. 77:12-14. 2 Ch 20:5-13. Is *26:8.

10. **According.** Ps 67:2. 113:3. 138:2-4. Ex *3:13-15. 34:5-7. Dt *28:58. Jsh 7:9. Ml *1:11, 14. **thy right.** Ps 11:7. 45:7. 99:4. 145:17. Re 19:2, 11.

11. **rejoice.** Ps *149:2. **daughters.** Ps 97:8. SS 1:5. 2:7. 3:5. 5:16. Is 37:22. Zc *9:9. Lk 23:28. **because.** Ps 58:10. 137:8, 9. Dt +32:43. Jg *5:31. 2 Ch 20:26, 27. Re *15:4. 16:5-7. 18:20. 19:1-3.

12. **Walk.** Ne 12:31-40. Mt *24:1, 2. **tell.** Ps 78:4, 6, 7. Is *33:18-20. He 12:22.

13. **Mark ye well.** Heb. Set your heart to. Ps 62:10. Ex 7:23. 1 S +4:20mg. 2 S 13:20mg. Jb 7:17. Pr 22:17. 24:32mg. 27:23mg. **her bulwarks.** Ps 10:10mg. 122:7. Is 26:1. 59:19. **consider.** or, raise up. Is 58:12. Am *9:11. Ac *15:14-16. **that ye.** Ps 71:18. 78:4. Dt 11:19. Jl 1:3.

14. **this God.** Ps 16:2. *31:14. *73:24, 26. La 3:24. **our God.** Ps 118:28. Ge 17:7. Jsh 24:18. Ro 8:15. Ga 4:6. Re 21:3. **for ever.** Heb. olam, Ps +21:4. **and ever.** Ps +9:18 (❋S#5703h). **guide.** Ps *23:3, 4. *25:9. +*32:8. *73:24. Ge 48:15. Pr √3:5, 6. *8:20. Is *58:11. Je 3:4. Jn *16:13. **unto death.** 1 C +*15:55.

PSALM 49

The psalmist calls on all mankind to attend to his instructions, 1-4. He shows that the righteous have no cause to fear in evil times, 5. He exposes the vanity of trusting in riches, 6-13. He contrasts the condition of the prosperous ungodly man with that of the believer, especially in respect of death and the resurrection, 14-20.

(Title.) A.M. cir. 3464. B.C. cir. 540. **A Psalm.** This psalm was probably written by one of the descendants of the sons of Korah during the Babylonian captivity. **for.** or, of. Ps 46, 48, titles.

1. **Hear.** Ps 34:11. 78:1. Pr *1:20-23. Mt *11:15. 13:9. Re 2:7, 11, 17, 29. **inhabitants.** Ps 50:1. Is 49:6. Ml 1:11. Mt 28:19, 20. Ro 3:29. 10:18.

2. **Both low.** Ps 62:9. 1 S 2:7, 8. Jb 34:19. Pr *22:2. Je 5:4, 5. Ja 1:9-11. *2:1-7. Re 6:15-17. **and poor.** ♪174, Ge +18:27.

3. **mouth.** Dt 32:2. Jb 33:3, 33. Pr 4:1, 2. *8:6-11. 22:17, 20, 21. Lk 4:22. 2 T √3:15-17. **wisdom.** ♪96F2, Ge +4:10. **meditation.** Ps *19:14. 45:1. 104:34. Mt *12:34, 35.

4. **incline.** Ps 78:2. Mt *13:34, 35. **parable.** Nu +23:7n. Ezk 20:49. Mt 13:11-15. **will open.** Da +*12:4, 9. **dark saying.** Ps 78:2. Nu +12:8. Pr 1:6. Da 8:23. Lk 12:3. 2 C 3:12.

5. **Wherefore.** Ps *27:1, 2. 46:1, 2. Is 41:10, 11. Ac 27:24. Ro *8:33, 34. Ph 1:28. **days.** Pr 24:10. Am 5:13. Ep 5:16. **iniquity.** Ps 38:4. Pr 5:22. Ho 7:2. **heels.** Ps 22:16. 56:6, 7. Ge 49:17. 1 S 26:20.

6. **trust.** Ps *52:7. *62:10. Jb *31:24, 25, 28. Pr 10:15. 23:5. Mk *10:24. 1 T *6:17. **boast.** Est 5:11. Je *9:23. Ezk 28:4, 5. Ho 12:8. Lk 12:19.

7. **None.** Ex 32:33. **give.** Mt *16:26. *20:28. 1 T *2:6. 1 P *1:18. **redeem.** ♪147C, Ge +3:4. **ransom.** 1 S +12:3 (❋S#3724h).

8. **the redemption.** Ex 21:30. Jb *36:18, 19. **soul.** Heb. nephesh, Ge +12:13. ver. 15, 18. **is precious.** Ps 72:14. 116:15. 139:17. 1 S 18:30mg. Jb *36:18, 19. Is 28:16. 1 P *1:18, 19. 2:7. 2 P 1:1, 4. **it ceaseth.** Ps 36:3. Ge 11:8. 18:11. 41:49. Dt 32:22. **for ever.** Heb. olam, Ex +*12:24.

9. **That he.** Ps *89:48. Pr *10:2. 11:4. Ec 8:8. Zc

1:5. Lk *16:22, 23. **for ever**. Jb +4:20 (❋S#5331h).
For a hidden indefinite time (Young). **not see**. Ps
+*16:10. 49:15. Jn *8:51, 52. Ac 2:27, 31. 13:33, 35-
37.

10. **wise**. Ec *2:16-21. 9:1, 2. Ro 5:12-14. He
+*9:27. **fool**. Ps 73:22. 92:6, 7. 94:8. Pr 12:1. 30:2.
Je 10:8. **leave**. ver. 17. Ps 17:14. *39:6. Pr *11:4. Ec
*2:18, 19, 21, 26. 5:13-16. Je 17:11. Lk 12:20. 1 T
+*6:6-10.

11. **Their inward**, etc. Or, "Their grave is their
house forever, their dwelling place through all generations, though their names are celebrated over countries." Ps 5:9. 64:6. Ezk 38:10. Lk 11:39. Ac 8:22.
thought. T#710. Ps +89:47 (T#726). +90:12 (T#727).
Pr +14:13 (T#479). 24:33. Is 28:15. 56:12. Am 6:3.
Lk *12:19. Ac *24:25. **houses**. ∫121J4, Ge +7:1. ∫132A,
Ge +4:23. **for ever**. Heb. *olam*, Ex +*12:24. **all generations**. Heb. generation and generation. Ps 10:6mg.
33:11mg. 45:17. **they call**. Ge 4:17. 1 S 15:12. 2 S
18:18. **lands**. Ps 83:10. 104:30. 105:35. **names**. Ge 4:17.
11:4. Jsh 19:47. 2 S *18:18.

12. **man**. Heb. *adam*. ver. 20. Ps 8:4. 11:4. 12:1.
in honor. ver. 20. Ps 37:35, 36. *39:5. 82:7. Est 1:4,
20. 6:3. Ja 1:10, 11. 1 P 1:24. **abideth**. ∫171J7. Synecdoche of the Species B631. To pass the night is used
for abiding. For another instance of this figure see Is
1:21. The word *yalin*, rendered "abideth," signifies
to lodge for a night. Man's continuance in the world,
or in honor or distinction, resembles a traveller's lodging at an inn, whence he removes in the morning;
and is frequently far more transient and evanescent.
S#3885h. Ps 25:13mg. 30:5. 55:7 (remain). 59:15
(grudge). 91:1mg. Ge 19:2. 32:13. He +*9:27. 1 J *2:17.
like. ver. 20. 28:1. 143:7. Nu +21:27. Is 14:10. **beasts**.
ver. 20. Ps 8:7. 36:6. 50:10. Ec 3:18-21. 9:12. **perish**.
or, cut off. ver. 20. Is 6:5mg.

13. **folly**. Lk *12:20. 1 C *3:19. **approve their sayings**. Heb. delight in their mouth. Ps *50:18. 51:16.
62:4. Je 44:17. Lk 11:47, 48. 16:27, 28.

14. **Like sheep**. Ps *44:11. Je *12:3. Ro *8:36. **they**.
Jb *17:13, 14. *21:13, 26. *30:23. Ec *12:7. Is *38:10,
11. **grave**. Heb. *sheol*, Ge +37:35. **death**. Jb *24:19,
20. **upright**. Ps *47:3. Da *7:22. Ml *4:3. Lk *22:30.
1 C *6:2. Re *2:26, 27. *20:4, 5. **have dominion**. Ps
+*145:13. *149:4-9. Ge +1:26. Lk *19:17. **in the morning**. Ps *30:5. +*46:5mg. +*59:16. 88:13. +*101:8.
110:3. *143:8. Is +*17:14. Ho *5:15. *6:3. Ml 3:17.
4:1-3. 2 P +*1:19. Re +*2:28. **their**. Ps *39:11. Jb
*4:21. **beauty**. or, strength. Is 45:16h. **in the grave**,
etc. or, the grave being an habitation to every one of
them. Jb *30:23. Pr 10:28. 14:32. Is +*24:21, 22. Re
+*20:5. **grave**. Heb. *sheol*, Ge +37:35. **dwelling**.
1 K 8:13. 2 Ch 6:2. Is 63:15. Hab 3:11.

15. **God**. Ps *31:5. 56:13. 73:24. Ho *13:14. Re 5:9.
*14:13. **soul**. Heb. *nephesh*, Ge +12:13. ∫121A8, Ps
+16:10. **from**. 1 C +*15:55. **power**. Heb. hand.
∫144A5, Ge +9:5. Ps 89:48. **the grave**. or, hell. Heb.
sheol, Ge +37:35. Ps +*16:10. *86:13. *89:48. **shall
receive me**. Ps *31:5. *73:24. Lk *23:46. Jn √14:3.
Ac *7:59.

16. **Be not**. ver. 5. Ps *37:1, 7. Est 3:1-6. Pr *28:12.
made rich. Lk 12:20. **glory**. Ge *31:1. Est *5:11. Re
*21:24, 26.

17. **he shall**. Jb *1:21. 27:19. Ec *5:15. Lk *12:20.
*16:24. 1 T *6:7. **his**. Is *5:14. *10:3. 1 C *15:43.

18. **while he lived**. Heb. in his life. Ps 7:5. 16:11.

17:14. 18:46. **blessed**. Dt *29:19. Ho 12:8. Lk *12:19.
soul. Heb. *nephesh*, Ge +34:3. **praise**. 1 S 25:6. Est
3:2. Ac *12:20-22. Re *13:3, 4.

19. **He**. Heb. The soul. Ec *3:21. *12:7. Lk *12:20.
*16:22, 23. **to the generation**. Ge *15:15. 1 K 16:6.
never. Ps *56:13. Jb +4:20 (❋S#5331h). *33:30. Mt
*8:12. *22:13. Ju *13. **see light**. Ps 36:9.

20. **Man**. ver. *12. Est *5:11-14. *7:10. **honor**. Pr
◖16:31. **understandeth not**. Ps *119:155. Jb *4:21.
*36:12. Pr 21:30. Is √8:20. *27:11. Mk √12:24. Lk
+*11:52. **is like**. ver. 12. Ps 32:9. *73:18, 19, 22. Nu
+21:27. Ec *3:18, 19.

PSALM 50

*The mighty God comes in awful majesty from Zion,
to judge his people in the sight of the assembled world,
1-4. He commands that the saints be gathered to him
and declares that the heavens shall declare his righteousness, 5, 6. He delights not in legal sacrifices but
in spiritual worship, 7-15. Hypocrites are rebuked and
silenced, 16-21. The ungodly are solemnly warned,
and salvation is promised to the upright, 22, 23.*

(Title.) **of Asaph**. or, for Asaph. Ps 73, 83, titles.
1 Ch 15:17. 16:37. 25:2, 6. 2 Ch 29:30.

1. **mighty God**. Heb. *El, Elohim, Jehovah*. Ps 145:3-
6. Ge 17:1. Jsh √22:22. Ne 9:6, 32. Is √9:6. Je 10:6.
*32:18, 19. **even**. 1 K 18:21, 36, 37. Is 37:20. 54:5.
hath spoken. Is 1:2. Am 3:8. **called**. Ps 49:1, 2. 113:3.
Ml 1:11. Mt *25:31, 32. He 1:1, 2.

2. **Out of Zion**. Ps 68:24. +*102:16. Is *12:6.
+*26:21. Ho +*5:15. Hab *2:20. He *12:22-26. **perfection**. Ps *48:2. 87:2, 3. 90:17. SS 5:16. Zc *9:17. **God**.
Ps 80:1. Dt +*33:2. Hab *3:3, 4. 2 C *4:6. Re 1:16.
21:23.

3. **Our**. Ps 48:14. 68:20. Re 22:20. **keep**. ver. 21.
Ps 83:1. Is *42:13, 14. *65:6, 7. **a fire**. Ps √21:9, 10.
97:3. Ex *19:18. Le 10:2. Nu *16:35. Dt 9:3. 1 K
19:11, 12. Da *7:10. Na 1:5-7. Hab 3:5. Ml *3:2, 3.
+√4:1. Mt *3:12. 1 Th 2:16. 2 Th √1:7-9. He 2:3.
10:28, 29. 12:18-21, *29. 2 P +√3:7, 13n. **it shall**. Ps
18:7-15. 97:4, 5.

4. **call**. ver. 6. Dt 4:36. 30:19. 31:28. 32:1. Is *1:2.
Mi 6:1, 2. **judge**. Ps 96:13. 98:9. Is 11:3, 4. Lk +*12:47.
Jn √5:22, 23. 2 C *5:10. 1 P *4:17. Ju 14, 15.

5. **Gather**. Mt *24:31. Jn 11:52. 1 Th √4:16, 17.
2 Th *2:1. **my saints**. Ps 97:10. Ex 8:23. Dt +*33:2,
3. Pr 2:8. Is 13:3. Jl 3:11. Zc +*14:5. Ml 3:16, 17.
1 C +*6:2, 3. 1 Th +*3:13. Ju *14. **made**. Ge *24:3-8.
Dt 26:17-19. Je *31:32. Mt 26:28. He 9:10-23. *12:22,
24. *13:20. **by sacrifice**. Je +*34:18n.

6. **heavens**. Ps *97:6. Ro 2:5. Re *16:5-7. 19:2. **God
is judge**. Ps +√94:2. **Selah**. Ps 7:3-5. +*9:16.

7. **Hear**. Ps 81:8. Is *1:18. Je 2:4, 5, 9. Mi 6:1-8.
O my. Ps 81:10-12. Ex 19:5, 6. Dt 26:17, 18. 1 S
12:22-25. **testify**. Dt 31:19-21. 2 K 17:13. Ne 9:29,
30. Mi *6:2, 3. Ml +*3:5. **I am**. Ex *20:2. 2 Ch 28:5.
Ezk 20:5, 7, 19, 20. Zc 13:9.

8. **I will not**. Ps 40:6-8. 51:16. Is *1:11, etc. Je *7:21-
23. Ho *6:6. Ro *2:25. He *10:4-10.

9. **take no**. Is 43:23, 24. Mi *6:6-8. Ac *17:25. He
10:4-6.

10. **every**. Ps 8:6-8. 104:24, 25. Ge 1:24, 25. 2:19.
8:17. 9:2, 3. 1 Ch 29:14-16. Jb 40:15, etc. Je 27:5, 6.
Da 2:38. **cattle**. Ps 104:14. Ge 31:9. Jon 4:11.

11. **know**. Ps 104:12. *147:9. Ge 1:20-22. Jb 38:41.

39:13-18, 26-30. Mt *6:26. *10:29-31. Lk 12:24. **wild.** Is 56:9. Ezk 14:15, 16. **mine.** Heb. with me.

12. **world.** Ps *24:1, 2. 115:15, 16. Ex 19:5. Dt *10:14. Jb *41:11. 1 C 10:26-28. **mine.** Ro +14:8. **fulness.** Ps 104:24. 145:15, 16. Ge 1:11, 12, 28-30. 8:17. 1 Ch 29:14.

13. **eat.** ver. 3. **flesh.** Ps 16:9. 27:2. 38:3. 56:4. **bulls.** lit. mighty ones. Ps 22:12. 68:30. 76:5. 78:25mg. **drink.** Ps 75:8. 78:44. 110:7. **blood.** Ps 5:6. 9:12. 16:4. 26:9. **goats.** ver. 9.

14. **Offer.** ver. 23. Ps 69:30, 31. 107:21, 22. 147:1. Le +*23:19. Ho *14:2. **thanksgiving.** Le 7:12. Pr 7:14. Am ◑4:5. Jon 2:9. 1 Th *5:18. He *13:15. Ja 5:13. 1 P 2:5, 9. **pay thy vows.** T#1425. Ps 56:12, 13. 61:8. 65:1. *76:11. 116:12-14, 17, 18. 132:1-5. Ge 28:20-22. Le +*23:38. 27:2, etc. Nu 21:1-3. 30:2, etc. Dt *23:21. 1 S 1:9-11. Jb 22:27. Pr 7:14. Ec *5:4, 5. Jon 1:15. 2:9. Na 1:15.

15. **call.** Ps 77:2. *91:14, 15. 107:6, 13, 19, 28. 2 Ch *33:12, 13. Jb 22:27. Pr 1:28. Zc 13:9. Lk 22:44. Ac *16:25. Ja *5:13. **day of trouble.** T#1159. Ps 20:1. 77:2. 86:7. 2 K 19:3, 4. Je +*30:7. **deliver.** Ps *34:3, 4. 54:6, 7. 66:13-20. Lk 17:15-18. **glorify.** ver. 23. Ps 22:23. Mt *5:16. Jn 15:8. 1 P 4:11, 14.

16. **But unto.** ♪34. Apodioxis; or, Detestation B935. An expression of feeling by way of detestation. For other instances of this figure see Is 1:12-15. Je 9:2. Mt 4:10. 16:23. Ac 8:20-23. **wicked.** T#589. Is 1:11-15. *48:22. √55:6, 7. Ezk 18:27. Am 5:21-23. Mt 15:7, 8. 18:3. 23:25, 26. Jn 3:3, 5, 7. He *11:6. **What hast.** ♪85K, Ge +3:9. 2 Ch ◑+*19:2. Pr 26:7. Is *1:11-15. 48:1, 2. 58:1-7. Je *7:4-7. 23:38. Mt 7:3-5, *22, *23. Mk +*1:25. +*3:12. Lk 5:14. Jn *4:24. Ac *19:13-16. Ro 2:17-24. 1 C *9:27. 2 P 2:15. **thou shouldest.** Ps *25:14. *78:35-38. Ezk 20:37, 38. He *8:9.

17. **hatest.** Pr *1:7, 28, 29. 5:12, 13. 8:36. 12:1. Jn 3:20. Ro 1:28. 2:21, 23. 2 Th 2:10-12. 2 T 4:3, 4. **castest.** Ne *9:26. Is 5:24. Je 8:9. 18:12. 36:23, etc.

18. **consentedst.** Pr *1:10-19. Is 5:23. Mi 7:3. Ro *1:32. Ep √5:11-13. **hast been partaker.** Heb. thy portion was. Le 20:10. Jb 31:9-11. Pr 2:16-19. 7:19-23. Je 5:8, 9. He 13:4. **partaker.** Mt 23:30. 1 T *5:22.

19. **givest.** Heb. sendest. Ps 52:2-4. 55:20. 78:25. Je *9:5, 9. **tongue.** Ps 5:9. 10:7. 12:2, 3. 36:3, 4. 52:2. 55:12, 21. 64:3-5. Jb *27:4. Is 59:3, 4. Ho 4:2. Ro 3:13, 14. Ja 3:5-9. Re +*21:8.

20. **speakest.** Ps 31:18. Mt 5:11. Lk 22:65. **slanderest.** Le *19:16. Pr 10:18. 1 T 3:11. T 2:3. Re 12:10. **thine own.** Mt 10:21.

21. **I kept.** ver. 3. Ps 109:1-3. Ec √8:11, 12. Is 26:10. 57:11. Ro *2:4, 5. 2 P √3:9. **thoughtest.** Ps 73:11. 94:7-11. Nu 23:19. Is 40:15-18. **that I was altogether such an one as thyself.** Or, as Bishop Horsley renders, "that I AM (*eheyeh*) is such an one as thyself." Ex +*3:14. **will.** ver. 8. Pr *29:1. Re *3:19. **set.** Ps *90:8. Ec *12:14. Am 8:7. 1 C 4:5.

22. **consider.** Dt 32:18. Ec 7:14. Ezk *18:28. Hg 1:5. Lk 15:17. **forget.** Ps +*9:17. *10:4. Jb *8:13. Is 51:13. Je 2:32. Ho 4:6. **I tear.** Ho 5:14. 13:8. Re 6:16, 17. **none.** Ps 7:2. 2 S 22:42. Is 42:22. Am 2:14. Mi 5:8.

23. **Whoso.** ver. *14, *15. Ps 22:23. 27:6. 86:9, 12. Ro √12:1. 15:6, 9. Ga 1:24. He *13:15. 1 P *2:9. **to him.** Ps 24:4, 5. *25:14. *85:9. *119:166. Jn √7:17. √8:31, 32. Ac *10:2-4. 11:14. 13:26. Ga 6:16. **ordereth his conversation.** Heb. disposeth his way. Ps *66:18.

*119:166. Is ◑+*66:4. Lk +*21:36. Jn +*9:31. Ph *1:27. 2:12, 13. Col +*1:10. 3:1-3. 1 Th 4:1. Ja *3:13. 1 P 1:15. 2 P *3:11. 1 J 3:3. **salvation.** Ps *91:16. Is *12:2. 45:17. 49:6. 51:5, 6. Lk *2:25, 29, 30. He +*9:28n. 1 P *1:13.

PSALM 51

David earnestly prays for mercy, humbly confesses his sins, and laments his original depravity, 1-6. He prays for forgiveness, sanctification, and renewed comfort, that he may glorify God and promote the conversion of sinners, 7-15. He shows that God delights more in a contrite heart than in legal sacrifices, 16, 17. He prays for the prosperity of Zion, 18, 19.

(*Title.*) A.M. 2970. B.C. 1034. **chief.** Ps 4, 5, 6, 8, 9, etc., titles. **when.** 2 S 12:1-13. **Nathan.** 2 S 11:2, etc. **Bath-sheba.** 2 S 11:3. 12:24. 1 K 15:5. 1 Ch 3:5. Mt 1:6. See 2 S 7:18-29. 12:16. 1 Ch 28:2-10.

1. **Have mercy.** Ps *4:1. 109:26. Ex 33:19. Ezk 18:23, 31. Lk 15:7, 10, 32. *18:13. Jn 8:11. Ro 11:32. 2 P *3:9. **O God.** Ps *25:6, 7. 103:17. 106:1. 109:21. *119:77, 124, 156. Ex 34:6, 7. Nu 14:18, 19. Da *9:9, 18. Mi *7:18, 19. Lk 1:78. Jn 1:17. Ro *5:20, 21. Ep 1:6-8. *2:4-7. **lovingkindness.** Ps *13:5. 17:7. **multitude.** Ps 5:7. *69:13, 16. 106:7, 45. Ne 9:19. Is 63:7, 15mg. La *3:32. **tender.** ♪22A18, Is +63:15. Ps *40:11. 69:16. 77:9. 145:9. **blot.** ♪22C34, Ex +32:33. ver. 9. Ps *25:11, 18. 69:28. 109:13. Ex *32:32, 33. Nu 5:23. 2 K 21:13. Ne 4:5. Is *1:16-20. *43:25. *44:22. *55:7. 59:1, 2. Je 18:23. Ho 14:2. Mt 4:17. Lk +*13:3, 5. 24:47. Ac +*3:19. 26:18. Ro 2:4-7. *3:24-31. √6:23. *8:1-13. Ep 1:6. Col *2:14. 1 J √1:7-9. 3:5-10. Re 2:5. **transgressions.** ver. 3. Ps 5:10. 19:13. *32:1. Jb 34:37. Pr 10:19.

2. **Wash.** T#32. ver. 7. Ps 65:3. Ex 19:10. Is *1:16. 4:4. Je *2:22. *4:14. Ezk 36:25. Zc 13:1. Ml 3:2, 3. Mt 3:11. 20:22. Lk 12:50. Jn 3:5. Ac 1:5. +*22:16. Ro 2:28, 29. 6:3-5. 1 C *6:11. 10:1, 2. √12:13. Ga 3:27. Col 2:11-13. T *3:5, 6. He 9:13, 14. *10:21, 22. 1 J *1:7-9. Ju 23. Re *1:5. 7:14. ♪22C24. Anthropomorphism B889. Human actions are attributed to God: washing. For other instances of this figure see Is 4:4. Ezk 36:25. **iniquity.** ver. 5, 9. Ps 18:23. 25:11. **cleanse.** ver. 7. Ps *19:12. Le 13:6, 13, 17, 23, 34. Je *33:8. Ezk 36:33. Zc 3:3, 4. 1 J *1:7. **sin.** ver. 3. Ps 25:7, 18. √32:5. 38:3.

3. **For I.** Ps √32:5. 38:17, 18. 41:4. Le 26:40, 41. Nu 5:7. Dt *4:29-31. 30:1-3. 1 K 8:33-36, 47. Ne 9:2. Jb *33:27, 28. Pr *28:13. Je 3:13. 31:18-20. Ezk 6:9. Da 9:3-20. Ho 5:15. Lk *15:18-21. 1 J √1:9. **acknowledge.** Ps 1:6. 4:3. +*9:10. 36:10. 39:4. 44:21. 46:10. Pr 3:6. Is 61:9. Je *3:13. *14:20. **my sin.** Ps 40:12. Ge 42:21. Is *59:12. Je 3:25. Da 9:5, 6. **ever.** Ps 16:8. 25:15. 34:1. *38:3. Is +*58:11 (continually).

4. **Against thee.** Ps *41:4. Ge 9:6. 20:6. 39:9. Ex 16:8. Le 5:19. 6:2-7. 1 S 8:7. 2 S *12:9, 10, 13, 14. 24:10. Pr *8:36. Is *59:2. Lk *15:21. Ac 5:4. Ja *2:9-11. **sinned.** Ps *78:32. 106:6. **evil.** Ge 38:7. Nu *32:13. 2 K 17:17. 21:6. Lk *15:21. **that.** Ge 18:19. **thou.** Ps *50:4, 6. Ru 3:19. Lk *7:29. Ro ◑3:4. **judged.** or, righteous. Ps 143:2. Ge 38:26. **when.** Ac *17:31. Ro 2:5. Re *15:3, 4. 16:5. 19:11. **clear.** or, pure. Jb 15:14. *25:4. Mi 6:11. **judgest.** Ps 10:18. *96:13.

5. **shapen.** Ps *58:3. Ge 5:3. *8:21. Jb 14:4. *15:14-16. Jn 3:6. *8:44. Ro *2:12-16. *5:12-21. 7:18. Ep 2:1-

3. 1 J *3:8. **iniquity.** Ro 7:17. **in sin.** ver. 9. Ps 103:10. Ge 41:9. Jb *25:4. Pr *20:9. Ec √7:20. Ep *2:1. **mother.** Ps 139:13. **conceive.** Heb. warm. Ge 30:38, 39, 41. 31:10. 1 K 1:1h (heat). *8:46. Jb *14:1, 4. 15:14, 16. 25:4, 5. Ec 4:11h (warm). Is 48:8. Lk ◑+*1:35.

6. **Behold.** Ps *26:2. Ge 20:5, 6. 2 K 20:3. 1 Ch *29:17. 2 Ch *31:20, 21. Jb 4:18. 15:15. 25:5. Pr 2:21. *11:20. Je *5:3. Jn 4:23, 24. 2 C *1:12. Ja *4:8. **desirest.** Ps *40:6, 8. Jb 33:32. **truth.** ver *15:2. 19:9. 25:5, 10. 145:18. Jsh 24:14. 1 K 2:4. 3:6. 2 K 20:3. Pr 12:17, 19. Mt 23:25. Jn 3:21. Ja 4:8. 1 J √2:4. 3 J 3. **inward.** Ps 5:9. 125:4. 1 S *16:7. Jb 38:36. Je 31:33. Mk *7:20-23. Lk 11:39. Ro 1:18-32. 2:29. 7:22. 1 C 6:9-11. 2 C 5:17, 18. Ga 5:19-21. Col 3:5-10. **in the hidden.** Ps 26:2. 2 K 20:3. Jb 32:8. Je 17:9. 32:40. Ezk 28:3. Da 12:9. Lk *11:39. Jn 1:47. 2 C 1:12. 1 P 3:4. **make.** Jb *28:28. 33:27, 28. *34:31. 35:11. 38:36. 39:17. Pr *2:6. Ec 2:26. Mt 11:19. Lk 7:35. 2 T √3:15. Ja √1:5. **to know.** Ps *16:11. 89:1. **wisdom.** T#1753. Ps *19:12. 37:30. *90:12. 104:24. Ex 4:10. 1 Ch *22:11, 12. 2 Ch *1:8-10. Jb *11:6. *34:32. 35:10, 11. Pr 28:5. Je *33:3. Da 2:20-23. 1 C *1:22-24. Ep 1:17, 18. Col *1:9, 10. Ja √1:5.

7. **Purge.** Ex 29:36. Le 8:15. 14:4-7, 49-52. Nu 19:18-20. Jb *9:30. Ezk *36:25. Ml 3:3. He *1:3. 9:, 14, 19. **hyssop.** ♪121B. Metonymy of the Cause B549. Hyssop is put for the sprinkling which was effected by it, i.e. *purge me with the atoning blood;* not with the herb. Ex *12:22. Le 14:4, 6. Nu 14:18. 19:6, 18. 1 K 4:33. Jn *19:29. He 9:19. **and.** He 9:13, 14. 1 J *1:7. Re 1:5. **clean.** Le 11:32. 12:7, 8. 13:6. Mt 26:28. Col 1:20. He *9:12, 14, 22. 13:12, 20. 1 J 5:8-10. **wash me.** T#1742. ver. +*2. Ps +19:12 (T#1453). Jn 13:8, 9. Ac 15:8, 9. *22:16. T *3:5, 6. **whiter.** Jb 38:22. Is √1:18. Da 11:35. Jl 1:7. Jn 13:10. *15:3. *17:17. Ep *5:26, 27. 1 Th 4:3. 5:23. Re *7:13, 14. **snow.** Ps 147:16. 148:8. Ex 4:6.

8. **Make.** Ps 13:5. 30:11. 119:81, 82. *126:5, 6. Mt +*5:4. **hear.** Ps 66:8. 76:8. Ac 16:14. **joy.** T#1586. ver. 12. Ps 32:11. 45:7. 67:4. 70:4. 85:6. 86:4. 90:14, 15. 105:43. 106:5. 109:28. *119:111. Is *35:10. Jl 1:16. Col *1:10, 11. **gladness.** Ps *4:7. *16:11. 21:6. 30:11. **bones.** Ps 6:2, 3. 22:14, 17. 31:10. 32:3. 34:20. 35:10. *38:3. Jb *5:17, 18. Pr *16:24. Is 57:15-18. Ho *6:1, 2. Lk *4:18. Ac 2:37-41. 16:29-34. **broken.** or, bruised. ver. 17. Ps 44:19. **rejoice.** Ps 9:14. *13:4, 5. Mt 5:4.

9. **Hide.** Ps 10:11. 13:1. 17:8. 22:24. Is *38:17. Je 16:17. Mi *7:18, 19. **face.** Nu 23:21. 2 C 3:18. **blot.** ver. 1. Ac *3:19. Col *2:14.

10. **Create.** or, Prepare. T#1669. ver. +7 (T#1742). Ps 57:7mg. Ge 41:32mg. Is 65:17. Ho +*6:3. Jn *3:6-8. 2 C √5:17. Ga 6:15. Ep *2:10. **clean.** Ps 12:6. 19:9. 24:4. 73:1. 1 S 10:9. Pr 15:26. √20:9. Je 13:27. *24:7. 31:21, 22, *33. 32:39, 40. Ezk 11:19. 18:31. *36:25-27, 37. Hab *1:13. Mt 5:8. Ac *15:9. 1 P 1:22. **heart.** Je 4:4. Zc *7:12. **renew.** Ps 104:30. La 5:21. Lk *22:32. Ro √12:2. Ep 4:22-24. Col 3:10. T √3:5. **right.** *or,* constant. or, steadfast. T#1711. Ps 5:9mg. 57:7. *78:8, 37. 86:11. 108:1. 112:7. Jsh 14:14. 1 K 15:3-5. Jb 42:7. Ac *11:23. 1 C √15:58. Ja 1:8. **spirit.** Heb. *ruach,* Ge +41:8. Is +√29:24. ♪121A2. Metonymy of the Cause B541. Spirit is put for his quickening, regenerating, and sanctifying work in man, in creating the new nature with its spiritual desires and powers. For other instances of this figure see ver. 17. Is 26:9. Ezk 11:19. 18:31. Mt +*5:3. 26:41. Jn *3:6. Ac 17:16. 19:21. 20:22.

Ro 1:9. +√8:1n. *8:2. 1 C 5:3, 4, 5. 6:20. Ep 4:23. 1 P 3:4. **within.** Ps 5:9. 49:11.

11. **Cast me not.** T#1443. Ps +27:9 (T#1500). 43:2, 3. 44:22, 23. 50:17. 60:1. *71:9, 10, 18. 74:1, 2. 77:7-10. 88:14, 15. 102:10. Ge 4:14. 37:24. Ex 1:22. Le 13:46. 1 S *16:13, 14. 2 K 13:23. 17:18-23. 23:27. 24:20. Est 4:15-17. 5:1, 2. Je 7:15. 2 Th *1:9. He 10:14, 19. **thy presence.** ♪22A4, Ge +19:13. T#1536. Ps 6:3, 4. 10:1. 13:1, 2. 22:1-6, +11 (T#1625). 25:16. 27:8-10. 31:16. 35:22, 23. 60:1. 63:1, 2. 69:16-19. 80:14-19. 88:14, 15. *91:15, 16. 144:5-8. Is 63:15-19. 64:1-4. Je 14:8, 9. 15:15. 31:18. La 5:20, 21. Mk 5:18. 15:34. Lk 24:28, 29. Jn 4:40. 11:32. 17:20-23. 2 C 13:14. Ep 3:16-19. 2 T 4:22. Re *3:20. **take not.** T#1562. Ge *6:3. Jg 13:25. 15:14. *16:20. 1 S 10:10. 16:14. 2 S *7:15. Is 63:10, 11. Jn *14:16. Ep *1:13. *4:30. **holy.** ver. 12. Ps *143:10. Ge +*41:38. Ne *9:20. Is 63:10-12. Ezk *36:27. Hg 2:5. Lk *11:13. Jn *14:16, 17, 26. Ro *1:4. *8:9. Ep *4:30. **spirit.** Heb. *ruach,* Ge +41:8.

12. **Restore.** Ps 54:7. 85:6-8. Ge 20:7. 2 K 8:6. Jb 20:10, 18. 29:2, 3. Is 41:13. 42:22. *57:17, 18. Je 31:9-14. **joy.** ver. 8. Ps 13:5. 21:1. 35:9. Is 49:13. *61:10. Mt *26:75. Lk *1:47. Jn *21:15-17. Ro 5:2-11. 1 P *1:8. **salvation.** Ps *18:2, 35, 46. *20:6. **uphold.** Ps *3:5. 17:5. *19:13. 37:17, *24. 41:3, 12. 54:4. 63:8. 119:116, 117, *133. Is *41:10. Je 10:23. Ro 14:4. 1 P 1:5. Ju *24. **free.** or, willing. Ps *54:6. *110:3. Ex 35:5, 22. 2 Ch 29:31. Mt 26:41. Ro 7:25. 8:2, 15. 2 C 3:17. Ga 4:6, 7. 2 T *1:7. **spirit.** Heb. *ruach,* Ge +41:8.

13. **Then.** Ps 18:26. *32:5, 8-10. 119:37. 2 Ch 6:27. Zc 3:1-8. Mk *5:19. Lk *22:32. Jn *21:15-17. Ac *2:38-41. *9:19-22. 2 C *5:8-20. **teach.** Ps *19:7, 8. *25:9. 34:11. 94:12. 126:1-3. Pr *11:30. 1 T *1:12-16. **transgressors.** Ps 37:38. Is *1:28. **ways.** Ps 5:8. *18:21, 30. *25:4, 8, 9. *32:8. Is 2:3. Ac 13:10. **sinners.** Ps *1:1, 5. 25:8. 26:9. 104:35. **converted.** or, turned. Ps 6:10. *19:7. 22:27. Is 1:27. 6:10. Je 31:18. Mt *13:15. *18:3. Mk *4:12. Lk *22:32. Jn 12:40. Ac *3:19. 15:3. *26:18-20. 28:27. Ja +*5:19, 20.

14. **Deliver.** T#1440. Ps 7:1. 22:20. *25:20. 26:9. 39:8. 55:23. Ge *9:6. 44:22. Dt 21:7, 8. 2 S 3:28. 11:15-17. *12:9. 21:1. Ezk 3:21. Jon 1:14. **bloodguiltiness.** Heb. bloods. ♪171I12, Le +20:9. Ps *5:6. 9:12. 16:4. 26:9. Ge +*4:10mg. 9:5, 6. Dt *21:8. 2 S 11:14-21. 12:9. 16:7mg. 2 K +*9:26mg. Ezk 33:8. Ho 4:2. Jon *1:14. Zc *12:10. Mt *27:25. Ac *5:28. *18:6. *20:26. **thou God.** Ge 24:5. *25:5. 38:22. *62:2, 7. *68:20. 88:1. Is *12:2. 45:17. Hab 3:18. Re *7:10. **salvation.** Ps 33:17. *37:39. 38:22. *40:10, 16. Pr 11:14. 21:31. 24:6. Is 45:17. Je 3:23. La *3:26. **tongue.** Ps 35:28. 40:9, 10. *71:15-24. 86:12, 13. **sing.** Ps *5:11. 20:5. 32:11. *59:16. 63:7. Is 53:4-6. 54:1. **righteousness.** Ps 145:1, 17. Ezr *9:13. Ne *9:33. Da *9:7, 16. Ro *10:3. Ph *3:9.

15. **O Lord.** Ge 44:16. 1 S *2:9. Ezk *16:63. Mt 22:12. Ro *3:19. **open.** T#1607. Ps 38:13. 39:9. 49:4. 78:2. Ex *4:11, 15. Is *6:5-7. *32:4. 35:6. Ezk *3:27. 29:21. Mk 7:34. **mouth.** Ps 63:3-5. 119:13. He *13:15. **show forth.** or, declare. Ps 9:14. *19:1. 22:31. 30:9. 38:18. **praise.** Ps *9:14. 22:3, 25. 33:1. *34:1. *50:14, 23.

16. **desirest.** ver. 6, 19. Ps *40:6. 50:8, 13. 69:31. Ex 21:14. Nu 15:27, 30, 31. *35:31. Dt 22:22. 1 S 15:22. Ho *6:6. Mi *6:6-8. **sacrifice.** ver. *17, 19. Ps *4:5. 27:6. **else would I.** *or,* that I should. **delightest.** or, acceptest. Ps *40:6. 50:8, 18. 69:30, 31. Pr *15:8.

21:27. Is *1:11-15. Je 7:22, 23, 27. Am 5:21-23. He *10:5, 6. **burnt offering**. ver. 19. Ps 20:3. Le 1:3-17. +*23:12. Ep *5:2.

17. **sacrifices**. ƒ96F2, Ge +4:10. ƒ108C7. Idiom B834: Plural noun for singular adjective. By using the plural instead of the singular, the meaning is the great sacrifice which God requires is a broken spirit and a contrite heart. Ps 107:22. Ho *6:6. Mk *12:33. Jn 6:28. Ro √12:1. Ph *4:18. He *13:16. 1 P *2:5. **a broken**. T#1412. Ps *34:18. 147:3. 2 K *22:19. Is *57:15. 60:1. *61:1-3. *66:2. Ezk *9:3, 4, 6. Mt +*5:3. Lk *18:11-14. **spirit**. Heb. *ruach*, Ge +41:8. ƒ121A2, ver. 10. **contrite**. or, bruised. T#1343. ver. 8. Ps 34:18. 131:1, 2. Is *57:15. 61:1. *66:2. **heart**. Ps *38:8. **thou**. Ps *22:24. 69:33. 73:20. 102:17. 2 Ch *33:12, 13. Am 5:21. Lk *7:39-50. *15:2-7, 10, 21-32. *18:9-14. **not**. ƒ175B, Ge +21:16.

18. **Do good**. Ps 25:22. 36:3. 49:18. *69:35, 36. *102:16. √122:6-9. 137:5, 6. Ex 20:24. Dt *30:1-10. Is 51:3. *62:1, 6, 7. Je 51:50. 2 C *11:28, 29. **thy**. Lk *12:32. Ep *1:5, 9, +11. Ph *2:13. 2 Th *1:11. **Zion**. T#1757. Ps 2:6. 9:11, 14. 14:7. 20:2. 50:2. 74:2. *102:13-17. *122:6, 7. Is +*24:23. **build**. Ps 28:5. *69:35. *78:69. 89:40. +*102:16. *127:1. *147:2. 2 S 5:9. 1 K 3:1. Ne 2:17. Is *58:12. Je 30:18. 31:4. Ezk *36:33. Da *9:25. Am +√9:11, 12, 14, 15. Mi 7:11. Zc 2:5. Ac √15:15, 16. **walls**. Ps 55:10. Ne 12:27. Is 22:10. *26:1. *60:10, 18. Re 21:14.

19. **pleased**. Ps 66:13-15. 118:27. Ep *1:6. *5:2. **sacrifices**. Ps 4:5. 27:6. Le 26:31. Dt 33:19. Ml 3:3. Ro *12:1. **burnt offering**. ver. 16. Ps 66:13, 15. Le 1:3. +*23:12. 2 Ch 7:4-7. Is 60:7. Ezk 43:18-27. 46:12-15. **whole burnt**. Le 6:22, 23. Dt 33:10. 1 S *7:9. **they**. Is 60:7. Zc *8:20-23. **bullocks**. Ps 22:12. 50:9. 69:31. **altar**. Ps 26:6. 43:4. 84:3. He *13:10.

PSALM 52

David contrasts the deceit and malice of Doeg with the goodness of God, 1-4. He predicts Doeg's ruin and the joy of the righteous, 5-7. He professes confidence in God and a full persuasion that he shall praise him forever, 8, 9.

(Title.) A.M. 2942. B.C. 1062. **Doeg**. Ps 54:3. 1 S *21:7. *22:9-19. **told**. Ps 59:7. Je 9:8. Ex 22:9.

1. **boastest**. Ps 10:2, 3. *94:4, 22, 23. Ro 1:30. 2 T 3:2. **mischief**. Ps 7:14. 10:7. 36:3-6. Pr 6:14, 18. Is 59:4. Mi 7:3. **O mighty**. Ge 6:4, 5. 10:8, 9. 1 S 21:7. **goodness**. Ps 37:32, 33. 103:17. 107:1. 137:1, 2. 140:11, 12. 1 J 4:7, 8. **God**. Heb. *El*, Ex +15:2.

2. **Thy**. Ps 50:19. 64:2-6. 140:2, 3. Pr 6:16-19. 30:14. Je 9:3, 4. 18:18. Mt 26:59. Ac 6:11-13. 24:1, 5. Re 12:10. **like**. Ps 57:4. 59:7. Pr 12:18. 18:21. **working**. Ps 109:2. 120:2. 2 C 4:2. 11:13.

3. **lovest**. Je 4:22. Mi 3:2. Ro 1:25. 2 T 3:4. **lying**. Ps 62:4. Je 9:3-5, 8. Mt 26:59. Jn *8:44. Re *22:15.

4. **devouring**. 1 S 22:18, 19. Ja 3:6-9. **O thou**. *or, and* the.

5. **God**. Ps 7:14-16. 55:23. 64:7-10. 120:2-4. 140:9-11. Pr 12:19. 19:5, 9. Re *21:8. **destroy thee**. Heb. beat thee down. Ps 58:6. Ex 34:13. Pr 2:22. 19:9. **for ever**. Jb +4:20 (*S#5331h). Mt +√25:46. **pluck**. Ps 37:35, 36. Jb 18:14. 20:6, 7. Lk 16:27, 28. **root**. Pr 2:22. **the land**. Ps 27:13. 116:9. Is 38:11.

6. **righteous**. Ps 37:34. *64:8, 9. 97:8. Jb 22:19. Ml 1:5. Re 15:4. 16:5-7. *18:20. 19:1, 2. **and fear**. Ps

40:3. 119:120. **laugh**. Ps 58:10, 11. Is 37:22.

7. **Lo**. Is 14:16, 17. Jn 19:5. **made**. Ps 146:3-5. Je 17:5. **trusted**. Ps 49:6, etc. 62:9, 10. Jb 31:24, 25. 1 T 6:17. **strengthened**. Ps 73:7-11, 18-20. Ec *8:8. Ho 12:7, 8. **wickedness**. *or*, substance. ver. 2. Ps 5:9. 38:12h.

8. **like**. Ps *1:3. *92:12-14. Je 11:16. Ho 14:6-8. Ro 11:24. **I trust**. Ps 13:5. 33:18. *147:11. **for ever**. Heb. *olam*, Ps +21:4. **and ever**. Ps +9:18 (*S#5703h).

9. **praise**. Ps 145:1, 2. 146:2. Ep 3:20, 21. **for ever**. Heb. *olam*, Ex +*12:24. **wait**. Ps 27:14. 40:1. 48:9, 10. 62:1, 5. 123:2, 3. 130:5, 6. Pr 18:10. La 3:25, 26. **for it is**. Ps 54:6. 73:25, 26, 28.

PSALM 53

The general corruption of mankind; the madness of persecutors; and the terrors which seize on them, 1-5. A prayer for the salvation of Israel, 6.

(Title.) A.M. cir. 3464. B.C. cir. 540. **Mahalath**. *S#4257h. Ps 88, title.

1. **fool**. Ps 14:1, etc. 92:6. Mt 5:22. Lk *12:20. **said**. Ps 10:*4, 6, 11, 13. *50:21, 22. 1 K 12:26. Ro 1:21, 28. **Corrupt**. Ge 6:5, 6, 11-13. Jb 14:4. 15:16. **have done**. Is 18:24-30. Dt 12:31. 1 K 14:24. Ezk 16:47, 51. Ep 5:12. 1 P 4:3. **there is**. Ro ɩ3:10-12.

2. **God**. ƒ66, Ge +9:3. **looked down**. Ps 11:4. *33:13, 14. 102:19. Ge 6:12. Jb 33:27. Je 16:17. 23:24. **to see**. ƒ22C1, Ge +18:21. **any that**. Ps 111:10. Dt 4:6. Jb 28:28. **seek**. Ps 10:4. 27:8. 1 Ch +*28:9. 2 Ch *15:2. 19:3. Pr 2:1-5. Is √55:6. Jn √3:19.

3. **Every**. Ps *14:3. 2 S 20:2. Is √53:6. √64:6. Je 8:5, 6. Zp 1:6. **filthy**. Jb 15:16. Ezk 36:25. 2 C *7:1. Re *22:11, 12. **none**. Ro 3:12. 1 J 2:29. 3 J 11.

4. **Have**. Here seventy MSS., several editions, and the ancient versions add *kol*, "all," as in Ps 14. Ps 94:8. Is *27:11. Je *4:22. Mt *23:17, etc. **who eat**. Ps *27:2. Je *10:25. Re *17:16.

5. **There**. Le *26:17, 36. Dt *28:65-67. 1 S *14:15. 2 K *7:6, 7. Jb *15:20, 21. Pr *28:1. **were they in great fear**. Heb. they feared a fear. ƒ147D, Ge +1:29. ƒ121R6, Ge +31:42. Ps *14:5mg. Is +8:12. **where no fear was**. Le 26:14, 17, 36. Pr 10:4. *28:1. **scattered**. Ps *141:7. Ezk 6:5. *37:1-11. **thou hast**. Ps *35:4, 26. *40:14. *83:16, 17. **because**. Ps *2:4. *73:20. Is 37:22, etc. Je 6:30. La 2:6.

6. **Oh**, etc. Heb. Who will give salvations, etc. ƒ96F2, Ge +4:10. Ps 14:7. *42:5. **the salvation**. Is +*25:9. He +*9:28n. **out of Zion**. Ps 50:2. Is 12:6. 14:32. +*51:11. Ro +*11:26. **God**. Instead of *elohim*, "God," more than twenty MSS. with the LXX., Syriac, and Chaldee, read *yehowah*, "Jehovah," as in Ps 14:7. **bringeth**. Ps 79:9. 85:1. *126:1-4. Jsh 7:8, 9. Jb *42:10. Je *30:18. 31:23. Jl 3:1. Am +*9:14, 15. **Jacob**. Ps 18:1. 20:1. 106:46-48. Ezr 3:11. Ne 12:43. Is *12:1-3.

PSALM 54

David complains of his enemies and prays for deliverance, 1-3. He glories in the help of God, predicts ruin to his foes, and vows sacrifices and praises, 4-7.

(Title.) A.M. 2943. B.C. 1061. **Ziphims**. i.e. *inhabitants of Ziph* (i.e. *borrowed*, Jsh +15:24), *S#2130h. 1 S *23:19, 20. 26:1. Mi 7:5, 6. Mt 10:21.

1. **by thy name**. Ps 20:1. 48:10. 79:9. Ex 3:14, 15.

23:21. 34:5, 6. Pr 18:10. Is 30:27. Mt 1:21, 23. Ac √4:12. **judge**. Ps 26:1. 43:1, 2. 99:4. Pr 23:11. Je *50:34.

2. **Hear**. Ps 5:1-3. 13:3. 55:1, 2. *91:14-16. 130:2. 143:7.

3. **strangers**. Ps 69:8. 86:14. Jb 19:13-15. **oppressors**. Ps 22:16. 59:3-5. Mt 27:20-23. **soul**. Heb. *nephesh*, Ge +12:13. **they have**. Ps *10:4. ❶16:8. *36:1. *53:4. Jb +*21:14, 15. Jn *16:3.

4. **God is**. Ps *118:6, 7, 13. 1 Ch 12:18. Is *41:10. 42:1. *50:7-9. Ro *8:31. He *13:6. **soul**. Heb. *nephesh*, Ge +12:13.

5. **reward**. Ps *31:23. 137:8. Ge +√6:13 (T#566). Je +*10:25. 2 T *4:14. Re *6:10. 18:6. **mine enemies**. Heb. those that observe me. Ps 5:8mg. 27:11mg. 37:32. *39:1. **cut them off**. Ps 89:49. *143:1, 12.

6. **freely**. Ps 66:13-16. 107:22. *116:17. Dt 12:6, 7. Ezr 8:28. Ezk 46:12. **sacrifice**. Ps 50:14, 15. **unto thee**. or, With a freewill offering will I sacrifice unto thee. Le +*23:38. Ps +119:108. **praise**. Ps 7:17. 21:13. 140:13. He *13:15. **for it**. Ps 52:9. *92:1. 147:1.

7. **For he**. Ps 18:2, 3. *34:19. Ge 48:16. 1 S 26:24. 2 S 4:9. 2 T 4:18. **and mine**. Ps 37:34. 58:10, 11. 59:10. 91:8. 92:11. 112:8.

PSALM 55

David prays in great distress and terror, 1-8. He describes the wickedness and predicts the ruin of his enemies, 9-15. He determines to persevere in prayer; and confiding in God to deliver him and confound his foes, he exhorts others to trust in God, 16-23.

(*Title*.) A.M. 2983. B.C. 1021. **Neginoth**. Ps 6, 54, titles.

1. **Give ear**. √22A8, Ps +10:17. Ps 5:1. 17:1. 64:1. 80:1. 84:8. Is 38:5. 1 P *3:12. **hide**. Ps 28:1. 80:4. 143:7. La 3:8.

2. **I mourn**. Ps 13:1, 2. 32:3. 38:6. 43:2. 102:9, 10. Is *38:14. **make a noise**. Mi 2:12. Ro 8:26.

3. **oppression**. Ps 12:5. 54:3. 73:8. La 3:34-36. **for they**. Ps 27:12. 35:11. 2 S 15:3. *16:7, 8. 19:19. Mt *26:59, 60.

4. **sore pained**. T#1358. Ps 6:3. 10:5h. 69:20. 88:3. 102:3-5. Mt *26:37, 38. Mk 14:33, 34. Jn 12:27. 2 C *1:8-10. **terrors**. Ps 18:4, 5. 116:3. Is 38:10-13. He *5:7.

5. **Fearfulness**. Ps 119:120. 2 S 15:14. Jb 6:4. 23:15, 16. **horror**. Ps 42:6. 61:2. 88:15, 16. Lk 22:44. **overwhelmed**. Heb. covered. Ps 32:5. 40:10. 44:15. 69:7. 78:53mg.

6. **Oh that**. √124, Dt +5:29. Ps 11:1. 139:9. Re 12:14. **wings**. T#1752. Is 40:31. Ezk 17:3. **rest**. T#1676. Ps 15:1. 16:9. 37:29. 65:4. Ru 1:9. Jb 14:5, 6.

7. **then would**. 1 S 27:1. 2 S 15:14. 17:21, 22. Pr 6:4, 5. Je 9:2. 37:12.

8. **the windy storm**. From the sweeping wind and tempest, Absalom and his rebellious party. Ps 18:4. Is 17:12, 13. Mt 7:25-27.

9. **divide**. That is, "Distract their counsels; and let their devices be confounded;" and the prayer was heard: See the Parallel Passages. Ge *11:7-9. 2 S √15:31. 17:1-14, *23. Jn 7:45-53. Ac 23:6-10. **I have**. Je 6:7. 23:14. Mt 23:37, 38. 1 Th 2:15, 16.

10. **Day**. Ps 59:6, 14, 15. 1 S 19:11. 2 S 17:1, 2. Ho 7:6. Mi 2:1, 2. Jn 18:3, 28. Ac 9:24. **mischief**. 2 S

16:21, 22. Is 59:6-15. Ezk *9:4. Zp 3:1-3.

11. **Wickedness**. Ezk 22:1-12. Ac 7:51, 52. **deceit**. Ps 109:2, 3. Is 59:7. Je 5:26, 27. 9:3-5. Mt 26:4.

12. **For**. Ps 41:9. **magnify**. Ps 35:26. 38:16. Is 10:15. **not an enemy**. T#1925. Mt *☀26:47-50. **then I**. Mt 26:21-23. Jn 13:18. 18:2, 3.

13. **a man mine equal**. Heb. a man according to my rank. Ex 40:4, 23. Le 5:15, 18. 6:6. **my guide**. 2 S 15:12. 16:23. Je 9:4. Mi 7:5. **mine acquaintance**. 2 K 10:11mg. Jb 19:13. Mt 26:47-50. Mk 14:44, 45. Lk 22:21, 47, 48.

14. **We took sweet counsel together**. Heb. Who sweetened counsel. Jb 20:12. Pr 27:9. **walked**. Ps 42:4. 122:1. Is 2:3. Ezk +*33:31.

15. **Let death**, etc. Or rather, "Death shall seize on them; they shall descend quickly into the grave;" which is a prediction of the sudden destruction which befell the ringleaders of this unnatural rebellion. Ps 59:13. 69:22-28. 109:6-20. 2 S 17:23. 18:9, 14. Mt 27:5. Ac 1:18-20. **them**. Nu 16:30-34. Mt 26:24. Ac 1:25. **go down**. Ps 17:16. 18:9. 49:17. **quick**. or, alive. Ps 124:3. Ge 1:20 (life). 2:7 (life, living). 2 S 12:21, 22. Pr 1:12. Ezk 7:13. **hell**. or, the grave. Heb. *sheol*, Ge +37:35. Ps 6:5. 9:17. +*16:10. 86:13. 116:3. 139:8. Pr 5:5. Is +*66:24. **for wickedness**. Ps 5:4. 7:4, 9. 10:6, 15. 15:3. **dwellings**. lit. sojournings. Ps 119:54. **among them**. Mt 27:5.

16. **As for**. Is 59:21. **I will call**. Ps 50:15. 73:28. 91:15. 109:4. Lk 6:11, 12. 22:37-44.

17. **Evening**. Ps 5:2, 3. 119:62, 147, 148, 164. Da *6:10, 13. Mt +14:23. Mk +*1:35. 6:46-48. Lk 6:12. 18:1-7. Ac 3:1. 10:3, 9, 30. Ep 6:18. 1 Th *5:17. **morning**. Ps +5:3. **at noon**. T#1167. Ps 119:164. Ac 10:9. Da 6:10, 13. **will I pray**. T#1922. Mk *14:34-36. **and cry**. T#1967. Mt ☀27:50. **aloud**. T#533. 1 K 8:22, 23, 28-30. Jb 19:7. La 3:8. Da 9:19-21. Ho 14:2. Jl 1:14. Mt 8:6. 26:39, 42. Jn 11:41, 42. Ac 1:24. 7:59, 60. 20:36, 37. 27:35. He *5:7.

18. **He hath**. Ps 3:6, 7. 27:1-3. 57:3. 118:10-12. 2 S 18:28. 22:1. Ac 2:33-36. **delivered**. √63H, Ge +12:15. **soul**. Heb. *nephesh*, Ge +12:13. **there**. 2 K *6:16. 2 Ch *32:7, 8. Mt 26:53. 1 J *4:4.

19. **hear**. Ps 65:5. 143:12. 1 Th 2:15, 16. Re 6:10, 11. **and afflict**. Ps 119:67, 71. **even**. Ps 90:1, 2. Dt *33:27. Mi *5:2. Col 1:17. **of old**. Ps 44:1. 68:33. 74:2, 12. 77:5, 11. Mi +*5:2 (✠S#6924h). **Because**, etc. or, With whom also there be no changes; yet they fear not God. **no changes**. Ps 73:5, 6. Jb 10:17. *14:14. Pr 1:32. Ec √8:11. Is 36:20. Je 48:11. Zp 1:12. **fear not**. Ps 76:8. 112:1. √119:63. Mk +4:19. Lk 18:2.

20. **put**. 1 S 22:17. 24:10. 2 S 18:12. Ac 12:1. **at peace**. Ps 7:4. 109:5. 120:6, 7. **broken**. Heb. profaned. Ps 74:7. 89:28, 31mg, 34, 38, 39h. 2 S 2:4. 5:3. 14:32, 33. 15:10-12. Ec 8:2. Ezk 17:16-19.

21. **The words**. Ps *28:3. 57:4. 62:4. 64:3. Pr 5:3, 4. *12:18. 26:24-26, 28. 27:6. Mt 26:25, *49. Lk 20:20, 21. 22:48. **war**. Jn 13:2. **his words**. T#1927. Mt ☀26:49, 50. Mk ☀14:45.

22. **Cast**. Ps *27:14. *37:5mg. 42:10, 11. *62:8. 63:8. Is *50:10. Mt 6:25, 31-34. √11:28. Ph *4:6, 7. 1 P √5:7. **burden**. or, gift. lit. which he hath given thee, i.e. thy lot. Zc 11:12 (give). Ga 6:2. **sustain**. Ru +4:15. Mt *6:25. **suffer**. Ps *16:8. *37:24. *62:2, 6. *121:3. 1 S *2:9. Jn √10:27-30. 1 P *1:5.

23. **O God**. Ps 7:15, 16. 58:9. 59:12, 13. **pit**. Heb. *be-er*, Ge +16:14. Ps 69:15. Ge 14:10. 16:14. 21:19.

Pr 15:11. 27:20. Is 38:17. **destruction**. Ps 7:15. 9:15. *16:10. *37:38. **bloody and deceitful men**. Heb. men of bloods and deceit. Ps 26:9mg. 2 S 16:7mg. 2 K +9:26mg. **deceit**. Ps 5:6mg. 10:7. 17:1mg. 24:4. **shall not**, etc. Heb. shall not halve their days. Ps 5:6. 2 S 3:27. 20:9, 10. 1 K 2:5, 6. Jb 15:32. Pr *10:27. Ec +*7:17. Is 30:28h (reach). +*38:10. Mt 27:4, 5.

PSALM 56

David prays for mercy, depending on the word of God, amidst the rage and malice of his enemies, 1-7. He comforts himself by the thoughts of the Lord's providential care and gracious promises and by praising him for past deliverances, 8-13.

(Title.) A.M. 2942. B.C. 1062. **upon Jonath-elem-rechokim**. Or, as it may be rendered, "concerning the dumb dove (or oppressed band) in distant places," i.e. *David, or his companions*; though some consider it as the name of a tune and others a musical instrument. i.e. *dove of silence among strangers,* *S#3128h. **Michtam**. *or,* a golden *psalm*. Ps 16, 57-60, titles. **when.** 1 S 21:11-15. 29:4.

1. **Be merciful**. Ps 31:9. 57:1-3. 59:10. 69:13-16. 136:10, 15, 17-20. 143:12. **swallow**. Ps 21:9. 27:2. 35:25. 57:3. 106:17. 124:3. Pr 1:12. La 2:2, 5, 16. Ho 8:8. Jn 15:20. Ac 4:25-27. 1 C 15:54.

2. **enemies**. Heb. observers. Ps 5:8mg. 54:5mg. **many**. Ps 3:1. 118:10-12. Ac 4:25-27. 9:1, 2. Re 16:14. **most**. Ps 9:2. 91:1. 92:1, 8. *93:4. Is 57:15. Da 5:18. Mi 6:6.

3. **What time**. Ps *34:4. *55:4, 5. 112:7, 8. 1 S 21:10, 12. *30:6. 2 Ch *20:3. Is 12:2. 2 C *1:8-10. *7:5, 6. 1 J 4:18.

4. **In God I will**. ♪53, 2 S +1:19. ver. *10, *11. Ps *12:6. *19:7, 8. 119:*89, 90, *160. *138:2. Nu 23:19. Jn *10:35. 2 P 1:4. **in God I have**. Ps *27:1. *46:1, 2. *118:6. Is 31:3. *41:10. Lk *12:4, 5. Ro *8:31-39. He *13:6. **my trust**. T#876. Ps 2:12. 18:30. 26:1. 27:14. 31:19, 24. 34:8, 22. *37:3, 9, 40. 40:4. 84:12. 112:7, 8. 125:1. 146:5. 1 S 30:6. Pr 16:3, 20. 28:25. 29:25. Is *26:3 (T#293), 4. *30:18. 49:23. 57:13. Je *17:7, 8. La *3:25, 26. Mi 7:7. Na 1:7. Ro 8:24. 1 P *5:7. **not fear**. Ps +*34:4. 118:6. Is *51:12. Mt +*10:28. Lk 12:4, 5. He ▶13:6. **flesh**. ♪171Q6, Ge +6:12. Ge +*6:3.

5. **they wrest**. Dt ●16:19. Is 29:20, 21. Mt 22:15. 26:61. Lk *11:54. Jn 2:19. 2 P *3:16. **all**. 1 S 18:17, 21, 29. 20:7, 33. Je 18:18. Lk 22:3-6.

6. **gather**. Ps 2:1-3. 59:3. 71:10. 140:2. Mt 26:3, 4, 57. 27:1. Ac 4:5, 6. 23:12-14. **hide**. Ps 10:8-10. 64:2-6. Da 6:4. **mark**. Ps 37:32, 33. 57:6. 89:51. Jb 14:16. 31:4. Je 20:10. Lk 20:20. **wait for**. Ps 71:10. **soul**. Heb. *nephesh,* Ge +12:13.

7. **escape**. Ps 94:20, 21. Ec *8:8. Is 28:15. Je 7:10. Hab 1:13. **in thine**. Ps 55:9, 15, 23. Je 10:25. 18:19-23.

8. **tellest**. Ps *105:13, 14. 121:8. Nu 33:2, etc. 1 S 19:18. 22:1-5. 27:1. Is *63:9. Mt *10:30. 2 C 11:26. He 11:8, 13, 38. **tears**. T#1298. Ps *30:5. 39:12. 69:3. 88:9. *126:5, 6. Ge 21:14-16. Dt 1:44, 45. Jg 20:21-23, 26. 21:2, 3. 1 S 1:9, 10. 2 S 15:30, 31. 2 K 20:1-3, 5. 22:19. Ezr 10:1. Ne 1:4. Jb *16:16, 20. Je 31:9. 50:4. La 2:18, 19. 3:48, 49. Ho 12:4. Jl 2:12. Re *7:17. **thy bottle**. Archeologists have discovered tiny narrow-necked "tear bottles" into which tears were anciently

collected. Ps 119:83. Jsh 9:4, 13. Jg 4:19. 1 S 16:20. **are they**. Ps *139:16. Ml √3:16. Mt 10:30. Re 13:8. *20:12. **thy book**. ♪22D5K1A, Ex +32:32. Ps 40:7. 69:28. 139:16.

9. **When**. Ps 118:11-13. Ex 17:9-11. Je *33:3. **then**. Ps 18:38-42. 27:2. Jn 18:6. **for**. Ps 46:7, 11. Is 8:9, 10. Ro *8:31.

10. **In God**. ♪53, 2 S +1:19. See on ver. 4. Ps 60:6. Ge 32:11. Mt 24:35. He *6:18. 2 P *1:4.

11. **I will not**. Ps 27:1. 112:7, 8. Is 51:7, 8, 12, 13.

12. **Thy vows**. Ps *66:13, 14. 76:11. 116:14-19. 119:106. Ge 28:20-22. *35:1-3. Le +*23:38. Nu 30:2, etc. 1 S 1:11, 24-28. Ec *5:4-6. **I will**. Ps 9:1-3. 21:13. 59:16, 17. Is 12:1.

13. **For**. Ps 86:12, 13. *116:8. 2 C 1:10. 1 Th *1:10. He 2:15. Ja *5:20. **soul**. Heb. *nephesh,* Ge +12:13. ♪121A7, Ge +9:5. **wilt not thou**. ♪85A. Erotesis; or, Interrogating B947: The asking of questions without waiting for the answer; here, in positive affirmation, where the answer must be in the affirmative. For other instances of this figure see Is 51:19. Lk 14:5. For the very important opposite of this figure, where the answer must be in the negative, see ♪85C, Ge +18:14. **deliver my feet**. Ps *17:5. 94:18. 145:14. 1 S *2:9. **falling**. T#1487. Ps *17:5. 2 P +*1:10. **walk**. Ps 116:9. Ge *17:1. Is 2:5. 38:3. **the light**. Jb 33:30. Jn *8:12. 12:35, 36. Ep 5:8-14. Re 21:23, 24.

PSALM 57

In extreme danger, David fervently prays to be delivered from his cruel foes, 1-6. He encourages himself by praising God and fervently prays that God may be universally glorified, 7-11.

(Title.) A.M. 2943. B.C. 1061. **Al-taschith**. *or,* destroy not. A golden psalm. This psalm is supposed to have been called *al tashcheth,* or "destroy not," because David thus addressed one of his followers when about to kill Saul in the cave; and *michtam,* or "golden," because written, or worthy to be written, in gold. Ps 58, 59, titles. **when**. Ps 142, title. 1 S 22:1. 24:3, 8.

1. **be merciful**. Ps 56:1. 69:13-16. 119:76, 77. **soul**. Heb. *nephesh,* Ge +34:3. **trusteth**. T#1408. Ps +√9:10. 13:5. 125:1. Is 50:10. **shadow**. Ps *17:7, 8. *36:7. 61:4. 63:7. 91:1, 4, 9. Ru 2:12. Lk 13:34. **wings**. ♪22G2, Ps +91:4. **refuge**. T#1668. Ps 9:9, 10. 11:1. *62:8. 71:3-7. 142:3-5. **until**. Is 10:25. 26:20. Mt 23:37. 24:22. Jn 16:20. Ja 5:10, 11. Re 7:14. 21:4.

2. **God most**. Ps 56:2. 136:2, 3. Is *57:15. **that performeth**. Ps *138:8. Jb 23:14. Is 26:12. Ph *1:6. *2:12, 13. He 13:21. **all things**. ♪63A2, 2 S +6:6.

3. **send**. Ps 18:6, etc. 144:5-7. Mt 28:2-6. Ac 12:11. **from the reproach of him**. *or,* he reproacheth him, etc. **swallow**. Ps 56:1, 2. 61:7. Nu 23:24. Jb 31:31. Mi 3:2, 3. **send**. Ps *40:11. 43:3. Jn 1:17.

4. **soul**. Heb. *nephesh,* Ge +12:13. **among**. T#1393. Ps 10:9. 17:12, 13. 22:13-16. 35:17. 58:6. Pr 28:15. Da 6:22-24. **set**. Jg 9:20. Ja *3:6. **whose**. Ps 58:6. Jb 4:10, 11. Pr 30:14. **tongue**. Ps 52:2. 55:21. 64:3. Pr 12:18. 25:18. Re 19:15.

5. **Be thou**. ver. 11. Ps 21:13. 108:4, 5. 1 Ch *29:11. Is 2:11, 17. 12:4. 37:20. Mt *6:9, 10. **above**. Ps 8:1. 113:4-6. **thy glory**. Ps 72:19. 148:13. Nu 14:21. Is 6:3. Hab 2:14. 3:3.

6. **a net**. Ps 7:15, 16. 9:15, 16. 35:7, 8. 140:5. 1 S 23:22-26. Pr 1:17. 29:5. Mi 7:2. **my soul**. Heb. *nephesh,*

Ge +34:3. Ps 42:6. 142:3. 143:4. Mt 26:37, 38. **they are fallen**. Pr 5:22.

7. **My**. ♪59, Ge +28:16. Ps 108:1, 2. 112:7. **fixed**. *or*, prepared. T#1347. Ps 5:9. 38:17. 51:10mg. 108:1. 112:7. Ge 41:32mg. 2 Ch 12:14mg. Ho +*6:3. **my**. ♪84, Ge +6:17. **I will**. Ps 34:1, √4. Is 24:15. Ro 5:3. Ep 5:20.

8. **Awake**. Jg 5:12. Is 52:1, 9. **my glory**. ♪121F, Ge +49:6. Ps *16:9n. +*30:12n. 108:1-3. Ac *2:26. **I myself will awake early**. Literally, "I will awaken the morning," or dawn; a highly poetical expression, which Milton and others have borrowed: "Cheerly rouse the slumbering morn" (*L'Allegro*).

9. **I will**. Ps 2:1. 18:49. 22:22, 23. 96:3. 138:1, 4, 5. 145:10-12. Ro 15:9.

10. **For**. Ps 36:5. 71:19. 85:10, 11. 89:1, 2. *103:11. 108:4. **truth**. Ge 9:9-17. Is 54:7-10. He 6:17, 18.

11. **Be thou exalted**. ver. 5. Ps 8:1, 9. Re *15:3, 4.

PSALM 58

David reproves unjust elders and judges, 1, 2. He describes the odious character of the wicked, 3-5. He predicts their ruin and the joy of the righteous on beholding the just judgments of God upon them, 6-11.

(*Title*.) **Al-taschith**. *or*, destroy not. A golden psalm. Ps 57, 59, titles.

1. **Do**. Ps 72:1-4. Dt 16:18, 19. 2 S 23:3. 2 Ch 19:6, 7. Is 11:3-5. 32:1. Je *23:5, 6. **O congregation**. Ps 82:1, 2. Nu 11:16. Dt 1:15, 16. 2 S 5:3. Mt 26:3. *27:1. Lk 23:50, 51. Ac 5:21. **O ye**. Ps 82:6, 7.

2. **in heart**. Ps *21:11. Ec 3:16. Is 59:4-6. Je 22:16, 17. Ezk 22:12, 27. Mi 3:1-3, 9-12. Jn 11:47-53. **weigh**. Ps √94:20. Is *10:1. 26:7.

3. **estranged**, etc. Ps *51:5. Jb *15:14. Pr *22:15. Is *48:8. Ep *2:3, 12. *4:18. **as soon**, etc. Heb. from the belly. Ps 22:10. Is 46:3. 48:8.

4. **poison**. Ps *140:3. Ec 10:11. Ro 3:13. Ja *3:8. **like**. Heb. according to the likeness of. **serpent**. Mt 3:7. *23:33. **the deaf**. Je 8:17. Ac 7:57. **adder**. *or*, asp. *Pethen* is no doubt the *baeten* of the Arabians, which M. Forskal (*Descript. Anim.* p. 15) describes as spotted with black and white, about one foot in length, nearly half an inch thick, oviparous, and its bite almost instant death. It is the aspic of the ancients, and is so called by the literati of Cyprus, though the common people call it *koupha*, "deaf" (compare Aelian, l. ix. c. 61). Ps 91:13. Dt 32:33. Jb 20:14, 16. Is 11:8.

5. **Which**. That serpents might be charmed or rendered harmless was well known to the ancients. Virgil (*Ecl.* viii. 71) and many others, state the fact: "In the meadows the cold snake is burst by incantation." **will not hearken**. T#373. Pr 1:24, 25. Zc 7:11-13. Mt 22:2-6. Lk 14:17-20. **charming never so wisely**. *or*, *be* the charmer never so cunning. Dt 18:11. Pr 21:9. 25:24. Is 19:3. 47:9, +*12. Ho 6:9. **so wisely**. Pr 30:24.

6. **Break their**. Ps 3:7. 10:15. Jb 4:10, 11. 29:17. Ezk 30:21, etc. **young**. Ps 17:12. 91:13. Nu 23:24. Is 31:4. Ho 5:14. Mi 5:8.

7. **melt**. Ps 22:14. 64:7, 8. *112:10. Ex 15:15. Jsh 2:9-11. 7:5. 2 S 17:10. Is 13:7.

8. **a snail**. *Shabbelool*, in Chaldee *tivlala*, the snail, is probably so called from the Arabic *balla*, to wet, moisten, because of the glutinous slime emitted from its body, by which it appears to waste itself away by

its own motion; in the same manner the actions of the wicked prove their own destruction. Nu +*32:23. **pass**. Ps *37:35, 36. Mt 24:35. Ja 1:10. **untimely**. Jb *3:16. Ec *6:3.

9. **thorns**. Ps 118:12. Ec 7:6. **as**. Ps 10:25. 55:23. *73:18-20. Jb 18:18. 20:5, etc. Pr 1:27. *10:25. +*14:32. Is 17:13. 40:24. Je 23:19. **both living**, etc. Heb. as living as wrath. Nu 16:30.

10. **righteous**. Ps 52:6. 64:10. 68:1-3. 107:42. Jg 5:31. Jb 22:19. Pr 11:10. Ezk 25:17. Re *11:17, 18. 18:20. 19:1-6. **rejoice when**. Dt +32:43. **seeth**. Ps *91:8. Is +*66:24. Je *11:20. Jn +*18:36. **the vengeance**. Ps 49:14, 15. 94:1. *101:8. Ge +*6:13. Dt 32:35. Is +*24:6. *34:8. 61:2. *63:4. Je 20:12. Mi 5:15. Ml +*4:3. Lk +*18:7, 8. √21:22. Re *6:10. **wash**. Ps 68:23. Jb 29:6. Re 14:20.

11. **Verily there is**. Ps 73:13-15. 92:15. Ml 3:14. Ro 2:5. **a reward for**. Heb. fruit of the, etc. T#630. Ps 1:1-3. 4:3. 5:12. 15:1-5. 37:*3, 9, 10, 17-20, *25, 26. *84:11. 92:12, 13. 112:1-3. Ge 19:15, 22. 2 Ch *16:9. Pr *3:3, 4, 32, 33. 10:9, 25, 29. 11:17-21, *30, *31. 13:6, 21, 22. *14:34. *16:8. 20:7. 21:21. 28:16, 18. Is *3:10, 11. 33:15, 16. 58:6-8. Da 3:18, 30. 6:21, 22, 28. Mt +*5:12. *6:33. Ro 6:21, 22. *8:28. 1 T +*4:8, 9. 6:6. He +*6:10. 1 P *3:10-13. **verily he**. Ps 9:8, 16. 64:9. 67:4. 83:18. 96:13. 98:9. Ml 2:17. 2 P 3:4-10.

PSALM 59

David, in great danger, prays to be saved from his enemies, complains of their cruelty, but still trusts in God, 1-10. He prays for and predicts their confusion and ruin and resolves to praise God continually, 11-17.

(*Title*.) A.M. 2942. B.C. 1062. **Al-taschith**. *or*, destroy not. A golden psalm. Ps 57, 58, titles. **Michtam**. The seven poems of the celebrated Arabian poets who flourished before the time of Mohammed called *Moalla-kat*, from being suspended on the walls of the temple of Mecca, were also called *Modhabat*, "golden," because they were written in letters of gold on the papyrus; probably this is another reason why the six poems of David were called "golden." **when**. Jg 16:2, 3. 1 S 19:11, etc. 2 C 11:32, 33.

1. **Deliver**. Ps 7:1, 2. *18:48. 71:4. 143:12. Lk 1:74, 75. 2 T 4:17, 18. **from mine enemies**. T#1475. Ps 7:1. 17:8, 9. +18:3. 25:19, 20. 44:4, 5. 60:11, 12. 80:6, 7. 1 S 12:10. 2 S 22:3, 4. La 3:52-58. **defend me**. Heb. set me on high. Ps 12:5. 91:14. Is 33:16.

2. **save**. Ps 26:9. 27:2. 55:23. 139:19.

3. **they**. Ps 10:9, 10. 37:32, 33. 38:12. 56:6. 1 S 19:1. Pr 12:6. Mi 7:2. Ac 23:21. **my soul**. Heb. *nephesh*, Ge +12:13. **the mighty**. Ps 2:2. Ac *4:26, 27. **not**. Ps 7:3-6. 69:4. 1 S 24:11, 17. 26:18. Jn 15:25.

4. **run**. 1 S 19:12-24. Pr 1:16. Is 59:7. Ac 23:15. Ro 3:15. **without**. Ps 109:3. 1 S 24:11. Da 6:4. Jn *15:24, 25. 19:6. **awake**. Ps 5:6. 35:23. 44:23. Is 51:9. **help me**. Heb. meet me. Ps 35:2.

5. **the God**. Ge 33:20. Ex 3:15. **visit**. Ex 20:5. **the heathen**. Ps 9:15. 54:3. Is 1:10. Am 9:7. Ro 2:28, 29. 9:6. **be not**. Ps 7:12, 13. +*9:17. 55:15. Is 27:11. Je 7:16. Ezk *18:27, 28. Ro 2:5. Ja *2:13. 2 T 4:14. 1 J 5:16. Re 6:10.

6. **return**. ver. 14. 1 S 19:11. Jn 18:3.

7. **belch**. Pr 15:2mg. Mt 12:34. **swords**. Ps 55:21.

57:4. 64:3-5. 109:2, 3. Pr *12:18. **who.** Ps 10:11, 13. 73:11. *94:7-10. Jb 22:12, 13. Je 33:24.

8. **thou.** Ps *2:4. 37:13. 1 S 19:15, 16. Pr *1:26. **heathen.** ver. 5. Mt 18:17.

9. **his strength.** Instead of *uzzo,* "his strength," fourteen MSS. and all the ancient versions read *uzzee,* "my strength:" "O my strength, I will wait upon thee." Ps 18:1, 2. 27:1, *14. ◑38:19. 46:1. 62:5, 6, 11. Is 12:2. 26:3, 4. 40:31. Mt 6:13. **God.** ver. 17. Ps 62:2. **defence.** Heb. high place. Ps +9:9mg. 20:1mg. 46:7mg. 62:2mg. 94:22. 144:2. Pr 2:8. Is 58:14. Hab 3:19. 2 T 4:18.

10. **The God.** ver. 17. 2 C *1:3. Ep 2:4, 5. 1 P 5:10. **prevent.** Ps 21:3. 79:8. Is +*65:24. 1 Th 4:15. **let me see.** Ps *37:24. 54:7. 91:8. 92:11. 112:8. 1 S 26:10. 2 S 1:11, 12, 17. Is +√66:24. Je *17:16, 18. Lk 19:41-44. Ro 10:2, 3. **enemies.** Heb. observers. Ps +5:8mg. 27:11mg. *54:5mg. 56:2, 6.

11. **Slay.** Ge 4:12-15. Jg 1:6, 7. Ec 9:5. Je *30:11. Ezk *12:15, 16. 14:22, 23. Re 9:6. **scatter.** Ps 44:11. 52:5. Le 26:33. Dt 4:27. 28:64. 30:3, 4. Ezk 12:15. Lk 1:51, 52. *21:24. **bring.** Jb 40:12. **our shield.** Ps 3:3. 84:11.

12. **For the.** Ps 64:7, 8. 79:12. 120:3, 4. 140:9, 10. Pr *12:13. *18:7. Mt 12:36, 37. 27:25, 63. **taken.** Ps 10:2. Pr 6:2. 11:6. **cursing.** Ps 109:17, 18. Ho 4:2. Lk 23:5.

13. **Consume.** ver. 11. Ps *7:9. Nu 14:34, 35. 32:13. Dt 2:14-16. 7:22, 23. Hab 1:12. **not be.** Ps +*115:17. +*146:4. **let them know.** Ps 46:10, 11. *83:18. 102:15. 135:5, 6. 1 S 17:46, 47. 1 K 18:36, 37. 2 K 19:19. Is +*24:21. Ezk *38:23. +*39:7. Da 4:25, 32-35. **God ruleth.** Ps 102:16. Is 54:5. Zc +*14:9.

14. **at evening.** ver. 6, ◐*16. Ps 22:16. Is 65:14. **return.** Ps +*6:10. Is +*24:22. Re +*20:5. **go around.** Re √20:9. **like a dog.** Re 22:15.

15. **wander.** Ps 109:10. Jb 15:23. 30:1-7. Is 8:21. **for meat.** Heb. to eat. Dt 28:48, *53-58. 2 K 6:25-29. La 4:4, 5, 9, 10. 5:9, 10. Mt 24:7, 8. **grudge.** etc. *or,* if they be not satisfied, then they will stay all night. Ps +49:12n. Pr 19:23. **if.** Is 56:11. Mi 8:5.

16. **But.** ver. 9, 10. Ps *21:13. 106:8. 145:11. Ex 15:6. Jb 37:23. **sing aloud.** Ps *31:7. 36:5. 86:13. *89:1. 101:1. Is 24:14, 16. +*51:11. Zc +*2:10. Ro 15:9. Ep *1:6, 7. **in the morning.** ver. ◐*14. Ps *5:3. +*30:5. +*49:14. 88:13. +*101:8. 143:8. 1 S *19:11, 12. Is +*26:19n. **for thou.** Ps 4:1. 61:2, 3. 1 S 17:37. 2 C *1:10. Ep *3:20. **day.** Ps *77:2. 116:1-5. 138:7. Je 30:7. He *5:7.

17. **O my.** Ps *18:1, 2. 46:1. **for.** ver. 9, 10.

PSALM 60

David complains of heavy judgments that God has inflicted on Israel, 1-3. He takes courage from present successes to pray for more complete deliverance and to exult in the prospect of subjugating all his enemies, according to the promises of God to him, 4-12.

(Title.) A.M. 2964. B.C. 1040. **Shushan-eduth.** Probably a hexachord harp or lute, for *aiduth* appears to be the same as the Arabic *ood,* a harp or lute: concerning *shushan,* see on Ps 45, 80, titles. i.e. *lily of testimony,* ✻S#7802h. **Michtam. or,** a golden *psalm.* Ps 59, title. **when he strove.** 2 S 8:3, 12, 13. 10:16. 1 Ch 18:3, 12, 13. 19:16-19. **Aramnaharaim.** i.e. *highland of two rivers,* ✻S#763h. Ge 24:10 (Mesopotamia).

Dt 23:4. Jg 3:8. 1 Ch 19:6. **Aramzobah.** i.e. *exalted station; exalted conflict,* ✻S#760h. **valley.** 2 K 14:7. 2 Ch 25:11.

1. **O God.** ver. 10. Ps 44:9. 74:1. 89:38. 108:11. 1 Ch +*28:9. Ro +*11:1, 2. **scattered.** Heb. broken. Ps 59:11. 80:12. 89:40. 1 S 4:10, 11, 17. 13:6, 7, 11, 19-22. *31:7. 33:1-7. 2 S 5:20. **O turn.** Ps 79:9. 80:3, 7, 19. 85:4. 90:13. Is *30:19. La *3:31, 32. Ho +*14:2. Zc 10:6.

2. **made.** Ps 104:32. 114:7. 2 S 22:8. Jb 9:6. Is 5:25. Je 4:24. 10:10. Am 8:8. Hab 3:10. Mt 27:51. **broken.** Ps 89:40. 2 S 2:8, etc. 3:11-14. Is 7:8. Je 14:17. 48:38. Hg 2:6, 7. **heal.** 2 Ch +√7:14. Jb 5:18. Is 30:26. Je *30:17. La 2:13. Ezk 34:16. Ho 6:1.

3. **showed.** Ps *71:20. Dt *28:28, 34. Ne 9:32. Da 9:12. **hard things.** Je +*30:7. Da +*12:1. **to drink.** Ps 75:8. Is *51:17, 22. Je 25:15. La 4:21. Ezk 23:31, 32. Hab 2:16. Re 16:19. 18:6.

4. **a banner.** ♪22D5Q, Ex +17:15. Ps 20:5. Ex +17:15. SS 2:4. Is 11:12. *49:22. 59:19. Jn *12:32. **because.** Ps 12:1, 2. 45:4. Is 59:14, 15. Je 5:1-3.

5. **That.** ver. 12. Ps 22:8. 108:6, etc. Dt *7:7, 8. *33:3. Is *41:8. Mt 3:17. 17:5. **save.** Ps *17:7. 18:35. 20:6. 74:11. Ex 15:6. Is *41:10. He *7:25.

6. **God hath.** Ps 89:19, 35. 108:7-13. 132:11. 1 S *16:1. 2 S 3:18. 5:2. Je 23:9. Am 4:2. **rejoice.** Ps 56:4. 119:162. 2 S 7:18-20. Lk 1:45-47. **divide.** Jsh 1:6. 2 S 2:8, 9. 5:1-3. **Shechem.** Ge 12:6, Sichem. Jsh +20:7n. 24:1, 32. **valley.** Jsh 13:27.

7. **Gilead.** Jsh 17:1, 5, 6. 1 Ch 12:19, 37. **strength.** Dt 33:17. 1 S 28:2. **Judah.** Ps 76:1. *108:8. 114:2. Ge +*49:10. Mt ✻1:2. He ✻7:14. Re ✻5:5. **lawgiver.** Ps 108:8. Ge +√49:10. Nu 21:18. Is *33:22.

8. **Moab.** Ps 83:6. 108:9. Ge 19:37. 2 S *8:2. 1 Ch 18:1, 2. **washpot.** or, pot for washing. **wash.** or, washing. ✻S#7366h. Ps 108:9h. Ge 18:4. ✻S#7364h, Ex +29:4. 2 K 3:11. **pot.** S#5518h. Ps 58:9. 108:9. Ex 16:3. 27:3. **over Edom.** Ge 25:23. 27:40. Nu 24:18. 2 S *8:14. 1 Ch 18:13. **cast.** Ps 2:3. 50:17. 51:11. 71:9. **shoe.** Ps 108:9. Ge 14:23. Ex 3:5. Jsh 10:24. Ru *4:7. Mt 10:14. Lk 10:11. Jn 1:27. 3:30. Ac 13:51. **triumph.** *or,* triumph thou over me. ♪60A, Irony, Ge +3:22. Ps *108:9, 10. Ex 8:9mg. 2 S 5:17, etc. *8:1. 21:15-22.

9. **Who.** ♪60A, Ge +3:22. Jg 1:12, 24, 25. 1 Ch 11:6, 17-19. **strong city.** Heb. city of strength. ♪27, Ge +3:22. Ps 31:21mg. 2 S 11:1. *12:26, etc. Is +37:25mg.

10. **Wilt.** Ps 20:7. 44:5-9. 118:9, 10. Is 8:17. 12:1, 2. **hadst.** ver. 1. Ps *108:11. Je 33:24-26. **didst.** Dt 1:42. 20:4. Jsh 7:12. 10:42. 1 S 4:6, 7, 10, 11. 1 Ch 10:1, etc.

11. **Give us help.** T#1558. Ps 25:22. 30:8-10. *40:17. 44:23-26. 54:1-3. 59:2-4. 61:2. 69:1-3. 70:1, 2. 77:1, 2. 81:7. *86:6, 7. 88:1-3. *102:1, 2. 109:21-26. 130:8. Ge 4:13, 14. 19:18-22. *28:20-22. 32:9-12. Ex 17:3, 4. 2 Ch *20:3, 4. Ne *2:2-4. 9:27. Is 33:2. *41:10. Je 17:17, 18. 26:19. La 2:18, 19. 5:1, 2, 4-6. Jl 1:19, 20. Hab 3:2. Ja +*5:4. **from trouble.** Ps 46:1. **vain.** Ps *118:8, 9. *124:1-3. *146:3. Is *30:7. 31:3. **help.** Heb. salvation. Ps 62:1. 146:3mg.

12. **Through God.** Ro *8:37. 1 C 15:57. Ep 6:10. Ph *4:13. **we shall.** Ps 18:32-42. 144:1. Nu *24:18, 19. Jsh 1:9. 14:12. 2 S 10:12. 1 Ch 19:13. **tread.** Ps 44:5. Is 10:6. *63:3. Zc 10:5. Ml 4:3. 1 C *15:25. Re *19:15.

PSALM 61

David encourages himself by past experience to persevere in prayer, 1-3. Because of former and in the prospect of future mercies, he purposes to praise and serve God forever, 4-8.

(*Title.*) **Neginah.** i.e. *a harp song,* ✱S#5058h. Instead of *neginath,* many MSS. have *neginoth;* and two MSS. supply *mizmor,* "a psalm." Some suppose this psalm was composed when David was driven by Absalom's rebellion beyond Jordan and from the sanctuary of God. Ps 4, 6, 54, 55, 67, titles. 69:12 (song). 76, title. 77:6 (song). Is 38:20. La 3:14. 5:14. Hab 3:19mg.

1. **Hear.** Ps 5:1-3. 17:1. 28:2. 55:1, 2. 130:2. Ph 4:6.

2. **From the end.** T#1188. Ps *42:6. 139:9, 10. Dt *4:27, 29. Jon 2:2-4. **when my heart.** T#1170. Ps 43:5. 55:5. 77:3. 142:3. 143:4. Is 54:11. Mk 14:33, 34. Lk 22:44. **overwhelmed.** T#1351. Ps +77:3 (✱S#5848). Ge 30:42 (feeble). La 2:19h. **the rock.** Ps 18:46. 27:5. 40:2. 62:2, 6. 2 S 15:14, 17. Is 32:2.

3. **thou.** Ps 4:6, 7. *116:2. 140:7. 1 S 17:37. Is 46:3, 4. 2 C *1:10. **strong.** Ps 18:2. Pr *18:10. **tower.** ♪22L6. Anthropomorphism B897. Certain elements are used as emblems of God: God is spoken of as a tower of strength. For other instances of this figure see 2 S 22:51. Pr 18:10.

4. **abide.** ver. 7. Ps 15:1. 23:6. *27:4. 90:1. 91:1. 92:13. Re *3:12. **for ever.** Heb. *olam* plural. ✙S#5769h: rendered "for ever:" Ps 61:4. 77:7. 1 K 8:13. 2 Ch 6:2. Rendered "everlasting:" Ps 145:13. Is 26:4. 45:17a. Da 9:24. Rendered "of ancient times" or "old time:" Ps 77:5. Ec 1:10. Rendered "of old:" Is 51:9. **trust.** *or,* make my refuge. Ps *17:8. *57:1. 62:7. 63:7. *91:4. 142:4, 5. Ru 2:12. Mt *23:37. He *6:18. **wings.** ♪22G2, Ps +91:4.

5. **hast heard.** Ps 56:12. 65:1. 66:19. **vows.** Le +*23:38. **heritage.** Ps 16:5, 6. 115:13. 119:111. Is *54:17. Ml *3:16-18. Ac 10:35.

6. **wilt prolong the king's life.** Heb. shalt add days to the days of the king. Ps *21:4, 6. 72:15-17. 2 S *7:16. Is *53:10. **many generations.** Heb. generation and generation. Ps 10:6mg. 33:11mg. 49:11mg. 89:36, 37.

7. **abide.** Ps 41:12. Is *9:6, 7. Lk *1:32, 33. He 7:21-25. 9:24. **for ever.** Heb. *olam,* Ex +*12:24. **prepare.** Ps 40:11. 43:3. 57:3. *85:10. Ge 24:27. 32:10. Pr *20:28. Mi 7:20. Lk 1:54, 55. Jn *1:17. 2 C 1:20. **and truth.** ♪174, Ge +18:27.

8. **sing.** Ps 30:12. 79:13. 145:1, 2. 146:2. **for ever.** Ps +9:18 (✱S#5703h). **that I.** Ps 65:1. *66:13-16. **vows.** Le +*23:38.

PSALM 62

David avows his confidence in God and warns his enemies of their danger, 1-7. He exhorts the people to trust in the Lord and not in men, nor in iniquity, nor in riches, 8-10; for power and mercy belong to God, 11, 12.

(*Title.*) **Jeduthun.** Ps 39, 77, titles. 1 Ch 16:41, 42. 25:1, 3.

1. **Truly.** *or,* Only. ver. 2, 5, 6, 9. **my soul.** Heb. *nephesh,* Ps 25:5. 27:14. 33:20. 40:1. 123:2. 130:5, 6. Ge +34:3. Is *30:18. 40:31. Lk 2:25, 38. Ja 5:7. **waiteth.** Heb. is silent. Ps 33:20. +37:7mg. 65:1mg. 131:2.

La 3:26. **from.** Ps 37:39. 68:19, 20. 121:2. Is *12:2. Je 3:23. Lk 2:30-32.

2. **He only.** ver. 6. Ps 18:2. 21:1. *27:1. 73:25, 26. Dt *32:30, 31. Is *26:4. 32:2. **defence.** Heb. high place. Ps +9:9mg. 59.9mg, 17. **I shall.** Ps +*37:24. Mi *7:8, 9. 1 C √10:13. 2 C *4:8, 9.

3. **How.** Ps 4:2. 82:2. Ex 10:3. 16:28. Pr 1:22. 6:9. Je 4:14. Mt 17:17. **imagine.** Ps 21:11. 38:12. 140:2. Ho 7:15. **ye shall.** Ps 73:18-20. 1 S 26:10. **bowing.** Is 30:13, 14.

4. **consult.** Ps 2:1-3. Mt 2:3, 4, 16. *22:15, 23, 34, 35. 26:3, 4. 27:1. Jn 11:47-50. Ac 4:16, 17, 25-28. **delight.** Ps 52:3. 119:163. Pr *6:16-19. 13:5. Ho 7:3. Jn *8:44. Ro 1:32. Re *22:15. **bless.** Ps 28:3. 55:21. Lk 20:20, 21. **inwardly.** Heb. in their inward parts. Ps 5:9. 51:6. Lk 11:39. Ro 7:22.

5. **soul.** Heb. *nephesh,* Ps 42:5, 11. 43:5. 103:1, 2. 104:1, 35. 146:1. Ge + 34:3. **wait.** ver. 1, 2. Ps 27:13, 14. 37:7, 34. Is *30:18. La 3:24-26. Mi 7:7. Hab 2:3. Zp 3:8. Lk 11:6. Jn 6:67-69. **my.** Ps 39:7. 71:5. 81:10. Je *17:17. Ml 3:10. Ph 1:20.

6. **rock.** ver. 2. Ps 18:31, 32. Is 45:17. Ho 1:7. **I shall.** Ps 16:8. 112:6. Pr 10:30. 12:7.

7. **In God.** Is *45:25. Je 3:23. *9:23, 24. 1 C *1:30, 31. Ga *6:14. **glory.** Ps 3:3. 4:2. **rock.** Ps 18:2, 31, 32, 46. 94:22. 95:1. Is 26:4.

8. **Trust.** Ps 22:4, 5. 34:1, 2. 46:1-3. Jb *13:15. Is 26:4. *50:10. 1 J 2:28. **pour out.** T#1353. Ps 42:4. 102, title. 142:2. 1 S *1:15. 1 K 10:2. Is 26:16. La *2:19. Jon 3:8. Ph √4:6. Ja +*5:16. **heart.** ♪121I1, Ge +3:7. **God.** Ps 18:2. 46:11. Pr *14:26. He *6:18.

9. **Surely.** Ps 39:5, 11. 1 S 18:5-7. 23:12, 19, 20. 2 S 15:6. Mt *21:9. Jn *19:15. **men.** ♪138C, Ge +22:14. **of high.** Ps 55:13, 14. 118:8, 9. 1 S 18:21-26. 26:21-25. 2 S 15:31. Ro 3:4. **laid.** Da 5:27. **altogether.** *or,* alike. **lighter.** Is 40:15, 17. **vanity.** Ps 31:6. *39:5, 6, 11. 78:33.

10. **Trust not.** Jb 20:19-29. Is 28:15. 30:12. 47:10. 59:4. Je 13:25. *17:11. **in oppression.** Ps +*12:5. Dt +*24:14. Ezk +*16:49. **riches.** Ps *39:6. 49:6, 7, 16, 17. *52:7. Dt 6:10-12. 8:12-14. Jb 27:16, etc. 31:24, 25. Pr 11:4, 28. 28:22. Mk 8:36, 37. 10:23, 24. Lk *12:15-21. 2 C *8:9. *9:8. 1 T +*6:9, 10, 17. Re 3:17. **set not.** Ps 91:14. Pr 23:5. Mt *6:19-21. Col *3:2. 1 T +*6:9. **heart.** ♪121I1, Ge +3:7.

11. **spoken once.** Jb *33:14. *40:5n. **power.** *or,* strength. Ps 24:8. 68:34, 35. 89:8. Ge *17:1. √18:14. 49:24. Dt *3:24. Is *26:4. 63:1. Da 2:20. Zp 3:17. Mt *6:13. √28:18, 19. Mk √10:27. Jn 19:11. 1 C 10:22. Ep *3:20, 21. 1 P 5:6. Re 18:8. *19:1, 6.

12. **power.** Ps +24:10. +102:24. **mercy.** Ps *86:15. *103:8-11, 17, 18. Ex 34:6, 7. La *3:22, 23. Da *9:9, 18. Mi 7:18. 2 C 1:3. Ep 2:4. **thou renderest.** Jb *34:11. Pr *24:12. Je *32:19. Ezk 7:27. 18:30. 33:20. Mt ❱16:27. Ro 2:6. 1 C 3:8. 2 C √5:10. Ep 6:8. Col 3:25. 1 P *1:17. Re *22:12. **his work.** Ec ❶9:5. Mt 16:27. Mk 13:34. Re 2:23.

PSALM 63

David earnestly thirsts for God and longs to behold his glory at the sanctuary, 1, 2. Regarding the love of God more than life, he determines to rejoice in praising him, 3-5. By meditation and prayer, he rises to full assurance of protection, success, and exulting joy in God; and predicts the ruin of his enemies, 6-11.

(*Title.*) A.M. 2913. B.C. 1061. **when.** 1 S 22:5. 23:14-16, 23-25. 26:1-3. 2 S 15:28.

1. **thou.** Ps 31:14. 42:11. 91:2. 118:28. 143:10. Ex 15:2. Je 31:1, 33. Zc 13:9. Jn 20:17. **early.** Ps 5:3. 78:34. Jb 8:5. Pr 1:27, 28. *8:17. SS 3:1-3. Ho 5:15. Mk +*1:35. **seek thee.** Ps 27:8. Dt 33:27. Mt √6:33. **my soul.** Heb. *nephesh*, Ps 42:6. 43:5. 88:3. Ge +34:3. Jb +*14:22. **thirsteth.** T#1289. Ps *42:1, 2. 68:9. *84:2. 107:4-6. 119:81. 143:6. Ex 15:23-25. 17:2-7. Nu 20:1-11. Jg 15:16-19. Jn 7:37. Re 7:16, 17. **flesh.** Ps 102:3-5. SS 5:8. **dry and thirsty land, where no water is.** Heb. weary land without water. Ex 17:3. Is 32:2. 35:7. 41:18. Mt 12:43.

2. **To see.** Ps *27:4. 78:61. 105:4. 145:11. Ex 33:18, 19. 1 S 4:21, 22. 1 Ch *16:11. 2 C 4:4-6. **thy glory.** T#1526. Ps 90:16, 17. Ex 33:13-18. **in the.** Ps 68:24. 73:17, 18. 77:13, 14. 84:2-11. 96:6. 134:2. Is 60:13.

3. **Because.** Ps *4:6. 21:6. *30:5. Ph *1:23. 1 J *3:2. **lips.** Ps 30:12. *51:15. 66:17. Ho *14:2. Ro *6:19. *12:1. 1 C *6:20. He *13:15. Ja *3:5-10. **shall praise thee.** T#1378. Ps 27:6. 30:12. 40:16. 54:6. 56:12. 61:8. 65:1. 69:34. *70:4. 86:12. 119:7. Is 12:1. Ac 16:25. Re 4:8-11. 5:11-14. 7:11, 12. 15:3, 4. 19:5.

4. **Thus.** Ps 104:33. 145:1-3. 146:1, 2. **I will lift.** Ps 134:2. 1 K 8:22, etc. Hab 3:10.

5. **My soul.** Heb. *nephesh*, Ps 17:15. 36:7-9. 65:4. 104:34. Ge +34:3. SS *1:4. Is 25:6. Je 31:4. **marrow.** Heb. fatness. or, milk. Ps 17:10. 73:7. **and fatness.** Ps *36:8. 65:11. Jg 9:9. **with joyful.** Ps *4:7. 43:4. 71:23. 118:14, 15. 135:3. 149:1-3. Ezr 3:11-13. Re 19:5-7.

6. **I remember.** Ps *42:8. 77:4-6. *119:55, 147, 148. *139:17, 18. *149:5. SS *3:1, 2. *5:2. La 2:19. **my bed.** Ps +4:4. **meditate.** Jb 35:10. **the night watches.** Ps 42:8. +119:55.

7. **Because.** Ps 54:3, 4. **therefore.** Ps 5:11. 21:1. 57:1. *61:4. 1 S 17:37. 2 C 1:10. **wings.** ſ22G2, Ps +91:4.

8. **My soul,** etc. Heb. *nephesh*, Ge +34:3. "My soul cleaveth (*davekah*) after thee," which not only shows the diligence of the pursuit and the nearness of the attainment, but also the fast hold he had on the mercy of God. **followeth.** ſ63H, Ge +12:15. T#1401. Ps *73:25. 143:6, 7. Ge 32:26-28. 2 Ch 31:21. SS 3:2. Is 26:9. Mt 11:12. Lk 13:24. 18:5-7. **thy.** Ps 18:35. 37:24. 73:23. 94:18. SS 2:6. Is *41:10. 42:1. Ph *2:12, 13. Col 1:29. **right hand.** ſ22A15B, Ps +18:35.

9. **seek.** Ps 35:4, 26. 38:12. 40:14. 70:2. 1 S 25:29. **to destroy.** Ps 35:8. Jb 30:3, 14 (desolation). **soul.** Heb. *nephesh*, Ge +12:13. **go.** Ps +*9:17. 55:15, 23. *86:13. 88:6. 139:15. Nu 16:30-33. 1 S 28:19. Jb 40:13. Is 14:9, 15, 19. Ezk 32:18-32. Ac 1:25.

10. **They shall fall,** etc. Heb. They shall make him run out, like water, by the hands of the sword. Ps 77:2mg. 1 S 26:10. 31:1-6. 1 K +16:12mg. Jb 5:20mg. Je 18:21mg. Ezk 35:5mg. **a portion.** SS 2:15. Ezk 39:4, 17-20. Re 19:17, 18.

11. **But,** etc. David shall come to the kingdom according to the promise of God. **the king.** Ps 2:6. 21:1. 1 S 23:17. 24:20. **sweareth.** Dt *6:13. Is 19:18. √45:23. *65:16. Je 4:2. Zp 1:5. He 6:13. **the mouth.** Ps 31:18. Ro 3:19. T 1:10, 11.

PSALM 64

David, praying for deliverance, describes the malice and subtlety of his enemies, 1-6. He predicts their ruin and the effects of it on the beholders, 7-10.

1. A.M. 2943. B.C. 1061. **Hear.** Ps 27:7. 55:1, 2. 130:1, 2. 141:1. 143:1-3. La 3:55, 56. **preserve.** Ps 17:8, 9. 31:13-15. √34:4. *56:2-4. Ac 18:9, 10. 27:24.

2. **Hide me.** ſ22C25, Ps +31:20. ſ121S2, Ge +21:6. i.e. *protect.* T#1559. Ps 17:8. *27:5. 31:20. 32:7. 61:3, 4. 143:9. Is 32:2. **secret.** Ps 56:6. 109:2, 3. Ge 4:6. 1 S 23:22, 23. 2 S 17:2-4. Je 11:19. 18:23. Mt 26:3, 4. Ac 23:14, 15. 25:3. **insurrection.** Ps 2:2. 3:1. Lk 23:18-23.

3. **whet.** Ps 57:4. Pr 12:18. 30:14. Is *54:17. Je *9:3. Ja 3:6-8. **bend.** Ps 11:2. 58:7. **bitter words.** Is 28:15.

4. **shoot.** Ps *10:8, 9. Ne 4:11. Hab 3:14. **the perfect.** Ps 59:3, 4. Jn 19:6. 1 P *2:22, 23. **suddenly.** ver. 7. 1 S 18:11. 19:10. 2 S 15:14.

5. **encourage.** Ex 15:9. Nu 22:6. Pr *1:11-14. Is *28:15. 41:6. Re 11:10. **matter.** or, speech. ver. 3. Ps 35:20. 45:1. 65:3mg. Ge 11:1. **commune.** 1 S 23:19-23. Mt 23:15. 26:3, 4. **of laying snares.** Heb. to hide snares. Ps 124:7. 140:5. **Who.** Ps 10:11. 59:7. 94:7. Pr *15:3. Ezk 8:12.

6. **search.** Ps 35:11. 1 S 22:9-13. 24:9. 25:10. Da *6:4, 5. Mt *26:59-66. Jn 18:29, 30. 19:7. **they accomplish,** etc. or, we are consumed by that which they have throughly searched. **a diligent search.** Heb. a search searched. ſ147D, Polyptoton, Ge +1:29. **both.** Ps 5:9. Pr 20:5. Is 29:15. Je √17:9, 10. 1 C 4:5.

7. **God.** Ps *7:12, 13. 18:14. Dt 32:23, 42. Jb 6:4. La 3:12, 13. **shoot.** ſ22C42. Anthropomorphism B890. Human actions are attributed to God: shooting with arrows. **arrow.** ſ22D5B, Dt +32:23. **suddenly.** ver. 4. Ps *73:19. Pr 6:15. 29:1. Is 30:13. Mt 24:40, 50, 51. 1 Th *5:2, 3. **shall they be wounded.** Heb. their wound shall be. 1 K 22:34. 1 Ch 10:3-7.

8. **tongue.** Ps 59:12. *94:23. 140:9. Jb 15:6. Pr 12:13. *18:7. Mt 21:41. *27:25. Lk 19:22. *21:23, 24. **all that.** Ps 31:11. 52:6. Nu *16:34. 1 S 31:3-7. Na 3:7. Re *18:4, 10.

9. **fear.** Ps 40:3. 53:5. 119:120. Je 50:28. 51:10. Re 11:13. **they.** Ps 58:11. 107:42, 43. Is 5:12. Ezk 14:23. Ho 14:9. Ro √15:4. 1 C *10:11.

10. **righteous.** Ps *32:11. 33:1. 40:3. 58:10. 68:2, 3. Ph 4:4. **upright.** Ps 97:11. 112:2. 1 C 1:30, 31. Ga 6:14.

PSALM 65

David praises God for answering prayer, taking away sin, blessing his chosen, and performing wonders on their behalf, 1-5; and for his providential goodness and bounty, 6-13.

1. **Praise.** Ps 21:13. 115:1, 2. **waiteth.** Heb. is silent. Ps +37:7mg. 62:1mg. Lk 2:25. **in Sion.** S#6726h, elsewhere rendered Zion, Ps 76:2. 78:68, 69. 2 S +5:7. 1 Ch 11:7. 15:29. 16:41, 42. 25:1, etc. Re 14:1-3. **unto.** Ps 56:12. 76:11. 116:17, 18. **vow.** Ps 66:13, 14. Le +*23:38.

2. **thou.** Ps 66:19. 102:17. 145:18, 19. 1 K 18:29, 37. 2 Ch 33:13. Is *65:24. Je 29:12, 13. Da 9:17-19. Lk √11:9, 10. Ac 10:31. 1 J √5:14, 15. **unto thee.** Ps 22:27. 66:4. 86:9. Is 49:6. 66:23. Jn 12:32. He *4:16. Re 11:15. **all flesh.** ſ171Q6, Ge +6:12. T#1818. Ps

2:8. 72:11. 86:9. Is *45:22, 23. 62:2. *66:23. Zp 3:8-10. Ml 1:11. Ro 14:11. Ph *2:10, 11. Re *5:13. 15:4.

3. **Iniquities.** Heb. Words. or Matters, of iniquities. ✝144A8, Ps +35:20. Ps +64:5mg. **prevail.** Ps *38:4. *40:12. 2 S 12:7-13. Je 5:25. Mi 7:8, 9. Ro *7:23-25. Ga 5:17. **transgressions.** Ps 51:2, 3, 7. *79:9. Is *1:18, 19. *6:7. Zc 13:1. Jn 1:29. He *9:14. 1 J √1:7-9. Re *1:5.

4. **Blessed.** ✝43, Dt +28:3. Ps 33:12. 84:4. Ep *1:3, 4. **choosest.** Ps 4:3. 33:12. 78:70, 71. 106:4, 5. 135:4. Dt +10:15. Jn 15:16. Ep *1:4, 5. 2 Th *2:13, 14. 1 P *2:4, 5. **causest.** Ps 15:1. 23:6. 24:7. Jn √6:44, 65. *15:16. Re 3:12. **we shall be satisfied.** T#808. Ps 17:15. *36:8, 9. 63:2-5. *84:4, 10, 11. 89:15, 16. *92:13. SS 2:3. Is 12:3. *48:17. *60:7. Je *31:12-14, 25. Mt *18:20. Jn 3:20. Re 7:16, 17. 21:3, 4.

5. **terrible.** Ps 45:4. 47:2, 3. 66:3. 76:3-9. Dt 4:34. 10:21. Is 37:36. **righteousness.** Ps 145:17. Ro 2:5. 1 P 4:17, 18. Re 15:3, 4. 16:5. 19:1-3. **answer.** Je *33:3. **O God.** Ps 68:19, 20. **the confidence.** Is 45:22. Mt 28:19, 20. Ro 15:10-12. **all.** Ps 22:27. **afar.** Is 51:5. 60:5. 66:19. Zp 2:11. Zc 9:10. Ac 28:28. Ro 15:12. Ep 2:17, 18.

6. **Which.** Ps 24:2. 119:90. Mi 6:2. Hab 3:6. **girded.** Ps 93:1. 1 S 2:4. Is 51:9.

7. **Which stilleth.** Ps 89:9. 107:29. Jon 1:4, 15. Mt *8:26, 27. **of the seas.** Ps 93:3, 4. Da 7:2. Hab 3:8. Re 13:1. 21:1. **noise of their.** Ps 93:3, 4. 104:6-9. Jb 38:8-11. **tumult.** Ps 2:1-4. *76:10. Is *17:12, 13. Jn *18:6.

8. **in the.** Ps 2:8. **afraid.** Thunder and lightning, storms and tempests, eclipses and meteors, tornados and earthquakes, are proofs to all that there is a supreme being who is wonderful and terrible in his acts. Ps 48:5, 6. 66:3. 126:2. 135:9. Ex 15:14-16. Jsh 2:9-11. Hab 3:3, etc. Ac 5:38, 39. Re 11:13. **outgoings.** ✝121N1, Ps 19:5. 74:16. 104:20-23. 136:8. Ge 8:22. +31:54. Dt 4:19. Jb 38:12. **the morning.** The rising and setting sun, the morning and evening twilight, the invariable succession of day and night, are all ordained by thee and contribute to the happiness and continuance of man and beast. **and.** ✝63F, Ge +33:10. **rejoice.** or, sing. ver. 13. Ps 32:11. 81:1. 148:3. Jb 29:13.

9. **visitest.** Ps 104:13, 14. Dt 11:11, 12. Ru 1:6. Jb 37:6-13. Je 14:22. Ac 14:17. **and waterest it.** or, after thou hadst made it to desire rain. Ps 63:1. **greatly.** ver. 11. Ps 68:9, 10. 104:13-15. 147:8, 9. Jb 5:10, 11. Je *5:24. Jl 2:23-26. **the river.** Ps *46:4. Dt 33:28. Re 22:1. **is full.** Ps 104:16. Dt 33:28. Jn 7:37-39. Ac 2:16, 17. 14:17. **thou preparest.** Ps 104:15. 107:37. Ge 26:12. 1 T 6:17, 18.

10. **waterest.** Ps 36:8mg. Pr 5:19mg. 7:18. **ridges.** Jb 31:38. 39:10. Ho 10:4. 12:11. **settlest the furrows thereof.** or, causest rain to descend into the furrows thereof. **settlest.** or, to go down. Ps 18:34 (broken). 38:2 (stick fast). 2 S 22:35. Jb 21:13. Je 21:13. Jl 3:11. **furrows.** Je 48:37h. **makest it soft.** Heb. dissolvest it. Ps 46:6. 75:3. Jb 30:22. with showers. Ps 72:6. Dt 32:2. Je 3:3. 14:22. Mi 5:7. **blessest.** Ps 85:12. 147:8. 1 C 3:6, 7. 2 C 9:10. **springing.** Ge 19:24. Is 4:2.

11. **crownest.** Ps 5:12mg. 103:4. Pr 14:18. He 2:7-9. **with thy.** Heb. of thy. **thy paths.** Ps 25:10. *104:3. 147:8. Jl 2:14, 21-26. Hg 2:19. Ml 3:10. **fatness.** Ps 36:8. Ro 11:17.

12. **drop.** Ps 104:10-13. Jb 38:26, 27. **rejoice.** Heb. are girded with joy. ver. 6. Is √55:9-13. 61:10, 11.

13. **pastures.** Ps 104:24-28. Zc 9:17. Ac 14:17. **they shout.** Ps 96:11-13. 98:7-9. Is 35:1, 2, 10. 52:9. *55:12. Je 48:33.

PSALM 66

The psalmist exhorts all men to observe the works of God and to praise him, with solemn awe and lively gratitude, 1-9. He shows how God had tried and delivered his people, 10-12. He determines to perform his vows and declares how God had answered his prayers, 13-20.

1. A.M. 3469. B.C. 535. **Make.** Ps 81:1. 95:1, 2. 98:4. 100:1. 1 Ch 15:28. **all ye lands.** Heb. all the earth. ✝121J17, Ps 96:1. 117:1, 2. 150:6. Ge +6:11. 1 Ch 16:23, 24. Is 24:16.

2. **Sing forth.** Ps 47:6, 7. 72:18. 96:3-10. 105:2, 3. *106:2. 107:15, 22. 1 Ch 29:10-13. Ne 9:5. Is 6:3. 12:4-6. 49:13. Re 4:8-11. 5:13. **his name.** Ac 15:14, 17.

3. **How terrible.** Ps 47:2. 65:5. 76:12. Ex 15:1-16, 21. Jg 5:2-4, 20-22. Is 2:19. 64:3. Je 10:10. **through.** Ps 18:44. 22:28, 29. 68:30. 81:15. **submit themselves.** or, yield feigned obedience. Heb. lie. Ps +18:44mg. 78:35, 36. 81:15mg. 2 S 22:45mg. Je 3:10mg.

4. **All.** Ps *22:27. 65:5. 67:2, 3. 96:1, 2. 117:1. Is 2:2-4. 11:9. 42:10-12. 49:22, 23. Da 7:14. Ml 1:11. Re 5:13. 7:9. 15:4. **earth.** ✝121J17, Ge +6:11.

5. **Come.** ver. 16. Ps *46:8. *111:2, 3. 126:1-3. Nu 23:23. **terrible.** ver. 3. Ps 99:3. Ezk 1:18.

6. **He turned.** Ps 78:13. 106:8-10. 114:5-7. 136:13, 14. Ex 14:21, 22. Is 63:13, 14. **they.** Jsh 3:14, 16. **there.** Ps 106:11, 12. Ex 15:1, etc. Re 15:2, 3.

7. **ruleth.** Ps 62:11. Da 4:35. 6:26, 27. Mt *6:13. 28:18. **for ever.** Heb. olam, Ex +12:24. **his eyes.** Ps *11:4. 33:13. 2 Ch 16:9. **let.** Ps *2:10-12. 52:1-5. 68:18. 73:3-12. 75:4, 5. Ex 18:11. Jb 9:4. Is 10:7-16. 37:28, 29. Da 5:20-28.

8. **O bless.** Dt 32:43. Ro 15:10, 11. **make.** ver. 2. Ps 47:1. Je 33:11. Re 5:11-14. 19:1, 5, 6.

9. **holdeth.** Heb. putteth. Ps 22:29. 104:3h. 1 S 25:29. Ac 17:28. Col 3:3, 4. **soul.** Heb. nephesh, Ge +12:13. **in life.** Ps 7:5. 16:11. 17:14. 18:46. Col 3:3. **suffereth.** Ps 37:23, 24. 62:2, 6. 94:18. 112:6. *121:3. 125:3. Nu 23:9. 1 S 2:9. Je 30:11.

10. **hast proved us.** ✝22C31, Ps +17:3. Ps 17:3. Dt *4:20. *8:2, 16. 13:3. **tried.** Jb *23:10. Pr 17:3. Is *48:10. Zc 13:9. 1 P *1:6, 7. **as silver.** Is 1:25. Ezk 22:19. Zc *13:9.

11. **broughtest.** Jb 19:6. La 1:13. 3:2, etc. Ho 7:12. Mt 6:13. **upon.** Dt 33:11.

12. **caused.** Ps 129:1-3. Is 51:23. **heads.** ✝171Q12, Jg +5:30. **through fire.** Da 3:27. **water.** Ex 14:22, 29. Is √43:1, 2. Ac *14:22. 1 Th 3:3, 4. **but thou.** Ps 33:19. 40:2, 3. Jb 36:16. Lk 16:25. Ja 5:11. Re 7:14, etc. **wealthy.** Heb. moist. Ps 23:5h. 107:35-37. Is 35:6, 7.

13. **go into.** Ps 51:18, 19. *100:4. 116:17. 118:19, 27. Dt 12:11, 12. He *13:15. **burnt offerings.** Le +*23:12. **pay.** Ps 22:25. 56:12. 116:14, 17-19. Ec *5:4. Jon 2:9. Na 1:15. **vows.** Ps 116:14. Le +*23:38.

14. **Which.** ✝63H, Ge +12:15. **uttered.** Heb. opened. ✝63H, Ge +12:15. S#6475h. Ps 22:13mg. 144:7h (rid), 10, 11. Jg 11:35, 36. **mouth.** Nu 30:2, 8, 12. **when.** Ge 28:20-22. *35:3. 1 S 1:11. 2 S 22:7.

15. **will offer.** Le 3:3. 9:14. **fatlings.** Heb. marrow.

Is 5:17. **with the**. Je 41:5. **I will offer**. 2 S 6:13, 17-19. 1 Ch 16:1-3.

16. **Come**. ver. 5. Ps 34:2, *11. 71:18. Ml √3:16. 1 T 1:15, 16. 1 J 1:3. **and I will declare**. T#957. Ps 22:23, 24. 32:5, 6. 34:8. 40:9, 10. 71:20. 89:9. 107:29-31. 2 S 1:27. 2:1. Is 49:23. Da 2:23. 6:20, 23. Mk 7:36, 37. Jn 11:40. 1 C 15:8-10. **soul**. Heb. *nephesh*, Ge +12:13.

17. **I cried**. Ps 30:8. 34:3, 4, 6. *50:15. 116:1, 2, 12. **he was**. Ps 30:1. 145:1.

18. **If I regard iniquity**. T#1380, 1801. Ps 5:5h. 6:8h. 7:14h. 10:7mg,h. Ge 35:2, 3. Jg 10:15, 16. 1 S 7:4-6. Jb *11:13-15. 22:23. *27:8, 9. Pr *15:8, 29. *21:13. *28:9. Is *1:15-17. *55:6, 7. Jn +*9:31. 2 T *2:19. Ja *4:3, 8-10. **my heart**. Ps 4:7h. 7:9, 10h. 9:1h. 10:6h, 11h. 1 S √16:7. 1 K 15:14. Re 2:23. **the Lord**. Ps 2:4. 16:2. 22:30. 35:17. **not hear**. √22C14, Ge +16:11. T#546. Ps 4:3h. 5:3h. 18:6h, 41. 34:2h. 38:13h. 50:16, 17. Jb 27:9. 35:12. Pr 1:28, 29. 15:8, *29. *28:9. Is 1:11-15. *59:1, 2. Mi 3:4. Zc 7:13. Mt 7:18. Jn +*9:31. He *11:6. 1 J ◐√5:14.

19. **verily God hath**. Ps 6:9. 34:6. *116:1, 2. La 3:55, 56. He *5:7. 1 J *3:20-22.

20. **hath not turned**. Ps 51:11. 86:12, 13. 2 S 7:14, 15. **prayer**. √63F, Ge +33:10.

PSALM 67

A prayer for an increase of God's blessings, that all nations may know and rejoice in God's salvation and submit to his righteous government, 1-7.

(Title.) A.M. cir. 3464. B.C. cir. 540. **Neginoth**. Ps 4, 6, 76, titles.

1. **God**. Nu √6:24-27. Dt 21:8. 2 C *13:14. **bless us**. T#1438. Ps 28:9. 109:28. Ge 32:24-26. Dt 26:13-15. 1 Ch *4:10. Ep *1:3. **cause**. Ps *4:6. *31:16. 80:1-3, 7, 19. *119:135. Ml 4:2. 2 C *4:6. **face to shine**. Ps 34:5. Ex 34:29. Nu *6:25. 2 C *3:18. **upon us**. Heb. with us.

2. **That**. Ps 98:2, 3. Est 8:15-17. Zc 8:20-23. Ac 9:31. **thy way**. Lk 3:3. Ac 13:10. 18:25. 22:4. **saving**. Ps *43:5. 66:1-4. 117:2. Is *49:6. Mt *28:19. Mk 16:15. Lk 2:30, 31. *3:6. T *2:11.

3. **Let**. ver. 5. Ps 45:17. *66:4. 74:21. 119:175. 142:7. Is *38:18, 19.

4. **O let**. Ps 97:1. 138:4, 5. Dt 32:43. Is 24:14-16. 42:10-12. 54:1. Ro 15:10, 11. Ga 4:27. **for thou**. Ps 9:8. *96:10-13. 98:9. Ge √18:25. Is *2:4. Ac √17:31. Ro 2:5. **govern**. Heb. lead. Ps 2:8. 82:6. Is 55:4. Re 11:15-17.

5. **Let the people**. ver. 3. Mt 6:9, 10.

6. **Then**. Ps *85:9-12. Le *26:3, 4. Is 1:19. 30:23, 24. Ezk *34:26, 27. Ho 2:21, 22. 1 C *3:6-9. **our own**. Ps *48:14. Ge *17:7. Ex 3:15. Je 31:1, 33. Ezk 34:24.

7. **God**. Ps 29:11. 72:17. Ge *12:2, 3. Ac 2:28. Ga 3:9, 14. **bless**. √84, Ge +6:17. **all the**. Ps *22:27. 65:5. 98:3. Is 43:6. *45:22. 52:10. Mi 5:4. Zc 9:10. Ml 1:11. Ac 13:47. Re 15:4. **earth**. √121J17, Ge +6:11. **fear**. Ml *4:2. Ac 13:26.

PSALM 68

David prays for, or predicts, the confusion and destruction of the wicked and the joy of the righteous, 1-3. He praises the mercy and majesty of God, especially as shown in bringing Israel out of Egypt into Canaan, 4-14. Under the type of the ark of God taking possession of Zion and the prosperity of Israel, he predicts the ascension of Christ, the rapid success of the gospel, and the punishment of obstinate opposers, 15-31. He exhorts all nations to praise the God of Israel, 32-35.

(Title.) A.M. 2962. B.C. 1042. This magnificent, truly sublime ode is supposed, with much probability, to have been composed by David and sung at the removal of the ark from Kirjath-jearim. 2 S 6:12.

1. **God arise**. √22C21, Nu +10:35. Ps 7:6, 7. 44:26. 78:65-68. 132:8, 9. Nu *10:35. 2 Ch 6:41. Is 33:3. 42:13, 14. 51:9, 10. **be scattered**. ver. 14, 30. Ps 59:11. 89:10. Is 41:15, 16. Ezk 5:2. 12:14, 15. Da 2:35. **that hate**. Ps 21:8. Ex 20:5. Dt *7:10. Jn 14:23, 24. **before him**. Heb. from his face.

2. **As smoke**. Ps 37:20. Is 9:18. Ho *13:3. **as wax**. Ps 97:5. Is 64:2. Mi 1:4. **in the presence**. Ps 76:7. 80:16. Na 1:5, 6. 2 Th √1:8, 9. Re 6:16, 17.

3. **But**. Ps *32:11. 33:1. 58:10. 64:10. 97:12. Re 18:20. 19:7. **rejoice**. Ps 95:1, 2. 98:8, 9. 100:1, 2. Dt 12:12. Ne 8:10. Is 65:14. Jn 15:11. 1 Th √5:16. Re *5:11. **exceedingly rejoice**. Heb. rejoice with gladness. Ps 21:1. 43:4. 1 P 1:8.

4. **Sing unto God**. Ps 34:1. *50:23. 66:4. 67:4. Is 12:4-6. **rideth**. ver. 33. Ps 18:10. 104:3. Dt *33:26. Is 19:1. **his name**. Ps ◐+*83:18. Ex *3:13, 14. *6:3, 8. Is +*42:8. Je ◐*10:16. Jn 8:28, 58. Re 1:8. **JAH**. Ps 115:17, 18. Is 12:2. *JAH* is an abbreviation of JEHOVAH and signifies *self-existence*: he who derives his being from none but gives being to all. ❋S#3050h, Ex +15:2. 17:16.

5. **A father**. Ps 10:14, 18. *82:3, 4. *146:9. Jb 31:16, 17. Je *49:11. Ho 14:3. **a judge**. Ps 72:2, 4. Dt *10:18. Jb *29:12, 13. Is 1:23. Je 5:28. Lk *18:2-7. Ep 5:1. **in his**. Ps 33:14. 2 Ch 6:2. 30:27mg. Is *57:15. 66:1. Ac 7:48, 49. **habitation**. Dt +26:15. Zc 2:13mg. Jn 14:10. 2 C 5:19.

6. **God**. Ps 107:10, 41. 113:9. 1 S 2:5. Ga 4:27. **solitary**. Ps 22:20mg. 25:16. 35:17mg. **families**. Heb. a house. ver. 12 (home). 23:6. +*113:9. Ge 6:14 (within). *7:1 (house). 12:1, 15, 17. 14:14. 15:2, 3. 17:12. Ex 28:26 (inward). 39:19 (inward). **he bringeth**. Ps 107:10, 14. *146:7. Is 61:1. Ac 12:6, etc. **the rebellious**. ver. 18. Ps 66:7. 78:8. 107:34, 40. Dt 28:23, 24. Ho 2:3. Ml 1:3. Mt 23:37, 38. Ep 2:12. **dry**. Ps 107:33, 34. Dt 8:14, 15.

7. **O God**. Ps 114:1, etc. Ex *13:21. Dt 4:34. Jg 4:14. Hab 3:3. **thou didst march**. Dt +*33:2. Jg 5:4. Is *16:1-5. √63:1-4. Mi 2:13. Hab 3:12. **the wilderness**. Je +√31:2.

8. **earth**. Ps 77:18. 114:7. Is 64:1, 3. Hab 3:13. He 12:26. Re 11:19. **the heavens**. Jg *5:4, 5. **Sinai**. Ex *19:16, 18. Dt 5:23-25. **the God**. ver. 35. Ps 41:13. Is 45:3.

9. **didst**. Ps 65:9, etc. 77:16, 17. *78:24-27. Dt 11:10-12, 14. Ezk 34:26. **send**. Heb. shake out. Ex 20:25. 29:24mg. Le 23:11. 2 K 5:11mg. Pr 7:17. Is 10:15, 32. 11:15. 13:2. **plentiful rain**. Ps ◐63:1. Ac 2:1-18. **confirm thine inheritance**. Heb. confirm it. Ps 8:3 (ordain). 9:7 (prepared). 11:2 (made ready). 40:2 (established). 99:4. 119:90. 2 S 9:5-7.

10. **Thy congregation**. Ps 74:1, 2, 19. Ex 19:5, 6. Nu 16:3. 1 P 5:3. **thou**. Dt *26:5, 9, 10. 32:8-14. 1 S 2:8. Jb 5:10, 11. Is 52:7. Mt 11:5. Lk 1:53.

11. **Lord**. Ps 40:3. Ex 14:15. 17:9, etc. Jg 4:6, etc.

Ep *4:11. **great was**. Is +*66:19. Re 7:3, 4. **company**. Heb. army. ver. 25. Ex 15:20, 21. Jg 5:1, etc. Is +*27:6. Re √7:3, 9, 14. 19:13, 14. **that published**. Is +*27:6. *52:7. Mi 4:2. Na *1:15. Mt +*24:14.

12. **Kings**. Ex 14:25. Nu 31:8, 9, 54. Jsh *10:16, 42. 12:7, 8, etc. Jg 5:19. 11:34. 1 S 18:6. Re 6:2, 15, 16. 19:17-20. **did flee apace**. Heb. did flee, did flee. **she**. Nu 31:27. 1 S 30:24.

13. **Though**. That is, probably, "Though ye have labored and lain down between the brick kilns in Egypt—a poor, enslaved, and oppressed people, yet ye shall gradually rise to dignity, prosperity, and splendor; as a dove, which has been defiled with dirt, disordered, and dejected, by washing herself in a running stream and trimming her plumage, gradually recovers the serenity of her disposition, the purity of her color, and the richness and varied elegance of her appearance." **ye have**. Ps *81:6. Ex *1:14. 1 C *6:9-11. 12:2. *15:49. Ep 2:1-3. T 3:3. **the wings**. Ps 74:19. *105:37. 149:4. 1 K 4:20, 21. Ezk 16:6-14. Lk 15:16, 22. Ep *5:26, 27. Re *1:5, 6. **gold**. Dt 7:6. 1 K 10:14, 27.

14. **When**. Nu 21:3, 21, etc. Jsh 10:10, etc. ch. 12. 24:31. Re *19:14-21. **in it, it was**. or, for her, she was. Jg 2:7. Je 2:3. **as snow**. Ps 51:7. Is *1:18.

15. **hill**. √24L, Ge +6:2. **of God**. Ps 2:6. 78:68, 69. 87:1, 2. Is 2:2, 3. Zc ◑14:10. **of Bashan**. Nu +21:33. Dt 3:10. Jsh 12:4n. Mi 7:14.

16. **Why**. Ps 114:4, 6. Is 2:2. **high hills**. √147G. Polyptoton B282: Nouns repeated in different numbers: in singular and plural. For other instances of this figure see Is 2:11. Je 15:16. Jn 17:8, 14, 17. **this is**. √63K, Ge +37:13. **the hill**. Ps *132:13, 14. Dt 12:5, 11. 1 K *9:3. He *12:22, 23. Re 21:2, 3. **for ever**. Jb +4:20 (✱S#5331h).

17. **chariots**. Ps 18:10. 104:3. 2 K 2:11. *6:16, 17. Ps 104:3. Is 19:1. Ezk 1:15, etc. Hab *3:8. √22D5G. Anthropomorphism B893. Chariots are attributed to God. For another instance of this figure see 2 K 6:16, 17. **thousands**. or, many thousands. Ne 7:71. Da *7:10. He 12:22. Re 5:11. *9:16. **of angels**. Mt +*13:41. *26:53. Re 5:11. **among them**. Ex 40:35, 38. Le 16:2. Is +*59:20. Zc √9:14. *12:8. Jn=1:14. +*14:2, 3. 1 J 3:2. **as in Sinai**. Ex *3:2-5. 19:22, 23. *24:15, 16. +*33:2. **in the holy place**. √22D3J1. Anthropomorphism B892. God is spoken of being in circumstances as to place: as dwelling in the sanctuary. Ex 25:20-22. 40:34-38. Le 16:2. 1 Ch 28:18.

18. **Thou hast**. Ep ▶4:8. **ascended**. Ps 24:3, 7-10. 47:5. *110:1. Mk *16:19. Lk ✱24:51. Ac ✱*1:2-9. Ep √4:8-10. Col *2:15. He *4:14. *6:20. *8:1. 1 P *3:22. **led**. Jg 5:12. **captivity**. √121N1, Ge +31:54. i.e. captives. Is 49:24. Je 29:14. **received**. √63H, Ge +12:15. 2 S *6:12. 1 Ch 29:16. Lk *24:49. Jn 1:16. 3:34, 35. *14:16, 17. *16:7, 13-15. Ac 1:4. *2:4, 33-38. Ep *4:8. **for men**. Heb. in the man. 1 C 15:45-47. Col 1:18, 19. *2:3, 9. He *1:3. **yea**. √81, Ps 145:9. Ge +15:13. Lk +*6:35. **rebellious**. Dt 9:7. Pr *1:22, 23. Is √55:7. Mt *9:13. Lk 24:47. Ac 2:23, 36, 38-41. *9:17. 1 C *6:9-11. 1 T *1:13-15. T *3:3-7. **that**. Ps 78:60. 132:13, 14. 2 Ch *6:18. Is *57:15. Ezk 48:35. Jn *14:17, 23. 2 C *6:16. Re 1:20. 2:1. *21:3. **dwell among**. √63I1A, Ps 135:21. Ex +12:4. Jn *14:23.

19. **Blessed**. Ps *72:17-19. 103:1, etc. Ep *1:3. **daily**. or, day by day. Ps 32:7. 61:8h. 139:17, 18. Ex 16:5h. Pr 8:30, 34h. La *3:23. 1 T +*4:8. **loadeth us**. or, beareth our burdens. Ps 37:5. *55:22. 81:6. Nu 11:11,

12. Is 46:3, 4. 1 P *5:7. **with benefits**. Ps *103:1, 2.

20. **our God**. Is *12:2. *45:17-22. Ho 1:7. 2:23. Jn *4:22. **unto**. Ps *118:17, 18. Dt *32:39. 1 S *2:6. Jn *5:21, 23, 28, 29. *11:25, 26. He *2:14, 15. Re *1:18. *20:1. **issues**. Pr *4:23.

21. **God**. Ps 110:6. Hab 3:13. Mk 12:4. **wound**. √22C40, Ps +110:6. **the hairy**. Ps 55:23. **of such**. ver. 18. Ps 7:12. Ex 34:7. Pr 1:24, etc. Ezk 18:27-30. Lk *13:5. He *2:1-3. 12:25. Re 2:14-16.

22. **Bashan**. Nu 21:33, 35. Is 11:11-16. 49:22. **the depths**. Ex *14:22, 29. Is 51:10, 11. Je *23:5-8. Ezk 36:24. Ho 1:10, 11.

23. **That**. Ps 58:10. **dipped**. Heb. red. Ex 14:30. Is *63:1-6. Heb. *machats*, ✱S#4272h: Kal, Preterite: Nu 24:17 (smite). Dt 32:39 (wound). Jg 5:26 (pierced). Jb 26:12. Ps 110:5 (strike through), 6 (wound). Hab 3:13. Kal, Imperative: Dt 33:11 (smite through). Kal, Future: Nu 24:8 (pierce through). 2 S 22:39 (wounded). Jb 5:18. Ps 18:38. 68:21 (wound), 23 (dipped). **the tongue**. 1 K 21:19. 22:38. 2 K 9:33-37. Re *19:17-21.

24. **even**. Ps 24:7-10. 47:5-7. 2 S *6:12-17. 1 Ch 13:8. 15:16-24. **sanctuary**. Ps 63:2.

25. **the singers**. 1 Ch 15:16, 28. Re 19:1, 2. **the players**. Ps 87:7. 150:3-5. 1 Ch 13:8. Re 14:2, 3. 15:2, 3. **among**. Ps 148:12, 13. Ex 15:20. Jg 11:34. 1 S 18:6. Je 31:4, 13. **damsels**. or, virgins. Ge +24:43. Ex 2:8. Pr 30:19. SS 1:3. 6:8. Is √7:14. Je 31:11, 13. **timbrels**. Na 2:7.

26. **Bless**. Ps 107:32. 111:1. 135:19-21. 1 Ch 16:7, 8, etc. **from the fountain**. or, ye that are of the fountain. Ps 36:9. Ge 35:11. Dt 33:28. Pr 5:16. Is 48:1. Ac 13:26.

27. **There**. 1 Ch 13:5. **little**. Ge 42:32. Jg 20:35, 48. 21:6, etc. 1 S 9:21. 1 Ch 12:16, 29. *15:3. 27:12. **princes**. Ps 47:9. 60:7. Is 11:13. Ezk 37:19-27. **and their council**. or, with their company.

28. **commanded**. Ps *42:8. 44:4. 71:3. Dt 28:8. Is 40:31. Mt 8:8. Jn 5:8, 9. Ac 3:6-8. 2 C 12:9, 10. **thy strength**. Ps 18:1. 144:2. **strengthen**. Ps 138:8. 1 Ch 29:12. Ep 3:17-20. Ph *1:6. 2 Th 1:11. √135. Paregmenon; or, Derivation B304: The repetition of words derived from the same root. For other instances of this figure see Mt 16:18. Jn 15:2. Ac 8:31. Ro 2:1. 5:19. 12:3. 1 C 11:29. 11:31, 32. 2 C 4:8. 5:4. 10:6. 2 Th 3:11. He 10:34. **hast wrought**. Ps 31:19. Is 26:12. Ph *2:13.

29. **Because**. 1 Ch 17:4-12. 22:7-11. 28:10, etc. 29:3. 2 Ch 2:5, 6. 6:8, 9. **shall**. Ps *72:10, 11. *76:11. 1 K *10:10, 24, 25. 2 Ch *32:23. Ezr *7:13-28. Ne 2:8. Is 60:6-11, 16, 17.

30. **Rebuke**. 2 S ch. 8, 10. 2 Ch ch. 14, 20. Is ch. 37. **company of spearmen**. or, beasts of the reeds. Je 51:32, 33. **multitude**. Ps 22:12, 13. Is 34:7. Je 50:11. **every**. Ps 2:12. 18:44. 2 S *8:2, 8-11. **scatter thou**. or, he scattereth. ver. 14. **delight**. Ps 120:7. Ro 7:22. Ja 4:1.

31. **Princes**. Ps 72:8-11. Is *19:18-25. *45:14. 60:6, 7. 66:19. **Ethiopia**. √121J14, Ge +47:15. Zp *3:10. Ac *8:27, etc. **stretch**. √121S3K, Ge +14:22. Ps 44:20. 88:9. 143:6. 1 K 8:22. 2 Ch +*30:8mg. **hands**. √155A, Ge +31:35. √121BD. Metonymy of the Cause B547. *Hand* is put for a gift given to anyone. ver. 29. Ps 22:27. 72:10. Is 49:7. 60:6, 9.

32. **ye kingdoms**. Ps 67:2-5. 100:1. 117:1, 2. Dt 32:43. Ro 15:10, 11. Re 15:4.

33. **rideth**. √22C18, Dt +33:26. ver. 4. Ps 18:10. *104:3. Ex 20:18. Dt *33:26. **heavens of heavens**. Dt

10:14. 1 K 8:27. 2 C 12:2. **of old.** Ps 44:1. 55:19. 74:2, 12. 77:5. 93:2. 102:25. Mi +5:2 (✛S#6924h). **send out.** Heb. give. ver. 11. Ps 14:7mg. 46:6. 53:6mg. 77:17. **his voice.** Ps 29:3-9. 77:17, 18. Ezk 10:5. Jn 12:28, 29. Re 11:12, 15, 19.

34. **Ascribe.** Ps 29:1, 2. 96:6-8. 1 Ch 16:28, 29. Re *19:6. **his excellency.** Dt 33:26. 2 P 1:17. **and his strength.** This refers to the phenomena of thunder and lightning. All nations have observed that the electric fluid is an irresistible agent, destroying life, tearing towers and castles to pieces, rending the strongest oaks, and cleaving the most solid rocks; and even the most enlightened nations have justly considered it as a special manifestation of the power and sovereignty of God. **clouds.** or, heavens. Ps 18:11. 36:5. 57:10. 77:17. 108:4mg.

35. **terrible.** Ps 45:4, 5. 65:5. *66:5. 76:12. Ex 15:1. Ne *1:5. He *12:24-29. Re 6:16, 17. **out of.** Ps 110:2. **the God.** Heb. *El*, Ex +15:2. **giveth strength.** ver. 28. Ps 18:1. 29:11. 71:16. 73:26. Dt *33:25. Is 40:+*29, 31. *45:24. Zc 10:12. *12:8. Ro 14:4. Ep 3:16. Ph *4:13. Col 1:11. **Blessed.** Ps 72:18, 19.

PSALM 69

David, as a type of Christ, mingles doleful complaints with fervent prayers for himself and for his people, 1-21. He, as the type of the Redeemer, consigns his enemies to destruction, 22-29. He engages to praise and bless God, calls on the whole creation to join him, and predicts the enlargement and prosperity of Zion, 30-36.

(*Title*.) **Shoshannim.** Ps 45, 60, 80, titles. **A Psalm.** It is uncertain when this psalm was composed; though it is probable that it was written by David during the rebellion of Absalom. It is an exceedingly fine composition; it evidently refers to the advent, passion, and resurrection of our Lord, to the vocation of the Gentiles, and the reprobation of the Jews: see the Marginal References.

1. **the waters.** ver. 2, 14, 15. Ps *18:4. 42:7. 69:15. Ge 7:19. Is 28:17. *43:2. La 3:54. Jon *2:3-5. Re 12:15, 16. *17:15. **soul.** Heb. *nephesh*, Ge +12:13.

2. **I sink.** Ps *40:2. Je 38:6, 22. **deep mire.** Heb. the mire of depth. Ps 68:22. **deep waters.** Heb. depth of waters. Ps 88:6, 7. Ezk 27:26-34. **the floods.** Ps 32:6. Ge 7:17-23. Mt 7:25. 26:37, 38.

3. **I am.** Ps 6:6. 13:1-3. 22:2. Mt 26:38. 27:46. He *5:7. **my throat.** ver. 21. Ps 22:15. Jn *19:28-30. **mine.** Ps *119:82, 123. Dt 28:32. Jb 11:20. 16:16. Is *38:14. La 2:11. **I wait.** S#3176h. William Wilson defines the Hebrew term rendered *wait* "to wait, to hope; importing properly a long and patient waiting, a lingering hope, still expecting and earnestly desiring, though hitherto with delay and disappointment" (*Old Testament Word Studies*, p. 470). Compare S#6960h, Ps 37:34; S#2442h, Is 30:18. Ps *25:21. *39:7. 2 K 6:33h. Jb 14:14h. 29:21, 23h. 30:26h. 32:11, 16h. Is 42:4h. Ezk *19:5h. Mi 5:7h. 7:7h. 1 P 1:10, 11.

4. **hate me without.** T#1937. Ps 109:2-5. Is 49:7. Jn ✱15:24, ▶25. 1 P 2:22. **more than.** Ps 40:12. **being.** ✯63K, Ge +37:13. Ps 7:3-5. 35:12, 19. 38:19, 20. 109:3-5. Mt 27:23. **then I.** Le 5:15, 16. 6:4, 5. Is *53:4-7. Jn +17:5. 2 C ✓5:21. 1 T +*2:6. 1 P *2:24. *3:18.

5. **and my sins.** Heb. and my guiltiness. Ps *17:3. *19:12. *44:20, 21. **hid.** Ps 38:9. Je 16:17.

6. **Let not.** T#1716A. Ps 7:7. 25:3. 35:26, 27. Is 49:23. Lk 24:19-21. Jn 16:20. Ac 4:7-16. Ep 3:13. **wait.** S#6960h, Ps 37:34n. ver. ◐3n. **O God of Israel.** Ps 72:18. 2 S 23:3. Ac 13:17, 23.

7. **Because.** Ps 22:6-8. 44:22. Je 15:15. Jn 15:21-24. **shame.** Is 50:6. ✓53:3. Mt *26:67, 68. 27:29, 30, 38-44. Lk 23:11, 35-37. He *12:2.

8. **stranger unto.** T#1911. Ps *31:11. Jb *19:13-19. Is *63:3. Mt *26:48-50, 56, 70-74. Jn ✱*1:11. ✱*7:3, 5. **and an alien.** Heb. *nokri*, S#5237h, Ge +31:15n. 1 S 17:28. Mi *7:5, 6. Mt *10:21, 22, 35, 36. Mk 6:3. Jn ✱*7:5. **mother's children.** Mt +*13:55. Mk *3:31n. +*6:3. Ac 1:14.

9. **zeal.** T#1905. Ps *119:139. 1 K *19:10. 1 Ch 15:27-29. *29:3. Is 56:7. Je 7:11. Mt ✱21:13. Mk *11:15-17. Lk ✱19:46. Jn ✱*▶2:14-17. **and the.** Ps *89:50, 51. Ro *▶15:3.

10. **I wept.** Ps 102:8, 9. 109:24, 25. Lk 7:33, 34. **soul.** Heb. *nephesh*, Ge +34:3. **chastened.** T#1398. Ps *35:13mg, 14. **with fasting.** Ps *35:13, 14. Jg 20:26n. 2 Ch +*7:14.

11. **I made.** Ps 30:11. 35:13, 14. 1 K 20:31. Is 20:2. 22:12. Jl 1:8, 13. 2 C *8:9. **sackcloth.** ✯121S3U, Jb 16:15. **I became.** Ps 44:13, 14. Dt 28:37. 1 K *9:7. Je *24:9.

12. **They.** Dt 16:18. Mt 27:12, 13, 20, 41, 42, 62, 63. Lk 23:2. Ac 4:26, 27. **gate.** ✯171S7B, Ge +14:7. **speak against.** Ps 22:6, 7. Mt 27:12, 63. Jn 8:48. **I was.** Ps 35:15, 16. Jb 30:8, 9. Mk 15:17-19. **drunkards.** Heb. drinkers of strong drink. Da 5:2-4, 23.

13. **my prayer.** Ps *55:16, 17. 91:15. Da 9:21, 23. Mt 26:36, etc. Lk 22:44. Jn 17:1, etc. He *5:7. 1 P *2:23. **acceptable time.** T#1150. Ps 30:5. 32:6. 62:12. 1 S 25:8. Est 5:2, 6. 7:2. Is *49:8. ✓55:6. 2 C *6:+2 (T#553). **in the.** Ps 40:10, 11. 98:3. Ge 24:27. Mi 7:20. Lk 1:72. Ac 13:32, 33. Ro 15:8, 9.

14. **Deliver.** Ps 40:1-3. Je 38:6-13. La 3:55. Jon 2:3-6. Jn 17:1. He 5:7. **let me.** Ps 25:18, 19. 35:19. 109:3, 21. Lk 19:14, 27. Ac 5:30, 31. **out of.** ver. 1, 2, 15. Ps 42:7. 124:4, 5. 144:7. Mk 14:34, etc. 15:34.

15. **waterflood.** Is 43:1, 2. Jon 2:2-7. Mt 12:40. Ac 2:23-27. Re 12:15, 16. **pit.** Heb. *be-er*, Ge +16:14. Ge=37:24. Ps +*16:10. 88:4-6. Nu 16:33, 34. Ac 2:24, 31.

16. **for thy.** Ps *36:7. *63:3. 109:21. **turn.** Ps 25:16. 26:11. 86:15, 16. Mi 7:19. **according.** ver. 13. Ps 51:1. Is *63:7.

17. **hide.** Ps 13:1. 22:24. *27:9. 44:24. *102:2. 143:9. Mt *27:46. **for I am.** Mt 26:38. **hear me speedily.** Heb. make haste to hear me. Ps 40:13. 70:1. Jb 7:21.

18. **Draw.** Ps 10:1. 22:1, 19. Je 14:8. **soul.** Heb. *nephesh*, Ge +12:13. **redeem.** Ps 31:5. 111:9. Jb 6:23. **because.** Ps 27:11. Dt 32:27. Jsh 7:9.

19. **my reproach.** ver. 7-9. Ps 22:6, 7. Is ✓53:3. Jn 15:24. He *12:2. 1 P *2:23. **my shame.** T#1962. Ps 80:45. Ga *3:13. He ✱*12:2. **dishonor.** Jn 8:49. **mine.** Ps 2:2-4. 38:9. Mt 27:39, 41. Lk 23:35-37.

20. **Reproach.** Ps 42:10. 123:4. He 11:36. **broken my.** Ps 147:3. Pr 25:15. Mt +26:67. Jn ◐16:22. **I am.** Ps 42:6. Mt 26:37, 38. Jn 12:27. **I looked.** Is 63:5. Mt 26:40, 56. Mk 14:37, 50. **for some.** ✯63K, Ge +37:13. **take pity.** Heb. to lament with me. Jb 2:11. 42:11. La 1:12. Ro 12:15. **but there.** Ps *142:4. Jn 16:32. 2 T 4:16, 17. **comforters.** 2 S 10:3. 1 Ch 19:3. Jb 16:2. 19:21, 22. Mt 26:56.

21. **gall for my meat.** Bochart, from a comparison

of this passage with Jn 19:29, thinks that *rosh* is the same herb as the Evangelist calls *hyssop*; a species of which, growing in Judea, he proves from Isaac ben Orman, an Arabian writer, to be so bitter as not to be edible. Theophylact expressly tells us that the hyssop was added as being deleterious, or poisonous; and Nonnus, in his paraphrase, says, "One gave the deadly acid mixed with hyssop." T#1965. Je 8:14. 9:15. 23:15. Mt 27:✱34, 48. **in my thirst.** T#1964. ver. 3. Ps 22:15. Jn ✱19:29, 30. **vinegar to drink.** T#1966. Mk 15:23, 36. Lk ✱23:36. Jn ✱19:29, 30.

22. **Let their table,** etc. Or rather, "Their table *shall* become a snare; their eyes *shall* be darkened," etc. in the future tense. Ps 35:8n. 40:14n. 71:13n. 109:6n. Pr 1:32. Je +*10:25. Ml 2:2. Ro ▶11:8-10. **a trap.** Is 8:14, 15. 1 P 2:8.

23. **Their eyes.** Is 6:9, 10. 29:9, 10. Mt 13:14, 15. Jn 12:39, 40. Ac 28:26, 27. Ro 11:25. 2 C 3:14. **make their.** Dt 28:65-67. Is 21:3, 4. Je 30:6. Da 5:6. Ro 11:10.

24. **Pour.** Ps 79:6. Le 26:14, etc. Dt 28:15, etc. 29:18-28. 31:17. 32:20-26. Ho 5:10. Mt 23:35-37. Lk 21:22. 1 Th 2:15, 16. Re 16:1. **take.** Ex 15:15. Is 13:8. Zc 1:6.

25. **Let their.** 1 K 9:8. Je 7:12-14. Mt 23:38. 24:1, 2. Ac ▶1:20. **habitation.** Heb. palace. Ge 25:16. Nu 31:10. Is 5:1. 6:11. **let none dwell.** Heb. let there not be a dweller.

26. **For.** Ps 109:16. 2 Ch 28:9. Jb 19:21, 22. Zc 1:15. 1 Th 2:15. **whom.** Is 53:4, 10. Zc 13:7. **they talk.** Mk 15:28-32. **those,** etc. Heb. thy wounded. Ps 88:5. 89:10. Ge 34:27.

27. **Add.** Ps 81:12. Ex 8:15, 32. 9:12. Le 26:39. Is 5:6. Mt 21:19. 23:31, 32. 27:4, 5. Ro 1:28. 9:18. 2 Th 2:11, 12. Re 22:10, 11. **iniquity.** *or,* punishment of iniquity. Ps 109:17-19. 2 T 4:14. **let them.** Ps 24:5. Is 26:10. Ro 9:31. 10:2, 3.

28. **blotted.** Ex 32:32, 33. Is 65:15. Ho 1:9. Re √3:5. 22:19. **book.** 𝒮22D5K1A, Ex +32:32. **be written.** 4:3. Ezk 1:39. 13:9. Lk 10:20. Ph *4:3. He 12:23. Re 13:8. 20:12-15.

29. **I am poor.** Ps 40:17. 109:22, 31. Is 53:2, 3. Mt 8:20. 2 C *8:9. **and sorrowful.** T#1704. Ps 13:2. 18:4-6. 2 S 22:6, 7. Da 10:+16 (T#1390), 17-19. Mt 26:37-39. **let thy.** Ps 18:48. 22:27-31. 89:26, 27. 91:14-16. Ep 1:21, 22. Ph *2:9-11.

30. **I will.** Ps 28:7. 40:1-3. 118:21, 28, 29. **magnify.** Ps 34:3.

31. **also shall.** Ps 50:13, 14, 23. Ho 14:2. Ep 5:19, 20. He 13:15. 1 P 2:5.

32. **The humble.** *or,* The meek. Ps *25:9. 34:2. Is 61:1-3. Jn 16:22. 20:20. **your heart.** Ps 22:26, 29. Is √55:6, 7. **live.** 𝒮108B, 1 S +10:24.

33. **the Lord.** Ps *10:17. +*34:6, 15. 72:12-14. *102:17, 20. Is 66:2. Lk 4:18. **his prisoners.** Ps *107:10. *146:7. Zc *9:11, 12. Ac 5:18, 19. 12:4-11. Ep 3:1. Re 2:10.

34. **Let.** Ps 96:11, 12. 98:7, 8. 148:1, etc. 150:6. Is 44:22, 23. 49:13. 55:12. Re 7:11-13. **moveth.** Heb. creepeth. Ge 1:20mg.

35. **save Zion.** Ps *51:18. +*102:13, 16. 147:12, 13. Is 14:32. +*24:23. 44:26. 46:13. +*51:11. +*52:8. +*59:20. Ob 17. Mi +*4:7. Zc *3:15. Re 14:1. **build.** Ps 48:11-13. +*147:2. Je 33:10, 11. Ezk 36:35, 36. Am +*9:11, 14. **dwell there.** Am +√9:15. **in possession.** Ob *17.

36. **The seed.** Ps 37:25, 26. 102:28. 112:2. Pr 11:21. 20:7. Is 65:23. **his servants.** Ps 90:16, 17. 102:28. Is 44:3, 4. *61:9. Ac +*2:39. **shall inherit.** Mt +*5:5. Ro +*4:13. 8:17. Ep +√1:11n. 1 P +*1:4. **love his name.** Ps *91:14. *145:20. Jn 14:23. Ro √8:28. 2 T √4:8. Ja 1:12. +*2:5. Re 21:27. **dwell therein.** ver. 35. Ps *23:6. Mt *8:11.

PSALM 70

David prays for speedy help, the confusion of his foes, and the triumph of the righteous, 1-5.

(Title.) A.M. 2983. B.C. 1021. **A Psalm.** This psalm is almost word for word the same as the last verses of Psalm 40, and it is written as a part of the succeeding psalm in about twenty-seven MSS. Both psalms appear to have been written by David during the rebellion of Absalom, probably at the crisis when he heard of the sanguinary counsel which Ahithophel had given respecting him; or, as some suppose, when beyond Jordan. 2 S 17:1-21. **to bring.** Ps 38, title.

1. **O God.** Ps *40:1, 13, +17. 69:18. *71:12. 143:7. **to help me.** Heb. to my help. Ps 38:22mg. 71:12.

2. **Let.** Ps 6:10. 35:4, 26. 71:13. 109:29. Is 41:11. **my soul.** Heb. *nephesh,* Ge +12:13. Rather, "my life," *naphshee;* for the word as frequently this meaning. **be turned.** Is 28:13. Jn 18:6.

3. **back.** Ps *40:15. Ac 1:18. **Aha, aha.** *Heach! heach!* a note of extreme contempt; marking insult and triumph at the same time. Ps 35:21, 25. Pr *24:17, 18. Ezk 25:3. 26:2. 36:2.

4. **Let all.** Ps 5:11. 35:27. 40:16. 97:12. Is 61:10. *65:13, 14. La 3:25. Jn *16:20. **rejoice.** 𝒮121G2, Ps +25:2.

5. **I am.** Ps +*40:17. 69:29. 109:22. **make.** Ps *141:1. 2 C 1:10. **O Lord.** Ps 13:1, 2. He *10:37. Re *22:20.

PSALM 71

The psalmist professes his trust in God and prays for help to the end and for the confusion of his enemies, 1-13. He resolves to confide in God and praise him, 14-16. He renews his petitions, that he may not be cast off in the decline of life, but may be enabled to transmit to posterity his views of the power and grace of God, 17, 18. He exults in the prospect of complete deliverance, joy, and triumph, 19-24.

1. **do I.** Ps 22:5. *25:2, 3. 31:1-3. *125:1. 146:5. 2 K 18:5. 1 Ch 5:20. Ro 9:33. 1 P 2:6. **let me.** Is 45:17. Je 17:18.

2. **Deliver.** Ps *31:1. *91:15. **in thy.** Ps 17:2. *34:15. 43:1. 143:1, 11. Da 9:16. 2 Th *1:6. **cause.** 1 C √10:13. **escape.** Lk +√21:36. Re *3:10. **incline.** Ps 10:17, 18. 17:6. 116:1, 2. **thine ear.** 𝒮22A8, Ps +10:17.

3. **my strong habitation.** Heb. to me for a rock of habitation. Ps 31:2, 3. 91:1, 2. Pr *18:10. Is *32:2. 33:16. **continually resort.** Mk 10:1. Jn 10:41. **thou hast.** Ps 44:4. 68:28. 91:11, 12. Ezk 9:6. Re 7:2, 3. **my rock.** Ps 18:2. 144:2. **fortress.** 𝒮22L5, Ps +31:3.

4. **Deliver.** ver. 2. Da 3:17. **out of the.** Ps 17:8, 9, 13. 59:1, 2. 140:1-4. 2 S 16:21, 22. 17:1, 2, 12-14, 21.

5. **For thou.** Ps 13:5. 39:7. 42:11. 119:81, 166. Je *17:7, 13, 17. Ro 15:13. **my hope.** 𝒮121R3. Metonymy of the Adjunct B600. *Hope* is put for God, (the object on which it is set). For other instances of this figure

see Pr 13:12. Is 20:5. Je 14:8. 17:7. 50:7. Ac *28:20. Ro 8:24. 1 T 1:1. T *2:13. **my trust.** ver. 17. Ps 22:9, 10. 1 S 16:13. *17:33-37, 45-47. Ec 12:1. Lk *2:40. 2 T √3:15.

6. **By thee.** Ps *22:9, 10. Pr 8:17. Is *46:3, 4. *49:1, 2. Je 3:4. **thou art.** Ps 139:15, 16. 145:1, 2. Is 49:1, 5. Je 1:5. Lk 1:31, 32. Ga 1:15. **my praise.** ver. 14. Ps 34:1. Ep 5:20.

7. **as a wonder.** *Kemopheth,* "as a prodigy:" my low estate, my slaying the lion and bear, conquering the Philistine, escaping the fury of Saul, being raised to the throne of Israel, enduring such uncommon trials and afflictions and experiencing such wonderful deliverances, all mark me out as the subject of *"wonder* unto many; but thou art my strong refuge." Is 8:18. Zc *3:8. Lk *2:34. Ac 4:13. 1 C *4:9. 2 C 4:8-12. 6:8-10. **thou art.** Ps 62:7. 142:4, 5. Je *16:19.

8. **Let my mouth.** T#1645. ver. *15, *24. Ps 34:1. *35:28. *51:14, 15. *107:2. *118:24. +*141:2. *145:1, 2. *146:2. **thy honor.** Ps 95:6. 1 Ch *16:29. Is 6:1-3. Da +*4:34. Mt +*6:9. 1 T +*1:17. Ju 25. Re 4:8, 11.

9. **Cast.** ver. 18. Ps 92:13-15. Is *46:4. 2 T 1:12. 4:18. **old age.** T#772, 1555. This determines the period when this psalm was composed, for it was in David's old age that the rebellion of Absalom took place. ver. 18. Pr 16:31. Is 46:4. **when.** Ps *73:26. 90:10. 2 S 19:35. 21:15-17. Ec 12:1-7.

10. **and they.** Ps 10:9. 56:6. Pr 1:11. **lay wait for.** Heb. watch *or* observe. Ps +5:8mg. +31:6. *37:32, 33. *54:5mg. 1 S 19:11. Pr 1:11. Je 5:26. 20:10. **soul.** Heb. *nephesh,* Ge +12:13. **take.** Ps 2:2. 83:3. 2 S 17:1, etc. Mt 26:3, 4. 27:1. Mk 15:1.

11. **God.** Ps 3:2. *37:25, 28. 41:7, 8. 42:10. Mt 27:42, 43, 46, 49. **for there.** Ps 7:2. 50:22. 2 Ch 32:13, 14. Da 3:15.

12. **O God.** Ps 22:11, 19. *35:22. 38:21, 22. 69:18. **make.** Ps *46:1. 70:1, 2. 143:7.

13. **Let them be,** etc. "They *shall* be confounded," etc.: these are prophetic denunciations. ver. 24. Ps 6:10. 35:4, *8n, 26. 40:14n, 15. 109:6n. Is 41:11. Je ☉+*10:25. 20:11. 1 C *16:22. **soul.** Heb. *nephesh,* Ge +12:13. **covered.** Ps 109:29. 132:18. 1 P 5:5.

14. **hope.** Ps 43:5. Jb 13:15. La *3:21, 26. Ac 26:6. Ro +√15:4. He 10:35. 1 P *1:3, 13. 1 J 3:3. **praise.** Ps 35:28. 51:15. 119:164. Is 12:1. +*61:3. Lk 19:37. Ac 2:47. 16:25. He *13:15. **more and more.** ver. 6. Ps 104:33. 145:1. Ph *1:9. 1 Th 4:10. 2 P +*3:18. Re 4:8. 5:13.

15. **My mouth.** ver. 8, 24. Ps 22:22-25. 30:12. 37:30. *40:9, 10. 145:2, 5-14. **all the day.** Ps 35:28. 89:16. **I know.** Ps *40:5, 12. 139:17, 18.

16. **I will go.** Ps 29:11. 68:35. 73:26. Dt 33:25. Jsh 1:9. Is *40:31. *45:24, 25. Zc 10:12. Hab *3:16. *6:10. Ph √4:13. 2 T 2:1. **I will make.** Is 26:13. 63:7. Ro *1:16. **thy righteousness.** ver. 2, 15, 19, 24. Ps *51:14. Mt *6:33. Ro √1:17. 3:21. *10:3. Ph *3:9. 2 Th 1:6.

17. **thou hast.** ver. *5. Ps *119:9, 102. **hitherto.** Ps *66:16. 1 S 17:36, 37. 2 S 4:9. 22:1, etc. 1 Ch 16:4, etc.

18. **Now.** ver. 9. Ge 27:1. 1 S 4:15, 18. Is *46:4. **when I am old and greyheaded.** Heb. unto old age and grey hairs. **until I.** Ps *78:4-6. 145:4, 5. Ex *13:8, 14-17. 1 Ch 29:10, etc. Ac 13:36. **strength.** Heb. arm. Ps 79:11mg. Is 51:9. 53:1.

19. **Thy righteousness.** Ps 36:5, 6. 57:10. 139:6. Pr

15:24. 24:7. Is 5:16. √55:9. Ro *3:26. **who hast.** Ps 72:18. 126:2, 3. Jb 5:9. **who is like.** God is alone, who can resemble Him? He is that eternal, illimitable, unimpartible, unchangeable, incomprehensible, uncompounded, ineffable Being, whose *essence* is hidden from all created intelligences, and whose *counsels* cannot be fathomed by any creature. Ps 8:5n. 35:10. *86:8. √89:6-8. Ex *15:11. Is 40:18, 25. +*57:15. Je 10:7. Ro *11:33.

20. **which.** Ps *40:1-3. 60:3. *66:10-12. *88:6, etc. *138:7. 2 S *12:11. Mk *14:33, 34. *15:34. 2 C 11:23-31. Re *7:14. **quicken.** Ps *80:17, 18. 143:11. Is *26:19. Ho *6:1, 2. Ac *2:24, 32-34. +*13:33. Ro 4:17. 8:29. Col 1:18. He 1:5, 6. 12:2. 1 P ✱3:18. Re 1:5. **shalt bring.** Ps +*16:10. *40:2. *86:13. Is *38:17. Ezk *37:12, 13. Jon *2:6. Jn *5:28, 29. Ac √17:31. Ep *4:9.

21. **increase.** Ps 72:11. 2 S 3:1. Is *9:7. 49:6. *53:10, 11. Re *11:15. **comfort.** Ps 32:10. 2 C 1:4, 5. *2:14. 7:6, 13. 1 Th 3:9.

22. **psaltery.** Heb. instrument of psaltery. Ps *92:1-3. 150:3-5. Hab √3:18, 19. **even.** Ps 25:10. 56:4. 89:1, 2. 98:3. 138:2. Mi 7:20. Ro 15:8. **O thou.** Ps 89:18. 2 K 19:22. Is 5:16, 19, 24. 12:6. 30:11, 12. 43:3. 57:15. 60:9.

23. **my lips.** Ps 63:5. 104:33. Lk 1:46, 47. **my soul.** Heb. *nephesh,* Ge +12:13. Ps *34:22. *103:2-4. Ge 48:16. 2 S 4:9. Re 5:9.

24. **My tongue.** ver. 8, 15. Ps 37:30. Dt 11:19. Pr 10:20, 21. Mt 12:35. Ep 4:29. **for they.** ver. 13. Ps 18:37-43. 92:11. 1 C +*15:25. Ep *6:12.

PSALM 72

David prays for Solomon and for the Messiah under the type of Solomon; and predicts the peace, righteousness, honor, extent, and duration of his kingdom, as typifying that of the Messiah, 1-17. He ardently blesses God on these accounts and prays that the earth may be filled with his glory, 18-20.

(Title.) A.M. 2989. B.C. 1015. **A Psalm.** This psalm seems to have been composed by David in his last days, when he had set his beloved son on the throne. "Then," says *Calmet,* "transported with joy and gratitude, he addressed this psalm to God, in which he prays Him to pour out His blessings on the young king, and upon the people. He then, wrapped up in a divine enthusiasm, ascends to a higher subject; and sings the glory of the Messiah, and the magnificence of his reign." **for.** *or,* of. Ps 127, title.

1. **Give.** 1 K 1:39, etc. 1 Ch *22:12, 13. 29:19. 2 Ch *1:10. Is *11:2. Jn *3:34. He +*1:8, 9. **thy judgments.** 2 S 23:3. 1 K *3:9-12. **the king's.** 1 K *1:47, 48. *2:1-4. Je *23:5, 6.

2. **He shall.** ver. 12-14. Ps +*45:6, 7. 1 K *3:5-10. Is *11:3-5. 32:1, 17. Je *33:15. Re *19:11. **thy poor.** Ps 12:5. *82:3, 4. Jb 34:19.

3. **mountains.** ver. 16. Is *32:16, 17. *52:7. Ezk *34:13, 14. Jl 3:18. **bring peace.** T#943. ver. 7. Is *2:4. *11:6-9. Jn 17:20-23. Ep 4:16. **little.** Ps 65:12. **by righteousness.** Ps *85:10, 11. *96:11-13. 98:8, 9. Is *32:17. Da *9:24. Ro *14:17. 2 C *5:19-21.

4. **He shall judge.** ver. 12-14. 109:31. Dt 32:36. Is *11:4. Ezk *34:15, 16. Zc 11:7, 11. Mt *11:5. **the poor.** Ja +*2:5. **the needy.** Mt +*5:3. *11:5. **break.** Ps *2:9. 94:5. Jb 19:2. *34:24. Pr 20:26. Je *51:20-23. Da 2:34, 35. **the oppressor.** ⨍108J, Ge +43:18. Is 9:4. *51:12,

13. Zc *9:8-10. Re *18:6-8, 20, 24. 19:2.

5. **They shall.** 1 S 12:18. 1 K 3:28. **as long.** ver. 7, 17. Ps *89:29, 36, 37. Ge +8:22. Ec +1:4. Is *9:7. Je +31:35, 36. Da *2:44. *7:14, 27. Lk 1:32, *33. 1 C +*15:24, 25. Ep 3:21. Re *11:15. **generations.** Ge +9:12.

6. **like rain.** T#620. Dt *32:2. 2 S *23:4. Pr 1:23. 16:15. 19:12. Is 5:6. 32:15. *44:3-5. Ezk *34:23-26. 39:29. Ho *6:3. 14:5-7. Jl *2:28, 29. Zc *12:10. 1 P 1:12. **mown grass.** Heb. *gaz*, more properly denotes pastured grass; it seems to be a reference to the thick night dews which in the summer fall on the pasturages and become the means of restoring the grass consumed in the day time. This is finely expressed by Virgil (*Georg.* ii. 201), "And as much as the flocks crop in the long days, so much shall the cold dew restore in one short night." Is +*26:19n.

7. **In his days.** Ps +*118:24. *132:15-18. Is *11:6-9. 32:3-8, 15-20. 35:1, etc. *54:11-17. 55:10-13. 60:1, 22. 61:3-6, 10, 11. Ml 4:2. Ac 4:32. **righteous flourish.** Ps 92:12. **abundance.** 1 K *4:25. 1 Ch 22:8, 9. Is *2:4. *9:6, 7. Da *2:44. Lk *1:33. *2:14. Ep 2:14-17. He 7:2. **as long as the moon endureth.** Heb. till there be no moon. ver. +*5, 17.

8. **He shall.** Ps *2:8. 80:11. *89:25, 36. 110:2. Ex 23:31. 1 K *4:21n-24. Zc *9:10. √14:9. Re *11:15. **the river.** ℐ32, Ge +31:21. ℐ171E12, Ge +14:22. Ge 15:18. 2 Ch +*9:26. Is +*27:12. **the ends.** Ps 2:8. *22:27, 28. 59:13. 67:7. Is +*43:6. Je +*31:8.

9. **They that.** 1 K 9:18, 20, 21. Is 35:1, 2. **his enemies.** Ps 2:9. 21:8, 9. 110:1, 6. Lk 19:27. **lick.** ℐ121Q3, 2 S +22:8. ℐ121S3W. Metonymy of the Adjunct B607. *Licking the dust* is put for defeat and submission. Is *49:23. Mi *7:17.

10. **The kings.** Ps *45:12. 68:29. 1 K *10:1, 10, 25. 2 Ch 9:21. Is 43:6. *49:7. *60:3, 6, 9. **Tarshish.** Ge +10:4. **bring presents.** Mt ✱*2:11, 12. **offer gifts.** Is *60:6. Mt ✱2:2, 11.

11. **all kings.** Ps 2:10-12. 138:4, 5. Is 49:22, 23. Re *11:15. *17:14. 21:24, 26. **all nations.** Ps 86:9. Is 11:9. 54:5. Ro 11:25. Re *20:1-6.

12. **For.** ver. 4. Ps 10:17. 82:3, 4. 102:17, 20. Jb 29:12. Is *41:17. Lk 4:18. 7:22. 2 C *8:9. He *7:25. Re 3:17, 18. **the needy.** T#1265. Ps 9:18. 22:11. *40:+17 (T#1626). 70:5. 86:1. 109:21, 22. Is *41:17. **the poor.** T#1643. Ps 10:9-12. 34:6. *40:17. 74:19-21. 86:1. 109:21, 22. **him.** Ec 4:1. Is 63:4, 5.

13. **shall save.** Ps 109:31. Jb 5:15, 16. Ezk 34:16. Mt 5:3. 18:11. Ja 2:5, 6. **souls.** Heb. *nephesh*, Ge +12:13.

14. **he shall.** Ps 25:22. 130:8. Ge 48:16. 2 S 4:9. Lk 1:68-75. T *2:14. **soul.** Heb. *nephesh*, Ge +12:13. **precious.** Ps √116:15. Mt *23:30-36. 1 Th 2:15, 16. Re 2:10. *6:9-11. 17:6. 18:20-24. 19:2.

15. **And he.** Ps 21:4. Jn 11:25. *14:19. 16:23. Ro *8:34. 1 J 1:2. Re *1:18. **to him.** 1 K 10:14. Mt 2:11. **shall be given.** Heb. one shall give. **gold.** ℐ171I3. Synecdoche of the Species B626. Gold is put for gifts. Here, gold as the principal gift is put for all other kinds of gifts. Is 60:5-7. **prayer.** ver. 19. Ps 45:4. Mt 6:10. 21:9. Jn 16:23, 24. 1 C 1:2, 3. 2 C 13:14. 1 Th 3:11. 2 T 4:22. He 10:19-22. **continually.** 1 Ch +16:11. **daily.** 2 Ch 2:11, 12. 9:1, 4-8, 23, 24. Jn √5:23. Ph *2:11. 2 P *3:18. Ju *25. Re *1:5, 6. *5:8-14. 7:9-12.

16. **There.** Jb 8:7. Is 30:23. 32:15, 20. Mt *13:31-33. Mk 16:15, 16. Jn *4:35. Ac 1:15. *2:41. 4:4. 1 C

3:6-9. Re 7:9. **upon.** Is *2:2, 3. **the fruit.** Ps 92:12-14. Is 29:17. *35:1, 2. Ho 14:5-7. **of the city.** ver. 6. 1 K 4:20. Is 44:3-5. Je 33:22. Re 7:14. 21:10, 24.

17. **His name.** Ps 45:17. *89:36. Is *7:14. Mi 5:2. Mt *1:21, 23. Lk *1:31-33. Ph *2:10. **shall endure.** Heb. shall be. Ps 104:31mg. **for ever.** Heb. *olam*, Ex +*12:24. **his name,** etc. Heb. shall be as a son to continue his father's name forever. Ep 3:14. Col 1:3. 1 P *1:3. **as long.** ver. +*5, 7. **men.** Ge *12:3. *22:18. Ac *3:26. Ga *3:14. Ep *1:3. **all nations.** Je *4:2. Lk 1:48. Re *15:4.

18. **Blessed.** Ps 41:13. 68:35. 106:48. 1 Ch 29:10, 20. **who only.** Ps 77:14. 86:10. 136:4. Ex *15:11. Jb 9:10. Da 4:2, 3.

19. **blessed.** Ne *9:5. Re 5:13. **for ever.** Heb. *olam*, Ex +*12:24. **and let.** Nu *14:21. Is 6:3. 11:9. Hab *2:14. Zc *14:9. Ml 1:11. Mt *6:10, 13. **Amen.** Ps 41:13. 89:52. Nu 5:22. 1 K 1:36. Je 28:6. Re 1:18. 22:20.

20. **The prayers.** This was probably the last psalm he ever wrote; with it ends the second book of the psalter. 2 S 23:1. Jb 31:40. Je 51:64. Lk 24:51.

PSALM 73

The psalmist, assured that God is good to his people, shows that his faith had almost failed, on seeing the prosperity of the wicked, 1-14. He states how he overcame the temptation in the sanctuary by learning their dreadful end, 15-20. With deep humility he avows his unreserved dependence on God and determines to cleave to him, expecting present support and future glory, 21-28.

(Title.) **of.** *or*, for. Ps 50, 74, 83, titles. 1 Ch 6:39. 15:17. 16:7, 37. 25:1-6. 2 Ch 29:30.

1. **Truly.** *or*, Yet. Ps 2:6. 42:11. **God.** ver. 18-28. Ps *84:11. Is 63:7-9. Lk 12:32. **to such.** Jn *1:47. Ro *2:28, 29. 4:16. *9:6, 7. **of a clean heart.** Heb. clean of heart. Ps 24:4. 51:10. Pr *20:9. Je 4:14. 32:39. Mt +*5:8. T *3:5. Ja *4:8.

2. **But.** Ps 5:7. 17:15. 35:13. Jsh 24:15. 1 S 12:23. 1 Ch 22:7. Jb 21:4. **feet.** Ps 116:8. 1 S 2:9. Ro 7:23, 24. **steps.** Ps 17:5. 38:16. 94:18. Jb 12:5.

3. **I was.** Ps *37:1, 7, 10. Jb *21:7, 29, 30. Pr 3:31. 24:1. Je *12:1-3. Ja *4:5. **I saw.** Ps *17:14.

4. **no.** Ps 17:14. Jb 21:23, 24. 24:20. Ec 2:16. 7:15. Lk 16:22. **firm.** Heb. fat. Ps 17:10. Ge 41:2, 4, 5, 7, 18, 20.

5. **They are.** ver. 12. Jb 21:6. Pr 3:11, 12. Je 12:1, 2. 1 C 11:32. He 12:8. Re 3:19. **in trouble as other.** Heb. in the trouble of other. **like.** Heb. with. 1 C ◖11:32.

6. **Therefore.** Dt 8:13, 14. 32:15. Est 3:1, 5, 6. 5:9-11. Jb 21:7-15. Ec √8:11. Je *48:11, 29. Ezk 28:2-5. Da 4:30. **as a chain.** Jg 8:26. Pr 1:9. SS 4:9. Is 3:19. Ezk 16:11. Ja *4:6. **violence.** Pr 3:31mg. 4:17. Mi 2:1, 2. 3:5. Ja +*5:4-6. **covereth.** Ps 61:2h (overwhelmed). 65:13. 102:t. 109:18, 29. 142:3. Jb 23:9 (hideth). 1 P 5:5.

7. **eyes.** Ps 17:10. 119:70. Jb 15:27. Is 3:9. Je 5:28. Ezk 16:49. **have,** etc. Heb. pass the thoughts of the heart. ver. 12. Ps 17:14. 1 S 25:2, 36. Lk 12:16-21.

8. **corrupt.** Ps *53:1-4. Pr 30:13, 14. **speak wickedly.** Ps 10:2, 10, 11. 12:4, 5. Ex 1:9, 10. 1 S 13:19. 1 K 21:7, etc. Je 7:9-11. Ho 7:16. **speak loftily.** 2 P 2:10, *18. Ju 16.

9. **set.** Ex 5:2. 2 Ch 32:15. Jb 21:14. Da 3:15. 7:25.

Re 13:6. **heavens.** ✒121J20. Metonymy of the Subject B580. *Heaven* is put for God, who dwells there. For other instances of this figure see 2 Ch 32:20. Da 4:26. Mt 3:2. 21:25. Lk 15:18. **tongue.** Ps 52:4. Lk 18:4. Ja 3:6. **walketh.** ✒155A, Ge +31:35.

10. **Therefore.** Je *2:19. Mt 24:12. 2 P √2:20. **waters.** Ps *75:8. 144:13. Ge 23:9mg.

11. **How.** ✒85P, Ge +27:46. ver. 9. Ps 10:11. 94:7. Jb 22:13, 14. Ezk 8:12. Zp 1:12. **God.** Heb. *El,* Ex +15:2. **is there.** Ps 44:21. 139:1-6. Ho *7:2.

12. **these.** Ps 37:35. 52:7. Je 12:1, 2. Lk 16:19. Ja 5:1-3. **prosper.** ver. 3. **world.** Heb. *olam,* Le +25:32. Ec 3:11. **they.** Ps 17:14. 62:10. Pr 11:4. Je 5:27, 28. Ho 12:7, 8.

13. **Verily.** Jb 9:27, 31. 21:15. 34:9. 35:3. Ml 3:14. Ac 24:16. 1 C 6:11. 1 J 3:3. 5:18. **in vain.** Jb 21:15. 34:9. *35:3. **washed.** Ps 24:4. 26:6. 51:10. Dt 21:6. He *10:19-22. Ja *4:8.

14. **For all.** Ps *34:19. *94:12, 13. Jb 7:3, 4, 18. 10:3, 17. Je 15:18. Am 3:2. He 12:5. 1 P 1:6. **chastened.** Heb. my chastisement was. Ps 38:14. **morning.** ✒171T4, Jb 7:18.

15. **offend.** 1 S 2:24. Ml 2:8. Mt 18:6, 7. Ro *14:13, 15, 21. 1 C 8:11-13. **generation.** Ps 22:30. 24:6. 1 P 2:9.

16. **When.** Ps 36:6. 77:19. 97:2. Pr 30:2, 3. Ec 8:17. Ro 11:33. **too painful for me.** Heb. labor in mine eyes. Ps 39:6. Lk 18:32-34. Jn 16:18, 19.

17. **Until.** Ps 27:4. 63:2. 77:13. 119:24, 130. **the sanctuary.** Ps *20:2. 68:35. 74:7. 78:69. 2 K *19:1. Is *37:14. **of God.** Heb. *El,* Ex +15:2. **then.** Ps *37:37, 38. Jb 27:8. Ps *119:130. Ec 8:12, 13. Je 5:31. Lk 12:20. *16:22, 23. 2 C *4:17, 18.

18. **Surely.** Ps 35:6. Dt *32:35. Je 23:12. **thou castedst.** Ps 37:20, 24, 35-38. 55:23. *92:7. 94:23. 2 Th 1:9.

19. **How.** Ps *58:9. Jb 20:5. Is 30:13. Ac *12:23. 1 Th 5:3. Re 18:10. **they are.** or, how are they. ✒63I1C2B, Jb 21:17. Ps 53:5. Nu 17:12, 13. 1 S 28:20. Jb 15:21. *18:11. 20:23-25. Pr 28:1. Is 21:3, 4. Da 5:6.

20. **As a.** Ps 90:5. Jb *20:8. Is *29:7, 8. **when.** Ps 7:6. 78:65. **despise.** or, tread down. Ps 44:5. Is 14:19. 63:18. **their image.** Ps *39:6. Re +*13:15.

21. **my heart.** ver. 3. Ps 37:1, 7. **in my.** Jb 16:13. La 3:13.

22. **So.** Ps 49:10h. 69:5. *92:6h. Pr 12:1h. *30:2. Ec 3:18. **ignorant.** Heb. I knew not. Ps 35:8mg. 39:6. 92:6. 101:4. **as a.** Ps 32:9. Is 1:3. **before thee.** Heb. with thee.

23. **Nevertheless.** Ps 16:8. 23:4. 46:7. 139:1-12, 18. Ge 17:1. Mt 1:23. 28:20. He +*13:5. **thou hast.** Ps *37:17, 24. 63:8. Is *41:10, 13. 42:1.

24. **Thou.** Ps *16:7. √25:9. √32:8. *48:14. *143:8-10. La 33:16. Pr √3:5, 6. 8:20. Is *30:21. *48:17. *58:8, 11. Lk 11:13. Jn *16:13. Ja √1:5. **receive.** Ps *49:15. *84:11. Lk *23:46. Jn √14:3. *17:5, 24. Ac *7:59. 2 C *5:1. 1 P *1:4, 5.

25. **Whom.** Ps 16:5, *11. *17:15. *37:4. 43:4. 63:3. 89:6. Mt +*5:8. Ph *3:8. 1 J *3:2. Re *21:3, 22, 23. **none upon.** Ps 9:2. 18:1. *42:1, 2. *104:34. 143:6-8. Is *26:8, 9. Hab *3:17, 18. Mt *10:37. Ph *3:8. **desire.** Ps 45:11. SS 5:10, 16. Jn 6:68.

26. **flesh.** Ps 63:1. 84:2. 119:81, 82. Jb 13:15. 2 C 4:8-10, 16-18. Ph *1:21. 2 T *4:6-8. 2 P 1:14. Re *21:7. **but.** Ps 18:2. 23:4. 27:14. 138:3. Is 40:29-31. 1 C

+*15:55. 2 C 12:9, 10. **strength.** Heb. rock. ✒22L3, Dt +32:31. Ps 18:2, 31, 46. 19:14mg. 68:35. 71:16. **portion.** Ps +*16:5, 6. *119:57. 142:5. Nu 18:20. SS 2:16. La *3:24. Re 21:3, 4, 7. **for ever.** Heb. *olam,* Ex +*12:24.

27. **lo.** Ps √119:155. Jb 21:14, 15. Is 29:13. Je 12:2. Mt 15:7, 8. Ep *2:12, 13, 17. **that go.** Ex 34:15. Nu 15:39. Ja *4:4. 1 J √2:15. Re 17:1-5. **whoring.** ✒63H, Ge +12:15.

28. **But.** Ps 65:4. 84:10. 116:7. La *3:25, 26. Lk 15:17-20. He *10:19-22. Ja *4:8. 1 P *3:18. **for me.** Jsh +*24:15. **draw near.** Ge 45:4. SS 1:4. Is 48:16. Je 30:21. La 3:57. Ho 11:4. Ja *4:8. **that I may.** Ps 66:16. 71:17, 24. *107:22. *118:17. The LXX., Vulgate, Arabic, and Ethiopic, add, "in the gates of the daughter of Zion," which makes a better conclusion; but it is not acknowledged by any Hebrew MS. yet collated.

PSALM 74

Heavy complaints to God, that in anger he had left his congregation without any encouraging token, while insulting conquerors desolated the sanctuary, 1-9. Earnest pleas, that he would help his people, according to his former powerful works for Israel and in remembrance of his covenant; and thus silence the blasphemies and reproaches of his enemies, 10-23.

(Title.) A.M. 3416. B.C. 588. **Maschil of Asaph.** or, a psalm for Asaph to give instruction. Ps 78, title.

1. **O God.** Ps +√9:10. 10:1. 42:9, 23. 44:9. 60:1, 10. 77:7. Je +√31:37. +√33:24-26. Ro +√11:1, 2. **for ever.** Jb +4:20 (✚S#5331h). **smoke.** ✒22K1, Dt +4:24. ✒46A, Le +26:30. "Smoke" is used by catachresis for the heat of anger. Ps 79:5. Dt 29:20. **the sheep.** Ps 79:13. 95:7. 100:3. Je 23:1. Ezk *34:8, 31. Lk 12:32. Jn √10:26-30.

2. **purchased.** Ex 15:16. Dt 9:29. Ac √20:28. **of old.** Mi +5:2 (✚S#6924h). **rod.** or, tribe. Ps 2:9. 23:4. 45:6. 78:55. **thine.** Ps 33:12. 106:40. 135:4. Dt 4:20. *32:9. Je 10:16. **redeemed.** Is 43:3-5. 51:11. 62:12. *63:9-11. T *2:14. Re 5:9. **this mount.** Ps 48:1, 2. 78:68, 69. 132:13, 14.

3. **Lift.** Ps 44:23, 26. Jsh 10:24. 2 S 22:39-43. Is 10:6. 25:10. 63:3-6. Mi 1:3. **feet.** ✒22A20. Anthropomorphism B881. Feet are attributed to God, to denote his presence in the earth, in power, in universal dominion. For other instances of this figure see Ps 110:1. Is 60:13. 66:1. **the perpetual.** Ps 102:13, 14. Ne 1:3. 2:3, 13. Jb +4:20 (✚S#5331h). Is *64:10, 11. Da 9:17. Mi 3:12. Lk *21:24. Re 11:2. **all.** Ps 79:1. Je 52:13. La 1:10. Da 8:11-14. 9:27. 11:31. Mk 11:17.

4. **Thine.** 2 Ch *36:17, 19. La *2:7. Lk 13:1. Re 13:6. **they set.** Je 6:1-5. Da 6:27. Mt 24:15. Lk 21:20.

5. **was famous.** 1 K *5:5, 6. 2 Ch 2:14. Je 46:22, 23.

6. **the carved.** 1 K 6:18, 29, 32, 35.

7. **cast fire into thy sanctuary.** Heb. sent thy sanctuary into the fire. 2 K 25:9. Is 64:11. Mt 22:7. **defiled.** Ps 89:39. Ezk 24:21. **dwelling.** Ex 20:24. Dt *12:5. 1 K 8:20.

8. **said.** Ps 83:4. 137:7. Est 3:8, 9. **destroy.** Heb. break. or, oppress. Ps 123:4. Je 25:38. **all the synagogues.** or, meeting places. 2 K 2:3, 5. 4:23. 2 Ch 17:9. 23:5. Mt 4:23. Ac 15:21.

9. **We see.** Ex *12:13. *13:9, 10. 23:14. Jg *6:17. Ezk *20:12. He *2:4. **no more.** 1 S *3:1. Ho *3:4.

Am *8:11, 12. Mi *3:6, 7. **knoweth**. 1 Ch ◐+12:32. Lk 12:56. **how long**. Da *9:2. Mt *24:36. Ac *1:6, 7.

10. **how long**. Ps 13:1, 2. 79:4, 5. 89:46, 50, 51. Is 63:6. 64:12. Da 9:17, 18. 12:6. Re *6:10. **for ever**. Jb +4:20 (✳S#5331h).

11. **withdrawest**. Is 64:12. La 2:3. **pluck it out**. As the outward habit of the easterns has no sleeves, the hands and arms are frequently covered with the folds of the robe; in order to do anything, the hand must be disentangled and drawn out. Ps 44:23. 78:65, 66. **bosom**. ⨍22A19. Anthropomorphism B881. A bosom is attributed to God to denote comfort and rest (Pr 19:24. 26:15). For other instances of this figure see Nu 11:12. Is 40:11. Jn 1:18.

12. **God**. Ps 44:4. Ex 15:2. 19:5, 6. Nu 23:21, 22. Is *33:22. **of old**. Mi +5:2 (✣S#6924h). **working**. Ps 106:43. Ex 15:2-15. Jg 4:23, 24. 1 S *19:5. Is *63:8. Hab 3:12-14.

13. **divide**. Heb. break. Ps 66:6. 78:13. 106:8, 9. 136:13-18. Ex 14:21. Ne 9:11. Is 11:15, 16. **brakest**. Ps 89:10. 104:9. Ex 14:28. 15:4. Jb 7:12. 26:12, 13. 38:8, etc. Pr 8:29. Is *51:9, 10. Je 5:22. Ezk 29:3. **dragons**. or, whales. Ps 91:13. 148:7. Ge 1:21. La 4:3mg. Ezk 32:2.

14. **leviathan**. Ps 104:25, 26. Jb 3:8mg. 41:1, etc. Is 27:1. Re 20:2. **meat**. Ps 72:9. Ex 12:35, 36. *14:30. Nu 14:9. **to the people**. Ps +*83:3. Je *31:2. Ezk 20:35. **inhabiting the wilderness**. Is +*16:3, 4. Je +*31:2. Ezk +*20:35. Ho *2:14. Mt 24:16. Re +*12:6, 14.

15. **cleave**. Ps 105:41. Ex *17:5, 6. Nu *20:11. Is 48:21. **fountain**. Heb. mayan, Ge +7:11 (✳S#4599h). ⨍121H. Metonymy of the Effect B567: the thing made is put for the material from which it is made or produced. Here, "fountain" is put for the rock from which the fountain flowed. For other instances of this figure see Is 28:28. 33:12. 47:2. **flood**. Jsh 3:13, etc. 2 K 2:8, 14. Is 11:16. 44:27. Hab 3:9mg. Re 16:12. **mighty rivers**. Heb. rivers of strength. Ps 24:2. 46:4. 66:6.

16. **The day**. Ps 136:7-9. Ge 1:3-5. **prepared**. Ps 8:3. 19:1-6. 136:7-9. Ge 1:14-18. Mt 5:45. **the light**. Ge 1:3. **and**. ⨍93A, Ge 1:26. i.e. sunlight.

17. **set**. Ps 24:1, 2. Dt 32:8. Ac *17:26. **made summer**. Heb. made them summer. Ge +*8:22. Je +*31:35, 36. Ac 14:17.

18. **Remember**. ver. 22. Ps 89:50, 51. 137:7. Is 62:6mg, 7. Re 16:19. **the foolish**. T#200-3. ver. 22. Ps 14:1. 39:8. 94:2-8. Dt 32:27. Is 37:23, 24. Ezk 20:14.

19. **soul**. Heb. nephesh, Ge +12:13. **turtledove**. Ps 68:13. SS 2:14. 4:1. 6:9. Is 60:8. Mt *10:16. **forget**. Ps *68:10. 72:2. Zp 3:12. Ja *2:5, 6. **for ever**. Jb +4:20 (✳S#5331h).

20. **Have respect**. Ps 89:28, *34-36, 39. *105:8, 9. *106:45. Ge *17:7, 8. Ex 24:6-8. Le *26:40-45. Dt 9:27. 2 S +*7:10-13, 15, 16. *23:5. Is +*55:3. Je *31:33. +√33:20-26. Zc 9:11. Ml 3:6. Lk *1:68-75. He *8:10. **the covenant**. Ps 105:8-10. 106:45. Dt 30:1n. 2 Ch +*20:7. Mi +*7:20. **the dark**. Dt 12:31. Ro *1:29-31. Ep *4:17, 18. **habitations**. Ps 5:8. Ge 49:5-7.

21. **O let not**. Ps *9:18. 12:5. 102:19-21. 109:22. Is *45:17. **poor**. Ps 102:21. Ezr 3:11. Je 33:11.

22. **Arise**. Ps 9:19, 20. 79:9, 10. **remember**. ver. 18. Ps 75:4, 5. *89:50, 51. Is 52:5.

23. **Forget**. ⨍22C4, Ps +13:1. Ps 10:11, 12. 13:1. **tumult**. ver. 4. Ps 2:1, 2. Is 37:29. La 2:16. Re 17:14. **increaseth**. Heb. ascendeth. Ge 28:12. Jon *1:2.

PSALM 75

The people bless God for the tokens of his presence, 1. The psalmist determines to judge uprightly, 2, 3. He expostulates with the wicked, warning them of the power and righteous vengeance of God, 4-8. He resolves to praise God and to administer justice impartially, 9, 10.

(*Title.*) A.M. 3294. B.C. 710. **Al-taschith**. or, Destroy not. Ps 57, 58, titles. **A Psalm**. Some consider this psalm to have been written by David on his accession to the throne over all Israel; others refer it to the time of the captivity, considering it as a continuation of the subject in the preceding; but Bp. Patrick and others are of opinion that it was composed by Asaph to commemorate the overthrow of Sennacherib's army, 2 K ch. 19. **of Asaph**. or, for Asaph.

1. **for that**. Ps 76:1. 138:2. Ex 23:21. *34:6, 7. Je 10:6. **wondrous**. Dt *4:7, 33, 34. **works declare**. T#207. Ps 9:16. *19:1, 2. Ac 14:17. Ro *1:20. 11:36. He 3:4.

2. **When**. Ps 78:70-72. 101:2. 2 S 2:4. 5:3. 8:15. 23:3, 4. **receive the congregation**. or, take a set time. Ec 3:17. Jn 7:6. Ac *1:7. √17:31. **uprightly**. ⨍24I, Is +21:7. Ps 17:2.

3. **earth**. Ps 60:1-3. 78:60-72. 1 S 31:1-7. Is 24:1-12. Ro 8:21, 22. **I bear**. 1 S 18:7. 25:28. 2 S 5:2. Is *49:8. He *1:3. **pillars**. 1 S 2:8.

4. **I said**. Ps 82:2, etc. 94:8. Pr 1:22. 8:5. 9:6. **Lift**. Ps 89:17. 148:14. Da 7:20, 21. Zc 1:21.

5. **speak**. Ex 32:9. Dt 31:27. 2 Ch 30:8. Is 48:4. Ezk 2:4. Ac 7:51. **not with**. ⨍63K, Ge +37:13. **stiff neck**. ⨍121S3C. Metonymy of the Adjunct B606. To be stiff-necked is put for pride and obstinacy. 2 Ch 30:8.

6. **promotion cometh**. 1 S *16:7. Mt *7:21, 23. **south**. Heb. desert. Ps 29:8. 55:7. 63:1. 65:12.

7. **God**. Ps 50:6. 58:11. **he putteth**. Ps *113:7, 8. 1 S *2:7, 8. 15:23, 28. 16:1. 2 S 3:17, 18. 5:2. 6:21. Je 27:4-8. Da 2:21, 22, 37. 5:18. Lk 1:52. Jn *15:16. Ro 11:15. Ga 1:15.

8. **For in**. Ps 11:6. *60:3. Jb *21:20. Is *51:17, 22. Je 25:15, 17, 27, 28. Hab 2:16. Re 14:9, 10. *16:19. **it is full**. Alluding to the medicated wine or potion of stupifying drugs given to criminals to drink previous to their execution. Pr 23:30. Is 5:22. **poureth**. Heb. nagar, ✳S#5064h. Niphal, Preterite: Ps 77:2 (ran). La 3:49 (trickleth down). Niphal, Participle: 2 S 14:14 (spilt). Jb 20:28 (flow away). Hiphil, Preterite: Mi 1:6 (pour down). Hiphil, Imperative: Je 18:21 (pour out). Hiphil, Future: Ps 63:10 (fall. mg, run out). 75:8 (poureth out). Ezk 35:5 (shed. mg, poured out). Hophal, Participle: Mi 1:4 (poured down). **but the dregs**. Ps 73:10. Is 25:6. Je 48:11. Zp 1:12.

9. **But**. Ps 9:14. 34:1. 104:33. *145:1, 2. **for ever**. Heb. olam, Ex +*12:24.

10. **All the horns**. Ps *101:8. Je *48:25. Zc 1:20, 21. **but the horns**. Ps 89:17. 92:10. 148:14. 1 S 2:10. Lk 1:69.

PSALM 76

The psalmist praises God, who had defended his people and crushed their enemies, 1-10. He exhorts all to serve God reverently, 11, 12.

(*Title.*) **Neginoth**. Ps 4, 54, 61, 67, titles. **A Psalm**.

This psalm is entitled in the Septuagint, which is followed by the Vulgate and Apollinarius, "An ode against the Assyrian," and it is considered by many of the best commentators to have been composed by Asaph after the defeat of Sennacherib. **of Asaph.** *or,* for Asaph.

1. **In Judah.** ♪132G, Ge +3:19. Ps *48:1-3. *147:19, 20. Dt 4:7, 8, 34-36. Ac 17:23. Ro 2:17, etc. 3:1, 2. **his.** Ps 98:2, 3. 148:13, 14. 1 Ch 29:10-12. 2 Ch 2:5, 6. Da 3:29. 4:1, 2.

2. **Salem.** Ge 14:18. He 7:1, 2. **dwelling.** Ps 132:13, 14. 2 Ch 6:6. Is 12:6.

3. **There.** Ps 46:9. 2 K *19:35. 2 Ch 14:12, 13. 20:25. 32:21. Is 37:35, 36. Ezk *39:3, 4, 9, 10. Col 2:15. **brake he.** ♪22D2C, Ex 15:3. **battle.** Zc 14:3.

4. **mountains.** SS 4:8. Je 4:7. Ezk 19:1-4, 6. 38:12, 13. Da 7:4-8, 17, etc. Hab 3:6.

5. **stouthearted.** Jb 40:10-12. Is *46:12. Da 4:37. Lk 1:51, 52. **they.** Ps *13:3. Is 37:36. Je *51:39. Da √12:2. Na 3:18. **and.** Is 31:8. Ezk 30:21-25.

6. **At thy.** Ps 18:15. 80:16. 104:7. Ex *15:1, 21. Zc 14:3. **both.** Ex 14:27, 28. 15:4-6, 10. 2 S 10:18. Is 37:36. Ezk 39:20. Na 1:6. 2:13. 3:18. Zc *12:4. **dead.** 1 S 26:12. Je 51:39, 57.

7. **even thou.** Ps 89:7. Je 10:7-10. Mt +*10:28. Lk *12:5. Re 14:7. 15:4. **who.** Ps 90:11. Na *1:6. 1 C 10:22. Re 6:16, 17. **when.** Ps *2:12.

8. **didst.** Ex 19:10. Jg 5:20. 2 Ch 32:20-22. Ezk *38:20-23. **still.** Ps 46:10. 2 Ch *20:29, 30. Hab √2:20. Zc 2:13.

9. **When.** Ps *9:7-9. 35:20. *72:4. 82:2-5. Is 11:4. Je 5:28. **to judgment.** Ps +*94:15. **to save.** Ps *25:9. +*149:4. Zp √2:3. Mt +*5:5. 1 P 3:4.

10. **Surely.** Ge 37:18-20, 26-28. √50:20. Ex +*9:16, 17. 15:9-11. 18:11. Da *3:19, 20, 28. Ac 2:36. 4:26-28. Ph +*1:12. Re +*11:18. **shall praise.** ♪121E2, Ge +42:38. **remainder.** Ps 46:6. *65:7. 104:9. Mt 2:13-16. 24:22. Ac 12:3, etc.

11. **Vow.** Ps 50:14. 119:106. Le +23:38. Nu 30:2. Pr 7:14. Ec *5:4-6. **and pay.** Supply ellipsis, "your vows," ♪63E1, Le +4:2. **let all.** Ps +68:29. *89:7. Dt 16:16. 2 Ch *32:22, 23. **bring presents.** Le 7:16. +*23:19. Dt *16:16. Pr 23:26. 2 C *8:5. **unto him.** Heb. to fear. Le 31:42. **be feared.** Ps 9:20. Is 8:12. Je 32:21. Ml 1:6.

12. **cut off.** ♪22C46. Anthropomorphism B890. Human actions are attributed to God: cutting off the spirit. Ps 2:5, 10. 48:4-6. 68:12, 35. Jsh *5:1. 2 Ch 32:21. Da 5:6. Zp 3:6. **spirit.** Heb. *ruach*, Ge +41:8. ♪121A10, Ge +26:35. **terrible.** Is 13:6-8. 24:21. Re *6:15. 19:17-21.

PSALM 77

The psalmist relates the sharp conflict against despondency he had sustained under affliction, 1-9; and how he baffled the temptation by meditating on the wondrous works of God for Israel, 10-20.

(*Title.*) A.M. cir. 3463. B.C. cir. 541. **Jeduthun.** Ps 39, 62, titles. 1 Ch 16:41, 42. 25:3, 6. **A Psalm.** This psalm is allowed by the best judges to have been written during the Babylonian captivity. **of Asaph.** *or,* for Asaph. Ps 50, title.

1. **I cried.** Ps *3:4. *34:6. *55:16, 17. 142:1-3. **gave.** Ps 116:1, 2. **ear.** ♪96B, Ge +8:5.

2. **In the.** Ps 18:6. +*50:15. 88:1-3. 102:1, 2. 130:1, 2. Ge 32:7-12, 28. 2 K 19:3, 4, 15-20. Is 26:9, 16.

Jon 2:1, 2. 2 C 12:7, 8. He *5:7. Ja *5:13. **my.** Ps 6:2, 3. 38:3-8. 2 Ch 6:28. Is 1:5, 6. Ho 5:13. 6:1. **sore.** Heb. hand. ver. 20. 78:42, 61. 80:17. 89:21. Ex 9:29. √17:11, 12. 1 K +16:12mg. **ran.** or, spread out. Ps 63:10mg. 2 S 14:14 (spilt). La 3:49 (trickleth down). 1 T +*2:8. **in the night.** Ps 63:6. +119:55 (T#1165). Is *26:9. **ceased not.** Ps 38:8 (feeble). Hab 1:4 (slacked). Ge 45:26 (fainted). Lk 18:1. 1 Th √5:16. Ja *5:16. **my soul.** Heb. *nephesh*, Ge +34:3. **refused.** Ps 78:10. **to be comforted.** Ge 37:35. Est 4:1-4. Pr 18:14. Je 31:15. Jn 11:31.

3. **I remembered.** Jb 6:4. 23:15, 16. 31:23. Je *17:17. **was troubled.** Ps 42:5, 11. 46:3. 83:2. Jb *23:15, 16. **I complained.** Ps 55:2. 88:3, etc. 102:3, etc. 142:2. Nu +*11:1. Ru +*1:13. Jb 7:11. 10:1. 23:2. Pr +√19:3. Is ◑√29:24. La 3:17, *39. Ezk +*18:25. Ro +*9:14. Ph +√2:14. +*4:11. He ◑+*13:5. **spirit.** Heb. *ruach*, Ps +106:33. ♪121A10, Ge +26:35. Ps 55:4, 5. 61:2. 142:2, *3. 143:4, 5. **overwhelmed.** or, feeble. ✳S#5848h. Ps *61:2. 65:13 (covered). 73:6. 77:3. 102:t. 107:5. 142:3. 143:4. Ge 30:42 (feebler). Jb 23:9 (hideth). Is 57:16 (fail). La 2:11 (swoon), 12 (swooned), 19 (faint). Jon 2:7 (fainted). **Selah.** Ps +9:16.

4. **holdest.** Ps 6:6. Est 6:1. Jb 7:13-15. **I am.** Jb 2:13. 6:3.

5. **have considered.** Ps 74:12-18. *143:5. Dt 32:7. Jb *29:2-4. Is 51:9. 63:9-15. Mi 7:14, 15. **of old.** Mi +5:2 (✦S#6924h). **of ancient times.** Heb. *olam* plural, Ps +61:4.

6. **my song.** Ps *42:8. Jb *35:10. Hab 3:17, 18. Jon 1:2. Ac *16:25. or, music. Ps 4:t (Neginoth). 61:t (Neginah). 69:12. Jb 30:9. La 3:14. 5:14. Hab +3:19mg. **night.** ver. 2. 78:14. 88:1. 90:4. Is *50:10. **commune.** Ps *4:4. 63:6. 104:34. Ec 1:16. **and.** Ps 139:23, 24. Jb 10:2. La 3:40. 1 C 11:28-32. **spirit.** Heb. *ruach*, Ps +106:33. ♪121A10, Ge +26:35. **search.** Ge 31:35h. 44:12h. Je *29:13. La √3:40. Am 9:3h. Zp 1:12h. Jn +√5:39. 1 C *11:31.

7. **Will.** ♪85P, Ge +27:46. **the Lord.** Ps 13:1, 2. 37:24. 74:1. 89:√30-34, 38, 46. √94:14. Je 23:24-26. La √3:31, 32. Ro +*11:1, 2. **for ever.** Heb. *olam* plural, Ps +61:4. **and will.** Ps 79:5. 85:1, 5.

8. **Is his.** ♪85P, Ge +27:46. Ps *103:17, 18. Is 27:11. Lk 16:25, 26. **for ever.** Jb +4:20 (✳S#5331h). **promise fail.** Nu 14:34. *23:19. Je 15:18. Hab +*3:9. Ml +*3:6. Ro *9:6. +*11:29. He *6:18. **for evermore.** Heb. to generation and generation. Ps +33:11mg.

9. **Hath.** ♪85P, Ge +27:46. **God.** Is 40:27. *49:14, 15. 63:15. La *3:22, 23. Ho 11:8. **gracious.** Ex 34:6. **anger.** Ps 78:21, 31, 38, 49. **shut up.** Ps 107:42. Jb 5:16. Lk 13:25-28. Ro 11:32mg. 1 J 3:17.

10. **This is,** etc. Or as Dr. Waterland renders, "This my affliction is a change of the right hand of the Most High," it proceeds from a change of God's conduct towards me. De Dieu renders, "To pray, this is my business: to change the right hand of the Most High." I can do nothing else than pray: God is the ruler of events. Mr. N.M. Berlin translates, "To grieve is my portion: to change (my condition) belongs to the right hand of the Most High." Ps *31:22. 73:22. 116:11. Jb 42:3. La 3:18-23. Mk 9:24. **the years.** ver. 5. Ex 15:6. Nu 23:21, 22. Dt 4:34. Hab 3:2-13. or, changes. Ps 78:33. Ge 1:14. 47:8, 9. Pr 3:2mg. **right hand.** ♪22A15A, Ex +15:6. Ps 44:3. 78:54. 80:15, 17. **most High.** Ps +*7:17. +78:17, 35, 56. *83:18.

11. **remember.** ver. 10. Ps 28:5. 44:1. 78:11. *111:4.

*143:5. 1 Ch 16:12. Is 5:12. *46:9. **of old**. Mi +5:2 (✣S#6924h).

12. **meditate**. Ps 104:34. 143:5. **talk**. Ps 71:24. 105:2. 145:4, 11. Dt 6:7. Lk 24:14-32.

13. **Thy way**. Ps *25:10. 27:4. 63:2. 68:25. *73:3, 16, 17. **who**. Ps 89:6-8. Ex *15:11. Dt *32:31. Is 40:18, 25. 46:5. Ro *11:33. Re *15:3, 4.

14. **the God**. Ps 72:18. 86:10. 105:5. 136:4. Ex 15:11. Re 15:3. **thou hast**. Ex 13:14. 15:6. Jsh 9:9, 10. Is 51:9. 52:10. Da 3:29. 6:27.

15. **with**. Ps 136:11, 12. Ex 6:6. Dt 9:26, *29. Is 63:9. **arm**. ✶22A12, Ex +15:16. **the sons**. Ge 48:3-20.

16. **The waters**. Ps 114:3-6. Ex *14:21. Jsh *3:15, 16. Hab 3:8-10, 15. **saw**. ✶155D, Ge +4:10. **waters**. ✶84, Ge +6:17. **afraid**. ✶155D, Ge +4:10.

17. **clouds**. Ge 9:13. **poured out water**. Heb. were poured forth with water. Ps 68:8, 9. Heb. *zaram*, ✳S#2229h: Kal, Preterite: Ps 90:5 (flood). Poal, Preterite: Ps 77:17. **thine**. Ps 18:14. 144:6. 2 S *22:15. Hab *3:11.

18. **voice**. Ps 29:3-9. Ex 19:16. Jb 37:1-5. Re 11:19. **lightnings**. Ps 97:4. Hab 3:4. Re 18:1. **earth**. Ex 19:18. 2 S 22:8, 14. Mt 27:51. 28:2. Re 20:11.

19. **way**. Ps 29:10. 97:2. Ne 9:11. Jb *26:14. Na 1:3, 4. Hab 3:15. **and**. ✶95, Ps +7:13. **footsteps**. ✶22A21. Anthropomorphism B882. Footsteps are attributed to God. Ps *89:51. Ex 14:28. Ro *11:33.

20. **Thou leddest**. Ps 78:52. 80:1. Ex *13:21. 14:19. Is *63:11, 12. Ho 12:13. Ac 7:35, 36.

PSALM 78

An exhortation to Israel to consider the works and word of God; that what they had learned from their fathers, they might teach their children for the benefit of even their remote posterity, 1-8. A rehearsal of God's love and longsuffering to the unbelieving and obstinate Israelites, 9-11. An abstract of Israel's deliverance from Egypt, passage through the wilderness, settlement in Canaan, and the subsequent events; in which the mercies of God to them are contrasted with an account of their unbelief, apostasies, and idolatries, 12-66. God at length chooses Judah, Zion, and David, 67-72.

(Title.) A.M. 3074. B.C. 930. **Maschil**. or, A Psalm for Asaph, to give instruction. Ps 74, title. This psalm was probably written, as Calmet and others suppose, by Asaph in the days of Asa, who had gained, by the aid of the Syrians, a great victory over the Israelites, and brought back to the pure worship of God many out of the tribes of Ephraim, Manasseh, and Simeon, 2 Ch ch. 15, 16. It is a poetical abstract or chronological poem of the ancient history of the Hebrews and must have greatly assisted the people in becoming better acquainted with the wonderful deeds of Jehovah in their behalf.

1. **Give ear**. Ps 49:1-3. 51:4. Jg 5:3. Pr 8:4-6. Is *51:4. 55:3. Mt 13:9. **my people**. ver. 20, 52, 62, 71. 2 K 4:13. Est 7:3, 4. **my law**. ver. 5, 10. **incline**. Ps 86:1. 88:2. **words**. Ps 5:1. 19:14.

2. **I will**. T#1898. Ps *49:4. Mt *13:34, ✱⟩35. **open**. ✶108H6A, Jg +11:35. **parable**. Nu 23:7n. Or, as Bp. Lowth renders *mashal*, a grave, sententious, and elevated discourse or a poetic composition, elevated and grave, weighty and powerful, highly ornamented with comparisons, figures, and imagery. **dark sayings**. Or,

"pointed sayings," for there is nothing dark or mystical in this psalm except the history of Israel, like the parables of Christ, was a picture or similitude of heavenly things. Nu +12:8. Jg 14:12. Pr 1:6. Mt 13:11-13. Mk 4:34. 1 C 10:11. **of old**. Mi +5:2 (✣S#6924h).

3. **Which we**. Ps 44:1. 48:8. Ex 12:26, 27. *13:8, 14, 15.

4. **We will**. Ps 145:4-6. Dt *4:9. 6:7. Jl 1:3. **showing**. Ps *71:17, 18. Dt 11:19. Jsh 4:6, 7, 21-24. **praises**. Ps 9:14. 105:1-5. 145:5, 6. Is *63:7, etc.

5. **For he**. Ps 81:5. 119:152. 147:19. Dt 4:45. *6:7. 11:19. Is √8:20. Ro 3:2. 1 J √5:9-12. **testimony**. The word *testimony* is used for the ark and for the law, written on tables of stone, put within the ark, and covered with the mercy seat. This testified the Lord's gracious presence with his people and seemed to point out to them both the way of access and acceptance and the standard or rule of their duty. Ex 16:34. 25:16, 21. 40:3, 20. **that they**. ver. 3, 4. Ge +*18:19. Dt +*6:20. Is *38:19. Ml 4:6. Ep +*6:4.

6. **That**. Note the cause/effect relationships expressed in this passage (ver. 5-8. See related note, Ps +√9:10). Ps 48:13. 71:18. *102:18. *145:4. Est 9:28. **who**. Ps 90:16. Dt *4:10. Jsh 22:24, 25. Jl 1:3.

7. **set their hope**. Ps 40:4. 62:5. 91:14. 130:6, 7. 146:5. Je 17:7, 8. Ac +*26:6. Ro +*15:4. 1 P 1:21. **not forget**. Ps 77:10-12. 103:2. 105:5. Ex 12:24-27. Dt 4:9. 7:18, 19. 8:2, 11. Est 9:27, 28. 1 C 11:24. **God**. Heb. *El*, Ex +15:2. **keep**. Dt *5:29. Jn +*13:17. 14:21-24. 1 J 3:22-24. *5:3. Re 14:12.

8. **as their fathers**. Ps 68:6. 106:7. Ex *32:9. 33:3, 5. 34:9. Dt 9:6, 13. *31:27. 1 K ◗*9:4. 22:52. 2 K 17:14. 2 Ch ◗*17:3. 22:3. ◗*26:4. Je 9:14. Ezk 2:3-8. *20:8, 18. Am 2:4. Mt 14:8. 23:31-33. Ac 7:51. 2 T ◗*1:5. **stubborn**. 1 S +*15:23. **rebellious**. Ps 68:6. Dt 31:27. 1 S +*15:23. **set not**. Heb. prepared not. ver. 37. 2 Ch *12:14. 19:3. *20:33. 30:19. **whose**. ver. 37. Dt 4:4. Jsh 14:8, 9. Ac *11:23. Ph 1:27. 4:1. **spirit**. Heb. *ruach*, Ge +41:8. Ezr 1:5. Da 5:12. 2 C +*12:18. **stedfast**. ver. 37. Ps 16:8. Nu +*14:24. Jsh *24:15. 2 K 22:2. Jn √8:31. 1 C √15:58. 16:13. He *3:14. 4:14. 10:23. **God**. Heb. *El*, Ge +15:2.

9. **The children**. ✶171R, Ex +12:40. Some think this refers to a defeat of the Ephraimites mentioned in 1 Ch 7:20-22; but it probably refers to the conduct and defeat of the ten tribes, of which Ephraim was the head. Nothing is recorded in the history of Israel concerning the cowardice of the Ephraimites as distinct from that of the other tribes: some therefore think that "the children of Ephraim" is put by a figure of speech (✶171R. Synecdoche of the Part, Ex +12:40) for the nation in general. ver. 21. Dt *1:41-44. Jsh 17:16-18. 1 S *4:10. 31:1. **carrying**. Heb. throwing forth. **turned**. Ps 30:11. 41:3mg. 66:6. 105:25. Jg 9:28, 38-40. Lk 22:33, 56-60.

10. **kept not**. Dt 31:16, 20. Jg 2:10-12. 2 K *17:14, 15. Ne 9:26-29. Je *31:32.

11. **forgat**. ver. 7. Ps 106:*13, 21, 22. Dt *32:18. Je *2:32.

12. **Marvellous**. ver. 42-50. Ps 105:27-38. 135:9. Ex ch 7-12. Dt 4:34. 6:22. Ne 9:10. **Zoan**. *Zoan*, the ancient capital of the Pharoahs, where Moses wrought so many miracles, is rendered by the Chaldee, *Tanim*, LXX. *Tanis*, Vulgate, *Tanis*, and Coptic, *Tane*, from the Coptic *ten*, "plain, flat, level;" being situated in the low ground of the Delta, on one of the eastern branches

of the Nile, bearing its own name, near a large lake, now called the lake of Menzala, 44 miles west of Pelusium and 169 miles east of Alexandria according to the *Antonine Itinerary*, and three miles from the Mediterranean, according to the *Geograph. Nubiens* (Clim. 3, par. 3). There are ruins still remaining to mark the site of *Zoan*, or *Tanis*, called *San* by the Arabs; comprising broken obelisks, capitals of the Corinthian order, a granite monument, etc. ver. 43. Ge 32:3. Nu *13:22. Is 19:11, 13. Ezk 30:14.

13. **He divided**. Ps 66:6. 106:9, 10. 136:13-15. Ex ch. 14, 15. Is 63:13. 1 C *10:2, 3. **made**. Ps 33:7. Jsh 3:16. Hab 3:15.

14. **the daytime**. Ps 105:39. Ex *13:21, 22. 14:24. 40:35-38. Ne 9:12, 19.

15. **clave**. Ps 105:41. 114:8. Ex *17:6. Nu *20:11. Is 41:18. 43:20. Jn 7:37, 38. 1 C *10:4. Re 22:1, 17.

16. **brought streams**. Ps 105:41. Dt 8:15. 9:21. Is *43:19.

17. **they sinned**. ver. 32. Ps 95:8-10. 106:13-32. Dt *9:8, 12-22. He 3:16-19. **provoking**. ver. 35, +40h, 56. Is 63:10. ✛S#4784h, Hiphil, Infinitive: Jb 17:2. Is 3:8. **most High**. ver. 35, 56. Ps *7:17. 82:6. *83:18. Ge +14:18. Is 14:14. Da 7:18. Mk +5:7. Ro √9:5. 1 C *10:9. 1 Th 3:13. He 7:1.

18. **God**. Heb. *El*, Ex +15:2. **by asking meat**. Ps 106:14, 15. Ex *16:2, 3. Nu 11:4. 1 C *10:6. Ja 4:2, 3.

19. **Yea**. Ex 16:8-10. Nu 21:5. 2 Ch 32:19. Jb 34:37. Ro 9:20. Re 13:6. **Can God**. Heb. *El*, Ex +15:2. Nu *11:4, 13. **furnish**. Heb. order. Ps 40:5. Jg 20:22. 1 S 17:8. Is 21:5 (prepare). **table**. √121J6, Ps +23:5.

20. **he smote**. Ex 17:6, 7. Nu 20:11. **can he give**. ver. 41. Ge *18:12-14. Nu 11:21-23.

21. **the Lord**. ver. 31. Nu 11:10. 1 C 10:5, 11. Ju 5. **a fire**. Nu *11:1-3. Dt 32:22. He 12:29.

22. **Because**. Ps 106:24. Is 7:9. He 3:12, *18, 19. √11:6. 1 J *5:10. Ju *5.

23. **Though**. Ps 33:9. Is 5:6. **opened**. √22C30. Anthropomorphism B889. Human actions are attributed to God: opening doors, windows. For other instances of this figure see Dt 28:12. Ml 3:10. **the doors**. Ge 7:11. 2 K 7:2, 19. Ml 3:10.

24. **had rained**. Ps 68:9. 105:40. Ex *16:4, 14. Dt 8:3. Ne 9:15, 20. Jn *6:31, =33, etc. 1 C *10:3. **the corn of heaven**. The manna fell about their camp in the form of seeds; and as it appeared to come down from the clouds, it was not improperly termed *degan shamayim*, "the corn of heaven," or "heavenly grain." See Notes on Ex 16:22, 31.

25. **Man**, etc. *or*, Every one did eat the bread of the mighty. *Lechem abberim*, "bread of the mighty:" they ate such food as could only be expected at the tables of the *rich* and *great*; the best, the most delicate food. Or, it might be so called, because it rendered the people healthy, vigorous, and fit for their marches. Ps 103:20. Jn 6:48-50. **he sent**. Ex 16:8. Mt 14:20. 15:37.

26. **He caused**. Ps 135:7. Nu 11:31. **east wind**. Ps 48:7. Ge 41:6, 23, 27. **blow**. Heb. go.

27. **He rained**. Ex 16:12, 13. Nu *11:18, 19, 31, 32. **feathered fowls**. Heb. fowl of wing. Ps 17:8. **as the sand**. √102B, √138B, Ge +13:16.

28. **he let**. Ex 16:13. **fall**. ver. 55. **camp**. Ps 27:3. 106:16. SS 6:13. **habitations**. or, tabernacles. ver. 60.

29. **for he gave**. Ps *106:15. Nu *11:19, 20.

30. **But**. Nu *11:33, 34. 22:20-22. Pr 1:32. Lk 16:19-23.

31. **smote down**. Heb. made to bow. **chosen men**. *or*, young men. ver. 63.

32. **they sinned**. Nu ch. 14, 16, 17. 21:1-6. ch. 25. 2 Ch *28:22. Ezk 20:13. Ho *13:2. **believed**. ver. 22. Lk 16:31. Jn *12:37.

33. **days**. Ps 90:7-9. Nu *14:29, 35. *26:64, 65. Dt 2:14-16. **years**. Ge 3:16-19. Jb 5:6, 7. 14:1. Ec 1:2, 13, 14. 12:8, 13, 14.

34. **When he slew**. Nu *21:7. Jg 3:8, 9, 12-15. 4:3. 10:7-10. Is *26:16. Je 22:23. Ho *5:15. *7:14. **returned**. T#1422. Dt 4:29-31. Jg 10:15, 16. La 3:39, 40. Ho 3:5. 12:6. *14:1, 2. **early**. Mk +1:35. **God**. Heb. *El*, Ex +15:2.

35. **remembered**. ver. 7, 11, 42. Ps 106:13, 21. **God was**. Dt 32:*4, 15, 30, 31. **the high**. *Ail elyon goalom*, "the strong God, the Most High, their redeemer," or kinsman: that One who possessed the right of redemption, the nearest kin to him who had forfeited his inheritance, as the word originally means; and hence is used for a redeemer; and here denotes he who redeemed them from Egyptian bondage. **high**. ver. 17, 56. Ge +14:18. Mk +5:7. **God**. Heb. *El*, Ex +15:2. **their redeemer**. Ex 6:6. 15:13. Dt 7:8. 15:15. Jb *19:25. Is *41:14. *44:6. 48:17. *63:8, 9. T *2:14.

36. **Nevertheless**. Ps 106:12, 13. Dt *5:28, 29. Is √29:13. Ezk √33:31. Ho 11:12. **lied**. Ps 18:44mg.

37. **their heart**. Ps 119:80. Ho 7:14, 16. 10:2. Ac 8:21. **stedfast**. ver. 8. Ps 44:17, 18. Dt 31:20. Ho 8:1.

38. **But he**. Ps 106:43-45. Ex 34:6-9. Nu *14:18-20. 16:44-48. Is 44:21, 22. **full of**. Jb 23:6. Mt 11:28-30. 28:18. **many**. Is *48:9. Ezk 20:8, 9, 13, 14, 17, 21, 22. **did not**. 2 K 21:29.

39. **remembered**. √22C3, Ge +8:1. **flesh**. Ps √103:14-16. Ge *6:3. Jn *3:6. **a wind**. Or, as the Hebrew *rooach holaich welo yashoov* may be rendered, "the spirit goeth away, and returneth not again." To this purpose the Arabic, "He remembered that they were flesh; and a spirit, which, when it departs, returneth not again." The human being is composed of flesh and spirit, or body and soul: these are easily separated, and when separated, the body turns to dust, and the spirit returns no more to animate the body in a state of probation. Ps *39:13. Jb *7:7, 16. Ja 4:14.

40. **How oft**. ver. 17. Ps *95:8-10. 106:14-33. Nu 14:11. Dt 9:21, 22. **provoke him**. *or*, rebel against him. ver. +17h. Jb 17:2. Is 3:8. ✛S#4784h: Hiphel, Future: Dt 1:26, 43. 9:23. Jsh 1:18. 1 S 12:14. Ne 9:26 (were disobedient). Ps 78:40, 53. 106:7, 43. Ezk 5:6 (changed). 20:8, 13, 21. For Kal, Participle, see Dt +21:20; for Kal, Preterite, see Ho +13:16. **grieve**. √22B, Ge +6:6. Ps 95:10. Is 7:13. +63:10. Ep √4:30. He √3:15-17.

41. **Yea**. Nu *14:4, 22. Dt 6:16. Ac *7:39. He 3:8-11. 2 P 2:21, 22. **God**. Heb. *El*, Ex +15:2. **limited**. ver. 19, 20. Ezk 9:4 (set). Mk 5:35, 36.

42. **remembered**. ver. 11, 21, 22. Ps 136:10-15. Ex 13:9. Is 11:11. Je 32:21. **the day**. Ps 106:7-10. Ex 14:12, 30, 31. **delivered**. Ps 31:5. **the enemy**. *or*, affliction. ver. 61, 66.

43. **How**. Ps *105:27-38. 135:9. Ex 3:19, 20. Dt 4:34. 6:22. Ne 9:10. **wrought**. Heb. set. ver. 5. Ps 19:4. 50:23. 54:3. 74:4. 81:5. 86:14. Ex +9:21mg. Jb 1:8mg. Zp 3:19mg. **wonders**. ver. 12. Ps 71:7. 105:5, 27. 135:9.

44. **turned**. Ps 105:29. Ex 7:17-21. Re 16:3-6. The miracles mentioned in this and the four subsequent verses evidently show the power of God over the elements of nature, which at that time were the objects of Egyptian worship.

45. **sent**. Ps 105:31. Ex 8:21-24. **frogs**. Ps 105:30. Ex 8:2-15. Re 16:13.

46. **gave also**. Ps 105:34, 35. Ex 10:12-15. Jl 1:4-7. 2:25. Am 7:1, 2. Re 9:2-11. **the caterpillar**. *Chasil*, from *chasal*, "to consume, eat up," is rendered *brouxos* by the LXX. in 2 Ch 6:28, and *Aquila* here, and also the Vulgate in 2 Chronicles and 1s 33:4, and *Jerome* here, *bruchus*, the chaffer, which every one knows to be a great devourer of the leaves of trees. The Syriac in Jl 1:4. 2:25. renders it *tzartzooro*, which *Michaelis*, from the Arabic *tzartzar*, a cricket, interprets the "mole-cricket," which in its grub state is also very destructive to corn, grass, and other vegetables, by cankering the roots on which it feeds. **labor**. *J*121C1H, Dt +28:33.

47. **destroyed**. or, killed. ver. 31. **with hail**. Ps 105:32, 33. Ex 9:18-34. **sycamore**. From the value of the sycamore in furnishing wood for various uses (see Shaw's Travels, p. 376, 436), from the grateful shade which its wide-spreading branches afforded, and on account of the fruit, which Mr. Maillet says the Egyptians hold in the highest estimation, we may conceive somewhat of the loss they sustained when "their vines were destroyed with hail, and their sycamore trees with frost." See Note on 1 Ch 27:28. 1 K 10:27. **frost**. or, great hailstones.

48. **gave up**. Heb. shut up. ver. 62. **hot thunderbolts**. or, lightnings. *S#7565h. Ps 76:3h (arrows). Ex 9:28. Dt +32:24 (*S#7565h).

49. **cast**. Ps 11:6. Jb 20:23. Is 42:25. La 4:11. Zp 3:8. Ro 2:8, 9. **fierceness of**. Ps 2:5. 58:9. 2 Ch +24:18. 30:8. **wrath**. Ps 7:6. 85:3. 90:9, 11. **indignation**. Ps 38:3. 69:24. 69:24. 102:10. **trouble**. Ps 9:9. 10:1. 22:11. **by sending**. Ex 12:13. 1 S 24:16. 1 K 22:21, 22. Jb 1:12. 2:6, 7. Zc 8:8. **evil angels**. or, messengers. Pr 16:14. Is 14:32. 33:7. 37:9.

50. **made a way**. Heb. weighed a path. Ps 58:2. Pr 5:6. Is 26:7. **he spared**. Jb 27:22. Ezk 5:11. 7:4, 9. 8:18. 9:10. Ro *8:32. 2 P 2:4, 5. **not**. *J*175B, Ge +21:16. **soul**. Heb. *nephesh*, Ge +12:13. **life over to the pestilence**. or, beasts to the murrain. Ex 9:3-6.

51. **smote**. Ps 105:36. 135:8. 136:10. Ex 12:12, 29, 30. 13:15. He 11:28. **the chief**. Ge 49:3. **tabernacles**. Ps 105:23. 106:22. Ge 9:22-25. 10:6.

52. **But**. Ps 77:20. 105:37. Ne 9:12. Is 63:11-14. **like a**. Ps 95:7. 100:3. Is *40:11. Je 23:2-4. Ezk 34:11, etc. Lk 15:4-6. Jn 10:11, etc.

53. **so that**. Ex *14:15, 19, 20. He 11:29. **but**. Ps 136:15. Ex *14:27, 28. *15:10. **overwhelmed**. Heb. covered. Ps *32:5. 40:10. 44:15. 55:5mg. 69:7.

54. **And he**. Ex *15:13, 17. Da 9:16-20. 11:45. **his right**. Ps *44:3. Ep 1:14.

55. **cast**. Ps 44:2. 105:44, 45. 135:10-12. 136:18-22. Jsh ch. 6-21. Ne 9:22-25. **divided**. Nu 33:54. Jsh 13:7. *19:51. **and made**. Dt 6:10-12.

56. **they tempted**. ver. 40, 41. Dt 31:16-20. 32:15-21. Jg *2:11, 12. 2 K 17:7, etc. Ne 9:25, 26. Ezk 16:15-26. **most high**. ver. 17, 35. Ge +14:18. Mk +5:7. **But**. ver. 41. Jg 3:5-7, 12. Ezk *20:27, 28. **they were**. ver. 8-10, 37. Ho *7:16.

58. **their high**. Le 26:30. Nu 33:52. Dt *12:2, 4.

moved. Ps 79:5. Ex 34:14. Dt *32:16, 17, 21. Jg 2:12, 20. Ezk 8:3-5. 1 C 10:22. **with**. Ps 97:7. Ex 20:4, 5. Dt 4:16-25. 27:15. Jg 2:11, 17. 10:6. 1 K 11:7, 10. 12:31. 2 Ch +34:3. Je 8:19. Ho 13:2.

59. **God**. Ps 11:4. 14:2-5. Ge 18:20, 21. **greatly**. Ps 106:40. Le 20:23. 26:44. La 2:7. Zc 11:8.

60. **he forsook**. Jsh 18:1. 1 S 1:3. 4:4-11. Je *7:12-14. 26:6-9.

61. **his strength**. *J*121M, Ex +8:23. By Metonymy of the Subject, whereby the thing signified is put for the sign, "strength" is put for the Ark of the Covenant. That is, *the ark, where his power and glory were displayed*. Ps 63:2. *132:8. Jg 18:30. 1 S *4:11. 5:1, 2. 1 Ch 16:11. 2 Ch 6:41. **glory**. Ps 24:7. Ex 40:34. 1 S *4:21, 22.

62. **gave**. 1 S *4:2, 10, 11. **wroth**. Ps 89:38. Is 64:9.

63. **fire**. ver. 21. Dt 29:20. 32:22. **maidens**. Ps 45:14. 148:12. Ge +24:16 (*S#1330h). Is 4:1. Je 7:34. 16:9. 25:10. **given to marriage**. Heb. praised. Ps 18:3. 48:1. 113:3. Ge 12:15. Pr 31:28, 31. SS 6:9. Je 7:34.

64. **priests**. 1 S 2:33, 34. *4:11, 17. *22:18, 19. **widows**. 1 S 4:19, 20. Jb 27:15. Ezk 24:23.

65. **Then**. Ps 7:6. 44:23. Is 51:9. **as one**. *J*105, Ml +4:2. **and like**. Is *42:13, 14. **that shouteth**. *J*22C9, Is +42:13.

66. **And he**. 1 S *5:6-12. *6:4. Jb 40:12. **he put**. Je 23:40. **perpetual**. ver. 69. Ge +*9:12. **reproach**. Ps 15:3. 22:6. 31:11.

67. **he refused**. 1 S 6:21. 7:1, 2. 2 S 6:2, 17. **tabernacle**. *J*121J16, Ge +13:5.

68. **chose**. Ge *49:8-10. Ru 4:17-22. 1 S 16:1. 2 Ch 6:6. **mount**. Ps *87:2. 132:12-14.

69. **And he**. Ps 48:2, 3. 1 K *6:2. 9:8. 2 Ch 3:4. **high**. 1 Ch 29:1, 19. 2 Ch 2:9. Ac 7:48, 49. **earth**. Ps 102:25. 104:5. 119:90, 91. 1 S 2:8. Jb 26:7. Is 48:13. 51:6. Col 1:16, 17. Re 20:11. **established**. Heb. founded. Ps 8:2mg. 89:11. Hab 1:12mg. **for ever**. Heb. *olam*, Ex +*12:24. Ps *89:36, 37. 104:5. 119:90, 91. Ec +*1:4.

70. **chose**. Ps 89:19, 20. 1 S *16:11, 12. 2 S 3:18. 6:21. Is +*55:3. Ac *13:22, 34. **and took**. Ps *75:6, 7. Ex *3:1, 10. 1 S 17:15, etc. 2 S *7:8. 1 K *19:19, 20. Pr *15:33. Am *7:14, 15. Mt *4:18-22. 1 C *1:26-29.

71. **From following**. Heb. From after. 2 S 7:8mg. Am +*7:15mg. **ewes**. Ge 33:13. Is 40:11. **great with young**. or, suckling ones. *S#5763h. Ge 33:13. 1 S 6:7 (milch), 10. Is *40:11mg. **brought**. Ps 75:6, 7. 113:7, 8. 1 S 2:7, 8. Je 27:5, 6. **feed**. 2 S *5:2. 1 Ch 11:2. Is *40:11. Ezk *34:23, 24. Mi 5:2-4. Zc 11:4, etc. Mt 2:6mg. Jn 21:15-17. 1 P 5:2.

72. **according**. Ps 28:9. 75:2. *101:1-8. 2 S 8:15. 1 K *9:4. 15:5. Is *11:1-4. Ac 13:22, 36. **guided**. Ps *32:8. 1 K 3:6-9, 28. Zc 11:15-17. 2 C *3:5, 6. 2 T √2:15. Ja *1:5.

PSALM 79

The psalmist complains to God of the desolations of Jerusalem and the cruel insults of the heathen, 1-5. He prays for deliverance and forgiveness; and that the Lord would glorify himself by avenging his people on their oppressors, 6-13.

(Title.) A.M. 3416. B.C. 588. **A Psalm**. This psalm is supposed, with much probability, to have been written on the destruction of the city and temple of Jerusalem by Nebuchadnezzar. **of Asaph**. *or*, for Asaph. Ps 74, title, mg.

1. **the heathen**. Ps 74:3, 4. 80:12, 13. 2 K 21:12-16. *25:4-10. 2 Ch 36:3, 4, 6, 7, 17. Zc *14:2. Lk *21:24. Re 11:2. **into**. Ps *74:2. 78:71. Ex 15:17. Is 47:6. **holy**. Ps *74:7, 8. 2 K 24:13. La 1:10. Ezk 7:20, 21. 9:7. **have laid**. 2 K 25:9, 10. 2 Ch 36:19. Je 26:18. 39:8. *52:13. Mi *3:12.

2. **dead bodies**. Je *7:33. 15:3. 16:4. 34:20.

3. **Their**. ver. 10. Mt 23:35. Ro 8:36. Re 16:6. 17:6. 18:24. **and there**, etc. Either there was no friend or relation left to bury them, or none was allowed to perform this last sad office. The despotism of eastern princes often proceeds to such a degree of extravagance as to fill the mind with astonishment and horror. In Morrocco, no person dares to bury the body of a malefactor without an order from the emperor; and Windus, speaking of a man who was to have been sawn in two, informs us that "his body must have remained to be eaten by the dogs, if the emperor had not pardoned him." Ps 141:7. Je 8:1, 2. *14:16. 15:3. *16:4. 25:33. 34:20. Re 11:9.

4. **become**. Ps 44:13, 14. 80:6. 89:41. Dt *28:15, 37. Je *24:8, 9. 25:18. 42:18. La 2:15, 16. 5:1. Ezk 35:12. 36:3, 15. Da *9:16. **scorn**. 1 K 9:7. Ne 2:19. 4:1-4.

5. **How long**. Ps 13:1, 2. 74:1, 9, 10. 80:4. 89:46. Re 6:10. **wilt**. Ps 85:5. *103:8-10. Is 64:9. Mi √7:18. **for ever**. Jb +4:20 (❋S#5331h). **jealousy**. Dt 29:20. 32:16, 22. Ezk 36:5. Zp *1:18. 3:8.

6. **Pour out**. Ps 69:24. Is 42:25. Re *16:1, etc. ℐ22C38. Anthropomorphism B890. Human actions are attributed to God: pouring out. For other instances of this figure see Ezk 9:8. 20:13, 21, 33. Jl *2:28, 29. Zc *12:10. Ac 2:17, 18, 33. Ro *5:5. T *3:6. **wrath**. ℐ121C1C. Metonymy of the Cause B550. Anger and wrath are put for punishment and various acts which flow from them. For other instances of this figure see 1 S 28:18. Mi 7:9. Ro *2:5. 4:15. 13:4, 5. Ep 5:6. **upon**. Is ch. 13, 21, 23. Je +√10:25. 25:29. ch. 46-51. **not known**. Ps 9:16, 17. Is 45:4, 5. Jn 16:3. 17:25. Ac 17:23. Ro 1:28. Ep *2:12. 2 Th √1:8. **not called**. Ps 14:4. 53:4. 145:18. Ro *10:12-14. 1 C 1:2.

7. **For they**. Ps 80:13. Is 9:12. Je 50:7. 51:34, 35. Zc 1:15. **Jacob**. ℐ121K1, Dt +9:1. **laid**. 2 Ch 36:21. Is 24:1-12. *64:10, 11.

8. **remember**. Ps 25:7. *130:3, 4. Ex 32:34. 1 K 17:18. Is *43:25. *64:9. Ho 8:13. 9:9. Re 18:5. **former iniquities**. *or*, the iniquities of them that were before us. Ge 15:16. Ezk 2:3. Da 9:16. Mt 23:32-36. **let thy**. Ps 21:3. 69:16, 17. **we are**. Ps 106:43. 116:6. 142:6. Dt 28:43.

9. **for the glory**. T#538. Ps 25:11. 115:1. +119:158 (T#662). 143:11. 1 K 18:36, 37. 2 Ch 14:11. Is 37:20. Da 9:17-19. Ml 2:2. Mt +6:13 (T#1126). Ep 1:6. 1 T +1:17 (T#300). **purge**. Ps 25:11. 65:3. Da 9:9, 19. **for thy**. Jsh *7:9. Is 43:25. 48:9. Je *14:7, 21. Ezk 20:9, 14.

10. **Wherefore**. ℐ85L, Ps 42:3, *10. 115:2. Ge +27:45. Jl 2:17. Mi 7:10. **let him**. Ps 9:16. 58:11. 83:17, 18. Ex 6:7. 7:5. Ezk 36:23. *39:21, 22. **by the**. Je 51:35. Re 18:20. **revenging**. Heb. vengeance. Ro 12:19.

11. **sighing**. Ps +*12:5. 35:10. *69:33. 102:20, 30. Ex *2:23, 24. Is 42:7. **prisoner**. T#1654. Ps *102:19, 20. Ac 12:5. Ep 6:18-20. **according**. Ps 146:6, 7. Nu 14:17-19. Mt 6:13. Ep 3:20. **thy power**. Heb. thine

arm. ℐ22A12, Ex +15:16. Ps 71:18mg. Is 33:2. Ezk 22:6mg. **preserve thou those that are appointed to die**. Heb. reserve the children of death. T#1472. Ps 102:19, 20mg. 1 S +20:31mg. Pr 31:8mg.

12. **render**. Ps *31:23. Ge 4:15. Le 26:21, 28. Is 65:5-7. Je 32:18. Lk 6:38. **wherewith**. See on Ps 44:16. 74:18, 22. Zc *2:8.

13. **thy people**. Ps 74:1. 95:7. *100:3. **for ever**. Heb. *olam*, Ex +*12:24. **we will**. Ps 43:21. 45:17. 74:15, 22. 80:1. 145:4. Is *43:21. **all generations**. Heb. generation and generation. Ps +10:6mg. 12:7. 14:5. +33:11mg. 49:11mg. 61:6mg. 77:8mg. 89:1mg. 100:5mg. 119:90mg.

PSALM 80

The psalmist prays for the tokens of God's special presence with his people and deprecates his displeasure, 1-7. The former and present state of Israel is represented by a vine, planted and flourishing heretofore, but now wasted and trodden down, 8-13. A prayer that the Lord would cause this vine again to prosper, 14-19.

(Title.) A.M. cir. 3463. B.C. cir. 541. **Shoshannim-Eduth**. i.e. *lilies of testimony*, ❋S#7802h. Ps 45, 60, 69, titles. **A Psalm**. This psalm is generally supposed to have been written during the Babylonian captivity; but some think it refers to the desolations made by Sennacherib. **of Asaph**. *or*, for Asaph. Ps 79, title.

1. **Give ear**. Ps 5:1. 55:1. 79:13. **O Shepherd**. Ps *23:1, 2. Is 40:11. Ezk 34:23. Jn 10:14. He 13:20. 1 P 2:25. 5:4. **leadest**. Ps *77:20. 78:52. Is 49:9, 10. 63:11. Jn 10:3, 4. **Joseph**. ℐ171R, Ex +12:40. By the figure Synecdoche of the Part, whereby an integral part of men (collectively) is put for the whole, or others associated with them, "Joseph" (whose son Ephraim was) is put for all Israel. **dwellest**. ℐ22D3H. Anthropomorphism B892. God is spoken of in circumstances as to place: sitting between the cherubims. Ps *99:1. Ex *25:20-22. 1 S 4:4. 2 S 6:2. 2 K 19:15. Is 37:16. Ezk 1:13. 10:4. **shine**. ver. 3, 7, 19. Ps *50:2. 94:1. Dt 33:2. Jb 10:3. Is 60:1. Ezk 43:2. Da 9:17. Re 21:23.

2. **Before**. These three tribes, in the wilderness, marched immediately after the ark and cherubim by divine appointment, to which this appears to be an allusion. Nu *2:18-24. 10:22-24. **Ephraim**. ℐ171R, Ex +12:40. By the figure Synecdoche of the Part, "Ephraim" includes the ten tribes, while "Benjamin" includes Judah, and "Manasseh" includes the two-and-a-half tribes. Ps 78:9n. **stir up**. Ps 35:23. 44:23-26. 78:38. Is 42:13, 14. **come and save us**. Heb. come for salvation to us. Is 11:11n. 25:9. 33:22. +*59:20. Ro +*11:26.

3. **Turn us**. ℐ53, 2 S +1:19. T#1734. ver. 7, 19. Ps 85:4. 1 K 18:37. Je 31:18, 19. La *5:19-21. **cause**. ver. 1. Ps *4:6. *67:1. 119:135. Nu √6:25, 26. **face**. ℐ22A4, Ge +19:13. **be saved**. Is *30:15. Je 4:14.

4. **how long**. Ps 85:5. Is 58:2, 3, 6-9. La 3:44. Ho 3:4, 5. 5:15. 6:1-3. Mi 5:3. Mt 15:22-28. Lk *18:1-8. Ac +*3:19-21. Ja 4:3. **be angry**. Heb. smoke. ℐ46A, Le +26:30. ℐ22K1, Dt +4:24. Ps 74:1n. Dt 29:20.

5. **feedest**. Ps 42:3. 102:9. Jb 6:7. Is 30:20. Ezk 4:16, 17.

6. **Thou**. Je 15:10. **our enemies**. Ps 44:13, 14. 79:4. Jg 16:25. Is 36:8, 12-20. 37:23. Je 48:27. Ezk 36:4. Re 11:10.

7. **Turn us.** ſ53, 2 S 1:19. ver. 3, 19. Ps 51:10. Lk 1:16, 17. **face.** ſ22A4, Ge +19:13. **we shall.** Is 30:15. 64:5. Je 4:14. Mk 4:12. 2 T +*2:25, 26.

8. **a vine.** Is *5:1-7. 27:2, 3. Je *2:21. Ezk 15:6. 17:6. 19:10. Mt 21:33-41. Jn 15:1-8. **thou hast cast.** Ps 44:2. 78:55. Je 18:9, 10. This most elegant allegory, which is well supported, is frequently employed by sacred writers: see the Parallel Passages.

9. **preparedst.** Ps 105:44. Ex 23:28-30. Jsh 23:13-15. *24:12. Ne 9:22-25. Is 5:5, 6. Je 12:10. Na 2:2. **to take.** Is *27:6. 37:31. Je 12:2. **and it.** 1 K *4:20, 25. 1 Ch 21:5. 27:23, 24.

10. **goodly cedars.** Heb. cedars of God. ſ24L, Ge +6:2. Ps 36:6mg. 104:16. Ge +*23:6mg. Jon 3:3mg.

11. **She sent.** Ps *72:8. Ge *15:18. Ex 23:31. 1 K 4:21, 24. 1 Ch 18:3. **river.** ſ171E12, Ge +14:22. ſ32, Ge +31:21.

12. **broken.** Ps 89:40, 41. Is *5:5. 18:5, 6. Na 2:2. Lk 20:16.

13. **The boar.** The wild boar, *chazir*, is the parent stock of our domestic hog. He is much smaller but stronger and more undaunted; color, an iron gray, inclining to black; snout, longer than that of the common breed; ears, comparatively short; tusks, very formidable; and habits, fierce and savage. He is particularly destructive to cornfields and vineyards. 2 K ch. 18, 19, 24, 25. 2 Ch ch. 32, 36. Je 4:7. 39:1-3. *51:34. 52:7, 12-14.

14. **Return.** Ps 7:7. 90:13. Is 63:15, 17. Jl 2:14. Ml *3:7. Ac 15:16. **look down.** Ps 33:13. Is 63:15. La 3:50. Da 9:16-19.

15. **vineyard.** ver. 8. Is 5:1, 2. Je 2:21. Mk 12:1. Jn 15:1. **right hand.** ſ22A15B, Ps +18:35. **the branch.** Or, "the Son," *ben*, or, as eighteen MSS., LXX., Vulgate, Syriac, Arabic, and Ethiopic read, *ben adam*, "Son of man;" which the Targumist renders *malka mesheecha*, "the King Messiah." Ps 89:21. Is 11:1. 49:5. Je 23:5, 6. Ezk 17:22-24. Zc 3:8. 6:12.

16. **burned.** Ps 79:5. Is 27:11. Ezk *20:47, 48. Jn 15:6. **cut down.** Am +*9:11. Lk 13:7, 9. Ac 15:16. **perish.** Ps 39:11. *76:6, 7. 90:7. 2 Th 1:9.

17. **Let thy.** ver. 15. Ps 89:21. 110:1. *132:11. Is *53:5. Da +*7:13, 14. Jn *5:21-29. **the man.** 2 S 7:19. 1 Ch 17:17. Ac 2:30. 17:31. Ro 1:3. 1 T 2:5. 2 J +*7n. **right hand.** ſ22A15B, Ps +18:35. 110:1. Ac 3:20, 21. Ro 8:34. He 1:3. 8:1. 1 P 3:22. **son of man.** Ps 8:4, 5. Da +*7:13. Mt +√16:27n. **madest strong.** Ps +*45:7. Is *41:10. *53:10. Mt *28:18. Ac 2:33.

18. **So will not.** Ps 79:13. Je +√32:40. Jn *6:66-69. He *10:38, 39. **quicken.** T#1663. Ps 71:20. 85:6. 119:25, 37, 40, *50, 88, 107, 149, 154, 156, 159. 143:11. SS 1:4. Is 57:15. Ho 6:2. Mt 24:13. Jn 5:21. Ro 4:17. 8:11. Ph *2:12, 13. Ep *2:1-5. 1 P 3:18. **will call.** Ps 3:4. 18:3, 6. 22:2. 27:7. Ge 4:26. Ac 15:17. **thy name.** Ps +√9:10. 105:1. Ac 2:21. Ro √10:13.

19. **Turn us.** ſ53, 2 S +1:19. ver. 3, 7. SS 1:4. Je 3:22, 23. **cause.** ver. 1. Ps 27:4, 9. 31:16. 44:3. **face.** ſ22A4, Ge +19:13.

PSALM 81

An exhortation to praise God with psalms and musical instruments, especially on the solemn feasts, 1-3. God ordained this when he delivered Israel from the Egyptians, 4-7. He commands the people to renounce idolatry and trust in him alone, and complains of their

disobedience, which had turned to their own loss, 8-16.

(Title.) A.M. 3489. B.C. 515. **Gittith.** Ps 8, title. **A Psalm.** Some suppose this psalm to have been composed to be sung at the Feast of Trumpets, before the time of David; others think it was written at the removal of the ark to Mount Zion; but the most probable opinion is that it was sung at the dedication of the second temple. **of Asaph.** *or*, for Asaph. Ps 79, title.

1. **Sing.** Ps 67:4. Je 31:7. **our strength.** Ps 18:1, 2. 28:7. 52:7. Ph *4:13. **make.** Ps 33:1-3. 46:1-7. 66:1. 100:1, 2. **the God.** Ps 46:11. Ge 50:17. Mt 22:32.

2. **a psalm.** Ps 92:3. 95:1, 2. 149:1-3. Mk 14:26. Ep *5:19. Col √3:16. Ja *5:13.

3. **Blow.** Ps 98:6. Nu 10:1-9. 1 Ch 15:24. 16:6, 42. 2 Ch 5:12. 13:12, 14. **trumpet.** Le 23:24. **new moon.** Le 23:24, 25. Nu *10:10. 28:11. 2 K 4:23. 2 Ch +2:4. Col *2:16. **solemn.** Nu 15:3. Dt 16:15. 2 Ch 2:4. 8:13. La 2:6. Na 1:15.

4. **statute.** Ps 2:7. 50:16. 94:20. **a law.** *or*, ordinance. Ps 1:5 (judgment). 7:6. Ge 18:19, 25 (right). Ex 15:25. Le 5:10mg. Nu 15:24mg. **God of Jacob.** ver. 1.

5. **in Joseph.** Ps 77:15. 80:1, 2. Am 6:6. **for a.** Ps 78:6. Ex 13:8, 9, 14-16. Dt 4:45. Ezk 20:20. **through.** *or*, against. Ex *12:12, 27, 29. **where.** Ps *114:1. Ge 42:23. Dt 28:49. Is 28:11. Je 5:15. 1 C 14:21, 22.

6. **I removed.** Ex *1:14. 6:6. Is 9:4. 10:27. Mt 11:29. **were delivered.** Heb. passed away. Ps 17:3. 37:36. 42:4. 57:1. **from the pots.** Or rather, as *dood* also signifies (see 2 K 10:7. Je 24:2), the basket: so LXX. and Symmachus, *kophinos*, and Vulgate and Jerome, *cophino*; and Diodati, "his hands were removed from the baskets," says he in a note, "from carrying earth to make bricks, Ex 1:14." Ps 68:13. 1 S 2:14. 2 K 10:7. 2 Ch 35:13. Jb 41:20.

7. **calledst.** Ps *50:15. 91:14, 15. Ex *2:23. *14:10, 30, 31. 17:2-7. **secret.** Ex 14:24. *19:16, 19. 20:18-21. **proved.** Ex *17:6, 7. Nu *20:13, 24. Dt 33:8. **Meribah.** *or*, strife. Ps 95:8. 106:32. Ge 13:8. Ex *17:7mg. **Selah.** Ps +9:16.

8. **Hear.** Ps 50:7. Dt 32:46. Is 55:3, 4. Jn 3:11, 32, 33. Ac 20:21. 1 J 5:9. **if thou wilt.** ver. 13. Ex 15:26. Dt 5:27. Is 1:19.

9. **There shall.** Ex 20:3-5. 1 C 8:5, 6. **strange.** Ps 18:44, 45. 137:4. 144:7, 11. Ex 12:43 (✳S#5236h). Dt 6:14. 32:12. Is 43:12. Ml 2:11.

10. **I am.** Ex *20:2, 3, 5. Je 11:4. 31:31-33. **open.** Ps *37:3, 4. Dt 15:10. Jn *7:37. *15:7. 16:23. Ep *3:19, 20. Re 21:6. 22:17. **fill it.** Ps 36:8, 9. 107:9. SS 5:1. Mt *5:6. Jn 10:10. 1 C *2:9. 1 T 6:17. Ja *1:5.

11. **people.** Ps *106:12, 13. Je *2:11-13. *7:23, 24, 26. Zc *7:11. **would none.** Ex *32:1. Dt *32:15, 18. Pr *1:29, 30. He 10:29.

12. **I gave.** Ge *6:3. Ho 4:17. Ac 7:42. *14:16. Ro *1:24, 26, 27. 2 Th √2:9-11. **their own hearts' lust.** *or*, the hardness of their hearts, *or* imaginations. Dt 29:19. Je 3:17. 7:24. **they walked.** Ex 11:9. Is *30:1. Je *7:24. *44:16, 17. **own counsels.** Jsh 9:14. Je 7:24. ◗*23:18, 22.

13. **Oh that.** ſ124, Dt +*5:29. *32:29. Is *48:18. Mt *23:37. Lk 19:41, 42. **had hearkened.** T#485. Ex 19:5, 6. Le 26:3-12. Dt 4:5, 6, *40. 28:1-13. **had walked.** Dt *10:12, 13.

14. **I should.** Nu 14:9, 45. Jsh 23:13. Jg *2:20-23. **turned.** Am 1:8. Zc 13:7. **hand.** ſ22A14.8G, Is +1:25.

15. **The haters.** Ps 18:45. 83:2, etc. Ex 20:5. Dt

7:10. Jn 15:22, 23. Ro 1:30. 8:7. **submitted themselves.** *or,* yielded feigned obedience. Heb. lied. Ps 18:44mg. 66:3mg. Dt 33:29mg. 2 S 22:45mg. Je 3:10mg. **time.** Ps 102:28. Is 65:22. Jl 3:20. **for ever.** Heb. *olam,* Ex +*12:24.

16. **fed.** Ps 23:2. 36:8. 147:14. Dt *32:13, 14. Jl 2:24. **finest of the wheat.** Heb. fat of the wheat. Ps 17:10. 63:5mg. 73:7. 147:14mg. Ge 30:14. Dt 32:14. **honey.** Jg 14:8, 9, 18. 1 S 14:25, 26. Jb 29:6. **the rock.** Ps 18:33. Ex 17:6. Dt 32:13. Jg 6:21. Jb 29:6. Ep 2:6.

PSALM 82

The psalmist reminds magistrates of God's authority over them, reproves their injustice, and urges them to do their duty, 1-4. He exposes their ignorance and wickedness and warns them of their approaching doom, 5-7. He prays for the establishment of God's kingdom, 8.

(*Title.*) A.M. 3108. B.C. 896. **A Psalm.** Some refer this psalm to the time of David and others to that of Hezekiah, but it is more probable that it was composed when Jehoshaphat reformed the courts throughout his kingdom, 2 Ch 19:6, 7. **of Asaph.** *or,* for Asaph.

1. **God,** etc. Or, "God standeth in the assembly of God (*El*), he judgeth among the judges" (*elohim*): God is among his own people and presides especially in those courts of justice which he himself has established. Ex +*18:21. 2 Ch *19:6, 7. Ec 5:8. **the gods.** ver. +*6n, 7. Ps 138:1. Ex 21:6. *22:28. Jn *10:35.

2. **How.** Ps 62:3. Ex 10:3. 1 K 18:21. Mt 17:17. **judge.** Ps 58:1, 2. Ex 23:6, 7. Le *19:15. Mi 3:1-3, 9-12. **accept.** Dt *1:17. 2 Ch *19:7. Jb 34:19. Pr *18:5. Ga 2:6.

3. **Defend.** Heb. Judge. Ps *10:18. Dt *10:18. Is *1:17, 23. **do.** Je 5:28. 22:*3, 16. Ja *1:27.

4. **Deliver.** Ps *72:12-14. Jb *29:12, 16, 17. Pr *24:11, 12. **rid.** Ps 140:12. Ne 5:1-13. Jb 5:15, 16.

5. **They.** That is, the judges know not. **know not.** Ps 53:4. Jb *21:14, 15. Pr *1:29. Je *4:22. Mi 3:1. Ro *1:28. **walk.** Pr 2:13. 4:19. Ec 2:14. Is ◐2:5. Jn √3:19. 12:35. 1 J 2:11. **all the,** etc. All the civil institutions of the land totter. Ps 11:3. 75:3. Ec 3:16. Is 5:7. 2 T *2:19. **out of course.** Heb. moved. Ps 10:6. 13:4. 15:5. 16:8.

6. **I have said.** ver. 1. Ex 21:6. 22:8, 9, √28. Jn *10:34-36. **gods.** Heb. *elohim.* Here there is a special use of *elohim* (just as at Ps 8:5 there is another and different special use of *elohim*), where *elohim* refers to divinely appointed magistrates, kings, or judges, as "gods." These officials were not considered deity, for it is explicitly stated (ver. 7) that they shall die like men and are rulers of the people, Ex 22:28. As rulers in Israel only, not the nations, they were "the Lord's anointed" and were thus types of Christ, the great anointed one. If Christ were not truly God, they could not in type have been called gods. In contrast, when Christ is called God, it is in reference to his true deity, in combination with an attribute or action belonging only to the supreme God. William Kay notes that they are called "gods" because God's word came to them (Jn 10:35), "investing them with his prerogative of judgment." Ps 82:1. 86:8. +*138:1. Ex +12:12. 22:8. Jn 1:1. +*10:30, ▶34. Ro *9:5. T *2:13. 1 J 5:20. **most High.** Ps *83:18. Ge +√14:18. Mk +5:7.

7. **But.** Ps *49:12. Jb 21:32. Ezk 31:14. **like men.**

Or, "like Adam," *keadam.* Jg 16:7. **and fall,** etc. Or, "and fall as one of them, O ye princes." Ps 83:11. Ho 7:16.

8. **Arise.** ♪38A, Ne +4:4. Ps 7:6. *44:26. 74:22. *96:13. +√102:13. Is 51:9. Mi 7:2, 7. Zp *3:8. **judge.** Ps *9:7, 8. +*96:10, 13. Ac +*24:10n. **earth.** ♪121J17, Ge +6:11. **for thou.** He 1:2. **inherit all nations.** Ps *2:8. *22:28. 69:36. 86:9. *96:10. +*149:5-9. Zc +*14:9. Mt +*5:5. Jn 10:16. Ro √8:17, 32. Re +*5:10. +√11:15. 15:4.

PSALM 83

The psalmist appeals to God concerning a formidable conspiracy of the enemies of Israel, 1-8. He prays that they may be confounded, for a warning to others and for the honor of God, 9-18.

(*Title.*) A.M. 3416. B.C. 588. **A Song.** Some refer this psalm to the confederacy against Jehoshaphat, as William Kay notes "Referred by Kimchi (with the highest probability) to the time of Jehoshaphat's prayer, 2 Ch 20:5-12, when Juda was threatened by a confederacy of Moab, Ammon, Edom, and others, acting in concert with Syria, compare Am ch. 1" (*The Psalms with Notes,* p. 272); and others to the destruction of Jerusalem by Nebuchadnezzar. **of Asaph.** *or,* for Asaph. Ps 79, title.

1. **Keep.** Ps 28:1. 35:22. 44:23. 50:3. *109:1, 2. **not.** ♪175B, Ge +21:16. **be not.** ♪175B, Ge +21:16. Is 42:14.

2. **For, lo.** Ps *2:1, 2. 74:4, 23. 2 K 19:28. Is 37:29. Je 1:19. Mt 27:24. Ac 4:25-27. 16:22. 17:5. 19:28, etc. 21:30. 22:22. 23:10. **tumult.** Ps 46:3. Is 17:12. **that hate.** Ps *81:15. Ro *1:30. **lifted.** ♪121S3E2, Jg +8:28. Ps 75:4, 5. 93:3. Is 37:23. Da 5:20-23. **the head.** Hab *3:13.

3. **crafty counsel.** Ps 10:9. 56:6. *64:2. 1 S 13:19. Is *7:6, 7. Lk *20:20-23. **against.** Ps ◐+*122:6. Ge 12:3. Pr ◐+*21:30. **thy people.** Dt +*32:43. 2 Ch 20:7. **consulted against.** Ps 17:7-9. 64:2. *143:7-9. **thy hidden ones.** Ps *27:5. *31:20. *91:1. 1 K 17:3. Is +*16:3-5. =18:2. +*26:20, 21. Ezk +*20:35. Da +*11:33. Hab +*3:4, 16. Zp +*2:3. Zc +*11:16mg. Ml +*3:16. Lk +*21:36. Col *3:3, 4. 1 Th +*1:10. 2 Th +*1:7.

4. **Come.** Ex *1:10. Est *3:6-9. Pr 1:12. Je *11:19. +*31:36. Da *7:25. Mt 27:62-66. Ac 4:17. *9:1, 2. *23:14. **from being a nation.** 2 Ch 20:11. Is *7:8. Zc *14:2.

5. **For.** Ps 2:2. Pr √21:30. Is 7:5-7. 8:9, 10. Jn 11:47-53. Ac 9:4. 23:12, 13. Re 17:13. 19:19. **consent.** Heb. heart. Ps 4:7. 7:10. **they are.** Jsh 10:3-5. 2 S 10:6-8. Is 7:2.

6. **The tabernacles.** Tents are mentioned because it was the custom of these people, particularly the Ishmaelites, to live a migratory or wandering life, camping sometimes in one place and sometimes in another, as they found convenience for themselves and cattle, a custom retained by their descendants to the present day. **Edom.** 2 Ch 20:1, 10, 11. **Hagarenes.** i.e. *fugitives,* ✱S#1905h. Ge 25:12-18. 1 Ch *5:10, 19, 20, Hagarites.

7. **Gebal.** i.e. *boundary,* ✱S#1380h. Jsh 13:5. Ezk 27:9h.

8. **Assur.** *Assur* is the same in the original as *Asshur,* or Assyria. Ge *10:11, Asshur. 25:3. **Holpen.** Heb.

been an arm to. Is 33:2. **the children**. Ge *19:37, 38. Dt 2:9.

9. **as unto**. Nu *31:7, 8. Jg *7:22-25. 2 Ch 20:23. Is 9:4. 10:26. Hab 3:7. **as to Sisera**. Jg *4:15-24. **of Kison**. i.e. *curved*, *S#7028h, Jg +5:21, Kishon. The variation of *Kison* and *Kishon* only exists in the translation; the original being uniformly *Kishon*. Jg *5:21.

10. **Endor**. Taanach and Megiddo (Jg 5:19) were near En-Dor (William Kay). Jsh 17:11. 1 S 28:7. **as dung**. 2 K *9:37. Je 8:2. 16:4. Zp 1:17.

11. **Oreb**. Jg *7:25. **Zebah**. Jg *8:12-21.

12. **Let us take**. ver. 4. Ps 74:7, 8. 2 Ch 20:11. **the houses**. Heb. *neoth*. The lands of which God has given the occupation to Israel (William Kay). Ps +23:2. 74:20.

13. **O my**. Ps 22:1. 44:4. 74:11, 12. **like**. Is *17:12-14. **as the**. Ps 35:5. 68:1, 2. Ex 15:7. Jb 13:25. 21:18. Is 40:24. 41:2. Je 13:24. Mt 3:12.

14. **as the fire**. Is 29:6. 30:33. 33:11, 12. 64:1, 2. Ezk 20:47, 48. Ml 4:1. 2 P +*3:7. **the flame**. Dt 32:22. Na 1:6, 10.

15. **persecute**. Ps 2:5. *11:6. 50:3. 58:9. Jb 9:17. 27:20-23. Is 28:17. 29:6. *30:30. Ezk 13:11-14. Mt 7:27. He 12:18.

16. **Fill**. Ps *6:10. *9:19, 20. *34:5. **thy name**. 2 Ch 20:9.

17. **Let them**. Ps *35:4, 26. *40:14, 15. *109:29. Is *24:21, 22. 26:21. +*66:24. Da 2:44. Zc 14:12-14. **for ever**. Ps +9:18 (*S#5703h).

18. **That men**. T#570. Ps *9:16. *59:13. Ex 9:15, 16. 14:4. 1 K *18:37. 2 K *19:19. Pr +16:4 (T#209). Is 5:16. Je *16:21. Ezk 25:17. 30:19. *38:23. Jn +11:42 (T#276). Ro 9:17, 22-24. **know**. T#1535. 2 Ch 6:32, 33. Is 64:1, 2. **whose name**. Ps 20:1. ◖+68:4. Ge *22:14. Ex 3:13, 14. *6:3. 2 Ch 20:9. Is *42:8. Je ◖*10:16. **the most high**. Ps +*7:17. 87:5. *92:8. Ge +√14:18. 2 Ch 20:6. Is *54:5. Da *4:25, 32. 7:18. Mi 4:13. Zc 4:14. Mt 11:10. Mk +5:7. Lk 1:76. 8:28. Ro √9:5. 1 C 10:9. 1 Th 3:13. **earth**. Ps 97:5.

PSALM 84

The psalmist expresses his strong affection for the courts of God, 1-3. He shows the blessedness of those who attend there or cordially resort thither, 4-7. He prays to be restored to them and celebrates the great goodness of God to his people, 8-12.

(*Title*.) A.M. 3469. B.C. 535. **Gittith**. Ps 8, 81, titles. **A Psalm**. Some suppose this psalm was composed by David when driven from Jerusalem by Absalom's rebellion, but it is more probable that it was written at the foundation of the second temple. **for**. *or*, of.

1. **How**. ♪59, Ps 26:8. *27:4. 48:1, 2. 87:2, 3. *122:1. Ge +28:16. He 9:23, 24. Re *21:2, 3, 22, 23. **O Lord**. Ps *103:20, 21. 1 K 22:19. Ne 9:6. Is 6:2, 3.

2. **soul**. Heb. *nephesh*, Ge +34:3. Ps 139:14. Is 26:9. Mt +*11:29. Lk 1:46. 2:35. Ac 14:2, 22. **longeth**. T#1402. Ps 13:1, 2. 27:8. *42:1, 2. *63:1, 2. 73:26. 107:9. 119:20, 81. 143:6. SS 2:4, 5. 3:1-4. 5:8. **my heart**. ♪121J21, Ps +24:4. 1 S 13:14. **crieth**. T#1345. Jb *23:3. Is 26:9. 64:1. La 2:18. Ho 7:14.

3. **Yea**, etc. Or, rather, "Even as the sparrow findeth a house, and the swallow (*deror* or the ring dove, according to some, but probably the bird which Forskal [*Descript. Anim.* p. 10] mentions among the migratory birds of Alexandria by the name of *dururi*) a nest for

herself where she may lay her young, (so I seek) thine altars, O Jehovah, God of hosts, my King and my God." That is, as nature inclines birds to seek and prepare their nests, so grace has taught me to desire thy altars and to worship there. **sparrow**. Ps 90:1. 91:1. 116:7. Mt 8:20. 23:37. **even**. Rather, supply ellipsis, (so hath my soul found). ♪63I1D, Nu 26:4. **my King**. Ps 5:2.

4. **Blessed**. ♪43, Dt +28:3. Ps 23:6. 27:4. *65:4. 134:1-3. **they will**. Ps 71:8, 15. 145:1, 2, 21. Is 12:4, 5. Re *4:8. 7:15.

5. **Blessed**. ♪43, Dt +28:3. **strength**. Ps 28:7, 8. Is 45:24. Zc 10:12. 2 C 3:5. *12:9. Ph *4:13. **in whose**. Ps *40:8. 42:4. 55:14. Is *26:9. Je 31:33. 50:4, 5. Mi 4:2.

6. **Who**. Ps 66:10-12. Jn *16:33. Ac 14:22. Ro 5:3-5. 8:37. 2 C 1:5. 4:17. Re 7:14. **Baca**, etc. i.e. *the weeper*, *S#1056h. Same as *S#1057h: 2 S 5:23 (mulberry trees), 24. 1 Ch 14:14, 15. Ps 84:6mg. *or*, mulberry trees, make him a well, etc. *Baca* is probably a large shrub, which the Arabs still call *baca* (see on 2 S 5:23); and this valley, as Celsius observes, seems to be one "embarrassed with (such) bushes and thorns, which could not be passed without labor and tears," *bacah*, as seven MSS., LXX., Aquila, and Vulgate read. But for an alternative view suggested by Robert Dick Wilson, see the note on 2 S √5:23n. 2 S 5:22-24. **the rain**. Ps 68:9. 2 K 3:9-20. *S#4175h: Jl 2:23mg. **well**. Heb. *mayan*, Ge +7:11 (*S#4599h), a spring or fountain. Ps 74:15. 87:7. 104:10. Is *12:3. **filleth**. Heb. covereth. Ps 71:13. 109:19, 29. Is 59:17. **pools**. S#1293h, elsewhere generally translated *blessing*, Ge 12:2. 2 Ch 20:26mg. Ps 3:8. 21:3, 6. Also rendered "liberal," Pr 11:25; "present," 1 S 25:27mg; "favor," 2 K 18:31mg. On this passage Matthew Poole suggests that reference is made to pools or cisterns which former pious persons dug in this valley for the assistance of future travelers on their way to Jerusalem to worship, as otherwise water was very scarce (Ge 26:15; Jg 1:15), and made the journey difficult.

7. **They**. Jb *17:9. Pr *4:18. Is *40:29, 31. Jn 1:16. √10:27, 28. 15:2. 2 C *3:18. Ph *3:13, 14. He *12:1. 2 P 3:18. **strength to strength**. Heb. company to company. Ps 18:32, 39. 33:16. Ezk 41:7mg. Lk 2:44. Ro 1:17. 2 C *3:18. **in Zion**. Ps 43:3. Dt 16:16. Is 46:13. Je 31:6. Zc 14:16. Jn 6:39, 40. 14:3. 1 Th 4:17. **appeareth**. Ps 42:2. 90:16. Is 47:3.

8. **Lord**. ver. 1, 2, 3, 11, 12, Jehovah. **God of hosts**. Ps 59:5. 80:4, 7, 19. **prayer**. Ps 4:1. 6:9. 35:13. 39:12. **give ear**. Ps 5:1. 17:1. 39:12. 49:1. **God of Jacob**. Ps 20:1. 46:7. 76:6. Ge 32:28. Ho 12:3-6. **Selah**. Ps +*9:16.

9. **our**. ver. 11. Ps 98:1. Ge *15:1. Dt 33:29. **the face**. Ps 45:12mg. 80:3. 119:58mg. 132:10. **thine anointed**. Ps 2:2, 6mg. *89:20. 132:17. 1 S 2:10. 16:6. 2 S 19:21. 23:1. 2 Ch 6:42. Ac 4:27.

10. **For**. ver. 1, 2. Ps 27:4. 43:3, 4. 63:2. Lk 2:46. Ro 8:5, 6. Ph 3:20. **thousand**. ♪63F, Ge +33:10. By ellipsis (relative: of contrary words), supply (elsewhere, *or* in any other place). Young renders "teacher," perhaps because the term "thousand" is used of the chiefs or leaders, as in Ex 18:21 and Mi +*5:2. **I had**. Heb. I would choose rather to sit at the threshold. 2 K +12:9mg. Je 52:24mg. Ja 2:3. **to dwell**. Ps 17:14, 15. 26:8-10. 141:4, 5.

11. **is**. ♪119, Ge +49:9. **a sun**. Ps *27:1. Le=16:12, 13. Is *60:19, 20. Hab 3:19. Ml *4:2. Jn *1:9, 10. *8:12. Re *21:23. **shield**. ♪22D5F, Ge +15:1. ver. 9.

Ps 3:3. 47:9. *115:9-11. *119:114. Ge *15:1. Le=16:12, 13. Pr *2:7. **the Lord.** Jn *1:16. Ro *8:16-18. 2 C *3:18. *4:17. Ph 1:6. **give grace.** T#798. Je 30:9. 31:33. Mt +*28:19n. Lk 1:74, 75. Jn 17:17, 19. Ro 5:15, 17, 20. 1 C 6:11. 2 C 3:5, 18. ◐+*8:9. Ep *2:10. Ph 2:13. *4:13. Col 1:12, 21, 22. 1 Th 5:23. 2 Th *2:13. T *2:11, 14. He ◐10:29. Ja 4:6. 1 P 5:10. **glory.** Ps *73:24. Ex 33:18. Ro *5:2. *8:30. **no good thing.** ʃ175B, Ge +21:16. T#751. Ps 3:8. 5:12. 16:6. 23:6. *34:9, 10. 58:11. 85:12. 106:15. Pr 3:32. 10:6, 24, 28. 11:18, 19, 28. 12:12. 13:9, 21. 21:21. Ec 8:12. Is 3:10. Je 5:25. +*29:11. Mt √6:33. Ro √8:32. 1 C 3:21, 22. Ph √4:19. 1 T +*4:8. Ja 4:3. **walk.** Ps *15:2. Pr 2:7. *10:9. *28:6, 18. Mi *2:7. Ga 2:14.

12. **blessed.** ʃ43, Dt +28:3. Ps 2:12. *34:8. *62:8. *146:5, 6. Is *30:18. *50:10. Je *17:◐5, 7, 8. Ro 15:13. 1 P 1:8.

PSALM 85

Thankful recollections of former mercies from God to Israel, 1-3. Earnest prayers for grace, mercy, and peace, 4-7. Prophetical assurances of a gracious answer, especially by the coming of the Messiah, and in his glorious salvation, 8-13.

(Title.) A.M. 3468. B.C. 536. **for.** *or,* of. Ps 42, title.

1. **Lord.** Le 26:42. Jl 2:18. Zc *1:16. **favorable unto.** *or,* well pleased with. Ps 77:7. **thou hast.** Ps *14:7. 126:1, 2. Ezr 1:11. *2:1. Je *30:18. 31:23. Ezk *39:25. Jl 3:1.

2. **forgiven.** Ps *32:1. 79:8, 9. Je *50:20. Mi *7:18. Ac 13:39. Col *2:13, 14.

3. **taken.** Is 6:7. *12:1. *54:7-10. Jn 1:29. **turned,** etc. *or,* turned thine anger from waxing hot. Ex 32:11, 22. Dt *13:17.

4. **Turn us.** The Israelites were not restored from their captivity all at once: a few returned with Zerubbabel, some more with Ezra and Nehemiah; but a great number still remained in Babylonia, Media, Assyria, etc.; therefore the psalmist prays for a complete restoration. Ps 80:3, *7, 19. 138:8. Je *31:18. La 5:21. Ml 4:6. **O God.** Ps 25:2. *27:1. Mi 7:7, *18-20. Jn 4:22. **cause.** Ps *78:38. Is 10:25. Da *9:16.

5. **angry.** Ps 74:1. 77:7, 9. 79:5. 80:4. 89:46. Is +*41:9. 64:9-12. Mi *7:18. Zc +*10:6. **for ever.** Heb. *olam,* Ex +*12:24. **draw.** Lk *21:24. Re 18:21-23.

6. **Wilt thou.** T#622, 1678. Ps 80:14-16, +18 (T#1663). *122:6. SS 4:16. Is 62:6, 7. 64:1, 2. Je 14:20, 21. Da 9:17. Hab 3:2. Mt 6:10. **revive.** Ps 80:18. 138:7. Ezr *9:8, 9. Is *57:15. Ho *6:1, 2. Hab *3:2. **people.** Ps 53:6. Ezr *3:11-13. Je *33:11.

7. **thy mercy.** Ps 98:3. 106:45. Dt +*32:43. Is √54:7, 8. Je 42:12. Mi *7:18, 20. Hab 3:2. Zc √10:6. Lk 1:50, 54, 55, 72, 78. **thy salvation.** Ps 50:23. 91:16. Is *25:9. Lk 1:69. 2:30. He +*9:28n.

8. **hear.** Hab *2:1. He 12:25. **God.** Heb. *El,* Ex +15:2. **for he.** Ps 29:11. Is 57:19. Je *29:11. Zc *9:10. Jn *14:27. 20:19, 26. Ac 10:36. 2 C 5:18-20. Ep 2:17. 2 Th 3:16. **to his.** Ps 50:5. Ep 1:1, 2. **but.** Ps *130:4. Jn *5:14. *8:11. Ac 3:26. Ga *4:9. 2 T *2:19. He *10:26-29. 2 P *2:20-22. Re 2:4, 5. 3:19. **folly.** Ge 34:7. 1 S 25:25. Pr *26:11. 27:22.

9. **Surely.** Ps 24:4, 5. *50:23. √119:155. Is 46:13. Mk *12:32-34. Jn √7:17. Ac *10:2-4. *11:13, 14. 13:26. Ro *10:8, 9. T *2:11-13. **that fear.** Ac *13:26. **that**

---

glory. Ps +*102:16. Ex *40:34, 35. 2 Ch 7:1, 3. Is 4:5. *46:13. Ezk 26:20. Hg *2:7-9. Zc *2:5, 8. Lk 2:32. Jn *1:14.

10. **Mercy.** Ps *89:14. 100:5. Ex 34:6, 7. Mi 7:20. Lk 1:54, 55. Jn *1:17. **and.** ʃ174, Ge +18:27. **met.** ʃ155F, Ge +4:7. **righteousness.** T#587. Ps +46:10 (T#277). 72:3. Is 32:16-18. *42:21. *45:24. Je *23:5, 6. Ho *2:19. Lk 2:14. Ro 3:25, 26, 31. *5:1, 21. *14:17. 2 C 4:6. Ep 3:8-11. 1 T 1:11. He *7:2. 1 P 1:12. **kissed.** ʃ155F, Ge +4:7.

11. **Truth.** Is 4:2. 45:8. *53:2. Jn 1:17. √14:6. 1 J *5:20, 21. **shall spring.** Mk 16:6. Ga 4:4, 5. **righteousness.** Dt 33:16. Is *32:17. 42:21. 45:24, 25. Je *23:5, 6. Mt *3:17. *17:5. Lk 2:14. Ro 3:25, 26. 5:1, 2. 2 C √5:21. Ep 1:6.

12. **the Lord.** Ps *84:11. Mi *6:8. Mt 7:11. Lk 11:13. 1 C 1:30. Ep *1:3. Ja √1:17. **our land.** Ps 67:6. 72:16. Is 30:23, 24. *32:15, 16. Mt *13:8, 23. Ac 2:41. 21:20g. 1 C *3:6-9.

13. **Righteousness.** Ps 72:2, 3. *89:14. Is 58:8. Ps 119:35. Mt *20:27, 28. Jn 13:14-16, 34. 2 C *3:18. Ga *2:20. Ep 5:1, 2. Ph *2:5-8. *3:9, 16, 17. He *12:1, 2. 1 P 2:18-24. 4:1. 1 J *2:1-3, 6.

PSALM 86

David pleads his indigence and the fervor of his devotion in imploring help from the God of grace and mercy, 1-7. He praises God as alone worthy of universal adoration and prophesies that all nations shall thus adore him, 8-10. He prays for teaching and grace, renders thanks for former mercies, complains of his haughty foes, and craves some special token of divine favor, 11-17.

(Title.) **A Prayer of David.** *or,* a prayer, being a psalm of David. This psalm is supposed to have been composed by David either when persecuted by Saul or driven from Jerusalem by Absalom. Ps 102, 142, titles.

1. **Bow.** Ps 31:2. Is 37:17. Da 9:18. **for I am.** Ps 10:14. *34:6. *40:17. 72:12-14. 102:17. 119:22. 140:12. Is *66:2. Mt 5:3. Lk 4:18. Ja 1:9, 10. 2:5.

2. **Preserve.** T#1707. Ps 4:3. 37:28. 119:94, 175. 145:19, 20. 1 S 2:9. Is 55:3. Jn √10:27-29. 17:11. 1 P *1:5. 5:3-5. **soul.** Heb. *nephesh,* Ge +12:13. **holy.** *or,* one whom thou favorest. Ps 18:19. +43:1mg. 145:17mg. Dt 7:7, 8. Ro 9:18, 23, 24. **save.** Ps 119:124, 125. 143:12. Jn 12:26. **trusteth.** Ps 13:5. 16:1. 31:1. Is √26:3, 4. Ro 15:12, 13. Ep 1:12, 13.

3. **Be merciful.** Ps 56:1. 57:1. **for I.** Ps 55:17. 88:9. Lk 2:37. 11:8-13. 18:7. Ep 6:18. **daily.** *or,* all the day. T#1154. Ps *25:5. *55:16, 17. 88:9. Is *58:2. Lk 18:1. Ro 12:12. Ep 6:18. 1 Th *5:17.

4. **Rejoice.** Ps *51:12. Is *61:3. 65:18. 66:13, 14. **soul.** Heb. *nephesh,* Ge +34:3. **do.** Ps 25:1. *62:8. 143:8. 1 S 1:15. **soul.** Heb. *nephesh,* Ge +34:3.

5. **thou.** ver. 15. Ps 25:8. 36:7. 52:1. 69:16. 119:68. 130:7. 145:8, 9. Ex 34:6. Jl 2:13. 1 J 4:8, 9. **ready to forgive.** Ps *32:5. Ne 9:17. Is *1:18. *43:25. *44:22. √55:6, 7. Da 9:9. Mi 7:18. Ro √10:13. **plenteous.** Ps 103:8. 130:4, *7. Jl *2:13, 18. Jon +4:2. Ro 5:20, 21. Ep 1:6-8. 2:4. **unto all.** Ps *145:9, 18. Je *33:3. Ezk 36:33, 37. Lk √11:9, 10. Jn 4:10. *6:37. Ac 2:21. Ro √10:12, 13. 1 J 4:8.

6. **Give ear.** Ps 5:1, 2. 17:1. 54:2. 55:1. 130:2.

7. **In the day.** Ps *18:6. *34:4-6. +*50:15. 55:16-

18. 77:1, 2. *91:15. 142:1, 2. Is 26:16. La *3:55-57. Jon *2:2. Lk 22:44. He *5:7.

8. **Among.** Ps *89:6, 8. Ex *15:11. Is 40:18, 25. Je 10:6, 7, 16. Da 3:29. 1 C √8:5, 6. **the gods.** Heb. *elohim.* Ps +*82:6n. Ex 21:6. 22:8, 9, √28mg. **neither.** Ps 136:4. Dt *3:24. 4:34.

9. **All.** Ps 22:27-31. 66:4. 67:7. 72:8, 19. 102:15, 18. Is *2:2-4. *11:9. 43:7. 59:19. 66:23. Zc 14:9. Ro 11:25. Re 11:15. *15:4. 20:3. **shall come.** Is 66:18. Zc 14:16. **and shall.** Re ꓘ15:4. **glorify.** Ro 15:9. Ep 1:12. 1 P 2:9.

10. **For.** ver. 8. Ps 72:18. 77:14, 15. 145:3-5. Ex 15:11. Jb 11:7. Da 6:26, 27. Ac 2:19-22. 4:30. Ro 15:18, 19. He 2:4. **God alone.** Dt +*6:3, 4. +*32:39. Is *37:16, 20. *44:6-8. Mk *12:29. 1 C √8:4. Ep *4:6.

11. **Teach me.** T#1719. Ps 5:8. *25:4, 12. +*27:11. *32:8. 90:12. 119:12, 26, *33, 73, 108, 124. *143:8-10. Jb 34:32. Lk 11:1. Jn 6:45, 46. Ep 4:21. Ja *1:5. **I will.** Ps 26:3. 119:30. Ml 2:6. 2 J 4. 3 J 3, 4. **unite.** Je 32:38, 39. Ho 10:2. 14:8. Zp 1:5. Mt *6:22-24. Jn 17:20, 21. Ac 2:46. 1 C 6:17. 10:21. 2 C 11:3. Ga *5:17. Col 3:17, 22, 23. **to fear.** T#1492. Ps 33:8. 99:1. 1 K 8:40. 2 Ch 6:31.

12. **praise.** Ps 34:1. *103:1-3. *104:33. 145:1-5. 146:1, 2. 1 Ch 29:13, 20. Is 12:1. Re 5:9-13. 19:5, 6. **with all.** Ps 9:1. Dt 6:5. Pr √3:5, 6. Ac 8:37. Ep *5:19. **glorify.** Ro *15:6. 1 C *6:20. *10:31. **for evermore.** Heb. *olam,* Ps +18:50.

13. **great.** Ps 57:10. 103:8-12. 108:4. Lk 1:58. **and thou.** Ps +*16:10. *56:13. 88:6. 116:8. 2 S *12:13. Jb 33:18, 22, 24, 28. Is 38:17. Jon 2:3-6. 1 Th √1:10. **soul.** Heb. *nephesh,* Ps +30:3. **lowest.** Dt +32:22. Mk +*12:40. **hell.** *or,* the grave. Heb. *sheol,* Ps +30:3; Ge +37:35. Ps 6:5. 9:17.

14. **O God.** Ps 36:11. *54:3. 119:51, 69, 85. 140:5. 2 S 15:1, etc. **assemblies.** 2 S 16:20-23. 17:1-4, 14. Mt 26:3, 4. 27:1, 2. Ac 4:27, 28. **violent.** Heb. terrible. ✻S#6184h. Ps 37:35 (great power). 54:3 (oppressors). Jb 6:23 (mighty). 15:20 (oppressor). 27:13. Pr 11:16 (strong). Is 13:11. 25:3, 4, 5. 29:5, 20. Je 15:21. 20:11. Ezk 28:7. 30:11. 31:12. 32:12. **soul.** Heb. *nephesh,* Ge +12:13. **and have.** Ps 10:*4, 11, 13. 14:4. *36:1. Ezk 8:12. 9:9.

15. **But thou.** ver. 5. Ps *103:8. 111:4. 130:4, *7. 145:8. Ex *34:6, 7. Nu 14:18. Ne *9:17. Jl 2:13. Mi 7:18. Ro 5:20, 21. Ep 1:7. 2:4-7. **God.** Heb. *El,* Ex +15:2. **full.** √22I4. Anthropomorphism B895. Multitude or fulness is attributed to God. For other instances of this figure see Ps 103:8. 130:7. **mercy.** Ps *85:10. 98:3. Jn *1:17. Ro 15:8, 9. **and truth.** √174, Ge +18:27. Ps 146:6. Dt +*32:4. Ro 3:4. T +*1:2. He *6:18.

16. **turn.** Ps 25:16. 69:16. 90:13. *119:132. **give thy strength.** T#1715. Ps 27:14. 28:7, 8. 84:5. 119:28. *138:3. Jg 16:28. 1 Ch +16:11 (T#1537). Ne 6:9. Is *40:29-31. 45:24. Da 10:16-18. Zc 10:12. Ep 3:14-16. 6:10. Ph *4:13. Col *1:10, 11. **the son.** Ps 116:16. 119:94. 2 T 1:5. **handmaid.** Is +7:14. Mt ✻1:23. Lk *1:38.

17. **Show.** Ps *41:10, 11. 74:9. Is 38:22. 1 C 5:5. **that they.** Ps 71:9-13. 109:29. Mi *7:8-10. Ph *2:7-10. **thou.** Ps 40:1. 71:20, 21.

PSALM 87

Zion is honorable above the rest of the land, 1-3; and the saints thereof above the nations of the earth, 4-7.

(*Title.*) A.M. 3468. B.C. 536. **A Psalm.** It is highly probable that this psalm was written by one of the descendants of Korah on the return from the Babylonian captivity. It seems to have been written in praise of Jerusalem and typically of the Christian church. **for.** *or,* of.

1. **His.** 2 Ch 3:1. Is *28:16. Mt *16:16, 18. 1 C *3:10, 11. Ep 2:20-22. He 12:22. 1 P 2:4-8. **the holy.** Ps *48:1, 2. 68:16. 121:1. Is 2:2, 3. 56:7. Zc 8:3. 2 P 1:18.

2. **The Lord.** Ps *78:67-69. *132:13, 14. Dt 12:5. 2 Ch 6:6. Is 14:32. 56:7. Jl 2:32. 1 C 3:16. Ep 2:21. **gates.** √171S6, Ge +14:7. **dwellings.** √121J16, Ge +13:5.

3. **Glorious.** T#940. Ps 45:13. 48:2, 3, 11-13. 125:1, 2. Is 12:6. 19:14, etc. 46:13. 49:14-23. 54:2, 11, 12. *59:20, 21. 60:1, 2, 13, 15, 19. 61:3, etc. 62:1-3, etc. Je 3:14-17. 31:12, 13. Ezk 36:2, 11, etc. *37:27, 28. ch. 40—48. He 12:22, 23. Re 14:1. 21:10-27.

4.—— **Rahab.** √146, Ge +10:10. Ps 89:10mg. Is 51:9. **Babylon.** Ps 137:1, 8, 9. 2 K 20:17, 18. Is 13:1, etc. 14:4-6. Je 25:9. ch. 50, 51. Da 2:47, 48. 4:30. Re 17:5. 18:2. **Philistia.** i.e. *watered,* ✻S#6429h. Ps 60:8. 108:9. **Tyre.** Ps 45:12. Is 23. Ezk ch. 27, 28. **Ethiopia.** 1 K 10:1, etc. 2 K +*19:9. Is 18:1, 7. Je 3:16n. Ezk *38:5. Ac *8:27. **this man.** Ps *68:31. 1 S 17:8. 2 S 21:16-22. Is 19:11, 23-25. Ezk 28:2. **born.** √22C23, Ps +2:7.

5. **of Zion.** Is *44:4, 5. *60:1-9. Zc 8:22. Jn 1:12-14. 3:3-5. Ga 3:26-28. He 11:32-40. 12:1, 2, 22-24. 1 P 1:23, 24. **highest.** Ezk *48:35. Mt 16:18. Ro *8:31.

6. **when.** Ps *22:30. Is *4:3. Ezk *9:4. *13:9. Lk 10:20. Ph 4:3. Re 13:8. **this man.** Je 3:19. Ga *4:26-31. Re √20:15.

7. **As well.** Ps 68:24, 25. 1 Ch 15:16, etc. 23:5. 25:1-6. Re 14:1-3. 15:3. **on instruments.** Ps 150:4. Re 14:1-3. **all my.** Ps 46:4. Dt 8:15. Is *12:3. Jn *1:16. 4:10, 14. *7:37-39. Ja *1:17. Re 21:6. 22:1, 17. **springs.** Heb. *mayan,* Ge +7:11 (✻S#4599h).

PSALM 88

The psalmist bewails before God his complicated sufferings with great energy and variety of expression, and pleads earnestly for deliverance, 1-18.

(*Title.*) A.M. cir. 2173. B.C. cir. 1531. **for.** *or,* of. **Mahalath.** Ps 53, title. **Maschil,** etc. *or, A Psalm* of Heman the Ezrahite, giving instruction. Supposed to have been written by *Heman,* son of Zerah, and grandson of Judah, on the oppression of the Hebrews in Egypt. **Heman.** 1 K 4:31. 1 Ch 2:6. **Ezrahite.** Ps 89, title. 1 K +4:31.

1. **Lord.** Ps 27:1, 9. 51:14. 62:7. 65:5. 68:19, 20. 79:9. 140:7. Ge 49:18. Is 12:2. Lk 1:47. 2:30. T 2:10, 13. *3:4-7. He 5:7. **day and night.** T#1155. Ps 22:2. 86:3. Ne 1:6. Is 62:6. La 2:18, 19. Lk 2:37. *18:7. 1 Th 3:10. 1 T 5:5. 2 T 1:3. Re 4:8.

2. **Let.** Ps 79:11. 141:1, 2. 1 K 8:31. La 3:8.

3. **soul.** Heb. *nephesh,* Ge +34:3. ver. 14, 15. Ps 22:11-21. 69:17-21. 77:2. 143:3, 4. Ge 25:8n, 9, 17. 35:18. 1 K *17:22. Jb 6:2-4. +*14:22. 33:18, 22. Is *53:3, 10, 11. La 3:15-19. Mt +*10:28. *26:37-39. Mk 14:33, 34. **life.** Ps 107:18. Jb 33:22. **grave.** Heb. *sheol,* Ge +37:35.

4. **counted.** Ps 15:4. 28:1. 30:9. 143:7. Jb 17:1. Is 38:17, 18. Ezk 26:20. Jon 2:6. Mt 27:42. 2 C 1:9. **down.** Ps +*146:4. **pit.** Heb. *bor,* Ge +37:20. **as a man.** Ps

31:12. 109:22-24. Ro 5:6. 2 C 13:4.

5. **Free among.** ƒ46A, Le +26:30. "Set at liberty" is put by catachresis for cast off, deserted. Jb 3:17. Is 14:9-12. 38:10-12. Ezk 32:18-32. **grave.** Heb. *qeber*, Ge +23:4. **whom.** Ps 136:23. Ge 8:1. 19:29. Jb 14:12. **cut off.** ver. 16. Ps *31:22. Jb 6:9. 11:10. Is *53:8. Mt 27:46, 66. **from thy hand.** *or*, by thy hand.

6. **lowest.** Ps 40:2. 86:13. Dt +*32:22. **pit.** Heb. *bor*, Ge +37:20. **darkness.** Ps 143:3. Pr 4:19. La 3:2. Jn 12:46. Ju 6, 13. **deeps.** Ps 69:15. 130:1.

7. **Thy wrath.** Ps 38:1-6. 90:7-11. 102:10. Jb 6:4. 10:16. Jn √3:36. Ro 2:5-9. Ga 3:13. 1 P 2:24. Re 6:16, 17. **with.** Ps 42:7. Jon 2:3.

8. **put.** ver. 18. Ps 31:11. 142:4. 1 S 23:18-20. Jb *19:13-19. Mt 26:21, 34, 56. Jn 11:57. **acquaintance.** 2 K 10:11mg. **made.** Is 49:7. *53:3. Zc 11:8. Mt 27:21-25. Jn 15:23, 24. **I am shut.** Jb 12:14. 19:8. La 3:7-9.

9. **Mine.** Ps 38:10. 42:3. 102:9. Jb 16:20. 17:7. La 3:48, 49. Jn 11:35. **called.** See on ver. 1. Ps 55:17. 86:3. **stretched out.** T#1249. Ps 44:20. 68:31. 143:6. Ge 48:14, 15. Ex 17:11. 1 K 8:54. 2 Ch 6:13. Ezr 9:5, 6. Jb *11:13-15. Is 1:15.

10. **Wilt thou.** The interrogations in these verses imply the strongest negations (compare ƒ85C, Ge +18:14). Ps *6:5. *30:9. 115:17. 118:17. Is *38:18, 19. Mk 5:35, 36. Jn *11:25. **shall.** Jb 14:7-12. Is +*26:19n. Ezk 37:1-14. Lk 7:12-16. 1 C 15:52-57.

11. **declared in.** Ps +*146:4. **grave.** Heb. *qeber*, Ge +23:4 (*S#6913h). **in destruction.** Ps 55:23. 73:18. Jb 21:30. +*26:6. Pr 15:11. Mt 7:13. Ro 9:22. 2 P 2:1.

12. **dark.** Ps 143:3. Jb 10:21, 22. Is 8:22. Mt 8:12. Ju 13. **in the land.** ver. 5. Ps 31:12. Jb *24:20. Ec 2:16. 8:10. √9:5.

13. **and in.** See on Ps +5:3. 119:147, 148. Mk +*1:35. **prevent thee.** "Come before thee:" see on Ps 21:3.

14. **Lord.** Ps 43:2. 77:7-9. Mt *27:46. **soul.** Heb. *nephesh*, Ge +12:13. **hidest.** Ps 13:1. 44:24. 69:17. Jb 13:24.

15. **afflicted.** Ps 73:14. Jb 17:1, 11-16. Is *53:3. **die.** Ge +49:33 (S#1478h). **while.** Ps 22:14, 15. Jb *6:4. 7:11-16. Is 53:10. Zc 13:7. Lk 22:44. **thy terrors.** Jn 12:27.

16. **fierce wrath.** Ps 38:1, 2. 89:46. 90:7, 11. 102:10. Is *53:4-6. Ro *8:32. Ga 3:13. Re 6:17. **cut me.** Is *53:8. Da 9:26.

17. **They.** Ps 22:16. 42:7. 69:1, 2. 116:3. Jb 16:12, 13. 30:14, 15. La 3:5-7. Mt 27:39-44. **daily.** *or*, all the day. ver. 9. Ps 25:5. 32:3. 35:28. 38:6.

18. **Lover.** ver. 8. Ps 31:11. 38:11. Jb 19:12-15. **mine acquaintance.** A figurative expression to denote that he now never saw them. 2 K 10:11mg.

PSALM 89

The psalmist praises God for his covenanted mercies to David, celebrating his greatness, excellency, and wonderful works and showing the felicity of his people, 1-18. He enlarges on the promises of the covenant made with David and his seed, 19-37. He complains of the afflicted state of David's kingdom with earnest prayers and expostulations, 38-51. He concludes with blessing the Lord, 52.

(Title.) A.M. cir. 3463. B.C. cir. 541. **Maschil**, etc. *or, A Psalm* for Ethan the Ezrahite, to give instruction.

This psalm is generally supposed to have been written during the Babylonian captivity when, the family of David being dethroned and the royal family ruined, the divine promises had apparently failed. **Ethan.** 1 K 4:31. 1 Ch 2:6.

1. **I will.** Ps 86:12, 13. *101:1. 106:1. 136:1, etc. **mercies.** ƒ96F2, Ge +4:10. Ro *12:1. 2 C *1:3. **for ever.** Heb. *olam*, Ex +*12:24. **with.** Ps *40:9, 10. 71:8, *15-19. **thy faithfulness.** ver. 5, 8, 33-49. Ps 36:5. 92:2. Is 25:1. La *3:23. Mi 7:20. T *1:2. **all generations.** Heb. generation and generation. ver. 4. Ps +33:11mg. 100:5mg. 119:90mg. Pr +*27:24mg.

2. **Mercy.** Ps *36:5. *103:17, 18. Ne 1:5. *9:17, 31. Lk 1:50. Ep *1:6, 7. **for ever.** Heb. *olam*, Ex +*12:24. **faithfulness.** ver. 5, *37. Ps *119:89. 146:6. Nu *23:19. Mt *24:35. He *6:18.

3. **made.** ver. 28, 34, 39. 2 S √7:8-16, 24-26. 23:5. 1 K 8:16. Is +√55:3. Je *30:9. √33:19-22, 25, 26. Ezk *34:23, 24. Ho *3:5. Lk +*1:32, 33. **covenant.** Ge +9:16. **my chosen.** ver. 19. Ps 78:70. Is *42:1. Mt 3:17. 12:18-21. He 1:5. **sworn.** ver. 35. Ps 132:11. 2 S 3:9. Ac +*2:30, 31. He 7:21. **David.** Ac +✱13:23.

4. **Thy seed.** ver. 1, 29, 36. Ps 72:17. 132:12. 2 S √7:12-16, 29. 1 K 9:5. 1 Ch √17:10-14. *22:10. Is *9:6, 7. Zc 12:8. Lk +*1:32, 33. 20:41-44. Ac 13:32-37. Ro *1:3, 4. 15:12. Ph 2:9-11. Re *22:16. **for ever.** Heb. *olam*, Ge +9:16. Ex +*12:24. **throne.** ƒ121S1, Ge +49:10. By Metonymy of the Adjunct, "throne" is put for those, especially One, who shall sit upon it. **generations.** Ge +9:12. **Selah.** Ps +9:16.

5. **heavens.** Ps 19:1. 50:6. *97:6. Is 44:23. Lk *2:10-15. Ep 3:10. 1 P 1:12. Re 5:11-14. *7:10-12. **in the congregation.** ver. 7. Ps 111:1. Dt +*33:2. Da *7:10, 22, 27. 2 Th 1:7. He 12:22, 23. Ju *14, 15. Re 19:1-6.

6. **For who.** ver. 8. Ps 40:5. 71:19. 73:25. *86:8. 113:5. Ex 15:11. Je 10:6. **the sons.** ƒ108H11, Ge +6:2. Ps 29:1mg. 52:1. 103:20. **mighty.** ƒ24L, Ge +6:2.

7. **God.** Heb. *El*, Ex +15:2. **is greatly.** Ps 76:7-11. Le *10:3. Is 6:2-7. 66:2. Je 10:7, 10. Mt +*10:28. Lk 12:4, 5. Ac 5:11. He *12:28, 29. Re *15:3, 4. **feared.** Ec +12:13. **in reverence.** 1 Ch 13:7n, 10. Hab 2:20.

8. **O Lord.** Ps 84:12. Jsh 22:22. Is 28:22. **a strong.** ver. 13. Ps 24:8. 147:5. 1 S 15:29. Jb 9:19. Is 40:25, 26. Je 32:17. Mt *6:13. **like.** ver. 6. Ps *35:10. 71:19. Ex *15:11. Dt 32:31. 1 S *2:2.

9. **Thou rulest.** Ps 29:10. *65:7. 66:5, 6. 93:3, 4. *107:25-29. Jb 38:8-11. Na 1:4. Mt *8:24-27. *14:32. Mk *4:39, 41.

10. **Thou hast.** Ps 78:43, etc. 105:27, etc. Ex ch. 7-15. **Rahab.** *or,* Egypt. ƒ146, Ge +10:10. Ps 87:4. Is 51:9. **scattered.** Ps 59:11. 68:30. 144:6. Is 24:1. **thy strong arm.** Heb. the arm of thy strength. ƒ22A12, Ex 3:19, 20. +15:16. Dt 4:34.

11. **The heavens.** Ps *24:1, 2. *50:12. 115:16. Ge 1:1. 2:1. 1 Ch *29:11. Jb 41:11. 1 C 10:26, 28.

12. **north.** Jb 26:7. **Tabor.** Jsh 19:22. Jg 4:6, 12. **Hermon.** Ps 133:3. Dt 3:8, 9. Jsh 12:1. **rejoice.** Ps 65:12, 13. Is 35:1, 2. 49:13. 55:12, 13.

13. **a mighty arm.** Heb. an arm with might. ƒ22A12, Ex +15:16. ver. 10. Ps 62:11. Da 4:34, 35. Mt 6:13.

14. **Justice.** Ps +*45:6, 7. *97:2. 99:4. 145:17. Dt 32:4. Re 15:3. **habitation.** *or*, establishment. Ps 33:14. 97:2mg. 104:5. Pr *16:12. Is 4:5. **mercy.** ver. 2. Ps *85:13. Jn *1:17. **and truth.** ƒ174, Ge +18:27.

15. **Blessed.** ✸43, Dt +28:3. **know.** Ps 90:6. 98:4-6. 100:1. Le 25:9. Nu *10:10. 23:21. Is 52:7, 8. Na 1:15. Lk *2:10-14. Ro *10:15, 18. **joyful sound.** or, trumpet sound. Le +*23:24. **shall walk.** or, walk habitually. Ps 55:14. 81:13. Lk +*11:28. **in the light.** Ps *4:6. 44:3. Nu *6:25, 26. Jb 29:3. Pr 16:15. Is 2:5. Jn *14:21-23. Ac 2:28. Re 21:23.

16. **name.** ver. 12. Ps 20:5, 7. 33:21. 44:8. Lk 1:47. Ph *4:4. 1 P *1:8. **righteousness.** Ps *40:10. 71:15, 16. Is *45:24, 25. 46:13. Je *23:6. Ro *1:17. *3:21-26. 2 C *5:21. Ph *3:8, 9.

17. **For thou.** Ps 28:7. 1 C 1:30, 31. 2 C 12:9, 10. Ph 4:13. **our horn.** ver. 24. Ps 75:10. 92:10. 112:9. 132:17. 148:14. 1 S 2:1, 10.

18. **the Lord is,** etc. *or,* our shield is of the Lord, and our king is of the Holy One of Israel. Ps 47:9. 62:1, 2, 6. *84:11. 91:1, 2. Ge 15:1. Dt *33:27-29. Pr 30:5. **Holy.** Ps *30:4. 71:22. Is 1:4. 12:6. 29:19. 30:11. 43:3, 14. **king.** Ps 44:4. Is 33:22.

19. **Then.** 1 S 16:1. 2 S 7:8-17. Lk *1:68-70. 2 P √1:21. 3:2. **to thy holy.** Mk 1:24. Re 3:7. **I have laid.** Ge=49:24. 1 S 16:18. Jb 33:24. Is *9:6. Je 30:21. **mighty.** Jsh 4:24. 1 S *16:18. Is *9:6. 63:1. Je 50:34. Am 5:12. Zp 3:17. **exalted.** ver. 3. 1 K 11:34. Ph *2:6-11. He 2:9-17.

20. **I have found.** 1 S *16:1, 12, 13. Is 61:1-3. Mk 1:10. Jn *3:34. Ac ❱13:22.

21. **With.** Ps *18:32-39. *80:15-17. 2 S 7:8-16. Is 42:1. 49:8. **mine.** ver. 13. Is 41:10. Ezk 30:24, 25. Zc 10:12.

22. **enemy.** Ps 129:2. 1 Ch 17:9. Mt *4:1-11. **son.** Jn *17:12. 2 Th 2:3.

23. **I will.** Ps *2:9. 2 S 3:1. *7:1, 9. 22:40-44. Re 2:27. **plague.** Ps 2:1-6. 21:8, 9. 109:3, etc. *110:1, 2. 132:18. Lk 19:14, 27. Jn 15:23.

24. **But my.** ver. 2-5, 28, 33. Ps 61:7. Jn 1:17. 2 C 1:20. **in my.** ver. 16, 17. Ps 20:1, 5. 91:14. 1 S 2:1. Jn 17:6, 11, 26.

25. **I will.** Ps 2:8. *72:8-11. 80:11. 1 K 4:21. Re *11:15. **his hand.** ✸121BA, Dt +32:36. That is, *his power, or authority,* as *hand* frequently signifies: for the accomplishment of these promises, see the parallel texts. 1 Ch 18:1, 3.

26. **Thou.** 2 S 7:14. 1 Ch 22:10. Mt *26:39, 42. Lk 23:46. Jn 11:41. 20:17. He 1:5. **God.** Heb. *El,* Ex +15:2. Ps 43:4. Mk 15:34. **rock.** Ps 18:46. 62:2, 6, 7. 95:1. 2 S *22:47. Is 50:7-9.

27. **Also.** Ps *2:7. Ro *8:29. Col *1:15, 18. **him.** ver. 20. **firstborn.** Ge +48:14. 2 Ch +26:10. Je +√31:9. Col +√1:15n. **higher.** Ps *2:10-12. *72:11. Nu 24:7. 2 Ch 1:12. 9:23, 24. Is 49:7. Re *19:16. 21:24. or, Most High. Heb. *Elyon.* William Kay notes the same term is used of Israel at Dt 28:1 (on high), rendering it "...then shall the Lord thy God make thee supreme *(elyon)* above the nations of the earth"—noting "Here again Israel had failed, through disobedience; but the Lord's Anointed—perfect in obedience—should attain the 'Name above every name.'" Ps +*7:17. Ge +√14:18. Re ❱1:5.

28. **mercy.** 2 S √7:15, 16. *23:5. Is +√54:9, 10. +√55:3. Ac *13:32-34. **for evermore.** Ps +*18:50. **covenant.** ver. 34. Ps 111:5, 9. 2 S 23:5. Je +√33:20, 21, 25, 26. **stand fast.** Jg +2:1.

29. **His seed.** ver. 4, 36. Ps 132:11. 1 Ch 17:11, 12. Is 59:21. Je *33:17-26. **for ever.** Ps +9:18 (✸S#5703h). **throne.** Ps +*45:6. 1 Ch 22:10. Is *9:7.

Ezk 37:24, 25. Da 2:44. Lk 1:32, 33. **days of heaven.** Ps 21:4. Dt +*11:21. Mt *6:10. Ac +√3:19, 21. He +√11:13.

30. **If.** Ps 132:12. 2 S *7:14. 1 Ch +*28:9. 2 Ch 7:17-22. **forsake.** ✸173, Ge +27:44. Ps 119:53. Pr 4:2. 28:4. Je *9:13-16. **walk.** Ezk 18:9, 17. 20:19. Lk 1:6.

31. **If.** Ge +4:7. **break.** Heb. profane. Ps 55:20mg.

32. **Then.** Ps +*9:10. Ex 32:34. 2 S 7:14. 1 K *11:6, 14, 31, 39. Pr 3:11, 12. Am *3:2. 1 C *11:31, 32. He *12:6-11.

33. **Nevertheless.** ✸127, Re +2:6. 2 S √7:13, 15. 1 K 11:13, 32, 36. Is +*54:8-10. Je +*33:20-26. La *3:31, 32. 1 C 15:25. **not utterly take.** Heb. not make void. ver. 39. Ps 33:10. √94:14. 1 S 15:29. Is +*41:9. +*55:3. **fail.** Heb. lie. He *6:18.

34. **My covenant.** ver. 28. Le 26:44. Jg +2:1. Je 14:21. +√33:20, 21. Ro *11:29. **not break.** Dt ◐31:16. **nor alter.** Nu 23:19. Ml +*3:6. Mt 24:35. Ro √11:29. Ja *1:17.

35. **Once.** Ps 14:3. 27:4. 34:20. 53:3. Jb +40:5n. **have I sworn.** Ps 110:4. 132:11. Am 4:2. 8:7. He 6:13, 17. **that I will not lie.** Heb. If I lie. 2 T 2:13. T *1:2. **David.** Ac +✸*13:23.

36. **seed.** ver. 4, 29. 2 S 7:16. Is 53:10. 59:21. Jn 12:34. **for ever.** Heb. *olam,* Ex +*12:24. Ec +1:4. **and.** Ps 72:5, 17. Is *9:7. Je +√33:20, 21. Lk *1:33. Jn *12:34.

37. **It shall.** As long as the sun and moon shall endure, as long as time shall last, his kingdom shall continue among men. The moon is properly termed "a faithful witness," because by her, particularly, time is measured. Her decrease and increase are observed by every nation, and by these time is generally estimated, especially among eastern nations: So many moons is a man old—so many moons since such an event happened; and even their years are reckoned by lunations. Or, the rainbow may be intended, that faithful sign which God has established in the clouds that the earth shall no more be destroyed by water (Ge +*8:22). Re +*11:15. **faithful witness.** Jb 16:19. Re ❱1:5. 3:14. **for ever.** Heb. *olam,* Ex +*12:24. Ps 72:7. 104:19. Ge 1:14-18. Je +√31:35, 36. **and as.** Ge *9:13-16. Is +√54:9, 10.

38. **But.** Ps 44:9, etc. 60:1, 10. 77:7. 1 Ch +*28:9. Je *12:1. Ho 9:17. Ro ◐+*11:1. **and.** Ps 78:59. 106:40. Dt 32:19. La 2:7. Zc 11:8. **wroth.** ver. 51. Ps 84:9. 2 S 1:21. 15:26. 2 Ch 12:1-12. La 4:20. Zc 13:7.

39. **void.** ver. 34-36. Ps 77:10. 116:11. Jn 13:7. **profaned.** ver. 44. Ps 74:7. 143:3. Is 25:12. 43:28. La 5:16. **crown.** ✸121S1, Ge +49:10. By Metonymy of the Adjunct, whereby the sign is put for the thing signified, "crown" is put for kingly position. i.e. *thou hast removed him from his kingly position.* **by casting.** ✸63H, Ge +12:15.

40. **broken.** Ps 80:12. Jb 1:10. Is *5:5, 6. **brought.** 2 Ch 12:2-5. 15:5. La 2:2, 5. Re 13:1-7.

41. **All.** Ps 44:10-14. 80:13. Is 10:6. Je 50:17. **he is.** Ps 74:10. 79:4. Dt 28:37. Ne 5:9. Je 24:9. 29:18. 42:18. 44:8, 12. La 5:1. Ezk 5:14, 15. Da 9:16.

42. **set up.** Le 26:17, 25. Dt 28:25, 43. La 2:17. Jn 16:20. Re 11:10.

43. **turned.** Ezk 30:21-25. **not made.** Le 26:36, 37. Nu 14:42, 45. Jsh 7:4, 5, 8-12. 2 Ch 25:8.

44. **Thou.** 1 S 4:21, 22. 1 K 12:16-20. 14:25-28. La 4:1, 2. 2 Th 2:3-10. **glory.** Heb. brightness. Ex 24:10. **cast.** ver. 39. Da 7:20-25.

45. **The days.** ver. 28, 29. 2 Ch 10:19. Is *63:18. **thou.** Ps 44:15, 16. 109:29. Mi 7:10.

46. **How.** Ps 13:1, 2. *79:5. 85:5. 90:13. **wilt.** Ps 10:1. 88:14. Jb 23:9. Is 8:17. 45:15. Ho 5:15. **for ever.** Jb +4:20 (✳S#5331h). **shall.** or, how long, Lord, shall. ✓63I1C2B, Jb +21:17. **thy wrath.** Ps *78:63. Je 4:4. 21:12. 2 Th ✓1:8. He 12:29.

47. **Remember.** Ps *39:5, 6. 119:84. Jb 7:7. 9:25, 26. 10:9. **how short.** T#726. Ps *90:12. Jb 14:1, 5. 1 C 7:29-31. Ep *5:16. Ja +4:14 (T#148). **wherefore.** Ps 144:4. Jb 14:1. Ja *4:14.

48. **What.** Ps 49:7-9. Jb *14:5. *30:23. Ec 3:19, 20. *8:8. 9:5. 12:7. He +*9:27. **see death.** Jn 8:51. He 11:5. **shall.** Ps 49:15. Ac 2:27. 2 C 4:14. **soul.** Heb. *nephesh,* Ps +30:3. **grave.** Heb. *sheol,* Ps +30:3. Ge +37:35.

49. **where.** Ps 77:9, 10. Is 63:7-15. **thou.** ver. 3, 4, 35. Ps 54:5. 132:11, 12. 2 S 3:9. *7:15. Is +✓55:3. He 7:21.

50. **Remember.** Ps 44:13-16. *69:9, 19, 20. 74:18, 22. 79:10-12. Ro 15:3.

51. **they have.** Mt 5:10-12. Ac *5:41. 1 C 4:12, 13. He 10:33. 11:36. **footsteps.** ✓22A21, Ps +77:19. Ps 56:5, 6. 57:3. 2 S 16:7, 8. Mt 12:24. 26:61. Jn 8:48. 1 P *2:20, 21. 3:16. 4:14-16. 2 P *3:3, 4.

52. **Blessed.** This verse ends the third book of the psalter and is thought to have been added by a later hand, as it is wanting in two MSS., in another written without points, and in three others written separately from the text; though it is found in all the versions. Ps 41:13. 72:18, 19. 104:35. 106:48. Ne 9:5. Jb *1:21. Hab ✓3:17-19. Mt 6:13. Ro 9:5. 1 T 1:17. **for evermore.** Ps +*18:50.

PSALM 90

The psalmist comforts himself by considering the favor of the eternal God to his people, 1, 2. He laments the frailty, sufferings, and shortness of human life as the effects of the wrath of God against the sins of men, 3-11. He prays that these considerations may be wisely improved by him and his people, and entreats God for the comforts of his mercy and for a sensible experience of his power, glory, and favor, with them and their children, 12-17.

(Title.) A.M. 2514. B.C. 1490. **A Prayer.** or, A prayer, being a psalm of Moses. This psalm is supposed to have been composed by Moses, when all the generation of the Israelites who had offended God were sentenced to fall in the wilderness at the age of seventy or eighty years, except Moses, Caleb, and Joshua. Nu ch. 13, 14. **the man.** Ex 33:14-19. Dt 33:1. 1 K 13:1. 1 T 6:11.

1. **Lord.** Ps *71:3. *91:1, 9, 10. Dt *33:27. Is 8:13, 14. Ezk 11:16. Jn *6:56. 1 J *4:15, 16. **all generations.** Heb. generation and generation. Ps 89:1mg.

2. **Before.** Jb 38:*4-6, 28, 29. Pr *8:25, 26. **or ever.** Ps *33:9. *146:6. Ge *1:1. **even from.** Ps *93:2. *102:24-27. *103:17. Pr 8:23. Is *44:6. +*57:15. Mi +*5:2. Hab *1:12. 1 T 6:15, 16. He 1:10-12. *13:8. Re *1:8. **everlasting to.** Heb. *olam* doubled, Ps +41:13. 102:11, 12. **thou art.** Dt ⬤32:17. Is 44:6. *45:22. 57:15. Je 10:10mg. La 5:19, 20. **God.** Heb. *El,* Ex 15:2.

3. **Thou.** Ps 104:29. +*146:4. Ge *3:19. 6:6, 7. Nu 14:35. Jb *12:10. 17:14. *34:14, 15. Ec *12:7. **Return, ye children of men.** Rather, "Return, ye children of

Adam." i.e. *to that dust out of which ye were originally formed.* Ho 7:10.

4. **thousand years.** Ec 6:6. Is 65:17-25. 2 P ✓3:8. Re *20:4-7. **is past.** or, when he hath passed them. **and as.** Mt 14:25. 24:43. Lk 12:38.

5. **Thou.** Jb *9:26. *22:16. *27:20, 21. Is 8:7, 8. Je 46:7, 8. **as a sleep.** Ps 73:20. Is *29:7, 8. **morning.** Ps *103:15, 16. Is *40:6. Ja *1:10, 11. 1 P *1:24. **groweth up.** or, is changed. Ps 102:26. Is 2:18mg.

6. **In the morning.** Ps *92:7. Jb *14:2. Mt 6:30. **groweth up.** Jg 5:26 (stricken through). 1 S 10:3 (forward). Jb 9:26 (passed away). SS 2:11 (is over).

7. **For we.** ver. 9, 11. Ps 39:11. 59:13. Nu 17:12, 13. Dt 2:14-16. He 3:10, 11, 17-19. 4:1, 2. **are we.** Ex 14:24. Ro 2:8, 9.

8. **Thou.** Ps 10:11. 50:21. 139:1-4. Jb *34:21. Je *2:22. 9:13-16. *16:17. *23:24. Ezk 8:12. Re 20:12. **our.** Ps *19:12. Pr 5:21. Ec 12:14. Lk 12:1, 2. Ro 2:16. 1 C 4:5. He *4:12, 13. 1 J 3:20. **in the.** Ps 80:16.

9. **For.** Ps *78:33. Is 57:16-18. **passed.** Heb. turned. Ps 40:4 (respecteth). 102:17 (regard). Dt 16:7. 31:18. Ec 2:11 (looked), 12 (turned). Is ✓53:6. **We spend.** The Vulgate has, "Our years pass away like those of the spider." Our plans and operations are like the spider's web. Life is as frail, and the thread of it as brittle, as one of those which constitute the well-wrought and curious but fragile habitation of that insect. All the versions have the word *spider,* but it is not found in any Hebrew MSS. or edition yet collated. The Hebrew might be rendered, "We consume our lives like a groan," *kemo hegeh.* **a tale.** Heb. a meditation. ver. *4. Ps *39:5. 49:3. Jb 37:2. Ezk 2:10.

10. **The days,** etc. Heb. As for the days of our years, in them *are* seventy years. ✓144A10, Ge +29:14. Ge *47:9. Ex +23:26. Dt 34:7. Je +28:3mg. **strength.** ✓96F2, Ge +4:10. **yet.** 2 S *19:35. 1 K 1:1. Ec *12:2-7. **for.** Ps *78:39. Jb *14:10mg. 24:24. Is 38:12. Lk *12:20. Ja *4:14.

11. **Who knoweth.** ✓121C2A1, Jb +19:25. Ps 2:12. *7:11, 12. *76:7. Le 26:18, 21, 24, 28. Dt 28:59. 29:20, etc. *32:29. Is +*33:14. Na 1:2, 3, 6. Lk 12:5. Jn ✓3:36. Ro *1:18. 1 C 10:22. 2 C ✓5:11. Ep 5:6. 1 Th *1:10. He *10:26, 27. Re *6:17. 19:15.

12. **So teach.** T#1501. Ps *39:4. Dt *32:29. Ec *9:10. Lk *12:35-40. Jn *9:4. Ep *5:16, 17. Col *4:5. **to number.** T#156. Ps 89:47. Ge 13:16h. 1 Ch 21:1h. Ec *9:10. Mt 24:44. Lk 12:35-37. 1 C 1:7, 8. 2 C 4:18. Ph 3:20. T 2:11-13. 1 P 4:7. 2 P 3:11. **that.** T#727. Ps +49:11 (T#710). 95:7-9. Jb 22:21. *28:28. 1 Ch +28:9 (T#555). Pr *2:2-6. *3:13-18. ✓4:5, 7. 7:1-4. *8:32-36. *16:16. 18:1, 2. *22:17. *23:12, 23. 27:1. Ec 9:10. Mt +16:27 (T#556). Lk +9:24 (T#554). 2 C +6:2 (T#553). He *2:1. **apply our hearts.** Heb. cause our hearts to come.

13. **Return.** Ps 6:4. 80:14. Ex 32:12. Dt 32:36. Je 12:15. Jl *2:13, 14. Zc 1:16. **how.** Ps 89:46. **let it.** Ps 106:45. 135:14. Ex 32:12, 14. Dt *32:36. Ho 11:8. Am 7:3, 6. Jon 3:9.

14. **satisfy.** T#1687. Ps 17:15. *36:7, 8. 63:3-5. 65:4. 91:16. 103:3-5. 107:9. 145:15, 16. Je *31:13, 14. La *3:22, 23. Zc 9:17. **early.** or, in the morning. Ps 30:5. +*46:5mg. *49:14. 59:16. *97:11. 101:8. 110:3. 143:8. 2 S 23:4. Ho 6:3. Zp 3:5. 2 P 1:19. **that we.** Ps *23:6. *85:6. 86:4. 149:2. Ph *4:4.

15. **Make us glad.** Ps *30:5. +*118:24. *126:5, 6. Is 12:1. *40:1, 2. 61:3. *65:18, 19. Je 29:11. 31:12,

13. Mt +*5:4. Jn *16:20. Re *7:14-17. **according to.** Ge +*18:25. Je 31:25, 28. √32:42. Mi 7:15. Zc 8:13. 10:6. Mt 5:11, 12. Mk 10:29, 30. Lk *6:20-23. Ro √8:18. 1 C *2:9. 2 C √4:17, 18. Ph 4:19. 1 J 3:2. **the days.** Nu 14:34. Dt 32:7. **thou hast afflicted.** Ps +√119:75. Dt 8:2. Ru +*1:13. Jb 1:12. Je 31:28. La √3:33. Am +*3:2, 6. Ja *1:17. 1 P 5:10. **the years.** Ps 31:10. Dt 2:14-16. **seen evil.** Jb 2:10. Is +45:7h.

16. **Let.** Ps 44:1. Nu 14:15-24. Hab *3:2. **and.** Nu 14:22, 30, 31. Dt 1:39. Jsh 4:22-24. 23:14.

17. **And let.** Ps 27:4. 50:2. 80:3, 7. *110:3. Ezk 16:14. 2 C *3:18. 1 J *3:2. **establish.** Ps 68:28. 118:25. Jb 22:28. Pr *16:3. Is 26:12. 1 C 3:7. Ph *2:12, 13. 2 Th *2:16, 17. 3:1.

PSALM 91

The believer's security under the divine protection, amidst enemies and dangers, 1-10. Angels charged to take care of him, 11, 12. Promises to him who loves, knows, and trusts in God, 13-16.

(*Title.*) This psalm is supposed by some to have been composed by Moses on the same occasion as the preceding, but others think it was written by David, after his advice to his son Solomon, 1 Ch ch. 28.

1. **dwelleth.** Ps 2:4. 9:11. 17:12mg. *32:7. 52:8. *61:3, 4. *90:1. Is 8:14. Ezk 11:16. Ho 14:5, 6. 1 Jn 4:15, 16. **secret place.** ƒ22C25, Ps +31:20. Ps 18:11. *27:5. 31:20. SS 2:14. Col *3:3. **abide.** Heb. lodge. Ps 25:13mg. +*49:12n. Ru 1:16. Jb 17:2mg. 39:28. **under.** Ps 5:12. *17:8. *36:7. 57:1. Jg 9:15. Ru 2:12. SS 2:3. Is 4:5, 6. 32:2. La 4:20. **shadow.** ƒ22L8, Ps +121:5.

2. **I will.** ver. 9. Ps *18:2. *46:1. 71:3. 142:5. Dt 32:30, 31. 33:27-29. Pr 18:10. **fortress.** ƒ22L5, Ps +31:3. **my God.** Ps 43:4. *48:14. 67:6, 7. Ge 17:7. Dt 26:17-19. Je 31:1. Mt 1:23. Lk 20:38. Jn 1:36. He *11:16. **in him.** Ps *62:5-8. 118:8, 9. Is *12:2. √26:3, 4.

3. **snare.** Ps *124:7. *141:9. Pr 7:23. Ec *9:12. Ho 9:8. Am 3:5. 1 T *6:9. 2 T *2:26. **and from.** ver. 6. Nu 14:37, 38. 16:46-48. 2 S *24:15. Jb 5:19-22.

4. **cover.** Ps 17:8. 57:1. 61:4. 63:7. Dt *32:11, 12. Ru 2:12. Mt *23:37. **feathers.** ƒ22G2. Anthropomorphism B895. Wings and feathers are attributed to God. For other instances of this figure see Ps 17:8. 36:7. 57:1. 61:4. 63:7. Mt 23:37. **his truth.** Ps 89:23, 24. *138:2. 146:5, 6. Ge 15:1. Nu *23:19. Is *43:1, 2. Mk *13:31. T *1:2. He *6:17, 18.

5. **Thou.** Ps 3:6. *27:1-3. 46:2. 66:12. *112:7. 121:6. Jb 5:19, etc. Pr 28:1. Is *43:2. Mt 8:26. He +*13:6. **terror.** Ps *3:5. 55:4. 2 K 7:6. Jb 4:13-15. 18:11. *24:14-16. Pr √3:23-25. Is 21:4. Lk 12:20, 39. 1 C +*15:55. **nor.** Jb 6:4. La 3:12, 13.

6. **pestilence.** Ps 121:5, 6. Ex 12:29, 30. 2 K 19:35. **destruction.** Nu 16:48. 2 S 24:15. Mt 24:6, 7. 1 C *10:6-10.

7. **A thousand.** Ps 32:6. Ge 7:23. Ex 12:12, 13. Nu 14:37, 38. Jsh 14:10.

8. **Only.** Ps 37:34. 58:10, 11. 92:11. Pr *3:25, 26. Ml 1:5. **and see.** Is +*66:24. **reward.** Ge +*6:13 (T#566). Is 3:11. Ro 6:23. He *2:2.

9. **Because.** ver. 2. Ps 142:4, 5. 146:5, 6. **most high.** ver. 1. Ps *71:3. 90:1.

10. **no evil.** T#767. Ps 31:23. 32:6, 7. 121:7. Jb 5:19. Pr *12:21. 15:19. Zp 3:15. Ro √8:28. **neither.**

Dt *7:15. Jb 5:24. **dwelling.** ƒ121J16, Ge +13:5. By Metonymy of the Subject, "dwelling" is put for those who dwell in it.

11. **For.** Ps *34:7. 71:3. 2 K *6:16, 17. Mt ▶4:6. *18:10. Lk ▶4:10, 11. He *1:14. **in all.** Pr *3:6. Is 31:1. Je 2:18.

12. **They.** Ex 19:4. Dt 1:31. Is 46:3. *63:9. Lk 4:11. **lest.** Ps +*37:24. Jb 5:23. Pr 3:23.

13. **tread.** Jg 14:5, 6. Jb *5:23. 1 S 17:37. Da 6:22. Ro *8:37. 2 T *4:17. **adder.** *or*, asp. Ps 58:4. Mk 16:18. Ac 28:3-6. Ro 3:13. 16:20. **the dragon.** Is 27:1. Re 12:9. 20:1, 2.

14. **set.** ver. 9. Dt 28:1. 1 Ch 29:3. Is 33:16. Jn *14:23. 16:27. Ro √8:28. Ja *1:12. 2:5. **I will set.** Ps 59:1mg. 89:16, 17. Is *33:15, 16. Ph *2:9-11. Ja 1:12. **known.** Ps +√9:10. Jn *17:3. Ga 4:9. **my name.** Ex ◑23:13.

15. **He shall.** Ps 10:17. 18:3, 4, 6, 15. +*50:15. Is 58:9. *65:24. Je √29:12, 13. √33:3. Ro *10:12, 13. He *5:7. **I will be.** Ps 23:4. 138:7. Ge 39:21, 23. Is *41:10. *43:1, 2. Mt 28:20. Jn *16:32. Ac 18:9, 10. 2 T 4:17. **deliver.** Ps +*34:4. 37:40. 2 C 1:9, 10. **honor.** 1 S *2:30. Jn 5:√23, 44. 12:*26, 43. 1 P 1:21. 3:22. *5:4. Re *3:21.

16. **With long life.** Heb. With length of days. T#151. Ps 21:4. +23:6mg. 93:5mg. 102:24. Ge 15:15. +*25:8n. Ex 20:12. Dt +4:40. +*5:16. Jb 5:26. Pr 3:2mg, 16. *4:10. *22:4. Is *38:18, 19. 65:20-22. Je 35:7. **satisfy.** Ps 90:14. **show.** Ps +*16:11. *50:23. Is 45:17. Lk 2:30. 3:6.

PSALM 92

The psalmist shows that it is good to be thankful, to praise God, and to celebrate his perfection and works, 1-5. He contrasts the judgments of God on the wicked with the abiding felicity of the righteous, 6-15.

(*Title.*) A.M. cir. 3464. B.C. cir. 540. **A Psalm.** Calmet and others suppose this psalm to have been composed by some of the Levites during or near the close of the Babylonian captivity, acknowledging the mercy of God and foreseeing the destruction of their enemies, with their own return to Jerusalem and temple service. **for.** Is +*58:13n, 14. He 4:9mg. Re 4:8-11.

1. **good.** Ps *33:1. √50:23. 52:9. 54:6. 73:28. 107:1, 8, 15, 21, 22. 135:3. *147:1. Ep *5:19. He *13:15. **most.** ver. 8. Ps 82:6. Is +*57:15. Da 4:34-37. 5:18. Ac 7:48, 49.

2. **show.** Ps 71:15. *89:1, 2. 145:2. Is 63:7. La *3:22, 23. Jn *1:17. **lovingkindness.** Ge 24:12. **morning.** Is 33:2. La 3:23. **faithfulness.** Ge 24:27. **every night.** Heb. in the nights. Ps *42:8. 77:2. Jb *35:10. Ac *16:25.

3. **instrument.** Ps 33:2. 57:8. 68:25. 81:2, 3. 149:3. 150:3-5. 1 Ch 15:16. 25:6. 2 Ch 23:5. 29:25. **the harp.** etc. *or*, the solemn sound with the harp. 2 Ch 13:8n. **a solemn sound.** Heb. *higgaion.* Ps 9:16mg.

4. **hast made.** Ps 9:2. 64:10. *104:31, 34. 106:47, 48. 126:3. 145:6, 7. Is 61:2-11. 65:13, 14. 66:10, 11. Je 31:7, 11-13. Zp 3:14-16. Lk 1:47. Jn 16:22. 2 C *2:14. Re 18:20. **thy work.** Nu 23:23. Ph *2:12, 13. 1 Th 5:23, 24.

5. **O Lord.** Ps *40:5. 66:3. 104:24. 111:2. 145:3, 4. Re 15:3. **thoughts.** ƒ22C5, Ge +50:20. Ps +*40:17. *139:17. Is 28:29. √55:8, 9. Je 23:20. Ro *11:33, 34. **deep.** Ps 64:6. Ec 7:24. 1 C 2:10.

6. **A brutish**. Ps 32:9. 73:22. 94:8. Pr 30:2. Is 1:3. Je 10:14. 1 C √2:14. **a fool**. Ps 14:1. 49:10. 75:4. Pr 1:22. 24:7. Lk *12:20.

7. **wicked**. Ps 37:1, 2, 35, 38. 90:5, 6. 103:15, 16. Is 37:27. 40:6, 7. Ja 1:10, 11. 1 P 1:24. **workers**. Ps *73:12, 18-20. Jb 12:6. 21:7-12. Je 12:1, 2. Ml 3:15. 4:1. **it is that**. Ps 37:35, 36, 38. 73:18-20. 1 S 25:36-38. Pr *1:32. Mk +4:19. Lk 16:19-25. **destroyed**. Dt 4:26. 7:23. 12:30. **for ever**. Ps +9:18 (*S#5703h). Mt +*25:41, 46.

8. **art most high**. Ps +*7:17. 56:2. +77:10. 83:18. 102:26, 27. Ex 18:11. Ec 5:8. Da 4:34, 35. Ac 12:1, 22-24. **for evermore**. Heb. *olam*, Ps +*18:50.

9. **For**. Ps 21:8, 9. 37:20. *68:1, 2. 73:27. 89:10. Jg 5:31. Lk 19:27. 2 Th 1:7-9. **scattered**. Ps 1:4. 59:11. 68:30. Le 26:33. Nu 10:35. Dt 28:64. Is 17:13. Ezk 5:12. Mt 7:23. Lk *21:24.

10. **But**. Ps *89:17, 24. 112:9. 132:17. 148:14. 1 S 2:1, 10. Lk 1:69. **an unicorn**. Nu 23:22. 24:8. **I shall**. Ps *23:5. +*45:7. 2 C 1:21. **anointed**. ♪22C47, Ps +23:5. 1 S 16:13. 2 C 1:21. 1 J *2:20, 27.

11. **Mine eye**. Ps *37:34. 54:7. 59:10. 91:8. 112:8. Is *66:24. 2 Th 1:6.

12. **righteous**. ver. *7. Ps *52:8. *72:8. Is *55:13. *65:22. Ho *14:5, 6. **like**. ♪105, Ml +4:2. **the palm tree**. The noble and beautiful palm tree affords an agreeable shade: its fruit makes a great part of the diet of the East, the stones of which are ground for the camels; the leaves are made into couches, baskets, etc.; its boughs, into fences; the fibers of the boughs, into ropes, and the rigging of small vessels; its sap, into arrack; and its wood serves for lighter buildings and fire wood (see Dr. Clarke's *Travels*, P. I. Sec. 2. p. 302). See notes on 1 K 4:33 and 6:29. **cedar**. Ps 104:16. 148:9. Am 2:9.

13. **Those**. Is 60:21. Ro 6:5. 11:17. Ep 3:17. Col *1:23. *2:7. **planted**. Ezk ◑18:26. **shall flourish**. Is 61:3. 2 P √1:10, 11. √3:18. **in the**. Ps 23:6. 100:4. 135:2. 2 Ch 4:9.

14. **fruit**. T#816. Ps 1:3. Mt 3:10. Jn *15:2-5. Ga *5:22, 23. Ph 1:11. Ju 12. **in old age**. Ps 71:18. 1 Ch 29:1, etc. Jb *17:9. Pr *4:18. Is *40:31. 46:4. Je 17:8. **flourishing**. Heb. green. Ezk 47:12.

15. **To show**. Jn √10:27-29. 15:1-3. 1 C *1:8, 9. 1 Th 5:23, 24. T 1:2. 1 P 1:4, 5. **my rock**. Ps 18:2. 62:6. Dt *32:4. **and**. Ps 5:4, 5. 145:17. Jb *34:10. Hab 1:13. Zp *3:5. Ro +*9:14. 2 Th *1:6, 7. Ja 1:13.

PSALM 93

The majesty, stability, power, and holiness of Jehovah's kingdom shown, with how he triumphs over all opposition, 1-4. His testimonies are sure, and holiness becomes his house, 5.

(*Title.*) It is highly probable that this psalm was written on the same occasion as the preceding, as a part of which it is written in twelve MSS.

1. **Lord**. Ps 59:13. 96:10. *97:1. 99:1. 103:19. 145:13. 1 Ch 29:12. Is *52:7. Da 4:32-34. Ml *6:13. He √1:8. Re *11:15-17. *19:6. **he is**. Ps 104:1, 2. Jb 40:10. Is 59:17. 63:1. **clothed**. ♪22D5P. Anthropomorphism B894. Raiment is attributed to God. For other instances of this figure see Ps 104:1, 2. Is 51:9. 59:17. **he hath**. Ps 18:32. 65:6. Is 11:5. **world**. Ps 75:3. 96:10. Is 45:12, 18. 49:8. 51:16. He 1:2, 3.

2. **Thy**. Ps +*45:6. 145:13. Pr *8:22, 23. Da 4:34.

Mi +*5:2. He √1:8. **of old**. Heb. from then. **thou**. Ps 90:2. 102:24-27. He 1:10-12. √13:8. Re *1:8, 11, 17, 18. 2:8. **everlasting**. Ge +*17:7.

3. **The floods**. Ps *18:4. 69:1, 2, 14-16. Is 17:12, 13. *43:2. *57:20. Je *12:5. 46:7, 8. Jon 2:3. Mt 14:29, 30. Mk 4:39. Re 12:15. 17:15. **the floods**. Ps 96:11. 98:8. Is 55:12. **lifted**. ♪144A12, Ge +22:13. **the floods lift**. Ps 2:1-3. 107:25, 26. 124:3-5. Ac 4:25-27.

4. **mightier**. Ps 65:7. 89:6, 9. 114:3-5. Jb 38:11. Je 5:22. Mk 4:37-39.

5. **Thy**. Ps *19:7, 8. 119:111, 129, 138, 144. Is √8:20. Mt √24:35. He *6:17, 18. 1 J √5:9-13. **holiness**. Ps 5:4-7. 99:5, 9. Le 10:3. 19:2. Is 52:11. Zc 14:20, 21. Jn *4:24. 1 C 3:16, 17. He √12:14. 1 P 1:16. Re *21:27. *22:14. **thine house**. Ep 5:25-27. 1 T *3:15. He *3:6. **for ever**. Heb. to length of days. Ps +23:6mg. +*91:16mg.

PSALM 94

The psalmist calls on God to take vengeance on the persecutors of his people, 1-4. He complains of their cruelty and impiety and sharply reproves their atheistical folly, 5-11. He shows the benefits of affliction, attended by divine teaching, and the security of God's people, 12-15. He calls for helpers against evil doers, declares his experience of God's goodness, and foretells the destruction of persecutors, 16-23.

(*Title.*) A.M. 3416. B.C. 588. Dr. Delaney supposes that this psalm was written by David on occasion of his war with the Ammonites, in consequence of the indignities shown to his messengers; but it is more probable that it was written to bewail the destruction of Jerusalem and the temple.

1. **God**. Heb. *El*, Ex +15:2. **to whom vengeance belongeth**. Heb. God of revenges. Ps 18:47. **O God**. Heb. *El*, Ex +15:2. **to whom**. Dt *32:35, 41, 42. Is 35:4. 59:17. Je 50:28. Na *1:2. Lk *18:7, 8. Ro *12:19. 2 Th *1:7, 8. He 10:30. **show thyself**. Heb. shine forth. Ps 80:1.

2. **Lift**. Ps 7:6. 68:1. *74:22. Mi 5:9. **judge of the earth**. Ps 7:8, 11. 9:4, 8, 13, 14. *50:6. 75:7. 76:9. 96:13. 97:1. Ge +*18:25. Is *30:18, 19. 42:4. Je +*23:5-8. Mi +*5:1, 2. Zc +*14:9. Jn √5:22, 23. Ro 14:9-12. 2 C √5:10. 2 T +*4:1. Re *20:11, 12. **render**. Ps *31:23. Jb 40:11, 12. Pr 16:5. Is *2:11, 12, 17. 10:12. 37:23, 29, 36-38. Je 50:31, 32. Da 4:37. 5:22-24. 1 P 5:5. Re 18:6-8.

3. **Lord**. Ps 43:2. 73:8. 74:9, 10. 79:5. 80:4. 89:46. Je *12:1, 2. 47:6. Re *6:9, 10. **how long**. ♪18, Dt +28:4. **the wicked**. Est 5:11, 12. 6:6-10. 7:6, 10. Jb *20:5. Ac 12:22, 23.

4. **How long**. ♪63IC2B, Jb +21:17. **shall**. Ps 31:18. 59:7, 12. 64:3, 4. 73:8, 9. 140:3. Pr 30:14. Je 18:18. Mt 12:24, 34. Ju *14, *15. **boast**. Ps 10:2-7. 52:1. Ex 15:9, 10. Jb 21:14, 15. Is 10:13-15. 37:24, 25. Da 7:8, 11, 25. 8:11. 11:36, 37. Re 13:5, 6.

5. **break**. Ps 7:2. 14:4. 44:22. 74:8, 19, 20. 79:2, 3, 7. 129:2, 3. Is 3:15. 52:5. Je 22:17. 51:20-23, 34. Mi 3:2, 3. Re 17:6. **afflict**. Ex 2:23, 24. Je 50:11. Re 11:3.

6. **They slay**. Is 10:2. 13:15-18. Je 7:6. 22:3. Ezk 22:7. Ml +*3:5. **stranger**. Ps 39:12. 119:19. 146:9. Ge +23:4 (*S#1616h). Ex 12:48mg. **fatherless**. Dt +10:18.

7. **they say**. Ps 10:11-13. *44:21. 59:7. Jb 22:12,

13. Pr *15:3. Is 29:15. Ezk 8:12. 9:9. Zp 1:12. Lk 18:2, 4.

8. **brutish**. Ps 49:10. 73:22. 92:6. Pr 12:1. Is 27:11. Je 8:6-8. 10:8. Ro 3:11. **fools**. Dt *32:29. Pr 1:22. 8:5. T *3:3.

9. **He that planted**. Ps 139:2, 4. Ex *4:11. 1 K +8:39. Pr 20:1, 12. Je 17:10. **hear**. Ps 11:4. 17:3. 44:21. 139:1-12. Je 23:23, 24.

10. **chastiseth**. Ps *9:5. *10:16. 44:2. 135:8-12. *149:7. Is 10:12. 37:36. Je +*10:25. Ezk 39:21. **he correct**. ♪63A2, 2 S +6:6. Supply ellipsis (absolute: of the accusative), the omission of the object or accusative after the verb: (you among the heathen). Is 10:5, 6. Am 3:2. Hab 1:12. 3:12. **teacheth man**. Ps *25:8, 9. 119:66. Ex 35:34. Jb 35:11. 36:22. Pr *2:6. Is 2:3. 28:26. 54:13. Jn 6:45. **shall**. ♪63E2, 1 S +13:8.

11. **The Lord**. 1 C ⟩3:20. **knoweth**. Ps 49:10-13. Jb 11:11, 12. Ro 1:21, 22. 1 C 1:19, 21, 25. 3:18-20. **the thoughts**. Ge 6:5. Is √55:8. Mi √4:12.

12. **Blessed**. ♪43, Dt +28:3. Ps *119:67, 71, 75. Jb *5:17. Pr *3:11. 1 C *11:32. He *12:5-11. **teachest**. Jb 33:16-25. Mi 6:9. Re 3:19.

13. **rest from**. Ps 27:5. 31:19, 20. 143:8mg. Is *16:3-5. +*26:20, 21. Hab +*3:16. Zp +*2:3. Lk +*21:36. 2 C 4:17, 18. 2 Th 1:7, 8. He *4:9. Re +*3:10. *14:13. **until the pit**. Ps 9:15. 55:23. Je 18:20, 22. 2 P *2:9. 3:3-7. Re 6:10, 11. 11:18.

14. **For**. Ps 37:28. 1 S *12:22. Is 49:14, 15. Je 32:39, 40. Jn √10:27-31. Ro *8:30, 38, 39. +√11:1, ⟩2. He +*13:5. **not cast**. Ps 89:28, 33, 37. +√132:11. Le *26:44. 1 S +*12:22. 2 S +*7:15. Is +*41:9. +√55:3. Je +*4:27. +√33:24-26. Ro +√11:1. **forsake**. ver. 5. Ps 33:12. Dt 32:9. 1 S +*12:22. Is +*60:10. Je +*4:27. 10:16. Zc √10:6. Ml +*3:6. Ep 1:18. He +*13:5. **his inheritance**. Ps 2:8. 28:9. Ex 15:17. Le 25:23. Dt 4:20. 9:26, 29. +*32:43. 1 S 10:1. 26:19. 2 S 20:19. 21:3. 1 K 8:51, 53. 2 K 21:14. Is √19:25. 63:17. 65:9. Da +*7:14. Zc 2:12. Lk +*1:32, 33. Ro *8:17. Col +*3:24. He 1:2. Re +*11:15.

15. **But judgment**. ver. 2, 3. Ps 7:8, 9. 9:16. 58:11. +*76:9. 125:3. Dt 32:35, 36. Jb 35:14. Is +*16:5. +*32:1. 42:4. Da √7:22. Mi 7:9. Ml 3:18. 2 P 3:8-10. Re *15:3, 4. 20:4. **and all**. Ps *37:5-7, 34. 125:4, 5. Jb *17:9. 23:11, 12. Ja 5:7-11. 1 J *2:19. **the upright**. Pr 8:15, 16. Je 33:26. 1 C +*6:2. **shall follow it**. Heb. shall be after it.

16. **rise up**. Ex 32:26-29. Nu 25:6-13. Jg 5:23. 1 K 18:39, 40. 2 K 9:32. 10:15. Is 59:16. 63:5. Je 5:1. Ezk 22:30. Mt 12:30. 3 J 8. **stand up**. Ne 5:7. Je 26:16-19. Jn 7:50, 51.

17. **Unless**. Ps 118:13. 124:1, 2. 125:1-3. *142:4, 5. Jn 16:32. 2 C *1:8-10. 2 T 4:16, 17. **soul**. Heb. *nephesh*, Ps +30:3. **almost**. or, quickly. Ps 2:12 (little). 8:5 (little). 37:10 (little while). 81:14 (soon). **dwelt**. Ps 13:3. 31:17. 115:17. **dwelt**. ♪88, Ge +15:15. **silence**. Heb. *dumah*, ✱S#1745. Ps 115:17, only.

18. **My foot**. Ps *17:5. √37:23, 24. 38:16. 119:116, 117. *121:3. 1 S *2:9. Jb 12:5. Is *41:10. Lk *22:32. 1 P *1:5. **held me up**. 2 P +*1:10.

19. **In the multitude**. Ps 43:2-5. 61:2. 63:5, 6. 73:12-16. 77:2-10. Je 20:7-11. Hab *3:16-18. Ro 5:2-5. 2 C *1:4, 5. 1 P 1:7, 8. **soul**. Heb. *nephesh*, Ge 34:3.

20. **throne**. Ps *52:1, 2. *82:1, 2. 1 S *22:17-19. Ec 3:16. +*5:8. Am *6:3. **fellowship**. 2 Ch 6:14-16. Is *1:11-20. Je *7:4-11. Jn 18:28. 2 C √6:14-16. Ep √5:11. 1 J *1:5, 6. **frameth**. Ps 58:2. Ex 1:17. 1 K

12:32. Est *3:6-12. Is *10:1. Da *3:4-7. *6:7-9. Mi 6:16. Jn *9:22. *11:57. Re *13:15-17.

21. **gather**. Ps 2:1-3. 22:16. 59:3. Pr 1:11, 16. Mt *27:1. Ac 4:5-7, 27, 28. **soul**. Heb. *nephesh*, Ge +12:13. **condemn**. Ex *23:7. 1 K 21:19. Pr *17:15. Je 26:15. Ezk 22:6, 12, 27. Mt 23:32-36. Ac 7:52, 58-60. Ja 5:6. Re 17:6. **blood**. ♪171Q10. Synecdoche of the Part B644. *Blood* is put for *man*. For other instances of this figure see Pr 1:11. Mt 27:4. Ac 17:26.

22. **But**. ver. 10. Ps 27:1-3. *59:9, 16, 17. *62:2, 6. **the rock**. Ps *18:2. Is 33:16.

23. **And he**. Ps *7:16. 9:16, 17. *55:23. 64:8. Est *7:10. Pr *1:11, 18, 31. 2:22. 5:22. Da 7:24. **cut them**. Ps *12:3. 1 S 26:10, 11. Pr 2:22. 5:22. 14:32. Ezk 18:24. Da 9:26.

PSALM 95

An exhortation with exulting joy to praise God the rock of our salvation for his greatness, as the Creator and Sovereign of the world, 1-5; and to worship him, as his creatures and his peculiar people, 6, 7: with a solemn warning not to tempt him, as Israel did in the wilderness, 8-11.

1. **Come**. Ps 34:3. 66:8. 107:8, 15, 21. 117:1. 118:1. 136:1-3. 148:11-13. 150:6. **sing**. Ps 47:6, 7. 66:1, 2. 81:1. 96:1, 2. 101:1. Ex 15:1, 21. 1 Ch 16:9. Ep *5:19. Col *3:16. Re *5:9. 14:3. 15:3. **let us make**. Ps 66:1. 98:4-8. 100:1. Ezr 3:11-13. Is 12:4-6. Je 33:11. Mt 21:9. Re 19:6. **the rock**. Ps 89:26. Dt 32:15. 2 S *22:47. Mt 16:16, 18. 1 C *10:4.

2. **Let us**. Ps 5:7. 100:2, 4. Je 31:12, 13. **come before his presence**. Heb. prevent his face. Ps 17:13mg. 18:18. 21:3. Mi 6:6. **psalms**. Ps 105:2. Ja *5:13.

3. **For**. Ps *86:8-10. *96:4. 97:9. 145:3. Je 10:6, 7. **a great**. Ps 47:2. 48:2. Je *10:10, 11. 46:18. 48:15. Da 4:37. Ml 1:11. *14. Mt 5:35. **above**. Ps 135:5. Ex 18:11. Is 44:8. Je 10:10-16. Mt *28:18. Ep *1:21. 1 P *3:22. **gods**. Ps +82:6n.

4. **In**. Ps 24:1. Jb 11:10. **his**. Heb. whose. **deep**. Ps 135:6. **the strength of the hills is his also**. or, heights of the hills are his. Ps 65:6. 97:5. Jb 9:5. Mi 1:4. Na 1:5. Hab 3:6, 10.

5. **The sea is his**. Heb. Whose the sea is. Ps 33:7. Ge 1:9, 10. Jb 38:10, 11. Pr 8:29. Je *5:22. **he made**. Jn *1:3. **hands**. ♪22A14.1, Nu +11:23. Pr 8:26.

6. **O come**. ver. 1. Ho 6:1. Mt 4:2. Re 22:17. **worship**. Ps 72:9. Ex 20:5. Mt *4:9. Mk 14:35. Ac 10:25, 26. Re 22:8, +*9. **let us**. T#1257. Ps 105:1-4. Ge 35:2, 3. Is *2:3. Jon 1:6. 3:6-9. Zc *8:21. He *4:16. **kneel**. 1 K 8:54. 2 Ch 6:13. Ezr 9:5. Da +6:10 (T#1259). Lk 22:41. Ac 7:60. 20:36. 21:5. 1 C 6:20. Ep *3:14. Ph *2:10. **Lord**. Ex +15:26. **our maker**. Ps 100:3. Jb *35:10. Ec *12:1. Is 54:5. Jn *1:3. 1 P 4:19.

7. **For he**. Ps *48:14. 67:6. 115:3. Ex *15:2. 20:2. Je *31:33. He *11:16. **people**. Ps *23:1. 79:13. 80:1. 100:3. Is 40:10, 11. Ezk 34:30, 31. Jn *10:3, 4, 14-16. Ac +*20:28. 1 P *2:25. **Today**. T#1172. He 3:⟩7-11, +*13, ⟩15. ⟩4:7. **if ye**. Pr 8:6. Is *55:3. Mt 3:2, 3. 17:5. Re √3:20.

8. **Harden**. Ex 8:15. 1 S 6:6. Da 5:20. Ac 19:9. Ro 2:5. He 3:⟩8, +√13. 12:25. **in the**. Ex *17:2, 7. Nu *14:11, 22, 27. 20:13. Dt 1:34, 35. 6:16. He 3:8, 9, 15-19. Ju 5. **provocation**. Heb. contention. ✱S#4808h. Ps 81:7mg. 95:8mg. 106:32. Ge 13:8. Ex 17:7mg. Nu 20:13mg, 24. 27:14, 14. Dt 32:51mg. 33:8. Ezk

47:19mg. 48:28mg. or, Meribah. i.e. *strife,* Ex +17:7. **temptation.** *S#4531h. Ps 95:8. Ex 17:7mg. Dt 4:34. 6:16. 7:19. 9:22. 29:3. 33:8. Jb 9:23. or, Massah. i.e. *trial,* Ex +17:7. **wilderness.** Ps 29:8. 55:7. 65:12.

9. **When.** Ps *78:17, 18, 40, 41, 56. 1 C *10:9, 11. **He** 3:8. **saw.** Nu 14:22. Mt 11:20-22. Jn 15:24.

10. **Forty.** Nu 14:33, 34. 32:13. Dt 1:3. 2:14-16. He 3:9, 10, 17. **grieved.** Ge 6:6. Ep +√4:30. He 3:10. **err.** Is *63:17. He *3:10, 17. **and they.** Pr 1:7, 22-29. Je 9:6. Jn *3:19-21. Ro 1:28.

11. **I sware.** Nu 14:23, 28-30. Dt 1:34, 35. He 3:11, *18. 4:3, 5. **that they should not enter.** Heb. if they enter. Ge +4:7. Nu 14:23. **my rest.** Ge 2:2, 3. Je 6:16. Mt *11:28, 29. Ro *5:1. He 4:4-11. Re *14:13.

PSALM 96

Israel and all nations are called on to celebrate the praises of God, to show forth his salvation, and to join in his worship, 1-10. The whole creation is excited to rejoice in the prospect of his coming and of his righteous judgment, 11-13.

1. A.M. 2962. B.C. 1042. **O sing.** Ps 33:3. 98:1. 149:1. 1 Ch 16:23-33. Is 42:10. Re 5:9. 14:3. **sing unto.** Ps 67:3-5. 68:32. Ro 15:11. **earth.** √121J17, Ge +6:11.

2. **bless.** Ps *72:17, 18. 103:1, 2, 20-22. 104:1. 145:1, 10. 1 Ch 29:20. Ep *1:3. Re *5:13. **show.** Ps *40:9, 10. 71:15. Is 40:9. 52:7, 8. Mk *16:15. Ac 13:26. Ro 10:14-18. 1 P 2:9.

3. **Declare.** Ps 22:27. 72:18, 19. ch. 117. Is 19:23-25. 49:6. Da 4:1-3. 6:26, 27. Mi 4:2. Zc 9:10. Mt 28:19. Mk *16:15. Lk 24:47. Re 14:6, 7.

4. **For the.** Ps 18:3. 86:10. 89:7. *145:3. Ex 18:11. 1 S 4:8. Ne *9:5, 6. **and greatly.** Ps 18:3. **he is.** Ps 66:3, 5. 76:7. 89:7. 95:3. Je 5:22. 10:6, 7. Mt +*10:28. Lk 12:5. Re 15:4.

5. **For.** Ps 115:3-8. 135:15-18. Is 44:8, etc. 46:1, 2. Je *10:3-5, 11, 12, 14, 15. Ac 19:26. 1 C √8:4. **but.** Ps 115:15. Ge √1:1. Is *42:5. Je 10:11.

6. **Honor.** Ps 8:1. 19:1. 63:2, 3. 93:1. 104:1. He *1:3. 2 P 1:16, 17. **strength.** Ps 27:4. 29:1, 2, 9. 50:2. **sanctuary.** 1 Ch 16:27.

7. **Give.** Ps 29:1, 2. 68:32-34. Lk 2:14. Ju *25. **O ye kindreds.** Ps 22:27. 66:1, 2. 67:3, 4. Ro 15:9, 10. Re 5:9. 19:6. **glory.** 1 Ch 29:11-13. Mt *6:13. Jn √5:23. 1 P 5:11. Ju *24, 25. Re *5:13. 7:12. 14:7. 19:1. **and.** √93A, Ge +1:26. i.e. *glory, yes—and great glory too.* **strength.** 121L3, Ps +8:2. Ps *29:1n.

8. **the glory.** Ps 108:3-5. *111:9. 148:13, 14. Ex +*34:5-9. Re *15:4. **due unto.** Heb. of. **his name.** Ps +√9:10. 68:4. 83:18. Mt *6:9. Jn √5:23. Ph *2:9, 10. **bring.** Is 60:6, 7. Ml *1:11. Ro √12:1. 15:16. Ph 2:17. 4:18. He 13:13, *15, 16. 1 P *2:5. Re 8:3, 4. **come.** Ps 100:4.

9. **in the beauty of holiness.** or, in the glorious sanctuary. Ps 29:2. *110:3. 2 Ch *20:21. Ezr 7:27. Ezk 7:20. Da 11:45. Lk 21:5, 6. **fear.** Ps 33:8. 76:7, 11.

10. **say.** Ps 18:49. 46:6, 10. 126:2. Ml 1:11, 14. Ga 1:16. **the Lord.** Ps 2:8-12. 59:13. 93:1. *97:1. 99:1. 1 Ch 16:31. Da 2:44. Mt 3:2. Re *11:15. *19:6. **the world.** Is 49:8. Col 2:7. He 1:3. **judge.** ver. 13. Ps 9:8. *67:4. 98:9. Is 11:3-5. Ac √17:31. Ro 2:5, 6. 3:5, 6. 15:9. Re 19:11. 20:13.

11. **the heavens.** Ps *69:34. 148:1-4. Is 44:23. 49:13. Lk *2:10, 13, 14. 15:10. Re 12:12. 19:1-7. **rejoice.**

√155D, Ge +4:10. **the earth.** Ro *8:21. **the sea.** Ps √69:34-36. *98:7-9.

12. **Let.** Ps 65:12, 13. Is 42:10, 11. 55:12, 13. Ro ●8:22. **joyful.** √155D, Ge +4:10. **rejoice.** √155D, Ge +4:10.

13. **he cometh.** Ps 98:9. Dt +*33:2. Is *25:8, 9. Ml 3:1, 2. 1 Th √4:16-18. 2 Th *1:10. 2 T 4:8. T *2:13. 2 P *3:8-10, 12-14. Re +*11:18. 22:20. **cometh.** √84, Ge +6:17. **to judge.** ver. 10. Ps 9:7, 8. *67:4. Is +√16:5. Je +*23:5-8. Jn *5:22, 23. Ac √17:31. 24:10n. Ju 14, 15. Re *19:11. **the earth.** Ps *67:4. √82:8. *98:9. Re +*5:10. **with righteousness.** Is *2:1-4. *11:3-9. Da +*7:13, 14. 1 C *6:2, 3. Re +*5:10. √20:4-6.

PSALM 97

The nations are called on to rejoice in the coming of the righteous kingdom of God and in the subversion of idolatry, 1-7. Zion rejoices because of his judgments and in his universal sovereignty, 8, 9. An exhortation to holiness and joy in God, 10-12.

1. A.M. 3000. B.C. 1004. **Lord.** Ps 93:1. 96:10, 11. 99:1. Ob +*21. Mt 3:3. 6:10, 13. Mk 11:10. Col 1:13. Re 11:17. **the earth.** Ps *2:11. 98:4-6. Is 49:13. Lk 2:10, 11. **let the multitude of isles.** Heb. let the many, or great isles. Ge 10:5. Is 11:11. 24:14-16. 41:5. 42:4, 10-12. 49:1. 51:5. *60:9. 66:19. Zp 2:11.

2. **Clouds.** Ps 18:11, 12. 77:19. Ge +9:13. Ex 20:21. 24:16-18. Dt 4:11, 12. 1 K 8:10-12. Na 1:3. **darkness.** Ex 20:21. 2 S 22:10. Jb 38:9. **righteousness.** Ps 45:6, 7. 89:14. 99:4. Ge +*18:25. He +*1:8, 9. **judgment.** Ro *11:33. **habitation.** or, establishment. Ps 89:14mg. Pr 16:12.

3. **A fire.** Ps 18:8. 21:8, 9. 50:3. Dt 4:11, 36. 5:4, 23, 24. *32:22. Is +*24:6. Da *7:10. Na 1:5, 6. Hab 3:5. Ml +*4:1. 2 Th *1:8. He *12:29. 2 P 3:7, 10-12. Re 11:5. 20:15.

4. **His.** Ps 77:18. 144:5, 6. Ex *19:16-18. **the earth.** Ps 18:7. *104:32. 114:7. Jb 9:6. Je 10:10. Mt 27:50, 51. 28:2, 3. Re 11:19. 19:11.

5. **hills.** Jg 5:4, 5. Is 24:19, 20. 64:1, 2. Mi 1:3, 4. Na *1:5, 6. Hab 3:6. **the Lord of.** Ps 47:2. 83:18. Is 54:5. Mi 4:13. Zc 4:14. Mk 11:3. 1 C 1:2.

6. **The heavens.** Ps *19:1. 36:5, 6. 50:6. 89:2, 5. Is 1:2. Re *19:1, 2. **all the.** Ps 67:4. 98:3. Nu 14:21. 2 S 22:47. Is 6:3. 45:6. 60:2, 3. Hab *2:14. Mt 6:9, 10.

7. **Confounded.** Ex +*20:4. Le 26:1. Dt 5:8. *27:15. Is *2:20, 21. 37:18, 19. 41:29. *42:17. 44:9-11. Je 10:14. Re 14:8-10. **of idols.** Ho +*14:8. Jn *5:43. 1 J *5:21. **worship.** Ex 25:20. Dt 32:43. 2 Ch 3:13. He *)1:6. 1 P 1:12. *3:22. Re 5:11-14. **gods.** Ps +8:5n. +82:6n. 96:4, *5. Ge 1:26. Ex 22:8, 9, 28. 2 Ch +*35:22n.

8. **Zion.** Ps 48:11. Is 51:3. 52:7-10. 62:11. Zp 3:14-17. Zc 9:9. Mt 21:4-9. **because.** Ps 52:6. 58:10. Re 18:20. 19:1-7.

9. **Lord.** Ex +15:26. **most high.** Ps +*7:17. 9:2. 18:13. +77:10. +78:17, 35, 56. *83:18. Ep 1:21. Ph *2:9-11. **far.** Ps *95:3. 96:4. 115:3-8. 135:5. Ex *18:11. Je 10:8, 10. **above all.** Is 44:6. Jn *3:31. Ro √9:5. **gods.** Ps +*8:5n. +*82:6n.

10. **Ye that.** Ps 91:14. Ro √8:28. 1 C 8:3. Ja 1:12. 2:5. 1 P 1:8. 1 J 4:19. *5:2, 3. **hate evil.** Ps 34:14. 36:4. 37:27. √101:3. 119:*104, 163. Pr *3:7. 8:13. Am 5:15. Ro 7:15, 24. *12:9. 2 T 2:19. Ju 23. **preserveth.** Ps *31:23. *37:28, 39, 40. *145:20. Pr 2:8. Is 45:17.

Jn √10:28-30. Ro √8:28-30. 2 T *4:17, 18. 1 P *1:5.
souls. Heb. *nephesh*, Ge +12:13. **delivereth.** Ps 125:3.
Je 15:21. Da 3:28. 6:22, 27. 2 Th 2:8-12. 3:2. 1 J 5:18.
Re 13:8.

11. **Light.** Ps *18:28. *112:4. Ge +1:3. Est 8:16.
Jb *11:14, 17. *22:28. Pr +*4:18. Is *60:1, 2. 62:1.
Mi *7:9. Jn *12:46. Re *21:23. *22:5. **sown.** Ps *126:5,
6. Pr *11:18. Jn *16:20. Ga *6:8. Ja 5:7-11.

12. **Rejoice.** Ps 32:11. *33:1. Hab √3:17, 18. Zp 3:14-
17. Ph *4:4. **give thanks.** Ps 30:4. 60:6. Hab 1:12,
13. He 12:10. **at the remembrance.** *or,* to the memorial. Ps 6:5. 9:6. *30:4mg. **holiness.** Is *57:15. 1 Th
4:3. He √12:14.

PSALM 98

*The psalmist calls on the whole world to praise the
Lord, for overcoming all opposition, in making known
his salvation to Israel to the ends of the earth, and
to rejoice in the prospect of his coming judgment,
1-9.*

1. **Sing.** Ps 33:3. 96:1. 149:1. Is 12:5. 42:10. Re
5:9. 14:3. **for he.** Ps 77:14. 86:10. *105:5. 136:4. 139:14.
Ex 15:6, *11. Is 43:18-20. Je 31:22. Lk 1:49. 2:10-14.
Ac 2:11. Re *15:3, 4. **hath done.** Mk 7:37. Lk 13:17.
his right. Ps 2:5, 6. 45:3-5. 110:2-6. Ge *3:15. Ex 15:6.
Is 52:10. *59:16. *63:5. Jn *16:33. Ac 2:32, 33. 19:20.
Ro *8:37. Col *2:15. He 2:14, 15. Re 3:21. 6:2. 17:14.
19:11-21.

2. **made.** Is *45:21-23. 49:6. 52:10. Mt *28:19. Mk
*16:15. Lk 2:30-32. 3:6. Ro 10:18. T *2:13. **righteousness.** Ps 22:31. 24:5. Is *45:24, 25. 46:13. 62:2. Je
*23:6. Jn 16:8-10. Ro *1:17. *3:21-26. 9:30. 10:3, 4.
2 C √5:21. Ph *3:9. 2 P 1:1. **openly showed.** *or,* revealed. Le 20:11, 17, 18. Ro *1:17.

3. **remembered.** Ps *106:45. Le 26:42. Dt *4:31.
Mi 7:20. Lk *1:54, 55, 72. Ro 15:8, 9. **mercy.** √121C1B,
Ge +20:13. **and.** √174, Ge +18:27. **all the ends.** ver.
2. Ps *22:27. 67:7. Is *45:22. *49:6. *52:10. Lk *2:30,
31. 3:6. Ac *13:46, 47. *28:28. Ro *10:12, 18. Re 5:9.

4. **Make.** Ps 47:1-5. 66:1, 4. 67:4. *95:1. 100:1. Is
12:6. 42:11. 44:23. Je 33:11. Zp 3:14. Mt 21:9. Re
19:1, 6.

5. **Sing.** √16, Ge +1:27. **with the harp.** Ps 33:2.
92:3, 4. 1 Ch +13:8n. 15:16. 25:1-6. 2 Ch 29:25. Re
5:8. 14:2, 3. **voice.** √144A, Ge +3:8.

6. **trumpets.** Ps 47:5. 81:2-4. Le +23:24. Nu *10:1-
10. 1 Ch *15:28. 2 Ch 5:12, 13. 29:27. **the King.** Ps
47:6, 7. Mt 25:34. Re 19:16.

7. **Let.** Ps +*96:11, etc. Ro 8:21, 22. **roar.** √155D,
Ge +4:10. **world.** Ps 97:1. Is 49:13. 61:11.

8. **Let the floods.** Ps 47:1. 2 K 11:12. Is 55:12. **clap.**
√155D, Ge +4:10. **hills.** Ps 65:12, 13. Is 55:12.

9. **for he cometh.** Ps +*96:10, 13. Re √1:7. **with
righteousness.** Ps *67:4. 72:2. +*96:13. Is 5:16. Ac
√17:31. 24:25. Ro 2:5, 6. 2 P *3:13, 14. Re √20:4-6.
with equity. Ps *9:8. 17:2. 58:1.

PSALM 99

*Exhortations to adore the power, equity, and holi-
ness of the Lord as reigning in Zion, 1-5. Encouragements to worship him from the examples of Moses,
Aaron, and Samuel, 6-9.*

1. **Lord.** Ps 2:6. 93:1. 96:10. 97:1. Lk 19:12, 14.
Re 11:17. **people.** Ps *2:11, 12. 21:8, 9. 97:4. Lk 19:27.

Ph 2:12. **he sitteth.** √22D3H, Ps +80:1. Ps 18:10. 80:1.
Ex *25:22. Ezk 10:1, etc. **earth.** Ps 82:5mg. Je 4:24.
*5:22. 49:21. 50:46. Re 6:14. 20:11. **be moved.** Heb.
stagger. Is 19:14. 24:19, 20.

2. **great.** Ps 48:1-3. 50:2. 76:1, 2. Is 12:6. 14:32.
He 12:22-24. Re 14:1, etc. **high.** Ps 66:7. *97:9. Is
6:1-7. Da 4:34, 35. He 12:18. Ja 4:6, 7.

3. **thy great.** Ps 66:3. 76:12. Dt 7:21. 28:58. Ne
1:5. 4:14. 9:32. Is 12:6. Je 20:11. **for it.** Ps 111:9. 145:17.
Jsh 24:19. 1 S 2:2. Is *6:3. Jn 17:11. Re 4:8.
*15:3, 4.

4. **strength.** √24J, Dt +32:42. Ps +*45:6, 7. 72:1,
2. Dt 32:3, 4. 2 S *23:3, 4. Jb *36:5-7. 37:23. Is *11:3-
5. Je *23:5. He +*1:8. Re 19:11, 16. **thou dost.** Is
*9:7. 42:4. 61:11. **executest.** Dt 10:18. Ju *15.

5. **Exalt.** ver. 9. Ps 21:13. 34:3. 108:5. Ex 15:2. Is
12:4. 25:1. Ho 11:7. **Lord.** Ex +15:26. **footstool.**
√22D3D1, Is +66:1. Ps *132:7. 1 Ch *28:2. Is 66:1.
he is holy. *or,* it is holy. ver. 3. Le *19:2. Is 6:3.

6. **Moses.** Ex 24:6-8. 29:11, etc. 40:23-29. Nu 16:47,
48. **his priests.** He=7:24. **they called.** Ex 14:15. *15:25.
*32:11-14. *33:12-15. Nu *14:13-20. 16:21, 22. 1 S
*7:9-12. *12:18-24. Je 15:1. He *7:25. **he answered.**
Prayers answered, examples of: Moses, Ex 14:15, 16.
15:25. 17:4-6. Nu 11:11-17. Abraham, Ge ch. 15. Abraham's servant, Ge 24:12-21. Isaac, Ge 25:21. Jacob,
Ge ch. 32. Ho 12:3, 4. Israelites, Ex 2:23-25. 14:10.
Jg 3:9, 15. 4:3, 23. 6:7-14. 10:10, 15, 16. 1 S 12:10,
11. 2 Ch 15:4, 15. Ne 9:27. Ps 106:15. Gideon, Jg
6:36-40. Manoah, Jg 13:8, 9. Samson, Jg 15:18, 19.
16:28-30. Hannah, 1 S 1:10-17. David, 1 S 23:10-12.
Ps +*27:7. Solomon, 1 K 3:1-13. 9:2, 3. Jabez, 1 Ch
*4:10. Abijah's army, 2 Ch 13:14-18. Asa, 2 Ch 14:11-
15. 2 Ch 15:15. Elijah, 1 K 18:36-38. Elisha, 2 K 6:18,
20. Jehoshaphat, 2 Ch 18:31. 2 Ch *20:6-27. Jehoahaz,
2 K 13:4. Levites, 2 Ch 30:27. Hezekiah and Isaiah,
2 K 19:14-20. 2 Ch 32:20, 21, 24. 2 K *20:1-6, 10,
11. Manasseh, 2 Ch 33:13, 19. Reubenites, etc.,
1 Ch 5:20. Jews, Ezr 8:21, 23. Zc 7:1-4. Daniel, Da
*9:20-23. 10:12. Zacharias, Lk 1:13. Ananias, Ac 10:4.

7. **He spake.** T#1767. **in the cloudy.** Ex 19:9. *33:9.
Nu 12:5. **kept.** Ex 40:16. Nu 16:15. Dt 4:5. 33:9. 1 S
*12:3-5. Pr 28:9. He *3:2. 1 J 3:21, 22.

8. **Lord.** Ex +15:26. **thou wast.** Ps *89:31-33. Nu
14:20. Dt 9:19. Je √46:28. Zp 3:7. **though.** Ex *32:2,
34, 35. Nu 11:33, 34. 14:20-34. 16:47-49. *20:12, 24.
Dt 3:26. 9:20. Re 3:19. **their inventions.** Ec 7:29. Ro
1:21.

9. **Exalt.** ver. 5. Ps 34:3. 118:28. Ex 15:2. **his holy.**
Ps 2:6. 48:1, 2. 87:1-3. **for the.** T#410. ver. 3, 5. Ps
107:8. 145:3. 148:13. 1 S 2:2. Is 5:16. 6:3. +*57:15.
Hab 1:12, 13. Lk 1:49. 1 P 1:15, 16. Re 3:7. 4:8. **Lord.**
Ex +15:26. **is.** √63B, Ge +2:10.

PSALM 100

*A solemn call to the joyful worship of God as our
Creator and Shepherd, and to adore his everlasting
goodness, mercy, and truth, 1-5.*

(*Title.*) **A Psalm.** Ps 145, title. **praise.** *or,* thanksgiving. ver. 4. Ps 26:7. 42:4. 50:14. 56:12.

1. **Make.** Ps 32:11. 47:1, 5. 66:1, 4. 95:1, 2. 98:4.
Is 24:14-16. 42:10-12. Zp 3:14. Lk 19:37. **all ye lands.**
Heb. all the earth. Ps 67:4. 68:32. ch. 117. Dt 32:43.
Zc +*14:9. Ro 15:10.

2. **Serve.** Ps *9:2. 63:4, 5. 71:23. 107:21, 22. Le

25:9. Dt 12:12. 16:11, 14. *28:47. 1 K 8:66. Ne 8:10. Lk 1:74. Ac 2:46, 47. Ph *4:4. Col *3:23. **come**. Ps 42:4. 95:2. 2 Ch 20:27, 28. 31:2. Ep *5:19. **presence**. ⌐22A4, Ge +19:13.

3. **Know**. Ps 46:10. 95:3, 6, 7. Dt 4:35, 39. 7:9. 1 S *17:46, 47. 1 K 18:36-39. 2 K 19:19. Je 10:10. Jn *17:3. Ac 17:23, 24. 2 C 4:6. Ga 4:8, 9. 1 J 5:20. **it is he**. Ps *95:6. *119:73. 139:13, etc. *149:2. Jb 10:8-13. Ec 12:1. Ep √2:10. 1 P 4:19. **not we ourselves**. *or,* his we *are*. Ps 12:4. 1 C 6:19, 20. **we are his**. Ps 74:1, 2. 78:52. 79:13. 95:7. Is 40:9-11. 63:11, 19. Ezk *34:11, 30, 31. Jn 10:14-16, √26-28. Ac √20:28, 29. 1 C 6:19, 20. 1 P 2:9, *25. 5:2-4.

4. **Enter**. Ps *65:1. 66:13. *116:17-19. Is +*35:10. **be thankful**. Ps 136:1. 1 Ch *29:13. Col +*3:17. 1 Th *5:18. He *13:15. **bless his name**. Ps 96:2. 103:1, 2, 20-22. 145:1, 2. 1 Ch *29:20. Jb 1:21. 1 P 2:9.

5. **is good**. Ps 52:1. *86:5. 106:1. 107:1, 8, 15, 22. 119:68. +*136:1. +145:9 (T#228). Je *33:11. Ro *2:4. *11:22. **his mercy**. Ps 36:5. 103:17. 118:1-4. 136:1, etc. Jon +*4:2. Lk 1:50. **everlasting**. Ge +*17:5. **and his truth**. Ps 85:10. 89:1, 2. 119:90, 91. *146:6. Ex +*34:6, 7. Dt 7:9. Je +*33:20, 21. Mi *7:20. Ro *15:8, 9. T +*1:2n. He 6:13-18. **all generations**. Heb. generation and generation. Ps +33:11mg. 89:1mg.

PSALM 101

David declares in what manner he purposes to rule his household and his kingdom, for the suppression of sin and the encouragement of piety, 1-8.

1. **I will sing**. Ps *89:1. 97:8. 103:6-8. 136:10-22. Re *15:3, 4. 19:1-3. **of mercy**. Ps +*100:5. Ro 9:15-18, 22, 23. +*11:22. **unto thee**. Ps 71:22, 23.

2. **behave**. ver. 6. Ps 75:1, 2. 119:106, 115. *143:8. 1 S *18:14, 15. 22:14. 2 S 8:15. 2 Ch 30:12. 31:20, 21. Je *23:5, 6. **O when**. Ps +*40:17. 143:7, 8. **walk within**. T#492. Ge +*18:19. Dt +*6:7. Jsh +*24:15. 2 S +6:20. Jb +1:5. Is √38:19. 1 T √3:4, 5. +4:12 (T#178). T 1:6. 2:7. **my house**. T#953. Jsh *24:15. Ec 4:9, 10. Is 41:13. Mt *6:33. Lk 16:13. 1 C 13:5. 2 C 3:5. Ep *4:32. Col 3:19. He 10:24. T 2:4. 1 P 3:7. **perfect heart**. 1 K 9:4. 11:4. 2 K +*20:3. 1 Ch 12:38n. 2 Ch 15:17. Is *38:3.

3. **set**. Ps *18:20-23. 26:4, 5. *39:1. *119:37, 113. Ex 20:17. 2 S *11:2-4. 1 K 21:2, etc. Jb *31:1. Pr *6:25. 23:31-35. Ec 6:9. Is *33:15. Je *22:17. Ezk ◐23:14, 16, 20. Ho 7:6, 7. Mi 2:2. Mt *5:28. Mk 7:20-23. Ro 1:21-32. *13:13, 14. 1 C *3:16, 17. +√6:9, 10. 2 C 12:21. Ga *5:19-21. Ep 4:19-23. √5:3-5, 11, 12. 1 Th √5:22. 1 T 1:9, 10. 2 T *2:22. Ja *1:13-15. 1 P 2:11. 4:3-5. 2 P ◐2:14. **wicked thing**. Heb. thing of Belial. Dt +15:9mg. Jg +19:22. 1 S +30:22. 1 K 21:13. **I hate**. Ps +*97:10. Ro *12:9. **the work**. ⌐24A, Ge +32:24. **them**. Ps *14:3. *36:3. *40:4. 78:*41, 57. *125:5. Ex 32:8. Jsh *23:6. 1 S *12:20, 21. 15:11. Is 30:11. Zp *1:5, 6. Ga *4:9. He *10:39. 2 P *2:21. 1 J *2:19. **it shall not**. Dt *13:17.

4. **A froward**. Pr 2:12-15. *3:32. 8:13. 11:20. **not know**. Ps 6:8. 119:√63, *115. Est +1:12. Pr 9:6. 22:24. Mt √7:23. 2 C *6:14-16. 15:33. 2 T *2:19.

5. **Whoso**. Ps 15:3. 50:20. Ex +*20:16. 23:1. Le *19:16. Pr 6:16, 17. 10:18. 20:19. 25:23. Ezk 22:9. 1 C 5:11. 1 T 3:11. T 2:3. **slandereth**. ⌐171E6, Ec +10:11. The literal Hebrew is "the tongue (i.e. *the slanderer*), in the secret places of his friend, him shall

I cut off." T#729. Ps +74:18. 141:3. Le *19:16. Pr 4:24. 10:8, +18 (T#417). 13:3. 21:23. 24:28. 25:23. +29:11 (T#200). Ro 1:22, 30. 14:10. 1 C 5:11. 15:33. Ep 4:29, 31. 5:3, *4. Col 3:8, +9 (T#417). 2 T 2:16. T 2:7, 8. 3:1, 2. Ja 4:11. 1 P *2:1, 2. 3:9. Ju 9. **an high**. Ps 10:2-4. *18:27. +*119:21. 138:6. 1 S 2:3. Jb 40:11, 12. Pr *6:16-19. 30:13. Is 2:11. Da 4:37. Ob 3, 4. Lk +*18:14. 1 P 5:5, 6. **suffer**. lit. I am not able (to bear). ⌐63BA, Ps +21:11.

6. **Mine**. Ps 15:4. 34:15. √119:63. Pr 28:28. 29:2. Mt +*24:45. Lk +*12:42-44. Ro 13:1-4. **that they**. Jn *12:26. √14:3. *17:24. Re √3:20, 21. *21:3. **in a perfect way**. *or,* perfect in the way. Ps *119:1mg, 2, 3. Ge +*17:1. Pr 11:20. 13:6. Ph √3:12-15.

7. **He that worketh**. 2 S 4:10-12. 2 K 5:26, 27. Pr 29:12. Ac 1:16-20, 25. 5:1-10. **tarry in my sight**. Heb. be established. Ps 89:21, 27. 93:1. Ec *8:11. Ep *5:11.

8. **early**. lit. at morning. ⌐171T4, Jb +7:18. By Synecdoche of the Part, "morning" is put for a more lengthened period or continuous time. Here it should not be rendered "early," as in the A.V., nor "morning by morning," as in the R.V., as though in millennial days each morning would commence with, and each day begin with, executions! It means more than that. It means *continually*; so that all through the Millennium all workers of iniquity will be continually cut off (B655, 656). Ps +*59:16. *90:14. Is +*17:14. Je *21:12. Zp √3:5. **destroy**. Ps *49:14, 15. +*58:10. Pr +*2:22. 16:12. 20:8, 26. Is ◐11:4. *17:14. +*24:6. √65:20. Mi ◐3:1-4, 9. **cut off**. Ps +*37:9. 75:10. Pr +*2:22. Ho 9:3. Mi 2:8-10. Re √21:27. 22:14, 15. **the city**. Ps *48:2, 8. √102:13, 16. Is 1:26. 26:1. 62:6, 7.

PSALM 102

The psalmist pours out doleful complaints before the Lord, 1-11. He takes comfort from the eternity of God, 12. He predicts the triumph of Zion, though then desolated, according to the promises of God, at the appointed time and in answer to the prayers of his people, 13-17. He records the mercies of the Lord for the benefit of posterity, 18-22. Conscious of his own weakness, he rests his hope on the unchangeableness of God our Savior, 23-28.

(Title.) A.M. cir. 3464. B.C. cir. 540. **A Prayer**. This psalm was evidently composed towards the close of the Babylonian captivity, probably by the prophet Daniel. **of**. *or,* for. **overwhelmed**. Ps 12:5. 61:2. 69:1, 2. 142:2, 3. 143:4. La 3:18-20. Mk 14:33, 34. Lk 22:44. He 5:7. **poureth**. Ps 42:4. *62:8. 77:3. 142:2. 1 S 1:15, 16.

1. **Hear**. Ps 5:2. 55:1-5. 57:1-3. 130:1, 2. 141:1, 2. 143:7. *145:19. **let my**. Ps *18:6. Ex 2:23. Jg 10:16. 1 S 9:16. 2 Ch 30:27. La 3:8, 44.

2. **Hide**. Ps 13:1. *27:9. 69:17. 88:14. 104:29. 143:7. Jb 34:29. Is 8:17. *43:2. 1 C √10:13. **incline**. Ps 71:2. 88:2, etc. **in the day**. Ps 22:19. 40:13. 70:1, 5. Jb 7:21. Is +*65:24. Ac 12:5, etc.

3. **my days**. Ps 37:20. 119:83. Ja *4:14. **like smoke**. *or,* (as some read) into smoke. **my bones**. Ps 22:14, 15. 31:10. 38:3. Jb 30:30. La 1:13. 3:4.

4. **heart**. Ps 6:2, 3. 42:6. 55:4, 5. 69:20. 77:3. 143:3, 4. Jb 6:4. 10:1. La 3:13, 20. Mt 26:37, 38. **withered**. ver. 11. Ps 37:2. Is 40:7. **so that**. ver. 9. 1 S 1:7, 8. Ezr 10:6. Ac 9:9. **bread**. ⌐171I8, Ge +3:19.

5. **the voice**. ⌐144, Ge +3:8. Ps 6:6, 8. 32:3, 4.

38:8-10. Jb 19:20. Pr 17:22. La 4:8. **skin**. *or*, flesh. √171N, Ge +8:13. Ps +*16:9. Jb 12:10mg. Is 10:18mg. Ezk 10:12mg.

6. **like**. Jb 30:29, 30. Is 38:14. Mi 1:8. **a pelican**. Is 34:11-15. Zp 2:14mg. Re 18:2.

7. **watch**. Ps 22:2. 77:4. 130:6. Dt 28:66, 67. Jb 7:13-16. Mk 14:33-37. **alone**. Ps *38:11. La 3:28-30.

8. **Mine**. Ps 31:11-13. 55:3. 69:9, 10, 20. 89:51. Ro 15:3. **mad**. Ps 2:1. Lk 6:11. Ac 7:54. 26:11. **are sworn**. or, do curse by me. Dt 21:33. Je 29:22. Ac 23:12, etc. **against me**. Ac 4:27.

9. **I have**. Ps 69:21. Is 44:20. La 3:15, 16. Mi 1:10. 7:17. **mingled**. Ps 42:3. 80:5. Jb 3:24. La 3:48, 49.

10. **Because**. Ps 38:3, 18. 39:11. 90:7-9. La 1:18. *3:39-42. 5:16. Da 9:8-14. Ro 3:19. **thou hast**. T#1923. Ps 30:6, 7. 73:18-20. 147:6. 1 S 2:7, 8. 2 Ch 25:8. Jn ✱12:32, 33. 2 C 4:9.

11. **My days**. √171T2B. Synecdoche of the Part B654. "Days" are used for time. For other instances of this figure see Ps 103:15. Is 4:1. 9:4. Ho 9:9. Mt 2:1. Ac 5:36. **like a shadow**. ver. 3. Ps 39:5, 6. 109:23. 144:4. Jb 14:2. Ec 6:12. Ja *4:14. **I am withered**. ver. 4. Ps 39:11. Is *40:6-8. Ja 1:10. 1 P 1:24.

12. **thou**. ver. 24-27. Ps *9:7. 90:1, 2. Dt 33:27. Is 44:6. 60:15. La *5:19. Ml *3:6. He √13:8. Re 1:17, 18. **for ever**. Heb. *olam*, Ex +*12:24. Re 5:14. **thy remembrance**. Ps 135:13. Ex 3:15. **generations**. Ge +9:12.

13. **Thou shalt arise**. √22C21, Nu +10:35. Ps 7:6. *44:26. *51:18. *69:35, 36. +*82:8. Is 14:32. *60:1, 10-14. Je 31:10-12, *23. Zp +*3:8. Zc 1:12, 13. √2:10-12. **the set time**. ver. +*16. Ge +17:21h. Ezr 1:1, etc. Is *40:2mg. Je √29:10, 12. Da *9:2, etc. *12:9, 12, 13. Ho *6:2. Mi +*5:3. Zp +*3:20. Ac √1:6n, 7. +*3:19. Ga *4:4. 2 P 3:8, 12. Re 11:15-18.

14. **thy servants**. Ps 79:1, 7-10. 137:5, 6. Ezr 1:5. 3:1-3. 7:27. Ne 1:3. 2:3, 17. 4:2, 6, 10. Da 9:16. **stones**. √171S4, Ge +14:7. By Synecdoche of the Part, whereby a part of a thing is put for the whole of the thing, *stones* is put for the restored buildings.

15. **heathen shall fear**. Ps 61:5. *67:2-4. 68:31, 32. *72:11. *86:9. *138:4. 1 K *8:43. Is *55:5. *60:3, etc. Je 25:12. Zc *8:20-23. Re *11:15. 21:24. **all the kings**. Ps *138:4. 148:11. **thy glory**. Is *59:19. Ezk 39:21.

16. **When**. ver. +*22. Is 2:2, 3. Ezk +*34:27. 39:28n. Ho 6:11. Zp 3:20. **shall build**. √108B, Ezk +26:14. Ps 51:18. *69:35. +*147:2. Is 16:5. *44:26. Je 31:4. *33:7. Am +√9:11-15. Mi 3:12. 4:1-7. +*5:3. Ac +√3:19, 21. +*15:16. **Zion**. Ps *14:7. +*50:2, 3. +*122:6. Is +√24:23. Zc √2:12. **he shall appear**. Ps +*42:5mg. 97:6. Is 40:5. 60:1, 2, 7. Je 31:3. Ezk +*20:35-38. Zc *2:6-13. *9:14. 2 T +*4:1n. **his glory**. Ps *85:9. 97:6. *145:11, 13. Is 61:3. 66:18. Mi 2:9. Hg *2:7n. Zc √2:8. +√6:13. 14:9. Mt *16:27n. Mk 8:38. Col +*3:4. 1 P +√1:11.

17. **He will**. Ps 4:1. 6:9. *9:18. +*34:6, 15. *72:12. Dt 4:29. 32:36. 1 S 2:8. Ne *1:6, 11. *2:1-8. Jb 34:28. 36:15. Is *30:19. Je *29:11-14. Da 9:3-21. Jl 2:18-20. Zc 10:6. **not despise**. T#49. Ps *22:24. 69:33.

18. **written for**. T#49. Ps 71:18. 78:4-6. *119:105, 130. Ex 17:14. Dt 9:10. 31:19, etc. Jb 19:23, 24. Is +√8:20n. Pr +*8:9. +*18:1n. Da 9:2. Jn √20:31. Ro √15:4. 1 C *10:11. 2 T √3:16, 17. 2 P 1:15, 18, 19. **the people**. Ps 22:30, 31. 45:16, 17. Is *43:5-7, 21. 65:17-19. 2 C √5:17, 18. Ep √2:10. 1 P 2:9, 10.

19. **For he**. Ps 14:2. *33:13, 14. Dt *26:15. 1 K

8:39, 43. 2 Ch 16:9. **the height**. Jb 22:12. He 8:1, 2. 9:23, 24.

20. **To hear**. Ps *79:11. 146:7. Ex *2:23-25. 3:7. 2 K 13:4, 22, 23. Jb 24:12. Is 14:17. *61:1-3. Je 51:34, 35. Zc 9:9-12. **to loose**. 2 Ch 33:11-13. Je 52:32-34. Ac 12:6-11. **those that are appointed to**. Heb. the children of. √181E, Ge +3:24. √108B, 1 S +20:31. Ps 79:11mg. Ep *2:2, 3.

21. **To declare**. Ps 9:13, 14. *22:22. 51:14, 15. 79:13. Is 51:11. Ep 2:4-7. 3:21. 1 P 2:9.

22. **When**. ver. *16. Ps *72:8-11. Ge +*49:10. Ezr 10:7. Est 2:8, 19. Ezk +*34:27. Zc *8:20-23. Ro 15:19. **gathered**. Ps +*147:2. Is *66:18. Ezk 37:11, 12. Ho 1:9-11. 2 Th +*2:1. **the kingdoms**. Ps 145:11-13. Ob +*21. Mt +*24:14. Re √11:15. **to serve**. Ps *72:11. Is 49:22, 23. 60:3-5.

23. **He weakened**. Heb. He afflicted. Ps 89:38-47. 2 Th 2:3-12. 1 T 4:1-3. 2 T 3:1, etc. Re 11:2, etc. 12:13, etc. **shortened**. Ps 110:3. Ex 12:5. Jb 21:21.

24. **I said**. Ps 39:13. Is *38:10, etc. **my God**. Ps +62:12. Ec +12:14. Ho 1:7. He 1:+*8, 10-12. **in the midst**. Ec +*7:17. Is +*38:10. **thy years**. √22D44, Jb +36:26. ver. 12. Ps 9:7. √90:1, 2. Hab 1:12. Re 1:4, 8. **generations**. Ge +9:12.

25. **Of old**. Ge *1:1. 2:1. Ex *20:11. Jb 38:4-7. Pr 8:23, etc. Je 32:17. He ▶1:10-12. 3:3, 4.

26. **They shall perish**. Ec ◑+*1:4. Is *34:4. *51:6. *65:17. 66:22. Lk 21:33. Ro *8:20. 2 P *3:7-12. Re 20:11. 21:1. **endure**. Heb. stand. ver. 12. Ex 3:14.

27. **thou art**. Ml +*3:6. Jn √8:58. He √13:8. Ja *1:17. Re *1:8, 17, 18. **thy years**. √22D4A, Jb +36:26. Ps *90:4. Jb 36:26.

28. **The children**. Ps 22:30, 31. 45:16, 17. *69:35, 36. 103:17. +*145:13. Is +*29:23. 53:10. *54:1. *59:20, 21. *65:22. *66:22. Ho 1:10. Jn 8:33-40. Ac 2:39. 2 P 3:13n. **of thy servants**. Ps 78:70. *89:3, 20. *105:6, 26, 42. Is 37:35. *41:8, 9. Je *33:21, 22, 26. Ezk 28:25. 34:23, 24. *37:24, 25. Mi 7:20. Zc ◑3:8. Ml 4:4. Ro ◑8:17, 19. **shall continue**. Ps 72:5. +*145:13. 146:10. Is 60:15. Je +*31:36. Ezk 37:25. Jl *3:20. Mt 24:34. Lk +*1:32, 33. **their seed**. Ps *69:36. *89:4, 29, 36, 37. 90:16, 17. 112:2. Is *65:23. *66:22. Ezk *37:25.

PSALM 103

David earnestly praises God for his plenteous mercy and goodness to him and to Israel, 1-10; for his fatherly compassion to the frailty of those who fear and obey him; and for his constant regard to their posterity, 11-18. He calls on men, angels, and all creatures, to join him in blessing the Lord, the universal sovereign, 19-22.

1. A.M. 2970. B.C. 1034. **Bless**. ver. 22. Ps *30:4. 68:19. 104:1. *146:1, 2. Lk 1:46, 47. O. √38C, Ps +42:5. **my**. Ps 104:1. 146:1. Is 42:1. Lk +1:46. **soul**. Heb. *nephesh*, Ge +34:3. √171Q2, Nu +23:10. √121A8, Ps +16:10. **all that**. √155A, Ge +31:35. Ps 47:7. 57:7-11. 63:5. 86:12, 13. 111:1. 138:1. Mk *12:30-33. Jn *4:24. 1 C 14:15. Ph *1:9. Col *3:16. **holy name**. Ps 99:3. Is 6:3. Re 4:8.

2. **soul**. Heb. *nephesh*, Ge +34:3. **forget not**. Ps 105:5. 106:7, 21. *116:12. Dt 8:2-4, 10-14. *32:6, 18. 2 Ch 32:25. Is 63:1, *7. Je 2:31, 32. Lk *17:15-18. Ep *2:11-13. **all**. √108E3. Idiom B836. In the New Testament the adjective *pas* ("all") is frequently used according to Hebrew idiom, being joined with the nega-

tive to the verb instead of the predicate. The Hebrews would say "everything is not," and this is put instead of the ordinary Greek idiom *nothing is* in the following unmarked passages, as not readily observable in English translation: Mt 24:22. Mk 13:20. Lk *1:37. Jn 3:15, 16. 6:39. 12:46. Ro *3:20. 1 C 1:29. Ga 2:16. 1 J 2:21. Re 18:22.

3. **forgiveth.** T#790. Ps *32:1-5. *51:1-3. +*130:8. 2 S 12:13. Is *43:25. Je 33:8. Ezk 33:16. Mt *9:2-6. Mk *2:5, 10, 11. Lk 7:47, 48. Ep *1:7. **healeth.** T#756. Ps 30:2. 38:1-7. 41:+3, 4, 8. *107:17-22. 147:3. Ex *15:26. +23:25. Nu 12:13. *21:7-9. Jsh 18:27, Irpeel. 2 K 20:5. Pr 3:7, 8. 4:22. Is 33:24. *53:5. Je *17:14. 33:6. Mt 8:16, 17. Ac 10:38. 2 T ◐4:20. Ja *5:15. 3 J 2.

4. **redeemeth.** Ps *30:3. 34:22. *56:13. 71:23. Ge 48:15, 16. Jb 33:19-30. Ho 13:9. Re *5:9. **crowneth.** Ps 5:12mg. *8:5. 21:3. 65:11. Ja *1:12. 1 P *5:4.

5. **satisfieth.** Ps 23:5. *36:8. 63:5. *65:4. 104:28. *107:9. 145:15, 16. 1 T *6:17. **thy youth.** Is *40:31. Ho 2:15. 2 C *4:16. **like the eagle's.** Dt 32:11, 12. Is +*40:31. Lk ◐+*17:37n.

6. **executeth.** Ps 9:9. 10:14-18. 12:5. 72:4, 12. *109:31. 146:7. Dt 24:14, 15. Jb *27:13, etc. Pr 14:31. *22:22, 23. 23:10, 11. Is 14:4, etc., 17-19. 58:6, 7. Je 7:6, etc. Ezk 22:7, 12-14. Mi 2:1-3. 3:2-4. Ja 2:6. +*5:1-6.

7. **He made.** Ps 77:20. 105:26, etc. Ex 19:8, 20. 20:21. 24:2-4. Nu *12:7, 8. Dt *29:29. 34:10. Ne 9:13, 14. Is 63:11, 12. Jn 5:45-47. Ac 7:35, etc. **his ways.** Ex √33:13. +*34:5, 6. Jn=5:20. **his acts.** Ps 78:5. *147:19.

8. **merciful.** Ps 86:5, 15. +*100:5. 130:7. *145:8. Ex +*34:6, 7. Nu 14:18. Dt 5:10. Ne *9:17. Is *55:7. Je 32:18. Ro 5:20, 21. Ep 1:7, 8. **slow.** Jl 2:13. Jon *4:2. Na 1:3. **plenteous in mercy.** Heb. great of mercy. √22I4, Ps +*86:15. Ps 18:16mg.

9. **not always.** Ps 30:5. Jb +4:20 (✱S#5331h). Is 27:4. Is +*41:9. Je 3:5. **neither.** Ps 30:5. Is 57:16. Je 3:5. Mi *7:18, 19. **his anger.** √63A2, 2 S +6:6. **for ever.** Heb. *olam*, Ex +*12:24.

10. **hath not dealt.** T#552. Ps 130:3. Ezr 9:13. Ne 9:31. Jb 11:6. Ec *8:11. 9:1, 2. La *3:22. Da 9:18, 19. Hab 3:2. Mt +6:5 (T#565). Ro 4:7, 8. **rewarded.** 1 S +1:22n (✚S#1580h).

11. **as the,** etc. Heb. according to the height of heaven. √170, Is +1:18. Ps 36:5. 57:10. 89:2. Jb 22:12. Pr 25:3. Is √55:9. Ep 2:4-7. *3:18, 19. **so.** √170, Is +1:18. **his mercy.** ver. 17. Lk 1:50.

12. **As.** √170, Is +1:18. **as the east.** Ps 50:1. 113:3. Le +=1:16. Is *45:6. **so far.** √170, Is +1:18. Is *43:25. Je *31:34. 50:20. Mi *7:18. He 10:2-4. 1 J *1:7. **removed.** Is 43:25. Je 33:8. Mi 7:19.

13. **Like.** Nu 11:12. Dt *8:5. Pr *3:12. Is 63:13, 15, 16. Je *31:9, 20. Mt 6:9, 32. Lk 11:11, 12. *15:21, 22. Jn 20:17. He *12:5-11. **as.** √170, Is +1:18. **so.** √170, Is +1:18. **them.** ver. 11, 17. Ps *147:11. Ml *3:16, 17. 4:2. Ac *13:26.

14. **he knoweth.** Ps 40:17. *78:38, 39. *89:47. **our frame.** Ps +*34:4. 38:10. 49:12. 1 S 20:3. Is 2:22. 64:6. Mk 8:3. Ro 7:15-25. 1 C *10:13. **remembereth.** √22C3, Ge +8:1. **we are.** √63B, Ge +2:10. **dust.** √121D10, Ge +3:19. Ps 104:29. +146:4. Ge +*3:19. Jb 7:5-7, 21. *10:9. 13:25. 14:2, 3. Ec 3:20. *12:7.

15. **his days.** √171T2B, Ps +102:11. Ps 90:5, 6. Is *40:6-8. 51:12. Ja 1:10, 11. 1 P 1:24. **as.** √160B, Ge

+25:31. **a flower.** Jb *14:1-3. Is 28:1, 4. Na 1:4. **so.** √160B, Ge +25:31.

16. **the wind.** Jb 27:20, 21. Is 40:7. **it is gone.** Heb. it *is* not. Ge 5:24. 42:36. Jb 14:10. **and the.** Jb 7:6-10. 8:18, 19. *20:9. **know.** √155D, Ge +4:10.

17. **the mercy.** Ps 89:1, 2. 100:5. 118:1. 136:1, etc. Je 31:3. Da 9:9. Ro √8:28-30. Ep 1:4-8. 2:4-7. 2 Th *2:13, 14. 2 T √1:9. **from everlasting to.** Heb. *olam* doubled, Ps +41:13. **his righteousness.** Ps 22:31. Is 46:13. 51:6. Da 9:24. Mi 6:5. Ro 1:17. 3:21-25. 2 P 1:1. **unto children's.** Ps 25:13. 90:16. +*102:28. Ex 20:6. Dt 10:15. Is 41:8. 59:20, 21. Je *33:24-26. Ac *13:32-34. Ro *15:8.

18. **To such.** Ps 25:10. 132:12. Ge 17:9, 10. Ex *19:5. 24:8. Dt *7:9. 2 Ch 34:31. He *8:6-13. **remember.** Ps √119:9-11. Dt 4:23. 6:6-9. Pr 3:1. Mt 28:20. Lk 1:6. Ac 24:16. 1 Th 4:1, 2. **to do them.** Lk +√6:46.

19. **prepared.** Ps 2:4. 9:7. 11:4. 115:3. Is 66:1. He *8:1. **his throne.** √22D3C1, Ps 9:4. +11:4. 47:8. 89:14. 97:2. 2 Ch 18:18. Mt 5:34. 23:22. Ac 7:49. He 8:1. 12:2. Re 1:4. +*3:21. 14:3. 19:4. 21:5. **in the heavens.** Ps 11:4. **his kingdom.** Ps 22:28. 47:2. 83:18. 2 Ch 20:6. Da *4:25, 34, 35. Mt +*6:10, 13. Ep 1:21, 22. Ph *2:9, 10. 1 P 3:22. **over all.** Ps 22:27. 59:13. 67:7. 1 C 15:24-28. Ep 1:10.

20. **Bless.** Ps 148:2. Lk 2:13, 14. Re 19:5, 6. **that excel in strength.** Heb. mighty in strength. Ps 78:25. 2 K 19:35. Is 6:2. Jl 2:11. Mt 26:53. **do his.** Mt *6:10. Lk 1:19. He *1:14.

21. **all ye his hosts.** Ps 33:6. Ge 32:2. Jsh 5:14. 1 K 22:19. 2 Ch 18:18. Lk 2:13. **ministers.** Ps 68:17. 104:4. Ne 9:6. Da 7:9, 10. Mt 13:41. 24:30, 31. 2 Th 1:7, 8. He *1:6, 7, 14. Re 22:8, 9.

22. **all his works.** Ps *145:10. 148:3-12. 150:6. Is 42:10-12. 43:20. 44:23. 49:13. Re 5:12-14. **bless the Lord.** ver. 1. Ps 104:1, 35. 146:1. **O my.** √38C, Ps +42:5. **soul.** Heb. *nephesh*, Ge +34:3.

PSALM 104

The psalmist celebrates the glory of the divine perfections as displayed in creation and providence, 1-32. He determines to meditate perpetually with delight on God and his works and predicts the destruction of the wicked, 33-35.

1. **Bless.** This sublime poem on the works of God in creation and providence is ascribed to David in the LXX., Vulgate, Ethiopic, Syriac, and Arabic; and as it opens and closes with the same words as the preceding psalm, it is probable that it was composed on the same occasion; it is written as part of it in nine MSS. See on ver. 35. Ps 103:1, 2, 22. **my.** Ps +103:1. Lk +12:19. **O my.** √38C, Ps +42:5. **soul.** Heb. *nephesh*, Ge +34:3. **O Lord.** Ps 7:1-3. Da 9:4. Hab 1:12. **art very great.** Ps *145:3. Je 23:24. *32:17-19. Re 1:13, etc. **clothed.** √22D5P, Ps +93:1. Ps 93:1. Is 59:17. Da 7:9. **honor.** Ps 29:1-4. 96:6. **and majesty.** Ps *93:1. 146:10. Ex 8:10, 11. 19:18. 20:18, 19. 1 Ch +*29:11. Jb *37:22-24. Da 7:9, 10. Is 2:10. +*57:15. Mi *5:4.

2. **with light.** Da *7:9. Mt *17:2. 1 T *6:16. 1 J *1:5. **garment.** √22D5P, Ps +93:1. **stretchest.** Is *40:22. 45:12. Zc 12:1. He *1:10-12.

3. **Who layeth.** Ps 18:10, 11. Am 9:6. **waters.** Ge 1:7. **maketh.** Is 19:1. Mt *26:64. Re *1:7. **clouds.** Ps 18:11, 12. 77:17. Ge +9:13. Na 1:3. Mt +*24:30.

*26:64. ƒ22D5H. Anthropomorphism B893. *Clouds* are represented as his chariots. For other instances of this figure see Ps 18:10, 11. Is 19:1. **his chariot**. Ps +*68:17. **walketh**. Ps 18:10. *139:9. 2 S 22:11. Na *1:3.

4. **Who maketh**. Ac *23:8. He *1:▸7, 14. **spirits**. Heb. *ruach*. Thus, *ruach* is used of invisible spirit beings, here, angels. For cherubim, see Ezk 1:12, 20, 20, 20, 21. 10:17. For neutral spirit beings, see Jb 4:15. Is 31:3. For evil spirit beings see Jg +9:23. For the other uses of *ruach*, see Ge 6:3n. **ministers**. 2 K *2:11. *6:17. Ezk 1:13, 14. **flaming fire**. Is +*24:6. Ho 7:6, 7. Zc 12:6. Mt *3:12. Mk 3:17. Lk *9:54. *12:49. 2 Th 1:8. Re *11:5. 16:8.

5. **Who laid the foundations of the earth**. Heb. He hath founded the earth upon her bases. Ps 24:2. 33:9. 136:6. Jb √26:7. 38:4-7. **should not**. Ps *72:5, 17. *78:69. *89:36, 37. 93:1. 96:10. 119:90, 91. 1 Ch √16:30. Ec +*1:4. Is *49:8. 51:16. 2 P ◐*3:7, 10, 11. Re 6:14. ◐20:11. **for ever**. lit. forever and ever. **and ever**. Ps +9:18 (*S#5703h).

6. **coveredst**. Ge *1:2-10. 7:19, 20. 2 P *3:5, 6. **stood above**. Ge 7:19.

7. **At thy**. Ge 1:9. 8:1. Pr 8:28, 29. Mk *4:39. **they fled**. Ps 114:3-7.

8. **They go up**, etc. *or*, The mountains ascend, the valleys descend. Ge 8:5.

9. **hast set**. Ps 33:7. Ge *9:11-15. Jb 26:10. 38:10, 11. Is +*54:9. Je 5:22.

10. **He sendeth**. Heb. Who sendeth. Ps 107:35. The waters of the sea are not only prevented from destroying the earth, but by the providence of God are rendered the means of preserving every living thing; partly ascending from the great deep through the strata of the earth, partly exhaled in vapor from the surface of the ocean and thence falling in rain, especially on the tops and sides of mountains, they break forth into fresh springs and form streams and rivers. Dt 8:7. Is 35:7. 41:18. **springs**. Heb. *mayan*, Ge +7:11 (*S#4599h). **run**. Heb. walk. Ps 131:1mg. Pr 8:20mg. Ec 1:7. Hab 3:11mg.

11. **They give**. Ps 145:16. **the wild**. Jb 39:5-8. **quench**. Heb. break. Ps 105:16. Ex 12:46. Is 42:3.

12. **the fowls**. ver. 16, 17. Ps 50:11. 84:3. 148:10. Mt 6:26. ▸13:32. Mk 4:32. Lk 13:19. **sing**. Heb. give a voice. Ps 147:9.

13. **watereth**. Ps 147:8. Dt 11:11. Jb 38:25-28, 37. Je *10:13. *14:22. Mt +5:45. Ac *14:17. **his chambers**. ver. 3. Ge 1:7. Am 9:6. **the earth**. Ps 65:9-13.

14. **causeth**. Ps 145:15, 16. 147:8, 9. Ge 1:11, 12, 29, 30. 2:5. 1 K 18:5. Je 14:5, 6. Jl 2:22. Mt +5:45. **herb**. Ge 1:29, 30. 2:9, 16. 3:18. 9:3. **that he**. Ps *136:25. Ge 4:12. Jb 28:5. 1 C 3:7. **food**. Heb. bread. ƒ171I8, Ge +3:19. ƒ121D14. Metonymy of the Cause B567. Bread is put for all food. The opposite of this figure, Metonomy of the Effect B567, may be seen at Is ◐28:28.

15. **wine**. Ps *23:5. Le +23:13. Jg 9:13. Pr 31:6, 7. Ec 10:19. Je 31:12. Zc 9:15-17. Mk 14:23. Ep *5:18. **oil to make his**, etc. Heb. to make his face shine with oil, *or* more than oil. Ps 92:10. Dt 28:40. Jg 9:9. Ec 8:1. 9:7, 8. SS 1:2-4. He 1:9. 1 J *2:20, 27. **bread**. Ps 105:16. Le 26:26. Dt 8:3. Is 3:1. Ezk 4:16. 5:16. 14:13.

16. **trees**. ƒ24L, Ge +6:2. Ps 29:5. 92:12. Nu 24:6. Ezk 17:23. **are full**. Ps 65:9. Dt 33:28.

17. **the birds**. ver. 12. Je 22:23. Ezk 31:6. Da 4:21. Ob 4. Mt 13:32. **as for**. Le 11:19. Je 8:7. **the stork**. The stork is a species of the *ardea* or *heron* genus, about the size of a goose in its body, but when erect, about three or four feet high; its general color is white; extremity of the wings, and small part of the head, black; legs, very long, red, and naked a great way up; the toes four, long and connected, with flat nails like those of a man; beak long, jagged, red, and somewhat compressed; the upper and under chaps both of a length, with a furrow from the nostrils: it feeds on serpents, frogs, and insects, on which account it might be deemed unclean; lays four eggs, and sits thirty days; migrates about August, and returns in spring; and is remarkable for its love to its parents, whom it never forsakes, but feeds and cherishes when old; whence it had the name *chaseedah*, which denotes "kindness" or "piety," and *stork*, from the Greek *storga*, "natural affection." Le 11:19. Dt 14:18. Jb 39:13mg. Je 8:7.

18. **the wild goats**. The *yaal* is the *ibex*, or rock goat, so called from *alah*, "to ascend," because it is famous for mounting to the tops of the highest rocks. Its general appearance is that of the tame goat, of a dusky brown color; but the male is larger, with long horns, bending backwards. 1 S 24:2. Jb 39:1. **the conies**. Dt 14:7. Pr *30:26.

19. **the moon**. Ps 8:3. 136:7-9. Ge *1:14-18. Dt 4:19. Jb 31:26-28. 38:12. Je 31:35. **seasons**. Ge +17:21h. **knoweth**. ƒ155D, Ge +4:10.

20. **makest**. Ps 74:16. 139:10-12. Ge 1:4, 5. +8:22. Is 14:7. Am 4:13. **darkness**. Jb +38:9. Is *45:7. **of the forest do creep forth**. Heb. thereof do trample on the forest. Ps 69:34mg. Ge 9:2. Le 20:25mg.

21. **The young**. Ps 34:10. Jb 38:39. Is 31:4. Ezk 19:2, etc. Am 3:4. **seek**. Ps 147:9. Jb 38:41. Jl 1:18, 20. 2:22.

22. **The sun**. Jb 24:13-17. Na 3:17. Jn 3:20. **together**. ƒ63H, Ge +12:15. Supply, by ellipsis (relative: of a combined word), "they gather themselves together, (depart, and) lay themselves down in their dens."

23. **goeth forth**. Ge *3:19. Jg 19:16. Ec 5:12. Ep 4:28. 2 Th 3:8-12.

24. **O Lord**. ƒ38A, Ne +4:4. **how**. Ps 8:3. 40:5. 107:31. Ne *9:6. Jb 5:9. **in wisdom**. Ps 136:5. Ge 1:31. Pr 3:19, 20. 8:22, etc. Je 10:12. Ro *11:33. Ep 1:8. 3:10. **the earth**. Ps 24:1. 50:10-12. 65:11. Ge 1:11, 12, 24, 25. 1 T *6:17.

25. **this great**. Ps 95:4, 5. Ge 1:20-22, 28. Dt 33:14-16, 19. **beasts**. Ge 3:1. Ac 28:5.

26. **There go**. Ps *107:23. Ge 49:13. **leviathan**. Ps 74:14. Jb 3:8mg. 41:1, etc. Is 27:1. **made**. Heb. formed. Ps 74:17. 94:9, 20. 95:5. Ge 2:7, 8. 19. **to play**. Jb 41:5, 29.

27. **wait**. Ps 36:6. 136:25. *145:15, 16. *147:9. Jb 38:41. Lk 12:24-28. **meat in**. Jb 36:31. Mt +√24:45. Lk +*12:42.

28. **gather**. Ex 16:4, 18, 22. Nu 11:8. **openest**. Ps 38:13. 39:9. 49:4. 51:15. ƒ22A14.8I. Anthropomorphism B880. To "open the hand" is to bestow or give bountifully. For another instance of this figure see Ps 145:16. **thine hand**. Ps +*37:24. Ru ◐+*1:13. ƒ22A14.4. Anthropomorphism B878. A *hand* is attributed to God, indicative of His providence. **filled**. ver. 13. **with good**. Ps +*145:9. 2 K ◐+*6:33. Je +*29:11. Ja +*1:17.

29. **hidest**. Ps 30:7. 31:20. 44:24. 64:2. 69:17. Jb 13:24. 34:29. Ro *8:20-22. **are troubled**. Ps 6:10. 48:5.

83:17. 90:7. **thou takest**. Ps +*146:4. Jb 34:14, 15. Ec *12:7. Ac 17:25, 28. **breath**. Heb. *ruach*, Ge +6:17. Jb 12:10. 27:3. 33:4. *34:14. +*146:4. Ec *8:8. *12:7. Is 2:22. *42:5. Ezk 37:9mg. Ac 17:25. **die**. Ge 6:17. 7:21. +*25:8n. 35:29. +*49:33. **return**. ver. 9. Ps 6:10. 7:12. 90:3. Ge +*3:19. **dust**. Ps 7:5. 18:42. *22:15. *30:9. Ec √3:20.

30. **sendest**. Ps 33:6. Jb 26:13. 33:4. Is *32:14, 15. Ezk 37:9. Jn ●7:39. Ep 2:1, 4, 5. T *3:5. **spirit**. Heb. *ruach*, Nu +16:22. **renewest**. 2 K 2:11. 6:17. Is 11:6-9. *65:17, 25. *66:22. Ho 2:18. Mk 11:2. Ro *8:21. Re 21:5. **the face**. Ge 1:2.

31. **The glory**. Ps 102:16. Ro 11:36. Ga 1:5. Ep 3:21. 2 T 4:18. He 13:21. 1 P 5:11. 2 P 3:18. Re 5:12, 13. **endure**. Heb. be. Ps 72:17mg. **for ever**. Heb. *olam*, Ex +*12:24. **rejoice**. T#223. Ge 1:31. Ex 31:17. Is *62:5. 65:18, 19. Je 9:24. 32:41. Ezk 5:13. Zp 3:17. Lk 15:5, 6, 22-24. √22B. Anthropomorphism B882. Rejoicing is attributed to God. For other instances of this figure see Dt 28:63. 30:9. Is 62:5. Je 32:41. Zp 3:17.

32. **looketh**. Ps 77:16. 97:4, 5. 114:7. Is 64:2. Je 4:23-26. 5:22. Am 8:8. Na 1:5, 6. Hab 3:5, 6, 10. Re 20:11. **he toucheth**. Ps 50:3. 144:5. Ex *19:18. Is 64:1, 2. Re 19:3. √22C16. Anthropomorphism B888. Human actions are attributed to God: tasting and touching. For other instances of this figure see Ps 144:5. Je 1:9. Ho 9:4.

33. **I will sing**. Ps 63:4. 145:1, 2. *146:2.

34. **meditation**. Ps *1:2. +*40:17. 63:5, 6. 77:12. 119:15, 16, 97, 103, 111, 127, 128, 167. *139:17, 18. Pr 24:14. **I will be**. Ps 32:11. Hab √3:17, 18. Lk 1:47. Ph *4:4.

35. **sinners**. Ps *1:4. *37:38. 59:13. 68:1, 2. 73:27. +*101:8. Jg 5:31. Pr *2:22. Ml +*4:1, 3. Re *19:1, 2. **the wicked**. Ps *37:9, 10. **Bless**. ver. 1. Ps 89:52. 103:1, 2, 22. Ro *9:5. **soul**. Heb. *nephesh*, Ge +34:3.

PSALM 105

An exhortation to praise God, to make known his works, to glory in him, and to seek his favor, 1-7. The story of God's providence over Abraham, 8-15; over Joseph, 16-22; over Jacob in Egypt, 23-25; over Moses delivering the Israelites, 26-36; over the Israelites brought out of Egypt, fed in the wilderness, and planted in Canaan, 37-45.

(*Title.*) A.M. 2962. B.C. 1042. It appears from 1 Ch 16, where the former part of this psalm as far as the 16th verse, is found with little variation, that David composed it at the removal of the ark to Mount Zion, and he himself probably enlarged it afterwards with the glorious detail of God's merciful dealings with Abraham and his posterity till their settlement in the land of promise. The *Hallelujah* which terminates the preceding psalm, is made the title of this by the Septuagint, Vulgate, Arabic, and Ethiopic; and the Syriac considers it a paraphrase on the words, "Fear not, Jacob, to go down into Egypt;" "and teaches us spiritually not to fear when we are obliged to contend with devils; for God is our shield, and will fight for us."

1. **Give**. Ps 136:1-3. 1 Ch ‖16:7-22. 25:3. 29:13, 20. **call**. Is 12:4. Jl 2:32. Ac 9:14. Ro √10:13. 1 C 1:2. **make known**. Ps 89:1. 96:3. *145:4-6, 11, 12. Nu 23:23. Is 12:4. 51:10. Da 3:29. 4:1-3. 6:26, 27.

2. **Sing unto**. Ps 47:6, 7. 96:1, 2. 98:1, 5. Jg 5:3. Is 12:5, 6. 42:10-12. Ep *5:19. Re 15:3, 4. **talk ye**. Ps 77:12. 78:4-6. *119:27. Ex 13:8, 9, 14. Dt 6:6-9. Lk 24:14, etc.

3. **Glory**. Ps 34:2. Is 45:25. Je 9:23, 24. 1 C 1:29, 31. Ga 6:14. **let the heart**. Ps +√9:10. Pr 8:17. Is 45:19. √55:6, 7. La 3:25. Lk √11:9, 10.

4. **Seek**. Am *5:4-6. Zp +*2:2, 3. **his strength**. Ps 78:61. 132:8. 2 Ch 6:41. **seek his face**. √22A4, Ge +19:13. Ps *27:8. 63:1.

5. **Remember**. Ps 77:11. 103:2. Dt *7:18, 19. 8:2. 32:7. Is 43:18, 19. Lk 22:19. 1 C 11:24-26. **the judgments**. Ps 119:13. Re 16:7. 19:2.

6. **ye seed**. Ex 3:6. Is *41:8, 14. 44:1, 2. Ro 9:4, etc. **his chosen**. Dt 7:6-8. Jn *15:16. 1 P 2:9.

7. **the Lord**. Ps 95:7. 100:3. Ge 17:7. Ex 20:2. Dt 26:17, 18. 29:10-15. Jsh 24:15-24. **judgments**. Ps 48:10, 11. Is √26:9. Re 15:4.

8. **He hath remembered**. √22C3, Ge +8:1. ver. 42. Ps *111:4, 5, 9. 1 Ch 16:15. Ne *1:5. Da 9:4. Lk *1:72-74. **for ever**. Heb. *olam*, Ex +*12:24. Ge +9:16. **a thousand**. Dt 7:9.

9. **covenant**. Ge 17:2. *22:16, 17. 26:3. 28:13. 35:11. Ne 9:8. Ac 7:8. He *6:17.

10. **an everlasting**. Ge +9:16. 17:+*7, 8. 2 S 23:5. He 13:20.

11. **Unto thee**. Ge 12:7. *13:15. *15:18. 26:3, 4. 28:13. **lot**. Heb. cord. √121B, Jsh +17:14. A "line" (or cord) is used for the territory divided up or marked out by it. Ps 16:5, +6. 18:4, 5mg. 78:55. Jsh 17:5, 14.

12. **a few**. Ge 34:30. Dt *7:7. 26:5. Is 51:2. Ezk 33:24, etc. **and strangers**. Ge 17:8. 23:4. Ac 7:5. He *11:9, 12.

13. **went from**. Ps 12:8. 39:6. Ge 13:17. **one nation to another**. Ge 12:10. 15:13-16. 20:1. 46:3, 6. Nu 32:13. **from one kingdom**. 1 Ch 16:20.

14. **He suffered**. Ge *12:14-17. *20:1-7. 26:14, etc. 31:24-29. *35:5. Ex 7:16, 17.

15. **Touch not**. √108B, +26:11. Ge +26:29. Zc *2:8. **mine anointed**. 1 K 19:16. 1 J *2:27. **and do**. Ge *20:7. 27:39, 40. 48:19, 20. 49:8, etc.

16. **Moreover**. Ge 41:25-32, *54. 42:5, 6. 2 K 8:1. Am +*3:6. 7:1-4. *8:11, 12. Hg 1:10, 11. 2:17. Mt 8:8, 9. Re 6:8. **famine**. Ru 1:1. Lk 15:14. **brake**. Ps 104:15. Ge 47:13, 19. Le 26:26. Is 3:1. Ezk 4:16. Ac 7:11.

17. **He sent**. Ge *45:5, 7, 8. √50:20. **Joseph**. Ge *37:27, 28, 36. 39:1. 45:4. Ac 7:9. **was sold**. Ge 39:1. Is=49:7. Ph=2:7.

18. **Whose**. √142, Ge +20:16. √106, Ge +31:7. Ge *39:20. 40:15. 41:12. Ps=22:16. Mt 27:2. Ac 16:24. **he was laid in iron**. Heb. his soul came into iron. Heb. *nephesh*, Ge +27:31. Ps 107:10. **iron**. √121D6, 2 K +6:5.

19. **his word**. Ps 44:4. Ge *41:11-16, 25, 39, 40. Pr 21:1. Da 2:30. Ac 7:10. **tried him**. 1 P 1:6, 7. 4:19.

20. **The king**. Ge 41:14. **loosed**. Ac=2:24.

21. **made**. Ge 41:40-44, 55. 45:8, 26. **substance**. Heb. possession. Ps 104:24. Ge 31:18.

22. **To bind**. Ge *41:44. Nu 30:2. Jg 15:10, 12, 13. **princes**. Ps 45:16. 68:27. 82:7. 119:23. **pleasure**. Heb. *nephesh*, Ex +15:9. **teach**. Ge 41:33, 38, 39. Is 19:11, 12. **senators**. or, elders. Ps 107:32. 119:100. 148:12. **wisdom**. Ps 119:98. Jb 35:11.

23. **Israel**. Ge 45:9-11. *46:2-7. Jsh 24:4. Ac 7:11-

15. **Jacob.** Ge 47:6-9, 28. **the land.** ver. 27. Ps 78:51. 106:22. Ge *10:6.

24. **And he.** Ge 13:16. 46:3. Ex *1:7. Dt 26:5. Ac 7:17, 18. He 11:12. **made.** Ge 26:16. Ex 1:8, 9. 12:37.

25. **He turned.** Ge 15:13. Ex *1:8-10. 9:16. 10:1. Dt +*2:30. Ro *9:17-19. **to hate.** Ex 1:11-14, 16. 2:23. Ac 7:19.

26. **sent.** Ps 77:20. Ex *3:10. 4:12-14. 6:11, 26, 27. Jsh 24:5. Mi 6:4. Ac 7:34, 35. **his servant.** Mt =12:18. **Aaron.** Ex *4:14, 16. 7:1, 12. 28:1, 2, 12, 29-38. 29:5, etc. Le 8:7, etc. Nu 16:5-11, 40, 47, 48. 17:5. 1 S 12:6.

27. **They.** Ps *78:43-51. 135:8, 9. Ex ch. 7-11. Dt 4:34. Ne 9:10, 11. Is 63:11, 12. Je 32:20, 21. **his signs.** Heb. words of his signs. ∫144A8, Ps +35:20. **wonders.** ver. 23. Ps 106:22.

28. **sent.** Ex *10:21-23. Jl 2:2, 31. Lk 23:44, 45. 2 P 2:4, 17. **rebelled.** Ps 99:7. Ezk 2:4-8.

29. **turned.** Ps 78:44. Ex *7:20, 21. Is 50:2. Ezk 29:4, 5. Re 16:3.

30. **brought.** Ps 78:45. Ex *8:3-14. Re 16:13, 14.

31. **there.** Ps 78:45. Ex *8:21-24. Is 7:18. **and lice.** Ex 8:16-18.

32. **He gave them hail for rain.** Heb. their rain hail. Ps 78:47, 48. Ex *9:18-28. Re 8:7. 11:19. 16:21.

33. **He smote.** Re 9:4.

34. **the locusts.** Ps 78:46. Ex *10:12-15. Jl 1:4-7. 2:25. Re 9:3-10.

35. **eat up.** Ps 18:8. 21:9. 22:26. Ex 10:15. **the herbs.** Ps 72:16. 92:7. 102:4, 11. **the fruit.** Ps 1:3. 21:10. 58:11mg. 72:16.

36. **He smote.** Ps 78:51. 135:8. 136:10. Ex 4:23. 11:4, 5. 12:12, *29, 30. He 11:28. **chief.** Ge 49:3.

37. **brought.** Ge 15:14. Ex 3:22. *12:35, 36. Ac 13:17. **and there.** Considering the immense number of men, women, children, and cattle, it must certainly have appeared extraordinary that there was none among them weak or feeble, none unable to perform the journey. The order was that "not a hoof should be left behind;" and he who commanded gave strength to obey. 2 Ch 28:15. Jb 4:4. Is 5:27.

38. **Egypt.** ∫121J14, Ge +47:15. **glad.** Ex 10:7. *12:33. **for.** Ge 35:5. Jsh 2:9.

39. **spread.** Ps 78:14. Ex *13:21, 22. 14:24. Nu 9:15-22. Ne 9:12, 19. Is 4:5. 1 C 10:1, 2.

40. **The people.** ∫63A1, Ge +14:20. **asked.** Ps 78:18, 26-28. Ex *16:12, 13. Nu 11:4-6, 31-33. **satisfied.** Ex 16:14-35. Nu 11:7-9. Dt 8:3. Jsh 5:12. Ne *9:20. **bread.** Ps 78:23-25. Jn 6:=31-33, 48-58.

41. **opened.** Ps 78:15, 16, 20. 114:8. Ex *17:6. Nu *20:11. Ne 9:15. Is 48:21. 1 C *10:4.

42. **For he.** See on ver. 8-11. Ge 12:7. 13:14-17. *15:14. Ex 2:24. Lk *1:54, 55, 72, 73. **remembered.** ∫22C3, Ge +8:1. Ml +*3:6. **Abraham.** Ex 32:13. Dt *9:5, 27. Mi *7:20.

43. **And he.** Ps 78:52, 53. *106:8-12. Ex 15:13. Dt 4:37, 38. Is 63:11-14. Ac 7:36. 13:17. **with joy.** Is 35:10. *51:10, 11. 55:12. Je 31:11, 12. **gladness.** Heb. singing. Ps 106:12. Ex 15:1, etc.

44. **gave.** Ps 44:2, 3. 78:55. 80:8. 135:10-12. 136:21, 22. Jsh 11:23. *21:43. 23:4. *24:8, 13. Ne 9:22-25. **inherited.** Dt 6:10, 11. Jsh 5:11. 13:7, etc. **the labor.** ∫121C1H, Dt +28:33. That is, "the produce of their labor;" the cities and houses they had built, the vineyards they had planted, etc.

45. **That.** Dt 4:40. 5:33. 6:1, 2, *21-25. Ezk 36:24-

28. Jn *15:12, 14. Ep √2:8-10. T *2:14. 1 J √2:3. *5:3. **Praise ye the Lord.** Heb. Hallelujah. Ps 106:1. 150:1mg. Re 19:3, 4.

PSALM 106

The psalmist praises God, admires the happiness of his people, and prays to partake of it, 1-5. He recapitulates Israel's provocations, from their bondage in Egypt to the time when they were settled in Canaan and imitated the idolatries of the Canaanites, 6-46. He concludes with prayer and praise, 47, 48.

(*Title.*) As part of the preceding psalm is found in 1 Ch 16, so the first and two last verses of this are found in the same place; and it is highly probable that they were composed upon the same occasion as the former, to which it seems to be a continuation; for as *that* celebrates the mercies of God to Israel, so *this* confesses and deplores the rebellions of Israel against Jehovah.

1. **Praise ye the Lord.** Heb. Hallelujah. Ps 105:45. **O give.** Ps 100:4, 5. 107:1. 118:1. 136:1. 1 Ch 16:34. Ezr 3:11. Je 33:11. 1 Th 5:18. **is good.** Ps 100:5. 119:68. √145:9. Mt 19:17. Lk *6:35. **his mercy.** Ps 103:17. Ro 5:20, 21.

2. **Who.** ∫85C, Ge +18:14. **utter.** Ps *40:5. 139:17, 18. 145:3-12. Jb 5:9. 26:14. Ro *11:33. Ep 1:19. 3:18-21. **all his praise.** Ne *9:5.

3. **Blessed.** ∫43, Dt +28:3. Ps *1:1-3. *84:11, 12. *119:1-3. Mk 3:35. Lk *6:47-49. +*11:28. Jn +√13:17. +*14:21. *15:14. Ja 1:25. Re 7:15. 22:14. **keep.** Ps *119:106, 112. Is 56:1, 2. Je 22:15, 16. Lk *11:42. Jn 14:21-23. **doeth.** Ps *15:2. 119:44. Is 64:5. Ezk *18:21, 22. Lk 1:74, 75. Ac *24:16. Ro 2:7. Ga √6:9. Ja *1:25. 2:17, 23. Re 2:10. *22:14. **at all times.** Ps 119:20, 112. Dt 5:29. *11:1.

4. **Remember.** Ps *25:7. *119:132. Ne +*5:19. 13:14, 22, 31. Lk *23:42. **the favor.** Ps 5:12. **visit.** Ps +*8:4. 65:9. *80:14. Ex +*3:16. Jb *10:12. Lk 1:68, 69. Ac 15:14. **thy salvation.** Ps 35:3. 119:123. Is 12:2. La 3:26. Mt 1:21. Ro *5:9. Ep √2:8. 2 C +*6:2. He +*9:28n.

5. **may see.** Ps 105:6, 43. Dt *7:6. Jn *15:16. Ac 9:15. Ep *1:4. 2 Th *2:13. Ja +*2:5. 1 P 2:9. Re 17:14. **thy chosen.** Ps 33:12. 65:4. Dt +10:15. Hg 2:23. **rejoice.** Ps +*14:7. *16:11. 48:11. +*118:24. Is 12:6. +*35:10. 66:10. Jl 2:23. Zp *3:14. Zc 9:9. Jn *16:22. Ph 3:3. **glory.** Is *45:25. Ep *1:17, 18. Col +*3:4. **thine inheritance.** Ps +*94:14. Is *19:25. Col +*3:24.

6. **have sinned.** Ps 78:8. Le *26:40, 42. Nu 32:14. 1 K 8:47. Ezr 9:6, 7. Ne 9:16, 32-34. Da *9:5-8. Mt 23:32. Ac 7:51, 52. **fathers.** ∫171G, Ge +13:8.

7. **Our.** Dt *29:2-4. 32:28, 29. Pr 1:22. Is 44:18. Mk 4:12. 8:17-21. 2 Th 2:10-12. **they.** Ps 78:42. 105:5. Dt 15:15. Ep 2:11. **multitude.** ver. 45. Ps 5:7. 51:1. Is 63:7. La 3:32. **but.** Ex *14:11, 12.

8. **Nevertheless.** ∫127, Re +2:6. **he saved.** Ps 143:11. Nu 14:13-16. Dt *32:26, 27. Jsh 7:9. Je 14:7, 21. Ezk 20:9, *14, 22, 44. Da 9:17-19. **that he.** Ps 111:6. Ex *9:16. 15:6. Ro 9:17.

9. **He rebuked.** In the descriptions of the psalmist, everything has life. The sea is an animated being, behaves itself proudly, is rebuked, and retires in confusion. Ps 18:15. 66:6. 78:13, 52, 53. 114:3-7. 136:13-16. Ex *14:21, 22, 27-29. Ne 9:11. Is 11:14-16. Na *1:4. Mt 8:26. **so he.** Ps 77:19, 20. Is 63:11-14.

10. **And he.** Ex 14:30. 15:9, 10. Dt 11:4. Ne 9:11. **redeemed.** Ps 107:2. 136:24. Ex 15:13. Jb 6:22, 23. Mi 6:4.

11. **the waters.** Ps 78:53. Ex 14:13, 27, 28. 15:5, 10, 19.

12. **believed.** Ex *14:31. *15:1, etc. 2 Ch *20:20. Lk +√8:13. Jn √8:30, 31. **they sang.** Ps +√9:10n. Ho +*2:15.

13. **They soon forgat.** Heb. They made haste, they forgat. Three days afterwards, at the waters of Marah. T#411. Ps 78:11. Ex 15:17, *24. 16:2. 17:2, 7. Ezk *33:31. **waited not.** 1 Ch 10:14. Pr 1:25, 30. Is 48:17, 18. Je *23:22. Ml 2:6.

14. **But.** Ps 78:18, 30. Nu *11:4, 33, 34. Dt 9:22. 1 C 10:6. **lusted exceedingly.** Heb. lusted a lust. √147D. Polyptoton, verb with cognate noun, Ge +1:29. 1 C 10:6. **tempted.** Ps 78:18-20, 40, 41. 95:8, 9. Ex 17:2. Nu 14:22. 1 C 10:9. He 3:8-10. **God.** Heb. *El*, Ex +15:2.

15. **he gave.** Ps 78:29-31. *84:11. Nu *11:31-34. 1 S 8:22. 12:13. Is 10:16. 24:16. 48:22. Ho 4:17. Ja 4:3. **but sent.** T#1791. Ge 19:20. Ex 32:31-35. Nu 11:18-20, 21-23, 30-33. *14:20-23. 16:44-49. 20:7-12. 21:6-9. Dt 3:23-27. Jg 20:23-25. 1 S 8:4-7. 2 S 24:10-15. 1 K 21:27-29. 2 K 22:18-20. 2 Ch 12:5-9. Is +*66:4. Je +*6:19. 15:1-4. 21:1-6. 37:3-10, 16, 17. Ezk 14:12-19. They despised the manna, calling it light or innutritive food. God gave them flesh as they desired, but no blessing accompanied it; and in consequence, they did not fatten but grew lean upon it; and many, surfeited by excess, died of disease. Instead of *razon*, "leanness," however, Bp. Lowth supposes we should read *zeraon*, "nausea or loathing," which appears to be supported by several ancient versions, and by Nu 11:20, where this portion of the history of the Israelites is recorded and where the word *zara* is used, and rendered, "it be loathsome." **soul.** Heb. *nephesh*, Ge +12:13.

16. **envied.** Nu *16:1, 3, etc. Mk=15:10. **the saint.** Ex 28:36. Le 21:6-8, 10-12. Nu 16:7.

17. **The earth opened.** Nu *16:29-33. 26:10. Dt 11:6.

18. **a fire.** Nu *16:35-40, 46. He 12:29.

19. **made a calf.** Ex 32:4-8, 35. Dt 9:12-16, 21. Ne 9:18. 1 C 10:7.

20. **Thus.** Ps 89:17. Je *2:11. Ro *1:22, 23. **their glory.** √182, Ge +18:22. That is, their God, who ought to have been the peculiar object of their glory. or, honor. √121E1, Ge +25:23. Ps 3:3. +*8:5. +*16:9. 26:8. 30:12mg,n. **into.** Ex 20:4, 5. Is 40:18-25.

21. **forgat.** ver. 13. Ps 78:11, 12, 42-51. Dt 32:17, 18. Je *2:32. **God.** Heb. *El*, Ex +15:2. Is 12:2. 45:21. 63:8. Ho 1:7. Lk 1:47. T 1:3. 2:10. *3:4-6. **which.** Ps 74:13, 14. 135:9. Dt 4:34. 6:22. 7:18, 19. Ne 9:10, 11.

22. **Wondrous.** The plagues he inflicted on the Egyptians. Egypt is called the *land of Ham*, or rather, *Cham*, because it was peopled by Mizraim, the son of Ham, and grandson of Noah. Plutarch (*De Iside and Osiride*) informs us that the Egyptians called their country *Chemia*, and the Copts give it the name of *Chemi* to the present day. Ps 78:51. 105:23, 27-36. **terrible.** Ex 14:25-28. 15:10.

23. **he said.** Ex *32:10, 11, 32. Dt *9:13, 14, 19, 25. 10:10. Ezk 20:13, 14. **his chosen.** Ps 105:6, 26. Nu 16:5. Is=42:1. Zc=13:7. Mt 12:18. Jn *15:16, 19.

stood. Ex 32:14. Je 5:1. Ezk 13:5. 22:30. Ja *5:16. **lest.** √22D1, Ge +32:28.

24. **they despised.** Ge 25:34. Nu 13:32. 14:4, 31. Mt 22:5. He 12:16. **the pleasant land.** Heb. a land of desire. Dt *8:7-9. 11:11, 12. Je +3:19mg. Ezk 20:6. **they believed not.** Nu 14:11. Dt 1:32. He *3:12-14, 18, 19. 4:2, 6, 14. Ju 5.

25. **murmured.** Ps 144:14. Nu +*11:1. 14:1-4, 27-29. Dt 1:26, 27. **hearkened.** Ps 95:7-9. Nu 14:22. He 3:7, 8, 15.

26. **Therefore.** Ps 95:11. Nu 14:28-35. Dt 1:34, 35. He *3:11, 18. **lifted.** √121S3, Ge +14:22. 14:22, 23. Ex 6:8. Dt 32:40-42. Ezk *20:15. Re 10:5, 6.

27. **overthrow.** Heb. make them fall. **to scatter.** Ps *44:11. Le *26:33. Dt 4:26, 27. 28:37, 64, 65. 32:26, 27. Ezk 20:23.

28. **joined.** Nu *25:1-3, 5. *31:16. Dt 4:3. 32:17. Jsh 22:17. Ho 9:10. Re *2:14. **of the dead.** The word *maithim* signifies dead men, for the idols of the heathen were generally men—warriors, kings, or lawgivers—who had been deified after their death, though many of them had been execrated during their life. Ps 115:4-8. Je 10:8-10. 1 C 10:19, 20.

29. **with their.** ver. 39. Ps 99:8. Dt 32:16-21. Ec 7:29. Ro 1:21-24. **the plague.** Nu 25:9. 1 C 10:8.

30. **Then stood.** Nu *25:6-8, 14, 15. Dt 13:9-11, 15-17. Jsh 7:12. 1 K 18:40, 41. Jon 1:12-15.

31. **was counted.** Nu 25:11-13. Dt 24:13. Mk 14:3-9. **generations.** Ge +9:12. **for evermore.** Heb. *olam*, Ps +*18:50.

32. **angered.** Ps 78:40. 81:7. Nu *20:2-6, 13. **so that.** Nu *20:12, 23, 24. 27:13, 14. Dt 1:37. *3:26. 4:21. **for their sakes.** Is=53:5.

33. **Because.** Nu *20:10, 11. **provoked.** ver. 7, 43. 78:17, 40. Jb 17:2. Is 3:8. Ep 4:26. Ja 1:20. **spirit.** Heb. *ruach*. √171Q24. Synecdoche of the Part: here, "spirit" is put by synecdoche for the whole person. ✚S#7307h. Ps 77:3, 6. Ezk 21:7. Da 2:1, 3. Ml 2:15, 16. For the other uses of *ruach*, see Ge 6:3n. **he spake.** Ps *39:1. *141:3. Ge *30:1. *35:16-18. Jb *2:10. *38:2. 40:4, 5. *42:7, 8. Mt +*12:36. Ja *3:2. As Matthew Poole notes, the psalmist here does not mention what Moses spake because that was fully known from the history, and because he would throw a veil over Moses's infirmity, imply rather than express his fault. Similar reticence is observed in Chronicles, where David's sin regarding Bathsheba is omitted from the account. This should inform us as to the need for extreme caution in any application we might make of such a passage as Ja 5:16, "confess your faults one to another," particularly since the Apostle Paul expressly forbids discussion of what has been done in darkness (Ep 5:11, 12).

34. **did not.** Jsh 15:63. 16:10. 17:12-16. 23:12, 13. Jg *1:19, 21, 27-35. Mt 17:19-21. **concerning.** Nu 33:52, 55, 56. Dt *7:2, 16, 23, 24. 20:16, 17. 1 S 15:3, 22, 23.

35. **But.** Jsh 15:63. Jg 1:27-36. *2:2, 3. **learned.** Is 2:6. Je √10:2. 1 C *5:6. *15:33.

36. **And.** Ps 78:58. Ex 34:15, 16. Jg *2:12, 13, 17, 19. *3:5-7. 10:6. 2 K 17:8-11, 16, 17. 2 Ch 33:2-9. Ezk 16:15, etc. 20:28-32. **which.** Ex 23:33. Dt 7:16. Jsh 23:13. Jg 2:3, 14, 15.

37. **they sacrificed.** However unnatural and horrid human sacrifices may appear, it is certain that they did not only exist but almost universally prevailed in

the heathen world, especially among the Canaanites and Phoenicians. Dt 12:30, 31. 18:10. 2 K *16:3. 17:17. 21:6. Is *57:5. Je 7:31. 32:35. Ezk *16:17, 20, 21. *20:26. 23:37, 47. **devils**. Le 17:7. Dt *32:17. 2 Ch 11:15. 1 C *10:20. Re *9:20.

38. **shed**. Dt 21:9. 2 K 21:16. 24:4. Je 2:34. **the land**. Nu *35:33. Is 1:15. 26:21. Ezk 7:23. 22:3.

39. **defiled**. Is 24:5, 6. 59:3. Ezk 20:18, 30, 31, 43. **went**. Ex 34:+15, 16. Le *17:7. 20:5, 6. Nu *15:39. Je 3:1, 2, 6-9. Ezk 16:15, etc. 23:3, etc. Ho 9:1. Re 17:1-6. **their own**. ver. 29. Is 1:4.

40. **the wrath**. Ps 78:59-62. Jg *2:14, 20. 3:8. Ne 9:27, etc. **insomuch**. Le 20:23. Dt *32:19. Zc 11:8. **his own**. Ps 74:1, 2. Dt 9:29. La 2:7.

41. **he gave**. Dt 32:30. Jg 2:14. 3:8, 12. 4:1, 2. 6:1-6. 10:7, etc. Ne *9:27, etc. **and they**. Dt 28:25, 29, 33, 48.

42. **enemies**. ver. 10. Ps 3:7. 6:10. 7:5. 8:2. 9:3. **oppressed**. Ex 22:21. 23:9. Nu 22:25. Jg 4:3. 10:12. **into subjection**. or, humbled. Le 26:41. Dt 28:25. Jg 3:30.

43. **Many**. Jg *2:16-18. 1 S 12:9-11. Ne 9:27, 28. **with their**. ver. 29. Ps *1:1. 81:12. **brought low**. or, impoverished, or weakened. Jg 5:8. 6:5, 6. 1 S 13:19-22.

44. **Nevertheless**. ʃ127, Re +2:6. **he regarded**. Jg 2:18. 3:9. 4:3. 6:6-10. 10:10-16. 1 S 7:8-12. 2 K 14:26, 27. 2 Ch 33:12. Ne *9:27-31.

45. **And he**. Ps 105:8. Le 26:40-42. 2 K *13:22, 23. Lk 1:71, 72. **remembered**. ʃ22C3, Ge +8:1. **repented**. ʃ22B, Ps 90:13. 135:14. Ge +6:6. Ex 32:14. Dt 32:36. Jg *2:18. 2 S 24:16. Ho 11:8. Am 7:3, 6. **the multitude**. Ps *51:1. 69:16. Is *63:7. La *3:32.

46. **He made**. 1 K 8:50. Ezr *9:9. Je 15:11. *42:12. Da 1:9.

47. **Save us**. Ps 14:7. 126:1-4. 1 Ch 16:35, 36. **gather**. Je *32:37-41. Ezk 36:24-28. 37:21-28. 39:25-29. **to give thanks**. Ps 107:1-3. Re 7:10-12. **triumph**. Ps 92:4. 2 C *2:14.

48. **Blessed**. Ps *41:13. 72:18, 19. 89:52. 1 Ch 29:10. 1 C 14:16. **from everlasting to**. Heb. olam doubled, Ps +41:13. **Praise ye the Lord**. Heb. Hallelujah. ver. 1. Ps 105:45mg.

PSALM 107

Exhortations to praise God for redemption from captivity and guidance in perilous journeys to a safe habitation, 1-9; for deliverance from prison, 10-16; for recovery from sickness, 17-22; for preservation when in imminent danger of shipwreck, 23-32; and for the care of his providence over the affairs of men, 33-43.

(*Title.*) A.M. 3468. B.C. 536. The author of this psalm is unknown, but it was evidently written to commemorate the return of the Jews from the Babylonian captivity. It may easily be perceived that it must have been sung in alternate parts, having a double burden or two *intercalary* verses often recurring. Bp. Lowth considers it as written "after the method of the ancient pastorals, where, he be the subject of their verse what it will, each swain endeavors to excel the other; and one may perceive their thoughts and expressions gradually to rise upon each other." "No doubt," he adds, "the composition of this psalm is admirable throughout, and the descriptive part of it adds at least its share of beauty to the whole: but what is most to be admired

is its conciseness, and withal the expressiveness of the diction, which strikes the imagination with inimitable elegance. The weary and bewildered traveller—the miserable captive in the dungeon—the sick and dying man—the seaman foundering in a storm—are described in so affecting a manner, that they far exceed any thing of the kind, though never so much labored."

1. **Give**. Ps 106:1. 118:1. 136:1, etc. 1 Ch 16:34, 41. 2 Ch 5:13. 7:3, 6. 20:21. **good**. Ps 106:1. *119:68. Mt *19:17. **for his mercy**. Ps 103:17. Lk 1:50. **for ever**. Heb. olam, Ex +*12:24.

2. **Let the redeemed**. Ps *31:5. 130:8. Ex 15:16. Dt *15:15. Is 35:9. 43:1. *44:22, 23. Lk *1:68. *24:21. Ga *3:13. T *2:14. 1 P *1:18, 19. **say so**. Ps 32:3. 39:3. 126:2. Ex 12:14. Mk +*5:19. *8:38. Ro ✓10:9, 10. **from**. Ps *106:10. Dt *7:8. Je *15:21. 31:11. Mi *4:10. Lk *1:74. **hand**. ʃ144A5, Ge +9:5.

3. **gathered**. Ps *106:47. Is 11:11-16. *43:5, 6. 49:12. Je *29:14. *31:8, 10. Ezk 36:24. 39:27, 28. Lk *13:29. Re 5:9. **south**. Heb. sea. ver. 23. Ps 8:8. 24:2. 106:7.

4. **wandered**. ver. 40. Ge 21:14-16. Nu 14:33. Dt 8:15. *32:10. Jb 12:24. Ezk 34:6, 12. He 11:38. Re 12:6. **solitary way**. Mk 1:35. **they found**. This is the first similitude, in which the Israelites in captivity are compared to travelers in a dreary, uninhabited, and barren desert, spent with hunger and thirst as well as by the fatigues of the journey. See ver. 10n, 17n, 23n.

5. **Hungry**. T#1254, 1566. Jg 15:18, 19. 1 S 30:11, 12. Is 44:12. Je 14:18. Lk 2:19. Mk 8:2, 3. **soul**. Heb. *nephesh*, Ge +34:3.

6. **trouble**. T#1418. ver. 13, 19, 28. Ps 9:13. *50:15. 88:3. 91:15. 107:17-19. Jg 10:9, 10. 2 Ch *15:4. Ne 9:32. Is *41:17, 18. Je 29:12-14. Ho *5:15. He 4:15, 16. **he delivered**. 2 C 1:8-10. 12:8-10. 2 T 3:11.

7. **he led**. Ps 77:20. 78:52. 136:16. Dt 32:11, 12. Ezr 8:21-23. Is 30:21. 35:8-10. *48:17. 49:8-11. 63:13, 14. Je 6:16. 31:9. 2 P 2:15, 21. **that they**. ver. 4, 36. Ne 11:3. Je 31:24, 38-46. 33:10-13. He 4:9. *11:9, 10, 16. *12:22, 23. Re 21:2-4, 10-27.

8. **Oh that men**. ver. 15, 21, 31. Ps *81:13-16. Dt *5:29. *32:39. Is *48:18. **praise**. Ps *34:3. 92:1, 2. 147:1. Is 63:7. **goodness**. Ps 106:1. **his wonderful**. Ps *40:5. *78:4. 111:4. Da 4:2, 3. 6:27.

9. **he satisfieth**. Ps *34:10. 36:8. 90:14. 132:15. *146:7. Is *55:1-3. Je *31:14, 25. Mt +*5:6. Lk *1:53. Re *7:16, 17. **soul**. Heb. *nephesh*, Ge +34:3. Pr 6:30. Is 5:14. 29:8. Re +*18:14. **and filleth**. Ps 81:10. Mt *5:6. *6:33. 1 P 2:2. **soul**. Heb. *nephesh*, Ge +34:3.

10. **Such**. Here begins the second comparison, in which the state of the captives in Babylon is illustrated by that of prisoners in a dreary dungeon. See ver. 4n. **as sit**. Jb 3:5. Is *9:2. Mt *4:16. *22:13. Lk 1:79. **bound**. Ps 105:18. Ex 2:23, 24. 2 Ch 33:11. Jb *36:8, 9. La 3:6, 7. Ro *6:20, 21. 2 P 2:19.

11. **Because**. Ps *68:6, 18. 106:43. Is *63:10, 11. La 3:39-42. 5:15-17. **God**. Heb. El, Ex +15:2. **contemned**. Ps *73:24. 113:7-9. 119:24. 2 Ch 25:15, 16. 33:10. Pr *1:25, 30, 31. Is 5:19. Je *23:22. 44:16. Lk *7:30. 16:14. Ac *20:27. Ro *1:28.

12. **he brought**. Ex 2:23. 5:18, 19. Jg 10:16-18. 16:21, 30. Ne 9:37. Is 51:19, 20, 23. 52:5. La 5:5, 6. Lk 15:14-17. **and there**. Ps 18:40, 41. 22:11. 142:4. 2 K 6:26, 27, 33. Jb 9:13. Is *63:5.

13. **they cried**. ver. 6, 19, 28. Ps 18:6. 116:3-6.

Ex 3:7, 8. Jg 4:3. 6:6-10. 10:10, etc. 2 Ch 33:12, 13, 18, 19. Je 31:18-20.

14. brought. ver. 10. Ps 68:6. Jb 3:5. 10:21, 22. 15:22, 30. 19:8. 33:30. 42:10-12. Is 42:16. 49:9. 60:1-3. Ep *5:8. He 2:15. 1 P 2:9. **brake.** Ps 102:20. 105:19, 20. 116:16. 146:7. Jb 36:8. Is 61:1. Je 52:31-34. Zc 9:11, 12. Lk 4:18. Ac 5:19, 25. 12:7-10. 16:26, etc.

15. Oh that. ver. 8, 21, 31. Ps 116:17-19.

16. For he. Jg 16:3. Is 45:1, 2. Mi 2:13. **bars of iron.** Ps 2:9. Jb 40:18. Is 45:2. **in sunder.** Ac 12:6, 7.

17. Fools. This is the third comparison; the captives being compared to persons in a dangerous malady as the consequence of their own sins. Ps 14:1. 92:6. Pr 1:22. 7:7, 22. 26:3. **because.** Ps 38:1-8. Nu 11:33, 34. 12:10-13. 21:5-9. Is 57:17, 18. Je 2:19. La 1:8. *3:39.

18. soul. Heb. *nephesh,* Nu +11:6. **abhorreth.** Jb *33:19-22. **meat.** ℐ17118. Synecdoche of the Species, meat put for all kinds of food. Jn 4:8, 32, 34. 6:27. 21:5. He 12:16. **and they.** Ps 9:13. 88:3. Is 38:10. **draw near.** Jb 33:22. Is *38:1. Ph 2:27. **the gates.** ℐ171S7B, Ps. 9:13. Ge +14:7. Jb +*38:17. **of death.** Pr +*7:27.

19. they cry. T#1238. ver. 6, 13, 18, 28. Ps 30:8-12. +*34:4-6. 78:34, 35. 116:4-8. Ge 48:14-16. Jg 16:28-30. 2 S *22:5-7. Is 57:17, 18. Je √33:3. Mt 27:46-50. Lk 23:33, 34, 39-42, 46. Ac 7:59, 60.

20. He sent. Ps 147:15, 19. 2 K *20:4, 5. Mt 8:8. **healed.** Ps 30:2, 3. 103:+*3, 4. 147:3. Nu 21:8, 9. Jb 33:23-26. Mt 8:8. **delivered.** Ps 49:15. 56:13. Jb *33:28-30.

21. Oh that. ver. 8, 15, 31. Ps 66:5. 2 Ch *32:25. Lk *17:17, 18.

22. sacrifice. Ps 50:14. 116:12, 17. Le *7:12. He *13:15. 1 P 2:5, 9. **declare.** Ps 9:11. 73:28. 105:1, 2. 118:17. Is 12:4. **rejoicing.** Heb. singing. Ps 17:1. +30:5mg. 42:4. 47:1.

23. They. This is the fourth comparison, their captivity was as dangerous and alarming as a dreadful tempest at sea, with a most natural and striking description of which we are here presented. **go down.** Ps 48:7. Ezk 27:26. Ac 27:9, etc. Re 18:17.

24. his wonders. Ps 95:5. 104:24-27. Jb 38:8-11. **deep.** Ge +1:2.

25. he commandeth. Ps 135:7. 148:8. Jon *1:4. **raiseth.** Heb. maketh to stand. **lifteth.** Ps 93:3, 4. Mt 8:24. Jn 6:18.

26. mount up. ℐ102, Ge +2:4. Dt 30:12. Ro ▶10:6. **their soul.** Heb. *nephesh,* Ge +34:3. **is melted.** Ps 22:14. 119:28. 2 S 17:10. Is 13:7. Na 2:10.

27. stagger. Jb 12:25. Is 19:14. 29:9, 10. **are at their wit's end.** Heb. all their wisdom is swallowed up. Jb 37:20. Is 19:3mg. 28:7. Ac 27:15-20.

28. they cry. T#1204. ver. 6, 13, 19. Jon 1:4-6, 13-15. Mt 8:23-26. 14:29-32. Mk 5:18. Ac 27:23-25, 33-37.

29. He maketh. Ps 65:7. *89:9. Jon 1:15. Mt *8:26. Mk 4:39-41. Lk 8:23-25.

30. he bringeth. Jn 6:21. Ac 27:44.

31. Oh that men. ver. 8, 15, 21. Ps 103:2. 105:1. Ho 2:8. Jon 1:16. 2:9. Mi 6:4, 5. Ro 1:20, 21. 2 T 3:2. He 13:15. **his wonderful.** Ps 71:17. 72:18, 19. 77:11, 14. 105:2. Re 15:3.

32. exalt. Ps 18:46. 46:10. 99:5, 9. Ex 15:2. Is 12:4. 25:1. **in the congregation.** Ps *22:22, 25. 40:9, 10. *66:16. *111:1. 119:46. Ac 4:8-12.

33. turneth. 1 K *17:1-7. Is 13:19-21. 19:5-10. 34:9, 10. 42:15. 44:27. 50:2. Ezk 30:12. Jl 1:20. Na 1:4. Zp

2:9, 13. **watersprings.** 1 K 18:5. Je 14:3. Am 4:7, 8.

34. A fruitful. Ge *13:10, 13. *19:25. Dt 29:23-28. Is 32:13-15. **barrenness.** Heb. saltness. Ge 14:3. Jb 39:6mg. Je 17:6. Ezk 47:11. **the wickedness.** Je 12:4.

35. turneth. Ps 114:8. Nu 21:16-18. 2 K 3:16-20. Is 35:6, 7. *41:17-19. 44:3-5. Ezk 47:6-12. **and.** ℐ148, Ge +8:22.

36. And. ℐ148, Ge +8:22. **there he.** Ps 146:7. Lk 1:53. **a city.** ver. 7. Ac 17:26.

37. And. ℐ148, Ge +8:22. **sow.** Is 37:30. Je 29:5. 31:5. Ezk 28:26. Am +*9:13-15. **which may.** Ps 65:9-13. Ge 26:12. Jl 1:10-12. Hg 1:5, 6, 10, 11. 2:16-19. Zc 8:12. Ac 14:17. 1 C 3:7. 2 C 9:10.

38. He blesseth. Ps 128:1-6. Ge 1:28. 9:1. 12:2. 17:16, 20. Ex *1:7. Dt 28:4, 11. 30:9. Je 30:19. Ezk 37:26. **suffereth.** Ps 144:13, 14. Ge 30:43. 31:9. Ex 9:3-7. 12:38. Dt 7:14. Pr 10:22. **not.** ℐ175B, Ge +21:16.

39. Again. The incidents detailed in these verses, which frequently occur and mark the superintendence of a benign providence and the hand of a just God, appear to be brought forward to illustrate the return of the Israelites from captivity and the punishment of their oppressors the Babylonians. Wherefore, at last, as in a common chorus, they conclude with exhorting each other to a serious consideration of these things, and to make a proper return to the Almighty. **they are.** Ps 30:6, 7. Ge 45:11. Ru 1:20, 21. 1 S *2:5-7. 2 K 4:8. 8:3. Jb 1:10-17. **oppression.** Ex 1:13, 14. 2:23, 24. Jg 6:3-6. 2 K *10:32. 13:7, 22. 14:26. 2 Ch 15:5, 6. Je 51:33, 34.

40. poureth. Jb *12:21, 24. Is 23:8, 9. **contempt.** Ps 78:66. Ex 8:3, 17, 24. Jsh 10:24-26. Jg 1:6, 7. 4:21. 1 S 5:9. 6:4. 1 K 21:19. 2 K 9:35-37. Da 4:33. 5:5, 6, 18-30. Ac 12:23. Re 19:18. **causeth.** ver. 4. Jb 12:24. Je 13:15-18. **wilderness.** *or,* void place. Ge 1:2. Dt 32:10.

41. setteth. Ps *113:7, 8. Ru 4:14-17. 1 S *2:8. Est 8:15-17. Jb 5:11. 8:7. 11:15-19. 42:10-12. Je 52:31-34. Ja 5:11. **from.** *or,* after. **maketh.** ℐ63E1, Le +4:2. Supply the ellipsis (relative: of cognate words) to read "and maketh like a flock the families (of the afflicted)." Ps 78:52. 128:6. Ge 33:5-7. 48:11. 1 S 2:21. Jb 21:11. 42:16. Pr 17:6. Is 49:20-22.

42. righteous. Ps 52:6. 58:10, 11. Jb 22:19. Is 66:10, 11, 14. **iniquity.** Ps 63:11. 112:10. Ex 11:7. Jb *5:15, 16. Pr 10:11. Ro 3:19. **shall stop.** ℐ96C2, Ge +45:9.

43. is wise. Ps 28:5. 64:9. Dt 32:29. Is 5:12. Je 9:12. Da 10:12. Ho *14:9. Lk 19:42. **observe.** Ps 47:7. **they shall understand.** Ps *25:14. 50:23. Je 9:24. Ep 3:18, 19.

PSALM 108

David earnestly praises God, 1-5. He fervently prays for help and expects great success according to the promises of God to him, 6-13.

(Title.) A.M. 2964. B.C. 1040. This psalm is composed of two psalms: ver. 1-5 being the same as Ps 57:7-11; and ver. 6-13 the same as Ps 60:5-12; it is probably to be referred to the same period as the latter. Ps 60, title.

1. my heart. Ps 57:7-11. **I will.** Ps 30:12. 34:1. 104:33. 138:1. 145:1, 2. 146:1, 2. Ex 15:1. **my glory.** Ps +*16:9. 30:12mg,n. 71:8, 15, 23, 24. *145:21.

2. Awake. Ps 33:2. 69:30. 81:2. 92:1-4. Jg 5:12. **I myself.** Ps 57:8. 103:22.

3. **praise**. Ps 22:22, 27. 96:10. 117:1, 2. 138:4, 5. Zp 3:14, 20.

4. **thy mercy**. Ps 36:5. *85:10, 11. 89:2, 5. 103:11. Is 55:9. Mi *7:18-20. Ep 2:4-7. **clouds**. *or*, skies. Ps 36:5. 68:34mg. 89:6, 37.

5. **Be thou**. Ps 8:1. 21:13. 57:5, 11. 148:13. 1 Ch 29:10-13. **thy glory**. Ps 72:19. Is 6:3. Mt 6:9, 10, 13.

6. **That thy**. Ps 60:5-12. Dt 33:12. 2 S 12:25. Mt 3:17. 17:5. Ro 1:7. Ep 1:6. Col 3:12. **save**. Ps 35:1-3. 54:1. 98:1, 2. 144:5-7. Ex 15:6. Is 51:2-11. **and answer me**. 1 K 18:24, 26, 29, 36, 37. 2 Ch 32:20-22. Is +*65:24. Je √33:3.

7. **spoken**. Ps 89:35, 36. Am 4:2. **I will rejoice**. Ps *16:9-11. 2 S 7:20, etc. 1 P 1:3, 8. 2 P 1:3, 4. **Shechem**. Jsh 17:7. 20:7. 24:1. **the valley**. Ge 33:17. Jg 8:5, 6.

8. **Gilead**. Jsh 13:8-11. 2 S 2:8, 9. 5:5. **Ephraim**. Dt 33:17. 1 S 28:2. **Judah**. Ps 60:7. 122:5. Ge +*49:10.

9. **Moab**. Ps 60:8-10. 2 S 8:1, 2. Jn 13:8, 14. **I cast**. Ru 4:7, 8. **over Philistia**. 2 S 21:15-22. Is 14:29-32.

10. **who will lead**. Ps 20:6-8. 60, title. Is 63:1-6. Je 49:7-16. Ob 3, 4.

11. **who hast**. Ps 44:9. 1 S ch. 29, etc. **go forth**. Nu 10:9. Dt 20:3, 4. 1 S 17:26, 36. 2 Ch 13:12. 14:11. 20:15.

12. **Give**. Ps 20:1, etc. **for vain**. Ps 146:3-5. Jb 9:13. 16:2. Is 2:22. 30:3-5. 31:3. Je 17:5-8. La 4:17.

13. **Through**. Ps 18:29-34. 118:6-13. 144:1. 2 Ch 20:12. Ro 8:37. 1 C 15:10. Ep 6:10-18. **valiantly**. Je 9:3. 1 T 6:12. **tread**. Ps 18:42. 60:12. Jg 15:8. Is 25:10. 63:3. Ro 16:20. 2 C *2:14.

PSALM 109

David, as the type of Christ, complains of the slanders, deceit, and malice of his enemies, 1-5. He predicts the doom of Judas by devoting one person in particular to destruction, 6-20. He complains of his sufferings, prays for relief, and determines to praise the Lord, 21-31.

(*Title.*) A.M. 2942. B.C. 1062. It is generally supposed that this psalm was composed by David while persecuted by Saul, who was rendered more implacable by the base and malicious calumnies of Doeg and others; though some are of opinion that it was written when David fled from Absalom, and that Ahithophel, rather than Doeg, is the typical person against whom it is principally directed.

1. **Hold**. Ps 28:1. 35:22, 23. 83:1. Is 42:14. **O God**. Ps 118:28. Ex 15:2. Dt 10:21. Je 17:14.

2. **the mouth**. Ps 31:13, 18. 64:3, 4. 140:3. 2 S 15:3-8. 17:1. Pr 15:28. Mt *26:59-62. **of the deceitful**. Heb. of deceit. Ps 5:6. 10:7. 17:1. 24:4. 52:4. **are opened**. Heb. have opened themselves. Ps 78:23. 105:41. **with**. Ps 120:3. Pr 6:17. 12:19. Je 9:3, 5. Ac 6:13.

3. **compassed**. Ps 17:11. 22:12. 32:7. 88:17. 2 S 16:7, 8. Ho 11:12. **fought**. Ps 35:7, 20. 59:3, 4. 69:4. 1 S 19:4, 5. 26:18. 2 S 15:12. Jn *15:24, 25. **without**. Ps 59:4. Da 6:4. Jn 19:6.

4. **For my**. Ps 35:7, 12. 38:20. 2 S 13:39. Jn 10:32. 2 C 12:15. **but I**. Ps 55:16, 17. 69:12, 13. 2 S *15:31, 32. Da 6:10. Lk *6:7, 11, 12. 23:34. **give myself unto**. *or*, I (am) prayer. √119, Ge +49:9. See Ps 120:7.

5. **they**. Ps 35:7-12. 37:7. Ge 44:4. Pr *17:13. **hatred**. Ps 55:12-15. 2 S 15:12, 31. Mk 14:44, 45. Lk 6:16. 22:47, 48. Jn 13:18. **love**. √63BA, Ge +26:7. Supply ellipsis, (saying). √108F. Idiom B837: idiomatic forms

of quotations. The Hebrews generally omitted the word *saying* whenever the words of another speaker were quoted. For other instances of this figure see Ps 2:2. 144:12. La 2:15.

6. **Set thou**. Dr. Sykes, Michaelis, and others contend that these imprecations are those of David's enemies against himself, and they would render, "Set, *say they*, a wicked," etc.: but this is rendered highly improbable by the eighth verse being applied by Peter to the traitor Judas, of whom David was certainly not a type (see ver. 20). Bp. Horsley and others, however, render the verbs in the future tense, the first verb alone being in the imperative, justly considering the psalmist as merely uttering prophetic denunciations of God's displeasure against sinners (see also Ps 35:8n. 40:14n. 71:13n). Mt 27:4. **and let**. Zc 3:1. Jn *13:2, 27. **Satan**. *or*, an adversary. ver. 4, 20, 29. Nu 22:22. 1 S 29:4. Zc 3:1mg. Mt 5:25.

7. **be condemned**. Heb. go out guilty, *or* wicked. Ro 3:19. Ga 3:10. **and let**. 2 S 15:7, 8. Pr 15:8. 21:27. 28:9. Is 1:15. 66:3. Mt 23:14. **become sin**. T#1648, 1814. Pr 15:8. *28:9. Mt 23:14. Lk 20:46, 47.

8. **his days**. Ps *55:23. Mt 27:5. **let**. Ac ⟩1:20. **another**. Ac *1:16-26. **office**. *or*, charge. ver. 6. Nu 3:32. 4:16. 16:29. 1 Ch 24:3. Zc 3:7mg.

9. **his children**. Ex *22:24. Je 18:21. La 5:3.

10. **Let his**. Ps 37:25. Ge 4:12-14. 2 S 3:29. 2 K 5:27. Jb 24:8-12. 30:3-9. Is 16:2.

11. **extortioner**. Jb 5:5. *18:5, 9-19. 20:18-20. **strangers**. Dt 28:29, 33, 34, 50, 51. Jg 6:3-6.

12. **none**. Is 27:11. Lk 6:38. Ja *2:13. **favor**. Ps 137:8, 9. Is 13:18. Mt 27:25. Lk 11:50, 51.

13. **Let his**. Ps *37:28. 1 S 2:31-33. 3:13. 2 K 10:10, 11. Jb *18:19. Is *14:20-22. Je 22:30. **their name**. Dt 9:14. 25:19. 29:20. Pr *10:7.

14. **Let the**. Ex +*20:5. Le 26:39. 2 S 3:29. 21:1, 8, 9. Mt 23:31-36. **let not**. 2 K 8:27. 9:27. 10:13, 14. 11:1. 2 Ch 22:3, 4. **blotted**. Ne *4:5. Is 43:25. Je *18:23.

15. **before**. Ps 51:9. 90:8. Dt 32:34. Je 2:22. Ho 7:2. Am *8:7. **cut off**. ver. 13. Ps *34:16. Jb 18:17. Is 65:15.

16. **he remembered**. 2 S 17:1, 2. Mt 5:7. 18:33-35. Ja 2:13. **persecuted**. Ps 10:2, 14. Ge 42:21. Jb 19:2, 3, 21, 22. Mt 27:35-46. **slay**. Ps *34:18. 69:20-29. 2 S 16:11, 12. Mk 14:33-36.

17. **loved**. √121C2C3. Metonymy of the Cause B556. "To love" is used not merely for the act itself but for the effect of it. Here, not merely loved to do it but did it. For other instances of this figure see Pr 8:36. 13:24. 17:19. **cursing**. Ps 52:4, 5. 59:12, 13. Pr 14:14. Ezk 35:6. Mt 7:2. 2 Th 2:10, 11. Re 16:6.

18. **As he**. Ps 73:6. Jb 29:14. Col 3:8, 12. 1 P 5:5. **so let**. Nu 5:22, 27. Jb 20:12-16, 20-23. Mt 26:24. 27:3-5. Ac 1:18, 25. **into his bowels**. Heb. within him. ver. 22. Ps 5:9. 36:1. 39:3.

19. **as the garment**. ver. 18, 29. Ps 35:26. 132:18.

20. **Let this**. Ps 2:5, 6, 12. 21:8-12. 40:14, 15. 110:1, 5, 6. 2 S 17:23. 18:32. 1 K 2:44. Lk 19:27. 1 Th 2:15, 16. **them**. Mt 11:19. 12:24. 26:66, 67. Mk 9:39. 1 C 12:3. **soul**. Heb. *nephesh*, Ge +12:13.

21. **But do**. √38A, Ne +4:4. Ps 25:11. 31:3. 69:29. 79:9, 10. 143:11, 12. Jn 17:1. Ph 2:8-11. **thy mercy**. Ps 36:7-9. 63:3. 86:5, 15.

22. **For I**. Ps 22:6. +*40:17. 86:1. *102:17-20. Mt *8:20. 2 C *8:9. **heart is wounded**. T#1362. ver. 16.

Ps 88:15, 16. 102:4. 2 K 4:27. Jb 6:4. Is *53:3. Lk 22:44. Jn 12:27.

23. **gone.** Ps 102:11. *144:4. 1 Ch 29:15. Jb 14:2. Ec 6:12. 8:13. Ja *4:14. **I am tossed.** Ps 102:10. Ex 10:13, 19.

24. **knees.** Ps 22:14. 35:13, 14. 69:10. Mt 4:2. 2 C 11:27. He *12:12. **are weak.** T#1944. Lk ✷23:26. Jn ✷19:17. **my flesh.** Ps 32:3, 4. 38:5-8. 102:4, 5. Jb 19:20.

25. **a reproach.** Ps 31:11-13. 35:15, 16. 69:9-12, 19, 20. Ro 15:3. He *12:2. 13:13. **when they.** Ps *22:6, 7. Jb 16:4. Is 37:22. Mt *27:39, 40.

26. **Help.** Ps 40:12, 13. 119:86. He *5:7. **save me.** Ps 57:1. 69:13, 16.

27. **they may know.** Ps *17:13, 14. *64:8, 9. 126:2. Ex 8:19. Nu 16:28-30. 1 S 17:46, 47. 1 K 18:36, 37. Jb 37:7. Is *53:10. Ac 2:32-36. 4:16.

28. **Let them.** ver. 17. Nu 22:12. 23:20, 23. 2 S *16:10-13. **but let.** Is 65:13-16. Jn 16:22. He 12:2.

29. **be clothed.** ver. 17-19. Ps 6:10. 35:26. *132:18. 140:9. Je 20:11. Da *12:2. Mi 7:10.

30. **greatly.** Ps 7:17. 9:1. 22:22, 25. 71:22, 23. 108:1-3. **I will praise.** Ps 22:22-25. 35:18. 107:32. 111:1. 116:12-18. 138:1, 4. He 2:12.

31. **For he.** Ps *16:8. 73:23. 110:5. *121:5. **poor.** ver. 16. Ps 68:5. 72:4, 12, 13. 140:12. **to save.** Ps 10:14. Ex 22:22-24. Pr 22:22, 23. Ec 5:8. Is 54:17. Ac √4:10-12. 5:30, 31. **those that condemn.** Heb. the judges of. **soul.** Heb. *nephesh,* Ge +12:13.

PSALM 110

A prophecy of the Messiah's kingdom, subjects, priesthood, triumphs, and sufferings as introducing them, 1-7.

(*Title.*) A.M. 2962. B.C. 1042. This psalm was probably composed by David after Nathan's prophetic address, and from the grandeur of the subject and the sublimity of the expressions, it is evident that it can only refer, as the ancient Jews fully acknowledged, to the royal dignity, priesthood, victories, and triumphs of the Messiah.

1. **The Lord.** Mt ▶22:44. Mk ▶12:36. Lk ▶20:42, 43. Ac ▶2:34, 35. He ▶1:13. **said.** Ps *8:1. Mt *22:42-46. Mk *12:35-37. Lk 20:41-44. **Sit.** Mk *16:19. Ac ▶2:34-36. Ep *1:20-22. He *12:2. 1 P *3:22. **right hand.** ʃ22A15C. Anthropomorphism B880. A right hand is attributed to God, used of the place accorded to Christ in his human nature as now exalted. For other instances of this figure see Mt 26:64. Mk 16:19. Ac 2:33, 34. 7:55, 56. Ro 8:34. Ep 1:20. Col *3:1. He ✷1:3. 8:1. **until.** Ps *2:6-9. +*45:6, 7. Is 7:14. 9:6. Mi 5:2. Ml 3:1. Mk 1:2. 1 C *15:25. He *1:3, 13. 10:12, 13. **footstool.** ʃ22A20, Ps +74:3. ʃ22D3D2. Anthropomorphism B892. God is spoken of as to place, having all enemies under his feet, denoting the completeness of their subjection. For other instances of this figure see Ps 8:6. 1 C *15:25n. Ep 1:22. He 1:13. 2:8.

2. **shall send.** Da +*7:13, 14. Mt 26:29. Lk 1:32. 19:15. 22:29. Re +*11:15. 22:3. **the rod.** ʃ22D5R, Ps +2:9. Ex 7:19. 8:5. Mi *7:14. Mt *28:18-20. Ac 2:34-37. Ro *1:16. 1 C *1:23, 24. 2 C *10:4, 5. 1 Th √2:13. 1 P 1:12. **out of Zion.** Is *2:3. Je 3:17. Ezk 47:1. Mi 4:2, 7. Zp 3:14, 15. **rule.** Ps *2:8, 9. 18:43. 22:28, 29. 45:5, 6. 2 S *23:3. Je 23:5, 6.

3. **Thy.** Ps *22:27, 28. Jg *5:2. Je 24:7. Ac *2:41. Ro *11:2-6. 2 C 8:1-3, 5, 12, 16. Ph *2:13. He 13:21.

day. Ac *1:8. 2:33, 41. 4:30-35. 19:20. 2 C 13:4. Ga 1:15, 16. **beauties.** Ps 96:9. Ezk 43:12. Ep 1:4. 1 Th 4:7. T *2:14. **from the womb,** etc. *or,* more than the womb of the morning: thou shalt have, etc. **morning.** Ps 30:5. 46:5. 49:14, 15. Ho 5:15. *6:3. 2 P +*1:19. Re +*2:28. **thou hast.** Ps 102:23, 24. Ex 12:5. Ac 4:4. 21:20. Re *7:9. **the dew.** ʃ121N1, Ge +31:54. By Metonomy of the Adjunct, the adjunct or accident is put for the subject, the abstract is put for the concrete. Here, "dew of thy youth" signifies that "thy young men shall be born to thee as dew is born in the morning" (B588). Is +*26:19n.

4. **Lord.** Ps 89:34-36. He 5:6. 6:13-18. 7:▶21, 28. **will not.** Nu 23:19. **Thou.** Ge 14:18-20. Zc +*6:13. He ▶5:6, 10. 6:20. 7:1-3, 11, ▶17, ▶21. Re 1:6. **for ever.** Heb. *olam,* Ex +*12:24. He 7:15, 16, 24, 25. **the order.** He ✷5:5, 6.

5. **at thy.** ver. 1. Ps 16:8. Mk 16:19. Ac 2:34-36. 7:55, 56. **strike.** Ps 2:2-6, 9-12. 45:4, 5. 68:14, 30. *149:7-9. Is 29:8. Zc 9:9, 10, 13-15. Re 17:12-14. 19:11-21. 20:8, 9. **in the day.** Ps 21:8, 9. Ezk 38:18, 19. Ro +*2:5. Re *6:15-17. *11:18.

6. **judge.** 1 S 2:10. Is 2:4. 11:3. 42:1, 4. 51:5. Jl *3:2, 12-16. Mi 4:3. Jn 5:22, 27. Re 19:11. **fill.** Is 34:2-8. *43:2-4. *66:16, 17. Ezk 38:21, 22. *39:4, 11-20. Re *14:19, 20. **wound.** Ps *68:21. Ge +*3:15. Is 9:4, 5. Hab 3:13. ʃ22C40. Anthropomorphism B890. Human actions are attributed to God: wounding the head. For other instances of this figure see Ps 68:21. Hab 3:13. **many.** *or,* great.

7. **He shall.** Ps 102:9. Jg 7:5, 6. Jb 21:20. Is 53:12. Je 23:15. Mt 20:22. 26:42. Jn 18:11. **drink.** 1 K 17:6. **therefore.** Is 53:11, 12. Lk 24:26. Ph *2:7-11. He *2:9, +10. 1 P 1:11. **lift.** Ps 3:3. 27:6. Je 52:31.

PSALM 111

The psalmist praises God for his glorious and gracious works, 1-9; and shows that the fear of God is the beginning of wisdom, 10.

1. A.M. 3468. B.C. 536. **Praise ye the Lord.** Heb. Hallelujah. Ps 106:1, 48. As this is an alphabetical psalm, every member of each verse beginning consecutively with a letter of the Hebrew alphabet, *Hallelujah,* which begins with the fifth, must be considered as the title. **I will.** Ps 9:1. 103:1. 138:1. **assembly.** Ps 22:25. 35:18. 40:9, 10. 89:5, 7. 107:32. 108:3. 109:30. 149:1. 1 Ch *29:10-20. 2 Ch 6:3, 4. 20:26-28.

2. **works.** Ps *92:4, 5. *104:24. 139:14. Jb 5:9. 9:10. *26:12-14. ch. 38, 41. Is 40:12. Je 32:17-19. Da 4:3. Ep 1:19, 20. 2:7-10. Re ▶15:3. **sought.** Ps 77:11, 12. 104:24, 34. *107:43. 143:5. Jb 37:7. Ec 3:11. 1 P 1:10-12. **that have.** Ps 92:4. Pr 17:16. 18:1, 2. 24:14. Ro 1:28. 8:6.

3. **honorable.** Ps 19:1. 145:4, 5, 10-12, *17. Ex 15:6, 7, *11. Ep 1:6-8. 3:10. Re 5:12-14. **righteousness.** Ps 103:17. 119:142, 144. Is 51:5, 6, 8. Da 9:24. **for ever.** Ps +9:18 (✷S#5703h).

4. **He hath.** Ps 78:4-8. Ex 12:26, 27. 13:14, 15. Dt 4:9. 31:19, etc. Jsh 4:6, 7, 21-24. 1 C 11:24-26. **gracious.** Ps *86:5, 15. *103:8. Ex 34:6, 7. Is 63:7. Mi 7:18, 19. Ro 5:20, 21. Ep 1:6-8. 1 T 1:14. **full.** Ps 78:38. 112:4. 145:8.

5. **hath given.** Ps 34:9, 10. 37:3. Is *33:16. Mt *6:26-33. Lk 12:30. **meat.** Heb. prey. Ps 104:21. 124:6. Ge 49:9. ʃ171I10. Synecdoche of the Species B628.

"Prey," that which is taken in hunting, one kind of food, is put for any and all kinds of food. For other instances of this figure see Pr 31:15. Ml 3:10. **he will**. Ps 89:34. 105:8. 106:45. Ne 1:5. Is +√55:3. Da 9:4. Ml +*3:6. Lk 1:72. **ever**. Heb. *olam*, Ps +5:11. **covenant**. ver. +*9. Ge +9:16.

6. **showed**. Ps 78:12, etc. 105:27, etc. Dt 4:32-38. Jsh *3:14-17. *6:20. *10:13, 14. **that he**. Ps 2:8. 44:2. 78:55. 80:8. 105:44.

7. **works**. Ps 85:10. 89:14. 98:3. Dt 32:4. 2 T 2:13. Re *15:3, 4. **all his**. Ps *19:7. *105:8. 119:86, 151, 160.

8. **They**. Is *40:8. Mt *5:18. Ro 3:31. **stand fast**. Heb. are established. Ps 112:8. Is *26:3. **for ever**. Ps +9:18 (✳S#5703h). **and ever**. Heb. *olam*, Ps +21:4. **are done**. Ps 19:9. 119:127, 128. Ro 7:12. Re 15:3.

9. **sent redemption**. Ps 130:7, 8. Ex 15:13. Dt 15:15. Is 35:10. 44:6. +*51:11. 63:9. Mt 1:21. Lk *1:68, 71, 72. Ep 1:7, +*14. T *2:14. He 9:12. 1 P 1:18-20. Re 5:9. **his covenant**. ver. 5. 2 S 23:5. 1 Ch 16:15. Is +√55:3. Je +√33:20, 21. Ga 3:15-17. He 13:20. **for ever**. Heb. *olam*, Ex +*12:24. **holy**. Ps 89:7. 99:3, 5, 9. Ex 15:11. Dt 28:58. Is *6:3. Ml 1:11. 2:2. Lk *1:49. Re *4:8.

10. **fear**. ∫138C, Ge +22:14. Jb *28:28. Pr *1:7. 8:13. *9:10. Ec *12:13. **a good understanding**. *or*, good success. Ps *1:3. Dt 4:6. Jsh *1:7, 8. Pr 3:4. 2 T *3:15-17. **do his commandments**. Heb. do them. Dt *4:6. Jn +*13:17. Re *22:14. **his praise**. Mt *25:21, 23. Jn 5:44. *12:43. Ro 2:7, *29. 1 C *4:5. 2 C *4:17. 1 P *1:7. **for ever**. Ps +9:18 (✳S#5703h).

PSALM 112

The believer's character, privileges, and final felicity, 1-9. The anguish and despair of the wicked, 10.

1. **Praise ye the Lord**. Heb. Hallelujah. Ps 111:1mg. 147:1mg. *148:11-14. 150:1mg. This is another of the alphabetical psalms, being formed exactly as the preceding in the division of its verses, and like it, was probably composed for the use of the Jews after their return from captivity. **Blessed**. ∫43, Dt +28:3. See on Ps *111:10. 115:7-13. *128:1. 145:19. Is *50:10. Lk *1:50. **the man**. ∫171G1, Ps +32:2. **delighteth**. Ps *1:1, 2. *40:8. *119:16, 35, 47, 48, 70-72, 97, 143. Ro *7:22. *8:6.

2. **His seed**. Ps *25:12, 13. 37:26. *102:28. Ge 17:7. 22:17, 18. Pr 20:7. Je 32:39. Ac 2:39.

3. **Wealth**. Pr 3:16. 15:6. Is 33:6. Mt *6:33. 2 C 6:10. Ph 4:18, 19. 1 T 6:6-8. **and riches**. Jb 22:23, 24. Pr 10:4, 22. Mt ◑6:19, 20. Lk 6:20, ◑24. 12:21. Ja 5:1-3. **and his**. ver. 9. Ps 111:3, 10. Is 32:17. 51:8. Da 9:24. Mt 24:22-24. Re 22:11. **for ever**. Ps +9:18 (✳S#5703h).

4. **there ariseth**. Ps 37:6. *97:11. 118:27. Jb 11:17. 18:5. Is 50:10. Mi *7:8, 9. Ml 4:2. Jn 12:46. **he is gracious**. Ps 106:1. Mi *6:8. Lk 6:36. 2 C *8:8, 9. Ep √4:32. 5:1, 2, 9, 15. Col 3:12, 13. **righteous**. T 2:11, 12. 1 J 2:29. 3:7, 10.

5. **good**. Pr 2:20. 12:2. Lk 23:50. Ac 11:24. Ro 5:7. **showeth**. Ps 37:25, 26. Dt *15:7-10. Jb 31:16-20. Lk +*6:35. **lendeth**. ∫171K1, Dt +19:5. By Synecdoche of the Species, one example or specimen is put for all kinds of similar things. Here, in human actions, "lending" is put as one kind of favor which a good man shows. The most rare is given as an example of

all kinds of merciful works (B634). **he will**. Pr 17:18. *18:9. 22:26, 27. 24:27, *30-34. *27:23-27. Jn *6:12. Ro *12:11. Ep 5:15. Col *4:5. **guide his affairs**. Pr +*22:3. Lk *14:28. **discretion**. Heb. judgment. Ps 1:5. 7:6. *9:4. 10:5. Ge +*18:19. Mi +*6:8. Ph *1:9.

6. **Surely**. Ps 15:5. *62:2, 6. 125:1. 2 P √1:5-11. **for ever**. Heb. *olam*, Ex +*12:24. **the righteous**. Ne 13:22, 31. Pr *10:7. Mt 25:34-40. He *6:10. **everlasting**. Heb. *olam*, Ge +*17:7.

7. **shall not**. Ps *27:1-3. +√34:4. *56:3, 4. Pr *1:33. *3:25, 26. Lk 21:9, 19, 26. **tidings**. lit. hearing. ∫121R1, Le +13:55. By Metonymy of the Adjunct, the senses are put for the object of them, or for the things which are perceived by the senses. Here, "hearing" is put for what is heard: rumor, common talk, or evil tidings. **heart**. Ps 57:7. 118:6. Is *26:3, 4. Da *3:16, 17. Ac *20:23, 24. 21:13. **fixed**. Ps 57:7mg. 2 Ch 12:14mg. **trusting**. Ps *62:8. 64:10. 118:8, 9. Jn *14:1. Ac 27:25.

8. **heart**. Ps 27:14. 31:24. He 13:9. **shall**. Pr *3:33. **until he see**. Ps 59:10. *91:2, 8. 92:11. 118:7. Is +*66:24.

9. **He**. 2 C ▶9:9. **dispersed**. Dt 15:11. Pr 11:24, 25. 19:17. Ec 11:1, 2, 6. Is 32:8. 58:7, 10. Mk 14:7. Lk 11:41. 12:33. 18:22. Jn 13:29. Ac 4:35. 20:35. Ro 12:13. 2 C *8:9. 9:10-15. 1 T 6:18. He 13:16. Ja 2:15, 16. 1 J 3:16-18. **righteousness**. See on ver. 3. Dt *24:13. Mt 6:4. Lk 14:12-14. 16:9. He 6:10. Re 22:11. **for ever**. Ps +9:18 (✳S#5703h). **horn**. Ps 75:10. 92:10. 1 S 2:1, 30.

10. **wicked**. Est 6:11, 12. Is 65:13, 14. Lk 13:28. 16:23. **gnash**. Ps 37:12. Mt 22:13. Lk *13:28. Re 16:10, 11. **melt**. Ps 58:7, 8. **desire**. Ps 36:12. Jb +*8:13. Pr +*10:28. 11:7. Is +*38:18. Lk 16:24-26. He +*9:27.

PSALM 113

The servants of Jehovah are exhorted to praise his glorious majesty, his condescension, and kindness in his kingdom of providence and grace, 1-9.

(*Title.*) This and the following five psalms form what is called by the Hebrews the great *Hallel*, or praise, which was sung on their most solemn festivals, particularly after the celebration of the Passover (see Mt 26:30. Mk 14:26). This and the following were probably composed after the return from the captivity.

1. **Praise ye the Lord**. Heb. Hallelujah. Ps 112:1. **Praise, O**. Ps 33:1, 2. 103:20, 21. 134:1. 135:1-3, 20. 145:10. Ep 5:19, 20. Re 19:5. **the name**. ∫144A4A, Is +30:27. i.e. *praise Jehovah himself*.

2. **Blessed**. Ps 41:13. *72:17-19. 106:48. 1 Ch 16:36. 29:10-13. Da 2:20. Ep 3:21. Re 5:13. **for evermore**. Heb. *olam*, Ps +18:50.

3. **the rising**. Ps 72:11, 17-19. 86:9. Is 24:16. 42:10-12. 49:13. *59:19. Hab 2:14. Ml *1:11. Ro 15:9, 10. Re 11:15.

4. **high**. Ps 97:9. 99:2. Is *40:15, 17, 22. **his glory**. Ps 8:1. 57:10, 11. 1 K 8:27. Is 66:1.

5. **like**. Ps *89:6, 8. Ex *15:11. Dt 33:26. Is 40:18, 25. 46:5. Je 10:6. **dwelleth**. Heb. exalteth himself to dwell. Ps 21:13.

6. **humbleth**. ∫138B, Ge +13:16. Ps 11:4. Jb 4:18. 15:15. Is 6:2. **in heaven**. Bp Lowth observes that the two members of this line are to be referred severally to the two preceding lines as if it were, "Who is exalted to dwell in the heavens; and who humbleth himself

to inspect the things on earth." **in the earth.** Ps 138:6. Is 57:15. 66:2.

7. **raiseth.** Ps 75:6, 7. 107:41. Jb 5:11, 15, 16. Ezk 17:24. 21:26, 27. Lk 1:52, 53. 1 C 1:27. Ja *2:5. **out of.** Ps 22:15. Is +*26:19n. Da +*12:2, 3. Ac 2:31-33. Ep 1:20, 21. 1 P 3:21, 22. **needy.** 1 S 2:7, 8. 24:14. 2 S 7:8, 9. Jb 2:8. 36:6, 7.

8. **may set.** Ps 45:16. 68:13. Ge 41:41. Ph *2:8-11. Re 5:9, 10. **the princes.** ♪16, Ge +1:27. Ps 47:9. Is +*32:1.

9. **maketh.** T#783. Ps *68:6. Ge 21:5-7. 25:21. 30:22, 23. 1 S 2:5. Is +*54:1. 56:4, 5. Lk 1:13-15. Ga 4:27. **barren.** Ge +*11:30. ◑29:31. **mother.** Ps +*127:3. Is +*54:1. **keep house.** Heb. dwell in an house. Ps 23:6. Is 60:7. Jn +*14:2, 3.

PSALM 114

The powerful presence of God with Israel when he brought them out of Egypt and led them through the wilderness into Canaan, admired and adored in exalted strains, 1-8.

(*Title.*) This short, only apparently imperfect psalm, for elegance and sublimity yields to few in the whole book. The composition of it is inexpressibly beautiful, in the highest style of poetry.

1. **Israel.** Ex 12:41, 42. 13:3. 20:2. Dt 16:1. 26:8. Is 11:16. **a people.** Ps 81:5. Ge 42:23.

2. **Judah.** Ex 6:7. 19:5, 6. *25:8. 29:45, 46. Le 11:45. Dt 23:14. 27:9, 12. Ezk 37:26-28. 2 C *6:16, 17. Re 21:3. **dominion.** Ex *19:6.

3. **sea.** Ps 77:16. 104:7. 106:9. Ex 14:21. 15:8. Is 63:12. Hab 3:8, 15. **Jordan.** Ps 74:15. Jsh 3:13-16. Hab 3:9.

4. **mountains skipped.** Ps 29:6. 68:8, 16. Ex *19:18. 20:18. Jg 5:4, 5. Je 4:23, 24. Mi 1:3, 4. Na 1:5. Hab 3:6, 8. 2 P 3:7-11. Re 20:11.

5. **What ailed.** Je 47:6, 7. Hab 3:8. **thou sea.** ♪38G, Dt +32:1.

6. **skipped.** ver. 4. Ps 29:6.

7. **Tremble.** Ps 77:18. 97:4, 5. 104:32. Jb 9:6. 26:11. Is 64:1-3. Je 5:22. Mi 6:1, 2.

8. **Which turned.** Ps 78:15, 16. 105:41. 107:35. Ex 17:6. Nu *20:11. Dt 8:15. Ne 9:15. Is 14:23. 1 C *10:4. **the flint.** Dt 8:15. 32:13. Jb 28:9mg. Is 50:7. **fountain.** Heb. *mayan*, Ge +7:11 (❋S#4599h). Jsh 15:9. 1 K 18:5. 2 K 3:19, 25.

PSALM 115

The psalmist calls on God to vindicate his own honor against the reproaches of idolaters, 1-3. He exposes the vanity of idols and the folly of idolaters, 4-8. He exhorts Israel to trust in the Lord, who will not fail to bless his people, 9-18.

(*Title.*) A.M. 3108. B.C. 896. This seems to be an *epinikion*, or triumphal song, in which the victory is wholly ascribed to Jehovah; to none can it be referred with more propriety than to that of Jehoshaphat over the confederated forces of his enemies, 2 Ch 20.

1. **Not unto us.** Ps 74:22. 79:9, 10. Dt 32:27. Jg 4:9. Jsh 7:9. Is *48:11. Je 17:5. Ezk 20:14. *36:32. Da 9:19. Ep 1:6. Re 4:10, 11. **thy name.** ♪121T1, Dt +28:58. **unto thy name.** Mt 6:9. **for thy mercy.** Ps 61:7. 89:1, 2. 2 Ch 32:25, 26. Mi 7:20. Jn 1:17. Ro 15:8, 9.

2. **Wherefore.** Ps 42:3, 10. 79:10. Ex 32:12. Nu

14:15, 16. Dt 32:26, 27. 2 K 19:10-19. Jl 2:17.

3. **But our.** Ps 2:4. 47:2. 68:4. *83:18. 93:1. 123:1. Dt 4:39. 1 Ch 16:25. Mt 6:9, 13. Ac 17:24. **he hath.** Ps 29:10. *135:6. Ex +33:19. Dt +*2:30. 1 Ch 29:12. Jb 9:12. 42:1, 2. Is 14:24, 27. 46:9-11. 55:11. Je 32:17. Da *4:35. Mt 19:26. *20:15. Ro 9:+18, 19. Ep +*1:11. **whatsoever.** Jb 42:2.

4. **Their idols.** ♪132G, Ge +3:19. They are metal, stone, and wood; and though generally made in the form of a man, they can neither see, hear, smell, feel, walk, nor speak! Even the wiser heathen made them the objects of their jests. Ps 97:7. 135:15-17. Dt 4:28. Is 40:19, 20. 42:17. 46:1, 2, 6, 7. Je *10:3-5. Ho 8:6. Da 5:4. Hab 2:18-20. Ac 19:26, 35. 1 C 10:19, 20. Re 9:20. **silver.** ♪121D5, Ge +23:9. **and.** ♪174, Ge +18:27.

5. **they speak not.** Is 46:7. Je 10:5. Hab 2:18, 19. **see not.** Ps 135:16.

6. **They have ears.** Ps 135:17. **smell not.** 1 C 10:19.

7. **hands.** ver. 4. Ps 8:6. 10:12. 17:14. **handle not.** 1 S 5:4. **feet.** Ps 8:6. 18:9. 22:16. 25:15. **walk.** Ps 55:14. 81:13. 85:13. 86:11. 1 S 5:3. Is 46:7. Ac 17:29. **neither speak.** Hab 2:18.

8. **make them.** Ps *135:18. Is *44:9-20. Je 10:8. Jon +*2:8. Hab *2:18, 19. Ro *1:23, 28. **are like.** 2 K 17:15. Je +*2:5.

9. **Israel.** Ps 118:2-4. 135:19, 20. Ex 19:5. **trust.** Ps *62:8. 125:1. 130:7. 146:5, 6. Je 17:7, 13. Ep 1:12. **he.** ♪76, Ge +13:6. **their help.** Ps 33:20, 21. *84:11, 12. Dt 33:29. Pr *30:5.

10. **house of Aaron.** Ex 28:1. Nu 16:5, 40. 18:7. **trust.** Ph *4:6. **he.** ♪76, Ge +13:6.

11. **Ye that.** Ps *33:18. 118:4. 147:11. Pr *14:26. 30:5. Ac 10:35. Re 19:5. **he.** ♪76, Ge +13:6.

12. **hath.** Ps 25:7. 136:23. Ge 8:1. Ex 2:24, 25. Jsh 17:14. 1 S 7:12. Is *44:21. 49:14-16. Ac 10:4. **mindful.** ♪22C3, Ge +8:1. **bless.** ♪16, Ge +1:27. **the house of Israel.** Ps 67:7. Ge 12:2, 3. 22:17, 18. Ac 3:26. Ga 3:14, 29. Ep *1:3. **will bless.** ♪18, Dt +28:4. Ep 1:3.

13. **He will bless.** Ps *29:11. 112:1. 128:1, 4, 5. Ml √3:16, 17. *4:2. Lk 1:50. Ac *13:26. Col 3:11. **both small.** Ac 26:22. Re 11:18. 19:5. 20:12. **and.** Heb. with. ♪174, Ge +18:27. Ps 104:25. Dt 25:13.

14. **increase.** Ge *13:16. 2 S 22:36mg. 24:3. Is 2:2, 3. *27:6. 49:20, 21. *56:8. 60:4, etc. Je 30:19. 33:22. Ho *1:10. Zc *8:20-23. 10:8. Col √1:10. 2:19. Ja 4:6. Re 7:4, 9. **you.** Ge 17:7. Je 32:38, 39. Ac *2:39. 3:25.

15. **blessed.** Ps *3:8. Ge 14:19. 32:26-29. Ep *1:3, 4. 1 P *3:9. **made.** Ps 96:5. 146:5, 6. Ge 1:1.

16. **heaven.** Ps 89:11. 144:5. 148:4. Is *66:1. La 3:66. Jn *14:2, 3. **but the earth.** Ps *50:12. Ge *1:28-30. 9:1-3. Dt 32:8. Je 27:5, 6. 1 C 10:26.

17. **dead.** Ps 6:5. 30:9. 31:12. 88:10-12. 106:28. 118:17. Pr +*21:16. Ec +*9:5. Is *38:18, 19. Ro *12:1, 2. Re √20:5. **praise not.** Ps +*146:4. **go down.** Ps 22:29. 28:1. 30:3. 31:17. 37:20. *49:14, ◑15, 19. *140:10, ◑13. *147:6. 1 S √2:9. Jb 27:13, 19. 40:12, 13. Pr 12:7. Is +*24:22. *26:14. *42:7, 22. 43:17, ◑21. **silence.** Heb. *dumah*, Ps 94:17 only.

18. **But we.** Ps 59:16. 102:18. Is 24:14, 16. **will bless.** Ps 113:2. 118:17-19. 145:2, 21. Is +*51:11. Da *2:20. Re 5:13. **for evermore.** Heb. *olam*, Ps +18:50. **Praise the Lord.** Ps 105:45.

PSALM 116

The psalmist avows his gratitude to God, who had answered his prayers and brought him out of deep distress, and resolves to worship and serve him all his days, 1-9. He records his temptation to unbelief and his victory over it, 10, 11. He determines to perform his vows and render thanks to God in the most public manner at the sanctuary, 12-19.

(*Title.*) A.M. 3468. B.C. 536. From several instances of the Chaldee dialect in this psalm, it appears to have been written after the Babylonian captivity.

1. **love.** T#1370. Ps 18:1-6. 91:14, 15. 119:132. Mk 12:33. Jn 21:17. 1 J *4:19. 5:2, 3. **because.** Ps 18:6. 31:22, 23. 34:3, 4. 40:1, 2. 66:19, 20. 69:33, 34. Ge *35:2, 3. 1 S 1:26, 27. Jn 16:24. **and.** ♪93A, Ge +1:26. By Hendiadys, "my supplicating voice," with emphasis on "supplicating."

2. **therefore.** Ps 55:16, 17. *86:6, 7. 88:1, 2. 145:18, 19. Jb 27:10. Lk 18:1. Ph *4:6. Col 4:2. **as long as I live.** Heb. in my days. 2 K 20:19.

3. **sorrows.** Ps *18:4-6. 88:6, 7. Jon 2:2, 3. Mk *14:33-36. Lk 22:44. He *5:7. **pains.** Ps 118:5. La 1:3. **hell.** Heb. sheol, Ge +37:35. **gat hold upon me.** Heb. found me. ♪155F, Ge +4:7. Ps 119: 143mg. Ge +44:34mg. **I found.** Ps 32:3, 4. 38:6. Is *53:3, 4.

4. **called.** Ps 22:1-3. 30:7, 8. 34:6. *50:15. 118:5. 130:1, 2. 2 Ch 33:12, 13. Is 37:15-20. 38:1-3. Jon 2:2. **O Lord.** Ps 6:4. 22:20. 25:17. 40:12, 13. 142:4-6. 143:6-9. Lk *18:13, 14. *23:42, 43. **deliver.** T#1462, 1705. Ps *56:1-3. 60:1-3. Ge 32:11, 12. Ex 14:10. 2 K 19:1, 2. Jon 1:4-6, 13, 14. Mt 8:23-25. 14:26-30. 24:19-21. Mk 4:38, 39. Lk *21:36. Ac 12:5. *16:23-25. Ep *6:18-20. Ph *4:6. 2 Th 3:1, 2. Phm 22. Ja *5:14, 15. **soul.** Heb. nephesh, Ge +12:13.

5. **Gracious.** Ps 86:5, 15. 103:8. 112:4. 115:1. 145:8. Ex 34:6, 7. Ne 9:17, 31. Da 9:9. Ro 5:20, 21. Ep 1:6-8. 2:4. 1 T 1:14. T 3:4-7. **and righteous.** Ps 119:137. 145:4-7, 17. Ezr 9:15. Ne 9:8, 33. Is 45:21. Da 9:7, 14. Ro *3:25, 26. 1 J √1:9.

6. **preserveth.** Ps *19:7. 25:21. Is 35:8. Mt 11:25. Ro 16:19. 2 C 1:12. 11:3. Col 3:22. **simple.** ♪108K54, Pr +1:4. **I was.** Ps 79:8. 106:43. 142:6.

7. **thy rest.** Ps 42:11. 95:11. Je *6:16. 30:10. Mt √11:28, 29. He 4:8-10. **soul.** Heb. nephesh, Ge +34:3. **hath dealt.** Ps *13:6. *119:17. Ho 2:7. **bountifully.** 1 S +1:22n (✚S#1580h).

8. **For thou.** Ps 56:13. 86:13. **soul.** Heb. nephesh, Ge +12:13. **mine eyes.** ♪132A, Ge +4:23. Is 25:8. 38:5. Re 7:17. *21:4. **and my feet.** Ps *37:24. 56:13. 73:23. *94:18. 1 S 2:9. Lk 22:31, 32. Ju *24.

9. **walk.** Ps 61:7. Ge *17:1. 1 K 2:4. 8:25. *9:4. Lk 1:6, 75. **in the land.** Ps 27:13. Is 53:8.

10. **I believed.** 2 C ▸4:13. *5:7. He *11:1. **therefore.** Nu 14:6-9. Pr 21:28. 2 P 1:16-21. **I was greatly.** ver. 3.

11. **in my.** Ps *31:22. 1 S 27:1. **All.** Ps 62:9. 2 K 4:16, 28. Je 9:4, 5. Ro 3:4.

12. **What shall.** Ps *51:12-14. *103:2, 3. Is 6:5-8. Ro √12:1. 1 C 6:20. 2 C √5:14, 15.

13. **I will take.** ver. 17. Ps 36:8. Nu 15:2-5. Lk 22:17, 18, 20. 1 C *10:16, 21. 11:25-27. **call.** ver. 2. Ps 105:1. Is 12:4.

14. **pay my vows.** ver. 18. Ps 22:25. 56:12. *66:13-15. Le +*23:38. Dt 23:21. Jon 1:16. *2:9. Na 1:15. Mt 5:33.

15. **Precious.** Ps *37:32, 33. 49:7, 8. *72:14. 126:5, 6. 139:17. 1 S *25:29. Jb *5:26. Is 28:16. Ho 11:4.

Lk *16:22. Re *1:18. √14:13. **the death.** Ge 4:10. 1 C +15:55.

16. **truly.** Ps 86:16. 119:125. 143:12. Jn *12:26. Ac *27:23. Ja 1:1. **the son.** Ps 86:16. **handmaid.** Ps 86:16. Mt ✱1:23. **thou hast.** Ps 107:14-16. 2 Ch 33:11-13. Is 61:1. Ro *6:22.

17. **the sacrifice.** Ps 50:14. 107:22. Le 7:12. He *13:15, 16. **call.** ver. 13. Ac 2:42.

18. **will pay.** ver. 14. Ps 22:25. 76:11. Le +*23:38. Ec 5:5.

19. **the courts.** Ps 96:8. 100:4. 118:19, 20. 122:3, 4. 135:2. 2 Ch 6:6.

PSALM 117

An exhortation to praise God for his mercy and truth, 1, 2.

(*Title.*) This Psalm, the shortest in the whole collection, is written as a part of the preceding in thirty-two MSS: it celebrates the deliverance from the Babylonian captivity, the grand type of the redemption of the world by the Messiah.

1. **O praise.** Ps 66:1, 4. 67:3. 86:9. Is 24:15, 16. 42:10-12. Ro ▸15:11. Ep *3:5, 6. Re *15:4. **praise him.** Ps 148:11-14. *150:6. Re *5:9. 7:9, 10.

2. **his merciful.** Ps *85:10. *89:1. 100:4, 5. Is 25:1. Mi *7:20. Lk *1:54, 55. Jn *14:6. Ro 15:8, 9. 1 J 5:6. **for ever.** Heb. olam, Ex +*12:24.

PSALM 118

The psalmist exhorts all orders of men in Israel to praise God, 1-4. He shows by his own experience how good it is to trust in the Lord, 5-18. In blessing him for deliverance and advancement, and in calling on the people to join in his triumphant praises, he predicts the coming and the kingdom of the Messiah, 19-29.

(*Title.*) A.M. 2962. B.C. 1042. This psalm was probably composed by David after Nathan's prophetic address and sung by alternate choirs at some public festival. It largely partakes of David's spirit and everywhere shows the hand of a master: the style is grand and sublime, the subject is noble and majestic.

1. **give thanks.** ver. 29. Ps 103:17. 106:1. 107:1. 136:1. 1 Ch 16:8, 34. Je 33:11. **his mercy.** ♪8. Amoebaeon; or, Refrain B343: the repetition of the same phrase at the end of successive paragraphs. For other instances of this figure see Ps 136:2. Is 9:12, 17, 21. 10:4. Am 4:6, 8, 9, 10, 11. Mt 6:2, 5, 16. Mk 9:46, 48. Lk 13:3, 5. Jn 6:39, 40, 44, 54. Re 2:7, 11, 17, 29. 3:6, 13, 22. 18:21, 22, 23. **for ever.** Heb. olam, Ex +*12:24.

2. **Let.** ♪51. Coenotes; or, Combined Repetition B345: the repetition of two different phrases, one at the beginning and the other at the end of successive paragraphs. For other instances of this figure see Ps 118:8, 9, 15, 16. 136:1, 2, 3. **Israel now say.** Ps 115:9-11. 135:19, 20. 145:10. 147:19, 20. Ga 6:16. He *13:15. 1 P 2:9, 10. **his mercy.** ♪8, ver. 1. **for ever.** Heb. olam, Ex +*12:24.

3. **the house of Aaron.** Ps 115:9-11. 134:1-3. 1 P 2:5. Re 1:6. 4:7-11. 5:8-10. **mercy.** ♪8, ver. 1. Ep 2:4. 1 P 1:3. **for ever.** Heb. olam, Ex +*12:24.

4. **Let them.** Ps 22:23. Re 19:5. **his mercy.** ♪8, ver. +1. **for ever.** Heb. olam, Ex +*12:24.

5. **called.** Ps 18:6. 40:1-3. 77:2. 107:13, 19. 116:3,

4. 120:1. 130:1, 2. Ge 32:7, 9-11. 1 S 30:6-8. Mk 14:34-36. **in distress.** Heb. out of distress. Ps 130:1. Jon 2:2. **and.** ſ63H, Ge +12:15. **set me.** ſ63K, Ge +37:13. Ps 18:19. 22:21. 31:8. He 5:7.

6. **The Lord.** Ps 27:1-3. 46:1, 11. 56:4, 9, 11. 146:5. Is 51:12. Je 20:11. Mi 7:8-10. Ro *8:31. He *▶13:6. **on my side.** Heb. for me. Ps 56:9. **not fear.** Ps 3:6. 27:1-3. +*34:4. *46:1, 2. 56:11. 146:5. Ge ◑19:30. Dt 31:6, 8. Jsh 8:1. 1 K 18:8-16. 2 K 6:15, √16. Pr 29:25. Is 41:√10, 13, 14. 43:1. 44:2, 8. 51:7, 12. Je 1:8. Ezk 2:6. Da 3:17, 18. 6:10. Mt +*10:28-33. Mk 4:40. Jn 14:27. Ac 4:13. 20:24. He *13:6. 1 P 3:13, 14.

7. **taketh.** Ps 54:4. 55:18. 1 Ch 12:18. **therefore.** Ps 54:7. 59:10. 92:11. 112:8.

8. **It is.** ſ51, ver. +2. **better to trust.** Ps 9:10. 20:7. 23:4-6. 27:1. 40:4. 49:6, 7. 56:4. *62:8, 9. 91:2. Pr 28:1, 26. Is *26:4. Je *17:5-7. Mi *7:5-7. Zc 4:6. Mk 10:24. Lk 12:19, 20. 2 C 1:9. Ga 6:7. 1 Th 5:2, 3. He 3:12, 14. 10:35, 36. 13:5. Ja 4:13-15. **than .** ſ76, Ge +13:5. ſ96E1. Heterosis of Degree B526: The positive is put for the comparative. Here, "It is good to trust in the Lord, *rather* than to put confidence in man": the one is good, the other is not; it is even accursed (see Je 17:5, 7). Where the positive is used with the comparative particle *ee* (in Greek), *than*, it implies that though there may be in one sense a comparison, yet in another and true sense, there is really no comparison at all. The use of the positive declares that the one case is so, rather than the other, which is not so. For other instances of this figure see Mt 12:7. 18:8. Mk 3:4. Lk 18:14. Jn 6:27. 15:22. 1 C 3:7. **put confidence.** 2 Ch 12:1. Is 30:2, 3.

9. **It is better.** ſ18, Dt +28:4. **trust.** Ps 91:2. Is 26:4. **than to put.** ſ76, Ge +13:5. Ps *146:3-5. Is 30:2, 3, 15-17. 31:1, 8. 36:6, 7. Ezk 29:7.

10. **All nations.** ſ171A, Ex +9:6. 2 S ch. 5, 8, 10. Zc 12:3. 14:1-3. Re 19:19-21. 20:8, 9. **but .** ſ76, Ge +13:5. **destroy them.** Heb. cut them off. ver. 11, 12. Ps 58:7. 90:6. Jb 14:2.

11. **They compassed.** Ps 22:12-16. 88:17. 1 S 23:26. 1 Ch 19:10. **they compassed.** ſ84, Ge +6:17. **but.** ſ76, Ge +13:5.

12. **They compassed.** ſ18, Dt +28:4. **like bees.** Dt 1:44. **quenched.** Ps 83:14, 15. Ec 7:6. Is 27:4. Na 1:10. **for .** ſ76, Ge +13:5. **in the name.** Ps 8:9. 20:1, 5. 1 S 17:45. 2 S 23:6. 1 Ch 14:10, 11, 14-16. 2 Ch *14:9, 11, 12. 16:7-9. 20:17-22. 22:7, 8. *32:7, 8. **destroy them.** Heb. cut them down. ver. 10, 11.

13. **Thou hast.** Ps 18:17, 18. 56:1-3. 1 S 20:3. 25:29. 2 S 17:1-3. Mi 7:8. Mt 4:1-11. He 2:14.

14. **is my strength.** Ps 18:2. Ex 15:2-6. Is *12:2. 45:17, 22-25. Mt 1:21-23. **and song.** ſ121R7, Ge +43:11.

15. **voice.** Ps 30:11, 12. 32:11. 33:1. 119:54, 111. Dt 12:12. Is 51:11. 65:13. Ac 2:46, 47. 16:34. Re 18:20. 19:1-5. **the right hand.** ſ22A15A, Ex +15:6. Ps 44:3. 45:4. 60:12. 89:13. 98:1. Is 51:9, 10.

16. **The right hand.** ſ84, Ge +6:17. Ex 15:6. Ac 2:32-36. **the right hand.** ſ22A15A, Ex +15:6.

17. **not die.** Ps 6:5. Is *38:16-20. Hab 1:12. Jn 11:4. Ro *14:7-9. **declare.** Ps 40:5, 10. 71:17, 18. 73:28. 107:22. 119:13. 145:4. Je 51:10.

18. **chastened.** ſ147B, Ge +2:16. Ps 66:10-12. 94:12, 13. 2 S 12:10. ch. 13, 16. Jb 5:17, 18. 33:16-30. Pr 3:11, 12. Je *10:24. *30:11. Jon 2:6. 1 C *11:32.

2 C *1:9-11. *6:9. He 12:10, 11. **not given.** Jb 2:6.

19. **Open.** Is *26:2. Re 22:14. **I will go.** Ps 9:13, 14. 66:13-15. 95:2. 100:4. 116:18, 19. Is 38:20, 22.

20. **This gate.** Dr. Kennicott supposes that this verse was sung by the priest, the next by the king, the three next by a chorus of people, the twenty-fifth by the king, the two next by the priest, the twenty-eighth by the king, and the last the grand chorus of the whole assembly. Ps 24:3, 4, 7, 9. Is 26:2. *35:8-10. Re *21:24-27. *22:14, 15.

21. **will praise.** Ps 22:23, 24. 69:33, 34. 116:1. **and art.** ver. 14. Ex 15:2. Is 12:2. 49:8.

22. **The stone.** ſ22L1. Anthropomorphism B896. God is figured by things which pertain to the earth: a stone. For other instances of this figure see Mt ▶21:42. Mk ▶12:10, 11. Lk ▶20:17. Ac ▶4:11. Ep *2:20-22. 1 P 2:4-6, ▶7, 8. **refused.** Mt *21:42. Jn *7:48. **the head.** Zc *4:7.

23. **This.** Mt ▶21:42. Mk ▶12:10-11. **the Lord's doing.** Heb. from the Lord. Ac 2:32-36. 3:14, 15. 5:31, 32. Ro *1:4. Ep *1:19-22. **it is.** Jb 5:9. Ac 4:13. 13:41.

24. **the day.** Ps 2:7. Dt *11:21. 33:12. Is √24:21, 22n. *25:9. 26:1. 49:8. Ho +*2:18. √6:2. Jl 3:18. Zc +*3:9, 10. 14:7, 8. Mt *28:1-8. Jn 8:56. 20:19, 20. Ac +*20:7. 1 C +*5:5. 2 C +*6:2. He 3:7, 13. Re +*1:10n. **we will rejoice.** Ps *84:10. *106:5. 1 K 8:66. 2 Ch 20:26-28. Ne *8:10. Is +*58:13n. Hab √3:17, 18. **glad.** Ps 97:11. Nu *10:10.

25. **Save now.** Ps 20:9. 22:21. 69:1, 13. ſ87. Euche; or, Prayer B920. An expression of feeling by way of prayer, curse, or imprecation. For other instances of this figure see Dt 28:67. Is 63:19. 64:1, 2. Ac 26:29. Ro 9:3. **send now.** Ps 90:17.

26. **Blessed.** Zc 4:7. Mt ▶21:9. ▶23:39. Mk ▶11:9, 10. Lk ▶13:35. ▶19:38. Jn ▶12:13. **we have.** Ps 134:3. Nu *6:23-26.

27. **God.** Heb. *El*, Ex +15:2. 1 K 18:21, 39. **showed.** Ps 18:28. 37:6. 112:4. Est *8:16. Is 9:2. 60:1. Mi 7:9. Ml 4:2. Jn *8:12. 1 P *2:9. **bind.** Ps 51:18, 19. 1 K 8:63, 64. +18:44mg. 1 Ch 29:21. Ro *12:1. He *13:15. **sacrifice.** lit. feast. ſ121P7, Ex 23:18. **the horns.** Ex 27:2. 38:2.

28. **my God.** Heb. *El*, Ex +15:2. Ps 22:1. 63:1. 89:26. 145:1. 146:2. Ex *15:2. Is *12:2. *25:1, 9.

29. **give thanks.** ver. 1. Ps 103:17. 106:1. Ezr 3:11. Is 63:7. **for ever.** Heb. *olam*, Ex +*12:24.

PSALM 119

This psalm contains a miscellaneous collection of wise maxims, pious ejaculations, holy purposes, gracious experiences, etc. which cannot with ease and simplicity be arranged under any particular heads. There frequently is little connection between one sentence and another, and the whole being, as Mr. Henry remarks, "rather a chest of gold rings, than a chain of gold links." The whole psalm is a majestic hymn to the written word of God, expressing David's love for it and a prayer for grace to carry himself according to it, with an account of God's law, institutions, commandments, testimonies, precepts, word, promises, ways, judgments, name, righteousness, and truth.

(Title.) A.M. 3560. B.C. 444. This psalm, probably composed by Ezra (though many, including Matthew Poole, think it was composed by David), is another of the alphabetical psalms: it consists of twenty-two parts, answering to the number of the Hebrew letters; every part being divided into eight verses, and each verse beginning with that letter which forms the title of the part; that is, the first part of eight verses, with *aleph*, the second with *beth*, etc. It is an elegant, important, and useful composition; the chief subjects of which are the excellence of God's laws, and the happiness of those who observe them.

ALEPH

1. ſ2. Acrostichion; or, Acrostic B182: the repetition of the same or successive letters at the beginnings of words or clauses. This device has been noted in the original language for the following passages, which are unmarked for this figure since this feature is not observable in English translation: Ps ch. 9, 10, 25, 34, 37. 96:11. ch. 145. Est 1:20. 5:4, 13. 7:7. Pr 31:10-31. La ch. 1, 2, 3, 4. **Blessed.** ſ43, Ps √1:1-3. 32:1, 2. *112:1. 128:1. Dt +28.3. Mt +*5:3-12. Lk +√11:28. Jn +√13:17. Ja *1:25. Re *22:14. **undefiled.** *or*, perfect, *or* sincere, Ps +101:6mg. T#504. ver. +3 (T#505), *165. Ps 11:7. 37:18n. 45:13. 73:1. *139:23, 24. *147:11. Ge 5:24. Dt +33:9 (T#672). Jsh +14:8, +14. 2 K +*20:3. 1 Ch 12:38n. 2 Ch 31:20, 21. Jb 1:1, 8. +36:7 (T#585). Pr *8:17. 11:20. Is +60:21 (T#441). Jn 1:+12 (T#584), +47 (T#659). 13:34. 16:27. +√17:6. Ac 24:16. Ro *13:8, 10. 2 C 1:12. Ep +5:25 (T#94). Ph √3:12. 1 Th 2:10. T *2:11, 12. 1 J +1:8 (T#507), 10. *3:3. 4:12, 17. Re *19:8. **walk.** Ps √1:1-3. 25:10. Ezk *11:20. Ho 14:9. Lk 1:6. 1 Th *4:1, 2.

2. **Blessed.** ſ43, Dt +28:3. **keep.** ver. 22, 146. Ps *25:10. 105:45. Dt 6:17. 1 K *2:3. Pr 23:26. Ezk ◐*33:31. 36:27. Jn +√13:17. *14:23. 1 J 3:20. **seek.** ver. *10. Ps +*9:10. 27:8. Dt *4:29. 2 Ch 31:21. Je 3:10. √29:13. Ho 10:2. He *11:6. **whole heart.** Dt *6:5. Jsh +*14:8. Je 24:7. *29:13.

3. **do no iniquity.** T#505. Ezk 33:26. Zp *3:13. Mt 6:24. Ro 6:14. 7:15. 13:10. 1 C 2:6 (T#503). Ga 5:16, 17. Ph *3:12. 1 J +√1:8 (T#507). *2:15. √3:6, 9. 4:18. *5:18. **they walk.** Ps *44:18. +*128:1. Jn *10:27. Col +*1:10. 1 Th *4:1.

4. **commanded.** Dt 4:1, *9. *5:29-33. 6:17. *11:13, 22. *12:32. +*26:16, 18. *28:1, etc. 30:16. Jsh 1:7. Je 7:23. Mt √7:21. *28:20. Lk √6:46. +*11:28. Jn 14:15, +√17, 21. Ph *4:8, 9. He √11:6. 1 J √2:3. *5:3.

5. **my ways.** ver. 32, 36, 44, 45, 131, 159, *173. Ps *51:10. Is *30:21. Je *31:33. Ro *7:22-24. 2 Th *3:5. He 13:21.

6. **shall I.** ver. *31, *80. Jb 22:23, 26. Da *12:2, 3. Ro 6:21. 1 J *2:28. 3:20, 21. **ashamed.** Is 45:17. Ro 9:33. **I have.** T#602. ver. *128. Mt *7:16-21. Jn 8:47. 13:35. 14:21, 23, 24. 15:14. Ro 8:9, 14. Ja *2:10, 17, +18 (T#186). 1 J *2:3-6. 3:14, 18, 19, 24. 5:1-4.

7. **I will.** ver. *171. Ps 9:1. 63:3. 86:12, 13. 1 Ch *29:13-17. **when.** ver. 12, *18, 19, *27, 33, 34, 64, 73, 124. Ps *25:4, 5, 8-10. 143:10. Is *48:17. Jn *6:45. **thy righteous judgments.** Heb. judgments of thy righteousness. ver. 138.

8. **I will.** ver. *16, 106, 115. Jsh +*24:15. **O forsake.** ver. 116, 117, *176. Ps 38:21, 22. 51:11. 2 Ch 32:30, 31. Is 54:7, 8. Ph *4:13. He +*13:5.

BETH

9. **shall.** Ps *25:7. 34:11. Jb *1:5. 13:26. Pr *1:4, 10. 4:1, 10-17. 5:7, etc. 6:20, etc. *7:7. Ec 11:9, 10.

*12:1. Lk 15:13. 2 T *2:22. T 2:4-6. **cleanse.** T#1045. Ps 19:9, 11, 12. Ex=30:18. Jn *15:3. *17:17. Ep *5:26, 27. He *10:22. **by taking.** ver. √11, √97-105. Ps *1:1-3. *17:4. √19:7-11. *74:4-8. Dt 6:6-9. 17:18-20. Jsh 1:7. Pr √4:23. Lk 22:61, 62. Jn √15:3. 17:17, 19. 2 T √3:15-17. Ja *1:21-25.

10. **my whole heart.** ver. 2, 34, 58, 69. Ps *78:37. 1 S 7:3. 2 Ch *15:15. Is 26:9. Je 3:10. Ho *10:2. Zp 1:5, 6. Mt *6:24. Col 3:22. He √11:6. 1 J *2:15. **O let me not wander.** T#1455, 1741. ver. 17, *18, 21, 33-35, 118, *133, 176. Ps 23:3. 125:5. *143:8-10. 1 Ch 29:18, 19. Pr 2:13. 21:16. Is *35:8. Ezk 34:6. 2 P *2:15-22.

11. **Thy word.** ver. *97, 105. Ps √1:2. √37:31. *40:8. Jb *22:22. Pr *2:1, 10, 11. Is 51:7. Je √15:16. 20:9. Lk 2:19, 51. Col √3:16. 1 J 2:14. **hid.** T#1070, 1088. Dt 6:6. 11:18. Jsh √1:8. Lk 8:15. **that I.** Ps *19:13. Ep 6:17, 18.

12. **Blessed.** 1 T 1:11. 6:15. **teach.** T#1096. ver. 26, 27, 33, 64, 66, 68, 71, 72, 108, 124, 125, 135. Ps *25:4, 5. *86:11. 143:10. Lk √24:45. Jn *14:26. 1 J *2:27.

13. **I declared.** ver. 46, 172. Ps *34:11. 37:30. 40:9, 10. 71:15-18. 118:17. Dt *11:18, 19. Mt 10:27. *12:34, 35. Ac 4:20.

14. **rejoiced.** ver. 47, 72, 77, 111, 127, 162. Ps *19:9, 10. 112:1. Jb √23:12. Is 35:8. Je √15:16. Mt 13:44. Jn +*5:39. √14:6. Ac 2:41-47. 1 C 3:21, 22.

15. **meditate.** ver. 23, 48, 78, 97, 131, 148. Ps √1:2. Ja 1:25. **have respect.** ver. 6, 117. Jb √23:11, 12.

16. **delight.** ver. 14, 24, 35, 47, 70, 77, 92. Ps 40:8. Ro 7:22. He 10:16, 17. **not forget.** T#1086. ver. √11, 83, 93, 109, 141, 176. Pr *3:1. Jn 14:26. He √2:1. Ja *1:23-25.

GIMEL

17 **Deal.** *Gemol*, "reward" thy servant: let him have the return of his faith and prayers. From this word is derived the name of the third letter of the Hebrew alphabet, *gimmel*, which is prefixed to every verse in this part: this is a stroke of the psalmist's art and ingenuity. ver. 65, 124, 132. Ps 13:6. 116:7. Jn 1:16. 2 C 9:7-11. Ph *4:19. **bountifully.** Ps 13:6. *116:7. 1 S +1:22n (✛S#1580h). **I may live.** Ro 8:2-4. 2 C *5:14, 15. Ep 2:4, 5, 10. T 2:11, 12. 1 J 2:29. 5:3, 4.

18. **Open.** Heb. Reveal. T#1482. Ps 146:8. Ge +3:7. 2 K 6:15-17, 20. Is 29:10-12, *18. 32:3. 35:5. 42:7. 43:8. Mt 13:13. 16:17. 20:30-34. Lk +24:16, *45. Jn 9:39. Ac 26:18. 2 C 2:11, 14. *3:14-18. 4:4-6. Ep *1:17, 18. Re 3:18. **that I.** Mt 11:25. Jn 3:27. 6:45. **wondrous.** ver. 96. Ho *8:12. 2 C 3:13. He 8:5. 10:1.

19. **a stranger.** T#1714. Ps 39:12. 94:6. 146:9. Ge +23:4 (✛S#1616h). *47:9. Ex 12:48mg. 1 K 8:41-43. 1 Ch 29:15. Mi 2:10. Mt 8:20. 2 C *5:6. Ph 3:20. He 11:13-16. 13:14. 1 P 1:1-4. 2:11. **hide.** ver. 10. Jb 39:17. Is 63:17. Lk 9:45. *24:45.

20. **soul.** Heb. *nephesh*, Ge +34:3. **breaketh.** T#1396. ver. 40, 131, 174. Ps 42:1. 63:1. 84:2. Pr 13:12. SS 5:8. Mt +*5:6. Re 3:15, 16. **thy judgments.** Is 26:8. **at all times.** Ps 106:3. Jb √23:11, 12. 27:10. Pr 17:17.

21. **rebuked.** ver. 78. Ps 138:6. Ex 10:3. 18:11. Jb 40:11, 12. Is 2:11, 12. 10:12. Ezk 28:2-10. Da 4:37. 5:22-24. Ml 4:1. Lk 14:11. 18:14. Ja 4:6. 1 P *5:5. **the proud.** Pr +*16:5. Ro +*12:3. Ph +*2:3. **cursed.** ver. 10, 110, 118. Ps 37:22. Dt 27:15-26. 28:15. 30:19.

Ne 9:16, 29. Pr +*3:33. Is 42:24. 43:28. Je *17:5. 44:9-11, 16, 28, 29. Zc +*5:3. Mt +*25:41. Ga 3:13. **do err.** Mk *12:24, 27.

22. **Remove.** ver. 39, *42. Ps 39:8. 42:10. 69:9-11, 19, 20. 123:3, 4. 1 S *25:10, 39. 2 S 16:7, 8. Jb 16:20. **reproach.** Jb 19:2, 3. He 13:13. 1 P 2:20. *4:14. **contempt.** T#1671. Ps 123:3, 4. **for I have.** Ps 37:3, 6. 1 P 2:20. 3:16, 17. 4:14-16.

23. **Princes.** Ps 2:1, 2. 1 S 20:31. 22:7-13. Lk 22:66. 23:1, 2, 10, 11. **thy servant.** ver. 15. Da *6:9, 10.

24. **testimonies.** ver. 16, 77, 92, 143, 162. Jb 27:10. Je *6:10. **my counsellers.** Heb. men of my counsel. ver. 97-100, 104, 105. Ps *19:11. 73:24. Dt *17:18-20. Jsh √1:8. Pr *6:20-23. Is √8:20. 40:13mg. 46:11mg. Col *3:16. 2 T √3:15-17.

DALETH

25. **soul.** Heb. *nephesh*, Ge +34:3. Ps 22:15. 44:25. Is *65:25. Mt 16:23. Ro *7:22-24. Ph 3:19. Col 3:2. **quicken.** ver. 37, 40, 88, 93, 107, 149, 154, 156, 159. Ps 71:20. 80:18. 143:11. Is *40:31. Hab 3:2mg. Jn *10:10. Ro 8:2, 3. **according.** T#1098. ver. 28, 41, 76, 169. Dt 30:6. 2 S 7:27-29.

26. **declared.** ver. 106. Ps 27:11. *32:5. 38:18. *51:1, etc. *69:5. 143:8, 10. Jb 31:33. Pr +*28:13. **thou heardest me.** Ps +*34:15, 17. 116:1, 2. Lk 15:18-22. Jn +*9:31. He 4:13-16. **teach.** ver. 12. Ps *25:4, 8, 9. 27:11. 86:11. 143:8-10. 1 K 8:36.

27. **understand.** T#1736. ver. 34, 73, 125, 144, 169. 1 K *3:9. 1 Ch *22:11, 12. Da *9:13. Col *1:9. 2:2. 2 T 2:7. **so shall I talk.** Ps *37:30. *71:17. 78:4. 105:2. 111:4. *145:5, 6. Ex 13:14, 15. Jsh 4:6, 7. Ac 2:11. Re 15:3.

28. **soul.** Heb. *nephesh*, Ge +34:3. **melteth.** Heb. droppeth. T#1404. Ps *22:14. 107:26-28. Jsh 2:11, 24. Jb 16:20h. Ec 10:18h. **strengthen.** Ps *27:14. 29:11. *68:28. Dt 33:25. Is *40:29, 31. Zc 10:12. Ep *3:16. Ph *4:13.

29. **Remove.** T#1614. ver. 37, 104, 128, 163. Ps *141:3, 4. Pr *30:7-9. Is 44:20. Je 16:19. Jon *2:8. Ep *4:22-25. 1 J 1:8. *2:4. Re *22:15. **grant me.** ver. 5. Je *31:33, 34. He *8:10, 11.

30. **chosen.** ver. 29, 11, *173. Jsh √24:15. Pr *1:29. Lk *10:42. Jn *3:19-21. 8:45. 1 P √2:2. 2 J 4. **thy judgments.** ver. 24, 52. Dt *11:18-20.

31. **stuck.** ver. 48, 115. Dt 4:4. *10:20. Pr *23:23. Jn √8:31. Ac *11:23. He 11:13. 2 P *2:21. **put me.** ver. 6, 80. Ps *25:2, 20. Is 45:17. 49:23. Je 17:18. Jl *2:27. Ro *5:5. 1 J *2:28.

32. **run.** SS 1:41. Is 40:31. 1 C *9:24-26. He *12:1. 1 J *5:3. **enlarge.** T#1549. ver. 45. Ps 18:36. 1 K 4:29. Ne 8:10. Jb 36:15, 16. Is 60:5. 61:1. Lk 1:74, 75. Jn 8:32, 36. 2 C 3:17. 6:11. 1 P 2:16.

HE

33 **Teach.** ver. 12, 26, 27. Is 54:13. Jn 6:45. **I shall keep.** ver. 8, 112. Je *32:40. Mt 10:22. 24:13. 1 C 1:7, 8. Ph 1:6. 1 J 2:19, 20, 27. Re *2:26.

34. **Give me.** ver. 73. Ps 111:10. Jb 28:28. Pr 2:5, 6. Jn *7:17. Ph *2:13. Ja *1:5. 3:13-18. **I shall.** Dt 4:6. Mt 5:19. 7:24. Ja 1:25. 2:8-12. 4:11. **observe.** ver. 10, 58, 69.

35. **Make me.** ver. 27, 36, 173. Ezk 36:26, 27. Ph 2:13. He 13:21. **the path.** Ps *23:3. Pr *3:13, 17. 4:11, 18. 8:20. Is 2:3. 48:17. **therein.** ver. 16. Is 58:13, 14. Ro 7:22. 1 J 5:3.

36. **Incline.** Ps 51:10. 141:4. 1 K 8:58. Je 32:29. Ezk 11:19, 20. **and not to.** Ps 10:3. Ex +*18:21. Ezk +*33:31. Hab 2:9. Mt *6:24. Mk *7:21, 22. Lk √12:15. 16:14. 2 C 4:18. Ep 5:3, 5. Col *3:5. 1 T *6:9, 10, 17. He +*13:5. 2 P 2:3, 14.

37. **Turn.** Heb. Make to pass. Nu *15:39. Jsh 7:21. 2 S *11:2. Jb *31:1. Pr *4:25. 23:5. Is *33:15. Mt *5:28. Ph *3:13, 14. 1 J *2:16. **quicken.** ver. 25, 40.

38. **Stablish.** ver. 49. 2 S 7:25-29. 2 C *1:20. **who is devoted.** Ps *103:11, 13, 17. 145:19. 147:11. Je 32:39-41.

39. **reproach.** T#1672. ver. 22, 31. Ps *39:8. 57:2, 3. 69:6-9, 19, 20. 79:4, 5. 109:25, 26. 2 S *12:14. Ne 4:4. Je 20:7-13. La 5:1. 1 T 3:7. 5:14. T 2:8. **for thy.** ver. 20, 43, 75, 123, 131. Ps 19:9. Dt 4:8. Is 26:8. Ro 2:2. 7:12. Re 19:2.

40. **I have.** ver. 5, 20. Ps *37:4. Mt 26:41. Ro 7:22, 24. 2 C *7:1. Ga 5:17. Ph 3:13, 14. **quicken.** ver. 25, 37, 88, 107, 149, 156, 159. Mk 9:24. Jn 5:21. 10:10. 1 C 15:45. Ep 2:5. 3 J 2.

VAU

41. **Let.** ver. 58, 76, 77, 132. Ps 35:3. 69:16. 106:*4, 5. Lk *2:28-32. Ja 1:21.

42. **So shall.** Ps 3:2, 3. 42:10. *71:10, 11. 109:25. Mt *27:40-43, 63. **have wherewith,** etc. *or,* answer him that reproacheth me in a thing. 2 S 16:7, 8. 19:18-20. 1 P *3:15. 2 P 1:16, 19. **for I trust.** T#1092. ver. 49, 74, 81. Ps *56:4, 10, 11. 89:19, etc. 2 S 7:12-16. 1 Ch 28:3-6. Mi 7:8. Ac *27:25.

43. **take not.** ver. 13. Ps 50:16. 51:14, 15. 71:17, 18. Is 59:21. Ep 1:13. Ja 1:18. **for I have.** ver. 52, 120, 175. Ps 7:6-9. 9:4, 16. 43:1. 1 P 2:23.

44. **So shall.** The language of this verse is very emphatic. Perfect obedience will constitute a large proportion of heavenly happiness to all eternity; and the nearer we approach to it on earth, the more we anticipate the felicity of heaven. **keep.** ver. 33, 34. Re *7:15. 22:11. **continually.** Ps 119:109, 117. Is +*58:11. **for ever.** Heb. *olam*, Ps +21:4. **and ever.** Ps +9:18 (*S#5703h).

45. **And I will.** ver. 133. Ps 12:8. 39:6. Is 26:12, 13. Lk 4:18. Jn *8:30-36. Ja 1:25. 2:12. 2 P 2:19. **at liberty.** Heb. at large. ver. 32, 96. Ps 101:5 (proud). 104:25. 118:5. Ne 7:4mg. Pr 4:12. Is 22:18mg. **for I seek.** ver. 19, 71, 94, 148, 162. Pr 2:4, 5. 18:1. Ec 1:13. Jn +√5:39. Ep 5:17.

46. **speak.** Ps 138:1. Da 3:16-18. 4:1-3, 25-27. Mt 10:18, 19. Ac 26:1, 2, 24-29. 1 T 6:13. **will not.** Mk √8:38. Ro √1:16. Ph 1:20. 2 T 1:8, 16. 1 P 4:14-16. 1 J 2:28.

47. **I will delight.** ver. 16, 24. Ps 112:1. Jn 4:34. Ph 2:5. 1 P 2:21. **which.** ver. 48, 97, 127, 140, 167, 174. Ps *19:7-10. Jb √23:11, 12. Ro 7:12, 16, 22.

48. **hands.** Ps 10:12. Ezk 44:12. Mi 5:9. **unto thy.** Mt √7:21. Jn +√13:17. 15:14. Ja 1:22-25. **and I will.** ver. 15. Ps *1:2.

ZAIN

49. **Remember.** ƒ22C3, Ge +8:1. T#1656. Ps 105:2, 42. 106:4, 45. Ge 8:1. 32:9-12. Jsh 23:14. 2 Ch 6:42. Ne 1:8, 9. Jb 7:7. Is 62:6mg. **upon which.** ver. 43, 74, 81, 147. Ps 71:14. 2 S 5:2. 7:25. Ro 15:13. 1 P 1:13, 21.

50. **This.** Ps *27:13. *28:7. 42:8, 11. 94:19. Je √15:16. Ro 5:3-5. *8:28. √15:4. He 6:17-19. 12:11, 12. **thy word.**

ver. 11, 38, 41, 58, 67, 76, 82, 103, 116, 123, 133, 140, 148, 158, 162, 170, 172. **hath quickened**. ver. +25, +40, 162. Ezk 37:10. Jn *6:63. Col 2:13. He *4:12. Ja *1:18. 1 P *1:23. *2:2.

51. **proud**. ver. 21, 69. Ps 123:3, 4. Je 20:7. Lk 16:14, 15. 23:35. 1 C 4:12, 13. 2 T *3:12. 1 P 2:23. **yet have**. ver. 31, 157. Ps 44:18. Jb 23:11. Is 38:3. 42:4. Ac 20:23, 24. He *12:1-3.

52. **remembered**. T#1382. Ps 42:6. 63:5, 6. 77:5, 11, 12. 78:34, 35. 105:5. 143:5. Ex 14:29, 30. Nu 16:3, etc. Dt 1:35, 36. 4:3, 4. Is 64:5. Jon 2:4. 2 P *2:4-9. **of old**. Heb. *olam*, Ge +*6:4. **comforted**. Is 25:4. Ro *15:4.

53. **Horror**. Ps 11:6. La 5:10mg. *Zilaphah* properly signifies the pestilential burning wind called by the Arabs *Simoom* (see Ps 11:6). It is here used in a figurative sense for the most horrid mental distress and strongly marks the idea the psalmist had of the corrupting, pestilential, and destructive nature of sin. ver. 136, 158. Ezr *9:3, 14. 10:6. Je 13:17. Da 4:19. Hab 3:16. Lk *19:41, 42. Ac 17:16, 17. Ro 9:1-3. 2 C 12:21. Ph 3:18. **the wicked**. 2 P *3:17.

54. **Thy statutes**. Ps 89:1. 101:1. Ge 47:9. He *11:13-16.

55. **night**. T#1165. ver. 62, 148. Ps 22:2. *42:8. *63:5, 6. *72:2. *77:6. *139:18. Ge 20:3, 4. 26:24. *32:24-28. Jb 35:9, *10. Is *26:9. La 2:19. Lk *6:12. Ac *16:25. **kept**. ver. 17, 34. Jn *14:21. *15:10.

56. **This**. ∫63A4, 1 K +3:22. Supply ellipsis (absolute: of connected words), "This (consolation) I had." Luther supplies the word *treasure*. **I kept**. T#1132. ver. 8, 22, 43, 47, 55, 58-60, 145, 146, 153, *165. Ps 18:18-22. *19:11. Dt 26:13-15. Is 32:17. Jn 14:23. 1 J 3:19-24.

CHETH

57. **my portion**. Ps +16:5. *73:25, 26. 142:5. Je 10:16. La 3:24. **I have**. ver. 106, 115. Ps 66:14. Dt 26:17, 18. Jsh 24:*15, 18, 21, 24-27. Ne 10:29, etc.

58. **I intreated**. ver. 10. Ps 4:6. 51:1-3. 86:1-3. Ge 32:26. Ho 7:14. He 10:22. **favor**. Heb. face. T#1525. Ps 27:8. 45:12mg. 102:12, 13. 106:4, 5. Jb +11:19mg. 33:26. **be merciful**. ver. 41, 65, 76, 170. Ps 56:4, 10. 138:2. Mt 24:35. **according to**. Ge 32:12. Ex 32:13. 2 S 7:25. 1 K 8:25.

59. **thought**. La 3:40. Ezk 18:28, 30. Hg *1:5, 7. Lk *15:17-20. 2 C *13:5. **turned**. T#600. ver. 112. Dt 4:30, 31. Je 8:4-6. 31:18, 19. La *3:40. Ezk 18:27, 28. 33:14-16, 19. Jl *2:13. Ac 17:28. 1 C 4:15. 2 C 12:21. Col 3:9, 10. 1 P 1:22.

60. **made**. Ps *95:7, 8. Ezr 10:6-8. Pr *27:1. Ec 9:10. Ac ◐24:25. Ga 1:16.

61. **The bands**. *or*, The companies. ver. 95. Ps 3:1. 1 S *30:3-6. Jb 1:17, 20, 21. Ho 6:9. He 10:34. **but I**. ver. 176. 1 S 24:9-11. 26:9-11. Pr 24:29. Mt *6:20. Ro *12:17-21.

62. **midnight**. T#1162. ver. 147, 164. Ps 42:8. 139:17, 18. 149:5. Mk *1:35. Ac *16:25. **thy**. ver. 7, 75, 106, 137. Ps 19:9. Dt 4:8. Ro 7:12.

63. **a companion**. ver. 79, 115. Ps *15:4. *16:3. 45:7. 55:14. 101:+*4, 6, 7. 142:7. Jg 20:11. 1 S 23:16. 2 Ch ◐*13:7. *19:2. Pr 2:20. 12:26. *13:20. 27:17. Ec 10:10. Ml *3:16-28. Mt +15:14. Lk 24:15, 32. Ro 1:12. *16:17. 1 C *12:13. 1 C +*15:33. 2 C *6:14-17. 7:6, 7. Ep 5:3, 7, 11. Col 2:2. 2 Th *3:6, 14. 1 T +6:5. 2 T *2:19. 3:5. He +*3:12, 13. 10:25. 1 P 3:8.

1 J 1:3. 3:14. **fear**. ver. 120. Ps 55:19. 76:8. 103:11, *17. 112:1. 118:4. 128:4. 135:20. Ex +*18:21. Pr 1:29. Ec 8:12. Ml *3:16. **keep**. ver. 2, 4. Ps *103:18. Pr 1:10. Lk +*11:28. 2 J 9-11. **precepts**. ver. 56. Ps 111:10.

64. **earth**. Ps 33:5. 104:13. *145:+9, 15, 16. **teach**. ver. 12, 26. Ps 27:11. Is 2:3. 48:17, 18. Mt *11:29.

TETH

65 **dealt well**. ver. 17. Ps 13:6. 16:5, 6. 18:35. 23:5, 6. 30:11. 116:7. 1 Ch 29:14.

66. **Teach me**. Rather, "Teach me (to have) good taste (Heb. *taam*) and discernment, that faculty of the mind by which I may discern, distinguish, judge rightly, and relish things moral and spiritual." ver *34. Ps 72:1, 2. 1 K *3:9, 28. Pr *2:1-9. 8:20. Is *11:2-4. Je *3:15. Mt 13:11. Ph √1:9, 10. *4:8, 9. Ja *3:13-18. **I have**. ver. *128, *160, 172. Ne 9:13, 14.

67. **Before**. ver. *176. Ps 73:5, etc. Dt *32:15. 2 S 10:19. *11:2, etc. 2 Ch *33:9-13. Pr *1:32. *22:21. **but now**. ver. *71, 75. Je *31:18, 19. La 3:27. Ho 2:6, 7. *5:15. *6:1. He *12:10, 11. Re *3:10.

68. **good**. T#224. Ps 5:4. *86:5. 106:1. 107:1. *145:7-9. Ex *33:18, 19. *34:6, 7. Dt 5:29. 32:29. Is 63:7. Ezk 18:32. Mt +*5:45. *19:17. Mk *10:18. Lk +*6:35. *18:19. Jn 3:14-17. Ro *2:4. *5:8. *8:32. *11:22. 1 Th 4:3. 1 T *2:3, 4. 2 P √3:9. 1 J *4:7-10. **teach**. ver. *12, 26. Ps *25:8, 9.

69. **proud**. Ps 35:11. *109:2, 3. Jb *13:4. Je 43:2, 3. Mt *5:11, 12. 10:25. *26:59, etc. Ac *24:5, 13. **I will**. ver. *51, 157. **with my whole**. ver. *34, *58. Mt *6:24. He √11:6. Ja 1:8.

70. **heart is as fat**. Ps 17:10. *73:7. Is *6:10. Ac *28:27. Ep 4:19. 1 T *4:2. **but I**. ver. *16, *35. Ps +*1:2. *40:8. Ro *7:22.

71. **good**. ver. *67. Ps *94:12, 13. Is 27:9. 1 C *11:32. He 5:8. *12:10, 11. 1 P 1:6, 7.

72. **better**. ver. 14, 111, 127, 162. Ps *19:10. Pr *3:14, 15. 8:*10, 11, 19. *16:16. Mt *13:44-46. Ep 3:8.

JOD

73. **Thy hands**. Ps *100:3. 138:8. *139:14-16. Jb *10:8-11. **give me**. ver. *34, 125, 144, *169. Ps *111:10. 1 Ch *22:12. 2 Ch 2:12. Jb *32:8. Pr *2:3-6. 2 T *2:7. 1 J *5:20. **that I may**. ver. *111:10. Ja 3:18. 1 J *2:3.

74. **fear thee**. ver. *79. Ps *34:2-6. *66:16. Ml *3:16. **I have**. ver. *42, *147. Ps 108:7. Ge 32:11, *12. Lk *21:33. Ro *15:4.

75. **I know**. ver. *7, *62, *128, *160. Le 10:3. Dt *32:4. Ezr 9:13. Jb 2:10. *34:23. Is 27:8. Je 12:1. La 3:39. Mi 7:18. **right**. Ne. righteousness. ver. 137. Ps *145:17. Ge √18:25. Ex ●9:27. Jg ◐1:7. 2 Ch ◐12:6. Je 10:24. Ro 3:4, 5. Ja ◐+*2:19. **thou in faithfulness**. Ps *25:10. 39:9. 89:30-33. *94:11, 12. 107:43. Dt *8:16. 1 S 3:18. 16:10-12. 2 K *4:19, 20, 23, 26, 27. Jb 1:21. *13:15. Is 39:8. Je +*29:11. 1 C *11:32. He *12:10, 11. Ja *5:11. 1 P *4:17, 19. Re *3:19. **afflicted me**. ver. 67, 71. Ps 77:2, 71:10. ●*34:19. +√90:15. 102:23mg. Ex 15:23-25. Ru +*1:13. Ezr 9:13. Jb 11:6. ●√37:23. Is 27:9. *48:10. 64:12. La +*3:33. Ho 2:6, 7, 14. Am 3:2. Na 1:12. Zc 13:9. Jn 15:2. 1 C *11:30, 31. He 12:6. Re 3:19.

76. **merciful**. Ps *86:5. 106:4, 5. 2 C *1:3-5. **for my comfort**. Heb. to comfort me. Ge 37:35. 2 S 10:2. Is *66:13.

77. **thy tender**. ver. *41. Ps *51:1-3. La *3:22, 23.

Da 9:18. **may live.** Jn *10:10. **for thy.** ver. *24, 47, 174. Ps *1:2. He *8:10-12.

78. **the proud.** ver. *21, 51, 85. Ps *35:26. *83:16-18. **dealt perversely.** Ps 139:21. Mt 5:11, 12. **without.** ver. 86. Ps *7:3-5. *25:3. *35:7. *69:4. 109:3. 1 S *24:10-12, 17. 26:18. Jn *15:24, 25. 1 P *2:20. **but I will.** ver. *23. Ps *1:2.

79. **Let those.** T#1491. ver. +√63, *74. Ps 7:7. 133:1. *142:7. Est 10:3. Ac 2:46, 47. Ro 15:7. 1 C 11:1. 2 T *4:16. He 10:24. 3 J 11, 12. **turn.** Ps 6:10. 7:12. 9:17. 18:37. Ga 6:2. **and those.** ver. +√63. **known.** Ps *36:10. 37:18. 44:21.

80. **heart.** Ps 51:6. 95:10, 11. **sound.** Ps 25:21. 32:2. Dt *26:16. 2 Ch *12:14. 15:17. *25:2. *31:20, 21. Pr +*4:23. Ezk 11:19. Jn 1:47. 2 C *1:12. 1 T *4:16. 2 T *2:15. 4:3. Re 3:1, 2. **that I be.** ver. *6. Ps 25:2, 3. 1 J *2:28.

CAPH

81. **soul.** Heb. *nephesh,* Ge +34:3. **fainteth.** T#1399. ver. 20, 40. Ps 42:1, 2. 73:26. *84:2. 106:4. 107:4-6. SS 5:8. Jon 2:7. Ph 1:23. Re 3:15, 16. **salvation.** Ps 35:3. Ge 49:18. 2 S 23:5. Is 25:9. 1 Th 5:8. **but I hope in.** T#1089. See on ver. *42, 74, *77, *114, 147. Ro 8:24.

82. **Mine eyes.** T#1084. ver. *123. Ps *69:3. Dt *28:32. Pr 13:12. Is *38:14. **fail.** √155A, Ge +31:35. **When wilt.** Ps *86:17. 90:13-15. Is 8:17. **comfort.** T#1454. ver. 76. Ps 71:21. *86:17. 2 Th 2:16, 17.

83. **like a bottle in the smoke.** As the bottles in the East were made of skin, it is evident that one of these hung up in the smoke must soon be parched, shrivelled up, lose all its strength, and become unsightly and useless. Thus the psalmist appeared to himself to have become useless and despicable through the exhausted state of his body and mind and by long bodily afflictions and mental distress. Ps 22:15. *102:3, 4. Jb 30:30. **yet do I.** ver. *16, 61, 176.

84. **How.** Ps *39:4, 5. *89:47, 48. *90:12. Jb 7:6-8. **when.** Ps 7:6. 2 Th 1:6. Re *6:10, 11.

85. **The proud.** This metaphor is taken from the mode in which wild beasts are caught in the East: deep pits are dug in the earth and slightly covered over with reeds or turf so as not to be discerned from the solid ground. The animals attempt to walk over them, the surface breaks, they fall in, and are taken alive. Thus the psalmist's enemies employed craft as well as power in order to effect his ruin. ver. 78. Ps *7:15. *35:7. *36:11. Pr *16:27. Je 18:20. **which.** Ps 58:1, 2.

86. **All thy.** ver. 128, 138, *142, 151. Ps *19:9. Ro *7:12. **faithful.** Heb. faithfulness. ver. 30, 75, 90, 138mg. **they.** ver. *78. Ps 7:1-5. *35:7, 19. *38:19. 59:3, 4. Je *18:20. **help.** Ps 44:4-6. *70:5. 142:4-6. 143:9. 2 Ch *14:11, 12.

87. **almost.** 1 S *20:3. 23:26, 27. 2 S *17:16. Mt +*10:28. **but I forsook not.** ver. 51, 61. 1 S 24:6, 7. *26:9, 24.

88. **Quicken.** ver. 25, 40, 159. Col 3:3. **so shall I.** ver. *2, 146. Ps *25:10. 78:5. *132:12. 2 C 3:5. **testimony.** Jg 3:20. 1 S 3:9.

LAMED

89. **For ever.** Heb. *olam,* Ex +*12:24. ver. 152, 160. Ps *89:2. Is *40:8. Mt *5:18. 24:34, *35. 1 P *1:25. 2 P *3:13. Or, as the Syriac reads, "Thou art

(or, existest) for ever, O Jehovah; thy word is established in the heavens." The word of God is as unchangeable and everlasting as his own existence: it is "established in the heavens" beyond the reach of the revolutions of this lower world; its accomplishment is as certain as the motions of the heavenly bodies, which are not and cannot be affected by the convulsions and vicissitudes of the earth and its inhabitants. Je +√33:20, 21, 25, 26. Ml *3:6. **O Lord.** √63B, Ge +2:10. Supply by ellipsis (absolute: of verb substantive), "For ever (art Thou) O Lord;!Thy word is settled in heaven.!Thy faithfulness (is) unto all generations;!Thou hast established the earth, and it abideth." In the first and third lines, we have Jehovah. In the second and fourth lines, we have what he has settled and established (B39). **thy word.** Is 45:23. 1 P *1:25. **is settled.** He *6:17-19. **in heaven.** Ep 1:4.

90. **faithfulness.** Ps 89:1, 2. Dt 7:9. Mi 7:20. **unto all generations.** Heb. to generation and generation. Ps +33:11mg. 89:*1mg, 2, 4. 100:5mg. 135:13mg. Pr +*27:24mg. **thou hast.** Ps 89:11. *93:1. 104:5. Jb 38:4-7. 2 P *3:5-7. **established.** Ps 8:3. 9:7. 40:2. **abideth.** Heb. standeth. Ps 10:1. 33:9. 38:11. 76:7. 78:69. 104:5. Ec +*1:4. He *1:3.

91. **They continue this.** Ps *148:5, 6. Ge +*8:22. Is 48:13. Je +*33:25, 26. **according to.** Ps 148:8. Jb 37:11, 12. **ordinances.** Jb +38:33. **all are.** Ge +50:20. Dt *4:19. Jsh *10:12, 13. Jg 5:20. Mt *5:45. 8:9.

92. **thy law.** ver. 24, 77, 143. Ro √15:4. **my delights.** Jb *23:12. Je +*15:16. **I should.** Ps *27:13. *94:18, 19. Pr *6:22, 23.

93. **will never.** ver. 16, 50. Jn √8:31. **with them.** Jn *6:63. 1 P *1:23. **thou hast.** 1 C *3:7. Ph *2:13. **quickened.** T#1036. ver. +50. Jn *6:63. Ro √10:17. He *4:12. Ja +*1:18.

94. **I am thine.** ver. 125. Ps *4:3. 74:2. *86:2. 143:12. Dt 32:9. Jsh 10:4-6. Is *41:8-10. 43:*1, 10-12. 44:2, 5, *21, *22. *64:8-10. Zp *3:17. Ml *3:17. Lk 11:21, 22. Jn √6:37. *10:29. *17:6-11. Ac √20:28. *27:23, 24. Ro *6:16. *8:7-9. 1 C *3:23. *6:19, 20. Ep *2:10. **save me.** T#1688. ver. 146. Ps 3:7. 6:4. 7:1. 54:1. 69:1. 71:2. 80:2, 3. 86:2mg, 16. 106:47. 109:26. 118:25. Je 17:14. Mt 8:25. 14:30. 1 Ch 16:35. **for I have.** ver. *27, 40, 173. Jn √10:27, 28. **sought.** ver. 10, 45, 155. Ps +*34:4. 109:10. Is 34:16. Jn +√5:39. He *11:6.

95. **wicked.** ver. *61, *69, 85-87. Ps 10:8-10. 27:2. *37:32. 38:12. 1 S 23:20-23. 2 S 17:1-4. Zc 2:8. Mt *26:3-5. Lk *21:17-19. Ac *12:11. *23:21. 25:3. **but I.** ver. *24, 31, 111, 125, 129, 167.

96. **I have seen.** That is, I have seen all that human wisdom or knowledge, however extensive, noble, and excellent, has its bounds, limits, and end, but thy law, a transcript of thine own mind, is infinite and extends to eternity. Ps *39:5, 6. 1 S 9:2. *17:8, 49-51. 31:4, 5. 2 S 14:25. 16:23. 17:23. 18:14, 17. Ec *1:2, 3. 2:11. √7:20. 12:8. Mt *5:18. *24:35. Ph 3:6, 7. Ja *2:10. **but thy.** Ps *19:7, 8. Pr 24:9. Mt *5:18, 28. *22:37-40. 24:35. Mk *12:29-34. Jn 6:28, 29. Ro *7:7, 9, 12, 14. Ga 3:13. He √4:12, 13. 1 J 3:23. **broad.** ver. 45h. Ge 34:21. Jb 11:9. Is 22:18mg. 33:21mg. 51:28. Ezk 23:32. Ro 3:22.

MEM

97 **O how.** T#1080. ver. *48, *113, 127, *159, 165, *167. Ps *1:2. √138:2. Dt *6:6-9. *17:18, 19. Jsh √1:8.

1 K ●22:8. Pr 2:10. 18:1. **meditation**. ver. 99. Jb 15:4. 1 T *4:15.

98. **Thou**. Ps 25:12. **through**. ver. 104. Dt *4:6, 8. 1 S *18:5, 14, 15, 30. Pr *2:6. Col *3:16. **wiser**. Ps 105:22. Jb 35:11. **they are ever**. Heb. it *is* ever. ver. √11, 30, √105. Ja *1:25. **ever**. Heb. *olam*, Ps +*5:11.

99. **understanding**. Jb *32:8. **than all**. Dt *4:6, 8. 2 S 15:24-26. 1 Ch 15:11-13. 2 Ch 29:15, etc. 30:22. Je 2:8. *8:8, 9. Mt *11:25. 13:11. *15:6-9, 14. 23:24, etc. Lk *2:46, 47. He *5:12. **teachers**. Ps 18:34. 94:10. 144:1. **for thy**. ver. 24. 2 T √3:15-17.

100. **understand**. 1 S 3:19. 1 K 12:6-15. Jb *12:12. 15:9, 10. 32:4, 10. **the ancients**. Ps +105:22. 107:32. 148:12. Jb *32:9. Ec 4:13. **because**. Ps *111:10. Jb 28:28. Is *64:5. Je *8:8, 9. Mt *7:24. Jn *7:17. 14:21-23. Ja 3:13.

101. **refrained**. ver. *59, *60, *104, *128. Ps *18:23. 139:24. Pr *1:15. 10:23. 16:17. Is √53:6. √55:7. Je 2:36. Ro *12:9. 1 C 9:25. 2 C *7:1. Ga 5:23. 1 Th *5:22. T *2:11, 12. 1 P *2:1, 2. *3:10, 11. 2 P 1:6. **keep**. Pr 7:2. Lk +√11:28.

102. **departed**. Ps *18:21. *86:11. Dt *17:20. Jsh 23:6. 1 K *15:5. Pr *5:7. Je 17:5. *32:40. **for thou**. Ps 27:11. *32:8. 86:11. 1 K 8:36. Is 30:20. *54:13. Je 31:33. Jn *6:45. Ep *4:20-24. 1 Th √2:13. 1 J *2:20, 27.

103. **sweet**. T#1082. Ps *19:10. 56:10. 63:5. Jb √23:12. Pr 3:17. *8:11. *24:13, 14. SS 1:2-4. 5:1. Je *15:16. **taste**. Heb. palate. Ps 137:6. Jb 6:30mg. 12:11mg. +31:30mg. 34:3mg. Pr 5:3mg. SS 2:3mg. Ho 8:1mg. **honey**. Ps 19:10. 34:8. 81:16. Ge 43:11. Pr 24:13, 14. 27:7. 2 C 2:14.

104. **Through**. ver. *98, *100. **precepts**. ver. 4, 15, 27, 35, 40, 45, 56. **get understanding**. ver. *130. Ps *19:7. Pr 2:10, 11. *8:9. 16:21. Lk 24:32, 45. He 6:1. 2 P *3:18. **therefore**. ver. *128. Ps *36:4. *97:10. *101:3. Pr *8:13. 13:5. Am *5:15. Ro *12:9. Ju 23. **false way**. ver. *29, *30, +*128. Ps 49:13. Pr *14:12. Je 44:4. Mt *7:13. Ep *5:11, 12. 1 Th *5:22. 2 Th *2:10-12. 2 J *9-11.

NUN

105. **word**. Ps 19:8. *43:3. Pr *6:23. Ep 5:13. 2 P √1:19. **lamp**. *or*, candle. ƒ22K2, 2 S +22:29. Ps +18:28mg. 132:17mg. Jb *29:3mg. **a light**. T#1095. ver. 130. Ps 4:6. 27:1. 36:9. 37:6. 38:10. Is √8:20. Mt 5:14. Jn 1:9. 1 J 1:5. **path**. ver. 9. Ps *17:4. 142:3. Jg 5:6. Jb 19:8. 24:13.

106. **sworn**. Ps 56:12. 66:13, 14. 2 Ch 15:13, 14. Ne *10:29. Ec *5:4, 5. Je 50:5. Mt 5:33. 2 C 8:5. **that I will**. ver. 115. 2 K 23:3.

107. **afflicted**. Ps 6:1-3. *22:14-18. *34:19. Ro 5:3-5. 2 C *4:17. **quicken**. ver. *25, *88. Ps 71:20. *143:11. Hab 3:2. Jn 5:21. 6:63.

108. **Accept**. Ps 19:14. 50:14. **freewill offerings**. Ps 54:6mg. Le 22:21, 23. +*23:38. Nu 15:3. 29:39. Dt 12:6. 16:10. 23:23. 2 Ch 31:14. Ezr 1:4. 3:5. 7:16. 8:28. **of my mouth**. Ps 69:30, 31. Ho *14:2. He *13:15. **teach**. ver. *12, 26, *130, *169.

109. **My soul**. Heb. *nephesh*, Ge +12:13. Rather, "My life (*naphshee*) is continually in my hand;" i.e. *it is in constant danger*; every hour I am on the confines of death. The LXX., Syriac, and Ethiopic read "in thy hand;" but this is a conjectural and useless alteration. Jg *12:3. 1 S *19:5. *20:3. Jb *13:14. Ro *8:36. 1 C 15:31. 2 C 1:9. *11:23. **yet do I not**. ver. 61,

*83, 93, 117, 141, 153, 176. Ja ●1:22-25. 2 P 1:12.

110. **wicked**. ver. *85. Ps 10:8-18. 124:6, 7. 140:5. 141:9. Pr 1:10-15. Je *18:22. **snare**. ver. +*128. 1 S 18:21. Mt 24:4. 2 C 11:13-15. **yet I erred not**. ver. *10, 21, 51, 87, 95. Da *6:10. Mk *12:24. Lk *20:19-26. Ep 4:14. Col 1:23. 2:7.

111. **Thy testimonies**. ver. *14, 127, 162. Ps *16:5, 6. Dt *33:4. Is *54:17. Ac *26:18. Col 1:12. He *9:15. 1 P *1:4. **heritage**. Ps 61:5. Is *54:17. **for ever**. Heb. *olam*, Ex +*12:24. 1 P 1:25. **for they**. ver. 77, 92, 174. Ps *19:8. Je √15:16. 1 P *1:8.

112. **inclined**. ver. *36. Ps *141:4. Jsh *24:23. 1 K *8:58. 2 Ch *19:3. Pr *4:23. Ph *2:12, 13. **perform**. Heb. do. Dt 4:13. Jn +*13:17. **alway**. Heb. *olam*, Ge +*6:3. **the end**. ver. 33, 44. 1 P 1:13. Re 2:10.

SAMECH

113. **hate**. Ps *94:11. Pr 24:9. Is *55:7. Je *4:14. Mk 7:21. 2 C *10:5. **vain thoughts**. Or, "divided thoughts," "*saiaphim*," or, as Gesenius renders, "ambiguities (or indecisions) in religion;" Luther, "inconstant fellows;" LXX., "transgressors," Vulgate, "iniquitous," and Jerome, "tumultuous." 1 K 18:21mg. Je 23:26, 28. Ja 1:8. **thy law**. ver. *97, *103.

114. **my hiding place**. ƒ22L4, Ps +32:7. Ps *32:7. *91:1, 2. 143:9. Is 25:4. *32:2. Col 3:3. **my shield**. Ps *3:3. 18:2. *84:11. Ge 15:1. **I hope**. ver. *81. Ps *130:5, 6.

115. **Depart**. Ps 6:8. 26:5, 9. *139:19. Mt *7:23. *25:41. 1 C 15:33. 2 C 6:14, 17. **for I will**. ver. 106. Jsh *24:15.

116. **Uphold**. Ps 37:17, *24. 41:12. 63:8. 94:18. Dt 33:25. Is *41:10. 42:1. **and let me**. Ps *25:2. Is 45:17. Ro *5:5. *9:33. 10:11. 1 P 2:6. **ashamed**. ƒ121G2, Ps +25:2.

117. **Hold**. Ps 17:5. 37:17. 51:12. 71:5, 6. 73:2, 23. 139:10. *145:14. SS 8:5. Is 41:*10, 13. Jn √10:28, 29. Ro 14:4. 1 P *1:5. Ju *24. **and I will**. ver. 6, 48, 111, 112.

118. **trodden**. Is 25:10. *63:3. Ml 4:3. Lk *21:24. Re 14:20. **err**. ver. 10, 21. Ps *95:10. Dt *29:18-20. Mk *12:24, 27. **their deceit**. ver. 29. Ps 78:36, 37, 57. Is *44:20. Ep 4:22. 5:6. 2 Th 2:9-11. 2 T 3:13. 1 J 2:21. Re 18:23.

119. **Thou**. When Thou triest them in the refining fire, they are burnt up, fly off in fumes, or in *scoriae*, which Thou sweepest away. **puttest away**. Heb. causest to cease. 1 S 15:23. Je 6:30. Ezk *22:18-22. Ml 3:2, 3. Mt 3:12. 7:23. 13:40-42, 49, 50. **therefore**. ver. 111, 126-128.

120. **My flesh**. ver. 53. Le 10:1-3. 1 S 6:20. 2 S 6:8, 9. 1 Ch 21:16, 17, 30. 2 Ch 34:21, 27. Is 66:2. Da 10:8-11. Hab *3:16. Ph *2:12. He 12:21, 28, 29. 1 J ●4:18. Re 1:17, 18. **trembleth**. ver. 161. Is *66:2. Ezk 9:4. **am afraid**. Ps *37:32, 33. Ro *8:1, 33, 34. 2 C 1:12. 1 J 3:21.

AIN

121. **I have**. Ps 7:3-5. *18:18-25. 75:2. 1 S 24:11-15. 25:28. 2 S 8:15. Ac 24:16. 25:10, 11. 2 C 1:12. **leave me**. Ps 37:33. 57:3, 4. Lk 18:7, 8. 2 P 2:9.

122. **surety**. T#1519. Ge 43:9. Pr 22:26, 27. Is 38:14. Phm 18, 19. He 7:22. **let not**. ver. 21. Ps 36:11. **oppress**. ƒ108J, Ge +43:18.

123. **Mine eyes fail**. ƒ155A, Ge +31:35. T#1328. ver. 81, 82. Ps 22:1. *69:3. 130:6. 143:7. La 4:17.

124. **Deal**. ver. 41, 76, 77, 132. Ps 51:1. 69:13, 16. 79:8. *103:10. 130:3, 4, 7. Da 9:18. Lk 18:13. 2 T 1:16-18. **teach**. ver. 12, 26. Ps 143:10-12. Ne 9:20.

125. **I am thy**. ver. 94. Ps 86:16. 116:16. Ro *6:22. **give**. ver. 34, 66. 2 Ch 1:7-10. 2 C 3:5, 6. 2 T 2:7. Ja *1:5. 3:13-17. **that I**. ver. 11, 18, 19, 29. Pr 9:10. 14:8.

126. **time**. Ps 9:19. 102:13. Ge 6:3. 22:10, 11, 14. Dt 32:36. Is 42:14. Ezk 9:4. **to work**. That is, "to take vengeance," as *asah* signifies, Je 18:23. Ml 3:17, by an ellipsis of the noun. ✓63A2. Figure of speech Ellipsis (Absolute: of the Object), 2 S +6:6. When infidels, profligates, and Pharisees "make void the law of God," generally, then it is time for God to arise to vindicate his own honor and maintain his cause among men. **they**. Je 8:8. Hab 1:4. Ml 2:8. Mt 15:6. Ro 3:31. 4:14.

127. **I love**. ver. 72. Ps *19:10. Pr 3:13-18. *8:11. 16:16. Mt 13:45, 46. Ep 3:8.

128. **I esteem**. ver. 6. Ps *19:7, 8. Dt 4:8. Jb 33:27. Pr *30:5. Ro *7:12, 14, 16, 22. **all things**. Lk 1:6. 2 C *7:1. Ph 1:9, 10. 2 T *3:16, 17. Ja *2:10. *Kol*, "all," seems to have been omitted by all versions except the Chaldee, which reads simply, "all thy precepts;" this renders the text more perspicuous and unembarrassed. **right**. Pr 3:6 (direct). 11:5. 15:21. Is 45:2, 13mg. **and I**. ver. *104, 118. **false way**. ver. +*63, 101, 104. Ps 1:6. Pr 14:12. Je 10:2. Lk +6:46. 16:15. Jn 3:19. 5:23, 43. 1 C 6:9-11. 12:3. 2 C 6:14-18. Ga 5:16-21. Ep 4:14. 5:3-7, 11, 12. He 10:25, 26. 1 J 1:10. 2:15-17. 2 J 9-11. Ju 3, 23.

PE

129. **testimonies**. ver. 18. Ps 139:6. Is *9:6. 25:1. Ro *11:33. Re 19:10. **doth**. ver. 2, 31, 146. Ps 25:10. **soul**. Heb. *nephesh*, Ge +34:3.

130. **entrance**. Or, "opening," *paithach*: the Scriptures give satisfactory light to the mind upon every subject of which they treat and speedily communicate more useful knowledge to the simplest believer upon the most important topics than the acutest philosophers have been able to develop through successive ages. ver. *105. Pr 6:23. Is ✓8:20. Lk 1:77-79. Ac *26:18. 2 C *4:4, 6. Ep *5:13, 14. Ph 2:15, 16. 2 P *1:19. **it giveth understanding**. T#1037. Ps *19:7. Pr *1:4, 22, 23. *8:8, 9. 9:4-6. Ro 16:18, 19. 2 T ✓3:15-17. **simple**. ✓108K54, Pr +1:4. Ps *19:7. 116:6. Pr 1:4. Mt 11:25.

131. **opened**. ver. 20. Ps *42:1. Is 26:8, 9. 1 P *2:2. **and panted**. Is +*42:14mg. **I longed**. ver. 40, 162, 174. He *12:14.

132. **Look**. ver. 124. Ps 25:18. Ex 4:31. 1 S 1:11. 2 S 16:12. Is 63:7-9. **as thou usest to do unto those**. Heb. according to the custom toward those. T#1139. Ps 22:4, 5. 71:4-6. 86:17. *106:4. Ge 19:19. Nu 14:19. 1 K 8:51-53. Da 9:15, 18. Jn 14:21, 23. 2 Th *1:6, 7.

133. **Order**. T#1097, 1713. ver. 116. Ps 17:5. *32:8. 121:3. 1 S *2:9. **let not**. Ps *19:13. Ro *6:12-14. 7:23, 24.

134. **Deliver**. T#1631. ver. 121, 122. Ps 17:8, 9. 44:24, 25. 56:1, 2, 13. 105:43-45. Jg 4:3. 10:7-10. Is 19:19, 20. 38:14. Ezk 11:17-20. 36:24-27. Lk 1:74, 75. Jn 8:36. Ac *9:31. **oppression**. ✓108J, Ge +43:18. T#1268. ver. 121, 122. Ps 17:8, 9. 44:23, 24. Ex +2:23 (T#1228). 2 Ch +6:37 (T#1232). Is 19:20. 38:14. 1 T 2:2.

135. **Make**. Ps *4:6. 80:1, 3, 7, 19. Nu *6:25, 26. Jb 33:26. Re *22:4, 5. **and teach**. ver. 12, 26. Jb 34:32.

35:11. 36:22. Lk 24:45. Jn 14:26. 2 C 4:6. He 8:10.

136. **Rivers**. T#1286. ver. 53, 158. Ps 126:6. 1 S 15:11. Je 9:1, 17, 18. *13:17. 14:17. La 1:16. 2:19. 3:48. Ezk *9:4. Lk *19:41. Ro 9:2, 3. 1 C 5:2. 2 C 2:4. Ph *3:18. **because**. Dt 9:18. Ezr 9:2, 3. Mk 3:5. 2 P 2:7.

TZADDI

137 **Righteous**. Ps 99:4. 103:6. 145:17. Dt 32:4. Ezr 9:15. Ne *9:33. Is 45:21. Je 12:1. Da 9:7, 14. Ro 2:5. 3:5, 6. 9:14. Re 15:3, 4. 16:7. 19:2.

138. **testimonies**. ver. 86, 144. Ps *19:7-9. Dt 4:8, 45. **righteous**. Heb. righteousness. ver. 75mg, 172. **and**. ✓93A, Ge +1:26. By the figure hendiadys, "thy testimonies, yes—thy exceeding faithful testimonies" (B661). **faithful**. Heb. faithfulness. ver. 75, 86mg.

139. **zeal**. Ps *69:9. 1 K 19:10, 14. Is 59:17. Jn 2:17. Ro 12:11. T *2:14. Re *3:16, 19. **consumed me**. *or*, cut me off. Ps 18:40. 54:5. 88:16. 101:5, 8. 143:12. La 3:53. **because**. Ps 53:4. Mt 9:13. 12:3-5. 15:4-6. 21:13, 16, 42. 22:29. Ac 13:27. 28:23-27.

140. **Thy word**. Gold has need to be refined, but thy word is purity itself, reflecting the holiness of Jehovah's character and government, both requiring and leading to purity of heart and life. **pure**. Heb. tried, *or* refined. ver. +128. Ps 12:6. 18:30. *19:8. Pr +*30:5. Ro 7:12, 16, 22. 1 P *2:2. 2 P *1:21.

141. **small**. Ps *22:6. +40:17. Pr 15:16. 16:8. 19:1. Is 53:3. Lk 6:20. 9:58. 2 C ✓8:9. *10:10. Ep *3:8. Ja *2:5. **yet do**. ver. 109, 176. Pr 3:1.

142. **Thy righteousness**. Men, as Bp. Horne observes, may decree wickedness by a law or they may change their decrees, and with them what is right today may be wrong tomorrow; but the law of God is righteousness and truth, today and forever. **an everlasting**. Heb. *olam*, Ge +*17:7. **righteousness**. ver. 144. Ps 36:6. Is 51:6, 8. Da 9:24. 2 Th 1:6-10. **and thy**. ver. 151. Ps *19:9. Jn *17:17. Ep *4:21.

143. **Trouble**. ver. 107. Ps 18:4, 5. 88:3, etc. 116:3. 130:1. Mk 14:33, 34. **taken hold on me**. Heb. found me. ✓155F, Ge +4:7. Ps 116:3. Ge +44:34mg. **yet thy**. ver. 16, 47, 77. Jb ✓23:12. Jn 4:34. 16:33. Ro *15:4.

144. **righteousness**. ver. 138, 152. Mt *5:18. 1 P 1:23-25. **everlasting**. Heb. *olam*, Ge +*17:7. **give me**. ver. 34, 66, 73, 169. 2 C 4:6. 1 J 5:20, 21. **understanding**. Pr 10:21. Is 6:9, 10. 27:11. Je 4:22. *9:23, 24. Da 12:10. Ho 4:6. Mt *13:19. Jn ✓17:3. Ja *1:5. **shall live**. 1 P *1:23.

KOPH

145. **cried**. ver. 10, 2. *62:8. 86:4. 102, title. *141:1, 2. *142:1, 2. 1 S 1:10, 15. 1 S +*7:8. Je ✓29:13. Lk +*18:1. **whole heart**. ver. 58. Ps 5:1-3. 17:1, 6. *19:14. *20:9. 22:2, 19. 27:7, 8. *28:1, 2. 38:9. 39:12. *55:1, 2, 16, 17. 57:2. *61:2. 84:8. 88:1, 2, 9, 13. 102:1, 2. 130:1, 2. Ge 18:32. *32:26. Ex 32:32. Dt 9:25. Jg 6:39. 16:28. 1 S 1:10. Ezr 9:5. Ne 1:6. Is *62:1, 6, 7. 64:12. Je ✓29:13. Da 9:3. Ho 12:3, 4. Jon 1:14. Mt *15:23. 20:31. Lk *18:7. Ac 12:5. Ro 8:26. 2 C 12:8. Ja +*5:17. **I will**. ver. 44, 106, 115.

146. **and I shall keep**. *or*, that I may keep. ver. 134. Jg 10:15, 16. Mt 1:21. T *2:14. *3:4-8.

147. **I prevented**. That is, *I anticipated*, or rose before the morning dawn and was beforehand with the light itself. Ps +*5:3. 21:3. 42:8. 88:13. *130:6. 139:17, 18. Ge +22:3. Is 26:9. Mk +*1:35. **dawning**.

T#1156. Ge 32:24. 1 S 30:17. 2 K 7:5. Jb 3:9. **and cried**. Lk 6:12. Ju *20. **hoped**. ver. 74, 81. Ps 56:4. 130:5. He *6:17-19.

148. **eyes**. ver. 62. Ps *63:1, 6. 139:17, 18. La *2:19. Lk *6:12. **the night watches**. The ancient Jews divided the night into three watches of four hours each, beginning at six o'clock in the evening; before the last of which, "the daybreak," or "morning watch," as the LXX. and Vulgate read, the psalmist was awake.

149. **Hear**. Ps 5:2, 3. 55:2. 64:1. **according unto**. Ps 51:1. 69:16. 109:21. Is 63:7. Jn *10:10. Ro √8:32. **quicken me**. ver. 25, 40, 154, 156. Is *30:18.

150. **draw nigh**. Ps 22:11-13, 16. 27:2. 1 S 23:26. 2 S 17:16. Mt 26:46, 47. **far from**. Ps 50:17. Jb 21:14. Pr 1:7, 22. 28:9. Ep 2:13, 14.

151. **near**. Ps *46:1. 75:1. 139:2. *145:18. Dt 4:7. Mt *1:23. Jn 16:32. Ep 2:13. Ph 4:5. **all**. ver. *138, 142.

152. **thy testimonies**. ver. 144, 160. Ps *89:34-37. *111:7, 8. Ec *3:14. Lk *21:33. **of old**. Mi +5:2 (✛S#6924h). **founded**. Ps 104:5. **for ever**. Heb. *olam*, Ex +*12:24.

RESH

153. **Consider**. ver. 159. Ps 9:13. 13:3, 4. 25:19. 31:7. Ex 3:7, 8. Ne 9:32. La 2:20. 5:1. **affliction**. T#1431. Ps 25:16-18. 30:2, 3. 44:22-25. 69:14, 15. 81:6, 7. 86:4-9. 89:14, 15. 106:43, 44. 107:17-19. 109:22-26. Ex 2:23. Dt 26:6, 7. Jg 6:2-6. 1 S 26:24. 2 K 4:18-22. 2 Ch 6:28-30. 33:11-13. Ne 1:3, 4. 9:36, 37. Jb 1:20-22. 34:28. Da 9:17, 18. Jon 2:2-7. Mt 26:38, 39. 2 C 12:7, 8. **deliver**. ver. 154. Ps 91:14, 15. **for I**. ver. 16, 98, 109, 141, 176.

154. **Plead**. Ps 35:1. 43:1. 1 S *24:15. Jb 5:8. Pr 22:23. Je 11:20. 50:34. 51:36. Mi *7:9. 1 P 2:23. 1 J *2:1. **quicken**. ver. 25, 40.

155. **Salvation**. Ps *73:27. *85:9. Jb 5:4. Is 46:12. 57:19. Lk *16:26. Ep *2:12, 13, 17, 18. **for they**. Ps *10:4, 5. Jb *21:14, 15. Pr *1:7. Lk 16:24. Ro *3:11.

156. **Great**. Heb. Many. ver. 157, 162, 165. Ps 3:1. **are thy**. Ps 51:1. 86:5, 13, 15. 1 Ch 21:13. Is *55:7. 63:7. Ep 2:4-6. **quicken**. ver. 149.

157. **Many**. Ps 3:1, 2. 22:12, 16. 25:19. 56:2. 118:10-12. Mt 13:20, 21. 24:9. 26:47. Ac 4:27. **yet do I**. ver. 51, 110. Ps *44:17. Jb 17:9. 23:11. Is 42:4. Ac *20:23, 24. 1 C √15:58.

158. **beheld**. ver. 53, 136. Ezk 9:4. Mk 3:5. **was grieved**. T#662, 1087. ver. 136. Ps +79:9 (T#538). Ezr 9:2-5. 10:6. Ezk *9:4. Ac 17:16. Ro 9:1-3. 2 P 2:7, 8. **kept not**. T#1106.

159. **Consider**. ver. 97, 153. 2 K 20:3. Ne 5:19. 13:22. Jb 1:8. Mt 5:6. **quicken**. ver. 88.

160. **Thy word is true from the beginning**. Heb. The beginning of thy word is true. Dathe renders, "The sum of thy word," and Abp. Secker, "The principles of thy word;" but the textual rendering, by understanding the preposition *mem*, "from," before *rosh*, "beginning," appears to be more correct, as it is supported by the following line. T#1026. ver. 86, 89, 90, 138. Pr +*22:21. *30:5. Jn *17:17. 2 T *3:16. **and every one**. ver. 75, 142, *144, 152. Ec *3:14. Mt *5:18. **for ever**. Heb. *olam*, Ex +*12:24.

SCHIN

161. **Princes**. ver. 23, 157. 1 S 21:23. 24:9-15. 26:18. Jn 15:25. 2 T *3:12. 1 P 3:17. **my heart**. T#1085. Ps

*4:4. Ge 39:9. 42:18. 2 K 22:19. Ne 5:15. Jb 31:23. Is *66:2. Je 36:23-25.

162. **rejoice**. ver. 72, 111. Je √15:16. **as one**. 1 S 30:16. Pr 16:19. Is 9:3. Mt 13:45, 46.

163. **hate**. ver. 29, 113, 128. Ps 101:7. Pr 6:16-19. 26:25. 30:8. Am 5:15. Ro 12:9. Ep 4:25. Re *22:15.

164. **Seven times**. That is, probably, *many times*, or *frequently*, as the term *seven* denotes (compare Jb 5:19n). Rabbi Solomon says that this is to be understood literally, for they praised God twice in the morning before reading the Decalogue and once after; twice in the evening before the same reading, and twice after; making in the whole seven times. ver. 62. Ps 55:17. Pr 24:16. Da 6:10. Mt 18:21. Lk 17:4. **praise**. Ps 34:1. **because**. Ps 48:11. 97:8. Re *15:3. 19:2.

165. **Great peace**. ∫171I9A, Ge +43:23. By Synecdoche of the Species, "peace" is put for every blessing. T#758. Ps 29:11. 125:5. 147:14. Le 26:6. Pr *3:1, 2, 13, 17. Is *26:3, 12. *32:17, 18. *57:21. Jn *14:27. Ga 5:22, 23. 6:15, 16. Ph *4:7. **nothing shall offend them**. Heb. they shall have no stumbling block. Is *8:13-15. *28:13. 57:14. Ezk √3:20. Mt *13:21. 24:24. 1 P *2:6-8.

166. **Lord**. ver. 81, 174. Ps 130:5-7. Ge 49:18. 1 J *3:3. **and done**. Ps 4:5. 24:3-5. *50:23. Jn *7:17. 1 J 2:3, 4.

167. **soul**. Heb. *nephesh*, Ge +34:3. **hath kept**. ver. 5-8, 97, 111, 159. Jn 14:21-24. 15:9, 10. He 10:17. **and I love**. Ps 40:8. Ro 7:22.

168. **for all my**. Ps 44:20, 21. 90:8. 139:3. Jb *34:21. Pr *5:21. Je 23:24. He *4:13. Re 2:23.

TAU

169. **Let my cry**. ver. 145. Ps 18:6. 2 Ch 30:27. **give me**. ver. 144. 1 Ch 22:12. 2 Ch 1:10. Pr 2:3-5, 7. Da 2:21. Ja *1:5.

170. **deliver me**. ver. 41. Ps 89:20-25. Ge 32:9-12. 2 S 7:25.

171. **My lips**, etc. Or, more literally, accordant with the context, "My lips shall pour forth (*tabbanah*) praise; for (*kee*) thou hast taught me thy statutes." ver. 7. Ps 50:23. *71:17, 23, 24.

172. **tongue**. T#1094. ver. 13, 46. Ps 37:30. 40:9, 10. 78:4. Dt 6:7. Mt √12:34-36. Ep *4:29. Col *4:6. **speak**. ∫171J11, Jb +3:1. **for all thy**. ver. 86, 138, 142, 144. Ro 7:12, 14.

173. **Let**. ver. 94, 117. Is 41:10-14. Mk 9:24. Jn *15:5. 2 C 12:9. Ep 6:10, etc. Ph *4:13. **hand**. T#1527. 1 Ch 4:10. Is 41:13. **I have chosen**. ver. 30, 35, 40, 111. Dt 30:19. Jsh *24:15, 22. 1 K 3:11, 12. Pr 1:29. Is ◑+*66:4. Lk *10:42.

174. **longed**. ver. 81, 166. Ge 49:18. 2 S 23:5. Pr 13:12. SS 5:8. Mt +*5:6. Ro 7:22-25. 8:23-25. Ph 1:23. **and thy law**. ver. 16, 24, 47, 77, 111, 162, 167. *1:2.

175. **Let my**. Ps 9:13, 14. 30:9. 51:14, 15. 118:18, 19. Is 38:19. **soul**. Heb. *nephesh*, Ge +12:13. **praise**. 1 P 1:3. **and let thy**. ver. 75. Is *26:8, 9. Ro √8:28. 1 C 11:31, 32. 2 C 4:17.

176. **gone astray**. T#1437. Ps *51:7-12. 80:3-7. 1 K 8:46-50. Is √53:6. 63:15-19. Je 3:21, 22. *14:+7 (T#1311), 8, 9. *31:18, 19. La 5:20, 21. Ezk 34:6, 16. Ho *14:2-4. Mt 10:6. 15:24. 18:12, 13. Lk 15:4-7. 22:61, 62. Jn 10:16. Ja *5:16. 1 P 2:25. **seek**. T#1518. SS 1:4. Je 31:18. Lk *19:10. Jn √10:27, 28. Ga 4:9. Ph *2:13. Ja 1:17. **for I do**. ver. 61, 93. Ho 4:6.

PSALM 120

The psalmist prays to be delivered from his calumniator, Doeg, and shows his doom from God, 1-4. He complains that his permanent abode is among the contentious and malicious, 5-7.

(*Title.*) **A Song of degrees.** Bp. Patrick and others suppose this psalm to have been composed by David, when the calumnies of Doeg and others forced him to flee his country. Ps 121-134, titles.

1. **my distress.** Ps 18:6. 30:7, 8. *50:15. 107:13. 116:3, 4. *118:5. Is 37:3, 4, 14, etc. 38:2-5. Jon *2:2. Lk 22:44. He *5:7.

2. **Deliver.** 2 T *4:18. **soul.** Heb. *nephesh*, Ge +12:13. Nu +*23:10. Mt +*12:18. **from lying lips.** Ps *5:6. 35:11. 52:2-4. 109:1, 2. 140:1-3. Mt 26:59-62. Re *21:8. **deceitful.** ♪76, Ge +13:6.

3. **What shall**, etc. *or*, What shall the deceitful tongue give unto thee? *or*, What shall it profit thee? Jb 27:8. Mt 16:26. Ro 6:21. **done.** Heb. added. Ps 10:18 (more). 41:8 (more). 61:6mg. 77:7 (more). Pr 3:2. **false tongue.** ♪76, Ge +13:6. Ps 7:11-13. Ja *3:6.

4. **Sharp**, etc. *or*, It is as the sharp arrows of the mighty man with coals of juniper. Ps 57:4. 59:7. Pr 11:9. 12:18. 16:27. 18:8, 21. Ja 3:5-8. **arrows.** Ps 7:13. 52:5. 140:9-11. Dt 32:23, 24. Pr 12:22. 19:5, 9. Re *21:8.

5. **Woe.** Je 9:2, 3, 6. 15:10. Mi 7:1, 2. 2 P 2:7, 8. Re 2:13. **Mesech.** i.e. *selection*, ✱S#4902h. Ge 10:2. Ezk 27:13, Meshech. 32:26. 38:2, 3. 39:1. (1) A son of Japheth, Ge 10:2; 1 Ch 1:5. (2) A son of Shem, 1 Ch 1:17. (3) A district inhabited by descendants of Meshech, the son of Shem, Ps 120:5. (4) The tribe descended from Meshech, the son of Japheth, Ezk 32:26. **the tents.** Ge 25:13. 1 S 25:1. SS 1:5. Is 60:6, 7. Je 49:28, 29.

6. **soul.** Heb. *nephesh*, Ge +27:31. **dwelt.** Ps 57:4. 1 S 20:30-33. Ezk 2:6. Mt 10:16, 36. Jn *15:18. T 3:3.

7. **am for.** ♪63B, Ge +25:28. or, am. ♪119, Ge +49:9. See Ps 109:4. **peace.** *or*, a man of peace. Ps 34:14. 35:20. 55:20. 2 S 20:19. Mt +5:9. Ro √12:18. Ep 2:14-17. He √12:14. **when.** 1 S 24:9-11. 26:2-4.

PSALM 121

The psalmist expects help from God and shows the security of Israel and every believer under the constant protection of the Almighty, 1-8.

(*Title.*) **A Song.** Ps 120, title.

1. **I will**, etc. *or*, Shall I lift up mine eyes to the hills? whence should my help come? Je *3:23. **lift up.** ♪144A12, Ge +22:13. Ps 2:6. 68:15, 16. 78:68. 87:1. *123:1. Is *2:3. ♪121S3E1. Metonymy of the Adjunct B606. To "lift up the eyes" is put for implore or pray. For other instances of this figure see Ps 123:1. Ezk 18:6, 15.

2. **My help.** ♪16, Ge +1:27. Ps *46:1. 124:8. *146:5, 6. Is *40:28, 29. 41:13. Je 20:11. Ho 13:9. He *13:6.

3. **will not suffer.** Ps *91:12. 1 S *2:9. Pr 2:8. *3:21, 23, 25, 26. 1 P *1:5. **thy foot.** Ps 66:9. **slumber.** ♪76, Ge +13:6. Ps 76:5.

4. **he that.** Ps *27:1. *32:7, 8. 127:1. Is *27:3. **shall.** Ps 127:2. 1 K *18:27. Ec 8:16. Re *7:15. **slumber.** ♪76, Ge +13:6. Is 5:27.

5. **The Lord is.** Nu 14:9. Pr 3:24. **thy shade.** Ps

*91:1. Ex *13:21. SS 2:3. Is *4:5, 6. 25:4. *32:2. Mt *23:37. ♪22L8. Anthropomorphism B897. God is spoken of as a shade or shadow. For other instances of this figure see Ps 91:1. Ex 33:23. Is 49:2. 51:16. Lk 1:35. **upon.** Ps *16:8. 109:31.

6. **The sun.** Ps *91:5-10. Is *49:10. Re *7:16.

7. **preserve.** Ps *91:9, 10. 1 Ch 4:10. Jb 5:19, etc. Pr *12:21. Mt *6:13. Ro 8:√28, *35-39. 2 T *4:18. **he shall.** Ps 34:22. *41:2. 97:10. *145:20. **soul.** Heb. *nephesh*, Ge +12:13.

8. **The Lord shall.** ♪18, Dt +28:4. **thy going out.** ♪171J3, Nu +27:17. Dt *28:6, 19. 2 S 5:2. Ezr 8:21, 31. Pr *2:8. *3:6. Jn 10:9. Ja *4:13-16. **from this time.** Ps 113:2. 115:18. **for evermore.** Heb. *olam*, Ps +*18:50.

PSALM 122

David expresses his joy at being called on to go up to the sanctuary; he extols the holy city, 1-5. He exhorts the people to pray for the peace of Jerusalem and resolves to seek her good, 6-9.

(*Title.*) **A Song of degrees.** Ps 120-134, titles.

1. **I was glad.** Ps 42:4. 55:14. 63:1-3. *84:1, 2, 10. 119:111. **Let us go.** Is *2:3. Je 31:6. 50:4, 5. Mi 4:2. Zc *8:21-23. He *10:25.

2. **Our feet.** Ps 84:7. 87:1-3. 100:4. Ex 20:24. Dt 12:5, 14. 2 Ch 6:6.

3. **Jerusalem.** ♪16, Ge +1:27. **builded.** 2 S 5:9. Ep 2:20, 21. *4:4-7. Re 21:10, etc. **as.** ♪160B, Ge +25:31. **compact.** lit. "coupled or joined together to itself" (Peters, *Theocratic Kingdom*, vol. 3, p. 50). Is 62:3. Je 31:38-40. Zc 14:10. Ac 4:32. Re 22:1, 2.

4. **Whither.** Ps 78:68. 132:13. Ex 23:17. 34:23, 24. Dt 12:5, 11. √16:16. **the testimony.** Ex 16:34. *25:21, 22. 26:33, 34. 32:15. **to give.** Ps 66:13-16. 107:1-3. 116:17-19. 118:19.

5. **there.** Dt *17:8, 18. 2 S 15:2. 2 Ch *19:8. **are set.** Heb. do sit. Ps 125:1. Jl 3:20. **the thrones.** 2 S 8:18. 2 Ch 11:22. Is +*2:3.

6. **Pray.** Ps *51:18. 137:6, 7. Is *62:1, 6, √7. Je 51:50. Jn *17:20, 21. Ep 4:3. 2 Th 3:16. **Jerusalem.** T#1568. Ps *51:18. +*147:2. Is 4:3, 4. +*24:23. *52:9, 10. 65:18, 19. Je *3:17. Da 9:16. Jl 3:17. Zc 1:12, 13. *2:10-13. 8:3, 15. **they shall.** Ge *12:3. Nu 24:9. 1 J 3:14. **prosper.** Dt +29:9.

7. **Peace.** ♪66, Ge +9:3. Ps *147:14. 1 Ch 12:18. Is 9:7. *54:13. Jn *14:27. Ja 3:18. **within thy palaces.** Ps 48:3.

8. **my brethren.** Ps 16:3. 42:4. +*119:63. Ep 4:4-6. Ph 2:2-5. Ja 3:13-18.

9. **the house.** Ps 26:8. 69:9. 84:1, 2, 10. 1 Ch 29:3. Jn 2:17. **I will seek.** Ps *102:13, 14. 137:5, 6. Ne *2:10. 13:14.

PSALM 123

The psalmist expresses confidence in God, and complains of the contempt of the proud, 1-4.

(*Title.*) A.M. cir. 3463. B.C. cir. 541. **A Song of degrees.** This psalm is probably a complaint of the captives in Babylon relative to the contempt and cruel usage they received. Ps 120-134, titles.

1. **lift I.** ♪144A12, Ge +22:13. ♪121S3E1, Ps +121:1. Ps 25:15. *121:1. 141:8. Lk 18:13. **O thou.** Ps 2:4. *11:4. 113:5, 6. 115:3. Is *57:15. 66:1. Mt *6:9.

2. **as the eyes.** ∫18, Dt +28:4. Jsh 9:23, 27. 10:6. **look unto.** Ps 27:8. 1 Ch 23:28. Mt 21:28. Lk 12:37. **so our eyes wait.** Ps 32:8. 33:18, 20. 40:1-3. 119:82, 123-125. 130:5, 6. Ge 32:26. 49:18. 2 Ch *20:12. Is 40:31. La *3:25, 26. Lk *18:1. He *12:2.

3. **Have mercy.** Ps 56:1, 2. 57:1. 69:13-16. Lk 18:11-13. **have mercy.** ∫18, Dt +28:4. **for we are.** Ps 44:13-16. 89:50, 51. Ne 4:2-4. Is *53:3. Lk 16:14. 23:35. **contempt.** ∫76, Ge +13:6.

4. **soul.** Heb. *nephesh*, Ge +34:3. **with the scorning.** Ps 73:5-9. 119:51. 1 S 17:42. Ne 4:2, 6. Jb 12:5. 16:4. Je 48:11, 27, 29. Ac 17:21, 32. 26:24. 1 C 4:13. **at ease.** Ezk +*13:10. Am *6:1. **contempt.** ∫76, Ge +13:6. Ps *80:6. 119:22. 1 S 17:28. Ne *2:19. 4:3. Mt 13:55. Jn *9:34. **the proud.** Ps +*119:21.

PSALM 124

Israel blesses God for marvellous deliverances and exults in his protection, 1-8.

(*Title.*) **A Song.** It is uncertain what the particular deliverance was which is celebrated in this psalm. Some refer it to the deliverance of Hezekiah from Sennacherib and others to the return from the Babylonian captivity, while Dr. A. Clarke refers it to that of the Jews from the massacre intended by Haman. Ps 120-134, titles.

1. **the Lord.** Ps 27:1. 46:7, 11. 54:4. 56:9. 118:6, 7. Ex 15:1. Is 8:9, 10. Ro *8:31. He *13:5, 6. **now may.** Ps 129:1.

2. **If it.** ∫18, Dt +28:4. **when men.** Ps 2:1, 2. 3:1. 22:12, 13, 16. 37:32. Nu 16:2, 3.

3. **Then they.** Ps 27:2. 35:25. 56:1, 2. *57:3. 74:8. 83:4. Est 3:6, 12, 13. **swallowed.** Nu 16:30-34. Pr 1:12. Je 51:34. Jon 1:17. **their wrath.** Ps 76:10. 1 S 20:30-33. Da 3:19. Mt 2:16. Ac 9:2. 26:11.

4. **the waters.** Ps 18:4. 42:7. 69:15. Is 8:7, 8. 28:2. *59:19. Je 46:7, 8. Da 9:26. Re 12:15, 16. 17:1, 15. **soul.** Heb. *nephesh*, Ge +12:13.

5. **Then.** ∫18, Dt +28:4. **the proud.** Ps 93:3, 4. Jb 38:11. Je 5:22. **soul.** Heb. *nephesh*, Ge +12:13.

6. **who hath not.** Ps 17:9-13. 118:13. 140:5, 6. Ex 15:9, 10. Jg 5:30, 31. 1 S 26:20. Is 10:14-19.

7. **Our soul.** Heb. *nephesh*, Ge +12:13. **is escaped.** 1 S 23:26, 27. 24:14, 15. 25:29. 2 S 17:2, 21, 22. **as a bird.** Ps 25:15. *91:3. Pr 6:5. Je 5:26. 18:22. 2 T 2:26.

8. **help.** Ps 115:15. 121:2. 134:3. 146:5, 6. Ge *1:1. Is 37:16-20. Je *32:17. Ac 4:24.

PSALM 125

The security of the faithful, 1-3. A prayer for them and a prediction of the ruin of apostates and of the ungodly, 4, 5.

(*Title.*) A.M. 3468. B.C. 536. **A Song.** Ps 120-124, titles.

1. **that trust.** Ps 20:7. 21:7. 25:2, 3. 34:22. 44:6. 62:2, 6. 118:8, 9. 147:11. 1 S 17:45. 1 Ch 5:20. 2 Ch 32:8. Pr √3:5, 6. Je *17:7, 8. Ep 1:12, 13. 1 P *1:21. Re 3:12. **be as mount.** Ps 132:13, 14. Is 12:6. 14:32. 51:3, 11, 16. 52:1, 7, 8. Ob +*21. Mi *4:2. Zc 1:14, 17. Re 14:1. **but abideth.** Mt 16:16-18. **for ever.** ∫76, Ge +13:6.

2. **As the mountains.** Is 54:10. La 4:12. **round about.** T#95. Ps 46:1-7. Pr 18:10. Is 43:2-6. 54:14, 17. **the Lord.** Ps 34:7. Dt *33:27. Is 4:5. Zc 2:5. Jn +*10:28,

29. **for ever.** ∫76, Ge +13:6.

3. **the rod.** Ps 103:9, 14. Pr 22:8. Is 9:4. 10:5. 14:5, 6. 27:8. 1 C √10:13. Re 2:10. **the wicked.** Heb. wickedness. Ps *5:4. 10:15. 45:7. *73:12-18. 89:22. **rest.** Ge 8:4. Ex 10:14. 20:11. **lot.** Ps +16:5. 22:18. 78:55. Le 16:8. Jsh +14:2n. **lest.** Ps 103:14. Mt *24:22. 1 C √10:13. Ju *24. **righteous.** Ps *1:5. 5:12. 7:9. 11:3. **put forth.** Ps 18:14, 16. 20:2. 55:20. 57:3. 1 S 24:10. Ac 12:1. **iniquity.** Ps 37:1. 43:1mg. 89:22. 92:15. Ec 7:7.

4. **Do good.** Ps 41:1-3. 51:18. 73:1. Is 58:10, 11. Ep 6:18. He *6:10. 1 J *3:17-24. **upright.** Ps 32:2. *84:11, 12. 119:80. La 3:25. Jn 1:47. Re 14:5.

5. **As for such.** Ps 40:4. 101:3. 1 Ch 10:13, 14. Pr 14:14. Je 2:19. Zp 1:6. 1 C +15:2. He +10:38. 2 P √2:20, 21. 1 J 2:19. **crooked.** Jg 5:6mg. Pr 2:15. Is 59:8. Ph 2:15. **lead them.** Ps 106:9. Ex +9:16. 14:21. Dt +2:30. 1 S +18:10n. Am +3:6. Ep +1:11. **with the workers.** Ps 5:5. 6:8. Mt √7:23. 24:48-51. He *10:26. 1 J 3:9. 5:18. **peace.** Ps *122:6. 128:6. Is 54:10, 13. Ezk 37:26. Ho 2:18. Jn *14:27. Ga *6:16. 1 P 1:2.

PSALM 126

The joyful surprise of the Jews when delivered from captivity, 1-3. A prayer for a more complete deliverance, with assurances of a happy event to all the sorrows of God's people, 4-6.

(*Title.*) **A Song of degrees.** This psalm evidently appears to have been composed in consequence of the proclamation of Cyrus in favor of the Jews, giving them leave to return to their own land and rebuild their city and temple. Ps 120-125, titles.

1. **turned again**, etc. Heb. returned the returning of Zion. Ps *53:6. *85:1. Ezr ch. 1. Jb 42:10. Je *31:8-10. Ho 6:11. Jl 3:1. **we were like.** Jb 9:16. Mk 16:11. Lk 24:11, 41. Ac 12:9, 14-16.

2. **Then was.** Ps 14:7. 53:6. 106:47, 48. 107:1, 2. 136:1. Ex 12:14. Ezr 3:11. Jb 8:21. Is *35:10. 49:9-13. Je 31:12, 13. 33:11. Re 11:15-17. **laughter.** ∫121S2, Ge +21:6. **then said.** ∫18, Dt +28:4. Nu 23:23. Jsh 2:9-11. 9:9, 10. Ne 6:16. Zc 8:22, 23. Ro 11:15. **hath.** Dt 16:13, 17. Zc 14:18. **done great things for them.** Heb. magnified to do with them. Ps 35:26. 38:16. 41:9mg. Je 48:26. Da +8:11. *11:36, 37. Jl *2:20mg. Zp 2:8, 10.

3. **great things.** ∫16, Ge +1:27. Ps 18:50. 31:19. 66:5, 6. 68:7, 8, 22. Ezr 7:27, 28. Is 11:11-16. 12:4-6. 51:9-11. 52:9, 10. 66:14. Lk 1:46-49. Ep 1:18-22. Re 12:10. 19:1-7. **whereof.** ∫63K, Ge +37:13.

4. **Turn again.** See on ver. 1. Ps 85:4. Ho 1:11. **as the streams.** Jsh 3:16. Is 41:18. 52:9, 10.

5. **that sow.** Ps *137:1. Is *12:1-3. Je *31:9-13. Jl *2:17, 23. Mt +*5:4. Jn 16:20-22. 2 C *7:8-11. **shall reap.** T#431. Pr *11:18, 30. Is 66:8. Da *12:3. Mk *1:17. Lk 1:16. Jn 17:20. Ja *5:20. **joy.** *or*, singing. Ps +30:5mg.

6. **that goeth.** Ps *30:5. Jb 11:13-17. Is *61:3. Je 50:4, 5. Ga *6:7, 8. **weepeth.** Ps 119:136. Lk 19:41. Ac *20:31. 2 C 11:28. Ga *4:19. Ph 3:18. He +*6:11. 13:17. **bearing.** Ec 11:1. **precious seed.** *or*, seed basket. ✱S#4901h. Jb 28:18h (price). Am 9:13 (S#4900h). **shall doubtless.** Is 9:2, 3. Lk *15:18-24. Ac *16:29-34. Re *7:15-17. **with rejoicing.** 1 Th +*2:19, 20. He +*13:17. **bringing his sheaves.** Pr +*11:30. Da +*11:33. +*12:3. **with him.** Mt √6:19, 20. Lk +*16:9. Ph +*4:17. He 10:34.

PSALM 127

*Every labor is vain without the blessing of God, 1,
2. Children are gifts of God to be valued highly, 3-5.*

(*Title.*) **A Song.** Ps 120-126, titles. **for Solomon.** *or,*
of Solomon. Ps 72, title.

1. **Except.** ſ18, Dt +28:4. **the Lord.** T#1869. Ps
*33:16-18. Pr *16:9. *21:30, 31. Ec *9:11. 1 C *3:6,
7. **build.** 1 Ch 22:10, 11. 28:10, *20. 29:19. Ne 2:17.
1 C √3:9-15. **they labor.** Ge 11:8, 9. 1 C *15:14. Ga
*4:11. **that build it.** Heb. that are builders of it in it.
Ps 118:22. 147:2. 1 K 5:18. **except.** Ps *121:3-5. Is
*27:3. Zc 2:4, 5. **the watchman.** SS 3:3. 5:7. Is 21:5-
12. *56:10. *62:6. Je 51:12, 31. Ezk *33:2-9.

2. **vain.** ſ16, Ge +1:27. Ps 39:5, 6. *121:4. Ec 1:14.
2:1-11, 20-23. 4:8. **rise up.** Pr *31:15-18. **the bread.**
Ge *3:17-19. Ec *6:7. **for.** ſ63K, Ga +37:13. **so he.**
Ps *3:5. *4:8. Ge 32:24. Pr *10:22. Ec *5:12. Is *32:17,
18. Je 31:26. Ezk 34:25. Ac 12:5, 6.

3. **children.** T#763. Ps +*113:9. 115:14. 128:3, 4.
Ge 1:28. 4:1. 15:4, 5. 24:60. 30:1, 2. 33:5. 41:51, 52.
48:4. Dt 7:13. *28:4. 30:9. Jsh 24:3, 4. 1 S 1:19, 20,
*27. 2:20, 21. 1 Ch 28:5. Jb 5:25. Is 8:18. **fruit.** Ge
◐+11:30. +*29:31. Dt 7:14. Ru 4:13.

4. **arrows.** Je 50:9. **so are children.** Pr *17:6. 31:28.

5. **Happy.** ſ43, Dt +28:3. Ge 50:23. Jb 1:2. *42:12-
16. **his quiver full of them.** Heb. filled his quiver
with them. Ps 107:9. Jb 29:23. Is 22:6. *49:2. Je 5:16.
La 3:13. **they shall.** Jb 5:4. Pr 27:11. **speak.** *or,* subdue.
Ps 18:47. *or,* destroy. **enemies.** Ps 3:7. 6:10. 7:5. 8:2.
9:3. 13:2. **gate.** ſ171S7B, Ge +14:7. Ps 9:13. 69:12.
87:2. Ge +*14:7. +22:17.

PSALM 128

*The blessedness of the righteous, personal and do-
mestic, temporal and spiritual, 1-6.*

(*Title.*) **A Song of degrees.** Ps 120-127, titles.

1. **Blessed.** ſ43, Dt +28:3. **every one.** Ps 103:1,
*13, *17. 112:1. *115:13. *147:11. Lk 1:50. **walketh.**
Ps *1:1-3. *44:18. 81:13. *119:1, 3. Pr 8:32. Lk 1:6.
Ac 9:31. Col +*1:10. 1 Th *4:1.

2. **thou shalt eat.** Ps 58:11. Ge *3:19. Dt 28:4, 11,
39, 51. Jg 6:3-6. Ec +*2:24. *5:18, 19. Is *62:8, 9.
65:13, 21-23. **labor.** ſ121C1H, Dt +28:33. Ps 109:11.
Pr 14:23. Is *65:22. Lk *10:7. **happy.** Ps 58:10. Dt
33:29. Pr *14:21. *16:20. 28:14. 29:18. Jn *13:17. **and
it shall.** Ec *8:12, 13. Dt +*4:40. Is *3:10. Je 22:15.
1 C √15:58. Ep +*6:3.

3. **a fruitful vine.** Ge 49:22. Pr 5:15-18. Ezk 19:10.
olive plants. Ps 52:8. 144:12. Je 11:16. Ho 14:6, 7.
Ro 11:24. **round about.** Ps 127:5.

4. **blessed.** Ps 112:2. Jg 5:24. **feareth.** Ps 111:10.
Pr 1:7.

5. **bless thee.** Ps 20:2. 118:26. Ep *1:3. **out of Zion.**
Ps 20:2. 134:3. 135:21. Is +*2:3. +*24:23. **thou shalt
see.** Ps +*122:6, 9. Is *33:20.

6. **thou shalt see.** ſ18, Dt +28:4. Ps +*102:28. Ge
*50:23. Jb *42:16. **peace.** Ps +*125:5. Is *66:12. Ga
*6:16.

PSALM 129

*An exhortation to praise God for saving Israel in
their great afflictions, 1-4. The utter ruin of Israel's
implacable enemies predicted, 5-8.*

(*Title.*) A.M. 3470. B.C. 534. **A Song of degrees.**

Ps 120-128, titles. This psalm was most probably composed in consequence of the opposition of the Samaritans, Ezr ch. 4.

1. **Many.** *or,* Much. ſ18, Dt +28:4. ver. 2. Ps 32:10.
34:19. 65:9. **have they.** Ex 1:12-14, 22. 5:7-19. Jg 2:15.
10:8-12. 1 S 13:19. La 1:3. **from.** Je 2:2. Ezk 23:3.
Ho 2:15. 11:1. **may.** Ps 124:1.

2. **yet they have.** Ps *34:19. 118:13. 125:1. Jb
5:19. Je 1:19. Mt *16:18. Jn 16:33. Ro *8:35-39. Re
12:8, 9.

3. **The plowers.** Ps 141:7. Is 50:6. 51:23. Mi 3:12.
Mt 27:26. Mk 15:15. Lk 22:63.

4. **The Lord.** Ezr 9:15. Ne 9:33. La 1:18. 3:22. Da
9:7. 2 Th *1:6, 7. **cut asunder.** Ps 124:6, 7. 140:5-11.
2 P *2:9.

5. **be confounded.** Ps 83:4-11. 122:6. Est 6:13. 9:5.
Is 10:12. 37:22, 28, 29, 35. Zc 1:14-17. 12:3, 6. 1 C
16:22.

6. **as the grass.** Ps *37:1, 2. 92:7. Je 17:5, 6. Mt
13:6.

7. **he that bindeth.** Ps 126:6. Is 17:10, 11. Ho 8:7.
Ga *6:8.

8. **The blessing.** Ps 118:26. Ru *2:4.

PSALM 130

*The psalmist, in deep distress, cries out unto God,
confessing his sin and determined to wait patiently
for his gracious forgiveness, 1-6. He exhorts Israel to
hope in God's mercy and plenteous redemption, 7, 8.*

(*Title.*) A.M. cir. 3464. B.C. cir. 540. **A Song.** Ps
120-129, titles.

1. **Out of.** T#1186. Ps 18:4-6, 16. 25:16-18. *40:1,
2. *42:7. *69:1, 2, 14, 15. 71:20. 88:6, 7. 116:3, 4.
La 3:53-55. Jon 2:2-4. He *5:7.

2. **hear.** ſ22C14, Ge +16:11. **let thine ears.** ſ22A8,
Ps +10:17. Ps 5:1, 2. 17:1. 55:1, 2. 61:1, 2. 2 Ch
6:40. Ne 1:6, 11. Is 37:17. Da 9:17-19.

3. **shouldest mark.** Ps *143:2. 1 K 8:46. 2 Ch 6:36.
Jb 9:2, 3, 20. 10:14. 15:14-16. Pr *20:9. Ec *7:20. Is
√53:6. *64:6. Jn 8:7-9. Ro *3:9-12, 20-24. Ja 3:2, 8.
1 J 1:8, 10.

4. **forgiveness.** T#788. Ps 25:11. *32:1, 2. 65:3.
86:5. 103:2, 3, 9-12. Ex 34:5-7. Is √1:18. 33:24. *44:22.
*45:25. √55:7. Je 31:34. Da *9:9. Ho 11:8, 9. Mi *7:18-
20. Mt 12:31, 32. Lk 7:47, 48, 50. Ro *8:1. 2 C *5:19.
Ep *1:7. +4:32 (T#203). Col *1:14. He 8:12. 10:17.
that thou mayest. Ps *2:11, 12. 1 K 8:39, 40. Je *33:8,
9. Ho 3:5. Ac 9:31. 2 T *2:19. He *12:24-28.

5. **I wait.** Ps *27:14. 33:20. *40:1. 62:1, 5. Ge 49:18.
Is *8:17. 26:8. *30:18. Lk 2:25, 38. **soul.** Heb. *nephesh,*
Ge +34:3. **and in his.** Ps 119:42, 49, 81, 114. He
6:18.

6. **soul.** Heb. *nephesh,* Ge +34:3. **waiteth.** T#1409.
Ps *63:1, 2, 5, 6. 119:147. 123:2. La 4:17. Ac 27:29.
He 12:2. **I say more than they that watch for the
morning.** *or,* which watch unto the morning. Ps 134:1.
Is 21:8.

7. **Let Israel.** Ps 40:3. 71:5. 115:9-13. 131:1, 3. Is
27:5. Zp 3:12. **for with.** ver. 4. Ps 86:5, 15. Is √55:7.
Ro *5:20, 21. 8:24. Ep 1:7, 8. 1 T 2:5, 6. He 10:35.
1 J *2:1, 2. Re 5:9. **plenteous.** ſ22I4, Ps +86:15.

8. **he shall redeem.** Ps *103:3, 4. Mt *1:21. Ro
*6:14. 11:26. T *2:14. 1 J 3:5-8. **from all.** Jb +5:24.
Is +*60:21. Je 32:40. 31:31-34. Ezk 36:27. Zp 3:13.
Ro 11:26. 1 C 15:24-28. Re 21:3-7. 22:3.

PSALM 131

David professes humility and resignation and exhorts Israel to hope in God, 1-3.

(*Title.*) **A Song of degrees.** Ps 122, 124, 133, titles. Some think that this psalm was composed by David when accused by Saul and his courtiers that he affected the crown, though others refer it to the time of the captivity and consider it a fair account of the manner in which the captives behaved themselves.

1. **my heart.** Nu *12:3. Dt 17:20. 1 S 16:13, 18, 22. 17:15, 28, 29. 18:23. Mt *11:29. Ac *20:19. 1 Th *2:6, 7, 10. **neither.** Ps *78:70-72. Je *17:16. *45:5. Am 7:14, 15. Ro *12:16. **exercise.** Heb. walk. Ps +104:10mg. **high for me.** Heb. wonderful for me. Ps *139:6. Jb *42:3. Ro *11:33.

2. **quieted.** Ps 42:5, 11. 43:5. 62:1mg. 1 S 24:10. 25:32, 33. 30:6. 2 S 15:25, 26. 16:11, 12. Is *30:15. La *3:26. **myself.** Heb. my soul. *nephesh,* Ex +15:9. Lk 21:19. Jn 14:1, 2. **as.** ſ160A, Ps +1:3. **a child.** Mt *18:3, 4. Mk 10:15. 1 C 14:20. **soul.** Heb. *nephesh,* Ge +34:3. **weaned.** ſ76, Ge +13:6. 1 S +1:22n. Is 11:8. 28:9. **even as.** ſ160A, Ps +1:3. **weaned.** ſ76, Ge +13:6.

3. **Let Israel.** Ps 115:9-11. 130:7. 146:5. Je 17:7, 8. **from henceforth.** Heb. from now. Ps 113:2. 115:18. Is *26:3, 4. **for ever.** Heb. *olam,* Ex +*12:24.

PSALM 132

The psalmist pleads David's pious care about a stated residence for the ark and entreats the Lord to take possession of the temple and to bless his priests and people, 1-10. He shows the promises of God to David and to his family, 11-18.

(*Title.*) A.M. 2962. B.C. 1042. **A Song of degrees**. Ps 120-131, titles. Some attribute this psalm to Solomon; others refer it to the building of the second temple, but it seems most probable that it was sung at the solemn induction of the ark into the tabernacle of Mount Zion, expressing the holy joy and triumph of that event.

1. **remember.** Ps 25:6, 7. Ge 8:1. Ex 2:24. La 3:19. 5:1. **all his afflictions.** ſ24A, Ge +32:24. 1 S ch. 18-30. 2 S ch. 15-20.

2. **he sware.** T#1266. Ps 56:12. *65:1. 66:13, 14. 116:14-18. 119:106. 2 S 7:1, 2. 2 Ch *15:12-15. **vowed.** Le +*23:38. **the mighty.** ſ76, Ge +13:6. ver. 5. Ps 46:11. 50:1. 146:5, 6. Ge *49:24.

3. **I will not.** ſ142, Ge +20:16. Ec *9:10. Hg *1:4. Mt *6:33. **go up.** Ge 49:4. Ex 8:3. 2 K +1:16n. Ec 10:20. Is 57:7.

4. **I will.** ſ142, Ge +20:16. **give sleep.** Ge 24:33. Ru 3:18. Pr 6:4.

5. **I find.** 2 S 6:17. 1 Ch 15:3, 12. Ac 7:46. **an habitation.** Heb. habitations. 1 K 8:27. 2 Ch 2:6. Is 66:1. Ac 7:47-49. Ep *2:22. **for the mighty.** ſ76, Ge +13:6. ver. 2.

6. **at Ephratah.** Ru 1:2. 1 S 17:12. Mi +*5:2. **we found.** 1 S 7:1. 1 Ch *13:5, 6. Jn=1:45.

7. **will go.** Ps *5:7. 66:13, 14. 118:19. *122:1. Is 2:3. **worship.** Ps *95:6. 99:5, 9. La 2:1. **footstool.** ſ22D3D1, Is +66:1.

8. **Arise.** Ps 68:1. Nu *10:35, 36. 2 Ch 6:41, 42. **the ark.** Ps 62:7. 71:7. *78:61n. 105:4.

9. **thy priests.** ver. 16. Ps 93:1. 104:1. Jb 29:14. Is

*61:10. Je=23:6. Ro *13:14. 1 C=1:30. 1 P 5:5. Re 19:8. **let thy saints.** Ps 35:26, 27. 68:3. 70:4. Jg 5:31. **shout.** Ps 47:1. Ezr 3:11, 12. Is 65:14. Zp 3:14. Zc 9:9. 2 C 1:24.

10. **thy servant.** T#1133. Ps 105:41, 42. Ex 32:13. Dt 9:27. 1 K *8:25. 11:12, 13, 34. 15:4, 5. 2 K 19:34. 2 Ch 6:16, 17, 42. Is *37:35. 42:1. Ho 3:5. **turn not.** Ps 84:9. 89:38, 39. 2 Ch 6:42. Jn 11:42. 1 J 2:20.

11. **sworn.** Ps √89:3, 4, 33-37. 110:4. 1 S 15:29. Je +*33:20-26. He *6:18. **unto David.** Je *23:5. Ac ♣13:23. Ro ♣1:3. **not turn.** Ps √89:28. Is √55:3. Ac √13:34. Ro 11:29. **Of the fruit.** 2 S *7:12. 1 K 8:25. 2 Ch 6:16. Lk 1:69, 70. Ac ♣2:30. **body.** Heb. belly. Dt 28:4, +11mg, 18. 30:9. Jb 19:17mg. Mi 6:7mg. **throne.** 2 S *7:13.

12. **If.** Ge +4:7. **thy children.** Ps 89:30-35. **teach them.** Ps *25:12, 13. **their children.** Ps 102:28. 115:14. Is *9:7. *59:21. Lk *1:32, 33. **thy throne.** Re 3:21. **for evermore.** Ps +9:18 (✱S#5703h).

13. **the Lord.** Ps 76:1, 2. 78:68, 69. Is 14:32. He 12:22. **Zion.** Ps 87:1, 2. Is 56:7. 1 C 3:16. Ep 2:21. **he hath desired.** Ps 48:1-3. 68:16. 87:2. 1 T 3:15.

14. **my rest.** ver. 8. Is 11:10. 66:1. Zp *3:16, 17. **for ever.** Ps +9:18 (✱S#5703h). **here will.** Ps 68:18. 76:2. 135:21. 1 K 8:13, 27. Is 8:18. 12:6. 57:15. Ezk 48:35. Jl 3:21. Ep 2:22. He 12:22. Re 21:23. **for I have.** Ps 87:2.

15. **abundantly.** *or,* surely. Ge 2:17. **bless her provision.** Ps 147:14. Ex 23:25. Le 26:4, 5. Dt 28:2-5. Pr 3:9, 10. Hg 1:6, 9. 2:16-19. Ml 2:2. Mt 14:19-21. Lk 1:53. 2 C 9:10, 11. **I will satisfy.** Ps 22:26. 33:18, 19. 36:8. 37:3, 19. 149:4. Dt 14:29. Is 33:16. Je 31:14. Zc 11:7. Mt +*5:6. 6:32, 33. Mk 8:6-9. Jn 6:57, 58.

16. **clothe.** ver. 9. Ps 149:4. 2 Ch 6:41. Is 61:10. Ga=3:27. **with salvation.** Ps=27:1. Lk=2:30. **her saints.** Ho 11:12. Zc 9:9, 15-17. Jn *16:24.

17. **will I make.** Ps 92:10. 148:14. Ezk 29:21. Lk 1:69. **I have ordained.** 1 K *11:36. 15:4. 2 Ch *21:7. Lk 2:30-32. **lamp.** *or,* candle. Ps +18:28mg. 119:105mg. Ge 15:17. 2 S 21:17mg. Jb 29:3mg. Lk 2:32.

18. **His enemies.** Ps 21:8, 9. 35:26. 109:29. Jb 8:22. Da *12:2. Lk *19:27. **but upon.** Ps 72:8-11. Is *9:6, 7. 58:10-12. Mt 28:18. Lk *1:32, 33. Re +*11:15. *17:14.

PSALM 133

A commendation, with a twofold illustration, of the excellency of harmony among brethren, 1-3.

(*Title.*) **A Song of degrees.** Ps 122, 124, 131, titles. This psalm was probably composed when David was made king over all Israel.

1. **how good.** ſ85E, Ge +17:17. Ps *122:6-8. Ge 13:8. 45:24. 2 S 2:26, 27. Is *11:6-9, 13. Je 32:39. Jn *13:35. *17:21. Ro 12:9, 10. 13:8-10. 1 C *1:10. Ga 5:13, 14. Ep *4:3-6. 5:1, 2. Ph √2:2-5. Col 2:2. 1 Th 3:12, 13. He 13:1. 1 P 1:22. *3:8. 1 J 2:9-11. *3:10, 11, 14-19. 4:20, 21. **pleasant.** Ps 45:8. SS 4:16. **together.** Heb. even together. **unity.** Mk 9:50.

2. **It is like.** Ps 141:5. Pr 27:9. SS 1:3. Jn 12:3. **ointment.** Le 8:12, 30. 1 J 2:20. **that ran down.** Ex 30:23-30. Le 8:12.

3. **As the dew of Hermon.** Mr. Maundrell says, "We were sufficiently instructed by experience what the holy Psalmist means by 'the dew of Hermon,' our

tents being as wet with it as if it had rained all night." Some suppose that *Zion* here means a part of Mount Hermon (Dt 4:48), but it is not written *Sion* here but *Zion*, which is at Jerusalem. Dt 3:8, 9. *4:48. Jsh 13:11. **for there the Lord**. Ps 42:8. Le 25:21. Dt *28:8. **even life**. Ps 16:11. 21:4. Jn 4:14. 5:24, 29. 6:50, 51, 68. 11:25, 26. Ro 5:21. √6:23. 1 C *12:12, 13. Ga 5:22. 1 J 2:25. *5:11. Re 1:18. **for evermore**. Heb. *olam*, Ps +*18:50.

PSALM 134

The psalmist exhorts the watchers in the sanctuary to bless the Lord; and they pray for a blessing on him, 1-3.

(*Title.*) A.M. 3468. B.C. 536. **A Song of degrees**. Ps 120-133, titles.

1. **bless ye**. Ps 103:21. 135:1, 2, 19-21. 1 Ch *23:30-32. Re 19:5. **which by night**. Ps 130:6. Le 8:35. 1 Ch 9:23, 33. Lk 2:37. Re *7:15.

2. **Lift up**. Ps 28:2. 63:4. 141:2. La 2:19. 3:41. **in the sanctuary**. *or, in* holiness. Ps 26:6. 1 T *2:8.

3. **Lord**. Ps *124:8. 146:5, 6. **bless thee**. Ps 14:7. 20:2. 110:2. *128:5. 135:21. Nu *6:24. Ro 11:26.

PSALM 135

Exhortations to praise God for his goodness, his special kindness to Israel, his power shown in the works of creation and providence, and his judgments on the enemies of his people, 1-14. The vanity of idols and the folly of idolaters exposed, 15-18. All orders of men in Israel are called on to praise the Lord, 19-21.

(*Title.*) A.M. 3000. B.C. 1004. Bp. Patrick supposes this to be the morning hymn which the precentor called upon the Levites to sing at the opening of the gates of the temple, as the foregoing was sung at the shutting in the evening; but it is more probable that it was composed by Solomon, to be sung at the dedication of the temple.

1. **Praise ye the Lord**. Ps 33:1, 2. 96:1-4. 106:1. 107:8, 15. 111:1. 112:1. 113:1. ch. 117. 150:6. **Praise ye the name**. Ps 7:17. 102:21. 113:2, 3. 145:1, 2. 148:13. See on Ex 34:5-7. Ne *9:5. **O ye servants**. Ps 113:1. 134:1. 149:1-3.

2. **that stand**. 1 Ch 16:37-42. 23:30. Ne 9:5. Lk *2:37. **the courts**. Ps 92:13. 96:8. 116:19.

3. **Praise**. T#882. Ps 69:30, 31. 92:1, 2. **for the Lord**. Ps 106:1. 107:1. 118:1. *119:68. 136:1. 145:7, 8. Is 63:7. Mt 19:17. **for it is**. Ps 33:1. 63:5. 92:1, 2. 147:1.

4. **the Lord**. Ps 33:12. Dt *7:6, 7. *10:15. 1 S 12:22. Is 41:8. *43:20, 21. Zc 2:10-12. Ac 13:48. 1 P 2:9. **Jacob**. √121A5, Ge +9:27. **Israel**. √121A5, Ge +9:27. **his peculiar**. Ex *19:5, 6. Dt 14:2. *26:18. 32:9. Je 13:11. Ml 3:17. T *2:14.

5. **I know**. Ps 48:1. 86:8-10. 89:6. 95:3. 96:4, 5. 97:9. Dt 10:17. Is 40:22, 25. Je 10:10, 11. Da 3:29. 6:26, 27. **great**. Ps 77:13. 104:1. 145:3. Is 12:6. Je 32:18, 19.

6. **Whatsoever**. Ps 33:9, 11. +115:3. Jb 42:2. Is *46:10. Da 4:35. Am 4:13. 9:6. Mt 20:15. 28:18. Ro +9:18. Ep +1:11. Re 4:11. **in the seas**. Ps 136:13-15. Mt 8:26, 27. 14:25.

7. **He causeth**. Ps 148:8. Ge 2:5, 6. 1 K 18:1, 41-45. Jb 5:10. Je 10:13. 14:22. 51:16. Zc 10:1. **he maketh**

lightnings. Dr. Russel (vol. ii. p. 285) informs us that seldom a night passes at Aleppo without much lightning in the northwest, but not attended with thunder; and when it appears in the west or soutwestern points, it is a sure sign of the approaching rain, which is often followed with thunder. See the Note on Jb 38:25. Jb 28:25, 26. 38:24-28, 35. **the rain**. Je 14:22. **he bringeth**. Ps 107:25. 148:8. Jb 38:22, 23. Jon 1:4. Jn 3:8. **treasuries**. √121.O, Ge +28:22. √22D5.O, Dt +28:12.

8. **smote**. Ps 78:51. 105:36. 136:10. Ex 12:12, *29, 30. 13:15. **both of man and beast**. Heb. from man unto beast.

9. **sent tokens**. Ps 78:43-50. 105:27-29. Ex ch. 7-15. Dt 4:34. Ne 9:10. Is 51:9, 10. Je 32:20, 21. Ac 7:36. **upon Pharaoh**. Ps 136:15.

10. **smote**. Ps 44:2, 3. 136:17-22.

11. **Sihon**. Nu 21:21, 35. Dt 2:30-37. 3:1, etc. Ne 9:22. **and all the**. Jsh ch. 10-12.

12. **gave their**. Ps *44:1-3. 78:55. 136:21, 22. Nu 33:54. Jsh 11:23. 12:7.

13. **Thy name**. Ps 8:1, 9. 72:17. 102:12, 21. Ex *3:15. 34:5-7. Ho 12:5. Mt 6:9, 13. **for ever**. Heb. *olam*, Ex +*12:24. **throughout all generations**. Heb. to generation and generation. Ps +33:11mg. 89:1mg. 102:12. Pr +*27:24mg.

14. **For**. He ▶10:30. **the Lord**. Ps 7:8. 50:4. 96:13. **he will repent**. Dt *32:36. Jg 10:16. 1 Ch 21:15. Ho 11:8, 9. Am 7:3, 6. Jon *4:2.

15. **idols**. √132G, Ge +3:19. Ps 115:4-8. Dt 4:28. Is 37:19. 40:19, 20. 44:9-20. 46:6, 7. Je 10:3, etc. Hab 2:18, 19. Ac 17:29.

16. **eyes have they**. Is 6:10. Mt 13:14-16.

17. **hear not**. Ps 115:6. 1 C 10:19. **neither**. Ps 115:7. Je 10:14. 51:17. Hab 2:19. **breath**. Heb. *ruach*, Ge +6:17.

18. **They that**. Ps 97:7. ‖115:8. Is 44:18-20. Je 10:8. 2 C 4:4. **are like**. Ps 115:8. 2 K 17:15. Je +*2:5.

19. **Bless**. Ps 115:9-11. 118:1-4. 145:10. 147:19, 20. 148:14. 2 C 1:3. Re 5:12. 19:5. **house of Aaron**. Ps 115:10.

20. **Bless**. Ps 72:18. 2 C 1:3. Re 5:12. **ye that fear**. Ps 22:23. 103:11, 13, 17. 115:11. 118:4. 119:+*63, 74. Pr 14:2.

21. **out of Zion**. Ps 76:2. 134:3. 2 Ch 6:6. **which dwelleth**. Ps 48:1, 9. 132:13, 14. Is 12:6. **Praise**. √74, Jg +5:31.

PSALM 136

Exhortations to praise the Lord for his everlasting mercy; for all the blessings of creation, providence, and redemption; and for his glory displayed in them, 1-9; for delivering the Israelites out of Egypt, and bringing them into the Promised Land, 10-26.

(*Title.*) This psalm is little else than a repetition of the preceding, with the addition of the burden, "for his mercy endureth for ever," at the end of each verse; it was doubtless composed on the same occasion. It seems evidently to have been a responsive song; the first part of the verse being probably sung by the Levites and the burden by the people.

1. **Give thanks**. Ps *100:4. 105:1. 106:1. 107:1. 118:1. 119:68. 2 Ch 7:3, 6. Ezr 3:11. Je 33:11. **is good**. Ps 4:6. 14:1. 16:2. 21:3. *25:8. *33:5. *34:8. 100:5. 106:1. 119:68. 126:1, 2. 145:7, +*9. Is 63:7. Je *33:11. Na 1:7. Mt *19:17. Ro *2:4. √11:22. **for his mercy**.

♪76, Ge +13:6. Ps 103:17. 1 Ch *16:34, 41. 2 Ch *20:21. Lk *1:50. Ju 21. **for ever**. Heb. *olam*, Ex +*12:24.

2. **O give**. ♪51, Ps +118:2. **the God**. Ps 82:1. 97:7, 9. Ex 18:11. Dt *10:17. Jsh 22:22. 2 Ch 2:5. Da 2:47. **for his**. ♪8, Ps +118:1.

3. **the Lord**. 1 T 6:15. Re 17:14. *19:16.

4. **who alone**. Ps 72:18. 86:10. Ex 15:11. Jb 5:9. Re 15:3.

5. **To him**. The contrivance of the celestial bodies, in their specific gravities, relations, connections, influences on each other, revolutions and in the wonderful adaptation of the atmosphere for the purposes of refracting the light, forming rain, dew, snow, are exhibited the most astonishing displays of the divine wisdom. Ps 33:6. *104:24. Ge 1:1. Pr *3:19, 20. 8:22-29. Je *51:15.

6. **To him**. Ps 24:2. 104:2, 3. Ge 1:9. Jb 26:7. 37:18. Is 40:22. 44:24. Je 10:12. Zc 12:1. 2 P 3:5-7.

7. **great lights**. Ps 74:16, 17. 104:19. Ge 1:14-19. Dt √4:19.

8. **The sun**. Ps 148:3. Je 31:35. Mt +*5:45. **to rule**. Heb. for the rulings. ver. 9. 103:22. 114:2. **by day**. Ps 49:5. 50:15. 59:16.

9. **The moon and stars**. The sun is the monarch of day, the state of light; the moon of the night, the state of darkness. The rays of the sun falling on the atmosphere are refracted and diffused over the whole of the hemisphere of the earth immediately under his orb; while those rays of that vast luminary which, because of the earth's smallness in comparison of the sun, are diffused on all sides beyond the earth, falling on the opaque disc of the moon, are reflected back on the lower hemisphere, or the part of the earth opposite the sun. But the reflected light being 50,000 times less in intensity than that of the sun, there is a sufficient distinction between day and night, though each is ruled and determined by one of these two *great lights*. Ps 8:3. 89:36, 37. Jb 31:26.

10. **smote Egypt**. Ps 78:51. 105:36. 135:8. Ex 11:5, 6. 12:12, 29. He 11:28.

11. **brought out**. Ps 78:52. 105:37. Ex 12:51. 13:3, 17. 1 S 12:6-8.

12. **With a strong hand**. Ex 6:6. 13:14. 15:6. Dt 11:2-4. Is 51:9, 10. Je 32:21. Ac 7:36. **arm**. ♪22A13, Is +52:10.

13. **which divided**. Ps 66:5, 6. 74:13. 78:13. 106:9-11. Ex 14:21, 22, 29. Is 63:12, 13. He 11:29.

14. **pass through**. Ps 78:13. 106:9. Ex 14:22.

15. **But overthrew**. Heb. But shaked off. Ps 78:53. 135:9. Ex 14:27, 28. 15:4, 5, 10, 11. Ne 9:10, 11. **for his mercy**. Ps 65:5. 79:6-9. 143:12. Ex 15:12, 13. Lk 1:71-74.

16. **which led**. Ps 77:20. Ex 13:18. 15:22. Nu 9:17-22. Dt 8:2, 15. Ne 9:12, 19. Is 49:10. 63:11-14.

17. **which smote**. Ps 135:10, 11. Jsh ch. 12. **great kings**. ver. 18, 19, 20. Ps 48:2. 135:10.

18. **And slew**. Ps 10:8. 59:11. 78:31. 94:6. **famous kings**. Ps 135:11.

19. **Sihon**. Nu 21:21, 23. Dt 2:30-36. 29:7. **Amorites**. Dt +20:17.

20. **Og**. Nu 21:33. Dt 3:1, etc. **Bashan**. Ps 22:12. Nu +21:33. Jsh 12:4n.

21. **gave their land**. Ps 44:2, 3. 78:55. 105:44. 135:12. Nu 32:33, etc. Dt 3:12-17. Jsh 12:1, etc. ch. 13-21. Ne 9:22-24.

22. **an heritage**. Ps 47:4.

23. **remembered**. Ps 102:17. *106:42-45. Ge 8:1. Dt 32:36. Is 63:9. Ezk 16:3-13. Lk 1:48, 52. **in our low estate**. Ps 72:12-14. 113:7. 116:6. 142:6. 1 S 2:7, 8.

24. **hath redeemed**. Ex 15:13. Dt 15:15. Pr 23:10, 11. Is *63:9. Lk 1:68-74. T *2:14.

25. **Who giveth food**. ♪171I8, Ge +3:19. Ps 104:27. +*145:15. 147:9. **flesh**. ♪171Q8, Ge +6:13.

26. **the God**. Heb. *El*, Ex +15:2. **of heaven**. ver. 1-3. Ps *115:3. 123:1. Jon 1:9. Re *11:13. **for ever**. Heb. *olam*, Ex +*12:24.

PSALM 137

The pious captives at Babylon bewail Zion's desolations, complain of the insults of their oppressors, and declare their strong and inviolable attachment to Jerusalem, 1-6. They pray that God would remember the conduct of Edom; and they predict the doom of Babylon, 7-9.

(Title.) A.M. cir. 3463. B.C. cir. 541. The author of this beautiful and affecting elegy is unknown, but the occasion is evident: it was most probably composed during or near the close of the captivity.

1. **the rivers**. Ge 2:10-14. Ezr 8:21, 31. Ezk 1:1. **there sat**. Ne 1:3, 4. 2:3. Jb 2:12, 13. Je 13:17, 18. 15:17. La 2:10. Ezk 3:15. **we wept**. Ps 42:4. 102:9-14. Is 66:10. Je 51:50, 51. La 1:16. 2:11, 18. 3:48-51. Da 9:3. 10:2, 3. Lk 19:41. Re 11:3.

2. **We hanged**. Willows were so plentiful at Babylon on the banks of the Euphrates that Isaiah calls it "the brook or river of willows" (Is 15:7). Ps 33:2. 81:2. Is 24:8. Ezk 26:13. Am 8:10. Re 18:22.

3. **For there**. Ps 123:3, 4. La 2:15, 16. **a song**. Heb. the words of a song. ver. 4. Ps 28:7. 33:3. 40:3. 42:8. **wasted us**. Heb. laid us on heaps. ✻S#8437h, only here. Ps *79:1. Ne 4:2. Je 9:11. 26:18. La *1:7. Mi 3:12. Lk 21:6. **the songs of Zion**. Ps 9:14. 65:1. 1 Ch 15:27, 28. 16:7. Is 35:10. 51:11. Je 31:12, 13. Re 14:1-3.

4. **How shall**. Ec 3:4. Is 22:12. La 5:14, 15. Ho 9:4. Am 8:3. **strange**. Ps 18:44, 45. 81:9. 144:7, 11. Ex 12:43 (✻S#5236h). **land**. Heb. land of a stranger. Is 49:21.

5. **I forget**. Ps 84:1, 2, 10. 102:13, 14. +*122:5-9. Ne 1:2-4. 2:2, 3. Is *62:1, 6, 7. Je 51:50. Da 6:10, 11. **let my right**. Zc 11:17. **forget**. ♪155A, Ge +31:35. **her cunning**. ♪63A2, 2 S +6:6.

6. **let my tongue**. Ps 22:15. Is 41:17. La 4:4. Ezk 3:26. **if I prefer**. Ps 84:10. Mt √6:33. Ac 20:24. Ph 1:20-25. 1 Th 3:7-9. **my chief joy**. Heb. the head of my joy. Ps 21:6.

7. **Remember**. ♪22C3, Ge +8:1. Ps 74:18. 79:8-12. Ex 17:14. 1 S 15:2. Ho 7:2. Zc 1:15. **the children**. Is 63:1-6. Je 49:7, etc. La *4:21, 22. Ezk *25:12-14. Jl 3:19. Ob *10-14, 18-21. **the day**. ♪121P4, Dt +4:32. **who said**. ♪122, Ex +15:9. Ob 12. **Rase it**. Heb. Make bare. Ps 141:8mg. Is 3:17mg. Hab 3:13mg. **rase**. ♪84, Ge +6:17.

8. **daughter**. ♪155E5, Nu +21:25. Is *47:1-5. Je 50:42. 51:33. Zc 2:7. **who art**. Is ch. 13. 14:4-24. 21:1-10. 47:1. Je √25:12-14. ch. 50, 51. Re 14:8-11. ch. 17. *18:6. **destroyed**. Heb. wasted. Ps 17:9mg. **happy**. ♪43, Dt +28:3. Ps +*149:6-9. Is 13:3-5. 44:28. Re 17:5, 6, 14. 18:6, 20. **rewardeth**, etc. Heb. recom-

penseth unto thee thy deed which thou didst unto us. Je 50:15-29. Re 18:6.

9. **Happy.** ♪43, Dt +28:3. Pr 17:5. **taketh.** Ps 48:6. 73:23. 77:4. 139:10. **and dasheth.** Ps *2:9. 1 K 5:9. 2 K *8:12. 15:16. Is *13:16. Je 13:14. Ho 10:14. *13:16. Am *1:13. Na *3:10. Zc 14:2. **little ones.** Ps 8:2. 17:14. 1 S 15:3. **the stones.** Heb. the rock. Ps 18:2. 31:3. 40:2. 42:9.

PSALM 138

David praises the mercy and truth of God, who has answered his prayers, 1-3. He prophesies that all kings shall praise God and rejoice in his ways, 4, 5. He shows the Lord's dealings with the humble and with the proud and professes full confidence in him, 6-8.

(Title.) A.M. 3485. B.C. 519. **A Psalm of David.** Five MSS. omit *ledawid;* and the LXX. and Arabic prefix also the names of Haggai and Zechariah; it is probable that it was composed to be sung at the dedication of the second temple.

1. **I will praise.** Ps *9:1. *86:12, 13. *103:1, 2. *111:1. 1 C 14:15. Ep *5:19. **with my whole.** The versions and several MSS. add, Jehovah. **before.** Ps *82:1, 6. *119:46. Ex *22:28. Jn +*10:34-36. Ac *23:5. He 1:14. **the gods.** Or, God, *Elohim.* Ps +*8:5n. +*82:6n. 96:4, 5. 2 S 19:21. Ro 13:1.

2. **toward.** Ps *5:7. 28:2. 99:5, 9. 1 K 8:29, 30. Da *6:10. **and praise.** Ps 36:5, 6. 85:10. *86:15. *89:1, 2. 100:4, 5. 115:1. Is *63:7. La 3:23. Mi *7:18-20. Lk 1:68-72. Jn 1:17. Ro 15:8, 9. **for thou hast.** Ps *56:4, 10. Is 42:21. Mt *5:18. *24:35. Jn *10:35. **magnified.** Ps 35:26. 38:16. 41:9mg. 55:12. Is *42:21. **thy word.** Ps 12:6. 17:6. 18:30. *56:4. 105:19. *119:11. Nu 11:23. Pr 13:13. **thy name.** Ps 8:9. +√9:10. Pr 18:10.

3. **In the day.** Ps 18:6. 34:4-6. 77:1, 2. 2 K +20:4. Is +*65:24. Da *9:23. Lk *17:5. He 5:7. **strengthenedst.** Ps 27:14. 29:11. 63:8. Is 12:2. 40:29-31. 41:10. Zc 10:12. 2 C √12:8-10. Ep √3:16. 6:10. Ph *4:13. Col 1:11. 1 P 5:10. **soul.** Heb. *nephesh,* Ge +34:3.

4. **All the kings.** Ps 72:11. *102:15, 22. Is 49:23. *60:3-5, 16. Re +*11:15. 21:24. **when they hear.** Ps 22:22, 27. 51:13. *68:11. 69:30-32. 71:18. Is *11:9. 54:13. Ro *10:18.

5. **they shall.** Is 52:7-10. 65:14. *66:10-14. Je 31:11, 12. Zp 3:14, 15. Mt 21:5-9. Lk 19:37, 38. **for great.** Ps 21:5. Ex 15:11. 33:18, 19. Is 6:1-3. Ml 1:11. Jn 13:31, 32. 17:1. 2 C 4:6. Ep 1:6, 12. Re 4:11. 5:12-14. 7:12. 19:1.

6. **Though.** Ps 51:17. *113:5, 6. 1 S 2:7, 8. Pr *3:34. Is +*57:15. 66:2. Lk 1:51-53. 14:11. *18:14. Ja 4:6. 1 P *5:5, 6. **yet hath.** Ps 34:18. Is 66:2. **but the proud.** Ps +*119:21. Ex 18:11. Jb 40:11, 12. Is *2:11, 17. Ezk 28:2-9. Da 4:37. 5:20-24. Ac 12:22, 23. **afar off.** Ps 139:2. Mt 25:41. 2 Th 1:9.

7. **Though I walk.** Ps *23:3, 4. 42:7, 8. 66:10-12. Jb *13:15. *19:25, 26. Is 57:16. **thou wilt.** Ps 71:20, 21. 85:6. 119:49, 50. **thou shalt stretch.** ♪22A14.8A, Ex +7:5. Ps 35:1-3. 56:1, 2, 9. 64:7, 8. 77:10. 144:1, 2. Is 5:25. 9:12, 17, 21. 10:4. Mi *7:8-10. **and thy right.** Ps 17:7. 18:35. 44:3, 5-7. 60:5. Is 41:10. Ac 2:33.

8. **perfect.** Ps 57:2. Is *26:12. *46:4. Je *32:39, 40. Jn *15:2. Ro 5:10. √8:28-30. Ph *1:6. 1 Th 5:24. 1 P 5:10. 2 P +*1:10. **thy mercy.** Ps *100:5. 103:17. Jon +4:2. **for ever.** Heb. *olam,* Ex +*12:24. **forsake.** Ps

71:6-9, 17, 18. Jb 10:3, 8. 14:15. Is *42:16. 43:21. He +*13:5. 1 P *1:3-5. *4:19. Ju 1. **the works.** Ps 100:3. Is 64:8.

PSALM 139

David contemplates with adoring surprise the omniscience and omnipresence of God, 1-12. He praises him as his all-wise and bountiful Creator and for his numberless mercies, 13-18. He avows his abhorrence of the wicked, prays to be searched, proved, and directed in the right way, 19-24.

(Title.) A.M. 2956. B.C. 1048. **A Psalm.** This psalm is supposed to have been composed by David when made king of Israel, though some think it was written by him when accused of traitorous designs against Saul. It is a most sublime ode on the wisdom, knowledge, presence, and justice of God: the sentiments are grand, the style highly elevated, and the images various, beautiful, and impressive.

1. **thou hast.** ver. 23. Ps 11:4, 5. 17:3. 44:21. 1 K 8:39. 1 Ch *28:9. Je *12:3. √17:9, 10. Jn 21:17. 1 C 2:10. He *4:13. Re 2:18, 23. **and known.** Jn 1:48.

2. **knowest.** Ps 56:8. Ge 16:13. 1 K +8:39. 2 K 6:12. 19:27. Jb 31:4. Pr *15:3. Is 37:28. Zc 4:10. **understandest.** Ps *94:11. Mt *9:4. Lk 9:47. Jn +*2:24, 25. 1 C *4:5. **afar off.** Ezk 38:10, 11, 17.

3. **compassest.** or, winnowest. Jb 13:26, 27. 14:16, 17. *31:4. Mt *3:12. **my path.** ver. 18. Ps *121:3-8. Ge 28:10-17. 2 S *8:14. 11:2-5, 27. **and art acquainted.** 2 S 12:9-12. Pr *5:20, 21. Ec *12:14. Is 29:15. Je *23:24. Jn 1:48, 49. 6:70, 71. 13:2, 21. Ac *5:3, 4.

4. **there is not.** Ps *19:14. Jb 8:2. *38:2. *42:3, 6-8. Zp 1:12. Ml *3:13-16. Mt √12:35-37. Ja *1:26. *3:2-10. **thou knowest.** Ps 50:19-21. Je 29:23. He *4:12, 13.

5. **beset me.** Dt *33:27. Jb 23:8, 9. **before.** Mi +5:2 (✜S#6924h). **and laid.** Ex 24:11. Re 1:17.

6. **knowledge.** Ps 40:5. 131:1. Jb 11:7-9. 26:14. 42:3. Pr 30:2-4. Ro *11:33. **cannot.** Lk 18:34. 1 C 2:10, 11. **attain.** ♪63BA, Ps +21:11.

7. **Whither.** 2 Ch 16:9. Je *23:23, 24. Jon 1:3, 10. Ac 5:9. **from thy.** Ps 51:11. Ge 1:2. Jb 26:13. Is 11:1, 2. Ac 5:3, 4. **spirit.** Heb. *ruach.* A reference to God as being invisible. Jn 4:24. Similar possible references include 2 S 23:2. Is 40:13. But this may be a reference to God the Holy Spirit, the third person of the Trinity, Is +48:16. **thy presence.** ♪22A4, Ge +19:13. God the Holy Spirit is omnipresent and possesses the attribute of immensity. Ps 51:11. Is *57:15. Je *23:23, 24. Mt +*28:19n. Jn 14:16, 17. 1 C 3:16. 6:19. Scripture teaches both the immanence of God (He is everywhere present at the same time) and the transcendence of God (He is separate from the universe, not a part of it, but entirely above it, so that to suppose man can become "God" or is "God" is, from a biblical standpoint, absurd (see Ps 8:5n). That men are called "god" or "gods" in Scripture does not suggest man can become or is divine or deity; rather, the Hebrew word "elohim" has multiple meanings and is sometimes used of false gods and idols (2 Ch 35:22n), of divinely appointed (though very mortal, Ps 82:7) judges and magistrates (Ps +82:6n), and is used of angels (Ps +8:5n).

8. **If I.** ♪102C, Mt +5:29. **ascend.** Ezk 28:12-17.

Am 9:2-4. Ob 4. Mt 22:31, 32. Mk 12:26, 27. **in hell**. Heb. sheol, Ge +37:35. Ps +*16:10. 30:3. Jb 14:13. *26:6. 34:21, 22. Pr *15:11. Is 38:10. Am 9:2-4. Jon *2:2.

9. **If I take**. Light has been proved, by many experiments, to travel at the astonishing rate of 194,188 (the more modern figure is 186,000) miles in one second of time. It comes from the sun to the earth, a distance of 95,513,794 miles, in 8 minutes and nearly 12 seconds! Yet, could I even fly upon the wings or rays of the morning light, which diffuses itself with such velocity over the globe from east to west, instead of being beyond thy reach, or by this sudden transition be able to escape thy notice, thy arm could still at pleasure prevent or arrest my progress, and I should still be encircled with the immensity of thy essence. The sentiment in this noble passage is remarkably striking, and the description truly sublime. **the wings**. Ps 18:10. 19:6. Ml 4:2. **dwell**. Ps 74:16, 17. Is 24:14-16.

10. **Even there**. Ps 63:8. *73:23. 143:9, 10. Is 41:13. **right hand**. ♪22A15A, Ex +15:6. **lead me**. Ps +32:8.

11. **Surely**. Ps 10:11-13. 94:7. Jb 22:12-14. Is 29:15. Je *23:24. **even the night**. Jb 12:22.

12. **the darkness**. Ex 14:20. 20:21. Jb *26:6. √34:22. Da *2:22. He *4:13. **hideth not**. Heb. darkeneth not. Ps 105:28. Is *29:15. Je 13:16. **shineth**. Ps 18:28. 67:1. 118:27. **the darkness**, etc. Heb. as *is* the darkness, so *is* the light.

13. **For thou**. Jb 10:9-12. **covered me**. Ps 22:9, 10. 71:6. Jb 31:15. Is 44:2. 46:3. Je 1:5.

14. **for I am fearfully**. lit. with fears and wonder. ♪24I, Is +21:7. ♪96F2, Ge +4:10. Ge *1:26, 27. **marvelous**. Ps 92:4, 5. *104:24. *111:2. Jb 5:9. Re *15:3. **soul**. Heb. *nephesh*, Ps +*84:2. Ge +34:3. Mt +*11:29. **right well**. Heb. greatly. Ps 6:3. 21:1. 31:11. 38:6.

15. **substance**. *or*, strength, *or* body. Dt 8:17. Jb 30:21mg. **when I**. ver. 13. Jb *10:8-11. Ec 11:5. **in the lowest**. Ps 63:9. Ep *4:9.

16. **in thy book**. Ps 56:8. 69:28. Ex 32:32. Ml *3:16. Re 13:8. *20:12. **all my members**. Heb. all of them. **written**. Ps 69:28. 102:18. Ezr 8:34. **which in continuance were fashioned**. *or*, what days they should be fashioned. Ps +*90:12. Jb 17:7. 33:29. **when**. Ac 13:48.

17. **How**. ♪85F, Ps +8:4. **precious**. Ps 40:5. 49:7, 8. 116:15. Jb 26:14. Pr 8:31. Is 28:16. √55:8, 9. Je 29:11. Ep 3:9, 10. 1 P *1:19. 2:7. 2 P 1:1, 4. **thy thoughts**. ♪22C5, Ge +50:20. **God**. Heb. *El*, Ex +15:2. **how great**. Ps 31:19. 36:7.

18. **they are more**. Ps 40:*5, 12. **than the sand**. ♪102B, ♪138B, Ge +13:16. **when I awake**. ver. 3. Ps *3:5. 16:8-11. 17:15. 63:6, 7. Is +*26:19n. Da *12:2. 1 Th *5:10.

19. **Surely**. Ps 5:6. +*9:17. *55:23. 64:7. 94:23. Is 11:4. Ju 14, 15. **depart from**. Ps 6:8. *26:5. *101:4. 119:+*63, 115. Mt *7:23. +*25:41. 2 C *6:17. Re 18:4. **ye bloody**. Ps 5:6. 26:9. 55:23. 59:2.

20. **For they speak**. Ps 73:8, 9. 74:18, 22, 23. Jb *21:14, 15. Is 37:23, 28, 29. Ju 15. Re 13:6. **thine**. Ps 2:1-3. Ex +*20:7.

21. **Do not I**. Ps 15:4. 31:6. *97:10. 2 Ch √19:2. 2 P 2:7, 8. Re *2:2, 6. **and am not**. Ps 119:136, 158. Je 13:17. Mk *3:5. Lk 19:41. Ro 9:1-3.

22. **hate them**. Ps *101:3-8. Lk *14:26.

23. **Search me**. T#1691. ver. 1. Ps 26:2. 44:21. Pr 30:7, 8. Jn *3:20, 21. **God**. Heb. *El*, Ex +15:2. **try**

me. T#1733. Ps 26:2. 1 J 3:21. **know**. Dt 8:2, 16. Jb *31:6. Pr 17:3. Zc 13:9. Ml 3:2, 3. 1 P 1:7.

24. **And see**. Ps 7:3, 4. *17:3. Pr 28:26. Je √17:9, 10. Jn 15:6. **wicked way**. Heb. way of pain, *or* grief. ♪100, Ge +10:9. ✳S#6090h. 1 Ch 4:9 (with sorrow). Is 14:3 (sorrow). 48:5 (Mine idol). He *12:15, 16. **and lead**. Ps *5:8. *25:8, 9, 12. 119:1, 32. *143:8, 10. **the way**. Ps 1:6. Mt √7:13, 14. Jn √14:6. Col *2:6. **everlasting**. Heb. *olam*, Ge +*17:7.

<h2 style="text-align:center">PSALM 140</h2>

David prays for deliverance from his malicious persecutors, Saul and Doeg, 1-7; and predicts their ruin, 8-11. He professes confidence that God will rescue and bless all his afflicted people, 12, 13.

1. A.M. 2942. B.C. 1062. **Deliver**. Ps 43:1. 59:1-3. 71:4. **violent man**. Heb. man of violences. ver. 4, 11. Ps 18:48mg. 25:19mg. Pr 3:31mg. Hab 1:2, 3.

2. **imagine**. Ps 2:1, 2. 21:11. 36:4. 38:12. 52:2. 62:3. 64:5, 6. Pr 6:14. 12:20. 16:27. Is 59:4. Ho 7:6, 15. Mi 2:1-3. Na 1:11. **continually**. Ps 56:6. 120:7. 1 S 23:19-24. 24:11, 12. 26:1, etc.

3. **sharpened**. Ps 52:2, 3. 57:4. 59:7. 64:3, 4. Pr 12:18. Is 59:3-5, 13. Je 9:3, 5. Ja 3:6-8. **like a serpent**. Ge 3:13. Pr 23:32. Mt 12:34. 2 C 11:3. **adders.'** Ps 58:4. Ro 3:▶13, 14.

4. **Keep me**. Ps 17:8, 9. 36:11. *37:32, 33-40. 55:1-3. 71:4. **preserve**. ver. 1. **overthrow**. Ps 17:5. Pr 18:5.

5. **The proud**. Ps 10:4-12. 17:8-13. 35:7. 36:11. 57:6. 119:69, 85, *110. 123:3, 4. 141:9, 10. 142:3. Pr 29:5. Je 18:18, 20, *22. Lk 11:53, 54. *20:20-23.

6. **I said unto**. Ps 16:2, 5, 6. 31:14. 91:2. 119:57. 142:5. La 3:24. Zc 13:9. **hear**. Ps 27:7, 8. 28:1, 2. 55:1, 2. 64:1.

7. **the strength**. Ps 18:1, 2, 35. 27:1. 28:7, 8. 59:17. *62:2, 7. 89:26. 95:1. Dt 33:27-29. Is 12:2. **thou hast covered**. Ps 144:10. Le 26:7, 8. Dt 32:30. 1 S 17:36, 37, 45-51. 2 S 8:6, 14. Zc 12:6, 8.

8. **Grant not**. Ps 27:12. 94:20, 21. 2 S 15:31. Jb 5:12, 13. **lest they exalt themselves**. *or*, let them not be exalted. Dt 32:27.

9. **let the mischief**. Ps *7:16. 64:8. *94:23. Est 5:14. 7:10. Pr 10:6, 11. *12:13. *18:7. Mt 27:25.

10. **burning coals**. Ps *11:6. 18:13, 14. 21:9. 120:4. Ge 19:24. Ex 9:23, 24. Re 16:8, 9. **let them**. Da 3:20-25. Mt 13:42, 50. **into deep**. Ps 55:23. Pr 28:10, 17. Re 20:15. *21:8.

11. **Let not**, etc. *or*, Let not an evil speaker, a wicked man of violence, be established in the earth: let him be hunted to his overthrow. **an evil speaker**. Heb. a man of tongue. ♪171E6, Ec +10:11. Ps +*12:3, 4. Pr 6:17. 12:13. 17:20. 18:21. **evil**. Ps 7:14-16. 9:16. 34:21. Pr *13:21. Is 3:11.

12. **maintain**. T#522. Ps *9:4, 18. *10:14, 17, 18. 22:24. 34:6. 72:4, 12-14. *102:17. +119:68 (T#224). 146:9. 1 K 8:45, 49. Jb 5:15, 16. Pr 22:22, 23. 23:10, 11. Is 11:4. Je 22:16. Da *10:18. Mt 11:5. Ja +5:11 (T#225).

13. **Surely**. Ps 32:11. 33:1. Is 3:10. **the upright**. Ps *16:11. *23:6. 73:24. Jn +*14:3. 17:24. 1 Th *4:17. Re *7:14-17. 21:24-27. **shall dwell**. Jn +*14:3. **thy presence**. T#825. Ps +*16:11. Ex 33:14. Nu 23:21. Dt 31:8. 2 Ch 15:2. Is +*24:23. 41:10. Ezk 34:30. Jl *2:27. Mt +*5:8. Jn *14:23.

PSALM 141

David earnestly requests that his prayers may be accepted; that he may be preserved from sinful words, works, and indulgences, 1-4. He desires the reproofs of the righteous, whom he will recompense by his prayers, and hopes to win on his people when afflicted, 5, 6. He complains that his friends were cruelly slain, professes confidence in God, and predicts the fall of the wicked, 7-10.

1. A.M. 2946. B.C. 1058. **make haste**. Ps 40:13. 69:17, 18. *70:5. 71:12. 143:7. Jb 7:21.

2. **Let my prayer**. David, who was now driven from Judea and far from the sanctuary, here prays that the devotion of his heart and the elevation of his hands might be accepted; that the one might ascend to heaven fragrant and well pleasing as the cloud of incense, and the other, in conjunction with it, be prevalent as the *minchah*, or evening oblation. Pr 15:8. **set forth**. Heb. directed. Ps 5:3. **as incense**. T#1649. Ex 30:+1, 7-9, 34-38. Le 10:1, 2. 16:11-13. Nu 16:35, 46-48. Dt 33:10. 1 K 18:29. 2 Ch=13:11. Ml 1:11. Lk 1:9, 10. 2 C=2:15. Re 5:8mg. *8:3, 4. **the lifting**. Ps 28:2. 63:4. 134:2. 1 T +2:8. **the evening**. Ex 29:39-42. 1 K 18:29, 36. Ezr 9:4, 5. Da 9:21. Mt=27:45, 46. Lk=23:44n. Ac 3:1. 10:2, 3, 30.

3. **Set a watch**. T#1743. Ps *17:3-5. 19:14. *39:1. *71:8. +101:5. Pr 21:23. Mi *7:5. Ja *1:26, 27. *3:2. **keep**. T#1606. Mi 7:5.

4. **Incline not**. Ps *119:36. Dt +2:30. 29:4. 1 K *8:58. 22:22. Is *63:17. Mt *6:13. Ja *1:13. **to practice**. 1 C *15:33. 2 C *6:17. Re *18:4. **with men**. Ps *26:4. +*119:63. 1 C 15:33. **and let me**. Nu 25:2. Pr *23:1-3, 6-8. Da *1:5-8. Ac 10:13, 14. 1 C *10:27, 28, 31.

5. **the righteous**. T#1703. 1 S *25:31-34. 2 S *12:7-13. 2 Ch *16:7-10. *25:16. Pr *6:23. *9:8, 9. *15:5, 22. *19:25. *25:12. *27:5, 6. Ga *2:11-14. *6:1. Re *3:19. **smite**, etc. *or*, smite me kindly and reprove me; let not their precious oil break my head, etc. **reprove**. T#1675. Pr 13:18. 15:5. *17:10. 25:12. **head**. ♪145, Jg +11:40. **for yet my**. Ps 51:18. 125:4. Mt *5:44. 2 T 1:16-18. Ja *5:14-16.

6. **When their judges**. 1 S 31:1-8. 2 S *1:17, etc. 1 Ch 10:1-7. **they shall hear**. 2 S 2:4. 5:1-3. 1 Ch 11:1-3. 12:38. **for they**. Ps 45:2. 2 S 2:5, 6. 23:1. 1 Ch 13:2. Lk 4:22.

7. **bones**. Ps 44:22. 1 S 22:18, 19. Ro 8:36. 2 C *1:8, 9. He 11:37. Re 11:8, 9. **grave's**. Heb. *sheol*, Ge +37:35.

8. **mine eyes**. Ps *25:15. 123:1, 2. 2 Ch *20:12, 14, 15. **leave not my soul destitute**. Heb. make not my soul bare. Ps 25:16, 17. *102:17. +137:7mg. 143:3, 4. Is 41:17. Jn 14:18. **soul**. Heb. *nephesh*, Ge +12:13.

9. **from the snares**. Ps 91:3. *119:110. 124:7. 140:5. 142:3. Pr 13:14. Je 18:22. Lk 20:20.

10. **the wicked**. Ps 7:15, 16. *9:15. 35:8. 37:14, 15. 64:7, 8. 140:9. Est 7:10. Pr 11:8. **escape**. Heb. pass over. Ps 17:3 (transgress). 37:36. 42:4 (had gone). 57:1. 81:6mg. 90:4. 104:9. 148:6.

PSALM 142

David complains of his persecutors and expresses his confidence and joy in God, 1-7.

(*Title.*) A.M. 2942. B.C. 1062. **Maschil of David**. *or*, a Psalm of David giving instruction. Ps 32, 54, 57, titles. 1 Ch 4:10. **A Prayer**. David was twice in great peril in caves: on one occasion in the cave of Adullam, when he fled from Achish king of Gath, and on another in the cave of Engedi, where he had taken refuge from the pursuit of Saul. It is not certain to which of these events this psalm refers; though probably to the former. **when he was**. 1 S 22:1, 2. 24:3. He 11:38.

1. **with my voice**. Ps 28:2. 77:1, 2. 141:1.

2. **poured out**. Ps 42:4. *62:8. 102, title. 1 S 1:15, 16. Is 26:16. Ro 8:26. **I showed**. Ps 18:4-6. Ph *4:6, 7. He *5:7.

3. **my spirit**. Heb. *ruach*, Ge +41:8. Ps 22:14. 61:2. 102:4. 143:4. Mk 14:33-36. **then thou**. Ps *1:6. 17:3. 139:2-4. Jb 23:10. **In the way**. Ps 31:4. 35:7, 8. 56:6. 140:5. 141:9. Je 18:22. Mt 22:15.

4. **I looked**, etc. *or*, Look on the right hand and see. **beheld**. ♪63G, Ge +50:23. Supply by ellipsis (relative: of analogous, or related words), "I looked on (my) right hand, and beheld (on my left hand)." **but there was**. Ps 31:11. *69:20. 88:8, 18. Jb 19:13-19. La *1:12. Mt 26:38, 40, 47, *56. 2 T 4:16. **know**. ♪121C2A2, Ge +39:6. **refuge**. 1 S 23:11-13, 19, 20. 27:1. **failed me; no man cared for my soul**. Heb. perished from me; no man sought after my soul. **soul**. Heb. *nephesh*, Ge +12:13.

5. **Thou art**. Ps *32:7. *46:1, 7, 11. 62:6, 7. *91:2, 9, 10. Jn 16:32. 2 T 4:17. **my portion**. Ps 16:5. 73:26. 119:57. La 3:24. **in the land**. Ps 27:13. 56:13.

6. **for I am**. Ps 44:24-26. 79:8. *116:6. 136:23. 143:3, 7. Ge 41:14. **for they**. Ps 3:1. 38:19. 57:3, 4. 59:3. 1 S 24:14. Ro 8:33, 37.

7. **my soul**. Heb. *nephesh*, Ps 142, Title. Ge +12:13. Ps 9:13, 14. 31:8. 88:4-8. 143:11. 146:7. Is 61:1. Ac 2:24. **prison**. T#1405, 1653. 2 Ch 33:11-13. Ac 12:5. 16:23-27. **the righteous**. Ps 7:6, 7. 22:21-27. *34:2. 107:41, 42. *119:74. **thou shalt**. Ps *13:6. 116:7. 119:17. Ja *5:10, 11.

PSALM 143

David earnestly deprecates the severity of God's judgment, 1, 2; complains of his enemies and distresses, 3, 4; and encourages his faith by meditating on the works of God, 5, 6. He fervently prays for comfort, guidance, quickening, and deliverance, 7-11; and foretells the destruction of his enemies, 12.

(*Title.*) **A Psalm**. The LXX., Vulgate, Ethiopic, and Arabic state that this psalm was composed by David on the rebellion of his son Absalom. There are several passages in it which agree remarkably well with that period: for then he had most reason to fear lest God should deal with him according to his sins; which he deprecates with such a deep sense of his unworthiness, that it has hence been numbered among the penitential psalms, of which it is the last. In it he prays to God for pardon, ver. 1; acknowledges the impossibility of being saved but by grace, ver. 2; deplores the lamentable effects of sin, ver. 3, 4; comforts himself with a retrospect of God's mercies of old, ver. 5; and prays, in a variety of expressions, for the remission of sin, sanctification, and redemption, ver. 6-12.

1. **in thy faithfulness**. T#1134. Ps *31:1. 71:2. 2 S 7:25. La *3:22, 23. Da 9:16. 1 J √1:9.

2. **enter not**. Ps 130:3. Jb 14:3. **in thy sight**. Ps +130:3. Ex 34:7. Jb 4:17. *9:2, 3. *15:14. 25:4. Pr *20:9. Ec √7:20. Ro *3:20. Ga 2:16. 1 J *1:10. **no man**.

T#576. Mt *18:11. Ac √4:12. 13:38, 39. Ro 3:19, 20. 5:6. 9:31, 32. Ga *2:16, 20, 21. 3:10-12, 18-24. Ph 3:4-7. He 9:23. Ja *2:10. **living**. √171E, Ge +3:20.

3. **the enemy**. Ps 7:1, 2. 17:9-13. 35:4. 54:3. 142:6. **soul**. Heb. *nephesh*, Ge +12:13. **smitten**. Ps 7:5. 2 S 2:22. 18:11. **made me**. Ps 31:12, 13. 88:4-6. Ezk 37:11. **long**. Heb. *olam*, Le +25:32. Ec 12:5.

4. **is my spirit**. Heb. *ruach*, Ge +41:8. Ps 55:5. 61:2. 77:3. 102, title. 124:4. 142:3. Jb 6:27. **my heart**. T#1346. Ps 25:16. 102:3, 4. 119:81-83. Lk 22:44.

5. **remember**. Ps 42:6. *44:1. 77:5, 6, *10-12. 111:4. Dt 8:2, 3. 1 S 17:34-37, 45-50. Is 63:7-14. Mi 6:5.

6. **stretch forth**. Ps 44:20. 88:9. Jb 11:13. **my soul**. Heb. *nephesh*, Ps *42:1, 2. 63:1. 84:2. Ge +34.3. Is 26:8, 9. 35:7. Jn 7:37.

7. **Hear me**. Ps 13:1-4. 40:13, 17. 70:5. 71:12. **my spirit**. Heb. *ruach*, Ge +41:8. Ps 40:12. 69:3. Is 57:16. Lk 21:26. **hide not**. Ps 22:24. 27:9. 69:17. Is 8:17. **lest I be like**, etc. *or*, for I am become like, etc. **like**. Nu +21:27. **unto them**. Ps 28:1. 88:4-6, 10, 11. +*146:4. Is 38:18. **pit**. Heb. *bor*, Ge +37:20. Ps 7:15. 28:1. 30:3. 40:2. 88:4.

8. **to hear**. Ps *30:5. *42:8. *46:5mg. *59:16. Ge *32:24-29. 2 Ch *20:20. Ho *6:3. **cause me**. ver. *10. Ps 5:8. *25:4, 5. *27:11. *32:8. *119:27, 33, 34, 73. Pr √3:5, 6. Is *30:21. *48:17. **for I lift up**. T#1403. Ps *25:1. 86:4. La *3:41. **soul**. Heb. *nephesh*, Ge +34:3.

9. **flee unto thee**. Heb. hide me with thee. Ps 31:2-4. 32:7. 56:9. 61:3, 4. 91:1, 4. 142:5. Pr 18:10. He 6:18.

10. **Teach**. T#1539. Ps *25:4, 5, 8, 9, 12. *32:8. 119:5-7, 12, 35. *139:24. Mi 4:2. Mt *28:20. Col *1:9, 10. 1 Th 4:1, 2. He *13:21. 1 J *2:27. **to do**. T#1627. Ps 86:11. 119:5, 10, 35, 133. **for thou art**. Ps 22:1. 31:14. *63:1. 118:28. 140:6. **thy spirit**. Heb. *ruach*, Ge +41:38. Is +*48:16. **is good**. Ne *9:20. Is 63:14. Mt +*28:19n. Mk ◑+*10:18n. Jn ◑+*10:11. *14:26. 16:13-15. Ro *5:5. *8:2, 14-16, 26. *15:13, 30. Ga *5:22, 23. Ep √4:30. 5:9. 2 T √1:7. **the land**. Ps 27:11, 13. Is *26:10.

11. **Quicken**. Ps 85:6. 119:25, 37, 40, 88, 107. 138:7. Hab 3:2. Ep 2:4, 5. **name's sake**. Ps 25:11. **for thy righteousness'**. ver. 1. Ps 9:7, 8. 31:1. 71:2. **bring**. Ps 25:17. *34:19. 37:39, 40. 91:15, 16. Re 7:14-17. **soul**. Heb. *nephesh*, Ge +34:3.

12. **of thy mercy**. Ps 54:5. 55:23. 136:15-20. 1 S 24:12-15. 25:29. 26:10. **soul**. Heb. *nephesh*, Ge +34:3. **for I am thy**. Ps 116:16. 119:94.

PSALM 144

David praises God for his goodness to him and his condescension to the human race, 1-4. He prays for the powerful interposition of Jehovah to deliver him from his enemies, 5-8. He promises to praise God, 9, 10. He renews his prayers for personal and public prosperity and shows the happiness of those "whose God is the Lord," 11-15.

(Title.) **A Psalm of David**. Calmet and others think that this psalm was composed by David after the death of Absalom, and from a collation of it with Ps 18 in which the same ideas and form of expression occur, there can be no doubt of both having proceeded from the same pen: that David was the author.

1. **my strength**. Heb. my rock. Ps 18:2, 31. 71:3.

95:1. Dt 32:30, 31. Is *26:4mg. 45:24. **teacheth**. Ps 18:34. *44:3, 4. 60:12. 2 S 22:35. 2 C 10:4. Ep 6:10, 11. **to war**. *or*, to the war, etc.

2. **My goodness**. *or*, mercy. Ps 52:1. 57:3. 59:10. **my fortress**. ♪22L5, Ps +31:3. 2 S 22:2, 3, 40-48. Je 16:19. **who subdueth**. Ps 18:47. *110:2, 3. 2 S *22:40.

3. **what is man**. ♪85F, Ps +8:4. Ps *8:4. Jb *7:17. 15:14. He 2:6, 9. **or the son**. Ps 146:3, 4.

4. **Man**. Ps *39:5, 6. 62:9. 89:47. Jb 4:19. *14:1-3. Ec 1:2, 14. 12:8. **vanity**. ♪121N1, Ge +31:54. **his days**. Ps 102:11. *103:15, 16. 109:23. 2 S 14:14. 1 Ch *29:15. Jb 8:9. Ec 8:13.

5. **Bow**. Ps 18:9. Is *64:1, 2. **come down**. T#1505. Is 64:1-4. Re 22:17, 20. **touch**. ♪22C16, Ps +104:32. Ps 104:32. Ex 19:18. Na 1:3-6. Hab 3:3-6. He 12:18.

6. **Cast forth**. Ps 18:13, 14. 77:17, 18. 2 S *22:12-15. **lightning**. ♪147D, Ge +1:29. **shoot out**. Ps 7:12. 21:12. 45:5. Dt 32:23, 42. **thine arrows**. ♪22D5C, Ps +18:14.

7. **Send**. Ps *18:16. 2 S 22:17. Mt 27:43. **hand**. Heb. hands. ♪96F2, Ge +4:10. ♪22A14.3, Ps +31:5. **deliver me**. Ps 69:1, 2, 14, 15. 93:3, 4. Re 12:15, 16. 17:15. **the hand**. ver. 11. Ps 54:3. Ne 9:2. Ml 2:11. **strange**. ver. 11. Ps 18:44, 45. 81:9. 137:4. Ex +12:43 (❉S#5236h). Is 56:3, 6.

8. **mouth**. Ps 10:7. 12:2. 41:6. 58:3. 62:4. 109:2, 3. Is 59:5-7. **their right hand**. Is 44:20. Mt 5:30. Re 13:16, 17.

9. **sing a new**. Ps 33:2, 3. *40:3. 98:1. 149:1. Re 5:9, 10, 12, 13. *12:10. 14:3. **upon**. Ps 81:1-3. 108:2, 3. 150:3-5. 1 Ch 25:1-6.

10. **that giveth**. Ps 18:50. 33:16-18. 2 S 5:19-25. 8:6, 14. 2 K 5:1. **salvation**. *or*, victory. 2 S 19:2. Pr 21:31mg. Is *45:1-6. Je 27:6-8. **who delivereth**. Ps 140:7. 1 S 17:45, 46. 2 S 21:16, 17.

11. **Rid**. T#1506. Ps 35:1-5. **and deliver me**. ver. 7, 8. 2 S 10:6, etc. 16:5, etc. 17:1, etc. La 1:3, 4. **strange**. ver. +7.

12. **That**. ♪122, Ex +15:9. ♪108F, Ps +109:5. ♪63BA, Ge +26:7. Supply by ellipsis, (say). **our sons**. T#1446. Ps 72:1. Ge 17:18. 27:26-29. 28:1-4. 43:13, 14. 48:14-16. 1 Ch 22:6, 11, 12. 29:19. Mt *19:13-15. 20:20-23. **as plants**. Ps 115:14, 15. 127:4, 5. 128:3. Is 44:3-5. La 4:2. **as corner stones**. Jb 42:15. Pr 31:10-27. Is 3:16-24. **polished**. Heb. cut. Zc 9:15. **the similitude**. SS 8:8, 9. 1 P 3:3-6.

13. **our garners**. T#1716B. Ps 37:34. 107:37, 38. Ge 24:12. *28:20. 43:14. Le 26:5, 10. Dt 28:8. 33:11, 13-16, 18, 19, 23. 1 Ch *4:10. Ne 1:11. Jb 8:5-7. 22:23-28. Jl 2:19. Ml 3:10. Lk 12:16-20. **all manner of store**. Heb. from kind to kind. 2 Ch 16:14. **our sheep**. Ge 30:29-31. Dt 7:13, 14. 8:3. 28:4.

14. **strong to labor**. Heb. able to bear burdens, *or*, loaden with *flesh*. **no breaking in**. Dt 28:7, 25. Jg 5:8. 6:3-6. 1 S 13:17-23. 31:7. Je 13:17-19. 14:18. La 1:4-6. Zc 8:3-5. **no complaining**. Ps 102:11. 109:23. Nu +11:1. Jb 8:9. 14:2. Pr +*19:3. Is 24:11. +√29:24. Je 14:2. 46:12. La 3:39. Jn *6:43. 1 C 10:10. Ph *2:14. **streets**. Am +5:16.

15. **Happy**. ♪43, Dt +28:3. **yea, happy**. Ps 33:12. 65:4. 89:15. 146:5. Dt 33:29. Ep *1:3.

PSALM 145

David zealously praises the greatness, power, goodness, and mercy of God, 1-8. He celebrates the glory of his kingdom and the bounty of his providence, 9-16; his justice, holiness, regard to the prayers of the upright, and care of those that love him, with his vengeance upon the wicked, 17-21.

(Title.) A.M. 2989. B.C. 1015. **David**'s. This incomparable song of praise, which is the last of the acrostic or alphabetical psalms, each verse beginning with a consecutive letter of the Hebrew alphabet, is supposed to have been composed by David towards the close of his life. **Psalm of praise.** Ps 100, title.

1. **extol thee.** Ps 30:1. 68:4. 71:14, etc. 103:1, 2. Da 4:37. **my God.** Ps 44:4. 45:1, 6. 47:6-8. 48:2, 3. 95:3. *149:2. Is 33:22. Ml 1:14. Mt 25:34. Re 19:16. **I will bless.** ver. 21. Ps 30:12. 52:9. 113:1, 2. 146:1, 2.

2. **Every day.** Ps 72:15. 119:164. Da 6:10. Re 7:15.

3. **Great.** Ps 48:1. 96:4. 147:5. Jb 5:9. *9:10. Re 15:3. **and his greatness is unsearchable.** Heb. and of his greatness there is no search. Ps 139:6. Jb 5:9. 9:10. 11:7-9. 26:14. Is 40:28. Ro *11:33.

4. **generation.** Ps 44:1, 2. 71:18. *78:3-7. Ex 12:26, 27. 13:14, 15. Dt 6:7. Jsh 4:21-24. Is *38:19.

5. **will speak.** Ps 40:9, 10. 66:3, 4. 71:17-19, 24. 96:3. 104:1, 2. 105:2. Is 12:4. Da 4:1-3, *37. **works.** Heb. things, *or* words. *144A8, Ps +35:20. Ps 72:18.

6. **And men.** Ps 22:22, 23, 27, 31. 98:2, 3. 113:3. 126:2, 3. Jsh 2:9-11. 9:9, 10. Ezr 1:2. Je 50:28. Da 3:28, 29. *6:25-27. Hab 2:14. **I will declare thy greatness.** Heb. thy greatness I will declare it. Ps 92:1, 2. 107:21, 22, 31, 32.

7. **abundantly.** Ps 36:5-8. Is 63:7. Mt 12:34, 35. 2 C 9:11, 12. 1 P 2:9, 10. **sing.** Ps 36:10. 51:14. 71:15, 16, 19. 72:1-3. 89:16. Is 45:24, 25. Je 23:6. Ph 3:7-9. Re *15:3, 4. 19:1-3.

8. **Lord is gracious.** Ps *86:5, 15. 100:5. 103:8. 116:5. Ex *34:6, 7. Nu 14:18. Da 9:9. Jon 4:2. Mi 7:18-20. Ro 5:20, 21. Ep 1:6, 8. 2:4. **of great mercy.** Heb. great in mercy. Ps 5:7. 6:4. 13:5. 17:7. 31:21.

9. **good to all.** T#228. ver. 7. Ps 8:3, 4. *25:8. 33:5. 36:6, 7. 52:1. 65:9-13. 68:18. *100:5. 104:27, 28. 107:8, 9. 113:4-6. 119:68. +136:1. Ge +*18:25. Ex +*34:6. 1 Ch 16:34. Is *57:15. Je +*29:11. Jon *4:11. Na +*1:7. Zc 9:17. Mt +*5:45. *19:17. Lk +*6:35. Ac *14:17. *17:25. Ro +*11:22. Ja +*1:17.

10. **All thy.** Ps *19:1. 96:11-13. 98:3-9. 103:22. *104:24. 148:1-13. Is 43:20. 44:23. Ro *1:19, 20. **and thy saints.** Ps 22:23. 30:4. 32:11. 97:12. 135:19-22. 148:14. Is *43:21. He *13:15. 1 P 2:5, 9. Re 7:9-12. 19:5, 6.

11. **the glory.** Ps 2:6-8. +*45:6, 7. 72:1, etc. 93:1, 2. 96:10-13. 97:1, etc. 99:1-4. +*102:16. 1 Ch *29:11, 12. Is 9:6, 7. +*24:23. *33:21, 22. Da +*7:13, 14. Zc 9:9. Mt *6:13. +*25:31. Mk 11:9, 10. Lk 1:31-33. 1 Th *2:12. 2 T 2:10. Re 5:12, 13. 11:15-17.

12. **make known.** Ps 98:1. 105:5. 106:2. 110:2, 3. 135:6-12. 136:4, etc. Da 4:34, 35. Mt 28:18. Ac 2:8-11. Ep 1:19-21. 3:7, 8. Re 12:10. 19:15, 16.

13. **kingdom.** Ps *146:10. Is *9:7. Da *2:44. +*7:14, 27. 1 T *1:17. Re √11:15. **everlasting kingdom.** Heb. kingdom of all ages. Ps 93:2. 100:5. 103:17. Lk +*1:32, 33. 1 C 15:21-28. **thy dominion.** Ps +*49:14. 72:8. Da 4:3, 34. Mi 4:8. Zc *9:10. 1 P *4:11. 5:11. Ju *25. Re 1:6. **all generations.** Ps 45:17. 72:5. +*102:28. *146:10. Is *34:17. 51:8. Ezk *37:25.

14. **upholdeth.** Ps *37:24. *94:18. 119:117. Lk 22:31, 32. **raiseth up.** Ps 38:6. 42:5. 146:8. Lk 13:11-13.

15. **The eyes.** ver. 9. Ps 104:21, 27. 136:25. 147:8, 9. Ge 1:30. Jb 38:39-41. Jl 2:22. Mt *6:26. Lk 12:24. Ac 17:25. **wait upon thee.** *or*, look unto thee. *155A, Ge +31:35. Ps 104:27. 119:166. Ru 1:13. **due season.** Mt +*24:45.

16. **openest.** *22A14.8I, Ps 104:21, 28. +104:28. 107:9. 132:15. 147:9. Jb 38:27, 41. **hand.** *22A14.4, Ps +104:28.

17. **righteous.** Ps 50:6. 89:14. 97:2. 99:3, 4. 103:6. Ge +*18:25. Dt 32:4. 1 S 2:2, 3. Ne 9:33, 34. Is 45:21. Da 9:7. Zp 3:5. Zc 9:9. Ro 3:5, 6, 25, 26. Re 4:8. *15:3, 4. 16:5-7. 19:2, 11. **holy.** *or*, merciful, *or* bountiful. Ps +43:1mg. Mi 7:2mg.

18. **nigh unto.** Ps 34:18. 46:1, 5. Dt *4:7. 1 K *18:27, 28. Is *58:9. Jn *14:23. Ac *10:34, 35. Ja *4:8. **call upon.** *16, Ge +1:27. Ps *17:1. 119:2. Pr *15:8. Is 1:15, 16. Je *29:12, 13. Ho 7:14. Mt *6:5-8. 23:14. Jn *4:24. 1 J *3:20-22. √5:14, 15. **in truth.** T#542. Dt 4:29. 1 S +16:7 (T#333). Is 29:13, 14. Je 29:13. Mt 15:7, 8. Jn *4:24.

19. **fulfill the desire.** Ps *20:4, 5. *34:9. 36:7, 8. *37:4, 19. ●140:8. Pr *10:24. Mt +*5:6. Lk 1:53. Jn *15:7, 16. *16:24. Ep 3:16-20. 1 J 5:15. **fear him.** Ps 147:11. Ml +*3:16. **will hear.** Ps 10:17. 20:1. +*34:15, 17. *37:39, 40. *91:15.

20. **preserveth.** Ps *31:23. *37:28. *97:10. Ex +*20:6. Jn √10:27-29. Ro √8:28-30. Ja +*2:5. 1 P *1:5-8. **all the wicked.** Ps *1:6. +*9:17. Mt √25:41.

21. **My mouth.** ver. 1, 2, 5. Ps 30:12. 51:15. 71:8, 15, 23, 24. 89:1. **let all flesh.** *171E1, *171Q6, Ge +6:12. Ps *65:2. 67:3, 4. *86:9. 103:22. ch. 117. 150:6. Re 5:11-14.

PSALM 146

The psalmist resolves to praise God while he has any being, 1, 2. He dissuades all from trusting in man, 3, 4. He encourages confidence in God from a view of his power and goodness, as displayed in all his works, 5-10.

1. A.M. 3489. B.C. 515. **Praise ye the Lord.** Heb. Hallelujah. Ps 105:45mg. **Praise the Lord.** Ps *103:1, 22. 104:1, 35. **O my.** *38C, Ps +42:5. **soul.** Heb. *nephesh*, Ge +34:3. Ps +103:1. Lk 12:19.

2. **While I live.** Ps 63:4. 71:14, 15. 104:33. 145:1, 2. Re 7:9-17.

3. **Put.** Ps 62:9. *118:8, 9. Is *2:22. 31:3. 36:6. Je *17:5, 6. **in princes.** Ps 107:40. Is 24:21. **son of man.** Ps 8:4. 80:17. 144:3. Ec 9:12. Is 51:12. 56:2. **no help.** *or*, salvation. Ps 33:17. 37:39. 40:10. 60:11mg. 108:12. Is *2:22. Ac √4:12.

4. **His breath.** Heb. *ruach*, Ge +6:17. T#993‡. Ps +31:5. *104:29. Ge +*2:7. *6:17. 7:15, 22. Jb *12:10. 14:10. 17:1. 27:3. Is 2:22. La 4:20. Da 5:23. Mt +*10:28. Ja 2:26. **goeth forth.** Ps 17:2. 41:6. 44:9. Ec *8:8. Mt *27:50. Ac *7:59. **in that very day.** Ps *37:9-13. +*118:24. Is 2:12, 17. +*24:21-23. Lk ●*23:43. **he returneth.** Ps 9:15, 17. *90:3. +*94:13. *103:14. *115:17. Ge +*3:19. Ec 3:20. *12:7. **earth.** Lk 12:16. **his thoughts.** Heb. *eshtonoth*, only here. William Kay notes that the Chaldi verb is used in Da 6:4 of the labored artifices of Daniel's enemies. Ps *6:5. +13:3. 28:1. 30:9. *33:10. √49:11. 88:4, 11. *94:11. +*115:17. 143:7. Jb 14:10, 21. √17:11. Pr ●10:7. √11:7. ●√14:32. Ec √9:5, 10. Is *2:22. *38:18. 55:7. La *4:20. Jn *9:4. 12:35. 1 C 2:6. He +*9:27. Ja 4:13, 14.

perish. Ps 9:6. 10:16. 41:5. 115:17. 119:92. 142:4. 1 S +*2:9. Est 4:16. Jb 4:7. 11:20mg. *18:17. 30:2. Pr √11:7. Ec 5:14. 9:6. Is √26:14. 29:14. 57:1. Je 6:21. 7:28. 9:12. La 3:18. Jon 4:10. Mi 7:2. Ja 4:14.

5. **Happy.** √43, Dt +28:3. Ps 33:12. 84:12. *144:15. Dt 33:29. **the God.** Ps 46:7, 11. 84:8. Ge 32:24-29. 50:17. Ex 3:6. **whose hope.** Ps 39:7. 71:5. +*94:13, 14. *115:18. Je *17:7, 8. Ac +√26:6. Ro +*15:4. T +*1:2. 1 P 1:21.

6. **made heaven.** Ps 33:6. 136:5, 6. 148:5, 6. Ge *1:1. 2:1, 4. Je 10:11, 12. 32:17. Jn *1:3. Ac ✝4:24. Col *1:16. Re 14:7. **the sea.** Ps 95:5. Ex 20:11. Jb 38:8-11. Pr 8:28, 29. **keepeth truth.** Ps 89:2, 33. 98:3. 100:5. Dt *7:9. Is +√55:3. Da 9:4. Mi √7:20. Ml +*3:6. Jn *10:35. Ro +*15:8. T +*1:2. He *6:18. **for ever.** Heb. *olam*, Ex +*12:24.

7. **executeth judgment.** Ps 9:16. 10:14, 15, 18. 12:5. 72:4. *94:15. 103:6. Pr 22:22, 23. 23:10, 11. Is 9:4. Ml +*3:5. Ac +24:10n. Ro *12:17, 19. **which giveth food.** √171I8, Ge +3:19. Ps *107:9. 136:25. 145:15, 16. Je 31:14. Mt ✱14:15-21. Lk 1:53. 9:17. **looseth.** T#784. Ps 68:6. *69:33. √102:20. 105:17-20. 107:10, 14-16. 142:7. Dt 30:4. Is 42:7, 22. *49:9, 25. 61:1. Je 15:11. Zc 9:11, 12. Lk *4:18. ✱13:16. Ac 5:19. 16:26. **the prisoners.** Ps 79:11. Jb 3:18. Is 42:22. *49:24mg. Ep +*4:8.

8. **openeth.** Is 35:5. 42:16, 18. Mt *9:30. ✱11:5. Lk 18:41, 42. +24:16. Jn *9:7, 32, 33. Ac 26:18. Ep 1:18. 1 P 2:9. **raiseth.** Ps 145:14. 147:6. Lk *13:11-13. 2 C *7:6. **loveth.** Ps 11:7. Dt 33:3. Jn *14:21-23. *16:27. 1 J *4:16.

9. **preserveth.** T#780. Ps 68:5. Dt 10:*18, 19. 16:11. *27:19. Pr 15:25. Je *7:6, 7. 49:11. Ezk *11:16. Ho 14:3. Ml +*3:5. Ja 1:27. **strangers.** Ps 39:12. 94:6. 119:19. Ge +23:4 (✱S#1616h). Ex 12:48mg. Is 14:1. **fatherless and widow.** √171I14, Ex +22:22. Ps 68:5. Ge +11:28. Ex +*22:22-24. Dt +*10:18. 14:29. Je *49:11. Ho 14:3. Ja 1:27. **the way.** Ps 1:6. 18:26. 83:13-17. 145:20. 147:6. 2 S 15:31. 17:23. Est 5:14. *7:10. 9:25. Jb *5:12-14. Pr 4:19. 1 C 3:19. **he turneth.** Is 24:18-20.

10. **reign.** Ps 10:16. +22:28. +*102:15, 16. *145:13. Ex *15:18. Is +*9:7. Da *2:44. 6:26. +*7:14. Zc +*14:9. 1 C *15:24. Re √11:15. **for ever.** Heb. *olam*, Ex +*12:24. **thy God.** Ps 147:12. Is 12:6. 40:9. 52:7. Jl *3:17. **O Zion.** Ps +*102:16. Is +√24:23. +*51:11. +*59:20. **unto all.** Ps 72:5. √102:28. 115:14. Ge *17:5-8. Is 34:17. 51:8. +*59:21. Je 32:39, 40. Ezk 37:25. 1 P 3:13n. **generations.** Ge +9:12. **Praise ye.** Ps 105:45mg.

PSALM 147

Exhortations to praise God for his goodness displayed in providence and in the care of Israel, 1-3; his power and wisdom, 4, 5; his mercy, 6; the changes of the weather and the revolving seasons, and his providential care of his creatures, 7-11; for his blessings upon the kingdom, 12-14; for his power over the elements, 15-18; and for giving Israel his word and ordinances, 19, 20.

1. **for it is good.** Ps 63:3-5. *92:1. 135:3. **and praise.** Ps *33:1. *42:4. 122:1-4. Re *5:9-14. 19:1-6.

2. **build.** Ps *51:18. √102:13-16. Ne 3:1, etc. 7:4. Is 14:32. 16:5. +*24:23. 52:9, 10. *62:7. Je 31:4. Da *9:25. Mt *16:18. **he gathereth.** Ps *102:20-22. 106:47. Ge +*49:10. Dt *30:3. Ezr 2:64, 65. 8:1, etc. Is

+√11:11n, 12. 27:13. +√52:12mg. √54:7. *56:8. Je 32:37. Ezk +*20:34, 35. +*34:13. 36:24, etc. 37:21, etc., +*25. 38:8. 39:27, 28. Zp *3:20. Ep 2:12-19. **the outcasts.** Is +*16:3. +*27:13.

3. **healeth.** √22D2E, Ex +15:26. Ps *51:17. Jb 5:18. Is +*57:15. 61:1. Je *33:6. Ho *6:1, 2. Ml 4:2. Mt *9:22. 12:20. Lk *4:18. **the broken.** Ps 69:20. **bindeth up.** √22C29, Jb +5:18. **wounds.** Heb. griefs. Ps 16:4. Jb 9:28. Pr 10:10. 15:13. Is *1:5, 6.

4. **He telleth.** Ps 8:3. 148:3. Ge 15:5. Is *40:26. **number.** ver. 5. Ps 40:12. 104:25. 105:12. **stars.** Ps 8:3. 136:9. 148:3. Ge 1:16.

5. **Great.** Ps 48:1. 96:4. 99:2. 135:5. 145:3. 1 Ch 16:25. Je 10:6. *32:17-19. Na 1:3. Re 15:3. **his understanding is infinite.** Heb. of his understanding there is no number. Ps 40:5. 139:17, 18. Is *40:28. Ro *11:33.

6. **lifteth up.** Ps 25:9. 37:11. 145:14. 146:8, 9. 149:4. 1 S 2:8. Jb 22:29. Zp +*2:3. Mt +*5:5. Ja 4:10. 1 P 3:4. 5:6. **he casteth.** Ps 55:23. *73:18, 19. 146:9. 2 P 2:4-9.

7. **Sing.** Ps 47:6, 7. 68:32. 92:1-3. 95:1, 2. 107:21, 22. Ex 15:20, 21. Re 5:8-10.

8. **covereth.** Ps 135:7. Ge 9:14. 1 K 18:44, 45. Jb 26:8, 9. 36:27-33. 38:25-27. Is 5:6. **clouds.** Ge +9:13. **prepareth.** Ps 65:9-13. 104:13, 14. Jb 5:10. Je 14:22. Jl 2:23. Am 5:7, 8. Mt *5:45. Ac *14:17. Ja 5:17, 18.

9. **He giveth.** Ps *104:27, 28. 136:25. *145:15, 16. Jb 38:41. Mt *6:26. Lk 12:24.

10. **delighteth.** Ps *20:7. *33:16-18. Jb 39:19-25. Pr *21:31. Is 31:1. Ho *1:7. **he taketh.** 1 S 16:7. 2 S 1:23. 2:18-23. Ec 9:11.

11. **taketh pleasure.** Ps 35:27. 149:4. Pr 11:20. 31:30. Is *62:4. Zp 3:17. Ml *3:16, 17. Col *1:10. He 11:5. 1 P 3:4. **that fear.** Ps 33:18, 22. *145:19. Ml +*3:16. 1 P 1:13, 17. **that hope.** Ps +*146:5.

12. **praise thy God.** Ps 135:19-21. 146:10. 149:2. Is 12:6. 52:7. Jl 2:23.

13. **he hath.** Ps 48:11-14. 51:18. 125:2. Ne 3:1, etc. 6:1. 7:1. 12:30. La 2:8, 9. 4:12. Da 9:25. **blessed.** Ps 115:14, 15. 128:3-6. 144:12. Is 44:3-5. Je 30:19, 20. Zc 8:3-5. Lk 19:42-44.

14. **He maketh peace,** etc. Heb. Who maketh thy border peace. Ps 29:11. 122:6. Le 26:6. 1 Ch 22:9. Is 9:6, 7. *60:17, 18. 66:12. Zc 9:8. **filleth.** Ps *132:15. Ge=42:25. Dt 8:7, 8. Ezk 27:17. **finest of the wheat.** Heb. fat of wheat. Ps 81:16mg. Dt 32:14.

15. **sendeth.** Ps *33:9. 107:20, 25. Jb 34:29. 37:12. Jon 1:4. Mt *8:8, 9, 13. **his word.** Ps 68:11. 2 Th 3:1mg.

16. **giveth.** Ps 148:8. Jb 37:6. Is 55:10. **scattereth.** Jb 37:9, 10. 38:29.

17. **casteth.** Ps 78:47, 48. Ex 9:23-25. Jsh 10:11. Jb 38:22, 23. **who can stand.** Jb 38:29, 30.

18. **He sendeth.** ver. 15. Jb 6:16, 17. *37:10, 17. 19. **showeth.** Ps 76:1. 78:5. *103:7. Dt 33:2-4. Ml 4:4. Ro *3:2. *9:4. 2 T √3:15-17. **word.** Heb. words. Ex 20:1, etc. Dt 4:12, 13mg. 5:22. **his statutes.** Ex ch. 21-23. Dt 4:1, 8, 45. 5:31. 6:1. Ml 4:4.

20. **not dealt so.** Dt *4:32-34. Pr 29:18. Is 5:1-7. Mt 21:33-41. Ac 14:16. 26:17, 18. Ro 3:1, 2. Ep 2:12. 5:8. He √4:1, 2. 1 P 2:9, 10.

PSALM 148

The psalmist calls on all celestial beings to praise God their Creator, 1-6; and on all terrestrial, 7-10;

especially on all the race of men, however distinguished, 11, 12; and this on account of his glory and his love to his people, 13, 14.

1. **Praise ye the Lord**. Heb. Hallelujah. Ps 89:5. 146:1mg. Is 49:13. Mk ⫶11:10. Lk 2:13, 14. Re *5:13. 19:1-6.

2. **Praise**. ƒ18, Dt +28:4. **all his angels**. Ps *103:20, 21. Jb 38:7. Is 6:2-4. Ezk 3:12. Lk *2:14. Re 5:11-13. **all his hosts**. Ge 2:1.

3. **Praise**. ƒ155D, Ge +4:10. **sun**. ƒ38G, Dt +32:1. Ps 8:1-3. *19:1-6. 89:36, 37. 136:7-9. Ge 1:14-16. 8:22. Dt 4:19. Je 33:20.

4. **heavens**. Ps 113:6. 1 K 8:27. 2 C 12:2. **waters**. Ps 104:3. Ge 1:7. 7:11.

5. **for he**. Ps *33:6-9. 95:5. Ge *1:1, 2, 6. Je 10:11-13. Am 9:6. Re 4:11.

6. **He hath also**. Ps 89:37. 93:1. ◑102:26. *119:90, 91. Jb 38:10, 11, 33. Pr 8:27-29. Ec +*1:4. Is 54:9. ◑65:17. Je +*31:35, 36. 33:25. 2 P ◑3:10. **for ever**. Ps +9:18 (✳S#5703h). **and ever**. Heb. *olam*, Ps +21:4.

7. **from the earth**. See on ver. 1. **ye dragons**. ƒ38F. Apostrophe B904: to animals. For another instance of this figure see Jl 2:22. Ps 74:13, 14. 104:25, 26. Ge 1:21. Jb 41:1, etc. Is 27:1. *43:20. 51:9, 10.

8. **Fire**. Ps 147:15-18. Ge *19:24. Ex *9:23-25. Le 10:2. Nu 16:35. Jsh 10:11. Jb 37:2-6. 38:22-37. Is 66:16. Jl 2:30. Am 7:4. Re 16:8, 9, 21. **stormy**. Ps *107:25-29. Ex 10:13, 19. *14:21. Am 4:13. Jon 1:4. Mt 8:24-27.

9. **Mountains**. Ps 65:12, 13. 96:11-13. 97:4, 5. 98:7-9. 114:3-7. Is 42:11. *44:23. 49:13. *55:12, 13. 64:1. Ezk 36:1, etc.

10. **Beasts**. Ps 50:10, 11. 103:22. 150:6. Ge 1:20-25. **flying fowl**. Heb. birds of wing. Ge 7:14mg. Ezk 17:23.

11. **Kings**. Ps 2:10-12. 22:27-29. 66:1-4. 68:31, 32. *72:10, 11. 86:9. 102:15. 138:4, 5. Pr 8:15, 16. Is 49:23. 60:3. Re 21:24.

12. **young men**. Ps 8:2. 68:25. 78:31, 63. Dt 32:35. Je 31:13. Zc 9:17. Mt *21:15, 16. Lk 19:37. T 2:4-6. **maidens**. Ps 45:14. 78:63. Ge +*24:16. **old men**. Ps +105:22. 107:32. +119:100. **children**. or, youths. Ps 37:25. 119:9. Ge 14:24. 2 K +2:23n.

13. **for his name**. Ps *8:1, 9. 99:3, 4, 9. SS 5:9, 16. Is 6:3. Zc 9:17. Ph 3:8. **excellent**. Heb. exalted. 1 Ch 29:11. Is *12:4. 33:5. Mt *6:13. **glory**. Ps 57:5. 72:19. 108:4. 113:4. Ep 4:10. 1 P 3:22.

14. **exalteth**. Ps 75:10. 89:17. 92:10. 112:9. 1 S 2:1. Lk 1:52. **the praise**. Ps *145:10. 149:9. Lk *2:32. Re 5:8-14. **a people**. Ex *19:5, 6. Dt *4:7. 33:29. Jn *4:23. Ep 1:4. *2:13, 17, 19. Ja *4:8. 1 P 2:9. **Praise**. Ps 105:45mg.

PSALM 149

Israel is exhorted to praise God and to rejoice in him, 1-5; and to prepare for victory and triumph over all their enemies, 6-9.

1. **Praise ye the Lord**. Heb. Hallelujah. Ps 148:1. **Sing**. Ps 33:3. 96:1. 98:1. 144:9. Is *42:10. Re 5:9. 7:10, 12. **in the congregation**. Ps 22:22, 25. 68:26. 89:5. 111:1. 116:18. He 2:12.

2. **rejoice**. Ps 100:1-3. *135:3, 4. Dt *7:6, 7. 12:7. **him that made**. Ps 100:3. 1 S √12:22. Jb 35:10. Is 17:7. 27:11. *54:5. Ep *2:10. **children of Zion**. Is *62:11, 12. Jl 2:23. **be joyful**. Is +*51:11. *52:7. Zc

*9:9. Mt 21:5. Lk 19:37, 38. Ph 3:3. *4:4. Re *19:6. **their King**. Ps 59:13. 114:2. Zp +*3:15. Zc *9:9. Mt 21:5. *25:34. Jn +*1:49. 19:15, 19-22.

3. **in the dance**. or, with the pipe. Ps 150:4mg. Ex +15:20n. Jg 11:34. 2 S 6:16. Je 31:13. **with the timbrel**. Ps 33:2. 81:2. 137:2-4. 150:3-5. 1 Ch 15:28, 29. 16:42. 25:6. 2 Ch 29:25. Ezr 3:10.

4. **taketh pleasure**. Ps 22:8. *35:27. 44:3. 47:4. 117:11. 147:11. Pr 11:20. Is 62:4, 5. Je 32:41. Zp *3:17. Col *1:10. He 11:5. **beautify**. Ps 90:17. *132:16. Is *61:1-3, 10. 2 Th +*1:10. He 12:10. 1 P 3:4. *5:5. Re 7:14. **the meek**. Ps 147:6. Mt +*5:5. **with salvation**. Ps 9:13, 14. *14:7. 37:39, 40. +*42:5mg. 53:6. 98:2, 9. 102:16. 132:11-16. Is +*25:9. He +*9:28n.

5. **the saints**. Ps 23:1. *118:14, 15. *145:10. Ro 5:2. 1 P *1:8. **sing**. Ps *42:8. 63:5, 6. 92:2. 119:55, 62. Jb *35:10. **upon their beds**. Peters notes these are couches, "expressive of couches around the divan of an Oriental prince," indicative of honor and exaltation (*Theocratic Kingdom*, vol. 2, p. 615). Ps 4:4. 36:4. 41:3. Ge 49:4. Re 7:15-17.

6. **the high**. Ps 96:4. Ne 9:5. Da *4:37. Lk *2:14. Re 19:6. **of**. ƒ181E, Ge +3:24. **God**. Heb. *El*, Ex +15:2. **mouth**. Heb. throat. Ps 5:9. 69:3. 115:7. *145:3-5. Is 58:1. **and a two-edged**. Pr 5:4. Is 41:15mg. 2 C 10:4. Ep 6:17. He *4:12. Re 1:16. *12:11. **in their hand**. Ne 4:17. Lk +*22:36. Jn 18:36.

7. **execute vengeance**. Ps 137:8, 9. Nu 31:2, 3. Dt *32:41. Jg 5:23. 1 S 15:2, 3, 18-23. Ezk 28:26. Mi +*5:8-15. Zc +*9:13-16. *12:6. 14:17-19. Ju √15. Re 19:11-21. **upon the heathen**. Ezk +*30:3. Mi 7:16, 17.

8. **To bind**. Jsh 10:23, 24. 12:7. Jg 1:6, 7. 2 Ch 33:11. **their kings**. Is 60:10.

9. **To execute**. Ps 137:8. Dt 7:1, 2. *32:42, 43. Jg 5:13, 31. Is 14:22, 23. Da +*7:22. Ju √15. Re 2:26, 27. *17:14-16. **the judgment**. Is *1:27. 10:17. 62:1. Mt *3:11. Jn 20:22, 23. Re 14:18. **written**. Jb 13:26. Is 26:9. **this honor**. Pr +*22:29. 1 C √6:2, 3. Re 3:21. **have all**. 1 S √30:24. Pr 19:22. Da 7:18. Ho +*11:12. Zc +*14:5. Jn +*10:16. Ac +√10:11. 1 C 12:11, √13. Ga √3:28. Ep +*4:4. 1 Th *3:13. Ju *14. Re 20:16.

PSALM 150

Repeated calls to praise God for his glorious excellences and mighty acts, 1, 2; with all kinds of musical instruments and the concurrence of all that breathe, 3-6.

1. **Praise ye the Lord**. Heb. Hallelujah. Ps 105:45mg. 149:1. **God**. Heb. *El*, Ex +15:2. **in his sanctuary**. Ps 29:9. 66:13-16. 116:18, 19. 118:19, 20. *134:2. **in the firmament**. Ge 1:6-8. Ezk 1:22-26. 10:1. Da *12:3.

2. **for his mighty**. Ps *145:5, 6. Re *15:3, 4. **according**. Ps *96:4. *145:3. Dt 3:24. Je *32:17-19.

3. **with the sound**. Ps 81:2, 3. 98:5, 6. Nu 10:10. 1 Ch 15:24, 28. *16:42n. Da 3:5. **trumpet**. or, cornet. Ps 47:5. 81:3. 98:6. 2 Ch +5:12. **the psaltery**. 33:2. 57:8. 71:22. 81:2. 92:3. 108:2. 149:3. 1 S +10:5. **harp**. Ps 33:2. 43:4. 49:4. 57:8. 1 Ch +13:8n. Re *14:2.

4. **with the timbrel**. Ps 81:2. 149:3. Ex +15:20n. **dance**. or, pipe. Ps 30:11. 149:3mg. Je 31:4, 13. La 5:15. **stringed instruments**. Ps 33:2. 45:8. 92:3. 144:9. Is *38:20. Hab 3:19. **organs**. Jb 30:31.

5. **the loud cymbals.** 2 S 6:5. 1 Ch +13:8. 15:16, 19, 28. 16:5. 25:1, 6. Jb 41:7. Is 18:1. **sounding.** Ps 18:44. Ge 29:13.

6. **Let everything.** Ps 103:22. 145:10. 148:7-11. Ep *5:19, 20. Col *3:16. Re *5:13, 14. **breath.** Heb. *neshamah*, Ge +2:7. **Praise ye.** Ps 105:45mg.

PROVERBS

PROVERBS 1

The title and subject and use of the book, 1-6. Exhortations to fear God, believe his word, and obey parents, 7-9. Exhortations to avoid the enticings and company of the wicked, 10-19. Wisdom's address to sinners, 20-23. She complains of being despised and denounces the doom of her despisers, 24-32; and shows the security of her disciples, 33.

1. **proverbs.** Pr 10:1. 25:1. 1 K *4:31, 32. Ec *12:9. Jn 16:25. **Solomon.** 2 S 12:24, 25. 1 K 2:12. 1 Ch 22:9. 28:5. 29:23.

2. **To know.** Pr √4:5-7. 7:4. 8:5. *16:16. *17:16. Dt *4:5, 6. 1 K *3:9-12. 2 T √3:15-17. **wisdom.** Ep ◑4:14. **instruction.** 2 P 1:6. **perceive.** Is ◑6:10. Ph 1:10. He 5:14.

3. **receive.** Pr *2:1-9. *8:10, 11. Jb *22:22. **instruction.** 2 P 1:6. **equity.** Heb. equities. 1 K 3:28.

4. **subtility.** ver. *22, *23. Pr 8:5. *9:4-6. Ps *19:7. *119:130. Is 35:8. Mt 10:16. **simple.** ♪108K54. Idiom, involving a change of usage in the English language B860. *Simple* meant, originally, "without guile, open, artless." But now, because a person who acts thus, is considered devoid of all sense, it has come to mean "foolish." In the Authorized Version of the Bible the word is used in its original sense, as the usage had not then changed. For other instances of this figure of speech involving this term see: ver. 22, 32. Pr 7:7. 8:5. 9:4, 13. 14:15, 18. 21:11. 22:3. Ps 19:7. 116:6. 119:130. Ezk 45:20. Ro 16:18, 19. For "simplicity," which has undergone a corresponding shift in meaning, see ver. 22. **to the young.** Pr *7:7-24. 8:17, *32. Ps *34:11. *119:9. Ec 11:9, 10. *12:1. 2 T *2:22. T *2:6. **discretion.** *or*, advisement. Pr 2:11. 3:21. 5:2. 8:12. Ps 17:4. 1 Th 5:21.

5. **wise.** Pr *9:9. *12:1. Ex *18:17, 24. Jb 34:10, 16, 34. Ps √119:98-100. 1 C 3:18. 10:15. Ph 3:12. **a man.** 1 S *25:32, 33. 2 Ch *25:16. **unto wise counsels.** Ps *119:18, 33, 34. Ac 8:34, 35. 18:24-26. 1 C 2:9, 10. He 13:9.

6. **a proverb.** Mt 13:*10-17, 51, 52. Mk 4:11, 34. Ac *8:30, 31. **the interpretation.** *or*, an eloquent speech. Hab 2:6. **the words.** Ec *12:11. **dark.** Ps 49:4. *78:2. Nu +12:8. Mt *13:34, 35. He *5:14. 2 P *3:16.

7. **fear.** ♪138C, Ge +22:14. **or.** Pr *9:10. 15:33. Dt 17:18-20. Jb *28:28. Ps 5:7. 25:12. *111:10. 112:1. Ec *12:13. Lk 23:40. Ro 3:18. He 12:28, 29. **of.** ♪181E, Ge +3:24. **beginning.** *or*, principal part. Pr 3:9. √4:7. 8:22. 17:14. **but.** ver. *22, *29, *30. Pr 5:12, 13. *15:5. 18:2. Ps 36:1. Je √8:9. Jn *3:18-21. Ro 1:28.

8. **My son.** ver. 10, 15. Pr 2:1. 3:1. 7:1. Mt 9:2, 22. **hear.** Pr *4:1-4. *5:1, 2. *6:20. *30:17. 31:1. Le *19:3. Dt *21:18-21. 1 S 2:25. Je 35:18, 19. Lk 2:51. Jn 19:27. Ep *6:2. Col *3:20. 2 T 1:5. *3:14, 15. He 1:6.

9. **they.** Pr *3:22. 4:9. *6:20, 21. 1 T 2:9, 10. 1 P *3:3, 4. **an ornament.** Heb. an adding. Ge 41:42. SS 1:10. 4:9. Is 3:19. Ezk 16:11. Da *5:7, 16, 29.

10. **if sinners.** Pr *7:21-23. *13:20. 20:19. Ge 3:6. 11:4. *39:7-13. Dt *13:6-8. Jg *16:16-21. 1 Ch 21:1. Ps *1:1. 50:18. 119:+√63, 101. Is 41:6. Ro 16:18. 1 C 15:33. 2 C 2:11. Ep *5:11. Ja 1:13-15. **consent thou not.** Est +*1:12. Ro 7:14-17, 20, 23.

11. **Come with.** ver. 14. Is 56:12. **let us lay.** ver. *16. Pr *12:6. 30:14. Ps 56:6. 64:5, 6. 71:10. Je 5:26. Mi 7:2. Ac 23:15. 25:3. **blood.** ♪117, Ge +19:8. ♪171Q10, Ps +94:21. ♪121L8, Is +33:15 **let us lurk.** ver. 18. Ps 10:8-10. 17:12. 35:7. Je 11:19. *18:18-20. Mt *26:3, 4. Jn *15:25.

12. **swallow.** Ps 35:25. *56:1, 2. *57:3. 124:3. Je 51:34. La 2:5, 16. Mi 2:2, 3. **as the.** Ps 5:9. Ro *3:13. **grave.** Heb. *sheol*, Ge +37:35. **whole.** Nu *16:30-33. *26:10. Ps 28:1. 143:7. **pit.** Heb. *bor*, Ge +37:20.

13. **We shall find.** ver. 19. Jb 24:2, 3. Is 10:13, 14. Je *22:16, 17. Na 2:12. Hab *2:9. Lk *12:15. 1 T *6:9, 10. Re 18:9-16.

14. **lot.** Pr 16:33. 18:18. Le 16:8, 9. **among us.** ver. 11. Ge 19:1. **purse.** Pr 16:11. 23:31. Dt 25:13.

15. **walk not.** Pr *4:14, 15. *9:6. *13:20. 1 K *13:15-19. Ps √1:1. *26:4, 5. +*119:63. 2 C √6:17. **refrain.** Pr *4:27. *5:8. Ps *119:101. Je 14:10.

16. **For their.** Pr *4:16. *6:18. Is *59:7. Ro *◑3:15. **feet.** ♪171Q21. Synecdoche of the Part B648: "feet" are put for the whole man, in respect to carefulness, quickness, etc. For other instances of this figure see Pr 6:18. Is 52:7. Ro 3:15.

17. **Surely.** ♪138C, Ge +22:14. **in vain.** Pr 7:23. Jb 35:11. Is 1:3. Je *8:7. **net.** Pr 29:5. Ex 27:4, 5. 38:4. Ps 57:6. **sight of any bird.** Heb. eyes of every thing that hath a wing. Pr 23:5.

18. **lay wait.** Pr *5:22, 23. *9:17, 18. *28:17. Est *7:10. Ps *7:14-16. *9:16. *55:23. Mt *27:4, 5. **lurk.** 1 K 21:20. Ps 10:8. **lives.** Heb. *nephesh*, Ge +44:30.

19. **every.** Pr 15:27. 23:3, 4. 2 S *18:11-13. 2 K *5:20-27. Je 22:17-19. Mi *2:1-3. 3:10-12. Hab *2:9. Ac *8:19, 20. 1 T 3:3. *6:9, 10. Ja *5:1-4. 2 P *2:3, 14-16. **greedy.** Pr 15:27. 1 K 21:4. Mt 26:14-16. 27:3, 5. Lk *12:15. **taketh.** Jb 31:39. Ps 7:15, 16. Ec *5:13. **life.** Heb. *nephesh*, Ge +44:30.

20. **Wisdom.** Heb. Wisdoms, that is, *excellent wisdom*. Mt 13:34, 35. Lk 11:49. 1 C *1:24, 30. Col *2:3. **crieth.** Pr *8:1-5. 9:3. Ps 40:9, 10. Jn *7:37. Re √3:20. **in the streets.** lit. "open places." Am +5:16. Ac 26:26. 2 P +1:16. Matthew Poole notes, not in corners and privily, as seducers persuade men to error or wickedness, being afraid of the light, but openly and publicly before all the world.

21. **She crieth.** Pr 9:3. Mt 10:27. 13:2. Lk 14:21, 23. Jn *18:20, 21. Ac 5:20. Ro 10:21. **gates.** ♪171S7B, Ge   +14:7.

22. **How.** Pr 6:9. Ex *10:3. 16:28. Nu *14:27. Mt *17:17. **ye simple.** ♪108K54, ver. +4. Pr *7:7. *9:4-6, 16-18. Ps 94:8. Mt *9:13. *11:29, 30. *23:37. Lk *19:42. Re *22:17. **simplicity.** ♪108K55. Idiom. The meaning of the English word "simplicity" has shifted in the same manner as the word "simple" (see Note

on ver. 4). 2 S 15:1. Ro 12:8. 2 C 1:12. 11:3. **the scorners.** Pr *3:34. *14:6. *15:12. 19:29. *21:11. Jb 34:7. Ps *1:1. 2 P *3:3. **delight.** or, have delighted. i.e. will delight. ✓96C2, Ge +45:9. **fools hate knowledge.** ver. 7, 29. Pr 5:12. Jb *21:14. 24:13. Mt 23:37. Lk 19:41, 42. Jn *3:20. Ro 1:20.

23. **Turn.** Is *1:18. *55:1-3, 6, 7. Je 3:14. Ezk *18:27-30. *33:11. Ho 14:1. Zc 9:12. Ac *3:19. 26:20. **my reproof.** ver. 25, 30. Pr *6:23. 10:17. 12:1. *29:1. Ps 141:5. Re *3:19. **behold.** T#840. Is 32:15. 45:8. 59:21. Jl *2:28. Zc *12:10. Lk 11:13. Jn 4:10, 14. 7:36, 37. *14:16, 17. Ac 2:36-38. 1 C 2:12. Ga 3:14. 2 T 1:14. Re *3:16-18. **pour.** Heb. *nabah*, *S#5042h: Kal, Participle: Pr 18:4 (flowing). Hiphil, Future: Ps 19:2 (uttereth). 59:7 (belch out). 78:2 (utter). 94:4. 119:171. 145:7 (abundantly utter). Pr 1:23. 15:2, 28. Ec 10:1 (send forth). **spirit.** Heb. *ruach*, Ge +41:38. ✓121A10, Ge +26:35. **make known.** Pr 28:5. Ps 25:12. 32:8. Jn *16:13. 1 J *2:27.

24. **I have called.** Is 50:2. *65:12. *66:4. Je 7:13. Ezk 5:11. 8:18. Zc *7:11, 12. Mt 22:5, 6. *23:37, 38. He 12:25, 26. **ye refused.** T#373. Ps 58:4, 5. +119:68 (T#224). +145:9 (T#228). Jon +4:2 (T#233). Zc 7:11-13. Mt 22:2-6. Lk 14:17-20. **stretched.** Ps *31:20. Ac 4:30. Ro *10:21. ✓22A14.8H, Anthropomorphism in Idiomatic Expressions B880: here, to call for the receiving of mercy, or invite to receive. Is 49:22. 65:2.

25. **ye.** ver. *30. 2 Ch *36:16. Ps 107:11. Je 23:22. Lk *7:30. **set at nought.** T#691. Ex 5:2. Dt 31:27. Ne *9:26. Ps 81:11. Is 1:2. 30:8, 9. 65:2, 3. Je 5:23. 25:4. Ezk 2:7, 8. **would.** ver. 30. Pr *5:12. *12:1. Ps 81:11.

26. **will laugh.** Jg *10:14. Ps *2:4. *37:13. 59:8. Lk *14:24. **calamity.** ✓132G, Ge +3:19. **fear.** ✓121R6, Ge +31:42.

27. **your fear.** ✓121R6, Ge +31:42. Pr *3:25, 26. *10:24, 25. Ps *69:22-28. Lk *21:26, 34, 35. 1 Th *5:3. Re *6:15-17. **as a.** Ps *58:9. Is 17:13. Na *1:3. **distress.** Lk *21:23-25. Ro *2:9.

28. **Then shall.** T#1787. Ge *6:3. 1 S 8:18. *15:24-26. 28:5, 6. Jb 27:8, 9. *35:12. Ps *18:41. Is 1:15. *50:15. ✓55:6. Je *11:11-14. 14:11, 12. *15:1. Ezk 7:25, 26. 8:18. 14:13-20. 20:1-3. Ho 5:6, 7. Am *8:11, 12. Mi *3:4-7. Zc 7:13, 14. Mt *7:22, 23. 25:10-12. Lk *13:25-28. *16:22-26. He *12:15-17. Ja *4:3. Re *6:15-17. **they shall seek.** Pr 8:17. 1 Ch +*28:9. Ps 78:34-36. Ho *5:15. 6:1-4. **not find.** Lk 13:24, 25.

29. **hated knowledge.** ver. *22. Pr 5:12. 6:23. Jb *21:14, 15. Ps *50:16, 17. Is 27:11. 30:9-12. Jn *3:20. Ac 7:51-54. **did not choose.** Ps *119:173. Is +✓66:4. Lk *10:42. He *11:25.

30. **would none.** ver. 25. Pr 15:32. Ps 81:11. 119:111, 173. Je *8:9. Lk *14:18-20.

31. **they eat.** Pr 14:14. *22:8. Dt 28:63. Jb *4:8. Is *3:10, 11. Je 2:19. *6:19. Ga ✓6:7, 8. He *10:26, 27, 31.

32. **For.** ✓138C, Ge +22:14. **the turning.** or, ease. Ec *8:11. Je 48:11, 12. Mk +4:19. **the simple.** ✓108K54, ver. 4. **shall slay them.** Pr 8:36. Jn ✓3:36. He *10:38, 39. *12:25. **prosperity.** Dt 32:15, etc. Ps 69:22. *92:6, 7. Lk *12:16-21. *16:19-25. He 12:8. Ja 5:5. **fools.** T#200-14. Pr +23:4 (T#626). Mk +4:19 (T#625). Lk 12:19-21.

33. **whoso.** Pr 8:32-35. 9:11. 12:15. Ps *25:12, 13. 81:13. Is 48:18. *55:3. Mt *17:5. Jn ✓10:27-29. 1 P 1:5. **dwell safely.** T#757. Pr *3:23, 24. 18:10. Ge 7:13,

16. 9:2. Dt 33:12. 1 S 2:9. Jb 4:7. 5:21, 23. *11:18. Ps ✓4:8. 16:8. 25:12, 13. 27:1. 34:20. *91:1, 2, 4, 10. *112:7. 121:1-8. 124:8. 125:2. Is 4:5, 6. 27:3. 33:16. ✓43:2, 3. Ezk 34:25, 28. Ho 2:18. Zc 2:5. 1 P 3:13. **and shall.** Pr *3:21-26. 14:26. 31:21. Ps *112:7. Is 14:3. *26:3. Ml 4:1, 2. Lk 21:9, 19, ●26, 28. Ro *8:35-39. 2 P 3:13. **fear.** Ge ●19:30.

PROVERBS 2

Wisdom promises the blessings of true religion to those who seek her from God, with prayer and diligence, 1-9; and to preserve them from the ruinous ways of bad men and women, by guiding them in the paths of righteousness, 10-22.

1. **if.** Pr 1:3. *4:1. 7:1. Jn *12:47, 48. 1 T 1:15. **hide.** Pr 3:1. *4:20-22. 6:21. Dt 6:6-9. Jb ✓23:12. Ps ✓119:9-11. Mt 13:44. Lk 2:19, 51. *9:44.

2. **thou.** Pr 18:1. Ps 119:111, 112. Is *55:3. Mt 13:9. **incline.** Zc ●7:11, 12. **apply.** T#1842. Pr 22:17-21. 23:12. Ps *90:12. Ec 7:25. 8:9, 16. Lk *14:28. Ac ✓17:11.

3. **if.** Pr ✓3:6. *8:17. 1 K *3:9-12. 1 Ch 22:12. Ps *25:4, 5. 119:*34, 73, 125, 169. Lk 11:13. Ep *1:17, 18. Ja ✓1:5. **liftest up thy voice.** Heb. givest thy voice. Pr 1:20. 8:1. Ps 46:6.

4. **thou.** Pr 3:14, 15. 8:18, 19. *16:16. 23:23. Ps 19:10. 119:14, 72, 127. Mt *6:19-21. 13:44. *19:21, 22, 29. **searchest.** Jb 28:12-20. Ec 4:8. Lk *16:8.

5. **shalt.** 2 Ch *1:10-12. Ho *6:3. Mt *7:7, 8. Lk ✓11:9-13. **the fear.** Pr *9:10. Jb *28:28. Je 32:40, 41. **find.** Je *9:24. 24:7. *31:34. Mt *11:27. Lk 10:22. Jn ✓17:3. 1 J 5:20. **knowledge.** T#803. ver. 9. Pr 28:5. Is 2:3. *29:18, 24. 32:3. *35:8. 42:7. 52:6. Je *31:34. Ho *6:3. Mt *11:20. Lk 1:77-79. 4:18. Jn *8:12. 1 C *2:14, 15. 2 C 4:6. 1 J 5:20.

6. **the Lord.** Ex *31:3. 1 K 3:9, 12. *4:29. 1 Ch 22:12. Jb *32:8. Is 54:13. Da *1:17. *2:21, 23. Lk *21:15. Jn *6:45. Ep *1:17, 18. Ja *1:5, 17. **wisdom.** T#804. Pr *8:9. Jb 28:20. Ps 16:7. 51:6. Ec 2:26. Ja *1:5. **out.** Pr *6:23. *8:5-9. Ps *19:7. *119:98, 104. Is ✓8:20.

7. **layeth.** Pr 8:14. 14:8. Jb 28:28. 1 C *1:19, 24, 30. 2:6, 7. 3:18, 19. Col 1:5. *2:3. 2 T ✓3:15-17. Ja 3:15-17. **a buckler.** Pr 28:18. *30:5. Ps *84:11. 144:2.

8. **keepeth.** Pr *8:20. Ps *1:6. *23:3, 4. *121:5-8. Is 35:9. 49:9, 10. Jn ✓10:28, 29. **and.** Pr *3:21-24. Dt *33:3, 26-29. 1 S *2:9. Ps *37:23, 24, 28, 31. 66:9. *145:20. Je 32:40, 41. Lk 8:15. 1 P 1:5. Ju ✓24.

9. **Then shalt.** Pr *1:2-6. Ps *25:8, 9. *32:8. *119:99, 105. *143:8-10. Is 35:8. *48:17. Je *6:16. Mt ✓7:13, 14. Jn ✓14:6. T 2:11, 12.

10. **wisdom entereth.** Pr 14:33. 18:1, 2. 24:13, 14. Jb ✓23:12. Ps *19:10. *104:34. *119:97, 103, 111, 162. Je ✓15:16. Jn 14:23. Ro 6:17, 18. Col *3:16. **heart.** ✓121I1, Ge +3:7. **soul.** Heb. *nephesh*, Ge +34:3. ✓121I1, Ge +3:7.

11. **Discretion.** Pr 4:6. 6:22-24. Ps 25:21. *119:9-11. Ec *9:15-18. 10:10. Ep *5:15.

12. **deliver.** Pr *4:14-17. *9:6. *13:20. Ps *17:4, 5. 26:4, 5. 141:4. 2 C ✓6:17. **from the man.** Pr 3:32. *8:13. 16:28-30. Ps *101:4. Is *59:3-5. Ac 20:30. 1 C 15:33.

13. **leave.** Pr *21:16. Ps 14:3. 36:3. 125:5. Ezk *18:26. *33:12, 13. Zp 1:6. Mt *12:43-45. 2 T 4:10. He +*3:13. *6:4-6. 2 P *2:20-22. 1 J *2:19. **walk.** Pr *4:19. Jb *24:13-16. Jn *3:19, 20. *12:35.

Ro *1:21. 1 Th *5:5-7. 1 J *1:6. *2:9-11.
14. **rejoice.** Pr *10:23. Je 11:15. Hab 1:15. Zp 3:11.
1 C *13:6. **and.** Ho 7:3. Lk *22:4, 5. Ro *1:32.
15. **Whose ways.** Dt 32:5. Ps *125:5. Is *30:8-13.
*59:8. Ph *2:15.
16. **deliver.** Pr *5:3-20. *6:24. *7:5-23. *22:14.
*23:27. Ge *39:3-12. Ne *13:26, 27. Ec *7:26. **flattereth.** Pr *7:21. *29:5.
17. **the guide.** Pr 5:18. Je *3:4. **forgetteth.** Ezk 16:8,
59, 60. Ml *2:14-16.
18. **her house.** Pr *5:4-14. *6:26-35. *7:22-27. *9:18.
1 C *6:9-11. Ga *5:19-21. Ep *5:5. Re √21:8. 22:15.
19. **None.** Ps *81:12. Ec *7:26. Je *13:23. Ho 4:14.
Mt *19:24-26. **take.** Pr *4:18. Ga *5:19, 21. Ep *5:5.
He *6:18. Re *21:8.
20. **mayest walk.** Pr *13:20. Ps 119:+*63, *115.
SS 1:7, 8. Je *6:16. He *6:12. 3 J √11.
21. **the upright.** Jb *1:1. 42:12. Ps 7:28. *37:3, 9,
11, 22, 29. *84:11. *112:4-6. Mt +*5:5.
22. **the wicked.** Pr *5:22, 23. Jb *18:16-18. *21:30.
Ps *37:20, 22, 28, 37, 38. 52:5. √101:8. *104:35.
*145:20. 147:7-9. Is 3:10, 11. 11:4. +*65:20. **rooted.**
or, plucked up. Pr +13:22. +28:8. Dt 7:22mg. *28:63.
Mt 3:10. +*13:30. 2 P 3:7.

PROVERBS 3

*Wisdom exhorts to obedience, as conducive to long
life, peace, and reputation, 1-4; to simple dependence
on God; with a promise of special guidance, 5, 6; and
avoiding self-wisdom, to fear God, to honor him, and
profit by his fatherly correction, 7-12. The happiness
and safety of him that finds wisdom, 13-26. Exhortations to justice, charity, peace, and contentment, 27-
32. The miserable state of the wicked, 33-35.*

1. **forget not.** Pr 1:8. *4:5. 31:5. Dt 4:23. Ps 119:*93,
153, 176. Ho *4:6. **let.** Dt *4:9. *6:6-9. 8:1. *30:16-
20. Ps 119:*11, 16, 34, 47, 48. Is 51:7. Je 31:33. Ezk
11:19. 36:26, 27. Jn *14:21-24. Ro 7:22. Re 22:14, 20.
2. **length.** ver. *16. Pr *4:10. 9:11. Dt +*5:16. Jb
5:26. Ps *34:11-14. +*91:16mg. 128:6. Ep *6:1-3.
1 T 4:8. **long life.** Heb. years of life. ver. 16. Dt 30:20.
Jb 12:12. Ps 21:4. 23:6mg. +*91:16mg. 93:5mg. **and
peace.** ver. *17. Ps *119:165. Is *32:17. 48:17, 18.
*57:19-21. Ro *5:1. *14:17. *15:13. Ep 2:14. Col 1:20.
3. **mercy.** Pr *16:6. 20:28. 2 S 15:20. Ps *25:10.
*85:10. 89:14. 117:2. Ho *4:1. Mi *7:18-20. Ml 2:6.
Mt *23:23. Ep 5:1, 2, 9. Col 3:12. **and truth.** √174,
Ge +18:27. **bind.** Pr 6:21. 7:3. Ex 13:9, 16. Dt 6:8.
*11:18-21. Ps *119:11. **write.** Je 17:1. 2 C *3:3. He
*10:16. **table of.** Ex +25:21.
4. **shalt.** √96B, Ge +20:7. **find favor.** Ge *39:2-4,
21. 41:39, 40. 1 S *2:26. Ps *111:10. Da 1:9. Lk *2:52.
Ac 2:47. Ro *14:17-19. **good understanding.** *or,* good
success. Pr 12:8. 13:15. 16:22. 19:11mg. 23:9. Jsh
√1:7mg, 8mg. Ps *111:10.
5. **Trust.** T#292. Pr 22:19. +25:19 (T#170). Jb
*13:15. Ps *4:5. +√9:10. *37:3, 5, 7. 42:5. *62:8. 115:9-
11. 125:1. 146:3-5. Is *12:2. *26:3, 4. 50:10. Je *17:7,
8. Ep 1:12. 1 P +1:21 (T#352). **lean not.** ver. *7. Pr
*23:4. 28:26. Ge 3:5, 6. Ps 78:18-21. Is 47:10, 11. Je
1:6-8. 2:13. 9:23. 10:23. *17:5. Ro 12:16. 1 C *3:18-
20. *8:1, 2. Ph 3:3.
6. **In.** Pr *16:3. 23:17. 1 S 23:4, 11, 12. 30:8.
1 Ch +*28:9. Ezr 7:27. *8:22, 23. Ne 1:11. 2:4. 1 C
√10:31. 2 C 8:16. Ph *4:6. Col *3:17, 23. **direct.** T#759.

Pr 11:5. *16:9. Ps *25:8, 9. √32:8. 37:23. 48:14. *73:24.
Is 28:26. *30:21. *42:16. *48:17. Je 10:23. Ja *1:5.
7. **Be.** ver. 5. Pr 26:12. Is *5:21. Ro 11:25. *12:16.
fear the Lord. T#877. Pr *14:26, 27. 16:6. 19:23. Ne
5:15. Jb 1:1. *28:28. Ps 25:14. 31:19. 34:11-14. 85:9.
103:11. 115:13. 128:1. 147:11. Ec 8:12. *12:13. Ml 4:2.
Lk 1:50. Ac 10:35. *13:26.
8. **shall.** Pr *4:22. *16:24. Ps 147:3. Is 1:6. Je 30:12,
13. **health.** Heb. medicine. ✱S#7500h, only here.
Compare ✱S#7499h: Je 30:13. 46:11. Ezk 30:21mg.
thy. Ezk 16:4, 5. **marrow.** Heb. watering, *or* moistening. Jb 21:24. Ho 2:5mg.
9. **Honor.** T#878. Pr *14:31. Ge *14:18-21. 28:22.
Ex *22:29. 23:19. 34:26. 35:20-29. Nu 7:2, etc. 31:50,
etc. Dt 26:2, etc. 1 S *2:30. Hg *1:4-9. Ml *3:8, 9.
4:2. Mt 6:1. Mk 14:7, 8, 10, etc. Lk *14:13, 14. 1 C
*16:2. 2 C *5:14, 15. 8:2, 3, 8, 9. Ph 4:17, 18. 1 J
*3:17, 18. **with thy substance.** T#917. Dt 14:29. Ml
*3:10-12. Ro 12:1. 1 C 6:20. 2 C √8:5. Ga *6:6-8. Ph
4:17-19. 1 T *5:17, 18. **firstfruits.** Le +*23:10.
10. **So shall.** Pr *11:24, 25. *19:17. *22:9. Le 26:2-
5. Dt 28:8. Ne 8:10. Ec 11:1, 2. Hg 2:19. Ml √3:10,
11. Mt *10:42. Lk +*6:38. 2 C *9:6-11. Ga 6:10. He
*6:10.
11. **My.** Jb *5:17. Ps 94:12. 139:23, 24. Je 5:3. La
3:40. 1 C *11:32. He *❱12:5, 6. Re *3:19. **neither.** Pr
*24:10. Jb 4:5. Ps 77:2, 7-10. Is *40:30, 31. 2 C *4:1,
16, 17. √12:8-10. He *12:3, 7-12. Ja 5:11. 1 P 1:6, 7.
weary. S#6973h, Is +7:6.
12. **For.** ✐138C, Ge +22:14. **whom the Lord.** Dt
8:2, 15, 16. Ps *119:75. Je 29:11. 1 P 5:6. Re √3:19.
he correcteth. Pr 13:24. Jb *5:17. Ps 103:10. Is 48:10.
Je 10:24. *30:11. La 3:31-33, 39. Zc 13:9. Ml 3:3. He
*❱12:5, 6. **as a father.** Pr *29:17. Dt *8:5. Ps *103:13.
*119:67, 71. He 12:10.
13. **Happy.** T#322. Pr √4:5-8. *8:+10 (T#391), 32-
35. +16:22 (T#392). 1 K *10:1-9, 23, 24. Ec *9:15-
18. **getteth.** Heb. draweth out. Pr 2:4. 8:35mg. 12:2.
18:1, 22. Ps 140:8.
14. **the merchandise.** Pr 2:4. *8:10, 11, 19. *16:16.
2 Ch *1:11, 12. Jb 28:13-19. Ps 19:10. *119:72, 111,
162. Mt *16:26. Ph *3:8, 9. Re 3:18.
15. **more.** Pr *8:11. *20:15. 31:10. Jb 28:15-18. Mt
*13:44-46. Ph *3:7, 12, 14. **all.** Ps 63:3. 73:25, 26.
Ro *8:18.
16. **Length.** ✐132G, Ge +3:19. **of days.** ver. *2.
Pr *4:10. Ps 21:4. *71:9. +*91:16mg. 1 T 4:8. **riches.**
T#762. Pr *4:6-9. *8:18-21. 15:6. Dt 11:14, 15. *28:11,
12. 30:9. 1 K 3:13. Jb 22:24, 25. Ps 19:11. 107:38.
*112:3. Is 30:23. Mk *10:30. 1 C 3:21-23. 2 C 6:10.
17. **ways of.** Pr 2:10. 22:18. Ps *19:10, 11. 63:3-5.
112:1. *119:14, 47, 103, 174. Mt *11:28-30. He 11:26.
all. Ps 25:10. *37:11. *119:165. Is √26:3. 57:19. Lk
1:79. Jn 16:33. Ro *5:1. Ph √4:8, 9.
18. **tree of life.** Pr √11:30. *13:12. Ge *2:9. *3:22.
Re 2:7. *22:2. **happy.** Jn 15:11. 17:13. 2 C 6:10. 8:2.
1 P 1:6-8.
19. **Lord.** Pr 8:27-29. Ps *104:24. 136:5. Je *10:12.
*51:15. Jn *1:3. **established.** *or,* prepared. Ex 15:17.
2 S 7:13.
20. **the depths.** Ge 1:9. 7:11. Jb 38:8-11. Ps 104:8,
9. **the clouds.** Ge 27:28, 37-39. Dt 33:28. Jb 36:27,
28. 38:26-28. Ps 65:9-12. Je *14:22. Jl *2:23. **dew.**
Dew is defined by Dr. Hutton "a thin, light, insensible
mist, or rain, descending with a slow motion, and falling
while the sun is below the horizon. It appears to differ

from *rain* as *less* from *more*. Its origin and matter are doubtless from the vapors and exhalations that rise from the earth and water." Like rain, it is wonderfully adapted, by an infinitely wise and gracious Providence, to invigorate and give life to the whole vegetable world. See on Ps 72:6n; Is +*26:19n.

21. **let.** ver. *1-3. Dt *4:9. *6:6-9. Jsh √1:8. Jn √8:31. *15:6, 7. He *2:1-3. 1 J *2:24, 27. **keep.** Pr 2:7. Dt *32:46, 47. 2 P 1:12.

22. **life.** Pr *4:22. Ec 7:12. Is *38:16. Jn *8:12. *12:49, 50. √17:3. **soul.** Heb. *nephesh*, Ge +34:3. **grace.** Pr *1:9.

23. **safely.** Pr 2:8. 4:12. 10:9. Ps *37:23, 24, 31. 91:11, 12. *121:3, 8. Zc *10:12.

24. **liest.** Pr *6:22. Le 26:6. Ps *3:5. *4:8. *121:4-7. Jb *11:19. Is 26:9. Ezk 34:15. **afraid.** Ge ◐19:30. Ezk 34:25-28. **and.** Ps *127:2. Je 31:26. Ac 12:6. 1 Th 4:13, 14.

25. **Be not.** Pr *1:33. Jb *5:21, 22. 11:13-15. Ps *27:1, 2. +34:4. *46:1-3. 91:5. *112:7. Is 8:12, 13. 14:3. *41:10-14. Da *3:17, 18. Mt *8:24-26. 24:6. Mk *4:40. Lk 21:9. Jn √14:1. 2 T *1:7. 1 P *3:14. **sudden.** ♪24E, Ge +30:33. **fear.** ♪121R6, Ge +31:42. **neither.** Pr 1:27. Ps *73:19. Is 57:20, 21. Mt 24:15. Lk 21:18-28.

26. **Lord.** Pr *14:26. Dt 33:27. Ps *91:1-3, 9, 10. Is 26:1, 20. Hab *3:17, 18. Lk 21:28, 36. Re 1:7. **shall keep.** Pr 11:8. 1 S *2:9. Ps 25:15.

27. **Withhold not.** T#1846. Pr 11:24, 26. 25:11. Ro *13:7. 2 C 9:7. Ga *6:10. T 2:14. Ja *2:15, 16. +*5:4. **them to whom it is due.** Heb. the owners thereof. Le +*19:13. **in the power.** Ge 31:29. Mi *2:1.

28. **Go, and come again.** Pr *27:1. Le +√19:13. Dt +√24:12-15. Ec *9:10. 11:6. 2 C 8:11. 9:3. 1 T *6:18.

29. **Devise not evil.** *or*, Practice no evil. Pr 6:14, 18. *16:29, 30. Dt 27:24. Ps *35:20. 55:20. 59:3. Je 18:18-20. Mi *2:1, 2.

30. **Strive not.** Ps 17:14. 18:6. *25:8, 9. *29:22. Mt *5:39-41. Ro *12:18-21. 1 C *6:6-8. Col 3:12-15. 2 T *2:24. He √12:14.

31. **Envy.** Pr *23:17. *24:1, 19, 20. Ps *37:1, 7-9. *73:3. Ga *5:21. **the oppressor.** Heb. a man of violence. Pr 16:29. 2 S 22:49. Ps 73:6. 140:1mg. Ec *5:8. **choose.** Pr *1:15-18. 2:12-15. *12:12. *22:22-25.

32. **the froward.** Pr 6:16-19. *8:13. *11:20. *17:15. Ps *18:26. Lk *16:15. **his secret.** Pr 14:10. Ge 18:17. Dt *29:29. Ps *25:14. Mt *11:25. 13:11. Jn √7:17. *14:21-24. 15:15. 1 C 2:12-15. Re *2:17.

33. **curse.** Pr *21:12. √26:2. Ge +*6:13 (T#566). Le 26:14, etc. Dt 7:26. √27:15-26. *28:15, etc. 29:19, etc. Jsh 6:18. *7:13. Ps *37:22. √119:21. Da 5:5, 6. +*9:11. Zc +*5:3, 4. Ml *2:2. Mt +*25:41. Ga √3:13. **the house.** Mi *6:10. **he blesseth.** Dt *28:2, etc. 2 S 6:11. 1 K 21:20-22. 2 K 10:1-11. Jb 8:6, 7. Ps *1:3. *31:23. *91:10.

34. **he scorneth.** Pr 9:7, 8, 12. *19:29. 21:24. Ex 14:13. Ps *2:1-4. *138:6. Is 37:33, 34. **he giveth.** Is *57:15. 66:2. Mt +*5:3. 15:27, 28. Lk *18:13, 14. Ja *▶4:6. 1 P *▶5:5.

35. **wise.** Pr *4:8. 1 S *2:30. Ps *73:24. **but.** Pr 13:18. Ps 132:18. Is 65:13-15. Da *12:2, 3. Ml 3:18. Mt 13:43. **shame.** Pr 6:33. 9:7. 11:2. 12:16. Da *12:2. Ro 6:21. **shall be the promotion of fools.** Heb. exalteth the fools. Pr 14:29. **fools.** Pr 1:22. 8:5. 10:1. 12:23.

PROVERBS 4

Solomon shows what good instruction he had received from his parents concerning the advantages of wisdom, in order to induce obedience, 1-13. He dissuades from the path of the wicked and contrasts it with that of the righteous, 14-19. Further admonitions and counsels of Wisdom, 20-27.

1. **ye.** Pr 1:8. *6:20-23. Ps *34:11. 1 Th 2:11, 12. **attend.** Pr *2:1-5. 5:1. 7:4. *8:32-36. *19:20. 22:17. He *2:1.

2. **good doctrine.** Pr *8:6-9. *22:20, 21. Dt 32:2. Jb 33:3. Ps 49:1-3. Je ◐*5:31. Jn *7:16, 17. 1 T 4:*6, √16. T *1:9. **forsake.** 1 Ch +*28:9. 2 Ch 7:19. Ps *89:30-32. Ga *1:6, 7.

3. **I was.** 2 S 12:24, 25. 1 K 1:13-17. 1 Ch 3:5. 22:5. 28:9. 29:1. Je *10:23. Ro *12:16.

4. **He.** Pr *22:6. Ge +*18:19. 1 Ch 22:11-16. +*28:9. Ep √6:4. 2 T 1:5. √3:15. **Let.** See on Pr *3:1. Dt *4:9. *6:6. Ps √119:11. **keep.** Pr *7:2. Le *18:3-5. Is *55:3. Jn *12:50. He *5:9. **live.** ♪96B, Ge +20:7.

5. **Get wisdom.** Pr *1:22, 23. 2:2-4. *3:13-18. 8:5. *17:16. *18:1. *19:8. *23:23. 1 K 3:5, 6, 9, 11, 12. Ja *1:5. **neither.** 2 Ch *34:2. Jb *23:11. Ps *44:18. *119:51, 157.

6. **love.** ver. *21, *22. Pr *2:10-12. Ep *3:17. 2 Th *2:10.

7. **Wisdom is.** Ec *7:12. 9:16-18. Mt 5:6. √6:33. *13:44-46. Lk 10:42. Ph *3:8. **with.** Pr *16:16. 21:6. Ps *49:16-20. Ec 2:4-9. 4:8. Mk *8:36, 37. Lk *12:20. **get understanding.** Ps *119:104.

8. **promote thee.** Pr 3:35. 22:4. 1 S *2:30. 1 K *3:5-13. Da *12:3.

9. **give.** Pr *1:9. 3:22. 1 T *2:9, 10. 1 P *3:4. **a crown,** etc. *or*, she shall compass thee with a crown of glory. Pr *16:31. Is *28:5. He *2:7-9. 1 P *5:4. Re 3:21.

10. **my.** Pr *8:10. *19:20. Jb *22:22. Je 9:20. Jn 3:32, 33. 1 Th √2:13. 1 T 1:15. **the years.** Pr *3:+2, 16. Dt +*5:16. *6:2. Ps +*91:16mg. 1 T 4:8. 1 P 3:10-12.

11. **taught.** ver. *4. Dt 4:5. 1 S *12:24. Jb 36:22. Ec *12:9. **led.** Pr *8:6, 9, 20. Ps *23:3. *25:4, 5. 32:8. Ac 13:10.

12. **thou goest.** Pr *6:22. 2 S 22:37. Jb 18:7, 8. Ps 18:36. **thou shalt.** ver. *19. Pr *3:23. Ps 91:11, 12. *119:165. Je 31:9. Jn *11:9, 10. Ro 9:32, 33. 1 P *2:8. 1 J *2:10, 11.

13. **Take.** Pr 3:18. *23:23. Is 48:17, 18. Ac *2:42. *11:23. 1 Th *5:21. He *2:1. Re 2:13. *12:11. **let.** Ge *32:26. SS *3:4. Lk *24:27-29. Jn *4:39-42. Ga 3:1. 2 T *3:14. **she.** Pr *3:22. Dt 32:47. Ps *34:12-14. Ec *7:12. Jn *6:68.

14. **Enter.** ♪173, Ge +27:44. **not into the path.** Pr *1:10, 15. 2:11, 12. *9:6. *13:20. Ps √1:1. 17:4. *26:4, 5. 119:+*63, 114, 115. 1 C 15:33.

15. **Avoid it.** Pr 1:15. *5:8. 6:5. Ex *23:7. Jb *11:14. *22:23. Is 33:15. 2 C *6:17. Ep √5:11. Col 2:8. 1 Th *5:22.

16. **they sleep not.** Pr 1:16. Ps *36:4. Is *57:20. Mi *2:1. Lk 22:66. Jn 18:28. 2 P *2:14.

17. **they eat.** Pr 9:17. *20:17. Jb 24:5, 6. Ps *14:4. Je 5:26-28. Ezk *22:25-29. Am 8:4-6. Mi 3:5. 6:12. Zp 3:3. Mt *23:14. Ja +*5:4, 5.

18. **But.** This comparison is extremely beautiful, and the sense highly instructive. As the light first tints

the east and increases till the sun has attained its meridian splendor, so is the course of a good man: his knowledge, purity, and holiness gradually increase, and the light of his pious example shines more and more, till he is exalted in the heavens to shine as a sun in the full blaze of endless felicity. But the path of the wicked, though they may amuse themselves with many glittering meteors, is thick, gloomy darkness, a compound of ignorance, error, sin, and misery, until at length it terminates, perhaps unexpectedly to themselves, in "the blackness of darkness for ever" (Ju *13). **the path.** ver. 11. Pr 2:9. 2 S 23:4. Jb 11:17. 22:28. *23:10. 33:28. Ps *16:11. *23:3. √25:10. 119:14, 35, +√105, *130. Is 2:3. 26:7. Ho *6:3. Zc 14:6, 7. Mt *5:14, 16, 45. Jn *8:12. Ac ◐20:30. 2 C √3:18. Ga ◐1:6, 7. Ep ◐4:14. Col 1:23. 2:3, 4, 6, 7. He 12:13. 2 P *1:19. ◐2:1, 2. *3:18. 1 J 2:3, 6. Re *21:23. *22:5. **the just.** Pr 3:32. 12:13. 20:7. Jb 36:7. Ps 34:15. 37:25. 92:12. Is 3:10. Mt 13:43. **shining light.** Ps 112:4. 119:147. 130:6. Is 58:8, 10. Da *12:3. Ph *2:15. **more and more.** T#817. 2 S 3:1. Jb *17:9. Ps 84:7. 92:12. 97:11. √119:105. Da 12:4. Ml 4:2. Mt 5:14. ◐√6:23. 13:12. ◐24:4. Mk 8:24, 25. Jn 1:46, 49-51. Jn *16:13. 1 C 13:12. 2 C *3:18. 4:6. ◐*11:13-15. Ep 3:17-19. Ph *3:12-15. 2 Th 1:3. 1 T √4:15, 16. 2 T ◐*3:13. Ja 4:6. 2 P √1:19. The Watchtower Bible and Tract Society of the Jehovah's Witnesses declares itself to be God's only true church or organization. It ventures to claim to itself the position of His faithful and wise servant (Mt +√24:45. Lk +*12:42), the sole and exclusive authorized dispenser of divine truth or authoritative Bible interpretation. Just how God got along for 1884 years prior to its founding is not explained. This group appeals to this verse in its literature and teaching to excuse or justify former errors in doctrine or prophetic speculation on the basis that new light has been received. Such an explanation is contrary to the clear teaching of other scripture which declares God is not the author of false prophecy (Dt √18:20-22. Je √14:14). We are commanded "not to be afraid of" the false prophet; rather, the source of spiritual and doctrinal truth and authority must be grounded solely in the written word of God, Is +√8:20, not in any humanly devised religious organization. While our understanding of the truths revealed in God's word must be subject to continual growth and correction as we continue to make His word our careful study, His truth never changes. **perfect day.** Jb 11:17. 19:25. Is 60:20. Ho +*6:3h (prepared). Mt 13:43. 1 C *1:8. Col 3:4. 1 Th 5:8. 2 T 1:12. 2 P 3:10-14. 1 J 3:2, 3. Re 21:23.

19. **The way of the wicked.** Pr 2:13. Dt 28:29. 1 S *2:9. Jb 5:14. 12:25. *15:23. 18:5, 6, 18. 24:13. Ps 35:6. *82:5. Is +√8:20. 59:9, 10. Je *13:16. 23:12. Zp 1:17. Mt √6:23. *7:23. +√15:14. Jn √3:19. 11:10. *12:35, 36. 1 J 1:6. *2:11. **as darkness.** Is +9:2. Mi 3:6. Jn 1:5. Ro 13:12. Ep 5:8. 1 Th 5:4. **know not.** Ps 73:18. Is 30:13. Je *13:16. Mt 7:26, 27. *23:13, 15. Mk √12:24, 27. Lk +*11:52. Jn *12:35, 36. 1 C 2:5. 10:12. **stumble.** Mt 18:6. Ro 9:32, 33. 1 P *2:8.

20. **attend.** Pr 5:1. 6:20, 21. *7:1. Ps 78:1. *90:12. Is 55:3. Mt *17:5.

21. **depart.** Pr *3:3, 21. **in the.** Pr 2:1. Ps 40:8mg. Je 31:33.

22. **life.** ver. *4, *10. **health.** Heb. medicine. Pr 3:8mg. 6:15. *12:18. 13:17. 16:24. Jsh 18:27, Irpeel. Je 33:6.

23. **Keep thy heart.** T#332. Pr 16:9. 22:5. *23:19. 28:26. Dt *4:9. 23:9. 2 S +*15:6. 1 K +*11:9. 2 K ◐10:31. Jb 15:12. 31:1. Ps 19:13. 25:20. *119:11, 37. *139:23, 24. *141:3, 4. Je +*6:19. *17:9. Ho 4:11. Mt +*5:8. 6:22. 12:34, 35. Mk 14:38. Lk 6:45. Ac 15:20, 29. Ro 6:17. Ep +*4:14. Ph +*4:7, 8. Col 1:22, 23. 2:6, 7. 1 T +*4:12. He *12:15. 13:9. Ja *4:8. 1 P *1:22. 4:19. **with all diligence.** Heb. above all keeping. ver. *7. Pr 3:21. 11:16. *13:3. Ex +*20:15n. +*15:26. Ec 5:13. 1 C 10:12. Ph 2:12, 13. Col 1:10. **for.** Pr 10:11. Mt *12:34, 35. *15:19. Mk √7:21-23. Jn 4:14. Ph *4:8. 1 T *4:12. Ja *1:14, 15. 3:5, 6.

24. **Put away.** Pr *11:14. Ps 19:13. 141:3, 4. Ezk 18:31. Ep *4:25-31. Col *3:8. Ja *1:21, 26. 1 P 2:1. **a froward,** etc. Heb. frowardness of mouth, and perverseness of lips. Pr *8:8, 13. 17:20. 1 T *6:5. T 2:9.

25. **thine eyes.** Pr 23:5, 33. Ex ◐2:12. Jb *31:1. Ps 119:37. Mt 6:22. Lk 9:62. **look straight.** 1 K 13:18-22.

26. **Ponder.** Pr 5:6. Ps *119:59. 143:8-10. Ezk *18:28. Hg 1:5, 7. Ep *5:15, 17. **let all thy ways be established.** or, all thy ways shall be ordered aright. Ps *37:23. *40:2. 1 Th *3:13. 2 Th *3:3. 1 P 5:10.

27. **Turn.** Nu 20:17. Dt *5:32. *12:32. *17:20. *28:14. Jsh *1:7. Ga 2:11-13. **remove.** Pr 16:17. Is *1:16. Ro *12:9. Ju 21, 24, 25.

PROVERBS 5

Exhortations to study wisdom, 1, 2. The seductions of harlots and the complicated mischiefs of their society, 3-14. A figurative commendation of marriage, and of affection to a man's wife and children, 15-19. A further dissuasive from whoredom, urging the Lord's continual presence, and the miserable end of wicked men, 20-23.

1. **attend.** Pr 2:1. 4:1, 20. Mt 13:9. Mk 4:23. Re 2:7, 11, 17, 29. 3:6, 13, 22. **bow.** Pr 22:17. Ja *1:19.

2. **thy lips.** Pr *10:21. 15:2, 7. *16:23. 20:15. Ps 45:2. 71:15. *119:9, 11, 13, 59. SS 4:11. Ml *2:6, 7.

3. **the lips.** T#403. Pr 2:16. 6:23-25. 7:10-18, *21. Re 17:2-6. **strange woman.** 1 K 11:1, 2, 6-8. Ne 13:26. **mouth.** Heb. palate. ∫121BE, Metonymy of Cause B546, whereby the "palate" is put for the words spoken, her speech. Jb +31:30mg. Ps 119:103mg. **smoother.** Ps 55:21.

4. **her.** Pr *6:24-35. 7:22, 23. *9:18. 23:27, 28. Ec *7:26. He *12:15, 16. **sharp.** Jg *16:4-6, 15-21. Ps 55:21. He *4:12.

5. **down.** Pr 1:12. *2:18, 19. *7:27. Ge 28:12. **death.** ✱S#4194h. Pr 2:18. 5:5. 7:27. 8:36. 10:2. 11:4, 7, 19. 12:28. 13:14. 14:12, 27, 32. 16:14, 25. 18:21. 21:6. 24:11. 26:18. Ge 21:16. 25:11. 26:18. 27:2, 7, 10. 50:16. Ex 10:17. Le 11:31, 32. 16:1. Nu 6:7. 16:29. 23:10. 26:10. 33:39. 35:25, 28, 32. Dt 19:6. 21:22. 22:26. 30:15, 19. 31:27, 29. 33:1. 34:7. Jsh 1:1. 2:13. 20:6. Jg 1:1. 2:19. 13:7. 16:30. Ru 1:17. 2:11. 1 S 5:11. 15:32, 35. 20:3, 31. 26:16. 2 S 1:1, 23. 3:33. 6:23. 12:5. 15:21. 19:28mg. 22:5, 6. 1 K 2:26mg. 11:40. 2 K 1:1. 2:21. 3:5. 4:40. 14:17. 15:5. 1 Ch 2:24. 22:5. 2 Ch 22:4. 24:15, 17, 22. 25:25. 26:21. 32:33. Est 2:7. Jb 3:21. 5:20. 7:15. 18:13. 27:15. 28:22. 30:23. 38:17. Ps 6:5. 7:13. 9:13. 13:3. 18:4, 5. 22:15. 33:19. 49:14, 17. 55:4, 15. 56:13. 68:20. 73:4. 78:50. 89:48. 107:18. 116:3, 8, 15. 118:18. Ec 3:19. 7:1, 26. 8:8. 10:1mg. SS 8:6. Is 6:1. 14:28. 25:8. 28:15, 18. 38:18. 53:9, 12. Je 8:3.

9:21. 15:2. 18:21, 23mg. 21:8. 26:11, 16. 43:11. 52:11, 34. La 1:20. Ezk 18:23, 32. 28:10. 31:14. *33:11. Ho 13:14. Jon 4:3, 8, 9. Hab 2:5. Ro *6:23. **steps.** Pr 4:12. 16:9. 30:29h. 2 S 6:13. **take hold.** Pr 4:4. 11:16. 28:17. **hell.** Heb. *sheol*, Ge +37:35. Pr 7:27. 9:18. 15:11, 24. 23:14. 27:20. Dt +32:22. Jb 26:6. Is 5:14. 14:9, 15. 28:15. Jon 2:2.

6. **ponder.** Pr *4:26. Ps *119:59. **the path.** Pr 11:19. Ps *16:11. **her.** Pr 6:12, 13. *7:10-21. 2 Th *2:9, 10.

7. **Hear.** Pr 4:1. *8:32-36. *22:17-21. He *12:25. **and depart.** Pr 3:21. *4:21.

8. **thy way.** Pr *4:15. 6:27, 28. Mt 6:13. Ep √5:11.

9. **Lest thou give.** Pr *6:29-35. Ge 38:23-26. Jg *16:19-21. Ne *13:26. Ho 4:13, 14. **years.** 121P3, Metonymy of the Adjunct B594. "Years" put for what happens in them.

10. **strangers.** 121C, Ge +4:12. Pr *6:35. Ho 7:9. Lk *15:30. **wealth.** Heb. strength. Pr 14:4. 20:29. 24:5, 10. +27:24mg. *31:3. 121C1I. Figure of speech Metonymy of the Cause: "strength" is put for that which it produces, Ge +4:12. 121N2, Metonymy of the Adjunct, Ge +34:29. "Strength" is put for that to which it pertains (wealth). **labors.** 121C1H, Dt +28:33.

11. **thou.** Pr 7:23. Dt 32:29. Je *5:31. Ro *6:21. He *13:4. Re *21:8. 22:15. **when.** Nu 5:27. 1 C *5:4, 5. √6:18.

12. **How.** Pr *1:7, 22, 29-30. 15:5. Ps *50:17. 73:22. Zc *7:11-14. Jn *3:19, 20. **and my.** Pr *1:25. *6:23. *12:1. *13:18. Ge 19:9. Ex 2:13, 14. 2 Ch *24:20-22. 25:16. *33:10, 11. *36:16, 17. Je 44:4, 5. Zc 1:4-6.

13. **not obeyed.** Lk *15:18. 1 Th *4:8. *5:12, 13. He *13:7.

14. **almost in all evil.** Pr *13:20. Nu 25:1-6. Ho 4:11-14. 1 C *10:6-8. 2 P 2:10-18. Ju 7-13.

15. **Drink waters.** ver. *18, *19. Pr 9:5. 23:7. Ge 24:14. Jn 4:14. 7:37, 38. 1 C *7:2-5. He *13:4. **cistern.** Heb. *bor*, Ge +37:20. Pr 1:12. 28:17. **running waters.** Ps 78:16. SS 4:15. Je 2:13. Jn 4:10. **well.** Heb. *be-er*, Ge +16:14. Pr 23:27. Ge 21:19.

16. **thy.** Dt *33:28. Ps 68:26. Is *48:1, 21. **fountains.** Heb. *mayan*, Ge +7:11 (✱S#4599h). **dispersed.** Ge *24:60. Jg 12:9. Ps *127:3. *128:3. **abroad.** Heb. *chuts*, Am 5:16n (✚S#2351h, highways). **streets.** Heb. *re-chob*, public square or broad street. Am 5:16n (✱S#7339h, streets).

17. **strangers'.** ver. 3, 10, 20. Ge 34:27. 1 K ◯11:1.

18. **rejoice.** Ec *9:9. Ml *2:14, 15.

19. **as the.** SS 2:9. 4:5. 7:3. *8:14. **satisfy thee.** Heb. water thee. ver. *15. Ps 36:8mg. 65:10. **be thou ravished always with her love.** Heb. err thou always in her love. 2 S *12:4.

20. **with.** Pr *2:16-19. 6:24. 7:5. *22:14. 23:27, 28, 33. 2 S 11:2, 3. 1 K *11:1.

21. **the ways.** Pr *15:3. 2 Ch *16:9. Jb *31:4. 34:21. Ps 11:4. 14:1-3. 17:3. *139:1-12. Je 16:17. *17:10. *23:24. 32:19. Ho 7:2. He *4:13. *13:4. Re 2:18, 23.

22. **His.** Pr *1:18, 31, 32. 11:3, 5. Ge 29:25. Nu +√32:23. 1 S 2:3. Jb 31:4. Ps 7:15, 16. 9:15, 16. Ec 12:14. Is 29:15. Je *2:19. Ho 4:11-14. Ga *6:7, 8. **holden with.** T#166. Pr 27:22. Ge 37:4. Ex 32:9. Jsh 24:19. Jb +21:15 (T#689). Ec 7:26. 9:3. Is 48:4. Je 2:22. 3:5. *6:10. *13:23. 17:1, *9. Mt 7:18. 12:34. +13:38 (T#690). 17:17. 23:33. Jn *6:44, 65. +17:14 (T#740). Ro 8:7, 8. **sins.** Heb. sin. 1 C 5:9, 10. Ga *5:19-21. Ep *5:5, 6. He 13:4.

23. **shall die.** Pr 10:21. 14:32. Jb *4:21. *36:12. **in the.** Pr 14:14. Ps *81:12. 2 P 2:15-22.

PROVERBS 6

Cautions against suretiship, and counsels to those who have rashly engaged in it, 1-5. The slothful sent to the ant for instruction, and shown how idleness tends to penury, 6-11. Some artful practices of wicked men exposed and their ruin denounced, 12-15. Seven things which the Lord hates, 16-19. Exhortations to obey parents and to walk in God's commandments, 20-23. Dissuasives from fornication and adultery, and· the fatal consequences of the latter especially stated, 24-35.

1. **if thou be.** Pr *11:15. *17:18. 20:16. *22:26. 27:13. Ge 43:9. 44:32, 33. Jb 17:3. Phm *18, *19. He 7:22. **thou hast.** To strike, or join hands, was an ancient form of entering into contracts in all countries and all ages.

2. **snared.** Pr 12:13. *18:7.

3. **when.** 2 S *24:14. 2 Ch 12:5. Ps 31:8. **go.** Ex 10:3. 2 Ch 36:12. Ja *4:10. **and make sure thy friend.** *or*, so shalt thou prevail with thy friend.

4. **Give not sleep.** ver. *10, *11. Ps *132:4. Ec *9:10. Mt 24:17, 18. Mk *13:35, 36.

5. **Deliver thyself.** Mt 5:25. **as a bird.** Pr *1:17. Ps 11:1. 124:7. **fowler.** Ps 91:3.

6. **Go.** 138C, Ge +22:14. **the ant.** The ant has been famous in all ages for its social habits, foresight, economy, and industry. Collecting their food at the proper seasons, they bite off the ends of the grain to prevent it germinating, and lay it up in cells till needed. Pr 1:17. Jb *12:7, 8. 35:11. Is 1:3. Mt *6:26. **thou sluggard.** ver. *9. Pr *10:26. *13:4. 15:19. *18:9. 19:*15, 24. 20:4. 21:25. 22:13. *24:30-34. 26:13-16. Mt *25:26. Ro *12:11. He *6:12. **consider.** T#132. Pr 4:26. Dt 4:39. 32:29. Jb 37:14. Ps +10:4 (T#693). 28:5. 50:21, 22. 111:4. Ec 7:13, 14. Is 1:3. 5:12, 13. Ho 7:2. Hg *1:5.

7. **no guide.** Jb 38:39-41. 39:1-12, 26-30. 41:4, etc.

8. **her meat.** Pr *30:25. 1 T *6:19.

9. **How.** Pr *1:22. *24:33, 34. Je *4:14. **when.** Ps 13:3. 94:8. Jon *1:6. Ro 8:13. 13:11-14. Ep 5:14. 1 Th *5:2-7. **arise.** SS 2:10. Is 60:1. Mk 10:49. Lk 22:46. Jn 5:8. Ep 5:14.

10. **a little sleep.** ver. *6. Pr *19:15. *‖24:33, 34. +25:28. 1 Th 5:6.

11. **poverty come.** Pr *10:4. *13:4. *20:4.

12. **naughty.** Heb. "A man of Belial." Pr 16:27mg. 19:28mg. 108K42, Idiom B859. The English word *naughty* meant "worth nought, worthless." Now we use it of any evil, and sometimes of some special form. Pr 17:4. Je 24:2. **person.** Pr 11:6. 17:4. 1 S 17:28. Je 24:2, 8-10. Ja *1:21. **walketh.** ver. *14. Pr 2:12. 4:24. *8:13. Ps *10:3, 7. *36:3. 52:2-4. 59:7. *73:8, 9. Mt *12:34. Ac *20:30. 1 T 5:13. T 1:10, 11. Ja *3:6.

13. **winketh.** Pr 5:6. 10:10. Jb 15:12. Ps *35:19. **speaketh with.** Is 3:16.

14. **Frowardness.** Pr 2:14. *16:28-30. *21:8. Mt 15:19. **he deviseth.** ver. *18. Ps *36:4. Is *32:7. *57:20. Ezk 11:2. Mi 2:1. **soweth.** Heb. casteth forth. ver. *19. Pr *16:28. 22:8. *26:17-22. Ho 8:7. Ro *2:8. *16:17. Ga √6:7, 8.

15. **shall his.** Pr *1:27. *29:1. Ps 73:18-20. Is 30:13.

1 Th *5:3. **he be**. 2 Ch *36:16. Ps *50:22. Je 19:11. Jn 3:7. T 3:3-5.

16. **six**. Pr *8:13. 30:18, 21, 24, 29. Am 1:3, 6, 9, 11. 2:1, 4, 6. **yea, seven**. ♪69B. Epanorthosis; or, Correction B910, where the retraction is partial or relative. For other instances of this figure see Mt 11:9. Jn 16:32. Ac 26:27. 1 C 7:10. 15:10. Ga 1:6. 2:20. 4:9. 2 T 4:8. 1 J 2:2. **an abomination**. Pr 3:32. *11:1, 20. *15:8, 9. *17:15. 20:10, 23. Dt *18:10-12. 23:18. 24:4. 25:16. Re *21:27. **unto him**. Heb. of his soul. Ps 11:5. Heb. *nephesh*, Ex +15:9. Le +26:11n.

17. **A proud look**. Heb. Haughty eyes. ♪171Q16, ·Ps +18:27. Pr 30:13. Ps *10:4. 18:27. 73:6-8. 101:5. 131:1. Is *2:11. 3:*9, 16. 1 P *5:5. **lying**. Pr *12:22. 14:5. 26:28. Ps 5:6. 120:2, 3. Ho *4:1, 2. Jn *8:44. Re *22:15. **and hands**. Pr 1:11. Ge 4:8. 9:6. Dt *27:25. 2 K 21:16. 24:4. Is 1:15. *59:3-7. Mt 23:37, 38.

18. **heart**. Pr 24:8. Ge *6:5. 2 S 16:20, 21. Ps *36:4. Je *4:14. Mi 2:1. Zc *8:17. **feet**. 171Q21, Pr +1:16. Pr *1:16. Is 59:7. Zc 5:4. Ro 3:15. Ju 19.

19. **A false**. Pr 12:17. 19:5, 9. 21:28. 25:18. Ex *20:16. *23:1. Dt *19:16-20. 1 K 21:10-15. Ps 27:12. 35:11. Ml +*3:5. Mt *15:19. 26:59. Ac 6:13. **that soweth**. ver. 14. Pr *16:28. 22:10. *26:20. Ro *16:17, 18. 1 C 3:3, 4. 2 T *2:23. Ja *3:14-16, 18. 3 J 9, 10. Ju 19.

20. **keep thy**. Pr *1:8, 9. 7:1-4. *23:22. 30:11. Dt *21:18. 27:16. Ep √6:1. **forsake not**. Pr 1:8.

21. **Bind them**. Pr *3:3. 4:6, 21. 7:3, 4. Ex 13:16. Dt 6:8. 2 C *3:3. **continually**. Is +*58:11.

22. **When thou goest**. Pr 2:11. *3:23, 24. Dt *11:18-21. Ps *17:4. 43:3. 119:*9, *11, 24, 54, *97, 148. **sleepest**. Pr 3:24. Le 26:6. Ps 3:5. 4:8. 121:4-7.

23. **the commandment**. Ps *19:8-11. 119:98-100, *105. Is √8:20. 2 T √3:16, 17. 2 P *1:19. **lamp**. *or*, candle. ♪22K2, 2 S +22:29. Pr 13:9mg. 20:20mg, 27mg. 24:20mg. Ps +18:28mg. *119:105mg. Re 2:5. **law**. ♪140, Paronomasia, Ge +4:25. The words for "law" and "light" contain similar sounds in Hebrew. **and reproofs**. Pr 5:12. *15:31, 32. 29:15. Le *19:17. Ps 141:5. **the way**. Pr 3:18. *4:4, 13. 15:24. Je *21:8.

24. **keep**. Pr 2:16. 5:3. 7:5. Ps 17:4, 5. Ec *7:26. **of the tongue of a strange woman**. *or*, of the strange tongue.

25. **Lust**. Ex 20:14, 17. Le 20:10. 2 S *11:2-5. Jb *31:1. Ps 119:37. Mt *5:28. Ja *1:14, 15. **take**. 2 K 9:30mg. SS 4:9. Is 3:16.

26. **by**. Pr 5:10. 29:3, 8. Lk *15:13-15, 30. **a piece**. 1 S *2:36. **the adulteress**. Heb. the woman of a man, *or*, a man's wife. **hunt**. Ge *39:14. Jb 2:4. Ezk *13:18. **life**. Heb. *nephesh*, soul, Ge +44:30.

27. **Can**. ♪138C, Ge +22:14. **take fire**. Jb *31:9-12. Ho 7:4-7. Ja *3:5.

28. **go upon**. Is 43:2. **hot coals**. Pr 25:22. 26:21. Ps 140:10. SS 8:6. **burned**. Is 43:2.

29. **he that**. Ge *12:18, 19. Le *20:10. 2 S *11:3, 4. *12:9, 10. 16:21. Je 5:8, 9. Ezk 22:11. Ml +*3:5. **toucheth**. ♪108B, Ge +20:6. Ge *20:4-7. 26:10, 11. 1 C *7:1.

30. **despise**. Pr 23:9, 22. 30:17. **thief**. Pr 29:24. Ex 22:2, 7. Dt 24:7. **steal**. Ge 31:19. 44:8. Ex 20:15. **to satisfy**. Charles Bridges notes, "Here is no excuse or impunity for the thief. The full restitution he is compelled to make (ver. 31)—perhaps sweeping away all his little substance—proves that no extremity can excuse 'the transgression of the law' (compare 1 C 6:10,

with 1 J 3:4)" (*Commentary*, p. 66). Jb 38:39. **soul**. Heb. *nephesh*, Nu +11:6. Ps 107:9. Is 5:14. 29:8. Re +*18:14. **hungry**. Pr 19:15. Ge 41:55.

31. **restore**. Ex 22:1, 3, 4. 2 S 12:6. Jb *20:18. Lk *19:8. **sevenfold**. Charles Bridges notes that *sevenfold* is not used literally. "Four or five-fold was the extent of the Divine requirement. Compare Lk 19:8. It means full (ver. 3) and satisfactory—an indefinite number. Compare Ge 4:15, 24; Ps 79:12, and *alia passim*. Compare Job 20:18" (*Commentary*, p. 66). **he shall give**. Mt *18:25.

32. **lacketh**. Pr *7:7. Ge *39:9, 10. *41:39. Ec *7:25, 26. Je 5:8, 21. Ro *1:22-24. **understanding**. Heb. heart. ♪12I11, Ge +3:7. Pr 17:18mg. Ho *4:11, 12. **destroyeth**. Pr *2:18, 19. *5:22, 23. *7:22, 23. *8:36. *9:16-18. Ezk *18:31. Ho 13:9. He *13:4. **soul**. Heb. *nephesh*, Ge +27:31.

33. **A wound**. Pr *5:9-11. Jg 16:19-21. Ps 38:1-8. 51:8. **and his**. Ge *49:4. 1 K *15:5. Ne *13:26. Ps 51, title. Mt *1:6.

34. **jealousy**. Pr 27:4mg. Nu 5:14. 25:11. Jg *19:29, 30. SS *8:6. 1 C 10:22.

35. **regard**. S#5375h. Heb. accept the face of. Pr 4:3. 7:13. 8:25. 18:5. 2 K 5:1mg. Is 2:9 (forgive). Ml 2:9mg.

PROVERBS 7

Repeated invitations to a familiar acquaintance with wisdom, as the preservative from strange women, 1-5. A fact related, to illustrate the artful way by which such women draw in the unwary to their destruction, 6-23. Another warning against all approaches to this vice, from its fatal effects on many eminent persons, 24-27.

1. **My son**. Pr 1:8. *3:1. **keep**. Lk *8:15. 11:28. Jn *14:23. 15:20. Re *1:3. 22:9. **lay**. Pr *2:1-7. 10:14. Dt 11:18. Jb *22:22.

2. **Keep**. Pr 4:4, 13. Le *18:5. Is √55:3. Jn 12:49, 50. 14:21. 15:14. 1 J *2:3, 4. 5:1-3. Re *22:14. **as the**. As the pupil of the eye, the hole or opening of the uveous coat, or iris, through which the rays of light pass, and falling upon the retina, there depict every object in its natural color, as upon a piece of white paper. Now the pupil of the eye being essentially necessary to sight, and easily injured, it is not only, in common with the other parts, deeply entrenched in the skull, ramparted with the forehead and cheek bones, defended by the eyebrows, eyelids, and eyelashes, and placed so as to be best protected by the hands, but by a wonderful mechanism is contracted or dilated by the muscular power of the iris, without which an excess of light would cause instant blindness. Dt 32:10. Ps 17:8. Zc *2:8.

3. **Bind them**. Pr *3:3. 6:21. Dt 6:8, 9. *11:18-20. Ps 143:10. Is 30:8. Je 17:1. *31:33. 2 C *3:3. **table of**. Ex +25:21.

4. **Say**. Pr *2:2-4. √4:6-8. **Thou**. Jb 17:14. SS 8:1. Mt *12:49, 50. Lk *11:27, 28.

5. **keep thee from**. Pr 2:16. 5:3. 6:24.

6. **at the**. Ge 26:8. 2 S 6:16. **casement**. *Eshnav*, rather a "lattice," so called from the Arabic *shanaba*, "to be cool," because of its use in keeping the apartments *cool*.

7. **the simple**. ♪108K54, Pr +1:4. Pr 1:4, 22, 32. 8:5. 14:*15, 18. 19:25. *22:3. 27:12. Ps *19:7. *119:130.

Ro 16:18, 19. **the youths**. Heb. the sons. **void**. Pr 6:32. 9:4, 16. 10:13. *12:11. *19:2. 24:30. Je *4:22. Mt 15:16. **understanding**. ♪12I1, Ge +3:7.

8. **street**. Heb. *shuk*, properly, "an alley," ✳S#7784h. Ec 12:4, 5. SS 3:2. See note at Am 5:16. **near her corner**. Pr *4:14, 15. *5:8. Jg 16:1. 2 S *11:2, 3. 1 C *6:18. 2 T *2:22. Ju 23.

9. **the twilight**. Ge *39:11. Jb *24:13-15. Ro 13:12-14. Ep *5:11, 12. 1 Th 5:7. 1 J 1:6. **evening**. Heb. evening of the day. Ex 12:6mg.

10. **the attire**. Ge 38:14, 15. 2 K 9:22, 30. Is *3:16-24. 23:16. Je 4:30. 1 T *2:9. Re 17:3-5. **subtil**. Ge *3:1. 2 C 11:2, 3.

11. **loud**. Pr *9:13. 25:24. 27:14, 15. *31:10-31. **her feet**. Ge 18:9. 1 T *5:13, 14. T *2:4, 5.

12. **without**. Heb. *chuts*, Am 5:16 (✛S#2351h, highways). Outside, or narrow streets. Pr 9:14, 15. *23:28. Je 2:20, 33, 36. 3:2. Ezk 16:24, 25, 31. Re 18:3, 23. **in the streets**. Heb. *rechob*, Am 5:16n (✳S#7339h, streets). Public square or broad streets. Pr 22:13.

13. **she**. Ge *39:7, 12. Nu 25:1, 6-8. 31:16. Ezk 16:33. Re *2:20. **with an impudent face said**. Heb. she strengthened her face and said. Is *50:7. Ezk *2:4, 6. *3:7-9. ♪121S3F1. Metonymy of the Adjunct B606, connected words and phrases. "To strengthen the face" is put for boldness or impudence.

14. **I have peace offerings with me**. Heb. Peace offerings are upon me. Pr *15:8. 17:1. *21:27. Le 7:15. +*23:19. Nu 15:3, 8. Dt 12:6, 7. Ps 50:14. Jon 2:9. **this**. 2 S 15:7-9. 1 K 21:9, 10. Jn *18:28. **vows**. Le +*23:38.

15. **came I forth**. 1 T 5:13-15. T ◐2:5. **meet**. ver. 10.

16. **decked**. SS 1:16. 3:7-10. Re *2:22. **fine linen**. Pr ◐31:22. 1 K 10:28. Is 19:9. Ezk 27:7.

17. **perfumed**. Ge 30:14, 15. SS *3:6. Is 57:7-9. **with**. Ps *45:8. SS 4:13, 14. 5:5.

18. **fill of love**. SS 1:2. 2:3. 4:10. **until morning**. Pr 27:14. Ge 1:5. 19:27. Jg 19:25-27. **with loves**. Pr 5:19. Ge 39:7, 12. Ho 8:9mg.

19. **the goodman**. Mt *20:11. *24:43. Lk 12:39. **he is gone**. Mt *24:48. Mk *13:34-36. Lk *12:45, 46.

20. **bag**. Pr 26:8. Ge 42:25. 1 S 25:29. **money**. Pr 2:4. 3:14. 8:10, 19. 10:20. **with him**. Heb. in his hand. **the day appointed**. *or*, the new moon. 2 Ch +2:4.

21. **With her**. ver. 5. Pr 5:3. Jg *16:15-17. Ps 12:2. **forced**. 1 S *28:23. 2 K 4:8. Mt 26:41. Lk *14:23. *24:29. Ac 16:15. 2 C 5:14.

22. **straightway**. Heb. suddenly. Pr 3:25. 6:15. 24:22. **as an ox**. Pr 14:4. Ac 14:13. **slaughter**. Pr 9:2mg. Ge 43:16mg. 1 S 25:11mg. **as a fool**. T#200-12. ver. 6-9, 23. Pr 1:7. 10:8, 14, 21. 11:29. 12:15. He +13:4 (T#405). Dr. Grey, making a slight alteration in the text, renders "as a dog to the chain, and as a deer, till a dart strike through his liver;" and Dr. Hunt, "Or as a hart boundeth into the toils, till a dart strike through his liver." The LXX., Chaldee, Syriac, and Arabic, concur in this interpretation. The circumstance of the dart, as applied to the deer, is beautiful and proper, which otherwise we are at a loss to dispose of; and this creature, of all others, was the most proper to be noticed on this occasion; for the usual representation which the Egyptians made of a man overthrown by flattery and fair speeches was the picture of a hart captivated and ensnared by the sound of music. **the correction**. Jb 13:27. Je 20:2. Ac 16:24.

23. **a dart**. Nu 25:8, 9. **as a bird**. Pr 1:17. Ec 7:26. *9:12. **knoweth**. Pr *9:18. Jg 16:6. Ho 4:11, 14. Ro 13:12, 13. **life**. Heb. *nephesh*, Ge +44:30.

24. **O ye children**. Pr 4:1. *5:7. *8:32, 33. 1 C 4:14, 15. Ga *4:19. 1 J *2:1.

25. **thine**. Pr *4:14, 15. *5:8. *6:25. 23:31-33. Mt *5:28. **go not astray**. Pr 5:23. Ps *119:176. Is √53:6.

26. **hath cast down**. Pr 6:33. Jg *16:21. 2 S 3:6-8, 27. *12:9-11. 1 K 11:1, 2. Ne *13:26. Ro 6:2, 3. 1 C 9:27. 10:8. 2 C 12:21. Ga 5:24. Col 3:1-5. 1 Th *4:3-5. 2 T *2:22. 1 P *2:11.

27. **Her house**. Pr *2:18, 19. *5:5. *9:18. Ec *7:26. **hell**. Heb. *sheol*, Ge +37:35. T#1009‡. 2 S 22:5, 6. Hab 2:5. Ro +6:23 (T#1010‡). 2 C +4:12 (T#1007‡). Re 6:8. **the chambers**. Pr 18:8mg. 20:27. 26:22mg. Dt 32:25mg. 1 K 20:30mg. 22:25mg. Is 14:18. Lk *16:23, 26. **death**. Pr 2:18. 5:5. 8:36. 14:12, 27. Jb +18:13. +38:17. Ps 55:4. 107:18. Is 28:15, 18. Hab 2:5. Re *21:8.

PROVERBS 8

Wisdom calls to the sons of men to hear her invaluable instructions, 1-11. She recommends herself as the giver of numberless blessings, 12-21. She declares her eternity: she was present at the Creation, as the foundation of Jehovah's counsels and the object of his delight, and as rejoicing in the sons of men, 22-31. She renews her exhortations to hear her words as the only way to obtain life and the favor of the Lord, and to avoid the willful ruin of men's own souls, 32-36.

1. **Doth not**. Pr *1:20, 21. 9:1-3. Is *49:1-6. *55:1-3. Mt 3:3. 4:17. *28:19, 20. Mk 13:10. *16:15, 16. Lk 24:47. Jn *7:37. Ac √1:8. 22:21. Ro *15:18-21. **wisdom**. T#1918. ver. 22-30. Mt 11:19. Lk 11:49. 1 C ✳1:24.

2. **standeth**. Ge 37:7. Ex 7:15. 15:8. Re *3:20. **the top**. ver. 23, 26. Pr 1:9, 21. 4:9. **high places** Pr 9:3, 14. Jg 5:18. **the way**. ver. 13, 22, 32. Pr 1:15, 31. **paths**. ver. 20. Pr 1:15. 3:17. 12:28.

3. **crieth**. Mt 22:9. Lk *14:21-23. Jn *18:20. Ac 5:20.

4. **Unto you**. Ps 49:1-3. *50:1. Mt 11:15. Mk *16:15. Jn *3:16. 7:37. 2 C 5:19, 20. Col *1:23, 28. 1 T *2:4-6. T *2:11, 12. Re *22:17.

5. **ye simple**. ♪108K54, Pr +1:4. Pr 1:22. 9:4. Ps *19:7. 94:8. Is 42:13. *55:1-3. Ac *26:18. 1 C 1:28. *6:9-11. Re 3:17, 18. **heart**. ♪121I1, Ge +3:7.

6. **for**. Pr *2:6, 7. *4:2, 20-22. *22:20, 21. Ps *19:7-11. 49:3. 1 C 2:6, 7. Col 1:26. **the opening**. Jb 33:1-3. Mt *5:2, etc. *7:28, 29. *13:35.

7. **my mouth**. Jb 36:4. Jn *1:17. *8:14, 45, 46. √14:6. *17:17. *18:37. Re 1:14. **an abomination to**. Heb. the abomination of. Pr *12:22. 16:12. 29:27.

8. **All**. Ps *12:6. Is *45:23. 63:1. **there**. ver. 13. Jn *7:46. **froward**. Heb. wreathed. Jb 5:13. **perverse**. Pr 2:15. 11:20. 17:20.

9. **all plain**. Pr 1:7. 2:6. *14:6. 15:14, 24. 17:24. 18:1, 2, 15. Dt 27:8. 30:11. Ps *19:7, 8. *25:12-14. *119:98-100, 104, 105, 130. Is *35:8. Am 3:10 (✳S#5228h). Mi *2:7. Mt *13:11, 12. Lk 10:21. Jn *6:45. √7:17. 1 C √2:14, 15. 2 T 2:7. Ja √1:5. 1 J 5:20. **that understandeth**. Pr 14:6. 17:10, +*24. 26:2, 7, 11. 28:+*5, 11. Da +*11:33n. **right**. Pr 2:7. 3:32. 11:3, 6, 11. **find knowledge**. Pr 11:27. 18:15.

10. **Receive my**. Pr *2:4, 5. *3:13, 14. 10:20. 16:16. *23:23. Ps 119:*72, 127, *162. Ec 7:11, 12. Lk *10:39.

Ac 3:6. 2 C 6:10. **knowledge**. T#391. Pr 4:*7-9, 13. 22:17. 23:12. Jb +21:14 (T#363). Lk +11:52 (T#633). **rather than**. Jb 28:15-28.

11. **wisdom**. T#344. Pr 3:13-18. √4:5-7. 16:16. 20:15. Jb 28:12-19, *28. Ps 19:10. +58:11 (T#630). 119:127. Mt *16:26. Jn 6:29. 1 C 1:20. 3:18. Ph *3:8, 9. He +*12:14.

12. **I wisdom**. Ps 104:24. Is 11:1, 2. √55:8, 9. Ro *11:33. Ep 1:*8, 11. 3:10. Col 1:19. *2:3. **prudence**. *or*, subtlety. ver. 5. Pr 1:4. Ex 21:14. Jsh 9:4. Mt 22:18-22. Jn 2:23, 24. Ep 1:7, 8. **knowledge**. Ex 31:3-6. 35:30-35. *36:1-4. 1 K 7:14. 1 Ch 28:12, 19. 2 Ch 2:13, 14. Is *28:26.

13. **The fear**. Pr *16:6. Ps *97:10. *101:3. *119:104, 128. Am 5:15. Ro *12:9. 1 Th *5:22. 2 T *2:19. **hate evil**. Ex 18:21. Ps 45:7. *97:10. 101:3. 119:104. 139:21, 22. Am 5:15. Mi ◐3:2. Ju 23. **pride**. Pr *6:16-19. 1 S *2:3. Ps *5:4, 5. 138:6. Zc *8:17. Mt 20:28. Lk 22:27. 1 P *5:5. **the froward**. Pr *4:24. 6:12. *10:31. **mouth**. ⨍171Q17. Synecdoche of the Part B647. The mouth is put for the whole man, in respect of his speaking.

14. **Counsel**. Is *9:6. 40:13, 14. Je 32:19. Jn 1:9. Ro *11:33, 34. 1 C *1:24, 30. Ep 1:11. Col *2:3. 1 J 2:1. Re 3:18. 19:16. **sound**. Pr *2:6, 7. Ro 1:22. **understanding**. Is 40:28, 29. **I have**. Pr 24:5. Jb *9:4. Ps 89:19. Ec *7:19. *9:16-18. Is *26:4. Col 1:24.

15. **By**. 1 S 9:17. *16:1. 1 Ch 28:5. Je *27:5-7. Da *2:21. *4:25, 32. 5:18, etc. *7:13, 14. Mt *28:18. Ro *13:1-6. Re 19:16. **decree**. 1 K *3:9, 28. 5:7. 10:9. Ps *72:1-4. 99:4. Is 1:26. *32:1, 2. Je *33:15. Re *19:11.

16. **princes**. Pr 19:10. 28:2. Ge 12:15. **rule**. Pr 29:4. 2 Ch 1:10. Est 1:22. Is 32:1. **nobles**. Pr 17:7, 26. 19:6. 25:7. **judges**. Pr 29:14. Ge *18:25. Ex 2:14.

17. **I love**. 1 S *2:30. Ps *91:14. Jn *14:21, 23. *16:27. 1 J *4:19. **those**. Ps 63:1. Ec *12:1. Is 45:19. √55:6. Je √29:13. Mt √6:33. *7:7, 8. Mk *10:14. Lk √13:24, 25. 2 C *6:2. Ja *1:5.

18. **Riches**. ⨍22D5I. Anthropomorphism B893. God is spoken of as to circumstances connected with His person: riches. For other instances of this figure see Ro 2:4. 9:23. 10:12. 11:33. 2 C *8:9. Ep 1:7, 18. 2:4, 7. 3:8, 16. Ph 4:19. Col 1:27. **and honor**. Pr *3:16. √4:7-9. Is 55:2. Ja *2:5. **durable**. Ps *39:6. Ec *5:14-16. Mt *6:19, 20. Lk *10:42. *12:20, 21, 33. *16:11, 12. Ro 5:17. 2 C 6:10. Ep *3:8. Ph √4:19. 1 T *6:17-19. Ja *5:1-3. Re *3:18. **and righteousness**. Pr *11:4. Mt √6:33. Ph *3:8, 9.

19. **My fruit**. ver. *10. Pr *3:14, 15. Ps *19:10. Ec *7:12.

20. **lead**. *or*, walk. Pr √3:6. *4:11, 12. *6:22. Ps *23:3. *25:4, 5. √32:8. +104:10mg. Is *2:3. *49:10. 55:4. Jn √10:3, 27, 28. Re *7:17. **in the midst**. Pr *4:25-27. Dt *5:32.

21. **to inherit**. ver. *18. Pr 1:13. 6:31. Ge *15:14. 1 S 2:8. Mt *25:46. Jn 1:1, etc. Ro *8:17. He *10:34, 35. 1 P *1:4, 5. **fill**. Ps *16:11. Ep *3:19, 20. Re *21:7.

22. **possessed**. Pr *3:19. Ge 4:1. 25:10. Jn *1:1, 2. Col *1:17. Heb. acquired. S#7069h. Rendered "possessed" at Ps 139:13; Pr 8:22; Je 32:15. This verb occurs elsewhere in Proverbs in the following passages: Pr 1:5. *4:5, 7. 15:32. 16:16. 17:16. 18:15. 19:8. 20:14. 22:23. It is frequently rendered by "get" or "buy" (Pr 4:5, 7; Ge 4:1. Pr 23:23; Ge 47:19; Ru 4:4, 8; Je 32:7, 8, 8, 25). The Syriac (compare Lamsa's rendering: "The Lord created me as the first of his creations") and LXX. (compare Charles Thomson's rendering: "The

Lord created me, the beginning of His ways, for His works" or the rendering in Bagster's LXX.: "The Lord made me the beginning of his ways for his works") render it "created." This rendering is significant to the Arian controversy of the fourth century and since: is Wisdom a personification of Christ? and if so, is Christ then a created being? If Christ is a created being, then he could not be eternal, or God, as the second member of the Trinity. Since the Hebrew verb does not mean "create," as an examination of its occurrences and renderings will show, this text does not furnish evidence to support the notion that Jesus Christ is, in his pre-incarnate nature, a created being. Compare Pr 8:30. Mi +*5:2. Lk 11:49. Jn √17:5. 1 C 1:24. He *13:8. Re ◐*3:14. **beginning**. Pr 1:7. 3:9. 4:7. 17:14. **before**. Mi +5:2 (✚S#6924h).

23. **set up**. *or*, anointed. Ge *1:26. Ps 2:6. Is 29:10. Mi +*5:2. Jn *17:24. Ep 1:10, 11. 1 J 1:1, 2. **everlasting**. Heb. *olam*, Ge +17:7. **from the beginning**. Jn *1:1-3, 14, 18. √8:58. +*10:30. √17:5. Ph *2:6-11. 1 P 1:20. 1 J 1:1, 2. Re 1:11. **or ever**. ver. 25. 2 K 19:25. Mi +5:2 (✚S#6924h). Jn 17:5.

24. **I was**. Ps 2:7. Jn *1:14. √3:16. 5:20. He *1:5, 6. 1 J *4:9. **fountains**. Heb. *mayan*, Ge +7:11 (✸S#4599h).

25. **Before the mountains**. Jb *15:7, 8. *38:4-11. Ps *90:2. *102:25-28. Is 53:8. He *1:10.

26. **as yet**. Ge 1:1, etc. **fields**. *or*, open places. Pr 1:20. 5:16. 7:12. **highest part**. *or*, chief part. ver. 2, 23.

27. **When**. Ge 1:6. **he prepared**. Ps *33:6. *103:19. *136:5. Je *10:12. Col *1:16. He *1:2. **compass**. *or*, circle. Jb 22:14. Is 40:11, 12, √22.

28. **established**. or, strengthened. Pr 31:17. Dt 15:7. **clouds**. Pr 3:20. Jb 35:5. 36:28. **strengthened**. Jg 3:10. 6:2mg. **the fountains**. Ge 7:11.

29. **he gave**. Ge *1:9, 10. Jb 38:8-11. Ps *33:7. *104:9. Je 5:22. **when he appointed**. Jb 38:4-7.

30. **Then**. Col 1:16. **one**. Jn *1:1-3, 18. 16:28-30. **I was daily**. Is *42:1. Mt *3:17. *17:5. Jn *12:28. Col 1:13.

31. **and my**. Ps *16:3. 40:6-8. Jn *4:34. *13:1. 2 C *8:9.

32. **for blessed**. Ps *1:1-4. *119:1, 2. 128:1, 2. Lk +*11:28.

33. **Hear**. Pr 1:2, 3, 8. *4:1. 5:1. +*19:20. Dt 10:12, 13. Is *55:1-3. Lk +*11:28. Ro *10:16, 17. Ja 1:25. **refuse**. Pr 1:21-23. 1 S +√25:17. Ps 81:11, 12. Je 6:16. *44:16, 17. Lk 19:14. Ac 7:35-37. *13:46. *12:25.

34. **that heareth**. Is 55:3. Jn √5:24. Re √3:20. **watching**. Pr 1:21-23. 2:3, 4. 3:13, 18. Ex 29:42. 33:11. 1 K 17:1. Ps *27:4. 84:10. *92:13. Mt *7:24. *18:20. Lk 1:6. 2:37. *10:39. +*11:28. Jn √8:31, 32. Ac *2:42. √17:11, 12. Ja *1:22-25. Re 3:2. **waiting**. 1 Ch 6:33.

35. **whoso**. Pr *1:33. *3:13-18. Jn 1:4. √3:16, 36. √14:6. Ph *3:8, 9. Col 3:3. 1 J √5:11, 12. **obtain**. Heb. bring forth. Pr 3:13mg. **favor**. Pr 12:2. Ep 1:6.

36. **sinneth against**. Pr *1:31. *15:32. 20:2. Jn *3:19, 20. Ac *13:46. He *2:3. *10:29. **soul**. Heb. *nephesh*, Ge +27:31. **all they**. ver. 33. Pr *5:11, 12, 22, 23. Ezk *18:31. *33:11. Jn *15:23, 24. 1 C *16:22. **love**. ⨍121C2C3, Ps +109:17. That is, so live and act as to injure life and accelerate death. **death**. Pr 21:6. 29:24.

PROVERBS 9

The feast prepared by Wisdom, and her invitations given, 1-6. The different reception given them: with instructions given to those who publish them; and the contrary end of the wise and scornful, 7-12. The foolish woman's feast and invitations, and the doom of her guests, 13-18.

1. **Wisdom.** The infinite and eternal *Wisdom* of God, which has so framed the universe as to exhibit a scene of grandeur and stability, and made ample provision for the innumerable beings by which it is inhabited. **builded.** Mt 16:18. 1 C *3:9-15. Ep 2:20-22. 1 T √3:15. He *3:3-6. 1 P *2:5, 6. **pillars.** 1 K 7:2, 3, 6, 21. Ga *2:9. Re *3:12.

2. **killed.** Is 25:6. Mt *22:3, 4, etc. 1 C 5:7, 8. **beasts.** Heb. *killing.* Pr 7:22. Ge +43:16mg. **mingled.** ver. 5. Pr 23:30. Lk *14:17.

3. **sent.** Mt *22:3, 4, 9. Lk 11:49. *14:17, 21-23. Ro 10:15. 2 C *5:20, 21. **maidens.** Pr 27:27. 31:15. Ge +*24:14 (✱S#5291h). **she crieth.** ver. 14. Pr *1:20-23. 8:1-3. Jn *7:37. *18:20. Re *3:20.

4. **simple.** √108K54, Pr +1:4. ver. *16. Pr 1:22. *6:32. 8:5. Ps *19:7. *119:130. Mt 11:25. Re 3:17, 18. *22:17. **understanding.** √121I1, Ge +3:7.

5. **eat.** ver. 2, 17. Ps *22:26, 29. SS 5:1. Is *55:1-3. Je 31:12-14. Mt *26:26-28. Jn 6:*27, 49-58.

6. **Forsake.** Pr 4:14, 15. *13:20. Ps 26:4-6. 45:10. *119:115. Ho 7:11. Ac 2:40. 2 C *6:17. Ja *4:4. Re 18:4. **in.** Pr *4:11. *10:17. Mt *7:13, 14. Lk 13:24.

7. **reproveth.** Pr 15:12. Ge 19:8, 9. 1 K 18:17. 21:20. *22:24, 27. 2 Ch 24:20-22. 25:15, 16. *36:16. Mt +*7:6.

8. **Reprove not.** Pr 23:9. *29:1. Nu 14:6-10. 1 K *22:8. Mt +*7:6. *15:14. He *6:4-8. **rebuke a wise man.** Pr *13:18. *28:23. Ex *18:17-24. Le +*19:17. 2 S 12:7-14. 1 K 1:23, 32-40. Ps 141:5. Ga 2:11-14. 2 P 3:15, 16.

9. **Give instruction.** Pr *1:5. 25:12. Ho *6:3. Mt *13:11, 12. 2 P *3:18. 1 J 2:20, 21. *5:13.

10. **The fear.** √138C, Ge +22:14. Pr *1:7. Jb *28:28. Ps *111:10. Ec 12:13. **the knowledge.** Pr *2:5. *30:3. 1 Ch +*28:9. Mt 11:27. Jn *17:3. 1 J 5:20.

11. **by me.** Pr 3:+*2, 16. 10:27. Dt 6:2.

12. **If thou.** Pr 16:26. Jb *22:2, 3, 21. 35:6, 7. Is 28:22. Ezk 18:20. 2 P *3:3, 4, 16. **thou alone.** Nu +*32:23. Ga *6:5, 7, 8.

13. **clamorous.** Pr *7:11. 21:9, 19. 1 T 6:4mg. **simple.** √108K54, Pr +1:4.

14. **she.** Pr 7:10-12. **in.** ver. 3.

15. **To call.** Pr *7:13-15, 25-27. *23:27, 28.

16. **Whoso is.** ver. *4. **understanding.** √121I1, Ge +3:7.

17. **Stolen.** Pr *20:17. 23:31, 32. Ge *3:6. Ro *7:8. Ja *1:14, 15. **eaten in secret.** Heb. *of secrecies.* Pr *7:18-20. *30:20. 2 K *5:24-27. Ep *5:12.

18. **he.** Pr *1:7. Ps 82:5. 2 P *3:5. **the dead.** Pr *2:18, 19. *5:5. 6:26. *7:27. **hell.** Heb. *sheol,* +Ge 37:35.

PROVERBS 10

Miscellaneous maxims, chiefly recommending righteousness, piety, industry; and the government of the tongue, and improvement of the gift of speech, 1-32.

1. **proverbs.** Pr *1:1. 25:1. 1 K *4:32. Ec *12:9. **A wise.** ver. 5. Pr 13:1, 24. *15:20. *17:21, 25. 19:13,

26. 20:20. 23:15, 16, 24, 25. *29:3, 15. Ec 2:19. √132B. Parallelism (Simple) B351, antithetic or opposite, when the words are contrasted in the two or more lines, being opposed in sense the one to the other. Here, "wise" contrasts with "foolish." For another instance of this frequent figure, see Pr 27:6. **glad father.** √63J1, Ge +13:9. Ge 45:28. 46:30. **heaviness of.** Ge *26:34, 35. 1 S 2:24. **mother.** √63J1, Ge +13:9.

2. **Treasures.** Pr *11:4. 1 K 21:4-24. 2 K 5:22-27. Ps *49:6-10. Is 10:2, 3. Zp 1:18. Lk *12:15-21. *16:22, 23. Ro 2:5. Ja *5:1-3. **profit nothing.** ver. 4, 15, 22. Pr 11:4, 24, 28. 13:8, 11. 14:20. 18:11, 23. 19:1, 4, 7, 22. 20:21. 21:6, 20. 22:27. Ezk *7:19. Mt *27:3-5. Ro *6:21. **but.** Pr *12:28. Da *4:27. Ro 5:21. Ph *3:9. **death.** √121G, Ge +31:1.

3. **will.** Jb 5:20. Ps 10:14. 33:19. 34:9, 10. *37:3, 19, 25. Is 33:16. Mt *6:30-33. Lk 12:22-24, 31. He *13:5, 6. **not suffer.** ver. 29. Pr 11:18, 21, 23, 25, 31. 12:2. 13:21, 22. 14:9, 11, 14. 15:6, 10, 25. 19:29. 20:30. 22:4. **soul.** Heb. *nephesh,* Ge +12:15. **to famish.** Mt *6:25, 26. Ph 4:18. **but.** Jb 20:5-8, 15, 20-22, 28. Hab 2:6-8. Zp *1:18. **the substance of the wicked.** *or,* the wicked for their wickedness. Pr *14:32.

4. **becometh poor.** T#1867. Pr *6:6-11. *11:24. 12:24. 19:15, 24. 20:4, 13. *24:30-34. Ec 10:18. Je 48:10. Mt *13:12. *25:29. Jn *6:27. He 6:11, 12. 2 P 1:5-10. **with a slack hand.** That is, slothfully and negligently. Je +*48:10. Ro +*12:11. **but.** Pr 13:4. 21:5. 1 C √15:58. **diligent.** T#922. Pr 12:11, 24, 27. 13:4, 11. 14:23. 21:5. 22:29. √28:19, 20. Ro +*12:11. Ep √6:5, 6. Col √3:22, 23. 1 Th 4:11. 2 Th *3:10. **maketh rich.** Thus "my responsibility," diligence; compare ver. ◐22. Ps √62:10. 1 T ◐+*6:9. 2 P √1:5-11.

5. **He.** √138C, Ge +22:14. **gathereth.** Pr *6:6-8. 30:25. Ge 41:46-56. Is √55:6, 7. Mt 20:30. Ga *6:10. **that sleepeth.** Mt 25:5, 8-10. **in harvest.** Je 8:20. **a son.** Pr 12:4. 17:2. 19:26.

6. **Blessings.** Pr *11:26. 24:25. *28:20. Dt *28:1-6. Jb 29:13. Mt +5:8. 2 T *1:16-18. **head.** √171Q12, Jg +5:30. **but.** ver. 11. Est 7:8. Ps *107:42. Ro *3:19. **violence covereth.** ver. 9, 10, 11, 16, 21, 25, 27, 30. Pr 11:5, 6, 8, 19, 30. 12:5, 26. 16:27, 28, 29, 30. 17:4. 21:8, 12, 26, 29. 22:10.

7. **memory.** 1 K 11:36. 2 K 19:34. 2 Ch 24:16. Ps ◐+13:3. *112:6. ◐+*146:4. Ob ◐16. Mt ◐*25:41. 26:13. Mk *14:9. Lk *1:48. 2 T 1:5. Re ◐20:4, 5. ◐21:4. **the name.** Jb 18:17. 27:23. Ps 9:5, 6. 109:13, 15. Ec *8:10. Je *17:13.

8. **wise in heart.** ver. 13, 14, 23. Pr 12:1, 8, 15, 23. 13:15, 16. 14:*6, 7, 8, 15, 16, 18, 24, 33. 15:7, 14, 21. 17:10, 12, 24. **will receive.** Pr *1:5. *9:9. *12:1. 14:8. Ps 119:34. 143:8-10. Ja 3:13. **but.** ver. *10. Pr *12:13. *13:3. *14:23. **prating fool.** Heb. a fool of lips. ver. 10. Jg +7:22mg. Ec *10:12. **fall.** *or,* be beaten. ver. 10mg. Pr *18:6, 7.

9. **that walketh.** Pr *28:18. Ps *23:4. 25:21. 26:11, 12. 37:37. *84:11. Is *33:15, 16. Da 3:19-29. Ga 2:13, 14. 1 J 3:18-22. **but.** Pr *17:20. Lk *12:1, 2. Ac 5:1-10. 1 C 4:5.

10. **that.** Pr *6:13. Jb 15:12. Ps 35:19. **but.** ver. *8. Pr *18:6, 7, 21. **prating.** ver. 8mg. Jg +7:22mg. **fall.** *or,* be beaten. ver. 8mg. Ho 4:14mg. 3 J 10.

11. **mouth of a.** ver. *20, *21, *32. Pr *13:14. *15:7. *16:22-24. 18:4. 20:15. Ps *37:30, 31. 45:2. Jn 4:14. 7:38. Ep *4:29. **but.** See on ver. *6. Ps 107:42. Ec *10:12-14. Mt *12:34-37. Ja *3:5-8.

12. **Hatred**. Pr 11:1, 2, 3, 9, 17. 12:9, 16, 25. 13:7. 14:17, 29. 15:12, 22, 33. 16:18. 17:9, 11, 17. 18:1, 12, 24. 19:2, 6, 11. 20:1, 6, 11, 22. 21:24. **stirreth up**. Pr *15:18. *16:27. *28:25. *29:22. Ja *4:1. **love covereth**. Pr *17:9. Ge 45:5, 8. Ps *106:33n. Mt 18:21-35. 1 C *13:4. Ga 6:1. Col 3:13. Ja *5:20. 1 P *4:8.

13. **In**. ⌐138C, Ge +22:14. **the lips**. ver. *11, *21. Pr *15:7, 23. 20:15. 2 S 12:9-11. 1 K 3:12. Ec *10:12. Is *50:4. Lk *4:22. **but**. 1 K 12:13-24. **a rod**. ver. 10. 7:22. *17:10. 26:3. *27:22. Ps *32:9. He 12:6, 7. **understanding**. Heb. heart. ⌐121I1, Ge +3:7. Pr 6:32mg.

14. **lay up**. Pr *1:5. *9:9. *18:1, 15. *19:8, Mt *12:35. *13:44, 52. 2 C *4:6, 7. **the mouth**. ver. 8, 10. Pr *13:3. *18:6, 7. *21:23. Ex 5:2. Ps 52:1, 4, 5. Lk 12:19, 20.

15. **rich**. Pr *‖18:11. Jb 31:24, 25. Ps *49:6. √52:7. Ec *7:12. Je *9:23. Mk *10:24. Lk 12:19. 1 T *6:17. **the destruction**. Pr 14:20. *19:7. *22:22, 23. Mi 2:1, 2. **poor**. T#521. Pr 14:20. 19:7. *22:7. Ec *9:16. Ja ◐2:5.

16. **labor**. Pr √11:30. Is *3:10, 11. Jn *6:27. Ro 8:13. 1 C 10:31. √15:58. Ga √6:7-9. Ph *2:12, 13. He √6:10. **the fruit**. Mt *7:17, 18. *12:33, 34. *15:19. Ro *6:23. 2 T 2:17, 18. 3:13.

17. **the way**. Pr *3:1, +2, 18. 4:4, 13. 12:1. *22:17-19. Mt *7:24-27. Lk +*11:28. He *2:1. 2 P *1:5-11. **he that**. Pr 1:25, 26, 30. 5:12. *15:10. *29:1. 2 Ch 25:15, 16. He 12:25. **refuseth reproof**. Pr +8:33. 13:13, 14, 18. 16:32. **erreth**. or, causeth to err. Ec 5:6. Is 3:12. 9:16. 30:28. Mi 3:5.

18. **that hideth**. Pr *26:24-26. 1 S 18:21, 22, 29. 2 S *3:27. *11:8-15. 13:23-29. *20:9, 10. Ezr 4:1-10. Ps *5:9. 12:2. *55:21. Lk *20:20, 21. Jn 13:34, 35. **that uttereth**. Ps 15:3. 50:20. +101:5. **slander**. Pr 18:8. 19:5, 9, 28. **fool**. T#200-17.

19. **In**. ⌐138C, Ge +22:14. **the multitude**. Ec *5:3. 10:13, 14. Ja *3:2. **but**. Pr *17:27, 28. Ps *39:1. Ja *1:19. 3:2. **refraineth**. ver. 20, 31, 32. Pr 11:12, 13. 12:6, 13, 14, 18. 13:2, 3. 14:3, 23. 15:1, 2, 4, 23, 28. 16:21, 23, 24. 17:27, 28. 18:4, 6, 7, 13, 20, 21. 20:19. 21:23. 22:11. Is +*58:13. **is wise**. Jb *13:5. Ps *141:3. Col *4:6. Ja *1:19. *3:2.

20. **tongue**. ⌐121BB, Ps +5:9. Pr *12:18. *15:2, 4. 16:13. *25:11, 12, 15. 31:26. Is 35:6. Mt *12:35. **the heart**. Pr *23:7. Ge *6:5. *8:21. Je *17:9. Mt *12:34.

21. **The lips**. Pr 15:7. Ep *4:29. Col *3:16. **feed many**. Pr 11:25. *12:18. *15:4. Jb *4:3, 4. √23:12. 29:21, 22. Ps 37:30. Ec *12:9, 10. Je *3:15. √15:16. Da *12:3mg. Jn 6:11. *21:15-17. 1 P *5:2. **fools**. Pr *1:29, 31. *5:12, 23. Ho *4:6. Mt *13:19. Jn *3:19, 20. Ro 1:28. **wisdom**. Heb. heart. ⌐121I1, Ge +3:7. Pr 6:32mg. *17:16.

22. **The blessing**. T#764. Pr *15:16. Ex 23:25. Dt 26:11. 28:3-6, 8. 1 Ch *13:14. Ps 3:8. *37:16. Ec *2:26. 3:13. *5:19, 20. **it maketh rich**. Thus "God's responsibility," compare ver. ◐4. Pr √28:20. Ge *12:2. 13:2. 14:23. *24:35. 26:12. Dt *8:17, 18. 1 S *2:7, 8. 2 Ch *25:24. Ps *37:22. 107:38. 113:7, 8. 1 T ◐+*6:9. **he**. Pr *20:21. 28:22. Jsh 6:18. 7:1, etc. 1 K 21:19. 2 K 5:26, 27. Jb *27:8, etc. Hab 2:6-12. Zc 5:4. Ro 8:38, 39. 1 T 6:6. Ja *5:1-5.

23. **as sport**. Pr *14:9. *15:21. *26:18, 19. Ec 7:6. *11:9. **fool**. T#200-20. Pr +14:13 (T#479). Ec *7:4. *11:9. **wisdom**. Heb. heart. ⌐121I1, Ge +3:7. Pr 6:32mg. *17:16.

24. **fear**. Jb +*3:25. 15:20, 21. Ps ◐+*34:4. Is 8:12. Je ◐+*10:5. He *10:27. **shall come**. ver. 28. Pr 11:27, 30. 12:3, 7, 12, 20, 21, 28. 13:6, 9, 10. 14:19, 22, 30,

32. 16:20. 17:19, 20. 18:3. 19:16. 20:7. 21:5, 16, 17, 18, 21. 22:5. **the desire**. Ps 21:2. *37:4. *145:19. Mt +*5:6. Jn 14:18. *16:24. 1 J √5:14, 15.

25. **the whirlwind**. Pr 1:27. Jb 27:19-21. Ps *37:9, 10. *58:9. 73:18-20. Is 40:24. Je 23:19. Ho 13:3. **an**. ver. *30. Ps *15:5. Mt *7:24, 25. *16:18. Ep *2:20. 1 T *6:19. 2 T *2:19. 2 P +*1:10. 1 J √2:17. **everlasting**. Heb. *olam*, Ge +17:7.

26. **vinegar**. Pr 25:13, 20. **as smoke**. As the acidity of vinegar causes unpleasantness and pain to the teeth, and by softening and dissolving the alkali of the bone, impairs their texture and renders them incapable of mastication; and as smoke, by irritating the tender vessels, causes the eyes to smart and prevents distinct vision; so a sluggish messenger is a continual vexation and loss to those by whom he is employed. Is 65:5. **so**. Mt *25:26. Ro *12:11. He *6:12. **the sluggard**. T#1822. Pr 12:11, 24, 27. 13:4. 14:4, 23. 15:19. 16:26. 18:9. 19:15, 24. 20:4, 13. 21:25. 22:13. Ex ◐22:29. Ec 11:4. Re *3:15, 16.

27. **fear**. Pr 3:2, 16. 9:11. 14:27. Ps 21:4. *34:11-13. *91:16. **prolongeth**. Heb. addeth. Pr +*3:2. **the years**. Jb 15:32, 33. 22:15, 16. Ps *55:23. Ec +*7:17. Is +*38:10. *65:20. Je *17:11. Lk *12:20.

28. **hope**. Ps *16:9. *73:24-26. *97:11. 147:11. Is 12:3. 35:10. Ro 5:2. *12:12. *15:13. 2 Th 2:16. T 1:2. He 6:19. **but**. Pr *11:7. *14:32. Jb +*8:13. 11:20. +36:18. Ps 112:10. Mt *7:22, 23. Lk *16:23-26. He +*9:27.

29. **way**. Ne 8:10. Jb 17:9. Ps 84:5, 7. Is *40:29, 31. Zc *10:12. Ph *4:13. **but**. Pr ‖21:15. Jb *31:3. Ps *1:6. *36:12. *37:20. *92:7. Mt *7:22, 23. Lk 13:26, 27. Ro *2:8, 9.

30. **never**. ver. *25. Ps 15:1, 2. *16:8. *37:22, 28, 29. 112:6. *125:1. Ro *8:35-39. 2 P √1:10, 11. **the wicked**. Ps *37:9, 10, 22. *52:5. Ezk 33:24-26. Mi 2:9, 10. Mt *21:41.

31. **mouth**. ver. *11, *13, *20, *21. Jb 6:25. Ps *37:30. Ja 3:13. **the froward**. Ps *31:18. *63:11. 120:3, 4.

32. **know**. ⌐155A, Ge +31:35. Ec *12:10. Da 4:27. T *2:8. **but**. Pr 11:11. *12:6, 18. *15:2, 28. *18:6-8. **frowardness**. Heb. frowardnesses. ver. 31. Pr 2:12, 14.

PROVERBS 11

Maxims of wisdom, chiefly contrasting honesty, humility, faithfulness, and liberality, with the opposite vices, 1-31.

1. **A false balance is**. Heb. Balances of deceit are. Pr 16:11. 20:10, 23. Le 19:35, 36. Dt *25:13-16. Ps *66:18. Ho 12:7. Am 8:5, 6. Mi 6:10, 11. Mt *7:12. Ph *4:8. 1 Th 4:6. **a just weight**. Heb. a perfect stone. ⌐121D7, Ex +7:19. Pr 16:11. 1 Ch 23:29n. Ezk 45:10-12.

2. **pride**. Pr *3:34, 35. 16:18, 19. 18:12. Da *4:30-32. Lk *14:8-11. *18:14. **cometh shame**. Ge 3:5, 7. Nu 12:2, 9, 10. **but**. Pr 15:33. Lk 14:10, 11. 1 C *8:1, 2.

3. **The integrity**. ver. 5. Pr 2:1, 2, 9. 3:3, 4. 4:23, 25-27. 10:9. 12:22. 13:6. 14:30. 15:21. 16:11. 19:1. 20:7. 21:3. Ps 15:1-5. 24:3-5. 25:21. *26:1. Is 33:15, 16. Ezk 18:5, 7-9. Mi +*6:8. Mt 6:22. Lk 3:13, 14. 6:31. 16:10. Jn *7:17. Ac +*6:3. 24:16. Ro 13:1. 2 C 4:1, 2. Ep 6:14. Ph 4:8. Col 3:22, 23. 1 T 1:5. T 1:7-9. 1 P 2:11,

12. 3:13. 1 J 5:18. **the perverseness.** Pr 21:7. 28:18. Ec 7:17. Is *1:28.

4. **Riches.** Pr *10:2. Jb *36:18, 19. Ps *49:6-8. Ezk *7:19. Zp +*1:11, 18. Mt *16:26. Lk *12:20. **day of wrath.** Jb 20:28. +*21:30. Ezk √7:19. Zp +*1:11, 18. Ro +*2:5. Ja +*5:1. **but.** Pr *12:28. Ge 7:1. 2 K 20:3-6. Ezk 14:20. 18:27. Ro 5:17. 1 T +*4:8.

5. **direct.** Heb. rectify. Pr 3:6. 9:6. 15:21. **but.** ver. *3. Pr 1:31, 32. *5:22. 2 S 17:23. Est *7:3-10. Ps *9:15, 16. Mt *27:4, 5.

6. **righteousness.** Ge 30:33. 31:37. 1 S *12:3, 4. **but.** Pr *5:22. Nu 22:32. 2 S 15:6. 18:14. 1 K *2:32, 33, 44. Ps *7:16. *9:15. Ec *10:8.

7. **expectation shall perish.** ƒ96C2, Ge +45:9. Pr +*10:28. 13:12, 19. *14:32. Ex 15:9, 10. Jb *8:13, 14. *11:20. Ps +*146:4. Ezk 28:9. Lk *12:19, 20. **the hope of unjust.** Ps 49:17-19. Is 1:28. Zp 1:18.

8. **righteous is delivered.** Pr *21:18. Ex 14:21-23, 26. Est 5:14. *7:9, 10. Is 43:3, 4. Da *6:23, 24. **out of trouble.** 2 K *22:20n. 23:29. 2 Ch 35:20-24. Is *57:1. Da 3:22. Lk +*21:36.

9. **An hypocrite.** Or rather, as *chanaiph* properly signifies, a wicked, profligate person, an infidel. 2 S +*15:6. 1 K *13:18-22. *22:6, 20-23. Jb *8:13. 34:30. Ps 55:12, 20, *21. Mt *7:15. *15:5-14. Ac *20:30. 2 C *11:13-15. 2 Th *2:8-10. 1 T *4:1-3. 2 P *2:1-3. **through.** Pr 2:10-16. *4:5, 6. *6:23, 24. 2 S 16:1-4. Mt 7:15. 24:11, 24. Mk *13:14, 22, 23. 2 C 11:3. Ep *4:13, 14. 2 P *3:16-18. 1 J 2:20, 21, 27.

10. **it goeth.** Pr 28:12, 28. Est 8:15, 16. **the righteous.** ver. 11, 14, 26. Pr 14:34. 21:15. **when.** Ex *15:21. Jg 5:31. Jb 27:23. Ps *58:10, 11. Re *19:1-7. **shouting.** Pr ◑29:2. Am ◐5:13.

11. **the blessing.** Pr *14:34. *29:8. Ge *41:38-42. *45:8. Jg 5:31. 2 Ch 32:20-23. Jb 22:30. Ec *9:15. **it.** 2 S 20:1. Est *3:8-15. *9:1-16. Ja *3:6.

12. **that.** Jg 9:27-29, 38. Ne 4:2-4. Ps 123:3, 4. Mt 7:3-5. Lk *16:14. *18:9. Jn *7:48-52. 1 C 4:7. **void of wisdom.** Heb. destitute of heart. Pr 6:32mg. 7:7. 9:4, 16. **a man.** Pr *10:19. 1 S 10:27. 2 K 18:36. Ga 6:1. 1 P *2:23.

13. **A talebearer.** Heb. He that walketh *being* a talebearer. Pr *20:19. Le *19:16, 17. 1 Th 4:11. 2 Th 3:10-12. 1 T 5:13. **revealeth.** Pr *25:9. *26:20-22. Ne 6:17-19. **he.** Pr *11:2. Jsh 2:14, 20. Je 38:27. **spirit.** Heb. *ruach*, Ge +41:8.

14. **no counsel is.** Pr *15:22. 16:22. ||24:6. 1 K *12:1-19. Ec 10:10. Is 19:11-14. Ac 15:6, etc.

15. **He.** ƒ138C, Ge +22:14. **that is surety.** Pr 6:1-5. 17:18. 20:16. *22:26, 27. **smart.** Heb. be sore broken. Pr 13:20. Is 1:27. *42:21. 53:10. Jn 10:15, 17, 18. Ga 3:13. Re 5:12. **suretiship.** Heb. those that strike hands. Pr 3:24 (sweet). 6:1. 17:18. 20:16. 22:26. 27:13. Jb 17:3.

16. **gracious.** ver. 22. Pr 12:4. 18:22. 19:14. 21:9, 19. *31:30, 31. Ru 3:11. 1 S 25:32, 33. 2 S 20:16-22. Est 9:25. Mt *26:13. Lk 8:3. *10:42. *21:2-4. Ac *9:39. *16:14, 15. Ro 16:2-4, 6. 1 P *3:1-4. 2 J 1. **and strong.** Ps +86:14 (✱S#6184h). Lk *11:21, 22.

17. **merciful.** Ps *41:1-4. *112:4-9. Is 32:7, 8. 57:1. *58:7-12. Da 4:27. Mt +*5:7. *6:14, 15. *25:34-40. Lk *6:36. 2 C *9:6-14. Ph 4:17. **soul.** Heb. *nephesh*, Ge +27:31. **but.** Pr *15:27. Jb 20:19-23. Ec 4:8. Ja 2:13. 5:1-5.

18. **wicked.** Pr 1:18. *5:22. Ge 3:4, 5. Jb 27:13-23. Ec 10:8. Is 59:5-8. Ro 6:21. Ep 4:22. **but.** Pr +*3:27.

22:8. Ps *126:5, 6. Ho *10:12, 13. Ga √6:8, 9. He *6:10. Ja 3:18. **righteousness.** Ps *112:9. 2 C 9:9.

19. **righteousness.** ver. 4. Pr 10:16. *12:28. *19:23. Ge 19:16. Is 3:10. Ac *10:35. 1 J 3:7, 10. **he that pursueth evil.** Pr 1:16-19. 7:22, 23. 8:36. 1 Ch +28:9. Ro *2:8, 9.

20. **of a froward.** Pr *6:14, 16-19. *8:13. Ps 18:25, 26. **abomination.** Pr 15:8, 9, 26, 29. Ps 11:5-7. **upright.** Pr *2:7. *15:8. 16:17. 21:29. Ps 11:7. *51:6. 140:13. **his delight.** Ps 147:11. Zp 3:17.

21. **hand.** Pr *16:5. Ge 11:1, 4, 6-8. Ex *23:2. Nu 16:1-33. Is 8:9. 41:7. **the seed.** Pr 13:22. Ge 7:1. 17:7, 8. Nu 14:24. Ps 37:26. *84:11. *112:1, 2. Is 27:4. Je 32:39. Ac *2:39. **be delivered.** ƒ96C2, Ge +45:9.

22. **a jewel.** Pr *31:30. Ezk 16:15, etc. Na 3:4-6. 1 P *3:3, 4. 2 P 2:22. **is without.** Heb. departeth from. Pr 7:10. 9:13.

23. **desire.** Ps *10:17. *27:4. *37:4. 39:7, 8. 73:25. *119:5, 10. Is *26:8, 9. Je 17:16. Mt +*5:6. Ro √7:15-17, 22. **expectation.** ver. *7. Pr *10:28. Jn *3:36. Ro *2:8, 9. He *10:27.

24. **that scattereth.** ver. *18. Pr *19:17. 28:8. Dt *15:10. Ps √112:9. Ec 11:*1, 2, 6. Lk *6:38. Ac *11:29, 30. 2 C *9:5-11. **yet increaseth.** Is 15:9mg. Lk +6:38. 16:9. **withholdeth.** Pr +√3:27. 10:19. 13:24. 17:27. 21:13. 28:27. 2 Ch 29:7. Ps +*10:3. Ec +*5:13. Ezk +*16:49. Mt 26:7, 8. Ac *5:1, 2. 1 J *3:17. **is meet.** or, uprightness. Pr 2:13. 4:11. 14:2. **but.** Hg 1:*6, 9-11. 2:16-19. **poverty.** Pr 6:11. 14:23. 21:5, 17.

25. **liberal soul.** Heb. soul of blessing. Heb. *nephesh*, Ge +12:5. Pr *28:27. Jb *29:13-18. 31:16-20. Is 32:8. *58:7-11. Mt +*5:7. *25:34, 35. 2 C *9:6-11. **that watereth.** Pr 10:21. 25:13, 25. Is 58:10. Da 12:3mg. **shall be.** Ro 2:21.

26. **that withholdeth.** Pr 15:27. Je 48:10h. Ezk 16:49. Am *8:4-6. Mt 25:26, 27. 1 J 3:17. **corn.** Is 3:11. **shall curse.** Pr 24:24. 28:27. Ex +*22:22-24. Jg 9:57. Ja +*5:4. **blessing.** Pr 10:6. Jb *29:13. 2 C 9:11. **that selleth.** Ge 41:53-57. =42:6. Is 55:1.

27. **diligently.** *Shochair*, properly, "rising early to seek" what is greatly desired. Jb +8:5 (✱S#7836h). **he that seeketh.** Pr 17:11. Est *7:10. Ps *7:14-16. 9:15, 16. 10:2. 57:6.

28. **that trusteth.** Pr 10:15. Dt *8:12-14. Jb 31:24, 25, 28. Ps *52:7. *62:10. Is 26:4. Mk *10:24. Lk *12:19-21. 1 T *6:17. **but.** Ps *1:3. 52:8. *92:12-14. Is 60:21. Je *17:7, 8.

29. **that troubleth.** Pr 15:27. 17:6. 18:19. 19:13. Ge 34:30. 49:7. Jsh *7:24, 25. 1 S 25:3, 17, 38. Je 29:28. Hab 2:9, 10. **inherit.** Ec *5:16. Ho *8:7. **the wind.** Heb. *ruach*. Ec 5:16. **servant to.** Pr 14:19. 17:2. *22:7. **wise of heart.** ƒ12I1, Ge +3:7. Pr 10:8. 16:21.

30. **fruit.** Pr 3:18. 10:16. 15:4. Je 17:8. Ezk 33:8, 9. Da 12:2, 3. Lk 13:7. Jn 15:8, 16. 1 T √4:16. 2 T √2:12. **tree of life.** Is +*61:3. Da +*12:3. **and.** Da *12:3. Mt *4:19. Jn *4:36. 1 C *9:19-23. 1 Th 2:19. Ja *5:19, 20. **winneth.** Heb. taketh. Pr 9:7h. Ge 19:14h. Ml 2:6. Mt 18:15. Lk 5:9, 10. Ja 5:19, 20. **souls.** Heb. *nephesh*, Ge +12:5.

31. **the righteous.** 2 S 7:14, 15. *12:9-12. 1 K 13:24. Je 25:29. 1 C *11:30-32. 1 P √4:17, 18.

PROVERBS 12

Maxims of wisdom; distinguishing the righteous from the wicked by their thoughts, words, and works; noting the different event of their conduct; and teaching discretion both in temporal and spiritual things, 1-28.

1. **loveth.** T#614. Pr 2:10, 11. 6:23. *8:17, 32. *10:17. 13:18. 15:5, 10, 31, 32. 18:1. 29:1. Ps 16:7. 119:27, *97-100. Ec *4:13. Je 31:18. 2 Th *2:10. **instruction.** or, discipline. Pr 1:2, 3, *7, 8. ●5:23. 6:23. 10:17. **he that.** Pr 5:12, 13. *9:7, 8. 15:10. Ps 32:9. 92:6. Is 1:2, 3. Je 6:8.

2. **good.** Pr *8:35. Ps 4:6. *5:12. 63:3. *112:5. Is 58:8-11. Ac 11:24. Ro 5:7. 2 C *5:9, 10. **a man.** Pr 1:31. *6:18. Ps 9:15. Is 32:5-7. 1 P 3:11, 12.

3. **shall not.** ✓175B, Ge +21:16. **be established.** Pr *10:25. Jb 5:3-5. 15:29. *20:5-9. 27:13-18. **the root.** ver. 12. Ps 15:5. 62:2. *125:1, 2. 1 S 25:33. Is *54:17. Mi 7:8. Ro *8:31. Ep *3:17. Col *2:7. **not.** ✓175B, Ge +21:16.

4. **virtuous woman.** T#906. Pr 11:16. 14:1. 19:13, *14. *31:10-25, 28, 30, 31. Ac 9:36. 1 C 11:7, 11. T *2:5. 1 P ✓3:1. **she.** Pr 21:9, 19. 27:15, 16. 1 K 21:25. **as.** Pr *14:30. Hab 3:16.

5. **thoughts.** Pr *11:23. *24:9. Ps 119:15. *139:23. Is *55:7. Je 4:14. Ro 7:15-23. **counsels.** Ps 12:2, 3. *36:2-4. 41:6, 7. 140:1-3. Mt 2:3-8, 16. 26:4. 1 C *4:5. 2 C *4:2.

6. **words.** Pr *1:11-19. Ge 37:18-20. 2 S 17:1-4. Ps 37:12, 22. Is *59:7. Je 5:26. Mi 7:1, 2. Mt 2:7, 8. Ac 23:12, 15. 25:3. **to lie.** ✓96B, Ge +8:5. **the mouth.** Pr 14:3. Est 4:7-14. 7:4-6. Mt 22:46. Lk 21:14, 15.

7. **wicked.** Pr *11:21. *14:11. 15:25. Ge 6:5. Est 9:6-10, 14. Jb 5:3, 4. *11:20. 18:15-20. 27:18-23. Ps *37:10, 35-37. 73:18, 19. Je 17:9. **the house.** T#766. Pr 3:33. 14:1, *11. *24:3, 4. 2 S 7:16, 26. 1 K 15:4. Jb 5:24. *8:6, 7. Ps *128:3-6. Mt *7:24-27. Re 3:12.

8. **commended.** Ge *41:39. 1 S *16:18. *18:30. Ec 8:1. Da 6:3. Lk *12:42-44. *16:8. 1 C *3:10-15. *4:5. 2 C *10:18. **he that.** Pr *1:26. 3:35. *5:23. 1 S 13:13. +*25:17. Ps 132:18. Da *12:2. Ml *2:8, 9. Mt 27:4, 5. Ac *12:23. **of a perverse heart.** Heb. perverse of heart. 1 S 20:30. Est 1:16. **despised.** Pr 18:3. Ge 38:23mg.

9. **He that is,** etc. Or, rather, as in the old translation, "He that is despised, and is his own servant, is better than he that boasteth himself and wanteth bread;" with which the versions generally agree. That is, it is better to be in lowness and obscurity, and to support one's self by manual labor, than to want the necessaries of life, through a foolish vanity, or the pride of birth, which refuses to labor. 2 Th 3:10. 1 T 5:8. **despised.** Pr *13:7. Lk *14:11.

10. **righteous.** Ge *33:13, 14. Ex 9:19. Nu *22:28-32. Dt *25:4. Jon 4:11. **regardeth.** T#1854. Pr 14:21, 31. 17:5. 19:17. 21:10, 13. 22:9. or, knoweth. ✓121C2A2, Ge +39:6. Pr 14:10. 17:27. 24:22. 28:2. **life.** Heb. *nephesh*, soul, Ge +✓2:19. 9:4. Dt 12:23. **beast.** Pr 30:30. Ge 1:24, 25, 26. 2:20. **but.** Ge *37:26-28. Jg 1:7. 1 S *11:2. Jn 19:31, 32. Ja *2:13-16. **tender mercies.** or, bowels. Ge 43:14, 30. Dt 13:17. 1 J *3:17. **cruel.** Ps 5:9. 11:17. 17:11. Is *13:9.

11. **tilleth.** Pr 13:23. *14:4, 23. 27:27. *28:19. Ge 2:15. *3:19. Ps 128:2. Ep *4:28. 1 Th *4:11, 12. 2 Th *3:8, 10-12. **be satisfied.** Ge 26:12. 31:40. 32:10. **he that followeth.** Pr +*1:10, etc. *4:14, 15. *9:6. *13:20. *24:21. Ex *23:2. Jg 9:4. 2 S 15:11. 2 Ch +*13:7. Ps *26:4. +✓119:63. Jon *2:8. Ac 5:36, 37. 20:29, 30. T 1:10, 11. **void.** Pr *6:32. *7:7. *9:13, 16.

12. **desireth.** Pr *1:17-19. *29:5, 6. Ps *9:15. 10:8-

10. Je *5:26-28. Mi *7:2. Hab *1:15-17. **net.** or, fortress. Pr 10:15. Ec 7:26. 9:14. Is 29:7. **the root.** Ps *1:3. Is 27:6. *37:31. Je *17:7, 8. Lk *8:13-15. Jn *15:4, 5, 16. Ro *6:22.

13. **The wicked is snared by the transgression of his lips.** Heb. snare of the wicked is in the transgression of lips. Pr *6:2. *15:2. *18:6, 7. 2 S 1:2-16. 1 K 2:23. Ps *5:6. *64:8. Da *6:7, 8, 24. Mt 27:25. **but.** Pr 11:8. Ge 48:16. 2 S 4:9. Ps *34:19. Ec 7:18. Ro *8:35-37. 2 P *2:9.

14. **satisfied.** Pr *13:2. *18:20, 21. Ps 63:5. Ml *3:16, 17. Ja 3:2, 13. **and.** Is *3:10, 11. Mt *10:41, 42. 16:27. Ga ✓6:7, 8. 2 Th 1:6, 7. He 2:2. *6:10. 11:26.

15. **way.** Pr *3:7. *14:12, 16. *16:2, 25. 21:2. 26:12, 16. *28:11. *30:12. Ps 32:9. Lk *18:11. Ga 6:3. **fool.** T#200-6. Pr 14:8. 26:12. 28:26. 1 S 25:17, 25. Ps +5:9 (T#702). Lk 11:39, 40. T 3:3. **is right.** T1835. 1 K *12:13, 14. **but.** Pr *1:5. *9:9. *19:20. 1 S ●+✓25:17. 1 K 12:6-15. 2 K *5:13, 14. Ec *4:13. Je 38:15, etc. **hearkeneth.** Pr 1:33. 8:33. **is wise.** Ja *1:5.

16. **fool's.** T#200-21. Pr 14:16. 18:6. *20:3. *25:28. 27:3. *29:11. 1 S 20:30-34. 1 K 19:1, 2. Jb 5:2. Ec 7:9. Ja +1:20 (T#735). **wrath.** S#3708h. Pr 17:25 (grief). 21:19. *27:3. Jb 5:2. 6:2. 10:17 (indignation). 17:7 (sorrow). Ec 1:18 (grief). 2:23. 7:3mg, *9. *11:10mg. **presently.** Heb. in that day. Ps 2:7. 18:18. 50:15. **but.** Pr *10:12. 16:22. *17:9. *29:11. 1 S 10:27. Ro 12:18-21. Ja *1:19.

17. **that.** Pr 14:5, 25. 1 S 22:14, 15. Ps 119:163. 1 J 4:2. **truth.** ver. 19, 22. Pr 13:5. 14:5, 25. 17:7. **but.** Pr *6:19. 19:*5, 28. *21:28. *24:28. Mt *15:19. 26:59. Ac 6:13. 1 P *3:16.

18. **that.** Pr 25:18. Ps 42:10. *52:2. *57:4. 59:7. 64:3. Ja *3:6-8. **like.** Compare Re 1:16. **but.** Pr 10:20, 21. 13:17. *15:7. *16:24. Da *11:33. Col 4:6. Re 22:2. **health.** Pr 4:22mg. 6:15. 13:17. 16:24.

19. **lip.** ✓121BD, Ge +11:1. **of truth.** T#926. ver. 22. Ps 15:1, 3. 34:12, 13. Zc 1:4-6. Mt *24:35. 1 P 3:10. **for ever.** Ps +9:18 (✱S#5703h). **but.** Pr *19:9. 2 K 5:25-27. Jb 20:5. Ps 52:5. Ac *5:9.

20. **Deceit.** ver. 12. Pr *26:24-26. Ge 37:31, 32. Je *17:16. Mi 2:1. Mk *7:21, 22. 12:14-17. Ro *1:29. **but.** Is 9:6, 7. Zc *6:13. Mt +*5:9. He *12:14. 1 P *3:8-13.

21. **no evil.** Ge +24:44n. Ps 34:19. +91:10. Ro ✓8:28. 1 C 3:22, 23. 2 C *4:17. **happen.** ✤S#579h. Ps 91:10 (befall). See also Ex 21:13 (deliver). 2 K 5:7 (seek). Young renders this clause, "No iniquity is desired by the righteous." **filled.** ✓96C2, Ge +45:9. Pr *1:31. *14:14. Ec 9:3. Je 13:12-14. Hab 2:16. Re 18:6.

22. **Lying.** Pr *6:16, 17. Ps 5:6. Is 9:15. Ezk 13:19, *22. Jn 3:20, 21. Re ✓21:8. 22:15. **lips.** ✓121BD, Ge +11:1. **deal truly.** T#1823. Pr ●20:14. Mt 7:12. Mk 10:19. Ep 4:1. **his delight.** Pr *11:1, 20. *15:8. Je *9:24.

23. **A prudent.** Pr *10:19. *11:13. *13:16. Ec 3:7. Am *5:13. Mt 17:9. Lk 2:19. **but.** Pr *15:2. Ec *10:3, 12-14.

24. **hand.** Pr *10:4. 13:4. 17:2. 22:29. 1 K *11:28. 12:20. Mt *25:21-23. **but.** ver. 27. Pr *19:15. 21:25, 26. 22:13. *24:30-34. *26:13-16. **slothful.** or, deceitful. T#1859. ver. 27. Pr 10:4, +26. 19:15. Jb 13:4. 27:4. Je +*38:10mg.

25. **Heaviness.** T#171. Pr 14:10. 15:13, 15, 23. 17:22. 18:14. Ge 37:34, 35. Jsh 7:6, 7, 10. Ne 2:1, 2. Ps 38:6. 42:*5, 11. Je 18:11, 12. Mt 27:5. Mk 14:33, 34. **but.** ver. 18. Pr 15:23. 16:24. 25:11. 27:9. Is *35:3,

4. 50:4. 61:1, 2. Zc 1:13. Mt *11:28. 2 C *1:4. 2:4-8.

26. **righteous.** ver. 13. Pr 17:27. Ps 16:3. Mt 5:16, 46-48. Lk 6:32-36. 1 P 2:18-21. 1 J 3:1. **excellent.** *or,* **abundant.** Jg 1:23 (descry). Ec 1:13 (search). 2:3 (sought). 7:25 (search). Young renders this clause, "The righteous searcheth his companion." That is, he carefully selects his companions. Pr *13:20. 18:24. 22:24. Ex 23:2. 2 Ch ◑*13:7. Ps +*119:63. Je 10:2. 1 C 15:33. 2 C *6:14, 17. **but.** Ps 81:12, 13. Is 44:20. Ja 1:13, 14. 2 P 2:18-22. 1 J 2:26. Re 12:9. 13:14.

27. **slothful.** Pr *13:4. 23:21. 26:15. Jsh 18:3. 2 J +*8. **but.** Pr *15:16. *16:8. Ps *37:16. Jn 15:8. Ph 1:11.

28. **In the way.** Pr *8:35. 9:11. 10:16. *11:19. Is 35:8. Ezk 18:9, *20-24. Mt √7:13, 14. Jn √14:6. Ro 5:21. *6:22, 23. T *2:11, 12. He *10:19-23. 1 J 2:29. 3:7. 3 J 11. **no death.** Jn √5:24. 1 C +*15:55.

PROVERBS 13

The advantages of prudence, diligence, piety, and sincerity; and the mischiefs resulting from the opposite vices, 1-25.

1. **wise.** Pr 4:1-14, 20-22. *10:1. 15:5, 20. He 5:8. **heareth.** ⌐63I2, Jsh +3:3. **but.** Pr *9:7, 8. *14:6. 1 S 2:25. Ps ◑1:1. Is *28:14, 15. **heareth not.** T#613. Pr *1:7, 25. *15:12. 1 S +*25:17. Je *5:3. Ezk +22:29 (T#488). Am 5:10. Mt +*7:6. Lk 3:19, 20. Jn *3:20. 7:7. **rebuke.** ver. 8. Pr 17:10. 2 S 22:16. Is 1:4, 5. He 12:5.

2. **eat.** Pr *12:14. 18:20. **the fruit.** Pr 1:31. 8:19. 11:30. 12:14. Mt 7:16-23. **the soul.** Heb. *nephesh,* Ge +27:31. **violence.** Pr *1:11-13, 18, 31. 4:17. *10:11. Ps 75:8. *140:11. Je 25:27-31. Hab 2:8, 17. Re 16:6.

3. **that keepeth.** Pr *10:19. 12:13. *17:28. *21:23. Ps *39:1. +101:5. +*141:3. Mt *12:36, 37. Ja *1:26. *3:2-12. **life.** Heb. *nephesh,* soul, Ge +44:30. **openeth wide.** Ezk 16:25h. **shall have.** 1 S *25:10, 11, 33.

4. **soul.** Heb. *nephesh,* Ge +34:3. **sluggard.** Pr 6:6, 9. 10:26. 15:19. **desireth.** Pr *10:4. *12:11, 24. 26:13. Nu 23:10. **soul.** Heb. *nephesh,* Ge +34:3. **diligent.** Pr *2:2-9. 8:34. 10:4. 12:24, 27. 21:5. Jn *6:27. He *6:11. 2 P √1:5-11. **shall be.** Ho 6:3. Mt 11:12. 25:14-29. **made.** Pr *11:25. *28:25. Ps 92:14. Is *58:11.

5. **righteous.** Pr 6:17. *30:8. Ps 19:14. 51:15. *119:29, 163. Ep *4:25. Col *3:9. **is.** Ezk *6:9. *20:43. 36:31. Zc 11:8. **and.** Pr 3:35. Da *12:2. Ac 12:21-23. Re *21:8.

6. **Righteousness.** Pr 11:3, 5, 6. Ge 7:1. 19:29. 39:9. Ps 5:8. 15:2. *25:21. *26:1. Is 33:15, 16. **wickedness.** Pr *5:22. 21:12. 2 Ch 28:23. Ps *140:11. **the sinner.** Heb. sin. Ge 4:7. Ex 29:14, 36. 30:10. ⌐121L5. Metonymy of the Subject: sin put for the sin offering, Ge +4:7. 2 C *5:21.

7. **There is.** Pr 11:24, 25, 30. Is 55:1-3. **maketh himself rich.** ver. 11. Pr 12:9. Lk *18:11-14. 1 C 4:8. 2 P 2:19. Re *3:17, 18. **that maketh himself poor.** Ec *11:1, 2. 1 C 4:10, 11. 2 C *4:7. +*6:10. Ph 3:7-9. Re *2:9. **yet.** Lk +6:38.

8. **ransom.** Pr 6:35. Ex 21:30. Jb *2:4. Ps *49:6-10. Je *41:8. Mt *16:26. 1 P *1:18, 19. **life.** Heb. *nephesh,* soul, Ge +44:30. **the poor.** 2 K 24:14. 25:12. Je 39:10. Zp *3:12. **rebuke.** ver. +1.

9. **light.** Pr *4:18. 1 K 11:36. Ps 97:11. *112:4. Mt 5:14, 16. **lamp.** *or,* candle. Pr +6:23mg. *20:20mg. *24:20mg. Jb 18:5, 6mg. *21:17mg. Ps *49:17-19. Is

50:*10, 11. Mt *22:13. 25:3, 8.

10. **Only.** Pr 21:24. Jg 12:1-6. 1 K 12:10, 11, 16. 2 K 14:10. Lk 22:24. 1 T 6:4. Ja 3:14-16. 4:1, 5, 6. 3 J 9, 10. **with.** Pr 12:15, 16. 17:14. 19:20. 20:18. 25:8. Jg 8:1-3. Mt +*5:5. Lk 14:28-32. Ac 6:1-5. Ph √2:3. Ja 3:17. **well advised.** Pr *20:18. 1 K +√12:7n.

11. **Wealth.** Pr 10:2. 20:21. 28:8. Jb 15:28, 29. 20:15, 19-22. 27:16, 17. Ec 5:14. Je 17:11. Hab 2:6, 7. Hg *1:6. Ja 5:1-5. **gotten.** Charles Bridges regards this as false ellipsis (⌐63K, Ge 37:13), stating in a footnote to this passage "The interpolation of our translators is uncalled for, and misleads the reader. The word '*vain*' is of very frequent occurrence, and always implies, not what is sinful, but what is empty and unsubstantial." Bridges states "This Proverb does not imply the means, by which *wealth has been gotten*; but the impoverishing use, to which it is applied. However large, *by vanity* it will soon *be diminished*" (*Commentary,* p. 157). **he.** ver. 22, 23. Pr 20:21. 27:23-27. Ps 128:2. **by labor.** Heb. with the hand.

12. **Hope.** ⌐121R3, Ps +71:5. **deferred.** Ge 15:2. Ps 42:1-3. 69:3. 119:81-83, 123. 143:7. SS 5:8. La 4:17. **when.** ver. 19. Ge 21:6, 7. 46:30. 1 S 1:26-28. Ps 17:15. 40:2, 3. Hg 2:7. Lk 2:29, 30. 24:17, 21. Jn 16:22. He 10:37. Re 21:4. 22:7, 12, 20. **a tree.** Pr 3:18. *11:30. Re 22:2.

13. **despiseth.** Pr 1:25, 30, 31. Ex 5:2. 14:28. 2 S *12:9, 10. 2 Ch *36:16. Je 36:23-32. 43:2. *44:16, 17. Ezk 20:13, 16, 24. Lk *16:31. He 2:2, 3. *10:28, 29. 12:25. **he.** Ezr *10:3. Ps 115:13. Is *66:2. Ml *3:16. **rewarded.** Heb. in peace. Ps *19:11. *119:165. Mt *5:12. 2 J *8.

14. **law.** Pr 9:11. 10:11. *14:27. 16:22. **to depart.** Pr 15:24. *16:6, 17. 2 S 22:6, 7. Ps 18:5. 116:3. √119:9, 11.

15. **Good understanding.** Pr *3:4. 14:35. 1 S 18:14-16. Ps 111:10. Lk *2:52. Ac 7:10. **way of transgressors.** Pr *4:19. 15:10. Ge +√6:13 (T#566). Nu 22:22-31. +*32:23. Ps *95:9-11. Is 57:20, 21. 59:8. Je *2:19. La 3:7. Ho 2:6. Ac 9:5. Ro *6:21, 23. Ga 6:7. Ja 4:6.

16. **prudent.** Pr *12:22, 23. 15:2. 21:24. Ezr 8:22. Ps 112:5. Is 52:13. Mt 10:16. Ac 16:37, 38. 22:25. Ro 16:19. 1 C 14:20. Ep *5:17. **with knowledge.** Lk 14:28-32. **a fool.** 1 S 25:10, 11, 17, 25. Ec *10:3. **layeth.** Heb. spreadeth. Ex 9:29, 33. 37:9. Is 37:14. **folly.** ver. 19, 20. Pr 1:22, 32. 3:25.

17. **wicked.** Pr 10:26. 26:6. 2 K 5:26, 27. Je 23:13-16, *28. Ezk *3:18. *33:7, 8. 2 C *2:17. **but.** Pr 25:13, 23. 1 C *4:2. 2 C 5:20. 1 T 1:12. 2 T *2:2. **a faithful ambassador.** Heb. an ambassador of faithfulness. **faithful.** or, stedfast. lit. stedfastnesses. Pr 14:5. 17:2. 20:6. Dt 32:20. 1 S 26:2mg. **ambassador.** Pr 25:13. 26:14. Ge 24:34, 37, 38, 51-56. Ac *20:27. 2 C 5:20. **health.** Pr 4:22mg. 6:15. 12:18. 16:24.

18. **Poverty.** ver. *13. Pr *5:9-14. 12:1. *15:5, 31, 32. *19:16. Je *5:3-9. Lk *15:12-16. He *12:25. **refuseth instruction.** ver. +1, 8. Pr 15:32. 1 S +√25:17. Je *5:3. **regardeth reproof.** Pr *9:9. 25:12. 2 K +√5:13. Ps 141:5. 1 T +*5:19n. He 12:11.

19. **The desire.** ver. *12. 1 K 1:48. Ps 17:15. 21:1, 2. SS *3:4. 2 T *4:7, 8. Re *7:14-17. **soul.** Heb. *nephesh,* Ge +34:3. **it is.** Pr *29:27. **fools.** T#200-7. Pr 27:22. Dt 32:5, 6. **depart.** Pr *3:7. *16:6, 17. Jb *28:28. Ps *34:14. *37:27. 2 T *2:19.

20. **walketh with wise.** T#899. Pr *2:20. 12:26. 27:17. 1 K 10:8. Ps +√119:63. SS 1:7, 8. Ml *3:16.

Ac *2:42. He *10:24. 3 J +*11. **but.** Pr *1:11-19. 2:12-19. 7:22, 23, 27. *9:6. +*12:11. 22:14. Ge 13:12, 13. 14:12. 1 K *12:8, 10. 22:4, 32. 2 Ch *13:7. *19:2. Ac 2:40. 1 C *15:33, 34. 2 C *6:14-18. Ep 5:11. Re 18:4. **destroyed.** Heb. broken.

21. **pursueth.** Pr +17:13. Ge 4:7. Nu +√32:23. 35:19. Jsh 7:20-26. Jg 9:24, etc. 1 K 21:19-23. 2 K 9:30-36. Est 7:7-10. 8:1. 9:10. Ps 32:10. 140:11. Ac *28:4. **righteous.** Pr *11:18. Jb ◐21:15. Is 3:10, 11. Mt *10:41, 42. Mk +*10:29, 30. Lk +*14:14. Ro *2:7-10. Ga *6:9. 1 T +*4:8. He *6:10.

22. **good.** ♪16, Ge +1:27. **leaveth an inheritance.** Ge 17:7, 8. 2 Ch *21:7. Ps *25:12, 13. 102:28. 112:2. 128:6. **to his.** Ge 48:15, 16, 20. Nu 14:24. Jsh 14:14. **the wealth.** Pr +*28:8. Ex 3:22. Est 8:1, 2. Jb 27:13, 16, 17. Ps 105:44. Ec *2:26. Is +*60:5mg. Lk 19:24-26. **for the just.** Ps +*37:9. Zc +*14:14. Mt +*5:5. Ro +*11:26.

23. **food.** Pr *12:11, 14. *27:18, 23-27. 28:19. Ec 5:9. **destroyed.** Pr *6:6-11. 11:5, 6. Ps 112:5. Ec *8:5, 6. Je *8:7-10. **for want.** Pr 17:15, 23, 26. 18:5, 17, 18. 21:28.

24. **spareth.** T#494. Pr 10:13. +√19:18. *22:15. *23:13, 14. 26:3. *29:15, 17. Dt +27:16 (T#54). He 12:9. **hateth.** Pr *8:36. Ge 29:30, 31, 33. Dt 21:15. Ml 1:2, 3. Mt 6:24. Mt ◐*10:37. Lk *14:26. 16:13. Jn 12:25. Ro 9:13. **he that.** Pr 3:12. Ps √94:12. 103:13. Ep +*6:4. He *12:6-8. **loveth.** ♪121C2C3, Ps +109:17. That is, his love takes effect, and is seen, in the chastening (B556).

25. **righteous.** Ps *34:10. *37:3, 16, 18, 19. Jn 6:35, 55. 1 T *4:8. He *13:5. **soul.** Heb. *nephesh,* Nu +11:6. **but.** Pr 15:27. 16:11. 20:10, 14, 23. **belly.** Pr 6:11. 24:34. Dt 28:48. 32:24. Is *65:13, 14. Ho *4:10. Mi 6:14. Lk 15:15-17. 2 Th *3:10.

PROVERBS 14

Integrity, prudence, piety, meekness, and diligence recommended: and the ruinous effects of pride, injustice, sloth, hypocrisy, anger, envy, and oppression; and the vanity of carnal mirth and ungodly prosperity, pointed out, 1-35.

1. **wise.** Pr 16:22. 20:5, 18. 21:22. *24:3, 4. *31:10-31. Ru 4:11. **the foolish.** Pr *9:13-15. 19:13. 21:9, 19. 1 K 16:31. *21:24, 25. 2 K 11:1.

2. **that walketh.** Pr *16:17. 28:6. 1 K *3:6. Jb 1:1. *28:28. Ps *25:21. 112:1. Ec *12:13. Ml *2:5, 6. Ac *9:31. 10:22, 35. 1 J 3:21. **feareth.** ver. 27. Pr 21:3, 4, 27. **but.** Pr 11:12. Jb 12:4. Ps 123:3, 4. Lk *10:16. 16:14. Ro 2:4, 5. 2 T *3:2, 3.

3. **the mouth.** Pr 18:6. 21:24. 22:8. 28:25. 1 S *2:3. Jb 5:21. Ps 10:5-14. *12:3, 4. 31:18. 52:1, 2. 57:4. Je *18:18. Da 7:20. Ja 3:5, 6. 2 P *2:18. Re 13:5, 6. **but.** Pr 12:6. Ps *141:3. Ro √10:9, 10. Re 3:10. *12:11.

4. **clean.** Am 4:6. 1 C 3:9. **but.** Pr 13:23. 1 C *9:9-11. **strength.** Le=1:5.

5. **faithful witness.** ver. *25. Pr 6:19. 12:17. 13:5. *19:5, 9. Ex 20:16. *23:1. 1 K 21:13. *22:12-14. Ps 51:6. **false witness.** 2 C *11:13-15.

6. **scorner.** Pr 18:2. 26:12. Is √8:20. Je *8:9. Mt *6:22, 23. 11:25-27. Ro *1:21-28. 9:31, 32. 1 C *3:18, 19. 8:2. 2 P 3:3-5. **findeth it not.** Ezk 14:3, 4. Jn 18:38. **knowledge.** Pr *8:9. *15:14. 17:24. 24:7. Ps *119:18, 98-100. Mt *7:7, 8. 13:11, 12. Jn 7:17. Ac 8:27-39. Ja *1:5. **hath understanding.** Pr +*19:25.

7. **Go from.** Pr *9:6. 13:20. *19:27. Ps 119:+*63, 114, 115. Mt +*7:6. 1 C *5:11. 15:33. Ep +*4:14. *5:11. 1 T 4:7. *6:3-5. 2 P 2:1, 2. 2 J √10. **lips.** ♪121BD, Ge +11:1.

8. **wisdom.** Pr 2:9. 8:20. Ps *111:10. 119:5, 34, 35, 73. *143:8. Ec 8:5. 1 C 7:20. Ep *5:17. Col √1:9, 10. 1 Th *4:11. 2 T √3:15-17. Ja 3:13. **folly.** Pr *11:18. 2 K 5:20-27. Je *42:20mg. Lk *12:19, 20. Ac 5:1-10. Ep 4:22. 2 T *3:13.

9. **Fools.** T#200-15. Pr *1:22. *10:23. 26:18, 19. *30:20. Jb *15:16. 34:7-9. Je 44:4, 5. Ju *18. **mock at sin.** T#706. Ge 3:12, 13. 1 S *15:13-15. Ps +58:5 (T#373). Je 7:9, 10. Ezk +33:20 (T#272). Mt 25:44. **among.** Pr *3:4. *8:35. *12:2. *13:15. Is *66:2-5. Ezk 9:4-6. Da 9:4-21. Mt 27:46. Ro *14:17, 18.

10. **heart.** ver. 13. Pr 15:13. 18:14. 1 S 1:10. 2 K 4:27. Jb 6:2-4. 7:11. 9:18. 10:1. Ezk 3:14. Mt 14:33, 34. Jn 12:27. 1 C 2:11. **his own.** Heb. *nephesh,* Ex +15:9. **bitterness,** etc. the bitterness of his soul. Ge 42:21. 2 K +4:27mg. Is 53:3. 63:9. Mk 14:34, 35. **and a.** Ps 25:14. Jn 14:18, 23. Ph *4:7. 1 P 1:8. Re 2:17.

11. **house.** ♪121J16, Ge +13:5. Pr +*3:33. 12:7. 21:12. Jb *8:15. 15:34. 18:14, 15, 21. 20:26-28. 21:28. 27:13-23. Zc +*5:4. Mt *7:24-27. **the tabernacle.** ♪121J16, Ge +13:5. Pr 11:28. 21:20. Jb 8:6. Ps 112:2, 3. 128:3. Is 40:29. 58:11, 12. He 11:9, 10.

12. **is a way.** Pr 12:15. 15:24. 16:12, 17, *‖25. 30:12. Is 53:6. Mt √7:13, 14. Lk 13:24. Ro 6:21. Ga 6:3. Ep *5:6. Ja *1:22. **seemeth right.** Jg 17:13. **the end.** ver. 13. Pr 5:4, 11. 16:25. **ways of death.** Pr 16:25. Je 21:8. Ro *6:21.

13. **in laughter.** T#479. Pr 5:4. 21:17. Jb 21:11-14. Ec 2:1, 2, 10, 11. 7:2-5, 6. 11:9, 10. Lk 6:25. *16:25. 1 C 10:7. Ep +2:3 (T#698). Ja 4:9. 1 P +4:7 (T#711). 2 P 2:13. Re 18:7, 8. **the end.** Pr 5:3, 4.

14. **backslider.** Pr 1:32. Je 2:19. 8:5. 17:5. Ho 4:16. Zp 1:6. He 3:12. 2 P *2:20-22. **filled.** Pr *1:31. *12:14. Ezk 22:31. **a good.** ver. 10. Jn 4:14. 2 C 1:12. Ga 6:4, 8.

15. **simple.** ♪108K54, Pr +1:4. Pr 4:26. +*22:3. 27:12. Ge 3:1-6. Ezk 14:10n. Ro 16:18, 19. Ep +*4:14. 5:17. 1 J *4:1. **believeth every.** Jsh 9:14. 1 K 13:15-24. Ep +*4:14. 2 T 3:6-8, 13. He 13:9. 2 P 2:2, 18-20. **the prudent.** See on ver. 8. Pr +*22:3. Am 5:13. Ac 13:7. Ro *14:12. 1 Th *5:21. **looketh well.** Pr +*15:14. 18:1n, 17. Is +*8:20n. Mt 7:15. Ac +*17:11. 20:28-30. 1 Th √5:21. 2 P *3:17. 1 J *4:1.

16. **feareth.** Pr *3:7. 16:6, 17. *22:3. Ge 39:9. 42:18. Ne 5:15. Jb 31:21-23. Ps 119:120. 1 Th 5:22. **the fool.** Pr 7:22. 28:14. 29:9. 1 K 19:2. 20:10, 11, 18. Ec 10:13. Mk 6:17-19, 24, 25. Jn 9:40.

17. **that.** ver. 29. Pr 12:16. 15:18. 22:24. 29:22. Ec 7:9. Ja 1:19. **a man.** Pr 6:18. 12:2. Est 3:6. 7:5, 6. Is 32:7. Je 5:26-29.

18. **simple.** ♪108K54, Pr +1:4. **inherit.** Pr 3:35. 11:29. Je 16:19. 44:17. Mt 23:29-32. 1 P 1:18. **the prudent.** Pr 4:7-9. *11:30. Da *12:3. 2 T 4:8. 1 P 5:4.

19. **The evil bow.** Ge 42:6. 43:28. Ex 8:8. 9:27, 28. 11:8. 2 K 3:12. Est 6:11. 7:7, 8. 8:1, 2. Ps 49:14. Is 60:14. Mi 7:9, 10, 16, 17. Ml 4:3. Ac 16:39. Re 3:9.

20. **poor.** Pr 10:15. *19:7. Jb 6:21-23. 19:13, 14. 30:10. **but.** Pr 19:4, 6. Est 3:2. 5:10, 11. **the rich hath many friends.** Heb. many are the lovers of the rich. ♪24B, Ge +23:16. Ru +3:10.

21. **that despiseth.** Pr 11:12. 17:5. 18:3. Jb 31:13-

15. 36:5, 6. Ps 22:24. Lk 18:9. Ja 2:5, 6, 14-16. **he that hath.** ver. 31. Pr 11:24, 25. 19:17. 28:27. Ps 41:1, 2. 112:5-9. Ec 11:1, 2. Is 58:7-12. Da 4:27. Mt 25:34, etc. Lk 6:30-36. Ac 20:35. He 6:*10, 12. 1 J 3:17-22.

22. **err.** ver. 17. Pr 12:2. Is 32:7, 8. **devise evil.** Pr 6:18. Ge 11:4, 5. Ps 2:1, 4. Mt 27:5. Ja 1:15. **but.** Ge 24:27. Ps 25:10. 61:7. Mt 5:7. Jn 1:17. **and truth.** ſ174, Ge +18:27. **devise good.** Pr 19:22. 1 K 8:17, 18. 2 Ch 6:8. Is 32:8.

23. **all labor.** Pr 12:24. +*22:29. 28:19. Ge *3:19. 1 K 11:28mg. Ps 90:17. Ec 2:24. Mt 11:12. Lk *10:7. Jn *6:27. 1 C +*15:58. Col *3:22-24. 2 Th 3:10, 12. He +*6:10, 11. **but.** Pr 10:10. Ec 5:3. Je 12:2. Lk +*6:46. 2 Th 3:10-12. 1 T 5:13.

24. **crown.** See on ver. 18. 1 K 3:13. Ps 112:9. Ec 7:11, 12. Is 33:6. Lk 16:9. **foolishness.** Pr 27:22. Ps *49:10-13. Lk 12:19, 20. 16:19-25.

25. **true witness.** See on ver. 5. Ac *20:21, 26, 27. 26:16-20. Ep 4:25. 1 T √4:16. **souls.** Heb. *nephesh,* Ge +12:5. **speaketh lies.** ver. 5. Je 5:31. 2 C *11:13-15. 2 T 4:1-3. 2 P 3:3.

26. **fear.** ver. 27. Pr *3:7, 8, 25, 26. *19:23. Ge 31:42. Ps *34:7-11. *112:1, 6-8. 115:13, 14. 130:4. Ec 7:18. Ml √3:16-18. *4:2. Ac *9:31. He 12:28. **confidence.** Pr 18:10. Hab *3:17-19. 1 J 4:18. **his children.** Pr *18:10. Ge 22:12. Ps +*83:3. Is *26:20, 21. Je *15:11. *32:39, 40. **refuge.** Ps *94:13. Is +*26:20. Je +*31:2. Zp +*2:3. Lk +*21:36. He=6:18, 19.

27. **The fear.** Pr 10:27. Ps 103:17. Ml 4:2. **a fountain.** Pr 13:14. Is 33:6. Jn 4:14. Re 21:6. **to.** Pr 2:10-18. 22:5. Ps 18:5. Ec 7:26.

28. **the multitude.** Ex 1:12, 22. Dt 1:11. 1 K 4:20, 21. 20:27. 2 K 10:32, 33. 13:7. Re 7:9, 10. **king's honor.** ver. 35. Pr 16:10, 12-15. 19:12. 20:2, 8, 9, 26, 28. 21:1.

29. **slow.** See on ver. 17. Pr 15:18. 16:32. Nu *12:3. Mt *11:29. 1 C *13:4, 5. Ja *1:19. 3:17, 18. 1 P 2:21-23. **but.** Pr 22:24, 25. 25:8, *28. Ec *7:9. Da 3:19, etc. Jon 4:9. Mt 2:16. **hasty.** Heb. short. Jb +21:4mg. **spirit.** Heb. *ruach,* Ge +41:8. **exalteth.** Pr *4:8. Ec 10:6. Mt 5:22. Ep 4:26, 27, 31.

30. **sound.** Pr *4:23. Ps *119:80. 2 T √1:7. **flesh.** ſ171Q5, Ge +17:13. **envy.** 1 S 18:9, 12, 29. 1 K 21:4. Jb 5:2. Ps 112:10. Ac 7:9. Ro 1:29. Ja 3:16. 4:5. **rottenness.** Pr 3:8. 12:4. *17:22.

31. **that oppresseth.** ſ108J, Ge +43:18. Pr 17:5. 22:2, 16, 22, 23. Jb 31:13-16. Ps +*12:5. Ec +*5:8. Mt 25:40-46. **but.** See on ver. 21. Pr 19:17. Le 25:35, 36. Dt 15:11. Mt 25:40. Jn 12:8. 2 C 8:7-9. 1 J 3:17-21. 4:21. **the poor.** Mt 11:5. 26:11. Ja +*2:5.

32. **wicked.** Pr +10:28. **driven.** Jb 18:18. 27:20-22. Ps *1:4. 58:9. Is 8:21, 22. Da 5:26-30. Jn *8:21, 24. Ro 9:22. 1 Th 5:3. **the righteous.** Ge 49:18. Jb 13:15. *19:25-27. Ps *23:4. *37:37. 39:7. Lk 2:29. 1 C √15:55-58. 2 C 1:9. +√5:8. Ph *1:22, 23. 2 T 4:6-8, 18. Re √14:13. **death.** 1 C +*15:55.

33. **Wisdom.** Pr 2:10. Mt 22:15-46. Jn 14:23. **resteth.** Pr 12:16, 23. 13:16. 15:2, +*28. 29:11. Ec 10:3. **fools.** Ec 5:3. 10:14.

34. **Righteousness.** Dt 4:6-8. 28:1-14. Jg 2:6-14. Is 58:13, 14. Je 2:2, etc. Ho 13:1. **but.** Dt 28:15, etc. 29:18-28. Ne 13:15-18. Ps 107:34. Ezk ch. 16, 22, 23. **sin.** or, sin offering. ſ121L5. Metonymy of the Subject: sin put for sin offering, Ge +4:7. Pr 5:22. 10:16. *13:6. 20:9. **reproach.** 2 S 12:14. **any people.** Heb. nations. Ge 27:29. Is 17:12.

35. **king's.** Pr 16:12, 13, *15. 20:8, 26. 22:11. 25:5. 29:12. Ps 101:4-8. Da 6:1-3. Mt *24:45-51. Lk *12:42-48. **wise servant.** T#907. Pr 17:2. 27:18. Mt *25:21. Lk 12:37. Ep 6:5-8. Col 3:+22 (T#680), 24. **him.** Pr 10:5. 17:2. 19:26.

PROVERBS 15

Maxims about bridling the passions; improving the gift of speech; receiving reproof; the omniscience of God; his dealings with the righteous and the wicked; the advantages of piety and peace; and the evil of sloth, rashness, and avarice, 1-33.

1. **A soft answer.** Pr *25:11, 15. Jsh 22:30. Jg 8:1-3. 1 S *25:21-33. 2 S 2:5. 20:16-22. Ac 23:6. 2 C 6:3. 12:6. Ja 3:17, 18. **turneth away.** Pr 16:7. 29:8. Je +2:24mg. **grievous.** ver. 18. Pr 10:12. *28:25. *29:22. Jg 12:3-6. 1 S 25:10, 11, 21, 22. 2 S 19:43. 1 K 12:13-16. Ec 7:8, 9. Ac 15:39. Ja 3:5.

2. **tongue.** ver. 23, 28. Pr 12:23. 13:16. *16:23. *25:11, 12. Ps 45:1. Ec 10:12, 13. Is 11:2. *50:4. Mt 22:15-46. Mk 4:33. Jn 7:46. 1 C 3:2. 2 T 2:15. **fools.** T#200-9. Pr 10:8. 18:7. Ps +101:5 (T#729). Ec 5:3. 10:12-14. **poureth.** Heb. belcheth, *or,* bubbleth. ver. 28. Pr 1:23. Jb 2:9, 10. Ps 19:2. *59:7. 145:7.

3. **eyes of.** ver. 11. Pr *5:21. 2 Ch *16:9. Jb *34:21, 22. Je 16:17. *23:24. *32:19. He *4:13. **every place.** T#220. God the Father is omnipresent. 1 K 8:27. Ps 139:3-10. Is +*57:15. Je 23:23, 24. Mt +18:20 (T#76-6). +*28:19n. Ac 17:27. Ep 1:23. **beholding.** 2 K 5:26. Ps 73:11. 139:23, 24. Is 29:15. Ho 7:2. Jn 1:48.

4. **A wholesome.** Heb. The healing of the. Pr 4:22mg. *12:18. 14:30. 16:24. Ec 10:4. Ml 4:2. Col *4:6. 1 T 6:3. **a tree.** Pr 3:18. Ge *3:22-24. Re *2:7. **a breach.** Pr *18:8, 14. 26:22. Ps 52:2-4. 109:22. **spirit.** Heb. *ruach,* Ge +41:8.

5. **fool.** T#200-5. ver. 20. Pr 10:1. *13:1, 18. 22:15. Ex 20:12. Dt +27:16 (T#54). 1 S 2:23-25. 2 S 15:1-6. 1 Ch *22:11-13. *28:9, 20. La 3:27. Ep 6:1, 2. **instruction.** ver. 31, 32. Pr 17:16. 18:15. 19:8, 18, 20, 27. 22:6, 15. **but.** ver. *31, *32. Pr *1:23. *6:23. *19:20. 25:12. Ps 141:5. T 1:13. 2:15.

6. **the house.** ver. 16. Pr *8:21. 13:22. 21:20. Ps *112:3. 1 C 2:9. 2 C 6:10. He *11:26. **treasure.** lit. strength. ſ121N2, Ge +34:29. By Metonymy of the Adjunct, "strength" is put for wealth or treasure. Pr 27:24mg. Ro 11:25n. **in the revenues.** Pr *10:22. *16:8. Jb *20:19-23. Ps *37:16. Ec *4:6. *5:10-14. Ja *5:1-3.

7. **lips.** Ps *37:30. 45:2. *51:13-15. *71:15-18. *78:2-6. 119:13. Ec 12:9, 10. SS 4:11. Mt *10:27. *28:18-20. Mk √16:15. Ac 18:9, 10. Ro *10:14-17. *15:18-21. Ep *4:29. 2 T *2:2. **disperse.** Jb 4:3, 4. Ps 40:9, 10. Mt 4:23. 2 C 9:6. 1 P 4:10. **the heart.** Pr 10:20, 21. Mt *12:34. Jn *3:6.

8. **sacrifice of the wicked.** Pr *21:4, 27. *28:9. Ge 4:3-5. 1 S 15:22. Ec 5:1. Is *1:10-15. 29:13, 14. 61:8. 66:3. Je 6:20. *7:21-23. Am 5:21, 22. Mt 15:8, 9. Jn *4:24. Ac 8:22. T 1:15. **the prayer.** ver. *29. 1 Ch *29:17. Ps 17:1. SS 2:14. Da 10:12. Ac 10:4. **the upright.** Pr 21:21. Jn +*17:6. Ph 3:12. **his delight.** Ps 141:2. SS 2:14. 4:11. Da *9:23. 10:12. Jn 4:23, 24. Ro 8:26, 27. He 4:16. 10:19-22. Re 8:4.

9. **The way.** Pr *4:19. 21:4, 8. Ps *1:6. *146:8, 9. Is 29:13, 14. Mt √7:13. **an abomination.** Je 44:4. Hab *1:13. **he loveth.** Pr *21:21. Is *26:7. *51:1, 7. Da 9:23. Ho *6:3. 1 T *6:11. 2 T *2:22.

10. **Correction.** *or,* instruction. ver. 5, 32, 33. Pr 12:1. 23:12. **grievous.** Pr *12:1. *13:1. 23:35. 1 K 18:17. 21:20. *22:8. 2 Ch 16:10. 36:16. Jn *3:20. 7:7. **and he.** Pr 1:30. 5:12. *10:17. Is *1:5, 6. Ezk 24:13, 14.

11. **Hell.** Heb. *sheol,* Ge +37:35. Pr 27:20. Jb *26:6. Ps 139:7, 8. Re 1:18. **destruction.** Jb 26:6. **the hearts.** 2 Ch 6:30. Ps 7:9. 44:21. 139:23, 24. Je *17:9, 10. Jn +*2:24, 25. 21:17. Ac 1:24. He *4:13. 1 J 3:20. Re *2:23.

12. **scorner.** ver. 10. Pr 9:7, 8. 1 K 22:8. Am *5:10. Jn *3:18-21. 7:7. 2 T *4:3. **neither.** 2 Ch 18:7. Jb 21:14.

13. **merry.** ver. *15, 30. Pr 17:22. 1 S 1:17, 18. Ps 32:1, 2, 11. Ac 6:15. 2 C 1:12. Ph 4:4. **by.** Pr 12:25. 18:14. Ne 2:2. Jn *14:1. 2 C *2:7-11. √7:10. **spirit.** Heb. *ruach,* Ge +41:8.

14. **heart.** *f*12I1I, Ge +3:7. Pr +*4:23. **hath understanding.** Pr *1:5. 9:9. **seeketh knowledge.** Pr 2:3-5. *4:7. +*14:15. 18:1, 15, 17. 23:23. 1 K 3:6-12. 10:1. 2 Ch 1:10. Jb 28:12, 20. Ps 90:12. *119:33, 34, 66, 97, 100. Ec 1:13. 7:25. 8:16. 12:9, 10. Da 9:2. Mt 5:6. 12:42. Lk *10:39. Jn 3:1, 2. *5:39. Ac *8:28, 31. 10:33. √17:11. Ph *1:9. He 5:14. 6:1. 1 P 1:11. 2 P √3:18. **the mouth.** ver. 21. Pr 12:23. 18:2. Is 30:10. 44:20. Ho 12:1. Ac 17:21.

15. **All.** Ge *37:35. 47:9. Ps 90:7-9, +*15. Mk +*10:30. 1 P *5:10. **but.** Pr 14:30. 16:22. 17:22. Jb 1:21. 15:11. Hab *3:17, 18. Ac 16:25. Ro 5:2, 3, 11. 12:12. 2 C 1:5, 12. 6:10. He 10:34. 1 P 1:6-8. 4:13. **feast.** Ps *4:6, 7. Ec 9:7. Jn 4:13, 14. 7:38, 39.

16. **little.** Pr 16:8. 28:6. Ps 37:16. Ph +4:11. 1 T 6:6. **great.** Pr 10:22. Ec 2:10, 11, 18-23. *4:6. 5:10-12.

17. **a dinner.** Pr 17:1. 21:19. Ps ch. 133. Ph 2:1. 1 J 4:16.

18. **wrathful.** Pr 10:12. 19:19. *22:24. 26:21. 28:25. 29:22. 2 S 19:43. 20:1. Ja 3:14-16. **stirreth up.** Pr 28:25. 29:22. **strife.** Pr 6:14. 16:28. 17:1, 14. 20:3. **slow to anger.** ver. 1. Pr *14:29. *16:32. 25:15. Ge 13:8, 9. Jg 8:1-3. 1 S 25:24, etc. Ps *103:8. Ec 10:4. Mt +*5:5, 9. Ac 6:1-5. Ja *1:19, 20. **appeaseth.** Jb 34:29. 37:17. Ec 10:4. **strife.** Pr 17:1, 14. 18:6, 17. 20:3.

19. **way of the slothful.** Pr 22:5, 13. 26:13. Nu 14:1-3, 7-9. Mt *25:26, 27. **the way of the righteous.** Pr √3:6. √8:9. Ps 5:8. *25:8, 9, 12. 27:11. Is 30:21. 35:8. Zc 4:7. Ph 4:13. **made plain.** Heb. raised up as a causey. Is 57:14. Je 18:15.

20. **wise.** Pr 10:1. 23:15, 16. 29:3. 1 K 1:48. 2:9. 5:7. Ph 2:22. **father.** *f*63J1, Ge +13:9. **despiseth.** Pr 23:22. 30:11, 17. Ex 20:12. Le 19:3. Dt 27:16. 2 K 2:23. Jb 19:18. Ezk *22:7. Mi *7:6. **mother.** *f*63J1, Ge +13:9.

21. **joy.** Pr *10:23. 14:9. 26:18, 19. **destitute of wisdom.** Heb. void of heart. Pr 6:32mg. 11:12mg. **a man.** Pr 14:16. Jb *28:28. Ps *111:10. Ep *5:15. Ja 3:13.

22. **Without counsel.** Pr *11:14. *20:18. Ec 8:6. **but in.** Pr 24:6.

23. **joy.** Pr 12:14. 16:13. 24:26. *25:11, 12. Ep *4:29. **in due season.** Heb. in his season. Ps *1:3. Ec 3:1. Is *50:4. 2 T 4:2. **how good.** 1 S 25:32, 33. Mt *18:15.

24. **way.** Pr 6:23. Ps *16:11. 139:24. Je 21:8. Mt √7:14. Jn √14:6. **above.** Mt *6:20. 2 C 4:18. Ph *3:20. Col *3:1, 2. He 11:16. 13:14. **that.** Pr 2:18. 5:5. 7:27. 9:18. 23:14. **hell.** Heb. *sheol,* Ge +37:35. **beneath.** *f*24E, Ge +30:33.

25. **destroy.** Pr 12:7. 14:11. Jb 40:11-13. Ps 52:1, 5. 138:6. Is 2:12. Da 5:20. Lk 1:51, 52. 1 P 5:5. **but**.

Dt *10:17, 18. Ps 68:5, 6. 146:9. Je 49:11. Ja 1:27.

26. **thoughts of the wicked.** Pr *6:16-19. 23:7. 24:9. Ps 94:11. Is 59:7. Je 4:14. Mt *15:19. He 4:13. **but.** ver. 23. Pr 22:11. Ps 18:26. 19:14. 24:4. *37:30, 31. 45:1. Ml *3:16, 17. Mt +*5:8. 12:34-37. **pleasant words.** Heb. words of pleasantness. ver. 8. Pr 3:17. 15:1. +*16:24. 1 T +*4:12.

27. **greedy of gain.** Pr 1:13, 19. 11:19, 29. 20:21. *21:26. Ge 13:10, 11. Dt 7:26. Jsh 6:18. 7:1, 11, 12, 15, 21, 24, 25. 1 S 8:3-5. √15:19, 23. 1 K 15:19, 23. 2 K *5:20-27. Ps *10:3. Ec 5:10. Is 5:8-10. *56:11. Je 17:11. Am 2:7. Mi 3:11. Hab 2:9-11. Zc *5:3, 4. 9:3. Mt 26:15, 16. Jn 12:6. Ac 16:19. 24:26. 1 T *6:9, 10. Ja 5:3. 2 P 2:15. **but.** Pr 28:16. 29:4. Ge *14:22, 23. Ex +*18:21. 23:8. Dt 16:19. Is 33:15, 16.

28. **heart.** ver. *2. Pr *16:23. 1 K *3:23-28. Ne 2:4. Ec *5:2, 6. 10:2. **studieth.** or, meditateth. Pr 8:7. 24:2. Jsh +√1:8. **to answer.** Ja *1:5. 1 P √3:15. **the mouth.** Pr *10:19. 13:16. *29:11, 20. Ec *10:12-14. Mt √12:34-36. T 1:10, 11. Ja *3:6-8. 2 P 2:18.

29. **far from.** Pr 28:9. Jb 21:14. Ps 10:1. *34:16. +*66:18. 73:27. *138:6. Is 1:11. 46:12, 13. Je 14:12. 18:17. ●23:24. Ezk *8:18. Am 9:4. Mi *3:4. Mt *25:46. Jn +*9:31. Ac 13:38-46. ●17:27, 28. Ep 2:12, 13. 2 Th 1:9. **wicked.** T#1813. ver. 8. Ps *50:14-17. Is *59:2. 1 P *3:12. **he heareth.** ver. *8. 1 S 1:13. Ps 6:8. 10:17, 18. +*34:15-17. 38:9. 65:2. √66:18, 19. *145:18, 19. Is 30:18. 38:14. 58:8, 9. La 3:56. Lk 18:1-7. Jn +*9:31. Ro *8:26, 27. Ja *5:16-18. 1 P *3:12. 1 J *5:14, 15. **righteous.** T#1385. Jb 8:5, 6. Ps *4:4, 5. +*34:15, 17, 18. Is 58:8, 9. 64:5. Je *17:16. Jn +*9:31. 17:6. Ja √5:16. 1 P *3:12. 1 J 2:1. *3:22.

30. **light.** Pr 13:9. Ezr 9:8. Ec 11:7. Re *21:23. *22:5. **a good.** Pr *17:22. *25:25. Ps 89:15. Lk 2:10-19. 1 Th 3:6-9. **the bones.** Pr 3:8. Is *58:11.

31. **ear.** ver. 5. Pr *1:23. 9:8, 9. 13:20. *19:20. 25:12. 2 S 12:13. Ps 141:5. Is 55:3. Mk 4:24. Lk 8:18. +*11:28. **abideth.** Pr 19:23. Ge 19:2. 24:23. Ps +*49:12n. Jn *15:3, 4. 1 J *2:19. **among.** Pr 14:33.

32. **refuseth.** Pr *1:24, etc. 5:11, 12. *8:+33-36. 1 S +*25:17. Ps 50:17. He 12:25. **instruction.** *or,* correction. Pr +12:1. *29:1. Is *1:5. Je 5:3. Ezk 24:13, 14. **soul.** Heb. *nephesh,* Ge +27:31. **heareth.** or, obeyeth. Pr 5:13. 25:12. Ge 22:18. 26:5. Dt 21:18, 20. Mt *7:24-27. Ja *1:22. Re 3:19. **reproof.** Pr 1:30. **getteth understanding.** Heb. possesseth an heart. *f*12I1I, Ge +3:7. ver. 14, 21mg. Pr *17:16. *18:15. 19:8mg.

33. **fear.** Pr *1:7. *8:13. Jb *28:28. Ps 34:11. *111:10. **and.** Pr ‖18:12. 25:6, 7. 29:23. Lk *14:10, 11. Ph *2:5-11. Ja *4:10. 1 P *5:5, 6.

PROVERBS 16

Maxims of wisdom, relating to the providence of God; the power and duty of kings; the evil of pride, calumny, discord, and violence; and the excellency of prudence, meekness, and integrity, 1-33.

1. **preparations.** *or,* disposings. *S#4633h, only here; compare S#4634h, Ex 39:37 (order); Le 24:6 (rows); Jg 6:26 (ordered places); 1 S 4:2 (army; mg, array); 1 Ch 12:38 (rank). ver. *9. Pr *19:21. 20:24. *21:1. 2 Ch 18:31. Ezr 7:27. Ne 1:11. Ps *10:17. 119:36. Je *10:23. 32:39, 40. Ezk 36:26, 27. 2 C 8:16. Ph *2:13. Ja *1:16-18. **heart.** Ps 10:17. Je 10:23. 31:33. Da 1:8. Am 4:12. Jn *6:44, 45. Ac 16:14. 2 C 3:3, 5. 1 T 5:22. **and.** Pr +15:28. Ex *4:11, 12, 15. Nu 22:18. Je *1:7-

9. Mt *10:19, 20. Lk 12:11, 12. *21:14, 15. **from the Lord.** ver. 2-7, 9, 33. Pr 17:3. 19:21. 20:12, 24, 27. 21:2, 30, 31. 22:12. Ph 2:13.

2. **the ways.** ver. *25. Pr *21:2. *30:12. 1 S *15:13, 14. Ps 36:2. Je 2:*22, 23. Lk *18:9-11. Ro 7:7-9. **clean.** Is *5:20. Mt *6:23. Jn 16:2. 18:28. Ac 26:9. **but.** Pr *5:21. *24:12. 1 S 2:3. √16:7. Is 26:7. Je √17:10. Da *5:27. Lk *16:15. Re 2:18, 23. 3:1. **spirits.** Heb. *ruach,* Ge +41:8.

3. **Commit.** Heb. Roll. Ps 22:8mg. 37:5mg. **thy works.** Ne 2:4-6. Jb 5:8. Ps 37:4, *5. *55:22. Mt *6:25, etc. Lk 12:22. Ph *4:6. 1 P *5:7. **thy thoughts.** Pr 4:23. Jb 22:28. Ps 112:7. 127:2. Is 7:5-7. √26:3. Ph *4:8. **established.** ver. 33.

4. **Lord.** Is *43:7, 21. Ro 11:36. Re *4:11. **for himself.** T#209. Ps +46:10 (T#277). +83:18 (T#570). Is 42:8. 43:7, 21. 48:11. Ezk 20:9. 36:32. Jn +11:42 (T#276). 1 C +√15:28. Col 1:16. Re *4:11. **yea even.** T#256. Ex *9:16. 14:17. Jb *21:30. Ezk ◑*33:11. Mk 4:11, 12. Ro *9:17, 22, 23. 2 C 2:15. 13:5, 6. 1 P 2:8. 2 P *2:3,'9, 12. Re 19:3.

5. **proud.** T#550. Pr *6:16, 17. *8:13. 15:26. Ge 3:5. Ex 5:2. 2 S 22:28. Jb 40:12. Ps 2:1. 12:3, 4. 18:27. +*119:21. 138:6. Is 2:12. 3:16-23. 13:11. 26:5. 45:9. 65:5. Je +20:11 (T#513). Ezk 28:2. Da 4:30-32. Mt 23:12, 29-31. Lk +*16:15. 2 Th 2:4, 8. Ja *4:6, 16. 1 P 5:5. **though.** Pr *11:21. Is 8:9, 10. **unpunished.** Heb. held innocent. Pr 6:29. 11:21. 17:5mg. 19:5mg. Ex +*20:7. Is 3:11. Ro *2:8, 9.

6. **mercy.** Pr 20:28. Ex 30:10. Le 4:20. Ps *85:10. 86:15. Da *4:27. Mi *7:18-20. Lk 11:41. Jn 1:17. *15:2. Ac *15:9. 1 P *1:22. **and truth.** ♪174. Ge +18:27. **purged.** Ps 65:3. **by the.** Pr *8:13. 14:16, 27. Ge 20:11. Ne 5:*9, 15. Jb 1:1-8. *28:28. Ec 7:18. 2 C *7:1. Ep 5:21.

7. **When.** T#737. Pr 10:12. +17:17 (T#204). 18:24. +19:11 (T#201). 25:15, 21, 22. *29:8. Mt 5:38-45. +10:16 (T#660). +11:29 (T#62). Lk 6:30, 35-37. Ro 12:14, *20, 21. Ga +6:1 (T#437). Ep +*4:32 (T#203). 1 P 3:8, 13. **please.** 2 Ch 14:3. Ps 69:31. Ro *8:31. Ph 4:18. Col √1:10. *3:20. He +*12:14(T#499). *13:21. Ja +1:4 (T#498). 1 J *3:22. **he maketh.** Ge 27:41. 32:6, 7, 28. *33:4. 43:14. Jb 1:9, 10. Je 15:11mg. Da 1:9. 3:26-30. 6:24, 28. Ac 9:1, 2, 19, 20. **enemies.** T#775. Dt *28:7. 2 K *6:16. *17:39. 2 Ch 14:11. Jb 8:22. Ps 17:7. 27:5, 6. 37:32, 33, 40. *76:10. *97:10. 112:8. 118:6, 7. *125:3. Is 25:5. *54:15, 17. Lk 1:71, 74, 75. *18:7, 8. Ac *18:10. He *13:6. **at peace.** Ge 31:55. 33:1, 4. 39:21. 2 Ch 20:30. Jb 34:29. Ps 105:13-15. Ac 9:31. Ro √8:28, 31. 1 P 3:13.

8. **Better is.** Pr *15:16. Ps *37:16. 1 T 4:8. *6:6-9. **little.** Pr 6:10. 10:20. 24:33. Ge 18:4. 1 K 17:10, 12. **with righteousness.** T#925. Pr 11:1. *12:21. 15:27. *28:20. Dt 16:20. 25:15. Ps 15:5. Is 33:15, 16. 56:1, 2. Ezk 18:5, 7-9. **than great revenues.** ver. 16, 19. Pr 13:11. 20:15. *21:6, 7. 22:1, 16. *28:8. 1 K 21:19. Je *17:11. Mi 6:10. Hab *2:6. Lk *19:8. 1 T *6:10. Ja 5:1-3. **without right.** ver. 10 (judgment), 11 (just), 33 (disposing). Ge 18:19, *25. Ps 112:15mg. 140:12. Is 1:17 (judgment).

9. **heart deviseth.** ver. *1. Pr 19:21. *20:24. *21:30. Ps *37:23. Is *46:10. **directeth.** Ge *45:5. Ps 33:11. *37:23. 107:7. Is *42:16. Je *10:23. La *3:37.

10. **A divine sentence.** Heb. Divination. ✱S#7081h. Nu 22:7. 23:23. Dt +*18:10. 1 S 15:23mg. 2 K 17:17. Pr 16:10mg. Je 14:14. Ezk 13:6, 23. 21:21, 22. Young

comments that here "a divine sentence" is to be taken in the sense of "an oath." ver. 12, 13. Ge 44:5, 15. Dt *17:18-20. 2 S 23:3, 4. Ps 45:6, 7. 72:1-4. 99:4. Is *32:1, 2. Je *23:5, 6. **transgresseth.** Ho 10:4. Am 5:7. 6:12.

11. **just.** Pr *11:1. 20:10, 23. Le *19:35, 36. Dt *25:13-15. Ezk 45:10. Ho 12:7. Am 8:5. Mi 6:11. **weights.** Heb. stones. Pr 11:1mg. 20:10mg. Le 19:36mg. Dt 25:13mg. **bag.** ✱S#3599h. Pr 1:14 (purse). 23:31 (cup). Dt 25:13. Is 46:6. Mi 6:11.

12. **an.** Pr *28:9. Dt *25:16. Lk +*12:48. **for.** Pr 20:18. *25:5. *29:14. 2 S 23:3, 4. 1 K 3:9. Ps 72:1. 99:4. Re *19:11.

13. **Righteous lips.** Pr *14:35. *22:11. 2 S 14:17. Ps *45:7. 101:5-7. Is 11:2-4.

14. **wrath.** Pr *19:12. *20:2. Est 7:7. Ec 8:3, 4. Da *3:13, etc. Mt 22:13. Lk *12:4, 5. Re 6:16, 17. **messengers.** Pr 17:11. 1 S 22:16. 1 K 2:25. 2 K 6:31-33. Da 2:12. Mk *6:27. **but.** Ec *10:4. Ac *12:20. 2 C *5:20.

15. **the light.** Pr *19:12. Jb 29:23, 24. Ps *4:6. 21:6. Ac *2:28. **his favor.** Pr 22:1. Est 5:2, 3. Jb 29:23. Ps 4:7. *30:5. 72:6. Ho *6:3. Zc 10:1. Col 1:20.

16. **better.** Pr *3:15-18. √4:7. *8:10, 11, 19. Jb *28:13, etc. Ps *119:27. Ec *7:12. Mt *16:26. Lk *12:21. Ph *3:7, 8. Col *2:3. Ja *1:5.

17. **highway.** Pr *4:24-27. Is *35:8. Ac *10:35. *24:16. T *2:10-14. **depart.** Pr +*3:7. *4:27. *14:16. Jb 28:28. Ps 18:23. *34:14. *97:10. Zc 7:10. Ro 12:9. 1 C 10:6. 1 Th √5:22. 2 T *2:19. 1 P 3:11. **he.** Pr *10:9. 19:16. Mt *24:13. He *10:39. Ju *21, *24. Re *3:10. **soul.** Heb. *nephesh,* Ge +27:31.

18. **Pride goeth.** T#551. Pr 11:2. 17:19. *18:12. 28:26. 29:23. Nu +*32:23 (T#733). 2 Ch 32:25. Est *3:5, 6. *6:6. *7:9, 10. Is 2:11, 12. 37:10-13, 38. Da *4:30-37. *5:22-24. Ob 3, 4. Mt 26:33-35, 74. Ac 12:21-23. Ro 11:20. 1 T *3:6. **haughty.** 2 S 22:28. **spirit.** Heb. *ruach,* Ge +41:8. **before a fall.** 1 C *10:12. 2 C ◑12:9.

19. **to be.** Ps 34:18. 138:6. Is *57:15. Mt +*5:3. Lk 1:51-53. *18:13, 14. Ph +*2:3. **spirit.** Heb. *ruach,* Ge +41:8. **than.** Ex 15:9. Is 9:3. 10:6, 13-15. 53:12.

20. **handleth.** *or,* understandeth. Pr 8:35. 13:15. 17:2. 19:8. 24:3-5. Ge 41:38-40. Da 1:19-21. Mt 10:16. **whoso.** Pr 22:19, 20. 1 Ch 5:20. Ps 2:12. 34:8. 125:1. 146:5. Is *26:3, 4. *30:18. Je *17:7, 8. Da 3:28. 6:23. Ep 1:12, 13.

21. **wise.** ver. 23. Pr 10:8. 23:15. 1 K 3:12. Ho *14:9. Ro 16:19. Ja *3:17. **in heart.** ♪121I1, Ge +3:7. **the sweetness.** ver. 24. Pr 15:7. 27:9. Ps 45:2. Ec 12:10. Is 50:4. Lk 4:22. Jn 7:46.

22. **Understanding.** T#392. Pr 2:10-12. 3:13-18, 35. *4:5-9. Ec 7:12. **a wellspring.** Pr 10:11. 13:14. 14:27. 18:4. Jn 4:14. √5:24. 6:63, 68. 7:38. **the instruction.** Pr 15:2, 28. Mt +*7:6. *15:14. 23:16-26. Lk *6:39, 40. Ro 1:22.

23. **heart.** ♪121I1, Ge +3:7. Pr 15:28. 22:17, 18. Ps 37:30, 31. 45:1. Mt 12:34, 35. Col *3:16. **teacheth.** Heb. maketh wise.

24. **Pleasant words.** T#896. Pr 12:6, 14, *18. 13:2. *15:4, 23, 26. 18:20, *21. 23:16. 25:*11, 12. 27:9. Dt 32:2. SS 4:11. Ml *3:16, 17. Jn 20:19-21. **an honeycomb.** Pr 24:13, 14. Ps *19:10. 119:103. Je √15:16. Lk *24:32. **soul.** Heb. *nephesh,* Ge +34:3. **health.** Pr 3:8mg. *4:22. 6:15. 12:18. 13:17. 29:1. 2 Ch 36:16mg. Je 8:15.

25. **a way.** Pr 12:26. *‖14:12. Ge 41:32. Is 28:15-

19. Da 5:20. Jn *7:47-49. 9:40. ◑√14:6. Ac 26:9. 1 C 10:12. 2 C *13:5. Re 3:11. 22:7. **seemeth right**. T#704. Pr +30:12 (T#510). Dt 11:16. Is *5:20. 44:20. Je ◑*6:16. La +3:40 (T#397). Mt *6:23. *7:22, 23. 24:4, 5. Lk 21:8. Jn √3:19. +5:43 (T#476). 1 C 3:18. Ga 6:3, 7. Ep 4:18. 5:6. 2 Th 2:3, 11, 12. Re +3:17 (T#25). **death**. Ge +2:17. Is 5:1-7. 27:10, 11. 28:15-19. Ezk 15:2-5. +18:4. Ml 4:1. Mt 3:10. 25:41. Jn 15:6. 2 C 13:5. Ph 3:19. He 6:8. 12:17. Ja 1:15. Re 20:15.

26. **He**. Heb. The soul of him. Heb. *nephesh*, Ex +15:9. **laboreth for**. Pr 9:12. 14:23. Ge 3:19. Ec *6:7. 1 Th *4:11, 12. 2 Th *3:8-12. **craveth it of him**. Heb. boweth unto him.

27. **An ungodly man**. Heb. A man of Belial. Pr 19:28mg. Dt +15:9. Jg +19:22. 1 S 25:17. 2 S 20:1. **diggeth**. Pr 2:4. Ps 7:14, 15. Is 5:18. Hab 2:13. **in**. Ps 7:14. 52:2-4. 57:4. Ja *3:6-8.

28. **froward**. Pr 6:14, 19. 15:18. 18:8. 26:20-22. 29:22. 30:33. 1 T 6:3-5. Ja 3:14-16. **soweth**. Heb. sendeth forth. Pr 6:14mg, 19. Ge 3:23. 8:7, 8, 12. **a whisperer**. Pr 17:9. Ge 3:1, etc. 1 S 24:9. Ro 1:29. 2 C 12:20.

29. **violent**. Pr *1:10-14. 2:12-15. 3:31. 1 S 19:11, 17. 22:7-9. 23:19-21. Ne 6:13. 2 P 3:17.

30. **shutteth**. Pr 6:12-14. 10:10. Is 6:10. Mt 13:15. Jn 3:20. **moving**. ver. 27. Mi 7:3. Mt 14:7, 8. 27:23-26.

31. **hoary**. Pr 20:29. Le *19:32. Jb 32:6, 7. Ps 92:13, 14. **if**. Ge 47:7-10. 1 S 12:2-5. 1 Ch 29:10, etc. Ec 4:13. Lk 1:6. 2:29, etc., 37, 38. Phm 9.

32. **that is**. Pr *14:29. 15:18. *19:11. Ps *103:8. Ep 5:1. Ja *1:19. **and he**. ver. 19. Pr 25:28. 1 S 25:32, 33. Ro *12:19, 21. Ja 3:2. Re 2:7. 3:21. **spirit**. Heb. *ruach*, Ge +41:8. **than he**. Pr 25:28.

33. **the lot**. Ge 24:44n. Nu 26:55, etc. Jsh 7:14. +14:2n. 18:5, 10. 1 S 14:41, 42. 1 Ch 24:5. Ne 11:1. Jon 1:7. Mt 10:29, 30. Ac 1:26. **whole disposing**. Ep +1:11.

PROVERBS 17

Cautions against many vices; a quiet, friendly, and cheerful spirit inculcated; and several wise and pious observations concerning the conduct and events of life, 1-28.

1. **a dry morsel**. Pr 15:17. Ps 37:16. 1 T 6:6. **an house**. Pr 7:14. **sacrifices**. *or*, good cheer. **with**. Pr 21:9, 19.

2. **wise**. Pr *11:29. 14:35. Ge 24:4, etc. 30:27. Ec *4:13. **that**. Pr 10:5. 19:26. *29:15. **have part**. Ge 31:1.

3. **fining pot**. Pr 27:21. Ps 26:2. 66:10. Is *48:10. Je *17:10. Zc 13:9. Ml 3:2, 3. 1 P *1:7. Re 2:23. **but**. Jb 23:10. 1 C *3:13.

4. **wicked doer**. Pr 28:4. 1 S 22:7-11. 1 K *22:6, etc. Is 30:10. Je *5:30, 31. Mi 2:11. 2 T *4:3, 4. 1 J 4:5. Re 13:3-8. **naughty**. √108K42, Pr +6:12.

5. **mocketh**. Pr 14:21, 31. Ps 69:9. 1 C 11:22. 1 J *3:17. **glad at calamities**. Pr *24:17, 18. Jb 31:29. Je *17:16. Ezk 26:2, 3. Am 5:18. Ob 11-13, 16. Ro *12:15, 20, 21. **unpunished**. Heb. held innocent. Pr +16:5mg.

6. **Children's**. Ge 48:11. 50:23. Jb 42:16, 17. Ps *127:3-5. 128:3-6. **the crown**. Pr 12:4. 16:31. **and the glory**. Ex *3:14, 15. 1 K 11:12. 15:4. Zc 10:7. Ml +*4:6. Mt 3:9.

7. **Excellent speech**. Heb. A lip of excellency. √121BD, Ge +11:1. Jg +7:22mg. Ep *4:29. Ph 1:27.

Col *4:6. **becometh not**. Pr *26:7. Ps *50:16, 17. Mt *7:5. **much**. Pr 16:10-13. *29:12. 2 S *23:3. Jb *34:12. Ps *101:3-5. **lying lips**. Heb. a lip of lying. √121BD, Ge +11:1. Pr *12:19.

8. **gift**. ver. 23. Pr *18:16. 19:6. 21:14. 29:4. Ex *23:8. Dt *16:19. **precious stone**. Heb. stone of grace. Pr 1:9. 3:4, 22, 34. 4:9. **whithersoever**. Ge 33:9-11. 43:11. 1 S *25:35. 2 S 16:1-4. Mi 7:3. **prospereth**. Dt +29:9.

9. **that covereth**. Pr *10:12. Ps *32:1. Ep 5:1, 2. 1 P *4:8. **seeketh**. *or*, procureth. ver. 19. Pr 21:6. 28:5. 29:26. **but**. Pr *16:28. **repeateth**. 1 T 5:13.

10. **A reproof**, etc. *or*, A reproof aweth more a wise man, than to strike a fool an hundred times. Pr *9:8, 9. 13:1. 15:5. *19:25. 27:22. 29:19. Ps 141:5. Ezk 36:26. Lk 22:61, 62. Re *3:19. **than**. 2 Ch 28:22. Je 5:3.

11. **An evil man**. ver. 13. Pr 19:19. 20:17. 21:7. 22:8, 16. 2 S 15:12. 16:5-9. 18:15, 16. 20:1, 22. 1 K 2:24, 25, 31, 46. Mt *21:41. *22:7. Lk *19:27. **rebellion**. Nu 17:10. Dt *21:18-23. 31:27. Or, "A rebel seeketh only evil." 1 S √15:23. **messenger**. Pr 16:14.

12. **a bear**. Pr 28:15. 2 S *17:8. 2 K *2:24. Ho 13:8. **rather**. Pr 27:3. 2 Ch *10:14-16. Mt *2:16.

13. **rewardeth evil**. Pr 20:22. 1 S *24:17. *25:21. *31:2, 3. 2 S 21:1, etc. Ps *35:12. *38:20. *55:12-15. *109:4-13. Je 18:20, 21. +*37:18. Mt 5:39. *27:5, 25. John *10:32. Ro *12:17. 1 Th *5:15. 1 P *3:9. **evil**. 1 S 20:7. *25:17. 2 Ch *25:16. Est 7:7. Is 28:22. Da 9:24-27. 11:36. Lk 22:22. **not depart**. Pr 13:21. Ex +*20:5. Nu +*32:23. 2 S *12:10. 21:1, etc. Ps 32:10. Je 18:20-23. Am 7:9. Mt 27:5. Ga *6:7. **his house**. Mt 23:37, 38. +24:8. Lk 13:35.

14. **beginning**. ver. *19. Pr *26:21. *29:22. Jg 12:1-6. 2 S 2:14-17. 19:41-43. 20:1, etc. 2 Ch 10:14-16. 13:17. 25:17-24. *28:6. **leave**. Pr *13:10. *14:29. *15:1. *16:32. *19:11. *20:3. *25:8. Ge *13:8, 9. Jg 8:1-3. Ec *7:8, 9. Mt *5:39-41. Ac 6:1-5. 15:2, etc. Ro *12:18. 14:19. 1 Th *4:11. 2 T 2:23, 24. Ja *3:14-18.

15. **that justifieth**. Pr *24:23, 24. Ge ◑+9:5. Ex *23:7. 1 K 21:13. Is 5:23. √55:8, 9. Ezk 22:27-29. Am 5:7, 12. 6:12. Lk *23:18-25. Jn 18:40. Ro *4:5. Ja 5:6. **condemneth the just**. Lk +*16:1n. Jn +*7:24, 51. **abomination**. Pr *6:16. *11:1. *15:8. 2 C √5:21.

16. **a price**. T#1833. Pr *1:22, 23. 8:4, 5. *9:4-6. Is *55:1-3. Ac 13:46. 2 C *6:1. **fool**. T#200-18. Ps +10:4 (T#693). Je *4:22. **seeing**. Pr 1:7, 25. *14:6. *18:15. 21:25, 26. Dt 5:29. Ps 81:11-13. Ho *4:11. Jn *3:20. Ac 28:26, 27.

17. **friend**. T#204. Pr +16:7 (T#737). *18:24. 19:6. 27:9. 2 S 1:26. **loveth**. Pr *18:24. 19:7. Ru *1:16, 17. 1 S 18:3. *19:2. *20:17. *23:16. 2 S *1:26. 9:1, etc. Est 4:14. Jb 6:14. Jn 13:1. *15:13, 14. 1 C *13:4, 7, 8. He 2:11. **a brother**. Pr *18:+19, 24. Ep 5:30. Ph 2:25.

18. **void**. Pr *7:7. *12:11. 18:2. *24:30. 28:16. Is 27:11. 44:19. Je *4:22. *5:21mg. +8:7. Mt *13:19. 2 C *4:4. **understanding**. Heb. heart. Pr +6:32mg. 10:13mg, 21mg. Je 5:21mg. Ho 7:11. **striketh hands**. Pr 6:1. 11:15mg. 22:26. Jb 17:3. **surety**. T#717. Pr *6:1-5. *11:15. 20:16. *22:26, 27. **friend**. Pr 3:28, 29. 6:1, 3, 29.

19. **loveth**. √121C2C3, Ps +109:17. ver. 14. Pr *29:9, 22. 2 C *12:20. Ja *1:20. *3:14-16. **he that**. Pr *16:18. *18:12. *24:27. 1 S 25:36-38. 2 S 15:1. 1 K *1:5. Je *22:13-15. Da 4:30, 31. Mk 9:33, 34. Lk 22:24. 1 C 3:3, 4.

20. He that hath a froward heart. Heb. The froward of heart. Pr *3:32. *6:12-15. *8:13. Ps *18:26. La 3:27. **and he.** Pr *10:10, 14, 31. *18:6, 7. Ec *10:12. Ja *3:6-8.

21. that. ver. *25. Pr *10:1. 15:20. *19:13. Ge 26:34, 35. 1 S 2:32-35. *8:3. 2 S 18:33. Ec 2:18, 19. **hath.** Pr *23:15, 16. 2 C 2:3. Phm 19, 20. 3 J *4. **no.** ƒ175B, Ge +21:16.

22. merry heart. Pr *12:25. *15:13, 15. *18:14. Ps 35:27. Ec 9:7-9. Ac 16:25. Ro *5:2-5. **like a medicine.** Heb. to a medicine. Pr 4:22mg. **a broken.** Ps *102:3-5. 2 C *2:7. *7:10. **spirit.** Heb. *ruach*, Ge +41:8. **drieth.** Jb 30:30. Ps 22:15. *32:3, 4. **bones.** ƒ96F1, Ge +3:8.

23. taketh a gift. T#1826. ver. 8. Pr *18:16. 28:21. 29:4. Ex *23:8. Dt *16:19. 1 S 8:3. *12:3. Is *1:23. 5:22, 23. 33:15, 16. Ezk *22:12. Mi 7:3. Mt 28:11-15. Mk *14:10, 11. Ac 8:18-20. **out of.** Pr *21:14.

24. before. Pr *14:6. *15:14. Dt 30:11-14. Ec 2:14. 8:1. Jn *7:17. **understanding.** Pr +*8:9. 28:2, +5. **the eyes.** Pr *12:11. *23:5. Ps *119:37. Ec *6:9. 1 J *2:16. **fool.** T#200-16. Pr ◐16:3. Dt *29:29. Ps ◐37:5. Ec 8:17. 11:5. Lk ◐+*10:42. 13:23, 24. Jn 21:21, 22. Ac 17:21. 2 C ◐*10:5. Ep 4:14. Col 2:18. 2 T 2:23.

25. foolish son. ver. 21. Pr *10:1. *15:20. 19:13. Ge 26:34, 35. 1 S *2:24, 25. 2 S 13:1, etc. 18:33. Ec *2:18, 19. **father.** ƒ63J1, Ge +13:9. **her.** ƒ63J1, Ge +13:9.

26. to punish. ver. 13, *15. Pr *18:5. Ge +*18:25. 1 K 21:11, etc. Je +*37:18. Mt 26:3, etc. **to strike.** 1 S 24:5, 6. 2 S 3:23-25, 39. 16:7, 8. 19:7. Jb 34:18, 19. Ec √10:20. Mi 5:1. Jn *18:22, 23. 2 P *2:10.

27. spareth his words. T#1858. Pr *10:19. 15:28. *18:13. Ps *39:1. Ec 9:17. Mt +*7:6. √12:36, 37. Col *4:6. Ja *1:19. *3:2. **an excellent spirit.** *or*, a cool spirit. Heb. *ruach*, Ge +41:8. Pr *16:32. 25:25h. Ec *9:17. Je 18:14h. Ja *3:18.

28. Even a fool. Pr 10:19. *15:2. Jb *13:5. Ec *5:3. *10:3, 14. **understanding.** Pr *1:5. 10:13. 14:*6, 33.

PROVERBS 18

Maxims about seeking wisdom; avoiding contention, governing the tongue; the mischiefs of pride and sloth; the strong tower of the righteous man, and of the rich man; and the trials or comforts arising from relations and friends, 1-24.

1. Through, etc. *or*, He that separateth himself seeketh, according to his desire, and intermeddleth in every business. Isaac Leeser translates, "He that separateth himself (from God) seeketh his own desires; at every sound wisdom is he enraged." Ralph Wardlaw observes that the verse is variously rendered, such that opposing translations express an opposite meaning. Wardlaw argues that since this verse is in contrast with verse two, this verse must be taken in a positive sense of a man who loves and pursues knowledge, whereas verse two speaks of the man who undervalues and despises it. Wardlaw explains "Through desire"—that is, the desire of knowledge—"a man having separated himself"—that is, having retired and secluded himself from interruption by the intrusion of companions and the engagements of social life—"seeketh and intermeddleth with all wisdom" (Ralph Wardlaw, *Lectures on The Book of Proverbs*, vol. 2, pp. 170, 171). To suggest this verse teaches that the individual has

no authority to read and understand Holy Scripture independently of the authority of a religious organization, as the Jehovah's Witnesses maintain in their claim to be Jehovah's exclusive vehicle of divine truth as the "faithful and wise servant" (Mt 24:45), is unacceptable, being in conflict with the direct teaching of Scripture elsewhere regarding the right of private judgment (Ga 1:8n) and the perspicuity of Scripture (Pr +*8:9. Is +*8:20n). **having separated.** Ge 32:24. Ex *33:16. Ps 55:7. Je 9:2. Zc 7:3. Mt *14:23. Mk +*1:35. +*6:31. Lk 5:16. 6:12. 9:10. Ro *1:1. 2 C *6:17. Ga 1:17. 1 Th 3:1. Ju 19. **seeketh.** Pr *2:1-6. +*14:15. +*15:14. Mt *13:11, 12, 44. Mk 4:11. Ep *5:15-17. **intermeddleth.** Pr 14:10. 17:14. *20:3, 19. 24:21. 26:17. Is *26:8, 9. Je *15:17. Mk *1:35.

2. fool. T#200-10. Pr *1:7, 22. 15:14. *17:16. Jb +21:14 (T#363). Ps *1:1, 2. 92:5, 6. Mt 8:34. 1 C *8:1. **but.** Nu 24:15, 16. Ac *8:9, 19, 21. 1 C 14:12. Ph 1:15. 2 P *2:15-19.

3. wicked cometh. Pr 11:2. 22:10. *29:16. 1 S 20:30. Ne 4:4. Ps *69:9, 20. *123:3, 4. Mt *27:39-44. 1 P *4:4, 14.

4. words. Pr *10:11. 13:14. 16:22. *20:5. Mt *12:34. Jn *4:14. *7:38, 39. Col *3:16. *4:6. **the wellspring.** Pr 5:18. 10:11. 13:14. 14:27. Ps 78:2. Mt 7:29. Lk 4:32. 24:32. Col 3:16.

5. not. ƒ175B, Ge +21:16. Pr *24:23. *28:21. Le *19:15. Dt *1:16, 17. 16:19. 2 Ch 19:7, 9. Jb 13:7, 8. 34:19. Mt *22:16. **to overthrow.** 1 K 21:9-14. Is 5:23. *59:14. Mi 7:3.

6. fool's. Pr *12:16. *13:10. *14:16. *16:27, 28. 17:14. *20:3. 27:3. Jg 8:6, 15, 16. 2 K *2:23, 24. Ps 52:1-5. Ec 10:12. **lips.** ƒ121BD, Ge +11:1. **his.** Pr 14:3. *19:19. *22:24, 25. 25:24. 29:9.

7. his destruction. Pr *10:8, 14. *12:13. *13:3. Ec *10:11-14. **his lips.** ƒ121BD, Ge +11:1. Pr *6:2. Jg 11:35. 1 S 14:24, etc. Mk 6:23-28. Ac 23:14, etc. **soul.** Heb. *nephesh*, Ge +12:13.

8. words. Pr *12:18. *16:28. *26:20-22. Le *19:16. Ps 52:2. 64:3, 4. **talebearer.** *or*, whisperer. Pr 16:28. 26:20mg, 22. **as wounds.** *or*, like as when men are wounded. Pr 12:18. ‖26:22. Col 3:12-14. **innermost parts.** Heb. chambers. Pr 7:27. 20:27, 30. **belly.** ƒ121J22, Jb +15:25.

9. that is slothful. T#1828. Pr 6:6. *10:4, 26. 12:24, 27. 13:4. 15:19. *19:15, 24. 20:4. 21:25. 22:13. 23:20, 21. *24:30-34. *26:13-16. ◐31:27. Je √48:10mg. Mt *25:25, 26. Ro *12:11. 1 T 5:13. T 1:12. He *6:12. **is brother.** Pr 28:24. Jb 30:29. Lk *15:13, 14. 16:1, 2.

10. name. ƒ121T1, Dt +28:58. Ge *17:1. Ex *3:13-15. *6:3. *34:5-7. Ps +√9:10. 20:1. Is *9:6. *57:15. Je *23:6. Mt *1:23. 2 C 1:3. 1 P 5:10. Re *1:8. **a strong tower.** ƒ22L6, Ps +61:3. Dt 33:27-29. 2 S *22:3, 51. Ps *18:2. *27:1. 61:3, 4. 91:2. 144:2. Is *26:4. **the righteous.** Ge 32:11, 28, 29. 1 S 30:6. 2 S 22:45-47. Ps *56:3, 4. Mi 7:18. **safe.** Heb. set aloft. Ps *91:14. Hab 3:19.

11. The rich. Pr *10:15. *11:4. Dt 32:31. Jb 31:24, 25. Ps *49:6-9. *52:5-7. *62:10, 11. Ec *7:12. Mt 7:24-27. Lk *12:19-21.

12. destruction. Pr *11:2. *16:18. *29:23. Ezk 16:49, 50. 28:2, 9. Da *5:23, 24. Ac *12:21-23. **and.** Pr ‖15:33. Ge 3:5, 6. Jb *42:6, etc. Ps 113:7, 8. Is *6:5, etc. Da 9:20, 23. Mt +*5:3. 23:12. Lk *14:11. 1 C 4:7. 1 P *5:5.

13. that. Dt *13:14. 2 S 16:4. 19:24-30. Est 3:10,

etc. 8:5, etc. Jb *29:16. Da 6:9, 14. Jn 7:24. **answereth a matter**. Heb. returneth a word. Pr 17:13. 24:26mg. 26:16. Jsh 22:16, 21n. 1 S 17:30mg. **before**. T#1829. ver. *17. Pr 14:8. 15:22, +28. Le +*19:15. Dt 19:15. Jb ●32:4, 10, 11. Jn +*7:51. 1 T +√5:19n. **folly**. Pr 5:2, 3. 12:23. 13:16. 14:1. **shame**. Jb 20:3. Ps 4:2. 35:26.

14. **spirit**. Heb. *ruach*, Ge +41:8. √121A10, Ge +26:35. Jb *1:20, 21. *2:7-10. Ps *147:3. Ro 5:3-5. 8:35-37. 2 C 1:12. *12:9, 10. Ja 1:2. 1 P *1:6. **a wounded**. Pr *17:22. Ge 4:13. 1 S 28:6, 15. 2 S 17:23. 1 K 16:18. Jb 6:4. 7:14, 15. 10:15-17. Ps 30:9, 10. *32:3, 4. *38:2-4. *42:10, 11. 55:3, 5. *77:2, 3. 88:14-16. 109:22. Mt 27:3-5. Mk *14:33, 34. Ro ●*8:35-37. 2 C 2:7. 1 Th 5:14g. He *12:15. **spirit**. Heb. *ruach*, Ge +41:8. √121A10, Ge +26:35.

15. **getteth knowledge**. Pr *1:5. √4:5, 7. *9:9. *10:14. +*15:14. *23:23. 1 K *3:9. Ps *119:97-104. Lk *8:8-10. *10:39. Ph 1:9. Col √1:10. 2 T √3:15-17. Ja *1:5. 2 P √3:18.

16. **gift**. Pr *17:8. *19:6. *21:14. Ge 24:30-33. *32:20. *33:10. 43:11, 12. 1 S 25:27. **bringeth**. Pr *22:29. 1 S 16:20. Jb 11:19. Ps 112:6. Mt 13:57. 23:12.

17. **He that is first**. ver. +*13. Pr 12:15. 2 S 16:1-3. 19:24-27. Ac *17:11. *24:5, 6, 12, 13. Ep *4:14. 1 Th *5:21. 2 T 3:14. 1 P 3:15. 2 P 1:16. **but**. Pr *14:15. Jn +*7:24, 51. Ac +*17:11. Ro 14:12. 1 Th √5:21.

18. **The lot**. Pr +*16:33. Ge +24:44n. Jsh +14:2n. 1 S *10:21, etc. *14:42. 1 Ch 6:63. 24:31. Ne *11:1. Ac 1:24-26.

19. **brother**. ver. +24. Pr 6:19. 17:17. Ge *4:5-8. *27:41-45. *32:6-11. *37:3-5, 11, 18-27. Nu 20:18. 2 S *13:22, 28. 19:43. 1 K *2:23-25. 12:16. 2 Ch 13:17. Ps 133:1. Lk 17:3-5. Ac *15:39. **than**. Pr 10:15. *16:32. **bars**. Ex 26:26, 27, 29. 35:11. Jg +*16:3. **castle**. 1 K 16:18. 2 K 15:25. 1 Ch +*27:25.

20. **satisfied**. Pr *12:13, 14. *13:2. *22:18, 21. *25:11, 12.

21. **Death**. ver. *4-7. Pr *10:20, 21, 31. √11:30. Ps *34:11-13. 51:15. *141:3. Mt *12:35-37. Ac 16:30, 31. Ro *10:9, 10, 14, 15. 2 C *2:16. *11:15. Ep *4:29. Col *4:6. T *1:10, 11. Ja *3:6-9. 2 P *2:18. **and**. Pr *10:19. Ec *10:12-14. Is 57:19.

22. **findeth a wife**. Pr 5:15, etc. *12:4. *19:14. 30:18, 19. *31:10, etc. Ge 2:18. ●+21:21. 24:57, 67. ●28:8, 9. 29:20, 21, 28. Ex 2:21. Nu 12:1. 36:6. Dt 21:10-14. Jg ●14:2, 3. 1 S 18:20-29. 2 S 3:12-16. Ec 9:9. SS 4:9. Ho 12:12. Mt 19:5. 1 C *7:2, 39. 14:35n. 2 C √6:14. He *13:4. **and**. Pr *3:4. *8:35.

23. **poor**. Ru 2:7. 1 S 2:36. 2 K *4:1, 2. Is *66:2. Mt +*5:3. Ja 1:9-11. **rich**. Ge *42:7, 30. Ex *5:2. 1 S 25:10-12, +√17. Ja 2:3.

24. **that hath friends**. √132D, Ge +19:25. Darby renders this verse: "A man of many friends will come to ruin, but there is a friend that sticketh closer than a brother." ver. 17. Pr 3:28, 29. 6:1. 12:26. 17:17. 22:24. 25:17. *27:9. 1 S *19:4, 5. 30:26, etc. 2 S *9:1, etc. 16:17. 17:27-29. 19:30-39. *21:7. 1 Ch 12:38-40. 2 Ch √13:7. Ps *38:11. Je *2:37. Mt *26:49, 50. **there**. Pr √27:10. 2 S *1:26. Jn 14:3, 18. *15:14, 15. Ro +*12:5. He 2:11, 14-18. 1 J 3:16. **brother**. ver. +19. Pr 17:17. *27:10.

PROVERBS 19

Commendations of wisdom, integrity, kindness, meekness: the fatal effects of rashness, impatience,

wrath, sloth; the punishments awaiting false witnesses, disobedient children, scorners; with pious and pruden-tial maxims and remarks of a more general nature, 1-29.

1. **Better**. ver. 22. Pr 12:26. *15:16. *16:8. 28:6. Ps 37:26. Mt *16:26. 1 T 6:17-19. He 11:37, 38. Ja *2:5, 6. **he that**. √63F, Ge +33:10. **perverse**. 1 S 25:+*17, 25. Is 59:3. Mt *12:31-34.

2. **that the**. Pr 10:21. Ec 12:9. Is 27:11. Ho *4:6. Jn *16:3. Ro *10:2. Ph *1:9. **soul**. Heb. 'nephesh,' Ge +34:3. **and**. Pr *1:16. *14:29. 21:5. *25:8. *28:22. Jb 31:5. Ec *7:9. Is 28:16.

3. **foolishness**. Ge 3:6-12. 4:5-14. Nu *16:19-41. 17:12, 13. 1 S *13:13. *15:23. 22:13, etc. 1 K 20:42, 43. 2 K 3:9, 10. +*6:33. 2 Ch *16:9, 10. Jb √2:10. Ac *13:45, 46. **fretteth**. Nu +*11:1. Ru +*1:13. Ps *37:1, 7. +*77:3. Is 8:21, 22. √29:24. Ph +*2:14. ●+*4:11. Re *16:9-11. **against**. Is 45:9. Ezk +*18:25. Ro *9:+*14, 20-24.

4. **Wealth maketh**. ver. *6, *7. Pr *14:20. Lk *15:13-15. 1 C 3:21-23. **the poor**. Pr 10:15. Jb 6:15-23. 19:13-17. Ja 2:5.

5. **false**. ver. *9. Pr *6:19. *21:28. Ex *23:1. Dt *19:16-21. Ps 120:3, 4. Da *6:24., **unpunished**. Heb. held innocent. Pr +16:5mg. Dt 5:11. 1 K 2:9. **speaketh lies**. ver. +*9. Re *21:8.

6. **will**. ver. 12. Pr 16:15. 29:26. Ge *42:6. 2 S 19:19, etc. Jb 29:24, 25. Ps *45:12. Mt *2:11. **favor**. √171Q, Ge +3:19. **and**. Pr 17:8. *18:16. 21:14. Ge 32:20. *43:15. Ro *6:23. **him that giveth gifts**. Heb. a man of gifts. Pr 18:16. 21:14. Ge 34:12.

7. **the brethren**. ver. *4. Pr *14:20. 27:10. Ps 38:11. 88:8, 18. 113:7, 8. Ec 9:15, 16. Ja 2:6. **go far**. Ps 38:11. **he pursueth**. Pr *21:13. Lk 18:38-40. **yet**. Pr 18:23. Ja *2:15, 16. 1 J *3:17, 18.

8. **that getteth**. T#884. Pr 1:*5, 6. 3:13-18, 35. *4:6-9. 8:35. 9:12. 10:17. 11:29. *12:8. *13:15. 15:24. 16:20, 22. 21:20. 24:3-5, 13, 14. 28:26. Ps 107:43. Ec 7:12. 8:1. 10:10. Ho 14:9. Da 2:21. *12:3, 10. **wisdom**. Heb. an heart. Pr 15:32mg. *17:16. Ezk *36:26. **loveth**. Pr *8:35, 36. Jn *12:25. 1 P *3:10. **soul**. Heb. 'nephesh,' Ge +27:31. **he that keepeth**. Pr *2:1-9. *3:18, 21. 4:4, 6, 21. *16:20. 22:18. Ps *19:11. Jn *14:21.

9. **false witness**. ver. *5. **and**. Is 9:15-17. Je *23:25-32. 27:15-17. *28:15-17. *29:31, 32. Ezk 13:22. 2 Th √2:8-10. 1 T *4:1, 2. 2 P *2:1-3. Re *19:20. +*21:8. *22:15. **lies**. T#418. Pr *6:16-19. 10:18. 12:19, 22. 21:6. Ge +6:6 (T#230). Ps 5:6. 59:12, 13. 62:3, 4. 63:11. Is 28:17. Zc 8:16, 17. Ac 5:3-5. Re *21:8. *22:15.

10. **Delight**. Pr *30:21, 22. 1 S 25:36. Est 3:15. Ps 32:11. ●33:1. Is *5:11, 12. *22:12-14. Ho 7:3-5. 9:1. Am *6:3-6. Lk *16:19, 23. Ja *4:9. **much**. 2 S 3:24, 25, 39. Ec *10:5-7. Is *3:5.

11. **discretion**. T#172. Pr 2:11, 12. 3:21-23. 8:12. 11:22. 12:16. Jn 6:12. *or*, prudence. Pr 3:4mg. 12:8 (wisdom). 13:15 (understanding). 16:22. 23:9. 1 S +*25:3 (*S#7922h). **deferreth**. T#201. Pr *12:16. *14:29. *15:18. *16:+7 (T#737), 32. 17:14. Ec ●8:11. Mt +5:5 (T#438). Ac +7:59 (T#439). 1 C *13:4, 5, 7. Ga +6:1 (T#437). Ep 4:1, 2, +32 (T#203). Col *3:12, 13. He +12:14 (T#499). Ja 1:+4 (T#498), *19. 1 P 2:18-23. 3:8, 9. **and**. Pr *16:32. *20:3. *25:21, 22. Ge 45:4-15. *50:15-21. 1 S 24:7-19. Mt *5:44, 45. *18:21, 22. Ro *12:18-21. Ep √4:32. 5:1. **pass over**. Le 19:18. Ps 38:12-14. Col *3:13. 1 P 3:9.

12. **king's.** Pr *16:14, 15. *20:2. *28:15. Est 7:8. Ec 8:4. Da *2:12, 13. *3:19-23. *5:19. *6:24. Mt 2:16-18. Lk *12:4, 5. **roaring.** Re 10:1-3. **his.** 2 S *23:3, 4. Ps *72:6. Ho *14:5.

13. **foolish.** Pr *10:1. *15:20. *17:21, 25. Dt *21:18, etc. 2 S ch. 13-18. Ec *2:18, 19. **calamity.** √121G, Ge +31:1. **the contentions.** Pr *21:9, 19. *25:24. 27:15, 16. Jb *14:19. 1 C 7:16. *14:34. Ep *5:22-24. Col *3:18. T 2:5. 1 P *3:1.

14. **the inheritance.** Pr *13:22. Dt *21:16. Jsh 11:23. 2 C *12:14. **prudent wife.** Pr *3:6. √18:22. *31:10, etc. Ge *24:7. *28:1-4. Ja *1:17.

15. **Slothfulness casteth.** ver. 24. Pr *6:6, 9-11. *20:13. *23:21. *24:33, 34. Is 56:10. Ro *13:11, 12. Ep *5:14. **an idle.** Pr *10:4, 5. *20:13. *23:21. 2 Th √3:10. **soul.** Heb. 'nephesh,' Ge +12:5.

16. **keepeth the commandment.** Pr *3:1. *29:18. Ps 103:17, 18. Ec *8:5. *12:13. Je *7:23. Lk *10:28. +*11:28. Jn +*13:17. *14:15, 21-23. *15:10-14. 1 C *7:19. 1 J √2:3, 4. *3:22. *5:3. Re *22:14. **keepeth his.** Pr *16:17. *21:23. *22:5. Ps 19:11. 119:165. Ezk 33:5. Mt *16:26. **soul.** Heb. 'nephesh,' Ge +27:31. **he that despiseth.** Pr *13:13. *15:32. Le *26:21. Je 10:23. Hg 1:5, 7. Ga √6:7, 8. Ja *1:14, 15.

17. **hath pity.** Pr *14:21. 28:8, 27. Dt *15:7-11. 2 S 12:6. Ec 11:1. Mt 25:34-40. Lk 10:33-37. 14:12-14. 1 J 3:17. **lendeth.** Pr *11:24, 25. *28:27. Dt *15:7-14. Is *58:7-11. Mt *10:41, 42. *25:40. 2 C 9:6-8. Ph 4:17. He √6:10. **that which he hath given.** or, his deed. Pr 12:14. Jg 9:16. 2 Ch 32:25. 2 C *9:6-9. **pay him.** Pr 6:31. 13:21. 20:22. Mt 10:42. Mk √10:30. Lk *6:38. Ro 11:35. 1 C 13:3.

18. **Chasten.** Pr +*13:24. *22:6, 15. *23:13, 14. *29:15, 17. Ex +13:8. Ps 39:10. 89:30-32. Is 66:13. La 3:33. Mt *12:7-10. 1 P 5:6. **while.** Pr 22:6. 29:1. 1 K *1:6. 2:24. Ps 103:13. Ec 1:15. 4:13. √8:11. √11:3. Col 3:21. 1 T 5:14g. He *3:12, 13. *12:15. Re 22:11. **soul.** Heb. 'nephesh,' Ge +34:3. **spare.** lit. lift not up thy soul. Pr 6:35 (regard). 9:12 (bear). 18:14 (bear). Ge 18:24, 26. Ps 25:1. 82:2 (accept). 86:4. Je 7:16. La 3:41. **for his crying.** Ex 2:23, 24. Jg 10:16. or, to his destruction, or, to cause him to die. Pr 23:13. Dt *21:18-21.

19. **man.** Pr *22:24, 25. *25:28. *29:22. 1 S 19:1-11. 20:30-33. 22:7, etc. *24:17, etc. *26:21, etc. 2 S 16:5, 6. **great wrath.** Pr 6:34. 15:1, 18. 16:14. Ge 4:5-8, 13. **deliver.** Pr 10:2. 11:6. 12:6. Ps 138:8. Mt *11:29. Ro *7:22-25. 2 C √12:9. **do it again.** Heb. add. ver. 4. Pr 1:5. 3:2. 9:9, 11. 10:22.

20. **Hear.** Pr 1:8. 4:1, 10. 5:7. 7:24. Mk 4:24. Lk 8:18. +*11:28. **counsel.** ver. 21. Pr 1:25, 30. 8:14. *12:15. 1 K ◐12:13. 2 Ch 25:16. Is 1:3. **receive instruction.** T#885. Pr *1:8. *2:1-9. 4:*7, 13. *8:17, +33, 34, 35. 1 S ◐+√25:17. 2 Ch 1:11, 12. Ho 6:3. **be wise.** Nu 23:10. Dt 8:16. *32:29. Ps *90:12, 14. **thy latter end.** Ps *37:37. Lk 16:19-23.

21. **many.** Pr 12:2. Ge 37:19, 20. Est *9:25. Ps 21:11. *33:10, 11. 83:4. Ec *7:29. Is *7:6, 7. Da 11:24, 25. Mt 26:4, 5. 27:63, 64. **nevertheless.** Pr *16:1, 9. *21:1, 30. Ge *45:4-8. √50:20. Jb 23:13. Ps 2:6. 21:11. 94:11. Is *14:24, 26, 27. 43:13. *46:10. Da *4:35. Ac *4:27, 28. *5:38, 39. Ep +*1:11. He *6:17, 18. 1 P *2:8. Ju *4.

22. **desire.** 1 S √30:24. 1 Ch 29:2, 3, 17. 2 Ch *6:8. Ps +149:9. Mk *12:41-44. *14:6-8. Lk 21:4. 2 C 8:2, 3, *12. **kindness.** +*31:26. **and.** ver. *1. Jb 6:15. *17:5.

Ps 62:9. Ac 5:1-5. T *1:2. **poor.** 2 C *8:9. **liar.** ver. +*9.

23. **fear of the Lord.** Pr *10:27. *14:26, 27. Ps *19:9. *33:18, 19. *34:9-11. 85:9. *103:17. *145:18-20. Ml √3:16, 17. *4:2. Ac *9:31. He *12:28. Re 15:4. **to life.** Pr 3:2, 18, *22. 10:16. **shall abide.** Ps *90:14. *91:16. Is *58:10, 11. Mt +*5:6. Ph *4:11, 12. 1 T *4:8. *6:6-9. He +*13:5, 6. **satisfied.** Pr 27:7. Ge 25:8. 35:29. **he shall.** Pr *12:21. Ro √8:28. 2 T *4:18.

24. **slothful man.** ver. *15. Pr *6:9, 10. 12:27. *15:19. *24:30-34. 26:13-16. Ps *74:11. Ec 4:5. Am *6:1. Ro *2:7. He *12:1, 2.

25. **Smite.** Pr 21:11. 23:13, 14. Ge 14:5, 7, 15. Dt 13:11. *21:21. Mt +5:39. Ac *13:9-11. **scorner.** ver. 29. Pr 1:22. 3:34. **simple.** Pr 1:4, 22, 32. 7:7. 8:5. 9:4. **beware.** Heb. be cunning. or, act prudently. Pr 15:5. Ex 18:10, 11. Dt *19:20. 1 S 23:22. Ps 83:3. Re 11:13. **reprove.** Pr 3:12. *9:8-10. 15:5. *17:10. *30:6. 1 S ◐+*25:17. Ps *141:5. Mt ◐+*7:6. Re *3:19. **hath understanding.** Pr 1:5. +*8:9. 10:13. 14:+*6, 33. +15:14. **knowledge.** ver. 2, 27. Pr 1:4, 7, 22, 29.

26. **wasteth.** Pr 10:1. 17:25. *23:22-25. 28:24. 30:11, 17. Dt 21:18-21. Lk *15:12-16, 30. Ro 1:30, 31. Ep 6:2, 3. **a son.** Pr 10:5. 17:2. *28:7.

27. **Cease.** Pr *14:7. Dt 4:2. *13:1-4. 1 K 22:22-28. 2 Ch 13:7. Ps +*119:63. Is 30:10. Je 5:31. Mt *7:15. +15:14. *16:6, 12. Mk *4:24. 7:6-14. Jn 10:5. Ro *16:17. 2 C 10:5. *11:13-15. Ga 1:6, 7. 3:1-4. 5:+*4, 7, 8. Ep *4:14. 1 T 4:7. *6:3-5. 2 T 2:16, 17. 4:3. He *13:9. 2 P 2:1, 2. 1 J *4:1. 2 J 10. Re 2:2. **to err.** Mk √12:24.

28. **An ungodly witness.** Heb. A witness of Belial. Pr +16:27mg. 1 S +30:22. 2 S 22:5mg. 1 K 21:10, 13. Ps 18:4mg. Ac *6:11-13. **scorneth.** Pr 14:9. Ps 10:5, 11. Is *28:14-18, 22. Lk *18:2-4. **the mouth.** Pr *15:14. Jb *15:16. 20:12, 13. 34:7. Ho 4:8.

29. **Judgments.** Pr *3:34. 9:12. Is *28:22. 29:20. √33:14. Je 31:18. Ezk 22:14. Ac *13:40, 41. He 10:31. 2 P *3:3-7. **scorners.** ver. 25. Ps 1:1. **and.** Pr *7:22. *10:13. *17:10. *26:3. He *12:6.

PROVERBS 20

The evils of intemperance, dishonesty, and many other vices and imprudences. The power of kings, and the good use to be made of it. The benefit of deliberation and good counsel. The deceitfulness of men, and the curse attending dishonest gain. The honor of young and old men. The advantage of correction; and man's obligation to trust in God, 1-30.

1. **Wine.** √121G, Ge +31:1. Pr 4:17. 9:2, 5. 21:17. Is 5:11, 13, 22. Ho 4:6-11. Hab 2:15. **a mocker.** Pr *23:29-35. 31:4. Ge 9:21-23. 19:31-36. 1 S 25:36-38. 2 S 11:13. 13:28. 1 K 20:16-21. Is *28:7. Ho *4:11. 7:5. Hab √2:15, 16. 1 C *6:10. Ga √5:21. Ep √5:18. **strong drink.** Pr 31:4, 6. Le 10:9. **raging.** or, noisy. Pr 1:21. 7:11. 9:13. 1 K 1:41. **deceived.** T#365. Pr 23:21, 29, 30, 34, 35. Ge 9:20, 21. Is 28:7, 8. 56:12. Je 25:27. Da 5:1, 4. Ho 4:11. 1 C 11:21. or, going astray. Ps 119:21, 118. Ezk 45:20. **not wise.** T#200-8. 2 S 13:28. 1 K 16:9. Is *28:7. Lk *21:34. Ep *5:18.

2. **fear.** Pr *16:14, 15. 19:12. Ec *10:4. Ho 11:10. Am 3:8. **sinneth.** Pr *8:36. 1 K 2:23. Est 7:7. Ps 2:12. **soul.** Heb. *nephesh*, Ge +27:31.

3. **honor.** Pr 3:16, 35. 8:18. 11:16. **to cease.** Pr 14:29. *16:32. 17:14. *19:11. 25:8-10. Ge 13:8. Ro 12:√18,

21. Ep 1:6-8. √4:32. 5:1. Col *3:12-15. **but every fool.** T#200-13. Pr 14:17. 18:6. 21:24. 2 K 14:9, 10. Ja 3:14-18. 4:1. **meddling.** Pr 17:14. 18:1. 1 P 4:15.

4. **sluggard.** Pr *10:4, 19:15, 24. 26:13-16. Mt 25:26-30. Ro 13:11. **cold.** or, winter. *S#2779h. Ge 8:22. Jb 29:4 (youth). Ps 74:17. Je 36:22. Am 3:15. Zc 14:8. **therefore.** Pr 6:10, 11. 19:15. 24:34. Mt 25:3-10, *24-28. 2 P √1:5-11.

5. **Counsel.** Pr *18:4. Ps 64:5, 6. Je 17:9. 1 C 2:11. **man of understanding.** Pr +*8:9. 14:6. +19:25. Ps *119:98.

6. **proclaim.** Pr *25:14. *27:2. 2 K 10:16, 31. Je 2:23, 35. Mt *6:2, 5, 16. Lk *16:15. *18:8, 11, 28. 22:33. Ro 2:17-23. 2 C 12:11. **goodness.** or, bounty. ver. 28 (mercy). Pr 3:3. 11:17. 14:22. **but.** Ps 12:1. Ec 7:28. Je *5:1. Mi 7:2. Lk *18:8. Jn 1:47. **faithful.** Pr 13:17. 14:5. Dt 32:20. Ps *12:1. Is 26:2. Lk √18:8. Ph +*2:12.

7. **just.** Pr 14:2. 19:1. Ge 17:1, 2. Ps *15:2. 26:1, 11. Is 33:15. Lk 1:6. 2 C *1:12. T *2:11, 12. 3 J *3, *4. **his children.** T#765. Pr 11:21. *13:22. 14:26. Ge 17:7. +*18:19. Dt *4:40. 5:29. Ps 25:12, 13. *37:25, 26. +*102:28. 112:2. *147:13. Je 32:39. Ac *2:39. 2 T *1:5.

8. **A king.** ver. *26. 16:12. *29:14. 1 S 23:3, 4. 2 S 8:15. *23:4. 1 K 10:9. Ps 72:4. 82:1. 89:14. 92:9. 99:4. *101:3-8. Is 32:1. **his eyes.** Ps 5:5. Re 1:14.

9. **Who.** 1 K 8:46. 2 Ch 6:36. Jb 14:4. 15:14-16. *25:4. Ps *51:5, 10. 130:3. 143:2. Ec √7:20. Is 6:5. 53:6. 64:6. Mt 11:28. Lk +*19:10. Ro 3:9-12. 1 C *4:4. 1 T 1:15. Ja 3:2, 8. 1 J √1:8-10. **can say.** √108B. Idiom B828. "Can say" is used of being able really and truly to affirm from the heart. For another instance of this idiom see 1 C 12:3. **clean.** Jb 8:6. Ps 24:4. 51:2, 7.

10. **Divers weights, and divers measures.** Heb. A stone and a stone, an ephah and an ephah. √171K1, Dt +19:5. Dt 25:13. **both.** ver. *23. Pr *11:1. 16:11. Le *19:35, 36. Dt *25:13-16. 32:4. Ps 5:6. 25:21. Am 8:4-7. Mi 6:10, 11. **abomination.** Dt *7:25, 26. Re *21:8.

11. **a child.** Pr 21:8. 22:15. 1 S 2:26. 3:19, 20. Ps *51:5. *58:3. Mt *7:16. Lk 1:15, 66. *2:46, 47, 50-52. *6:43, 44. 2 T √3:14, 15.

12. **hearing ear.** T#1831. Ex *4:11. Ps *94:9. *119:18. Mt *13:13-16. Mk +*4:24. 8:25. Lk +*8:18. Ac *26:18. Ep *1:17, 18. **seeing eye.** Ge +*3:7. Lk +*24:31. **the Lord.** Pr 2:6. Ex 4:11. Jn 16:14, 15. 1 C 4:7. 2 T 2:25.

13. **Love not sleep.** T#924. Pr *6:9-11. *10:4, 5. *12:11. 13:4. *19:15. *24:30-34. 1 K 19:5. Ps 127:2. Ro *12:11. 1 C 9:24, 25. 1 Th 5:6. 2 Th *3:10. **open.** Jon *1:6. Ro *13:11. 1 C *15:34. Ep *5:14.

14. **It is naught.** ver. 14, 20. Pr 1:16, 33. Le 19:18. *25:14. Ec 1:10. Is *5:20. Ho 12:7, 8. Mt 5:37. Ac *24:16. 1 Th *4:6. **naught.** √84, Ge +6:17. **boasteth.** Ja 4:16.

15. **There is gold.** Mt 19:22. 1 T 6:9, 10. **but.** Pr *3:15. *8:11. *10:20, 21. *15:7, 23. *16:16, 21, 24. *25:12. 1 K 3:9. Jb *28:12-19. Ec *12:9-11. Mt 13:45, 46. Ro *10:14, 15. Ep *4:29.

16. **Take his.** Pr *11:15. *22:26, 27. 27:13. Ex *22:26, 27. **a strange.** Pr 2:16. 5:3. 7:5, 10. *23:27.

17. **deceit.** Heb. lying, or falsehood. Pr 4:17. **is sweet.** Pr *9:17, 18. Ge *3:6, 7. 2 K 5:20, 26, 27. Jb √20:12-20. Ec *11:9. He *11:25. **afterwards.** He 12:11. **his.** La 3:15, 16.

18. **purpose.** Pr *15:22. *24:5, 6. 1 K 22:6. Is 9:6. **good advice.** Pr *13:10. 1 K +*12:7n. **make war.** Pr *25:8. Jg *1:1, 2. 9:29. 20:7, 18, 23, 26-28. 2 S 2:26, 27. 2 Ch 25:17-23. Ps 144:1. Lk *14:31. +*22:36.

19. **that goeth.** Pr *11:13. *18:8. *26:20-22. Le *19:16. 1 T 5:13. **meddle.** Pr 24:21. **flattereth.** or, enticeth. Pr *16:29. Ro *16:18.

20. **curseth.** Pr *30:11, 17. Ex *20:12. *21:15, 17-21. Le 20:9. Dt 27:16. Mt *15:4. Mk *7:10-13. **his.** Pr *13:9. *24:20. Jb *18:5, 6, 18. Mt *22:13. 25:8. Ju *13. **lamp.** or, candle. ver. *27mg. Pr +6:23mg. **put out.** Pr 13:9. 24:20. **obscure.** *S#380h. Pr 7:2 (apple), 9 (black). Dt 32:10. Ps 17:8. Ju 13. **darkness.** Pr 2:13. Ge 1:2, 4, 5, 18. Ex 10:21, 22. Is 5:30. 8:22. 13:10. Je 4:28. +8:15. 13:16. La 3:2. Ezk 32:7, 8. Jl 2:*2, 10. Am 4:13. *5:18, 20. 8:9. Mi *7:8. Mt *24:29. √27:45. Mk 13:24. 2 P 2:4. Ju *6, *13. Re 8:12. 9:2.

21. **gotten.** Pr *23:4. *28:20, 22. 2 S 15:10. 1 T *6:9. **but.** Pr *13:22. *28:8. 2 S 18:9-17. 1 K 21:1-15. Jb *27:16, 17. Je 17:11. Hab 2:6. Zc 5:4. Ml *2:2.

22. **I will recompense.** Pr *17:13. *24:29. Ge 27:41. Dt *32:35. Ro *12:17-19, 21. 1 Th *5:15. He 10:30. 1 P *3:9. **wait.** 2 S 16:12. Ps *27:14. *37:5, 34, 40. Is *40:31. La *3:25, 26. Mt 5:38, 39. 1 P 2:23. *4:19. Re 6:10.

23. **weights.** See on ver. 10. Ezk *45:10. **a false balance.** Heb. balances of deceit. Ho *12:7. Am 8:5. Mi 6:10, 11.

24. **Man's.** Ps *37:23. 119:32. Is 30:21. Je *10:23. Da 5:23. Ac 17:28. **how.** Pr *14:8. *16:9. Ps *25:4, 12. 37:23. 73:24. Is 10:6, 7. Ro 1:10. Ph *2:13.

25. **a snare.** Pr 18:7. Le *5:15. 22:10-15. 27:30. Jsh 6:18. Ml *3:8-10. **after.** Le *27:9, 10, 31. Nu *30:2, etc. Dt 23:21. Ec *5:4-6. Mt *5:33.

26. **wise.** ver. *8. Pr 17:15. Ge +9:5. 2 S 4:9-12. 1 K 14:14. Ps 1:4. *101:5-8. Ml 3:2. **bringeth.** 2 S 12:31. Is 28:27, 28.

27. **spirit.** Heb. neshamah, breath, Ge +*2:7. Jb *32:8. Ro 1:19-21, 32. *2:14, 15. 1 C *2:11. 2 C *4:2-6. 1 J *3:19-21. **candle.** or, lamp. ver. +20mg. Ps *119:105mg. **searching.** ver. 30. Ac 24:16. He *4:12, 13. 1 J 3:20. **belly.** √121J22, Jb +15:35.

28. **Mercy.** Pr *16:6. See on Ps 61:7. 85:10. 89:14. 101:1. **and truth.** √174, Ge +18:27. **his.** Pr 16:12. *29:14. Ps 21:7. 26:1. Is *16:5. Mi √7:18.

29. **glory.** Is 40:29. Je *9:23, 24. 1 J *2:14. **the beauty.** See on Pr *16:31. Le *19:32.

30. **cleanseth away evil.** Heb. is a purging medicine against evil. Pr 4:22mg. Ps *119:9, 11. Is 27:9. **stripes.** Pr *19:25. *22:15. Ps 103:14. 119:75. Is 27:9. Je 10:24. He *12:10, 11.

PROVERBS 21

All hearts are in the hands of the Lord, 1. The evil of pride, hypocrisy, injustice, sloth, voluptuousness, falsehood, and cruelty to the poor; commendations of diligence, prudence, equity, and mercy: and the misery of domestic contention, 2-29. All events are at the Lord's disposal, 30, 31.

1. **The king's.** Pr *16:1, 9. *20:24. 28:2. Ge *20:6. Ezr 1:1. *7:27, 28. Ne 1:11. *2:4. Ps 76:10. 105:14, 25. 106:46. Je 52:3. Da *4:35. Ac *7:10. Re 17:17. **rivers.** *S#6388h. Pr 5:16. Jb 29:6. Ps 1:3. 46:4 (streams). 65:9. 119:136. Is 30:25. 32:2. La 3:48. **of water.** √63I1D, Nu +26:4. Supply ellipsis (in the hand

of the gardener). Ps *1:3. 74:15. 93:4. 114:3, 5. Is *43:19. 44:27. Je 17:8. Re *16:4, 12. turneth. Dt +*11:10n. Is 37:25. Ezk 32:2. whithersoever. Pr *16:9, 33. Ezr 6:22. Ne 2:4. Est 4:11. 5:3. Je *10:23. Ep +*1:11.

2. right. Pr *16:2, 25. 20:6. *30:12. Ps 36:2. Mt *19:20. Lk *18:11, 12. Ga *6:3. Ja *1:22. the Lord. Pr *24:12. 1 S √16:7. Ps 139:23, 24. Je √17:9, 10. Lk *16:15. Jn +*2:24, 25. Re *2:23.

3. do justice. T#629. Pr *15:8. 24:23. Le *19:15, 36. Dt 6:18. 16:20. 1 S 12:1-4. *15:22. Ps 50:8. *51:6. Is *1:11-17. 56:1. Je 7:21-23. Ho *6:6. Mi *6:6-8. Zc *7:9, 10. Mt *23:23. Mk *12:32-34. Lk 20:25. Jn +1:47 (T#659). +8:50 (T#56). Ac 10:35. Ro *12:1. 13:7, 8. 2 C +7:1 (T#501). Ep 6:14. 1 Th 2:10. +4:6 (T#732). 1 T 6:11. T 2:11, 12.

4. An high look. Heb. Haughtiness of eyes. Pr 6:17. *8:13. 30:13. Ps *10:4. Is 2:11, 17. 3:16. 10:12. Je 48:29. Lk *18:14. 1 P 5:5. and the. ver. *27. Pr *15:8. Ro *14:23. proud. Pr 28:25. Ge 34:21 (large). Ex 3:8. plowing of the wicked. or, light of the wicked. Pr 20:27. Jb 4:8. Mt *6:23. Ro 2:4. 1 C 2:11.

5. thoughts. Pr *10:4. 13:4. 27:23-27. Ep 4:28. 1 Th 4:11, 12. He √6:11, 12. 12:1. tend. √63BC, Ge +9:20. of every. Pr 14:29. 20:21. 28:22. that is. √63BC, Ge +9:20.

6. getting. Pr *10:2. *13:11. 20:14, 21. 22:8. 30:8. Je *17:11. 1 T *6:9, 10. T 1:11. 2 P 2:3. seek. Pr *8:36. Ezk 18:31. Ro 6:23.

7. robbery. Pr *1:18, 19. 10:6. *22:22, 23. Ps 7:16. 9:16. Is 1:23, 24. Je 7:9-11, 15. Ezk 22:13, 14. Mi 3:9-12. destroy them. T#489. Nu +*32:23 (T#733). Is 30:12, 13. Heb. saw them, or, dwell with them. Je 30:23mg. Zc 5:3, 4. because. ver. *21. Ezk 18:18. Ep *5:6.

8. way. Ge *6:5, 6. Jb *15:14-16. Ps *14:2, 3. Ec 7:29. *9:3. 1 C 3:3. Ep *2:2, 3. T 3:3. but. Pr 15:26. 30:12. Da *12:10. Mt +*5:8. 12:33. Ac *15:9. T *1:15. *2:14. *3:5. 1 P *1:22, 23. 1 J 2:29. *3:3.

9. better. ver. *19. Pr 12:4. 19:13. *25:24. 27:15, 16. brawling woman. Heb. woman of contentions. Pr 25:24. in a wide house. Heb. in a house of society. Pr *15:17. *17:1. 25:24. Is +*47:12h. 1 P ○*3:3, 4.

10. soul. Heb. nephesh, Ge +34:3. desireth. Pr *3:29. 12:12. Ps *36:4. 52:2, 3. Ec √8:11. Mk *7:21, 22. 1 C 10:6. Ja *4:1-5. 1 J *2:16. findeth no favor. Heb. is not favored. ver. *13. 1 S 25:8-11. Ps *112:5, 9. Is *32:6-8. Mi 3:2, 3. Ja 2:13. 5:4-6.

11. the scorner. Pr *19:+25, 29. Nu 16:34. Dt 13:11. *21:21. Ps 64:7-9. Ac *5:5, 11-14. 1 C *10:6-11. He *2:1-3. *10:28, 29. Re 11:13. punished. Ex 21:22. Ec 8:11. Is 26:9. simple. √108K54, Pr +1:4. when the wise. Pr *1:5. 8:33. *9:9. *15:14. *18:1, 15. 19:20. Ps *94:12. 119:71. instructed. Ne 8:13mg.

12. wisely. Jb *5:3. 8:15. *18:14-21. *21:28-30. *27:13-23. Ps *37:35, 36. 52:5. *58:10, 11. *107:43. Ho *14:9. Hab 2:9-12. overthroweth. Pr *11:3-5. *13:6. *14:32. Ge *19:29. Am *4:11. 1 C 10:5. 2 P *2:4-9. *3:6, 7.

13. stoppeth. T#687. Pr 24:11, 12. *31:8, 9. Le +25:35 (T#526). Jb +27:13 (T#490). Ps +12:5. 58:4. *82:34. Is *1:17. *16:3, 4. Je 21:12. Zc 7:11. Mt +5:7 (T#527). Lk *6:38. Ac 7:57. 1 J *3:17. at. Pr *28:27. Dt *15:7-11. Ne 5:1-5, 13. Is *1:15-17. 58:6-9. Je 34:16, 17. Zc *7:9-13. Mt 6:14. 7:2. *18:30-35. *25:41-46. Ja *2:13-16. cry himself. See on Pr *1:28. Ps 18:41. Lk

13:25. 16:24. but shall. T#543. Is 58:7, 9. Col 3:12. not be heard. T#1807. Is √58:7-11. Jn +*9:31.

14. gift. Pr *17:8, 23. *18:16. *19:6. Ge *32:20. *43:11. Ex 23:8. Dt 16:19. 1 S 25:35. Ec 10:19. in secret. Mt *6:3, 4.

15. joy. Pr 10:29. Jb 29:12-17. Ps 32:11. *40:8. 112:1. 119:16, 92. Ec 3:12. Is *32:17. *64:5. Mt 11:30. Jn *4:34. Ro *7:22. destruction. ver. 12. Pr 5:20. *10:29. Mt *7:23. *13:41, 42. Lk *13:27, 28.

16. wandereth. Pr *13:20. 1 S +16:14. Ps *125:5. Je *14:10. Zp 1:6. Jn *3:19, 20. He √6:4-6. *10:26, 27, 38. 2 P √2:21, 22. 1 J *2:19. remain. Pr *2:18, 19. 7:26, 27. 9:18. Je 22:17-19, 28-30. Ep *2:1. Ju *12. Re √20:5. the dead. or, Rephaim. *S#7496h. Pr 2:18. 9:18. Jb 26:5. Ps 88:10. Is 14:9. 26:14, 19. Compare Ge +*14:5 (*S#7497h). Dt +2:20. Jsh +17:15mg.

17. loveth. √121C2C1, Ps +11:5. ver. *20. Pr 5:10, 11. *23:21. Lk *15:13-16. *16:24, 25. 1 T *5:6. 6:17. 2 T *3:4. pleasure. Heb. sport. or, mirth. ver. 15. Pr 10:28. 12:20. 14:10, √13. 15:*21, 23. *26:19. Ge 31:27. Jb *20:5. Ec 2:1, 2. 7:4. 8:15. Is 32:11. 47:8, 9. Lk 8:13. 12:19. 21:34. Ep 5:4. 2 P 2:13. Re 18:7. wine. Pr 20:1. 23:20, *21, 29-35. and oil. ver. 20. Pr 5:3. 27:9, 16. Ge 28:18. rich. Pr 10:4, 22. *23:21. 1 S 17:25.

18. wicked. Pr *11:8. Jsh 7:25. Ps 49:7, 8. Is 43:3, 4. *53:4, 5. √55:8, 9. 1 P *3:18.

19. better. See on ver. *9. Ps *55:6, 7. 120:5, 6. Je *9:2. 1 C 7:15. wilderness. Heb. land of the desert.

20. treasure. Pr *10:22. *15:6. Ge 41:48. Ps *112:3. Ec *5:19. 7:11. 10:19. Mt *6:19, 20. Lk *6:45. oil. Ps *23:5. Je 41:8. Mt *25:4, 5. desired. √24C, 2 K +18:21. but. T#200-19. Mt *25:3, 4, 8. Lk *15:14. 16:1, 19-25.

21. that. Pr *15:9. Ps 63:8. Is 32:17. 33:15-17. 51:1. Ho *6:3. Mt *5:6. Ro *14:19. Ph *3:12-14. 1 Th *5:15. 1 T *6:11. 2 T *2:22. He *12:14. findeth. Pr *22:4. Mt 10:41, 42. Jn 12:26. Ro *2:7-10. 1 C √15:58. 2 T *4:7, 8. He *6:10. 1 P *1:7.

22. wise. 2 S *20:16-22. Ec *7:19. *9:13-18. 2 C 10:4. Ep 6:10-12.

23. keepeth. T#897. Pr *10:19. *12:13. *13:3. 14:3. *17:27, 28. *18:21. Ps *34:12, 13. +101:5. Mt 12:37. Ja *1:26. *3:2-13. 1 P 3:10. soul. Heb. nephesh, Ge +27:31.

24. haughty. Pr 6:17. *16:18. *18:12. 19:29. Est *3:5, 6. Ec *7:8, 9. Is 2:12. Ml 4:1. Mt 2:16. proud wrath. Heb. the wrath of pride. Jb 38:11mg. Is ○66:2.

25. desire. Pr *6:6-11. 12:24, 27. *13:4. 15:19. 19:24. 20:4. 22:13. *24:30-34. 26:13, 16. Mt *25:26. slothful. Ec +*10:18. refuse. Pr 19:15. 1 Th 4:11. 2 Th 3:10, 11. 1 T 5:13.

26. coveteth. Ex +*20:17. Ac *20:33-35. Ph +2:21 (T#136). Col +*3:5. 1 Th *2:5-9. greedily. Pr +*15:27. the righteous. Ps *37:26. 112:9. Lk *6:30-36. Ac *20:35. 2 C 8:7-9. 9:9-14.

27. sacrifice. Pr *15:8. *28:9. 1 S 13:12, 13. *15:21-23. Ps 50:8-13. Is *1:11-16. 66:3. Je 6:20. 7:11, 12. Am 5:21, 22. Ml 1:7, 8. Mt 15:7-9. Jn √14:6. with a wicked mind. Heb. in wickedness. Mt *23:14. Jn 10:1.

28. false witness. Heb. witness of lies. Pr 6:19. *19:5, 9. 25:18. Ex *23:1. Dt *19:16-19. Is 29:21. the man. Pr 1:33. 8:34. 12:19. Ac *12:15. 2 C 1:17-20. *4:13. T *3:8. 1 J 1:1, 3. constantly. Pr *12:19. Jb +4:20 (*S#5331h). Jn 3:11. 2 P √1:16-18.

29. **hardeneth**. Pr *28:14. *29:1. 1 S +√25:17. Je 3:2, 3. *5:3. 8:12. *36:25. *44:16, 17. **he directeth**. *or*, he considereth. Pr *11:5. Ps *119:59. 2 K +*5:13, 14. Ezk *18:28. Hg *1:5, 7. 2:15, 18, 19. Mt 6:22. Lk *15:17, 18. 1 Th 3:11.

30. **no wisdom**. Pr *19:21. Is 7:5-7. 8:9, 10. *14:27. *46:10, 11. Je *9:23. Jon 1:13. Ac *4:27, 28. *5:39. 1 P 2:8. **nor understanding**. Is 44:25. Ro 11:33-36. **nor counsel**. Pr +*19:21. 2 S 15:31. 16:23. 17:14, 23. 1 K 11:11, 40. 21:21. 22:30-34. 2 K 10:1-7. 11:2. Ezr 4:15. Jb 5:13. 12:21, 22. Ps 33:10, 11. Is +*7:7. *14:27. **against**. Nu 23:23. Ge 11:8. Jb 5:12. 12:17. 42:2mg. Is 37:27. 40:23. 41:11. 44:25. 45:16. Je 20:11. Lk *20:26. 2 C 13:8.

31. **horse**. Ps *20:7. *33:17, 18. 147:10. Ec *9:11. Is *31:1. Ho 14:3. **but**. Ps 3:3, 8. *68:20. **safety**. *or*, victory. Ps 144:10mg.

PROVERBS 22

The worth of a good name and the dependence of both rich and poor on God, 1, 2. Commendations of prudence, humility, piety, charity, and the proper tuition of children; and cautions against frowardness, iniquity, sloth, intimacy with bad women, and oppression, 3-16. An address to the reader, calling his attention to wisdom; again exhorting him to avoid oppression, friendship with angry men, suretiship, and removing ancient landmarks; and showing the advantages of diligence, 17-29.

1. **good name**. T#616. Pr 25:18. 1 K 1:47. Ps +101:5 (T#729). Ec 7:1. Lk *10:20. Ph *4:3. He *11:39. Ju +8 (T#730). **loving favor rather than**. *or*, favor is better than, etc. Pr 16:15. Ac 7:10.

2. **rich**. Pr *29:13. 1 S *2:7. Ps 49:1, 2. Lk 16:19, 20. 1 C 12:21. Ja *2:2-5. **and**. ƒ174, Ge +18:27. **poor**. Ex +23:3. **meet together**. Jb 3:19. Is *53:6. 1 C *12:13. Ga 3:28. Re 20:12. **the Lord**. Pr 14:31. Jb 31:15. *34:19. Ac *17:25, 26, 28.

3. **prudent**. Pr 12:16, 23. 13:16. 14:8, 15, *16, 18. *15:5. 16:21. *18:15. *||27:12. Ex *9:20, 21. Ps 112:5. Is 26:20, 21. Je +8:7. Ho *14:9. Mt +*7:6. *24:15-18. 1 Th *5:2-6. He 6:18. *11:7. **forseeth**. T#1843. Pr 6:8. 14:15. 24:27. 2 Ch 34:21. Ps +*34:4. +*112:5. Lk 12:33. √14:28. Ro 11:20. 2 C 5:9-11. He 4:1, 11. 11:7. **the evil**. Is 50:11. Mt 25:41. **hideth**. Pr 14:16. 18:10. 27:12. *28:12. Ex 12:12, 13, 21-23. Nu 5:13. 35:11-13. Jsh 20:7n. 1 S 19:12, 18. 20:5, 19. +21:10, 14. 23:19-21. 26:1. *27:1. 1 K 17:3. 19:3. Is 26:20. Je +*36:19. *37:12. Am 5:13. Mt +*10:23. 24:15-18. Mk 3:6, 7. Lk +4:30. Jn *8:59. 10:39. *12:36. Ac 4:12. 9:23-25. 17:14. 23:12-24. He *6:18. **the simple**. ƒ108K54, Pr +1:4. Pr 1:4, 22, 32. *7:7, 22, 23. *9:16-18. *14:15, 16. *29:1. Ps 116:6. Is 26:11. **punished**. Pr 27:12. Ex 21:22. Mt 25:46.

4. **By**, etc. Heb. The reward of humility, etc. Pr 3:16. *21:21. Ps *34:9, 10. 112:1-3. Is 33:6. *57:15. Ml 3:14. Mt +*5:3. *6:33. Lk 18:13, 14. 1 T *4:8. Ja *4:6, 10.

5. **Thorns**. Pr *13:15. 15:19. Jsh 23:13. Jb *18:8. Ps *11:6. *18:26, 27. Je 23:12, 13. **he**. Pr *13:3. *16:17. *19:16. Ps *91:1. 1 J *5:18. Ju *20, *21. **soul**. Heb. *nephesh*, Ge +27:31.

6. **Train up**. ƒ138C, Ge +22:14. T#493, 904. Pr +*19:18. Ex 10:2. +13:8. Dt 6:6-9. 11:18-21. 32:46. Jsh +1:8 (T#48). Is *28:9. Ep *6:4. *or*, Catechize.

❋S#2596h. Dt 20:5 (dedicated), 5 (dedicate). 1 K 8:63. 2 Ch 7:5. **a child**. Ge +*18:19. Dt 4:9. *6:7. Ps *78:3-6. La 3:27. Ep *6:4. 2 T +√3:15. **the way**. Heb. his way. lit. mouth of the way. i.e. *entrance on life*. ƒ144A2, Ge +34:26. **when**. 1 S *1:28. *2:26. *12:2, 3. **not depart**. T#496. Pr *20:7. Ge *18:19. 1 K +8:36h. Ps 37:26. 102:28. Ac +2:39 (T#120). Ph +*2:12. 2 T *1:5.

7. **rich**. ver. *16, *22. Pr *14:31. 18:23. Am 2:6. 4:1. *5:11, 12. 8:4, 6. Ja 2:6. *5:1, 4. **the borrower**. T#1825. Dt 15:6. *28:12. 2 K 4:1, √7n. Ne 5:3-5. Ps *37:21. Is 24:2. Mt *18:24, 25. Lk 16:5, 6. Ro *13:8. **servant to**. 2 K 4:1-7. 1 C 6:12. **lender**. Heb. man that lendeth. Pr 19:17. 28:8. Dt 15:6. 24:6. +√28:12. 2 K 4:1. Jb 24:3. Ps 37:26. 112:5. Is 24:2. Mt 5:42. Lk 6:34, 35.

8. **that**. Jb *4:8. Ho 8:7. *10:12, 13. Ga *6:7, 8. **the rod of his anger shall fail**. *or*, with the rod of his anger he shall be consumed. Pr *14:3. Ps 125:3. Is 9:4. 10:5. 14:29. 30:31.

9. **He that hath a bountiful eye**. Heb. Good of eye. Pr *11:25. *19:17. *21:13. Dt *15:7-11. 28:56. Jb 31:16-20. Ps *41:1-3. 112:9. 145:16. Ec 11:1, 2. Is 32:8. *58:7-12. Mt 20:15. *25:34-40. Mk 7:22. Lk *6:35-38. *14:14. Ac 20:35. 2 C 8:1, 2. *9:6-11. 1 T *6:17-19. He *6:10. 13:16. 1 P 4:9.

10. **Cast out**. Pr 21:24. *26:20, 21. Ge 21:9, 10. Ne 4:1-3. *13:28. Ps 1:1. *101:5. Mt *18:17. 1 C *5:5, 6, 13.

11. **that**. Pr *16:13. Ps *101:6. Mt +*5:8. **for the grace of his lips**. *or*, and hath grace in his lips. Ps 45:2. Lk *4:22. **the king**. Ge *41:39, etc. Ezr *7:6, etc. Ne *2:4-6. Est 10:3. Da *2:46-49. *3:30. *6:20-23.

12. **eyes**. 2 Ch *16:9. Ps *34:15. Is *59:19-21. Mt 16:16-18. Ac *5:39. 12:23, 24. Re 11:3-11. 12:14-17. **he**. Jb *5:12, 13. Ac 8:9-12. *13:8-12. 2 Th *2:8. 2 T 3:8, 9. **words**. *or*, matters. Jb 33:13. Ps 64:5. 63:5mg. Ec 12:13. Je 7:22mg. 52:34mg. Ezk 9:11mg. Da 1:14.

13. **The slothful**. That is, the slothful man uses any pretext, however improbable, to indulge his love of ease and indolence. Pr *15:19. *26:13-16. Nu 13:32, 33. **without**. Heb. *chutz*, Am +5:16n (✦S#2351h, highways), outside, or narrower streets. **the streets**. Heb. *rechob*, Am +5:16n (❋S#7339h, streets), public square or broad streets.

14. **mouth**. Pr *2:16-19. *5:3, etc. *6:24-29. *7:5, etc. 23:27. Jg 16:20, 21. Ne *13:26. Ec *7:26. **a deep pit**. That is, it is like a deep pit, or pitfall, in which animals are often taken alive. Heb. *shuchah*, ❋S#7745h. Pr 23:27 (ditch). Je 2:6 (pits). 18:*20, 22. **abhorred**. Dt 32:19. Ps 81:12. Ro 1:28.

15. **Foolishness**. Jb 11:12. *14:4. Ps *51:5. Jn *3:6. Ep *2:3. **a child**. Pr +*19:18. Ex +13:8. 2 K 2:23, 24. **but**. Pr +*13:24. +*19:18. *23:13, 14. *29:13-17. He *12:7, 10, 11.

16. **oppresseth**. ƒ108J, Ge +43:18. **the poor**. ver. *22, *23. Pr *14:31. *21:13. *28:3. Jb 20:19, etc. Ps +*12:5. Ezk +*16:49. Mi 2:2, 3. Zc *7:9-14. Ja *2:13. *5:1-5. **to increase**. Lk +*6:35. 1 T +*6:9. **he that giveth**. Lk *6:33-35. *14:12-14. 16:24.

17. **Bow**. Pr *2:2-5. *5:1, 2. **and hear**. Pr 1:3. *3:1. *4:4-8. *8:33, 34. Is *55:3. Mt *17:5. **apply**. Pr *23:12. Ps *90:12. Ec 7:25. 8:9, 16. **heart**. ƒ12111, Ge +3:7.

18. **it is**. Pr *2:10. *3:17. 24:13, 14. Ps 19:10. *119:103, 111, 162. Je √15:16. **keep them**. Col 3:16.

within thee. Heb. in thy belly. Jb 32:18mg, 19. Jn *7:38. **fitted.** Pr 8:6. *10:13, 21. 15:7. 16:21. *25:11. Ps *119:13, 171. Ml *2:7. He *13:15.

19. **thy.** Pr *3:5. Ps *62:8. Is *12:2. *26:4. Je *17:7. 1 P *1:21. **even to thee.** or, trust thou also.

20. **written.** Pr 8:6. Ps *12:6. Ho *8:12. 2 T √3:15-17. 2 P *1:19-21.

21. **I.** Lk *1:3, 4. Jn √20:31. 1 J √5:13. **certainty.** Pr *19:27. 21:30. *S#7189h, Ps 60:4h (truth). 119:160. Is √8:20. Lk 1:1-4. Jn 4:42. 20:25-28. Ac √17:11. 1 C 2:5. 1 Th 1:5. 2 T 1:12. √3:15. 2 P √1:15, 16. **words of truth.** Pr 8:8, 9. 30:5. Ps 119:160. Ec 12:10. Da 10:21. Jn *17:17. Ja 1:18. **answer.** Pr 8:6. 15:28. 1 P √3:15. **them that send unto thee.** or, those that send thee. Pr 10:26. 15:23. 25:13. 26:6. Ml 2:7. 1 T *4:16. 2 T *2:2.

22. **Rob not.** T#636. Pr 21:7. 23:10, 11. 28:24. Ex +*20:15. Le +*19:13. Nu +*32:23 (T#733). Jb +27:13 (T#490). Is 61:8. Ezk 22:29-31. Mt +26:52 (T#736). 1 Th +4:6 (T#732). 1 T +1:10 (T#682). **oppress.** ver. *16. Ex *23:6. 2 S 12:1-6. Jb 29:12-16. 31:16, 21. Ps +12:5. Is 3:15. Ezk 22:29. Zc *7:9, 10. Ml +*3:5. **in the gate.** That is, in the court of justice, which, as we have already seen, was held at the gates of cities in the East. Ge +14:7. 2 S 19:8n.

23. **the Lord.** Pr *23:11. 1 S 24:12, 15. *25:39. Ps 12:5. 35:1, 10. *43:1. *68:5. 140:12. Je 50:34. 51:36. Mi 7:9. Ml +*3:5. **spoil.** Is 33:1. Hab 2:8. **soul.** Heb. nephesh, Ge +12:5.

24. **Make no friendship.** Pr 21:24. *29:22. Ps +*119:63. 2 C *6:14-17. 1 T 5:22. **angry man.** Pr 11:22h (snout). 14:17, 29. 16:32. 19:11. 29:8, 22. **furious man.** Pr 6:34. 15:1, 18. *19:19. 25:28. 27:4.

25. **Lest thou learn.** Pr *13:20. Ps *106:34-36. Je +*10:2. 1 C *15:33. **soul.** Heb. nephesh, Ge +34:3.

26. **strike hands.** Pr *6:1-5. *11:15. *17:18. 27:13. **sureties.** Pr 17:18. 20:16. Ne 5:3. Ezk 27:27. **debts.** Ex 22:26, 27. Dt 24:10, 12, 14.

27. **why should.** Pr 20:16. Ex *22:26, 27. 2 K 4:1. **he.** √63A1, Ge +14:20.

28. **Remove not.** Pr *23:10. Dt 19:14. 27:17. 1 K +*12:7, 8, 13. Jb 24:2. **ancient.** Heb. olam, Jb +22:15. **landmark.** or, bound. Pr 23:10mg. Ge 10:19. 23:17. Dt 32:8. Jg ⬤21:25. Jb 38:10, 11. Ho 5:10. 2 T 3:7. *4:3, 4.

29. **Seest thou.** √85D, Ps +25:12. Pr 26:12. 29:20. **a man diligent.** T#1839. Pr *10:4. *12:24. 13:4. ⬤25:14. Ge 47:6. 1 K *11:28. Ezr 7:6. Ps 45:1. Ec *9:10. Is +16:5. Mt *25:21, 23. Lk 19:13. Jn 12:26. Ro *12:8, 11. Ep 5:16. Col 4:5. 2 T *2:15. *4:2. He *6:11. *11:6. 2 P +*1:10. *3:14. **he shall stand.** That is, he shall have the honor of serving kings, as the phrase denotes. Pr 18:16. Ge 39:3-6. 41:40, 42. 1 S 16:21. 1 K 10:8. Ne 1:11. 2:1. Est 6:11. Jb 11:19mg. 29:7-12. Ps +*149:9. Da 2:48. 3:30. 5:29. 6:1-3, 28. Lk 10:7. +*21:36. Re 7:15. 22:3, 4. **mean men.** Heb. obscure men. *S#2823h, only here.

PROVERBS 23

Cautions against self-indulgence before rulers; against avarice; visiting a churl; speaking before a fool; and oppression, 1-11. Exhortations to study wisdom and to correct children for their good, 12-14. The joy of teachers and parents over wise children; with cautions against envy, intemperance, and whoredom; and

exhortations to buy the truth, to honor parents, and to give God the heart, 15-26. The infatuation of drunkards, 27-35.

1. **sittest.** Ge *43:32-34. Ju *12.

2. **put a knife.** Mt *18:8, 9. 1 C *9:27. Ph *3:19. **appetite.** √121A9, Ge +23:8.

3. **not desirous.** ver. *6. Ps *141:4. Da *1:8. Lk *21:34. Ro *13:14. 1 C √10:31. Ep *4:22. 2 P 1:5, 6.

4. **Labor not.** T#626. Pr *28:20, 22. Jb 9:29h. Is 5:8. 40:28h. Mt *6:20. Lk *12:15. Jn *6:+27 (T#742). Ph +4:11 (T#133). 1 T *6:8-10, 17. He 10:34. Ja 5:2, 3. 2 P 2:14-16. 1 J +5:4 (T#743). **cease.** Pr *3:5. 26:12. Is 5:21. Ro 11:25. 12:16. 1 C 1:30, 31.

5. **thou.** Ps *119:36, 37. Je 22:17. 1 J *2:16. **set thine eyes upon.** Heb. cause thine eyes to fly upon. "He expresses it in such a way," says Abp. Tillotson, "as if a rich man sat brooding over an estate till it was fledged, and gotten itself wings to fly away." Col *3:1-4. **that which.** Ge 42:36. Ec 1:2. 12:8. Is *55:2. 1 C *7:29-31. **riches.** Pr *27:24. Jb 1:14-17. Ps *39:6. Ec 5:13, 14. Mt *6:19. 1 T *6:17. Ja 5:1, 2. **they fly away.** T#627. Ec 1:2, 14. 2:4-11, 17-19. 5:10, 11. Ge 31:9. Jb 1:14-17. Ja +4:14 (T#148).

6. **an evil eye.** ver. 5, 26, 29, 31, 33. Pr *22:9. Dt *15:9. 28:56. Mt *20:15. Mk *7:22. 1 C 5:11. **desire.** ver. *3. Ps *141:4. Da *1:8-10. Col 3:2.

7. **as.** Pr 19:22. Je +*6:19. Mt 9:3, 4. Lk 7:39. **heart.** Heb. nephesh, soul, Ex +23:9. 1 K +8:18. **Eat.** Jg *16:15. 2 S 13:26-28. Ps *12:2. *55:21. Da 11:27. Lk 11:37, etc.

8. **morsel.** Pr 17:1. 28:21. Ge 18:5. **vomit up.** √102, Ge +2:24. Le 18:25, 28. 20:22. **lose.** or, marr. Pr 9:8. Ge 38:9. Ex 21:26. Ec 3:7. **sweet.** Pr 22:18. 24:4. 2 S +1:23mg.

9. **Speak.** Pr 9:7, 8. 26:4, 5. Is 36:21. Mt +*7:6. Ac 13:45, 46. 28:25-28. **he.** Lk 16:14. Jn 8:52. *9:30-34, 40. 10:20. Ac *17:18, 32. 1 C 1:21-24. 4:10-13.

10. **Remove.** Pr *22:28. Dt *19:14. *27:17. Jb 24:2. **old.** Heb. olam, Jb +22:15. **landmark.** or, bound. Pr 15:25. 22:28mg. **fatherless.** √171I14, Ex +22:22. Ex +√22:22-24. Dt +10:18. Jb 6:27. 22:9, 10. 24:3, 9. 31:21-23. Ps 94:6. Je 7:5. *22:3. Zc 7:10. Ml +*3:5. Ja *1:27.

11. **their redeemer.** Pr *22:23. Ex *22:22-24. Dt 27:19. Ps +12:5. 103:6. 136:1. Je 50:33, 34. 51:36.

12. **Apply.** ver. 19. Pr *2:2-6. 5:1, 2. 15:28. *22:17. Ps 119:*18, 72. Is 28:13. 34:16. Ezk *33:31. Mt *13:52. Jn +√5:39. 2 T √2:15. +√3:15. Ja *1:21-25. **words of.** Pr 2:5. 5:1. +22:21.

13. **Withhold not correction.** T#905. Pr +*13:24. +*19:18. *29:15, 17. Ex +13:8. Le +*19:17. 1 S 2:23-25. ⬤*3:13. 1 K ⬤*1:6. 2:24. La ⬤3:33. Ep 6:4. 1 T 2:8. He 12:10. **from the child.** Jb 11:12. Ps 58:3. Ec 11:10.

14. **Thou shalt.** Ex +13:8. **beat him.** Pr *22:15. 1 C *5:5. *11:32. **rod.** ver. 13. Pr 10:13. +*13:24. 22:8. *29:15, 17. **deliver.** 1 C 5:5. 11:32. He 12:10. **soul.** Heb. nephesh, Ps +30:3. **hell.** Heb. sheol, Ge +37:35. Pr +30:3.

15. **My son.** Pr *1:10. *2:1. *4:1. Mt 9:2. Lk 15:18-20. Jn 21:5. 1 J *2:1. **if.** ver. *24, *25. Pr 10:1. *15:20. 29:3. 1 Th *2:19, 20. 3:8, 9. 2 J *4. 3 J *3, *4. **even mine.** or, even I will rejoice. Pr 29:3. Je *32:41. Zp *3:17. Lk *15:23, 24, 32. Jn *15:11. 2 T *1:2-5.

16. **thy.** Pr 8:6. Ep *4:29. *5:4. Col 4:4. Ja *3:2.

17. **not.** Pr 3:31. *24:1. Ps *37:1-9, 35, 36. 73:3-7.

be thou. Pr 15:16. 28:14. Ps *111:10. 112:1. Ec 5:7. *12:+13, 14. Ac *9:31. 2 C 7:1. 1 P 1:17.

18. **surely.** Ps *37:37. Je *29:11. Lk *16:25. Ro *6:21, 22. **end.** *or,* reward. Pr *24:14. He *10:35. ✓121P6. Metonymy of the Adjunct B595. "End" is put for that which takes place at the end, here for the *reward* which comes at the end. For other instances of this figure see Je +*29:11. Ja *5:11. 1 P 1:9. **thine.** Ps *9:18. Je +*29:11. Ph *1:20.

19. **Hear.** Mt 13:9. Mk *4:24. Lk +*8:18. **and guide.** ver. *12, *26. Pr *4:10, 23. **in the way.** That is, *in the right way.*

20. **not.** ver. *29-35. Pr +*20:1. 28:7. 31:6, 7. Is *5:11, 12, 22. 22:13. Mt 24:49. Lk *15:13, 14. *16:19. *21:34. Ro *13:13. Ep ✓5:18. 1 P *4:3, 4. **flesh.** Heb. their flesh.

21. **the drunkard.** Pr *21:17. Dt *21:20. Is 28:1-3. Jl 1:5. 1 C *5:11. *6:10. Ga *5:21. Ph *3:19. **drowsiness.** ✓121N1, Ge +31:54. "Drowsiness" is put by Menonymy of the Adjunct for the sluggard. Pr *6:9-11. *19:15. *24:30-34.

22. **Hearken.** Pr *1:8. *6:20. Ex +*20:12. Dt *21:18-21. *27:16. Mk *7:10. Ep *6:1, 2. **despise.** Pr *30:11, 17. Le *19:3. Mt *15:4-6. Jn *19:26, 27.

23. **Buy.** Pr *2:2-4. *4:5-7. 10:1. *16:16. *17:16. Jb *28:12-19. Ps *119:72, 162. Is *55:1. Mt *13:44, 46. Ph *3:7, 8. Re 3:18. **sell.** Mt *16:26. Ac 20:23, 24. He *11:26. Re *12:11.

24. **father.** ✓63J1, Ge +13:9. ver. *15, *16. Pr *10:1. *15:20. 1 K 1:48. 2:1-3, 9. Ec *2:19. **shall have.** Phm *19, *20.

25. **and she.** Pr *17:25. 1 Ch *4:9, 10. Lk *1:31-33, 40-47, 58. *11:27, 28.

26. **My son.** ver. *15. **give me.** Pr *4:23. Dt *6:5. 1 Ch 29:14. Ps 76:11. Mt *10:37, 38. Lk *14:26. 20:25. Ro *12:1. 1 C 6:20. 2 C *5:14, 15. *8:5. Ep *3:17. **let.** Pr *4:25-27. Ps *107:43. *119:2, 9-11, 105. Ho *14:9. Ro *8:13. Ga *5:6. 2 P *1:19.

27. **deep ditch.** Pr +*22:14 (❋S#7745h). **strange woman.** Ec 7:26. Je 10:2. **pit.** Heb. *be-er,* Ge +16:14.

28. **as for a prey.** *or,* as a robber. Pr *2:16-19. *7:12, 22-27. *9:18. *22:14. Jg *16:4, etc. Ec *7:26. Je 3:2. **increaseth.** Nu *25:1. Ho *4:11. 1 C 10:8. Re *17:1, 2.

29. **Who hath woe.** ver. *21. Pr ✓20:1. 1 S *25:36, 37. 2 S 13:28. 1 K 20:16. Is *5:11, 22. *28:7, 8. Na 1:10. Mt *24:49, 50. Lk *12:45, 46. Ep *5:18. **redness.** Ge 49:12.

30. **tarry long.** Pr +*20:1. Ge *9:21. Ps 127:2. Is *5:11. Am 6:6. Ep ✓5:18. **mixed.** Not wine diluted and lowered with water, but made stronger and more inebriating, by the addition of more powerful ingredients, as honey, spices, myrrh, defrutum, opiates, etc. Pr 9:2. Ps 75:8. Is 65:11.

31. **Look not.** Pr *6:25. Ge 19:32. 2 S *11:2. Jb *31:1. Ps 75:8. *119:37. Jl 1:5. Mt *5:28-30. Mk *9:47. Ro 13:13. Ep *5:18. 1 P 4:3. 1 J *2:16. **color.** lit. eye. ✓121R1, Le +13:55.

32. **At the last.** Pr 5:11. Is *28:3, 7, 8. Je 5:31. Ezk 7:5, 6, 12. Lk *16:25, 26. Ro *6:21. **biteth.** Ec *10:8. Je *8:17. Am 5:19. *9:3. **an adder.** *or,* a cockatrice. Is 11:8mg. 59:5mg. Je 8:17.

33. **eyes.** Ge *19:32, etc. **and.** Pr *31:5. Ps 69:12. Da *5:4. Ho *7:5. Ju *12, *13.

34. **thou.** 1 S 25:33-38. 30:16, 17. 2 S 13:28. 1 K 16:9. 20:16, etc. Jl *1:5. Mt *24:38. Lk *17:27-29.

*21:34. 1 Th *5:2-7. **midst.** Heb. heart. ✓144A7, Ex +15:8. Pr 30:19mg. Ex 15:8. Je 51:1mg.

35. **stricken.** Pr *27:22. Je *5:3. 31:18. **I felt it not.** Heb. I knew *it* not. Jb 20:20mg. Ec 8:5mg. Ep *4:18, 19. **I will.** Pr *26:11. Dt *29:19. Is 22:13. *56:12. 1 C *15:32-34. 2 P *2:22.

PROVERBS 24

Cautions against envy, discontent, sinful thoughts, neglect of doing good, or deferring to do it; rejoicing over an enemy's calamity; respect of persons, flattery, revenge, and sloth: with recommendations of the knowledge and fear of God, and obedience to the king; and declarations of the safety of the righteous, 1-34.

1. **not.** ver. *19. Pr 3:31. *23:17. Ps *37:1, 7. 73:3. Ga *5:19-21. Ja 4:5, 6. **neither.** Pr 1:11-15. *13:20. Ge 13:10-13. 19:1, etc. Ps *26:9. +*119:63.

2. **their heart.** ver. 8. Pr *6:14. 1 S 23:9. Est 3:6, 7. Jb *15:35. Ps *7:14. 10:7. *28:3. *36:4. 64:2-6. 140:2. Is *59:4. Mi 7:3. Mt *26:3, 4. Lk 23:20, 21. Ac 13:10.

3. **wisdom.** Pr 9:1. 14:1. 1 C 3:9, 10. **house builded.** Je 22:13-18. **it is.** 2 S 7:26. Je 10:12. Col *2:7.

4. **by knowledge.** Pr *15:6. 20:15. 21:20. *27:23-27. 1 K 4:22-28. 1 Ch 27:25, etc. 29:2, etc. 2 Ch 4:18-22. *26:4-11. Ne 10:39. *13:4-13. Mt *13:52.

5. **A wise.** Pr *8:14. *10:29. 21:22. Ec *7:19. *9:14-18. **strong.** Heb. in strength. **increaseth strength.** Heb. strengtheneth might. Ps 84:7. Is *40:31. Col *1:11.

6. **by.** Pr 15:22. *20:18. Lk *14:31. 1 C *9:25-27. Ep *6:10, etc. 1 T *6:11, 12. 2 T *4:7. **and.** Pr *11:14. *15:22.

7. **too.** Pr *14:6. 15:24. 17:24. Ps *10:5. *92:5, 6. Mt 11:25. 1 C *2:14. **openeth not.** ✓108H6B, Ps +38:13. Pr *22:22. *31:8, 9. Jb 29:7, etc. *31:21. Is *29:21. Am 5:10, 12, 15. **in the gate.** Ge +14:7n. Ps 127:5.

8. **that deviseth.** ver. *2, *9. Pr 6:14, 18. *14:22. Ge 3:1. 1 K 2:44. Ps 21:11. Is 10:7-13. *32:7. Ezk 38:10, 11. Na 1:11. Ro *1:30.

9. **thought.** ver. 8. Pr 23:7. Ge 6:5. 8:21. Ps *119:113. Is *55:7. Je 4:14. Ho +*6:9 (❋S#2154h, lewdness). Mt *5:28. 9:4. *15:19. Ac *8:22. 2 C *10:5. **the scorner.** Pr 22:10. 29:8. Ps 1:1.

10. **thou faint.** Pr 3:11, 12. Ex 15:1, 24. 16:3. 17:3. Nu 11:4-6. 14:3. Dt 33:27. 1 S 27:1. Jb *4:5. 5:7. 7:1-4. Ps 78:19, 20. 91:15. Is *40:28-31. *54:7. 61:3. Je ✓12:5. Jon 4:8. Mt 10:30. 14:30. 2 C 4:1. 12:9. Col 1:11. Ep 3:13. 2 T 1:15. 4:16. He 10:32-35. *12:1-5. +*13:5. Ja 1:4. Re 2:3, 13. **day of.** Jb 5:17. Ps *50:15. Mt 13:20, 21. Lk +*8:13. He 12:5. **small.** Heb. narrow. Pr 23:27. Ge 12:10-13. 20:2. Ex 4:10-13. Nu 11:11. 22:26. Jsh 7:6-10. 1 S 27:1. 1 K 19:3, 4. Jb 41:15. Ps 31:1, 22. 116:11. Je 20:7-18. Jon 4:8, 9. Mt 26:35, 36, 56, 69-74.

11. **forbear.** 1 S 26:8, 9. Jb 29:17. Ps 82:4. Is *58:6, 7. Lk *10:31, 32. *23:23-25. Ac 18:17. 21:31, 32. 23:10, 23, etc. 1 J *3:16, 17.

12. **doth not he that.** Pr *5:21. 21:2. 1 S ✓16:7. Ps 7:9. 17:3. 44:21. Ec *5:8. Je ✓17:10. Ro 2:16. 1 C *4:5. He ✓4:12, 13. Re 2:18, 23. **that keepeth.** Pr 22:5. 1 S *2:6. 25:29. Ps +36:6. *66:9. *121:3, 8. Da 5:23. Ac *17:28. Re 1:18. **soul.** Heb. *nephesh,* Ge +12:13. **doth not.** ✓63I1C1, Ge +2:6. **and shall.** Jb *34:11. Ps *62:12. Je *32:19. Mt +*)16:27. Ro ⟩2:6. 2 C *5:10. Re 2:23. *20:12-15. *22:12. **not.** ✓63I1C1, Ge +2:6.

13. **eat**. Pr 25:16, 27. SS 5:1. Is *7:15. Mt 3:4. **to thy taste**. Heb. upon thy palate. Jb +31:30mg.

14. **shall the**. Pr 22:18. Ps *19:10, 11. *119:103, 111. Je √15:16. **soul**. Heb. *nephesh*, Ge +34:3. **when**. Pr 2:*1-5, 10. *3:13-18. **there**. Pr 23:18. Mt *19:21, 29. Ph 4:7. Ja *1:25.

15. **Lay**. Pr 1:11. 1 S *19:11. 22:18, 19. 23:20-23. Ps 10:8-10. *37:32. 56:6. 59:3. 140:5. Je *11:19. Zc 2:8. Mt 26:4. Ac *9:24. *23:16. *25:3. **spoil**. Ps *22:28. Is 32:18.

16. **a just**. Jb *5:19. Ps *34:19. *37:24. Mi *7:8-10. 2 C 1:8-10. *4:8-12. 11:23-27. **falleth**. Pr 11:5, 14. 13:17. 17:20. 27:27. 28:10, 14, 18. The just man rising from his fall is most unwarrantably applied to the perseverance of the saints. The word *fall* frequently occurs in this book; but always in reference to trouble, not sin (see the parallel passages). The antithesis obviously fixes this meaning (Charles Bridges). "There are plain texts enough to prove every scriptural doctrine. But pressing texts into any particular service, contrary to their plain meaning, not only serves to deceive the inconsiderate, but to rivet the prejudices, and confirm the suspicions of opposers; just as bringing forward a few witnesses of suspicious character would cause all those, however deserving of credit, who should be examined in the same cause, to be suspected also, and create a prejudice against it in the minds of the court and of all present" (Scott). **seven times**. Ps 119:164n. Mt 18:21. Lk 17:4. **and riseth**. Pr 31:28. Ge 37:7. 41:30. Ps *37:24, 39, 40. Ju *24. **but**. Pr *13:17. 28:14-18. 1 S *26:10. *31:4. Est *7:10. Jb 15:30. Ps *7:16. 52:5. Am 5:2. 8:14. Ac *12:23. 1 Th 5:3. Re 18:20, 21.

17. **Rejoice not**. Pr ●11:10. *17:5. Ex ●15:1. Jg 16:25. 2 S 1:11, 12. 16:5-7, etc. Jb ●22:19. *31:29. Ps 35:13-16, 19. 42:10. ●58:10. Ezk 35:15. Ob 12. Zc 1:15. Mt 5:44. Lk 19:41-44. 1 C *13:6, 7. Re ●15:3, 4. ●*18:20. ●19:1-6.

18. **displease him**. Heb. be evil in his eyes. Ge +38:10mg. Nu 11:1mg. 1 S 8:6mg. 2 S *11:27mg. Is 59:15mg. **and he**. La 4:21, 22. Zc 1:15, 16. **turn away**. Jg 16:25-30. Ps 137:7-9. Is *51:22, 23. Je 48:26, 27. La *1:21. Ezk 25:1-7. 26:2. *35:15. 36:5-7. Ob 10-14. Mi 7:10. **him**. √63F, Ge +33:10. Supply by ellipsis (relative: of contrary words), "(to thee)."

19. **Fret**. *or*, Keep not company with the wicked. Pr 12:26n. *13:20. Nu *16:26. Ps *1:1. *26:4, 5. √37:1. 119:+√63, 115. 2 C √6:17. Ep √5:11. 2 T *3:2-5. Re *18:4. **evil**. √132D, Ge +19:25. Note the alternate parallelism: evil, wicked, evil, wicked, in this verse and the next. **neither**. ver. *1. Pr *23:17. Ps *37:1. 73:3.

20. **there**. Ps *9:17. *11:6. Is *3:11. **candle**. *or*, lamp. Pr +6:23mg. *13:9. *20:20, 27mg. Jb *18:5, 6. *21:17. Mt *8:12. 25:8. Ja 2:26. Ju *13.

21. **fear**. Ex 14:31. 1 S 24:6. Ec 8:2-5. Mt *22:21. Ro 13:1-7. 1 T *2:1, 2. T *3:1. 1 P *2:17. **and the king**. 1 S 22:17, 18. Ec √10:20. Da 3:16-18. Mt 17:24-27. Ac 4:18, 19. 5:27-29. Ro 13:1-7. T 3:1. 1 P 2:13-17. **meddle**. Ge 49:6. Nu *16:1-13. 1 S *8:5-7. 12:12-19. 2 S *15:10-13, etc. 1 K 12:16. **given to change**. Heb. changers. Pr 17:9. 26:11. *31:5mg. 1 S 10:27. 1 K 16:8-22. Est 1:7. 3:8. Da 2:21. 7:25. Ro 13:2. Ep +*4:14. 2 T √3:14. 2 P 2:10. Ju ●+*3, 8.

22. **their**. Nu *16:31-35. 1 S *31:1-7. 2 S 15:13. 18:7-16. 2 Ch 13:16, 17. Ho 5:11. 13:10, 11. **who**. Pr 16:14. *20:2. Ps *90:11. 2 S 18:7, 8. 20:1, 2, 22. 2 K 17:21, 23. Ec 8:2-5. Ac 5:36, 37.

23. **things**. Ps *107:43. Ec *8:1-5. Ho *14:9. Ja *3:17. **It**. Pr *18:5. 28:21. Le *19:15. Dt *1:17. *16:19. 2 Ch *19:7. Ps *82:2-4. Jn *7:24. 1 T 5:20, 21. Ja 2:4-6. 1 P 1:17. **have respect**. √121C2A1, Jb +19:25. "It is not good to know (or discern) faces in (giving) the judgment": i.e., to have respect or show favor to them (B552).

24. **that**. Pr *17:15. Ex *23:6, 7. Le *19:15. Dt 1:17. 16:19. Ps 82:2-4. Is *5:20, 23. Je 6:13, 14. 8:10, 11. Ezk *13:22. **unto the wicked**. √63A2, 2 S +6:6. Supply by ellipsis (absolute: of accusative), "(king)." This is clear from the context, ver. 21-25, which concerns the subject not to flatter a wicked king (B10). **him shall**. Pr *11:26. *28:27. *30:10. Is *66:24.

25. **them**. Le *19:17. 1 S *3:13. 1 K 21:19, 20. Ne 5:7-9. 13:8-11, 17, 25, 28. Jb *29:16-18. Mt 14:4. 1 T *5:20. 2 T *4:2. T *1:13. 2:15. **a good blessing**. Heb. a blessing of good. Pr *28:23.

26. **shall kiss**. Pr 15:23. 16:1. *25:11, 12. Ge 41:38, etc. Da 2:46-48. Mk *12-17, 28, 32-34. **giveth a right answer**. Heb. answereth right words. Pr 18:13mg. Jb *6:25.

27. **Prepare**. Pr +*22:3. 1 K 5:17, 18. *6:7. Mt 18:17, 18. Lk 6:48. *14:28-30. 1 C 3:10-15. Ep 2:21, 22. 3:17. 4:11-16. Col *1:23. *2:7. 1 T *4:16. 2 T 2:2.

28. **not**. Pr *14:5. *19:5, 9. *21:28. Ex *20:16. *23:1. 1 S 22:9, 10. 1 K 21:9-13. Jb *2:3. Ps 35:7-11. 52:title. Mt 26:59, 60. 27:23. Jn *15:25. **without cause**. √24E, Ge +30:33. **deceive**. Ps 52:4. 120:2-4. Ep *4:25. Col *3:9. Re *21:8. *22:15.

29. **Say**. Pr *20:22. 25:21, 22. Mt *5:39-44. Ro *12:17-21. 1 Th *5:15. 1 P 2:21-23. **I will do**. Jg *15:11. 2 S 13:22-28.

30. **went**. Pr *6:6, etc. Jb *4:8. 5:27. 15:17. Ps *37:25. 107:42. Ec 4:1-8. 7:15. 8:9-11. **void**. Pr *10:13. *12:11.

31. **it was**. Ge *3:17-19. Jb 31:40. Je *4:3. Mt *13:7, 22. He *6:8. **and the stone wall**. Pr 19:23. *20:4. 22:13. *23:21. Ec *10:18.

32. **considered it**. Heb. set my heart. Jb 7:17. 1 S +4:20mg. Ps *4:4. +48:13mg. Je +31:21. Lk *2:19, 51. **I looked**. Dt *13:11. *21:21. *32:29. 1 C *10:6, 11. Ju *5-7.

33. **a little sleep**. Pr *6:4-11. +25:28. Ro *13:11. Ep 5:14. 1 Th *5:6-8.

34. **thy poverty**. Pr *10:4. 13:4. **come**. Ge 3:19. **armed man**. Heb. a man of shield. Pr ‖6:11. 30:5.

PROVERBS 25

Of kings and those who minister to them, 1-7. Of avoiding contention and receiving reproof, 8-12. Of faithful messengers and vain boasters, 13, 14. Of forbearance, temperance, and prudent conduct towards neighbors, 15-17. Of false witnesses, unfaithful friends, and unseasonable mirth, 18-20. Of kindness to enemies, frowning away backbiters, and domestic discord, 21-24. Of the righteous falling before the wicked; of vain glory and an ungoverned temper, 25-28.

1. **proverbs**. Pr 1:1. 10:1. 1 K *4:32. Ec *12:9. **which**. Is 1:1. 36:22. 37:2. Ho 1:1. Mi 1:1.

2. **the glory**. Dt √29:29. Jb *11:7, 8. 26:14. 38:4, etc. ch. 39. *40:2. 42:3. Ps 18:11. 77:19. Ro *11:33, 34. 1 T 6:16. **the honor**. 1 K *3:9-28. *4:29-34. Ezr

4:15, 19. 5:17. 6:1. Jb *29:16. **kings.** ver. 3-7.

3. **heaven.** Ps *103:11. Is *7:11. *55:9. Ro *8:39. **is unsearchable.** Heb. *there is* no searching. 1 K *4:29.

4. **Take away.** Pr 17:3. Le 6:28. Is 1:25-27. Ml 3:3, 8, 17, 18. 2 C 4:10, 11. 2 T *2:20, 21. 1 P *1:7.

5. **away.** Pr *20:8. 1 K 2:33, 46. Est *7:10. 8:11, etc. Ps 101:7, 8. **his.** Pr 16:12. 20:28. *29:14. Is *9:7. *16:5. Mt *13:41-43.

6. **Put not forth thyself.** Heb. Set not out thy glory. ver. *27. Pr *27:2. Is 39:1-8. +63:1. **in the presence.** Pr *16:19. Ex 3:11. 1 S 9:20-22. *15:17. 18:18-23. 2 S 7:8, etc. Ps *131:1. Je *1:6-10. Am 7:12-15.

7. **that it.** Pr *16:19. Mt 11:29. Lk *14:8-10. **Come.** Be humble; affect not high things; keep thyself quiet; and thou shalt live at ease, in safety, and in peace. "Why was it," says a wise heathen on this subject, "that Daedalus winged his way safely, while Icarus his son fell, and gave name to the Icarian sea? Was it not because the son flew aloft, and the father skimmed the ground? For both were furnished with the same kind of wings. Believe me, that he who lives privately, lives safely; and every one should live within his own income. Envy no man; pray for a quiet life, though it should not be dignified; seek a friend, and associate with thine equals" (Ovid, Trist. l. III. El. 4. v. 21-28). 1 T *2:2. Re 4:1. **than.** Lk *18:14. 1 P *5:5.

8. **hastily.** Pr 17:14. 18:6. 30:33. 2 S 2:14-16, *26. 2 K 14:8-12. Mt 5:25. Lk 14:31, 32. **what.** Pr *14:12. Je *5:31. Mt 5:25. **neighbor.** ver. 9-11, 18, 23. Pr 26:22.

9. **with.** Mt *18:15-17. **a secret to another.** *or,* the secret of another. Pr *11:13. *20:19.

10. **thine.** Ps *119:39.

11. **word.** Pr 15:23. 24:26. Jb 6:25. Ec 12:10. Is *50:4. **fitly spoken.** Heb. spoken upon his wheels. **is like.** Rather, "is like golden apples (*tappuchim,* in Arabic, *tuffach*) in baskets (*maskeeyoth,* in Arabic, *shakeekat*) of silver." A word fitly spoken with propriety, opportunely, and suitably to the occasion, is as much in its place, and as conspicuously beautiful, as the golden fruit which appears through the apertures of an exquisitely wrought silver basket.

12. **an earring.** Jb 42:11. **a wise.** Pr 1:8, 9. *9:8. 15:5, *31, *32. *27:5, 6. 1 S 25:31-34. Ps 141:5. Mt +*7:6. 2 T 2:15. 4:2. **wise reprover.** Pr 15:1. 27:17. 29:1, 15, 17, 19, 21. Ro 12:8n. **obedient ear.** Mt 7:24, 25. Lk +*11:28. 1 Th √2:13. He 2:1. Ja 1:22-25.

13. **the cold.** ver. *25. Pr 13:17. 25:25. 26:6. Ph *2:25-30. **faithful.** Nu 12:7. 2 Ch 19:9. 34:12. Da *12:3. 3 J 5. **messenger.** ver. 14-17, 19. Pr 27:9, 10, 12. 28:27. **he refresheth.** Pr 11:25. **soul.** Heb. *nephesh,* Ge +34:3.

14. **boasteth.** Pr *20:6. 1 K 22:11. Lk *14:11. *18:10-14. 2 C *11:13-18, 31. 2 P *2:15-19. Ju *12, *13, *16. **of a false gift.** Heb. in a gift of falsehood. T#1840. ver. 18. Pr 6:17, 19. 10:18. Ge 3:3-5. Je 5:31. Mt 4:8-10. *7:22, 23. Jn 8:44. 1 C 13:8. 2 C *2:17. *4:2. 6:8. √11:13-15. Ga 1:6, 7.

15. **long forbearing.** Pr *15:1. 16:14. Ge 32:4, etc. 1 S 25:14, 24, etc. Ps 69:20. Ec 10:4. Mt 11:29. Jn 16:22. Ja 1:19. **tongue.** ⌐121BB, Ps +5:9. By Metonymy of the Cause, "tongue" is put for what is *spoken* by it, signifying that gentle speech overcomes obstinacy. **the bone.** Rather, "*a bone;*" that is, *soft and conciliating language will often accomplish the most difficult things.*

16. **Hast.** Pr 24:13, 14. Jg 14:8, 9. 1 S 14:25-27. Is

7:15, 22. **sufficient.** Ph 4:5. 1 T 4:4. **lest.** ver. *27. Pr 23:8. Lk *21:34. Ep *5:18.

17. **Withdraw thy foot from thy neighbor's.** *or,* Let thy foot be seldom in thy neighbor's house. Pr ●8:34. 20:19. 27:8. Ge 19:2, 3. Jg 19:18-21. 1 T √5:13. T 2:4, +*5. **weary.** Heb. full. Pr 27:20. 30:9. SS ●5:1. Lk ●11:5-10. ●*18:1. Ro 15:24. Ep ●3:12. He ●4:16.

18. **beareth false.** Pr *12:18. Ps 52:2. *55:21. 57:4. 120:3, 4. 140:3. Je *9:3, 8. Ja *3:6.

19. **Confidence.** 2 Ch 28:20, 21. Jb 6:14-20. Is 28:16. *30:1-3. *36:6. Ezk 29:6, 7. 2 T *4:16. **unfaithful.** T#170. Pr 28:26. Ps 146:3, 4. Is 2:22. Je 17:5, 6. Mi 7:5.

20. **that taketh.** Dt *24:12-17. Jb 24:7-10. Is *58:7. Ja *2:15, 16. **vinegar.** Pr *10:26. Is 61:2, 3. Lk 10:34. **nitre.** Je 2:22. **so is.** ver. 26-28. Pr 26:13-16. 27:4, 8, 13, 20. 28:22, 23. 29:22, 23. **that singeth.** 1 S 16:23. 2 K 3:15. Jb 2:11-13. 30:31. Ps 103:14. *137:3, 4. 2 C *3:4. Da *6:18. Mt 8:17. Ro *12:15. 2 C 1:4-6. He 4:15. 13:3. Ja 5:13. **heavy heart.** Pr 31:6. Ps 104:15.

21. **thine enemy.** Pr *24:17. 27:5, 6. Ex *23:4, 5. Le *19:18. Mt 5:44, 45. Lk *10:33-36. Ro *12:)20, 21. Col 3:12, 13. 1 P 3:9. **give him.** ⌐171K2, Ex +23:4.

22. **For thou.** Not to *consume,* but to *melt* him into kindness; a metaphor taken from smelting metallic ores. **coals of fire.** ⌐121S1, Ge +49:10. By Metonymy of the Adjunct, whereby the sign is put for the thing signified, "coals of fire" are put for cruel words and hard speeches. Pr 6:28. 26:21. Le 16:12. Ps 140:9, 10. **heap.** ⌐63H, Ge +12:15. The coals of fire which tine enemy casts at thee, thou shalt take them and put them upon his head: he will thus get what he intended for thee. The "burning coals" are put by Metonymy for cruel words and hard speeches (see Pr 16:27; 26:23). But if thou doest good to him who uses cruel words of you, that will burn him as coals of fire (B65). Pr 6:27h. Is 30:14. 52:5h. **the Lord shall reward thee.** Pr 6:31. +*13:21. 2 S 16:12. Mt 10:13. 1 C √15:58. 1 T +*4:8.

23. **north.** Jb *37:22. **driveth,** etc. *or,* bringeth forth rain; so doth a backbiting tongue an angry countenance. Monconys (p. 353) says, that when travelling on the second of January, 1648, from Tripoli in Syria, between Lebanon and the sea, it rained without ceasing, while the *north wind* blew directly in his face. **so.** Pr *26:20. Ps *15:3. +101:5. Ro 1:30. 2 C 12:20.

24. **better to dwell.** Pr 19:13. *21:9, 19. 27:15, 16. 1 T 2:11-14. **wide house.** Pr +21:9mg.

25. **cold.** ver. 13. Ge *21:16-19. Ex 17:2, 3, 6. Jg *15:18, 19. 2 S 23:15. Ps *42:1, 2. 63:1. Is *55:1. Lk 18:14. Jn *7:37. Re *21:6. *22:17. **thirsty.** Pr 11:25. **soul.** Heb. *nephesh,* Ge +12:5. **so.** Pr 15:30. Is *52:7. Na 1:15. Lk *2:10, 11. Ro *10:15. 1 T 1:15.

26. **righteous.** Pr 10:11. Ge 4:8. 1 S 22:14-18. 2 Ch 24:21, 22. Mt *23:34-37. 26:69-74. 27:21. Ac *7:52. 1 Th 2:15. Re 17:6. **falling down.** Charles Bridges comments, in this place Satan thus makes more effective use of God's people than of his own. The gross wickedness of the ungodly passes in silence. But makes the neighborhood ring with the failings of Christian professors. Godly consistency so grates upon the conscience of the world, that at any breach of it they clap their hands with Satanic joy; to see the Lord "wounded in the house of his friends" (Zc 13:6). Ge 12:18-20. 20:10. 26:10. 2 S 11:2. 12:14. 13:11-14. 16:22. 1 K 11:1-8. 2 K 18:5, 6, 13-16. 23:13. Ga ●*2:4, 5,

11-14. Col 4:14. 2 T *4:10. Phm 24. **before the wicked.** 2 S √12:14. Ps *39:1. Col 4:5. **troubled.** Est 3:15. Ezk 32:2. 34:18, 19. **fountain.** Heb. *mayan*, Ge +7:11 (✱S#4599h). 26:18-22. Dt 8:7. Jsh 15:18, 19. 2 K 2:21, 22. Mt 5:13-16. Ja 2:11, 12.

27. **not good.** ver. 16. **so.** Pr *27:2. Ge 11:4. Da 4:30. Jn *5:43, 44. 2 C 12:1, 11. Ph +*2:3. **not.** ʃ63I1C1, Ge +2:6.

28. **He that.** Pr *16:32. 22:24. 1 S 20:30. +*25:17. Est 3:5, 6. 5:13. **no rule.** Ge 4:5-8. Jg 16:1-19. 1 S 25:33. 2 S 11:2-4. Da 3:13, 19. **spirit.** Heb. *ruach*, Ge +41:8. T#994‡. Ge 41:7, *8. Mk 14:38. **city.** Ge +=11:4. Ne 1:3. 2:17. **broken down.** Pr 6:10, 11. 17:14. 24:*31, 33, 34. Ro ◐*6:14. 1 C ◐*10:13. 1 Th 5:6.

PROVERBS 26

Divers maxims, concerning fools, 1-12; sluggards, 13-16; intermeddlers with strife, those who do mischief in sport, talebearers, dissemblers, liars, and flatterers, 17-28.

1. **in summer.** 1 S 12:17, 18. **so.** ver. 3. Pr 28:16. Jg 9:7, 20, 56, 57. Est 3:1, etc. 4:6-9. Ps *12:8. 15:4. 52:title, 1-4. Ec *10:5-7. **fool.** ver. 3-11. Pr 27:3, 22. 29:9.

2. **so.** Nu 23:8. Dt *23:4, 5. 1 S 14:28, 29. *17:43. 2 S 16:12. Ne *13:2. Ps 109:28. Ro 8:1. 1 C 15:22. Ga 3:13. **curse.** Pr +*3:33. 29:24. Da *9:11. Zc +*5:3. Ga √3:13. **causeless.** Nu 22:4-6. 23:8. Dt 23:4, 5. Jsh ◐6:26. Jg ◐9:56, 57. 1 K ◐16:34. 2 K ◐2:24. **shall not come.** 1 S 17:43. 2 S 16:12. Je 15:10.

3. **A whip for.** According to our notions, we should rather say a bridle for the horse and a whip for the ass; but it should be considered that the Eastern asses are not only much more beautiful but better goers than ours; and being active and well broken, they need only a bridle to guide them; whereas their horses, being scarce, and often caught wild, and badly broken, are much less manageable, and need the correction of the whip. Pr *10:13. *17:10. *19:25. *27:22. Jg 8:5-7, 16. Ps *32:9. 1 C 4:21. 2 C 10:6. 13:2. **a rod.** T#311. Pr +*13:24 (T#494). 20:8, 30. Dt 13:10, 11. *19:18-20. 2 Ch 9:8. Is 1:26. 1 T *1:8-10.

4. **Answer not.** Pr 17:14. Jg 12:1-6. 2 S 19:41-43. 1 K *12:14, 16. 2 K *14:8-10. 18:36. Ec 3:7. Mt +*7:6. 16:1-4. 1 P *2:21-23. *3:9. Ju 9.

5. **Answer a fool.** 1 K *22:24-28. Je 36:17, 18. Mt *15:1-3. *16:1-4. *21:23-27. *22:15-32. Lk *12:13-21. *13:23-30. Jn *8:7. *9:26-33. T *1:13. **lest.** ver. *12. Pr *28:11. Ro 11:25. **conceit.** Heb. eyes. Pr *3:7. Is *5:21. Ro *12:16.

6. **sendeth.** Pr 10:26. 13:17. *25:13. Nu 13:31. Ps *50:16, 17. 2 T 2:15. **by the hand.** 1 K +16:12mg. **damage.** *or*, violence. Pr 3:31mg. 4:17. 10:6. 13:2. *25:19.

7. **legs.** ʃ12I1I, Ge +3:7. By Metonymy of the Subject, "legs" are put for the clothes which being lifted up expose the lameness. So when a fool attempts to utter a parable, he soon exposes himself (B568). **not equal.** Heb. lifted up. 2 S ◐22:34mg. Jb 28:4. Ps 78:9. 116:6. Is 19:6. 38:14. **so.** ver. *9. Pr 17:7. Ps *50:16-21. 64:8. Mt 7:4, 5. Lk 4:23. **parable.** Nu 23:7n.

8. **bindeth a stone in a sling.** Heb. putteth a *precious stone* in a heap of stones. This probably refers, as Coverdale understands it, to the custom of throwing a stone to the heap under which a criminal was buried.

So the Vulgate, "As he who throws a stone to Mercury's heap, so is he who gives honor to a fool." Mercury was a heathen god of highways; and stones were erected in different parts to guide the traveler: hence those lines of Dr. Young,

> Death stands like Mercuries in every way;
> And kindly points us to our journey's end.

so. ver. 1. Pr 19:10. 30:22.

9. **a thorn.** Pr *23:35.

10. **The great,** etc. *or*, A great man grieveth all; and he hireth the fool, he hireth also the transgressors. **both.** Pr *11:31. Lk +*12:47, 48. Ro *2:6. Re 15:4.

11. **As.** ʃ138C, Ge +22:14. **a dog.** Ex 8:15. Mt *12:45. 2 P *♭2:22. **vomit.** Jb 20:15. **returneth to his folly.** Heb. iterateth his folly. Pr 17:9. 24:21. Ps 85:8. Mt 12:43-45.

12. **Seest.** Pr 22:29. *29:20. Lk 7:44. **a man.** ver. 5, 16. Pr 28:*11, 26. *29:20. Mt *21:31. Lk *18:11. Ro *12:16. 1 C *3:18, 19. *8:1, 2. Ga 6:3. Re *3:17.

13. **slothful.** Pr 15:19. *19:15. *22:13.

14. **the door.** Pr *6:9, 10, 11. 12:24, 27. *24:33. He *6:12.

15. **slothful.** Pr *19:24. Ec 4:5. **it grieveth him.** *or*, he is weary. Ex 7:18. Ps 68:9.

16. **wiser.** ver. *12. Pr *12:15. 1 P √3:15. **seven.** A perfect number (Young).

17. **passeth.** Pr 17:11. 18:6, 7. *20:3. Lk 12:14. 2 T *2:23, 24. **meddleth.** *or*, is enraged. Pr 14:16. 20:2. **strife.** ver. 20, 21. **belonging not.** 1 K 22:4, 32. 1 P 4:15, 16.

18. **mad.** Pr 27:14. **casteth.** 1 Ch 10:3. 2 Ch 35:23. Ho 6:3 (former rain; perhaps, as the latter rain sprinkling the earth). **firebrands.** Heb. flames, *or* sparks. **arrows.** Pr 7:23. 25:18. Ge 49:23.

19. **and.** Pr *10:23. *14:9. *15:21. Ep *5:4. 2 P 2:13.

20. **Where no wood is.** Heb. Without wood. ver. 21. Pr 3:18. 11:30. **so.** ver. *22. Pr *16:28. 22:10. Ps 52:1-5. Ja *3:6. **talebearer.** *or*, whisperer. ver. 22. Pr 16:28. 18:8mg. Ps 41:7. **ceaseth.** Heb. is silent. Ps 37:7mg. 107:30. Jon 1:11mg, 12.

21. **As coals.** Pr *10:12. *15:18. *29:22. *30:33. 2 S 20:1. 1 K 12:2, 3, 20. Ps *120:4.

22. **words.** Pr *18:8. 20:19. Ezk 22:9. **innermost parts.** Heb. chambers. Pr +7:27. 18:8mg. **belly.** ʃ121J22, Jb +15:35.

23. **Burning lips.** Ardent professions of friendship from a wicked heart, however smooth, shining, and splendid they may appear, are like a vile vessel covered over with base metal. ver. 24-26. Pr *10:18. 29:5. 2 S *20:9, 10. Ps 55:12-14. Ezk *33:31. Lk *22:47, 48. **silver.** ʃ100, Ge +10:9.

24. **hateth.** Pr 11:15. 12:1. 13:24. **dissembleth.** *or*, is known. **deceit.** Pr 11:1. 12:5, 17, 20. 14:8.

25. **speaketh fair.** Heb. maketh his voice gracious. Ps *12:2. *28:3. Je *9:2-8. Mi *7:5. **believe.** Je *12:6. Mt *24:23. **seven.** Pr *6:16-19.

26. **Whose hatred is covered by deceit.** *or*, Hatred is covered in secret. Ge *4:8. 1 S 18:17, 21. 2 S *3:27, etc. *13:22-28. Ps *55:21-23. **showed before.** Lk 12:2.

27. **diggeth.** Pr *28:10. Est *7:9, 10. Ps 7:15, 16. 9:15. 10:2. 57:6. Ec 10:8. **shall fall.** Pr 27:18. 28:10, 17-20, 25. Jb 5:13. Da 6:24.

28. **lying.** He that injures another hates him in proportion to the injury. *Proprium humani ingenii est, odisse quem laeseris*, says Tacitus; and strange to say,

in proportion to the innocence of the injured. Je 14:14-16. Jn *8:40, 44-49. 10:32, 33. *15:22-24. **a flattering.** Pr 6:24. 7:5, 21-23. 27:1, 2. 29:*5, 11, 20. Lk 20:20, 21.

PROVERBS 27

Maxims against procrastination, carnal security, vain glory, wrath, and envy, 1-4; concerning reproof, contentment, steadiness, friendship, and prudence, 5-12; against suretiship, lavish commendations, and domestic discord, 13-16; concerning industry, the conformity of one man's heart to another's, insatiable desires, the effects of praise, and the obstinacy of fools, 17-22; and recommending diligence, good management, and rural plenty, 23-27.

1. **Boast not.** Ps 95:7. Is 56:12. Lk *12:19, 20. 17:29. 2 C *6:2. Ja *4:13-16. **tomorrow.** Heb. tomorrow day. ✓24E, Ge +30:33. Pr 3:28. Ge +30:33mg. **thou.** 1 S 28:19. Ps 37:5. Mt 24:48-51. 25:13.

2. **Let another.** Pr *25:27. Mt 5:16. 2 C *10:12, 18. 12:11. Ja 5:16.

3. **heavy.** Heb. heaviness. Ex 15:5. Is 21:15. 30:27mg. Na 3:3. **but.** Pr 17:12. Ge 34:25, 26. *49:7. 1 S 22:18, 19. ●25:32, 33. 2 S 13:22, 23. Est 3:5, 6. Da *3:19. Mt 2:16. Ep 4:26. 1 J 3:12.

4. **cruel, and anger is outrageous.** Heb. cruelty, and anger an overflowing. 1 S 25:13, 21. Ja *1:19-21. **but.** Pr 14:30. Ge 26:14. 37:11. Jb 5:2. Mt *27:18. Ac 5:17mg. *7:9. *17:5. Ro 1:29. Ja *3:14-16. 4:5, 6. 1 J 3:12. **envy.** *or,* jealousy. Pr 6:34. Ge 4:5-8. 26:14. 1 S 18:6-9, 16, 17. Ps 73:3. Ec *4:4. SS 8:6. Da 6:3-5. Mk 7:21-23. Ro 1:29, 30. 2 C 12:20. Ga 5:20, 21. T 3:3. Ja 3:14, 16. 4:5.

5. **rebuke.** Pr *28:23. Le *19:17. Mt *18:15. Ga 2:14. 1 T 5:20.

6. **Faithful.** ✓138C, Ge +22:14. Le +*19:17. Ps +*141:5. Ga +*2:11. 1 T +*5:19n. **the wounds.** 2 S *12:7, etc. Jb *5:17, 18. Ps 141:5. He 12:10. Re 3:19. **but.** ✓132B, Pr +10:1. Ps 55:21. Lk 22:48. **the kisses.** Pr 10:18. 26:23-26. 2 S 20:9, 10. Mt *26:48-50. **deceitful.** *or,* earnest, *or,* frequent. Ezk 35:13 (multiplied).

7. **full.** ✓138C, Ge +22:14. Nu *11:4-9, 18-20. *21:5. **soul.** Heb. *nephesh,* Ge +12:5. **loatheth.** Heb. treadeth under foot. Ps 44:5. 60:12. 108:12. **honeycomb.** Ex 16:31. **to.** Jb *6:7. Lk *15:16, 17. Jn 6:9. **hungry.** Pr 28:3, 6, 8, 11. 29:13. **soul.** Heb. *nephesh,* Ge +12:5. **every.** Ph 4:11. 1 T 6:6.

8. **a bird.** Jb 39:14-16. Is 16:2. **nest.** Dt 22:6, 7. **man.** Pr *21:16. Ge 4:16. 16:6-8. 1 S 22:5. 27:1, etc. 1 K *19:9. Ne 6:11-13. Jon 1:3, 10-17. 1 C *7:20, 24. 1 T 6:6. Ju 13. **wandereth.** Pr 26:17. Ge 34:1, 2. 1 T 5:13. T 2:5. **his place.** Pr 14:8. Ne 10:39. SS 1:7, 8. Zc 11:7. Mk 9:38-40. Lk 16:2. Col 2:5. 1 Th 4:11. 5:21. 2 T 3:7. 4:3, 4. He √10:25.

9. **Ointment.** Pr 7:17. Jg 9:9. Ps *45:7, 8. *104:15. *133:2. SS 1:3. 3:6. 4:10. Jn *12:3, 7. Ro 12:15. 2 C *2:14-16. **so.** Pr *15:23. *16:21, 23, 24. Ex 18:17-24. 1 S *23:16, 17. Ezr 10:2-4. Ps 55:14. Ac *28:15. **by hearty counsel.** Heb. from the counsel of the soul. Heb. *nephesh,* Ex +15:9.

10. **own.** 2 S 19:24, 28. 21:7. 1 K *12:6-8. 2 Ch 24:22. Is *41:8-10. Je 2:5. **father's friend.** Ge 48:15, 16. 1 K 5:1-10. 1 Ch +*28:9. Jn 15:15. **neither.** Pr ●17:17. 19:7. Jb 6:21-23. Ob *12-14. **better.** Pr *17:17. *18:24. 2 S 1:26. Lk *10:30-37. Ac 23:12, 23, etc. **neigh-**

bor. Pr ●25:17. **brother.** Pr ●17:17. **far off.** Ge 39:4, 21. 41:39-45. 37:4-18. 1 S 17:28. ch. 20. Mt 13:57. Lk 4:24. 22:28. Jn 4:44. 7:3-5.

11. **be wise.** Pr 10:1. *15:20. *23:15, 16, 24, 25. Ec 2:18-21. Phm 7, 19, 20. 2 J *4. 3 J *4. **make.** Pr 28:7, 24. 29:3. **that I.** Ps *119:42. 127:4, 5.

12. **prudent.** Pr *18:10. +*‖22:3. Ex *9:20, 21. Ps 57:1-3. Is 26:20, 21. Je +*8:7. Mt *3:7. He *6:18. *11:7. 2 P *3:7, 10-14.

13. **his garment.** Pr *6:1-4. ‖20:16. *22:26, 27. Ex 22:26.

14. **He that.** 2 S 15:2-7. 16:16-19. 17:7-13. 1 K 22:6, 13, 14. Je 28:2-4. Ac *12:22, 23. **with.** ✓171K1, Dt +19:5. By Synecdoche of the Species, whereby one example or specimen is put for all kinds of similar things, "blessing" a friend with a loud voice is here put for all kinds of flattery (B634).

15. **A continual.** Pr *19:13. *21:9, 19. *25:24. Jb *14:19.

16. **the ointment.** Mt 26:73. Jn *12:3.

17. **Iron sharpeneth.** ✓138C, Ge +22:14. As iron or steel will bring a knife to a better edge when properly whetted, so one friend may excite another to reflect deeply, furnish useful hints, and invigorate and improve each other by mutual intercourse. So Horace (Ars Poet. 304), *Ergo fungar vice cotis, acutum reddere quae ferrum valet, exors ipsa secandi,* "But let me sharpen others as the hone/Gives edge to razors, though itself has none" (Francis). 1 S *13:20, 21. **so.** ver. *9. Jsh 1:18. 2:24. 1 S *9:27. 11:9, 10. *23:16. 2 S 10:11, 12. Jb *4:3, 4. Ec *4:10. Is *35:3, 4. 41:6. Ml *3:16. 1 Th 3:3, 4. 2 T *1:8, 12. *2:3, 9-13. He +*3:12, 13. *10:24. Ja *1:2. 1 P *4:12, 13.

18. **keepeth.** SS 8:12. 1 C *9:7, 13. 2 T 2:6. **so.** Pr *17:2. 22:29. Ge 24:2, 3. *39:2-5, 22, 23. Ex 24:13. 2 K 3:11. *5:2, 3, 25, 27. Mk *10:43. Ac 10:7. Col *3:22. **waiteth.** Ps 33:20. 123:2. **shall be.** 1 S *2:30. Ps *123:2. Mt *24:45, 46. *25:21, 22. Lk *12:37, 43, 44. Jn *12:26. 1 P *2:18, 21.

19. **in.** Ja 1:22-25. **so.** Ge *6:5. Ps 33:15. Mk *7:21.

20. **Hell.** Heb. *sheol,* Ge +37:35. Pr 15:11. 30:15, 16. Jb 26:6. Is 5:14. Hab *2:5. **destruction.** Jb +26:6. **never.** Heb. not. **so.** Pr *23:5. Ps 4:6. Ec *1:8. 2:10, 11. 5:10, 11. 6:7. Je 22:17. 1 J *2:16.

21. **the fining.** Pr *17:3. Ps *12:6. 66:10. Zc *13:9. Ml 3:3. 1 P *1:7. *4:12. **so.** 1 S 18:7, 8, 15, 16, 30. 2 S 14:25. 15:6, etc. 1 C 4:7.

22. **Though thou.** ✓102C, Mt +5:29. Pr *23:35. Ex 12:30. 14:5. 15:9. 2 Ch *28:22, 23. Is *1:5. Je *5:3. *44:15, 16. Re 16:10, 11. **will not.** T#569. Is +9:13 (T#9). Je *13:23. Re 16:9-11, 21.

23. **diligent.** Ge 30:32-42. *31:38-40. 33:13. 1 S 16:11. *17:28. 1 Ch 27:29-31. 2 Ch 26:10. Ru 2:4, 5. 3:7. Ps 78:70, 71. Ezk *34:22-24, 31. Jn *21:15-17. Ro *12:11. Col *3:22-24. 1 P *5:2. **know the state.** T#1830. Pr 20:4. Ac 20:28. He +*3:12, 13. +*12:15. √13:20. 1 P 2:25. 5:*2, 4. **look well.** Heb. set thy heart. Pr 24:32mg. Ex 7:23. Dt *32:46. 1 S +4:20. Ps +48:13mg.

24. **For.** Pr *23:5. Zp *1:18. 1 T *6:17, 18. **riches.** Heb. strength. *✓121N2, Ge +34:29. Pr 5:10mg. 15:6. Is 10:14. 30:6. 33:6. Je 20:5. Ezk 22:25. Ja *1:10. **for ever.** Heb. *olam,* Ex +*12:24. **doth.** 2 S *7:16. Ps *89:36. Is *9:7. **every generation.** Heb. generation and generation. Pr 30:11, 12, 13, 14. Ps 10:6mg. +33:11mg. 49:11mg. 61:6mg. 72:5mg. 77:8mg.

79:13mg. 89:1mg. 90:1mg. 100:5mg. 102:12mg. 119:90mg. 135:13mg. Je 50:39. La 5:19. Jl 2:2mg. 3:20.

25. **hay.** Rather, "herbage," as *chatzir* uniformly denotes. Pr 10:5. Ps 104:14. 1 K 18:5. 2 K 19:26.

26. **lambs.** Jb 31:20.

27. **enough.** Pr *30:8, 9. Mt √6:33. **food.** Je √15:16. *23:28. Am 8:11. Mt +*25:45. He 5:12-14. 1 P 2:2. **household.** Ps 36:7. Ga *6:10. Ep 2:19. He 3:6. **maintenance.** Heb. life. √121F, Ge +49:6. Dt 24:6n. Is 57:10mg. **maidens.** Pr 9:3. 31:15. Ge +*24:14.

PROVERBS 28

Maxims concerning faith, piety, integrity, charity, humility, industry, and fidelity; against oppression, usury, hypocrisy, pride, violence, covetousness, bribery, flattery, robbery of parents, and self-confidence, 1-28.

1. **wicked.** Ge 3:9, 10. Le 26:17, 36. Dt 28:7, 25. 2 K *7:6, 7, 15. Ps 53:5. Is 7:2. Je 20:4. **the righteous.** Ex 11:8. Ps 27:*1, 2. 46:2, 3. *112:7. Is *26:3, 4. Da *3:16-18. 6:10, 11. Ac 4:13. 14:3. Ro 1:15, 16. 1 Th *2:2.

2. **For the.** Pr 21:1. Je 52:3. Ro 13:1-7. **the transgression.** 1 K 15:25, 28. 16:8-29. 2 K 15:8-31. 2 Ch 36:1-12. Is 3:1-7. Ho 13:11. **land.** √121J17, Ge +6:11. **but.** Ge *45:5-8. 2 Ch *32:20-26. Jb *22:28-30. Ec 9:15. Is 58:12. Da *4:27. **by a man,** etc. *or,* by men of understanding *and* wisdom shall they likewise be prolonged. Pr 11:11.

3. **poor man.** Jb 20:10mg. Mt *18:28-30. **oppresseth.** √108J, Ge +43:18. ver. 16. **which leaveth no food.** Heb. without food.

4. **that.** 1 S 23:19-21. Ps 10:3. 49:18. Je 5:30, 31. Ml 3:15. Ac 12:22. 24:2-4. Ro *1:32. 1 J *4:5. **but.** 1 S *15:14-24. 22:14, 15. 1 K *18:18, 21. 20:41, 42. 21:19, 20. *22:19-28. 2 K 3:13, 14. Ne 5:7, etc. 13:8-11, 17-20, 23-26, 28. Mt *3:7. 14:4. Ac 15:2. 19:9. Ga 2:3-6. Ep *5:11. 1 Th 2:2. Ju 3. **contend.** Ne +13:11.

5. **Evil men.** Pr 15:24. 24:1. Jn *3:19. **understand not.** Pr 14:6. *24:7. Ps *10:4. *25:14. 82:5. 92:6. Jb *21:14. Is 5:20. Je *4:22. Mt 13:12. 25:29. Mk 4:10-13. Jn *3:19. √7:17. 1 C √2:14, 15. Ep 4:18. 2 Th *2:10-12. Ja *1:5. 2 P 3:5. 1 J *2:20, 27. **but they.** Ps 119:100. **that seek.** Ps +*9:10. 97:11. 105:4. 119:4, 5, 8, *10, 32, 173. Is 26:9. 55:6. Je *29:13. Mt 13:12. 25:29. Jn *6:37. Ph 2:12, 13. He *11:6. **understand all.** Pr 1:23. +8:9. 14:6. Dt 29:29. Jb 32:7-9. Ps *25:9, 12, 14. 97:11. 119:*98-100, 104, *130. Mt 11:25. Lk 7:35. 10:21. 2 C 4:6. 2 T 2:7. √3:15-17. 1 J *2:20.

6. **Better.** ver. *18. Pr *16:8. 19:1, 22. Dt 5:32. Lk *16:19-23. Ac 24:24-27.

7. **keepeth.** Pr *2:1, etc. *3:1, etc. Dt 4:6. Ps √119:9, 11. **but.** ver. 24. Pr 19:26. *23:19-22. 29:3, 15. Ps 119:+√63, 115. Lk *15:13, 30. 1 P *4:3, 4. **is a companion of riotous men.** *or,* feedeth gluttons. Pr 23:20, 21. Dt 21:20. **shameth.** Pr 25:8. Ru 2:15mg. 1 S 20:34. Ps 44:9.

8. **that by usury.** Pr *13:22. Jb *27:16, 17. Ec *2:26. Is +*24:2. **unjust gain.** Heb. by increase. ver. 20, 22, 24. Pr 10:2. 11:24, 26. 13:7. 15:16, 17, 27. 16:8. 21:6, 7. 22:16. Le *25:36, 37. Je 17:11. +*22:13. Ezk *18:8, 13, 17. *22:13. Ja *5:1-6. **increaseth.** Lk 12:15. **gather it for.** Pr *2:21, 22. 10:30. 11:31. 12:7. +*13:22. 14:11, 19. 15:25. **pity.** Pr *19:17. 2 S 12:6. Ps 140:12. Mt 5:3-7.

9. **turneth away.** T#1803. Pr *21:13. Jb *21:14. 22:17. Ps *50:16, 17. Is *1:15, 16. *58:7-11. Ezk 33:31, 32. Zc *7:11-13. Mt 15:8. 2 T *4:3, 4. **even.** Pr 1:28, 29. *15:8. Ps √66:18. *109:7. Mt 25:41. Lk 13:25-27. Jn +*9:31.

10. **causeth.** Nu *31:15, 16. 1 S 26:19. Mt 5:19. *18:6. Mk 9:42. Lk 17:1, 2. Ac *13:8-10. Ro *16:17, 18. 2 C *11:3, 4, 13-15. Ga *1:8, 9. 2:4. *3:1-4. 2 P 2:18-20. Re *2:14. **he shall.** Pr *26:27. Ps *7:15, 16. *9:15. Ec *10:8. **but.** Pr *10:3. *15:6. *21:20. Dt *7:12-14. Ps *37:11, 25, 26. Mt √6:33. Ro 8:39. 1 C 2:9. 1 P 1:4.

11. **rich.** Pr *18:11. *23:4. Is 10:13, 14. Ezk 28:3-5. Lk *16:13, 14. 1 C 3:18, 19. 1 T *6:17. **wise.** 1 C 10:12. **his own conceit.** Heb. his eyes. Pr 26:16. Is *5:21. Ro 11:25. *12:16. **the poor.** Pr 18:17. 19:1. Jb *32:9. Ec *9:15-17.

12. **righteous.** ver. *28. Pr 11:10. *29:2. 1 Ch 15:25-28. *16:7, etc. 29:20-22. 2 Ch 7:10. 30:22-27. Est 8:15-17. Jb 29:11-20. Lk *19:37, 38. **but.** 1 S *24:11. 1 K 17:3, etc. 18:4, 13. 19:3. Ec 10:6, 16. Je 36:26. He *11:37, 38. **hidden.** sought for. Pr +*22:3. Je *5:1. +*36:19. Am 5:13.

13. **covereth.** Pr *10:12. 17:9. 30:20. Ge 3:7, 12, 13, 21. 4:9. 31:34, 35. 37:31-35. Ex 32:21-24. 1 S *15:13, 20, 21, 24. 2 S 11:15, 25. Jb *31:33. Ps *32:1, 3-5. 90:8. Is 5:20. Je *2:22, 23. Mt *23:25-28. Mt 26:70. 27:24-26. Ac 5:1-8. **not prosper.** Pr 13:15. Ge 3:9. +6:13 (T#566). 4:10-12. 42:21. Nu +*32:23. 1 S 15:21, 23. 2 K 5:27. Jb 34:21, 22. Ps 1:3, 4. *66:18. Ec *12:14. Is 30:1. Lk *12:2, 3. Jn 8:9. 1 C *4:5. **whoso confesseth.** T#124. Le 26:40-42. Jsh 7:19, 20. 1 K 8:47-49. Jb *33:27. 40:4. 42:6. Ps 25:11. *51:1-5, 10. 119:26. Is 43:25, 26. Je 3:12, 13. Da 9:20-23. Ho 5:14, 15. Lk 15:18-24. +18:14 (T#537). 2 C +7:10 (T#603). Ac +*19:18. Ja +*5:16. 1 J √1:8-10. **and forsaketh.** Ex 10:16, 17. 1 S 15:30. Jb *34:32. Ps *85:8. Is √55:7. Je 3:7. Mt 3:6-10. 27:4, 5. Ac *26:20. **shall have.** Le 26:40-42. 2 Ch +*7:14. Jb 33:27, 28. Ps *32:5. *85:2. Is 1:16-18. √55:7. Je 31:18-20. Ezk 18:21, 22. Ho 5:15. Lk 15:20. 23:43. 1 J √1:9.

14. **Happy.** Pr *23:17. Ps 2:11. *16:8. 112:1. Is *66:2. Je *32:40. Ro 11:20. He 4:1. 1 P 1:17. **that feareth.** T#898. Mk 13:35-37. Lk *12:37, 38. 1 C *10:12. Re 16:15. **but.** Pr *29:1. Ex 7:22, 23. 14:23, etc. Jb *9:4. Ro *2:4, 5.

15. **a roaring.** Pr *20:2. Ho 5:14. 1 P *5:8. **a ranging.** Pr 17:12. 2 K *2:24. Ho *13:8. **so.** Ex *1:14-16, 22. 1 S *22:17-19. 2 K 15:16. 21:16. Est *3:6-10. Mt *2:16. **wicked ruler.** T#318. ver. 16. Pr *29:2, 4. 1 K 4:16. 2 Ch 33:9-11. Ps *12:8. 94:20, 21. Zp *3:3.

16. **prince.** 1 K *12:10, 11, 14. Ne *5:15. Ec 4:1. Is *3:12. Am 4:1. **oppressor.** √108J, Ge +43:16. **but.** √63F, Ge +33:10. **hateth covetousness.** T#137. Ex +*18:21. +29:17. Ps +37:1 (T#174). Is *33:15, 16. Je *22:15-17. Lk 12:15-21. Ga +5:14 (T#413). Ep 5:3. Ph 2:4. Col *3:5. He 13:5.

17. **doeth violence.** Ge *9:6. Ex *21:14. Nu *35:14, etc. 1 K 2:28-34. 21:19, 23. 2 K 9:26. 2 Ch 24:21-25. Mt *27:4, 5. Ac *28:4. Ro 5:20. **person.** Heb. *nephesh,* Jsh +10:28. **pit.** Heb. *bor,* Ge +37:20.

18. **walketh.** Pr *10:9, 25. 11:3-6. Ge 17:1. Ps 11:7. 15:1, 2. 25:21. *26:11. *84:11. 97:11. *125:4. Ga *2:14. **but.** ver. *6. Nu *22:32. Ps 73:18-20. *125:5. 1 Th *5:3. 2 P *2:1-3. Re *3:3.

19. **that tilleth.** Pr *‖12:11. 14:4. *27:23-27. Ec 9:10.

Ro 12:11. **but**. Pr *13:20. *23:20, 21. Jg 9:4. Lk *15:12-17.

20. **faithful**. T#1836. Pr √10:4. *20:6. Ge 24:35. 1 S 22:14. 1 Ch 28:7. Ne 7:2. Ps 101:6. 112:4-9. Mt *25:21, 23. Lk +√12:42. *16:1, 10-12. ◐*17:10. 1 C 4:2-5. √15:58. Ja 1:6-8. Re 2:10, 13. **abound with blessings**. Pr √10:22. 11:28, 31. Mt *25:21, 23. Mk +*10:30. Lk *14:14. √16:10. Ph +*4:17n. Ja +*2:5. **but**. ver. 22. Pr 13:11. 20:21. 23:4. 2 K 5:20-27. 1 T 6:9, 10. **innocent**. *or*, unpunished. Pr 6:29. 11:21. 16:5mg. 17:5mg. 19:5mg, 9. Ge 24:41. Je 25:29. 49:12.

21. **To**. √138C, Ge +22:14. **respect**. T#1824. Pr 18:5. 24:23. Ex 23:2, 8. **persons**. √171Q, Ge +3:19. **for**. Erasmus observes that this expression probably originated from the circumstance of holding out a piece of bread to a dog, in order to soothe him. For a similar expression see A. Gellius (Noct. At. l. 1. c. 15). Ezk *13:19. Ho 4:18. Mi 3:5. 7:3. Ro 16:18. 2 P 2:3.

22. **that hasteth**, etc. Heb. that hath an evil eye, hasteth to be rich. ver. 20. Pr 19:2. 23:5. Ge ◐13:2. Lk 12:15. 1 T 6:9, 10, 17. **an evil**. Pr 23:6. Mt 20:15. Mk 7:22. 1 J 2:16. **and**. Ge 13:10-13. 19:17. 1 K 21:2, 18, 19. Jb 20:18-22. 27:16, 17. Je *17:11. *22:13-19. Lk *12:19, 20.

23. **that rebuketh**. T#610, 919. ver. 4. Pr 6:23. 13:18. 15:31, 32. +*19:25. *24:24, 25. 25:12. *27:5, 6. Le +*19:17. 2 S 12:7. 1 K 1:23, 32-40. Ps *141:5. Ezk 16:1. Mt *18:15. Lk 17:3. Ga 2:11. +6:1 (T#109). Ep *5:11. Col *3:16. 1 Th 5:14. 2 P 3:15, 16. **afterwards**. T#612. Pr 25:12. Ps *141:5. Mt ◐+*7:6. 1 P 2:12.

24. **robbeth**. Pr 19:26. Ge 31:19, 34, 35. Jg 17:2. Mt 15:4-6. **the same**. ver. 7. Pr 13:20. 18:9. **a destroyer**. Heb. a man destroying. Pr 6:32. *18:9. Ge 6:13.

25. **that is**. Pr 10:12. 13:10. 15:18. 21:24. 22:10. 29:22, 23. **heart**. Heb. *nephesh*, soul, Ex +23:9. **he that putteth**. Ps 37:5-7. 84:12. Je *17:7, 8. 1 T 6:6. 1 P 5:7. **made**. Pr 11:25. 13:4. 15:30. Is 58:11.

26. **that**. Pr *3:5. Ge 3:6. 2 K 8:13. Je √17:9. Mt 26:33, 35, 41, 69, 70. Mk *7:21-23. 14:27-31. Ro 8:7. **heart**. √121I1, Ge +3:7. **but**. Jb *28:28. Ep 5:16, 17. Col √1:10. 4:5, 6. 1 Th 4:1. 2 T √3:15. Ja *1:5. 3:13-18.

27. **that giveth**. Pr 19:17. 22:9. Dt 15:7, 10. Ps 41:1-3. 112:5-9. 2 C 9:6-11. He 13:16. **hideth**. Is *1:15. **shall**. Pr 11:26. 24:24. Mt 25:41-45. Ja 2:13.

28. **the wicked**. ver. *12. Pr 29:2. Is 51:12. **hide**. Jb 24:4. Is 26:20. Am 5:13. **they perish**. Est 8:17. Ac *12:23, 24.

PROVERBS 29

Miscellaneous maxims, concerning a man being hardened against reproof, and of good government, wisdom, and righteousness; against flattery, profligacy, injustice, scornfulness, loquacity, rashness, indulging children, improperly treating servants, pride, and the fear of man; and of the goodness and sovereignty of the Lord, 1-27.

1. **He, that being often reproved**. Heb. A man of reproofs. Pr *1:24-31. 1 S 2:25, 34. 1 K 17:1. *18:18. 20:42. 21:20-23. 22:20-23, 28, 34-37. 2 Ch *25:16. 33:10. 36:15-17. Is 48:8. Je *25:3-5. *26:3-5. 31:18. 35:13-16. Zc 1:3-6. Mt 26:21-25. Jn 6:70, 71. 13:10, 11, 18, 26. Ac *1:18, 25. **hardeneth**. Ex *9:34. 2 Ch 36:13. Ne 9:29. Is 48:4. Je *17:23. **neck**. Ex 32:9. Ac 7:51. **shall**. Pr 6:15. *28:18. Is 30:13, 14. Zc *7:11-

14. Ro √11:32. 1 Th 5:3. **without remedy**. 2 Ch 36:16. He *6:4-6.

2. **the righteous**. Pr 11:10. 28:12, 28. Est 8:15. Ps 72:1-7. Is 32:1, 2. Je *23:5, 6. Re 11:15. **in authority**. *or*, increased. ver. 16. Ge 7:17. Ex 11:9. Ec 5:11. **when the wicked**. Est 3:15. Ec 10:5. Mt *2:3, 16. **people mourn**. Pr ◐11:10. Am 5:13.

3. **loveth**. Pr 10:1. 15:20. 23:15, 24, 25. 27:11. Lk 1:13-17. **he**. Pr 5:8-13. *6:26. 21:17, 20. 28:7, 19. Lk *15:13, 30.

4. **king**. ver. *14. Pr 16:12. 20:8. 1 S *13:13. 2 S 8:15. 1 K 2:12. 2 Ch 1:1. Ps 89:12, 14. 97:2. 99:4. Is *9:7. 32:1, 2. 49:8. **he that receiveth gifts**. Heb. a man of oblations. 2 K 15:18-20. Je *22:13-17. Da 11:20. Mi *7:3.

5. **flattereth**. Pr 7:5, *21. *20:19. *26:24, 25, 28. 2 S 14:17, etc. 15:1-14. 16:1-4. Jb 17:5. Ps *5:9. 12:2. Da 11:21. 1 Th *2:5. **spreadeth**. Pr 1:17. La 1:13. Ho 5:1. Lk *20:20, 21. Ro 16:18.

6. **the transgression**. Pr *5:22. 11:5, 6. *12:13. Jb 18:7-10. Ps 11:6. Is *8:14, 15. 2 T *2:26. **but**. Ps *97:11. *118:15. 132:16. Is 35:10. Ac 16:25. Ro *5:2, 3. 1 C 15:55-57. Ja *1:2. 1 P *1:8. 1 J *1:4. Re 5:8-10.

7. **considereth**. lit. knoweth. √121C2A2, Ge +39:6. Le +*19:15. Jb *29:11-16. 31:13, 21. Ps 31:7. *41:1. Ga *6:1. **but**. Pr *21:13. 1 S 25:9-11. Je 5:28. *22:15-17. Ezk 22:7, *29-31. Mi 3:1-4.

8. **scornful**. Pr *11:11. Is *28:14-22. Mt 27:39-43. Jn *9:40, 41. 11:47-50. 1 Th *2:15, 16. **bring a city into a snare**. *or*, set a city on fire. Ja *3:5, 6. **wise**. Ex *32:10-14. Nu *16:48. *25:11. Dt *9:18-20. 2 S *24:16, 17. Je *15:1. Ezk *22:30. Am 7:2-6. Jon 3:5-10. Ja *5:15-18. **turn away**. Pr 15:1. Ex 32:10-14. Nu 16:48. Je +2:24mg. Ja 5:18.

9. **contendeth with**. Pr *26:4. Ec 10:13. Mt +*7:6. *11:17-19.

10. **The bloodthirsty**. Heb. Men of bloods. Ge *4:5-8, +10mg. 1 S 20:31-33. 22:11, etc. 1 K 21:20. *22:8. 2 K +*9:26mg. 2 Ch *18:7. Mt 5:12. Mk *6:18, 19, 24-27. Jn 7:7. *15:18, 19. Ac 7:52. Ga 4:29. 2 T 3:12. 1 J *3:12, 13. Re 17:6. **but**. 1 S *15:11. Je *13:15-17. *18:20. 40:14-16. Lk *23:34. Jn 5:34. Ac *7:60. Ro *10:1. soul. Heb. *nephesh*, Ge +12:13.

11. **fool uttereth**. T#200-2. ver. 20. Pr *12:16, 23. 13:16. 14:16, 17, *33. 15:2. 18:7, +13. Jg *16:17. 1 S ◐16:1, *2n. Ps +101:5 (T#729). Am 5:13. Mi *7:5. Ep 5:4. **mind**. Heb. *ruach*, spirit, Ge +26:35. √121A10, Ge +26:35. **wise man**. Pr 10:14. *16:32. 17:28. 30:32. Ps 141:3. **till afterwards**. 1 S *25:36.

12. **ruler hearken**. Pr *20:8. 25:23. 1 S 22:8, etc. 23:19-23. 2 S 3:7-11. *4:5-12. 1 K +*12:8. 16:2. 21:11-13. 2 K 10:6, 7. Ps 52:2-4. *101:5-7. Je 37:2. Zp 1:9. 1 T *5:19. **his servants**. 2 K ◐+*5:13. **wicked**. Ho +7:3.

13. **The poor**. Pr 10:4. 13:8, 23. 14:20. Ezk 18:25. **the deceitful man**. *or*, the usurer. *⊛S#8501h, only here. Is +24:2. Mt 9:9. 1 C *6:10. **meet**. Pr *22:2. Ex *22:25, 26. Le *25:35-37. Ne 5:5-7. **Lord**. Jb 25:3. Ps 13:3. 145:9. Mt +*5:45. Ep *2:1.

14. **king**. T#908. ver. 4. Pr 16:12. 20:28. *25:5. *28:16. Dt 17:18-20. Jb 29:11-18. Ps 72:2-4, 12-14. 82:2, 3. 89:2. Is *1:17. 11:4. 28:6. Je 5:28. *22:16. Da *4:27. **his throne**. Is *9:6, 7. Lk *1:32, 33. He *1:8, 9. **for ever**. Ps +9:18 (*⊛S#5703h).

15. **rod**. ver. *17, *21. Pr 10:13. *13:24. +*19:18. 22:+*6, 8h, *15. *23:13, 14. Mi 6:9. **and reproof**. Pr

10:17. 15:5, 10. 17:10. 25:12. 27:5. *29:1. Ex +13:8. Ps *141:5. Ec 7:5. He 12:5. **give wisdom**. 2 Ch *33:12. Ps 119:67, 71, 75. He 12:9-11. **a child**. Pr 10:1, 5. 17:21, 25. √22:6. 1 S *3:13. 1 K *1:6. **left to himself**. Ex 4:24-26. 1 S +*3:13. 1 K *1:6. Est ◑*2:11. Is 16:2, 27:10. 2 C ◑+*12:14. 1 T +*5:8. **to shame**. Pr 10:5. 12:4. 14:35. 17:2. *19:26.

16. **the wicked**. ver. 2mg. Ezk 16:49. **but**. Ps *37:34, 36. 58:10. 63:10. 91:8. 92:9, 11. 112:8. Re 11:15. 15:4. 18:20.

17. **Correct thy son**. ver. *15. Pr *13:24. +*19:18. *22:15. *23:13, 14. Ex +13:8. **soul**. Heb. *nephesh*, Ge +34:3.

18. **there**. 1 S 3:1. 1 Ch 17:15. 2 Ch 15:3-5. Ps *74:9. La *2:9. Ho *4:6. Am 8:*11, 12. 9:11, 12. Ml 2:7. Mt 9:36. Ro 10:13-15. **perish**. *or*, is made naked. Ex 32:25. 2 Ch 28:19. **but**. Pr 19:16. Ps 19:11. *119:2. Lk +*11:28. Jn +*13:17. 14:21-23. Ro 2:13. Ja *1:25. Re 22:14. **happy**. T#324. Ps +58:11 (T#630). 119:1, 2. +*128:2. Ro +7:12 (T#286).

19. **servant**. Pr 26:3. 30:22. T 2:9. **though**. Jb *19:16.

20. **Seest thou**. ƒ85D, Ps +25:12. ver. *11. Ec *5:2. Ja *1:19. **words**. *or*, matters. Pr *14:29. 21:5. **more**. Pr 26:12.

21. **servant**. ver. 19. La 3:27. Ep *6:9. Col 4:1. **become**. Pr 30:21, 22. Jn 15:15. **length**. Pr 5:4, 11. 14:12, 13.

22. **angry**. Pr 10:12. 15:18. 17:19. 26:21. 30:33. Ep 4:26. **strife**. 1 T 6:4. 2 T 2:23, 24. Ja 3:16. **a furious**. Pr 17:19. 22:24. Ja 3:16.

23. **man's**. Pr 18:12. 2 Ch 32:25, 26. 33:10-12, 23, 24. Jb 22:29. 40:12. Ps 39:5. Is 2:11, 12, 17. Da 4:30-37. 5:20, 21. Lk 14:11. 18:14. Ac 12:23. Ja 4:6-10. 1 P 5:5. **pride**. ƒ138B, Ge +13:16. Ps +*119:21. **honor**. Pr 15:33. Ge 18:27. Dt 8:2, 3, 16. Jb 22:29. Is +*57:15. 66:1, 2. Mt +*5:3. 18:4. 23:12. **spirit**. Heb. *ruach*, Ge +41:8.

24. **partner**. Pr 1:11-19. Ex 22:8. Ps 50:18-22. Is 1:23. Mk 11:17. **hateth**. Pr 6:32. 8:36. 15:32. 20:2. **soul**. Heb. *nephesh*, Ge +27:31. **he**. Le 5:1. Nu 5:21. Jg 17:2. 1 K 22:16. Mt 26:63. Ep *5:11.

25. **fear**. Ge 12:11-13. *20:2, 11. 26:7. Ex *32:22-24. 1 S *15:24. 27:1, 11. 1 K 19:3. Is 57:11. Je 38:19. Mt +*10:28. 15:12. 26:69-74. Jn 3:2. 9:22. *12:42, 43. 19:12, 13. Ga *2:11-13. 2 T 4:16, 17. **whoso**. Pr *16:20. 18:10. *30:5. 2 K 6:31, 32. 1 Ch 5:20. Ps *118:8. 125:1. Ec 7:18. Da *3:28. *6:23. Ac 4:13, 19. 1 P *1:21. **safe**. Heb. set on high. Ps 69:29. *91:14.

26. **seek**. Pr 19:6. Ps 20:9. **ruler's favor**. Heb. face of a ruler. Pr 17:9, 19. 28:5. **but**. Pr *16:7. 19:21. 21:1. Ge 43:14. Ezr *7:27, 28. Ne 1:11. Est *4:16. Ps 20:9. 62:12. Is *46:9-11. Da *4:35.

27. **unjust**. Pr *24:9. Ps 119:115. *139:21, 22. Zc 11:8. Jn *7:7. 1 J 3:13. **just**. T#647. Mt *5:45. **and he**. Jn *15:17-19, 23. Ro 8:7. 1 J 3:12, 13.

PROVERBS 30

The title, 1. Agur's confession of sin and ignorance; his inquiry after God, and his cautions about the word of God; his prayer to be delivered from vanity and lies, and from the temptations of wealth and of poverty, 2-9. A caution against accusing servants; and concerning four sorts of wicked persons, 10-14. Four things insatiable, 15, 16. The punishment of those who mock their parents, 17. Four things wonderful and not to be traced out, 18-20. Four things exceedingly trouble-some, 21-23. Four things small but wise, 24-28. Four things comely in going, 29-31. A counsel for men to check themselves, when conscious of being wrong, and to avoid forcing wrath and strife, 32, 33.

1. **Agur**. i.e. *gatherer*, ✲S#94h. Agur was probably a public teacher, and Ithiel and Ucal, his pupils; and this was the *massa*, or oracle, which he delivered, not by his own wisdom but by the Holy Spirit, for the benefit of man; and which, it is probable, was added by "the men of Hezekiah." **Jakeh**. i.e. *obedient*, ✲S#3348h. **even**. Pr 31:1. 2 P *1:19-21. **Ithiel**. i.e. *God has arrived; God is with me*, ✲S#384h. Pr 30:1, 1. Ne 11:7. (1) One of the children or disciples of Agur, Pr 30:1. (2) A Benjamite, son of Jesaiah, Ne 11:7. **Ucal**. i.e. *prevailing; devoured; I shall be completed, I shall be enabled*, ✲S#401h.

2. **I am**. Jb *42:3-6. Ps *73:22. Is *6:5. Ro 11:25. 1 C *3:18. *8:2. Ja *1:5. **brutish**. Pr 5:12. Ps 92:6. Je 10:14. 2 P 2:12-16.

3. **neither**. Je 10:7. Am *7:14, 15. Mt *16:17. **nor**. Jb *11:7-9. Mt *11:27. Jn *17:3. Ro *11:33. Ep *3:17-19. **have**. Heb. know. Pr 5:6. 10:32. 24:12. **the holy**. Is 6:3. 30:11. *57:15. Re 3:7. 4:8.

4. **Who hath ascended**. Dt 30:12. Jn *3:13. Ro 10:6. Ep *4:9, 10. **who hath gathered**. Jb 11:7-9. *38:4, etc. Ps 104:2, etc. Is *40:12, etc. 53:8. **what is his name**. Ex *3:13-15. *6:3. 34:5-7. Dt *28:58. **and what**. Ge *32:29. Jg *13:18. Ps *2:7. Is *7:14. *9:6. Je *23:6. Mt *1:21-23. 11:27. Lk *10:22.

5. **word**. Ps *12:6. 18:30. *19:8. 119:140. Ro *7:12. Ja *3:17. **pure**. Heb. purified. T#1025. 2 S 22:31. Ps 12:6. 18:30. 119:140mg. **shield**. Ge *15:1. Ps *84:11. 91:2. 115:9-11. 119:114. 144:2. Ep 6:16.

6. **Add**. T#50, 1032. Ge 3:3. Dt *4:2. 12:32. Is +42:21 (T#284). 2 P 3:15, 16. Re *22:18, 19. **and**. Ge 3:3. Jb 13:7-9. 1 C 15:15.

7. **have**. 1 K *3:5-9. 2 K 2:9. Ps 27:4. Lk *10:42. **deny me them not**. Heb. withhold not from me. Pr 3:27. 23:13. Ge 30:2. 2 S 13:13. Ps 21:2.

8. **vanity**. T#1738. Pr *21:6. 22:8. Ps *62:9, 10. 119:37. Ec 1:2. Is 5:18. *59:4. Jon *2:8. Ac 14:15. 1 J 2:16. **and lies**. Ps *119:29. **neither**. Ge 28:20. Jb 1:21. Je *45:5. Ph *4:11, 12. 1 T 6:6-10. **poverty**. T#1644. Pr 6:11. +10:15 (T#521). 11:24. 20:13. 21:17. 23:21. 24:34. 28:19. Le +25:35 (T#526). Dt ◑15:11. Ps +12:5 (T#523). +140:12 (T#522). Is 3:7. Am 8:11. Mt +5:7 (T#527). Lk +16:25 (T#525). 2 C +6:10. Ja +2:5 (T#524). **nor riches**. T#1679. Pr 23:4, 5. 1 K ◑3:13. Ec 5:10. Hab 2:5. Mt *13:22. Mk +4:19. Ph 4:11, 12. 1 T +*6:5, 9, 10. **feed**. Ge 28:20. 48:15, 16. Ex *16:15, 18, 21, 22, 35. Mt *6:11, 33. Lk 11:3. 1 T *6:6-8. **convenient for me**. Heb. of my allowance. ƒ171E9, Ge +47:22. 1 K 4:27. 2 K 25:30. Je 37:21. 52:34. Mt *6:11.

9. **I be full**. Dt 6:10-12. *8:10-14, 17. 31:20. 32:15. Ne *9:25, 26. Jb *31:24-28. Je 2:31. Ezk 16:14, 15, 49, 50. Da 4:17, 30. Ho *13:6. Mk +4:19. Ac *12:22, 23. Ja 4:3. **deny thee**. Heb. belie thee. Jsh 24:27. Jb 8:18. 21:13, 14. 22:17, 18. 31:28. Je 5:12. **Who**. Ex *5:2. 2 Ch *32:15-17. **or**. Pr *6:30, 31. Ps 125:3. **lest**. Ps +√9:10n. **and steal**. T#1712. Ex +√20:15. Dt 23:24. Ep *4:28. 1 P 4:15. **and take the name**. Pr 29:24. Ex *20:7. Le *5:1. Mt 26:72, 74.

10. **Accuse not**. Heb. Hurt not with thy tongue. Pr 17:20. *24:23. Ge ◑21:25, 26. Le 19:16, ◑17. Dt

23:15. 1 S 22:9, 10. 24:9. 26:19. *30:15. 2 S 16:1-4.
19:26, 27. Ps +101:5. Ec 7:21. Da *3:8, etc. *6:13,
24. Mt 7:3-5, 12. 18:15. Ro *14:4. Ep 4:31, 32. Col
3:12, 13. T 3:2. Phm 8-10. Ja 2:13. **lest.** Pr 11:26.
*24:24. *26:2. 28:27. Dt *15:9. 1 S 26:19. 2 Ch 24:22-
24. Ec *7:21. **and thou.** Jn 8:3-9. Ro 2:1, 3, 21, 22.
  11. **a generation.** ver. *12-14. Mt *3:7. 1 P *2:9.
that curseth. ver. *17. Pr *20:20. Le *20:9. Dt *21:20,
21. *27:16. Mt *15:4-6. Mk *7:10-13. **doth.** 1 T *5:4,
8.
  12. **that are pure.** T#510. Pr +16:25 (T#704). 21:2.
Jg 17:5, 13. 1 S *15:13, 14. Jb 33:9. Ps +10:4 (T#696).
36:2. 51:10. Is *65:5. Je 2:*22-24, 35. 17:9. Mt 19:20-
22. Lk 11:39, 40. *16:+15 (T#703). *18:11. 2 T *3:5.
T *1:15, 16. 1 J √1:8-10. **not.** Ps *51:2, 7. Is *1:16.
Je *4:14. Ezk 36:25. Zc 13:1. 1 C 6:11. T √3:5. 1 J
*1:7. Re *1:5.
  13. **how lofty.** Pr 6:17. *21:4. Ps *101:5. 131:1. Is
*2:11. 3:16. Ezk *28:2-5, 9. Da *11:36, 37. Hab *2:4.
Ph ◑2:5-8. 2 Th *2:3, 4.
  14. **whose.** Pr 12:18. Jb 29:17. Ps 3:7. 52:2. *57:4.
58:6. Da 7:5-7. Re 9:8. **to devour.** Pr 22:16. 28:3. Ps
10:8, 9. 12:5. *14:4. Ec 4:1. Is *32:7. Am 2:7. 4:1.
8:4. Mi 2:1, 2. 3:1-5. Hab 3:14. Zp 3:3. Mt *23:14.
Ja *5:1-4.
  15. **The horseleach.** Is 57:3, 4. Ezk 16:44-46. Mt
23:32. Jn *8:39, 44. **Give.** Is 56:11, 12. Ho 4:18. Mi
7:3. Ro *16:18. 2 P *2:3, 13-15. Ju *11, *12. **There.**
ver. 21, 24, 29. Pr 6:16. Am 1:3, 6, 9, 11, 13. 2:1, 4.
never satisfied. Pr 27:20. Ec 1:8. 4:8. 5:10. Ezk 16:28,
29. Am 4:8. Hab 2:5. **It is enough.** Heb. Wealth. ver.
16. Ps 44:12.
  16. **The grave.** Heb. *sheol,* Ge +37:35. Pr *27:20.
Hab *2:5.
  17. **eye that mocketh.** ver. 11. Pr *20:20. *23:22.
Ge 9:21-27. Le *20:9. Dt *21:18-21. 2 S 18:9, 10,
14-17. 2 K 2:23. Jb 19:18. **father.** ſ63J1, Ge +13:9.
By ellipsis (of repetition: complex, of single words),
supply "mother" in this clause, and "father" in the
next, for what is said of one is applicable to the other.
This figure applies to a number of passages in Proverbs:
Pr 10:1. 15:20. 17:25. 23:24. **mother.** ſ63J1, Ge +13:9.
the ravens. 1 S 17:44, 46. 2 S 21:10. **valley.** or, brook.
Nu +13:23mg. Jg +16:4mg.
  18. **too wonderful.** Jb *42:3. Ps *40:5. 131:1mg.
139:6. Ro 11:33.
  19. **way of an eagle.** Jb 39:27. Is *40:31. **midst.**
Heb. heart. ſ144A7, Ex +15:8. Pr 23:34mg. **and the.**
Pr *14:12, 13. Ex *22:16. 1 Th 5:22. 1 T 4:12. 5:2.
6:11. 2 T 2:22. He 3:13. 1 J 2:16.
  20. **the way.** Pr *7:13-23. Nu *5:11-30. **no wickedness.** He +*3:13.
  21. **For three.** Jb 40:5n. **disquieted.** Pr 29:9. Dt
2:25. **bear.** Pr 18:5. Ge 4:13. 36:7.
  22. **a servant.** Pr *19:10. *28:3. Ec 10:7. Is *3:4,
5. 1 C 14:40. **a fool.** 1 S 25:3, 10, 11, 25, 36-38. 30:16.
  23. **an odious.** Pr *19:13. *21:9, 19. *27:15. **an handmaid.** Pr 29:21. Ge 16:4.
  24. **little.** Jb 12:7. **upon.** ſ181E, Ge +3:24. **exceeding wise.** Heb. wise, made wise. ſ147D, Ge +1:29.
Pr 1:5, 6. 3:7, 35. 9:8, 9.
  25. **The ants.** The ants may truly be called a *people,*
as they have houses, towns, public roads, etc.; and
show their wisdom and prudence by preparing their
meat in due season. Pr *6:6-8. Mt *6:20. Jn 6:27. **not.**
ſ175B, Ge +21:16.

  26. **The conies.** The *shaphan,* a creature like a rabbit, though but a feeble animal and incapacitated by
its soft, tender feet, from digging, yet, by its sagacity
and judgment builds its house in the holes and clefts
of the rock; far more inaccessible than the burrows of
the rabbit. See on Le 11:5n. Ps 104:18. **rocks.** Ps 18:2.
91:1, 2. Je 48:28.
  27. **The locusts.** Ex 10:4-6, 13-15. Ps 105:34. Jl 1:4,
6, 7. *2:7-11, 25. Re *9:3-11. **by bands.** Heb. gathered
together. Ezk 1:21-26.
  28. **palaces.** Ps 144:12. Is 13:22. Da 1:4. Ep 2:6.
  29. **three.** ver. 21. Jb +40:5n. **go well.** Ph *4:8.
  30. **A lion.** Nu 23:24. Jg *14:18. **among.** ſ108C1.
Idiom B833. This is an idiomatic degree of comparison
using a preposition after an adjective to emphasize
and make the adjective superlative. "Strong among
beasts" signifies the strongest of beasts. The same Hebrew idiom is found in the New Testament at Lk 1:42,
where "Blessed art thou among women" signifies the
most blessed of women.
  31. **greyhound.** or, horse. Heb. girt in the loins.
ſ142, Ge +20:16. **against.** Pr *16:14. *20:2. Da *3:15-
18.
  32. **thou hast done.** Pr *26:12. Ec 8:3. **thought evil.**
Pr 16:3. Ec 10:20. Mt 5:28. 2 C 10:5. Ph *4:8. **lay.**
ſ121S3N, Jg +18:19. Pr *17:28. Jb 21:5. *40:4, 5.
Ec 8:4. Mi 7:16, 17. Ro *3:19.
  33. **so.** Pr *15:18. 16:28. 17:14. *26:21. *28:25.
*29:22.

PROVERBS 31

*King Lemuel instructed by his mother to avoid
whoredom and drunkenness and to use his wealth and
authority for the relief and protection of the poor and
oppressed, 1-9; and concerning the character and value
of the virtuous woman, 10-31.*
  1. **the prophecy.** Pr 30:1. **his.** Pr *1:8. *6:20. 2 T
*1:5. √3:15, 16.
  2. **the son of my womb.** Is *49:15. **the son of my
vows.** 1 S *1:11, 28.
  3. **strength.** Pr *5:9-11. *7:26, 27. Ho *4:11. **to that.**
Dt *17:17. Ne *13:26.
  4. **not for kings.** T#369. Le *10:8-11. Nu 6:1-4.
1 K 20:12, 16-20. Est 3:15. Ec *10:17. Is *28:7, 8. Da
*5:2-4. Ho *4:11, 12. *7:3-5. Hab *2:5. Mt +10:16
(T#457). Mk *6:21-28. **Lemuel.** i.e. *for whom is a
mighty one; by God; unto God,* *S#3927h. ver. 1.
drink. ſ108H7. Idiom B842. To drink or taste wine
is a Hebraism for drinking wine to excess, as Da 5:2.
ſ108B. Idiom B828. "Drink" is a Hebraism for good
living and drinking wine. For other instances of this
idiom see Mt 11:18, 19. Lk 7:33, 34.
  5. **drink.** Ec 10:17. **pervert.** Heb. alter. 1 S 21:13.
Est 2:9mg. Ps *89:34. **any of the afflicted.** Heb. all
the sons of affliction. Hab *2:5.
  6. **strong.** Ps 104:15. 1 T *5:23. **of heavy hearts.**
Heb. bitter of soul. Jg +18:25mg. 1 S 1:10mg. *30:6mg.
2 K 4:27mg. Heb. *nephesh,* Ex +23:9.
  7. **drink.** Ep √5:18. **remember his.** Je 16:7.
  8. **Open.** Pr *24:7, 11, 12. 1 S 19:4-7. 20:32. 22:14,
15. Est *4:13-16. Jb 29:9-17. Ps *82:3, 4. Je 26:16-
19, 24. 38:7-10. Jn *7:51. **such,** etc. Heb. the sons of
destruction. or, change. ſ171E7, Jb +14:14. 1 S
20:31mg. Ps 79:11mg.
  9. **judge righteously.** ſ24I, Is +21:7. Pr 16:12. 20:8.

Le *19:15. Dt 1:16. *16:18-20. 2 S 8:15. Jb 29:12, 15, 16. Ps 58:1, 2. 72:1, 2, 12-14. Is 1:*17, 23. *11:4. 31:1, 2. Je 5:28. *22:3, 15, 16. 23:5. Da *4:27. Am 5:11, 12. Zc 7:9. *9:9. Jn *7:24. He 1:9. Re 19:11.

10. **Who.** This is the commencement of an alphabetical poem, each verse beginning consecutively with a letter of the Hebrew alphabet; in which we are presented with an admirable picture of a good wife, according to the primitive manners of the East. **can.** Pr 12:4. *18:22. *19:14. Ru 3:11. Ec 7:28. SS 6:8, 9. Ep *5:25-33. **her.** Pr 3:15. *8:11. 20:15. **price.** Ml 3:17.

11. **heart.** 2 K 4:9, 10, 22, 23. 1 P *3:1-7. **no need.** SS 4:16.

12. **will do.** Ge 2:18. 1 S *25:18-22, 26, 27. Ro 7:18, 25. 1 C 7:34. Ep 5:31, 32.

13. **worketh.** Ge 18:6-8. *24:13, 14, 18-20. 29:9, 10. Ex 2:16. Ru *2:2, 3, 23. Is 3:16-24. *32:9-11. Ac *9:39, 40. 1 Th *4:11. 2 Th *3:10-12. 1 T *5:10, 14. T *2:5. **willingly.** Ro 6:19. **from afar.** Jn 6:33.

14. **is like.** ver. 24. 1 K 9:26-28. 2 Ch 9:10, 21. Ezk 27:3, etc.

15. **riseth.** Jsh 3:1. 2 Ch 36:15. Ps *119:147, 148. Ec *9:10. Mk *1:35. Ro *12:11. **and giveth.** Mt *24:45. Lk *12:42. **meat.** lit. prey. *171I10, Ps +111:5mg. **portion.** Lk +12:42. **maidens.** Pr 9:3. 27:27. Ge 24:14.

16. **considereth.** Jsh 15:18. SS 8:12. Mt *13:44. **buyeth.** Heb. taketh. Pr 1:19. Nu 21:25. Ps 6:9. Is 55:1.

17. **girdeth.** 1 K 18:46. 2 K 4:29. Jb *38:3. Ps 18:32. Lk *12:35. Ep *6:10, 14. 1 P *1:13. **strengtheneth.** Ge 49:24. Is 44:12. Ho 7:15.

18. **perceiveth.** Heb. tasteth. 1 S 14:24, 29, 43. **her candle.** Ge 31:40. Ps *127:2. Mt 5:15, 16. Mk *25:3-10. 1 Th *2:9. 2 Th *3:7-9.

19. **She layeth.** She takes the spindle in her right hand and twists the thread while she holds the distaff, on which the wool or flax is rolled, in the guard of the left arm, and draws down the thread with the fingers of the left hand. Ex *35:25, 26. **her hands.** Ep 4:28.

20. **She stretcheth.** Heb. She spreadeth. Pr 1:24. Ro 10:21. **to the poor.** Mt 25:36. **she reacheth.** Pr *19:17. *22:9. Jb 31:16-20. Ps *41:1. 112:9. Ec 11:1,

2. Mk *14:7. Ac *9:39-41. *20:34, 35. Ep *4:28. He *13:16.

21. **not afraid.** Pr 1:33. *25:20. **scarlet.** or, double garments. Ge 38:28, 30. 45:22. Ex 25:4.

22. **coverings.** Pr *7:16. **clothing.** Ge 41:42mg. Est 5:1. 8:15. Ps *45:13, 14. Ezk 16:10-13. 1 P *3:3, 4. **silk.** *Shesh,* rather fine linen, or cotton (see on Ex 39:27n). *Sadin,* rendered *fine linen,* ver. 24, is probably the same as the Arabic *sidn,* and *sudl,* a veil or an inner covering of fine muslin.

23. **husband.** Pr *12:4. **in the gates.** *171S7, Ge +14:7. Pr 24:7. Dt 16:18. 21:19. Ru 4:1, 2. Jb 29:7.

24. **She maketh.** ver. 13, 19. 1 K 10:28. Ezk 27:16. Lk *16:19. Re 19:8.

25. **Strength.** Jb 29:14. 40:10. Ps 132:9, 16. Is *61:10. Ro *13:14. Ep *4:24. 1 T *2:8-10. 1 P 3:3, 4. *5:5, 6. **and she.** Ps *97:11, 12. Is 65:13, 14. Mt *25:20, 21. Jn 16:20.

26. **openeth.** *108H6A, Jg +11:35. ver. 8, 9. Jg *13:23. 1 S *25:24-31. 2 S *20:16-22. 2 K *22:15-20. Est 4:4. 5:8. 7:3-6. 8:3-6. Lk *1:38, 42-56. Ac *18:26. Ep *4:29. Col *4:5, 6. Ja 3:17. **in her.** Pr *12:18. 15:4. *16:24. *25:15. Ge *24:18-20. SS 2:14. 4:11. Ml *2:6. Ac 16:15. 1 P *3:1, 4, 5, 8, 9. **law of kindness.** Pr. 19:22. Lk. +*6:35. Ep. √4:32. 6:4. Col. 3:17, 21.

27. **looketh well.** Pr *14:1. Ph 2:12. 1 Th 4:11. 2 Th *3:6-12. 1 T *5:10, ◐13, 14. T *2:4, 5.

28. **children.** ver. 1. 1 K *2:19. Ps 116:16. 2 T *1:5. √3:15-17. **her husband.** SS 7:1-9. Is 62:4mg, 5mg. **praiseth.** 1 C 4:5.

29. **done virtuously.** or, gotten riches. ver. 3, 10. Pr 12:4. 13:22. **thou.** SS 6:8, 9. Ep *5:27.

30. **Favor.** Pr *6:25. *11:22. 2 S 14:25. Est 1:11, 12. Ezk *16:15. Ja *1:11. 1 P *1:24. **a woman.** Pr *1:7. 8:13. Ex *1:17-21. Ps *147:11. Lk *1:6, 46-50. 1 P *3:4, 5. **she.** Ec 7:18. *12:13. Ro *2:29. 1 C *4:5. 1 P *1:7. *3:4.

31. **of the.** ver. 16. Pr *11:30. Ps *128:2. Mt *7:16, 20. Ro *6:21, 22. Ph 4:17. **and let.** Mk *14:7-9. Ac *9:39. Ro *16:1-4, 6, 12. 1 T *5:10, 25. He *6:10. Re *14:13.

ECCLESIASTES

ECCLESIASTES 1

The writer and subject of the book, 1, 2. The vanity of earthly things illustrated by the shortness of life; the restless motions of the sun, wind, and waters, the correspondent toil of man; and the want of satisfaction, and of novelty, experienced in everything, for nothing is permanent, 3-11. The writer shows his royal authority, his pursuit of wisdom, and the vexation that he found in it, 12-18.

1. A.M. 3027. B.C. 977. **the Preacher.** ver. 12. Ec 7:27. *12:8-10. Ne 6:7. Ps 40:9. Is 61:1. Jon 3:2. 2 P 2:5. **king.** ver. 12. 1 K 11:42, 43. 2 Ch 9:30. 10:17-19.

2. **Vanity.** *66, Ge +9:3. **of vanities.** *147H, Ge +9:25. Ec 2:11, 15, 17, 19, 21, 23, 26. *3:19. 4:4, 8, 16. 5:10. *6:11. 11:8, 10. 12:8. Ps *39:5, 6, 11. 62:9, *10. *144:4. Ro 8:20, 21. **vanity of.** *113, Nu +9:20.

3. **profit.** Ec 2:22. 3:9. *5:15, 16. Pr *23:4, 5. Is

*55:2. Hab 2:13, 18. Mt *16:26. Mk 8:36, 37. Jn *6:27. **under.** Ec *2:11, 19. 4:3, 7. *5:18. 6:12. 7:11. 8:15-17. 9:3, 6, 13.

4. **One generation.** Ec 6:12. Ge 5:3-31. 10:1-32. 11:10-32. 36:9, etc. *47:9. Ex 1:6, 7. 6:16, etc. Ps *89:1, 2, 47, 48. *90:9, 10. Zc 1:5. **but.** Ge +8:22. Ps 78:69. 89:36, 37. *102:24-28. *104:5. 119:90, 91. Mt *24:35. 2 P *3:10-13. **abideth.** 1 Ch √16:30. Ps ◐+102:25, *26. **for ever.** Heb. *olam,* Ge +9:12. Ex +*12:24. Ps *72:5, 7, 17. *89:36, 37. 104:5. *148:6. Is +*9:6, 7. Ezk +*37:25.

5. **sun.** Ge *8:22. Ps *19:4-6. *89:36, 37. 104:19-23. Je *33:20. **hasteth.** Heb. panteth. Jsh *10:13, 14. Ps 42:1. 119:131. Is +42:19mg. Am 2:7. Hab 3:11.

6. **The wind.** This verse should be connected with the preceding and rendered, "The sun also ariseth, and the sun goeth down, and hasteth to his place where he arose; going toward the south, and turning about unto the north. The wind whirleth about continually,"

etc. Alluding, in the former part, to the apparent daily motion of the sun from east to west and to his annual course through the signs of the zodiac. Jb 37:9, 17. Ps 107:25, 29. Jon 1:4. Mt *7:24-27. Jn *3:8. Ac 27:13-15.

7. **the rivers run**. Jb 38:10, 11. Ps 104:6-9. **return again**. Heb. return to go.

8. **full**. Ec 2:11, *26. Ge 3:19. Mt *11:28-30. Ro *8:22, 23. **man**. Ec 4:1-4. *7:24-26. **the eye**. Ec *4:8. *5:10, 11. Ps 63:5. Pr *27:20. 30:15, 16. Is 55:2. Mt +*5:6. Re *7:16, 17.

9. **that hath**. Ec *3:15. *7:10. 2 P *2:1. **and there**. Is 43:19. Je 31:22. Re *21:1, 5.

10. **it hath**. Mt *5:12. 23:30-32. Lk *17:26-30. Ac 7:51, 52. 1 Th 2:14-16. 2 T *3:8. **of old time**. Heb. *olam* plural, Ps +61:4.

11. **There is**. Ec *2:16. Ps 9:6. Is *41:22-26. 42:9.

12. **the Preacher**. See on ver. 1. 1 K 4:1, etc.

13. **I gave**. ver. 17. Ec 7:25. 8:9, 16, 17. Ps 111:2. Pr 2:2-4. √4:7. 18:1, 15. 23:26. 1 T 4:15. **by wisdom**. 1 C 1:20. **this sore**. Ec 3:10. 4:4. 12:12. Ge 3:19. **to be exercised**. *or*, to afflict them.

14. **have seen**. ver. 17, 18. Ec 2:11, 17, 26. 1 K 4:30-32. Ps 39:5, 6. **spirit**. Heb. *ruach*, Ge +41:8.

15. **crooked**. ſ138C, Ge +22:14. Ec 3:14. 7:12, *13. Est 5:11-13. Jb 11:6. 34:29. Pr +19:18. Is 40:4. La 3:37. Da 4:35. Mt 5:36. 6:27. Re +*22:11. **cannot**. Jb 12:14. Is 14:27. Da +*10:12. **wanting**. Heb. defect. 1 K 21:4. Jb 20:22.

16. **communed**. 2 K 5:20. Ps 4:4. 77:6. Is 10:7-14. Je 22:14. Ezk 38:10, 11. Da 4:30. **Lo**. Ec 2:9. 1 K *3:12, 13. *4:29-31. 10:6, 7, 23, 24. 2 Ch 1:10-12. 2:12. 9:22, 23. **great experience of**. Heb. seen much. He *5:14.

17. **I gave**. See on ver. 13. Ec 2:3, 12. 7:23-25. 1 Th *5:21. **I perceived**. Ec 2:10, 11. **spirit**. Heb. *ruach*, Ge +41:8.

18. **For**. ſ138C, Ge +22:14. **in much**. Ec 2:15. *7:16. *12:12, 13. Jb *28:28. Pr 3:13. 1 C *3:18-20. Ja *3:13-17.

ECCLESIASTES 2

Solomon shows from his own experiments and reflections, the vanity and vexation of mirth, pleasure, riches, and magnificence, 1-11; of wisdom and knowledge, though far preferable to folly, 12-17; of the most successful labors of man; except as the things of the world are used in a proper manner, according to the will of God, and by his special gift, 18-26.

1. **said**. ver. 15. Ec 1:16, 17. 3:17, 18. Ps 10:6. 14:1. 27:8. 30:6, 7. Lk *12:19. **Go to**. Ge 11:3, 4, 7. 2 K 5:5. Is 5:5. Ja 4:13, 14. 5:1. **I will**. Ec 8:15. 11:9. Is 50:5, 11. Lk 16:19, 23. Ja 5:5. T 3:3. Re 18:7, 8. **pleasure**. T#321. ver. 10, 11. Pr +23:5 (T#627).

2. **I said**. Solomon is not speaking here of a sober enjoyment of the things of the world, but of intemperate pleasure, whose two attendants, laughter and mirth, are introduced by a beautiful prosopopoeia as two persons, whom he treats with the utmost contempt. **laughter**. ſ155F. Personification; here, abstract human actions are spoken to as persons. For other instances of this figure, see Ge +4:7; Compare ſ155D, Ge +4:10. **It is**. Ec 7:2-6. Pr 14:13. Is 22:12, 13. Am *6:3-6. 1 P 4:2-4.

3. **sought**. Ec 1:17. 1 S 25:36. **give myself unto wine**. Heb. draw my flesh with wine. **yet**. Pr +*20:1. *31:4,

5. Ep *5:18. **and to lay**. Ec 7:18. Pr *20:1. *23:29-35. Mt *6:24. 2 C 6:15-17. **till**. Ec 6:12. 12:13. **all**. Heb. the number of. Ge 47:9. Ex +23:26. Jb 14:14. Ps *90:9-12.

4. **made**. Ge 11:4. 2 S 18:18. Da 4:30. **I builded**. Dt 8:12-14. 1 K 7:1, 2, 8-12. 9:1, 15-19. 10:19, 20. 2 Ch 8:1-6, 11. Ps 49:11. **I planted**. 1 Ch 27:27. 2 Ch 26:10. SS 1:14. 7:12. 8:11, 12. Is 5:1.

5. **me**. SS 4:12-16. 5:1. 6:2. Je 39:4. **I planted**. Ge 2:8, 9. Lk 17:27-29.

6. **pools**. Ne 2:14. SS 7:4. **to water**. Ps *1:3. Je *17:8.

7. **servants**. 1 K 9:20-22. Ezr 2:58. Ne 7:57. **and had**. Ge 17:12, 13. **servants born in my house**. Heb. sons of my house. Ge 15:3. **also**. Ge 13:2. 2 K 3:4. 1 Ch 27:29-31. 2 Ch 26:10. 32:27-29. Jb 1:3. 42:12.

8. **silver**. 1 K 9:14, 28. 10:10, 14, 15, 21-28. 2 Ch 9:11, 15-21. **men singers**. 2 S 19:35. Ezr 2:65. **musical instruments**, etc. Heb. musical instrument and instruments. 1 Ch 25:1, 6. Jb 21:11, 12. Ps 150:3-5. Da 3:5, 7, 15. Am 6:5. The difficult words *shiddah weshiddoth* are variously rendered. The LXX. have "male and female cup-bearers," with which the Syriac and Arabic and Parkhurst agree; Aquila, "a cup and smaller cups;" Jerome, *scyphos et urceolos* (Vulgate, *urceos*), "goblets and pots;" Targum, "warm and cold baths;" others, as M. Desvoeux, "male and female captives;" others, "cooks and confectioners;" others, "a species of musical compositions," derived from *Sido*, a celebrated Phoenician woman to whom Sanchoniatho attributes the invention of music; but others, with more probability, "wives and concubines;" and *siddoth* may be in this sense synonymous with the Arabic *seedat*, *conjux* from *sada*, in Conj. V. *conjugium inivit*. Of the former, Solomon had three hundred, and of the latter, seven hundred; and if they are not mentioned here they are not mentioned at all, which is wholly unaccountable.

9. **I was great**. Ec 1:16. 1 K 3:12. 10:7, 23. 1 Ch 29:25. 2 Ch 1:1. 9:22, 23.

10. **whatsoever**. Ec 3:22. 6:9. 11:9. Ge 3:6. 6:2. Jg 14:2. Jb *31:1. Ps *119:37. Pr 23:5. 1 J *2:16. **kept not from**. T#180. 1 K 11:1-3. Lk 15:13, 17, 18. 16:19, 22, 23. Mk +4:19 (T#625). Ph +3:19 (T#199). 1 T +2:9 (T#173). **my heart rejoiced**. ver. 22, 24. Ec 3:22. 5:18. 9:9. Ps 128:2.

11. **I looked**. Ec 1:14. Ge 1:31. Ex 39:43. 1 J *2:15-17. **behold**. ver. 17-23. Ec 1:3, 14. 11:8. Hab *2:13. 1 T *6:6-11. **spirit**. Heb. *ruach*, Ge +41:8.

12. **I turned**. Ec 1:17. *7:25. **even that which hath been already done**. *or*, in those things which have been already done. ver. 25.

13. **I saw**. Ec *7:11, 12. 9:16. Pr 4:5-7. 16:16. Ml *3:18. 4:1, 2. **that wisdom excelleth folly**. Heb. that there is an excellency in wisdom more than in folly, etc. **light**. Ec 11:7. Ps *119:105, 130. Pr *4:18, 19. Mt 6:23. Lk 11:34, 35. Ep 5:8.

14. **wise**. Ec 8:1. 10:2, 3. Pr 14:8. *17:24. Jn 13:7. 1 J 2:11. **walketh in darkness**. 1 J *2:9. **one**. Ec 9:1-3, 11, 16. Ps 19:10. 49:10.

15. **even to me**. Heb. to me, even to me. **and why**. Ec 1:16, 18. 1 K 3:12. **Then I**. ver. 1. Ec 1:2, 14.

16. **there is**. Ec 1:11. Ex 1:6, 8. Ps 88:12. 103:16. Ml √3:16. **for ever**. Heb. *olam*, Ex +*12:24. **how**. Ec 6:8. 2 S 3:33. Ps *49:10. Is *57:1, 2. Lk *16:22, 23. He +*9:27.

17. **I hated.** Nu *11:14, 15. 1 K 19:4. Jb 3:20-22. 7:15, 16. 14:13. Je 20:14-18. Jon 4:3, 8. Ph 1:23-25. **work.** Ec 1:14. 3:16. Ezk 3:14. Hab 1:3. **for.** ver. 11, 22, 23. Ec 6:9. Ps 89:47. **spirit.** Heb. *ruach*, Ge +41:8.

18. **I hated.** ver. 4-9. Ec 1:13. 4:3. 5:18. 9:9. **taken.** Heb. labored. **I should.** ver. 26. Ec 5:13, 14. 1 K 11:11-13. Ps 17:14. 39:6. *49:10. Lk *12:20. 16:27, 28. Ac 20:29, 30. 1 C *3:10.

19. **who knoweth.** Ec 3:22. 1 K 12:14, etc. 14:25-28. 2 Ch 10:13-16. 12:9, 10. Jn ◑3:17. Ja 1:5. **labor.** √121C1H, Dt +28:33. **wise under.** Ec 9:13. Lk 16:8. Ja 1:17. 3:17.

20. **to cause.** Ge 43:14. Jb 17:11-15. Ps 39:6, 7. 1 C 15:19. 2 C 1:8-10. 1 Th 3:3, 4.

21. **whose.** ver. 17, 18. Ec 9:18. 2 Ch 31:20, 21. 33:2-9. 34:2. 35:18. 36:5, etc. Je 22:15, 17. **leave.** Heb. give. Je 40:11.

22. **hath man.** Ec 1:3. 3:9. 5:10, 11, 17. 6:7, 8. 8:15. Pr 16:26. 1 T 6:8. **and of the.** Ec 4:6, 8. Ps 127:2. Mt 6:11, 25, 34. *16:26. Lk 12:22, 29. Ph *4:6. 1 P *5:7.

23. **all.** Ec 1:18. Ge 47:9. Jb 5:7. 14:1. Ps *90:7-10, +*15. *127:2. **travail.** Ec 1:13. 3:10. **his heart.** Ec 5:12. Est *6:1. Jb *7:2, 3, 13, 14. Ps ◑*4:8. *6:6, 7. 32:4. 77:2-4. Je ◑*31:26. Da *6:18. Ac +*14:22.

24. **nothing.** ver. 10. Ec 3:12, 13, 22. 5:18. 8:15. 9:7-9. 11:9, 10. Dt 12:12, 18. Ne *8:10. Ac 14:17. 1 T *6:8, 17. **make his soul.** Heb. *nephesh*, Ge +34:3. **enjoy good.** *or*, delight his senses. Ps +*128:1, 2. Is 9:3. Jon 4:6. **his labor.** Lk 10:7. **that it.** Ec 3:13. 5:19. 6:2. Dt *8:18. Pr *10:22. Ml 2:2. Lk *12:19, 20.

25. **who can.** ver. 1-12. 1 K 4:21-24.

26. **in his sight.** Heb. before him. Ge 7:1. Lk 1:6. Ac 11:24, 25. **wisdom.** 2 Ch *31:20, 21. Pr *3:13-18. Is *3:10, 11. Jn *16:24. Ro *14:17, 18. 1 C *1:30, 31. Ga *5:22, 23. Col *1:9-12. *3:16, 17. He 13:21. Ja *1:5. 3:17. **to the sinner.** Jb *27:16, 17. Pr *13:22. *28:8. **may give.** Jb 27:16, 17. Ps 39:6. Is 65:13, 14. **spirit.** Heb. *ruach*, Ge +41:8.

ECCLESIASTES 3

The mutability of human affairs, as resulting from the unsearchable, wise, and everlasting purposes of God, and connected with man's duty and interest, 1-15. The abuse commonly made of power; the future account to be rendered; and the way in which men live and die like beasts, without properly considering their immortal souls, 16-21. Men should rejoice in their present duties and comforts, being unable to know things future, 22.

1. **every thing.** ver. *17. Ec 7:14. *8:5, 6. 2 K *5:26. 2 Ch 33:12. Pr *15:23. Mt *16:3. **season.** Ezr 10:14. Ne 2:6. Est 9:27, 31. Je +8:7. **time.** Lk 22:14. Jn 17:1. Ga 4:4. **under.** Ec 1:13. 2:3, 17.

2. **time to be born.** Heb. time to bear. Ge 17:17, 21. 18:14. 21:1, 2. 1 S 2:5. 1 K *13:2. 2 K 4:16. Jb 7:1. Ps +*113:9. Is 54:1. Lk 1:13, 20, 36. Jn *16:21. Ac 7:17, 20. Ga *4:4. **and a time to die.** Ec +*7:17. Ge 5:5. 47:29. Ex 1:6. Nu 20:24-28. 27:12-14. Dt *3:23-26. 34:5. Jb *7:1. *14:5, 14. Ps 31:5, 15. Is *38:1, 5, +*10. Jn *7:30. He +*9:27. **a time to plant.** Ps 44:2. 52:5. 80:8, 15. Is *5:2-5. Je *1:10. *18:7-10. 45:4. Am √9:15. Mt *13:28, 29, 41. *15:13. **to pluck up.** Je 18:7, 9.

3. **time to kill.** Ge *9:5, 6. Dt *32:29. 1 S 2:6, 25.

1 K 2:23, 24, 28, 29, 34, 36, 37, 46. Ps 78:31, 34. Je 12:3. Ho *6:1, 2. Ro 13:4. **a time to heal.** Nu *21:6-9. Ps 107:20. 147:3. Is *38:5, 21. 57:18. Je 33:6. Lk *9:54-56. Ac *5:15, 16. **a time to break.** Is *5:5, 6. 44:26. Je *31:28. 39:2, 8. 45:4. Ezk 13:14. 33:21. Da *9:25-27. Zc 1:12-17. Ml 1:4. **build up.** Ne 2:17, 18, 20. Ps 102:13-16. Is 45:13. 58:12. 60:10. Da 9:25. Am √9:11.

4. **time to weep.** Ge 23:2. 43:30. 2 S 12:21. Ne 8:9-12. 9:1, etc. Ps *30:5. 126:1, 2, *5, *6. Is 22:12, 13. Je 22:10. Jl 2:17. Mt 9:15. 11:17. Lk 6:25. Jn *16:20-22. Ro *12:15. 2 C *7:10. Ja 4:9. **a time to laugh.** Ec 2:1, 2. Ge 21:6. Ne*8:9. Ps 2:4. 37:13. Lk 1:13, 14, 58. *6:21-25. **to mourn.** Ge 23:2. 1 S 16:1. Pr 29:2. Is 38:14. 61:2. Jl 1:9. Zc 12:10, 12. Mt +*5:4. 9:15. **to dance.** Ex *15:20n. 2 S *6:14, 16. Ps 30:11. 149:3. 150:4. Je 31:13.

5. **to cast.** Le 14:40, 45. Jg 20:16. Jsh 4:3-9. 10:27. 2 S *18:17, 18. 1 K 15:22. 2 K 3:25. Is 5:2. La 4:1. **gather stones.** Ec 2:4. Ge 31:45, 46, 51, 52. Dt 27:4, 5. Jsh 4:3, 8, 20. 1 S *17:40. 1 K 18:31, 32. Ps 102:14. Is 54:11. **a time to embrace.** Ec 2:3. Ge 29:13. 33:4. 48:10. Ex 19:15. 1 S 21:4, 5. 2 K 4:16. SS 2:6, 7. Jl 2:16. Zc 7:3. 1 C *7:5. He 13:4. 1 P *3:7. **refrain from.** Heb. be far from. Ex 19:15. Pr 5:20. Jl 2:16. 1 C 7:5.

6. **time to get.** *or*, time to seek, or, to buy, or acquire. Ec 2:8. Ge 30:30, etc. 31:18. 42:2, 7, 10. Ex *12:35, 36. Dt *8:17, 18. Ru 4:5. 2 S *24:21. 2 K *5:26. 8:9. Pr 23:23. Is *55:1. Je 32:7. Ep 4:28. **and a time to lose.** Ge 31:39. Is 47:9. Mt 10:39. *16:25, 26. *19:29. Mk 8:35-37. *10:28-30. Lk 9:24, 25. **to keep.** 1 S 16:11. Pr *7:1. Lk *8:15. +*11:28. Jn 2:10. 12:7. 2 T *1:14. **and a time to cast.** Ec *11:1. Jg 15:17. 2 K 7:15. Ps 112:9. Is *2:20. *31:7. Ho *9:17. Jon *1:5. Ac 27:19, 38. Ph *3:7, 8. He 10:34, 35.

7. **time to rend.** Ge 37:29, 34. 1 S *15:27, 28. 2 S 1:11. 3:31. 1 K 11:11, 31. *13:3, 5. 14:8. *21:27. 2 K 5:7. 6:30. Je 36:24. Jl *2:13. Jn 19:24. Ac 9:39. **to sew.** Ezr 4:12mg. Ezk 37:17, 22. **time to keep silence.** Le 10:3. Dt +3:26. 2 K 18:36. Jb 2:13. Ps 32:3. 38:13, 14. 39:*1, 2. √50:16. Pr +12:23. 17:27, 28. 26:4, 5. Is 36:21. Je 8:14. La *3:28. Am *5:13. 8:3. Mi *7:5. Mt +*7:6. 27:12. Mk 1:25, 34. 3:12. Lk 1:19, 20, 22. *4:41. 1 T *2:11, 12. 1 P *2:15. **and a time to speak.** Ge 44:18-34. Ex 7:2. Le +19:17. Nu 22:8. 1 S *19:4, 5. *25:24, etc. 2 S 7:17. Est *4:13, 14. 7:4. Jb 32:4, etc. Ps 2:5. *107:2. 145:6, 11, 21. Pr *24:11, 12. *25:11. *31:8, 9. Ezk *2:7. *3:18. Lk *19:37-40. Jn *16:13. Ac *4:20.

8. **time to love.** Je 2:2. Ezk *16:8. Da 1:9. Ga 5:13. Ep 3:19. *5:25, 28, 29. 2 Th 1:3. T *2:4. **a time to hate.** 2 S 13:15. 2 Ch *19:2. Ps 105:25. *139:21. Pr 11:15. 15:27. 25:17. 28:16. Lk *14:26. Jn 12:25. Ju 23. Re 2:2. **a time of war.** Ge *14:14-17. Ex 17:16. Nu 1:3, 20, 22. Dt 3:18. Jsh 8:1, etc. *11:23. Jg 3:2. 2 S 3:1. 10:6, etc. +*11:1n. 1 K 5:4. 1 Ch +5:22. +*20:1. 2 Ch 20:1, etc., 30. Jb 7:1mg. 38:23. Je 6:4. Lk *14:31. Re 12:7. 19:11, 19. **of peace.** Le 26:6. Jsh 11:23. 14:15. Jg 4:17. 1 S 7:14. Ps 72:3. 85:8. Pr +*16:7. Is 9:7. Zc 9:10. Ro *5:1. Ep 4:3. He 12:13.

9. **What profit.** Ec 1:3. 2:11, 22, 23. 5:16. Pr 14:23. Mt 16:26.

10. **have seen.** Ec 1:13, 14. 2:26. Ge 3:19. 1 Th 2:9. 2 Th 3:8.

11. **hath made.** Ec 7:29. Ge 1:31. Dt 32:4. Ps 111:2.

Mk 7:37. **also.** Mt 13:22. Ro 1:19, 20, 28. **world.** Heb. *olam*, Le +25:32. Ps 73:12. **so.** Ec 8:17. Jb 11:7-9. 37:23. Ps 104:24. Mt 11:27. Ro *11:33.

12. **but.** ver. 32. Ec 9:7-9. Dt 28:63. Ps 37:3. Is 64:5. Lk 11:41. Ac 20:35. Ph 4:4-9. 1 Th 5:15, 16. 1 T 6:18.

13. **should eat.** Ec 2:24. 5:18-20. 6:2. 9:7. Dt 28:30, 31, 47, 48. Jg 6:3-6. Ps 128:2. Is 65:21-23.

14. **whatsoever.** Ps 33:11. 119:90, 91. Is 46:10. Da 4:34, 35. Ac 2:23. 4:28. Ro 11:36. Ep 3:11. T *1:2. Ja 1:17. **it shall be.** Is +31:2. Ml +3:6. Ja +1:17. **for ever.** Heb. *olam*, Ex +*12:24. **nothing.** Ps 76:10. Pr 19:21. 21:30. 30:6. Is 10:12-15. Da 8:8. 11:2-4. Jn 19:10, 11, 28-37. Ac 5:39. **God doeth it.** Ps 64:9. Is 59:18, 19. Re 15:4.

15. **which hath.** Ec 1:9, 10. 1 C *10:13. **past.** Heb. driven away.

16. **I saw.** Ec 4:1. 5:8. 1 K 21:9-21. Ps 58:1, 2. 82:2-5. 94:21, 22. Is 5:7. 59:14. Je 5:5. Mi 2:2. 7:3. Zp 3:3. Mt 26:59. Ac 23:3. Ja 2:6.

17. **said.** Ec 1:16. 2:1. **God.** Ec 12:14. Ge +*18:25. Ps 98:9. Mt 10:15. 16:27. 25:31-46. Jn 5:22, 26-29. Ac *17:31. Ro *2:5-9. 1 C 4:5. 2 C *5:10. 2 Th *1:6-10. Re √20:11-15. **for.** ver. 1. Je 29:10, 11. Da 11:40. 12:4, 9, 11-13. Ac 1:7. 1 Th 5:1. 2 P 3:7, 8. Re 11:2, 3, 18. 17:12-17. 20:2, 7-9.

18. **I said.** √96D1. Heterosis of Person B524. The First Person is put for the Third. Here, "I said" means "Man says in his heart." For other instances of this figure see Ro 7:7. 10:18. **concerning.** Ge 3:17-19. Jb 14:1-4. 15:16. Ps 49:14, 19, 20. 73:18, 19. 90:5-12. He +*9:27. 1 P 1:24. **sons.** √144A3, Ge +11:5. **that God**, etc. *or*, that they might clear God, and see, etc. Jb 40:8. Ps 51:4. Ro 3:4. 9:23. **and that.** Ge 3:19. Jb 14:1. Ps 73:22. 2 P 2:12. **they.** √84, Ge +6:17.

19. **that which.** Ec 2:16. Ps 49:12, *20. 92:6, 7. **one thing.** Ps 27:4. Mk 10:21. Lk 10:42. Jn 9:25. Ph 3:13. 2 P 3:8. **as the.** 2 S 14:14. Jb 14:10-12. Ps 104:29. Is 2:22. **breath.** Heb. *ruach*, Ge +6:17. T#991‡. Ec +*12:7 (T#992‡). Ge *7:22. Nu 27:16. Jb 27:3, 4. Ps 104:29. +*146:4. Re 16:3. **no preeminence.** Animal life is the same both in man and beast: they respire in the same way; and when they cease to respire, life becomes extinct, and they return to the dust whence they were taken; so that in these things "man hath no preeminence above a beast; for all is vanity." But, as none can fully comprehend, so alas, few properly consider, the difference between the rational and immortal soul of man, which after the death of the body ascends to God who gave it (Ec +*12:7), and the spirit or life of the beast, which is extinct with the body when it returns to the earth. Ge 5:22, +*24. 15:15. +*25:8n. 35:29. 37:35. Nu 20:24. 27:13. Mt +*10:28n. √22:32. Lk 16:26. Jn 5:24. *8:51. 11:25. 12:25. 1 Th 5:23n. 2 T √1:10. He 11:16, 26. Ju 14, 15. **for.** Ec 2:20-23. Ps 39:5, 6. 89:47, 48.

20. **go.** ver. 21. Ec 6:6. 9:10. Ge 25:8, 17. Nu 27:13. Jb 7:9. 17:13. 30:24. Ps 49:14. **all are.** Ge 3:19. Jb 10:9, 10. 34:15. Ps 104:29. +*146:4. Da *12:2.

21. **Who.** √85C, Ge +18:14. √182, Ge +18:22. **knoweth.** Ec 12:7. Lk 16:22, 23. Jn *14:3. Ac 1:25. 2 C 5:1, 8. Ph *1:23. **spirit.** Heb. *ruach*, Nu +16:22. T#152. Ec 12:7. Jb +14:22. 32:8. Da 7:15. Mt √22:32. Mk 2:8. Lk *16:22, 23. 23:43, 46. Ac *7:59. 1 C 2:11. 2 C √5:8. Ph *1:23. 2 T +1:10 (T#422). He *12:23. Re *6:9. 16:3. **of man.** Heb. of the sons of man. ver.

18, 19. **that.** √88, Ge +15:15. **goeth upward.** Heb. is ascending. Ec *12:7. **spirit.** Heb. *ruach*, Nu +16:22.

22. **nothing.** ver. 11, 12. Ec 2:10, 11, 24. 5:18-20. 8:15. 9:7-9. *11:9. Dt 12:7, 18. 26:10, 11. 28:47. Ro 12:11, 12. Ph 4:4, 5. **who.** Ec 6:12. 8:7. 9:12. 10:14. Jb 14:21. Da 12:9, 10, 13. Mt 6:34.

ECCLESIASTES 4

The miseries arising from oppression; and the vanity resulting from envy, idleness, and avarice, 1-8. The advantages of friendship and social affections, 9-12. The vanity of royal dignity, through the folly of princes, and the fickleness of their subjects, 13-16.

1. **I returned.** Jb 6:29. Ml 3:18. **and considered.** Ec *3:16. +*5:8. 7:7. Ex 1:13, 14, 16, 22. 2:23, 24. 5:6-19. Dt 28:33, 48. Jg 4:3. 10:7, 8. Ne 5:1-5. Jb 24:7-12. Ps 10:9, 10. Pr 28:3, 15, 16. Is 5:7. 51:23. 59:7, 13-15. Ml +*3:5. **oppressions.** √108J, Ge +43:18. **the tears.** Ps 42:3, 9. 80:5. 102:8, 9. Ml 2:13. Ja +*5:4. **they had.** Jb 16:4. 19:21, 22. Ps 69:20. 142:4. Pr 19:7. La 1:2, 9. Mt 26:56. 2 T 4:16, 17. **side.** Heb. hand. Ex 2:5.

2. **I praised.** Ec 2:17. 9:4-6. Jb *3:17-21. Ph *1:23. Re *14:13.

3. **better.** Ec 6:3-5. Jb 3:10-16. 10:18, 19. Je 20:17, 18. Mt 24:19. Lk 23:29. Ro *8:28. 2 C 4:17. **who.** Ec 1:14. 2:17. Ps 55:6-11. Je 9:2, 3.

4. **every,** etc. Heb. all the rightness of work, that this *is* the envy of a man from his neighbor. Ge 4:4-8. 37:2-11. 1 S 18:8, 9, 14-16, 29, 30. Pr 27:4. Mt 27:18. Ac 7:9. Ja 4:5. 1 J 3:12. **This is.** ver. 16. Ec 1:14. 2:21, 26. 6:9, 11. Ge 37:4, 11. **spirit.** Heb. *ruach*, Ge +41:8.

5. **fool.** Pr *6:9-11. 12:27. 13:4. 20:4. 24:33, 34. **eateth.** That is, with envy (see ver. 4), though too idle to follow his neighbor's example. Jb 13:14. Pr 11:17. Is 9:20.

6. **an handful.** Ps 37:16. Pr *15:16, 17. 16:8. 17:1. **spirit.** Heb. *ruach*, Ge +41:8.

7. **I returned.** ver. 1. Ps 78:33. Zc 1:6.

8. **Two.** 1 K 22:4. **one.** ver. 9-12. Ge 2:18. Is 56:3-5. **he hath.** Ge 15:2, 3. **no.** Is 5:8. **eye satisfied.** Ec 1:8. 5:10. Pr *27:20. Hab 2:5-9. 1 J *2:16. **For.** Ps *39:5, 6. Is 44:19, 20. Lk *12:20. **soul.** Heb. *nephesh*, Ge +27:31. **it is.** Ec 1:13. 2:23. Is 55:2. Mt 11:28.

9. **are.** Ge *2:18. Ex 4:14-16. Nu *11:14. Pr *27:17. Hg 1:14. Mk 6:7. Ac 13:2. 15:39, 40. 1 C 12:18-21. **a good.** Ru 2:12. Jn 4:36. 2 J 8.

10. **if.** Ex 32:2-4, 21. Dt 9:19, 20. 1 S 23:16. 2 S 11:27. 12:7, etc. Jb 4:3, 4. Is 35:3, 4. Lk 22:31, 32. Ga 2:11-14. 6:1. 1 Th 4:18. 5:11. **but.** Ge 4:8. 2 S 14:6.

11. **if two.** 1 K 1:1, 2.

12. **And if.** This is well illustrated by the fable of the dying father, who, to show his sons the advantage of union, gave them a bundle of twigs, which could not be broken when bound together, but were easily snapped asunder one by one. **and a.** 2 S 23:9, 16, 18, 19, 23. Da 3:16, 17. Mt *18:20. Ep 4:3.

13. **is a poor.** Ec 9:15, 16. Ge 37:2. Pr 19:1. 28:6, 15, 16. **will no more be.** Heb. knoweth not to be. 1 S +*25:17. 1 K 22:8. 2 Ch 16:9, 10. 24:20-22. 25:16.

14. **For out.** This is probably an allusion to some fact with which we are unacquainted. History furnishes many instances of mean persons raised to sovereign

authority, and of kings being reduced to the meanest offices and to a morsel. Agrippa mounted the throne of Israel after having been long in prison; and similar instances are not wanting in modern times. Ge=41:14, 33-44. 2 S 7:8. Jb 5:11. Ps 113:7, 8. **also.** 1 K 11:43. *12:13-20. 14:26, 27. 2 K 23:31-34. 24:1, 2, 6, 12. 25:7, 27-30. La 4:20. Da 4:31.

15. **child.** 2 S 15:6.

16. **no end.** 2 S 15:12, 13. 1 K 1:5-7, 40. 12:10-16. **they also.** Jg 9:19, 20. 2 S 18:7, 8. 19:9. **this.** Ec 1:14. 2:11, 17, 26. **spirit.** Heb. *ruach,* Ge +41:8.

ECCLESIASTES 5

Cautions against those things which render men's devotions and vows vain and sinful, 1-7; and against being stumbled by beholding oppression, 8. The vanity of riches, in the getting, keeping, or loss of them, 9-17. The proper use of them in the fear of God is the only remedy against vanity, 18-20.

1. **thy foot.** Ge 28:16, 17. Ex 3:5. Le 10:3. Jsh 5:15. 2 Ch 26:16. Ps 89:7. Is 1:12, etc. 1 C 11:22. He 12:28, 29. **thou goest.** Ep 2:18. He *4:16. 7:25. 10:22. *11:6. **ready.** Ac 10:33. √17:11. Ja 1:19. 1 P √2:1, 2. **give.** Ge 4:3-5. 1 S 13:12, 13. *15:21, 22. Ps 50:8-18. Pr *15:8. 21:27. Is *1:10-15. 66:3. Je 7:21-23. Ho *6:6, 7. Ml 1:10, 11. He 10:26. **for.** Am 5:21-23.

2. **not rash.** Ge 18:27, 30, 32. 28:20-22. Nu 30:2n-5. Jg *11:30-36. 1 S 14:24-45. 25:10, +*17. Pr 77:7-10. Pr 20:25. Mt 20:21, 22. Mk 6:23. **to utter.** Jb 37:20. **thing.** *or,* word. **for.** Ps 115:3. Is 55:9. Mt 6:9. **let thy.** T#1231. ver. 3, 7. 1 S ❍+*23:4. Jb +*6:24. Ps ❍+25:5 (T#1758). Pr 10:19. 17:27. Is +*58:13. Ml 3:5. Mt *6:7. *23:14. Mk *12:40. Lk ❍+6:12 (T#1759). ❍*18:1. Ja 3:2.

3. **dream.** ver. 7. Ge 20:3, 6. 31:10. Jb 20:8. 33:15. Je 23:25. **multitude.** ver. 7. Ec 1:18. 11:1. **business.** ver. 14. Ec 1:13. 2:13, 16. **a fool's.** Ec 10:12-14. Pr 10:19. 15:2. 18:2. **by.** Pr 17:28.

4. **vowest.** Ge 28:20. 35:1, 3. Nu 30:2n. Dt 23:21-23. Ps *50:14. 56:12. 76:11. 119:106. Is 19:21. Mt 5:33. **vow.** Le +*23:38. **for.** Ps 147:10, 11. Ml 1:10. He 10:6. **pay.** Ps *66:13, 14. 116:14, 16-18. Jon 2:9.

5. **Better.** Dt 23:22. Pr 20:25. Ac 5:4. **vow.** Le +*23:38.

6. **thy mouth.** ver. 1, 2. Ja 1:26. 3:2. **before.** Or, whose business it was to take cognizance of vows and offerings. See Le 5:4, 5. Ge 48:16. Nu 22:34. Ps +*35:6. Ho 12:4, 5. Ml 2:7. 3:1. Ac 7:30-35. 1 C 11:10. 1 T 5:21. He 1:14. **it was.** Le 5:4-6. 27:9, 10. **wherefore.** √85L, Ge +27:45. **destroy.** Hg 1:9-11. 2:14-17. Mt *10:28. 1 C 3:13-15. 2 J 8. **but fear.** Ec *12:13. Dt 28:58. Ml *1:6. He *12:28, 29.

7. **in the.** ver. 3. Mt 12:36. **vanities.** √96F2, Ge +4:10. **but.** Ec 7:18. 8:12. 12:13. Pr 23:17. Is 50:10, 11.

8. **thou seest.** Pr 29:12, 24. Ep +*5:11. **oppression of the poor.** √108J, Ge +43:18. Ec *3:16. 4:1. Le +*19:13. Ps +*12:5. Ezk +*16:49. Am 2:7. +*5:12. Mt 23:14. **violent.** Ps 55:9. 58:2. Ezk 8:17. Hab 1:2, 3, 13. **perverting of judgment.** Ec 3:16. Le +*19:15. Dt 24:17. Ps 82:2. Pr 29:27. 31:4, 5. Mi ❍+*6:8. Hab +*1:4. Lk +*16:10. **and justice.** Dt +*16:20. Lk +*16:10. Ph *4:8. **marvel.** Zc 8:6. 1 J 3:13. Re 17:6, 7. **matter.** Heb. will, *or* purpose. Is 10:5-7, 12. 46:10, 11. Hab 1:12. Ac 4:27, 28. Ro 11:33. **for.** Is 57:15.

Lk 1:32, 35, 76. **regardeth.** Ex *3:9. 1 K 21:19, 20. Jb 20:19-29. 27:8-23. Ps 10:17, 18. 12:5. 58:10, 11. 82:1. 83:18. 140:11, 12. Is 3:15. 5:7. 59:13-16. Je 22:17-19. Ezk 22:6-14. Am 5:12. 6:2-6, 12. 8:4-7. Mi 2:1-3, 9. 3:1-4, 9-12. 6:10-13. Zc 7:9-13. Ml +*3:5. Ja 2:13. *5:2-7. **higher than they.** 1 Ch 21:15, 16. Ps 95:3. Pr 8:15, 16. Is 37:36. Mt 13:41, 42. Ac 12:7-10, 23.

9. **the profit.** Ge 1:29, 30. 3:17-19. Ps 104:14, 15. 115:16. Pr 13:23. 27:23-27. 28:19. Je 40:10-12. **the king.** 1 S 8:12-17. 1 K 4:7-23. 1 Ch 27:26-31.

10. **He that.** The more he gets, the more he would get; for *Crescit amor nummi, quantum ipsa pecunia crescit,* "The love of money increases, in proportion as money itself increases." Ec 4:8. 6:7. Ps 52:1, 7. 62:10. Pr 30:15, 16. Hab 2:5-7. Mt 6:19, 24. Lk 12:15. 1 T *6:9, 10. Ja 5:1-3. **this.** Ec 1:17. 2:11, 17, 18, 26. 3:19. 4:4, 8, 16.

11. **they.** Ge 12:16. 13:2, 5-7. 1 K 4:22, 23. 5:13-16. Ne 5:17, 18. Ps 119:36, 37. **what.** Ec 6:9. 11:9. Jsh 7:21-25. Pr 23:5. Je 17:11. Hab 2:13. 1 J *2:16.

12. **sleep.** Ps *4:8. 127:2. Pr *3:24. Je 31:26. **abundance.** Ps *62:10. Mk +4:19.

13. **a sore.** Ec 4:8. 6:1, 2. **riches kept.** Ec 8:9. Ge 13:5-11. 14:16. 19:14, 26, 31, etc. Pr 1:11-13, 19, 32. 11:4, 24, 25. 21:13. 28:27. Is 2:20. 32:6-8. Zp 1:18. Lk 12:16-21. 16:1-13, 19, 22, 23. 18:22, 23. 19:8. Jn 12:5. Ac +*5:2. 1 T +*6:9, 10. Ja *2:5-7. *5:1-4.

14. **those.** Ec 2:26. Jb 5:5. 20:15-29. 27:16, 17. Ps 39:6. Pr 23:5. Hg 1:9. 2:16, 17. Mt 6:19, 20. **and he.** 1 S 2:6-8, 36. 1 K 14:26. Ps 109:9-12.

15. **came forth.** Jb *1:21. Ps *49:16, 17. Lk 12:20. 1 T *6:7.

16. **a sore.** ver. 13. Ec 2:22, 23. **what.** 1 S 12:21. Je 2:8. Mk 8:36. **for.** Ec 1:3. Pr 11:29. Is 26:18. Ho 8:7. Jn 6:27.

17. **he eateth.** Ge 3:17. 1 K 17:12. Jb 21:25. Ps 78:33. 102:9. 127:2. Ezk 4:16, 17. **much.** 2 K 1:2, 6. 5:27. 2 Ch 16:10-12. 24:24, 25. Ps 90:7-11. Pr 1:27-29. Ac 12:23. 1 C 11:30-32.

18. **it is good and comely.** Heb. there is a good which is comely, etc. Ec *2:24. 3:12, 13, *22. 8:15. *9:7. 11:9. 1 T *6:17-19. **the days.** Heb. the number of the days. Ec 2:3mg. **it is his.** Ec *2:10. 3:22. Je 52:34.

19. **to whom.** Ec 2:24. *3:13. *6:1, 2. Dt 8:18. 1 K 3:13. **this is.** Ec 2:24-26.

20. **For he shall not much remember.** *or,* Though he give not much, yet he remembereth, etc. Ps 37:16. **because.** Dt 28:8-12, 47. Ps 4:6, 7. Is 64:5. 65:13, 14, 21-24. Ro 5:1-5, 11.

ECCLESIASTES 6

The vanity of riches without power to enjoy them; and of large families and long life, 1-6. The little advantage that a wise man has above a fool, or one man above another, 7, 8. The vanity of restless desires; the frailty of man; and the emptiness and uncertainty of all his enjoyments, 9-12.

1. **an evil.** Ec 5:13.

2. **man.** Ec 5:19. 1 K 3:13. 1 Ch 29:25, 28. 2 Ch 1:11. Da 5:18. **so.** Ec 2:4-10. Dt 8:7-10. Jg 18:10. Jb *21:9-15, 17. Ps *17:14. 73:7. Lk *12:19, 20. **soul.** Heb. *nephesh,* Ge +27:31. **yet.** A man may possess many earthly goods and yet have neither the heart nor power to enjoy them. Possession and fruition are

not necessarily joined together; and this is also among the vanities of life, and was and still is a very "common evil among men." It belongs to God as much to give the power to enjoy as it does to give earthly blessings. This a wise heathen clearly saw and well expressed: "The gods have given thee riches, and the art to enjoy them" (Horace, Ep. l. i. ep. 4. v. 7). **but**. Ec 4:8. Dt 28:33, 43. Ps 39:6. La 5:2. Ho 7:9. **vanity**. Ec 4:4, 8. 5:16.

3. **a man**. Ge 33:5. 1 S 2:20, 21. 2 K 10:1. 1 Ch 28:5. 2 Ch 11:21. Est 5:11. Ps 127:4, 5. Pr 17:6. **so**. Ec 5:17-19. Ge 47:9. **soul**. Heb. *nephesh*, Ge +34:3. **not filled**. ver. 6. **and also**. 2 K *9:35. Est 7:10. 9:14, 15. Is 14:19, 20. Je *22:19. 36:30. **burial**. Heb. *qeburah*, Ge +35:20 (*S#6900h). **that an**. Ec 4:3. Jb 3:16. Ps 58:8. Mt 26:24.

4. **his name**. Ps 109:13.

5. **this**. Jb 3:10-13. 14:1. Ps 58:8. 90:7-9. **more rest**. That is, the abortion, or untimely birth, which seems to come into the world in vain, leaves it in obscurity and disgrace, has no name to be remembered, and has neither seen the sun, nor known anything,—even "this hath more rest than the other,"—the miser, who with his coffers filled, should have lived a thousand years, and had a hundred children, "whose soul was not filled with good," who never could have enough, nor yet enjoy what he had. It had rest in the womb, and now rests in the grave: its pain was transient; its unhappiness a mere negation of pleasure; and it lived not, as the miser, to incur guilt and misery.

6. **though**. Ge 5:5, 23, 24, 27. Is 65:22. **yet**. ver. 3. Jb 7:7. Ps 4:6, 7. 34:12. Is +*65:20. Je 17:6. **do**. ♪85B, Ge +13:9. Ec 3:20. 12:7. Jb 1:21. 30:23. He +*9:27.

7. **the labor**. Ge 3:17-19. Pr *16:26. Mt 6:25. Jn 6:27. 1 T 6:6-8. **appetite**. Heb. soul. *nephesh*, Nu +11:6. ver. 3. Ec 5:10. Is 56:11mg. Lk 12:19.

8. **what hath the wise**. Ec 2:14-16. 5:11. 1 T 6:6, 7. **the poor**. Ge 17:1. Ps 101:2. 116:9. Pr 19:1. Lk 1:6. 1 T 6:17. **living**. ♪108B, 1 S +10:24.

9. **Better**. Ec 2:24. 3:12, 13. 5:18. **wandering of the desire**. Heb. walking of the soul. Heb. *nephesh*, Ex +15:9. Jb 31:7. Pr 30:15, 16. Je 2:20. **this**. ver. 2. Ec 1:2, 14. 2:11, 22, 23. 4:4. **spirit**. Heb. *ruach*, Ge +41:8.

10. **which**. Ec 1:9-11. 3:15. **and it**. Ge 3:9, 17-19. Jb 14:1-4. Ps 39:6. 82:6, 7. 103:15. **neither**. Jb 9:3, 4, 32. 33:10, 11, 13. 40:2. Is *45:9, 10. Je 49:19. Ezk *22:14. Ro *9:19, 20. 1 C 10:22.

11. **many things**. Ec 1:6-9, 17, 18. 2:3-11. 3:19. 4:1-4, 8, 16. 5:7. Ps 73:6. Ho 12:1.

12. **who knoweth**. Ec 2:3. 12:13. Ps 4:6. 16:5. 17:15. 47:4. La 3:24-27. **good for**. Mi *6:8. **the days of his vain life**. Heb. the number of the days of the life of his vanity. Ec 8:13. 9:6. 1 Ch 29:15. Jb *8:9. 14:2. Ps *39:5, 6. 89:47. √90:10-12. 102:11. 109:23. 144:4. Ja √4:14. **for who can**. Ec 2:18, 19. 3:22. 8:7. Jb 14:21.

ECCLESIASTES 7

The benefit of a good name; of death above life; and of sorrow and rebuke above vain mirth, 1-6. Observations concerning oppression, bribery, pride, anger, and discontent, 7-10. The advantages of wisdom; of accommodating to circumstances; and of avoiding extremes, and occasions of offense, 11-22. The dangers

to the wisest arising from bad women, with Solomon's own experience in that respect, 23-28. Man was created upright but ruined by his own devices, 29.

1. **good**. ♪66, Ge +9:3. Pr 22:1. SS 2:13. **name**. Pr 15:30. *22:1. Is 56:5. Lk 10:20. He 11:2, 39. **precious**. Ec 10:1. Ps 133:2. Pr 27:9. SS 1:3. 4:10. Jn 12:3. **the day**. Ec 4:2. Jb 3:17. 5:7. Is 57:1, 2. Lk 16:22, 23. 2 C 5:1, 8. Ph 1:21-23. Re *14:13.

2. **better**. Ge 48:1, etc. 49:2, etc. 50:15-17. Jb 1:4, 5. Is 5:11, 12. 22:12-14. Am 6:3-6. Mt +*5:4. 14:6, etc. 1 P 4:3, 4. **that**. Nu 23:10. Dt 32:29. Ro 6:21, 22. Ph 3:19. He +*9:27. **living**. Dt 32:46. Is 47:7. Hg 1:5mg. Ml 2:2.

3. **Sorrow**. or, Anger. ver. 9. Ec 1:18. 2:23. 2 C *7:10. **is better**. Ne ♦8:10. Ps 119:67, 71. *126:5, 6. Je 31:8, 9, 15-20. 50:4, 5. Da *9:3, etc. 10:2, 3, 19. Zc 12:10-14. Lk 6:21-25. Jn 16:20-22. 2 C 7:9-11. Ph ♦*4:4. Ja 4:8-10. **by**. Ro 5:3, 4. 2 C 4:16, 17. He 12:10, 11. Ja 1:2-4.

4. **heart**. Ne 2:2-5. Is 53:3, 4. Mt 8:14-16. Mk 5:38, etc. Lk 7:12, 13. Jn 11:31-35. **the heart**. 1 S 25:36. 30:16. 2 S 13:28. 1 K 20:16. Is 21:4. Je 51:39, 57. Da 5:1-4, 30. Ho 7:5. Na 1:10. Mk 6:21, etc.

5. **better**. Ps *141:5. Pr 9:8. *13:18. *15:31, 32. 17:10. 27:6. Re 3:19. **the song**. Ps 69:12.

6. **as**. Ec 2:2. Ps 58:9. 118:12. Is 65:13-15. Am 8:10. Lk 6:25. 16:25. 2 P 2:13-17. Ju 12, 13. **crackling**. Heb. sound. Ec 5:3, 6. *10:20. 12:4. **the laughter**. Pr 29:9.

7. **oppression**. ♪108J, Ge +43:18. T#491. Dt 28:33, 34, 65. Am 3:10. 2 P +3:5 (T#707). **a gift**. Ex 23:8. Dt *16:19. 1 S 8:3. 12:3. Pr 17:23. Is 1:23. 33:15.

8. **Better**. Ps *126:5, 6. Is 10:24, 25, 28-34. Lk 16:25. He *12:11. Ja 5:11. 1 P 1:13. **the patient**. Ps *25:9. Pr *14:29. 15:18. 16:32. Mt +*5:3, 5. Lk *21:19. Ro 2:7, 8. He 10:36. Ja 5:8, 10, 11. 1 P 2:20, 21. 5:5, 6. **in spirit**. Heb. *ruach*, Ge +41:8. **the proud**. Ps 31:23. +*119:21. Pr 13:10. 28:25. Ro 12:3, 16. Ph +*2:3. **in spirit**. Heb. *ruach*, Ge +41:8.

9. **hasty**. 1 S 25:21, 22. 2 S 19:43. Est 3:5, 6. Ps *37:8. Pr *14:17. 16:32. Jon 4:9. Ep *4:26, 27. Ja *1:19, 20. **spirit**. Heb. *ruach*, Ge +41:8. ♪121A10, Ge +26:35. **anger**. Ge 4:5, 6, 8. 34:7, 8, 25, 26, 30, 31. 2 S 13:22, 28, 32. Pr 26:23-26. Mk 6:19, 24.

10. **What**. Jg 6:13. Je 44:17-19. Mt 24:38, 39. Ac 17:30. 2 T 3:13. **wisely**. Heb. out of wisdom. Ge 6:11, 12. Ps 14:2, 3. Is 50:1. Ro 1:22-32. 3:9-19.

11. **good with an inheritance**. or, as good as an inheritance, yea, better too. Ec 9:15-18. 1 K 3:6-9. Lk *16:8, 9. 1 T *6:17-19. **by it**. ♪63I1D, Nu +26:4. EWB (B100) renders this verse: "Wisdom [is] good, as an inheritance [is good], and more excellent to them that see the sun" [i.e., for living men, Jb 3:23]. "For [to be] in the shelter of wisdom [is more excellent than to be] under the shelter of money; and the advantage of wisdom [is] that wisdom preserveth the life of them that possess it." Thus wisdom has this advantage over money; it can preserve life, while an inheritance or money cannot. **them**. Ec 11:7.

12. **wisdom**. Jb *1:10. *22:21-25. Pr *2:7, 11. 8:11. 14:20. 16:16. *18:10, 11. Is *33:6. **is**. ♪63B, Ge +2:10. **a defence**. Heb. a shadow. Jg 9:15. Ps *57:1. Is *30:2. *32:2. **money is**. Jb 22:25. **the excellency**. Dt *30:19, 20. *32:47. Pr *3:18. *8:35. *9:11. *11:4. Jn *12:50. *17:3. Ph *3:8. 2 T *3:15.

13. **Consider**. Dt 8:2, 5. Jb 37:14. Ps 8:3. 107:43. Is 5:12. Ro √8:28. **who**. Ec 1:15. Jb 9:12. 11:10. 12:14.

34:29. Is 14:27. 43:13. 46:10, 11. Da 4:35. Ro 9:15, 19. Ep +*1:11.

14. **the day.** Ec 3:4. Dt *28:47, 48. Ps 30:11, 12. 40:3. 73:25. Mt 9:13. Jn 16:22, 23, 33. Ja 5:13. **but.** Dt 8:3. 1 K 8:47. 17:17, 18. 2 Ch 33:12, 13. Jb 10:1, 2. Ps 94:12, 13. 119:71. Is 22:12-14. 26:11. 42:25. Je 23:20. Mi 6:9. Hg 1:5-7. Lk 15:17, 18. Ac 14:22. **set.** Heb. made. 2 Ch 2:18. **to the.** Ec 12:8, 13. Ho 2:6, 7.

15. **have I.** Ec 2:23. 5:16, 17. 6:12. Ge 47:9. Ps 39:6. Jn 13:7. **there is a just.** Ec 3:16. 8:14. 9:1, 2. 1 S 22:18, 19. 1 K 21:13. 2 Ch 24:21, 22. Jb 9:22, 23. Is *57:1. Mt 23:34, 35. Lk 16:25. Jn 16:2. Ac 7:52, 59. **there is a wicked.** Ec 8:12, 13. Jb 21:7-15. Ps 73:3-13. 92:7. Is *65:20. Je 12:1, 2.

16. **Be not.** This verse is probably the language of an ungodly man to which Solomon answers, as in the following verse, "Do not multiply wickedness; do not add direct opposition to godliness, to the rest of your crimes. Why should you provoke God to destroy you before your time?" Pr 25:16. Mt ☻*5:48. 6:1-7. 9:14. 15:2, etc. 23:5, 23, 24, 29. Lk 18:12. Ro *10:2. Ph 3:6, 12. 1 T 4:3. **neither.** Ec 12:12. Ge 3:6. Jb 11:12. 28:28. Pr 23:4. Ro 11:25. *12:3. 1 C 3:18, 20. Col 2:18, 23. Ja 3:13-17. **destroy thyself.** Heb. be desolate. Mt 23:38. Re 18:19.

17. **not.** Je 2:33, 34. Ezk 8:17. 16:20. Ja *1:21. **why.** ✓85L, Ge +27:45. Ge 38:7-10. 1 S 25:38. Jb 15:32, 33. Ps *55:23. Pr *10:27. Ac 5:5, 10. 12:23. **before thy time.** Heb. not in thy time. 1 S 25:38. Jb *14:5, 14. 15:32, 33. 21:21. 22:15, *16. Ps *55:23. Pr *10:27. Is +*38:10. Mt 8:29. Jn 7:8, 30. 1 C *11:30, 32.

18. **good.** Ec 11:6. Pr 4:25-27. 8:20. Lk 11:42. **for.** Ec *8:12, 13. 12:13. Ps 25:12-14. 145:19, 20. Pr 16:6. Je 32:40. Ml *4:2. Mt *10:28. Lk 1:50.

19. **strengtheneth the wise.** Ec *9:15-18. 2 S 20:16-22. Pr *21:22. *24:5. Col ✓1:9-11.

20. **there.** 1 K *8:46. 2 Ch 6:36. Jb 15:14-16. Ps 130:3. *143:2. Pr *20:9. Is ✓53:6. Ro ✓3:23. *7:18, 19. Ja 3:2, 8. 1 J ✓1:8-10. **doeth.** Is *64:6.

21. **take no heed.** Heb. give not thine heart. 2 S 19:19. Pr 19:11. 20:3. **unto.** 2 S 16:10. Is 29:21. 1 C 13:5-7.

22. **also.** 1 K 2:44. Mt 15:19. 18:32-35. Jn 8:7-9. Ja 3:9.

23. **I said.** Ge 3:5. 1 K 3:11, 12. 11:1-8. Ro *1:22. 1 C 1:20.

24. **which is far off.** Dt 30:11-14. Jb 11:7, 8. 28:12-23, 28. Ps 36:6. 139:6. Is ✓55:8, 9. Ro *11:33. 1 T 6:16. **deep.** ✓84, Ge +6:17.

25. **I applied mine heart.** Heb. I and my heart compassed. Ec 1:13-17. 2:1-3, 12, 20. **the reason.** ver. 27mg. Ec 2:15. 3:16, 17. 9:1, 2. Je 12:1, 2. 2 P 2:3-9. 3:3-9. **know.** Ec 9:3. 10:13. Ge 34:7. Jsh 7:13. 2 S 13:12. Pr 17:12. 26:11.

26. **I find.** Jg 16:18-21. Pr 2:18, 19. 5:3-5. 7:21-27. 9:18. *22:14. 23:27, 28. **whoso pleaseth God.** Heb. he that is good before God. Ec 2:26.

27. **saith.** Ec 1:1, 2. 12:8-10. **counting one by one, to find out the account.** or, weighing one thing after another, to find out the reason. ver. 25.

28. **yet.** ver. 23, 24. Is 26:9. **one.** Jb 33:23. Ps 12:1. **soul.** Heb. nephesh, Ge +34:3. **one man.** 1 K 19:14, 18. **but.** Solomon, instead of seeking one rational, virtuous woman, had collected an immense multitude, of various countries and religions, for magnificence and indulgence; among whom, as might have been expected, he had not found one who was thoroughly faithful, upright, and pious. He here uses the language of a penitent, warning others of the errors into which he had been led; and not that of a waspish satirist, lashing indiscriminately one half of the human species. 1 K 11:1-3.

29. **God.** Ge +*1:26, 27. *3:6. 5:1. **they.** The descendants of Adam have sought out an immense number of inventions in order to find happiness in the world without God, which have only proved so many variations of impiety and iniquity. Ge *3:6, 7. 6:5, 6, 11, 12. 11:4-6. Ps 99:8. 106:29, 39. Je 2:12, 13. 4:22. Ezk 22:6-13. Mk 7:8, 9. Ac 7:40-43. Ro *1:21-32. 3:9-19. Ep *2:2, 3. T 3:3.

ECCLESIASTES 8

A commendation of wisdom, 1. The king must be obeyed from prudence and for conscience sake, 2-5. The misery of men for want of foresight, neglect of opportunities, and the unavoidable stroke of death, 6-8. Men abuse power, and the patience of God, to the increase of wickedness and misery, 9-11. The righteous happy, and the wicked miserable, notwithstanding contrary appearances, 12-15. The unsearchableness of God's counsels and works, 16, 17.

1. **as the.** Ec 2:13, 14. 1 C 2:13-16. **who knoweth.** Ge 40:8. 41:15, 16, 38, 39. Jb 33:23. Pr 1:6. Is ✓8:20. Da 2:28-30, 47. 4:18, 19. Mk +*12:24. Jn +*5:39. Ac 8:30, 31. ✓17:11. 1 T *4:16. 2 T *2:15. 2 P +*1:20. 1 J *2:20, 27. **a man's.** Ex 34:29, 30. Pr 4:8, 9. 17:24. 24:5. Mt 17:2. Ac 6:15. Ja 3:17. **face.** ✓171Q, Ge +3:19. ✓121S3E3, Nu +6:26. **and the.** Dt 28:50. Ac 4:13, 29. Ep 6:19. **boldness.** Heb. strength. 2 T 4:17.

2. **I counsel.** ✓63B, Ge +25:28. Ec 12:13. Pr 24:21. Ro 13:1-4. T 3:1. 1 P 2:13-17. **in regard.** 1 K 2:43. 1 Ch 29:24. Ezk 17:13-20. Ro *13:5.

3. **not hasty.** Ec *10:4. Pr 14:29. **stand.** 1 K 1:50-52. 2:21-24. Ps 68:21. Is 48:4. Je 44:16, 17. Ac 5:8, 9. **for.** Pr 16:14, 15. 30:31. Da 4:35. 5:19.

4. **Where.** Ge 1:3. Mk 4:39. Jn 2:5. 1 C 4:20. **the word.** 1 K 2:25, 29-34, 46. Pr 19:12. 20:2. 30:31. Da 3:15. Lk 12:4, 5. Ro *13:1-4. 1 T +*2:1, 2. **What.** Jb 33:12, 13. *34:18, 19. Da 4:35. Ro 9:20.

5. **keepeth.** ver. 2. Ex 1:17, 20, 21. Ps 119:6. Ho 5:11. Lk 20:25. Ac 4:19. 5:29. Ro 13:5-7. 1 P *3:13, 14. **feel.** Heb. know. Jb 20:20mg. Pr 23:35mg. **a wise.** Ec 2:14. 10:2. 1 Ch +*12:32. Pr 17:24. Lk 12:56, 57. 1 C 2:14, 15. 2 C 6:2. Ep *5:15-17. Ph 1:9, 10. Col 1:9. He *5:14.

6. **to every.** Ec *3:1, 11, 17. 7:13, 14. **therefore.** Ec 11:9, 10. 12:1. Is 3:11-14. 22:12-14. Lk 13:25. 17:26-30. *19:41-44. He 3:7-11.

7. **he knoweth.** Ec 6:12. *9:12. 10:14. Pr *24:21, 22. 29:1. Mt *24:44, 50. 25:6-13. 1 Th 5:1-3. **when.** or, how.

8. **is no.** Ec 3:21. 2 S 14:14. Jb 14:5. 34:14. Ps *49:6-9. 89:48. He +*9:27. **power.** 1 C 15:43. 2 C 13:4. **spirit.** Heb. ruach, Nu +16:22. Ec 11:5. Pr 30:4. **to retain.** Ps *31:15. Lk *12:20. **the spirit.** Heb. ruach, Nu +16:22. **neither hath.** Ec 3:19. 9:2. **discharge.** or, casting off weapons. Dt 20:1-8. 2 K 7:15. **neither.** Ps 9:17. 52:5-7. 73:18, etc. Pr 14:32. Is 28:15, 18.

9. **this.** Ec 1:14. 3:10, 16. 4:7, 8. 7:25. **there is.**

Ec 5:8, 13. Ex 14:5-9, 28. Dt *2:30. 2 K 14:10-12. 25:7.

10. **so.** 2 K 9:34, 35. Jb 21:18, 32, 33. Lk 16:22. **the place.** Ps 122:1-5. Ac 6:13. **they were.** Ec 2:16. 9:5. Ps 31:12. Pr 10:7. Je 17:13. He 10:38.

11. **Because.** Ps +√9:10n. **sentence.** Ex 8:15, 32. Jb 21:11-15. Ps *10:6. *50:21, 22. Is 5:18, 19. √26:10. 57:11. Je 48:11. Mt 24:49, 50. Ro √2:4, 5. 2 P √3:3-10. **fully.** Je 42:15.

12. **a sinner.** Ec 5:16. 7:15. 1 K 2:5-9. 21:25. 22:34, 35. Pr 13:21. Is *65:20. Ro 2:5. 9:22. 2 P 2:9. **surely.** Ec 7:18. Ps *37:11, 18-20. 112:1. 115:13. Pr *1:32, 33. Is *3:10, 11. 65:13, 14, 20-24. Mt +*10:28. *25:33, 34, 41-46. Lk 1:50. **fear before.** Ec 3:14. 1 Ch 16:30. Ps 96:9.

13. **it shall.** Jb 18:5. 20:5. 21:30. Ps 11:5. Is 57:21. Ml *3:15, 17, 18. Mt 13:49, 50. Jn 5:29. **neither.** Ps 55:23. Is 30:13. 2 P 2:3. **as a.** Ec 6:12. Jb 7:6, 7. 14:2. Ps 39:5. 144:4. Ja 4:14.

14. **a vanity.** Ec 4:4, 8. 9:3. 10:5. **there be just.** Ec *2:14. *7:15. 9:1-3. Jb 9:22-24. 21:17, etc. 24:21-25. Ps 73:13, 14. Ml 3:15. Ro √8:28. 1 C 15:19.

15. **Then I.** Some consider this as the cavil of an infidel objector, equivalent to the Epicurean maxim, *Ede, bibe, lude; post mortem nulla voluptas,* "Eat, drink, and play: there is no pleasure after death." But it may be regarded as a recommendation of a moderate use of worldly things, with a cheerful and contented mind; which may justly be considered as the greatest advantage which can be made of all below the sun: and amidst all changes, such a frame of mind, if the result of right principles, may and ought to be preserved; and it will be the recompense and solace of all our labors and toils. Ec 2:24. 3:12, 13, 22. 5:18. 9:7-9. 1 T *4:3-5. *6:17.

16. **When I.** Solomon here records the result of his perplexing inquiries into the affairs of men and the purposes, providence, and works of God. When he examined with great attention and diligence into the works of God, he found he could neither comprehend nor explain them; and was persuaded that no application or capacity would enable a man to fathom the depth of the divine dispensations in this lower world. How vain, then, are all cavils against divine providence when we can neither understand nor comprehend it! ver. 9. Ec 7:25. **there is that.** Ec 2:23. 4:8. 5:12. Ge 31:40. Ps 127:2.

17. **that a man.** Ec √3:11. 7:23, 24. 11:5. Jb *5:8, 9. 11:7-9. Ps *40:5. 73:16. 104:24. Pr 30:3, 4. Is 40:28. Ro *11:33, 34.

ECCLESIASTES 9

Like things happen to good and bad men till death, 1-3. The near approach of death should induce men to use cheerfully the comforts of life and diligently to perform its duties, 4-10. In all human affairs, probabilities are often strangely crossed, and great calamities befall men unawares, 11, 12. A fact recorded showing that wisdom and usefulness procure little respect or gratitude, notwithstanding the excellency and efficacy of wisdom, 13-18.

1. **considered in my heart.** Heb. gave, *or* set to my heart. Ec 1:17. 7:25. 8:16. 12:9, 10. **to declare.** Though Solomon could not "find out the whole work of God," yet his inquiries led him to make many useful

conclusions, which he *declared* for the benefit of others. And he was assured, from what he had seen and from the well known character of God, "that the righteous, and the wise, and their works" were all "in the hand of God," protected by His power, under his especial care, and safe in His approbation; but that the events of human life were so intricately and mysteriously arranged, that no one could decide from them who were the objects of God's love or displeasure. Mt +*5:45. Lk +*6:35. *13:2, 3. Jn *9:3. **that the.** Ec 8:14. Dt 33:3. 1 S 2:9. 2 S 15:25, 26. Jb 5:8. Ps 10:14. 31:5. 37:5, 6. Pr 16:3. Is 26:12. 49:1-4. Je 1:18, 19. 9:23, 24. Jn √10:27-30. 1 C *3:5-15. 2 T *1:12. 1 P *1:5. **no man.** Ec 7:15. Ps 73:3, 11-13. Ml 3:15-18.

2. **alike.** Ec 2:14-16. Jb 9:22. 21:7-9, 12-15, 17, 18. Ps 73:2, 3, 12, 13. Ezk 21:3. Ml 3:14, 15. Mt +*5:45. He 13:15, 16. **as is.** Ec 2:26. 7:18. 8:12-14. **feareth.** Ge 24:3, 8, 9. Jsh 2:17-20. 1 S 14:26. Ezk 17:18, 19. Zc 5:3, 4. Ml 3:+5, 18.

3. **also.** Ec *8:11. Ge *6:5. 8:21. 1 K +8:18. Jb 15:16. Ps 51:5. Pr 20:9. Je *17:9. Mt 15:19, 20. Mk *7:21-23. Jn 3:19. Ro 1:29-31. 6:21. 8:7, 8. 1 C 2:14. Ep 4:17-19. 5:8. T 1:15. 3:3. **and madness.** Ec 1:17. 7:25. Lk 6:11. 15:17. Ac 26:11, 24. 2 P 2:16. **after.** Ec 12:7. Pr 14:32. Ac 12:23.

4. **to him.** Jb 14:7-12. 27:8. Is 38:18. La 3:21, 22. Lk *16:26-29. **hope.** Ec ●8:8. **for.** ⨍138C, Ge +22:14. **living dog.** Is 38:19. Mt 15:27. Ph 3:2. **dead lion.** 2 Ch 35:24. Pr 30:30.

5. **the living.** Ec 7:2. Ge 3:19. 47:30. Jb 30:23. Ro 5:12. He +*9:27. **the dead.** Jb 14:21. Ps 6:5. 88:10, 11. Is 63:16. **know not.** T#998‡, 1008x. ver. +10. Dt +*18:10, 11. 1 S 20:39. *28:7-20. 2 S 15:11. Jb *14:21. Ps 31:17. 115:17. 139:7, 8. +*146:4. Pr 15:11. Is ☾*14:10, 16. *38:18. *63:16. Mt 8:6. Lk 16:19-31. Jn 11:11. He 11:36, 37. 1 J +4:18 (T#1012‡). **reward.** Ec ◐2:26. ◐3:21. ◐12:7. Jb +14:22. Ps 6:5. +13:3. 62:12. 91:8. Mt ☾*16:27. ☾*25:41. **for the.** Ec 2:16. 8:10. Jb 7:8-10. Ps 31:12. 88:5, 12. 109:15. Is 26:14. **forgotten.** Ec 6:4. 8:10. Dt *32:26. Jb 18:17. Ps +9:5. 34:16. 109:15.

6. **their love.** Ex 1:8. Jb 3:17, 18. Ps 146:3, +*4. Pr 10:28. Mt 2:20. **neither have they.** Ec 2:18-23. 6:12. ◐8:8. **portion.** ver. 9. Ec 2:10, 21. 3:22. Ps 17:14. Lk 16:25. 1 P ◐1:3, 4. **for ever.** Heb. *olam,* Ex +*12:24.

7. **Go.** Ge 12:19. Mk 7:29. Jn 4:50. **eat.** Ec 2:24-26. 3:12, 13, 22. 5:18. 8:15. 10:19. Dt 12:7, 12. 16:14, 15. 1 K 8:66. 1 Ch 16:1-3. 29:21-23. 2 Ch 30:23-27. Ne 8:10-12. Ac 2:46, 47. **for.** Ge 4:4, 5. Ex 24:8-10. Lk 11:41. Ac 10:35. Ro 5:1, 2. 1 T 6:17. 1 P 2:5.

8. **thy garments.** 2 S 19:24. Est 8:15. Re 3:4, 5. 7:9, 13, 14. 16:15. 19:8, 14. **let thy head.** Ru 3:3. 2 S 14:2. Da 10:3. Am 6:6. Mt 6:17. Lk 7:46.

9. **Live joyfully.** Heb. See, *or* enjoy life. Ec 1:10. 2:1. 7:13. **with the wife.** Pr 5:18, 19. 18:22. 19:14. Ml 2:15. **all the days of the life.** Ec 6:12. Ps 39:5. 144:4. **given thee.** T#635. Mt 19:6. Ep 6:4. **for.** Ec 2:10, 24. 3:13, 22. 5:18.

10. **thy hand findeth.** T#1857. Nu 13:30. Jg 9:33mg. 1 Ch 22:19. 28:20. 29:2, 3. 2 Ch 31:20, 21. Ezr 6:14, 15. Ne 2:12-20. 3:1, etc. 4:2, 6, 9-13, 17-23. 13:8-31. Ps 71:15-18. Pr 10:29. +22:29. Is 40:29-31. Je √29:13. Mt √6:33. Jn 4:34. Ac 9:6. Ro √12:11. 15:18-20. 1 C 9:24, 26. 15:10. 16:10. Ep √5:16. Col √3:23. 2 P 1:12-15. **do it with.** Ec 11:6. 2 Ch 31:21. Ph 2:12. Col *3:23. 1 Th +4:11. **for.** ver. 5, 6. Ec +*11:3. Jb 14:7-

12. Ps 6:5. 88:10-12. Is 38:18, 19. Ho 13:9. Jn *9:4. Ac 20:25-31. **no work**. Ps +*146:4. Jn *9:4. **nor knowledge**. Ec 1:16, 18. 2:21, 26. Is 38:18. **nor wisdom**. ver. 13, 15, 16, 18. Ec 1:13. Ps +*146:4. **grave**. Heb. *sheol*, Ge +37:35. 42:38. 44:29. Nu 16:33. 1 K 2:6. Jb 30:23. Is 5:14. ◐*14:10, 16. Lk 16:31. **whither**. Jb *30:23. Ps 115:17.

11. **returned**. Ec 2:12. 4:1, 4. Ml 3:18. **that the race**. 1 S 17:50. 2 S 2:18-23. 17:14, 23. Ps 33:16, 17. *75:6, 7. 147:10, 11. Je 9:23. 46:6. Am 2:14-16. Ro *9:16. **bread**. ᶠ17l18, Ge +3:19. **but**. Ec 2:14, 15. 3:14, 17. 7:13. 1 S 2:3-10. Jb 5:11-14. 34:29. Pr 21:30, 31. La 3:37, 38. Da *4:35. Ep +*1:11. **chance**. The Hebrew word means "an occurrence, incident" (Wilson). Ge +24:44n. 1 K 5:4h (occurrent). 22:34. Est 6:1-11. Lk 10:31. **happeneth**. Ec 2:14, 15. Nu 11:23.

12. **man**. Ec 8:5-7, 11. Lk 19:42-44. 2 C 6:2. 1 P 2:12. **as the fishes**. Pr 7:22, 23. Hab 1:14-17. 2 T 2:26. **as birds**. Mt *10:29, 30. **the sons**. Jb 18:8-10. Ps 11:6. 73:18-20. Pr 6:15. 29:6. Is 30:13. Lk 12:20, 39. *17:26-31. +*21:34-36. 1 Th *5:2, 3. 2 P 2:12. **it falleth suddenly**. T#149. 1 S *20:3. Ps 102:23, 24. Mt +25:13 (T#385).

13. **This wisdom**. ver. 11. Ec 6:1. 7:15. 8:16.

14. **There was**. This passage receives a fine illustration from the case of Archimedes, who defended the city of Syracuse from all the Roman forces which besieged it by sea and land. He destroyed their ships by his burning glasses; lifted up their galleys out of the water by his machines, dashing some to pieces and sinking others. Yet this wise man was not remembered but was slain by a Roman soldier while deeply engaged in demonstrating a problem (See Plutarch in Marcell, etc.). 2 S *20:15-22. 2 K 6:24-33. 7:1, etc.

15. **delivered**. Pr 11:11. **yet**. Ge=40:23. Est 6:2, 3.

16. **Wisdom**. ver. 18. Ec *7:19. Pr 21:22. 24:5. 1 C 12:31. **the poor**. Pr 10:15. Mk *6:2, 3. Jn 7:47-49. 9:24-34. 1 C 1:26-29. Ja 2:2-6. **not heard**. 1 C 2:8.

17. **of wise**. Ge 41:33-40. 1 S 7:3-6. Pr 28:23. Is 42:2, 4. Ja 1:20. 3:17, 18.

18. **better**. ver. *16. **sinner**. Jsh *7:1, 5, 11, 12. *22:20. 1 S 14:28, 29, 36-46. 2 S 20:1, 2. 1 C 5:6. Ga 5:9. 2 Th 2:8-12. 2 T 2:16-18. 3:8. *4:3, 4. T 1:10, 11. He *12:15, 16. 3 J 10.

ECCLESIASTES 10

The care requisite to preserve a reputation for wisdom, and the different conduct of a wise man and a fool, 1-3. Observations on the duties and errors of rulers and subjects, with various maxims for the prudent conduct of affairs, 4-15: of riot, 16, 17; slothfulness, 18, and money, 19. Men's thoughts of kings to be reverent, 20.

1. **Dead flies**. Heb. Flies of death. ᶠ138C, Ge +22:14. **the ointment**. Ex 30:34, 35. **a little**. 2 Ch 19:2. Ne 6:13. 13:26. Mt *5:13-16. Ga 2:12-14.

2. **wise**. Ec +*9:10. Pr 14:8. Lk *14:28-32. **right hand**. Ge +48:13. **but**. ver. 10, 14. Pr *17:16. Lk 12:18-20. **left**. Ge +48:13. Jg +20:16.

3. **wisdom**. Heb. heart. Jb +12:3. **and he**. Ec 5:3. Pr 13:16. 17:28. 18:2, 6. 1 P 4:4.

4. **spirit**. Heb. *ruach*, Ge +41:8. **leave**. Ec 8:3. **for**. 1 S 25:23, 24, 32, 33. Pr 25:15.

5. **an evil**. Ec 4:7. 5:13. 6:1. 9:3. **as an**. Ec 3:16. 4:1. **from**. Heb. from before.

6. **Folly**. Jg 9:14-20. 1 K 12:13, 14. Est 3:1. Ps 12:8. Pr 28:12, 28. **dignity**. Heb. heights. Jg 5:18. 2 S 22:17. **the rich**. Ja 2:3-5.

7. **have seen**. Pr 19:10. 30:22.

8. **that**. Jg 9:5, 53-57. 2 S 17:23. 18:15. Est 7:10. Ps 7:15, 16. 9:15, 16. Pr 26:27. *28:10. **a serpent**. Am 5:19. 9:3.

9. **stones**. Ec 3:5. Ge 2:12. 11:3. **hurt**. Ge 45:5. 1 S 20:3. Ne 8:10, 11. **cleaveth**. Ps 141:7. Is 63:12.

10. **wisdom**. ver. 15. Ec 9:15-17. Ge 41:33-39. Ex +*18:19-23. 1 K 3:9. 1 Ch +*12:32. 2 Ch 23:4-11. Mt 10:16. Ac 6:1-9. 15:2, etc. Ro 16:19. 1 C 14:20. Ep 5:15-17. Col *4:5. Ja *1:5.

11. **the serpent**. Ps 58:4, 5. Je 8:17. **a babbler**. Heb. the master of a tongue. Ps 34:13. 52:2. 64:3. Pr 18:21. Ja *3:6-8. ᶠ171E6. Synecdoche of the Genus B621. The "tongue" is put for the man. For other instances of this figure see Ps 101:5. 140:11mg.

12. **words**. Jb 4:3, 4. 16:5. Ps 37:30. 40:9, 10. 71:15-18. Pr 10:13, 20, 21, 31, *32. 12:*13, 14, 18. 15:2, 23. 16:21-24. 22:17, 18. 25:11, 12. 31:26. Mt *12:35, 36. Lk 4:22. Ep *4:29. Col *4:6. **wise man's**. Pr +*1:5. **gracious**. Heb. grace. Ec 9:11. Ge 6:8. 18:3. 1 S ◐+*25:17. 2 K +*5:13. Ep +*6:9. **but**. 2 S 1:16. 1 K 20:40-42. Ps 64:8. 140:9. Pr 10:8, 10, 14. 18:6-8. 19:5. 26:9. Lk 19:22.

13. **beginning**. Jg 14:15. 1 S 20:26-33. 22:7, 8, 16-18. 25:10, 11. 2 S 19:41-43. 20:1. 2 K 6:27, 31. Pr 29:9. Mt 2:7, 8, 16. Lk 6:2, 11. 11:38, 53, 54. Jn 12:10. Ac 5:28-33. 6:9-11. 7:54-59. 19:24-28. **talk**. Heb. mouth. **mischievous madness**. ver. 5. Ec *1:13. 2:17, 21.

14. **fool**. Ec 5:3. Pr 10:19. *15:2. **is full of words**. Heb. multiplieth words. Jb 34:37. 35:16. Ezk 35:13. **a man**. Ec 3:22. 6:12. 8:7. Ja 4:13, 14.

15. **labor**. ver. 3, 10. Is 44:12-17. 47:12, 13. 55:2. 57:1. Hab 2:6, 13. Mt 11:28-30. **because**. Ps 107:4, 7. Is 35:8-10. Je 50:4, 5.

16. **when**. 2 Ch 13:7. 33:1, etc. 36:2, 5, 9, 11. Is 3:4, 5, 12. **and**. Pr 20:1, 2. Is *5:11, 12. 28:7, 8. Ho 7:5-7. **in the**. Je 21:12.

17. **Blessed**. ᶠ43, Dt +28:3. **when**. ver. 6, 7. Pr 28:2, 3. Je 30:21. **and thy**. Pr *31:4, 5. **due season**. Mt +*24:45. Lk 12:42, 45. **drunkenness**. Lk 12:45.

18. **slothfulness**. Pr 12:24. 14:1. 18:9. 19:15. 20:4. 21:25. 22:13, ◐+29. 23:21. 24:30, 31. 26:13. Mt 25:26. Ro *12:11. 2 Th 3:11. He 6:11, 12. 2 P ◐√1:5-10.

19. **feast**. ᶠ171I8, Ge +3:19. Ec 2:1, 2. 7:2-6. Ge 43:34. Da 5:1, etc. 1 P 4:3. **and wine**. Ec 9:7. 1 S 25:36. 2 S 13:28. Ps *104:15. Is 24:11. Lk 12:19. Ep *5:18, 19. **maketh merry**. Heb. maketh glad the life. **but**. Money which would have answered every good purpose and served for every emergency, is too often spent in feastings and revelings. Ec 7:11, 12. 1 Ch 21:24. 29:2, etc. 2 Ch 24:11-14. Ezr 1:6. 7:15-18. Ne 5:8. Ps 112:9. Is 23:18. Mt 17:27. 19:21. Lk 8:3. *16:9. Ac 2:45. 11:29. Ph 4:15-19. 1 T *6:17-19.

20. **Curse**. Ex 22:28. Is 8:21. Ac 23:5. 1 P 2:13. 2 P 2:10. **thought**. *or*, conscience. Ec 7:21, 22. Lk 19:40. Ro 13:5. **curse not**. Pr 11:24-26. **in thy bedchamber**. Ex 3:8. 2 S 4:7. 2 K 1:16n. *6:11, 12. 11:2. 2 Ch 22:11. Est 2:21-23. Hab 2:11. Lk 10:40. 12:2, 3. **hath wings**. Ps 15:3. Pr 1:17mg. Ezk *11:5. *33:20. Lk 12:2, *3. 19:40.

ECCLESIASTES 11

An exhortation to be liberal and unwearied in doing good, 1-6. The prosperous should expect affliction and death, and beware of future misery, 7, 8; and young persons should remember judgment in their most cheerful hours, 9, 10.

1. **Cast.** That is, says Bp. Lowth, "Sow thy seed or corn on the face of the waters;" in plain terms, sow without any hope of a harvest:—do good even to them on whom your benefactions seem thrown away. Dr. Jubb has well illustrated it by the following passages:

Vain are the favors done to vicious men;
Not vainer 'tis to sow the foaming deep.
The deep no pleasant harvest shall afford,
Nor will the wicked ever make return.
Theognis, *Gnome,* 105.
To befriend the wicked is like sowing in the sea.
Phocylides, v. 141.

These, indeed, invert this precept; nor is it extraordinary that they should, "The one, frail human power alone produced, The other, God." **thy bread.** ſ121G, Ge +31:1. Dt *15:7-11. Pr 11:24, 25. 22:9. Is 32:8. **waters.** Heb. face of the waters. Is 32:20. **for.** ver. 6. Dt 15:10. Ps *41:1, 2. *126:5, 6. Pr 3:9, 10. 11:18. *19:17. Is 32:8. Mt 10:13, *42. 25:40. Mk 4:8. Lk √6:35. *14:14. +*16:9. 2 C 9:6, 8, 9. Ga √6:8-10. He √6:10. Ja *5:7.

2. **a portion.** Ne 8:10. Est 9:19, 22. Ps *112:9. Lk *6:30-35. 1 T 6:18, 19. **seven.** Jb 5:19n. Ps 119:164n. Pr 6:16. Mi 5:5. Mt 18:22. Lk 17:4. **for.** Da 4:27. Ac 11:28-30. Ga 6:1. Ep 5:16. He 13:3.

3. **the clouds.** Ge +9:13. 1 K 18:45. Ps 65:9-13. Is 55:10, 11. 1 J 3:17. **if the tree.** Ec 7:13. Pr +*19:18. 20:4. Mt 3:10. 7:19, 20. Lk 13:7. 16:22-26. Ja 2:15-17. Re 22:11.

4. **that observeth.** Pr 3:27, 28. 20:4. 22:13. **wind.** Ge +9:14. **clouds.** Ge +9:13.

5. **thou knowest not what.** Jn 3:8. **spirit.** Heb. *ruach,* Nu +16:22. Ec 1:6. **nor.** Ps *139:14, 15. **even.** Ec 7:24. 8:17. Jb 5:9. 26:5-14. 36:24-33. 37:23. 38:4, etc. ch. 39-41. Ps 40:5. 92:5. 104:24. Is 40:28. Ro *11:33.

6. **In.** ſ138C, Ge +22:14. **morning.** ſ171T4, Jb +7:18. **sow.** Ec +*9:10. Is 55:10. Ho 10:12. Mk 4:26-29. Jn 4:36-38. 2 C 9:6. Ga *6:9. 2 T 4:2. **thou knowest.** Ec 9:1. Hg 1:6-11. 2:17-19. Zc 8:11, 12. Ac 11:20, 21. 1 C 3:5-7. 2 C 9:10, 11. **prosper.** Heb. be right. ✻S#3787h. Ec 10:10 (direct). Est 8:5 (right).

7. **the light.** Jb 33:28, 30. Ps 56:13. Pr 15:30. 29:13. **a pleasant.** Ec 7:11. Ps *84:11. Mt +*5:45.

8. **if a man.** Ec 6:6. 8:12. **rejoice.** Ec 3:12, 13. 5:18-20. 8:15. **yet.** Ec 7:14. 12:1-5. Dt 32:29. Jb 10:22. 14:10. 15:23. 18:18. Je 13:16. Jl 2:2. Mt 22:13. Jn 12:35. Ju 18. **All that.** Ec 2:1-11, 15, 17, 19, 21-23, 26. 4:8, 16. 5:15, 16. 6:11.

9. **Rejoice.** ſ60A, Ge +3:22. ſ83, 1 K +22:15. 1 K 18:27. 22:15. Lk 15:12, 13. **in thy youth.** Ec *12:1. 1 K 18:12. La 3:27. **walk.** Nu 15:39. 22:32. Dt *29:19, 20. Jb 31:7. Ps 81:12. Je 7:24. 23:17. 44:16, 17. Ac 14:16. Ep 2:2, 3. 1 P 4:3, 4. **in the sight.** Ec 2:10. Ge 3:6. 6:2. Nu 15:39, 40. Jsh 7:21. 2 S 11:2-4. Mt 5:28. 1 J *2:15, 16. **know.** Ec 3:17. *12:14. Ps 50:4-6. Ac *17:30, 31. 24:25. Ro *2:5-11. 14:10. 1 C 4:5. 2 C *5:10. He +*9:27. 2 P 3:7. Re *20:12-15.

10. **remove.** Ec *12:1. Jb 13:26. Ps 25:7. 2 P 3:11-14. **sorrow.** or, anger. Ps 90:7-11. **and put.** Jb 20:11. 2 C *7:1. 2 T *2:22. **for.** Ec 1:2, 14. Ps *39:5. Pr 22:15.

ECCLESIASTES 12

An exhortation to early piety, 1. A description of the infirmities of old age and the approach and consequences of death, 2-7. A repeated declaration that "all is vanity;" the preacher's purpose and care in his instructions and the solemn conclusion of his subject, in a charge to fear and obey God as the whole of man, and thus to prepare for judgment, 8-14.

1. **Remember.** Ec 11:10. Ge 39:2, 8, 9, 23. Dt 8:18. 1 S 1:28. 2:18, *26. 3:19-21. 16:*7, 12, 13. 17:36, 37. 1 K *3:6-12. 14:13. 18:12. 2 Ch *34:2, 3. Ne 4:14. Ps 22:9, 10. *34:11. *63:6. *71:17, 18. 78:35. *119:55. Pr *8:17. +*22:6. Is 26:8. Je 51:50. La *3:27. Da *1:8, 9, 17. Lk 1:15. *2:40-52. *18:16. Ep *6:4. 2 T √3:15. **youth.** Je *3:4. **while.** Ec 11:8. Jb *17:1. 30:2. Ps *90:10. Ho 7:9. **when.** 2 S *19:34, 35.

2. **the sun.** Ec 11:7, 8. Ge 27:1. 48:10. 1 S 3:2. 4:15, 18. **nor.** Ps 42:7. 71:20. 77:16-20. **clouds.** Ge +9:13.

3. **keepers.** ſ142, Ge +20:16. **strong.** 2 S 21:15-17. Ps *90:9, 10. 102:23. Zc 8:4. He 12:12. **and those.** ver. 2. Ge 48:10.

4. **all.** 2 S 19:35.

5. **the almond.** Ge 42:38. 44:29, 31. Le 19:32. Jb 15:10. Ps 71:18. Pr *16:31. 20:29. Is 46:4. Je 1:11. **desire.** ſ88, Ge +15:15. ſ117, Ge +19:8. The Hebrew is literally "and the caper berry shall be powerless." Almost every part of the caper berry plant was used to make condiments but the berries were specially provocative of appetite, though not restricted to sexual desire. Here, then, we have first the plant or berry put for the condiments made from it, and then the condiments put for the desire they created. The meaning is that not only shall appetite or desire fail, but that the condiments and stimulants shall be powerless to produce their usual effect (B609, 610). **because.** Ec +*9:10. Jb 17:13. 30:23. Ps 49:10-14. He +*9:27. **long.** Heb. *olam,* Le +25:32. Ps 143:3. **the mourners.** Ge 50:3-10. Je *9:17-20. Mk 5:38, 39.

6. **Or ever.** ver. 1, 2. **silver cord.** ſ142, Ge +20:16. 2 S 8:2. 17:13. 22:6. **golden bowl.** Ec 2:8. Ge 2:11, 12. 13:2, etc. SS 5:11. **broken.** Is 42:4. **pitcher.** Ge 24:14-18, 20, 43. **fountain.** Jb 21:24. Is 35:7. 49:10. **wheel.** Ps 83:13. Is 5:28. **cistern.** Heb. *bor,* Ge +37:20. 40:15. 41:14.

7. **Then shall.** 1 S 20:3. Ezk *33:11. He +*9:27. **dust.** ſ121D10, Ge +3:19. Ec +*3:20. Ge +2:7. +*3:19. 15:15. 18:27. Jb 4:19, 20. 7:21. 20:11. 34:14, 15. Ps 90:3. *104:29. +*146:4. Is 25:8. Da *12:2. Jn *6:40. Ro *8:23. Ph *3:21. **the spirit.** Heb. *ruach,* Nu +16:22. T#992‡. Ec 3:+19 (T#991‡), +*21. +*9:5. Ge +*2:7. Nu +*27:16n. 1 K √17:17, 21, 22. Jb 14:22. 27:3, 4. 32:8. 33:4. +*34:14. Ps 104:29. Pr 20:27. Da *7:15. Zc +*12:1n. Mk 2:8. Lk √23:46. Ac √7:59. Ro +8:10. 1 C 2:11. 5:3, 5. *6:20. 2 C 4:16. 1 Th *5:23. Ja 2:26. Re 11:11. **return unto God.** Ge +*2:7. Nu 16:22. 27:16. Jb 20:8. Is 57:16. Je 38:16. Ezk +*18:4n. Zc 12:1. Lk 16:22-25. √20:37, 38. *23:43. 1 C *8:4. 2 C √5:6-8. T 2:13. **who gave.** Ge +*2:7. Jb 27:3mg. Is 42:5. Zc *12:1. He 12:+9, 23.

8. **of vanities.** Ec 1:2, 14. 2:17, 26. 4:4. 6:12. 8:8. Ps 62:9.

9. **moreover, because the Preacher was wise.** *or,* the more wise the Preacher was, etc. **he still.** 1 K 8:12, etc. 10:8. **he gave.** 1 K *4:32. Pr 1:1. 10:1. 25:1.

10. **Preacher.** Ec 1:1, 12. **sought.** Pr 16:21. **acceptable words.** Heb. words of delight. Pr 15:23, 26. 16:21-24. 25:11, 12. Is 50:4. Lk 4:22. Jn 7:46. 1 C 2:4. 1 T 1:15. **written.** Pr 1:1-6. 8:6-10. 22:17-21. Lk *1:1-4. Jn 3:11. Col 1:5. **words of truth.** Pr +*22:21. Da 10:21. Ja 1:18.

11. **as goads.** Je 23:29. Mt 3:7. Ac 2:37. 2 C 10:4. He √4:12. 1 P 1:10, 11. 2 P 3:1, 2. **by.** or, are the words. √63I1A, Ex +12:4. **masters.** Jn 3:10. **which.** or, both of these. √63I1A, Ex +12:4. **given.** Ge 49:24. Ps *23:1. 80:1. Is 40:11. Ezk 34:23. Jn 10:14. He *13:20. 1 P 5:4.

12. **by these.** Lk *16:29-31. Jn √5:39. √20:31. 21:25. 2 P *1:19-21. **of.** √138C, Ge +22:14. **study.** or, reading.

*S#3854h, only here. **weariness.** Ec *1:18.

13. **Let us hear the conclusion of the whole matter.** *or,* The end of the matter, even all that hath been heard is. **Fear God.** T#290. Ec 5:7. 8:12. Ge *22:12. Dt 6:2, 24. *10:12, 20. Jsh *24:14. 2 K 17:35, 36. Ps 33:8. *89:7. *111:10. 112:1. 145:19. *147:11. Pr *1:7. *23:17. Is 8:13. Mt +*10:28. Lk +10:42. *12:5. Ac *10:2, +*35. 1 P 2:17. Re 19:5. **keep.** T#295. Dt 13:4. Ps 95:6-8. 96:9. 99:5. Mt +4:10 (T#744). +5:48 (T#285). Ac +4:32 (T#661). Ro 12:1. Col 3:23, 24. He +10:25 (T#745). 1 J +*2:3. Ju +21 (T#288). **for.** Ec 2:3. 6:12. Dt *10:12, 13. Jb *28:28. Ps 115:13-15. Pr *19:23. Lk 1:50. **whole duty.** Mi +*6:8.

14. **God shall.** Ec *11:9. Ps *96:13. Mt 10:15. √12:36. *25:31-46. Lk 12:1, 2. Jn *5:29. Ac √17:30, 31. Ro √2:12, 16. *14:10-12. 1 C *4:5. 2 C √5:10. Re √20:11-15. **every work.** T#389. Ec 11:9. Ne +*9:6. Ps +62:12. +102:24. Mt *12:36. Lk 12:2, 3. Ro 2:16. 1 C 3:13. *4:5. 2 T 4:1. **every secret.** 1 C 4:5. **whether good.** 2 C *5:10.

SONG OF SOLOMON

SONG OF SOLOMON 1

The title, 1. The church, or the believer, desires of Christ the tokens of his love, praises him, and expresses her delight in communion with him; confesses that her comeliness is very defective; complains that she had met with ill treatment, and prays to be directed to the resting place of his people, 2-7. He instructs her to follow the footsteps of his flock and comforts her with commendations and promises, 8-11. Mutual gratulations and professions of love between Christ and the church, 12-17.

1. **song.** Ps 14, title. Is 5:1. **of songs.** √147H, Ge +9:25. Ps 33:1-3. 34:1-3. 51:15. 92:1-3. 104:34. 147:7. Ep *5:19. Col *3:16. Re 5:9. 15:2-4. **Solomon's.** 2 S 12:24. 1 K *4:32. 1 Ch 22:7-10. Ne 13:26. Is 9:6, 7. Da 7:13, 14. Mt 3:17. Lk 1:31-33. 11:31. 24:31. Jn 21:7. Re 19:16.

2. **him.** SS 5:16. 8:1. Ge 27:26, 27. 29:11. 45:15. Ps 2:12. Lk 15:20. Ac 21:7. Ep 5:29. 1 P 5:14. **his mouth.** 1 S 3:9. Jb *23:12. Ps 119:103. Je *15:16. Mt *4:4. 11:28-30. Mk 10:14. Lk 4:22. Jn 7:37, 46. 8:11. 20:15. 1 P 2:22. **thy love.** Heb. thy loves. ver. 4. SS 2:4. 4:10. 7:6, 9, 12. 8:2. Ps 36:7. 63:3-5. Is 25:6. 55:1, 2. Je *31:3. Mt 26:29. Jn 13:1. 15:9. Ro *8:38, 39. 1 J 4:8, 16, 18, 19.

3. **the savor.** SS 3:6. 4:10. 5:5, 13. Ex 30:23-38. Ps 45:7, 8. 133:2. Pr 27:9. Ec 7:1. Is 61:3. Jn 12:3. Ac 4:13. 2 C 2:14-16. Ep *5:2. Ph 4:18. Col 2:9. 1 P 2:7. **thy name.** Ex 33:12, 19. 34:5-7. 1 S 18:30mg. Ps 8:1. +*9:10. 45:17. 89:15, 16. Pr 18:10. Is 7:14. 9:6, 7. Je *23:5, 6. Mt 1:21-23. Jn=16:23. Ac 3:16. √4:12. Ph *2:9-11. **ointment.** ver. 12. 1 Ch=9:30. **the virgins.** ver. 4. SS 6:8. Ge +*24:43. Ex 2:8. Ps 45:14. Mt 25:1. 2 C 11:2. Re 14:1-5.

4. **Draw me.** Ps 73:28. Je 30:21. 31:3. Ho 11:4. Jn *6:37, 44. *12:32. 2 C 5:14. Ph 2:12, 13. 1 J 4:19. **we will.** Ps 45:14, 15. 119:32, 60. Ph 3:12-14. He 12:1. **the king.** SS 2:3-5. 3:4. Ps 45:14, 15. Mt 25:10. Jn *14:2, 3. Ep 2:6. He 6:20. **his chambers.** Ps 27:4, 5. 65:4. Re 22:4, 5. **we will be glad.** Ps 4:6, 7. 45:15.

98:4-9. 149:2. Is 25:8, 9. 45:25. 61:3, 10. Mi 4:2. Hab *3:17, 18. Zp 3:14-17. Zc 9:9. Lk 2:10. Ph 3:3. 4:4. 1 P 1:8. **remember.** ver. 2. Ps 42:4. 48:9. 63:5, 6. 103:1, 2. 104:34. 111:4. Is 63:7. Lk 22:19. 1 C 11:23-26. Re 1:5. **thy love.** SS 2:4. 8:6. Ps 63:3. Jn 15:9. Ro 5:5. 1 J 4:9. **the upright love thee.** *or,* they love thee uprightly. ver. 3. SS 8:7. Ps *84:11. Jn 21:15-17. Ro 12:9. Ep 6:24. Ju 21.

5. **black.** ver. 6. Ge 8:21. Le 13:45. Jb 40:4. 42:6. Ps 51:5. Is 1:5, 6. 6:5. 53:2. Je 17:9. Ezk 16:6. Mt 10:25. Lk 5:8. Ro 3:10. 7:14, 18, 21, 23, 24. 1 C 4:10-13. 1 J 3:1. or, dark. SS 5:11. Le 13:31, 37. Zc 6:2, 6. **but comely.** ver. 8-10. SS 2:10, 14. 4:1, 7. 6:4-10. Nu +23:21. 2 S 12:13. Ps 51:7. 90:17. 149:4. Is 6:7. 61:10. Ezk 16:14. Mt 9:2. 22:11. Lk 15:22. Ro 7:22. 13:14. 2 C 5:21. 6:9, 10. 12:10. Ep 1:6. 5:26, 27. Ph 3:9. Col 1:28. 2:10. Ja 2:5. Re 7:14. 19:7, 8. **O ye.** SS 2:7. 3:5, 10, 11. 5:8, 16. 8:4. Ps 45:9. Lk 13:34. Ga 4:26. **as the tents.** Ps 120:5.

6. **Look.** Ru 1:19-21. Ob 12, 13. Mt 18:10. **because I.** Jb 30:30. Je 8:21. La 4:8. 5:10. Mk 4:6, 17. Ac 14:22. **looked.** √155D, Ge +4:10. **my mother's.** Ps +*69:8. Je 12:6. Mi 7:6. Mt 10:22, 25, 35, 36. Lk 12:51-53. Ga 4:29. **were angry.** 2 T 3:12. **keeper.** SS 8:11, 12. Lk +*10:42. 12:35, 36, 38. 2 T 4:2. 2 P *3:14. **not kept.** Pr 24:30, 31. 1 C 9:27. 11:28, 31. He 12:15.

7. **O thou.** SS 2:3. 3:1-4. 5:8-10, 16. Ps 18:1. 116:1. Is 5:1. 26:9. Mt 10:37. Jn 21:17. 1 P 1:8. 2:7. **where.** Jb 23:3, 4, 8-12. Ps 25:4, 5. 27:11. 43:3. 119:105. **thou feedest.** Ge 37:16. Ps 23:1, 2. 80:1. Is 40:11. Mi 5:4. Jn 10:11, 28, 29. Re 7:17. **rest.** Ps 23:2, 3. 73:24, 25. 119:176. **for.** 1 S 12:20, 21. Ps 28:1. Jn 6:67-69. 1 J 2:19, 20. **turneth aside.** *or,* is veiled. Ge 38:15. 2 C 3:14-18.

8. **know not.** Ps 25:8, 9. *32:8. Pr 8:17-21. Is 30:21. Jn +*5:39. 14:6. 16:13. He 13:22. Ja *1:5. 1 P 3:12. **O thou.** ver. 15. SS 2:10. 4:1, 7, 10. 5:9. 6:1, 4-10. 7:1, etc. Ps 16:3. 45:11, 13. Ep 5:27. Re 19:7, 8. **go thy way.** Pr 6:22, 23. Lk 1:78, 79. Ep 5:1. 1 P 2:21. 25. 2 P 1:19. **forth by.** Pr 8:34. Je 6:16. 1 C 11:1. He

6:12. 11:4, etc. 13:7. Ja 2:21, 25. 5:10. 1 P 3:6. **feed.** Jn 21:15. 1 P 5:2. **the shepherd's.** Zc 13:7. He 13:20, 21. 1 P 5:4.

9. **O my.** SS 2:2, 10, 13. 4:1, 7. 5:2. 6:4. Jn 15:14, 15. **to a.** 1 K 10:28. 2 Ch 1:14-17. Jb 39:21-25. Is 31:1. Zc 10:3.

10. **thy cheeks.** Ge 24:22, 47. Is 3:18-21. Ezk 16:11-13. 2 P 1:3, 4. **thy neck.** SS 4:9. Ge 41:42. Nu 31:50. Pr 1:9. 1 P 3:4.

11. **We will.** SS 8:9. Ge 1:26. Ps 45:9, 13, 14. 149:4. Is 61:10. Je 2:32. Ep 5:25-27. Ph 3:21.

12. **the king.** SS 7:5. Ps 45:1. Mt 22:11. 25:34. Jn 18:37. Re 19:16. **sitteth.** SS 4:16. Mt 18:20. 22:4. 26:26-28. Lk 12:37. 24:30-32. 1 C 10:16. Re 3:20. **my.** SS 4:13-16. Jn 12:1-3. Ph 4:18. Re 8:3, 4. **spikenard.** 1 Ch=9:30. **sendeth.** Mk 7:24. Jn 12:3. **smell.** ver. 3. SS 4:10. Ex +30:1. Mt=26:7. Jn=12:3.

13. **bundle.** SS 4:6, 14. 5:1, 5, 13. Ge 43:11. Ex 30:22-25. Ps 45:8. Jn 19:39. **he shall.** SS 2:7. 3:5. 8:3, 4. Ep 3:17.

14. **beloved.** See on ver. 13. SS 2:3. Mt 12:18. 17:5. 1 P 2:7. **camphire.** *or,* cypress. SS 4:13, 14. **En-gedi.** Jsh 15:62. 1 S 23:29. 24:1.

15. **thou art fair.** See on ver. 8. SS 4:1, 7, 10. 5:12. 7:6. Nu 23:21. Jb ●40:4. Ps 45:11. Je 6:2. Ep 1:4, 5. 5:27. Ju 24. **my love.** *or,* my companion. Ml 2:14. **thou hast.** SS 4:1. 5:12. 2 C 11:2, 3. Ep 1:17, 18.

16. **thou art.** SS 2:3. 5:10-16. Ps 45:2. 90:17. Zc 9:17. 1 C 1:30. Ph 3:8, 9. Re 5:11-13. **also.** SS 3:7. Ps 110:3.

17. **beams.** SS 8:9. 2 Ch 2:8, 9. Ps 92:12. 1 T *3:15, 16. He 11:10. 1 P 2:4, 5. **our house.** Ps 23:6. 92:13. Jn 14:20. 17:21. 1 C 3:9. Ep 2:19, 20, 22. He 3:6. 1 P 2:4-7. Re 21:22. **cedar.** SS 5:15. 8:9. Le 14:4, 49. 1 K 5:8. 6:15-18. **rafters.** *or,* galleries. SS 7:5. Ezk 41:16. 42:3.

SONG OF SOLOMON 2

The glory of Christ, the excellency of the church, and the mutual actings of love between them, 1-7. The church hears the voice of her Beloved and has discoveries of his glory, 8, 9. His gracious invitations and encouragements and his command to guard against subtle and mischievous enemies, 10-15. The church glories in her relation to him and longs for the completion of the sacred union, 16, 17.

1. **the rose.** Ps 85:11. Is 35:1, 2. **lily.** ver. 16. SS 6:3. Is 57:15. Mt 6:28, 29. **valley.** 2 C 8:9. Ep 4:2. Ph 2:7. Ja 1:9-11. 2:5.

2. **lily.** Is 55:13. Ho 14:5. Mt 6:28, 29. 10:16. Ph 2:15, 16. 1 P 2:12. **among thorns.** Nu 33:55. Mt 10:16. 13:3, 7, 24-28. Ph 2:15. **daughters.** Is 32:9, 11.

3. **the apple tree.** SS 8:5. Is 4:2. Ezk 17:23, 24. Jn 15:1-8. **my beloved.** SS 5:9, 10, 16. Ps 45:2. 89:6. Jn 1:14-18. 3:29-31. He 1:1-6. 3:1-6. 7:23-26. 12:2. **among the sons.** SS 5:10. Jg 9:8-15. Jn 7:46. Ph 2:11. **I sat,** etc. Heb. I delighted and sat down, etc. Dt 33:3. Jg 9:15, 19, 20. Ps 57:1. 91:1. Is 4:6. 25:4. 32:2. Lk 10:39. 1 P 1:8. 1 J 1:3, 4. **his shadow.** Ps 91:1. Is 32:2. **his fruit.** ver. 5. Ge 3:22-24. Ps 63:1. Ezk 47:12. Jn 1:16. 6:55, 57. Re 22:1, 2. **taste.** Heb. palate. SS 5:16mg. Jb +31:30mg. Ps 34:8. 119:103. Je *15:16.

4. **brought.** SS 1:4. 5:1. Ps 23:5. 40:2. 63:2-5. 65:4. 84:10. Is 25:6. 55:1, 2. Lk 14:17. Jn 14:21-23. Re 3:20.

22:17. **banqueting house.** Heb. house of wine. SS 1:1, 4. 1 Ch 9:33. Est 7:7. Ps 16:11. 36:8. Re 19:9. **his banner.** ⌐22D5Q, Ex +17:15. SS 6:4. Ex 17:15. Jb 1:10. Ps 60:4. Is 11:10. Jn 15:9-15. Ro 5:8-10. 8:28-39. 1 C 15:57.

5. **Stay.** SS2:3. Ps 4:6, 7. 42:1, 2. 63:1-3, 8. 104:15. Is 26:8, 9. Lk 22:20. 24:32. Jn 6:55, 57. Ph 1:23. **flagons.** 2 S 6:19. Ho 3:1. **comfort me.** Heb. straw me. Ps 55:6. 73:25. Is 40:1. He 4:9. Re 22:3, 4. **for.** SS 5:8. 2 S 13:1, 2. Ps 84:1, 2. 119:130, 131. Is 6:11. Ga 2:20. Re 22:20.

6. **left hand.** SS 8:3-5. Ge 13:9. Is 54:5-10. 62:4, 5. Je 32:41. Zp 3:17. Jn 3:29. Ep 5:25-29. **under.** Dt 33:27. Ps *37:24. 55:22. Is *26:3. 40:11. *41:10. Mt 14:30, 31. 1 P 5:7. **right hand.** Dt 33:12. Ps 31:5. Is 40:29. Jn √10:28-30.

7. **charge you.** Heb. adjure you. Mt 26:63. **O ye.** SS 1:5. 5:8, 16. **by the roes.** SS 3:5. Pr 5:19. **ye stir.** SS *8:4. Ep 5:22-33. **till he please.** Mt 6:9, 10. 2 Th 3:5. 1 T 6:14-17. Ja 1:4. 5:8. Re 13:10.

8. **voice.** SS 5:2. Jn 3:29. 10:4, 5, 27. Re 3:20. **behold.** Nu 23:9. Is 33:17. Ju 14. Re 1:7. **he cometh.** Mt 25:6. Jn 11:28, 29. 1 Th 5:1, 2. T 2:13. Re 16:15. **leaping.** 2 S 6:16. Is 35:6. Je 48:27. Lk 6:23. Ac 3:8. 14:10. **the mountains.** Is 40:3, 4. 44:23. 49:11-13. 55:12, 13. Lk 3:4-6.

9. **like.** ver. 17. SS 8:14. Ps 70:5. **behold.** Re 22:7, 20. **he standeth.** 1 C 13:12. 2 C 3:13-18. Ep 2:14, 15. Col 2:17. He 9:8, 9. 10:1, 19, 20. **showing.** Heb. flourishing. Lk 24:35. Jn 5:39, 46. 12:41. 1 P 1:10-12. Re 19:10.

10. **spake.** ver. 8. 2 S 23:3. Ps 85:8. Je 31:3. **Rise.** ver. 13. SS 4:7, 8. 5:2. Ge 12:1-3. Ps 45:10, 11. Pr 6:9. Is 52:1, 2. 60:1-5. Mi 2:10. Ml 4:2. Mt 4:19-22. 9:9. Mk 10:49. Lk 22:46. Jn 5:8. 2 C 6:17, 18. 11:2. Ep 5:14. Re 19:7-9. 22:17. **come away.** Ex 33:15. Je 29:11. Jn 14:2, 3. He 13:14.

11. **the winter.** Ec 3:4, 11. Is 12:1, 2. 40:2. 54:6-8. 60:1, 2. Mt +*5:4. Ep 5:8. Re 11:14, 15. **is past.** Is 44:22. Je 50:20. 2 C 5:17. Ep 2:1. 5:8. **rain.** Ge 8:13. 9:15. Ps 126:5. Re 7:17. 21:3, 4.

12. **flowers.** SS 6:2, 11. Is 35:1, 2. Ho 14:5-7. **appear.** Ps 90:17. 92:12, 13. **time.** Ps 40:1-3. 89:15. 148:7-13. Is 42:10-12. 55:12. Je +*8:7. Mt 16:3. Ep 5:18-20. Col 3:16. **of the turtle.** Ro 15:9-13. Ep 1:13, 14.

13. **fig tree.** SS 6:11. 7:8, 11-13. Is 18:5. 55:10, 11. 61:11. Ho 14:6, 8. Hg 2:19. Mt 24:32, 33. Lk 13:6, 7. **vines with.** or, the vines (are) blossoms. ⌐119, SS +49:9. **smell.** SS 4:13, 14. Ex 30:8, 34. Ph 4:18. **Arise.** ver. 10. Pr 8:17. Mt 18:10. 19:14. Lk 19:42. 2 C 5:20. 6:1, 2. **and come.** 1 Th 4:17. He 6:10.

14. **my dove.** SS 5:2. 6:9. Ps 68:13. 74:19. Is 60:8. Ezk 7:16. Mt 3:16. 10:16. **that art.** Ex 3:6. 4:11-13. Ezr 9:5, 6. Jb 9:16. Is 6:5. Da 9:7. Lk 8:47, 48. **clefts.** Ex 33:22, 23. Ps 71:3. Is 2:21. 33:16. Je 49:16. Ob 3. **secret.** Dt 13:6. 27:15, 24. Ps 27:5. 91:1. Is 26:20. **stairs.** Ezk 38:20. **let me hear.** Ec 8:13. Ps 50:14, 15. Pr 15:8. He 4:16. 10:22. **for sweet.** Ps 22:3. 50:23. Is 51:3. Re 4:8-10. 5:8. 7:9, 10. **voice.** SS 8:13. Ps 29:3. Jn *10:3. **thy countenance.** SS 1:5, 8. 6:10. Ps 17:15. 45:11. 110:3. Ep 5:27. Col 1:22. 1 P 3:4. Ju 24.

15. **the foxes.** Ps 80:13. Ezk 13:4-16. Lk 13:32. 2 P 2:1-3. Re 2:2. **the little.** Ps 19:12. Pr 4:23. Mt 16:6, 12. 1 C 5:6-8. Ga 5:7. Re 2:4, 7. **that spoil.** Pr 17:14. 1 T 6:10, 11. 2 T 2:21-23. He 12:1, 15. 1 J

2:15, 16. **tender.** ver. 13. SS 7:12. Mt 12:20. Lk 8:14. Re 3:2, 8.

16. **beloved.** SS 6:3. 7:10, 13. Ps 48:14. 63:1. Pr 8:31. Je 31:33. Jn 4:32, 34. 1 C 3:21-23. 6:20. Ga 2:20. Re 21:2, 3. **I am his.** T#832. SS 7:10. Nu 18:20. Ps 73:25, 26. Is 9:6. 42:6. 55:4. Ezk 34:23. Ml 4:2. Jn *3:16. √6:37. Ro 14:7, 8. He *10:22. **he.** ver. 1. SS 1:7. 6:3. Mt 18:20.

17. **Until.** Ps 42:8. 1 Th 5:2, 4-6. 2 Th 2:3. **the day.** SS 4:6. Lk 1:78. Ro 13:12. 2 P 1:19. Re 22:20. **the shadows.** 1 C 13:10, 12. Col 2:16, 17. He 8:5. 10:1. **beloved.** ver. 9. SS 8:14. **Bether.** *or*, division. *S#1335h. Ge 15:10 (piece). Je 34:18, 19 (parts).

SONG OF SOLOMON 3

The spouse relates the pains she took to recover the company of her Beloved; her success and care not to lose his gracious presence, 1-5. Her companions admire her zeal and heavenly affections, 6. All the company unite in admiring the glory of the Beloved, 7-11.

1. **night.** Ps +4:4. 6:6. 22:2. 63:6-8. 77:2-4. Is 26:9. Am 6:1. Ro 13:11. Ep 5:14. **him whom.** SS 1:7. 5:8. Jn 21:17. 1 P 1:8. **soul.** Heb. *nephesh*, Ge +34:3. **I sought.** SS 5:6. Jb 23:8, 9. Ps 30:7. 130:1, 2. Is 55:6. Lk 12:37. 13:24. Ro 12:11. 1 P 1:13. 2 P 3:13, 14.

2. **will rise.** SS 5:5. Is 64:7. Jon 1:6. Mt 26:40, 41. Ro 13:11. 1 C 15:34. Ep 5:14. **and go.** SS 1:8. Lk 15:18-20. **the streets.** Heb. *shuk*, Am 5:16n (alleys). Pr 1:20, 21. +7:8 (*S#7784h). 8:2, 3, 34. Mk 6:56. Lk 14:21-23. **broad ways.** Heb. *rechob*, Am 5:16n (*S#7339h, streets), public square or broad streets. **seek him.** Jb 23:8, 9. Ps 22:2. Is *26:9. Je *29:13. Jn *5:39. **soul.** Heb. *nephesh*, Ge +34:3. **loveth.** SS 1:4. Jn 21:15-17. Ep 6:24. **I sought.** Ps 22:1, 2. 42:7-9. 43:2-5. 77:7-10. Jn 6:68, 69.

3. **watchmen.** SS 5:7. Is 21:6-8, 11, 12. 56:10. *62:6. Je 6:17. Ezk *3:17. 33:2-9. Ml 2:7. He 13:17. **Saw.** Jn 12:20-22. 20:15. **soul.** Heb. *nephesh*, Ge +34:3.

4. **but.** SS 6:12. Pr 8:17. Is 45:19. *55:6, 7. Je √29:13. La 3:25. Mt *7:7. **found him.** Ge 24:27. Ps 145:18. Pr 8:17. Is 45:19. *55:6, 7. Mt 7:7. Jn 20:11-16. Ga *6:9. **soul.** Heb. *nephesh*, Ge +34:3. **I held.** SS 7:5. Ge 32:26. Pr 4:13. Ho 6:1-3. 12:3, 4. Mt 28:9. Jn 20:16, 17. Re 3:11, 12. **I had.** Is 49:14-18. 54:1-3. Ga 4:26. **conceived me.** Jn 1:12, 13. 3:5-8. Ja 1:18. 1 P 1:23. 1 J 5:1, 4-7.

5. **charge.** SS 2:7. 8:4. Mi 4:8. **till he.** 2 C 13:14. 1 J 1:3.

6. **this.** SS 8:5. Dt 8:2. Is 43:19. Je 2:2, 3. 31:2. Re 12:6, 14. **that cometh.** Ge 24:63. Nu 23:21. Dt 32:12. **like.** Probably the clouds of incense arising from the palanquin, which seemed like pillars of smoke. Ex 13:21, 22. Nu 10:35. Jl 2:29-31. Ac 2:18-21. Col 3:1, 2. **perfumed.** SS 1:3, 13. 4:12-14. 5:5, 13. Ex 30:1-9, 34-38. 2 C 2:14-16. Ph 4:18. Re 5:8.

7. **his bed.** ver. 9mg. SS 1:16. **threescore.** These were the guards about the pavilion of the bridegroom; which were required both for the security and state of the prince. 1 S 8:16. 14:52. 28:2. 1 K 9:22. 14:27, 28. 2 K 6:17. He 1:14. **the valiant.** 1 K 4:26, 27. 10:26-29. Ps 68:17, 18.

8. **all.** Ps 45:3. 149:5-9. Is 27:3. 2 C 10:4. Ep 6:12, 16-18. 1 P 5:8. 1 J *3:8. Re 19:14. **because.** Ne 4:21, 22. Ps +34:4. 1 Th 5:6-8.

9. **a chariot.** *or*, a bed. *Appiryou*, rendered by Montanus, *sponsarum thalamum*, "a nuptial bed;" but probably it denotes a kind of palanquin, perhaps synonymous with the Arabic *farfar*, a species of vehicle for women. ver. 7. 2 S 23:5. Re 14:6. **Lebanon.** 1 K 5:13-16.

10. **the pillars.** 1 K 7:21. Ps 87:3. 1 T *3:15, 16. Re *3:12. **the midst.** That is, probably, amatory verses, expressive of the amiable qualities of the bride and bridegroom, wrought either on the coverlet or embroidered carpet. Lady M. W. Montague (let. 29) informs us that the inside even of Turkish coaches are "painted with baskets and nosegays of flowers, intermixed commonly with little poetical mottos." Ro 5:8. Ep 3:18, 19. Re 1:5. **for.** Re 21:9-11, 21.

11. **Go.** SS 7:11. He 13:13. **O ye.** SS 1:5. 2:7. Ps 9:14. 45:14, 15. 48:11. **daughters.** Is 62:11, 12. Zp 3:14-17. Zc 2:10. 9:9. Jn 12:12-15. **of Zion.** Ps 2:6. 76:1, 2. Is 62:1-5. **behold.** Is 9:6. Mt 12:42. Ph 2:9-11. He 2:9. Ju 24. Re 1:7. 19:12, 16. **his mother.** SS 8:5. Col 1:18. Re 5:9, 10. **in the day of his.** Is 62:5. Je 2:2. Ho 2:19, 20. Jn 3:29. Re 19:7. 22:9, 10. **in the day of the.** Is 53:11. Je 32:41. Zp 3:17. Lk 15:6, 7, 23, 24, 32. Jn 15:11. 1 C *2:9. Re 22:5.

SONG OF SOLOMON 4

Christ commends the comeliness of the spouse by various similes, invites her to accompany him, 1-7; and shows the warmth of his affection, 8-15. The spouse desires supplies of divine influences to invigorate her holy affections, to be made fit for his presence, 16.

1. **thou art fair.** ver. 9, 10. SS 1:15. 2:10, 14. Ps 45:11. Ezk 16:14. 2 C 3:18. **thou hast.** SS 5:12. Mt 11:29. Ph 2:3-5. **dove's.** SS 1:15. 2:14. 5:2, 12. Mt 5:5. 6:22. 10:16. 11:29. Ph 2:15. **within.** ver. 3. SS 6:7. **thy hair.** SS 5:11. 6:5, 7. 7:5. **flock.** Lk 12:32. Jn 10:16. 1 P 5:2. **appear from.** *or*, eat of, etc. **mount.** Ge 31:25. Nu 32:1, 40. Dt 3:12.

2. **teeth.** SS 6:6. Je *15:16. Jn 15:7. Col 1:4-6. 1 Th √2:13. 2 P 1:5-8. **flock.** Ps 78:52. 79:13. 95:7. **came up.** SS 6:6. Ge 19:15, 28. **washing.** SS 6:6. Is 1:18. Zc 13:1. Jn 15:3. 1 C 6:11. T *3:5. He +*10:22. Re +1:5. 7:14. Heb. *rachtsah*, *S#7367h. SS 6:6. **bear twins.** SS 7:3. Ge 25:24. 38:27. **and none.** Ex 23:26. Dt 7:13, 14. **barren.** SS 6:6. 2 S 17:8. Ps +113:9. +127:3. Pr 17:12. Je 18:21. Ho 13:8.

3. **lips.** ver. 11. SS 5:13, 16. 7:9. Ps 37:30. 45:2. 119:13. Pr 10:13, 20, 21. 16:21-24. Mt 12:35. Lk 4:22. 1 C 1:23. 2 C 5:18-21. Ep 4:29. Col *3:16, 17. 4:6. **scarlet.** Le 14:4, 6, 49-52. Nu 4:8. 19:6. Jsh 2:18. Pr 31:26. He 9:19. Re 5:9, 12. **thy temples.** SS 6:7. Ge 32:10. Ezr 9:6. Ezk 16:63.

4. **neck.** SS 1:10. 7:4. 2 S 22:51. Ep 4:15, 16. Col 2:19. 1 P 1:5. **tower.** SS 5:13. 7:4. 8:10. Ge 11:4. Ps 144:12. **an armoury.** Ne 3:19. **there hang.** Ezk 27:10, 11. Is 22:23, 24. **a thousand.** 2 Ch 9:15, 16. 12:9-11. **shields.** 2 S 8:7-11. 2 K 11:10. 2 Ch 23:9. **mighty men.** 2 S 23:8-39. 2 Ch 11:10, etc. ch. 12. Lk 11:21, 22. Ro 8:37. Ep 6:10. 1 J 5:4.

5. **two breasts.** SS 1:13. 7:3, 7. 8:1, 10. Pr 5:19. Is 66:10-12. 1 P *2:2. **feed.** SS 2:16. 6:3. Ps 133:1, 2. Ro 12:9, 10. 1 C 1:10. 10:16, 17. Ep 4:3.

6. **Until.** Mt 28:20. He +*13:5. **day.** SS 2:17. Ml 4:2. Lk 1:78. 2 P *1:19. 1 J 2:8. Re 22:16. **break.** Heb. breathe. SS 2:17. Ezk 21:31. **the mountain.** Ex

20:24. 30:8, 23-26. 37:29. Dt 12:5, 6. Ps 66:15. Is 2:2.
Ml 1:11. Lk 1:9, 10. Re 5:8.

7. **all fair.** ver. 1. SS 5:16. 6:10. Nu 24:5. Jb ◑40:4.
Ps 45:11, 13. 90:17. Ep 5:25-27. Col 1:22. 2 P 3:14.
Ju 24. Re 21:2. **no spot.** Ep ▶5:27.

8. **with me.** SS 2:13. 7:11. Ps 45:10. Pr 9:6. Lk
9:57. Jn 12:26. Col 3:1, 2. Re 14:4. **from Lebanon.**
Dt 3:25. **look from.** Ge 19:17. Mt 4:8, 9. Lk 22:31.
1 P 5:8. **Amana.** i.e. *support, confirmation, faithful-*
ness; constancy, a settled provision, *S#549hl. SS 4:8.
2 K 5:12. **Shenir.** Dt +3:9. Jsh 12:1. 1 Ch +5:23.
Hermon. Dt +3:8. **from the lion's.** Ge 49:9. Nu 23:24.
Ps 76:1, 4. **leopards.** Is 11:6. Je 5:6.

9. **ravished.** *or,* taken away, etc. Ro 8:35. Ep 3:19.
my sister. ver. 10, 12. SS 5:1, 2. Ge 20:12. Mt 12:50.
1 C 9:5. He 2:11-14. **my spouse.** SS 3:11. Ps 45:9. Is
54:5. 62:5. Ezk 16:8. Ho 2:19, 20. Jn 3:29. 2 C 11:2.
Re 19:7, 8. 21:2, 9, 10. **thou hast.** SS 6:12. 7:5, 6,
10. Pr 5:19, 20. Zp 3:17. **with one of.** SS 1:15. 6:5.
one chain. SS 1:10.

10. **love.** Heb. loves. SS 1:2mg. Mt 11:19. Ep 2:4-
7. 5:25, 32. **how much.** SS 1:2, 4. **the smell.** SS 1:3,
12. 3:6. 5:5. Mt 26:6-12. Lk 7:36-50. 2 C 1:21, 22.
Ga 5:22, 23. Ph 4:18. Re 5:8. **ointments.** SS +1:3.
1 Ch +=9:30.

11. **lips.** ver. 3. SS 5:13. 7:9. Ps 71:14, 15, 23, 24.
Pr 16:24. Ho 14:2. He 13:15. **drop.** Dt 32:2. 1 P 3:15,
16. **honey.** SS 5:1. Pr 24:13, 14. Is 7:15. **and milk.**
✓174, Ge +18:27. **the smell.** ver. 10. Ge 27:27. Ps
45:8. Ho 14:7. **thy garments.** Ex 22:9, 26. Dt 24:13.
29:5. Ps 45:13, 14. Is 61:10. Ezk 16:14. Mt 22:11. Lk
15:22. Ph 3:8, 9. Col 1:12. Ju 24, 25. Re 19:7, 8.

12. **garden.** ver. 15, 16. SS 5:1. 6:2, 11. Ge 2:8-
10. Ps 1:3. 80:8-16. 92:12, 13. 125:2. Pr 5:15-18. Is
58:11. 61:10, 11. Je 31:12. Ho 6:3. 14:5. Zc 2:5. Jn
15:19. 17:9. 1 C 6:13, 19, 20. 7:34. Ph 2:15. 1 J 5:19.
Re 21:27. **inclosed.** Heb. barred. Jg 3:23, 24. 2 S 13:17,
18. Ps 91:1. **fountain.** Heb. *mayan,* Ge +7:11
(*S#4599h). ver. 15. Ge 8:2. Pr 5:15. Is 27:3. **sealed.**
Dt 32:34. Ne 9:38. 2 C 1:22. Ep +*1:13. *4:30. Re
7:3.

13. **are an orchard.** SS 6:11. 7:12. 8:2. Ps 92:14.
Ec 2:5. Is 60:21. 61:11. Jn 15:1-3. Ph 1:11. **pleasant.**
ver. 16. SS 2:13. 6:2. *7:13. Ex 30:8, 34. Dt 33:13-
16. **fruits.** ver. 16. SS 2:3. 8:11, 12. Je 17:7, 8. Mt
7:16, 17. Jn 15:2, 8. Ro 6:22. Ga *6:7, 8. Ep 5:9. Ja
5:7. **camphire.** *or,* cypress. ver. 14. SS 1:14mg. **spike-**
nard. SS 1:12. Mk 14:3. Jn 12:3.

14. **calamus.** Ex 30:23. Ezk 27:19. **cinnamon.** Ex
30:23. Pr 7:17. Re 18:13. **trees.** 1 K 4:33. **of frankin-**
cense. ver. 6. SS 3:6. 5:1. Ex 30:34. Nu 24:6. **myrrh.**
ver. 6. SS 3:6. Ex 30:34. Jn 19:39. **aloes.** Nu 24:6. Ps
45:8. Pr 7:17. **the chief.** 1 C 12:4-6. 15:41. **spices.** SS
6:2. Ge 43:11. 1 K 10:10. 2 Ch 9:9. Ps 141:5. Mk
16:1.

15. **fountain.** Heb. *mayan,* Ge +7:11 (*S#4599h).
ver. 12. Ps 42:1. 63:1. Ec 2:6. Is 12:3h. Re 21:6. **of**
gardens. ver. 12, 16. SS 5:1. 6:2. **a well.** Heb. *be-er,*
Ge +16:14. Ge 14:10. 21:19. Ps 36:8, 9. 46:4. Jn 4:10,
14. Re 22:1. **living waters.** Ge 26:19. Le 14:5, 6, 51,
52. 15:13. Nu 19:17. Pr 5:15, 16. Is 58:11. Je 2:13.
17:13. Zc 14:8. Jn 4:14. 7:37, 38. **streams.** Ge 2:10.
Ex 15:8. Ps 78:16. Is 32:2. Je 18:13, 14. Ezk 47:1-10.
Jl 3:18. Ja 1:17. Re 22:1.

16. **Awake.** SS 1:4. Jg 5:12. Ps 7:6. Ec 1:6. Is 51:9-
11. 64:1. Ezk 37:9. Jn 3:8. Ac 2:1, 2. 4:31. **north wind.**

Pr 25:23. **south.** Ex 26:18, 35. 27:9. 36:23. **blow.** Ge
1:2. Ezk 37:9. Zc 4:6. Jn 3:8. 6:63. 14:26. Ac 9:31.
1 C 12:11. **garden.** ver. 12, 15. SS 5:1. 6:2. **the spices.**
ver. 13, 14. SS 7:12, 13. Ps 45:8. 133:1, 2. 2 C 9:10-
15. Ph 1:9-11. Col 1:9-12. 1 Th 2:12, 13. He 13:20,
21. 2 P ✓3:18. **may flow.** Nu 24:7. Dt 32:2. **Let.** SS
5:1. 8:12. Mt 25:14-30. 26:10, 12. Jn 15:8. Ro 15:16,
28. 1 P 2:5, 9, 10. **his garden.** Lk 13:6-9. **pleasant**
fruits. ver. 13. SS *7:13. Dt 33:13-16. Ps 23:3. 119:67.
Pr 31:11. Is 42:3. Lk 4:18. 2 C 7:11. Ga 5:22, 23. He
12:11.

SONG OF SOLOMON 5

Christ visits his garden, expresses his delight in it,
and invites his friends to feast with him, 1. The spouse
relates her drowsiness and vain excuses when visited
by her Beloved; and that he was withdrawn when she
arose to open to him, 2-6. The hard usage she met
with from the watchmen, 7. She charges her compan-
ions to inform her Beloved that she was sick of love,
8. They inquire after her Beloved; and she describes
his manifold excellences, 9-16.

1. **come.** SS 4:16. 6:2, 11. 8:13. Is 5:1. 33:17. 45:19.
51:3. 58:11. 61:11. 66:14. Hg 2:7. Jn *10:10. 14:21-
23. Re 3:11. **my sister.** SS 4:9-12. 8:1. Mt 15:28. He
2:12-14. **I have gathered.** SS 4:13, 14. Ps 80:12h.
147:11. Is 53:11. **myrrh.** ver. 5, 13. SS 1:13. 3:6. 4:6.
honey. SS 4:11. Ge 43:11. Ex 3:8. 1 S 14:27. **wine.**
Pr 9:5. **eat.** Dt 16:13-17. 26:10-14. 2 Ch 31:6-10. Ps
16:3. Is 23:18. 55:1, 2. 62:8, 9. 65:13. 66:14. Mt 25:40.
Jn 6:53-57. Ac 11:29. 2 C 9:11-15. Ep *5:18. 1 Th
3:8, 9. **O friends.** Jg 14:20. Ps 23:5. Lk 12:4. 15:6, 7,
9, 10. Mt 9:15. Jn 3:29. 15:14, 15. Re 19:9. **drink.**
Mt 5:6. Jn 1:16. **yea, drink abundantly, O beloved.**
or, and be drunken with loves. Pr 7:18. Zc 9:15-17.
Ro 14:17. Ph 4:19. 2 P *1:11. Re 22:17.

2. **sleep.** SS 3:1. 7:9. Da 8:18. Zc 4:1. Mt 25:4, 5.
26:40, 41. Lk 9:32. Ro 13:11. Ep 5:14. 1 Th 5:6. He
6:12. 1 P 1:13. **but.** Ro 7:21:23. Ga 5:17. He 12:1.
the voice. SS 2:8, 10. Ps 119:50. Jn 5:28, 29. 10:+*4,
27. **knocketh.** Re *3:20. **Open.** Ps 24:7-10. 81:10. Pr
23:26. **my dove.** SS 2:14. 6:9. Ps 119:1. Re 3:4. 14:4.
my head. SS 8:7. Ge 29:20. 31:40, 41. Is 50:6. 52:14.
53:3-5. Mt 8:17. 25:35-45. Mk 1:35. Lk 6:12. 22:44.
2 C 5:14, 15. Ga *2:20.

3. **have put.** Pr 3:28. 13:4. 22:13. Mt 25:5. 26:38-
43. Lk ✓11:7. Ro 7:22, 23. **I have washed.** Ge 18:4.
19:2. 24:32. 43:24. Ex 29:+4, 17. 30:19n, 21n. 40:31.
Jg 19:21. 1 S 25:41. 2 S 11:8. Lk 7:38, +44n. Jn 13:5.
1 T 5:10. As the Orientals only wear sandals, they
are obliged to wash their feet previously to their lying
down. Hence a Hindoo, if called from his bed, often
makes his excuse that he shall daub his feet. **how shall.**
Ps 123:4. Is 32:9. Is 47:8. 64:7. Am 6:1. Zp 1:12. Mt
22:5. Mt 24:12. Lk 9:59. ✓14:18-20.

4. **put.** SS 1:4. Ps 38:2. 44:21. 110:3. Ac 16:14.
2 C 8:1, 2, 16. Ph 2:13. **hole.** or, network. 1 S 14:11.
2 K 12:9. Ezk 8:7. **my bowels.** Ge 15:4. 25:23. 43:30.
1 K 3:26. Is 26:8, 9. Lk 22:61, 62. 1 J 3:16, 17. **were**
moved. Ps 46:6. Je *31:20. 51:55. Zc 9:15. **for him.**
or, (as some read,) in me.

5. **rose.** ver. 2. Ps 119:59. Lk 12:36. Ep 3:17. Ph
1:6. 2:13. Re *3:20. **open.** Dt 15:8, 11. Ne 8:5. **my**
hands. ver. 13. SS 3:6. 4:13, 14. 2 C 7:7, 9-11. **sweet**
smelling. Heb. passing, *or* running about. **myrrh.** Ps
45:8.

6. **but my.** Ps 30:7. Is 8:17. 12:1. 50:2. 54:6-8. Ho 5:6, 15. Mt 15:22-28. Re 3:19. **withdrawn.** Jb 29:2, 3. **my soul.** Heb. *nephesh*, Ge +34:3. ver. 2, 4. Ge 42:28. 2 S 16:10. Ps 69:3. 77:3. Is 57:16. Mt 26:75. Mk 14:72. Lk 22:61, 62. **I sought.** SS 3:1, 2. 1 S 28:6. Jb 23:3-9. Ps 22:1, 2. 28:1. 80:4. 88:9-14. Is 26:9. 58:2-4, 7-9. La 3:8. Zc 7:13. **not find.** Je 2:17. **I called.** Ps 143:7. **no answer.** Jb 30:20. La *3:8, 44.

7. **watchmen.** SS 3:3. Is 56:10, 11. 62:6. Ezk 3:17. Ho 9:7, 8. Ac 20:29, 30. 2 C 11:13. He 10:25. **they smote.** Ps *141:5. Pr 9:8. Ho 6:5. Jn 16:2. Ac 26:9, 10. 2 C 7:10. Ga 2:11. Ph 3:6. 1 T 5:20, 21. T 1:13. 2:15. Ja 5:16. 1 P 1:6, 7. Re 3:19. 17:5, 6. **the keepers.** SS 8:11. Is 62:6. Mt 21:33-41. 23:2, 29-36. He 13:17. **took away.** Lk 6:22. Ac 5:40, 41. 1 C 4:10-13. He 11:36, 37. 12:2. 1 P 4:14-16. or, lifted up. Ge 13:6 (bear). 18:26 (spare). 19:21 (accepted). Ex 6:8mg. Ezr 9:2. Ps 123:1. Is 5:26. **veil.** Is 3:23.

8. **charge.** See on SS 2:7. 3:5. 8:4. Ro 15:30. **daughters of Jerusalem.** ver. 16. SS 1:5. 2:7. 3:5, 10. 8:4. **if ye.** Ge 32:36. Ro 15:30. Ga 6:1, 2. Ja 5:16. **that ye.** Heb. what ye. Ps 42:1-3. 63:1-3. 77:1-3. 119:81-83. Pr 13:12.

9. **What is.** Is 53:2. Mt 16:13-17. 21:10. Jn 1:14, 46. 7:41-43. 2 C 4:3-6. **O thou.** SS 1:8, 15. 6:1, 9, 10. Ps 45:13. 87:3.

10. **beloved.** SS 2:1. Dt 32:31. Ps 45:17. Is 66:19. He 7:26. **white.** or, clear. Is 18:4. 32:4. Je 4:11. La 4:7. Da 7:9. Mt 17:2. Re 1:14. **ruddy.** Ge 25:30. Nu 19:2. 1 S +16:12. 17:42. **the chiefest.** Heb. a standard bearer. SS 6:4, 10. Ps 45:2, 7. 73:25. 89:6. Is 10:18. 59:19. Mt 13:46. Mk 10:44. Jn 6:68. Ro 8:29. √9:5. Ph *2:9-11. Col *1:15-18. T *2:13. He 1:2. +*2:10. 4:14. 7:26. 13:20. 1 P 2:6. 5:4. Re 1:5, 8. **ten thousand.** Ge 24:60. Le 26:8. 2 S 18:3. Ec 7:28.

11. **head.** Da 2:37, 38. 1 C 11:3. Ep 1:21, 22. Col 1:18. **his locks.** Ps 7:5. Da 7:9. Re 1:14. **bushy.** or, curled.

12. **His eyes.** Rather, "His eyes are as doves"—the deep blue pigeon, the common dove in the East, whose brilliant plumage vibrates around his neck every sparkling hue, every dazzling flash of color. This pigeon, standing amid "the torrents of water," or the foam of a waterfall, would be a blue center with a bright space, like the iris of the eye, surrounded by the white. SS 1:15. 4:1. 2 Ch 16:9. Ps 32:8. Pr 15:3. He 4:13. **fitly set.** Heb. sitting in fulness, that is, *fitly placed*, and set as a precious stone in the foil of a ring.

13. **cheeks.** SS 1:10. Is 50:6. **as a.** Ps 4:6, 7. 27:4. 89:15. Re 21:23. **sweet flowers.** or, towers of perfumes. SS 3:6. **his lips.** SS 4:11. Ps *45:2. 85:8. 89:15. Pr 8:6-10. Is 50:4. Lk 4:22. Jn 6:63. **dropping.** ver. 5.

14. **hands.** Ex 15:6. Jb 10:8. Ps 31:5. 45:4-7. 99:4. 104:24. 139:9, 10. 145:15, 16. Is 9:7. 49:16. 52:13. Mt 14:31. 2 T 1:12. 1 P 4:19. **his belly.** SS 7:2. Ex 24:10. Is 54:11. Ezk 1:26-28.

15. **legs.** Re 1:15. **pillars.** Dt 32:4. Ps 75:3. 80:17. Pr 8:22, 23. **sockets.** Ex 26:19. **his countenance.** SS 2:14. Nu *6:25, 26. Jg 13:6. Ps 4:6. 31:16. 44:3. Mt 17:2. 28:3. Ac 2:28. Re 1:16. **as Lebanon.** SS 4:11. Ps 92:12. Ho 14:7. Zc 9:17. 1 T 3:16.

16. **mouth.** Heb. palate. SS 1:2. 2:3mg. Jb +31:30mg. Ps 19:10. 119:103mg. Je *15:16. Jn 7:46. **most.** SS 1:16. 2:1, 3. Ps 45:2. 89:6. 148:13. Is 9:6, 7. Ph 3:8. 1 P 2:6, 7. **altogether lovely.** Ge=39:6. Ps 8:9. 24:10. 34:2. Col 2:9. **my beloved.** SS 2:16. 6:3.

Ps 73:25. Jn 6:68. Ga *2:20. **friend.** Pr 17:17. 18:24. Je 3:20mg. Ho 3:1. Jn *15:14, 15. He 2:11. Ja 2:23. 4:4.

SONG OF SOLOMON 6

The daughters of Jerusalem purpose to seek Christ: the spouse answers them, and professes her faith in him, 1-3. Christ repeats his commendations, declares his fervent love, shows his conduct, and describes her character, 4-13.

1. **O thou.** ver. 4, 9, 10. SS 1:8. 2:2. 5:9. **that.** SS 1:4. Ru 1:16, 17. 2:12. Is 2:5. Je 14:8. Zc 8:21-23. Jn 6:24. Ac 5:11-14. **seek him.** Pr 8:17. La 3:25. Mt 7:7, 8. Jn 20:15, 16. Ro 10:6, 8. He √11:6.

2. **gone.** ver. 11. SS 4:12-16. 5:1. Ec 2:5. Is 58:11. 61:11. Mt 18:20. 28:20. **the beds.** SS 5:13. **feed.** SS 1:7, 8. Is 40:11. Ezk 34:23. Zp 3:17. Jn 4:34, 35. Re 7:17. **and to gather.** SS 2:2. Is 57:1. Mk 4:29. Jn 14:3. 17:24. Ph 1:21-23. 1 Th 4:13, 14. Re 14:15.

3. **my beloved's.** SS 2:16. 7:10. Ps 23:1. 63:1. La 3:24. Lk 1:46, 47. Jn √20:28. He 8:10. Re 21:2-4. **he feedeth.** SS 2:2, 16.

4. **beautiful.** ver. 10. SS 2:14. 4:7. 5:2. Ezk 16:13, 14. Ep 5:27. **as Tirzah.** Nu +26:33. Jsh 12:24. 1 K 14:17. 15:21, 33. 16:8, 15, 23. **comely.** Ps 48:2, 13. La 2:15. Re 21:2. **as Jerusalem.** Ps 50:2. 122:3. 125:2. Lk 12:22. **terrible.** ver. 10. SS 4:4. Nu 24:5-9. Ps 144:4-8. Zc 12:3. 2 C 10:4. Re 19:14-16.

5. **away.** SS 4:9. Ge 32:26-28. Ex 32:10. Ps 25:15. 123:2. Je 15:1. Mt 15:27, 28. **overcome me.** or, puffed me up. Ge 32:28. Ps 138:3. Pr 8:31. Ho 12:4. Lk 24:29. Ja 5:16. **thy.** SS 4:1-3.

6. **teeth.** SS +*4:2. Mt 21:19. 25:30. Lk 12:32.

7. **a piece.** SS 4:3.

8. **are.** Ge +4:19. **threescore.** SS 3:7. Ge 5:15, 18, 20. 1 K 11:1. 2 Ch 11:21. Ps 45:14. Re 7:9. **queens.** ver. 9. 1 K 10:1, 4, 10. **fourscore.** Ge 5:25, 26, 28. 16:16. **concubines.** ver. 9. Ge 22:24. 1 K 11:1, 3. 1 Ch +2:48. **virgins.** SS 1:3. Ge +24:43. Ex 2:8. **without number.** Ge 34:30.

9. **My dove.** SS 2:14. 5:2. **but one.** Ge 2:23. Mt 19:4-6. Jn 10:16. 17:22. 1 C 15:48. Ep 4:4. 1 T 3:2. **only one.** Nu 23:9. Ps 45:9. Ga 4:26. Ep 4:3-6. **the choice.** Pr 31:29. **The daughters.** Dt 4:6, 7. 33:29. Ps 45:12-15. 126:2. Pr 31:28, 29. 2 Th 1:10. Re 21:9, 10. **praised her.** Pr 31:10-31. Re 21:26.

10. **Who.** SS 3:6. 8:5. Is 63:1. Re 21:10, 11. **looketh.** 2 S 23:4. Jb 11:17. Pr 4:18. Is 58:8. Ho 6:5. 2 C *3:18. Ph 2:16. Re 22:16. **morning.** 2 S 23:4. Jn 17:22. **fair.** Jb 31:26. Ep 5:27. **moon.** Ge 1:16. **clear.** Ps 14:5. Pr *4:18. Ml 4:2. Mt 13:43. 17:2. Re 10:1. 12:1. 21:23. 22:5. **the sun.** 2 P 1:19. Re 12:1. **terrible.** ver. 4. Ro 8:37.

11. **the garden.** ver. 2. SS 4:12-16. 5:1. Ge 2:9. Ps 1:3. 92:12-15. Jn 15:16. **to see the.** SS 7:12. Is 5:2-4. Mk 11:13. Lk 13:7. Ac 15:36. **fruits.** Mk 4:28, 29. Jn 15:5. 1 P 3:4.

12. **Or ever I was aware.** Heb. I knew not. **my soul.** Heb. *nephesh*, Ge +34:3. Le +26:11n. Je 31:18-20. Ho 11:8, 9. Lk 15:20. **made me like the chariots of Amminadib.** or, set me on the chariots of my willing people. Ge 41:43. 46:29. Ps 110:3. Is 6:8. Ho 2:1. Ac 9:6.

13. **return.** SS 2:14. Je 3:12-14, 22. Ho 14:1-4. **Shulamite.** i.e. *complete, having peace; the perfect, the*

peaceful; that recompenses, *S#7759h. **What.** SS 1:6. Lk 7:44. 15:10. 2 Th 1:10. **see in.** Ac 4:13. **Shulamite.** Ge 49:10. Ps 76:2. Is 8:6. Jn 9:7. He 7:2. **As.** Jn 10:16. Ro 3:29. Ep 2:14-17. **two armies.** *or,* Mahanaim. Ge 32:2. Ps 34:7. Ro 7:23. Ga 5:17. Ep 6:10-19.

SONG OF SOLOMON 7

The church commended under various similitudes, 1-5. Christ expresses his love to her and delights in her company, 6-9. The church expresses her delight in him, and seeks more intimate communion with him, 10-13.

1. **thy feet.** Ex 12:11. Is 52:7. Lk 15:22. Ep 6:15. Ph 1:27. **with shoes.** Dt 33:25. **O prince's.** 1 S 2:8. Ps 45:13. Lk 8:48. Ro 8:17. 2 C *6:17, 18. 1 J 3:1. Re 21:7. **the joints.** Da 2:32. Ep 4:15, 16. Col 2:19. **the work.** Ex 28:15. 35:35.

2. **navel.** Pr 3:8. **goblet.** Ex 24:6. Ps 23:5. Is 22:24. **wanteth not.** Dt 33:23. Ps 23:5. 34:9, 10. **liquor.** Heb. mixture. **thy belly.** SS 5:14. Ps 45:16. Is 46:3. Je 1:5. Ro 7:4. **wheat.** Ps 147:14. Mt 3:12. 13:30.

3. **Thy two.** SS 4:5. 6:6.

4. **neck.** SS 1:10. 4:4. **ivory.** SS 5:14. 1 K 10:18, 22. 22:39. Ps 45:8. 144:12. **thine eyes.** That is, "Thine eyes are dark, deep, clear, and serene, as the fishpools in Heshbon." SS 4:1, 9. 6:5. Ep 1:17, 18. 3:18, 19. **Heshbon.** Nu 21:25. Is 15:4. **gate.** Ge +14:7. 19:1. 22:17. 23:10. **Bath-rabbim.** i.e. *daughter of many* (a village dependent on a city, Nu +21:25mg), *S#1337h. **thy nose.** That is, "Thy nose is as finely formed as the tower of Lebanon." Ph 1:9, 10. He 5:14. **the tower.** SS 4:8. 5:15. 1 K 7:2. 9:19. 2 Ch 8:6. **Damascus.** Ge 15:2. 2 S 8:6.

5. **head.** Is 35:2. Ep 1:22. 4:15, 16. Col 1:18. 2:19. **Carmel.** *or,* crimson. Is 35:2. Mi 7:14. **the hair.** SS 4:1. 5:11. Re 1:14. **the king.** Ge 32:26. Ps 68:24. 87:2. Mt *18:20. 28:20. **held.** Heb. bound. Ge 32:26. Ex 32:10, 11, 14. Re 21:3. **galleries.** SS 1:17mg. Ge 30:38, 41. Ex 2:16.

6. **fair.** ver. 10. SS 1:15, 16. 2:14. 4:7, 10. Ge 12:11, 14. *24:16. *29:17. Dt 21:11. 2 S 13:1. 14:27. 1 K 1:3, 4. Est *2:7. Jb 42:15. Ps 45:11. Is 62:4, 5. Am 8:13. Zp 3:17. **pleasant.** Ge 49:15. 2 S 1:26. **O love.** Ac 20:28. Ep 5:32. Re 21:9. **delights.** Ps 104:31. Pr 19:10. Ec 2:8. Mi 1:16. 2:9. Zp 3:17.

7. **thy stature.** Ps 92:12. Je 10:5. Ep 4:13. He 6:1. **thy breasts.** ver. 3, 8. SS 1:13. 4:5. 8:8. Is 66:10, 11. Ep 3:17-19. **clusters.** Re 7:9.

8. **I will go.** SS 4:16. 5:1. Je 32:41. Jn 14:21-23. **the vine.** Jn 15:1-5. **the smell.** SS 1:3. 2:3. 2 C 2:14.

9. **the roof.** SS 2:3mg, 14. 5:16mg. Jb 6:30mg. Pr 16:24. Ep 4:29. Col 3:16, 17. 4:6. He 13:15. **thy mouth.** Nu 12:6. 24:2-4. Jb 33:14-17. Je √23:28, 29. 2 C 12:1-4. **the best wine.** Is 62:8, 9. Zc 9:15-17. Jn 2:10. Ac 2:11-13, 46, 47. 4:31, 32. 16:30-34. Ep *5:18, 19. 2 P *1:21. **that goeth.** Ge 2:4. 13:5. 15:2. Pr 23:31. **sweetly.** Heb. straightly. SS 1:4mg. 1 Ch 29:17. Pr 23:31. **those that are asleep.** *or,* the ancient. SS 5:2. 1 S 26:7, 12. 1 K 3:20. Ro 13:11. 1 Th 4:13, 14. Re 14:13.

10. **my.** SS 2:16. 6:3. Ps 116:16. 119:94, 125. Ac 27:23. 1 C *6:19, 20. Ga *2:20. 2 T *1:12. **his desire.** ver. 5, 6. Jb 14:15. Ps 45:11. 147:11. Is 26:8. Lk 22:15. Jn 15:9. 17:24. Ro *8:38, 39. Ep 2:4. 1 J 4:16-19.

11. **let us go.** SS 1:4. 2:10-13. 4:8.

12. **get.** Pr 8:17. Ec 9:10. Mk +1:35. 6:31. **let us see.** SS 6:11. Pr 24:30, 31. Ac 15:36. 2 C *13:5. 1 Th 3:5, 6. He *12:15. **the tender.** SS 2:13, 15. Is 18:5. **appear. open.** Jb 12:18. 30:11. 39:5. Mk 4:28. 2 P *1:8. **there will I give thee.** ver. 6. SS 4:16. Ex 25:22. Ps 43:4. 63:3-8. 73:25. 122:5. Pr 8:17. Ezk 20:40, 41. Mk 10:13, 14, 16. Ro 5:11. 2 C *5:14, 15. Ep 6:24. He 4:16.

13. **mandrakes.** Ge 30:14-16. Je 24:1. **at our.** SS 4:16. 5:1. Jn 15:8. Ga 5:22, 23. Ep 5:9. Ph 1:11. **new.** Mt 13:52. **I have.** 1 Ch 28:12. Ps *16:11. 36:8. Is 23:18. 60:6, 7. Mt 6:20. 25:40. Ro 15:25-27. 1 C *2:9, 10. 16:2. 2 C 8:8, 9. Col 3:17. 1 P 4:11. Re 22:14.

SONG OF SOLOMON 8

The spouse desires to be instructed by her Beloved and to have near communion with him; and charges the virgins not to disturb him, 1-4. She is beheld with admiration, as "coming up from the wilderness leaning on her Beloved," 5. She owns her obligations, desires to continue in his love; and shows the strength and vehemency of love and jealousy, 6, 7. The calling of the Gentiles requested and foretold, 8-10. Solomon's vineyard and its fruits, 11, 12. The concluding words of Christ and of the spouse, 13, 14.

1. **that thou.** Is 7:14. 9:6. Hg 2:7. Zc 9:9. Ml 3:1. Mt 13:16, 17. Lk 2:26-32, 38. 10:23, 24. 1 T 3:16. He 2:11, 12. **my brother.** Pr 17:17. 18:24. Jn 1:14. He 2:17. 4:15, 16. **sucked.** Is 66:11, 12. Ga 4:26. **find thee.** Ps 63:1-5. Jn 1:14. 3:13. 8:42. 13:3. 16:28. He 2:9-14. 9:26-28. **I would.** SS 1:2. Ps 2:12. 45:10, 11. Lk 7:45-48. 9:26. 12:8. Jn 7:46-52. 9:25-38. Ga 6:14. Ph 3:3, 7, 8. **yea.** Ps 51:17. 102:16, 17. Mk 12:42-44. 14:6-9. **I should not be despised.** Heb. they should not despise me. Is 60:14. Lk 10:16. 18:9. 1 C 1:28.

2. **bring.** SS 3:4. Ga 4:26. **who.** Lk 16:29-31. Jn √5:39, 46, 47. Ac √17:11, 12. 2 T √3:15. 1 P *1:10-12. 2 P *1:19. Re 19:10. **instruct.** Mt 10:20. Lk 12:12. Jn 14:26. 16:13. Ac 6:5, 6. **I would cause.** SS 4:10-16. 5:1. 7:9, 12. **spiced.** Pr 9:2.

3. **left hand.** SS 2:6. Ge 13:9. Dt 33:27. Is 62:4, 5. 2 C 12:9. **under.** Dt 33:27. Ps 145:14. **right hand.** Ps 63:7, 8. **embrace.** SS 2:6. Ge 29:13. 33:4. Ps 55:22.

4. **charge.** SS 2:7. 3:5. 5:8, 9. **daughters of Jerusalem.** SS 1:5. 2:7. 3:5, 10. **that ye stir not up.** SS 2:7. 3:5. Pr 10:12. **nor awake.** Heb. why should ye stir up, *or,* why awake, etc. SS 2:7. 3:5. Dt 32:11. **love.** ver. 6, 7. SS 2:4, 5, 7. 3:5. **he please.** or, she please. SS 2:7. 3:5. Dt 25:7.

5. **Who is this.** SS 3:6. 6:10. Ge 24:65. **cometh up.** Dt 33:2. Ps 50:5. Zc 14:5. 1 C 15:52. 1 Th 3:13. 2 Th 1:10. Ju 14. Re 21:9. **from the wilderness.** SS 3:6. 4:8. Ge 14:6. 16:7. Ps 45:10, 11. 107:2-8. Is 40:3. 43:19. Je *2:2. Ho 2:14. Ac 7:38. Re 12:6. **leaning.** 2 Ch 32:8mg. Ps 63:8. Is 26:3, 4. 36:6. Mi 3:11. Jn 13:23. Ac 27:23-25. 2 C 12:9, 10. Ep 1:12, 13. 1 P 1:21. **I raised.** SS 2:3. Ho 12:4. Jn 1:48-51. **there she.** ver. 1. SS 3:4, 11. Is 49:20-23. Ro 7:4. Ga 4:19.

6. **as a seal.** Ge 28:9-12, 21, 29, 30. Is *49:16. Je 22:24. Hg 2:23. Zc 3:9. 2 C 1:22. Ep +*1:13. +*4:30. 2 T *2:19. **upon thine heart.** Ex 28:30. Pr 23:26. **love.** SS 5:8. Ps 42:1, 2. 63:1. 84:2. Jn 21:15-19. Ac 20:24. 21:13. 2 C 5:14, 15. Ph 1:20-23. Re 12:11. **is strong.** Ro *8:35, 38, 39. **jealousy.** Ex 20:5. 34:14. Nu 5:14.

25:11. Dt 32:21. Pr 6:34. Na 1:2. 2 C 11:2. **cruel.** Heb. hard. Pr 27:4mg. **grave.** Heb. *sheol,* Ge +37:35. **coals.** Dt 32:24. Jb 5:7. Ps 120:4. Pr 25:22. Ro 12:20. **of fire.** Ge 15:17. 19:24. 22:6, 7. **which hath.** ℐ63K, Ge +37:13. **vehement.** ℐ24L, Ge +6:2. **flame.** Le 6:13.

7. **Many waters.** Ps 93:4. Is 43:2. Mt 7:24, 25. Ro 8:28-39. **quench.** Ezk 32:7mg. **love.** ver. 4, 6. SS 2:4, 5, 7. 3:10. Je 31:3. Jn *3:16. Ro 5:7, 8. 1 C ch. 13. Ep 2:4. 1 J 4:9, 10. **floods.** Ge 2:10, 13, 14. 15:18. **drown.** Jb 14:19. Ps 69:15mg. **if a man.** Pr 6:31, 35. Ro 13:8-10. **substance.** Ps 44:12. 112:3. 119:14. **be contemned.** or, tread. ver. 1. Pr 6:30. 23:9, 22.

8. **a little.** Ezk 16:46, 55, 56, 61. 23:33. Lk 8:14. Jn 10:16. Ac 15:14-17. Ho 15:9-12. 1 C 3:1, 2. 11:30. He 5:12-14. **she hath.** ver. 10. SS 4:5. 7:3. Ps 147:19, 20. Ac 7:38. Ro 3:1, 2. Ep 2:12. **what.** Ps 2:8. 72:17-19. Is 49:6. 60:1-5, 10, 11. Ac ch. 10. 11:1-18. 16:9. *18:26. 22:21. 26:17, 18. Ro 10:12-15. 14:1. 15:1. Ep 2:13-15, 19-22. 1 Th 2:7. **in the day.** Lk 19:44. 1 P 2:12.

9. **a wall.** SS 2:9. Re 21:12-19. **we will.** Is 58:12. 60:17. 61:4. Zc 6:12-15. Mt 16:18. Ac 15:16. 1 C 3:10-12. Ep 2:20-22. **build upon.** Ph 1:6. Ep 2:19-22. He 6:1. 1 P 2:5. Ju 20. **a door.** Ac 14:27.

10. **a wall.** ver. 9. Ne 12:27-43. Re 21:10-21. **my.** SS 4:5. 7:3, 4, 7, 8. Ezk 16:7. Col 2:7. **then.** Ge 6:8. Dt 7:7, 8. Pr 3:4. Is 60:10. Lk 1:30. Ep 1:6-8. 1 T 1:16. **in his eyes.** Mt 5:48. Lk 6:40. Jn +*17:6. 1 C 11:1. 2 C 13:9. Ph 3:14-17. **favor.** Heb. peace. or,

grace. Ge 15:15. 26:29, 31. Ro 5:1-10. 8:33. 1 C 15:10. 1 J 3:21.

11. **Solomon.** Calmet thus translates these verses: "Solomon has a vineyard at Baal-hamon; he has let it out to keepers, each of whom for the fruit of it was to bring a thousand pieces of silver. As for me, my vineyard is before me; keep thyself, O Solomon, thy thousand pieces of silver," etc. **vineyard.** ver. 12. SS 1:6, 14. 2:15. 4:13, 16. 7:12. Ec 2:4, 5. Is 5:1-7. 27:2, 3. Mt 21:33-43. Mk 12:1-9. Lk 20:9-16. 1 C 9:7. **Baal-hamon.** i.e. *lord of the multitude; place of the sun,* *S#1174h. **he let.** Ps 80:8. Mt 21:33. Lk 20:9, etc. **keepers.** ver. 12. SS 1:6. Na 1:2. **fruit.** ver. 12. SS 2:3. 4:3, 16. Mk 13:34. Lk 19:13. **a thousand.** Ge 20:16. Is 7:23. **silver.** ver. 9. SS 1:11. 3:10.

12. **vineyard.** SS 1:6. Pr 4:23. Ac 20:28. 1 T *4:15, 16. **thou.** Ps 72:17-19. Ro 14:7-9. 1 C 6:20. 2 C 5:15. **those.** 1 Th 2:19, 20. 1 T 5:17, 18.

13. **dwellest.** SS 2:13. 4:16. 6:2, 11. 7:11, 12. Mt *18:20. 28:20. Jn 14:21-23. **the companions.** SS 1:7. 3:7-11. 5:9-16. Jg 11:38. 14:11. Ps 45:14. **voice.** SS 2:14. 1 S 3:9. Ps 29:3. Is 40:2. Ho 2:14. Jn *10:+3, 27. **cause.** SS 2:14. Ps 50:15. Jn 14:13, 14. 15:7. 16:24. **to hear.** Is 30:21. Hab 2:1. Mt 13:9. Re 2:29.

14. **Make haste.** Heb. Flee away. SS 2:17. Ge 16:6, 8. Ps 70:1, 5. Lk 19:12. Ph 1:23. 3:20, 21. 2 P *3:9. Re *22:17, 20. **be thou like.** SS 2:9, 17. **young.** SS 2:9, 17. 4:5. 7:3. **hart.** SS 2:9, 17. Dt 12:15, 22. **spices.** SS 4:10, 14, 16. Ex 25:6.

ISAIAH

ISAIAH 1

The title, 1. God, by his prophet, charges Judah and Jerusalem with base ingratitude and atrocious wickedness; and describes their deplorable condition, 2-9. He shows his abhorrence of their sacrifices, calls them to repentance with promises of forgiveness, and warns them against obstinate rebellion, 10-20. He laments Zion's degeneracy and the iniquity of her princes; denounces severe vengeance; yet intimates a subsequent recovery of the nation to purity and prosperity, 21-31.

1. A.M. 3244. B.C. 760. **vision.** Is 21:2. Nu *12:6. 24:4, 16. 2 Ch 26:22. *32:32. Ps 89:19. Je 23:16. Ezk 1:1. Na 1:1. Hab 2:2. Mt 17:9. Ac 10:17. 26:19. 2 C 12:1. **Isaiah.** i.e. *safety of Jahu* or *a safety (is) Jahu; salvation of the Lord; the salvation of Jehovah,* *S#3470h. 2 K 19:2, 5, 6, 20. 20:1, 4, 7, 8, 9, 11, 14, 16, 19. 2 Ch 26:22. 32:20, 32. Is 1:1. 2:1. 7:3. 13:1. 20:2, 3. 37:2, 5, 6, 21. 38:1, 4, 21. 39:3, 5, 8. See for the same Hebrew name belonging to other persons, rendered "Jesaiah," 1 Ch +3:21; "Jeshaiah," 1 Ch +25:3. **Amoz.** 2 K +19:2. **saw.** Is 2:1. 13:1. 2 P *1:21. **the days.** Is 6:1. 2 Ch ch. 26-32. Ho 1:1. Am 1:1. Mi 1:1. **Uzziah.** 2 K 15:1. 2 Ch +26:1. **Jotham.** Jg +9:5. 2 K 15:32. **Ahaz.** 2 K 16:1. 1 Ch +8:35. **Hezekiah.** 2 K +16:20. 18:1.

2. **Hear.** Dt *4:26. *30:19. 32:1﹀℘. Ps 50:4. Je 2:12. 6:19. 22:29. Ezk 36:4. Mi 1:2. 6:1, 2. This is a reference to the Pentateuch (℘). Such frequent references to the very words of the Pentateuch prove that the books of Moses existed as such in Isaiah's time, contrary to

the popular but very mistaken documentary hypothesis which asserts a later, even post-exilic, and non-mosaic authorship. Other instances of citation of the technical terms of the Pentateuch in Isaiah are noted at Is 1:4, 9, 10, 12, 13, 24, 26. 2:3, 6, 8, 22. 3:7. 4:5. 5:6, 24, 25. 6:6, 8. 7:14, 18. 8:13, 16, 17, 18. 9:13, 15, 20. 10:13, 15, 21, 22. 11:9. 12:2, 3, 5. 13:1, 19. 14:4, 21, 24, 25. 17:6, 8, 10. 18:2. 19:3, 9. 20:3. 21:9. 22:14, 25. 23:3. 24:2, *5, 10, 15, 18. 25:1. 26:4, 8, 17, 21. 29:22. 30:6, 8, 9, 17, 22, 29. 31:1, 5. 32:1, 9. 33:15, 19, 20, 24. 34:11. 35:9. 37:30, 32. 38:11. 39:2. 41:3, 9, 10, 11, 14. 42:4, 8, 16, 17, 20. 43:2, 12, 16, 20. 44:*2, 4, 6, 8. 45:12, 18, 19, 23. 46:3, 8, 11. 47:4, 7. 48:1, 4, 11, 16, 19, 21. 49:23, 24, 26. 50:1, 2. 51:2, 3, 10, 13, 16. 52:4, 12. 53:10, 12. 54:4, 5, 8, 9, 11. 56:2. 57:5, 6. 58:3, 7, 8, 13, 14. 59:19. 60:10, 16. 61:6. 62:8, 9. 63:4, 9, 10, 11, 12, 16, 17, 18. 64:3, 5, 7. 65:1, 3, 4, *6, 16, 21, 23. 66:3, 17, 20, 21, 23. For references to the Pentateuch in the other prophets, see references at Je +1:5; La +1:3; Ezk +1:28; Da +1:2; Ho +1:2; Jl +1:3; Am +1:11; Ob ver. +4; Jon +1:2; Mi +1:2; Na +1:2; Hab +1:5; Zp +1:5; Hg +1:1; Zc +2:6; Ml +1:2. **O heavens.** ℐ38G, Dt +32:1. **for the Lord.** Je 13:15. Am 3:1. Mi 3:8. Ac 4:20. Ro 3:1, 2. 9:4. He 1:1. **I have.** Is 5:1, 2. 46:3, 4. Dt 1:31. 4:7, 8. 7:6. Ps 147:20. Je 31:9. Ezk 16:6-14. 20:5, etc. Ro 3:1, 2. 9:4, 5. He 12:7. **they have.** Is 63:9, 10. Dt 9:22-24. 32:5, 6, 15. Je 2:5-13. Ml 1:6.

3. **ox.** Pr 6:6. Je +*8:7. Ho 11:4. **but Israel.** Is 5:12. 27:11. 44:18. Dt 29:2, 4. 32:28, 29. Ps 94:8. Je 4:22. 9:3-6. 10:8, 14. Mt 13:13-15, 19. Ro *1:28. 2 P 3:5. **know.** ℐ121C2A1, Jb +19:25.

4. **Ah.** *f*59, Ge +28:16. **sinful.** *f*173, Ge +27:44. ver. 23. Is 10:6. 30:9. Ge 13:13. Mt *11:28. Ac 7:51, 52. Re 18:5. **people.** *f*12, Ps +1:1. **laden with iniquity.** Heb. of heaviness. **a seed.** Is 57:3, 4. Nu 32:14. Ps 78:8. Je 7:26. 16:11, 12. Mt 3:7. 23:33. **children.** Je 2:33. Ezk 16:33. **corrupters.** Dt 32:5♪𝒫. **forsaken.** F/L ver. 28. Is 6:12. 7:16. 10:3 (leave), 14 (left). 17:2, 9. 18:6 (left). 27:10. 32:14. 41:17. 49:14. 54:6. 55:7. 58:2. 60:15. 62:4, 12. 65:11. Dt 28:20♪𝒫. 29:25. 31:16♪𝒫. Jg 10:10. Je 2:13, 17, 19. **provoked.** Is 3:8. 65:3. Nu 14:11, 23♪𝒫. 16:30♪𝒫. Dt 31:20♪𝒫. 32:19. Ps 78:40. Je 7:19. 1 C 10:22. **the Holy one of Israel.** F/L Is 5:19, 24. 10:20. 12:6. 17:7. 29:19. 30:11, 12, 15. 31:1. 37:23. 41:14, 16, 20. 43:3, 14. 45:11. 47:4. 48:17. 49:7. 54:5. 55:5. 60:9, 14. 2 K 19:22. Ps 71:22. 78:41. 89:18. Je 50:29. 51:5. Ezk 39:7. **gone away backward.** Heb. alienated, *or* separated. Ps 58:3. Je 2:5, 31. Ro 8:7. 10:21. Col 1:24.

5. **Why should.** *f*38B, 2 S +1:24. Is 9:13, 21. Je 2:30. 5:3. 6:28-30. Ezk 24:13. He 12:5-8. Re 3:17-19. **ye will.** 2 Ch 28:22. Je 9:3. Re 16:8-11. **revolt more and more.** Heb. increase revolt. Je +28:16mg. **the whole.** ver. 23. Ne 9:34. Je 5:5, 31. Da 9:8-11. Zp 3:1-4. **head.** *f*155E1. Personification B867. Things represented as persons, here involving kingdoms, countries, and states, whereby a whole people is represented as an individual man, the whole Jewish nation is elegantly addressed as one man. For other instances of this figure see Is 7:20. 30:28.

6. **From the.** *f*105, Ml +4:2. **the sole.** Dt 28:35. 2 S 14:25. Jb *2:7, 8. Lk 16:20, 21. **no soundness.** Ps 38:7, 8. **bruises.** 2 Ch 6:28, 29. Ps 77:2. Je 6:14mg. 30:12. Na 3:19. **sores.** Lk 16:20. **they have.** Jb 5:18. Ps 38:3-5. Je 6:14. 8:21, 22. 33:6. Ho 5:12, 13. Ml 4:2. Mt 9:12, 13. Lk 10:34. **ointment.** *or*, oil. Is 5:1mg. 10:27 (anointing). 25:6 (fat). 28:1, 4. 39:2. 41:19 (oil tree). 59:9. 61:3. Dt +*33:24.

7. **country.** Is 5:5, 6, 9. 6:11. 24:10-12. Le 26:34. Dt 28:51, 52. 2 Ch 28:5, 16-21. Ps 107:34, 39. Je 6:8. **desolate.** F/L Is 6:11. 17:9. 33:8. 49:8, 19. 54:1, 3. 61:4. 62:4. **burned.** Is 9:5. 34:9. Je 2:15. **strangers.** Is 5:17. Dt 28:33, 43, 48-52. La 5:2. Ezk 30:12. Ho 7:9. 8:7. **as.** *f*160B, Ge +25:31. **overthrown by strangers.** Heb. the overthrow of strangers.

8. **daughter.** *f*155E5, Nu +21:25. Is 4:4. 10:32. 37:22. 62:11. Ps 9:14. La 2:1. Zc 2:10. 9:9. Jn 12:15. **cottage.** Jb 27:18. La 2:6. **besieged.** Is 8:8. 10:32. Je 4:17. Lk 19:43, 44.

9. **left.** La 3:22. Hab 3:2. Ro ♪9:29. **a very.** Is 6:13. 10:22. 17:6. 24:13. 37:4, 31, 32. 1 K 19:18. Ezk 6:8. 14:22. Jl 2:32. Zc 13:8, 9. Mt 7:14. Ro 9:27. 11:4-6. **remnant.** Is +10:21, 22. 11:11. 37:32. Le +23:22. Jb 1:12. Zc 13:9. Jn +6:12. Re ◐6:16, 17. 12:12-17. 13:7. **we should.** Ge 18:26, 32. 19:24. Dt 29:23. La 4:6. Am 4:11. Zp 7:9. Lk 17:29, 30. 2 P 2:6. **as.** *f*160B, Ge +25:31. **Sodom.** Ge 19:1-29♪𝒫. Dt 29:23♪𝒫. **like.** *f*160B, Ge +25:31.

10. **Hear.** 1 K 22:19-23. Am 3:1, 8. Mi 3:8-12. **Sodom.** Ge 13:13. Dt 32:32. Je 9:26. 23:14. Ezk 16:46-48. Am 9:7. Re 11:8. **the law.** A general reference to the whole Pentateuch. Is 2:3. 5:24. 8:16, √20. 24:5. 30:9. 42:4, 21, 24. 51:4, 7.

11. **To what purpose.** *f*105, Ml +4:2. Is 66:3. 1 S *15:22. Ps 50:8, 9. *51:16, 17. Pr *15:8. *21:27. Je 6:20. 7:21. Am *5:21, 22. Mi 6:7. Mt 9:13. **saith the Lord.** F/L Is 1:11, 18. 33:10. 40:1, 25. 41:21, 21. 66:9.

Ps 12:5. **burnt offerings.** Le +23:12. **the fat.** *f*168. Synathroesmos; or, Enumeration B436. The enumeration of the parts of a whole which has not been mentioned. One sentence would have expressed the whole, "your sacrifices are not pleasing to me." But by the figure *Synathroesmus*, all kinds of sacrifices are enumerated, and the sense is thus amplified and emphasized to show that, with all their outward show of "religion," there was no true worship of the spirit and heart. For other instances of this figure see Is 3:16-23. 58:6, 7. Ps 15:2-5. Mi 6:8. Ro 1:29-31. 1 T 4:1-3. 2 T 3:1-7. 1 P 4:3. **he goats.** Heb. great he goats. Is 14:9mg.

12. **When.** Is 58:1, 2. Ex 23:17. 34:23. Dt *16:16. Ec *5:1. Mt 23:5. **to appear.** Heb. be seen. Ex 23:15♪𝒫. 34:20♪𝒫. **required.** Ps 40:6. Mi *6:6-8. **tread.** Ezk 26:11. *34:18. Da 8:7, 10.

13. **Bring no more.** *f*34, Ps +50:16. **vain.** Ezk 20:39. Ml 1:10. Mt 15:9. Lk 11:42. **oblations.** *f*168, ver. +11. **incense.** Is 66:3. Pr 21:27. **the new.** Le ch. 23. Nu ch. 28-29. Dt ch. 16. La 2:6. Jl 1:14. 2:15. **assemblies.** or, convocations. *S#4744h. Is 4:5. Ex 12:16, 16♪𝒫. Le 23:2♪𝒫, 3, 4, 7, 8, 21, 24, 27, 35, 36, 37. Nu 10:2♪𝒫. 28:18, 25, 26. 29:1, 7, 12. Ne 8:8. **cannot.** *f*22D1, Ge +32:28. **away with.** *f*63BA, Ps +21:11. i.e. *I am not able to endure.* Je 44:22. **it is.** 1 C 11:17. Ph 1:15. **iniquity.** or, grief. Ps 78:40. Ep *4:30. **even.** *f*93A, Ge +1:26. "I am not able (to endure) your iniquity and assembly": i.e. *your iniquity, yes—your iniquitous assemblies, or your festal iniquity* (B661). **solemn.** Nu 10:10.

14. **new moons.** 2 Ch +2:4. **appointed feasts.** Ge +17:21h. Le 23:2n. **my soul.** Heb. *nephesh*, Ge +34:3. *f*22A1, Le +26:11n. Is 61:8. Am *5:21. **hateth.** *f*22B, Ex +15:7. **I am weary.** Is 43:24. Ps 50:8, 9. Am 2:13. Zc 11:8. Ml 2:17.

15. **when.** Is 59:2. 1 K 8:22, 54. Ezr 9:5. Jb 27:8, 9, 29. Ps *66:18. 134:2. Pr 1:28. Je 14:12. Ezk 8:17, 18. Mi 3:4. Zc 7:13. Lk 13:25-28. 1 T *2:8. **your hands.** *f*121BA, Dt +32:36. **I will hide.** Is 58:7. Ps 27:9. 30:7. *55:1. 77:7-9. **make many prayers.** Heb. multiply prayer. Mt 6:7. 23:14. **not hear.** Is *59:2. Ps +66:18. Pr 1:28. Mi 3:4. Jn +*9:31. **your hands.** T#734. Is 10:13. Ge 6:11. 2 K 19:11. Ezk +22:29 (T#488). Ezk 33:25, 26. Mi 3:4. Lk 13:25-27. Ro +3:15 (T#701). **full of.** T#1794. Is 59:2, 3. Je 7:8-10. Ezk 7:23-26. Mi 3:9-11. **blood.** Heb. bloods. *f*171112, Le +20:9. Is 26:21mg. Ge +4:10mg. 2 K +*9:26mg.

16. **Wash.** Ge 18:4. 19:2. 2 S 11:8. 2 K *5:13. Jb *11:13, 14. Ps *26:6. Je *4:14. Ac +*22:16. 2 C *7:1. Ja *4:8. Re *7:14. **put away.** Is √55:6, 7. Ezk *18:30, 31. Zc *1:3, 4. Mt *3:8. Ep *4:22-24. T *2:11-14. 1 P *2:1. **mine eyes.** *f*22A6, Ps +11:4. **cease.** Jg 2:19. Ps *34:14. *37:27. Am *5:15. Ro *12:9. Ep *4:25-29. 1 P *3:11.

17. **seek.** ver. 23. Is 58:6. Ps *82:3, 4. Pr 31:9. Je *22:3, 15, 16. Da *4:27. Mi *6:8. Zp 2:3. Zc *7:9, 10. *8:16. Lk 3:8. **relieve.** *or*, righten. Pr 23:19. **judge.** Je 22:3. **fatherless.** ver. 23. Dt +10:18. **plead.** Ps 35:1. **widow.** *f*171I14, Ex +22:22. Ex 22:22. Dt 14:29. 24:17. 26:12. Je 22:3. *49:11. Mt 23:14. Lk 2:37. 4:26. 7:12. 18:3, 5. 21:2, 3. Ac 6:1. 9:39, 41. 1 C 7:8. 1 T 5:3-5, 9, 11, 16. Ja 1:27. Re 18:7.

18. **Come now.** Ps +119:68 (T#224). Pr 1:20-23. Je 22:29. Ezk *33:11. Mi 6:1-3. Mt +14:14 (T#60). Ja +5:11 (T#225). **and let us reason.** lit. "clear up."

It means the putting an end to all reasoning, rather than an invitation to commence reasoning (CB). Is *41:21. 43:24-26. Jsh 20:4. 1 S *12:7. Ec ❍*3:11. Je 2:5. Mi 6:2, 3. Ac +*17:2. *18:4. *24:25. **though your.** T#789. Is *44:22. Ps *51:7. Mi *7:18, 19. Ro *5:20. Ep *1:6-8. Re *7:14. **sins.** ♪121N2, Ge +34:29. As it is the sinner himself who is made "whiter than snow" (Ps 51:7), it may be that "sins" is here put for *sinners*, for it is not easy to think of "sins," as such, becoming white, for certainly persons are spoken of. **as scarlet.** ♪170. Syncrisis; or, Repeated Simile B734. The repetition of a number of resemblances, note here "as scarlet," "as white as snow," "like crimson," "as wool." For other instances of this figure see Is *24:2. 32:2. 66:12. **they shall be.** Ps 51:7. **snow.** 2 K +5:27.

19. **If.** Ge 4:7. **willing.** Is 3:10. 55:1-3, 6, 7. Je 3:12-14. 31:18-20. Ho 14:1-4. Jl 2:26. Mt 21:28-32. **obedient.** Lk ✓6:46. Jn 3:36. +*13:17. He *5:9.

20. **if.** Ge +4:7. **ye refuse.** Is 3:11. 1 S 12:25. 2 Ch 36:14-16. He *2:1-3. **sword.** ♪121B, Ex +5:3. **for the mouth.** F/L Is +21:17. 40:5. 58:14. Le 26:33. Nu *23:19. 1 S 15:29. T *1:2.

21. **How.** ♪85P, Ge +27:46. **the faithful.** Is 48:2. Ne 11:1, 18. Ps 46:4. 48:1, 8. Ho 11:12. Zc 8:3. He 12:22. **become.** Ps 73:23. Je 2:20, 21. 3:1. La 1:8, 9. Ezk ch. 16, 22, 23. Lk 13:34. Re 11:2, 8. **harlot.** ♪155E3, Is +32:9. **it was full.** Is 5:7. 2 S 8:15. 1 K 3:28. 2 Ch 19:9. Ezk 22:3-7. Mi 3:2, 3. Zp 3:1-3. **lodged.** ♪171J7, Ps +49:12. **but now.** Ac 7:52. ♪31. Antithesis; or, Contrast B715. A setting of one phrase in contrast with another. It is a figure by which two thoughts, ideas, or phrases, are set over one against the other, in order to make the contrast more striking, and thus to emphasize it. When this contrast consists of *words* rather than of sentences, it is called *Epanados* (♪68, Ex +9:31) and *Antimetabole* (♪25, Ge +4:4). For other instances of Antithesis see Is 59:9. 65:13, 14. La 1:1. Lk 2:14. Ro 5:18, 19. 6:7, 8. 8:5, 13. 15:12. 2 C 4:17, 18. 6:8-10. Ph 3:7. 2 P 2:19.

22. **silver.** Je 6:28-30. La 4:1, 2. Ezk 22:18-22. Ho 6:4. **wine.** Pr 6:17. Ho 4:18. 2 C 2:17. Re 14:10.

23. **Thy princes.** ♪95, Ps +7:13. Is 3:14. 2 K 17:9-11. 2 Ch 24:17-21. 28:22. 36:14. Je 5:5. Ezk 22:6-12. Da 9:5, 6. Ho 7:3-5. 9:15. Mi 3:1-3, 11. Ac 4:5-11. **companions.** Pr 29:24. Mt 21:13. Mk 11:17. Lk 19:46. **every.** Is 33:15. Ex 23:8. Dt 16:19. Pr 17:23. Je 22:17. Ezk 22:12. Ho 4:18. Mi 7:3. **they judge not.** Is 10:1, 2. Je 5:28, 29. Zc 7:10. Ml +*3:5. Lk 18:2-5. **widow.** ♪171I14, Ex +22:22.

24. **the mighty One of Israel.** Is 30:29. 49:26. 60:16. Ge 49:24♪℗. Je 50:34. Re 18:8. **Ah.** Dt *28:63. 32:43. 2 K 15:37. Pr 1:25, 26. Ezk 5:13. 16:42. 21:17. He 10:13. **avenge.** ♪22B, Ex +15:7. Dt 32:41. Jg 16:28.

25. **And I.** Zc 13:7-9. Re 3:19. **turn.** Ps 81:14. Am 1:8. **hand.** ♪22A14.8G. Anthropomorphism B880. A hand is attributed to God in the idiomatic expression "to turn the hand upon," meaning to repeat the punishment. For other instances of this figure see Ps 81:14. Am 1:8. Zc 13:7. **purely.** Heb. according to pureness. 2 S 22:21, 25. Jb 9:30. 22:30. Ps 18:20, 24. **purge.** ver. 22. Is *4:4. 6:11-13. Je 6:29. 9:7. Ezk 20:38. Zp 3:11. Ml 3:3. Mt 3:12. **thy dross.** Nu 31:22, 23. Ps 66:10. Ezk *22:18-22. Zc *13:9. 1 C *3:13, 15.

26. **And I will.** Is *32:1, 2. *60:17, 18. Nu *12:3. *16:15. 1 S *12:2-5. Je *33:7, 15-17. Ezk *34:23, 24. *37:24, 25. *45:8. **judges.** Ex 18:16-26♪℗. Nu 25:5♪℗.

Dt 1:16♪℗. 16:18♪℗. 19:17-19♪℗. 21:2♪℗. **afterward.** Is 59:20, 21. Ezk +*38:8, 16. Da +*9:24n. Zc 12:10. 13:1. **thou shalt.** ver. *21. Is +*60:21. 62:1. Je 31:23. Zp *3:9, 13. Zc *8:3, 8. Re *21:27. **righteousness.** Da +*9:24n.

27. **redeemed.** Is 5:16. 10:21. 45:21-25. Ro *3:24-26. 11:26, 27. 2 C ✓5:21. Ep 1:7, 8. T 2:14. 1 P 1:18, 19. **with judgment.** Re 3:19. **her converts.** or, they that return of her. 1 C *1:30.

28. **the destruction.** Heb. the breaking. Is 15:5mg. +51:19mg. Jb 31:3. Ps 1:6. 5:6. 37:38. 73:27. 92:9. *104:35. 125:5. Pr *29:1. Lk 12:45, 46. 1 Th 5:3. 2 Th ✓1:8, 9. 2 P 3:7. Re *21:8. **they that.** Is 30:13, 14. 50:11. 65:11, 12. 1 S 12:25. 1 K 9:6-9. 1 Ch +*28:9. Zp 1:4-6. Zc 3:9.

29. **ashamed.** Is 30:22. 31:7. 45:16. Dt 16:21. Ezk 16:63. 36:31. Ho 14:3, 8. Ro *6:21. **the oaks.** ♪132D, Ge +19:25. Is 57:5mg. 65:3. 66:17. 2 K +16:4n. +17:10. Ezk 6:13. Ho 4:13. **ye.** ♪96D2. Heterosis of Person B524. The Second Person put for the Third. For other instances of this figure see Is 42:20. Je 29:19. Ga 6:1. **the gardens.** Is 65:3. 66:17. Je 2:20. 3:6. **chosen.** F/L Is 7:15, 16. 14:1. 40:20. 41:8, 9, 24. 43:10. 44:1, 2. 48:10. 49:7. 56:4. 58:5, 6. 65:12. 66:3, 4.

30. **ye shall be.** Is *5:6. Je 17:5, 6. Ezk 17:9, 10, 24. Mt 21:19, 20. **an oak.** Is 6:13. Ezk 6:13. **garden.** Is 58:11. Je 31:12. Ezk 31:4, etc.

31. **the strong.** Ezk 32:21. **as tow.** Is 27:4. 43:17. 50:11. Jg 15:14. Ps 68:1, 2. He 12:29. Re 6:14-17. **the maker of it.** or, his work. **and they.** Is 9:18. *30:33. 34:9, 10. ✓66:24. 2 S 23:6, 7. Ps *37:20. Ezk 20:47, 48. Ml *4:1. Mt 3:10, 12. Mk 9:43-49. Lk 12:5. Re 14:10, 11. 19:20. 20:10, 15. **quench.** Je 4:4. 21:12. Am 5:6. Mt *3:12.

ISAIAH 2

Predictions of the establishment, extent, and peace of Zion, in the days of the Messiah, 1-5; of the rejection of the Jews for their iniquities and idolatries, 6-9; and of divine judgments, which would be employed to humble their pride, cure them of idolatry, and cause them to cease from confidence in man, 10-22.

1. **saw.** Is 1:1. 13:1. Am 1:1. Mi 1:1. 6:9. Hab 1:1.

2. **And it shall.** Mi 4:1-3. **in the last days.** Ge 49:1. Nu 24:14. Jb *19:25. Je 23:20. 30:24. 33:15, 16. 48:47. 49:39. Ezk 38:16. Da 2:28. 10:14. Ho 3:5. Am 9:13-15. Ac *2:17. 2 T *3:1. He 1:2. 2 P 3:3. **the mountain.** Is 30:29. Ps 68:15, 16. Da 2:35, 45. Zc 8:3. Re *20:4. 21:10, etc. **the Lord's house.** Is +*60:13n. Ezk +*37:26. 40:2n. Jl 2:1. Mi 4:1, 2. Zc *1:16. ✓6:12, 13. **established.** or, prepared. Is 16:5. 45:18. 54:14. Ge 41:32mg. Ps 48:8. 57:8mg. **the hills.** Ps 68:15. Zc 14:10. **and all.** *♪171A, Ex +9:6. i.e. many from all nations. ver. 3. Is 11:10. *27:13. 49:6. 60:11, 12. Ps *2:8. *22:27. 72:*8, 17-19. 86:9. Je 3:17. Mi 4:1, 2. Ml 3:12. Re *11:15.

3. **Come ye.** Je 31:6. *50:4, 5. Zc *8:20-23. Lk 24:47. Jn 4:22. Ep 2:13. **up.** ♪180A, Ge +4:20. **he will teach.** Dt 6:1. Ps *25:8, 9. Mt *7:24. Lk +*11:28. Jn ✓7:17. Ac 10:33. Ja *1:25. **paths.** F/L Is 3:12. 26:7, 8. 30:11. 33:8 (highways). Is 40:14. 41:3. out of Zion. Is *24:23. 51:4, 5. Ps 110:2. *122:6. Lk 24:47. Ac ✓1:8. 13:46-48. Ro 10:18. **the law.** Is +1:10n♪℗. **and the word.** ♪164, 1 S +17:7. Here the facts, or premises, are stated (Out of Zion shall, etc.; he shall judge; shall

rebuke; they shall beat their swords into plowshares, etc.), but it is left for us to draw the conclusion as to the marvellous results of this wonder-working word, which going out of Zion shall bring about. That "Word of the Lord" by which the heavens and earth were created shall presently be spoken and bring peace and prosperity to the nations (B166).

4. **And.** ƒ148, Ge +8:22. **he shall judge.** Is 11:3, 4. 1 S 2:10. Ps *82:8. *96:13. 110:6. Jn 16:8-11. Ac √17:31. Re *19:11. **rebuke.** Is 11:4. 37:4. Ge 21:25. **and they shall.** ƒ121S4, 2 K +4:29. Is 9:7. 11:6-9. Ps *46:9. Ho *2:18. Jl 3:10. Mi 4:3. Zc *9:10. **swords.** ƒ121S1, Ge +49:10. By Metonymy of the Adjunct, whereby the sign is put for the thing signified, swords and plowshares, etc., are used for war and peace, of which they were the signs and symbols. Is 1:20. 3:25. 13:15. **plowshares.** ƒ121S1, Ge +49:10. 1 S 13:20, 21. Jl 3:10. Mi 4:3. **pruning hooks.** or, scythes. Is 18:5. Jl 3:10mg. Mi 4:3mg. **neither.** Is 60:17, 18. Ps *72:3-7.

5. **house of Jacob.** F/L ver. 6. Is 8:17. 10:20. 14:1. 29:22. 46:3. 48:1. 58:1. **come ye.** ver. 3. Is 50:10, 11. *60:1, 19. Ps *89:15. Lk *1:79. Jn *12:35, 36. Ro *13:12-14. Ep *5:8. 1 Th 5:5, 6. 1 J *1:7. Re *21:23, 24. **walk.** Is 50:11. Ps 82:5. 1 Th 1:3. 1 J 1:7.

6. **Therefore.** Dt *31:16, 17. 2 Ch 15:2. 24:20. 28:16-19. La 5:20. Ro +√11:1, 2, 20. **from the east.** or, more than the east. Nu 23:7. ƒ171.O.6, 1 K +4:30. **and are.** Is 8:19. 47:12, 13. Ex 22:18. Le *19:31. 20:6. Dt +*18:10-14. 1 Ch 10:13. **soothsayers.** F/L Is 2:6. 57:3 (sorceress). Le 19:26⫾℗. Dt 18:10, 14⫾℗. 2 K +*21:6 (✻S#6049h, observed times). **and they.** Ex 34:16. Nu 25:1, 2. Dt 21:11-13. 1 K 11:1, 2. Ne 13:23. Ps *106:34, 35. Je +√10:2. **please themselves in.** or, abound with, etc. Pr 29:21. or, strike hands. Pr 6:1. Ezk 17:18.

7. **land.** Dt 17:16, 17. 1 K 10:21-27. 2 Ch 9:20-25. 27:5, 6. Je 5:27, 28. Ja 5:1-3. Re 18:3, 11-17. **their land is.** ƒ70, Ex +16:35. Is 30:16. *31:1. Dt 17:16. 1 K 4:26. 10:26. Ps *20:7. Ho 14:3. **horses.** Is 31:1. Mi 5:10. **neither.** ƒ167. Symploce; or, Intertwining B297. The repetition of different words in successive sentences in the same sense. Here, "their land" and "neither" are repeated in verses 7 and 8. For other instances of this figure see Is 65:13, 14. Je 9:23. 1 C 12:4, 5, 6. 14:15. 15:42-44. 2 C 9:6. Re 18:22.

8. **Their land.** ƒ70, Ex +16:35. **is full.** Is 57:5. 2 Ch 27:2. *28:1-4, 23-25. 33:3-7. Je *2:28. 11:13. Ezk 16:23-25. Ho 12:11. Ac 17:16. **idols.** lit. empty, vain things; nothings. Le 26:1⫾℗. Dt 27:14, 15⫾℗. **worship.** Is 37:19. 44:15-20. Dt 4:28. Ps 115:4-8. Ho 8:6. 13:2. *14:3. Hab 1:16. Re 9:20.

9. **the mean.** Is 5:15. Ps 49:2. Je 5:4, 5. Ro √3:23. Re 6:15-17. **humbleth.** Is 57:9. Col 2:18, 23. **therefore.** Is *27:11. Jsh 24:19. Je 18:23. Mk 3:29.

10. **Enter.** ver. 19-21. Is 10:3. 42:22. Jg 6:1, 2. Jb 30:5, 6. Ho 10:8. Lk 23:30. Re *6:15, 16. **hide.** ƒ60A, Ge +3:22. **for fear.** Is 6:3-5. Jb 31:23. 37:22-24. Ps 33:8. 90:11. Je 10:7, 10. Lk 12:5. Re 15:3, 4.

11. **lofty.** ƒ173, Ge +27:44. ver. 17. Is 5:15, 16. 13:11. 24:21. Jb 40:10-12. Ps 18:27. Je 50:31, 32. Ml 4:1. Lk 18:14. 1 P 5:5. **of man.** ƒ147G, Ge +68:16. **humbled.** ƒ173, Ge +27:44. **and.** ƒ148, Ge +8:22. **of men.** ƒ147G, Ps 68:16, **and the Lord.** Is 5:16. 12:4. Je 9:24. 1 C 1:29-31. 2 C 10:17. **in that day.** Is 4:1. 11:10, 11. 12:1, 4. 24:21. 25:9. 26:1. 27:1, 2, 12, 13.

28:5. 29:18. 30:23. 52:6. Jb +21:30. Je 30:7, 8. Ezk 38:14, 19. 39:11, 22. Ho 2:16, 18, 21. Jl 3:18. Am 9:11. Ob 8. Mi 4:6. 5:10. 7:11, 12. Zp 3:11, 16. Zc 9:16.

12. **the day of the Lord.** Is 13:+*6, 9. +*34:8. Ps 92:6-9. Je *46:10. La 2:22. Ezk 13:5. +*30:3. Jl 1:15. +*2:1, 11. 3:14. Am +*5:18, 20. Ob 15. Zp 1:7, 8, +*14, 18. +*2:2, 3. Zc √14:1. Ml *4:5. 1 C +*3:13. *5:5. 1 Th *5:2. 2 Th +*1:10. 2:2. 2 P √3:10. Re +*1:10n. **be upon.** Is *23:9. Ps *119:21. Pr *6:16, 17. *16:5. Da *4:37. *5:20-24. Mt *23:12. Lk 14:11. Ja *4:6. **and.** ƒ148, Ge +8:22.

13. **And.** ƒ148, Ge +8:22. **upon all.** Is 10:33, 34. 14:8. 37:24. Ezk 31:3-12. Am 2:5. Zc 11:1, 2.

14. **And.** ƒ148, Ge +8:22. **high mountains.** Is 30:25. 40:4. Ps 68:16. 110:5, 6. 2 C 10:5.

15. **And.** ƒ148, Ge +8:22. **high tower.** lit. great place. Zp 1:16. **fenced wall.** Is 25:2. 27:10. 36:1.

16. **And.** ƒ148, Ge +8:22. **the ships of Tarshish.** F/L Is 23:1, 14. 60:9. Ge +10:14. 1 K 10:22. 22:48n, 49. Ps 48:7. Re 18:17-19. **pleasant pictures.** Heb. pictures of desire. Nu 33:52. Re 18:11, 12.

17. **And.** ƒ148, Ge +8:22. **the loftiness.** See on ver. 11. Is 13:11. 24:21. Ps 9:19, 20. 37:13, 35, 36. Pr 6:16, 17. 8:13. 16:18, 19. Je 9:24. 48:29, 30. Ezk 28:2-7. Zc 11:2. Lk *18:14. 1 C 1:29-31. 1 P 5:5. **of man.** ƒ147, Ps +68:16. **exalted.** Is 5:15, 16.

18. **And.** ƒ148, Ge +8:22. **the idols.** Is 10:10, 11. 27:9. Ezk 36:25. 37:23. Ho 14:8. Zp 1:3. Zc 13:2. **he shall utterly abolish.** or, shall utterly pass away. Mi 1:7.

19. **And.** ƒ148, Ge +8:22. **they shall go.** See on ver. 10, 21. 1 S 13:6. 14:11. Je 16:16. Ho 10:8. Mi 7:17. Lk 23:30. He 11:38. Re *6:15. 9:6. **holes.** or, caverns. Is 32:14. Ge 19:30. **caves.** lit. pierced places. ✻S#4247h, only here. **earth.** Heb. dust. ver. 10. Is 25:12. 26:5, 19. Ge 2:7. 3:14, 19. **for fear.** See on ver. 10. 2 Th *1:9. **when he ariseth.** ƒ22C21, Nu +10:35. **to shake.** Is 30:32. Ps 7:6. 18:6-15. 76:7-9. 114:5-7. Mi 1:3, 4. Na 1:3-6. Hab 3:3-14. Hg 2:6, 21, 22. He +*12:26. 2 P *3:10-13. Re 6:12-14. 11:13, 19. 16:18. 20:11.

20. **cast.** Is 30:22. 31:7, 27. 46:1, 2. Le 1:16. 14:40. Nu 19:6. Ho 14:8. Ph 3:7, 8. **his idols of silver.** Heb. the idols of his silver, etc. Is 31:7. 46:6. **they.** ƒ96F4, Ex +10:2. **each one for himself to.** or, for him to. **worship.** lit. bow themselves to. Ge 37:10. Le 26:1. Jg 2:19. **bats.** Le 11:19. Dt 14:18.

21. **go into.** See on ver. 10, 19. Ex 33:22. Jb 30:6. SS 2:14. **clefts.** Ex 33:22. **tops.** lit. boughs. Is 17:6. 27:10. 57:5. **for fear.** Ps 9:19, 20. 33:8. *90:11. Mt +*10:28. **when he ariseth.** ƒ22C21, Nu +10:35. Na 1:5, 6. Ml 4:5. 1 Th *5:2, 3. 2 P *3:10-13. Re 6:15, 16. 20:11. **shake terribly.** or, terrify. Ps 10:18. Ho 10:8. Hg 2:6. Mt 7:26, 27. Lk 23:30. He +*12:26.

22. **Cease.** Is 1:16. Ex 14:12. Ps *62:9. 118:8, 9. 146:3, +4. Je *17:5, 6. **whose.** Ge +*2:7⫾℗, Is +1:2. Ge 7:22. Jb 27:3. **breath.** Heb. neshamah, Ge +2:7. F/L Is 30:33. 42:5. 57:16 (soul). Ps +*146:4. **for wherein.** ƒ85N, 1 K 9:13. Is 40:17. Jb 7:15-21. Ps *8:4. *144:3, 4. Je 17:5.

ISAIAH 3

A prediction, that Jerusalem and Judah should be deprived of every support, and reduced to abject dis-

tress, because of their daring impiety, 1-9. The happiness of the righteous, and the misery of the wicked declared, 10, 11. A rebuke of the princes and elders for oppression, 12-15. The pride, wantonness, and gaudy apparel and ornaments of the daughters of Zion described; with predictions of terrible judgments on them, 16-26.

1. **behold.** Is 2:22. **the Lord.** Is 1:24. 36:12. 51:22. **the stay.** Le *26:26. Ps 105:16. Je *37:21. *38:9. Ezk 4:16, 17. 14:13. **bread.** ♪171I8, Ge +3:19.

2. **mighty.** Is 2:13-15. 2 K *24:14-16. Ps 74:9. La 5:12-14. Am 2:3. **prophet.** Ps +*74:9. **prudent.** 1 Ch 12:32n. Pr 16:10. **the ancient.** Is 9:15. Ezk 8:12. 9:5, 6.

3. **captain.** Ex +18:21. Dt 1:15. 1 S 8:12. 2 K 1:9, 14. **the honorable man.** Heb. a man eminent in countenance. Jg 8:18. 2 K +5:1mg. **cunning artificer.** Is 5:21. 19:11. 1 S 13:19, 20. 2 K 24:14. **eloquent orator.** *or*, skilful of speech. Ex 4:10, 14-16. Heb. the skilful of charm. Is +26:16 (✻S#3808h). Pr 16:10. Ec 10:11. Je 8:17. Ho 3:4.

4. **children.** 1 K 3:7-9. 2 Ch 26:1. 33:1. 34:1. 36:2, 5, 9, 11. Ec *10:16.

5. **the people.** Is 9:19-21. 11:13. Je 9:3-8. 22:17. Ezk 22:6, 7, 12. Am 4:1. Mi 3:1-3, 11. Zc 7:9-11. Ml +*3:5. Ja 2:6. +*5:4. **child.** Is 1:4. Le *19:32. 2 K 2:23. Jb 19:18. 30:1-12. Pr 30:17. **base.** 2 S 16:5-9. Ec 10:5-7. Mt 26:67, 68. 27:28-30, 44. Mk 14:65. Lk 22:64.

6. **a man.** Is 4:1. Jg 11:6-8. Jn 6:15. **clothing.** ♪171I13. Synecdoche of the Species B629. "Clothing" is put for all necessary things. **ruler.** Is 1:10. Jsh 10:24. **ruin.** Zp 1:3.

7. **swear.** Heb. lift up *the hand.* ♪121S3, Ge +14:22. Ge 14:22♪𝒫. Ex 6:8♪𝒫. Nu 14:30♪𝒫. Dt 32:40♪𝒫. Re 10:5, 6. **healer.** Heb. binder up. Is 58:12. Je 14:19. La 2:13. Ho 5:13. 6:1. **neither bread.** Princes and great men in the East, as Sir J. Chardin testifies, are obliged to have a great stock of clothes in readiness for presents on all occasions; and a great quantity of provisions for the table is equally necessary (see 1 K 4:22, 23. Ne 5:17, 18). Hence the person desired to undertake the government, alleges as an excuse that he is not able to support the dignity of his station. 2 S 19:31-40. Je 41:17, 18.

8. **Jerusalem.** 2 Ch 28:5-7, 18, 19. 33:11. 36:17-19. Je 26:6, 18. La 5:16, 17. Mi 3:12. **because.** Is 5:18, 19. 57:4. Ps 73:8, 9. Ezk 8:12. 9:9. Ho 7:16. Ml 3:13-15. Mt 12:36, 37. Ju 15. **to provoke.** Is 65:3-5. Dt 31:16-18. 2 Ch 33:6, 7. Jb 17:2. Ps 78:17. Ezk 8:4-6, 17, 18. Hab 1:13. 1 C 10:22. **the eyes.** 1 K 9:3. Hab *1:13.

9. **The show.** ver. 16. 1 S 15:32. 2 K 9:30. Ps 10:4. 73:6, 7. Pr 30:13. Je *3:3. 6:15. Da 7:20. **and they declare.** Ge *13:13. *18:20, 21. 19:5-9. Je 44:16, 17. Ezk 23:16. **hide it not.** ♪144D, Ge +40:23. **Woe.** La *5:16. Ho *13:9. **soul.** Heb. *nephesh*, Ge +12:3.

10. **Say ye.** Is 26:20, 21. Ec *8:12. Je 15:11. Ezk *9:4. 18:9-19. Zp 2:3. Ml *3:18. Ro 2:5-11. **they shall eat.** Ps *1:3-5. 18:23, 24. *128:1, 2. Ga *6:7, 8. He *6:10.

11. **Woe.** ♪110, Ezk +34:2. Is 48:22. 57:20, 21. 65:13-15, 20. Ps *1:3-5. *11:5, 6. Ec *8:13. **for the reward.** Ps 28:4. 62:12. Pr 1:31. Mt +16:27. 2 C *5:10. Ja 2:13. **given him.** Heb. done to him. Ps 120:3, 4. Ro *2:6-9.

12. **children.** ver. +4. 2 K 15:8-25. Ec 10:16. Ho 7:3-7. **women rule over them.** Jg 4:4. 1 K 10:1-13. 2 K 11:1-16. 2 Ch 9:1-9, 12. 22:2, 3, 10-12. 23:1-15. Ne 2:6. Na *3:13. Zc 5:7, 8. Mt 13:33. Ac 8:27. 1 T √2:12. Re ch. 17. 19:2. **lead thee.** *or*, which call thee blessed. Is 9:15, 16. Nu *6:23-27. Je 5:31. Mt 15:14. **destroy.** Heb. swallow up. Is 9:16mg. 25:7mg, 8. 28:4mg. Ps 35:25. La 2:5, 16. Mt 23:14. **paths.** Is 2:3.

13. **standeth up.** Ps *12:5. Pr 22:22, 23. 23:10, 11. Ho 4:1, 2. Mi 6:2.

14. **enter.** Jb 22:4. 34:23. Ps *143:2. **the ancients.** See on ver. 2, 3. **ye have eaten.** *or*, ye have burnt. Is *5:5, 7. Jb 24:2-7. Je 5:27. Am 4:1. Mi 2:2. 6:10. Mt 21:33-41. **the spoil.** Ja *5:2-5. **of.** ♪181E, Ge +3:24.

15. **What mean.** Ezk 18:2. Jon 1:6. **ye beat.** Is 58:4. Ex 5:14. Am 2:6, 7. 8:4-6. Mi 3:2, 3. **faces.** ♪171Q, Ge +3:19.

16. **the daughters.** Is 1:8. *4:4. SS 3:11. Mt 21:5. Lk 23:28. **are haughty.** Is 24:4. 32:9-11. Pr *6:16, 17. *16:5, 18. *21:4. 30:13. Ec 7:8. Ezk 16:49, 50. Zp 3:11. Ml 3:15. Ja *4:4-6. 1 P 3:3, 4. **walk with.** ♪86. Ethopoeia; or, Description of Manners B449. For other instances of this figure see Lk 18:11, 13. 1 P 3:3. **wanton eyes.** Heb. deceiving with their eyes. Pr 7:10, 11. 29:3. Lk 15:30. Ja 5:5. 2 P 2:√14, 18. Or, as *mesakkaroth ainayim* is rendered in the Targum, "painting their eyes with stibium:" for *sakar* is probably the same as the Chaldee *sekar*, of that import. **mincing.** *or*, tripping nicely. **and making.** The Eastern ladies wear on their ankles large rings, to which smaller ones are attached, which make a tinkling sound as they move nimbly.

17. **smite.** Le 13:29, 30, 43, 44. Dt 28:27. Re 16:2. **daughters.** ♪155E3, Is +32:9. **and.** ♪148, Ge +8:22. **discover.** Heb. make naked. ver. 24. Is 20:4. 47:2, 3. Ge 24:20. 2 Ch 24:11. Ps +137:7mg. 141:8. Je 13:22. Ezk 16:36, 37. 23:25-29. Mi 1:11. Na 3:5. Zc 14:2.

18. **tinkling ornaments.** ♪168, Is +1:11. ver. 16. **and.** ♪148, Ge +8:22. **cauls.** *or*, networks. *Shevisim*, probably the rich *embroidered kerchiefs* used to bind on their caps on the head, described by Lady M. W. Montague, Let. 32. **round tires.** Jg 8:21mg.

19. **chains.** *or*, sweet-balls. *Neteephoth*, earrings or drops; in Arabic, *netafat.* Jg 8:26. **and.** ♪148, Ge +8:22. **the bracelets.** Ge 24:22, 30, 53. 38:18, 25. Ex 35:22. Nu 31:50. Ezk 16:11. **mufflers.** *or*, spangled ornaments.

20. **bonnets.** F/L Is 61:3, 10. Ex 39:28. Ezk 24:17, 23. **and.** ♪148, Ge +8:22. **ornaments.** lit. steppings. ✻S#6807h. 2 S 5:24 (a going). 1 Ch 14:15 (going). **tablets.** Heb. houses of the soul. Heb. *nephesh*, Nu +23:10. Probably perfume boxes, as rendered by Bp. Lowth. **the earrings.** *Lechashim*, probably amulets. Ge 35:4. Ex 32:2. Ezk 16:12. Ho 2:13.

21. **rings.** Ge 41:42. Est 8:2. SS 5:14. Lk 15:22. Ja 2:2. **and.** ♪148, Ge +8:22. **nose jewels.** Ge 24:47. 1 T 2:9, 10. 1 P 3:3, 4.

22. **The changeable suits.** *Machalatzoth*, probably loose robes, used according to the weather. Zc 3:4. 1 T 2:8-10. 1 P *3:3, 4. 5:5. **and.** ♪148, Ge +8:22. **mantles.** Ru 3:15. **crisping pins.** or, purses. 2 K 4:23.

23. **glasses.** Ex 38:8. **and.** ♪148, Ge +8:22. **fine linen.** Ge 41:42. 1 Ch 15:27. Ezk 16:10. Lk 16:19. Re 19:8, 14. **vails.** Ge 24:65. Nu 3:35. SS 5:7.

24. **And.** ♪148, Ge +8:22. **instead.** Is 57:9. Pr 7:17. **baldness.** ♪121S3V, Mi +1:16. ver. 17. Is 15:2. 22:12. Le 13:40. 21:5. Jb 1:20. Ezk 7:18. 27:31. Am 8:10. Mi 1:16. **a girding.** Is 15:3. 32:9-11. Jb 16:15. Je 4:8.

6:26. 48:37. 49:3. La 2:10. Ezk 27:31. Jl 1:8. Am 8:10. Re 11:3. **burning**. Is 4:4. Le 26:16. Dt 28:22. 32:24. Re 16:9. 18:9.

25. **Thy men**. 2 Ch 29:9. Je 11:22. 14:18. 18:21. 19:7. 21:9. 39:1-10. La 2:21. Am 9:10. Zc 14:2-5, 14. Re 19:11-21. **and**. ƒ148, Ge +8:22. **mighty**. Heb. might. Is 11:2. 28:6. 30:15. Jg 5:31. Je 41:2, 3.

26. **And**. ƒ148, Ge +8:22. **her gates**. Is 24:12. Je *14:1, 2. La *1:4. **lament**. ƒ155D, Ge +4:10. **mourn**. F/L Is 19:8. 24:4, 7. 33:9. 57:18. 60:20. 61:2, 3. 66:10. Jb 1:20. 2:13. **desolate**. *or*, emptied. Heb. cleansed. ✛S#5352h. Ge 24:8 (clear). Ex 21:19 (be quit). Nu 5:28 (be free), 31 (guiltless). Jg 15:3 (blameless). Ps 19:13 (innocent). Je 2:35. Zc 5:3mg (guiltless). **shall sit**. ƒ121S3Y, La +2:10. Is 47:1. Jb 2:8, 13. Ps 137:1. La *2:10. 3:28. Je 6:26. Ezk 26:16. Mi 1:10. Lk 19:44.

ISAIAH 4

Predictions, that women would irregularly seek to be married, as few men would be left, 1; but that glorious times, for holiness, peace, and security, would follow, 2-6.

1. **And**. ƒ148, Ge +8:22. **in that day**. ƒ171T2B, Ps +102:11. See on Is 2:11, 17. 10:20. 17:7. Lk 21:22, 23. **seven**. Is 3:25, 26. 13:12. An indefinite number of persons (Young). Jb 5:19n. **women**. Is 24:6. Je *15:8. **one man**. Is 3:25, 26. +*24:6. **We will eat**. 2 Th 3:12. **only**. ƒ164, 1 S +17:7. **let us be called by thy name**. Heb. let thy name be called upon us. Nu 6:27. Dt 28:10. **to take away**. *or*, take thou away. **reproach**. Ge *30:22, 23. 1 S 1:6. Ps 78:63. Lk *1:24, 25.

2. **that day**. Is 2:12. **the branch**. Is *11:1. 60:21. Je 23:5. *33:15. Ezk 17:22, 23. Zc *3:8. *6:12. Lk 1:78. ƒ22H1A. Anthropomorphism B895. Certain plants are used as figures of God: a branch or sprout. For other instances of this figure see Is 11:1, 10. Je 23:5. 33:15. Zc 3:8. 6:12. Lk 23:31. Ro 15:12. Re 5:5. 22:16. **beautiful and glorious**. Heb. beauty and glory. Ex 28:2. Zc 9:17. Jn *1:14. 2 C *4:6. 2 P 1:16, 17. Re 22:16. **the fruit**. ƒ22H1B. Anthropomorphism B895. Certain plants (as to genus) are used as figures of God: the fruit of the earth. Is *27:6. *30:23. 45:8. Le 23:10. Ps 67:6. *85:9-13. Ezk 34:29. Ho 2:22, 23. Jl 2:23-25. 3:18. Am 9:11-15. Zc 9:17. **them that are escaped**. Heb. the escaping. Is 10:20-22. 27:12, 13. 37:31, 32. Je 44:14, 28. Ezk 7:16. 9:4. Jl 2:32. Ob 17. Mt 24:22. Lk √21:36. Ro 11:4, 5. Re 7:9-14. 14:1-5.

3. **Zion**. Ps 87:5, 6. **Jerusalem**. Ga 4:26. He 12:22. **shall be**. Is 1:27. 52:1. *60:21. Ezk 36:24-28. 43:12. Zc *14:20, 21. 1 C 1:2. Ep 1:4. Col 3:12. He *12:14. 1 P *2:9. **written**. ƒ22C43, Ex +31:18. 32:32, 33. Ezk 13:9. Da 12:1. Lk *10:20. Ph *4:3. Re 3:5. *13:8. 17:8. √20:12, 15. 21:27. **among the living**. *or*, to life. Ps *69:28. 87:5, 6. Ml *3:16. Ac √13:48.

4. **When**. Is 52:1. Re 21:27. **washed away**. ƒ22C24, Ps +51:2. Is 3:16, etc. La 1:9. Ezk 16:6-9. 22:15. √36:25-27, 29. Jl 3:21. Zp 3:1. Zc 3:3, 4. *13:1, 9. Ml 3:2, 3. *or*, bathed. Ex 29:4, 17. 30:19, 21. **filth**. lit. outgoing. Is 28:8. 36:12. 2 K 18:27. Pr 30:12. **have purged**. Is 26:20, 21. Ex 40:38. 2 Ch 4:6. Ezk 24:7-14. Mt 23:37. **blood**. lit. bloods. Is 1:11, 15. 9:5. Ge +4:10mg. 2 K +*9:26mg. **spirit**. Heb. *ruach*, Ex +15:8. **of judgment**. Is 9:5. Ezk 22:18-22. Ml *3:2, 3. 4:1. Mt *3:11, 12. Jn 16:8-11. **spirit**. Heb. *ruach*, Ex +15:8. **of burning**. ƒ24A, Ge +32:24. Is 5:5. 40:16. 44:15. 2 Ch 4:20.

13:11. Ne 10:34. Mt *3:11. 1 C *3:13-15. 2 P +*3:7.

5. **upon every**. Is 32:18. 33:20. Ps 87:2, 3. 89:7. 111:1. Mt *18:20. 28:20. **assemblies**. Is +*1:13. Le 23:2)℘. **a cloud**. Ex 13:21, 22. 14:19, 20, 24. 40:34-38. Nu *9:15-22. Ne 9:12. Ps 78:14. Zc *2:5-10. **upon**. *or*, above. **all the glory**. Is 31:4, 5. 37:35. 46:13. Ps 85:9. 87:3. **a defence**. Heb. a covering. Is 62:4. Ex 26:1, 7. Ps 19:5. Jl 2:16.

6. **tabernacle**. Is 8:14. 25:4. Ps 27:5. 91:1. *121:5, 6. Pr 18:10. Ezk 11:16. He 6:18. Re *7:16. *or*, covering. lit. "booth." Is 1:8. Ge 33:17. Le 23:34. **place**. ƒ22L4, Ps +32:7. **for a covert**. Is *32:2, 18, 19. Mt 7:24-27. He 11:7. Re *21:2-4. **rain**. Is 5:6. 30:23. Ex 9:33.

ISAIAH 5

A parable of a well-cultivated vineyard, which bare corrupt fruit; explained of the advantages and conduct of Israel, 1-7. Their atrocious sins stated by an induction of particulars, and the correspondent judgments which were coming on them, 8-25. The invasion of the land by the Assyrians, or Chaldeans, predicted, 26-30.

1. **Now**. Dt 31:19-22. Jg 5:1, etc. Ps 45:1. 101:1. **well–beloved**. SS 2:16. 5:2, 16. 6:3. Mk 1:11. **touching his**. ƒ7. Allegory by continued Hypocatastasis, Ga 4:24. Is 27:2, 3. Ps 80:8. SS 8:11, 12. Je 2:21. Mt 21:33. Mk 12:1. Lk 20:9. Jn 15:1. **a very fruitful hill**. Heb. the horn of the son of oil. Is 21:10mg. Dt 8:7-9. Zc 4:14mg.

2. **fenced it**. *or*, made a wall about it. Ex 33:16. Nu 23:9. Dt 32:8, 9. Ps 44:1-3. 105:44, 45. Ro 9:4. **gathereth out**. Is 62:10. 2 S 16:6, 13. **planted**. Je 2:21. +*11:17. **the choicest vine**. *Sorek*, in Arabic, *sharik*, certainly denotes an *excellent vine*; but some, with Bp. Lowth, retain it as a proper name. *Sorek* was a valley lying between Askalon and Gaza, so called from the excellence of its vines. Is *27:2-6. Jg 16:4. Ps 44:1, 2. *80:8. SS 8:12. Je *2:21. 12:10. Ho *10:1. 14:5-7. Jn 15:1. **and built**. Is 1:8. Mi 4:8. **made**. Heb. hewed. Is 22:16. Dt 6:11. Pr 9:1. Ho 6:5. **a winepress**. Is 63:2, 3. Ne 13:15. Re 14:18-20. **he looked**. ver. 7. Is 1:2-4, 21-23. Dt 32:6. Mt *21:33, 34. Mk 11:13. 12:2. Lk *13:7. 20:10, etc. 1 C 9:7. **wild grapes**. Dt 32:32, 33. Ho 10:1.

3. **And now**. ƒ14. Anacoenosis; or, Common Cause B968. An appeal to others as having interests in common. For other instances of this figure see Jg 23:23. Ml 1:6. Lk 11:19. Ac 4:19. 1 C 4:21. 10:15. 11:13, 14. Ga 3:1, 2, 5. 4:21. **O inhabitants**. ƒ7. Allegory by continued Metaphor or Substitution, Ga 4:24, no longer implication. **judge**. Ps 50:4-6. *51:4. Je 2:4, 5. Mi 6:2, 3. Mt 21:40, 41. Mk 12:9-12. Lk 20:15, 16. Ro 2:5. *3:4.

4. **What could**. ƒ85K, Ge +3:9. Is 1:5. 2 Ch 36:14-16. Je 2:30, 31. 6:29, 30. Ezk 24:13. Mt √23:37. Ac 7:51, etc. Ro 1:24, 28. 2 Th 2:7.

5. **go to**. Ge 11:4, 7. **my vineyard**. Ps 80:9. Je 12:10. Na 2:2. **I will take**. ƒ96B, Ge +8:5. Is 27:10, 11. Le 26:31-35. Dt 28:49-52. 2 Ch 36:4-10. Ne *2:3. Ps 74:1-10. *80:12-16. La 1:2-9. 4:12. Lk *13:7. **trodden down**. Heb. for a treading. Is 10:6. 25:10. 28:3, 18. La 1:15. Da 8:13. Mt *23:38. Lk *21:24. Re *11:2.

6. **I will lay**. ver. 9, 10. Is 6:11, 12. 24:1-3, 12. ◖27:3. 32:13, 14. Le 26:33-35. Dt 29:23. 2 Ch 36:19-21. Je 25:11. 45:4. Lk *21:24. **it shall**. Is 7:23-25. Ho

3:4. **I will also**. Is 30:23. Le 26:19)✸. Dt 28:23, 24)✸. Am 4:7. Zc 14:16, 17. He 6:6-8. Re 11:6. **clouds**. Ge +9:13.

7. **the vineyard**. ♪132G, Ge +3:19. Ps 80:8-11, 15. Je 12:10. **the Lord of hosts**. Is 1:9. 1 S 1:3. **house of Israel**. F/L Is 14:2. 46:3. 63:7. **his pleasant plant**. Heb. plant of his pleasures. Is 62:5. Ps 147:11. 149:4. SS 7:6. Zp 3:17. **he looked**. ver. 2. Is 58:6-8. Ex 22:22-27. Mi 6:8. Zc 7:9-14. Mt 3:8-10. 23:23. Jn 15:2. 1 C 6:8-11. 1 J 3:7, 8. **but**. The *paronomasia*, or play of words, is very remarkable here: "he looked for *mishpat*, "judgment," but behold *mispach*, "oppression;" for *tzedakah*, "justice," but behold *tzeakah*, "a cry." **oppression**. Heb. a scab. Is 1:6. 3:17. **a cry**. Ge *4:10. Ex *2:23, 24. 3:7. 22:21-24, 27. Dt 15:9. Ne 5:1-5. Jb 31:38, 39. 34:28. Pr 21:13. Lk 18:7. Ja +*5:4.

8. **Woe**. ♪70. Ex +16:35. **them**. Ps 10:3. Je 22:13-17. Ezk 33:31. Mi *2:2. Hab *2:9-12. Mt 23:14. Lk *12:15-24. Ep 5:3. He 13:5. 2 P 2:14. **field**. 1 K 21:16, 20. **no place**. F/L Is 34:12. 40:17. 41:12, 29. 45:6, 14. 46:9. 47:8, 10. 52:4. 54:15. **they**. Heb. ye. **placed**. Ezk 11:15. 33:24.

9. **In mine ears, said**. *or*, This *is* in mine ears, *saith*, etc. ♪63BA, Ge +26:7. Is 22:14. Am *3:7. **Of a truth**, etc. Heb. If not many houses desolate, etc. **desolate**. ver. 6. Is 27:10. 2 Ch 36:21. Am 5:11. 6:11. Mt 22:7. 23:38.

10. **one bath**. Le 27:16. Ezk 45:10, 11. Jl 1:17. Hg 1:9-11. 2:16.

11. **Woe**. ♪70. Ex 16:35. **rise**. ver. *22. Is *28:1. Pr *23:29, 30. Ec *10:16, 17. Ho *4:11. 7:5, 6. Hab *2:15. Lk *21:34. Ro *13:13. 1 C *6:10. Ga *5:21. Ep *5:18, 19. 1 Th *5:6, 7. **inflame**. *or*, pursue. Is 28:7, 8. Pr +*20:1. *23:32.

12. **the harp**. Is 22:13. Ge 31:27. Jb *21:11-14. Da *5:1-4, 23. Am *6:4-6. Lk 16:19. Col 3:16. Ja 5:13. Ju *12. **are in**. or, are. ♪119, Ge +49:9. **they regard**. ver. 19. Jb *34:27. Ps *28:5. 92:5, 6. Ho *4:10, 11.

13. **my people**. Is 1:7. *42:22-25. 2 K 17:6. 2 Ch 28:5-8. **because**. Is *1:3. 27:11. Je +*8:7. Ho √4:6. Mt *23:16-27. Lk 19:44. Jn √3:19, 20. Ro *1:28. 2 P *3:5. **honorable men are famished**. Heb. glory *are* men of famine. Is 3:8. 4:2, 5. 6:3. Je 14:18. La √4:4, 5, 9. **multitude**. Je 14:3. Am 8:13.

14. **hell**. Heb. *sheol*, Ge +37:35. Is 14:9-15. 30:33. Ps 49:14. Pr 27:20. Ezk 32:18-30. Hab 2:5. Mt √7:13. Re 6:8. *20:13-15. **enlarged**. ♪155D, Ge +4:10. **herself**. Heb. *nephesh*, Ex +15:9. Re +*18:14. **opened**. Nu *16:30-34. Pr 1:12. **he that rejoiceth**. Is 21:4. 1 S 25:36-38. 2 S 13:28, 29. Ps 55:15. Da 5:3-6, 30. Na 1:10. Lk *12:19, 20. *16:20-23. 17:27. *21:34. Ac 12:21-23. **shall descend**. Ge +*3:19. Ec +*3:18-20.

15. **the mean**. Is 2:9, 11, 17. 9:14-17. 24:2-4. Ps 62:9. Je 5:4, 5, 9. Ja 1:9-11. Re 6:15, 16. **the eyes**. Is 10:12. 13:11. 37:23, 29. Ex 9:17. Jb 40:11, 12. Da 4:37. 1 P 5:5.

16. **the Lord**. Is 12:4. 1 Ch 29:11. Ps 9:16. 21:13. *46:10. Ezk 28:22. 38:22, 23. Ro *2:5. Re 19:1-5. **God that is holy**. *or*, the holy God. Heb. the God the holy. Heb. *El*, Ex +15:2. Is *6:3. √57:15. 1 P 1:16. Re 3:7. *4:8-11. *15:3, 4. **sanctified**. Is *8:13. 29:23. Le 10:3. Ezk 36:23. 1 P 1:16. 2:15. Re 19:11.

17. **shall the lambs**. Is 7:21, 22, 25. 17:2. 32:14. 40:11. 65:10. Zp 2:6, 14. **the waste**. Is 10:16. Dt 32:15. Ps 17:10, 14. 73:7. 119:70. Je 5:28. Am 4:1-3. **strangers**.

Is 1:7. Le 26:43. Dt 28:33. 2 Ch 36:21. Ne 9:37. La 5:2. Ho 8:7. Lk *21:24.

18. **Woe**. ♪70, Ex +16:35. **draw**. Is 28:15. Jg 17:5, 13. 2 S 16:20-23. Ps 10:11. 14:1. 36:2. 94:5-11. Je 5:31. *8:5-9. 23:10, 14, 24. 28:15, 16. 44:15-19. Ezk 13:10, 11, 22. Zp 1:12. Jn 16:2. Ac 26:9.

19. **Let him**. ♪60D, Ge +37:19. Is 66:5. Je 5:12, 13. *17:15. *36:20-26. Ezk 12:22, 27. Am *5:18, 19. 2 P √3:3, 4, 9. **let the**. Is 30:11. Je 23:18, 36.

20. **Woe**. ♪70. Ex +16:35. **them**. Pr 17:15. Ml 2:17. 3:15. Mt *6:23. 15:3-6. 23:16-23. Lk √11:35. 16:15. 2 T *3:1-5. 2 P 2:1, 18, 19. **call evil good**. Heb. say concerning evil, **It** is good, etc. Nu 11:5, 6. Pr 24:24. Je *44:16-18. Jn 16:2. Ro 3:8. **evil**. ♪25, Ge +4:4. **put darkness**. Jb 10:22. Pr 16:25. Mt +*6:23. 15:12-14. Jn √3:19, 20.

21. **Woe**. ♪70. Ex +16:35. **wise**. Is 47:10. Jb 11:12. 37:24. Pr *3:7. *26:12, 16. Lk *16:15. Jn *9:41. Ro *1:22. 11:25. *12:16. 1 C *3:18-20. **in their own sight**. Heb. before their face. ♪121I1, Ge +3:7. Ge 19:21mg. 23:4, 8. Dt 4:37. 2 S 7:9mg.

22. **Woe**. ♪70, Ex +16:35. **mighty**. ver. *11. Is 28:1-3, 7. Pr 23:19, 20. Hab √2:15.

23. **justify**. Ex 23:6-9. Pr *17:15. 24:24. *31:4, 5. **for reward**. Is 1:23. Dt *16:19. 2 Ch 19:7. Pr 17:23. Mi 3:11. 7:3. **take**. Is 10:2. 1 K 21:13. Ps 94:21. Mt 23:35. 27:24, 25. Ja *5:6.

24. **fire**. Heb. tongue of fire. Jn 15:6. **devoureth**. Is 47:14. Ex *15:7. Jl 2:5. Na 1:10. Ml 4:1. 1 C 3:12, 13. **the flame**. Mt *3:12. Lk 3:17. **their root**. Is 9:14-17. Jb 18:16. Ho 9:16. Am 2:9. **cast away**. 1 S √15:22, 23, 26. 2 K 17:14, 15. Ne 9:26. Ps 50:17. Je 6:19. 8:9. Lk 7:30. Jn *12:48. He *10:28, 29. **the law**. Is +1:10n)✸. **despised**. Is *30:12, 14. 2 S 12:9, 10. Lk *10:16. Ac *13:41. 1 Th *4:8.

25. **the anger**. Dt *31:17. 32:19-22. 2 K 13:3. √22:13-17. 2 Ch *36:16. Ps 106:40. La 2:1-3. 5:22. 1 Th *2:16. **stretched forth**. ♪22A14.8A, Ex +7:5. Is 14:26, 27. **the hills**. Ps 18:7. 68:8. 77:18. 114:7. Je 4:23-26. La 3:2. Ezk 32:7, 8. Jl 2:10. Mi 1:4. Na 1:5. Hab 3:10. Mt 24:7. Re 20:11. **tremble**. ♪102, Ge +2:24. **torn**. *or*, as dung. 1 K 14:11. 16:4. 21:24. 2 K 9:37. Ps 83:10. Je 8:2. 9:22. 15:3. 16:4. 25:33. Zp 1:17. **For all this**. Is 9:12, 13, 17, 21. 10:4. Le 26:14, 18, 21, 23, 24, 28)✸. Ps 78:38. Da 9:16. Ho 14:4. Re 9:12. **stretched out still**. Ex 6:6)✸. Dt 4:34)✸. 5:15)✸. 7:19)✸. 9:29)✸. 11:2)✸. 26:8)✸.

26. **he will**. Is 11:12. 18:3. Je 51:27. **ensign**. ♪22D5Q, Ex +17:15. **from afar**. Is 39:3. Dt *28:49. Je 5:15, 16. **hiss unto**. or, will whistle for them. Will gather them together by his word, as shepherds gather their sheep (Matthew Poole), or as men hiss for swarming bees, according to others (J. A. Alexander); Is 7:18. 1 K 9:8. Jb 27:23. Je 19:8. 49:17. 50:13. La 2:15, 16. Ezk 27:36. Zp 2:15. Zc 10:8. ♪22C6. Anthropomorphism B887. Human actions are attributed to God: hissing. For other instances of this figure see Is 7:18. Zc 10:8. **end**. Is 39:3. Dt 28:49. Ps 72:8. Je 5:15. Ml 1:11. **they shall come**. ♪105, Ml +4:2. Is 30:16. Je 4:13. La 4:19. Jl 2:7. Hab 1:6-10.

27. **shall be**. Jl 2:7, 8. **neither**. Is 11:5. 45:1, 5. 1 K 2:5. Jb 12:18, 21mg. Ps 18:32. 93:1. Da 5:6. Ep 6:13, 14. **nor the latchet**. Dt 32:25.

28. **arrows**. Ps 45:5. 120:4. Je 5:16. Ezk 21:9-11. **their horses**. Jg 5:22. Je 47:3. Mi 4:13. Na 2:3, 4. 3:2.

29. **roaring**. Is 31:4. Ge 49:9. Nu 24:9. Je 4:7. 49:19. 50:17. Ho 11:10. Am 3:8. Zc 11:3. **lion**. Da 7:2-4, 7. Mt ch. 24. Jn 11:48. **lay hold**. Is 42:22. 49:24, 25. Ps 50:22. Mi 5:8. **none shall**. Ps 50:22. Je 32:5, 28. *37:8-10.

30. **like**. Ps 93:3, 4. Je 6:23. 50:42. Lk 21:25. **if one look**. Is 8:22. 13:10. Ex 10:21-23. Je 4:23-28. La 3:2. Ezk 32:7, 8. Jl 2:10. Am 8:9. Mt 24:29. Lk 21:25, 26. Re 6:12. 16:10, 11. **darkness**. Is 8:22. 13:10. Pr +*20:20. **sorrow**. *or*, distress. Is 25:4. 26:16. **and the light**, etc. *or*, when it is light, it shall be dark in the destructions thereof. Jl 3:15. Zc 14:6.

ISAIAH 6

Isaiah, by a vision of Jehovah's glory and the adoring Seraphim, is greatly dismayed: but encouraged by a Seraph touching his lips with a coal from the altar, 1-7. He receives a commission, showing the awful event of his prophetical labors, in the obduracy and ruin of the people; with an intimation of a remnant to be spared, and a holy seed to spring from them, 8-13.

1. A.M. 3245. B.C. 759. **the year**. 2 K 15:7, Azariah. 2 Ch *26:22, 23. **I saw also**. Ex *24:10, 11. Ex ❏33:20. Nu *12:8. Ezk 1:1, 25-28. Jn *1:18. 12:41, *45. 1 T ❏√6:16. **sitting**. Is 66:1. 1 K *22:19. Ezk 10:1. Da *7:9. Mt *25:31. Re 3:21. *4:2, 10. 5:1, 7. 6:16. 7:15-17. *20:11. **high**. Is 12:4. *57:15. Ps 46:10. 108:5. 113:5. Ezk 1:26. Ep 1:20, 21. **his train**. *or*, the skirts thereof. Ex 28:33, 34. 39:24-26. Je 13:22, 26. La 1:9. Na 3:5. **filled**. 1 K 8:10, 11. Re 15:8.

2. **stood**. 1 K 22:19. Jb 1:6. Da *7:10. Zc 3:4. Lk 1:19. Re 7:11. **seraphims**. Ps 104:4. Ezk 1:4. He 1:7. **wings**. Ex 25:20. 37:9. 1 K 6:24, 27. 8:7. Ezk 1:6, 9, 24. 10:21. Re 4:8. **covered his face**. Ge 17:3. Ex 3:6. 1 K 19:13. Ps 89:7. **his feet**. Jb 4:18. 15:15. Ezk 1:11. **did fly**, ver. 6. Ps 18:10. 103:20. Ezk 10:16. Da 9:21. Re 8:13. 14:6.

3. **one cried unto another**. Heb. this cried to this. Ex 15:20, 21. Ezr 3:11. Ps 24:7-10. **Holy**. Ex *15:11. Ps 99:3, 5, 9. 145:17. Mt 6:9. Re *4:8, 9. *15:3, +4. **holy**. √84, Ge +6:17. **the Lord**. Is 40:10, 11. Ne +9:6. **the whole earth**, etc. Heb. his glory *is* the fulness of the whole earth. Is 11:9, 10. 24:16. *40:5. Nu 14:21. Ps 19:1-3. 57:11. *72:19. Hab 2:14. Zc 14:9. Ep 1:18-23. **his glory**. Jn *12:41.

4. **posts**. Ezk 1:24. 10:5. Am 9:1. **door**. Heb. thresholds. 1 K +14:17. 2 K +12:9mg. **the house**. Ex *40:34. 1 K *8:10-12. 2 Ch 5:13, 14. 6:1. Ps 18:8. Ezk 1:28. Re 11:19. 15:8. **filled**. √22D3J5, Ex +13:21.

5. **said I**. Ex 33:20. Jg 6:22. 13:22. Jb 42:5, 6. Da 10:6-8. Hab 3:16. Lk 5:8, 9. Re 1:16, 17. **Woe**. √59, Ge +28:16. **undone**. Heb. cut off. Is 15:1mg. Ps 31:17mg, 22. **a man**. Ex 4:10. 6:12, 30. Jb *42:5, 6. Je 1:6. Zc 3:1-7. Mt 12:34-37. Lk *5:8. Ja 3:1, 2. **I dwell**. Is 29:13. Je 9:3-8. Ezk 2:6-8. 33:31. Ja 3:6-10. **mine eyes**. Is *33:17. Jg 6:22. 13:22. Re *1:5-7, 17. **the King**. Is 44:6. **the Lord of hosts**. Is 54:5. Je 10:16. 50:34. 51:19. Jn 12:37-41. Ac 5:3, 4. 28:25, 26. Ro *9:29. Ja +*5:4.

6. **flew**. ver. 2. Da 9:21-23. He *1:7, 14. **having**, etc. Heb. and in his hand a live coal. Ezk 10:2. Mt 3:11. Ac 2:3, 4. Re 8:3-5. **which**. Le 16:12. He 9:22-26. 13:10. Re 8:3-5. **tongs**. Ex 25:38)℘. 37:23 (snuffers)℘. **the altar**. Le 6:9. 1 K 18:38.

7. **he laid it upon**. Heb. caused it to touch. Je *1:9.

Da 10:16. **thine iniquity**. Is 43:25. *53:5, 10. Mt 9:2. Ro 8:1. He *1:3. *9:13, 14. 1 J *1:7. *2:1, 2. **thy sin**. Is 38:17. 43:25. Lk 1:77. 24:47. Ro 5:11, 18, 19. 2 C √5:21. He +*9:22.

8. **I heard**. Ge 3:8-10. Dt 4:33-36. Ezk 1:24. 10:5. Ac 28:25-28. **the voice of the Lord**. Ex 16:7 w He 3:7-9. Ac 5:3, 4. 28:25-27. **Whom**. √85G. Erotesis B952. Questions asked *in wishes*. For other instances of this figure see 2 S 23:15h. Ro 7:24. **send**. Ex *4:10-13. 1 K 22:20. Ac 22:21. 26:16, 17. **who will go**. Ezk *22:30. **us**. T#211. Ge +√1:26)℘. 3:22)℘. 11:7)℘. Da 4:17. Mi +5:2 (T#76-3). Mt +9:4 (T#76-7). +18:20 (T#76-6). *28:19. Jn +5:18 (T#75). 1 C +1:24 (T#76-5). 2 C √13:14. Ep 2:18. Col +1:16 (T#76-2). +2:10 (T#76-1). He +9:14 (T#346). +13:8 (T#76-4). 1 P 1:2. 1 J 5:7. **Then**. Mt 4:20-22. Ac *20:24. Ep *3:8. **Here am I**. Heb. Behold me. Is 65:1. Ge 22:1mg. Jb 38:35mg. **send me**. T#1516. Ezk *22:30. Ac *9:6.

9. **Go**. √38E. Apostrophe B904: in prophecies. In certain solemn prophecies, the prophet is told what to say directly (instead of indirectly or obliquely). For other instances of this figure see Is 23:16. 47:1. **and tell**. Is 29:13. 30:8-11. Ex 32:7-10. Je 15:1, 2. Ho 1:9. **Hear ye**. Is *43:8. 44:18-20. Mt ▶13:14, 15. Mk ▶4:12. Lk ▶8:10. Jn 12:40. Ac ▶28:26, 27. Ro ▶11:8. **indeed**. *or*, without ceasing. Heb. in hearing. √147B, Ge +2:16. **indeed**. Heb. in seeing. **perceive not**. Dt 29:4. Je 5:21. Jn *8:43. Ac 7:51. 2 Th *2:11, 12.

10. **Make**. √121I2, Ge +2:17. √108A3. Idiom B822. Active verbs are used to declare that the thing has been or shall be done, and not the actual doing of the thing said to be done. Here, "Make" is used by this idiom to mean "declare" or "foretell" that the heart of this people will be fat, etc. Note that when this passage is cited in Mt ▶13:15, this idiomatic use of the verb is not literally translated, but is idiomatically rendered "the heart of this people is waxed gross." So in Ac ▶28:27. But in John ▶12:40, it is rendered literally according to the Hebrew idiom: "He hath blinded," etc. See Ps +*16:9n. For other instances of this figure see Je 1:10. Ezk 22:2. 43:3. Mt 13:15. Jn 12:40. Ac 10:15. See the closely related figure √108A4, Ge +31:7, and Am +√3:6. **the heart**. √132G, Ge +3:19. Is 29:10. 63:17. Ex 7:3. 10:27. 11:10. 14:17. Dt 2:30. Ezk 3:6-11. Jn ▶12:40. 2 C *2:16. **fat**. Dt 32:15. Ps 17:10. 119:70. **ears heavy**. Je 6:10. Zc 7:11. Ac 7:51. **eyes**. √68, Ge +10:1. Ps 69:23. **lest**. Je 5:21. Jn √3:19, 20. 12:40. He 3:8-11. **convert**. Is 19:22. Mt 13:15. Ac 3:19. 28:27.

11. **Lord**. Ps 74:10. 90:13. 94:3. Je 4:21. Da 8:13. Hab 1:2. Re *6:10. **how long**. Ezk 11:13. Ro 11:25. Re 11:1, 2. **Until the**. Is 1:7. 3:26. 24:1-12. 27:10. 32:13, 14. 2 Ch 36:21. Je 26:6, 9, 18. Mi 3:12. Lk *21:24. **utterly desolate**. Heb. desolate with desolation.

12. **the Lord**. Is 26:15. 2 K 25:11, 21. Je 15:4. 52:28-30. **a great**. Je 4:29. 12:7. La 5:20. Ro +*11:1, 2, 15.

13. **But yet**. Is 1:9. 4:3. 10:20-22. Ezk 11:16. Mt 24:22. Mk 13:20. Ro 11:5, 6, 16-29. **and it shall return**, etc. *or*, when *it* is returned, and hath been broused. "Broused" is apparently an obsolete form of the word *browsed*. **teil tree**. The teil tree is the linden or lime tree, a species very common in Palestine, the leaf of which resembles that of the laurel, and its flower that of the olive. But the original, *ailah*, which our translators render the *oak*, (but here distinguised from *allon*, the oak), and Bp. Lowth the *ilex*, in Is 1:29, 30, probably

denotes, as Celsius contends, the *terebinth*. It is an evergreen of moderate size, but having the top and branches large in proportion to the trunk; leaves, like those of the olive, but green intermixed with red and purple; flowers, like those of the vine, growing in bunches, and purple; fruit, of a ruddy purple, the size of a juniper berry, hanging in clusters, very juicy, and containing a single seed of the size of a grape stone; wood, hard and fibrous, from which a resin distills; with an excrescence scattered among the leaves, of the size of a chestnut, of a purple color, variegated with green and white. **substance**. *or*, stock, *or* stem. Jb *14:7-9. **so the holy**. Is 11:1. 27:6. *65:8, 9. Ge 22:18. +*49:10. Ezr 9:2. Ml 2:15. Mt 1:23. Lk +*1:35. Jn *5:26. 15:1-3. Ac 4:27. Ro *9:5. 11:5, 24. Ga 3:16-19, 28, 29. Re 22:16.

ISAIAH 7

Ahaz and his people are greatly terrified by hearing that the Syrians and Israelites had confederated against them, 1, 2. Isaiah is sent to assure Ahaz that they should not accomplish their purpose; but be speedily ruined, 3-9. Ahaz refuses to ask a sign of God; and Isaiah predicts the miraculous birth of Immanuel, as a sign or pledge of preservation to David's family, 10-16. A prophecy of judgments to be executed on the land by the Egyptians and Assyrians, 17-25.

1. **the days**. 2 K 16:1-6. 2 Ch 28:1-6. **Rezin**. Is 8:6. 2 K 15:27, 37. 16:5. Ps 83:3-5. **war against**. ♪24H, Jg +16:23. **but could**. ver. 4-9. Is 8:9, 10. Ps 27:1, 2. 112:7, 8. Pr 28:1.

2. **the house**. ver. 13. Is 6:13. 37:35. 2 S 7:16. 1 K 11:32. 12:16-20. 13:2. Je 21:12. **is confederate with**. Heb. resteth on. ver. 17. Is 11:13. 2 Ch 25:10. 28:12. Ezk 37:16-19. Ho 12:1. **Ephraim**. ♪171R, Ex +12:40. Ephraim is named, because in that tribe was Samaria, the royal city; and because out of that tribe was Jeroboam, the first king of Israel. But by Synecdoche all the ten tribes are included (B649). **And his heart**. Is 8:12. 37:27. Le 26:36, 37. Nu 14:1-3. Dt 28:65, 66. 2 K 7:6, 7. Ps 11:1. 27:1, 2. 112:7, 8. Pr 28:1. Mt 2:3.

3. **Then said**. Is 65:24. Ja 5:11. **Go forth**. Ex 7:15. Je 19:2, 3. 22:1. **Shear-jashub**. that is, *The remnant shall return*. *S#7610h. Is 6:13. 10:21, 22. 55:7. Ro 9:27. **the end**. Is 36:2. 2 K 18:17. 20:20. **conduit**. lit. a thing causing to go up. Is 36:2. 2 K 20:20. **upper**. Is 22:9, 11. 2 K √18:17. 20:20. Ne 2:14. 3:16. **pool**. lit. "blessing," because of the value of water. **highway**. *or*, causeway. F/L Is 11:16. 19:23. 33:8. 35:8. 36:2. 40:3. 49:11. 57:14. 59:7. 62:10. **fuller's**. or, washerman. Is 36:2. 2 K 18:17.

4. **Take heed**. Is 28:16. *30:7, 15. Ex *14:13, 14. 2 Ch 20:17. La *3:26. **fear not**. Is 8:11-14. *35:4. *41:14. 51:12, 13. Mt +*10:28. 24:6. **neither be fainthearted**. Heb. let not thy heart be tender. Dt 20:3. 1 S 17:32. 2 S 3:39mg. **the two tails**. ver. 8. Is 8:4. 2 K 15:29, 30. Am 4:11.

5. **Syria**. Ps 2:2. 83:3, 4. Na 1:11. Zc 1:15. **Ephraim**. ♪171R, Ex +12:40. **the son**. Is 8:6.

6. **go up**. Is 2:3. 5:24. 14:8, 13. **vex**. *or*, waken. lit. disgust. *S#6973h. Ge 27:46 (weary). Ex 1:12 (grieved). Le 20:23 (abhorred). Nu 21:5 (loatheth). 22:3 (distressed). 1 K 11:25 (abhorred). Pr *3:11 (weary).

Is 7:16 (abhorrest). **Tabeal**. i.e. *goodness of God; good is God.; good for nothing*, *S#2870h. Is 7:6. Ezr 4:7. (1) A Persian governor in Samaria, Ezr 4:7; (2) He whose son the Syrians and Ephraimites intended to place on the throne of Jerusalem, Is 7:6.

7. **It shall not**. Is *8:10. 10:6-12. 37:29. *46:10, 11. Ps 2:4-6. 33:11. *76:10. Pr +*21:30. La √3:37. Da *4:35. Ac 4:25-28.

8. **For the head**. Dr. Jubb transposes the former part of ver. 9, and renders, "Though the head of Syria be Damascus; and the head of Damascus Retzin; and the head of Ephraim be Samaria; and the head of Samaria Remaliah's son; yet within threescore and five years Ephraim shall be broken, that he be no more a people." This renders the passage perfectly clear; and the prophecy received its full accomplishment when Esarhaddon carried away the remains of the ten tribes. 2 S 8:6. **Syria**. i.e. *sublime, deceiving; exalted*, *S#758h. Is 7:1, 2, 4, 5, 8. 17:3. Jg 10:6. 2 S *8:6, 12. 15:8. 1 K 10:29. 11:25. 15:18. 19:15. 20:1, 20, 22, 23. 22:1, 3, 31. 2 K 5:1, 1, 5. 6:8, 11, 23, 24. 7:5. 8:7, 9, 13, 28, 29. 9:14, 15. 12:17, 18. 13:3, 4, 7, 17, 19, 19, 22, 24. 15:37. 16:5, 6, 7. 2 Ch 1:17. 16:2, 7, 7. 18:10, 30. 20:2. 22:5, 6. 24:23. 28:5, 23. Ezk 16:57. 27:16. Ho 12:12. Am 1:5. **within**. Is 8:4. 17:1-3. 2 K 17:1-6, etc. 19:17. Ezr 4:2. **Ephraim**. ♪171R, Ex +12:40. **that it be not a people**. Heb. from a people. Ho 1:6-10.

9. **the head**. 1 K 16:24-29. 2 K 15:27. **Ephraim**. ♪171R, Ex +12:40. **If ye**, etc. *or*, ye not believe? *it is because ye are not stable*. 2 Ch +*20:20. Ac 27:11, 25. Ro 11:20. He √11:6. Ja 1:8. 1 J *5:10.

10. **Moreover**, etc. Heb. and the Lord added to speak. Is 1:5, 13. 8:5. 10:20. Ho 13:2mg.

11. **Ask**. Is 45:11. Dt 4:32. 32:7. Ml 3:10. Mt 7:7. **sign**. or, "token." T#1697. F/L ver. 14. Is 8:18. 19:20. 20:3. 37:30. 38:7, 8, 22. 44:25. 55:13. 66:19. Ge 1:14. 15:7, 8. 24:14. Ex 4:1, 8, 9. 12:13. Jg *6:36-40. 2 K *20:8-11. Ps 86:17. Je 19:1, 10. 51:63, 64. Mt 12:38-40. 16:1-4. Lk *21:7. Jn 2:18. 6:30, 31. Ac 4:29, 30. **ask it either in the depth**. *or*, make *thy* petition deep. **the height**. Ezk 21:26.

12. **I will not ask**. 2 K 16:◑7, 8, 15. 2 Ch *28:22. **neither**. Ezk 33:31. **tempt**. Dt 6:16. Ml 3:15. Ac 5:9. 1 C 10:9.

13. **O house**. ver. 2. 2 Ch 21:7. Je 21:12. Lk 1:69. **Is it a small**. Ge 30:15. Nu 16:9, 13. Ezk 16:20, 47. 34:18. **to weary**. 2 Ch *36:15, 16. Je 6:11. **will ye**. Is 1:14, 24. *43:24. *63:10. 65:3-5. 2 Ch 28:5, 6. Ps 78:40. Am 2:13. Ml 2:17. Ac 7:51. He 3:10, 11.

14. **sign**. ver. 11. Is 38:7. **Behold**. Ge +√3:15. Ps 22:10. 69:8. 86:16. 116:16. Je √31:22n. Mi 5:3. Mt ✶+*1:23. Lk +*1:35. **a virgin**. Young notes, "not 'a virgin,' but 'the virgin.'" *S#5959h. T#1886. Ge +*24:43. Ex 2:8. Ps 68:25. Pr 30:19. SS 1:3. 6:8. Mt *1:18, 20, 21, ▶23, 25. Lk *1:27 (S#3933g), 34, 38. ✶2:7. Ga *4:4. For related words, see *S#1330h, Ge +24:16; *S#1331h, Le +21:13; *S#3207h, Ge +34:4; *S#5291h, Ge +24:14; S#5291h w 1330h, Dt +22:23; *S#3933g, Mt +1:23. **shall**. Is ◑37:22. Ge 38:24. **conceive**. *S#2030h. Ge 16:11▶P. 38:24, 25. Ex 21:22. Jg *13:5, 7▶P. 1 S +*4:19. 2 S 11:5. 2 K 8:12. 15:16. Is 7:14. 26:17. Je 20:17. 31:8. Am 1:13. **a son**. Is +*9:6. **shall call**. *or*, thou, *O virgin*, shalt call. Ge *4:1, 2, 25. *16:11. 29:32. 30:6, 8. 1 S *1:20. 4:21. **Immanuel**. i.e. *with us (he is) God; God with us*, *S#6005h. Is

8:8h, 10. *9:6. 44:6. Mt ✻1:22, 23. Jn √1:1, 2, 14. Ro √9:5. 1 T √3:16.

15. **Butter**. Connecting this verse with the preceding and following, we may render with Dr. Jubb and Lowth, "Behold *the virgin* (*haalma*, as the word uniformly signifies: Ge 24:43. Ex 2:8. Ps 68:26. Pr 30:19. SS 1:3. 6:8) shall conceive and bear a son, and thou shalt call his name Immanuel; butter and honey shall he eat *when* he shall know to refuse the evil and choose the good. For," etc. ver. 22. Mt 3:4. **know**. Ps 51:5. Am 5:15. Lk +*1:35. *2:1-5, 40, 52. Ro 12:9. Ph 1:9, 10.

16. **before**. Dt 1:39. Jon 4:11. **the land**. Is 8:4. 9:11, 12. 17:1-3. 2 K *15:29, 30. *16:9.

17. **bring upon**. Is 8:7, 8. 10:5, 6. ch. 36, 37. 2 K ch. 18, 19. 2 Ch *28:19-21. ch. 32. 33:11. 36:6-20. Ne 9:32. **the day**. 1 K *12:16-19. 2 Ch 10:16-19.

18. **hiss**. ♪22C6, Is +5:26. Is +*5:26. **fly**. Is 30:1, 2. 31:1. Ex 8:21, 24. Dt 1:44. 7:20. Jsh 24:12. Ps 118:12. **rivers of Egypt**. Ex 7:19♪𝒫. 8:5♪𝒫. 2 K 19:24. Jb 28:10. Ps 78:44. **bee**. ver. 17. Dt 1:44. Jg 14:8. 2 K 23:29, 33, 34. Ps 118:12.

19. **desolate valleys**. Le 26:31-33. **in the holes**. Is 2:19, 21. 2 Ch 33:11. Je 16:16. Mi 7:17. **bushes**. *or*, commendable trees.

20. **shave**. Is 10:6. 2 K 15:19. 16:7, 8, 17, 18. 17:3. 2 Ch *28:20, 21. Je 27:6, 7. Ezk 5:1-4. *29:18, 20. **the head**. ♪155E, Is +1:5. Is 1:5, 6. 9:14-17. 24:2.

21. **a man**. ver. 25. Is 5:17. 17:2. 37:30. Je *39:10.

22. **butter and honey**. ver. 15. 2 S 17:29. Mt 3:4. **land**. Heb. midst of the land.

23. **shall come to**. ♪144A11, Ge +38:11. **a thousand vines**. SS *8:11, 12. Mt 21:33. **be for briers**. Is 5:6. 32:12-14. Je 4:26. He *6:8.

24. **arrows**. Is 5:28. 37:33. 49:2. Ge 27:3. Jg 5:6, 11.

25. **but it**. ver. 21, 22. Is 13:20-22. 17:2. Le 26:34, 35. Zp 2:6.

ISAIAH 8

By the name given to a son of the prophet, the speedy ruin of Syria and Israel, and the invasion of Judah by the king of Assyria, are predicted, 1-8. A formidable confederacy against Judah would be defeated, 9, 10. The Jews are exhorted to fear and trust God, and not to fear man, as the way to safety, when numbers would be ensnared and destroyed, 11-15. The prophet (as a type of Christ), with his disciples, are signs to the people, 16-18. He warns them against diviners; directs them to the word of God as the only test and standard of truth; and predicts the blasphemy and despair of the rebellious, 19-22.

1. **Take thee**. Is 36:2, 28, 32. **write**. Is *30:8. Jb 19:23, 24. Hab √2:2, 3. **a man's pen**. Re 13:18. 21:17. **Maher-shalal-hash-baz**. Heb. in making speed to the spoil, he hasteneth to the prey. *Or*, Make speed, etc. hasten, etc. i.e. *hasting the prey*, ✻S#4122h.

2. **I took**. Ru 4:2, 10, 11. 2 C 13:1. **Uriah**. i.e. *light of Jah*. 2 S +11:3. 2 K *16:10, 11. 18:2. **Zechariah**. i.e. *remembered of Jah*. 2 K 18:2. Zc +1:1. **Jeberechiah**. i.e. *Jah blesses; he will be blessed of the Lord*, ✻S#3000h.

3. **went**. Heb. approached. Ge 27:41. 37:18. **the prophetess**. Ex 15:20. Jg 4:4. 2 K 22:14. 2 Ch 34:22. Ne 6:14. **she conceived**. Ho 1:3-9. **Call his name**. Is

7:13, 14. **Maher-shalal-hash-baz**. ver. 1.

4. **before**. Is 7:15, 16. Dt 1:39. Jon 4:11. Ro 9:11. **the riches of Damascus**, etc. *or, he that is* before the king of Assyria shall take away the riches, etc. Is 10:6-14. 17:3. 2 K 15:29. *16:9. *17:3, 5, 6.

5. A.M. 3263. B.C. 741. **spake**. Is 7:10.

6. **refuseth**. 1 K 7:16. 2 Ch 13:8-18. **the waters of**. Ne *3:15. Jn *9:7, Siloam. **Shiloah**. i.e. *thing sent; sent forth*, ✻S#7975h. Is 8:6. Ne 3:15. **that go softly**. 2 S 18:5. 1 K 21:27. Jb 15:11. Je *2:13, 18. 18:14. **rejoice**. Is 7:1, 2, 6. Jg 9:16-20.

7. **the Lord bringeth**. Is 17:12, 13. 28:17. 59:19. Ge 6:17. Dt 28:49-52. Je 46:7, 8. Da 9:26. 11:10, 22. Am 8:8. 9:5. Na 1:8. Lk 6:48. Re 12:15, 16. 17:15. **strong**. Ezr 4:10. Ps 72:8. **the king**. Is 7:1-6, 17. 10:8-14. Ezk 31:3, etc. **he shall come**. 2 K 17:3-6, 23, 24. 18:9-16. **banks**. Nu 34:12.

8. **he shall pass**. Is 10:28-32. 22:1-7. 28:14-22. 29:1-9. ch. 36, 37. **reach**. Is 30:28. **the stretching**, etc. Heb. the fulness of the breadth of thy land shall be the stretchings out of his wings. Ezk 17:3. **O Immanuel**. Is 7:14. Mt 1:23, Emmanuel. *28:20.

9. **Associate**. ♪60A, Ge +3:22. Is 7:1, 2. 54:15. Je 46:9-11. Ezk 38:9-23. Jl 3:9-14. Mi 4:11-13. Zc 14:1-3. Re 17:12-14. 20:8, 9. **and ye**. *or*, yet ye. Is 14:5, 6. 28:13. Ps 37:14, 15. Pr 11:21. **gird yourselves**. F/L Is 45:5. 50:11. **be broken**. Is 37:36. 1 K 20:11.

10. **Take**. ♪96B, Ge +20:7. **counsel**. Is 7:5-7. 2 S 15:31. 17:4, 23. Jb *5:12. Ps 2:1, 2. 33:10, 11. 46:1, 7. 83:3, etc. Pr +*21:30. La *3:37. Na 1:9-12. Ac 5:38, 39. **for God**. Heb. *El*, Ex +15:2. **with us**. Is 7:14. 9:6. 41:10. Dt 20:1. Jsh 1:5. 2 Ch 13:12. 33:7, 8. Ps *46:7, 11. Pr 11:21. Mt 1:23. 28:20. Ac *5:39. Ro 8:13, √31. 1 J 4:4.

11. **with a strong hand**. Heb. in strength of hand. Je 20:7, 9. Ezk 3:14. Ac 4:20. **instructed**. Ps +*32:8. Pr 1:15. Je 15:19. Ezk 2:6-8.

12. **Say ye not**. Is 7:2-6. 51:12, 13. 2 K 16:5-7. **A confederacy**. ♪115, 2 K +19:7. 2 K +*11:14. **neither fear ye**. ♪147D, Ge +1:29. Is 7:4. 51:12, 13. +*36:18n. 57:9-11. Jb +*3:25. Ps 53:5. Je 1:17-19. Mt 28:2-5. Lk 12:4, 5. 21:9. 1 P ❭3:14, 15.

13. **Sanctify**. ♪108B, Je +12:3. Is √26:3, 4. 29:23. Le 10:3. Nu 20:12❭𝒫, 13. 27:14❭𝒫. Ro 4:20. 1 P 2:5-8. **and let him**. Ge 31:53. Ps 76:7. Ml 2:5. Mt +*10:28. Lk 12:5. 1 P ❭3:13-15. Re *15:4. **fear**. ♪121R6, Ge +31:42. "Fear" is here put for "the God Whom ye shall fear." Ec +12:13.

14. **he shall be**. Is *26:20. Ps *46:1, 2. Pr *18:10. Ezk *11:16. **a stone**. Is 28:16. Lk *2:34. Ro ✻9:32, ❭33. 11:9-11, 35. 1 P ✻)2:8. ♪22L2. Anthropomorphism B897. God is figured by things which pertain to the earth: a cornerstone, foundation, and *stumbling stone*. For other instances of this figure see Is 28:16. Zc 3:9. Lk 2:34. Ro 9:32, 33. Ep 2:20, 21. 1 P 2:4, 6, 8. **a snare**. Ps 11:6. 69:22. Mt 13:57. Lk 21:35.

15. **stumble**. Mt *11:6. 15:14. 21:44. Lk *20:17, 18. Jn *6:66. Ro 11:25. 1 C *1:23. 1 P 2:7, 8.

16. **Bind up**. Is *29:11. Da 12:4. **the testimony**. ver. √20. Dt 4:45. 2 K 11:12. Jn 3:32, 33. He 3:5. 1 J √5:9-12. Re +*19:10. **seal**. Da 9:24. Re 5:1, 5. 10:4. **law**. Is +1:10n❭𝒫. **among**. Is 54:13. Ps √25:14. Pr +*8:8, 9. Da 12:9, 10. Mt √13:11. Mk 4:10, 11, 34. 10:10. 1 C √2:14. 2 C *3:14-16. Re 2:17. **disciples**. lit. taught ones. ✻S#3928h. Is *50:4 (learned; lit. disciples). 54:13 (taught). Je 2:24 (used; mg, taught).

13:23 (accustomed; mg, taught).

17. **I will.** Is *25:9. 26:8. 33:2. *64:4. Ge 49:18◑𝒫.
Ps *27:14. 33:20. 37:34. 39:7. 40:1. 130:5. La 3:25,
26. Ho 12:6. Mi 7:7. Hab 2:3. 1 Th 1:10. 2 Th 3:5.
He *9:28. 10:36-39. **hideth.** Is 54:8. √59:2. 64:7. Dt
*31:17, 18. 32:20. Ezk 39:23, 24. Mi 3:4. **I will look.**
Is *50:10. Lk 2:38. He ◑2:13a. *9:28.

18. **I and the.** ver. 3. Is 7:3, 16. 53:10. Ps 22:30.
He 2:◑13b, 14. **for signs.** Is 20:3. Ex 7:3◑𝒫. Dt 4:34◑𝒫.
6:22◑𝒫. 7:19◑𝒫. 13:1, 2◑𝒫. 26:8◑𝒫. 28:46◑𝒫. 29:3◑𝒫.
34:11◑𝒫. Ps 71:7. Zc 14:8. Zc 3:8. Lk 2:34. 1 C *4:9-
13. He *10:33. **which.** Is 12:6. 14:32. 24:23. 1 Ch 23:25.
Ps 9:11. Zc 8:3. He 12:22.

19. **Seek.** Is 2:6. 19:3. Le *19:31. 20:6. Dt +*18:10-
12. 1 S 28:8. 1 Ch *10:13, 14. 2 Ch 33:6. **familiar
spirits.** lit. bottles. Dt +*18:11. 2 K +21:6. **wizards.**
Dt +*18:11. 2 K +21:6. **that peep.** Is 10:14. 29:4.
should not. 1 S 28:16. 2 K 1:3. 2 P *2:1. **for the living.**
Ps 106:28. Je 10:10. 1 Th *1:9.

20. **the law.** ver. +16. Ezr 10:3. Mt 4:7. Lk *10:26.
*16:29-31. Jn √5:39, 46, 47. Ac √17:11. Ro 4:3. Ga
3:8, etc. 4:21, 22. 2 T √3:15-17. 2 P *1:19. **if they
speak not.** Ps +√119:63. Pr +*19:27. Mt 24:4. Mk
+4:24. Lk +8:18. Ac *20:28-32. 2 C 4:2. Ga 1:6, 7.
3:1. Ep 4:14. 2 T +3:5. 2 P 2:1. 3:16. 2 J 9, 10. **according.** Here we learn the absolute importance of basing
every doctrine, every belief, on the written word of
God. No error is more fundamental, nor more disastrous, than depending upon some external source of
authority, whether extra-Biblical writings, or an organization claiming to dispense God's truth. The only
source of authority is the written word of God. This
word is declared in many ways to be perspicuous—
that is, understandable (Dt 30:11n; Ps +102:18, T#49;
Pr +*8:9) to the ordinary person, who, with the assistance of the Holy Spirit, together with careful study,
may be trusted to come to just and sound conclusions
as to the meaning of Scripture. Otherwise how could
spiritual truth be made known to "babes and sucklings"
(Ps 8:2. Mt 11:25), and how could ordinary listeners
be commended for checking up on the accuracy and
truthfulness of an apostle (Ac √17:11), and be charged
with the responsibility of judging the message of an
apostle, to determine that it was the true gospel (Ga
1:8)? Note that the great doctrinal epistles are specifically addressed to the "saints," that is, the ordinary
believers, not to the pastors, bishops, theologians, or
authorities of the church (Ro 1:6, 8; 1 C 1:2; Ep 1:1;
Ph 1:1; Col 1:2). We shall be judged on the basis of
our belief or disbelief in the written word of God (Jn
5:24-47. 12:48); in that day we will not be able to
excuse our wrong belief, if such it should prove to
be, by an appeal claiming "But I believed what my
church, pastor, organization, etc., taught me" (Ezk
√14:10. Mt 7:21-23; Mk 12:24, 27. Ro √14:12). T#46.
Is 29:11-13. Mt 15:3-6, 9. Mk *7:7-9. Jn *12:48. Ro
2:16, 18. 2 C 10:12. 11:4. Col 2:8. **to this word.** Dt
+*4:2. Pr *30:5, 6. Je √23:28, 29. Mk √12:24. Jn *8:31,
32. **it is.** Is 30:8-11. Ps √19:7, 8. √119:130. Je *8:9.
Mi 3:6. Mt √6:23. √22:29. Mk *7:7-9. Ro 1:22. 2 P
*1:9. **light.** Heb. morning. lit. darkness, either of morning or of evening (Young). Is +*17:14. Ge 32:25, 27.
Jsh 6:15. 1 S 9:26. Jb 24:16. 38:12. Ps *101:8. *119:105,
130. 139:9. Pr +*4:18, 19. 20:20. Ho 6:3. Ml *4:2.
Mt *6:23. *8:12. Jn 1:9. 3:19. 8:12. 2 C *4:3, 4. 2 P
*1:19. 1 J 1:5, 7. 2:11. Ju *13.

21. **through.** ver. 7, 8. **hardly bestead.** Is 9:20. Dt
28:33, 34, 53-57. 2 K *25:2, 3. Je 14:18. 52:6. La 4:4,
5, 9, 10. **hungry.** Mt 4:4. 5:6. 2 P 2:2. **they shall fret.**
Pr 19:3. Re 16:11, 21. **curse.** Ex 22:28. 2 K 6:33. Jb
1:11. 2:5, 9. Re 9:20, 21. *16:9-11. **look upward.** 2 S
+*22:42.

22. **look.** Is 5:30. 9:1. 2 Ch 15:5, 6. Je 13:16. 30:6,
7. Am 5:18-20. Zp 1:14, 15. Mt 8:12. 24:29. Lk 21:25,
26. Ju 13. **and darkness.** Is 13:10. Pr +*20:20. **dimness.**
Pr 20:20. **driven to darkness.** Is 3:11. Jb 18:18. Pr
14:32. Je 23:12. Mi *3:6. Mt *22:13.

ISAIAH 9

*Predictions of deliverance and joy to the people of
God, through the incarnation, salvation, and kingdom
of Christ, 1-7; of dreadful vengeance on Israel, for
their pride, hypocrisy, and impenitent wickedness, and
through the success of their enemies, and their own
furious contentions, 8-21.*

1. A.M. 3264. B.C. 740. **the dimness.** Is 8:22. **when.**
1 K *15:19, 20. 2 K *15:29. 2 Ch 16:4. **afterward.**
Le *26:23, 24, 28. 2 K 17:5, 6. 1 Ch 5:26. **by the
way.** Mt 4:15. **Galilee of the nations.** or, Galilee the
populous. Mt ✱4:12-16, 23.

2. **walked.** Is 50:10. *60:1-3, 19. Ec 2:14. Mi 7:8,
9. Mt ◑4:14-16. Lk *1:78, ◑79. *2:32. Jn 1:4, 5, 9.
*8:12. 9:5. *12:35, 36, 46. Ep 5:8, 13, 14. 1 P 2:9.
1 J *1:5-7. Re 21:23, 24. *22:5. **darkness.** Is 42:16.
50:10. Mt 4:16. 6:22, +*23. Lk 1:79. Jn 1:5. *3:19,
21. 8:12. 11:9, 10. 12:35. Ac 26:18. Ro 1:21. 13:12,
13. 1 C 4:5. 2 C 4:6. 6:14. Ep 5:8, 11. 1 Th 5:4, 5.
1 P 2:9. 1 J 1:5-7. 2:8-11. **seen.** ✓96C1, Ge +4:1. **in
the land.** Jb 10:21. Ps *23:4. 107:10, 14. Am 5:8. **shadow
of death.** Jb 3:5. 10:21, 22. 12:22. Mt 4:16. **the light
shined.** T#1894. Jb 22:28. Mt ✱4:12-16.

3. **hast multiplied.** Is 26:15. 49:20-22. Ne 9:23. Ps
107:38. Ho 4:7. Zc 2:11. 8:23. 10:8. **not increased
the joy.** or, to him increased the joy. **they joy.** Is
12:1. *25:9. *35:2, 10. 54:1. 55:12. 61:7, 10. 65:18.
66:10. Ps 4:7. *126:5, 6. Je 31:7, 12-14. Ac 8:8.
Ph *4:4. 1 P 1:8. **according.** Is 16:9, 10. **and as
men.** Jg 5:30. 1 S 30:16. 2 Ch 20:25-28. Ps 119:162.
Lk 11:22.

4. **For thou hast broken.** or, When thou brakest.
Is 14:25. 47:6. Ge 27:40. Le 26:13. Je 30:8. Na 1:13.
the staff. Is 10:5, 27. 14:3-5. 30:31, 32. **the rod.** Ps
+*125:3. **as in the day.** ♪171T2B, Ps +102:11. Is
*10:26. Jg 6:1-6. 7:22-25. 8:10-12. Ps *83:9-11.

5. **For every battle,** etc. or, When the whole battle
of the warrior was, etc. **confused noise.** Is 13:4. 1 S
14:19. Je 47:3. Jl 2:5. Na 3:2. **garments.** Is *63:1-3.
Re 19:13. **but this shall be.** or, and it was, etc. **burning.**
Is 4:4. 10:16, 17. 30:33. 37:36. *66:15, 16. Ps 46:9.
50:3. Ezk 39:8-10. Hab 3:5. Ml 3:2, 3. Mt 3:11. Ac
2:3, *19. 2 Th √1:8. He 12:29. 2 P +*3:7. **fuel.** Heb.
meat. ver. 19. Le 3:11, 16.

6. **For unto.** Is √7:14. Lk *1:35. *◑2:11. **us.** Lk 2:4.
3:23. Jn *4:22. Ro 9:5. **a child.** Is 2:6. 8:18. 29:23. **is
born.** Is +*7:14. 44:6. Mt 1:23. Lk 1:35. 2:11. **a son.**
lit. a builder up. Is 1:1, 2. **is given.** Jn *1:14. √3:16,
17. +*8:35. 16:30. Ro *8:32. He 1:2. 1 J *4:10-14.
and. Is 6:12. Lk 4:18, 21. **the government.** Is *22:21,
22. Ge=41:40. +*49:10. Ps *2:6-12. 8:6. *110:1-4. Je
*23:5, 6. Zc *6:12, 13. *9:9, 10. Mt 2:6. *11:27. *28:18.
Lk 22:29. 1 C *15:25. Ep *1:22, 23. Re 1:6. 2:27.

*19:16. **upon his shoulder.** Is *22:22. **his name.** Is +*7:14. Jg 13:18. Ps +*9:10. +*20:1. Je 31:22. Mt +*1:23. 1 T *3:16. **Wonderful.** Is 28:29. Jg *13:18mg. Mt 21:15. Ac 2:22. **Counsellor.** Is 11:2. *28:29. Pr 8:14. Je 32:19. Zc *6:13. Mt 7:28, 29. 12:42. Lk *21:15. Jn *1:16. 1 C *1:30. Ep +*1:11. Col *2:3. 1 J 2:1. Re 3:18. **The mighty.** Is 1:24. +10:21 (✱S#1368h). 44:6, 8. 49:26. 60:16. Dt 7:21. 10:17. Ne 1:5. 4:14. 9:32. Ps 45:3. 50:1. √89:19. Mt 11:21. Lk 9:43. Ep √1:21, 22. Re *1:8. 7:10, 12. **God.** Heb. *El*, Ex +15:2. Is *45:24, 25. Ps *45:3, 6. *50:1. Je *23:5, 6. Zc 13:7. Mt *1:23. Lk *1:47, 76. Jn √1:1, 2. +*8:24, 58. +*20:28. Ac √20:28. Ro √9:5. Col 2:9. 1 T *6:14-16. T √2:13. He 1:2, 3, +√8. 1 J *5:20. **The everlasting.** Is *40:28. *63:16. Ps +9:18 (✱S#5703h). Pr 8:27. Jn +*1:1-3. +*8:58. Col +*1:17. **Father.** Is 8:18. *53:10. 64:8. Pr +*8:23. Jn +*10:30. 1 C 15:22. He 2:13, 14. 9:12. Re 1:18. **The Prince of Peace.** T#1904. Is *11:6-9. *53:5. Ps *72:3, 7. *85:10. Da *9:24, 25. Mi *5:4, 5. Lk *2:14. Jn *14:27. Ac *10:36. Ro *5:1-10. 2 C *5:19. Ep √✱2:14-18. Col √1:20, 21. 2 Th 3:16. He *7:2, 3. √13:20.

7. **the increase.** 2 S *7:16. Ps *2:8. *72:8-11. *89:35-37. *145:13. Je *33:15-21. Da *2:35, 44. 4:3. *7:14, 18, 27. Lk ▶1:32, 33. 1 C +*15:24-28. **no end.** Ge 9:+12, +16. Ps *89:4. Da 2:44. +*7:14. Lk ✱1:32, 33. **throne of David.** Ps +*132:11. Lk √1:32. Ac +*2:30. ✱+*13:23. Re 3:7. **to establish it.** Is *11:3-5. *32:1, 2. Ps *45:4-6. *72:1-3, 7. He √1:8. Re *19:11. **for ever.** Heb. *olam*, Ex +*12:24. Ge 9:+12, +16. Mi 4:7. 1 P 4:11. Re 11:15. **The zeal.** √22B. Anthropomorphism B883. Human affections and feelings are attributed to God: zeal. For other instances of this figure see Is *37:32. *59:16, 17. 63:4-6. 2 K *19:31. Ezk *36:21-23.

8. **sent a word.** Is 7:7, 8. 8:4-8. Mi 1:1-9. Zc 1:6. 5:1-4. Mt 24:35.

9. **And all.** Is 26:11. 1 K 22:25. Jb 21:19, 20. Je 30:24. 44:28, 29. Ezk 7:9, 27. 30:19. 33:33. **even Ephraim.** √171R, Ex +12:40. Is 7:9. 10:9-11. **in the pride.** Is 46:12. 48:4. Pr 16:18. Ml 3:13. 4:1. 1 P 5:5.

10. **bricks.** 1 K 7:9-12. 10:27. Ml 1:4. **fallen down.** √132U, Ge +19:25. **but we.** Le 26:18. Pr 16:18. Ezk 7:9. Ml ◐1:4. 1 P 5:5.

11. **set up.** Is 8:4-7. 10:9-11. 17:1-5. 2 K 15:29. 16:9. **join.** Heb. mingle. Is 19:2mg.

12. **Syrians.** 2 K 16:6. 2 Ch 28:18. Je 35:11. **devour Israel.** Dt 31:17. Ps 79:7. 129:3-6. Je 10:25. **open mouth.** Heb. whole mouth. **For all.** ver. 17, 21. Is 5:25. 10:4. Je 4:8. **stretched.** √22A14.8A, Ex +7:5. —**still.** Je 44:28. Mt *24:35.

13. **the people.** Is *1:5. 26:11. 57:17. 2 Ch 28:22. Jb *36:13. Je *5:3. *31:18-20. Ezk 24:13. Ho *5:15. *7:10, 16. **turneth not.** T#9. Is 1:5. Dt 4:29, 30♪. Jb 10:15-18. 16:12. Pr +27:22 (T#569). Je *5:3. La 1:12, 13. 3:10-12. Am 4:6, 7-11. Ju +16 (T#700). **neither.** Is 31:1. Dt *4:29. Je +*29:11. 50:4, 5. Ho 3:4, 5.

14. **will cut.** Is 3:2, 3. 19:15. 2 K 17:6-20. Ho 1:4, 6, 9. 4:5. 5:12-14. 8:8. 9:11-17. 13:3. Am 2:14-16. 3:12. 5:2, 3. 6:11. 7:8, 9, 17. 9:1-9. Mi 1:6-8. **rush.** F/L Is 19:15. 58:5. Jb 41:2, 20. **in one day.** Is 10:17. 30:13. Ho 10:15. Re 18:8, 10, 17.

15. **ancient.** Is 3:5. 5:13. 1 S 9:6. **head.** Dt 28:13, 44♪. **the prophet.** Is 28:17. 29:10. 1 K 13:18. 22:22-24. Je 5:31. 14:14, 15. 23:9, 14, 15, 25-27. 27:9, 10,

14, 15. 28:15, 16. 29:21, 31, 32. Ezk *13:1-16, 19, 22. Ho 9:8. Ml 2:9. Mt *7:15, 16. 24:24. 2 C 11:13-15. Ga 1:8, 9. 2 Th √2:9-12. 2 T 4:2, 3. 2 P *2:1-3. 1 J *4:1. Re 19:20. **tail.** Dt 28:13, 44♪.

16. **the leaders.** etc. *or*, they that call them blessed. Is 3:12mg. **cause them to err.** Is 3:12. 30:28. Je 50:6. Mi 3:5. Mt +*15:14. 18:6. *23:2, 3, 15, 16, etc. Mk 9:42. +*12:24, 26. Lk 17:1, 2. 1 T 4:2. 6:3, 4. 2 T *4:3. T 1:11. 2 P *2:1. **led of them.** *or*, called blessed of them. Nu √6:23-26. 1 K 8:55, 56. 2 Ch 30:27. He 7:7. **destroyed.** Heb. swallowed up. Is +3:12mg.

17. **have no joy.** Is 10:2. 13:18. 27:11. 62:5. 65:19. Ps 147:10, 11. Je 18:21. Zc 9:17. **for every.** Is 10:6. Jb 15:34. Je 5:1, 2. Mi 7:2. Mt 16:3, 4, 12. **every mouth.** Is 32:6, 7. Mt 12:34. **folly.** *or*, villany. ✱S#5039h. Is 32:6. Ge 34:7. Dt 22:21. Jsh 7:15mg. Jg 19:23, 24mg. 20:6, 10. 1 S *25:25. 2 S 13:12. Jb 42:8. Je 29:23. **For all.** √8, Ps +118:1. ver. 12, 21. Is 5:25. 10:4. Ezk 20:33. **stretched.** √22A14.8A, Ex +7:5.

18. **wickedness.** Is 1:31. 30:30, 33. 33:12. 34:8-10. 66:16, 17. Nu 11:1-3. Dt 32:22. Jb 31:11, 12. Am 7:4. Na 1:6, 10. Ml *4:1. Mt 13:49, 50. √25:41. Mk 9:43-50. Re *14:11. **it shall.** Is *10:16-18. 27:4. He *6:8. **thorns.** 2 S 23:6. Mi 7:4. **shall kindle.** Ezk 20:47, 48. **mount.** Is 5:24. Ps 37:20. Ho 13:3. Jl 2:30. Re 14:11.

19. **is the land.** Is 5:30. 8:22. 24:11, 12. 60:2. Je 13:16. Jl 2:2. Am 5:18. Mt 27:45. Ac 2:20. **fuel.** Heb. meat. ver. 5. **no man.** Is 13:18. Ezk 9:5. Mi 7:2, 6. 2 P 2:4.

20. **And he.** Is 49:26. Le *26:26-29. Je *19:9. La 4:10. **snatch.** Heb. cut. 2 K 6:4. Jb 22:28 (decree). Hab 3:17. **right hand.** Ge +48:13. Ec 10:2. **shall eat.** Le 26:26♪♪. **left hand.** Ge +48:13. Jg +20:16. **not be satisfied.** Is 1:11. 66:11. Dt 6:11. **they shall.** Is 49:26. Ec 4:5.

21. **Ephraim.** Jg 7:22. 1 S 14:20. 2 K 15:30, 37. 2 Ch 28:6-8. Mt 24:10. Ga 5:15. **For all this.** √8, Ps +118:1. ver. 12, 17. Is 5:25. 10:4. Je 4:8. **stretched.** √22A14.8A, Ex +7:5.

ISAIAH 10

Woes denounced against the rulers for their iniquitous laws and decrees, 1-4. God commissions the Assyrian to punish the Jews; describes and rebukes his insolence and impiety, and predicts the ruin of him and his army, 5-19. He promises mercy to a remnant, attended with righteous judgments on the nations, 20-23. The people are encouraged not to fear the Assyrians; and a prophetical description is given of Sennacherib's progress, and the sudden ruin of his army, 24-34.

1. A.M. 3291. B.C. 713. **Woe.** Is *3:11. *5:8, 11, 18, 20-22. Je *22:13. Hab 2:6, 9, 12, 15, 19. Mt *11:21. 23:13-16, 23, 27, 29, 33. *26:24. Lk *11:42-44, 46, 47, 52. Ju *11. **them.** 1 K 21:13. Est *3:10-13. Ps 58:2. *94:20, 21. Da *6:8, 9. Mi *3:1-4, 9-11. *6:16. Jn *9:22. *19:6. **that write grievousness.** *or*, to the writers that write grievousness.

2. **turn aside.** Is 29:21. La 3:35, 36. Am 2:7. 5:11, 12. Ml +*3:5. **that widows.** Is 1:23. 3:14. 5:7. Je 7:6. Ezk 22:7. Mt 23:14, 33.

3. **And what.** Is 20:6. *33:14. Jb *31:14. Je 5:31. Ezk 24:13, 14. Re *6:15-17. **the day.** Is 26:21. Je +*8:12. Ho *9:7. Lk *19:44. 1 P 2:12. **in the desolation.** Is 5:26. 30:27, 28. 39:3, 6, 7. Dt 28:49. **to whom.** Is

30:1-3, 16. 31:1-3. Ho 5:13. **where**. Is 2:20, 21. 5:14. Ge 31:1. 2 K 7:6-8, 15. Ps 49:16, 17. Pr *11:4. Zp 1:18. **glory**. ⨍121G, Ge +31:1.

4. **Without me**. Le *26:17, 18, 36, 37. Dt *31:15-18. *32:29, 30. Je 37:10. Ho *9:12. **For all this**. ⨍8, Ps +118:1. Is 5:25. 9:12, 17, 21. **stretched**. ⨍22A14.8A, Ex 7:5.

5. **O Assyrian**. *or*, Woe to the Assyrian. Heb. O Asshur. Ge 10:11. **the rod**. ver. 15. Is 5:26. 7:18. 8:4. 13:5. 14:5, 6. 41:15. Dt *28:49, 50. Jg 3:12. 1 K 11:14. Ps *17:13, 14. 125:3. Je 5:15. 6:22. 27:8. *51:20-24. Ezk 23:24. *29:19, 20. Da 2:37. Lk 19:43. **and**. *or*, though. **indignation**. ver. 25. Is 13:5. +*26:20. Da +*8:19 (✱S#2195h).

6. **against**. Is 9:17. 19:17. 29:13. 30:9-11. 33:14. Je 3:10. 4:14. Mt 15:7. **will I give**. ver. 13, 14. Is 37:26, 27. 41:25. 45:1-5. Je 25:9. 34:22. 47:6, 7. **tread them**. Heb. lay them a treading. Is 22:5. 63:3, 6. 2 S 22:43. Mi 7:10. Zc 10:5.

7. **he meaneth**. Ge √50:20. Mi *4:11, 12. Ac *2:23. *13:27-30. **but**. 2 K 18:13-37. 19:1-37. **in his heart**. Is 36:18-20. 37:11-13.

8. **Are not**. Is 36:8, 9. 2 K 18:24. 19:10. Ezk 26:7. Da 2:37.

9. **Calno**. i.e. *his perfection; fortified dwelling*, ✱S#3641h. Ge 10:10. Am 6:1, 2, Calneh. **Carchemish**. i.e. *fortress of refuge; fortress of Chemosh* i.e. (as if departing, as if feeling; the swift, i.e. the sun, Nu +21:29) the head (or lamb) as if departed, ✱S#3751h. 2 Ch 35:20. Je 46:2. **Hamath**. Is 36:19. 37:13. 2 S 8:9. 2 K 17:24. Je 49:23. Am 6:2. **Samaria**. Is 7:8, 9. 17:3. 2 K 16:9, 10. 17:5, 6. 18:9, 10.

10. **my hand**. Is 46:10, 11. Ps 76:10. Mt 23:37. 1 P 4:17. **the kingdoms**. ver. 14. 2 K 18:33-35. 19:12, 13, 17-19. 2 Ch 32:12-16, 19.

11. **as I have**. Is 36:19, 20. 37:10-13.

12. **when the Lord**. ver. 5, 6. Is 14:24-27. 27:9. 46:10, 11. Ps *76:10. 1 P *4:17. **I will**. ver. 16-19, 25-34. Is 17:12-14. 29:7, 8. 30:30-33. 31:5-9. 37:36-38. 50:15. Je 50:18. **punish**. Heb. visit upon. Is 24:21mg. Je +9:25mg. Zc 10:3mg. **the fruit of the stout heart**. Heb. visit upon the fruit of the greatness of the heart. Is 2:11. 9:9. 2 K 19:36, 37. Jb 40:11, 12. Ps 21:10. 62:9. Pr 18:12. 21:4, 24. Je 50:18. Mt 12:33. 15:19. 1 P 5:5. **king of Assyria**. Da 11:40n. Mi +*5:5n, 6. Hab *3:16. **the glory**. Is 2:11. 5:15. Ps 18:27. Pr 30:13. Ezk 31:10, 14. Da 4:37. **high looks**. Da *11:36, 37.

13. **For he saith**. ver. 8. Is 37:23, 24. Dt 8:17. 2 K 19:20-24. Ezk 25:3. 26:2. 28:2-9. 29:3. Da *4:30. Am 6:13. Hab 1:16. **I have removed**. 2 K 15:29. 17:6, 24. 18:11, 32. 1 Ch 5:26. Am 5:27. 6:1, 2. **bounds**. Dt 32:8⟩𝒫. **robbed**. 2 K 16:8. 18:15. Ho 13:15, 16. **a valiant man**. *or*, many people.

14. **And my**. Is 5:8. Jb 31:25. Pr 18:12. 21:6, 7. Ho 12:7, 8. Na 2:9-13. 3:1. Hab 2:5-11. **riches**. ⨍121N2, Ge +34:29. **peeped**. That is, *chirped*, from the Latin *pipio*. We still use the term *pipe* to express the note of the bullfinch.

15. **the axe**. ver. +5. Ps 17:13, 14. Je 51:20-23. Ezk 28:9. Jn 19:11. Ro 9:20, 21. **boast itself**. F/L Is 44:23. Ex 8:9⟩𝒫. **or shall**. ⨍85S, Jb +4:17. **against him**. T#1845. Pr 3:27. 25:11. **the rod should shake itself against them**. *or*, a rod should shake itself. **itself, as if it were no wood**. *or, that which is* not wood.

16. **the Lord of hosts**. Is 5:17. 14:24-27. 29:5-8. 37:6,

7, 29, 36. 2 Ch 32:21. Ps 106:15. Ac 12:23. **and under**. Is 9:5. 30:30-33. 33:10-14.

17. **the light**. Is 60:19. Ps 27:1. *84:11. Re 21:23. 22:5. **fire**. ⨍22K1, Dt +4:24. Is 9:19. Ps *21:9. Ml +*4:1. Lk 12:49. **for a flame**. Is 30:27, 28. 33:14. 64:1, 2. 66:15, 16, 24. Nu 11:1-3. 16:35. Ps 18:8. 21:9. 50:3. 83:14, 15. Je 4:4. 7:20. Ml 4:1-3. Mt *3:12. 2 Th √1:7-9. He *12:29. **devour**. Is *27:4. 37:36. Ps *97:3. Na 1:5, 6, 10. **in one day**. Is 9:14. 2 K 19:35.

18. **consume**. ver. 33, 34. Is *9:18. 2 K 19:23, 28. Je *21:14. Ezk 20:47, 48. **both soul and body**. Heb. from the soul and even to the flesh. Heb. *nephesh*, Ge +12:13. Jb +*14:22. Da *7:15. Mt +*10:28n. **fainteth**. Ps 27:1, 2.

19. **few**. Heb. number. Is 37:36. Nu 9:20. Dt 33:6. 1 S 27:7mg. 2 S 2:11mg. 1 Ch 16:19mg. Jb 16:22mg. Ezk 12:16mg.

20. **that day**. ver. 27. Is 11:10, 11. 12:1, 4. 19:18, 19. 24:21. 28:5. 52:6. Zc 9:16. **the remnant**. Is 1:9. 4:2, 3. 6:13. 37:4, 31, 32. Ezr 9:14. Ezk 7:16. Ro 9:27-29. **no more**. 2 K *16:7. 2 Ch *28:20. Ezk 23:12. Ho *5:13. 14:3. **but shall stay**. Is 17:7, 8. √26:3, 4. 48:1, 2. *50:10. 2 Ch *14:11. Je 21:2. Ho *3:5. 6:1. Mi 3:14. 7:7. **Holy One**. Is 1:4. 5:24. 12:6. 41:14, 16. *57:15. Le 11:44. 19:2. Jb 6:10. Ps 71:22. 89:18. Ho 11:9. **in truth**. F/L Is 16:5. 38:3. 48:1. 61:8.

21. **remnant**. Is +1:9. *11:11. Jl 2:32. 3:1, 2. Mi *4:7. Ro 9:29. **return**. Is 1:27mg. *7:3. 9:13. 19:22. √55:7. 65:8, 9. 2 Ch ✱30:1-13. Ho *6:1. 7:10, 16. 14:1-3. Ac 26:20. 2 C 3:14-16. **the mighty**. ✱S#1368h. Ge 6:4. 10:8, 9, 9. Dt 10:17. Jsh 1:14. 6:2. 8:3. 10:2, 7. Jg 5:13, 23. 6:12. 11:1. Ru 2:1. 1 S 2:4. 9:1. 14:52 (strong). 16:18. 17:51 (champion). 2 S 1:19, 21, 22, 25, 27. 10:7. 16:6. 17:8, 10. 20:7. 22:26 (man). 23:8, 9, 16, 17, 22. 1 K 1:8, 10. 11:28. 2 K 5:1. 15:20. 24:14, 16 (strong). 1 Ch 1:10. 5:24. 7:2, 5, 7, 9, 11. 8:40. +9:13mg, 26 (chief). 11:10, 11, 12, 19, 24, 26. 12:1, 4, 8, 21, 25, 28, 30. 19:8. 26:6, 31. 27:6. 28:1. 29:24. 2 Ch 13:3, 3. 14:8. 17:13, 14, 16, 17. 25:6. 26:12. 28:7. 32:3, 21. Ezr 7:28. Ne 3:16. 9:32. 11:14. Jb 16:14 (giant). Ps 19:5 (strong man). *24:8. 33:16. *45:3. 52:1. 78:65. *89:19. 103:20mg. 112:2. 120:4. 127:4. Pr 16:32. 21:22. 30:30 (strongest). Ec 9:11 (strong). SS 3:7 (valiant), 7. 4:4. Is 3:2. 5:22. +√9:6. +10:21. 13:3. 21:17. 42:13. 49:24, 25. Je 5:16. 9:23. 14:9. 20:11. 26:21. √32:18. 46:5, 6, 9, 12, 12. 48:14, 41. 49:22. 50:9, 36. 51:30, 56, 57. Ezk 32:12, 21, 27, 27. 39:18, 20. Da 11:3. Ho 10:13. Jl 2:7. 3:9, 10, 11. Am 2:14, 16. Ob 9. Na 2:3. Zp 1:14. √3:17. Zc 9:13. 10:5, 7. **God**. Is +√9:6. 45:22. 49:26. 60:16. Ex 3:6. Dt 7:21. *10:17⟩𝒫. Ps *24:8. *45:3. Je √32:18. Zp √3:17. Mt 11:21. Lk 9:43. Ep 1:21. Re 7:10, 12.

22. **though thy**. 1 K 4:20. Ho *1:10. Ro ⟩9:27, 28. *11:5, 6. Re 20:8. **as the sand**. ⨍102B, ⨍138B, Ge +13:16. Ge 22:17⟩𝒫. 32:12⟩𝒫. **yet a remnant**. Is 6:13. **of**. Heb. in, *or*, among. **the consumption**. Is 6:11. 8:8. 27:10, 11. 28:15-22. Dt 28:65⟩𝒫. Da *9:27. Ro 9:28. **with**. *or*, in. Ge +*18:25. Ac √17:31. Ro *2:5. 3:5, 6.

23. **consumption**. Is 28:22. **determined**. Is *14:26, 27. 24:1, etc. Da 4:35. *8:19. Ro 9:28. **midst**. ⨍144A6, Ge +45:6.

24. **O my people**. Is 4:3. 12:6. 30:19. 46:13. 61:3. He 12:22-24. **be not afraid**. Is 8:12, 13. 33:14-16. *35:4. 37:6, 22, 33-35. **smite thee**. ver. 5. Is 9:4. 14:29. 27:7. **and shall lift his staff against thee**. *or*, but he shall

lift up his staff for thee. **after the manner.** Ex 1:10-16. 14:9, 21-31. 15:6-10.

25. **For yet.** ver. 33, 34. Is 12:1, 2. 14:24, 25. 17:12-14. 30:30-33. 31:4-9. 37:36-38. √54:7. 2 K 19:35. Ps *37:10. Da 11:36. He √10:37. 2 P *3:8. **the indignation.** ver. +5. Da +*8:19.

26. **stir up.** See on ver. 16-19. 2 K 19:35. Ps 35:23. **according.** Is 9:4. Jg *7:25. Ps 83:11. **his rod.** See on ver. 24. Is 11:16. *51:9, 10. Ex *14:25-27. Ne 9:10, 11. Ps 106:10, 11. Hab 3:7-15. Re 11:18. 19:15.

27. **his burden.** Is 9:4. 14:25. 2 K 18:13, 14. Na 1:9-13. **be taken away.** Heb. remove. **because.** Is *37:35. 2 S 1:21. Ps *2:1-3, 6mg. 20:6. +*45:7. 84:9. *89:20-22, etc. *105:14, 15. 132:10, 17, 18. Da √9:24-26. Lk *4:18. Jn *1:41mg. Ac 4:27. 1 J √2:20, 27. **anointing.** ſ121N2, Ge +34:29.

28. **He is come.** This is a prophetical description of the march of Sennacherib's army approaching Jerusalem in order to invade it, and of the terror and confusion spreading and increasing through the several places as he advanced; expressed with great brevity, but finely diversified. *Aiath*, or *Ai*, was situated a little east of Bethel, about twelve miles north of Jerusalem; *Michmash* about three miles nearer, where there was narrow pass between two sharp hills; *Geba* and *Ramah* about three miles more to the south; *Gibeah* a mile and a half more southward; *Anathoth* within three miles of Jerusalem; to the westward of which, towards Lydda, was *Nob*, from which place Sennacherib might have a prospect of Zion, and near which, it would appear, his army was destroyed. 2 K 17:5. **Aiath.** i.e. *a heap of ruins,* ✸S#5857h. Jsh 7:2, Ai. Ne 11:31, Aija. **Migron.** 1 S 14:2. **Michmash.** 1 S 13:2, 5. 14:5, 31.

29. **the passage.** 1 S 13:23. 14:4. **Geba.** Jsh 21:17. 1 K 15:22. **Ramah.** Jsh 18:24, 25. 1 S 7:17. 15:34. Je 31:15. Ho 5:8. **Gibeah.** Jg 19:12-15. 1 S 11:4. 13:2. Ho 9:9. 10:9.

30. **Lift up thy voice.** Heb. Cry shrill with thy voice. **Gallim.** 1 S 25:44. **Laish.** Jg 18:7, 29. **Anathoth.** Jsh 21:18. 1 K 2:26. Je 1:1. 32:8.

31. **Madmenah.** i.e. *dunghill,* ✸S#4088h, only here. Is 25:10mg. Jsh 15:31, Madmannah. **Gebim.** i.e. *trenches, pits; beams, locusts,* ✸S#1374h. See ✸S#1356h, Je +14:3.

32. **Nob.** 1 S 21:1. 22:19. Ne 11:32. **shake.** ver. 24. Is 11:15. 13:2. 19:16. Zc 2:9. **hand.** ſ22A14.8C, Is +19:16. **the mount.** Is 2:2. 37:22. **daughter.** ſ155E5, Nu +21:25.

33. **lop.** ver. 16-19. Is 37:24-36, 38. 2 K *19:21-37. 2 Ch 32:21. **the high ones.** Am 2:9. **and the haughty.** Is 2:11-17. Jb 40:11, 12. Da *4:23, 37. Lk 14:11.

34. **cut down.** ver. 18. Is 37:24. Je 22:7. 46:22, 23. 48:2. Na 1:12. **Lebanon.** Zc 11:1, 2. **by a mighty one.** *or,* mightily. Is 31:8. 37:36. Ps 89:6. *103:20. Da 4:13, 14, 23. 2 Th *1:7. He 1:13. 2 P 2:11. Re 10:1. 18:21.

ISAIAH 11

Predictions of Christ, as springing from the root of Jesse; his endowments for his work; and the equity of his government, 1-5; of the peace and holiness produced by his gospel, 6-9; of the conversion of the Gentiles, and the gathering of Israel to him by the marvelous power of God, 10-16.

1. **And there.** ſ3, Ge +49:10. **shall come.** ſ96C2, Ge +45:9. The prophet having described the destruc-

tion of the Assyrian army under that of a mighty forest, here takes occasion to represent the great Person, who makes the subject of this chapter, as a slender twig, shooting out of the trunk of an old tree; which tender twig, though weak in appearance, should become fruitful and prosper. Is 53:2. Zc 6:12. Re *5:5. *22:16. **of Jesse.** T#1880. ver. 10. Ru 4:17. 1 S 17:58. Mt +*✸1:6-16. Lk 2:23-32. ✸3:23-32. Ac *13:22, 23. Ro 15:12. **a Branch.** ſ22H1A, Is +4:2. Is 4:2. Ps 80:15, 17. Je *23:5, 6. *33:15. Zc *3:8. *6:12, 13. **his roots.** Jn 1:1, 14. Ro 15:12. Col 1:17.

2. **the Spirit.** Heb. *ruach,* Ge +41:38. Is 42:1. *57:15. 59:21. *61:1. Ge 1:2. Nu 11:25, 26. Jb 26:13. Ps 51:11. 139:7. Mt 3:16. Lk 4:16-21. Jn *1:32, 33. √3:34. Ac 6:10. 10:38. 1 C 2:10. 12:8. Ep 1:17. Col 1:9. 2:3. Ja 3:17. **rest upon.** Is 61:1. Ps +*45:7. Mt ✸3:16. Jn ✸3:34. Ac ✸10:38. **the spirit.** Heb. *ruach,* Ge +41:38. **of wisdom.** Ex 31:2, 3. Dt 34:9. Mt +*28:19n. Jn 14:17. 15:26. 16:13. 1 C *1:30. Ep 1:17, 18. Col 1:8, 9. 2:2, 3. 2 T +*1:7. Ja 3:17, 18.

3. **shall make him.** Is 33:6. Pr 2:5, 9. Lk *2:46, 47, 52. **understanding.** Heb. scent, *or,* smell. Ge=42:23. Jb 12:11. 34:3. Ph *1:9, 10. He *5:14. **and he shall not judge.** 1 S √16:7. 2 S 14:17. 1 K 3:9, 28. Jn *5:22, 23, 27, 30. 7:24. 8:15, 16, 28, 38. 1 C 2:13-15. 4:3-5.

4. **But with righteousness.** Is 32:1. 2 S 8:15. *23:2-4. 1 K 10:8, 9. Ps +*45:6, 7. 72:*1-4, 12-14. 82:2-4. Je *23:5, 6. 33:15. Mt 11:5. Jn 7:24. Re 19:11. **reprove.** *or,* argue. Is 1:17. Pr 31:8, 9. Je 5:28. **for the meek.** Is 29:19. 61:1. Zp +*2:3. Mt +*5:5. 2 C 10:1. Ga 5:23. T 3:2. Ja 3:13. **he shall smite.** ſ132G, Ge +3:19. Jb 4:9. Ps 2:9. 110:2. Ml 4:6. Ep *6:17. 2 Th *2:8. Re *1:16. *2:16. 19:15. **mouth.** ſ22A10, Nu +12:8. **with the breath.** Heb. *ruach,* Ex +15:8. Is *30:33. Ps 18:8. Ac 9:1. 2 Th +*2:8. **slay the wicked.** Paul cites and applies this verse to the personal Antichrist in 2 Th *2:8. Ps ◐101:8. Pr +*2:22.

5. **righteousness.** Is *59:17. Ps 93:1. Ro 14:17. 2 C 6:7. Ep 6:14. 1 P 4:1. Re 1:13. 15:3. **and faithfulness.** Is 25:1. Ho 2:20. He *2:17. 1 J √1:9. Re *3:14. 19:11, 13.

6. **The wolf.** ſ11, Ge +2:23. The Oriental poets elegantly apply the same ideas to show the effects of justice impartially administered. "Through the influence of righteousness, the hungry wolf becomes mild, though in the presence of the white kid" (Ibn Onein). Is *55:13. *65:17, +*25. Jb 5:23. Ps 8:6-8. Ezk *34:25. Ho +*2:18. Jl *2:22. Mt 19:28. Ac +3:21. 9:13-20. Ro 8:19-21. 14:17. 1 C +*6:9-11. 2 C *5:14-21. Ga 3:26, 27. Ep *4:22-32. Col 3:3-8. T *3:3-5. Phm 9-16. He 2:8. Re 5:9, 10.

7. **cow.** Ge 32:15. 41:2-4, 18-20. **feed.** Is 27:10. 30:23. 40:11. **young ones.** lit. children. Is 2:6. **the lion.** Is *35:9. **ox.** Jb 40:15. Ho 2:18.

8. **weaned child.** Is *28:9. 1 S +1:22n. Ps 131:2. Mt 18:3. 1 C 14:20. **cockatrice'.** *or, adder's.* F/L Is 59:5mg. Ps 91:13. 140:3. Pr 23:32mg. Mk 16:18.

9. **not hurt.** ver. 13. Is *2:4. 35:9. *60:18. Jb 5:23. Ho 2:18. Mi 4:2-4. Mt +*5:44, 45. Ac 2:41-47. 4:29-35. Ro 12:17-21. Ga *5:22-24. Ph 2:14, 15. 1 Th 5:15. Re 21:27. **in all.** Zc 14:9. Ac 4:32. **holy mountain.** F/L Is 27:13. 56:7. 57:13. 65:25. **for the earth.** Is 30:26. 49:6. 59:19. 60:1, etc. Ps *22:27-31. 72:19. 98:2, 3. Ec +*1:4. Hab √2:14. Zc +*14:9. Mt +*5:5. Ro *11:25, 26. Re *20:2-6. **be full.** Je *31:34. He √8:11. **the knowl-**

edge. Is 1:3. 6:3. Nu *14:21⃗𝒫. Ps +*9:10. Jn *17:3. 1 C 13:8, 12.

10. **in that day.** ver. 1. Is 2:11. Ro ▸15:12. Re 22:16. **root.** 𝒥22H1D. Anthropomorphism B895. Certain plants are used as figures of God: a root. For other instances of this figure see Ro 15:12. Re 5:5. 22:16. **Jesse.** ver. +1. **which shall.** Is 59:19. Ge +√49:10. Jn *3:14, 15. *12:32. **ensign.** 𝒥22D5Q, Ex +17:15. **to it shall the Gentiles.** Is 42:1. 60:3, 5. 66:12, 19. Ge 49:22. Mt 2:1, 2. *8:11. ✱12:17, 21. Lk *2:32. Jn 3:14, 15. ✱10:16. 12:20, 21, *32. Ac ✱10:45, 47. 11:18. 26:17, 18. √28:28. Ro √15:9-12. **his rest.** Is 32:17, 18. 66:10-12. Ps 91:1, 4. 116:7. Je 6:16. Zp 3:17. Hg 2:9. Mt √11:28-30. 2 Th √1:7-12. He 4:1, 3, 6, 8, 9, etc. 1 P 1:7-9. 5:10. **glorious.** Heb. glory. Ps 149:5. Mt 25:31. Ro 8:18, 21. 1 C *2:9, 10. 2 C 3:10. 4:17. Ph 4:19. T *2:13. 1 P 5:1, 10.

11. **set his hand.** 𝒥22A14.1, Nu +11:23. Is 26:19-21. ch. 60-66. Le 26:40-42. Dt 4:27-31. 30:3-6. Ps 68:22. Je 23:7, 8. 30:8-11. 31:36-40. 33:24-26. Ezk 11:16-20. 34:23-28. 36:24, etc. ch. 37-48. Ho 1:11. 3:4, 5. Jl ch. 3. Am √9:9, 14, 15. Mi 7:14, 15. Zc 10:8-12. ch. 12-14. Ro *11:15, 25, 26. 2 C 3:16. **the second time.** Some interpreters suggest the *first time* was Israel's exodus from Egypt, making the *second time* refer to Israel's return from the Babylonian captivity. This is not correct. Israel's full restoration was not accomplished with the return from the Babylonian captivity but is still future (Dt 30:4n). The second regathering (the Bible does not predict a third) precedes the restoration. The regathering brings Israel back to the land in unbelief (Zp 2:1, 2) before the rapture (Zp +*2:3) and the great tribulation (Je +*30:7. Da +*12:1). The initial regathering of Israel to the land (Is 54:7. Ezk +*34:13. +*37:25) sets the stage for the further working out of God's prophetic purposes, for even Christ in the Olivet discourse assumes Israel is in the land (Mt 24:15) before the tribulation. The purpose of the regathering and final restoration is to make possible the fulfillment of the Abrahamic and Davidic covenants (Is +*55:3. Ac +*7:5). This regathering (Mt 24:31n) must be distinguished carefully from the final restoration. The following predictions were not fulfilled by the return from Babylon, and therefore relate to the initial regathering in unbelief, the future glorious restoration and final regathering. The regathered and/or restored nation will (1) speak Hebrew (Ne ◐√13:24. Je 31:23. Zp 3:9); (2) return the *second time* (Is √11:11); (3) no more be removed (Is 60:21. Ezk 37:23-27. Am +√9:15). Since Israel was removed in A.D. 70, long after the return from Babylon, these predictions cannot refer to the return from Babylon, but must refer to a future return. (4) The return of Christ in the first stage of the Second Advent, unobserved by the world, takes place with the resurrection of the righteous dead and the rapture of living believers (1 Th +*4:16n, 17n). (5) The restoration of Israel is contingent upon their final repentance and spiritual awakening (Ezk 39:22. Ho 5:15. Ml 3:7), and will come at the height of the great tribulation when Jerusalem is taken and all hope of survival is gone (Zc 14:2). (6) God responds to the cry of an apparently very small believing remnant (Is +*17:6. 24:13, 14. 30:19. Ps 80:2mg. Zc √13:9). (7) This believing remnant, probably accounting for one third or less of the Jews at that time (Zc 13:8. 14:2) may have been prepared spiritually by careful students

of the Bible among them who taught others (Da +*11:33) apart from any officially recognized ecclesiastical organizations, and some of these may be the Jewish evangelists to the world during the tribulation (Is +*27:6). This spiritual response may also be directly related to the appearance of Elijah (Ml 4:5). (8) The repentance of this remnant determines the timing of the Second Advent (Ho 6:1. Ac +*3:19-21). (9) In the final moments of tribulation crisis the question is asked, "Where is their God?" (Jl 2:17). (10) Israel shall cry, "My God, we know thee" (Ho 8:2. Zc 13:9). (11) When Israel's cry ascends, God will hear (Is *30:19). In answer to this prayer the Lord will (12) be jealous for his land and pity his people (Jl 2:18). (13) God will remove the northern army (Jl 2:20). (14) God will put Israel's enemies to flight (Is 59:19). All this is contingent upon Israel's final repentance (Ho 5:15. Ml 3:7, 16, 17. 4:2). (15) When Israel turns from transgression, the Messiah will come to deliver her (Is +√59:19, 20. Lk 21:28. Ac +√3:19-21. Ro +√11:26). (16) God awaits (Is +*30:18) and will plead with them in the wilderness (Ezk 20:35, 36. Ho 2:14) *till* they acknowledge their guilt and call upon Him (Is +√59:20. Ho 5:15. Jl √2:12, 17, 18). Thus it appears that a portion of the Jews will be in Jerusalem (Ezk 22:19, 20. Zc *14:2) and the rest of the land of Israel, while another portion of the Jews will be in the wilderness (Ezk 20:35, 36. Ho 2:14. Re +*12:6, 14) at this time. A third portion will be scattered throughout the nations of the earth. (17) The words of the prayer (Ps 60:1. Ho 14:2). (18) The swift answer to the prayer (Is +*65:24). (19) God will immediately answer (Is *30:19. Je √33:3). (20) God will defend Judah and Jerusalem against the armies of Antichrist (Zc +*12:8), delivering the tents of Judah first (Zc 12:7). (21) The Lord will be literally seen over them, protecting and defending them, and defeating their enemies (Zc 9:14). (22) They shall know from then on that the Lord is their God (Ezk 39:22. Jl 2:27). Upon this repentance God will (23) take away Israel's judgments, cast out the enemy, be the king of Israel, the Lord in the midst of them, and Israel shall not see evil any more (Zp 3:15). (24) The Messiah will return to the earth before the open manifestation of the Second Advent (Re 11:17n. 16:5) to the region of Sinai (Dt +*33:2. Ps +*68:7, 8. Is +*16:1-5) to organize his kingdom; proceed with judgment upon the enemies of Israel, to Bozrah (Is 34:1-10), for they have sought refuge and have been hidden there (Is +*16:1-5), perhaps at Petra (2 K 14:7n. Is 16:1mg. Je 49:16n. Ezk 35:9n. Ob +*3); Christ proceeds to destroy His enemies (Is 63:1-3), and to march victoriously (Dt 33:2) to Jerusalem, where he will ascend the mount of Olives (Zc 14:4) and come to Zion (Is +*51:11). Israel's return from the wilderness at the start of the Millennium (Ho 2:14-23), led by God, may be referred to this time. (25) All the saints will return with God and Christ at the visible final stage of the Second Advent (Ps +*149:9. Ho +*11:12. Jl 3:11. Ob +*21). (26) This will be a time of great singing and rejoicing (Is 24:14-16. Ho +*2:15. Jl 2:23. Zc +*2:10). (27) As a result of the earthquake at the Second Advent of Christ, the physical features of the land and mount Zion experience topographical changes which will raise Jerusalem to a more eminent position, making it "beautiful for situation" (Ps 48:2), leveling the present surrounding towering mountains like a plain (or, the Arabah, a hollow depression), providing the space needed for the millennial temple (Ezk 42:16n. Zc √14:4, 10). (28) Israel will at last possess the full geographical extent of the land covenanted to Abraham (1 K 4:21n. Is +*26:15. Je +*7:7. +*33:21n. Ac +*7:5. He +*11:13, 39). (29) The captivity will be ended, the commencement of the final and complete regathering begins, and Israel will be a name and a praise among all the nations of the earth (Zp 3:20). (30) Israel will experience a supernatural return, apparently after the tribulation just prior to the millennium (Is 27:12. Ezk 34:12. Am 9:9), to be distinguished from the initial regathering in unbelief. (31) This will be a complete return (Ezk 39:28). (32) Unlike the return from Babylon, this is a worldwide return (Is 43:6. Je 31:8. Ezk 38:8n). (33) It is a return in joy without sorrow (Is 65:19). (34) It includes the return of the resurrected (Ezk 37:12). (35) The land will be crowded (Is 49:19. Zc 2:4. 8:4, 5. 10:9, 10). (36) The millennium is preceded by the universal cleansing of the earth by fire to rid the world of the wicked (Ps 97:3. Is 24:1-6. +*66:24. Jl 2:30. Zp 2:3. Ml 4:1. Mt 3:11, 12. +*13:40-42. 2 Th *1:8. He *10:27. 2 P √3:10-13n). (37) In the land of Israel preparatory cleansing of the land will take place so the millennial temple can be built (Zc 13:1). (38) The millennial temple will be built by the Messiah (Zc 6:12, 13). (39) Christ in victory will judge the nations to determine which nations will be permitted to enter the millennium (Mt +*10:15n. √25:31-46). (40) Jewish evangelists will travel throughout the world to preach the gospel among the unconverted Gentile nations at the beginning of the millennium (Is +√66:19). (41) Thereafter knowledge of the Lord will be universal (Is 54:13. Hab 2:14. Jn +*6:45. He +*8:11). (40) Israel will be the spiritual center of the world (Mi 4:1, 2. Zc *8:3, 22, 23. 14:16). (42) Israel will never suffer God's wrath or fury again (Is 51:22). (43) Israel will dwell in supernatural righteousness (Is +*60:21). (44) Israel will be as though God had never cast them off (Jl +*2:25. Zc +√10:6. Ml 3:4). (45) Through Messiah Israel will be "head of the heathen," with Messiah as king over all the earth, ruling from Jerusalem (Ps 18:43. 110:2. Je 3:17. Mi 4:7. Zp 3:15. Zc *14:9). (46) Israel will "eat the riches of the Gentiles" (Is 61:6). (47) This is what marks the "fulness of the Gentiles" (Ro 11:25). (48) Israel will be a praise among all people of the earth (Is 60:15. 61:9, 11. Zp *3:20. Zc 8:13. Ml 1:11. 3:12). (49) Israel will no more be a reproach among the heathen (Jl 2:19. Zc 8:13). (50) Israel shall never be invaded by foreign powers again (Jl +*3:17. Ml 4:1-3), pertaining of course to the restoration, not necessarily the initial regathering. (51) Israel will "take them captives whose captives they were" (Is 14:2. 60:14. 61:5). (52) Israel will not depart from the Lord (Is 59:21. Je 32:40). The restoration of Israel (53) inaugurates universal peace and righteousness on earth (Is 2:4. Mi 4:3-5. Zc 9:10); (54) results in the restoration of all nature and the removal of the curse (Is √11:6-9. 24:6. 65:25. Ezk 34:25. Ml 4:6. Ac +*3:19. Ro 8:19-23. Re 22:3); and (55) is accompanied by the universal removal of all false religion (Is 45:22. Ho 2:17. Mi ☾*4:5. *5:8, 12, 13. Zc *13:2. Ml *1:11). Ex 15:16, 17)♇. Je +*23:8. 29:14. +*31:36. Am +√9:14, 15. Zc 8:7, 8. Ml 3:4, 6, 12, 18. Ro +*11:1. **from Assyria.** ver. 16. Is *27:12, 13. Mi 7:12. Zc 10:10. **Egypt.** Is 19:23. Je 44:1. **Pathros.** i.e. *extension of ruin; a morsel moistened,* ✳S#6624h.

Is 11:11. Je 44:1, 15. Ezk 29:14. 30:14. **Cush.** Is 45:14. Ge 10:6, 7. **Elam.** Ge 10:22. Je 25:25. Da 8:2. **Shinar.** Ge +10:10. 11:2. Zc 5:11. **Hamath.** Is 10:9. Je 49:23. Zc 9:2. **the islands.** F/L Is 20:6. 23:2, 6. 24:15. 40:15. 41:1, 5. 42:4, 10, 12, 15. 49:1. 51:5. 59:18. 60:9. 66:19. Ge 10:5. Ps 72:10. Je 31:10. Ezk 27:6. Da 11:18. Zp 2:11.

12. **set up.** ver. 10. Is 18:3. 59:19. 62:10. Re 5:9. **shall assemble.** Is 27:13. *43:6. 49:11, 12. 56:8. Dt 32:26. Ps 68:22. +*147:2. Zp 3:10. Jn 7:35. Ja *1:1. **outcasts of Israel.** Is +*16:3. Ps +*147:2. **gather together.** Ps +*147:2. Ezk *11:17. +34:13. **corners.** Heb. wings. Is +24:16mg. Jb 37:3mg.

13. **the envy.** Is 7:1-6. 52:7, 8. 60:14. Je *3:18. Ezk *37:16-24. Ho *1:11. Jn 11:52. 13:34, 35. **the adversaries.** Nu 24:17.

14. **the Philistines.** Ob 19. Zp 2:5. Zc 9:5-7. **toward.** Is 59:19. 66:19, 20. Mt +*8:11. **spoil.** Is 33:1. Je 49:28. Ezk ch. 38, 39. **them of the east.** Heb. the children of the east. Is 2:6. Ge 25:6. 29:1. Nu 23:7. Jg 6:3, 33. 7:12. 8:10, 11. 1 K 4:30. Jb 1:3. Je 49:28. Ezk 25:4, 10. **they shall lay,** etc. Heb. Edom and Moab *shall be* the laying on of their hand; the children of Ammon their obedience. Is 25:10. 34:5, 6. 60:14. Nu 24:17. Da 11:41. Jl 3:19. Am 9:12. Ob 18. Re 15:3, 4.

15. **the Lord shall.** T#379. Is 27:12. Re 16:12. **utterly.** Is 50:2. 51:9, 10. Zc 10:11. Re 21:1. **with his mighty.** Ex 14:16, 21, 29. **he shake.** Is 19:16. **his hand.** ♪22A14.8C, Is +19:16. **shall smite.** Is 19:5-10. Ex 7:19-21. Ps 74:13-15. Ezk 29:10. 30:12. Zc *10:11. Re *16:12. **go over.** or, tread it. Jg 20:43. Jb 28:8. Pr 4:11h. **dryshod.** Heb. in shoes, ✳S#5275h. Is 5:27. 20:2. Ge 14:23. Ex 3:5. 12:11. Dt 25:9, 10. 29:5. Jsh 5:15. 9:5, 13. Ru 4:7, 8. 1 K 2:5. Ps 60:8. 108:9. SS 7:1. Ezk 24:17, 23. Am 2:6. 8:6.

16. **And there shall.** ver. 11. Is 19:23. 27:13. *35:8-10. 40:3, 4. 49:12. 57:14. **like as it was.** Is 42:15, 16. 48:20, 21. 51:10. 63:12, 13. Ex 14:22)♇, 26-29. **in the day.** ♪171T2, Ge +2:17. Ge 2:4, 17. 1 K 2:37. Ezk 36:33.

ISAIAH 12

A joyful thanksgiving of the faithful for the mercies of God, on the accomplishment of the preceding prophecies, 1-6.

1. **And in that.** Is 2:11. 11:10, 11, 16. 14:3. 26:1. 27:1-3, 12, 13. *35:10. Zc 14:9, 20, 21. **O Lord.** Is 25:1, 9. 49:13. 60:18, 19. Ps 34:1, etc. 67:1-4. 69:34-36. 72:15-19. 149:6-9. Ro 11:15. Re 15:3, 4. 19:1-7. **though.** Is 10:4, 25. *40:1, 2. 51:3. *54:8. *57:15-18. *66:13. Dt 30:1-3. Ps 30:5. 85:1-3. Je 31:18-20. Ezk 39:24-29. Ho 6:1. 11:8. *14:4-9. **thou comfortedst.** Is *49:13.

2. **God.** Heb. *El,* Ex +15:2. Is 7:14. +*9:6, 7. *45:17, 22-25. Ps *27:1. Je 3:23. *23:6. Jon *2:9. Mt *1:21-23. Lk 2:30-32. Ro *1:16. 1 T *3:16. Re 7:10. **I will trust.** Is 8:17. 2 S 22:3. Ps 56:3. He ♭2:13. **not be afraid.** T#814. Is 35:3, 4. 40:29-31. 42:3. Jb 11:15. Ps *31:24. +*34:4. 68:35. Jl 3:16. Zc 10:12. 12:8. 2 C *12:9. 2 T √1:7. 1 J 4:18. **the Lord.** Is √26:4. Ex +*15:2. Ps 83:18. *118:14. Ho 1:7. **Jehovah.** Is 26:4. Ex *3:13, 14. *6:3. Ps 83:18. **my strength.** Ex 15:2)♇. Nu 23:22. Jb 9:19. Ps *27:1. 89:8, 13. **my salvation.** Is 52:9, 10. Je 3:23. Mt 1:21. Ac √4:12.

3. **with joy.** Is 49:10. *55:1-3. Ps 36:9. 51:12. SS 2:3. Je *2:13. Jn 1:16. *4:10-14. *7:37-39. Re 7:17. 21:6. 22:1, 17. **wells.** Heb. *mayan,* Ge +7:11 (*S#4599h). **salvation.** Ge 49:18)𝒫. Ex 14:13)𝒫. 15:2)𝒫. Dt 32:15)𝒫.

4. **in that day.** ver. 1. Ps 65:1. 106:47, 48. 113:1-3. ch. 117. **call upon his name.** *or,* proclaim his name. Ex 33:19. 34:5-7. 1 Ch 16:8. Ps 105:1. **declare.** Is 66:19. Ps 9:11. 22:31. 40:5. 71:16-18. 73:28. 96:3. 107:22. 145:4-6. Je 50:2. 51:9, 10. Jn 17:26. 2 Th 1:10. **his name.** Is 2:11, 17. 25:1. 33:5. Ex 15:2. 1 Ch 29:11. Ne 9:5. Ps +*9:10. 18:46. 21:13. 34:3. 46:10. 57:5. 97:9. 113:5. Ph √2:9-11.

5. **Sing.** Ex 15:1, 21)𝒫. Ps 68:32-35. 98:1. 105:2. Re *15:3. 19:1-3. **excellent things.** Mk 7:37. Lk 13:17. **this is known.** Is 40:9. Ps 72:19. Hab *2:14. Re 11:15-17.

6. **Cry out.** Is 40:9. 52:7-10. 54:1. Zp 3:14. Zc 9:9. Lk 19:37-40. **thou.** Is 10:24. 24:23. 30:19. 33:24. Zc 8:3-8. **inhabitant.** Heb. inhabitress. Je 10:17mg. Mi 1:11mg. **for great.** Is 8:18. 24:23. 25:9. 41:14, 16. Ps 9:11. 47:2. 68:16. 71:22. 89:18. 102:16. 132:14. Je 23:5, 6. Ezk 43:7. *48:35. Zp 2:5. 3:15-17. Zc 2:5, 10, 11. **in the midst.** Ps +*16:11. Jl *2:27. Zp 3:14, 15, 17. Zc *2:5, 10. 12:10. Jn 12:35, 36. Re 21:23.

ISAIAH 13

God musters the armies of his indignation, 1-5. The terrible destruction of Babylon by the Medes, 6-18. The final devastation of Babylon, 19-22.

1. A.M. 3292. B.C. 712. **burden.** ∫121L4, Is +22:1. Is 14:28. 15:1. 17:1. 19:1. 21:1, 11, 13. 22:1, 25. 23:1. Nu 24:3)𝒫. Je 23:33-38. Ezk 12:10. Na 1:1. Hab 1:1. Zc 9:1. 12:1. Ml 1:1. **of Babylon.** Is 14:4, etc. 21:1-10. 43:14. 44:1, 2. 47:1, etc. Ge 10:10. Je 25:12-26. ch. 50, 51. Da 5:28-31, etc. Re 16:19. ch. 17, 18. **which Isaiah.** Is 1:1.

2. **Lift ye up.** Is 5:26. 11:12. 18:3. Je 50:2. 51:27, 28. **upon the high.** Je 51:25. **shake.** Is 10:32. 11:15. **hand.** ∫22A14.8C, Is +19:16. **go into.** Is 45:1-3. Je 51:58.

3. **commanded.** Is 23:11. *44:27, 28. *45:1, 4, 5. Ezr 1:1-4. Ps *149:5-7, +9. Je 50:21, etc. Re 19:14-16. **mighty ones.** Je 51:20-24. Jl +*3:11. Mt *13:41. Re 17:12-18. 18:1, 2, etc. **them that.** Ezr ch. 1, 6. 7:12-26. Ps √149:2, 5-9. Re 18:4-8, 20-24. 19:1-7.

4. **noise.** Is 22:1-9. Je 50:2, 3, 21, etc. 51:*11, 27, 28. Ezk 38:3-23. Jl 3:14. Zc 14:1-3, 13, 14. Re *19:11-21. **like as.** Heb. the likeness of. Jl 2:4-11. Re 9:7-10, 14-19. **the Lord.** Is 10:5, 6. 45:1, 2. Je 50:14, 15. 51:6-25. Jl 2:1-11, 25. Re 18:8. **mustereth.** 1 S +11:8.

5. **from a far country.** ver. 17. Je 50:3, 9. 51:11, 27, 28. Mt 24:31. **end of heaven.** ∫121Q3, 2 S +22:8. i.e. from where the earth seems to touch the heaven. Dt 4:32. 30:4. Ne 1:9. Mt 24:31. **and the weapons.** Je 51:20, etc. **his indignation.** Da +*8:19. **the whole land.** ∫171.O.3, Ge +41:57.

6. **Howl ye.** Is 14:31. 23:1. 52:5. 65:14. Je 25:34. 49:3. *51:8. Ezk 21:12. 30:2. Jl 1:5, 11, 13. Zp 1:14. Ja *5:1. Re 18:10. **for the.** ver. 9. Is +*2:12. *34:8. Ezk *30:3. Jl *2:11, 31. Am 5:18. Zp *1:7. *2:2, 3. Ml *4:5. 1 C +*3:13. 1 Th *5:2, 3. Re *6:17. **day of the Lord.** ∫121P4, Dt +4:32. ver. 9. Ezk 13:5. Jl *1:15. 2:1, 11, 31. 3:14. Am 5:18, 18, 20. Ob 15. Zp 1:7, 14, 14. Ml 4:5. 1 Th +*5:2. 2 Th ◑2:2. 2 P +*3:10.

Re 1:10n. **as a.** Jb 31:23. Jl 1:15.

7. **shall all.** Is 10:3, 4. 37:27. 51:20. Je 50:43. Ezk 7:17. 21:7. Na 1:6. **be faint.** *or,* fall down. Zp 3:16mg. **every.** Is 19:1. Ex 15:15. Na 2:10.

8. **pangs.** Is 21:3, 4. 26:17. Ps 48:5, 6. Je +*30:6, 7. *50:43. 51:30, 31. Da *5:5, 6, 30, 31. 1 Th *5:3. **be amazed one at another.** Heb. wonder every man at his neighbor. Ge 43:33. **flames.** Heb. faces of the flames. Jb +41:21. Jl 2:6. Na 2:10. 3:3mg.

9. **the day.** ver. 6. Is +*34:8. **cruel.** ver. 15-18. Is 47:10-15. Je 6:22, 23. 50:40-42. 51:35-58. Na 1:2, *6. Ml +*4:1. Re 17:16, 17. 18:8. 19:17-21. **the land.** Re 16:2. **destroy the sinners out.** Is +*24:6. Ps *37:9, 10, 20. *104:35. Pr *2:22. 2 P +*3:7.

10. **the stars.** Is 5:30. 14:13. 24:21, 23. 47:13. Ge 1:16. Ezk 32:7, 8. Jl 2:10, *31. *3:15. Am 8:9, 10. Zp 1:15, 16. Mt 24:29. Mk 13:24, 25. Lk 21:25. Re 6:12-14. 8:12. **constellations.** Jb 9:9. Am 5:8. **give their light.** F/L Is 38:18 (celebrate). 41:16. 45:25 (glory). 62:9. 64:11 (praise). 2 S 22:29. Ps 18:28. 19:1-3. 145:10. Jl 2:30, 31. Zc 14:6. Re 6:12. **darkened.** Is 5:30. 34:4. Jb 18:6. Pr 20:20. Jl 2:10. 3:15. Mt *)24:29. Mk 13:24-26. Lk 21:25-27. **going forth.** Is 37:28. Ge 8:7. **to shine.** 2 S 22:29. Ps 18:28.

11. **I will punish.** Is 14:21. 24:4-6. Je 51:34-38. Re 12:9, 10. 18:2, 3. **the world.** ∫171.O.2. Synecdoche of the Whole B638. "World" is put for a primary part of it. Here, a primary reference to Babylon (ver. 1). For other instances of this figure see Is 14:17. Lk 2:1. **and I will cause.** Is 2:17. 5:15. 14:12-16. *47:1. Ps 110:5. Je 50:29-32. Da *5:22, 23.

12. **a man.** ver. 15-18. Is √4:1. 10:19. √24:6. Ps 137:9. **more precious.** or, rare. Is 24:6. Pr 8:12, 14-16, 18, 19. Ezk ◑22:18. **Ophir.** 1 K +9:28n. 2 Ch +8:18n.

13. **Therefore.** He 12:26. **I will.** Jl 3:16. Hg *2:6, 7, 21, 22. Mt 24:29. He 12:26, 27. Re 6:13, 14. **the earth.** Je 4:23, 24. Mt 24:35. 2 P *3:10. Re *20:11. **in the wrath.** Ps 110:5, 6. La 1:12. Na 1:4-6. Re 19:17-19, 21. **fierce anger.** Je 51:1-4, 6. He 12:28, 29.

14. **as the.** Is 17:13. 1 K 22:17, 36. **they shall.** Is 47:15. Je *50:16. 51:9. Re *18:9, 10.

15. **that is found.** Is *14:19-22. 47:9-14. Je 50:27, 35-42. 51:3.

16. **children.** Ps *137:8, 9. Ho 10:14. Na *3:10. **and their.** La 5:11. Zc 14:2.

17. **I will.** ver. 3. Is *21:2. 41:25. Je 50:9. *51:11, 27, 28. Da *5:28-31. **shall not regard.** Pr 6:34, 35.

18. **shall dash.** ver. 16. 2 K 8:12. Ho 13:16. Na 2:1. 3:10. **their eye.** ∫155A, Ge +31:25. 2 Ch 36:17. Ezk 9:5, 6, 10.

19. **Babylon.** Babylon, whose destruction and utter ruin are here predicted, was situated in the midst of a large plain, having a very deep and fruitful soil, on the Euphrates, about 252 miles south-east of Palmyra, and the same distance north-west of Susa and the Persian gulf, in lat. 32 degrees 30 minutes North and long. 44 degrees 20 minutes East. According to Herodotus, it formed a perfect square, each side of which was 120 stadia, and consequently its circumference 480 stadia, or sixty miles; enclosed by a wall 200 cubits high, and fifty wide, on the top of which were small watch towers of one story high, leaving a space between them, through which a chariot and four might pass and turn. On each side were twenty-five gates of solid brass, from each of which proceeded a street, 150 feet broad, making in all fifty streets; which, crossing each

other at right angles, intersected the city into 676 squares, extending four stadia and a half on each side, along which stood the houses, all built three or four stories high, and highly decorated towards the street; the interior of these squares being employed as gardens, pleasure grounds. Its principal ornaments were the temple of Belus, having a tower of eight stories, upon a base of a quarter of a mile square; a most magnificent palace, and the famous hanging gardens, or artificial mountains raised upon arches, and planted with large and beautiful trees. Cyrus took it by diverting the waters of the Euphrates, which ran through the midst, and entering by the channel; and the river being never restored to its proper course, overflowed the whole country and made it a morass. Darius Hystaspes afterwards depopulated the place, lowered the walls, and demolished the gates; Xerxes destroyed the temples; the building of Seleucia nearly exhausted it of its inhabitants; a king of the Parthians carried a number of them into slavery, and destroyed the most beautiful parts; so that modern travelers describe it as a mass of shapeless ruins, the habitation of wild beasts. Is 14:4-6, 12-15. Je 51:41. Da 2:37, 38. *4:30. Re 14:8. *18:10, 21. **when God overthrew.** Heb. the overthrowing of. Ge 19:24, 25♪♫. Dt 29:23. Je 49:18. *50:40. Zp 2:9, 10. 2 P *2:6.

20. **never.** Jb +4:30 (*S#5331h). **be inhabited.** Is *14:23. 15:6, 7. 21:9. 34:11. 46:1. 47:1-11. Je 25:12-14. *50:3, 13, 21, 39, 45. *51:25, 29, 43, 62-64. Zp 3:6. Re 18:21-23.

21. **But.** Is 34:11-15. Re 18:2. **wild beasts.** Heb. *Ziim.* **doleful creatures.** Heb. *Ochim.* **owls.** *or,* ostriches. Heb. daughters of the owl. Is +34:13mg. **satyrs.** Le 17:7. 2 Ch 11:15. 25:14.

22. **the wild beasts.** Heb. *Iim.* **desolate houses.** *or,* palaces. Ezk 19:7. **dragons.** Is 35:7. **her time.** Dt 32:35. Je *51:33. Ezk 7:7-10. Hab *2:3. 2 P 2:3. *3:9, 10.

ISAIAH 14

A prediction of Jacob's deliverance, as the effect of Babylon's ruin, 1, 2. A prophetical exultation over the royal family, and the last king of Babylon; and over the desolations of that city, 3-23. The ruin of Sennacherib's army predicted, 24-27. The burden of the Philistines, 28-32.

1. **the Lord.** Is 40:1, 2. 44:21, 22. *54:7, 8. Le √26:40-45. Dt 4:29-31. Ne 1:8, 9. Ps 98:3. *102:13. 136:10-24. 143:12. Je 50:4-6, 17-20, 33, 34. 51:4-6, 34-37. Lk 1:54, 72-74. **choose.** Is 27:6. Zc 1:17. 2:12. **set.** Dt *30:3-5. Je 24:5-7. 29:14. 30:18-22. 31:8-12. *32:37-41. Ezk *36:24-28. 39:25-29. **the strangers.** Ge +23:4 (*S#1616h). Ex 12:48mg. Ps 146:9. Je 7:6. **be joined.** Is 19:24, 25. 49:16-23. *56:6-8. *60:3-5, 10. 66:20. Ru 1:14-18. Est ✷8:17. Je 12:15, 16. Zc 2:11. *8:22, 23. Ml 1:11. Lk 2:32. Ac *15:14-17. Ep *2:12-19.

2. **and the house.** Is 18:7. *60:9-12. *61:5. Ezr 2:65. Ro *15:27. 2 C 8:4, 5. Ga 5:13. **for servants.** Is 49:22, 23. **and they.** Ps 68:18. 2 C 10:5. Ep 4:8. **whose captives they were.** Heb. that had taken them captives. **they shall rule over.** Is *60:14. Je 30:16. Da 7:18, 25-27. Zc 14:2, 3. Re 3:9. 11:11-18. 18:20-24.

3. **rest.** Is 12:1. *32:18. Dt 28:48, 65-68. Ezr 9:8, 9. Je *30:10. 46:27, 28. 50:34. Ezk 28:24. Zc 8:2, 3,

8. Mt *11:28. Re 18:20. 19:1-3. **thy fear.** Ps +*34:4. Pr *1:33. 3:25.

4. **take up.** ♪48, Ps +2:4. Nu 23:7, 18♪♫. 24:3, 15, 20, 21, 23♪♫. Jb 27:1. 29:1. Mi 2:4. Hab 2:6. **proverb.** *or,* taunting speech. Je 24:9. Ezk 5:15. Hab 2:6. **Babylon.** ♪146, Ge +10:10. **How.** ver. 6, 17. Is 47:5. 49:26. 51:23. Je 25:9-14. 27:6, 7. 37:6, 7. *50:22, 23. 51:20-24, 34, 35. Da 7:19-25. Hab 1:2-10. 2:6-12, 17. Re 13:15-17. 16:5, 6. 17:6. 18:5-8, 20. **golden city.** *or,* exactress of gold. Is *13:19. 45:2, 3. 2 Ch 36:18. La 4:1. Da *2:38. Re *18:16.

5. **broken the staff.** ver. 29. Is 9:4. 10:5. Ps *125:3. 129:4. Je 48:15-17.

6. **who smote.** Is 33:1. 47:6. 2 Ch 36:17. Je 25:9. Da 7:19-21. Ja 2:13. **continual stroke.** Heb. a stroke without removing. lit. turning aside. Is 1:5. 31:6. **is persecuted.** Is 13:14-18. 21:1-10. 47:1, etc. Je 25:26. 50:2, 31. 51:25. Re 17:16, 17. 18:8-10. **and none.** ♪175B, Ge +21:16. Is 46:10, 11. Jb 9:13. Pr +*21:30. Da 4:35. Ja *2:13.

7. **they.** Is 49:13. Ps 96:11-13. 98:7-9. *126:1-3. Pr 11:10. Je 51:48. Re *18:20. *19:1-6. **break forth.** F/L Is 44:23. 49:13. 52:9. 54:1. 55:12.

8. **fir trees.** Is 37:24. 41:19. 55:13. 60:13. Ezk *17:2, 3, 11, 12. **rejoice.** ♪155D, Ge +4:10. Is 55:12, 13. Ezk *31:16. Zc 11:2. **saying.** ♪63BA, Ge +26:7.

9. **Hell.** *or,* The grave. Heb. *sheol,* Ge +37:35. The Hebrew word *sheol,* which our translation renders "hell," or "the grave," signifies the state of the dead in general, Jb 13:14, and is indifferently applied to the good and bad. Here it is taken in the worst sense, and denotes the infernal mansions of deceased tyrants (Lowth, cited by Scott). Ps 16:8-11. Pr 15:24. **from beneath.** Is *30:33. Pr *15:24. Ezk *32:21. Mt +12:40. Ju *6. **is moved.** The scene here changes. The regions of the dead are laid open to the imagination, and their inhabitants are seen in commotion, at the approach of this proud monarch to join their company: and the mighty kings and captains (especially they whom the kings of Babylon had destroyed), are represented as leaving their several thrones in order to meet him: not to condole with him, or to welcome him; but to insult him as now become like one of them; and as bereft of all his pomp, luxury, music, and mirth; while his poor remains on earth are become company and food for the worms. "This is one of the boldest prosopopoeias that ever was attempted in poetry; and is executed with astonishing brevity and perspicuity, and with that peculiar force, which in a great subject naturally results from both" (Bp. Lowth, cited by Scott). Ezk 32:18-32. Mk 9:43-50. Doubtless this is a poetical description, and the imagery is taken from external objects: but we must remember that it has truth for its basis; that the wicked remove at death to a place of misery; and that proud malignant spirits do insult and torment each other (Scott). Lk 16:27-31. **the dead.** Heb. *rephaim,* S#7496h, Pr +*21:16. The word *rephaim,* rendered *the dead,* signifies *giants* (Dt +*2:20. Jsh +17:15); and Mr. Mede seems to think that the rebels of the old world, who perished in the deluge, were especially intended (Scott). **chief ones.** Heb. leaders, *or,* great goats. Matthew Poole notes, which lead and govern the flock. Is 1:11mg. Je 50:8.

10. **speak.** ♪155D, Ge +4:10. **Art thou also.** Jb *30:23. Ps *49:6-14, 20. 82:6, 7. Ec *2:16. Lk √16:20-23. **become like.** Nu +21:27.

11. **pomp.** Is 21:4, 5. 22:2. Jb *21:11-15. Ezk *26:13. 32:19, 20. Da *5:1-4, 25-30. Am *6:3-7. Re *18:11-19. **grave.** Heb. *sheol*, Ge +37:35. **viols.** Is 5:12. **the worm.** Is *66:24. Ge +*3:19. Jb *17:13, 14. √19:26. *21:26. *24:19, 20. Mk *9:43-48. **spread.** Est 4:3. Ps 139:8. **worms.** Is 41:14. 66:4. Dt 28:39. **cover.** Is 23:18. Le 9:19. Jb *21:26.

12. **How art thou fallen.** ♪48, Ps +2:4. This language may refer to the fall of Satan and his angels, as the king of Babylon greatly resembled that arch-apostate in his character and fate (Scott). Is 13:10. 34:4. La 2:1. Ezk √28:13-17. Lk *10:18. 2 P 2:4. Re 8:10. *12:7-10. **from heaven.** From the height of thy glory and royal majesty. As kings are sometimes called *gods* in Scripture (Ps +82:6n), so their palaces and thrones may be fitly called their *heavens* (Matthew Poole). **Lucifer.** *or*, day star. i.e. *morning star*, ✳S#1966h, only here. 2 P 1:19. Re 2:28. 22:16. This properly is a bright and eminent star, which ushers in the sun and the morning; but is here metaphorically taken for the high and mighty king of Babylon. And it is a very usual thing, both in prophetical and profane writers, to describe the princes and potentates of the world under the title of the sun or stars of heaven. Some understand this place of the devil; to whom indeed it may be mystically applied; but as he is never called by this name in Scripture, so it cannot be literally meant of him, but of the king of Babylon, as is undeniably evident from the whole context, which certainly speaks of one and the same person, and describes him as plain as words can do it (Matthew Poole). **son of the morning.** The title of *son* is given in Scripture not only to a person or thing begotten or produced by another, but also in general to any thing which is any way related to another; in which sense we read of *a son of stripes*, Dt 25:2; *the son of a night*, Jon 4:10; *a son of perdition*, Jn 17:12; and, which is more agreeable to the present case, *the sons of Arcturus*, Jb 38:32 (Matthew Poole). **weaken.** ver. 4-6. Je 50:23. 51:20-24.

13. **thou.** Is 47:7-10. Ezk 27:3. 28:2. 29:3. Da 4:30, 31. Zp 2:15. Re 18:7, 8. **hast said.** ♪122, Ex +15:9. **I will ascend.** ♪102, Ge +2:24. Jb 20:6. Je 51:53. Ezk √28:9, 12-16. Da *3:1, 13-15. *8:10-12. Am 9:2. **I will exalt.** Da 8:10. Ob 4. Ezk 28:2. 2 Th *2:4. **of God.** Heb. *El*, Ex +15:2. **the mount.** Is 2:2. Ps 75:2. +82:1. Ezk 28:14. **sides.** lit. thighs. ver. 15h. Is 37:24. 1 S 24:3. Ezk 32:23. **of the north.** Jb 26:7. Ps *48:2. 75:6.

14. **ascend.** ♪102, Ge +2:24. Is 37:23, 24. **clouds.** Ge +9:13. **I will be.** Is 47:8. Ge 3:5. 2 Th 2:4.

15. **thou.** ver. 3-11. Ezk 28:8, 9. Mt 11:23. Ac 12:22, 23. Re *19:20. **brought.** ♪142, Ge +20:16. **hell.** Heb. *sheol*, Ge +37:35. **to the sides.** ver. 13. Ezk 32:23. **pit.** Heb. *bor*, Ge +37:20 (✳S#953h).

16. **shall narrowly.** Ps 58:10, 11. 64:9. **saying.** ♪56. Dialogue B957. For other instances of this figure see Is 63:1-6. Mi 2:4. Zc 8:21. Mt 25:37-39. Lk 13:6-9. 15:20-32. 1 C 9:24. **Is this.** ver. 4, 5. Ps *52:7. Je 50:23. 51:20-23. Da 4:30, 31, 33. Ac 12:23.

17. **made.** Is 13:19-22. 64:10. Ezk 6:14. Jl 2:3. Zp 2:13, 14. **world.** ♪171.O.2, Is +13:11. **opened not the house of his prisoners** *or*, did not let his prisoners loose homewards. Is 45:13. 58:6. 2 Ch 28:8-15. Ezr 1:2-4. Ep 4:8.

18. **all of.** Is 22:16. 2 Ch 24:16, 25. Ec 6:3. Ezk 32:18, etc. **house.** Jb 30:23. Pr 7:27. Ec 12:5.

19. **thou.** The prophet having briefly set forth, in

the beginning of this chapter, the deliverance of Judah from captivity, in consequence of the destruction of Babylon, then introduces this triumphant song, the beauties of which are excellently illustrated by Bp. Lowth. A chorus of Jews is first introduced, expressing their astonishment at the sudden downfall of Babylon, and the great reverse of fortune that had befallen the tyrant, who had, like his predecessors, oppressed his own, and harassed the neighboring kingdoms; who, with their rulers, are represented under the images of the fir trees and cedars of Lebanon; and who, while the whole earth shouts for joy, utter a severe taunt over the fallen tyrant, and boast their security now he is no more, ver. 3-8. The scene is then changed to the regions of the dead; and Hades is represented as rousing up the shades of the departed monarchs, who rise from their thrones to meet the king of Babylon at his coming, and insult him on his being reduced to the same low state of impotence and dissolution as themselves, ver. 9-11. The Jews then resume the speech; address him as the morning star fallen from heaven; and introduce him as uttering the most extravagant vaunts of his power and ambitious designs; which are strongly contrasted with his present low and abject condition, ver. 12-15. Then certain persons are introduced, who light upon the corpse of the king of Babylon, cast out and lying naked on the ground among the slain, covered with wounds, and so disfigured that it is some time before they know him; they accost him with the bitterest taunts, and reproach him with his destructive ambition and cruelty, which have deservedly brought him and his posterity to this ignominious end, ver. 16-20. And, to complete the whole, God is introduced, declaring the utter extirpation of the royal family, the total desolation of the city, the deliverance of his people, and the destruction of their enemies, which He confirms by the awful sanction of His oath, ver. 21-27. **cast out.** 1 K 21:19, 24. 2 K 9:25, 34-36. Je 8:1, 2. 16:6. 22:19. **grave.** Heb. *qeber*, Ge +23:4 (✳S#6913h). **go down.** Je 41:7, 9. Ezk 32:23, 24. **pit.** Heb. *bor*, Ge +37:20 (✳S#953h). ver. 15. A rock-hewn burying place. Ps 28:1. 30:3. 88:6. The Hebrew term *bor* is rendered *cistern* four times (2 K 18:31. Pr 5:15. Ec 12:6. Is 36:16), *dungeon*, thirteen (Ge 40:15. 41:14. Ex 12:29. Je 37:16. 38:6, 6, 7, 9, 10, 11, 13. La 3:53, 55), *fountain*, one (Je 6:7), *well*, nine (Dt 6:11. 1 S 19:22. 2 S 3:26. 23:15, 16. 1 Ch 11:17, 18. 2 Ch 26:10. Ne 9:25), *pit*, forty-one times (Ge 37:20, 22, 24, 24, 28, 29, 29. Ex 21:33, 33, 34. Le 11:36. 2 S 23:20. 2 K 10:14. 1 Ch 11:22. Ps 7:15. 28:1. 30:3. 40:2. 88:4, 6. 143:7. Pr 1:12. 28:17. Is 14:15, 19. 24:22. 38:18. 51:1. Je 41:7, 9. Ezk 26:20, 20. 31:14, 16, 18, 23, 24, 25. 32:29, 30. Zc 9:11).

20. **not be joined.** Ec 6:3. **burial.** Heb. *qeburah*, Ge +35:20 (✳S#6900h). **the seed.** Is 13:15-19. Jb 18:16, 19. Ps 21:10. 37:28. 109:13. 137:8, 9. Da 5:18, 20, 22, 23, 30, 31.

21. **slaughter.** Ex 20:5. Le 26:39. Mt *23:35. **iniquity of their fathers.** Ex +*20:5)℘. **do not.** Is 27:6. Ps 140:8, 10. Hab 2:8-12. **face.** ♪144A1, Ge +11:8. Ge +1:2.

22. **I will.** Is 13:5, 6. 21:9. 43:14. 47:9-14. Je 50:26, 27, 29-35. 51:3, 4, 56, 57. **Babylon.** T#44. Is 13:17-22. 45:1-3. ch. 47. Je 50:23-40. 51:30-44. Ezk *26:7-11. 29:18-20. Da 2:31-35. 7:24, 25. ch. 7-12. Na ch. 2, 3. Zp 2:13-15. Mt 24:1, 2, 15, 16, 21. Lk 19:43,

44. 2 Th 2:3, 4. **the name**. Jb *18:5, 6, 16-19. Ps *21:10. *37:28. *109:13. Pr *10:7. Je 51:62-64. **remnant**. 1 K 14:10.

23. **make**. Pr 13:21, 22. 34:11-15. Je 50:39, 40. 51:42, 43, 61, 62. Zp 2:14. Re 14:8. 18:2, 21-23. **I will sweep**. ✠22C45. Anthropomorphism B890. Human actions are attributed to God: sweeping. 1 K 14:10. 2 K 21:13. Je 51:25, 26.

24. **Lord**. Ex 17:16. Ps 110:4. Je 44:26. Am 8:7. He 4:3. 6:16-18. **hath sworn**. F/L Is 45:23. 54:9. 62:8. Dt 1:8)𝒫. 2:14)𝒫. 4:31)𝒫. **Surely**. Is 46:10, 11. Jb 23:13. Ps 33:10. 92:5. Pr 19:21. 21:30. Je 23:30. 29:11. La 3:37. Mt 11:25, 26. Ac 4:28. Ep 1:9, +*11. **purposed**. Is 46:9-11. *55:11. Ps +115:3.

25. **I will**. Is 9:4. 10:16-19, 32-34. 17:12-14. 30:30-33. 31:8, 9. 37:36-38. 2 K ✱19:35-37. Ezk 39:4. **break**. Ge 27:40)𝒫. **then**. ver. 5. Is 10:24-27. Na 1:13.

26. **the purpose**. ✠132D, Ge +19:25. Is 5:19, 25. 8:10. 11:2. Jb +14:5. Zp 3:6-8. **hand**. Ac *4:28.

27. **the Lord**. Is 23:9. 44:13. *46:10, 11. Jb 40:8. Je 4:28. 51:29. Ro *8:28, 31. **purposed**. Is 46:9-11. *55:11. Ps +115:3. **his hand**. Is 9:12. **stretched**. ✠22A14.8A, Ex +7:5. **who shall**. Is 43:13. 2 Ch *20:6. Jb *9:12. *23:13. Ps 33:11. Pr *19:21. +*21:30. Da *4:31-35. Mt *24:35. Ep +*1:11.

28. A.M. 3278. B.C. 726. Is 6:1. 2 K *16:20. 2 Ch 28:27.

29. **Rejoice**. Pr 24:17. Ezk 26:2. 35:15. Ho 9:1. Ob 12. Mi 7:8. Zp 3:11. **whole**. Jsh 13:3. 1 S 6:17, 18. **because**. 2 Ch 26:6. 28:18. **for**. 2 K *18:8. **cockatrice**. or, adder. Is 11:8mg. **a fiery**. Is 30:6.

30. **the firstborn**. i.e. *the poorest of the poor* (CB). Jb +*18:13. **the poor**. Is 5:17. 7:21, 22. 30:23, 24. 33:16. 37:30. 65:13, 14. **and I**. ch. 47. Ezk 25:15-17. Jl 3:4-8. Am 1:6-8. Zp 2:4-7. Zc 9:5-7.

31. **Howl**. Is 13:6. 16:7. **O city**. ✠121J19, 1 S +22:19. **for**. Is 20:1. Je 1:14. 25:16, 20. **none shall be alone**. or, *he shall* not *be* alone. **appointed times**. or, assemblies. ✠S#4151h, only here; compare ✱S#4150h, Ge +17:21; Ex +27:21n. Is 5:27. 40:29-31. Ge 18:14.

32. **shall one**. Is 39:1. 2 S 8:10. 2 K 20:12, etc. **the Lord**. Is 12:6. 37:32. Ps *87:1, 5. 102:√16, 28. *132:13-15. Mt 16:18. **and the poor**. Is 11:4. 25:4. Zp *3:12. Zc 11:7, 11. Ja *2:5. **trust in it**. or, betake themselves unto it. Pr 18:10. Mt 24:15, 16. He *12:22.

ISAIAH 15

The beginning of a prophecy against Moab, 1-9.

1. **burden**. This and the following chapter form one entire prophecy; which was most probably delivered, as Bp. Lowth supposes, soon after the foregoing (Is 14:28-32), in the first year of Hezekiah, and accomplished in his fourth year when Shalmaneser invaded Israel. Is 13:1. 14:28. **Moab**. Is 11:14. 25:10. Ge *19:37. Dt 34:5, 6. Je 9:26. ch. 48. Ezk 25:8-11. Am *2:1-3. Zp 2:8-11. **in the night**. Ex 12:29, 30. 1 Th *5:1-3. **Ar**. Nu 21:28. Dt 2:9, 18. **brought to silence**. or, cut off. Is 6:5mg. Je 47:5. 48:2mg. **Kir**. Is 16:7, Kir-hareseth. ver. 11, Kir-haresh. 2 K 3:25, Kir-haraseth. Je 48:31, 36, Kir-heres.

2. **is gone**. Is 16:12. Jsh 13:17. Je 48:18, 22, 23. **Bajith**. i.e. *the house*, ✱S#1006h. **Moab**. ver. 3. Is 14:31. 16:7. Je 48:31, 39. **Nebo**. Nu 32:3, 38. Dt 34:1. Je 48:1. **Medeba**. Nu 21:30. Jsh 13:16. **all**. Is 3:24.

22:12. Le 19:27, 28. 21:5. Dt 14:1. Jb 1:20. Je 7:29. 47:5. 48:1, 37, 38. Ezk 7:18.

3. **their streets**. 2 S 3:31. 2 K 6:30. Jon 3:6-8. Mt 11:21. **on the**. ver. 2. Is 22:1. Dt 22:8. Je 19:13. 48:38, 39. **weeping abundantly**. Heb. descending into weeping; *or*, coming down with weeping. ver. 5.

4. **Heshbon**. Is 16:8, 9. Nu 21:27-30. 32:3, 4. Je 48:34. **Jahaz**. Nu 21:23. Dt 2:32. Jsh 13:18. Jg 11:20. **his**. Ge 27:46. Nu 11:15. 1 K 19:4. Jb 3:20-22. 7:15, 16. Je 8:3. 20:18. Jon 4:3, 8. Re 9:6. **life**. Heb. *nephesh*, soul, Ge +44:30.

5. **My heart**. Is 16:9-11. Je 8:18, 19. 9:10, 18, 19. 13:17. 17:16. 48:31-36. Lk 19:41-44. Ro 9:1-3. **his fugitives**, etc. or, to the borders thereof, even *as* an heifer. **Zoar**. Ge 13:10. 14:2. 19:22. **three**. Is 16:14. Je 48:34. **the mounting**. Je 48:5, 34. **Luhith**. i.e. *tables made of boards; tabular; pertaining to the table*, ✱S#3872h. Is 15:5. Je 48:5. **with**. 2 S 15:23, 30. **Horonaim**. i.e. *two caverns*, ✱S#2773h. Is 15:5. Je 48:3, 5, 34. **destruction**. Heb. breaking. Is 1:28mg. 22:5. +51:19mg. Je 4:20.

6. **waters**. ver. 9. Is 1:22, 30. 3:1. **Nimrim**. i.e. *rebellious ones; leopards*, ✱S#5249h. Nu 32:3, 36, Nimrah, Beth-nimrah. Jsh 13:27, Beth-nimrah. Je 48:34h. **desolate**. Heb. desolations. Je 48:34mg. 51:62mg. **the grass**. Is 16:9, 10. Jl 1:10-12. Ps 129:6-8. Hab *3:17, 18. Re 8:7.

7. **the abundance**. Is 5:29. 10:6, 14. Na 2:12, 13. **to the**. Ps 137:1, 2. **brook of the willows**. *or*, valley of the Arabians. Jg +16:4mg.

8. **the cry**. ver. 2-5. Je 48:20-24, 31-34. **Eglaim**. i.e. *two pools; double reservoir*, ✱S#97h. Ezk 47:10, En-eglaim. *Eglaim* is called *Agallim* by Eusebius, who places it eight miles south from Ar or Areopolis. **Beer-elim**. i.e. *well of heroes, strong ones, princes, or oaks; well of the gods* or *mighty ones*, ✱S#879h.

9. **Dimon**. i.e. *silence; undisturbed silence, secure rest*, ✱S#1775h. Some have *Dibon*; and Jerome says that the same town was called both *Dibon* and *Dimon*. **more**. Heb. additions. Le 26:18, 21, 24, 28. Je 48:43-45. **lions**. ✠171I5. Synecdoche of the Species B626. A "lion" is put for all kinds of wild beasts. Le 26:22. 2 K 17:25. Je 15:3. Am 5:19. **him**. Bp. Lowth, upon the authority of the LXX., renders, "upon the escaped of Moab, and Ariel, and the remnant of Admah." Is 4:2. Jg 3:28-30. 2 K 17:25. Je 49:19.

ISAIAH 16

Moab is counselled to submit to the kings of Judah, and show kindness to the Lord's distressed people, 1-5. Farther predictions of the miseries of Moab, for his excessive pride and wickedness, 6-14.

1. **Send**. Is +*59:20. Ac √3:20. **the lamb**. 2 S *8:2. 2 K *3:4, 5. Ezr 7:17. **from**. 2 K 14:7. **Sela**. or, Petra. Heb. a rock. i.e. *fortress*, ✱S#5554h. 2 K *14:7n. **to the wilderness**. Ps +*68:7. Je +√31:2. **the mount**. Is 10:32. 59:20. Mi 4:8. **daughter**. ✠155E5, Nu +21:25.

2. **as**. Is 13:14. Pr 27:8. **cast out of the nest**. or, a nest forsaken. **the fords**. Nu *21:13-15. Dt 2:36. 3:8, 12. Jsh 13:16. Jg 11:18.

3. **Take**. Heb. Bring. **execute**. Is 1:17. Ps 82:3, 4. Je 21:12. 22:3. Ezk 45:9-12. Da 4:27. Zc 7:9. **make**. Is +*9:6. 25:4. 32:2. Jg 9:15. Jon 4:5-8. **hide**. Is

+*26:20. Zp +*2:3. Mt 25:35. Lk +√21:36. He 13:2.
the outcasts. Is *11:12. +*27:13. 56:8. Ps +*147:2.
Ob 12-14. **bewray.** i.e. expose, reveal, make known.
that wandereth. Mt √24:16-21. Re √12:6, 14.

4. **mine.** Dt 23:15, 16. 24:14. Je 21:12. **Moab.** Da
√11:41. **for.** Is 14:4. 33:1. 51:13. Je 48:8, 18. Zc 9:8.
extortioner. Heb. wringer. *S#4160h, only here. **op-**
pressors. Heb. treaders down. Is 15:6. 25:10. Zc 10:5.
Ml 4:3. Lk *21:24. Ro 16:20mg. Re 11:2.

5. **in mercy.** Ps 61:6, 7. *85:10. 89:1, 2, 14. 2 S
*23:3. Ps 89:14. Pr 20:28. 29:14. Mt *25:31, 32, 34-
37, 40. Lk 1:69-75. **throne.** √22D3C2, Ps +45:6. **estab-**
lished. *or,* prepared. Is 30:33. **in the tabernacle.** Is
+*9:6, 7. 2 S 5:9. *7:16. Je *23:5, 6. Da 7:14, 27.
Am 9:11. Mi 4:7. Lk 1:31-33. Ac √15:16, 17. **of David.**
Is +√55:3. Ac √13:34. **judging.** Is *11:1-5. 32:1, 2.
2 S *23:3. 1 K 10:9. 2 Ch *31:20, 21. Ps *72:2-4.
*94:15. 96:13. 98:9. 99:4. Je *23:5, 6. 33:15. Am *9:11.
Zc 9:9. Ac +*24:10n. 1 C +*6:2. He +*1:8, 9. **hasting.**
2 P 3:11, 12.

6. **have.** Is 2:11. Je 48:26, 29, 30, 42. Am 2:1. Ob
3, 4. Zp 2:9, 10. 1 P 5:5. **Moab.** Ps 60:8. **very proud.**
Jb 40:11, 12. Ps 12:3. 31:23. Pr *6:16, 17. *16:5. **but.**
Is 28:15, 18. 44:25. Je 50:36.

7. **shall Moab.** Is 15:2-5. Je 48:20. **Kir-hareseth.**
i.e. *an earthen wall; city or wall of brick,* *S#7025h.
ver. 11. Is 15:1. 2 K 3:25. **mourn.** *or,* mutter. Is *8:19.
33:18 (meditate). 38:14. 59:3. **stricken.** 2 K *3:24-27.
Ps 119:21.

8. **the fields.** Is 15:4. 24:7, 8. 2 S 1:21. **languish.**
√155C, Le +19:23. Is 19:8. **the vine.** ver. 9. **Sibmah.**
i.e. *river of water; sweet smell; why hoary?* *S#7643h.
ver. 9. Nu 32:3, Shebam, 38, Shibmah. Jsh 13:19. Je
48:32. **the lords.** Is 10:7. Je 27:6, 7. **Jazer.** Nu 32:3.
Jsh 13:25. 21:39. 2 S 24:5. 1 Ch 6:81. 26:31. Je 48:32.
stretched out. *or,* plucked up. Is 33:23. Jg 15:9. Am
5:2.

9. **I will bewail.** See on Is 15:5. Je 48:32-34. **O**
Heshbon. Is 15:4. **for.** Is 9:3. Jg 9:27. Je 40:10, 12.
the shouting for. *or,* the alarm is fallen upon, etc.
ver. 10. Je 25:30. 48:33. **summer.** √121P9. Metonymy
of the Adjunct B596. "Summer" is put for the fruits
gathered in it. For other instances of this figure see
2 S 16:1. Je 40:10, 12. Am 8:1. Mi 7:1. **harvest.** √121P9,
Metonymy of the Adjunct.

10. **gladness.** Is 24:8, 9. 32:10. Je 48:33. Am 5:11,
17. Hab *3:17, 18. Zp 1:13.

11. **my.** Is 15:5. 63:15. 2 K 8:11. Je 4:19. *13:17.
31:20. 48:36. Ho 11:8. Lk 19:41. Ph 2:1. **Kir-haresh.**
i.e. *the wall is earthen,* *S#7025h. ver. 7, Kir-hareseth. Je 48:31, 36.

12. **when.** Is 15:2. 26:16. Nu 21:29. 22:39, 41. 23:1-
3, 14, 28. 24:17. Jg 11:24. Pr 1:28. Je 48:7, 13, 35.
he shall. Is 37:38. 1 K 11:7. 2 K 3:27. Je 48:7, 13,
46. **sanctuary.** Is 16:12. Le 26:31. Ezk 21:2. Am 7:9.
but. Is 47:13. 2 K 19:12, 16-19. Ps *115:3-8. Je 10:5.

13. **since.** Is 44:8. Nu 24:15-17.

14. **But now.** Ac *1:6, 7. **three.** That is, exactly
three years; which are to be computed from the death
of Ahaz, and end the third year of Hezekiah, three
years before the taking of Samaria by Shalmaneser;
who did not ruin Moab completely, but left the final
desolation of it to Nebuchadnezzar. Is 7:16. 15:5. 21:16.
Dt 15:18. **the glory.** Is 17:4. 23:9. Ge 31:1. Est 5:11.
Je 9:23. Na 2:9, 10. **and the remnant.** Je 48:46, 47.
feeble. *or,* not many.

ISAIAH 17

*A prophecy against Syria and Israel; and intimations
of mercy to a remnant of Israel, 1-11. The destruction
of Sennacherib's army foretold, 12-14.*

1. A.M. cir. 3263. B.C. cir. 741. **burden.** Is 15:1.
19:1. **Damascus.** Is 7:8. Ge 14:15. 15:2. 1 K 11:24.
1 Ch 18:5. 2 Ch 28:5, 23. Je *49:23-27. Am *1:3-5.
Zc 9:1. Ac *9:2. **Damascus is.** Is 8:4. 10:9. 2 K 16:9.
a ruinous. Is 25:2. 37:26. Je 49:2. Mi 1:6. 3:12.

2. **Aroer.** Nu 32:34. Dt 2:36. 3:12. Jsh 13:16. 2 K
10:32, 33. Je 48:19. **they shall.** Is 5:17. 7:23-25. 1 K
22:3. Ezk 25:5. Zp 2:6. **none.** Je 7:33.

3. **fortress.** Is 7:8, 16. 8:4. 10:9. 2 K *16:9. *17:6.
Ho 1:4, 6. 3:4. 5:13, 14. 8:8. 9:16, 17. 10:14. 13:7, 8,
15, 16. Am 2:6-9. 3:9-15. 5:25-27. 6:7-11. 8:14. 9:1-
10. Mi 1:4-9. **Damascus.** 1 K 15:18, 19. 20:34. **they**
shall. √60A, Ge +3:22. Is 16:14. 28:1-4. Ho 9:11.

4. **the glory.** Is 9:8, 21. 10:4. Ho 9:11. 12:2. Mi
1:5. **the fatness.** Is *10:16-19. 24:13, 16. 28:1. Dt 32:15-
27. Ezk 34:20. Zp 2:11mg.

5. **as when.** Ps 129:6, 7. Je 9:22. 51:33. Ho 6:11.
10:12-14. Jl 3:13. Mt 13:30, 39-42. Re 14:15-20. **corn.**
lit. harvest. √121P10, Dt +24:19. **the valley.** Jsh *15:8.
18:16, the valley of the giants. 2 S 5:18, 22.

6. **gleaning grapes.** Is 1:9. 10:22. 24:13. Dt *4:27.
24:20. Jg 8:2. 1 K 19:18. Ezk 36:8-15. 37:19-25. 39:29.
Ob 5. Mi 7:1. Ro 9:27. *11:4-6, 26. **Lord God.** Is
●29:23. Ex 32:27)℗. Jsh 9:18, 19. 10:40, 42. **of Israel.**
F/L Is 47:17. 45:3, 15. 48:2. Ex 24:10)℗. Nu 16:9)℗.

7. **shall a man look to.** √132D, Ge +19:25. Is
+*26:9. **to his Maker.** Is 10:20, 21. 19:22. 22:11. 24:14,
15. 29:18, 19, 24. Jg 10:15, 16. 2 Ch *30:10, 11, 18-
20. 31:1. 35:17, 18. Je 3:12-14, 18-23. 31:4-10. Ho
3:5. 6:1. 14:1-3. Mi 7:7. **have respect.** Zc 9:1.

8. **he shall.** Is 1:29. 2:18-21. 27:9. 30:22. 2 K 16:10,
11. *23:11, 12. 2 Ch *34:4, 6, 7, 33. Ezk *36:25. Ho
*14:8. Zp 1:3. Zc 13:2. **look to.** √132D, Ge +19:25.
the work. Is 2:8. 31:6, 7. 44:15, 19, 20. Ho 8:4-6.
10:1, 2. 13:1, 2. Mi 5:13, 14. **the groves.** Is 27:9. Ex
34:13)℗. Dt 7:5)℗. 12:3)℗. 16:21)℗. 2 K +17:10. 21:3n.
23:6. Mi 5:14. **images.** *or,* sun images. Is 27:9. Le
+26:30)℗. 2 Ch 14:5. 34:4mg.

9. **In that day.** ver. 4, 5. Is 6:11-13. 7:16-20. 9:9-
12. 24:1-12. 27:10. 28:1-4. Ezr 9:7. Ho 10:14. 13:15,
16. Am 3:11-15. 7:9. Mi 5:11. 6:16. 7:13.

10. **thou hast forgotten.** Is 51:13. Dt 6:12. 8:11,
14, 19. Ps 9:17. 106:13, 21. Je *2:32. 17:13. Ho 2:13,
14. 4:6. 8:14. 13:6, 7. **the God.** Is +*12:2. 1 Ch 16:35.
Ps 65:5. *68:19, 20. 79:9. 85:4. Hab 3:18. **the rock.**
Is *26:4. Dt 32:4, 15)℗, 18, 30, 31. Ps 18:2. 31:2, 3.
1 C 10:4. **shalt thou.** Is 65:21, 22. Le 26:16, 20. Dt
28:30, 38-42. Je 12:13. Am 5:11. Zp 1:13.

11. **the harvest.** Is 18:5, 6. Jb *4:8. Je 5:31. Ho
8:7. 9:1-4, 16. *10:12-15. Jl 1:5-12. Ga √6:7, 8. **a heap**
in the day of grief and of desperate sorrow. *or,* removed in the day of inheritance, and *there shall be*
deadly sorrow. Is 65:13, 14. Mt *8:11, 12. Ro 2:5, 8,
9. 2 C √7:10.

12. **multitude.** *or,* noise. Is 9:5. **make a noise.** Is
5:26-30. *8:7, 8. 28:17. 2 K 15:29. 17:3. Ps 18:4. 46:1-
3. 65:6, 7. *93:3, 4. Je 6:23. Ezk 43:2. Lk 21:25. **mighty.**
or, many. Ps 29:3. Re 17:1, 15.

13. **shall rush.** Je 6:23. **but.** Is 10:15, 16, 33, 34.
14:25. 25:4, 5. 27:1. 30:30-33. 31:8, 9. 33:1-3, 9-12.
37:29-38. Ps 9:5. 46:5-11. **rebuke.** Jb 38:11. Mk 4:39-

41. **shall be**. Is 29:5. 41:15, 16. Jb 21:18. Ps 1:4. 35:5. 83:13-15. Da 2:35. Ho 13:3. **a rolling thing**. *or*, thistledown. Ps 83:13 (wheel).

14. **at eveningtide**. Is 10:28-32. 2 K *19:3, 35. Ps 37:36. **before the morning**. Is *8:20mg. *37:29, 33-36. Ps 9:5. +*46:5. *59:16. 78:65, 66. Ml 4:1, 2. **he is not**. Is +*24:22. Ps +*37:9, 10. +*101:8. Pr 13:9. **the portion**. Is 33:1. Jg 5:31. Jb 20:29. Pr 22:23. Je 2:3. 13:25. Ezk 39:10. Hab 2:16, 17. Zp 2:9, 10. Zc 14:2, 3, 12-15. **that spoil us**. Zc 14:1, 2.

ISAIAH 18

A message to Egypt and Ethiopia, probably showing the event of the Assyrian invasion; and a prediction, that they would present oblations to the Lord, 1-7.

1. A.M. cir. 3290. B.C. cir. 714. **Woe**. Bp. Lowth renders, after Bochart, "Ho! to the land of the winged cymbal;" which he thinks is a periphrasis for the Egyptian sistrum; and consequently, that Egypt, "which borders on the rivers of Cush," is the country to which the prophecy is addressed. If we translate "shadowing with wings," it may allude to the multitude of its vessels, whose *sails* may be represented under the notion of *wings*. **the land**. Is 20:3-6. 30:2, 3. 31:1. **shadowing**. Ru 2:12. Ps 17:8. 36:7. 57:1. 61:4. 63:7. 91:4. Mt 23:37. **which**. 2 K 19:9. Ezk 30:4, 5. Zp 2:12. 3:10. **Ethiopia**. 2 Ch 14:9. 16:8.   •

2. **sendeth**. Is 30:2-4. Ezk 30:9. **vessels**. It is well known that the Egyptians commonly used on the Nile a light sort of ships or boats made of the papyrus. See Note on Ex 2:3. **bulrushes**. Is 35:7. Ex 2:3✦. Jb 8:11. Ps=83:3. **saying**. ✦63BA, Ge +26:7. **to a nation**. ver. 7. **scattered and peeled**. *or*, outspread and polished. Or, as Bp. Lowth renders, "stretched out in length and smoothed." *Egypt*, which is situated between 24 degrees and 32 degrees N. latitude and 30 degrees and 33 degrees E. longitude, being bounded on the south by Ethiopia, on the north by the Mediterranean, on the east by the mountains of Arabia, and on the west by those of Lybia, is one long vale, 750 miles in length (through the middle of which runs the Nile), in breadth from one to two or three days' journey, and even at the widest part of the Delta, from Pelusium to Alexandria, not above 250 miles broad. **to a people**. Ge 10:8, 9. 2 Ch 12:2-4. 14:9. 16:8. Hebrew. **meted out and trodden down**. *or*, that meteth out and treadeth down. Heb. of line and line and treading under foot. This is an allusion to the frequent necessity of having recourse to mensuration in Egypt, in order to determine their boundaries, after the inundation of the Nile had *smoothed* their land and effaced their landmarks; and to their method of throwing seed upon the mud, when the waters had subsided, and treading it in by turning their cattle into the fields. **have spoiled**. *or*, despise. Is 19:5-7.

3. **All ye**. Is 1:2. Ps 49:1, 2. 50:1. Je 22:29. Mi 6:2. **see ye**. Is *5:26. 7:18. 13:2, 4. 26:11. Am 3:6-8. Mi 6:9. Zc 9:14. Mt 13:9, 16. **trumpet**. Le +23:24. Re 8:2, 13. **hear ye**. Mt 11:15.

4. **I will take**. Is 26:21. Ps 132:13, 14. Ho *5:15. **consider my dwelling place**. *or*, regard my set dwelling. ver. 7. Is 12:6. 14:32. 31:9. 46:13. Nu 24:8, 9. 2 K 19:6-14. Jl 3:17. **like a clear**. 2 S 23:4. Ps 72:6. **upon herbs**. *or*, after rain. 2 K 4:39.

5. **afore harvest**. See on Is 17:11. SS 2:13, 15. Ezk 17:6-10.

6. **shall be left**. Is 14:19. 34:1-7. Je 7:33. 15:3. Ezk 32:4-6. 39:17-20. Re 19:17, 18. **fowls**. ✦132D, Ge +19:25.

7. **shall the present**. Is 16:1. 23:17, 18. 45:14. 2 Ch *32:23. Ps 68:29-31. 72:9-15. 87:4. Je 3:16n. Ezk 39:10. Zp *3:10. Ml *1:11. Mt 2:11. Ac *8:27, 28. Ro +*11:25. **scattered and peeled**. *or*, outspread and polished. ver. 2. **to the place**. See on ver. 4. Is 60:6-9. Ps 132:13, 14. Mi 4:13. Zc *14:16, 17.

ISAIAH 19

Predictions of terrible judgments, which God was about to inflict on Egypt, 1-17; and that the Egyptians would at length join in the worship of the Lord, and share the blessings of his salvation, 18-25.

1. **Egypt**. Je 25:19. *43:8-13. 44:29, 30. ch. 46. Ezk ch. 29-32. Jl 3:19. Zc 10:11. 14:18, 19. **rideth**. ✦22C18, Dt +33:26. Dt 33:26. Ps *18:10-12. 68:4, +*17, 33, 34. *104:3. Mt *26:64, 65. Re *1:7. **swift cloud**. ✦22D5H, Ps +104:3. 2 Ch +*5:13. Mt +*24:30. **the idols**. Is 21:9. 46:1, 2. Ex *12:12. 1 S 5:2-4. Je 43:12. 46:25. 50:2. 51:44. Ezk 30:13. **the heart**. ver. 16. Ex 15:14-16. Jsh 2:9, 11, 24. Je 46:5, 15, 16.

2. **I will**. ver. 13, 14. Is 9:21. Jg *7:22. 9:23. 1 S *14:16, 20. 2 Ch *20:22, 23. Ezk 38:21. Mt √12:25. Re 17:12-17. **set**. Heb. mingle. Is 9:11mg.

3. **the spirit**. Heb. *ruach*, Ge +41:8. This is a prophecy of what took place in Egypt about twenty-two years after the destruction of Sennacherib's army; when, upon the death of Tirhakah (B.C. 688), not being able to settle about the succession, they continued for two years in a state of anarchy, confusion, and civil wars; which was followed by the tyranny of twelve princes, who, dividing the country among them, governed it for fifteen years; and at last, by the sole dominion of Psammiticus, which he held for fifty-four years. See on ver. 1, 11-13. Is 57:16. 1 S 25:37. Ps 76:12. Je 46:15. Ezk 21:7. 22:14. **fail**. Heb. be emptied. Is 24:1, 3. 44:25. Jsh 2:11. Jb 5:12, 13. Da 5:7-9. Na 2:2. **and I**. Is 14:27. 2 S 15:31. 17:14, 23. 2 Ch 25:16-20. Jb 5:12, 13. Pr +*21:30. 1 C 3:19, 20. **destroy**. Heb. swallow up. Ps 107:27mg. **and they**. Is +*8:19. 15:2. 44:25. 47:12. 1 Ch 10:13. Da 2:2. 4:6, 7. 5:7. **familiar spirits**. Le 19:31. 20:6, 27✦. Dt +*18:11✦✦. 2 K +21:6. **wizards**. Dt +*18:11. 2 K +21:6.

4. **give over**. *or*, shut up. 1 S 23:7. Ps 31:8. **a cruel lord**. Rather, "cruel lords," agreeably to the LXX., Syriac, Vulgate, and the original, *adonim kasheh*. Nebuchadnezzar, who first conquered and ravaged Egypt, B.C. 573, and the following year; and then, not only his successors, but Cambyses (who invaded Egypt, B.C. 526), the son of Cyrus, and the whole succession of Persian kings till the time of Alexander, who were in general hard masters, and grievously oppressed the country. ver. 2. Is 20:4. Je 46:26. Ezk 29:19. Da 11:5-45.

5. **the waters**. Is 11:15. Je 51:36. Ezk 30:12. Zc 10:11. 14:18. **fail**. F/L Is 41:17. Je 51:30.

6. **and the**. Is 37:25. 2 K 19:24. **the reeds**. Is 18:2. Ex 2:3. Jb 8:11.

7. **every thing sown**. Is 32:20. Dt 11:10n. Je 14:4. Ezk 19:13. Jl 1:17, 18. **be no more**. Heb. shall not be.

8. **fishers.** Ex 7:21. Nu 11:5. Ezk 30:10-12. 47:10. Hab 1:15. **mourn.** *12, Ps +1:1. **angle.** Jb 41:1. **upon.** *144A1, Ge +11:8. **shall languish.** Is 16:8.

9. **work.** 1 K 10:28. Pr 7:16. Ezk 27:7. **weave.** F/L Is 38:12. 59:5. Ex 28:32}*P*. 35:35}*P*. 39:22}*P*. **networks.** *or*, white works.

10. **purposes.** Heb. foundations. Ps 11:3. **make.** Ex 7:19. 8:5. Dt 11:10. **for fish.** *or*, of living things. Heb. *nephesh*, Ge +2:19. Nu 11:5.

11. **the princes.** ver. 3, 13. Is 29:14. 44:25. Jb 5:12, 13. *12:16, 17. Ps 33:10. Je 49:7. Ezk 7:26. 1 C *1:19, 20. **Zoan.** Is 30:4. Nu 13:22. Ps 78:12, 43. Ezk 30:14. **brutish.** Ps 73:22. 92:6. Pr 30:2. Je 10:14, 21. **say ye unto.** *63I2, Jsh +3:3. Supply "(the wise) Pharaoh." **I am.** Ge 41:38, 39. 1 K 4:30. Ac 7:22. **the son.** Ps 72:1. **ancient.** Heb. *kedem*, Mi +5:2 (✦S#6924h).

12. **where are thy.** Is 5:21. 47:10-13. Jg 9:38. Je 2:28. 1 C 1:20. **let them.** Is 40:13, 14. 41:22, 23. 44:7. Jb 11:6, 7. Ro 11:33, 34.

13. **princes of Zoan.** See on ver. 11. Ro 1:22. **Noph.** i.e. *presentability*, ✦S#5297h. Is 19:13. Je 2:16. 44:1. 46:14, 19. Ezk 30:13, 16. **stay.** *or*, governors. Heb. corners. Is 28:16. Ex 27:2. Nu 24:17. Jg 20:2. 1 S 14:38mg. Zc 10:4. 1 P 2:7.

14. **hath mingled.** See on ver. 2. Is 29:10, 14. 47:10, 11. 1 K 22:20-23. Jb 12:16. Ezk 14:7-9. 2 Th 2:11, 12. **perverse spirit.** Heb. spirit of perverseness *or*, perversities. ✦S#5773h, only here; the root is S#5753h, which occurs at Is 24:1mg. 1 S 20:30. 2 S 19:17. Pr 12:8. **as a drunken.** Is 28:7, 8. 29:9. Jb 12:25. Je 25:15, 16, 17, 19, 27. 48:26.

15. **Neither shall.** Is 9:14, 15. Ps 128:2. Pr 14:23. Hab *3:17. Hg 1:11. 1 Th 4:11, 12. **head or tail.** Is 9:15.

16. **like.** Is 30:17. Ps 48:6. Je 30:5-7. 50:37. 51:30. Na 3:13. **the shaking.** Is 10:32. 11:15. 30:30-32. Zc 2:9. **hand.** *22A14.8C. Anthropomorphism B879. A *hand* is attributed to God in certain idiomatic expressions: to shake the hand. For other instances of this figure see Is 10:32. 11:15. 13:2.

17. **the land.** Is 31:1-5. 36:1. Je 25:19, 27-31. 43:8-13. 44:28-30. Ezk 29:6, 7. **because.** Is 14:24, 26, 27. 20:2-5. 46:10, 11. Da 4:35.

18. **that day.** ver. 19, 21. Is 2:11. Zc 2:11. **shall five.** Is 11:11. 27:13. Ge +43:34n. 2 K +7:13. Ps 68:31. **speak.** Zp *3:9. **language.** Heb. lip. Ge 11:1mg. Jg +7:22mg. Zp 3:9mg. **and swear.** Is *45:23, 24. Dt 10:20. Ne 10:29. Ps 68:31. Je *12:16. Ph √2:9-11. **destruction.** Heb. Heres, *or*, the sun. Instead of *heres*, "destruction," which is also the reading of Aquilla, Theodotion, and the Syriac, fifteen MSS. and seven editions have *cheres*, "the sun;" agreeably to Symmachus, the Arabic, and Vulgate; while the Chaldee takes in both readings; and the LXX. reads *polis asedek*, "the city of righteousness," a name apparently contrived by the party of Onias, to give credit to his temple. As, however, *heres* in Arabic signifies a *lion*, Conrad Ikenius is of opinion that the place here mentioned is not Heliopolis, as is commonly supposed, but Leontopolis in the Heliopolitan nome, as it is termed in the letter of Onias to Ptolemy (Josephus, Ant. l. xiii. c. 3). The whole passage, from this verse to the end, contains a general intimation of the propagation of the knowledge of the true God in Egypt and Syria, under the successors of Alexander, and the early reception

of the gospel in the same countries. Je 43:13mg. Ezk 30:17mg.

19. **an altar.** T#1176. Is *66:23. Ge 12:7, 8. 13:4. 26:25. *28:18. Ex 24:4. Jsh √22:10, 26, 27. 1 K 18:35, 36. Zc 6:15. He 13:10. **pillar.** ✦S#4676h, Ex +*34:13. Ge *28:18. 35:14. Le ●26:1mg. Dt ●12:5. ●16:22mg. Not a reference to the Great Pyramid, as some wrongly suppose, but to an altar for sacrifices in Egypt in the millenium (ver. 21). Mention here of "altar" and "pillar" are reminiscent of the pre-mosaic patriarchal worship practices reflected in the references.

20. **for a.** Is 55:13. Jsh 4:20, 21. 22:27, 28, 34. 24:26, 27. **they shall.** See on ver. 4. Is 20:4. 52:5. Ex 2:23. 3:7. 2 K 13:4, 5. Ps 50:15. Ja +*5:4. **he shall send.** Is 37:36. *45:21, 22. Lk *2:11. T √2:13.

21. **the Lord shall.** Is *11:9. 37:20. 55:5. 1 S 18:46. 1 K 8:43. Ps 67:2. *98:2, 3. Je 16:19-21. Hab 2:14. Jn √17:3. Ga 4:8, 9. **and shall.** Zp *3:10. Ml 1:11. Jn √4:21-24. Ro 15:27, 28. 1 P *2:5, 9. **shall vow.** Is 44:5. Le +*23:38. Ec *5:4. Jon 1:16.

22. **he shall smite.** ver. 1, etc. Dt +*32:39. Jb *5:17, 18. Ho *5:15. *6:1, 2. He *12:11. **they shall.** Is 6:10. √55:7. Ho 14:1. Am *4:6-12. Ac 26:17-20. 28:26, 27.

23. **a highway.** Is 11:16. *35:8-10. √40:3-5. Ep *2:18-22. 3:6-8.

24. **shall.** Is 6:13. 49:6, 22. 65:8, 22. 66:12, 19-21. Dt 32:43. Ps ch. 117. Zc 2:10, 11. 8:20-23. Lk 2:32. Ro √10:11-13. 15:9-12, 27. **a blessing.** Is 65:8. Ge +*12:2. Ezk 34:26. Zc 8:13. Ga 3:14.

25. **the Lord.** Is 61:9. 65:23. Nu *6:24, 27. 24:1. Ps *67:6, 7. 115:15. Ro *11:12. Ep *1:3. 2:14. **Blessed.** Is 29:23. Ps 100:3. 138:8. Ho 2:23. Ro 3:29. 9:24, 25. Ph *1:6. Col 3:10, 11. 1 P *2:10. **my people.** Ho 2:23. **the work.** Ro 10:12. Ga 6:15. Ep *2:10. **and Israel.** See on Dt 32:9. **mine inheritance.** Is +*60:21n. Dt +*32:43. Ps +*94:14. Zc +*2:12.

ISAIAH 20

The prophet goes uncovered and barefoot, as a sign or type prefiguring the shameful captivity of Egypt and Ethiopia by the Assyrians, 1-4. He predicts the terror of those who had expected help from them, 5, 6.

1. **Tartan.** *Tartan* was one of the generals of *Sennacherib*, who, it is probable, is here called *Sargon*, and in the book of Tobit, *Sacherdonus* and *Sacherdan*, against whom Tirhakah, king of Cush or Ethiopia, was in league with the king of Egypt. 2 K *18:17. **Ashdod.** 1 S 6:17. Je 25:20. Am 1:8. **Sargon.** i.e. *the legitimate king; stubborn rebel; prince of the sun*, ✦S#5623h. **and took.** Je 25:29, 30.

2. **Isaiah.** Heb. by the hand of Isaiah. 1 K +16:12mg. **Go.** Je 13:1-11. 19:1, etc. Ezk 4:5, 6. Mt 16:24. **the sackcloth.** 2 K 1:8. Zc 13:4. Mt 3:4. Re 11:3. **put.** Ex 3:5. Jsh 5:15. Ezk 24:17, 23. **naked.** *171N, Ge +8:13. ✦S#6174h. ver. 3, 4. Is 58:7. Ge 2:25. 1 S 19:24. 2 S 6:20. Jb *1:20, 21h. 22:6. 24:7, 10. 26:6. Ec 5:15. Ho 2:3. Am 2:16. Mi *1:8h, 11. Jn 21:7. Ac 19:16. 1 C 4:1, 2, 9-13.

3. **naked.** *171N, Ge +8:13. Ex 32:25n. 2 S 6:20n. Jb 22:6. 24:10. Mt 25:43. Jn 21:7n. **barefoot.** 2 S 15:30. Je 2:25. **three years.** Is 16:14. 37:30. Nu 14:34. 1 K 2:11. Ezk 4:5, 6. Re 11:2, 3. **a sign.** Is +7:11. 8:18. Ex 7:3}*P*. Dt 4:34}*P*. 1 C 4:9. **upon Egypt.** Is 18:1, etc.

4. **shall**. Is 19:4. Je 9:25, 26. 46:26. Ezk 30:18. **Egyptians**. Heb. captivity of Egypt. **and old**. *ſ*174, Ge +18:27. **with their**. Is 3:17. 2 S 10:4. Je 13:22, 26. Mi 1:11. **uncovered**. ver. 2, 3. Is 58:7. ✱S#2834h: Is 20:4. 30:14 (take). 47:2 (make bare). 52:10 (made bare). Ps 29:9 (discovereth). Je 13:26 (discover). 49:10 (bare). Ezk 4:7 (uncovered). Jl 1:7. Hg 2:16 (draw out). **shame**. Heb. nakedness. ✱S#6172h. Is 47:3. Ge 9:22, 23, 23. 42:9, 12. Ex 20:26. 28:42. Le 18:6, 7, 8, 9, 10, 11, 11, 12, 13, 14, 15, 15, 16, 17, 17, 18, 19. 20:11, 17, 17, 18, 19, 20, 21. Dt 23:14mg. 24:1mg. 1 S 20:30. La 1:8. Ezk 16:8, 36, 37. 22:10. 23:10, 18, 29. Ho 2:9. Re 3:18.

5. **afraid**. Is *30:3, 5, 7. *36:6. 2 K *18:19-21. Ezk 29:6, 7. **their expectation**. *ſ*121R3, Ps +71:5. Je 37:7, 8. 42:13-22. 43:7. 46:26. La 5:6. Ezk 17:15. **their glory**. Is 2:22. Je 9:23, 24. *17:5. 1 C 3:21.

6. **isle**. *or*, country. Jb 22:30. Je 47:4. **whither**. Is 28:17. 30:1-7, 15, 16. 31:1-3. Jb 6:20. **and how**. Mt 23:33. 1 Th 5:3. He 2:3.

ISAIAH 21

A prophecy of the destruction of Babylon by the Medes and Persians, 1-10. The burden of Dumah, 11, 12. The burden of Arabia, 13-17.

1. **The burden**. The first ten verses of this chapter contain a prediction of the taking of Babylon by the Medes and Persians; which is here denominated "the desert of the sea," because the country around it, and especially towards the sea, was a great morass, often overflowed by the Tigris and Euphrates, and only rendered habitable by being drained by a number of canals. Is 13:1. 14:4, 23. 17:1. Je 50:1, etc. 51:1, etc. **the desert**. Is 13:20-22. 14:23. Je 51:42. **As whirlwinds**. Jb 37:9. Da 11:40. Zc 9:14. **from**. Is 13:4, 5, 17, 18. Ezk 30:11. 31:12.

2. **grievous**. Heb. hard. Is 48:4mg. Ps 60:3. Pr 13:15. **the treacherous**. Is 24:16. 33:1. 1 S 24:13. Je 51:44, 48, 49, 53. Jn *8:44. Re *13:10. **Go up**. Is 13:2-4, 17, 18. Je 50:14, 34. 49:34. *51:11, 27, 28. Da 5:28. *8:20. **all the sighing**. F/L Is 14:1-3. 35:10h. 47:6. 51:11h. Ps *12:5. *79:11. *137:1-3. Je 31:11, 12, 20, 25. 45:3. 51:3, 4. La 1:22. Mi 7:8-10. Zc 1:15, 16.

3. **are**. Is 15:5. 16:9, 11. Hab 3:16. **pangs have**. Is 13:8. 26:17. Ps 48:6. Je 48:41. 49:22. *50:43. Mi 4:9, 10. 1 Th 5:3. **I was bowed**. Dt 28:67. Ps 38:6. Da 5:5, 6.

4. **heart panted**. *or*, mind wandered. Is 16:8 (wandered). √53:6 (gone astray). Ps 119:110 (erred), 176 (gone astray). **the night**. Is 5:11-14. 1 S 25:36-38. 2 S 13:28, 29. Est 5:12. 7:6-10. Jb 21:11-13. Je *51:30, 39, 57. Da *5:1, 5, 30. Na 1:10. Lk *21:34-36. **turned**. Heb. put.

5. **Prepare**. *ſ*60A, Ge +3:22. **eat**. Is 22:13, 14. Da *5:1-5. 1 C 15:32. **arise**. Is 13:2, 17, 18. 45:1-3. Je *51:11, 27, 28.

6. **Go**. Is 62:6. 2 K 9:17-20. Ps *127:1. Je *51:12, 13. Ezk *3:17. 33:2-7. Hab 2:1, 2.

7. **And he saw**. ver. 9. Is 37:24. **he hearkened**. Je 51:31. He *2:1. **diligently**. 1 K 18:29. **heed**. *ſ*24I. Antimereia of the Noun B496: a noun for an adverb, i.e. *most attentively*. For other instances of this figure see Ps 75:2. 139:14. Pr 31:9. La 7:3. Mk 7:3. Jn 7:26. 10:24. 11:14, 54. 16:25, 29. 18:20. Ac 4:31.

8. **cried. A lion**. *or*, cried as a lion. Is 5:29. Je 4:7.

25:38. 49:19. *50:44. Da *7:2-4. 1 P *5:8. **I stand**. Is 56:10. 62:6. Ps 63:6. 127:1. Hab 2:1, 2. **whole nights**. *or*, every night.

9. **behold**. Je 50:3, 9, 29, 42. 51:27. **Babylon**. Is *13:19. 14:4. Je 50:2. *51:8, 64. Re *14:8. *18:2, 21. **is fallen**. *ſ*84, Ge +6:17. **all**. Is *46:1, 2. Je *50:2, 38. *51:44, 47, 52. **graven images of**. Dt 7:25*ꝗꝓ*. 12:3*ꝗꝓ*.

10. **my threshing**. Is 41:15, 16. 2 K 13:7. Je 51:33. Mi 4:13. Am *9:9. Hab 3:12. Mt *3:12. Re *14:14, 15. **corn**. Heb. son. Is 5:1mg. **floor**. or, threshing floor. Ge +50:10. Dt +*16:13mg. **that which**. 1 K 22:14. Ezk 3:17-19. Ac *20:26, 27.

11. **burden**. *ſ*3, Ge +49:10. Is 13:1. **Dumah**. *Dumah* is probably the same as *Dumatha*, a city of Arabia, mentioned by Stephanus, and the modern *Dumah* and *Dumathalgandel*, on the borders of Arabia and Syria, in a rocky valley. The Edomites, says Bp. Lowth, as well as Jews, were subdued by the Babylonians. They enquire of the prophet how long their subjection is to last; he intimates that the Jews should be delivered from their captivity; not so the Edomites. "The morning cometh, and also the night." Ge +25:14. 1 Ch 1:30. **to me out of Seir**. Is ch. 34. 63:1-6. Nu 24:18. Dt 2:5. Ps 137:7. Je 49:7-22. Ezk ch. 35. Jl 3:19. Am 1:6, 11, 12. Ob 1, etc. Ml 1:2-4. **Watchman**. *ſ*41, Ge +10:1. Ezk *3:17. 33:1-9. Mt *13:35-37. **what**. ver. 6. Je 37:17.

12. **The morning**. Is 17:14. Je 50:27. Ezk 7:5-7, 10, 12. **if**. Is √55:7. Je 42:19-22. Ezk *14:1-6. 18:30-32. Ac 2:37, 38. 17:19, 20, 30-32. **enquire**. Is 63:1. Je 49:7-22. Ezk 35:1-15. Ob 1-21. **return**. 2 S 23:4. 1 Th 5:1, 2, 5, 6. Re 22:16. **come**. SS 2:17. Re *22:17, 20.

13. **Arabia**. 1 K 10:15. Je 25:23, 24. 49:28-33. Ga 4:25. **O ye**. Is 13:20. Ge *25:3. 1 Ch *1:9, 32. Ezk 27:15, 20, 21. **Dedanim**. i.e. *leading forward; inhabitants of Dedan*, ✱S#1720h, only here. 1 Ch 1:9, 32.

14. **Tema**. Ge 25:15. 1 Ch 1:30. Jb 6:19. **brought**. *or*, bring ye. Is *16:3, 4. Jg 8:4-8. Pr 25:21. Je 12:9mg. Ro 12:20. 1 P 4:9.

15. **from the swords**. *or*, for fear of the swords. Heb. from the face of. Jb 6:19, 20.

16. **according**. Is *16:14. Jb *7:1. **Kedar**. Is 42:11. *60:7. Ge *25:13. 1 Ch 1:29. Ps *120:5-7. SS 1:5. Je *49:28. Ezk 27:21.

17. **archers**. Heb. bows. Is 22:3mg. **the mighty**. Is 10:18, 19. 17:4, 5. Ps 107:39. **for**. Is 1:20. Nu *23:19. Je 44:29. Zc 1:6. Mt *24:35. **hath spoken**. Is +1:20. 22:25. 24:3. 25:8.

ISAIAH 22

Prophecies of calamities coming on the Jews; with a rebuke of their impious and sensual behavior, when threatened with divine judgments, 1-14; and concerning the ruin of Shebna the treasurer, and the advancement of Eliakim, 15-25.

1. A.M. cir. 3292. B.C. cir. 712. **burden**. *ſ*121L4. Metonymy of the Subject B584. The object is put for that which pertains or relates to it: "burden" is put for the prophecy. For other instances of this figure see Is 13:1. 23:1. Na 1:1. Hab 1:1. Ml 1:1. **the valley**. Jerusalem being situated in the midst of surrounding hills, and the seat of divine revelation, is here termed "the valley of vision." The prophecy foretells the inva-

sion of Jerusalem by the Assyrians under Sennacherib; and probably also, by the Chaldeans under Nebuchadnezzar. Ps *125:2. Je 21:13. **of vision.** 1 S 3:1. Ps 147:19, 20. Pr 29:18. Mi 3:6. Ro 3:2. 9:4, 5. **What.** Ge 21:17. Jg 18:23. 1 S 11:5. 2 S 14:5. 2 K 6:28. Ps 114:5. **that thou.** The eastern houses are built with a court within, into which chiefly the windows open; those on the street being so obstructed with lattice work, that no one can see through them. Whenever, therefore, anything is to be seen or heard in the streets, any public spectacle, or any alarm, every one immediately goes up to the housetop to satisfy his curiosity. Hence all the people running to the top of their houses, gives a lively image of a sudden general alarm. Is 15:3. Dt 22:8. Je 48:38.

2. **that art.** ver. 12, 13. Is 23:7. 32:13. Am 6:3-6. **thy slain.** Is 37:33, 36. Je 14:18. *38:2. 52:6. La 2:20. 4:9, 10.

3. **thy rulers.** Is 3:1-8. 2 K *25:2-7, 18-21. Je 39:4-7. 52:24-27. **by the archers.** Heb. of the bow. Is 21:17mg.

4. **Look.** Ru 1:20, 21. Ezr 9:3. Je 4:19. *9:1. 13:17. Lk 1:2. **weep bitterly.** Heb. be bitter in weeping. Is 33:7. Je 6:26. Mi 1:8. Mt 26:75. ♪141. Pathopoeia; or, Description of Feelings B450. The description or the expression of feeling or emotion (B450, 916). For other instances of this figure see Is 49:15. Je 9:1. 23:9. 31:20. Ho 11:8. Mk 3:5. 5:33. 7:34. 10:14, 21. Lk 19:41. Ac 7:54, 57. 2 C 2:4. Ga 4:19, 20. 2 T 1:16-18. **labor.** Ps 77:2. Je 8:18. 31:15. Mt 2:18.

5. **a day.** Is 37:3. 2 K 19:3. Je 30:7. Am 5:18-20. **treading.** Is 5:5. 10:6. 25:10. **perplexity.** Est 3:15. Mi 7:4. **breaking.** 2 K *25:8-10. La *1:5. *2:2. **crying.** Ho 10:8. Mt 24:16. Lk 23:30. Re 6:16, 17.

6. **Elam.** Is 21:2. Ge 10:22. Je *49:35-39. **quiver.** F/L Is 49:2. **Kir.** Is *15:1. 2 K *16:9. Am 1:5. 9:7. **uncovered.** Heb. made naked. Is +3:17mg. 21:5. Hab 3:9. Zp 2:14mg.

7. **thy choicest valleys.** Heb. the choice of thy valleys. Is 37:24. Ge 23:6. Ex 15:4. **full.** Is 8:7, 8. 10:28-32. 37:34. 2 K *24:10. Je 39:1-3. **at.** or, toward.

8. **he discovered.** Is 36:1-3. **the armor.** 1 K 7:2. *10:17. 14:27, 28. 2 Ch 12:10. SS 4:4.

9. **have seen.** 2 K 20:20. 2 Ch 32:1-6, 30. **breaches.** or, "clefts." Am 6:11. **gathered.** Is 11:12. 40:11. 43:5. **lower.** Is ◐7:3. A reference to the pool of Siloam, the "old pool." Is 7:3. 8:6. 36:2. 2 S 5:8. 2 K *20:20. 2 Ch 32:3-5, 30. Ne 2:14. Ps 46:4. **pool.** lit. blessing. ver. 11. Is 7:3. 36:2.

10. **numbered.** Le 15:13, 28. 23:15. **broken.** Ex 34:13. Dt 7:5.

11. **a ditch.** or, reservoir. Ne *3:16. **old pool.** ver. ◐9. Is 7:3. Ne 2:13-15. 7:1-4. **ye have.** Is 8:17. 17:7. 31:1. 37:26. 2 Ch 6:6. 16:7-9. Je *33:2, 3. Mi 7:7.

12. **call.** 2 Ch 35:25. Ne 8:9-12. 9:9. Ec 3:4, 11. Je *36:22-24. Jl 1:13. *2:17, 18. Ja *4:8-10. 5:1. **to baldness.** Is 15:2. Ezr 9:3. Jb 1:20. Am 8:10. Jon 3:6. Mi 1:16.

13. **behold.** Is 5:12. 21:4, 5. 56:12. Am 6:3-7. Lk *17:26-30. **wine.** ♪63BA, Ge +26:7. Supply (saying). **let.** Is 56:12. 1 C 15:32. Ja 5:5.

14. **it was.** Is 5:9. 1 S 9:15. Am 3:7. **Surely.** Nu *15:25-31. 1 S *3:14. 2 K 24:4. Ezk 24:13. Mt √12:31, 32. Jn √8:21-24. He √10:26, 27. 1 J √5:16. Re *22:11, 12. **iniquity shall not be purged.** Is ◐6:7. ◐27:9. Ex 30:10♪𝒫. Le 4:20♪𝒫.

15. **treasurer.** 1 Ch 27:25. Ac 8:27. **Shebna.** Is 36:3. 37:2. 2 K 18:18, 37. 19:2. **which.** 1 K 4:6. 2 K 10:5.

16. **What hast.** Is 52:5. Mi 2:10. **hewed.** There are some monuments still remaining in Persia, of great antiquity, says Bp. Lowth, called Naksi Rustam, which give a clear idea of Shebna's pompous design for his sepulchre. They consist of several sepulchres, each of them hewn in a high rock near the top. The front of the rock to the valley below is adorned with carved work in relief, being the outside of the sepulchre. Some of these sepulchres are about thirty feet in the perpendicular from the valley, which is itself raised perhaps about half as much by the accumulation of the earth since they were made. Is 14:18. 2 S 18:18. 2 Ch 16:14. Jb 3:14. Mt *27:60. **sepulchre.** Heb. qeber, Ge +23:4. **as he.** or, O he.

17. **will carry,** etc. ♪147D, Ge +1:29. or, who covered thee with an excellent covering, and clothed thee gorgeously, shall surely violently turn, etc. ver. 18. **a mighty captivity.** Heb. the captivity of a man. **cover.** Est 7:8. Jb 9:24. Je 14:3.

18. **surely.** Is 17:13. Am 7:17. **a large country.** Heb. a land large of spaces. Is 33:21mg. Ps 119:45mg.

19. **I will drive.** Jb 40:11, 12. Ps *75:6, 7. Ezk 17:24. Lk 1:52.

20. **Eliakim.** Is 36:3, 11, 22. 37:2. 2 K 18:18, 37.

21. **clothe.** Ge 41:42, 43. 1 S 18:4. Est 8:2, 15. Jn 1:14. Ph 2:7, 8. 1 T 3:16. He 2:8-14, 16. **thy girdle.** Is 11:5. Ex 28:4, 39, 40♪𝒫. 29:9♪𝒫, +39. 39:29♪𝒫. Le 8:7, 13♪𝒫. 16:4♪𝒫. Lk 17:8. **a father.** Is +*9:6, 7. Ge 45:8.

22. **And the key.** As the robe and the baldric, mentioned in the preceding verse, were the ensigns of power and authority; so likewise was the *key* the mark of office, either sacred or civil. To comprehend how the key could be borne on the shoulder, it will be sufficient to observe, that the ancient keys were of considerable magnitude, and much bent. Jg 3:25. 1 Ch=9:27. Mt *16:18, 19. Lk +*11:52. Re *1:18. ♪165. Symbol B769. A material object substituted for a moral or spiritual truth. The stages by which a symbol is reached are: (1) either by *Metonymy* or *Metaphor*, one thing is used to *represent* another; then (2) by *Hypocatastasis* the one is used to *imply* the other; and finally (3) it becomes permanently *substituted* for it as a *symbol* of it. Here, "key" is used as a symbol of power and authority. With regard to leaven, we have first the thing itself causing fermentation, and therefore forbidden to be used in connection with any sacrifice or offering to the Lord. Then it is used by *Metonymy* for that which is corrupt (1 C 5:6-8). Then by *Implication* for corrupt or evil doctrine (Mt 16:6). And finally it is used as the permanent *symbol* of it (Mt *13:33). Indeed, "leaven" is always used in a bad sense, and of that which is corrupt. In the case of the two wave-loaves, where leaven was to be put into one and not into the other, the exception is significant, and proves the rule. For one represented Christ, and the other his people (B770). **so he.** Jb 12:14. Mt √18:18, 19. 28:18. Re *3:7. **open.** ♪121S3B, Jb +12:14.

23. **I will.** Ezr 9:8. Ec 12:11. Zc 10:4. Jn *10:18. Ro 1:4. **a nail.** ver. 25. Is 33:20. 54:2. Ezk 15:3. Zc 10:4. **a glorious.** Ge 45:9-13. 1 S 2:8. Est 4:14. 10:3. Jb 36:7. Lk *1:31-33. 22:29, 30. Ac 2:29-31. Re 3:21.

24. **hang.** Ge 41:44, 55. 47:11-25. Da 6:1-3. Mt 28:18. Jn 5:22-27. 20:21-23. Re 5:12, 13. 19:12.

offspring. F/L Is 34:1. 42:5. 44:3. 48:19. 61:9. 65:23. Jb 5:25. 21:8. 27:14. 31:8. **and the issue.** Ezk 4:15. **vessels of small.** Ezk 15:3. Ro *9:22, 23. 2 T *2:20, 21. **vessels of cups.** Ex 24:6. **vessels of flagons.** *or,* instruments of viols. J. A. Alexander notes that the old interpretation represented by the marginal reading, that the underlying Hebrew term denotes musical instruments, though justified by usage, is forbidden by the context. Je 48:12. La 4:2.

25. **the nail.** ver. 15, 16, 23. **cut down.** Is 53:8. Jn 19:11. Ac 2:23. 3:17, 18. 8:33. 1 C 1:23. 2 C 13:4. **and fall.** Lk *24:21, 25-27. Jn 19:30. Ph 2:8. **the burden.** Est 9:5-14, 24, 25. Ps 52:5-7. 146:3, 4. Je 17:5, 6. **for the.** Is 46:11. 48:15. Je 4:28. Ezk 5:13, 15, 17. Mi 4:4.

ISAIAH 23

A prediction of the ruin of Tyre, and the extensive consternation occasioned by it, 1-14; of the restoration of Tyre's prosperity, and the conversion of the Tyrians, 15-18.

1. A.M. 3289. B.C. 715. **burden.** *121L4, Is +22:1. Tyre, whose destruction by Nebuchadnezzar is here foretold, was a city of Phoenicia, on the shore of the Mediterranean, twenty-four miles south of Sidon, and thirty-two north of Accho or Ptolemais, according to the Antonine and Jerusalem Itineraries, about lat. 33 degrees 18 minutes N. long. 35 degrees 10 minutes E. There were two cities of this name; one on the continent called Palae Tyrus, or Old Tyre, according to Strabo, thirty stadia south of the other, which was situated on an island, not above 700 paces from the main land, says Pliny. Old Tyre was taken by Nebuchadnezzar, after a siege of thirteen years, B.C. 573, which he so utterly destroyed, that it never afterwards rose higher than a village. But previous to this, the inhabitants had removed their effects to the island which afterwards became so famous by the name of Tyre, though now consisting only of about 800 dwellings. Je 25:15, 22. 47:4. Ezk ch. 26-28. Jl 3:4-8. Am 1:9, 10. Zc 9:2, 4. **Howl.** Is 15:2, 8. Re 18:17-19. **ye ships.** *121J10. Metonymy of the Subject B577. "Ships" are put for the souls in them. Is 2:16. 60:9. 1 K 22:48n. 2 Ch *9:21n. Ps 48:7. Ezk 27:25. **Tarshish.** Ge +10:4. **for it is.** Is 15:1. Je 25:10, 11. Re 18:22, 23. **the land.** ver. 12. Nu 24:24. Je 2:10. Ezk 27:6. Da 11:30.

2. **still.** Heb. silent. Is 41:1. 47:5. Ps *46:10. Je 47:6. Hab √2:20. **the isle.** Ezk 27:3, 4. 28:2. **the merchants.** Ezk 27:8, etc.

3. **great waters.** Ps 29:3mg. 32:6. **Sihor.** 1 Ch 13:5. Je *2:18. **the harvest.** Is 32:20. Dt 11:10. **river.** *121.O, Ge +28:22. Is 7:18. Ex 7:19𝔓. 8:5𝔓. **she is.** ver. 8. Ezk 27:33. 28:4, 5. Jl 3:5, 6. Re 18:11-13. **mart.** ver. 18. Is 45:14. Pr 3:14. 31:18.

4. **I travail.** Je 47:3, 4. Ezk 26:3-6. Ho 9:11-14. Re 18:23.

5. **at the.** Is *19:16. Ex 15:14-16. Jsh 2:9-11. **so shall.** Ezk 26:15-21. 27:29-36. 28:19. Re 18:17-19.

6. **Pass.** ver. 10, 12. Is 21:15. Jon 1:3. **Tarshish.** Ge +10:4. **howl.** ver. 1, 2. Is 16:7.

7. **your.** Is 13:3. 22:2. 24:8. 32:13. **whose.** Jsh *19:29. **antiquity.** ✲S#6927h. Is 23:7. Ps 129:6 (afore). Ezk 16:55, 55 (former). 36:11 (former estate). **ancient.** Heb. *kedem,* Mi 5:2 (✥S#6924h). Is 19:11. **her own.** Is 47:1,

2. Ec 10:7. **carry.** Ps 60:9. 68:29. 76:11. **afar off.** Heb. from afar off. Is 5:26.

8. **Who hath.** Dt 29:24-28. Je 50:44, 45. Re 18:8. **the crowning.** Ezk 28:2-6, 12-18. Zc 9:3. **merchants.** Is 10:8. 36:9.

9. **Lord.** Is 10:33. 14:24, *27. 46:10, 11. Je 47:6, 7. 51:62. Ac *4:28. Ep +*1:11. 3:11. **to stain.** Heb. to pollute. Is *2:11, 12, 17. 5:15, 16. 13:11. Jb 40:11, 12. Da *4:37. Ml 4:1. Ja 4:6. **bring.** Jb 12:21. Ps 107:40. 1 C 1:26-29.

10. **O daughter.** ver. 12. **Tarshish.** Ge +10:4. **no more.** ver. 14. 1 S 28:20. Jb 12:21. La 1:6. Hg 2:22. Ro 5:6. **strength.** Heb. girdle. Ps 18:32. 109:19.

11. **stretched.** Is 2:19. 14:16, 17. Ex 15:8-10. Ps 46:6. Ezk 26:10, 15-19. 27:34, 35. 31:16. Hg 2:7. **the Lord.** Is 10:6. Ps 71:3. Je 47:7. Na 1:14. **against the merchant city.** *or,* concerning a merchantman. ver. 3. Ho 12:7, 8. **the merchant city.** Heb. Canaan. Ge 9:25. 10:15-19. Zc 14:21. Mk 11:17. Jn 2:16. **strongholds.** *or,* strengths. Zc 9:3, 4.

12. **Thou shalt.** ver. 1, 7. Ezk 26:13, 14. Re 18:22. **thou oppressed.** Is 37:22. 47:1, 5. Je 14:17. 46:11. La 1:15. **daughter.** *155E5, Nu +21:25. "The Sidonians," says Justin, "when their city was taken by the king of Ascalon, betook themselves to their ships; and landed and built Tyre;" Sidon was therefore the mother city. ver. 2. Ge 10:15-19. 49:13. Jsh 11:8. **pass.** ver. 1. Nu 24:24. Ezk 27:6. **there also.** Dt 28:64-67. La 1:3. 4:15.

13. **land.** Is 13:19. Ge 11:28, 31. Jb 1:17. Hab 1:6. Ac 7:4. **the Assyrian.** Ge 2:14. 10:10, 11. 11:9. 2 K *17:24. 20:12. 2 Ch 33:11. Ezr 4:9, 10. Da 4:30. **for them.** Ps 72:9. **and he.** Ezk 26:7, etc. *29:18.

14. **Howl.** ver. 1, 6. Ezk 27:25-30. Re 18:11-19. **ships.** *121J10, ver. 1. **Tarshish.** Ge +10:4.

15. **Tyre shall.** Je *25:9-11, 22. *27:3-7. 29:10. Ezk 29:11. **one.** Heb. *echad,* Dt +*6:4. A compound unity; here, a dynasty, the Babylonian dynasty. **king.** Da 7:14. 8:21. Re 17:10. **seventy years.** Je 25:9-11. 27:2-7. 29:10. **shall Tyre sing as an harlot.** Heb. it shall be unto Tyre as the song of an harlot. *155E3, Is +32:9. Ezk 27:25. Ho 2:15.

16. **go about.** Pr 7:10-12. Je 30:14. **thou harlot.** *38E, Is +6:9.

17. **visit.** Je 29:10. Zp 2:7. Ac 15:14. **and she shall.** Dt 23:18. Ezk 16:31. 22:13. 27:6, etc. Ho 12:7, 8. Mi 1:7. 3:11. 1 T 3:3, 8. 1 P 5:2. **shall commit.** Na 3:4. Re 17:2-5. 18:9-14. 19:2. **the face.** Ge +1:2.

18. **her merchandise.** Is 60:6, 7. 2 Ch 2:7-9, 11-16. Ps *45:12. 72:10. 87:4. Zc 14:20, 21. Mt 21:31. Mk *3:8. Lk 7:47. Ac *21:3-5. **it shall.** Mt 6:19-21. Lk 12:18-20, 33. 16:9-13. **for them.** Dt 12:18, 19. 26:12-14. Pr *3:9, 10. 13:22. 28:8. Ec 2:26. Ml 3:10. Mt *6:19. 25:35-40. Lk 8:3. Ac 9:39. Ro 15:25-27. Ga √6:6. Ph 4:17, 18. **durable.** Heb. old. Pr 8:18.

ISAIAH 24

Terrible judgments denounced against the whole land, 1-12. A remnant of Israel would escape and join with Gentiles in glorifying God, 13-15. His vengeance would overtake the rest, even the mightiest of them, 16-21. A day of visitation in mercy, and a glorious event to Zion and Jerusalem, 22, 23.

1. A.M. 3292. B.C. 712. **maketh the.** Is 1:7-9. 5:6. 6:11, 12. 7:17-25. 27:10. 32:13, 14. 42:15. Je √4:7, 23, 26. Ezk 5:14. 6:6. 12:20. 24:11. 35:14. Na 2:10. Lk

*21:24. **turneth it upside down.** Heb. perverteth the face thereof. Is 29:16. 2 K 21:13. Ps 146:9. Ac 17:6. **scattereth.** Dt 4:27. 28:64. 32:26. Ne 1:8. Je 9:16. 40:15. 50:17. Ezk 5:2. Zc 13:7-9. Ja 1:1.

2. **as.** ♪160B, Ge +25:31. **with the people.** Is 2:9. 3:2-8. 5:15. 9:14-17. 2 Ch *36:14-17, 20. Je 5:3-6. 23:11-13. 41:2. 42:18. 44:11-13. 52:24-30. La 4:13. 5:12-14. Ezk 7:12, 13. √14:8-10n. Da 9:5-8. Ho *4:9, 10. Ro *2:11. 1 C 7:29-31. Ep 6:8, 9. **so.** ♪160B, Ge +25:31. **priest.** or, prince. Ge 41:45mg, 50mg. Ex 2:16mg. 2 S 8:18mg. 20:26mg. **as.** ♪170, Is +1:18. **servant.** Ex 21:2. Mt 6:24. Col 3:22. 4:1. **master.** Col +*4:1. **maid.** Ge 16:1. 2 S 6:22. 14:6. **the buyer.** Pr 20:14. Ezk 7:12. Ho 12:7. **lender.** Ex 22:25, 27)♪. Dt 15:2)♪. 24:10, 11)♪. *28:12. Pr √22:7. **taker of usury.** Ex +*22:25. Le 25:36, 37. Dt ◐*15:3. 23:19, ◐20. Ne 5:2-5, 7, 11n. Ps 15:5. Pr 28:8. 29:13mg. Je 15:10. Ezk 18:8, 13, 17. 22:12. Mt 5:42. √25:27n. Lk 6:34, 35. 14:28. *16:8-10. *19:22, 23.

3. **shall.** ver. 1. Is 6:11. Le 26:30-35. Dt 4:27. 29:23, 28. 2 Ch 36:21. Ezk 36:4. Lk *21:24. Ja 1:1. **emptied.** ♪112. Merismos; or, Distribution B435: an enumeration of the parts of a whole which has been mentioned. Here, after stating that the Lord maketh the earth empty, the statement is amplified, and the way in which God will do this and scatter the people is afterwards enumerated. For other instances of this figure see Ezk 36:4. Ro 2:7. Ga 5:19-21. 5:22, 23. **the Lord.** See on Is 21:17. 22:25. Nu *23:19. Je 13:15. Mi 4:4.

4. **mourneth.** ♪155D, Ge +4:10. Is 3:26. 28:1. 33:9. √64:6. Je 4:28. 12:4. Ho 4:3. **haughty people.** Heb. height of the people. See on Is 2:11, 12. **earth.** ♪68, Ge +10:1.

5. **earth.** ♪16, Ge +1:27. **defiled.** Ge 3:17, 18. 6:11-13. Le 18:24-28. 20:22. Nu *35:33, 34. 2 Ch 33:9. Ps 106:36-39. Je 3:1, 2. Ezk 7:20-24. 22:24-31. Mi 2:10. Ro 8:20-22. **because.** Is 1:2-5. 50:1. 59:1-3, 12-15. Dt 32:15, 20. 2 K *17:7-23. 22:13-17. 23:26, 27. Ezr *9:6, 7. Ezk 20:13, 24. Da *9:5, 10. **changed.** Jsh 24:25. Da 7:25. Mk 7:7-9. Lk 1:6. He 9:1. **broken.** T#86. Is 55:3. 59:13-15. Ge 17:13, 14. 2 S 23:5. Ps 14:2, 3. 105:10. Je 50:5. Ezk 37:26. Jl 3:13. Am 8:11. Mt *24:24. Lk 18:8. Ro *3:9, 10, 23. 2 Th *2:3, 4, 7. 2 T *3:1-5. He 13:20. 2 P *2:1, 2. 3:3, 4. Ju 17-19. Re 3:10. 11:3, 7, 10. 12:12. 13:3, 4. 16:13, 14. **everlasting.** Heb. olam, Ge +17:7. Is √55:3. Ge +9:16)♪. 2 S √23:5. Je 50:5.

6. **hath.** Is 42:24, 25. Dt *28:15-20. *29:22-28. 30:18, 19. Jsh *23:15, 16. Zc +*5:3, 4. Ml 2:2. 3:9. *4:1, 6. Mt 27:25. **the curse.** Ge 3:17. Pr +*3:33. Zc +*5:3. **that dwell.** Re +*3:10. **are desolate.** or, found guilty. Ps *5:10mg. **are burned.** Is 1:31. 4:4. *31:9. 42:25. √66:15, 16, 24. Dt 32:22. Ps √21:9, 10. +*50:2, 3. *97:3. +*104:4. Da 7:10, 11. Ml +√4:1. 2 P +√3:7. Re *16:9. 19:20. **and few.** ver. 13. Is *4:1. 13:12. 45:20. *66:16. Le 26:22. Dt 4:27. *28:62. *29:20. Ps 92:7-9. Ezk 5:3. 36:36. Zc 13:8—14:5. Mt +*7:14. Lk 18:8. Ro 9:27. 1 Th 4:15n. 2 P 3:10. Re 6:4, 8. *8:9, 11. *9:15, 18. *11:13. 13:15. 14:15, 16, 20. 16:*3, 18, *21. 18:8. 19:15, 18, *21.

7. **new wine.** Is 16:8, 10. 32:9-13. Ho 9:1, 2. Jl 1:10-12. **mourneth.** ♪155D, Ge +4:10. **the vine.** Jl 1:7.

8. **mirth.** Is 23:15, 16. Je *7:34. 16:9. 25:10. Ezk 26:13. Ho *2:11. Re 18:22.

9. **drink wine.** Is 5:11, 12. Ps 69:12. Ec 9:7. Am 6:5-7. 8:3, 10. Zc 9:15. Ep √5:18, 19.

10. **city.** ver. 12. Is 25:2. 27:10. 32:14. 34:13-15. 2 K 25:4, 9, 10. Je 39:4, 8. 52:7, 13, 14. Mi 2:13. 3:12. Lk 19:43, 44. *21:24. **of confusion.** Heb. tohu, Ge 1:2)♪. F/L 29:21 (naught). 34:11. 40:17, 23. 41:29. 44:9 (vanity). 45:18, 19 (in vain). 49:4 (naught). 59:4 (vanity). Ge 11:9mg. Je 9:25, 26. Mt 23:34, 35. Re 11:7, 8. 17:5, 6. 18:2.

11. **a crying.** Pr 31:6. Ho 7:14. Jl 1:5. **all joy.** ver. 7-9. Is 8:22. 9:19. Je 48:33. La 5:14, 15. Am 5:16-20. Mt 22:11-13. Lk 16:25.

12. **the city.** Is 32:14. Je 9:11. *25:11. La 1:1, 4. 2:9. 5:18. Mi 1:9, 12. Mt 22:7. **the gate.** Is 3:26. 14:31. 45:2. Ge +*14:7n. 2 K 25:10. Lk *21:24.

13. **there.** Is *1:9. 6:13. 10:20-22. *17:5, 6. Le *19:9, 10. Je 44:28. Ezk 6:8-11. 7:16. *9:4-6. 11:16-20. 14:22, 23. Mi 2:12. Mt 24:22. Ro *11:2-6. Re 3:4. 11:2, 3.

14. **shall lift.** Is 12:1-6. 25:1. 26:1. 27:2. *35:2, 10. 40:9. 42:10-12. 44:23. 51:11. *52:7-9. 54:1. Je 30:19. 31:12. 33:11. Zp 3:14-20. Zc 2:10. **sea.** ♪63BA, Ge +26:7. Supply (saying).

15. **glorify.** ver. 23. Jb 35:9, 10. Da *3:16-18. Hab *3:17, 18. Zc *13:8, 9. Ac 16:25. 1 P 1:7. √3:15. *4:12-14. Re 15:2-4. **fires.** or, valleys. J. A. Alexander suggests that the reference is to in the east (as the region of sunrise, or of dawning light) in opposition to the sea or west. Is 44:16mg. *59:19. Ps +*49:14. +*59:16. **God of Israel.** Is +29:23. Ge 33:20)♪. Ex 24:10)♪. Nu 16:9)♪. **isles.** Is 11:11, 12. 41:5. 42:4, 10. 49:1. 51:5. 60:9. Ge 10:4, 5. Zp 2:11. Zc 10:9-12. Ml 1:11.

16. **From the.** Re 26:15. 45:22-25. 52:10. 66:19, 20. Ps *2:8. *22:27-31. 67:7. 72:8-11. 98:3. ch. 117. Mi 5:4. Mk *13:27. Ac 13:47. **uttermost part.** Heb. wing. Is 11:12mg. Ge 7:14mg. 1 K 6:24. Jb 37:3mg. Ezk 5:3mg. 39:4mg. **heard songs.** Is *35:10. +*51:11. Ho +*2:15. Hab *3:3. Zc +*2:10. **glory.** ver. 23. Ex 15:11. Ps 58:10, 11. Re 15:3. 16:5-7. *19:1-6. **the righteous.** ver. 15. Is 26:2. Ac 3:14. 7:52. 22:14. **But.** Is 10:16. 17:4. Ps 106:15. **My leanness.** Heb. Leanness to me. or, My secret to me. ♪84. Figure of speech Epizeuxis; or, Duplication: the repetition of the same word in the same sense. F/L Used in the "former" portion here and Is 26:3; 29:1. Used in the "latter" portion at Is 41:27; 65:1. For other instances of this figure see Ge +6:17. **the treacherous.** ♪147E. Combined Polyptoton B280. Verbs with other parts of speech. For other instances of this figure see Ho 10:1. 2 C 10:12. Ga 5:7. Ep 1:3. **have dealt.** Is 21:2. 33:1. 48:8. 63:5. Je 3:20. *5:11. 12:1, 6. La 1:2. Ho 5:7. 6:7. Hab 1:3.

17. **and the pit.** Le 26:21, 22. 1 K 19:17. Je 8:3. 48:43, 44. Ezk 14:21.

18. **he who fleeth.** Dt 32:23-26. Jsh 10:10, 11. 1 K 20:29, 30. Jb 18:8-16. 20:24. Am 5:19. **noise.** ♪144, Ge +3:8. **for the.** Ge 7:11. 19:24. 2 K 7:2. **snare.** Je 48:43, 44. Lk 21:35. **the windows.** Ge 7:11)♪. 2 P 3:5-7, 10. **the foundations.** Is 40:21. Dt 32:22. Ps 18:7, 15. 46:2, 3.

19. **utterly broken.** ver. 1-5. Is 34:4-10. Je 4:23-28. Na 1:5. Hab 3:6. Mt *24:3. Re 20:11. **dissolved.** 2 P *3:11.

20. **reel.** Is 19:14. 29:9. Ps 18:7. 107:27. **removed.** Is 1:8. 38:12. **the transgression.** Is 5:7-30. Ps 38:4. La 1:14. Ho 4:1-5. Mt 33:35, 36. **shall fall.** Je 8:4. 25:27. Da *11:19. Am *8:14. Zc 5:5-8. Re 18:21.

21. **in that day.** Is +*2:11. Da +*12:1. Re 12:7, 8, 12, 13. *20:1-3. **the Lord.** Is 10:25-27. 14:1, 2. 25:10-

12. *34:2, 4, 5, etc. Ps 76:12. √149:6-9. Ezk ch. 38, 39. Jl 3:9-17, 19. Hg 2:21, 22. Zc 14:12-19. Re 6:14-17. 17:14. 18:9. *19:17-21. 20:1-3. **punish**. Heb. visit upon. Nathaniel West cites Nagelsbach to the effect that the Hebrew word *pakad* signifies "a 'visiting' which consists in a looking again after some one who, long time, has remained neglected" (*The Thousand Years in Both Testaments*, pp. 40, 41). Is 10:12mg. 23:17. Je +9:25mg. 27:22. Zc 10:3mg. Re √20:7. **high ones**. Ep 2:2. *6:12. Re 12:7-9. 20:1-3. **the kings**. Ps 2:2. *76:12. Zc *14:2. 2 Th 2:8. Re *19:11-21.

22. **they shall**. ver. 17. Is *2:19. Jsh 10:16, 17, 22-26. **be gathered**. Is +*17:14. Ps +*37:9. *101:8. Mi *4:11-13. Zp *3:8. Mt 13:28, 30, √40-42. **as prisoners are gathered**. Heb. with the gathering of prisoners. **pit**. *or*, dungeon. Heb. *bor*, Ge +37:20. F/L Is 14:15, 19. 36:16. 38:18. 51:1. **shut up in the prison**. Heb. *masger*, ✱S#4525h. Rendered (1) prison: Is 42:7. Ps 142:7. (2) smiths: 2 K 24:14, 16. Je 24:1. 29:2. Re √20:1-7. **after many days**. This expression is identical in reference to (1) the *thousand years* of Re √20:2-7. (2) *many days* of Ezk ?38:8. (3) the *third day* of Ho 6:2. (4) *for ever*, Heb. *leolam*, of Ezk 37:25, 26, 28. **shall they**. Je 38:6-13. Zc 9:11, 12. **visited**. *or*, found wanting. Is 10:3. *23:17. 26:14, 16. 29:6. Ps +*6:10. *109:28. Je *27:22. Ezk +*38:8. Re *20:7-10.

23. **the moon**. lit. the pale. ♪24G, Ge 1:9. Is 4:5. *13:10. 30:26. *60:19. Ezk 32:7, 8. Jl *2:31. *3:15. Hab 3:11. Mt √24:29. Mk √13:24-26. Re 6:12-14. 20:11. *21:23. **confounded**. ♪155D, Ge +4:10. **ashamed**. ♪155D, Ge +4:10. **shall reign**. Is 52:7. Ex 15:21. Ps 18:43. 97:1. Je +√23:5. Mi +*4:7. Zc +*9:9. +*14:9. Mt *6:10, 13. Lk √1:32, 33. Re 11:15. 19:4, 6. **in mount Zion**. Is +*2:3. *4:3, 4. 12:6. +*51:3, 11. *60:14, 15. 62:1-4. Ps 2:6, 8. 69:35, 36. +*102:13, 16. 110:2. +*122:6. √132:13, 14. Je *3:17. Jl 3:17. Mi *4:7. Zc 2:10-13. *8:2, 3, 15. He 12:22. Re 14:1. **in Jerusalem**. Is *2:3. *62:7, 12. √65:17-19. *66:13. Ps 51:18. *122:5, 6. +*147:2. Je +*3:17. Zc √2:12. *8:15, 22. 12:6. 14:17-21. Lk +*19:11. **before his ancients gloriously**. *or, there shall be* glory before his ancients. ver. 16. Ps +*102:16. 145:10, 11. Col +*3:4. 1 P +*1:11. **before**. Lk +*21:36. **his ancients**. Is *35:10. Jb 38:4-7. Ps *140:13. Da *7:9, 10, 18, 22, 27. Jl *3:11. Zc +*14:5. Mt *8:11. +*13:43. Re 4:4. +*5:10. *20:4-6. 22:4, 5.

ISAIAH 25

The prophet praises God, for abasing his haughty foes, and protecting his afflicted people, 1-5. He predicts the saving benefits of Christ, 6-8; the success of the gospel, and his triumph over all opposers, 9-12.

1. **thou art**. Is 26:13. 61:10. Ex 15:2)♀. 1 Ch 29:10-20. Ps 99:5. *118:28. 145:1. SS 6:3. 2 T *1:12. Re 5:9-14. 7:12. **my God**. Heb. *Elohim*. ver. 9. **exalt**. Ps 96:1-13. 98:1-9. 146:2. Re 15:3. **thou hast**. Ps *40:5. 46:10. 78:4. 98:1. 107:8, 15, 21, 31. 111:4. Da 4:2, 3. Re 15:3. **thy counsels**. Is 28:29. 46:10. Nu 23:19. Ps *33:10, 11. Je 32:17-24. Ezk 38:17-23. Ro 11:25-29. Ep +*1:11. He *6:17, 18. Re *19:11.

2. **For**. ver. 12. Is 14:23. 17:1. 21:9. 23:13. Dt 13:16. Je 51:26, 37, 64. Na 3:12-15. **palace**. Is 13:22. Re 18:1-3, 19, 21-24. **never be built**. Is √13:20. 14:22, 23. Je *50:3, 39. 51:26, *29, 37, *62. Re 14:8. 16:19-21. 17:15-18. 18:2, 19, 21. 19:1-3.

3. **shall the strong**. Is 49:23-26. 60:10-14. 66:18-20.

Ps 46:10, 11. 66:3. 72:8-11. Ezk 38:23. 39:21, 22. Zc 14:9, 16. Re 11:13, 15-17.

4. **thou hast**. Is 11:4. 14:32. 29:19. 33:2. *66:2. Jb 5:15, 16. Ps *12:5. *35:10. 72:4, 13. 107:41. 119:31. Zp 3:12. Ja 2:5. **a refuge**. Is 4:5, 6. 32:2. **when**. Is 32:18, 19. 37:3, 4, 36. Ezk 13:11-13. Mt 7:25-27. **shadow**. Is 4:6. 26:20. 32:2. Ps 121:6. Da 3:24, 25. 6:19-22. **blast**. Heb. *ruach*, Ge +26:35. Is 37:7. Ex 15:8. 2 K 19:7.

5. **shalt bring**. Is 10:8-15, 32-34. 13:11. 14:10-16. 17:12-14. 30:30-33. 49:25, 26. 54:15-17. 64:1, 2. Ps 74:3-23. 79:10-12. Je 50:11-15. 51:38-43, 53-57. Ezk 32:18-32. 38:9-23. 39:1-10. Da *5:30. 7:23-27. 11:36-45. Re ch. 16-19. 20:8, 9. **as the heat**. Is 18:4. 49:10. Ps 105:39. Jon 4:5, 6. **branch**. Is 14:19, 20. Jb 8:16-19.

6. **in this mountain**. ver. 10. Is 2:2, 3. *24:23. Ps 72:14-16. 78:68. Mi 4:1, 2. Zc *8:3. He *12:22. **make**. Is *55:1, 2. Ps *63:5. Pr *9:1-5. SS *2:3-5. 5:1. Je *31:12, 13. Zc 9:16, 17. Mt *22:1-10. Lk 14:16-23. *22:29, 30. Re *19:9. **all people**. Is 49:6-10. Da *7:14. Mt +*8:11. Mk √16:15, 16. **of wines**. SS 1:2, 4. Je 48:11. Mt *26:29. Lk 5:39.

7. **he will**. Is *60:1-3. Mt *27:51. Lk *2:30-32. Ac *17:30. 2 C √3:13-18. Ep 3:5, 6. *4:18. *5:8. He *9:8, 24. *10:19-21. **destroy**. Heb. swallow up. ♪22C35, Ex +15:7. ver. 8. Is 3:12mg. Ps 35:25. La 2:2, 5, 16. **cast**. Heb. covered. ✱S#3874h. 1 S 21:9 (wrapped). 1 K 19:13. **the vail**. 2 C *3:15. √4:3, 4. Ep √4:18. Re 20:1-3.

8. **He will**. Da +*12:2. Ho *13:14. Jn 19:30. 1 C *15:26, 54, +*55. 2 T √1:10. He *2:14, 15. Re *20:14. *21:4. **swallow up**. ♪22C35, Ex +15:7. An example of double reference in prophecy (Ho +*11:1. Mt +*16:23), for the *time* the prophecy will be fulfilled is applied by Paul in 1 C 15:54 to the rapture (1 C 15:51, 52), but it is applied here by Isaiah to the Second Advent of Christ. ver. 7 (destroy). Nu 16:30. Ps 69:15. 106:17. Jon 1:17. **victory**. Heb. *nezach*, Jb +4:20 (✱S#5331h). F/L Is 13:20. 28:28. 33:20. 34:10. 57:16. 1 S 15:29mg. 1 Ch 29:11. 1 C▸15:54. **wipe away tears**. Is 35:10. Je √31:15-17. Ezk +16:49, 55, 60. Re *7:17. 21:4. **rebuke of his people**. Is 30:26. 37:3. +√54:4-10. *60:15. 61:7. 66:5. Dt +*32:43. Ps 69:9. *89:50, 51. Jl *2:19. Am *9:9. Zp +*3:20. Mt 5:11, 12. Ro √11:25, 26, 29, 32-36. 1 P 4:14. **take away**. Is *65:17. Jl +*2:25. Zp +√3:15. Zc √8:13-15. √10:6. Ml 3:4. **off**. Ml 3:17, 18.

9. **it shall**. Is 12:1. Zp 3:14-20. Re *1:7. 19:1-7. **in that day**. Ps +*118:24. Ho 2:18. Jl 3:18. **Lo**. Is 8:17. 26:8, 9. 30:18, 19. Ge 49:18. Ps 27:14. *37:5-7. 62:1, 2, 5-7. Mi 7:7. Zp 3:17. Lk *2:25, 28-30. Ro *8:23-25. T *2:13. 2 P 3:12, 13. Re 22:20. **our God**. ver. 1. Is 52:7. Jb +19:26. Ps +√45:6, 7. Jn √1:1. +*20:28. Ro √9:5. 2 C 5:19. Col *2:8, 9. 1 T *3:16. T √2:13. He +*1:8. 2 P 1:1. Ju 4. Re 21:7. **we have waited**. Is 33:2. Ge 49:18)♀. Nu 24:17. Jb +19:26. Ps 92:2. 130:5, 6. La 3:23. Mi 7:7, 8. Mt 24:27. Ac 1:9-11. 1 Th *4:16, 17. T 2:13. He *9:28. Ja 5:7, 8. Re 1:7. 22:20. **we will**. Is 12:2-6. 66:10-14. Ps 9:14. 20:5. 21:1. 95:1. 100:1. +*118:24. Zc 9:9. Ro 5:2, 3. Ph 3:1, 3. 1 P *1:6, 8, 9. **his salvation**. Is *12:2. 26:1. 33:16-22. *35:4. 45:17. 49:8-11, 26. *59:16-21. 60:18. 61:10. 62:1. 63:5. Ps 9:14. *14:7. +*37:9, 39. *42:5mg. *53:6. 74:12, 20. *85:7, 9. 98:2, 9. 118:14. *132:11, 16. *149:4. Is 23:6. *30:7. Ezk 37:23. Mi 7:7. Lk 2:25, 30. Ro *13:11.

1 Th 5:9. 2 T *2:10. He +*9:28n.

10. **in this.** ver. 6. Is 11:10. 12:6. 18:4. Ps 132:13, 14. Ezk 48:35. Zp 3:15-17. Zc 9:9-11. **Moab.** Is 11:14. ch. 15, 16. Nu *24:17. Zp 2:9. **trodden down.** or, threshed. Is 41:15, 16. Mi 4:13. **even.** Is 5:25. 10:6. 14:19. 26:6. Ps 83:10. La 1:15. **for the dunghill.** or, in Madmenah. Is +10:31. Je 48:2.

11. **he shall spread.** Is 5:25. 14:26. 65:2. Col *2:15. **he shall bring.** ver. 5. Is *2:11. 10:33. 13:11. 14:12. 16:6. 53:12. Ps 2:5, 8-12. ch. 110. Je 48:29, 42. 50:31, 32. 51:44. Da 4:37. Ja *4:6. Re 18:6-8. 19:18-20.

12. **the fortress.** Is 26:5. Je 51:58, 64. 2 C 10:4, 5. He 11:30. Re *18:21. **to the dust.** Is 13:19-22. 14:23.

ISAIAH 26

A song of praise, with animating exhortations to trust in God, who gives his people peace, and victory over their most haughty foes, 1-6. The conduct of the righteous and the wicked, when under divine judgments, 7-11. Recollections of past mercies to Israel, for an encouragement under present trials, 12-18. A call to the people of God, to wait in faith and hope for his salvation, and for the punishment of the wicked, 19-21.

1. **that day.** Is 2:11, 20. 12:1. 24:21-23. 25:9. **this song.** Is 5:1. 27:1, 2. Ex 15:2-21. Nu 21:17, 18. Jg ch. 5. 2 S 22:1, etc. Je 33:11. Ep *5:19, 20. Re 5:9-14. 7:9-17. 11:15-18. 14:3. 15:3, 4. 19:1-7. **in the land.** Ezr 3:11. Ps 137:3, 4. **strong city.** Ps 48:11-13. **salvation.** Is 60:18. 62:11. Ps 31:21. 48:12, 13. 125:1, 2. Ezk 48:35. Zc *2:4, 5. Mt 16:18. Re 21:12-22. **God.** ✓63A1, Ge +14:20.

2. **Open.** Is *60:11. 62:10. Ps *118:19, 20. Ezk 48:31-34. Zc 8:20-23. Ac 2:47. Re *21:13, 24-27. **righteous.** Is +*60:21. Ex 19:6. Dt 4:6-8. Ps 106:5. Ph *3:8, 9. 1 P 2:9. 2 P *3:13. Re 5:9. 19:8. 21:27. 22:14, 15. **truth.** Heb. truths. ✓96F2, Ge +4:10. Dt 32:20. Pr 13:17. Ju *3.

3. **wilt keep.** Is +*9:6, 7. *57:19-21. Dt 32:10. Ps 12:7. *85:7, 8. Mi 5:5. Jn *14:27. *16:33. Ro *5:1. Ep 2:14-16. Ph *4:7. **in perfect peace.** Heb. peace, peace. F/L Is *57:19. ✓84. Figure of speech Epizeuxis, Ge +6:17. Is 24:16. ✓24K. Antimereia B497. A noun is put for an adjective. A noun is sometimes repeated in order to express the adjective in the highest or superlative degree. **mind.** or, thought, or, imagination. Is 29:16. Ge 6:5. 8:21. 2 C 10:5. **stayed.** Is *31:1. 48:2. *50:10. 2 Ch +*20:20. 29:18. Ps 111:8mg. 112:8. **because.** 1 Ch 5:20. 2 Ch 13:18. *16:8. Ps +✓9:10. 84:11, 12. 146:3-6. Je *17:7, 8. Ro *4:18-21. **he trusteth.** T#293. 2 S 22:31. Ps 2:12. 17:7. *28:7. 31:19, 20, 24. 32:10. 34:8, 22. *37:3. 38:15. 40:4. 112:6-8. 118:8, 9. 125:1. 146:5. Pr *18:10. 28:25. 29:25. *30:5. Je *17:7, 8.

4. **Trust.** Is ✓12:2. *50:10. 2 Ch 13:18. +*20:20. 32:8. Ps 46:1. 55:22. *62:8. 91:2. 115:9-11. 118:8, 9. Pr ✓3:5, 6. Ro 4:20, 21. **for ever.** Heb. *olam* plural, Ps +61:4; Ps +9:18 (❋S#5703h, *ad*). **in the Lord Jehovah.** Is 12:2. 45:17, 24. 63:1. Ex 3:13, 14. 6:3. Jb 9:19. Ps 46:1. 62:11. 66:7. 83:18. 93:1. 125:1. Mt 6:13. 28:18. Ph *4:13. **everlasting strength.** Heb. the Rock of ages. ✓22L3, Dt +32:31. F/L Is 17:10. 30:29. 32:2. 44:8. Dt 32:4, 15, 18, 30, 31}✓. 1 S 2:2. 2 S 23:3. Ps 18:2, 46. 62:1, 2. 144:1mg. Hab 1:12. Mt 6:13. =16:18. 1 C=10:4. Ph *4:13. He ✓13:8.

5. **bringeth.** Is 2:12. 13:11. 14:13-15. 25:11. Jb 40:11-13. 2 C *10:5. **the lofty.** Is *25:12. 32:19. *47:1. Je 50:31, 32. 51:25, 26, 37, 64. Re 18:2.

6. **foot.** Is 25:10. 37:25. 60:14. Jsh 10:24, 25. Je 50:45. Da *7:27. Zp *3:11, 12. Ml 4:3. Lk 1:51-53. 10:19, 20. Ro *16:20. 1 C *1:26, 27. Ja *2:5. Re *2:26, 27. 3:9.

7. **way.** Is 35:8. 1 Ch 29:17. Jb 27:5, 6. Ps 18:23-26. *37:23. Pr 20:7. 2 C 1:12. Ep ✓2:10. 1 J 3:7, 10, 22. **uprightness.** 1 Ch 29:17. Ps *143:10. **most.** 1 S 2:2-4. Jb 31:6mg. Ps *1:6. 11:4, 7. Zp 3:5. 1 C 4:5. **dost weigh.** 1 S *2:3. Jb 1:8. 31:6.

8. **in.** Is 64:4, 5. Nu 36:13. Jb 23:10-12. Ps 18:23. 44:17, 18. 65:6. 106:3. 119:102, Ml 4:4. Lk 1:6. 1 C *4:5. 2 C *1:12. **we.** Is 25:9. ✓30:18. 33:2. Ps *37:3-7. 63:1. Mi 7:7. Ac 1:4, 14. 2:1. Ro 8:25. 2 Th *3:5. Ja *5:7-11. **desire.** 2 S 23:5. Ps 13:2. 42:1, 2. 63:1-3. 73:25. 77:10-12. 84:2. 143:5, 6. SS 1:2-4. 2:3-5. 5:8. 7:10. **soul.** Heb. *nephesh*, Ge +34:3. **remembrance.** Ex 3:15}✓. Ps 102:12. 135:13. Ho 12:5.

9. **With my.** T#1392. 2 S 23:5. Ps 42:1, 2. **soul.** Heb. *nephesh*, Ge +34:3. Ps +*84:2. Mt +*11:29. **have I desired.** Ps *63:6, 7. *73:25. *77:2, 3. 119:62. 130:6. SS *3:1-4. 5:2-8. Mk *1:35. Lk *6:12. **the night.** Ps 63:6. +119:55. Pr +3:24. SS 3:1. **spirit.** Heb. *ruach*, Ge +41:8. ✓121A2, Ps +51:10. Mk +*2:8. **seek thee.** Ps *63:1. Pr *8:17. Ho *5:15. Mt ✓6:33. He ✓11:6. **early.** Ge +19:27. Mk +*1:35. **for when.** Is 27:9. Nu 14:21-23. Ps 58:11. *64:9, 10. *83:18. *105:7. *119:155. Ho 5:15. 1 T +*2:6. Re 7:14-17. 11:13. 15:4. **will learn.** Ps 119:67, 71. Re 15:4.

10. **favor.** Is *63:9, 10. Ex 8:15, 31, 32. *9:34. Dt 32:15. 1 S *15:17-23. Ps 106:43. Pr *1:32. Ec 3:16. ✓8:11. Ho *13:6. Ro *2:4, 5. Re 2:21. **in the.** Is 3:10. 24:5. 27:13. Ps *78:54-58. *143:10. Je *2:7. 31:23. Ezk 22:2, etc. Ho 9:3. Mi 2:10. *3:10-12. Mt 4:5. 23:37. 24:15. **and will not.** Is 2:10. *5:12. 22:11. Ps 28:4, 5. Ho *11:7. Jn *5:37, 38.

11. **when.** Ps 10:12. 106:26. Mi 5:9. **will not see.** Is 18:3. Ex 7:23. 1 S 6:9. Jb 34:27. Je 5:3. 44:17-23. Mi 6:9. Ac 28:27. Re *9:20. **they shall see.** Ex 9:14. 11:6, 7. 14:25. 1 S 5:6-11. 1 K 22:25. Ps 37:32-34. Je 44:28. Mi 6:9. Zc 1:6. Lk 16:23. **be ashamed.** Is 11:13. 60:14. 66:5. Ps 76:17. 1 P *3:16. Re 3:9. **at the.** or, towards *thy* fire. Is 5:24. 30:27, 33. 64:2. ✓66:24. Dt 32:22. Ps 21:8, 9. Ml *4:1. Mt *25:41. Mk ✓9:43-49. 2 Th ✓1:8. He 12:29. Re *19:20. 20:15.

12. **ordain.** ver. 3. Is *57:19, 21. Ps *29:11. *37:37. 85:8. Pr +*16:7. Je 33:6. Mi 5:5. Jn *14:27. 20:19, 21. 2 Th 3:16. He *13:20, 21. **for.** Dt 30:6. Ps 51:10. Je 31:33. 32:39, 40. Ezk *36:25-27. Jn 3:21. Ep *2:10. Ph 2:13. He 13:20, 21. **hast wrought.** Ps 68:28. Ph 2:13. **in us.** or, for us. Ps *57:2. Ezk 20:9, 14, 22. 1 C 15:10. Ph *2:13.

13. **other.** Is 51:22, 23. 2 Ch 12:8. Ne 9:28, 36, 37. Je 50:17. La 5:8. Mt *6:24. Jn *8:32-36. Ro *6:20, 22. Ep 2:1-3. 1 T 1:12-15. T 3:3-7. **by thee.** Is *12:4. 48:1. Ex 23:13. Jsh *23:7. Am 6:10. 1 C 4:7. 15:10. 2 T ✓2:19. He *13:15.

14. **dead.** ver. 19. Is *8:19. 51:12, 13. Ex 14:30. Ps 106:28. Hab 2:18-20. Mt 2:20. Jn 5:28, 29. Re 18:2, 3. 19:19-21. 20:5. **deceased.** Heb. *rephaim*. ver. 19. Is 14:9. 17:5. Jb 26:5. Ps 88:10. Pr 2:18. 9:18. 21:16. **shall not rise.** 1 P 3:19. 2 P 2:4. Ju 6. **visited.** or, inspected. ver. 16. Is 13:11. 34:16. **destroyed.** Is *13:9. Nu 33:52. Jb 19:10. Ps 37:1, 2, 9, 10, 20, 35, 36, 38.

and made. Is 14:19-22. 33:14. Ps 9:6. 109:13. +*146:4. Pr *10:7. Ec +*9:5. Mt +*10:28.

15. increased. Is 9:3. 10:22. Ge 12:2. 13:16. Nu 23:10. Dt 10:22. Ne 9:23. Je 30:19. thou art glorified. Is 44:23. 49:18-21. 60:7-10, +*21. Ps *86:9, 10. Jn 12:23-28. 13:31, 32. 15:8. 17:1, √5, 24. Re 11:15-18. thou hadst. Is 6:12. Dt 4:27, 28. 28:25, 64. 32:26, 27. 1 K 8:46, 47. 2 K 17:6, 23. 23:27. Je 32:37. Ezk 5:12. 36:24. Lk *21:24. Ro 11:12. removed it far. Rather, "thou hast extended far all the borders of the land" (Peters, *Theocratic Kingdom*, vol. 2, p. 146). Ge 15:18. Ex 23:31. Dt 11:24. Je +*7:7. Ac +*7:5. He +*11:13, 39. The original grant of land to the Jews will be confirmed in the millennium, and extended. The boundaries given are the Mediterranean, the Nile and the Euphrates; thus including places *not before* possessed (Peters, vol. 2, p. 144). See related notes (Is 60:21n. 1 K 4:21n. Jsh 21:43n. Je 33:21n. Ac 7:5n).

16. in trouble. Dt √4:29-31. Jg 10:9, 10. 2 Ch 6:37, 38. 33:12, 13. Ps *50:15. 77:1, 2. 91:15. Je 22:23. Ho *5:15. 7:14. Re *3:19. they poured. 1 S *1:15. Ps 42:4. 142:2. La 2:19. Da *6:10. Heb. *tzook*, *S#6694h: Kal, Preterite: Is 26:16. Kal, Future: Jb 28:2 (molten). 29:6 (poured). prayer. Heb. secret speech. *S#3908h. Ec 10:11 (enchantment). Is 3:3 (orator; mg, skilful of speech), 20 (earrings). Je 8:17 (charmed).

17. as a woman. Is 13:8. 21:3. 37:3. 42:14. 66:7, 9. Ge 3:16)℘. Ps 48:6. Je 4:31. 6:24. 30:6. Mt +24:8. Jn 16:21. 1 Th *5:3.

18. we have been in. Is 37:3. 2 K 19:3. Ho 13:13. brought forth wind. Ec 2:11, 17. we have not. Ex 5:22, 23. Jsh 7:7-9. 1 S 11:13. 14:45. the inhabitants. Ps 17:14. Jn 7:7. 1 J 5:19.

19. dead men. Is 25:8. 1 S +*2:6. Jb 14:14. Ezk *37:1-14. Da 12:2. Ho 6:2. *13:14. Jn √5:28, +*29. Ac *24:15. Ro 11:15. 1 C *15:22, 23. 1 Th *4:14, 15. Re *20:5, 6, 12. my dead. Mt 27:+*52, 58. Jn *11:25, 26. 1 C 15:20, 23. Ph *3:10, 21. my dead body. T#1901. Jb +*19:25, 26. Ezk 37:11-14. Ho *13:14. Mt 12:38-40. Mk 8:31-33. 9:9, 10. 10:32-34. Jn +*2:19, +√21. √10:18. 12:31-34. 20:6-10. shall they arise. T#1900. Ezk *37:1-8. Da *12:1-4. Mt +*)11:5. Mk 12:18-27. Lk)7:22. Jn *5:28, 29. Awake. Is 51:17. 52:1, 2. 60:1, 2. Ps *17:15. 22:15. +*71:20. 139:18. Da √12:2. Ep 5:14. Re 11:8-11. thy dew. Is *66:14. Ge 2:5, 6. Dt 32:2. 33:13, 28. 2 S 17:12n. Jb 29:19. Ps *72:6n. *110:3. Pr 3:20n. Ho *14:5. Zc 8:12. *Dew* is here an apt type or symbol of bodily resurrection from the dead, the comparison centering upon the revitalizing effect of dew upon herbs being like the revivifying effect of the resurrection upon once dead bodies. See the reference passages and their Notes given above. the earth. Re 20:13. cast out. Ho 13:14. Zc 9:12. Ac 24:15. the dead. Heb. *rephaim*. ver. 14 (deceased). Is 17:5. Ge 14:5. 15:20. Pr +21:16 (*S#7496h).

20. my. Is 51:4, 16. Je 7:23. 31:14. enter. Is 32:18, 19. Ge 7:1, 16. Ex *12:22, 23. Ps 32:6, 7. 91:4. Pr 14:26. 18:10. +*27:12. Ezk 11:16. Zc *9:12. Mt 23:37. Re *14:13. shut. Mt 6:6. hide. Is 16:1-5. 42:11-13. 63:1-5. Ps *17:8. *27:5. *31:19, 20. 32:7. 60:6-12. *94:12, 13. 108:8-13. 143:9. Pr +*27:12. Ezk 20:33-44. Da 11:36-45. Ho 2:14-23. Ml 3:16-18. Mt 24:15-22. Lk +*21:36. Col 3:3, 4. Re 12:6, 14. for a little. Is 54:7, 8. Ps 30:5. 57:1. 2 C 4:17. moment. *S#7281h. Is 27:3. 47:9. 54:7, 8. Ex 33:5. Nu 16:21, 45. Ezr 9:8mg. Jb 7:18. 20:5. 21:13. 34:20. Ps 6:10 (suddenly). 30:5.

73:19. Je 4:20. 18:7 (instant), 9. La 4:6. Ezk 26:16. 32:10. until the indignation. Jb *14:13. Ps *57:1. Da +8:19 (*S#2195h). 9:27. 11:36. Mt 24:15-22. Lk +√21:36. 1 Th 4:13, 14. 5:9. 2 P 2:9. Re √3:10.

21. Lord cometh. Is 18:4. Ps 9:12. 50:2, 3. +*102:16. Ezk 8:6. 9:3-6. 10:3-5, 18, 19. Ho *5:14, 15. Mi *1:3-8. Zc 8:3. 2 Th √1:7-10. Ju *14, *15. his place. ℘22D3A, 1 K +8:39. punish. Is +*24:21. also. Ge 4:10, 11. Nu *35:32, 33. Jb 16:18. Ps 79:10. Ezk 24:7, 8. Lk 11:50, 51. Re *6:9-11. *16:6, 7. 18:24. blood. Heb. bloods. Ge 4:10, 11)℘. 2 K +*9:26mg.

ISAIAH 27

God's judgment on leviathan, and his care over his vineyard, Israel, 1-6. He chastises his people in measure, and for their reformation, 7-9. Desolation, and punishment without mercy are threatened, because the people had no understanding, 10, 11. The Lord will gather his dispersed, to worship in his holy mount, 12, 13.

1. that day. Is 26:21. with his. Is 34:5, 6. *66:16. Dt 32:41, 42. Jb 40:19. Ps 45:3. Je 47:6. Ep 6:17. He *4:12, 13. Re 1:16. 2:16. 19:13, 15, 21. sword. ℘22D5D, Dt +32:41. leviathan. Jb 12:1, etc. Jb 41:1, 33, 34. Ps 74:14. 104:26. piercing. *or*, crossing like a bar. *S#1281h. Is 43:14mg. Jb 26:13 (crooked). crooked. Is 65:25. Jb 26:13. serpent. Ge 3:1, 14, 15. the dragon. Is *51:9. Ps *74:13, 14. Je 51:34. Ezk 29:3. 32:2-5. Re *12:3-17. 13:1, 2, 4, 11. 16:13. *20:2. in the sea. Je 51:13. Re 13:1. 17:1, 15.

2. sing. Is *5:1-7. Nu 21:17. A vineyard. Ps 80:8, 14, 15. Je 2:21. Mt 21:33, etc. Lk 20:9, etc. red wine. Ge 49:11, 12.

3. I the Lord. Is 46:4, 9. 60:16. Ge 6:17. 9:9. Ezk 34:11, 24. 37:14, 28. do keep. Dt 33:26-29. 1 S 2:9. Ps 46:5, 11. 121:3-5. Jn √10:27-30. *15:1, 2. water. Is ●5:6. 35:6, 7. *41:13-19. √55:10, 11. 58:11. every moment. Jb 7:18. will keep. Is 42:6. Dt *11:12. Ps 34:15. *121:4, 5. Pr *15:3. SS 4:12-16. Zc *4:10. 2 T *1:12. 1 P 3:12.

4. Fury. Is 12:1. *26:20, 21. 54:6-10. Ex 34:6, 7. Ps 85:3. *103:9. Ezk 16:63. Na *1:3-7. 2 P 2:9. not in me. Ezk *18:23. Lk +*6:35. 2 P √3:9. who would. Is 5:6. 9:18. 10:17. 2 S *3:6. Ml 4:3. Mt *3:12. Lk 6:44. √14:31, 32. He √6:8. briers and thorns. Is 5:6. He 6:8. go through. *or*, march against. burn them. Is *9:18.

5. let him. Is 25:4. 26:3, 4. 45:24. 56:2. 64:7. Ge *32:24-28. Jsh 9:24, 25. 10:6. Jb *22:21. Lk 13:34. 14:32. 19:42. Ep √2:8. He 6:18. and he. Is *57:19. Le 3:2, 3, 5. Ezk *34:25, 26. Ho 2:18-20. Lk *19:42. Ro 5:1-10. 2 C *5:19-21. Ep 2:16, 17. Col *1:20, 21.

6. cause them. Is *6:13. *37:31. 49:20-23. *54:1-3. *60:22. Ge 49:22. Ps *92:13-15. Je *30:19. Ho *2:23. *14:5, 6. Zc *2:11. 6:12. 10:8, 9. Ro *11:12, 16-26. Ga 3:29. Ph 3:3. Re *11:15. Israel shall. Ezk 39:25. take root. Is 4:2. 11:10. 37:31. 2 K 19:30. Ps 80:9. Ho 14:5. blossom and bud. Is *35:1, 2. Ge 40:10. and fill. Ge 49:10. Ps *68:11. Na 1:15. Hab *2:14. Mt +*24:14. Ac 5:28. 1 T +*2:6. Re 11:15. face. Ge +1:2. the world. Is 42:12. 48:20. 49:6. 61:6. +*66:19. Ge +*12:3. Mt +√24:14. 28:19, 20. Mk 16:15. Ac +*1:8. 17:6. with fruit. Is 37:31. 52:7. 2 K 19:30. Ps 68:11. 72:16. Pr +*11:30. Ezk 17:23. 36:8. Da +*11:33.

+*12:3. Ho 14:5, 6, 8, 9. Na 1:15. Jn √15:5, 16. Col 1:6. Re √7:3, 9, 14.

7. Hath he smitten. Is 10:20-25. 14:22, 23. 17:3, 14. Je 30:11-16. 50:33, 34, 40. 51:24. Da 2:31-35. Na 1:14. 3:19. **as he smote.** Heb. according to the stroke of.

8. measure. Is *57:16. 2 S 24:14. Jb *23:6. Ps 6:1. 38:1. 78:38. *103:9, 10, 14. Je *4:27. 10:24. √30:11. 46:28. Ml 3:17. Jn 3:34. 1 C √10:13. 1 P 1:6. **it shooteth forth.** or, thou sendest it forth. **thou wilt.** Is 1:5, 18-20. *5:3, 4. Jg 10:10-16. Je 2:17-37. Ho 4:1. 6:1, 2. 11:7-9. Mi 6:2-5. **debate.** or, strive. Is 1:17. 3:13. 49:25. 50:8. 51:22. Je 2:9, 29. 12:1. 50:34. Mi 7:9. **he stayeth,** etc. or, when he removeth it. Pr 25:4, 5. **his rough.** Is 10:5, 6, 12. Ps 76:10. 78:38. Je 4:11, 27. Ezk 19:12. Ho 13:15.

9. this therefore. Is 1:24, 25. 4:4. 48:10. Ps *119:67, 71. Pr 20:30mg. Ezk 20:38. 24:13. Da 11:35. Ml 3:2, 3. 1 C *11:32. He 12:6, 9-11. **be purged.** Is +*60:21n. Nu √35:33. Dt √32:43. Ps +*130:8. Da +√9:24n. Jl √3:21. Zc √13:1. **this is.** He 12:11. **take away his sin.** Is +*60:21. Ro ▶11:27. **when.** Is 64:10, 11. 2 K *25:8, 9, 13-17. 2 Ch 36:19. Ezr 3:2, 3. Ezk 11:18. 24:11-14. **the groves.** Is 1:29. 2:12-21. *17:8. 2 K +17:10. 21:3n. 23:6. Ho 14:8. Mi 5:13, 14. Zc 13:2. **images.** or, sun images. Is 17:8mg. Le +26:30. 2 Ch 14:5mg. 34:4mg. **shall not stand.** Le 26:30. Ho 14:8.

10. the defenced. Is 5:9, 10. 6:11, 12. 17:9. 25:2. 64:10. Le 26:31-35. Je 26:6, 18. La 1:4. 2:5-9. 5:18. Ezk 36:4. Mi 3:12. Lk *19:43, 44. *21:20-24. **there shall.** Is 7:21, 22, 25. 17:2. 32:13, 14. Je 39:10. **the branches.** Is 17:6.

11. the boughs. Ps 80:15, 16. Ezk 15:2-8. 20:47. Mt 3:10. Jn *15:6. **withered.** Jn *15:6. **broken off.** Ro 11:17, 18, 20. **on fire.** Jn *15:6. **for it is.** Is *1:3. 44:18-20. Dt 4:6. *32:28, 29. Je *4:22. 5:4, 5, 21, 22. +*8:7. Ho 4:6. Mt 13:15, 19. Ro 1:28, 31. **no understanding.** Ps +49:20. **therefore.** Is 43:1, 7. 44:20, 21, 24. Ge 6:6, 7. Dt 32:18-25. 2 Ch 36:16, 17. Ps *106:40. Ezk *9:5, 10. 1 Th *2:16. 2 Th √1:8, 9. Ja 2:13. **no favor.** T#559. Ge +6:6 (T#230). Ex 34:6, 7. Jb +27:8 (T#572). Ezk 7:9. Da +12:2 (T#573-7). Na 1:3.

12. beat off. Is 11:11-16. *24:13-16. 56:8. Ge 15:18. Dt *24:20. Jg 6:11. Ps 68:22. 72:8. **the channel.** Jg 12:6. **the river.** Is 7:20. 8:7. 11:15. Ge +15:18. 31:21. Ex 23:31. Jsh 24:2. 1 K 4:21, 24. 2 Ch +9:26. Ps 72:8. **stream of Egypt.** Ge 15:18. Nu 34:5. Jsh 13:3. 15:4, 47. 1 K *8:65. 2 K 24:7. 2 Ch 7:8. Ezk 47:19. 48:28. **ye shall be.** Dt *30:3, 4. Ne 1:9. Je *3:14. 43:7. Am *9:9. Mt 18:12-14. Lk *15:4. Jn √6:37. 10:16. **gathered.** or, gleaned. Is 17:6. Le +23:22.

13. And it. Is 2:11. **the great trumpet.** Is 18:3. Le +23:24. =*25:9n, 52n. Nu 10:2-4. 1 Ch 15:24. Ps 47:5. 81:3. *89:15. Zc 9:13-16. Mt *24:31. Lk 4:18. Ro *10:18. 1 Th √4:16, 17. Re 8:2, 6-13. 9:1, 14. 10:7. *11:15-18. 14:6. **and they.** Is 11:16. *19:23-25. 2 K 17:6. Ho 9:3. 11:11. Zc 10:8-12. **Assyria.** 2 K 17:6. **the outcasts.** Is 11:12. *16:3, 4. 56:8. Ps *147:2. Je 43:7. 44:28. Ho 8:13. **and shall.** Is *2:2, 3. 25:6, 7. 66:18-21. Zc *14:16. Ml 1:11. Jn *4:21-24. He *12:22, 23.

ISAIAH 28

The prophet threatens the speedy ruin of Ephraim for its pride and drunkenness, 1-4. God will be the Glory and Strength of the residue of his people, 5,

6. The Jews are severely reproved for drunkenness, 7, 8; unteachableness, 9-13; and carnal security, 14, 15. Christ, as the sure Foundation, is promised, 16. The presumptuous security of scorners will end in destruction, 17-22. The wisdom of Providence is illustrated, by the discretion of the husbandman as given by God, 23-29.

1. A.M. 3279. B.C. 725. the crown. This chapter begins a new subject, chiefly relating to the devastations of Israel and Judah by the Assyrian kings. The ancient Samaria being beautifully situated on the top of a round hill, and surrounded immediately with a rich valley, and then a circle of other hills around it, suggested the idea of a chaplet, or wreath of flowers. ver. 3. Ho 5:5. 6:10. **drunkards.** ver. 7. Is √5:11, 22. Pr +*23:29. Ho 4:11. *7:5. Am 2:8, 12. *6:6. **whose.** ver. 4. Is *7:8, 9. 8:4. 2 K 14:25-27. 15:29. 18:10-12. 2 Ch 28:6. 30:6, 7. Ho 13:1. Am *6:1. **overcome.** Heb. broken. *S#1986h. Is 16:8. 41:7 (smote). Jg 5:22, 26mg. 1 S 14:16 (beating down). Ps 74:6. 141:5. Pr 23:35 (beaten).

2. the Lord. Is 9:9-12. 27:1. Ezk 30:10, 11. **as a tempest.** ver. 15-19. Is *8:7, 8. 25:4. 29:6. 30:30. 2 K *15:29. *17:5, 6. Ezk 13:11. Na 1:8. Mt 7:25-27. Re 18:8.

3. The crown. ver. 1. **shall.** Is 25:10. 26:6. 2 K 9:33. La 1:15. Da 8:13. He 10:29. Re 11:2. **under feet.** Heb. with feet.

4. shall be. ver. 1. Is 1:30. Ps 73:19, 20. Ho 6:4. 9:10, 11, 16. 13:1, 15. Mt √21:19, 20. Ja 1:10, 11. **the hasty.** "No sooner," says Dr. Shaw (p. 370), "doth the boccore (or early fig) draw near to perfection in the middle or latter end of June, than the kermez, or summer fig, begins to be formed, though it rarely ripens before August; about which time the same tree frequently throws out a third crop, or winter fig, as we may call it. This is usually of a much longer shape and darker complexion than the kermez, hanging and ripening upon the tree, even after the leaves are shed; and, provided the winter proves mild and temperate, is gathered as a delicious morsel in the spring." Mi 7:1. Na 3:12. Re 6:13. **eateth.** Heb. swalloweth. Is 3:12mg. 9:16mg.

5. shall the. Is 41:16. 45:25. 60:1-3, 19. 62:3. Je 9:23, 24. Zc 6:13-15. Lk 2:32. 1 C *1:30, 31. 2 C 4:17. 1 P 5:4. **crown of glory.** T#824. Is 62:3. 2 Th 1:10. **for a diadem.** Jb 29:14. Ps 90:16, 17. 149:4. **residue.** Is 10:20, 21. 11:16. 37:31, 32. Ro 11:5, 6.

6. for a spirit. Heb. ruach, Ex +15:8. Is 11:2-4. 32:15, 16. Ge 41:38, 39. Nu 11:16, 17. 27:16-18. 1 K 3:28. 2 K *18:1-7. Ps 72:1-4. Pr 20:8. Jn *3:34. *5:30. 1 C 12:8. **and for strength.** Dt *20:4. Jsh 1:9. Ps 18:32-34. 46:1, 11. 144:1, 2, 10.

7. priest and the prophet. Ml 2:7. **erred through wine.** Is 19:14. *56:10-12. Le 10:9, 10. 2 K 17:18, 19. Pr +√20:1. 31:4, 5. Ec 10:17. Ezk 44:21. Ho *4:11. Mi 2:11. Mt 24:29. Lk 21:34. Ep +*5:18. **are swallowed.** Is 19:3mg. Ps *107:27mg. **err in vision.** Is 3:12. 9:16. Je 14:14. 23:13, 16. La 2:14. Ezk √13:7. Ho *4:12.

8. all tables. Pr 26:11. Je 48:26. Hab √2:15, 16.

9. Whom. ♪63BA, Ge +26:7. Supply (say they). **shall he teach.** Is 30:10-12. Ps ❶*25:9. 50:17. Pr 1:29, 30. Je 5:31. 6:10. Jn √3:19. 12:38, 47, 48. **weaned.** 1 S +1:22n. Ps 131:2. Mt *11:25. *21:15, 16. Mk *10:15. 2 T *3:15. 1 P √2:2. **to understand.** Is +√29:24.

doctrine. Heb. the hearing. ſ121R1, Le +13:55. Is 53:1mg.

10. **For precept.** ver. 13. Is 5:4. Dt 6:1-6. 2 Ch 36:15, 16. Ne 9:29, 30. Je 11:7. 25:3-7. Mt 21:34-41. Ph 3:1. 2 T 3:7. He *5:12. 6:1. **must be.** *or,* hath been. **upon precept.** ſ84, Ge +6:17. **line.** ſ84, Ge +6:17. **little.** ſ84, Ge +6:17.

11. **with.** Dt *28:49. Je 5:15. 1 C ✓14:21. **stammering lips.** Heb. stammerings of lips. *S#3934h. Ps 35:16 (mockers). For the related root, *S#3932h, see Is +33:19mg. **will he speak.** *or,* he hath spoken.

12. **This.** Is *30:15. 2 Ch 14:11. 16:8, 9. Je *6:16. Mt *11:28, 29. **rest.** ſ121G, Ge +31:1. **yet.** Ps 81:11-13. Je ✓6:10. 44:16. Zc 7:11-14. Jn ✓3:19. He *12:25.

13. **the word.** 2 Ch 36:15, 16. Ne 9:30. **precept upon precept.** ver. 10. Je 23:36-38. Ho 6:5. 8:12. Ph 3:1. 2 T *3:7. **that.** Is 6:9, 10. 8:14, 15. Ps *69:22. Mt 13:14. 21:44. Ro 11:9. 2 C *2:15, 16. 1 P *2:7, 8. 2 P 3:16.

14. **ye.** ver. 22. Is 1:10. 5:9. 29:20. *30:10. Pr 1:22. *3:34. *29:8. Ho 7:5. Ac 13:41.

15. **have said.** ſ122, Ex +15:9. **We have.** To be in covenant with a thing, says Bishop Lowth, is a proverbial expression to denote perfect security from mischief or evil of which it is the cause. Is 5:18, 19. Jb 5:23. 15:25-27. Ec 8:8. Je *36:21-24. 37:9, 10. 44:17. Ezk 8:12. Ho 2:18. Zp 1:12. **made a covenant.** F/L Is 24:5. 33:8. 54:10. 55:3. 56:4, 6. 59:21. 61:8. **hell.** Heb. *sheol,* Ge +37:35. **when.** Is 8:7, 8. Da 11:22. **we have made.** Is 30:10. Je 5:31. 14:13, 14. 16:19. 28:15-17. Ezk 13:16, 22. Am 2:4. Jon 2:8. 2 Th ✓2:9-12.

16. **Behold.** Is 8:14. Ge *49:+10, 42. Ps *118:22. Zc 3:9. Mt 21:42. Mk 12:10. Lk 20:17, 18. Ac ✓4:11, 12. Ro ▶9:33. ▶10:11. 1 C 3:11. Ep 2:20. 1 P ▶2:6-8. **foundation.** Ep 2:19-22. Col 1:17. **a stone.** Is 26:4mg. Ge 49:24▶9ᵉ. Ps 62:1, 2. **precious.** Ps 49:7, 8. 116:15. 139:17. 1 P 1:19. 2:7. 2 P 1:11, 4. **corner stone.** 1 P *2:6, 7. **foundation.** ſ22L2, Is +8:14. **he that.** Is *30:18. Ps 22:4, 5. *112:7, 8. Hab 2:3, 4. Ja 5:7, 8. 1 P 3:6. **make haste.** ſ121G2, Ps +25:2. Is 35:4mg.

17. **Judgment.** Is 10:22. 2 K 21:13. Ps 94:15. Am 7:7-9. Ro 2:2, 5, 6, 25. 9:28. Re *19:2. **and the hail.** ver. 2, 15. Is 25:4. 32:2, 18, 19. Ex 9:18, 19. Jsh 10:11. Je 7:4-8, 14, 20. 23:19. 30:23, 24. Ezk 13:10-16. 38:22. Re 8:7. 11:19. 16:21. **and the waters.** Is 30:28. Jb 22:16. Da 11:22. Mt 7:27. 2 P 3:6, 7.

18. **your covenant.** Is 7:7. 8:10. Je 44:28. Ezk 17:15. Zc 1:6. **shall be disannulled.** For *kuppar,* Houbigant, Archbishop Secker, and Bishop Lowth, would read *tupper;* but the former may well have the sense ascribed to it here, as it signifies in Chaldee and Syriac, *abstersit, diluit, abolevit.* **your agreement.** Je 19:7. Da +*9:27. **hell.** Heb. *sheol,* Ge +37:35. Is 57:9. Ezk 31:16, 17. 32:21, ✓27. **when.** ver. 2, 15. Is 8:8. +*10:5, 6. Je 47:2. Da 8:9-13. 9:26, 27. 11:40. Re 12:15, 16. 17:15. **trodden down by it.** Heb. a treading down to it. ver. 3. Ml 4:1-3.

19. **the time.** Is 10:5, 6. 2 K *17:6. 18:13. Ezk 21:19-23. **morning by.** 2 S 13:4mg. **and it.** Is 33:7. 36:22. *37:3. 1 S *3:11. 2 K *21:12. Je 19:3. Da 7:28. 8:27. Hab *3:16. Lk *21:25, 26. **to understand the report.** *or, when* he shall make *you* to understand doctrine. lit. hearing. ſ121R1, Le +13:55. ver. 9mg. Is 53:1mg.

20. **the bed.** ſ7. Allegory as repeated Hypocatastasis B750, Ga +4:24. Here only one part of the figure is mentioned, the bed and its covering, and not the people to whom it refers. The prophet is speaking of the great fear which ought to agitate the people of Judea at the speedy coming of Sennacherib; but they preferred to be left in their false security. By this beautiful allegorical illustration they are informed that their rest should be restless, and their sleep should be soon disturbed. Is 57:12, 13. 59:5, 6. *64:6. 66:3-6. Je 7:8-10. Mt 5:20. Ro 9:30-32. 1 C 1:18-31. Ph 3:8, 9.

21. **in mount Perazim.** i.e. *breaches; defeats,* *S#6556h, as a name only here; compare *S#1188h, 2 S +5:20. 2 S *5:20. 1 Ch 14:11. **the valley.** Jsh *10:10, 12. 2 S 5:25, Geba. 1 Ch 14:16. Ps 18:13-15. These incidents happened too long before for them to have been a matter of memory; this furnishes clear evidence that the books in which these events were recorded were extant in Isaiah's day, not written afterwards. **his strange work.** ver. 19. Dt 29:21-24. Is 29:13, 14. Je 30:14. La 2:15. 3:33. Ezk 33:21. Hab *3:11. Lk *19:41-44. Ac 13:41. The parallel passages and context show that his "strange work" was the turning of God against his own people.

22. **be ye.** ver. 15. 2 Ch 30:10. *36:16. Je 15:17. 20:7. Mt 27:39-44. Ac *13:40, 41. 17:32. 2 P ✓3:3-12. **lest.** 2 Ch 33:11. Ps 107:16. Je 39:7. La 1:14. Re 22:18, 19. **a consumption.** Is 10:22, 23. *24:1, 3, 4, etc. 32:12-14. Je 25:11. Da ✓9:26, 27. Lk ✓21:24.

23. **Give ye ear.** Is 1:2. Dt 32:1. Je 22:29. Mt 11:15. 13:3-43. Re 2:7, 11, 14, 17, 29.

24. **plow.** 1 C 3:9. 9:9, 10. **break.** Je 4:3. Ho 10:11, 12.

25. **made plain.** or, level, or, equal. Is 38:13. Mt *3:12. **cast abroad.** or, scatter. Is 24:1. Ge 11:9. **scatter.** or, sprinkle. Ex 9:10. 24:8. Le 7:2. **in the principal,** etc. *or,* the wheat in the principal *place,* and the barley in the appointed *place.* **rye.** *or,* spelt. Ex 9:31, 32. Ezk 4:9. **place.** Heb. border. *S#1367h. Is 10:13 (bounds). Nu 32:33 (coasts). 34:2, 12. Dt *32:8 (bounds). Jsh 18:20. 19:49. Jb 24:2 (landmarks). Ps 74:17 (borders).

26. **For his God,** etc. *or,* And he bindeth it in such a sort as his God doth teach him. Ex 28:3. 31:3-6. 36:2. Jb 35:11. 39:17. Ps 144:1. Da 1:17. Ja 1:17. **doth instruct.** Is 30:21. 42:16. Ps 5:8. 25:5, ✓9. *27:11. *32:8. 48:14. 73:24. 119:102. 139:9, 10. *143:10. Pr *1:23. Jn *7:16, 17. Ja *1:5.

27. **threshed.** Is 41:15. 2 K 13:7. Am 1:3. **threshing instrument.** F/L Is 41:15. **the fitches.** Is 27:7, 8. Je 10:24. 46:28.

28. **Bread.** ſ121H, Ps +74:15. By Metonymy of the Effect, the thing made is put for the material from which it is made or produced. Here, "bread is bruised" signifies the corn of which it is made. The sense is clear from verse 27 and Job 28:5. In Ps 104:14, we have the opposite of this in the Metonymy of the Cause (ſ121D14). Is 21:10. Jb 28:5. Ps ◖104:14. Am 9:9. Mt 3:12. 13:37-43. Lk 22:31, 32. Jn 12:24. 1 C 3:9. 9:9, 10. **bruised.** Is=53:5. Ex +27:20. Nu 11:8. He +=2:10. **ever.** Jb +4:20 (*S#5331h). **the wheel.** ver. 27.

29. **cometh.** ver. 21, 22. Is +*9:6. Jb 5:9. 37:23. Ps 40:5. *92:5. Je *32:19. Da 4:2, 3. Ro *11:33. **wonderful in.** Is +*9:6. Mt 21:15. Ac 2:22. **excellent.** Jb 37:23. 1 C 15:35-38, 42-44, 51-54.

ISAIAH 29

A prediction of the distress of Jerusalem by a siege; and of the sudden destruction of the besiegers, 1-9. The Jews are reproved for their insensibility and hypocrisy, and threatened with judgments, 10-16. A promise of happier times, for the scorner and oppressor being cut off, the rest shall be converted, 17-24.

1. A.M. 3292. B.C. 712. **Woe**, etc. *or*, O Ariel, *that is*, the lion of God. ❋S#740h: Is 29:1, 1, 2, 2, 7. Ezr 8:16. ver. 15. Is 31:9. Ge 49:9. Ezk 43:15mg, 16. **Ariel**. ✓60A, Ge +3:22. ✓146, Ge +10:10. **the city**. *or*, of the city. 2 S *5:7-9. **add**. Is *1:11-15. Ps *50:8-17. Je 7:21. Ho 5:6. 8:13. 9:4. Am 4:4, 5. Mi *6:6-9. He 10:1. **let**. ✓60A, Ge +3:22. **kill**. Heb. cut off the heads. Is 66:3. Mi 6:6, 7. **sacrifices**. lit. feasts. ✓121P7, Ex +23:18.

2. **I will**. Is 5:25-30. 10:5, 6, 32. 17:14. 24:1-12. 33:7-9. 36:22. 37:3. Je 32:28-32. 39:4, 5. **heaviness**. Is 10:32. 37:3. Je 7:14. Ezk 9:6. **and it shall**. Or, as Bp. Lowth renders, "and it shall be unto me as the *hearth of the great altar;*" that is, it shall be the seat of the fire of God, which shall issue from thence to consume his enemies. The hearth of the altar is expressly called *Ariel* by Ezekiel, Ezk 43:15; which is put, in the former part of the verse, for Jerusalem, the city in which the altar was. The subject of this and the four following chapters, says Bp. Lowth, is the invasion of Sennacherib; the great distress of the Jews while it continued; their sudden and unexpected deliverance by God's immediate and miraculous interposition on their behalf; the subsequent prosperous state of the kingdom under Hezekiah; interspersed with severe reproofs and threats of punishment for their hypocrisy, stupidity, infidelity, their want of trust in God, and their vain reliance on the assistance of Egypt; and with promises of better times, both immediately to succeed, and to be expected in the future age. Is 34:6. Ezk 22:31. 24:3-13. 39:17. Zp 1:7, 8. Re 19:17, 18.

3. **camp against**. 2 K *18:17. 19:32. 24:11, 12. *25:1-4. Ezk 21:22. Mt 22:7. Lk *19:43, 44.

4. **thou shalt**. Is 2:11-21. 3:8. 51:23. 2 K 18:26, 36, 37. Ps 44:25. La 1:9. **whisper**. Heb. peep, *or* chirp. See on Is +8:19. **out of the dust**. 1 S 13:6. 14:11. Je 41:9.

5. **the multitude**. Is 10:16-19. 25:5. 31:3, 8. 37:36. **as chaff**. Is *17:13. Jb *21:18. Ps *1:4. 35:5. **at an**. Is 30:13. Nu 6:9. Ps 46:5, 6. 76:5, 6. 1 Th *5:3.

6. **visited**. Is 5:26-30. 28:2. 30:30. 33:11-14. 1 S 2:10. 12:17, 18. 2 S 22:14. Mt 24:7. Mk 13:8. Lk 21:11. Ne 11:13, 19. 16:18. **with earthquake**. Mt +*24:7. **storm and tempest**. Ps 83:15. **devouring fire**. Is *30:30. Ps 83:14. 97:3-5. He 10:27. *12:29. 2 P +√3:7.

7. **the multitude**. Is 37:36. 41:11, 12. Je 25:31-33. 51:42-44. Na 1:3-12. Zc 12:3-5. 14:1-3, 12-15. Re 20:8, 9. **that distress**. See on ver. 2. **shall be**. Is √54:17. Jl 3:11. **as a dream**. Jb 20:8. Ps 73:20.

8. **as when**. Is 10:7-16. 2 Ch 32:21. **dreameth**. Is 37:36. Jb *20:8. Ps 73:20. **he awaketh**. 2 S 4:31. Ps 3:5. 73:20. 139:18. **soul**. Heb. *nephesh*, Nu +11:6. Ps 107:9. Pr 6:30. Is 5:14. Re +*18:14. **behold**. Is 44:12. **soul**. Heb. *nephesh*, Nu +11:6. **hath appetite**. Is 33:4. Ps 107:9. Pr 28:15. **so shall**. Ezk 38:3-23. 39:8-29. 2 P *2:9. Re 20:9.

9. **Stay**. ✓96B, Ge +20:7. **and wonder**. Is 1:2. 33:13,

14. Je 2:12. Hab 1:5. Ac 13:40, 41. Re 17:6. **cry ye out, and cry**. *or*, take your pleasure and riot. Is 22:12, 13. Mt 26:45. Mk 14:41. **they are**. ver. 10. Is 19:14. 28:7, 8. 49:26. 51:21, 22. Je *23:9. 25:27. 51:7. La 4:21.

10. **the Lord**. ver. 14. Is 6:9, 10. Dt +*2:30. 1 S 26:12. Ps 69:23. Mi *3:6. Ac *28:26, 27. Ro ⟩11:8. **poured out**. Is 40:19. 44:10. **spirit**. Heb. *ruach*, Ge +41:8. ✓121A10, Ge +26:35. **deep sleep**. Ge 2:21. 15:12. Jb 4:13. **hath closed**. Is *44:18. Ge +19:11. Ezk 14:9. 2 C *4:4. 2 Th √2:9-12. **rulers**. Heb. heads. Is 3:2, 3. Mi 3:1. **the seers**. Is 30:10. 1 S 9:9. Je 26:8-11. Am 7:12, 13. **he covered**. Je 26:8.

11. **book**. *or*, letter. 2 S 11:14. **that is sealed**. Is 8:16. **I cannot**. Da *12:4, 9. Mt 11:25. 13:11. 16:17. Re *5:1-9. 6:1.

12. **I am not**. ver. 18. Is 28:12, 13. Je 5:4. Ho *4:6. Lk *14:18. Jn *5:40. 7:15, 16.

13. **Forasmuch**. Is 10:6. *48:1, 2. 58:2, 3. Ps 17:1. Je 3:10. 5:2. 12:2. *42:2-4, 20. Ezk √33:31-33. Mt *⟩15:7-9. Mk ⟩7:6. **mouth**. ✓121II, Ge +3:7. **their fear**. 2 Ch ch. 29-31. Pr 30:6. Mt *15:2-6. Mk *7:2-13. Col *2:22. **taught by**. Is +*8:20.

14. **I will**. ver. 9. Is 28:21. Hab *1:5. Jn 9:29-34. **proceed**. Heb. add. Is 38:5. Dt 5:25mg. **for the wisdom**. ver. 10. Is 6:9, 10. 19:3, 11-14. Jb 5:13. Je *8:7-9. 49:7. Ob 8. Lk 10:24. Jn *9:39-41. Ac 28:26, 27. Ro 1:21, 22, 28. 1 C 1:⟩19-24. *3:19.

15. **Woe**. Is 30:1, 2. **seek**. Is 5:18, 19. 28:15, 17. 30:1. Jb 22:13, 14. Ps 10:11-13. 64:5, 6. *139:1-8. Je 23:24. Ezk 8:12. 9:9. Zp *1:12. Re *2:23. **to hide**. Jb 34:22. Ps 94:7, 9. **and their works**. Jb 24:13-17. 34:22. Lk *12:1-3. Jn √3:19. 1 C *4:5. 2 C *4:2, 5. **in the dark**. Ep +*5:11. **Who seeth**. Is 47:10. Ps 59:7. 73:11. 94:7-9. Ml 2:17.

16. **your turning**. Is 24:1. Ac 17:6. **as the potter's**. Is *45:9, 10. Je 18:1-10. Ro *9:19-21. **or shall**. Is 45:11. Ps 94:8, 9.

17. **yet a very**. Is 63:18. Hab 2:3. Hg 2:6. He 10:37. **Lebanon**. Is *32:15. 35:1, 2. 41:19. 49:5, 6. 55:13. 65:12-16. Ho 1:9, 10. Mt 19:30. *21:43. Ro *11:11-17. **the fruitful**. Is 5:6. Ezk 20:46, 47. Ho 3:4. Mi *3:12. Zc 11:1, 2. Mt 21:18, 19. Ro 11:19-27.

18. **the deaf**. ver. 10-12, 24. Is *35:5. *42:16-18. Dt 29:4. Ps √119:18. Pr 20:12. Je 31:33, 34. Mt *11:5. *13:14-16. 16:17. Mk 7:37. Lk *4:18. 7:22. Jn *6:45. Ac *26:18. 2 C *3:14-18. √4:2-6. Ep 1:17-19. 5:14. 1 P 2:9. Re 3:18. **the words of the book**. Ne √8:8. Ps √119:18. Jn +√5:39. Ac √17:11. **shall see**. Ep *1:18. 1 P *2:9.

19. **meek**. Is 61:1. Ps √25:9. *37:11. 149:4. Zp 2:3. Mt +*5:5. *11:29. Ga *5:22, 23. Ep 4:2. Ph *2:1-3. Ja *1:21. *2:5. 3:13-18. 1 P *2:1-3. **increase**. Heb. add. Is 15:9mg. 26:15. **the poor**. Is 41:17, 18. *57:15. 66:2. Ps 9:18. *12:5. Zp 3:12-18. Mt +*5:3. 11:5. 1 C 1:26-29. Ja *1:9. *2:5. **rejoice**. Is 41:16. 61:10. Hab 3:18. Ph 3:1-3. *4:4.

20. **the terrible**. ver. 5. Is 10:24-26. 13:3. 14:12. 25:4, 5. 49:25. 51:13. Jb 1:6-12. 2:1-7. Ps 109:6. Da 7:7, 19-25. Hab 1:6, 7. Zc 3:1, 2. Lk 22:31. Ro 16:20. **is brought**. Lk 10:18. 1 Th 2:18. Re 12:10. **the scorner**. See on Is 28:14-22. Lk 16:14. 23:11, 35. **and all**. Mi 2:1. Mk 2:6, 7. 3:2-6. Lk 6:7. 13:14-17. 20:20-23. Re 12:10.

21. **make**. Jg 12:6. Mt 22:15. Lk 11:53, 54. **and lay**. Je 18:18. 20:7-10. 26:2-8. Am 5:10-12. 7:10-17.

Mi 2:6, 7. **reproveth**. Je 17:19, 20. 19:2. Am 5:10. **gate**. ✓171S7B, Ge +14:7. **and turn**. Is 30:10. Pr 28:21. Ezk 13:19. Am 5:11, 12. Ml +*3:5. Mt *22:15. 26:15. Ac 3:14. Ja *5:6. **nought**. Is 59:4. Mt 26:14, 15. Lk 6:7.

22. **the Lord**. Jn *8:56. **who redeemed**. Is 41:8, 9, 14. 44:21-23. 51:2, 11. 54:4. Ge 48:16▶𝒫. Jsh *24:2-5. Ne 9:7, 8. Lk 1:68. 1 P 1:18, 19. Re 5:9. **Jacob shall**. Is 44:21-26. *45:17, 25. 46:3, 4. 49:7, etc. 60:1-9. 61:7-11. Je 30:5-7, 10. 31:10-12. 33:24-26. Ezk 37:24-28. 39:24-29. ch. 40-48. Jl *2:26, 27. Ro 11:11, etc. **face**. ✓121S3F3. Metonymy of the Adjunct B606. The sign is put for the thing signified, in connected words and phrases: the "face to wax pale" is put for being afraid.

23. **But when**. Ezk 36:25n. +*39:28n. **seeth his children**. Is +*26:19n. Mt +*8:11. +*19:28. Ac +*2:39. **the work**. Is 19:25. 43:21. 45:11. 60:21. Ps 100:3. Ep ✓2:10. **sanctify my name**. Is *5:16. *8:13. Le 10:3. +*22:32. Ps +*9:10. Mt +✓6:9. 2 C 5:5. Re 11:15-17. **shall fear**. Is 41:17. Ex 24:10. Ho 3:5. Mt 15:31. Ac 2:36-39. 8:14, 15. 10:44, 45. 11:18. Re 15:4. 19:5. **the God of Israel**. Is 41:17. 45:3, 15. 48:1, 2. 52:12. Ge 33:20. Ex 24:10. Nu 16:9. Jsh 22:16. 1 S 1:17. 5:7, 8, 10, 11. 6:3, 5. 2 S 23:3. 1 K 8:26. 1 Ch 4:10. 5:26. 17:24. 2 Ch 29:7. Ezr 3:2. 7:15. 8:35. 9:4. Ps 69:6. 72:18. Ezk 8:4. 9:3. 10:19, 20. 11:22. 43:2.

24. **They also**. ver. *10, *11. Is *28:7. Ps 95:10. Pr 12:8. Ho 3:5. Zc *12:10. Mt *21:28-32. Lk *7:47. *15:17-19. Ac *2:37. 6:7. 9:19, 20. Ro 11:26. 1 C *6:11. 1 T 1:13-15. He 5:2. Re 20:2, 3. **that erred**. Those going astray (Young). Ge 37:15. Ex 23:4. Jb *6:24. Ps *95:10. ▪Pr 21:16. Mk +✓12:24. 1 T 5:13-15. 2 T 3:6-8. 2 P ✓3:16, 17. **in spirit**. Heb. *ruach*, Ge +41:8. Ps +*51:10. **shall come**. Notice the implicit cause/effect relationships which point to the Biblical medicine (Pr 4:22mg) to cure a wrong spirit and murmurings (Ps +✓9:10n). Ps 18:28. +*119:130. Pr *29:13. Ac 26:18. 2 C 4:6. Ep 1:18. 1 P 2:9. **to understanding**. Heb. know understanding. Is *32:4. 41:20. Ps +✓9:10. 94:10. ✓111:10. +*119:97-105. Pr 1:1-6. *4:7. Jn 17:3. 1 C 2:14. Col +✓1:10. 2 T *2:15. +✓3:15-17. He +*8:11. **they that murmured**. Nu +*11:1. Ru +*1:13. Ps +*77:3. 106:25. 144:14. Pr +✓19:3. Je ◑+✓29:11. Ezk +*18:25. Ro ◑+*9:14. Ph ◑+4:11. Ju +*16. **shall learn**. Is 28:9. 42:16. Ps +*25:9. Pr *16:21, 23. Je 42:3. Mt 13:23. Lk *10:39. Ac 2:41. ✓17:11. 1 Th ✓2:13. **doctrine**. Is 28:9. Jb 11:4. Pr 4:2. Ac 2:42. 1 T +*4:16. 2 T +✓3:16.

ISAIAH 30

The prophet threatens the people for confiding in Egypt, 1-7, and for despising God and his word, 8-17. Promises of returning mercies and glorious times to Israel, 18-26. A prediction of the destruction of the army and king of Assyria; involving still greater events yet future, 27-33.

1. A.M. cir. 3291. B.C. cir. 713. **Woe**. Is 31:1. **the rebellious**. ver. 9. Is 1:2. *63:10. 65:2. Dt *9:7, 24. 29:19. 1 S ✓15:22, 23. Je 4:17. *5:23. Ezk 2:3. 3:9, 26, 27. 12:2, 3. Ho 7:13. Ac 7:51, 52. **that take**. Is *8:19. 29:15. Jsh 9:14. 1 Ch *10:13, 14. Ho 4:10-12. **cover**. Is 4:5mg. *28:15, 20. 32:2. Ps 61:4. 91:1-4. Ezk 28:14. **spirit**. Heb. *ruach*, Ge +41:38. **add**. Is 1:5. 5:18. Nu 32:14. Ho 13:2. Ro *2:5. 2 T 3:13.

2. **walk**. Is 20:5, 6. *31:1-3. *36:6. Dt 28:68. 2 K *17:4. Je *37:5-7. 43:7. Ezk 29:6, 7. **and have**. Nu 27:21. Jsh 9:14. 1 K 22:7. Je 21:2. 42:2, 20. **strengthen themselves**. 2 Ch 12:1. to trust. Ps 60:11, 12. *118:8, 9. **the shadow**. Is 16:3. 18:1. Jg 9:15. La 4:20.

3. **the strength**. ver. 5-7. Is 20:5. Je 37:5-10. **the trust**. Je 42:1-3, 13-16, 20. **your confusion**. Is 45:16, 17. Je *17:5, 6. Ro 5:5. 10:11.

4. **his princes**. Is 57:9. 2 K 17:4. Ho 7:11, 12, 16. **Zoan**. Is 19:11, 13. Nu *13:22. Ps 78:12, 43. Ezk 30:14. **Hanes**. i.e. *grace has fled; ensign of grace*, ✱S#2609h, only here. Je 2:16. *43:7, Tahpanhes. Ezk 30:18, Tehaphnehes.

5. **ashamed**. ver. 16. Is 20:5, 6. 31:1-3. Je *2:36.

6. **burden**. Is 46:1, 2. 57:9. Ho 8:9, 10. 12:1. **beasts**. 1 K 10:2. Mt 12:42. **the south**. Heb. Negeb. ✤S#5045h. Is 21:1. Ge 12:9. 13:1. 20:1. 24:62. Nu 13:29. Dt 1:7. Jsh 15:21. Jg 1:9. 1 S 27:10. Ps 126:4. Je 13:19. 17:26. 32:44. 33:13. Ezk 20:46, 47. 21:4. **into the land**. Or, as Bishop Lowth renders, "through a land of distress and difficulty:" the same deserts are here spoken of which the Israelites passed through. Is 19:4. Ex 1:14. 5:10-21. Dt 4:20. *8:15. 17:16. Je 11:4. **the viper**. F/ L Is 59:5. Nu *21:6, 7. Dt 8:15▶𝒫. Je 2:6. **and old**. ✓174, Ge +18:27. **riches**. ✓121N2, Ge +34:29. 2 Ch 9:1. 16:2. 28:20-23.

7. **the Egyptians**. Is 31:1-5. Je 37:7. **in vain**. Ps 60:11. 118:8, 9. **concerning this**. *or*, to her. **Their**. ver. 15. Is 2:22. 7:4. 28:12. *41:10. Ex 14:13. Ps 76:8, 9. 118:8, 9. La 3:26. Ho 5:13. **strength**. ✓121N2, Ge +34:29. **sit still**. Is 7:3, 4. 46:10. Ex *14:13, 14. La 3:26. Mt 8:25, 26.

8. **write**. Is 8:1. Dt 31:19, 22. Jb 19:23, 24. Je 36:2, 28-32. 51:60. Hab *2:2. **note**. Ex 17:14▶𝒫. 24:4▶𝒫. 34:27, 28▶𝒫. Nu 33:2▶𝒫. Dt 31:9, 24▶𝒫. **the time to come**. Heb. the latter day. Is 2:2. Nu 24:14. Dt 4:30. 31:29. Jb *19:25. Je 23:20. 48:47. Ezk 38:16. Ho 3:5. 1 T 4:1. 2 P 3:3. Ju 18. **for ever**. Ps +9:18 (✱S#5703h). **and ever**. Heb. *olam*, Ps +21:4. Mt *24:35. 1 P *1:23-25.

9. **this is**. See on ver. *1. Is *1:4. Dt *31:27-29. *32:20. Je *44:2-17. Zp *3:2. Mt 23:31-33. Ac 7:51. **lying**. Is 59:3. 63:8. Je *9:3-5. Ho 4:2. Re +*21:8. 22:15. **will not**. 2 Ch 33:10. *36:15, 16. Ne *9:29, 30. Pr *28:9. Je 7:13. Zc 1:4-6. *7:11, 12. Ro 2:21-23. **the law**. Is 1:10n▶𝒫.

10. **say**. T#466-3. 1 K 21:20. 2 Ch 16:9, 10. *18:7-27. ✓24:19-21. 25:16. Je *5:31. *11:21. 26:11, 20-23. 29:27. 38:4. Am *2:12. 7:13. Mi 2:6. Ac 4:17, 18. 5:28, *40. Ro *8:7. 1 Th 2:15, 16. Re 11:7. **speak**. 1 K *22:8-13, 27. Je 6:13, 14. 8:10, 11. 23:17, 26-29. Ezk 13:7-10, 18-22. Mi 2:11. Jn *7:7. *8:45. Ro 16:18. Ga 4:16.

11. **Get you out**. Is 29:21. Am 7:13. **cause**. Jn 15:23, 24. Ro 1:28, 30. 8:7. Ep 4:18.

12. **Because**. ver. 1, 7, 15-17. Is *5:24. 31:1-3. 2 S 12:9, 10. Am 2:4. Lk *10:16. 1 Th *4:8. **and trust**. Is 28:15. 47:10. Ps 52:7. 62:10. Je 13:25. **oppression**. *or*, fraud. ✱S#6233h. Is 54:14. 59:13. Le 6:4 (thing). Ps 62:10. 73:8. 119:134. Ec 5:8. 7:7. Je 6:6. 22:17. Ezk 18:18. 22:7mg, 12 (extortion), 29. **perverseness**. ✤S#3868h. Pr 2:15. 3:32. 14:2.

13. **as a breach**. 1 K 20:30. Ps *62:3. Ezk 13:10-15. Mt *7:26, 27. Lk 6:49. **cometh**. Is 29:5. Jb 36:18. Ps *73:19, 20. Pr 6:15. *29:1. 1 Th *5:1-3.

14. **he shall break**. Ps *2:9. Je *19:10, 11. Re 2:27. **potter's vessel**. Heb. bottle of potters. **he shall not**.

Is *27:11. Dt 29:20. Jb 27:22. Je *13:14. Ezk 5:11. 7:4, 9. 8:18. 9:10. 24:14. Zc *7:13. Ro 8:32. *11:21. 2 P 2:4, 5. so that. Is 47:14. Ps 31:12. Je 48:38. La 4:2. Ezk 15:3-8.

15. the Holy One. ver. 11. Je 23:36. In returning. ver. 7. Is 7:4. 26:3, 4. 32:17. 1 Ch 5:20. 2 Ch *16:8, 9. 32:8. Ps 125:1, 2. Je 3:22, 23. Ho 14:1-3. and rest. Ex 14:13. Mt 8:25, 26. in quietness. Jb *34:29. and ye. Ps 80:11-13. *81:13, 14. Je *6:16. 44:16, 17. Mt 22:3. 23:37. Lk *13:34. Jn *5:40. He *12:25.

16. for we will. Is 5:26-30. 10:28-32. *31:1. Dt 28:25. 2 K 25:5. Ps *33:17. 147:10. Je 52:7. Am 2:14-16. 9:1. Mi 1:13. horses. Dt *17:16. therefore. Dt *28:49. Je 4:13. *39:4, 5. La *4:19. Hab 1:8.

17. thousand. Le 26:8)℘, 36. Dt *28:25)℘. *32:30)℘. Jsh 23:10. Pr 28:1. Je 37:10. ye flee. ⨍63G, Ge +50:23. Supply by ellipsis, "One thousand shall flee at the rebuke of one; at the rebuke of five shall ye (all) flee." till ye. Is 1:7, 8. 37:3, 4. Ne 1:2, 3. Zp 3:12. Zc 13:8, 9. Mt 24:21, 22. a beacon. or, a tree bereft of branches, or, boughs, or, a mast. Is 6:13. 27:11. Jn 15:2-6. Ro 11:17-19.

18. therefore. Is 32:2. *55:8, 9. Ex *34:6, 7. Ho 2:14. Ro *5:20. *9:15-18. wait. S#2442h. William Wilson defines the Hebrew term rendered *wait* "to look for, to wait, to desire" (*Old Testament Word Studies*, p. 470). Compare S#6960h, Ps 37:34n; S#3176h, Ps 69:3n. Is 8:17h. 18:4. 57:17, 18. *64:4h. Jb 32:4h. Ps 33:20h. 106:13h. Da 12:12h. Ho *5:15. 6:1, 2, 9h. Hab *2:3h. Zp *3:8h. Mt +*23:39. Lk +*21:31. Ac +*3:19-21. be gracious. Ex +*34:6. Je *31:18-20. Jon *3:4-10. Zp 3:15. Zc *10:6. Mt *15:22-28. Lk *6:35. *15:20. Ro 9:22, 23. 2 P *3:9, 15. be exalted. Is 33:10-12. Ps 46:*10, 11. 76:5-10. Lk *24:26, 27. Ac *2:33-39. *5:31. Ep *1:6, 20-23. have mercy. T#827. Is 48:9. 60:10. Ex 33:19. 34:6, 7. Dt 4:31. Jb *11:6. Ps 62:11, 12. *85:10. 98:3. 100:5. 103:13, 17. *130:4, 7. 147:10, 11. Je *31:20. Ho 2:23. *11:8, 9. Zc √10:6. Ja *2:13. 2 P 3:√9, 15. God of judgment. Is *33:5. *42:1-4. 45:21. √55:8. Ge +*18:25. Dt +*32:4. 1 S *2:3. Jb *35:14. Ps 92:15. +*94:2. *99:4. 103:6. Je +*10:24, 25. Mi √7:18-20. Zp *3:5. Ml *2:17. Jn *5:30. Ro *2:2-10. Ep *1:8. blessed. ⨍43, Dt +28:3. Is 32:20. 56:2. Ps *2:12. *28:6, 7. *34:8. *84:12. Pr *16:20. Je *17:7. wait for him. Is *8:17. 25:9. *26:7, 8. 33:2. *40:31. Ps *27:14. *37:7, +*34. *40:1-3. *62:1, 2, 5-8. *130:5, 6. La *3:25, 26. Mi *7:7-9. Lk *2:25. Ac 1:4. Ro *8:25-28. Ja *5:7, 11.

19. dwell. Is 10:24. 12:6. 46:13. 65:9. Je *31:6, 12. 50:4, 5, 28. 51:10. Ezk 20:40. √37:25-28. Zp 3:14-20. Zc *1:16, 17. 2:4-7. *8:3-8. Ro 11:26. thou shalt weep. Is 12:3-6. 25:8. *35:10. *40:1, 2. 54:6-14. *60:20. 61:1-3. *65:18, 19. Je 30:12-19. 31:9-17. Mi 4:9, 10. Lk 6:21. Re 5:4-6. 7:17. *21:4. gracious unto thee. Zc √12:10. voice of thy cry. Ps *60:1. Ho +*5:15. *8:2. +*14:2. Zc √13:9. he will answer. Is *58:9. √65:24. Ps 38:15mg. *50:15. Je 29:11-13. √33:3. Ezk *36:37. Mt *7:7-11. Ep 3:20. 1 J √5:14, 15.

20. the bread. Dt 16:3. 1 K *22:27. 2 Ch 18:26. Ps 30:5. *80:5. 102:9. *127:2. Ezk *4:13-17. 24:22, 23. Jn 16:33. Ac *14:22. affliction. or, oppression. Ex 3:9. Jg 2:18. yet shall. Ps *74:9. Am *8:11, 12. Mt *9:38. Ep *4:11. thy teachers. 2 Ch +15:3. 35:3n. Je 3:15. 23:3, 4. Ezk 34:23. Da +*11:33n.

21. thine ears. Is *35:8, 9. *42:16. *48:17. *58:11. Ps *25:8, 9. *143:8-10. Pr √3:5, 6. Je *6:16. Jn *14:26.

15:26, 27. *16:13, 14. 1 J *2:20, 27. shall hear. Jn +*10:4. This is. Ps *32:8. Je 3:15. 42:3. when ye turn to the right. Dt *5:32. Jsh *1:7. *23:6. 2 K *22:2. Ps *32:8. Pr *4:27.

22. defile. Is *2:20, 21. 17:7, 8. 27:9. *31:7. 2 K *23:4-20. 2 Ch *31:1. 34:3-7. Ezk 36:31. Mi 5:10-14. Zc 13:2. Re 19:20. covering. Ex 38:17, 19)℘. Nu 16:38, 39)℘. thy graven images of silver. Heb. the graven images of thy silver. Is 31:7mg. 46:6. Ex 32:2-4. Jg 17:3, 4. ornament. Ex 28:8 (ephod))℘. 39:5)℘. cast. Heb. scatter. Is 41:16. Ex 32:20. Nu 16:37. Je 15:7. Ezk 5:2. as a. La 1:17. Ezk 18:6. Get. Ho *14:8. 1 J *5:21.

23. shall he. Is 5:6. 32:20. 44:2-4. √55:10, 11. 58:11. Ps 65:9-13. 104:13, 14. 107:35-38. Je 14:22. Ezk 36:25, 26. Ho 2:21-23. Jl *2:21-26. Am 4:7, 8. Zc 8:11, 12. *10:1. Ml *3:10. Mt √6:33. 1 T *4:8. it shall. Is 4:2. Le *26:9, 10. Dt 28:3-12. Ps 36:8. thy cattle. Ge 41:18, 26, 47. Ps 144:12-14. Ho 4:16. Ml 4:2.

24. oxen. Dt 25:4. 1 C 9:9, 10. ear the ground. Ge 45:6. Ex 34:21. Dt 21:4. 1 S 8:12. clean. or, savory. Heb. leavened. *S#2548h, only here.

25. upon every high. Is 2:14, 15. 35:6, 7. *41:18, 19. 43:19, 20. *44:3, 4. Ezk 17:22. 34:13, 26. Jn 7:38. Re *22:1. high. Heb. lifted up. Is 2:14. streams. F/L Is 44:4. Ezk 47:1-12. in the day. Is 34:2-10. 37:36. 63:1-6. Ezk 39:17-20. Re ch. 16-19. when. Is 32:14. Na 3:12. 2 C *10:4. towers. lit. great places. Is 2:15. 5:2. 33:18.

26. the light of the moon. Is 11:9. 24:23. *60:19, 20. Zc 12:8. 14:7. Re *21:23. 22:5. bindeth. Is 1:6. Dt 32:39. Jb 5:18. Je 33:5, 6. La 2:13. Ho 6:1, 2. Am *9:11. Re *21:4. healeth. Re *22:2.

27. the name. ⨍121T1, Dt +28:58. ⨍144A4A. Pleonasm; or, Redundancy B409. Involving certain idiomatic words: *name*. This word appears to be redundant in the phrase "the name of God." It means *God Himself*, and has greater emphasis than if the simple word God were used. For other instances of this figure see Ps 20:1. 113:1. Je 44:26. Mi 5:4. cometh. Is 63:1. Re 19:11-13. burning. Is 9:5. 10:16, 17. 33:12. 34:9. Dt 32:22. 33:2. Ps 18:7-9. 79:5. La 1:12, 13. Da 7:9. Na 1:5, 6. 2 Th *2:8. He 12:29. the burden thereof. or, the grievousness of flame. Is 13:8mg. heavy. Heb. heaviness. Pr +27:3mg. lips. ⨍22A10, Nu +12:8. indignation. Is +*26:20. Da +*8:19 (*S#2195h).

28. his breath. Heb. *ruach*, Ex +15:8. Is *11:4. Ps 18:15. Lk 22:31. 2 Th √2:8. He √4:12. Re 1:16. *2:16. an overflowing. Is 8:8. 28:17, 18. 29:6. Hab 3:12-15. neck. ⨍155E1, Is +1:5. to sift. Bp. Lowth renders, "to toss the nations with the van of perdition;" that is, says Kimchi, nothing useful shall remain behind, but all shall come to nothing and perish. The van of the ancients was a large instrument, somewhat like a shovel, with a long handle, with which they tossed the corn mixed with the chaff and chopped straw into the air, that the wind might separate them. Is 19:12-14. 33:10-12. Ho 13:3. Am 9:9. Mt 3:12. a bridle. Is *37:29. 2 K 19:28. Ps 32:9. Pr 26:3. causing. Is 19:3, 13, 14. 2 S 17:14. 1 K 22:20-22. Jb 39:17. Ezk 14:7-9. 2 Th √2:11.

29. Ye shall. Is 12:1. 26:1. Ex 15:1, etc. 2 Ch 20:27, 28. Ps 32:7. Je 33:11. Re *15:3, 4. *19:1-7. in the night. Le 23:32. Dt 16:6, 14. Ps 42:4. 81:1-4. Mt 26:30. holy solemnity. Le 23:2n)℘. with a pipe. 1 Ch 13:7, 8. Ps 42:4. 95:1, 2. 150:3-5. the mountain. Is 2:3. mighty

One. Heb. Rock. Is 26:4mg. Dt 32:4, 15, 18, 30, 31⸱𝒫. Ps 18:31.

30. **the Lord.** Is 29:6. Ps 2:5. 18:13, 14. 46:6. **his glorious voice.** Heb. the glory of his voice. ✗100, Ge +10:9. Jb 37:2-5. 40:9. Ps 29:3-9. *46:6. Ezk 10:5. Re 1:15. ✗22A11. Anthropomorphism B876. A voice is attributed to God. For another instance of this figure see Ps 29:3. **the lighting.** Is *51:9. 62:8. Ex 15:16. Ps *98:1. Lk 1:51. **arm.** ✗22A12, Ex +15:16. **indignation.** Na 1:6. **the flame.** Is 28:2. 32:19. Jsh 10:11. 1 S 7:10. Ps 18:13, 14. 50:1-3. 76:5-8. 97:3-5. Ezk 38:19-22. Da *7:9, 10. Mi 1:4. Na 1:2-6. Mt *24:7. 2 Th √1:8. Re 6:12-17. 11:19. 14:16-20. 16:18-21. **devouring fire.** Is 10:16. Mt *3:12. 2 Th √1:8. He *12:29. **the tempest.** Na 1:2, 3. **hailstones.** Jsh *10:11. Re *16:21.

31. **the voice.** ver. 30. Is *37:32-38. **the Assyrian.** Is 10:12. 31:8. **which smote.** Is 9:4. *10:5, 15, 24. Ps 17:13, 14. 125:5. Mi *5:5, 6.

32. **every place,** etc. Heb. every passing of the rod **founded. grounded staff.** Young renders, settled staff *or* "founded rod." Is 9:4. 10:5, 15, 24, 26. 14:5. J. A. Alexander renders, "rod of doom" or "rod of destiny." The general sense of the passage is that God has determined to violently overthrow Assyria in raging battle, and his victory will be attended by the rejoicing of the spectators, those who had been subject to oppression. **lay.** Heb. cause to rest. **it shall be.** ver. 29. Is 24:8. Ge 31:27. 1 S 10:5. Jb 21:11, 12. Ps 81:1, 2. Re 14:2, 3. 19:5, 6. **shaking.** Is 2:19. 11:15. 19:16. Jb 16:12. He 12:26. **with it.** *or*, against them.

33. **Tophet.** Jsh +*15:8n. 2 K 23:10. Je *7:31, 32. *19:6, 11-14. Mt 4:22. 18:8, 9. Re *19:20. 20:10. **ordained.** Mt √25:41. 1 P 1:8. Ju 4. **of old.** Heb. from yesterday. Ge +31:2mg. Ex +4:10mg. Jsh 3:4mg. 1 S 4:7mg. 10:11. 14:21. He *13:8. **for the king.** "The king" is a title of the antichrist (Da 11:36). Is *14:9-20. 37:38. Ezk 32:22, 23. Re 19:18-20. **fire.** Lk +16:24. **the breath.** Heb. *neshamah,* Ge +2:7. ✗22K3, Jb +4:9. ver. 27, 28. Ps 40:5, 6. 2 Th *2:8. Re 14:10, 11. **brimstone.** Ge 19:24. Re 9:17. 14:10, 11. **doth kindle.** Is 1:31. Dt +32:22. Mt 25:41. Ja 3:6.

ISAIAH 31

The folly and misery of those who depended on the Egyptians, 1-3. The Lord will defend Zion, 4, 5. A call to turn unto God and renounce idols, 6, 7. The ruin of the Assyrian, 8, 9.

1. **Woe.** Is 30:1. **to them.** Is 30:1-7. *36:6. 57:9. Ezk 17:15. Ho 11:5. **go down.** Is 30:2. Jg 4:8. 1 S 17:39. Ho 1:7. Zc *4:6. 2 C 10:4. **stay on horses.** Is 2:7. 30:16. 36:9. Dt 17:16. Ps *20:7. *33:16, 17. Mi 5:10. **they look.** Is 5:12. 17:7, 8. 22:11. 2 Ch 16:7. Je 2:13. *17:5. Ho 14:3. **neither seek.** Is 9:13. 30:2. 64:7. Dt *17:16⸱𝒫. Da *9:13. Ho 7:7, 13-16. Am 5:4-8.

2. **he also.** 1 S 2:3. Jb 5:13. Je 10:7, 12. 1 C 1:21-29. Ju 25. **will bring.** Is *19:11, 12. 30:13, 14. *45:7. Jsh 23:15. Am +√3:6. **will not.** Nu *23:19. Jb 23:13. Ps 33:11. Pr 19:21. Ec *3:14. 7:13. Je 36:32. *44:29. Zc 1:6. Ml +3:6. Mt *24:35. He 6:17, 18. Ja +1:17. **call back.** Heb. remove. Is 18:5. 36:7. 2 K 17:23. 18:4. **arise.** Is 28:21. 63:4-6. Nu 10:35. Ps 12:5, 6. 68:1, 2. 78:65, 66. Zp 3:8. **against the help.** ver. 3. Is 20:4-6. 30:3. Je 44:29, 30. Ezk 29:6, 7.

3. **the Egyptians.** Is 20:5. 36:6. Dt 32:30, 31. Ps 9:20. *146:3-5. Ezk 28:9. Ac 12:22, 23. 2 Th 2:4-8.

men. ✗132D, Ge +19:25. **and not.** ✗144D, Ge +40:23. **God.** Heb. *El,* Ex +15:2. **their horses.** Ps 33:17. **not spirit.** Heb. *ruach,* Ps +104:4. **stretch.** ✗22A14.8A, Ex +7:5. Is 9:17. Jsh *23:15. Je 15:6. Ezk 20:33, 34. **both.** Je 37:7-10.

4. **Like as.** Nu 24:8, 9. Je 50:44. Ho 11:10. Am *3:8. Re 5:5. **shepherds.** Lk 2:8. **noise.** *or,* multitude. Is 29:5, 7, 8. 63:15mg. Je +10:13mg. **so shall.** Is 10:16. 12:6. 37:35, 36. *42:13. 2 Ch 20:15. Ps 46:5, 8, 9. 125:1, 2. Zc 2:5. 9:8, 15. +*12:8. +*14:3.

5. **as birds flying.** ✗6312, Jsh +3:3. "As mother-birds fluttering (see Dt 32:11), or as fluttering birds (defend their young: supplied by ellipsis from the next clause), so will the Lord of hosts defend Jerusalem" (B105). Is 10:14. Ex 19:4. Dt 32:11⸱𝒫. Ps 46:5. *91:4. Zc √9:14. **defend.** Is 37:35. 38:6. 2 K 19:34. 20:6. Zc 9:15. 12:8. **defending.** 2 K 19:34. 20:6. Ps 37:40. **passing.** Or rather, as Bishop Lowth renders, "leaping forward," *pasoach.* As the mother bird spreads her wings to cover her young, throws herself before them, and opposes the rapacious bird that assaults them; so shall Jehovah protect, as with a shield, Jerusalem from the enemy, protecting and delivering, *springing forward* and rescuing her. Ex 12:13, 23, 27⸱𝒫.

6. **Turn.** Is √55:7. Je 3:10, 14, 22. *31:18-20. Ho 14:1-3. Jl *2:12, 13. Ac *3:19. 26:20. **deeply.** Is 1:4. 29:15. 48:8. 2 Ch 33:9-16. 36:14. Je 5:23. Ho 9:9.

7. **in that.** Is *2:20. *30:22. Dt 7:25. Ezk *36:25. Ho *14:3, 8. **his idols of gold.** Heb. the idols of his gold. Is 30:22mg. **for a sin.** 1 K 12:28-30. Ho 8:11.

8. **shall the.** Is 10:16. 19:33, 34. 14:25. 29:5, 8. 30:27-33. 37:35, 36. 2 K *19:34-37. 2 Ch 20:15. 32:21. Ps 37:40. Ho 1:7. **Assyrian.** Is 30:31. **he shall flee.** Is 37:37, 38. **from the sword.** *or,* for fear of the sword. Is 1:20. 2:4. 3:25. **discomfited.** *or,* tributary. Ge 49:15. Pr 12:24. Heb. for melting, *or* tribute. Is 10:18. 13:7.

9. **he shall pass over to his strong hold for fear.** Heb. his rock shall pass away for fear. **his strong hold.** *or,* his strength. **the ensign.** Is 11:10. 18:3. **whose fire.** Is 4:4. *10:17. 29:6. Le *6:13. 10:2. Ps *50:2, 3. Ezk *22:18-22. Zc *2:5. Ml +*4:1. **in Zion.** Ps +*50:2, 3. **his furnace.** Ps *21:9. La 5:10.

ISAIAH 32

A prophecy of Christ and his kingdom, 1-8; of desolating judgments on the Jews, 9-14; of the pouring out of the Spirit, and the surprising and happy change which would then take place, 15-20.

1. **king.** Is +*9:6, 7. *40:1-5. Dt 17:14, 15⸱𝒫. 2 S *23:3. 2 Ch 31:20, 21. Ps *45:1, 6, 7. 72:1, 2. 99:4. Je *23:5, 6. 33:15. Ho 3:5. Zc *9:9. Ro 5:21. He *1:8, 9. Re 19:11. **princes.** Is 28:6. Ps *45:16. 47:9. 113:8. Je 33:26. Mt +*19:28. Lk +*22:30. 1 C +*6:2. 2 T 2:12. Re 2:26, 27. 3:21. *17:14. *20:4.

2. **a man.** Is +*7:14. 8:10-14. +*9:6. Ps 146:3-5. Mi 5:4, 5. Zc *13:7. 1 T *2:5. *3:16. **as.** ✗170, Is +1:18. **an hiding.** ver. 18, 19. Is *4:5, 6. *25:4. *26:20, 21. 28:17. 30:18. 44:3. Ps *32:7. 91:1. 143:9. Mt *7:24-27. **rivers of water.** Is 35:6, 7. 41:18. 43:20. Ex 17:6. Ps *1:3. Pr +*21:1. Jn *7:37. 19:34. Re 22:1. **the shadow.** SS 2:3. **great.** He heavy. Is 36:2. 2 K 6:14mg. **rock.** Ps 31:2, 3. Ex 33:22. **weary.** Ps *63:1mg.

3. **the eyes.** Is 29:18, 24. 30:26. *35:5, 6. *54:13. 60:1, 2. Je 31:34. Mt 13:11. Mk 7:37. 8:22-25. Ac *26:18. 2 C *4:6. 1 J 2:20, 21. **the ears.** Mt 13:9.

4. **heart.** Is 29:24. Ne 8:8-12. Mt 11:25. 16:17. Ac 6:7. 26:9-11. Ga 1:23. **rash.** Heb. hasty. Is 35:4mg. Jb 5:13. Hab 1:6. **the tongue.** Ex 4:11. SS 7:9. Lk 21:14, 15. Ac 2:4-12. 4:13. **plainly.** *or,* elegantly. ✳S#6703h. Is 18:4 (clear). SS 5:10 (white). Je 4:11 (dry).

5. **vile.** Is 5:20. Ps 15:4. Ml 3:18. Re 20:12. 22:11, 12. **nor.** 1 S 25:3-8. Pr 23:6-8.

6. **the vile.** 1 S 24:13. 25:10, 11. Je 13:23. Mt 12:34-36. 15:19. Ja 3:5, 6. **will speak.** Is 5:20. Lk *6:45. Re +*22:11. **and his heart.** Ps 58:1, 2. Ho 7:6, 7. Mi 2:1, 2. Ac 5:3, 4. 8:21, 22. Ja 1:14, 15. **empty.** Jb 22:5-9. 24:2-16. Pr 11:24-26. Am 2:6, 7. 8:6. Mi 3:1-3. Mt 23:14. Ja 1:27. **soul.** Heb. *nephesh,* Ge +34:3.

7. **instruments.** Is 1:23. 5:23. Je 5:26-28. Mi 2:11. 7:3. Mt 26:14-16, 59, 60. **the churl.** 1 S 25:10, 11. **deviseth.** Ps 10:7-10. 64:4-6. 82:2-5. Je 18:18. Mi 7:2. Mt 26:4. **to destroy.** Mt 23:14. **lying.** Is 59:3, 4. 1 K 21:10-14. Mt 12:34, 35. Ac 6:11-13. **the needy speaketh right.** *or,* he speaketh *against* the poor in judgment. Ml +3:5. Ja +*5:4.

8. **the liberal.** 2 S *9:1, etc. Jb 31:16-21. Ps 112:9. Pr *11:24, 25. Lk +*6:33-35. Ac 9:39. 11:29, 30. 2 C 8:2. *9:6-11. **stand.** *or,* be established. Is 14:24. 40:8. Dt 19:15. Pr 15:22. 19:21.

9. **ye women.** ver. 11. Is 3:16. 47:7, 8. Dt 28:56. SS 2:2. Je 6:2-6. 48:11, 12. La 4:5. Am *6:1-6. ♪155E3. Personification B868. A whole people or state personified as a woman. For other instances of this figure see Is 1:21. 3:17-26. 23:15-17. 57:3. Dt 31:16. Jg 2:17. Je 3:1, 2, 3. 4:30. Ezk 16:13. 23:2. Mi 7:8-10. Na 3:4. **give ear.** Is 28:23. Dt 4:33, 36▶♪. Jg 9:7. Ps 49:1, 2. Mt 13:9.

10. **Many days and years.** Heb. Days above a year. Is 3:17-26. 24:7-12. Je 25:10, 11. Ho 3:4, 5. Mi 7:15. Mt +*25:19. **for.** Is 7:23. 16:10. Dt 8:8. Je 8:13. Ho 2:12. Jl 1:7, 12. Hab 3:17. Zp 1:13.

11. **Tremble.** ♪96B, Ex +20:8. **ye women.** ver. 9. Is 3:16, 17, 24. **be troubled.** Is 2:19, 21. 22:4, 5. 33:14. Lk 23:27-30. Ja 5:5. **strip.** Is 20:4. 47:1-3. Dt 28:48. Ho 2:3. Mi 1:8-11. **and gird.** Is 3:24. 15:3. Je 4:8. 6:26. 49:3.

12. **lament.** Dt 28:48. Ps 137:1. La *2:11. *4:3, 4. Lk *23:28. **pleasant fields.** Heb. fields of desire. ♪121R5, Ge +27:15. Is 54:12. Dt 8:7, 8. 11:11, 12. Jb 33:20mg. Je +25:34mg. La 1:7. Ezk 20:6, 15. +*26:12mg. Am 5:11mg.

13. **come.** Is 6:11. 7:23. 34:13. Ps *107:33, 34. Ho *9:6. 10:8. **yea, upon.** *or,* burning upon, etc. Je 39:8. Re 18:7, 8. **in the.** Is 22:2, 12, 13.

14. **the palaces.** Is 5:9. 24:1-3, 10, 12. 25:2. *27:10. 2 K 25:9. Ps 106:40-42. Lk *21:20, 24. **forts and towers.** *or,* clifts and watchtowers. 2 K +5:24mg. Ne 2:11-15. **for.** Is 13:19-22. 34:11-17. Re 18:2, 3. **for ever.** Heb. *olam,* Ex +*12:24.

15. **Until.** Is 62:1, 2. Ezk 36:24-26, 31. Jl 2:28n. Zp 3:8-10. **the spirit.** Heb. *ruach,* Ge +41:38. Is 11:2, 3. *44:3, 4. 45:8. 59:19-21. 63:11. Ps 104:30. 107:33. Pr 1:23. Ezk 37:9. 39:29. Jl *2:28, 29. Zc *12:10. Lk 24:49. Jn 7:39. Ac 2:17, 18, 33. 2 C 3:8. T *3:5, 6. **poured.** F/L Is 3:17. 22:6. 53:12. Heb. *arah,* ✳S#6168h: Niphal, Future: Is 32:15. Piel, Preterite: Is 22:6 (uncovered. mg, made naked). Zp 2:14 (uncover). Piel, Infinitive: Hab 3:13 (discovering. mg, making naked). Piel, Imperative: Ps 137:7 (rase. mg, make bare), 7.

Piel, Future: Ge 24:20 (emptied). 2 Ch 24:11 (emptied). Ps 141:8 (destitute. mg, bare). Is 3:17 (discover. mg, make naked). Hiphil, Preterite: Le 20:18 (discovered. mg, made naked), 19 (uncovereth). Is 53:12 (poured out). Hithpael, Future: La 4:21 (shalt make thyself naked). Hithpael, Participle: Ps 37:35 (spreading himself). **wilderness.** Is *29:17. 35:2, 7. *54:1-3. 55:11-13. 60:1, etc. 61:3-5. Ho *1:10, 11. Ro 11:18-26.

16. **judgment.** Is 35:8. 42:4. 56:6-8. +*60:21. Ps 94:14, 15. Ho 3:5. 1 C 6:9-11. T 2:11, 12. 1 P 2:9-12. 4:1-4.

17. **the work.** Is 26:3. *48:18. *54:13, 14. 55:12. *57:19. 66:12. Ps 72:2, 3. *85:8. *119:165. Ro *14:17. Ph 4:6-9. Ja *3:17, 18. **quietness.** Is 2:3, 4. 9:7. 11:6-9, 15. Ps 112:6-9. Pr 14:26. Ezk 37:21, 22, 25. 39:29. Mi 4:3, 4. 2 C 1:12. He 6:11. 2 P 1:10, 11. 1 J 3:18-24. *4:17. **for ever.** Heb. *olam,* Ex +*12:24.

18. **my people.** Is *33:20-22. 35:9, 10. 60:17, 18. Je *23:5, 6. 33:16. Ezk *34:25, 26. Ho 2:18-23. Zc 2:5, 8. He 4:9. 1 J 4:16. **sure dwellings.** Am +√9:14, 15. Ob +*17. **resting places.** Dt 33:12. Je 50:6. Mt 9:36mg.

19. **it shall.** Is 25:4. 26:20, 21. 28:2, 17. 30:30. 37:24. Ex 9:18-26. Ezk 13:11-13. Mt 7:25. Re 8:7. **on the.** Zc 11:2. **the city shall be low.** *or,* the city shall be utterly abased. Is 14:22, 23. 26:5. Na 1:1, 8. 2:10-13. Re 18:21.

20. **Blessed.** Is 19:5-7. 30:*18, 23. √55:10, 11. 56:2. Dt *28:8. Ps 3:8. Pr +*10:22. Ec *11:1. Ac 2:41. 4:4. 5:14. 1 C 3:6. 9:11. Ga *6:7-10. Ja 3:18. **that sow.** T#910. Is *49:4. Dt 10:9. 33:11. Ps 132:16. Je 1:7, 8, 19. 15:19-21. *20:11. 31:14. Ezk 3:8, 9. Da *12:3. Mt 10:19, 20. *28:20. Lk +*12:42-44. *21:15. Jn *4:36. 1 T √4:16. 1 P 5:1-4. Re 2:1. **the ox.** Is 30:24. 1 C 9:9-11.

ISAIAH 33

The doom of Sennacherib, 1. The prayers of the pious Jews, 2. The haughty invader, when scattering the nations, becomes a spoil to the invaded, 3, 4. God exalted, and Jerusalem reformed and established, by means of Hezekiah's wisdom and piety, 5, 6. The Jews dismayed and distressed, by the ravages and menaces of the invaders; whom God determines to destroy, that all men may know his might, 7-13. The terror of the hypocrites, contrasted with the confidence of believers, 14-16. The happy event of these dangers and terrors; and the security of Zion, under the protection of God, 17-24.

1. **thee that.** Is 10:5, 6. 17:14. 24:16. 2 K 16:17, 18. *18:13-17. 2 Ch 28:16-21. Hab *2:5-8. **when thou shalt cease.** Is 10:12. *21:2. *37:36-38. Jg 1:7. 2 K *19:6, 7. Je 25:12-14. 27:7. Ob 10-16. Zc 14:1-3. Mt 7:2. Re *13:10. 16:6. 17:12-14, 17.

2. **be gracious.** Is *25:9. *26:8. 30:18, 19. Ps 27:13, 14. 62:1, 5, 8. *123:2. *130:4-8. La 3:25, 26. Ho 14:2. **be thou.** Is 25:4. Ex 14:27. Ps 25:3. 83:8mg. 143:8. La 3:23. **morning.** ♪171T4, Jb +7:18. Is 17:14. 37:36. **our salvation.** Is 26:16. Ps *37:39. 46:1, 5. *50:15. 60:11. 90:15. 91:15. Je 2:27, 28. *14:8. 2 C √1:3, 4.

3. **the noise.** Is 10:13, 14, 32-34. *17:12-14. 37:11-18, 29-36. Ps 46:6.

4. **your spoil.** ver. 23. 2 K 7:15, 16. 2 Ch 14:13. 20:25. **the running.** Jl 2:9, 25.

5. **The Lord.** ver. 10. Is 2:11, 17. 12:4. 37:20. Ex

9:16, 17. 15:1, 6. 18:11. Jb 40:9-14. Ps 21:11-13. *46:9, 10. 97:8, 9. 115:1, 2. 118:16. Da 4:37. Ro 3:26. Re 19:1-6. **he dwelleth**. Is 57:15. 66:1. Ps *113:5, 6. 123:1. Ep 1:20, 21. **he hath**. Is 1:26, 27. 4:2-4. 32:1, 15-18. 52:1. 54:11-14. 60:21. 61:3, 11. 62:1, 2. 2 Ch *31:20, 21. Ro 11:26.

6. **wisdom**. Is 11:2-5. 38:5, 6. 2 Ch 32:27-29. Ps 45:4. Pr 14:27. 24:3-7. 28:2, 15, 16. 29:4. Ec *7:12, 19. 9:14-18. Je 22:15-17. **strength**. Ps 27:1, 2. 28:8. 140:7. **salvation**. Heb. salvations. Is 26:18. Ps 28:8mg. **fear**. 2 Ch 32:20, 21. Ps *112:1-3. Pr 15:16. 19:23. Mt √6:33. 2 C 6:10. 1 T 4:8. 6:6. **treasure**. ſ22D5.O, Dt +28:12.

7. **valiant ones**. or, messengers. Is 29:1 (Ariel). **the ambassadors**. ſ41, Ge +10:1. Is 36:3, 22. 2 K *18:18, 37. *19:1-4.

8. **highways**. Is 10:29-31. Jg 5:6. La 1:4. **he hath broken**. 2 K 18:14-17. **he hath despised**. Is 10:9-11. 36:1. 2 K 18:13. **he regardeth**. Is 10:13, 14. 1 S 17:10, 26. 2 K 18:20, 21. Ps 10:5. Lk 18:2-4.

9. **earth**. Is 1:7, 8. 24:1, 4-6, 19, 20. Je 4:20-26. **mourneth**. ſ155D, Ge +4:10. **languisheth**. Is 16:8. **Lebanon**. Is 14:8. 37:24. Zc 11:1-3. **hewn down**. or, withered away. Is 19:6. **Sharon**. F/L Is 35:2. 65:10. SS 2:1. **Bashan**. Nu +*21:33. Dt 3:4. Jsh 12:4n. 1 K 4:13. Je 50:19. Mi 7:14. Na 1:4. **Carmel**. Jsh +15:55. **shake off**. F/L ver. 15. Is 52:2.

10. **Now will I rise**. ſ22C21, Nu +10:35. Is 10:16, 33. 42:13, 14. 59:16, 17. Dt 32:36-43. Ps 12:5. 78:65. 102:13-18. Zp 3:8. **now will I be exalted**. Is 30:17, 18. Ex 14:18. 15:9-12. Ps 46:10. Am 6:1. **will I lift**. Dt 32:36. 2 K 19:7, 8. Ps 7:6. *12:5. 46:9. *102:13.

11. **conceive**. Is 8:9, 10. 10:7-14. 17:13. 29:5-8. 59:4. Jb 15:35. Ps 2:1. 7:14. 83:5-18. Ac 5:4. Ja 1:15. **your breath**. Heb. ruach, Ge +41:8. Jb 19:17. **shall devour**. Is 5:24. 30:30-33. 31:8, 9. 37:23-29. Na 1:5-10.

12. **the people**. 2 K 19:32-35. **the burnings**. ſ121H, Ps +74:15. i.e. as fuel for lime-kilns. Am 2:1. **thorns**. Is 9:18. 27:4. 37:36. 2 S 23:6, 7.

13. **Hear**. Is 18:3. *37:20. *49:1. 57:19. Ex 15:14, 15. Jsh 2:9-11. 9:9, 10. 1 S 17:46. Ps 46:6-11. 48:10. 98:1, 2. Da *3:27-30. 4:1-3. 6:25-27. Ac 2:5-11. Ep 2:11-18. **ye that are near**. Ps 97:8. 99:2, 3. 147:12-14. 148:14. **acknowledge**. Da 4:37.

14. **sinners**. Is 7:2. *28:14, 15, 17-22. *29:13. *30:8-11. Nu 17:12, 13. Jb 15:21, 22. *18:11. Ps *53:5. Pr *28:1. Re *6:15-17. **fearfulness**. Jb 4:14. Ps 2:11. 48:6. **the hypocrites**. Is 9:17. 10:6. Mt 22:12. *24:50, 51. **Who among us shall dwell with the**. Is *5:24. 29:6. *30:27-33. Dt 4:24. *5:24, 25. 9:3. *32:21-24. Ps *11:6. *21:9. *50:3. Na *1:6. He *12:29. **fire**. Lk +16:24. **everlasting**. Heb. olam, Ge +17:7. 2 Th 1:9. **burnings**. Is 26:11. 34:9, 10. +√66:24. Mt *18:8. √25:41, 46. Mk √9:43-49. Lk *16:23-26. 2 Th √1:8, 9. Re *14:10, 11. *20:10.

15. **that walketh**. Is 56:1, 2. Ps *1:1-3. *15:1, 2. *24:4, 5. *26:1, 2, 11. *106:3. Ezk *18:15-17. Ml *2:6. Lk 1:6. Ro *2:7. T *2:11, 12. 1 J *3:7. **righteously**. Heb. in righteousnesses. Is 45:24mg. Jg +5:11mg. 1 K 3:6. **uprightly**. Heb. in uprightnesses. lit. upright things. Is 26:7. 45:19. 1 Ch 29:17. **despiseth**. Ex +*18:21. Ne 5:7-19. Jb 31:13-25. Lk *3:12-14. *19:8. Ja +*5:4. **oppressions**. or, deceits. Pr 28:16. **shaketh**. Ex *23:6-9. Nu 16:15. Dt 10:17♪℘. *16:19♪℘. 27:25♪℘. 1 S *12:3. Je 5:26-28. Mi 7:3, 4. Mt *26:15. Ac *8:18-23. 2 P 2:14-16. **stoppeth**. 1 S 24:4-7. *26:8-11. Jb

*31:29-31. Ps *26:4-6, 9-11. Je 40:15, 16. Ep *5:11-13. **blood**. Heb. bloods. ſ96F2, Ge +4:10. ſ117, Ge +19:8. By the figure Metalepsis, "bloods" is first put for blood-shedding, and then blood-shedding is put for the murderers who shed it. Is 1:15mg. 26:21mg. Ge +4:10mg. 2 K +*9:26mg. Pr 1:11. ſ121L8. Metonymy of the Subject B585. "Blood" is put for bloodshedding. For another instance of this figure see Pr 1:11. **shutteth**. Ps *119:37.

16. **shall dwell**. Is 32:18. Ps 15:1. *90:1. 91:1-10, 14. 107:41. Pr *1:33. 18:10. Hab 3:19. **high**. Heb. heights, or high places. ver. 5. Is 22:16. Dt 28:1. Jg 5:18. Ps +*91:14. 102:19. 148:1. Pr 8:2. 9:3. Hab 3:19. Re 3:10. **his place**. Is 26:1-5. Ps 18:33. bread. ſ171I8, Ge +3:19. Ps 33:18. *34:10. √37:3. 111:5. Mt *6:11. Lk √12:29-31. **waters**. 2 Ch 32:30.

17. **eyes**. Is 32:1, 2. 37:1. 2 Ch 32:23. Ps 45:2. SS 5:10. Zc 9:17. Mt √17:2. Jn *1:14. 14:21. 17:24. 1 J √3:2. **shall see**. Jb +*19:27. Ps *17:15. **beauty**. *S#3308h. Is 3:24. Est *1:11. Ps 45:11. 50:2. Pr 6:25. 31:30. La 2:15. Ezk 16:14, 15, 25. 27:3, 4, 11. *28:7, 12, 17. 31:8. Zc *9:17. **that is very far off**. Heb. of far distances. Is 39:3. Ps 31:8. Je 8:19. 2 C 4:18. He 11:13-15.

18. **heart**. Is 38:9, etc. 1 S 22:33-36. 30:6. 2 K 19:14. 2 Ch 32:17-21. Ps 31:7, 8, 22. 71:20. 2 C 1:8-10. 2 T 3:11. **Where is the scribe**. 1 C 1:20. **receiver**. Heb. weigher. Ge 23:16. 2 K 15:19, 20. 18:14, 15, 31. **where is he**. Is 10:16-19. Ps 48:12, 13.

19. **shall not**. Ex 14:13. Dt 28:49, 50. 2 K 19:32. **fierce**. Dt 28:49, 50♪℘. **deeper**. Is 28:11. Je 5:15. Ezk 3:5, 6. 1 C 14:21. **speech**. ſ121BD, Ge +11:1. **stammering**. or, ridiculous. ſ24C, 2 K +18:21. Is 28:11mg. *S#3932h. Is 37:22 (scorn). 2 K 19:21. 2 Ch 30:10 (mocked). Ne 2:19. 4:1. Jb 9:23 (laugh). 11:3. 21:3. 22:19. Ps 2:4 (derision). 22:7. 59:8. 80:6 (laugh). Pr 1:26 (mock). 17:5. 30:17. Je 20:7.

20. **Look**. Is 26:1-3. Ps *48:12, 13. **the city**. Dt 12:5. Ps 78:68, 69. **solemnities**. Is 1:14. 14:13. Ge +17:21h. Ex +27:21n. Le 23:2n♪℘. **thine eyes**. Ps *46:5. 125:1, 2. *128:5, 6. **quiet habitation**. Is *32:17, 18. **a tabernacle**. Is *16:5. Am +*9:11. Ac *15:16. Re 21:3. **not be taken down**. Am +√9:15. **not one**. Is 37:33. 54:2. Ezk 48:35. Mt 16:18. He 12:28. Re 3:12. **be removed**. Am +√9:15. **ever**. Jb 4:20 (*S#5331h).

21. **the glorious**. Ps 29:3. Ac 7:2. 2 C 4:4-6. **a place**. Ps 46:4, 5. **broad rivers and streams**. Heb. broad of spaces, or hands. Is 22:18mg. Ne 7:4. Ezk 47:1-5. Re 22:1.

22. **the Lord is our judge**. Ge +*18:25. Ps 50:6. 75:7. 98:9. 2 C √5:10. Re 20:12. **lawgiver**. Heb. statute-maker. Dt 33:2. Ne 10:14. Ps 147:19, 20. Ja *4:12. **the Lord is our king**. Ps 44:4. *74:12. 89:18. Je *23:5, 6. Zc *9:9. Mt 21:5. *25:31-34, 46. Re *19:16. **he will**. Is *12:2. +*25:9. Zp 3:15-17. Mt *1:21-23. Lk 2:11. Ac *5:31. T 3:4-6. He *5:9.

23. **Thy tacklings are loosed**. or, They have forsaken thy tacklings. ver. 21. Ezk 27:26-34. Ac 27:19, 30-32, 40, 41. **then**. ver. 1-4. 2 Ch 20:25. Re 19:17, 18. **prey**. ſ144B, Dt +33:19. **the lame**. 1 S 30:10, 22-24. 2 K 7:8. 19:35. Ps 68:12. 1 C 1:27.

24. **the inhabitant**. Is 58:8. Ex 15:26. Dt 7:15. 28:27. 2 Ch 30:20. Je 33:6-8. Ezk 47:6, 7, 12. Ja *5:14, 15. Re 21:4. *22:2. **shall be forgiven**. Is 44:22. Ex 23:21♪℘. 32:32♪℘. Nu 14:19♪℘. Je *50:20. Mi 7:18, 19. 1 J √1:7-9.

ISAIAH 34

Predictions of dreadful vengeance and perpetual desolations against Idumea and the enemies of Zion, 1-15. The certainty of the prophecy, 16, 17.

1. **Come**. This and the following chapter, as Bishop Lowth observes, form one distinct prophecy; an entire, regular, and beautiful poem, consisting of two parts; the first containing a denunciation of Divine vengeance against the enemies of the people or church of God; the second describing the flourishing state of that church consequent upon those judgments. The event foretold is represented as of the highest importance, and of universal concern; *all nations* are called upon to attend to the declaration of it; and the wrath of God is denounced against all the nations who had provoked to anger the Defender of the cause of Zion. By a figure frequently occurring in the prophetical writings, the cities and people mentioned here, who were remarkably distinguished as the enemies of the people of God, are put for those enemies in general. Is 18:3. 33:13. 41:1. 43:9. 49:1. Jg 5:3, 31. Ps 49:1, 2. 50:1. 96:10. Mk *16:15, 16. Re 2:7. **to hear**. ♪105, Ml +4:2. **let the**. Is 1:2. Dt 4:26. *32:1. Je *22:29. Mi 6:1, 2. **all that is therein**. Heb. the fulness thereof. Ps 24:1. 1 C 10:26, 28.

2. **the indignation**. Is 24:1, etc. Je *25:15-29. Jl 3:9-14. Am ch. 1. 2:1-6. Zp 3:8. Zc 14:3, 12-16. Ro *1:18. Re 6:12-17. 14:15-20. *19:15-21. 20:9, 15. **and his**. Is 30:27-30. Na 1:2-6. **destroyed**. or, devoted. ver. 5. Is 3:4. 8:18. *11:15. 22:22. Le *27:29n. Nu 21:2. Jsh 6:17mg. Jg 21:11. Ezr 10:8mg. **hath delivered**. Je 27:2-6. Re 16:14.

3. **slain**. Is 14:19, 20. *66:24. 2 K 9:35-37. Je 8:1, 2. 22:19. Ezk 39:4, 11. Jl 2:20. Re 19:17, 18. **and the mountains**. ♪102, Ge +2:24. ver. 7. Ezk 32:5, 6. Re 14:20. 16:3, 4.

4. **all the host**. ♪102, Ge +2:24. Is 13:10. 14:12. Ps *102:25, 26. Je 4:23, 24. Ezk 32:7, 8. Jl *2:10, 30, 31. 3:15. Mt *24:29, 35. Mk 13:24, 25. Ac 2:19, 20. 2 P *3:7-12. Re *6:13, 14. 8:12. 20:11. **heavens**. ♪101, Dt +32:42. Here (in the Hebrew) the word "heavens" is emphasized by being, by Hyperbaton, put last: "And they shall be rolled together as a scroll—the heavens" (B694).

5. **my sword**. ♪22D5D, Dt +32:41. Dt *32:41, 42. Ps 17:13. Je *46:10. 47:6. Ezk 21:3-5, 9-11. Zp 2:12. Re 1:16. 19:15. **bathed**. ♪102, Ge +2:24. ♪155D, Ge +4:10. Heb. *ravah*, ❋S#7301h. Kal, Preterite: Je 46:10 (made drunk). Kal, Future: Ps 36:8 (abundantly satisfied. mg, watered). Pr 7:18 (take our fill). Piel, Preterite: Is 34:5 (bathed), 7 (shall be soaked. mg, drunken). Je 31:14 (satiate). Piel, Imperative: Ps 65:10 (waterest...abundantly). Piel, Future: Pr 5:19 (satisfy. mg, water). Is *16:9 (water). Hiphil, Preterite: Is 43:24 (filled. mg, drunk, abundantly moistened). 55:10 (watereth). Je 31:25 (satiated). La 3:15 (drunken). Hiphil, Participle: Pr 11:25 (watereth). **upon Idumea**. i.e. *earthy*, ❋S#123h. ver. 6. Ezk 25:12-14. 35:15. 36:5. or, Edom. Is 63:1. Ps 137:7. Je 49:7-22. Ezk 25:12. etc. 29:18-21. Mt 25:41. 1 C 16:22. Ga 3:10. 2 P 2:14. **of**. ♪181E, Ge +3:24. **my curse**. ver. 2. Is 43:28. Le *27:29n. Zc 14:11. Ml 4:6.

6. **sword**. ♪22D5D, Dt +32:41. **filled**. ♪102, Ge +2:24. Is 63:3. Je 49:13. Ezk 21:4, 5, 10. **made fat**.

♪132D, Ge +19:25. **the fat**. Dt 32:14. **for**. ♪95, Ps +7:13. **the Lord hath**. ver. 5. Is 63:1. Ps 37:20. Je 50:27. 51:40. Ezk 39:17-20. Zp *1:7. Re 19:17, 18. **Bozrah**. Is 63:1-3. **great slaughter**. Jl 3:13, 14. Re 14:19, 20. **Idumea**. ver. 5. Je 49:7-22.

7. **unicorns**. or, rhinoceroses. Nu 23:22. 24:8. Dt 33:17. Jb 39:9, 10. Ps 92:10. **the bullocks**. Ps 68:30. Je 46:21. 50:11, 27. **soaked**. or, drunken. ♪102, Ge +2:24. ver. 3. Is +43:24mg. **with blood**. Ezk 32:5, 6. **fatness**. ❋S#2459h. ver. 6. Is 1:11. 43:24. Ge 4:4. 45:18. Ex 23:18. Le 3:3, 4, 9, 17, etc. Nu 18:12. Dt 32:14, 38. Jg 3:22. 1 S 15:22. Jb 15:27. Ps 17:10. 63:5. 73:7. 81:16mg. 119:70. 147:14mg. Ezk 34:3. 39:19. 44:7, 15.

8. **the day**. Is 26:21. *35:4. 49:26. 59:17, 18. 61:2. *63:4. Dt 32:35, 41-43. Ps *94:1. Je +*46:10. Ezk +*30:3. Mi 6:1. Lk *18:7. Ro 2:5, 8, 9. 1 Th +*5:2. 2 Th *1:6-10. Re 6:10, 11. 9:15. *18:20. 19:2. **vengeance**. Is +*61:2. +*63:4. Ezk +*30:3. **year of recompences**. Is *63:4. Ho +*9:7. **Zion**. Ps √102:13, 16.

9. **the streams**. Is 11:15. 27:12. 30:28. **pitch**. ❋S#2203h. Ex 2:3. **brimstone**. Ge 19:28. Dt 29:23. Jb 18:15. Ps 11:6. Lk 17:29. Ju *7. Re *19:20. *20:10. +*21:8.

10. **shall not**. Is 1:31. +*66:24. Je 7:20. Ezk 20:47, 48. Mk √9:43-48. **the smoke**. Re *14:10, 11. *18:18. *19:3. **from**. Is 13:20. Ezk 29:11. Ml 1:3, 4. **for ever**. Heb. *olam*, Ex +12:24. **and ever**. Jb +4:20 (❋S#5331h, doubled here).

11. **cormorant**. or, pelican. Is 13:20-22. 14:23. Zp 2:14. Re 18:2, 21-23. **stretch**. 2 S 8:2. 2 K 21:13. La 2:8. Ml 1:3, 4. **the line**. Zc 1:16. **confusion**. Heb. *tohu*. Ge 1:2❵℗. **stones**. ♪121D7, Ex +7:19. i.e. *the stones which characterize wasteland*. **emptiness**. Heb. *bohu*. Ge 1:2❵℗. Je 4:23.

12. **call**. Is 3:6-8. Ec 10:16, 17. **nothing**. Is 41:24. 1 C +*8:4. 13:2. 2 C 12:11.

13. **thorns**. Is 32:13, 14. Ho 9:6. Zp 2:9. **an habitation**. See on Is 13:21, 22. 35:7. Je 9:11. 10:22. 49:33. 50:39, 40. 51:37. Ml *1:3. Re 18:2, 20-24. **owls**. or, ostriches. Heb. daughters of the owl. Is 13:21mg. 43:20mg. Jb +*30:29n.

14. **The wild beasts of the desert**. Heb. Ziim. Is 13:21mg. **the wild beasts of the island**. Heb. Ijim. Is 13:22mg. **satyr**. or, goat. lit. hairy one. ❋S#8163h. Is 13:21. Ge 27:11, 23 (hairy). 37:31 (kid). Le 4:23, 24 (goat). Nu 7:16, etc. 2 Ch 11:15 (devils). 29:23 (he goats). Ezk 43:22, 25. 45:23. Da 8:21 (rough). **screech owl**. or, night monster.

15. **nest**. Ps 104:17. Je 48:28. Ezk 31:6. **lay**. lit. letteth escape. Is 46:4. **hatch**. lit. cleave. Ne 9:11. **gather under**. Je 17:11. **the vultures**. Dt 14:13.

16. **Seek**. Is 1:17. 8:19, +√20. 28:13. 55:16. Dt 31:21. Jsh 1:8. Pr 23:12. Da 10:21. Am 3:7. Ml √3:16. Mt 4:10. Mk +*12:24. Jn +√5:39. *10:35. Ac √17:3, 11. 2 T 3:15. 2 P *1:19. **book**. roll or scroll. ver. 4. Is 19:11. 30:8. Ex +*17:14. Da 9:2. 2 T +*3:16. **read**. lit. "call," for reading in the east is generally done aloud (Young). T#1063. Is 8:3 (call). 12:4mg. 29:11, 12. 40:2 (cry), 6. *55:6. 58:1. Dt 17:19. Re 1:3. **no one**. Is 55:11. Mt *5:18. Lk 21:33. **shall fail**. F/L Is *40:26. **want her mate**. 1 S 20:6. 25:15. **my mouth**. Is 46:10. Ge 6:17. Nu 23:19. Ps 33:6, 9. **spirit**. Heb. *ruach*, Ex 15:8.

17. **he hath cast**. Ge +24:44n. Jsh +14:2n. *18:8. **divided**. Dt *32:8, 9. Ps 78:55. Ac 13:19. *17:26. **they**

shall. See on ver. 10. Is 13:20-22. **for ever**. Heb. *olam*, Ex +*12:24.

ISAIAH 35

Great prosperity predicted to Israel, 1, 2. The weak to be encouraged in hope, 3, 4. The miracles of Christ and the effects of his gospel foretold, 5-7; with the peace, holiness, and triumphant joy of his people, 8-10.

1. **wilderness**. Is 29:17. *32:15, 16. 40:3. *51:3. 52:9, 10. Ezk 36:35. **be glad**. Dt 28:63. 30:9. Ps 48:11. 97:8. Je 32:41. Re 19:1-7. **desert**. Is 4:2. 27:6. *55:12, 13. *61:10, 11. 66:10-14. Ho 14:5, 6.
2. **blossom abundantly**. T#444. Is 25:6. 41:18. 60:5-7, 13. Ps 72:16. Jl 2:21-26. 3:18. Ac +3:21 (T#446). **and rejoice**. Is 42:10-12. 49:13. 55:12, 13. 1 Ch 16:33. Ps 65:12, 13. 89:12. 96:11-13. 98:7-9. 148:9-13. Zc 10:7. Ro 10:15. *15:10. Re 14:2, 3. **the glory**. Is 33:9. 41:19. 60:13, 21. *61:3. 65:8-10. Ps 72:16. Ho 14:6, 7. **the excellency**. Is 60:13. Ezk 34:25, 26. Am 9:13-15. Mi 7:14, 15. Zp 3:19, 20. Zc 14:20, 21. Ac 4:32, 33. **Sharon**. i.e. *a great plain*, *S#8289h. Is 33:9. 35:2. 65:10. Jsh 12:18. 1 Ch 5:16. 27:29. SS 2:1. **they shall**. Is 6:3. *40:5. *60:1-3, 19. 66:18, 19. Ex 33:18, 19. Ps 50:2. 72:19. 97:6. *102:15, 16. Hab *2:14. Jn 12:41. 17:24. 2 C 3:18. *4:6. Re 21:23.
3. **Strengthen**. Is *40:1, 2. 52:1, 2. *57:14-16. Jg 7:11. Jb 4:3, 4. 16:5. Lk 22:32, 43. Ac 18:23. He *12:12.
4. **fearful**. Heb. *hasty*. Is 28:16. 32:4mg. Ps 116:11. Hab 2:3. **Be strong**. Is 44:2. Jsh 1:6, 7. 1 Ch 28:20. Da 10:19. Hg 2:4. Ep *6:10. 2 T 2:1. **fear not**. Is *41:10-14. *43:1-6. 54:4, 5. Zp 3:16, 17. Jn ▶12:15. Re *2:10. **behold**. Is *25:9. 26:20, 21. 34:8. 40:9, 10. 52:7-10. 61:2. 66:15. Dt *32:35-43. Ps 50:3. Ho 1:7. Hab 2:3. Zc 2:8-10. Ml 3:1. Mt *1:21-23. Lk 21:28. T *2:13. He 9:28. 10:37, 38. Ja 5:7-9. Re *1:7. 22:20. **with vengeance**. Is 34:8. Ps 94:1. Lk *21:22. Ro 3:5, 6. 12:19. 2 Th 1:6-8.
5. **the eyes**. T#1896. Is *29:18, 19. *32:3, 4. *42:6, 7, 16. 43:8. Ps 146:8. Mt 9:27-30. *√11:2-6. 12:22. 20:30-34. 21:14. Mk 8:22-25. 12:37. Lk 4:18. 7:22. Jn 9:1-7, 39-41. 11:37, *47. Ac 9:17, 18. *26:18. Ep *1:17, 18. 5:14. **the ears**. Is 48:8. Ex 4:11. Jb 33:16. Pr 20:12. Je 6:10. Mk 7:32-37. 9:25, 26. Lk 7:20-23.
6. **shall the lame**. Mt *11:5. 15:30, 31. 21:14. Jn *5:8, 9. Ac 3:2, 6-8. 8:7. 14:8-10. **the tongue**. Is 32:4. Ps 51:15. Mt *9:32, 33. 12:22. 15:30. Mk 7:32-37. 9:17-25. Lk 1:64. 11:14. Col *3:16. **for**. Is 41:17, 18. 43:19, 20. 48:21. 49:10, 11. Ex 17:6. Nu 20:11. Ne 9:15. Ps 46:4. 78:15, 16. Ezk 47:1-11. Zc 14:8. Jn 7:37-39. Re 22:1, 17.
7. **the parched**. Is 29:17. 44:3, 4. Mt 21:43. Lk 13:29. Jn 4:14. 7:38. 1 C +√6:9-11. **springs**. Is 41:18. 43:20. 44:3, 4. 49:10. Je 31:12. Jn 7:38, 39. Re 22:17. **in the habitation**. Is 34:13. Ho 1:10, 11. Ac 26:18. 1 J 5:19, 20. Re 12:9-12. 18:2. 20:2, 3. **grass with reeds**. *or*, a court for reeds, etc. Is 19:6.
8. **an highway**. Is *11:16. 19:23. *40:3, 4. *42:16. 49:11, 12. 57:14. *62:10. Je 31:21. Jn *14:6. He *10:20-23. **The way**. Is 7:3. 59:8. Ep *2:10. 1 Th *4:7. 2 T *1:9. T *2:11-14. He *10:19-22. √12:14. 1 P *1:14, 15. *2:9, 10. **the unclean**. Is 52:1, 11. *60:21. Ezk 43:12. *44:9. Jl *3:17. Zc 14:20, 21. Jn √14:6. 2 P *3:13. Re *21:27. **but it shall be for those**. *or*, for he

shall be with them. Is *49:10. Ps *23:4. Mt *1:23. Re *7:15-17. **the wayfaring**. Is *30:21. Ps *19:7. √25:8, 9. √119:130. Pr +√4:18. *8:8, 9, 20. Je *32:39, 40. *50:4, 5. Jn *7:17. 1 J *2:20, 27. **not err**. Nu 35:32n. Dt +27:8. Pr +*8:8, 9. Je 31:21. Hab 2:2. Lk 10:21. Ja 2:5.
9. **No lion**. Is *11:6-9. 65:25. Le 26:6⟩𝒫. Ezk *34:25. Ho 2:18. 1 P 5:8. Re *20:1-3. **but**. Is 62:12. Ex 15:13. Ps *107:2. Ga *3:13. T *2:14. 1 P *1:18. Re 5:9. 14:1-4.
10. **the ransomed**. Is *51:10, 11. Jb 33:24. Ho 13:14. Mt *20:28. 1 T √2:5, 6. **and come**. Ps 84:7. Je *31:11-14. 33:11. Jn 16:22. Ju 21. Re 14:1-4. 15:2-4. 18:20. 19:1-7. **with songs**. Is *24:14, 16. +*51:11. Ho 2:15. Hab *3:3. Zc +*2:10. **everlasting**. Heb. *olam*, Ge +*17:7. **joy**. T#445. Is 25:8. 52:9. 65:18, 19. Zp 3:14-17. **heads**. *√171Q12*, Jg +5:30. **and gladness**. Ps 51:8. **and sorrow**. Is *25:8. 30:19. 60:20. 65:19. Re *7:9-17. *21:4.

ISAIAH 36

Sennacherib invades Judah, 1-3. He sends a blasphemous message by Rabshakeh, to persuade the Jews to revolt, 4-20; Hezekiah's servants return no answer, but report his words to the king, 21, 22.

1. **it came**. 2 K 18:13, 17. 2 Ch 32:1. **that Sennacherib**. Is 1:7, 8. 7:17. *8:7, 8. 10:28-32. 33:7, 8. This account is parallel to 2 K 18:13—20:19 and 2 Ch 32:1-33.
2. A.M. 3294. B.C. 710. **sent**. 2 K 18:17, etc. 2 Ch 32:9, etc. Is 7:3. 22:9-11. **great**. 2 K 6:14mg. **upper pool**. *or*, blessing. Is 7:3. 2 K 18:17. **fuller's**. *or*, washerman. Is 7:3. 2 K 18:17.
3. **Eliakim**. Is *22:15-21. **house**. *√121J4*, Ge +7:1. **Shebna**. 2 S 8:16, 17. 20:24, 25. **scribe**. *or*, secretary. 2 S 8:17mg. 2 K 18:18mg. 22:3. Je 52:25. **Joah**. i.e. *whose helper is Jehovah*, *S#3098h. 2 K 18:18, 26, 37. 1 Ch 6:21. 26:4. 2 Ch 29:12. 34:8. Is 36:3, 11, 22. (1) A son of Asaph the recorder, 2 K 18:18, 37; Is 36:3. (2) A descendant of Gershom, the son of Levi, 1 Ch 6:21. (3) A son of Obed-edom, 1 Ch 26:4. (4) A Levite who aided Hezekiah in his reforms, 2 Ch 29:12. (5) A Levite commissioned by Josiah to repair the house of the Lord, 2 Ch 34:8. **recorder**. *or*, remembrancer. ver. 22. Is 62:6. 66:3. 2 S 8:16mg.
4. **Thus saith**. Is 10:8-14. 37:11-15. Pr 16:18. Ezk 31:3, etc. Da 4:30. Ac 12:22, 23. Ju 16. **the great king**. Ps ◑47:2. **Assyria**. *Assyria* proper, now *Kurdistan*, was bounded by Armenia on the north, Media and Persia on the east, Babylonia on the south, and the Tigris, which divides it from Mesopotamia, on the west, between 33 and 38 degrees N. lat. and 42 and 46 degrees E. long. But the Assyrian empire, the bounds of which were different at different times, in its most flourishing state, according to the descriptions of the Greek and Roman writers, comprehended all the countries and nations between the Mediterranean on the west, and the Indus on the east, and between the deserts of Scythia on the north, and the Indian Ocean on the south. **What**. 2 K 18:5, 19, etc. 19:10. 2 Ch 32:7-10, 14-16. Ps 42:3, 10. 71:10, 11. **trustest**. Ps 121:3. 125:1, 2. 127:1. 130:5-8.
5. **vain words**. Heb. a word of lips. Jg 7:22mg. Pr 14:23. **I have counsel and strength for war**. *or*, *but counsel and strength are for the war*. Pr 21:+*30,

31. 24:5, 6. **that**. 2 K 18:7, 19, 20. 24:1. Ne 2:19, 20. Je 52:3. Ezk 17:15.

6. **thou trustest**. Is 20:5, 6. *30:1-7. 31:3. 2 K 17:4. 18:21. Je 37:5-8. Ezk *29:6, 7.

7. **We trust**. 2 K 18:5, 22. 1 Ch 5:20. 2 Ch *16:7-9. 32:7, 8. Ps 18:1, 2, 50. *22:4, 5. 42:5, 10, 11. **is it not**. Dt 12:2-6, 13, 14. 2 K *18:4, ‖22. 2 Ch *30:14. 31:1. 32:12. 1 C 2:15.

8. **pledges**. *or*, hostages. 2 K 14:14. **and I**. Is 10:13, 14. 1 S 17:40-43. 1 K 20:10, 18. 2 K 18:23. Ne 4:2-5. Ps 20:7, 8. 123:3, 4.

9. **face**. ♪171Q, Ge +3:19. **the least**. Is 10:8. 2 K 18:24. **and put**. ver. 6. Is 30:16, 17. 31:1, 3. Dt 17:16. Ps *20:7, 8. Pr *21:31. Je 2:36.

10. **am I now**. ✱10:5-7. 37:28. 1 K 13:18. 2 K 18:25. 2 Ch √35:21. Ps *94:20. 115:2-4. Da 3:15, 17. Am +*3:6. Jn 19:11.

11. **in the Syrian**. 2 K 18:26, 27. Dt 28:49. Ezr 4:7. Je 5:15. Da 2:4. **in the Jews' language**. Is 19:18.

12. **that sit upon**. 2 K ‖18:27. **that they may**. Is 9:20. Le 26:29. Dt 28:53-57. 2 K 6:25-29. 31:18. Je 19:9. La 4:9, 10. Ezk 4:16.

13. **cried**. 1 S 17:8-11. 2 K 18:28-32. 2 Ch 32:18. Ps 17:10-13. 73:8, 9. 82:6, 7. **Hear**. ver. 4. Is 8:7. 10:8-13. Ezk 31:3-10. Da 4:37.

14. **Let not**. Is 37:10-13. 2 K 19:10-13, 22. 2 Ch 32:11, 13-19. Da 3:15-17. 6:20. 7:25. 2 Th 2:4. Re 13:5, 6.

15. **make you trust**. ver. 7. Is 37:23, 24. Ps 4:2. 22:7, 8. 71:9-11. Da 3:14, 15. Mt 27:43.

16. **Make an agreement with me by a present.** *or,* Seek my favor *by* a present. Heb. Make with me a blessing. Ge 32:20. 33:11. 1 S 25:27. 2 S 8:6. 2 K 5:15. 18:31. 2 C 9:5mg. **come out**. 1 S 11:3. 2 K 24:12-16. **eat ye**. 1 K 4:20, 25. Mi 4:4. Zc 3:10. **cistern**. Heb. *bor*, Ge +37:20.

17. **I come**. 2 K 17:6, etc. 18:9-12. 24:11. Pr 12:10. **a land of corn**. ♪121D4, Ge +27:28. Ex 3:8. Dt *8:7-9. 11:12. Jb 20:17. The other copy in 2 K 18:32, adds here, "a land of oil olive, and of honey; that ye may live, and not die: and hearken not unto Hezekiah when he seduceth you." **and**. ♪174, Ge +18:27. **wine**. ♪121D13, Ge +27:28. **and vineyards**. ♪174, Ge +18:27.

18. **lest**. ver. 7, 10, 15. Is 37:10. Ps 12:4. 92:5-7. **Hath**. Is 37:12, 13, 17, 18. 2 K 18:33-35. 19:12, 13, 17, 18. 2 Ch 32:13-17. Ps 115:2-8. 135:5, 6, 15-18. Je 10:3-5, 10-12. Da 3:15. Hab 2:19, 20. **gods of the nations**. Note that Rabshakeh holds the pagan notion of Jehovah being merely a tribal deity, a god who has power only in the land of the Hebrews, comparable to the deities worshipped by other lands he has conquered, unable to grant victory over his superior armed forces. Jg 11:24n. 1 K *20:23n.

19. **Hamath**. Nu 34:8. 2 S 8:9. **Arphad**. i.e. *firmly laid; resting place,* ✱S#774h. 2 K 18:34. 19:13. Is 10:9. 36:19. 37:13. Je 49:23. The variation of *Arphad* and *Arpad* exists only in the translation; the original is uniform. Is 10:9. Je 49:23, Arpad. It is probably the same as *Arvad* (Ezk +27:8). **Sepharvaim**. Calmet is of opinion that *Sepharvaim* was the capital of the *Saspires,* who, according to Herodotus (l. i. 103. iii. 94. vii. 79), were the only people that inhabited between the Colchians and Medes; and probably the *Sarapases,* whom Strabo (l. x.) places in Armenia. Hiller considers the name as denoting Sephar of the Parvaim, i.e.

Mount Sephar adjacent to the regions of Arabia called Parvaim. But it is more probable, as Wells and others suppose, that *Sepharvaim* is the *Sipphara* of Ptolemy, the city of the *Sippareni,* mentioned by Abydenus (in Eusebius, Praep. Evang. l. ix. 41), and probably the *Hipparenum* of Pliny (l. vi. c. 30), a city of Mesopotamia, situated upon the Euphrates, near where it is divided into two arms, by one of which, it is probable, it was divided into two parts. 2 K 17:24. **and have**. Is 10:10, 11. 2 K 17:5-7. 18:10-12.

20. **that the Lord**. Is 37:18, 19, 23-29. 45:16, 17. Ex 5:2. 2 K 19:22, etc. 2 Ch 32:15, 19. Jb 15:25, 26. 40:9-12. Ps 50:21. 73:9. Da 3:15.

21. **they held**. 2 K 18:36, 37. Ps *38:13-15. √39:1. Pr *9:7. 26:4. Ec 3:7. Am *5:13. Mt +*7:6.

22. **Then came**. 2 K ‖18:37. **Eliakim**. ver. 3, 11. **recorder**. ver. 3mg. 2 S +8:16mg. **with their**. Is 29:2. 33:7. 37:1, 2. 2 K 5:7. Ezr 9:3. Mt 26:65. The history of the invasion of Sennacherib, observes Bp. Lowth, and the miraculous destruction of his army, which makes the subject of so many of Isaiah's prophecies, is very properly inserted here; as affording the best light to many parts of these prophecies; and as almost necessary to introduce the prophecy in the 37th chapter, being the answer of God to Hezekiah's prayer, which could not be properly understood without it. Sennacherib succeeded his father, Shalmaneser on the throne of Assyria, A.M. 3290, B.C. 714, and reigned only about eight years.

ISAIAH 37

Hezekiah sends to Isaiah entreating him to pray for the people, 1-5. Isaiah encourages him, 6, 7. Sennacherib, going to meet the Ethiopian king, sends a blasphemous letter to Hezekiah, who spreads it before God with fervent prayer, 8-20. Isaiah describes the arrogant impiety, and predicts the ruin, of Sennacherib, 21-35. An angel slays 185,000 of the Assyrians; and Sennacherib is murdered at Nineveh by two of his own sons, 36-38.

1. **it came**. 2 K ‖19:1, etc. **he rent**. Is 36:22. 2 K 22:11. Je 36:24. Jon 3:5, 6. Mt 11:21. **and went**. Ezr 9:5. Jb 1:20, 21. Ps 26:8. 73:16, 17. *122:1, 9. 134:1, 2. Da 6:10. **the house**. 1 K 8:26-30. 9:3.

2. **sent Eliakim**. ver. 14. Is 36:3. See on 2 K 18:18. 19:2. 22:12-14. 2 Ch +*20:20. Ps 50:15. 91:15. Ja 5:16-18. Jl 1:13. **elders of the priests**. 2 K 19:2. Je 19:1.

3. **This day**. Is 25:8. 33:2. 2 K 19:3. 2 Ch 15:4. Ps *50:15. 91:15. 116:3, 4. Je 30:7. Ho *5:15. 6:1. Re 3:19. **blasphemy**. *or,* provocation. Ps 95:8mg. 120:2, 3. 123:3, 4. **for the**. Is 26:17, 18. 66:9. Ho 13:13.

4. **It may**. Jsh 14:12. 1 S 14:6. 2 S 16:12. Am 5:15. **to reproach**. ver. 23, 24. Is 36:20. 51:7, 8. 1 S 17:26, 36. 2 K 19:4, 22, 23. 2 Ch 32:15-19. **and will**. ver. 23. Ps 50:21. **lift up**. 1 S 7:8. 12:19, 23. 2 Ch 32:20. Ps 106:23. 120:1. 123:1-3. 130:1, 2. Jl 2:17. Ja 5:16. **for the**. Is 1:9. 8:7, 8. 10:5, 6, 22. 2 K *17:18. 18:9-16. 2 Ch 28:19. Je *33:3. Ezk 36:37. Ro 9:27. **left**. Heb. found. Jg +20:48mg. 2 K 19:4mg.

6. **Thus shall**. 2 K 19:5-7. 22:15-20. **Be not**. Is 7:4. 10:24, 25. 35:4. *41:10-14. 43:1, 2. *51:12, 13. Ex *14:13, 14. Le 26:8. Jsh 11:6. 2 Ch 20:15-20. Mk 4:40. 5:36.

7. **I will**. Is 10:16-18, 33, 34. 17:13, 14. 29:5-8. 30:28-

33. 31:8, 9. 33:10-12. 2 K *7:6. Jb 4:9. *15:21. Ps 58:9. **send a blast upon him.** *or,* put a spirit into him. Heb. *ruach,* Ex +15:8. ʃ121A10, Ge +45:27. **I will cause.** ver. 36-38. 2 Ch 32:21.

8. **Rabshakeh.** 2 K 19:8, 9. Nu 33:20, 21. **Libnah.** Jsh 10:29, 31-34. 21:13. 2 K 8:22. 2 Ch 21:10. **Lachish.** Jsh 12:11. 15:39.

9. **he heard.** 1 S 23:27, 28. **Ethiopia.** *Cush,* which is generally rendered *Ethiopia,* is applied in Scripture to at least three distinct and different countries. (1) The country watered by the Gihon or Araxes (Ge 2:13), also called *Cuth,* 2 K 17:30. (2) A country of Arabia Petraea, bordering upon Egypt, which extended from the northern extremity of the Red Sea along its eastern shore (Compare Ex 3:1 with Nu 12:1. Hab 3:7). (3) *Ethiopia* Proper, an extensive country of Africa, comprehending Nubia and Abyssinia; being bounded on the north by Egypt, on the east by the Red Sea and Indian Ocean, and on the south and west by various nations of Africa, and extending from about 6 to 24 degrees N. lat. and 25 to 45 degrees E. long. It is probable that it was this latter *Cush,* or *Ethiopia,* of which Tirhakah was king; he being in league with his kinsman Sevechus, son of So, or Sabacon, king of Egypt, against Sennacherib, the king of Assyria.

10. **Let not.** Is 36:4, 15, 20. 2 K 18:5. 19:10-13. 2 Ch 32:7, 8, 15-19. Ps 22:8. Mt 27:43.

11. **thou hast heard.** ver. 18, 19. Is 10:7-14. 14:17. 36:18-20. 2 K 17:4-6. 18:33-35.

12. **the gods.** Is 36:18n, 20. 46:5-7. **Gozan.** 2 K 17:6. 18:11. 19:12. **Haran.** *Haran,* the *Carrhae* of the Greeks and Romans, is situated in the northwest part of Mesopotamia, between the Euphrates and the river Chebar; about 110 miles west of Nisibis, 90 east of Bir, 100 south of Diarbekir, and 170 north of Palmyra. Ge 11:31. 12:14. 28:10. 29:4. Ac 7:2. **Eden.** It is probable that this Eden is the country near Diarbekir, on the Tigris, called *Madon,* according to Asseman. Ge 2:8. Ezk 27:23. 28:13. Am 1:5. **Telassar.** i.e. *hill of Assur; Assyrian hill; weariness of the prince,* *S#8515h. 2 K 19:12. *Telassar* is probably the same as *Ellasar,* Ge 14:1, as the Jerusalem Targum reads; for both of which the Syriac has *Dolassar;* and perhaps, as Doederlein supposes, the same as *Sharra,* a city of Mesopotamia, half a mile from the Euphrates. 2 K 19:12, Thelasar.

13. **Hamath.** Is 10:9. 36:19. Je 49:23. **Hena.** i.e. *shaken,* *S#2012h. 2 K 18:34. 19:13. *Hena* is probably the same as *Anah,* a city of Mesopotamia, situated on an island in the Euphrates. **Ivah.** 2 K 17:24, 30, 31, Ava, Avites. +18:34. 19:13.

14. **received.** 2 K 19:14. **and Hezekiah went.** ver. 1. 1 K 8:28-30, 38, *44, *45. 9:3. 2 Ch 6:20, etc. Ps 27:5. 62:1-3. 74:10, 11. 76:1-3. 123:1-4. 143:6. Jl 2:17-20. **and spread.** 1 S 23:4.

15. **prayed.** 1 S *7:8, 9. 2 S 7:18-29. 2 K 19:15-19. 2 Ch *14:11, 12. *20:5-12, 22. Da 9:3, 4. Ph √4:6, 7. Ja 5:13.

16. **Lord.** Is 6:3. 8:13. 2 S 7:26. Ps *46:7, 11. **dwellest.** Ex *25:22. 1 S 4:4. Ps 80:1. 99:1. He *4:16. **thou art.** ver. 20. Is 43:10, 11. 44:6. 45:22. 54:5. 1 K 18:39. 2 K 5:15. Ps 86:10. Re 11:15-17. **thou hast.** Is 40:28. 44:24. Ge 1:1. Ps 121:1, 2. 123:1. 124:8. 134:3. 146:6. Je 10:10-12. Jn 1:3. Col *1:16.

17. **Incline.** 2 Ch 6:40. Jb 36:7. Ps 17:6. 71:2. 130:1, 2. Da 9:17-19. 1 P *3:12. **hear.** ver. 4. 2 S 16:12. Ps

*10:14, 15. *74:10, 22. 79:12. *83:1-4, 17, 18. 89:50, 51. *93:3, 4.

18. **the kings.** 2 K 15:29. *16:9. *17:5, 6, 24. 1 Ch *5:26. Na 2:11, 12. **laid waste.** 2 K 19:17. Je 51:36. **nations.** Heb. lands. This is an example of how the Hebrew text in Isaiah varies from the text in 2 Kings. Here, the repetition of *lands* and *land* has much perplexed interpreters, as J. A. Alexander notes. Young in his translation follows Gesenius who follows J. D. Michaelis and Augusti in giving the masculine suffix a reflexive sense, translating "laid waste all the land and their land," indicating that they had destroyed not only other countries but their own, agreeing with the charge against the king of Babylon in Is 14:20, "thou hast destroyed thy land and slain thy people." But it is better to take this passage in the sense of 2 K 19:17, and regard the differing construction here as a combination of the figures of speech Paronomasia (ʃ140, Ge +4:25) and Metonymy of Adjunct (ʃ121J17, Ge +6:11), where the latter word "land" is put for the people inhabiting the lands. For other instances of this figure see Ge +6:11. **countries.** ʃ145, Jg +11:40.

19. **And have.** Is 10:9-11. 36:18-20. 46:1, 2. Ex 32:20. 2 S 5:21. Ps 86:8. 89:6. *96:5, 6. Je 10:15, 16. **cast.** Heb. given. Is 36:8. 61:3. **no gods.** Is 40:19-21. 41:7. 44:9, 10, 17. Ps *115:4-8. Je *10:2-6, 11. Ho 8:6. 1 C +*8:4.

20. **that all.** Is 42:8. Ex *9:15, 16. Jsh 7:8, 9. 1 S 17:45-47. 1 K 8:43. 18:36, 37. Ps 46:10. 59:13. *67:1, 2. 83:17, 18. Ezk 36:23. Ml 1:11. **even.** ver. 16. **thou only.** Is *43:11. Dt +*6:4. +*32:39. Ps 83:18. 86:10. Mk 12:29. Jn 20:17. 1 C 8:6. Ep 1:17. 4:5, 6. 1 T 2:5.

21. **Whereas.** Is .38:3-6. 58:9. *65:24. Ge 32:28. 2 S 15:31. 17:23. 2 K 19:20, 21. Jb 22:27. Ps 91:15. Da *9:20-23. Ac 4:31. 1 Th *5:17. Ja *5:16. 1 J √5:14, 15.

22. **The virgin.** Is 23:12. Ge +24:16. Je 14:17. 18:13. La 1:15. 2:13. Ezk ◯16:35. Am 5:2. **the daughter.** ʃ155E5, Nu +21:25. Is 1:8. 10:32. 55:2. 62:11. Ps 9:14. Zp 3:14. Zc 2:10. 9:9. Mt 21:5. **hath despised.** ʃ151, Ge +1:28. Is 8:9, 10. 1 S 17:36, 44-47. Ps 2:2-4. 27:1-3. 31:18. 46:1-7. Jl 3:9-12. **shaken.** Jb 16:4. Ps 22:7, 8. *105:14, 15. Mt 27:39.

23. **Whom hast.** ver. 10-13. Ex 5:2. 2 K 19:4, 22. 2 Ch 32:17. Ps 44:16. 73:9. 74:18, 23. Re 13:1-6. **against whom.** Is 10:13-15. 14:13, 14. Ex 9:17. Pr 30:13. Ezk 28:2, 9. Da 5:20-23. 7:25. 2 Th 2:4. **the Holy One.** Is 10:20. 12:6. 17:7. 30:11, 12. 41:14, 16. 43:3, 14. Ex *15:11. Ezk *39:7. Hab √1:12, 13.

24. **By thy.** Heb. By the hand of thy. 1 K +16:12mg. 2 K 14:25. 19:23mg. **servants.** ver. 4. Is 36:15-20. 2 K 19:22, 23. **By the.** Is 10:13, 14. 36:9. Ex 15:9. Ps *20:7. Da 4:30. **Lebanon.** Is *14:8. **tall cedars thereof, and the choice fir trees thereof.** Heb. tallness of the cedars thereof *and* the choice of the trees thereof. Is 10:18. 14:8. Ezk 31:3, etc. Da 4:8-14, 20-22. Zc 11:1, 2. **of his Carmel.** *or, and* his fruitful field. Is 29:17. Mi 7:14.

25. **digged.** 2 K 19:24. **with the sole.** Is 36:12. 1 K 20:10. 2 K 19:23, 24. **my feet.** Dt +11:10n. Pr 21:1. **dried up.** Is 19:5. 44:12. 51:17. Ex 17:6. **rivers.** arms, or canals. Is *19:6. Mi 7:12. **besieged.** *or,* fenced and closed. 2 K 19:24mg. Ps 31:21mg. 60:9mg. Je 10:17. Mi 7:12. Zc 9:3. "Besieged places" are here put for Egypt by use of the figure of speech ʃ121.O, Metonymy

of the Adjunct, where the contents of a place are put for the place itself. For other instances of this figure see Ge +28:22. In some versions this figure is translated "the rivers of Egypt." Is +*27:12.

26. **long ago**, etc. *or, how* I have made it long ago, *and* formed it of ancient times? Should I now bring it to be laid waste, *and* defenced cities *to be* ruinous heaps? **how I.** Is 10:+5, 6, 15. 45:7. *46:10, 11. Ge √50:20. Ps *17:13. 76:10. Am +√3:6. Ac 2:23. 4:27, 28. 15:18. 1 P 2:8. Ju 4. **ancient.** Mi +5:2 (✛S#6924h). **formed.** or, purposed. Is 10:5, 15. 30:32. **lay waste.** Is 54:16. 2 K 19:25. **defenced cities.** Is 25:2. **ruinous heaps.** Is 10:30. 25:2. 37:26. 48:18.

27. **their inhabitants.** Is 19:16. Nu 14:9. 2 K 19:26. Ps 127:1, 2. Je 5:10. 37:10. **of small power.** Heb. short of hand. Jb 14:1. Pr 14:17, 29. **as the grass of.** Is 40:6-8. Ps 37:2. 90:5, 6. 92:7. 103:15. *129:5-7. Ja 1:10, 11. 1 P 1:24.

28. **I know.** Ps *139:2-11. Pr *5:21. 15:3. Je 23:23, 24. Jn +*2:24, 25. Ac 1:24. He *4:12, 13. Re 2:13. **abode.** or, sitting. Is 40:22. 44:13. **going out.** √171J3, Nu +27:17. Is 13:10. Ge 8:7. 12:4. **coming in.** Is 2:21. 13:22. 14:9.

29. **rage.** ver. 10. Is 36:4, 10. 2 K 19:27, 28. Jb 15:25, 26. Ps 2:1-3. 46:6. 93:3, 4. Na 1:9-11. Jn 15:22, 23. Ac 9:4. **tumult.** Ps 74:4, 28. 83:2. Am 6:1. Mt 27:24. Ac 22:22. **will I.** Is 30:28. Jb 41:2. Ps 32:9. 92:5-8. Ezk 29:4. 38:4. Am 4:2. **turn thee back.** Ps 129:4, 5.

30. **this shall.** Is +*7:14. 38:7. Ex 3:12. 1 K 13:3-5. 2 K 19:29. 20:9. **Ye shall.** Is 7:21-25. Le *25:4, 5, 20-22. Ps 126:5, 6. 128:2. **groweth of itself.** Le 25:5, 11)᾽𝒫. 2 K 19:29. Jb 14:19. **third year.** Is 20:3. **sow.** √96B, Ge +20:7.

31. **remnant that is escaped of the house of Judah.** Heb. escaping of the house of Judah that remaineth. Is 1:9. 6:13. 10:20-22. Je 44:28. **shall.** 2 K 19:30-34. Ps 121:2-8. 124:1-3, 6. 125:2. 126:2, 3. 127:1. **take root.** Is 11:1, 10. *27:6. 65:9. 2 K 19:30, 31. Ps 80:9. Je 30:19. Ro 9:27. 11:5. Ga 3:29. Re 22:16. **upward.** Zc 3:8. 6:12. Jn 15:5.

32. **a remnant.** Ro 11:5. **they that escape.** Heb. the escaping. **the zeal.** √22B, Is +9:7. ver. 20. Is *9:7. *59:17. Ex 20:5. Nu 25:11 (my sake, jealousy))᾽𝒫. 2 K 19:31. Jl 2:18. Zc 1:14.

33. **He.** Is 8:7-10. 10:32-34. 17:12, 14. 33:20. 2 K 19:32-35. Da 4:34, 35. **shields.** Heb. shield. 2 K 19:32. **cast.** Ezk 21:22. Lk 19:43, 44.

34. **the way.** ver. 29. Pr +*21:30.

35. **I will.** Is 31:5. 38:6. 2 K 20:6. **for mine.** Is 43:25. 48:9-11. Dt 32:27. Ezk 20:9. 36:22. Ep 1:6, 14. **and for.** 1 K 11:12, 13, 36. 15:4. Je *23:5, 6. 30:9. 33:15, 16. Ezk 37:24, 25. **my servant.** Is 41:8. 42:1. **David's sake.** Is +*9:7. 2 S *23:1, 5. Ps 132:1, 10. Je +√33:20, 21. Lk 1:31-33.

36. **the angel.** Is 10:12, 16-19, 33, 34. 17:13, 14. 29:7, 8. *30:30-33. 31:8. 33:10-12. Ex 12:23. 2 S 24:16. 2 K 19:35. 1 Ch 21:12, 16. 2 Ch 32:21, 22. Jb 4:9. Ps 35:5, 6. 73:18, 19. 90:5, 6. 92:1. 98:1. Ac 12:23. **and when.** Ex 12:30. Jb 20:5-7. 24:24. Ps 46:6-11. 76:5-7. 1 Th 5:2, 3.

37. **Sennacherib.** ver. 7, 29. Is 31:9. **and.** √148, Ge +8:22. **Nineveh.** Ge 10:11, 12. Jon 1:2. 3:3. Na 1:1. Mt 12:41.

38. **his god.** ver. 10. Is 14:9, 12. 36:15, 18. 2 K 19:36, 37. 2 Ch 32:14, 19, 21. **smote him.** Is 14:12.

Ps 94:20-23. **Armenia.** Heb. Ararat. Ge 8:4. Je 51:27. **Esar-haddon.** *Esar-haddon*, called *Asar-addinus* in the *Canon* of Ptolemy, was the third son of Sennacherib; and having reigned twenty-nine years over the Assyrians, he took advantage of the anarchy and confusion which followed the death of Mesessimordacus, and seized upon Babylon; which he added to his former empire, and reigned over both for thirteen years; when he was succeeded by his son Saosduchinus, A.M. 3336, B.C. 668. Ezr 4:2.

ISAIAH 38

Hezekiah, being sick unto death, prays, and is assured that his life shall be prolonged; and that he shall be delivered from the Assyrians, 1-6. The sun goeth back ten degrees, as a sign to him, 7, 8. His recollection of his thoughts and prayer when he was sick; and his thanksgivings for recovery, 9-20. The means appointed for that end, 21, 22.

1. **A.M. 3291. B.C. 713. was Hezekiah.** 2 K ‖*20:1-11. 2 Ch ‖32:24. **sick unto death.** 2 K 13:14. Ps 107:18. Jn 11:1-5. Ac 9:37. Ph 2:27-30. 2 T +*4:20. **And Isaiah.** Is 37:21. 39:3, 4. **Set thine house in order.** Heb. Give charge concerning thy house. 2 S 17:23mg. 2 K 20:1mg. Ec +*9:10. Lk 9:61. **for thou.** Je 18:7-10. Jon 3:4, 10. **not live.** √144D, Ge +40:23.

2. **turned.** Hezekiah's couch was probably placed in a corner, which is the place of honor in the East; in which, turning on either side, he must turn his face to the wall; by which he would withdraw himself from those attending him in his apartment. 1 K 8:30. Ps *50:15. *91:15, 16. Mt 6:6. **and prayed.** Is 37:4, 14. ◖39:2.

3. **Remember.** Ne 5:19. 13:14, 22, 31. Ps 18:20-27. 20:1-3. He *6:10. **I have.** Ge 5:22, 24. *6:9. *17:1. 1 K 2:4. *3:6. 2 Ch *31:20, 21. Jb 23:11, 12. Ps 16:8. 18:23, 24. 32:2. Jn *1:47. 2 C *1:12. 1 J *3:21, 22. **in truth.** 2 J 4. 3 J 3, ◖4. **a perfect heart.** 1 K ◖11:4. 15:14. 2 K +*20:3. 1 Ch 12:38n. *29:9, 19. 2 Ch *16:9. ◖25:2. Ps 37:18n. *101:2. *119:80. 2 C 13:9. **have done.** 2 Ch 31:20, 21. **good.** Ne 13:14. **wept.** 2 S 12:21, 22. Ezr 10:1. Ne 1:4. Ps 6:8. 102:9. Ho 12:4. He *5:7. **sore.** Heb. with great weeping. Jg 21:2. 2 S 13:36mg. 2 K 20:3mg.

5. **and say.** 2 S 7:3-5. 1 Ch 17:2-4. **God.** Is 7:13, 14. 1 K 8:25. 9:4, 5. 11:12, 13. 15:4. 2 Ch 34:3. Ps 89:3, 4. Mt 22:32. **of David.** Is *55:3. 2 S 7:12-16. Ps +*132:11. Ac *13:34. **I have heard.** Is *65:24. 2 K 19:20. ‖20:5. Ps 34:5, 6. 55:1. Da 9:21, 22. Mt 7:7, 8. Lk 1:13. 1 J √5:14, 15. **I have seen.** Ps 6:6. 39:12. *56:8. 147:3. 2 C 7:6. Re 7:17. **I will.** Jb 14:5. Ps 116:15. Ac 27:24.

6. **I will deliver.** Is 10:12. 12:6. 14:25. 31:4. 37:35. 2 Ch 32:22. 2 T 4:17. **I will defend.** Is 31:5. Lk 18:7, 8.

7. **this shall be a sign.** ver. 22. Is *7:10-14. 37:30. Ge 9:13. Jg 6:17-22, 37-39. 2 K 20:8, etc.

8. **I will bring.** Jsh √10:12-14. 2 K 20:11. 2 Ch 32:24, 31. Mt 16:1. **the sun dial.** Heb. the degrees by, *or*, with the sun. Or, as the Hebrew might be rendered, "the steps of Ahaz." The researches of curious travelers in Hindostan, observes Bp. Stock, have lately discovered in that country, three observatories of similar form, the most remarkable of which is to be seen within four miles of Delhi, the ancient capital of the Mogul

empire. A rectangled triangle, whose hypotenuse is a staircase (apparently parallel to the axis of the earth), bisects a zone, or coping of a wall, which wall connects the two terminating towers at right and left. The coping itself is of a circular form, and accurately graduated, to mark, by the gnomon above, the sun's progress, before and after noon.

9. **writing**. Is 12:1, etc. Ex 15:1, etc. Jg 5:1, etc. 1 S *2:1-10. Ps 18, title. 30:11, 12. 107:17-22. *116:1-4. 118:18, 19. Jon 2:1-9. **he had**. Dt 32:39. 1 S 2:6. Jb 5:18. Ho 6:1, 2. We have here Hezekiah's thanksgiving song, which he penned by divine direction, after his recovery. He might have used some of the Psalms of David his father, as he had appointed the Levites to praise the Lord with *the words of David* (2 Ch 29:30), but the occasion here was extraordinary. His heart being full of devout affections, he would not confine himself to the compositions he had, though of divine inspiration, but offered up his praises in his own words. The Lord put a new song into his mouth. He put his thanksgiving in writing, that he might review it himself afterwards, for the reviving of the good impressions made upon him by the providential interference—and that it might be recommended to others also for their use upon the like occasion. This verse contains the superscription of the song, as verse 20 contains the subscription, as is frequent in the titles of the psalms.

10. **in the cutting off of my days**. ver. 1. Jb 6:11. 7:7. 17:11-16. Ps 31:22. 88:1-7. 130:1. 2 C 1:9. **the gates**. ♪171S7B, Ge +14:7. ♪88, Ge +15:15. Jb 38:17. Ps 9:13. 107:18. Mt 16:18. **grave**. Heb. *sheol*, Ge 37:35. Jb +14:13. Ps +*16:10. 30:3. 139:8. **deprived**. Jb 17:11, 15. 2 C 1:9. **residue**. Is 40:24. *65:15, 20. 1 S 25:38. Jb *14:5, 14. 15:32, 33. 21:21. 22:15, *16. Ps 37:22, 28. *55:23. 90:10, *12. √102:24. Pr +*10:27. Ec 3:2. +*7:17. Je 17:11. Mt 8:29. Lk 12:20. Jn 7:8, 30. 1 C *11:30, 32.

11. **I shall not**. Jb 35:14, 15. Ps 6:4, 5. 27:13. 31:22. 116:8, 9. Ec +*9:5, 6. **see**. or, appear before. Is 1:12. Ex 23:15♪℘. 34:20♪℘. **the land of the living**. Jb 28:15. Ps 27:13. 142:5. Ezk +26:20. **behold man**. Ps 88:8, 9, 18.

12. **departed**. Ja *4:14. **is removed**. Jb 4:19. 7:7. Ps 89:45-47. 102:11, 23, 24. 2 C *5:1. **as a**. Is 1:8. 13:20. **I have** Jb *7:6. 9:25, 26. 14:2. Ja *4:14. **cut off**. or, rolled up. Is 34:4. He 1:12. The allusion is to a weaver's mode of finishing his work (J. A. Alexander). 2 T 4:7. Note the directive in ver. 1 to "set thine house in order"; Hezekiah says here he has "rolled up his life," as directed, in preparation for death. **a weaver**. ♪63G, Ge +50:23. i.e. I have cut off my life as a weaver (his thread). **he will cut**. Jb *6:9. 7:3-5. 17:1. Ps 31:22. 32:4. 109:23. **with pining sickness**. or, from the thrum. i.e. the ends of the threads by which the web is fastened to the beam. or, loom. **from day**. Jb 4:20. Ps 73:14. Commonly explained to mean *before tomorrow*, within the space of one day (J. A. Alexander).

13. **as a lion**. 1 K 13:24-26. 20:36. Jb 10:16, 17. 16:12-14. Ps 39:10. 50:22. 51:8. Da 6:24. Ho 5:14. 1 C 11:30-32. **break**. ♪22C32, Ps +2:9. Jb 9:17. 30:17. Ps 10:10mg. 51:8. La 3:4. **from day**. ver. 12n. Jb 4:20. Ps 88:13. 130:6. **an end**. Is 27:4, 5. Ps 55:4, 6.

14. **a crane**. Jb 30:29. Ps 102:4-7. **I did mourn**. Is 59:11. Ps 55:1, 2. Ezk *7:16. Na 2:7. **dove**. Is 59:11.

Le=1:14. Mt=10:16. **mine eyes**. Ps 69:3. 119:82, 123. *123:1-4. La 4:17. Jn 17:1. **O Lord**. Mt 6:9. **I am**. Ps 119:122. 143:7. **undertake for me**. or, ease me. Is *40:29. Jb *17:3. Ps 6:2-4. 61:1, 2. 2 C √12:9, 10.

15. **What**. Jsh 7:8. Ezr 9:10. Ps 39:9, 10. Jn 12:27. **spoken**. Mi *6:8. Mt *11:28-30. **himself hath done**. Ps 39:9. Ezk 14:23. Mk 7:37. Jn 13:7. **I shall**. Ph *4:6, 7. 1 P 5:6, 7. **go softly**. 1 K *21:27. **in the bitterness**. 1 S +1:10mg. 2 K 4:27. Jb *7:11. *10:1. 21:25. **soul**. Heb. *nephesh*, Ge +34:3.

16. **by these**. Is 64:5. Dt √8:3. Jb 33:19-28. Ps 71:20. Mt √4:4. 1 C 11:32. 2 C 4:17. He *12:10, 11. **life of**. Ps 119:25, 37, 40, 88, 107, 149, 156, 159. Mt +*10:28. 1 C 5:5. He +*12:23. Ja *1:18, 21. 2:26. 5:20. **spirit**. Heb. *ruach*, Ge +41:8. **so wilt**. Is 53:10. Jb 23:10. Ps 119:75. Mt 10:24, 25. 2 C 4:17. He 2:10. 1 P 5:10. **to live**. ♪96B, Ge +8:5.

17. **for peace I had great bitterness**. or, on my peace *came* great bitterness. Jb 3:25, 26. 29:18. Ps 30:6, 7. **in love to my soul delivered it from the pit**. Heb. loved my soul from the pit. Heb. *nephesh*, Ps +30:3. 40:2. 86:13. 88:4-6. Jon 2:6. **delivered**. Ge=37:24. Jb 33:24, 28. Ps 40:2. *103:3-5. 118:17, 18. 1 C +*15:55-57. Ph 2:27. **pit**. Heb. *shachath*, Jb +9:31. 33:18. **thou hast cast**. Is *43:25. Ex 34:6, 7. Ps 10:2. √32:1, 2. 51:9. 85:2. Je 31:34. Ezk 18:31. Mi *7:18, 19. Mk 2:5, 6. Ac 5:31. 13:38. Ep 1:7. Col 1:14. Ja *5:15. Re 7:14. **all my sins**. Ps 130:4, 7, 8. Je +*50:20. 1 J √1:7-9. **behind**. Contrast unforgiven sins said to be "before His face." Ps ●90:8. ●109:14, 15. Je ●16:17. Ho ●7:2.

18. **the grave**. Heb. *sheol*, Ge +37:35. ♪121J15. Metonymy of the Subject B578. The *grave* is put for the dead buried in it. **cannot praise**. Ps *6:5. 30:9. 88:10-12. *115:17, 18. +*146:4. Ec +*9:5, 6, 10. **not**. ♪63I1C1, Ge +2:6. **they that**. Nu 16:33. Pr *14:32. Mt *8:12. *25:46. Lk *16:26-31. **pit**. Heb. *bor*, Ge 37:20. **cannot hope**. Jb +*8:13. 11:20. 27:8. +*36:18. Ps *36:12. *112:10. Pr +*10:28. *11:7. ●14:32. Ezk ●x16:49, +*55, +60. Lk 16:26. Ac ●x3:21. 2 C *5:11. He +*9:27. Ju √7. Re 22:11.

19. **the living**. Ps 103:1, 2. *146:2. Ec +*9:10. Jn *9:4. **the father**. Ge +*18:19. Ex 12:26, 27. +*13:8, 14, 15. Dt *4:9, 10. +*6:6, 7, 20. Jsh *4:21, 22. Ps √78:3-8. 145:4. Jl 1:3. This affords sufficient clue to the nature of Hezekiah's predicament, and his need of a sign: he was "sick unto death" (ver. 1), surrounded by the Assyrian army, and childless. Hezekiah directs his prayer to the "God of David" (ver. 5), laying claim to the "sure mercies of David" which promised to him an heir for the throne as a provision of the unconditional and irrevocable Davidic Covenant (2 S +*7:15; Ps +*89:28, 33, 37; +*132:11; Is +*55:3; Ac +*13:34; Ro +*11:1, 2, 29). God furnished him a miraculous sign in his distress (whereby the shadow on the dial of Ahaz retreated ten degrees), granted him recovery from sickness and fifteen additional years of life, utterly defeated his enemies, and gave him a son three years later (Manasseh, i.e. *one who forgets*, a king of Judah remarkable for idolatry and cruelty. 2 K 20:21. 21:1-18. 2 Ch 33:1-20.) Note here Hezekiah's joyful anticipation of providing his son spiritual guidance, and compare a corresponding sentiment of joy upon the birth of children in his song of degree, Ps 128:3. Compare the central Psalm of the song of degrees, Ps +*127:3, selected by Hezekiah for his collection of fifteen songs

celebrating the fifteen years promised him.

20. **ready to save.** Ps 21:4. 116:9. Jn 11:25. **therefore.** Ps 9:13, 14. 27:5, 6. 30:11, 12. 51:15. 66:13-15. 145:2. **we will sing.** Is 26:19. Ps 16:11. 33:1. 89:1. 95:1, 2. 101:1. 105:1. **my songs.** Hezekiah's songs are the "songs of degrees," ten of which he composed himself (Ps 120, 121, 123, 125, 126, 127, 128, 129, 130, 132), and five others were taken as ready to hand (composed by David: Ps 122, 124, 131, 133; by Solomon, Ps 127): ten being the number of degrees the sun went backwards, and fifteen being the number of years added to his life. The word "degrees" means "steps," as noted in verse 8 above, the steps of the dial of Ahaz. There are numerous points of comparison between the experience of Hezekiah and the subject matter of these songs, as may be seen by consulting the references. **to the stringed.** This verse constitutes the subscription of the psalm or song of Hezekiah, as noted in verse 9 above, which contains the superscription. Ps 150:4. Hab 3:19, 21. **stringed instruments.** Jb 30:9. Ps 4, 61, 67, titles. 69:12. 76, title. 77:6. 150:4. Hab 3:19. **in the house.** Ps 122:1, 9. 134:1, 2.

21. **For Isaiah.** ♪107, Ge +10:5. 2 K 20:7. Mk 7:33. Jn 9:6. **lump of figs.** 1 S 25:18.

22. **said.** ♪107, Ge +10:5. **What.** 2 K 20:8. Ps 42:1, 2. 84:1, 2, 10-12. 118:18, 19. 122:1. Jn 5:14.

ISAIAH 39

The king of Babylon sends ambassadors to Hezekiah, who shows them all his treasures, 1, 2. Isaiah, hearing it, foretells the Babylonian captivity, and that his descendants would be eunuchs in the king of Babylon's palace, 3-7. Hezekiah submits to the sentence, 8.

1. A.M. cir. 3292. B.C. cir. 712. **Merodach-baladan.** i.e. *baal worshipper; baal is lord; thy rebellion, Merodach is not a lord; death and slaughter, Mars is a worshipper of Baal,* ❋S#4757h, only here. 2 K *20:12, etc., *Berodach-baladan. Merodach-baladan* (called *Berodach-baladan* by the mutation of the Hebrew letters *mem* and *baith*) is called *Mardock-empadus* in the *Canon of Ptolemy,* who says he began to reign at Babylon 26 years after the era of Nabonassar, A.M. 3283. B.C. 721. For, after the death of Belesis, Baladan, or Nabonassar, his father, several other princes succeeded in Babylon before the crown came to him (see Prideaux, sub an. 724). **king.** Is 13:1, 19. 14:4. 23:13. **sent letters.** 2 S 8:10. 10:2. 2 Ch 32:23.

2. **was glad.** 2 Ch 32:25, 31. Jb 31:25. Ps 146:3, 4. Pr 4:23. Je 17:9. **showed.** Is 10:13. 14:13. 47:10. 2 K 5:11. ‖20:13. Ex 5:2. 2 Ch 26:16. *32:25, 27, ‖31. Est 2:20. 3:5. Pr 11:2. 15:33. *16:18. 18:12. 25:6mg. Da 4:30. *5:23. Ob 3. Lk *12:15-21. **precious things.** *or,* spicery. 1 K 10:2, 10, 15, 25. 2 Ch 9:1, 9. **the silver.** Dt 17:17)Ϸ. **armor.** *or,* jewels. Heb. vessels, *or* instruments. 2 K 19:35. 20:15mg. 2 Ch 32:22, 23, *27. **and all.** Is 33:1, 23. 2 K ◐18:15, 16. **there was.** Ec 7:20. 2 C 12:7. 1 J 1:8. **nor in all.** Ge +√7:19 (♪102, Hyperbole/Overstatement). 1 K √18:10. Mt √5:29. **dominion.** 2 K 20:13. 2 Ch 8:6.

3. **came Isaiah.** Is 38:1, 5. 2 S 12:1. 2 K 20:14, 15. 2 Ch 16:7. 19:2. 25:15, 16. Je 22:1, 2. **What.** ♪22C2, Ge +3:9. **They are.** Dt 28:49. Jsh 9:6, 9. Je 5:15.

4. **What.** ♪22C2, Ge +3:9. **All that.** Jsh 7:19. Jb 31:33. Pr 23:5. √28:13. 1 J √1:9.

5. **Hear.** 1 S 13:13, 14. 15:16. **the Lord of hosts.** 1 S 1:3.

6. **that all.** Is 46:11. Dt 28:49-51. 2 K 20:17-19. 24:12, 13. 25:13-15. 2 Ch 36:10, 18. Je *20:5. 27:21, 22. 52:17-19. Da 1:2.

7. **of thy sons.** 2 K 24:12. 25:6, 7. 2 Ch 33:11. 36:10, 20. Je 39:7. Ezk 17:12-20. **they shall be.** Da ❋1:2-7. **eunuchs.** Ge +37:36mg. 2 K +8:6mg.

8. **Good.** Le *10:3. 1 S +*3:18. 2 S 15:26. Jb *1:21. 2:10. Ps 39:9. La *3:22, 39. Ja 5:10, 11. 1 P 5:6. **For.** 2 Ch *32:26. 34:28. Zc 8:16, 19.

ISAIAH 40

God commands his prophet and servants to comfort his people, by the assurance that their sins are forgiven, 1, 2. The ministry of John the Baptist foretold and described, 3-8. The glad tidings of the gospel proclaimed; and the tender care of the good Shepherd, 9-11. A sublime representation of the majesty of God, contrasted with the insignificance and vanity of the human race, as exposing the folly of attempting to liken any to him, 12-26. A gentle rebuke of God's people, for desponding in trouble; and encouraging thoughts suggested to them, 27-31.

1. **comfort.** ♪84, Ge +6:17. Is 3:10. 35:3, 4. 41:10-14, 27. 49:13-16. 50:10. 51:3, 12. √57:15-19. 60:1, etc. 61:1-3. 62:11, 12. 65:13, 14. 66:10-14. Ne 8:10. Ps 85:8. *94:19. Je 31:10-14. Zp 3:14-17. Zc 1:13. 9:9. Jn *14:26. 2 C √1:3, 4. 1 Th 4:18. He 6:17, 18.

2. **Speak ye.** Is 49:13. 61:2. 65:16-19. 66:10-13. Re 21:4, 5. **comfortably.** Heb. to the heart. Ge 34:3mg. 50:21mg. Jg 19:3mg. 2 Ch *30:22mg. 32:6mg. Ho 2:14mg. **warfare.** *or,* appointed time. 2 S +*11:1n. Jb +7:1mg. Ps 102:13, etc. SS 2:11-13. Je 29:11. Da *9:2, 24-27. 11:35. +*12:4, 9. Hab 2:3. Ac √1:7. Ga *4:4. Re 6:10, 11. 11:15-18. **that her iniquity.** Is *12:1. 33:24. 43:25. 44:22. 61:7. Ps 32:1. Je 31:33, 34. 33:8, 9. 1 C +*6:9-11. **double.** ♪121L9, Ge +43:12. ❋S#3718h. Is ◐+*61:7h. Ge 43:22. Jb 11:6h. 41:13h. √42:10-12. Je 16:18. 17:18. Da 9:12. Zc 1:15. 9:12. Ro 5:15, *20. 1 C *2:9. 2 C √4:17, 18. Ga 6:7-9. Ep 3:20. 1 T *5:17. Re 18:6.

3. **The voice.** Mt ▶3:1-3. Mk ▶1:2-5. Lk ▶3:2-6. Jn ▶1:23. **of him.** Ml *4:5, 6. Mt 11:10-12. **wilderness.** Je +*31:32n. **Prepare.** T#1892. Is 35:8. 54:17. 62:10, 11. Ml *3:1. 4:5, 6. Mk *❋1:2-4. Lk 1:16, +*❋17, 76, 77. Jn *1:19-25. **the Lord.** Heb. Jehovah; applied repeatedly to Jesus the Messiah in the New Testament, showing that in Scripture, Jesus is identified as Jehovah. Ne +*9:6. Ps 24:7, 10. Jn √5:23. *8:24. 1 C *12:3. 1 P +*2:3n. **make.** Is 11:15, 16. 43:19. 49:11. Ps 68:4. These words are ascribed to Isaiah by the Holy Spirit in Mt 3:3; Is 42:1-4 is so ascribed in Mt 12:17-21; Is 53:1 in Jn 12:38. Ro 10:16; Is 53:4 in Mt 8:17; Is 53:7, 8 in Ac 8:32, 33. Is 61:1 in Lk 4:18, 19. These statements of Scripture itself as to the authorship of this portion of this book are sufficient to settle the issue for all who accept Scripture as the Word of God. **desert.** Heb. *arabah,* Dt +11:30. Am +*6:14.

4. **valley.** Is *42:11, 15, 16. 1 S 2:8. Ps 113:7, 8. Ezk 17:24. 21:26. Lk 1:52, 53. 3:5. 18:14. **every mountain.** Is 2:12-15. Jb 40:11-13. **and the.** Is 42:16. 45:2. Pr 2:15. Ac 9:1-22. **straight.** *or,* a straight place. **plain.** *or,* a plain place.

5. **the glory.** Is 6:3. 11:9. 35:2. 60:1. Ex 33:18. Nu

14:21. Ps 72:19. 96:6. 102:16. Hab 2:14. Lk 2:10-14. Jn *1:14. *12:41. 2 C *3:18. 4:6. He +*1:3. Re 21:23. **all flesh.** ✍171E1, Ge +6:12. Is 49:6. *52:10. 66:16, 23. Je 32:27. Jl 2:28. Zc 2:13. Lk 2:32. 3:6. Jn 1:9. 17:2. Ac 2:17. T 2:11. **for the mouth.** Is 1:20. 58:14. Nu *23:19. Je 9:12. Mi 4:4.

6. **Cry.** See on ver. 3. Is 12:6. 58:1. 61:1, 2. Je 2:2. 31:6. Ezk 33:2-9. Ho 5:8. **All flesh.** ✍171Q6, Ge +6:12. Is 37:27. Ge +*6:3. Jb *14:2. Ps *90:5, 6. 92:7. *102:11. 103:15, 16. Ja 1:10, 11. 1 P ▶1:24, 25.

7. **withereth.** ver. 8. Is 15:6. 19:5. **the flower.** 1 P 1:23, 24. **fadeth.** ver. 8. Is 24:4. Ps 39:11. Pr 30:32. **spirit.** Heb. *ruach*, Ex +15:8. **bloweth upon.** Ps 103:16.

8. **the word.** T#41. Is 25:1. 46:10, 11. √55:10, 11. Ps 19:9. 93:5. *119:89-91, 142. Zc *1:5, 6. Mt √5:18. √24:35. Mk *13:31. Jn +*10:35. 12:34. Ro *3:1-3. 1 P *1:25. **for ever.** Heb. *olam*, Ex +*12:24.

9. **O Zion, that bringest good tidings.** or, O thou that tellest good tidings to Zion. Is *41:27. *52:7. Ezr 1:1, 2. Lk *24:47. Ro 10:18. **get.** Jg 9:7. 1 S 26:13, 14. 2 Ch 13:4. **O Jerusalem, that bringest good tidings.** or, O thou that tellest good tidings to Jerusalem. Ps +*122:6. 128:5. **lift up.** ✍144A12, Ge +22:13. Is 52:8. 58:4. Je 22:20. Ac 2:14. **be not.** Is 35:3, 4. 51:7, 12. Ac 4:13, 29. 5:41, 42. Ep *6:18, 19. Ph 1:28, 29. 1 P 3:14. **Behold.** Is +*9:6. *12:2. +*25:9. Ps +*45:6. 47:7, 8. Zc 9:9. 13:7. Jn √1:1, 14. +√20:28. 1 C 15:24, 25. Ph 2:5, 6. 1 T *3:16. He +√1:6, 8. 1 J 5:20, 21. Re 11:15. 19:16.

10. **the Lord God.** Is +*9:6, 7. 59:15-21. 60:1, etc. Zc 2:8-11. Ml 3:1. Jn 12:13, 15. **will come.** Jn 1:18. **with strong hand.** or, against the strong. Is 49:24, 25. 53:12. Mt 12:29. He 2:14. 1 J *3:8. **his arm.** Is *59:16. Ps *2:8, 9. 66:3. 110:1, 2, 6. Mt *28:18. Ep 1:20-22. Ph *2:10, 11. Re 2:26, 27. 17:14. *19:11-16. 20:11. **his reward.** Is 62:11. Mt +*16:27. Lk +*14:14. Re +*11:18. *22:12. **with him.** Mt *25:10, 31-46. Lk +*14:14. Ju 14, 15. Re +*11:18. **his work.** or, recompence for his work. Is 49:4. Ro 2:5, 6. 14:10. 2 C √5:10.

11. **feed.** T#838. Is 42:3. *49:9, 10. 63:11. Ge 49:24. Ne +*9:6. Ps *23:1, etc. 77:20. 78:52, 53, 71, 72. 80:1. Pr 16:4. SS 1:7. Ezk 34:12-14, 23, 31. 37:24. Mi 5:4. Jn *10:11-16. Ep 5:25-27, 29. He *13:20. 1 P *2:25. 5:4. Re 2:1. 7:17. **his flock.** Lk 12:32. **like a shepherd.** Zc 13:7. Mt 26:31. Jn 10:11. **he shall gather.** Is 42:3. Ge 33:13. Ezk 34:16. Jn 21:15-17. 1 C 3:1, 2. **and carry.** Is 46:4. 63:9. **his bosom.** ✍22A19, Ps 74:11. **shall gently lead.** A beautiful image, as Bp. Lowth remarks, expressive of the tender attention of the shepherd to his flock. That the greatest care in driving the cattle, in regard to the dams and their young, was necessary, appears clearly from Jacob's apology to his brother Esau, Ge 33:13; which is set in a still stronger light by the following remarks of Sir J. Chardin: "Their flocks feed down the places of their encampments so quick, by the great numbers that they have, that they are obliged to remove them often, which is very destructive to their flocks, on account of the young ones, who have not strength enough to follow." **gently.** T#1909. Is *42:3. Mt 11:28. 12:15, 20. He ✱4:15. **lead.** T#1902. Is 11:1-9. 42:1-4. Mt ✱12:15, 20. Jn 10:+*4, ✱11-18. He ✱4:15. **are with young.** or, give suck. Ps +*78:71.

12. **Who hath.** Ps 33:8, 9. 93:1, 2. **measured.** Is 48:13. Jb 11:7-9. 38:4-11. Ps 102:25, 26. 104:2, 3. Pr

8:26-28. 30:4. He 1:10-12. Re 20:11. **span.** ✍22A16, Ex +8:19. **measure.** Heb. tierce. i.e. *a third*. Ps 80:5. Probably the third part of an ephah (CB). **weighed.** Jb 28:25.

13. **Who.** ✍85C, Ge +18:14. **hath directed.** Jb 21:22. 36:22, 23. Lk 10:22. Jn 1:13. *3:8. Ro ▶11:34. 1 C 2:9-11, ▶16. Ep +*1:11. **Spirit.** Heb. *ruach*, Is +48:16. God the Holy Spirit is unequaled (Je ◐+*10:6. Mt ◐+*8:27. +*28:19n). Is 11:2. 42:1. **being.** ✍63I1A, Ex +12:4. or, who as. **his counsellor.** Heb. man of his counsel. lit. "and a man, his counsellor." Compare for similar grammatical construction the renderings of the following passages (Ge 13:8mg. Ex 2:14mg. Le 22:12mg. Jsh 2:1n. Jg 6:8mg. 11:1mg. 15:15n. 16:1. 19:1mg. 21:12mg. 1 K 1:2mg. 2 K 9:4n. Je 3:3. 20:15mg. Lk 2:15mg). Is +*9:6. 41:28. Jb 15:8. 29:4. Ps *119:24mg. Je 23:18.

14. **With.** ✍85C, Ge +18:14. **counsel.** Is +*9:6. Ro *11:33-36. Ep +*1:11. **instructed him.** Heb. made him understand. Jb 40:2. 42:1-3. **understanding.** Heb. understandings. 1 C 12:4-6. Col 2:3. Ja 1:17.

15. **the nations.** ver. 22. Jb 34:14, 15. Je 10:10. **are as.** 1 S 14:16. **drop.** ✍111, Ge +18:27. **small dust.** ✍111, Ge +18:27. Ps 103:14. **the isles.** Is 11:11. 41:5. 59:18. 66:19. Ge 10:5. Da 11:18. Zp 2:11.

16. **not sufficient.** Ne 10:39. **nor.** Ps 40:6. *50:10-12. Mi 6:6, 7. He 10:5-10.

17. **as nothing.** ✍111, Ge +18:27. F/L Is +5:8 (no). 1 S 14:16. Jb 25:6. Ps 62:9. Da *4:34, 35. 2 C 12:11. **vanity.** ver. 23. Is 24:10. Ge 1:2.

18. **To whom.** ver. 25. Is *46:5, 9. Ex 8:10. 9:14. *15:11. *20:4. Dt 4:15, 16. 33:26. 1 S 2:2. Jb 40:9. Ps 8:5n. 86:8-10. 89:6, 8. 113:5. Je *10:6, 16. Mi 7:18. Ac *17:29. Col +√1:15. He +*1:3.

19. **workman.** Is 37:18, 19. 41:6, 7. 44:10-12. 46:6, 7. Ex 32:2-4. Jg 17:3, 4. Ps 115:4-8. 135:15, 18. Je 10:3-5, 9. Ho 8:6. Hab 2:18, 19.

20. **is so impoverished that he hath no oblation.** Heb. *is* poor of oblation. **chooseth.** Is 2:8, 9. 44:13-19. Je 10:3, 4. Da 5:23. **shall not.** Is 41:7. 46:7. 1 S *5:3, 4.

21. **not known.** Is 27:11. 44:20. 46:8. Ps 19:1-5. 115:8. Je 10:8-12. Ac *14:17. Ro *1:19-21, 28. 3:1, 2.

22. **It is he that sitteth.** or, Him that sitteth, etc. Is 19:1. 66:1. Ps 2:4. 29:10. 68:33. **sitteth.** ✍22D3I. Anthropomorphism B892. God is spoken of as being in circumstances of place: sitting upon the circle or horizon of the earth, and the arch of heaven, as it appears to us, high above all. **the circle.** Jb 22:14 (circuit). Ps 8:27 (compass). This is a reference to the fact that the earth is round, just as in Job 26:7 we have the statement that "he hangeth the earth upon nothing," both remarkable declarations since proved scientifically accurate. **the inhabitants.** ver. 15, 17. Nu 13:33. Ps 33:13, 14. **stretcheth.** Is 42:5. 44:24. 51:13. Jb 9:8. 37:18. 38:4-9. Ps 102:25, 26. *104:2. Je 10:12. Zc 12:1. He 1:10-12. **as a curtain.** Or, "as a thin veil," as Bp. Lowth renders; which he illustrates from the following passage from Dr. Shaw (Travels, p. 274). "It is usual in the summer season, and upon all occasions when a large company is to be received, to have the court sheltered from heat, or inclemency of the weather, by a *velum*, umbrella, or veil, as I shall call it; which, being expanded on ropes from one end of the parapet to the other, may be folded or unfolded at pleasure. The Psalmist seems to allude

to some covering of this kind, in that beautiful expression of spreading out the heavens as a curtain."

23. **bringeth**. Is 19:13, 14. 23:9. 24:21, 22. Jb 12:21. 34:19, 20. Ps 76:12. 107:40. Je 25:18-27. Lk 1:51, 52. Re 19:18-20.

24. **they shall not be planted**. Is 14:21, 22. 17:11. 1 K 21:21, 22. 2 K 10:11. Jb 15:30-33. 18:16-19. Je 22:30. Na 1:14. **he shall also**. ver. 7. Is 11:4. 30:33. 37:7. 2 S 22:16. Jb 4:9. Hg 1:9. **and the**. Is 17:13. 41:16. Jb 21:18. Ps 58:9. Pr 1:27. Je 23:19. Ho 13:3, 15. Zc 7:14. 9:14. **as stubble**. Is 5:24. Jb *21:17, 18. Ps 83:13. Na 1:10. Ml 4:1.

25. **To whom**. ver. 18. Is √55:9. Dt 4:15-18, 33. 5:8. Ps 8:5n. 147:5. **liken me**. Ge ◐1:26. ◐3:5, 22. ◐5:1.

26. **Lift**. ⌐144A12, Ge +22:13. Is 51:6. Dt 4:19. Jb 31:26-28. Ps *8:3, 4. 19:1. **who hath**. Is 44:24. 45:7. 48:13. Ge *1:1. 2:1, 2. Ps 33:6. 102:25. 148:3-6. Je 10:11, 12. Jn *1:1-3. Col *1:16, 17. **bringeth**. Ps 147:4, 5. **by the greatness**. Ps 89:11-13. Je 32:17-19. **faileth**. F/L Is 34:16. 1 S 30:19. 2 S 17:22.

27. **sayest**. Is *49:14, 15. *54:6-8. 60:15. 1 S 12:22. Jb 3:23. Ps *31:22. *77:7-10. Je 33:24. Ezk 37:11. Ro +*11:1, 2. **my judgment**. Is *49:4. Jb 27:2. 34:5. Ml 2:17. Lk *18:7, 8.

28. **Hast thou not known**. Je *4:22. Mk *8:17, 18. 9:19. +*12:24. *16:14. Lk *24:25. Jn *14:9. 1 C *6:3-5, 9, 16, 19. **the everlasting**. Heb. *olam*, Ge +*17:7. Is √57:15. Ge *21:33. Dt *33:27. Je *10:10. Ro *16:26. 1 T *1:17. He *9:14. **the Lord**. Ne +*9:6. Jn *1:3. **the ends**. Is *45:22. 49:6. 1 S *2:10. Ac *13:47. **fainteth**. Is 59:1. 66:9. Ps *138:8. Jn 5:17. Ph *1:6. **no searching**. Is √55:8, 9. Ps 139:6. *147:5. Ro *11:33, 34. 1 C *2:16.

29. **giveth power**. Is 38:14. 41:10. Ge 18:14. 49:24. Dt 33:25. Jb 26:2. Ps 29:11. 68:35. *119:28. Zc 10:12. 2 C √12:9, 10. Ph *4:13. Col 1:11. He *11:34. **to the faint**. Is 50:4. Je 31:25. **no might**. ver. 26. Ho 12:3. **increaseth strength**. ver. 31. Is 41:10. Ex 15:2. 1 S *2:4. 2 S 22:33, 40. Ps 18:32, 39. 28:8. 29:11. 46:1. 68:35. 73:26. 81:1. 84:5. 86:16. 89:21. *138:3. Zc *12:8. Ro 14:4.

30. **youths shall**. Is 9:17. 13:18. Ps 33:16. *34:10. 39:5. Ec 9:11. Am 2:14. **faint**. Dt 20:8. Ml 1:13. Ro 2:7. 1 C √15:58. Ga *6:9. 2 Th 3:13.

31. **they that wait**. Is 8:17. 25:9. +√30:18. Ps 25:3, 5, 21. *27:14. 37:34. *40:1. 84:7. 92:1, 13. *123:2. La *3:25, 26. Ro 8:25. 1 Th 1:10. **renew**. Heb. change. Jg 16:28. Jb 17:9. 33:24-26. Ps 103:5. 138:3. 2 C 1:8-10. *4:8-10, 16. √12:9, 10. **strength**. Ps 18:1, 2. 68:35. **mount up**. Ex 19:4. Ps 84:7. SS 8:5. Zc 10:12. 2 C 11:5. 12:11. He 4:7. **as eagles**. Ex ◐19:4. Dt 32:11, 12. Ps 103:5. Mt ◐+*24:28. Lk ◐+*17:37. **run**. Ep 3:8. **walk**. ⌐45. Catabasis; or, Gradual Descent B432. The figure *Catabasis* here illustrates the effect of growth in grace. At first the believer *flies*; but as his experience increases, he *runs*, and at the end of his course he *walks*. Like Paul, who first said "I suppose I was not a whit behind the very chiefest *apostles*" (2 C 11:5. 12:11). Later he writes, I "am less than the least of all *saints*" (Ep 3:8); while at the end of his life he says, "I am the chief of *sinners*!" (1 T 1:15). For other instances of this figure see Je 9:1. La 4:1, 2. Ezk 22:18. Da 2:38, 39. Am 9:2, 3. Ph 2:6-8. **not faint**. Ps *27:13. Lk 18:1. 2 C 4:1, 16. Ga √6:9. He *12:1. Re 2:3.

ISAIAH 41

Jehovah calls on the nations to consider his works for Israel, and describes the zeal of the idolaters about their idols, 1-7. He gives many promises and predictions of assistance, victory, and prosperity to his people; and of the conversion of the Gentiles, 8-20. He challenges the idols of the nations to foretell future events and accomplish them, as he did; and predicts the conquests of Cyrus, and the deliverance of the Jews from captivity, 21-29.

1. **Keep silence**. Is 49:1. Ps 37:7mg. *46:10. Hab √2:20. Zc *2:13. **islands**. Is +*11:11. ⌐121J5. Metonymy of the Subject B574. Islands are put for their inhabitants. For other instances of this figure see Is 42:4. 51:5. **let the people**. ver. 6, 7, 21, 22. Is 8:9, 10. Jb 38:3. 40:7. Jl 3:10, 11. **strength**. Jb 26:2. Ro 5:6. **let us**. Is √1:18. Jb 23:3-7. 31:35, 36. 40:8-10. Mi 6:1-3.

2. **Who raised**. ver. 25. Is 45:13. 46:11. Ge 11:31. *12:1-3. *17:1. Ps 47:7-9. 105:5, 6. He 11:8-10. **the righteous man**. Heb. righteousness. ver. 10. **his foot**. Jg 5:15mg. **kings**. Ge 14:1, 8, 9. **gave**. ver. 45. Is 45:1. Ge 14:14, 15. Ezr 1:2. Ga 3:18. He 7:1. **as the dust**. ver. 15, 16. 2 S 22:43. 2 K 13:7. **as driven**. Is 40:24.

3. **pursued**. Is 5:11. Ge *14:14, 15⌐P. **safely**. Heb. in peace. Is 57:2. Jb 5:24.

4. **hath**. ver. 26. Is 40:12, 26. 42:24. 46:11. **calling**. Is *44:7. 46:10. 48:3-7. Dt *32:7, 8. Ac *15:18. 17:26. **I the Lord**. Is 43:10. *44:6. *48:12. Re 1:11, *17. *2:8. *22:13. **the first**. Is *44:6. *48:12. **with the**. Is 46:3, 4. Mt 1:23. 28:20. **I am**. Is 43:10, 13. 46:4. 48:12. 52:6. Dt 32:39. 1 Ch ◐21:17. Jn +*8:58.

5. **isles**. Ge 10:5. Ezk 26:15, 16. **the ends**. Ex 15:14, 15. Jsh 2:10, 11. 5:1. Ps 65:8. 66:3, 4. 67:7.

6. **helped**. Is 40:19. 44:12. 1 S *4:6-9. 5:3-5. Da 3:1-7. Ac 19:24-28. **said to**. 1 Th 4:18. **of good courage**. Heb. strong. Is 35:4. Jl 3:9-11.

7. **the carpenter**. Is 40:19. 44:12-15. 46:6, 7. Je 10:3-5, 9. Da 3:1, etc. **goldsmith**. *or*, founder. Jg 17:4. **him that smote the anvil**. *or*, the smiting. **saying, it is ready for the sodering**. *or*, saying of the solder, It *is* good. **that it**. Is 40:20. 46:7. Jg 18:17, 18, 24.

8. **thou**. Is 43:1. 44:1, 2, 21. 48:12. 49:3. Ex 19:5, 6. Le 25:42. Dt 7:6-8. 10:15. 14:2. Ps 33:12. 105:6, 42-45. 135:4. Je 33:24. **the seed**. Mt 3:9. Lk 1:54, 55. Jn 8:33-44. Ro 4:12, 13. 9:4-8. Ga 3:16, 19. 4:22-31. He 2:16. **my friend**. Ge 18:17. 2 Ch 20:7. Mt=17:5. Jn *15:14, 15. Ja ▶2:23.

9. **whom**. ver. 2. Jsh 24:2-4. Ne 9:7, etc. Ps 107:2, 3. Lk 13:29. Re 5:9. **called**. Dt 7:7. 1 C 1:26-29. Ja *2:5. **I have chosen**. Ge 12:1. Dt *7:6▶P. *10:15▶P. 14:2▶P. Jsh 24:2-4. Ne 9:7. Ac 7:2-7. Ro +*11:29. **not cast**. Is 42:3. +*55:3. 1 S √12:22. 1 K √11:39. Ps √94:14. Je +√33:25, 26. Zc *10:6. Ro +*11:1, 2.

10. **Fear thou not**. ver. 13, 14. Is *12:2. 43:1, 5. 44:2. *51:12, 13. Ge *15:1. Dt 20:1. 31:6-8▶P. Jsh *1:9. 2 Ch 20:17. 32:8. Ps *27:1. +*34:4. *46:1, 2, 7, 11. 56:3, 4. Lk 1:13, 30. *2:10, 11. Ro √8:31. 2 T +*1:7. **for I am thy God**. T#822. Is 52:7. 54:5. 60:19. Ge 17:7. Le 26:12. 1 Ch 12:18. Ps 48:14. 147:12. Je 30:22. Ezk 34:24, 31. Ho *1:9. Zc *13:9. Jn *8:54, 55. 2 C 6:16. He *8:10. 11:16. Re *21:3. **I will strengthen**. Is 12:2. 40:29-31. Dt *33:27-29. Ps 27:1. 29:11. Zc 10:12. 2 C √12:9. Ep *3:16. Ph √4:13. **will**

help. Is 30:7. 2 Ch 32:8. Ps 60:11. Ro √8:31. **I will uphold**. Ps *37:17, 23, 24. 41:12. *63:8. 119:117. *145:14. **the right**. Ge +48:13. Ps 65:5. *89:13, 14. 99:4. 144:8, 11.

11. **all they**. Is 45:24. 49:26. 54:17. 60:12-14. Ex 11:8. 23:22)𝒫. Zc 12:3. Ac 13:8-11. 16:39. Re 3:9. **ashamed**. Je +20:11. **as nothing**. ver. 24, 29. Is 40:17. Da 4:35. **they that strive with thee**. Heb. the men of thy strife. Jb 31:35. **shall perish**. Is 60:12. Ps 37:1, 2, 7.

12. **shalt seek**. Jb 20:7-9. Ps *37:35, 36. **them that contend with thee**. Heb. the men of thy contention. **they that war against thee**. Heb. the men of thy war.

13. **will hold**. Is 43:6. 45:1. 51:18. Dt 33:26-29. Ps 63:8. 73:23. 109:31. 2 T 4:17. **Fear not**. T#955. ver. +10. Is 43:2. 46:4. Ps *32:8. 91:15. Mt *11:28. *28:20. 2 C 1:20. Ph *4:6, 7. He +*13:5. Re 1:17. **help thee**. Is 50:9. Ps 119:173.

14. **thou worm**. ♪111, Ge +18:27. Jb 25:6. Ps *22:6. **Jacob**. Is 43:1. 44:1, 2. **men**. or, few men. Dt 7:7. Mt √7:14. Lk *12:32. Ro 9:27. **help thee**. Is 50:9. **saith**. Is 43:14. 44:6, 24. 47:4. 48:17. 49:7, 26. 54:5, 8. 59:20. 60:16. 63:16. Jb +*19:25. Ps 19:14. Je 50:34. Ga 3:13. T *2:14. Re 5:9. **thy redeemer**. Ge 48:16)𝒫. Ex 6:6)𝒫. 15:13)𝒫.

15. **I will make**. Is 21:10. 28:27. Mi 4:13. Hab 3:12. **teeth**. Heb. mouths. Ps 149:6 (two–edged). **thou shalt**. Ps 18:42. Mi 4:13. Zc 4:7. 2 C 10:4, 5.

16. **shalt fan**. Is 17:13. Ps 1:4. Je 15:7. *51:2. Mt *3:12. **thou shalt rejoice**. Is 12:6. 25:1-3. *45:24, 25. 61:10, 11. 1 S 2:1, 2. Je *9:23, 24. Hab 3:18. Lk 1:46, 47. Ro 5:11. 1 C 1:30, 31. 2 C 10:17. Ph 3:3g.

17. **the poor**. T#1271. Is 61:1. 66:2. Ex 22:25-27. Dt +*24:14, 15. Jg 6:6. 2 K 4:1. Jb 34:28. Ps 9:18. 34:6. *40:17. 68:9, 10. 69:29, 33. 70:5. 72:12, 13. 86:1. 102:16, 17. 109:22. Mt +*5:3. **needy**. Ps *40:17. +72:12. **seek water**. T#1744. Is 55:1. Ge *21:15, 16. Ex 17:3, 4, 6. Nu 20:5, 6. Jg 15:16-18. Ps 42:2. 63:1, 2. Am 8:11-13. Mt +*5:6. Lk *16:22-24. Jn *4:10-15. *7:37-39. Re 21:6. 22:17. **their tongue**. Ps 22:15. La 4:4. Lk 16:24. **I the Lord**. Is 30:19. Jg 15:18, 19. Ps 34:6. *50:15. 102:17. 107:5, 6. 2 C √12:9. **not forsake**. ver. +9. Is 42:16. Ge 28:15. 1 S +*12:22. Ps +√94:14. He +*13:5, 6.

18. **open**. Is 45:8. 53:7. Ge 8:6. **rivers**. Is *12:3. 30:25. 32:2. *35:6, 7. 43:19, 20. *44:3. 48:21. 49:9, 10. 58:11. Ps 46:4. 78:15, 16. 105:41. 107:35. Ezk 47:1-8. Jl 3:18. Zc 14:8. Re 7:17. 22:1. **fountains**. Heb. mayan, Ge +7:11 (✲S#4599h). **I will make**. Ex 17:6. 2 K 3:16. Ps 114:8.

19. **plant**. Is 27:6. 32:15. 37:31, 32. 51:3. *55:11, 13. 60:21. *61:3, 11. Ps *92:12-14. Ezk 17:22-24. 47:12.

20. **may see**. Is 43:7-13, 21. 44:23. 45:6-8. 66:18. Ex 9:16. Nu 23:23. Jb 12:9. Ps 109:27. Ep *2:6-10. 4:24. Col 3:10. 2 Th *1:10. Re *4:11.

21. **Produce**. Heb. Cause to come near. Is 1:18. Jsh *20:4. Jb 23:3, 4. 31:37. *38:3. 40:7-9. Mi 6:1, 2.

22. **and show**. Is 42:9. *43:9-12. 45:21. 48:14. Jn 13:19. 16:14. **happen**. Nu 11:23. Ru 2:3mg. **consider them**. Heb. set our heart *upon them*.

23. **that we may know**. Is 42:9. *44:7, 8. 45:3. 46:9, 10. Ps +*82:1, 6, 7. Ezk *33:33. Jn 13:19. *14:29. Ac 15:18. **do good**. Is +*45:7. 46:7. Je 10:5.

24. **ye are**. ver. 29. Is *44:9, 10. Ps 115:8. Je 10:8, 14. 51:17, 18. 1 C √8:4. **of nothing**. or, *worse* than nothing. **of nought**. or, *worse* than of a viper. Is 30:6.

59:5. **an abomination**. Is *66:24. Dt 7:26. *27:15. Re 17:5.

25. **I have**. Jehovah here, by the mouth of the prophet, predicts the victories of Cyrus over the Chaldeans and their allies, at least 150 years before the event, as one instance of his foreknowledge and invincible power. Media lay north of Babylon, and Persia eastward; and Cyrus commanded the forces of both these nations; and, by his wonderful success, he trampled down mighty monarchs as mortar, and as the potter treads the clay. **raised**. Is 21:2. 44:28. 45:1-6, 13. 46:10, 11. Je 51:27-29. **he shall come**. Ml 4:2, 3. **the rising of the sun**. Jg 5:31. **shall he call**. Is 45:3, 4. 2 Ch 36:22, 23. Ezr *1:2, 3. **come upon**. ver. 2. Is 10:6. 2 S 22:43. Mi 7:10. Zc 10:5. **princes**. Heb. *seganim*, the title of Babylonian governors and prefects of provinces, only occurrence in Isaiah (CB). Ezr 9:2 (rulers). Ne 2:16, 16. 4:14, 19. 5:7, 17. 7:5. 12:40. 13:11. Je 51:23, 28, 57. Ezk 23:6, 12, 23. **as the potter**. Je *18:1-6.

26. **declared**. ver. 22. Is 43:9. 44:7. 45:21. Hab 2:18-20. **righteous**. ver. 23.

27. **first**. ver. 4. Is 43:10. 44:6. 48:12. Re 2:8. **I will give**. Is *40:9. 44:28. 52:7. Ezr 1:1, 2. Na 1:15. Ml 3:1. Lk 1:76-80. 2:10, 11. Ro *10:15.

28. **I beheld**. Is *45:21. *63:5. Da 2:10, 11. 4:7, 8. 5:8. **answer**. Heb. return. Ex 19:8.

29. **they are all**. ver. 24. Is 44:9-20. Ps 115:4-8. 135:15-18. Je *10:2-16. Hab *2:18, 19. **vanity**. Is 58:9. Ps 10:7. **molten images**. 2 Ch +34:3. Je 10:14. 51:17. **wind**. Je 5:13.

ISAIAH 42

Jehovah calls on men to behold the Messiah; and predicts his character, ministry, and kingdom, 1-4, and states his commission to Jews and Gentiles, 5-7. He declares that he will glorify himself in fulfilling his predictions, and calls on the nations to rejoice in and praise him, 8-12; promises to remove every obstacle to the conversion of the Gentiles, and denounces the confusion of idolaters, 13-17; predicts the blind and obstinate unbelief of the Jews, and their rejection and consequent miseries, 18-25.

1. **my servant**. Is 43:10. *49:3-6. *52:13. *53:11. Ex +28:39 (girdle). Ps=106:23. Mt ▶12:18-21. Lk 23:35. Ph *2:6-8. **whom I**. Is 49:7, 8. 50:4-9. Jn 16:32. **mine elect**. Ps 89:19, 20. Jn *6:27. 1 P 2:4, 6. **my soul**. Heb. *nephesh*, Ge +34:3; Le +26:11n. ♪22A1, Le +26:11. Je 9:9. Am 6:8h. Mt *3:17. *17:5. Mk 1:11. Lk 3:22. Ep *1:4, 6. Col 1:13mg. He 10:38. **I have**. Is *11:2-5. 59:21. 61:1. Mt 3:16. Mk 1:10. Lk 3:22. Jn 1:32-34. √3:34. Ac 10:38. **my spirit**. Heb. *ruach*, Ge +6:3; +41:38. Is +*48:16. Ac +*5:4n. The Trinity is seen here, for we have the Father as the speaker; the Son as the servant, the Messiah; and the Holy Spirit. All three persons of the Trinity are also mentioned together in Mt 3:16, +*17; +√28:19n; Lk 1:35; Jn 14:16, 26; 15:26; Ro *15:30; 1 C *12:4-6; 2 C 13:14; Ep 2:18; 4:4-6; 2 Th 3:5; He 9:14; 1 P 1:2; 1 J 5:7; Ju 20, 21; Re 1:4, 5. **he shall**. Is 32:16. 49:6. Ml *1:11. Mt 12:18. Ac 9:15. 11:18. 26:17, 18. 28:28. Ro 15:8-16. Ep *3:8. **to the Gentiles**. Is 11:10. Mt ✱12:17, 21. Jn ✱10:16. Ac ✱10:45, 47.

2. **not cry**. T#1907. Zc *9:9. Mt *11:29. ✱12:15-20. Lk 17:20. 2 T *2:24. 1 P *2:23.

3. **bruised**. Is 35:3, 4. 40:11, 29-31. 50:4, 10. *57:15-18. +58:6mg. 61:1-3. 66:2. Ps 103:3, 10, *13, 14. 147:3. Je 30:11-17. 31:18-20, 25. Ezk 34:16. Mt 11:28. 18:11-14. Mk 1:40, 41. Lk 22:31, 32, 60-62. Jn 8:10, 11. *20:19-21, 27. Ro 5:6, 8, 9. He 2:17, 18. **not break**. ſ175B, Ge +21:16. Is 40:11. Mt ✲12:15, 20. He ✲4:15. **smoking**. *or*, dimly burning. 1 S 3:2. **flax**. ſ121D9. Metonymy of the Cause B560. "Flax" is put for the *wick* made of it. For another instance of this figure see Is 43:17. **not**. ſ175B, Ge +21:16. **quench**. Heb. quench it. 2 S 21:17. 2 Ch 29:7. **he shall**. Is *11:3, 4. Ps 72:2-4. 96:13. 98:9. Mi 7:9. Jn 5:30. 18:37, 38. 1 T 6:13. Re 19:11.

4. **shall not**. Is +*9:7. +*49:5-10. 52:13-15. *53:2-12. Jn 17:4, 5. He 12:2-4. 1 P 2:22-24. **discouraged**. Heb. broken. Is 58:6mg. Ec 12:6. **and the isles**. ſ121J5, Is +41:1. ver. 12. Is 2:2-4. 11:9-12. 24:15, 16. 41:5. 55:5. 60:9. 66:19. Ge +*49:10. Ps *22:27. 72:8-11. 98:2, 3. Mi 4:1-3. Zc 2:11. Mt 12:21. Ro 16:26. 1 C 9:21. He 12:2. Ju 24, 25. **law**. Is +1:10nⱽℙ.

5. **he that created**. T#139. Is 40:12, 22, 28. *44:24. 45:12, 18. 48:13. Ge +*1:1. Jb 26:13, 14. Ne 9:6. Ps 33:*6, 9. 102:25, 26. 104:2, etc. Je 10:12. 32:17. Am 4:13. 9:6. Zc *12:1. Jn 1:+*1, *3, 14. Ep 3:9. Col *1:16. He 1:2, 10-12. 3:4. Re 4:11. **and stretched**. lit. they that stretched. Ge +1:26. **he that spread**. Ge 1:10-12, 24, 25. Ps 24:1, 2. *136:6. **he that giveth**. Ge +*2:7. Jb 12:10. 27:3. 33:4. 34:14. Jb *14:10. Ps 33:6. Ezk 37:5, 6. Da *5:23. Ac *17:25. **breath**. Heb. *neshamah*, Ge +2:7. **spirit**. Heb. *ruach*, Nu +16:22. Jb 32:8. Ec +*12:7. He +*12:9.

6. **called**. Is 32:1. 43:1. 45:13. 49:1-3. Ps +*45:3, 6, 7. Je *23:5, 6. 33:15, 16. Ro 3:25, 26. He +*1:8, 9. 7:2, 26. **and will hold**. ver. 1. Is 41:13. **will keep**. Is 27:3. **and give**. Is 49:8. Mt +*26:28. Lk 1:69-72. Ro +*15:8, 9, 2 C *1:20. Ga 3:15-17. He 8:6. 9:15. *12:24. 13:20. **for a covenant**. Is *49:8. Ge +*3:15. Ho ◐+*6:7. Ml *3:1. Mt √26:28. Ro 8:3. 1 C ◐+*15:45. Ga 3:21. He *10:5-10. +*13:20. **a light**. Is 49:6. 51:4, 5. 60:1-3. Lk ⅃2:32. Jn 8:12. Ac 13:47. 26:23. 1 P 2:9.

7. **open**. ver. 16. Is 29:18. 35:5. Ps 146:8. Mt 11:5. Lk 24:45. Jn 9:39. Ac *26:18. 2 C 4:6. Ep 1:17, 18. Re 3:18. **to bring**. ver. 22. Is *9:2. 49:9. 61:1. Ps 107:10-16. 146:7. Zc 9:11, 12. Lk *4:18-21. Ep *5:8. Col *1:13. 2 T *2:26. He *2:14, 15. 1 P 2:9. **sit**. Lk 1:79. ſ171J12. Synecdoche of the Species B633. To *sit* is used of a permanent condition in which one is *placed*. For other instances of this figure see Mt 4:16. Ac 18:11.

8. **I am**. Is *48:11. Ex 3:15ⱽℙ. Ne +*9:6. Jn √8:24. **that is**. Is 3:13-15. 4:5. +*6:3. Ps 29:1, 2. 83:18. 115:1. Jn +*8:58. 1 C +*12:3. **my name**. Ps +√9:10. +*68:4. +*83:18. Je 10:16. **my glory**. Is 48:11. Ex 20:3-5. 34:14. Jn √5:23. √17:5. 1 C +*2:8. Ja +2:1. Re *5:12, 13. **not give**. Ex 20:5ⱽℙ. **praise**. Heb. *halal*. F/L Is 13:10. 38:18.

9. **the former**. Ge *15:12-16. Jsh *21:45. 23:14, 15. 1 K 8:15-20. 11:36. **new things**. Is *41:22, 23. 43:19. 44:7, 8. 45:11. 46:9, 10. 48:5, 6. Je 1:5. Da 2:28, 29. Jn 13:19. Ac +2:23. *15:18. 1 P *1:10-12. 2 P *1:19-21. **I tell**. Dt +*29:29.

10. **Sing**. Is 24:14-16. 44:23. 49:13. 65:14. Ps 33:3. *40:3. 96:1-3. *98:1-4. ch. 117. 149:1. Ro 15:9-11. Re 5:9. 14:3. **ye that go**. Ps *107:23-32. 148:1-14. 150:6. **all that is therein**. Heb. the fulness thereof. **the isles**. ver. 4. Is 51:5. 60:9. Ps 97:1. Zp 2:11.

11. **Let the wilderness**. Is 32:16. *35:1, 2, 6. 40:3.

41:18, 19. 43:19. Ps *72:8-10. **lift**. ſ144A12, Ge +22:13. **Kedar**. Is 60:7. Ge *25:13. Ps 120:5. **let the inhabitants**. Je 21:13. 48:28. 49:16. Ob 3.

12. **give glory**. Is 24:15, 16. 66:18, 19. Ps *22:27. 96:3-10. ch. 117. Ro 15:9-11. Re 5:9, 10, *13. 7:9-12.

13. **go forth**. Is 41:15, 16. Re 6:2. 19:11. **as a mighty**. Is 59:16-19. 63:1-4. Ex 15:1-3. Ps *78:65, 66. 110:5, 6. Je 25:30. **stir up**. Pr 10:12. SS 2:7. **jealousy**. Ex 20:5ⱽℙ. Na 1:2. Zp 1:18. 3:8. **shall cry**. Is *31:4. Ho 11:10. Jl 3:16. Am 1:2. ſ22C9. Anthropomorphism B887. Human actions are attributed to God: crying out. For other instances of this figure see ver. 14. Ps 78:65. **roar**. ſ22F1. Anthropomorphism B894. Actions of certain animals are attributed to God: to bellow or roar. For other instances of this figure see Je 25:30. Ho 11:10. Jl 3:16. Am 1:2. **prevail**. *or*, behave himself mightily. Jb 15:25. 36:9. Ps *118:16. Re *1:7. 19:11.

14. **long time**. Heb. *olam*, Le +25:32. Jb 32:18, 20. Ps 50:21. 83:1, 2. Ec √8:11, 12. Je 15:6. 44:22. Lk 18:7. 2 P √3:9, 10, 15. **refrained**. Is 63:15. 64:12. Ge +45:1. 1 S 13:12. Est 5:10. **cry**. ſ22C9, ver. +13. **like a travailing**. Is 13:8. Je 6:24. Mt +24:8. **devour**. Heb. swallow, *or* sup up. Ob 16mg. Lk 12:49. ✲S#7602h. Jb 5:5. 7:2mg. 36:20. Ps 56:1, 2. 57:3. 119:131. Ec 1:5mg. Je 2:24. 14:6. Ezk 36:3. Am 2:7. 8:4.

15. **will make**. Is 2:12-16. 11:15, 16. 44:27. 49:11. 50:2. Ps 18:7. 107:33, 34. 114:3-7. Je 4:24. Na 1:4-6. Hab 3:6-10. Hg 2:6. Zc 10:11. Re 6:12-17. 8:7-12. 11:13. 16:12, 18. 20:11. **waste**. ſ102, Ge +2:24.

16. **I will bring**. Is 29:18, 24. 30:21. 32:3. 35:5, 8. 48:17. 54:13. 60:1, 2, 19, 20. Je 31:8, 9. Ho 2:14. Lk 1:78, 79. Ep 5:8. **lead**. Is 41:3. 58:11. Jsh 3:4. Ps 23:2. 25:12. *32:8. 43:3. Pr +*8:9. Ho 2:6. Lk *1:78, 79. Jn 9:25. 16:13. 2 C 4:3. **darkness**. Is 9:2. **crooked**. Is 40:4. 45:2. Ec 1:15. 7:13. Lk 3:5. **straight**. Heb. into straightness. Is 40:4. **These things**. Dt 31:6ⱽℙ. **not forsake**. Is +*55:3. Ps +√94:14. Je 32:39-41. Ezk 14:23. Ro 5:8-10. 8:29-31. 2 Th 2:13, 14. He +*13:5. 1 P 1:3-5.

17. **be greatly**. Is 1:29. 44:11. 45:16, 17. Ps *97:7. Je 2:26, 27. Hab 2:18-20. Re *22:15. **say to**. See on Is 44:17. Ex 32:4, 8ⱽℙ.

18. **ye deaf**. Is 29:18. 43:8. Ex 4:11. Pr 20:12. Ezk 12:2. Mk 7:34-37. Lk 7:22. Jn *8:43. *9:39. 2 C *3:15. Re 3:17, 18.

19. **Who is blind**. Is 6:9. 29:9-14. 56:10. Je 4:22. 5:21. Ezk 12:2. Mt 13:14, 15. 15:14-16. 23:16-24. Mk 8:17, 18. Jn 7:47-49. 9:39, 41. 12:40. Ro 2:17-23. 11:7-10, 25. 2 C 3:14, 15. 4:4. **my messenger**. Ml 3:1. Lk 7:23. **perfect**. i.e. *an intimate friend or trusted one* (CB). Heb. *meshullam*, to be at peace with. Nu 23:21. 2 S 20:19. Jb 22:21. Ps 7:4.

20. **Seeing**. Is 1:3. 48:6-8. Nu 14:22. Dt 4:9. 29:1-4ⱽℙ. Ne 9:10-17. Ps 106:7-13. 107:43. Jn 9:37-40. 11:47-50. **but thou**. ſ96D2, Is +1:29. Ro 2:21. **opening**. Is 58:2. Je 42:2-5. Ezk 33:31. Mk 6:19, 20. Ac 28:22-27. **heareth not**. Je 5:21. 6:10. Ezk 12:2. Mt 13:14. Jn 12:40.

21. **well**. Is 1:24-27. 46:12, 13. Ps 71:16, 19. 85:9-12. Da *9:24-27. Mt *3:17. 5:17. 17:5. Jn 8:29. 15:10. Ro 3:25, 26. 2 C *5:19-21. Ph 3:9. **he will magnify**. T#284. Is *66:2. Ps *40:8. √138:2. Pr +30:6 (T#50). Mt +*3:15. +*5:18 (T#42). Ro 3:31. 7:12. 8:3, 4. *10:4. Ga 3:13, 21. *5:22, 23. He *8:10. 1 J *3:4, 5. **it**. Heb. *or*, him. Jn 13:31, 32. 17:4, 5.

22. **a people.** Is 1:7. 18:2. 36:1. 52:4, 5. 56:9. 2 K *24:11-13. *25:9. Je 50:17. 51:34, 35. 52:4, etc. Lk 19:41-44. 21:20-24. **they are all of them snared.** *or,* in snaring all the young men of them. **are hid.** See on ver. 7. Is 14:17. 45:13. Ps 102:20. Je 52:31. **a spoil.** Heb. a treading. Is 51:23. Dt 28:29-33. Ps 50:22.

23. **will give.** Is √1:18-20. 48:18. Le 26:40-42. Dt 4:29-31. √32:29. Pr 1:22, 23. Je 3:4-7, 13. Mi *6:9. Mt *13:9. 21:28-31. Ac 3:19, 22, 23. 1 P 4:2, 3. **time to come.** Heb. after-time. Pr 29:11.

24. **gave Jacob.** Is 10:5, 6. 45:7. 47:6. 50:1, 2. 59:1, 2. 63:10. Dt 28:49. *29:24-28. 32:30. Jg 2:14. 3:8. 10:7. 2 Ch 15:6. 36:17. Ne 9:26, 27. Ps 106:40-42. Je 5:15. 25:8, 9. La 1:14, 18. Am +*3:6. Mt 22:7. **Israel.** Ge 32:28. 43:6. 45:26, 28.

25. **he hath poured.** Le 26:15, etc. Dt 32:22. Ps 79:5, 6. Ezk 7:8, 9. 20:34. 22:21, 22. Na 1:6. Re 16:1, etc. **and it hath.** 2 K 25:9. **he knew.** Is 9:13. Je 5:3. Ho 7:9. Re 9:18-21. 16:9. **yet he laid.** Is 57:11. Ml 2:2.

ISAIAH 43

Promises to Israel of support, deliverance out of trouble, and abundant honor and increase, 1-7. A challenge to idolaters and idols to equal these prophecies, or the miracles wrought by Jehovah for his people, 8-13. Predictions of deliverance from Babylon, attended with the ruin of that city; and of spiritual redemption, 14-21. Heavy charge against Israel, contrasted with the freeness of God's pardoning mercy to them, 22-28.

1. **created.** ver. 7, 15, 21. Is 44:2, 21, 24. Ps 100:3. 102:18. Je 31:3. 33:24, 26. Ep *2:10. **O Jacob.** Ge 32:27, 28. **Fear.** ver. 14. Is 35:9, 10. 41:+*10, 14. 44:6, 22-24. 48:17. 54:4, 5. 62:12. 63:16. Ex 15:13. Dt 31:8. Je *50:34. T *2:14. Re 5:9. **I have called.** Is 42:6. 44:5. 45:4. 49:1. Ex 33:17. Ac 27:20, 25. **thou art mine.** Ex 19:5, 6. Dt 32:9. Ezk 16:8. Zc 13:9. Ml 3:17. 2 T *2:19. He *8:8-10.

2. **When.** Mt *14:29, 30. **passest.** Is 8:7-10. 11:15, 16. Ex 14:29. Dt 31:6, 8)𝒫. Jsh 3:15-17. Ps *66:10, 12. *91:3, 5-7. Am 9:8, 9. Mt 7:25-27. He 11:29. **I will be with.** Is 41:10, 14. Dt 31:6-8. Jsh 1:5, 9. Ps *23:4. *46:4-7. *91:15. Da *3:25. Mt *1:23. Ac 18:9, 10. 2 C √12:9, 10. 2 T *4:17, 22. **not overflow.** Jb 28:11. Ps 93:3, 4. **when thou walkest.** Ps 23:4. Da *3:25-27. Zc 13:9. Ml 3:2, 3. 4:1. Lk 21:12-18. 1 C 3:13-15. He 11:33-38. 1 P 4:12, 13.

3. **the Lord.** Ex +*6:2, 3. **the Holy One.** Is 6:3. 30:11. 41:14. 45:15, 21. 49:26. 60:16. Le 19:2. Ps 22:3. *145:17. Ho *13:4. T *2:10-14. 3:4-6. Ju 25. **thy Savior.** Is +*63:16. T *3:5. **I gave.** Ex *10:7. 2 Ch 14:9-14. Pr 11:8. 21:18. **Egypt.** 𝒥121J14, Ge +*47:15. Ps 68:31. **Ethiopia.** 𝒥121J14, Ge +*47:15. Is 20:3. **Seba.** 𝒥121J14, Ge +*47:15. Ps 72:10. **for thee.** Pr 11:8. 21:18.

4. **precious.** Ex 19:5, 6. Dt *7:6-8. 14:2. 26:18. 32:9-14. Jb 28:10. Ps 135:4. Ml 3:17. T *2:14. 1 P *2:9. **thou hast been.** Ge *12:2. Ps 112:9. Jn *5:44. 1 P 1:7. **I have.** Je 31:3. Ho 11:1. Ml 1:2. Jn 16:27. 17:23, 26. Ro *8:32. Re 3:9. **life.** *or,* person. Heb. *nephesh,* soul, Ge +*44:30.

5. **Fear not.** ver. 2. Is 41:10, 14. 44:2. Je *30:10, 11. 46:27, 28. Ac 18:9, 10. **I will.** Is √11:11, 12. 27:12, 13. 49:12. 60:1-11. 66:19, 20. Dt 30:3. 1 K 8:46-51. Ps 22:27-31. *50:5. 106:47. 107:3. Je 30:18, 19. 31:8,

9. Ezk √36:24-27. *37:21-28. 39:25-29. Mi 2:12. Zc 8:7. Lk 13:29. Jn 10:16. **gather thee.** Mt 24:31. Mk 13:27.

6. **to the north.** Je +*23:8. Ezk +*38:6, 15n. **bring my sons.** Is √11:11. 18:7. Je 3:14, 18, 19. Ho 1:10, 11. Ro 9:7, 8, 25, 26. 2 C 6:17, 18. Ga 3:26-29. **ends of the earth.** Ps 72:8. Je +*31:8. Ezk 38:8n.

7. **every one.** Ho 1:10. Ac 11:26. Ep 3:14, 15. 2 T *2:19. **called.** Is 62:2-5. 63:19. Je 33:16. Ac *11:26. Ja 2:7. Re 3:12. **for I.** ver. 1. Is 29:23. Ps 95:6, 7. *100:3. Jn √3:3-7. 2 C √5:17. Ga *6:15. Ep *2:10. Ph *1:6. T *3:5-7. He *13:20, 21. **for my.** ver. *21. Is 48:11. Ps *50:23. Jn 15:8. Ro 9:23. Ep *1:5, 6, 12. *2:4-7. 1 P *2:9. *4:11, 14. Re 4:11.

8. **Bring forth.** Is *6:9. 42:18-20. 44:18-20. Dt 29:2-4. Je 5:21. Ezk *12:2. 2 C √4:4-6. **the blind people.** Is 6:10. 42:19, 20. Je 5:21. Ezk 12:2. Mt 13:14. Ac 28:26, 27. **the deaf.** Mt 13:43.

9. **all the.** Is 45:20, 21. 48:14. Ps 49:1, 2. 50:1, 4. Jl 3:11. **who among.** Is 41:21-26. 44:7-9. 46:10. 48:5, 6. **that they may.** ver. 26. Jsh 24:15-24. 1 K 18:21-24, 36-39. Ro 3:4. **truth.** Jn 18:37, 38.

10. **my witnesses.** ver. 12. Is 44:8. Jn 1:7, 8. 15:27. Ac +*1:8. 5:32. 10:41. Ro 3:1, 2. 1 C √15:15. He 12:1. The disciples in the New Testament emphatically gave their witness of the bodily resurrection (there is no other kind of resurrection!) of Jesus Christ. Ac √1:8. 2:24, 32. 3:15, 26. 4:10, 33. 5:30. 10:40. 13:30, 33, 34. *17:30, 31. Ro 4:24. 1 C 6:14. 2 C 4:14. Ga 1:1. Ep 1:20. Col 2:12. 1 Th 1:10. 2 T 2:8. He 13:20. 1 P 1:21. Notice the single, consistent note present in all their witness as seen in the above passages: the resurrection of Christ. Belief in the resurrection of Christ's physical body (which He himself predicted in Jn +*2:19, 21) is made a matter essential to salvation by the apostle Paul in Ro +√10:9, 10. Any religious faith which claims to be Biblical must share the same emphasis and declare the same truth the Bible itself contains. **saith the Lord.** Ne +*9:6. 1 C +*12:3. **and my servant.** Is 42:1. *55:4. Ph *2:7. Col 1:7. Re 1:2, *5. 3:14. **ye may know.** Is 40:21, 22. 41:20. 45:6. 46:8, 9. Jn 8:12. 10:9, 14. *17:3. √20:31. **I am he.** Is 41:4. 44:6-8. Mk ◉13:6. Jn 4:26. *8:19, 20, +√24, 45, +√58. 13:19. **before me.** Ps 90:2. 93:2. Pr 8:22, 23. Mi +*5:2. Jn +√8:58. Col √1:17. **no God formed.** *or,* nothing formed of God. Heb. *El,* Ex +15:2. **no God.** Dt *32:39. Mk +*12:32. Jn +*1:1. **formed.** Ph +*2:6, 11. Re +*3:14.

11. **I, even I.** ver. 25. Ne +*9:6. 1 C *12:13. **am the Lord.** ver. 3. Is *12:2. *45:21, 22. Dt 6:4. Ho 1:7. 13:4. Lk 1:47. 2:11. Jn √10:28-30. Ac √4:12. T *2:10, √13. *3:4-6. 2 P 3:18. 1 J 4:14. 5:20, 21. Ju 25. Re 1:11, 17, 18. 7:10-12. **beside me.** Dt *32:39. Ps 49:7. Pr 8:22-31. **no savior.** Is +*63:16. 1 S ◉14:45. 2 K ◉13:5. Ne ◉9:27. Ho *13:4. Ob ◉21. Lk *1:46, 47. *2:11. Ac √4:12. 1 T 1:1. 2:3. 4:10. 2 T 1:10. T 1:3. 2:10. 3:4. 2 P 2:20. 1 J *4:14. Ju *25.

12. **declared.** Is 37:7, 35, 36. *46:10. 48:4-7. **no strange.** Dt *32:12, 16)𝒫. Ps *81:8-10. **my witnesses.** ver. 10. Is 37:20. 44:8. 46:9.

13. **before.** Is *57:15. Ps 90:2. 93:2. Pr 8:23. Mi +*5:2. Hab 1:12. Jn +*1:1, 2. *8:58. 1 T 1:17. He √13:8. Re +*1:8. **none that can.** Dt 28:31. 32:39. Ps 50:22. Ho 2:10. 5:14. Jn √10:27, 28. **I will work.** Is 46:10. Jb 9:12. 34:14, 15, 29. 42:2. Pr +*21:30. Da *4:35. Ro 9:18, 19. Ep +*1:11. Ph *2:13. **let it.** Heb.

turn it back. Is 1:25, 26. *14:27. Jb *9:12. Je +2:24mg.
Am 1:3, 6, 9, 11, 13. 2:1, 4, 6.

14. **the Lord.** ver. 1. Is 44:6. 54:5-8. Ps 19:14. Re
5:9. **For.** ver. 3, 4. Is 44:24-28. *45:1-5. Je 50:2-11,
17, 18, 27-34. 51:1-11, 24, 34-37. Re 18:20, 21. **nobles.**
Heb. bars. Is +27:1mg. 45:2. Je 50:36mg. **whose cry.**
Ezk 27:29-36. Re 18:11-19.

15. **the Lord.** ver. 3. Is 30:11. 40:25. 41:14, 16.
45:11. 48:17. Je 51:5. Hab 1:12. Re 3:7. **your Holy
One.** 2 Ch 12:8. Ps 44:4. 89:18. Ac 27:23. **the creator.**
ver. 1, 7, 21. Is 33:22. 40:21-24. 44:2, 21, 28. 45:11-
13, 18. 51:13. 54:5. Je 27:5. 31:35, etc. 33:25, etc.
Mt 25:34. **your King.** Is 33:17, 22. Ps 74:12. 98:6. Jn
18:36, 37. Re 19:12, 16.

16. **maketh.** ver. 2. Is 11:15, 16. *51:10, 15. 63:11-
13. Ex *14:16, 21, 22, 29♦𝒫. Jsh *3:13-16. Ne 9:11.
Ps 74:13, 14. *77:19. 78:13. 106:9. 114:3-5. 136:13-
15. Je 31:35. Re 16:12.

17. **bringeth.** Ex *14:4-9, 23-28. 15:4. Ps *46:8, 9.
76:5, 6. Ezk 38:8-18. **they shall.** Is 14:20-22. Re 19:17-
24. 20:8, 9. **they are.** Is 1:31. **tow.** lit. flax. 𝒥121D9,
Is +42:3. Flax is put for the wick made of it.

18. **Remember ye not.** Is 46:9. *65:17. Dt 7:18.
8:2. 1 Ch 16:12. Je 16:14, 15. *23:7, 8. 2 C 3:10.

19. **I will do.** Is 42:9. 48:6. Je 31:22. Re *21:5. **I
will even.** Is *35:6-10. 40:3, 4. 48:21. Lk 3:4, 5. **rivers.**
Is *41:18, 19. 48:21, 22. Ex 17:6. Nu 20:11. Dt 8:15.
Ps 78:15-20. 105:41. Ezk 47:7, 8. Jl 3:18. Jn *4:10.
*7:37-39.

20. **beast.** Is 11:6-10. Ps 104:21. 148:10. Lk 10:17,
19. **owls.** or, ostriches. Heb. daughters of the owl. Is
+34:13mg. **I give waters.** Ex 17:6♦𝒫. Nu 20:11♦𝒫. **to
give drink.** ver. 19. Is 41:17. 48:21. 49:10. *55:1, 2.
Ge 24:19. Je 31:9. Jl 3:18. Jn *4:10, 14. *7:37-39. Re
21:6. 22:17. **my chosen.** Is 42:1. 65:15. 1 Ch 16:13.
Ps 33:12. Mk 13:20. 1 P ♦2:9. Re 17:14.

21. **This people.** ver. 1, 7. Is 50:7. 60:21. 61:3. Ps
4:3. *102:18. Pr *16:4. Lk 1:74, 75. 1 C √6:19, 20.
*10:31. Ep *1:5-12. 3:21. Col 1:16. T *2:14. He 13:15.
1 P *2:9.

22. **thou hast not.** Is 64:7. Ps 14:4. 79:6. Je 10:25.
Da 9:13. Ho 7:10-14. 14:1, 2. Ja *4:2, 3. **called.** 𝒥171J6,
Ge +4:26. **thou hast been.** Jb 21:14, 15. 27:9, 10. Je
2:5, 11-13, 31, 32. Mi 6:3. Ml *1:12-14. 3:14. Jn 6:66-
69.

23. **hast not.** Am 5:25. Ml 1:7, 8, 13, 14. 3:8. **small
cattle.** Heb. lambs, or, kids. Is 66:3. Ex 12:3mg,n.
honored. Is 1:11-15. 25:3. 66:3. Pr *15:8. *21:27. Am
5:21, 22. Zc 7:5, 6. Mt *11:30. **thy sacrifices.** T#1277.
Is 56:7. 1 K 18:33-36. Ps 20:1-4. Jon 1:16. **nor wearied.**
Is 1:14. Mi 6:3. Mt *11:30.

24. **no sweet.** Ex 30:7, 23, 24, 34. Je 6:20. **neither.**
Le 3:16. 4:31. Ps 50:9-13. **filled me.** Heb. made me
drunk, or, abundantly moistened. Is 34:5 (bathed),
7mg. 55:10 (watereth). Je 31:25 (satiated). La 3:15.
thou hast made. Is 1:14, 24. 63:10. Ps 95:10. Ezk 6:9.
16:43. Am 2:13. Ml 1:17. 2:13-17. **to serve.** 𝒥121E2,
Ge +42:38. Put by Metonymy of the Effect (of the
verb) for the judicial consequences of their sins. i.e.
*thy sins have caused the hard service and passion which
I endured on account of them* (B562). **wearied me.**
Is *7:13. Ml 2:17.

25. **even I.** ver. 11. Is √1:18. 44:22. Ne +*9:6. Ps
51:9. Je +*50:20. Da 9:9. Mi *7:18, 19. Mk +√2:7.
Ac *3:19. Ro *5:20. **am.** 𝒥63B, Ge +2:10. **blotteth
out.** 𝒥22C34, Ex +32:33. Is *44:22. Hab 1:13. Ro *3:26.

thy transgressions. Ps *103:12. Je 33:8. **for mine.** Is
37:35. 48:8-10. Ps 25:7, 11. 79:9. Ezk 20:9, 14, 22.
36:22, 32. Ep 1:6, 8. **will not remember.** 𝒥22C3, Ge
+8:1. Is √55:7. Ps *32:5. 79:8. Je 31:34. Mi *7:19.
Ep 1:7. He 8:12. 9:14. 10:17. 1 J √1:7, 9. Re *1:5, 6.

26. **Put.** Is √1:18. Ge 32:12. Jb 16:21. 23:3-6. 40:4,
5. Ps 141:2. Je 2:21-35. Ezk 36:37. Ro 11:35. **declare.**
ver. 9. Jb 40:7, 8. Ps *32:5, 6. Mt *7:7, 8. Lk 10:29.
*11:2, 4. 16:15. 18:9-14. Ro 3:24-26. 5:1. 8:33. 10:3.

27. **first father.** Nu 32:14. Dt 26:5. Ps 78:8. 106:6,
7. Je 3:25. Ezk 16:3, 45. Zc 1:4-6. Ml 3:7. Ac 7:51.
Ro √5:12. **and thy.** Is 3:12. 28:7. 56:10-12. Je 5:31.
23:11-15. La 4:13, 14. Ezk 22:25-28. Ho 4:6. Mi 3:11.
Ml 2:4-8. Mt 15:14. 27:1, 41. Jn 11:49-53. Ac 5:17,
18. Ro 3:19. **teachers.** Heb. interpreters. ✤S#3887h.
Ge 42:23. 2 Ch 32:31mg. Jb 16:20 (scorn). 33:23.

28. **I have.** Is 47:6. 2 S 1:21. Ps 89:39. La *2:2, 6,
7. 4:20. **princes.** or, holy princes. Ps 82:+*6, 7. Ge
12:15. Ex 1:11 (taskmasters). 2:14. 18:21, 25 (rulers).
and have. Is 42:24, 25. 65:15. Dt 28:15-20. 29:21-28.
Ps *79:4. Je 24:9. Da 9:*11, 14. Zc 8:13. Lk *21:21-
24. 1 Th *2:16. **to the curse.** Je 24:9. Da +*9:11. Zc
*8:13.

ISAIAH 44

*Jehovah promises to pour out his Spirit on the seed
of Israel, and to convert them to himself, 1-5. He declares himself to be the only true and eternal God,
and exposes the gross and stupid folly of idolaters, 6-
20. He calls on Israel to remember these things; and
promises forgiveness and many blessings; especially
deliverance by Cyrus from the Babylonian captivity,
21-28.*

1. **now.** Is 42:23. 48:16-18. 55:3. Ps *81:11-13. Je
4:1. Lk 13:34. He *3:7, 8. **O Jacob.** Is *41:8. 43:1.
Ge 17:7. Dt 7:6-8. Ps 105:6, 42, 43. Je 30:10. 46:27,
28. Ro 11:5, 6.

2. **that made.** ver. 21. See on Is 43:1, 7, 21. **formed.**
ver. 24. Is 46:3, 4. 49:1. Ps 46:5. 71:6. Je 1:5. Ezk
16:4-8. 20:5-12. He *4:16. **Fear.** Is *41:10, 14. 43:1.
Je 30:10. 46:27, 28. See on Lk +*12:32. Ro 8:30. Ep
*1:4. 1 Th 1:4. **Jesurun.** i.e. *upright; the righteous
one, a little righteous,* ✱S#3484h. Dt 32:15♦𝒫. 33:5,
Jeshurun, 26.

3. **pour.** "Roberts thinks there is an allusion here
to one mode of bathing practiced by Orientals, which
is to have water poured on the body by an attendant.
The Egyptian monuments give evidence that this mode
was practiced in Egypt" (James M. Freeman, *Manners
and Customs of the Bible*, Note 515, page 269). See
related notes (2 K 3:11n). Ezk 36:25. Ac +1:5. Re
19:13. **water.** 𝒥22K4, Je +2:13. Is *41:17, 18. 59:21.
Ezk 34:26. Jl 3:18. Jn 4:14. 7:37-39. Re 21:6. 22:17.
thirsty. Ps 42:2. Mt +*5:6. **floods.** Is 32:2. 35:6, 7.
43:19, 20. 48:21. 49:10. Ps 78:15, 16. 107:35. **dry
ground.** Ps 63:1. Mt 12:43g. **I will.** 𝒥95, Ps +7:13.
pour my. Is 32:15. 59:21. Pr 1:23. Ezk 36:25-30. 39:29.
Jl *2:28, 29. Zc 12:10. Ac *2:16, 17, 18, 33, 39. 10:45.
◗28:25, 26. T √3:5, 6. **spirit.** Heb. ruach, Ge +41:38.

4. **spring up.** Is 58:11. 61:11. Ge 39:3, 23. Dt 29:9.
Jsh +*1:8. Ps +*1:3. 92:13-15. Je 17:7, 8. Ac 2:41-
47. 4:4. 5:14. Col 1:6. **willows.** Nu 24:6♦𝒫. Ps 137:1,
2. Ezk 17:5. **water courses.** F/L Is 30:25.

5. **shall say.** T#107. Dt 26:17, 18. Mt 5:15, 16.
*10:32, 33. 26:27. Lk 12:8, 9. 22:19. Mk 8:38. 16:16.

Ro √10:9, 10. 1 C 11:26. 2 T 2:12. 1 J 4:15. **I am**. Dt 26:17-19. Ps 22:27. 116:16. Je *50:5. Mi 4:2. Zc *8:20-23. 13:9. **subscribe**. Ne 9:38. 10:1-29. 2 C *8:5. **the name**. Ga 6:16. 1 P 2:9.

6. **the Lord**. Ex 3:14. Dt +*32:39. **the King**. Is 33:22. 43:15. Ml 1:14. Mt 25:34. 27:37, 42. Mk 15:32. Jn √1:49. *12:13. **his redeemer**. ver. 24. Is 41:14. 43:1, 14. 48:17. 54:5. 59:20. Ge 48:16⊮℗. Ex 6:6⊮℗. 15:13⊮℗. Je 50:34. **the Lord of hosts**. Is *6:5. 54:5. Ex 15:26n. 1 S +1:3. Ps +24:10. Je 10:16. 50:34. 51:19. Zc 13:7. Jn *12:37-41. Ro 9:29. Ja 5:4. **I am**. ⨍63B, Ge +2:10. **the first**. Is 41:4. 48:12. Re +*1:8, 11, ▸17, 18. 2:8. 22:13. **am**. ⨍63B, Ge +2:10. **beside me**. ver. 8. Is 37:16, 20. 42:8. 43:+*10, 11. 45:6, 21, 22. Dt 4:*35, 39⊮℗. +*6:4. +*32:39⊮℗. Ps 86:10. Mk +*12:32. 1 T *3:16. **there is**. ⨍63B, Ge +2:10.

7. **who**. See on Is 41:22, 26. 43:9, 12. 45:21. 46:9, 10. 48:3-8. **since**. Is 41:4. Ge 17:7, 8. Dt 32:8. Ac *17:26. 2 Th 2:13. **ancient**. Heb. *olam*, Jb +22:15. lit. the everlasting nation. Ge +17:7. Ps 111:5, 7, 8. Ro +*11:1, 2.

8. **neither**. See on ver. 2. Is 41:10-14. Pr 3:25, 26. Je 10:7. 30:10, 11. Jn 6:10. **have declared**. Is 42:9. 48:5. Ge 15:13-21. 28:13-15. 46:3. 48:19. *49:1-28. Le ch. 26. Dt 4:25-31. ch. 28. **ye are**. Is 43:+*10, 12. Ezr 1:2. 8:22. Da 2:28, 47. 3:16-28. 4:25. 5:23-30. 6:22. Lk 24:48. Ac +*1:8. 14:15. *17:23-31. He *12:1. 1 J *1:2. **Is there**. See on ver. 6. Is 45:5, 6. *46:9, 10. Dt 4:35, 39. +*32:39. 1 S 2:2. 2 S 22:32. Je 10:6. Jn +√1:1. √10:30. **beside me**. ver. +6. Dt 4:35, 39. +32:39. Mk +*12:32. **no God**. Heb. no rock. F/L Is +26:4. Dt 32:4⊮℗, 31. Ps 18:31. 1 C 10:4.

9. **They that**. ⨍105, Ml +4:2. **make**. Is 41:24, 29. Dt 27:15. Ps 97:7. Je *10:2-8, 14, 15. **vanity**. Heb. *tohu*. Ge 1:2⊮℗. F/L Is +24:10. **and their**. Is 2:20, 21. 37:18-20. 46:1, 2, 6, 7. Jg 10:14. 1 K 18:26-40. Je 2:11, 27, 28. 14:22. 16:19, 20. Da 5:23. Ho 8:4-6. Hab 2:18-20. 1 C +*8:4. **delectable**. Heb. desirable. ⨍121R5, Ge +27:15. Da 11:38. **their own**. ver. 18, 20. Is 42:18. 43:8, 9. 45:20. Ps *115:8. 135:18. Ro 1:22, 23. 2 C √4:4. Ep 4:18. 5:8.

10. **formed a god**. 1 K 12:28. Je *10:5. Da 3:1, 14. Hab *2:18. Ac 19:26. 1 C +*8:4.

11. **all his**. Is 1:29. 42:17. 45:16. 1 S *5:3-7. 6:4, 5. Ps 97:7. Je 2:26, 27. 10:14. 51:17. **let them all**. See on Is 41:5-7. Jg 6:29-31. 16:23-30. 1 K 18:19-29, 40. Da 3:1, etc. 5:1-6. Ac 19:24-34. Re 19:19-21.

12. **The smith**. Is *40:19. 41:6, 7. 46:6, 7. Ex 32:4, 8. Je 10:3, etc. Ac 19:24, 25. **the tongs**. or, an ax. Je 10:3. **with hammers**. 1 K ◐6:7. **yea, he is**. Hab 2:13.

13. **he marketh**. Ex 20:4, 5. Dt 4:16-18, 28. Ac 17:29. Ro 1:23. **that it may**. Ge 31:19, 30, 32. 35:2. Dt 27:15. Jg 17:4, 5. 18:24. Ezk 8:12.

14. **heweth**. Is 40:20. Je 10:3-8. Ho 4:12. Hab 2:19. **strengtheneth**. or, taketh courage. **nourish**. Ho 9:12.

15. **he maketh a god**. See on ver. 10. Is 45:20. Jg 2:19. 2 Ch 25:14. Re 9:20.

16. **part thereof**. or, half of it. ver. 19. Ex 24:6. Je 10:3-5. **seen the fire**. lit. seen light. Is 24:15mg.

17. **Deliver me**. Is 36:19, 20. 37:38. 1 K *18:26. Da 3:17, 29. 6:16, 20-22, 27.

18. **have not**. ver. 9, 20. Is 45:20. 46:7, 8. Je 10:8, 14. Ro 1:21-23. **for he hath**. Is 6:10. 29:10. Ge +*19:11. Dt +*2:30. Ps 81:12. Mt 13:14, 15. Ac 14:16. Ro 1:28. 11:8-10. 2 C 4:3, 4. 2 Th √2:9-12. **shut**. Heb. daubed. Le 14:42. Ezk 13:10, 12, 14. 22:28. **cannot understand**.

Is 56:11. Ps 92:6. Pr 2:5-9. 28:5. Je 5:21. Da 12:10. Ho 14:9. Mt *12:34. Jn *5:44. √8:43. √12:39, 40. 2 P *2:14.

19. **considereth in his heart**. Heb. setteth to his heart. Is 46:8. Ex 7:23. Dt 32:46. Pr 24:32mg. Je +31:21. Ezk 40:4. Hg 1:5mg. Ho 7:2. **an abomination**. Dt 27:15. 1 K 11:5, 7. 2 K 23:13. **the stock of a tree**. Heb. that which comes of a tree.

20. **feedeth**. Jb 15:2. Ps 102:9. Pr 15:14. Ho 12:1. Lk 15:16. **a deceived**. 1 K 22:20-23. Jb 15:31. Ps 14:1-3. 97:7. Ho 4:12. Ro *1:20-22, 28. 2 Th √2:11. 2 T 3:13. 1 J 5:21. Re 12:9. 13:14. 14:9-11. 18:23. 20:3. **turned him**. Is 42:17. 45:16. **soul**. Heb. *nephesh*, Ge +12:13. **Is there**. Is 28:15-17. Je 16:19. Hab 2:18. 2 Th √2:9-11. 1 T *4:2.

21. **Remember**. Is 42:23. 46:8, 9. Dt 4:9, 23. 31:19-21. 32:18. ⨍121C2B. Metonymy of the Cause B554. Verbs of remembering are used to show a strong desire or wish for the thing mentioned or remembered. For other instances of this figure see Ezk 23:19. Ho ◐4:6. Jon 2:7, 8. 2 T 2:8. He 11:15. **thou art**. ver. 1, 2. Is 41:8, 9. 43:1, 7, 15. **O Israel**. Ge 32:26. **thou shalt**. Is +*41:9. *49:14-16. Ro 11:28, 29. He +13:5.

22. **blotted out**. ⨍22C34, Ex +32:33. Is √1:18. *43:25. Ne 4:5. Ps *32:1, 2. *51:1, 9. 103:12. 109:14. Je 18:23. 31:34. 33:8. Mi *7:18, 19. Ac 3:19. **as a thick**. Jb 37:11. La 3:42-44. **return**. Is 1:27. 43:1. 48:20. 51:11. √55:6, 7. 59:20, 21. Je 3:1, 12-14. Ezk *33:11. Ho *14:1-4. Lk 1:73, 74. 22:61, 62. 24:47. Ac *3:18, 19. 1 C √6:20. Ep *1:7. T *2:12-14. 1 P *1:18, 19. **have redeemed**. Is 38:17. Je 50:20. He 9:12. Re *1:5, 6.

23. **Sing**. Is 42:10-12. 49:13. 55:12, 13. Ps 69:34. 96:11, 12. 98:7, 8. Je 51:48. Lk 2:10-14. Ro 8:19. Re 5:8-14. 12:12. 18:20. 19:1-6. **glorified**. Is 26:15. 49:3. 60:21. Ezk 36:1, 8. 39:13. Ep 1:6, 7. 3:21. 2 Th *1:10-12. 1 P 4:11.

24. **thy redeemer**. ver. 6. Is 43:14. 48:17. 49:7, 26. 54:5, 8. 59:20. 60:16. 63:16. Ps 78:35. Je 50:34. Re 5:9. **and he**. ver. 2. Is *43:1, 7. 46:3, 4. 49:1. Jb 31:15. Ps 71:6. 139:13-16. Ga 1:15. **I am**. Is *40:22. 42:5. 45:12. 48:13. 51:13. Jb *9:8. 26:7. Ps *104:2. Je 51:15. **maketh all**. Col *1:16, 17. He 1:2. **by myself**. Jn *1:3. Ep 3:9. Col *1:16, 17. He *1:2, 10-12.

25. **frustrateth**. Is *47:12-14. 1 K 22:11, 12, 22-25, 37. 2 Ch 18:11, 34. Je 27:9, 10. 28:9-17. *50:36. **maketh**. Ex 9:11. Da 1:20. 2:10-12. 4:7. 5:6-8. **diviners**. Nu 24:1. ✹S#7080h: Is 3:2 (prudent). 44:25. Dt *18:10 (that useth), 14 (diviners). Jsh 13:22mg. 1 S 6:2. 28:8. 2 K 17:17 (and used). Je 27:9. 29:8. Ezk 13:9, 23. 21:21, 23, 29. 22:28. Mi 3:6, 7, 11. Zc 10:2. **turneth**. Is 19:11-14. 29:14. 2 S 15:31. 16:23. 17:23. Jb 5:12-14. Ps 33:10. Je 49:7. 51:57. Da 5:8. 1 C *1:20-27. *3:19, 20. **wise**. ⨍27, Ge +3:22. **knowledge**. ⨍27, Ge +3:22.

26. **confirmeth**. Is 42:9. Ex 11:4-6. 12:29, 30. 1 K 13:3-5. 18:36-38. Ezk 38:17. Da 4:14, 28, 29. Zc *1:6. Mt 26:56. Lk +*24:44. Ac 2:25-28. 2 P *1:19-21. **that saith**. Is 54:3, 11, 12. 60:10. Ezr 2:70. Ps 102:13-16. 147:2. Je 30:18. 31:4, 38-40. 33:7. Ezk 36:33-36. Da *9:25. Zc 2:4. 12:6. 14:10, 11. **and I will**. Is 58:12. Ne 1:3. 2:3. 3:1, etc. Am 9:14. **decayed places**. Heb. wastes. Is 61:4. Ezk 36:10.

27. **Be dry**. Is 11:15, 16. 42:15. 43:16. 51:15. Ps 74:15. Je *50:38. *51:31, 32, 36. Re *16:12.

28. **Cyrus**. Is 41:25. 45:1, 3. 46:11. 48:14, 15. Da 10:1. **my shepherd**. Is 63:11. Ps 78:71, 72. **shall per-**

form all. Ac ‖13:22. saying. Is *45:13. 2 Ch *36:22, 23. Ezr *1:1-3. 6:3, etc. foundation. Ezr 3:11.

ISAIAH 45

God promises Cyrus signal success, that he may liberate the Jews, 1-6. He declares his eternal Deity, as the Creator of all things; and promises glorious prosperity to his people, and sharply rebukes those who contended against his appointments, 7-14. The prophet declares his deep counsels, pronounces the confusion of idolaters, and assures Israel of salvation, 15-20. Jehovah reveals himself as "a just God and a Savior;" and swears by himself, that all shall bow to him, and that Israel shall be justified and glory in him, 21-25.

1. to his. Is 13:3. 44:28. 1 K 19:15. Je 27:6. Cyrus. i.e. *supreme power; the sun; spiritual sense,* *S#3566h. Is 44:28. 45:1. 2 Ch 36:22, 22, 23. Ezr 1:1, 1, 2, 7, 8. 3:7. 4:3, 5. Da 1:21. 10:1. whose. Is 41:13. 42:6. Ps 73:23. holden. *or,* strengthened. Ezk 16:49. 30:21-24. to subdue. Is 41:2, 25. Ezr 1:1. Je 50:3, 35-37. 51:11, 12, 20-24. Da 5:6, 28-30. 7:5. 8:3. to loose the loins. Jb 12:18, 21mg. Da 5:6, 30, 31. ♪22C39. Anthropomorphism B890. Human actions are attributed to God: loosening the loins. For another instance of this figure see Jb 12:21mg. Matthew Poole notes that this action signifies to weaken them, or it may signify to take away their girdle, which was about their loins, to wit, their power and authority, whereof that was an ensign, of which see on Jb 12:18; Is 22:21. This is the figure Metonymy of the Adjunct, ♪121S3AA B606. to open. All the streets of Babylon, leading on each side to the river, were secured by two-leaved brazen gates, and these were providentially left open when Cyrus's forces entered the city in the night, through the channel of the river, in the general disorder occasioned by the great feast which was then celebrated; otherwise, says Herodotus (i. 180. 191), the Persians would have been shut up in the bed of the river, as in a net, and all destroyed. The gates of the palace were also imprudently opened to ascertain the occasion of the tumult; when the two parties under Gobrias and Gadatas rushed in, got possession of the palace, and slew the king (Xenophon, lib. vii). Na 2:6. shut. Is 60:11. Nu 12:14, 15.

2. go before. Is 13:4-17. make. Is 40:4. 42:16. Ec 1:15. Lk 3:5. straight. ♪22C37, Ps +5:8. break. ♪22C32, Ps +2:9. Ps *107:16.

3. I will give. Ezr 1:7, 8. Je 27:5-7. 50:37. 51:53. Ezk 29:19, 20. Da 6:28. that thou. Is 41:23. Ezr 1:2. which call. Is 43:1. 48:15. 49:1. Ex 33:12, 17. by thy name. Ge 17:19. 1 K *13:2. 1 Ch 22:9.

4. Jacob. Is 41:8, 9. 42:1. 43:3, 4, 14. 44:1. Ex 19:5, 6. Je 50:17-20. Mt 24:22. Mk 13:20. Ro 9:6. 11:7. mine elect. Is 65:9, 22. Mt *24:21-31. Mk 13:22, 27. Lk 18:7, 8. 1 P 1:2. 2 J +1. I have even. ver. 1. Is 44:28. though. Ac 17:23. Ga 4:8, 9. Ep *2:12. 1 Th *4:5.

5. the Lord. ver. 14-18, 21, 22. Is 44:8. 46:9. Dt 4:35, 39. +*32:39. 1 K 8:60. Jl 2:27. Jn +*1:1. He +*1:8, 9. no God. Dt +*6:4. I girded thee. Is 22:21. Ezr 1:2. Jb 12:18, 21mg. Ps 18:32, 39.

6. they may know. Is 37:20. 1 S 17:46, 47. Ps 46:10. 83:18. *102:15, 16. Ezk 38:23. 39:21. Ml *1:11. none else. Dt 4:35, 39. +*32:39.

7. form. Ge 1:3-5, 17, 18. Ps 8:3. 104:20-23. Je

31:35. 2 C 4:6. Ja 1:17. light. Ge +1:3. create darkness. Ex 10:21-23. 14:20. Jb +38:9. Ps +104:20. Je 13:16. Ezk 32:8. Jl 2:2. Am 4:13. Na 1:8. Ju 6, 13. I make peace. Is 10:5, 6. Jb 2:10. *34:29. Ps 29:11. 75:7. Ec 7:13, 14. Je 18:7-10. 51:20. Ezk 14:15-21. Am +*3:6. 5:6. Ac 4:28. create. Heb. *bara,* Poel Participle, which with "evil" requires the rendering "bring about" (CB). evil. S#7451h. Is 47:11n. Ge 2:9, 17. 3:5, 22. 6:5 (wickedness), 5 (evil). 8:21. 13:13 (wicked). 19:19. 24:50 (bad). 28:8mg. Ex 23:2. Nu 11:1mg. 2 S *17:14. Jb 1:1. Ps 5:4. 7:4. 23:4. 28:3 (mischief). Pr 1:16, 33. Ec 8:11, 12. Am +√3:6. This Hebrew word is never rendered "sin"; it is rendered "calamity" in Ps 141:5; "adversity" in 1 S 10:19; Ps 94:13; Ec 7:14; "grief" in Ne 2:10; Pr 15:10; Ec 2:17; Jon 4:6; "affliction" in Nu 11:11; "misery" in Ec 8:6, besides several other renderings elsewhere. do all. Dt +*2:30. Ep +*1:11.

8. Drop down. Is 32:15. 44:3. Ps *72:3, 6. *85:9-12. Ezk *34:26. Ho *10:12. 14:5-8. Jl 2:28, 29. 3:18. Ac *2:33. T *3:3-6. let the earth. Is 4:2. 11:1. *53:2. 61:3, 11. 1 C *3:6-9. open. Nu ◑16:32. ◑26:10. Ps ◑106:17. I the Lord. Is 65:17, 18. 66:22. Je 31:22. 2 C √5:21. Ep √2:10. *4:24.

9. unto him. Is *64:8. Ex 9:16, 17. Jb 15:24-26. 40:8, 9. Ps *2:2-9. Pr +*21:30. Je *50:24. 1 C 10:22. Shall the clay. Is 10:15. *29:16. Je *18:6. Ro *9:20, 21.

10. that saith. Dt +*27:16. Ml 1:6. He *12:9.

11. the Holy One. Is 43:3, 7, 15, 21. 48:17. Ask me. Ge 32:26. Est 8:8. Je √33:3. Ezk 36:37. Da 2:18. 9:2, 3, 24-27. Mt 7:7, 9-11. Mk √11:24. Lk 8:9, 10. 12:41. *13:23, 24. 18:26-30. 20:1-8, 27-35. 21:7-9. Jn 3:4-9. 9:36-38. 10:24, 25. *15:7. things to come. T#1596. Da 8:13-15. 9:20-23. Mt 24:3. Ac ◑1:6, 7. Re 1:3. concerning my sons. Je 3:19. 31:1, 9. Ho 1:10. Ro 9:4-8. 2 C 6:18. Ga *3:26-29. concerning the work. Is 29:23. 43:7. 60:21. Ep *2:10. command. Some, as Isaac Leeser, render these statements as questions: "About events to come will you ask me? concerning my sons, and concerning the work of my hands will ye command me?" However, J. A. Alexander discusses the difficulties in terms of Hebrew syntax of so translating (involving, as it does, an abrupt change from affirmation to interrogation), and concludes "By far the simplest syntax is the common one, which makes the first verb an imperative...and to understand both verbs as conceding an indulgence to those who are addressed. You may ask me concerning things to come, for I am able to inform you; you may trust my children to my care, for I am abundantly able to protect them." "Command" is used in the sense of "giving one authority over any thing or person, or in other words committing it to him, and leaving it at his disposal" (J. A. Alexander). It hardly means for us to boss God around in our prayers, as some mistakenly have understood. Is 5:6. 10:6. +*62:7. Ge 2:16. 32:26. Jg 16:23. Jsh 10:12. Jb 22:28. Ho 12:4.

12. made the earth. ver. 18. Is 40:28. 42:5. Ge 1:1, 26, 27‖𝒫. Ps 102:25. Jn 1:3. He *11:3. Re 4:11. my hands. Is 40:12, 22. 44:24. Je 27:5. 32:17. Zc 12:1. all their host. Ge 2:1. Ne +9:6. Je 31:35.

13. raised him. ver. 1-6. Is 41:2, 25. 46:11. 48:14, 15. in righteousness. Is 42:6. Ps 65:5. direct. *or,* make straight. ♪22C37, Ps +5:8. ver. 1, 2. he shall build. Is √44:28. 49:23. 52:2, 3. 60:10, 16. 2 Ch ✱36:22, 23. Ezr ✱1:1-3. Ro 3:24-26. 1 P *1:18, 19. price. Is 13:17.

14. **The labor**. *f*121C1H, Dt +28:33. Is 18:7. 19:23-25. 23:18. 49:23. 60:5, 6. 61:5, 6. 66:19, 20. Ps *68:30, 31. *72:10-15. 138:4. Zc *8:22, 23. **the Sabeans**. i.e. *drunkards*, ✻S#5436h. Is 45:13. Ezk 23:42. That the *Sabeans* were of a most majestic appearance is particularly remarked by Agatharchides, an ancient Greek historian quoted by Bochart (Phaleg. l. ii. c. 26). Jb 1:15. Ezk 23:42. Jl 3:8. **men of stature**. Is 10:33. Nu 13:32. 2 S 21:20. Ezk 31:3. **come after**. Mt +*8:11. **in chains**. Is 14:2. 49:23. Ps 149:6, 8. **they shall fall**. Is *60:14. 61:5, 9. Ex 11:8. Est 8:17. Ac 10:25, 26. 1 C 14:24, 25. Re 3:9. **Surely**. ver. 24. Je 16:19. Zc 8:20-23. 1 C 8:4-6. 14:25. 1 Th 1:9. **and there**. ver. 5, 6. Is 44:8.

15. **a God**. Is 8:17. 57:17. Ex 20:21. Ps 44:24. 77:19. *97:2. Jn 12:35, 36. *13:7. Ro *11:33, 34. **O God**. ver. 17. Is *12:2. 43:3, 11. 46:13. 60:16. Ps 68:26. Mt *1:22, 23. Jn 4:22, 42. Ac 5:31. 13;23. 2 P *3:18.

16. **be ashamed**. ver. 20. Is 41:29. 42:17. 44:9, 11. Ps *97:7. Je 2:26, 27. 10:14, 15. 1 J 5:21. Re 14:9, 10.

17. **Israel**. ver. 25. Is 26:4. Ho 1:7. Ro 2:28, 29. 8:1. *11:26. 1 C 1:30, 31. 2 C *5:17-21. Ph 3:8, 9. 1 J 4:15. √5:11, 12. **in the Lord**. Jn 14:20. **an everlasting**. Heb. *olam* plural, Ps +61:4. Is 51:6, 8. 54:8. 60:19. Ps 103:17. Je 31:3. Jn √5:24. 6:40. √10:28. 2 Th 2:13, 14, 16. He *5:9. 1 J √5:11-13. **ye shall not**. Is 29:22. 49:23. 54:4. Ps 25:3. Jl +*2:26, 27. Zp 3:11. Ro 8:1. 9:33. √10:11-13. 1 P 2:6. **without end**. lit. unto the ages of perpetuity. Ps +9:18 (✻S#5703h).

18. **that created**. Is 42:5. Je 10:12. 51:15. Heb. *bara*, ✻S#1254h: Kal, Preterite: Ge 1:1, 27. 2:3. 5:2. 6:7. Dt 4:32. Ps 89:12, 47. Is 4:5. 40:26. 41:20. 43:7. 45:8, 12, 18. 54:16, 16. Je 31:22. Ml +2:10. Kal, Infinitive: Ge 5:1. Kal, Imperative: Ps 51:10. Kal, Future: Ge 1:21, 27. Nu 16:30 (make. mg, create). Kal, Participle, Poel: Ec 12:1 (Creator). Is 40:28. 42:5. 43:1, 15. 45:7, 18. 57:19. 65:17, 18, 18. Am 4:13. Niphal, Preterite: Ex 34:10 (been done). Ps 148:5. Is 48:7. Ezk 21:30. Niphal, Infinitive: Ge 2:4. 5:2. Ezk 28:13, 15. Niphal, Future: Ps 104:30. Niphal, Participle: Ps 102:18. Piel, Preterite: Jsh 17:15, 18. Piel, Infinitive: Ezk 23:47. Piel, Infinitive: Ezk 21:19 (choose), 19. Hiphil, Infinitive: 1 S 2:29 (make yourselves fat). **God himself that**. Pr 8:22, 23, 30, 31. Jn √1:1-3. **he created**. ver. 12. Ge 1:1, 28▶𝒫. 9:1. Ps 115:16. Ezk 36:10-12. **in vain**. Heb. *tohu*, ✻S#8414h. Is 24:10 (confusion). 29:21 (thing of nought). 34:11 (confusion). 40:17, 23 (vanity). 41:29 (confusion). 44:9. 45:18, 19 (vain). 49:4 (for nought). 59:4. Ge 1:2 (without form). Dt 32:10 (waste). 1 S 12:21, 21 (vain). Jb 6:18 (to nothing). 12:24 (wilderness). 26:7 (empty place). Ps 107:40mg. Je *4:23 (without form). **I am**. ver. 5, 6.

19. **spoken**. Is 43:9, 10. 48:16. Dt *29:29. *30:11-14. Pr 1:21. 8:1-4. Am *3:7. Jn 7:26, 28, 37-39. 18:20. Ac 2:4-8. **Seek**. Is *1:15. *8:19. √55:6, 7. 58:1-3. Dt 30:11▶𝒫. 1 Ch 28:8. 2 Ch 15:2. Ezr 8:22. Ps 24:6. 69:13, 32. 116:1, 2. Pr 15:8. Je 29:13. Am 5:4. Ml 3:13, 14. Mt 15:8, 9. Ja *4:3. **speak righteousness**. Is 63:1. Nu 23:19, 20. Dt 32:4. Ps +√9:10. 12:6. 19:7-10. 111:7, 8. 119:137, 138. Pr *8:6, 8, 9. +*30:5.

20. **yourselves**. Is 41:5, 6, 21. 43:9. **and come**. Mt 11:28. Ro 3:29. **escaped**. Is 4:2. Je 25:15-29. 50:28. 51:6-9. Ep 2:12, 16. Re 18:3-18. **they**. Is 42:17, 18. 44:17-20. 46:7. 48:7. 1 K 18:26-29. Ps 115:8. 135:15-

18. Je 2:27, 28. 10:8, 14. 51:17, 18. Hab 2:18-20. Ro 1:21-23. **god**. Heb. *El*, Ex +15:2.

21. **Tell ye**. Ps 26:7. 71:17, 18. 96:10. Je 50:2. Jl 3:9-12. **and bring**. Is 41:1-4. **who hath declared**. Is 41:22, 23. 43:9. 44:7, 8. 46:9, 10. 48:3, 14. **ancient**. Heb. *kedem*, Mi +5:2 (✤S#6924h). Is 19:11. 23:7. 37:26. 46:10. 51:9. **and there is**. ver. 5, 14, 18. Is 44:8. **a just**. ver. 25. Is 43:3, 11. 63:1. Ge +*18:25. Ps 116:5. Je *23:5, 6. Zp 3:5, 17. Zc *9:9. Ro *3:25, 26. 4:5. T *2:13, 14. 1 J √1:9. **God**. Heb. *El*, Ex +15:2. **none beside**. Dt 4:35▶𝒫. 6:4. Mk ▶12:32.

22. **Look**. Nu *21:8, 9. 2 Ch 20:12. Ps 22:27. 65:5. Mi 7:7. Zc 12:10. Lk 23:42, 43. Jn 1:29. √3:13-16. 6:40. *12:32. 19:37. He *12:2. **for**. ver. 21. Jn √10:28-30. T *2:13. 2 P *1:1. **ends of the earth**. Ps 65:5. **God**. Heb. *El*, Ex +15:2. **none else**. *f*144D, Ge +40:23. *f*64, Ps +1:1.

23. **sworn**. Ge 22:15-18▶𝒫. Je 22:5. 49:13. Am 6:8. He *6:13-18. **the word**. ver. 19. Is √55:11. Nu *23:19. **That unto**. Is +43:10. *48:11. Ne +*9:6. Ro 11:4. ▶14:10-12. Ph √▶2:10. **bow**. *f*121S3H. Metonymy of the Adjunct B607. To bow the knee is put for compulsory submission. For other instances of this figure see Ro 14:11. Ph 2:10. **every tongue**. Is 19:18-21. 44:3-5. 65:16. Ge 31:53. Dt 6:13. 2 Ch 15:14, 15. Ne 10:29. Ps 63:11. 132:2.

24. **Surely**, etc. *or*, Surely he shall say of me, In the Lord *is* all righteousness and strength. **in the Lord**. ver. 25. Is 54:17. *61:10. Je *23:5, 6. 1 C *1:30. 2 C √5:21. 2 P 1:1mg. **righteousness**. Heb. righteousnesses. Is 33:15mg. Jg +5:11mg. 1 S 12:7mg. Da 9:18. **strength**. Dt 31:23. Ps 18:1, 2. Jl 3:10. Zc *10:6, 12. 2 C √12:9, 10. Ep *3:16. Ph √4:13. Col *1:11. 2 T *4:17, 18. **even**. Is 55:5. 60:9. Ge +*49:10. Mt *11:27, 28. Jn *7:37. √12:32. Ro 11:26. Ep *6:10. Re 22:17. **and all**. Is 41:11. Ps √2:1-12. 21:8, 9. 72:9. 110:2. Lk 13:17. 19:27. Re 11:18.

25. **the Lord**. ver. 17, 24. Ac 13:39. Ro 3:24, 25. 5:1, 18, 19. 8:1, 30, 33, 34. 1 C 6:11. 2 C √5:21. **the seed**. ver. 19. Is 61:9. 65:9, 23. 1 Ch 16:13. Ps 22:23. Ro 4:16. 9:6-8. Ga 3:27-29. **be justified**. T#787. Is *53:11. +*60:21. Nu 23:21. Ezk *36:25. Ac *13:39. Ro *3:24. 5:1, 9, 18, 19. 8:1, 33, 34. 2 C √5:21. T 3:7. 1 J +2:12 (T#583). **glory**. Is 41:16. Ps 64:10. Je *9:23, 24. 1 C *1:31. 2 C 10:17. Ga 6:14. Ph 3:3g.

ISAIAH 46

The idols of Babylon unable to preserve themselves from captivity, 1, 2. The powerful care of God over his people, even to the end, 3, 4. Idols, made with great expense, not to be compared with God, who declares his purposes before he executeth them, especially the deliverance of the Jews by Cyrus, 5-11. The stouthearted far from righteousness, but salvation near to Israel, 12, 13.

1. **Bel**. i.e. *lord, master*, ✻S#1078h. Is 46:1. Je 50:2. 51:44. *Bel*, called *Belus* by the Greek and Roman writers, is the same as *Baal*; and *Nebo* is interpreted by Castell and Norberg of *Mercury*; the two principal idols of Babylon. When that city was taken by the Persians, these images were carried in triumph. Is 21:9. 41:6, 7. Ex 12:12. 1 S 5:3, 4. Je 48:1, etc. 50:2. 51:44, 47, 52. **Nebo**. i.e. *a prophet*, the Mercury of the Babylonians, "Anubis, Hermes, Mercury." Is 15:2.

Nu 32:3, 28. Ac 14:12. **their idols**. lit. grievous things. Is 10:11. 21:9. Da 3:1. **your carriages**. Am 5:26. **a burden**. Is 2:20. Je 10:5.

2. **they could**. Is 36:18, 19. 37:12, 19. 44:17. 45:20. **but**. Jg 18:17, 18, 24. 2 S 5:21. Je 43:12, 13. 48:7. **themselves are**. Heb. their soul is. Heb. *nephesh*, Ge +27:31.

3. **Hearken**. See on Is 44:1, 21. 48:1, 17, 18. 51:1, 7. Ps 81:8-13. **the remnant**. See on Is 1:9. 10:22. 11:11. 37:4. **borne**. Is 44:1, 2. 49:1, 2. 63:9. Ex 19:4♭𝒫. Dt 1:31♭𝒫. 32:11, 12♭𝒫. Ps 22:9, 10. 71:6. Ezk 16:6-16.

4. **even to your**. Is 41:4. 43:13, 25. Ps 92:14. 102:26, 27. Ml 2:16. *3:6. Ro √11:29. He 1:12. √13:8. Ja *1:17. **even to hoar**. Ps *48:14. 71:18. **hairs**. Ru +4:15. **will I carry**. Is 40:11. *63:9. Dt 33:27.

5. **To whom**. See on Is 40:18, 25. Ex 15:11. Ps *86:8. 89:6, 8. 113:5. Je 10:6, 7, 16. Ph 2:6. Col +√1:15. He *1:3. **compare**. Nu 21:27.

6. **lavish**. ♪105, Ml +4:2. Is 40:19, 20. 41:6, 7. 44:12-19. 45:20. Ex 32:2-4. Jg 17:3, 4. 1 K 12:28. Je 10:3, 4, 9, 14. Ho 8:4-6. Hab 2:18-20. Ac *17:29. **maketh it a god**. T#360. Ps *115:4-8. **they fall**. Is 2:8. 44:17. Da 3:5-15.

7. **they carry him**. 1 S *5:3. Je *10:5. Da 3:1. **one shall cry**. Is 37:38. *45:20. Jg 10:12-14. 1 K 18:26, 40. Je 2:28. Jon 1:5, 14-16.

8. **Remember**. Is 44:18-21. Dt 32:7♭𝒫, 29. Ps 115:8. 135:18. Je 10:8. Ac 7:51. 1 C 14:20. **bring**. Is 47:7. Ezk 18:28. Hg 1:5, 7. Lk 15:17. Ep 5:14.

9. **the former**. Is 42:9. 65:17. Dt 32:7. Ne 9:7, etc. Ps ch. 78, 105, 106. 111:4. Je 23:7, 8. Da *9:6-15. **of old**. Heb. *olam*, Ge +*6:4. **I am God**. See on Is 45:5, 6, 14, 18, 21, 22. **and there is none like**. See on ver. 5. Dt 33:26.

10. **the end**. Is √41:21-23. 44:7. 45:21. Ge +√3:15. *12:2, 3. +*49:10, 22-26. Nu *24:17-24. Dt 4:25-31. 28:15, etc. Ac 15:18. **ancient**. Mi +5:2 (✚S#6924h). **My counsel**. ver. 11. Is 43:13. Ps *33:11. 135:6. Pr *19:21. +*21:30. Da *4:35. Ac 3:23. 4:27, 28. *5:39. Ro *11:33, 34. Ep *1:9-11. He 6:17. **will do my**. Is *55:11. Ex +33:19. Dt +*2:30. Ps +*115:3. Mt *20:15. Ep +*1:11.

11. **Calling**. Is 13:2-4. 21:7-9. 41:2, 25. 45:1-6. Je 50:29. 51:20-29. **a ravenous bird**. Or, "an eagle," a very proper emblem for Cyrus, says Bp. Lowth, as in other respects, so particularly because the ensign of Cyrus was a golden *eagle, aetos xrusous,* the very word *ayit,* which the prophet uses here, expressed as near as may be in Greek letters. Ezk 39:4. **the man**. Is 44:28. 45:13. 48:14, 15. Ezr 1:2. Ps *76:10. Da 7:2-4. Ac 4:28. **that executeth my counsel**. Heb. of my counsel. Ps 119:24mg. **I have spoken**. Is 14:24-27. 38:15. Nu *23:19♭𝒫. Jb 23:13. Je 50:45. Ac *5:39. Ep +*1:11. 3:11.

12. **Hearken**. See on ver. 3. Is 28:23. 45:20. Ps 49:1. Pr *1:22, 23. 8:1-5. Je 50:45. Ep 5:14. Re 3:17, 18. **ye stouthearted**. Is 48:4. Ps *76:5. Zc 7:11, 12. Ml 3:13-15. Ac 7:51. **that**. Ps 119:150, 155. Je 2:5. Ep 2:13.

13. **bring**. Is *51:5. 61:11. Ro 1:17. *3:21-26. *10:3-15. **shall not tarry**. Ps 14:7. 46:1, 5. Hab *2:3. He 10:37. **salvation**. Is *12:2, 6. 28:16. 61:3. 62:11. Jl 3:17. Lk *2:11. 1 P 2:6. **Israel**. Is 43:7. 44:23. 60:21. 61:3. Je 33:9. Hg 1:8. Jn 17:10. Ep 1:6. 2 Th 1:10, 12.

ISAIAH 47

Predictions of terrible judgments upon the inhabitants of Babylon, for their pride, luxury, and cruelty to the Jews, 1-11. Their diviners and counselors shall not help them, 12-15.

1. **Come**. ♪38E, Is +6:9. **down**. Is 3:26. 26:5. 52:2. Jb 2:8, 13. Ps 18:27. Je 13:18. 48:18. La 2:10, 21. Ezk 26:16. 28:17. Ob 3, 4. Jon 3:6. **O virgin**. Is 37:22. Je 46:11. **daughter**. ♪155E5, Nu +21:25. Is 13:1. Ps 137:8. Je 50:42. 51:33. Zc 2:7. **there is**. Is 14:13, 14. Ps 89:44. Hg 2:22. **thou shalt**. ver. 7-9. Is 32:9-11. Dt 28:56, 57. La 4:5. Ne 16:19. 17:1-6. 18:7.

2. **the millstones**. Ex 11:5. Jg 16:21. Jb 31:10. Je 27:7. La 5:13. Mt *24:41. Lk 17:35. **grind meal**. ♪121H, Ps +74:15. i.e. *corn,* from which meal is made. Ex 11:5. Mt 24:41. **make bare**. Is 3:17. 20:4. Je 13:22, 26. Ezk 16:37-39. Ho 2:3. Mi 1:11. Na 3:5, 6. **uncover**. Is 20:2.

3. **I will take**. Is 13:6. 34:1-8. 59:17, 18. 63:4-6. Dt 32:35, 41-43. Ps 94:1, 2. 137:8, 9. Je 13:22, 26. 50:27, 28. 51:4, 11, 20-24, 34-36, 56. Na 3:5. Ro *12:19. He 10:30, 31. Re 6:9, 10. 16:19. 17:14, 16, 17. 18:5-8, 20.

4. **our redeemer**. T#1920. Is 41:14. 43:3, 14. *44:6. *49:26. 54:5. 59:20. 62:11. 63:1. Je 31:11. 50:33, *34. Mt 1:21. Lk 2:11. Jn 1:29. 4:42. Ac ✱5:31. Ro ✱11:26. Re 5:9. **Lord of hosts**. Is 44:6. **his name**. Ex 3:15♭𝒫. 15:3♭𝒫.

5. **silent**. Is 13:20. 14:23. 1 S *2:9. Ps 31:17. 46:10. Je 25:10. La 1:1. Hab *2:20. Zc 2:13. Mt 22:12, 13. Ju 13. Re 18:21-24. **for**. After Babylon was taken by Cyrus, instead of being "the lady of kingdoms," the metropolis of a great empire, and mistress of all the East, it became subject to the Persians; and the imperial seat being removed to Susa, instead of having a king, it had only a deputy residing there, who governed it as a province of the Persian empire. ver. 7. Is 13:19. 14:4. Da *2:37, 38. Re *17:3-5, 18. *18:7, 16-19.

6. **wroth**. Is 10:6. 42:24, 25. 2 S 24:14. 2 Ch *28:9. Ps *69:26. Zc *1:15. **I have polluted**. Is *43:28. La 2:2. Ezk 24:21. 28:16. **thou didst**. Is 13:16-18. 14:17. Ps 137:1-3. Ob 10, 16. Mt 7:2. Ja *2:13. **no mercy**. 2 K 25:5, 6, 26. Je 50:17. 51:34. **upon**. Dt 28:50. **the ancient**. La 4:16.

7. **thou saidst**. ver. 5. Ezk 28:2, 12-14. 29:3. Da 4:29, 30. 5:18-23. Re *18:7. **for ever**. Heb. *olam,* Ex +*12:24. **so that**. Is 46:8, 9. Dt 32:29♭𝒫. Je 5:31. Ezk 7:3-9.

8. **given**. Is 21:4, 5. 22:12, 13. 32:9. Jg 18:7, 27. Je 50:11. Da 5:1-4, 30. Zp 2:15. Re 18:3-8. **I am**. ver. 10. Je 50:31, 32. 51:53. Da 4:22, 30. 5:23. 11:36. Hab 2:5-8. 2 Th 2:4. **none else**. Is ❍45:6, 14. ❍46:9. **I shall not**. Ps 10:5, 6. Na 1:10. Lk 12:18-20. 17:27-29. Re 18:7.

9. **these two**. Is 51:18, 19. Ru 1:5, 20. Lk 7:12, 13. **in a moment**. Is 13:19. Ps *73:19. Da 5:30. 1 Th *5:3. Re *18:8-10. **they shall come**. Is 13:20-22. 14:22, 23. Je 51:29, 62-64. Re 14:8. 18:21-23. **for the multitude**. ver. 12, 13. Da 2:2. 4:7. 5:7. Na 3:4. 2 Th √2:9, 10. Re 9:20, 21. 18:23. +*21:8. 22:15.

10. **thou hast trusted**. Is 28:15. 59:4. Ps *52:7. 62:10. **thou hast said**. Is *29:15. Jb 22:13, 14. Ps *10:11. 64:5. *94:7-9. Ec +*8:8. Je 23:24. Ezk 8:12. 9:9. **Thy wisdom**. Is 5:21. Ezk 28:2-6. Ro 1:22. 1 C 1:19-21.

3:19. **perverted thee**. *or*, caused thee to turn away. Je 50:6. **I am**. ver. 8.

11. **evil**. S#7451h, Is +45:7. The word often means, when used as a noun, calamity, disaster, adversity, bad thing: Ge 19:19; 44:4; Jb 20:12; Ps 97:10. **thou shalt not know**. Is 37:36. Ex 12:29, 30. Ne 4:11. Re 3:3. **from whence it riseth**. Heb. the morning thereof. Is +*8:20. *14:12. 17:14. **thou shalt not be**. Ps 50:22. Je 51:39-42. Da 5:25-30. 1 Th *5:3. Re 18:9, 10. **put it off**. Heb. expiate. Nu 35:33. Mt 18:34. Lk 12:59. **desolation**. Is 10:3. Jb 30:3, 14. Ps 35:8. **suddenly**. Pr 6:15. 24:22. *29:1. Ec 9:12. Is 29:5. 30:13. Je 15:8. 1 Th *5:3. Re 18:21. **not know**. Pr 5:6.

12. **Stand now**. ver. 9, 10. Is *8:19. 19:3. 44:25. Ex 7:11. 8:7, 18, 19. 9:11. Je 2:28. Ezk *21:21-23. Da *5:7-9. Na 3:4. Ac 13:8-12. 2 Th √2:9-12. Re 17:4-6. **enchantments**. ✱S#2267h. Is 47:9, 12. Dt +18:11 (charmer). Ps 58:5 (charmers). Pr 21:9mg. 25:24 (wide). Ho 6:9 (company). **sorceries**. ✱S#3785h. Is 47:9, 12. 2 K 9:22 (witchcrafts). Mi 5:12. Na 3:4, 4. Compare S#3786h, Je 27:9. Re *18:23.

13. **wearied**. Is 57:10. Ezk 24:12. Hab 2:13. **Let now**. Is 44:25. Da 2:2, 10. 5:7, 8, 15, 16, 30. **astrologers, the stargazers**. Heb. viewers of the heavens. J. A. Alexander renders "the dividers of the heavens," noting "i.e. the astrologers, so called because they divided the heavens into houses with a view to their prognostications." S#8064h, the usual word for "heavens," and S#2374h, the usual word for "seer." **stargazers**. ✱S#2374h. Is 28:15 (agreement). 29:10 (seers). 30:10 (prophets). 2 S 24:11 (seer). 2 K 17:13. 1 Ch 21:9. 25:5. 29:29. 2 Ch 9:29. 12:15. 19:2. 29:25, 30. 33:18, 19. 35:15. Ezk 13:9 (that see), 16 (which see). 22:28 (seeing). Am 7:12 (seer). Mi 3:7 (seers). **the monthly prognosticators**. Heb. that gave knowledge concerning the months. **monthly**. Ge 7:11. 8:4. 29:14. **prognosticators**. ✦S#3045h (Hiphil, participle): 2 Ch 23:13 (taught). Je 16:21 (cause them to know). Da 8:19 (make thee know). They pretended to know the future by observing the shape of the moon, or at the new moon made known their monthly predictions. From Isaiah's challenge, it can be seen that Scripture regards astrology and horoscopes as worthless and false, practices forbidden to the people of God.

14. **they shall**. Is 40:24. 41:2. Ex 15:7. Ps 83:13-15. Jl 2:5. Ob 18. Na 1:10. Zp 3:8. Ml *4:1. Mt 3:12. 2 Th √1:8. He 10:27. 2 P 3:7. Re 19:3. **themselves**. Heb. their souls. Heb. *nephesh*, Nu +23:10. Mt +√10:28. 16:26. **there shall**. Is 30:14. Je 51:25, 26. Re 18:21.

15. **thy merchants**. Is 56:11. Ezk 27:12-25. Re *18:11-19. **they shall**. Babylon was replenished from all nations, by a concourse of people, whom Jeremiah (Je 50:37) calls "the mingled people." All these, at the approach of Cyrus, sought to escape to their several countries. Je 51:6-9. Re 18:15-17.

ISAIAH 48

The Lord, foreseeing the obstinate idolatry of Israel, had foretold what he was about to do, that his works might not be ascribed to idols, 1-8. He promises to save his people, for his own name's sake, by his almighty power, and by raising up and prospering Cyrus, 9-15. He pathetically shows how happy obedience would have rendered them, 16-19. He calls on the captive

Jews to leave Babylon, remembering how their fathers had been supplied in the wilderness; and declares that there is no peace for the wicked, 20-22.

1. **Hear**. Mt 13:9. **house of Jacob**. F/L Is +2:5. **which are**. Ge 32:28)𝒫. 35:10)𝒫. 2 K 17:34. Jn *1:47. Ro 2:17, 28, 29. 9:6, 8. Re 2:9. 3:9. **come**. Nu 24:7. Dt 33:28. Ps 68:26. Pr 5:16. **which swear**. Is 44:5. 45:23. 65:16. Dt 5:28. *6:13)𝒫. 10:20. Ps 63:11. Zp *1:4, 5. **make mention**. Is 26:13. 62:6. Ex 23:13. **not in truth**. Is 1:10-14. Le 19:12. Ps 50:16-20. 66:3mg. Je 4:2. *5:2, 3. 7:9, 10. Ml +*3:5. Mt *15:7-9. 23:14. Jn √4:24. 1 T *4:2. 2 T 3:2-5.

2. **they call**. Is 52:1. 64:10, 11. Ne 11:1, 18. Ps 48:1. 87:3. Da *9:24. Mt 4:5. 27:53. Re 11:2. 21:2. 22:19. **and stay**. Is 10:20. Jg 17:13. 1 S 4:3-5. Je 7:4-11. 21:2. Mi *3:11. Jn *8:33, 40, 41. Ro *2:17. **The Lord**. Is 47:4. 51:13. Je 10:16.

3. **declared**. Is 41:22. 42:9. 43:9. 44:7, 8. 45:21. 46:9, 10. **and I**. Is 10:12-19, 33, 34. 37:7, 29, 36-38. Nu *23:19. Jsh *21:45. 23:14, 15. Ps 89:2. *119:89, 90.

4. **I knew**. Is 46:12. Ps 78:8. Zc 7:11, 12. **obstinate**. Heb. hard. Is 14:3. 19:4. 21:2mg. 27:1, 8. 2 S 3:39. Je 5:3. Ezk 3:4-7. Da 5:20. Ro 2:5. He +√3:13. **and thy neck**. Ex *32:9)𝒫. 33:3, 5. Dt 10:16. 31:27. 2 K 17:14. 2 Ch 30:8. 36:13. Ne 9:16, 17, 28. Ps 75:5. Pr *29:1. Je 7:26. 19:15. Zc 7:12. Ac *7:51, 52. **thy brow**. Je 3:3. Ezk 3:7-9.

5. **even**. ver. 3. Is 44:7. 46:10. Lk 1:70. Ac 15:18. **before**. Ɫ151, Ge +1:28. **Mine idol**. Is 42:8, 9. Ex 32:4. Je 44:17, 18.

6. **hast heard**. Ps 107:43. Je 2:31. Mi 6:9. **and will**. Is 21:10. 43:8-10. Ps 40:9, 10. 71:15-18. 78:3-6. 119:13. 145:4, 5. Je 50:2. Mt 10:27. Ac +*1:8. **showed**. Is 42:9. Da 12:8-13. Am +*3:6. Jn 15:15. Ro 16:25, 26. 1 C 2:9. 1 P √1:10-12. Re *1:19. 4:1. 5:1, 2. 6:1, etc. **new things**. Is 65:17. Ro 16:25. **hidden things**. Is 42:9. 49:6. 1 P √1:10-12. **not know**. Dt 1:31, 32. 4:9.

7. **created**. or, produced. lit. prepared. Ex 34:10. Ps 148:5. Ezk 21:30. **now**. Is 65:17, 18. **not from**. Is 45:21. **I knew**. Is 43:10. 46:10. Ex 6:7. Ezk 39:6. Jl 3:17.

8. **thou heardest**. Is 6:9, 10. 26:11. 29:10, 11. 42:19, 20. Je 5:21. Mt 13:13-15. Jn 12:39, 40. **thine ear**. Is 50:5. Ps 40:6. 139:1-4. Je 6:10. I knew. ver. 4. Is 21:2. Je 3:7-11, 20. 5:11. Ho 5:7. 6:7. Ml 2:11. **a transgressor**. Ex 32:8. Dt 9:7, 24. Ps *51:5. √58:3. Ezk 16:3-5. Ep *2:3.

9. **my name's**. ver. 11. Is 37:35. *43:25. Jsh 7:9. 1 S +*12:22. Ps 25:11. 79:9. *106:8. 143:11. Je 14:7. Ezk 20:9, 14, 22, 44. Da 9:17-19. **defer**. Nu 14:17-21. Ne 9:30, 31. Ps *78:38. 103:8-10. Pr *19:11.

10. **I have refined**. Is 1:25, 26. Jb 23:10. Ps 66:10. Pr 17:3. Je 9:7. Ezk 20:38. 22:18-22. Zc 13:8, 9. Ml 3:2, 3. He 12:10, 11. 1 P 1:7. 4:12. Re 3:19. **with silver**. or, for silver. **I have chosen**. Dt 4:20. **affliction**. Ps 119:67. 118:18. 2 C *4:17, 18. He 12:6.

11. **mine own**. ver. 9. **for how**. Is 52:5. Nu 14:15, 16. Dt 32:26, 27. Ezk 20:9, 39. Ro 2:24. **my name**. *Shemi*, "my name," is supplied by one MS. and the LXX. **I will not give**. ver. 5. Is 42:8. 45:23. Ex 20:5)𝒫. Ne +*9:6. Ps 115:1. Je 23:5. Jn √5:23. +*17:5.

12. **Hearken**. Is 34:1. 46:3. 49:1. 51:1, 4, 7. 55:3. Pr 7:24. 8:32. **O Jacob**. Three MSS. and two old editions add *avdi*, "my servant." **my called**. Dt 7:6. Mt 20:16. Ro 1:6. √8:28. 1 C 1:24. 1 P *2:9. Re 17:14. **I am he**.

Is 41:4. 44:6. Dt +*32:39. Jn +√8:24. Re +*1:8, 11, 17, 18. 2:8. *22:13. **the first**. Is 41:4. 44:6. Re *22:13, 14.

13. **hand**. Is 42:5. 45:18. Ge 1:1. Ex *20:11. Ps 102:25. Jn *1:3. He *1:10-12. **and**. Is 40:12. **my right hand hath spanned**. *or*, the palm of my right hand hath spread out. ♩22A15A, Ex +15:6. Is 40:22. Jb 37:18. **spanned**. ♩22A16, Ex +8:19. **when**. Is *40:26. Ps 119:89-91. 147:4. 148:5-8.

14. **assemble**. Is 41:22. *43:9. 44:7. 45:20, 21. **a-mong them**. Instead of *bahem*, "among them," thirty-five MSS. and two editions have *bachem*, "among *you*." **The Lord**. Rather, "He whom the Lord hath loved, will execute his will on Babylon:" that is, Cyrus. Is *45:1-3. Mk 10:21. **he will do**. Is 13:4, 5, 17, 18. *44:28. 46:11. Je 50:21-29. 51:20-24.

15. **prosperous**. Jsh +*1:8. Ps *45:4. Ezk 1:2.

16. **Come ye near**. Ge 45:4. Ps 73:28. Ja 4:8. **I have not**. See on ver. 3-6. Is *45:19. Dt 30:11)♆. Jn 18:20. **there am I**. Ex 3:14. Jn +√1:1. 1 P 1:10, 11. **the Lord God**. Is *11:1-5. 61:1-3. Zc 2:8-11. Lk 4:18. Jn √3:34. 20:21, 22. The doctrine of the Trinity can be seen here by the distinct mention of three divine persons: "I," in the first person, the Messiah the Son, who is speaking; the Lord God, the Father, and "his Spirit," the Holy Spirit. See Is +42:1n. **and his**. Ge +1:26. **Spirit**. Heb. *ruach*, ✛S#7307h. Here, a reference to the Holy Spirit, the Third Person of the Trinity. Is 40:13. 59:19, 21. *61:1. 63:10, 11-14. Ge 6:3. 2 S 23:2. 1 K 18:12. 22:24. 2 K 2:16. 2 Ch 18:23. Ne 9:20, 30. Jb 26:13. 33:4. Ezk 3:12, 14a. 8:3. 11:1, 24. 37:1, 14. 43:5. Ho 9:7mg. Mi 2:7. 3:8. Zc *4:6. 6:8. 7:12. Ml 2:15. For the other uses of *ruach*, see Ge 6:3n.

17. **the Lord**. See on ver. 20. Is 43:14. 44:6-24. 54:5. **which teacheth**. Is 2:3. 30:20. 54:13. Dt 8:17, 18. 1 K 8:36. Jb 22:21, 22. *36:22. Ps *25:8, 9, 12. 71:17. 73:24. Je 31:33, 34. Mi 4:2. Jn *6:45. Ep 4:21. **which leadeth**. Is 43:16. 49:9, 10. Dt 32:12. Ps 23:2. +*32:8. Je *6:16.

18. **O that**. ♩124, Dt +5:29. **thou hadst**. Dt *5:29)♆. *32:29. Ps *81:13-16. Mt 23:37. Lk *19:41, 42. **heark-ened to**. Jn +*13:17. **then had**. Is 32:15-18. 66:12. Ps 36:8. *119:165. Am 5:24. Ro *14:17.

19. **seed**. Is 10:22. Ge 13:16. *22:17)♆. 32:12)♆. Je 33:22. Ho *1:10. Ro *9:27. **as the sand**. ♩102B, ♩138B, Ge +13:16. **his name**. ver. 9. Is 9:14. 14:22. Jsh 7:9. Ru 4:10. 1 K 9:7. Ps 9:5. 109:13. Zp 1:4.

20. **ye forth**. Is *52:11. Je *50:8. *51:6, 45. Zc *2:6, 7. Re *18:4. **with a voice**. Is 12:1. 26:1. 45:22, 23. 49:13. 52:9. Ex 15:1, etc. 19:4-6. Ps 126:1, 2. Je 31:12, 13. 51:48. Re 18:20. 19:1-6. **utter it even**. ver. 6. 2 S 7:23. Je 31:10. 50:2.

21. **they thirsted**. Is 30:25. 35:6, 7. *41:17, 18. *43:19, 20. 49:10. Je 31:9. **he led them**. Dt 8:2)♆. **he caused**. Ex 17:6)♆. Nu 20:11)♆. Ne 9:15. Ps 78:15, 20. 105:41.

22. **no peace**. Is *57:20, 21. Jb 15:20-24. Mt *12:43. Lk 19:42. Ro *3:16, 17. Re 14:11.

ISAIAH 49

The Messiah declares to the nations his appointment and qualifications for his work; complains of ill success among the Jews, and receives assurances of being "the Light of the Gentiles," and the source of salvation and consolation to vast numbers, 1-13. Zion thinks

herself forgotten of God; but is assured of his unchange-able love, and the kings and nations shall be her chil-dren, to show her honor and to do her service, 14-23. The redemption of sinners from Satan's power, and Israel from that of Antichrist is predicted, with allusion to the deliverance of the captive Jews, 24-26.

1. **Listen**. Is 41:1. 42:1-4, 12. 45:22. 51:5. 60:9. 66:19. Zp 2:11. **and hearken**. Is 55:3. 57:19. Ep 2:17. He 12:25. **The Lord**. ver. 5. Ps 71:5, 6. Je *1:5. Mt 1:20, 21. Lk 1:15, 31-35. 2:10, 11. Jn *10:36. Ga 1:15. 1 P *1:20. **mother**. Is +*7:14. Mt ✱1:23.

2. **he hath made**. Is 11:4. 50:4. *51:16. Ps 45:2-5. Je 1:6-10. Ho 6:5. Jn *6:63. He √4:12. Re *1:16. 2:12, 16. *19:11, 13, 15. **in the shadow**. ♩22L8, Ps +121:5. Is 42:1. 51:16. Ps 91:1. Lk 23:46. **made me**. The polished shaft, says Bishop Lowth, denotes the same efficacious word which is before represented by the sharp sword. The doctrine of the gospel pierced the hearts of its hearers, "bringing into captivity every thought to the obedience of Christ" (2 C 10:5). Is 50:4. 61:1-3. Ps 45:5. Je 1:18. 15:19, 20.

3. **my servant**. Is 42:1. 43:21. 44:23. 52:13. 53:10, 11. Zc 3:8. Mt 17:5. Lk 2:10-14. Jn √5:23. *12:28. *13:31, 32. 15:8. *17:1, 4, 5. Ep 1:6. Ph *2:6-11. 1 P 2:9. **glorified**. Ga 1:24.

4. **I have labored**. Is 65:2. Ezk 3:19. Mt 17:17. 23:37. Jn √1:11. *7:5. Ro *10:21. Ga 4:11. **spent**. Le 26:20. 2 C 12:15. **yet**. Is *53:10-12. Ps 22:22-31. Mt 11:25-27. Lk 24:26. Jn +*17:4, 5. 2 C 2:15. Ph *2:9, 10. He *12:2. **work**. *or*, reward. Is *40:10mg. 61:8. +*62:11mg.

5. **that formed**. ver. 1. Ph *2:6, 7. **to bring**. Is 56:8. Mt *15:24. Ac 10:36. Ro 15:8. **Though**, etc. *or*, That Israel may be gathered to him, and I may, etc. Is 9:3. Ge +*49:10. Mt *23:37. Jn 6:37. 17:1, 2, 12. Ep 1:5, 6. **Israel**. Mt 21:37-41. 23:37. Lk 19:42. 1 Th 2:15, 16. **yet**. Ps 110:1-3. Mt 3:17. 11:27. 17:5. 28:18. Jn 3:35. 5:20-27. Ep 1:20-22. 1 P 3:22.

6. **It is a light thing that**. *or*, Art thou lighter, than that, etc. 2 K 3:18. 20:10. **restore**. Is 62:1, 2. Ezk *34:11-14. Ac +*1:6. +*3:19, 21. +*15:26. **preserved**. *or*, desolations. ♩121M, Ex +8:23. i.e. *the land and the cities of Israel which have been reduced to desola-tion*. Here, by Metonymy of the Subject, the thing signified is put for the sign. Is 1:8. 48:6. +*65:4h (monu-ments). **I will also**. Is *42:6, 7. *60:3. Lk ⅃2:32. Jn 1:4-9. Ac ⅃13:47. 26:18. Ro 15:10. **that thou mayest**. Is 11:10. 24:14-16. 46:13. 52:10. Ps 98:2, 3. Lk 24:46, 47. **salvation**. ♩121E1, Ge +25:23. **the end**. Ge=41:57.

7. **the Redeemer**. See on Is 48:7. Re 3:7. **to him**. ♩96B, Ge +8:5. **whom man despiseth**. *or*, to him that is despised in soul. **man**. Heb. *nephesh*, Ex +15:9. Is 52:14. *53:3. Ps 22:6-8. 42:5, 6. 69:4, 7-9, 19, 20. Zc 11:8. Mt *26:67. 27:38-44. Lk 23:11, 18, 23. Jn ✱15:25. 18:40. 19:6, 15. 1 C 2:14. **the nation abhorreth**. T#1943. Mt ✱27:17-22. Lk ✱4:27-30. **to a**. Mt 20:28. Lk 22:27. **servant of rulers**. Ge=39:1. Ps 2:2. Mt 27:41. Ph=2:7. **Kings**. ver. 23. Is 52:15. 60:3, 10, 16. Ps *2:10-12. 68:31. 72:10, 11. Re 11:15. **princes shall wor-ship**. Ps *72:10, 11. Mt ✱2:1, 2, 11. **and he**. Is 42:1. Lk 23:35. 1 P 2:4.

8. **In an**. Ps 69:13. Lk 2:14. Jn *11:41, 42. 2 C ⅃6:2. Ep 1:6. He 5:7. √7:25. **day of salvation**. Ps 102:13. +*118:24. Ho 6:3. **have I helped**. Is 42:1. 50:7-9. Ac 2:24-32. **give thee**. Is 42:6. Mt 26:28. He 8:6. 12:24. **for a covenant**. ♩121M, Ex +8:23. The Messiah is

called the *covenant* by a known metonymy, whereby the sign is put for the thing signified. Matthew Poole notes additional examples of this figure. At Ge 17:10, circumcision, the sign of the covenant, is called God's *covenant*. The paschal lamb is called *the passover*, Ex 12:11, and the sacramental cup is called *the new testament*, Lk 22:20, and *the communion of the blood of Christ*, 1 C 10:16. to establish. or, raise up. Is *51:16. 1 Ch √16:30. Ps 75:3. to cause. ver. 19. Is 51:3. 54:3. 58:12. 61:4. Ps *2:8. Ep 2:12-19.

9. to the. Is 42:7. 61:1. Ps 69:33. 102:20. 107:10-16. 146:7. Zc 9:11, 12. Lk 4:18. Col 1:13. 1 P 2:9. go forth. Jn 5:25. 11:25. to them. Is 9:2. 42:16. 60:1, 2. Lk 1:79. Jn 8:12. Ac 26:18. 2 C 4:4-6. Ep 5:8, 14. 1 Th 5:5, 6. They shall feed. Is 5:17. 55:1, 2. 65:13. Ps 22:26. *23:1, 2. SS 1:7. Ezk 34:13-15, 23, 29. Jl 3:18. Jn 6:53-58. *10:9. high. Dt 32:13.

10. shall not hunger. Mt +*5:6. Jn *6:35. Re *7:16, 17. nor thirst. Jn 4:14. neither. Is 4:6. 25:4. 32:2. Ps *121:5, 6. he that. Is 54:10. Ps *23:2-4. Je *31:9. Ezk 34:23. shall lead. Jn +*10:3, 4. even by. Jn 7:38, 39. guide. Is 58:11. Ps 25:9, 10. 34:5, 11. Lk 10:21. Jn *14:26. 1 J *2:27.

11. I will make. Is 11:16. 35:8-10. *40:3, 4. 43:19. 57:14. 62:10. Ps 107:4, 7. Lk *3:4, 5. Jn √14:6. highways. F/L Is +7:3.

12. these shall. Is 2:2, 3. 11:10, 11. *43:5, 6. 60:9-14. 66:19, 20. Ps *22:27. 72:10, 11, 17. Mi 4:2. Zc 2:11. 8:20-23. Mt +*8:11. Lk +*13:29. Re 7:9. 11:15. Sinim. i.e. *thorns*, *S#5515h, only here. Understood by some to be a possible reference to China. Others refer the name to "Sin," mentioned in Ezk 30:15; to Syene, Ezk 30:6; or "Sin" in Sinai, Ex 16:1. Compare Sinite, Ge 10:17; 1 Ch 1:15.

13. O heavens. Is 42:10, 11. 44:23. 52:9. 55:12. Ps 96:11-13. 98:4-9. Lk 2:13, 14. 15:10. Re *5:8-13. *7:9-12. 14:3. break forth. F/L Is +14:7. the Lord. Is *12:1. 40:1, 2. 51:3. 61:2, 3. 66:13, 14. Je 31:13. 2 C 7:6. 2 Th 2:16, 17. have mercy. Is +*54:8.

14. Zion said. 152B. Prolepsis; or, Anticipation B981. The answering of an argument by anticipating it before it is used, when the anticipated objection is both answered and stated. For other instances of this figure see Mt 3:9. Ro 3:3. 4:2. 6:1, 2. 7:7. 9:14, 15. 9:19. 11:20, 21. 1 C 14:35. 15:35, 36. The Lord. Is *40:27. Ps 22:1. 31:22. *31:22. *77:6-10. 89:38-46. Ro +*11:1-5. forsaken. F/L Is +1:4. my Lord. Ps 13:1. Je 23:39. La 5:20.

15. a woman. 1 K *3:26, 27. Ps *103:13. Ml *3:17. Mt 7:11. forget. Je 2:32. suckling. Is 65:20. that she should not have compassion. Heb. from having compassion. √141, Is +22:4. they may. Le 26:29. Dt 28:56, 57. 2 K 6:28, 29. Mi 1:1, 2. Ps 27:10. La 4:3, 10. Ro 1:31. yet. Is 44:21. Je *31:20. Ho 11:1. Ro +*11:28, 29. not forget. √22C4, Ps +13:1. Is +*41:9. Ps 77:9. +94:14. Ro *8:38, 39. He +*13:5.

16. I have. Ex 13:9. 28:9-30. SS 8:6. Je 22:24. Hg 2:23. Re ●13:16. palms. √12I1I, Ge +3:7. thy walls. Is 26:1. 54:12. 60:18. Re 21:10-21.

17. children. Is 51:18-20. 62:5. Ezr 1:5. Ne 2:4-9, 17. Ezk 28:24. haste. Or, by a slight change of points, "Thy builders shall make haste:" those appointed to build the city and walls of Zion shall speedily begin and accomplish the work. thy destroyers. ver. 19. Is 51:13, 22, 23. 60:10, 18.

18. Lift up. √144A12, Ge +22:13. Is 60:4. Ge 13:14.

Mt 13:41, 42. Re 22:15. all these. ver. 12, 22. Is 43:5, 6. 54:1-3. 60:5-11. 66:12, 13, 20. Je 31:8. Ga 3:28, 29. As I live. Is 54:9. Ge 22:16. Nu 14:28. Je 22:24. Ezk 5:11. Ro ▶14:11. He 6:13-18. thou shalt. Is 61:10. Pr 17:6. as a bride. Je 2:32. Re *21:2. doeth. Bp. Lowth adds from the LXX., "her jewels."

19. thy waste. ver. 8. Is 51:3. *54:1, 2. Je 30:18, 19. 33:10, 11. Ezk 36:9-15. Ho *1:10, 11. Zc *2:4, 11. 10:10. Ro 11:11, 12. they that. ver. 17, 25, 26. Ps 56:1, 2. 124:3. Pr 1:12. Je 30:16. 51:34, 44. Ezk 36:3.

20. children. Is 60:4. Ho 1:10. Mt 3:9. Ga 4:26-28. The place. Is 51:3. 54:1, 2. Jsh 17:14-16. 2 K 6:1.

21. Who hath. √164, 1 S 17:7. seeing. Je 31:15-17. Mt 3:9. Ro 11:11-17, 24. Ga 3:29. 4:26-29. am desolate. Is 3:26. 51:17-20. 52:2. 54:3-8. 60:15. 62:4. 64:10. La 1:1-3. Mt 24:29, 30. Lk *21:24. Ro 11:26-31. Ep 2:13.

22. Behold. ver. 12. Is 2:2, 3. 11:10, 11. 42:1-4. 60:3-11. *66:7-12, 18-20. Ps 22:27. 67:4-7. 72:8, 17. 86:9. Ml 1:11. Lk +*13:29. Ro 11:15. lift up. √22A14.8H, Pr +1:22. set up. Is 62:10. shall bring. Is 14:2. 60:9. Ps 126:2. Jn 3:14, 15. 12:32. arms. Heb. bosom. Ne 5:13. Ps 129:7. daughters. Is 60:4. carried upon. Is 66:12.

23. kings. Cyrus, Darius, Artaxerxes, and other Persian monarchs, as well as Alexander the Great and his successors, particularly Demetrius, conferred many privileges and immunities on the Jewish people, and were munificent benefactors to their temple. But the prophecy was more remarkably and fully fulfilled in the favor which Constantine the Great, and other Christian princes and princes and princesses from his time to the present day, have shown to the church of Christ; though it cannot be disputed, that the grand and signal accomplishment of these predictions is yet future. ver. 7. Is 52:15. *60:3, 10, 11, 16. 62:2. Ezr 1:2-4. 6:7-12. 7:11-28. Ne 2:6-10. Est ch. 8-10. Ps *2:10-12. 68:31. *72:10, 11. 138:4. Re 21:24-26. nursing fathers. Heb. nourishers. lit. steadfast ones or supporters. Nu 11:12. 2 K 10:15. 1 Th 2:7. queens. Heb. princesses. or, king's daughters. 1 K 11:3. Est 1:18. La 1:1. bow. Is 45:14. 60:14. Ge 43:26. Ps 72:9. Re 3:9. lick up. √121S3W, Ps +72:9. Nu 22:4. Ps *72:9. Mi *7:17. shalt know. Ex 6:7▶𝒫. for they. Is 25:9. 50:7. 64:4. Ro 25:3. 34:22. 69:6. Ro 5:5. 9:33. 10:11. 1 P 2:6. wait. Is 40:31. Ge 48:18▶𝒫. Ps 27:14. 37:9. 62:5.

24. Shall. Ezk 37:3, 11. prey. Is 42:22. 53:12. Nu 31:11, 12, 26, 27, 32▶𝒫. Ps 22:15. 124:6, 7. 126:1-3. Zp +*3:8. Mt 12:29. Lk 11:21, 22. lawful captive. Heb. captivity of the just. Ezr 9:9, 13. Ne 9:33, 37. Ps 68:18. *69:33. 79:11. +*102:13, 16, 20. *116:8, 9. Je 25:6-9, 11-14. 29:14.

25. Even. Is 10:27. 52:2-5. Je 29:10. 50:17-19, 33, 34. Zc 9:11. He 2:14, 15. 1 J 3:8. captives. Heb. captivity. Is 61:1. Nu 31:12, 19, 26mg. 2 Ch 28:17mg. Ps 68:18. Je 48:46mg. Da 11:8. Am 4:10mg. I will contend. Is 41:11, 12. 54:15-17. Ge √12:3. Nu 23:8, 9. Je 50:34. 51:35, 36. Zc 9:13-16. 12:3-6. 14:3, 12. Ro *8:31-39. Re 18:20. I will save. Is +*24:13. *25:9. 33:22. 41:1, 2, 9, 10, 11. 54:13. Ps 50:2-5. Je +*30:7. Ga 4:26.

26. I will feed. Is 9:20. Ex 4:22, 23. 14:8, 27, 30, 31. 15:1. Jg 7:22. drunken. Re *14:19, 20. *16:6. 17:6. sweet wine. or, new wine. SS 8:2. Jl 1:5. and all. Is 41:14-20. 45:6. 60:16. Ps *9:16. 58:10, 11. 83:18. Ezk 39:7. Da 7:21-27. Re 15:3, 4. thy Savior. Is 12:2. 25:9.

26:1. 35:4. 63:1. Je 23:6. 30:7. Da 4:37. Mt 12:29. Lk 11:21, 22. He 2:14, 15. 9:28. **the mighty.** Is +*9:6. +*10:21. 60:16. Je 32:18. Mt 11:21. Lk 9:43. Ep 1:21. Re 7:10, 12. **One of Jacob.** Is 60:16. Ge 49:24)℗. Ps 132:2, 5.

ISAIAH 50

The Lord Messiah shows that the Jews were rejected through their obstinate wickedness and unbelief; declares his power and fitness for his work; and speaks of his voluntary humiliation and patient sufferings, as assured of being delivered, justified, and rendered victorious over all enemies, 1-9. He encourages afflicted and tempted believers, and denounces the ruin of presumptuous transgressors, 10, 11.

1. **the bill.** Dt 24:1-4. Je 3:1, 8. Ho 2:2-4. Mk 10:4-12. **divorcement.** Dt 24:1, 3)℗. Je 3:8. **put away.** √132G, Ge +3:19. **or which.** Ex 21:7. Le 25:39. Dt 32:30. 2 K 4:1. Ne 5:5. Est 7:4. Ps 44:12. Mt 18:25. **Behold.** Husbands often sent bills of divorcement to their wives on slight occasions; and fathers, oppressed with debt, sold their children till the year of release. But this, saith God, cannot be my case: I am not governed by any such motives, nor am I urged by any such necessity. Your captivity and afflictions are the fruits of your own folly and wickedness. **for your iniquities.** Is *52:3. *59:1, 2. 1 K 21:25. 2 K 17:17. Je 3:8. 4:18. 31:31, 32. **your mother.** √155E4, 2 S +20:19. Ga 4:26.

2. **when I came.** Is 59:16. 63:3, 5. 65:12. 66:4. Pr 1:24. Je 5:1. 7:13. 8:6. 35:15. Ho 11:2, 7. Jn 1:11. 3:19. **no man.** Je 5:1. Jn 1:11. Ac 13:46. 18:6. 28:28. **Is my.** √85B, Ge +13:9. Is *59:1. Ge 18:14. Nu 11:23)℗. **have I.** Is 36:20. 2 Ch 32:15. Da 3:15, 29. 6:20, 27. **at my.** Ps 106:9. 114:3, 5, 7. Na 1:4. Mk 4:39. **I dry.** Is 42:15. 43:16. 51:10. 63:13. Ex 14:21, 29)℗. Jsh 3:16. Ps 107:33. 114:3-7. **their fish.** Ex 7:18, 21)℗. **rivers.** Plural of majesty: i.e. the great river, the Jordan. Is 44:27. Jsh 4:7, 18)℗. Ps 107:33.

3. **I clothe.** Ex *10:21. Ps 18:11, 12. Mt *27:45. Re *6:12.

4. **God.** Is 49:2. Ex 4:11, 12. Ps 32:3, 8. 45:2. Je 1:9. Mt 10:19. 22:46. Mk 13:11. Lk 2:46, 47, 52. 4:22. 21:15. Jn 7:46. 1 C 1:30. Col 2:3. 3:16. **learned.** Is +*8:16. **that I should know.** Jb 4:3, 4. Jn 7:16. *8:28, 38, 46, 47. 12:49. 14:10, 24. 17:8. 2 C *1:4. **a word.** Is 57:15-19. Pr 15:23. 25:11. Mt 11:28. 13:54. **weary.** Jn 4:6, 7. **morning by.** Is 28:19. 2 S 13:4mg. **waketh mine ear.** √22A8, Ps +10:17. 1 S 9:15, 17. *15:22. Ps 78:1. Ezk *3:10. Hab 2:1. **learned.** Is +*8:16. Jn *7:15-17.

5. **opened mine ear.** Is 48:8. Ex=21:2-6. Ps *40:6-8. Mt √26:39. Jn 8:29. 14:31. 15:10. Ph *2:8. He *5:8. *10:5-9. **not rebellious.** Mt 26:39. Jn 4:34. *14:31. He 5:8. 10:5.

6. **gave.** Le +=1:3. Jn=√10:18. He *12:2. **my back.** Mi 5:1. Mt 27:26. Mk 14:65. Lk 22:63, 64. Jn 18:22. ✶19:1. He *12:2. **the smiters.** Zc 3:7. Mt 26:31. **my cheeks.** The eastern people have always held the beard in great veneration; and to pluck a man's beard is one of the grossest indignities that can be offered. D'Arvieux (tom. iii. p. 214) gives a remarkable instance of an Arab, who, having received a wound in his jaw, chose to hazard his life rather than suffer the surgeon to cut off his beard. See Note on 2 S 10:4. 2 S 20:9n. Jb

16:10. La 3:30. Mi 5:1. Mt √5:39. Mk 15:19. **that plucked.** Ne 13:25. **I hid.** Another instance of the utmost contempt and detestation. Throughout the East it is highly offensive to spit in any one's presence; and if this is such an indignity, how much more spitting in the face? **spitting.** T#1946. Mt +*✶26:67. ✶27:30. Mk ✶14:65.

7. **the Lord.** ver. 9. Is 42:1. 49:8. Ps 89:21-27. 110:1. Lk *22:43. Jn 16:33. He *13:6. **I set.** Je 1:18. Ezk 3:8, 9. Mt 23:13-36. *26:53, 54. Lk *9:51. 11:39-54. Ro √1:16. 1 P 4:1, 16. **ashamed.** Is 49:23.

8. **near that.** Is *53:6. Ro *8:32-34. 1 T *3:16. **let us.** Is 41:1, 21. Ex 22:9. Dt 19:17. Jb 23:3-7. Mt 5:25. **mine adversary.** Heb. the master of my cause. Ge +*3:14, 15. Zc 3:1, etc. Mt 4:10, 11. Jn 12:31. Re 12:10.

9. **help me.** Is 41:13, 14. 42:1. 1 P 2:21-23. **who is.** Ro *8:33, 34. **they all.** Is 51:6-8. Jb 13:28. Ps 39:11. 102:26. Mt 24:35. He *1:11, 12.

10. **is among.** Pr 25:12, 14. 111:10. 112:1. 128:1. Ec 12:13. Ml √3:16. **obeyeth.** Is 42:1. 49:3. *53:11. He +*5:9. **that walketh in darkness.** T#1322. Is 9:2. 59:9. Jb 29:3. Ps *23:4. La 3:2. Mi 7:8. Jn *8:12. √12:46. **hath no light.** Ps 112:4. Mi 7:8. **let him trust.** T#1419. Is 26:3, 4. 1 S 30:6. 1 Ch *5:20. 2 Ch 13:18. 20:12, +√20. Jb 13:15. 23:8-10. Ps *4:5. +√9:10. 10:14. 22:4, 5. 25:20. 27:13, 14. 28:7. 31:1. *37:5, 6. 40:1-4. 42:11. 46:1. *57:1. *62:8. 71:5. 73:28. 112:7, 8. *118:8, 9. 141:8. 145:21. La 3:25, 26. Mi 7:7-9. Hab *3:17, 18. 2 C 1:8-10. He *10:35. 1 P *5:7. **the name.** Ps +√9:10. **and stay.** 2 Ch *13:18.

11. **all ye.** Is 28:15-20. 30:15, 16. 55:2. Ps 20:7, 8. Je 17:5-7. Jon 2:8. Mt 15:6-8. Ro 1:21, 22. 10:3. **that kindle.** Is 64:2. Dt 32:22. Je 15:14. 17:4. **compass.** or, gird. F/L Is +8:9. **walk.** √60A. Figure of speech Divine Irony, Ge +3:22. Here, showing the vanity of striving for light and happiness apart from God. Is ◐2:5. Ec *11:9, 10. Ezk 20:39. Am 4:4, 5. 1 Th ◐1:3. 1 J ◐*1:7. **This shall.** Jn 9:39. **ye shall.** Is 8:22. 65:13-16. Ps 16:4. *32:10. Mt 8:12. 22:13. Lk √16:22, 23. Jn √8:24. 1 C +*6:9. 2 Th √1:8, 9. Re *19:20. √20:15.

ISAIAH 51

God encourages his people, by the example of Abraham, to trust in him; and promises them comfort, 1-3. He contrasts the certainty and perpetuity of his righteousness and salvation with the short continuance of the visible creation and the feebleness of persecutors; and warns his people against the dread of reproach, 4-8. The redeemed call on God to renew his wonderful works in their behalf; and receive assurances of comfort and prosperity, with a rebuke for Zion's unbelief and fear of man, 9-16. Israel, in past and present distresses, is assured of deliverance, and the punishment of her oppressors, 17-23.

1. **Hearken.** ver. 4, 7. Is 46:3, 4. 48:12. 55:2, 3. **ye that follow.** ver. 7. Ps 94:15. Pr 15:9. 21:21. Mt +*5:6. √6:33. Ro 9:30-32. *14:19. Ph *3:13. 1 T 6:11. 2 T *2:22. He √12:14. **ye that seek.** Is 45:19. √55:6. Ps 24:6. 105:3, 4. Am 5:4, 6. Zp +*2:3. **look.** Ge 17:15-17. Jsh 24:2. Ep *2:11, 12. **pit.** Heb. *bor,* Ge +37:20. Jb 33:30. Ps 40:2.

2. **Look unto.** √95, Ps +7:13. **Abraham your father.** Ge 15:1, 2)℗. 17:17. *18:11-13. Jsh 24:3. Ro 4:1-5, 16-24. **for.** Ge √12:1-3. 13:14-17. 15:4, 5. 22:17. *24:1,

35, 36)✐. Ne 9:7, 8. Ezk 33:24. Ga 3:9-14. He 11:8-12. **alone.** Ge 12:4. Ex ◑12:38. Ne ◑13:3. Ezk 33:24. Ml 2:15. Mt 10:37.

3. **the Lord.** ver. 12. Is *12:1. 40:1, 2. 49:13. *54:6-8. *61:1-3. *66:10-14. Ps 85:8. +*102:13. Je 31:12-14, 25. Zp 3:14-20. 2 C 1:3, 4. **all.** Is 44:26. 49:8. 52:9. 61:4. Ps 102:13, 14. Je 33:12, 13. **waste places.** Is 40:1. 49:13. **make.** See on Is 35:1, 2, 7-10. 41:18, 19. Am +*9:13. **like the garden.** Ge 2:8, 9)✐. 13:10)✐. Ezk 31:8-10. *36:35. Jl 2:3. Re *10:7. 22:3. **joy.** Je 33:11. 1 P 1:8. Re 19:1-7. **melody.** Ps 98:5.

4. **Hearken.** ✓18, Dt +28:4. **O my.** Is 26:2. Ex 19:6. 33:13. Ps 33:12. 106:5. 147:20. 1 P 2:9. **a law.** Is 2:3. Mi +*4:2. Ro 8:2-4. 1 C 9:21. **I will make.** See on Is 42:1-4, 6. *49:6. Ps ✓119:105. Pr *6:23. Mt 12:18-20. Lk 2:32. Jn *1:9. 16:8-11.

5. **righteousness.** Is 46:13. 56:1. Dt 30:14. Ps *85:9, 10. Mt 3:2. Ro *1:16, 17. ✓10:6-10. **my salvation.** Is 2:2, 3. Ezk 47:1-5. Mt *28:18, 19. Mk *16:15. Lk 24:47. Ro *10:17, 18. **mine.** 1 S 2:10. Ps 50:4-6. 67:4. 96:13. 98:9. 110:6. Jl 3:12. Jn *5:22, 23. Ac ✓17:31. Ro 2:16. 2 C ✓5:10. **the isles.** ✓121J5, Is +41:1. See on Is 42:4. 49:1. 60:9. Zp 2:11. Ro ✓1:16. 15:9-12.

6. **Lift up.** ✓144A12, Ge +22:13. Is 40:26. Dt 4:19. Ps 8:3, 4. **the heavens.** Is 34:4. 50:9. Ps *102:26, 27. Mt *24:35. He 1:11, 12. 2 P *3:10-12. Re 6:12-14. 20:11. **my salvation.** ver. 8. Is 45:17. Ps 103:17. Da *9:24. Jn ✓3:15, 16. ✓5:24. ✓10:27-29. 2 Th 2:16. He ✓5:9. 9:12, 15. **for ever.** Heb. *olam,* Ex +*12:24.

7. **Hearken.** ✓18, Dt +28:4. See on ver. 1. **ye that.** Ph 3:8-10. T *2:11, 12. **in whose.** Ps *37:31. *40:8. Je +*31:33, 34. 2 C 3:3. He 10:16. **fear.** Je 1:17. Ezk 2:6. Mt *5:10, 11. +*10:28. Lk 6:22. 12:4, 5. Ac *5:41. 1 P *4:4, 14.

8. **For.** Je +20:11. **the moth.** Is 50:9. *66:24. Jb 4:19. 13:28. Ho 5:12. **my righteousness.** See on ver. 6. Is 45:17. 46:13. Lk 1:50. **for ever.** Heb. *olam,* Ex +*12:24. **generation.** Ge +9:12.

9. **Awake.** ver. 17. Is 27:1. Ps 7:6. 44:23. 59:4. 78:65. Hab 2:19. **awake.** ✓84, Ge +6:17. **put on.** ✓22D5P, Ps +93:1. Is 52:1. 59:17. Ps 21:13. 74:13, 14. 93:1. Re 6:10. *11:17. **O arm.** ✓22A12, Ex +15:16. ver. 5. Is 53:1. 59:16. 62:8. Lk 1:51. Jn 12:38. **as in.** Jg 6:13. Ne 9:7-15. Ps *44:1. **ancient.** Mi +5:2 (✛S#6924h). **of old.** Heb. *olam* plural, Ps +61:4. **Art thou.** Jb 26:12mg. Ps *87:4. *89:10. **Rahab.** ✓146, Ge +10:10. Is 30:6. Jb 9:13. **the dragon.** Is 27:1. Ps 74:13, 14. Ezk 29:3. Hab 3:13. Re *12:7-9.

10. **dried.** Is 42:15. 43:16. 50:2. 63:11, 12. Ex 14:21, 22, 29)✐. 15:13. Ps 74:13. **deep.** Ge +1:2.

11. **the redeemed.** Is 35:10. *44:23. 48:20. 49:13. Ps 111:9. Je 30:18, 19. 31:11, 12. 33:11. Ac 2:41-47. Ep +*1:14. Re *5:9-13. 7:9, 10. 14:1-4. 19:1-7. **shall return.** Is +*52:12mg. +*54:7. **and come.** Ho 2:15. **with singing.** Is 24:14-16. Ho +*2:15. Jl 2:23. Zp *3:17. Zc +*2:10. **unto Zion.** Is +*24:23. ✓52:8. +*59:20. +*66:5-8. Ps 51:18. ✓102:13, 16-22. 122:6. *132:10-14. Zc *8:2-8. **everlasting.** Heb. *olam,* Ge +17:7. Is 60:19. 61:7. 2 C 4:17, 18. 2 Th 2:16. Ju *24. **and sorrow.** Is 25:8. 60:20. 65:19. 2 C *4:17. Re 7:17. 21:1, 4. 22:3.

12. **I, even I.** Ge 6:17. **that comforteth.** T#956. ver. *3. Is *43:25. 53:3. 57:15-18. 61:1. *66:13. Dt 33:27. Jb 20:14. Je 8:18. La 3:22, 33. Jn 13:7. *14:16-18, 26, 27. Ac 9:31. 2 C *1:3-5. *7:5, 6. Ja 5:11. **afraid of.** ver. 7, 8. Is 2:22. 1 S *15:24. Ps *118:6. 146:4.

Pr *29:25. Da *3:16-18. Mt +*10:28. Lk *12:4, 5. **son of man.** Is 56:2. Ps +*146:3. **made as grass.** Is *40:6, 7. Ps *90:5, 6. *92:7. *103:15, 16. Ja *1:10, 11. 1 P *1:24.

13. **forgettest.** See on Is 17:10. Dt *6:12. 32:18. Ps +*9:17. Je 2:32. **that hath stretched.** Is 40:22. 42:5. 44:24. 45:12. Ge 1:1)✐. Jb 9:8. 37:18. Ps 102:25, 26. 104:2. Je 10:11, 12. 51:15. He 1:9-12. **feared.** Is 8:12, 13. 57:11. He *2:15. **were ready.** *or,* made *himself* ready. Is 10:29-32. Ex 14:10-13. 15:9, 10. Est 5:14. Da 3:15, 19. Re 20:9. **where is.** Is 10:33, 34. 14:16, 17. 16:4. +*25:8. 33:18, 19. 37:36-38. Ex 14:13. Est *7:10. Jb *20:5-9. Ps 9:6, 7. *37:35, 36. 76:10. Da *4:32, 33. Mt 2:16-20. Jn *14:27. Ac 12:23. 1 C 1:20. +*15:55. 2 C *1:3, 4. Re 19:20.

14. **captive.** Is 48:20. 52:2. Ezr 1:5. Ac 12:7, 8. Ro *7:24. *8:19. 2 C +*5:2. **die.** Je 37:16. 38:6-13. La 3:53, 54. Zc 9:11.

15. **that divided.** See on ver. 10. Ne 9:11. Jb 26:12. Ps 74:13. 114:3-5. 136:13. Je 31:35. Am 9:5, 6. **The Lord.** Is 47:4. 48:2. 54:5. Je 10:16.

16. **I have put.** Is 50:4. 59:21. Dt ✓18:18)✐. Jn ✓3:34. 8:38-40. *17:8. Re 1:1. **my words.** Je ✓23:28. **I have covered.** See on Is 49:2. Dt 33:27. **shadow.** ✓22L8, Ps +121:5. **plant.** Is 45:18. 60:21. 61:3. *65:17. *66:22. Ps 92:13. 2 P *3:13. **the heavens.** "Heaven" and "earth" are here put by symbolic language for "a *political universe.* That is, that I might make those who were but scattered persons and slaves in Egypt before, a kingdom and polity, to be governed by their own laws and magistrates" (Horne, *Introduction,* vol. 4, "Index of Symbolical Language of the Scriptures," p. 523, entry number 3). Hg +*2:6n. **and lay.** Is 48:13. 49:8. Ps 75:3. **Thou art.** Is 60:14, 15. Je 31:33. *32:38. Zc 8:8. *13:9. He *8:10.

17. **awake.** ✓84, Ge +6:17. See on ver. 9. Is 52:1. 60:1, 2. Jg 5:12. 1 C 15:34. Ep 5:14. **which hast.** Dt 28:28, 34. Jb 21:20. Ps 11:6. *60:3. *75:8, 22. Je 25:15-17, 27. Ezk 23:31-34. Zc 12:2. Re 14:10. 18:6.

18. **none.** Is 3:4-8. 49:21. Ps 88:18. 142:4. Je 5:30, 31. La *2:9. Zc 1:5. Mt 9:36. 15:14. **that taketh.** Is 41:13. 45:1. Jb 8:20mg. Je 31:32. Mk 8:23. Ac 9:8. 13:11. He 8:9.

19. **two things.** Is 47:9. Ezk 14:21. **are come.** Heb. happened. Ge +24:44n. Jg 14:5mg. 2 S 1:6mg. Ps 59:4mg. **who shall.** ✓85A, Ps +56:13. Jb 2:11. Ps 69:20. Je 9:17-21. La 1:9, 12, 17. Am 7:2. **destruction.** Heb. breaking. Is 1:28mg. 15:5mg. 59:7mg. 65:14mg. Jg +7:15mg. Je 4:6mg. 6:14mg. **by whom.** Is 22:4. 61:2. Jb 42:11. Ec 4:1. La 1:16. Am 7:2. 2 C 7:6, 7, 13. 2 Th 2:16, 17.

20. **sons.** ✓132D, Ge +19:25. Is 40:30. Je 14:18. La 1:15, 19. *2:11, 12. 4:2. 5:13. Am 7:2. **a wild.** Is 8:21. Ezk 12:13. 17:20. Re 16:9-11. **full.** ver. 17, 21. Is 9:19-21. Ps 88:15, 16. La 3:15, 16. Re 14:10. **the rebuke.** Ps 39:10, 11.

21. **hear.** ver. 1. **thou afflicted.** Is 3:14, 15. 10:2. *54:11. **drunken.** Is 29:9. Re ◑17:6. **but.** Is 29:9. 49:26. Ezk 39:19.

22. **pleadeth.** Is 41:13. 1 S 25:39. Ps 35:1. Pr 22:23. Je *50:34. *51:36. Jl 3:2. Mi *7:9. **I have.** ver. 17. Is +*54:7-10. 62:8. Ezk 39:29. Zc *12:2. **no more drink it again.** This refers, therefore, to the final restoration of Israel. Is ✓11:11. 52:1. +54:7. Je *31:40. Ho +*2:19. Am +✓9:15. Zc +*9:8. Lk 1:71.

23. **I will.** Is 49:25, 26. Pr 11:8. 21:18. Je 25:17-

29. Zc 12:2. Re 17:6-8, 18. **soul**. Heb. *nephesh*, Ge +27:31. **Bow**. Jsh 10:24. Ps *66:11, 12. Re 11:2. 13:16, 17.

ISAIAH 52

A call to captive Zion to assert her liberty, accompanied by promises of deliverance, 1-6. The joy occasioned by the gospel; and the knowledge, peace, and purity of Zion, with suitable exhortations, 7-12. The humiliation and exaltation of Christ and the success of his cause, 13-15.

1. **awake**. ℐ84, Ge +6:17. See on Is 51:9, 17. Da 10:9, 16-19. Hg 2:4. Ep 6:10. **put on thy beautiful**. See on Is 61:3, 10. SS 6:4, 10. Ezk 16:14. Lk 15:22. Ro 3:22. *13:14. Ep 4:24. Re *19:7, 8, 14. **the holy**. Is 1:21, 26. 48:2. Ne 11:1. Je 31:23. Zc 14:20, 21. Mt 4:5. Re *21:2, 27. **henceforth**. Is +60:21. Jb +5:24. Ps +130:8. **there shall**. Is 1:26. 26:2. 35:8. 60:21. 2 Ch 23:19. Ezk 44:9. Na *1:15. Zp 3:13. Zc 14:9. Re 20:9. *21:27. **unclean**. Is 35:8-10.

2. **Shake**. Is 3:26. 51:23. Je 51:6, 45, 50. Zc 2:6, 7. Re 18:4. **arise**. The common mode of sitting in the East is upon the floor, with the legs crossed; and when sitting is spoken of as a posture of more than ordinary state, it means sitting on high, on a chair of state, or throne. Re 18:7. Jona 4:5. **loose**. Is 45:13. 49:21. 51:14. 61:1, 3. Lk 4:18. *21:24.

3. **have sold**. Is 45:13. *50:1. Ps 44:12. Je 15:13. 1 P *1:18, 19. Ro 7:14-25.

4. **My people**. Ge 46:6ℐℙ. Ac 7:14, 15. **the Assyrian**. Is 14:25. ch. 36, 37. Ex *1:8. Je 50:17. Ac *7:18. **without**. Jb 2:3. Ps 25:3. 69:4. Jn 15:25.

5. **what**. Is 22:16. Jg 18:3. **people**. ver. 3. Ps 44:12. **make**. Is *47:6. 51:20, 23. Ex 1:13-16. 2:23, 24. 3:7. Ps 137:1, 2. Je 50:17. La 1:21. 2:3. 5:13-15. Zp 1:10. **my name**. Is 37:6, 28. Ps 44:16. 74:10, 18, 22, 23. Ezk 20:9, 14. *36:20-23. Ro ♭2:24. **blasphemed**. 1 T 6:1.

6. **my people**. Ex 33:19. *34:5-7. Ps 48:10. Ezk 20:44. 37:13, 14. 39:27-29. Zc 10:9-12. He *8:10, 11. **know my name**. Ex 3:14, 15. Ps +√9:10. **I am he**. Is 42:9. Nu *23:19. He *6:14-18.

7. **How beautiful**. This is a highly poetical expression, for, How welcome is his arrival! how agreeable are the tidings which he brings! Is 40:9. 61:1-3. 2 S 18:26. SS 7:1. Na *♭1:15. Lk *♣2:10. Ro 10:12-♭15. **feet**. ℐ171Q21, Pr +1:16. By Synecdoche of the Part, the feet are put for the whole man, in respect to carefulness, quickness, etc. How beautiful or pleasant is the coming of him who brings good news. **that bringeth**. Jn 1:41, 45. 4:29. **good tidings**. 2 K 7:9. Re 22:17. **publisheth**. Ps 68:11. SS 2:8. Mk 13:10. *16:15. Lk 24:47. Ac 10:36-38. Re *14:6. **Thy God**. Is 24:23. 25:9. 33:22. Jb +*19:26. Ps +*45:6. 59:13. 93:1. 96:10. 97:1. 99:1. Mi +*4:7. Zc *9:9. Mt 25:34. 28:18. Jn +√1:1. +√20:28. Ac +√20:28. Ro √9:5. 2 C 5:19. Col 2:8, *9. 1 T *3:16. T √2:13. He +√1:8. 2 P √1:1. Ju 4. Re *11:15. 21:7.

8. **Thy**. Is 56:10. *62:6, 7. SS 3:3. 5:7. Je 6:17. 31:6, 7. Ezk 3:17. 33:7. He 13:17. **lift**. ℐ144A12, Ge +22:13. Is 24:14. 40:9. 58:1. **with**. Is 12:4-6. 26:1. 27:2. 35:10. 48:20. Je *33:11. Ac 2:46, 47. Re 5:8-10. 18:20. 19:4. **sing**. Is +*51:11. **see**. Is 30:26. Je 32:39. Zp 3:9. Zc 12:8. Ac 2:1. *4:32. 1 C 1:10. 13:12. Ep 1:17, 18. **eye to eye**. That is, *face to face*. This expres-

sion has nothing to do with agreement in opinion, but with seeing the heralds of the coming King, and the King himself, face to face. Zc 9:14. 12:10. Jn 1:51n. **shall bring again**. or, returneth to. Is √59:20. Ps +*102:16. Ho +*5:15. +*6:3. Mi +*2:13. +*5:3, 4. Mt +*23:39. Ac +√3:19-21. **Zion**. Is +*24:23. +*51:11. +*59:20. Mi +*4:7.

9. **Break**. Is 14:7. 42:10, 11. 44:23. 48:20. 49:13. 54:1-3. 55:12. 65:18, 19. 66:10-13. Ps 96:11, 12. Zp 3:14, 15. Ga 4:27. **ye waste**. Is 44:26. 51:3. 61:4.

10. **made**. Is 51:9. 66:18, 19. ℐ Ps *98:1-3. Ac 2:5-11. Re *11:15-17. 15:4. **arm**. ℐ22A13. Anthropomorphism B877. An *arm* is attributed to God, denoting power executed in judgment, as well as making known his grace in wondrous power. For other instances of this figure see Is 53:1. Ps 136:12. Jn 12:38. **eyes**. Is 40:5. 49:26. **all**. Is 49:6. Ps 22:27. Lk 3:6. Ac 13:47. Re 11:15. 14:6. 19:1-3.

11. **depart ye**. Is 48:20. Je *50:8. *51:6, 45. Zc 2:6, 7. 2 C *♭6:17. Re *18:4. **touch**. Le 5:2, 3. 11:26, 27, 45, 47. 15:5, etc. Ezk 44:23. Hg 2:13, 14. Ac 10:14, 28. Ro *14:14. Ep +*5:11. 1 P 1:14-16. 2:5, 11. **be ye clean**. Le 10:3. 11:45. 22:2, 3. Ezr 1:7-11. 8:25-30. **that bear**. 1 P 2:5, 9. Re 5:9, 10.

12. **ye shall**. Is 28:16. 51:14. Ex 12:33, 39♭ℙ. 14:8. Dt 16:3♭ℙ. **for**. Is 45:2. Ex 13:21, 22. 14:19, 20. Dt 20:4. Jg 4:14. 1 Ch 14:15. Ezr 1:1-11. Mi 2:13. Jn +*10:4. **the God of Israel**. Is 17:6. 21:10, 17. +29:23. **be your rereward**. Heb. gather you up. Is 11:16. 14:1-3. 24:13, 14, 23. 25:6. 26:1, 2, 9, 13, 15. 27:6, 12, 13. *30:19. √33:20. +*35:10. 43:5. 44:23. 46:13. 49:6, 12, 19. +*54:7. *56:8. 58:8mg. 60:4. Ex 14:19♭ℙ. Nu 10:25. Jsh 6:9, 13. Ps 27:10mg. 147:2. Je 3:17. √16:14, 15. 23:3. *24:6. 30:3, 10. 31:8, 10. *32:37-40. 33:7, 26. 46:27. 50:19. Ezk *11:17. 20:33, 34. 34:+*13-16, *23-31. *36:24. 37:19-28. Am +*9:14, 15. Ob 17. Mi 2:12. 4:1-6. 5:7. Zp 3:18, 20. Zc 2:12. 8:7, 8. 9:16. *10:6-12.

13. **my servant**. Is *11:2, 3. +37:35. *42:1. 49:3, 6. *53:11. Ezk 34:23. Zc 3:8. Ph *2:7, 8. **deal prudently**. or, prosper. T#1899. Is *53:10. Jsh +*1:7mg, 8mg. 1 S 18:14mg. Je *23:5. Mt ♣22:34-40. **he shall**. Is +*9:6, 7. 49:6. Ps *2:6-9. 110:1, 2. Mt 28:18. Jn 3:31. √5:22, 23. Ep 1:20-23. Ph *2:5, 9-11. Col 1:19. *2:3, 9. He +*1:3. 2:7, 8. Re *5:6-13. **exalted**. ℐ173, Ge +27:44. Is 53:12.

14. **many**. Ps 71:7. Mt 7:28. 22:22, 33. 27:14. Mk 5:42. 6:51. 7:37. 10:26, 32. Lk 2:47. 4:36. 5:26. **astonied**. Archaic for "astonished," as in Jb 17:8. T#1960. Ps 22:17. Lk ♣23:35. **marred**. T#1947. Is 50:6. *53:2-5. Ps *22:6, 7, 15, 17. 102:3-5. Zc 13:6. Mt *♣26:67. *♣27:29, 30. Lk *♣22:64. Jn ♣19:5. 1 T 3:16.

15. **sprinkle**. Heb. *nazah*, Nu +19:21. Is 63:3h. Le 14:7. Nu *8:7. 2 K ◑9:33. Ezk *36:25. Jl 2:28. Mt *28:19. Ac +1:5. 2:17, 33. *8:36n. T *3:5, 6. He *9:13, 14. +*10:22. *11:28. *12:24. 1 P 1:2. Young notes, an eastern token of welcome. Samuel J. Baird, noting that the LXX. reads "astonish" here, suggests "this only shows how willingly those writers would have obliterated from the text the promise of salvation for the Gentiles, which it contains" (*A Bible History of Baptism*, pp. 140, 141). **kings**. T#946. Is 49:7, 23. 60:3, 10, 11, 16. Jb 21:5. 29:9, 10. 40:4. Ps *72:9-11. Mi *7:16, 17. Zc 2:13. **for**. Is 51:5. 55:5. Ro *15:20, ♭21. 16:25, 26. 1 C ♭2:9. Ep *3:5-9.

ISAIAH 53

The unbelief of the Jews predicted, 1. The meanness of Christ's external appearance; and the contempt and sufferings which he would endure, 2, 3. He would suffer as a sacrifice for the sins of his people; but in perfect holiness and patience, 4-7. Several circumstances predicted, which attended his death, burial, resurrection, and glory; and his success in justifying and saving sinners as his spiritual progeny, 8-10. As a recompense of his sufferings, and the fruit of his intercession, he should rescue a numerous people from Satan's bondage and rule over them as his willing subjects, 11, 12.

1. **Who hath believed.** lit. remained steadfast. Ge +*15:6. 45:26. Ex 4:8. Jn *1:7, 12. 7:5. *▶12:38. Ro *▶10:16, 17. 1 C 1:18, 24. 2 C √4:3, 4. This chapter declares the circumstances of our Savior's sufferings so exactly that it seems rather a history of his passion than a prophecy. And it is so undeniable a proof of the truth of Christianity that the bare reading of it, and comparing it with the gospel history, hath converted some infidels (Lowth). **report.** *or,* doctrine. Heb. hearing. ꟊ121R1, Le +13:55. Is 28:9mg, 19mg. 37:7. 1 S 2:24. **the arm.** ꟊ22A13, Is +52:10. Is 51:9. *52:10. 62:8. Mt *11:25. 13:11. *16:17. Ro √1:16. 1 C *1:18, 24. Ep *1:18, 19. **revealed.** Is *40:5. Mt *11:25. *16:17. Ro *1:17, 18.

2. **he shall grow.** Is *11:1. Je *23:5. Ezk 17:22-24. Zc *6:12. Mk *6:3. Lk √2:7, 39, 40, 51, 52. 9:58. Ro *8:3. Ph *2:6, 7. 1 T 3:16. **and as.** ꟊ105, Ml +4:2. **dry ground.** Mt ✱6:3. Lk ✱9:58. **he hath no form.** Is *52:14. Mk +*14:44. Lk +*4:30. Jn +*8:59. 18:4-8. **no beauty that.** Mk 9:12. Jn *1:10-14. 7:24. *9:28, 29. *18:40. *19:5, 14, 15. 1 P 2:4.

3. **despised.** Is *49:7. *50:6. Ps *22:6-8. 69:10-12, 19, 20. Mi *5:1. Zc 11:8, *12, *13. Mt *26:67. *27:39-44, 63. Mk 3:21, 30. 6:3. 9:12. *15:19. Lk 4:22, 24. *8:53. *9:22, 58. *16:14. *23:18, etc. Jn *8:48. 9:16, 24. He *12:2, 3. **and rejected.** T#85. Ge 6:5. Mt√27:25. Lk √19:14. *20:13-15. Jn ✱1:10, √11. 7:41, 52. ✱8:48. 10:20. Ac 7:51, 52. √13:46. **a man of sorrows.** ver. 4, 10. Ge=49:23. 1 Ch 4:9. Ps 69:29. Mt *26:37, 38. Mk *14:34. Lk *19:41. Jn *11:35. He *2:15-18. *4:15. *5:7. **we hid as it were our faces from him.** *or,* he hid as it were, *his* face from us. Heb. as a hiding of faces from him, *or* from us. lit. "making secret," as if he were ashamed; as in Is 8:17. Is 50:6. Ps 22:6, 7. Mk 3:20, 21. Jn 8:48. 18:40. **we esteemed.** T#1942. Dt 32:15. Ps 69:8. 118:22. Zc *11:13. Mt ✱21:42, 43. 26:15. *27:9, 10. Jn √✱1:10, 11. ✱7:5, 48. 18:40. Ac *3:13-15.

4. **he hath.** ver. 5, 6, 11, 12. Mt *▶8:17. Lk 4:2. Jn 11:35. Ga *3:13. He 2:17, 18. +*4:15. *9:28. 1 P *2:24. *3:18. 1 J *2:2. **borne.** ꟊ121C1E, Ge +19:15. Ex 28:38, 43▶ꟼ. Ezk +4:4. **our griefs.** Da 9:26. Mt ✱20:28. **yet.** Mt 26:37. Jn 19:7. **smitten.** T#1945. Is +*50:6. Mi *5:1. Mt ✱26:67, 68. ✱27:30. Jn ✱19:3.

5. **But he was.** ver. 6-8, 11, 12. Da *9:24. Zc *13:7. Mt *20:28. Ro *3:24-26. *4:25. 5:6-10, 15-21. 1 C +√15:3. 2 C √5:21. Ga 3:13. Ep *5:2. He *9:12-15, 28. *10:10, 14. 1 P *3:18. **wounded.** *or,* tormented. Is 51:9. Ps 109:22. **for our.** Ps=106:32. **transgressions.** Le +=5:6. **bruised.** T#1948. ver. 10. Ge +√3:15. Ex +=27:20. Le=2:1. +=23:13. Mt ✱27:26-29. He +=2:10. **iniquities.** 1 J *3:5. **the chastisement.** 1 P

*2:24. **peace.** Le 7:29, 30. +=23:19. Ro *5:1. Ep *2:14. **stripes.** Heb. bruise. Is 1:6. Ge 4:23. Ex 21:25. **with his.** 1 P ▶2:24. **healed.** T#1895. Ex +15:26. Le 13:18, 37. 14:3. Nu 21:9. Ps *103:3. Mt ✱*▶8:17. Jn 3:14, 15. Ac *10:38. 3 J 2.

6. **All.** Is *64:6. 1 K 8:46. 2 Ch 6:36. Jb 15:14-16. Ps 130:3. 143:2. Pr *20:9. Ec √7:20. Ro 3:9-12, √23. 1 J √1:8, 10. **we like sheep.** Ps 23:1, 3. *119:176. Mt *18:12-14. Lk *15:3-7. Ro *3:10-19. 1 P *2:25. **turned.** That is, turned the face. Is 8:21. 56:11. **his own.** Is √55:7. *56:11. Pr √14:12. Ezk √3:18. Ro *4:25. Ja *5:20. 1 P *3:18. **the Lord hath.** T#581. ver. 10. Jn √3:16. Ro 3:25. Ga 4:4, 5. 1 J 4:9, 10. **laid on him the iniquity of us all.** Heb. made the iniquities of us all to meet on him. Is 50:8. Le +=23:19. Ps 69:4. **the iniquity.** T#578. Je 23:6. Da 9:24. Jn *3:17. 6:51, 55. 10:9. Ro *1:16, 17. 3:21, 22. 5:10, 11, 15-21. *10:3, 4. 2 C √5:14, 15. Ep 5:2. Ph 3:9. 1 J *2:2. *3:5. 4:9, 10. Re 5:9.

7. **yet.** Ps 38:13. Mt 12:19. *26:63. *27:12-14. Mk *14:61. *15:5. Lk *23:9. Jn *19:9. 1 P *2:23. **opened not.** ꟊ108H6B, Ps +38:13. **he is brought.** T#1938. "The Savior was neither 'driven' nor 'dragged,' but *led*: thereby the Holy Spirit informs us, once more, of His *willing submission*" (Pink, *Comm. on John,* vol. 3, p. 176). Ge ◐3:24. Le=17:5. Jn *18:13. Ac *▶8:32, 33. **as a lamb.** T#1908. Ex 12:5, 13. Ac ✱8:32-35. Re 13:8. **sheep.** Le=1:10. **is dumb.** T#1939. Mt ✱27:12-14. 1 P ✱2:23.

8. **from prison and from judgment:** *and. or,* by distress and judgment: but, etc. T#1941. Ps 22:12-21. 69:12. Mt *26:65, 66. ✱27:23, 24. Jn *19:4, 7. Ac ✱8:33. **who shall declare.** Mt *1:1. 12:50. Jn *7:27. Ac *8:33. Ro *1:4. 2 C 5:16. **his generation.** Or, as Bishop Lowth renders, "his manner of life (Heb. *doro*) who would declare?" None was called, or admitted to bear witness to his character, as was customary in criminal causes. Da +*9:26. Jn 16:32. **cut off.** T#1973. Ps 102:23, 24. Da +*9:24-26. Mk ✱14:41. Lk 3:1, 2, 23. Jn 8:20. *11:49-52. 13:1. ✱18:13, 14. **for the transgression.** Jn *11:51, 52. **was he stricken.** Heb. *was* the stroke upon him. 1 P *3:18.

9. **And he.** Rather, as Bp. Lowth and others render, "And his grave was appointed with the wicked; but with the rich man was his tomb;" regarding the Hebrew letter *beth* in *bemothaiv* as a radical, and deriving it from *bamoth,* a high or elevated place, or a *tumulus,* the sepulchres among the Hebrews being generally erected on *eminences.* **made.** or, appointed. lit. gave. Is 7:14. 55:4. Ge 15:18. Ps 72:15. Ec 2:21mg. Je 1:4. Mt *27:57-60. Mk *15:43-46. Lk *23:50-53. Jn *19:38-42. 1 C *15:4. **grave.** Heb. *qeber,* Ge +23:4. Is 14:19. 22:16. 65:4. **wicked.** or, wrong ones. Is 3:11. Lk 23:32. **with the rich.** T#1974. Mt ✱*27:57-60. Mk 15:43, 46. Lk 23:53. Jn 19:40-42. **death.** Heb. deaths. i.e. *most bitter death.* Mk 15:42-47. Jn 19:38, 39. **done no violence.** T#1940. Jn ✱19:4. **neither.** T#1906. Jn ✱8:46. 1 P ✱2:22, 23. **deceit.** T#1910. Ex 12:5. Le 1:3, 10. 2 C √5:21. He +*4:15. *7:26. *9:14. 1 P ✱*▶2:22. 1 J *3:5. **in his mouth.** Ja *3:2.

10. **pleased.** Is *42:1. Mt *3:17. *17:5. **bruise.** ver. +*5. Le +=23:13. **he hath.** Ps *69:26. Zc *13:7. Mt 27:46. Lk 22:44. Jn 12:27. 18:11. Ro *8:32. Ga *3:13. 1 J *4:9, 10. **when thou shalt make his soul.** Heb. *nephesh,* Ge +12:13. *or,* when his soul shall make. Da *9:24. Lk +*9:24. Ro 8:3. 2 C √5:21. Ep 5:2. 1 T

2:6. He *7:27. *9:14, 25, 26. 10:6-12. 13:10-12. 1 P
*2:24. **an offering.** Heb. *asham*, the trespass offering.
Le +*=5:6n. +=23:19. This is a particularly Levitical
word (Le 14:12, 21), and cannot be understood apart
from the institution described in the Pentateuch, making this a very remarkable reference to the Pentateuch.
Le 14:12, 21▶♉. **he shall see.** Ps 22:30. 45:16, 17. 110:3.
Jn *12:24. He *2:13. **he shall prolong.** Is +*9:7. Ps
√16:9-11. *21:4. *72:17. *89:29, 36. Ezk *37:25. Da
*7:13, 14. Lk *1:33. 23:42, 43. Ac *2:24-28. Ro *6:9.
Re *1:18. **the pleasure.** Is √55:11-13. 62:3-5. Ps *72:7.
*85:10-12. *147:11. *149:4. Je *32:41. Ezk 33:11. Mi
*7:18. Zp *3:17. Lk 15:5-7, 23, 24. Jn √6:37-40. *10:17,
18. Ep *1:5, 9. 2 Th *1:11. **shall prosper.** Ge=39:3.
Ps 22:30. 110:3. Mt 12:20. Lk 1:33. Jn *6:40. 12:23,
24. Ro 6:9. Ep 1:5. He 2:13. Re 1:18. 14:3, 4.

11. **see.** Lk *22:44. Jn *12:24, 27-32. 16:21. Ga
*4:19. He *12:2. Re *5:9, 10. 7:9-17. **travail.**
Ge=41:51. Ga 4:19. **soul.** Heb. *nephesh*, Ge +12:13.
satisfied. Ps 17:15. Jn 19:30. **by his knowledge.**
T#1897. Jn 4:39-42. √17:3. 2 C *4:6. Ph *3:8-10. 2 P
*1:2, 3. *3:18. *ſ*121C2A3. Metonymy of the Cause
B554. Verbs of *knowing* are used also of *experiencing*,
either by saving faith or personal dealing. For other
instances of this figure see Mt 7:11. Mk 5:29. Lk 1:77.
1 C 4:19. 2 C 1:9. **my righteous.** Is 42:1. 49:3. 1 J
√2:1. 2 J 1, 3. **justify.** Is *45:25. 61:10. Le +=23:12.
Ps 85:10. Lk +*19:10. Ro *3:22-24. *4:24, 25. 5:1, 9,
18, 19. 1 C *6:11. Ph 3:9. T 3:6, *7. **bear.** See on
ver. 4-6, 8, 12. Mt √20:28. He *9:28. 1 P *2:24. *3:18.

12. **will I.** Is 49:24, 25. *52:15. Ge +√3:15. Ps *2:8.
24:7-10. Da 2:45. Mt *12:28, 29. Ac *26:18. Ep 4:8-
10. Ph √2:8-11. Col *1:13, 14. *2:15. He *2:14, 15. **a
portion.** *ſ*63A2, 2 S +6:6. "Therefore will I (Jehovah)
divide (or apportion) to him a great multitude (*for
booty*), and the strong ones will he (i.e., Messiah) divide
as spoil" (B11). The "many nations" of Is 52:15 answer
to the "great multitudes" of Is 53:12; and "the kings"
of Is 52:15 answer to the "strong ones" of Is 53:12.
Thus the two passages explain each other. The first
line of verse 12 is what Jehovah divides to his servant;
and the second line is what he divides as victor for
himself and his host. Compare Ps 110:2-5 and Re 19:11-
16. **spoil.** Mk 3:27. Ro 16:20. 1 J 3:8. **the great.** Ac
2:33, 36. 2 C 13:4. Ph 2:9. Re 17:14. 19:12. **poured.**
F/L Is 32:15. Le=4:30. +=23:19. Ps *22:14. Ph
2:17mg. He *12:2. **soul.** Heb. *nephesh*, Ge +12:13.
unto death. Mt ✱27:50. **numbered with.** T#1952. Mk
✱*)15:28. Lk *)22:37. *23:25, 32, 33. **he bare.** See
on ver. *11. Le 10:17▶♉. Nu 9:13▶♉. 18:32▶♉. 1 T
√2:5, 6. T *2:14. He *9:26, 28. **of many.** √*ſ*171F. Synecdoche of the Species B623. When the species is put
for the genus, or when particulars are put for universals.
Many is sometimes put for *all*. Contrast *ſ*171B, Ge
+24:10. For other instances of this figure see Da 12:2.
Mt 20:28. √26:28n. Jn 6:50. Ro √5:15, 19. 8:29. He
2:10. 9:28. **made intercession.** T#1953. Ps 109:4. Lk
✱*23:34. Ro *8:34. He √7:25. √9:24. 1 J *2:1, 12. **for
the transgressors.** T#1748. Lk 23:43. Jn 17:20. Ro
5:8.

ISAIAH 54

*Predictions that Israel shall be exceedingly enlarged
by the conversion of the Gentiles: with promises of
great honor and happiness to her, as espoused by God,*

*1-5. Encouraging assurances of deliverance from afflic-
tion, perpetual mercy, prosperity, and victory over
every enemy, to Israel and to every servant of God,
6-17.*

1. **Sing.** *ſ*96B, Ge +20:7. **O barren.** Is 62:4. Ge
+*11:30. 2 S 2:1, 5. SS 8:8. Je 3:20. Ezk 16:15, 20,
21, 36, etc. Ho 2:4. 4:6. 5:7. *9:14-17. 10:1. Ga ▶4:27.
He 11:11, 12. **thou.** lit. she. *ſ*96D3, Ge +49:4. **break.**
F/L Is +14:7. 42:10, 11. 44:23. 49:13. 52:9. 55:12,
13. Ps 67:3-5. 98:3-9. Zp *3:14. Zc *9:9. Re 7:9, 10.
into singing. Is 12:6. 49:13. Zp 3:14. Zc +*2:10. **for
more.** Is 27:6. 49:17, 18, 20. Ge +*22:16-18. 1 S 2:5.
Ps +*113:9. Je 31:27, 28. 33:22. Ezk 36:10, 11, 37,
38. Ho 1:10. Zc 2:3-5. He 11:11, 12. 12:22, 23. Re
21:2. **are the children.** Ps +*102:28. Ho 1:10. **of the
desolate.** Is *62:4. **than the children.** Mt +*7:14. Lk
√20:35, 36. Ro 8:23. **married wife.** 2 C *11:2. Ep *5:27.
Re *19:7-9.

2. **Enlarge.** Is 33:20. *49:19, 20. Je 10:20.

3. **thou shalt.** T#380. Is *2:2-4. *11:9-12, 14. *35:1,
2. 42:1-12. 43:5, 6. 49:12. 60:3-11. Ge +*49:10. Ps
*72:8-11. Am +*9:11, 12. Ob 18-20. Ro 9:25, 26. 10:18.
11:12. Col *1:23. **and thy.** Is 49:18. *55:5. *60:10-13.
*61:5-9. **make.** Is 49:8, 19. 52:9. Ezk *36:35, 36.

4. **Fear not.** Is 41:10, 14. *45:16, 17. 61:7. Le
26:6▶♉. 1 P *2:6. **thou shalt forget.** Je 31:19. Ezk 16:22,
43, 60-63. Ho 3:1-5. **shame of thy youth.** Je 3:24, 25.
the reproach. Is 50:1. Je 3:14.

5. **thy Maker.** Ps 45:10-17. Je 3:14. 31:32. Ezk *16:8.
Ho *2:19, 20. Jn 3:29. 2 C *11:2, 3. Ep *5:25-27, 32.
the Lord of hosts. Is 6:5. +44:6. 48:2. 51:15. 1 S +1:3.
Je 10:16. 50:34. 51:19. Lk 1:32. Jn 12:37-41. Ro 9:29.
thy Redeemer. or, kinsman-Redeemer. Ja 5:4. **the Holy One of Israel.**
48:16▶♉. Ex 6:6▶♉. 15:13▶♉. **the Holy One of Israel.**
F/L Is +1:4. **The God.** Jsh 3:11, 13. Zc 6:5. *14:9.
Ro *3:29, 30. 11:12. Re *11:15. A reference to the
triune Jehovah (CB). Is 42:1n.

6. **a woman.** Is 49:14. *62:4. Ho 2:1, 2, 14, 15.
Mt *11:28. 2 C 7:6, 9, 10. **forsaken.** F/L Is 1:4. **grieved.**
1 S +1:10. **spirit.** Heb. *ruach*, Ge +41:8. **a wife.** Pr
5:18. Ec 9:9. Ml 2:14.

7. **a small.** Is *26:20. 60:10. Ps 30:5. 2 C *4:17.
2 P *3:8, 9. **forsaken thee.** Is ◑+*41:9. *61:15. Dt
31:17. 1 S +*12:22. 2 K 21:14. 1 Ch +*28:9. 2 Ch
15:2. Je 6:30. La 5:20. Re 11:2. **with.** Is 11:11. 14:1.
40:11. 49:18. 60:4. 66:18. Ps 119:156. Je 29:10. Da
9:18. Mt 23:37. Ep *1:10. **gather thee.** Is 11:12. 27:12,
13. 43:5, 6. +√52:12mg. +*56:8. Dt *30:3, 4. 1 Ch
16:35. Ne 1:9. Ps 106:47. 107:3. +*147:2. Je 16:15.
23:3. *24:6. 29:14. 30:3. 31:8, 10. *32:37. 50:19. Ezk
11:17. 20:34, 41. 28:25. 34:13. *36:24. 37:21. 39:27,
28. Mi 2:12. 4:6. Zp √3:19. Zc √10:6, 8, 10.

8. **a little.** Is 47:6. *57:16, 17. 60:10. Ps 30:5. Zc
1:15. **I hid.** Is 8:17. 45:15. 53:3. 64:7. Dt 31:17, 18▶♉.
Ps 13:1. 27:9. Ezk 39:23, 24. **but.** Is +√55:3. Ps *103:17,
18. Je *31:3. 2 Th 2:16. 1 T 1:16. **everlasting.** Heb.
olam, Ge +*17:7. Ge +9:16. **have mercy.** Is 49:13-
17. Ho √2:14, 16mg, 19. **the Lord.** ver. 5. Is 48:17.
49:26. He 9:12.

9. **For this.** Je +√33:25, 26. Ro +√11:1, 2. **the waters
of Noah.** Is 12:1. √55:11. Ge +√8:21, 22. 9:11-16▶♉.
1 Ch 1:4. Ps *104:9. Je +*5:22. +√31:35, 36. +√33:20-
26. Ezk *14:14, 20. *39:29. He 6:16-18. Re 4:3. **no
more.** Ge +8:21, 22. +9:16. **so have.** Ge +*22:16-
18. Je 31:35-37. Lk 1:73. He 6:13, 14. **sworn that.** Is
*55:11. Ps *119:89, 90. Mi 7:20. He *6:18.

10. **the mountains.** Is 51:6, 7. Ps 46:2. 125:2. Mt *5:18. 16:18. *24:35. Ro 11:29. 2 P 3:10-13. **not depart.** Is +*41:9, 17. +*55:3. Ge +8:22. +9:16. 1 S +*12:22. Ps +√94:14. Je +*31:36. +*33:24-26. Ezk 16:60. Ro +√11:1, 2. He +*13:5. **the covenant.** Is +*55:3. 2 S 23:5. Ps 89:33, 34. Ezk 37:26. Ml 2:5. He 8:6-13. 13:20, 21. **that hath.** Is 49:10. Ep 2:4, 5. T *3:5.

11. **thou afflicted.** ver. 6. Is 49:14. 50:10. 51:17-19, 23. 52:1-5. 60:15. Ex 2:23. 3:2, 7. Dt 31:17. Ps *34:19. 129:1-3. Je 30:17. Jn *16:20-22, 33. Ac *14:22. Re 7:13, 14. 11:3-10. 12:13-17. **tossed.** Mt 8:24. Ac 27:18-20. **not comforted.** La 1:1, 2, 16, 17, 21. **I will lay.** 1 K 5:17. 1 Ch 29:2. Ezk ch. 40-42. 1 C *3:12, 13. Ep *2:20. 1 P *2:4-6. Re *21:18-21. **sapphires.** Ex 24:10. 28:17-20. 39:10-14. SS 5:14. Ezk 1:26. 10:1.

12. **windows.** or, pinnacles. Is 14:31. 22:7. 24:12. **agates.** Ezk 27:16. Re 21:21. **pleasant stones.** or, stones of delight. lit. desire, pleasure. Is 32:12mg. 44:28. 46:10. 48:14.

13. **all.** Is *2:3. 11:9. Ps 25:8-12. 71:17. Je 31:34. Mt *11:25-29. 16:17. Lk 10:21, 22. *24:45. Jn)6:45. √14:26. 1 C *2:10. Ep 4:21. 1 Th *4:9. He +*8:10, 11. 1 J *2:20, 27. **taught.** Is +*8:16. 48:17, 18. Mi 4:2. 1 J 2:27. **great.** Is √26:3. *32:15-18. *55:12. Ps *119:165. Je 33:6. Ezk 34:25, 28. 37:26. Ho 2:18. Jn 14:27. 16:33. Ro 5:1. 14:17. 15:13. Ga 5:22. Ph 4:7. **of thy children.** Dt +*29:11n. Ne +*12:43. Jl *2:16. Mt 14:21. 15:38. 19:13-15. Mk *9:36, 37. Lk *18:15. 2 T +*3:15.

14. **righteousness.** Is 1:26, 27. 45:24. 52:1. +*60:21. 61:10, 11. 62:1. Je *23:6. 31:23. Ezk 36:27, 28. 37:23-26. Jl *3:17-21. Zc 8:3. 2 P *3:13. **thou shalt be.** T#776. Is 51:13. Ex *22:26, 27. Ps 12:5. 35:10. 72:4, 14. 109:31. *146:7. Ec *5:8. Zc 9:8. **for thou.** Is *2:4. 60:18. Pr *3:25, 26. Je 23:3, 4. 30:10. Mi 4:3, 4. Zp 3:13-16. Zc *2:4, 5.

15. **they shall.** Ps 56:7. 59:4. Ezk *38:8-23. Jl √3:9-14. Re 16:14. 19:19-21. *20:8, 9. **shall fall.** Is 43:3, 4, 14. Ps *37:12, 13. Pr 15:25. Zc 2:8. 12:3, 9. 14:2, 3.

16. **I have.** Is 10:5, 6, 15. 37:26. +*45:7, 8. 46:11. Ex +*9:16. Pr +*16:4. Da 4:34, 35. Jn *19:11.

17. **no weapon.** ver. *15. Ps *2:1-6. Pr +*21:30. Ezk 38:9, 10. Mt *16:18. Jn √10:28-30. Ro *8:1, 28-39. **every.** Is 50:8, 9. Jb 1:11. 2:5. 22:5, etc. *42:7, 8. Ps *32:6. Je +20:11. Zc *3:1-4. Re *12:10. **the heritage.** Is *58:14. Jb 20:29. Ps 16:6. *61:5. 119:111. Da 3:26-28. 6:20-22. Ro *6:22, 23. **and their.** Is *45:24, 25. *61:10. Ps *24:5. 71:16, 19. Je *23:6. Ro *3:22. *10:4. 1 C *1:30. 2 C *5:21. Ph *3:9. 2 P *1:1.

ISAIAH 55

Enlarged and urgent invitations to partake freely of spiritual blessings, with expostulations and promises of the sure mercies of David, 1-3. Christ proposed to mankind as he whom the nations would obey, 4, 5. A call to the prayer of faith and repentance, with promises of abundant mercy, 6, 7: because God's ways are not like man's, 8, 9. The success of the gospel, the joy of believers, and the happy change which was about to take place in the world, 10-13.

1. **Ho.** Ru 4:1. Pr 1:21-23. 8:4. Zc 2:6. **every.** Is *41:17, 18. Ps 42:1, 2. 63:1. 143:6. Jn *4:10-14. *7:37, 38. Re 21:6. *22:1, 17. **waters.** Γ22K4, Je +2:13. **buy, and.** Ps 31:16. Mt 13:44-46. Ph 3:7. Re 3:18. **buy wine.**

Ps *104:15. SS 1:2, 4. 5:1. Zc 9:15. 10:7. Mt 26:29. Jn 2:3-10. **milk.** Jl 3:18. 1 C 3:2. 1 P *2:2. **without money.** Is 52:3. Ge=47:25. Ro *3:24. 11:6. Ep *2:4-8.

2. **do ye.** Is *44:20. Je *2:13. Ho 8:7. 12:1. Hab 2:13. Mt *15:9. Lk 15:15, 16. Ro 9:31. *10:2, 3. Ph *3:4-7. He *13:9. **spend.** Heb. weigh. Is 46:6. Ge 23:16. Je 32:9. **hearken.** Is 51:1, 4, 7. Ex *15:26. Dt 11:13. Ps 34:11. Pr *1:33. 7:24. 8:32. Mk 7:14. Ro √10:17. **eat.** Is 25:6. Ps *22:26. 36:8. 63:5. Pr 9:5. Je 31:14. Mt 22:4. Lk *15:23. Jn *6:48-58. **soul.** Heb. *nephesh*, Ge +34:3. **delight.** Is 58:14. Jb 22:26. 27:10. **fatness.** Is 25:6. ✱S#1880h: Is 55:2. Jg 9:9. Jb 36:16. Ps 36:8. 63:5. 65:11. Je 31:14. See also ✱S#1880h: Le 1:16 (ashes). 4:12, 12. 6:10, 11. 1 K 13:3, 5. Je 31:40.

3. **Incline.** Ps 78:1. 119:112. Pr 4:20. **come.** Mt *11:28. Jn 6:√37, 44, 45. 7:37. **hear.** Mt 13:16. 17:5. Jn √5:24, 25. 8:47. √10:27. **soul.** Heb. *nephesh*, Ge +12:13. **and I will.** Is 54:8. 61:8. Ge 17:7. 2 S 23:5. Je 31:33, 34. 32:40. *50:5. He *13:20. **everlasting.** Heb. *olam*, Ge +17:7. Ge +9:16. **covenant.** Jg 2:1. 2 S *7:10-16. Ps +*74:20. √89:34. **the sure mercies.** Is +*41:9. +*54:8-10. +*59:21. 2 S +√7:10, 15. Ps +*89:28, 33, 35-37. +*132:11. Je +*33:20, 21, 25, 26. Ezk √37:24, 25. Ac +√13:34. **of David.** Γ181E, Ge +3:24. Is 38:5. Ac ✱+*13:23.

4. **I have.** Jn √3:16. 18:37. 1 T 6:13. Re +*1:5. +√3:14. **a leader.** Is 49:8-10. =63:12, 13. Jsh 5:14. Ps *2:6. 67:4mg. 77:20. Je 30:9. Ezk 34:23, 24. Da *9:25. Ho 3:5. Mi +*5:2-4. Mt 2:6. 28:18-20. Jn *10:3, 27. 12:26. *13:13. Ac 5:31. 2 Th √1:8. Ep 5:24. He +*2:10. *5:9. Re 19:16.

5. **thou shalt.** Is 11:10, 11. 52:15. 56:8. Ge +*49:10. Ps *18:43. Ro 15:20, 21. Ep 2:11, 12. 3:5, 6. **nations.** Is 49:5, 6. *60:5. Ho 1:10. Zc 2:11. *8:20-23. Ep 2:13. **Holy One of Israel.** F/L Is +1:4. 5:19, 24. 54:5. 60:9, 14. Ps 71:22. 78:41. 89:18. Je 50:29. 51:5. **hath glorified.** Is 60:9. Ps 110:1-3. Lk 24:26. Jn *12:28. *13:31, 32. 17:1. Ac *3:13. 5:31. He *5:5. 1 P 1:11.

6. **Seek.** Is 45:19. 1 Ch +*28:9. 2 Ch +*19:3. Jb 8:5. Ps *14:2. 27:8. *32:6. 95:7. Pr 8:17. Je *29:12-14. Am *5:6. Mt 5:25. *7:7, 8. *25:11, 12. Lk *13:25. Jn *7:33, 34. *8:21. *12:35, 36. 2 C *6:1, 2. He *2:3. +√3:13. Ja *4:8. **while he may.** T#1174. Ps *32:6. Lk √13:24. **while he is near.** T#1173. Is *12:6. *46:13. Ge +6:3. Dt *4:7. Ps *75:1. *145:18. 148:14. Pr 1:28. Ezk 8:6. Ho 5:6. 9:12. 2 C +6:2. Ep 2:13, 17.

7. **the wicked.** Is 1:16-18. 2 Ch +√7:14. Pr √28:13. Je 3:3. 8:4-6. Ezk 3:18, 19. 18:21-23, 27-32. 33:11, 14-16. Ho *14:1, 2. Jon *3:10. Mt 9:13. Lk 15:10, 24. Ac +*3:19. 26:20. 1 C +*6:9-11. Ja 4:8-10. **forsake.** T#1421. 2 Ch +√7:14. Jb *34:31, 32. Ps ◐37:11. Pr √28:13. Jon 3:7, 8. **unrighteous man.** Heb. man of iniquity. **his thoughts.** Ge 6:5. Jb √17:11. Ps 66:18. +*146:4. Je 4:14. Zc 8:17. Mt 15:18, 19. 22:25, 26. Mk 7:21, 23. Lk 11:39, 40. Ac 8:21, 22. Ja 1:15. **have mercy.** Ex 34:6. Jn ◐+*3:36. **for.** Is *43:25. 44:22. Ex 34:6, 7. Nu 14:18, 19. Ps *51:1. 130:7. Je 3:12, 13. Lk 7:47. Ro 5:16-21. Ep 1:6-8. 1 T *1:15, 16. **abundantly.** Heb. multiply to. Is 1:15mg. Ge 3:16. Ps 18:35mg. Lk 15:20. Ro *5:20. **pardon.** Mi *7:18, 19.

8. **my thoughts.** Γ132G, Ge +3:19. Γ25, Ge +4:4. Γ22C5, Ge +50:20. 2 S 7:19. Ps 25:10. 40:5. 92:5. √94:11. Pr 21:8. 25:3. Je 3:1, 4. Ezk 18:29. Da 4:37. Ho 14:9. Mi √4:12.

9. **the heavens.** Ps 36:5-7. 77:19. 89:2. *103:11, 12.

Mt 11:25, 26. Ro *11:31-36. **ways higher.** Is 57:15. 64:4. Ps +8:5n. Ec *3:11. 8:17. 1 C *2:9. **your ways.** 2 S 7:19. 1 J 4:10. **my thoughts.** ver. 8. Ps 40:5, +17.

10. **as the rain.** ♪160B, Ge +25:31. Is 5:6. 30:23. 61:11. Dt 32:2. 1 S 23:4. Ps 65:9-13. 72:6, 7. Ezk 34:26. Ho 10:12. Mt +*5:45. Re 11:6. **returneth not.** Ps ◗135:7. Je ◗10:13. ◗51:16. That is, not in the same form, or void, or without effect, or immediately: it abides for a time upon the earth until it does that for which it is sent, as Poole and others note. **that it.** 2 C ♪9:10. **give seed.** Ge=47:23. 2 C 9:9-11. **eater.** Jg 14:14.

11. **So.** ♪160B, Ge +25:31. **shall my word.** Is +*54:9. Nu *23:19. Dt 8:3♪?. 32:2♪?. Ps *119:89. *138:2. Ezk *12:25. Mt *24:35. Lk 8:11-16. Jn 6:63. Ro √10:17. 1 C 1:18. 3:6-9. Ep 6:17. 1 Th √2:13. He 6:7. Ja √1:18. 1 P *1:23. **my mouth.** ♪22A10, Nu +12:8. **not return.** 1 S 3:19. **it shall accomplish.** Is 44:26-28. 45:23. 46:10. Ep 1:9-11. **please.** Ps +*115:3.

12. **ye shall.** Is 35:10. 48:20. 49:9, 10. 51:11. 65:13, 14. Ps 105:43. Je 30:19. 31:12-14. 33:6, 11. Zc 2:7-10. Ro 5:1, 11. 15:13. Ga 5:22. Col 1:11-13. **the mountains.** Is 14:8. 35:1, 2. 42:10, 11. 44:23. 49:13. Ps 65:13. 96:11-13. 98:7-9. 148:4-13. Lk 15:10. Re 19:1-6. **singing.** ♪155D, Ge +4:10. **the trees.** Is 41:19, 20. 61:3. Ps 92:12. 104:16. **clap.** ♪155D, Ge +4:10. 1 Ch 16:32, 33. Ps 47:1.

13. **Instead.** Is *11:6, 7. *65:25. Ac +3:21. **of the thorn.** Is 11:6-9. 41:19. 60:13, 21. 61:3. Mi 7:4. Ro 6:19. 1 C +*6:9-11. 2 C √5:17. **for a.** Is *43:21. Je 13:11. 33:9. Lk 2:14. Jn 15:8. Ep 3:20, 21. 1 P 2:9, 10. 4:11. **an everlasting.** Heb. *olam,* Ge +17:7. Is 54:10. Je 50:5.

ISAIAH 56

An exhortation to justice and piety, in the prospect of the near approach of God's salvation, 1, 2. Encouragement to strangers and eunuchs to expect spiritual blessings in the way of faith and obedience, 3-8. A severe rebuke of blind and wicked watchmen, or teachers and rulers, 9-12.

1. **Keep.** Is 1:16-19. 26:7, 8. √55:7. Ps 24:4-6. 50:23. Je 7:3-11. Ml 4:4. Mt 3:2. Jn +*7:17. **judgment.** *or,* equity. Is 1:17. 26:9. 59:8mg. **for.** Is 46:13. 51:5. Ps 50:23. 85:9. Mt 3:2. 4:17. Mk 1:15. Lk 3:3-9. Ro *1:16. *10:6-10. 13:11-14. **my righteousness.** Ro *1:17. 3:21, 22.

2. **Blessed.** Ps *1:1-3. 15:1-5. 106:3. 112:1. *119:1-5. 128:1. Lk +*11:28. 12:43. Jn +*13:17. Re *22:14. **layeth hold.** ver. 4. Pr *4:13. Ec 7:18. **keepeth the sabbath.** Is √58:13n. Ex +*20:8-11♪?. *31:13-16. Le 19:30. Ne 13:17, 18. Je 17:21, 22. Ezk 20:12, 13, 20, 21. **keepeth his.** Ps 34:14. 37:27. 119:101. Pr 4:27. 14:16. 16:6, 17. Ro 12:9.

3. **the son.** Nu 18:4, 7. Dt 23:1-3. Zc 8:20-23. Mt +*8:10, 11. Ac 8:27. 10:1, 2, 34. 13:47, 48. 17:4. 18:7. Ro 2:10, 11. 15:9-12, 16. Ep 2:12-22. 1 P 1:1. **stranger.** ver. 6. Is 60:10. 61:5. 62:8. Ex 12:43 (✻S#5236h). Ps 144:7, 11. **joined.** Je *50:5. Zp 2:11. 1 C +*6:17. **The Lord hath.** Mt 15:26, 27. Lk 7:6-8. Ro 2:10, 11. Ep *2:19. **neither.** ver. 4, 5. Is 39:7. Ge +37:36mg. Dt 23:1. Je 38:7-13. 39:16, 17. Da 1:3, etc. Mt 19:12, etc. Ac 8:26-40. **dry tree.** Le 21:20. Ezk 17:24. Mt 19:12.

4. **choose.** Is ◗+*66:4. Jsh √24:15. Ps 119:111. Lk

10:42. **take hold.** Is 27:5. +*55:3. 2 S 23:5. Je 50:5. He 6:17, 18.

5. **will I.** Mt *16:18. Ep *2:22. 1 T √3:15. He √3:6. **give.** Is 27:5. Mt 15:26, 27. **mine house.** Ezk 43:7. Zc *6:12, 13. Mt 21:13. **a place.** Ex 33:21. Dt +16:16. Jsh 20:4. Zc 3:7. *or,* station. lit. hand. Is 1:12. 1 S 15:12n. 2 S *18:18n. **and a name.** Is 62:12. 65:15. Lk *10:20. Jn √1:12. Ro 8:15-17. 1 J √3:1. Re 2:17. *3:12. 21:7. **better.** 1 S 1:8. **everlasting.** Heb. *olam,* Ge +17:7. **name.** Ex ◗32:32. **that shall.** Is 48:19. *55:13. 65:23. *66:22. Je 33:18. 35:19. Re *3:5.

6. **stranger.** ver. +3. Is 60:10. Ac 10:34, 35. 17:4. Re 7:9. **join.** ver. +3. Is 44:5. Je 50:5. Ac 2:41. 11:23. 2 C 8:5. 1 Th *1:9, 10. He 12:23. 1 P 1:1, 2. **to love the name.** Ps +√9:10. Mk 12:30-34. Ro √8:28. 1 C 16:22. Ga 5:6. Ep 6:24. Ja 1:12. *2:5. **every.** ver. 2. Is 58:13. Re 1:10.

7. **them will.** Is 2:2, 3. 66:19, 20. Ps *2:6. Ezk 20:40. Mi 4:1, 2. Zc 8:3. Ml 1:11. Jn 12:20, etc. Ep 2:11-13. He 12:22. 1 P 1:1, 2. **house of prayer.** Zc *8:22. Mk 11:17. **their burnt offerings.** Ezk 43:18, 24, 27. 45:15-25. 46:11-15. Lk 22:15-18, 30. **sacrifices.** Ps 50:14, 23. Je 33:18. Ro *12:1. He 13:15. 1 P 2:5. **for mine house.** Ps 132:13. Ml 1:11. Mt ♪21:13. ◗*23:38. Mk ♪11:17. Lk ♪19:46. Jn *4:21-23. 1 T 2:8. **for all.** 1 T +*2:2.

8. **which.** Is +*11:11, 12. 27:12, 13. 54:7. Ps 106:47. 107:2, 3. *147:2. Je 30:17. 31:10. Ho 1:11. Mi 4:6. Zp 3:18-20. Zc 10:8-10. **Yet.** Is 43:6. 49:12, 22. 60:3-11. 66:18-21. Ge +*49:10. Jn +*10:16. *11:51, 52. Ep *1:10. 2:14-16. **beside those that are gathered.** Heb. to his gathered.

9. **ye beasts.** Dt 28:26. Je *12:7-9. Ezk 29:5. 39:17. Da *7:2-28. Re 13:1-18. 19:17, 18.

10. **watchmen.** Is 52:8. Ezk *3:17, 18. **are blind.** Is 29:10. Je 14:13, 14. Ho 4:6. 9:7, 8. Mt *15:14. *23:16-26. Lk 6:39, 40. **they are all dumb dogs.** Is *58:1. Je 6:13, 14. 23:13, 14. Ezk 3:15-18, 26, 27. 13:16. 33:6. Ph *3:2. **sleeping.** *or,* dreaming, *or,* talking in their sleep. **loving.** Pr 6:4-10. 24:30-34. Jon 1:2-6. Na 3:18. Mk 13:34-37.

11. **Yea, they are.** Ex +*18:21. 1 S 2:12-17, 29. Ezk 13:19. *34:2, 3. Mi *3:5, 10, 11. Ml 1:10. Ac *20:29, 33, 34. Ph 3:2, 19. 1 T *3:2, 3, 8. T 1:7, 11. 1 P *5:2, 3. 2 P *2:3, 14, 15. Ju 11, 16. Re 22:15. **greedy.** Heb. strong of appetite. Heb. *nephesh,* Nu +11:6. Ec 6:7mg. Ph +*3:19. **can never have enough.** Heb. know not to be satisfied. Ec 5:10. Ph ◗4:11. **are shepherds.** Mi 3:6. Zc 11:15-17. Mt 13:14, 15. Jn 8:43. 2 C √4:4. **all look.** Ex 23:3. Je 22:17. 2 P 2:15, 16. **his gain.** Ex +*18:21. Ps *10:3. Lk 16:13, 14. 1 C +*6:10. Ep √5:5. Col +*3:5. 1 T +√6:5, 17-19. 2 T 3:1, 2.

12. **I will.** Is 5:22. 28:7, 8. Pr *23:29-32. 31:4, 5. Ho 4:11. Am 6:3-6. Mt 24:49-51. Lk 12:45, 46. 21:34. 1 C √6:10. Ep +*5:18. 1 Th 5:6-8. T 1:7. **tomorrow.** Is 22:13, 14. Ps 10:6. Pr 23:35. *27:1. Je 18:18. Lk *12:19, 20. 1 C 15:32. Ja *4:13, 14.

ISAIAH 57

The disregarded yet happy death of the righteous a token of approaching judgments, 1, 2. Idolaters, hypocrites, and wicked men cited before God's tribunal, convicted, and threatened with destruction; while none could help them, and while those who trusted

God would be saved, 3-14. Promises to the broken-hearted; causes of the sufferings of God's professed people; and the free grace of the gospel, from which the impenitent are excluded, 15-21.

1. righteous. 2 Ch 32:33. 35:24. Ec 7:15. **no man.** ver. 11. Is 42:25. 47:7. Ml *2:2. **merciful men.** Heb. men of kindness, *or* godliness. Ps *12:1. Mi *7:2. **the righteous.** 1 K 14:13. 2 K *22:20. 2 Ch 34:28. Lk 19:43, 44. **taken away.** 2 K 22:20n. 23:29. Ps 7:7. Jl 2:32. Zp +*2:3. Mt 24:40. Lk +*21:36. Ro *5:9. 1 Th √1:10. 4:17. √5:9, 10. Re +*3:10. **the evil to come.** *or,* that which is evil. Is +45:7. Je √22:20. 1 Th *1:10. 2 T 3:1. 1 J 2:18. Re 8:13.

2. He shall. Jb *3:17. Ec *12:7. Mt *25:21. Lk *16:22. 1 C 15:18. 2 C *5:1, 8. Ph *1:23. Re +*14:13. **enter into.** *or,* go in. Lk *2:29. 7:50. **rest.** Is 14:18. 2 Ch 16:14. Ezk 32:25. **in his uprightness.** *or,* before him. Ge *17:1. Am +3:10 (❋S#5228h). Lk *1:6.

3. draw. Is 45:20. Jl 3:9-11. **sons.** Ge +*3:15. Ho *1:2. Mt 3:7. 12:34. *16:4. 23:33. Lk 3:7. Jn *8:40-44. Ja √4:4. 1 J 3:10. Re *17:1-5. **sorceress.** ♪155E3, Is +32:9. F/L Is 2:6. Le 19:26ɥᛈ. Dt 18:10, 14ɥᛈ. 2 K +*21:6h (❋S#6049h, observed times).

4. Against. Is 10:15. 37:23, 29. Ex 9:17. 16:7, 8. Nu 16:11. Lk 10:16. Ac 9:4. **sport.** Jg 16:25-27. Ps 69:12. Mt 27:29, 39-44. 2 P 2:13. **make.** Ps 35:21. **draw.** Jsh 10:21. Jb 16:9, 10. Ps 22:7, 13, 17. La 2:15, 16. **are ye.** Is 1:4. 30:1, 9. Ezk 2:4. Ho 10:9. Mt 13:38. Ep 2:2, 3. 5:6. Col 3:6.

5. Inflaming. Ex 32:6. Nu 25:1, 2, 6. Je 50:38. 51:7. Ho 4:11-13. 7:4-7. Am 2:7, 8. Re 17:1-5. 18:3. **with idols.** *or,* among the oaks. Is *1:29. Ge 12:6. 13:18. 14:13. 18:1. 21:33. 35:4. Jsh 24:26. Jg 6:11, 19. 9:6, 37. 1 S 10:3. 22:6. 31:13. Ho *4:13. **under every green tree.** Dt 12:2. 1 K 14:23. 2 K 16:3, 4n. +17:10. Je *2:20. 3:6, 13. 17:2. Ezk 6:13. **slaying the children.** Le 18:21ɥᛈ. 20:2-5. 1 K 11:7. 2 K 16:3. 17:16, 17. 23:10. 2 Ch 28:3. Ps 106:37. Je *7:31. 19:5. 32:35. Ezk *16:20. 20:26, 31. 23:39. Ho 13:1. **valleys.** or, brooks. Is 15:7mg. Jg +*16:4mg.

6. the smooth. Je 3:9. Hab 2:19. **to them.** Is 65:11. Dt 32:37, 38. Je 7:18. 19:13. 32:29. 44:17-25. **drink offering.** Ex 29:40. Le +*23:13. Nu 15:5, 10. **meat offering.** Ex 29:41. Le +*23:13. Nu 15:6, 9. **Should.** Is 66:3. 1 K 12:32, 33. Ezk 20:39. **comfort.** ♪22B. Anthropomorphism B883. *Comfort* is spoken of God. For another instance of this figure see Ezk 5:13.

7. a lofty. Je 2:20. *3:2. Ezk 16:16, 25. 20:28, 29. 23:17, 41.

8. the doors. Ezk 8:8-12. 23:14, 41. **also and the posts.** ♪93A. Figure of speech Hendiadys, Ge +1:26. Here, the sense is "door posts." **for.** Ezk 16:32. **made thee a covenant with them.** *or,* hewed it for thyself *larger* than theirs. **thou lovedst.** Ezk 16:25-28. 23:2-20. **where thou sawest it.** *or,* thou providedst room. or, station. lit. hand. Is +56:5.

9. thou wentest to the king. *or,* thou respectedst the king. Is *30:1-6. 31:1-3. 2 K *16:7-11. 2 Ch 28:22, 23. Ezk 16:33. 23:16. Ho *7:11, 12. 12:1. or, the idol. Is 30:33. 1 K 11:7. **perfumes.** Pr 7:17. **and didst debase.** ♪102, Ge +2:24. Is 2:9. Col 2:18. **unto hell.** Heb. *sheol,* Ge +37:35. Is 5:14. The world of spirits (Young).

10. wearied. Is 47:13. Je 2:36. 9:5. Ezk 24:12. Hab 2:13. **There is.** 2 Ch 28:22, 23. Je *2:25. 44:17, 18. Ro 7:9. **life.** *or,* living. Pr 27:27mg. **therefore.** Je 3:3. 5:3.

11. of whom. Is *51:12, 13. Pr *29:25. Mt 26:69-75. Ga 2:12, 13. **that thou.** Is 30:9. 59:3, 4. Je 9:3-5. 42:20. Ezk 13:22. Ho 11:12. Ac 5:3. 2 Th 2:9. 1 T 4:2. Re +*21:8. 22:15. **and hast.** See on Je *2:32. 3:21. **nor.** See on ver. 1. **have not.** Is √26:10. Ps *50:21. Ec √8:11. **of old.** Heb. *olam,* Ge +6:4.

12. I. ♪60A, Ge +3:22. **will declare.** Is *1:11-15. 58:2-6. 59:6-8. 64:5. 66:3, 4. Je 7:4-11. Mi 3:2-4. Mt 23:5, 14. Ro 3:10-20. *10:2, 3. **thy righteousness.** ♪27, Ge +3:22. Is √64:6. T *3:5. **not profit.** Mk 8:36.

13. let. ♪60A, Ge +3:22. ver. 9, 10. Jg *10:14. 2 K 3:13. Je 22:22. Zc 7:13. **but the wind.** Is 40:24. 41:16. Jb *21:17, 18. Ps *1:4. 37:9. 58:9. 115:8. Ho 13:3. **vanity.** ♪121N1, Ge +31:54. i.e. vain men. Ps 144:4. Ja 4:14. **but he.** Is √26:3, 4. Ps +√9:10. +*37:3, 9. 84:12. 118:8, 9. 125:1. Pr 28:25. Je *17:7, 8. **my holy.** Is 11:9. 56:7. 65:25. 66:20. Ezk 20:40. Jl 3:17.

14. Cast. Is 35:8. *40:3, 9. *62:10. Lk 3:3-6. **take.** Ro 14:13. 1 C 1:23. 8:9, 13. 10:32, 33. 2 C 6:3. He 12:13.

15. the high. Is *6:1. Ps +8:5n. *83:18. *97:9. *138:6. *139:7n. Da 4:17, 24, 25, 34. Ho 11:9. **that inhabiteth.** Is *40:28. Ge *21:33. Dt *33:27. Ps *90:2. *93:2. Pr *8:23. Je *10:10. Mi *5:2. Ro *1:20. 1 T *1:17. **He** *9:14. **eternity.** Heb. *ad,* Ps +9:18 (❋S#5703h). **whose.** Is *6:3. Ex *15:11. 1 S *2:2. Jb 6:10. Ps *99:3. 111:9. Lk *1:49. Ac *3:14. Re *3:7. *4:8. *15:4. **I dwell.** Is 66:1. 1 K *8:27. Jb 22:12. Ps *68:4, 5. 113:4-6. *115:3. 123:1. 138:*6, 8. 139:7. Zc 2:13. Mt *6:9. Jn 1:38. 1 T *6:16. **with.** Is *66:1, 2. 2 Ch *33:12, 13. *34:27. Ps *34:18. *51:17. *138:6. Ezk *9:4. 16:63. Mt +*5:3, 4. Ja *4:6. 1 P *5:5. **contrite.** Ps 51:10, 11, 17. Jl 2:13. 2 C +*7:10. **humble.** 2 Ch +*7:14. Pr 16:19. Mt +*5:3. Ja 4:6. **spirit.** Heb. *ruach,* Ge +41:8. **to revive.** Is *61:1-3. 2 K 5:7h. Ps *147:3. Ezk 13:22mg. Mt +*5:4. Lk *4:18. *15:20-24. 2 C *1:4. 2:7. 7:6. **the spirit.** Heb. *ruach,* Ge +41:8. **contrite ones.** T#604. Dt +33:9 (T#672). Ps 34:18. Lk 15:7, 21, 22.

16. I will not. Ps *78:38, 39. 85:5. *103:9-16. Je *10:24. Mi *7:18. **for ever.** Heb. *olam,* Ex +*12:24. **neither.** Is *54:7, 8. Ps 30:5. **always.** Heb. *nezach,* Jb +4:20 (❋S#5331h). **the spirit.** Heb. *ruach,* Ge +41:8. **should fail.** 2 C 2:7. Col 3:21. **the souls.** lit. breathing things. Heb. *neshamah,* Ge +2:7ɥᛈ. F/L Is 2:22. 30:33. 42:5. Ge 6:3. Nu 16:22. Jb 34:14, 15. Ec +*12:7. Je 38:16. Zc 12:1. He +*12:9.

17. the iniquity. Is 5:8, 9. 56:11. Je *6:13. 8:10. 22:17. Ezk 33:31. Mi 2:2, 3. 3:10, 11. Lk √12:15. Ep 5:3-5. Col *3:5. 1 T 6:9, 10. 2 P 2:3, 14, 15. **I hid.** Is 8:17. *45:15. **and he.** Is *9:13. Je *2:30. √5:3. Lk 15:14-16. **frowardly.** Heb. turning away. ❋S#7726h. Is 57:17. Je 3:14 (backsliding), 22. 50:6 (turned them away). **in the.** Ec 6:9.

18. have. Is *1:18. *43:24, 25. 48:8-11. Je *31:18-20. Ezk 16:60-63. 36:22, etc. Lk 15:20. Ro 5:20. **will heal.** Je *3:22. 31:3. 33:6. Ho 14:4-8. **will lead.** Is 49:10. Ps *23:2. Re 7:17. **restore.** ver. 15. Is *12:1. *61:2, 3. *66:10-13. Ps *51:12. Ro 15:5. 2 C √1:4. *7:6. Re 7:17. **to his.** Je 13:17. Ec 9:4.

19. I create. "The sacrifice of praise," says St. Paul, "is the fruit of the lips." God creates this fruit of the lips, by giving new subject and cause of thanksgiving by His mercies conferred on His people. The great subject of thanksgiving is peace, reconciliation and pardon offered to them that are nigh, and to them that are far off—not only to the Jew, but also to the Gentile. **the fruit.** Ex *4:11, 12. Ho *14:2. Lk 21:15. Ep *5:18, 19. 6:19. Col 4:3, 4. He *13:15. **Peace.** Mt 10:13. Mk *16:15. Lk 2:14. 10:5, 6. Ac *2:39. *10:36. 2 C *5:20, 21. Ep *2:14-17. 171I9B. Synecdoche of the Species B627. Peace is used of all heavenly and spiritual blessing. For other instances of this figure see Jn 14:27. 20:19, 21, 26. Ro 1:7. 5:1. 14:17. **near.** Ps 148:14. **will heal.** Is *1:5, 6. Ex +*15:26. Ps +*103:3. *147:3.

20. **like.** Is 3:11. Jb *15:20-24. 18:5-14. 20:11, etc. Ps 78:18-20. Pr *4:16, 17. Ju *12, *13.

21. **no peace.** Is 3:11. *48:22. 2 K 9:22. Ro 3:16, 17.

ISAIAH 58

The prophet is commanded boldly to reprove hypocrisy, 1, 2. He shows that pride, injustice, and oppression render fasts unprofitable, and he declares the nature of an acceptable fast, 3-7. Most encouraging promises to those who attend on these duties, 8-12; and who duly hallow the sabbath, 13, 14.

1. **aloud.** Heb. with the throat. ſ121BF2. Metonymy of the Cause B546. "Throat" is put for loud speaking. Ps 149:6. **spare.** Is 56:10. Ps 40:9, 10. Je 1:7-10, 17-19. 7:8-11. 15:19, 20. Ezk 2:3-8. 3:5-9, *17-21. 20:4. 22:2. Mi 3:8-12. Mt *3:7-9. Ac 7:51, 52. 20:26, 27. T 2:15. Re 14:9, 10. **lift up.** See on Is 40:9, 10. **like.** Is 27:13. Ho 8:1. Re 1:10. 4:1. **trumpet.** Le +23:24. **and show.** Mt 23:1-3, 33. Lk 20:45-47. Ac 7:51. *20:26, 27. 2 C 13:2.

2. **they seek.** Is 1:11-15. 29:13. 48:1, 2. Dt 5:28, 29. 1 S 15:21-25. Pr *15:8. Ezk 33:30-33. Mt *15:7-9. Mk *4:16, 17. 6:20. Jn 5:35. T √1:16. He *6:4-6. Ja 1:22. **they ask.** Je *42:2, 3, 20. Mk 12:14, 15. Ja 1:21, 22. 1 P 2:1, 2.

3. **Wherefore.** ſ85, Ge +3:9. **have we fasted.** Nu 23:4. Mi 3:9-11. Zc 7:5-7. Ml *3:14. Mt 20:11, 12. Lk 15:29. 18:9-12. **afflicted.** Le 16:29, 31)℗. 23:27, 32)℗. Nu 29:7)℗. Ps 69:10. **soul.** Heb. *nephesh,* Ge +27:31. **in the day.** Da 10:2, 3. Jon 3:6-8. **exact.** Ne 5:7. Pr 28:9. Je 34:9-17. Mt 18:28-35. **labors.** *or,* things wherewith ye grieve others. Heb. griefs. ✲S#6092h, only here. Is 47:6. Ex 2:23, 24.

4. **ye fast.** Jg +20:26n. 1 K 21:9-13. 2 Ch +*7:14. Pr 21:27. Mt 6:16. 23:14. Lk 20:47. Jn 18:28. **and to smite.** Ac 23:1, 2. Ph 1:15, 16. **shall not fast as ye do this day.** *or,* fast not as this day. Pr 21:27. Lk 18:9-14. **to make.** Jl 2:13, 14. Jon 3:7. Mt 6:16-18.

5. **Is it such.** 2 Ch 20:3. Ezr 10:6. Ne 9:1, 2. Est 4:3, 16. Da 9:3, etc. Zc *7:5, 6. **a day for a man to afflict his soul.** *or,* to afflict his soul *for* a day. Heb. *nephesh,* Ge +27:31. ſ171Q2, Nu +23:10. See on ver. 3. Le 16:29. **to spread.** 1 K 21:27-29. 2 K 6:30. Jb 2:8. Jon 3:5-8. **an acceptable.** Is 49:8. 61:2. Ps 69:13. Lk 4:19. Ro *12:2. 1 P 2:5.

6. **Is not this.** ſ168, Is +1:11. Mi +*6:8. **the fast.** Mt 6:17, 18. 1 P 2:5. **to loose.** T#1299. Ne *5:10-12. Je *34:8-11. Mi 3:2-4. **bands.** or, pangs. Ps 73:4. **heavy burdens.** Heb. bundles of the yoke. **to let.** Lk ⅃4:18. **oppressed.** Heb. broken. Is 42:3 (bruised), 4mg. 2 K 18:21 (bruised). 2 Ch 16:10mg. Jb 20:19mg. **go free.** Ex 21:2. Le 25:39, 50. **ye break.** 1 T 6:1.

7. **to deal.** Jb 42:11. La 4:4. Ezk 18:7. 24:17. Ho 9:4. Lk 24:30, 35. Ac 2:42, 46. 20:7, 11. 27:35. 1 C 10:16. 11:24. lit. divide or break. ſ108H4. Idiom B839.

Idiomatic phrases: "breaking of bread" means to partake of food, and is used of eating, as in a meal. For other instances of this figure see Dt 26:14. Jb 42:11. Je *16:7mg. La 4:4. Ezk *18:7. 24:17. Ho 9:4. Mt 14:19. 15:36. 26:26. Mk 8:6, 19. 14:22. Lk 22:19. 24:30, 35. Ac 2:46. 20:7. 27:35. 1 C 10:16. 11:24. **bread.** ſ171i8. Figure of speech Synecdoche of the Species, whereby bread is put for all kinds of food. For other instances of this figure, see Ge +3:19. **to the hungry.** ver. 10. Jb 22:7. 31:18-21. Ps 112:9. Pr 22:9. 25:21. 28:27. Ec 11:1, 2. Ezk 18:7, 16. Da 4:27. Mt 25:35-40. Lk 11:41. 19:8. Ro +*12:20, 21. 2 C 9:6-10. 1 T 5:10. Phm 7. Ja √2:15, 16. 1 J √3:17, 18. **bring.** Is 16:3, 4. Ge 18:2-5. 19:2. Jg 19:20, 21. Ac 16:15, 34. Ro 12:13. He 13:2, 3. **the poor.** Ps 41:1. **cast out.** *or,* afflicted. ✲S#4788h. La 1:7 (miseries). 3:19 (misery). **to thy house.** Ps 68:6mg. **the naked.** 2 Ch 28:15. Jb 31:19, 20. Ezk 18:7. Mt √25:35-45. Lk 3:11. **hide not thyself.** Ps 55:1. Dt √22:1, 3, 4. Jb 6:16. Mt 15:5. Mk 7:11-13. **thine own.** Ge 29:14)℗. 37:27. Jg 9:2. 2 S 19:12, 13. Ne 5:5. Mt 22:39. Lk *10:26-36. Ro 11:14. Ga *6:10. Ep 5:29. 1 T 4:10. +√5:8. 1 J √3:17. **flesh.** that is, kindred. 1 T √5:8mg.

8. **thy light.** ver. 10, 11. Jb 11:17. Ps 37:6. *97:11. *112:4. Pr +√4:18. Ho 6:3. Ml 4:2. **and thine health.** Heb. thy healing. Referring to the healing of wounds. lit. prolongation. Is 57:18. Je +*8:22. 33:6. 38:17. Ho 6:2. 14:4. Mt 13:15. **and thy.** Ps 85:13. Ac *10:4, 31, 35. **the glory.** Is 52:12. Ex 14:19. **be thy rereward.** Heb. gather thee up. Is 40:11. +52:12mg. Ge 42:17mg. Ex 14:19, 20)℗. Ps 27:10mg.

9. **shalt thou.** Is 1:15. 30:19. *65:24. Ps *34:15-17. 37:4. *50:15. +*66:18, 19. 91:15. 118:5. Je 29:12, 13. Mt *7:7, 8. 1 J √3:21-23. **Here.** Ge 27:18. 1 S 3:4-8. **the yoke.** See on ver. 6. **the putting.** Is 57:4. Pr 6:13. **speaking vanity.** Is 59:3, 4. Ps *12:2. *36:3. 1 S 25:10, 11. Pr 18:23. Ezk 13:8. Zc 10:2. Mt *12:34. Ep 4:31. ſ121G1. Figure of speech Metonymy of the Effect; the effect put for the thing or action causing or producing it; here, "vanity" or "affliction" is put for the words which vex or grieve. For other instances of this figure see Ge +31:1.

10. **if thou.** ſ26, Ro +11:19. **draw out.** ver. 7. Dt *15:7-10. Ps *41:1, 2. *112:5-9. Pr *11:24, 25. 14:31. *28:27. Lk *18:22. **thy soul.** Heb. *nephesh,* Ge +34:3. Instead of *naphshecha,* "thy soul," eleven MSS. read *lachmecha,* "thy bread," which is adopted by Bishop Lowth; but "to draw out the soul" in relieving the poor, probably means to do it not of constraint, but cheerfully. 1 C 16:2. 2 C 8:3, 11. *9:7. **satisfy.** ver. 11. Dt 15:7, 8. **soul.** Heb. *nephesh,* Ge +34:3. ſ145, Jg +11:40. **shall thy.** ſ26, Ro +11:18. **light rise.** ver. *8. Is 60:1. Ex 22:3. Dt 33:2. **in obscurity.** Is *29:18. 59:9. Ge +1:2 (darkness). **thy darkness.** ſ125, Jb +22:6. Is 9:2. 42:7, 16. 49:9. 60:2. Ps 107:10. Mi *7:8. **noon day.** Is *16:3. 59:10. Ge 43:16. Jb *11:17. Ps *37:6.

11. **guide thee.** Is *49:10. 62:20. Ge *24:27. Ex 13:17. Ps √25:9. +*32:8. *48:14. *73:24. Jn *16:13. 1 Th *3:11mg. **continually.** ✲S#8548h. Is 21:8. 49:16. 51:13. 52:5. 58:11. 60:11. 62:6 (never; lit. not *ever*). 65:3. Ex 25:30 (always). 27:20. 28:29, 30, 38. 29:38, 42. 30:8 (perpetual). Le 6:13 (ever), 20. 24:2, 3, 4, 8. Nu 4:7, 16 (daily). 9:16. 28:3, 6, 10, 15, 23, 24, 31. 29:6 (daily), 11, 16, 19, 22, 25, 28, 31, 34, 38. Dt 11:12 (always). 2 S 9:7 (continually), 10, 13. 1 K 10:8.

2 K 4:9. 25:29 (continually), 30 (continual). 1 Ch 16:6, 11, 37, 40. 23:31. 2 Ch 2:4. 9:7. 24:14. Ezr 3:5. Ne 10:33. Ps 16:8 (always). 25:15 (ever). 34:1 (continually). *35:27. 38:17. *40:11, 16. 50:8. 51:3 (ever). 69:23. *70:4. *71:3, 6, 14. *72:15. *73:23. 74:23. 105:4 (evermore). 109:15, 19. *119:44, 109, 117. Pr 5:19 (always). *6:21. 15:15. 28:14. Je 6:7. 52:33, 34. Ezk 38:8 (always). 39:14mg. 46:14, 15. Da 8:11 (daily), 12, 13. 11:31. 12:11. Ho 12:6. Ob 16. Na 3:19. Hab 1:17. **and satisfy.** Is *33:16. Jb *5:20. Ps *33:18, 19. *34:9, 10. *37:19. Je *17:8. Ho 13:5. **soul.** Heb. *nephesh*, Ge +34:3. **drought.** Heb. droughts. *S#6710h, only here. √96F2. Heterosis of Number: the plural put for the singular. For other instances of this figure, see Ge +4:10. Plural form for plural of majesty, indicating great drought. Ps 68:6. **make fat.** Ps *92:14. Pr *3:8. +*11:25. 13:4. *28:25. **be like.** Is *61:11. SS 4:15. Je *31:12. Ezk *36:35. **a spring.** Is 41:18. **whose waters.** Jn *4:14. **fail.** Heb. lie, *or* deceive. Is 57:11. Jb 6:15-20.

12. **build.** Is 51:3. *61:4. Ne *2:5, 17. 4:1-6. Je 31:38. Ezk 36:4, 8-11, 33. Am +√9:14, 15. **old.** Heb. *olam*, Jb +22:15. **waste.** Is 51:3. 52:9. **The repairer.** Ne 4:7. 6:1. Da *9:25. Am 9:11.

13. **turn.** Is *56:2-7. Ge 2:3. Ex 16:23. +*20:8-11♪𝒫. 31:13-17. 35:2, 3. Dt 5:12-15. Ne 9:14. *13:15-22. Je *17:21-27. Ezk 20:20. 44:24. **from doing thy pleasure.** Here is the main difficulty: so long as sensual repose, instead of spiritual; intellectual effort, instead of devotional; the pleasure of the mere appetites, instead of the pleasure of the soul of God, is the governing principle in our religion, the sabbath will never be kept aright (Daniel Wilson, *The Lord's Day*, p. 155). As these prophecies evidently relate, or extend, to the times of the Christian dispensation; a cogent argument may be deduced from them, for hallowing the Lord's day. The rule here given implies, that men must not profane that day by doing their ordinary work, or seeking their secular interest; or by spending it in worldly pleasures and recreations, or sloth and animal indulgence; or by vain and trifling conversation: but that they should delight in the sabbath, as a holy day especially consecrated to the Lord, to be spent in the public and private duties of religion; honor it above all other days, and honor God on it and for it. In proportion as we are spiritually minded, we shall hallow, honor, and delight in the sabbaths of God; and, laying aside all employments, pleasures, or discourse which can interrupt our sacred rest in him, we shall seek communion with him in his public and private ordinances: without any other remission, than what is really necessary, or what is a work of love to the souls and bodies of our neighbors and fellow Christians (Scott). If the Divine command was actually delivered at the creation, it was addressed, no doubt, to the whole human species alike, and continues, unless repealed by some subsequent revelation, binding upon all who come to the knowledge of it (William Paley, *Moral and Political Philosophy*, Book V, ch. 7). See Notes on Ge 2:3n. 4:3n. 29:27n. Ex 16:26n. Mt 23:23n. Lk +*13:14n. Ro 14:5n. **call.** Ps *27:4. √37:4. 42:4. 84:2, 10. 92, title, 1, 2. *122:1. Re 1:10. **honor him.** Is 8:13. 25:1. Ps 29:2. 34:3. 57:5. *71:8. 107:32. 145:5. Pr *3:9. *14:31. Ml 1:6. Mt 15:8. Mk 7:6. 11:8. Lk 4:15. 19:35. Jn *5:+√23, 44. 8:◖49, 54. 12:13. Re *5:13. 19:7. **own ways.** Is *55:8. 66:3. Am *8:5. Ep 5:8. **nor speaking.** Is 59:3, 13. **words.** Of complaint or expostulation

(Young); vain words: or keep making talk (CB). Is 29:24. Nu +11:1. Pr 10:19. +19:13. Ec *5:1, 2. Hab √2:20. Mt 6:7. √12:36. 1 C 14:34. Ep 5:4. 1 T 2:11, 12.

14. **delight.** Jb 22:26. 27:10. 34:9. Ps 36:8. 37:4, 11. Hab 3:18. Ph *4:4. 1 P 1:8. **cause thee to ride.** Is 33:16. Dt 32:13♪𝒫. 33:29♪𝒫. Ps 45:4. Hab 3:19. Re 6:2. **and feed.** Is 1:19. Ge 28:14. Ps 105:9-11. 135:12. 136:21, 22. Je 3:19. **the mouth.** Is 1:20. 40:5. √55:10, 11. Mi 4:4. Mt 24:35.

ISAIAH 59

Sin separates God and us, 1, 2. Murder, theft, falsehood, injustice, and cruelty assigned as the causes of all the calamities endured by the professed people of God, 3-15. Promises that God would rescue his people; take vengeance on his enemies; widely diffuse truth and holiness; stop the torrent of impiety and wickedness; and preserve true religion, by his word and Spirit, to the end of time, 16-21.

1. **the Lord's.** Is 50:2. Ge 18:14. Nu 11:23. Je *32:17. **that it cannot save.** Is 63:1. 1 S 17:37. 2 C 1:10. 2 T *4:17. He √7:25. 2 P 2:9. **his ear.** Is 6:10. *65:24. Da *9:21. Mt 13:15.

2. **your iniquities.** See on Is 50:1. Dt 32:19. Jsh 7:11, 12. Pr 15:29. Je 5:25. **have separated.** Ge 4:16. Je 44:4. Lk *16:26. **your sins.** Ho 14:4. 1 J √1:9. **hid.** *or,* made *him* hide. T#26. Is 57:17. Dt 31:17, 18. 32:20. Jb 23:8, 9. Ezk 39:23, 24, 29. Mi 3:4. Mt 6:22, +*23. 2 P +3:5 (T#707). **not hear.** T#1810. 1 S 14:36-38. Jn +*9:31.

3. **your hands.** Is √1:15, 21. Je 2:30, 34. *22:17. Ezk 7:23. 9:9. 22:2-6. 35:6. Ho 4:2. Mi 3:10-12. 7:2. Mt 27:4, 25. **your lips.** Je 7:8. 9:3-6. *42:20. *44:16. Ezk 13:8. Ho 7:3, 13. Mi 6:12. 1 T 4:2.

4. **calleth.** ver. 16. Je *5:1, 4, 5. Ezk 22:29-31. Mi 7:2-5. **trust.** Is 30:12. Jb 15:31. Ps 62:10. Je 7:4, 8. **and speak.** ver. 3. Ps 62:4. **they conceive.** ver. 13. Jb 15:35. Ps 7:14. Pr 4:16. Mi 2:1. Mt *23:27, 28. Ja √1:15.

5. **cockatrice'.** *or,* adder's. Is 11:8mg. 14:29mg. Pr 23:32mg. **eggs.** √132D, Ge +19:25. **crushed breaketh out into a viper.** *or,* sprinkled *is as if* there brake out a viper. Mt 3:7. 12:34.

6. **webs.** Is *28:18-20. 30:12-14. Jb *8:14, 15. **garments.** Is 61:10. **neither.** Is 30:1. 57:12. √64:6. Ro *3:20-22. 4:6-8. Re 3:17, 18. **their works.** Is 5:7. Ge 6:11. Ps 58:2. Je 6:7. Ezk 7:11, 23. Am 3:10. 6:3. Mi 2:1-3, 8. 3:1-11. 6:12. Hab 1:2-4. Zp 1:9. 3:3, 4.

7. **feet.** Pr *1:16. 6:17, 18. Ro ◖3:15-17. **and they.** ver. 3. Je 22:17. La 4:13. Ezk 9:9. 22:6. Mt 23:31-37. Re 17:6. **innocent blood.** Dt 19:10, 13♪𝒫, 9♪𝒫. 27:25♪𝒫. **their thoughts.** Pr *15:26. 24:9. Mt √15:18, 19. Mk √7:21, 22. Ac 8:20-22. **wasting.** Is 60:18. Ro ◖3:16. **destruction.** Heb. breaking. Is 51:19mg. **paths.** F/L Is +7:3.

8. **way.** Is *57:21. Ps 120:7. Pr 3:17. Lk 1:79. Ro ◖3:17. **no.** ver. 14, 15. Is 5:7. Je 5:1. Ho 4:1, 2. Am 6:1-6. Mt 23:23. **judgment.** *or,* right. Is 56:1mg. Ps 58:1, 2. **crooked.** Ps 125:5. Pr 2:15. 28:18. **whosoever.** Is 48:22. 57:20, 21.

9. **is judgment.** La 5:16, 17. Hab 1:13. **we wait.** Is 5:30. Jb 30:26. Je 8:15. 14:19. Am 5:18-20. Mi 1:12. 1 Th 5:3. **but.** √31, Is +1:21. **we walk.** Pr +*4:19. Je *13:16.

10. **grope.** Dt +28:29♪𝒫. Jb 5:14. Pr +*4:19. Je

*13:16. La 4:14. Am 8:9. Jn 11:9, 10. 12:35, 40. 1 J 2:11. **the blind.** 1 S 3:1. 28:6. Mt +*15:14. 2 P 1:9. **night.** A Hebrew homonym with two meanings: (1) darkness, as here; Is 5:11. 21:4. Jb 24:15. Pr 7:9. 2 K 7:5, 7. Je 13:16. (2) daylight, 1 S 30:17. Jb 7:4. Ps 119:147. **in desolate.** La 3:6.

11. **roar.** Is 51:20. Ps 32:3, 4. *38:8. Ho 7:14. **mourn.** Is *38:14. Jb 30:28, 29. Je 8:15. 9:1. Ezk *7:16. **like doves.** Le=1:14. Mt=10:16. **for salvation.** Ps *85:9. √119:155.

12. **our transgressions.** Is 1:4. Le 16:21. Ezr *9:6. Je 3:2. 5:3-9, 25-29. 7:8-10. Ezk 5:6. 7:23. 8:8-16. 16:51, 52. 22:2-12, 24-30. 23:2, etc. 24:6-14. Ho 4:2. Mt 23:32, 33. 1 Th 2:15, 16. **our sins.** Le 16:21. Je 14:7. Ho 5:5. 7:10. Ro *3:19, 20. **testify.** √155F, Ge +4:7. **iniquities.** Le 16:21. Note that the three words for "sin" in this verse occur together in Le 16:21. **we know.** Ezr 9:13. Ne *9:33. Da *9:5-8.

13. **lying.** Is 32:6. 48:8. 57:11. Ps 78:36. Je 3:10. 42:20. Ezk 18:25. Ho 6:7. 7:13. 11:12. Ac *5:3, 4. **departing.** Is 31:6. Ps 18:21. Je 2:13, 19-21. 3:20. 17:13. 32:40. Ezk 6:9. Ho 1:2. He +*3:12. **speaking.** Je 5:23. 9:2-5. Mt √12:34-36. Mk √7:21, 22. Ro *3:10-18. Ja *1:15. *3:6.

14. **judgment.** ver. 4. Is 5:23. 10:1, 2. Ps 82:2-5. Ec 3:16. Je 5:27, 28, 31. Am 5:7, 11, 12. Mi 3:9-11. 7:3-5. Hab 1:4. Zp 3:1-3. **standeth.** √155F, Ge +4:7.

15. **truth.** Is 48:1. Ps 5:9. *12:1, 2. Je 5:1, 2. 7:28. Ho 4:1, 2. Mi 7:2. Mt +*23:13, 14. **faileth.** Is 34:16. **he that.** Hab 1:13, 14. Ac 9:1, 23. Ro 8:36. He 11:36-38. 1 J 3:11, 12. **maketh himself a prey.** *or*, is accounted mad. 1 S 21:14mg. 2 K 9:11. Je 29:26. Ho 9:7. Mk 3:21. Jn 8:52. 10:20. Ac 26:24. 2 C 5:13. 2 T ☉+*1:7. **displeased him.** Heb. was evil in his eyes. Ge 38:10mg. 2 S 11:27mg. 2 Ch 21:7mg. Pr +24:18mg.

16. **he saw.** Is 50:2. 64:7. Ge 18:23-32. Ps 106:23. Je 5:1. Ezk √22:30. Mk 6:6. **no man.** Is 63:3. **wondered.** Ps 143:4. Mk 6:6. **intercessor.** Is 53:12. Je 15:11. **therefore.** Is *52:10. *63:3-5. Jb 40:14. Ps *98:1. **his arm.** √22A12, Ex +15:16. Is 40:10.

17. **he put on righteousness.** Is 11:5. 51:9. Jb 29:14. Ro *13:12-14. 2 C 6:7. Ep 6:14, 17. 1 Th 5:8. Re *19:11. **breastplate.** √22D5A, Ps +35:2. **the garments.** √22D5P, Ps +93:1. Dt *32:35-43. Ps 94:1. 2 Th √1:7, 8. He *10:30. **vengeance.** Is 61:2. 63:4. **and clad.** Ep *6:13. **with zeal.** Is +*9:7. 63:15. Ps +*69:9. Zc 1:14. Jn *2:17.

18. **According.** Is 63:6. Jb 34:11. Ps 18:24-26. 62:12. Je √17:10. 50:29. Mt *16:27. Ro *2:6. Re *20:12, 13. **deeds.** Heb. recompences. 2 S 19:36. Je 51:56. **fury.** Is 1:24. 49:25, 26. *63:3, 4, 6. 66:15. Ps 21:8, 9. La 4:11. Ezk 5:13. 6:12. 38:18. Na *1:2. Lk 19:27. *21:22. Re 16:19. *19:15.

19. **fear the name.** Is *11:9-16. 24:14-16. 49:12. 66:18-20. Ps *22:27. *102:15. *113:3. Da 7:27. Zp 3:8, 9. Ml *1:11. Re *11:15. **his glory.** Is 66:18. Ps +*102:15, 16. Ezk 39:21. **the rising.** Is +*24:15. Ps 113:3. Ml *1:11. **When.** This all the Rabbins refer to the coming of the Messiah. If, say they, ye see a generation which endures much tribulation, then expect Him, according to what is written, "When the enemy shall come in like a flood," etc. Ezk +*39:28n. **the enemy.** Is 29:19, *20. Re 12:10, 15-17. 17:14, 15. **like a flood.** Ezk +*38:15, 16. Jl *3:2, 11, 14. Zc √14:2-4. Mt +*24:8. **the Spirit.** Heb. *ruach*, Is +48:16. Is *11:10. Ge +41:38. Ps 51:12. Jl 2:28-32. 3:1, 7-17. Zc √4:6. 2 Th

√2:8. Re 20:1-3. **lift up a standard against him.** *or*, put him to flight. √22D5Q, Ex +17:15. T#944. ver. 17. Is 10:18. *11:4. 27:1. 41:11, 12, 15, 16. 49:22, 24-26. *60:14. *62:10. Ex 17:15♯♪. Ps 92:7. 110:2, 5, 6. Ezk √38:4. √39:2-4. Jl √2:20. Re *20:9.

20. **the Redeemer.** Is 25:9. Ob *17-21. Ro *♭11:26, 27. **shall come.** Is +*16:1. √52:8. Ps 85:9. +*102:16. Jl 2:12, 17-21. Zc *12:8. +*14:3, 4. Ac +*3:20. **to Zion.** Is *1:27. +*24:23. +*51:11. √52:8. Ps 14:7. *132:13. Ho 2:14, 15. Jl *3:16. Zc *1:16, 17. Ro ♭11:26. **turn from.** Is *44:21-23. 62:1. Dt *30:1-10. Je 31:2, 3. Ezk 18:30, 31. Da 9:13. Ho √5:15. *14:2. Jl √2:17, 18. Zc +*13:9. Ac 2:36-39. +√3:19, 26. 26:20. T *2:11-14. He *9:28. √12:14. 2 P √3:14.

21. **As for me.** Ps 55:16. **this.** Is *49:8. +*55:3. Je *31:31-34. 32:38-41. Ezk *36:25-27. 37:25-27. 39:25-29. He *8:6-13. *10:16. **My spirit.** Heb. *ruach*, Is +48:16. Is *11:1-3. 32:15. 44:3. *61:1-3. Ezk *37:14. *39:29. Pr *1:23. Jn *1:33. √3:34. *4:14. *7:39. Ac 2:38. Ro √8:9. 1 C √12:13. 2 C 3:8, 17, 18. **my words.** Is *51:16. Jn √7:16, 17. 8:38. 17:8. 1 C +*15:3. 1 P 1:25. **shall not depart.** Is +*41:9. +*55:3. Je 3:19. √32:40. Ezk *16:63. Am +*9:15. **for ever.** Heb. *olam*, Ex +*12:24. Ge +9:12. Since this deliverance is spoken of as final, it has not yet taken place (CB).

ISAIAH 60

Predictions of glorious light, holiness, and prosperity to Israel, and an immense accession of converts; till all kings and nations should either serve her or utterly perish, 1-14. All her trials shall terminate in peace and felicity, resembling those of heaven, 15-22.

1. **Arise.** √132G, Ge +3:19. Is 52:1, 2. Pr 6:9. SS 2:10. Mt 5:16. Mk 10:49. Lk 22:46. Jn 5:8. Ep 5:8, 14. Ph 2:15. **shine; for thy light is come.** *or*, be enlightened, for thy light cometh. √121R7, Ge +43:11. ver. 19, 20. Is 9:2. 2 S *23:4. Ml *4:2. Mt 4:16. Lk 1:78, 79. Jn *1:9. *3:19. *8:12. *9:5. *12:46. Ep *5:8. 1 J *1:5. Re 1:16. 21:23. 22:5. **is come.** Ge 6:13. Mt 12:28. He 12:22. **the glory.** Is 4:2, 5. 6:3. 35:2. 40:5. 58:8. Ps 106:20. Je 2:11. Hg 2:3, 7, 9. Ml 4:2. Lk *2:32. 1 P 4:14.

2. **the darkness.** Ps *74:20. Mt +*15:14. 23:19, 24. Jn √3:19. 8:55. Ac 14:16. 17:23, 30, 31. *26:18. Ro *1:21-32. Ep 4:17-20. 1 P *2:9. **gross darkness.** Je *13:16. Lk 18:8. Jn +=21:3. Ep 5:8. Col *1:13. 1 P *2:9. **the Lord.** Le 9:23. Nu 16:19. 1 K 8:11. Ps 80:1. Ezk 10:4. Hab 3:3, 4. Hg *2:7-9. Ml 4:2. Jn √1:1, 14, 18. 2 C 3:18. 4:4-6. He +*1:2, 3.

3. **the Gentiles.** Is 2:2-5. 11:10. 19:23-25. 45:14. 49:6, 12, 23. 54:1-3. 66:12, 19, 20. Ge +*49:10. Ps 22:27. 67:1-4. 72:17-19. 98:2, 3. ch. 117. Am 9:12. Mi 4:1, 2. Zc 2:11. 8:20-23. Mt *2:1-11. 28:19. Lk 24:47. Jn 12:20, 21, 32. Ac √13:47, 48. 15:17. Ro 11:11-15. 15:9-12. **kings.** ver. 10, 16. Is 49:7, 23. Ps *2:10. 68:29. 72:11. 138:4. Re *11:15. *21:24.

4. **Lift.** √144A12, Ge +22:13. Is 49:18. Jn 4:35. Ac 13:44. **they gather.** Ge +√49:10. **they come.** Is 42:6. 49:20-22. 66:11, 12. Mt +*8:11. Ga *3:28, 29. **thy sons.** Je *31:10. Ezk *34:11-15. **nursed.** Is 49:22mg.

5. **thou shalt see.** Is 11:10. 49:6-23. 61:6. 66:10-12. Je 33:9. Ho 1:10, 11. 3:5. Ac 10:45. 11:17. **fear.** Heb. *pahad*. A Hebrew homonym with two meanings: (1) to fear, as in Dt 28:66. Jb 23:15. (2) to rejoice, here and Ho 3:5 (praise). **be enlarged.** Is 54:2. 1 S 2:1.

2 C 6:1-13. 10:15. Re 21:26. **abundance of the sea shall be converted unto thee**. or, noise of the sea shall be turned towards thee. Is 24:14, 15. 42:10. Ps 96:7-9. 98:7-9. Je 51:16mg. Ro +*11:25. **forces.** or, wealth. ♪121N2, Ge +34:29. Metonymy of the Adjunct, whereby the abstract is put for the concrete, an adjunct for the subject to which it pertains, here "forces" is put for "wealth." ver. 11. Is 10:3. 23:18. 61:6. Jb 36:19. Pr *13:22. Mi 4:13. Zc *14:14. Ac 24:17. Ro √)11:25. 15:26. ♪121G1. Figure of speech Metonymy of the Effect, Ge +31:1. By Metonymy of the Effect, whereby the effect is put for the thing or action producing it, "forces" is put for *wealth*. Peters notes, "The nations, and especially the Jews, will enjoy the wealth accumulated and stored up by Gentile domination" (*Theocratic Kingdom*, vol. 2, p. 143).

6. **multitude**. Is 30:6. Jg 6:5. 7:12. 1 K 10:2. 2 K 8:9. **Midian**. Ge 25:4, 13. **all**. Is 45:14. Ge 10:7. 25:3. 2 Ch 9:1. Ps *72:10, 15. **they shall bring**. T#1889. Is *61:6. Ps *72:10. Ml 1:11. Mt ✱2:2, +11. **they shall show**. Ro 15:9. Ph 2:17. 1 P 2:5, 9. Re 5:9, 10. 7:9-12.

7. **the flocks**. Is 42:11. Ge 25:13. **of Kedar**. Is 21:16, 17. 42:11. Ge 25:13. Ps 120:5. SS 1:5. **Nebaioth**. i.e. *high places; heights; prophecies; increasings; fruitful-nesses,* ✱S#5032h. Is 60:7. 1 Ch 1:29. See also Ge +25:13. 28:9. 36:3 (Nebajoth). **they shall**. Is 56:7. Jb 42:8. Ro *12:1. 15:16. He 13:10, 15, 16. **I will**. Hg *2:7-9.

8. **fly**. ver. 4. Is 2:3, 5. 45:22. Zc *8:21. Lk +*13:29. Re 7:9. **a cloud**. He *12:1. **as the**. Ge 8:8-11.

9. **the isles**. Is *42:4, 10. 49:1. *51:5. 66:19, 20. Ge 9:27. *10:2-5. Ps 72:10. Zp *2:11. **the ships**. See on Is 2:16. 1 K 10:22. 22:48. 2 Ch +*9:21n. **thy sons**. See on ver. 4. Ps *68:30, 31. Zc *14:14. 2 C *8:4, 5. Ga 3:26. 4:26. **unto**. Ex 33:19. 34:5-7. Jsh 9:9. 1 K 8:41. 10:1. Pr 18:10. Je *3:17. Jn 17:26. Ac 9:15. **because**. Is 14:1, 2. 43:4. 52:1-6. *55:5. 57:17. Je 30:19. Lk 2:32. Jn *17:4.

10. **the sons**. Is 61:5. 66:21. Zc *6:15. **of strangers**. Is 56:3, 6. 61:5. 62:8. Ex +12:43)Ρ (✱S#5236h). Le 22:25)Ρ. **their kings**. See on ver. 3. Is *49:23. Ezr *6:3-12. *7:12-28. Ne 2:7-9. Re 21:24, 26. **in my wrath**. Is *12:1. √54:7, 8. 57:17, 18. 1 S +*12:22. Ps *30:5. Zc *1:15. **in my favor**. Is √14:1. 49:8. Re 69:13. 77:7. 85:1. +*102:13. 106:4. **had mercy**. Is +√55:3. Ps 106:46. Je 12:15. 31:20. +√33:25, 26. *42:12. La 3:32. Ezk *39:25. Ho 1:7. 2:23. Mi 7:19. Zc 1:16. √10:6.

11. **Therefore**. The subject of this chapter, says Bp. Lowth, is the great increase and flourishing state of the church of God, by the conversion and accession of the heathen nations to it; which is set forth in such ample and exalted terms, as plainly show that the full completion of this prophecy is reserved for future times. This subject is displayed in the most splendid colors, under a great variety of images highly poetical, designed to give a *general* idea of the glories of that perfect state of the church of God, which we are taught to expect in the latter times; when the fulness of the Gentiles shall come in, and the Jews shall be converted and gathered from their dispersions, and the "kingdoms of this world shall become the kingdom of our Lord and of His Christ." **thy gates**. Ne 13:19. Re 21:25. **forces**. or, wealth. ver. +*5mg.

12. **For**. ♪136. Parembole; or, Insertion B476. A parenthetic independent addition complete in itself,

which makes complete sense when separated from the sentence which it divides. For other instances of this figure see Mk 7:3, 4. Lk 17:9. Ac 2:8-11. Ro 3:27-31. 6:13-17. 8:2-15. 1 C 15:20-28. 2 C 3:7-16. Ep 1:19-23. 3:2-13. Ph *3:18, 19. 1 T 5:22, 23. He 12:18-29. 1 P 3:19-21. 1 J 1:2. Re 16:15. **the nation**. Is 41:11. 54:15. Ps *2:12. Da 2:35, 44, 45. Zc 12:2-4. *14:12-19. Mt *21:44. Lk *19:27. Re 2:26, 27.

13. **The glory**. That is, the *cedar*; and as the choice timber of Lebanon beautified Solomon's temple, that *footstool* of Jehovah; so shall the peculiar advantages of every nation, and of every description of men, concur to beautify the church of Christ, which He has determined to make glorious. The language then becomes more energetic, and the images employed more grand and magnificent; and nothing can answer to the glorious description but some future exalted state of the church on earth, or the church triumphant in heaven; though several expressions seem to limit it to the church below. Is 35:2. 41:19, 20. 55:13. Ho 14:6, 7. **to beautify**. Is 41:19. 51:3. Ezr *7:27. Re 3:12. **my sanctuary**. A reference to the millennial temple which will be built on earth when Christ returns. Ezk +*37:26. 43:7. Zc *1:16. √6:12, 13. **the place**. Is 35:2. *66:1. 1 Ch *28:2. Ps 96:6. 99:5. *132:7. **my feet**. ♪22A20, Ps +74:3. Ezk 43:7. Zc 14:4.

14. **sons**. Is 14:1, 2. 45:14. 49:23. Je 16:19. Re 3:9. **afflicted**. or, oppressed. Is 1:7, 8. 6:12. 7:16. **shall come bending**. Ml 1:11. Mt +*8:11. Re *3:9. **The city**. Is 62:12. Ps 87:3. He *12:22. Re *3:12. *14:1.

15. **thou**. Is 49:14-23. 54:6-14. Ps 78:60, 61. Je 30:17. La 1:1, 2. Re 11:2, 15-17. **forsaken**. Is 1:+4, 7-9. 6:11-13. 54:6. 62:4. Je 30:17. Zc *10:6. Ro 11:15. **and hated**. Is *66:5. Dt 21:15. Ps 9:13. 25:19. 35:19. 38:19. 69:4. 109:3. 119:78, 86. Mt *10:22. **eternal**. Heb. *olam*, Le +25:32. **excellency**. Ps 47:4. **a joy**. Is 35:10. 61:7. Je 33:11. Re 21:2.

16. **suck the milk**. Is 49:23. 61:6. 66:11, 12. **thou shalt know**. See on Is 43:3, 4. 66:14. Ezk 34:30. **thy Redeemer**. Is 41:14. 43:14. 44:6, 24. 47:4. 48:17. 49:7, 26. 54:5, 8. 59:20. 60:16. 63:16. Ge 48:16)Ρ. Ex 6:6)Ρ. 15:13)Ρ. Pr 23:11. **the mighty**. Is +*9:6. +10:21. 49:26. Je 32:18. Mt 11:21. Lk 9:43. Ep 1:21. Re 7:10, 12. **One of Jacob**. Is 49:26. Ge 49:24)Ρ. Ps 132:2-5.

17. **brass**. Is 30:26. 1 K 10:21-27. Zc 12:8. He 11:40. 2 P 3:13. **make**. Is 1:26. 32:1, 2. **thine exactors**. Is 3:12. Lk 3:13.

18. **Violence**. Is *2:4. 11:9. Ps 72:3-7. Mi 4:3. Zc 9:8. **but**. See on Is *26:1. Re 19:1-6. **thy walls**. Re 21:18. **Salvation**. Re 19:1. **Praise**. Is 61:11. Ps 89:16.

19. **sun**. Ps 36:9. Re *21:23. *22:5. **everlasting**. Heb. *olam*, Ge +17:7. **thy God**. Ps 3:3. 4:2. 62:7. Zc *2:5. Lk *2:32.

20. **sun**. Ps 27:1. *84:11. Am 8:9. Ml *4:2. **the Lord shall**. Is 58:11. **everlasting**. Heb. *olam*, Ge +17:7. **the days**. Is 25:8. 30:19. 35:10. 65:19. Re 7:15-17. *21:4.

21. **people**. Is 4:3, 4. 52:1. 62:4. Zc *14:20, 21. 2 P *3:13. Re *21:27. **all righteous**. T#441. Is +*27:9. 35:8-10. 45:25. 52:1. *61:3. 62:2. 65:25. Dt +30:6 (T#506). Jb +5:24. Ps +130:8. Je *31:33, 34. Ezk *36:25-29. 37:23, 24. Da +*9:24n. Na 1:15. Zp *3:13. Zc 14:20. Lk 1:68. Ro 11:25-27. Re 21:27. **inherit**. Ps 37:9, 11, 22. Mt +*5:5. Re 5:10. 21:7. **the land**. 2 Ch +*20:7. Zc 3:9. Mt +*5:5. Ac +*7:5. **for ever**. Heb. *olam*, Ex +*12:24. Note the straightforward promise here that Israel is to inherit the land forever.

Such a promise requires a literal fulfillment, which has not yet been accomplished (He +*11:39); but since God cannot lie (T 1:2), the fulfillment is reserved for the future. This promise, repeated many times and in many ways (Is +*41:9. +*55:3. Ge +*17:8. 2 Ch +*20:7), renders the "church-kingdom" theory (often reflected in the headnotes and chapter or page running heads of various editions of the Authorized Version) utterly false, since such a theory denies the literal fulfillment of these promises to Israel and applies them to the church, or to "spiritual Israel." The inconsistency of such a method of interpretation is readily seen when the blessings are eagerly applied to the church, but the curses are literally applied to Israel! Peters (*Theocratic Kingdom*, vol. 2, p. 90, footnote 5) states "The great spiritual blessings are promised to *the identical* people that suffered dispersion from their land, and are so repeatedly linked with a return to *the same land* from which they were driven, that it is folly to apply these to the Church as now constituted, and not to the time, place, and people for whom they are intended." Peters notes that the multiplicity of prophetic detail forbids any spiritualized application to the Church: "The election of the nation, the rejection for a time, the Theocratic relationship, the absolute promises, the gathering from all countries and bringing into their own land, the personal appearance of the Messiah and effect upon them, the time of this Advent, the distressed condition of the nation, the miraculous attending the conversion and restoration, the aid tendered by Gentiles, the formation into a State, the union of the two nations, the vast multiplication, and a hundred more particulars, *are all* of such a nature, and *so connected*, that they forbid any other view." Biblical references for each of these details of predictive prophecy named by Peters will be found in the note for Is 11:11n, or in the index, particularly entries under "Israel." Each school of prophetic interpretation seems quite aware of the interpretative mistakes of the opposing school, while remaining unaware of its own. There are two extremes to be avoided: spiritualization and speculation. Amillennialists wisely caution against speculation, premillennialists rightly caution against spiritualization. Is 11:11n. Am +√9:15. **the branch.** Is 4:2, 3. 29:23. 43:7. 45:11. 61:3. Ps *92:13. Mt *15:13. Jn 15:2. **the work.** Is 29:23. 43:21. Hab *3:2. Ep √2:10. **that I.** Is 43:21. 44:23. 49:3. Ep *1:6, 12. 2:7. 2 Th *1:10.

22. **little.** Is 66:8. Da *2:35, 44. Mt *13:31, 32. Mk 4:28, 29. Ac *2:41. 5:14. Re 7:9. **I the Lord.** Is 5:19. Hab *2:3. Lk 18:7, 8. He 10:36, 37. 2 P *3:8, +*9.

ISAIAH 61

The Messiah declares his anointing, his office, and the effects of his fulfilling it, 1-3. The honor and excellency of Zion, 4-9. Her joy in God's salvation, 10, 11.

1. **Spirit.** Heb. *ruach*, Is +48:16. Is *11:2-5. *42:1. 59:21. Mt *3:16. Lk *⸜4:18, 19. Jn *1:32, 33. √3:34. **anointed.** ♪22D51, Ps +45:7. Is 11:2. 1 S 16:13. Ps 2:6mg. +*45:7. Da *9:24. Jn 1:41. Ac 4:27. ❋*10:38. He 1:9. **to preach.** Is 52:9. Ps 22:26. *25:9. 69:32mg. 149:4. Mt +*5:3-5. 11:5. Lk ❋4:16-21, 43. 7:22. **to bind.** ♪22C29, Jb +5:18. Is +*57:15. 66:2. Ps *34:18.

51:17. *147:3. Ho 6:1. 2 C 7:6. **to proclaim.** The proclaiming of perfect liberty to the bound, and the year of acceptance with Jehovah, is a manifest allusion to the proclaiming of the year of jubilee by sound of trumpet (Le 25:11n, 52n); and our Savior, by applying this text to himself (Lk ⸜4:18, 19), plainly declares the typical design of that institution. T#1903. Is 42:7. 49:9, 24, 25. Ex=9:13. Ps 102:20. Je 34:8. Zc 9:11, 12. Lk ❋4:16-22. Jn √8:32-36. Ac *26:18. Ro 6:16-22. 7:23-25. 2 C 3:17. 2 T 2:25, 26. He 2:8-10.

2. **the acceptable year.** ♪171T1. Synecdoche of the Part B652. A part of time is put for the whole time: a *year* is put for *time*, definite and indefinite. For other instances of this figure see Is 63:4. Je 11:23. 48:44. Compare ♪171T2, Ge +2:4, where "day" is put for "time," definite and indefinite, and the light this sheds upon 2 P 3:7, "day of judgment," and Peter's comment immediately following in 2 P 3:8, as if to reinforce the significance of this figure, by alerting his readers to the fact, citing Ps 90:4, that "one day is with the Lord as a thousand years." Is 49:8. Le *25:9-13⸜9. Lk ⸜4:19. 2 C √6:2. A reference to the year of acceptance, or jubilee year (Le 25:11n, 52n). Jesus ends his quotation of this passage with this clause. He stated that "this day is this scripture fulfilled in your ears." He did not quote the next clause (so "rightly dividing the word," 2 T 2:15), for it relates to a future time. There are a number of such passages in Scripture where a period of time intervenes historically or prophetically between adjacent statements: Ps 118:22. Is 9:6. 53:10, 11. La 4:21, 22. Da 2:39-45; 7:3-28; 8:3-25; *9:26, 27; 11:20, 21; 12:2. Ho 2:13, 14. 3:4, 5. Am 9:10, 11. Ob 21. Mi 2:12, 13. 5:2, 3. Hab 2:13, 14. Zp 3:7, 8. Zc 8:2, 3. 9:9, 10. Ml 3:1-3. Mt 10:23. 12:20. Lk 1:31, 32. 21:24, 26. Jn 1:5, 6. 5:28, 29. 1 P 1:11. Re 1:19; 4:1. 12:5, 6. **and the day of vengeance.** Is 34:8. 35:4. 59:17, 18. 63:1-6. 66:14. Dt *32:41. Ps 110:5, 6. Je 46:10. Na *1:2. Ml *4:1-3. Lk *21:22-24. 1 Th 1:10. 2:16. 2 Th √1:7-9. He *10:30, 31. **to comfort.** Is *25:8. 40:1. 57:18. 66:10-12. Je 31:13. Mt +*5:4. Lk *6:21. *7:44-50. Jn 16:20-22. 2 C 1:4, 5. 2 Th 2:16, 17. **mourn.** F/L Is +3:26. Mt +*5:4.

3. **mourn.** Ezk 26:15, 16. Mt +*5:4. **beauty.** Is *12:1. Est 4:1-3. 8:15. 9:22. Ps *30:11. Ezk 16:8-13. **for ashes.** 2 S 13:19. **the oil.** Ps *23:5. +*45:7. 104:15. Ec 9:8. Jn 16:20. He 1:9. **the garment of praise.** ver. 10. Zc 3:5. Lk 15:22. Re *7:9-14. **the spirit.** Heb. *ruach*, Ge +41:8. **of heaviness.** ❋S#3544h: Is 42:3 (smoking; mg, dimly burning). Le 13:6 (somewhat dark), 21, 26, 28, 39 (darkish), 56. 1 S 3:2 (wax dim). Compare ❋S#3543h, 1 S +3:13 (restrained). 2 T +*1:7. 1 P ⬤*4:14. **be called.** Is 60:21. Ps 92:12-15. Je *17:7, 8. Mt 7:17-19. **trees of righteousness.** Is 41:19, 20. ⬤57:5. +*60:21. Ps +*1:3. Pr +*11:30. Je +*31:2. Da +*12:3. **the planting.** Is 5:2. 60:21. Ex 15:17. Nu 24:6. 2 S 7:10. 1 Ch 17:9. Ps +*1:3. 44:2. 80:8. 92:12, 13. Je 2:21. 11:17. √24:6. 32:41. 42:10. Ezk 19:10. Mt *7:19. *15:13. Jn √15:1, 2. 1 C 3:9. **that he.** Is 26:15. 44:23. 49:3. +*60:21. Ex 14:18. Le 10:3. Ezk 28:22. 39:13. Hg 1:8. Mt *5:16. Jn *15:8. 1 C √6:20. Ph *1:11. 2 Th *1:10. 1 P 2:9. √4:9-11, 14.

4. **shall build.** ♪132D, Ge +19:25. Is 49:6-8. 58:12. Ezk 36:23-26, 33-36. Am √9:14, 15. **old.** Heb. *olam*, Jb +*22:15. **raise up.** Am *9:11, 12. Ac +*15:16. **desolations.** F/L Is +1:7. Ps 74:3.

5. **strangers.** Is *14:1, 2. 56:3, 6. 60:10-14. 62:8. Ex 12:43 (✳S#5236h). Jsh *9:21. Ep 2:12-20.

6. **named.** Is 60:17. 66:21. Ex 19:6)✳℗. Ro *12:1. 1 P *2:5,)9. Re 1:6. 5:10. *20:6. **call.** Ezk 14:11. 1 C 3:5. 4:1. 2 C 6:4. 11:23. Ep *4:11, 12. **Ministers.** Ex 28:35)✳℗. Nu 16:9)✳℗. Dt 10:8)℗. 17:12)℗. 1 C *4:1. **ye shall eat.** Is 23:18. *60:5-7, 10, 11, 16. 66:12. Ac 11:28-30. Ro 15:26, 27. **riches of the Gentiles.** Is +*60:5. Mi 4:13. Zc *14:14. Ro +*11:25.

7. **your shame.** Is 40:2. Dt √21:17. 2 K 2:9. Jb *42:10. Zc √9:12. Ro *5:20, 21. 2 C 4:17. **ye shall have.** ♪63B, Ge +25:28. Jl +*2:25. Zc *10:6. **double.** or, double (honor). ♪121L9, Ge +43:12. Here we have the "double" denoting not full punishment (as in Is 40:2), but complete compensation. And this is marked in the alternation of the four lines: where we have this completeness in the first and third lines; and the consequent joy and rejoicing in the second and fourth lines: (A) For your shame ye shall have complete compensation or full acquittal. (B) And for confusion they shall rejoice in their portion. (A) Therefore in their land they shall possess the complete pardon. (B) Everlasting joy shall be unto them (B586). S#4932h. Is 61:7, 7. Ge 41:43. 43:12, 15. Ex 16:5, 22. Dt 15:18. 17:18 (copy). 1 S 8:2 (second). 15:9mg. 17:13 (next). 23:17. 2 S 3:3. 2 K 22:14mg. 23:4. 25:18. 1 Ch 5:12. 15:18. 16:5. 2 Ch 28:7mg. 31:12. 34:22mg. 35:24. Ezr 1:10. Ne 11:9, 17. Est 10:3. Jb √42:10mg. Je 16:18. 17:18. 52:24. Zp 1:10. Zc *9:12. Not the same as Is +*40:2h. Zc *9:12. 1 T 5:17. **everlasting.** Heb. *olam,* Ge +17:7. Is *35:10. +*51:11. +*60:19, 20. Ps +*16:11. Mt +√25:46. 2 Th 2:16.

8. **I the Lord.** Ps *11:7. 33:5. 37:28. +*45:7. 99:4. Je +*9:24. Zc 8:16, 17. **I hate.** Is *1:11-13. 1 S *15:21-24. Je 7:8-11. Am 5:21-24. Mt 23:14. **I will direct.** Ps *25:8-12. +*32:8. Pr +√3:6. 8:20. 2 Th 3:5. **I will make.** Is +*55:3. Ge *17:7. 2 S 23:5. Ps 50:5. Je 32:40. He *13:20, 21. **everlasting.** Heb. *olam,* Ge +*17:7. **covenant.** Ge +9:16. Je *31:33.

9. **their seed.** Is *44:3. Ge *22:18. Zc 8:13. Ac +*2:39. √3:25. Ro 9:3, 4. **they are.** Is 65:23. Ps 115:14. Zc *8:13. Ac √3:26. Ro 11:16-24.

10. **will greatly.** Is 35:10. 51:11. 1 S *2:1. Ne 8:10. Ps 28:7. *97:12. Hab 3:18. Zc 10:7. Lk 1:46, 47. Ro 5:11. Ph 3:1-3. 4:4. 1 P 1:8. Re 19:7, 8. **rejoice.** Zp ◑*3:17. **soul.** Heb. *nephesh,* Ge +34:3. T#983‡. Ge 23:8. Le 26:43. 1 S *18:1. Ps 119:28. **clothed me.** ver. 3. Is *52:1. 2 Ch 6:41. Jb 29:14. Ps 132:9, 16. Ezk ◑26:15, 16. Zc 3:4. Lk 15:22. Ro 3:22. √13:14. *14:17. Ga √3:27. Ph *3:9. Re 4:4. *7:9-14. 21:2. **covered me.** Is ◑59:6. Re *19:7, 8. **as a bridegroom.** Is *49:18. Ps 45:8, 9, 13, 14. Je 2:32. Ezk 16:8-16. Re 19:7, 8. *21:2, 9. **decketh himself.** Heb. decketh as a priest. Ex 28:2, etc. Or, as Bishop Lowth renders, "as the bridegroom decketh himself with a priestly crown." An allusion, he observes, to the magnificent dress of the high priest, when performing his functions; and particularly to the mitre and crown, or plate of gold, in the front of it. Ex 28:40. **with her.** Ge 24:53.

11. **as the earth.** Is √55:10, 11. 58:11. SS 4:16. 5:1. Mt 13:3, 8, 23. Mk 4:26-32. **so.** Is 45:8. 62:1. Ps 72:3, 16. *85:11. *97:11. 2 C 1:20. **righteousness.** T#942. Is *4:3, 4. 32:15, 16. 33:5, 6. 45:8. +*60:21. Ps 72:5. *85:10, 11, 13. Zc 14:20, 21. Ml 3:3, 4. Re *19:8. **praise.** Is 60:18. 62:7. 1 P 2:9.

ISAIAH 62

The prophet, as a type of Christ, shows his zeal in interceding for the performance of God's glorious promises to Israel, 1-5. Vigilant watchmen are promised; who, with believers in general, are excited to the same zeal, 6, 7. God confirms his promises by an oath, 8, 9. Preparations to be made for the coming of his salvation, 10-12.

1. **Zion's.** ver. 6, 7. Ps 51:18. √102:13-16. √122:6-9. 137:6. Zc 2:12. Mt *24:27. Lk 10:2. 21:24. 2 Th 3:1. He 7:25. **the righteousness.** Is 1:26, 27. 32:15-17. 51:5, 6, 9. 61:10, 11. Ps 98:1-3. Pr +√4:18n. Mi *4:2. Mt *5:16. Lk *2:30-32. Ph *2:15, 16. 1 P *2:9. **lamp.** Zc 4:2. Re 21:23, 24.

2. **the Gentiles.** Is 49:6. 52:10. *60:1-3. 61:9. 66:12, 19. Mi 5:8. Mt *24:27. Ac 9:15. 26:23. Col 1:23. **thy righteousness.** Is +*60:21. **all kings.** Is 49:23. 60:11, 16. Ps 72:10, 11. 138:4, 5. **thou shalt.** ver. 4, 12. Is 65:15. Ge 17:5, 15. 32:28. Je 11:16. √33:16. Ezk √48:35. Ac 11:26. Ga 4:26. He 12:22. Re 2:17. 21:2, 9, 10.

3. **crown.** Ps 132:18. Pr 12:4. SS 3:11. Re 19:12. **of glory.** Is 28:5. Zc 9:16. Lk 2:14. 1 Th *2:19.

4. **shalt no more.** ver. 12. Is 32:14, 15. 49:14. 50:1. 54:1, 6, 7. Je 3:8. Ho 1:9, 10. 2:2. Ro 9:25-27. He +*13:5. 1 P 2:10. **Hephzibah.** that is, *My delight is in her.* ♪32, Ge +31:21. ✿S#2657h. ver. 5. Ps 16:3. 149:4. 2 K *21:1h. Je 32:41. Zp *3:17. **Beulah.** that is, *Married.* Is 54:5. *61:10. Ps 48:2. SS 4:7. Je 3:14. Ezk *16:8, 14. Ho √2:19, 20. Mt 23:39. Jn 3:29. 2 C 11:2. Ep *5:25-27. Re 21:2, 9, 10. ✿S#1166h. Is 54:1. 62:4. Ge 20:3mg. Dt 22:22. Pr 30:23.

5. **shall thy sons.** ♪46A, Le +26:30. Is 49:18-22. Ps 45:11-16. Je 32:41. **as.** ♪170, Is +1:18. **the bridegroom rejoiceth.** Heb. with the joy of the bridegroom. ver. 4. Is 65:19. Ps 45:11. SS 3:11. Jn 3:29. 2 C 11:2. He *12:2. 1 P 1:8. Re 21:2. **so.** ♪170, Is +1:18. **rejoice.** ♪22B, Ps +104:31.

6. **set watchmen.** Is 21:11, 12. 52:8. 56:10. 2 Ch 8:14. SS 3:3. 5:7. Je 6:17. Ezk √3:17-21. 33:2-9. 1 C 12:28. Ep √4:11, 12. He √13:17. **which.** ver. 1. Ps 134:1, 2. Re 4:6-8. **make mention of the Lord.** or, are the Lord's remembrancers. Is 26:13. *43:26. Ge 32:12. Nu 14:17-19. 2 S +8:16. Ps 74:2, 18. 137:5, 6. Ac 10:4, 31. **keep.** Ge 32:26. Ps 83:1. Mt 15:22-27. Lk *11:5-13. *18:1-8, 39. 1 Th √5:17. Re *6:10.

7. **give him.** Is +45:11n. Mt 6:9, 10. Lk +*18:1-8. 1 Th +*5:17. **no rest.** Heb. silence. ver. 6. Ps 83:1. **till he make.** See on ver. 1-3. 61:11. 64:9-12. Ps +*102:13, 16. +*122:6. Je *33:9. Zp *3:19, 20. Mt *6:9, 10, 13. Re +*11:15. **Jerusalem.** Is +*24:23. Zc +*2:12. **a praise.** Zp √3:20. Zc ◑*12:2.

8. **sworn.** Dt 32:40. Ezk 20:5. **arm.** ♪22A12, Ex +15:16. **Surely I will no more give.** Heb. if I give, etc. Is *65:21-23. Le 26:16. Dt 28:30, 31, 33)℗. Jg 6:3-6. Je *5:17. **stranger.** Is 56:3, 6. 60:10. 61:5. Ex 12:43 (✳S#5236h). Je 5:19.

9. **gathered it.** Dt 20:6)℗. 28:30)℗. Je 31:5. **shall eat.** Dt 12:7, 12. 14:23-29. 16:11, 14. **and praise.** Dt 14:23, 26)℗. 16:11, 14)℗. **brought it together.** Dt 12:12)℗.

10. **go through.** Is 18:3. ◑*40:3. 48:20. 52:11. *57:14. Ex 17:15. Mt 22:9. He 12:13. **highway.** F/L Is +7:3. **gather out.** Jn 11:39. **lift up.** Is *11:12. *49:22.

11. **the Lord.** Ps 98:1-3. √102:18, 21, 22. Je 33:9. Zp 3:20. Mk *16:15. Ro √10:11-18. **Say.** Is 40:9. Zc

*9:9. Mt ‣21:5. Jn 12:15. **his reward**. See on Is *40:10. 49:4. Re *22:12. **work**. *or*, recompence. Is 40:10mg. 49:4mg. 61:8. Le +*19:13.

12. **The holy**. Is +*60:21. Dt 7:6. 26:19. 28:9. 1 P 2:9. **The redeemed**. Is 35:9. *43:1. Ps *107:2. 1 P *1:18, 19. Re 5:9. **Sought out**. Is 65:1. Ezk 34:11-16. Zc √8:23. *14:16. Mt 18:11-13. Lk 15:4, 5. +*19:10. Jn *4:23. +*10:16. **not forsaken**. See on ver. 4. Is +√41:9. *49:14-16. 1 S +*12:22. Ps 87:3. +*94:14. Mt 16:18. 28:20. He +*13:5.

ISAIAH 63

Christ shows his power to save; and his victories over his enemies and vengeance on them, 1-6. A thankful commemoration of God's ancient mercies to Israel, 7-14. A prayer for the return of his mercy to them, 15-19.

1. **Who**. ♪85E, Ge +17:17. **is this**. Ps 24:7-10. SS 3:6. 6:10. 8:5. Mt 21:10. **from Edom**. Is 34:5, 6. Ps 137:7. Ob 1, 8, 9, 21. **with**. ♪154, Mt +3:4. **dyed**. ver. 2, 3. Is 9:5. Re 19:13. ✲S#2556h. Ex 12:19, 20, 34, 39 (leavened). Ps 71:4 (cruel). 73:21 (grieved). Ho 7:4 (leavened). **Bozrah**. Am 1:11, 12. **glorious**. Heb. decked. ✲S#1921h. Is 45:2 (crooked places). Ex 23:3 (countenance). Le 19:15 (honor), 32. Pr 25:6mg. La 5:12 (honored). **travelling**. Ps *45:3, 4. Re 11:17, 18. **I that**. ♪56, Is +14:16. **speak**. Is 45:19, 23. Nu *23:19. **mighty**. Jsh 4:24. Ps *89:19. Am ◐5:12. Zp 3:17. Lk 1:49. Jn √10:28-30. He √7:25. 1 P *1:5. Ju *24, *25.

2. **Wherefore**. ♪85E, Ge +17:17. **art thou**. Re *19:13. **red**. Ge 25:30. Nu 19:2. **treadeth**. Ps *68:23. La 1:15. Re *14:19, 20. *19:15. **winefat**. Jg 6:11. Ne 13:15. Jl 3:12-14.

3. **trodden**. ♪96C8, Ex +15:5. Is 25:10. La 1:15. Ml 4:3. Re 14:19, 20. 19:13-15. **alone**. Ps +69:8. Jn 1:11. ✲7:3, 5. He 9:7. **and of the people**. The very remarkable passage contained in the first six verses of this chapter seems in a manner detached from the rest, and to stand by itself; containing a prophetical representation of the victories of the Messiah over the enemies of his church, here designated by the names of Edom and Bozrah. Though, as Bishop Lowth observes, this prophecy must have its accomplishment, there is no necessity for supposing that it has been already accomplished. There are prophecies which intimate a great slaughter of the enemies of God and his people, which remain to be fulfilled: those in Ezk ch. 38 and Re ch. 20 are called Gog and Magog. This prophecy of Isaiah may possibly refer to the same or the like event. See related note (Is 11:11). **none with me**. Is 59:16. **tread**. Is 22:5. 28:3. Ps 60:12. **and trample**. ver. 6. Is 34:2-5. 2 K 9:33. Ezk 38:18-22. Mi 7:10. Zc 10:5. **fury**. Is 59:18. **sprinkled**. 2 K 9:33. Re 19:13.

4. **day of vengeance**. ♪171T2, Ge +2:17. Is +*24:6. *34:8. *35:4. 59:17. *61:2. Ps +*58:10. Je 51:6. Zp +*3:8. Lk √21:22. 2 Th 1:8. 2 P 3:7. Re 6:9-17. 11:13. 18:20. **the year of**. ♪171T1, Is +61:2. Is *34:8. Dt 32:35‣𝒫. Ps 97:8. 98:9. +*102:13. Ro *11:25-29.

5. **looked**. ver. 3. Is *41:28. 50:2. *59:16. Jn *16:32. Ac √4:12. He √7:25. **mine own**. Is 40:10. 51:9. *52:10. 59:16. Ps 44:3. *98:1. Ho 1:7. 1 C 1:24. He 2:14, 15. **my fury**. Is 59:16-18.

6. **in mine anger**. Ps *76:7-9. 99:1. **make**. ver. 2,

3. Is 49:26. 51:21-23. Jb 21:20. Ps 60:3. 75:8. Je 25:16, 17, 26, 27. La 3:15. Re *14:10. *16:6, 19. 18:3-6. **I will bring**. Is 25:10-12. 26:5, 6. Re 18:21.

7. **mention**. Is 41:8, 9. 51:2. Ne 9:7-15, 19-21, 27, 31. Ps 63:3. 78:11, etc. 105:5, etc. 107:*8, 15, 21, 31. 136:1, etc. *147:19, 20. Je 2:2. Ezk 16:6-14. Ho 2:19. **the great goodness**. 1 K 8:66. 2 Ch 7:10. Ne 9:25, 35. Zc *9:17. Ro √2:4. **according to his**. Is √55:7. Ex 34:6, 7. Nu 14:18, 19. Ps *51:1. 86:5, 15. La 3:32. Ro *5:20. Ep 1:6, 7. 2:4. 1 T 1:14. T *3:4-7.

8. **Surely**. Is 41:8. Ge *17:7. Ex 3:7. 4:22, 23. *6:7. 19:5, 6. Ro +√11:1, 2, 28. **children**. Is 57:11. Ex 24:7. Ps 78:36, 37. Zp 3:7. Jn *1:47. Ep 4:25. Col 3:9. **so he**. Is *12:2. *19:20. *43:3, 11. *45:21, 22. Dt *33:29. Ps 106:21. Je *14:8. Ho 13:4. 1 J 4:14. Ju 25.

9. **all their**. Ex *3:7-9. Jg *10:16. La 3:33. Zc *2:8. Mt 25:40, 45. Ac 9:4. Ne 2:18. +*4:15. **the angel**. Ge 22:11-17. 48:16. Ex 14:19‣𝒫. *23:20, 21‣𝒫. 32:34. 33:2, *14‣𝒫. Ho 1:7. 12:3-5. Ml 3:1. Ac 7:30-32, 34, 35, 38. 12:11. 1 C 10:9. **his presence**. ♪22A4, Ge +19:13. **in his love**. Dt *7:7, 8. Ps *78:38. *106:7-10. Jn 16:27. T *2:14. 1 J *4:9, 10. Re +*1:5. *5:9. **redeemed them**. Ex 15:13‣𝒫. **bare them**. Ex 19:4‣𝒫. Dt 1:31‣𝒫. 4:37. 32:11‣𝒫. Ac 13:18. **carried**. Is 40:11. 46:3, 4. Ex 19:4. Dt 1:31. 32:11, 12. Lk 15:5. **of old**. Heb. *olam*, Ge +6:4.

10. **they rebelled**. Is *1:2. 65:2. Ex 15:24‣𝒫. 16:8. 32:8. Nu 14:9, 11, 34‣𝒫. 16:1, etc. Dt *9:7, 22-24. Ne 9:16, 17, 26, 29. La 1:18, 20. Ezk 2:3, 7. 20:8, 13, 21. **vexed**. ♪22B, Ge +6:6. Is *7:13. 43:24. Ge *6:3, 6. Ex *23:21, 22. Jg 10:16. Ps 78:8, 40, 49, *56. *95:9-11. Ezk 6:9. 16:43. Mk 3:5. Ac *7:51. Ep +√4:30. **his holy**. Ne 9:20. Hg 2:4, 5. **Spirit**. Heb. *ruach*, Is +48:16. **he was**. Ex 23:21. Le *26:17, etc. Dt 28:15, etc. 32:19-25. Je 21:5. 30:14. La 2:4, 5. Mt 22:7.

11. **he remembered**. Le *26:40-45. Dt 4:30, 31. Ps 25:6. 77:5-11. 89:47-50. 143:5. Lk 1:54, 55. **of old**. Heb. *olam*, Ge +6:4. **Where is he that brought**. ver. 15. Is 51:9, 10. Ex 14:30. 32:11, 12. Nu 14:13, 14, etc. Je 2:6. **shepherd**. *or*, shepherds. Ex=3:1. Ps *23:1, 2. 77:20. *79:13. 80:1. Jn *10:11, 14. He *13:20. 1 P 2:25. 5:4. **where is he that put**. Nu 11:17‣𝒫, 25, 29. Ne *9:20. Da 4:8. Hg *2:5. Zc √4:6. Jn √3:34. **Spirit**. Heb. *ruach*, Is +48:16.

12. **That led**. Is=55:4. Nu 24:8. Ps 77:20. **with**. Ex 15:6, 13, 16‣𝒫. Ps 80:1. **dividing**. Ex 14:21‣𝒫. Jsh 3:16. Ne 9:11. Ps 78:13. 114:5-7. 136:13-16. **to make**. Is 55:13. Ex 14:16, 17. 2 S *7:23. Ro 9:17. **everlasting**. Heb. *olam*, Ge +17:7.

13. **led them**. Ps *106:9. Hab *3:15. **deep**. Ge +1:2.

14. **the Spirit**. Heb. *ruach*, Is +48:16. Jsh 22:4. 23:1. He 4:8-11. **to make**. ver. 12. Nu 14:21. 2 S 7:23. 1 Ch 29:13. Ne 9:5. Lk 2:14. Ep 1:6, 12, 14.

15. **Look down**. Dt 26:15. Nu 14:17-20. Ps 33:14. 80:14. 102:19, 20. La 3:50. **the habitation**. Is +*57:15. 66:1. 1 K 8:27. 2 Ch 30:27. Ps *113:5, 6. *123:1. *138:6. **where**. Is 51:9, 10. Ps 89:49. **sounding**. *or*, multitude. Is 31:4mg. Ps 51:1. **thy bowels**. ver. 9. Is 49:15. Ps 25:6mg. Je 31:20. Ho 11:8. Lk 1:78mg. Ph 2:1. 1 J 3:17. ♪22A18. Anthropomorphism B881. Bowels are attributed to God to denote his mercies and his pity. This is also the figure Metonymy, whereby a movement of the bowels is put for the feeling itself which caused the movement, Metonymy of the Effect, ♪121G1, Ge +31:1. For other instances of this figure see Ge 43:30. 1 K 3:26. Ps 51:1. Je *31:20. Ho 11:8. Mt 9:36. 14:14.

15:32. Mk 1:41. 6:34. Lk *1:78mg. Ph 2:1. Col 3:12. **Are.** Ps 77:7-9.

16. **thou art.** Is √64:8. Ex 4:22. Dt *32:6)ℙ. 1 Ch *29:10. Je *3:19. 31:9. Ml 1:6. 2:10. Mt *3:9. *6:9. **our father.** Dt 32:6. Ml 1:6. 2 C 1:21. **though Abraham.** Mt +*8:11. Ga 3:16, 26-29. **be ignorant of us.** 2 K 2:9n. Jb +*14:21. Ec +*9:5. Mt ◑*22:32. Lk ◑+*16:23. **Israel.** ♪171H. Synecdoche of the Species B625. A proper name is put for a common; an individual is put for many; the particular is put for the universal. Here, the individuals Abraham and Israel are put for the great majority of the people of Israel, for the patriarchs named were long since dead. For other instances of this figure see 1 C 3:6. 7:16. **redeemer; thy name is from everlasting.** or, Redeemer from everlasting *is* thy name. ver. 12. Is 41:14. 43:14. 44:6. 54:5. 60:16. He +*13:8. 1 P 1:18-21. Re *1:8. 4:8. 11:17. 16:5. **everlasting.** Heb. *olam,* Ge +17:7.

17. **why hast.** Ps *119:10, 36. 141:4. Ezk 14:7-9. 2 Th √2:11, 12. **made us to err.** Is +√45:7. 2 K 21:9. La 3:9. Am +*3:6. **and hardened.** Is *6:10. Dt +√2:30. Jsh 11:20. Jn *12:40. Ro *9:18-20. **Return.** ♪87, Ps +118:25. Nu 10:36)ℙ. Ps 74:1, 2. 80:14. 90:13. Zc 1:12.

18. **people.** Is 62:12. Ex *19:4-6. Dt *7:6)ℙ. 26:19)ℙ. Da *8:24. 1 P *2:9. **our.** Is 64:11, 12. Ps 74:3-7. *79:1. La 1:10. 4:1. Mt *23:38. *24:2. Lk *21:24. Re 11:2.

19. **are thine.** Ps 79:6. *135:4. Je 10:25. Ac 14:16. Ro √9:4. 11:28. Ep 2:12. **they were not called by thy name.** or, thy name was not called upon them. Is *65:1. Dt 28:10. Je +14:9mg. Am 9:12. Ac 15:17.

ISAIAH 64

The Israelites earnestly beseech God powerfully to interpose for the nation, according to his wonderful works of old in their behalf, and according to his abundant mercies, 1-5. They humbly confess their unworthiness, refer themselves to his disposal, bewail the desolations occasioned by their iniquities, and deprecate the severity of his indignation, 6-12.

1. **Oh that.** ♪124, Dt +5:29. ♪87, Ps +118:25. Ps 18:7-15. 144:5, 6. Mk 1:10mg. **rend.** Ml 3:10. **that thou wouldest come.** Is 63:15. Ex 3:8. 19:11, 18, 19. Ps 144:5. Da 7:13. Mi 1:3, 4. Hab 3:1-13. Mt 26:64. Ac √1:9-11. *3:20, 21. Re *1:7. 22:17, 20. **that the.** Jg 5:4, 5. Ps 46:6. 68:8. 114:4-7. Am 9:5, 13. Na 1:5, 6. 2 P 3:10-12. Re 20:11.

2. **melting fire.** Heb. fire of meltings. Mi 1:4. 2 P *3:10. **to make.** Is 37:20. 63:12. Ex 14:4. 1 S 17:46, 47. 1 K 8:41-43. Ps 46:10. 67:1, 2. 79:10. 83:13. 98:1, 2. 102:15, 16. 106:8. Ezk 38:+*16, 22, 23. 39:27, 28. Da 4:1-3, 32-37. 6:25-27. Jl 3:16, 17. Hab *3:2. **that the nations.** Ex 15:14-16. Dt 2:25. Ps 9:20. 48:4-6. 99:1. Je 5:22. 33:9. Mi 7:15-17. Re 11:11-13.

3. **thou didst.** Ex 34:10)ℙ. Dt 4:34. 10:21. Jg 5:4, 5. 2 S 7:23. Ps 65:5. 66:3, 5. *68:8. 76:12. 105:27-36. 106:22. He 12:21. **the mountains.** ver. 1. Ex 19:18. Na 1:5, 6. Hab 3:3, 6.

4. **beginning of the world.** Heb. *olam,* Le +25:32. **have not.** Ps 31:19. 1 C 2:)9, 10. Ep 3:5-10, 17-21. Col 1:26, 27. 1 T *3:16. 1 J *3:1, 2. 4:10. Re 21:1-4, 22-24. 22:1-5. **seen,** etc. *or,* seen a God besides thee, *which* doeth so for, etc. **prepared.** Ps 31:19. Mt 25:34. Jn √14:2, 3. He 11:16. **waiteth.** Is 25:9. Ge 49:18. Ps

62:1. 130:5. La *3:25, 26. Lk 2:25. Lk 2:25. Ro 8:19, 23-25. 1 C 1:7. 1 Th *1:10. Ja 5:7.

5. **meetest.** Ge 32:1)ℙ. Ex 20:24. 25:22. 29:42, 43. 30:6. He *4:16. **rejoiceth.** Ps 25:10. 37:4. 112:1. Ac *10:2-4, √35. Ph 3:13-15. **worketh righteousness.** Zp +*2:3. **those that.** Is 26:8, 9. 56:1-7. **remember thee.** Ml +*3:16, 17. **thou art wroth.** Is 63:10. Ps 90:7-9. **in those.** Ps *103:17, 18. Je 31:18-20. Ho 6:3. 11:8, 9. Ml √3:6. **continuance.** Heb. *olam,* Le +25:32. Is 63:9, 11, 16, 19. Jn √6:54n. Ep 1:21. 3:21. **we shall be saved.** Ro *8:38, 39. +*11:26.

6. **are all.** Is 6:5. √53:6. Jb 14:4. 15:14-16. 25:4. *40:4. 42:5, 6. Ps +*51:5. Ro *7:18, 24. Ep *2:1, 2. T 3:3. **unclean thing.** Le 5:2. Ezk 36:17. **all our righteousnesses.** Is *57:12. Dt 6:12. Je *23:6. Ezk +*33:13. Zc 3:3, 4. Ph √3:8, 9. Re 3:17, 18. 7:13, 14. **filthy.** ✱S#5708h, only here. Le 12:2. 15:20. rags. S#899h. Is 51:6, 8 (garment). *59:6. Ge 24:53 (raiment). 27:15, 27. 38:14, 19. Ex 28:2. Zc *3:5. **we all.** Is *40:6-8. Ps *90:5, 6. Ja *1:10, 11. 1 P *1:24, 25. **our iniquities.** ♪144A5, Ge +9:5. Is 57:13. Ps *1:4. Je 4:11, 12. Ho 4:19. Zc 5:8-11.

7. **there is.** Is 50:2. 59:16. Ps 14:4. Ezk 22:30. Ho 7:7, 14. **to take hold.** T#1413. Is *27:5. 56:4. +62:7. 2 Ch +*7:14. Ezk *22:30. **hast hid.** Is 45:15. 53:3. 54:8. *57:17. √59:2. Dt √31:17, 18, 20)ℙ. 32:19-25. Ho 5:15. **consumed.** Heb. melted. Ps 46:6. *90:7-9. Je 9:7. Ezk 22:18-22. 24:11. Am 9:5. **because.** Heb. by the hand, as Jb 8:4mg.

8. **thou art.** Is *63:16. Ex 4:22. Dt *32:6. Ga 3:26, 29. **are the clay.** Is 29:16. *45:9. Je 18:2-6. Jn 9:6. Ro *9:20-24. **all are.** Is 43:7. 44:21, 24. Jb 10:8, 9. 26:13. Ps 100:3. 119:73. 138:8. Jn *1:3. Ac 17:24, 26. 2 C 6:1. Ep *2:10.

9. **wroth.** Ps 6:1. 38:1. *74:1, 2. *79:5-9. Je *10:24. Hab 3:2. **remember.** Je 3:12. La 5:20. Mi *7:18-20. Ml 1:4. 2 P 2:17. Re 20:10. **for ever.** Heb. *ad,* Ps +9:18 (✱S#5703h). **we are.** Is *63:19. Ps *79:13. 119:94.

10. **holy cities.** Is 1:7. 2 K 25:9. 2 Ch 36:19-21. Ps *79:1-7. La 1:1-4. 2:4-8. 5:18. Da *9:26, 27. 12:7. Mi 3:12. Lk *21:21, 24. Re 11:1, 2. **desolation.** Mt 23:38. 24:2.

11. **holy.** 2 K *25:8, 9. 2 Ch *36:19, 20. Ps *74:5-7. Je 52:13. La 2:7. Ezk 7:20, 21. 24:21, 25. Mt *24:2. **house.** T#1529. 2 Ch 6:19, 20. 7:12. Ps 74:2-8. 79:1-7. **where.** 1 K 8:14, 56. 2 Ch 6:4. 7:3, 6. 29:25-30. **all our.** La 1:7, 10, 11. **pleasant things.** 2 Ch 36:19.

12. **refrain thyself.** Is 42:14. 63:15. Ge 43:31. 45:1. Ps 10:1. *74:10, 11, 18, 19. 79:5. 80:3, 4. *83:1. 89:46-51. Zc 1:12. Re *6:10.

ISAIAH 65

Jehovah declares his free mercy in the conversion of the Gentiles, and his justice in casting off Israel for unbelief, idolatry, and wickedness, 1-7; shows that he preserved the nation for the sake of a chosen seed to arise out of it; and contrasts the blessedness of his servants with the miseries coming on the unbelieving Jews, 8-15; and predicts the glories and privileges of Jerusalem in the latter days, 16-25.

1. **I am sought.** ♪108A2. Idiom B822. Active verbs are sometimes used to denote the effect of the action expressed. Here, the meaning is "I am found of them that sought me not," as cited in Ro ▶10:20. Note that

the New Testament citation of this passage interprets rather than literally translates the figure (see related note, Ps +*16:9). Another instance of this figure is Jn *16:5. Is 2:2, 3. 11:10. 55:5. Ps *22:27, 28. Mt *8:10. *15:21-28. Ro *9:24-26, 30. ▶10:20, 21. Ep *2:12, 13. **Behold.** Is 40:9. 41:27. *45:22. Jn *1:29. **unto.** Is 43:1. 63:19. Ho 1:10. Zc 2:11. 8:22, 23. 1 P *2:10. **a nation.** Dt 32:21▶𝒫.

2. **I have.** Ro ▶10:21. **spread.** ♪22A14.8H, Pr +1:24. Pr *1:24. Mt √23:37. Lk 13:34. 19:41, 42. Ro 10:21. **a rebellious.** Is 1:2. 63:10. Dt 9:7. 31:27. Je 5:23. Ezk 2:3-7. Ac *7:51, 52. 1 Th 2:15, 16. **which.** Is 59:7, 8. Ps 36:4. Pr 16:29. **after.** Is √55:7. Ge 6:5. Nu 15:39. Dt 29:19. Ps *81:11, 12. Je 3:17. 4:14. 7:24. Mt *12:33, 34. *15:19. Ro *2:5. Ja *1:14, 15.

3. **A people.** Is 3:8. Dt 32:16-19, 21▶𝒫. 2 K *17:14-17. 22:17. Ps *78:40, 58. Je 32:30-35. Ezk 8:17, 18. Mt 23:32-36. **to my face.** Jb 1:11. 2:5. **that sacrificeth.** Is 1:29. 57:5. 66:17. Le 17:5▶𝒫. Je 2:20. 3:6. Ezk 20:28. **altars.** Heb. bricks. Is 9:10. Ex 20:24, 25. 30:1-10. 2 K 23:12.

4. **remain.** Nu *19:11, 16-20. Dt 18:11. 2 Ch 34:5n. Mt 8:28. Mk 5:2-5. Lk 8:27. **graves.** Heb. qeber, Ge +23:4. **monuments.** ✚S#5341h. Is 1:8 (besieged). 48:6 (hidden things). 49:6mg (preserved). Pr 7:10 (subtil). Ezk 6:12 (besieged). This term has been variously interpreted to mean monuments, caves, or temples where idolatrous abominations took place. **which eat.** Is 66:3, 17. Le *11:7▶𝒫. Dt 14:8▶𝒫. **broth.** or, pieces. Ex 23:19. 34:26. Dt 14:3, 21. Jg 6:19, 20. Ezk 4:14. **abominable things.** Le 7:18▶𝒫. 19:7▶𝒫. Ezk 4:14.

5. **Stand.** Mt 9:11. Lk 5:30. 7:39. 15:2, 28-30. 18:9-12. Ac 22:21, 22. Ro 2:17, etc. Ju 19. **I am holier than thou.** Those caught up in false doctrine and false cults often possess a superiority complex because of their supposed superior experience or knowledge. The fundamental error of the first is that of being "experience centered" instead of "Bible centered" or "Christ centered," and leads to instability, with repeated spiritual "ups and downs." The fundamental error of the latter is that of gnosticism—the claim to exclusive or superior spiritual knowledge or authority (Pr +4:18n. Mt *23:13, 15. +24:45. Lk +*11:52. +12:42. 1 C 8:2. Ga 6:3. Ep 4:14. Ph 3:15. 1 T 6:3, 4. 2 T *3:6, 7. T 1:11. 2 P 2:14). Such distortions are the mark of the false, not the true, and can have no place in the genuine believer (Ps 138:6. Pr 8:13. Mk *12:34. Ph *2:3. 3 J *9-11). The remedy for the "experienced centered" error is to become Bible and Christ centered (Jn +*5:39); the remedy for gnosticism is to adopt the Bible as the exclusive spiritual authority (Is +*8:20n), and separate entirely from the literature, fellowship and influence of false teachers (Ps +√119:63; Pr +√19:27. Mk +√4:24. 2 J 9-11; Ju +*3). **These.** Pr 6:16, 17. 10:26. 16:5. Ja 4:6. 1 P 5:5. **nose.** or, anger. **a fire.** Dt 29:20. 32:20-22.

6. **it is written.** Is 30:8. Ex 17:14. 32:33▶𝒫. Dt 32:34▶𝒫. Ps 56:8. Ml √3:16. Re 20:12. **I will.** Is 42:14. 64:12. Ps 50:3, 21. **but.** Ps 79:12. Je 16:18. Ezk 11:21. 22:31. Jl 3:4. **recompense.** Dt 32:35▶𝒫. 1 Th 2:16.

7. **Your iniquities.** Ex *20:5. Le 26:39. Nu 32:14. Ps 106:6, 7. Da 9:8. Mt *23:31-36. **burned.** Is 57:7. 1 K 22:43. 2 K 12:3. 14:4. 15:35. 16:4. Ezk 18:6. **blasphemed.** Ezk 20:27, 28. **therefore.** See on ver. 6. Je 5:9, 29. 7:19, 20. 13:25. Mt *23:32. 1 Th *2:16.

8. **a blessing is.** Jb 14:7. Jl 2:14. Lk 13:6-9. **not**

destroy. Is 6:13. 10:21, 22. Je √30:11. +*31:37. √46:28. Am *9:8, 9. Mt 24:22. Mk 13:20. Ro *9:27-29. 11:+√1, 5, 6, 24-26.

9. **I will.** Is 10:20-22. 11:11-16. 27:6. Je 31:36-40. 33:17-26. Ezk 36:8-15, 24. 37:21-28. 39:25-29. Am √9:11-15. Ob 17-21. Zp 3:20. Zc 10:6-12. **a seed.** Is 26:2. 66:7, 8. Mt 21:43. **mine elect.** ver. 15, 22. Mt 24:22. Ro 11:5-7, 28.

10. **Sharon.** F/L Is +33:9. 35:2. Ezk *34:13, 14. 35:2. **fold of flocks.** Ps 23:1. SS 1:7. Jn 10:11. **valley of Achor.** Jsh 7:24-26. Ho 2:15. **for my people.** Is 6:13. Ga 3:29.

11. **they that forsake.** F/L Is 1:+4, 28. Dt 28:20▶𝒫. 29:25. 1 Ch +*28:9. Je 2:28. 17:13. Jn 1:11. 1 C 10:21. **my holy.** ver. 25. Is 2:2. 11:9. 56:7. 57:13. Ps 132:13, 14. He 12:22. Re 21:2, 3. **prepare.** Is 57:5-10. Dt 32:17. Je 2:28. Ezk 23:41, 42. 1 C 10:20, 21. **troop.** or, Gad. or, fortune. Ge 30:11. Jsh 11:17. The disquisitions and conjectures of the learned, says Bp. Lowth, concerning *Gad* and *Meni*, are infinite and uncertain: perhaps the most probable may be, that Gad means good fortune, and Meni, the moon. "But why should we be solicitous about it," says Schmidius. "It appears sufficiently, from the circumstances, that they were false gods; either stars, or some natural object; or a mere fiction. The Holy Scriptures did not deign to explain more clearly what those objects of idolatrous worship were; but chose rather that the memory of the knowledge of them should be utterly abolished. And God be praised, that they are so totally abolished, that we are now quite at a loss to know what sort of things they were." Ge +24:44n. **drink offering.** Is 5:22. Pr 23:30. Je 7:18. 19:13. 44:17. **number.** or, Meni. or, fill up mingled wine unto Destiny. Thus a reference to the gods of Fortune and Fate. Arthur Carr, *Horae Biblicae*, "The Exclusion of Chance from the Bible," remarks that this passage "contains a direct protest by the prophet Isaiah against the worship of Fortune or Good Luck as a divinity," further noting that Isaiah plainly indicates that the Jews of the Exile had been attracted by the cult of Fortune. Evidence of this worship is found in Palestine in the place names of Baal-Gad (Jsh 11:17. 12:7. 13:5) and Migdal-Gad (Jsh 15:37). The name Azgad ("strong is Gad," Ezr 2:12), may indicate that a Jewish family had at one time devoted itself to the service of Fortune. Carr cites Prof. G. A. Smith that this practice of "preparing a table for Gad, and filling up mixed wine to Meni," may be closely connected with the commercial spirit which the Jews imbibed for the first time during the Exile. "The merchants of Mesopotamia had their own patron gods. In completing business contracts a man had to swear by the idols, and might have to enter their temples" (G. A. Smith, *Book of Isaiah*, ii. 62). In this way the Jewish trader would be drawn into idolatry.—If this conjecture be true, and it carries with it the highest probability, how closely does the whole subject connect itself not only with the commercial transactions of the present day on their speculative side, but with the spirit of gambling generally. It was quite in accordance with the teaching of Holy Scripture that games of chance were repudiated by the stricter Jews (Schurer, ii. 1, 36). It has sometimes been thought difficult to discover a principle on which to base a general condemnation of games of chance. However this may be, a sufficient justification will be found for discountenanc-

ing and condemning what Bishop Cosin calls "inordinate gaming," not only in the stern reproof of the prophet (Is 65:11), but in the whole of the remarkable and suggestive contrast presented to the life and literature of pagan civilization by the thought, and utterance, and silence of the Bible (Arthur Carr, pp. 38-46). See Note on Ge 24:44n.

12. **will I.** Is 3:25. 10:4. Le 26:25. Dt 32:25. Je 18:21. 34:17. Ezk 14:17-21. Zp 1:4-6. Mt 22:7. **because.** Is 50:2. 66:4. 2 Ch *36:15, 16. Pr √1:24, etc. Je 7:13. Zc 7:7, √11-13. Mt 21:34-43. 22:3. Jn *1:11. **did evil.** ver. 3. Is *1:16. Je 16:17. **and did.** Is 66:3, +√4. Pr *1:29.

13. **Behold.** √167, Is +2:7. **my servants shall eat.** Ps *34:10. 37:19, 20. Ml 3:18. Lk 14:23, 24. 16:24, 25. **but ye.** √31, Is +1:21. **be hungry.** Lk 6:25. **my servants shall rejoice.** Is 26:2. 61:7. 66:5, 14. Da +*12:2. Mt 21:43.

14. **my servants.** Is 24:14. 52:8, 9. Jb 29:13. Ps 66:4. Je 31:7. Ja *5:13. Re *14:3. **but ye shall.** √31, Is +1:21. Mt +*8:12. +*13:42. *22:13. +*24:51. Lk +*13:28. *16:22, 23. Ja *5:1. **heart.** √76, Ge +13:6. **vexation.** Heb. breaking. Is +51:19mg. Pr *15:4. Je 4:6mg. **spirit.** Heb. *ruach*, Ge +41:8.

15. **ye shall.** Pr *10:7. Je 29:22. Zc 8:13. **my chosen.** ver. 9, 22. **the Lord.** ver. 12. Is 66:15, 16. Mt *21:41. *22:7. 1 Th *2:16. **shall slay thee.** Is +√38:10. **his servants.** Is 42:1. 62:2. Ac *11:26. Ro 9:26. 1 P 2:9, 10. **another name.** Is 60:18. 62:2, 4, 12. Ge ◐+*17:5. Dt ◐+*7:24. Jb *34:24. Je 23:6. 33:16. Ezk 48:35. Re 2:17.

16. **he who blesseth.** Ge 22:18)᛬ᐝ. 26:4)ᐝ. Ps 72:17. Je *4:2. **in the God.** Dt 32:4. Ps 31:5. 86:15. Je 10:10. Jn 1:14, 17. √14:6. He *6:17, 18. 1 J 5:20. Re 3:14. **of truth.** or, faithfulness. 2 C 1:20. **he that.** Is 19:18. 45:23-25. 48:1. Dt 6:13. 10:20. Ps 63:11. Je 12:16. Zp 1:5. Ro 14:11. Ph 2:11. **shall swear.** Dt 6:13)ᐝ. **because.** ver. 19. Is 11:16. 12:1. 35:10. 54:4. Je 31:12. Ezk 36:25-27. Da *12:1, 11, 12. Zp 3:14-20. Re *20:4. **are hid.** Is 64:4. 1 C *2:9. **mine eyes.** √22A6, Ps +11:4.

17. **I create.** Is 51:16. 66:22. Ps 102:25, 26. 2 P √3:13. Re *21:1-5. **the former.** Je 3:16. **not be remembered.** Is *25:8. **into mind.** Heb. upon the heart. Je 3:16mg.

18. **be ye glad.** Is *12:4-6. 42:10-12. *44:23. 49:13. 51:11. 52:7-10. 66:10-14. Ps 67:3-5. 96:10-13. ch. 98. Zp 3:14. Zc *9:9. 1 Th *5:16. Re 11:15-18. 19:1-6. **for ever.** Heb. *ad*, Ps +9:18 (✳S#5703h).

19. **I will.** Is *62:4, 5. SS 3:11. Je 32:41. Zp 3:17. Lk 15:3, 5. **my people.** Is 51:16. √66:22. **the voice of weeping.** Is 25:8. *35:10. *51:3, 11. 60:20. Je 31:12. Re *7:17. *21:4.

20. **There shall.** "That is," says Kimchi, "the people shall live to three or five hundred years of age, as in the days of the patriarchs; and if one die at one hundred years, it is because of his sin; and even at that age he shall be reputed an *infant*; and they shall say of him, An infant is dead. These things shall happen to Israel in the days of the Messiah." **an infant of days.** Dt +*4:40. Jb *5:26. Ps 34:12. Jn *3:36. *10:10, 28. *17:3. Ro √6:23. **the child.** Je 31:17. **but the sinner.** Is *3:11. 11:2-4. Pr +*10:27. Ec +*7:17. *8:12, 13. Je 31:30. Zp ◐*3:13. Ro *2:5-9. **accursed.** or, cut off. Ne +13:25. Ps 37:22. √101:8. Pr *2:22. 3:33. Is √11:4. La 3:65. or, lightly esteemed. Jb *24:18h (cursed). Ro *2:5. √6:23.

21. **they shall build.** Is 62:8, 9. Le 26:16)ᐝ. Dt 28:30-33, 41)ᐝ. Jg 6:1-6. Je 31:4, 5. Am +*9:14. **inhabit.** √132E. Alternate Parallelism B355. Repeated alternation: here, build/inhabit and plant/eat are repeated in ver. 22. For another instance of this figure see 1 J 2:15, 16, where world/Father is repeated.

22. **for as the days.** ver. 9, 15. Ge 5:5, 27. Le 26:16. Ps 92:12-14. Re √20:3-5. **of a tree.** It is commonly supposed, observes Bp. Lowth, that the oak, one of the most long-lived of the trees, lasts about 1000 years; being 500 years growing to full perfection, and as many decaying; which seems to be a moderate and probable computation (See Evelyn, Sylva, B. iii. c. 3). The prophet's idea seems to be that they shall live to the age of the antediluvians; which seems to be very justly expressed by the days of a tree, according to our notions. **elect.** ✳S#972h. ver. 9, 15 (chosen). Is 42:1. 43:20. 45:4. 2 S 21:6. 1 Ch 16:13. Ps 89:3. 105:6, 43. 106:5, 23. **long enjoy.** Heb. make them continue long, or, shall wear out. Ge 18:12. Jb 13:28. 21:13. *36:11. **the work.** Ps 90:17.

23. **not labor in vain.** Is 49:4. 55:2. 61:9. Le 26:3-10, 20, 22, 29. Dt 28:3-12, 38-42)ᐝ. Ho 9:11-14. Hg 1:6, 9. 2:19. Ml 3:10, 11. 1 C √15:58. Re 22:3. **bring forth.** Dt 28:41. **for trouble.** Ps 78:33. **for they.** Is 61:9. Ge *12:2. +*17:7. Ps 115:14, 15. Je 32:38, 39. Zc 10:8, 9. Ac 2:39. 3:25, 26. Ro 4:16. 9:7, 8. Ga 3:29.

24. **before they call.** Is √30:19. *58:9. Ge +*24:15, 45. 2 K +20:4. Ps *32:5. *50:15. 91:15. *138:3. Da √9:20-23. *10:12. Ho +*5:15. *8:2. Mt *6:8. Mk√11:24. Lk 15:18-20. Ac *4:31. 10:30-32. 12:5-16. 1 J √5:14, 15. **I will answer.** Is *30:19. Ge +*17:20. Ps +*27:7. 38:15mg. *50:15. +*99:6. Je √33:3. Ac +*3:20. **I will hear.** √22C14, Ge +16:11. Is √30:19. Ps 38:15. 65:2. Je √33:3. Jn +*9:31. Ja +*5:16. 1 J *5:14, 15.

25. **wolf.** Is *11:6-9. 35:9. Ezk *34:25. Ho +*2:18. Jl *2:22. Ac 9:1, 19-21. Ro √8:19-21. 1 C +*6:9-11. T *3:3-7. **shall feed.** Is *11:6, 7. *55:13. Ac +*3:21. **together.** i.e. "as one," one of others. Heb. *echad*, Dt +*6:4 (one). F/L Is 4:1. 5:10. 6:2, 6. 9:14. 10:17. 19:18. 23:15. 27:12. 30:17, 17. 34:16. 36:9. 47:9. 51:2. 65:25. 66:8, 8, 17. **dust.** Ge *3:14, 15. Ps *72:9. Pr 20:17. Ro *16:20. He *2:14. Re 12:7-9. *20:2, 3. **the serpent's meat.** Ge 3:14. Re 20:1-3. **shall not.** Is 2:4. 11:9. Mi 4:3. **my holy mountain.** ver. 11. F/L Is +11:9. Ezk 43:11, 12. Zc 8:3. 14:20, 21. Re 14:1.

ISAIAH 66

God regards a broken heart more than he did the temple itself, and he abhors hypocritical and unbelieving sacrifices, 1-4. The confusion and ruin of the persecuting Jews, 5, 6. The rapid enlargement and great prosperity of Israel, 7-14. The vengeance of God on the wicked, 15-17. The people of the Gentile nations from throughout the new earth shall participate in the temple worship at Jerusalem, 18-23; who shall see the eternal punishment of the wicked, 24.

1. **The heaven.** T#971‡. Dt 10:14. 1 K *8:27, 30. 1 Ch 28:2. 2 Ch 6:18. Ps *11:4. 99:9. 132:7. Mt 5:34, 35. 23:21, 22. Ac)7:49, 50. 17:24. Ep 1:20. He 9:24. **my throne.** √22D3C1, Ps +11:4. **footstool.** √22A20, Ps +74:3. √22D3D1. Anthropomorphism B892. God is represented as to circumstances of place as having a *footstool*, the earth. The Ark of the Covenant is also

spoken of as his footstool. For other instances of this figure see 1 Ch 28:2. Ps 99:5. 132:7. La 2:1. Mt 5:35. **where is.** 2 S 7:5-7. Je 7:4-11. Ml *1:11. Mt *24:2. Jn *4:20, 21. Ac 7:48-50. Re *21:22. **the house.** Is 2:2. 60:13n. Ezk +*37:26. 40:2n. Jl 2:1. Mi 4:1, 2. Hg 2:7. Zc 1:16. *6:12, 13.

2. **For all those.** Is *40:26. Ge *1:1, etc. Ac ✝7:50. Col *1:17. He *1:2, 3. **to this.** Is √57:15. *61:1. 2 K 22:19, 20. 2 Ch 34:27, 28. **will I look.** Jn *4:23, 24. **poor.** Mt +*5:3. Ja *2:5. **contrite.** Ps *34:18. *51:17. 138:6. Je 31:19, 20. Ezk *9:4-6. Mt +*5:3, 4. Lk *18:13, 14. **spirit.** Heb. *ruach*, Ge +41:8. **trembleth.** T#890. ver. 5. Ezr 9:4. 10:3. Ps *119:120, 161. Pr *13:13. 28:14. Je ◑*36:23, 24. Ezk *9:4, 6. Hab +*3:16. Ac *9:6. *16:29, 30. Ph *2:12.

3. **killeth.** Is *1:11-15. Pr 15:8. 21:27. Am 5:21, 22. **lamb.** or, kid. Is 43:23mg. Ex 12:3mg,n. **cut off.** Ex 13:13. Dt *23:18. **as if he offered.** ver. 17. Is 65:3, 4. Le 11:7✝℘. Dt *14:8℘. **burneth.** Heb. maketh a memorial of. Is 62:6mg. Le 2:2. 2 S 8:16mg. **they have.** Is 65:12. Jg 5:8. 10:14. **own ways.** Is 58:13. **soul.** Heb. *nephesh*, Ge +34:3.

4. **I will choose.** 2 S 22:27. 1 K 22:19-23. Ps 81:12. Pr *1:31, 32. Ezk 14:9. Mt 24:24. 2 Th +√2:10-12. **delusions.** or, devices. Is 3:4 (babes). Je +*6:19. **will bring.** Pr 10:24. **fears.** Ps +*34:4. **when I called.** Is 50:2. 65:12. Pr *1:24. Je 7:13. Mt 22:2-7. **not hear.** 2 K 21:9. Je 7:13. 13:11. 25:3. 26:5. **they did evil.** Is 65:3. 2 K 21:2, 6. **and chose.** Is 56:4. 58:10, 13. 65:12. Ge 19:20. Dt +*30:19. Jsh 24:√15, 22. 1 K *3:11, 12. +*18:21. Jb 36:21. Ps ◑+*50:23. 106:15. 119:+√63, 111, *173. Pr √1:29. Je *9:6. *21:8. Da ◑*1:8. ◑*3:16-18. ◑*6:10. Ml ◑*3:16. Mt ◑*16:24. 27:25. Lk +*10:42. 19:14. Jn √3:18. 18:40. Ro *1:28. +*12:1, 2. *14:19. 1 C +*6:9, 10. 2 C +*6:17. 2 Th √2:10-12. He ◑*11:25. Ja *4:4. 1 J √2:15-17. Re ◑√3:20. **delighted not.** *145, Jg +11:40. Is ◑+*58:13, 14. Jb 34:9. Ps ◑+*37:4. Pr ◑11:1, 20. ◑12:22. ◑*15:8. *18:2. Je ◑9:24.

5. **ye that.** ver. 2. Pr 13:13. Je 36:16, 23-25. **Your.** Ps 38:20. SS 1:6. Ml √3:16-18. Mt 5:10-12. 10:22. Lk *6:22, 23. Jn 9:34. 15:18-20. 16:2. Ac 26:9, 10. 1 Th 2:15, 16. 1 J 3:13. **Let.** Is 5:19. **but.** Ac 2:33-47. 2 Th *1:6-10. T *2:13. He +*9:28. 1 P *4:12-14.

6. **voice of noise.** ✟63B, Ge +25:28. Supply by ellipsis (is heard). Is 5:14. 13:4. 42:14. Je 51:55. Zc 12:3-6. 14:3. **voice from.** Re 19:1-3. **a voice of the Lord.** Is 34:8. *59:18. 65:5-7. Jl 3:7-16. Am 1:2, etc.

7. **travailed.** Is 54:1. Mt +*24:8. Jn +*16:21. Ga 4:26. Re *12:1-4. **delivered.** ver. 8. Da 12:1. **man child.** Re +*12:5.

8. **hath heard.** Is 64:4. 1 C 2:9. **the earth.** A reference to the future conversion of the remnant of Israel after the tribulation. Zc 12:10-13. 13:9. Mt 24:15-22. Ro 11:25-29. **shall a nation.** Is 26:2. 49:20-22. Mt 21:43. Ac 2:41. 4:4. 21:20. Ro 15:18-21. **travailed.** ver. 7. Da 12:1. Mi +*5:3. Zc 12:10—13:1. Mt +*24:8, 15-22. Re *12:1-6, 14. **brought forth.** Ro 8:14. Ga 3:26. 4:26. 1 J *3:1.

9. **bring to.** Is 37:3. Ge 18:14. **cause to bring forth.** or, beget. Ge 11:27. **saith.** F/L Is +1:11. **shut.** Ge 16:2. **the womb.** Ge 20:18.

10. **Rejoice ye.** Is 44:23. 65:18. Dt 32:43. Ro 15:9-12. **all ye that love.** Ps 26:8. 84:1-4. +*122:6. 137:5, 6. Re 20:9. **that mourn.** Is 57:18. 61:2, 3. Ezk *9:4. Mt *23:37. Jn 16:20-22. Re 11:3-15.

11. **ye may suck.** Is 49:23. 60:5, 16. Nu 11:12. Ps 36:8. Je *3:15. Jl 3:18. 1 P *2:2. **and be satisfied.** Is 49:23. Mt +*5:3, 6. Lk *18:13, 14. ✟93B. Figure of speech Hendiadys of Verbs: two words used, but one thing meant; here, meaning "suck to satiety" and "milk out with delight." For other instances of this figure see Mt 13:23 ("heareth...and understandeth" means "hears with understanding," two words, but one act). Lk 6:48. Jn 11:25, 26. Ac 9:31. 13:41. 1 H *4:1. Ja 4:2. 2 P √3:12. Re 20:4. Re 22:17. **breasts of.** Ge 49:25. **abundance.** or, brightness. Is 25:6. Ps 50:11h (wild beasts). 80:13h. **her glory.** Is 60:1, 2. 62:2. Lk 2:32.

12. **I will.** Is +*9:7. *48:18. *60:4, 5. Ps 72:3-7. **like.** ✟170, Is +1:18. **the glory.** ver. 19, 20. Is 45:14. 49:19-23. 54:3. 60:4-14. **then.** ver. 11. Is 49:22. 60:16. **ye shall.** Is 60:4.

13. **one.** Is 40:1, 2. *51:3. 1 Th 2:7. **comfort you.** Is *51:12. Ps 103:13. 2 C +*1:4. **ye shall.** ver. 10. Is 65:18, 19. Ps 137:6. Mt +*5:4. **in Jerusalem.** Is +*24:23. Zc *2:12.

14. **your heart.** Zc 10:7. Jn 16:22. **your bones.** Is +*26:19n. 58:11. Pr 3:8. 17:22. Ezk *37:1-14. Ho *14:4-8. Ro 11:15. **like an herb.** Is +*26:19n. Dt 32:2. **the hand.** ver. 5. Is 65:12-16. Ru +*1:13. Ezr 7:9. 8:18, 22, 31. Ps *37:24. Ml 3:18. He 10:27. **toward.** Is 54:7-9. Ps +*102:13. Zc *8:15. **his servants.** Is 54:17. **indignation.** Is 10:5. 13:5. 30:27, 30. *34:2. Ps 69:24. 78:49. 102:10. Je *10:10. Na *1:6. Zp *1:18. *3:8. He *10:27. Re 14:10.

15. **the Lord.** Is 10:17. 30:27, 28, 33. 31:9. Dt 4:24. Ps *11:6. 21:9. 50:3. 97:3. Ezk 20:38. 38:16-23. Am 7:4. Mt 22:7. 24:29-31. 25:31. 2 Th +√1:6-10. He 12:29. 2 P √3:10-12. **with fire.** Is +*24:6. 30:30. Ezk 38:22. Na 1:5. Hab 3:5. 2 Th 1:8. He 10:27. 2 P +√3:7. **with his chariots.** Is 5:28. Dt 33:2. 2 K 6:16, 17. Ps +*68:17. Je *4:13. Da 7:10. 11:40. Hab 3:8. He 12:22. Re 9:16. **like a whirlwind.** Is 21:1. Ps 50:3. Je 25:32. Zc *9:14. **with fury.** Is 59:18. **with flames.** Nu 16:35. 2 Th *1:8. 2 P +*3:7.

16. **by fire.** Is 30:30. Jb *36:18. Ezk 38:22. Zc 13:9. **by his sword.** Is 27:1. 34:5-10. 65:12. Je 15:2. Ezk 38:21, 22. 39:2, etc. Jl 3:13. Re *19:11-21. **plead with.** Is 59:4. **flesh.** ✟171E1, Ge +6:12. **the slain.** Is 22:2. 34:3. Je *25:33. Zc 13:8, 9. 14:2, 3. Re 19:18. **be many.** Jl 3:14. Re 19:21.

17. **in the gardens.** Is 1:29. 65:3, 4. **behind one tree in the midst.** or, one after another. Or, as Bishop Lowth renders, "after the rites of Achad;" which is supposed to be the same as the Syrian god *Adad*, whom they held to be the highest and greatest of the gods and the same with Jupiter and the sun; and whose name, says Macrobius (Sat. i. 23), signifies *one*; as does also the word *Achad* in this passage. See Pliny, l. xxxvii. c. 11. **tree.** or, Asherah. Dt 16:21, grove, or Asherah. 2 K 21:3n. The Asherah was often a wooden pole or pillar, an image of wood, perhaps like a totem pole. It was an idol involved in pagan fertility worship (Ex 34:13), erected beside the altar of Baal (Jg 6:25, 28). It degenerated into phallic worship (Ezk 16:17), the worship of male organs of procreation. In the Authorized Version the word is always rendered "grove" or "groves," but that it cannot be a whole grove of trees may be seen by the fact that the "grove" was brought out of the temple (2 K 23:6), and that they were forbidden to be set up "under any green tree" (2 K +*17:10). Women wove hangings for the Asherah

in the temple (2 K 23:7). Male and female prostitutes (Sodomites, Dt 23:17mg) were consecrated to the cult of this goddess. In Ahab's time Elijah slew the prophets of the Asherah along with those of Baal at the river Kishon (1 K 16:33; 18:19-40). eating. Is 65:4. Le 11:2-8. Dt *14:3-8. abomination. Heb. *shakaz.* Le 7:21. 11:10, 11, 11, 12, 13, 13, 20, 23, 41, 42, 43. 20:25. Dt 7:26⟩℘. Ezk 8:10. the mouse. Le 11:29⟩℘. 1 S 6:4, 5, 11, 18. consumed together. Is 1:28, 31. Est 9:28. Ps *37:20, 38.

18. I know. Is *37:28. Dt 31:21. Am 5:12. Jn 5:42. Re 2:2, 9, 13. their thoughts. Is 59:7. 65:2. Jb 42:2. Ezk 11:5. 38:10. Mt 9:4. 12:25. Lk 5:22. Jn +*2:25. 1 C 3:20. He *4:12, 13. that I. Is *2:2. Ps 67:2. 72:11, 17. 82:8. 86:9. Jl 3:2. Ro 15:8-12. 16:26. Re 11:15. will gather. Is 45:22-25. Je *3:17. Jl 3:2. Zp *2:11. 3:8. shall come. Ps *86:9. Zc *14:16-19. see my glory. ver. *19. Is 40:5. *59:19. Ps +*102:15, 16. Ezk +*39:21. Lk +*9:32. Jn 1:14. *17:24. 2 C 4:4-6.

19. I will set. Is *11:10-12. 18:3, 7. 30:17. 31:9. 49:22. 59:19. 62:10. Lk *2:34. sign. F/L Is +7:11. I will send. ver. 12, 20. Is 49:7, 8, 9, 18. *52:7-10. 55:5. 56:6-8. 60:3-5, 14, 15. 61:4, 6, 9. 62:2. Zc 13:9. Mk *16:15. Ro *11:1-6, 15. Ep 3:8. Re *21:24-26. 22:2. Tarshish. *Tarshish* (See Note on 2 Ch 9:21) seems to be used here for the East, *Pul* and *Lud* (two African nations) for the south, *Tubal* and *Javan* (the Tiberenians and Grecians) for the north, and "the isles afar off" for the west. Is 2:16. 60:9. Ge 10:+4, 13. 1 K 10:22. 1 Ch 1:7, 11. Ezk 27:10. *30:5. Lud. Ezk 27:10. that draw the bow. Bishop Lowth suspects that the words "*moshechey kesheth,*" "who draw the bow," are a corruption of *Mesheck*, the *Moschi,* a nation situated between the Euxine and Caspian seas, and properly joined to *Tubal,* the Tibarini (See Bochart, Phaleg. l. iii. c. 12). The LXX. have "Mosox," as a proper name without "*kesheth,*" "the bow," which is also omitted by one MS. Ezk 38:2. Tubal. Ge 10:2. Ezk 27:13. 38:2, 3. 39:1. the isles. F/L Is +11:11. 24:15, 16. 42:4. 43:6. 49:1, 12. 51:5. 60:9. Ps 72:10. Zp 2:11. that have. Is 29:24. 52:15. 55:5. 65:1. Ml *1:11. Mt +*8:11, 12. 28:19. Ro 15:21. Re ❶1:7. they shall declare. Is 12:4. 42:12. 43:10-12, 21. 44:22, 23. 52:7. 53:1. 1 Ch *16:24. Ps 9:11. ch. 47, 97. 98:1-3. 118:17. 138:1-5. Ml *1:11. He 2:4. my glory. ver. +*18. Hg 2:9. Re 15:4. among the Gentiles. Is 25:6-9. +*27:6. *48:20. 60:1-3. 62:1-4. Dt 32:43. Ps ch. 67. *96:3. 102:15, 21, 22. Je *3:17. Ezk 36:36. *37:28. 38:16, 23. 39:7,

21-23. Mi 4:1-3. Zc *8:20-23. Mt +*24:14.

20. shall bring. Is 14:2. all your brethren. Is 43:6. 49:12, 22. 54:3. 60:3-14. an offering. Reference to the "meat offering," or meal offering, or gift offering. Le +*23:13. Ro *12:1, 2. 15:16. Ph 2:17. 1 P 2:5. upon horses. Is 60:9. litters. *or,* coaches. Nu 7:3. "*Tzabbim*" signifies some kind of covered vehicle, probably *palanquins.* SS 3:9. mules. 2 S *13:29. 18:9. swift beasts. "*Kirkaroth,*" rendered by the LXX. "shaded vehicles," and by the Vulgate *carrucis,* "cars," probably denotes the same as "kar," the *coune* or *pannier* used for riding in. See on Ge 31:34n. my holy mountain. Is 2:2, 3. 11:9. 27:13. 56:7. 65:11, 25. bring an offering. Le 2:1n, 14-16⟩℘. +*23:13. clean vessel. Is 52:11.

21. I will also take. Is 61:6. Ex 19:6. Je 13:18-22. 1 P √2:5, 9. Re *1:6. *5:10. √20:6. for Levites. Dt 17:9⟩℘. Jsh 3:3. 8:33. 2 Ch 30:27. Ne 11:20. Je 33:21. Ezk 43:19. 44:10, 13, 15.

22. the new heavens. Is *65:17. He 12:27, 28. 2 P √3:13. Re *21:1. shall remain. or, are standing. Is 3:13. 6:2. 11:10. Ec +*1:4. your seed. Is 53:10. 61:8, 9. 65:22, 23. Mt 28:20. Jn √10:27-29. 1 P *1:4, 5. your name. Is 56:5. remain. T#948. Is *59:21. Ps √72:17. Je +*31:35-37. +*33:20-22, 25, 26. Da *2:44. 7:14. Mt 28:20. Lk *1:33. Re 11:15.

23. that from. Is 1:13, 14. Nu 10:10⟩℘. 28:11-15⟩℘. 2 K *4:23. Ps 81:3, 4. Ezk 46:1, 6. Col 2:16, 17. one new, etc. Heb. new moon to his new moon, and from sabbath to his sabbath. 2 Ch +2:4. shall all. ver. +18. Ps *65:2. +*86:9. Zc 8:20-23. *14:14, 16, 17. Ml 1:11. Jn √4:23. He 4:9. Re 15:4. flesh. ∫171E1, Ge +6:12. worship before me. Is 19:21, 23. 27:13. 49:7.

24. and look. ver. 16. Jb 34:26. Ps 37:24. *58:10, 11. 59:10. 91:8. +*112:8. Je +*11:20. 20:12. 51:24. Ezk *28:17. *39:9-16. Zc 14:12, 18, 19. Lk +13:28. ❶16:23. Re *14:10. *19:17-21. carcasses. Is 5:25. *34:3, 8. Zc 14:12. Mt +*24:28. transgressed. Is 1:28. *24:20-22. their worm. The worm that died on the dead bodies in Gehenna died, and the fire, which consumed them, was soon extinguished; but in the figurative Gehenna the means of punishment are everlasting (Mt +√25:41, 46. Re 20:10). *S#8438h. Is *14:11b. 41:14. Ex 16:20. Dt 28:39. Jb 25:6b. Ps 22:6. Jon 4:7. Mk √9:44-49. Re *14:10, 11. not die. Is 14:9, 10. *30:33. Jb 36:18. Ezk 32:21. Da +*12:2. their fire. Is 1:31. +*33:14. *34:10. Mt *3:12. Re +*21:8. and they. Is 34:3. 65:15. Da *12:2. 1 Th 2:15, 16.

JEREMIAH

JEREMIAH 1

Some account of Jeremiah; and of the times during which he prophesied, 1-3. His calling and commission, 4-10. His visions, of an almond tree and of a seething pot, explained to him, 11-16. He is encouraged by promises of protection and assistance, 17-19.

1. A.M. 3375. B.C. 629. words. 2 Ch 36:21. Is 1:1. 2:1. Am 1:1. 7:10. Jeremiah. i.e. *Jah is the exalted one; high one of Jah,* *S#3414h. Je 1:1, 11. 7:1. 11:1. 14:1. 18:1, 18. 19:14. 20:1, 2, 3, 3. 21:1, 3. 24:3. 25:1, 2, 13. 26:7, 8, 9, 12, 20, 24. 28:12. 29:27, 29, 30. 30:1. 32:1, 2, 6, 26. 33:1, 19, 23. 34:1, 6, 8, 12. 35:1,

3, 12, 18. 36:1, 4, 4, 5, 8, 10, 19, 26, 27, 27, 32, 32. 37:2, 3, 4, 6, 12, 13, 14, 14, 15, 16, 16, 17, 18, 21. 38:1, 6, 6, 6, 7, 9, 10, 11, 12, 12, 13, 13, 14, 14, 15, 16, 17, 19, 20, 24, 27, 28. 39:11, 14, 15. 40:1, 2, 6. 42:2, 4, 5, 7. 43:1, 2, 6, 8. 44:1, 15, 20, 24. 45:1, 1. 46:1, 13. 47:1. 49:34. 50:1. 51:59, 60, 61, 64. 52:1. 2 K 23:31. 24:18. 1 Ch 12:13. 2 Ch 35:25. 36:12, 21, 22. Also *S#3414h: Je 27:1. 28:5, 6, 10, 11, 12, 15. 29:1. 1 Ch 5:24. 12:4, 10. Ezr 1:1. Ne 10:2. 12:1, 12, 34. Da 9:2. (1) The father of Hamutal, wife of King Josiah, 2 K 23:31; 24:18; Je 52:1. (2) Head of a family in Manasseh, 1 Ch 5:24. (3) A valiant man who joined David in Ziklag, 1 Ch 12:4. (4, 5) Gadite warriors who joined David at Ziklag, 1 Ch 12:10, 13. (6) A priest who sealed the covenant, Ne 10:2; 12:1, 12, 34. (7) A descendant of Jonadab, the son of Rechab, Je 35:3. He was one of the Rechabites. (8) Jeremiah, one of the four great prophets, a son of Hilkiah of Anathoth, in the land of Benjamin. Jeremiah began his prophetic ministrations at an early age, in the thirteenth year of the reign of Josiah, B.C. 626, and continued it for a period of forty-two years, until after the destruction of Jerusalem and the beginning of the captivity. **Hilkiah.** i.e. *portion of Jah.* 2 K +18:18. **of the priests.** Ezk 1:3. **in Anathoth.** i.e. *answers, responses.* Je 11:21. 32:7-9. Jsh 21:17, 18. 1 Ch 6:60. +7:8.

2. **the word.** ver. 4, 11. 1 K 13:20. Ho 1:1. Jon 1:1. Mi 1:1. **in the days.** 2 K 21:25, 26. ch. 22, 23. 2 Ch 2 Ch ch. 34, 35.

3. **It came also.** Je 25:1-3. ch. 26, 35, 36. 2 K 24:1-9. 2 Ch 36:5-8. **unto the end.** Je ch. 21, 22, 28, 29, 34, 37-39, 52. 2 K 24:17-20. ch. 25. 2 Ch 36:11-21. **in the fifth.** Is 52:12, 15. 2 K 25:8. Zc 7:5. 8:19.

4. **the word.** See on ver. 2. Ezk 1:3. 3:16.

5. **Before I.** Ps *71:5, 6. Is 49:1, 5. Lk 1:76. Ga *1:15, 16. **I knew.** ✗121C2A2, Ge +39:6. Ex *33:12, 17✗. Jn *10:14. Ro *8:29. 2 T *2:19-21. Other references to the Pentateuch in Jeremiah are: 1:6, 7, 8, 16. 2:2, 3, 5, 6, 17, 18, 21, 28. 3:1, 3, 8, 13, 16, 17. 4:2, 4, 23, 27, 28. 5:1, 1, 7, 7, 15, 17, 24, 24, 28, 28. 6:2, 10, 12, 13, 18, 19. 7:6, 7, 9, 12, 19, 22, 23, 25, 31, 33, 34. 8:10, 19. 9:4, 13, 14, 15, 16, 24, 25, 26. 10:2, 16. 11:3, 4, 5, 12, 14. 12:14. 13:9, 11. 14:1, 9, 11, 12, 22. 15:1, 3, 4, 10, 14, 19. 16:6, 10, 11, 12, 13, 14, 21. 17:4, 14, 21, 26, 27. 18:18. 19:4, 5, 7, 9. 20:5, 7, 8, 10, 14, 16, 21. 22:8, 13. 23:2, 6, 7, 14, 20, 30, 31. 24:7, 9, 10. 25:7, 9, 16, 29. 26:2, 4, 8, 15, 19. 27:5, 8. 28:9, 14, 16. 29:13, 17, 18, 32. 30:11, 16, 21, 24, 31. 31:2, 5, 9, 15, 20, 32, 35. 32:7, 17, 18, 20, 21, 22, 27, 29, 35, 37, 40, 41. 33:2, 18, 20, 22, 25. 34:8, 16, 17, 18. 35:7. 36:30. 40:3. 41:5. 42:2, 6, 10, 15, 22. 44:3, 7, 11, 12, 17, 26. 46:10, 16, 27, 28. 47:6. 48:7, 16, 40, 45, 46. 49:13, 18, 22, 31. 50:40. 52:31. See related note at Is 1:2. **and before.** Lk 1:15, *41n. Ro 1:1. **and I ordained.** Heb. and I gave. Jn ✓15:16. 20:21-23. Ac ✓1:8. Ep 1:22. 4:11, 12.

6. **Ah, Lord.** Is 4:10. 14:13. 32:17. **I cannot speak.** T#1708. Ex 4:1, *10-16✗. 6:12, 30. 1 S 16:2. 1 K *3:7. 18:14. Is 6:5. Ep +6:19 (T#1441). **for I am.** 1 K 3:7-9. Mk *10:15. Lk *10:21. 2 C *3:5.

7. **for thou shalt.** ver. 17, 18. Ex 4:12. 7:1, 2. Nu 22:20✗, 38. Dt 4:2. 1 K 22:14. 2 Ch 18:13. Is ✓55:11. Ezk *2:3-5. *3:17-21, 27. Mt *10:19, 20. 28:20. Mk 16:15, 16. Ac 20:27. T 2:15.

8. **not afraid.** ver. 17. Is 51:7, 12. Ezk *2:6, 7. 3:8, 9. Mt *10:26, 28. Lk 12:4, 5. Ac 4:13, 29. Ep 6:20. **for I am.** Je 15:20, 21. 20:11. Ex *3:12✗. Dt 31:6, 8✗. Jsh 1:5, 9. Is 43:2. Mt 28:20. Ac 7:9, 10. 18:10. *26:17. 2 C 1:8-10. 2 T 4:17, 18. He +*13:5, 6.

9. **and touched.** ✗22C16, Ps +104:32. Ex *4:11, 12. Is *6:6, 7. 49:2. 50:4. Lk *21:15. **Behold.** Je *5:14. Ex 4:15, 16. Is *51:16. Ezk 3:10. Mt 10:19. Lk 12:12.

10. **I have.** ✗108A3, Is +6:10. Je *25:15-27. 27:2-7. ch. 46-51. 1 K 17:1. Re *11:3-6. **to root out.** ✗121I2, Ge +2:17. Je *18:7-9. 1 K 19:17. Ezk 32:18. 43:3. Am ✓3:7. Zc 1:6. Mt 18:18. 2 C ✓10:4, 5. Re 19:19-21. **to build.** Je 18:9. 24:6. 31:4, 5, 28. Is 44:26-28. Ezk 36:36. Am 9:11.

11. **what seest thou.** Am 7:8. *8:2. Zc 4:2. 5:2. **I see a rod.** Nu *17:8. Ezk *7:10, 11.

12. **Thou hast.** Dt 5:28. 18:17. Lk 10:28. 20:39. **I will hasten.** Je ch. 39, 52. Dt 32:35. 2 K 24:2. Ezk 12:22, 23, 25, 28. Am 8:2. Re *22:10.

13. **the second time.** Ge +22:15. +*41:32. 2 C *13:1, 2. **I see.** Ezk *11:2, 3, 7. *24:3-14. **seething.** Jb 41:20. Ezk 22:21. **pot.** Je 52:18, 19. Ex 16:3. 27:3. Ezk 24:3. **toward the north.** Heb. from the face of the north. ✗171.O.9, Je +13:20. ver. 14, 15. Je 3:12, 18. 4:6.

14. **Out of the north.** ✗171.O.9, Je +13:20. Je *4:6. *6:1, 22. 10:22. 31:8. 46:20. 50:9, 41. Is *41:25. Ezk 1:4. +*38:6. Jl +*2:20. Zc 2:6. **break forth.** Heb. be opened. Ne 7:3. Jb 12:14.

15. **I will call.** Je *5:15. 6:22. 10:22, 25. 25:9, 28, 31, 32. **of the north.** ✗171.O.9, Je +13:20. **and they.** Je 39:3. *43:10. Is 22:7. **and against.** Je 4:16. 9:11. 33:10. 34:22. 44:6. *52:4, 5. Dt 28:49-53. La 5:11. Mt 23:37-39.

16. **And I.** Je 4:12, 28. 5:9, 29. Ezk *24:14. Jl 2:11. Mt 23:35, 36. **who have.** Je 2:13, 17. *15:6. 16:11. *17:13. 19:4. Dt 28:20✗. 31:16, 17. Jsh 24:20. 2 K 22:17. 2 Ch 7:19. 15:2. 34:25. **and have.** Je 7:9. 11:12, 17. 44:17. Is 65:3. Ezk 8:9-11. Ho 11:2. **worshipped.** Je 10:8, 9, 15. 51:17. Is 2:8. 37:19. 44:15-17. Ho 8:6. Ac 7:41. Ja *4:4. Re *2:20-23.

17. **gird up.** 1 K 18:46. 2 K 4:29. 9:1. Jb 38:3. Ps 18:32n. Lk *12:35. 1 P 1:13. **and speak.** ver. 7. Je 23:28. Ex 7:2. Ezk 3:10, 11. Jon 3:2. Ac 20:20, 27. **be not.** See on ver. 8. Je 17:18. Ex 3:12. Ezk *2:6, 7. Mt +*10:28. 1 Th 2:2. **confound thee.** or, break thee to pieces. Ezk 3:14-18. 33:6-8. 1 C 9:16.

18. **I have.** Je 6:27. 15:20. Is *50:7. Ezk *3:8, 9. Mi 3:8, 9. Jn 1:42. **against.** ✗18, Dt +28:4. Je 21:4-14. ch. 22. 26:12-15. 34:3, 20-22. 36:27-32. 37:7-10. 38:2, 18-23. 42:22.

19. **And they.** Je 11:19. 15:10-21. 20:1-6. 26:11-24. 29:25-32. 37:11-21. 38:6-13. **fight.** ✗102, Ge +2:24. **not prevail.** Ps *129:2. Ac *5:39. 2 T 4:17, 18. **for I am.** See on ver. 8. Je 15:20, 21. Jsh 1:9.

JEREMIAH 2

God reminds Judah and Israel of his former kindnesses; and expostulates with them on their ungrateful, unreasonable, and unexampled apostasies and idolatries, 1-13. Their calamities originate from their crimes, 14-19. Their conduct is a breach of solemn engagements; degeneracy from their pious ancestors; undeniable, and inexcusable; the effect of impetuous lusts, and desperately persisted in, 20-30. It is connected with folly and weary labor, murder and persecution, useless self-justification, and continual changes from one false confidence to another, 31-37.

1. **the word.** Je 1:11. 7:1. 23:28. Ezk 7:1. He 1:1. 2 P 1:21.

2. **Go.** ✗96B, Ex +20:8. **cry.** Je 7:2. 11:6. 19:2. Pr 1:20. 8:1-4. Is 58:1. Ho 8:1. Jon 1:2. Mt 11:15. Lk *12:3. **I remember.** This expression used in a good sense in Ne 5:19. 13:14, 22, 31. Ps 98:3. 106:45. 132:1. Used in bad sense in Ne 6:14. 13:29. Ps 79:8. 137:7. Probably both senses here: the good on Jehovah's part (ver. 3. Ho 2:19, 20. 11:1. Am 2:10); and the evil on Israel's part, for even in the wilderness Israel was unfaithful (Am 5:25, 26. Ac 7:39-43), CB. Nu 23:19-21.

Re 2:2-4. **thee.** *or,* for thy sake. **the kindness.** Ex 14:31. 15:1-20. Is 63:7. SS 6:3. Ezk 16:8, 22, *60. 23:3, 8, 19. Ho *2:15, 19, 20. **thine espousals.** Ex 24:3-8. SS 3:11. Ezk 16:8. **when.** ver. 6. Dt 2:7)𝒫. *8:2, 15, 16)𝒫. Ne 9:12-21. Is 63:7-14.

3. **holiness.** Ex 19:5, 6)𝒫. Dt *7:6-8. 14:2. 26:19. Zc *14:20, 21. Ep 1:4. 1 P *2:9. **the firstfruits.** Ex 22:29. 23:16, 19)𝒫. Le +*23:10. Nu 18:12. Dt 18:4)𝒫. 26:10)𝒫. Am 6:1mg. Ro *11:16. 16:5. Ja *1:18. Re 14:4. **all that.** Je 12:14. 50:7. Ex 4:22, 23. Ps 81:14, 15. *105:14, 15, 25-36. Is *41:10, 11. 47:6. Jl 1:3, 7, 8. Zc *1:15. 2:8. 12:2-4. Ac 9:4, 5. **offend.** Le 4:13, 22, 27)𝒫. 5:2, 3, 4, 5, 17, 19)𝒫. 6:4)𝒫. Nu 5:6, 7)𝒫. **evil.** Is +45:7.

4. **Hear ye.** Je 5:21. 7:2. 13:15. 19:3. 34:4. 44:24-26. Is 51:1-4. Ho 4:1. Mi 6:1. **house of Jacob.** Je 5:20. **all the families.** Je 31:1. 33:24. **house of Israel.** ver. 26. Je 3:18, 20. 5:11, 15. 9:26. 10:1. 11:10, 17. 13:11. 18:6, 6. 23:8. 31:27, 31, 33. 33:14, 17. 48:13.

5. **What.** ver. 31. Dt 32:4)𝒫. Is *5:3, 4. 43:22, 23. Mi *6:2, 3. **fathers.** ver. 7. Jg 2:10. **are gone.** Je 12:2. Is 29:13. Ezk 11:15. Mt 15:8. **walked.** Je 10:8, 14, 15. 14:22. 16:19, 20. Dt 32:21. 1 S 12:21. 2 K 17:15. Jon 2:8. Ac 14:15. 1 C 8:4. **vanity.** ⨍121N1, Ge +31:54. **are become vain.** Je +*10:2, 3, 5. 51:17, 18. 2 K *17:15. Ps √115:8. 135:18. Is 44:9. Ro *1:20-23. 2 C ◑*3:18.

6. **Where.** ver. 8. Je 5:24. Jg 6:13. 2 K 2:14. Jb 35:10. Ps 77:5. Is 64:7. **brought us up.** Ex ch. 14, 15. Nu 13:27)𝒫. 14:7, 8)𝒫. Dt 6:10, 11, 18)𝒫. Is *63:9, 11-13. Ho 12:13. *13:4. **led us.** See on ver. 2. Dt 8:14-16)𝒫. 32:10)𝒫. **deserts.** Je 5:6. 17:6. 50:12. Mt 12:43. **pits.** Je 18:20, 22. Pr +22:14 (S#7745h). 23:27. **drought.** Is 35:1. **the shadow.** Je 13:16. See on Jb 3:5. 10:21, 22. Ps *23:4. Mt 4:16.

7. **brought.** Nu 13:27. 14:7, 8. Dt 6:10, 11, 18. 8:7-9. *11:11, 12. Ne 9:25. Ezk 20:6. 1 C *2:9, 10. **a plentiful country.** *or,* the land of Carmel. Je 4:26. 48:33. Jsh +15:55. **ye defiled.** Je 3:1, 9. 16:18. Le *18:24-28. Nu 35:33, 34. Dt 21:23. Ps *78:58, 59. 106:38, 39. Ezk 36:17, 18. Mi *2:10. **my land.** Je 16:18. Le +*25:23n. Dt +*32:43. Ho 9:3.

8. **priests.** ver. 6. Je *5:31. 8:10, 11. 23:9-15. 1 S 2:12. Is *9:16. 28:7. √29:10-12. 56:9-12. Ho 4:6. Mt +*15:14. **and they that.** Je 8:8, 9. Le 10:11)𝒫. Dt 17:11)𝒫. 33:10)𝒫. Ml 2:6-9. Lk *11:46, 52. Jn 8:55. 16:3. Ro 2:17-24. 2 C 4:2. **handle the law.** Such a statement reveals that the law was extant, well known, and that the priests were the custodians of it. 2 K *14:6n. 22:8n. **the pastors.** Je 10:21. 12:10. 23:1, 2. **prophets.** Je 23:13. 1 K 18:19, 22, 40. **do not.** ⨍75B, Ge +21:16. ver. 11. Je 7:8. 1 S 12:21. Is 30:5. Hab 2:18. Mt 16:26.

9. **I will.** ver. 29, 35. Is 3:13. 43:26. Ezk 20:35, 36. Ho 2:2. Mi 6:2. **with your.** Ex *20:5. 34:6, 7. Le 20:5.

10. **over.** *or,* over to. **the isles.** Ge 10:4, 5. Nu 24:24. 1 Ch 1:7. 23:1, 12. Ps 120:5. Ezk 27:6. Da 11:30. **Kedar.** Ge 25:13. **and see.** Je 18:13, 14. Jg 19:30. 1 C 5:1.

11. **a nation.** ver. 5. Mi 4:5. 1 P 1:18. **no gods.** Je 16:20. Ps 115:4. Is 37:19. 1 C +√8:4. Ga 4:8. **changed their glory.** ⨍182, Ge +18:22. ver. 8. Dt 33:29. Ps 3:3. *106:20, 21. Ro 1:23. **not profit.** ⨍175B, Ge +21:16.

12. **Be astonished.** Je 6:19. 22:29. 30:2-1. Is *1:2. Mi 6:2. Mt 27:45, 50-53. **ye heavens.** ⨍38G, Dt +32:1.

13. **For my.** ver. 31, 32. Je 4:22. 5:26, 31. Ps 81:11-13. Is 1:3. 5:13. 63:8. Mi 2:8. 6:3. **forsaken me.** ver. 17, 19. Je 1:16. 15:6. Jg 10:13. 1 S 12:10. Jn 18:40. **the fountain.** Je 17:13. 18:14. Ps *36:9. Is 55:1, 2. Jn *4:14. 7:37-39. Re 21:6. 22:1, 17. **waters.** ⨍22K4. Anthropomorphism B896. Certain elements are used as emblems of God: God is spoken of as *water*, as is the Holy Spirit. For other instances of this figure see Je 17:13. Ps 36:8, 9. Is 44:3. 55:1. Ezk 36:25. Jl 2:28, 29. Zc 12:10. 14:8. Jn 4:10, 14. 7:38. Ac 2:17, 18, 33. T 3:5, 6. **broken cisterns.** ver. 11, 26, 27. Ps 115:4-8. 146:3, 4. Ec 1:2, 14. 2:11, 21, 26. 4:4. 12:8. Is 44:9-12. 46:6, 7. 55:2. 2 P 2:17.

14. **Israel.** Ex *4:22, 23. Is *50:1. **he a homeborn.** Ge 14:14. 15:3. Ec 2:7. **spoiled.** Heb. *become* a spoil.

15. **young lions.** Je 5:6. 25:30. 50:17. Jg 14:5. Jb 4:10, 11. Ps 57:4. Is 5:29. Ho 5:14. 11:10. 13:7, 8. Am 3:4, 8, 12. Na 2:11, 12. **yelled.** Heb. gave out their voice. Je 4:16. **they made.** See on Is 1:7. 24:1. Ezk 5:14. **his cities.** Je 4:7. 9:11. 26:9. 33:10. 34:22. 44:22. Is 5:9. *6:11. Zp 1:18. 2:5. 3:6.

16. **Also the.** 2 K *18:21. 23:33. Is 30:1-6. *31:1-3. **Noph.** Je 44:1. 46:14, 19. Is 19:13. Ezk 30:13, 16. **Tahapanes.** i.e. *beginning of the age or world; thou wilt fill hands with pity,* *S#8471h, only here. Je 43:7-9, 11. 44:1. 46:14, Tahpanhes. **have broken the crown.** *or,* feed on thy crown. Dt 33:20. Is 1:6, 7. 8:8.

17. **Hast thou.** ver. 19. Je 4:18. Le *26:15, 17, etc. Nu +√32:23. Dt 28:15, etc. Jb *4:8. Is 1:4. Ho 13:9. Ga *6:7, 8. **in that.** ver. 13. 1 Ch +*28:9. 2 Ch 7:19, 20. **when he.** Dt 32:10, 12, 19)𝒫. Ps 77:20. 78:53, 54. 107:7. 136:16. Is 63:11-14.

18. **what hast.** ver. 36. Je 37:5-10. Is *8:6, 7. 30:1-7. 31:1-3. La 4:17. Ezk 17:15. Ho 7:11. **the way of Egypt.** Dt 17:16)𝒫. **Sihor.** i.e. the Nile. Jsh 13:3. **or what hast.** 2 K 16:7-9. 2 Ch 28:20, 21. Ho 5:13.

19. **Thine.** ver. 17. Pr *1:31. *5:22. Is *3:9. 5:5. 50:1. Ho 5:5. **and thy.** Je 3:6-8, 11-14. 5:6. 8:5. Ho 4:16. 11:7. 14:1. Zc 7:11. **bitter.** Je 4:18. Jb *20:11-16. Am 8:10. **and that my.** Je 5:22. 36:23, 24. Ps 36:1. Ro 3:18. **Lord God of Hosts.** Je ◑+6:6. 46:10. 49:5. 50:25, 31.

20. **For of.** Je 30:8. Ex 3:8. Le *26:13. Dt 4:20, 34. 15:15. Is 9:4. 10:27. 14:25. Na 1:13. **old time.** Heb. *olam,* Jsh +*24:2. **and thou saidst.** Ex 19:8. 24:3. Dt 5:27. 26:17. Jsh 10:16. 24:16-24. 1 S *12:10. **transgress.** *or,* serve. Je 5:19. 16:11. 22:9, 13. Ge 25:23. 29:18. Ex 3:12. 20:9 (labor). 34:21 (work). Jg 2:7, 11, 17. **when upon.** Je *3:6. Dt 12:2. 1 K 12:32. Ps 78:58. Is *57:5-7. Ezk 16:24, 25, 31. 20:28. **high hill.** Je 17:2. 1 K 14:23. 2 K 16:4n. +17:10. **green tree.** Je 3:6, 13. 17:2. 2 K 16:4n. +17:10. **playing.** Je 3:1, 6-8. Ex 34:14-16. Dt 12:2. Is 1:21. Ezk 16:15, 16, 28, 41. 23:5. Ho 2:5. 3:3.

21. **Yet I.** Ex 15:17. Ps 44:2. *80:8. Is *5:1, 2, 4. 60:21. 61:3. Mt 21:33. Mk 12:1. Lk 20:9. Jn 15:1. **noble vine.** Ge 49:11)𝒫. Is 5:2. **wholly.** Ge +*18:19. 26:3-5. 32:28. Dt 4:37. Jsh 24:31. Ps 105:6. Is 41:8. **into the degenerate.** Dt 32:32. Is 1:21. *5:4. La 4:1.

22. **For though.** Jb *9:30, 31. Ps *51:1, 2. Ml *3:2. **yet thine iniquity.** Je 16:17. 17:1. Dt 32:34. Jb 14:17. Ps 90:8. 130:3. Ho 13:12. Am 8:7.

23. **How canst.** ver. 34, 35. Ge *3:12, 13. 1 S √15:13, 14. Ps 36:2. Pr √28:13. *30:12, 20. Ml 3:7, 8, 13. Lk 10:29. Ro 3:19. 1 J √1:8-10. Re *3:17, 18. **see.** Je 3:2. Ps 50:21. Ezk ch. 16, 23. **valley.** Je 7:31. Is 57:5, 6.

thou art a swift. *or*, O swift. Est 8:16.

24. **A wild ass.** *or*, O wild ass, etc. Je 14:6. Jb 11:12. 39:5-8. **used.** Heb. taught. Je 13:23mg. Is +8:16. **her pleasure.** Heb. the desire of her heart. or, her soul. Heb. *nephesh*, Ge +2:19. **turn her away.** *or*, reverse it. Je 15:19. 23:22. 32:44. Pr 15:1. 29:8. Is 43:13mg. La 3:21mg. Ezk 16:34. **in her month.** ver. 27. Ho 5:15.

25. **Withhold.** Je 13:22. Dt 28:48. Is *20:2-4. La 4:4. Ho 2:3. Lk 15:22. 16:24. **There is no hope.** *or*, Is the case desperate? Je 18:12. Is 57:10. **for I have.** Je 3:13. Is 2:6. **after.** Je 44:17. Dt *29:19, 20. 32:16. 2 Ch 28:22. Lk 15:21-24. Ro *2:3-5. 8:24.

26. **the thief.** ver. 36. Je 3:24, 25. Ezr 9:6. Pr 6:30, 31. Is *1:29. Ro 2:21. 6:21. **their kings.** Je 32:32. Ezr 9:7. Ne 9:32-34. Da *9:6-8.

27. **to a stock.** Je 10:8. Ps 115:4-8. Is 44:9-20. 46:6-8. Hab *2:18-20. **stone.** ℐ121D7, Ex +7:19. i.e. an idol made of stone. **brought me forth.** *or*, begotten me. Je 14:5 (calved). 15:10 (borne). 17:11 (hatcheth). 20:14 (bare). 22:26. Ge 4:18 (begat). Is 66:7, 8. **for they.** Ezk 8:16. 23:35. **their back.** Heb. the hinder part of the neck. Je 7:26. 17:23. **but in the time.** ver. 24. Je 22:23. Jg *10:8-16. Ps *78:34-37. Is 26:16. Ho *5:15. 7:14.

28. **But where.** ℐ83, 1 K 22:15. Dt *32:37, 38↦𝒫. Jg *10:14. 2 K 3:13. Is *45:20. 46:2, 7. **trouble.** Heb. evil. ver. 3. Je 1:14. Is +*45:7. 57:1. **to the number.** ver. 32. Je 11:13. 44:28. 2 K 17:30, 31. Ho 10:1.

29. **will ye plead.** See on ver. 23, 25. Je 3:2. **ye all have.** Je 5:1. 6:13. 9:2-6. Da 9:11. Ro *3:19. 1 J 2:1.

30. **In vain.** Je 5:3. 6:29, 30. 7:28. 31:18. 2 Ch 28:22. Is *1:5. 9:13. Ezk 24:13. Zp 3:2. Re *9:20, 21. 16:9. **your own sword.** Je 26:20-24. 1 K 18:4, 13. 19:10, 14. 2 K 21:16. 2 Ch 24:21. 36:16. Ne *9:26. Mt 21:35, 36. 23:29, 34-37. Mk 12:2-8. Lk 11:47-51. 13:33, 34. Ac *7:52. 1 Th *2:15.

31. **O generation.** Once chosen (Ps 22:30. 24:6. 112:2. Is 53:8), now perverse (Je 7:29. Dt 32:5. Ps 78:8). Mt 3:7. 11:16. 12:34, 39, 41-45. 16:4. 17:17. **see ye.** Am 1:1. Mi 6:9. **Have I been.** See on ver. 5, 6. 2 S 12:7-9. 2 Ch 31:10. Ne 9:21-25. Ho 2:7, 8. Ml 3:9-11. **darkness.** ℐ24L, Ge +6:2. **We are lords.** Heb. We have dominion. Dt 8:12-14. 31:20. *32:15. Ps 10:4. *12:4. Pr 30:9. Ho 13:6. 1 C 4:8. Re 3:15-17.

32. **a maid.** ver. 11. Je 14:17. 18:13. 31:4. Ge 24:+*16 (✻S#1330h), 22, 30, 53. 2 S 1:24. Ps 45:13, 14. Is *61:10. Ezk *16:10-13. 1 P 3:3-5. Re *21:2. **forget.** Is 49:15. **yet my people.** Je 3:21. 13:10, 25. 18:15. Ps 9:17. 106:21. Is 17:10. Ezk 22:12. Ho 8:14.

33. **Why.** ver. 23, 36. Je 3:1, 2. 7:3. Is *57:7-10. Ho 2:5-7, *13. **love.** ℐ121R4. Metonymy of the Adjunct B600. "Love" is put for the person or object loved. For other instances of this figure see Je 12:7. Ho 9:10. **hast.** 2 Ch *33:9. Ezk *16:27, 47, 51, 52. Ro 1:32.

34. **Also.** Je 7:31. 19:4. 2 K *21:16. 24:4. Ps *106:37, 38. Is 57:5. 59:7. Ezk 16:20, 21. 20:31. Lk *11:49, 50. Re 17:6, 7. **blood of.** T#990‡. Ge 9:5. Ezk 22:27. **souls.** Heb. *nephesh*, Jsh +*10:28. **I have.** Je 6:15. 8:12. Ezk 24:7. **secret search.** Heb. digging. Ex 22:2. Mt 24:43.

35. **Because.** See on ver. 23, 29. Jb 33:9. Pr √28:13. Is 58:3. Ro 7:9. **I will.** See on ver. 9. 1 J √1:8-10. Re 3:16-18.

36. **gaddest.** ver. 18, 23, 33. Je 31:22. Ho 5:13.

*7:11. 12:1. **thou also shalt.** Je 37:7. Is 20:5. *30:1-7. 31:1-3. La 4:17. 5:6. Ezk 29:7. **as thou wast.** 2 Ch *28:16, 20, 21. Ho 5:13. 10:6. 14:3.

37. **thine hands.** ℐ121S3M, 2 S +13:19. 2 S 13:19. **for the Lord.** ver. 36. Je 17:5. 37:7-10. 1 S √15:22, 23. Is 10:4. Ezk *17:15-20. **and thou.** Je 32:5. Nu 14:41. 2 Ch 13:12.

JEREMIAH 3

God invites Judah to return to him, with intimations of mercy; but with rebukes and expostulations, 1-5. Israel, though rejected for sin, is less criminal than Judah, who had not profited by the judgments inflicted on Israel, 6-11. Both are called to repentance, with gracious promises and predictions, 12-19. The people being sharply reproved, are prophetically represented, as repenting and confessing their sins, 20-25.

1. **They say.** Heb. Saying. Jg 16:2. **If a man.** See on Dt 24:1-4↦𝒫. **put away.** Ml 2:16. **return unto her.** 1 Ch 8:9n. Ho 2:7. **shall not that.** ver. 9. See on Je 2:7. Le 18:24-28. Is 24:5. Mi 2:10. **but thou hast.** Je *2:7, 20, 23. Dt 22:21. Jg 19:2. Ezk 16:26, 28, 29. 23:4, etc. Ho 1:2. 2:5-7. **harlot.** ℐ155E3, Is +32:9. **yet return.** ver. 12-14, 22. Je 4:1, 14. 8:4-6. Dt 4:29-31. Is *55:6-9. Ezk 33:11. Ho 14:1-4. Zc 1:3. Ml 3:7. Lk *15:16-24.

2. **Lift.** Je 2:23. Ezk *8:4-6. Lk 16:23. **unto.** Je 2:20. Dt 12:2. 1 K 11:3. 2 K 23:13. Ezk *16:16, 24, 25. 20:28. **In the.** Ge 38:14. Pr 7:11, 12. 23:28. Ezk 16:24, 25. **thou hast.** See on ver. 1, 9. Je 2:7. **whoredoms.** Ex +34:16.

3. **the showers.** Je 9:12. 14:4, 22. Le *26:19↦𝒫. Dt 11:17↦𝒫. 28:23↦𝒫, 24. Is 5:6. Jl 1:16-20. Am 4:7. Hg 1:11. **withholden.** Je 5:24, 25. Am 4:7. Zc 14:17. Ml 3:10. **latter rain.** Je 5:24. Zc 10:1. **a whore's.** Je 5:3. 6:15. 8:12. 44:16, 17. Ezk 3:7. 16:30-34. Zp 3:5. **thou refusedst.** Je 5:3. Ne 9:17. Zc 7:11, 12. He 12:25.

4. **Wilt thou.** ver. 19. Je 31:9, 18-20. Ho 14:1-3. **My father.** See on Je 2:27. Ro 8:15. Ga 4:6. **the guide.** Je 2:2. Ge 48:15. Ps 48:14. *71:5, 17. 119:9. Pr 1:4. *2:16, 17. Ho 2:15. Ml 2:14. **youth.** T#1175. Je +2:2. Ps 129:1. Ezk 16:22. 23:3. Ho 11:1.

5. **Will he.** Ps 30:5. 103:9. **reserve.** ver. 12. Ps *77:7-9. 85:5. *103:8, 9. Is 57:16. 64:9. **his anger.** ℐ63A2, 2 S +6:6. **for ever.** Heb. *olam*, Ex +*12:24. **the end.** Heb. *netsach*, Jb +4:20. **thou hast spoken.** Ezk *22:6. Mi 2:1. 7:3. Zp 3:1-5.

6. A.M. 3292. B.C. 612. **backsliding.** ver. 8, 11-14. See on Je 2:19. 7:24. 2 K 17:7-17. Ezk *23:11. **she is.** See on Je 2:20. Is 57:7. Ezk *16:24, 25, 31. *20:28. 1 K 14:23. **played.** See on ver. 1.

7. **Turn thou.** 2 K 17:13, 14. 2 Ch 30:6-12. Pr 28:13. Ho 6:1-4. 14:1. **her treacherous.** ver. 8-11. Ezk *16:46. *23:2-4. 37:16, 17.

8. **when for.** See on ver. 1. 2 K 17:6-18. 18:9-11. Ezk 23:9. Ho 2:2, 3. 3:4. 4:15-17. 9:15-17. **and given her.** Dt 24:1↦𝒫. Is 50:1. **feared not.** 2 K 17:19. Ezk 23:11-21. Ho 4:15.

9. **lightness.** *or*, fame. Ge 18:21. Ezk 23:10. **she defiled.** See on ver. 2. Je 2:7. **committed.** Je 2:27. 10:8. Is 57:6. Ezk 16:17. Ho 4:12. Hab 2:19.

10. **Judah.** 2 Ch 34:33. 35:1-18. Ps 78:36, 37. Is 10:6. Ho 7:14. **feignedly.** Heb. in falsehood. Je 27:15mg. 29:9mg. Dt +33:29mg. 2 S 22:45mg. Ps 18:44mg. 66:3mg. 81:15mg.

11. **The backsliding**. ver. 8, 22. Ho *4:16. 11:7. **justified**. Ezk *16:47, 51, 52. 23:11. **herself**. Heb. *nephesh*, Ge +27:31.

12. **toward the north**. ver. 18. Je 23:8. 31:8. 2 K 15:29. 17:6, 23. 18:11. **Return**. ✓53, 2 S +1:19. ver. 1, 7, 22. Je 4:1. Is *44:21-23. Ezk *33:11. Ho 6:1. 14:1-3. **backsliding**. Ho 4:16. **for I am**. Je 30:11. 31:20. 33:26. Dt 4:29-31. 2 Ch 30:9. Ps *86:5, 15. *103:8, 17. 145:8. Ezk 16:60. 39:25. Ho 11:8, 9. Mi 7:18-20. Ro *5:20, 21. **will not keep**. ver. 5. Ps 79:5. **anger**. ✓63A2, 2 S +6:6. **for ever**. Ex +*12:24.

13. **acknowledge**. ver. 25. Je 31:18-20. Le *26:40-42)ⱣＰ. Dt 30:1-3. 2 S 12:13. Jb *33:27, 28. Pr ✓28:13. Lk *15:18-21. 1 J ✓1:8-10. **and hast scattered**. ver. 2, 6. Je 2:20, 25. Ezk 16:15, 24, 25. **under every**. Dt 12:2. **green tree**. 2 K 16:4n. +17:10. Is +*66:17n.

14. **Turn**. T#28. ver. 22. Ho 10:12. 14:1, 2. Re 2:4, 5. 3:1, 2, 3. **O backsliding**. ver. 22. See on Je 2:19. Is +57:17mg. **for I am married**. ver. 1, 8. Je 2:2. *31:32. Is *54:5. Ho *2:19, 20. **one of a city**. Je 23:3. 31:8-10. Is 1:9. 6:13. 10:22. *11:11, 12. 17:6. 24:13-15. 27:13. Ezk *34:11-14. Zc 13:7-9. Ro 9:27. 11:4-6.

15. **will give**. T#807. Je *23:4. 31:12, 14. 1 S 13:14. Ps 23:2. Is *30:20, 21. 41:18. 49:9, 10. 52:7, 8. 56:7. 62:6. Ezk *34:15, 23. *37:24. Mi 5:4, 5. Jn *10:1-5. *21:15-17. Ep *4:11, 12. 1 P *5:1-4. **pastors**. T#101. Lk 1:2. Ac 15:6, 23. 20:28. Ep *4:11 (T#447), 12. Ph 1:1. 1 T 2:7. 3:1. 2 T 1:11. 1 P *5:1-3. **which shall**. Je 23:3, 4. Pr *10:21. Is 30:20, 21. Ezk 34:23. Lk 1:31, 32. +*12:42. Jn 10:11. 21:15, 17. Ac 2:34-36. ✓20:28. 1 C *2:6, 12, 13. *3:1, 2. He *5:12-14. 1 P *2:2. 5:2.

16. **when**. Je 30:19. 31:8, 27. Is 60:22. 61:4. Ezk 36:8-12. 37:26. Ho 1:10, 11. Am 9:9, 14, 15. Zc 8:4, 5. 10:7-9. **say**. Je 7:4. Zp 3:11. Mt 3:9. **The ark**. Some believe the Ark of the Covenant has been preserved in Ethiopia, and suggest it is the present which the Ethiopians will bring to the Lord of Hosts (Ps 87:4. Is ✓18:7). Ex 25:22)ⱣＰ. 2 Ch 35:3. Ezr 1:7n. Is 65:17. 66:1, 2. Ml 1:11. Jn ✓4:20-24. He 9:9-12. 10:8, 9, 19-21. **to mind**. Heb. upon the heart. Je 7:31mg. 19:5. 2 K 12:4mg. Is 65:17mg. **visit**. or, inspect. Je 5:9. 9:9. *29:10. 2 K 25:9, 13-15. **neither shall**. Or, as Dr. Blayney renders, "neither shall it be made any more:" the ark once lost was never to be made again. Ezr 1:7n. **that be done**. or, *it* be magnified. S#6213h. Je 5:13. Ge 20:9. 29:26. 34:7. Ex 12:16. 31:15. Le 23:3. Ezk 12:11, 25, 28. 15:5mg. 2 C 3:7, 8, 11. He 9:3, 4, 11, 12.

17. **call Jerusalem**. Ps 87:2-7. Is 60:1. 65:18. 66:7-13, 20. **the throne**. Je 14:21. 17:12. 31:23. 1 S 2:8. Ps 47:8. 87:3. Is 6:1. 12:6. 24:23. 46:13. 66:1. Ezk 1:26. 37:24-28. 43:7. Jl 3:16, 17, 20, 21. Zp 3:8, *14-17. Zc 2:10-13. 8:3. Mt 25:31. Ga 4:26. **and all the nations**. Is 2:2-4. 49:18-23. 60:3-9. 66:20. Mi 4:1-5. Zc 2:11. *8:20-23. **to the name**. Je 26:8. 56:6. 59:19. 60:9. **walk**. Je 7:24. 9:14. 11:8. 16:12. 18:12. Ge *8:21. Nu 15:39. Ro 1:21. 6:14. 2 C 10:4, 5. Ep 4:17-19. **imagination**. *or*, stubbornness. Je 7:24mg. 9:14mg. 11:8mg. Dt 29:19mg)ⱣＰ. Jg 2:19. Ps 78:8. 81:12.

18. **In**. Je 30:3. 50:4, 20. Is *11:11-13. Ezk *37:16-22. 39:25-28. Ho *1:11. 11:13. Zc ✓10:6. **house of Judah**. Je 5:11. 11:10, 17. 12:14. 13:11. 22:6. 31:27, 31. 33:14. 36:3. **with**. *or*, to. **land of the north**. See on ver. 12. Je ✓23:7, 8. 31:8. Am 9:15. **to the land**. Je +*7:7.

Am +✓9:15. Zc 3:9. **given**, etc. *or*, caused your fathers to possess. Zc 8:12.

19. **How**. Je 5:7. Ho 11:8. **put thee**. ver. 4. Je 31:9, 20. Jn *1:11-13. 2 C 6:17, 18. Ga 3:26. *4:5-7. Ep *1:5, 6. 1 J *3:1-3. **pleasant land**. Heb. land of desire. ✓121R5, Ge +27:15. Je 12:10mg. Ps 106:24mg. Ezk 20:6. Da 8:9. 11:16mg, 41mg, 45mg. Zc 7:14mg. **goodly heritage**. Heb. heritage of glory, *or* beauty. Pr 3:35. 1 P *1:3, 4. **Thou shalt**. See on ver. 4. Is 63:16. *64:8. Mt *6:8, 9. Ro 8:15-17. Ga 4:5. **shalt not**. Je +*32:39, 40. He *10:39. **from me**. Heb. from after me. Je +17:16mg. 32:40mg.

20. **husband**. Heb. friend. SS 5:16. Ho 3:1. **so have**. ver. 1, 2, 8-10. Je 5:11. Is 48:8. Ezk 16:15, etc. Ho 5:7. 6:7. Ml 2:11.

21. **A voice**. Je 30:15-17. 31:9, 18-20. 50:4, 5. Is 15:2. Ezk 7:16. Zc 12:10-14. 2 C 7:10. **for they have**. Nu 22:32. Jb 33:27. Pr 10:9. 19:3. Mi 3:9. **and they have**. See on Je 2:32. Is 17:10. Ezk 23:35. Ho 8:14. 13:6.

22. **Return**. ✓53, 2 S +1:19. ver. 14. Ho *6:1. *14:1, 4. **backsliding**. Je 50:6. Is +57:17mg. **will heal**. Jn +*12:40. Ac +*3:19-21. **Behold**. Je 31:18. Ps 27:8. SS 1:4. Ho 3:5. 6:1, 2. 13:4. 14:8. Zc 13:9.

23. **in vain**. ver. 6. Je 10:14-16. Ps 121:1, 2. Is 44:9. 45:20. 46:7, 8. Ezk *20:28, 29. Jon 2:8, 9. **mountains**. ✓121J7B. Metonymy of the Subject B575. "Mountains" are put for idols worshipped there, or for other inhabitants. For other instances of this figure see Ezk 18:6, 11, 15. Mi 1:4. **in the Lord**. Je 14:8. Ps 3:8. 37:39, 40. 121:1, 2. Is *12:2. 43:11. 45:15, 17. 63:1, 16. Ho 1:7. Jn *4:22.

24. **shame**. ✓121G, Ge +31:1. Je 11:13. Ezk 16:61, 63. Ho *2:8. 9:10. 10:6. Ro 6:21. **labor**. ✓121C1H, Dt +28:33.

25. **lie down**. Je 2:26. 6:26. Ezr *9:6-15. Ps 109:29. Is 50:11. La 5:16. Ezk 7:18. Da +*12:2. Ro *6:17, 18, 20, 21. **for we have sinned**. Je 2:17, 19. Dt 31:17, 18. Ezr 9:6. Ezk 36:32. **we and our**. Je 2:2. Ezr 9:7. Ne 9:32-34. Ps 106:7. Is 48:8. La 5:7. Da 9:6-9. **and have not**. Je 22:21. Jg 2:2. Pr 5:13. Da 9:10.

JEREMIAH 4

Israel and Judah are called to repent, with gracious promises and solemn warnings, 1-4. A prediction of the invasion of Judah and the ravages of war, for the wickedness and hypocrisy of the inhabitants, 5-18. The prophet bitterly laments the sins and miseries of his people, 19-31.

1. **wilt return**. ver. 4. Je 3:12, 22. **return**. Je 3:1, 14. Is 31:6. Ho 7:16. 14:1. Jl *2:12. **put away**. Ge 35:2. Dt 27:15. Jsh ✓24:14. Jg 10:16. 1 S 7:3. 2 K 23:13, 24. 2 Ch 15:8. Ezk 11:18. 18:13. 20:7, 8. 43:9. Ho 2:2. Ep 4:22-31. **then shalt**. Je 15:4. 22:3-5. 24:9. 25:5. 36:3. 2 Ch 33:8.

2. **shalt swear**. Je 5:2. Dt *10:20)ⱣＰ. Is *45:23-25. 48:1, 2. 65:16. Ph *2:10, 11. **in truth**. Je 9:24. 1 K 3:6. Ps 99:4. Ho 2:19. Zc 8:8. **in righteousness**. ✓94. Hendiatris; or, Three for One B673. Three words used, but one thing meant. Here, the meaning may be understood to be "thou shalt swear, in truth (i.e. truly, yes— justly and righteously)." In swearing by Jehovah in truth, justice and righteousness is included; not only that people swear the truth (Le 19:12. Nu 30:3. Je 5:2. Mt 5:33), but also that they swear by Jehovah

alone (i.e., justly and righteously), and not by idols also, as, according to Zp 1:5, they did in his day. For other instances of this figure see Da 3:7. Mt 6:13. Jn √14:6. **and the nations.** Ge +*22:18. Ps *72:17. Is 65:16. Ga *3:8. **and in him.** Je 9:24. Is 45:25. 1 C *1:29-31. 2 C 10:17. Ph 3:3g.

3. **Break.** Ge *3:17, 18. Ho *10:12. Mt *13:7, 22. Mk 4:7, 18, 19. Lk 8:7, 14. Ga *6:7, 8.

4. **take.** Je 9:26. Dt *10:16⊮𝒫. *30:6⊮𝒫. Ezk 18:31. Ro *2:28, 29. Col *2:10, 11. **lest.** Je 21:5, 12. 23:19. 36:7. Le 26:28. Dt 32:22. Is 30:27, 38. 51:17. La 4:11. Ezk 5:13-15. 6:12. 8:18. 16:38. 20:33, 47, 48. 21:17. 24:8, 13. Am 5:6. Na 1:2. Zp 2:2. Mk 9:43-50. **evil.** Is +*45:7.

5. **Declare ye.** Je 5:20. 9:12. 11:2. **Blow.** Je 6:1. Ezk 33:2-6. Ho *8:1-4. Am 3:6, 8. **Assemble.** Je 8:14. 35:11. Jsh 10:20.

6. **the standard.** ver. 21. Je 50:2. 51:12, 27. Is 62:10. **retire.** *or,* strengthen. ✻S#5756h. Je 6:1 (gather). Ex 9:19 (gather). Is 10:31 (gather). **for I will.** Je 1:13-15. 6:1, 22. 21:7. 25:9. **and a great.** Je 50:22. 51:54. **destruction.** Heb. breaking. Je 6:14 (mg. hurt). Is +51:19mg. Zp 1:10.

7. **lion.** ⨍103, Ge +3:13. Je 5:6. 25:38. 49:19. 50:17, 44. 2 K *24:1. 25:1. Da *7:4. **destroyer.** Je 25:9. 27:8. Ezk 21:19-21. 26:7-10. 30:10, 11. Da 5:19. **to.** Je 2:15. 9:11. 26:9. 33:10. 34:22. Is *1:7. 5:9. *6:11-13.

8. **gird.** Je 6:26. Is 15:3. *22:12, 13. 32:11. Jl *2:12, 13. Am 8:10. **howl.** Je 48:20. Is 13:6. 15:2, 3. Ezk 21:12. 30:2. **the.** Is 5:25. 9:12, 17, 21. 10:4. 12:1.

9. **that the heart.** Je *39:4-7. 52:7. 1 S 25:37, 38. 2 K *25:4-7. Ps 102:4. Is 19:3, 12, 16. 21:3, 4. 22:3-5. **and the priests.** Je 5:31. 6:13, 14. 37:19. Is 29:9, 10. Ezk 13:9-16. Ac *13:40, 41.

10. **Ah.** Je 1:6. 14:13. 32:17. Ezk 11:13. **surely.** Je 14:13, 14. 1 K *22:20-23. Is 63:17. Ezk √14:9, 10. Ro 1:24, 26, 28. 2 Th √2:9-12. **deceived.** ⨍12112, Ge +2:17. √⨍108A4, Ge +31:7. i.e. prophesied that this people shall be deceived. By the figure Metonymy of the Subject, the action is put for the declaration concerning it: or where what is said *to be done* is put for what is declared, or permitted, or foretold as *to be* done: or where an action, said *to be done*, is put for *the giving occasion* for such action. This is also the figure Idiom, whereby active verbs were used by the Hebrews to express, not the doing of the thing, but the *permission* of the thing which the agent is said to do. Thus here, "thou hast greatly deceived this people" is an idiom for "thou hast suffered this People to be greatly deceived, by the false prophets, saying: Ye shall have peace, etc." Am +√3:6. **Ye shall have.** Je 5:12. 6:14. 8:11. 23:17. Is 30:10. 37:35. Ezk *13:2, 10. **the sword.** ver. 18. Ex 9:14. La 2:21. **soul.** Heb. *nephesh,* Ge +12:13. Ps 69:1.

11. **A dry wind.** Je 23:19. 30:23, 24. 51:1. Is 27:8. √64:6. Ezk 17:10. 19:12. Ho 13:3, 15. **daughter.** Je 8:19. 9:1, 7. 14:17. Is 22:4. La 2:11. 3:48. 4:3, 6, 10. **not to fan.** Je 51:2. Is 41:16. Mt *3:12. Lk 3:17.

12. **a full wind from those.** *or,* a fuller wind than those. **give sentence.** Heb. utter judgments. Je 1:16. 39:5mg. 2 K 25:6mg. Ezk 5:8. 6:11-13. 7:8, 9.

13. **Behold.** Is 13:5. 19:1. Na *1:3. Mt √24:30. Re *1:7. **as.** ⨍102B, Ge +13:16. **clouds.** Je +9:13. **his chariots.** Is 5:28. 66:15. Na 2:3, 4. **as a whirlwind.** ⨍102B, Ge +13:16. **his horses.** Dt *28:49. La 4:19. Da 7:4. Ho 8:1. Hab 1:8. **swifter than.** ⨍102B, Ge

+13:16. **Woe.** See on ver. 31. Je 9:19. 10:19.

14. **wash.** Is *1:16-19. √55:7. Ezk *18:31. Mt 12:33. *15:19, 20. 23:26, 27, *37-39. Lk 11:39. Ja *4:8. **How long.** Je +6:19. 13:27. Ps √66:18. 119:113. Pr 1:22. Ac +*8:22. Ro 1:21. 1 C 3:20. **vain thoughts.** Je +*6:19.

15. **a voice.** Je 6:1. 8:16. Jg 18:29. 20:1. **mount Ephraim.** Jsh 17:15. 20:7.

16. **ye.** Je 6:18. 31:10. 50:2. Is 34:1. **watchers.** ver. 17. Je 5:6. 16:16. 39:1. **from.** Je 5:15. Dt 28:49-52. Is 39:3, 4. **give out.** Je 2:15. Ezk 21:21, 22.

17. **keepers.** Je 6:2, 3. 2 K *25:1-4. Is *1:8. Lk 19:41, 43, 44. 21:20-24. **because.** Je 5:23. Ne *9:26, 30. Is 1:20-23. 30:9. La 1:8, 18. Ezk 2:3-7. Da 9:7, etc.

18. **Thy way.** See on Je *2:17, 19. 5:19. 6:19. 26:19. Jb 20:5-16. Ps 107:17. Pr 1:31. 5:22. Is 50:1. **it reacheth.** See on ver. 10.

19. **My bowels.** Je *9:1, 10. 13:17. 14:17, 18. 23:9. 48:31, 32. Ps *119:53, 136. Is 15:5. *16:11. 21:3. 22:4. La 1:16. 2:11. 3:48-51. Da 7:15, 28. 8:27. Hab *3:16. Lk √19:41, 42. Ro *9:2, 3. 10:1. Ga 4:19. **my bowels.** ⨍84, Ge +6:17. **my very.** Heb. the walls of my. **hast heard.** ⨍105, Ml +4:2. **O my.** Ge 49:6. Jg 5:21. Ps 16:2. 42:5, 6. 103:1. 116:7. 146:1. **soul.** Heb. *nephesh,* Ge +27:31. **sound.** See on ver. 5, 21. Am +*3:6. Zp 1:15, 16.

20. **upon destruction.** See on ver. 6. Je 17:18. Le 26:18, 21, 24, 28. Ps *42:7. Is 13:6. La 3:47. Ezk *7:25, 26. 14:21. Jl 1:15. Mt +*10:28. 2 Th √1:9. **suddenly.** Je 10:19, 20. Is 33:20. 54:2. La 2:6-9. Hab 3:7. **curtains.** ⨍121D3, 2 S +7:2. **a moment.** Ex 33:5. Nu 16:21, 45. Ps 73:19. Is 47:9. 2 Th *5:2-5.

21. **How long.** See on ver. 14. **shall I.** See on ver. 5, 6, 19. Je 6:1. 2 Ch 35:25. 36:3, 6, 7, 10, 17.

22. **For my.** Je 5:4, 21. 8:7-9. Dt 32:6, 28. Ps *14:1-4. Is *1:3. *6:9, 10. 27:11. 29:10-12. 42:19, 20. Ho *4:1, 6. Mt 23:16-26. Ro *1:22. 3:11. 1 C 1:18. **they have.** Ho 5:4. Jn 16:3. Ro 1:28. 1 C 1:20, 21. **known me.** Je 9:24. Ho 4:1. **they are wise.** 2 S 13:3. 16:21-23. Mi 2:1. Lk 16:8. Ro 16:19. 1 C 14:20.

23. **the earth.** Je 9:10. Ge √1:2. Dt 32:10. Is 24:19-23. Re *20:11. **void.** Ge +*1:2⊮𝒫. Is 34:11. 45:18. **the heavens.** Is 5:30. 13:10. Ezk 32:7, 8. Jl 2:10, 30, 31. 3:15, 16. Am 8:9. Mt 24:29, 35. Mk 13:24, 25. Lk 21:25, 26. Ac 2:19, 20.

24. **I beheld.** ⨍18, Dt +28:4. **mountains.** Je 8:16. 10:10. Jg 5:4, 5. 1 K 19:11. Ps 18:7. 77:18. 97:4. 114:4-7. Is 5:25. Ezk 38:20. Mi 1:4. Na 1:5, 6. Hab 3:6, 10.

25. **there was no man.** Ho 4:3. Zp *1:2, 3.

26. **the fruitful.** Je 12:4. 14:2-6. Dt *29:23-28. Ps 76:7. 107:34. Is 5:9, 10. 7:20-25. 24:18-20. Mi 3:12. Mt 24:29, 30. Ac 2:16-21. Re 21:23-25.

27. **The.** See on ver. 7. Je 7:34. 12:11. 18:16. 2 Ch 36:21. Is 6:11, 12. 24:1, 3-12. Ezk 6:14. 33:28. **yet.** Je 5:10, 18. √30:11. *46:28. Le √26:44⊮𝒫. 1 S +*12:22. Is 24:12, 13. +60:10. Ezk *11:13. Am √9:8, 9. Mi *7:18. Zc *10:6. Ro 9:27-29. +*11:1-7.

28. **the earth.** See on ver. 23-26. Je 12:4. 23:10. Is 24:4. 33:8, 9. Ho *4:3. Jl 1:10. **mourn.** ⨍155D, Ge +4:10. **the heavens.** Is *5:30. 34:4. 50:3. Jl 2:30, 31. Mt 27:45. Mk 15:33. Lk 23:44. Re 6:12. **black.** Pr +20:20. **because.** Je 7:16. 14:11, 12. 15:1-9. Nu *23:19⊮𝒫. 1 S 15:29. Is 14:24-27. 46:10, 11. Ezk 24:14. Ho +*13:14. Ep 1:9, +*11. He 7:21.

29. **city.** ⨍121J19, 1 S +22:19. **shall flee.** Je 39:4-

6. 52:7. 2 K 25:4-7. Is 30:17. Am 9:1. **they shall go.** 1 S 13:6. 2 Ch 33:11. Is 2:19-21. Lk 23:30. Re 6:15-17. **thickets.** ✓102, Ge +2:24. *Lit.,* into the clouds; to express inaccessible places (B425). **every.** See on ver. 27.

30. **And when.** Je 5:31. 13:21. Is 10:3. 20:6. 33:14. He +*2:3. **Though.** Ezk *23:40, 41. 28:9, 13. Re 17:4. **thyself.** ✓155E3, Is 32:9. **face.** Heb. eyes. 2 K 9:30mg. Ezk 23:40. **in vain.** Je 22:20-22. La *1:2, 19. 4:17. Ezk 16:36-41. 23:9, 10, 22-24, 28, 29. Re 17:2, 13, 16-18. **lovers.** Ezk 23:5. **will despise.** Je 30:14. La *1:2, 19. **life.** Heb. *nephesh,* Ge +44:30.

31. **I have heard.** Je 6:24. 13:21. 22:23. 30:6. 48:41. 49:22, 24. 50:43. Is 13:8. 21.3. Ho 13:13. 1 Th *5:3. **the voice.** Je 6:2, 23. Mt 21:5. **daughter.** ✓155E5, Nu +21:25. **spreadeth.** Is *1:15. La *1:17. **saying.** ✓63BA, Ge +26:7. **Woe.** Je 10:19. 15:18. 45:3. Ps 120:5. Is 6:5. Mi 7:1. 1 C 9:16. **for my.** Ge 27:46. Jb 10:1. **soul.** Heb. *nephesh,* Ge +34:3. **because.** Je 14:18. 18:21. La 1:20. 2:21. Ezk 9:5, 6. 23:46, 47. Re *17:3-6.

JEREMIAH 5

The judgments of God on the Jews for the incorrigible wickedness of all ranks and orders among them, 1-6; for adultery, 7-9; impious contempt of God's word, 10-14; idolatry, 15-19; blindness, presumption, and ingratitude, 20-25; injustice and oppression, 26-29; and the favor shown to false prophets, 30, 31.

1. **Run ye.** 2 Ch 16:9. Da *12:4. Jl 2:9. Am 8:12. Zc 2:4. **streets.** Heb. *chuts,* Am 5:16n (✛S#2351h, highways), outside or narrow streets. Je 6:11. **broad places.** Heb. *rechob,* Am +5:16n (*S*7339h, streets), public square or broad streets. Je 9:21. 48:38. Pr 8:3. SS 3:2. Lk 7:32. 14:21. **if ye can find.** Ge 18:26🙼𝒫. 1 K 19:10. Pr 20:6. Ezk 22:30. Mt +✓7:14. Lk ✓18:8. **if there.** Ge *18:23-32. Ps 12:1. 14:3. 53:2-4. Ezk ✓22:30. Mi *7:1, 2. Ro 3:10. **that seeketh.** Pr 2:4-6. 23:23. Is 59:4, 14, 15. 2 Th ✓2:10. **will pardon.** Ge 18:24-32🙼𝒫.

2. **though.** See on Je 4:2. 7:9. Le 19:12. Is 48:1. Ho 4:1, 2, 15. 10:4. Zc 5:3, 4. Ml +*3:5. 1 T 1:10. 2 T 3:5. T *1:15, 16.

3. **are not thine.** Je 32:19. 2 Ch 16:9. Ps 11:4-7. 51:6. Pr 22:12. Ro 2:2. **thou hast stricken.** Je 2:30. 7:28. 2 Ch 28:22. Pr 23:35. *27:22. Is *1:5, 6. *9:13. 42:25. Ezk 24:13. Zp 3:1, 2, 7. Ml *3:13, 14. **not grieved.** Mt 11:16, 17. **refused.** 1 S +*25:17. Pr +8:33. 13:+1, 18. **they have made.** Pr 21:29. Is 48:4. Ezk 3:7-9. Zc 7:11, 12. Ro 2:4, 5. He 12:9.

4. **Surely.** Je 4:22. *7:8. 8:7. Is 27:11. 28:9-13. Ho 4:6. Mt 11:5. Jn *7:48, 49.

5. **get me.** Am 4:1. Mi *3:1. Ml 2:7. **but these.** Je 6:13. Ps *2:2, 3. Ezk 22:6-8, 25-29. Mi 3:1-4, 11. 7:3, 4. Zp 3:3-5. Mt 19:23-26. Lk 18:24. 19:14. Ac 4:26, 27. Ja 2:5-7.

6. **a lion.** Je 2:15. 4:7. 25:38. 49:19. Ezk 14:16-21. Da 7:4. Ho 5:14. *13:5-8. Am 5:18, 19. Na 2:11, 12. **and a wolf.** Ps 104:20. Ezk 22:27. Hab 1:8. Zp 3:3. **evenings.** *or,* deserts. Je 50:12. Jsh 18:18mg. Ezk 47:8mg. **a leopard.** Da 7:6. Ho 13:7. Re 13:2. **because.** See on Je 2:17, 19. 9:12-14. 14:7. 16:10-12. 30:24. Nu 32:14. Ezr 9:6. 10:10. Is 59:12. La 1:5. Ezk 16:25. 23:19. **increased.** Heb. strong. Je 15:8. 30:14, 15. Is 31:1.

7. **How shall.** Je 3:19. Ho 11:8. Mt 23:37, 38. **for-saken me.** Dt 32:15, 21🙼𝒫. **sworn by.** Je 12:16. Jsh 23:7. Ho 4:15. Am 8:14. Zp 1:5. **no gods.** See on Je 2:11. Dt 32:21. 1 C +*8:4. Ga 4:8. **I had fed.** See on Je 2:31. Dt 32:15. Ezk 16:49, 50. Ho 13:6. Ja *5:1-5. **they then.** Je 9:2. 13:27. 23:10. 29:22, 23. Ex 20:14🙼𝒫. Le 20:10. Dt 5:18🙼𝒫. Ps 50:18. Ezk 22:11. Ho 4:2, 13, 14. 7:4. Ml +*3:5. 1 C +*6:9. He +*13:4. Ja +*4:4. **committed adultery.** Je 7:30, 31. 19:4, 5. 32:34, 35. Is +66:17n. Ezk 16:17. Ho 4:12-14. Am 2:7-9. **by troops.** Nu *25:1-3.

8. **every one.** Je 13:27. Ge 39:9. Ex 20:14, 17. Dt 5:18, 21. 2 S 11:2-4. Jb 31:9. Mt *5:27, 28.

9. **I not visit.** ver. 29. Je 9:9. 23:2. La 4:22. Ho *2:13. 8:13. **and shall.** ✓85S, Jb +4:17. Je 44:22. Le 26:25. See on Dt 32:35, *39-41, 43. Is *1:24. Ezk 5:13-15. *7:9. Na 1:2. **soul.** Heb. *nephesh,* Ge +34:3. Le +26:11n. ✓22A1, Le +26:11.

10. **Go ye up.** ✓38B, 2 S +1:24. Je 6:4-6. 25:9. 39:8. 51:20-23. 2 K 24:2-4. 2 Ch 36:17. Is 10:5-7. 13:1-5. Ezk 9:5-7. 14:17. Mt 22:7. **but make.** ver. 18. See on Je 4:27. 30:11. 46:28. Ezk *12:15, 16. Am ✓9:8, 9. **they are not.** Je 7:4-12. Ps 78:61, 62. Ho 1:9.

11. **the house.** See on Je *3:6-11, 20. Is *48:8. Ho 5:7. 6:7.

12. **have belied.** ver. 31. Je 4:10. 14:13, 14. 23:14-17. 28:15-17. 43:2, 3. Dt 29:19. 1 S 6:9. 2 Ch *36:16. Is 28:14, 15. Ezk 12:22-28. *13:6. Mi 2:11. 3:11. Hab 1:5, 6. 1 J ✓5:10. **neither.** Je 23:17. 28:4. Ps 10:6. 1 Th 5:2, 3.

13. **the prophets.** Je *14:13-15. 18:18. 20:8-11. 28:3. Jb 6:26. 8:2. Ho 9:7. 1 C *2:14-16.

14. **the Lord God of hosts.** Je *15:16. 35:17. 49:5. **I will make.** Je 1:9. 23:29. 28:15-17. 2 K *1:10-15. Ho 6:5. Zc 1:6. Re *11:3, 5, 6. **fire.** Je 20:9. *23:29.

15. **I will.** See on Je 1:15. 4:16. 6:22. 25:9. Dt *28:49🙼𝒫. Is *5:26. *39:3, 6. **O house.** ver. 11. Je 2:26. 9:26. Is 5:7. Ezk 18:31. Mt 3:9, 10. **a mighty.** Da 2:37, 38. 7:7. Hab 1:5-10. **ancient.** Heb. *olam,* Jb +22:15. Ge 10:10. **a nation.** Is 28:11. 33:19. 1 C 14:21-25. **language.** The Chaldee, which, though a dialect of the Hebrew, is so very different in its words and construction, that in hearing it spoken they could not possibly understand it.

16. **quiver.** Ps 5:9. Is 5:28. Ro 3:13. **sepulchre.** Heb. *qeber,* Ge +23:4.

17. **And they.** Le *26:16🙼𝒫. Dt *28:30, 31, 33. Jg 6:3, 4. Is 62:9. 65:22. Hab 3:17, 18. **they shall eat.** ✓18, Dt +28:4. **they shall impoverish.** See on Je 2:15. 4:7, 26. La 2:2. Ezk 36:4. Zp 3:6. Ml 1:4.

18. **I will not make.** See on ver. 10. Je 4:27. Ezk 9:8. 11:13. Ro +✓11:1-5.

19. **Wherefore.** See on Je 2:35. 13:22. 16:10. 22:8, 9. Dt *29:24-28. 1 K *9:8, 9. 2 Ch 7:21, 22. **Like as.** See on Je 2:13. Dt *4:25-28. 28:47, 48. La 5:8. **strange.** Je 8:19. Ex 12:43 (*S#5236h). Is 62:8.

21. **O foolish.** See on ver. 4. Je 4:22. 8:7. 10:8. Dt 29:4. 32:6. Ps 94:8. Is 6:9, 10. 27:11. 44:18. Ezk *12:2. Mt *13:13-15. Jn *12:40. Ac 28:26. Ro *11:8. **under-standing.** Heb. heart. Pr 17:16. Ho 7:11. **which have eyes.** Mk 🙼8:18.

22. **Fear ye not.** Je 10:7. Dt 28:58. Ps 119:120. Mt +*10:28. Lk *12:5. Re *15:4. **tremble.** Ps 99:1. 119:120. Is 66:5. Da 6:26. **placed.** Jb ✓26:10. *38:10, 11. Ps 33:7. 93:3, 4. 4✓104:9. Pr 8:29. Is 50:2. +✓54:8-10. Am 9:6. Na 1:4. Mk 4:39. **perpetual.** Ge +*9:12.

toss. Je 46:7. **roar.** Je 51:55. Ps 46:3.

23. **a revolting.** See on ver. 5. Je 6:28. 17:9. Ps 95:10. Is 1:5. 31:6. Ho 4:8. 11:7. He +*3:12.

24. **Let us now.** See on ver. 22. Je 50:5. Is 64:7. Ho 3:5. 6:1. **that giveth rain.** Je 3:3. *14:22. Dt 11:13, 14⏵ℙ. 28:12. 1 K 17:1. Jb 5:10. 36:27, 28. 38:37. Ps 147:8. Jl *2:23. Am 4:7. Zc 10:1. Ml 3:10. Mt +*5:45. Ac *14:17. Ja 5:7, 17, 18. Re 11:6. **former.** Dt +11:14⏵ℙ. **the appointed.** Ge +√8:22⏵ℙ.

25. **iniquities.** See on Je *2:17-19. 3:3. Dt 28:23, 24. Ps 107:17, 34. Is √59:2. La 3:39. 4:22. **withholden good.** Ps 84:11.

26. **For.** Je 4:22. Is 58:1. Ezk 22:2-12. **lay wait.** or, pry as fowlers lie in wait. Je 18:22. 1 S 19:10, 11. Ps 10:9, 10. 64:5. 71:10. Pr *1:11, 17, 18. Hab *1:14, 15. **catch.** Lk 5:10.

27. **cage.** or, coop. This is, without doubt, a reference to a decoy or trap-cage, as Dr. Blayney renders; in which fowlers place several tame birds, to decoy the others into the snare prepared for them. Re *18:2-4. **so are.** Pr 1:11-13. Ho 12:7, 8. Am 8:4-6. Mi 1:12. 6:10, 11. Hab 2:9-11.

28. **waxen.** Dt *32:15⏵ℙ. Jb 15:27, 28. 21:23, 24. Ps 73:6, 7, 12. 119:70. Am 4:1. Ja 5:4, 5. **overpass.** Je 2:33. Ezk 5:6, 7. 16:47-52. 1 C 5:1. **judge.** Je 22:15-19. Jb 29:12-14. Ps 72:4. 82:2-4. Is 1:23. Zc 7:10. **yet.** Je *12:1. Jb *12:6. Ps *73:12. **prosper.** Dt 10:18⏵ℙ. 24:17⏵ℙ. 27:19⏵ℙ.

29. **not visit.** See on ver. *9. Je 9:9. Ml +*3:5. Ja +*5:4. **shall not.** √85S, Jb +4:17. **soul.** Heb. nephesh, Ge +34:3. Le +26:11n. √22A1, Le +26:11.

30. **A wonderful and horrible thing.** or, Astonishment and filthiness. Je 2:12. 23:14. Is 1:2. Ho 6:10.

31. **prophets.** Je 14:14. 23:25, 26. La 2:14. Ezk 13:6. Mi 3:11. Mt 7:15-17. 2 C √11:13-15. 2 P 2:1, 2. **bear rule.** or, take into their hands. Ne 9:28. Ps 49:14. 72:8. La 1:13. **my people.** Is *30:10, 11. Mi 2:6, 11. Jn √3:19-21. 2 Th √2:9-12. 2 T *4:2-4. **and what.** Je 4:30, 31. 22:22, 23. Dt 32:29. Is 10:3. 20:6. 33:14. La 1:9. Ezk 22:14. Zp *2:2, 3.

JEREMIAH 6

The eagerness of Zion's enemies prophetically described, 1-5. Because of her sins and impenitency, God will prosper them, 6-9. The prophet pathetically declares the sins and miseries of the people, 10-15. Having in vain warned them to repent, he denounces the judgments of God; calls the people to mourning; and predicts their incorrigible obduracy, 16-30.

1. **O ye.** Jsh 15:63. 18:21-28. Jg 1:21. **Benjamin.** √171R, Ex +12:40. "Benjamin" is put for all Judah, on account of their close connection with the Gibeathites (Jg 19:16. Ho 9:9. 10:9). **gather.** Je 4:29. 10:17, 18. **blow.** See on Je 4:5, 6, 19, 20. **Tekoa.** 2 S 14:2. 2 Ch 11:6. Am 1:1. **Beth-haccerem.** i.e. the vineyard house, ✻S#1021h. Ne 3:14. **evil.** See on ver. 22. Je 1:14, 15. 4:6. 10:22. 25:9. Ezk 26:7, etc. **north.** √171.O.10. Synecdoche of the Whole B639. The north is put for Media and Persia, with respect to Babylon. For other instances of this figure see Je 50:3, 41.

2. **daughter.** √155E5, Nu +21:25. See on Je 4:31. Is 1:8. 3:16, 17. La 2:1, 13. **comely and delicate woman.** or, a woman dwelling at home. Dt 28:56⏵ℙ. 2 K 4:13.

3. **shepherds.** Na 3:18. **they shall.** Je 4:16, 17. 39:1-3. 2 K 24:2, 10-12. 25:1-4. Lk *19:41-44.

4. **Prepare.** Je 5:10. 51:27, 28. Is *5:26-30. 13:2-5. Jl *3:9. **at noon.** Je 15:8. 2 S 4:5. SS 1:7. Is 32:2. Zp 2:4. **for the.** Je 8:20. **shadows.** SS 2:16, 17.

5. **let us destroy.** Je 9:21. 17:27. 52:13. 2 Ch *36:19. Ps 48:3. Is 32:14. Ho 8:14. Am 2:5. 3:10, 11. Zc 11:1.

6. **Lord of hosts.** ver. 9. Je 8:3. 9:7, 17. 10:16. 11:17, 20, 22. 19:11. 20:12. 23:15, 16, 36. 25:8, 28, 29, 32. 26:18. 27:18, 19. 29:17. 30:8. 31:35. 32:18. 33:11, 12. 46:18. 48:15. 49:7, 26, 35. 50:33, 34. 51:5, 14, 19, 57, 58. Ex 15:26n. 1 S +1:3. Ps +24:10. Is 44:6. **Hew.** Dt *20:19, 20. **cast a mount.** or, pour out the engine of shot. Je 32:24. 33:4. 52:4. Is 37:33. Ezk 21:22. **this.** See on Je 5:9, 29. **wholly.** 2 K 21:16. Is 59:13, 14. Ezk 7:23. Am 4:1. 8:5, 6. Zp 3:1-3. Ja *5:1-5. **oppression.** √108J, Ge +43:18.

7. **a fountain.** Heb. bor, Ge +37:20. A well, bored or hewn out. Ge 21:19. 2 S 23:15, 16. 1 Ch 11:17. Pr 4:23. Is *57:20, 21. Ja *3:10-12. **violence.** Je 20:8. Ps 55:9-11. Ezk 7:11, 23. 22:3-12. 24:7. Mi 2:1, 2, 8-10. 3:1-3, 9-12. 7:2, 3.

8. **Be thou.** See on Je 4:14. 7:3-7. 17:23. 31:19. 32:33. 35:13-15. Le 26:33-35. Dt *32:29. Ps *2:10-12. 50:17. 94:12. Pr 4:13. Zp 3:7. **lest.** Ezk 23:18. Ho 9:12. Zc 11:8, 9. **soul.** Heb. nephesh, Ge +34:3. **depart.** Heb. be loosed, or disjointed. Ge 32:25. Ezk 23:17mg, 18. **lest I.** See on Je 2:15. 7:20, 34. 9:11. Le 26:34.

9. **They shall.** Je 16:16. 49:9. 52:28-30. Ob 5, 6. Re *14:18-20. **vine.** Jn 15:1, 5, 6.

10. **To whom.** See on Je *5:4, 5. Is *28:9-13. *53:1. **give.** Ezk *3:18-21. 33:3, 9. Mt *3:7. Col *1:28. He 11:7. **their ear.** Je *4:4. *7:26. Ex *6:12. Dt *29:4. Is *6:9, 10. 42:23-25. Ac *7:51. **is uncircumcised.** Ex 6:12, 30⏵ℙ. Le 26:41⏵ℙ. **cannot hearken.** Jn *8:43, 47. Ro *8:7. 1 C √2:14. **the word.** Je *20:8, 9. 2 Ch *36:15, 16. Am 7:10. Lk *11:45. *20:19. Jn *7:7. *9:40. 2 T *4:3. **a reproach.** Je 8:9. 17:15. 23:36. **delight.** Je +*15:16. Ps √1:2. *40:8. 112:1. *119:16, 24, 35, 70, 77, 174. Ho 4:6. Ro *7:22.

11. **Therefore.** Je 20:9. Jb *32:18, 19. Ezk 3:14. Mi 3:8. Ac *4:20. *17:16. 18:5. **I will.** Je 9:21. 18:21. Re *16:1. **stretch.** √22A14.8A, Ex +7:5. **for even.** Ezk 9:6. Lk *17:34-36.

12. **And their.** Je 8:10. Dt *28:30-33⏵ℙ, 39-43. Is *65:17, 18, 21, 22. La 5:3, 11. Zp 1:13. **I will.** 1 Ch 21:16. Is 5:25. 9:12, 17, 21. 10:4. La 2:4, 5, 8. 3:3.

13. **For.** Je 8:10. 14:18. 22:17. 23:11. Is *56:9-12. 57:17. Ezk 22:12. 33:31. Mi 2:1, 2. 3:2, 3, 5, 11. Zp *3:3, 4. 1:8. *16:13, 14. 1 T *3:2, 3. 2 P 2:3, 14, 15. **covetousness.** Ex +*18:21⏵ℙ. Col *3:5, 6. 1 T *6:10. **and.** Je 2:8, 26. 5:31. 23:11, 14, 15. 26:7, 8. 32:32. Is 28:7. La 4:13. Ezk 22:25-28. Zp 3:4.

14. **healed.** Je *8:11, 12. Ezk *13:10. **hurt.** Heb. bruise, or breach. Je 4:7mg. 14:17. Is 1:6. 30:26. Am 6:6mg. **Peace.** Je 4:10. 5:12. 14:13. 23:17. 28:3. La 2:14. Ezk 13:22. Mi 2:11. 2 P 2:1, 18, 19. **peace.** √84, Ge +6:17. **no peace.** T#500. Ezk 13:10. 2 T +3:5 (T#191).

15. **Were.** Je 3:3. 8:12. Is *3:9. **blush.** Ezk 2:4. *16:24, 25. *24:7. Zp *3:5. Ph *3:19. **therefore.** Je 23:12. Pr *29:1. Is 10:4. Ezk 14:9, 10. Mi 3:6. Mt +*15:14. **at the time.** See on Je 5:9, 29. Ex 32:34. Ezk 7:6-9. Ho 9:7. Mi 7:4.

16. **Stand.** Je *18:15. Dt *32:7. SS 1:7, 8. Is +√8:20n. Ml *4:4. Lk *16:29. Jn √5:39, 46, 47. Ac

√17:11. Ro 4:1-6, 12. He *6:12. 11:2, etc. *12:1. **and walk.** Je *7:23. Is 2:5. *30:21. Jn *12:35. +*13:17. Col *2:6. **old.** Heb. *olam,* Jb +22:15. Ps 139:24. **paths.** Ps *25:10. **ye shall.** Is *28:12. Mt √11:28, 29. **souls.** Heb. *nephesh,* Ge +34:3. **We will not.** Je 2:25. *18:12. *22:21. *44:16. Mt *21:28-32. Lk √19:14, 27.

17. **I set watchmen.** Je 25:4. Is 21:11. 56:10. Ezk *3:17-21. 33:2-9. Hab 2:1. Ac *20:27-31. He *13:17. **Hearken.** Is 58:1. Ho 8:1. Am *3:6-8. **We will not.** ver. +16. Zc 7:11.

18. **hear.** See on Je 4:10. 31:10. Dt 29:24-28. Ps 50:4-6. Is 5:3. Mi 6:5. **congregation.** Je 30:20. Ex 12:3, 6, 19, 47₽. Ho 7:12.

19. **O earth.** Je 22:29. Dt *4:26. 30:19. 32:1. Is 1:2. Mi 6:2. **I will bring evil.** Is +*45:7. Am +*3:6. **even.** Je 4:4. *17:10. Pr *1:24-31. 15:26. Is 59:7. 66:18. Ho 10:13. Ac *8:22. **fruit of their thoughts.** Nu +*32:23. Pr 1:31. 4:23. √23:7. Is 66:4. Ezk 33:31, 32. 38:10mg. Mt 5:28. Mk *7:21-23. Ac 5:4. 2 C +*10:5. Ph √4:8, 9. 2 P 2:14. **not hearkened.** Je *29:19. Dt +*28:15. Lk +*8:18. **nor to.** See on ver. 10. Je 8:9. 1 S 15:23, 26. Pr 28:9. Ho 4:6. Jn √3:19-21. *12:48. **my law.** Is +1:10n₽. **rejected.** Ho 4:6.

20. **To what.** 1 S *15:22. Ps *40:6. 50:7-13, 16, 17. 66:3. Is *1:11. 66:3. Ezk 20:39. Am *5:21, 22. Mi *6:6-8. **Sheba.** 1 K 10:1, 2, 10. Is 60:6. Ezk 27:22. **sweet cane.** Is 43:23, 24. **your burnt offerings.** See on Je 7:21-23. Le +*23:12.

21. **I will.** Je 13:16. Is *8:13, 14. Ezk *3:20. Mt *21:42-44. Ro *9:33. 11:9. 1 C +11:19. 1 Th √2:11. 1 P *2:7-9. **fathers.** Je 9:21, 22. 15:2-9. 16:3-9. 18:21. 19:7-9. 21:7. 2 Ch 36:17. Is 9:14-17. 24:2, 3. La 2:20-22. Ezk 5:10. 9:5-7.

22. **a people.** ver. 1. Je 1:14, 15. 5:15. 10:22. 25:9. 50:41-43. **the north.** Je 1:14. 10:22. Zc 2:6.

23. **They shall.** Je 5:16. 50:42. Is 13:18. Ezk 23:22-25. Hab 1:6-10. **cruel.** Je 30:14. Is 13:18. 19:4. **their.** Je 4:13. Is 5:26-30. Lk √21:25-28. **horses.** Re 9:2, 3, 7.

24. **We have.** Je 4:6-9, 19-21. Is 28:19. Ezk 21:6, 7. Hab 3:16. **anguish.** Je 4:31. 13:21. 22:23. 30:6. 49:24. 50:43. Ps 48:6. Pr 1:27, 28. Is 21:3. Mi 4:9, 10. 1 Th √5:2-6.

25. **Go not.** Je 4:5. 8:14. 14:18. Jg 5:6, 7. **the sword.** Je 4:10. 20:3mg, 4, 10. 49:29. 2 Ch 15:5. Jb 18:11. Ps 31:13. Is 1:20. Lk 19:43. **fear is.** Je 20:3, 10. 46:5. 49:29. La 2:22.

26. **daughter.** ver. 14. Je 4:11. 8:19, 21, 22. 9:1. 14:17. Is *22:4. La 2:11. 3:48. 4:3, 6, 10. **gird.** Je 4:8. 25:33, 34. Is *32:11. Ezk 27:30, 31. Mi *1:8-10. **make thee.** Je 9:1, 10, 17-22. 13:17. Is 22:12. La 1:2, 16. Ezk 7:16-18. Zc *12:10. Lk 7:12. Ja 4:9. 5:1. **for the.** Je 4:20. 12:12. 15:8. Is 30:13.

27. **set thee.** See on Je 1:18. 15:20. Ezk 3:8-10. 20:4. 22:2.

28. **all grievous.** See on Je 5:23. Is *1:5. *31:6. **walking.** Je 9:4. 18:18. 20:10. Ps 50:20. **they are brass.** ver. 30. Ezk *22:18-22. **corrupters.** Is 1:4. Re 11:18. 19:2.

29. **the founder.** Je 9:7. Pr *17:3. Zc 13:9. Ml *3:2, 3. 1 P *1:7. *4:12. **in vain.** Is 49:4. Ezk 24:13. Ho 11:7.

30. **Reprobate silver.** *or,* Refuse silver. Ps *119:119. Pr *25:4, 5. Is 1:22, 25. Ezk *22:18, 19. Mt *5:13. **the Lord.** Je 14:19. Is +*54:7. La 5:22. Ho *9:17. Ro +√11:1.

JEREMIAH 7

JEREMIAH is sent to the temple, to call the Jews to repentance, that they might not be removed, 1-3, to reprove their presumptuous confidence in the temple, while living in gross wickedness, 4-11; and to predict that Jerusalem would be desolated, like Shiloh; and the people carried captive, as Israel had been, 12-15. God directs the prophet not to pray for them. He shows him their idolatries, and the judgments about to come on them, 16-20. He rejects with disdain the sacrifices of the disobedient; and exposes the perverse conduct of the nation, from their departure out of Egypt, 21-28. A call to mourning for the prevailing abominations, and a denunciation of desolating judgments, 29-34.

2. A.M. 3394. B.C. 610. **Stand.** Je 17:19. 19:2, 14. 22:1. 26:2. 36:6, 10. Pr *1:20-22. 8:2, 3. Jn *18:20. Ac *5:20, 42. **Hear.** Je 2:4. 10:1. 19:3. 34:4. 44:24. 1 K 22:19. Is 1:10. Ezk 2:4, 5. Ho 5:1. Am 7:16. Mi 1:2. 3:1, 9. Mt *13:9. Re *2:7, 11, 17, 29. 3:6, 13, 22. **that enter.** Je 17:19, 20. 22:2.

3. **the Lord of hosts, the God of Israel.** ver. 21. Je 9:15. 16:9. 19:3, 15. 25:27. 27:4, 21. 28:2, 14. 29:4, 8, 21, 25. 31:23. 32:14, 15. 35:13, 18, 19. 39:16. 42:15, 18. 43:10. 44:2, 11, 25. 46:25. 48:1. 50:18. 51:33. **Amend.** ver. 5-7. Je 18:11. 26:13. 35:15. Pr √28:13. Is *1:16-19. √55:7. Ezk *18:30, 31. 33:4-11. Mt 3:8-10. Ja *4:8.

4. **Trust.** ver. 8. Je 6:14. 28:15. 29:23, 31. Ezk 13:19. Mt *3:8-10. **The temple.** ver. 9-12. 1 S 4:3, 4. Mi 3:11. Zp 3:11. Lk 3:8. 1 C 1:12. 3:3, 4.

5. **For if.** Je 12:16, 17. 15:19. 17:24-27. 18:8-10. 22:4, 5. 26:3, 4. Ge +*4:7. Ezk 33:18, 19. Zc 3:7. Ml 2:2. 2 P +*1:10. **throughly amend.** ver. 3. Je 4:1, 2. Is 1:19, 20. **throughly execute.** Je 5:1. 21:12. 22:3. 1 K 6:12, 13. Is 16:3. Ezk 18:8, 17. Mt 22:37-40.

6. **oppress.** Je 22:3, 4, 15, 16. Ex +*22:21-26. Dt 24:17₽. 27:19. Jb 31:13-22. Ps 82:3, 4. Zc 7:9-12. Ml +*3:5. Ja 1:27. **stranger.** Je 14:8. 22:3. Ge 23:4 (✱S#1616h). Ex 12:48mg. Is 14:1. Ezk 14:7. **the fatherless.** Dt +10:18. **the widow.** ↗171I14, Ex +22:22. Is +1:17. **and shed.** Je 2:30, 34. 22:17. 26:15, 23. 2 K 21:6. 24:4. Ps 106:38. Is 59:7. La 4:13. Ezk 22:3-6. Mt 23:35-37. 27:4, 25. **innocent blood.** Dt 19:10₽. Is 59:7. **neither walk.** Je 13:10. Dt 6:14, 15₽. 8:19₽. 11:28. Ezk 18:6.

7. **will I.** Je 17:20-27. 18:7, 8. 25:5. Ex 15:17, 18. Le 26:42. Is 25:6, 7, 10. Mi 4:1, 2. Zc 14:4. **in the land.** See on Je 3:18. Dt 4:40₽. 2 Ch 33:8. Am +*9:15. Zc 1:17. 3:9. Ac +√7:5. **that I gave.** Ge +*13:15. Am +*9:15. Ac +*7:5. **for ever and.** Heb. *olam* doubled, Da +2:20. Je *25:5.

8. **ye trust.** See on ver. 4. Je 4:10. 5:31. 8:10. 14:13, 14. 23:14-16, 26, 32. Is 28:15. 30:10. Ezk 13:6-16.

9. **steal.** ↗96B, Ge +8:5. Je 9:2-9. Ex 20:7-15₽. Ps 50:16-21. Is 59:1-8. Ezk 18:10-13, 18. 33:25, 26. Ho 4:1-3. Mi 3:8-12. Zp 1:5. Zc 5:3, 4. Ml +*3:5. Ro *2:2, 3, 17. 1 C +*6:9-11. Ga 5:19-21. Ep 5:5-7. 2 T 3:2-5. Ja 4:1-4. Re 21:8. 22:15. **and burn.** Je 11:13, 17. 32:29. 1 K 18:21. **and walk.** ver. 6. Je 13:10. 44:3. Ex 20:3. Dt 32:17. Jg 5:8.

10. **come.** Pr 7:14, 15. 15:8. Is 1:10-15. 48:2. 58:2-4. Ezk 20:39. 23:29, 37-39. 33:31. Mt 23:14. Jn 13:18, 26, 27. 18:28. **which is called,** etc. Heb. whereupon my name is called. ver. 11, 14, 30. Je +14:9mg. 32:34.

34:15. 2 K 21:4. 2 Ch 33:4, 7. **abominations.** Ezk 33:25, 26.

11. **this.** 2 Ch *6:33. Is *56:7. Mt ▸21:13. Mk ▸11:17. Lk ▸19:45, 46. Jn 2:16. **even.** Je 2:34. 16:16, 17. 23:24. He *4:13. Re 2:18, 19.

12. **my place.** Jsh *18:1. Jg *18:31. 1 S 1:3. **where.** Dt *12:5, 11▸℘. **and see.** Je 26:6. 1 S *4:3, 4, 10, 11, 22, etc. Ps *78:60-64.

13. **and I spake.** ver. *25. Je *11:7. 25:3. 35:15. 44:4. 2 Ch *36:15, 16. Ne 9:29, 30. **rising up early.** ver. 25. Je 11:7. 25:3, 4. 26:5. 29:19. 32:33. 35:14, 15. 2 Ch 36:15. **and I called.** Pr *1:24. Is 50:2. *65:12. +√66:4. Ho 11:2, 7. Zc 7:13. Mt 23:37.

14. **wherein.** See on ver. 4, 10. Dt 28:52. Mi 3:11. Ac 6:13, 14. **as.** Je 26:6-9, 18. 52:13, etc. 1 S 4:10, 11. 1 K 9:7, 8. 2 K 25:9. 2 Ch 7:21. 36:18, 19. Ps 74:6-8. 78:60. Is 64:11. La 2:7. 4:1. Ezk 7:20-22. 9:5-7. 24:21. Mi 3:12. Mt 24:1, 2.

15. **I will.** Je 3:8. 15:1. 23:39. 52:3. 2 K *17:6, 18-20, 23. 24:20. Ho 1:4. 9:9, 16, 17. 13:16. **the whole.** 2 Ch 15:9. Ps *78:67, 68. Ho 9:3.

16. **pray not.** T#1788. Je *11:14. *14:11, 12. *15:1. 18:20. Ex *32:10. Dt +28:32mg,n. 1 S 2:25. Ezk *14:3, 14-20. 1 J *5:16. **I will.** 1 S 8:18. Is *1:15. Mi 3:4.

17. **Seest thou not.** See on Je 6:27. Ezk *8:6-18. 14:23.

18. **children.** See on Je 44:17-19, 25. 1 C 10:22. **queen of heaven.** *or,* frame, *or* workmanship of heaven. Though several MSS. and editions have *melachath,* "workmanship," instead of *melecheth,* "queen," yet the latter reading seems the true one, as the LXX. in the parallel place, and the Vulgate uniformly, have "the queen of heaven;" by which there can be little doubt, is meant the *Moon.* Je 44:17, 18, 19, 25. Dt √4:19. 1 K ●11:5. 1 Ch ●11:44. Jb √31:26-28. **to pour.** Je 19:13. 32:29. Dt 32:37, 38. Ps 16:4. Is 57:6. 65:11. Ezk 20:28. **drink offerings.** Le +23:12. **that they.** Je 25:7. Is 3:8. 65:3.

19. **they provoke.** ♪145, Jg +11:40. Je 2:17, 19. Dt 32:16, 21, 22▸℘. Is 1:20, 24. Ezk 8:17, 18. 1 C *10:22. **the confusion.** Je 20:11. Ezr 9:7. Is 45:16. Da *9:7, 8.

20. **Behold.** Je 4:23-26. 9:10, 11. 12:4. 14:16. 42:18. 44:6. Is 42:25. La 2:3-5. 4:11. Ezk *20:47, 48. 22:22. Da 9:11. Na 1:6. Ml 4:1. Re *14:10, 18, 19. 16:1-21. **and shall.** See on Je 17:27. 2 K 22:17. Is *66:24. Mk *9:43-48.

21. **Put.** ♪60A, Ge +3:22. See on Je 6:20. Is *1:11-15. Ho *8:13. Am 5:21-23.

22. **nor.** Ex 15:26▸℘. 19:5▸℘. 1 S 15:22. Ps 40:6. 50:8-17. 51:16, 17. Is 1:11-17. Ho *6:6. Am 5:21-24. Mi 6:6-8. Mt 9:13. 12:7. 23:23. Mk 12:33. **burnt offerings.** Heb. the matter of burnt offerings. Le +*23:12.

23. **Obey.** Je 11:4, 7. Ex *15:26. *19:5, 6. Le *26:3-12▸℘. Dt 5:29, 33. *6:3. 11:27. 13:4. 30:2, 8, 20. Jn +*13:17. Ro 16:26. 2 C *10:5. He *5:9. **and I.** See on Je 31:33. **that it.** Je 42:6. Dt 4:10. 5:16, 33.

24. **they.** ver. 26. Je 11:7, 8. Ex 32:7, 8. Ne *9:16-20. Ps *81:11, 12. 106:7, etc. Ezk 20:8, 13, 16, *21. **walked.** Je 23:17. Dt 29:19. **counsels.** Je 23:18, 22. **imagination.** *or,* stubbornness. Je 3:17mg. **went.** Heb. were. **backward.** ver. 26. Je 2:27. 8:5. 32:33. Ne 9:29. Ho 4:16.

25. **the day.** Je 32:30, 31. Ex ch. 12-15▸℘. Dt 9:7, 21-24. 1 S 8:7, 8. Ezr 9:7. Ne 9:16-18, 26. Ps 106:13-22. Ezk 2:3. 20:5, etc. 23:2, 3. **sent.** ver. 13. Je 25:4.

2 Ch *36:15. Ne 9:30. Mt *21:34-36. Lk *20:10-12.

26. **they hearkened not.** See on ver. 24. Je 6:17. 11:8. 17:23. 25:3, 7. 26:5. 29:19. 34:14. 44:16. 2 Ch *33:10. Ne 9:16. Da 9:6. **but.** Je 19:15. 2 K 17:14. 2 Ch 30:8. Ne 9:17, *29. Pr 29:1. Is 48:4. Ac 7:51. Ro 2:5. **they did.** Je 16:12. Mt *21:36-39. *23:32, 33.

27. **thou shalt speak.** Je 1:7. 26:2. Ezk 2:4-7. 3:17, 18. Ac 20:27. **hearken.** Je 1:19. Is 6:9, 10. Ezk 3:4-11. **also.** Is 50:2. 65:12. Zc 7:13.

28. **nor.** Je 2:30. 5:3. 6:29, 30. Is *1:4, 5. Zp 3:2. **correction.** *or,* instruction. Je 6:8. 32:33. Ps 50:17. Pr *1:7. Zp 3:7. **truth.** Je 5:1. 9:3-8. Is *59:14, 15. Ho 4:1. Mi *7:2-5.

29. **Cut.** Je 16:6. 47:5. 48:37. Jb 1:20. Is *15:2, 3. Mi *1:16. **and take.** Je 9:17-21. Ezk 19:1. 28:12. **for.** See on Je 6:30. 2 K *17:20. Zc 11:8, 9. **generation.** Dt *32:5. Mt *3:7. 12:39. 16:4. *23:36. Ac *2:40.

30. **they.** Je 23:11. 32:34. 2 K *21:4, 7. 23:4-6, 12. 2 Ch 33:4, 5, 7, 15. Ezk 7:20. *8:5-17. 43:7, 8. Da √9:27.

31. **the high.** Je 17:3. 19:5, 6. 32:35. 2 K +21:3. 23:20. 2 Ch 33:6. Is 15:2. 16:12. **of Tophet.** i.e. contempt; a spitting (as an object of contempt); place of burning, burial, or of drums, ✱S#8612h. Je 7:31, 32, 32. 19:6, 11, 12, 13. 2 K 23:10. Is +*30:33. **the valley.** Je 19:2. Jsh +*15:8n. 18:16. 2 K *23:10. 2 Ch 28:3. 33:6. Ne 11:30. **to burn.** Dt 12:31. 2 K 17:17. Ps 106:37, 38. Ezk *16:20, 21. **which I.** Le 18:21▸℘. 20:1-5. Dt 17:3▸℘. 18:10▸℘. Pr *30:6. **came it into.** Heb. came it upon. lit. ascend upon. ♪171J1, 2 K +12:4. T#1011‡. Je 3:16mg. 19:5. 32:35.

32. **the days.** Je 19:6. Le 26:30. Ezk 6:5-7. **Tophet.** ver. +31. Is +*30:33. **the valley.** ver. +31. Je 19:5. **slaughter.** Je 12:3. 19:6. Zc 11:4, 7. **for.** Je 19:11, 13. 2 K 23:10.

33. **the carcasses.** Je 8:1, 2. 9:22. 12:9. 16:4. 22:19. 25:33. 34:20. Le *26:30. Dt 28:26▸℘. Ps *79:1-3. Is 14:19, 20. Ezk 39:4, 18-20. Re *19:17, 18. **none shall.** Je 9:22. 14:16. Is 17:2.

34. **to cease.** Je 16:9. 25:10. 33:10, 11. Is *24:7, 8. Ezk *26:13. Ho *2:11. Re *18:23. **for.** Je 4:27. Le *26:31, 33▸℘. Is 1:7. 3:26. 6:11. Mi 7:13.

JEREMIAH 8

A prediction of the indignities, which would be shown to the bones of the idolatrous Jews; and of such miseries, that men would prefer death to life, 1-3. Severe reproofs of the obstinacy, avarice, and shameless wickedness of the people, 4-12. A prophetical description of the dismay occasioned by the Chaldean invasion, 13-17. The grief of the prophet in the prospect of these calamities, 18-22.

1. **At that time.** Je 7:32-34. 1 K 13:2. 2 K 23:16, 20. 2 Ch 34:4, 5. Ezk *6:4, 5. 37:1, 3. Am 2:1. **bring out the bones.** This was no uncommon practice at the sacking of cities; and it was the highest expression of hatred and contempt. Horace (Epod. xvi. 11) refers to it, "And her great founder's hallowed ashes spurn, That slept uninjured in the sacred urn" (Francis). See Note on 2 Ch 34:5n. **graves.** Heb. *qeber,* Ge +23:4.

2. **and all.** Je 7:18. 19:13. 44:17-19. Dt 4:19. 17:3. 2 K 17:16. 21:3, 5. *23:5, 11. 2 Ch 33:3-5. Ezk 8:16. Zp 1:5. Ac 7:42. **they shall be.** Je 9:22. 16:4. 22:19. 25:33. 36:30. 2 K 9:36, 37. Ps 83:10. Ec 6:3. Zp 1:17. **face.** Ge 1:2.

3. **death shall be chosen**. Je 20:14-18. 1 K *19:4. Jb 3:20-22. 7:15, 16. Jon *4:3. 2 C *5:4. Ph *1:23-25. Re *6:16. √9:6. **evil family**. Am 3:1. Mi 2:3. **in all**. Je 23:3, 8. 29:14, 28. 32:36, 37. 40:12. Dt 30:1, 4. Da 9:7.

4. **Moreover**. Blayney justly observes, that the change of speakers here requires careful attention. The prophet first, in the name of God, reproves the people, and threatens them with grievous calamities, ver. 4-13. Then, apostrophising his countrymen, he advises them to retire with him to some fortified city, ver. 14-16. God then threatens to bring foes against them, that are irresistible, ver. 17. The prophet next commiserates the daughter of his people, who is heard bewailing her forlorn case; whilst the voice of God breaks in upon her complaints, and shows that all this ruin is brought upon her by her infidelities, ver. 18-20. The prophet regrets that her wounds had not been healed, and laments over her slain, ver. 21—Je 9:1. **Shall they**. Pr *24:16. Ho *14:1. Am *5:2. Mi √7:8. Ro *11:11. **shall he**. √63A2, 2 S +6:6. or, "Shall they return (to the Lord)/And He not return (to them)?" This agrees with Ml 3:7, and with the context, and brings out the parallel between the two lines as well as exhibiting more clearly the figure of Polyptoton (see B12). **turn**. √147A, Ge +50:24. Je 3:1, 22. 4:1. 23:14. 36:3. 1 K 8:38. Is *44:22. √55:7. Ezk 18:23. Ho *6:1, 2. *7:10. Lk 15:32.

5. **slidden**. Je 2:32. 3:11-14. 7:24-26. Ho 4:16. *11:7. **they hold**. Je 9:6. Pr 4:13. Is *30:10. *44:20. 1 Th √5:21. 2 Th √2:9-12. Re 2:25. **they refuse**. Je 5:3. Is 1:20. Zc 7:11. Jn 5:40. He 12:25.

6. **hearkened**. Jb *33:27, 28. Ps *14:2. Is √30:18. Ml √3:16. 2 P √3:9. **no man**. √171C, Ex +20:10. Je *5:1. Is 59:16. Ezk *22:30. Mi 7:2. **saying**. Jb *10:2. Ezk *18:28. Hg *1:5, 7. Lk *15:17-19. **as**. Je *2:24, 25. See on Jb *39:19-25.

7. **stork**. Jb 39:13mg. Pr *6:6-8. Is *1:3. **appointed times**. Ge +17:21h. Le 23:2n. Nu 28:2n. Ec 3:1. Mt +*24:44, 45. **turtle**. SS *2:12. **people**. Je *5:4, 5. Is *1:3. *5:12. **know not**. Je *5:4, 5. 1 Ch +*12:32. Is 27:11. Da *12:4, 9, 10. Lk +*11:52.

8. **We**. Jb *5:12, 13. 11:12. 12:20. Jn *9:41. Ro *1:22. 2:17, etc. 1 C *3:18-20. **the law**. Ps 147:19, 20. Ho *8:12. **Lo**. Mt *15:6. **in vain**, etc. or, the false pen of the scribes worketh for falsehood. Pr 17:16. Is 10:1, 2. Lk +*11:52. 2 C *2:17mg. *4:2. *11:13. 2 T √2:15. 2 P *3:16. **pen**. Je 17:1. Jb 19:24. Ps 45:1. **scribes**. 1 Ch 2:55. 2 Ch +15:3. *17:7-9. 34:13. Ezr *7:6, 12. Ne 13:13. Mt 2:4.

9. **The wise men are**. or, Have they been, etc. Je 6:15. 49:7. Jb 5:12, 13. Is 19:11, 12. Ezk *7:26. 1 C *1:26-29. **lo**. Dt *4:6. Ps √19:7. √119:98-100. Is +√8:20n. 1 C 1:18-29. 2 T √3:15. **rejected**. T#1104. Je *6:10. 20:8. 36:23. 2 Ch 36:16. Ps 50:17. Is *5:24. 30:12. Zc 7:12. Mk +*7:9, 13. Ac 13:46. **what wisdom**. Heb. the wisdom of what thing, etc. Pr 1:7. +*21:30. 1 C 1:20.

10. **will I**. Je 6:12. Dt *28:30-32)℘. Am *5:11. Zp *1:13. **for**. See on Je 6:13. Ex +*18:21. Is 56:10-12. Ezk 33:31. Mi 3:5, 11. Ac *20:33, 34. 2 C *12:14. T 1:7, 11. 2 P *2:1-3. **from the prophet**. See on Je 5:31. 23:11-17, 25, 26. 32:32. Is 28:7. La 4:13. Ezk 22:27, 28.

11. **they**. See on Je 6:14. 14:14, 15. 27:9, 10. 28:3-9. 1 K *22:6, 13. La 2:14. Ezk *13:10-16, 22. Mi 2:11.

12. **ashamed when**. Je 3:3. 6:15. Ps *52:1, 7. Is

*3:9. Zp 3:5. Ph *3:18, 19. **therefore**. Is 9:13-17. 24:2. Ezk 22:25-31. Ho 4:5, 6. **in the time**. Je 10:15. 11:23. 23:12. 46:21. 48:44. 50:27. 51:18. Dt *32:35. Is 10:3. Ho *5:9. 9:7. Mi 7:4. Lk *19:44.

13. **I will surely consume**. or, In gathering I will consume. Is 24:21, 22. Ezk 22:19-21. 24:3-11. Zp *1:2, 3. **there**. Le 26:20. Dt 28:39-42. Is 5:4-6, 10. Ho 2:8, 9. Jl *1:7, 10-12. Hab 3:17. Hg 1:11. 2:17. Mt *21:19. Lk *13:6-9. **the leaf**. Je *17:8. Ps +*1:3, 4. Ja 1:11.

14. **do**. 2 K 7:3, 4. **enter**. Je 4:5, 6. 35:11. 2 S 20:6. **be silent**. Je 48:2. 49:26. 50:30. 51:6. Le 10:3. 1 S *2:9. Ps 39:2. La 3:27, 28. Am 6:10. Hab *2:20. Zc 2:13. **to silence**. √145, Jg +11:40. **water**. Je 9:15. 23:13. 22:15, 17. Nu 5:18-24. Mt 27:34. **gall**. or, poison. Je 9:15. 23:15. Dt 29:18. *32:32. Ps 69:21. La 3:19.

15. **We looked**. Je 4:10. 14:19. Jb 30:26. Mi *1:12. 1 Th *5:3. **health**. Je 14:19. 33:6. 2 Ch +*21:18. **trouble**. or, terror. ✳S#1205h, only here and Je 14:19. Jb 3:26. 19:8. 23:17. 30:26. Pr +*20:20. Ec 6:4. Is 59:9. La 3:2.

16. **The snorting**. Grotius observes, after Jerome, that Nebuchadnezzar, having subdued Phoenicia, passed through Dan, in his way to Jerusalem. **was heard**. Je 4:15, 16. Jg 18:29. 20:1. **the whole**. Je 4:24. Hab 3:10. **trembled**. Je 49:21. Jg 5:4. Ps 68:8. Ezk 38:20. Jl 2:10. 3:16. Na 1:5. **at the**. Je 6:23. 47:3. Jg 5:22. Na 1:4, 5. 3:2. **of his strong ones**. Of his **war-horses**. This is a fine image; so terrible was the united neighings of the cavalry of the Babylonians, that the reverberation of the air caused the ground to tremble. **all that was in it**. Je. the fulness thereof. Je 47:2mg. Dt 33:16. Ps 24:1. 1 C 10:26, 28.

17. **I will**. Dt 32:24. Is *14:29. Am 5:19. *9:3. Re *9:19. *12:9. **which**. Ps 58:4, 5. Ec 10:11.

18. **comfort**. Is 51:12. **my**. Je 6:24. 10:19-22. Jb 7:13, 14. Is 22:4. La *1:16, 17. Da *10:16, 17. Hab *3:16. **in**. Heb. upon.

19. **the voice**. See on Je 4:16, 17, 30, 31. Is 13:5. 39:3. **them**, etc. Heb. the country of them that are afar off. **the Lord**. Je 14:19. 31:6. Ps 135:21. Is *12:6. 52:1. Jl *2:32. 3:21. Ob 17. Zc *14:3, 4. Re 2:1. **her king**. Ps 146:10. 149:2. Is 33:22. Lk 1:32, 33. **Why**. See on ver. 5, 6. Dt 32:16-21. Is 1:4. **provoke**. Je 7:19. Dt 32:21)℘. 1 K 15:30. 21:20. **graven images**. Dt 7:5)℘. 2 Ch +34:3. **strange**. Je 5:19. Ex 12:43 (✳S#5236h). Ezk 44:7, 9. **vanities**. Je 2:5. 10:3, 8, 15. 14:22. 16:19. 51:18. Dt 32:21)℘. 1 K 16:13, 26. 2 K 17:15. Ps 31:6. Jon 2:8. 1 C 8:4.

20. **harvest is past**. Le +*23:22. Pr 10:5. Mt 13:30. *25:1-13. Lk 10:2. *13:25. √19:43, 44. Jn *4:35. 1 Th 4:16, 17. He +*3:7-15. Re 14:15.

21. **the hurt**. Je 4:19. 9:1. 14:17. 17:16. Ne 2:3. Ps *137:3-6. Lk *19:41. Ro 9:1-3. **I am black**. Je 4:28. 14:2. SS *1:5, 6. Jl 2:6, 10. 3:15. Mi 3:6. Na 2:10.

22. **no balm**. Je 46:11. 51:8. Ge *37:25. 43:11. Ezk 27:17. **Gilead**. Je 22:6. 46:11. 50:19. Ge +31:23. **no physician**. Ge 50:2. Mt *9:11-13. Lk 5:31, 32. *8:43, 46, 48. **why**. Je 30:12-17. **health**. lit. prolongation. ✳S#724h. Je *30:17. 33:6. 2 Ch 24:13mg. Ne 4:7 (made up; lit. *healing* went up to the walls). Is *58:8. **recovered**. Heb. gone up. Is 1:5, 6.

JEREMIAH 9

The prophet shows the excess of his grief for the miseries of his people, and his abhorrence of their crimes; and also the justice of God in his dealings with them, 1-16. He calls them to lamentation, 17-22. Warnings not to glory in wisdom, strength, riches, or external distinctions, but in the knowledge of God, and of his grace, 23, 24. Wicked Israelites, and uncircumcised Gentiles, will be punished together, 25, 26.

1. **Oh that.** Heb. Who will give, etc. Je 4:19. 13:17. 14:17. Ps *119:136. Is 16:9. 22:4. La *2:11, 18, 19. *3:48, 49. Ezk 21:6, 7. **waters.** ſ45, Is +40:31. **weep.** ſ141, Is +22:4. Ps *42:3. **the daughter.** See on Je 6:26. 8:21, 22.

2. **that I had.** Ps *55:6-8. 120:5-7. Mi 7:1-7. **for they.** ſ34, Ps +50:16. **all adulterers.** T#402. Je 5:7, 8. 23:10. Ge 19:5. Le 18:22-25. 1 S 2:22. Ezk *22:9-11. Ho *4:2. *7:4. Mt 12:39. Jn 8:7, 9. Ga 5:19. Ja *4:4. 1 P 4:3, 4. **an assembly.** Je 12:1, 6. Ho 5:7. 6:7. Mi 7:2-5. Zp 3:4. Ml 2:11.

3. **they bend.** ver *5, *8. Ps 52:2-4. *64:2-4. 120:2-4. Is *59:3-5, 13-15. Mi *7:3-5. Ro *3:13. **valiant.** Mt *10:31-33. Mk *8:38. Ro ✓1:16. Ph *1:28, 29. Ju +✓3. Re *12:11. **for they.** Je *7:26. 2 T *3:13. **they know.** Je *4:22. *22:16. +*31:34. Jg 2:10. 5:23. 1 S 2:12. Ho 4:1-3. Jn *8:54, 55. ✓17:3. Ro 1:28. 2 C *4:4-6.

4. **ye heed.** Je 12:6. Ps *12:2, 3. 55:11, 12. Pr 26:24, 25. Mi *7:5, 6. Mt *10:17, 21, 34, 35. Lk 21:16. **neighbor.** or, friend. Ge 38:12. **every brother.** Ge 25:26)ℙ. 27:35, 36)ℙ. 32:28. 1 Th 4:6. **walk.** See Je 6:28. Le *19:16. Ps *15:3. Pr 6:16, 19. 10:18. 25:18. Ezk 22:9. 1 P 2:1, 2.

5. **they will.** See on ver. 5, 8. Is 59:13-15. Mi 6:12. Ep 4:25. **deceive.** or, mock. Ge 31:7. Jg 16:10. Jb 11:3. **taught.** ver. 3. Jb 15:5. Ps 50:19. 64:3. 140:3. 1 T *4:1-3. **weary.** Ge 19:11. Ps 7:14. Pr 4:16. Is *5:18. 41:6, 7. 44:12-14. 57:10. Ezk 24:12. Mi 6:3. Hab 2:13.

6. **habitation.** Je *11:19. *18:18. *20:10. Ps *120:2-6. **refuse.** Je *13:10. Jb ✓21:14, 15. Pr *1:24, 29. Ho ✓4:6. Jn ✓3:19, 20. Ro *1:28. 1 C 15:34. 2 Th +*2:10.

7. **I will.** Je 6:29, 30. Pr *1:23-27. Is 1:25. 48:10. Ezk 22:18-22. 24:11, 12. Zc 13:9. Ml *3:3. 1 P 1:7. 4:12. **shall.** Je 31:20. 2 Ch 36:15. Ho 6:4, 5. 11:8, 9. Zc 1:14-16.

8. **tongue.** ver. 3, 5. Ps *12:2. 57:4. 64:3, 4, 8. 120:3. Ro 3:13. **one.** 2 S 3:27. 20:9, 10. Ps 28:3. *55:21. Pr 26:24-26. Mt *26:48, 49. **in heart.** Heb. in the midst of him. Ge 41:21mg. **his wait.** or, wait for him.

9. **visit them.** See on Je 5:9, 29. Is 1:24. **soul.** Heb. nephesh, Ge +34:3. Le +26:11n. **avenged.** ſ22B, Ex +15:7.

10. **the mountains.** Je 4:19-26. 7:29. 8:18. 13:16, 17. La 1:16. 2:11. **habitations.** or, pastures. lit. comely places. Je 23:10. 25:37. Ps ✓23:3. **because.** Je 12:4, 10. 14:6. 23:10. Jl 1:10-12. **burned up.** or, desolate. ver. 12. Je 2:15. 10:22. 46:19. **so.** Je 2:6. Is 34:19. Ezk 14:15. 29:11. 33:28. **both**, etc. Heb. from the fowl even to, etc. See on Je 4:25. Ho 4:3.

11. **Jerusalem.** Je 26:18. 51:37. Ne 4:2. Ps 15:2. Mi 1:6. 3:12. Mt 24:1, 2. Mk 13:1, 2. Lk 21:6. **a den.** Je 10:22. Is 13:22. 34:13. Re 18:2. **the cities.** Je 34:22. Is 44:26. La 2:2, 7, 8. **desolate.** Heb. desolation. Je 10:22. 25:11, 18. La 3:47. Mi 6:16.

12. **Who.** ſ85D, Ps +25:12. **the wise.** Dt 32:20, 29-31. Ps *107:43. Ho 14:9. Mt *24:15. Re 1:3. **for.** Je 5:19, 20. 16:10-13. 22:8, 9. Dt 29:22-28. 1 K 9:8, 9. Ps 107:34. Ezk 14:23. 22:25-31. Ho *13:9.

13. **Because.** Je 22:9. Dt 31:16, 17. 32:15, 21)ℙ.

2 Ch 7:19. Ezr *9:10. Ps 89:30. 119:53. Pr 28:4. Zp 3:1-6. **my law.** Ex ch. 20)ℙ.

14. **walked.** Je 3:17. 7:24. Ge *6:5. Ro *1:21-24. Ep *2:3. 4:17-19. **imagination.** or, stubbornness. Je +3:17mg. Dt +29:19)ℙ. **which.** Je 44:17. Zc 1:4, 5. Ga 1:14. 1 P 1:18.

15. **the Lord of hosts.** Je 7:3. **I will.** See on Je 8:14. 23:15. 25:15. Ps *60:3. 69:21. *75:8. *80:5. Is 2:17, 22. La 3:15, 19. Am 6:12. Re *8:11. **wormwood.** Dt 29:18)ℙ. **water of gall.** Je 8:14.

16. **scatter.** Je 13:24. Le 26:33)ℙ. Dt 4:27. 28:25, 36, 64)ℙ. 32:26. Ne *1:8. Ps 106:27. Ezk 11:17. 12:15. 20:23. Zc *7:14. Ja *1:1. **and I.** Je 15:2-4. 24:10. 25:27. 29:17. 44:27. 49:36, 37. Ezk 5:2, 12. 14:17.

17. **Lord of hosts.** ver. 7. Je 2:19. +6:6. **call for.** ſ121S4, 2 K +4:29. Je 22:18. 34:5. 1 S 1:24. 2 Ch *35:25. Jb 3:8. Ec 12:5. Am *5:16, 17. Mt *9:23. Mk 5:38. **the mourning women.** Those whose office it was to sing mournful dirges, and make public lamentations at funerals.

18. **take.** ver. 10, 20. **our eyes.** See on ver. 1. Je 6:26. 13:17. 14:17. Is 22:4. La 1:2. *2:11, 18. Lk 19:41.

19. **a voice.** Je 4:31. Ezk 7:16-18. Mi 1:8, 9. **Zion.** ſ63BA, Ge +26:7. Supply by ellipsis, (saying). **we are.** Je 2:14. 4:13, 20, 30. Dt *28:28, 29. La 5:2. Mi 2:4. **our.** Le 18:25, 28. 20:22. Jb 8:18. La 4:15. Ezk 19:12. Da 8:11. Mi 2:10.

20. **hear.** Is *3:16, 18-24. *32:9-13. Lk *23:27-30. **receive.** Jb 22:22. **and teach.** See on ver. 17, 18.

21. **death is come.** Je 6:11. 15:7. 2 Ch 36:17. Ezk *9:5, 6. 21:14, 15. Am 6:10, 11. **windows.** lit. pierced places. Je 22:14. Ge 8:6. 26:8. Jl *2:9. **from without.** Heb. *chuts*, Am 5:16n (✚S#2351h, highways), outside or narrow streets. **streets.** Heb. *rechob*, Am 5:16n (✳S#7339h, streets), public square or broad streets.

22. **fall.** Je 7:33. 8:2. 16:4. 25:33. 2 K 9:37. Ps 83:10. Is 5:25. Zp 1:17.

23. **Let not.** ſ167, Is +2:7. Pr +*21:30. **wise.** Jb *5:12-14. Ps 49:10-13, 16-18. Ec 2:13-16, 19. *9:11. Is *5:21. *10:12, 13. Ezk 28:2-9. Ro 1:22. 1 C *1:19-21, 27-29. ✓3:18-20. Ja *3:14-16. **neither.** Dt 8:17. 1 S 17:4-10, 42. 1 K 20:10, 11. Ps 33:16, 17. Is 10:8. 36:8, 9. Ezk 29:9. Da 3:15. 4:30, 31, 37. 5:18-23. Am 2:14-16. Ac 12:22, 23. **rich.** Jb 31:24, 25. Ps 49:6-9. 52:6, 7. 62:10. Pr 11:4. Ezk 7:19. Zp 1:18. Mk 10:24. Lk ✓12:19, 20. 1 T *6:10.

24. **let him.** Je 4:2. Ps 44:8. Is 41:16. *45:25. Ro *5:11g. 1 C *)1:31. 2 C *)10:17. Ga *6:14. Ph 3:3. **knoweth me.** ſ121C2A1, Jb +19:25. Jn ●4:22. *31:33, 34. Ps *91:14. Pr 2:5. Ho 4:1. Mt *11:27. Lk 10:22. Jn ✓17:3. 2 C *4:6. 1 J *5:20. **lovingkindness.** Ezk *34:5-7)ℙ. Ps 36:5-7. *51:1. 107:43. 145:7, 8. *146:7-9. Ro *3:25, 26. **for.** 1 S ✓15:22. Ps 99:4. Is 61:8. Mi +*6:8. *7:18. **I delight.** Is ●+66:4.

25. **that.** Ezk 28:10. 32:19-32. Am 3:2. Ro *2:8, 9, 25, 26. Ga ✓5:2-6. **punish.** Heb. visit upon. Je +11:22mg. 21:14mg. 23:34mg. 30:20. 36:31mg. 44:13. 51:47mg. Ho 4:9mg. 12:2mg. Zp 1:8mg. **circumcised.** Je 4:4. 6:10. Le 26:41, 42)ℙ. Dt 10:16)ℙ. 30:6)ℙ. Ezk 44:7, 9. **with the.** Ro 2:25-29.

26. **Egypt.** Je 25:9-26. 27:3-7. ch. 46-52. Is ch. 13-24. Ezk ch. 24-32. Am ch. 1, 2. Zp ch. 1, 2. **Judah.** Is 19:24, 25. **in the utmost corners.** Heb. cut off into corners; *or,* having the corners *of their hair* polled. Dr. Durell and others justly consider the marginal reading as far preferable; as being descriptive of the

mode in which the Arabians cut their hair and beard. See Notes on Le 21:5. Je 25:23. 49:32. Le 19:27ᴵᵐᵍℙ. **nations.** Dt 32:8, 9. **uncircumcised in.** Je 4:4. Le *26:41. Dt 30:6. Ezk 44:7, 9. Ac 7:51. Ro *2:28, 29.

JEREMIAH 10

Warnings against the idolatry and superstition of the heathen, 1-5. None like to Jehovah the Creator and Lord of all, 6-16. Prophecies concerning the captivity, with suitable lamentations and prayers, 17-25.

1. A.M. 3397. B.C. 607. **Hear.** Je 2:4. 13:15-17. 22:2. 42:15. 1 K 22:19. Ps 50:7. Is 1:10. 28:14. Ho 4:1. Am 7:16. 1 Th √2:13. Re 2:29.

2. **Learn not.** Le *18:3ᴵᵐᵍℙ. *20:23ᴵᵐᵍℙ. Ex *23:2, +*13. Dt √12:30, 31. 18:14. 20:18. 22:5. Jg 6:10. 1 S 8:19, 20. 2 K 5:18. *17:15. Ps *16:4. 106:35. Pr 22:25. Is *2:6. Ezk *20:32. Jon 2:8. Mt 23:2, 3. 1 C ◑11:1. Ph ◐*4:8. **be not dismayed.** ver. +5. Dt *18:10, 14. Is +*8:12. *47:12-14. Jl 2:30, 31. Mt 24:7. Lk *21:11, 25-28.

3. **customs.** Heb. statutes, *or* ordinances, are vanity. T#143. ver. +*2, 8. Je +*2:5. *13:23. Le 18:30. Jg 11:39mg. 1 K *18:26-28. 2 K 17:15. Pr +5:22 (T#166). Mt 6:7. Mk +*7:9. Ro 1:21, 22. *7:19-24. 1 P 1:18. 1 J +1:8 (T#507). **vain.** or, a breath. Pr 21:6. Is 49:4. *57:13. Mt 6:7. Ro 1:21. **one cutteth a tree.** Not a reference to a Christmas tree, but to the manufacture of idols, such as the Asherah (Is +*66:17n). See on Is 40:19, etc. *44:9-20. 45:20. Ho 8:4-6. Hab 2:18, 19. **work of the hands.** 1 P ◐*1:18, 19.

4. **deck.** Ps 115:4. 135:15. Is 40:19, 20. **fasten.** Is *41:6, 7. 44:12. *46:7.

5. **speak not.** Ps *115:5-8. 135:16-18. Hab *2:19. 1 C *12:2. Re 13:14, 15. **be borne.** Is 46:1, 7. **not afraid.** ver. +2. Jb +*3:25. Ps 53:5. Is +*8:12. **do evil.** Is 41:23, 24. 44:9, 10. 45:20. 1 C +*8:4.

6. **none like.** Ex 8:10. *9:14. *15:11. Dt *32:31. 33:26. 2 S 7:22. 1 K 8:23. Jb 36:22, 23. Ps *35:10. 77:13, 14. 86:8-10. 89:6-8. 96:4, 5. Is 40:◑13, ◑14, 18, 25. 46:5, 9. 55:8, 9. Mt ◐+*8:27. +*28:19n. **thou.** Je 32:18. Ne 4:14. 9:32. Ps 48:1. 96:4. 145:3. 147:5. Is 12:6. Da 4:3, 34, 35. Ml 1:11, 14.

7. **would.** Je 5:22. Jb 37:23, 24. Lk 12:5. Re ▶15:4. **O King.** Ps 22:28. 72:11. 86:9. 89:6. Is 2:4. Zc 2:11. Re *11:15. ▶15:3. **to thee.** or, it liketh thee. Ps 76:7. **among.** See on ver. 6. Ps 89:6. 1 C *1:19-21.

8. **altogether.** Heb. in one, **or** at once. Nu 10:4. Dt +√6:4. Jb 33:14. Pr 28:18. Is +65:25. **brutish.** ver. 14. Je +*2:5. 51:17, 18. Ps +*115:8. 135:18. Is 41:29. Hab 2:18. Zc *10:2. Ro *1:21-23. **the stock.** Je 2:27. Is 44:19. Ho 4:12.

9. **Silver.** See on ver. 4. **Tarshish.** Ge +10:4. 1 K 10:22. Ezk 27:12. **Uphaz.** i.e. *island of gold; desire of fine gold; pure gold,* *S#210h. Je 10:9. Da *10:5. Compare Ophir, 1 K +9:28n. 2 Ch +8:18n. **are all.** Ps *115:4.

10. **the Lord.** 1 K 18:39. 2 Ch *15:3. Jn √17:3. 1 Th 1:9. 1 J *5:20. **true God.** Heb. God of truth. Dt *32:4. Ps *31:5. *100:5. *146:6. **the living.** Je *23:36. 44:26. Dt *5:26. 1 S 17:26, 36. Ps *42:2. 84:2. Is 37:4, 17. Da *6:26. Mt *16:16. *26:63. Ac *14:15. 1 T *6:17. He *10:31. **everlasting king.** Heb. king of eternity. Heb. *olam,* Ge +17:7. Ps *10:16. *90:2. *93:2. *145:13. Is *57:15. Da *4:3, 34. *7:14. 1 T *1:17. **wrath.** Is 10:5, 6. +66:14. Da 8:19. Mi 7:9. Jn +3:36. 1 Th

+5:9. Re *14:10. **tremble.** Jg 5:4. Jb 9:6. Ps *18:7. 68:11. 77:18. 97:4. 104:32. 114:7. Mi 1:4. Na *1:6. Hab 3:*6, 10. Mt *27:51, 52. Re *20:11. **the nations.** Ps *76:7. *90:11. Jl *2:11. Na *1:6. Ml *3:2. **his indignation.** Is +*26:20. +*66:14. Da +*8:19 (*S#2195h).

11. **Thus.** "In the Chaldean language." **The gods.** Ps *96:5. **they.** ver. 15. Je 51:18. Is *2:18. Zp 2:11. Zc *13:2. Re *20:2, 3. **under.** La 3:66.

12. **hath made.** Je 32:17. 51:15-19. Ge 1:1, 6-9. Jb *38:4-7. Ps *33:6. 136:5, 6. *146:5, 6. 148:4, 5. Jn √1:1-3. Col √1:16. **established.** Ps 24:2. 78:69. 93:1. 119:90. Pr 3:19. 30:4. Is 45:18. 49:8. **by his wisdom.** T#142. Ps 19:1, 2. *104:24. Pr 3:19, 20. Ro +11:33 (T#222). **stretched.** Jb 9:8. 26:7. Ps 104:2, 24. Is 40:22. 42:5. 44:24. 45:12. 48:13. Zc 12:1.

13. **uttereth.** Jb 37:2-5. 38:34, 35. Ps 18:13. 29:3-10. 68:33. **multitude.** *or,* noise. Je 3:23. 47:3 (rumbling). 51:16mg. Is 31:4mg. Ezk 7:11mg. 39:11mg. **he causeth.** 1 K 18:41, 45, 46. Jb 36:27-33. Ps *135:7. 147:8. **maketh.** Ex *9:23. 1 S *12:17, 18. Jb 38:25-27, 34, 35. Zc 10:1mg. **with.** *or,* for. **bringeth.** Jb 38:22. Ps 135:7. **treasures.** ♪22D5.O, Dt +28:2.

14. **man.** See on ver. 8. Je 51:17, 18. Ps 14:2. 92:6. 94:8. Pr 30:2. Is 44:18-20. 46:7, 8. Ro 1:22, 23. **brutish in his knowledge.** *or,* more brutish than to know. ver. 21. Je 51:17mg. Is 19:11. **founder.** Je 51:17. Ps 97:7. Is *42:17. *44:10, 11. *45:16. **falsehood.** Hab 2:18. Ro 1:25. **and.** Ps *115:4-8. 135:16-18. Hab *2:18, 19. **breath.** Heb. *ruach,* Ge +6:17.

15. **vanity.** ver. 8. Je 8:19. 14:22. 51:18. Dt 32:21. 1 S 12:21. Is *41:24, 29. Jon +*2:8. Ac *14:15. **in the.** ver. 8. Is *12:17-21. Zp 1:3, 4. Zc 13:2. **time of their visitation.** Je +*8:12.

16. **portion.** Je 51:19. Nu 18:20ᴵᵐᵍℙ. Dt *32:9ᴵᵐᵍℙ. Ps +*16:5, 6. *73:26. 119:57. 142:5. La 3:24. **former.** See on ver. 12. Pr +*16:4. Is +√45:7. **Israel.** Ex 19:5, 6. Dt 32:9. Ps 74:2. 135:4. Is 47:6. **The Lord of hosts.** Je 31:35. 32:18. 50:34. 51:19. Is +6:5. 44:6. *47:4. 51:15. *54:5. Jn 12:37-41. Ro 9:29. Ja 5:4. **is his name.** Ex +√6:3n. Ps +√9:10. +68:4. +*83:18. Is 42:8. 54:5.

17. A.M. 3404. B.C. 600. **thy wares.** Je 6:1. Ezk *12:3-12. Mi 2:10. Mt *24:15-18. Re 18:4. **inhabitant.** Heb. inhabitress. Je 21:13mg. 48:19mg. 51:35mg. Is 12:6mg. Mi 1:11mg.

18. **I will.** ♪121S4, 2 K 4:29. Je 15:1, 2. 16:13. Dt *28:63, 64. 1 S *25:29. **that.** Je 23:20. Ezk *6:10. Zc *1:6.

19. **Woe.** See on Je 4:19, 31. 8:21. 9:1. 17:13. La 1:2, *12, etc. 2:11, etc. 3:48. **Truly.** Ps *39:9. 77:10. Is 8:17. La *3:18-21, 39, 40. Mi *7:9. Ja *1:2.

20. **tabernacle.** Je 4:20. Is 54:2. La 2:4-6. **my children.** Je 31:15. Jb 7:8. Pr 12:7. Is 49:20-22. **there.** Je 4:20. Is 51:16.

21. **the pastors.** See on ver. 8, 14. Je 2:8. 5:31. *8:9. 12:10. 22:22. 23:9, etc. 25:34. √50:6. Is *9:16. *56:10-12. Ezk 22:25-30. *34:2-10. Zc 10:3. Mt +*15:14. Jn √10:12, 13. **brutish.** ver. 8, 14. Je 5:31. 51:17. Ps 94:8. Is 19:11. 44:18. **not sought.** ver. +*25. Je 2:5. ◐*8:2. 1 Ch +*28:9. 2 Ch ◐+*7:14. **not prosper.** Je 20:11. 22:30. Ps ◐*1:3. **their.** Je 9:16. *23:1. 49:32. 50:17. Ezk 34:5, 6, 12. Zc 13:7.

22. **the noise.** Je 1:15. 4:6. 5:15. 6:1, 22. Hab 1:6-9. **bruit.** Na 3:19. **Archaic** for report, rumor. **north country.** Je 1:14. 5:15. 6:22. Zc 2:6. **a den.** See on Je 9:11. Ml 1:3.

23. **I know.** Ps √17:4, 5. √37:23, 24. 119:116, 117.

Pr +*16:1. *20:24. **the way.** Pr *14:12. *16:25. Mt
√7:22, 23. **direct his steps.** Pr *16:9.
24. **correct me.** T#1457. Je 30:11. See on Ps *6:1.
38:1. Pr +*19:18. 29:17. Hab *3:2. **lest.** Je *30:11.
Jb 6:18. Is 40:23. 41:11, 12. **bring me to nothing.** Heb.
diminish me. Ex 30:15mg. Le 25:16. Ezk 5:11.
25. **Pour out.** Je 6:6. Jg 6:20. See on Ps ⟩79:6, 7.
Jn +*17:9. 2 Th 1:6-8. For other instances of imprecatory prayer see: Je 11:20. 12:3. 15:15. 17:18. 18:21-
23. 20:12. Nu 16:15. Dt 33:11. Jsh 8:33, 34. Jg 16:28.
1 S 26:19. Ne 4:4, 5. 5:13. Jb 27:7. Ps 5:10. 6:10.
9:20. 10:2, 15. 28:4. 31:17, 18. 35:4, 8◑n, 9, 26.
40:14◑n, 15. 54:5. 55:9, 15. 56:7. 58:7. 59:5, 11, 15.
68:1, 2. 69:22◑n, 23, 24, 27, 28. 70:2, 3. 71:13◑n.
79:10, 12. 83:13-17. 94:2. 109:6◑n, 7, 9-20, 28, 29.
119:78, 84. 129:5. 140:9, 10. 143:12. 144:6. La 1:22.
3:64-66. Ga 1:8, 9. 1 C 16:22. 2 T 4:14. Re 6:10. **that
know thee not.** Jb 18:21. Jn 17:25. Ac 17:23. 1 C 15:34.
1 Th 4:5. 2 Th √1:8. **call not.** T#548. ver. 21. Ge
+6:6 (T#230). Jsh +*9:14 (T#1820). Jb *15:4. √21:15.
+27:10 (T#547). Ps *10:4. *14:4. *53:4. *79:6. Is
*43:22. *64:7. 65:1. *66:4. Da 9:13. Ho *7:7. Jon 1:6.
Zp *1:6. Ja √4:2. **thy name.** ∫144A4, Ge +4:26. ∫121T1,
Dt +28:58. **eaten.** Je 8:16. 50:7, 17. 51:34, 35. Ps
27:2. La 2:22. Ezk 25:6-8. 35:5-10. Ob 10-16. Zc 1:15.

JEREMIAH 11

*The prophet is sent to proclaim the covenant of God,
and to reprove the Jews for breaking it, 1-10. He denounces vengeance against them, 11-17; and against
the men of Anathoth, who devised his death, 18-23.*

2. A.M. 3406. B.C. 598. **the words.** ver. 6. Je 34:13-
16. Ex *19:5. 2 K *11:17. √23:2, 3. 2 Ch 23:16. 29:10.
34:31.
3. **the Lord God of Israel.** Je 13:12. 21:4. 23:2.
24:5. 25:15. 30:2. 32:36. 33:4. 34:2, 13. 37:7. 42:9.
45:2. **Cursed be.** Je +*10:25. Dt *27:26⟩𝒫. *28:15,
etc. 29:19, 20. Jsh *24:19-22. Ga *3:10-13.
4. **I commanded.** Je 31:32. Ex 24:3-8. Dt 5:2, 3.
29:10-15. Ezk 20:6-12. He 8:8-10. **in the day.** ∫171T2,
Ge +2:17. **iron.** Dt 4:20⟩𝒫. 1 K *8:51. Is 48:10. **Obey.**
See on Je 7:22, 23. 26:13. Ex 15:26⟩𝒫. 20:6. 23:21,
22. Le 26:3, 12. Dt 11:27. 28:1, etc. 1 S √15:22. Zc
6:15. Mt *28:20. He √5:8, 9. **ye be.** Je 24:7. 30:22.
31:31, 33. 32:28. Ge 17:8. Le 26:12. Ezk 11:20. 14:11.
36:28. 37:23, 27. Zc 8:8. 13:9. 2 C 6:16. He *8:9, 10.
I will be. Le 26:3-12⟩𝒫.
5. **perform.** Ge *22:16-18. 26:3-5. Ps *105:9-11. Ac
+*7:2-5. **the oath.** Dt 7:12⟩𝒫. **a land.** Je 32:22. See
on Ex 3:8, 17⟩𝒫. 13:5⟩𝒫. Le 20:24⟩𝒫. Nu 13:27⟩𝒫.
14:8⟩𝒫. 16:13, 14⟩𝒫. Dt 6:3⟩𝒫. 7:12, 13. 11:9⟩𝒫. 26:9,
15⟩𝒫. 27:3⟩𝒫. 31:20⟩𝒫. Jsh 5:6. Ezk 20:6, 15. **milk
and.** ∫174, Ge +18:27. **honey.** ∫171I7, Ex +3:8. **So
be it.** Heb. Amen. lit. steadfast. ✱S#543h. Je 28:6.
Nu 5:22. Dt 27:15, 16, 17, 18, 19, 20, 21, 22, 23, 24,
25, 26⟩𝒫. 1 K 1:36. 1 Ch 16:36. Ne 5:13. 8:6. Ps 41:13.
72:19. 89:52. 106:48. Is 65:16, 16 (truth). Mt 6:13.
Lk 10:21. 1 C 14:16. Re 7:12.
6. **Proclaim.** Je 3:12. 7:2. 19:2. Is *58:1. Zc 7:7.
Hear. See on ver. 2-4. Ps 15:5. Jn +*13:17. Ro *2:13.
Ja √1:22.
7. **I earnestly.** 1 S 8:9. Ep 4:17. 2 Th 3:12. **in the
day.** See on Je 7:13, 23-25. 25:4. 35:15. Ex *15:26.
23:21, 22. Dt 4:6. 5:29. 6:2. 8:6. 10:12, 13. 11:26-28.
12:32. 28:1, etc. 30:20.

8. **obeyed.** Je 3:17. 6:16, 17. 7:24, 26. 9:13, 14.
35:15. 44:17. Ne *9:16, 17, 26, 29. Ezk *20:8, 9, 18-
21. Zc *7:11, 12. **imagination.** *or,* stubbornness. Je
+3:17mg. 7:24mg. **therefore.** Le 26:16, etc. Dt 28:15,
etc. 29:21-24. 30:17-19. 31:17, 18. 32:20-26. Jsh 23:13-
16. Ezk 20:37, 38.
9. **A conspiracy.** Je 5:31. 6:13. 8:10. 2 K +11:14.
Ezk *22:25-31. Ho 6:9. Mi 3:11. 7:2, 3. Zp 3:1-4. Mt
*21:38, 39. *26:3, 4, 15. Jn *11:53. Ac *23:12-15.
10. **turned.** Je 3:10. 1 S *15:11. 2 Ch 34:30-33. Ho
*6:4. 7:16. Zp 1:6. **iniquities.** Jg *2:17, 19. Ps 78:8-
10, 57, 58. Ezk 20:18-21. Zc *1:4. Ac *7:51, 52. **the
house of Israel.** See on Je 3:6-11. 31:32. Le 26:15.
Dt 31:16. 2 K 17:7-20. Ezk 16:59. 44:7. Ho 6:7. 8:1.
He 8:9.
11. **I will bring.** ver. 17. Je 6:19. 19:3, 15. 23:12.
35:17. 36:31. 2 K *22:16. 2 Ch *34:24. Ezk *7:4, 5.
which. Je 15:2, 3. Pr √29:1. Is *24:17. Am 2:14, 15.
5:19. 9:1-4. 1 Th *5:3. He 1:3. Re 6:16, 17. **escape.**
Heb. go forth of. Je 29:2. 38:17, 21. Ge 8:7mg. 1 S
14:41. Ezk 26:18. Lk +*21:36. **cry.** Je 14:12. Ps 18:41.
+*66:18. Pr *1:28. Is *1:15. Ezk *8:18. Mi 3:4. Zc
7:13. Lk √13:24-28. Jn +*9:31.
12. **go.** See on Je 2:28. 44:17-27. Dt *32:37, 38⟩𝒫.
Jg *10:14. 2 Ch 28:22, 23. Is 45:20. **trouble.** Heb.
evil. ver. 8, 11, 14. Is +*45:7.
13. **For according.** Je 2:28. 3:1, 2. Dt 32:16, 17.
2 K √23:4, 5, 13. Is *2:8. Ho *12:11. **set up altars.**
Je 19:5. 32:35. 2 K *21:4, 5. **shameful thing.** Heb.
shame. ∫121G1, Ge +31:1. "Shame" is put for an idol
or for idolatry. Je 2:26. 3:24. 48:13. Nu 25:1-3. Jg 6:32.
Is 66:17n. Ho 9:10.
14. **pray not.** See on Je 7:16. 14:11. 15:1. Ex
*32:10⟩𝒫. Pr 26:24, 25. 1 J +√5:16. **for.** See on ver.
11. Ps +*66:18. Ho 5:6. **trouble.** Heb. evil. ver. 11.
Is +*45:7.
15. **What,** etc. ∫60A, Ge +3:22. Heb. What is to
my beloved in my house? Lk 8:28g. **my beloved.** ∫27,
Ge +3:22. Je 2:2. 3:14. 12:7. Ho 3:1. Mt *22:11, 12.
Ro 11:28. **to do.** Je 3:8. 7:8-11. 15:1. Ps 50:16. Pr
15:8. 21:27. 28:9. Is *1:11-15. 50:1. **seeing.** Je 3:1, 2.
Ezk +*16:25, etc. 23:2, etc. **the holy flesh.** Je 7:21.
Hg *2:12-14. T *1:15. **thou doest evil.** *or,* thy evil *is.*
Pr *2:14. 10:23. 26:18, 19. Ro *1:32. 1 C *13:6. Ja
*4:16.
16. **A green.** Ps *52:8. Ro *11:17-26. **with.** Ps 80:16.
Is 1:30, 31. *27:11. Ezk 15:4-7. *20:47, 48. Mt *3:10.
Jn +*15:6.
17. **the Lord of hosts.** Je +6:6. **that planted.** See
on Je 2:21. 12:2. 24:6. 42:10. 45:4. 2 S +√7:10. Ps
44:2. *80:8, 15. Is *5:1, 2. 61:3. Ezk 17:5. **pronounced.**
See on ver. 11. Je 16:10, 11. 18:8. 19:15. 26:13, 19.
35:17. 36:7. 40:2. **to provoke.** Je 7:18.
18. **the Lord.** ver. 19. 1 S *23:11, 12. 2 K 6:9, 10,
14-20. Ezk 8:6, etc. Mt *2:13. Ac *27:23, 24. Ro 3:7.
hath given me knowledge. ∫38B, 2 S +1:24. Is=11:2.
Jn +=2:25.
19. **I was.** Pr 7:22. Is=53:7, 8. **and I.** Je 18:18.
20:10. Ps 31:13. *35:15. 37:32, 33. Is 32:7. Mt *26:3,
4. **saying.** ∫63BA, Ge +26:7. Je 50:5. **destroy.** "Let
us kill the prophet and burn his prophecies." **tree
with the fruit.** Heb. stalk with his bread. or, dish in
his food. ∫100, Ge +10:9. i.e. the food in his dish.
let us cut. Ps *83:4. Is=*53:8, ◑=10. Da √9:26. Lk
*20:10-15. **from.** Jb 28:13. Ps *27:13. 52:5. 116:9. 142:5.
that his name. Ps √109:13. 112:6. Pr 10:7. Is 38:11.

Na 1:14. **no more remembered.** Jb 24:20. Ezk 21:32.

20. judgest righteously. Je 12:1. Ge +*18:25. Ps *98:9. Ac √17:31. **triest.** *22, Ge +3:9. Je √17:10. 20:12. 1 S √16:7. 1 Ch +*28:9. 29:17. Ps *7:9. 26:2. Is ☾=53:11. Re √2:23. **reins.** *12I1, Ge +3:7. **let.** Je +*10:25. 15:15. 17:18. 18:20-23. 2 T √4:14. Re 6:9, 10. *18:20. **see.** Dt +32:43. Ps *58:10. Is +*66:24. **revealed.** 1 S *24:9, 15. Jb 5:8. Ps 10:14, 15. 35:1. 43:1. 57:1. Ph *4:6. 1 P *2:23.

21. that seek. Je 12:5, 6. 20:10. Mi 7:6. Mt 10:21, 34-36. 13:57. Lk 4:24. **life.** Heb. *nephesh*, soul, Ge +44:30. **Prophesy not.** Is *30:9, 10. Am 2:12. 7:13-16. Mi 2:6, 11. **thou.** Je 20:1, 2. 38:1-6. Mt 21:35. 22:6. *23:34-37. Lk 13:33, 34. Ac 7:51, 52.

22. punish. Heb. visit upon. S#6485h. Je 9:25mg. 13:21mg. 23:2. 25:12mg. 29:32. 44:29. 46:25. 50:18. Ex +20:5n. +32:34. 34:7. Nu 14:18. Dt 5:9. Am 3:2mg. Zc 10:3mg. Young renders, "seeing after," commenting "not 'punish,' as in C.V. (A.V.)." **young.** Je 9:21. 18:21. 2 Ch ✱*36:17. La *2:21. 1 Th √2:15, 16.

23. no. ver. 19. Je 44:27. Is 14:20-22. **the year.** *171T1, Is +61:2. Je 5:9, 29. +*8:12. 23:12. 46:21. 48:44. 50:27. Ho 9:7. Mi 7:4. Lk *19:43, 44.

JEREMIAH 12

The prophet pleads with God concerning the prosperity of the wicked; appeals to him for his integrity; and prays that they, for whose sins the land was visited, might be selected for punishment, 1-4. God reproves his impatience, warns him to expect heavier trials, describes the wickedness of the people, and denounces sentence against them, 5-13. A prophecy of heavy judgments on the oppressors of the Jews, who would be restored to their own land; and of the calling of the Gentiles; the privileges of the obedient, and the destruction of the disobedient, 14-17.

1. Righteous. *169. Synchoresis; or, Concession B970: making a concession of one point in order to gain another. The figure Synchoresis is used when we make a *concession* of one point in order to gain another. In this case the concession or admission is made, and may be rightly made, in order to gain a point. *Synchoresis* thus differs from *Epitrope* (*83, 1 K 22:15), where we admit something that is wrong in itself for the sake of argument. Synchoresis, therefore, is *concession*, while Epitrope is *admission* or *surrender*. For other instances of this figure see Hab *1:13. Ro 2:17-20. 1 C 4:8. 2 C 10:1. 12:16. Ga 4:15. Ja *2:19. **art thou.** Je 11:20. Ge +*18:25. Dt 32:4. Ezr *9:15. Ps 51:4. 119:75, 137. *145:17. La 1:18. Da 9:7. Hab √1:13-17. Zp 3:5. Ro 3:5, 6. **talk.** *or,* reason the case. Je 39:5mg. Jb 13:3. Ps 127:5mg. Is 41:21. **Wherefore doth.** Je 5:28. Jb 12:6. 21:7-15. Ps *37:1, 35. *73:3-5, 7. *92:7. 94:3, 4. Pr 1:32. Hab 1:4. Ml 3:15. **deal.** ver. 6. Je 5:11. Is 48:8. Ho 6:7.

2. hast. See on Je 11:17. 45:4. Ezk *17:5-10. 19:10-13. **grow.** Heb. go on. **near.** Is √29:13. Ezk 33:31. Mt *15:8. Mk *7:6. T *1:16. **reins.** *12I1, Ge +3:7.

3. knowest. Je 11:20. 2 K +*20:3. 1 Ch 29:17. Jb *23:10. Ps *17:3. 26:1. 44:21. *139:1, 23. Jn *21:17. 1 J *3:20, 21. **toward.** *or,* with. **pull.** Je 17:18. 18:21-23. 20:12. 48:15. 50:27. 51:4. **prepare.** or, sanctify. Je 6:4. *108B. Idiom B831. "To sanctify" often means to make ceremonially clean. It means to *set apart*, fit, or prepare for a particular purpose. For other in-

stances of this idiom see Is 8:13. Mt 6:9. 1 C 7:14. 1 P 3:15. **the day.** Je 11:19. Ps 44:22. Ja *5:5.

4. long. Je 9:10. 14:2. 23:10. **mourn.** *155D, Ge +4:10. **the herbs.** Ps *107:33, 34. Jl *1:10-17. **the beasts.** Je 4:25. 7:20. Ho *4:3. Hab 3:17. Ro *8:22. **He.** Je 5:13, 31. Ps 50:21. Ezk 7:2-13.

5. if. Heb. 12:1. **thou hast.** Pr *3:11. *24:10. He *12:3, 4. 1 P *4:12-14. **canst.** Je 26:8. 36:26. *38:4-6. **then how wilt.** Mt *7:14-23. 25:14-30, 34-40. Lk *16:10. Ro *8:18. 1 C 2:9. 3:13-15. 9:24-27. He *6:11, 12, 18. 2 P *3:14. **swelling.** Je 49:19. 50:44. Jsh *3:15n. 1 Ch 12:15. Jb 41:34. Ps 42:7. *69:1, 2. Zc *11:3.

6. thy brethren. Je 9:4. 11:19, 21. 20:10. Ge 37:4-11. Jb *6:15. Ps +*69:8, 9. Ezk 33:30, 31. Mi 7:5, 6. Mt *10:21. Mk 13:12. Jn *7:5. **yea.** Is 31:4. Ac 16:22. 18:12. 19:24-29. 21:28-30. **have called,** etc. *or,* cried after thee fully. **believe them not.** Ro *3:13. **though.** Ps *12:2. Pr 26:25. Mt *22:16-18. **fair words.** Heb. good things. 2 K 25:28mg.

7. have forsaken. Je 11:15. 51:5. Is 2:6. Ps *78:59, 60. Ho 9:15. Jl 2:17. 3:2. **house.** *121.O, Ge +28:22. **I have given.** Je 7:14. La 2:1, etc. Ezk *7:20, 21. 24:21. Lk *21:24. **dearly beloved.** Heb. love. *121R4, Je +2:33. **soul.** Heb. *nephesh*, Ge +34:3.

8. crieth out. *or,* yelleth. Heb. giveth out his voice. Je 2:15. 51:38. **therefore.** Ho 9:15. Am *6:8. Zc *11:8.

9. Mine. Or rather, as the learned Bochart renders, "Is then my heritage (people) to me as a fierce hyena? Is there a wild beast all around upon her?" i.e. the land of Canaan. The *hyena* is a kind of wolf, a little bigger than a mastiff; color grey, streaked with black: it is of a solitary and savage disposition. **speckled bird.** *or,* a bird having talons. **the birds.** Je 2:15. 2 K 24:2. Ezk 16:36, 37. 23:22-25. Re *17:16, 17. **come ye.** Je 7:33. Is *56:9. Ezk *39:17-20. Re *19:17, 18. **come.** *or,* cause them to come. Is 21:14mg.

10. pastors. See on Je 6:3. 25:9. 39:3. **my vineyard.** Ps *80:8-16. Is *5:1-7. Na 2:2. Lk *20:9-16. **trodden.** Is *43:28. *63:18. La 1:10, 11. Lk 21:14. Re *11:1, 2. **pleasant portion.** Heb. portion of desire. See on Je 3:19mg.

11. made it. Je 6:8. 9:11. 10:22, 25. 19:8. **it mourneth.** See on ver. 4-8. Je 14:2. 23:10. La ch. 1-5. Zc *7:5. **layeth.** Ec 7:2. Is 42:25. 57:1. Ml *2:2.

12. spoilers. See on Je 4:11-15. 9:19-21. **the sword.** Je 15:2. 34:17. 47:6. 48:2. Le 26:33. Is 34:6. 66:15, 16. Ezk 5:2. 14:17. Am 9:4. Zp 2:12. Ep 6:17. He 4:12. Re 1:16. 2:16. 19:16-21. **no.** Is *57:21. Mt 24:21, 22. Re *6:4.

13. sown. Le 26:16. Dt 28:38. Mi 6:15. Hg 1:6. 2:16, 17. **shall reap.** Nu +*32:23. **put.** See on Je 3:23-25. Is 30:1-6. 31:1-3. *55:2. Hab *2:13. Ro *6:21. **they.** *or,* ye.

14. A.M. 3401. B.C. 603. against. Je 48:26, 27. 50:9-17. 51:33-35. Ezk *25:3-15. Am 1:2-15. Zp 2:8-10. **that touch.** *108B, Ge +26:29. Je 2:3. 49:1, 7. Ps *105:14, 15. Ob 10-16. Zc *1:15. *2:8. 12:2-4. **to inherit.** Je 3:18. Ex 32:13⑨. **I will.** Je ch. 48-51. Ezk ch. 25-32, 35. **and pluck.** Je 3:18. 32:37. Dt *30:3. Ps 106:47. Is *11:11-16. Ezk 28:25. 34:12, 13. 36:24. 37:21. *39:27, 28. Ho 1:11. Am √9:14, 15. Zp *3:19, 20. Zc 10:6-12. 2 C *3:15, 16.

15. after. Je 48:47. 49:6, 39. Dt 30:3. Is 23:17, 18. Mi *7:19. **heritage.** Je 48:47. 49:6, 39. Nu 32:18. Dt 3:20.

16. if. Je +7:5. **my name.** See on Je 4:2. 5:2. Dt

*10:20, 21. SS 1:8. Is 9:18-22. 45:23. 65:16. Ro 14:11. **as they.** Jsh 23:7. Ps 106:35, 36. Zp 1:5. **built.** Is 19:23-25. 56:5, 6. Zc *2:11. Ro 11:17. 1 C 3:9. Ep 2:19-22. 1 P 2:4-6.

17. **if.** Je +7:5. Ps *2:8-12. Is *60:12. Zc *14:16-19. Lk *19:27. 2 Th √1:8. 1 P 2:6-8. **pluck.** ver. 14-17. Je 18:7. 31:28. Ezk 19:12. Da 7:4-8. 11:4.

JEREMIAH 13

The prophet, by the sign of a linen girdle, first worn by him, and then buried and spoiled near Euphrates, and by the simile of bottles filled with wine, predicts the approaching captivity, and the miseries attending it, 1-14. He calls the king, the rulers, and the people to repentance; and mourns over their pride, and in the prospect of their calamities, 15-21. He expostulates with them, concerning their incorrigible obstinacy, 22-27.

1. A.M. 3405. B.C. 599. **Go.** ver. 11. Je 19:1. 27:2. Ezk 4:1, etc. 5:1, etc. He *1:1, 2.

2. **according.** Pr *3:5. Is 20:2. Ezk *2:8. Ho 1:2, 3. Jn *13:6, 7. +*15:14.

3. **the word.** ver. 3, 8. **second time.** Ge +41:32.

4. **go.** Intending to point out, by this distant place, the country, Chaldea, into which they were to be carried captive. Je 51:63, 64. Ps *137:1. Mi *4:10.

5. **as.** Ex 39:42, 43. *40:16. Mt 21:2-6. Jn 2:5-8. Ac 26:19, 20. 2 T 2:3. He *11:8, 17-19.

6. **Arise.** See on ver. 2-5.

7. **it was.** ver. 10. Je 24:1-8. Is √64:6. Ezk 15:3-5. Zc 3:3, 4. Lk 14:34, 35. Ro *3:12. Phm *11.

9. **After.** Je 18:4-6. La 5:5-8. **the pride.** ver. 15-17. Le 26:19)꜠. Jb 40:10-12. Pr *16:18. Is *2:10-17. *23:9. Ezk 16:50, 56. Na *2:2mg. Zp 3:11. Lk √18:14. Ja √4:6. 1 P *5:5. **the great.** Je 48:29. Is 16:6.

10. **evil.** Je 5:23. 7:25-28. 8:5. 11:7, 18. 15:1. 25:3-7. 34:14-17. Nu 14:11. 2 Ch 36:15, 16. He *12:25. **walk.** Je 7:24. 9:14. 11:8. 16:12. Ec 11:9. Ep 4:17-19. **imagination.** *or,* stubbornness. See on Je +3:17mg. Ps 78:8. Ac 7:51. **shall.** See on ver. 7. Je 15:1-4. 16:4. Is 3:24.

11. **I caused.** Ex *19:5, 6)꜠. Dt *4:7. 26:18. 32:10-15. Ps *135:4. *147:20. **for a name.** Je 33:9. Is *43:21. 55:13. +*62:12. 1 P *2:9. **but.** ver. 10. Je 6:17. Ps 81:11. Jn 5:37-40.

12. **Every bottle.** or, jar. ❋S#5035h. Je 48:12. 1 S 1:24. 10:3. 25:18꜠n. 2 S 16:1. Jb 38:37. Is *30:14mg. La *4:2 (pitchers). Here, not wineskins, leathern or skin bottles, but earthenware jars (according to CB and Vine, *Expository Dictionary of Old Testament Words,* pg 37, 38). Jsh ꜠9:4n. **shall be filled.** Je 25:15. Ge 6:11. **and they shall.** Ezk 11:2, 3. *24:19.

13. **I will.** Je 25:15-18, 27. 51:7. Ps *60:3. *75:8. Is 29:9. 49:26. 51:17, 21. 63:6. Hab 2:16. **with drunkenness.** Ezk 23:33. 39:19.

14. **I will dash.** Je 19:9-11. 48:12. Jg 7:20-22. 1 S *14:16. 2 Ch 20:23. Ps +√2:9. Is *9:20, 21. **one against another.** Heb. a man against his brother. 1 S 10:11mg. **even.** See on Je 6:21. 47:3. Ezk *5:10. Mt *10:21. Mk *13:12. **I will not.** Je 21:7. Dt 29:20. Is 27:11. Ezk 5:11. 7:4, 9. 8:18. 9:5, 10. 24:14. **but destroy.** Heb. from destroying. Je 15:3. 51:11.

15. **and.** Is *42:23. Jl *1:2. Re *2:29. **be.** Is *28:14-22. Ja *4:10. **for.** Je *26:15. Am 7:15. Ac *4:19, 20.

16. **Give.** Jsh 7:19. 1 S 6:5. Ps 96:7, 8. 1 T +1:17.

before. Je 4:23. Ec 11:8. 12:1, 2. Is 5:30. 8:22. 59:9. Am 8:9, 10. Jn √12:35. **cause.** Am +*3:6. 5:8. **darkness.** Pr +*20:20. **your.** Pr +*4:19. 1 P *2:7, 8. 1 J *2:8-11. **while.** Je 8:15. 14:19. Is 59:9. La 4:17. **the shadow.** Ps 44:19. **gross darkness.** Ex 10:21. Is +*60:2. Mt +*6:23. +*8:12.

17. **if.** Je 22:5. Ml 2:2. **my soul.** Heb. *nephesh,* Ge +34:3. Je 9:1. 14:17. 17:16. 1 S 15:11, 35. Ps *119:136. La *1:2, 16. 2:18. Lk 19:41, 42. Ro 9:2-4. **weep.** ♪174, Ge +27:44. **pride.** See on ver. 15. Jb 33:17. Ps +*119:21. **mine eye.** Je 9:1. **run down.** Mt=26:38. Lk=19:41. =22:41, 44, 45. **because.** ver. 19, 20. Ps 80:1. Is 63:11. Ezk *34:31. 36:38.

18. **unto.** Je 22:26. 2 K √24:12, 15. Ezk 19:2, etc. Jon 3:6. **Humble.** Ex 10:3. 2 Ch 33:12, 19, 23. Mt 18:4. Ja *4:10. 1 P *5:6. **sit.** Is 3:26. 47:1. La 2:10. **principalities.** *or,* head tires. lit. first estates. ❋S#4761h, only here. Compare S#7218h, Jsh 11:10. 19:51. 22:21, 30. 2 S 23:8, 13, 18. 1 K 21:9mg. 2 K *9:30. Ezk 24:23.

19. **cities.** Je 17:26. 33:13. Dt *28:52. Jsh 18:5. Ezk 20:46, 47. **south.** ♪171.O.7, Da +11:5. Ge 12:9. 13:1, 3. Dt 1:7. Ps 126:4. Is +*30:6. **shut.** Dt 28:52. Jb 12:14. **Judah.** Je 39:9. 52:27. Le 26:31-33. Dt *28:15, 64-68. 2 K *25:21.

20. **Lift.** ♪144A12, Ge +22:13. **and.** Je 1:14. 6:22. 10:22. Hab 1:6. **north.** Je 1:13. 3:12. 6:1. ♪171.O.9. Synecdoche of the Whole B639. The "north" is put for *Chaldea* and its chief city *Babylon,* because all armies from beyond the Euphrates crossed high up and entered Palestine from the North. For other instances of this figure see Je 1:13-15. 47:2. Zp 2:13. **where.** ver. 17. Je 23:2. Is 56:9-12. Ezk *34:7-10. Zc *11:16, 17. Jn *10:12, 13. Ac *20:26-29.

21. **wilt.** Je 5:31. 22:23. Is 10:3. Ezk 28:9. **punish.** Heb. visit upon. Je +11:22mg. **for.** 2 K 16:7. Is 39:2-4. **shall not.** Je 4:31. 6:24. +√30:6, 7. 48:41. Is 13:8. 21:3. 1 Th +*5:3.

22. **if.** Dt 7:17. 8:17. 18:21. Is 47:8. Zp 1:12. Lk 5:21, 22. **Wherefore.** See on Je 5:19. 16:10, 11. **the greatness.** See on Je 2:17-19. 9:2-9. Ho 12:8. **skirts.** ver. 26. Is 3:17. 20:4. 47:2, 3. La *1:8. Ezk 16:37-39. 23:26-29. Ho 2:3, 10. Na 3:5, 6. Re *3:18. **heels.** Ge 3:15. Ro 16:20. **made bare.** *or,* shall be violently taken away. La 2:6. Mt 11:12.

23. **Can.** ♪138C, Ge +22:14. ♪85R, Jb +4:17. **Ethiopian.** i.e. *descendants of Cush,* ✛S#3569h. Je 38:7, 10, 12. 39:16. Nu +*12:1, Jn 2 Ch 14:9. **change his skin.** Je 2:*22, 30. 5:3. 6:29, 30. √17:9. Pr *27:22. Is *1:5. Mt *19:24-28. **then may.** Jb 14:4. Mt 7:16-18. 12:33. Jn 6:44, 65. Ro 11:35, 36. 1 C √2:14. 4:7. 2 C 3:5. **accustomed.** Heb. taught. Je 2:24mg. 9:5. Is +*8:16.

24. **will.** Le 26:33. Dt 4:27. 28:64. *32:26. Ezk 5:2, 12. *6:8. 17:21. Lk *21:24. **as.** Je 4:11, 12. Ps √1:4. 83:13-15. Is 17:13. 41:16. Ho *13:3. Zp 2:2.

25. **thy lot.** Le 16:8-10. Nu 26:55. Jb 20:29. Ps 11:6. Is 17:4. Mt 24:51. **because.** See on Je 2:13, 32. Dt 32:16-18. Ps +*9:17. 106:21, 22. **trusted.** See on Je 7:4-8. 10:14. Dt *32:37, 38. Is 28:15. Mi 3:11. Hab 2:18, 19.

26. **I discover.** See on ver. 22. La 1:8. Ezk 16:37. 23:29. Ho 2:10.

27. **thine adulteries.** Je 2:20-24. 3:1, 2. 5:7, 8. Ezk 16:15, etc. 23:2, etc. Ho 1:2. *4:2. 2 C 12:21. Ja *4:4. **neighings.** Je 5:8. 8:16. **lewdness.** Je 11:15. **abomina-**

tions. See on Je 2:20. 3:2, 6. Is 57:7. *65:7. Ezk 6:13. 20:28. **Woe.** Je 4:13. Ezk 2:10. 24:6. Zp 3:1. Mt *11:21. Re *8:13. **wilt.** Je 4:14. Ps 94:4, 8. Ezk 24:13. *36:25, 37. Lk √11:9-13. 2 C *7:1. **when,** etc. Heb. after when yet? **shall.** Pr 1:22. Ho 8:5.

JEREMIAH 14

A terrible famine in Judah, 1-6. The prophet calls on God to deliver the people, though deeply guilty, for his own name's sake, 7-9. The Lord shows him their wickedness, and forbids him to pray for them, 10-12. The prophet charges the blame on the false prophets, and the Lord includes them also in the threatened vengeance, 13-16. The prophet is ordered to mourn over his people; and he perseveres in interceding for them, 17-22.

1. A.M. 3399. B.C. 605. **The word.** ✸101, Dt +32:42. This discourse is supposed to have been delivered after the fourth year of Jehoiakim. The Hebrew *batzaroth*, rendered *dearth*, signifies *restraint*, that is, "when the heaven is shut up that there is no rain;" which Houbigant thinks happened early in the reign of Zedekiah. **the dearth.** Heb. the words of the dearths, *or* restraints. ✸121C1L. Metonymy of the Cause. The holding back of rain is put for the famine caused by it. Je 17:8mg.

2. **mourneth.** See on Je 4:28. 12:4. Is 3:26. Ho 4:3. Jl 1:10, 12. **the gates.** Is 24:4, 7. 33:9. Ge +*14:7. **they.** Je 8:21. La 2:9. 4:8, 9. 5:10. Jl 2:6. **are black.** or, sit in black. Je 8:21. 13:18. Jb 2:8, 13. Ps 35:14. Is 3:26. 15:3. **the cry.** Je 11:11. 18:22. 46:12. Ex +*2:24. 1 S 5:12. 9:16. Jb 34:28. Ps 144:14. Is 5:7. 15:5. Zc 7:13.

3. **their nobles.** 1 K *18:5, 6. **pits.** Je 2:13. 1 K 17:7. 2 K 18:31. Ps *63:1. Jl 1:20. Am *4:8. or, cisterns. ✸S#1356h. 1 K 6:9 (beams). 2 K 3:16. Is 10:31 (Gebim, or, the ditches, ✸S#1374h). **they were.** Je 2:26, 27. 20:11. Ps 40:14. *109:29. Is 45:16, 17. **covered.** ver. 4. 2 S 15:30. 19:4. Est 6:12.

4. **the ground.** Le 26:19, 20. Dt *28:23, 24. 29:23. Jl 1:19, 20. **the plowmen.** Jl 1:11, 17. **ashamed.** Jb 29:23. **they covered.** ✸121S3F2, 2 S +15:30.

5. **the hind.** Jb *39:1-5. Ps 29:9. **forsook.** ✸96B, Ge +8:5.

6. **the wild.** Je 2:24. Jb 39:5, 6. **they.** They sucked in the air, for want of water, to cool their internal heat. **their.** 1 S 14:29. La *4:17. 5:17. Jl *1:18.

7. **though.** Is 59:12. Ho 5:5. 7:10. **testify.** ✸155F, Ge +4:7. **do.** ver. 20, 21. Dt 32:27. Jsh 7:9. Ps *25:11. *115:1, 2. Ezk *20:9, 14, 22. Da 9:9, 18, 19. Ep 1:6, 12. **for our backslidings.** T#1311. See on Je 2:19. 3:6. 5:6. Ezr 9:6, 7, 15. Ne 9:33, 34. Ps 51:7, 12. Ps +119:176 (T#1437). Da 9:5-16.

8. **the hope.** ✸121R3, Ps +71:5. Je 17:13. 50:7. Jl 3:16. Ac 28:20. 1 T 1:1. **savior.** Is *43:3, 11. 45:15, 21. **in time.** Ps 9:9. 37:39, 40. 46:1. *50:15. 91:15. 138:7. 2 C *1:4, 5. **why.** Ps 10:1. **stranger.** Je 7:6. 22:3. Ge +*23:4 (✸S#1616h). **a wayfaring.** Jg 19:17. **tarry.** Lk *24:28, 29.

9. **cannot.** Nu 11:23. 14:15, 16. Ps 44:23-26. Is *50:1, 2. 51:9. *59:1. **in the midst.** Ex 29:45, 46✸𝒫. Le 26:11, 12✸𝒫. Dt 23:14. Ps 46:5. *84:1. Is 12:6. Zc 2:5. 2 C *6:16. Re *21:3. **we are called by thy name.** Heb. thy name is called upon us. Je 7:10mg, 11. √15:16mg. 25:29mg. Is 63:19mg. 65:1. Da 9:18mg, 19. Am 9:12mg.

leave. 1 S +*12:22. Ps 27:9. 119:121. He +*13:5.

10. **have they.** See on Je 2:23-25, 36. 3:1, 2. 8:5. Ho 11:7, 9. **wander.** T#1798. ver. +11. Je 50:6. Jg 9:9, 11, 13. Ps 119:176. Pr 21:16. 27:8. Is *53:6. La 4:14. Ezk 34:6. 1 T 1:6. 1 P 2:25. 2 P 2:15. Ju 13. **refrained.** Je 2:25. Ps 119:101. **the Lord.** Je 6:20. Is *1:13, 14. Am *5:21, 22. Ml 1:8-13. **he will.** Je 31:34. 44:21, 22. 1 S 15:2. 1 K 17:18. Ps 109:14, 15. Ho 8:13. 9:9. He 8:12.

11. **Pray not.** See on Je +*7:16. 11:14. 15:1. Ex 32:10✸𝒫, *31-34.

12. **they fast.** Je 11:11. Pr *1:28. *28:9. Is *1:15. √58:3. **not hear.** Je +7:16. 11:14. Am 5:23. Zc 7:13. **and when.** Je 6:20. 7:21, 22. Pr 15:8. 21:27. Is 1:11-15. **burnt offering.** Le +*23:12. **not accept.** Ezk *8:18. Mi *3:4. **but.** See on Je 9:16. 15:2, 3. 16:4. 21:7-9. 24:10. 29:17, 18. Ezk 5:12-17. 14:21. **sword.** ✸121B, Ex +5:3. Je 21:6, 7, 9. 24:10. 42:22. Le 26:6, 25, 33, 36✸𝒫. Dt 28:22✸𝒫.

13. **Ah.** See on Je 1:6. 4:10. **behold.** Je 5:31. 6:14. 8:11. 23:17. 28:2-5. Ezk *13:10-16, 22. Mi 3:11. 2 P *2:1-3. **sword.** ✸121B, Ex +5:3. **assured peace.** Heb. peace of truth. Je 4:10. 23:17.

14. **The prophets.** Je 23:25, 26. 27:10, 14. 28:13. 29:21. 37:19. Dt √18:20-22. Pr +4:18n. Is 9:15. Zc 13:3. 1 T √4:1-3. Re *13:13-15. **I sent.** Je 23:14-16, 21-32. 27:15. 28:15. 29:8, 9, 31. Is 30:10, 11. 2 Th √2:9-11. **false vision.** There are several marks of false cults. False cults typically: (1) Appeal to the wrong basis of authority, Is +*8:20n. (2) Make exclusive claim to the truth, Pr +*4:18n. (3) Claim superior experience or knowledge, Is 65:5n. (4) Distort the balance of Biblical truth, Is 43:10n. (5) Deny the perspicuity of Scripture, Is +*8:20n; Pr +*8:9. (6) Deny the sufficiency of Scripture, 2 T +*3:17. (7) Deny the right of private or individual judgment and interpretation, Pr 18:1n; Ro 14:12; 2 P ◗1:20n. (8) Deny the full, eternal deity of Jesus Christ as the Second Person of the triune Godhead, or Trinity, Pr 8:22n. (9) Add to the written word of God additional revelation, whether in the form of authoritative writings or publications, or unwritten traditions, or new revelation, as from supernatural dreams, and supposed revelation through supernatural gifts of the Spirit, Je +*23:28n. (10) Approach Scripture deductively with their closed system of belief, rather than inductively to learn its truth, 2 P 1:20n. (11) Possess an innate, tenacious inability to receive new or corrective spiritual insight based upon additional light received from the continuing inductive study of Scripture, Ps 25:9; 119:18; Pr +*4:18n; 2 P 1:20n. (12) Wrest Scripture, and handle it deceitfully, in a persistent effort to ignore, suppress, explain away, circumvent, or evade those texts which do not "fit" their deductively developed, arbitrarily imposed, system of belief upon Scripture, 2 C 4:2; 2 P 3:16. (13) Exert lordship over their follower's faith, 2 C +*1:24, rather than encouraging submission to the Lordship of Christ, Ac +√10:36. (14) Fail to teach the obligation of each believer to carefully judge the truth of what is being taught, Ro 14:12; 1 C 14:29; Ga 1:8, 9; 1 Th 5:21. (15) Fail to encourage the right of each believer to independently submit to the written word of God, Ps 119:18, 105; Ac 17:11, 12; 2 T 2:15; +*3:15-17; 1 P 2:2. (16) Impose a uniform system of belief upon all followers, rather than allow for individual differences in depth of knowledge to be reflected in honestly held differences of

interpretation of Scripture and doctrinal understanding, Jn 16:12; Ac 18:24-26; Col 1:10; He 5:12; 2 P 3:18. (17) Deny legitimate Christian liberty by restricting the reading of followers to their own group's publications, providing no open forum for the discussion of doctrinal differences, and not allowing participation in Bible studies not conducted by their own group, Jn 8:31, 32; 1 C 14:29; Ga 5:1; 3 J 9. **divination**. Je 27:9, 10. 29:8, 9, 31. Pr +16:10mg. Is +44:25. Ezk 12:24. 13:6, 7, 23. 21:29. Mi 3:11. Zc 10:2. **and the**. Je 23:26. Is 30:10. La 2:14. **their heart**. Nu +16:28.

15. **Sword**. ⌁121B, Ex +5:3. **and famine shall not**. Je 5:12, 13. 6:15. 8:12. 20:6. 23:14, 15. 28:15-17. 29:20, 21, 31, 32. 1 K 22:25. Ezk √14:9, 10. Am 7:17. 2 P *2:1-3, 14-17. Re 19:20.

16. **the people**. Je 5:31. Is *9:16. Mt +*15:14. **be cast**. See on Je 7:33. 9:22. 15:2, 3. 16:4. 18:21. 19:6, 7. Ps *79:2, 3. **sword**. ⌁121B, Ex +5:3. **for**. Je 2:17-19. 4:18. 13:22-25. Pr 1:31. Re *16:1. **wickedness**. ⌁121C1E, Ge +19:15.

17. **Let mine**. Je 8:18, 21. 9:1. 13:17. Ps 80:4, 5. 119:136. La 1:16. 2:18. 3:48, 49. **for**. Is 37:22. La 1:15. 2:13. Am *5:2. **with a very**. Je 30:14, 15. Ps *39:10. Mi 6:13.

18. **go forth**. Je 52:6, 7. La *1:20. 4:9. Ezk *7:15. **yea**. Je 6:13. 8:10. 23:21. Dt 28:36, 64. Is 28:7. La 4:13-16. **go about**, etc. *or*, make merchandise against a land, and *men* acknowledge *it* not. Je 2:8. 5:31. Ge 34:10. Mi 3:11. 2 P 2:3. **into a land**. Je 9:16. 15:14. 19. **utterly**. Je 6:30. 15:1. 2 K 17:19, 20. Ps 78:59. 80:12, 13. 89:38. La 5:22. Ro +*11:1-6. **hath**. Je 12:8. Zc 11:8, 9. **soul**. Heb. *nephesh*, Ge +34:3. Le +26:11n. **no healing**. See on Je 8:22. 15:18. 2 Ch 36:16. La 2:13. **we**. See on Je 8:15. Jb 30:26. La 4:17. 1 Th *5:3.

20. **We acknowledge**. Je 3:13, 25. Le 26:40-42. Ezr 9:6, 7. Ne 9:2. Ps √32:5. *51:3. 106:6, etc. Da 9:5-8. 1 J √1:7-9. **for**. 2 S 12:13. 24:10. Jb 33:27. Ps 51:4. Lk 15:18-21.

21. **not abhor**. ver. 19. Le 26:11, 30. Dt 32:12, 19. Ps *51:11. 106:40. La 2:7. Am 6:8. **for**. See on ver. 7. Ps *79:9, 10. Ezk 36:22, 23. 39:25. Da *9:7, 15-19. Ep *2:4-7. **disgrace**. See on Je 3:17. 17:12. Ps 74:3-7, 20. 106:45. La 1:10. 2:6, 7, 20. Ezk 7:20-22. 24:21. 43:7. Da 8:11-13. Lk *21:24. Re 11:2. **throne**. ⌁22D3C1, Ps +11:4. **remember**. T#1460. Ex 32:13. Le 26:42-45. Ps 74:2, 18-20. 89:39, 40. 106:45. Is 64:9-12. Zc 11:10, 11. Lk 1:72. He 8:6-13.

22. **Are**. Je 10:15. 16:19. Dt 32:21. Is 41:29. 44:12-20. **vanities**. ⌁121N1, Ge +31:54. Je +*2:5. +√8:19. +*10:3mg, 8. 16:19. 51:18. Dt *32:21. 1 K 16:13, 26. *17:1. *18:1, 41, 44, 45. 2 K 17:15. Ps 31:6. 74:1, 2. Jon +*2:8. Zc 10:1, 2. Ac 14:15-17. 1 C +*8:4. **Art**. Je 5:24. 10:13. 51:16. Dt 28:12. 1 K 8:36. 17:14. 18:39-45. Jb 5:10. 38:26-28. Ps 147:8. Is 30:23. Jl 2:23. Am 4:7. Mt +*5:45. **wait upon**. Ge 49:18⌁𝒫. Ps 25:3, 21. 27:14. 130:5. 135:7. Is √30:18, 23. La 3:25, 26. Mi 7:7. Hab *3:17-19.

JEREMIAH 15

God determines (let who will intercede) to pour out many heavy judgments on the Jews, 1-9. Jeremiah complains that he is generally hated; and God promises good to him amidst the calamities of the nation, 10-14. The prophet professes his integrity, and renews

his complaints, 15-18. God recalls him to his work, and promises to support and deliver him in the due discharge of it, 19-21.

1. **Then said**. Je *7:16. 1 J 5:16. **Though**. Je 7:16. 11:14. 14:11. Ezk *14:14-21. **Moses**. Ex 17:11⌁𝒫. *32:11-14⌁𝒫. Nu *14:13-20⌁𝒫. 1 S 7:9. 8:6. 12:23. Ps √99:6. Ezk √14:14. He ◑=7:25. **stood**. Je 18:20. Ge 19:27. Ps 106:23. Zc 3:3. He 9:24. **my mind**. Heb. *nephesh*, soul, Ge +23:8. ⌁22A1, Le +26:11. Le +26:11n. Jg 5:9. Pr 14:35. **not be toward**. T#1790. Je 21:1-7. 37:3-10. Ex 32:30-35. Nu 16:44-46. Dt 3:23-26. Jg 10:10-14. 1 S *15:10, 11. *16:1. Ezk *14:1-3. 14:13-21. Mt *20:20-23. Mk *5:18, 19. Lk 9:59-62. 12:13-15. *13:23, 24, √25-27. 16:24, 25, 27-30. Ac *1:6, 7. 2 C √12:7-9. **cast**. See on Je 7:15. 23:39. 52:3. 2 K 17:20.

2. **for death**. Je 14:12. 24:9, 10. 43:11. 2 S 8:2. 12:31. Is *24:18. Ezk *5:2, 12. *14:21. Da 9:12. Am *5:19. Zc *11:9. Re *6:3-8. √13:10. **to death**. Ge +2:17. Nu 15:30. 16:26-32. 1 S 2:25. Pr +16:25. Da *12:2, 3. Mt *12:31, 32. Mk 3:28-30. Ro 6:21-23. 2 T 4:14. He *6:4-6. √10:26-31. 2 P √2:20-22. Ja *5:20. 1 J +*5:16. Re 2:11. 20:6, 14. +*21:8.

3. **I will**. Je 7:33. Le *26:16, 22, 25⌁𝒫. Dt 28:26. 1 K 21:23, 24. 2 K 9:35-37. Is 18:6. *56:9, 10. Ezk 14:21. Re 6:8. *19:17, 18. **kinds**. Heb. families. Je 1:15. 2:4.

4. **cause them to be removed**. Heb. give them for a removing. See on Je 9:16. 24:9mg. 29:18. 34:17mg. Le 26:33. Dt 28:25⌁𝒫, 64. La 1:8mg. Ezk 23:46mg. **because**. 2 K √21:3, 11-13. *23:26, 27. *24:3, 4.

5. **For who**. Je 16:5. 21:7. Jb 19:21. Ps 69:20. Is 51:19. La 1:12-16. *2:15, 16. Na 3:7. Mt *23:37-39. **how thou doest**. Heb. of thy peace. Ex 18:7mg. Jg +18:15mg. 1 S 10:4mg. 17:22mg. 25:5mg.

6. **forsaken**. See on Je 1:16. 2:13, 17, 19. **thou art**. Je 7:24. 8:5. Is 1:4. 28:13. Ho 4:16. 11:7. Zc 7:11. **stretch**. Ezk 14:9. 25:7. Zp 1:4. **I am**. Je 6:11. 20:9. Ps *78:38-40. *106:43-45. Ezk 12:26-28. Ho 13:14. Am 7:3-8.

7. **I will fan**. Je 4:11, 12. 51:2. Ps +*1:4. Is 41:16. Mt *3:12. ⌁22C44. Anthropomorphism B890. Human actions are attributed to God: fanning. For other instances of this figure see Mt 3:12. Lk 3:17. **gates**. ⌁171S6, Ge +14:7. **bereave**. Je 9:21. 18:21. Dt 28:18, 32, 41, 53-56. Ho 9:12-17. **children**. *or*, whatsoever is dear. Ge 42:36. Ezk 24:21, 25. **since**. See on Je 5:3. 8:4, 5. Is *9:13. Am 4:10-12. Zc *1:4.

8. **widows**. Je 7:6. 18:21. 22:3. Is 3:25, 26. +*4:1. **sand**. ⌁102B, ⌁138B, Ge +13:16. **the mother**, etc. *or*, the mother *city* a young man spoiling, etc. *or*, the mother *and* the young men. Je 6:11. **a spoiler**. Je 4:16. 5:6. 6:4, 5, 26. Lk 21:35. **at noon day**. Je 6:4. **suddenly**. Is 47:11. 1 Th 5:3. **terrors**. Le 26:16. Ps 78:33. Is 65:23.

9. **She that hath**. She that hath had a numerous offspring—*Jerusalem*, the mother city, the parent of so many cities, villages, and families in the land. 1 S 2:5. Is 47:9. La *1:1. *4:10. **seven**. Ru 4:15n. 1 S 2:5. Jb 1:2. **languisheth**. Je 14:2. 1 S 2:5. **given up**. Jb 11:20. **ghost**. Heb. *nephesh*, soul, Nu +23:10. **her sun**. Am 8:9, 10. **and the**. See on ver. 2, 3. Je 44:27. Ezk 5:12.

10. **my**. Je 20:14-18. Jb *3:1-3, etc. **a man**. ver. 20. Je 1:18, 19. 20:7, 8. 1 K *18:17, 18. 21:20. 22:8. Ps *120:5-7. Ezk 2:6, 7. 3:7-9. Mt *10:21-23. 24:9.

Lk *2:34, 35. *21:17. Ac 16:20-22. 17:6-8. 19:8, 9, 25-28. 28:22. 1 C 4:9-13. **neither.** ♪171K1, Dt +19:5. **lent on usury.** Ex 22:25♪℘. Dt 23:19, 20. Ne 5:1-6. Ps 15:5. Is +*24:2. **curse.** Ps 109:28. Pr 26:2. Mt 5:44. Lk 6:22.

11. **The Lord said.** Je 46:25. Lk 11:39. 12:42. 18:6. 22:31. **Verily it.** Ps √37:3-11. Ec √8:12. **verily I.** Je 29:11-14. 39:11, 12. 40:2-6. Ps *106:46. **cause the enemy to entreat thee.** or, entreat the enemy for thee. Pr +*16:7. *21:1.

12. **Shall iron.** Je 1:18, 19. 21:4, 5. Jb 40:9. Is *45:9. Hab *1:5-10.

13. **substance.** ver. 8. Je 17:3. 20:5. **without.** Ps 44:12. Is 52:3, 5.

14. **pass.** ver. 4. Je 14:18. 16:13. 17:4. 52:27. Le 26:38, 39. Dt 28:25, 36, 64. Am *5:27. **a fire.** Je 4:4. Dt 29:23. 32:22♪℘. Ps 21:9. Is 42:25. 66:15, 16. Na 1:5, 6. He 12:29.

15. **thou.** Je 12:3. 17:16. Jb 10:7. Ps 7:3-5. 17:3. Jn 21:15-17. 2 C √5:11. **remember.** Je 11:18-20. 20:12. Ne *5:19. 6:14. 13:22, 31. Ps 106:4. 109:26-29. 119:84, 132-134. Lk *18:7, 8. Ro *12:19. 2 T √4:14. Re *6:10. *18:20. **visit.** T#1521. Ps 59:5. 80:14, 15. 106:4. **revenge me.** Je +*10:25. 11:20. Jg 16:28. **take.** Ps 39:13. 102:24. Is 38:3. **know.** ver. 10. Je 11:21. 20:8. Ps 69:7-9. Mt √5:10-12. 10:22. 19:29. Lk 6:22, 23. 21:17. Ro 8:35. 1 P 4:14-16.

16. **Thy words.** ♪147G, Ps +68:16. **found.** 2 K +*22:8. 2 Ch +*34:14n, 15. **I did.** Ezk *3:1-3. Re *10:9. **eat them.** Jb +*23:12. Ps *119:92, 103. Jn 6:63. He *5:12-14. 1 P √2:2. Re 10:10. ♪108B. Idiom B826. To "eat or drink" may denote the operation of the mind in receiving, understanding, and applying doctrine or instruction of any kind. For other instances of this figure see Ezk 3:1. Jn 6:51, 53n. 1 C 12:13. **thy word.** Je ❍*6:10. Jb √23:12. Ps *19:10. *119:72, 97, 101-103, 111. Mi 2:7. **rejoicing.** T#1091. Ps *119:111, 162. **I am called by thy name.** Heb. thy name is called upon me. Je +14:9mg. 2 Ch +√7:14. Jn 17:14. **O Lord God of hosts.** Je +5:14.

17. **sat not.** Ps √1:1. *26:4, 5. 2 C +*6:17, 18. **sat alone.** Le 13:17. La 3:28. Ezk 3:24, 25. Da 7:28. **for.** Je 1:10. 6:11. See on Je 20:8, 9. **indignation.** Da +*8:19 (❋S#2195h).

18. **my pain.** Je 14:19. Ps *6:3. *13:1-3. La 3:1-18. **perpetual.** Jb +4:20 (❋S#5331h). **my wound.** Je 30:12, 15. Jb 34:6. Mi 1:9. **as a.** Je 1:18, 19. 20:7. Ezk 5:22, 23. **and as.** Je 14:3. Jb 6:15-20. Is 58:11. **fail.** Heb. be not sure. Ps 78:8, 37. ❍93:5. Pr ❍11:13. Is 7:9mg. ❍22:23. Mi 1:14mg.

19. **If.** Je +*7:5. **return.** ver. 10-18. Je 20:9. Ex 6:29, 30. Jon 3:2. **stand.** ver. 1. 1 K 17:1. 18:15. 2 K 3:14. Pr 22:29. Zc 3:7. Lk 1:19. +*21:36. Ju √24, 25. **take.** Ge +*18:25. Le 10:10♪℘. Is *32:5, 6. Ezk 22:26. *44:23. He *5:14. **as my.** Ex 4:12, 15, 16. Lk 10:16. 12:12. 21:15. **let them.** Je 38:20, 21. Ezk 2:7. 3:10, 11. Ac 20:27. 2 C 5:16. Ga 1:10. 2:5.

20. **I will.** See on Je 1:18, 19. 6:27. Ezk *3:9. Ac *4:8-13, 29-31. *5:29-32. **fight.** ♪102, Ge +2:24. **but.** Je 20:11, 12. Ps *124:1-3. 129:1, 2. Ro 8:31-39. **for.** Je 20:11, 12. Ps 46:7, 11. Is +*7:14. 8:9, 10. 41:10. Ac 18:9, 10. 2 T 4:16, 17, 22.

21. **deliver.** Ge 48:16. Ps 27:2. 37:40. Is *49:24, 25. 54:17. Mt *6:13. Lk +*21:36. Ro *16:20. 2 C *1:10. **redeem.** Ex 6:6. 13:13. **the terrible.** Is 13:11. 25:3-5. 29:5, 6, 20.

JEREMIAH 16

JEREMIAH, as a sign to the people, is forbidden to marry; to enter into the house of mourning; and to go to any feast, 1-9. The greatness of the people's crimes assigned as the reason of their heavy afflictions, 10-13. Predictions both of mercies and judgments to Israel and to the Gentiles, 14-21.

1. **The word.** See on Je 1:2, 4. 2:1.

2. **not take.** Ge 19:14. Mt *24:19. Lk *21:23. 23:29. 1 C *7:26, 27.

3. **thus saith.** ver. 5, 9. **their fathers.** Je 6:21. **that begat.** Is 66:9.

4. **die.** Je 14:16. 15:2, 3. Ps 78:64. **not.** ver. 5-7. Je 22:18. 25:33. Am 6:9, 10. **neither.** Je 7:33. 22:19. 36:30. Ps √79:1-3. **as dung.** Je 8:1-3. 9:22. 25:33. 1 K 14:10, 11. 21:23, 24. 2 K 9:10, 36, 37. Ps 83:10. Is 5:25. Zp *1:17. **consumed.** Je 14:15. 34:17. 44:12, 27. Ezk 5:12. **meat.** Je 34:20. Ps 79:2. Is *18:6. Ezk *39:17-20. Re *19:17, 18.

5. **Enter.** ver. 6, 7. Ezk *24:16-23. **mourning.** or, mourning feast. Am 6:7. **neither go to lament.** Mt 8:22. Lk 9:60. **I have.** Je 15:1-4. Dt 31:17. 2 Ch 15:5, 6. Is 27:11. Zc *8:10. Re *6:4. **taken away.** Heb. asaph. A homonym, with two meanings: (1) to protect, or heal, Nu 12:14, 15; 2 K 5:6; Ps 27:10; (2) to snatch away, Je 16:5; Ps 26:9.

6. **the great.** Je 13:13. Is 9:14-17. *24:2. Ezk *9:5, 6. Am *6:11. Re *6:15. *20:12. **they.** See on ver. 4. Je 22:18, 19. **nor cut.** Je 7:29. 41:5. 47:5. 48:37. Le 19:28♪℘. 21:5♪℘. Dt 14:1♪℘. Is 22:12.

7. **tear themselves.** or, break bread. ♪63A2, 2 S +6:6. ♪108H4, Is +58:7. Dt 26:14. Jb *42:11. Is *58:7. Ezk 18:7, 16. *24:17n. Ho 9:4. Mt 25:35. **cup.** Pr *31:6, 7.

8. **the house.** Je 15:17. Ps 26:4. Ec *7:2-4. Is 22:12-14. Am 6:4-6. Mt 24:38. Lk 17:27-29. 1 C 5:11. Ep +*5:11. **to sit.** Am *6:1.

9. **the Lord of hosts, the God of.** Je +7:3. **I will.** Je 7:34. 25:10. Is *24:7-12. Ezk *26:13. Ho *2:11. Re *18:22, 23. **the voice.** ♪144, Ge +3:8. **the bride.** Je 7:34. 25:10. 33:11.

10. **Wherefore.** See on Je 2:35. 5:19. 13:22. 22:8, 9. Dt *29:24, 25♪℘. 1 K *9:7-9. Ho 12:8. **evil.** Is +45:7.

11. **Because.** Je 2:8. 5:7-9. Jg *2:12, 13. 10:13, 14. Ne *9:26-29. Ps √106:35-41. Da 9:10-12. **walked.** Je 8:2. 9:14. Ezk 11:21. 1 P 4:3. **my law.** Ex ch. 20♪℘.

12. **worse.** See on Je 7:26. 13:10. Jg *2:19. Mt 23:32. 2 T *3:13. **imagination.** or, stubbornness. Je +3:17mg. 7:24mg. 9:14mg. 13:10mg. Dt 9:27. 29:19mg♪℘.

13. **will I.** Je 6:15. 15:4, 14. 17:4. Le 18:26-28. Dt 4:26-28. 28:36, 63-65. 29:28, 29. 30:17, 18. Jsh 23:15, 16. 2 Ch 7:20. **into a.** Je 14:8. 17:4. 22:28. **and.** Dt 4:26-28♪℘. 28:36♪℘. Ps 81:12.

14. **behold.** Je 23:7, 8. Is 43:18, 19. Ho 3:4, 5. **that brought.** See on Ex 20:2♪℘. Dt 15:15. Mi 6:4.

15. **that brought.** Je 3:18. 24:6. *30:3, 10. 31:8. 32:37. 50:19. Dt 30:3-5. Ps 106:47. Is √11:11-16. *14:1. *27:12, 13. 43:5, 6. Ezk 34:12-14. *36:24, 27, 28. *37:21-24. *39:28, 29. Am √9:14, 15. Lk √21:20-24. **the land of the north.** Babylon and Chaldea; the restoration from which, as the more recent mercy, and in every respect interesting and remarkable, would be more remembered than their former deliverance from

Egypt. Je 3:12, 18. 6:22. 10:22. 23:8. 31:8. Is 41:25. **bring them again.** Je 24:6. 30:3. 32:44. Is 11:12. 56:8. Ezk 38:14. Jl 3:1. **I gave.** Dt 30:3.

16. **I will send.** I will raise up enemies against them, some of whom shall destroy them by *wiles*, and others shall ruin them by *violence*. The Chaldeans shall make an entire conquest of the whole land, and strip it of its riches and inhabitants; and those who may escape one party shall fall into the hands of another. Je 25:9. Ezk 12:13. Am *4:2. Hab 1:14, 15. Mk ◑1:17. **fish them.** Jb 19:6. Ezk *32:3. Ho *7:12. Mt +*13:47. **hunters.** Ge 10:9. 1 S 24:11. 26:20. Mi 7:2. **every mountain.** Is 24:17, 18. Am 5:19. 9:1-3. Lk 17:34-37. Re 6:15-17. **holes of the rocks.** Je 13:4. Ge +19:30. Is 7:19.

17. **mine eyes.** Je 23:24. 32:19. 2 Ch 16:9. Jb 34:21, 22. Ps 90:8. *139:3, 4. Pr 5:21. 15:3. Is 29:15. Ezk 8:12. 9:9. Mt *12:36. Lk *12:1-3. 1 C 4:5. He *4:13.

18. **first.** Je 17:18. Is 40:2. 61:7. Re 18:6. **double.** √121L9, Ge +43:12. Is +*40:2. *61:7. **they have defiled.** Je 2:7. 3:1, 2, 9. Le 18:27, 28. Nu 35:33, 34. Ps 106:38. Is 24:5. Mi 2:10. Zp 3:1-5. **my land.** Je 2:7. Le +*25:23n. Dt +*32:43. Ho 9:3. **the carcases.** Either meaning the *idols* themselves, which were *carcases* without life; or the *sacrifices*, especially those of their sons and daughters, which were made to them (Le 18:21). Le 26:30. Ezk 11:18, 21. 43:7-9.

19. **my strength.** √121E1, Ge +25:23. Je 17:17. Ps 18:1, 2. 19:14. 27:5. *46:1, 7, 11. 62:2, 7. 91:1, 2. 144:1, 2. Pr *18:10. Is 25:4. *32:1, 2. Ezk 11:16. Na 1:7. Hab 3:19. **fortress.** √22L5, Ps +31:3. **Gentiles.** Je 3:16, 17. Ps *22:27-30. 67:2-7. 68:31. *72:7-12. 86:9. Is *2:2, 3. 11:9, 10. *49:6. 60:1-3. 62:2. Mi 4:1, 2. Zc *2:10, 11. *8:20-23. Ml 1:11. Lk *1:31-33. *2:32. Re 7:9-11. *11:15. *21:23, 24. **Surely.** See on Je 3:23. 10:14, 15. Hab 2:18, 19. 1 P 1:18. **wherein.** See on Je 2:11. 10:5. Is 44:10.

20. **make gods.** Ps 115:4-8. 135:14-18. Is 36:19. 37:19. Ho 8:4-6. Ac 19:26. Ga *1:8. *4:8-11.

21. **I will this.** Ex 9:14-18. 14:4. Ps 9:16. Ezk 6:7. 24:24, 27. 25:14. **and they.** Je 33:2. Ex +15:3. Ps 83:18. Is *43:3. Am *5:8. **my name.** Ex 3:15𝒫. +*6:3n. 15:3𝒫. **The Lord.** *or,* JEHOVAH. Ps *83:18.

JEREMIAH 17

The Jews are convicted of idolatry, and condemned to captivity, 1-4. They who trust in man are cursed, and those who trust in God are blessed, 5-8. None but God can search out the extreme deceitfulness and desperate wickedness of the heart, 9, 10. The doom of those who grow rich by injustice, 11. The glory of God, as dwelling among his people, an aggravation of the guilt of such as forsake him, 12, 13. The prophet prays for comfort and salvation; complains of ill usage; protests his fidelity and love to the people; and calls for vengeance on his persecutors, 14-18. A message to the rulers concerning hallowing the sabbath, with conditional promises and threatenings, 19-27.

1. **written with.** Jb 19:23, 24. Ps 45:1. **point.** Heb. nail. **graven.** Pr 3:3. 7:3. 2 C 3:3. **table of.** Ex +25:21. **and upon.** Le *4:7, 18, 25. Ho 12:11.

2. **their children.** Je 7:18. Ho 4:13, 14. **their altars.** See on Je 2:20. Jg 3:7. 2 Ch 24:18. 33:3, 19. Ps 78:58. Is 1:29. *17:7, 8. Ezk 20:28. **groves.** Dt 16:21. 2 K +17:10. 21:3n. Is 66:17n. **green trees.** 2 K 16:4n. +17:10. **high hills.** 2 K 16:4n. +17:10.

3. **my.** Je 26:18. Is 2:2, 3. La *5:17, 18. Mi *3:12. 4:1, 2. **I will.** Je 15:13. 52:15-20. 2 K 24:13. 25:13-16. Is 39:4-6. La *1:10. Ezk 7:20-22. **give.** √101, Dt +32:42. Here (in Hebrew) the verb is emphasized by being put last: "All thy substance and all thy treasures to the spoiler—will I give" (B694). **and thy.** Je 12:12. Le 26:30. Is 27:9. Ezk 6:3. 16:39. Mi 1:5-7.

4. **thyself.** Heb. in thyself. **shalt.** Je 16:13. 25:9-11. Le 26:31-34. Dt 4:26, 27. 28:25. Jsh 23:15, 16. 1 K 9:7. 2 K 25:21. **and I.** Je 5:29. 27:12, 13. Dt 28:47, 48. Ne 9:28. Is 14:3. **for.** Je 7:20. 15:14. Dt 29:26-28. 32:22-25. Is 5:25. 30:33. +*66:24. La 1:12. Ezk 20:47, 48. *21:31, 32. Na 1:5, 6. Mk √9:43-49. **for ever.** Heb. *olam,* Ex +*12:24.

5. **Cursed.** Jg 4:9. Ps 62:9. *118:8, 9. *146:3, 4. Is *2:22. *30:1, etc. *31:1, etc. 36:6. Ezk 29:6, 7. **the man.** √171G1, Ps +32:2. **flesh.** Ge +*6:3. **his arm.** 2 Ch *32:8. Is *31:3. **whose.** 2 Ch 12:1. Ps *18:21. Is 59:15. Ezk 6:9. Ho 1:2. He +*3:12.

6. **like.** Je 48:6. Jb *8:11-13. 15:30-34. Ps +*1:4. *92:7. 129:6-8. Is 1:30. **and shall.** 2 K *7:2, 19, 20. Jb 20:17. **a salt.** Dt 29:23. Jg 9:45. Ezk 47:11. Zp 2:9.

7. **Blessed is.** Ps *2:12. *34:8. 40:4. *84:12. *125:1. 146:5. Pr *16:20. Is √26:3, 4. +*30:18. Ep 1:12. **the man.** √171G1, Ps +32:2. **hope.** √121R3, Ps +71:5.

8. **he shall.** Jb 8:16. Ps +*l:3. *92:10-15. Pr 11:28. Is *58:11. Ezk 31:4-10. *47:12. Re *22:2. **the waters.** *or,* rivulet. Je 15:18. Is 58:11. Jn 4:13, 14. **drought.** *or,* restraint. Je 14:1mg.

9. **The heart.** Je 16:12. Ge *6:5. 8:21. Jb 14:4. *15:14-16. Ps *51:5. 53:1-3. Pr *28:26. Ec *9:3. Mt 12:34, 35. *15:19. Mk √7:21, 22. Jn *3:19. Ro 8:7, 8. 1 C 2:14. Ep 4:17-19. 5:8. T *1:15. He +*3:12. Ja *1:14, 15.

10. **the Lord.** Ne +9:6. **search the heart.** √121I1, Ge +3:7. "Heart" put by Metonymy of the Adjunct for the mind, or intellect. Je 11:20. 20:12. 1 S √16:7. 1 Ch +*28:9. 29:17. 2 Ch *6:30. Ps 7:9. *139:1, 2, 23, 24. Pr 17:3. Jn +*2:25. Ro ▶8:27. He √4:12, 13. Re *▶2:23. **reins.** √121I1, Ge +3:7. Put by Metonymy of the Adjunct for the thoughts, or affections. **even.** Je 32:19. Ps *62:12. Mt +16:27. Ro 2:6-8. Re *20:12. 22:12. **fruit.** Je 6:19. 21:14. 32:19. Is 3:10, 11. Mi 7:13. Ro *6:21. Ga √6:7, 8.

11. **sitteth,** etc. *or,* gathereth *young* which she hath not brought forth. **he that.** Je 5:27, 28. 22:13, 17. Pr *1:18, 19. 13:11. 15:27. *21:6. 28:8, 16, 20, 22. Is 1:23, 24. Ezk 22:12, 13. Ho 12:7, 8. Am 3:10. 8:4-6. Mi 2:1, 2, 9. 6:10-12. 7:3. Hab *2:6-12. Zp 1:9. Zc 5:4. 7:9-13. Ml +*3:5. Mt *23:14. 1 T *6:8, 9. T 1:11. Ja +*5:3-5. 2 P 2:3, 14. **shall leave.** Ps 55:23. Pr 23:5. Ec 5:13-16. **in the midst.** Ps 102:24. Pr *10:27. Ec +*7:17. Is +*38:10. **a fool.** T#200-11. Lk √12:20.

12. **glorious high.** Je 3:17. 14:21. 2 Ch 2:5, 6. Ps 96:6. 103:19. Is 6:1. 66:1. Ezk *1:26. 43:7. Mt *25:31. He √4:14, 16. *12:1, 2. Re *3:21, 22.

13. **the hope.** √121R3, Ps +71:5. ver. 7, 17. Je 14:8. Ps *22:4, 5. Jl 3:16. Ac 28:20. 1 T 1:1. **all that.** Je 2:26, 27. Ps 97:7. Is *45:16, 17. 65:11-14. 66:5. Ezk 16:63. 36:32. Da √12:2. **they that.** See on ver. 5. Ps 73:27. Pr 14:14. Is 1:28. **written.** Pr 10:7. Lk 10:20. Jn 8:6-8. Re 20:15. **forsaken.** Je 2:13, 17. Ps 36:8, 9. Jn *4:10, 14. *7:37, 38. Re *7:17. 21:6. *22:1, 17. **waters.** √22K4, Je +2:13.

14. **Heal.** T#1546. Je 15:18. 31:18. 33:6. Ge 20:17.

Nu 12:10-13. Dt +*32:39. 1 K 13:6. 2 K *20:1-3. 2 Ch 16:12. Ps 6:2, 4. 12:4. 30:+2 (T#1695), 3. 41:4. 60:1, 2. +*103:3. *107:17-19. Is 6:10. 57:18, 19. Mt 8:2, 3, 5-7. 14:35, 36. 15:22. 17:14-18. Mk 1:40, 41. 7:32-35. Lk *4:18. 5:12, 13. 17:12-18. **save.** Je 15:20. Ps 60:5. 106:47. Mt 8:25. 14:30. **thou.** Dt 10:21⟩𝒫. Ps 109:1. 148:14.

15. **Where is the word.** Je 20:7, 8. Is 5:19. Ezk 12:22, 27, 28. Am *5:18. 2 P √3:3, 4.

16. **I have.** Je 1:4-10. 20:9. Ezk 3:14-19. 33:7-9. Am 7:14, 15. Ja *1:19. 3:1. **to follow thee.** Heb. after thee. Je 3:19mg. 13:27mg. 48:2mg. 2 S 7:8mg. Ps 78:71mg. Ezk 13:3mg. Am 7:15mg. **neither.** Je 4:19, 20. 9:1. 13:17. 14:17-21. 18:20. Ro 9:1-3. **desired.** Jb 36:20. Am √5:18. **woeful.** ver 9 (desperately wicked). Jb +34:6 (※S#605h). **day.** ver. +18. **that.** Ac *20:20, 27. 2 C *1:12. 2:17. *4:3, 4.

17. **a terror.** Jb 31:23. Ps *77:2-9. 88:15, 16. **thou.** See on ver. 7, 13. Je 16:19. Ps 41:1. *59:16. Na 1:7. Ep *6:13.

18. **Let them.** Je +*10:25. **confounded.** Je 20:11. Ps *35:4, 26, 27. 40:14. 70:2. 83:17, 18. **but let not me be confounded.** Ps 25:2, 3. 71:1. **the day of evil.** ver. 16, 17. Je *18:19-23. Is +*45:7. **destroy them with double destruction.** Heb. break them with a double breach. Je 11:20. 14:17. 16:18. Jb 16:14. Ezk 21:6. Re *18:5, 6. **double.** 𝒥121L9, Ge +43:12. Je 16:18. Is +*40:2. +*61:7. Zc 9:12.

19. A.M. cir. 3393. B.C. cir. 611. **Go and stand.** Je 7:2. 19:2. 26:2. 36:6, 10. Pr 1:20-22. 8:1-4. 9:3. Ac 5:20, 25. **gate.** 𝒥171S7B, Ge +14:7.

20. **Hear.** Je 13:18. 19:3. 22:2. Ps 49:1, 2. Ezk 2:7. 3:17. Ho 5:1. Am 4:1. Mi 3:1. Re 2:29.

21. **Take.** Dt 4:9, 15, 23. 11:16. Jsh 23:11. Pr √4:23. Is 65:5n. Mk +√4:24. Lk +√8:18. Ac √20:28. He √2:1-3. *12:15, 16. **yourselves.** Heb. *nephesh*, Ge +27:31. **bear.** ver. 22-27. Ex 20:8⟩𝒫. 23:12⟩𝒫. 31:13⟩𝒫. Nu 15:32-36. Ne *13:15-21. Jn ◐*5:9-12. Ga ◐*4:9-11. Col ◐*2:16, 17.

22. **neither do.** Ge *2:2, 3. Ex *16:23-29. *20:8-10. 23:12. 31:13-17. Le *19:3. *23:3. Dt 5:12-15. Is 56:2-6. +√58:13n. Ezk 20:12, 20, 21. 22:8. Lk *6:5, 9-11. 23:56. Re *1:10.

23. **they obeyed.** Je 7:24-26. 11:10. 16:11, 12. 19:15. Is 48:4. Ezk 20:13, 16, 21. Zc 7:11, 12. Ac 7:51. **made.** Pr *29:1. **nor.** Je 6:8. 32:33. 35:15. Ps 50:17. Pr 1:3, 5. 5:12. 8:10. Zp 3:7. Jn √3:19-21.

24. **if.** Je +7:5. **diligently hearken.** Ex *15:26. Dt 11:13, 22. +*26:16. Ezr +*7:10. Is 21:7. 55:2. Zc 6:15. Lk +*11:28. He *11:6. 2 P √1:5-10. **to bring.** See on ver. 21, 22. Ne 13:15, 19. Jn 5:10. **sabbath day.** T#642. Is *56:2, 6, 7. +*58:13n, 14. **but hallow.** Is +√58:13n, 14.

25. **shall there.** Je 22:4. **sitting.** Je 13:13. 22:30. 33:15, 17, 21. 2 S *7:16. 1 K 9:4, 5. Ps *89:27, 29-37. √132:11, 12. Is +*9:6, 7. Lk 1:32, 33. Ac 2:34-36. **riding.** Dt 17:16. 1 S 8:11. 2 S 8:4. **and this.** Ex 12:14. Ps *132:13, 14. Am *9:11, 15. He 12:22. **for ever.** Heb. *olam*, Ex +*12:24.

26. **from the cities.** Je 32:44. 33:13. Jsh 15:21, etc. **the plain.** Jsh 15:33. Zc 7:7. **the south.** Je 13:19. 32:44. Ge 13:1. Is +*30:6. **bringing.** See on Le ch. 1-7. Ezr 3:3-6, 11. **burnt offerings.** Le 1:1, 2⟩𝒫. +*23:12. **sacrifices.** Ge 46:1. Ex 18:12. Jg 2:5. 1 S 1:21. 6:15. 11:15. 2 S 6:13. 1 Ch 21:28. 29:21. 2 Ch 5:6. Jon 1:16. **meat offerings.** Le +*23:13. **incense.** Je 6:20. 41:5. Le 2:1.

5:11. 6:15. 24:7. Nu 5:15. 1 Ch 9:29. Ne 13:5. Is 60:6. 43:23. 66:3. **sacrifices of praise.** Je 33:11. Le 7:12. 22:29. 2 Ch 33:16. Ps √50:23. *65:1. 107:22. 116:17. He √13:15. 1 P 2:5, 9, 10. Re *1:5, 6.

27. **if.** Je +7:5. **ye will not hearken.** ver. 24. Je 6:17. 26:4-6. 44:16. Is 1:20. Zc 7:11-14. He 12:25. **hallow the sabbath.** "We cannot possibly conceive anything more decisive, on the importance of hallowing the sabbath day" (Scott). ver. +*21, +*22. Is +*58:13n, 14. Ezk 22:8. **then.** See on ver. 4. Je 21:12, 14. 32:29. 38:21-23. 49:27. Dt 32:22. Is 9:18, 19. La 4:11. Ezk 16:41. 20:47, 48. Am 1:4, 7, 10, 12, 14. 2:2, 4, 5. **shall devour.** Je 39:8. 52:13. 2 K 25:9. 2 Ch 36:19. Am 2:5. **shall not.** Je 7:20. 2 K 22:17. Is 1:31. Ezk 20:47. Mk √9:43-48.

JEREMIAH 18

By the emblem of a potter and his clay, God shows his absolute right and power over Israel; and the method of his righteous and merciful dealings with the nations, 1-10. The prophet warns the people to repent; expostulates with them on their folly and wickedness, and denounces divine judgments, 11-17. The devices which they devised against him; and his prophetical prayers against them, 18-23.

2. A.M. 3396. B.C. 608. **and go.** Je 13:1. 19:1, 2. Is 20:2. Ezk 4:1, etc. 5:1. Am 7:7, 8. He 1:1. **cause.** Je 23:22. Ac 9:6.

3. **I went.** Jon 1:3. Jn 15:14. Ac 26:19. **wheels. or,** frames, or, seats. Ex 1:16.

4. **made of clay was marred in. or,** made was marred, as clay in. **made it again.** Heb. returned and made. Nu 11:4mg. **as.** ver. 6. Is *45:9. Ro *9:20-23.

6. **cannot I do.** ver. 4. Is *64:8. Da 4:34, 35. Mt *20:15. Ro *11:32-36.

7. **to pluck.** See on Je 1:10. 12:14-17. 25:9, etc. 45:4. Am 9:8. Jon 3:4.

8. **If.** Je +7:5. **that nation.** Je 7:3-7. 36:3. Jg 10:15, 16. 1 K 8:33, 34. 2 Ch 12:6, 7. Is *1:16-19. Ezk 18:21. 33:11, 13. Jon 2:5-10. Lk *13:3-5. **I will repent.** 𝒥22B, Ge +6:6. Je 15:6. 26:3, 13. 42:10. Ge +6:6. Ex 32:12. Dt *32:36. Jg 2:18. Ps 90:13. 106:45. 135:14. Ho 11:8. Jl 2:13, 14. Am 7:3-6. Jon *3:9, +10. 4:2.

9. **to build.** Je 1:10. 11:17. 30:18. 31:4, 28, 38. 32:41. Ec *3:2, 3. Am √9:11-15.

10. **If.** Je +7:5. **do evil.** See on Je 7:23-28. Ps 125:5. Ezk 3:20. 18:24. 33:18. Zp 1:6. **then.** Nu *14:22, 23, 34. 1 S *2:30. √13:13, 14. 15:11, 35. **repent.** Ge +6:6. Jon +3:10.

11. **go to.** Ge 11:3, 4, 7. 2 K 5:5. Is 5:5. Ja 4:13. 5:1. **and devise.** ver. 18. Je 4:23. 11:19. 51:11. Mi 2:3. **return.** Je 3:1, 22. 7:3. 25:5. 26:3, 13. 35:15. 36:3, 7. 2 K 17:13. 27:13. Is *1:16-19. √55:6, 7. La 3:39-41. Ezk 13:22. 18:23, 30-32. Zc 1:3. Ac 26:20.

12. **There.** See on Je 2:25. 2 K *6:33. Is 57:10. Ezk *37:11. **we will walk.** Je 3:17. *7:24. *11:8. 16:12. 23:17. √44:17. Ge *6:5. *8:21. Dt 29:19. Mk *7:21, 22. Lk 1:51. **imagination.** Je 3:17.

13. **Ask.** See on Je 2:10-13. **who.** 1 S 4:7. Is 66:8. 1 C 5:1. **virgin.** 𝒥155E5, Nu +21:25. Je 2:13. 14:17. 31:4. Is 36:22. La 1:15. **a very.** Je 5:30. 23:14. Ho *6:10.

14. **Will.** Jn 6:68. **the snow,** etc. *or,* my fields for a rock, *or for* the snow of Lebanon? shall the running

waters be forsaken for the strange cold *waters*? Parkhurst renders, "Will the snow of Lebanon fail from the rock of the field? or will the issuing cold flowing waters (from that mountain namely) be exhausted?" (See Targ. LXX. and Vulg.) No more could I fail my people if they trusted in me (Compare Je 2:13). Maundrell says, "The chief benefit the mountain of Lebanon serves for, is, by its exceeding height, it proves a conservatory for abundance of snow, which thawing in the heat of summer, affords supplies of water to the rivers and fountains in the valleys below." Jb 9:30. **which cometh.** ⸓63B, Ge +25:28. "Will (a man) leave the snow (water) of Lebanon for the rock of the field? Or shall the cold flowing waters (be forsaken) for strange waters?"

15. **my people.** See on Je 2:13, 19, 32. 3:21. 13:25. 17:13. **burned.** Je 10:15. 16:19. 44:15-19, 25. Is 41:29. 65:7. Ho 2:13. 11:2. **caused.** Is *3:12. 9:16. Ezk √14:10. Ml *2:8. Mt √15:6-9. *23:13, 15. Mk +*12:24. Ro *14:21. **from.** ⸓63F, Ge +33:10. **the ancient.** Heb. *olam*, Jb +*22:15. **paths.** See on Je 6:16. **to walk.** Je 19:5. Is 57:14. **a way.** Pr 15:19. Is 57:14. 62:10.

16. **make.** See on Je 9:11. 19:8. 25:9. 49:13. 50:13. Le *26:33, 34, 43. Dt 29:23. Is 6:11. Ezk *6:14. 12:19. 33:28, 29. **a perpetual.** Heb. *olam*, Ge +*9:12. 1 K 9:8. 2 Ch 7:20, 21. La 2:15, 16. Mi 6:16. **shall be.** Dt 28:59. Ps 22:7. 44:14. Is 37:22. Mt 27:39. Mk 15:29.

17. **scatter.** Je 13:24. Dt *28:25, 64. Jb 27:21. Ps 48:7. Ho *13:15. **show.** Je 2:27. 32:33. Dt 31:17. Jg 10:13, 14. **the day.** Je 46:21. Dt 32:35. Pr 7:25, 26.

18. **come.** ver. 11. Je 11:19. Ps 21:11. Is 32:7. Mi *2:1-3. **for the law.** Je 13:13, 14. 14:14-16. 29:25-29. Le 10:11⸒𝒫. 1 K 22:24. Ml *2:7. Lk 11:45. Jn 7:47-49. 9:40. **counsel.** 2 S 15:31. 17:14. Jb 5:13. **Come and let us smite.** Je 26:11. Ps 52:2. 57:4. *64:2, 3. Pr 18:21. **with.** or, for. **tongue.** ⸓121BB, Ps +5:9. **and let us not.** Je 5:12, 13. 43:2. 44:17.

19. **Give.** Je 20:12. Ps 55:16, 17. *56:1-4. 64:1-4. 109:4, 28. Mi 7:8. Lk *6:11, 12. **hearken.** 2 K 19:16. Ne 4:4, 5. 6:9.

20. **evil.** 1 S 24:17-19. Ps *35:12. 38:20. *109:4, 5. Pr 17:13. Jn *10:32. *15:25. **digged.** ver. 22. Jb 6:27. Ps 7:15. 35:7. 57:6. 119:95. Pr 26:27. Ec 10:8. **pit.** Heb. *shuchah*, Pr +22:14 (⸙S#7745h). **soul.** Heb. *nephesh*, Ps +30:3. **Remember.** Je 7:16. 11:14. 14:7-11, 20-22. 15:1. Ge *18:22-32. Ps 106:23. Ezk 22:30, 31. Zc 3:1, 2.

21. **deliver.** Je +*10:25. 11:20-23. 12:3. 20:1-6, 11, 12. Ps 109:9-20. 2 T √4:14. **pour out their blood.** Heb. pour them out. Ps 63:10mg. Ezk 35:5. **let their wives.** See on Je 15:2, 3, 8. 16:3, 4. Ex 22:24. Dt *32:25. La 5:3. **let their young.** Je 9:21. 11:22. 2 Ch 36:17. Am *4:10.

22. **a cry.** Je 4:19, 20, 31. 6:26. 9:20, 21. 25:34-36. 47:2, 3. 48:3-5. Is 10:30. 22:1-4. Zp *1:10, 11, 16. **for.** See on ver. 20. **pit.** Heb. *shuchah*, Pr +22:14 (⸙S#7745h). **and hid.** Je 20:10. Ps 38:12. 56:5-7. *64:4, 5. 140:5. Mt *22:15.

23. **thou.** See on ver. 18. Je 11:18-20. 15:15. Ps *37:32, 33. **their counsel.** Jn=11:53. **to slay me.** Heb. for death. Je 15:2. **forgive not.** Ne 4:4, 5. Ps 35:4. 59:5. 69:22-28. 109:14, 15. Is 2:9. Mt 18:18. Lk ◑=23:34. Jn 20:23. **in the time.** Je 8:12. 11:23. Is 10:3. Lk 21:22. Ro 2:5.

JEREMIAH 19

The prophet is sent to Tophet, with an earthen bottle, and attended by the elders; to denounce the judgments of God on the Jews and on Jerusalem, and there to break the bottle as an emblem of their destruction, 1-13. He returns to the temple, and declares the same to the people, 14, 15.

1. **A.M.** 3397. **B.C.** 607. **Go.** ver. 10, 11. Je 18:2-4. 32:14. Is 30:14mg. La 4:2. 2 C *4:7. **bottle.** ⸙S#1228h. ver. 10. 1 K 14:3mg. Compare Je ◑+13:12n. **take.** ⸓63B, Ge +25:28. **the ancients of the people.** Je 26:17. Ex 3:16. 12:21. 18:12, +21. 24:1. Nu *11:16, 17. Jsh +20:4. 1 K 8:1. 1 Ch 24:4-6. Ezk 8:11, 12. 9:6. Mt 26:3. 27:1, 41, 42. Ac 4:5, 6. **ancients of the priests.** Dt 21:2. 2 K 19:2. Is 37:2. Ac 5:21.

2. **the valley.** See on Je 7:31, 32. 32:35. Jsh +*15:8n. 2 K 23:10. 2 Ch 28:3. 33:6. Ne 2:13n. **east gate.** Heb. sun gate. Ne 3:29. or, the gate of potsherds. i.e. the pottery gate. Is 30:14. Thus the pottery dump was accessed through the "east gate" to the valley of Hinnom. **and proclaim.** Je 1:7. 3:12. 7:2. 11:6. 26:2. Pr 1:20-22. Ezk 3:10, 11. Jon 3:2. Mt 10:27. Ac 5:20. 20:27.

3. **Hear.** Je 13:18. 17:20. Ps *2:10-12. 102:15. 110:5. Mt 10:18. Re 2:29. **I will bring.** Je +6:19. Am +*3:6. **evil.** Is +45:7. **his ears.** 1 S *)3:11. 4:16-18. 2 K)21:12, 13. Is 28:19.

4. **they have.** Je 2:13, 17, 19, 34. 5:6, 7, 19. 15:6. 16:11. 17:13. Dt 28:20⸒𝒫. 31:16-18. 32:15-23⸒𝒫. 2 K 22:16, 17. Is *65:11. Da 9:5-15. **estranged.** 2 K 21:4, 5, 7. 23:11, 12. 2 Ch 33:4-7. **burned.** Je 7:9. 11:13. 18:15. 32:29-35. Dt 13:6, 13. 28:36, 64. 32:17. **whom neither.** Dt *32:17⸒𝒫. **filled.** Je 2:30, 34. *7:31, 32. 22:17. 26:15, 23. 2 K 21:6, 16. 24:4. Is 59:7. La 4:13. Mt √23:34, 35. Lk 11:50. Re *16:6.

5. **the high.** Nu 22:41. **to burn.** Je 7:31. Dt 12:31. 2 K 17:17. 2 Ch 28:3. Ps 106:37, 38. Ezk *16:20, 21. 20:26. **which.** See on Je 7:31, 32. 32:35. Le 18:21⸒𝒫. **neither.** Ezk 38:10. Da 2:29. **mind.** ⸓22A17, Ge +6:6.

6. **this.** See on ver. 2, 11. Je *7:32, 33. Jsh 15:8. Is +*30:33.

7. **I will make void.** Jb 5:12, 13. Ps 33:10, 11. Pr +*21:30. Is *8:10. *28:17, 18. 30:1-3. La 3:37. Ro 3:31. 4:14. **the counsel.** Is +*28:18. Da +*9:27. **I will cause.** Le 9:21. 15:2, 9. 18:21. 22:25. 46:26. Le 26:17⸒𝒫. Dt 28:25⸒𝒫. **lives.** Heb. *nephesh*, Ge +44:30. **and their.** Je 7:33. 8:2. 9:22. 16:4. 22:19. 34:20. Dt 28:26. Ps 79:2, 3. Re 19:18-21.

8. **desolate.** See on Je 9:9-11. 18:16. 25:18. 49:13. 50:13. Le 26:32. 1 K *9:8. 2 Ch *7:20, 21. La 2:15, 16. Zp *2:15.

9. **eat the.** Le 26:29⸒𝒫. Dt *28:53-57⸒𝒫. 2 K *6:26-29. Is 9:20. La *2:20. *4:10. Ezk 5:10. **lives.** Heb. *nephesh*, Ge +44:30.

10. **break the bottle.** Je 48:12. 51:63, 64.

11. **Lord of hosts.** Je +6:6. **Even.** Je *13:14. Ps *2:8, 9. Is *30:12-14. La 4:2. Re *2:26, 27. **made whole.** Heb. healed. Je 15:18. **bury.** ver. 6. See on Je 7:31, 32.

12. **make.** lit. give. Je 10:13. 11:5. **as Tophet.** Je +7:31. 2 K *23:10. Is +*30:33.

13. **defiled.** 2 K 23:10, 12, 14. Ps *74:7. *79:1. Ezk *7:21, 22. **upon.** Je 32:29. 2 K 23:12. Zp 1:5. **have poured.** Je 7:18. **drink offerings.** Le +*23:13.

14. **from.** ver. 2, 3. **he stood.** Je 17:19. 26:2. 2 Ch

20:5. 24:20, 21. Lk 21:37, 38. Ac 5:20.

15. **because**. See on Je 7:26. 17:23. 35:15-17. 2 Ch 36:16, 17. Ne 9:17, 29. Zc √7:11-14. Ac *7:51, 52. **hardened**. This is a metaphor taken from unruly and unbroken oxen, who resist the yoke, and break and run away with their gears. Dt 10:16. 2 Ch 30:8mg. **that they**. Je 7:13. 11:7, 8, 10. 13:10, 11. 16:12. 17:23. 18:12. 22:21. 25:3. Ps 58:2-5.

JEREMIAH 20

Pashur, a chief priest, smites Jeremiah and sets him in the stocks, 1, 2. Jeremiah gives him a new name, and predicts the doom of him and his friends, 3-6. The prophet complains bitterly, but is constrained to speak in the name of God, 7-9. He recovers his confidence, and rejoices in God, 10-13. He curses the day of his birth, 14-18.

1. **Pashur**. i.e. *prosperity round about; freedom,* ✱S#6583h. Je 20:1, 2, 3, 3, 6. 21:1. 38:1, 1. 1 Ch 9:12. Ezr 2:38. 10:22. Ne 7:41. 10:3. 11:12. (1) Son of Immer, a priest who persecuted Jeremiah, Je 20:1-6. (2) Son of Melchaiah, who suggested Jeremiah's imprisonment, Je 21:1; 38:1. (3) One whose children came up from Babylon, Ezr 2:38; Ne 7:41. (4) One whose sons took strange wives, Ezr 10:22. (5) One who sealed the covenant, Ne 10:4. **son of**. Here "son" is put for descendant, in this instance descended from him through many generations (Matthew Poole). 1 Ch 7:15n, 17n. **Immer**. 1 Ch +9:12. *24:14. Ezr 2:37, 38. Ne 7:40, 41. **chief**. 2 K 25:18. 2 Ch 35:8. Ac *4:1. 5:24.

2. **smote**. Je 1:19. 19:14, 15. 26:8. 29:26. 36:26. 37:15, 16. 38:6. 1 K 22:27. 2 Ch 16:10. 24:21. Am 7:10-13. Mt √5:10-12. 21:35. 23:34-37. Ac 4:3. 5:18, 40. 7:52. 16:22-24. He *11:36, 37. Re 2:10. 17:6. **the stocks**. *Hammahpecheth,* from *haphach,* "to overturn, subvert, distort," generally denotes an *overthrow* (Dt 29:22. Is 1:7. 10:19), and seems to signify here a sort of stocks, by which the limbs were distorted into uneasy postures. So the Chaldee *keephtha,* and Jerome, *nervus,* which he explains in his comment as "a kind of wooden fetter, into which the feet were thrust," *vinculi lignei genus, cui pedes inseruntur.* Some learned men understand it as merely signifying a place of confinement, or *house of correction*; but the word is never used for any of the prisons into which the prophet was afterwards cast; and the punishment seems to have been public and ignominious. **in the high gate**. Je 37:13. 38:7. Zc 14:10.

3. **Pashur**. Ac 4:5-7. 16:30, 35-39. **hath**. Je 7:32. 19:2, 6. Ge 17:5, 15. 32:28. Is 8:3. Ho 1:4-9. **Magormissabib**. that is, *Fear round about.* i.e. *terror on every side,* ✱S#4036h, only here. ver. 10. Je 6:25. 46:5. 49:29. Ps 31:13. La 2:22.

4. **I will make**. Dt *28:65-67. Jb 18:11-21. 20:23-26. Ps *73:18, 19. Ezk 26:17-21. Mt 27:4, 5. **thine**. Je 29:21. 39:6, 7. Dt 28:32-34. 1 S 2:33. 2 K 25:7. **I will give**. Je 19:15. 21:4-10. 25:9. 32:27-31.

5. **I will deliver**. Je 3:24. 4:20. 12:12. 15:13. 24:8-10. 27:19-22. 32:3-5. 39:2, 8. 52:7-23. 2 K *20:17, 18. *24:12-16. 24:12-16. 25:13, etc. 2 Ch *36:10, 17-19. La 1:7, 10. 4:12. Ezk 22:25. Da *1:2. **strength**. ╱121N2. Metonymy of the Adjunct, Ge +34:29. *Strength* is put for all the riches which are procured by strength. **labors**. The word *labors* is here used for the *produce*

of labor. ╱121N2. Metonymy of the Adjunct, Ge +34:29. ╱121C1H, Dt +28:33. Metonymy of the Cause, labor is put for that which is produced by it.

6. **thou, Pashur**. Je 28:15-17. 29:21, 22, 32. Ac *13:8-11. **thy friends**. ver. 4. Je 5:31. 6:13-15. 8:10, 11. 14:14, 15. 23:14-17, 25, 26, 32. Is 9:15. La 2:14. Ezk 13:4-16, 22, 23. 22:28. Mi 2:11. Zc 13:3. 2 P *2:1-3. **thou hast**. Le 26:17. Dt 28:25.

7. **deceived**. *or,* enticed. Je 1:6-8, 18, 19. 4:10. 15:18. 17:16. Ex *5:22, 23. 22:16. Nu *11:11-15. 1 K 22:20mg. Ezk 14:9. or, induced or persuaded. The word is used in a good sense at Ge 9:27 (enlarge). Pr 25:15. Ho 2:14 (allure). The adjective means "persuasible," generally in a good sense, Ps 19:7; rendered "simple" at Ps 19:7; 116:6; 119:130. Pr 1:4; 8:5; 21:11, CB. **thou art**. ver. 9. Ezk 3:14. Mi 3:8. 1 C 9:16. **I am**. Je 15:10. 29:26. 2 K 2:23. Ps 22:6, 7. 35:15, 16. 69:9-12. La 3:14. Ho 9:7. Lk 16:14. 22:63, 64. 23:11, 35, 36. Ac 17:18, 32. 1 C *4:9-13. He *11:36.

8. **I cried**. Je 4:19, etc. 5:1, 6, 15-17. 6:6, 7. 7:9. 13:13, 14. 15:1-4, 13, 14. 17:27. 18:16, 17. 19:7-11. 28:8. **the word**. See on ver. 7. Je 6:10. 2 Ch 36:16. La 3:61-63. Lk 11:45. He *11:26. *13:13, 14. 1 P *4:14.

9. **I will not**. Ex 4:13. 1 K 19:3, 4. Jon 1:2, 3. 4:2, 3. Lk 9:62. Ac 15:37, 38. **was in**. Je 6:11. Jb *32:18-20. Ps 39:3. √119:11. Ezk 3:14. Ac *4:20. *17:16. *18:5. 1 C *9:16, 17. 2 C *5:13-15. **fire**. Je 5:14. *23:29. **could not**. Ac 4:20.

10. **I heard**. Ps *31:13. 57:4. 64:2-4. Mt 26:59, 60. **defaming**. Ge 39:16. Ps 37:12. **fear**. See on ver. 3. **Report**. Je 18:18. Ne 6:6-13. Pr 10:18. Is 29:21. Ezk 22:9. Lk 20:20. Ac 6:11-15. 24:1-9, 13. **All my familiars**. Heb. Every man of my peace. Je 38:22mg. Jb 19:19mg. Ps 41:9mg. 55:13, 14. Lk 11:53, 54. 12:52, 53. **we shall**. 1 K 19:2. 21:20. 22:8, 27. Mk 6:19-28. Ac *5:33. 7:54. *23:12-15.

11. **the Lord**. See on Je 1:8, 19. 15:20. Is *41:10, 14. Ro √8:31. 2 T 4:17. **a mighty**. Ps 47:2. 65:5. 66:5. **my**. Je 17:18. Dt *32:35, 36. Ps 27:1, 2. Jn 18:4-6. **not prevail**. T#513. Je 1:19. 15:20. +*17:18. Ps 37:+9 (T#87), 12-15. 47:3. Pr +16:5 (T#550). Is *41:11. *51:7, 8. √54:17. 60:14. +66:5n. Da +12:2 (T#573-7). Mi 7:9, 10. Ml 4:2, 3. Lk +16:25 (T#525). Ro 16:20. 2 Th 1:4-8. Re 3:9. 18:20. 19:3. **everlasting**. Heb. *olam,* Ge +17:7. Je 23:40. Ps 6:10. 35:26. 40:14. Is 45:16. Da +*12:2, 3.

12. **Lord of hosts**. Je +6:6. **that**. Je +*17:10. Ps *7:9. 11:5. 17:3. 26:2, 3. *139:23. Re *2:23. **reins**. ╱121I1, Ge +3:7. **let me see**. Je +*10:25. +*11:20. 12:3. 17:18. 18:19-23. 2 Ch 24:22. Ps 54:7. +*58:10. 59:10. 109:6-20. Is +*66:24. Re *6:10. *18:20. 19:2, 3. **for**. 1 S 1:15. Ps 62:8. 86:4. Is 37:14. 38:14. 1 P *2:21-23. √4:19.

13. **for**. Ps *34:6. *35:9-11. 69:33. 72:4. 109:30, 31. Is 25:4. Ja *2:5, 6. **soul**. Heb. *nephesh,* Ge +12:13.

14. **Cursed be the day**. See on Je 15:10. Jb *3:3-16. **let not**. ╱144D, Ge +40:23.

15. **A man child**. lit. a son, a male. Je 1:5. Ge 21:5, 6. Is 40:13mg. Lk 1:14. Re 12:5.

16. **as**. Ge 19:24, 25⟋P. Dt 29:23. Ho 11:8. Am 4:11. Zp 2:9. Lk 17:29. 2 P 2:6. Ju 7. **repented not**. Je 18:8. 26:13. Jon 3:4, 9, 10. 4:2. **let him**. Je 4:19. 18:22. 48:3, 4. Ex 32:17, 18. Ezk 21:22. Ho 10:14. Am 1:14. 2:2. Zp 1:16.

17. **he slew**. Jb 3:10, 11, 16. *10:18, 19. Ec *6:3.

He √10:36, 37. **grave.** Heb. *qeber*, Ge +23:4. **always.** Heb. *olam*, Ge +6:3.

18. **Wherefore.** Ge 27:46. Jb *3:20. 6:11. 7:6. 10:1. Ec 2:17. 4:1, 2. Jon 4:8. **came.** Jb *3:20. 14:1, 13. La 3:1. **to see.** Je 8:18. Ge *3:16-19. Ps *90:10. La 1:12. Jn 16:20. He 10:36. **with.** Ps 69:19. Is 50:6. 51:7. Ac 5:41. 1 C 4:9-13. 2 T 1:12. He √10:36, 37. 11:36. *12:2. 13:13. 1 P 4:14-16.

JEREMIAH 21

Zedekiah sends to inquire concerning Nebuchadnezzar's invasion, 1, 2. He is told that the city shall be destroyed, and that God will fight against both king and people, and show them no mercy, 3-7. The prophet counsels the people to fall to the Chaldeans, as the only way of preserving their lives, 8-10. He exhorts the king and his family to execute justice, 11, 12. He again predicts, that the city would certainly be destroyed, 13, 14.

1. A.M. cir. 3415. B.C. cir. 589. **The word.** This discourse was delivered about the ninth year of the reign of Zedekiah. This chapter, observes Dr. Blayney, contains the first of those prophecies which were delivered *subsequent* to the revolt of Zedekiah, and the breaking out of war thereupon; and which are continued on to the taking of Jerusalem, related in Je ch. 39 in the following order: Je ch. 21, 34, 32, 33, 38, 39. **when.** Je 32:1-3. 37:1. 52:1-3. 2 K *24:17-20. *25:1, 2. 1 Ch 3:15. 2 Ch *36:9-13. **Pashur.** Je 38:1. 1 Ch 9:12. Ne 11:12. **Melchiah.** i.e. *the Lord is king,* *S#4441h. For *S#4441h, Malchiah, see Je +38:1. For *S#4441h, Malchijah, see 1 Ch +9:12. **Zephaniah.** Je 29:25. 37:3. 52:24. 2 K 25:18-21. **Maaseiah.** i.e. *work of Jehovah; whose refuge is Jehovah,* *S#4641h. Je 21:1. 29:21, 25. 37:3. Ezr 10:18, 21, 22, 30. Ne 3:23. 8:4, 7. 10:25. 11:5, 7. 12:41, 42. Also *S#4641h: Je 35:4. 1 Ch 15:18, 20. 2 Ch 23:1. 26:11. 28:7. 34:8. (1) A priest who helped to bring up the ark from Obed-edom, 1 Ch 15:18, 20. (2) Son of Adaiah, taken in covenant by Jehoiada, 2 Ch 23:1. (3) A priest whose son was sent by Zedekiah to Jeremiah, Je 21:1; 29:25; 37:3. (4) Grandfather of Baruch, Je 32:12. (5) Grandfather of Seraiah, a quiet prince, Je 51:59. (6, 7, 8) Three priests who had taken foreign wives, Ezr 10:18, 21, 22. (9) A descendant of Pahath-moab who took a foreign wife, Ezr 10:30. (10) The father of Azariah, Ne 3:23. (11) A priest or Levite who assisted Ezra when he read the law to the people, Ne 8:4. (12) A Levite who expounded the law to the people, Ne 8:7. (13) A Jew whose descendants sealed the covenant made by Nehemiah, Ne 10:25. (14, 15) Two Jews whose descendants lived in Jerusalem after the captivity, Ne 11:5, 7. (16, 17) Two priests who assisted in the ceremonial of purifying the wall of Jerusalem, Ne 12:41, 42. (18) The father of Zedekiah the false prophet, Je 29:21. (19) One of the principal officers under Uzziah, king of Judah, 2 Ch 26:11. (20) A son of Ahaz, king of Judah, 2 Ch 28:7. (21) The governor of Jerusalem in the time of King Josiah, 2 Ch 34:8. (22) An officer of the Temple, Je 35:4.

2. **Inquire.** Je 37:3, 7. 38:14-27. 42:4-6. Jg 20:27. 1 S 10:22. 28:6, 15. 1 K 14:2, 3. 22:3-8. 2 K 1:3. 3:11-14. 22:13, 14. Ezk 14:3-7. 20:1-3. **for.** Je 32:24. 39:1, 2. 52:3-6. 2 K *25:1, 2. **Nebuchadrezzar.** i.e. *Nebo, the fire of brightness; may Nebo protect the crown,*

*S#5019h. Je 21:2, 7. 22:25. 24:1. 25:1, 9. 29:21. 32:1, 28. 35:11. 37:1. 39:1, 22. 43:10. 44:30. 46:2, 13, 26. 49:28, 30. 50:17. 51:34. 52:4, 12, 28, 29, 30. Ezk 26:7. 29:18, 19. 30:10. **according.** Ex ch. 14, 15. Jsh ch. 10, 11. Jg ch. 4, 5. 1 S 7:10-12. 14:6-14. 17:45-50. 2 Ch 14:9-13. 20:1-30. 32:21. Ps 44:1-4. 46:8-11. 48:4-8. 105:5, etc. 136:1, etc. Is *59:1, 2.

4. **Behold.** Je 32:5. 33:5. 37:8-10. 38:2, 3, 17, 18. 52:18. Is 10:4. Ho 9:12. **and I.** Je 39:3. Is *5:5. 13:4, 14. La 2:5, 7. Ezk 16:37-41. Zc 14:2. Mt *22:7.

5. **I myself.** Is *63:10. La 2:4, 5. **with an.** Je 32:17. Ex 6:6)𝓟. 9:15. Dt 4:34)𝓟. Is 5:25. 9:12, 17, 21. 10:4. Ezk 20:33, 34. Na 1:5, 6. **strong arm.** Je 20:5, 7.

6. **I will.** Je 7:20. 12:3, 4. 33:12. 36:29. Ge 6:7. Is *6:11. 24:1-6. Ezk 14:13, 17, 19, 21. *33:27-29. Ho 4:3. Mi 3:12. Zp 1:3. Lk *21:24. **they.** Je 32:24. 34:17. 42:22. Ezk 5:12, 13. 7:15. 12:16.

7. **I will.** Je 24:8-10. 34:19-22. 37:17. 38:21-23. 39:4-7. 52:8-11, 24-27. 2 K *25:5-7, 18-21. 2 Ch 36:17-20. Ezk 12:12-16. 17:20, 21. 21:25, 26. **life.** Heb. *nephesh,* Ge +44:30. **he shall.** Je 13:14. Dt 28:50)𝓟. 2 Ch 36:17. Is 13:17, 18. 27:11. 47:6. Ezk 7:9. 8:18. 9:5, 6, 10. Hab 1:6-10.

8. **I set.** Dt *11:26. *30:15, *19)𝓟. Is *1:19, 20. Re +3:20. **life.** √121G, Ge +31:1. **death.** √121G, Ge +31:1.

9. **that abideth.** See on ver. 7. Je 27:13. 38:2, 17-23. **falleth.** √96C2, Ge +45:9. **life.** Heb. *nephesh,* Ge +44:30. **a prey.** Je 38:2. 39:18. 45:5.

10. **I have.** Je 44:11, 27. Le 17:10)𝓟. 20:3-5. 26:17. Ps 34:16. Ezk 15:7. Am 9:4. **face.** √22A4, Ge +19:13. **it shall.** Je 17:27. 26:6. 32:28-31. 34:2, 22. 37:8-10. 38:3, 18, 23. 39:8. 52:13, 14. 2 Ch *36:19. Zc 1:6.

11. **the house.** Je 13:18. 17:20. Mi 3:1.

12. **house.** Is 7:2, 13. Lk 1:69. **Execute.** Heb. Judge. Je 5:28. 22:2, 3, 15-17. 23:5. 2 S 8:15. Ps 72:1-4, 12-14. 82:2-4. Is 1:17. 16:3-5. 32:1, 2. Zc 7:9-11. **morning.** Ex 18:13. Ps 101:8. Ec 10:16, 17. Zp 3:5. **deliver.** Jb 29:17. Ps 82:4. Pr 24:11, 12. 31:8, 9. Is 1:17. Lk 18:3-5. Ro 13:4. **lest.** ver. 5. Je 4:4. 5:14. 17:4. 23:19. 36:7. Le 26:28. Dt 32:22. La 2:3, 4. 4:11. Ezk 20:47, 48. 22:18-22, 31. 24:8-14. Na 1:6. Zp 1:18. **none.** See on Je 7:20. Is 1:31. Mk √9:43-48.

13. **I am.** ver. 5. Je 23:30-32. 50:31. 51:25. Ex 13:8, 20. **inhabitant.** Heb. inhabitress. √142, Ge +20:16. Je +10:17mg. **of the valley.** Jsh 15:8. Ps 125:2. Is 22:1. **Who.** Je 7:4. 49:4, 5, 16. 2 S 5:6, 7. La *4:12. Ob *3, 4. Mi *3:11.

14. **punish.** Heb. visit upon. Je +9:25mg. 11:22mg. Is 10:12mg. 24:21mg. Zc 10:3mg. **according.** Je 6:19. 17:10. 32:19. Pr *1:31. Is *3:10, 11. Ga 6:7, 8. **kindle a fire.** Je 52:13. Dt 32:22)𝓟. 2 K 25:9. 2 Ch 36:19. Is +*30:33. **in the.** Je *22:7. Is 10:18, 19. 27:10, 11. 37:24. Ezk 20:46-48. Zc 11:1. **forest.** √121D12. Metonymy of the Cause B560. Forest or wood is put for the *houses* made of its trees. For another instance of this figure see Je 22:7. **shall.** Je ✱52:13. 2 Ch 36:19.

JEREMIAH 22

The prophet is sent to the king's palace, to exhort him and his people to various duties, with conditional promises and threatenings, 1-9. The people are told not to weep for Josiah; but to lament for Shallum, who was carried captive to return no more, 10-12. Severe rebukes of Jehoiakim, and a dreadful sentence against him, 13-19. The Jews, who had been rebellious in prosperity, would be rendered more pliant by suffering, 20-23. The doom of Jeconiah, and others of David's family, 24-30.

1. A.M. cir. 3406. B.C. cir. 598. **Go.** Je 21:11. 34:2. 1 S *15:16-23. 2 S 12:1. 24:11, 12. 1 K 21:18-20. 2 Ch 19:2, 3. 25:15, 16. 33:10. Ho 5:1. Am 7:13. Mk 6:18. Lk 3:19, 20.

2. **Hear.** ver. 29. Je 13:18. 17:20, etc. 19:3. 29:20. 1 K 22:19. Is 1:10. 28:14. Ezk 34:7. Am 7:16. **that sittest.** ver. 4, 30. Je 17:25. 29:16, 17. 36:30. Is +*9:7. Lk *1:32, 33. **enter.** Je 7:2. 17:20.

3. **Execute.** Je 5:28. 9:24. See on Je 21:12. Ex √23:6-9. Le +*19:15. Dt 16:18-20. 25:1. 2 S 23:3. Jb 29:7-17. Ps 72:2-4. Mi 3:11. +*6:8. Zc 7:9-11. **judgment and.** √93A, Ge +1:26. By Hendiadys, execute righteous judgment. **do no wrong.** See on ver. 17. **do no violence.** Dt 10:18. 24:17. 27:19. Jb 22:9. 24:9. 29:12. Ps 68:5. 94:6. Pr 23:10. Is 1:23. Ezk 22:7. Ml +*3:5. Ja *1:27. **stranger.** Je 7:6. 14:8. Ge 23:4 (✴S#1616h). Ex 12:48mg. Ezk 14:7. **fatherless.** Dt +10:18. **widow.** √171I14, Ex +22:22. Is 1:17. **neither.** ver. 17. Je 7:6. 26:16. Dt 19:10-13. 2 K 24:4. Ps 94:21. Pr 6:17. Is *1:15-20. Jl 3:19.

4. **if.** Je +7:5. **then.** See on Je *17:25. **upon the throne of David.** Heb. for David upon his throne.

5. **if.** Je +7:5. 17:27. 2 Ch 7:19, 22. Is *1:20. **I swear.** Ge 22:16. Nu 14:28-30. Dt 32:40-42. Ps 95:11. Am 6:8. 8:7, 8. He 3:18. *6:13, 17. **that.** See on Je 7:13, 14. 26:6-9. 39:8. Mi 3:12.

6. **unto.** ver. 24. Je 21:11. Ge 37:25. Dt 3:25. SS *5:15. **house of Judah.** Je +3:18. **Thou.** *Gilead* was the most fertile part of the country, and renowned for its rich pastures; and Lebanon was the highest mountain in Israel, celebrated for its stately cedars; and both were, therefore, proper emblems of the reigning family. "But though thou art the richest and most powerful, I, who raised thee up, can bring thee down, and make thee a wilderness." **surely.** Je 4:20. 7:34. 9:11. 19:7, 8. 21:14. 25:9, 10. 26:6-9, 18. Ps 107:34. Is 6:11. 24:1-6. 27:10. Ezk 33:27, 28.

7. **I will.** Je 4:6, 7. 5:15. 6:4. 50:20-23. 51:27, 28. Is 10:3-7. 13:3-5. √54:16, 17. Ezk *9:1-7. Mt *22:7. **cut.** Je 21:14. Is 10:33, 34. 27:10, 11. 37:24. Zc 11:1. **cedars.** √121D12, Je +21:14.

8. **many nations.** Dt *29:23-25⟩𝒫. 1 K *9:7-9. 2 Ch *7:20-22. La *2:15-17. 4:12. Da 9:7.

9. **they shall answer.** Je 2:17-19. 40:2, 3. 50:7. Dt *29:25-28. 1 K *9:9. 2 K *22:17. 2 Ch *34:25. Da *9:7.

10. **Weep ye not.** 2 K 22:20. 23:30. 2 Ch √35:23-25. Ec 4:2. Is 57:1. La 4:9. Lk √23:28. **weep.** √113, Nu +9:20. **sore.** √147B, Ge +2:16. ver. 11. 2 K 23:30-34. Ezk 19:3, 4.

11. **Shallum.** 1 Ch *3:15. 2 Ch 23:30. 36:1-4, Jehoahaz.

12. **he shall die.** ver. 18. 2 K √23:34.

13. **unto.** ver. 18. 2 K *23:35-37. 2 Ch 36:4. **buildeth.** T#1851. Le +√19:13⟩𝒫. +√Dt 24:14, 15. Jb *24:10, 11. Mi *3:10. Hab *2:9-11. Ml +*3:5. 1 T +*5:18. Ja +*5:4. **work.** lit. wages. √121C1F, Le +19:13. Lk √10:7.

14. **I will.** Pr *17:19. *24:27. Is *5:8, 9. 9:9, 10. Da 4:30. Ml *1:4. Lk 14:28, 29. **large.** Heb. through aired. **windows.** *or,* my windows. lit. "holes." Je 9:21. Ex 8:6. **ceiled with cedar.** 2 S 7:2. 2 Ch 3:5. SS 1:17.

Hg 1:4. **vermilion.** Ezk *23:14. Na 2:3.

15. **thy.** ver. 18. 2 K 23:25. 1 Ch 3:15. **eat.** 1 K 4:20-23. 2 Ch 35:7, 8, 12-18. Ec 2:24. 9:7-10. *10:16, 17. Is 33:16. Lk *11:41. Ac *2:46. 1 C √10:31. **and do.** See on ver. 3. Je 21:12. 23:5. 2 S 8:15. 1 K 10:9. 2 K 22:2. 23:25. 2 Ch 34:2. Pr 20:28. 21:3. 25:5. 29:4. 31:9. Is +*9:7. **judgment and justice.** √93A, Ge +1:26. i.e. execute ye judgment, yea—and righteous judgment too. **then.** Je 42:6. See on Dt 4:40. Ps 128:1, 2. Ec *8:12. Is 3:10.

16. **judged.** √147D, Ge +1:29. Je 5:28. Jb *29:12-17. Ps *72:1-4, 12, 13. 82:3, 4. 109:31. Pr *22:22, 23. *24:11, 12. Is *1:17. **was not.** Je *9:3, 16, 24. *31:33, 34. 1 S 2:12. 1 Ch +*28:9. Ps +√9:10. Jn *8:19, 54, 55. 16:3. 17:√3, 6. T *1:16. Ja *1:27. 1 J √2:3, 4.

17. **thine eyes.** Jsh *7:20, 21. Jb 31:7. Ps 119:36, 37. Ezk 19:6. *33:31. Mk √7:21, 22. Ja *1:14, 15. 2 P *2:13, 14. 1 J √2:15, 16. **covetousness.** Ex +*18:21. Ps *10:3. Lk √12:15-21. *16:13, 14. Ro 1:29. 1 C +*6:9, 10. Ep +*5:3-5. Col *3:5. 1 T *6:9, 10. 2 P 2:3, 14. **shed.** ver. 3. Je 6:11. 26:22-24. 1 K 21:19. 2 K 24:4. 2 Ch 36:8. Ezk 19:6. Zp 3:3. **violence.** *or,* incursion. Je 8:6. 23:10mg. 2 S 18:27.

18. **They.** ver. 10. Je 16:4, 6. 2 K *23:34-37. 2 Ch 21:19, 20. 35:25. **Ah my brother.** 2 S 1:26. 3:33-38. 1 K *13:29, 30.

19. **buried.** √125, Jb +22:6. Figure of speech Oxymoron, which gives the meaning that he was not buried at all (for asses have no funerals). i.e. not buried at all; he shall have an unburied burial! Jehoiakim is the only king of Judah whose burial is not recorded. Je 36:30. 2 Ch 36:6. **burial.** Heb. *qeburah,* Ge +35:20. **of an ass.** Je 15:3. *36:6, 30. 1 K 14:10, 11. 21:23, 24. 2 K 9:35-37. √24:6. 2 Ch 36:6. Is 14:19. Ec 6:3.

20. **Go.** √60A, Ge +3:22. **lift.** √144A12, Ge +22:13. **and cry.** Je 2:36, 37. 30:13-15. 2 K 24:7. Is 20:5, 6. *30:1-7. 31:1-3. **Bashan.** Nu +21:33. Jsh 12:4n. 1 K 4:13. **passages.** Nu 27:12. 33:47, 48. Dt 32:49. **for.** ver. 22. Je 4:30. 25:9, 17-27. La 1:2, 19. Ezk 23:9, 22.

21. **I spake.** Je 2:31. 6:16, 17. 35:15. 36:21-26. 2 Ch 33:10, 11. *36:16, 17. Pr 30:9. **prosperity.** Heb. prosperities. √96F2, Ge +4:10. Ps ❶*119:67. 122:7. Mk +4:19. Plural of majesty for great prosperity. **will not hear.** Pr *1:24-30. **This.** Je 3:25. 7:22-28. 32:30. Dt *9:7, 24. 31:27. *32:15-20. Jg *2:11-19. Ne *9:16, etc. Ps *106:6, etc. Is *48:8. Ezk *20:8, 13, 21, 28. 23:3-39.

22. **wind.** Je 4:11-13. 30:23, 24. Is √64:6. Ho 4:19. 13:15. **thy pastors.** Je 2:8. 3:15. 5:30, 31. 10:21. 12:10. 23:1, 2. Ezk 34:2-10. Zc 11:8, 17. Ac 7:51, 52. **thy lovers.** See on ver. 20. **surely.** See on Je 2:26, 27, 37. 20:11. **wickedness.** Is +45:7.

23. **inhabitant.** Heb. inhabitress. Je 10:17mg. Is 12:6mg. **Lebanon.** ver. 6. Zc *11:1, 2. **makest.** Je 21:13, 14. 48:28. 49:16. Nu 24:21. Am *9:2, 3. Ob *4. Hab 2:9. **how gracious.** √91, 2 S +6:20. Je 3:21. 4:31. 6:24. 30:5, 6. 50:4, 5. Ho 5:15. 6:1. 7:14. **when.** See on Je 4:30, 31.

24. **As I live.** Nu 14:28. Is 49:18. Ezk 5:11. Ro ▶14:11. **Coniah.** √33, 1 Ch +11:13. i.e. *made ready of Jah; established of the Lord; Jehovah has established,* ✴S#3659h. Je 22:24h, 28h. 37:1h. 2 K 24:6-8, Jehoiachin. 1 Ch *3:16, Jeconiah. Mt *1:11, 12, Jechonias. **the signet.** √22D5N. Anthropomorphism B894. A seal

is attributed to God. For another instance of this figure see Hg 2:23. ver. 6. SS *8:6. Hg 2:23.

25. I will give. ver. 28. Je 21:7. 34:20, 21. 38:16. 2 K *24:15, 16. **life.** Heb. *nephesh*, Ge +44:30. **whose.** Pr 10:24.

26. I will cast. Je 15:2-4. 2 K 24:15. 2 Ch *36:9, 10. Is 22:17. Ezk 19:9-14.

27. to the. ver. 11. Je 44:14. 52:31-34. 2 K *25:27-30. **desire.** Heb. lift up their mind. Heb. *nephesh*, Ex +15:9. Je 44:14mg. Ps 86:4. Ezk 24:25mg.

28. Is this man. This appears to be the application of the whole discourse to Zedekiah; for it is to be observed, that Jeconiah is spoken of as *absent*, and *already in captivity.* Now if he and his seed had been for their sins thrown aside as a broken idol, or as a vessel which a man despises, how could Zedekiah, who copied and far exceeded them, expect to prosper on the throne of David? **Coniah.** See on ver. 24. **a despised.** Je 48:38. 1 S 5:3-5. 2 S 5:21. Ps 31:12. Ho *8:8. 13:15. Ro *9:21-23. 2 T *2:20, 21. **his seed.** ver. 30. 1 Ch 3:17-24. Mt 1:12-16. **which.** See on Je 14:18.

29. O earth. ♪84, Dt +32:1. Je 6:19. Dt *4:26. 31:19. 32:1. Is 1:1, 2. *34:1. Mi *1:2. *6:1, 2. **earth.** ♪84, Ge +6:17.

30. Write. Zedekiah was taken prisoner by Nebuchadnezzar; his sons slain before his eyes; and his eyes being put out, he was carried to Babylon; and we read no more either of him or his posterity. 1 Ch 3:16, 17. Mt 1:12-16. **childless.** Coniah did have children (1 Ch 3:16, 17. Mt 1:12), but this prediction asserts that he would not have any children who would prosper, sitting upon the throne of Judah. Their title to the throne was not lost, but the experience of occupying the throne at length and prosperously has never been granted to Coniah's descendants. For a fuller discussion see W. W. Barndollar, *Jesus' Title to the Throne of David,* pp. 88-99. **sitting.** The line of the Messiah is traced for Joseph's genealogy to David through his son Solomon to Jeconiah, upon whom Jeremiah records the curse that no descendant of his should sit (at length or prosperously) upon the throne of David. But Luke traces Mary's genealogy through David's son Nathan, so that through the virgin birth Jesus's right to "sit upon the throne of David" is unimpaired by this prophecy, as Jeconiah is not in Mary's line to David. The legal title to the throne of David can only be established through the genealogy as given by Matthew, for only Solomon was chosen heir, by divine appointment (1 Ch 22:8-10), of the Davidic throne (1 Ch √28:5), not Nathan. As Jesus was the legal son of Joseph, though not the natural son because of the virgin birth, the legal claim of Jesus as the Messiah to the throne of David through the line of Solomon is unimpaired. See on Je *36:30. Ps 94:20. Mt 1:1, 11, 12, 16. Lk 1:27, 32, 33. 3:23, ◐*31.

JEREMIAH 23

A woe is denounced on the corrupt pastors, and the restoration of the scattered flock is predicted, 1-4. A prophecy of the kingdom and righteousness of Christ, and of the gathering of the people to him, 5-8. The wickedness of the nation charged on the priests and false prophets, 9-15. The people are cautioned against hearkening to false prophets, and instructed how to distinguish them; with sharp rebukes and terri-ble threatenings against them, 16-32. A rebuke of those who made a scoff at the words of the true prophets, 33-40.

1. Woe. Je 2:8, 26. Ezk √13:3. *34:2. Zc *11:17. Mt *23:13-29. Lk 11:42-52. **pastors.** ver. 2, 11-15. Je 2:8. 10:21. 12:10. 22:22. 25:34-36. 50:6. Is *56:9-12. Ezk 22:25-29. 34:2-10, 21. Mi 3:11, 12. Zp 3:3, 4. Zc 11:5-7, 15-17. Mt 9:36. +*15:14. Jn *10:10, 12-15.

2. not visited. T#463. 1 S *12:23. Jl 2:17. Mt *25:36, 42, 43-45. Ac 20:31. Ro 1:9. 2 C 11:2. 12:14, 15. Ga 4:19, 20. Ph *1:3-5, 8. Col *1:9-11, 28. 4:12, 13. 1 Th 2:6-12. 3:7-10. Ja √1:27. **visit upon.** ver. 34mg. Je 5:9, 29. 8:12. +11:22mg. 13:21mg. Ex 32:34₽. Ho 2:13. Mi 7:4.

3. I will gather. Je 29:14. 30:3. 31:8, 10. 32:37. Dt √30:3-5. Ps 106:47. Is √11:11-16. *27:12, 13. *43:5, 6. Ezk *11:17. *34:12, 13, etc. *36:24, 37. *37:21-27. 39:27, 28. Am √9:14, 15. Mi 7:12. Zp *3:19, 20. Zc *10:8-12.

4. set up shepherds. Je 3:14, 15. 33:26. Ps 78:70-72. Is 11:11. 30:20, 21. 40:11. Ezk 34:23, etc. Ho 3:3-5. Mi 5:2, 4, 5. 7:14. Jn *21:15-17. Ac √20:28, 29. 1 P *5:1-4. **neither.** Nu 31:49. Jn 6:39, 40. √10:27-30. 17:12. 18:9. 1 P 1:5.

5. the days. Je *30:3. *31:27, 31, 38. *33:14. He *8:8. **the Lord.** Ne +9:6. **I will raise.** Je *33:15. Ps 72:1, 2. Is *32:1, 2. *40:10, 11. Da *9:24. Am 9:11. Zc √9:9. Re *19:11. **righteous.** Zc 13:7. 1 C 1:30. **Branch.** ♪22H1A, Is +4:2. Ps 80:15. Is 4:2. *11:1-5. *40:9, 11. *53:2. Ezk 17:2-10, 22-24. *34:29. Zc *3:8. *6:12, 13. Jn *1:45. **shall reign.** Ps 47:8. 96:10. 146:10. Is +*9:7. +*24:23. 32:1. 52:7. Mi +*4:7. Zc +*14:9. Lk +*1:32, 33. 1 C +*15:25n. 2 T 2:12. Re *11:15, 17. 19:6. +*20:4. **and prosper.** Je 22:30. Ps 45:4. Is 52:13mg. 53:10. **and shall.** See on Je 22:3, 15. Ps *72:2. Is 32:1, 2. 40:10, 11. **judgment and justice.** ♪93A. Hendiadys, Ge +1:26. Je 22:15. Da √9:24. Am 9:11. Zc 9:9. Re 19:11. **in the earth.** Is 26:9. Re +*5:10.

6. Judah. Dt *33:28, 29. Ps 130:7, 8. Is *12:1, 2. *33:22. *45:17. Ezk *37:24-28. Ho 1:7. Ob 17, 21. Zc *10:6. Mt √1:21. Lk *1:71-74. √19:9, 10. Ro *11:26, 27. **dwell.** Je 30:10. *32:37. Le 25:18, 19₽. 26:5₽. Dt 33:12, 28₽. 1 K 4:25. Is *2:4. 35:9. Ezk *34:25-28. Ho *2:18. Zp +*3:13. Zc *2:4, 5. 3:10. *14:9-11. **and this.** Is +*7:14. +*9:6. Mt +*1:21-23. **THE LORD OUR RIGHTEOUSNESS.** Heb. *Jehovah-tsidkenu.* ♪121E1, Ge +25:23. Je *33:15, 16. Ex +15:26. Dt 6:25. Is *45:24, 25. *54:17. 64:6. Da *9:24. Ro √3:22. 5:19. *10:2-4. 1 C *1:30. 2 C √5:21. Ph *3:9. 2 P 1:1.

7. the days come. ver. 3. See on Je 16:14, 15. 31:31-34. Is *43:18, 19. **which brought.** Ex ch. 12-15₽.

8. which brought. ver. 3. Is √11:11n. *14:1. *27:12, 13. √43:5, 6. 65:8-10. Ezk +*34:13. *36:24. +√37:25. √39:28, 29. Am √9:14, 15. Zp *3:20. **the house of Israel.** Je +2:4. **the north country.** Is √43:6. Ezk +*38:6, 15n. Da *11:44. **they shall dwell.** Is 65:9, 10. Ezk √37:25. Am +√9:14, 15. Zc 8:7, 8. **own land.** Dt +*32:43. Is +*60:21.

9. A.M. 3399. B.C. 605. heart. Je 9:1. 14:17, 18. 2 K 22:19, 20. Ezk *9:4, 6. Da *8:27. Hab *3:16. **broken.** ♪141, Is +22:4. **because.** See on Je 5:31. **like a drunken.** Je 25:15-18. Ps *60:3. Is *6:5. 28:1. *29:9. 51:21. La 3:15. Ro *7:9.

10. full. Je 5:7, 8. 7:9. 9:2. Ezk 22:9-11. 23:9-12. Ho 4:2, 3. Ml +*3:5. Mt *5:27, 28. 1 C +*6:9, 10.

Ga +*5:19-21. He +*13:4. Ja *4:4. **because**. Zc 5:3, 4. 1 T 1:10. **swearing**. Heb. cursing. Je 29:18mg. Ge 24:41 (oath). Le 5:1. Pr 29:24. Is 24:6. **the land**. Je 12:3, 4. 14:2. La 1:2-4. Jl 1:10. **the pleasant**. Je 9:10. Ps 107:34. Is 24:6. **course**. or, violence. Je 8:6. 22:17. 2 S 18:27.

11. **both**. ver. 15. Je 5:31. 6:13. 8:10. Ezk *22:25, 26. Zp *3:4. **in**. Je 7:10, 11, 30. 11:15. 32:34. 2 Ch 33:5, 7. 36:14. Ezk 7:20. 8:5, 6, 11, 16. 23:39. Mt *21:12, 13.

12. **as**. Je 13:16. Ps 35:6. 73:18. Pr +*4:19. **in the**. Jb 18:18. Is 8:22. Jn *12:35. 1 J *2:11. Ju 13. **the year**. Je +*8:12. 11:23. 23:12. 48:44. 50:27. Ex 32:34. Mi 7:4.

13. **folly**. or, an absurd thing. Heb. unsavory. Jb 1:22. 24:12. La 2:14. **prophets**. Ho *9:7, 8. **prophesied**. Je 2:8. 1 K 18:18-21, 25-28, 40. **and caused**. 2 Ch 33:9. Is *9:16. **to err**. ver. 32. Je 42:20.

14. **in the**. Je 5:30, 31. 14:14. 26:32. Ezk *13:2-4, 16. 22:25. Is 41:6, 7. Mi 3:11. Zp 3:4. 2 P *2:1, 2. **an horrible thing**. or, filthiness. Je 5:30. 18:13. **they commit**. Je 29:23. 2 P 2:14-19. **walk**. ver. 17, 25, 26, 32. Je 14:14. Ezk 22:25. 2 Th √2:9-11. 1 T 4:2. Re 19:20. +*21:8. 22:15. **strengthen**. See on Ezk 13:22, 23. **Sodom**. Ge 13:13. 18:20. 19:24℘. Dt 32:32. Is 1:9, 10. Ezk 16:46-52. Ml 1:1. Mt 11:24. 2 P 2:6. Ju 7. Re 11:8.

15. **Lord of hosts**. Je +6:6. **will**. Je 8:14. 9:15. Ps 69:21. La 3:5, 15, 19. Mt 27:34. Re *8:10, 11. **profaneness**. or, hypocrisy. *S#2613h, only here. Is 32:6.

16. **Hearken**. Je 27:9, 10, 14-17. 29:8. Pr 19:27. Mt *7:15, 16. 2 C √11:13-15. Ga *1:8, 9. 1 J *4:1. **they make**. Je +*2:5. 2 K 17:15. Ro 1:21. **a vision**. ver. 21, 26. Je 14:14. Ezk *13:3, 6, 16, 23. 22:28. Mi 2:11. **own heart**. ver. 26. Nu +16:28.

17. **say still**. √147B, Ge +2:16. **that despise**. Nu 11:20. 1 S *2:30. 2 S 12:10. Ml *1:6. Lk √10:16. Ju √5:23. 1 Th *4:7, 8. **Ye**. Je 4:10. 6:14. 8:11. 14:13, 14. 28:3-9. Is *3:10, 11. *57:21. La 2:14. Ezk 13:10, 15, 16, 22. Mi 3:5, 11. Zc 10:2. **imagination**. or, stubbornness. Je 3:17mg. 7:24mg. 9:14mg. 13:10mg. Dt 29:19mg. **No**. Je 18:18. Am 9:10. Mi 3:11. Zp 1:12.

18. **who**. ver. 22. Nu 9:8. 1 K *22:24. Jb 15:8-10. 2 Ch 18:23. Is *40:13, 14. 1 C *2:16. **counsel**. or, secret. Je ●7:24. Ps 25:14. ●81:12. Am 3:7. Jn 15:15.

19. **a whirlwind**. As whirlwinds are sometimes fatal to travelers, who overwhelmed by them in the desert, they are elegantly employed to denote the certainty, as well as suddenness, of the destruction of the wicked. Mr. Morier (Second Journey, p. 202), describing the whirlwinds of Persia, says they swept along the country in different directions, in a manner truly terrific, carrying away in their vortex sand, branches, and the stubble of the fields, and really appearing to make a communication between the earth and the clouds. Je 4:11. 25:32. 30:23. Ps *58:9. Pr *1:24-27. 10:25. Is 5:25-28. 21:1. 40:24. 66:15, 16. Am 1:14. Na 1:3-6. Zc 9:14.

20. **until**. Je 30:24. Is 14:24. Zc 1:6. 8:14, 15. **in the latter days**. Ge *49:1℘. Dt *31:29, 30. 1 K 8:47. Pr 5:11-14. +*21:30. Ho *3:4, 5.

21. **not sent**. ver. 32. Je 14:14. 27:15. 28:15. 29:9, 31. Is 6:8. Jn 20:21. Ac 13:4. Ro *10:15.

22. **if**. See on ver. *18. Ezk *27:3. *3:17. Ac *20:27. **my counsel**. ver. 18. Je ●7:24. Ps ●81:12. 106:13. 107:11. Pr 1:25. **had caused**. ver. √28. **then**. Je *25:5. *35:15. 36:3. Ezk *13:22. *18:30. Zc *1:4. Ac *26:18-

20. 1 Th *1:9, 10. *5:6. **turned them**. Ml *2:6.

23. **Am I**. √14, Is +5:3. **a God at hand**. 1 K +*20:23, 28. Ps 113:5, 6. *139:1-10. Ezk 20:32-35. Jon *1:3, 4.

24. **Can**. √85C, Ge +18:14. **hide**. Je 49:10. Ge *16:13. Jb *22:13, 14. *24:13-16. Ps *10:11. *90:8. 139:7, 11-16. Pr *15:3. Is *29:15. Ezk *8:12. 9:9. Am 9:2, 3. **Do not I fill**. √85B, Ge +13:9. For the omnipresence of God the Father, see Pr +15:3 (T#220). God the Father possesses the incommunicable divine attribute of immensity (Mt +*28:19n). Shedd categorizes this attribute as one of the immanent or intransitive attributes "which do not go forth and operate outside of the Divine essence, but remain internal. Such are immensity, eternity, simplicity, self-existence, etc." (Dogmatic Theology, Vol. 1, p. 337). "The Immensity of God is his essence as related to space. The Divine essence is not measurable, because not included in the limits of space. God's immensity is spiritual, having no extension of substance. By virtue of God's immensity, he is Omnipresent" (Shedd, Dogmatic Theology, vol. 1, pp. 339, 340). 1 K 8:27. 2 Ch 2:6. 6:18. Ps 148:13. Is √57:15. 66:1. Da 4:35. Mt +*28:19n. Ep *1:22, 23.

25. **heard**. Je 8:6. 13:27. 16:17. 29:23. Ps *139:2, 4. Lk *12:3. 1 C *4:5. He √4:13. Re *2:23. **dreamed**. The false prophets professed that they had revelations from God in supernatural dreams; and they caused this to be rumored abroad. But the Lord declared that it was an imposture: for they only spake their own conjectures, the result of the pride and presumption of their own deceitful hearts. Their purpose, as well as the tendency of their lying predictions, was to seduce the people into forgetfulness of God, and contempt of his word; that they might graft idolatry and superstition on their infidelity, and so render them their attached and submissive followers (Scott). ver. 28, 32. Je 29:8. Ge 37:5, 9. Nu 12:6. Jl 2:28. Mt 1:20.

26. **How**. Je 4:14. 13:27. Ps *4:2. Ho 8:5. Ac *13:10. **shall this be**. Je 31:6, 16, 17. Pr 8:21. 18:24. Lk 7:25. **prophets of**. See on Je 14:14. 17:9. Is *30:9, 10. 2 Th √2:9-11. 1 T √4:1, 2. 2 T √4:3. 2 P 2:13-16. **own heart**. ver. 16. Nu +16:28.

27. **think**. Dt 13:1-5. Ac 13:8. 2 T *2:17, 18. 3:6-8. **as**. See on Je 3:7. 8:33, 34. 10:6. 2 K 21:3.

28. **that hath**. Heb. with whom is. **a dream**. ver. 32. Ezk 13:7. The contrast is between the false prophets who have their dreams and the true prophet who has God's word. The opposition between chaff and wheat which follows shows these alleged supernatural dreams for what they are—not divine revelation, but a dream of their own heart, mere chaff, unsuitable and valueless for spiritual sustenance. This is perhaps the clearest and strongest appeal to the perspicuity of Scripture to be found in the Bible, for an appeal is here made for the ordinary believer to discern the difference between the false and the true. A mark of false religion is placement of spiritual and doctrinal authority in any other source than the written word of God found in the Bible—whether the source be an organization and its literature, the writings of a particular teacher or prophet, or a claim to divine authority based upon apostolic succession, or even a line of succession through valid baptisers traced back to John the Baptist! Is +*8:20n. **speak my word**. Pr *14:5. Mt +*24:45. Lk +*12:42. 1 C *4:2. 2 C √2:17. 1 T 1:12. 1 P 2:2. A mark of the false is adding to the written word of

God supposed new revelation from whatever source— whether supernatural dreams, or alleged supernatural gifts of the Spirit. Pr +*30:6. Jn 16:8-14. 2 T +√3:15-17. 2 P *1:21. **faithfully**. Da +*11:33n. 1 T +*4:16. 2 T +√2:15. *4:2. **What**. ƒ138C, Ge +22:14. That is, when the dreamers declare their dreams, and the true prophets faithfully declare their message, the difference between them will be as evident as that between "the chaff and the wheat." 1 C *3:11-13.

29. **Is not**. As *fire* penetrates, enlivens, illuminates, purifies, consumes, or transforms every substance into its own nature; so the Sacred Word, applied by the Spirit of God, penetrates the conscience, quickens and illuminates the mind, softens and melts the heart, purifies the affections, consumes the dross of sin, and transforms the believer's soul into its own holy nature; and as a *hammer*, it breaks down the presumptuous confidence of the proud and stouthearted. Dr. Adam Clarke thinks there may be an allusion to the practice, in some countries, of roasting *stones* containing ore, before they are subjected to the *hammer*, in order to pulverize them. In Cornwall, they roast the tin stones, by which the arsenic is separated from the ore, and they are then easily reduced to powder in the stamp mill; and, being afterwards washed, the grains of tin sink to the bottom, while the lighter parts go off with the water, and the metal is then procured clean and pure. **my word**. Je +*15:16. **like as**. Je *5:14. 20:9. Lk *24:32. Jn *6:63. Ac 2:3, *37. 2 C *2:16. √10:4, 5. He √4:12. Re *11:5.

30. **I am against**. Je 14:14, 15. 44:11, 29. Le 20:3. 26:17. Dt √18:20⸰℘. 29:20. Ps 34:16. Ezk 13:8, 9, 20. 15:7. 1 P 3:12. God was against the false prophets for attaching His name to their falsehoods to lend them authority. **that steal**. Lk *8:12. God's word is stolen when we substitute for it our own values, message, program, and authority.

31. **use**. *or*, smooth. Is 30:10. Mi √2:11. **He saith**. See on ver. 17. Ge 22:16⸰℘. Nu 14:28⸰℘. 24:3, 4, 15, 16⸰℘. 2 Ch 18:5, 10-12, 19-21.

32. **false dreams**. ver. +*28. **to err**. See on ver. 16. Je 27:14, etc. 28:15-17. 29:21-23, 31. Dt *13:1, etc. √18:20. Is 3:12. Ezk √13:7-18. Zc 13:2, 3. Mk +*12:24. Re *19:20. **and by**. Zp 3:4. 2 C 1:17. **therefore**. See on ver. 22. Je 7:8. La 2:14. Mt +*15:14.

33. **What**. ƒ85.O. Erotesis B955: in reproaches. For another instance of this figure see ver. 35, 36. **the burden**. Je 17:15. 20:7, 8. Is 13:1. 14:28. Na 1:1. Hab 1:1. Ml 1:1. **forsake you**. See on ver. 39, 40. Je 12:7. Dt 31:17, 18. 32:19, 20. 2 Ch 15:2. Ps *78:58-60. Ho 9:12.

34. **punish**. Heb. visit upon. See on ver. 2. Je +9:25mg.

35. **every one**. Je 31:34. He +*8:11. **What**. ƒ85.O, ver. 33.

36. **for every**. Ps 12:3. 64:8. 120:3. 140:9. Pr 17:20. Is 3:8. Mt √12:36. Lk *19:22. 2 P *2:17-19. Ju 15, 16. **for ye**. Is 28:13, 14, 22. Ga 1:7-9. 6:5. 2 P 3:16. **of the**. See on Je 10:10. Dt 5:26. 1 S 17:26, 36. 2 K 19:4. Ac 14:15. 1 Th 1:9.

37. **What hath**. ver. 35. Je 33:3. 42:4.

38. **ye say**. 2 C +*11:13, 14. **the burden**. ver. +30n. Is +*8:20n. **ye shall not say**. Ps +*50:16. Mk +*3:12.

39. **I, even I**. Ge 6:17. Le *26:28. Dt 31:17. 32:39. Is 48:15. 51:12. Ezk 5:8. 6:3. 34:11, 20. Pr 13:13. Ho 4:6. 5:14. **forget**. ƒ22C4, Ps +13:1. **forsake you**. See

on ver. 33. Je 32:28-35. 35:17. 36:31. Is ◐+*41:9. +*54:7. La 5:20. Ezk 8:18. 9:6. Ho 9:12-17. Mt *21:43. **cast**. Je 52:3. Ps 51:11. Mt +*25:41. 2 Th √1:8, 9.

40. **everlasting**. Heb. *olam*, Ge +17:7. **reproach**. See on Je 20:11. 24:9. 42:18. 44:8-12. Dt *28:37. Ezk *5:14, 15. Da 9:16. +*12:2. Ho 4:7. **perpetual**. Ge +*9:12.

JEREMIAH 24

A vision of two baskets of figs, one very good, the other very bad, 1-3. This is explained of the reformation and restoration of the Jews who had been carried captive with Jeconiah; and the increasing wickedness and total ruin of those who remained in the land, 4-10.

1. A.M. 3406. B.C. 598. **Lord**. Am *3:7. 7:1, 4, 7. *8:1, 2. Zc 1:20. 3:1. **two**. Dt *26:2-4. **after**. Je 22:24-28. 29:2. 2 K *24:12-16. 2 Ch 36:10. Ezk 19:9. **Jeconiah**. i.e. *he will be established of the Lord; Jehovah will establish*, ✳S#3204h. Je 24:1. 27:20. 28:4. 29:2. 1 Ch 3:16, 17. Est 2:6. Variant of the name Jehoiachin, 2 K +24:8, and Coniah, Je +22:24. **carpenters**. Je 10:3, 9. 29:2. Ex 28:11. **smiths**. Je 29:2. 1 S 13:19, 20. 2 K 24:14.

2. **One basket**. ver. 5-7. Ho *9:10. Mi 7:1. **first ripe**. The *boccore*, or figs of the *early sort*; perhaps those which are ripe about six weeks before the full season, which are reckoned a great dainty. See Note on Is 28:4. **naughty**. ƒ108K42, Pr +6:12. The *winter* fig, probably, then its *crude* or unripe state. ver. 8-10. Is *5:4, 7. Ezk *15:2-5. Ml 1:12-14. Mt *5:13. **they were so bad**. Heb. for badness.

3. **What**. Je 1:11-14. 1 S 9:9. Am 7:8. 8:2. Zc 4:2. 5:2, 5-11. Mt *7:17, 19. 25:32, 33.

5. **God of Israel**. Je +11:3. **I acknowledge**. lit. know. ƒ121C2A2, Ge +39:6. Na *1:7. Zc *13:9. Mt 25:12. Jn √10:27. 1 C 8:3. Ga 4:9. 2 T *2:19. **them that are carried away captive**. Heb. the captivity. Je 28:4mg. **for**. Dt *8:16. Ps *94:12-14. 119:67, 71. Ro √8:28. He 12:5-10. Re *3:19.

6. **For I will**. Je 21:10. Dt *11:12. 2 Ch √16:9. Ne 5:19. Jb 33:27, 28. Ps *34:15. 1 P *3:12. **and I will bring**. Je 12:15. 23:3. 29:10. 32:37. Ezk 11:15-17. 36:24. **I will build**. Je 1:10. 18:7-9. 32:41. 33:7. 42:10.

7. **I will give**. Je 31:33, 34. 32:39. Dt *30:6⸰℘. Ezk *11:19, 20. *36:24-28. **and they**. Je 30:22. 31:33. 32:38. Le 26:12⸰℘. Dt 26:17-19. Ezk *37:23, 27. Zc *8:8. 13:9. He *8:10. +*11:16. **for they**. Je 3:10. 29:12-14. Dt 4:29-31. 30:2-5. 1 S 7:3. 1 K 8:46-50. 2 Ch 6:38. Is √55:6, 7. Ho 14:1-3. Ro *6:17. 2 C *3:16, 17.

8. **as**. See on ver. 2, 5. Je 29:16-18. **So will**. Je 21:10. 32:28, 29. 34:17-22. 37:10, 17. 38:18-23. 39:2-9. 52:2-11. Ezk *12:12-16. *17:11-21. **and them**. See on Je 43, 44.

9. **to be removed**. Heb. for removing, *or* vexation. Je 15:4mg. 34:17mg. Dt *28:25⸰℘, 37, 65-67. Ezk 5:1, 2, 12, 13. **to be a**. Je 19:8. 25:18. 26:6. 42:18. 44:12, 22. 1 K 9:7. 2 Ch 7:20. Ps *44:13, 14. La 2:15-17. Ezk 25:3. 26:2. 36:2, 3. **a taunt**. Dt 28:37 (byword)⸰℘. **a curse**. Je 29:18, 22. Ps 109:18, 19. Is 65:15.

10. **I will send**. Je 5:12. 9:16. 14:15, 16. 15:2. 16:4. 19:7. 34:17. Le 26:25, 26⸰℘. Dt 28:21-24⸰℘. Is *51:19. Ezk 5:12-17. 6:12-14. 7:15. 14:12-21. 33:27.

JEREMIAH 25

A summary review of the messages sent by Jeremiah to the Jews, during twenty-three years; and a reproof of their contempt of them, 1-7. A prediction of the desolations of the land for seventy years; after which the Chaldean empire would be subverted, 8-14. A prediction of the devastation of the surrounding kingdoms; under the figures of an intoxicating cup, a destroying sword, a lion wasting a sheepfold, and the howlings of the shepherds, 15-38.

1. A.M. 3398. B.C. 606. **in the.** Je 36:1. 46:2. 2 K *24:1, 2. Da 1:1, 2. **the first.** Nebuchadnezzar was associated with his father Nabopollasar two years before the death of the latter; and from this time the Jewish computation of Nebuchaddnezzar's reign begins; and, from the end of the third year of Jehoiakim; and therefore, according to them, the fourth year of Jehoiakim was the first year of Nebuchadnezzar. But the Babylonians date the commencement of his reign two years later, that is, on the death of his father; which computation is followed by Daniel, who wrote in Chaldee. See Prideaux, sub. an. 607 & 562.

2. **spake unto.** Je 18:11. 19:14, 15. 26:2. 35:13. 38:1, 2. Ps 49:1, 2. Mk 7:14-16.

3. **thirteenth.** Je 1:2. 1 K 22:3. 2 Ch 34:3, 8. **rising.** ver. 4. Je 7:13. 11:7. 29:19. 35:15. 44:4. Ge +*19:27. *22:3. Ex 8:20. 2 Ch 36:15. Ps 81:13. Is 55:2. Mk +*1:35. Jn 8:2, 47. 2 T *4:2. **not hearkened.** Ps *81:13. Jn *8:47.

4. **all his.** Urijah the son of Shemaiah, and Huldah the prophetess, lived about this time. Zephaniah also prophesied during part of the time; and it is probable that Habakkuk was contemporary with them. **rising early.** That is, "sending them diligently." ver. 3. *7:25. 11:7. *26:5. 29:19. 32:33. *34:14, 15. *44:4, 5. 2 Ch *36:15, 16. **not hearkened.** ver. 3, 7. Je *7:24-26. 11:8-10. *13:10, 11. *16:12. *17:23. 18:12. 19:15. 22:21. 36:31. Zc *7:11, 12. Mt *21:32-40. Jn √1:11, 12. Ac *7:51, 52. He *12:25.

5. **Turn.** See on Je 18:11. 35:15. 2 K 17:13, 14. Is √55:6, 7. Ezk *18:30. 33:11. Jon 3:8-10. Zc 1:4, 5. Lk √13:3-5. Ac 26:20. Ja √4:8-10. **for.** Je 7:7. 17:25. Ge 17:8. Ps 37:27. 105:10, 11. **ever and for.** Heb. *olam* doubled, Da +2:20.

6. **go not after.** Je 7:6, 9. +*10:2. 35:15. Ex +*20:3, 23. Dt *6:14. 8:19. 13:2. 28:14. Jsh 24:20. 1 K 11:4-10. 14:22. 2 K 17:35.

7. **that ye.** See on Je 7:18, 19. 32:30-33. Dt *32:21⅌. 2 K 17:17. *21:15. Ne 9:26. Pr *8:36.

8. **the Lord of hosts.** Je +6:6.

9. **I will.** Je 1:15. 5:15, 16. 6:1, 22-26. 8:16. Le *26:25, etc. Dt 28:45-50. Pr +*21:1. Is *5:26-30. *10:5. 39:7. Hab *1:6-10. **Nebuchadrezzar.** Je 27:6. 40:2. 43:10. Is 13:3. 44:28. 45:1. Ezk 29:18-20. **my servant.** Je *27:6. 43:10. Is +*10:5. 44:24, 28. **against.** ver. 17-26. Je 27:3-8. Ezk 26:7. 29:19. 30:10, 11. **an astonishment.** See on Je 18:16. 24:9. Dt 28:37⅌. 1 K *9:7, 8. **perpetual.** Ge +*9:12.

10. **take from.** Heb. cause to perish from. Est 3:13. 7:4. 8:11. **voice of mirth.** Je 7:34. 16:9. 33:10, 11. Is *24:7-12. Ezk 26:13. Ho 2:11. Re *⟩18:22, 23. **the sound.** Sir J. Chardin remarks, that in the East, every where in the morning may be heard the *noise of the mills,* which often awakens people; for they generally grind every day just as much as may be necessary for the day's consumption. Where, then, the noise of the mill is not heard in the morning, nor the light of the candle seen in the evening, there must be an utter desolation (See Harmer, ch. iv. Ob. 15). Ec 12:2-4.

11. **seventy years.** This prophecy was delivered in the fourth year of Jehoiakim, and began to be accomplished immediately; and it was exactly *seventy* years from this time to the proclamation of Cyrus for the return of the Jews. Beginning B.C. 606, 2 K 14:1; ending B.C. 536, Ezr 1:1; Da 9:2. ver. 12. 2 Ch *36:21, 22. Is 23:15-17. Da √9:2. Zc 7:5.

12. **it shall come.** Is 44:26-28. **when.** Je 29:10. 2 K 24:1. Ezr 1:1, 2. Da √9:2. **that I.** ver. 14. Je ch. 50, 51. Dt *32:35-42. Is ch. 13, 14, 21, 46, 47. Da ch. 5. Hab ch. 2. Re ch. 18. **punish.** Heb. visit upon. Je +11:22mg. See on Je 23:2. **perpetual.** Je 50:3, 13, 23, 39, 40, 45. 51:25, 26, 62-64. Ge +*9:12. Is √13:19. 14:23. 15:6. 20:1, etc. *47:1. Ezk *35:9.

13. **hath.** See on Je 1:5, 10. Da 5:28, 31. Re 10:11.

14. **many.** Je 27:7. 50:9, 41. 51:6, 27, 28. Is *14:2. *45:1-3. Da *5:28. Hab *2:8-16. **I will recompense.** Je 50:29-34. 51:6, 20-27, 35-41. Ps 137:8. Is 66:6. Re *18:20-24.

15. **Lord God of Israel.** Je +11:3. **Take.** Je 13:12-14. Jb *21:20. Ps *11:6. *75:8. Is *51:17, 22. Zc 12:2. Re *14:9, 10, 19, 20. **all.** ver. 27-33.

16. **shall drink.** ver. 27. Je 51:7, 39. La *3:15. 4:21. Ezk *23:32-34. Na 3:11. Re *14:8, 10. 16:9-11. 18:3. **because of.** Le 26:25, 33⅌.

17. **and made.** ver. 28. Je 1:10. 27:3. ch. 46-51. Ezk *43:3.

18. **Jerusalem.** Je 1:10. 19:3-9. 21:6-10. Ps *60:3. Is *51:17, 22. Ezk *9:5-8. Da 8:12. *9:12. Am 2:5. *3:2. 1 P *4:17. **to make.** See on ver. 9, 11. Je 24:9. Jsh 6:18. 2 K 22:19. **as it.** Je 44:22. Jsh +*4:9. 1 K 8:24. Ezr 9:7. Ne 9:32, 36.

19. **Pharaoh.** Je 43:9-13. 46:2, 13-26. Ezk ch. 29-32. Na 3:8-10.

20. **the mingled.** ver. 24. Je 50:37. Ex 12:38. Ezr 9:2. Ps 106:35. Ezk 30:5. Da 2:43. **Uz.** Ge 10:23. 22:21. 1 Ch 1:17. Jb 1:1. La *4:21. **Philistines.** Je ch. 47. Ezk *25:15-17. Am *1:6-8. Zp *2:4-7. Zc *9:5-7. **Ashkelon.** 1 S 6:17, Askelon, Gaza. **remnant.** Ne *13:23-27. Is 20:1. Am 1:8.

21. **Edom.** Je 27:3. 49:7-22. Ps *137:7. Is ch. 34. *63:1-6. La *4:21, 22. Ezk √25:12-14. 32:29. ch. 35. Am 1:11, 12. Ob 1-16, 18. Ml 1:2-4. **Moab.** Je 9:26. ch. 48. Is ch. 15, 16. *25:10. Ezk *25:8-11. Am 2:1-3. Zp 2:8-10. **the.** Je 49:1-6. Ezk *25:2-7. Am *1:13-15.

22. **Tyrus.** i.e. *rock, strength; to distress,* ✛S#6865h. Je 27:3. 47:4. Ezk 26:2, 3, 4, 7, 15. 27:2, 3, 3, 8, 32. 28:2, 12, 18, 18. *29:18, 18. Ho 9:13. Am *1:9, 10. Zc *9:2, 3. See on 1 K +7:13, Tyre. **Zidon.** Ezk *28:22, 23. 32:30. Jl *3:4-8. **isles which are beyond the sea.** or, region by the seaside. Je 49:23-27. Am 1:3-5. Zc 9:1.

23. **Dedan.** Je 49:8. Ge *10:7. 22:21. *25:15. 1 Ch 1:30. Jb *6:19. Is *21:13, 14. Ezk *25:13. *27:20. **in the utmost corners.** Heb. cut off into corners, *or* having the corners of the hair polled. Je +9:26n. 49:32.

24. **Arabia.** 1 K 10:15. 2 Ch 9:14. Is 21:13. Ezk 27:21. **the mingled.** See on ver. 20. Je 49:28-33. 50:37. Ge 25:2-4, 12-16. 37:25-28. Ezk 30:5.

25. **Zimri.** Ge 25:2, Zimran. **Elam.** Je 49:34-49. Ge 10:22. 14:1. Is √11:11. 22:6. Ezk 32:24. Da 8:2. **Medes.** Je 51:11, 28. Is *13:17. Da *5:28.

26. **all the kings.** ver. 9. Je 50:9. Ezk *32:+27, 30. **and the.** Je 51:41. **Sheshach.** ʃ146, Ge +10:10. i.e. *thy fine linen; confusion; gates of iron; house of the*

prince, ✱S#8347h. Je 25:26. 51:41. A cypher (or secret code, constructed on a system known as Athbash) for *Babel,* arrived at by numbering the Hebrew alphabet from 1 to 24 forwards and backwards; then exchanging the forward place value of each letter with the letter occupying the position of the equivalent reverse numbering place value. Thus, in English, "b" being the second letter, could in a cypher be replaced by the second from the last letter, or "y." In Hebrew here, "B. B. L." (Babel) becomes "Sh. Sh. K." (Sheshach). Another possible cryptogram occurs in Je 51:1, where the Hebrew underlying "me" is said in a Massoretic note to mean "the Chaldees" (CB). **drink.** ver. 12. Je ch. 50, 51. Is ch. 13, 14, 47. Da ch. 5. Hab 2:16. Re ch. 18.

27. **Lord of hosts, the God of Israel.** Je +7:3. **Drink.** Is *51:21. *63:6. La 4:21. Hab *2:16. **because.** ver. 16. Je 12:12. 46:10, 14. 47:6, 7. 50:35. Dt 32:42. Ezk 21:4, 5. 24:21-25.

28. **if.** Jb 34:33. **Ye.** Je 4:28. 51:29. Is *14:24-27. *46:10, 11. Da *4:35. Ac 4:28. Ep +*1:11.

29. **I begin.** Je 49:12. Pr *11:31. Ezk √9:6. 38:21. Ob 16. Lk 23:31. 1 P *4:17. **which is called by my name.** Heb. upon which my name is called. Je +14:9mg. 1 K 8:43mg. Da 9:18mg, 19. **Ye shall.** Je 30:11. 46:28. 49:12. Pr 11:21. 17:5. **unpunished.** Ex 20:7)℗. 34:7)℗. Nu 14:18)℗. **I will.** Ezk *14:17, 21. 38:21. Zc *13:7.

30. **roar.** ∫22F1, Is +42:13. Is *42:13. Ho *5:14. 13:7, 8. Jl *2:11-13. 3:16. Am 1:2. 3:8. **his holy.** Je 17:12. Dt 26:15. 1 K 9:3. 2 Ch 30:27. Ps 11:4. 68:5. 132:14. Zc *2:13. **give.** Je 48:33. Ps 78:65. Is 16:9. *63:1-3. Re *14:18-20. *19:15.

31. **A noise.** The dreadful devastations made by the Chaldeans through all the nations of the East, and afterwards the destruction of Babylon by the Medes and Persians, are here primarily foretold in this awful language; but it also accords very much with the passages in which the ruin of all the anti-christian powers is evidently predicted. Je 45:5. Is *34:8. Ho *4:1. 12:2. Mi *6:2. **plead.** See on Is 66:16. Ezk 20:35, 36. 38:22. Jl 3:2.

32. **evil.** 2 Ch *15:6. Is *34:2. +*45:7h. *66:18. Lk *21:10, 25, 26. **and a.** See on Je 23:19. 30:23. Is 5:28. 30:30. Zp 3:8.

33. **the slain.** ver. 18-26. Je 13:12-14. Is 34:2-8. *66:16. Zp 2:12. Re *14:19, 20. *19:17-21. **they shall not.** See on Je 8:2. 9:21, 22. 16:4-7. Ps 79:3. 83:10. Ezk 39:4-20. Re *11:9. **they shall be.** 2 K 9:37. Is 5:25mg.

34. **Howl.** ver. 23, 36. Je 4:8, 9. Ezk 34:16. Ja 5:1, 2. **ye shepherds.** Ye kings and chiefs of the people. Ezk *34:10. **wallow.** Je 6:26. 48:26. Ezk 27:30, 31. **ye principal.** Ezk 34:17, 20. **the days of your.** Heb. your days for. ver. 12. Je 27:7. 51:20-26. Is 10:12. 33:1. La 4:21, 22. **ye shall.** Je 19:10-12. 22:28. Ps +*2:9. Is *30:14. **pleasant vessel.** Heb. vessel of desire. Je 3:19mg. 12:10mg. 2 Ch 36:10mg. Is 2:16mg. 32:12mg. Ezk 26:12mg. Da +10:3mg. 11:8mg. Ho 13:15mg. Am 5:11mg. Na 2:9mg.

35. **the shepherds,** etc. Heb. flight shall perish from the shepherds, and escaping from, etc. Je 32:4. 34:3. 38:18, 23. Jb *11:20. Is 2:12-22. 24:21-23. Ezk 17:15, 18. Da 5:30. Am 2:14. 9:1. Re 6:14-17. 19:19-21. **nor.** Je 48:44. 52:8-11, 24-27. Am 9:1-3.

36. **cry of.** See on ver. 34. Je 4:8. Zc 11:3.

37. **peaceable habitations.** Is *27:10, 11. 32:14.

38. **hath.** Je 4:7. 5:6. 49:19. 50:44. Ps 76:2. Ho *5:14. 11:10. 13:7, 8. Am 8:8. Zc 2:3. **desolate.** Heb. a desolation. ver. 12. Je 44:6, 22.

JEREMIAH 26

JEREMIAH delivers an awful message from God at the temple, and is persecuted by the priests and prophets, 1-9. He pleads his cause before the princes, exhorts them to repent, and warns them not to shed innocent blood, 10-15. The princes acquit him, referring to the example of Micah, 16-19. Urijah, having prophesied in like manner, was persecuted; and having fled into Egypt, was fetched thence by Jehoiakim and slain, 20-23. But Ahikam protects Jeremiah, 24.

1. A.M. 3394. B.C. 610. **the beginning.** Je 1:3. 25:1. 27:1. 35:1. 36:1. 2 K √23:34-36. 2 Ch *36:4, 5.

2. **Stand.** Je 7:2. 19:14. 23:28. 36:10. 2 Ch 24:20, 21. Lk 19:47, 48. 20:1. 21:37, 38. Jn 8:2. 18:20. Ac 5:20, 21, 25, 42. **court.** This was the great outer court, where the people assembled for the purpose of religious worship on ordinary occasions, when they brought no sacrifices; but when they offered a sacrifice, they were to bring it into the inner court, or that of the priests. **cities.** ∫121J19, 1 S +22:19. **all the words.** Je 1:17. 42:4. Is *58:1, 2. Ezk *3:10, 17-21. Mt *28:20. Ac *20:20, 27. **diminish.** Dt +4:2)℗. 12:32)℗. Re √22:19.

3. **If.** Je +7:5. **so.** Je 18:7-10. 36:3. Is *1:16-19. Ezk 18:27-30. Jon 3:8-10. 4:2. **that I.** ver. 13. See on Je 18:7-10. 1 K 21:27, 29. **repent.** ∫22B, Ge +6:6. Ge +6:6. Jon +3:10.

4. **If.** Je +7:5. **will not hearken.** Le 26:14)℗, etc. Dt 28:15)℗, etc. 29:18-28. 31:16-18, 20. 32:15-25. Jsh 23:15, 16. 1 K 9:6, 7. 2 Ch 7:19, 20. Ne 9:26-30. Is 1:20. 42:23-25. **my law.** Ex ch. 20)℗. **which.** Je 44:10. Dt 4:8, 44. 11:32. He 6:18.

5. **my.** Je 7:13, 25. 11:7. 2 K 9:7. 17:13, 23. 24:2. Ezr 9:11. Ezk 38:17. Da *9:6-10. Am 3:7. Zc 1:6. Re 10:7. 11:18. **whom.** See on Je 25:3, 4. Mk 12:2.

6. **will I.** See on Je 7:12-14. 1 S 4:10-12, 19-22. Ps *78:60-64. **a curse.** Je 24:9. 25:18. 29:22. 42:18. 44:8-12, 22. 2 K 22:19. Is *43:28. *65:15. Da 9:11. Ml *4:6.

7. **the priests.** Je 5:31. 23:11-15. Ezk 22:25, 26. Mi 3:11. Zp 3:4. Mt *21:15. Ac *4:1-6. 5:17.

8. **the priests.** Je 2:30. 11:19-21. 12:5, 6. 18:18. 20:1, 2, 8-11. 2 Ch *36:16. La 4:13, 14. Mt *21:35-39. *22:6. 23:31-35. 26:3, 4, 59-66. Ac 5:33. *7:52. Re *18:24. **Thou shalt.** Dt 18:20)℗. **surely die.** ∫147B, Ge +2:16. Ge 2:17)℗.

9. **Why.** 2 Ch 25:16. Is 29:21. 30:9-11. Am *5:10. 7:10-13. Mi 2:6. Mt *21:23. Ac 4:17-19. *5:28. 6:14. **And all.** *∫171A, Ex +9:6. Mt 27:20. Mk 15:11. Ac *13:50. *16:19-22. *17:5-8. 19:24-32. 21:30. 22:22. **in the.** Je 8:20, 59.

10. **the princes.** ver. 16, 17, 24. Je 34:19. 36:12-19, 25. 37:14-16. 38:4-6. Ezk *22:6, 27. **in the entry.** *or,* at the door. **the new gate.** ∫171S7B, Ge +14:7. Je 36:10. 2 K *15:35.

11. **saying.** Dt 18:20. Mt=26:65, 66. Lk *23:1-5. Jn *18:30. 19:7. Ac *22:22. *24:4-9. *25:2-13. **This man is worthy to die.** Heb. The judgment of death *is* for this man. ∫121C1D, Ex +6:6. ver. 16. Dt 19:6. 21:22. 22:26. Ac 23:29. 25:11, 25. 26:31. **for he.** Je 38:4. Ac 6:11-14.

12. **The Lord**. ver. 2, 15. Je 1:17, 18. 19:1-3. Am *7:15-17. Ac +*4:19, 20. +*5:29.

13. **amend**. See on Je 7:3-7. 35:15. 36:3. 38:20. Is *1:19. √55:7. Ezk √33:11. Ho *14:1-4. He *5:9. **repent**. See on ver. 3, 19. Je 18:8. 42:10. Ge +6:6. Ex 32:14. Dt *32:36. Jg 2:18. Jl 2:14. Jon *3:9, +10. *4:2. **evil**. Is +*45:7.

14. **As for**. Je 38:5. Jsh *9:25. Da *3:16. **as seemeth good and meet unto you**. Heb. as it is good and right in your eyes. 2 S *15:26.

15. **ye shall**. Je 2:30, 34. 7:6. 22:3, 17. Ge 4:10. *42:22. Nu *35:33. Dt 19:10, 13)𝒫. 2 K *24:4. Pr *6:17. Mt *23:30-36. 26:4, 25. =27:4, 25. Ac 7:60. 1 Th *2:14-16. Re 16:6. **for of**. See on ver. 12.

16. **Then said**. Je 36:19, 25. 38:7-13. Est 4:14. Pr +*16:7. Mt *27:23, 24, 54. Lk=23:13-15, 41, 47. Jn=10:21. Ac *5:34-39. 23:9, 29. 25:25. *26:31, 32.

17. **Then rose**. Mi 1:1. Ac 5:34. **elders of**. Je 19:1. 29:1. Ge 50:7. 2 Ch 34:29. Ezk 8:1, 12.

18. **Micah**. S#4320h. Mi 1:1. The prophet whose book is called after his name. Contemporary with Hosea and Amos in Israel, and with Isaiah in Judah (CB). **Morasthite**. i.e. *native of Moresheth* (i.e. *possession*), *S#4183h. Je 26:18. Mi 1:1. **Lord of hosts**. Je +6:6. **Zion**. Josephus relates (Bell. l. vii. c. 18) that Titus, after he had taken Jerusalem, ordered his soldiers to demolish it, except three of the largest and most beautiful towers, and the western wall of the city; all the rest was levelled, so that they who had never before seen it, could scarcely persuade themselves it had been inhabited. The Jewish writers also inform us, that Turnus Rufus, whom Titus had left in command, *ploughed* up the very foundations of the temple. When Dr. Richardson visited this sacred spot in 1818, he found one part of Mount Zion supporting a crop of barley, and another undergoing the labor of the *plough*: the soil turned up consisted of stone and lime mixed with earth, such as is usually met with in foundations of ruined cities. It is nearly a mile in circumference; is highest on the west side, and, towards the east, falls down in broad terraces on the upper part of the mountain, as it slopes down towards the brook Kedron (*Travels*, vol. ii. p. 348). See on Mi ‣3:12. This is the only instance in the Old Testament of one writer specifically naming the source of a citation from another writer. **Jerusalem**. See on Je 9:11. 51:37. 2 K 19:25. Ne *4:2. Ps *79:1. **the mountain**. Je 17:3. Is 2:2, 3. Mi *4:1. Zc *8:3.

19. **did he**. 2 Ch 29:6-11. 32:20, 25, 26. 34:21. Is 37:1, 4, 15-20. **fear the Lord**. Ac 5:39. 23:9. **besought the Lord**. Heb. besought the face of the Lord. Ex 32:11mg. 1 S 13:12mg. 1 K 13:6mg. 2 K 13:4. Jb 11:19mg. Ps 45:12mg. Pr 19:6. Da 9:13mg. Ml 1:9mg. **and the Lord**. See on ver. 3. Ex 32:14)𝒫. 2 S *24:16. **repented**. Ge +6:6. Jon +3:10. **Thus**. ver. 15. Nu *16:38. 35:33, 34. Is 26:21. La 4:13, 14. Mt 23:35. 27:24, 25. Lk 3:19, 20. Ac 5:39. Re 6:9, 10. 16:6. 18:20-24. **souls**. Heb. *nephesh*, Ge +12:13.

20. **Urijah**. i.e. *light of the Lord; my light is Jehovah*, ✛S#223h. ver. 20, 21, 23. 2 K 16:10, 11, 11, 15, 16. Ne 3:4, 21. 8:4. (1) A priest in Jerusalem in the time of King Ahaz, 2 K 16:10, 11. (2) The son of Shemaiah, a prophet slain by order of Jehoiakim, Je 26:20-23. (3) A priest, the father of Meremoth, Ne 3:4, 21. (4) One who stood by Ezra while he addressed the people, Ne 8:4. **Kirjath-jearim**. Jsh +9:17. 15:60. 18:14. 1 S 7:2.

21. **the king sought**. Je 32:3. 36:26. Ex 10:28. Nu 24:11. 1 K 13:4. 22:27. 2 K 5:12. 2 Ch *16:10. 24:21. 26:19. Ps 119:109. Mt 14:3, 5. Mk *6:19. **he was**. 1 K *19:1-3. Pr +*22:3. 29:25. Mt 10:23, 28, 39. *16:25, 26.

22. **men**. Ps 12:8. Pr *29:12. **Achbor**. 2 K *22:12, 14.

23. **who**. See on ver. 15. Je 2:30. Ezk 19:6. Mt 14:10. 23:34, 35. Ac 12:1-3. 1 Th 2:15. Re *11:7. **and cast**. Je 22:19. 36:30. **graves**. Heb. *qeber*, Ge +23:4. **common people**. Heb. sons of the people. Ezk 23:42mg.

24. **Ahikam**. Je 39:14. 40:5-7. 2 K *22:12-14. 25:22. 2 Ch 34:20. **the son of**. Je 29:3. 36:10. **that**. Je 1:18, 19. 15:19-21. 1 K 18:4. Is 37:32, 33. Ac *23:10, 20-35. 25:3, 4. *27:43. Re *12:16.

JEREMIAH 27

JEREMIAH is directed to make yokes and bonds; to wear them on his own neck, and to send them to several kings by their ambassadors; with a command to each of them from the Creator of the world, to submit to the king of Babylon, if they would escape destruction, 1-11. He counsels Zedekiah to the same effect; warns him and the people against false prophets; and predicts further desolations, 12-22.

1. A.M. 3409. B.C. 595. **the beginning**. ver. 3, 12, 19, 20. Je 26:1. 27:1. 28:1. Ge 1:1.

2. **saith the Lord**. *or*, hath the Lord said. Am 7:1, 4. **Make**. ver. 12. Je 28:10-14. **put**. Je 13:1-11. 18:2-10. 19:1-11. 28:10. 1 K 11:30, 31. Is 20:2-4. Ezk ch. 4, 5, 12. 24:3-12.

3. **Edom**. See on Je 25:19-26. ch. 47-49. Ezk ch. 25-28. 29:18. Am *1:9-15. *2:1-3. **the messengers**. 2 Ch 36:13. Ezk 17:15-21.

4. **to say unto their masters**. Thus. *or*, concerning their masters, saying, Thus. **the Lord**. Je 10:10, 16. 25:27. 51:19. Ex 5:1.

5. **made**. Je 10:11, 12. 32:17. 51:15. Ge 1:1)𝒫. *9:6. Ex *20:11. Jb 26:5-14. 38:4, etc. Ps 102:25. 136:5-9. 146:5, 6. 148:2-5. Is 40:21-26. 42:5. 44:24. 45:12. 48:13. 51:13. Jn +*1:1-3. Ac 14:15. 17:24. Col +*1:16. He *1:2, 10, 11. Re *4:11. **great power and**. Ex 6:6)𝒫. Dt 4:34)𝒫. 5:15)𝒫. 7:19)𝒫. 9:29)𝒫. 11:2)𝒫. 26:8)𝒫. **and have**. Ge 1:29, 30. 9:2, 3. Dt 2:7, 9, 19. 5:16. 32:8. Jsh 1:2, 3. Ezr 1:2. Ps 115:15, 16. 135:10-12. Da 2:21. 4:17, 25, 32, 35.

6. **have I given all**. Je 28:14. Da *2:37, 38. *5:18, 19. **my servant**. Je 24:1. 25:9. 43:10. 51:20-23. Is 44:28. Ezk *29:18-20. **the beasts**. Je 28:14. See on Ps 50:10-12. Da 2:38.

7. **all**. Je 25:11-14. 50:9, 10. 52:31. 2 Ch *36:20, 21. **until**. Je 25:12. 50:27. Ps 37:13. *137:8, 9. Is 13:1, 8, etc. *14:22, 23. *21:9. 47:1-5. Da *5:25-31. Hab 2:7. Zc 2:8, 9. Re 13:5-10. 14:8, 15-20. 16:19. 17:16, 17. 18:2-8. **many**. Je 25:14. ch. 50, 51. Is 14:4-6. **great kings**. Da 2:39.

8. **And it**. There is a peculiar grandeur, as well as propriety, in this method of predicting Nebuchadnezzar's rapid successes. The God of Israel, declaring himself to be the Lord of armies, and the Creator and Owner of the whole earth, with all its inhabitants and productions, and claiming full sovereignty over his creatures, avows his determination, for reasons he does not deign to assign, to give all the countries to the

king of Babylon, whom he calls his *servant*, because he would accomplish an important part of his righteous designs. They, therefore, who would escape the most dreadful judgments, must submit to the God of Israel, by submitting to Nebuchadnezzar; they must hearken to the prophets of Israel, and not to their own diviners; and they must observe, that Nebuchadnezzar, his son, and his grandson, would, whatever opposition should be made, possess the full dominion of these countries, till the appointed time was expired; and then, these haughty conquerors would in their turn become the prey of other powerful conquerors; all of which was most exactly fulfilled. **that nation**. Je 25:28, 29. 38:17-19. 40:9. 42:10-18. 52:3-6. Ezk 17:19-21. **with the sword**. Je 24:10. Le 26:25, 26↓𝒫. Dt 28:21-24↓𝒫. Ezk *14:21.

9. **hearken not**. ver. 14-16. Je 14:14. 23:16, 25, 32. +*29:8. Ex 7:11. Dt *18:10-12, 14. Jsh 13:22mg. Is *8:19. Mi 3:7. Zc 10:2. Ml +*3:5. Ac 8:11. Re 9:21. *18:23. +*21:8. *22:15. **diviners**. Ge +30:27. **dreamers**. Heb. dreams. Je 23:27, *28n. +*29:8. Is 47:12-14. **enchanters**. 2 K 21:6h (*S#6049h, observed times). **sorcerers**. *S#3786h, only here. Compare *S#3784h, Ml +3:5; *S#3785h, Is 47:12.

10. **they**. See on ver. 14. Je 28:16. Ezk *14:9-11. **to**. Je 32:31. La *2:14. **I**. See on ver. 15.

11. **bring**. ver. 2, 8, 12. **those**. Je 21:9. 38:2. 40:9-12. 42:10, 11.

12. **Zedekiah**. ver. 3. Je 28:1. 38:17. 2 Ch *36:11-13. Pr +*1:33. Ezk *17:11-21. **Bring**. See on ver. 2, 8.

13. **Why**. ſ85L, Ge +27:45. Je 38:20. Pr *8:36. Ezk *18:24, 31. *33:11. Jn *5:40. **by the sword**. ver. 8. Je 24:9. 38:2. Ezk 14:21.

14. **hearken not**. See on ver. 9. Is 28:10-13. 2 C √11:13-15. Ph 3:2. **they**. ver. 10. Je 14:14. 23:21, 25. 28:15. 29:8, 9. 1 K 22:22, 23. Ezk 13:6-15, 22, 23. Mi 2:11. Mt 7:15. 2 P *2:1-3. 1 J *4:1.

15. **a lie**. Heb. in a lie, *or* lyingly. Je +3:10mg. 29:9mg. **that I**. ver. 10. 2 Ch 18:17-22. 25:16. Ezk 14:3-10. Mt 24:24. 2 Th √2:9-12. 2 T 2:17-19. *4:3, 4. Re *13:7, 8, 12-14. **ye**. Je 6:13-15. 8:10-12. 14:15, 16. 20:6. 23:15. 28:16, 17. 29:22, 23, 31, 32. Mi 3:5-7. Mt +*15:14. Re 19:20.

16. **Behold**. Je 28:3. 2 K *24:12, 13. 2 Ch *36:7-10. Da 1:2. **for**. ver. 10, 14. Is 9:15. *44:24, 25.

17. **serve**. See on ver. 11, 12. **wherefore**. ſ85L, Ge +27:45. ver. 13. Je 38:17, 23.

18. **they**. 1 K *18:24, 26. **let them**. Je 7:16. 15:1. 18:20. 42:2. Ge *18:24-33. 20:17. 1 S *7:8. *12:19, 23. 2 Ch 32:20. Jb 42:8, 9. Ezk *14:14, 18-20. 22:30. Ml 1:9. Ja *5:16-18. **the Lord of hosts**. Je +6:6.

19. **the pillars**. Je 52:17-23. 1 K *7:15, etc. 2 K *25:13, 17. 2 Ch 4:2-16.

20. **when**. Je 22:28, Coniah. 24:1. 2 K 24:14-16, Jehoiachin. 2 Ch 36:10, 18.

21. **the vessels**. Je 20:5.

22. **carried**. Je 29:10. 34:5. 52:17-21. 2 K *24:13-17. 2 Ch *36:17, 18. Da *5:1-4, 23. **until**. Je 25:11, 12. 29:10. 32:5. 2 Ch *36:21-23. Ezr *1:1-5. Pr +*21:30. Da *9:2. **then**. Ezr ✱1:7, 11. ✱5:13-15. 7:9, 19.

JEREMIAH 28

Hananiah confidently predicts the speedy ruin of Babylon, and the return of the sacred vessels and the *captive Jews, 1-4. Jeremiah expresses his desire that it may prove true; but appeals to the event, 6-9. Hananiah breaks the yoke from Jeremiah's neck, who is sent with yokes of iron to confirm his former prophecies, 10-14. He foretells Hananiah's death, which takes place accordingly, 15-17.*

1. **the same**. Je 27:1. **Hananiah**. ver. 11. Je 36:12. 37:13. **Azur**. i.e. *helpful*, *S#5809h. Je 28:1. Ne 10:17, Azzur. Ezk 11:1. (1) Father of Hananiah, the false prophet of Gibeon, Je 28:1. (2) Father of Jaazaniah, Ezk 11:1. (3) A Jew who sealed the covenant of Nehemiah, Ne 10:17. **the prophet**. Je 23:28. Is 9:15. Zc 13:2-4.

2. **Thus speaketh**. This false prophet imitated the style and manner of the true prophets; but he *unconditionally* promised prosperity to an abandoned generation. **I have**. See on Je 27:2-12. Ezk 13:5-16. Mi 3:11.

3. **two full years**. Heb. two years of days. Ge 47:8, 28mg. Ps 90:10mg. Am 4:4mg. **all the**. Je 27:16-22. **that**. 2 K 24:13. 2 Ch 36:10. Da *1:2.

4. **I will bring**. This was doubtless grateful news to the people, who looked upon Zedekiah only as Nebuchadnezzar's deputy. Hananiah seems to have been more desirous of *popular* than *regal* favor; for this prediction could not be altogether agreeable to Zedekiah. But he was evidently a weak as well as a wicked prince, and very generally despised. **Jeconiah**. Je 22:24, 28, Coniah. 24:1. 52:31-34. 2 K *25:27-30, Jehoiachin. **captives**. Heb. captivity. Je 24:5mg. 29:22. Ezk 1:1mg. **I will break**. ver. 2, 10. Je 2:20. 30:8. Ge 27:40. Is 9:4. Na *1:13.

5. **unto the prophet**. ſ121Q1. Metonymy of the Adjunct B597. The appearance of a thing, or an opinion about it, is put for the thing itself, in nouns. Here, Hananiah is probably called a prophet, because he was reputed to be one. ver. 1. For other instances of this figure see Ezk 21:4. Mt 8:12. 9:13. Lk 2:48. 1 C 1:21, 25. 2 C 4:4. Ga 1:6. T 1:12. Ja 2:14, 17, 20, 24, 26. **the house**. ver. 1. Je 7:2. 19:14. 26:2.

6. **Amen**. Nu *5:20, 22. Dt *27:15-26. 1 K 1:36. 1 Ch 16:36. Ps 41:13. 72:19. 89:52. 106:48. Mt *6:13. 28:20. 1 C 14:16. 2 C 1:20. Re 1:18. +*3:14. 5:14. 19:4. *22:20, 21. **the Lord perform**. ver. 3. Je 11:5. 17:16. 18:20.

7. **Nevertheless hear**. 1 K √22:28.

8. **The prophets**. As Hosea, Joel, Amos, Isaiah, Micah, Nahum, Habakkuk, Zephaniah, and others, all of whom had denounced similar evils against a corrupt people. So that they who opposed Jeremiah also opposed those who preceded him; and it was altogether unprecedented for a true prophet to promise deliverance to a guilty nation, without calling them to repentance. **of old**. Heb. *olam*, Ge +*6:4. **prophesied**. Le 26:14, etc. Dt 4:26, 27. 28:15, etc. 29:18-28. 31:16, 17. 32:15, etc. 1 S 2:27-32. 3:11-14. 1 K 14:7-15. 17:1. 21:18-24. 22:8. Is 5:1-8. 6:9-12. 13:18. ch. 24. Jl 1:2, etc. 3:1-11. Mi 3:8-12. Na ch. 1-3. Am 1:2.

9. **which**. Je 4:10. 6:14. 8:11. 14:13. Ezk *13:10, 16. **then**. Dt *18:21, 22↓𝒫. Ezk 13:10-16.

10. **look**. ver. 2, 4. Je 27:2. 36:23, 24. 1 K 22:11, 24, 25. Ml 3:13.

11. **Thus**. Je 23:17. 29:9. 1 K 13:18. 22:6, 11, 12. 2 Ch *18:10, 22, 23. Pr 14:7. Ezk 13:7. **Even**. See on ver. 2-4. Je 27:2-12.

12. **the word**. Je 1:2. 29:30. 2 K 20:4. 1 Ch 17:3. Da 9:2.

13. **Thou hast**. Je 27:15. Ps *149:8. La 2:14. **thou shalt**. By encouraging an unavailing resistance to Nebuchadnezzar.

14. **I have put**. Je 27:4, 7. 40:4. Dt 4:20. 28:48๒𝒫. Is *14:4-6. **that they**. See on Je 25:9-26. Re *17:12, 13. **and I**. Je 27:6, 7. Da *2:38.

15. **The Lord hath not sent thee**. This was a bold speech, in the presence of those priests and people who were prejudiced in favor of the false prophets, who prophesied to them smooth things. ver. 11. Je 14:14, 15. 23:21. 27:15. 29:23, 31, 32. Dt 18:21, 22. 1 K *22:23. Ezk *13:2, 3, 22. 21:28, 29. 22:28. La *2:14. Zc *13:3.

16. **I will**. Ge 7:4. Ex 32:12. Dt 6:15. 1 K *13:34. Am *9:8. **face**. Ge +1:2. **this year**. ver. 3. Je 20:6. Nu *14:37. *16:28-35. 29:32. Dt 13:5-11. **die**. Dt 18:20๒𝒫. **because**. Dt 13:5๒𝒫. Ezk 13:11, 12. Ac 13:8-11. **rebellion**. Heb. revolt. Je 29:32. Dt 13:5mg. 2 K 24:17. 2 Ch 36:13. Ezk 17:15, 18.

17. **Hananiah**. Is √44:24-26. Zc *1:6. **the seventh month**. The prophecy was delivered in the *fifth* month (ver. 1), and Hananiah died in the *seventh* month; exactly *two* months after he had delivered his false prophecy, which he declared, in the name of God, would be fulfilled in *two* years. Here then the true prophet was demonstrated, and the false prophet detected. The death of Hananiah, thus predicted, was God's *seal* to the words of His prophet, and must have gained his other predictions great credit among the people; though it is evident that it did not induce them to forsake their sins and return to the God of Israel.

JEREMIAH 29

JEREMIAH, by letter, requires the captives at Babylon to accommodate themselves to their condition, and not to believe the false prophets, who assured them of a speedy deliverance, 1-9. He promises them in the name of God, a gracious restoration at the end of seventy years, 10-14. He foretells the destruction of those who remained at Jerusalem, 15-19; and shows the dreadful end of two false prophets at Babylon, 20-23. Shemaiah writes a letter from Babylon, against Jeremiah, 24-29; by whom Shemaiah's doom is foretold, 30-32.

1. Cir. A.M. 3407. B.C. 597. **Now**. This transaction is supposed to have taken place in the first or second year of Zedekiah. **words**. Je 25:1. 26:1. 27:1. 30:1. **of the letter**. ver. 25-29. 2 Ch 30:1-6. Est 9:20. Ac 15:23. 2 C 7:8. Ga 6:11. He 13:22. Re ch. 2, 3. **the elders**. See on Je 24:1-7. 28:4. Ezk 8:1. 14:1. 20:1. **the prophets**. Ezk 1:1. Da 1:6.

2. **Jeconiah**. Je 22:24-28, Coniah. 27:20. 28:4. 2 K 24:12-16. 2 Ch 36:9, 10, Jehoiachin. **the queen**. Je 13:18. 22:26. 2 K 24:12, 15. **eunuchs**. *or*, chamberlains. Je 34:19. 38:7. 41:16. 52:25. 2 K +8:6mg. 9:32mg. 20:18. Da 1:3, etc. **carpenters**. Je 10:3, 9. 24:1. Ex 28:11. **the smiths**. 2 K *24:14.

3. **Shaphan**. Je 26:24. 39:14. 2 K 22:8. Ezk 8:11. **Gemariah**. Je 36:25. 2 K 22:12. 2 Ch 34:20.

4. **whom I have caused**. Je 24:5. Is *5:5. 10:5, 6. +*45:7. *59:1, 2. Am +*3:6.

5. **Build ye houses**. The prophet here corrects the false expectation of a speedy return to their own land, which their false prophets had excited in the minds

of the Jews at Babylon; and which had led them to neglect their personal and domestic interests and comforts, and the good of the nation; and also tended to excite the jealousy of their victors, and to increase their own miseries. ver. 10, 28. Ezk *28:26.

6. **Take ye**. Je 16:2-4. Ge 1:27, 28. 9:7. 1 T 5:14. **take wives**. Ge 21:21. 24:3, 4, 51, 60. 28:1-4. 29:19. 34:4. Jg 1:12-14. 12:9. 14:2. 1 C *7:36-38. **that ye**. Je +*30:19. Ge 1:28. 15:5. 22:17.

7. **seek**. Da *4:27. 6:4, 5. Ro 13:1, 5. 1 P 2:13-17. **pray**. T#1634. Nu 6:26. Ezr 6:10. 7:23. Is 26:12. Da 4:19. Lk 10:5, 6. Ro 1:7. 15:13. 2 C 1:2. Ga 1:3. Ep 6:23. Ph 1:2. Col 1:2. 1 Th 1:1. 2 Th 1:2. 3:16. 1 T 1:2. +√2:1, 2. T 1:4. 1 P 1:1, 2. 5:14. 2 P 1:2. 2 J 3. Re 1:4.

8. **Let not**. Je 14:14. See on 23:21. 27:14, 15. 28:15. Ezk +*14:10n. Zc 13:4. Mt *24:4, 5, 24. Mk 13:5, 6, 22, 23. Lk 21:8. Ro 16:18. 2 C +*11:13-15. Ep +*4:14. 5:6. 2 Th √2:3, 9-11. 2 T 3:13. 2 J +*7-9. Re *13:13, 14. 19:20. **diviners**. Pr +16:10mg. Is +44:25. **deceive you**. Mt 24:4. **neither hearken** Je +*23:28n. +*27:9. Jb 20:8. Ps 73:20. Ec *5:3. Is *29:7, 8. Zc 10:2. **your dreams**. Je 5:31. +*23:28n. Mi 2:11. Lk 6:26. 2 P 2:2, 3.

9. **falsely**. Heb. in a lie. ver. 23, 31. Je 27:15mg.

10. **after**. Je 25:12. 27:7, 22. 2 Ch *36:20-23. Ezr 1:1, 2. Da +*9:2. Zc *7:5. **I will**. See on Je 24:6, 7. 32:42-44. Zp *2:7.

11. **I know**. Jehovah had this plan before Him; and neither the impatience of the Jews, nor the power of the Chaldeans, could alter it. He had determined that the Chaldean monarchy should continue till the seventy years expired, and so long the Jews must remain in captivity, and have no enlargement till that period was terminated. Jb *23:13. Ps *33:11. *40:5. Is +*46:10, 11. √58:8-12. Mi 4:12. Zc 1:6. 8:14, 15. **thoughts**. 𝒥22C5, Ge +50:20. Je 3:12-19. 23:5, 6. 30:9, 10, 18-22. ch. 31-33. Ps 40:5, +*17. Is ch. 40-46. Ezk 34:11-31. ch. 36, 37, 39. Ho *2:14-23. *3:5. *14:2-9. Jl *2:28-32. Am *9:8-15. Mi *5:4-7. √7:14-20. Zp *3:14-20. Zc *9:9-17. √12:5-10. 14:20, 21. Re 14:8-14. **of peace**. Ps 85:8. Ezk 11:5. **not of evil**. Ge 50:20. Ex +*34:6. Ru ◐+*1:13. Ps +√9:10. √55:22. 66:9-12. +*84:11. 89:33. 97:10. +*104:28. *121:3, 7. +*145:9. Pr 10:3. Is +*45:7. Mt *6:25-34. ◐*25:24. Lk +*6:35. Ro √8:28. +*9:14. 2 C *9:8. 2 T 3:11. Ja √1:13, 17. *5:11. **expected end**. Heb. end and expectation. 𝒥93A, Ge +1:26. By Hendiadys, this should be understood to mean "to give you the end, yes—the end you hope for": i.e., the end which I have promised and on which I have caused you to hope and depend. All this, and more, is contained in and expressed by the figure Hendiadys. Pr 3:5, 6. La *3:26. ⅃C 2:9. 1 J 3:2. **expectation**. *S#8615h. Jsh 2:18, 21 (line). Ru 1:12 (hope). Jb 4:6 (hope). 5:16. 6:8mg. 7:6. 8:13. 11:√18, 20. 14:7, 19. 17:15. 19:10. 27:8. Ps *9:18. *62:5. *71:5. Pr *10:28. 11:7. +*19:18. √23:18. *24:14. 26:12. 29:20. Je +*31:17. La 3:29. Ezk 19:5. 37:11. Ho +*2:15. Zc 9:12. or, hope in your latter end. **hope**. Ro +√15:4. **latter**. Ps +*118:24. Am √9:11-15. Zc *9:12. √10:6. Ja +*5:11. **end**. 𝒥121P6, Pr +23:18. By Metonymy of the Adjunct, "end" is put for that which takes place at the end, and thus signifies the *reward* which comes at the end.

12. **Then shall**. Je 31:9. √33:3. Ne 2:4, etc. Ps *10:17. +*50:15. *102:16, 17. Is *30:19. +*65:24. Ezk 36:37.

Da 9:3, etc. Zc √13:9. Mt *7:7, 8. 2 C √3:14-16.

13. **seek me**. T#880. Le *26:40-45. Dt √4:29-31⟩℘. *30:1, 2⟩℘, etc. 1 K *8:47-50. 1 Ch +*28:9. 2 Ch 6:37-39. 15:2. Ezr 8:22. Jb 8:5, 6. Ps +√9:10. 69:32. *91:15. Is 45:19. √55:6, 7. La 3:25. Ho *5:15. *6:1-3. 10:12. Am 5:4-6. Zp √2:1-3. Lk √11:9, 10. **with**. Je *3:10. *24:7. Dt 30:2, 10. 1 K 2:4. 2 K *23:3. 2 Ch 22:9. *31:21. Ps *119:2, 10, 58, 69, 145. Jl 2:12. Ac *8:37. 17:27. He *11:6.

14. **I will be**. Dt *4:7. 1 Ch +*28:9. 2 Ch *15:12-15. Ps *32:6. 46:1. Is *45:19. √55:6. Ro *10:20. **and I will turn**. Je *16:14, 15. *23:3-8. *24:5-7. *30:3, 10. *31:8, etc. *32:37, etc. *33:7, etc. *46:27, 28. 50:4, 5, 19, 20, 33, 34. 51:10. Ps 126:1, 4. Ezk *11:16-20. ch. 34, 36-39. Am √9:14. Mi 4:12. Zp 3:20. **your captivity**. √121N1, Ge +31:54. T#1180. Dt 4:27-29. Ezr 8:21-23. Ps 68:18. Is 49:24. Ezk 3:15, 16. Da 9:17, 18. 10:12. **will gather**. Je 23:3. 32:37. Ps 107:3. **whither**. ver. 18. Je 8:3. 23:3, 7, √8. Is √11:11, 12. 43:5, 6. **bring you again**. ver. 10. Je 3:14. *12:15. 16:15. 23:3. 24:6. 30:3. 31:10. 32:37. Dt 30:3. Ezk +*37:21.

15. **The Lord hath**. ver. 8, 9. Je 28:1, etc. Ezk 1:1, 3.

16. **of the king**. ver. 3. Je 24:2. 38:2, 3, 17-23. Ezk ch. 6-9. 17:12-21. 21:9-27. *22:31. 24:1-14.

17. **the Lord of hosts**. Je +6:6. **Behold**. ver. 18. Je 15:2, 3. 24:8-10. 34:17-22. 43:11. 52:6. Ezk 5:12-17. 14:12-21. Lk √21:11, 23, 25-27. **the sword**. Je 14:12. 24:10. Le 26:25, 26⟩℘. Dt 28:21-24⟩℘. Ezk 14:21. **them like**. See on Je 24:1-3, 8.

18. **will deliver**. Je 15:4. 24:9. 34:17. Le *26:33. Dt *28:25⟩℘, 64. 2 Ch *29:8. Ps *44:11. Ezk 6:8. *12:15. 22:15. 36:19. Am √9:9. Zc *7:14. Lk +*21:24. **to be a curse**. Heb. for a curse. ver. 22. See on Je 19:8. 25:9. 26:6. 42:18. Dt 29:21-28. 1 K 9:7, 8. 2 Ch 7:19-22. 29:8. Is 65:15. La 2:15, 16.

19. **not hearkened**. Je +*6:19. 7:13, 24-26. 25:3-7. 26:5. 32:33. 34:17. 35:14-16. 44:4, 5. Dt +√28:15. Zc *1:4-6. 7:11-13. Lk +*8:18. He *12:25. **rising up early**. Je +7:13. 25:3. 2 Ch 36:15. ye. √96D2, Is +1:29. **would not hear**. Je +6:16. 7:13. 11:8, 10. *13:10, 11. *16:12. *17:23. *18:12. *19:15. *22:21. 25:3. Jb +*21:14. Lk 19:14. Ac 7:39. Ro 1:28. 2 P 3:5.

20. **Hear**. Dr. Blayney thinks there were two letters written by the prophet to the captives in Babylon, and the first ends with this verse. That having heard, on the return of the embassy, that the captives had received his advices favorably, and because they were deceived by false prophets, who promised them a speedier deliverance, he therefore wrote a second letter, beginning with the fifteenth verse, and going on with the twenty-first, etc. (in which order these verses are read in the Septuagint), in which he denounces God's judgments on the three chief of those, Ahab, Zedekiah, and Shemaiah. **all ye**. Ezk *3:11, 15. **whom**. See on Je 24:5. Mi *4:10.

21. **which**. See on ver. 8, 9. Je 14:14, 15. La *2:14.

22. **shall be**. Ge 48:20. Ru 4:11. Is *65:15. 1 C *16:22. **roasted**. Da 3:6, 21.

23. **and have**. Je 7:9, 10. 23:14, 21. Ps +√50:16-18. Zp *3:4. 2 P *2:10-19. Ju *8-11. **lying**. See on ver. 8, 9, 21. La *2:14. **even I**. Je 13:27. 16:17. 23:23, 24. Pr 5:21. Ml 2:14. +*3:5. He *4:13. Re *1:5. +*3:14.

24. **Shemaiah**. ver. 31, 32. **Nehelamite**. or, dreamer. ✳S#5161h. ver. 31, 32. See on ver. 8.

25. **Because**. 1 K 21:8-13. 2 K 10:1-7. 19:9, 14.

2 Ch 32:17. Ezr 4:7-16. Ne 6:5, 17, 19. Ac 9:2. **Zephaniah**. ver. 29. Je 21:1, 2. 37:3. 52:24. 2 K *25:18-21.

26. **officers**. Je 20:1, 2. 2 K 11:15, 18. Ac 4:1. 5:24. **for every**. 2 K 9:11. Ho *9:7. Mk 3:21. Jn=7:20. =10:20, 39. Ac 26:11, 24. 2 C *5:13-15. 2 T +1:7. **and maketh**. ver. 27. Dt *13:1-5. Zc 13:3-6. Mt=21:11, 23. Lk=7:39. Jn +*5:18. =*8:53. +*10:33. **that thou**. Je 20:1, 2. 38:6, 28. 2 Ch 16:10. 18:26. Ac 5:18. 16:24. 2 C 11:23. Re 2:10.

27. **therefore**. Nu 16:2. 2 Ch 25:16. Am 7:12, 13. Jn 11:47-53. Ac 4:17-21. 5:28, 40. **which**. ver. 26. Je 43:2, 3. Nu 16:3. Mt 27:63. 2 T 3:8.

28. **This captivity is long**. See on ver. 1-10.

29. **Zephaniah the priest**. ver. 25.

31. **Send**. ver. 20. **Because**. See on ver. 9, 23. Je 14:14, 15. 23:21. 28:15-17. Ezk *13:8-16, 22, 23. 2 P *2:1.

32. **punish**. Je +11:22mg. 20:6. Ex +*20:5. Nu 16:27-33. Jsh 7:24, 25. 2 K *5:27. Ps *109:8-15. Is √14:20-22. Am *7:17. **he shall**. Je 22:30. 35:19. 1 S *2:30-34. **behold**. See on ver. 10-14. Je 17:6. 2 K 7:2, 19, 20. **rebellion**. Heb. revolt. Je 28:16mg. Dt 13:5mg⟩℘.

JEREMIAH 30

Prophecies of the restoration of the Jews, and the rebuilding of their city and temple; notwithstanding their extreme calamities, the justice of their punishment, the failure of all human help, and their own desponding thoughts, 1-18; of their subsequent increase and prosperity under their own rulers; and of the destruction of their enemies and the wicked, 19-24.

1. Cir. A.M. 3417. B.C. 587. **The word**. Dahler supposes that this prophecy was delivered about a year after the taking of Jerusalem; which appears highly probable. Dr. Blayney justly supposes this and the following chapter to refer to the future restoration of the Jews and Israelites in the times of the Gospel; though also touching at the restoration from the Babylonian captivity. The ninth verse is expressly referred to the times of the Messiah by the Chaldee paraphrast; who renders, "They shall serve before Jehovah their God, and shall obey Messiah the son of David, whom I shall raise up to them." Je 1:1, 2. 26:15.

2. **Write**. Je 36:2-4, 32. 51:60-64. Ex *17:14. Dt *31:19, 22-27. Jb 19:23, 24. Is 8:1. *30:8. Da 12:4. Hab *2:2, 3. Ro +*15:4. 1 C 10:11. 2 P √1:21. Re *1:11, 18, 19.

3. **the days**. Je 23:5, 7. 31:27, 31, 38. 33:14, 15. Lk 17:22. 19:43. 21:6. He *8:8. **that I**. ver. 10, 18. Je 27:22. 29:14. 31:23. 32:37, 44. 33:7-11, 26. Dt *30:3. Ps 53:6. Ezk *39:25, 26. Jl 3:1, 2. Am √9:14, 15. Ob 19, 20. Zp *3:20. **and I**. Je 16:15. 23:8. 27:11. Ezr 3:1, 8, 12. Ezk 20:42. *28:25, 26. *36:24. *37:21-25. 39:27, 28. 47:14.

4. **concerning Israel and**. Je 31:6. Is 11:13. Ho 1:11. Ezk *20:40.

5. **a voice**. Je 4:15-20, 31. 6:23, 24. 8:19. 9:19. 25:36. 31:15, 16. Is 5:30. 59:11. Am *5:16-18. 8:10. Zp 1:10, 11. Lk *19:41-44. √21:25-27. *23:28-30. **of fear, and not of peace**. or, *there is* fear, and not peace. Je 46:5.

6. **a man**. Heb. a male. Ge 1:27. Ezk 16:17mg. **every**. Je 4:31. 6:24. 13:21. 22:23. 49:24. 50:43. Ps 48:6. Is *13:6-9. 21:3. 42:14. +*66:7, 8. Da 5:6. Ho *13:12, 13. Mi 4:9, 10. 5:3. Zc 12:10—13:1. 14:1-15.

Mt +*24:8. Jn 16:21, 22. Ro 11:25-29. 1 Th *5:3. Re 12:2. **paleness**. Is 29:22. Jl 2:6. Na 2:10.

7. **Alas**. Jg +6:22. **that day is great**. Is *2:12-22. Ezk *7:6-12. Ho 1:11. Jl *2:11, 18, 31. Am 5:18-20. Zp *1:14-18. Zc √14:1-4. Ml *4:1. Ac *2:20. Re *6:17. **none is like it**. La 1:12. 2:13. 4:6. Da 9:12. √12:1. Mt +√24:21, 22. Mk *13:19, 20. **even the time**. Ge 32:7, 24-30. 43:6. 45:26, 28. Ezk ●+*30:3. Da +*12:1. Ho 12:2-4. **Jacob's trouble**. Thus pertaining exclusively to natural Israel, not spiritual Israel, having no reference to the church, but to the time of the Great Tribulation. Ezk 20:33. 22:17. Da 9:27. 11:40-45. 12:1-7. Ho* 12:2-4. Mt 24:15-31. Re 12:1—20:6. **but he**. See on ver. 10. Je 50:18-20, 33, 34. Ps 25:22. 34:19. Is 14:1, 2. *49:25. Ro 11:26. **out of**. Lk +*21:36. Ro *11:26.

8. **come to pass**. Dt 30:1-6. **in that day**. Is 2:11. **Lord of hosts**. Je +6:6. **I will break**. Je 27:2. *28:4, 10, 11, 13, 14. Is 9:4. *10:27. *14:25. Ezk *34:27. Na *1:13. **serve**. Je 25:14. 27:7.

9. **David their king**. Is +*55:3-5. Ezk √34:23-25. √37:24, 25. Ho *3:4, 5. Lk 1:69. Ac *2:30, 34. 13:34.

10. **fear**. Je 46:27, 28. Ge *15:1. Dt *31:6-8. Is *41:10-15. *43:5. 44:2. *54:4, 5. Zp *3:16, 17. Jn *12:15. **I will save**. See on ver. 3. Je 3:18. 23:3, 8. 29:14. 46:27. Is 46:11, 13. 49:25. 60:4, etc. Ezk 16:53. **and shall**. Je 23:6. 33:16. Is 35:9. Ezk 34:25-28. 38:11. Ho 2:18. Mi 4:3, 4. Zp 3:15. Zc 2:4, 5. 3:10. 8:4-8.

11. **I am**. Je 1:8, 19. 15:20. 46:28. Is *8:10. 43:25. Ezk *11:16, 17. Mt *1:23. 28:20. Ac *18:10. 2 T *4:17, 18, 22. **though**. Je +*4:27. 5:10, 18. 46:27, 28. Ezk 11:13. Am *9:8, 9. Ro *9:27-29. 11:5-7. **not make**. Je 31:10. 1 K √11:39. Is +√41:9. Am +*9:8, 9, 14, 15. Ro 11:+√1, 10, 12. **but I**. See on Je 10:24. Ps 6:1. Is 27:7, 8. **unpunished**. or, guiltless. Ex 20:7)𝒫. 34:7)𝒫. Nu 14:18)𝒫.

12. **Thy bruise**. See on ver. 15. Je 14:17. 15:18. 2 Ch *36:16. Is *1:5, 6. Ezk 37:11.

13. **none**. Ps 106:23. 142:4. Is 59:16. Ezk *22:30. 1 T √2:5, 6. 1 J *2:1. **that**, etc. Heb. for binding up, or pressing. Lk 10:30-34. **no healing medicines**. ver. 17. Je +*8:22. 17:14. 33:6. Ex +*15:26. Dt 32:29. Jb 5:18. 34:29. Is 1:6. Ho 6:1. 14:4. Na 3:19. 1 P 2:24.

14. **lovers**. Je 2:36. 4:30. 22:20, 22. 38:22. La *1:2, 19. Ezk *23:9, 22. Ho *2:5, 6, 10-16. Re 17:12-18. **I have wounded**. Jb 13:24-28. 16:9. 19:11. 30:21. La 2:5. Ho 5:14. **because**. See on ver. 15. Je 5:6. Ps *90:7, 8. Ezk *9:8-10.

15. **Why**. Je 15:18. Jsh *7:10, 11. La *3:39. Mi *7:9. **thy sorrow**. ver. 12, 17. Je 46:11. Jb 34:6, 29. Is 30:13, 14. Ho 5:12, 13. Mi 1:9. Ml 4:1, 2. **for the multitude**. ver. 14. Je 2:19, 28-30. 5:6-9, 25-31. 6:6, 7, 13. 7:8-11. 9:1-9. 11:13. 32:30-35. 2 Ch 36:14-17. Ezr 9:6, 7, 13. Ne 9:26-36. Is 1:4, 5, 21-24. 5:2. 59:1-4, 12-15. La 1:5. 4:13, 14. 5:16, 17. Ezk ch. 16, 20, 22, 23. Zp *3:1-5.

16. **all they**. Je 10:25. 12:14. 25:12, 26-29. 50:7-11, 17, 18, 28, 33-40. 51:34-37. Ex *23:22)𝒫. Ps *129:5. *137:8, 9. Is *14:2. 33:1. *41:11, 12. *47:5, 6, 11. 54:15, 17. La 1:21. 4:21, 22. Ezk *25:3, etc. *26:2, etc. 29:6, 7. 35:5, etc. Mi 4:11-13. 7:10-17. Na 1:8-14. Hab 2:16, 17. Zp 2:8-10. Zc 1:14, 15. 2:8, 9. 12:2-4. 14:2, 3. Re *13:10. **shall be**. Ge +*12:3.

17. **restore health**. See on ver. 13. Je 3:22. +*8:22. 31:20. 33:6. Ex +*15:26. Ps *23:3. +*103:3. *107:20. Is *30:26. 33:24. 35:5, 6. 42:3. Ezk 34:16. Ho 6:1. Ml 4:2. 1 P *2:24. Re *22:2. **they**. Ne 4:1-4. Ps +*12:5.

44:13-16. 79:9-11. Is *11:12. La 2:15-17. Ezk 35:12, 13. *36:2, 3, 20.

18. **Behold**. See on ver. 3. Je 23:3. 29:14. 33:7, 11. 46:27. 49:6, 39. Ps *85:1. √102:13, 16. **the city**. Je 31:40. Ne ch. 3. 7:4. Is *44:24, 26. Zc 12:6. *14:10, 11. **heap**. or, little hill. Je 21:10. 31:38, 39. 34:2. 37:10. Ezk 48:30-35. **the palace**. 1 Ch *29:1, 19. Ezr 6:3-15. Ps *78:69. Is *44:28. Ezk 7:20-22. Hg *2:7-9. Zc 1:16, 17.

19. **out**. Je 31:4, 12, 13. 33:10, 11. Ezr 3:10-13. 6:22. Ne 8:12, 17. 12:43-46. Ps *53:6. 126:1, 2. Is *12:1. 35:10. 51:11. 52:9. Zp *3:14-20. Zc 8:19. **and I**. Je 31:27. 33:22. Is *27:6. 60:22. Ezk *36:10-15, 37. *37:26. Zc *2:4, 5. *8:4, 5. 10:8. **I will**. Je 33:9. Is 60:19. 62:2, 3. Zp 3:19, 20. Zc 9:13-17. 12:8. Jn 17:22. 1 P 1:7.

20. **children**. Je 32:39. Ge 17:5-9. Ps 90:16, 17. 102:18, 28. Is 1:26, 27. **aforetime**. Heb. *kedem*, Mi +*5:2. Je 33:7. **and I**. See on ver. 16. Je 2:3. 50:33, 34. Is *49:25, 26. 51:22, 23. **punish**. Je +9:25mg. **all that**. Ge +*12:3.

21. **nobles**. Ge +*49:10. Ezr 2:2. 7:25, 26. Ne 2:9, 10. 7:2. **governor**. Je +*23:5, 6. 33:15. Dt +*18:18. 33:5. 2 S +*7:13. Ps *89:29. *110:1-4. Is +*9:6, 7. Ezk *34:23, 24. *37:24. Mi +*5:2-4. Zc *9:9, 10. Mt *2:2. *21:5-11. *27:37. Mk 11:9, 10. Lk *1:32, 33. Jn 18:36, 37. 19:19-22. Ac 2:34-36. *5:31. Re *19:16. **the midst**. Ge +*49:10. Dt +17:15. **and I**. Nu 16:5)𝒫, 40. 17:12, 13. Ps 110:4. Am +*9:11, 14, 15. Zc 6:12, 13. Mt 3:17. Lk 24:26. Ro 8:34. He +*1:3. 4:14-16. *7:21-26. 9:15-24. 1 J *2:2. Re 5:9, 10. **draw near**. Ps 73:28. SS 1:4. Ho 11:4. **for**. Je 49:19. 50:44. Is *63:1. Mt 21:10. **engaged**. Ge *18:27, 30, 32. Jb 23:3-5. 42:3-6. He *7:26. *9:24.

22. **ye shall**. Je 24:7. 31:1, 33. 32:38. Dt 26:17-19. SS 2:16. Ezk *11:20. 36:28. 37:27. Ho 2:23. Zc *13:9. Mt 22:32. He +*8:10. Re *21:3.

23. **the whirlwind**. See on Je 23:19, 20. 25:32. Ps 58:9. Pr 1:27. Zc *9:14. **continuing**. Heb. cutting. Pr 21:7mg. **fall**. or, remain. 2 S 3:29mg. Ho 11:6.

24. **fierce**. Je 4:28. 1 S 3:12. Jb 23:13, 14. Is *14:24, 26, 27. 46:11. Ezk *20:47, 48. 21:5-7. **in the latter days**. See on Je 23:20. 48:47. 49:39. Ge *49:1)𝒫. Nu *24:14. Dt 4:30. 31:29. Ezk *38:16. Da *2:28. *10:14. Ho *3:5. Mi 4:1.

JEREMIAH 31

God declares his love to all the race of Israel, 1-7; and promises to restore and abundantly bless them, 8-14. Rachel's mourning for her children is turned into joy, 15-17. Ephraim repents and is assured of mercy, 18-20. Predictions of blessings to Judah and Israel, as connected with the birth of Christ, 21-28. Every man shall answer for his own sins only, 29, 30. A new and better covenant is promised, 31-34. The stability of God's favor to Israel, 35-37. The rebuilding and extent of Jerusalem foretold, 38-40.

1. **same time**. See on Je 30:24. **will I**. ver. 33. Je 30:22. 32:38. Ge √17:7, 8. Le 26:12. Ps 48:14. 144:15. Is *41:10. Ezk 11:20. 34:31. 36:28. *39:22. Zc 13:9. Jn 20:17. He +*11:16. **of all**. Je 3:18. 23:6. 30:3, 10. 33:7, 14, 24-26. 50:4. Is *11:12, 13. Ezk *37:16-27. Ho 1:11. Zc 10:6, 7. Ro *11:26-29. **they shall**. Je 30:22. 32:28. Le 26:12)𝒫.

2. **The people**. Ex 1:16, 22. 2:23. 5:21. 12:37. 14:8-

12. 15:9, 10. 17:8-13. **were left**. Je 3:14. Is 24:6, 13. Zc 13:8. Mt 24:13. Lk 13:23. 18:8. Ro 11:5. **found grace**. Je 2:2. Dt 1:30, 33. *2:7. *8:2, 3, 16. Ne 9:12-15. Ps 78:14-16, 23-29, 52. 105:37-43. 136:16-24. Is 32:16. 63:7-14. Ezk 20:14-17. **in the wilderness**. Dt +*33:2, 3. Jg 5:4, 5. Ps √68:7. +*74:14. Is +*16:1. *32:15, 16. 35:1, 6. *40:3. 41:19, 20. *61:3. Ezk √20:35, 36. Ho √2:14. Mt 24:16. Re +*12:6, 14. **when**. Nu 10:33▶𝒫. Dt 1:33▶𝒫. 12:9. Ps 23:2. 95:11. Is 63:14. Ezk *34:15. Mt *11:28, 29. He *4:8, 9. **rest**. Ps +*94:13. Hab +*3:16. 2 Th *1:7.

3. **of old**. Heb. from afar. **I have**. Dt *7:7-9. *10:15. 33:3, 26-29. Ps 139:16. Ho 11:1. Ml +*1:2, 3. Jn √3:16. Ro 9:13. Ep 1:4. 1 J *4:19. **an**. Ps 103:17. Is 45:17. 54:8, 9. Ro 11:28, 29. 2 Th √2:13-16. 2 T √1:9. **everlasting**. Heb. *olam*, Ge +17:7. **with lovingkindness have I drawn**. *or*, have I extended lovingkindness unto. SS 1:4. Ezk +*20:35, 36. Ho +*2:14. 11:4. Jn √6:44, 45. Ro *8:30. Ep *1:3-5. *2:4, 5. T *3:3-6. Ja *1:18. 1 P *1:3, 4.

4. **build**. Je 1:10. 30:18. 33:7. Ps 51:18. *69:35. 102:16. 147:2. Am *9:11. Ac *15:16. Ep 2:20-22. Re 21:10, etc. **O virgin**. 𝒥155E5, Nu +21:25. ver. 21. Je 14:17. 18:13. Ge +24:16. 2 K *19:21. Is *37:22. La *1:15. *2:13. Am 5:2. **again**. ver. 13. Ex 15:20, 21. Jg 11:34. 1 S 18:6, 7. Ps 149:3. 150:3-6. Lk 15:23-25. Re 19:1-8. **tabrets**. *or*, timbrels. Ge 31:27. Ex +*15:20n.

5. **yet**. Dt 28:30. Is 62:8, 9. *65:21, 22. Am √9:14, 15. Mi *4:4. Zc *3:10. **mountains**. Ezk *36:8. Ob 19. Ac 8:5. **eat**. Heb. profane. Le 19:23-25▶𝒫. Dt 20:6▶𝒫. 28:30▶𝒫. 1 S 21:5.

6. **a day**. Je 6:17. Is *40:9. *52:7, 8. 62:6. Ezk 3:17. 33:2. Ho *9:8. **upon**. Je 50:19. 2 Ch 13:4. 30:5-11. Ac 8:5-8. **Arise**. Je 50:4, 5. Ezr 1:5. 8:15-20. Is *2:2-4. 11:11-13. Ho 1:11. Mi *4:1-3. Zc *8:20-23.

7. **Sing**. Dt *32:43. Ps ch. 67. 96:1-3. *98:1-4. ch. 117. *138:4, 5. Is *12:4-6. 24:14-16. 42:10-12. 44:23. Zp 3:14-20. **O Lord**. Ps 14:7. 28:9. 69:35. 106:47. 118:25. Ho 1:7. **remnant**. Je 23:3. Is 1:9. *11:11. 37:4, 31. Ezk 6:8. Jl 2:32. Am 5:15. Mi 2:12. 7:18. Zp 2:9. 3:13. Ro 9:27. 11:5, 6.

8. **I will**. Je 3:12. 29:14. 30:3, 18. Ps 107:3. Zc *2:6. **from the north country**. Je 3:18. 23:8. Ps 107:3. Is √43:6. Ezk +*38:6. Zc *2:6. **gather them**. Is +*52:12mg. Ezk *20:34, 41. +*34:13. +*37:25. **coasts of the earth**. Ps 65:5. 72:8. 98:3. Is √43:6. *45:22. √49:6. *52:10. **the blind and**. Is *40:11. *42:16. Ezk 34:16. Mi 4:6. Zp 3:19. Mt *12:20. Jn *21:15. 1 C 8:10. 1 Th 5:14. He √4:15. 12:12, 13.

9. **come**. Je 3:4. 50:4. Ps √126:5, 6. Ho 12:4. Da *9:17, 18. Zc *12:10. Mt +*5:4. Lk 6:21. Ro *8:26. 2 C √7:9-11. He *5:7. **supplications**. *or*, favors. Je *3:21, 22. 2 Ch 6:21. Zc √12:10. **I will**. Ps *23:2. Is *35:6-8. *41:17-19. *43:16, 19. *49:9-11. Re *7:17. **in a**. Is *40:3, 4. 57:14. 63:13. Mt *3:3. Lk 3:4-6. He *12:13. **for I**. ver. *20. Je 3:4, 19. Ex 4:22. Dt *32:6. 1 Ch 29:10. Is 63:16. 64:8. Mt *6:9. 2 C +*6:17, 18. He 12:23. **Ephraim**. Ex 4:22▶𝒫. Ezk *34:12-14. **my firstborn**. 1 Ch +*5:1. +26:10. Ps *89:20. 27. Col +√1:15n.

10. **declare**. Ge 10:5. Ps 72:10. Is 24:14, 15. 41:1. 42:4, 10-12. 48:20. 49:1. 51:5. *60:9. 66:19. Zp 2:11. **He**. Je 50:17-20. Dt *30:4. 32:26, 27, 36. Is *27:12, 13. 40:11. 54:7. Ezk 5:2, 10-12. 11:16, 17. 20:34, 41. Mi 2:12. 4:6. Zp 3:19. Jn 11:52. **and keep**. Je +30:11. Is 40:11. Ezk *34:12. 37:24. Mi 5:4, 5. Zc 9:16. Lk

*12:32. Jn √10:26-29. Ac *20:28, 29.

11. **redeemed**. Je 15:21. 50:33, 34. Is 44:23. *48:20. *49:24-26. Ho 13:14. Mt 20:28. T *2:14. He 2:14, 15. **stronger**. Ps 142:6. Mt 12:29. 22:29. Lk *11:21, 22.

12. **Therefore**. See on ver. 4. Je 33:9-11. Is ch. 12. *35:10. 51:11. **the height**. Is 2:2-5. Ezk 17:23. 20:40. Mi *4:1, 2. **and shall**. Je 33:9. Ps 130:4. Ho 3:5. Ro 2:4. **wheat**. Ho *2:20-23. Jl *3:18. Zc *9:15-17. **and their**. Is 1:30. 58:11. **soul**. Heb. *nephesh*, Ge +34:3. **watered garden**. Is 58:11. **and they**. Is 35:10. 60:20. *65:19. Jn *16:22. Re *7:17. *21:4.

13. **shall**. See on ver. 4. Ne *12:27, 43. Ps *30:11. 149:3. Zc *8:4, 5, 19. **and old**. 𝒥174, Ge +18:27. **for**. Ezr 6:22. Est 9:22. Is 35:10. 51:3, 11. 60:20. 61:3. 65:18, 19. Jn 16:22.

14. **satiate**. Dt 33:8-11. 2 Ch 6:41. Ne 10:39. Ps *132:9, 16. Is *61:6. Jn=6:35. 1 P *2:9. Re *5:9, 10. **soul**. Heb. *nephesh*, Ge +34:3. **my people**. ver. 25. Je 33:9. Ps *17:15. *36:8, 10. 63:5. *65:4. 90:14. *107:9. SS 5:1. Is *25:6. +*55:1-3. 66:10-14. Zc 9:15-17. Mt +*5:6. Ep *1:3. 3:19. Re 7:16, 17.

15. **A voice**. Ge 35:19▶𝒫. Ezk 2:10. Mt ✱2:16-18. **Ramah**. i.e. *high place*, ✱S#7414h. Je 40:1. Jsh 18:25. 19:8 (Ramath), 29, 36. Jg 4:5. 19:13. 1 S 1:19. 2:11. 7:17. 8:4. 15:34. 16:13. 19:18, 19, 22, 22, 23, 23. 20:1. 22:6. 25:1. 28:3. 1 K 15:17, 21, 22. 2 K 8:29. 2 Ch 16:1, 5, 6. 22:6. Ezr 2:26. Ne 7:30. 11:33. Is 10:29. Ho 5:8. Mt ▶2:18, Rama. (1) A city of Benjamin, where captives captured by Nebuchadnezzar were guarded, Je 31:15; 40:1. (2) A town in Mount Ephraim, also called Ramathaim-zophim, the birthplace of the prophet Samuel, 1 S 1:19. (3) A town on the boundary of Asher, Jsh 19:29. (4) A fortified place in Naphtali, Jsh 19:36. (5) Another name for the city of Ramoth-Gilead, 2 K 8:28, 29. (6) A place where some Benjamites returned after the captivity, Ne 11:33. **bitter weeping**. Je *6:26. Ho 12:14. **Rahel**. i.e. *ewe*, ✱S#7354h. See Ge +29:28, Rachel. **weeping**. 𝒥155D, Ge +4:10. **refused**. Ge 37:35. Ps 77:2. Is 22:4. **her children**. 2 S √12:23. **because**. T#1888. Ge 42:13, 36▶𝒫. Jb 7:21. Ps 37:36. La 5:7. Mt *✱2:16-18.

16. **Refrain**. Ge 43:31. 45:1. Ps 30:5. Mk 5:38, 39. Jn 20:13-15. 1 Th *4:13, 14. **from weeping**. Is +*25:8. Re +*21:4. **for thy work**. Je 2:2. Ru *2:12. 2 Ch 15:7. Ec 9:7. 1 C √15:58. He √6:10. √11:6. **they**. ver. 4, 5. See on Je 23:3. 29:14. 30:3, 18. 33:7, 11. Ezr 1:5-11. Ezk 11:17, 18. 20:41, 42. Ho 1:11. 2:15. **the enemy**. 1 C +*15:26.

17. **there is hope**. Je 29:11-16. 46:27, 28. Ps +*102:13, 14. Pr +*14:32. Is 6:13. √11:11, etc. +*26:19n. La *3:18, 21, 26, 27. Ezk √37:11-14, 25. √39:28. Ho 2:15. 3:5. Am √9:8, 9. Mt 24:22. Ro *11:23-26. 2 C *3:14-16. **thy children**. 2 S √12:23. Is 65:20. Ac +*2:39. **come again**. Dt +*32:39-43. 1 S *2:6. Ps 27:13. 79:11. 102:13-22. 116:9. 142:5-7. Is +*26:19n.

18. **surely**. Jb 33:27, 28. Ps 102:19, 20. Is √57:15-18. Ho *5:15. 6:1, 2. Lk *15:18-20. **Ephraim**. ver. 6, 9. Je 3:21, 22. 50:4, 5. Ho *11:8, 9. *14:4-8. **Thou hast**. Je 2:30. 5:3. Jb 5:17. Ps 39:8, 9. *94:12. *119:75. Pr 3:11. Is *1:5. 9:13. 57:17. Ho 5:12, 13. Zp 3:2. He *12:5. Re *3:19. **as a**. Ps 32:9. Pr 26:3. *29:1. Is 51:20. 53:7. La 3:27-30. Ho 10:11. **the yoke**. Mt 11:29. **turn**. Je 17:14. Ps 80:3, 7, 19. 85:4. La 5:21. Ml 4:6. Lk 1:17. Ac 3:26. Ph *2:13. Ja *1:16-18. **for**. See on Je 3:22, 25. Is 63:16.

19. **Surely after**. Dt 30:2, 6-8. Ezk 36:26, 31. Zc

12:10. Lk *15:17-19. Jn √6:44, 45. Ep *2:3-5. 2 T 2:25. T *3:3-7. **I smote.** ✓121S3X. Metonymy of the Adjunct B607. "Smiting the thigh" is put for grief. Ezk 21:12. Lk *18:13. 2 C *7:10, 11. **I was ashamed.** Je 3:25. Le 26:41, 42. Ezr 9:6. Ezk 6:9. 16:61-63. 20:43, 44. 36:31, 32. Ro 6:21. **I did.** Je 3:25. 22:21. 32:30. Jb 13:26. 20:11. Ps 25:7. Is 54:4, 7. Ezk 23:3. Lk *15:30.

20. **Is Ephraim.** ver. 9. Je 3:19. Ps *103:13. Pr 3:12. Lk *15:20, 24, 32. **for.** Dt 32:36)⊱𝒫. Jg 10:16. Is *57:16-18. La 3:31, 32. Ho 11:8, 9. **my bowels.** ✓22A18, Is 63:15. Ge 43:30. 1 K 3:26. SS 5:4. Is *63:15, 16. Ph 1:8. **are troubled.** Heb. sound. ✓141, Is 22:4. Je 48:36. Is 16:11. 63:15. **I will.** Is √55:7. 57:18. Ho *14:4. Mi *7:18, 19. **have mercy.** Je 30:17. Ezk 34:16. Lk +*19:10.

21. **Set thee.** Is *57:14. *62:10. **waymarks.** Nu 35:32n. Dt +27:8. Jsh +*20:7n. 2 K 23:17. Is 35:8. Ezk +*39:15. Hab *2:2. **set thine.** Je 50:5. Dt 32:46. 1 Ch 29:3. 2 Ch 11:16. 20:3. Ps 62:10. 84:5. Pr 24:32mg. Is 44:19mg. 57:14. Ezk 40:4. Hg 1:5mg. **even.** Je 6:16. **turn.** Je 51:6, 50. Is 48:20. 52:11, 12. Zc 2:6, 7. **O virgin.** ✓155E5, Nu +21:25. See on ver. 4. Je 3:14. Zc 10:9.

22. **How.** Je 2:18, 23, 36. 4:14. 13:27. Ho 8:5. **go about.** SS 5:6. **backsliding.** Je 3:6, 8, 11, 12, 14, 22. 7:24. 8:4-6. 14:7. 49:4. Ho 4:16. 11:7. 14:4. Zc 7:11. **created.** Nu 16:30. **new thing.** Je 30:14. Dt 24:4. Is +*7:14. Ho 2:19. Mt ✱1:23. **A woman.** ver. 21. ✱S#5347h. Ge 1:27. 5:2. 6:19. 7:3, 9, 16. Le 3:1, 6. 4:28, 32. 5:6. 12:5, 7. 15:33. 27:4, 5, 6, 7. Nu 5:3. 31:15. Dt 4:16. Literally, "A female ('one who is only a woman, not a wife, namely a virgin,' says Cocceius) shall encompass a man," or a male child: compare Jb 3:3. Which, together with the addition of a *new creation*, may well be understood to denote the miraculous conception. Hence the Jews have applied it determinately to the Messiah. In Berashith Rabba (Parash 89) it is said, that as God punished Israel in a virgin, so would he also heal; and in Midrash Tillim, on Ps ch. 2, R. Huna, in the name of R. Idi, speaking of the sufferings of the Messiah, says, that when his hour is come, God shall say, "I must create him with a *new creation*; and so he saith, This day have I begotten thee." Ge +*3:15. Is +*7:14. Mt +*1:21. Lk *1:34, 35. Ga √4:4. **compass.** Ps 7:7. 26:6. Jon 2:5. **a man.** Ps *10:15-18. La 3:1. Zc *13:7.

23. **As yet.** See on Je 23:5-8. 33:15-26. Is *1:26. +*60:21. Zc *8:3. In this day this portion of the prophecy is receiving a remarkable fulfillment, for Israel has her own land, and Hebrew is the official language. This restoration to contemporary use of an ancient language is unparalleled in history. See related note (Is √11:11n). **The Lord.** Je +7:3. Ru 2:4. Ps 28:9. +√122:5-8. 128:5. 129:8. 134:3. **O habitation.** Je 50:7. Is 1:21. **and mountain.** Ps 48:1, 2. 87:1-3. Ob 17. Mi 4:1. Zc 8:3.

24. **in Judah.** Je 33:11-13. Ezk *36:10, 11. Zc *2:4. *8:4-8.

25. **satiated.** See on ver. 14. Ps *107:9. Is *32:2. *50:4. Mt +*5:6. *11:28. Lk *1:53. Jn *4:14. 2 C 7:6. **soul.** Heb. *nephesh*, Ge +34:3.

26. **I awaked.** Ps *127:2. Zc 4:1, 2.

27. **the days.** See on ver. 31. **that I.** Je 30:19. Ezk *36:9. Ho *2:23. Zc *10:9, 10.

28. **And.** ✓148, Ge +8:22. **that like.** Je 44:27. Da 9:14. **to pluck.** See on Je 1:10. 18:7-9. 45:4. **so.** Je

24:6. 32:41, 42. Ps 69:35. 102:16. 147:2. Ec *3:2, 3. Da *9:25. Am √9:11. Ac *15:16.

29. **no more.** ✓138A, Ge +10:9. **The fathers.** ver. 30. La *5:7. Ezk √18:2-4. **children's.** ✓171G, Ge +13:8. **on edge.** Ec 10:10.

30. **every one.** Ex +*20:5. Dt *24:16. Is *3:10, 11. Ezk *3:18, 19, 24. √18:4, 20. 33:8, 13, 18. Ga *6:5, 7, 8. Ja *1:15. **his own.** 2 K +14:6.

31. **Behold.** He)8:8-12.)10:16, 17. **the days.** ver. 27. Je *23:5, 7. 30:3. 33:14-16. Am 9:13. **new covenant.** Je 32:40. Ge +*9:16. Ezk *37:26. Mt *26:28. Mk 14:24. Lk 22:20. 1 C *11:25. 2 C *3:6. He *8:6-13. *9:15. *10:16, 17. *12:24. *13:20. **with.** Je 50:4, 5. Ga 6:16. Ph 3:3.

32. **Not according.** See on ver. 1. Je 34:14. Ex *19:5, 6. *24:6-8. Dt 5:3, 4. 29:1, 10. Jsh 24:22. 1 K 8:9. Ezk 16:8, 60-62. He 9:18-22. **that I made.** Ex 24:3-8)⊱𝒫. **in the day.** ✓171T2, Ge +2:17. Dt 1:31)⊱𝒫. 32:11, 12)⊱𝒫. Ps 73:23. SS 8:5. Is 41:13. 51:18. 63:12-14. Ho 11:1, 3, 4. Mk 8:23. **which.** Je 11:7-10. 22:9. Le 26:15. Dt 29:21, 25. 31:16, 20. Is 24:5. Ezk 16:59. 20:37. He)8:9. **although I was.** *or*, should I have continued? Je 2:2. 3:14. Is 54:5. Ezk 16:8. 23:4. Ho 2:2. 3:1. Jn 3:29. 2 C *11:2. **husband.** Heb. *baal*, a homonym with two meanings: (1) to be lord or master, hence to be a husband; (2) to disdain, or reject. If the latter is the intended meaning here, the last clause could be rendered "and I rejected (or abhorred) them, declareth Jehovah." So the Syriac and other ancient interpreters, and so quoted in He)8:9.

33. **But this shall be.** Je 32:40. **covenant.** Ge +*9:16. **I will.** Dt 30:6. Ps 37:31. *40:8. Is 51:7. Ezk *11:19, 20. √36:25-27. Ro 7:22. *8:2-8. 2 C *3:3, 7, 8. Ga √5:22, 23. He *8:10. 10:16. **in their.** Ex +25:21. **write.** ✓22C43, Ex +31:18. **and will.** See on ver. 1. Je 24:7. 30:22. 32:38. Ge +*17:7, 8. Ezk 11:20. 37:27. Zc 13:9. Jn 20:17. Re 21:3, 7.

34. **teach no more.** 1 Th *4:9. He *5:12. 8:12. 1 J *2:27. **Know the Lord.** See on 1 S 2:12. 1 Ch +*28:9. Jn √17:3. **for they.** Je *24:7. Is *11:9. 30:26. *54:13. *60:19-21. Hab *2:14. Mt *11:27. Jn *6:45. +*17:6. 1 C 2:10. 2 C *4:6. 1 J *2:20. *5:20. **know.** ✓121C2A1, Jb +19:25. **from the least.** Je 6:13. **for I.** Je *33:8. *50:20. Ps 32:1. Is 33:24. *43:25. *44:22. Am ●8:7. Mi *7:18, 19. Ac *10:43. *13:38, 39. Ro *11:26, 27. Ep 1:7. He *8:12. *)10:17, 18. **remember.** ✓22C3, Ge +8:1. **no more.** Ge +9:16. Zc +*10:6.

35. **which giveth.** T#141. Ge 1:14-18)⊱𝒫. *8:22. Dt 4:19. Jb 38:33. Ps 19:1-6. 72:5, 17. 74:16. 89:2, 36, 37. 119:89. 136:7-9. Mt +*5:45. Ro 1:20. He 11:3. **ordinances.** Ge 8:22)⊱𝒫. Jb +38:33. **which divideth.** Ex 14:21, 22. Jb 26:12. Ps 74:13. 78:13. 106:9. 114:3-5. Is 51:15. 63:12. **when.** Je 5:22. Jb 38:10, 11. Ps 93:3, 4. 107:25-29. Is 51:15. Mt 8:25, 26. **The Lord of hosts.** Je +6:6. 10:16. 32:18. 46:18. 50:34. 51:19. Is 48:2. 54:5. **is his name.** Je +*10:16. Ex +*6:3n.

36. **If.** Ge √8:22. 13:15. **those.** Je 33:20-26. Ps 72:5, 17. √89:36, 37. 102:28. 119:89. 148:6. Is +√54:9, 10. **then.** Je 33:26. 2 S *7:24. Ps 72:5, 7, 18. 102:28. Is 11:11. √54:9, 10. Am √9:14, 15. Ro +√11:1. **cease.** Is 46:28. Dt 32:26. Am √9:8, 9. **for ever.** Heb. *olam*, Ge +9:12.

37. **If.** Je 33:22. Jb *11:7-9. Ps +*89:2, 28, 34. Pr 30:4. Is 40:12. **I will cast.** Je 30:11. 33:24-26. 46:28. Dt ●*4:31. Ro *11:2-5, 26-29.

38. **the days.** ver. 27. See on Je *23:5. **that.** Je

30:18. Ne 2:17-20. 12:30-40. Is 44:28. Ezk 48:30-35. Da *9:25. **the tower.** Ne 3:1. 12:39. Zc *14:10. **the gate of.** 2 K *14:13. 2 Ch *26:9.

39. measuring line. 1 K 7:23. Ezk 40:3, 8. Zc 1:16. *2:1, 2. Re 11:1. **Gareb.** i.e. *scabby, leprous; reviler,* ✳S#1619h, 2 S +23:38. 1 Ch 11:40. (1) One of David's valiant men, 2 S 23:38. (2) A hill near Jerusalem, Je 31:39. **Goath.** i.e. *lowing; fatigue,* ✳S#1601h, only here.

40. the whole. Je 7:32. 19:11-13. 32:36. Ezk *37:2. **the brook.** 2 S *15:23. 2 K *23:6, 12. Jn 18:1, Cedron. **unto.** 2 K 11:16. 2 Ch 23:15. Ne 3:28. **shall be holy.** Ezk *45:1-6. 48:35. Jl 3:17. Zc *14:20, 21. **not be plucked up.** See on Je 18:7. Is √51:22. Ezk 37:25. *39:28, 29. Am +√9:15. Zc +*9:8. **for ever.** Heb. *olam,* Ex +*12:24.

JEREMIAH 32

JEREMIAH is imprisoned, for predicting the destruction of Jerusalem, and the captivity of Zedekiah, 1-5. By the command of God he purchases a field, as a token that the Jews should be restored to their inheritances, 6-15. He prays to be further instructed concerning these transactions, 16-25. He is informed of the approaching calamities for the sins of the people, 26-35; and encouraged by predictions and promises of most extensive blessings, spiritual and temporal, to the nation of Israel and to the Israel of God, 36-44.

1. A.M. 3415. B.C. 589. **in the.** Je *39:1, 2. 52:4, 5. 2 K *25:1, 2. 2 Ch 36:11. **the eighteenth.** See on Je 25:1.

2. then. The siege had commenced on the tenth month of the preceding year, and continued a year after, ending in the fifth month of the following year; consequently the siege must have lasted eighteen months and twenty-seven days. See 2 K 25:18. **Jeremiah.** ver. 3, 8. Je 33:1. 36:5. 37:21. 38:6. 39:13-15. Mt *5:12. **in the.** Ne 3:25.

3. Zedekiah. Je 2:30. 5:3. 2 K 6:31, 32. 2 Ch 28:22. **Wherefore.** ver. 9. 38:4. Ex 5:4. Am 7:13. Lk *20:2. Ac 6:12-14. **Behold.** ver. 28, 29. See on Je 21:4-7. 27:8. 34:2, 3. 37:6-10. 38:3.

4. shall not escape. Je 37:17. 38:18, 23. 39:4-7. 52:8-11. 2 K *25:4-7. Ezk *12:12, 13. 17:13-21. *21:25-27. **delivered into.** Je 34:3. **shall speak.** Je 34:3mg.

5. until. Je 27:22. 34:4, 5. **though.** Je 2:37. 21:4, 5. 33:5. 37:10. Nu 14:41. 2 Ch *13:12. 24:20. Pr +*21:30. Ezk 17:9, 10, 15.

7. Behold. 1 K 14:5. Mk 11:2-6. 14:13-16. **Hanameel.** i.e. *gift of God; place of God's favor; God is a rock or safety,* ✳S#2601h. ver. 8, 9, 12. **my field.** Nu 35:5. **Anathoth.** Je 1:1. 11:21. Jsh 21:18, 19. **for.** Le *25:23-25, 32-34, 49↑𝒫. Nu 35:2. Ru *4:4-9. Re 5:1-5.

8. court. ver. 2. Je 33:1. **Anathoth.** See on ver. 7. 1 K *2:26. 1 Ch 6:60. **Then I.** 1 S 9:16, 17. 10:3-7. 1 K 22:25. Zc *11:11. Jn 4:53. Ac *10:17-28. **that this.** That it was by His appointment that I was to make this purchase; the whole of which was designed as a symbolical act, to show the people, that although Judah and Jerusalem should be desolated, and the inhabitants carried captive to Babylon, yet there should be a restoration, when lands and possessions should be again enjoyed by their legal owners, in the same manner as formerly. During the famine that prevailed in the

city, Hanameel probably wanted money to purchase bread, and his field would not be thought of much value in such circumstances, which may account for the stipulated sum being so very small; for at 2s. 6d. the shekel, it would only amount to about 2l. 2s. 6d.

9. weighed. Ge 23:15, 16. 1 K 20:39mg. Est 3:9mg. Is 55:2mg. **seventeen shekels of silver.** *or,* seven shekels, and ten *pieces* of silver. Ge 37:28. Ho *3:2. Zc *11:12, 13.

10. I. ver. 12, 44. Is 44:5. **subscribed the evidence.** Heb. wrote in the book. Jsh 18:9. Is 30:8. **and sealed.** Dt 32:34. Jb 14:17. SS 8:6. Da 8:26. Jn 3:33. *6:27. 2 C 1:22. Ep 1:13. 4:30. Re 7:2. 9:4. **and took.** ver. 12, 25, 44. Ru 4:9-11. Is 8:1, 2.

11. according. Lk 2:27. Ac 26:3. 1 C 11:16.

12. Baruch. i.e. *bent of knee* or *blessed,* ✳S#1263h. Je 32:12, 13, 16. 36:4, 4, 5, 8, 10, 13, 14, 14, 15, 16, 17, 18, 19, 26, 27, 32. 43:3, 6. 45:1, 2. Ne 3:20. 10:6. 11:5. (1) Friend and companion of Jeremiah the prophet employed as his amanuensis when he was in prison, Je 32:12. 43:6, 7. (2) A Jew who rebuilt part of the wall of Jerusalem, Ne 3:20; 10:6. (3) A descendant of Pharez, Ne 11:5. **Neriah.** i.e. *light of Jah; lamp of the Lord; my lamp is Jehovah,* ✳S#5374h. Je 32:12, 16. 36:4, 8. 43:3. 45:1. *51:59. Also Je 36:14, 32. 43:6. **and in.** 2 C *8:21.

14. Lord of hosts, the God of. Je +7:3. **Take.** ver. 10-12. **sealed.** Jb 14:17. **earthen vessel.** Je +19:1. Le 6:28.

15. Houses. ver. 37, 43, 44. See on Je 30:18. 31:5, 12, 24. 33:12, 13. Am √9:14, 15. Zc 3:10.

16. I prayed. Je 12:1. Ge 32:9-12. 2 S *7:18-25. Ezk 36:35-37. Ph *4:6, 7.

17. Ah. Je 1:6. 4:10. 14:13. Jg +6:22. Ezk 9:8. 11:13. **thou.** Je 10:11, 12. 27:5. 51:15, 19. Ge +*1:1↑𝒫, etc. Ex *20:11. 2 K 19:15. Ne +*9:6. Ps 102:25. +115:3. 136:5-9. 146:5, 6. Is 40:26-28. 42:5. 44:24. 45:12. 48:12, 13. Da 4:35. Zc 12:1. Jn +*1:1-3. Ac 7:49, 50. 14:15. 17:24. Col +*1:15, 16. He *1:2, 3, 10-12. Re 4:11. **there.** ver. 27. Ge *18:14↑𝒫. Jb 42:2. Mt √19:26. Lk 1:37. *18:27. **great.** ♪22I2, Ex +15:26. **too hard for thee.** *or,* hid from thee. Is 46:9, 10. Da 2:22. Ac 15:18. Ep 3:9-11.

18. showest. Ex *20:5, 6↑𝒫. 34:7↑𝒫. Nu 14:18. Dt *5:9, 10↑𝒫. 7:9, 10. **recompensest.** Jsh *7:24-26. 2 S *21:1-9. 1 K 14:9, 10. 16:1-3. 21:21-24. 2 K 9:26. Mt 23:31-36. √27:25. **the Great.** ♪22I2, Ex +15:16. Ge 49:24. Dt 7:21. 10:17. Ne 1:5. Ps 50:1. 145:3-6. Is +*9:6. 10:21. √57:15. Hab 1:12. **Mighty.** Dt 10:17↑𝒫. Is +*9:6. +10:21. 49:26. 60:16. Mt 11:21. Lk 9:43. Ep 1:21. Re 7:10, 12. **God.** Heb. *El,* Ex +15:2. Je 51:56. **the Lord of hosts.** Je +6:6. See on 10:16. 31:35. **is his name.** Je +10:16. Ex +*6:3n. Ps +68:4. +*83:18. Is 42:8.

19. Great. ♪22I2, Ex +15:16. Pr 8:14. Is +*9:6. 28:29. 40:13. 46:10, 11. Ro *11:33, 34. Ep +*1:11. Col 2:3. 1 J 2:1. Re 3:18. **work.** Heb. doing. Ex *15:11. Da 4:35. **for.** See on Je 16:17. 23:24. 2 Ch 16:9. Jb 34:21. Ps 33:13-15. 34:15. Pr 5:21. He *4:13. **to give.** See on Je 17:10. 1 K 8:32. Ps 62:12. Ec 12:14. Is 3:10, 11. Mt +*16:27. Jn 5:29. Ro 2:6-10. 2 C *5:10. Re *2:23. 22:12.

20. hast set. Ex *7:3↑𝒫. 10:2. Dt 4:34↑𝒫. *6:22↑𝒫. 7:19↑𝒫. 13:1, 2↑𝒫. 26:8↑𝒫. 28:46↑𝒫. 29:3↑𝒫. 34:11↑𝒫. Ne 9:10. Ps 78:43-51. 105:27-36. *135:8, 9. Ac 7:36.

and hast. Ex 9:16▸𝒫. 2 S 7:23. 1 Ch 17:21. Ne 9:10. Is *63:11, 12. Da 9:15.

21. **brought.** Ex *6:6. *13:14, 15. Ps √105:37, 43. *106:8-11. **with a strong.** Je +27:5. Ex 6:1, 6▸𝒫. 13:9. Dt 26:8. 1 K 8:42. Ps 89:8-10. *136:11, 12.

22. **which.** Ge *13:15. *15:18-21. *17:7, 8. 24:7. *28:13-15. 35:11, 12. +*50:24. Ex 13:5. Nu 14:16, 30. Dt 1:8, 35. 6:10, 18, 23. 7:13. 8:1. Jsh 1:6. 21:43. Ne 9:15. Ps 105:9-11. Ac +√7:5. **milk and.** 𝒥174, Ge +18:27. **honey.** 𝒥17117, Ex +3:8. Je +11:5. Ex 3:8, 17▸𝒫. 13:5. 33:1-3. Dt 26:9-11. Ezk 20:6, 15.

23. **possessed.** Ne *9:15, 22-25. Ps 44:2, 3. 78:54, 55. 105:44, 45. **but.** See on Je 7:23, 24. 11:7, 8. Jg 2:11-13. 10:6, etc. Ezr 9:7. Ne 9:26-30. Ezk 20:8, 18, 21. Da 9:4-6, 10-14. Zc 1:2-4. **they have.** Lk 17:10. Jn +*15:14. Ga 3:10. Ja √2:10. **therefore.** Le 26:14, etc. Dt 28:15, etc. Jsh 23:16. Ezr 9:7. La 1:8, 18. 5:16, 17. Da 9:11, 12. **evil.** Is +*45:7. **come.** 2 S +1:6.

24. **mounts.** or, engines of shot. Je 6:6. 33:4. Ezk *21:21, 22. The *mounts* were huge terraces raised up to plant their engines on; and so formed as to be capable of being moved forwards towards the city. See Note on 2 S 20:15. **the city is.** ver. 3, 25, 36. Je 21:4-7. 37:6-10. **because.** Je 14:12-15. 15:1-3. 16:4. 24:10. 52:6. La 2:21, 22. 4:3-10. Ezk 14:21. **what.** Dt 4:26. 31:16, 17. 32:24, 25. Jsh 23:15, 16. Zc *1:6. Mt √24:35.

25. **thou.** ver. 8-15. **for.** or, though. ver. 24. Ps 77:19. 97:2. Jn *13:7. Ro 11:33, 34.

27. **God.** Nu +*16:22▸𝒫. 27:16. Ps *65:2. Is *64:8. Lk 3:6. Jn √17:2. Ro 3:29, 30. **is there anything.** See on ver. *17. Je *33:3. Mt *19:26. Mk 9:23. 11:22. Lk 18:27.

28. **Behold.** ver. 3, 24, 36. Je 19:7-12. 20:5.

29. **and set.** Je 17:27. 21:10. 27:8-10. 37:7-10. 39:8. 52:13. 2 K √25:9. 2 Ch √36:19. Is *64:10, 11. La *4:11. Mt √22:7. **upon.** Je 7:18. 19:13. 44:17-19, 25. **to provoke.** Dt 4:25▸𝒫. 9:18▸𝒫. 31:29▸𝒫. 32:21▸𝒫.

30. **children.** Je 2:7. 3:25. 7:22-26. Dt *9:7-12, 22-24. 2 K 17:9-20. Ne 9:16, etc. Ps *106:6, 7. Is √63:10. Ezk 16:15, etc. 20:8, 28. 23:43, 44. Ac *7:51-53. **from.** Je 22:21. Ge 8:21. Ezk 23:3.

31. **this city.** Je 5:9-11. 6:6, 7. 23:14, 15. 1 K 11:7, 8. 2 K *21:4-7, 16. 22:16, 17. 23:13, 15. Ezk 22:2-22. Mt 23:37. Lk √13:33, 34. **a provocation of mine anger.** Heb. for my anger. ver. 37. Je 2:35. 4:8. **that I.** See on Je 27:10. 2 K 23:27. 24:3, 4. La 1:8.

32. **they.** Je 2:26. Ezr 9:7. Ne 9:32-34. Is *1:4-6, 23. 9:14, 15. Ezk *22:6, 25-29. Da *9:6, 8. Mi 3:1-5, 9-12. Zp *3:1-4.

33. **turned.** See on Je 2:27. 7:24. 18:17. Ezk *8:16. Ho *11:2, 7. Zc *7:11, 12. **back.** Heb. neck. **rising.** Je 7:13. 25:3, 4. 26:5. 35:15. 44:4. 2 Ch *36:15, 16. Jn 8:2.

34. **set their abominations.** See on Je 7:30. 23:11. 2 K *21:4-7. 23:6. 2 Ch √33:4-7, 15. Ezk *8:5-16. **which is called.** Je 7:10mg.

35. **they built.** See on Je 7:31. 19:5, 6. 2 K 23:10. 2 Ch *28:2, 3. 33:6. Ps *106:37, 38. Is *57:5. Ezk 16:20, 21. 23:37. **the valley.** Jsh +*15:8n. **which.** Je +*7:31. Le *18:21▸𝒫. *20:2-5. Dt +*18:10-12. 1 K 11:33. **neither came.** Je +*7:31. 19:5. **to cause.** Ex 32:21. Dt 24:4. 1 K 14:16. 15:26, 30. 16:19. 21:22. 2 K 3:3. 21:11. 23:15. 2 Ch 33:9.

36. **now.** Je 16:12-15. Is *43:24, 25. *57:17, 18. Ezk

*36:31, 32. Ho 2:14. Ro √5:20. Ep √2:3-5. **the Lord, the God of.** Je +11:3. **It shall.** See on ver. 3, 24, 28.

37. **I will gather.** "This promise," says Jerome, "taken in its full extent, was not made good to those that returned from captivity; because they were frequently infested with wars, as well by the kings of Syria and Egypt as by the rest of their neighbors; and they were finally subdued and destroyed by the Romans." God's word cannot fail; therefore there remaineth yet a rest for the ancient people of God. Je 23:3, 8. 29:14. 30:18. 31:10. 33:7. Dt √30:3-6▸𝒫. Ps 106:47. Is √11:11-16. Ezk 11:17. *34:12-14. 36:24. 37:21-25. 39:25-29. Ho *1:11. *3:5. Am +√9:14, 15. Ob 17-21. Zp *3:20. **I will cause.** See on Je +*23:6. 33:16. Le 23:43▸𝒫. Ezk 34:25-28. 36:11, 33. Ho 11:11. Jl 3:20. Zc 2:4, 5. 3:10. √10:6. 14:11.

38. **they shall.** Je 24:7. 30:22. 31:1, 33. Ge 17:7. Dt 26:17-19. Ps 144:15. Ezk *11:19, 20. *36:28. 37:27. 39:22, 28. Zc 13:9. He +*8:10. +*11:16. 1 J *3:1, 2. Re 21:7.

39. **I will.** 2 Ch 30:12. Is 52:8. Ezk 11:19, 20. 36:26. 37:22. Jn 17:21. Ac 4:32. 2 C 13:11. Ph 2:1, 2. **one way.** Je 6:16. Is 35:8. Jn √14:6. He 10:20. **they may fear.** T#802. ver. 40. Ge 22:12. Ps 112:1. Pr 14:26, 27. 23:17. Ac 9:31. **for ever.** Heb. all days. Je 33:18. 35:19. Ge +9:12. Lk 1:75. **for the.** Ge 17:7. 18:19. Dt 5:29. 11:18-21. Ps 115:13-15. 128:6. Ezk 37:25. Ac +*2:39. 3:39. 13:33. Ro 11:16. 1 C 7:14.

40. **I will make.** Je *31:31-33. 50:5. Ge *17:7-13. 2 S *23:4, 5. Ps +*89:34-36. Is *24:5. +*55:3. *61:8. Ezk 16:60. Lk *1:72-75. Ga *3:14-17. He 6:13-18. 12:24. *13:20. **everlasting.** Heb. olam, Ge +17:7. **covenant.** Ge +9:16▸𝒫. **that I.** Ezk *39:29. Jn √10:27-30. Ro √8:28-39. **will not.** Je +*31:36. +*33:25, 26. Ps *94:14. Is +*41:9. *51:22. 54:7. Ro +*11:1. √15:8. He +*13:5. **from them.** Heb. from after them. Je 3:19mg. 2 K 10:29. **but I.** Je *31:33. Ezk *36:26. Ro √15:8. 2 C 3:14. He 4:1. Ja 1:17. 1 P *1:5. **not depart.** Since Israel *did* depart after their return from the Babylonian captivity and was scattered to many nations, this must refer to the time of the millennium. Je √3:19. Jb *5:24. Ps 80:18. +*130:8. Is +√11:11n. +*41:9. +*55:3. +*59:21. Ezk *16:63. Zp *3:13.

41. **Yea, I.** Dt 30:9▸𝒫. Is *62:5. *65:18, 19. Zp *3:17. **rejoice.** 𝒥22B, Ps +104:31. **do them good.** Ezk 36:11. Zc √10:6. **and I.** Je 18:9. 24:6. 31:28. Am √9:15. **assuredly.** Heb. in truth, or stability. Je 2:21. 26:15. 28:9. Ho *2:19, 20. **heart.** 𝒥22A17, Ge +6:6. **soul.** Heb. nephesh, Ge +34:3. Le +26:11n.

42. **Like.** Je 31:28. Jsh *23:14, 15. Zc *8:14, 15. Mt √24:35. **so.** Je +*31:28. 33:10, 11. **promised.** Je 29:10. 33:17, 20, 21, 22, 25, 26. Is +*55:3. Ro *11:29. +*15:8.

43. **ye say.** See on ver. 36. Je 33:10. Ezk +*12:19. √37:11-14.

44. **buy.** See on ver. 6-15. **in the land.** Je 17:26. **for I.** See on ver. 37. Je 33:7, 11, 26. Ps *126:1-4. As an earnest of these promises, houses and lands shall again take a good price in Judah and Jerusalem; and though they now are almost valueless, there shall again be a sufficiency of purchasers. Trade shall revive, for they shall have money enough to buy land with; husbandry shall revive, for those that have money, shall covet to lay it out upon lands; laws shall again have their due course, for they shall *subscribe evidences, and seal them.*

JEREMIAH 33

Predictions concerning the return of the Jews from captivity; the rebuilding of Jerusalem; and the pardon, holiness, comfort, and prosperity connected with those events, 1-13; concerning the coming of Christ; and the performance of the covenant-engagements of God to the Levites, and to David, in him, 14-26.

1. A.M. 3416. B.C. 588. **Moreover**. This was the eleventh year of Zedekiah, Jeremiah being still shut up in prison; but he was now in the court of the prison, where the elders and the king's officers might consult him with the greater ease. **he**. See on Je 32:2, 3, 8. 37:21. 38:28. 2 T *2:9.

2. **the maker**. *Osah*, rather, "the Doer of it:" that is, he who is to perform that which he is now about to promise; thus rendered by Dahler: *Voice ce qui dit l'Eternel, qui fast ce* qu'il a dit. "Thus saith the Eternal, who doeth that *which he hath said."* Ps 87:5. 102:16. Is 14:32. 37:26. 43:1, 21. 62:7. He 11:10, 16. Re 21:2, 10. **the Lord**. *or*, Jehovah. See on Je 32:18. Ex 3:14, 15. 6:3. 15:3Ɫ. Am 5:8. 9:6.

3. **Call**. T#879. Je 29:12. Ex *34:24. Dt 4:7, 29. 1 K 8:47-50. Jb *22:21. *33:26. Ps *6:9. *10:17. 18:3. *50:15. *55:17. *73:28. *86:5, 7. 91:15. *145:18. Is √55:6, 7. +*65:24. Jl *2:32. Lk √11:9, 10. Ac 2:21. Ro √10:12, 13. 1 C 1:2. He *4:14-16. Ja *4:8. 1 J +√5:14 (T#797). **will answer**. Ps 65:5. Is +*65:24. **show**. Je 32:27. Jb 28:11. Ps +*51:6. Mi 7:15. Ep 3:20. **great and**. T#1786. Ge 32:9-11. 33:1-4. 32:24-30. Ex 14:10, 21-29. 34:8-10. Nu 11:11-23, 31. Jg 6:15, 16. 16:28-30. 1 S 7:8-12. 30:8-10, 18-20. 2 S 22:7-18. 24:17-19, 25. 1 K 18:36-39, 42-45. 2 K *4:1-7. 19:15, 16, 20, 32-36. 1 Ch 5:18-22. 14:13-17. 2 Ch 1:7-12. 2 Ch 13:14-18. *17:3-5. 20:13-17, 22-25. 26:3-8. Jb *42:10-13. Ps 2:8. 21:2-6. Is 38:1-6. 40:27-31. *41:17, 18. 49:14-16. +*55:1-3. *64:4. Ho 14:2-7. Mk 10:35-40. Lk 3:21, 22. *8:24, 25. *12:31. 15:17-24. 18:13, 14. 23:42, 43. Ac 4:23-33. 9:6, 10-17. 10:1-6. 2 C *12:7-11. Ep √3:20, 21. Ja 5:17, 18. Re 3:20, 21. **mighty**. Heb. hidden. or, fenced things, hitherto unrevealed. or, inaccessible, too high for Jeremiah to know, apart from revelation (CB). S#1219h. Je 15:20 (fenced). Nu 13:28 (walled). Dt 1:28 (walled). 3:5 (fenced). 9:1. 28:52. Jsh 14:12 (fenced). Is 2:15. 25:2 (defenced). 27:10. 36:1. 37:26. Ezk 21:20. 36:35. Ho 8:14. Zp 1:16. Zc 11:2mg. **things**. Mt *21:22. Ro +*8:32. **which thou**. Ps 25:14. Is 45:3. *48:6. Am √3:7. Mt 13:35. 1 C *2:7-11. Re 2:17.

4. **the Lord, the God of**. Je +11:3. **thrown**. Je 32:24. Ezk 4:2. 21:22. 26:8. Hab 1:10.

5. **come**. Je 21:4-7. 32:5. 37:9, 10. **I have hid**. Je 18:17. 21:10. Dt 31:17. 32:20. Is *1:15, 16. *8:17. 64:7. Ezk 39:23, 24, 29. Mi 3:4.

6. **I will bring**. Je 17:14. 30:12-17. Dt 32:39. Ps 67:2. Is 30:26. 58:8. Ho *6:1. 7:1. **health**. *Aruchah*; not a *plaister*, as some, or *progress*, as others; but *health*, or the *health*, or the *healing* or closing of a wound, as the cognate Arabic *areekat* signifies, from *araka*, to heal. Je +*8:22. 17:14. 30:17. Ps *103:3. Mt 14:36. **and will**. Ex 34:6. Ps 37:11. 72:7. 85:10-12. Is 2:4. 11:5-9. √26:2-4. 30:26. 33:15-18. 39:8. 48:17, 18. 54:13. 55:7. 66:12. Mi 4:3. Jn √10:10, 11. Ga 5:22, 23. Ep 6:23. T *3:5, 6. He 6:17, 18. 1 P 1:3.

7. **will cause**. ver. 11, 26. See on Je 23:3. 29:14. 30:3. 32:44. Ps *14:7. *85:1. *126:1, 2, 4. Is *11:12, etc. Zp *3:20. **and will**. Je 24:6. 30:20. 31:4, 28. 42:10.

Is 1:26. Ho 2:15. Am √9:14, 15. Mi 7:14, 15. Zc 1:17.

8. **will cleanse**. Je 31:34. 50:20. Ps 51:2. 65:3. 85:2, 3. Is 40:2. 44:22. 56:7. Ezk 36:25, 33. Jl 3:21. Mi *7:18, 19. Zc 13:1. He *9:11-14. 1 J √1:7-9. Re *1:5, 6. **will pardon**. Ps 103:12. Is 43:25. Mi 7:19.

9. **a name**. Je 13:11. 31:4. Ps *126:3, 4. Is *62:2, 3, 7, 12. Zp 3:17-20. Zc *8:20-23. 12:2, 3. **before**. Je 26:6. 29:1. 44:8. **fear**. Ex 15:14-16. 2 Ch 20:29. Ne 6:16. Est 8:17. Ps 40:3. Is 60:5. Ho 3:5. Mi 7:16, 17. Zc 12:2.

10. **which ye**. See on Je 32:36, 43. Ezk *37:11.

11. **voice of joy**. Je 7:34. 16:9. 25:10. Jn 3:29. Re 18:23. **the voice of them**. Je 31:12-14. Ezr 3:11-13. 6:22. Ne 8:12. 12:43. Is 12:1-6. 51:11. 52:9. Zp *3:14, 15. Zc 8:19. 9:17. *10:7. **Praise the**. 1 Ch 16:8, 34. 2 Ch 5:13. 7:3. 20:21. Ezr 3:11. Ps *106:1, 2. *107:1, 21. 118:1-4. 136:1-26. **Lord of hosts**. Je +6:6. **for ever**. Heb. *olam*, Ex +12:24. **sacrifice**. Le 7:12, 13. 22:29. 2 Ch 29:31. 33:16. Ps 107:22. 116:17. Ezk 43:27mg. 45:17mg. Am 4:5. **of praise**. Je 17:26. Ps 107:22. 116:17. 119:108. Jon 2:9. He *13:15. **For I**. See on ver. 7, 26.

12. **without**. Je 32:43. 36:29. 51:62. **in all**. See on Je 17:26. 31:24. 32:44. 50:19, 20. Is *65:10. Ezk *34:12-14. 36:8-11. Ob 19, 20. Zp 2:6, 7. Jn *10:2, 3.

13. **shall**. Le 27:32. Lk *15:4-7. Jn 10:3, 4, *14.

14. **the days come**. Je 23:5. 29:10. 31:27, 31-34. 32:38-41. Ge *22:18. +*49:10. 1 Ch 17:13, 14. Is +*7:14. +*9:6, 7. 32:1, 2. Ezk 34:23-25. Da 2:44. 7:13, 14. 9:25. Am 9:11. Mi +*5:2. Zp *3:15-17. Hg 2:6-9. Zc *9:9, 10. Ml 3:1. Lk *1:32, 33, 69, 70. *2:10, 11. 10:24. Ac 13:32, 33. 2 C *1:20. He 11:40. 1 P *1:10-12. Re *19:10.

15. **the Branch**. ♃22H1A, Is +4:2. See on Je +*23:5, 6. Is 4:2. *11:1-5. 53:2. 61:11. Ezk 17:22, 23. Zc 3:8. 6:12, 13. **unto David**. 2 S 7:12. **and he**. 2 S 23:2, 3. Ps +*45:4, 7. 72:1-5. Is +*9:7. 11:2-5. 32:1, 2. *42:21. Jn *5:22-29. He +*1:8, 9. 7:1, 2. Re 19:11.

16. **In those days**. Zc √12:8. **shall Judah**. See on Je +*23:6. Is *45:17, 22. Ro 11:26. **dwell safely**. T#947. Je 32:37. Dt 33:12, 28. Ps 102:*13, 14, 16. Is 4:5, 6. 27:2, 3. *33:20-22. 51:3. *54:14, 15, 17. 65:18, 19. 66:10-12. Ezk 28:26. 34:25-28. 38:8. Da *7:27. **The Lord our righteousness**. *Jehovah-tsidkenu*. Je *23:6. Ex +15:26. Is *45:24, 25. Ro 3:22. 5:19. 10:4. 1 C *1:30. 2 C √5:21. Ph *3:8, 9. 2 P *1:1.

17. **David shall never want**. Heb. There shall not be cut off from David. Je 35:19. 2 S 3:29. √7:14-16. 1 K *2:4. 8:25mg. 1 Ch *17:11-14, 27. Ps √89:29-37. Is +*9:7. Lk 1:32, 33.

18. **Neither shall**. Is 56:7. 61:6. Ezk 43:19-27. 44:9-11. *45:4, 5. Ml 3:3. Ro 12:1, 2. 15:16. 1 C=2:2. Ep 1:6, 7. He *13:15, 16. 1 P 2:5, 9. Re 1:6. *5:9, 10. **the priests the Levites**. Nu 25:10-13ᴾƗ. Dt 17:9ᴾƗ. Is 66:21. Ezk *43:18, 19. 44:10, 14, 15. Ml 2:5. **sacrifice**. Is +56:7. That there will be blood sacrifices in the future millennial Temple service is set forth in such detail in Scripture that it is not possible to deny their literality. Apparently such sacrifices look back upon the finished work of Christ, as they once looked forward, just as the present ordinances of baptism and the Lord's supper look back upon the cleansing of the blood and the death of Christ in history on our behalf. To suggest these references are all to be spiritualized, or to attempt to include them all under the figure of hypocatastasis (ſ103, Ge +3:13), as suggested by Peters

(Theocratic Kingdom, vol. 3, Prop. 172, Ob. 7, pp. 89, 90, and note 1, p. 90), is to misread the nature and misapply the purpose of the rhetorical figures of speech found in Scripture. Such a misreading is a double-edged sword, which can be unleashed to undo every other prophetic declaration to prove that it cannot be literally understood, the very opposite of what Peters masterfully argues everywhere else (contrast, e.g., the discussion of the deliverance of the animal kingdom, or lower creation, vol. 2, Prop. 146, Ob. 3, pp. 483-488, and note 4, p. 487) in his most excellent study. See Note on Ge 24:10n. **continually**. He=13:15, 16.

20. **If ye can break**. ver. 25, 26. See on Je 31:35, 36. Ge +*8:22)𝒫. Jb 38:12. Ps *89:30-37. 104:19-23. Is +*54:9, 10. Ro +√11:1. **covenant**. Ge +9:16.

21. **may**. 2 S √23:5. 2 Ch 7:18. *21:7. Ps √89:34-36. +*132:11, 12, 17. Is +*55:3. Mt 24:35. Lk 1:69, 70. **covenant**. Ge +9:16. **with David**. The Davidic covenant was wholly unconditional. It is this aspect of the Davidic covenant that constitutes it the "sure mercies of David." Many interpreters have failed to understand that while every covenant has conditions set upon it, yet this covenant is unconditional as to its ultimate fulfillment, though conditional with respect to any one individual, other than David himself. So in the New Testament, many promises which are unconditional to the body of believers, the elect, or the church as a whole, may yet be conditional with respect to individual believers within that body (Ep 4:30, note that "ye" is plural, thus postulated of the elect as a whole, not of every individual separately, for an occasional individual believer may become an unbeliever through moral [1 C +*6:9, 10. He +*10:26] or doctrinal [1 C +*15:2. 2 J 8-11] apostasy, and so forfeit the benefit promised [He 10:39]: Lk +*8:13. 1 C +*15:2. He +*3:12-14. 2 P +*1:10. *2:20, 21). 2 S √7:10-16. Ps 89:3, 4, 20-37. +*132:11. Is +√55:3. He=6:17, 18. **that he**. From the destruction of Jerusalem to the present time, a period of nearly eighteen hundred years, the Jews have had neither a king nor any form of government whatever; nor has the office of high priest, or priest of any kind offering sacrifice, been exercised among them during the same period. Hence this must be understood of the spiritual David, Jesus Christ, both the King and High Priest of his church, "the Israel of God" (Ga 6:16), in whom the covenant of royalty with David and his seed, and that of priesthood with Aaron and his seed, have received their full accomplishment; and all the sacrifices of that dispensation were superseded by his "one oblation of himself," the efficacy of which remains for ever. Scott suggests, "Probably, a more literal accomplishment will hereafter be witnessed: but I do not presume to state particularly the events which may be expected." Taking into account the Parallel Passages (ver. 20, 25, 26. Je 31:35-37. Is +*54:9, 10) which so strongly affirm the literal fulfillment of these covenant promises to natural Israel, and understanding their relationship to the Abrahamic Covenant, which has never been literally fulfilled (Je +7:7. Is +26:15. Ac +*7:5. He *11:13, 39), we must understand the fulfillment to be yet future, during the millennium, when the Jews are literally and fully restored to their land, Abraham (Mt +*8:11) and other patriarchs resurrected to experience the fulfillment of the covenanted kingdom in that age. Thus a spiritual fulfillment to the Church intimated in the note above

must not be permitted to displace, abrogate, or supersede the covenanted fulfillment to literal restored Israel. See the related notes (Jsh 21:43n. 1 K √4:21n. Is 60:21n. Ac 7:5n). Is +*9:6, 7. Da 7:14. Lk 1:32, 33. **and with**. See on ver. 18. Re 5:10.

22. **the host**. Je 31:37. Ge 13:16. 15:5)𝒫. 22:17)𝒫. 28:14. Ho *1:10, 11. He 11:12. Re *7:4, 9, 10. **sand of the sea**. √102B, 138B, Ge +13:16. Ge 22:17)𝒫. Ho *1:10. **so**. Ps 22:30. 89:3, 4, 29. Is *53:10-12. Ezk *37:24-27. Zc 12:8. **multiply**. Ac 9:31. He 2:10. **the Levites**. Is +*66:21, 22. Ezk 44:15.

24. **The two**. ver. 21, 22. Ps +√94:14. Ro +√11:1-6. **thus**. Ne 4:2-4. Est 3:6-8. Ps 44:13, 14. 71:11. 83:4. 123:3, 4. La 2:15, 16. 4:15. Ezk 25:3. 26:2. 35:10-15. 36:2.

25. **If my**. See on ver. 20. Ge +*8:22. 9:9-17. **and if**. Je +*31:35, 36. Ps *74:16, 17. 104:19. **ordinances of heaven**. Jb +38:33.

26. **Then**. Je 31:36. Dt 4:31. Jg 2:1. Is +√54:9, 10. Ro +√11:1. **will I**. See on Je 31:37. Ge +*49:10. **cast away**. Je 23:39. Is +√41:9. +*54:7. **I will cause**. See on ver. 7-11. Ezr 2:1, 70. **Abraham**. Ge 50:24. Ex 2:24. 3:6. 6:3, 4. Ps *105:9, 10. Mt +*8:11. +*22:32. Mk +*12:26, 27. Lk 1:72, 73. **for I**. Je *31:36, 37. Is 11:11. Am √9:14, 15. Ro +√11:1. **and have**. Je 31:20. Is *14:1. +*41:9. *54:8. Ezk *39:24, 25. Ho 1:7. 2:23. Zc √10:6. Ro *11:32.

JEREMIAH 34

The prophet is sent to assure Zedekiah, that the city will certainly be taken and burned; and that he will be carried to Babylon, and there die in peace, 1-7. The princes and people, having covenanted to set free their enslaved brethren, again reduce them to bondage, 8-11. God by the prophet proclaims liberty to the sword, pestilence, and famine; and predicts the return and success of the Chaldeans, 12-22.

1. A.M. 3415. B.C. 589. **The word**. This chapter contains two discourses, one concerning the taking of the city, and Zedekiah's captivity and death, ver. 1-7; and the other containing an invective against the inhabitants of Jerusalem for retaining their Hebrew slaves, ver. 8-22; both of which were delivered in the tenth year of Zedekiah. **when**. ver. 7. Je 32:2. 39:1-3. 52:4, etc. 2 K *25:1-9. 2 Ch √36:11-17. **all the kingdoms**. Je 1:15. 27:5-7. Da 2:37, 38. 4:1, 22. 5:19. **of his dominion**. Heb. the dominion of his hand.

2. **Go**. Je 22:1, 2. 37:1-4. 2 Ch 36:11, 12. **Behold**. ver. 22. See on Je 21:4, 10. 32:3, 28, 29. 37:8-10. 38:23. 39:8.

3. **And thou**. ver. 21. Je 21:7. 32:4. 37:17. 38:18. 39:4, 5. 52:7-9. 2 K √25:4, 5. **and thine**. Je 39:6, 7. 52:10, 11. 2 K *25:6, 7. Ezk *12:13. *17:18-20. 21:25. **he shall speak with thee mouth to mouth**. Heb. his mouth shall speak to thy mouth.

4. **Yet hear**. Je 38:17, 20.

5. **But thou**. 2 K *22:20. 2 Ch 34:28. Ezk *17:16. **and with**. 2 Ch *16:13, 14. 21:19. **so**. Da 2:46. **and they**. See on Je 22:18. 2 Ch 21:20. La 4:20.

6. **spake**. 1 S 3:18. 15:16-24. 2 S 12:7-12. 1 K 21:19. 22:14. Ezk 2:7. Mt 14:4. Ac 20:27.

7. **fought against**. See on ver. 1. Je 4:5. 8:14. 11:12. Dt *28:52. **Lachish**. Jsh 10:3, 11. 12:11. 15:35, 39. 2 K 18:13, 14. 19:8. Mi 1:13. **for**. 2 Ch *11:5-10. 27:4.

8. **had**. 2 K 11:17. 23:2, 3. 2 Ch *15:12-15. 23:16.

29:10. 34:30-33. Ne 9:38. 10:1, etc. **to proclaim.** See on ver. 14, 17. Ex 21:2-4♪𝒫. 23:10, 11. Le 25:*10, 39-46♪𝒫. Dt 15:12♪𝒫. Ne 5:1-13. Is 9:4. 10:27. 14:25. *61:1, 2. Ezk 46:17. 1 C 7:21.

9. **Hebrew.** Ge 14:13. 40:15. Ex 2:6. 3:18. Dt *15:12. 1 S 4:6, 9. 14:11. 2 C 11:22. Ph 3:5. **Hebrewess.** i.e. *a Hebrew woman*, ✢S#5680h, with this rendering only here. For ✢S#5680h, Hebrew, see Ge +14:13. **serve.** ver. 10. Je 25:14. 27:7. 30:8. 1 C *6:6-8.

10. **when.** Je 26:10, 16. 36:12, 24, 25. 38:4. **then.** Je 3:10, 11. Is *29:13. Mk *6:20.

11. **afterward.** ver. 21. Je 37:5. Ex *8:8, 15. 9:28, 34, 35. 10:17-20. 14:3-9. 1 S *19:6-11. 24:19. 26:21. Ps 36:3. *78:34-36. 125:5. Pr 26:11. Ec √8:11. Ho *6:4. 7:16. Zp 1:6. Mt 12:43-45. Ro 2:4, 5. 2 P √2:20-22.

12. **from the Lord.** Ge +*19:24.

13. **I made.** Je 31:32. Ex *24:3, 7, 8. Dt *5:2, 3, 27. 29:1. He +*8:10, 11. **in the day.** ♫171T2, Ge +2:17. See on Je 7:22. 11:4, 7. Dt 7:8. *15:15. *16:12. *24:18. Jsh 24:17. Jg 6:8. **out of.** Ex 13:3, 14. Dt 5:6. 6:12. 8:14. 13:10. Jsh 24:17. Jg 6:8.

14. **At the.** ver. 8, 9. Ex 21:1-4. 23:10, 11. Dt 15:12. 1 K *9:22. 2 Ch *28:10. Is *58:6. Am 2:6. 8:6. **been sold.** *or*, sold himself. 1 K 21:25. Is 50:1. Ro 7:14-17, 24. **but.** It appears from this and several other passages, that the sabbatical year had been wholly neglected some centuries before the captivity; and the author of the second book of Chronicles (2 Ch 36:21) assigns this as a reason for the captivity—"that the land might enjoy her sabbaths." Now, if we reckon the seventy years' captivity as a punishment for this neglect, it will follow that the law on this subject had been disregarded for about 490 years. Je 7:25, 26. 11:8-10. 32:30. 1 S 8:7, 8. 2 K 17:13, 14. 2 Ch 36:16. Ne 9:30. Ezk 20:4, 8. Zc *7:11, 12.

15. **ye.** 1 K *21:27-29. 2 K 10:30, 31. 12:2. 14:3. Is *58:2. Mt *15:8. **now.** Heb. today. **in proclaiming.** See on ver. 10, 11. **ye had.** See on ver. 8. 2 K *23:3. Ne 10:29. Ps 76:11. 119:106. **which is called by my name.** Heb. whereupon my name is called. See on Je 7:10mg, 11.

16. **ye turned.** See on ver. 11. 1 S *15:11. Ezk 3:20. *18:24. 33:12, 13. Lk +*8:13-15. **polluted.** Ex 20:7. Le *19:12♪𝒫. Ezk 17:16-19. 20:39. 39:7. Ml 1:7, 12. **pleasure.** Heb. *nephesh*, Ex +15:9. ♫121A9, Ge +23:8. **and brought.** Mt *18:28-34.

17. **behold.** When they proclaimed *liberty* to their slaves, God restrained the sword from cutting them off; but now having resumed their authority over them, He proclaimed *liberty* to these dire judgments to seize upon, and destroy them. Le 26:34, 35. Dt 19:19. Jg 1:6, 7. Est 7:10. Da 6:24. Mt *7:1, 2. Lk 6:37, 38. Ga √6:7. Ja *2:13. Re *16:6. **liberty.** ♫145, Jg +11:40. Le ●25:42, 55. **to the sword.** Je 15:2. 21:7. 24:10. 32:24, 36. 47:6, 7. Ezk *14:17-21. **I will.** See on Je 15:4. 24:9, 10. 29:18. Dt 28:25, 64. **to be removed.** Heb. for a removing. Je +15:4mg. Dt 28:25mg, 64♪𝒫. La 1:8mg. Ezk 23:46mg.

18. **have transgressed.** Dt *17:2. Jsh *7:11. 23:16. Ho 6:7. 8:1. **when.** This was the ancient mode of making a covenant (See on Dt 29:12mg,n. Jsh 9:7). Ge +*15:10, 17, 18♪𝒫. Ps 50:5.

19. **princes.** ver. 10. Ezk *22:27, etc. Da 9:6, 8, 12. Mi 7:1-5. Zp *3:3, 4. **the eunuchs.** Je 29:2. 38:7. 2 K 24:12mg, 15mg.

20. **and into.** Je 4:30. 11:21. 21:7. 22:25. 38:16.

44:30. 49:37. **life.** Heb. *nephesh*, Ge +44:30. **and their.** Je 7:33. 16:4. 19:7. 1 S 17:44, 46. 1 K *14:11. 16:4. 21:23, 24. 2 K 9:34-37. Ezk 29:5. 32:4. 39:17-20. Re *19:17-21.

21. **Zedekiah.** See on ver. 3-5. Je 39:6. 52:10, 24-27. 2 K *25:18-21. La *4:20. Ezk *17:16. **life.** Heb. *nephesh*, Ge +44:30. **which are.** Je 37:5, 11.

22. **I will command.** 2 S *16:11. 2 K *24:2, 3. 2 Ch *36:17. Is *10:5-7. 13:3. *37:26. 45:1-3. Am +*3:6. Mt √22:7. **cause.** They did return, and re-invested the city; and, after an obstinate defence, took it, plundered it, and burnt it to the ground, taking Zedekiah, his princes, and people, captive. See on Je 37:8-10. **shall fight.** See on Je 21:4-10. 32:29. 38:23. 39:1, 2, 8. 52:7, 13. **and I will.** Je 9:11. 33:10. 44:2-6, 22. Is *6:11. 24:12. *64:10, 11. La 1:1. Ezk *33:27, 28. Mi 7:13. Zc *1:12. 7:14.

JEREMIAH 35

JEREMIAH invites the Rechabites to drink wine; who answer, that, obeying their ancestor Jonadab, they drank none, and lived in tents, etc, 1-11. The disobedience of the Jews is contrasted with this example, 12-17. Promises made to the Rechabites, 18, 19.

1. A.M. 3397. B.C. 607. **The word.** This discourse was probably delivered in the fourth year of Jehoiakim's reign, when the king of Babylon made war against him. **in the.** Je 1:3. 22:13-19. 25:1. 26:1. 36:1, 9, 29. 46:2. 2 K 23:35. 24:1-6. 2 Ch *36:5-8. Da 1:1.

2. **the house.** ver. 8. 2 K *10:15, 16. 1 Ch *2:55. **Rechabites.** i.e. *descendants of Rechab* (i.e. horseman, 2 S +4:2), ✲S#7397h, Je 35:2, 3, 5, 18h. Nu 10:29. Jg 1:16. 4:11-17. 5:24. 1 S 15:6. **into one.** ver. 4. Je 36:10. 1 K 6:5, 6, 10. 1 Ch 9:26, 27. 23:28. 2 Ch 3:9. 31:11. Ezr 8:29. Ne 13:5, 8, 9. Ezk 40:7-13, 16. 41:5-11. *42:4-13.

3. **Habaziniah.** i.e. *God's light; the hiding of God's thorn; whom the Lord makes a buckler or shield,* ✲S#2262h.

4. **into the chamber.** Je 36:10-12. **Igdaliah.** i.e. *Great is Jah; Jehovah will wax great,* ✲S#3012h. **a man.** Dt 33:1. Jsh 14:6. 1 S 2:27. 9:6-8. 1 K 12:22. 13:1, 26. 17:18, 24. 20:28. 2 K 1:9, 11-13. 5:14, 20. 6:10. 7:2, 17. 8:2-8. 23:16, 17. 2 Ch 8:14. 25:7-9. 1 T 6:11. 2 T 3:17. **the princes.** Je 26:10. **the keeper.** Je 52:24. 2 K 12:9. 25:18. 1 Ch 9:18, 19, 27. 2 Ch 8:14. 31:14. Ps 84:10. **door.** Heb. threshold, *or* vessel. 1 K +14:17. 2 K +12:9mg. Ezk 43:8.

5. **Drink.** ver. 2. Ec *9:7. Am *2:12. 2 C *2:9.

6. **Jonadab.** i.e. *the Lord gave freely; Jehovah is a willing giver; whom Jehovah impels,* ✲S#3122h. Je 35:6, 10, 19h. 2 S 13:3, 3, 32, 35h. 2 K +10:15. 1 Ch 2:55. (1) A son of Shimeah, the brother of David, 2 S 13:3, 5, 32, 35. (2) The form of name given several times in Je 35 for Jehonadab, the son of Rechab, Je 35:8, 14, 16, 18; 2 K +10:15. **Ye shall.** Jonadab, a man of fervent zeal for the pure worship of God, and who lived about three hundred years before this time (2 K 10:15, 16, etc.), had probably practiced these rules himself; and having trained up his children to habits of abstemiousness, he enjoined them and their posterity to adhere to them. In these regulations he seems to have had no religious, but merely a prudential view, as is intimated in the reason annexed to them, "that ye may live many days in the land where ye be

strangers." And this would be the natural consequence of observing these rules; for their temperate mode of living would very much contribute to preserve health and prolong life; and they would avoid giving umbrage, or exciting the jealousy or envy of the Jews, who might have been provoked, by their engaging and succeeding in the principal business in which they themselves were engaged, agriculture and vinedressing, to expel them their country; by which they would have been deprived of the religious advantages they enjoyed. In 1 Ch 2:55, they are termed scribes, which intimates that they were engaged in some kind of literary employments. Le *10:9. Nu *6:2-5. Jg 13:7, 14. Lk 1:15. 1 C 7:26-31. **for ever**. Heb. *olam*, Ex +*12:24.

7. **all**. ver. 10. Ge 25:27. Le *23:42, 43. Ne 8:14-16. Ep +*5:18. He *11:9-13. 1 P *2:11. **live many**. Ex 20:12)℘. Dt +*5:16. Ps +*91:16mg. Ep 6:2, 3. **land where**. Ge 36:7. 1 Ch 16:19. Ps 105:12.

8. **we obeyed**. Ex 20:12. Pr 1:8, 9. 4:1, 2, 10. 6:20. 13:1. Col *3:20. **Jonadab**. S#3082h, 2 K +10:15. ver. 14, 16, 18.

9. **neither have**. ver. 7. Nu 16:14. 2 K 5:26. Ps 37:16. 1 T *6:6, 9.

10. **we have**. ver. 8.

11. **when**. 2 K 24:2. Da 1:1, 2. **Come**. Je 4:5-7. 8:14. Mk 13:14. Lk 21:20, 21. **Syrians**. Is 9:12.

13. **Will**. Je 5:3. 6:8-10. 9:12. 32:33. Ps *32:8, 9. Pr 8:10. 19:20. Is 28:9-12. 42:23. He *12:25.

14. **words**. See on ver. 6-10. **rising**. Je +7:13, 25. 11:7. 25:3, 4. 26:5. 29:19. 32:33. 2 Ch *36:15, 16. Pr *1:20-33. **but ye**. See on Je 7:24, 26. Ne *9:26, 30, 31. Is +*30:9. *50:2.

15. **I have**. Lk √10:16. 1 Th 4:8. **Return**. See on Je 3:14. 4:14. 7:3-5. 17:20-23. 18:11. 25:5. 26:13. 44:4, 5. Is *1:16-19. Ezk *18:30-32. Ho *14:1-4. Zc *1:3, 4. Ac 26:20. **ye shall dwell**. See on Je 7:5-7. 17:24, 25. 22:4. 25:5, 6. Dt 30:20. **ye have**. Lk *13:34, 35.

16. **the sons**. ver. 14. Is 1:3. Ml *1:6. Mt *11:28-30. Lk 15:11-13, 28-30.

17. **Therefore**. God having, by the conduct of the Rechabites, convicted the Jews of ingratitude and rebellion, He now proceeds to pass sentence against them. **Lord God of**. Je 38:17. 44:7. **Behold**. See on Je 11:8. 15:3, 4. 19:7-13. 21:4-10. Ge 6:17. Le *26:14, 21, etc. Dt *28:15, etc. 29:19-28. *31:20, 21. *32:16-42. Jsh 23:15, 16. Mi 3:12. **evil**. Is +*45:7. **because**. See on Je 7:13, 26, 27. 26:5. +*29:19. 32:33. Pr *1:24-31. 13:13. *16:2. Is 50:2. 65:12. 66:4. Lk 13:34, 35. Ro 10:21.

18. **Because**. Ex *20:12. Dt +*5:16. Ep *6:1-3.

19. **Jonadab**, etc. Heb. There shall not a man be cut off from Jonadab the son of Rechab to stand, etc. See on Je 33:17mg. 1 Ch *2:55. **stand**. Je 15:19. 33:17, 18. Ps 5:5. Lk +*21:36. Ju *24.

JEREMIAH 36

JEREMIAH, at God's command, causes Baruch to write in a roll all his threatening prophecies, 1-7. Baruch reads the roll publicly; and afterwards to the princes, who counsel him and Jeremiah to hide themselves, 8-19. Jehudi reads it before Jehoiakim, who cuts it in pieces, and casts it into the fire, contrary to the request of the princes; and orders Jeremiah and Baruch to be apprehended: "but the Lord hid them," 20-26. Jeremiah is directed to again write the

same things, with *"many like words,"* and a dreadful sentence against the king; which he does by the hand of Baruch, 27-32.

1. **fourth year**. See on Je 25:1. 35:1. 2 K 24:1, 2. 2. **a roll**. ver. 6, 23, 29. Je 30:2. 45:1. 51:60. Ex 17:14. Dt 31:24. Ezr 6:2. Jb 31:35. Ps 40:7. Is 8:1. 30:8, 9. Ezk 2:9. 3:1-3. Hab 2:2, 3. Zc 5:1-4. Re 5:1-9. **write**. See on Je 30:2. Ho 8:12. **against Israel**. Je 2:4. 3:3-10. 23:13, 14. 32:30-35. 2 K 17:18-20. **against all**. Je 1:5, 10. 25:9-29. ch. 47-51. **from the days**. See on Je 1:2, 3. 25:3.

3. **may be**. ver. 7. Je 18:8. 26:3. Dt *5:29. Ezk 12:3. Zp 2:3. Lk √20:13. 2 T *2:25, 26. 2 P √3:9. **hear**. Ezk 18:27, 28. 33:7-9, 14-16. Mt 3:7-9. Lk 3:7-9. **they may**. Je 18:8, 11. 23:14. 24:7. 35:15. Dt 30:2, 8. 1 S 7:3. 1 K 8:48-50. 2 Ch 6:38, 39. Ne 1:9. Is √55:6, 7. Ezk 18:23. Jon 3:8-10. Ac 26:20. **that I**. Is 6:10. Mt 13:15. Mk 4:12. Ac *3:19. 26:18. 28:27.

4. **Baruch**. ver. 26. Je 32:12. 43:3, 6. 45:1-5. **wrote**. *Baruch* is supposed to have been a disciple of Jeremiah; and being a ready scribe, he was employed by the prophet as his amanuensis. ver. 17, 18, 32. Je 45:1, 2. Ro 16:22. **upon**. ver. 21, 23, 28, 32. Is 8:1. Ezk 2:9. Zc 5:1.

5. **I am shut**. Je 20:2. 32:2. 33:1. 37:15. 38:6, 28. 40:4. 2 C 11:23. Ep 3:1. 6:20. 2 T *2:9. He 11:36.

6. **and read**. ver. 8. Ezk *2:3-7. **the words**. See on Je 7:2. 18:11. 19:14. 22:2. 26:2. **upon**. See on ver. 9. Le 16:29-31. 23:27-32. Ac 27:9. **fasting day**. This is supposed to have been the great day of expiation, called by way of eminence, the *fast*, which was kept on the tenth day of the month *Tisri*, answering to our September. Immediately after this Nebuchadnezzar invaded Judea; and, having besieged Jerusalem, made himself master of it, on the 18th of the ninth month *Cisleu*, corresponding to our November. Jehoiakim, having been taken prisoner, submitted to become tributary to Nebuchadnezzar; and was again restored to his kingdom, 2 K 24:1. 2 Ch 36:6.

7. **It may**. See on ver. 3. Je 26:3. 1 K *8:33-36. 2 Ch 33:12, 13. Ezk 12:3. Da 9:13. Ho *5:15. 6:1. *14:1-3. Am 5:15. Zp +*2:3. **they will present their supplication**. Heb. their supplication shall fall. Je 37:20mg. 38:26. 42:2mg, 9. **and will**. See on Je 1:3. 25:5. Jon 3:8. Zc 1:4. **for**. Je 4:4. 16:10. 19:15. 21:5. Dt *28:15, etc. 29:18-28. 2 K 22:13, 17. 2 Ch 34:21. La 4:11. Ezk 5:13. 8:18. 13:13. 20:33. 22:20. 24:8-13.

8. **did**. ver. 4. Je 1:17. Mt 16:24. 1 C 16:10. Ph 2:19-22. **in the**. Ne 8:3. Lk *4:16, etc.

9. **A.M. 3398. B.C. 606. in the fifth year**. See on ver. 1. **they proclaimed**. Le *23:27. 2 Ch *20:3. Ne 9:1. Est 4:16. Is 58:1-3. Jl 1:13. 2:12-17. Jon *3:5. Zc 7:5, 6. 8:19. **a fast**. This fast was held in commemoration of the calamities they had suffered on the taking of Jerusalem in the preceding year; and which has ever since been annually observed by the Jews on the 18th day of the month *Cisleu*. It evidently appears that Baruch read the roll twice; once in the fourth year of Jehoiakim, when it was little noticed; and now again in the fifth year after the taking of Jerusalem (See Prideaux, sub an. 606, 605). **came**. ver. 6.

10. **Then**. ver. 6, 8. **in the chamber**. See on Je 35:4. **Gemariah**. i.e. *perfected of the Lord; completeness of Jah*, *S#1587h. ver. 11, 12, 25. Je 29:3. (1) A son of Hilkiah the priest who was sent by Zedekiah,

king of Judah, as an ambassador to Nebuchadnezzar, king of Babylon, Je 29:3. (2) A prince of Judah in the time of Jehoiakim, king of Judah, Je 36:10, 11, 12, 25. **Shaphan.** See on ver. 11. Je 26:24. 29:3. **the scribe.** Je 52:25. 2 S 8:17. 20:25. 2 K 18:37. **entry.** *or,* door. Je 26:10. 2 K 15:35. **gate.** ✓171S7B, Ge +14:7.

11. **Shaphan.** ver. 10. 2 K *22:12-14. *25:22. 2 Ch *34:18-20.

12. **Elishama.** ver. 20, 21. Je 41:1. **Delaiah.** i.e. *drawn up of the Lord; Jah has delivered,* *S#1806h. Je 36:12, 25. 1 Ch 3:24. 24:18. Ezr 2:60. Ne 6:10. 7:62. (1) Head of the twenty-third temple-course of priests in the time of David, 1 Ch 24:18. (2) Founder of a family who, on their return from captivity, could not prove their genealogy, Ezr 2:60; Ne 7:62. (3) Father of Shemaiah, Ne 6:10. (4) A prince of Judah in the time of King Jehoiakim, Je 36:12, 25. **Elnathan.** ver. 25. Je 26:22. 2 K 22:12, 14. 24:8. **Gemariah.** ver. 10, 11. 2 K 22:3, 12. **Hananiah.** Je 28:1, etc.

13. **declared.** 2 K 22:10, 19. 2 Ch 34:16-18, 24. Jon 3:6.

14. **Jehudi.** i.e. *a Jew; praise of the Lord,* *S#3065h. ver. 21, 21, 23. **Nethaniah.** Je 40:8. 41:1, 2, 16, 18. 2 K 25:23. **Cushi.** Zp 1:1. **took.** See on ver. 2. Ezk 2:6, 7. Mt 10:16, 28.

15. **and read.** See on ver. 21.

16. **they were.** ver. 24. Ac *24:25, 26. **We.** Je 13:18. 38:1-4. Am *7:10, 11.

17. **Tell.** Jn 9:10, 11, 15, 26, 27.

18. **He pronounced.** ver. 2, 4. Je 43:2, 3. Pr +*26:4, 5. **with ink.** *Baddeyo* is rendered by some, *after him;* but *deyo* (in Chaldee and Syriac *deyootha,* and in Welsh *du*) certainly denotes *ink;* whence are derived the Arabic *dawat* and *deeweet,* and Persian *deeveet,* an *ink-holder;* the Syriac *dayowo,* and Persian *div,* the *devil.* So the Alexandrian copy of the LXX. has *en melani,* and Vulgate *atramento,* "with ink." Perhaps the princes supposed that Baruch had written his roll from memory; and that it was rather to be considered as his composition, than the substance of Jeremiah's prophecies; and they might ask this apparently frivolous question in order to allay the alarms excited by considering it as the word of God. But Baruch, with great simplicity, so answered their question, as to show that he only acted as Jeremiah's amanuensis, and wrote verbatim what he had dictated.

19. **Go, hide.** ver. 26. Je 26:20-24. 1 K *17:3. *18:4, 10. 2 Ch 25:15. Pr +*22:3. *28:12. Am *7:12. Lk ✓13:31. Ac *5:40. *23:16, etc.

20. **laid up.** ver. 12, 21.

21. **Jehudi.** ver. 14. **And Jehudi.** ver. 15. Je +✓23:28n. 26:2. 2 K *22:10. 2 Ch ◐✓34:18-20. Ezk *2:4, 5, 7.

22. **the winterhouse.** A warm apartment suited to the season of the year (December, when snow is often upon the ground in Palestine), in which was a *pan* or *brazier* (*ach,* or *ikhkh,* as it is pronounced in Arabic) of burning charcoal; for we learn from Bp. Pococke (vol. i. p. 87) and Dr. Russel (vol. i. pp. 82, 85), that this was the mode in which the Orientals warmed their apartments. Je 22:14-16. Jg 3:20. Am *3:15.

23. **he cut.** ver. 29-31. Dt 29:19-21. 1 K 22:8, 27, 28. Ps 50:17. Pr *1:30. 5:12. 13:13. 19:21. +*21:30. *29:1. Is 5:18, 19. 28:14, 15, 17-22. Re *22:19.

24. **they were not afraid.** ver. 16. Jb *15:4. Ps *36:1. *64:5. Is ✓26:11. Ro *3:18. **nor rent.** Je 5:3. 1 K 21:27.

2 K 19:1, 2. ◐*22:11-19. 2 Ch 34:19-31. Is 36:22. 37:1. Jon 3:6. Mt *12:41.

25. **Elnathan.** ver. 12. Je 26:22. **made.** Je 13:15-17. Ge 37:22, 26-28. Mt 27:4, 24, 25. Ac ✓5:34-39. **but.** 1 S +✓25:17. Pr 21:29.

26. **Hammelech.** *or,* the king. i.e. *the king; counselor,* *S#4429h. Je 38:6mg. 1 K 22:26. 2 K 10:2. Zp 1:8. The father of Jerahmeel, Je 36:26. The word suggests that Jerahmeel was of royal blood, son of the king. **Abdeel.** i.e. *servant of God,* *S#5655h. **to take.** Je 2:30. 26:21-23. 1 K *19:1-3, 10, 14. Mt *23:34-37. 26:47-50. Jn 7:32. *8:20. 11:57. **but.** ver. 5, 19. Je 1:19. 15:20, 21. 1 K 17:3, 9. 18:4, 10-12. 2 K 6:18-20. Ps 27:5. *31:20. 32:7. 57:1. 64:2. 91:1. 121:8. Pr +*22:3. Is *26:20. Jn *8:59. Ac 12:11.

27. **after that.** See on ver. 23. 2 T 2:9. **and the words.** ✓93A, Ge +1:26. i.e. the roll, yes—and the roll that contained the words of Jehovah too.

28. **another roll.** Je *28:13, 14. 44:28. Jb 23:13. Zc *1:5, 6. Mt ✓24:35. 2 T *2:13.

29. **Thou hast.** Dt 29:19. Jb 15:24-27. *40:8-10. Is *45:9. Ac ✓5:39. 1 C *10:22. **Why.** Je 26:9. 32:3. Is 29:21. 30:10. Ac 5:28. **The king.** Je 21:4-7, 10. 28:8. 32:28-30. 34:21, 22.

30. **He shall.** Je 22:30. Dt ✓29:19, 20. 2 K *24:12-15. **and his dead body.** Je +*22:18, 19. **in the day.** Sir J. Chardin (as cited by Harmer, ch. i. Ob. 32) observes, "In the Lower Asia, in particular, the day is always hot; and as soon as the sun is fifteen degrees above the horizon, no cold is felt in the depth of winter itself. On the contrary, in the height of summer the nights are as cold as at Paris in the month of March. It is for this reason that in Persia and Turkey they always make use of furred habits in the country, such only being sufficient to resist the cold of the nights. I have travelled in Arabia, and in Mesopotamia (the theater of the adventures of Jacob), both in winter and in summer, and have found the truth of what the Patriarch said, 'That he was scorched with the heat in the day, and stiffened with cold in the night' (Ge 31:40). This contrariety in the qualities of the air in twenty-four hours is extremely great in some places, and not conceivable by those that have not felt it; one would imagine that he had passed in a moment from the violent heats of summer to the depth of winter. Thus it hath pleased God to temper the heat of the sun by the coldness of the night, without which the greatest part of the East would be barren, and a desert." Ge 31:40.

31. **punish.** Heb. visit upon. T#1109. Je +9:25mg. 23:34mg. Ex 32:34❂. **will bring.** Je 11:8. 17:18. 19:15. 29:17-19. See on 35:17. 44:4-14. Le 26:14, etc. Dt *28:15, etc. Pr *29:1. **but.** Je +*29:19. Mt ✓23:37-39.

32. **took.** See on ver. 28-30. **who wrote.** ver. 4, 18. Ex 4:15, 16. Ro 16:22. **were added.** Le 26:18, 21, 24, 28. Da 3:19. Re +✓22:18, 19. **like words.** Heb. words as they.

JEREMIAH 37

The Chaldeans having left the siege of Jerusalem to meet the Egyptians, Zedekiah sends to desire Jeremiah's prayers; who predicts the certain return and victory of the Chaldeans, 1-10. He is taken up as a deserter, beaten, and put in prison, 11-15. Being privately consulted by Zedekiah, he confirms his former prediction, expostulates with the king, and prevails for some indulgence, 16-21.

1. A.M. 3406-3416. B.C. 598-588. **Zedekiah.** 2 K *24:17. 1 Ch *3:15. 2 Ch *36:10. **Coniah.** ✓33, 1 Ch +11:13. Je 22:24, 28. 24:1, Jeconiah. 52:31. 2 K 24:12-16. 1 Ch 3:16, 17. 2 Ch 36:9, Jehoiachin. **made king.** See on Ezk 17:12-21.

2. **neither.** 2 K *24:19, 20. 2 Ch 36:12-16. Pr *29:12. Ezk 21:25. 1 Th *4:8. **by the prophet.** Heb. by the hand of the prophet. Je 50:1mg. Ex 4:13. Le 8:36. 2 S 10:2. 12:25. 1 K 14:18. 16:7, +*12mg. 2 Ch ✓34:14mg,n. Pr 26:6. Ho 12:10mg.

3. **Jehucal.** i.e. *potent; he will be made strong; Jehovah will prevail,* ✱S#3081h. **Zephaniah.** Je 21:1, 2. 29:21, 25. 52:24. **Pray now.** T#1816. Je 2:27. 21:1, 2. 42:2-4, 20. Ge 27:38. Ex *8:8, 28. 9:27, 28. 10:16, 17. Nu 12:10-13. *21:6, 7. 1 S 7:8. *12:19. 1 K *13:6. 2 K *2:9. 4:27. 19:3, 4. Jb *42:8, 9. Ml 1:9. Lk *23:42. Ac *8:24. Ro 15:30-32. 2 C 1:11. Ep *6:18-20. Col 4:3, 4. 1 Th 5:25. 2 Th 3:1, 2. He 13:18, 19. Ja 5:14, 15.

4. **for.** ver. 15. Je 32:2, 3.

5. **Pharaoh's.** This was *Pharaoh Hophra, or Apries,* as he is called by Herodotus (l. ii. c. 161), who succeeded his father Psammis on the throne of Egypt, A.M. 3410, B.C. 594, and reigned twenty-five years. Having entered into a confederacy with Zedekiah (Ezk 17:25), he marched out of Egypt with a great army to his relief, which caused Nebuchadnezzar to raise the siege of Jerusalem to meet him; during which period the transactions detailed here took place. ver. 7. 2 K *24:7. Ezk *17:15. **they.** ver. 11. Je 34:21.

7. **Thus.** ver. 3. Je 21:2. 2 K 22:18. **the Lord, the God of.** Je +11:3. **Pharaoh's.** Je 17:5, 6. Pr +*21:30. Is *30:1-6. *31:1-3. La *4:17. Ezk *17:17. *29:6, 7, 16.

8. **fight against.** See on Je 32:29. 34:21, 22. 38:23. 39:2-8.

9. **Thus saith.** Ezk *24:14. **Deceive not.** Ob *3. Mt *24:4, 5. Ga *6:3, 7. Ep ✓5:6. 2 Th ✓2:3. Ja +*1:22. **yourselves.** Heb. your souls. Heb. *nephesh,* Ex +15:9. Est 9:31mg.

10. **though.** Je 21:4-7. 49:20. 50:45. Le *26:36-38. Is 10:4. *30:17. **wounded men.** Heb. men thrust through. Is 14:19. lit. "pierced." ✱S#1856h. Je 51:4. Nu 25:8. Jg 9:54. 1 S 31:4. 1 Ch 10:4. Is 13:15. La 4:9. Zc *12:10. 13:3. **yet.** Jl 2:11.

11. **that.** See on ver. 5. **broken.** Heb. made to ascend. Je 34:21. Ex 40:36.

12. **Then.** Lk *21:20, 21. **went.** 1 K *19:3, 9. Pr +*22:3. Ne *6:11. Mt *10:23. 1 Th 5:22. **the land.** Je 1:1. Jsh 21:17, 18. 1 Ch 6:60. **separate himself thence.** *or,* slip away from thence. or, receive a portion thence. Je 32:9. 1 S 30:24. Isaac Leeser renders, "to make his escape thence." Pr +*22:3. **in the midst.** Lk +*4:30.

13. **in the gate.** Je 38:7. 2 K 14:13. Ne 8:16. Zc 14:10. **Irijah.** i.e. *fear of Jah; protection of the Lord; he will see the Lord,* ✱S#3376h. ver. 14. **Hananiah.** Je 28:1, 10-17. 36:12. **Thou.** Je 18:18. 20:10. 21:9. 27:6, 12, 13. 28:14. 38:4, 17. Am 7:10. Lk 23:2. Ac 6:11. 24:5-9, 12, 13. 2 C *6:8-10.

14. **said.** Je 40:4-6. Ne *6:8. Ps 27:12. *35:11. 52:1, 2. Mt ✓5:11, 12. Lk 6:22, 23, 26. 1 P 3:16. *4:14-16. **false.** Heb. falsehood, *or,* a lie. Je 3:10mg, 23 (in vain).

5:2, 31. 8:8mg. 10:14. **princes.** Je 26:16. 38:1.

15. **the princes.** Je 20:1-3. 26:16. Mt 21:35. 23:34. 26:67, 68. Lk 20:10, 11. 22:64. Jn 18:22. Ac 5:28, 40. 16:22-24. 23:2, 3. 2 C 11:23-27. He 11:36-38. **put.** Ge 39:20. 2 Ch 16:10. 18:26. Ac 5:18. 12:4-6. Re *2:10. **in the.** ver. 20. Je 38:6, 26.

16. A.M. 3415. B.C. 589. **into the dungeon.** Heb. *bor,* Ge +37:20. lit. house of the pit. Je 6:7. 38:6, 10-13. Ge 21:19. *40:15. Is 14:19. La 3:53, 55. **cabins.** *or,* cells. **remained.** ver. 21. Je 38:13, 28.

17. **asked.** Je 38:5, 14-16, 24-27. 1 K 14:1-4. **secretly.** Je 38:16. 40:15. Dt 13:6. **Is there.** ver. 3. Je 21:1, 2. 1 K *22:16. 2 K *3:11-13. Pr 8:21h. 18:24h. Mk *6:20. Lk 7:25g. **thou shalt.** Je 21:7. 24:8. 29:16-18. 32:3-5. 34:21, 22. 39:6, 7. Ezk 12:12, 13. *17:19-21. 21:25-27.

18. **What have I offended.** Je 26:19. Ge 31:36. 1 S 24:9-15. 26:18-21. Pr *17:13, 26. Da *6:22. Jn *10:32. Ac 23:1. 24:16. 25:8, 11, 25. 26:31. Ga *4:16.

19. **Where.** Je 2:28. Dt 32:36, 37. 2 K 3:13. **your prophets.** Je 6:14. 8:11. 14:13-15. 23:17. 27:14-18. 28:1-5, 10-17. 29:31. La *2:14. Ezk *13:10-16.

20. **be accepted before.** Heb. fall before. Je 36:7mg. 42:2mg. Da 9:18mg. **lest.** Je 26:15. 38:6-9, *26. Ac 23:16-22. 25:10, 11. 28:18, 19.

21. **into the.** Je 32:2, 8. 38:13, 28. **and that.** 1 K 17:4-6. Jb 5:20. Ps 33:18, 19. 34:9, 10. 37:3, 19. Pr +*16:7. *21:1. Is 33:16. Mt ✓6:33. **daily.** Mt +*6:11. **piece.** lit. cake. Je 52:6. Ex 29:23. Jg 8:5. Lk 11:5. **until.** Je 38:9. 52:6. Dt 28:52-57. 2 K 25:3. La 2:11, 12, 19, 20. 4:4, 5, 9, 10. 5:10. **were spent.** or, till the consumption. Je 1:3. 24:10. 27:8. **Thus.** Je 38:13, 28. 39:14, 15. Ac 12:5. 24:27. 28:16, 30. Ep 4:1. 6:20. 2 T 1:8. *2:9.

JEREMIAH 38

JEREMIAH, being accused of disheartening the people by his prophecies, is cast into the miry dungeon of Malchia, 1-6. He is taken out at the suit of Ebedmelech, an Ethiopian, and by him, 7-13. In a private conference, he counsels Zedekiah to save himself and the city, by surrendering, 14-23. Zedekiah requiring him, he conceals what had been discussed in the conference from the princes; and remains in the court of the prison, till the taking of the city, 24-28.

1. **Shephatiah.** Ezr 2:4. Ne 7:9. **Jucal.** i.e. *mighty; he will be made able,* ✱S#3116h. Je 37:3, Jehucal. **Pashur.** Je 21:1. **Malchiah.** i.e. *Jehovah's king,* ✱S#4441h. Je 21:1. 1 Ch 6:40. 9:12, Malchijah. 24:9. Ezr 10:25, 25, 31. Ne 3:11, 14, 31. 8:4. 10:3. *11:12. 12:42. (1) An ancestor of Asaph, 1 Ch 6:40. (2, 3) Two Jews who had taken foreign wives, Ezr 10:25, 31. The last mentioned is probably same as Malchija in Ne 3:11. (4, 5) Two Jews who repaired the wall of Jerusalem, Ne 3:14, 31. (6) A priest who stood beside Ezra while he read the law to the people, Ne 8:4. (7) A priest who was the father of Pashur, Ne 11:12. (8) An officer into whose dry cistern the prophet Jeremiah was thrown, Je 38:6. Dry cisterns were used as dungeons in Palestine. **heard.** Ac 4:1, 2, 6-10. 5:28.

2. **He that.** ver. 17-23. Je 21:8, 9. 24:8, 9. 27:13. 29:18. 34:17. 42:17, 22. 44:13. Ezk *5:12-17. *6:11, 12. 7:15. 14:21. Mt *24:7, 8. Re *6:4-8. **shall have.** Je 21:9. 39:18. 45:5. **life.** Heb. *nephesh,* Ge +44:30.

3. **This city.** See on Je 21:10. 32:3-5.

4. the princes. Je 26:11, 21-23. 36:12-16. 2 Ch *24:21. Ezk *22:27. Mi *3:1-3. Zp 3:1-3. **thus.** Ex 5:4. 1 K 18:17, 18. 21:20. Ezr 4:12. Ne 6:9. Am 7:10. Lk *23:2. Jn 11:46-50. Ac *16:20. *17:6. *24:5. 28:22. **weakeneth.** Ezr 4:4. **welfare.** Heb. peace. Je +*29:7. 33:9. Ge 43:27mg. Ex 18:7mg. 2 S 11:7mg. 1 Ch 18:10mg. Ps 69:22. **hurt.** Is +*45:7.

5. for. 1 S *15:24. 29:9. 2 S *3:39. 19:22. Pr *29:25. Jn *19:12-16.

6. took. Je 37:21. Ps 109:5. Lk *3:19, 20. **into.** See on Je 37:16. La 3:55. Ac *16:23, 24. 2 C *4:8, 9. He *10:36, 37. **dungeon.** Heb. *bor*, Ge +37:20. Je 37:16. **Hammelech.** *or*, the king. Je +36:26mg. **and they.** ver. 11, 12. **And in.** This dungeon, which seems to have belonged to one of Zedekiah's sons, appears to have been a most dreadful place; the horrors of which were probably augmented by the cruelty of the jailor. "The eastern people," observes Sir J. Chardin (cited in Harmer, ch. ix. Ob. 84), "have not different prisons for the different classes of criminals; the judges do not trouble themselves about where the prisoners are confined, or how they are treated, considering it merely as a place of safety; and all that they require of the jailor is, that the prisoner be forthcoming when called for. As to the rest, he is master to do as he pleases; to treat him well or ill; to put him in irons or not; to shut him up close, or hold him in easier restraint; to admit people to him, or to suffer nobody to see him. If the jailor and his servants have large fees, let the person be the greatest rascal in the world, he shall be lodged in the jailor's own apartment, and the best part of it; and on the contrary, if those that have imprisoned a man give the jailor greater presents, or that he has a greater regard for them, he will treat the prisoner with the greatest inhumanity." This adds a double energy to those passages which speak of "the sighing of the prisoner," and to Jeremiah's supplicating that he might not be remanded to the dungeon of Jonathan (ver. 26. Je 37:20). ver. 22. Ge 37:24. Ps *40:2. *69:2, 14, 15. La 3:52-55. Zc *9:11. **dungeon.** Heb. *bor*, Ge +37:20.

7. Ebed-melech. i.e. *servant of the king*, ✻S#5663h. ver. 8, 10, 11, 12. Je *39:16-18. **Ethiopian.** Je 13:23. Ps 68:31. Mt 8:11, 12. 20:16. Lk √10:30-37. *13:29, 30. 23:26. Ac *8:27-39. **eunuchs.** Je 29:2mg. 34:19. 2 K 24:15mg. **dungeon.** Heb. *bor*, Ge +37:20. **the king.** Je 37:13. Dt 21:19. Jb 29:7-17. Am 5:10.

9. these. ver. 1-6. Est 7:4-6. Jb 31:34. Pr 24:11, 12. 31:8, 9. **dungeon.** Heb. *bor*, Ge +37:20. **is like to die.** Heb. will die. **for there.** Je 37:21. 52:6.

10. the king. Est 5:2. 8:7. Ps 75:10. Pr *21:1. **with thee.** Heb. in thine hand. Je 39:11mg. 43:9. 2 S 18:2.

11. let them. ver. 6.

12. Ebed-melech. Je *39:16-18. Mt 10:40-42. 25:34-40. **the Ethiopian.** ver. 7. **Put.** Ro *12:10, 13, 15. Ep √4:32.

13. So. ver. 6. **Jeremiah.** ver. 28. Je 37:21. 39:14-18. 1 K 22:27. Ac 23:35. *24:23-27. 28:16, 30. **dungeon.** Heb. *bor*, Ge +37:20. **remained.** Je 37:16.

14. sent. Je 21:1, 2. 37:17. **third.** *or*, principal. 1 K 10:5. 2 K 16:18. **I will.** Je 42:2-5, 20. 1 S 3:16-18. 1 K *22:16. 2 Ch 18:15.

15. wilt thou not surely. √147B, Ge +2:16. Lk *22:67, 68.

16. sware secretly. Je 37:17. Jn *3:2. **that made.** Nu 16:22. 27:16. Ec +*12:7. Is 57:16. Zc 12:1. He

+*12:9. **soul.** Heb. *nephesh*, Ge +12:5. **of these.** See on ver. 1-6. Je 34:20. **life.** Heb. *nephesh*, soul, Ge +44:30.

17. the God of hosts. Je +35:17. Ps 80:7, 14. Am *5:27. **the God of Israel.** 1 Ch *17:24. Ezr 9:4. **If thou.** ver. 2. Je 7:6, 7. 21:8-10. 27:12, 17. 39:3. Jb *23:13. **soul.** Heb. *nephesh*, Ge +12:13.

18. if thou. 2 K 24:12. 25:27-30. **then.** ver. 3, 23. Je 24:8-10. 32:3-5. 34:2, 3, 19-22. 39:3, 5-7. 52:7-11. 2 K *25:4-10. Ezk 12:13. 17:20, 21. 21:25-27.

19. I. ver. 5. 1 S 15:24. Jb 31:34. Pr *29:25. Is *51:12, 13. 57:11. Jn √12:42. 19:12, 13. **mock.** ver. 22. Jg 9:54. 16:25. 1 S *31:4mg. Is 45:9, 10.

20. Obey. Je 26:13. 2 Ch +*20:20. Da 4:27. Ac 26:29. 2 C √5:11, 20. +*6:1. Phm 8-10. Ja *1:22. **and thy.** Is +*55:3. **soul.** Heb. *nephesh*, Ge +12:13.

21. if thou refuse. Je 5:3. Ex 10:3, 4. 16:28. Jb 34:33. Pr *1:24-31. Is *1:19, 20. He *12:25. **to go.** ver. 2, 17. Je 27:12. 2 K 24:12. **this is.** Je 15:19-21. 26:15. Nu *23:19, 20. 24:13. Jb 23:13. Ezk 2:4, 5, 7. 3:17-19. Ac 18:6. √20:26, 27.

22. all. Je 41:10. 43:6. La 5:11. **and those.** Mr. Harmer (ch. ix. Ob. 70) would render, "and *here* (*hennah*, or reading *hinneh*, behold), the women (wont to sing on public occasions) shall say," etc.; observing "that these bitter speeches much better suit the lips of women belonging to the conquering nation, singing before a captive prince, than of his own wives and concubines." This he illustrates by the following extract from Della Valle (Let. xvi. tom. vi. pp. 32, 33): When he was at Lar, in Persia, the king of Ormuz was brought thither in triumph; and "this poor unfortunate king entered Lar, with his people, in the morning, music playing, and *girls* and *women* singing and dancing before him, according to the custom of Persia, and the people flocking together with a prodigious concourse, and conducting him in a pompous and magnificent manner, particularly with colors displayed, like what the Messenians formerly did to Philopoemen, the general of the Athenians, their prisoner of war, according to the report of Justin." **Thy friends.** Heb. The men of thy peace. ver. 4-6. Je 20:10mg. Ps 41:9mg. Ob 7mg. **have set.** ver. 19. La 1:2. Mi *7:5. **thy feet.** See on ver. 6. Ps *69:2, 14. **they are.** Je 46:5, 21. Is 42:17. La 1:13.

23. they shall. ver. 18. Je 39:6. 41:10. 52:8-13. 2 K *25:7, 9, 10. 2 Ch *36:20, 21. **shalt cause,** etc. Heb. shalt burn, etc. √12112, Ge +2:17. √121E2, Ge +42:38. Je 21:10. 27:12, 13. Ezk 14:9. 43:3.

24. Let no man know. Je 37:17. 1 S √16:2n. We are not bound to speak all we know to gratify our enemies, when no good end can be answered: and a partial evasive answer, if not contrary to truth, is sufficient for an impertinent and malicious inquiry. We have then need to be "wise as serpents, and harmless as doves" (Mt 10:16), Scott. Mt ❶*10:32, 33. Lk *16:8. 1 C ❶*12:3.

25. if the princes hear. See on ver. 4-6, 27.

26. I presented. Je 37:15, 20. 42:2. Est 4:8.

27. and he told. 1 S *10:15, 16. 15:16. √16:2-5. 2 K *6:19. Mt *2:8, 12, 16. Ac *23:6. **according.** Jeremiah answered them according as the king had directed. A man is not bound in all cases to speak the whole truth, much less to those who have nothing to do to inquire of us, which these princes had not. By this means the princes never knew the matter of this discourse (Matthew Poole). **left off speaking with him.** Heb. were silent from him. 1 S 7:8mg.

28. **abode.** ver. 13. Je 15:20, 21. 37:21. 39:14. Ps *23:4. 2 T 3:11. *4:17, 18.

JEREMIAH 39

Jerusalem is taken, and burnt; Zedekiah is made prisoner, his sons slain, his eyes put out, and himself carried in chains to Babylon, with the remnant of the Jews; a few poor people excepted, 1-10. Jeremiah is kindly used, by orders from Nebuchadnezzar, 11-14. A message from God to Ebed-melech, assuring him of protection, 15-18.

1. A.M. 3414. B.C. 590. **the ninth.** Je 52:4-7. 2 K 25:1, 2, etc. Ezk 24:1, 2. Zc 8:19. **the tenth.** This was the month *Tebeth* (Est 2:16), which began with the first moon of January; and it was on the 10th of this month that Nebuchadnezzar invested the city.

2. A.M. 3416. B.C. 588. **the fourth.** This was the month *Tammuz*, which commences with the first moon of July: the siege had lasted just eighteen months. 2 K 25:3. **was.** Je 5:10. 52:6, 7. 2 K 25:4. Ezk 33:21. Mi 2:12, 13. Zp 1:10.

3. **all the.** Je 1:15. 21:4. 38:17. **Nergalsharezer.** i.e. *fire prince; the splendor of brightness,* ✳S#5371h. ver. 13. 2 K 17:29, 30. A name applied to two princes of Babylon when Jerusalem was taken by Nebuchadnezzar, Je 39:3, 13. **Samgar-nebo.** i.e. *warrior; sword of Nebo,* ✳S#5562h. **Sarsechim.** i.e. *prince of the coverts,* ✳S#8310h. **Rab-saris.** i.e. *chief eunuch,* ✳S#7249h. An eminent Assyrian or Babylonian officer, 2 K 18:17; Je 39:3, 13. **Rab-mag.** i.e. *chief soothsayer; much melting,* ✳S#7248h. These were the principal commanders; but Dr. Blayney thinks that, instead of *six* persons, we have in reality but *three,* as the name that follows each is the title of office. Thus *Nergal-sharezer,* who was *Samgar-nebo,* or keeper, i.e. priest of Nebo; *Sarsechim,* who was *Rab-saris,* or chief eunuch; and *Nergal-sharezer,* who was *Rabmag,* or chief magi; as the words *mog* in Persian, *magoos,* in Arabic, *magooshai,* in Syriac, and *magos,* in Greek, signify; and we learn from Justin and Curtius that the magi attended the king in war.

4. **when.** Je 38:18-20. Le *26:17, 36. Dt *28:25. *32:24-30. 2 K 25:4, etc. Is *30:15, 16. Ezk 12:12. Am 2:14. **betwixt.** Je 52:7, etc. 2 Ch 32:5.

5. **Chaldeans'.** See on Je 32:4, 5. 38:18, 23. 2 Ch 33:11. La 1:3. 4:20. **in the plains.** Je 52:8. Jsh 4:13. 5:10. **Riblah.** Je 52:9, 26, 27. 2 K *23:33. *25:5, 6. **Hamath.** Nu 13:21. Jsh 13:5. Jg 3:3. 2 S 8:9. 2 K 17:24. **gave judgment upon him.** Heb. spake with him judgments. Je 4:12mg. 2 Ch 36:10, 13. Ezk 17:15-21.

6. **slew the.** Je 52:10. 2 K *25:7. **before.** Ge 21:16. 44:34. Dt *28:34. 2 K 22:20. 2 Ch 34:28. Est 8:6. Is *13:16. **slew all.** Je 21:7. 24:8-10. 34:19-21.

7. **he put.** Je 32:4, 5. 52:11. 2 K *25:7. Ezk √12:13. **chains.** Heb. two brasen chains, *or* fetters. Je 40:1. Jg 16:21. Ps 107:10, 11. 149:8. **to carry him.** Je 52:11. 2 K 25:7. 2 Ch 36:6.

8. **burned.** Je 7:20. 9:10-12. 17:27. 21:10. 34:2, 22. 37:10. 38:18. *52:12, 13. 2 K *25:9. 2 Ch *36:19. Is *5:9. La 1:10. 2:2, 7. Am 2:5. Mi 3:12. **and brake.** Je 52:14. 2 K 25:10. Ne 1:3.

9. **Nebuzar-adan.** ver. 13. Je 40:1. 52:12-16, 26. 2 K *25:11, 20. **captain of the guard.** *or,* chief marshal.

Heb. chief of the executioners, *or* slaughter-men; *and so* ver. 10, 11, etc. Ge 37:36mg. 39:1. 2 K 25:8mg. **carried.** Je 10:18. 16:13. 20:4-6. 52:28-30. Le 26:33. Dt *4:27. 2 K 20:18. Is *5:13.

10. **left of.** Je 40:7. 2 K 25:12. Ezk 33:24. **at the same time.** Heb. in that day.

11. **Now.** Nebuchadnezzar must have frequently heard of Jeremiah's predictions, many of which were now fulfilled, which would dispose him to respect his character and treat him with kindness. **gave.** Je 15:11, 21. Jb *5:19. Ac *24:23. **to.** Heb. by the hand of. Je 37:2mg.

12. **look well to him.** Heb. set thine eyes upon him. Je 24:6. 40:4mg. Pr 23:5. Am 9:4. 1 P *3:12. **do him.** Ps *105:14, 15. Pr +*16:7. *21:1. Ac *7:9, 10. 1 P *3:13.

13. **Nebuzar-adan.** See on ver. 3, 9. **Nebushashban.** i.e. *deliverance of Nebo,* ✳S#5021h.

14. **took.** ver. 15. Je 37:21. 38:13, 28. 40:1-4. Ps 105:19. **committed.** Je 40:5-16. 41:1-3. 2 K *25:22-25. **Ahikam.** See on Je 26:24.

15. **while.** ver. 14. Je 32:1, 2. 36:1-5. 37:21. 2 T *2:9.

16. **Ebed-melech.** See on Je 38:7-13. **the Lord of hosts, the God of Israel.** Je +7:3. **Behold.** Je 5:14. 19:11, 12. 21:7-10. 24:8-10. 26:15, 18, 20. 32:28, 29. 34:2, 3, 22. 35:17. 36:31. 44:28, 29. Jsh *23:14, 15. 2 Ch √36:20, 21. Da *9:12. Zc 1:6. Mt √24:35. **evil.** Is +45:7. **before thee.** Ps 91:8, 9. 92:11.

17. **I will.** Je 1:19. Jb 5:19-21. Ps 41:1, 2. *50:15. *91:14-16. Da 6:16. Mt *10:40-42. *25:40. 2 T 1:16-18. **of whom.** Je 38:1, 9. Ge 15:1. 2 S 24:14.

18. **but.** Je 21:9. 38:2. 45:4, 5. **life.** Heb. *nephesh,* Ge +44:30. **a prey.** or, spoil. Je 21:9. 38:2. 45:5. **because.** Je 17:7, 8. Ru 2:12. 1 Ch 5:20. Ps *2:12. 25:2. 33:18. 34:22. *37:3, 39, 40. *84:12. 146:3-6. 147:11. Is √26:3, 4. Ep 1:12, 13. 1 P *1:21.

JEREMIAH 40

JEREMIAH, being dismissed by the Chaldeans, returns to Gedaliah, 1-8. The fugitive Jews resort to Gedaliah, who encourages them to cultivate the land, 7-12. Johanan, informing Gedaliah that Ishmael designed to slay him, and proposing to kill Ishmael, is not believed, 13-16.

1. **The word.** This, and the four following chapters, record the events which occurred in Judea from the taking of Jerusalem to the retreat of the remnant of the people to Egypt; and contain several prophecies of Jeremiah concerning them there; which were "the word which came to Jeremiah from the Lord." It appears that Jeremiah, after being freed from prison, continued among the Jews, till he was bound, with others of them, and carried to Ramah; where he was set at liberty in the manner related. **after.** Je 39:11-14. **Ramah.** Je 31:15. Jsh 18:25. 1 S 7:17. **bound.** Ps 68:6. 107:16. Ac 12:6, 7. 21:13. 28:20. Ep 6:20mg. **chains.** *or,* manacles. ver. 4. Je 39:7. Ps 149:8. **that were.** Je 28:4.

2. **of the guard.** Je +39:9mg. **The Lord.** Je 22:8, 9. Dt *29:24-28. 1 K *9:8, 9. 2 Ch 7:20-22. La 2:15-17. **evil.** Is +45:7.

3. **because.** Je 50:7. Dt *29:24, 25➧𝒫. Ne *9:28, 33. Da *9:11, 12. Ro 2:5. *3:19.

4. **were upon thine hand.** *or, are* upon thine hand.

ver. 1mg. **look well unto thee.** Heb. set mine eye upon thee. See on Je 39:11, 12mg. **all the.** Ge 13:9. 20:15. 47:6.

5. **Go back.** Je 39:14. 41:2. 2 K 25:22-24. **Ahikam.** Je 26:24. 2 K 22:12, 14. 2 Ch 34:20. **or go.** ver. 4. Je 15:11. Ezr 7:6, 27. Ne 1:11. 2:4-8. Pr +*16:7. *21:1. **gave him.** Je 52:31-34. 2 K 8:7-9. Jb 22:29. Ac *27:3, 43. 28:10. He 13:6. **victuals and a reward.** Rather, "victuals (*aruchah*, a stated allowance, sufficient for the journey), and a present," *masseath*. 2 K 25:30.

6. **Then.** It has been doubted whether Jeremiah acted prudently in this decision, as the event seems to indicate the contrary, and as it was the evident meaning of all his predictions that the Jews should not prosper in their own country till the expiration of seventy years. But he was evidently influenced by the most unbounded love to his country, for whose welfare he had watched, prayed, and lived; and he now chose rather to share her adversities, her sorrows, her wants, her afflictions, and her disgrace, than to be the companion of princes, and to sit at the table of kings. His patriotism was as unbounded as it was sincere: he only ceased to live for his country when he ceased to breathe. Je 39:14. **Mizpah.** Je 41:5-9. Jsh 15:38. 18:26. Jg *20:1. 21:1. 1 S *7:5, 6, Mizpeh. 10:17. 1 K 15:22.

7. **all the.** Je 39:4. 2 K *25:4, 22, 23, etc. **governor.** Ezk 17:15-19. **the poor.** ♪121N2, Ge +34:29. Je 39:10. Ezk 33:24-29. 52:16.

8. **came.** ver. 6, 11, 12. **even.** ver. 14. Je 41:1-16. 2 K *25:23, 25. **Johanan.** Je 41:11, 16. 42:1, 8. 43:2-5. **Jonathan.** Je 37:15, 20. 38:26. **Kareah.** i.e. *bald*, ✛S#7143h. Je 40:8, 13, 15, 16. 41:11, 13, 14, 16. 42:1, 8. 43:2, 4, 5. **Ephai.** i.e. *languid; wearying of the Lord; great languishing*, ✱S#5778h. **Netophathite.** 2 S 23:28, 29. 1 Ch 2:54. 11:30. Ezr 2:2, 22. Ne 7:26. **Jezaniah.** i.e. *the Lord hears*, ✱S#3153h. Je 42:1. **Maachathite.** Dt 3:14. Jsh 12:5. 2 S 10:6, 8. 23:34. 1 Ch 2:48.

9. **sware.** 1 S 20:16, 17. 2 K *25:24. **Fear.** Je 27:11. 38:17-20. Ge 49:15. Ps *37:3. 128:2.

10. **serve.** Heb. stand before. See on Je 35:19. Dt 1:38. Pr 22:29. Lk +*21:36. **gather.** Je 39:10. **summer.** ♪121P9, Is +16:9. ver. 12. Je 48:32. 2 S *16:1. Is 16:9. Mi 7:1.

11. **all the Jews.** Je 24:9. Is *16:4. Ezk 5:3, 12. 25:2, 6, 8, 12. 35:5, 15. Ob *11-14.

12. **returned.** Je 43:5. **driven.** Je 43:5. 49:5. **unto Mizpah.** Je 41:1. **summer fruits.** ♪121P9, Is +16:9. ver. 10. Je 8:20. 48:32.

13. **Johanan.** Johanan and his companions seem to have acted honestly in this affair. They had received intelligence of designs formed against Gedaliah's life, and consequently against the whole new settlement. Ishmael, being a branch of David's family, was probably displeased that another was preferred above him; and the king of the Ammonites, out of hatred to the Jews, employed him to slay Gedaliah. But Gedaliah, conscious of his own integrity and benevolence, took the portrait of others from his own mind; and therefore believed evil of no man, because he felt none towards any in his own breast. He may be reproached for being too credulous and confiding; but this only serves to show the greatness of his soul; for a little mind is always suspicious, and ready to believe the worst of every person and thing. See on ver. 6-8.

14. **Baalis.** i.e. *son of exultation; lord of the banner*,

✱S#1185h. **Ammonites.** Je 25:21. 41:10. 49:1-6. 1 S *11:1-3. 2 S 10:1-6. Ezk *25:2-6. Am *1:13-15. **Ishmael.** See on ver. 8. Je 41:2, 10. Pr 26:23-26. Is 26:10. Mi *7:5. **slay thee?** Heb. strike thee in soul? Heb. *nephesh*, Jsh +10:28. ♪121A7, Ge +9:5. ver. 15. Ge 37:21. Dt 19:6mg. **believed.** 1 C 13:5-7.

15. **Let.** 1 S 24:4. 26:8. Jb 31:31. **wherefore.** Je 12:3, 4. 2 S 18:3. 21:17. Ezk 33:24-29. Jn 11:50. **slay thee.** Heb. *nephesh*, Jsh +10:28. ver. +14.

16. **Thou shalt.** Je 41:2. Mt *10:16, 17. Ro 3:8. **falsely.** Je 3:10, 23. 5:2, 31. *37:14. 2 K 9:12.

JEREMIAH 41

Ishmael treacherously murders Gedaliah and many other Jews; and attempts to lead the rest over to the Ammonites, 1-10. Johanan rescues them, drives away Ishmael, takes the command, and purposes to go into Egypt, 11-18.

1. **the seventh month.** This was the month *Tisri*, answering to the new moon of September, the seventh of the sacred, but the first of the civil year; on the third day of which the Jews keep a fast, in commemoration of the death of Gedaliah, to which the prophet Zechariah refers, Zc 8:19. Je 39:2. 52:6. 2 K *25:3, 8, 25. Zc 7:5. 8:19. **Ishmael.** See on Je 40:6, 8. **Elishama.** Je 36:12, 20. **of the.** Pr 13:10. 27:4. Ja 4:1-3. **seed royal.** 2 K *11:1. 2 Ch *22:10. Ezk 17:13. **they did.** Je 40:14-16. 2 S 3:27. 20:9, 10. Ps 41:9. 109:5. Pr 26:23-26. Da 11:26, 27. Lk 22:47, 48. Jn *13:18.

2. **and smote.** 2 K 22:25. **whom.** Je 40:7.

3. **slew all.** See on ver. 11, 12. 2 K 25:25. Ec 9:18. La 1:2.

4. **after.** 1 S 27:11. Ps 52:1, 2.

5. **came.** 2 K 10:13, 14. **Shechem.** Ge 33:18. 34:2. Jsh 24:32. Jg 9:1. 1 K 12:1, 25. **Shiloh.** Je 7:12, 14. 26:6, 9. Jsh 18:1. **Samaria.** 1 K 16:24, 29. **their beards.** All these were signs of deep mourning; which, though forbidden on funeral occasions, were customary, and perhaps counted allowable, on seasons of public calamity; and this mourning was probably on account of the destruction of Jerusalem. Le 19:27, 28. Dt 14:1. 2 S 10:4. Is *15:2, 3. **offerings.** Le 2:1♪9. Le +*23:13. **to bring.** Le 23:23, 34. Nu 29:12. Dt 16:13. **to the house.** 1 S 1:7. 2 K 25:9. Ps 102:14.

6. **weeping,** etc. Heb. in going and weeping. Je 50:4. 2 S *1:2, etc. 3:16. Pr *26:23-26.

7. **slew.** 1 K 15:28, 29. 16:10-12. 2 K 11:1, 2. 15:25. Ps 55:23. Pr 1:16. Is 59:7. Ezk 22:27. 33:24-26. Ro 3:15. **cast them.** Ps 74:7. 89:39. 118:5. **pit.** Heb. *bor*, Ge +37:20. ver. 9.

8. **Slay.** Jb 2:4. Ps 49:6-8. Pr 13:8. Mt 6:25. 16:26. Mk 8:36, 37. Ph 3:7-9. **treasures.** These "treasures hid in the field" were doubtless laid up in subterranean pits, similar to the *mattamores* in Barbary, in which, Dr. Shaw (p. 139) informs us, they deposit the grain when winnowed; two or three hundred of them being sometimes together, and the smallest holding four hundred bushels. The same mode of keeping corn prevails in Syria and the Holy Land. Jg 6:11.

9. **the pit.** Heb. *bor*, Ge +37:20. Je 37:16. 1 K 15:22. 2 K 10:14. 2 Ch 16:6. This was probably a large reservoir for receiving rain water, which Asa had caused to be made in the midst of the city, in case of a siege. **because of Gedaliah.** or, near Gedaliah. Heb. by the

hand, *or* by the side of Gedaliah. Je 38:10mg. 46:6. **was it.** Jsh 10:16-18. Jg 6:2. 1 S 13:6. 14:11, 22. 24:3. 2 S 17:9. He 11:38. **for fear.** 1 K 15:17-22. 2 Ch 16:1-10.

10. **all the.** See on Je 40:11, 12. **king's daughters.** Je 22:30. 38:23. 39:6. 43:5-7. 44:12-14. **whom.** Je 40:7. **to the.** Je 40:14. Ne 2:10, 19. 4:7, 8. 6:17, 18. 13:4-8.

11. **Johanan.** ver. 2, 3, 7. See on Je 40:7, 8, 13-16. 42:1, 3. 43:2-5.

12. **to fight.** Ge 14:14-16. 1 S 30:1-8, 18-20. **the great waters.** 2 S *2:13.

13. **that when.** They appear to have been weary of the tyranny of Ishmael, and glad of an opportunity to abandon him. **and all.** ver. 13, 16. Je 40:13. **were glad.** Pr 29:2.

14. **So all.** ver. 10, 16. **cast about.** or, turn round. Je 52:21. Ge 37:7.

15. **escaped.** 1 S 30:17. 1 K 20:20. Jb 21:30. Pr 28:17. Ec √8:11, 12. Ac *28:4. **eight men.** ver. 2. 2 K 25:25.

16. **even.** ver. 10. Je 42:8. 43:4-7.

17. **habitation.** or, inn. 2 S *19:31-40. Lk 2:7. **Chimham.** 2 S 19:37, 38. **to go.** As Johanan and the other princes had taken a decided part against Ishmael, they had no sufficient reason to fear that the Chaldeans would revenge on them the murder of Gedaliah; but perhaps Johanan was unwilling to be superseded in the command which he had rightly assumed, and so used his influence to induce the whole company to take refuge in Egypt; and their old attachment to the Egyptians rendered them more ready to concur in this ruinous measure. Je 42:14, 19. 43:7. Is *30:1-3.

18. **for they.** Je 42:11, 16. 43:2, 3. Ge +*19:30. 2 K *25:25. Ps +*34:4. Is 30:16, 17. *51:12, 13. 57:11. Lk *12:4, 5. **because.** See on ver. 2. **whom.** Je 40:5.

JEREMIAH 42

Johanan and his company desire Jeremiah to inquire of God for them, and promise implicit obedience, 1-6. He assures them of safety if they continued in Judah, but of dreadful miseries if they go into Egypt, 7-18. He charges them with hypocrisy, in asking counsel which they did not mean to follow, 19-22.

1. **all the.** See on ver. 8. Je 40:8, 13. 41:11, 16. 43:4, 5. **Jezaniah.** 2 K *25:23. Ezk *8:11. 11:1, Jaazaniah. **from.** ver. 8. Je 5:4, 5. 6:13. 8:10. 44:12. Ac 8:10. **came.** ver. 20. Is 29:13. 48:1. 58:1, 2. Ezk 14:3, 4. 20:1-3. 33:31. Mt 15:8.

2. **be accepted before thee.** Heb. fall before thee. Je 36:7mg. 37:20mg. **and pray.** Je 17:15, 16. 21:2. 37:3. Ex 8:28. 9:28. 1 S 7:8. 12:19, 23. 1 K 13:6. Is *1:15. 37:4. Ac 8:24. Ja +*5:16. **left.** Le 26:22)𝒫. Dt 4:27. 28:62. Is 1:9. La 1:1. Ezk 5:3, 4. 12:16. Zc 13:8, 9. Mt 24:22.

3. **may show us.** Je 6:16. Dt *5:26, 27, 29. 1 K 8:36. Ezr 8:21. Ps *25:4, 5. 27:11. 86:11. 143:8-10. Pr √3:6. Is *2:3. Mi *4:2. Mk 12:13, 14.

4. **Jeremiah.** The princes seem to have wholly neglected Jeremiah, till on this occasion they wanted his sanction to their purpose of going to Egypt. In order to induce him to favor them, they applied to him with one consent, in the most respectful and plausible manner: they used language to prepossess him with a favorable opinion of them, and to move his

compassion; and, in words expressing great humility, they entreated his prayers in their behalf, and that he would inquire of the Lord what he would have them to do. The prophet readily acquiesced; and doubted not but that he should receive an answer from God, which he would unreservedly declare to them; and they called the Lord to witness that they would implicitly follow his directions. **I will pray.** Ex *8:29. 1 S √12:23. Ro 10:1. **whatsoever.** Je +*23:28n. 1 K *22:14-16. 2 Ch *18:13-15. Ezk √2:7. **I will keep.** 1 S 3:17, 18. Ps 40:10. Ac √20:20, 27.

5. **The Lord be.** Je 5:2. Ge +*31:49, 50. Ex 20:7. Jg 11:10. 1 S *12:5. 20:42. Mi *1:2. Ml 2:14. +*3:5. Ro 1:9. Re *1:5. *3:14. **if we.** Ex 20:19. Dt 5:27-29.

6. **it be good.** Ro 7:7, 13. 8:7. **evil.** Is +45:7. **that it.** See on Je 7:23. Dt 5:29, 33. 6:2, 3)𝒫. Ps *81:13-16. 128:2. Is *3:10, 11. Ro *8:7, 8. 1 J *3:2, 3, 22, 23.

7. **after ten days.** At this time he was waiting for a revelation from God in answer to the inquiries of the people; who probably thus delayed to make known his will, in order to show them that Jeremiah did not speak of his own mind, but when and as he was directed. The delay was also suited to give time for consideration, and to retard their rash project; and, as it would render them impatient, it tended to detect their hypocrisy, and to show more clearly their determined rebellion against God. Ps *27:14. Is 28:16. Hab *2:3.

8. **Johanan.** See on ver. 1. Je 40:8, 13. 41:11-16. 43:2-5.

9. **the Lord, the God of Israel.** Je +11:3. **unto.** See on ver. 2. 2 K *19:4, 6, 20, etc. 22:15-20.

10. **abide.** Ge *26:2, 3. Ps *37:3. **then.** Je 24:6. 31:28. 33:7. Ps 69:35. 102:16. Ezk *36:36. Ac *15:16. **build.** Je 1:10. **for I repent.** Je 18:7-10. 26:19. Ge 6:6)𝒫. Ex 32:14. Dt 32:36)𝒫. Jg 2:18. 2 S 24:16. Ps *106:45. Ho 11:8. Jl 2:13. Am 7:3, 6. Jon *3:10. *4:2.

11. **afraid.** Je 27:12, 17. 41:18. 2 K 25:26. Mt +*10:28. **for I.** Je 1:19. 15:20. Dt 20:4. Jsh *1:5, 9. 2 Ch 32:7, 8. Ps *46:7, 11. Is 8:8-10. *41:10. 43:2, 5. Mt 28:20. Ac *18:9, 10. Ro √8:31. 2 T *4:17, 18.

12. **that he.** Ne 1:11. Ps *106:45, 46. Pr +*16:7.

13. **But if ye.** ver. 10. Je 44:16. Ex *5:2.

14. **we will go.** Je 41:17. 43:7. Dt *29:19. Is *30:15, 16. *31:1. **nor hear.** Je 4:19, 21. Ex *16:3. 17:3. Nu 11:5. 16:13.

15. **Lord of hosts, the God of Israel.** ver. 18. Je +7:3. **If.** If ye are determined to go into Egypt, the evils which ye dreaded by staying in your own land shall overtake and destroy you there; "and there ye shall die." God turned the policy of the wicked to their own destruction; for while they thought themselves safe in Egypt, there Nebuchadnezzar destroyed both them and the Egyptians. ver. 17. Je 44:12-14. Ge 31:21. Dt 17:16)𝒫. Da 11:17. Lk 9:51.

16. **that the sword.** ver. 13. Je 44:13, 27. Dt *28:15, 22, 45. Pr *13:21. Ezk *11:8. Am 9:1-4. Zc 1:6. Jn 11:48. **follow close.** Heb. cleave after you. 2 K 5:27. **there ye.** Je 44:11, 12, 27.

17. **it be with all the men.** Heb. all the men be. **they shall.** ver. 22. Je 24:10. 44:14. **none.** Je 44:28.

18. **As mine.** The people had witnessed the tremendous effects of the wrath of God, in the siege and destruction of Jerusalem; and had they not been past feeling, this denunciation must have made their ears tingle, and appalled their very souls. Je 6:11. 7:20.

39:1-9. 52:4, etc. 2 K 25:4, etc. 2 Ch 34:25. 36:16-19. La 2:4. 4:11. Ezk 22:22. Da 9:11, 27. Na 1:6. Re *14:9, 10. 16:2, etc. **ye shall be.** Je 18:16. 24:9. 25:9. 26:6. 29:18, 22. 44:12. Dt 29:21, 22. 1 K 9:7-9. Is 65:15. Zc 8:13. **and ye shall see.** Je 22:10-12, 27.

19. **Go.** God knew, that such was their miserable propensity to idolatry, that they would adopt the idolatrous worship of Egypt. Add to which, their going thither for protection was in effect refusing to submit to the king of Babylon, to whom God had decreed the rule of Judah and the neighboring kingdoms. Dt *17:16↟℗. Is *30:1-7. 31:1-3. Ezk 17:15. **know.** Je 38:21. Ezk 3:21. Ac *20:26, 27. **admonished you.** Heb. testified against you. Dt 31:21. 2 Ch 24:19. Ne 9:26, 29, 30. Ac 2:40. Ep 4:17. 1 Th 4:6. **this day.** Dt +4:26. Lk ◐23:43. Ac 20:26.

20. **For ye.** God made known to the prophet their dissimulation; which he shunned not to declare to them. Je 3:10. √17:10. 41:17. Ps 139:2. Ezk 14:3, 4. √33:31. Mt *22:15-18, 35. Jn 1:48. +*2:24, 25. Ga √6:7. **dissembled in your hearts.** Heb. have used deceit against your souls. Heb. *nephesh*, Ex +23:9. Nu 16:38. Ps 18:44mg. 65:3mg. Pr 14:8. Ja *1:22. **Pray.** See on ver. 2.

21. **I have.** Dt 11:26, 27. Ezk 2:7. 3:17. Ac 20:20, 26, 27. **this day.** ver. 19. Dt +*4:26. Lk ◐23:43. Ac 20:26. **but.** See on Je 7:24-27. Dt 29:19. Zc 7:11, 12.

22. **know.** See on ver. 17. Je 43:11. Ezk 5:3, 4. 6:11. **by the sword.** Je 24:10. Le 26:6, 25, 33, 36↟℗. Dt 28:22↟℗. Ezk √6:11, 12. **in the.** Ho *9:6. **to go and sojourn.** or, to go to sojourn. ver. 15. Je 44:12, 14.

JEREMIAH 43

Johanan and the captain, despising the prophet's counsel, take him, and Baruch, and the people, and go into Egypt, 1-7. Jeremiah, by a sign, predicts the conquest of Egypt by the Chaldeans, 8-13.

1. **had made.** Je 26:8. 42:22. 51:63. **all the words.** Je 1:7, 17. 26:2. 42:3-5. Ex 24:3. 1 S 8:10. Mt 28:20. Ac 5:20. 20:27.

2. **Azariah.** See on Je 40:8. 42:1, Jezaniah. **Johanan.** See on Je 40:13-16. 41:16. **all the.** Je 13:15. Ex +*5:2. 9:17. Ps 10:4, 5. 12:3. 119:21. 123:4. Pr 6:17. 8:13. 16:5, 18, 19. 30:9. Is 9:9, 10. Hab 2:4, 5. Ja 4:6. 1 P 5:5. **Thou speakest.** They had no other color for their rebellion than flatly to deny that God had spoken what the prophet had declared,—the constant method of hypocrites and infidels, who pretend that they are not satisfied of the truth of Divine revelation, when the true cause of their unbelief is, that the commands of God contradict their lusts and appetites. Je 5:12, 13. 2 Ch 36:13. Is 7:9.

3. **Baruch.** ver. 6. Je 32:12. 36:4, 10, 26. 45:1-3. **to deliver.** Je 38:4. Ps 109:4. Mt +*5:11, 12. Lk *6:22, 23, 26.

4. **obeyed not.** See on Je 42:5, 6. 44:5. 2 Ch 25:16. Ec *9:16. **to dwell.** Je 42:10-13. Ps *37:3.

5. **took.** See on Je 40:11, 12. 41:15, 16. 1 S 26:19.

6. **the king's.** Je 41:10. 52:10. **every.** Je 39:10. 40:7. **person.** Heb. *nephesh*, soul, Ge +12:5. **Jeremiah.** Ec 9:1, 2. La 3:1. Jn 21:18.

7. **So.** 2 Ch 25:16. **Tahpanhes.** i.e. *beginning of the age* or *world; thou wilt fill hands with pity; temptation,* *S#8471h. ver. 8, 9. Je 2:16, Tahapanhes. 44:1.

46:14. Is 30:4, Hanes. Ezk 30:18, Tehaphnehes.

8. **Then came.** Ps 139:7. 2 T *2:9.

9. **great.** Je 13:1, etc. 18:2, etc. 19:1, etc. 51:63, 64. 1 K 11:29-31. Is 20:1-4. Ezk 4:1, etc. 5:1, etc. 12:3, etc. Ho *12:10. Ac 21:11. Re *18:21. **in the brick-kiln.** Ex 1:14. 2 S 12:31. Na 3:14. Rather, brick pavement, a platform made of beaten clay, edged with bricks. Certainly not a brickkiln, which would have no place at the entrance to Pharaoh's house, and would not suit the conditions of the prophecy and its fulfillment, for how would Nebuchadnezzar spread his pavilion over stones hidden in a brickkiln?

10. **Lord of hosts, the God of Israel.** Je +7:3. **I will send.** Je 1:15. 25:6-26. 27:6-8. Ezk *29:18-20. Da *2:20, 21. 5:18, 19. **my servant.** Je +*25:9. 27:6. 46:27, 28. Is +*10:5. *44:27, 28. 45:1. Mt *22:7. **will set.** This prophecy was fulfilled to the letter. Josephus records it (Ant. x. 9, 10), CB. **his royal.** 1 K 20:12, 16. Ps 18:11. 27:5. 31:20.

11. **he shall smite.** Je 25:19. 46:1-26. Is ch. 19. Ezk 29:19, 20. **ch.** 30-32. **such as are for death.** See on Je 15:2. 44:13. 2 S *12:31. Jb *20:29. Ezk *5:12. Zc *11:9. Mt √25:31-46.

12. **in the.** Je 46:25. 48:7. 50:2. 51:44. Ex *12:12. 2 S 5:21. Is 19:1. 21:9. 46:1. Ezk *30:13, 15, 16. Zp 2:11. **array.** Est 6:9. Jb 40:10. **putteth.** Ps 109:18, 19. 132:16, 18. Is 49:18. *52:1. 59:17. *61:5, 10. Ro *13:12. Ep 4:24. 6:11. Col 3:12, 14.

13. **images.** Heb. statues, *or* standing images. 2 K +17:10. Is +66:17n. **Beth-shemesh.** or, the house of the sun. or, temple of the sun. Is 19:18mg. Ezk 30:17mg. *S#1053h: Je 43:13. Jsh 15:10. 19:22, 38. 21:16. Jg 1:33, 33. 1 S 6:9, 12, 12, 13, 15, 19, 20. 1 K 4:9. 2 K 14:11, 13. 1 Ch 6:59. 2 Ch 25:21, 23. 28:18. **that is in.** To distinguish it from the Beth-shemesh of Jsh 15:10. Jg 1:33. 1 S 6:9, 19. **and the.** See on ver. 12.

JEREMIAH 44

God, by his prophet, expostulates with the Jews in Egypt, for persisting in idolatry, after all that they had heard, suffered, and witnessed, 1-10. He denounces their destruction, 11-14. The Jews impiously avow their purpose of cleaving to their idols, and ascribe their miseries to the neglect of them, particularly the "queen of heaven," 15-19. The prophet shows the falsehood of their plea; and, in the name of God, predicts their utter ruin, 20-28; and, for a sign, that also of the king of Egypt, 29, 30.

1. Cir. A.M. 3433. B.C. 571. **The word.** Dahler supposes this discourse to have been delivered in the 17th or 18th year after the taking of Jerusalem. **concerning.** Je 42:15-18. 43:5-7. **Migdol.** See on Je 46:14. Ex 14:2. Ezk 29:10h. **Tahpanhes.** *Tahpanhes,* rendered "Taphnae" and "Taphnai" by the LXX., is no doubt the "Daphnai" of Herodotus, a royal city of Lower Egypt, situated, according to the Itinerary of Antoninus, sixteen miles south from Pelusium, from which it was called *Daphnae Pelusiacae.* Forster (in Michaelis Spicileg. Geog. Heb. Ex. P. ii.) says, that there is now a place situated in the vicinity of Pelusium called *Safnas,* which may be a vistige of the ancient name. It appears to have been the very first town in Egypt, in the road from Palestine, that afforded tolerable accommodation for the fugitives. It was at this place

that, according to Jerome and several of the ancients, tradition says the faithful Jeremiah was stoned to death by these rebellious wretches, for whose welfare he had watched, prayed, and suffered every kind of indignity and hardship. Je 43:7. Ezk 30:18. **Noph**. Je 2:16. 46:14, 19. Is 19:13. Ezk 30:13, 16. **Pathros**. Ge 10:14, Pathrusim. Is √11:11. Ezk *29:14. 30:14.

2. **Lord of hosts, the God**. Je +7:3. **Ye have**. See on Je 39:1-8. Ex 19:4. Dt 29:2. Jsh 23:3. Zc 1:6. **a desolation**. ver. 22. Je 4:7. 7:34. 9:11. 25:11. 34:22. Le 26:32, 33, 43. 2 K 21:13. Is 6:11. 24:12. 64:10, 11. La 1:1, 16. 5:18. Mi 3:12.

3. **of their**. Je 2:17-19. 4:17, 18. 5:19, 29. 9:12-14. 11:17. 16:11, 12. 19:3, 4. 22:9. Ezr 9:6-11. Ne 9:33. La 1:8. 4:13. Ezk *8:17, 18. 9:9. *22:25-31. Da 9:5-8. Zc 7:12, 13. **gods**. Dt 13:6)𝒫. 29:26. 32:17)𝒫.

4. **I sent**. Je 7:+13, 25. 25:3, 4. 26:5. 29:19. 32:33. 35:17. 2 Ch *36:15. Zc *7:7. **this abominable**. Je 16:18. Ezk *8:10. 16:36, 47. Ep *5:5. Col *3:5, 6. 1 P *4:3. Re *17:4, 5.

5. **they**. See on Je 7:24. 2 Ch *36:16. Ps *81:11-13. Is *48:4, 18. Zc 7:11, 12. Re *2:21, 22. **burn**. ver. 17-21. See on Je 19:13.

6. **my fury**. Je 4:4. 7:20. 21:5, 12. 36:7. 42:18. Le *26:27, 28. Is 51:17, 20. Ezk 5:13. 6:12. 8:18. *20:33. 24:8, 13. Da 9:12. Na 1:2. **wasted**. See on ver. 2, 3. Is *6:11.

7. **the Lord, the God of hosts**. Je +35:17. **against**. Je 7:19. 25:7. 42:20mg. Nu *16:38)𝒫. Pr 1:18. 5:22. 8:36. 15:32. Ezk √33:11. Hab *2:10. **souls**. Heb. *nephesh*, Ge +12:13. **to cut**. ver. 8, 11. Je 9:21. 51:22. Jsh 6:21. Jg 21:11. **child**. Dt 32:25. 1 S 15:3. 22:19. La 2:11. **Judah**. Heb. the midst of Judah. Je 50:8. 51:6. **to leave**. ver. 12, 14, 27, 28.

8. **ye provoke**. See on Je *25:6, 7. Dt *32:16, 17. 2 K 17:15-17. Is 3:8. 1 C *10:21, 22. He 3:16. **that ye might cut**. See on ver. 7. Ezk 18:31, 32. **a curse**. ver. 12. Je 18:16. 24:9. 26:6. 29:18. 42:18. 1 K 9:7, 8. 2 Ch 7:20. Is 65:15. La *2:15, 16.

9. **ye forgotten**. Jsh *22:17-20. Ezr *9:7-15. Da 9:5-8. **wickedness**. Heb. wickednesses, *or* punishments, etc. Is +45:7. **the wickedness of your**. ver. 15-19. Je 7:17, 18.

10. **are not**. Je 8:12. Ex 9:17. 10:3. 1 K 21:29. 2 Ch 12:6-12. 32:26. 33:12, 19. 34:27. Da 5:20-22. Ja *4:6-10. 1 P *5:6. **humbled**. Heb. contrite. 2 K 22:19. Ps 34:18. +*51:17. Is √57:15. 66:2. Ezk +*9:4. **neither**. Je 10:7. 36:24. Ex 9:30. Pr 8:13. 14:16. 16:6. 28:14. Ec *8:12, 13. Ml *4:2. Mt 27:54. Lk 23:40. Ro *11:19, 20. Re *15:4.

11. **I will**. Je 21:10. Le *17:10)𝒫. 20:3, 5, 6)𝒫. 26:17. Ps *34:16. Ezk *14:7, 8. 15:7. Am 9:4. **for evil**. Is +45:7.

12. **I will take**. See on Je 42:15-18, 22. **from the**. Ho *4:6. **and they shall be**. See on ver. 8. Je 29:22. Is *65:15. **by the sword**. Je 14:12. 42:16. 46:19. Le 26:6, 25, 33, 36)𝒫. Dt 28:22)𝒫. **an execration**. Je 42:18. 46:19. **a curse**. ver. 8. Je 42:18.

13. **I will punish**. ver. 27, 28. Je +9:25mg. See on 11:22. 21:9. 24:10. 42:18. 43:11. **by the sword**. Je 14:12. 42:16. 46:19. Ezk *6:11, 12.

14. **So**. It is evident from ver. 28, that some Jews were to escape the general destruction in Egypt, and to return into their own country, though but a few; and the same thing is implied in the latter clause of this verse. But the former part excludes from the num-

ber of those who should escape every individual of those who are properly termed "the remnant of Judah," those who had willingly and rebelliously "set their faces to go into the land of Egypt to dwell there," on a presumption that they knew better than God how to consult their own restoration. The few, then, who were destined to escape, were to be such as had come into the land of Egypt with Johanan by compulsion, or had previously fled thither, or in some other less offensive manner, and chanced to be there when the storm burst upon them. **which are**. Is *30:1-3. **shall escape**. ver. 27. See on Je 42:17. Mt 23:33. Lk +*21:36. Ro 2:3. He *2:3. **which they**. Je 22:26, 27. 42:22. **have a desire**. Heb. lift up their soul. Heb. *nephesh*, Ex +15:9. Je 22:27mg. **for none**. ver. 28. Is 4:2. 10:20. Ro 9:27. 11:5, 6.

15. **all the**. Je 5:1-5. Ge 19:4. Ne *13:26. Pr 11:21. Is *1:5. Mt √7:13. 2 P 2:1, 2.

16. **the word**. Ps 19:7, 8. Ho 8:12. 1 C 15:1-4. **we will not hearken**. Je 6:15-17, +*19. *8:6, 12. *18:18. +29:19. 38:4. Ex 5:2. Jb 15:25-27. *21:14, 15. Ps 2:3. *73:8, 9. Is *3:9. Da 3:15. 7:25. Mt 15:6. Lk *19:14, 27.

17. **we will**. T#699. Ex +22:30 (T#362). 32:1. Dt 31:16, 20. **certainly do**. Da 11:36. Mk *7:5-13. Ro 1:16, 25. Ga 1:8. 2 Th 2:4, 9-12. **whatsoever**. ver. 25. Nu 30:2, 12)𝒫. Dt 23:23)𝒫. Jg *11:36. Ps 12:4. Mk *6:26. **queen of heaven**. *or*, frame of heaven. As the *Sun* was worshipped, not only under the name of *baal shamayim*, "Lord of heaven," but also by that of *Molech*, or *King*; it is likely also that the *Moon* was adored as *melecheth hashshamayim*, "the Queen of heaven." So the Orphic hymn addressed to the Moon begins, "Kluthi thea basileia," Hear, goddess *Queen*. And "Ho Xaire, anassa, thea," All hail, *Queen*, goddess. In Epiphanius, we find some *women* of Arabia, towards the end of the fourth century, had set up another *queen of heaven*, the Virgin Mary, too well known since under that name and character, whom they likewise worshipped as a goddess, by holding stated assemblies every year to her honor, and by offering a *cake* of bread in her name; whence these heretics were called *Collyridians*, from the Greek *kolluris*, a *cake*. Je 7:18mg. 2 K *17:16. **drink offerings**. Le +*23:13. **as we**. Je *19:13. 32:29-32. 2 K 22:17. Ne 9:34. Da 9:6-8. **our fathers**. Ne 9:34. Ps 106:6. Ezk *20:8. Da 9:5, 6, 8. 1 P *1:18. **in the cities**. See on ver. 9, 21. **then**. Ex *16:3. Is 48:5. Ho *2:5-9. Ph *3:19. **victuals**. Heb. bread. 1 K 11:18.

18. **we have**. See on Je 40:12. Nu 11:5, 6. Jb +*21:14, 15. Ps 73:9-15. Ml 3:13-15.

19. **we burned**. See on ver. 15. Je 7:18. **without**. Ge *3:6, 11, 12, 16, 17. Dt *7:3, 4. 1 K *21:25. 2 Ch 21:6. Pr 11:21. Mk *6:19-27. **men**. *or*, husbands. ver. 15. Nu 30:6.

20. **the men**. Je 43:6.

21. **and in**. ver. 9, 17. Je 11:13. Ezk *16:24. **did**. Je 14:10. 1 S 15:3. 1 K *17:18. Ps 79:8. Is 64:9. Ezk *21:23, 24. Ho 7:2. Am 8:7. Re *16:19. 18:5.

22. **So that**. Je 5:9, 29. **could**. Je 15:6. Ge *6:3, 5-7. Ps *95:10, 11. 101:5. Is *1:24. 7:13. 43:24. Ezk *5:13-15. Am 2:13. Ml 2:17. Ro 2:4, 5. 9:22. 2 P 3:7-9. **your land**. See on ver. 2, 6, 12. Je 18:16. 24:9. 25:11, 18, 38. 26:6. 29:19. 1 K 9:7, 8. La 2:15, 16. Da *9:11, 12. **without an inhabitant**. Je 4:7. Is 6:11. **as at this day**. Je +25:18.

23. **ye have burned**. See on ver. 8, 18, 21. Je 32:31-33. 2 Ch *36:16. La *1:8. 1 C *10:20. 2 C *6:16-18. **nor walked**. Ps 119:150. **nor in his statutes**. Ps 119:155. **nor in his testimonies**. Ps 78:56. **therefore**. 1 K 9:9. Ne 13:18. Da 9:11, 12. **is happened**. 2 S +1:6. **as at**. ver. +22.

24. **Hear**. ver. 16. Je 42:15. 1 K 22:19. Is *1:10. 28:14. Ezk 2:7. Am 7:16. Mt 11:15. **all Judah**. ver. 15, 26. Je 43:7. Ezk 20:32, 33.

25. **Ye and**. See on ver. 15-19. Is +*28:15. Ju 13. **We will**. Mt *14:9. Ac *23:12-15. **vows**. Le ◑+*23:38. **ye will**. Jb 34:22. Ja *1:14, 15.

26. **I have sworn**. Je 46:18. Ge 22:16)𝒫. Nu 14:21-23, 28. Dt 32:40-42. Ps 89:34. Is 62:8. Am 6:8. 8:7. He 3:18. *6:13, 18. **great name**. ∫144A4A, Is 30:27. **that my name**. Ps 50:16. Ezk 20:39. Am 6:10. **The Lord God**. Je 4:2. 5:2. 7:9. Is 48:1, 2. Zp 1:4, 5.

27. **will watch**. Je 1:10. See on 21:10. 31:28. Ezk *7:5, 6. **shall be**. See on ver. 12, 18. 2 K 21:14.

28. **a small**. ver. 14. Is 10:19, 22. 27:12, 13. **shall know**. ver. 16, 17, 25, 26, 29. Nu 14:28, 29, 41. Ps 33:11. Is 14:24-27. 28:16-18. 46:10, 11. La *3:37, 38. Zc *1:5, 6. Mt *24:35. **mine, or theirs**. Heb. from me or them.

29. **a sign**. ver. 30. 1 S 2:34. Mt √24:15, 16, 32-34. Mk *13:14-16. Lk *21:20, 21, 29-33. **punish**. Je +11:22mg. **my words**. Pr *19:21. Is √40:8.

30. **I will**. Je 43:9-13. 46:13-26. Ezk ch. 29, 30. *31:18. ch. 32. **Pharaoh-hophra**. i.e. *Pharaoh, priest of the sun; his nakedness, covering evil,* ✻S#6548h. Grandson of Pharaoh-Necho (Young). **as I**. Je 34:21. 39:5-7. 52:8-11. 2 K 25:4-7. **life**. Heb. *nephesh*, Ge +44:30.

JEREMIAH 45

Baruch being dismayed, Jeremiah, in the name of God, warns and instructs him, and assures him of protection, 1-5.

1. A.M. 3397. B.C. 607. **Baruch**. Je 32:12, 16. 43:3-6. 51:59. 2 Ch 34:8. **when**. Je 36:1, 4, 8, 14-18, 26, 32. **in the**. Je 25:1. 26:1. 36:1, 9. **the fourth year**. The *Companion Bible* states this "is to be dated 496 B.C., instead of the usually "received" date of 606 B.C. or thereabout" (Ap. 86, p. 124). Ivan Panin places this date at (A.M.?) 3428, in his *Bible Chronology*, p. 126. Young gives B.C. 607. But Edwin R. Thiele places this date in 605 B.C. in his *The Mysterious Numbers of the Hebrew Kings*, Table XIV, p. 162. This appears to be in agreement with Jack Finegan, *Handbook of Biblical Chronology*, Section 314, pp. 201, 202, and Table 90, p. 202, who places this date at Tishri (Sep/Oct) 606—Elul (Aug/Sep) 605 B.C. Je 25:1-3. 46:2. Da 1:1.

2. **the Lord, the God of Israel**. Je +11:3. **unto**. Is √63:9. Mk 16:7. 2 C 1:4. 7:6. He 2:18. 4:15.

3. **Woe**. Je 9:1. 15:10, etc. 20:7, etc. Ps 120:5. **added**. Ge 37:34, 35. 42:36-38. Nu 11:11-15. Jsh 7:7-9. Jb *16:11-13. 23:2. Ps *42:7. La 3:1-19, 32. **I fainted**. Je 8:18. Ps 27:13. 77:3, 4. Pr 24:10. La 1:13, 22. 2 C 4:1, 16. Ga 6:9. 2 Th 3:13. He 12:3-5.

4. **that which**. See on Je 1:10. 18:7-10. 31:28. Ge 6:6, 7. Ps 80:8-16. Is *5:2-7.

5. **seekest**. 2 K 5:26. Ps 131:1. Lk *6:26. Ro *12:16. 1 C *7:26-32. 1 T √6:6-9. He +*13:5. **seek them not**. 1 K 3:11. Hab 2:6. Mt *6:25-33. Mk 9:33-37. 10:35-

45. 12:38, 39. Jn 5:44. 1 J √2:16. 3 J 9, 10. **I will bring**. Je 25:26. Ge 6:12. Is 66:16. Zp 3:8. **evil**. Is +45:7. **thy life**. Heb. *nephesh*, Ge +44:30. ∫121A7, Ge +9:5. Je 21:9. 38:2. 39:18.

JEREMIAH 46

Predictions of the destruction of Pharaoh-necho's army, near the Euphrates, by the Chaldeans, 1-12; and of the invasion and conquest of Egypt by Nebuchadnezzar, 13-26. A word of encouragement to Jacob, 27, 28.

1. **The word**. This is a general title to the prophecies contained in this and the following chapters, concerning different nations which had less or more connection with the Jews, either as enemies, neighbors, or allies. These prophecies were not delivered at the same time: to some the date is annexed; in others it is left uncertain. **against**. Je 1:10. 4:7. 25:15-29. Ge 10:5. Nu 23:9. Zc 2:8. Ro *3:29.

2. **Against Egypt**. ver. 14. Je 25:9, 19. Ezk ch. 29-32. **Pharaoh-necho**. i.e. *Pharaoh the lame,* ✻S#6549h. 2 K *23:29, 33, 34, 35h, Pharaoh-nechoh. 2 Ch *35:20, 29, Necho. **Carchemish**. Is *10:8, 9. **in the fourth year**. Je 25:1. 36:1. +*45:1n.

3. **Order ye**. This is a poetical and ironical call to the Egyptians to muster their forces; and implies that all their courage and efforts would be vain. Je 51:11, 12. Is 8:9, 10. 21:5. Jl 3:9. Na 2:1. 3:14.

4. **furbish**. Ezk *21:9-11, 28. **brigandines**. or, coats of mail. Je 51:3. 1 S 17:5, 38. 2 Ch 26:14. Ne 4:16.

5. **and their**. Re *6:15. **beaten down**. Heb. broken in pieces. Jb 4:20mg. **fled apace**. Heb. fled a flight. ver. 15. Ge 19:17. 2 K 7:6, 7. Na 2:8. **fear**. Je +6:25. 20:3, 4mg, 10. 49:29. Is 19:16. Ezk 32:10. Re *6:15-17.

6. **not**. Jg 4:15-21. Ps *33:16, 17. 147:10, 11. Ec *9:11. Is 30:16, 17. Am *2:14, 15. *9:1-3. **stumble**. ver. 12. Je 20:11. 50:32. Jg *5:26, 27. Ps 27:2. Is *8:15. Da 11:19, 22. **toward**. ver. 10. Je 1:14. 4:6. 6:1. 25:9.

7. **Who**. Is. SS 3:6. 8:5. Is 63:1. as a flood. Je 47:2. Is *8:7, 8. Da 9:26. 11:22. Am *8:8. Re 12:15.

8. **riseth**. Ezk 29:3. 32:2. **I will go**. Ex *15:9, 10. Is *10:13-16. *37:24-26.

9. **Come**. ∫60A, Ge +3:22. **rage**. Na 2:3, 4. **Ethiopians**. Heb. Cush. Zp 3:10. **Libyans**. Heb. Put. i.e. *afflicted,* ✛S#6316h, so rendered only here. Ge 10:6, Phut. 1 Ch 1:8. Ezk 27:10, Phut. 30:5. Ac 2:10. **Lydians**. i.e. *a magnet; to firebrand, travailing,* ✻S#3866h. Ge 10:13h. 1 Ch 1:11h, Ludim. Is *66:19. Ezk 27:10, Lud. 30:5. Na 3:9, Lubim.

10. **the day**. Je 51:6. Is +*13:6. 34:6, 8. 61:2. 63:4. Ezk +*30:3. Jl 1:15. 2:1. Zp *1:14, 15. Lk *21:22. 1 Th *5:1-5. 2 P *3:10. **the sword**. Dt 32:42)𝒫. Is 34:5-8. Ezk 39:17-21. Zp *1:7, 8. Re *19:17-21. **drunk**. ∫155D, Ge +4:10. Dt 32:42. **hath a sacrifice**. Is 34:6. Ezk 39:17. **the north**. See on ver. 2, 6. 2 K 24:7.

11. **Go**. ∫60A, Ge +3:22. **Gilead**. Je +8:22. 51:8. Ge 37:25. 43:11. Ezk 27:17. **O virgin**. ∫155E5, Nu +21:25. See on Je 14:17. Is 47:1. **in vain**. Is 30:12-15. Ezk 30:21-25. Mi 1:9. Na *3:19. Mk *5:25-28. Lk *8:43, 44. **thou shalt not be cured**. Heb. no cure *shall be* unto thee.

12. **heard**. Ezk *32:9-12. Na 3:8-10. **thy cry**. Je 14:2. 48:34. 49:21. 51:54. 1 S 5:12. Is 15:5-8. Zp 1:10. **stumbled**. See on ver. 6. Is 10:4. 19:2.

13. Cir. A.M. 3398. B.C. 606. **Nebuchadrezzar**. Je 43:10-13. 44:30. Is ch. 19. Ezk ch. 29-32.

14. **Migdol**. See on Je 43:9. 44:1. Ex 14:2. Ezk 30:16-18. **Stand**. See on ver. 3, 4. Je 6:1-5. Jl *3:9-12. **the sword**. See on ver. 10. Je 2:30. 12:12. 2 S 2:26. Is *1:19, 20. 31:8. 34:6. Na 2:13.

15. **thy**. ver. 5, 21. Jg 5:20, 21. Is 66:15, 16. **the Lord**. Ex 6:1. Dt 11:23. Ps 18:14, 39. 44:2. 68:2. 114:2-7.

16. **made many to fall**. Heb. multiplied the faller. Ps 78:38. **one**. Le *26:36, 37)𝒫. **they said**. ver. 21. Je 51:9.

17. **Pharaoh**. Ex *15:9. 1 K 20:10, 18. Is *19:11-16. *31:3. 37:27-29. Ezk 29:3. 31:18. **hath passed**. Je 37:7. 2 S 20:5. **time appointed**. Ge +*17:21h.

18. **saith**. Je 10:10. 44:26. 48:15. 51:57. Is *47:4. 48:2. Ml 1:14. Mt 5:35. 1 T 1:17. **the Lord of hosts**. Je +6:6. **Tabor**. Jsh 19:22. Jg 4:6. Ps 89:12. **Carmel**. 1 K 18:42, 43.

19. **thou**. Je 48:18. **dwelling**. or, inhabitress of. Je 48:18. Ezk 12:2. **furnish thyself to go into captivity**. Heb. make thee instruments of captivity. Is *20:4, 5. Ezk 12:3mg, 4-12. **Noph**. *Noph*, or *Moph*, is the celebrated city of *Memphis*, as the Chaldee and LXX. render; long the residence of the ancient Egyptian kings, and situated fifteen miles above where the Delta begins, on the western side of the Nile (Strabo, l. xvii. Pliny, l. v. c. 9). It was in the neighborhood of Memphis that the famous pyramids were erected, whose grandeur and beauty still astonish the modern traveler: they are about twenty in number; the largest of which is 481 feet perpendicular height, and the area of its basis is on 480,249 square feet, or something more than eleven acres, being exactly the size of Lincoln's Inn Fields in London. The immense ruins between the northern and southern pyramids, and about fourteen miles from Cairo, still called *Memf*, or *Menf*, or *Menouf*, seem to mark the site of this city (See Maillet, p. 265. Savary, etc.). See on Je 44:1. Ezk *30:13, 16. **waste**. Je 26:9. 34:22. 51:29, 37. Zp 2:5.

20. **a very**. Je 50:11. Ho *10:11. **heifer**. Probably an allusion to *Apis*, the sacred bull (CB). ver. 15. **it cometh**. See on ver. 6, 10. Je 1:14. 25:9. 47:2.

21. **her hired**. ver. 9, 16. 2 S 10:6. 2 K 7:6. Ezk 27:10, 11. 30:4-6. **like**. Je 50:11, 27. Is *34:7. **fatted bullocks**. Heb. bullocks of the stall. Pr 15:17. Am 6:4. **they did**. See on ver. 5, 15, 16. **the day**. Je 18:17. Dt *32:35. Ps 37:13. Is *10:3. Ezk 35:5. Ho 9:7. Ob 13. Mi 7:4. **time of**. Je +*8:12.

22. **voice**. Is 29:4. Mi 1:8. 7:16, 17. **and come**. Je 51:20-23. Is *10:15, 33, 34. 14:8. 37:24. Zc 11:2.

23. **cut**. Is 10:18, 19. Ezk 20:46, 47. **because**. Jg *6:5, 6. 7:12. Jl 2:25. Re 9:2-10.

24. **daughter**. See on ver. 11, 19. Ps *137:8, 9. **she shall**. ver. 20. Je 1:15. Ezk ch. 29-32.

25. **Lord of hosts, the God of**. Je +7:3. **punish**. Je +11:22mg. **multitude**. or, nourisher. Pr 8:30. Heb. Amon. Na 3:8mg. **No**. Ezk *30:14-16. Na *3:8-10. **with their**. Je 43:12, 13. Ex 12:12. Is 19:1. Ezk 30:13. Zp 2:11. **and their**. Ezk 32:9-12. Na 3:9. **and all**. Je 17:5, 6. 42:14-16. Is 20:5, 6. 30:2, 3. 31:1-3. Ezk 39:6, 7.

26. **I will**. See on Je 44:30. Ezk *32:11. **lives**. Heb. *nephesh*, souls, Ge +44:30. **and afterward**. Je 48:47. 49:39. Ezk 29:8-14. **old**. Heb. *kedem*, Mi +5:2.

27. **fear**. See on Je 30:10, 11. Is *41:13, 14. *43:1-5. 44:2. **I will save**. Je 23:3, 4. 29:14. 31:8-11. 32:37.

Is √11:11, etc. Ezk *34:10-14. 36:24. 37:21, 22. 39:25. Am √9:14, 15. Mi 7:11-16. **and be**. Je +*23:6. 33:16. 50:19. Ezk 34:25, 26. 39:25.

28. **Fear thou not**. Je 30:10, 11. Ge 26:24)𝒫. Dt 31:8. **for I am**. Je 1:19. 15:20. 30:11. Jsh *1:5, 9. Ps *46:7, 11. Is *8:9, 10. 41:10. *43:2. Mt +*1:23. *28:20. Ac 18:10. 2 T *4:17, 22. **make**. Je 25:9. Is 45:23. Da *2:35. **but I will not**. Je +*4:27. 5:10, 18. 10:24. +*30:11. 32:42-44. 33:24-26. Le √26:44. 1 S +*12:22. Is +*41:9. +60:10. Am √9:8, 9. Zc *10:6. Ro 11:+√1, 15-17. **correct**. See on Je 10:24. Hab 3:2. 1 C 11:32. **will I**. Is 27:7, 9. He 12:5-10. Re *3:19. **not leave thee wholly unpunished**. or, not utterly cut thee off. Ex 20:7)𝒫. 34:7)𝒫. Nu 14:18)𝒫.

JEREMIAH 47

A prophecy against the Philistines, 1-7.

1. Cir. A.M. 3387. B.C. 617. **against**. Je 48:1. 49:1, 7, 23. Ezk 25:15-17. Am 1:6-8. Zp *2:4-7. Zc *9:5-7. **Gaza**. Heb. Azzah. Je 25:20. Ge +10:19mg. 1 K 4:24.

2. **waters**. Je 46:7, 8. Is 8:7, 8. *28:17. 59:19. Da 11:22. Am 9:5, 6. Na 1:8. Re 12:15, 16. 17:1, 15. **out of**. See on Je *1:14. 46:6, 20. **north**. ∫171.O.9, Je +13:20. **all that is therein**. Heb. the fulness thereof. Je 8:16mg. Ps 24:1. 50:12. 96:11. 98:7. Am 6:8mg. 1 C 10:26, 28. **then the**. Je 46:12. 48:3-5, 39. Is 15:2-5, 8. 22:1, 4, 5. Zp 1:10, 11. Ja 5:1. **shall howl**. Am 8:3.

3. **the noise**. Je 8:16. 46:9. Jg *5:22. Jb *39:19-25. Ezk 26:10, 11. Na 2:4. 3:2, 3. **rumbling**. Je +10:13mg. **the fathers**. Dt 28:54, 55. La 4:3, 4.

4. **the day**. See on Je 46:10. Ps 37:13. Is 10:3. Ezk 7:5-7, 12. 21:25, 29. Ho 9:7. Lk 21:22. **Philistines**. i.e. *wanderers; wallowing; watered*, S#6430h. Je 25:20. 47:1, 4, 4. Ge 21:32. 26:1, 8, 14, 15, 18. Ex 13:17. 23:31. Jsh 13:2, 3. Jg 3:3, 31. 10:6, 7, 11. 13:1, 5. 14:1, etc. 15:5, etc. 16:5, etc. 1 S 4:1, etc. 2 S 1:20. 3:14, 18. 5:17, etc. 1 K 4:21. 15:27. 2 K 8:2, 3. 18:8. 1 Ch *1:12. 10:1, etc. 2 Ch 9:26. 17:11. 21:16. 26:6, 7. 28:18. Is 2:6. 9:12. 11:14. Ezk 16:27, 57. 25:15, 16. Am 1:8. 6:2. 9:7. Ob 19. Zp 2:5. Zc 9:6. **Tyrus**. Je 25:20-22. Is ch. 23. Ezk ch. 26-28. Jl 3:4-8. Am 1:9, 10. Zc 9:2-5. **every**. Jb 9:13. Is 20:6. 31:3. Ezk 30:8. **the remnant**. Ezk 25:16. Am 1:8. *9:7. **country**. Heb. isle. Jb 22:30. Is 20:6. **Caphtor**. i.e. *crown; hollow goblet*, ✱S#3731h. Ge 10:13, 14, Caphtorim. Dt 2:23h. 1 Ch 1:12, Caphthorim. Am 9:7h.

5. **Baldness**. ∫121S1, Ge +49:10. By Metonymy of the Adjunct, whereby the sign is put for the thing signified, "baldness" is put for grief, from the practice of shaving the head in grief. Je 16:6. 48:37. Is *15:2. Ezk 7:18. Mi 1:16. **Gaza**. ∫121J14, Ge +47:15. See on ver. 1. Am *1:6-8. Zp *2:4-7. Zc 9:5-7. **the remnant**. ver. 4. Je 25:20. Ezk 25:16. **how**. Je 16:1. 41:5. 48:37. Le 19:28. 21:5. Dt 14:1. 1 K 18:28. Mk 5:5.

6. **thou sword**. ∫38G, Dt +32:1. Je 12:12. 15:3. 25:27. 51:20-23. Dt *32:41, 42)𝒫. Ps 17:13. Is 10:5, 15. Ezk 14:17. *21:3-5. **how long**. See on Je 4:21. 12:4. 2 S 2:26. **put up thyself**. Heb. gather thyself. Je 4:5. Ge 49:1. into. 1 Ch 21:27. Eze 21:30. Jn 18:11.

7. **can it**. Heb. canst thou. **the Lord**. 1 S 15:3. Is 10:6. 13:3. 37:26. 45:1-3. 46:10, 11. Ezk 14:17. Am +*3:6. **the sea**. Ezk 25:16. Zp 2:6, 7. **hath he**. Mi *6:9.

JEREMIAH 48

A prophecy against Moab, for presuming on her wealth, 1-10; her uninterrupted prosperity, 11-13, and her strength for war, 14, 15; and for her contempt of God and his people; and her great pride, etc., 16-46. The restoration of Moab, 47.

1. A.M. cir. 3420. B.C. cir. 584. **Moab.** Je 9:26. 25:21. 27:3. Ge 19:37. Nu +*24:17. Jg 3:12, 28. 1 S 14:47. 2 S 8:2. 2 K 1:1. 3:4-27. 13:20. 2 Ch √20:10-12. Is ch. 15, 16. 25:10. 27:3. Ezk 25:8-11. Am 2:1, 2. Zp 2:8-11. **thus saith.** Nu 21:28, 29. 24:17. Am 2:2. Zp 2:8, 9. **the Lord of hosts, the God of Israel.** Je +7:3. **Nebo.** ver. 22, 23. Nu 32:3, 37, 38. 33:47. Is 15:2. **Kiriathaim.** i.e. *double city*, ✛S#7156h. Je 48:1, 23. Ezk 25:9. See also ✛S#7156h, Nu 32:37, Kirjathaim. Compare ✳S#7741h, Ge 14:5, Shaveh Kiriathaim. **Misgab.** or, The high place. i.e. *height, safety*, ✳S#4870h.

2. **no more.** ver. 17. Is 16:14. **Heshbon.** ver. 34, 45. Nu *21:+25-30. 32:37. Is 15:5. 16:8, 9. **come.** ver. 42. Je 31:36. 33:24. 46:28. Est 3:8-14. Ps 83:4-8. **thou shalt.** Je 25:15, 17. **cut down.** or, brought to silence. Je 8:14. Ps 31:17mg. Is 15:1mg. **Madmen.** i.e. *dunghill*, ✳S#4086h, only here. Is 25:10mg, Madmenah. **pursue thee.** Heb. go after thee. Je +17:16mg.

3. **voice.** See on Je 4:20, 21. 47:2. Is *15:2, 8. *16:7-11. 22:4. **Horonaim.** ver. 5, 34. Is 15:5.

4. **Moab.** This prophecy against Moab, as well as the following ones concerning Ammon, Edom, and the neighboring countries, seem to have been fulfilled during the long siege of Tyre by Nebuchadnezzar. Josephus places these events five years after the destruction of Jerusalem. Nu 21:27-30. **her.** Est 8:11. Ps 137:9.

5. **Luhith.** *Luhith* is placed by Eusebius between Areopolis, or Ar, and Zoar (See ver. 34). It was evidently situated upon a height, as was also *Horonaim*, which was probably not far from Luhith. Is *15:5. **continual weeping.** Heb. weeping with weeping. ♪147D. Polyptoton, Ge +1:29. 2 S 13:36.

6. **Flee.** Je *51:6. Ge 19:17. Ps 11:1. Pr 6:4, 5. Mt *24:15-18. Lk 3:7. *17:30-33. He +*6:18. **lives.** Heb. *nephesh*, Ge +44:30. **be like.** Je 17:6. Jb 30:3-7. **the heath.** or, a naked tree. Je 17:6.

7. **because.** Je 9:23. 13:25. Ps *40:4. 49:6, 7. *52:7. *62:8-10. Is 59:4-6. Ezk *28:2-5. Ho 10:13. 1 T √6:17. Re 18:7. **Chemosh.** ver. 13, 46. Je 43:12. Nu 21:29ἢℙ. Jg 11:24. 1 K 11:7, 33. 2 K 23:13. Is 46:1, 2. **his priests.** Je 49:3.

8. **the spoiler.** ver. 18. Je 6:26. 15:8. 25:9. 51:56. **and no.** ver. 20-25. Ezk *25:9. **city.** ♪121J19, 1 S +22:19.

9. **wings.** ver. 28. Ps 11:1. 55:6. Is *16:2. Re 12:14. **the cities.** See on Je 46:19. Zp 2:9.

10. **Cursed.** Je 50:25. Nu *31:14-18. Jg *5:23. 1 S *15:3, 9, 13, etc. 1 K *20:42. 2 K 13:19. **work of the Lord.** 1 C √15:58. He *6:10. **deceitfully.** or, negligently. The immediate reference in context is to the work of judgment pronounced against Moab, but the spiritual principles stated remain true for all time. Ge +*27:12. Ex ◐+*15:26. 2 Ch 24:5. Ne 3:5. Jb 13:7. Ps 32:2. 78:57. Pr +*10:4. 12:24mg. Ezk *33:31. Mi 6:12. Mt 25:26. Lk *16:10. Ro *12:11, 17. 1 Th √5:22. He +*6:12.

11. **hath been.** Ps *55:19. 73:4-8. 123:4. Pr 1:32mg. Zc 1:15. **he hath.** Is 25:6. Zp *1:12. **emptied.** Je 51:34.

Is 24:3. Na 2:2, 10. **therefore.** ver. 29. Is 16:6. Ezk 16:49, 50. **remained.** Heb. stood.

12. **wanderers.** ver. 8, 15. Je 25:9. Is 16:2. Ezk 25:9, 10. **empty.** ver. 11, 38. Je 14:3. 19:10. 25:34. Ps *2:9. Is *30:14. Na 2:2.

13. **ashamed.** ver. 7, 39, 46. Jg 11:24. 1 S 5:3-7. 1 K 11:7. 18:26-29, 40. Is *2:20. *16:12. *45:16, 20. 46:1, 2. **as the.** 1 K *12:28, 29. Ho 8:5, 6. *10:5, 6, 14, 15. Am 5:5, 6. **house of Israel.** Je +2:4.

14. **How.** Je 8:8. Ps 11:1. Is *36:4, 5. **We.** Je 9:23. 49:16. Ps 33:16. Ec 9:11. Is *10:13, 16. 16:6. Ezk 30:6. Zp 2:10.

15. **spoiled.** See on ver. 8, 9, 18, 25. **his chosen.** Heb. the choice of his, etc. Is √40:30, 31. **gone.** ver. 4. Je 50:27. 51:40. Is 34:2-8. **saith.** Je 46:18. 51:57. Ps 24:8-10. 47:2. Da 4:37. Zc 14:9. Ml 1:14. Re 19:16. **whose name is.** Je +10:16. Ex +*6:3n. Ps +68:4. +*83:18. **Lord of hosts.** Je +6:6. Ja +5:4.

16. **near.** Je 1:12. Dt 32:35. Is 13:22. *16:13, 14. Ezk 12:23, 28. 2 P 2:3.

17. **bemoan.** ver. 31-33. Je 9:17-20. Is 16:8. Re *18:14-20. **How.** ver. 39. Is 9:4. 10:5. 14:4, 5. Ezk 19:11-14. Zc 11:10-14.

18. **daughter.** Je 46:18, 19. Is 47:1. **Dibon.** ver. 22. Nu *21:30. 32:3. Jsh 13:17. Is 15:2. **and sit.** Ge 21:16. Ex 17:3. Jg 15:18. Is 5:13. Ezk 19:13. **the spoiler.** ver. 8.

19. **inhabitant.** Heb. inhabitress. Je +10:17mg. 21:13. **Aroer.** Nu *32:34. Dt 2:36. 2 S 24:5. 1 Ch 5:8. **ask.** 1 S 4:13, 14, 16. 2 S 1:3, 4. 18:24-32.

20. **confounded.** ver. 1-5. Is *15:1-5, 8. 16:7-11. **Arnon.** Nu *21:13, 14, 26-28. Dt 2:36. Jsh 13:9. Jg 11:18. Is 16:2.

21. **the plain.** ver. 8. Ezk 25:9. Zp 2:9. **Jahazah.** Jsh 13:18, Jahaza. 21:36, 37. Is 15:4, Jahaz.

22. **Dibon.** ver. 1, 18. Nu 32:34. **Beth-diblathaim.** i.e. *house of two fig cakes*, ✳S#1015h, only here. Nu 33:46, Almon-diblathaim. Ezk 6:14, Diblath.

23. **Kiriathaim.** ver. +1. Ge 14:5, Shaveh Kiriathaim. Jsh 13:19, Kirjathaim. **Beth-gamul.** i.e. *house of the weaned; house of recompense; house of the rewarded*, ✳S#1014h, only here. **Beth-meon.** i.e. *house of habitation*, ✳S#1010h. Nu 32:38, Baal-meon. Jsh 13:17, Beth-baal-meon.

24. **Kerioth.** ver. 41. Am 2:2. **Bozrah.** Dt 4:43, Bezer. Jsh 21:36, Bezor. Zp *2:8-10.

25. **horn.** Ps 75:10. La 2:3. Da 7:8. 8:7-9, 21. Zc 1:19-21. **and his.** Nu 32:37. Jb 22:9. Ps 10:15. 37:17. Ezk 30:21-25.

26. **ye him.** Je 13:13, 14. 25:15-17, 27-29. 51:7, 39, 57. Ps 60:3. *75:8. Is 29:9. 51:17. 63:6. La 3:15. 4:21. Ezk 23:31-34. Na 3:11. Re 16:19. **for he.** ver. 42. Ex 5:2. 9:17. Jb 9:4. Is 10:15. Ezk 35:12, 13. Da 5:23. 8:11, 12. 11:36. Zp 2:8-10. 2 Th 2:4. **wallow.** Is 19:14. 29:9. Hab 2:16. **and he also.** ver. 39. Ps *2:4. 59:8. La 1:21. Ezk 23:32.

27. **was not.** Ps *44:13. 79:4. Pr 24:17, 18. La 2:15-17. Ezk 25:8. 26:2, 3. 35:15. 36:2, 4. Ob *12, *13. Mi 7:8-10. Zp 2:8, 10. Mt 7:2. **was he found.** Je 2:26. Mt 26:55. 27:38. **skippedst.** or, movedst thyself. Je 31:18. Is 24:20.

28. **leave.** ver. 9. Jg 6:2. 1 S 13:6. Is 2:19. Ob 3, 4. **dwell in.** Pr 30:26. **like.** Je 49:16. Ps 55:6, 7. SS *2:14.

29. **heard.** Pr 8:13. Is 16:6. Zp 2:8-10, etc. **pride.** ♪173, Ge +27:44. **his loftiness.** Jb 40:10-12. Ps 138:6.

Pr 18:12. 30:13. Is *2:11, 12. Da 4:37. Lk *14:11. Ja *4:6.

30. **know.** Is 16:6. *37:28, 29. **his lies shall not so effect it.** or, those on whom he stayeth (Heb. his bars) do not right. *Baddim*, as Lowth observes, sometimes means those who pretend to the art of divination. Though the soothsayers of Moab, upon whose skill she relies, promise him success, yet in the event it will appear there was no truth in what they said. Je 50:36. Jb 9:12, 13. Ps *33:10. Pr +*21:30.

31. **will I howl.** See on Is 15:5. *16:7-11. **Kir-heres.** i.e. *city or wall of brick; the wall is earthen,* ✛S#7025h. ver. 36. 2 K 3:25, Kar-haraseth. Is 16:7, Kir-hareseth, 11, Kir-haresh.

32. **vine.** Nu *32:37, 38, Shibmah. Jsh 13:19. Is *16:8, 9. **Jazer.** Nu 21:32, Jaazer. 32:1, 35. Jsh 21:39. **the spoiler.** ver. 8, 15, 18. Je 40:10.

33. **joy.** Je 25:9, 10. Is 9:3. 16:9. 24:7-12. 32:9-14. Jl *1:12, 16. Re 18:22, 23. **caused.** Is 5:10. 7:23. 16:10. Jl 1:5, 12, 13. Hg 2:16.

34. **the cry.** See on ver. 2. Is √15:4-6. **Elealeh.** Nu 32:37. **Jahaz.** See on ver. 21, Jahazah. **Zoar.** ver. 3, 5. Dt 34:3. Is 15:5. **as an heifer of.** As a young cow, when deprived of her first calf; which runs about from place to place, filling the air with loud and repeated lowings, expressive of the deepest distress. **Nimrim.** Nu 32:3, Nimrah, 36, Beth-nimrah. Is 15:6. **desolate.** Heb. desolations. Is 15:6mg.

35. **him that offereth.** ver. 7. Nu *22:40, 41. 28:14, 28-30. Is *15:2. *16:12. **high places.** 2 K +21:3.

36. **mine heart.** Je 4:19. Is 15:5. 16:11. 63:15. **like pipes.** Mt 9:23. **Kir-heres.** See on ver. 31. **the riches.** Je 17:11. Pr *11:4. 13:22. 18:11. Ec 5:13, 14. Is 15:7. Lk *12:20, 21. Ja *5:2, 3.

37. **every head.** Je 16:6. 41:5. 47:5. Is *3:24. 15:2, 3. Ezk *7:18. 27:31. Am 8:10. Mi 1:16. **clipped.** Heb. diminished. **cuttings.** Le 19:28. 1 K 18:28. Mk 5:5. **upon the loins.** Ge 37:29, 34. 1 K 21:27. 2 K 6:30. Is 20:2. 37:1. Am 8:10. Re 11:3.

38. **upon.** Is *15:3. 22:1. **broken.** Je 22:28. 25:34. Ps *2:9. Is 30:14. Ho 8:8. Ro 9:21, 22. 2 T 2:20, 21. Re *2:26, 27.

39. **How is it.** See on ver. 17. La 1:1. 2:1. *4:1. Re 18:9, 10, 15, 16. **back.** Heb. neck. Je 46:5. **a derision.** See on ver. 26, 27. Is 20:4-6. Ezk 26:16-18. **dismaying.** Je 49:37. Ezk 32:23mg.

40. **he shall.** Je 4:13. Dt 28:49. La 4:19. Ezk 17:3. Da 7:4. Ho 8:1. Hab 1:8. **as an eagle.** Dt 28:49➧℗. **spread.** Je 49:22. Is 8:8.

41. **Kerioth.** or, The cities. ver. 24. **as the heart.** Je 4:31. 6:24. 30:6. 49:22, 24. 50:43. 51:30. Is 13:8. 21:3. 26:17, 18. Mi 4:9, 10. 1 Th *5:3.

42. **Moab.** Moab has long since ceased to be a nation; while the Jews, agreeably to the Divine promise (Je +*46:28), though successively subdued and oppressed by the Egyptians, Assyrians, Babylonians, Syro-Macedonians, and Romans, (which have also all passed away, and are no more), and dispersed over the face of the earth, subsist to this day as a distinct people from all the nations of the world! **from.** See on ver. 2. Je *30:11. Est 3:8-13. Ps 83:4-8. Is 7:8. Mt 7:2. **magnified.** See on ver. 26-30. Pr *16:18. Is *37:23. Da *11:36. 2 Th *2:3, 4. Re *13:5, 6.

43. **Fear.** Dt 32:23-25. Ps *11:6. Is *24:17, 18. La 3:47.

44. **that fleeth.** Je 16:16. 1 K *19:17. 20:30. Is 37:36-

38. Am 2:14, 15. 5:19. 9:1-4. **and he that.** Is *24:17, 18. **the year.** ʃ171Tl, Is +61:2. Je +*8:12. 10:15. 11:23. 23:12. 46:21. 51:18. Is 10:3. Ho 9:7. Mi 7:4.

45. **a fire.** Nu *21:28➧℗. Am 2:2. **devour.** Nu 24:17➧℗. Zc 10:4. Mt 21:42. **tumultuous ones.** Heb. children of noise.

46. **Woe.** ʃ110, Ezk 34:2. Nu 21:29. **the people.** ver. 7, 13. Jg 11:24. 1 K 11:7. 2 K 23:13. **of Chemosh.** Nu 21:29➧℗. **captives.** Heb. in captivity. Is 49:25mg.

47. **Yet will I bring.** Many of the Moabites were afterwards restored to their country by Cyrus, as we learn from Josephus; but they were never restored to their national consequence; and perhaps their restoration in the *latter days* refers to the conversion of their scattered remnants to the gospel. The Moabites are one of several nations promised to be regathered in the latter days: Elam, Je 49:39; Ammon, Je 49:6; Israel, Je 46:27, 28. Moab and Ammon were the children of Lot. Je 46:26. 49:6, 39. Is *18:7. *19:18-23. 23:18. Ezk 16:+*49, 53-55, 60. **in the latter.** See on Je 23:20. 30:24. Nu 24:14. Dt 4:30. 31:29. Jb +*19:25. Ezk 38:8. Da 2:28. 10:14. Ho 3:5.

JEREMIAH 49

Prophecies concerning the Ammonites, 1-6; Edom, 7-22; Damascus, 23-27; Kedar and Hazor, 28-33; and Elam, 34-39.

1. A.M. 3421. B.C. 583. **Concerning.** or, Against. ver. 7, 23, 28. Je 48:1. **Ammonites.** Je 25:9, 21. 27:3. Ge *19:38. Dt *2:19. *23:3. 2 Ch 20:1, 23. Ps 83:7. Ezk 21:28-32. *25:2-10. Am *1:13-15. Zp *2:8-11. **their king.** or, Melcom. Jg 10:7, 8. 11:13-15. 1 S 11:1-3. 2 K 10:33. +23:13. 24:2. Ne 2:19. 4:7. 13:1, 2. **cities.** Ps 9:6.

2. **that I will.** Je 4:19. Ezk 25:4-6. Am *1:14. **Rabbah.** Dt 3:11. Jsh 13:24, 25. Ezk 21:20, Rabbath. **her daughters.** Nu +*21:25mg. 2 S 11:1. 12:27-29. Ps 48:11. 97:8. Ezk 16:46-55. **shall Israel.** ver. 1. Is *14:1-3. Ob 19.

3. **Howl.** Je 48:20. 51:8. Is 13:6. 14:31. 15:2. 16:7. 23:1, 6. Ja *5:1. **gird.** Je 4:8. 6:26. See on 48:37. Is *32:11, 12. **run.** Jb 30:3-7. Is 15:2. **their king.** or, Melcom. ver. 1. 1 K 11:5, 33. 2 K 23:13, Milcom. Zp 1:5, Malcham. **shall go.** Je 46:25. 48:7. Am 1:15.

4. **gloriest.** Je +*9:23. Is 28:1-4. 47:7, 8. Re *18:7, 8. **thy flowing valley.** or, thy valley floweth away. **O backsliding.** Je 3:14. 7:24. Ho 4:16. **trusted.** Je 48:7. Ps 49:6. 52:7. 62:10. Pr 10:15. Ezk 28:4-7. 1 T 6:17. **Who.** ver. 16. Je 21:13. Ob 4, 5.

5. **I will.** ver. 29. Je 15:8. 20:4. 48:41-44. Jsh *2:9. 2 K 7:6, 7. 19:7. Jb 15:21. Pr *28:1. **Lord God of hosts.** Je +2:19. **ye shall.** Je 46:5. Am 4:3. **none.** Is 16:3. Ob 12-14.

6. **afterward.** ver. 39. Je 46:26. 48:47. Is 19:18-23. 23:18. Ezk *16:53.

7. **Edom.** Je 25:9, 21. Ge *25:30. 27:41. *36:8. Nu *20:14-21. +*24:17, 18. Dt *23:7. Ps 83:4-10. 137:7. Is ch. 34. 63:1-6. Ezk 25:12-14. ch. 35. Da 11:41. Jl 3:19. Am 1:11, 12. Ob 1, etc. Ml 1:3, 4. **Lord of hosts.** Je +6:6. **Is wisdom.** Je 18:18. Jb 5:12-14. Is 19:11-13. 29:14. Ob 8. Ro 1:22, 23. **Teman.** ver. 20. Ge 36:11, 15. 1 Ch 1:53. Jb 2:11. 4:1. Ezk 25:13. Am 1:12. Ob 9. Hab 3:3.

8. **Flee.** ver. 30. Je 6:1. 48:6. Mt 24:15-18. Re 6:15. **turn back.** or, they are turned back. Ezk 9:2mg. **dwell**

deep. This is an allusion to the custom of the Arabs, who, when attacked by a powerful foe, withdraw into the *depths* of the wilderness, *au fond du desert*, as Niebuhr expresses it (*Descript. de l'Arabie*, p. 329. *Voyage*, tom. ii. p. 199) whither none can follow them. So M. Savary (Lettre i. sur l'Egypte, tom. ii. p. 8), says, speaking of the Bedouins, "Always on their guard against tyranny, on the least discontent that is given them, they pack up their tents, lade their camels with them, ravage the flat country, and, laden with plunder, *plunge* (s' enfoncent) into the burning sands, where none can pursue them." Je 48:28. Jg 6:2. 1 S 13:6. Is 2:21. Am 9:1-3. Ob 3, 4. **Dedan.** Je 25:23. Is *21:13, 14. Ezk 25:13. **for.** ver. 32. Je 46:21. 48:44. La 4:21, 22.

9. **grapegatherers.** Is *17:6. Ob *5, 6. **till they have enough.** Heb. their sufficiency. Ex 36:7.

10. **I have made.** Ml +*1:2-4. Ro +*9:12, 13. **his secret.** Je 23:24. Is 45:3. Am 9:3. **his seed.** Ps 37:28. Is 14:20-22. Ob 9. **he is not.** Ps 37:35, 36. Is 17:14.

11. **the fatherless.** Dt +*10:18. Ps 10:14-18. *68:5. 82:3. *146:9. Pr 23:10, 11. Ho 14:3. Jon 4:11. Ml +*3:5. Ja *1:27. **let thy.** 1 T 5:5.

12. **they whose.** See on Je 25:28, 29. 30:11. 46:27. Pr 17:5. La *4:21, 22. Ob 16. 1 P *4:17, 18. **cup.** ♪121J13. Metonymy of the Subject B577. "Cup" is put for the wine in it. For other instances of this figure see Ezk 23:32. Lk 22:17, 20. 1 C 10:16, 21. 11:25, 26, 27, 28. **not go unpunished.** Ex 34:7.

13. **I have.** See on Je 44:26. Ge 22:16♪℘. Is 45:23. Ezk 35:11. Am 6:8. **Bozrah.** ver. 22. Ge 36:33. Is *34:6. *63:1. Am *1:12. **a desolation.** ver. 17, 18. Is 34:9-15. Ezk 25:13, 14. 35:2-15. Jl *3:19. Ob 18, 19. Ml 1:3, 4. **perpetual.** Ge +*9:12.

14. **heard.** Je 51:46. Is 37:7. Ezk 7:25, 26. Ob 1. Mt 24:6. **an ambassador.** Is 18:2, 3. 30:4. **Gather.** Je 50:9-16. 51:11, 27, 28. Is 13:2, 3.

15. **I will make.** 1 S *2:7, 8, 30. Ps 53:5. Ob 2. Mi 7:10. Lk *1:51.

16. **terribleness.** Or, monstrous thing; i.e. an Edomite Asherah, CB. Je 48:29. Pr *16:18. 18:12. 29:23. Is 25:4, 5. 49:25. 66:17n. Ob 3. **dwellest.** SS 2:14. Is 2:21. **the rock.** Probably *Sela,* or Petra. 2 K 14:7n. **though.** Je 48:28. Jb 39:27, 28. Is *14:13-15. Ezk *28:11-19. Am 9:2. Ob 4.

17. **Edom.** ver. 13. Is 34:9-15. Ezk *25:13, 14. 35:7, 15. **every.** ver. 18. Is 16:16. 50:13. **shall hiss.** 1 K 9:8. 2 Ch 7:20, 21. La 2:15, 16. Mi 6:16. Zp 2:15.

18. **in the overthrow.** Je 50:40. Ge *19:24, 25♪℘. Dt 29:23♪℘. Ps 11:6. Is 13:19-22. Am 4:11. Zp 2:9. Lk *17:28-30. 2 P 2:6. Ju +*7. Re *11:8. **no man.** ver. 33. Jb 18:15-18. Is 34:10. Re 18:21-23.

19. **he shall come.** Je 4:7. 50:44, etc. Zc 11:3. **the swelling.** Je +*12:5. Jsh *3:15. 1 Ch *12:15. **who is like.** See on Ex *15:11. Ps 89:6, 8. 113:5, 6. Is 40:25. **appoint me the time.** *or,* convent me in judgment. Jb 9:19-21. 23:3-7. 40:2-8. 42:3-5. Ps 143:2. **that shepherd.** See on Je 30:21. Jb 41:10. Ps 76:7. Na 1:6. Re 6:17.

20. **the counsel.** Je 50:45. Ps *33:11. Pr *19:21. Is 14:24-27. 46:10, 11. Ac 4:28. Ep +*1:11. **Teman.** See on ver. 7. Jb 6:19, 20. **Surely.** The prophet having given the name of the *shepherd* to the generals of the army, pursues the same metaphor, calling the common soldiers "the least of the flock;" who shall have strength and courage enough to defeat the Idumean

forces. Je 37:10. 50:45. Zc √4:6. 1 C 1:27-29. **make.** See on ver. 13, 17, 18. Ml 1:3, 4.

21. **earth.** Je 50:46. Is 14:4-15. Ezk 26:15, 18. 31:16. 32:10. Re *18:10. **Red sea.** Heb. Weedy sea. 1 K 9:26.

22. **he shall.** Je 4:13. 48:40, 41. Dt *28:49♪℘. Da *7:4. Ho *8:1. **Bozrah.** See on ver. 13. **the heart of the.** ver. 24. Je 4:31. 6:24. 13:21. 22:23. 30:6. 48:41. Ps 18:5. Is 13:8. 21:3. 26:17. 1 Th *5:3.

23. **Damascus.** Ge 14:15. 15:2. 1 K 11:24. Is 17:1-3. 37:13. Am *1:3-5. Zc 9:1, 2. 2 C 11:32. **Hamath.** ♪121J19, 1 S +22:19. Nu 13:21. 2 S 8:9. 2 K 17:24. 18:34. 19:13. Is 10:9. *11:11. 36:19. 37:13. **evil.** Is +45:7. **fainthearted.** Heb. melted. Dt 20:8mg. Jsh 2:11. 14:8. 2 S 17:10. Is 13:7. Na 2:10. **sorrow.** Is 57:20. **on the sea.** *or,* as on the sea. Ps 107:26, 27. Lk 8:23, 24. *21:25, 26. Ac 27:20. Re 15:2.

24. **anguish.** See on ver. 22.

25. **How.** Je 33:9. 48:2, 39. 51:41. Ps 37:35, 36. Is 1:26. 14:4-6. Da 4:30. Re *18:10, 16-19. **not left.** Not restored, strengthened, or fortified. A Hebrew homonym with two meanings: (1) to leave, or forsake, as at Ge 2:24; 39:6; Ne 5:10; Ps 49:10; Ml 4:1. (2) to help, or restore, strengthen or fortify, as at Ex 23:5; Dt 32:36; 1 K 14:10; 2 K 14:26; Ne 3:8; Je 49:25.

26. **young men.** Je 9:21. 11:22. 50:30. 51:3, 4. La *2:21. Ezk 27:27. Am *4:10.

27. **I will.** See on Am *1:3-5. **Ben-hadad.** 1 K 15:18-20. 20:1, etc. 2 K 13:5.

28. **Kedar.** Je 2:10. Ge *25:13. 1 Ch *1:29. SS 1:5. Is *21:13, 16, 17. 42:11. Ezk 27:21. **Hazor.** ver. 30, 33. **Arise.** ver. 14, 31. Je 50:14-16. Is 13:2-5. **spoil.** Ge 25:6. Jg 6:3. Jb 1:3. Is 11:14.

29. **tents.** Ps *120:5. Is 13:20. *60:7. **curtains.** Je 4:20. 10:20. Hab *3:7. **camels.** Ge 37:25. Jg 6:5. 7:12. 8:21, 26. 1 Ch 5:20, 21. Jb 1:3. **Fear.** ver. 24. Je 6:25. 20:3mg, 4, 10. 46:5. Ps 31:13. La 2:22. 2 C *4:8-10. 7:5.

30. **get you far off.** Heb. flit greatly. Je 50:8. Ps 11:1. **dwell.** See on ver. 8. **for.** Je 25:9, 24, 25. 27:6. Is *10:7.

31. **wealthy nation.** *or,* nation that is at ease. Je 48:11. Jb 16:12. Ps 123:4. Is 32:9, 11. Ezk 23:42. **that.** Jg 18:7-10, 27. Is 47:8. Ezk 30:9. 38:11. 39:6. Na 1:12. Zp 2:15. **which dwell.** Nu *23:9♪℘. Dt *33:28♪℘. Jg 18:28. Ezk 38:11, 12. Mi 7:14.

32. **their camels.** See on ver. 29. **I will scatter.** ver. 36. Dt *28:64. Ezk *5:10, 12. 12:14, 15. **winds.** ♪121.O, Ge +28:22. **in the utmost corners.** Heb. cut off into corners, *or,* that have the corners *of their hair* polled. Je 9:26mg. 25:23mg.

33. **Hazor.** *Hazor,* as well as *Kedar,* with which it is joined (ver. 28), was no doubt situated in Arabia, and a place of considerable importance; but it is now no more, and its very name seems to have perished. **a dwelling.** ver. 17, 18. Je 9:11. 10:22. 50:39, 40. 51:37. Is *13:20-22. 14:23. 34:9-17. Zp 2:9, 13-15. Ml 1:3. Re 18:2, 21, 22. **for ever.** Heb. *olam,* Ex +*12:24.

34. Cir. A.M. 3406. B.C. 598. **Elam.** *Elam,* the *Elymais* of the Greeks and Romans, was properly a province of the Persian empire, between Media and Susiana; but sometimes the name Elam is used in a larger sense, including Susiana and other provinces (see Da 8:2), all of which were subdued by Nebuchadnezzar, and afterwards restored and raised to dignity by Cyrus. Je 25:25. Ge *10:22. 14:1. Ezr *4:9, 10. Is 21:2. Ezk 32:24, 25. Da *8:2. Ac *2:8, 9.

35. **break**. Je 50:14, 29. 51:56. Ps 46:9. Is 22:6. **the bow**. Strabo says that the mountainous part of *Elymais* chiefly bred archers; and Livy (l. xxxvii. c. 40) speaks of *Elymaei sagittarii*, "the Elymean archers."

36. **the four winds**. Da 7:2, 3. 8:8, 22. 11:4. Re *7:1. **scatter**. ver. 32. Dt 28:25, 64. Ezk 5:10, 12. Am 9:9. **the outcasts**. Je 30:17. Ps 147:2. Is 11:12. 16:3, 4. 27:13. 56:8.

37. **to be**. ver. 5, 22, 24, 29. Je 43:39. 48:39. 50:36. Ps 48:4-6. Ezk 32:23mg. **their enemies**. See on Je 34:20, 21. **life**. Heb. *nephesh*, Ge +44:30. **I will send the sword**. Je 9:16. 48:2. Le 26:33. Ezk 5:2, 12. 12:14.

38. **will set my throne**. Je 43:10. Da 7:9-14.

39. **in the**. Je 48:47. Is 2:2. Ezk 38:16. Da 2:28. 10:14. Ho 3:5. Mi 4:1. **I will**. See on ver. 6. Jb 42:10. Ezk 16:53-55. 29:14. 39:25. Am √9:14.

JEREMIAH 50

Prophecies against Babylon, for all her idolatries and iniquities, but particularly for her oppression of God's people, 1-3; 9-17; 21-32; 35-46; intermixed with many and great mercies to Israel, 4-8; 18-20; 33, 34.

1. A.M. 3409. B.C. 595. **against Babylon**. Je 25:26, 27. 27:7. 51:1, etc. Ps *137:8, 9. Is 13:1-3. 14:4. 21:1-10. ch. 47. Hab 2:5-20. Re ch. 18. **the land**. Ge 11:31. Jb 1:17. Is 23:13. Ac 7:4. **Jeremiah**. Heb. the hand of Jeremiah. Je +37:2mg. 2 S 23:2. 1 K +16:12mg. Zc 7:7, 12. 2 P *1:21.

2. **Declare**. Je 6:18. 31:10. 46:14. Ps 64:9. 96:3. Is 12:4. 48:6. 66:18, 19. Re *14:6-8. **set up**. Heb. lift up. Je 4:5, 6. 46:14. Is 13:2. **Babylon is taken**. Je 51:8. Is 21:9. Re 14:8. 18:2, 6, 10, 21. **Bel**. Je 51:44. Is 46:1. **Merodach**. i.e. *death and slaughter; warlike*, *S#4781h, only here. Je 52:31. Is 39:1. **her idols**. ver. 47. See on Je 43:12, 13. Is 37:19. Zp 2:11. **images**. Le 26:30. Xerxes, after his return from his unsuccessful expedition into Greece, partly out of religious zeal, being a professed enemy to image worship, and partly to reimburse himself after his immense expenses, seized the sacred treasures, and plundered or destroyed the temples and idols of Babylon, thereby accomplishing the prophecies of Isaiah and Jeremiah (Is 21:9. 46:1. Je 50:2. 51:44, 47, 52). What God declares, "I will punish Bel in Babylon, and I will bring forth that which he has swallowed," was also literally fulfilled, when the vessels of the house of God, which Nebuchadnezzar had brought from Jerusalem and placed in the temple of the temple of Bel, Da 1:2, were restored by order of Cyrus, Ezr 1:7, and again carried to Jerusalem (Bp. Newton, Dis. X).

3. **out of the**. The *Medes*, who formed the greatest part of the army of Cyrus. *Media* lay N.E. of Babylon. ver. 9, 41. Je 51:11, 27, 48. Is 13:5, 17, 18. **north**. ∫171.O.10, Je +6:1. **which**. ver. 12, 13, 35-40. Je 51:8, 9, 25, 26, 37-44, 62. Is *13:6-10, 19-22. *14:22-24. Re 18:21-23. **both**. Je 7:20. 21:6. Ge 6:7. Ex 12:12. Ezk 14:13-31. Zp 1:3.

4. **those**. ver. 20. Je 3:16-18. 33:15. 51:47, 48. Is 63:4. **the children of Israel**. ver. 19, 20, 33, 34. Je 3:18. 23:6-8. 30:10, 11. 31:6, 7, 31. 33:7. Is *11:12, 13. *14:1. Ezk 37:16-22. *39:25. Ho *1:11. **going**. Je 31:9, 10, 18. Ezr 3:12, 13. Ps 126:4-6. Jl 2:12. Zc 12:10-14. Ja 4:9. Re 1:7. **seek the**. Je 29:12-14. Ps 105:4. Is 45:19. 55:6. Ho 3:5. Zc 8:21-23.

5. **ask**. Je 6:16. Ps 25:8, 9. *84:7. Is 35:8. Jn 7:17.

saying. ∫63BA, Ge +26:7. **Come**. Je 31:31-36. Is *2:3-5. Mi 4:1, 2. Ac 11:23. 2 C 8:5. **join**. Is +56:3. 1 C +*6:17. **in a**. Je 32:40. Ge 17:7. 2 S 23:5. Is +*55:3. 56:6, 7. **perpetual**. Heb. *olam*, Ge +9:12. Je 3:18—4:2. 11:1-6. 31:31. **that shall**. Je 32:40. 1 K 19:10, 14. He 8:6-10.

6. **people**. ver. 17. Ps 119:176. Is √53:6. Mt *9:36. *10:6. *15:24. 18:11-13. Lk 15:4-7. Ro 11:26. 1 P 2:25. **their shepherds**. Je 10:21. 23:11-15. Is 56:10-12. Ezk 34:4-12. Zc 11:4-9. **turned**. Je 3:14, 22. Is +57:17mg. **on the**. Je 2:20. 3:6, 23. Ezk 34:6. **have forgotten**. Je 2:32. Ps 32:7. 90:1. 91:1. 116:7. Is 30:15. 32:2. **resting place**. Heb. place to lie down in. Ps *23:2. SS 1:7, 8. Is 32:18. Ezk 34:14, 25-28. Mt 9:36mg.

7. **have devoured**. ver. 17, 33. Je 12:7-11. Ps 79:7. Is 9:12. 56:9. **We offend**. ver. 15, 23, 29. Je 2:3. 25:14, 15. 40:2, 3. 51:11, 24, 56. Is 10:5-7, 12. *47:6. 54:15-17. Da 9:6, 16. Zc 1:14-16. 11:5. **the habitation**. Je 31:23. Ps 90:1. 91:1. **the hope**. ∫121R3, Ps +71:5. Je 14:8. Ps 22:4, 5. 1 T 1:1.

8. **out of the midst**. Je 51:4, 6, 45. Nu 16:26. Is 48:20. 52:1. Zc 2:6, 7. 2 C √6:17. 2 Th *2:7, 8. Re *18:4. **he goats**. Pr 30:31.

9. **I will raise**. ver. 3, 21, 26, 41, 42. Je 15:14. 51:1-4, 11, 27, 28. Ezr 1:1, 2. Is 13:2-5, 17. 21:2. 41:25. 45:1-4. **an assembly**. The army of Cyrus was composed of Medes, Persians, Armenians, Caducians, Sacae, etc.; all of which, arranged under the Medes, came from the *north*. **they shall**. ver. 14, 29. **expert man**. *or*, destroyer. or, successful. Je 10:21. 23:5. 1 S 18:14. **none**. 2 S 1:22. Is 13:18.

10. **Chaldea**. i.e. *occultism, astrologer; clod breakers; land of the Chaldeans*, ✛S#3778h. Je 25:12. 27:7. 51:24, 35. Ezk 11:24. Re 16:29. 23:15, 16. **all that**. Is 33:4, 23. 45:3. Re *17:16.

11. **ye were**. Pr √17:5. La *1:21. *2:15, 16. 4:21, 22. Ezk 25:3-8, 15-17. 26:2, 3. Ob 12. **ye destroyers**. ver. 17. Je 51:34, 35. Ps 74:2-8. 79:1-4. 83:1-5. Is 10:6, 7. 47:6. Zc 2:8, 9. 14:1-3, 12. **ye are**. ver. 27. Je 46:21. Dt 32:15. Ps 22:12. Ho 10:11. Am 4:1. **fat**. Heb. big, *or* corpulent. Je 5:28. **bellow as bulls**. *or*, neigh as steeds. Je 5:8.

12. **mother**. Je 49:2. Ga *4:26. Re 17:5. **the hindermost**. ver. 17. Je 25:26. Is 23:13. **a wilderness**. ver. 35-40. Je 25:12. 51:25, 26, 43, 62-64. Is 13:20-22. 14:22. Re 18:21-23. **desert**. Je 5:6mg.

13. **Because**. Zc *1:15. **not be inhabited**. ver. +*39. 1 P 5:13. **every**. Je 18:16. 19:8. 25:12. 49:17. 51:37. Jb 27:23. Is 14:4-17. La 2:15, 16. Hab 2:6, etc. Zp *2:15.

14. **in array**. ver. 9. Je 51:2, 11, 12, 27. 1 S 17:20. 2 S 10:9. Is 13:4, 17, 18. **bend**. ver. 29, 42. Je 46:9. 49:35. Is 5:28. **for she**. ver. 7, 11, 29. Ps 51:4. Hab 2:8, 17. Re 17:5.

15. **Shout**. Je 51:14. Jsh 6:5, 20. Ezk 21:22. **she hath**. 1 Ch +*29:24mg. 2 Ch 30:8mg. La 5:6. Ezk 17:18. **hand**. ∫121S3I, 1 Ch 29:24. **her foundations**. Je 51:25, 44, 58, 64. **for it**. ver. 14, 28. Je 46:10. 51:6, 11, 36. Dt 32:35, 41, 43. Ps 94:1. 149:7. Is 59:17. 61:2. 63:4. Na 1:2. Lk *21:22. Ro *3:5. √12:19. 2 Th √1:8. **as she**. ver. 29. Jg 1:6, 7. 1 S 15:33. Ps 137:8, 9. Mt *7:2. Ja 2:13. Re *16:6. 18:6. 19:2.

16. **the sower**. Je 51:23. Jl 1:11. Am *5:16. **sickle**. *or*, scythe. Jl 3:13. **they shall turn every one**. Je 46:16. 51:9. Is *13:14.

17. **a scattered**. ver. 6. Je 23:1, 2. Ezk 34:5, 6,

12. Jl 3:2. Mt 9:36-38. Lk 15:4-6. Jn *10:10-12. 1 P 2:25. **the lions.** Je 2:15. 5:6. 49:19. 51:38. **first.** 2 K 15:29. 17:6, etc. 18:9-13. 2 Ch 28:20. 32:1, etc. 33:11. Is 7:17-20. 8:7, 8. 10:5-7. ch. 36, 37. **this.** Je ch. 39. 51:34, 35. 52:1. 2 K ch. 24, 25. 2 Ch ch. 36. Is 47:6. Da 6:24.

18. **Lord of hosts, the God of Israel.** Je +7:3. **will punish.** Je +11:22mg. **as I.** Is 37:36-38. Ezk *31:3-17. Na ch. 1-3. Zp *2:13-15.

19. **bring.** ver. 4, 5. Je 3:18. 23:3. 24:6, 7. 30:10, 18. 31:8-10. 32:37. 33:7-12. Is *65:9, 10. Ezk √11:17. *34:13, 14. 36:24, 33. 37:21, 22. 38:8. 39:25-29. Am √9:14, 15. Ob 17-21. **he shall.** Is 33:9. 35:2. Mi 7:14, 18. **his soul.** Heb. *nephesh*, Ge +34:3. See on Je 31:14, 25. **mount.** Je 31:6. Jsh 17:15. **Gilead.** Nu 32:1. SS 6:5. Ob 19.

20. **In those.** See on ver. 4. Je 33:15. **the iniquity.** Je 31:34. Nu +*23:21. Is 11:1, 2. *43:25. *44:22. Mi *7:19. Ac 3:19, 26. Ro 8:33, 34. He 8:10-12. *10:17, 18. **and there.** Ps 103:12. Ro 5:16. 2 P *3:15. **I will pardon.** Je *31:34. 44:14. Ps 32:1. *103:12. Is 1:9. Mi 7:19. Ro 5:16. 6:13. 11:6, 26, 27.

21. **up.** See on ver. 3, 9, 15. **Merathaim.** *or*, the rebels. i.e. *double rebellion; double bitterness,* ❋S#4850h, only here. So called, here, because the empire was founded in a double rebellion. See Prideaux, *Connection*, vol. i. p. 1. A symbolic name for Babylon, as Pekod is also and Sheshack, Je 25:26; 51:41 (CB). **Pekod.** *or*, visitation. Ezk 23:23. **and do.** Je 34:22. 48:10. Nu 31:14-18. 1 S 15:3, 11-24. 2 S 16:11. 2 K 18:25. 2 Ch 36:23. Is *10:6. 44:28. 48:14.

22. **A sound.** Je 4:19-21. 51:54-56. Is 21:2-4.

23. **How is.** Je 51:20-24. Is *14:4-6, 12-17. Da 2:40. Re 18:16-19, 21.

24. **snare.** Ec *9:12. **and thou wast.** Je 51:8, 31-39, 57. Is 21:3-5. Da 5:30, 31. Re *18:7, 8. **because.** Ex 10:3. Jb 9:4. 40:2, 9. Is 13:11. *45:9. 2 Th 2:4.

25. **opened.** ver. 35-38. Je 51:11, 20. Ps *45:3, 5. Is 13:2-5, 17, 18. 21:7-9. **armory.** ♩22D5.O, Dt +28:12. **weapons.** ♩22D5A, Ps +35:2. **indignation.** Da +*8:19 (❋S#2195h). **this.** See on ver. 15. Je 51:12, 25, 55. Is 14:22-24. *46:10, 11. 48:14, 15. Am +*3:6. Re *18:8. **Lord God of hosts.** Je +2:19.

26. **against.** ver. 41. Je 51:27, 28. Is 5:26. **the utmost.** Heb. the end. Je 51:31. **open.** ver. 10. Je 51:44. Is 45:3. **cast her up.** *or*, tread her. Ps 119:118. Is 10:6. 25:10. 63:3, 4. La 1:15. Mi 7:10. Re 14:19, 20. *19:15. **destroy.** ver. 13, 15, 23. Je 51:25, 26, 64. Is 14:23. Re *18:21-24.

27. **bullocks.** ver. 11. Je 46:21. Ps 22:12. Is 34:7. Ezk 39:17-20. Re 19:17, 18. **their day.** ver. 31. Je 27:7. See on 48:44. Ps *37:13. La 1:21. Ezk *7:5-7. Re 16:17-19. *18:10. **time of.** Je +*8:12.

28. **voice.** Je 51:50, 51. Is *48:20. **to declare.** ver. 15. Je 51:10, 11. Re +*149:6-9. Da *5:3-5, 23, 26, 27. Zc *12:2, 3. **vengeance of his.** ♩181E, Ge +3:24. Je 51:11. La 1:10. 2:6, 7. Da 5:3.

29. **the archers.** ver. 9, 14, 26. **recompense.** See on ver. 15. Je 51:56. Ps 137:8, 9. Re *16:6. 18:6. **for she hath.** ver. 24, 32. Ex 10:3. Is √14:13, 14. 37:23. 47:10. Da 4:37. 5:23. 11:36. 2 Th 2:4. Re 13:5, 6.

30. **Therefore.** Gobrias and Gadates, when they entered Babylon, marched directly to the palace, killing all they met (Xenophon, Cyr. vii.). **her young.** Je 9:21. 18:21. 48:15. 49:26. 51:3, 4. Is *13:15-18. **all her.** ver. 36. Je 51:56, 57. Re *6:15-17. 19:18.

31. **I am.** Je 21:13. 51:25. Ezk *5:8. 29:3, 9, 10. 38:3. 39:1. Na 2:13. *3:5. **O thou.** ver. 29, 32. Je 48:29. 49:16. Jb 40:11, 12. Da *4:30, 31. Hab *2:4, 5. Ja *4:6. 1 P *5:5. **most proud.** Heb. pride. ver. 32mg. **for.** See on ver. 27.

32. **the most proud.** Heb. pride. ver. 31mg. Pr *16:18, 19. *18:12. Is 10:12-15. *14:13-15. Ezk *28:2-9. Da *5:20, 23-30. **none.** Je 51:26, 64. Re *18:8, 21. **kindle.** Je 21:14. 49:27. Dt *32:22. Am 1:4, *7, 10, 12, 14. 2:2, 5.

33. **and all.** ver. 7, 17, 18. Je 51:34-36. Is 14:17. *47:6. 49:24-26. 51:23. 52:4-6. Zc 1:15, 16. **they refused.** Je 34:15-18. Ex 5:2. 8:2. 9:2, 3, 17, 18. Is 14:17. *58:6.

34. **Redeemer.** Ex 6:6. Pr *23:11. Is *41:14. *43:14, 15. 44:6, 23, 24. *47:4. *54:5. Mi 4:10. Re 18:8. **strong.** Ps 89:19. **Lord of hosts.** Je +6:6. Is +6:5. **is his name.** Je 10:16. Ex +*6:3n. Ps +68:4. +*83:18. Is 42:8. **plead.** Je 51:36. Ps 35:1. 43:1. Pr +*22:23. Is 51:22. Am 5:12. Mi *7:9. Ja +*5:4. **that he.** Is 14:3-7. 2 Th 1:6, 7. Re 19:1-3.

35. **sword.** Je 47:6. Le 26:25. Is *66:16. Ezk 14:2. Ho *11:6. Zc 11:17. **upon her princes.** ver. 27, 30. Je 51:39, 57. Is 41:25. Da 5:1, 2, 30. **her wise men.** Je 8:9. 10:7. Is 19:11-13. 29:14. 44:25. 47:13, 14. Da 5:7, 8. 1 C *1:25.

36. **A sword.** ♩18, Dt +28:4. **upon the liars.** *or*, upon the chief stays. Heb. bars. Je 48:30. Is 43:14mg. *44:24, 25. 2 Th √2:9-11. 1 T *4:2. 1 J 2:22. Re 19:20. +*21:8. *22:15. **dote.** 2 S 15:31. 17:14. 2 Ch 25:16. Is 47:10-15. 1 T 6:4. **her mighty.** See on ver. 30. Je 49:22. 51:23, 30, 32. Na 2:8. 3:7, 13, 17, 18.

37. **their horses.** Je 51:21. Ps *20:7, 8. 46:9. 76:6. Ezk 39:20. Na 2:2-4, 13. Hg 2:22. **all the.** Je 25:20, 24. Ezk 30:5. **as women.** See on Je 48:41. 51:30. Is 19:16. Na 3:13. **her treasures.** ver. 26. Is 45:3.

38. **A drought.** ver. 12. Je 51:32-36. Is *44:27. Re *16:12. *17:15, 16. **the land.** ver. 2. Je 51:44, 47, 52. Is 46:1-7. Da ch. 3. *5:4. Hab 2:18, 19. Re *17:5. **mad.** See on Je 51:7. Is 44:25. Ac *17:16.

39. **wild beasts.** ver. 12, 13. Je 25:12. 51:26, 37, 38, 43, 62-64. Is √13:20-22. 14:23. 34:11-17. Re 16:17-21. *18:2, 21-24. **no more inhabited.** ver. 3, 13. Je 25:12. 51:29, 43, 62. Is √13:20. **for ever.** Jb +4:20 (❋S#5331h).

40. **overthrew Sodom.** Je 49:18. 51:26. Ge 19:24, 25ᵠ﹒. Dt *29:23. Is 1:9. *13:19, 20. Ho 11:8, 9. Am 4:11. Zp 2:9. Lk 17:28-30. 2 P 2:6. Ju +*7. Re *11:8. 18:8, 9.

41. **a people shall.** ver. 2, 3, 9. Je 6:22, 23. 25:14. 51:1, 2, 11, 27, 28. Is *13:2-5, 17, 18. Re 17:16. **north.** ♩171.O.10, Je +6:1.

42. **hold.** See on Je 6:22, 23. **they are cruel.** Ps 74:20. 137:8, 9. Is 13:17, 18. 14:6. 47:6. Hab 1:6-8. Ja 2:13. Re 16:6. **their voice.** Ps 46:2, 3, 6. Is 5:30. **shall ride.** Je 8:16. 47:3. Is 5:28. Hab 1:8. Re *19:14-18.

43. **king.** Je 51:31. Is 13:6-8. 21:3, 4. Da ❋5:5, 6. **pangs.** See on Je 49:22, 24.

44. **like a lion.** Je 25:38. 49:19-21. **the swelling.** Je +*12:5. **who is a.** Jb 41:10, 11. Is 41:25. 46:11. **for who.** See on Ex 15:11. Ps 89:6, 8. Is *40:18, 25. 43:10. **appoint me the time.** *or*, convent me to plead. Je 49:19mg. Jb 9:19. **who is that.** See on Je 49:19. Jb *41:10.

45. **hear.** Je 51:10, 11. Ps *33:10, 11. Is *14:24,

etc. 46:10, 11. Ac 4:28. Ep +*1:11. Re 17:16, 17. **the least.** Je 37:10. 49:20. **surely he.** We have already adverted to the completion of the prophecies respecting the final destruction of Babylon (on Is 13:19n), and shall only add a few more observations, in order to show more clearly the full accomplishment of some of these predictions. Strabo says (l. xvi.) that in his time (about the Christian era) a great part of it was a desert. Jerome says that in his time (cir. A.D. 340) it was quite in ruins, the walls merely serving for an inclosure for *wild beasts*, for the hunting of the kings of Parthia: and modern travelers universally concur in describing it in a state of utter desolation, and the habitation of *wild beasts* and noxious reptiles (See Benjamin of Tudela, Itin. p. 76. Texeira, c. 5. Rauwolff, P. ii. c. 6. Della Valle, P. ii. ep. 17. Tavernier, vol ii. b. ii. c. 5. Rich's Two Memoirs on the ruins of Babylon; and Sir R. K. Porter's Travels, vol. ii., pp. 308-400).

46. **the noise.** Je 49:21. Is +*14:9, 10. Ezk *26:18. *31:16. 32:10. Re 18:9-19.

JEREMIAH 51

Further copious and varied predictions of terrible judgments on Babylon, for her enormous wickedness, 1-58. Jeremiah delivers the book of this prophecy to Seraiah, who is ordered to take this prophecy to Babylon, and to read it there; and then to sink the book in the Euphrates; as a sign that Babylon should thus fall, and rise no more, 59-64.

1. **I will.** See on Je 50:9, 14-16, 21. Is 13:3-5. Am +*3:6. **midst.** Heb. heart. Pr 23:34mg. **rise.** See on Je 50:24, 29, 33. Zc 2:8. Ac 9:4. **a destroying wind.** See on Je 4:11, 12. 49:36. 2 K *19:7. Ezk 19:12. Ho 13:15.

2. **fanners.** Je 15:7. Is 41:16. Ezk 5:12. Mt *3:12. **fan.** ſ147D, Ge +1:29. **in the day.** ver. 27, 28. Je 50:14, 15, 29, 32.

3. **let the.** See on Je 50:14, 41, 42. **brigandine.** Je 46:4. **spare.** Je 9:21. 50:27, 30. Dt 32:25. Ps 137:9. Is 13:10-18. Ja *2:13. **destroy.** Je 50:21.

4. **thrust.** Je 49:26. 50:30, 37. Is *13:15. 14:19.

5. **Israel.** Je +*30:11. 33:24-26. 46:28. 50:4, 5, 20. 1 S +*12:22. 1 K 6:13. Ezr 9:9. Ps +√94:14. Is 44:21. *49:14, 15. +*54:3-11. 62:12. La 3:31. Ho 1:10. Am √9:8, 9. Ro +√11:1, 2. **nor.** Zc √2:12. 12:6, 8. **Lord of hosts.** Je +6:6. **though.** Je 16:18. 19:4. 23:15. 31:37. 2 K 21:16. Ezr 9:13. Ne 9:17, 31. Ezk 8:17. 9:9. 22:24-31. Ho 4:1, 2. Mi *7:18, 20. Zp 3:1-4. Jn *6:37. Ro *5:8.

6. **Flee.** ver. 9, *45, 50. Je *50:8, 28. Is *48:20. Zc *2:6, 7. 2 C +*6:17. Re √18:4. **soul.** Heb. *nephesh*, Ge +12:13. **be not.** Ge *19:15-17. Nu *16:26. Pr *13:20. 1 T 5:22. **for this.** ver. 11. Je 27:7. 46:10. See on 50:8, *15, 28, 31. Dt 32:35, 41, 43. Re 16:19. 18:5, 6. **he will render.** Je 25:14, 16.

7. **a golden.** Is *14:4. Da *2:32, 38. Re *17:4, 5. **the nations.** See on Je 25:9, 14-27. Da *3:1-7. Hab 2:15, 16. Re 14:8. *17:2. 18:3, 23. 19:2. **are mad.** Je 25:16. 50:38.

8. **suddenly fallen.** This must refer to a future fulfillment, for the present condition came gradually (CB). ver. 41. Je 50:2. Is *21:9. 47:9, 11. Re *14:8. 18:2, 8, 10, 17, 19. **howl.** See on Je 48:20, 31. Is 13:6, 7. Ezk 27:30-32. 30:2. Da 5:24, 31. Re 18:9-11, 17-19.

take balm. ſ60A, Ge +3:22. Je +*8:22. 30:12-15. 46:11. Na 3:19.

9. **would have.** Je 23:22. 1 S 13:13, 14. Ps *81:13, 14. Is +30:15. Mt 26:53, 54. Lk *13:34. **forsake.** Je 8:20. 46:16, 21. 50:16. Is *13:14. 47:15. Mt 25:10-13. **her judgment.** 2 Ch 28:9. Ezr 9:6. Da 4:20-22. Re *18:5. **reacheth.** ſ102, Ge +2:24.

10. **brought.** Ps *37:6. Is *54:17. Mi *7:9, 10. 2 C √5:21. **let us.** Je 31:6-9. 50:28. Ps 9:14. 102:19-21. 116:18, 19. 126:1-3. Is 40:2. 51:11. 52:9, 10. Re 14:1-3. *19:1-6.

11. **Make.** Je 46:4, 9. 50:9, 14, 25, 28, 29. Is 21:5. **bright.** Heb. pure. or, cleanse. Je 4:11. **the Lord hath.** ver. 27, 28. 1 K 11:14, 23. 1 Ch 5:26. 2 Ch 36:22. Ezr 1:1. Is 10:26. 13:17, 18. 21:2. 41:25. 45:1, 5. 46:11. Re *17:16, 17. **the spirit.** Heb. *ruach*, Ge +41:8. ſ121A10, Ge +26:35. Of *Cyaxares* king of Media, called "Darius the Mede" in Scripture; and of *Cyrus* his nephew, king of Persia, presumptive heir of the throne of his uncle. **his device.** ver. 12, 29. Je 50:45. **the vengeance.** ver. 24, 35. Je 50:15, 28. Ps 74:3-11. 83:3-9. Hab 2:17-20. Zc 12:2, 3. 14:2, 3, 12.

12. **the standard.** Je 46:3-5. Pr +*21:30. Is 8:9, 10. 13:2. Jl 3:2, 9-14. Na 2:1. 3:14, 15. **make the watch.** Is 21:5, 6. **ambushes.** Heb. liers in wait. Jsh 8:4, 13mg, 14. **the Lord hath both.** ver. 11, 29. La *2:17.

13. **dwellest.** ver. *36. Re *17:1, 15. **upon many waters.** ver. *36, 42. Je 50:38. Nu 24:7. Jn +3:23. Re 17:1, 15. **abundant.** Je 50:37. Is 45:3. Hab 2:5-10. Re *18:11-17. **thine.** Je 17:11. 50:27, 31. Ge 6:13. La 4:18. Ezk 7:2-12. Da 5:26. Am 8:2. 1 P *4:7. **and the.** Hab 2:9-11. Lk *12:19-21. 2 P 2:3, 14, 15. Ju 11-13. Re 18:19.

14. **sworn.** See on Je 49:13. Am 6:8. He *6:13. **himself.** Heb. his soul. Heb. *nephesh*, Ge +27:31. ſ22A1, Le +26:11n. **as with.** Je 46:23. Jg 6:5. Jl 1:4-7. 2:3, 4, 25. Na 3:15-17. **lift up.** Heb. utter. See on Je 50:15. Ex 32:18.

15. **hath made.** Je 10:12-16. 32:17. Ge 1:1-6↑ℙ. Ps 107:25. *146:5, 6. 148:1-5. Is 40:26. Ac 14:15. 17:24. Ro 1:20. Col +*1:16, 17. He +*1:2, 3. Re *4:11. **by his wisdom.** Ps 104:24. 136:5. Pr 3:19. Ro 11:33. **and hath.** Jb 9:8. Ps 104:2. Is 40:22. 42:5. 44:24. 45:12. 48:13. 51:13.

16. **he uttereth.** See on Je 10:12, 13. Jb *37:2-11. 40:9. Ps 18:13. 29:3-10. 46:6. 68:33. 104:7. Ezk 10:5. **there is.** Jb 36:26-33. 37:13. 38:34-38. Ps 135:7. Am 9:6. **multitude.** or, noise. Je +10:13mg. Is 60:5mg. Ezk 7:11mg. Am 5:23. **and he causeth.** Ps 135:7. **bringeth.** Ge 8:1. Ex 10:13, 19. 14:21. Jb 38:22. Ps 78:26. 135:7. 147:18. Jon 1:4. 4:8. Mt *8:26, 27. **treasures.** ſ22D5.O, Dt +28:12.

17. **Every.** Je 10:14. Ps *14:2. *53:1, 2. 92:5, 6. *115:5, 8. 135:18. Is 44:18-20. Ro *1:20-23. 1 C *1:19-21. **brutish by his knowledge.** or, more brutish than to know. Je 10:14mg. **for his.** See on 10:14. 50:2. Ps 135:17. Hab 2:18, 19. **breath.** Heb. *ruach*, Ge +6:17.

18. **vanity.** See on Je 10:8, 15. Jon +*2:8. Ac *14:15. **in the.** Je 43:12, 13. 46:25. 48:7. 50:2. Ex 12:12. Is 19:1. 46:1. Zp 2:11. **time of.** Je +*8:12. 1 P 2:12.

19. **portion.** See on Je 10:16. Ps *16:5. *73:26. 115:3. La *3:24. **the former.** See on ver. 15. **Israel is.** ſ63A1, Ge +14:20. **the rod.** Je 12:7-10. 50:11. Ex *19:5, 6. Dt *32:8, 9. Ps 33:12. 74:2. 135:4. 1 P *2:9. **the Lord of hosts.** Je +6:6. See on 10:16. 50:34. Is +6:5. 44:6.

47:4. 54:5. Jn 12:37-41. Ro 9:29. Ja +5:4. **is his name.**
Je 10:16. Ex +*6:3n. Ps +68:4. +*83:18. Is 42:8.

20. **art.** Je 50:23. Is *10:5, 15. 13:5. 14:5, 6. 37:26.
*41:15, 16. Mi 4:13. Zc 9:13, 14. Mt *22:7. **weapons.**
*22D5A, Ps +35:2. **with thee.** or, in thee, or, by
thee. **break.** See on Je 25:9, 11. 27:5-7.

21. **the horse and.** Je 50:37. Ex *15:1, 21. Ps 46:9.
76:6. Ezk 39:20. Mi 5:10. Na 2:13. Hg 2:22. Zc 10:5.
12:4. Re 19:18. **and with thee.** *18, Dt +28:4.

22. **man and.** *174, Ge +18:22. Je 6:11. Dt *32:25.
1 S *15:3. 2 Ch 36:17. Is 20:4. La 2:11. Ezk *9:5, 6.
old and. *174, Ge +18:27.

24. **I will render.** ver. 11, 35, 49. Je 50:15, 17,
18, 28, 29, 33, 34. Ps *137:8, 9. Is *47:6-9. *51:22,
23. *61:2. *63:1-4. 66:6. 1 Th 2:15, 16. Re 6:10. 18:20,
24. 19:2-4. **in your sight.** Is +*66:24.

25. **I am.** See on Je 50:31. **O destroying.** ver. 53,
58. Ge 11:4. Is 13:2. Da 4:30. Zc *4:7. **which destroyest.**
ver. 7, 20-23. Je 25:9, 18-27. Re 8:8. 17:1-6. **and will.**
2 P 3:10. Re *8:8. 18:9, 19.

26. **shall not.** See on ver. 37, 43. Je 50:12, 13. Is
√13:19-22. *14:23. This is clearly future, for all ancient
cities were plundered for building materials in the
past. The materials of ancient Babylon were used for
building purposes in the building of four capital cities:
Seleucia by the Greeks; Ctesiphon by the Parthians;
al Maiden by the Persians; and Kufa by the Caliphs.
For some reason not explained here, the building materials of a future Babylon will never be used again.
desolate for ever. Heb. everlasting desolations. Je
50:40, 41. Is 34:8-17. Re 18:20-24. **for ever.** Heb. *olam*,
Ex +*12:24.

27. **Set ye up.** ver. 12. Je 6:1. 50:2, 41. Is 13:2-5.
18:3. Am +*3:6. Zc *14:2-4. **prepare.** Je 25:14. **Ararat.**
Bochart (Phaleg, l. i. c. 3. l. iii. c. 9.) reasonably concludes *Ararat* and *Minni* to be the greater and less
Armenia; and *Ashchenaz* he thinks formed part of
Phrygia near the Hellespont, part of that country being
called *Ascania* by Homer (Il. ii. 370, 371). Cyrus had
conquered Armenia, defeated Croesus king of Lydia
(B.C. 548), and subdued several nations from the Aegean sea to the Euphrates, before he marched against
Babylon; and Xenophon also informs us that there were
not only Armenians, but both Phrygians and Cappadocians in the army of Cyrus (Cyr. l. iii.-vii.). Ge 8:4.
Minni. i.e. *division; from me; part*, *S#4508h. **Ashchenaz.** i.e. *fire that spreads*, *S#813h. Ge *10:3, Ashkenaz. 1 Ch 1:6. **cause.** See on ver. 14. Je 46:23. 50:41,
42. Jg 6:5. Jl 2:2, 3. Na 3:15-17. Re 9:7-11. After Cyrus
had been the instrument in the hands of God of taking
Babylon, he marched against Tomyris, queen of the
Massagetae, a Scythian nation, and was totally defeated
(B.C. 530). The victorious queen, who had lost her
son in a previous battle, was so incensed against Cyrus,
that she cut off his head, and threw it into a vessel
filled with human blood, exclaiming, *Satia te sanguine,
quem sitisti.*

28. **the kings.** ver. 11. Je 25:25. Ge 10:2. 1 Ch 1:5,
Madia. Est 1:3. 10:2. Is 13:17. 21:2. Da 5:28-30. 6:8.
*8:3, 4, 20. *9:1, 2.

29. **the land.** See on Je 8:16. 10:10. 50:36, 43. Is
13:13, 14. 14:16. Jl 2:10. Am *8:8. **every purpose.** Pr
+*21:30. Ep +*1:11. **without an inhabitant.** Like ver.
8n and 26n, this must be yet future. ver. 11, 12, 43,
62-64. Je 50:13, 39, 40, 45. Is √13:19, 20. 14:23, 24.
46:10, 11. ch. 47. Re *18:2, 21-24.

30. **The mighty.** Accordingly the Babylonians, after
the loss of a battle or two, never recovered their courage
to face the enemy in the field: they retired within
their walls; and the first time that Cyrus came with
his army before the place he could not provoke them
to venture forth, though he challenged the king to
fight a duel with him; and the last time he came he
consulted with his officers respecting the best mode
of carrying on the siege, "since," said he, "they do
not come out to fight" (Xenophon, l. v. vii). ver. 32,
57. Je 48:41. 50:36, 37. Ps 76:5. Is *13:7, 8. 19:16.
Na *3:13. Re 18:10. **her bars.** Je 50:36mg. Ps *107:16.
147:13. Is 45:1, 2. La 2:9. Am 1:5. Na 3:13.

31. **post.** Je 4:20. 50:24. 1 S 4:12-18. 2 S 18:19-31.
2 Ch 30:6. Est 3:13-15. 8:10, 14. Jb 9:25. **to show.** Je
50:43. Is 21:3-9. 47:11-13. Da *5:2-5, 30. **one.** or, each.
*63A4, 1 K +3:22.

32. **the passages.** Je 50:38. Is 44:27. **the men.** See
on ver. 30. Je 50:37.

33. **Lord of hosts, the God of Israel.** Je +7:3. **is
like.** Is 21:10. 41:15, 16. Am 1:3. Mi *4:13. Hab 3:12.
threshingfloor. Ge +50:10. Dt +*16:13mg. **it is time
to thresh her.** or, in the time that he thresheth her.
Is 21:10. **the time.** Is 17:5. 18:5. Ho 6:11. Jl 3:13. Mt
*13:30, 37-39. Re *14:15-20.

34. **the king.** See on ver. 49. Je 39:1-8. 50:7, 17.
La *1:1, 14, 15. **he hath made.** Je 48:11, 12. Is 24:1-
3. 34:11. Na *2:2, 9, 10. **swallowed.** ver. 44. Jb 20:15.
Pr 1:12. La 2:16. Ezk 36:3. Am 8:4. Mt 23:14.

35. **The violence.** Heb. My violence. Je 50:29. Jg
9:20, 24, 56, 57. Ps 9:12. 12:5. 137:8, 9. Is 26:20, 21.
Zc *1:15. Mt *7:2. Ja *2:13. Re *6:10. 16:6. *18:6,
20. **flesh.** or, remainder. Le 18:6mg. **inhabitant.** Heb.
inhabitress. Je +10:17mg.

36. **I will plead.** See on Je 50:33, 34. Ps 140:12.
Pr 22:23. 23:11. Is *43:14. 47:6-9. 49:25, 26. Mi 7:8-
10. Hab 2:8-17. **take.** Dt 32:35, 43. Ps 94:1-3. Ro
*12:19. He *10:30, 31. Re *19:1-3. **and I will.** See
on Je 50:38. Ps 107:33, 34. Is 44:27. Re 16:12.

37. **become.** ver. 25, 26, 29. Je 25:9, 12, 18. 50:12,
13, 23-26, 38-40. Is √13:19-22. *14:23. 34:8-17. Re
*18:2, 21-23. **an hissing.** Je 18:16. 19:8. 29:18. 2 Ch
29:8. La 2:15, 16. Mi 6:16. Zp 2:15. **without an inhabitant.** ver. 29n. 1 P 5:13.

38. **roar.** Je 2:15. Jb *4:10, 11. Ps 34:10. *58:6. Is
35:9. Na 2:11-13. Zc 11:3. **yell.** or, shake themselves.
Jg 16:20.

39. **their heat.** Je 25:27. Is 21:4, 5. *22:12-14. Da
*5:1-4, 30. Na *1:10. 3:11. **and sleep.** ver. 57. Ps 13:3.
76:5, 6. **perpetual.** Heb. *olam*, Ge +9:12.

40. **like lambs.** Je 50:27. Ps *37:20. 44:22. Is 34:6.
Ezk *39:18.

41. **Sheshach.** *Sheshach* was probably an idol worshipped at Babylon, from which the city derived this
name; and the festival which was held when the city
was taken, when they were *heated* with wine, was
perhaps observed in honor of it (Da 5:1-3; Herodotus,
l. i. c. 191. Xenophon, l. vii). Sir H. Rawlinson has
observed that the name of the moon-god, which was
identical, or nearly so, with that of the city of Abraham,
Ur (or Hur), "might have been read in one of the
ancient dialects of Babylon as *Shishaki*," and that consequently "a possible explanation is thus obtained of the
Sheshach of Scripture" (Rawlinson's *Herodotus*, vol.
i. p. 616). Sheshach may stand for Ur, Ur itself, the
old capital, being taken (as Babel, the new capital,

was constantly) to represent the country. (George Rawlinson in Smith's *Dictionary of the Bible*, vol. iv. p. 2991.) Je 25:26n. Da 5:1-3. **the praise**. Je 49:25. 50:23. Is 13:19. *14:4. Da 2:38. 4:22, 30. 5:4, 5. Re *18:9-19. **an astonishment**. ver. 37. Je 50:46. Dt 28:37. 2 Ch 7:21. Ezk 27:35.

42. **The sea**. Ps 18:4, 16. 42:7. 65:7. 93:3. Is 8:7, 8. Ezk 27:26-34. Da *9:26. Lk √21:25. Re *17:15, 16.

43. **cities**. See on ver. 29, 37. Je 50:39, 40. **a land**. Je 2:6. Is √13:20. Ezk 29:10, 11.

44. **I will punish**. ver. 18, 47. Je 50:2. Is *46:1, 2. **I will bring**. See on ver. 34. 2 Ch 36:7. Ezr 1:7. Da *1:2. *5:2-4, 26. **the nations**. Is 2:2. 60:5. Da 3:2, 3, 29. 4:1, 22. 5:19, 31. Re 18:9-19. **the wall**. ver. 53, 58.

45. **go**. ver. 6, 10, 50. Je 50:8. Is *48:20. Zc *2:7. Re 14:8-11. *18:4. **deliver**. Ge 19:12-16. Nu *16:26. Ac 2:40. 2 C +*6:17. **soul**. Heb. *nephesh*, Ge +12:13.

46. **lest**. *or*, let not. 2 K *19:7. Mt √24:6-8. Mk 13:7, 8. Lk 21:9-19, 28. **a rumor shall**. Is 13:3-5. 21:2, 3. **ruler against**. Jg 7:22. 1 S 14:16-20. 2 Ch 20:23. Is 19:2.

47. **I will**. ver. 52. See on Je 50:2. Is *21:9. *46:1, 2. **do judgment upon**. Heb. visit upon. ver. 18. Je +9:25mg. 11:22mg. 13:21mg. 23:34mg. 25:12mg. **her whole**. ver. 24, 43. Je 50:12-16, 35-40.

48. **the heaven**. ver. 10. Ps +*58:10, 11. Pr *11:10. Is 44:23. 48:20. 49:13. Re 15:1-4. 16:4-7. 18:20. 19:1-7. **sing**. √155D, Ge +4:10. **the spoilers**. See on ver. 11. Je 50:3, 9, 41.

49. **As Babylon**, etc. *or*, Both Babylon *is* to fall, O ye slain of Israel, and with Babylon shall fall the slain of all the country. **hath**. ver. 10, 11, 24, 35. Je 50:11, 17, 18, 29, 33, 34. Jg *1:7. Ps *137:8, 9. Mt *7:2. Ja *2:13. Re *18:5, 6. **of all**. Is 14:16, 17. **the earth**. *or*, the country.

50. **escaped**. ver. 6, 45. Je 31:21. 44:28. 50:8. Is 48:20. 51:11. *52:2, 11, 12. Zc 2:7-9. Re *18:4. **remember**. Je 29:12-14. Dt 4:29-31. 30:1-4. Ezr 1:3-5. Ne 1:2-4. 2:3-5. Ps 102:13, 14. *137:5, 6. Da 9:2, 3, 16-19. **Jerusalem**. Ps +√122:6.

51. **are confounded**. Je 3:22-25. 31:19. Ps *74:18-21. 79:4, 12. 123:3, 4. 137:1-3. La 2:15-17. 5:1. Ezk 36:30. **shame**. Je 3:25. 14:3. Ps *44:13-16. 69:7-13. 71:13. 109:29. Ezk 7:18. Mi 7:10. **for strangers**. Je 52:13. Ps 74:3-7. 79:1. La 1:10. 2:20. Ezk 7:21, 22. 9:7. 24:21. Da 8:11-14. *9:26, 27. 11:31. Re *11:1, 2.

52. **that I**. See on ver. 47. Je 50:38. **her graven images**. This was verified when Xerxes destroyed all the temples of Babylon, B.C. 479 (Herodotus, l, i. c. 183., etc.). **the wounded**. Is 13:15, 16. Ezk 30:24. Da *5:30, 31.

53. **mount**. √102, Ge +2:24. ver. 25, 58. Je 49:16. Ge *11:4, 9. Ps *139:8-10. Is √14:12-15. 47:5, 7. Ezk 31:9-11. Da 4:30. Am *9:2, 4. Ob *3, *4. **from**. ver. 1-4, 11, 48. Je 50:9, 10, 21, 25, 31-34, 45. Is *10:6, 7. 13:2-5, 17. 41:25. 45:1-5.

54. **A sound**. √144, Ge +3:8. Je 48:3-5. 50:22, 27, 43, 46. Is *13:6-9. 15:5. Zp 1:10. Re *18:17-19.

55. **destroyed**. ver. 38, 39. Je 25:10. 50:10-15. Is 15:1. 24:8-11. *47:5. Re *18:21-23. **her waves**. Ps 65:7. 93:3, 4. Is 17:13. Ezk 26:3. Lk 21:25. Re 17:15.

56. **the spoiler**. ver. 48. Je 50:10. Is *21:2. Hab *2:8. Re *17:16. **her mighty**. See on ver. 30. 50:36. **every**. Je 49:35. Ge 49:24. 1 S 2:4. Ps 37:15. 46:9. 76:3. Ezk 39:3, 9. **the Lord**. See on ver. 6, 24. Je

50:28, 29. Dt *32:35. Ps 94:1, 2. 137:8. Is 34:8. 35:4. 59:18. 2 Th *1:6. Re *18:5, 6, 20. *19:2. **God**. Heb. *El*, Ex +15:2.

57. **I will**. See on ver. 39. Je 25:27. Is 21:4, 5. Da 5:1-4, 30, 31. Na *1:10. Hab 2:15-17. Re *18:6, 7, 9. **sleep a**. Ps 76:5, 6. Is 37:36. **perpetual**. Heb. *olam*, Ge +9:12. **the king**. See on Je 46:18. 48:15. Ml 1:14.

58. **The broad walls of Babylon**. *or*, The walls of broad Babylon. According to the testimony of Herodotus (l. i. c. 178), the circumference of the walls of Babylon was 480 stadia, or 60 miles, their breadth 50 cubits, and their height 200 cubits; but when Darius became master of the place, B.C. 516, he took away all their 100 gates of brass, and beat down their walls to 50 cubits (Herod. l. iii. c. 159); and now not a vestige of these immense fortifications remains, to mark the site of this once mighty city! ver. 44. Je 50:15. **utterly**. √147B. Polyptoton, Ge +2:16. lit. being broken shall be broken. **broken**. *or*, made naked. *S#6209h. Is 23:13. 32:11. **high gates**. ver. 30. Is *45:1, 2. **the people**. ver. 9, 64. Ps *127:1. Is 65:23. Hab 2:13.

59. **Neriah**. See on Je 32:12. 36:4. 45:1. **with**. *or*, on the behalf of. **quiet prince**. *or*, prince of Menucha, *or*, chief chamberlain. lit. prince of rest. Je 45:3, 5. Ps 23:2. Is 32:18.

60. **wrote in a book**. Je 30:2, 3. 36:2-4, 32. Is 8:1-4. 30:8. Da *12:4. Hab *2:2, 3. Re *1:11, 19. **evil**. Is +45:7.

61. **and shalt see**. Mt 24:1, 2. Mk 13:1, 2. **read**. Je 29:1, 2. Col *4:16. 1 Th *4:18. *5:27. Re √1:3.

62. **to cut**. See on ver. 25, 26, 29, 37. Je 50:3, 13, 39, 40. Is √13:19-22. 14:22, 23. Re 18:20-23. **desolate**. Heb. desolations. ver. 26. Je 25:9, 12. 48:34mg. Is 15:6mg. Ezk 35:9. **for ever**. Heb. *olam*, Ex +*12:24.

63. **thou shalt bind**. This was the emblem of its overthrow and irretrievable ruin; and the same emblem is employed in Re 18:21, to denote the utter ruin of mystical Babylon. Je 19:10, 11. Re √18:21.

64. **Thus shall**. ver. 42. Je 25:27. Na *1:8, 9. Re *14:8. 18:2, 21. **not rise**. Is √13:20. **evil**. Is +45:7. **they shall**. ver. 58. Ps 76:12. Hab *2:13. **Thus far**. Jb *31:40. Ps *72:20.

JEREMIAH 52

Zedekiah's wicked reign, and rebellion against the king of Babylon, 1-3. Jerusalem is taken; Zedekiah made prisoner; his sons and nobles are slain; his eyes are put out, and he is carried in chains to Babylon, 4-11. The temple and city are burnt, the sacred treasures, etc. are, with the people, carried to Babylon, 12-23. The nobles are slain at Riblah, 24-27. The numbers, at different times carried captive, 28-30. Evil-merodach shows kindness to Jehoiachin, 31-34.

1. A.M. 3406-3416. B.C. 598-588. **one and twenty**. 2 K *24:18. 2 Ch 36:11. **began to reign**. Heb. reigned. **Libnah**. Jsh 10:29. 15:42.

2. **he did**. 1 K 14:22. 2 K *24:19, 20. 2 Ch *36:12, 13. Ezk *17:16-20. 21:25. **according**. Je 26:21-23. 36:21-23, 29-31.

3. **through**. 2 S 24:1. 1 K 10:9. Pr +21:1. *28:2. Ec 10:16. Is 3:4, 5. 19:4. **Zedekiah**. 2 Ch 36:13. Ezk 17:15-21.

4. A.M. 3414. B.C. 590. **the ninth year**. Je 39:1.

2 K 25:1. Ezk *24:1, 2. **in the tenth month.** Zc 8:19. **pitched.** ver. 7. Je 6:3-6. 32:24. Le 26:25. Dt 28:52-57. Is 29:3. 42:24, 25. Ezk 4:1-7. 21:22. Lk *19:43. *21:20.

6. A.M. 3416. B.C. 588. **the fourth month.** Je 39:2. 2 K *25:3. Zc 8:19. **the famine.** Je 15:2. 19:9. 21:9. 25:10. 38:9. Ge +12:10. Le 26:26. Dt *28:52, 53. 32:24. Is *3:1. La 4:4-6. 5:10. Ezk 4:9-17. 5:10-12. 7:15. 14:21. **bread.** Je 37:21.

7. **the city.** Je 34:2, 3. 2 K 25:4. **all the men.** See on Je 39:4-7. 49:26. 51:32. Le 26:17, 36. Dt 28:25. 32:30. Jsh 7:8-12.

8. **overtook Zedekiah.** Je 21:7. 32:4. 34:21. 37:18. 38:23. 39:5. Is 30:16, 17. La 4:19, 20. Ezk 12:12-14. 17:20, 21. Am 2:14, 15. 9:1-4.

9. **they took.** Je 32:4, 5. 2 Ch 33:11. Ezk *21:25-27. **Riblah.** Je 39:5. 2 K *23:31-33. *25:4-6. **Hamath.** Nu 13:21. Jsh 13:5. 1 K 8:65. 2 Ch 8:3.

10. **slew.** Je 22:30. 39:6, 7. Ge 21:16. 44:34. Dt 28:34. 2 K *25:7. **he slew.** ver. 24-27. 2 K *25:18-21. Ezk *9:6. 11:7-11.

11. **put out the eyes of Zedekiah.** Heb. blinded Zedekiah. Je 32:4. 34:3-5. 2 K 25:6, 7mg. Ezk 12:13. **chains.** *or*, fetters. Je 39:7mg. **prison.** Heb. house of the wards.

12. **fifth month.** 2 K *25:8. Zc 7:3-5. 8:19. **the tenth.** It appears from the parallel passage of Kings, that Nebu-zar-adan came from Riblah to Jerusalem on the *seventh* of the fifth month; but it seems that he did not set fire to the temple and city till the *tenth* day, being probably occupied on the intervening days in taking the vessels out of the house of the Lord, and collecting together all the riches that could be found. In memory of this calamity, the Jews keep two fasts to this day; the seventeenth of the fourth month, which falls in June, for the destruction of Jerusalem, and the ninth of the fifth month, which falls in July, for the destruction of the temple; both of which are mentioned by Zechariah as kept from this event till his time, a period of seventy years, under the names of the fast of the fourth month, and the fast of the fifth month. **the nineteenth.** ver. 29. 2 K 24:12. ☽25:8. **captain of the guard.** *or*, chief slaughtermen, and so ver. 14. Je 39:9mg. Ge 37:36mg. **served.** Heb. stood before. Je 40:10.

13. **burned.** Je 7:14. 2 K *25:9. 2 Ch 36:19. Ps 74:6-8. 79:1. Is 64:10, 11. La 2:7. Ezk 7:20-22. 24:21. Mi 3:12. Zc 11:1. Mt √24:2. Ac *6:13, 14. **the king's.** Je 22:14. 34:22. 37:8-10. 38:23. 39:8, 9. Ezk 24:1-14. Am 2:5. 3:10, 11. 6:11.

14. **brake.** 2 K *25:10. Ne 1:3.

15. **carried.** Je 15:1, 2. Zc *14:2. **the poor.** 2 K *25:11, 12. Pr 10:15. 14:31. 19:4, 17. 22:9, 16, 22. 28:3, 8, 11, 15. 29:7, 14.

16. **certain.** Je 39:9, 10. 40:5-7. 2 K *25:12. Ezk 33:24. **the poor.** Mt 11:5. Ja 2:5.

17. **pillars.** ver. 21-23. Je 27:19-22. 1 K 7:15-22, 27, 50. 2 K *25:13-17. 2 Ch 4:12, 13. 36:18. La 1:10. Da *1:2. **the bases.** 1 K 7:23-26. 2 Ch 4:14, 15.

18. **caldrons.** Ex 27:3☽. 38:3. 2 K 25:14-16. Ezk 46:20-24. **the shovels.** *or*, instruments to remove the

ashes. Nu 4:14. 1 K 7:40, 45. 2 Ch 4:11, 16. **the snuffers.** Ex 37:23. 2 Ch 4:22. **bowls.** *or*, basons. Ex 25:29. 37:16. Nu 4:7, 14. 1 K 7:+40, 50. 1 Ch 28:17. 2 Ch 4:8. Ezr 1:10. **the spoons.** Nu 7:13, 14, 19, 20, 26, 32, 38, 44, 50, 56, 62, 84, 86. 2 Ch 24:14.

19. **basons.** 1 K +14:17. **firepans.** *or*, censers. Le 26:12. Nu 16:46. 2 K *25:15. Re 8:3-5. **bowls.** 1 K +7:40. **and the candlesticks.** Ex 25:31-39. 1 K 7:49. 2 Ch 4:6-23.

20. **two.** ver. 17. **the brass.** Heb. their brass. **without.** 1 K 7:47. 2 K *25:16. 1 Ch 22:14. 2 Ch 4:18.

21. **concerning.** 1 K 7:15-21. 2 K *25:17. 2 Ch 3:15-17. **fillet.** Heb. thread.

22. **with network.** Ex 28:14-22, 25. 39:15-18. 1 K 7:17. 2 Ch 3:15. 4:12, 13.

23. **all the.** 1 K 7:20.

24. **the captain.** See on ver. 12, 15. 2 K *25:18. **Seraiah.** Je 51:59. 2 K 25:18. 1 Ch 6:14. Ezr 7:1. **Zephaniah.** Je 21:1. 29:25, 29. 37:3. 2 K 25:18. **door.** Heb. threshold. Je 35:4. 1 K +14:17. 2 K +12:9mg. 1 Ch 9:19-26. Ps 84:10mg.

25. **an eunuch.** 2 K 25:19. **seven.** 2 K ☽25:19. **were near the king's person.** Heb. saw the face of the king. 2 K 25:19mg. Est 1:14. Mt 18:10. **principal scribe of the host.** *or*, scribe of the captain of the host.

27. **the king.** Je 6:13-15. 2 K *25:20, 21. Ezk 8:11-18. 11:1-11. **Riblah.** See on ver. 9. Nu 34:8-11. 2 S 8:9. **Thus.** Je 24:9, 10. 25:9-11. 39:10. Le 26:33-35. Dt 4:26. 28:36, 64. 2 K 17:20, 23. 23:27. 25:21. Is 6:11, 12. 24:3. 27:10. 32:13, 14. Ezk 33:28. Mi 4:10.

28. A.M. 3404. B.C. 600. **in the seventh year.** 2 K 24:2, 3, 12-16. Da 1:1-3.

29. A.M. 3415. B.C. 589. **the eighteenth year.** ver. 12. Je 39:9. 2 K 25:11. 2 Ch 36:20. **persons.** Heb. souls. Heb. *nephesh*, Ge +12:5. 14:21. 36:6. Ex 1:5.

30. **carried.** ver. 15. Je 6:9. 41:18. **persons.** Heb. *nephesh*, souls, Ge +12:5.

31. A.M. 3442. B.C. 562. **it came.** 2 K *25:27-30. **Jehoiachin.** Je 22:24, 28, Coniah. 24:1. 29:2, Jeconiah. **in the twelfth.** Nearly answering to our 25th of April, A.M. 3442. 2 K ☽25:27. **king of Babylon.** Pr +21:1. **lifted up.** This phrase is founded on the observation that those in sorrow *hold down* their heads; and, when comforted, or the cause of their sorrow removed, they *lift up* their heads. Ge 40:13, 20☽. Jb 22:29. Ps 3:3. 27:6.

32. **kindly unto him.** Heb. good things with him. Pr 12:25. **set.** Gave him a more respectable *seat* than any of the captive princes. Je 27:6-11. 2 K *25:28. Da 2:37. 5:18, 19.

33. **changed.** Presented him with a *caftan*, or robe, as a mark of favor, as is still the practice in the East. Ge 41:14, 42. 2 K *25:29. Ps 30:11. Is 61:1-3. Zc 3:4. **he did.** 2 S 9:7, 13. 1 K 2:7. **continually.** Is +*58:11. **bread.** ʃ17ı18, Ge +3:19.

34. **there was.** 2 S 9:10. Mt *6:11. **continual.** 1 K 8:59. 2 K *25:30. Is +*58:11. Da 1:5. **every day a portion.** Heb. the matter of the day in his day. Ex +*5:13mg. 2 Ch 31:16. Ne 11:23. Lk *11:3.

LAMENTATIONS

LAMENTATIONS 1

The miseries of Jerusalem, and of the Jews, pathetically lamented, with confessions of their sins, 1-11. The attention and compassion of beholders demanded to this unprecedented case, 12-17. The justice of God acknowledged, and his mercy supplicated, with prayers against insulting foes, 18-22.

1. **How doth.** ♪85M. Erotesis B954: in pity and commiseration. For another instance of this figure see Mt 23:37. The LXX. have the following words as an introduction: "And it came to pass after Israel had been carried captive, and Jerusalem was become desolate, that Jeremiah sat weeping, and lamented with this lamentation over Jerusalem and said." La 2:1. 4:1. Is 14:12. Je 50:23. Zp 2:15. Re 18:16, 17. **sit.** La 2:10. 3:28. Is *3:26. 47:1, 5. 52:2, 27. Je 9:11. Ezk 26:16. **that was.** ♪31, Is +1:21. **full.** Ps 122:4. Is 22:2. Zc 8:4, 5. **as a.** Is *47:7-9. 54:4. Re 18:7. **great.** 1 K 4:21. 2 Ch 9:26. Ezr 4:20. **how is.** ♪63I1C2B, Jb +21:17. La 5:16. 2 K 23:33, 35. Ne 5:4. 9:37.

2. **weepeth.** ver. 16. La 2:11, 18, 19. Jb *7:2, 3. Ps 6:6. 77:2-6. Je 9:1, 17-19. 13:17. **lovers.** ver. 19. Je 2:17, 27, 36, 37. 4:30. 22:20-22. 30:14. Ezk 16:37. 23:22-25. 29:6, 7, 16. Ho 2:7. Re 17:13, 16. **none.** ver. 9, 16, 17, 21. Is 51:18, 19. **all her friends.** Jb 6:15. 19:13, 14. Ps 31:11. Pr 19:7. Mi 7:5. **enemies.** Je 12:14.

3. **gone.** 2 K 24:14, 15. 25:11, 21. 2 Ch 36:20, 21. Je 39:9. 52:15, 27-30. **because of great servitude.** Heb. for the greatness of servitude. **she.** La 2:9. Le 26:36-39. Dt *28:64-67♪𝒫. Je 24:9. Ezk 5:12. Note the reference to the Pentateuch. Other references to the Pentateuch in Lamentations are La 1:5, 10, 14, 20. 2:9, 17, 20. 3:25. 4:6, 10, 11, 14, 15, 19. See related note at Is 1:2. **all.** La 4:18, 19. Je 16:16. 52:8. Am 9:1-4. **between the straits.** Ps 116:3. 118:5.

4. **ways.** Je 2:6, 7. 5:13. Is 24:4-6. Je 14:2. Mi 3:12. **mourn.** ♪155D, Ge +4:10. **solemn feasts.** La 2:6. Ge +17:21h. Le *23:2n. Ps 74:8. **all her gates.** La 2:9. Je 9:11. 10:22. 33:10-12. **her priests.** ver. 11, 12, 18-20. La 2:10, 11, 19-21. Is 32:9-14. Jl 1:8-13. **bitterness.** Je 7:34. 16:9. 25:10. 31:13. 33:11.

5. **adversaries.** La 2:17. 3:46. Le 26:17. Dt 28:13, 43, 44♪𝒫. Ps 80:6. 89:42. Is 63:18. Je 12:7. Mi 7:8-10. **for.** ver. 18. La 3:39-43. Le 26:15, etc. Dt 4:25-27. 28:15, etc. 29:18-28. 31:16-18, 29. 32:15-27. 2 Ch 36:14-16. Ne 9:33, 34. Ps 90:7, 8. Je 5:3-9, 29. 23:14. 30:14, 15. 44:21, 22. Ezk 8:17, 18. 9:9. 22:24-31. Da *9:7-16. Mi 3:9-12. Zp 3:1-8. **her children.** La 2:11, 19, 20. 4:4. Je 39:9. 52:27-30.

6. **from.** 2 K 19:21. Ps 48:2, 3. Is 1:21. 4:5. 12:6. Zp 3:14-17. **daughter.** ♪155E5, Nu +21:25. **all.** La 2:1-7. 2 S 4:21, 22. Ps 50:2. 96:9. 132:12, 13. Je 52:8, 11, 13. Ezk 7:20-22. 11:22, 23. 24:21, 25. **her princes.** Le 26:36, 37. Dt 28:25. 32:30. Jsh 7:12, 13. Ps 44:9-11. Je 29:4. 48:41. 51:30-32. 52:7. **harts.** Je 14:5, 6. 47:3.

7. **remembered.** Jb 29:2, etc. 30:1. Ps 42:4. 77:3, 5-9. Ho 2:7. Lk 15:17. 16:25. **all her.** Dt 4:7, 8, 34-37. 8:7-9. Ps 147:19, 20. Is 5:1-4. **pleasant.** *or*, desir-

able. ♪121R5, Ge +27:15. ver. 10mg. 1 K +20:6mg. Is 32:12mg. **old.** Heb. *kedem*, Mi +5:2. **the adversaries.** La 2:15, 16. Ps 79:4. 137:3, 4. Mi 4:11. **sabbaths.** Is +*58:13n. Je 17:21-23, √27. Ezk 22:8, 26. 23:38.

8. **hath.** ver. 5, 20. 1 K 8:46, 47. 9:7, 9. Is 59:2-13. Je 6:28. Ezk 14:13-21. 22:2-15. **grievously sinned.** lit. sinned a sin. ♪24I, Is +21:7. **removed.** Heb. become a removing, *or*, wandering. Je 15:4mg. 24:9mg. 34:17mg. Ezk 23:46mg. **all.** La 4:15, 16. 5:12-16. 1 S 2:30. **they.** La 4:21. Is 47:3. Je *13:22, 26. Ezk 16:37-39. 23:29. Ho 2:3, 10. Re 3:18. **she sigheth.** ver. 4, 11, 21, 22. La 2:10. Je 4:31.

9. **filthiness.** ver. 17. Je 2:34. 13:27. Ezk 24:12, 13. **she remembereth.** Dt *32:29. Is 47:7. Je 5:31. 1 P 4:17. **came.** ver. 1. La 4:1. Is *3:8, 9. Je 13:17, 18. **wonderfully.** ♪96F2, Ge +4:10. **she had.** ver. 2, 17, 21. La 2:13. Ec 4:1. Is 40:2. 54:11. Ho 2:14. Jn 11:19. **behold.** Ex 3:7, 17. 4:31. Dt 26:7. 1 S 1:11. 2 S 16:12. 2 K 14:26. Ne 9:32. Ps 25:18. 119:153. Da 9:17-19. **for.** Dt 32:27. Ps 74:8, 9, 22, 23. 140:8. Is 37:4, 17, 23, 29. Je 48:26. 50:29. Zp 2:10. 2 Th 2:4-8.

10. **spread.** ver. 7. Is 5:13, 14. Je 15:13. 20:5. 52:17-20. **pleasant.** *or*, desirable. ♪121R5, Ge +27:15. ver. 7mg. Ps 74:4-8. 79:1-7. Is 63:18. 64:10, 11. Je 51:51. 52:13. Ezk 7:22. 9:7. **whom.** Dt *23:3♪𝒫. Ne 13:1. Ezk 44:7. Mk 13:14.

11. **seek.** ver. 19. La 2:12. 4:4-10. Dt 28:52-57. 2 K 6:25. Je 19:9. 38:9. 52:6. Ezk 4:15-17. 5:16, 17. **relieve the soul.** Heb. make the soul to come again. Heb. *nephesh*, Ge +12:13. Ge +*2:7n. 1 S √30:11, 12. **see.** ver. 9, 20. La 2:20. Jb 40:4. Ps 25:15-19. **for I.** La 3:45. Je 30:17.

12. **Is it nothing.** *or*, It is nothing. Am=6:6. **pass by.** Heb. pass by the way. La 2:15mg. **if.** The church in distress here magnifies her affliction, and yet no more than there was cause for; her groaning was not heavier than her strokes. She appeals to all spectators: "See if there be any sorrow like unto my sorrow." This might perhaps be truly said of Jerusalem's griefs; but we are apt to apply it too sensibly to ourselves when we are in trouble and more than there is cause for. Because we feel most from our own burden, and cannot be persuaded to reconcile ourselves to it, we are ready to cry out, Surely never was *sorrow like unto our sorrow*; whereas, if our troubles were to be thrown into a common stock with those of others, and then an equal dividend made, share and share alike, rather than stand to that we should each of us say, "Pray, give me my own again" (Matthew Henry). La 2:13. 4:6-11. Da *9:12. Mt 24:21. Lk 21:22, 23. 23:28-31. **be.** or, exists. Heb. *yesh*. Ge 18:24. Pr 8:21 (substance; i.e. what exists). 18:24 (there is; i.e. there exists). **my sorrow.** Ps +*45:7. He 12:2, 3.

13. **above.** La 2:3, 4. Dt 32:21-25. Jb 30:30. Ps 22:14. 31:10. 102:3-5. Na *1:6. Hab +*3:16. 2 Th √1:8. He *12:29. **he hath spread.** La 4:17-20. Jb 18:8. 19:6. Ps 66:11. Ezk *12:13. *17:20. 32:3. Ho 7:12. **he hath turned.** Ps 35:4. 70:2, 3. 129:5. Is 42:17. **desolate.** ver. 22. La 5:17. Dt 28:65. Je 4:19-29.

14. **yoke.** Dt √28:47, 48♪𝒫. Pr 5:22. Is 14:25. 47:6. Je 27:8-12. 28:14. **delivered.** Je 25:9. 34:20, 21. 37:17.

39:1-9. Ezk 11:9. 21:31. 23:28. 25:4, 7. Ho 5:14.

15. **trodden.** 2 K 9:33. 24:14-16. 25:4, etc. Ps 119:118. Is 5:5. 28:18. Je 50:26mg. Da 8:13. Mi 7:10. Ml 4:3. Lk *21:24. He 10:29. **crush.** La 3:34. Dt 28:33. Jg 10:8mg. Je 51:34. **the virgin,** etc. *or,* the winepress of the virgin, etc. Je 14:17. **as in.** Is 63:3. Re 14:19, 20. *19:15.

16. **I weep.** ver. 2, 9. La 2:11, 18. 3:48, 49. Ps 119:136. Je 9:1, 10. *13:17. 14:17. Lk *19:41-44. Ro 9:1-3. **relieve.** Heb. bring back. ver. +11, 19. Ho 9:12. **soul.** Heb. *nephesh,* Ge +12:13. **my children.** ver. 5, 6. La 2:20-22. 4:2-10. Je 9:21.

17. **spreadeth.** 1 K 8:22, 38. Is 1:15. Je *4:31. **none.** ver. 2, 9, 16, 19, 21. **commanded.** La 2:1-8, 17-22. 2 K 24:2-4. 25:1. Je 6:3. 16:6. 21:4, 5. 34:22. Ezk 7:23, 24. Ho 8:8. Lk *19:43, 44. **Jerusalem.** ver. 9. La 4:15. Le 15:19-27. Ezk 36:17.

18. **Lord.** Ex 9:27. Dt 32:4. Jg 1:7. Ezr 9:13. Ne *9:33, 34. Ps 119:75. 145:17. Je 12:1. Da 9:7, 14. Zp 3:5. Ro 2:5. 3:19. Re 15:3, 4. 16:5-7. **for I.** La 3:42. 1 S 12:14, 15. √15:23. Ne 1:6-8. 9:26. Ps 107:11. Da 9:9-16. **commandment.** Heb. mouth. 1 K *13:21. **hear.** ver. 12. Dt 29:22-28. 1 K 9:8, 9. Je 22:8, 9. 25:28, 29. 49:12. Ezk 14:22, 23. **my virgins.** ver. 5, 6. Dt 28:32-41.

19. **for.** ver. 2. La 4:17. Jb 19:13-19. Je 2:28. *30:14. 37:7-9. **my priests.** ver. 11. La 2:20. 4:7-9. 5:12. Je 14:15-18. 23:11-15. 27:13-15. **ghost.** Heb. *gava,* Ge +49:33 (S#1478h). **while.** ver. 11. **souls.** Heb. *nephesh,* Ge +12:13.

20. **Behold.** ver. 9, 11. Is 38:14. **my bowels.** La 2:11. Jb 30:27. Ps 22:14. Is 16:11. Je 4:19. 31:20. 48:36. Ho 11:8. Hab 3:16. **for.** ver. 18. Le 26:40-42. 1 K 8:47-50. Jb 33:27. Ps 51:3, 4. Pr √28:13. Je 2:35. 3:13. Lk 15:18, 19. *18:13, 14. **abroad.** La 4:9, 10. Dt *32:25ᵐᵍ. Je 9:21, 22. 14:18. Ezk 7:15.

21. **have heard that.** ver. 2, 8, 11, 12, 16, 22. **they are.** La 2:15. 4:21, 22. Ps 35:15. 38:16. 137:7. Je 48:27. 50:11. Ezk 25:3, 6, 8, 15. 26:2. Ob 12, 13. **thou wilt.** Is ch. 13, 14, 47. Je 25:17-29. ch. 46-51. Ezk ch. 25-32. Am ch. 1. **the day.** Ps 37:13. Je 25:17-26. Jl 3:14. **called.** *or,* proclaimed. ver. 15, 19. Je 3:12. 12:6mg. 36:6 (read), 9, 14. 51:61 (read). **they shall.** La 4:22. Dt 32:41-43. Ps 137:8, 9. Is 51:22, 23. Je 50:15, 29, 31. *51:24, 49. Mi 7:9, 10. Hab 2:15-17. Re 18:6.

22. **Let.** Je +*10:25. **all their.** Ne 4:4, 5. Ps 109:14, 15. 137:7-9. Je +*10:25. 18:23. 51:35. Lk 23:31. Re *6:10. **my heart.** ver. 13. La 5:17. Is 13:7. Je 8:18. Ep 3:13.

LAMENTATIONS 2

The prophet describes, and mourns over, the desolations of Jerusalem and the miseries of the Jews, as brought on them by the just indignation of God, 1-12. He laments over the unequalled sufferings of the people, who, by hearkening to false prophets, are exposed to the cruel insults of their enemies; and he calls on the sufferers to join with him in tears and prayers, 13-19. Zion refers her doleful case to the compassionate consideration of God, 20-22.

1. **How.** La 1:1. 4:1. **covered.** La 3:43, 44. Ezk 30:18. 32:7, 8. Jl 2:2. **daughter.** ⌐155E5, Nu +21:25. **and cast.** ⌐102, Ge +2:24. Is 14:12-15. Ezk 28:14-16. Mt 11:23. Lk 10:15, 18. Re 12:7-9. **the beauty.** 1 S 4:21. 2 S 1:19. Is 64:11. Ezk 7:20-22. 24:21. **his foot-**

stool. ⌐22D3D1, Is +66:1. 1 Ch 28:2. Ps 99:5. 132:7. Is 60:13.

2. **swallowed.** ver. 17, 21. La 3:43. Jb 2:3mg. Ps 21:9. Is 27:11. Je 13:14. 21:7. Ezk 5:11. 7:4, 9. 8:18. 9:10. Zc 11:5, 6. Mt 18:33. **he hath thrown.** ver. 5, 17. Je 5:10. Mi 5:11, 12. Ml 1:4. 2 C *10:4. ⌐155E5, Nu +21:25. **brought them down to.** Heb. made to touch. Ps *89:39. Is 25:12. 26:5. **polluted.** See on Ps *89:39, 40. Is 23:9mg. 43:28. 47:6.

3. **the horn.** Jb 16:15. Ps 75:5, 10. 89:24. 132:17. Je 48:25. Lk 1:69. **he hath.** Ps 74:11. **he burned.** Dt 32:22. Ps 79:5. *89:46. Is 1:31. 42:25. Je 4:4. 7:20. Ml 4:1. Lk 3:17.

4. **bent.** ver. 5. La 3:3, 12, 13. Jb 6:4. 16:12-14. Is +*63:10. Je 21:5. 30:14. **bow.** ⌐22D5B, Dt +32:23. **like an enemy.** Ru +*1:13, 21. Jb +*13:24. **that were pleasant to the eye.** Heb. the desirable of the eye. ⌐121R5, Ge +27:15. Ezk 24:25. **he poured.** La 4:1. 2 Ch 34:21, 25. Is 42:25. 51:17-20. 63:6. Je 4:4. 7:20. 21:5, 12. 36:7. Ezk 5:13. 6:12. 22:22. 36:18. Na 1:2, 6.

5. **was.** ver. 4. Je 15:1. 30:14. **he hath swallowed up Israel.** ver. 2. 2 K *25:9. 2 Ch 36:16, 17. Je 52:13. **mourning.** Ezk 2:10.

6. **he hath violently.** "He hath destroyed the temple, as if it had been no better than a cottage erected in a garden, while the fruit is gathering, and then removed, or suffered to decay." Ps 80:12. 89:40. Is *5:5. 63:18. 64:11. **tabernacle.** *or,* hedge. Jb 27:18. Is 1:8. **as if.** Is 1:8. **caused.** La 1:4. Zp 3:18. **solemn feasts.** Ge +17:21h. Le *23:2n. **sabbaths.** Is 1:13. **the king.** La 4:16, 20. 5:12. Is 43:28. Je 52:11-27. Ezk 12:12, 13. 17:18. Ml 2:9.

7. **cast off.** ver. 1. Le 26:31, 44. Ps 78:59-61. Is 64:10, 11. Je 7:12-14. 26:6, 18. 52:13. Ezk 7:20-22. 24:21. Mi 3:12. Mt *24:2. Ac 6:13, 14. **given up.** Heb. shut up. ver. 5. 2 Ch 36:19. Je 32:29. 33:3, 4. 39:8. Ezk 7:24. Am 2:5. **they have.** Ps 72:4, etc. *74:3-8. Ezk 7:21, 22. **solemn feast.** Ge +17:21h. Le *23:2n.

8. **purposed.** ver. 17. Is 5:5. Je 5:10. **stretched.** 2 S 8:2. 2 K *21:13. Is 28:17. 34:11. Am 7:7, 8. **he hath not.** Jb 13:21. Ezk 20:22. **destroying.** Heb. swallowing up. ver. 2, 5. **he made.** Is 3:26. Je 14:2. **lament.** ⌐155D, Ge +4:10.

9. **gates.** Ne 1:3. Je 39:2, 8. 51:30. 52:14. **her king.** La 1:3. 4:15, 20. Dt *28:36ᵐᵍ. 2 K 24:12-16. 25:7. Je 52:8, 9. Ezk 12:13. 17:20. **the law.** 2 Ch +*15:3. Ezk 7:26. Ho 3:4. **her prophets.** Ps +*74:9. Am 8:11, 12. Mi 3:6, 7.

10. **elders.** La 4:5, 16. 5:12, 14. Jb 2:13. Is 3:26. 47:1, 5. **sit.** ⌐121S3Y. Metonymy of the Adjunct B607. The sign is put for the thing signified, in connected words and phrases. "Sitting on the ground" is put for grief. For other instances of this figure see Jb 2:13. Is 3:26. *Sitting on the ground* was a posture of mourning and deep distress. Hence the coin struck by Vespasian, on the capture of Jerusalem, has on the obverse side a palm tree, the emblem of Judea, and under it a woman, the emblem of Jerusalem, sitting down, with her elbow on her knee, and her head supported by her hand, with the legend *Judaea capta.* See La 1:1. **and keep.** La 3:28. Je 8:14. Am 5:13. 8:3. **cast up.** Jsh 7:6. 2 S 13:19. Jb *2:12, 13. Re 18:19. **they have girded.** Is *15:3. 36:22. Ezk 7:18. 27:31. Jl 1:8, 13. **sackcloth.** ⌐121S3U, Jb 16:15. **the virgins.** La 1:4. Am 8:13.

11. **eyes**. La 1:16. 3:48-51. 1 S 30:4. Ps *6:7. 31:9. 69:3. Is 38:14. **tears**. ver. 19. Zc 8:5. **my bowels**. La 1:20. Je 4:19. **my liver**. Jb 16:13. Ps *22:14. **poured**. *102, Ge +2:24. **for**. La 4:10. Is 22:4. Je 8:19-22. 9:1. 14:17. **because**. ver. 19, 20. La 4:3, 4, 9, 10. Lk 23:29. **swoon**. *or*, faint. Is 57:16.

12. **Where is**. La 1:11. **corn**. *121D4, Ge +27:28. **and**. *174, Ge +18:27. **wine**. *121D13, Ge +27:28. **as the wounded**. Ezk 30:24. **soul**. Heb. *nephesh*, Ge +12:13. Is 53:12.

13. **shall I take**. La 1:12. Da 9:12. **daughter**. *155E5, Nu +21:25. **for thy breach**. 2 S 5:20. Ps 60:2. Je 14:17. Ezk 26:3, 4. **who can**. Is 51:19. Je 8:22. 30:12-15. 51:8, 9.

14. **prophets**. Is 9:15, 16. Je 2:8. *5:31. 6:13, 14. 8:10, 11. 14:13-15. 23:11-17. 27:14-16. 28:15. 29:8, 9. 37:19. Ezk *13:1-16. Mi 2:11. 3:5-7. 2 P 2:1-3. **they have**. Is 58:1. Je √23:22. Ezk 13:22. **false**. Je *23:14-17, 31, 32. 27:9, 10. Ezk 22:25, 28. Mi 3:5. Zp 3:4. **banishment**. *121G, Ge +31:1.

15. **All**. The combination of scorn, enmity, rage, and exultation, which the conquerors and spectators manifested at the destruction of Jerusalem and the temple, are here described with peculiar pathos and energy. The whole scene is presented to view as in an exquisitely finished historical painting. **that pass**. Dt 29:22-28. 1 K 9:7-9. 2 Ch 7:21. Je 18:16. **by**. Heb. by the way. La 1:12mg. **clap**. La 1:8. Jb 27:22, 23. Ezk 25:6. Na 3:19. **they**. ver. 16. Je 19:8. 25:9, 18. 29:18. 51:37. Mi 6:16. Zp 2:15. **wag**. 2 K 19:21. Ps 22:7. *44:14, 15. Is 37:22. Je 18:16. Mt 27:39. Mk 15:29. **saying**. *108F, Ps +109:5. **Is this**. ver. 6. Ps *48:2. *50:2. Is 64:11.

16. **thine**. La 3:46. Jb 16:9, 10. Ps *22:13. 35:21. 109:2. **gnash**. Ps 35:16. 37:12. 112:10. Ac 7:54. **We have swallowed**. Ps 56:2. 57:3. 124:3. Is 49:19. Je 50:7, 17. 51:34. Ezk 25:3, 6, 15. 36:3. Ho 8:8. Zp 2:8-10. **we have seen**. Ps 35:21. 41:8. Ob 12-16.

17. **done**. ver. 8. Le *26:14, 16, 17)·Ͼ. Dt *28:15)·Ͼ, etc. 29:18-23. 31:16, 17. 32:15-27. Je 18:11. Mi 2:3. **old**. Heb. *kedem*, Mi +5:2. **he hath thrown**. ver. 1, 2. Ezk 5:11. 7:8, 9. 8:18. 9:10. **he hath caused**. La 1:5. Dt 28:43, 44. Ps *38:16. *89:42.

18. **heart**. Ps 119:145. Is 26:16, 17. Ho 7:14. **O wall**. ver. 8. Hab 2:11. **let tears**. La 1:2, 16. 3:48, 49. Ps 119:136. Je 4:31. 9:1, 17, 18. 13:17. 14:17. **the apple**. Bath ayin, which sometimes means the *pupil* of the eye, seems here to denote *tears*, the produce of the eye; and therefore elegantly termed the *daughter of the eye*. Ps 17:8.

19. **cry out**. Ps 42:8. *62:8. *119:+55, 147, 148. *130:6. Is √26:9. Mk +*1:35. Lk 6:12. **watches**. Jg 7:19. Mt 14:25. Mk 13:35. **pour**. 1 S 1:15. 7:6. Jb 3:24. Ps *62:8. 142:2. **heart**. *121I1, Ge +3:7. **like water**. ver. 11. Zc 8:5. **lift up**. Ps 28:2. 63:4. 134:2. 141:2. 1 T +*2:8. **life**. Heb. *nephesh*, Ge +44:30. **that faint**. ver. 11, 12. La 4:1-9. Is 51:20. Ezk 5:10, 16. Na 3:10.

20. **consider**. Ex 32:11. Dt 9:26. Is 63:16-19. 64:8-12. Je 14:20, 21. **Shall the women**. *85P, Ge +27:46. La *4:10. Le *26:29)·Ͼ. Dt *28:53-57)·Ͼ. 2 K 6:28, 29. Je 19:9. Ezk 5:10. **of a span long**. *or*, swaddled with their hands. ver. 22. **shall the priest**. *85P, Ge +27:46. La 1:19. 4:13, 16. Ps 78:64. Is 9:14-17. Je 5:31. 14:15-18. *23:11-15. Ezk *9:5, 6.

21. **young**. Dt 28:50. Jsh 6:21. 1 S 15:3. 2 Ch 36:17.

Est 3:13. Je 51:22. Ezk 9:6. **and the old**. *174, Ge +18:27. **my virgins**. La 1:15, 18. Ge +*24:16h. Ps 78:63. Je 9:21. 11:22. 18:21. Am 4:10. **by the sword**. Jb *27:14. **thou hast killed**. ver. 2, 17. La 3:43. Is 27:11. Je 13:14. 21:7. Ezk 5:11. 7:4, 9. 8:18. 9:5, 10. Zc 11:6.

22. **solemn day**. ver. +6. Ge +17:21h. **my terrors**. Ps 31:13. Is 24:17, 18. Je *6:25. 20:3, 10. 46:5. 49:29. Am 9:1-4. **those**. Dt 28:18. Je 16:2-4. Ho 9:12-16. Lk 23:29, 30.

LAMENTATIONS 3

The prophet bitterly bewails his complicated sufferings, 1-20. He acknowledges the mercy and truth of God, and the benefit of afflictions, to be a proper ground of patient hope, 21-36. He exhorts his people to submit to the sovereignty of God, and humbly to turn unto him, 37-41. He mingles complaints with confessions of sin, 42-54. He appeals to God against his enemies, and beseeches him to execute judgment upon them, 55-66.

1. **the man**. *155E2. Personification B867. A whole nation is spoken of as a man, or speaks as a man. For another instance of this figure, see Da 2:31. **hath**. lit. he hath. *96D3, Ge +49:4. **seen affliction**. La 1:12-14. Jb 19:21. Ps 71:20. 88:7, 15, 16. Is *53:3. Je 15:17, 18. 20:14-18. 38:6. **his wrath**. That is, the wrath of God. Jb 9:34. 21:9. Ps *2:9. 88:7. 89:32. Is +*10:5.

2. **brought**. ver. 53-55. La 2:1. Dt 28:29. Jb 18:18. 30:26. Is 59:9. Je 13:16. Am 5:18-20. Ju 6, 13. **darkness**. Pr +*20:20.

3. **and brought**. La 2:4-7. Dt 29:20. Jb 31:21. Is 1:25. 63:10. **darkness**. *Darkness* denotes calamity, and light signifies prosperity. Pr +*20:20.

4. **My flesh**. Jb *16:8, 9. Ps 31:9, 10. 32:3. 38:2-8. 102:3-5. **he hath**. Ps 22:14. *51:8. Is 38:13. Je 50:17.

5. **builded**. ver. *7-9. Jb *19:8. **compassed**. Ps 32:7, 10. **gall**. ver. *19. Ps *69:21. Je *8:14. *9:15. 23:15.

6. **in dark**. Ps 88:5, 6. *143:3, 7. **of old**. Heb. *olam*, Ge +*6:4.

7. **hedged**. ver. 9. Jb 3:23. 19:8. Ps 88:8. Pr +*13:15. Je 38:6. Ho *2:6. **made**. La 1:14. 5:5. Da 9:12. **chain**. lit. brass. *121D2, Jg +16:21. Jg 16:21. 2 K 25:7. 2 Ch 33:11. 36:6. Je 39:7.

8. **when I cry**. ver. 44. Jb 19:7. *30:20. Ps *22:2. 80:4. Hab 1:2. Mt=27:46.

9. **enclosed**. Je 36:5. **made**. ver. *11. Is *30:28. *63:17. Je 36:5.

10. **unto**. Jb *10:16. Is 38:13. Ho 5:14. 6:1. 13:7, 8. Am 5:18-20. **in secret**. Ps 10:9. 17:12.

11. **pulled**. Jb 16:12, 13. Ps 50:22. Je 5:6. 51:20-22. Da 2:40-44. 7:23. Mi 5:8. Ho *6:1. **he hath made**. La 1:13. Jb 16:7. Is 3:26. Je 6:8. 9:10, 11. 19:8. 32:43. Mt 23:38. Re 18:19.

12. **bent**. Jb 6:4. 7:20. 16:12, 13. Ps 7:12, 13. *38:2. **bow**. *22D5B, Dt +32:23.

13. **arrows**. Heb. sons. *22D5B, Dt +32:23. Jb *6:4. 41:28.

14. **a derision**. ver. 63. Ne 4:2-4. Jb 30:1-9. Ps 22:6, 7. 35:15, 16. 44:13. 69:11, =12. 79:4. 123:3, 4. 137:3. Je *20:7, 8. 48:27. Mt 27:39-44. 1 C 4:9-13. **song**. ver. 63. Ps 69:12.

15. **filled**. ver. 19. Ru 1:20. Jb 9:18. Ps 60:3. Is 51:17-22. Je *9:15. 23:15. 25:15-18, 27. **bitterness**. Heb. bitternesses. Ex 12:8. Nu 9:11. 1 S +1:10.

16. **broken.** Jb 4:10. Ps 3:7. 58:6. **gravel.** Pr 20:17. Mt 7:9. Lk 11:11. **hath.** Ps 102:9. **covered me with ashes.** *or,* rolled me in the ashes. Jb 2:8. Je 6:26. Jon 3:6.

17. **thou.** La 1:16. Ps 119:155. Is 38:17. 54:10. 59:11. Je 8:15. 14:19. 16:5. Zc 8:10. **soul.** Heb. *nephesh,* Ge +34:3. **I forgat.** Ge 41:30. Jb 7:7. Je 20:14-18. **prosperity.** Heb. good. Ge 1:4. Jb 2:10. Ec 7:14, 18, 20, 26. Je 18:20.

18. **I said.** 1 S 27:1. Jb 6:11. 17:15. Ps *31:22. 116:11. Is 40:27. Ezk 37:11. **strength.** 1 S 15:29. Jb +4:20 (✻S#5331h). Is 63:3.

19. **Remembering.** *or,* Remember. Ne 9:32. Jb 7:7. Ps 89:*47, 50. *132:1. **the.** ver. *5, *15. Je *9:15.

20. **My.** ∫182, Ge +18:22. **soul.** Heb. *nephesh,* Ge +34:3. ∫22A1, Le +26:11n. **hath.** Jb 21:6. **humbled.** Heb. bowed. Ps 42:5, 6, 11. 43:5. 146:8.

21. **recall to my mind.** Heb. make to return to my heart. Ps 77:7-11. Je 2:24mg. **therefore.** ver. 24-29. Ps 119:81. 130:7. Hab 2:3.

22. **of.** Ezr *9:8, 9, 13-15. Ne *9:31. Ps *78:38. 106:45. Ezk 20:8, 9, 13, 14, 21, 22. Ml *3:6. **mercies.** ∫96F2, Ge +4:10. **because.** Ps *77:8. *86:15. Mi *7:18, 19. Lk 1:50.

23. **new.** Ps *30:5. Is 33:2. Zp 3:5. **morning.** ∫171T4, Jb +7:18. Ps 92:2. Is 33:2. **great.** Ex 34:6, 7. Ps 36:5. *89:1, 2, 33. 146:6. T *1:2. He *6:18. *10:23. **faithfulness.** Ps 143:1.

24. **my portion.** Dt 32:9. Ps +*16:5. *73:26. *119:57. 142:5. Je *10:16. 51:19. **soul.** Heb. *nephesh,* Ge +34:3. **therefore.** ver. 21. 1 S *30:6. 1 Ch *5:20. Jb *13:15, 16. Ps *31:24. *33:18. *42:11. 43:5. *62:8. *84:12. 130:7. Ro 15:12, 13. 1 P *1:21.

25. **good.** Ex +*34:6. Ps 25:8-10. 86:5. Je +*29:11. Na *1:7. Mt +*5:45. Lk +*6:35. **that wait for.** ver. *26. Ge 49:18∥₽. Ps *25:8. *27:14. *37:7, 34. 39:7. *40:1-5. 62:1, 5. *130:5, 6. Is *25:9. *30:18. *40:31. 49:23. *64:4. Mi 7:7, 8. Zp 3:8. 1 Th *1:10. Ja *5:7. **soul.** Heb. *nephesh,* Ge +12:5. **that seeketh.** 1 Ch +*28:9. 2 Ch *15:2. *19:3. *30:19. *31:21. Ps +*9:10. *22:26. 27:8. *69:32. 105:3, 4. *119:2. Is √26:9. √55:6. Ho *10:12. Lk 11:9, 10. He √11:6.

26. **good.** Ps 52:9. 54:6. *73:28. *92:1. Ga *4:18. **hope.** Ro 8:25. He +*3:14. *10:35. 1 P *1:13. **quietly.** Ge *49:18. Ex 14:13. 2 Ch *20:17. Ps *37:7, 34. *119:166, 174. *130:5. Is *30:7, 15.

27. **bear.** Ps √90:12. *94:12. *119:71. Ec 12:1. Mt √11:29, 30. He *12:5-12.

28. **sitteth alone.** La 2:10. Ps 39:9. 102:7. Je *15:17.

29. **putteth.** 2 Ch 33:12. Jb 40:4. *42:5, 6. Ezk 16:63. Ro 3:19. **if.** Jl 2:14. Jon 3:9. Zp +*2:3. Lk *15:18, 19. *18:13.

30. **his cheek.** Jb 16:10. Is *50:6. Mi 5:1. Mt *5:39. ✻+26:67. Lk 6:29. 2 C 11:20. **filled.** La 1:12. Ps 69:9, 20. 123:3.

31. **not cast off.** 1 S +*12:22. Ps 77:7. +*94:14. 103:8-10. Is +*54:7-10. 57:16. Je +√31:37. +*32:40. 33:24. Mi *7:18, 19. Ro +√11:1-6. He +*13:5. **for ever.** Heb. *olam,* Ex +*12:24.

32. **though he cause.** ver. 22. Ex 2:23-25. 3:7. Jg 10:16. 2 K 13:23. Ps 30:5. 78:38. 103:11-13. 106:43-45. Je 31:20. Ho 11:8, 9. Mi *7:19. Lk 15:20.

33. **afflict.** Jb *37:23. Ps +*90:15. +*119:75. Is 28:21. 63:9. Ezk *18:32. √33:11. Jn 16:27. He *12:9, 10. **willingly.** Heb. from his heart. Nu 16:28. Je 14:14. 23:16. 31:20. Ezk 13:17. Jn 5:30. 6:38. **nor grieve.**

Ru ◐+*1:13. Is 55:7. Mt 23:37. Lk +*6:35. 1 C *10:13. Ja 1:13, 17.

34. **crush.** Is 51:22, 23. Je 50:17, 33, 34. 51:33-36. **all.** Ps 69:33. 79:11. 102:20. Is 14:17. 49:9. Zc 9:11, 12.

35. **turn aside.** Dt 16:19∥₽. 24:17∥₽. 27:19∥₽. Ps +*12:5. 140:12. Pr 17:15. 22:22, 23. 23:10, 11. Zc 1:15, 16. **the most High.** *or, a* superior. Dt 26:19.

36. **the Lord.** 2 S *11:27. Is *59:15. Hab √1:13. **approveth.** Heb. seeth. Ps 54:7.

37. **saith.** Ps *33:9-11. Pr *16:9. 19:21. +*21:30. Is *46:10, 11. Da *4:35. Ro *9:15, 16. Ep +*1:11. Ja *4:13-15.

38. **most High.** Ge +14:18. **proceedeth not evil and good.** Jb *2:10. Ps 75:7. Pr 29:26. Is +*45:7. Am +*3:6. Mt +*5:45.

39. **doth.** ver. 22. Nu 11:11. Pr *19:3. Is 38:17-19. **complain.** *or,* murmur. Nu +*11:1. Ps 144:14. Is *29:24. 58:13. Ju +*16. **a man.** Ge 4:5-7, 13, 14. Le 26:41, 43. Nu 16:41. 17:12, 13. Jsh 7:6-13. 2 S 6:7, 8. 2 K 3:13. 6:32, 33. Ezr 9:13. Jb 11:6. Is 51:20. Jon 2:3, 4. 4:8, 9. Mi *7:9. He 12:5-12. Re 16:9.

40. **Let us search.** T#397. 1 Ch 15:12, 13. Jb 11:13-15. 34:31, 32. Ps 4:4. 119:59. 139:23, 24. Pr +16:25 (T#704). Je √29:13, 14. Ezk 18:28. Hg 1:5-9. 1 C +5:8 (T#105). 11:28, 31. 2 C √13:5. Ga 6:4. **turn.** Dt *4:30. 2 Ch 30:6, 9. Is √55:7. Ho *6:1. 12:6. 14:1-3. Jl 2:12, 13. Zc 1:3, 4. Ac +*3:19-21. 26:20.

41. **lift.** T#1349. Ps 25:1. *86:4. 116:4. *119:48. 143:6-8. **with.** Ps 28:2. 63:4. 141:2. 1 T +*2:8. **God.** Heb. *El,* Ex +15:2. **heavens.** ∫63BA, Ge +26:7. By ellipsis, supply (saying).

42. **transgressed.** La 1:18. 5:16. Ne 9:26. Jb 33:27, 28. Je 3:13. Da *9:5-14. Lk 15:18, 19. **thou.** 2 K 24:4. Je 5:7, 9, 29. Ezk 24:13, 14. Zc 1:5, 6.

43. **covered.** La 2:1. Ps 44:19. **persecuted.** ver. 66. Ps 83:15. **thou hast slain.** La 2:2, 17, 21. 2 Ch 36:16, 17. Ezk 7:9. 8:18. 9:10.

44. **covered.** Ps 97:2. **that.** See on ver. 8. Ps 80:4. Je 14:11, 12. 15:1. Zc 7:13.

45. **as.** ver. 14. La 2:15. 4:14, 15. Dt 28:13, 37, 44. 1 C *4:11-13.

46. **have.** La 2:16. Ex 11:7. Jb 30:9-11. Ps 22:6-8. 44:13, 14. 79:4, 10. Mt 27:38-45.

47. **Fear.** Is *24:17, 18. 51:19. Je *48:43, 44. Lk 21:35. **desolation.** See on La 1:4, 13. 2:1-9.

48. **Mine eye runneth.** La 2:11, 18. Ps 119:136. Je 4:19. *9:1, 18. 13:17. Lk=19:41. Ro *9:1-3.

49. **and.** See on La 1:16. Ps *77:2. Je 14:17.

50. **Till the Lord look down.** La 2:20. 5:1. Ps 80:14-16. 102:19, 20. Is 62:6, 7. *63:15. 64:1. Da 9:16-19.

51. **eye.** Ge 44:34. 1 S 30:3, 4. Je 4:19-21. 14:18. Lk 19:41-44. **mine heart.** Heb. my soul. Heb. *nephesh,* Ex +23:9. **because of all.** *or,* more than all. **the daughters.** La 1:18. 2:21. 5:11. Je 11:22. 14:16. 19:9.

52. **chased.** Je 37:15, 16. 38:4-6. **without.** 1 S 24:10-15. 25:28, 29. 26:18-20. Ps 35:7, 19. *69:4. 109:3. 119:161. Je 37:18. Jn 15:25.

53. **cut.** Ps 88:6. Je 37:20. *38:6, 9, 10. **in the.** Je 37:16. 38:6, 9, 10. **dungeon.** Heb. *bor,* Ge +37:20. **and.** Da *6:17. Mt 27:60, 66.

54. **Waters.** Ps 18:4. *69:1, 2, 15. 124:4, 5. Jon 2:3-5. **I said.** See on ver. 18. Jb 17:11-16. Ps *31:22. Is 38:10-13. Ezk 37:11. 2 C 1:8-10.

55. **called upon.** 2 Ch 33:11, 12. Ps 18:5, 6. 40:1, 2. 69:13-18. 116:3, 4. *130:1, 2. 142:3-7. Je 38:6. Jon

*2:2-4. Ac 16:24-28. **thy name.** Ps +√9:10. 20:1. **dungeon.** Heb. *bor*, Ge +37:20. T#1187.

56. **hast.** 2 Ch 33:13, 19. Jb 34:28. Ps 3:4. 6:8, 9. 34:6. 66:19. *116:1, 2. Is 38:5. **hide.** Ps 55:1. 88:13, 14. Ro 8:26. **at my breathing.** Ml √3:16.

57. **drewest.** Ps 69:18. 73:28. 145:18. Is 58:9. Ja *4:8. **thou saidest.** Is 41:10, 14. 43:1, 2. Je 1:17. Ac 18:9, 10. 27:24. Re 1:17. 2:10.

58. **thou hast pleaded.** 1 S 25:39. Ps *35:1. Je *51:36. **soul.** Heb. *nephesh*, Ge +12:13. **thou hast redeemed.** Ge 48:16. Ps 34:22. *71:23. 103:4.

59. **thou hast.** Je 11:19-21. 15:10. 18:18-23. 20:7-10. ch. 37, 38. **judge.** √147D, Ge +1:29. Ge 31:42. Ps 9:4. 26:1. *35:1, 23. 43:1. 1 P 2:23.

60. **hast seen.** ver. 59. Ps 10:14. *56:6. Je 11:19, 20.

61. **hast heard.** ver. 30. La 5:1. Ps 74:18. 89:50. Zp 2:8.

62. **lips.** Ps 59:7, 12. 140:3. Ezk 36:3. **and.** Je 18:18.

63. **their sitting.** Ps *139:2. **I am.** ver. 14. Jb 30:9.

64. **Render.** Ps 28:4. Je +*10:25. *11:20. 50:29. 2 T *4:14. Re *6:10. 18:6.

65. **sorrow.** *or*, obstinacy. Dt +*2:30. Is 6:10. **thy curse.** Ge +*12:3. Dt *27:15-26. 28:20. 2 K 22:19. Ps √37:22. *109:17, 18. Pr +*3:33. Is 65:20. Je 17:5. Da *9:11. Ml 1:14. 2:2. 3:9. 1 C *16:22.

66. **Persecute.** ver. 43. Ps 35:6. 83:15. **under.** Dt 7:24. *25:19. 29:20. 2 K 14:27. Je 10:11. **heavens.** Ps 8:3. 115:16. Is 66:1.

LAMENTATIONS 4

The prophet deplores the ruin of the city and temple; and the extreme misery of the people, especially by famine, 1-12. He ascribes these calamities to the sins of the prophets and priests, and shows how their allies disappointed them, and their enemies pursued them, 13-20. He predicts the termination of Zion's calamities, and judgments upon insulting Edom, 21, 22.

1. **How is the gold.** ♪45, Is +40:31. 2 K 25:9, 10. Is 1:21, 22. 14:12. Ezk 7:19-22. **the stones.** La 2:19. Je 52:13. Mt *24:2. Mk 13:2. Lk 21:5, 6.

2. **sons.** Is 51:18. Zc 9:13. **how.** La 2:21. 5:12. Is *30:14. Je 19:11. 22:28. Ro 9:21-23. 2 C *4:7. 2 T 2:20. **earthen.** Je 18:1-6. 19:1-10. **pitchers.** Is 22:24. Je 48:12.

3. **sea monsters.** *or*, sea calves. Ps 74:13mg. Je 9:11. **the daughter.** ver. 10. La 2:20. Le 26:29. Dt 28:52-57. 2 K 6:26-29. Is 49:15. Je 19:9. Ezk 5:10. Lk 23:28, 29. **like.** Jb *39:13-16. Ro 1:31.

4. **tongue.** ♪105, Ml +4:2. Ps *22:15. 137:6. **the young.** La 1:11. 2:11, 12. Dt 32:24. Mt 7:9-11. **breaketh.** ♪108H4, Is +58:7.

5. **that did.** Dt 28:54-56. Is 3:16-26. 24:6-12. 32:9-14. Je 6:2, 3. Am 6:3-7. Lk 7:25. 1 T 5:6mg. Re 18:7-9. **brought.** 2 S 1:24. Pr 31:21. Lk 16:19. **embrace.** Jb *24:8. Je 9:21, 22. Lk 15:16.

6. **punishment of the iniquity of the daughter**, *or*, iniquity of the daughter, etc. Is 1:9, 10. Ezk 16:48-50. Mt 11:23, 24. Lk 10:12. *12:47. **greater than.** Lk +*12:48. **the punishment.** ver. 9. Ge *19:25♪℘. Da 9:12. Mt 24:21.

7. **Nazarites.** Nu *6:2, etc. Jg 13:5, 7. 16:17. Am 2:11, 12. Lk 1:15. **purer.** 1 S 16:12. Ps 51:7. 144:12. SS 5:10. Da 1:15. **than.** ♪102B, Ge +13:16. **their polishing.** *Gizrathom*, rendered by Dr. Blayney, "their vein-

ing," from *gazar*, to divide, intersect, as the *blue veins* do the surface of the body. This is approved by Dr. A. Clarke, who remarks, "Milk will most certainly well apply to the *whiteness* of the *skin*; the beautiful *ruby* to the ruddiness of the flesh; and the *sapphire*, in its clear, transcendent *purple*, to the *veins* in a fine complexion."

8. **visage.** La 5:10. Jb 30:17-19, 30. Jl 2:6. Na 2:10. **blacker than a coal.** Heb. darker than blackness. ♪102B, Ge +13:16. Or, as Dr. Blayney renders, "duskier than the dawn;" *shacar* signifying "the dawn of the day, when it is neither light nor dark, but between both, at which time objects are not easily distinguished." **they.** ver. 1, 2. Ru 1:19, 20. Jb 2:12. Is 52:14. **their skin.** Jb 19:20. 33:21. Ps 32:4. 38:3. *102:3-5, 11. 119:83.

9. **for.** Le 26:39. Ezk 24:23. 33:10. **pine away.** Heb. flow out. Ps 78:20.

10. **hands.** See on ver. 3. La 2:20. 2 K 6:26-29. **pitiful.** Is *49:15. **in.** La 3:48. Dt *28:56, 57♪℘. 2 K *6:29.

11. **Lord.** ver. 22. La 2:8, 17. Dt 32:21-25. Je 6:11, 12. 7:20. 9:9-11. 13:14. 14:15, 16. 15:1-4. 19:3-11. 23:19, 20. 24:8-10. Ezk 20:47, 48. 22:31. Da 9:12. Zc 1:6. Lk 21:22. **kindled.** Dt *32:22♪℘. Je 21:14.

12. **kings of.** Dt 29:24-28. 1 K 9:8, 9. Ps 48:4-6. *79:1.

13. **the sins.** La 2:14. Je 5:31. 6:13. 14:14. 23:11-21. Ezk 22:26-28. Mi 3:11, 12. Zp 3:3, 4. **that.** Je 2:30. 26:8, 9. Mt √23:31, 33-37. Lk 11:47-51. Ac 7:52. 1 Th 2:15, 16.

14. **have wandered.** Dt 28:28, 29. Is 29:10-12. 56:10. 59:9-11. Mi 3:6, 7. Mt +*15:14. Ep 4:18. **they have polluted.** Nu 35:33. Is *1:15. Je 2:34. **with blood.** Nu *19:11, 16♪℘. 2 K *21:16. **so that men could not touch.** *or*, in that they could not *but* touch. Nu 19:16. Ho 4:2.

15. **Depart ye.** Nu 16:26. 19:16. Ps 6:8. 139:19. Mi 2:10. 2 C +*6:17. **it is unclean.** *or*, ye polluted. Le *13:45♪℘.

16. **anger.** *or*, face. ♪22A4, Ge +19:13. Jb 23:15. **hath divided.** Ge 49:7. Le 26:33-39. Dt 28:25, 64, 65. 32:26. Je 15:4. 24:9. **he will.** Ps 106:44. He 8:9. **they respected.** La *5:12. 2 K 25:18-21. 2 Ch 36:17. Is 9:14-16.

17. **our eyes.** La 1:19. 2 K 24:7. Is 20:5, 6. *30:1-7. 31:1-3. Je 2:18, 36. 8:20. 37:7-10. Ezk *29:6, 7, 16. **watched for.** For the *Egyptians*, who were their pretended allies; but who were neither able nor willing to help them. Ps 130:6.

18. **hunt.** La 3:52. 1 S 24:14. 2 K *25:4, 5. Jb 10:16. Ps 140:11. Je 16:16. 39:4, 5. 52:7-9. **our end is near.** Je 1:12. 51:33. Ezk *7:2-12. 12:22, 23, 27. Am *8:2.

19. **persecutors.** Dt *28:49♪℘. Is 5:26-28. 30:16, 17. Je *4:13. Ho 8:1. Hab 1:8. Mt 24:27, 28. **than.** ♪102B, Ge +13:16. **the eagles.** The *eagle*, whose wings are of an extraordinary length, darts with amazing rapidity through the voids of heaven. **they pursued.** Am 2:14. 9:1-3.

20. **breath.** Heb. *ruach*, Ge +6:17. La 2:9. Ge 2:7. 44:30. 2 S 18:3. Ps +146:4. **the anointed.** 1 S 12:3, 5. 16:6. 24:6, 10. 26:9, 11, 16, 23. 2 S 1:14, 16, 21. 19:21. Ps 89:20, 21. **was taken.** Je 39:5. *52:8, 9. Ezk 12:13. 17:18-20. *19:4, 8. **pits.** Ps 107:20. Je 2:6. 18:20, 22. **we shall live among.** There is an unannounced time gap between this verse and the next (Is 61:2n).

21. **Rejoice.** ſ60A, Ge +3:22. **be glad.** Ps 83:3-12. 137:7. Ec 11:9. Ezk 25:6, 8. 26:2. 35:11-15. Ob 10-16. **the land.** Ge 36:28. Jb 1:1. **the cup.** Is ch. 34. 63:1-6. Je 25:15-29. 49:12, 13. Ezk 25:12-14. 35:3-9. Am 1:11, 12. Ob 1, *10, etc. Ml 1:2-4. **and shalt.** 2 Ch 28:19. Mi 1:11. Re 16:15.

22. **The punishment of thine iniquity.** or, Thine iniquity. ver. 6mg. Is √40:1, 2. Je 46:27, 28. 50:20. **no more carry.** Is 52:1. 60:18. Je +*32:40. Ezk 37:28. **he will visit.** ver. 21. Ps *137:7, 8. **discover thy sins.** or, carry thee captive for thy sins. Na 2:7mg.

LAMENTATIONS 5

The Jews complain to God of the greivous calamities which they endured for their sins; and of the desolations of Zion, 1-18. They earnestly pray him to return unto them in mercy, 19-22.

1. **Remember.** La 1:20. 2:20. 3:19. Ne 1:8. Jb 7:7. 10:9. Je 15:15. Hab 3:2. Lk 23:42. **behold.** La 2:15. 3:61. Ne 1:3. 4:4. Ps 44:13-16. 74:10, 11. 79:4, 12. *89:50, 51. 123:3, 4.

2. **inheritance.** Dt 28:30, etc. Ps *79:1, 2. Is 1:7. 5:17. 63:18. Je 6:12. Ezk 7:21, 24. Zp 1:13.

3. **orphans.** Ex 22:24. Je 18:21. Ho 14:3. **fatherless.** Dt +*10:18.

4. **have.** Dt √28:47, 48. Is 3:1. Ezk 4:9-17. **for money.** lit. silver. Ge 13:2. **is sold.** Heb. cometh for price.

5. **Our necks are under persecution.** Heb. On our necks are we persecuted. La 1:14. 4:19. Dt *28:48, 65, 66. Je 27:2, 8, 11, 12. *28:14. Mt *11:29. Ac 15:10. **labor.** Ne 9:36, 37.

6. **given.** Ge +*24:2. 47:29. 2 K 10:15. 1 Ch +*29:24mg. 2 Ch *30:8mg. Ezr 10:19. Je 50:15. Ezk 17:18. **hand.** ſ121S3I, 1 Ch +29:24. **to the Egyptians.** Is 30:1-6. 31:1-3. 57:9. Je 2:18, 36. 44:12-14. Ho 5:13. 7:11. 9:3. *12:1.

7. **fathers.** Ex +*20:5. Je 16:12. 31:29. Ezk *18:2. Mt 23:32-36. **and are.** Ge 42:13, 36. Jb 7:8, 21. Je 31:15. Zc 1:5. **borne.** Is 53:4, 11. Mt 27:25.

8. **Servants.** Ge 9:25. Dt 28:43. Ne 2:19. *5:15. Pr 30:22. **there.** Jb 5:4. 10:7. Ps 7:2. 50:22. Is 43:13. Ho 2:10. Zc 11:6.

9. **gat our bread.** Jg 6:11. 2 S 23:17. Je 40:9-12. 41:1-10, 18. 43:14, 16. Ezk 4:16, 17. 12:18, 19. **lives.** Heb. *nephesh,* souls, Ge +44:30. ſ121A7, Ge +9:5. **sword.** ſ121S1, Ge +49:10. By Metonymy of the Adjunct, whereby the sign is put for the thing signified, "sword" is put for the fightings. Ezk 21:3, 4.

10. **skin.** La 3:4. 4:8. Jb 30:30. Ps *119:83. Re 6:5,

6. **black.** or, burning. Ge 43:30. 1 K 3:26. Ho 11:8. **terrible famine.** or, terrors, or storms, of famine. Ps 11:6mg.

11. **ravished.** Dt 28:30. Is 13:16. Zc 14:2. **women.** Ge 2:22, 23. Ps 58:8. **maids.** Ge +24:16.

12. **Princes.** La 2:10, 20. 4:16. Is 47:6. Je 39:6, 7. 52:10, 11, 25-27. **hanged up.** Ge 40:19. Dt 21:22, 23. Est 2:23. 7:9mg, 10. **faces.** ſ171Q, Ge +3:19. **elders.** ver. 14. La 4:16. **not honored.** La 2:6. 4:16. Le +*19:32.

13. **the young men.** Ex 11:5. Jg *16:21. Jb 31:10. Is 47:2. **grind.** Ec 12:3, 4. Mt ◑*24:41. **fell.** Ex 1:11. 2:11. 23:5. Jsh *9:27. Ne 5:1-5. Is 58:6. Mt 23:4.

14. **elders.** La 1:4, 19. 2:10. Dt 16:18. Jb 29:7-17. 30:1. Is 3:2, 3. **the gate.** ſ171S7B, Ge +*14:7. Jsh 20:4. **the young.** Jb 30:31. Is √24:7-11. Je *7:34. 16:9. 25:10. Ezk 26:13. Re 18:22.

15. **our dance.** Ps 30:11. Am 6:4-7. 8:10. Ja 4:9, 10.

16. **The crown.** La 1:1. Jb *19:9. Ps *89:39. Je 13:18. Ezk 21:26. Re 2:10. 3:11. **is fallen from our head.** Heb. of our head is fallen. **woe.** La 1:8, 18. 2:1. 4:13. Pr *14:34. Is 3:9-11. Je 2:17, 19. 4:18. Ezk 7:17-22. 22:12-16. 2 P 2:4-6.

17. **our heart.** La 1:13, 22. Le 26:36. Is 1:5. Je 8:18. 46:5. Ezk 21:7, 15. Mi 6:13. **our eyes.** La 2:11. Dt 28:65. Jb 17:7. Ps 6:7. 31:9. 69:3. Is 38:14.

18. **of the.** La 2:8, 9. 1 K 9:7, 8. Ps 74:2, 3. Je 17:3. 26:9. 52:13. Mi 3:12. **the foxes.** Ps 63:10. Is 32:13, 14. Je 9:11.

19. **remainest.** Dt 33:27. Ps 9:7. 10:16. 29:10. *90:2. *102:12, 25-27. Hab 1:12. 1 T 1:17. 6:15, 16. He 1:10-12. +*13:8. Re 1:4, +*8, 17, 18. **for ever.** Heb. *olam,* Ex +*12:24. **thy throne.** Ps +*45:6. 145:13. 146:10. Da 2:44. 7:14, 27. He +*1:8, 9.

20. **dost.** Ps *13:1, 2. 44:24. 74:1. 77:7-10. 79:5. 85:5. 89:46. 94:3, 4. +*102:13, 16. Is 64:9-12. Je 14:19-21. Ac +*1:6. **for ever.** Jb +4:20 (❋S#5331h). **so long time.** Heb. for length of days. Ps +23:6mg. Mt +√25:19.

21. **Turn.** T#1456. Ex 25:21, 22. 33:15, 16. Dt √4:30. *30:1-10. 1 K 8:28, 29. 18:37. Jb *23:3, 4. Ps 22:1, 2. *42:1, 2. *51:11, 12. 63:1, 2, *4-6. *80:3, 7, 19. 84:2-4. *85:4. 139:17, 18. Is 64:6-12. Je *31:18. +*32:39, 40. Ezk 11:19, 20. 36:25-27, 37. Hab 3:2. Ep *3:16-19. Re *3:20. **renew.** Ps *51:10. Is 60:20-22. Je 31:4, 23-25. 33:10, 13. Zc 8:3-6. Ml *3:4. **old.** Mi +5:2 (❋S#6924h).

22. **But thou hast utterly rejected us.** or, For wilt thou utterly reject us? Ps 44:9. 60:1, 2. Is +√41:9. +*54:7. Je +*4:27. 14:19. 15:1-5. 23:39. Ezk 37:11. Ho 1:6. Zc √10:6.

EZEKIEL

EZEKIEL 1

The time, place, and manner, in which Ezekiel was called to the prophetical office, 1-3. The vision of four living creatures, and four wheels, 4-25; and of the glory of God above them, 26-28.

1. **A.M. 3409. B.C. 595. in the thirtieth year.** Nu 4:3. Lk 3:23. **as I.** 2 K *24:14. Ec 9:1, 2. Je 24:5-7. **captives.** Heb. captivity. Je 28:4mg. **by the river.** ver. 3. Ezk 3:15, 23. 10:15, 20, 22. 43:3. Ps *137:1. **Chebar.**

i.e. *abundant, vehement,* ❋S#3529h. Ezk 1:1, 3. 3:15, 23. 10:15, 20, 22. 43:3. **Chebar,** called now *Khabour,* is a river of Mesopotamia, which taking its rise in the Mysian mountains, falls into the Euphrates near Carchemish, or Circesium, now Karkisia, about 35 degrees 20 minutes N. lat. and 40 degrees 25 minutes E. long. 2 K 17:6. 1 Ch 5:26. **the heavens.** Mt 3:16. Lk 3:21. Jn 1:51. Ac 7:56. 10:11. Re 4:1. 19:11. **I saw.** Ezk 8:3. 11:24. Ge 15:1. 46:2. Nu 12:6. Is 1:1. Da 8:1, 2. Ho 12:10. Jl 2:28. Mt 17:9. Ac 9:10-12. 10:3. 2 C 12:1.

2. **the fifth year.** Ezk 8:1. 20:1. 29:1, 17. 31:1. 40:1. 2 K *24:12-15.

3. **word.** Je 1:2, 4. Ho 1:1. Jl 1:1. 1 T 4:1. **Ezekiel.** Heb. Jehezkel. i.e. *God will strengthen*, *S#3168h. Ezk 1:3. 24:24. 1 Ch 24:16. **Buzi.** i.e. *sprung from Buz* (i.e. *contempt*), *to disrespect*, *S#941h, only here. **and the hand.** ✓22A14.8L, 1 K +18:46. Ezk 3:14, 22. 8:1. 33:22. 37:1. 40:1. 1 K *18:46. 2 K *3:15.

4. **a whirlwind.** Is 21:1. Je 1:13, 14. 4:6. 6:1. 23:19. 25:9, 32. Na 1:3. Hab 1:8, 9. Ac 2:2. Re 4:5. **a great.** Ezk 10:2-4. Ex 14:19, 20. 19:16-18. 24:16, 17. 40:34. Dt 4:11, 12. 2 Ch 5:13, 14. 6:1. 7:1-3. Ps 18:11-13. 50:3. *97:2, 3. 104:3, 4. Is 19:1. Na 1:3-6. Hab 3:3-5. He 12:29. **infolding itself.** Heb. catching itself. **color.** lit. eye. ✓121R1, Le +13:55. ver. 27. Ezk 8:2. 10:8, 9. Re 1:15. **midst of the fire.** 2 Ch 5:13, 14. Is *4:5.

5. **the likeness.** Re *4:6. 6:6g.

6. **And every one had four faces.** These *living creatures* were probably hieroglyphical representations of the holy angels, the attendants on "the King of glory," and the ministers of his providence. They were *four*, apparently to denote that they were employed in the four quarters of the world; and they had the *likeness of a man*, to signify that they were intelligent and rational creatures. ver. 10, 15. Ezk 10:10, 14, 21, 22. Re 4:7, 8. **every one had four wings.** ver. 8-11. Ex 25:20. 1 K 6:24-27. Is 6:2.

7. **straight feet.** Heb. a straight foot. **like the sole.** Le 11:3, 47. **the color.** ver. 13. Ps 104:4. Da 10:6. Re 1:15.

8. **the hands.** Ezk 8:3. 10:2, 7, 8, 18, 21. Is 6:6.

9. **joined.** ver. 11. 2 Ch 3:11, 12. 1 C 1:10. **they turned.** ver. 12. Ezk 10:11, 22. Pr 4:25-27. Lk 9:51, 62.

10. **for the.** Ezk 10:14. Re *4:7. **the face of a man.** Nu 2:10. Is 46:8. Lk 15:10. 1 C 14:20. **the face of a lion.** Nu 2:3. Jg 14:18. 1 Ch 12:8. Re 5:5. **the face of an ox.** Ezk 10:14, Cherub. Nu 2:18. Pr 14:4. 1 C 9:9, 10. **the face of an eagle.** Nu 2:25. Dt 28:49. Jb 39:27. Is 40:31. Da 7:4.

11. **and their.** Ezk 10:16, 19. **stretched upward.** *or*, divided above. **and two.** ver. 23. Ge 3:24. Ex 26:1. 1 K 6:23-29. Is *6:2. Re 4:6-8. 5:8-10.

12. **they went every.** ver. 9, 17. Ezk 10:22. **whither.** ver. 20, 21. Jn 17:22. Ro 8:14. 1 C 3:16. 6:17, 19. 12:6. 2 C 6:16. He *1:14. **spirit.** Heb. *ruach*, Ps +104:4.

13. **their appearance.** ver. 7. Ge 15:17. Ps *104:4. Is 6:2. Da 10:5, 6. Mt 28:3. Ac 2:3. Re *4:5. 10:1. 18:1.

14. **ran and.** ✓96B, Ge +8:5. Ps 147:15. Da 9:21. Zc 2:3, 4. 4:10. Mt *24:27, 31. Mk 13:27.

15. **one.** ver. 19-21. Ezk 10:9, 13-17. Da 7:9. **with.** ver. 6. Re 4:7.

16. **the color.** Ezk 10:9. Ex 39:13. Da 10:6. **a wheel.** Ezk 10:10. Jb 9:10. Ps 36:6. 40:5. Ro *11:33. 1 C *2:9, 10, 16. Ep 3:10.

17. **and.** ver. 9, 12. Ezk 10:11. Is 55:11.

18. **they were so.** Jb 37:22-24. Ps 77:16-19. 97:2-5. Is 55:9. **rings.** *or*, strakes. 1 K 7:33. **full.** Ezk 10:12. 2 Ch *16:9. Ps *34:15. Pr *15:3. Zc *4:10. Re 4:6, 8.

19. **And when.** Ezk 10:16, 17. Ps 103:20.

20. **Whithersoever.** Jn *6:63. Ro 8:1, 2, 5, 9, 11, 16, 26, 27. Ep +*1:11. **the spirit.** Heb. *ruach*, Ps +104:4. ver. 12. 1 C 14:32. **spirit.** Heb. *ruach*, Ps +104:4. **for the.** Ezk 10:17. Zc 6:1-8. **spirit.** Heb. *ruach*, Ps +104:4. **of the living creature.** *or*, of life.

21. **When.** ver. 21-26. Pr 30:27. Lk 2:27. Mt 4:1. Ac 2:4. 8:29. 10:19. 16:7. **those went.** ver. 19, 20. Ezk 10:17. **spirit.** Heb. *ruach*, Ps +104:4. **of the living creature.** *or*, of life. Ro 8:2.

22. **the likeness.** ✓142, Ge +20:16. ver. 26. Ezk 10:1. Ge 1:6. Ex 24:10. Jb 37:22. Re *4:3, 6. 21:11. **crystal.** The Hebrew *kerach*, which generally denotes *ice*, doubtless here signifies *crystal* (krustallos, from kruos, *cold, ice*, and stellomai, to *concrete*), as it is rendered by the LXX. and Vulgate. It is a very large class of silicious minerals, hard, pellucid, naturally colorless, of regularly angular figures, and of simple plates; not flexible, nor elastic, but giving fire with steel; not fermenting by acid menstrua, but calcinable in a strong fire. There are three orders of pure crystal: the first is perfect columnar crystals, with double pyramids, of eighteen planes, in an hexangular pyramid at each end; the second is that of perfect crystals without a column, of twelve or sixteen planes, in two hexangular pyramids; and the third is that of imperfect crystals, with single pyramids, of ten or twelve planes, in an hexangular or pentangular column. *Terrible crystal* seems to denote that which was well cut and polished, vividly refracting the rays of light.

23. **their wings.** ver. 12, 24. **which.** ver. 11. Jb 4:18. Ps 89:7. Lk 17:10.

24. **like.** Ezk 43:2. Re 1:15. 19:6. **as the voice.** Ezk 10:5. Jb 37:2, 4, 5. Ps 18:13. 29:3-9. 68:33. Re *1:10. *16:17, 18. **as the noise.** 2 K 7:6. Da 10:6.

25. **and had.** ver. 24.

26. **And above.** Abp. Newcome judiciously observes, "We need not allegorize the circumstances of this august vision too minutely. Many of them augment the splendor of the scene, while others, no doubt, have much significance; which should be pointed out rather by a correct judgment, than a luxuriant imagination." ver. 22. Ezk 10:1. **over.** Mt 28:18. Ep 1:21, 22. Ph 2:9, 10. 1 P 3:22. **the likeness of a throne.** Ps +*45:6. Is 6:1. Da 7:9, 10, 14. Zc 6:13. Mt *25:31. Ac 7:56. He +*1:8. 8:1. *12:2. Re *3:21. 4:2, 3. 5:13. *20:11. **as the.** Ex 24:10. Is 54:11. **the appearance of a man.** Ge 32:24-30. Jsh 5:13-15. 6:1, 2. Is +*9:6, 7. Je +*23:5, 6. Da 10:18. Jn 6:62. Ro 8:3. Ph *2:7, 8. Col *2:9. 1 T ✓2:5. *3:16. He 2:14. Re 1:13. 3:21. 5:6. 14:14.

27. **as the color.** ver. 4. Ezk 8:2. **the appearance of fire.** Dt 4:24. Ps 50:3. 97:2, 3. Is 6:1. Da *7:9. 10:6. 2 Th ✓1:8. He *12:29. Re *1:14-16. **brightness.** Ps 80:1. 99:1. Mt *17:2. Ph *3:21. 1 T ✓6:16. He *1:2, 3. 1 J 1:5.

28. **the appearance of the bow.** Ge *9:13-16▶𝒫. Ex *24:10. Is +✓54:8-10. Re *4:3. 10:1. Note the reference to the Pentateuch. Other references to the Pentateuch in Ezekiel are Ezk 2:4, 5. 3:7. 4:3, 4, 14, 16, 17. 5:2, 10, 11, 13, 14, 15, 16, 17. 6:3, 4, 6, 10, 14. 7:13, 26. 8:3, 10, 18. 11:12, 17, 20. 12:15, 16, 20. 14:8, 9, 10, 13, 15, 17. 16:10, 19. 18:6, 7, 8, 9, 10, 13, 20. 19:10. 20:5, 6, 7, 9, 10, 11, 12, 13, 15, 16, 18, 23, 26, 33, 36, 37. 22:4, 7, 8, 9, 11, 12, 26, 29. 23:37, 38. 24:7. 31:8. 32:8. 33:10, 15, 24. 34:4. 36:5, 7, 13, 17, 19, 20, 22, 27, 28. 37:27. 43:18, 19, 21, 27. 44:7, 11, 17, 18, 20, 21, 22, 23, 24, 25, 26, 28, 29, 30, 31. 45:10, 12, 18. 46:13. 47:13, 14, 19. See related note, Is 1:2. **This.** Ezk 8:4. 10:19, 20. 43:3. Ex 16:7, 10. 24:16. 33:18-23. Nu 12:6-9. 1 K 8:10, 11. 1 C 13:12. **the glory.** Ezk 3:12, 23. 8:4. 9:3. 10:4, 18, 19. 11:22, 23.

43:2, 4, 5. 44:4. Jn +*17:5. 1 T *3:16. **I fell.** Ezk *3:23. 43:3. 44:4. Ge +17:3, 17. Le 9:24. Nu 14:5)♔. 16:4, 22, 45)♔. Da *8:17. 10:7-9, 15-17. Mt 17:5, 6. Ac 9:4. 10:10. Re *1:17, 18.

EZEKIEL 2

EZEKIEL receives his commission and instructions, as a prophet to rebellious Israel, 1-5. He is warned neither to fear them, nor to imitate their rebellion, 6-8. He receives a roll, full of "lamentations, and mourning, and woe," 9, 10.

1. **Son of man.** ver. 3, 6, 8. Ezk 3:1, 4, 10, 17. 4:1. 5:1. 7:2. 12:3. 13:2. 14:3, 13. 15:2. 16:2. 17:2. 20:3. 37:3. Ps *8:4. Da 8:17. Mt 8:20. √16:13-16. Jn *3:13, 16. Ac 7:56. He 2:6. Re 14:14. **stand.** Ezk 1:28. Da 10:11, 19. Mt 17:7. Ac 9:6. 26:16. Re 1:17. **I will speak.** Ex 25:17-22. Nu 7:89.

2. **the spirit.** Heb. *ruach,* Ge +41:38. **entered.** Ezk 3:12, 14, 24. 36:27. Nu 11:25, 26. Jg 13:25. 1 S 16:13. Ne 9:30. Jl *2:28, 29. Re 11:11. **and set.** Ezk 3:24. Da *10:11.

3. **I send.** Ezk 3:4-8. 2 Ch 36:15, 16. Is 6:8-10. Je 1:7. 7:2. 25:3-7. 26:2-6. 36:2. Mk 12:2-5. Lk 24:47, 48. Jn 20:21, 22. Ro 10:15. **a rebellious nation.** Heb. rebellious nations. Ezk ch. 16, 20, 23. **rebelled.** Ezk 17:15. 20:18-30, 38. Nu 20:10. 32:13, 14. Dt *9:24, 27. 1 S 8:7, 8. 2 K 17:17-20. Ezr 9:7. Ne 9:16-18, 26, 33-35. Ps 106:16-21, 28, 32-40. Je *3:25. 16:11, 12. 44:21, 22. Da 9:5-13. Ac 7:51.

4. **they.** Ezk 3:7. Dt 10:16. 31:27. 2 Ch 30:8. 36:13. Ps 95:8. Is 48:4. Je 3:3. 5:3. 6:15. 8:12. Mt √10:16. **impudent.** Heb. hard of face. Pr 21:29. **stiffhearted.** Ex 32:9)♔. 33:3, 5. 34:9. Dt 9:6, 13)♔. 10:16. 31:27. Jg 2:19. Is 48:4. Ac *7:51. **Thus.** 1 K 22:14. Je *26:2, 3. Ac *20:26, 27.

5. **whether.** ver. 7. Ezk 3:10, 11, 26, 27. Mt *10:12-15. Mk *6:11. Ac 13:46. Ro 3:3. 2 C 2:15-17. 2 T √4:2, 3. **rebellious.** Nu 17:10)♔. Dt 31:27)♔. 1 S 15:23. Ne 9:17. Jb 23:2. Pr 17:11. Is 30:9. **yet.** Ezk 3:19. 33:9, 33. Lk 10:10-12. Jn 15:22.

6. **be not.** Ezk 3:8, 9. 2 K 1:15. Ps *56:3, 11. Is 51:12. Je *1:8, 17. Mi 3:8. Mt +*10:28. Lk 12:4. Ac 4:13, 19, 29. Ep 6:19. Ph 1:28. 2 T +√1:7. **of them.** ʃ12, Ps +1:1. **briers.** *or,* rebels. 2 S 23:6, 7. Is 9:18. Je 6:28. Mi 7:4. **scorpions.** Lk 10:19. Re 9:3-6. **though they.** Ezk 3:9, 26, 27. Pr 30:13, 14. Is 51:7. Je 18:18. Am 7:10-17. He 11:27. 1 P 3:14.

7. **thou.** Ezk *3:10, 17. Ge ●3:2, 3. Je *1:7, 17. +√23:28n. *26:2. Jon *3:2. Mt *28:20. **whether.** ver. 5. 2 T √4:2. **are.** ʃ119, Ge +49:9. **most rebellious.** Heb. rebellion. ʃ24J, Dt +32:42. ver. 5. Ps 107:11. Is *30:9.

8. **hear.** Jb +*37:2. Lk +*8:18. Re 2:7, 11, 17, 29. **Be.** Le 10:3. Nu 20:10-13, 24. 1 K 13:21, 22. Is 50:5. 1 P 5:3. **open.** Ezk 3:1-3, 10. Ps *119:130, 131. Je 1:7, 9. √15:16. 1 T 4:14-16. Re 10:9.

9. **an hand.** Ezk 8:3. Je 1:9. Da 5:5. 10:10, 16-18. **a roll.** All ancient books were written so as to be *rolled* up: hence *volumen,* a volume, from *volvo,* I roll. Ezk 3:1. Ps 40:7. Je 36:2. He 10:7. Re 5:1-5. 10:8-11.

10. **spread.** Is 30:8-11. Hab 2:2. **was written within and without.** Contrary to the state of rolls in general, which are written on the *inside* only. Re 5:1. **lamentations.** Is 3:11. Je 36:29-32. Re 8:13. 9:12. 11:14.

EZEKIEL 3

EZEKIEL, being made to eat the roll, finds it very sweet, 1-3. God encourages him for the works assigned him, and warns him to be faithful, 4-11. He is carried by the Spirit, in great bitterness, to the captive Jews, and remains with them seven days, 12-15. He is shown his duty and responsibility as a watchman to Israel, 16-21. He is ordered to shut himself up; and is further instructed concerning the hardships which awaited him, and the shutting and opening of his mouth, 22-27.

1. **eat.** ʃ108B, Je +15:16. This must have passed in a vision; but the meaning is plain: Receive my word into thy mind, let it enter into thy soul; *digest* it, let it be thy *nourishment,* thy meat and thy drink, to do the will of thy Father who is in heaven. ver. 10. Ezk 2:8, 9. 1 T *4:15. Re *10:9, 10. **go.** ver. 11, 15, 17-21. Ezk 2:3. Je 24:1-7. **house.** ʃ121J4, Ge +7:1.

2. **opened my mouth.** Je 25:17. Ac 26:19.

3. **and fill.** Ezk 2:10. Jb 32:18, 19. Je 6:11. 20:9. Jn 7:38. Col √3:16. **Then.** Ps √119:11. Je √15:16. Jn *6:53, 63. **it was.** Jb √23:12. Ps *19:10. *119:97, 103. Pr 2:10, 11. Re *10:9, 10.

4. **go.** ver. 11. Ezk 2:3, 7. Mt *10:5, 6. 15:24. Jn *20:21. Ac √1:8. **speak with.** Mt 12:34, 35. Jn *3:34. *7:16. 1 C *11:23.

5. **thou.** Jon 1:2. 3:2-4. Ac 26:17, 18. **of a strange speech and of an hard language.** Heb. deep of lip and heavy of tongue: and so ver. 6. Jg +7:22mg. Ps 81:5. Is 33:19.

6. **of a strange speech and of an hard language.** Heb. deep of lip, and heavy of language. ver. +5mg. **Surely,** etc. *or,* If I had sent thee to them, would they not have hearkened? etc. Jon 3:5-10. Mt +*11:20-24. *12:41, 42. Lk 11:30-32. Ac √28:28. Ro 9:30-33.

7. **Israel will not.** 1 S 8:7. Je 25:3, 4. 44:4, 5, 16. Mt *23:37. Lk 10:16. 13:34. 19:14. Jn *1:11. √5:40-47. 10:20. 15:20-24. **all the.** Ezk 2:4. 24:7. Is 3:9. Je 3:3. 5:3. **impudent and hardhearted.** Heb. stiff of forehead and hard of heart. Ezk 2:4mg. Ex 32:9)♔. Dt 9:6, 13)♔.

8. **I have made.** T#470. Ex 4:15, 16. 11:4-8. 1 K 21:20. Ps +58:11 (T#630). Is 50:7. Je *1:18, 19. *15:19-21. Mi 3:8. Mt 28:20. Lk 6:22, 23. *21:15. Ac 7:51-56. 2 T 4:7, 8. He 11:27, 32-37.

9. **adamant.** Zc 7:12. **fear.** Ezk 2:6. Is 41:10, 14. 50:7. Je *1:8, 17. 17:18. Mi 3:8. 1 T 2:3. 2 T 2:6.

10. **all my words.** Is 50:4. **receive.** ver. 1-3. Ezk 2:8. Jb 22:22. Ps √119:11. Pr 8:10. 19:20. Lk 8:15. 1 Th √2:13. 4:1. 1 T *4:15. **and hear.** Lk +*8:18.

11. **get.** ver. 15. Ezk 11:24, 25. Da 6:13. **the children.** Ezk 33:2, 12, 17, 30. 37:18. Ex 32:7. Dt 9:12. Da *12:1. **speak.** ver. 27. Ezk 2:5, 7. Ac √20:26, 27. **whether.** Jn *3:11. 2 T *4:2.

12. **spirit.** Heb. *ruach,* Is +48:16. ver. 14. Ezk 2:2. 8:3. 11:1, 24. 40:1, 2. 1 K *18:12. 2 K *2:16. Ac *8:39. **a voice.** Ac 2:2. Re 1:10, 15. **Blessed.** Ps 72:18, 19. *103:20, 21. 148:2. Is *6:3. Re *5:11-14. 19:6. **glory.** Ezk *9:3. 10:4, 18, 19. 11:22, 23. Ex 10:34, 35. 1 S 4:21, 22.

13. **the noise.** Ezk 1:24. 10:5. 2 S 5:24. Jn *3:8. Ac *2:2-4. 4:31. **touched.** Heb. kissed. Ge 33:4. **and the noise.** Ezk 10:16, 17.

14. **the spirit.** Heb. *ruach,* Is +48:16. ver. 12. Ezk 8:3. 37:1. **lifted.** 1 K 18:12. Ac 8:39, 40. 2 C 12:4. Re

1:10. **took me away.** Jb 20:9. **and I went.** Ex 4:13. **in bitterness, in the heat of my spirit.** Heb. bitter in hot anger. Heb. *ruach,* Ge +41:8. Nu 11:11-19. Ps 32:3. 51:14. Je 6:11. 20:14-18. Jon 4:1, 3, 9. **but.** Ezk 1:3. 8:1. 37:1. 1 K 18:46. 2 K 2:16. 3:15. Je 20:7-9. 1 C *9:16.

15. **Telabib.** i.e. *corn hill, heap of green ears,* ✳S#8512h, only here. **that dwelt.** ver. 23. Ezk 1:1, 3. 10:15. 43:3. **sat.** Ge 50:10. Jb 2:13. Ps 137:1. Je 23:9. Hab 3:16.

16. **And it came to pass.** Je 42:7.

17. **I have.** Ezk 33:2-9. 1 C 12:28. Ep *4:11. **a watchman.** Ezk *33:2, 6, 7h. SS 3:3. 5:7. Is 21:6, 8, 11, 12. 52:8h. 56:10h. *62:6. Je *6:17h. 31:6. Ac √20:28-31. He √13:17. **hear.** Ezk 33:6-8. 2 Ch 19:10. Is 58:1. Je 6:10. Hab 2:1. Mt 3:7. 1 C 4:14. 2 C √5:11, 20. Col 1:28. 1 Th 5:14. **give them warning.** ver. 18-21. Ezk 33:3-9. Je 6:1 (sign of fire).

18. **I say.** Ezk √18:4n, 13, 20n. *33:6, 8. Ge *2:17. *3:3, 4. Nu *26:65. 2 K 1:4. Is 3:11. Lk *13:3, 5. Ep *5:5, 6. **surely.** √147B, Ge +2:16. **to save.** Ezk 18:30-32. Ac 2:40. +*3:19. 1 T √4:16. Ja *5:19, 20. **the same.** Ezk 33:6, 9, 10. Pr 14:32. Jn *8:21, 24. **but.** Ezk 34:10. Ge *9:5, 6. 42:22. 2 S 4:11. Lk 11:50, 51. Ac √20:26, 27. 1 T 5:22.

19. **if thou.** 2 K 17:13, etc. 2 Ch 36:15, 16. Pr *29:1. Je 42:19-22. 44:4, 5. Lk 10:10, 11. Ac 18:5, 6. *20:31. 1 Th 4:6. He *2:1-3. *12:25. **he shall.** ver. 18. Jn +*8:21, 24. 2 Th √1:8, 9. He +*10:26, 27. **but thou.** ver. *21. Ezk *14:14, 20. *33:5, 9. Is *49:4, 5. Ac 13:45, 46. 18:6. √20:26. 2 C 2:15-17. 1 T √4:16. **soul.** Heb. *nephesh,* Ge +12:13.

20. **When.** Ezk *18:24, 26. 33:12, 13. 2 Ch 24:2, 17-22. Ps 36:3. 125:5. Zp 1:6. Mt *13:20, 21. 2 T √2:15. He *10:38. 2 P *2:18-22. 1 J √2:19. **righteousness.** Heb. righteousnesses. Is √64:6. Da 9:18. **and I lay.** Ezk 7:19. 14:3, 7-9. Dt 13:3. Ps √119:165mg. Is 8:14. Je 6:21. Lk 2:34. Ro 9:32, 33. 11:9. 1 C 1:23. +*11:19. 2 Th *2:9-12. 1 P 2:8. **because.** ver. 18. Le 19:17. 2 S 12:7-13. 2 Ch 19:2-4. 25:15, 16. Pr 25:12. Mt 18:15. **and his.** Ezk 18:24, 26. 33:12, 13. Mt 12:43-45. Lk 8:15. Ro 2:7, 8. He 10:38. 2 P 2:21. **but his.** ver. 18. Ezk 33:6. He √13:17.

21. **if thou.** Mt *24:24, 25. Ac *20:31. 1 C 4:14. 10:12. Ga 1:6-10. 5:2-7. Ep 4:17-21. +*5:5, 6. Col 1:28. 3:5-8. 1 Th 4:6-8. 5:14. 2 T √4:1, 2. T 2:15. 1 J 3:6-9. Re 3:19. **he shall.** ver. 20. Ps *19:11. Pr 9:9. 17:10. Ga 2:11-13. Ja +*5:20. **also.** ver. *19. Ps 51:14. 1 T √4:6, 16. **soul.** Heb. *nephesh,* Ge +12:13.

22. **the hand.** ver. 14. Ezk 1:3. 37:1. **Arise.** Ezk 8:4. Ac 9:6.

23. **the glory.** Ezk 1:4, 28. *8:4. 9:3. 10:18. Nu 16:19, 42. Jn 1:14. Ac 7:55. **as the.** Ezk 1:24. **river.** Ezk 1:1-3. **and I fell.** Ezk 1:28. Da 8:17. 10:8, 9. Re 1:17. 4:10. 5:8, 14.

24. **the spirit.** Heb. *ruach,* Ge +41:38. Ezk 2:2. 37:10. Da 10:8-10, 19. **Go.** √60A, Ge +3:22. Ezk 4:1-4.

25. **they shall.** Ezk 4:8. Mk 3:21. Jn 21:18. Ac *9:16. 20:23. 21:11-13.

26. **I will.** Ezk 24:27. Ps 51:15. 137:6. Je 1:17. Lk 1:20-22. **and shalt.** Ps 36:13, 14. La 2:9. Ho 4:17. Am 5:10. 8:11, 12. Mi *3:6, 7. **a reprover.** Heb. a man reproving. Is 29:21. **for.** Ezk 2:3-8. Is 1:2.

27. **I will.** Ezk 11:25. 24:27. 29:21. 33:22, 32. Ex 4:11, 12. Lk 21:15. Ep 6:19. **Thus.** ver. 11. Ezk 2:5.

Mt 11:15. 13:9. Re +*22:10, 11. **for they.** ver. 9, 26. Ezk 12:2, 3.

EZEKIEL 4

The prophet is directed to portray Jerusalem on a tile; and by an iron pan, and by lying on his side before it for a number of days, to represent the siege and taking of that city, 1-8; and to represent the famine, to which the inhabitants of Jerusalem, and the captives, would be reduced, by his own coarse, scanty, and ill-dressed diet during those days, 9-17.

1. **take.** Ezk 5:1, etc. 12:3, etc. 1 S 15:27, 28. 1 K 11:30, 31. Is 20:2-4. Je 13:1-14. 18:2, etc. 19:1, etc. 25:15, etc. 27:2, etc. Ho 1:2, etc. ch. 3. 12:10. **a tile.** *Levainah* generally denotes a *brick,* and Palladius (*De Re Rustica,* l. vi. c. 12) informs us that the bricks in common use among the ancients were "two feet long, one foot broad, and four inches thick;" and on such a surface the whole siege might be easily portrayed. Perhaps, however, it may here denote a flat *tile,* like a Roman brick, which were commonly used for tablets, as we learn from Pliny, *Hist. Nat.* l. vii. c. 57. **even.** Je 6:6. 32:31. Am 3:2.

2. **lay.** Je 39:1, 2. 52:4. Lk *19:42-44. **battering rams.** *or,* chief leaders. Ezk 21:22.

3. **an iron pan.** *or,* a flat plate, *or,* slice. Le 2:5. **set thy face.** Le 17:10🕊𝒫. 20:3, 5, 6🕊𝒫. 26:17🕊𝒫. Je 21:10. 44:11. **besieged.** 2 K 25:1-10. Je 21:3-10. 37:8. **This.** Ezk *12:6, 11. 24:24-27. Is *8:18. 20:3. Lk 2:34. 1 C *4:9. He 2:4.

4. **upon.** ver. 5, 8. **and lay.** 2 K 17:21-23. **according to the number.** Nu 14:34🕊𝒫. **thou shalt bear.** Ezk 16:54. 18:19, 20. 23:49. 32:24, 25, 30. 44:10, 12. Ex 28:38, 43🕊𝒫. Le 10:17🕊𝒫. 16:22🕊𝒫. 17:16🕊𝒫. Nu 5:31🕊𝒫. *14:34🕊𝒫. 18:1. 30:15🕊𝒫. Is *53:11, 12. La 5:7. Mt 8:17. He 9:28. 1 P *2:24.

5. **I have.** Is √53:6. **three.** This number of years will take us back from the year in which Judea was finally desolated by Nebuzar-adan, B.C. 975, to the establishment of idolatry in Israel by Jeroboam, B.C. 584. "Beginning from 1 K 12:33. Ending Je 52:30."

6. **forty days.** This represented the forty years during which gross idolatry prevailed in Judah, from the reformation of Josiah, B.C. 624, to the same final desolation of the land. Some think that the period of 390 days also predicts the duration of the siege by the Babylonians (ver. 9), deducting from it five months and twenty-nine days, when the besiegers went to meet the Egyptians (2 K 25:1-4. Je 37:5); and that *forty* days may have been employed in desolating the temple and city. "Beginning from 2 K 23:3, 23. Ending Je 52:30." **each day for a year.** Nu √14:34. Da *9:24-26. 12:11, 12. Re 9:15. 11:2, 3. 12:14. 13:5.

7. **set.** ver. 3. Ezk 6:2. **and thine.** Is 52:10.

8. **I will.** Ezk *3:25. Ac *9:16. 2 C *11:23-27. **from one side to another.** Heb. from thy side to thy side.

9. **wheat.** ver. 13, 16. **millet.** Heb. *dochan.* *Dochan,* in Arabic *dokhu.* the *holcus dochna* of Forskal (*Flora Egyptio-arab.* p. 174), is a kind of *millet,* of considerable use as food; the cultivation of which is described by Browne (*Travels,* p. 291). **fitches.** *or,* spelt. *Kussemim* is doubtless *dzea,* or *spelt,* as Aquila and Symmachus render here; and so LXX. and Theodotion, *olura.* In times of scarcity it is customary to mix several kinds of coarser grain with the finer, to make it last the longer. Ex

9:32. Is 28:25. **three**. ver. 5.

10. **by weight**. ver. 16. Ezk 14:13. Le 26:26. Dt 28:51, etc. Is 3:1.

11. **shalt drink**. ver. 16. Is 5:13. Jn 3:34. **by measure**. Le 19:35. **hin**. Ezk 45:24. 46:5, 7, 11, 14.

12. **cake**. lit. a "round" thing. Ge 18:6. **dung**. or, filth. lit. "outgoing." Dt 23:13. **in their sight**. Ezk 12:3.

13. **Even thus**. Is 30:20. Da √1:8. Ho 9:3, 4.

14. **Ah**. ✶59, Ge +28:16. Ezk 9:8. 20:49. Je 1:6. **my soul**. Heb. *nephesh*, Ge +27:31. Ac *10:14. **from my youth**. Mt 19:20. Mk 10:20. Lk 18:21. Ac 10:14. 26:4. **have I eaten**. Ex 22:31✶℘. Le 11:39, 40✶℘. 17:15✶℘. **which dieth**. Le 11:1-47. 21:1, etc. 22:1, etc. Dt 14:3. **abominable**. Le 7:18✶℘. 19:7✶℘. Dt 14:3. Is 65:4. 66:17.

15. **cow's dung**. Dried cow-dung is a common fuel in the East, as it is in many parts of England to the present day; but the prophet was ordered to prepare his bread with human ordure, to show the extreme degree of wretchedness to which the besieged should be exposed, as they would be obliged literally to use it, from not being able to leave the city to collect other fuel. Am 7:6.

16. **I will break**. Ezk 5:16. 14:13. Le *26:26✶℘. Ps *105:16. Is 3:1. **eat**. The prophet was allowed each day only twenty shekels weight, or about ten ounces, of the coarse food he had prepared, and the sixth part of a hin, scarcely a pint and a half, of water; all of which was intended to show that they should be obliged to eat the meanest and coarsest food, and that by weight, and their water by measure. ver. 10, 11. Ezk 12:18, 19. Ps 60:3. La 1:11. 4:9, 10. 5:9.

17. **bread and**. ✶174, Ge +18:27. **and consume**. Ezk 24:23. 33:10. Le 26:39✶℘.

EZEKIEL 5

The prophet is ordered to shave off his hair; and to divide, burn, cut, and scatter it, as an emblem of the dealings of God with the Jews, 1-4. The sign applied to Jerusalem and its inhabitants: their enormous crimes exposed, and dreadful judgments denounced, 5-17.

1. **son**. In this expressive emblem, the prophet represents the Jewish nation; his hair, the people; the razor, the Chaldeans; the cutting of the hair, the calamities and disgrace coming upon them; the balances, the exact distribution of the Divine judgments; the third part of the hair burnt, those destroyed in the city; the third part smitten with a knife, those slain in attempting to escape; the third part scattered to the winds, those who escaped to other countries; the few hairs in his skirt, those left with Gedaliah; and the burning of these, their destruction in Egypt. **take**. Ezk 44:20. Le *21:5. 2 S 14:26. Is *7:20. **then**. Da 5:27.

2. **shalt burn**. ver. 12. Je 9:21, 22. 15:2. 24:10. 38:2. Jg 9:15, 19, 20. Zc √13:8, 9. Lk *12:49. **the city**. Ezk 4:1-8. **I will draw**. ver. 12. Ezk 12:14. Le 26:33✶℘. Je 9:16. Am 9:2, 3.

3. **a few**. 2 K 25:12. Je 39:10. 40:6. 52:16. Mt √7:14. Lk √13:23, 24. 1 P *4:18. **skirts**. Heb. wings. Is +24:16mg.

4. **take**. 2 K 25:25. Je ch. 41-44. 52:30. **shall a fire**. Je 4:4. 48:45.

5. **This**. Ezk 4:1. Ps 48:2. Je 6:6. Lk 22:19, 20.

1 C *10:4. **I have**. Ezk 16:14. Dt *4:6. Mi 5:7. Mt 5:14.

6. **she hath**. Ezk 16:47. Dt 32:15-21. 2 K 17:8-20. Ps 106:20. Ro *1:23-25. 1 C 5:1. Ju 4. **changed**. or, rejected or rebelled against. Ezk 20:8, 13, 21. Nu 20:24. 27:14. Dt *32:6. Is *1:2. **for they**. Ne 9:16, 17. Ps 78:10. Je 5:3. 8:5. 9:6. 11:10. Zc 7:11.

7. **neither have done**. ver. 11. Ezk 16:47, 48, 54. 2 K *21:9-11. 2 Ch 33:9. Is 5:2, 4. Je *2:10, 11.

8. **even I**. Ezk 15:7. 21:3. 26:3. 28:22. 35:3. 39:1. Le 26:17, etc. Dt 29:20. Is *5:5-7. Je 21:5, 13. La 2:5. 3:3. *4:6. Am √3:2. Zc 14:2, 3. Mt *22:7. **in the**. Ezk 25:2-6. 26:2. 29:6, 7. 35:10-15. Dt 29:23-28. 1 K 9:8, 9. Je 22:8, 9. 24:9. 50:7. La 2:15-17.

9. **that which**. La 4:6, 9. Da 9:12. Am 3:2. Mt 24:21. The sentence here passed upon Jerusalem is very dreadful, and the manner of expression makes it yet more so: the judgments are various, the threatenings of them varied, reiterated; so that one may well say, Who is able to stand in God's sight when he is angry?

10. **the fathers**. Le *26:29✶℘. Dt *28:53-57, 64✶℘. 2 K *6:29. Is 9:20. 49:26. Je *19:9. La *2:20. *4:10. **the whole**. ver. 2, 12. Ezk 6:8. 12:14. 20:23. 22:15. 36:19. Le 26:33. Dt 4:27. 28:64. 32:26. Ne 1:8. Ps 44:11. Je 9:16. 44:12. 50:17. Am 9:9. Zc *2:6. 7:14. Lk √21:24.

11. **as I live**. Nu 14:28-35. Ps 95:11. Is 49:18. Je 22:24. Am 8:7. Ro 14:11. He 6:13. **thou hast**. Ezk *8:5, 6, 16. *23:38. 44:7. 2 K *21:4, 5, 7. 23:12. 2 Ch 33:4, 7. *36:14. Je 7:9-11. 32:34. **detestable**. Ezk *7:20. 11:18, 21. Dt 7:25, 26. Je 16:18. 44:4. **will I**. Ezk 16:27. 29:15. Ps 107:39. Je 10:24mg. Ro 11:12. **neither shall**. Ezk 7:4, 9. 8:18. 9:5, 10. 24:14. Dt 13:8✶℘. 29:20. La 2:21. Zc 11:6. Ml 3:17. Ro *8:32. 11:21. 2 P 2:4, 5. **eye**. ✶22A7, Dt +11:12.

12. **third part of**. ver. 2. Ezk 6:12. Je *15:2. *21:9. 44:14. Zc 13:7-9. **and I will scatter**. ver. 2, 10. Ezk 6:8. Je *9:16. Zc 7:14. **winds**. ✶121.O, Ge +28:22. **and I will draw**. This was particularly fulfilled in the destruction of those who retired to Egypt; and has been remarkably verified in the many persecutions and miseries which the Jews have suffered at different times, in the various countries into which they are dispersed. ver. 2. Ezk 12:14. Le 26:33. Dt 28:65. Je 42:16, 17, 22. 43:10, 11. 44:27. Am 9:4.

13. **shall mine**. Ezk 6:12. 7:8. 13:15. 20:8, 21. Pr 1:26. Je 25:12. La *4:11, 22. Da 9:2. 11:36. **I will cause**. Ezk *16:42, 63. 21:17. 23:25. 24:13. Is 1:21. **I will be comforted**. ✶22B, Is +57:6. Dt *32:36✶℘. Is *1:24. Zc 6:8. **spoken**. Ezk 6:10. 36:5, 6. 38:18, 19. Is +*9:7. 59:17.

14. **I will**. Ezk 22:4. Le *26:31, 32✶℘. Dt *28:37. 2 Ch 7:20, 21. Ne 2:17. Ps 74:3-10. *79:1-4. Is 64:10, 11. Je 19:8. 24:9, 10. 42:18. La 1:4, 8. *2:15-17. *5:18. Mi 3:12. **the nations**. ver. 8.

15. **reproach**. Dt 28:37✶℘. **an instruction**. Dt *29:22-28. 1 K *9:7-9. Ps 79:4. Is √26:9. Je 22:8, 9. 1 C 10:11. **when**. Ezk 25:17. Is 66:15, 16. Na 1:2.

16. **the evil**. Dt 32:23, 24✶℘. Ps 7:13. 91:5-7. La 3:12. **and will**. Ezk 4:16. 14:13. Le *26:26✶℘. 2 K 6:25. Is 3:1.

17. **and evil**. Ezk 14:15, 21. 33:27. 34:25-28. Ex 23:29. Le *26:22✶℘. Dt *32:23, 24✶℘. 2 K *17:25. Je 15:3. Re *6:7, 8. **and pestilence**. ver. 12. Ezk 14:19. 38:22. **and I**. Ezk 6:3, 12. 11:8. 14:17. 21:3. 23:47. 29:8. 33:2. Le 26:25✶℘. **I the Lord**. ver. 13, 15. Ezk

17:21, 24. 21:32. 22:14. 24:14. 26:14. 30:12. 37:14. Is *14:27. Je *1:12. *44:28. Mt *24:35.

EZEKIEL 6

A prediction of the destruction of the idols and idolaters of Israel, and that a remnant shall be saved, 1-10. The prophet is ordered to use vehement expressions, to show his detestation of the sins, and his sorrow for the calamities, of his people, 11-14.

1. **And the word.** This is a new prophecy, and was probably given after the 430 days of his lying on his left and right side were accomplished. By *Israel* here Judea is simply meant; not the *ten tribes*, who had long before been carried captive.

2. **set.** Ezk 4:7. 13:17. 20:46. 21:2. 25:2. 38:2, 3. **the mountains.** Ezk 19:9. 33:28. 34:14. 35:12. 37:22. Dt 11:11. Jsh 11:21. Ps 87:1. 125:2. Mi 6:1, 2.

3. **Ye.** Ezk 36:1-4, 8. Je 22:29. Mi 6:2. **to the mountains.** Je 2:20. 3:6, 23. **rivers.** Ezk 36:4, 6. 2 S 22:16. **bring a sword.** Ezk +5:17. Le 26:25)℘. **and I will.** Le 26:30)℘. Is 27:9. **high places.** 1 K 3:3, 4. 11:7, 8. 12:28-31. 2 K 15:4. +21:3.

4. **images.** *or,* sun images: and so ver. 6. Le +26:30)℘. 2 Ch 14:5mg. 34:4mg. Is 17:8. 27:9. Je 43:13mg. **and I.** ver. 5, 13. Le *26:30. 1 K 13:2. 2 K 23:14, 16-20. 2 Ch 34:5. Je 8:1, 2.

5. **lay.** Heb. give. ver. 13, 14. Ezk 5:14. 7:3. **carcases.** lit. "faint ones." Ezk 43:7, 9. **I will scatter.** 2 K 23:14. **the bones.** Ps 53:5. 2 Ch 34:5n. Je 7:32.

6. **all your.** Is 6:11. Je 9:19. Zp 3:7. **laid waste.** Le 26:31)℘. **the cities.** Ezk 5:14. Is 24:1-12. 32:13, 14. 64:10. Je 2:15. 9:11. 10:22. 34:22. Mi 3:12. Zp 1:2-6, 18. 3:6. **and the.** Ezk 16:39. Le 26:30. Je 17:3. Ho 10:8. **your altars.** Ezk 30:13. Is 2:18, 20. 27:9. Ho 10:2. Mi 1:7. 5:13. Zp 1:3, 4. Zc 13:2. **images.** ver. 4mg. **your works.** Ps +*115:8. Is 1:31. Hab 2:18.

7. **slain.** Ezk 9:7. Je 14:18. 18:21. 25:33. La 2:20, 21. 4:9. **and ye shall know.** ver. +10, 13, 14. Ezk 7:4, 9, 27. 11:10, 12. 12:15, 16, 20. 13:9, 14, 21, 23. 14:8. 15:7. √16:62. 17:21, 24. 20:12, 20, 38, 42, 44. 21:5. 22:16, 22. 23:49. 24:24, 27. 25:5, 7, 11, 17. 26:6. 28:22, 23, 24, *26. 29:6, 9, 16, 21. 30:8, 19, 25, 26. 32:15. 33:29. *34:27, 30. 35:4, 9, 12, 15. 36:√11, 23, 36, 38. *37:6, 13, 14, 28. *38:16, 23. 39:6, *7, 22, *23, 28. Ex 7:5)℘. 10:2. 14:4, 18. 1 K 20:28. 2 K 19:19. Ps 83:17, 18. Je 24:7. Da *4:35-37. 6:26, 27. Jl 2:27. *3:17.

8. **leave a remnant.** Ezk 5:2, 12. 12:16. 14:22. Is 6:13. 27:7, 8. Je 30:11. *31:7. 44:14, 28. 46:28. Ro *9:27. *11:5, 6.

9. **remember.** Le *26:40, 41. Dt 4:29-31. *30:1-3. Ps 137:1. Je 51:50. Da 9:2, 3. Zc 10:9. **I am.** Ezk 5:13. 16:43. Ps 78:40. Is 7:13. 43:24. 63:10. Je 3:6, 13. Am 2:13. **their eyes.** Ezk 14:4-7. 20:7, 24, 28. 23:14-16. Nu 15:39. 2 K 16:10. 2 P 2:14. **they shall.** They shall humble themselves on account of their abominations, forsake their idolatry, and worship ME alone: and this they have done from the Babylonish captivity to the present day. Ezk 7:16. 12:16. 16:63. 20:43. 36:31, 32. Le 26:39. Jb *42:6. Is √64:6. Je 30:18, 19. 2 C 7:11.

10. **they shall know.** ver. +*7, 14. Ezk 12:15. 14:22, 23. 20:26. 30:8. 32:15. Ex 7:5)℘. Le 23:43)℘. 1 S 17:46, 47. 1 K 8:43. 18:37. 2 Ch 6:33. Ps 59:13. 83:18. 109:27. Is 19:12. 41:20. 45:6. Je 5:12-14. 31:34. 44:28. Da 9:12.

Zc 1:6. **not said in vain.** Nu *23:19. **evil.** Is +45:7.

11. **Smite.** Ezk 21:14-17. Nu 24:10. Is 58:1. Je 9:1, 10. **Alas.** Ezk +*9:4. Je +*30:7. Jl 1:15. Am 5:16. Re 18:10, 16-19. **fall.** Ezk 5:12. 14:21. Je 15:2, 3. 16:4. 24:10. **sword.** lit. mouth of the sword. ƒ144A2, Ge +34:26.

12. **far off.** Da 9:7. **thus.** Ezk 5:13. Le 26:14-39. Dt 28:15-68. Is 40:2. La 4:11, 22.

13. **when.** ver. 4-7. Is 37:20, 36-38. **upon.** Ezk 20:28. 1 K 14:23. 2 K 16:4. Is 1:29. *57:5-7. 65:3, 4. 66:17. Je *2:20. 3:6. Ho *4:13.

14. **will I stretch.** Ezk 16:27. 20:33, 34. Ex 7:5)℘. Is 5:25. 9:12, 17, 21. 10:4. 26:11. **more desolate than the wilderness.** *or,* desolate from the wilderness. **Diblath.** i.e. *fertile; place of the fig-cakes,* ✳S#1689h, only here. Nu 33:46, Almon-diblathaim. Je 48:22, Beth-diblathaim. *Diblath* was a city of Moab, and appears from the parallel passages to have been situated between Dibon and Abarim or Nebo. **shall know.** ver. +√7. Ps *83:16-18. Am *3:2.

EZEKIEL 7

Predictions that the desolations of Israel will immediately take place, 1-15. The penitent mourning and distress of them that escape, 16-19. The sanctuary given up to be defiled, for the abominations there committed, 20-22. Under the type of a chain is shown the miserable captivity of all orders of men, 23-27.

2. **unto.** Ezk 12:22. 21:2. 40:2. 2 Ch 34:7. **An end.** Two or three MSS. read *ketz ba, ba haketz,* "the end cometh, come is the end;" which is supported by all the ancient versions. ver. 3, 5, 6. Ezk 11:13. Ge 6:13. Dt 32:20. Je 5:31. 51:13. La 1:9. 4:18. Am *8:2, 10. Mt *24:6, 13, 14. 1 P *4:7.

3. **and I.** ver. 8, 9. Ezk 5:13. 6:3-7, 12, 13. **will judge.** ver. 8, 27. Ezk 11:10, 11. 16:38. 18:30. 33:20. 34:20-22. 36:19. Re 20:12, 13. **recompense.** Heb. give. ver. 4, 8, 20, 21.

4. **mine eye.** ƒ22A7, Dt +11:12. ver. 9. Ezk 5:11. 8:18. 9:10. 24:14. Je 13:14. Zc 11:6. **but.** Ezk 11:21. 16:43. 22:31. 23:49. Je 16:18. 25:14. Ho 9:7. 12:2. He 10:30. **and ye.** ver. 27. Ezk 6:7, 14. 12:20.

5. **An evil.** Ezk 5:9. 2 K 21:12, 13. Da 9:12. Am 3:2. Na 1:9. Mt *24:21.

6. **An end.** This is similar to the second verse, but there is a Paronomasia (ƒ140, Ge 4:25), or play upon the words, here, deserving of notice: *keiz ba, ba hakketz, haikeetz ailayich,* "the end cometh, come is the end: it waketh for thee." *Ketz* is an end; *haikeetz* is to *wake* or *watch.* ver. 3. Je 44:27. *watcheth for thee.* Heb. awaketh against thee. 2 K +4:31. Zc 13:7. **behold.** ver. 10. Ezk 21:25. 39:8. 2 P 2:5.

7. **morning.** Ge 19:15, 24. Is 17:14. Am 4:13. **the time.** ver. 12. Ezk 12:23-25, 28. Is 13:22. Zp *1:14-16. 1 P 4:17. **the day of trouble.** Is 22:5. Je +*30:7. **sounding again.** *or,* echo. Is 16:9. 22:5. Je 25:30.

8. **pour.** Ezk 9:8. 14:19. 20:8, 13, 21, 33. 22:31. 30:15. 36:18. 2 Ch 34:21. Ps 79:6. Is 42:25. Je 7:20. La 2:4. 4:11. Da 9:11, 27. Ho 5:10. Na 1:6. Re 14:10. 16:2, etc. **accomplish.** Ezk 6:12. **and I.** ver. 3, 4.

9. **recompense.** Je 51:56. **thee.** Heb. upon thee. **and ye.** ver. 4. **that I am.** Ex 15:26. **the Lord.** Is 9:13. Mi 6:9. Ga *6:7. Re 20:13. **that smiteth.** Ho 6:1.

10. **behold, it.** ver. 6. 1 Th *5:3. **the morning.** ver.

7. **the rod.** Ezk 19:14. 21:10, 13. Nu 17:8. Is 10:5. **pride.** Le *26:18, 19. Pr 14:3. 16:18. Is 28:1. Da 4:37. Ja *4:6.

11. **Violence.** ver. 23. Is 5:7. 9:4. 14:29. 59:6-8. Je 6:7. Am 3:10. 6:3. Mi 2:2. 3:3. 6:12. Ja *2:13. **none.** ver. 2, 16. Ezk 5:4, 11. 6:11. Ps *50:16-22. Zp 1:18. **multitude.** *or*, tumult. **theirs.** *or*, their tumultuous persons. Je +10:13mg. **neither.** Ezk 24:16-24. Ps 78:64. Je 16:5, 6. 22:18. 25:33.

12. **time.** ver. 5-7, 10. 1 C 7:29-31. Ja 5:8, 9. **let.** Is 24:1, 2. Je 32:7, 8, 24, 25. **for.** ver. 13, 14. Ezk 6:11, 12. Is 5:13, 14.

13. **the seller.** Le 25:24-28, 31)⅌. Ec 8:8. **they were yet alive.** Heb. their life *were* yet among the living. **neither.** Ezk 13:22. 33:26, 27. Jb 15:25. Ps 52:7. **in**, etc. *or*, whose life is in his iniquity. **the iniquity of his life.** Heb. his iniquity.

14. **have.** Je 4:5. 6:1. 51:27. **for.** ver. 11, 12. Is 24:1-7. Je 6:11. 7:20. 12:12.

15. **The sword.** ſ121S1, Ge +49:10. i.e., war, or destruction. Ezk 5:12. Dt 32:23-25)⅌. Je 14:18. 15:2, 3. 29:17, 18. 34:1. La 1:20.

16. **they.** Ezk 6:8. Ezr 9:15. Is 1:9. 37:31. Je 44:14, 28. **like.** Ezk 6:9. Is *38:14. 59:11. **mourning.** Ezk 36:31. Pr 5:11-14. Je 31:9, 18, 19. 50:4, 5. Zc 12:10-14.

17. **hands.** Ezk 21:7. Is 13:7, 8. Je 6:24. He 12:12. **be weak as water.** Heb. go into water. Ezk 21:7mg.

18. **shall also.** Is 3:24. 15:2, 3. Je 48:37. Am 8:10. **and horror.** Ge *15:12. Jb 21:6. Ps 35:26. 55:4, 5. Je 3:25. Re 6:15-17. **and baldness.** Is *22:12.

19. **shall cast.** 2 K 7:7, 8, 15. Pr *11:4. Is 2:20. 30:22. Zp 1:18. Mt 16:26. **removed.** Heb. for a separating, *or*, uncleanness. **deliver.** Pr +*11:4. Zp +*1:11, 18. **day of the wrath.** Jb 20:28. +*21:30. Pr +*11:4. Zp +*1:18. Ro +*2:5. Ja +*5:1. **they shall not.** Jb 20:12-23. Ps 78:30, 31. Ec 5:10. Is 55:2. Lk *12:19, 20. **souls.** Heb. *nephesh*, Ge +34:3. **it is the stumblingblock of their iniquity.** *or*, their iniquity is *their* stumblingblock. Ezk 14:3, 4, 7. 44:12. Ps ❂119:165mg. Ro 11:9.

20. **the beauty.** Ezk 24:21. 1 Ch 29:1, 2. 2 Ch 2:9. **ch.** 3. Ezr 3:12. Ps 48:2. 50:2. 87:2, 3. Is 64:11. Hg 2:3. **but.** Ezk 5:11. 8:7-10, 15, 16. 2 K 21:4, 7. 23:11, 12. 2 Ch 33:4-7. 36:14. Je 7:30. **set it far from them.** *or*, made it unto them an unclean thing. ver. 22. Ezk 9:7. 24:21. Je 7:14. La 1:10. 2:1, 7.

21. **I will give it.** 2 K *24:13-15. 25:9, 13-16. 2 Ch 36:18, 19. Ps 74:2-8. 79:1. Je 52:13, etc.

22. **face.** Ps 10:11. 35:22. 74:10, 11, 18-23. Je 18:17. **my secret place.** He 9:3. **robbers.** *or*, burglers. Ezk 18:10. Ps 17:4. Je 7:11. Da 11:14.

23. **a chain.** Ezk 19:3-6. Je *27:2. 40:1. La 3:7. Na 3:10. **for.** Ezk 9:9. 11:6. 22:3-6, 9, 13, 27. 2 K *21:16. 24:4. Is 1:15. 59:3, 7. Je 2:34. 7:6. 22:17. Ho 4:2. Mi 2:2. 7:2. Zp 3:3, 4.

24. **I will bring.** Ezk 21:31. 28:7. Ps 106:41. Je 4:7. 12:12. Hab 1:6-10. **they shall.** That is, "the Chaldeans shall possess the houses of the Jews." The antecedents of pronouns are thus frequently understood in Hebrew poetry. Je 6:12. La 5:2. **I will also.** Ezk 33:28. Is 5:14. **the pomp.** That is, the magnificence of their greatest and haughtiest princes. **their holy places shall be defiled.** *or*, they shall inherit their holy places. Ezk 21:2. 22:16. Jsh 14:1. 2 K 24:20. 25:8, 9. 2 Ch 7:19. Ps 83:12.

25. **Destruction.** Heb. Cutting off. Is 38:12. **and they.** Is 57:21. 59:8-12. Je 8:15, 16. La 4:17, 18. Mi 1:12.

26. **Mischief.** or, Accident. Is 47:11. **shall come.** Le 26:18, 21, 24, 28. Dt *32:23)⅌. Je 4:20. **rumor.** lit. hearing. ſ121R1, Le +13:55. **then.** Ezk 14:1. 20:1-3. 33:31. Je 21:2. 37:17. 38:14, etc. **but the law.** Dt 17:8-13. 33:10. Ps +*74:9. La 2:9. Am √8:11, 12. Mi 3:6. **ancients.** Ezk 8:1. 14:1. 20:1. Je √18:18.

27. **king.** Ezk 12:10-22. 17:15-21. 21:25. Je 52:8-11. **desolation.** ſ121M, Ex +8:23. That is, with his garments rent, which was the sign of his mourning. **I will.** ver. 4-8. Ezk 18:30. Is 3:11. Ro 2:5-10. **according to their deserts.** Heb. with their judgments. Mt *7:2. Ja *2:13. **and they.** ver. 4. 1 K 20:28. Ps 9:16. Jl 3:17.

EZEKIEL 8

The prophet is, in vision, brought to Jerusalem and to the temple, 1-4. He sees "the image of jealousy" by the gate of the altar; the elders of Israel worshipping base idols in a secret chamber of the temple; women weeping for Tammuz; and men with their backs to the temple, worshipping the sun, 5-16. The Lord appeals to him, whether such abominations do not deserve the severest punishment, 17, 18.

1. **in the sixth year.** Ezk 1:2. 20:1. 24:1. 26:1. 29:1, 17. 31:1. 32:17. 40:1. **and the.** Ezk 14:1, 4. 20:1. 33:31. Ml 2:7. Ac 10:33. **that the hand.** ſ22A14.8L, 1 K +18:46. Ezk 1:3. 3:12, 14, 22. 37:1.

2. **I beheld.** Ezk 1:4, 26, 27. Da 7:9, 10. Re 1:14, 15. **brightness.** Da 10:6. Mt 17:1, 2. Ac 26:13. 1 T 6:16. He 1:2, 3. 1 J *1:5. Re 1:15. **amber.** *Amber* is a hard, inflammable, bituminous substance, of a beautiful yellow color, very transparent, and susceptible of an exquisite polish. When rubbed it is highly endowed with electricity; a name which the moderns have formed from its Greek name *elektron*. But, as *amber* becomes dim as soon as it feels the fire, and is speedily consumed, it is probable that the original *chasmal*, which Bochart derives from the Chaldee *nechash*, copper, and *melala*, gold, was a mixed metal, similar to that which the Greeks called *elektron, electrum*, as the LXX. and Vulgate render, from its resemblance to amber in color.

3. **he put.** Ezk 2:9. Da *5:5. 10:10, 18. **the spirit.** Heb. *ruach*, Is +48:16. **lifted me up.** Ezk 3:14. 11:1, 24, 25. 40:2, 3. 1 K 18:12. 2 K 2:16. Ac *8:39. 2 C *12:2-4. Re 1:10, etc. 4:2, etc. 17:3. 21:10. **to the door.** ver. 5. 2 K 16:14. **the image.** Ezk 5:11. 7:20. 2 K 21:7. Je *7:30. *23:11. *32:34. **of jealousy.** Dt 4:16)⅌. 2 Ch 33:7, 15. **provoketh.** Ex +*20:5)⅌. 34:14. Dt 4:24. 5:9. 6:15. *32:16, 21)⅌. Jsh 24:19. Ps 78:58. 1 C 10:21, 22. **to jealousy.** ſ22B, Ex +20:5.

4. **the glory.** Ezk *1:26-28. 3:22, 23. 9:3. 10:1-4. 11:22, 23. 43:2-4. Ex 25:22. 40:34, 35. 2 C 3:18. 4:4-6. He *1:3.

5. **lift.** ſ144A12, Ge +22:13. Je 3:2. Zc 5:5-11. **at the.** ver. 3. Ps 48:2. **this image.** 2 K 21:7. Is +*66:17n.

6. **seest.** ſ85D, Ps +25:12. ver. 12, 17. Je 3:6. 7:17. **even.** ver. 9, 17. Ezk 5:11. 7:20-22. 23:38, 39. 2 K *23:4-7. Pr 5:14. Je 7:30. 23:11. 32:34. *44:17n. **that I.** Ezk 10:19. 11:22, 23. Dt 31:16-18. 2 Ch 36:14-17. Ps 78:60. Je 26:6. La 2:6, 7. **greater.** ver. 11, 14, 16.

7. **the door.** 1 K 7:12. 2 K 21:5.

8. **dig now.** Jb 34:22. Is 29:15. Je 2:34mg. 23:24. Am 9:2, 3.

9. **that they.** Ezk 20:8.

10. **and behold.** These images portrayed on the wall were no doubt the objects of Egyptian idolatry—the ox, ape, crocodile, ibis, beetle, etc.—as we find these idols were painted on the walls of the tombs of kings and nobles. **every.** Ex 20:4. Le 7:21𝒫. 11:10-12, 29-31, 42-44𝒫. 20:25𝒫. Dt 4:18. 7:26𝒫. 14:3, 7, 8. Is 57:6-10. +*66:17. Je 2:26, 27. 3:9. 16:18. Ro *1:21-23.

11. **stood.** ſ121S2, Ge +21:6. **seventy.** Ex 24:1, 9. Nu *11:16, 25. 2 Ch 19:8. Je 5:5. 19:1. 26:17. Da 9:8. **Jaazaniah.** 2 K +25:23. **Shaphan.** 2 K 22:+3, 8, 12, 14. 25:22. 2 Ch 34:20. Je 26:24. 29:3. 36:10. **every.** Nu 16:17, 35. 2 Ch 26:16, 19. Je 7:9.

12. **hast.** ver. 6, 15, 17. **ancients.** ver. 11. Ezk 14:1. 20:1. Ep *5:12. **in the dark.** ver. 7, 8. Jb 24:13-17. Jn √3:19, 20. Ep +*5:11, 13. **The Lord seeth.** Ezk *9:9. Jb 22:12, 13. Ps 73:11. *94:7-11. Is 29:15.

13. **greater.** ver. 6, 15. Je 9:3. Ro 1:24, 25. Ep *5:12. 2 T 3:13.

14. **toward.** Ezk 44:4. 46:9. **Tammuz.** i.e. *sprout of life; hidden; giver of the vine; dissolution; shrivelled up,* ✱S#8542h, only here. A Syrian idol, corresponding to the Adonis of the Greeks and Osiris of the Egyptians, the husband-brother of Ishtar (Asherah, fertility goddess, Is +*66:17n), and otherwise identified as Nimrod and Bacchus (See A. Hislop, *The Two Babylons*, p. 56). Ps 106:28. Is 17:10. Je 22:18. Am 8:10. Zc 12:10.

15. **Hast.** ver. 6, 12. 2 T 3:13. **greater.** ver. 9, 13.

16. **the inner.** Ezk 10:3. 40:28. 43:5. 45:19. **at the door.** 2 K 16:14. 2 Ch 7:7. Jl 2:17. **about.** Ezk 11:1. **with their.** Ezk 23:35. 1 K 8:29. 2 Ch 29:6. Je 2:27. 32:33. **their faces.** Dt *4:19. 17:3. 2 K *23:5, 11. 2 Ch 14:5. Jb *31:26-28. Je *8:1-3. *44:17n. Ac 7:42, 43. **and they.** It seems that the Jews had incorporated every species of idolatry into their worship,—Egyptian, Phoenician, and Persian; for this evidently was the Magian worship of the sun.

17. **Is it a light,** etc. *or,* Is there *any* thing lighter than to commit, etc. **for.** Ezk 7:23. 9:9. 11:6. Ge 6:13. 2 K 21:16. 24:4. Je 6:7. 19:4. 20:8. Am 3:10. 6:3. Mi 2:2. 6:12. Zp 1:9. **to provoke.** Je 7:19. **they put.** So the Vulgate has *applicant ramum ad nares suas*, "they apply the branch to their nose;" which Jerome explains by "a branch of a palm tree with which they adored the idols;" and it seems plainly to allude to the Magian fire-worshippers, who, Strabo (l. xv) tells us, held a little bunch of twigs in their hand, when praying before the fire (See Hyde, *Hist. Rel. Pers.* l. i. c. 27). **the branch.** The Asherah (Is +*66:17n), represented by a branch cut to a certain shape (CB). **their nose.** ſ182, Ge +18:22. ſ22A8, Ps +10:17. This is one of the eighteen emendations of the Sopherim, by which they record their change of *aphphi* (My nostrils) of the primitive text, to *apham*, (their nostrils), in order to remove what was thought to be an indelicate and derogatory *Anthropomorphism* (CB).

18. **will I also.** Ezk 5:11-13. 7:4-9. 9:5, 10. 16:42. 24:13. Na 1:2. **mine eye.** Ezk 5:11. 7:4, 9. 9:5. Dt 13:8𝒫. Je 21:7. **and though.** Jg 10:13, 14. Pr *1:28. Is 1:15. 59:2. Je 11:11. 14:12. Mi *3:4. Zc *7:13. Lk 13:25. **mine ears.** ſ22A8, Ps +10:17.

EZEKIEL 9

The destroyers of Jerusalem are called forth; the visible glory removes to the threshold of the temple; and one is appointed to set a mark on those who mourned over the prevailing abominations, 1-4. The destroyers, by God's command, slay the rest, beginning at the sanctuary, 5-7. God answers the prophet's intercession by showing the people's enormous wickedness, 8-10. The person, employed to mark the remnant, reports that he has executed his commission, 11.

1. **cried.** Ezk 43:6, 7. Is 6:8. Am 3:7, 8. Re 1:10, 11. 14:7. **Cause.** Ex 12:23. 2 K 10:24. 1 Ch 21:15, 16. Is 10:6, 7. He 1:7, 14.

2. **six.** Je 1:15, 16. 5:15-17. 8:16, 17. 25:9. **the higher.** 2 K 15:35. 2 Ch 27:3. Je 26:10. **lieth.** Heb. is turned. Je 49:8mg. **slaughter weapon.** Heb. weapon of his breaking in pieces. **and one.** Ezk 10:2, 6, 7. Le 16:4. Re 15:6. **inkhorn.** *Keseth* (in Chaldee *kista*, Syriac, *kesto*, Ethiopic, *kasut*), denotes a *bottle*, or *vessel* to hold any fluid; and being here united to *sophair*, a writer, is not improperly rendered an *inkhorn*: so one of the editions of Aquila, *melandoxeion*, and Vulgate *atramentarium*. Dr. Shaw informs us (p. 227), that among the Moors, "the *Hojas*, i.e. writers or secretaries, suspend their *inkhorns* in their *girdles*." **by his side.** Heb. upon his loins. **beside.** Ex 27:1-7. 40:29. 2 Ch 4:1.

3. **the glory.** Ezk 3:23. 8:4. 10:4, 18. 11:22, 23. 43:2-4. **from the cherub.** Ps 18:10. 80:1. **clothed with linen.** Da 10:5, 6. Re 1:13.

4. **set a mark.** Heb. mark a mark. Ex 12:7, 13. Jsh 2:18. 1 S 21:13mg. Jb 31:35mg. Ps 78:41. Ml √3:16. Jn *6:27. 2 C 1:22. Ep √4:30. 2 T *2:19. Re *7:2, 3. 9:4. 13:16, 17. 14:1. 20:4. **that sigh.** T#868. Ezk 6:11. 2 K *22:13, 19, 20. Ps +12:5. *119:53, 136. Is √57:15. *66:2. Je 13:17. 2 C 12:21. 2 P 2:8, 9.

5. **hearing.** Heb. ears. 1 S 9:15. Is 5:9. 22:14. **Go.** ver. 10. Ezk 5:11. 7:4, 9. 8:18. 24:14. Ex 32:27. Nu 25:7, 8. Dt 32:39-42. 1 K 18:40.

6. **Slay.** Ge 19:22. **utterly.** Heb. to destruction. Ezk 23:47. 26:8, 11, 15. **old.** Nu 31:15-17. Dt 2:34. 3:6. Jsh 6:17-21. 1 S 15:3. 2 Ch *36:17. **and.** ſ174, Ge +18:27. **young.** Ezk 23:6. **maids.** Ezk 44:22. **but.** Ex 12:23. Jsh 2:18, 19. 6:22-25. 2 T *2:19. He *11:28. Re 7:3. *9:4. 14:4. **and begin.** Ezk 8:5-16. 2 K 10:23. Is 10:12. Je 25:29. 49:12. Am 3:2. *9:9. Ml +*3:5. Lk +*12:47. 1 P √4:17, 18. **at the.** Ezk 8:11, 12, 16. 11:1, 13.

7. **Defile the house.** Ezk 7:20-22. 2 Ch 36:17. Ps 79:1-3. La 2:4-7. Lk 13:1.

8. **that I.** Nu 14:5. *16:4, 21, 22, 45. Dt 9:18. Jsh *7:6. 1 Ch 21:16. Ezr 9:5. Ga 3:19. **Ah.** ſ59, Ge +28:16. Ezk 4:14. 11:13. Ge 18:23. Je 4:10. 14:13, 19. Am 7:2-5. **pouring out.** ſ22C38, Ps +79:6.

9. **The iniquity.** Ezk 7:23. 22:2-12, 25-31. Dt 31:29. 32:5, 15-22. 2 K 17:7, etc. 2 Ch 36:14-16. Is 1:4. 59:2-8, 12-15. Je 5:1-9. 7:8, 9. Mi 3:9-12. Zp 3:1-4. **and the land.** Ezk 8:17. Ge 4. 2 K 21:16. 24:4. Je 2:34. 22:17. La 4:13, 14. Mt *23:35-37. Lk 11:50. **full of.** Heb. filled with. 2 K 15:35. **perverseness.** *or,* wresting of *judgment.* Ezk 22:27-29. Mi 3:1-3. 7:3, 4. Hab +1:4mg. **The Lord hath.** Ezk 8:12. Jb 22:13. Ps *10:11. *94:7. Is *29:15.

10. **mine.** ver. 5. Ezk 5:11. 7:4. 8:18. 21:31, 32. 2 K 24:4. **but.** Ezk 7:8, 9. 11:21. 22:31. Dt 32:41.

2 Ch 6:23. Is 65:6. Ho 9:7. Jl 3:4. He 10:30.

11. **reported the matter**. Heb. returned the word. **I have**. Ps *103:20. Is 46:10, 11. Zc 1:10, 11. 6:7, 8. Re *16:2, 17.

EZEKIEL 10

The man clothed in linen takes coals of fire from between the wheels, and scatters them over the city, 1-7. A vision of the living creatures and the wheels; and the removal of the divine glory from the temple, 8-22.

1. **I looked**. Is 21:8, 9. Hab 2:1. **in the**. Ezk 1:22-26. Ex 24:10. Ep 1:22. Re 4:2, 3. **above**. ver. 20. Ezk 11:22. Ps 18:10. 68:17, 18. Ep 1:20. 1 P 3:22. **as the**. Ezk 1:22, 26. Ge 18:2, 17, 22, 31. 32:24, 30. Jsh 5:13-15. 6:2. Jg 13:6, 8, 18-22. Jn *1:18. Re 1:13-18. **throne**. Ex 24:10. He +*1:8. Re 3:21. 4:1-10.

2. **unto**. ver. 7. Ezk 9:2, 3, 11. **Go**. ver. 8-13, 16. Ezk 1:15-20. **thine hand**. Heb. the hollow of thine hand. **coals**. Ezk *1:13. Ex 9:8-10. Ps 18:12, 13. 140:10. Is 6:6, 7. Re 8:5. **scatter**. Ezk 20:47, 48. 24:9-14. 2 K 25:9. Is 30:30. Je 24:8-10.

3. **and the cloud**. ver. 8. Ezk 9:3. 43:4. Ex 19:9. 24:15, 16, 18. Nu 9:19. 12:10. 1 K *8:10, 11.

4. **the glory**. ver. 18. Ezk 1:28. 9:3. 11:22, 23. Nu 16:19. **went up**. Heb. was lifted up. **and the house**. Ezk 43:5. Ex *40:34, 35. Nu *9:15. 1 K 8:10-12. 2 Ch 5:13, 14. Hg 2:9. Re 15:8.

5. **the sound**. Ezk *1:24. **outer**. Ezk 46:21. 1 K 7:9. 2 Ch 4:9. **the voice**. Ezk 19:16, 19. 20:18, 19. Dt 4:12, 13. Jb 37:2-5. 40:9. Ps *29:3-9. 68:33. 77:17. Jn 12:28, 29. He 12:18, 19. Re 10:3, 4.

6. **that when**. ver. 2. Ps 80:1. 99:1.

7. **stretched forth**. Heb. sent forth. **unto the**. ver. 6. Ezk 1:13. **and went**. Ezk 41:23-28. Is 6:6. Mt 13:41, 42, 49, 50. 24:34, 35. Re 8:5.

8. **the form**. ver. 21. Ezk 1:8. Is 6:6.

9. **behold**. Ezk 1:15-17. **as the**. Da 10:6. Re 21:20. **a beryl**. or, a stone of Tarshish. *Tarshish* is generally rendered by the LXX. and the Vulgate, the *chrysolite*, so called by the ancients (from *xrusos*, gold, and *lithos*, a *stone*), because of its fine gold yellow color. It is now called by the moderns the *topaz*; it is a very beautiful and valuable gem in its pure and perfect state, though very rarely found so; and the finer pieces of it are in hardness second only to the diamond. The Vulgate, however, in Ezk 1:16, renders, *quasi visio maris*, "as the appearance of the seas," i.e. *azure*; and Dr. Geddes (on Ex 28:10) says, that, with Abarbanel, he believes the *beryl* to be intended. It is a pellucid gem, called by our lapidaries *aqua marina*, of a sea or bluish green color, found in the East Indies and about the gold mines of Peru. The genuine beryl never receives any other mixture of color; and in its perfect state approaches to the hardness of the garnet.

10. **as if**. Ezk 1:16. Jb *23:13. Ps 36:6. 97:2. 104:24. Ro 11:33.

11. **they went upon**. ver. 22. Ezk 1:17. **whither**. Ezk 1:20. Mt 8:8-10.

12. **body**. Heb. flesh. Ps 102:5mg. **were**. Ezk 1:18. Col 1:12. Re *4:6, 8.

13. **it was cried**, etc. *or*, they were called in my hearing, Wheel, *or*, Galgal. ver. 2. Ezk 23:24. 26:10. Ps 77:18. 83:13. Ec 12:6. Is 5:28. 17:13. Je 47:3. Da 7:9.

14. **every**. ver. 21. Ezk 1:6-10. 1 K 7:29, 36. Re *4:7. **the face of a cherub**. In Ezk 1:10, instead of "the face of a cherub," it is "the face of an ox:" hence a *cherub* was in the likeness of an *ox*, at least as to its *head*. The extraordinary shape of these angelic beings, which appeared to the prophet in vision, is manifestly symbolical; for it is not to be supposed that these heavenly beings are really thus formed. The four faces, wings, and arms of a man, denote the sublime qualities of these immediate ministers of the Deity; qualities entirely essential to fill up the extent of their duty. The face of a *man* denotes their intelligence; of a *lion*, their intrepid courage; of an *ox*, their patience and perseverance in labor; and of an *eagle*, their great penetration, their sublime sight into heavenly things, and their readiness to rise up into all that is great and divine. The *wings* being *stretched* out, signifies their readiness and rapidity in obeying the commands of their Master; the *wings bent down*, denotes their profound respect before the Lord of the universe; and the *man's arms* under the wings, show that zeal produces application and labor (See a Dissertation by the Continuator of Saurin's Historical Discourses).

15. **lifted**. ver. 18, 19. Ezk 8:6. 11:22. Ho 9:12. **This**. ver. 20. Ezk 1:5, 13, 14. 43:3.

16. **And when**. Ezk 1:19-21.

17. **When**. Ep +*1:11. **for**. Ezk 1:12, 20, 21. **spirit**. Heb. *ruach*, Ps +104:4. **of the living creature**. *or*, of life. Ge 2:7. Ro 8:2. Re 11:11.

18. **the glory**. ver. 4. Ezk 7:20-22. Ps 78:60, 61. *80:1. Je 6:8. 7:12-14. Ho 9:12. Mt 23:37-39. **and stood**. ver. 3, 4. Ge 3:24. 2 K 2:11. Ps 18:10. 68:17, 18.

19. **the cherubims**. Ezk 1:17-21. 11:22, 23. Ps 99:1. **of the east**. Ezk 8:16. 43:4. **and the glory**. ver. 1. Ezk 1:26-28.

20. **the living**. ver. 15. Ezk 1:22-28. 3:23. **the river**. Ezk 1:1. **and I**. 1 K 6:29-35. 7:36.

21. **had four**. ver. 14. Ezk 1:8-10. 41:18, 19. Re 4:7. **and the**. ver. 8.

22. **the likeness**. Ezk 1:10. Ex 25:18-20, 40. **they went**. ver. 11. Ezk 1:12. Ho 14:9.

EZEKIEL 11

The prophet is shown the persons, who gave wicked counsel, and despised the word of God, 1-3. He prophesies against them, 4-12. He is alarmed at the sudden death of Pelatiah, 13. Encouraging promises are given to the captive Jews and Israelites, with denunciations of wrath on the impenitent, 14-21. The glory of God removes from the city, 22, 23. The prophet, in vision, is brought back into Chaldea, and reports what he had seen to the captive Jews, 24, 25.

1. **the spirit**. Heb. *ruach*, Is +48:16. ver. 24. Ezk 3:12, 14. 8:3. 37:1. 40:1, 2. 41:1. 1 K 18:12. 2 K 2:16. Ac 8:39. 2 C 12:1-4. Re 1:10. **the east gate**. Ezk 10:19. 43:4. **eastward**. ✳S#6921h. Ezk ◐17:10. 40:6, 10, 19, 22, 23, 32, 44. 41:14. 42:9, 10, 12, 15, 16. 43:1, 2, 4, 17. 44:1. 45:7. 46:1, 12. 47:1, 2, 3, 18. 48:1, 2, 3, 4, 5, 6, 7, 8, 10, 16, 17, 18, 21, 23, 24, 25, 26, 27, 32. Ge ◐+41:6. **behold**. Ezk 8:16. **gate**. ⌁171S7B, Ge +14:7. **five and**. Is ◐43:28. Je 38:4. **Jaazaniah**. 2 K 25:23. **Pelatiah**. ver. 13. Ezk 22:27. Is 1:10, 23. Ho 5:10.

2. **these are**. Est 8:3. Ps *2:1, 2. 36:4. 52:2. Is 30:1. 59:4. Je 5:5. 18:18. Mi 2:1, 2.

3. **Which say.** Je 28:1-17. **It is not**, etc. *or, It is not for us* to build houses near. Ezk 7:7. √12:22, 27. Is 5:19. Je 1:11, 12. Am *6:3, 5. 2 P √3:4. **this city.** ver. 7-11. Ezk 24:3-14. Je 1:13.

4. **prophesy against.** Ezk 13:2, etc., 17, etc. 20:46, 47. 21:2. 25:2. Is 58:1. Ho 6:5. 8:1.

5. **the Spirit.** Heb. *ruach,* Ge +41:38. Ezk 2:2. 3:24, 27. 8:1. Nu 11:25, 26. 1 S 10:6, 10. Ac 10:44. 11:15. **Speak.** Ezk 1:3. 2:4, 5, 7. 3:11. Is 58:1. 2 P √1:21. **Thus have.** Ezk 28:2. 29:3. 38:11. Ps 50:21. Is 28:15. Ml 3:13, 14. Mk 3:22-30. Ja 3:6. **for I know.** Ezk 38:10. 1 Ch +*28:9. Ps 7:9. 139:2, 3. Is 66:18. Je 16:17. *17:10. 29:11. Mk 2:8. Jn +*2:24, 25. 21:17. He *4:13. Re *2:23. **mind.** Heb. *ruach,* spirit, Ge +26:35.

6. **have multiplied.** Ezk 7:23. 9:9. 22:2-6, 9, 12, 27. 24:6-9. 2 K *21:16. Is *1:15. Je 2:30, 34. 7:6, 9. La 4:13. Ho 4:2, 3. Mi 3:2, 3, 10. 7:2. Zp 3:3. Mt 23:35.

7. **Your.** Ezk *24:3-13. Mi *3:2, 3. **but.** ver. 3, 9-11. 2 K *25:18-22. Je 52:24-27. **bring.** √96B, Ge +8:5.

8. **have feared.** Jb 3:25. 20:24. Pr *10:24. Is 24:17, 18. 30:16, 17. 66:4. Je 38:19-23. *42:14-16. 44:12, 13. Am 9:1-4. Jn 11:48. 1 Th 2:15, 16.

9. **and deliver.** Ezk 21:31. Dt 28:36, 49, 50. 2 K 24:4. Ne 9:36, 37. Ps 106:41. Je 5:15-17. 39:6. **and will.** Ezk 5:8, 10, 15. 16:38, 41. 30:19. Ps 106:30. Ec √8:11. Jn *5:27. Ro 13:4. Ju 15.

10. **fall.** 2 K 25:19-21. Je 39:6. 52:9, 10, 24-27. **in.** Nu 34:8, 9. Jsh 13:5. 1 K 8:65. 2 K 14:25. 25:18-21. Je 52:24-27. **and ye.** Ezk 6:7. 13:9, 14, 21, 23. Ps 9:16. Je 9:24.

11. **This city.** ver. 3, 7-10. **the border.** 1 K 8:65. 2 K 14:25. Je 39:5-7, 18-21. *52:9, 10.

12. **shall know.** Ps 9:16. **for ye have not walked.** *or,* which have not walked. ver. 21. Ezk 20:16, 21, 24. Le 26:40. 1 K 11:33. 2 K 21:22. Ezr 9:7. Ne 9:34. Ps 78:10. Je 6:16. Da 9:10. **but.** Ezk 8:10, 14, 16. 16:44-47. Le *18:3, 24-28)ᵱ. Dt √12:30, 31)ᵱ. 2 K 16:3, 10, 11. 17:11, etc. 18:12. 21:2. 2 Ch 13:9. 28:3. 33:2-9. 36:14. Ps 106:35-39. Je +√10:2.

13. **And it.** Whilst the prophet, in vision, was delivering this message to the princes, Pelatiah suddenly died; and it is highly probable that he was actually struck dead at this very time, in so remarkable a manner as to render the vision much noticed. The prophet, alarmed and distressed for the welfare of his people, anxiously inquired whether the Lord meant to destroy the remnant of Israel. **when.** ver. 1. Ezk 37:7. Nu 14:35-37. Dt 7:4. 1 K 13:4. Pr 6:15. Je 28:15-17. Ho 6:5. Ac 5:5, 10. 13:11. **Then.** Dt 9:18, 19. Jsh 7:6-9. 1 Ch 21:16, 17. Ps 106:23. 119:120. **Ah.** √59, Ge +28:16. Ezk 9:8. Am 7:2, 5. **full end.** Je +*4:27. 5:10, 18. Ro *11:4, 5.

15. **thy brethren.** Je 24:1-5. **Get.** 1 S *26:19. Is 65:5. 66:5. Jn 16:2. **unto.** Ezk 33:24.

16. **Thus saith.** Le 26:44. Dt *30:3, 4. 2 K 24:12-16. Ps 44:11. *84:11. Je 24:5, 6. *30:11. *31:10. **as a.** Ps 31:20. *61:3. 90:1. 91:1, 9, etc. Pr *18:10. Is 4:5. *8:14. Je 29:7, 11. 42:11.

17. **gather you.** Ezk 28:25. +*34:13. 36:24. 37:21, etc. 39:27-29. Dt *30:3)ᵱ. Is √11:11-16. +*52:12mg. Je 3:12, 18. 24:5. 30:10, 11, 18. 31:8-10. +*32:37-41. Ho 1:10, 11. Am √9:14, 15. Mk *13:27. 2 Th ◑*2:1. **the land of Israel.** Ezk +*21:2. +*37:25.

18. **shall take away.** ver. 21. Ezk 5:11. 7:20. 37:23.

43:7, 8. Is 1:25-27. 30:22. Je 16:18. Ho 14:8. Mi 5:10-14. Col 3:5-8. T 2:12.

19. **I will give.** Ezk √36:26, 27. Dt *30:6. 2 Ch 30:12. Je *24:7. *32:39, 40. Zp 3:9. Jn 17:21-23. Ac 4:32. 1 C 1:10. Ep 4:3-6. Ph 2:1-5. **I will put.** Ezk *18:31. 2 K 22:19. Ps *51:10. Je *31:33. Lk 11:13. Jn √14:26. Ro +*12:2. 2 C √5:17. Ga *6:15. Ep *4:23. **spirit.** Heb. *ruach,* Ge +41:38. *121A2, Ps +51:10. **I will take.** Ezk 36:26, 27. Is 48:4. Zc 7:12. Ro *2:4, 5. **heart of flesh.** 2 C 3:3.

20. **they may.** ver. 12. Dt *12:30, 31)ᵱ. Ps 105:45. 119:4, 5, 32. Lk 1:6, 74, 75. Ro 16:26. 1 C 11:2. T *2:11, 12. **and they.** Ezk *14:11. *36:28. *37:27. Je 11:4. 24:7. 30:22. 31:33. 32:38. Ho 2:23. Zc 13:9. He +*8:10. +*11:16.

21. **whose.** Ec 11:9. Je √17:9. Mk √7:21-23. He +*3:12, 13. *10:38. Ja *1:14, 15. Ju 19. **their detestable.** ver. 18. Je 1:16. 2:20. **I will.** Ezk 9:10. 20:31, 38. 22:31. Ex 34:7. Is *63:10. Je 29:16-19. Ga *6:7.

22. **the cherubims.** Ezk 1:19, 20. 10:19. 2 S 22:11.

23. **the glory.** Ezk 8:4. 9:3. 10:4, 18. 43:4. Ho 9:12. Zc 14:4. Mt 23:37-39. 24:1, 2. **went up.** Lk 24:50. Ac 1:9. **which.** Ezk 43:2. Zc *14:4.

24. **the spirit.** Heb. *ruach,* Is +48:16. ver. 1. Ezk *8:3. 2 K 2:16. Ac *8:39. 2 C *12:3. **into.** Ezk 1:3. 3:12, 15. Ps 137:1. **So.** Ge 17:22. 35:13. Ac 10:16.

25. **I spake.** Ezk 2:7. 3:4, 17, 27.

EZEKIEL 12

EZEKIEL is ordered, by removing his goods, and breaking through the wall of his house, to give the people a sign of the taking of Jerusalem, of Zedekiah's flight, and of the captivity of the Jews, 1-16; by eating and drinking with trembling and anxiety, to prefigure the famine, and the consternation of the Jews during the siege, 17-20; and to declare that this ruin was near at hand; as a rebuke to those who profanely spake of it as distant, 21-28.

2. **thou.** Ezk 2:3, 6-8. 3:9, 26, 27. *17:12. 24:3. 44:6. Dt 9:7, 24. 31:27. Ps 78:40. Is 1:23. 30:1, 9. 65:2. Je 4:17. 5:23. 9:1-6. Da 9:5-9. Ac 7:51, 52. **which have.** T#421. Dt 29:4. Pr 18:1. Is *6:9, 10. 29:9-12. 42:19, 20. Je 5:21. Mt *13:13, 14. Mk 4:12. 8:17, 18. Lk 8:10. Jn *9:39-41. 12:40. Ac 28:26, 27. Ro 11:7, 8. 2 C 3:14. 4:3, 4. 8:12. Ep *4:18. 2 Th 2:10, 11. He *5:14. 6:1. 2 P +3:18 (T#667). **for.** Ezk 2:5.

3. **prepare.** ver. 10-12. Ezk 4:1, etc. Je 13:1, etc. 18:2, etc. 19:1, etc. 27:2. **stuff.** *or,* instruments. By *stuff* our translators meant *furniture* or *goods*, as the word frequently denotes in our early writers; but the original, *keley*, has not only this sense (as in ver. 4), but is also used for any kind of *utensils* or *instruments* whatever; and here probably denotes *carriages*, or other means for removing goods. This was intended to signify that the *captivity* was at hand. Je 46:19mg. **it may.** Ezk *33:11. Dt 5:29. 32:29. Ps 81:13. Je 18:11. 25:4-7. 26:3. 36:3, 7. Lk 13:8, 9, 34. 20:13. 2 T 2:25.

4. **at even.** ver. 12. 2 K 25:4. Je 39:4. 52:7. **they that go forth into.** Heb. the goings forth of.

5. **Dig thou.** Heb. Dig for thee. This was to show that Zedekiah should escape from the city through *a breach in the wall.* 2 K 25:4. Je 39:2-4.

6. **thou shalt.** This intimated, that Zedekiah should steal out of the city in the twilight, carrying on his shoulders some of his property, with his head covered,

not only as in distress, but to escape detection. These prophecies, which were accurately fulfilled, are supposed to have been delivered in the *sixth* year of Zedekiah, *five* years before the taking of Jerusalem. **cover**. Ge +27:16. 1 S 28:8. 2 S 15:30. Jb 24:17. **for I**. ver. 11. Ezk 2:8. 4:3. 24:24. Is *8:18. *20:2-4.

7. **I did so**. Ezk 2:8. 24:18. 37:7, 10. Je 32:8-12. Mt 21:6, 7. Mk 14:16. Jn 2:5-8. +*15:14. Ac 26:19. **I brought**. ver. 3-6. **digged**. Heb. digged for me. **in their sight**. Ps 71:7.

9. **the rebellious**. ver. 1-3. Ezk 2:5-8. **What**. Ezk *17:12. 20:49. 24:19. Re *3:15, 16.

10. **This**. 2 K 9:25. Is 13:1. 14:28. Ml 1:1. **prince**. That is, Zedekiah king of Judah. Ezk 7:27. 17:13-21. 21:25-27. Je 21:7. 24:8. 38:18.

11. **I am**. ver. 6. **remove and go**. Heb. by removing go. Je 15:2. 52:15, 28-30.

12. **the prince**. ver. 6. 2 K 25:4. Je 39:4. 52:7.

13. **My net**. This was to intimate, that though he escaped out of the city, the Chaldeans should overtake him, and carry him to Babylon. Jeremiah had predicted that his "eyes should see the eyes of the king of Babylon," and here Ezekiel foretold that he should not see Babylon, though he should die there; and Josephus says that he thought the two prophecies so inconsistent with each other, that he believed neither; yet both were exactly fulfilled, and the enigma of Ezekiel explained, when Zedekiah was brought to Nebuchadnezzar at Riblah, where he had his eyes put out, and was then carried to Babylon, and there died. Ezk 17:16, 20. 19:8, 9. 32:3. Jb *19:6. Ps *9:16. 11:6. Is 24:17, 18. Je 50:24. La 1:13. 3:47. 4:19, 20. Ho 7:12. Lk 21:35. **and I**. 2 K *25:5-7. Je *34:3. 39:7. *52:8-11. **bring him**. J9, 2 K +5:19.

14. **I will scatter**. Ezk 5:10-12. 17:21. 2 K 25:4, 5. **I will draw**. Ezk 5:2, 12. 14:17, 21. Le 26:33. Je 42:16, 22.

15. **they shall know**. ver. 16, 20. Ezk 5:13. 6:7, 14. 7:4. 11:10. 24:27. 25:11. 26:6. 28:26. 33:33. 39:28. Ex 14:18. Ps *9:16. **scatter**. Le 26:33)𝒫. Dt 4:27)𝒫. *28:64)𝒫.

16. **I will leave**. Ezk *6:8-10. 14:22, 23. Dt 4:27)𝒫. 2 K 24:14. 25:12. Is 1:9. 6:13. 10:22. 24:13. Je 4:27. 30:11. Am *9:8, 9. Mt J7:14. 24:22. Ro 11:4, 5. **a few men**. Heb. men of number. Ge 13:16. 34:30. Is 10:19, +20mg. Ro 9:27. **that they**. Ezk 14:22, 23. 36:31. Le 26:40, 41. Je 3:24, 25. Da 9:5-12. **and they**. Dt 29:24-28. 1 K 9:6-9. Je 22:8, 9.

18. **eat thy bread with**. Ezk 4:16, 17. 23:33. Le 26:26, 36. Dt 28:48, 65. Jb 3:24. Ps 60:2, 3. 80:5. 102:4-9.

19. **with carefulness**. 1 K 17:10-12. **that her**. Ezk 6:6, 7, 14. 36:3. Is 6:11. Je +*4:27. 9:10, 11. 10:22. 18:16. 32:43. 33:10, 12. Mi 7:13. Zc *7:14. **all that is therein**. Heb. the fulness thereof. Ps 24:1. 1 C 10:26, 28. **because**. Ezk 7:23. Ge 6:11-13. Ps 107:34. Je 6:7. Mi 3:10-12.

20. **the cities**. Ezk 15:6-8. Le 26:31)𝒫. Is 3:26. 7:23, 24. 24:3, 12. 64:10, 11. Je 4:7, 23-29. 12:10-12. 16:9. 19:11. 24:8-10. 25:9. 34:22. La 5:18. Da 9:17.

22. **what**. J85K, Ge +3:9. Ezk 18:2, 3. Je 23:33-40. **The days**. ver. 27. Ezk 11:3. Is 5:19. Je 5:12, 13. Am *6:3. 2 P J3:3, 4.

23. **I will**. Ezk 18:3. Is 28:22. **proverb**. Nu +*21:27. **The days**. ver. 25. Ezk 7:2, 5-7, 10-12. Jl *2:1. Zp *1:14. Ml 4:1. Mt *24:34. Ja 5:8, 9.

24. **no more**. Ezk 13:23. 1 K 22:11-13, 17. Pr 26:28. Je 14:13-16. J23:14-29. La *2:14. Zc 13:2-4. Ro 16:18. 1 Th 2:5. 2 P *2:2, 3.

25. **I will**. ver. 28. Ezk 6:10. Nu 14:28-34. Is 14:24. J55:11. La 2:17. Da *9:12. Zc 1:6. Mt *24:35. Lk *21:13, 33. **in your**. Je 16:9. Hab 1:5. Mk 13:30, 31. **O rebellious**. ver. 1, 2.

27. **for**. ver. 22. Is 28:14, 15. Da 10:14. 2 P J3:4.

28. **There shall**. ver. 23-25. Nu 23:19. Je 4:7. 44:28. Mt *24:48-51. Mk 13:32-37. Lk *21:34-36. 1 Th *5:2, 3. Re 3:3.

EZEKIEL 13

EZEKIEL is ordered to prophesy against the false prophets, 1-9; and to expose their folly and wickedness, and the fatal effects of their delusions, to others and themselves, under the emblem of a wall daubed with untempered mortar, and beaten down by a violent storm, 10-16; and against the prophetesses, who, by their signs and lying prognostications, encouraged the wicked in sin, and discouraged the righteous: and to predict their disgrace and ruin, 17-23.

2. **prophesy against**. Ezk 14:9, 10. 22:25, 28. 2 Ch 18:18-24. Is 9:15. 56:9-12. Je *5:30, 31. 6:13, 14. 8:10. 14:13-15. *23:2, 11-22, 25, 26. 27:14, 18. 28:12-17. 29:8, 9, 22, 23. 37:19. La 4:13. Mi 3:6, 11. Zp 3:4. 2 P 2:1-3. **prophesy out of**. Heb. are prophets out of. ver. 3, 17. Nu +16:28. Je 14:14. J23:16, 26. **Hear**. Ezk 34:7, 9. 1 K 22:19. Is 1:10. 28:14. Je 28:15. 29:20-24, 31, 32. Am 7:16, 17.

3. **Woe**. ver. 18. Ezk 34:2. Is 23:1. Mt 23:13-29. Lk 11:42-47, 52. 1 C 9:16. **foolish**. Pr 15:2, 14. La 2:14. Ho 9:7. Zc 11:15. Mt 23:16-26. Lk 11:40. 1 T 6:4. 2 T 3:9. **follow**. Heb. walk after. Je +17:16mg. **spirit**. Heb. *ruach*, Ge +41:8. J121A10, Ge +26:10. Mk +*2:8. **have seen nothing**. or, *things which they have not seen*. ver. 6, 7. Je J23:28-32.

4. **prophets**. Crafty, mischievous, and ravenous; always scheming something for their own interest; while they would not risk their persons to avert the mischief which they had caused. **like**. SS *2:15. Mi 2:11. 3:5. Mt *7:15. Ro 16:18. 2 C J11:13-15. Ga 2:4. Ep J4:14. 2 Th J2:9, 10. 1 T *4:1, 2. T 1:10-12. Re 13:11-14. 19:20.

5. **have not**. Ezk J22:30. Ex 17:9-13. 32:11, 12. Nu 16:21, 22, 47, 48. 1 S 12:23, 30. Ps *106:23, 30. Je 15:1. 23:22. 27:18. Ml 1:9. **gaps**. or, breaches. Is 58:12. La 2:13, 14. Am 4:3. **made up the hedge**. Heb. hedged the hedge. J147D. Polyptoton, Ge +1:29. Nu 22:24. Ps 80:12. Is 5:5. Ho 2:6mg. **to stand**. Jb 40:9. Ps 76:7. Is 27:4. Ep 6:13, 14. Re 16:14. 20:8, 9. **the day**. Ezk 7:7. +*30:3. Is +*2:12. +*13:6, 9. 34:8. Jl 1:15. 2:1, 31. 3:14. Am 5:18-20. Zp 1:14-18. 2:2, 3. Ml 4:5. 1 Th *5:2. 2 P +*3:10. Re 6:17.

6. **have seen**. ver. 23. Ezk 12:23, 24. 22:28. La *2:14. 2 P 2:18. **lying**. Ezk 21:23, 29. Je 14:14. 29:8. Zc 10:2. **saying**. ver. 7. Je 23:31, 32. 28:2, 15. **made**. ver. 22. 1 K 22:6, 27, 37. Pr 14:15. Je 29:31. 37:19. Mk 13:6, 22, 23. 2 Th 2:11.

7. **The Lord**. ver. 2, 3, 6. Ezk 2:5-7. Je 23:21. Mt 24:23, 24.

8. **behold**. Ezk 5:8. 21:3. 26:3. 28:22. 29:3, 4, 10. 35:3. 38:3, 4. 39:1. Ps 5:6. Je 50:31, 32. 51:25. Na 2:13. 3:5, 6. 1 T 4:1, 8. 1 P 3:12.

9. **mine**. Ezk 11:13. 14:9, 10. Ps 101:7. Je 20:3-6.

28:15-17. 29:21, 22, 31, 32. Re 19:20. **assembly**. *or*, secret, **or** council. Je *23:18mg. **neither shall they be**. Ex *32:32, 33. Ezr 2:59, 62, 63. Ne 7:62, 64. Ps 69:5, 28. 87:6. Is 4:3. Da *12:1. Ho 9:3. Lk 10:20. Ph 4:3. He 12:23. Re 3:5. 13:8. 17:8. 20:12, 15. **neither shall they enter**. Ezk 20:38. **and ye**. ver. ◐14. Ezk ◐+*6:7. 11:10, 12. 12:20. 23:49h. 24:24h. 1 K 22:24, 25. Je 23:20.

10. **seduced**. 2 K 21:9. Pr 12:26. Je 23:13-15. 1 T *4:1. 2 T 3:13. 1 J 2:26. Re 2:20. **Peace**. ver. 16. Ezk 23:42. 1 K 13:9n, 18n. Ps 123:4. Is 57:21. Je 4:10. *6:14. *8:11, 15. 14:13. 23:17. 28:9. Am 6:1. Ml 3:15. **and one**. These false prophets pretend to be a *wall of defence*; but their *wall* is bad, and their *morter* is worse. One gives a *lying vision*; another pledges himself that it is *true*; and the people believe what *they* say, and trust not in God, nor turn from their sins. **a wall**. *or*, a slight wall. **others**. ver. 11, 14, 15. Ezk 22:28. Le 14:42. 2 Ch 18:12. Is 30:10. 44:18mg. Je 5:31. Mi 2:11. Mt 23:27. Ac 23:3.

11. **there shall**. It shall wash off this bad morter, sweep away the wall, and level it with the earth. In the East, where the walls are often built with unbaked bricks, desolations of this kind are frequently occasioned by tempestuous rains. Ezk 38:22. Jb 27:21. Ps 11:6. 18:13, 14. 32:6. Is 25:4. 28:2, *15-18. 29:6. 32:19. Na 1:3, 7, 8. Mt 7:25, 27. Lk 6:48, 49. **hailstones**. ſ38G, Dt +32:1. ver. 13. Jsh 10:10, 11.

12. **Where**. Dt 32:37. Jg 9:38. 10:14. 2 K 3:13. Je 2:28. 29:31, 32. 37:19. La 2:14, 15.

13. **a stormy**. Le 26:28. Ps 30:30. 107:25. 148:8. Je 23:19. Jon 1:4. **and great hailstones**. ver. 11. Ex 9:18-29. Ps *18:12, 13. 105:32. 148:8. Is *30:30. Hg 2:17. Re 8:7. 11:19. *16:21.

14. **the foundation**. Ps 11:3. Mi 1:6. Hab 3:13. Mt 7:26, 27. Lk *6:49. 1 C √3:11-15. **ye shall be**. Je 6:15. 8:12. 14:15. 23:15. **and ye shall know**. ver. 9, 21, 23. Ezk 14:8.

15. **The wall**. Ne 4:3. Ps 62:3. Is 30:13.

16. **see visions**. ver. 10. Je 5:31. 6:14. 8:11. 28:1, 9, etc. 29:31. 1 Th *5:3. **and there**. Is 48:22. *57:20, 21.

17. **set thy**. Ezk 4:3. 14:8. 20:46. 21:2. 29:2. 38:2. **the daughters**. Is *3:16, etc. 4:4. **prophesy**. Ex +*15:20n. Jg 4:4. 2 K 22:14. Lk 2:36. 2 P 2:1. **out of**. ver. +2. Nu +16:28. Ne 2:20.

18. **Woe**. ver. 3. **that sew**. Rather, "that fasten *cushions*;" by which they intimated that they might indulge and repose themselves in security, for no enemy would disturb them. The apartments of the easterns are well supplied with *cushions*, on which they sit, lean, rest their heads, and prop up their arms. ver. 10, 16. 2 K 23:7. Is 26:11. 52:10. Je 4:10. 6:14. 2 T 4:3. **armholes**. *or*, elbows. **hunt souls**. Heb. *nephesh*, Ge +12:5. Ezk 22:25. Pr *6:26. Ep √4:14. 2 P √2:14. **will ye save**. ver. 22. **souls**. Heb. *nephesh*, Ge +12:13.

19. **pollute**. Ezk 20:39. 22:26. **for handfuls**. 1 S 2:16, 17. Pr 28:21. Mi 3:5, 11. Ml 1:10. Ro 16:18. 1 P 5:2. 2 P 2:2, 3. **to slay**. ſ12112, Ge +2:17. ver. 22. Pr +√19:27. Mt √23:15. Ro 14:15. 1 C 8:11. **souls**. Heb. *nephesh*, Ge +12:13. **to save**. ſ12112, Ge +2:17. Je *23:14, 17. **souls**. Heb. *nephesh*, Jsh +10:28. **by your lying**. Pr 21:6.

20. **I am against**. ver. 8, 9, 15, 16. Pr 6:16-19. Am 6:1. **to make them fly**. *or*, into gardens. Ezk +8:14.

Nu 17:8. SS 6:11. 7:12. Is +*66:17n. **and will**. 2 T 3:8, 9.

21. **and ye shall**. See on ver. 9.

22. **with lies**. T#568. Ezk 9:4. Ge *3:4. Dt 29:19. Ps +14:1 (T#22). Pr 12:19, 22. Je 4:10. 14:13-17. 23:9, 14. La 2:11-14. Jn *8:44. He +3:12 (T#708). 2 P *3:5. Re +*21:8. **and strengthened**. Je *23:14. 27:14-17. 28:16. 29:32. **by promising him life**. *or*, that I should save his life. Heb. by quickening him. ſ12112, Ge +2:17. ver. 16. Ge 3:4, 5. Je 6:14. 8:11. *23:17. Mt +*6:23. +*23:15. 2 P √2:18, 19.

23. **ye shall see**. ver. 6, etc. Ezk 12:24. Dt 18:20. Mi 3:6, 7. Zc 13:3, 4. 2 T 3:9. **for I**. ver. 21. Ezk 34:10. Mt 24:24. Mk 13:22. 1 C 11:19. Ju *24. Re 12:9, 11. 13:5, 8. 15:2. **and ye**. ver. 9, 21. Ezk 14:8. 15:7.

EZEKIEL 14

The elders, who inquired of God, while their hearts were set on idols, are sharply reproved, and warned, 1-5. A call to repentance, with threatenings of temporal and spiritual judgments on many, in order to the reformation of Israel, 6-11. No righteousness of a few individuals would avert the judgments of famine, noisome beasts, sword, or pestilence, from a guilty land; much less these four sore judgments from Jerusalem, 12-21. A promise that a remnant should be preserved, for the instruction and comfort of the captives, 22, 23.

1. **certain**. Ezk 8:1. 20:1. 2 K 6:32. Ac 4:5, 8. **and sat**. Ezk 33:31. Jg 20:26. Is 29:13. Lk 10:39. Ac 22:3.

2. **the word**. 1 K 14:4, 5. Am +*3:7.

3. **these men**. ver. 4, 7. Ezk 6:9. 11:21. 20:16. 36:25. Je 17:1, 2, 9. Ep 5:5. **idols in their heart**. T#1800. Ezk 8:17, 18. 20:31. Is 16:12. Je *11:11-14. Ho 5:6, 7. Mk 7:21-23. Ep *5:5. Ph +*3:19. Col √3:5. 1 T +*6:9-11, 17-19. 1 J *5:21. **and put**. Ezk 3:20. 7:19. 44:12. Je 44:16-18. Zp 1:3. 1 P 2:8. Re 2:14. **should**. Ezk 20:3. 1 S 28:6. 2 K *3:13. Ps 66:18. 101:3. Pr 15:8, 29. 21:27. 28:9. Is *1:15. 33:15. Je 7:8-11, +*16 (T#1788). 11:11. *42:20, 21. Zc 7:13. Lk 20:8.

4. **speak**. Ezk 2:7. 3:4, 17-21. **I the Lord**. ver. 7. 1 K 21:20-25. *22:19-22. 2 K 1:16. Is 3:11. 66:4.

5. **I may**. ver. 9, 10. Ho 10:2. Zc 7:11-14. 2 Th √2:9-11. **estranged**. Dt 32:15, 16. Is 1:4mg. Je 2:5, 11-13, 31, 32. Zc 11:8. Ro 1:21-23, 28, 30. 8:7. Ga *6:7. Ep 4:18. Col 1:21. He +*3:12. **through**. Col √3:5, 6. 2 Th √2:11, 12.

6. **Repent**. Ezk 18:30. 1 S 7:3. 1 K 8:47-49. Ne 1:8, 9. Is √55:6, 7. Je 8:5, 6. 31:18-20. 50:4, 5. La 3:39-41. Ho 14:1-3, 8. Jon 3:7-9. Mt 3:8-10. Ac +*3:19. *8:22. 17:30. 26:20. Ja *4:8-10. **yourselves**. *or*, *others*. **turn**. ver. 4. Ezk 8:16. 16:63. 36:31, 32. 2 Ch 29:6. Is 2:20. 30:22. Je 13:27. Zp 3:11. Ro 6:21.

7. **of the stranger**. Ezk 22:7, 29. 47:22, 23. Ge +23:4 (✱S#1616h). Ex 12:48mg, 49. 20:10. Le 16:29. 20:2. 24:22. Nu 15:15, 16, 29. Je 22:3. **separateth**. Ho 4:14. 9:10. Ju 19. **and setteth**. ver. 3, 4. **and cometh**. Ezk 33:30-32. 2 K 8:8, etc. Is *58:1, 2. Je 21:1, 2. 37:1-3, 9, 10, 17. 38:14-23. **by**. ver. 4, 7, 8.

8. **I will set**. Ezk 15:7. Le 17:10♪℗. 20:3-6. 26:17♪℗. Ps 34:16. Je 21:10. 44:11. **a sign**. Ezk 5:15. Nu 26:10♪℗. Dt 28:37♪℗. Ps 37:22. 44:13, 14. Is 65:15. Je 24:9. 29:22. **I will cut**. Ge 17:14♪℗. Ex 12:15, 19♪℗. 30:33, 38♪℗. Le 7:20, 21, 25, 27♪℗. 17:4, 9♪℗. 19:8♪℗. 20:3.

22:3. 23:29♪℘. Nu 9:13♪℘. 19:20. Ro 11:22. 1 C 10:11. **and ye.** Ezk 6:7. 13:23.

9. **if the.** Ezk 20:25. 2 S 12:11, 12. 1 K *22:20-23. Jb *12:16. Ps 81:11, 12. Is 63:17. 66:4. Je 4:10. 2 Th √2:9-12. **I the Lord have deceived.** That is, I have suffered him to be deceived; I have given him up to "strong delusions to believe a lie," as a just judgment upon him for going after idols, and setting up false pretensions to inspiration. God, according to the genius of the Hebrew language, is often said to *do* a thing which he only *suffers* or *permits*. √𝄢108A4, Ge +31:7. Is +45:7. Je 20:7. Am +√3:6. **and I will.** Ezk 16:27. Ex 3:20♪℘. Is 5:25. 9:12, 17, 21. 10:4.

10. **they shall bear.** Ezk 17:18-20. 23:49. Ge 4:13. Ex 28:38♪℘. Le 5:1, 17♪℘. Nu 5:31. 14:34♪℘. 31:8. Mi 7:9. Ga 6:5. **the punishment.** ver. 4:7, 8. Dt *13:1-10. 17:2-7. Je 6:14, 15. 8:11, 12. 14:15. Re *19:19-21. **punishment of him that seeketh.** Note the awesome principle stated here: those who follow false prophets will receive the same punishment as the false prophets who lead them. How important it is to discern the false from the true, and to base this discernment on the only authority God has provided—his written word. Pr +*19:27. Is +√8:20n. Je +18:15. Mt ◐*10:41. +*15:14. Mk +*4:24. Ro √14:12. 1 C 11:19. 1 T ◐*4:16. 2 P √3:17.

11. **the house.** Ezk 34:10, etc. 44:10, 15. 48:11. Dt 13:11. 19:20. Ps 119:67. Is 9:16. Je 23:15. 50:6. 2 P 2:15, 25. **neither be.** Ezk 11:18-20. 36:25-29. *37:23. **that they.** Ezk 34:30. 36:28. 37:27. 39:22. Ge *17:7. Je 11:4. +*31:33. 32:38. Zc 13:9. He +*8:8, 10. +*11:16. Re 21:7.

13. **when.** Ezk 9:9. Ezr 9:6. Is 24:20. La 1:8, 20. Da 9:5, 10-12. **land.** 𝄢121J17, Ge +6:11. **trespassing.** Le 5:15♪℘. 6:2♪℘. 26:40♪℘. Nu 5:6, 12, 27♪℘. **break.** Ezk 4:16. 5:16. Le *26:26♪℘. Is 3:1. Je 15:2, 3. La 4:9, 10. Re 6:5, 6. **and will cut.** ver. 17, 19, 21. Ezk 25:13. Ge 6:7. Je 7:20. 32:43. 36:29.

14. **these.** ver. 16, 18, 20. **Noah.** Ge *6:8, 9. 7:1. 8:20, 21. He 11:7. **Daniel.** Ezk 28:3. Da 9:21. *10:11. William Whitla, in his Introduction to Sir Isaac Newton's *Daniel and the Apocalypse* remarks that "The date and genuineness of the book of Ezekiel has not been seriously disputed. He mentions Daniel in chapter 14:14 and following verses, where he is bracketed between two other great Biblical worthies—Noah, Daniel and Job—singled out for their righteousness. And again, in chapter 28:3, when censuring the vanity and presumption of the Prince of Tyre, he ironically says, "Behold, thou art wiser than Daniel; there is no secret that they can hide from thee." Note that Daniel is here singled out for his wisdom and his faculty of revealing secrets. It strikes me that had the prophet only wanted a representative of wisdom he would have chosen Solomon; but no other personality in Biblical history so fitly represents the double qualification of deep knowledge and the power of finding out the most profound or mysterious truths as does Daniel. Thus we have absolutely incontestable testimony that there existed before or during the lifetime of Ezekiel somewhere in Israel a man endowed with these two gifts which are so strikingly manifested in the book whose veracity is challenged, and the name of this person was Daniel. The date of the book of Ezekiel is between 500 and 600 B.C." (p. 75). Mt √24:15. **Job.** Jb *1:5, 8. 42:8, 9. Je +*7:16. 11:14. *14:11, 12. √15:1. **deliver.**

ver. 20. Pr 10:2. 11:4. 2 P *2:9. **souls.** Heb. *nephesh*, Ge +12:13.

15. **noisome.** Ezk 5:17. Le *26:22♪℘. 1 K 20:36. 2 K 17:25. Je 15:3. **spoil.** *or*, bereave. Ezk 36:12. Le 26:22.

16. **these.** ver. 14, 18. Mt √18:19, 20. Ja √5:16. **in it.** Heb. in the midst of it. ver. 9, 14, 18, 20. **as I live.** ver. 20. Ezk 33:11. Nu 14:28, 29. **they shall.** Ge √18:23-33. 19:29. Jb 22:30. Ac 27:24. He 11:7.

17. **I bring.** Ezk 5:12, 17. 21:3, 4, 9-15. 29:8. 32:11. 38:21, 22. Le *26:25, 33♪℘. Jb 27:14. Je 25:9. 47:6. Re *6:3, 4. **a sword.** 𝄢121B, Ex +5:3. **so that.** ver. 13. Ezk 25:13. Je 33:12. Ho 4:3. Zp 1:3.

18. **Though.** ver. +14.

19. **if I.** Ezk 5:12. 38:22. Nu 14:12. 16:46-50. Dt *28:21, 22, 59-61. 2 S *24:13, 15. 1 K 8:37. 2 Ch 6:28. 7:13. 20:9. Ps 91:3, 6. Is 37:36. Je 14:12. 21:6, 9. 24:10. Am 4:10. Mt *24:7. **and pour.** Ezk 7:8. 36:18. Re 16:3-6.

20. **Noah.** ver. 14, 16. **Daniel.** Daniel, says Abp. Newcome, was "taken captive in the third year of Jehoiakim (Da 1:1). After this, Jehoiakim reigned eight years (2 K 23:36). And this prophecy, as appears from Ezk 8:1, was uttered in the sixth year of Jehoiachin's captivity, who succeeded Jehoiakim, and reigned only three months (2 K 24:6, 8). Therefore, at this time, Daniel had been fourteen years in captivity;" and was, as is generally supposed, about thirty years of age. **souls.** Heb. *nephesh*, Ge +12:13. **by.** Ezk 18:20, 22. Jb 5:19-24. Ps 33:18, 19. Is 3:10. Ho 10:12. Zp 2:3. Ac 10:35. 1 J 2:29. 3:7, 10.

21. **How much more when.** *or*, Also when. **my four.** ver. 13, 15, 17, 19. Ezk 5:12, 17. 6:11, 12. 33:27. Pr 10:2. Je 15:2, 3. +29:17. Am 4:6-12. Re *6:4-8.

22. **behold, therein.** Ezk 6:8. Dt 4:31. 2 Ch 36:20. Is 6:13. 10:20-22. 17:4-6. 24:13. 40:1, 2. 65:8, 9. Je 4:27. 5:19. 30:11. 52:27-30. Mi 5:7. Mk 13:20. He 12:6-11. **ye shall see.** Ezk 6:9, 10. 16:63. 20:43. 36:31. Je 31:17-21. **ye shall be.** Je 3:21-25.

23. **shall comfort.** Is *40:1, 2. **that I have not.** Ezk 8:6-18. 9:8, 9. Ge √18:22-33. Dt 8:2. Ne 9:33. Pr 26:2. Je 7:17-28. *22:8, 9. Da 9:7, 14. Ro *2:5. Re *15:4. 16:6. **have done.** Ps 39:9. Is 38:15. Mk 7:37. Jn 13:7.

EZEKIEL 15

The unfitness of the wood of a vine for anything but the fire, 1-5; an emblem of the character and doom of the Jews, 6-8.

2. **What.** The vine is only noble and useful while producing fruit; for, when cut down, its wood is fit only for fuel. So Israel, having ceased to be *fruitful*, they are good for nothing, but, like a withered branch of a vine, to be burnt. Dt 32:32, 33. Ps 80:8-16. SS 2:13, 15. 6:11. 7:12. 8:11, 12. Is *5:1-7. Je 2:21. Ho 10:1. Mt 21:33-41. Mk 12:1-9. Lk 20:9-16. Jn *15:1-6. **among.** Is 44:23. Mi 3:12. Zc 11:2.

3. **wood.** Je 24:8. Mt *5:13. Mk 9:50. Lk 14:34, 35. **men take.** Jn 15:5, 6.

4. **it is cast.** Ps *80:8, 14-16. Is 27:11. Jn *15:6. He 6:8. **the fire.** Is 1:31. Am 4:11. Ml 4:1. Mt *3:12. He *12:28, 29. **Is it meet.** Heb. Will it prosper.

5. **meet.** Heb. made *fit*. Je +3:16mg.

6. **As the vine.** ver. 2. Ezk 17:3-10. 20:47, 48. Is 5:1-6, 24, 25. Je 4:7. 7:20. 21:7. 24:8-10. 25:9-11, 18. 44:21-27. Zc 1:6. **so will I give.** 2 K ✱25:9.

7. **I will see.** Ezk 14:8. Le 17:10. 20:3-6. 26:17. Ps 34:16. Je 21:10. **they shall.** 1 K 19:17. Is 24:18. Je 48:43, 44. Am 5:19. 9:1-4. **and ye shall.** Ezk 6:7. 7:4. 11:10. 20:38, 42, 44. Ps *9:16.

8. **I will.** Ezk 6:14. 14:13-21. 33:29. Is 6:11. 24:3-12. Je 25:10, 11. Zp 1:18. **committed a trespass.** Heb. trespassed a trespass. Ezk 14:13. 2 Ch 36:14-16.

EZEKIEL 16

The original state of Jerusalem is shown under the emblem of an exposed infant, 1-5; whom God is represented, as rescuing, educating, espousing, and richly providing for, 6-14; but she commits the most abandoned and multiplied adulteries, 15-43. Her crimes shown to equal those of her mother, the Hittite, and to exceed those of her sisters, Sodom and Samaria, 44-59. Yet at length she will be received to favor, and be deeply ashamed of her base conduct, 60-63.

2. **cause.** Ezk *20:4. 22:2. 23:36. 33:7-9. Is 58:1. Ho 8:1. **abominations.** Ezk 8:9-17.

3. **Thy birth.** Heb. Thy cutting out, *or* habitation. ver. 45. Ezk 21:30. 29:14. Ge 11:25, 29. Jsh 24:14. Ne 9:7. Is 1:10. 51:1, 2. Mt 3:7. 11:24. Lk 3:7. Jn *8:44. Ep *2:3. 1 J 3:10. **the land.** Ge 15:18-21. **Amorite.** Ge +10:16. 15:16. Dt 20:17. 1 K 21:26. 2 K 21:11. **Hittite.** Ge +15:20. Ezr 9:1.

4. **And.** ∫154, Mt +3:4. **for.** Ezk 20:8, 13. Ge 15:13. Ex 1:11-14. 2:23, 24. 5:16-21. Dt 5:6. 15:15. Jsh 24:2. Ne 9:7-9. Ho 2:3. Ac 7:6, 7. **to supple thee.** *or,* when I looked *upon thee.* **not salted.** Salt was anciently used for cleansing a newborn child. **nor swaddled.** La 2:20mg., 22. Lk 2:7, 12.

5. **eye.** Ex 2:6. Is 49:15. La 2:11, 12, 19. 4:3, 4, 10. **but thou.** Ge 21:10. Ex 1:22. Nu 19:16. Je 9:21, 22. 22:19. **person.** Heb. *nephesh,* soul, Ge +12:5. In ancient paganism female babies were sometimes abandoned and left to die, so Israel at its founding was exposed to death, none but God helping her.

6. **and saw.** Ex 2:24, 25. *3:7, 8. Ex *20:2. Ho *11:1. Ac 7:34. **polluted.** *or,* trodden under foot. Is 14:19. 51:23. Mi 7:10. Mt *5:13. He *10:29. Re 14:20. **Live.** Ezk 20:5-10. Ex 19:4-6. Dt 9:4, 5. Ps 105:10-15, 26-37. Jn 5:25. Ho 6:2. 13:9. Ep 2:4, 5. T 3:3-7. **when thou wast.** Canaanite cities were founded in blood, as proved today by human sacrifices discovered on the foundations (CB).

7. **caused,** etc. Heb. made thee a million. Ge 22:17. Ex 1:7. 12:37. Ac 7:17. **excellent ornaments.** Heb. ornament of ornaments. ver. 10-13, 16. Ex 3:22. Dt 1:10. 4:8. 32:10-14. 33:26-29. Ne 9:18-25. Ps 135:4. 147:20. 148:14. 149:2-4. Is 61:10. 62:3. **hair.** Is 7:20. **whereas.** ver. 22. Jb 1:21. SS 4:5. Ho 2:3, 9, 10. Re 3:17, 18.

8. **thy time.** ver. 6. Dt 7:6-8. Ru 3:9. 1 S +*12:22. Is +*41:8, 9. 43:4. 63:7-9. Je *2:2, 3. *31:3. Ho *11:1. Ml 1:2, 3. Ro *5:8. 9:10-13. **and I.** Dt 22:30. Ru *3:9. **I sware.** Ezk 20:5, 6. Ex *19:4-8. 24:1-8. 32:13. Dt 4:31. Je 2:2, 3. 31:32. Ho 2:18-20. Ml *2:14.

9. **washed.** ver. 4. Ezk 36:25. Ru 3:3. Ps 51:7. Is 4:4. Jn 13:8-10. 1 C 6:11. 10:2. He 9:10-14. 1 J 5:8. Re *1:5, 6. **blood.** Heb. bloods. ver. 6. Ezk 18:13mg. 2 K +*9:26mg. **anointed.** Ps *23:5. 2 C 1:21. 1 J *2:20, 27.

10. **clothed.** ver. 7. Ps 45:13, 14. Is 61:3, 10. Lk 15:22. Re 21:2. **broidered.** ver. 13, 18. Ex 28:5. 1 P

3:3, 4. **badgers' skin.** Ex 25:5)℘. 26:14)℘. Nu 4:6)℘. **I girded.** Ex 39:27, 28. Re 7:9-14. 19:8. **covered.** Ezk 27:7. Ge 41:42mg. Pr 31:22. Re 18:12. 19:8.

11. **I put.** Ge 24:22, 47, 53. **a chain.** Ge 41:42. Pr 1:9. 4:9. SS 1:10. 4:9. Is 3:19. Da 5:7, 16, 29.

12. **forehead.** Heb. nose. Ge 24:22mg. Is 3:21. **earrings.** Ge 35:4. Ex 32:2. 35:22. Nu 31:50. Jg 8:24. Jb 42:11. Pr 25:12. Ho 2:13. **and a.** Le 8:9. Est 2:17. Is 28:5. La 5:16. Re 2:10. 4:4, 10. **crown.** Jn 19:2.

13. **wast thou.** ∫155E3, Is +32:9. **thou didst.** ver. 19. Dt 8:8. 32:13, 14. 1 S 12:13. Ps 45:13, 14. 81:16. 147:14. Ho 2:5. **honey.** ∫17117, Ex +3:8. **and thou wast.** ver. 14, 15. Ps 48:2. 50:2. Is 64:11. Je 13:20. **and thou didst.** Ge 17:6. 1 S 12:12. 2 S 8:15. 1 K 4:21. Ezr 4:20. 5:11. Ps 50:2. La 2:15.

14. **thy renown.** Dt 4:6-8, 32-38. Jsh 2:9-11. 9:6-9. 1 K 10:1, etc., 24. 2 Ch 2:11, 12. 9:23. La *2:15. **beauty.** Ps 48:2, 12, 13. 90:17. SS 6:4. **perfect.** Ep 1:6. **through.** 1 C 4:7. **put upon.** Is 52:1.

15. **thou didst.** Ezk 33:13. Dt *32:15. Is 48:1, 2. Je 7:4. Mi 3:11. Zp 3:11. Mt 3:9. **and playedst.** Ezk 20:8. 23:3, 8, 11, 12, etc. Ex 32:6, etc. Nu 25:1, 2. Jg 2:12, 13. 3:6. 10:6. 1 K 11:5-8. 12:28. 2 K 17:7. 21:3-11. Ps 106:35-39. Is 1:21. 57:8. Je 2:20, 23-28. 3:1, 2, 6, 20. 7:4. Ho *1:2. 4:10-14. Re 17:5. **because.** Raised from the most abject state to dignity and splendor by Jehovah, Israel became proud of her numbers, riches, strength, and reputation, forgetting that it was "through his comeliness which he had put upon them;" and thus departing from God, made alliances with heathen nations, and worshipped their idols. **and pouredst.** ver. 25, 36, 37.

16. **of thy garments.** ver. 17, 18. Ezk 7:20. 2 K 23:7. 2 Ch 28:24. Ho 2:8. **and playedst.** Is *1:21.

17. **hast also.** Ezk 7:19. 23:14, etc. Ex 32:1-4. Ho 2:13. 10:1. **men.** Heb. a male. Is *57:8. 66:17n. Je 30:6mg. Da 3:1. **and didst.** Is 44:19, 20. 57:7, 8. Je 2:27, 28. 3:9. +5:7.

18. **And tookest.** This seems to intimate that the Israelites not only spent their own wealth and abundance in building and decorating idol temples, and in maintaining their worship, but that they made use of the holy vestments, and the various kinds of offerings which belonged to Jehovah, in order to honor and serve the idols of the heathen. ver. 10. Ho *2:8.

19. **meat.** See on ver. 13. Dt 32:14-17. Ho 2:8-13. **honey.** ∫17117, Ex +3:8. **a sweet savor.** Heb. a savor of rest. Ezk 6:13. 20:28, 41. Ge 8:21mg)℘. Le 1:9.

20. **thy sons.** ver. 21. Ezk 23:4. Ge *17:5. Re 13:2, 12. Dt 29:11, 12. **and these.** Ezk 20:26, 31. 23:37, 39. Jsh 15:8n. 2 K 16:3. 2 Ch 33:6. Ps 106:37, 38. Is 57:5. Je 7:31. 32:35. Ho +13:2mg. Mi 6:7. **be devoured.** Heb. devour. **Is this.** Ezk 8:17. Nu 16:9. Je 2:34, 35.

21. **my children.** Ps 106:37. **to pass.** Le 18:21)℘. 20:1-5. Dt +*18:10. 2 K 17:17. +21:6. 23:10.

22. **not remembered.** ver. 3-7, 43, 60-63. Je 2:2. Ho 2:3. 11:1.

23. **woe.** Ezk 2:10. 13:3, 18. 24:6. Je 13:27. Zp 3:1. Mt 11:21. 23:13-29. Re 8:13. 12:12. **woe.** ∫109, Ps +42:2. ∫47. Cataploce; or, Sudden Exclamation B475. Parenthetic addition by way of exclamation. For another instance of this figure see Ro 9:3.

24. **thou hast.** ver. 31, 39. Ezk 20:28, 29. 2 K 21:3-7. 23:5-7, 11, 12. 2 Ch 33:3-7. **eminent place.** *or,* brothel house. **and hast.** Le 26:30. Ps 78:58. Is 57:5, 7. Je 2:20. 3:2. 17:3.

25. **at every.** ver. 31. Ge *38:14, 21. Pr 9:14, 15. Is 3:9. Je 2:23, 24. 3:2. 6:15. *11:13. **hast made thy beauty to be abhorred.** As the beauty of a shameless whore is abhorred by them to whom she offers herself. In her high places every passenger might meet his own god, and worship his own idol, and then satisfy his lust with lewd women, common as the street; and this made men abhor that beauty they would have admired, dressed in modesty and dwelling retired (Matthew Poole). Ezk 23:9, 10, 32. Re 17:1-5, 12, 13, 16. **opened thy feet.** A modest expressing of the most immodest practice of lewd and insatiable adulteresses and whores, which are ready for every comer, and tempt such as tempt not them (Matthew Poole). ♪88. Euphemism, Ge +15:15. Ge 38:14. Dt 28:57. Jg +3:24. Pr 9:14. 23:28.

26. **with the.** Ezk 8:10, 14. 20:7, 8. 23:3, 8, 19-21. Ex 32:4. Dt 29:16, 17. Jsh 24:14. Is 30:21. Je *2:33. **neighbors.** lit. "settlers down." Ex 3:22. **great of flesh.** or, appetite. ♪88, Ge +17:11. A reference to the great physical size of the Egyptians, with a graphic reference (in Hebrew) to the genital organs. Thus Matthew Poole observes, "naturally of big make, and men of great stature, and such as insatiable adulteresses would covet." This strong language indicates the utter disgust of Ezekiel, and God, with the idolatry of Israel. ver. +17. Ezk 23:20. Le 15:2, 3.

27. **I have.** Ezk 14:9. Is 5:25. 9:12, 17. **stretched.** ♪22A14.8A, Ex +7:5. **and have.** Dt 28:48-57. Is 3:1. Ho 2:9-12. **thine ordinary.** ♪171E9, Ge +47:22. *Chukkach*, "thy portion;" the household provision of a wife—food, clothes, and money. **delivered.** The Jews, under Manasseh, and the succeeding kings of Judah, made the temple itself the scene of their open and abominable idolatries, in addition to all their idol-temples! which appears to be what is meant by "the eminent place," and "high places in every street," ver. 24. Allured by the prosperity of the Egyptians, they also connected themselves with them, and joined in their multiplied and abominable idolatries. And when Jehovah punished them by wars and famines, and by the Philistines, whose daughters are represented as ashamed of their enormous idolatries, instead of being amended, they formed alliances with the Assyrians, and worshipped their gods: and they even followed every idol which was worshipped between Canaan and Chaldee. ver. 37. Ezk 23:22, 25, 28, 29, 46, 47. Ps 106:41. Je 34:21. Re 17:16. **will.** Heb. *nephesh*, Ex +15:9. **daughters.** or, cities. Nu +*21:25mg. 2 K 24:2. 2 Ch *28:18, 19. Is 9:12. Je 49:2. **which.** ver. 47, 57. Ezk 5:6, 7.

28. **hast played.** Ezk 23:5-9, 12, etc. Jg 10:6. 2 K 16:7, 10-18. 21:11. 2 Ch 28:23. Je *2:18, 36. Ho 10:6.

29. **in the land.** Ezk 13:14-23. Jg 2:12-19. 2 K 21:9. **unto.** Ezk 23:14, etc.

30. **How.** ♪85E, Ge +17:17. **weak.** Pr 9:13. Is 1:3. Je 2:12, 13. 4:22. **the work.** Jg 16:15, 16. Pr 7:11-13, 21. Is 3:9. Je 3:3. Re 17:1-6.

31. **In that thou buildest thine.** or, In thy daughters *is* thine, etc. See on ver. 24, 39. **makest.** ver. 25. Ho 12:11. **in that thou scornest.** See on ver. 33, 34. Is 52:3.

32. **as a wife.** ver. 8. Ezk 23:37, 45. Je 2:25, 28. 3:1, 8, 9, 20. Ho 2:2. 3:1. 2 C 11:2, 3.

33. **give.** Ge 38:16-18. Dt 23:17, 18. Ho 2:12. Jl 3:3. Mi 1:7. Lk 15:30. **but thou.** Is 30:3, 6, 7. 57:9.

Ho 8:9, 10. **hirest.** Heb. bribest.

34. **thou givest.** Ho 8:9. **reward.** ver. 31, 33, 41. Dt 23:18♪℗. Is 23:17, 18. Ho 9:1. Mi 1:7. **no reward.** ver. 36.

35. **O harlot.** Is 1:21. 23:15, 16. Je 3:1, 6-8. Ho 2:5. Na 3:4. Jn 4:10, 18. Re 17:5. **hear.** Ezk 13:2. 20:47. 34:7. 1 K 22:19. Is 1:10. 28:14. Ho 4:1. Am 7:16.

36. **Because.** ver. 15, etc. Ezk 22:15. 23:8. 24:13. 36:25. La 1:9. Zp 3:1. **filthiness.** Heb. brass. Ezk 24:11. **and thy.** Ezk 23:10, 18, 29. Ge 3:7, 10, 11. Ps 139:11, 12. Je 13:22-26. Re 3:18. **idols.** lit. "rolled or dungy ones." Ezk 6:4, 5, 6, 9, 13. 2 K +*23:24 (❋S#1544h). **and by.** See on ver. 20, 21. Je *2:34.

37. **I will gather.** Ezk 23:9, 10, 22-30. Je 4:30. 13:22, 26. 22:20. La 1:8, 19. Ho 2:3, 10. 8:10. Na 3:5, 6. Re 17:16.

38. **as women.** Heb. with judgments of women, etc. ver. 40. Ezk 23:45-47. Ge *38:11, 24. Le *20:10. Dt 22:22-24. Mt 1:18, 19. Jn *8:3-5. **shed.** ver. 20, 21, 36. Ge √9:6. Ex 21:12. Nu 35:31. 2 K *24:3, 4. Ps 79:3-5. Je 18:21. Na 1:2. Zp 1:17. Re 16:6.

39. **And I.** For the enormous idolatries and cruelties of Judah and Jerusalem, Jehovah determined to gather together the surrounding nations,—both those with whom they had formed alliances, as the Egyptians and the Assyrians, and such as had always been inimical to them, as Edom, Ammon, Moab, and Philistia,—to inflict, or to witness, his judgments upon them. Having exposed their enormous crimes to view, He would pass sentence upon them: He would give Jerusalem into the hands of the Chaldeans, who would destroy the city and temple which they had polluted; level their cities and high places with the ground; slay, plunder, and enslave the people. **they shall throw.** ver. 24, 25, 31. Ezk 7:22-24. Is 27:9. **shall strip.** ver. 10-20. Ezk 23:26, 29. 2 K *25:13-15. Is 3:16-24. Ho 2:3, 9-13. **thy fair jewels.** Heb. instruments of thine ornament. ver. 17.

40. **shall also.** Hab 1:6-10. Jn 8:5-7. **and thrust.** Ezk 23:10, 47. 24:21. Je 25:9.

41. **burn.** Dt 13:16. 2 K 25:9. 2 Ch *36:19. Je *39:8. 52:13. Mi 3:12. **and execute.** Ezk 5:8. 23:10, 48. Dt 13:11. 22:21, 24. Jb 34:26. **and I.** Ezk 23:27. 37:23. Is 1:25, 26. 2:18. 27:9. Ho 2:6-17. Mi 5:10-14. Zc 13:2. 1 T 5:20.

42. **will I.** Ezk 5:13. 21:17. 2 S 21:14. Is 1:24. Zc 6:8. **my jealousy.** Ex 34:14. **and will.** Ezk 39:29. Is 40:1, 2. +*54:9, 10.

43. **thou hast.** ver. 22. Ps 78:42. 106:13. Je 2:32. **but hast.** Ezk 6:9. Dt 32:21. Ps *78:40, 58, 59. 95:10. Is +63:10. Am 2:13. Ac 7:51. Ep 4:30. **I also.** Ezk 7:3, 4, 8, 9. 9:10. 11:21. 22:31. Ro 2:8, 9. **thou shalt not.** Le 19:29♪℗.

44. **every.** Ezk 18:2, 3. 1 S 24:13. **proverb.** Nu +21:27. **saying.** ♪138A, Ge +10:9. **As is.** ver. 3, 45. 1 K 21:26. 2 K 17:11, 15. 21:9. Ezr 9:1. Ps 106:35-38.

45. **that lotheth.** ver. 8, 15, 20, 21. Ezk 23:37-39. Dt 5:9. 12:31. Is 1:4mg. Zc 11:8. Ro 1:30, 31. **your mother.** ver. 3. **Amorite.** Ge +10:16.

46. **elder.** ver. 51. Ezk 23:4, 11, 31-33. Je 3:8-11. Mi 1:5. **thy younger sister.** Heb. thy sister lesser than thou. ver. 48, 49, 53-56, 61. Ge 13:11-13. 18:20, etc. 19:24, 25. Dt 29:23. *32:32. Is *1:9, 10. Je 23:14. La 4:6mg. Lk 17:28-30. 2 P 2:6. Ju +*7. Re 11:8. **her**

daughters. ver. 27mg. Ezk 26:6. Ge 14:8. 19:29. Ho 11:8.

47. **as if that were a very little thing.** or, that was lothed as a small *thing*. Ezk 8:17. 1 K 16:31. Pr 5:14 (almost). The word denotes "quickly, shortly, in a little time." **thou wast.** ver. 48, 51. Ezk 5:6, 7. 2 K *21:9, 16. Jn 15:21, 22. 1 C 5:1.

48. **Sodom thy sister.** Mt +*10:15. +*11:23, 24. Mk 6:11. Lk 10:12. Ac 7:52.

49. **Sodom.** Mt 10:15. 11:23, 24. Lk +*12:48. Mk 6:11. Ju √7. **pride.** Ezk 28:2, 9, 17. 29:3. Ge 19:9. Ps 138:6. Pr 16:5, 18. 18:12. 21:4. Is 3:9. 16:6. Da 4:30, 37. 5:23. Ob 3. 1 P 5:5. **fulness.** Ge 13:10. 18:20. Dt 32:15. Pr 30:9. Is 22:13, 14. Je 5:28. 50:11mg. Am 6:3-6. Mk +*4:19. Lk 6:25. 12:16-20. *16:19. 17:28. 21:34. Re 3:17. **abundance of idleness.** or, prosperous ease. T#709. Dt 6:11, 12. 11:21. Pr 1:32. 10:4. 19:15. ◐+22:29. Is 56:10. Je +*48:10mg. Mt 12:36. 20:6, 7. 25:18, 26-30. Lk *12:19. 13:6, 7. 19:20-24. Ac 17:21. Ro +*12:11. 2 Th √3:10, 11. 1 T +*5:13 (T#358). He +*6:12. **neither.** Ezk *18:12. 34:4. Dt +*24:14. Jb 24:4. Ps +*12:5. +*62:10. 109:16. Pr √21:13. *22:16. 30:14. Ec +*5:8. Is 3:14, 15. 32:7. Am 2:6. 5:11, 12. 8:4-6. Mi 3:2-4. Hab 3:14. Zc 7:10. 11:16. Mt +*5:7 (T#527). 25:43. Lk 16:20, 21. Ja +*4:17.

50. **and committed.** Ge *13:10, 13. 18:20. 19:5. Le 18:22. Dt 23:17. 2 K 23:7. Pr 16:18. 18:12. Ro 1:26, 27. Ju +√7. **therefore.** Ge 19:24. Dt 29:23. Jb 18:15. Is 13:19. Je 20:16. 49:18. 50:40. La 4:6. Am 4:11. Zp 2:9. 2 P 2:6. Re 18:9.

51. **Samaria.** Lk +*12:47, 48. Ro 3:9-20. **justified.** Ezk 23:11. Je *3:8-11. Mt 12:41, 42. Re 2:20-22.

52. **which hast.** ver. 56. Mt 7:1-5. Lk 6:37. Ro 2:1, 10, 26, 27. **bear thine.** ver. 54, 63. Ezk 36:6, 7, 15, 31, 32. 39:26. 44:13. Je 23:40. 31:19. 51:51. Ho 10:6. Ro 1:32. 6:21. **they are more.** Ge 38:26. 1 S 24:17. 1 K 2:32.

53. **bring.** ver. 60, 61. Ezk 29:14. 39:25. Dt 30:3. Jb 42:10. Ps 14:7. 85:1. 126:1. Is 1:9. Je 20:16. 31:9, 10, 23. *48:47n. 49:6, 39. Jl 3:1. **captivity of Sodom.** With the millennial healing of the Dead sea these sites will be inhabited again. Ezk 47:8. Zc 14:8. **in the midst.** Is 19:24, 25. Je 12:16. Ro 11:23-31.

54. **thou mayest.** ver. 52, 63. Ezk 36:31, 32. Je 2:26. La *4:6. **in that.** Ezk 14:22, 23.

55. **Sodom.** Is 1:9, 10. 3:9. Je 23:14. Zp 2:9. Re *11:8. **her daughters.** Mi 4:8. Zp 3:10, 14. Zc 9:9. **former estate.** ver. 53n. Ezk 37:1-14. Is 25:7, 8. Je 48:47n. Ho 13:14. Ju ◐√7. **then.** ver. 53. Ezk 36:11. Is *1:9. Ml 3:4.

56. **was not.** Is 65:5. Zp 3:11. Lk 15:28-30. 18:11. **mentioned.** Heb. for a report, *or* a hearing. Ezk 7:26. Heb. prides, *or* excellencies.

57. **thy wickedness.** ver. 36, 37. Ezk 21:24. 23:18, 19. Ps 50:21. La 4:22. Ho 2:10. 7:1. 1 C 4:5. **reproach.** 2 K *16:5-7. 2 Ch 28:5, 6, 18-23. Is 7:1. 14:28. **Syria.** Heb. Aram. Ge 10:22, 23. Nu 23:7. **the daughters.** ver. 27mg. **despise.** or, spoil. Je 33:24.

58. **hast.** Ezk 23:49. Ge 4:13. La 5:7. **borne.** Heb. borne them. ⌐121C1E, Ge +19:15. Ezk 3:14. 32:8.

59. **I will.** Ezk 7:4, 8, 9. 14:4. Is 3:11. Je 2:19. Mt 7:1, 2. Ro 2:8, 9. **which.** Ezk 17:13-16, 19. Ex 24:1-8. Dt 29:10-15, 25◐℈. 2 Ch 34:31, 32. Is 24:5. Je 22:9. 31:32.

60. **I will remember.** ver. 8. Le 26:42, 45. Ne 1:5-11. Ps 105:8. *106:45. Je 2:2. √32:40. 33:20-26. Ho

2:15. Lk 1:72. **I will establish.** Ezk 37:26, 27. 2 S *23:5. Is *54:9, 10. +*55:3. Je *31:31-34. *32:38-41. 50:5. Ho 2:19, 20. He *8:10. 12:24. 13:20. **everlasting.** Heb. *olam*, Ge +17:7. **covenant.** Ge +9:16. Is 44:7.

61. **remember.** ver. 63. Ezk 20:43. 36:31, 32. Jb 42:5, 6. Ps 119:59. Je 31:18-20. 50:4, 5. **be ashamed.** Le 26:40, 41. **when.** ver. 53-55. SS 8:8, 9. Is 2:2-5. 11:9, 10. Ho 1:9-11. Ro 11:11. 15:8, 9, 16. Ga 4:26, 27. Ep 2:12-14. 3:6. **I will.** Is 49:18-23. 54:1, 2. 60:4. 66:7-12. Ga 4:26, etc. **but not.** Je 31:31, etc. Jn 15:16. He 8:13.

62. **I will.** ver. 60. Je 31:31, 32. *50:5. Da *9:27. Ho *2:18-23. He 8:8. **and thou.** Ezk 6:7. 39:22. Je 24:7. Jl 3:17.

63. **remember.** ver. 61. Ezk 36:31, 32. Ezr 9:6. Da 9:7, 8. **and never.** Jb 40:4, 5. Ps 39:9. Is +*59:21. Je *3:19. *31:34. √32:40. La 3:39. Zc +*10:6. Ro 2:1. *3:19, 27. 9:19, 20. **open thy mouth.** Ezk +24:27. 29:21. **when.** Ps +*102:13, 16. Ho √5:15. Ac +√3:19-21. **pacified.** Pr 16:14. Zc *10:6. Ro *5:1, 2. 1 C 4:7. Ep *2:3-5. T 3:3-7.

EZEKIEL 17

A parable of two eagles and a vine, 1-10: explained of the captivity of Jeconiah; and of Zedekiah, who had broken his covenant confirmed by an oath, with the king of Babylon, and made an alliance with the king of Egypt; and of the judgments that were coming upon him, 11-21. An emblematic prediction of the person and kingdom of Christ, 22-24.

2. **put forth.** Ezk 20:49. Jg 9:8-15. 14:12-19. 2 S 12:1-4. Ho 12:10. Mt 13:13, 14, 35. Mk *4:33, 34. 1 C 13:12mg. **riddle.** √3, Ge +49:10. Nu +12:8. **parable.** Nu +21:27. +23:7n.

3. **A great.** Nebuchadnezzar, so called from his towering ambition and rapaciousness. ver. 7, 12, etc. Dt *28:49. Je 4:13. *48:40. 49:16, 22. La 4:19. Ho 8:1. Mt 24:28. **great wings.** Extensive empire, both in length and breadth. Da 2:38. 4:22. 7:4. **full.** Numerous subjects, of various nations, and of different languages and manners. **divers colors.** Heb. embroidering. 1 Ch 29:2. **came.** Came against Judah and Jerusalem. ver. 12. 2 K 24:10-16. 2 Ch 36:9, 10. Je 22:23-28. 24:1. **the highest.** Jeconiah, whom he took captive to Babylon. ver. 12. Je 22:23, 24. **branch.** or, foliage. lit. "pruned" thing. Ezk 8:17. Nu 13:23. **the cedar.** The royal and ancient family of David. Ezk 31:3, 10.

4. **the top.** The princes of Judah. **into.** Is 43:14. 47:15. Je 51:13. Re 18:3, 11-19. **a land.** Chaldea. **a city.** Babylon, which by means of the Euphrates and Tigris, had communication with the richest and most distant nations. 2 K *24:12.

5. **the seed.** Zedekiah, brother to Jeconiah. ver. 13. 2 K *24:17. Je 37:1. **planted it in a fruitful field.** Heb. put it in a field of seed. Made him king of Judea. Dt *8:7-9. **he placed.** Made him dependent on Babylon, the city of great waters, as the willow is on humidity. Ezk 19:11, 12. Is 15:7. 44:4.

6. **it grew.** ver. 14. Pr 16:18, 19. Je 52:10. **whose.** The Jewish state had then no height of dominion; and Zedekiah was wholly dependent on Nebuchadnezzar.

7. **another.** Pharaoh-hophra, or Apries, king of Egypt. ver. 15. 2 K *24:20. 2 Ch 36:13. Je *37:5-7. **did bend.** Looked to him for support, in his intended rebellion.

8. soil. Heb. field. ver. 5, 6. **and that.** Though he was dependent on Babylon, yet he was in such a situation as would have enabled him to reign in credit, and be useful to his people.

9. Shall it. Shall he succeed in casting off the yoke of the king of Babylon, to whom he had *sworn* fealty? ver. 10, 15-17. Nu 14:41. 2 Ch 13:12. 20:20. Is 8:9, 10. 30:1-7. 31:1-3. Je 32:5. **shall he.** He shall come and dethrone him, and carry him captive. 2 K 25:4-7. Je 21:4-7. 24:8-10. 39:4-7. 52:7-11. **the fruit.** The children of Zedekiah. Je 52:10. **all the leaves.** All the nobles, who shall perish with Zedekiah. **even.** Je 37:10.

10. shall it. The *regal* government shall be finally destroyed, like a tree blasted by the east wind: Zedekiah shall be the *last king*; and the monarchy shall terminate with him. Ezk 19:12-14. Is *20:5. Ho 12:1. 13:15. Mt 21:19. Mk 11:20. Jn *15:6. Ju 12. **toucheth.** ƒ108B, Ge +26:29.

12. to the. Ezk 2:5, 8. 3:9. 12:9. Is 1:2. **Know.** Ezk 24:19. Ex 12:26. Dt 6:20. Jsh 4:6, 21. Mt 13:51. 15:16, 17. 16:11. Mk 4:13. Lk 9:45. Ac 8:30. **Behold.** ver. 3. Ezk 1:2. 2 K *24:10-16. 2 Ch 36:9, 10. Je 22:24-28. **and led.** Is 39:7. Je 52:31-34.

13. hath taken. ver. 5. 2 K 24:17. Je *37:1. **taken an oath of him.** Heb. brought him to an oath. Ezk 16:59. 2 Ch 36:13. Je 5:2. **he hath also.** 2 K 24:15, 16. Je 24:1. 29:2.

14. the kingdom. ver. 6. Ezk 29:14. Dt 28:43. 1 S 2:7, 30. Ne 9:36, 37. La 5:16. Mt 22:17-21. **base.** Or, *low*; a tributary kingdom, dependent on the king of Babylon. **but that by keeping of his covenant it might stand.** Heb. to keep his covenant, to stand to it. Je 27:12-17. 38:17-21.

15. he rebelled. ver. 7. 2 K 24:20. 2 Ch *36:13. Je 52:3. **in.** Dt 17:16. Is 30:1-4. *31:1-3. 36:6-9. Je 37:5-7. **Shall he prosper.** See on ver. 9. Dt 29:12-15. Je 22:29, 30. **shall he escape.** ver. 18. Ezk 21:25. Pr 19:5. Je 32:4. 34:3. 38:18, 23. Mt 23:33. He √2:3. **or shall.** Ps 55:23.

16. whose oath. See on ver. 18, 19. Ezk 16:59. Ex +*20:7. Nu 30:2. Jsh 9:20. 2 S 21:2. Ps √15:4. Ec 8:2. Ho 10:4. Zc 5:3, 4. Ml +*3:5. Ro 1:31. 1 T 1:10. 2 T 3:3. **even.** ver. 10. Ezk 12:13. Je *32:4, 5. √34:2-5. 39:7. 52:11.

17. hath. Ezk 29:6, 7. 2 K 24:7. Is *36:6, 9. Je 37:7. La 4:17. **by.** Ezk 4:2. Je 33:5. *52:4. **persons.** Heb. *nephesh*, souls, Jsh +10:28.

18. Seeing. Though Zedekiah's oath had been given to a heathen, a conqueror, and a tyrant, yet God considered the violation of it a most aggravated sin against Him, and determined to punish him. Nu √30:2. Jsh *9:19, 20. **lo, he.** 1 Ch +*29:24mg. 2 Ch 30:8mg. La 5:6. **given his hand.** ƒ121S3I, 1 Ch +29:24. 2 K 10:15. Ezr 10:19. Je 50:15. **he shall.** See on ver. 15.

19. surely. Ezk 21:23-27. Dt 5:11. Je 5:2, 9. 7:9-15. **hath broken.** Ps 33:10. 89:33mg.

20. I will spread. Ezk 12:13. 32:3. Jsh 10:16-18. 2 S 18:9. 2 K *25:5, 7. 2 Ch 33:11. Jb 10:16. Ec 9:12. Je 39:5-7. La 1:13. 4:20. Ho 7:12. Lk 21:35. **plead.** Ezk 20:35, 36. 38:22. Je 2:9, 35. 50:44. Ho 2:2. Mi 6:2. **trespass.** Ezk +15:8.

21. all his fugitives. Ezk 5:12. 12:14. 2 K 25:5, 11. Je 48:44. 52:8. Am 9:1, 9, 10. **shall know.** See on Ezk 6:7, 10. 13:14, 23. 15:7. Is 26:11.

22. highest branch. Ezk 34:29. Ps 80:15. Is 4:2. *11:1-5. Je *23:5, 6. 33:15, 16. Zc *3:8. 4:12-14. 6:12,

13. Mt *1:11, 12, 16. **a tender.** See on Is 53:2. **upon.** Ezk 20:40. 40:2. Ps *2:6. 72:16. Is *2:2, 3. Da 2:35, 44, 45. Mi *4:1.

23. and it. Ps 92:12, 13. Is 27:6. Jn 12:24. 15:5-8. **cedar.** ƒ22H2A, Is +4:2. **under.** Ezk 31:6. Ge +*49:10. Ps 22:27-30. 72:8-11. Is 2:2. 11:6-10. 49:18-23. 60:4-12. Da 4:10-14, 21-23. Ho 14:7. Mt 13:32, 47, 48. Lk 14:21-23. Jn √12:32. Ac 10:11, 12. Ga 3:28. Ep *1:10. Col *3:11. 2 Th +*2:1. Re 11:15.

24. all the trees. Ps 96:11, 12. Is 55:12, 13. Da 2:44, 45. ch. 4. **have brought.** 1 S 2:7, 8. Jb 5:11. 40:12. Ps 75:6, 7. 89:38-45. Is 2:13, 14. +*9:6, 7. *11:1, etc. 26:5. Am 9:11. Lk *1:33, 52, 53. 1 C 1:27, 28. **dry tree.** Is 56:3. **I the Lord have spoken.** Ezk 12:25. 22:14. 24:14. Mt √24:35. Lk 23:31.

EZEKIEL 18

God reproves the Jews for using the proverb of sour grapes, 1-4. He shows his dealings with a righteous man, 5-9; with the wicked son of a righteous father, 10-13; and with the righteous son of a wicked father, 14-18. He will deal with each individual according to his character, 19, 20. The wicked, if he repent, shall live, 21-23; and the righteous, if he apostatize, shall die, 24. He shows the equity of his dealings, and the iniquity of the Jews, 25-29. He earnestly exhorts them to repent, in the prospect of being judged according to their ways, 30-32.

2. What. ƒ85K, Ge +3:19. **mean.** Ezk 17:12. Is 3:15. Ro 9:20. **proverb.** ƒ147D, Ge +1:29. Nu 21:27. **the land.** Ezk 6:2, 3. 7:2. 25:3. 36:1-6. 37:11, 19, 25. **The fathers.** Je 15:4. √31:29, 30. La *5:7. Mt *23:36. **the children's.** Ex +*20:5. *34:7. Dt 5:9. ◑√24:16. La *5:7.

3. ye shall not. ver. 19, 20, 30. Ezk 33:11-20. 36:31, 32. Je *31:31, 32. Ro 3:19. **proverb.** Nu +21:27.

4. all souls. Heb. *nephesh*, Ge +12:5. Nu 16:22. 27:16. Zc 12:1. He +*12:9. **are mine.** Ro +14:8. **as the soul of.** Heb. *nephesh*, Ge +12:5. √ƒ171Q1, Ge +12:5. **the soul.** Heb. *nephesh*, +√Ge +12:5. 17:14. **that sinneth.** ver. 20. Ro √6:23. Ga 3:10-13, 22. **it shall die.** Dt +√24:16. Je *31:30. Mt +*10:28. ◑√22:32. Mk 12:26. Lk 9:60. 15:24. Ga √6:5, 7. Ep 2:1. 1 T 5:6. T#981‡: Nu 23:10. Jsh +11:11 (T#982‡). Ps 78:50. Is 53:12. Mt *10:28. Mk 14:34. Lk 6:9. Ac 3:23. The question here is not whether "soul" designates that immortal part of man's being which consciously outlasts the physical body (Ezk +*18:20n; Ec +*3:19n; +*12:7), is simply another designation for "person," or whether "soul" has reference merely to the physical body. But these issues, while not settled here, are clearly settled elsewhere, and consulting the references will lead to their solution. The immediate question before the prophet is not whether this death is spiritual or physical, whether it is simply a statement that disobedience to the Mosaic law requires capital punishment, but rather whether the children are punished for the sins of their fathers, the mistaken point of the proverb he is disputing. He gives a new proverb to replace the old one: the soul that sinneth, it itself will die. That is, individuals will receive the punishment due for their own sin. Of course it may be legitimately argued that since accounts are not equitably balanced in this life, this necessitates reward and punishment in a future life, in order for God's ways to be "equal" (Ezk 18:25). Therefore the "death" spoken of here is not annihilation, unconsciousness, or extinction, but spiritual death. All persons presently experience physical death: if death were merely a painless extinction, all sinners would suffer precisely the same lack of punishment, and God's ways would not be equal. Rather, Scripture teaches future punishment, punishment which varies in severity according to the degree of responsibility of the individual (See on Lk +*12:48), punishment which is conscious (Lk +16:24; Re 19:20; 20:10) and eternal (Mt +25:46). Ro 6:23. 14:12.

5. **if.** Ps 15:2-5. 24:4-6. Mt *7:21-27. Ro 2:7-10. Ja 1:22-25. 2:14-26. 1 J *2:3, 4, 29. 3:7, 8, 24. 5:2-5. Re 22:14. **that,** etc. Heb. judgment and justice. Ezk +*33:14mg. Ge +*18:19. Pr *21:3. Je 22:15.

6. **not.** ver. +*11, 15. Ezk 6:13. 20:28. 22:9. Ex 34:15. Nu 25:2, 3. Dt 12:2)℗. 1 C 10:20, 21, 28. **mountains.** ∫121J7B, Je +3:23. **neither hath lifted.** ∫144A12, Ge +22:13. ∫121S3E1, Ps +121:1. ver. 12, 15. Ezk 20:7, 8, 24. 33:25, 26. Dt 4:19. Ps 121:1. 123:1, 2. **neither hath defiled.** Ezk 22:10, 11. Le 18:19, 20)℗. 20:10, 18)℗. Dt 22:22, etc. Je 5:8, 9. Mt 5:28. 1 C +*6:9-11. Ga *5:19-21. He *13:4. **come near.** Le 18:19)℗. 20:18)℗. **menstrous.** La 1:17.

7. **hath not oppressed.** ver. 12, 16, 18. Ezk 22:12, 13, 27-29. Ex +*22:21-24)℗. 23:9. Le +*19:13, 15. 25:14)℗. Dt 23:16)℗. 1 S 12:3, 4. Jb 31:13-22. Pr 3:31. 14:31. 22:22, 23. Is 1:17. 5:7. 33:15. 58:6. Je 7:6, 7. Am 2:6, 7. 8:4-6. Mi 2:1, 2. 3:2-4. Zc 7:9-11. Ml +*3:5. Ja +*5:1-6. **hath restored.** Ezk 33:15. Ex *22:26)℗. Dt *24:6, 10, 12, 13, 17)℗. Jb 22:6. 24:3, 9, 10. Am 2:8. **hath spoiled.** Ezk 7:23. Ge 6:11, 12. Is 59:6, 7. Je 22:3, 16, 17. Am 3:10. 5:11, 12. 6:3. Zp 1:9. **hath given.** ver. 16. Dt √15:7-11)℗. Jb 31:16-20. Ps 41:1. 112:4, 9. Pr 11:24, 25. 28:8, 27. Is 58:7-11. Mt √25:34-46. Lk 3:11. 2 C 8:7-9. 9:6-14. Ja *2:13-17. 1 J *3:16-19. **bread.** ∫108H4, Is +58:7. **to the hungry.** Jb *31:17. Pr 25:21. Ec 11:1. Is 58:7, 10. Mt 25:35. Lk 3:11. Ja 2:15, 16. **covered the naked.** Jb *31:19. Is +58:7. Mt *25:36. Lk 3:11. Ja *2:15, 16.

8. **hath not.** ver. 13, 17. Ezk 22:12. Ex +*22:25)℗. Le 25:35-37)℗. Dt 23:19, 20)℗. Ne 5:1-11. Ps 15:5. Pr 28:8. Is +*24:2. Je 15:10. **hath withdrawn.** 2 S 22:24. Ne 5:15. Is 33:15. Ep +*5:11. 1 Th *5:22. **hath executed.** Le *19:15, 35)℗. Dt 1:16, 17)℗. 16:18-20)℗. Jb 29:7-17. Pr 31:8, 9. Is 1:17. Je 22:15, 16. Zc 7:9, 10. 8:16. Mt *7:2. Jn *7:24.

9. **walked.** ver. 17. Ezk 20:13. 33:15. 36:27. 37:24. Le 18:5)℗. Dt 4:1)℗. 5:1. 6:1, 2. *10:12, 13)℗. 11:1)℗. Ne 9:13, 14. Ps *19:7-11. 105:44, 45. *119:1-6. Lk 1:6. Jn +*14:21. Ac *24:16. Ja *1:22-25. **is just.** Ps 24:4-6. Mi *6:8. Hab 2:4. Ro *1:17. Ja *2:18-26. 1 J 2:29. 3:7. **he shall.** Ezk *20:11. Le 18:5)℗. Am *5:4, 14, 24. Lk *10:27-29.

10. **that is.** Ex 22:2)℗. Le +*19:13)℗. Ml 3:8, 9. Jn 18:40. **a robber.** or, a breaker up of an house. Ezk 7:22. Ex *22:2. Da +11:14mg. **a shedder.** Ge +*9:5, 6)℗. Ex *21:12)℗. Nu 35:31)℗. Ro 13:3, 4. 1 J *3:12-15. **the like to any one of these things.** or, to his brother besides any of these.

11. **that.** ver. 7-9. Mt *7:21-27. Lk +*11:28. Jn +*13:17. *15:14. Ph *4:9. Ja 2:17. 1 J 3:22. Re 22:14. **eaten.** ver. 6, 15. Ezk 6:3. *22:9. Ex 34:15. Nu *25:2. Dt 12:2. 1 K *13:8, 22. Is 65:7. Je 3:6. Ho 4:13. 1 C *10:20. **mountains.** ∫121J7B, Je +3:23.

12. **oppressed.** ver. 7, 16. Ezk +*16:49. 22:29. Ho

12:7. Am 4:1. Zc *7:10. Ja *2:6. **lifted.** ∫144A12, Ge +22:13. **hath committed abomination.** ver. 6. Ezk 8:6, 17. Le 18:22, 26-30. 2 K 21:11. 23:13.

13. **given.** ver. 8, 17. **shall he.** ver. 24, 28, 32. **he shall.** ∫144D, Ge +40:23. **surely.** ∫147B, Ge +2:16. **blood.** Heb. bloods. Ezk 3:18. *33:4. Le 20:9, 11-13, 16, 27)℗. 2 K +9:26mg. Ac *18:6.

14. **if he.** ver. 10. Pr 17:21. 23:24. **that seeth.** Ezk 20:18. 2 Ch 29:3-11. 34:21. Je 9:14. 44:17. Mt 23:32. 1 P 1:18. **considereth.** ver. 28. Ps 119:59, 60. Is 44:19. Je 8:6. Ho 7:2. Hg 1:5, 7. 2:18. Lk 15:17-19.

15. **not eaten.** ver. +6, 7, 11-13. **mountains.** ∫121J7B, Je +3:23. **lifted.** ∫144A12, Ge +22:13. ∫121S3E1, Ps +121:1.

16. **withholden the pledge.** Heb. pledged the pledge, or taken to pledge. ver. 7, 12. Jb 22:6. **but hath.** ver. 7. Jb *22:7. 31:19. Pr 22:9. 25:21. 31:20. Ec 11:1, 2. Is 58:7-10. Mt √25:34-46. Lk 11:41. 14:13. Ja √2:15, 16. 1 J *3:17.

17. **hath taken.** ver. 8. Jb 9:33. *29:16. Pr 14:31. 29:7, 14. Je 22:16. Da 4:27. Mt 18:27-35. Lk 19:8. **that hath not.** ver. +*8, 9, 13. Le 18:4, 26, 30. **he shall not.** ver. 19, 20. Ezk 20:18, 30. Dt √24:16. Je 16:11-13, 19. Ml 3:7. Mt 23:29-33. **he shall surely.** ver. 9, 19, 21, 28. Ezk 3:21. 33:13, 15, 16. Is *3:10.

18. **cruelly oppressed.** Ec *5:8. **even he shall die.** ver. 4, 20, 24, 26. Ezk 3:18. Is *3:11. Jn +*8:21, 24.

19. **Why.** Ex +*20:5. Dt *5:9. 2 K 23:26. 24:3, 4. Je 15:4. La *5:7. **When.** Ezk 20:18-20, 24, 30. Zc 1:3-6.

20. **the soul.** Heb. nephesh, Ge +√12:5. √∫171Q1, Ge +12:5. Scripture clearly and emphatically teaches that the "soul" is eternal and immortal, for (1) Christ by his resurrection brought immortality to light, 2 T +*1:10. (2) Christ taught the resurrection of both the righteous and unrighteous, Jn +*5:29. (3) Christ taught that those who had died long before were still alive, Mt +√22:32. Moses and Elijah talked with Christ at the Transfiguration, Mt 17:3. (4) Christ taught that the soul cannot be killed, Mt +*10:28, though the body can, thus proving that they are different, as elsewhere taught in Scripture, Jb +*14:22. (5) Christ taught that the dead are conscious, can suffer torment, and can communicate, Lk 16:23, 24, as intimated elsewhere in Scripture, Le 18:27; Dt +*18:10, 11; 1 S 28:7-20; Is 14:9, 11, 16; He 12:23; Re 6:9, 10. (6) At death believers go immediately to be with Christ, 2 C +*5:8; Ph +*3:21; at death the spirit goes immediately to God, Ec +*3:21; +*12:7; Lk +*23:46; Ac 7:59, 60. (7) Eternal life and eternal punishment require the immortality or eternal nature of the soul, Ezk +*18:4n; Mt +*25:46. (8) Since Christ by his death and resurrection abolished death (2 T 1:10), all will be resurrected: some to eternal bliss, and some to eternal shame and everlasting contempt, but both classes will live forever (Da +*12:2): the less undesirable option of annihilation is not offered in Scripture. **that sinneth.** ver. +*4n, 13. Dt √24:16)℗. 1 K 14:13. 2 K 14:6. 22:18-20. 2 Ch 25:4. Je √31:29, 30. **not bear.** Ezk 4:4. Le 5:1, 17. 10:17. 16:22. 19:8. Nu 18:1. Ps 49:7. Is *53:11. Ga +*6:5. He *9:28. 1 P *2:24. **iniquity.** ∫121C1E, Ge +19:15. **righteousness.** ver. 30. Ezk *14:14. 33:10. 1 K 8:32. 2 Ch 6:23, 30. Is *3:10, 11. Mt 16:27. Ro 2:6-9. 2 C √5:10. Re 2:23. 20:12. 22:12-15.

21. **if the.** ver. 27, 28, 30. Ezk 33:11-16, 19. 2 Ch

33:12, 13. Pr √28:13. Is *1:16-20. √55:6, 7. Lk *24:47. Ac +*3:19. 26:18-20. 1 T 1:13-16. Ja *4:8-10. **and keep.** ver. 9. Ezk 36:27. Ge 26:5. Ps 119:80, 112. Lk 1:6. Ja 2:14, 26. **and do.** ver. 5, 19, 27. Ps *119:1. Ga √5:22-24. T *2:11-14. **he shall surely.** ver. 17, 28. Ezk 3:21. Ro 8:13. **not die.** Lk 3:7. Re 2:11.

22. **his transgressions.** ver. 24. Ezk 33:16. 1 K 17:18. Ps 25:7. √32:1, 2. *51:1. 103:12. Is 43:25. Je 31:34. 50:20. Mi *7:19. Ro √8:1. He √8:12. 10:3, 4. **not be mentioned.** Is √43:25. Jn √5:24. +*17:6. Ro *4:3-5, 20-25. √5:1. √8:1. 2 C √5:21. Col √1:22. 1 J √1:9. Ju √24. **in his.** 2 Ch 6:23. Ps 18:20-24. 19:11. Ro *2:6, 7, 10. Ga *6:7, 8. Ja 2:21-26. 2 P √1:5-11. 1 J 3:7.

23. **any pleasure.** ver. 32. Ezk √33:11. La 3:33. Ho 11:8. 1 T √2:4. 2 P √3:9. **not that.** Ex *34:6, 7. Jb 33:27, 28. Ps 147:11. Je 31:20. Mi 7:18. Lk 15:4-7, 10, 22-24, 32. Ja *2:13.

24. **But when.** ver. 26. Ezk *3:20, 21. 33:12, 13, 18. 1 S 15:11. 1 Ch +√28:9. 2 Ch 24:2, 17-22. Ps 36:3, 4. 125:5. Zp 1:6. Mt *13:20, 21. Lk +*8:13. Jn 6:66-70. 1 C +*15:2. Ga *5:7. Col +*1:23. He +*10:26, 29, 38, 39. 2 P +*1:10. √2:18-22. 1 J √2:19. 5:16-18. Ju 12. **and doeth.** ver. 10-13. Mt 12:43-45. Ro 1:28-31. 2 C 12:20, 21. 2 T 3:1-5. He 10:26. **All his.** ver. 22. Mk 13:13. Ga 3:4. He *6:4-6. √10:26-31. 2 J +*8. Re 2:10. 3:11. **in his.** ver. 18. Pr 14:32. 21:16. Mt √7:22, 23. Jn +*8:21, 24.

25. **way.** ver. 29. Ezk 33:17, 20. Jb *32:2. *34:5-10. √35:2. *40:8. *42:4-6. Ml 2:17. 3:13-15. Mt 20:11-15. Ro 3:5, 20. 9:20. 10:3. **not equal.** Ru +*1:13. 2 K +*6:33. Jb 12:6. 21:7. Ps 73:14. +*77:3. Pr ◑+√19:3. Ec *7:15. 9:2. Is ◑+√29:24. Je √12:1. Hab *1:2. Mt *20:12. 25:24n. Ro +*9:14. Ph +*4:11. He ◑+*13:5. **my way equal.** Ge +*18:25. Dt *32:3, 4. Ps 50:6. 145:17. Is √55:8, 9. Je 12:1. Zp 3:5. Lk +*6:35. Ro *2:5, 6. **are not.** √23. Anticategoria; or, Tu Quoque B966: the use of a countercharge, or recrimination. The figure is used when we retort upon another their very insinuation or accusation which he has made against us. For other instances of this figure see ver. 29. Ezk 33:17. **your ways unequal.** Ps 50:21. Je 2:17-23, 29-37. 16:10-13.

26. **When.** ver. 24. **turneth away.** Ho ◑6:3. 1 C 11:28-32. 1 J 5:17.

27. **when.** ver. 21. Is *1:18. √55:7. Mt 9:13. 21:28-32. Ac +*3:19. 20:21. 26:20. **he shall.** Ezk 33:5. Ac 2:40. 1 T +*4:16. **soul.** Heb. *nephesh,* Ge +12:13.

28. **he considereth.** ver. 14. Ezk 12:3. Dt 32:29. Ps 119:1, 6, 59. Je *31:18-20. Lk 15:17, 18. **turneth.** ver. 21, 31. Ezk 33:12. 1 S 7:3, 4. Col 3:5-9. T *2:14. Ja √2:10-12.

29. **The way.** ver. 2, +*25. Pr +√19:3. **your ways.** √23, ver. +25.

30. **I will.** Ezk 7:3, 8, 9, 27. 33:20. 34:20. Ec 3:17. 12:14. 1 P 1:17. Re 20:12. **every.** Ml 3:18. Mt 16:27. 25:32. 2 C 5:10, 11. Ga 6:4, 5. Re 22:12. **Repent.** ver. 21. Ezk 14:6. 33:9, 11. Da 9:13. Ho 12:6. Jl 2:12, 13. Mt 3:2, 8. Ac 26:20. Re 2:5, 16. **yourselves.** *or, others.* ver. 32mg. Da *12:3. 1 T +*4:16. **so.** ver. 21. Lk *13:3, 5. Ro *2:5. Ja *1:15. Re 2:21-23. **ruin.** Ezk 21:15. Is 3:6.

31. **Cast away.** Ezk *20:7. Ps *34:14. Is *1:16, 17. 30:22. 38:17. √55:7. Ro *8:13. Ep *4:22-32. Col *3:5-9. Ja *1:21. 1 P 1:14. 2:1. 4:2-4. **make.** Ezk *11:19. *36:26. Ps *51:10. Je 32:39. Mt *12:33, 34. *23:26.

Ac +*3:19. Ro *8:13. *12:2. 2 C √5:17. Ja *4:8. 1 P *1:22. **spirit.** Heb. *ruach,* Ge +41:8. *121A2, Ps +51:10. Lk 1:46, 47. Jn 4:24. 6:63. **for why.** *85L, Ge +27:45. Ezk √33:11. Dt *30:15, 19. Pr *8:36. Je *21:8. 27:15. Ac *13:46.

32. **I have.** ver. 23. La *3:33. Mt *18:14. 1 T +√2:4. 2 P +√3:9. **yourselves.** *or, others.* ver. 30mg. Da *12:3. 1 T +*4:16.

EZEKIEL 19

A lamentation over the ruin of the royal family of Judah, under the emblem of young lions taken in a net to be destroyed, 1-9; and of a vine and its branches, once flourishing, but now rooted up, withered, and burnt, 10-14.

1. **take.** ver. 14. Ezk 2:10. 26:17. 27:2. 32:16, 18. Je 9:1, 10, 17, 18. 13:17, 18. **the princes.** 2 K 23:29, 30, 34. 24:6, 12. 25:5-7. 2 Ch 35:25. 36:3, 6, 10. Je 22:10-12, 18, 19, 28, 30. 24:1, 8. 52:10, 11, 25-27. La 4:20. 5:12.

2. **A lioness.** Judea, which possessed strength, courage, and sovereignty. Na 2:11, 12. Zp 3:1-4. **she lay.** Had confederacy with the neighboring kings, and learned their manners. **her whelps.** The sons of Josiah, who learned to be oppressive tyrants from the surrounding princes. **whelps.** Ge 49:9. Re 5:5. **young lions.** Jb 4:11. Ps 58:6. Is 5:29. 11:6-9. Zc 11:3.

3. **one.** Jehoahaz, made king instead of Josiah, who became cruel and oppressive. **it became.** ver. 6. 2 K *23:31, 32. 2 Ch 36:1, 2.

4. **He was.** Taken prisoner by Pharaoh-necho, and brought into Egypt. 2 K 23:31, 33, 34. 2 Ch 36:4, 6. Je 22:11, 12, 18.

5. **another.** Jehoiakim. ver. 3. 2 K 23:34-37. 2 Ch 36:4. **a young lion.** King of Judah.

6. **he went.** Became a perfect heathen: he reigned eleven years, a monster of iniquity. 2 K *23:35, 37. 24:1-7. 2 Ch 36:5. Je *22:13-17. ch. 26, 36. **he became.** ver. 3.

7. **knew.** *88, Ge +15:15. Ge +4:1. 2 Ch 36:8. **desolate palaces.** *or,* widows. Is 13:22mg. **he laid waste.** *121E2, Ge +42:38. **and the land.** Ezk 22:25. Pr 19:12. 28:3, 15, 16. **the fulness.** Ezk 12:19mg. 30:12mg. Am 6:8mg. Mi 1:2mg.

8. **the nations.** 2 K 24:1-6. 2 Ch 36:6. **and spread.** ver. 4. Ezk 12:13. 17:20. La 4:20.

9. **chains.** *or,* hooks. ver. 4. Ezk 29:4. 38:4. Ex 35:22 (bracelets). 2 K 19:28. Is 37:29. **and brought.** 2 Ch 36:6. Je *22:10-12, 18, 19. 36:30, 31. **that his.** ver. 7. Ezk 6:2. 36:1.

10. **mother.** ver. 2. Ho 2:2, 5. **like.** Ezk 15:2-8. 17:6. Is 5:1-4. Mt 21:33-41. **blood.** *or,* quietness, *or,* likeness. Ezk 16:6, 22. **she was.** Nu 24:6, 7. Dt 8:7, 9♪𝒫. Ps 80:8-11. 89:25-29. **full.** Many princes.

11. **she had.** Many powerful sovereigns, who rendered Judah very considerable among the nations. ver. 12, 14. Ezk 21:10, 13. Ge +*49:10. Nu 24:7-9, 17. Ezr 4:20. 5:11. Ps *2:8, 9. 80:15, 17. 110:2. Is *11:1. **her stature.** Ezk 31:3. Da 4:11, 20, 21.

12. **she was.** The kingdom was entirely ruined, and her princes cut off. Ezk 15:6-8. Ps 52:5. *80:12, 13, 16. 89:40-45. Is *5:5, 6. Je 31:28. **the east.** Ezk 17:10. Je 4:11, 12. Ho 13:15. **strong.** ver. 11. 2 K 23:29, 34. 24:6, 14-16. 25:6, 7. Je *22:10, 11, 18, 19, 25-27, 30.

the fire. Ezk 15:4. 20:47, 48. Dt 32:22. Is 27:11. Mt *3:10. Jn +*15:6.

13. **now.** Ezk 1:3. 2 K *24:12-16. **she is.** ver. 10. Dt 28:47, 48. Je 52:27-31. **in the wilderness.** In Chaldea, whither they were carried captive. **in a dry.** Ps 63:1. 68:6. Ho 2:3.

14. **fire.** The treachery of Zedekiah hath caused her utter ruin. Ezk 17:18-20. Jg 9:15. 2 K 24:20. 2 Ch 36:13. Is 9:18, 19. Je 38:23. 52:3. **she hath.** ver. 11. Ezk 21:25-27. Ge +*49:10. Ne 9:37. Ps 79:7. 80:15, 16. Je 22:28-30. Ho 3:4. 10:3. Am 9:11. Jn 19:15. **This is.** ver. 1. La *4:20. Lk 19:41. Ro 9:2-4.

EZEKIEL 20

God refuseth to be inquired of by certain elders of Israel, 1-3. He recapitulates his dealings with the people; and their rebellions in Egypt, 4-9; in the wilderness, 10-26; and in Canaan, 27-29; as imitated by that generation, 30-32. While the rebels will be rigorously punished, a chosen remnant shall be gathered into their own land, as accepted worshippers and humble penitents, 33-44. The destruction of Jerusalem is foretold by a parable of a forest, 45-49.

1. **A.M. 3411. B.C. 593. in the seventh.** The seventh year of the captivity of Jeconiah, and according to Usher, Monday, August 27, 3411. Ezk 1:2. 8:1. 24:1. 26:1. 29:1, 17. 30:20. 31:1. 32:1. 40:1. **that certain.** Ezk 14:1-3. 33:30-33. 1 K 14:2-6. 22:15, etc. 2 K 3:13. Is 29:13. 58:2. Je 37:17. Mt 22:16. **and sat.** Ezk 8:1. Jg +20:26. Lk 2:46. 8:35. 10:39. Ac 22:3.

3. **Are.** Is 1:12. Mt 3:7. Lk 3:7. **As I.** ver. 31. Ezk 14:3, 4, 7, 8. 1 S 28:6. Ps 50:15-21. Pr 1:24-31. 15:8. 21:27. 28:9. Is *1:15. Mi 3:7. Mt 15:8, 9. Jn √4:24.

4. **judge them.** *or,* plead for them. Ezk 14:14, 20. 22:2. 23:36, 45. Is 5:3. Je 7:16. 11:14. 14:11-14. 15:1. *22:21. 1 C +*6:2, 3. **cause.** Ezk 16:2, 3. Mt 23:29-37. Lk 11:47-51. 13:33-35. Ac 7:51, 52.

5. **In the day.** ♪171T2, Ge +2:17. Ex 6:6, 7)♔. 19:4-6. 20:2)♔. Dt 4:37. 7:6)♔. 14:2. Ps 33:12. Is 41:8, 9. 43:10. 44:1, 2. Je 33:24. Mk 13:20. **lifted up mine hand.** *or,* sware (and so ver. 6, etc. Ex 6:8, 9). ♪22A14.8K, Ex +6:8. ver. 15, 23. 47:14. Ge *14:22. Dt 32:40. Ps 106:26. Re 10:5. **and made.** Ezk 35:11. Ex 3:8. 4:31. 6:3)♔. Dt 4:34. 11:2-7. Ps 103:7. **I am.** Ex 3:6, 16. 20:2, 3.

6. **In the day.** ♪171T2, Ge +2:17. **lifted.** ♪22A14.8K, Ex +6:8. ver. 5, 15, 23, 42. **to bring.** Ge 15:13, 14. Ex 3:8, 17)♔. ch. 14, 15. **into.** Dt 8:7-9)♔. 11:11, 12. 32:8. **flowing.** ver. 15. Ex 13:5)♔. 33:3)♔. Le 20:24)♔. Nu 13:27)♔. 14:8. Dt 6:3)♔. 11:9)♔. 26:9, 15)♔. 27:3)♔. 31:20)♔. 32:13, 14. Jsh 5:6. Je 11:5. 32:22. **milk and.** ♪174, Ge +18:27. **honey.** ♪171I7, Ex +3:8. **which is.** ver. 15. Ps 48:2. Da 8:9. 11:16, 41. Zc 7:14.

7. **Cast.** ♪155A, Ge +31:35. ver. 8. Ezk 18:6, 15, 31. Is 2:20, 21. 31:7. **the abominations.** Ezk 6:9. 14:6. 2 Ch 15:8. **of.** ♪181E, Ge +3:24. ver. 24. **defile.** Ezk 23:3, 8. Le 17:7. 18:3)♔. Dt 29:16-18. Jsh 24:14. **I am.** ver. 19. Ex 16:12. Le 11:44. 20:7.

8. **they rebelled.** Dt 9:7. Ne 9:26. Is √63:10. **they did not.** ver. 7. Ezk 32:4-6. Ex 32:3, 4. **then I.** ver. 13, 21. Ezk 5:13. 7:8. **accomplish.** ♪22, Ge +3:9.

9. **I wrought.** ver. 14, 22. Ezk 36:21, 22. 39:7. Ex 32:12)♔. Nu 14:13)♔, etc. Dt 9:28. *32:26, 27. Jsh *7:9. 1 S +*12:22. **in whose.** Jsh 2:10. 9:9, 10. 1 S 4:8.

10. **I caused.** Ex 13:17, 18)♔. 14:17-22. 15:22. 20:2.

11. **I gave.** Dt *4:8)♔. Ne 9:13, 14. Ps *147:19, 20. Ro 3:2. **showed them.** Heb. made them to know. Ezk 16:2. **judgments.** Dt 4:1)♔. **which.** ver. 13, 21. Le 18:5)♔. Dt 30:15, 16. Lk 10:28. Ro *10:5. Ga *3:12.

12. **I gave.** Ge *2:3. Ex *16:29. +*20:8-11)♔. 31:13)♔. 35:2. Le 23:3, 24, 32, 39. 25:4. Dt 5:12-15. Ne 9:14. Is +*58:13n. Mk 2:27, 28. Col 2:16. **to be.** ver. 20. Ex 31:13-17. **know.** Ezk +6:10. **I am.** Ezk 37:28. Ex 19:5, 6. Le 20:8. 21:8, 15, 23. Jn 17:17-19. 1 Th *5:23. Ju 1. **Lord.** Ex +15:26.

13. **rebelled.** ver. 8. Ex 16:28. 32:8. Nu 14:22. Dt 9:12-24. 31:27. 1 S 8:8. Ne 9:16-18. Ps *78:40, 41. *95:8-11. 106:13-33. Is *63:10. **and they.** ver. 16, 24. Le 26:15, 43. 2 S 12:9. Pr 1:25. 13:13. Am 2:4. 1 Th 4:8. He *10:28, 29. **which.** ver. 11. **and my.** ver. 21. Ex 16:27, 28. Nu 15:31-36. Is 56:6. **I said.** ver. 8, 21. Ex 32:10. Nu 14:11, 12, 29)♔. 16:20, 21, 45. 26:65)♔. Dt 9:8. Ps 106:23. **pour out.** ♪22C38, Ps +79:6.

14. **I wrought.** ver. 9, 22. Ezk 36:22, 23. Ep 1:6, 12.

15. **I lifted.** ver. 23. Nu 14:23-30)♔. 26:64, 65. Dt 1:34, 35. Ps 95:11. 106:26. He 3:11, 18. 4:3. **flowing.** ver. 6. **milk and.** ♪174, Ge +18:27. **honey.** ♪171I7, Ex +3:8.

16. **they.** ver. 13, 14. **for their.** They still had a hankering after the idolatries they had learned in Egypt, to which they added new idols, which they had seen in the countries through which they had traveled, as those of the Midianites, Amorites, etc. ver. 8. Ezk 14:3, 4. 23:8. Ex 32:1-8, 23)♔. Nu 15:39. 25:2. Am *5:25, 26. Ac 7:39-43. 1 C *10:5, 6.

17. **mine.** Ezk 8:18. 9:10. Dt 4:31, 32. 1 S 24:10. Ne 9:19. Ps *78:37, 38. **eye.** ♪22A7, Dt +11:12. **neither.** Ezk 7:2. 11:13. Je +*4:27. 5:18. Na 1:8, 9.

18. **I said.** Nu 14:32, 33)♔. 32:13-15)♔. Dt 4:3-6)♔. Ps 78:6-8. **the statutes.** Mi 6:16. Zc 1:2-4. Lk 11:47, 48. Ac 7:51. 1 P 1:18. **defile.** ver. 7. Je 2:7. 3:9.

19. **the Lord.** Ex +*20:2, 3. Dt 5:6, 7. 7:4-6. Ps 81:9, 10. Je 3:22, 23. **walk.** Ezk 11:20. 36:27. 37:24. Dt 4:1. 5:1, 32, 33. 6:1, 2. 11:1. 12:1, etc., 32. Ne 9:13, 14. Ps *19:7-11. 105:45. T *2:11-14.

20. **hallow my sabbaths.** T#902. ver. 12. Ezk 44:24. Ex +*20:11. 31:13-17. Ne 13:15-22. Ps *118:24. Is 56:2, 6, 7. +*58:13n, 14. Je 17:22, 24, 25, 27n. Mk *2:27. Jn 20:19. Ac *20:7. Col ❶*2:16. Re 1:10, 11.

21. **the children.** Nu 21:5. 25:1-8)♔. Dt 9:23, 24)♔. *31:27)♔. Ps 106:29-33. Ac 13:18. **if a man.** ver. 11, 13. **I would.** ver. 8, 13. Ezk 21:31. 2 Ch 34:21, 25. Re 16:1. **poor out.** ♪22C38, Ps +79:6. **accomplish.** Ezk 7:8. 13:15. La 4:11. Da 11:36.

22. **I withdrew my hand.** ♪22A14.8F. Anthropomorphism B880. A *hand* is attributed to God in the idiomatic expression, "to withdraw the hand," meaning to take away the punishment. ver. 17. Jb 13:21. Ps 78:38. La 2:8. **wrought.** ver. 9, 14, 22. Ps 25:11. 79:9, 10. 115:1. Is 48:9-11. Je 14:7, 21. Da 9:17, 19.

23. **lifted.** ver. 15. Dt 32:40. Re 10:5, 6. **that I.** The predictions of the dispersion of Israel, delivered by Moses just before his death, are evidently here referred to: they received a partial accomplishment at the Babylonian captivity, but are more exactly fulfilling at this day. Le 26:33)♔. Dt *28:64-68)♔. 32:26, 27. Ps 106:27. Je 15:4.

24. **they had.** ver. 13, 16. **their eyes.** Ezk 6:9. 18:6,

12, 15. Dt 4:19. Jb 31:26, 27. Am 2:4.

25. I gave. ✻12112, Ge +2:17. ✓✻108A4, Ge +31:7. The simple meaning of this place is, that when the Israelites had rebelled against God, despised his statutes, and polluted his sabbaths,—in effect cast him off, and given themselves up wholly to their idols,—then He, in a just judgment for their disobedience, abandoned them, "gave them up to a reprobate mind" (Ro 1:28), and suffered them to walk after the idolatrous, cruel, and impious customs and ordinances of the heathen; by which they were ripened for the destruction which he intended to bring upon them, that they might learn to know God by his judgments, seeing they had despised his mercies. In the same sense God is said judicially to "send a strong delusion, that they should believe a lie," to those who "received not the love of the truth but had pleasure in unrighteousness" (2 Th ✓2:10, 11). Here, the Hebrew idiom means God suffered others to give them statutes in their captivity which were not good. The verb "give" has this sense in Ge 31:7. Jg 15:1. 1 S 24:7. 2 S 21:10. It sometimes means "permission," as in Ezk 14:9. Ex 4:21. 5:22. Ps 16:10. Je 4:10. The same idiom occurs in the New Testament (Mt 6:13. 11:25. 13:11. Ro 9:18. 11:7, 8. 2 Th 2:11). ver. 26, 39. Ezk 14:9-11. Dt 4:27, 28. 28:36. Ps 81:12. Is 66:4. Ro 1:21-28. 2 Th ✓2:9-11. **judgments.** ✻145, Jg +11:40.

26. polluted. ver. 31. Ps *106:15. Is 63:17. Ro 11:7-10. 2 Th ✓2:11. **in that.** Ezk 16:20, 21. Ex ⬤13:12. Le 18:21⬥℘. Dt 18:10⬥℘. 2 K 16:3. 17:17. 21:6. 23:10. 2 Ch 28:3. 33:6. Je 32:35. Ho +*13:2mg. **all that.** Ex 13:12. Lk 2:23. **to the end.** Ezk 6:7.

27. speak. Ezk 2:7. 3:4, 11, 27. **Yet.** Ro *2:24. Re 13:5. **committed.** Heb. trespassed. Ezk 14:13. 15:8.

28. when I. Jsh 23:3, 4, 14. Ne 9:22-26. Ps 78:55-58. **the which.** ver. 6, 15. Ge 15:18-21. 26:3, 4. Ps 105:8-11. **they saw.** Ezk 6:13. Ps 78:58. Is 57:5-7. Je 2:7. 3:6. **their sweet.** Ezk 16:19. **savor.** ✻22C15, Ge +8:21. **drink offerings.** Le +*23:13.

29. I said, etc. *or,* I told them what the high place *was, or,* Bamah. **And the.** Ezk 16:24, 25, 31.

30. Are ye. Nu 32:14. Jg 2:19. Je 7:26. 9:14. 16:12. Mt 23:32. Ac 7:51.

31. ye offer. ver. 26. Dt +*18:10-12. Ps 106:37-39. Je 7:31. 19:5. **and shall.** ver. 3. Ezk 14:3, 4. 1 S 28:5, 6. 2 K 3:13, 14. Jb 27:8, 10. Ps 66:18. Pr 1:27, 28. 28:9. Is *1:15. Je 14:12. Zc 7:13. Mt 25:11, 12. Ja *4:1-3.

32. that which. Ezk 11:5. 38:10. Ps *139:2. Pr *19:21. +*21:30. La 3:37. **mind.** Heb. *ruach,* Ge +26:35. **We will.** 1 S 8:5. Je +*10:2. *44:16, 17, 29. Ro *12:2. **to serve.** Dt 4:28. 28:36, 64. 29:17. Is 37:19. Da 5:4. Re 9:20.

33. surely. Ezk 8:18. Dt 4:34⬥℘. Je 21:5. 42:18. 44:6. La 2:4. Da 9:11, 12. **with fury.** Am *3:2. **poured out.** ✻22C38, Ps +79:6.

34. I will bring. ver. 38. Ezk 11:17. 28:25. +*34:16. Is 27:9-13. Am *9:9, 10. Mi 2:12, 13. Zp *3:15. **will gather.** Ezk 22:20. Ps +*147:2. Zc 10:8. 2 C ⬥6:17.

35. I will. ver. 36. Ezk 19:13. +*38:8. Ho ✓2:14. Mi 4:10. *7:13-15. Re 12:14. **into the wilderness.** Ps 74:14. Is +*26:20, 21. Je +*31:2. Zp +*2:3. Re +*12:6, 14. **of the people.** Ps +*74:14. +*83:3. Is +*16:3, 4. **and there.** Ezk 17:20. 38:22. Je 2:2, 3, 9, 35. 25:31. Ho 4:1. Mi *6:1, 2. **plead with.** Je *2:9. Ho ✓2:14. **face to face.** Zc *12:10. Mk +*1:2n.

36. Like as. This comparison with the wilderness experience under Moses is thought to imply a like period of time, forty years, during which the rebels are purged, during the personal presence of Jesus Christ in the wilderness with this portion of Israel before his open victorious manifestation in power and glory of the public stage of the Second Advent when he comes with all his saints (Peters, *Theocratic Kingdom,* vol. 2, p. 86). Even E. W. Bullinger supposes that these events will take longer than the seven years of Daniel's final or seventieth week, suggesting that the "Suntelia" is a longer period, which ends with Daniel's last week, the "Telos" (*Apocalypse,* p. 348; see also pp. 53, 88, 89, 248, 249, 558, 559). Just as John the Baptist held the office of Elijah at the first advent, and introduced Jesus as the Lamb of God, so at the second advent Elijah will be upon the earth (Is 40:3. Ml 4:5, 6), preparing the way of the Lord, for a period of time before the open manifestation, and like the first advent, Jesus will be upon the earth for a period of time before the public manifestation. Some writers suppose that the forty years of Israel in the wilderness is to be combined with the thirty years Christ was upon earth before commencing his public ministry to indicate a period of seventy years or more, with which idea Peters concurs (Vol. 2, p. *108, *315, 318, *336, *338. Vol. 3, p. 18), as necessary to allow time for the necessary events to transpire. Peters alludes to events which "follow the Advent before the overthrow of Antichrist, such as the development of the confederation, the return of a portion of the Jews to Palestine, the doom of the harlot" (Vol. 2, p. 315); he also refers to the "concealed, hidden Coming for specific purposes (viz., to raise, translate, and glorify His saints, to inaugurate the preliminaries of his Kingdom: Da 2:44. Lk 17:20, etc.) which takes place *before* the events predicted as pertaining to His visible manifestation" (Vol. 2, p. 319). Just as Sinai was the site of the original organization of Israel's theocracy and the giving of the law, etc., so it is possible, in view of the many hints given in Scripture, that this wilderness will be the location of such activity again (Dt +*33:2). Mi +*7:15. **I pleaded.** ver. 13, 21. Ex 32:7, etc. Nu ch. 11. 14:21-23, 28, 29⬥℘. ch. 16, 25. Ps 106:15, etc. 1 C 10:5-10.

37. pass. Ezk 34:17. Le 27:32⬥℘. Je *33:13. Am *9:9. Mt *25:32, 33. **I will.** Ezk 16:59, 60. Le 26:25. Ps 89:30-32. Am *3:2. **the bond.** *or,* a delivering.

38. I will purge. Ezk 11:21. 34:17, 20-22. Nu 14:28-30. Am 9:9, 10. Zc 13:8, 9. Ml 3:3. 4:1-3. Mt 3:9, 10, 12. 25:32, 33. Ro 9:27-29. **they shall.** Ezk 13:9. Nu 14:30. Ps *15:1. 95:11. Je 44:14. 1 C 10:5. He *3:19. 4:6. Ju 5. **and ye.** Ezk 6:7. 15:7. 23:49. Ps *9:16.

39. Go ye. ✻60A, Ge +3:22. ver. 25, 26. Jg 10:14. 2 K 3:13. Ps 81:12. Ho 4:17. Am 4:4, 5. Ro 1:24-28. 2 Th *2:11. **but.** Ezk 23:37-39. Pr 21:27. Is *1:13-15. *61:8. 66:3. Je 7:9-11. Zp 1:4, 5. Mt ✓6:24. Re 3:15, 16.

40. in mine. These predictions received a partial accomplishment by the restoration of the Jews from the Babylonian captivity; but they seem chiefly to relate to the establishment of the Christian church, and more especially to the future conversion of the Jews, and their restoration to their own land. Ezk 17:23. Ps *2:6. 68:15, 16. Is 2:2, 3. 54:1-7. 62:1-9. 65:17-25. 66:20-23. Je 31:12. Jl 3:17, 18. Ob 16. Mi 4:1, 2. He 12:20-

22. Re 21:10. **there shall**. Ezk 37:22-28. Is 56:7. *60:7. 66:23. Zc 8:20-23. Ml 1:11. 3:4. Ro *12:1. He *13:15. 1 P 2:5. **offerings**. i.e. heave offerings. Ex 29:27n. Ezr +8:25. **firstfruits**. or, chief. Le +*23:10. Pr 3:9.

41. **with your**. ver. 28. Ezk 6:13. Ge 8:21. Le 1:9, 13, 17. Ml *3:4. Ep 5:2. Ph 4:18. **sweet savor**. Heb. savor of rest. ∫22C15, Ge +8:21. ver. 28. Ezk 16:19mg. Ge 8:21mg. Ep 5:2. **I bring**. Ezk 11:17. 34:19. 36:24. 37:25. 38:8. Is *11:11-16. 27:12, 13. Je *23:3. 30:3, 18. 32:37. Am √9:14, 15. Ob 17-21. Mi 7:12-16. **gather**. ver. +34. **and I will**. Ezk 28:22, 25. 38:23. 39:27-29. Le 10:3. Is 5:16. Lk 2:14. Ro *12:1. 1 P +*3:15.

42. **ye shall**. ver. 38, 44. Ezk 24:24. 26:33. 36:23. 38:23. Je 24:7. 31:34. Jn √17:3. 1 J *5:20. **when I**. Ezk 11:17-20. 34:13. 36:24. 37:21, 25. **for the which**. ver. 15. Le *26:44, 45. Dt *30:4, 5.

43. **shall ye**. Ezk 6:9. Le 26:39-41. Ezr 9:5, 6, 15. Ne 1:8-10. ch. 9. Ho *5:15. **and ye shall**. Ezk 16:61-63. 36:31. Jb 42:6. Je 31:18. Zc 12:10-14. Lk *18:13. 2 C 7:11.

44. **And ye shall**. ver. 38. Ezk 24:24. **when I**. ver. 9, 14, 22. Ezk 36:21, 22. Ps 79:9. 115:1. Ep 1:6. 1 T 1:16.

45. **Moreover**. This is the beginning of another prophecy, and properly belongs to the following chapter.

46. **set**. Ezk 4:7. 6:2. **toward**. Towards *Judea*, which lay *south* of Mesopotamia, where the prophet now dwelt. **south**. Heb. Negeb, Is +30:6. ∫171.O.8, Ge +12:9. **and drop**. Ezk 21:2. Dt 32:2. Jb 29:22. Is 55:10. Am 7:16. Mi 2:6mg. **the forest**. The city of *Jerusalem*, as full of inhabitants as the forest is of trees. Je 13:19. 22:7. Zc 11:1, 2.

47. **south**. ∫171.O.8, Ge +12:9. **I will kindle**. I will send *war*; and it shall destroy all ranks and characters of the people. Ezk 15:6, 7. 19:14. 22:20, 21. Dt 32:22. Is 9:18, 19. 30:33. Je 21:14. **green**. Ezk 17:24. Lk 23:31. **the flaming**. Is +*30:33. +*66:24. Mk +*9:43-49. He 12:29. **from the south**. Ezk 21:3, 4. Is 24:1-6.

48. **all flesh**. Dt 29:24-28. 2 Ch 7:20-22. Is 26:11. Je 40:2, 3. La 2:16, 17.

49. **Doth he not speak**. Is it not his usual custom to deal in enigmas? His figures are not to be understood; we should not trouble ourselves with them. God therefore commands the prophet to declare, in the next chapter, the same things in the *plainest* terms, so that they should not complain of his parables. Mt *13:11, 13-15. Jn 16:25. Ac 17:18. **parables**. Nu +21:27. 23:7n.

EZEKIEL 21

The prophet, predicting the indiscriminate slaughter made by the Lord's sword, in Israel, is commanded to sigh bitterly, for a sign, 1-7. Another prophecy of the sharp and bright sword, to the same effect, 8-17. Nebuchadnezzar in suspense, whether to attack Rabbath or Jerusalem, is determined by divination to march against Jerusalem, 18-24. Sentence denounced against profane Zedekiah, 25-27. The destruction of Ammon predicted, 28-32.

2. **set**. Ezk 4:3, 7. 20:46. 25:2. 28:21. 29:2. 38:2. Ep 6:19. **and drop**. Dt 32:2. Am 7:16. Mi 2:6mg, 11. **holy places**. Le 26:31. Is 16:12. Am 7:9. **against**. Ezk 4:7. 6:2. 20:46. 36:1. Je 26:11, 12. Ac 6:13, 14. **the land**. Ezk 11:17. 12:19, 22. 13:9. 18:2. 20:38, 42. 25:3, 6. 33:24. 36:6. 37:12. 38:18, 19.

3. **to the land**. ver. +2. Ezk 7:2. ◐+27:17. **Behold**. Ezk 5:8. 26:3. Je 21:13. 50:31. 51:25. Na 2:13. 3:5. **will draw**. ver. 9-11, 19. Ezk 5:12. 14:17, 21. Ex 15:9. Le 26:25, 33. Dt 32:41, 42. Ps 17:13. Is 10:5. 34:5. Je *47:6, 7. 51:20. Zp 2:12. Zc 13:7. **the righteous**. Ezk *9:5, 6. Jb 9:22, 23. Ec 9:2. Je 15:2-4.

4. **the righteous**. ∫121Q1, Je +28:5. **against**. Ezk 6:11-14. 7:2. 20:47. Ps 16:4.

5. **all**. Ezk 20:48. Nu 14:21-23. Dt 29:24-28. 1 K 9:7-9. **it shall**. ver. 30. 1 S 3:12. Is 45:23. √55:11. Je 23:20. Na 1:9.

6. **Sigh**. ver. 12. Ezk 6:11. *9:4. Is 22:4. Je 4:19. 9:17-24. Jn 11:33-35. **with the**. Is 16:11. *21:3. Je *30:6. Da 5:6. 8:27. Na 2:10. Hab 3:16. **before**. Ezk 4:12. 12:3-5. 37:20. Je 19:10.

7. **Wherefore**. Ezk 12:9-11. 20:49. 24:19. **For the**. Ezk 7:26. 2 K 21:12. Is 7:2. 28:19. Je 6:22-24. 49:23. **and every**. Ex 15:15. Dt 20:8mg. Jsh 2:9-11. 5:1. 2 S 17:10. Na 2:10. **all hands**. Jb 4:3, 4. Is 35:3. Je 50:43. Lk 21:26. He 12:12. **spirit**. Heb. *ruach*, Ps +106:33. **faint**. Le 26:36. Is 13:7. Je 8:18. La 5:17. **weak as water**. Heb. go into water. Ezk 7:17mg. **it cometh**. Ezk 7:2-12. 12:22-28. 1 P √4:7.

9. **A sword**. ∫22D5D, Dt +32:41. ver. 3, 15, 28. Dt *32:41, 42. Jb 20:25. Is 66:16. Je 12:12. 15:2. Am 9:4. **a sword**. ∫84, Ge +6:17. **sharpened**. Ps *7:11-13. Is 27:1. 34:5, 6. He *4:12. Re 19:15.

10. **it is furbished**. Je 46:4. Na 3:3. Hab 3:11. **should**. Est 3:15. Ec 3:4. Is 5:12-14. 22:12-14. Am 6:3-7. Na 1:10. Lk 21:34, 35. **it contemneth the rod of my son**, as every tree. or, *it is* the rod of my son, it despiseth every tree. ver. 25-27. Ezk 19:11-14. 20:47. 2 S 7:14. Ps 2:7-9. 89:26-32, 38-45. 110:5, 6. Re 2:27.

11. **to give**. ver. 19. Je 25:9, 33. 51:20-23.

12. **howl**. ver. 6. Ezk 9:8. 30:2. Je 25:34. Jl 1:13. Mi 1:8. **terrors by reasons of the sword shall be upon my**. or, they are thrust down to the sword with my. **smite**. This was an expression of deep affliction. ver. 14. Ezk 6:11. Je 31:12.

13. **Because**, etc. or, When the trial *hath been*, what then? shall they not also belong to the despising rod? Je 12:5. 1 C 4:21. **a trial**. Jb 9:23. 2 C 8:2. **contemn**. ver. 10, 25. **it shall**. ver. 27. Is *1:5.

14. **smite**. ver. 17. Ezk 6:11. Nu 24:10⟩℘. **hands together**. Heb. hand to hand. ver. 17. **let the**. Le 26:21, 24. 2 K 24:1, 10-16. 25:1, etc. Da 3:19. **entereth**. Ezk 8:12. 1 K 20:30. 22:25. Am 9:2.

15. **point**. or, glittering, or fear. **against**. ver. 22. Ezk 15:7. Je 17:27. *32:3. **that their**. ver. 7. Ezk 20:47. **ruins**. lit. stumblingblocks. Ezk 3:20. 7:19. Je 18:23. **it is made**. ver. 10, 28. **wrapped up**. or, sharpened. ver. 9-11.

16. **Go**. ver. 4, 20. Ezk 14:17. 16:46. **either**. Ge 13:9. **or on the left**. Heb. set thyself, take the left hand.

17. **smite**. ver. 14. Ezk 22:13. Nu 24:10. **hands**. ∫22A14.8J. Anthropomorphism B880. A "hand" is attributed to God in idiomatic expressions to clap or smite the hands together, to express derision or disdainful anger. For another instance of this figure see Ezk 22:13. **and I**. Ezk 5:13. 16:42. Dt 28:63. Is *1:24. Zc 6:8.

19. **appoint thee two**. Ezk 4:1-3. 5:1, etc. Je 1:10. **the sword**. Ps 17:13. Is +*10:5. **a place**. lit. Heb. hand. i.e. a signpost. Nu 35:32n. Dt 23:12mg.

20. **Rabbath**. Ezk 25:5. Dt 3:11. 2 S 12:26. Je 49:2.

Am *1:14, Rabbah. **the defenced**. 2 S 5:9. 2 Ch 26:9. 32:5. 33:14. Ps *48:12, 13. 125:1, 2. Is 22:10. La 4:12.

21. **the king**. Pr 16:33. +*21:1. **parting**. Heb. mother. Mt 22:9. **at the head of**. Ezk 16:24, 25. Ge 38:14. Pr 9:14. Je 3:2. **to use divination**. Nu 23:23. Dt +*18:10. 1 S 15:23. Pr 16:10mg. Ac 16:16. **he made his**. Or, as the Vulgate, "he mingled his arrows:" "They wrote on several arrows," says Jerome, "the names of the cities they intended to assault; and then putting them altogether promiscuously in a quiver, they drew them out thence as lots are drawn; and that city whose name was written on the arrow first drawn, was the city they first made war on." Jsh 14:2n. Pr 16:33. The arrows were drawn out, one with each hand. The arrow selected by the right hand represented a good omen (Ge +48:13); the left, ill (Jg +20:16). **arrows**. *or,* knives. **images**. Heb. teraphim. Ge 31:+19mg, 30. Jg 17:5. 18:14, 18, 20, 24. 1 S 19:13-16. 2 K 23:24mg. Ho 3:4. 4:12. Zc 10:2mg. **the liver**. A third means of divination, mentioned nowhere else in Scripture. Its position and color were supposed to bode ill or well of future events.

22. **captains**. *or, battering* rams. Heb. rams. Ezk 4:2. **to lift**. Ex 32:17, 18. Jsh 6:10, 20. 1 S 17:20. Jb 39:25. Je 51:14. **to appoint**. Ezk 4:2. Je 32:24. 33:4. 52:4.

23. **as a**. Ezk 11:3. 12:22. Is 28:14, 15. **to them that have sworn oaths**. *or,* for the oaths made unto them. Ezk √17:13-19. 2 Ch 36:13. **but**. 2 K 24:20. 25:1-7. Je 52:3-11. **call**. ver. 24. Ezk 29:16. Nu 5:15. 1 K 17:18. Re 16:19. **remembrance**. 2 S 8:16mg. Ps *90:8. He *4:13.

24. **your transgressions**. Ezk 16:16, etc. 22:3-12, 24-31. 23:5, etc. 24:7. Is 3:9. Je 2:34. 3:2. 5:27, 28. 6:15. 8:12. 9:2-7. Ho 4:2. Mi 3:10-12. *or,* rebellion (plural of majesty, √96F2, Ge +4:10), indicating "great rebellion." **your sins**. Plural of majesty, indicating "great sins." **ye shall**. 2 K *25:1-4. 2 Ch *36:17. Is 22:17, 18. Je 15:2. Am 9:1-3.

25. **profane**. Ezk *17:18n, 19. 2 Ch 36:13. Je 24:8. 52:2. *or,* wounded. lit. "pierced through." ver. 14, 29. i.e. deadly wounded one. Zedekiah a type of the future Antichrist (CB). Re=13:3. **whose**. ver. 29. Ezk 7:6. 30:3. 35:5. Ps 7:9. 9:5, 6. Je 51:13.

26. **Remove**. Ezk 12:12, 13. 16:12. 2 K *25:5-7, 27, 28. Je 13:18. 39:6, 7. 52:9-11, 31-34. La 5:16. **diadem**. √121S1, Ge +49:10. Here, by Metonymy of the Adjunct, whereby the sign is put for the thing signified, the diadem and crown are put for the symbols of royalty of him who wears them. **exalt**. Ezk 17:24. 1 S 2:7, 8. Ps 75:7. 113:7, 8. Lk 1:52.

27. **I will overturn, overturn, overturn, it**. Heb. Perverted, perverted, perverted, will I make it. √84, Ge +6:17. Hg 2:21, 22. He 12:26, 27. **until he come**. ver. 13. Ezk 17:22, 23. 34:23. 37:24, 25. Ge +*49:10♦℗. Nu 24:19. 2 S 3:17, 18. 5:1, 2. Ps *2:6. 72:7-10. Is +*9:6, 7. 42:1. Je +*23:5, 6. 30:21. 33:15-17, 21, 26. Da 2:44. *9:25. Ho 3:5. Am *9:11, 12. Mi +*5:2. Hg 2:7. Zc 6:12, 13. *9:9. 14:9. Ml 3:1. *4:2. Mt 28:18. Lk 1:32, 69. 2:11. Jn 1:49. Ac 15:14-17. Ep 1:20-22. Ph 2:9, 10. 1 P 3:22. 4:13. Re 6:2. *11:15. *19:11-16. 20:1-10.

28. **concerning the**. ver. 20. Ezk 25:2-7. Je *49:1-5. Am 1:13-15. Zp *2:8-10. **The sword**. ver. 9, 10.

29. **they see**. Ezk 12:24. 13:23. 22:28. Is 44:25. 47:13. Je 27:9. **to bring**. Ezk 13:10-16. La 2:14. **whose**.

ver. 25. Jb 18:20. Ps 37:13. **day**. √121P4, Dt +4:32. **iniquity**. √100, Ge +10:9.

30. **Shall I cause it to return**. *or,* Cause *it* to return. ver. 4, 5. Je 47:6, 7. **I will**. Ezk 16:38. 28:13, 15. Ge 15:14. **in the**. Ezk 16:3, 4.

31. **pour**. Ezk 7:8. 14:19. 22:22. Is +66:14. Na 1:6. **I will blow**. Ezk 22:20, 21. Ps 18:15. Is +*30:33. 37:7. 40:7. Hg 1:9. **brutish**. *or,* burning. **and skilful**. Is 14:4-6. Je 4:7. 6:22, 23. 51:20, 21. Hab *1:6-10.

32. **for fuel**. Ezk 20:47, 48. Ml 4:1. Mt *3:10, 12. **thy blood**. ver. 30. Is 34:3-7. **thou shalt be no**. This prophecy against the Ammonites was fulfilled about five years after the taking of Jerusalem; and their name has utterly perished from the face of the earth. Ezk *25:9, 10. Zp 2:9. **for I**. Nu *23:19. Mt √24:35. 1 P *1:23.

EZEKIEL 22

A catalog of the crimes committed in Jerusalem, for which judgment was awarded against the Jews, 1-16. God will prove them as metals in the furnace, 17-22. The wickedness of the prophets, priests, princes, and people, shown to be the combined causes of their ruin, 23-31.

2. **wilt thou**. √108A3, Is +6:10. **judge**. *or,* plead for. Ezk 20:4mg. 23:36mg. **judge**. √84, Ge +6:17. **bloody city**. Heb. city of bloods. √96F2, Ge +4:10. Ezk 23:45. 24:6, 9. 2 K +9:26mg. *21:16. *24:3, 4. Je 2:30, 34. Ho 4:2. Na 3:1. Hab 2:12mg. Mt 23:35. 27:25. Lk 11:50. Ac 7:52. **thou shalt**. Ezk 16:2. Is 58:1. 1 T 5:20. **show her**. Heb. make her know. ver. 26. Ezk 20:11mg. **her abominations**. Ezk 8:9-17. ch. 16, 23.

3. **sheddeth**. ver. 27. Ezk 24:6-9. Zp 3:3. **that her**. ver. 4. Ezk 7:2-12. 12:25. Ro *2:5. 2 P *2:3. **and maketh**. 2 K 21:2-9. Je ch. 2, 3.

4. **that thou**. ver. 2. 2 K 21:16. **and thou hast**. Nu 32:14. Mt 23:32, 33. 1 Th 2:16. **days**. √121P4, Dt +4:32. **have I**. Ezk 5:14, 15. 16:57. 21:28. Le 26:32. Dt 28:37♦℗. 29:24. 1 K 9:7. 2 Ch 7:20. Ps 44:13, 14. *79:4. 89:41, 42. Je 18:16. 24:9. 44:8. La 2:15, 16. Da 9:16.

5. **infamous and much vexed**. Heb. polluted of name, much in vexation. Je 15:2, 3.

6. **the princes**. ver. 27. Ne 9:34. Is 1:23. Je 2:26, 27. 5:5. 32:32. Da 9:8. Mi *3:1-3, 9-11. Zp *3:3. **power**. Heb. arm. Ps 79:11mg. Mi 2:1.

7. **set**. Ex 21:17. Le 20:9. Dt *27:16♦℗. Pr 20:20. 30:11, 17. Mt 15:4-6. Mk 7:10. Ep 6:2. **dealt**. ver. 29. Ezk 18:12. Ex *22:21, 22♦℗. Dt 27:19. Pr 22:22, 23. Je 7:6. Zc 7:10. Ml +*3:5. **oppression**. *or,* deceit. ver. 29mg. Le 6:4. Is 30:12mg. **stranger**. ver. 29. Ezk 14:7. 47:22, 23. Ge 23:4 (*S#1616h). Ex 12:48mg. **widow**. √171I14, Ex +22:22.

8. **despised**. ver. 26. **profaned my sabbaths**. Ezk 20:13, 16, 21, 24. 23:38, 39. Le 19:30♦℗. Is +*58:13n, 14. Je √17:21-27n. Am 8:4-6. Ml 1:6-8, 12.

9. **men that carry tales**. Heb. men of slanders. Ex +*20:16. 23:1. Le +*19:16♦℗. 1 K 21:10-13. Ps 50:20. +*101:5. Pr 10:18. 18:8. 26:22. Je 6:28. 9:4. 37:13-15. 38:4-6. Mt 26:59. Ac 6:11-13. 24:5, 13. Re 12:9, 10. **they eat**. Ezk *18:6, +11, 15. Ps 106:28. 1 C 10:18-21. **they commit lewdness**. Ezk 16:43. 24:13. Jg 20:6. Pr +5:3. Je +9:2. Ho 4:2, 10, 14. 6:9. 7:4. Ac +15:20. He +13:4.

10. **discovered**. Ge 35:22. 49:4. Le 18:7, 8, 9♦℗.

20:11)𝒫. Dt 27:20, 23. 2 S 16:21, 22. 1 Ch +*5:1. Am 2:7. 1 C 5:1. **humbled**. Ezk 18:6. 36:17. Le 18:19)𝒫. 20:18.

11. **one**. *or*, every one. ver. 6. **committed**. Ezk 18:11. Ex +*20:14. Le 18:19, 20)𝒫. 20:10)𝒫. Dt 22:22. Jb 31:9-11. Je 5:7, 8. +*9:2. 29:23. Ml +*3:5. Mt *5:27, 28. 1 C +*6:9. Ga *5:19. He +*13:4. **another**. *or*, every one. ver. 6. **hath lewdly**. *or*, hath by lewdness. ver. +*9. Le 18:15)𝒫. 20:12, 17)𝒫. **his sister**. Le 18:9. 20:17. Dt 27:22. 2 S 13:1, 14, 28, 29.

12. **taken gifts**. Ex 23:7, 8)𝒫. Dt +*16:19)𝒫. *27:25)𝒫. Is 1:23. Mi 7:2, 3. Zp 3:3, 4. **to shed blood**. ver. 3. **thou hast taken usury**. Ezk 18:8, 13. Ex √22:25, 26)𝒫. Le 25:35, 36)𝒫. Dt 23:19)𝒫. Ne √5:1-7. Ps *15:5. Is +√24:2. **greedily gained**. Pr 1:19. Is 56:11. Mt 23:14, 25. Lk 3:13. 18:11. 19:8. 1 C 5:11. +*6:10. 1 T 3:3. *6:9, 10. Ja +*5:1-4. Ju *11. **extortion**. 𝓕108J, Ge +43:18. **and hast forgotten me**. Ezk 23:35. Dt 32:18)𝒫. Ps *50:21, 22. 106:21. Je 2:32. *3:21.

13. **I have**. Ezk 21:14, 17. Nu 24:10. **hand**. 𝓕22A14.8J, Ezk +21:17. **thy dishonest gain**. ver. 27. Pr 28:8. Is 33:15. Je 5:26, 27. 7:9-11. Am 2:6-8. 3:10. 8:4-6. Mi 2:1-3. 6:10, 11. Ep *5:5, 6. Col *3:5, 6. 1 Th +*4:6. **and at**. ver. 2-4.

14. **thine heart**. Ezk 21:7. 28:9. Jb 40:9. Is 31:3. 45:9. Je 13:21. 1 C 10:22. He 10:31. **I the**. Ezk 5:13. 17:24. 24:14. Nu *23:19. 1 S 15:29. Mk 13:31.

15. **scatter**. Ezk 5:12. 12:14, 15. 34:6. 36:19. Le 26:33. Dt *4:27)𝒫. *28:25, 64)𝒫. Ne 1:8. Je 15:4. Zc 7:14. **consume**. ver. 18-22. Ezk 20:38. 23:47, 48. 24:6-14. Is 1:25. Zc 13:9. Ml 3:3. *4:1. Mt *3:12. 1 P *4:12.

16. **take thine inheritance in thyself**. *or*, be profaned in thyself. Ezk 7:24. 25:3. Is 43:28. 47:6. **thou shalt know**. Ezk 6:7. 39:6, 7, 28. Ex 8:22. 1 K 20:13, 28. Ps *9:16. 83:18. Is 37:20. Da 4:25, 32-35. Am √3:2.

18. **the house**. Ps *119:119. Is *1:22. Je 6:28-30. **dross**. Is 1:25. ◖13:12. **brass**. 𝓕45, Is +40:31. ver. 20. Is 48:4. La *4:1, 2. **in the midst**. Pr 17:3. Is 31:9. 48:10. **dross**. Heb. drosses. ver. 19.

19. **dross**. Ps 66:10. Is 1:25. Zc 13:9. Ml *3:2, 3. **I will**. Jerusalem is here represented as the *fining pot*; all the people, who had become *dross*, are to be gathered together in it; and the **fire** of the Chaldeans, blown by the wrath of God, is to **melt** the whole. No ordinary means will avail to purge their impurities; the most violent must therefore be resorted to. Ezk 11:7. 24:3-6. Mi 4:12. Mt 12:30, 40-42.

20. **As they gather**. Heb. *According* to the gathering. to blow. ver. 21. Ezk 21:31, 32. Is 54:16. **will I gather**. Ezk +20:34. Zc 10:8. **in mine**. Ezk 24:13. Je 4:11, 12, 20. **you there**. 𝓕63K, Ge +37:13. If the preceding words are understood to be not "I will leave" but "I will blow," reversing a misreading of the primitive text (the letter *Pe* was mistaken for *nun*), the parallelism is perfectly restored, and the corrected sense no longer requires the ellipsis (you there) B122.

21. **and blow**. Ezk 15:6, 7. 20:47, 48. 22:20-22. Dt 4:24. 29:20. 32:22. 2 K 25:9. Ps 21:9. 50:3. Is +*30:33. Je 21:12. Na 1:6. Zp 1:18. 1 C *3:13. He *12:29. **and ye**. Ps 68:2. 112:10. Is 64:2mg, 7mg. Je 9:7.

22. **ye shall know**. ver. 16, 31. Ezk 20:8, 33. Ho 5:10. Re 16:1.

24. **Thou art**. 2 Ch 28:22. 36:14-16. Is *1:5. 9:13. Je 2:30. 5:3. 6:29. 44:16-19. Zp 3:2.

25. **a conspiracy**. Ezk 13:10-16. 1 K 22:11-13, 23. 2 K +11:14. Je 5:30, 31. 6:13. La 2:14. 4:13. 2 P *2:1-

---

3. **like**. ver. 27-29. Is 56:11. Ho *6:9. Mi +*3:5-7. Re 13:11, 15. **ravening**. That is, from the Saxon *reafian*, seizing and devouring it with eagerness and rapacity. ✥S#2963h. ver. 27. Jb 18:4 (teareth). Ps 22:13. Na 2:12 (tear in pieces). Mt 7:15. Lk 11:39. **they have devoured**. Ezk 13:19. Je 2:30, 34. Mt 23:14. Mk 12:40. Lk 20:47. Re 17:6. 18:13. **souls**. Heb. *nephesh*, Jsh +10:28.

26. **priests**. 1 S 2:12-17, 22. Je 2:8, 26, 27. La 4:13. Mi 3:11, 12. Zp 3:3, 4. Ml 1:6-8. *2:1-3, 7, 8. **violated**. Heb. offered violence to. Zp 3:4. **profaned**. Le 22:2, etc. 1 S 2:15, 29. **put no difference**. Ezk *44:23. Le *10:1-3, 10)𝒫. 11:47)𝒫. 20:25. 22:22)𝒫. Ps +*119:63. Je *15:19. Hg 2:11-13. Ac 10:14. 15:29. 2 C +*6:14-17. He *5:14. **hid their**. ver. +8. Ezk 20:12, 13. **I am profaned**. Ezk 36:20-23. Ro 2:24.

27. **princes**. ver. 6. Ezk 19:3-6. 22:6. 45:9. Is 1:23. Ho 7:1-7. Mi 3:2, 3, 9-11. 7:8. Zp 3:3. Ja 2:6, 7. **souls**. Heb. *nephesh*, Jsh +10:28. **to get**. ver. 13. Mt 21:13. Ja +*5:1-4.

28. **prophets**. The prophets employed all their ingenuity to varnish over the crimes of the princes (the antecedent to *them*), to palliate their offences, and to conceal their faults, while they were like ravening wolves, and took bribes to shed innocent blood. By these means they shared the dishonest gains with the princes, or availed themselves of their authority to gratify their avarice or revenge. ver. 25. Ezk *13:10-16. Is 30:10. Je 8:10, 11. **seeing**. Ezk 13:22, 23. 21:29. Je 23:25-32. La 2:14. Zp 3:4. **Thus saith the Lord**. Ezk 13:6, 7. Je √23:21. 28:2, 15. 29:8, 9, 23. 37:19.

29. **people**. ver. 7. Ezk 18:12. Is 5:7. 10:2. 59:3-7. Je 5:26-28, 31. 6:13. Am 3:10. Mi 2:2. 3:3. Ja +*5:4. **oppression**. *or*, deceit. 𝓕108J, Ge +43:18. T#488. ver. +*7mg. Ezk +27:13 (T#681). Ex 5:15-19. Pr +13:19 (T#200-7). Mi 3:2, 3. Na 3:1. 1 T +1:10 (T#682). **oppressed**. ver. 7. Ex *22:21)𝒫. *23:9)𝒫. Le *19:33)𝒫, 34. Ps 94:6. Mt 25:43. **stranger**. ver. +7. Ezk 47:22. **wrongfully**. Heb. without right. Je +*22:13.

30. **I sought**. God, speaking after the manner of men, sought for some Moses, Phinehas, or Samuel, to stand in the gap on this occasion; but as he found none, its destruction was inevitable. Is 41:28. *59:16. 63:5. Je *5:1. **make**. Ezk 13:5. Ge *18:23-32. Ex 32:10-14. Ps 106:23, 30. Je 15:1. **found none**. Ps *14:3. Mt +√7:14. Lk √18:8.

31. **Therefore**. Pr *1:24, 31. Mt *23:37, 38. **have I poured**. ver. 21, 22. **their own**. Ezk 7:3, 8, 9. 9:10. 11:21. 16:43. Ro 2:8, 9.

EZEKIEL 23

The idolatry of Israel in Egypt exposed by a parable of two sisters, Ahola, and Aholiab, 1-4. The subsequent whoredoms of Aholah, and her punishment, 5-10. The whoredoms and punishment of Aholibah, 11-35. As involved in the same guilt, they are visited by similar judgments, 36-49.

2. **two women**. 𝓕155E3, Is +32:9. Ezk 16:44, 46. Je 3:7-10. **mother**. 𝓕155E4, 2 S +20:19.

3. **in Egypt**. Ezk 20:8. Le 17:7. Dt 29:16, 17. Jsh 24:14. **in their**. ver. 8, 19, 21. Ezk 16:22. Ho 2:15.

4. **the names**. The kingdom of Israel, of which Samaria was the capital, containing ten tribes, and occupying a larger extent of country than that of Judah, is therefore called "her elder sister;" and *Aholah*, the

name given to her, implies that the whole religious establishment in Israel was a human invention, a temple and service of their own, and not God's appointment. *Aholibah*, the name given to Judah, implies that the worship established there was from God, and that His temple was truly at Jerusalem. **Aholah.** *ſ*146, Ge +10:10. **the elder.** Ezk 16:40. 1 K 12:20. **Aholibah.** *ſ*146, Ge +10:10. **they were.** Ezk 16:8, 20. Ex 19:5, 6. Ps 45:11-16. Je 2:2, 3. Ro 7:4. **Samaria.** Is 7:9. **Aholah.** *that is*, His tent, *or* tabernacle. i.e. *her own tent*, *S#170h. ver. 4, 4, 5, 36, 44. 1 K 12:26-33. Jn 4:22. **Jerusalem.** 1 Ch 11:4, 7. **Aholibah.** *that is*, My tabernacle in her. *S#172h. ver. 4, 4, 11, 22, 36, 44. 1 K 8:29. Ps 76:2. 132:13, 14.

5. **Aholah.** The Israelites, in addition to their former gross idolatries, received the impure idolatrous worship of the Assyrians, who became their *neighbors* by the conquest of Syria. 1 K 14:9, 16. 15:26, 30. 16:31, 32. 21:26. 2 K 17:7-18. **doted.** ver. 7, 9, 12, 16, 20. Ezk 16:37. Je 50:38. **on the.** Ezk 16:28. 2 K *15:19. *16:7. *17:3. Ho 5:13. *8:9, 10. 10:6. 12:1.

6. **all of.** ver. 12-15.

7. **committed her whoredoms with them.** Heb. bestowed her whoredoms upon them. Ezk 16:15. **the chosen men of Assyria.** Heb. the choice of the children of Asshur. Ge 10:22. **with all their.** ver. 30. Ezk 20:7. 22:3, 4. Ps 106:39. Ho 5:3. 6:10.

8. **whoredoms.** ver. 3, 19, 21. Ex *32:4. 1 K 12:28. 2 K 10:29. 17:16.

9. **I have delivered.** 2 K 15:29. *17:3-6, 23. *18:9-12. 1 Ch 5:26. Ho 11:5. Re 17:12, 13, 16.

10. **discovered.** ver. 29. Ezk 16:37-41. Ho 2:3, 10. **they took.** ver. 47. **famous.** Heb. a name. ver. 48. Je 22:8, 9.

11. **her sister.** ver. 4. Je 3:8. **was more corrupt in her inordinate love than she.** Heb. she corrupted her inordinate love more than she. **her sister in whoredoms.** Heb. the whoredoms of her sister. Ezk 16:47-51. Je *3:8-11.

12. **upon.** ver. 5. Ezk 16:28. 2 K *16:7-15. 2 Ch *28:16-23. **captains.** ver. 6, 23.

13. **that they.** ver. 31. 2 K 17:18, 19. Ho 12:1, 2.

14. **portrayed.** Ezk *8:9, 10. +16:17. Is 46:1. Je 50:2. **vermilion.** Je *22:14. Na 2:3.

15. **with girdles.** 1 S 18:4. Is 22:21. **all of.** Jg 8:18. 2 S 14:25. **look to.** That is, "princes in appearance;" which seem to have been the deified men worshipped by the Chaldeans. The inhabitants of Judah, like the Israelites, connnected themselves with the Assyrians, and were enamored with their idols; and then with the Chaldeans, and followed their idols; still retaining their attachment to the Egyptians and their idolatrous rites.

16. **as soon as she saw them with her eyes.** Heb. at the sight of her eyes. Ezk 16:29. Ge +*3:6. 6:2. *39:7. 2 S *11:2. 2 K 20:12-19. Jb √31:1. Ps +*101:3. 119:37. Pr 6:25. 23:33. Mt √5:28. 1 J √2:16. 2 P *2:14. **she doted.** ver. 20. **and sent.** ver. 40, 41. Ezk 16:17, 29.

17. **Babylonians.** Heb. children of Babel. Ge 10:10. 11:9. **and her.** ver. 22, 28. Ezk 16:37. 2 S 13:15. **mind.** Heb. *nephesh*, Ge +23:8. ver. 22, 28. Ezk ❍20:32. Ge +2:7n. **alienated.** Heb. loosed, *or* disjointed. Je 6:8mg.

18. **discovered.** Ezk 16:36. 21:24. Is 3:9. Je 8:12. Ho 7:1. **then.** Dt 32:19. Ps 78:59. 106:40. Je *6:8.

12:8. 15:1. La 2:7. Ho 2:2. Am 6:8. Zc 11:8. **my mind.** Heb. *nephesh*, Ge +23:8. Le +26:11n. **alienated.** *ſ*22D1, Ge +32:28.

19. **multiplied.** ver. 14. Ezk 16:25, 29, 51. Am 4:4. **in calling.** ver. 3, 8, 21. Ezk 16:22. 20:7. **remembrance.** *ſ*121C2B, Is +44:21.

20. **she doted.** ver. 16. **paramours.** Ezk 16:20, 26n. **whose flesh.** *ſ*88, Ge +17:11. Je 2:23, 24. 5:8. 13:27. **as the flesh.** Ezk +16:26n. **issue.** *S#2231h, only here. Strong defines "a *gushing* of fluid (semen)." Ge 38:9. Le 15:16-18, 32. 18:20h. 19:20h. 22:4. Nu 5:2. Dt 23:10. 2 S 3:29. Mt 9:20. **horses.** Ezk 17:15. Je 5:8.

22. **I will raise.** ver. 9, 28. Ezk 16:37. Is 10:5, 6. 39:3, 4. Hab *1:6-10. Re 17:16. **from.** ver. 17. **mind.** Heb. *nephesh*, Ge +23:8. ver. 17, 28. **and I.** Je 6:22, 23. 12:9-12.

23. **Babylonians.** Ezk 21:19, etc. 2 K 20:14-17. 25:1-3. **the Chaldeans.** 2 K 24:2. Jb 1:17. Is 23:13. Ac 7:4. **Pekod.** i.e. *punishment*, *S#6489h. Je 50:21. **Shoa.** i.e. *opulent, noble, free; cry; fruitful*, *S#7772h, only here. **Koa.** i.e. *alienation; curtailment; a prince*, *S#6970h, only here. **the Assyrians.** Ge 2:14. 25:18. Ezr 6:22. **desirable.** ver. 6, 12.

24. **with chariots.** Ezk 26:10. Je 47:3. Na 2:3, 4. 3:2, 3. **I will set.** ver. 45. Ezk 16:38. 21:23. Dt *28:49, 50. 2 S 24:14. Je 39:5, 6.

25. **I will set.** Ezk 5:13. ch. 8. 16:38-42. Ex 34:14. Dt 29:20. 32:21, 22. Pr 6:34. SS 8:6. Zp 1:18. **they shall take away.** This refers to the severe vengeance which enraged husbands took on their faithless wives: and implies that God would employ the Chaldeans to destroy the princes and priests of Judah, for violating their covenants and treaties. Such punishments were anciently common; and such is the present practice in the South Sea islands. **fall by the sword.** 2 Ch *36:17. **they shall take thy.** ver. 47. Ho 2:4, 5. **thy residue.** Ezk 15:6, 7. 20:47, 48. 22:18-22. Re 18:8.

26. **strip.** ver. 29. Ezk 16:37, 39. Je 13:22. Ho 2:3, 9, 10. Re 17:16. 18:14-17. **fair jewels.** Heb. instruments of thy decking. Is 3:17-24. 1 P 3:3, 4.

27. **will I.** Ezk 16:41. 22:15. Is 27:9. Mi 5:10-14. Zc 13:2. **and thy.** ver. 3, 19. **so that.** These severe judgments shall effectually deter you from idolatry, and make you abhor the least approaches to it. This often repeated prediction has received a most wonderful accomplishment. For neither the authority, frowns, examples, or favor of their conquerors or powerful neighbors, nor their own fears, hopes, interests, or predilection for the sensual worship of idols, could prevail with them to run into gross idolatry, either during the captivity, or ever afterwards, to the present day, a period of 2414 years! **from the land.** Is 31:1.

28. **whom thou.** ver. 17, 22. Ezk 16:37. Je 21:7-10. 24:8. 34:20. **mind.** Heb. *nephesh*, Ge +23:8. ver. 22.

29. **deal.** ver. 25, 26, 45-47. Ezk 16:39. Dt 28:47-51. 2 S 13:15. **labor.** *ſ*121C1H, Dt +28:33. **the nakedness.** ver. 18. Ezk 16:36, 37.

30. **thou hast.** ver. 12-21. Ezk 6:9. Ps ◐*16:4. 106:35-38. Je 2:18-20. 16:11, 12. 22:8, 9. **because thou art.** ver. 7, 17.

31. **walked.** ver. 13. Ezk 16:47-51. Je 3:8-11. **her.** 2 K 21:13. Je 7:14, 15. Da 9:12. **cup.** Is *51:17. Re *14:9, 10.

32. **drink.** Ps 60:3. Is 51:17. Je *25:15-28. 48:26. Mt 20:22, 23. Re 16:19. 18:6. **cup.** *ſ*121J13, Je +49:12.

thou shalt be. Ezk 22:4, 5. 25:6. 26:2. 35:15. 36:3.
Dt 28:37. 1 K 9:7. Ps 79:3. Je 25:9. La 2:15, 16. Mi
7:8.

33. **filled**. Je 25:27. Hab 2:16. **with the cup of astonishment**. Is *51:17, 22.

34. **drink**. Ps *75:8. Is *51:17. **and pluck**. ver. 3,
8. Mt 5:29, 30. Re 18:7. Scott suggests "as one drunken,
frantic, and in despair." *Companion Bible* notes, "(to)
destroy the occasions of their idolatry."

35. **Because**. Ezk 22:12. Is 17:10. Je *2:32. *3:21.
*13:25. 23:27. 32:33. Ho 8:14. 13:6. Ro 1:28. He *10:29.
and cast. 1 K *14:9. Ne *9:26. **therefore**. ver. 45-49.
Ezk 7:4. 44:10. Le 24:15. Nu 14:34. 18:22. **bear**.
√121C1E, Ge +19:15.

36. **wilt**. Ezk 20:4. 22:2. Je 1:10. 1 C 6:2, 3. **judge**.
or, plead for. Ezk 22:2mg. Je 11:14. 14:11. **Aholah**.
ver. 4. **declare**. Ezk 16:2. Is *58:1. Ho 2:2. Mi 3:8-
11. Mt 23:13-35. Lk 11:39-52. Ac 7:51-53.

37. **they have**. ver. 5. Ezk 16:32. Ho 1:2. 3:1. **and
blood**. ver. 39, 45. Ezk 16:36, 38. 22:2-4. 24:6-9. 2 K
24:4. Ps 106:37, 38. Is *1:15. Je 7:6, 9. Ho 4:2. Mi
3:10. Lk 13:34. **have also**. ver. 4. Ezk 16:20, 21, 36,
45. 20:26, 31. Le 18:21)℘. 20:2-5)℘. Dt 12:31. 2 K
17:17. 21:6. Je 7:31. 32:35.

38. **they have**. Ezk 7:20. 8:5-16. 2 K 21:4, 7. 23:11,
12. **defiled**. Jn 2:13-16. **and have**. Ezk 20:13, 24. 22:8.
Ex *31:13, 14. Le 19:30)℘. Ne 13:17, 18. Is +*58:13n,
14. Je √17:27n.

39. **they came**. Ezk *33:31. Is 3:9. *66:3. Je 7:8-
11. 11:15. Mi 3:11. Jn 18:28. **thus**. ver. 38. Ezk 44:7.
2 K 21:4. 2 Ch 33:4-7. Je 23:11.

40. **ye have**. ver. 16. Is 57:9. **to come**. Heb. coming.
2 K 20:13-15. **thou didst**. Ru 3:3. Est 2:12. **paintedst**.
Kachalt aineycha, rendered by the LXX. *estibidzou
tous ophthalmous sou*, "thou didst paint thine eyes
with stibium," and Vulgate, *circumlinisti stibio oculos
tuos*, "thou didst paint round thine eyes with stibium,"
or lead ore; whence it is called in Arabic *kochl*, and
in Syriac *kecholo*, and *koochlo*. 2 K 9:30mg. Je 4:30mg.
and deckedst. Ezk 16:13-16. Pr 7:10. Is 3:18-23.

41. **stately**. Heb. honorable. Est 1:6. Pr 7:16, 17.
Is *57:7-9. Am 2:8. 6:4. He ◐+*13:4. **a table**. Ezk
44:16. Is 65:11. Ml 1:7. **whereupon**. Ezk 16:18, 19.
Pr 7:17. Je 44:17. Ho 2:8, 9.

42. **a voice**. This seems to be an account of an idolatrous festival, perhaps that of Bacchus; in which a
riotous and drunken multitude assembled, adorned
with bracelets and chaplets, accompanied with music,
songs, and dances. Ezk 32:6, 18, 19. Ho 13:6. Am
6:1-6. **common sort**. Heb. multitude of men. Je
26:23mg. **were brought**. Ge 10:7, 28. 25:3. 1 K 10:1.
Sabeans. *or*, drunkards. *S#5433h, only here. Compare *S#5436h, Is 45:14; *S#7614h, Jb 1:15;
*S#7615h, Jl 3:8. Jb 1:15. Jl 3:8. **bracelets**. Ezk 16:11,
12. Re 12:3.

43. **old**. or, worn out. lit. "faded" one. Jsh 9:4, 5.
Ezr 9:7. Ps 106:6. Je 13:23. Da 9:16. **whoredoms with
her**. Heb. her whoredoms. Ezk 16:15, 19.

44. **so went**. ver. 3, 9-13. Ps 106:39.

45. **the righteous**. The Chaldeans, so called, because
appointed by God to execute his judgment on these
criminals. ver. 36. Je 5:14. Ho 6:5. Zc 1:6. Jn 8:3-7.
after the manner of adulteresses. ver. 37-39. Ezk
16:38-43. Le 20:10)℘. 21:9. Dt 22:21-24. Jn *8:7. Re
*16:5, 6. *19:2, 3. **because**. ver. 37.

46. **I will**. ver. 22-26. Ezk 16:40. Je 25:9. **to be

removed and spoiled. Heb. for a removing and spoil.
Je +15:4mg. 24:9mg. 34:17mg. La 1:8mg.

47. **the company**. ver. 25, 29. Ezk *9:6. 16:41. Dt
*22:24. Je 33:4, 5. **dispatch them**. *or*, single them
out. Ezk 24:6. **shall slay**. Ezk 24:21. 2 Ch *36:17-19.
and burn. Dt 13:16. Je 39:8. 52:13.

48. **I cause**. ver. 27. Ezk 6:6. 22:15. 36:25. Mi 5:11-
14. Zp 1:3. **that**. Ezk 5:15. 16:41. Dt *13:11. Is √26:9.
+*66:24. Ro *15:4. 1 C *10:6-11. 2 P *2:6.

49. **they shall**. Ezk 7:4, 9. 9:10. 11:21. 16:43. 22:31.
Is 59:18. **ye shall bear**. ver. 35. Ps 106:43. **sins**.
√121C1E, Ge +19:15. **and ye shall know**. Ezk +6:7.
13:9. 20:38, 42, 44. 24:24. 25:5. Ps *9:16.

EZEKIEL 24

*The prophet is informed of the day when Nebuchad-
nezzar laid siege to Jerusalem, 1, 2. He is shown the
miseries of the Jews, and the destruction of the city,
by the parable of the boiling pot, 3-14. He is forbidden
to mourn for the sudden death of his wife; to denote,
that the calamities of the people should exceed all expressions of sorrow, 15-24. When tidings were brought
him of these events, his mouth would be opened and
he should be no more dumb, 25-27.*

1. A.M. 3414. B.C. 590. **the ninth year**. This was
the *ninth* year of Zedekiah, about Thursday, January
30, A.M. 3414, the very day in which Nebuchadnezzar
began the siege of Jerusalem. Ezk 1:2. 8:1. 20:1. 26:1.
29:1, 17. 31:1. 32:1, 17. 33:21. 40:1. 2 K 24:12.

2. **write**. Is 8:1. 30:8, 9. Hab 2:2, 3. **of this**. 2 K
*25:1. Je *39:1. 52:4.

3. **utter**. Ezk 17:2. 19:2, etc. 20:49. Ps 78:2. Mi
2:4. Mk 12:12. Lk 8:10. **parable**. Nu +23:7n. **the rebellious**. Ezk 2:3, 6, 8. 3:9. 12:2, 25. 17:12. Is 1:2. 30:1,
9. *63:10. Ac 7:51. **Set**. ver. 6. Ezk *11:3. 17:12. Je
*1:13, 14.

4. **the pieces**. Ezk 22:18-22. Mi 3:2, 3. Mt *7:2.

5. **the choice**. Ezk 20:47. 34:16, 17, 20. Je 39:6.
52:10, 11, 24-27. Re 19:20. **burn**. *or*, heap. ver. 9,
10.

6. **Woe**. ver. 9. Ezk 11:6, 7. 22:2, 3, 6-9, 12, 27.
23:37-45. 2 K 21:16. 24:4. Mi 7:2. Na *3:1. Mt 23:35.
Re 11:7, 8. 17:6. 18:24. **to the pot**. ver. 11-13. Je 6:29.
bring. Ezk *9:5, 6. 11:7-9, 11. Jsh 10:22. **let no**. Jsh
7:16-18. 1 S 14:40-42. 2 S 8:2. Jl 3:3. Ob *11. Jon
1:7. Na *3:10. **let no lot**. Indicative of total destruction;
it would not be divided. Jsh 14:2n.

7. **her blood**. 1 K 21:19. Is 3:9. Je 2:34. 6:15. **she
poured**. Le 17:13)℘. Dt 12:16, 24. Jb 16:18. Is 26:21.

8. **it might**. Ezk 5:13. 8:17, 18. 22:30, 31. Dt 32:21,
22. 2 K 22:17. 2 Ch 34:25. 36:16, 17. Je 7:18-20. 15:1-
4. **I have set**. Ezk 16:37, 38. 23:45. Dt 29:22-28. Je
22:8, 9. Mt *7:2. 1 C √4:5. Re 17:1-6. 18:5-10, 16-20.

9. **Woe**. See on ver. 6. Na 3:1. Hab 2:12. Lk 13:34,
35. Re 14:20. 16:6, 19. **I will**. Ezk 22:19-22, 31. Is
+*30:33. 31:9. 2 Th √1:8. 2 P *3:7-12. Ju +*7. Re
+*21:8.

10. **Heap on wood**. Is +*30:33. **spice it well**. Ezk
43:24. Le *2:13. Jb 6:6. Mt *5:13. Mk +*9:50. Lk
14:34, 35. Ep *4:29. Col *4:6. He +*3:12, 13. **and
let**. 2 Ch +*34:5n. Je 17:3. 20:5. La 1:10. 2:16.

11. **set it**. Je 21:10. 32:29. 37:10. 38:18. 39:8. 52:13.
that the filthiness. Ezk 20:38. 22:15, etc. 23:26, 27,
47, 48. 36:25. Is 1:25. 4:4. 27:9. Mi 5:11-14. Zc 13:1,
2, 8, 9. Ml *4:1. Mt *3:12. 1 C √3:12, 13. **The *pot*
was Jerusalem; the *flesh*, the inhabitants in general:

every good piece, the thigh and the shoulder, Zedekiah, his family, and princes; the *bones,* the soldiers; the *fire* and *water,* the calamities they were to suffer; and the *setting on* of the pot, the commencement of the siege.

12. **wearied.** Is 47:13. 57:9, 10. Je 2:13. *9:5. 10:14, 15. 51:58. Ho 12:1. Hab *2:13, 18, 19. **her great.** ver. 6, 13. Ge 6:5-7. *8:21. Is *1:5. Je 5:3. 44:16, 17. Da 9:13, 14. **her scum.** The pot being polluted with the scum, must be heated, melted, and even burned with fire till purified; that is, Jerusalem shall be entirely levelled with the ground, as nothing short of this will purify it from the relics of its idolatrous abominations. 2 Ch +*34:5n. 1 P 4:12, 17. 2 P 3:10-14.

13. **thy filthiness.** ver. 11. Ezk 23:36-48. 2 C *7:1. **because.** Ezk 22:24. 2 Ch *36:14-16. Is *5:4-6. 9:13-17. Je 6:28-30. 25:3-7. 31:18. Ho 7:1, 9-16. Am 4:6-12. Zp 3:2, 7. Mt 23:37, 38. Lk *13:7-9. Re +*22:11. **have purged.** ∫108A1, Ex +8:18. **till I.** Ezk 5:13. 8:18. 16:42. Ro 2:8, 9.

14. **the Lord.** Nu *23:19. 1 S *15:29. Ps *33:9. Is √55:11. Je *23:20. Mt √24:35. **neither will I spare.** Ezk 5:11. 7:4, 9. 8:18. 9:10. Je 13:14. **according to thy ways.** Ezk 16:43. 18:30. 22:31. 23:24, 29, 49. Is 3:11. Je 4:18. Mt 16:27. Ro 2:5, 6.

16. **the desire.** ∫142, Ge +20:16. ∫121R5, Ge +27:15. ∫155A, Ge +31:35. ver. 18, 21, 25. 1 K 20:6mg. Ps 45:11. Pr *5:19. SS √7:10. La 2:4mg. **with a.** Jb 36:18. Ps 39:10. **stroke.** ❋S#4046h. Ex 9:14 (plagues). Nu 14:37 (plague). 16:48, 49, 50. 25:8, 9, 18. 26:1. 31:16. 1 S 4:17. 6:4. 2 S 17:9 (slaughter). 18:7. 24:21, 25. 1 Ch 21:17, 22. 2 Ch 21:14mg. Ps 106:29, 30. Zc 14:12, 15, 15, 18. This Hebrew term is elsewhere used of various plagues (Ex 9:14), including outbreaks of venereal disease (Nu 25:1, 2, 8, 9; Dt 4:3, 4). Note the measures taken to prevent the spread of the disease, including strict quarantine (Nu 31:15-24). Other physical symptoms of venereal diseases included baldness in women, Is 3:16, 24; evidence of congenital syphilis such as blindness, stunting, bone malformations dating from birth, Le 21:18-20; deformed stillbirths, Nu 12:12; crooked teeth in children because of the sins of their fathers, Je 31:29; perhaps alluded to in Ex 20:5. The devastating effects of homosexual practices are referred to in Ro 1:27, and may be related to God's threats of incurable disease (Ex 15:26. Dt 7:15. 28:60, 61. 2 Ch 21:18) for disobedience to his word, of which a contemporary example might be AIDS (Acquired Immune Deficiency Syndrome). Ezekiel's wife, however, is not connected with any of this. The word is used in connection with her because of the suddenness of her death. **yet.** ver. 21-24. Je 10:2, 3. Je 22:10, 18. 1 Th 4:13. **thy tears.** Je 9:1, 18. 13:17. La 2:18. **run.** Heb. go.

17. **Forbear to cry.** Heb. Be silent. Ps 37:7mg. 39:9. 46:10. Am 8:3. Hab √2:20mg. **make.** Je *16:4-7. **bind.** ver. 23. Le *10:6)℘. 13:45)℘. 21:10)℘. **put.** ver. 23. 2 S 15:30. Is 20:2. **cover.** ver. 22. Le 13:45. Mi 3:7. **lips.** Heb. upper lip, and so ver. 22. Le 13:45. 2 S 19:24. **eat.** Ho 9:4. **the bread of men.** ∫108H4, Is +58:7. Je 16:5mg. *Lechem anoshim,* not "the bread of mourners," as some render, but "the bread of *other* men," i.e. such as was commonly sent to mourners on such occasions by their friends. See on Je 16:7. Ho 9:4.

18. **and at.** Mt *19:29. 1 C 7:29, 30.

19. **Wilt thou.** Ezk 12:9. 17:12. 20:49. 21:7. 37:18. Ml 3:7, 8, 13.

21. **I will.** Ezk 7:20-22. 9:7. Ps *74:7. 79:1. Is *64:10, 11. Je *7:14. La 1:10. 2:6, 7. Da 11:31. Ac 6:13, 14. **the excellency.** Ps 96:6. 105:4. 132:8. **the desire.** ∫142, Ge +20:16. ∫155A, Ge +31:35. ver. 16. Ps 27:4. 84:1. **that which your soul pitieth.** Heb. the pity of your soul. Heb. *nephesh,* Ge +34:3. Jb 31:30. **your sons.** Ezk 23:25, 47. Je 6:11. 9:21. 16:3, 4.

22. **ye shall do.** ver. 16, 17. Jb 27:15. Ps 78:64. Je 16:4-7. 47:3. Am 6:9, 10.

23. **tires.** Je 13:18mg. **shall not.** Je *16:4-7. **But.** Ezk 4:17. 33:10. Le *26:39. **and mourn.** Is 59:11.

24. **Ezekiel.** Ezk 4:3. *12:6, 11. Is *8:18. *20:3. Ho 1:2, etc. 3:1-4. Lk 11:29, 30. 1 C *4:9. **when.** 1 S 10:2-7. Je 17:15. Lk 21:13. Jn 13:19. 14:29. 16:4. **ye shall know.** Ezk 6:7. 7:9, 27. 17:24. 25:5, 7, 11, 14, 17.

25. **take from.** Ps 78:64. **their strength.** ver. 21. Ps 48:2. 50:2. 122:1-9. Je 7:4. **desire.** ∫142, Ge +20:16. **that whereupon they set their minds.** Heb. the lifting up of their soul. Heb. *nephesh,* Ge +23:8. ∫142, Ge +20:16. Je 22:27mg. **their sons.** Dt 28:32. Je 11:22. 52:10.

26. **he that escapeth.** Ezk ❋33:21, 22. 1 S 4:12-18. Jb *1:15-19.

27. **thy mouth.** Ezk 3:26, 27. 29:21. 33:22. Ex 6:11, 12. Ps *51:15. Lk 21:15. Ep 6:19. **be opened.** ∫108H6A, Jg +11:35. **no more dumb.** Ezk 33:22. Lk 1:20, 62-65. **shalt be.** ver. 24. **they shall know.** Ezk +6:10.

EZEKIEL 25

God's vengeance, for their insolency against the Jews, upon the Ammonites, 1-7; upon Moab and Seir, 8-11; upon Edom, 12-14; and upon the Philistines, 15-17.

2. **thy face.** Ezk 6:2. 20:46. 21:2. 35:2. **the Ammonites.** Ezk *21:28-32. Ge 19:38. Je 9:25, 26. 25:21, 27. 27:3. *49:1-6. Am *1:13-15. Zp 2:8-11.

3. **Ammonites.** Ezk 21:28. Je 40:14. 41:10, 15. **thou saidst.** ver. 6, 8. Ezk 26:2, etc. 35:10-15. 36:2. Ps *40:15. 70:2, 3. Pr *17:5. 24:17, 18. La 1:21, 22. 4:21. Mi 7:8. **the land.** Ezk +11:17.

4. **men.** Heb. children. Jg 6:3, 33. 7:12. 8:10. 1 K 4:30. Josephus (Ant. l. x. c. 2) expressly states, that five years after the destruction of Jerusalem, Nebuchadnezzar turned his arms against the *Ammonites* and *Moabites,* and entirely subjugated them; and it is probable, that the Arabs, and other nations *east* of Judah, then took possession of their cities, and enjoyed the fruits of their land. The country of Moab and Ammon is now inhabited by the Bedouin Arabs; where they pasture their flocks, and, no doubt, make the ruins of *Rabbah,* their once proud capital, "a stable for camels," and other cattle. See Note on 2 S 12:26. **of the east.** ∫171.O.6, 1 K +4:30. Ezk 21:19, 20. Ge 29:1. Nu 23:7. Is 41:2. Je 25:21. 49:28. **they shall eat.** Le 26:16. Dt 28:33, 51. Jg 6:3-6. Is 1:7. 62:8, 9. 65:22.

5. **Rabbah.** Ezk *21:20, Rabbath. Dt 3:11. 2 S *12:26, 27. **a stable.** Is 17:2. 32:14. Zp 2:14, 15. **and ye.** ver. 8. Ezk +6:7. 24:24. 26:6. 30:8. 35:9. 38:23. Ps 83:18. Is 37:20.

6. **thou hast.** Jb 27:23. 34:37. Je 48:27. La 2:15. Na 3:19. Zp 2:15. **hands.** Heb. hand. **stamped.** Ezk

6:11. **feet.** Heb. foot. **rejoiced.** ver. 15. Ezk 35:15. 36:5. Ne 4:3, 4mg. Pr 24:17. Ob 12. Zp 2:8, 10. **heart.** Heb. soul. Heb. *nephesh*, Ex +23:9. **against.** Je *40:14. 41:10.

7. **I will stretch.** ℐ22A14.8A, Ex +7:5. ver. 13, 16. Ezk 14:9. 35:3. Zp 1:4. 2:10. **and will.** Je 49:2. Am 1:14. **a spoil.** *or*, meat. **thou shalt know.** Ezk 16:62. 22:16. 35:4. Jn +11:42.

8. **Moab.** Ge 19:37. Nu 24:17, 18. Ps 83:4-8. Is ch. 15, 16. 25:10. Je 25:21. ch. 48. Am *2:1-3. Zp *2:8-11. **Seir.** ver. 12-14. Ezk ch. 35. Dt 2:5. Is ch. 34. 63:1-6. Je 27:3. 49:7-22. Am 2:11, 12. Ob 1, etc. **Seir.** Ezk 35:2, 14, 15. **the house.** Is 10:9-11. 36:18-20.

9. **side.** *or*, shoulder. Ezk 3:16. 33:2, etc. Jsh 18:12. **Beth-jeshimoth.** i.e. *house of the desolations.* Nu 33:49. Jsh 12:3. 13:20. **Baal-meon.** i.e. *lord of a habitation.* Nu 32:37, 38. Jsh 13:17, 19. 1 Ch 5:8. Je 48:23. **Kiriathaim.** i.e. *two cities.* Je 48:1, 23.

10. **the men.** ver. 4. **with the Ammonites.** *or*, against the children of Ammon. ver. 2-7. **may.** Ezk 21:32. Ps 83:3-6. Is 23:16.

11. **I will.** ver. 17. Ezk 5:8, 10, 15. 11:9. 16:41. 30:14, 19. 39:21. Ps *9:16. *149:7. Ju 15. **upon.** Je 9:25, 26. 25:21. ch. 48. **and they.** ver. 5. Ezk +6:10. 35:15.

12. **Because.** ver. 8. Ezk ch. 35. Ge 36:8. 2 Ch *28:17, 18. Ps *137:7. Je 49:7, etc. La 4:21, 22. **taking vengeance.** Heb. revenging revengement. ℐ147A. Polyptoton, Ge +50:24. Ge 27:41, 42. Am 1:11, 12. Ob 10-16.

13. **I will also.** ver. 7, 16. Is ch. 34. 63:1-6. La 4:21, 22. Ob 1, etc. Ml 1:3, 4. **and will.** Ezk 14:8, 13, 17, 19-21. 29:8. Ge 6:7. Je 7:20. **Teman.** Ge 36:11. Je *49:7, 20. Am 1:12. Ob 9. Hab 3:3. **of Dedan shall fall by the sword.** *or*, shall fall by the sword unto Dedan. Je 25:23. 49:8.

14. **by the hand.** This was fulfilled by the Maccabees, who not only entirely subjugated them, but obliged them to receive circumcision (Josephus, Ant. l. xiii. c. 17; 1 Mac 5:65. 2 Mac 10:16). Ge 27:29. Nu *24:17-19. Is 11:14. 63:1, etc. Je *49:2. **and they shall know.** Dt 32:35, 36. Ps 58:10, 11. Na 1:2-4. He 10:30, 31. Re 6:16, 17.

15. **Because.** ver. 6, 12. Ge 26:14, 15. 1 S 4:2. 2 S 5:17. 23:8-17. 2 Ch 28:18. Is 14:29-31. Je 25:20. ch. 47. Jl 3:4, etc. Am 1:6-8. Zp 2:4-7. Zc 9:5-8. **dealt.** 2 Ch 28:18. Ps 83:7. Is 9:12. **heart.** Heb. *nephesh*, Ex +23:9. **to destroy.** Jg ch. 14-16. 1 S ch. 4-6, 13, 14, 17, 31. 2 S 8. 1 Ch 7:21. **for the old hatred.** *or*, with perpetual hatred. Ezk 35:5mg. Heb. *olam*, Jb +22:15.

16. **I will stretch.** These predictions against the Philistines, Edomites, and others, seem to have been fulfilled by Nebuchadnezzar during the siege of Tyre. Berosus (apud Josephus, Cont. Ap) states that he subdued Syria, Arabia, Phoenicia, and Egypt; and now their very names have no existence, except in history. ver. 7, 13. Ps 60:8, 9. *108:9, 10. Is *11:14. Je 47:1-7. Am 1:6-8. **Cherethims.** i.e. *exterminators, executioners,* *S#3774h. 1 S 30:14. 2 S 15:18. Zp *2:4, 5, etc., Cherethites. **and destroy.** Je 47:4. **sea coasts.** *or*, haven of the sea. Ge 49:13. Je 47:7.

17. **I will.** ver. 11. Ezk 5:15. **vengeance.** Heb. vengeances. ℐ96F2, Ge +4:10. Ps 94:1. **they shall.** ver. 5, 11, 14. Ezk 6:7, +10. Ps *9:16.

EZEKIEL 26

The ruin of Tyre, for insulting over Jerusalem, is foretold, 1-6. The siege and taking of that city by Nebuchadnezzar, 7-14; and the consternation occasioned by its fall, 15-21.

1. **the eleventh year.** Ezk 1:2. 8:1. 20:1. Je 39:2.

2. **Tyrus.** Ezk ch. 27, 28. Jsh 19:29. Ps *83:5, 7. Is ch. 23. Je 25:22. 27:3. 47:4. Jl 3:4. Am 1:9, 10. Zc 9:2-4. **Aha.** Ezk 25:2, 3, 6. 36:2. Ps 35:21-23. *40:15. 70:3. 83:2-4. Pr *17:5. **the gates.** Ge +14:7. La 1:1. Ac 2:5-10. **she is.** Ezk 35:10. Je 49:1.

3. **Behold.** These verses (ver. 3-6) contain a summary prediction of what befell both the continental and insular Tyre, during a long succession of ages. The former was totally destroyed by Nebuchadnezzar, after a siege of thirteen years, B.C. 573; and the latter, which arose out of its ruins, after seventy years recovered its ancient wealth and splendor, as foretold by Isaiah (Is 23:15-17). After it was taken and burnt by Alexander, B.C. 332, it speedily recovered its strength and dignity, and nineteen years afterwards withstood both the fleets and armies of Antigonus. Agreeably to the prophetic declarations (Ps 45:12. 72:10. Is 23:18. Zc 9:1-7), it was early converted to Christianity; and after being successively taken by the Saracens, Christians, Mamalukes, and Turks, in whose hands it still remains, it became "a place for the spreading of nets." **I am against.** Ezk 5:8. 21:3. 28:22. 38:3. Je 21:13. 25:15, 17, 22. 50:31. Na 2:13. **many.** Mi 4:11. Zc 14:2. **as the sea.** Ezk 27:26, 32-34. Ps 93:3, 4. 107:25. Is 5:30. Je 6:23. 51:42. Lk 21:25.

4. **destroy.** ver. 9. Is 23:11. Je 5:10. Am 1:10. Zc 9:3, 4. **scrape her dust.** ℐ102, Ge +2:24. ver. 12. Le 14:41-45. **make her like.** Ezk 24:7, 8.

5. **the spreading of nets.** ℐ121.O, Ge +28:22. ver. 14, 19. Ezk 27:32. 47:10. **and it.** Ezk 25:7. 29:19.

6. **her daughters.** ver. 8. Ezk 16:27mg, 46, 48. Nu +21:25mg. Je 49:2. **and they.** Ezk 25:5, 7, 11, 14, 17.

7. **I will.** ver. 3. Ezk 28:7. 29:18-20. 30:10, 11. 32:11, 12. Je *25:9-11, 22. 27:3-6. **Nebuchadrezzar.** Ezk 29:18, 19. 30:10. **a king of kings.** ℐ147H, Ge +9:25. Ezk 17:14-16. Ezr 7:12. Is 10:8. Je 52:32. Da *2:37, 38, 47. Ho 8:10. **with horses.** ver. 10, 11. Ezk 23:23, 24. Je 4:13. 6:23. Na 2:3, 4. 3:2, 3.

8. **he shall make.** Ezk 21:22. 2 S 20:15. Je 52:4. **cast a mount.** *or*, pour out the engine of shot. Je 6:6mg. 32:24mg. 33:4. Lk 19:43.

9. **engines.** ℐ142, Ge +20:16. 2 Ch 26:15. **he shall.** Zc *9:3, 4.

10. **By reason.** Ezk 29:18-20. **the abundance.** ver. 7. Je 47:3. **shake.** ver. 15. Ezk 27:28. Na 2:3, 4. **enter.** Jsh 6:5, 20. **as men enter into a city wherein is made a breach.** Heb. according to the enterings of a city broken up.

11. **hoofs.** Is 5:28. Je 51:27. Hab 1:8. **and thy.** Is 26:5. **garrisons.** Heb. pillars, 2 K +17:10.

12. **make a spoil.** ver. 5. Mt 6:19, 20. **thy merchandise.** Ezk 27:3-36. Is *23:8, 11, 17, 18. Zc *9:3, 4. Re 18:11-13. **destroy.** Am *1:9, 10. **thy pleasant houses.** Heb. houses of thy desire. 2 Ch 32:27mg. 36:10mg. Is 32:12mg. Je +25:34mg. Da 9:23mg. 11:8mg. Ho 13:15mg. Am 5:11mg. Na 2:9mg. Zc 7:14mg. **they shall lay.** The ruins of old Tyre contributed much to the taking of the new city; for with the stones, timber,

and rubbish, Alexander built a bank, or causeway, from the continent to the island, thereby literally fulfilling the words of the prophet (Q. Curtius, l. iv. c. 2. Diodorus, l. xvii).

13. **the noise.** Ezk 28:13. Is 14:11. 22:2. 23:7, 16. 24:8, 9. Je 7:34. 16:9. 25:10. Ho 2:11. Am 6:4-7. Ja +*5:1-5. Re 18:22, 23. **to cease.** Je 47:4.

14. **I will make.** Old Tyre was never rebuilt after its destruction by Nebuchadnezzar; and there are no traces left to mark its site (see Pococke, vol. ii. b. i. c. 20). The new city, when visited by Maundrell, Bruce, and other travelers, was literally "a place for fishers to dry their nets on." Maundrell states "On the north side it has an old Turkish ungarrisoned castle: besides which you see nothing here, but a mere Babel of broken walls, pillars, vaults, and there being not so much as one entire house left: its present inhabitants are only a few poor wretches, harboring themselves in the vaults, and subsisting chiefly upon fishing, who seem to be preserved in this place by divine Providence, as a visible argument, how God has fulfilled his word concerning Tyre, viz. that 'it should be, as the top of a rock, a place for fishers to dry their nets on'" Maundrell's Journal, quoted by Bp. Newton, cited by Scott). **like.** ver. 4, 5, 12. **be built no more.** ⨍108B. Idiom B827. "To build" is an idiom used for the restoration of anything to all its former glory. For another example of this figure see Ps 102:16. Dt 13:16. Jb 12:14. Ml 1:4. Even to this day the prophecy holds true; for an excellent modern discussion, see Peter W. Stoner, *Science Speaks*, pp. 72-79. **for I.** Ezk 5:13, 15, 17. 17:21-24. 21:32. 22:14. 30:12. Nu *23:19. Jb 40:8. Is 14:27. Mt √24:35.

15. **shake.** ver. 18. Ezk 27:28, 35. 31:16. 32:10. Is 2:19. Je 49:21. He 12:26, 27. **when.** Is ❶61:3, 10.

16. **all the princes.** Ezk 27:29-36. 32:21-32. Is 14:9-13. 23:1-8. Re 18:11-19. **come.** Ex 33:4, 5. Jb 2:12. Jon 3:6. **clothe.** Ezk 7:8. Jb 8:22. Ps 35:26. 109:18, 29. 132:18. 1 P 5:5. **trembling.** Heb. tremblings. **sit.** Jb *2:13. Is 3:26. 47:1. 52:2. La 2:10. **tremble.** Ezk 32:10. Ex 15:15. Da 5:6. Ho 11:10, 11. Re 18:15. **be astonished.** Ezk 27:35.

17. **take.** Ezk 19:1, 14. 27:2, 32. 28:12, etc. 32:2, 16. Je 6:26. 7:29. 9:20. Mi 2:4. **How art.** 2 S 1:19, 25-27. Is 14:12. La 1:1. Jl 1:18. Ob 5. Zp 2:15. Re 18:9, 10, 16-19. **seafaring men.** Heb. the seas. **strong.** Ezk 27:3, etc. 28:2, etc. Jsh 19:29. Is 23:4, 8.

18. **the isles tremble.** ver. 15. Ezk 27:28-30. **at thy.** Is 23:5-7, 10-12. Zc *9:5.

19. **bring.** ver. 3. Is 8:7, 8. Da *9:26. 11:40. Re 17:15.

20. **I shall bring.** Ezk 32:18-32, 34. Nu 16:30, 33. Ps 28:1. Is 14:11-19. Lk 10:15. **pit.** Heb. *bor*, Ge +37:20. **of old time.** Heb. *olam*, Jsh +24:2. **in places.** Jb 30:3-6. Ps 88:3-6. Is 59:10. La 3:6. **of old.** Heb. *olam*, Ge +6:4. **pit.** Heb. *bor*, Ge +37:20. **and I shall set.** Ezk 28:25, 26. 39:7, 25-29. Is 4:5. Zc 2:8. **in the land of the living.** Ezk 32:23, 26, 27, 32. Ps 27:13. Is *38:11.

21. **a terror.** Heb. terrors. ver. 15, 16. Ezk 27:36. 28:19. **though.** ver. 14. Ps *37:36. Je 51:64. Re 18:21. **yet shalt.** T#945. ver. 19. Da 7:24-26. Mt *11:21, 22. 2 Th *2:8. Re 18:2. 19:19, 20. 20:7-9.

EZEKIEL 27

The riches and extensive commerce of Tyre shown, 1-25. Her dreadful and irrecoverable fall predicted, 26-36.

2. **take up.** ver. 32. Ezk 19:1. 26:17. 28:12. 32:2. Je 7:20. 9:10, 17-20. Am 5:1, 16.

3. **O thou.** Tyre was situated in the Mediteranean, at the nearest *entrance* to it from the interior and eastern part of Asia. ver. 4, 25. Ezk 26:17. 28:2, 3. Is 23:2. **a merchant.** ver. 12, etc. Is 23:3, 8, 11. Re *18:3, 11-15. **I am.** ver. 4, 10, 11. Ezk 28:12-17. Ps 50:2. Is 23:9. **of perfect beauty.** Heb. perfect beauty. La 2:15. Ezk 28:12.

4. **midst.** Heb. heart. ⨍144A7, Ex +15:8. Ezk 26:5. Ps 46:2mg. **builders.** Is 62:5. **perfected thy.** Jsh 19:29. Ho 9:13.

5. **made.** Heb. built. **of Senir.** Dt *3:9. SS 4:8, Shenir. **cedars.** 1 K 5:1, 6. 2 S 5:11. Ps 29:5. 92:12. 104:16. Is 14:8.

6. **the oaks.** Is 2:13. Zc *11:2. **Bashan.** Ezk 39:18. Nu +21:33. Jsh 12:4n. 1 K 4:13. Ps 22:12. **the company,** etc. *or,* they have made thy hatches of ivory well trodden. Rather, "thy benches have they made of ivory inlaid with box, from the isles of Chittim." Vulgate, *de insulis Italiae,* "from the islands of Italy," which were always famous for *box trees* (cypress). **company.** Heb. daughters. **the isles.** Ge 10:4, Kittim. Nu 24:24. Je 2:10.

7. **linen.** 1 K *10:28. Pr *7:16. Is 19:9. **blue and purple.** *or,* purple and scarlet. Ex 25:4. Je 10:9. **Elishah.** *Elis,* part of the Peloponnesus, extending along the western coast, west of Arcadia, north of Messenia, and south of Achaia. Ge *10:4. 1 Ch 1:7.

8. **Zidon.** Ge *10:15, Sidon. 49:13. Jsh 11:8. **Arvad.** i.e. *place of fugitives,* ✳S#719h. ver. 11h. Ge *10:18. 2 K ❶18:34. Is 10:9. Je 49:23, Arpad. **wise.** ver. 28. 1 K 5:6. 9:27. 2 Ch 2:13, 14.

9. **Gebal.** Jsh 13:5. 1 K 5:18mg. Ps *83:7. **calkers.** *or,* stoppers of chinks. Heb. strengtheners. ver. 27. 2 K 12:5. **mariners.** lit. "salt" men. ver. 27, 29. Jon 1:5.

10. **Persia.** Ezk *38:5. Da 5:28. **of Lud.** Ezk 30:5. Ge *10:6, 13, +22. 1 Ch 1:8, 11, 17. Is 66:19. Je *46:9. Na 3:9. **Phut.** Ezk 30:5mg. 38:5mg. Ge +10:6. Je 46:9mg. Na +*3:9. **they hanged.** ver. 11. SS 4:4.

11. **of Arvad.** ver. 8. **Gammadims.** i.e. *dwarfs; courageous; deserters; cutters,* ✳S#1575h, only here. **they hanged.** ver. +10. **thy walls.** 2 S 24:7. **they have.** ver. 3, 4.

12. **Tarshish.** Ezk 38:13. Ge +10:4. 1 K *10:22. 22:48, Tharshish. 2 Ch 20:36, 37. Ps 72:10. Is 2:16. 23:6, 10, 14. 60:9. Je 10:9. Jon 1:3. **fairs.** ver. 14, 16, 19, 22, 27, 33 (wares).

13. **Javan.** Ge *10:2, 4. 1 Ch 1:5, 7. Is 66:19. Da 8:21. 10:20. 11:2. **Tubal.** Ezk 32:26. √38:2, 3. √39:1. Ge 10:2. 1 Ch 1:5. **traded the persons.** Heb. *nephesh,* souls, Ge +12:5. T#681. Ezk +22:29 (T#488). Pr +22:22 (T#636). Jl *3:3-8. 2 P 2:3. Re *18:2, 11-13. A reference to the slave trade (CB). **brass.** 1 K 7:14. **market.** *or,* merchandise. ver. 9, 17, 19.

14. **house.** ⨍121J4, Ge +7:1. **Togarmah.** Ezk 38:6. Ge *10:3. 1 Ch 1:6. **with horses and.** 1 K 10:29.

15. **Dedan.** ver. 20. Ge *10:7. 25:3. 1 Ch 1:9, 32. Je 25:23. 49:8. **of ivory.** 1 K 10:22. Re 18:12.

16. **Syria.** Ge 10:22, Aram. 28:5. Jg 10:6. 2 S 8:5.

10:6. 15:8. Is 7:2. **the wares of thy making.** Heb. thy works. ver. 18. Ne 13:16. Ac 12:20. **occupied.** or, traded. ver. +21, 27. Lk 19:13. **agate.** *or,* chrysoprase. Is 54:12.

17. **land of Israel.** Ezk ❶11:17. ❶+21:2, 3. 40:2h. 47:18h. **traded.** ver. 16. 1 K 5:8-11, 18. 9:11-13. **wheat.** Dt 8:8. 32:14. 1 K 5:9, 11. 2 Ch 2:10, 15. Ezr 3:7. Ac 12:20. **Minnith.** Jg 11:33. **Pannag.** i.e. *preparing of affliction; pastry,* ✱S#6436h. **oil.** Ezr 3:7. **balm.** or, rosin. Ge *43:11. Je +*8:22. *46:11.

18. **Damascus.** Ge 15:2. 1 K 11:24, 25. 2 K *8:9. Is 7:8. *8:4. Ac 9:2. **Helbon.** i.e. *the fat one; very fat,* ✱S#2463h, only here. The *Chalybon* of the Greeks and Romans, now called by the natives *Haleb,* and by us *Aleppo,* said to have been so celebrated for its wine, that the Persian kings would drink no other. It was a celebrated city of Syria, situated about 90 miles from the Mediterranean by way of Antioch, and 100 from the Euphrates, in lat. 36 degrees 11 minutes 25 seconds north, long. 37 degrees 9 minutes east; and previous to its destruction by an earthquake in 1822, occupied, including its suburbs, eight small hills, with the intermediate valleys, comprehending a circuit of about seven miles; and its inhabitants were variously estimated at from 100,000 to 258,000 souls.

19. **Dan.** Jg *18:28, 29. **going to and fro.** *or,* Meuzal. Ge 10:27. **cassia.** Ex 30:23, 24. Ps 45:8. SS 4:13, 14.

20. **Dedan.** ver. 15. Ge *25:3. **precious clothes.** Heb. clothes of freedom. or, clothes of freedom for riding. Rendered "saddle clothes, saddle blankets, rich saddles" by others.

21. **Arabia.** 1 K 10:15. Je 25:24. Ac 2:11. Ga 4:25. **Kedar.** Ge *25:13. 1 Ch 1:29. Ps *120:5. SS 1:5. Is 21:16. 42:11. *60:7. Je 49:28. **occupied with thee.** Heb. *were* the merchants of thy hand. ver. 15. Ezk 17:18. Ge +24:2. 1 Ch +29:24mg. Lk 19:13. **in lambs.** 2 Ch 17:11. Is 60:7.

22. **Sheba.** Ge *10:7. 1 K *10:1-13. 1 Ch 1:9. 2 Ch 9:1, etc. Ps *72:10, 15. Is *60:6. **and gold.** Ge 2:11, 12.

23. **Haran.** Ge *11:31, 32. 12:4. 2 K 19:12. Is 37:12. Ac 7:4, Charran. **Canneh.** i.e. *surname; flattering title,* ✱S#3656h, only here. Ge 10:10, 22, Calneh. Is 10:9, Calno. Am 6:2, Calneh. **Eden.** Ge 2:8. 2 K *19:12. Is 37:12. Am 1:5. Sheba. Ge 25:3. Jb 1:15. **Asshur.** Ezk 32:22. Ge 10:22. Nu 24:22. Ps 83:8, Assur. Is 7:18, 20. **Chilmad.** i.e. *complete clothing; defense; seven; complete measure; enclosure, fortress,* ✱S#3638h, only here.

24. **all sorts of things.** or, excellent things. **clothes.** Heb. foldings. 2 K 2:8.

25. **ships of Tarshish.** 1 K *10:22. 2 Ch +9:21n. *20:36. Ps *48:7. Is *2:16. *23:14. 60:9. **glorious.** ver. 4.

26. **rowers.** Is 33:23. **great.** Ezk 26:19. Ps 93:3, 4. Re 17:15. **the east wind.** ver. 34. Ezk 17:10. 19:12. Ge +*41:6. Ps 48:7. Je 18:17. Ho +*12:1. Ac 27:14, 41. **midst.** Heb. heart. ver. 4mg.

27. **Thy riches.** In these beautiful and expressive figures, Tyre is represented as a ship at sea, wrecked through the mistakes of her pilots and rowers; that is, destroyed by Nebuchadnezzar, and afterwards by Alexander, in consequence of her rulers having pertinaciously resolved to withstand those haughty conquerors. This vast ship, laden with all kinds of valuable wares, being wrecked, all her valuables, sailors, offi-

cers, etc., went to the bottom. ver. 7-9, 12, 18, 19, 22, 24, 34. Ezk 26:12. Pr 11:4. Re 18:11, etc. **occupiers.** or, traders. ver. 15, 21mg. Mt 25:16. Lk 19:13. **and in all.** or, even with all. **shall fall.** Ezk 26:14, 21. **midst.** Heb. heart. ver. 26mg.

28. **suburbs.** or, waves. ♪102, Ge +2:24. Is 57:20. **shake.** ver. 35. Ezk 26:10, 15-18. 31:16. Ex 15:14. Na 2:3.

29. **all that handle.** Re 18:17, etc. **shall come.** Ezk 26:16. 32:10.

30. **shall cause.** All that were on land, seeing this gallant ship perishing with all her men and goods, are here represented as setting up a dismal cry at the heart-rending sight. ver. 31, 32. Ezk 26:17. Is 23:1-6. Re *18:9-19. **cast.** 1 S 4:12. 2 S 1:2. Jb 2:12. La 2:10. Re 18:19. **shall wallow.** Est 4:1-4. Jb 2:8. 42:6. Je 6:26. 25:34. Jon 3:6. Mi 1:10.

31. **they shall make.** Ezk 7:18. Le 21:5. Dt 14:1. Is 15:2. 22:12. Je 16:6. *47:5. 48:37. Am 8:10. Mi *1:16. **they shall weep.** Is 16:9. 22:4. Mi 1:8. **bitterness.** 1 S 1:10mg. **heart.** Heb. *nephesh,* Ex +23:9.

32. **take up.** ver. 2. Ezk 26:17. **What city.** La 1:12. 2:13. Re *18:9-18. **the destroyed.** ver. 26. Ezk 26:4, 5.

33. **thy wares.** ver. 3, 12, etc. Is 23:3-8. Re *18:3, 12-15, 19. **with the.** ver. 27. Ezk 28:16.

34. **be broken.** ver. 26, 27. Ezk 26:12-15, 19-21. Zc *9:3, 4.

35. **the inhabitants.** Ezk 26:15-18. Is *23:5-11. **their kings.** Ezk 28:17-19. 32:10. Re 18:9, 10.

36. **hiss.** Ezk 26:2. 1 K 9:8. Je 18:16. 19:8. La 2:15. Zp 2:15. **thou shalt.** Ezk *26:14, 21. **a terror.** Heb. terrors. **never shalt be any more.** Heb. *shalt* not *be* for ever. Heb. *olam,* Le +25:32. Ps *37:10, 36.

EZEKIEL 28

The judgments of God on the prince of Tyre, for his impious pride, 1-10. A lamentation over him, as fallen from his height of grandeur through iniquity, 11-19. A prophecy against Zidon, 20-23. The restoration of Israel foretold, 24-26.

2. **the prince.** Josephus states, on the authority of Menander, who translated the Phoenician annals into Greek (Cont. Ap. l. i. sec. 20, 21) and Philostratus (Ant. l. x. c. ii. sec. 1) that this prince was Ithobal. **Because.** ver. 5, 17. Ezk 31:10. Dt 8:14. 2 Ch 26:16. Pr 16:18. 18:12. Is 2:12. Da 5:22, 23. Hab 2:4. 1 T 3:6. 1 P *5:5. **I am a god.** ver. 6, 9. Ge *3:5. Ac *12:22, 23. Re *17:3. **I sit.** ver. *12-14. Is √14:13, 14. Da *4:30, 31. 2 Th √2:4. **in the midst.** Heb. in the heart. Ezk 27:3, +4mg, 26mg, 27mg. ♪147F. Polyptoton B281. Nouns repeated in different cases. For other instances of this figure see Jn 3:13. Ro 4:18. 11:36. Ga 2:19, 20. **yet.** ver. 9. Ps 9:20. +*82:6, 7. Is 31:3. **and not.** ♪144D, Ge +40:23. **thou set.** ver. 6. 2 Th √2:3, 4.

3. **thou art wiser.** ♪60A, Ge +3:22. Da *1:17, 20. 2:48. 5:11, 12. Zc *9:2, 3. ♪60A, Divine Irony, Ge +3:22. **Daniel.** Ezk 14:14n. **no secret.** 1 K 4:29-32. 10:3. Jb 15:8. Ps 25:14. Ec *10:20. Da *2:22, 27, 28, 47. *5:12.

4. **With thy wisdom.** Ezk 29:3. Dt 8:17, 18. Pr 18:11. 23:4, 5. Ec 9:11. Hab 1:16. Zc *9:2-4. **riches.** lit. strength. ♪121N2. Metonymy of the Adjunct, Ge +34:29. ver. 5.

5. **thy great wisdom.** Heb. the greatness of thy wis-

dom. Pr 26:12. Is 5:21. Ro *12:16. **and by.** Ezk 27:12, etc. Ps 62:10. Is *23:3, 8. Ho 12:7, 8. Zc *9:3. Ja *4:13, 14. **and thine.** ver. 2. Ezk +*16:49. Dt 6:11, 12. 8:13, 14. 2 Ch 25:19. 32:23-25. Jb 31:24, 25. Ps 52:7. √62:10. Pr 11:28. 30:9. Is 10:8-14. Da *4:30, 37. Ho 13:6. Lk *12:16-21. 1 T *6:17. **because of.** Mk +4:19. **riches.** lit. strength. ver. 4.

6. **Because.** ver. 2. Ge *3:4, 5. Ex 9:17. Jb 9:4. 40:9-12. 1 C 10:22. 2 Th √2:4. Ja 1:11.

7. **I will.** Ezk *26:7-14. Is *23:8, 9. Je *27:2-7. Am +*3:6. **the terrible.** Ezk 30:11. 31:12. 32:12. Dt *28:49, 50. Is 25:3, 4. Da 7:7. Hab 1:6-8. **defile.** ver. 15-17.

8. **shall bring.** Ezk 32:18-30. Jb 17:16. 33:18, 28. Ps 28:1. 30:9. 55:15. 88:4, 5. Pr 1:12. 28:17. Is √14:12. 38:17. **are slain.** Ezk 27:26, 27, 34.

9. **yet say.** ver. 2. Is *45:9. Da *4:31, 32. 5:23-30. Ac 12:22, 23. 2 Th √2:4. **I am God.** ver. +2. Ps +8:5n. 82:6n. **thou shalt.** Ps 82:7. Is 31:3. **slayeth.** *or*, woundeth.

10. **the deaths.** ℐ96F2, Ge +4:10. Ezk 31:18. 32:19, 21, 24-30. 44:7, 9. Le 26:41. Jg 8:21n. 9:54n. 1 S 17:26, 36. 31:4. Je 6:10. 9:25, 26. Jn +*8:24. Ac 7:51. Ph 3:3. **by the.** ver. 7. Ezk 11:9. Je 25:9.

12. **take up.** ver. 2. Ezk 19:1, 14. 26:17. 27:2, 32. 32:2, 16. 2 Ch 35:25. Is 14:4. Je 9:17-20. **Thou sealest.** ver. 2-5. Ezk 27:3, 4. Ro 15:28. 2 C 1:22. **full.** Jb 38:3, 4, 7. Pr +*21:30. Is 10:13. Je *9:23. Lk *2:40. Ac 6:3. 1 C 1:19, 20. 3:19. Col *1:9. 2:3. Ja *3:13-18. **beauty.** Is +*33:17.

13. **in Eden.** Ezk 31:8, 9. 36:35. Ge *2:8. *3:23, 24. 13:10. Is 51:3. Jl 2:3. Re 2:7. **the garden.** lit. "covered, protected" place. ℐ24L, Ge +6:2. Ezk 31:8, 9. **every.** Ezk 27:16, 22. Ge 2:11, 12. Ex 28:17-20. 39:10-21. Is 54:11, 12. Re 17:4. 21:19, 20. **sardius.** *or*, ruby. Ex 28:17. 39:10. Re 4:3. **topaz.** Jb 28:19. Re 21:20. **diamond.** Ex 28:18. 39:11. **beryl.** *or*, chrysolite. Ex 1:16. 10:9. Re 23:20. 39:13. SS 5:14. Da 10:6. **onyx.** Ge 2:12. Ex 25:7. 28:9, 20. 35:9, 27. 39:6, 13. 1 Ch 29:2. Jb 28:16. **jasper.** Ex 39:13. Re 4:3. 21:19. **sapphire.** Ezk 1:26. 10:1. Re 21:19. **emerald.** *or*, chrysoprase. Ezk 27:16mg. Re 4:3. 21:19. **carbuncle.** Ex 28:17. 39:10. **gold.** Ge 2:12. **the workmanship.** Ezk 26:13. Is 14:11. 23:16. 30:32. **tabrets.** Ps ◐150:4. Is 5:12. 24:8. 30:32. Je 31:4. **pipes.** lit. things "pierced" with holes. **thou wast.** ver. 15. Ezk 21:30.

14. **the anointed.** ver. 16. Ex *25:17-20. 30:26. 40:9. **that covereth.** ver. 16. Ex 25:20 (covering). 37:9. 1 Ch 28:18. Is 30:1. Na 2:5mg. **and I.** Ex 9:16. Ps 75:5-7. Is 10:6, 15. 37:26, 27. Da 2:37, 38. 4:35. 5:18-23. Jn 11:51. Ro 9:17. **upon.** ver. 2, 16. Ezk 20:40. Is √14:12-15. 2 Th √2:4. **the stones.** ver. 13, 17. Ex *24:9, 10. Re 18:16.

15. **Thou wast.** The irony (see ver. 3) is still continued. Thou hast been like the angels,—like Moses,—like the Cherubs,—like Adam,—like God,—till thy iniquity was found out. **perfect.** An exact description of the angelic purity in which the devil was created: and in which he continued, till being lifted up with pride, he fell from his first estate (Lowth). ver. 3-6, 12. Ezk 16:14. 27:3, 4. **till iniquity.** ver. 17, 18. Ge √1:26, 27, 31. 6:5, 6. Pr 14:34. Ec *7:29. Is √14:12. La 5:16. Ro 7:9. 2 P √2:4. The expressions used, in this poetical description of the excessive pride of this monarch, seem to allude to the fall of angels, and to that of Adam in Paradise; and they intimated that his ruin would be owing to the same cause, and attended

with similar effects to him. He is likewise supposed to have been a type of the Roman antichrist, of whom similar things are spoken in the New Testament; and almost the whole of this description may be accommodated to that proud enemy of God and his truth (Scott).

16. **the multitude.** Ezk 27:12, etc. Is *23:17, 18. Ho 12:7. Lk 19:45, 46. Jn 2:16. 1 T *6:9, 10. **filled.** Ezk 8:17. Ge 6:11. Am 3:9. Mi 2:2. 6:12. Hab 2:8, 17. Zp 1:9. **thou hast sinned.** Ro √6:23. **therefore.** Ge 3:24. Le 18:24-28. Is 22:19. 23:9. Mi 2:10. 2 P √2:4-6. Ju *6. Re √12:9. **O covering.** ver. 14.

17. **heart.** ver. 2, 5. Ezk 16:14, 15. 31:10. Pr 11:2. 16:18. Lk 14:11. Ja *4:6. **beauty.** Is +*33:17. **thou hast.** Is 19:11-13. Je 8:9. Ro 1:22-25. 1 C 1:19-21. **I will cast.** Jb 40:11, 12. Ps 73:18. 147:6. **I will lay.** Ezk 16:41. 23:48. 32:10. Is √14:9-11. **may behold.** Is +√66:24.

18. **defiled.** ver. 2, 13, 14, 16. **by the iniquity.** Mk 8:36. **therefore.** Ezk 5:4. Jg 9:15, 20. Am 1:9, 10, 14. 2:2, 5. Re *6:15-17. *18:8. **I will bring.** Ml 4:3. 2 P 2:6.

19. **they.** Ezk 27:35, 36. Ps 76:12. Is 14:16-19. Re 18:9, 10, 15-19. **thou shalt.** Ezk 26:14, 21. 27:36. Je 51:63, 64. Re 18:21. **a terror.** Heb. terrors. Ezk 27:36mg. **any more.** Heb. *olam*, Le +25:32. Ps *37:10.

21. **set.** Ezk 6:2. 25:2. 29:2. **Zidon.** Tyre was a colony of the Zidonians (see on Is 23:12); and consequently *Zidon* was a more ancient, though a less considerable city than Tyre; and it is probable that it was taken by the Chaldeans soon after the destruction of the latter. It was afterwards burnt to the ground by the inhabitants, to prevent it falling into the hands of Ochus (see Prideaux, an. 351). Ezk 27:8. 32:30. Ge *10:15, Sidon. Is *23:2-4, 12. Je 25:22. 27:3. 47:4. Jl 3:4-8. Zc 9:2.

22. **I am against.** Ezk 5:8. 21:3. 26:3. 29:3, 10. 38:3. 39:1-3. Je 21:13. 50:31. Na 1:6. 2:13. 3:5. **I will.** ver. 25. Ezk 39:13. Ex 9:16. 14:4, 17. 15:21. Le 10:3. 1 S 17:45-47. Ps *9:16. 21:12, 13. 83:17, 18. Is 5:15, 16. 37:20. Re 19:1, 2. **shall be.** Ezk 20:41. 36:23. 38:23.

23. **I will send.** Ezk 5:12. 38:22. Je 15:2. Hab *3:5, 6. **and they shall.** Ezk 25:7, 11, 17. 26:6.

24. **a pricking.** Nu 33:55. Jsh 23:13. Jg 2:3. 2 S *23:6, 7. Is 35:9. 55:13. Je 12:14. Mi 7:4. Zc √14:21. 2 C 12:7. Re 21:4. **and they.** ver. 23, 26. Ezk 36:36-38. 39:28.

25. **When.** Ezk 11:17. 20:41. 34:13. 36:24. 37:21. 39:27. Le 26:44, 45. Dt *30:3, 4. Ps 106:47. Is √11:11-13. 27:12, 13. Je 30:18. 31:8-10. 32:37. Ho 1:11. Jl 3:7. Am √9:14, 15. Ob 17-21. Mi 7:11-14. Zp 3:19, 20. **be sanctified.** ver. 22. Ezk 36:23. 38:23. Is 5:16. **then shall.** Ezk 36:28. 37:25. Je 23:8. 27:11. **to my.** Ge 28:13, 14.

26. **and they shall dwell.** Ezk 34:25-28. 38:8. Le 25:18, 19. Dt 12:10. Je *23:6-8. 33:16. Ho 2:18. Zc 2:4, 5. **safely.** *or*, with confidence. Ezk +*38:8h, 11mg. 1 K 4:25mg. Pr 14:26. **build.** Is *65:21, 22. Je 29:5, 6, 28. *31:4, 5. 32:15. Am *9:13, 14. **when I.** ver. 24. Ezk ch. 25-32, 35. Is ch. 13-21. Je ch. 46-51. Zc 1:15. **despise.** *or*, spoil. Ezk 39:10. Is 17:14. 33:1. Je 30:16. La 1:8. Hab 2:8. Zp 2:8, 9. **and they.** ver. 22, 24. Ezk 34:40. 36:22, 23. Ex 29:46.

EZEKIEL 29

Prophecies of the ruin of Pharaoh and Egypt, for their pride and treachery to Israel, 1-7; the desolations of Egypt, *during forty years, 8-12; the restoration of that country, and its base and abject condition through succeeding generations, 13-16. Nebuchadnezzar should be rewarded, for his labor in besieging Tyre, with the spoils of Egypt, 17-20. Israel shall again flourish, 21.*

1. A.M. 3415. B.C. 589. **tenth year**. ver. 17. Ezk 1:2. 8:1. 20:1. 26:1. 40:1.

2. **set**. Ezk 6:2. 20:46. 21:2. 25:2. 28:21, 22. **Pharaoh**. This was *Pharaoh hophra*, or *Apries*, who, Herodotus (l. ii. c. 169) informs us, agreeably to the character given him by the prophet, "proudly and wickedly boasted of having established his kingdom so securely, that it was not in the power of any God to dispossess him of it." Je 44:30. **against all**. Ezk ch. 30-32. Is ch. 18. 19:1-17. ch. 20. Je *9:25, 26. 25:18, 19. 43:8-13. 46:2-26. Jl 3:19. Zc 14:18, 19.

3. **I am**. ver. 10. Ezk 28:22. Ps 76:7. Je 44:30. Na 1:6. **the great**. Ezk 32:2. Ps 74:13, 14. Is *27:1. *51:9. Re 12:3, 4, 16, 17. 13:2, 4, 11. 16:13. 20:2. **My river**. ver. 9. Ezk 28:2. Dt 8:17. Is 10:13, 14. Da 4:30, 31.

4. **I will put hooks**. Ezk *38:4. 2 K 19:28. Jb 41:1, 2. Is 37:29. Am 4:2. **the fish**. Hab 1:14, 15.

5. **I will leave**. Ezk 31:18. 32:4-6. 39:4-6, 11-20. Ps 110:5, 6. Je 8:2. 16:4. 25:33. **open fields**. Heb. face of the field. Je 9:22. **I have**. 1 S 17:44. Ps 74:14. Je 7:33. 34:20. Re *19:17, 18.

6. **know**. Ezk 28:22-24, 26. Ex 9:14. 14:18. **a staff**. 2 K 18:21. Is *20:5, 6. 30:2-7. *31:1-3. 36:6. Je 2:36. 37:7. La 4:17.

7. **they took**. Ezk 17:15-17. Je 37:5-11. **thou didst**. Ps 118:8, 9. 146:3, 4. Pr 25:19. Je 17:5, 6.

8. **I will**. ver. 19, 20. Ezk 5:17. 6:3. 11:8. 14:17. 29:8. 30:4, 5, 10, 11. 33:2. Le 26:33. Je 46:13, etc. **cut**. Ezk 25:13. *32:10-13. Ge 6:7. Ex 12:12. Je 7:20. 32:43.

9. **the land**. ver. 10-12. Ezk 30:7, 13-17. Je 43:10-13. **because**. ver. 3. Jb *41:1, 34. Pr 16:18. 18:12. 29:23.

10. **I will**. ver. 11. Ezk 30:12. Hab 3:8. **utterly waste**. Heb. wastes of waste. **desolate**. Jl 3:19. **from the tower of**. *or*, from Migdol to Syene. Ezk 30:6-9. Ex 14:2. Je 44:1. 46:14. **Syene**. Heb. Seveneh. i.e. *opening, key; seven*, ✻S#5482h. Now *Essnan*, situated at the southern extremity of Egypt (as *Migdol* was at the northern), on the confines of Ethiopia, near the tropic of Cancer, and about lat. 24 degrees N., long. 32 degrees E. Ezk 30:6.

11. **foot of man**. Ezk 30:10-13. 31:12. 32:13. 33:28. 36:28. Je 43:11, 12. **forty**. 2 Ch 36:21. Is 23:15, 17. Je 25:11, 12. 29:10. Da 9:2.

12. **desolate in**. Ezk 30:7. Je 25:15-19. 27:6-11. Na 3:8, 9. **and I will scatter**. We learn from Berosus (apud. Josephus, l. ix. c. 11, sec. 1) that Nebuchadnezzar sent several captive Egyptians to Babylon; and from Megasthenes (apud. Euseb. Praep. Evang. l. ix. c. 41) that he transplanted others to Pontus; and it is probable, that at the dissolution of the Babylonian empire, about forty years after, Cyrus permitted them to return to their native country. Ezk 30:23, 26. Je 46:19.

13. **At the**. Is 19:22, 23. Je 46:26.

14. **Pathros**. Ezk 30:14. Ge 10:14. 1 Ch 1:12, Pathrusim. Is √11:11. Je 44:1. **habitation**. *or*, birth. Ezk 16:3mg. **base**. Heb. low. ver. 15. Ezk 17:6, 14. Zc *10:11.

15. **the basest**. Ezk 17:6, 14. 30:13. Is *19:23. Zc *10:11. **rule**. Ezk 31:2. 32:2. Da *11:42, 43. Na 3:8, 9.

16. **the confidence**. ver. 6, 7. Ezk 17:15-17. Is 20:5. 30:1-6. 31:1-3. 36:4-6. Je 2:18, 19, 36, 37. 37:5-7. La 4:17. Ho 5:13. 7:11. 12:1. 14:3. **bringeth**. Ezk 21:23. Nu 5:15. 1 K 17:18. Ps *25:7. 79:8. Is 64:9. Je 14:10. Ho 8:13. 9:9. He 10:3, 17. Re 16:19. **remembrance**. 2 S 8:16mg. **but**. ver. 6, 9, 21. Ezk 28:22-24, 26.

17. A.M. 3432. B.C. 572. **the seven and twentieth year**. ver. 1. Ezk 1:2.

18. **Nebuchadrezzar**. Ezk *26:7-12. Je 25:9. *27:6. **a great service**. Nebuchadnezzar was thirteen years employed in the siege. During this long siege, the soldiers must have endured great hardships; their heads would become bald by constantly wearing their helmets; and their shoulders be peeled by carrying materials to form the works. **yet**. St. Jerome asserts (on Is 23:6), on the authority of the Assyrian histories, that when the Tyrians saw their city must fall, they put their most valuable effects on board their ships, and fled with them to the islands, and their colonies, "so that, the city being taken, Nebuchadnezzar found nothing worthy of his labor."

19. **I will**. ver. 8-10. Ezk 30:10-12. Je 43:10-13. **take her spoil, and take her prey**. Heb. spoil her spoil, and prey her prey. Ezk 38:12mg.

20. **labor**. *or*, hire. **served**. 2 K 10:30. Is *10:6, 7. 45:1-3. Je 25:9. Da *4:32.

21. **I cause**. Ezk *28:25, 26. 1 S 2:10. Ps 92:10. 112:9. *132:17. 148:14. Is *4:2. *11:1. 27:6. Je *23:5. Zc 3:8. *6:12. Lk 1:69. **the opening**. Ezk 3:26, 27. 24:27. 33:22. Ps 51:15. Am 3:7, 8. Lk 21:15. Col 4:3, 4. **they shall know**. ver. 6, 9, 16.

EZEKIEL 30

The desolation of Egypt and her allies, 1-19. The arms of Pharaoh incurably broken; and those of Nebuchadnezzar strengthened, to execute the judgments of God on Egypt, 20-26.

2. **Howl**. Ezk 21:12. Is 13:6. 14:31. 15:2. 16:7. 23:1, 6. 65:14. Je 4:8. 47:2. Jl 1:5, 11. Zp 1:11. Zc 11:2. Ja *5:1. Re 18:10.

3. **the day is**. Ezk 7:7, 12. Ps 37:13. Ob 15. Jl 2:1. Zp 1:7, 14. Mt 24:33. Ph 4:5. Ja 5:9. Re 6:17. **the day of the Lord**. Is 2:12h. +*13:6. +*34:8. Jl 2:1. Zp 1:7. Zc 14:1h. 1 Th +*5:2. 2 Th 2:2. 2 P *3:10. Re 1:10. 3:3, 11. 16:15. **a cloudy**. ver. 18. Ezk 32:7. 34:12. Ge +9:13. Ex 14:20, 24. Is 19:1. Jl 2:1, 2. Am 5:16-20. **the time of the heathen**. Ezk 29:12. Ps 110:6. +*149:7-9. Is 24:21-23. 34:2, etc. Je 25:15-29. ◐+*30:7. Da 9:27. 12:7. Jl 3:11-14. Zp 3:6, 7. Zc 14:3-19. Lk +21:24. Ro +11:25. Re 19:13-21.

4. **the sword**. Ezk 29:8. Is 19:2. Je 50:35-37. **pain**. *or*, fear. ver. 9. Ex 15:14-16. Ps 48:6, 7. Is 19:16, 17. Re 18:9, 10. **in Ethiopia**. ver. 9. Je 46:9. **and they**. ver. 10. Ezk 29:12, 19. **and her**. Is 16:7. Je 50:15.

5. **Ethiopia**. Is 18:1. 20:4. Je 46:9. Na 3:8, 9. **Libya**. Heb. Phut. i.e. *heart of the sea; afflicted*, ✚S#6316h. Ezk ◐27:10. *38:5mg. Na ◐+*3:9. **Lydia**. Heb. Lud. i.e. *birth; travail*, ✻S#3865h. Ezk 27:10h. Ge 10:6, 22h. 1 Ch 1:17h. Is 66:19h. Je 46:9. Na 3:9. **all the**. Je *25:15-17, 20, 24. 50:37. **Chub**. i.e. *Christ's thorn; bearing fruit; clustered; a horde*, ✻S#3552h, only here.

men. Heb. children. **that is**. Je 44:27. **by the sword**. Je *12:12.

6. **They also**. Jb 9:13. Is 20:3-6. 31:3. Na 3:9. **from the tower of Syene**. *or*, from Migdol to Syene. Ezk 29:10mg. **by the sword**. Jg 7:18. Ps *7:11-13.

7. **they shall**. Ezk 29:12. 32:18-32. Je 25:18-26. ch. 46-51.

8. **shall know**. Ezk 28:24, 26. 29:6, 9, 16. Ps 58:11. **when I**. ver. 14, 16. Ezk 22:31. Dt 32:22. Is 42:25. *66:15. La 4:11. Am 1:4, 7, 10, 12, 14. 2:2, 5. Na 1:5, 6. **destroyed**. Heb. broken. ver. 6.

9. **messengers**. ver. 5, 6. Is 18:1, 2. 20:3-5. Zp 2:12. **careless**. Ezk 38:11. 39:6. Jg 18:7. Is 32:9-11. 47:8. Je 49:31. Zp 2:15. 1 Th *5:2, 3. **great**. ver. 4. Ezk 26:16. 27:35. 32:9, 10. Is 19:17. 23:5. Je 49:21. Zc 11:2, 3. **lo**. Ezk 33:33. Am 4:2.

10. **I will**. Ezk 29:4, 5, 19. 32:11-16. **by the**. ver. 24, 25.

11. **the terrible**. Ezk 28:7. 31:12. 32:12. Dt 28:50. Is 14:4-6. Je 51:20-23. Hab 1:6-9. **and fill**. Ezk 35:8. 39:4, 11-20. Is 34:3-7. Zp 1:17, 18. Re 14:20. 19:18.

12. **I will make**. Ezk 29:3. Is 19:4-10. 44:27. Je 50:38. 51:36. Na 1:4. Re 16:12. **dry**. Heb. drought. Ge 7:22. Ex 14:21. **sell**. Jg 2:14. Is 19:4. **all that is therein**. Heb. the fulness thereof. Ezk +19:7. 1 C 10:26. **by the hand**. Ezk 28:10. 31:12.

13. **I will also**. Ex 12:12. Is *19:1, etc. Je *43:12, 13. *46:25. Zp 2:11. Zc 13:2. **idols**. 2 K +23:24. **images**. ✱S#457h. Le 19:4 (idols). 26:1. 1 Ch 16:26. Jb 13:4 (no value). Ps 96:5. 97:7. Is 2:8, 18, 20, 20. 10:10, 11. 19:1, 3. 31:7, 7. Je 14:14 (thing of nought). Hab 2:18. Zc 11:17. **Noph**. Is 19:13. Je 2:16. 44:1. 46:14. Ho 9:6, Memphis. Heb. Moph. **there shall**. Ezk 29:14, 15. Zc *10:11. **put**. Is *19:16. Je 46:5.

14. **Pathros**. Ezk 29:14. **Zoan**. *or*, Tanis. Nu *13:22. Ps *78:12, 43. Is 19:11. 30:4. **will execute**. Je 46:25. Na 3:8-10.

15. **I will pour**. Ps 11:6. Na 1:6. Re 16:1. **Sin**. i.e. *thorn; clay, mire*, ✱S#5512h. ver. 16. Ex 16:1. 17:1. Nu 33:11, 12. (1) A city of northern Egypt, Ezk 30:15, 16. (2) The Wilderness of Sin is on the east shore of the Gulf of Suez and between Elim and Sinai, Ex 16:1; Nu 33:11. *or*, Pelusium. Now *Tinch*, a town of Egypt, situated at the eastern extremity of the Delta, twenty stadia from the Mediterranean, near the lake of Menzaleh, and upon a branch of the Nile, to which it gave name. It was the key of Egypt on the side of Judea and Syria, and was therefore strongly fortified and garrisoned; but it is now quite in ruins. **the multitude of No**. Je 46:25. Na *3:8-10.

16. **set fire**. ver. 8, 9. Ezk 28:18.

17. **Aven**. i.e. *vanity; perverseness; nothingness*, ✱S#206h. *or*, Heliopolis. (1) Egyptian city of On, or Heliopolis, Ezk 30:17. (2) A plain, probably of Lebanon, Am 1:5. (3) Same as Beth-aven, Ho 10:5, 8. Ge 41:45, On. **Pibeseth**. i.e. *mouth of loathing*, ✱S#6364h, only here. *or*, Pubastum. Situated on the Pelusiac branch of the Nile, near the top of the Delta. **by the sword**. Is *66:16.

18. **Tehaphnehes**. i.e. *beginning of the age or world; thou wilt fill hands with pity*, ✱S#8471h. Je *2:16, Tahapanes. *43:7-9. 44:1. 46:14, Tahpanhes. **the day**. Ex 10:15, 22, 23. Is 5:30. 9:19. 13:10. Jl +3:15. Mt +*24:29. **darkened**. *or*, restrained. **I shall break**. Ezk 29:15. Is 9:4. 10:27. 14:25. **the pomp**. Ezk 31:18. 32:18, etc. Is 14:11. Je 46:20-26. **a cloud**. ver. 3. Is 19:1.

19. **execute judgments**. ver. 14. Ezk 5:8, 15. 25:11, 17. 39:21. Nu 33:4. Ps *9:16. 149:7. Ro *2:5, 6. Re 17:1.

20. A.M. 3416. B.C. 588. **eleventh year**. Ezk 1:2. 26:1. 29:1, 17.

21. **Son of man**. This prophecy was delivered soon after the Egyptians under Pharaoh-hophra had come to relieve Jerusalem, and some months before that city was taken, being the eleventh year of Jeremiah's captivity, and answering to April 26, A.M. 3416. When the king of Babylon took from the king of Egypt, in the days of Pharaoh-necho, all his dominions in Asia, one of his arms was broken. God now declared that he should never recover these territories, or gain any ascendancy in that part of the world; nay, that his other arm, which was now strong, should soon be broken, and rendered utterly useless. This was fulfilled when Hophra was dethroned and driven into Upper Egypt by Amasis; and then Nebuchadnezzar, taking advantage of this civil discord, invaded and conquered that kingdom, and enslaved, dispersed, and carried captive the Egyptians. **I have**. ver. 24. Ps 10:15. 37:17. Je 48:25. **it shall not**. Is 1:6. Je 30:13. 46:11. 51:8, 9. Na 3:19. Re 18:21.

22. **I am**. Ezk 29:3. Je 46:25. **will break**. Ps 37:17. **the strong**. Ezk 34:16. **and that**. 2 K 24:7. Je 37:7. 46:1-12. **I will**. Je 46:21-25.

23. **scatter the Egyptians**. ver. 17, 18, 26. Ezk 29:12, 13. Da *4:35.

24. **I will**. ver. 25. Ne 6:9. Ps 18:32, 39. *37:17. 144:1. Is 45:1, 5. Je 27:6-8. Zc 10:11, 12. **and put**. Dt 32:41, 42. Ps 17:13. Is 10:5, 6, 15. Zp 2:12. **he shall**. Ezk 26:15. Jb 24:12. Je 51:52.

25. **I will strengthen**. Ps *75:7. Da *4:32, 37. **they shall know**. ver. 19, 26. Ezk 29:16, 21. 32:15. 38:16, 23. 39:21, 22. Ps *9:16. **put my sword**. Ps *17:13, 14. Da 4:17.

26. **I will**. ver. 17, 18, 23. Ezk 6:13. 29:12. Da 11:42. **they shall**. ver. 8.

EZEKIEL 31

The prophet is ordered to show Pharaoh the prosperity and pride of the king of Assyria; and his dreadful fall, 1-17; and that he would be destroyed in like manner, 18.

1. **in the eleventh**. On Sunday, June 19, A.M. 3416, according to Usher; and about a month before the capture of Jerusalem. Ezk 1:2. 30:20. Je 52:5, 6.

2. **speak**. Je 1:5, 17. Pr 27:19. Re 10:11. **to his**. Ezk 29:19. 30:10. Na 3:8-10. **Whom**. ver. 18. Is 14:13, 14.

3. **the Assyrian**. Na 3:1, etc. Zp 2:13. **a cedar**. Ezk 17:3, 4, 22. Is 10:33, 34. 37:24. Da *4:10, 20-23. *5:20. Zc 11:2. **with fair branches**. Heb. fair of branches. Ezk 33:32mg. **of an high**. ver. 6. Jg 9:15. Da 4:12.

4. **waters**. Ezk 17:5, 8. Pr 14:28. Je 51:36. Re 17:1, 15. **made him great**. *or*, nourished him. **set**. *or*, brought. **little rivers**. *or*, conduits.

5. **his height**. The Assyrian king, to whom Pharaoh is compared, from his great power, extensive dominion, and the protection he afforded, resembled the spreading branches, thick shade, and high stature of a flourishing cedar on mount Lebanon. The fruitful lands of Assyria; the immense revenues he drew from vast multitudes in his extensive territories; his lucrative

commerce, by the river Tigris, with the countries on the Indian ocean; and all the various sources of his wealth and prosperity, resembled the rivers and streams which cause the trees planted by them to grow and flourish exceedingly; and hence the empire and its head were exalted above all the kingdoms of the earth. Ps 37:35, 36. Is 10:8-14. 36:4, 18, 19. 37:11-13. Da 4:11. **multitude of waters.** ver. 7. Dt +11:10. **he shot forth.** *or*, it sent *them* forth.

6. **the fowls.** Ezk 17:23. Da 4:12, 21. Mt 13:32.

7. **his branches.** ver. 9, 12. Ezk 17:6. Da 4:14. **great waters.** lit. "many waters." Ezk 29:3. Jn +*3:23.

8. **cedars.** Ezk 28:13. Ge *2:8୨ℙ. 13:10. Ps 80:10. Is 51:3. **nor any.** Ps 37:35. Is 10:7-14. 36:4-18. 37:11-13. **garden of God.** ♪24L, Ge +6:2. Ezk 28:13. Ge 2:8. 13:10.

9. **made.** Ezk 16:14. Ex 9:16. Ps 75:6, 7. Je *46:20. Da 2:21, 37, 38. 4:22-25. 5:20-23. **all the trees.** Ezk 17:22-24. Jg 9:8-20. Ps 96:12, 18. Is 55:12, 13. Zc 11:2. **of Eden.** Ge *2:8୨ℙ. **garden of God.** ♪24L, Ge +6:2. **envied.** Ge 26:14. 37:11. 1 S 18:15. Ps *73:3. Pr 27:4. Ec 4:4. Ja 4:5, 6.

10. **Therefore.** The allegory and its interpretation are here combined; and the Assyrian monarch, though already destroyed, is poetically addressed. **Because.** Mt 23:12. **and his.** ver. 14. Ezk 28:17. 2 Ch 25:19. 32:25. Jb 11:11, 12. Pr 8:13. 11:2. *16:18. 18:12. Is 14:13-15. Da 4:30. 5:20. Ob 3. Ja *4:6.

11. **delivered.** Ezk 11:9. 21:31. 23:28. Jg 16:23. Je 43:8-10. 44:30. 46:22-24. 1 T 1:20. **the mighty.** Nebuchadnezzar, the subverter of the Assyrian empire. Ezk *32:11, 12. Je 25:9. Da 5:18, 19. **he shall surely deal with him.** Heb. in doing he shall do unto him. Jg 1:7. Ps *39:11. Mt *7:1, 2. Ja *2:13. **I have driven.** Le 18:24-28. 20:22, 23. Dt 18:12. La 1:21. Na 3:18.

12. **strangers.** Ezk 28:7. 30:11. Is *19:4. Hab *1:6, 11. **upon.** Ezk 32:4, 5. 35:5, 8. 39:4. Is 34:5-7. **rivers.** or, torrents. ✥S#650h. Ezk 6:3. 32:6. 34:13. 35:8. 36:4, 6. 2 S 22:16. Jb 6:15. Ps 18:15. 42:1. 126:4. SS 5:12. Is 8:7. Jl 1:20. 3:18. A watercourse, constrained by rocks or pipes or rocky channels (CB). **gone.** Da 4:12-14. Na 3:17, 18. Re 17:16.

13. **his ruins.** Ezk 29:5. 32:4. Is 18:6. Re 19:17, 18.

14. **the end.** Dt 13:11. 21:21. Ne 13:18. Da 4:32. 5:22, 23. 1 C 10:11. 2 P 2:6. **the trees.** ♪142, Ge +20:16. **stand up in their height.** *or*, stand upon themselves for their height. **delivered.** Ps *82:7. Ec +*12:7, 8. He +*9:27. **the nether.** or, lowest. Dt +32:22 (✱S#8482h). Ezk 32:18-32. Ps 63:9, 10. **pit.** Heb. *bor*, Ge 37:20.

15. **grave.** Heb. *sheol*, Ge +37:35. Ezk √32:27. **I caused a.** The deep and all the mighty rivers which cherished this fair tree are here described as mourning at his downfall: they stop their usual courses to bewail his fate; and Lebanon with all its stately trees (his confederates and allies), sympathize with him in his misfortunes. Na 2:8-10. Re 18:9-11, 18, 19. **mourn.** Heb. be black. Ml 3:4.

16. **made.** Ezk 26:10, 15. 27:28. Na 2:3. Hg 2:7. He 12:26, 27. Re 11:13. 18:9, etc. **when I.** Ezk 32:18, etc. Is 14:15. **hell.** Heb. *sheol*, Ge +37:35. Ezk √32:27. **pit.** Heb. *bor*, Ge +37:20 (✱S#953h). Is 14:19. **and all.** ver. 9, 18. Is 14:8. Hab 2:17. **of Lebanon.** Is 10:12, 13, 17-19, 33, 34. **shall be comforted.** ver. 14. Ezk

32:31. Is 14:15. **nether.** ver. 14. Dt +32:22 (✱S#8482h).

17. **went.** Ezk 32:20-30. Ps 9:17. Is √14:9-15. **into.** ver. 15, 16. Ezk 32:21. **hell.** Heb. *sheol*, Ge +37:35. Ezk √32:27. **that were.** Ezk 30:6-8, 21-25. Na 3:17, 18. **dwelt.** ver. 3, 6. Ezk 32:31. La 4:20. Da 4:11, 12. Mk 4:32.

18. **To whom.** Pharaoh is here called upon to look in this mirror, and see the termination of his glory and greatness. **art thou.** ver. 2. Ezk 32:19. **among the trees.** Ps *37:35, 36. Is 14:18-20. Ezk 46:24, 26. **with the.** ver. 9, 16. **thou shalt.** Ezk +*28:10. 32:10, 19, 21, 24, etc. 1 S 17:26, 36. 2 S 1:20. Je 9:25, 26. **This is.** That is, the judgment that befell the king of Assyria, is an exact representation of the destruction that remains for Pharaoh and all his people. 2 Ch 28:22. Ps 52:7. Mt 13:19. 26:26-28. 1 C *10:4.

EZEKIEL 32

A lamentation over the dreadful fall of Pharaoh and Egypt, 1-10, as destroyed by the sword of the king of Babylon, 11-16. Pharaoh and his subjects brought to hell, with the nations of the uncircumcised, 17-32.

1. A.M. 3417. B.C. 587. **in the twelfth.** On Wednesday, March 22, A.M. 3417, the twelfth year of Jeconiah's captivity, about a year and a half after the destruction of Jerusalem, and at a time when Pharaoh was in power and prosperity. ver. 17. Ezk 1:2. 29:1, 17. 30:20.

2. **take up.** ver. 16, 18. Ezk 19:1. 27:2, 32. 28:12. Je 9:18. **Thou art like.** Ezk 19:2-6. 38:13. Ge 49:9. Nu 24:9. Pr 28:15. Je 4:7. Na 2:11-13. **and thou art as.** Ezk *29:3. Ps 74:13, 14. Is 27:1. 51:9. **whale.** or, dragon. lit. long "extended" object. Ezk 29:3. Jb 30:29. **and troubledst.** Ezk 34:18. **with thy feet.** Dt 11:10. Pr +21:1. **fouledst.** Ezk 34:18, 19. Nu ❶19:17mg. Ro 6:4. **rivers.** lit. "flowings." ver. 14. S#5104h. Ezk 1:1, 3. 31:4, 15. Ge 2:10, 13, 14. 15:18. Ex 7:19 (streams). Jsh 24:2 (flood). Jg 3:8mg. Jb 20:17mg. Ps 24:2 (floods). Zc 9:10.

3. **I will.** Ezk 12:13. 17:20. Ec 9:12. Je 16:16. La 1:13. Ho 7:12. Hab 1:14-17. Mt +*13:47.

4. **leave thee upon.** Ezk 29:5. 31:12, 13. 39:4, 5, 17-20. 1 S 17:44-46. Ps 63:10. 74:14. 79:2, 3. 83:9, 10. 110:5, 6. Is *14:19. 18:6. 34:2-7. +*66:24. Je 8:2. 25:33. Jl 3:19. Re *19:17, 18.

5. **And I.** To represent the power, rapaciousness, and cruelty of Pharaoh, he had been compared to a fierce young lion, and also to an immense, overgrown sea monster, or crocodile; and it is predicted that God would cast a net over him, by which many companies of people should drag him out of his rivers, and cast him into the open field, mountains, valleys, etc. to be devoured by birds and beasts of prey; that is, his ruin would be complete, and attended with terrible miseries to the Egyptians, and afford a large booty to their enemies. **height.** ♪102, Ge +2:24.

6. **water.** ♪102, Ge +2:24. Ex 7:17. Is 34:3, 7. Re √14:19, 20. 16:6. **the land.** Egypt, so called because interspersed by numerous canals, and overflowed annually by the Nile. **wherein thou swimmest.** *or*, of thy swimming. **rivers.** 2 S +22:16. **full.** ♪102, Ge +2:24.

7. **put thee out.** *or*, extinguish thee. 2 S 14:7 (quench). 21:17. 2 Ch 29:7. Jb *18:5, 6. Pr *13:9. SS

8:7h (quench). Is *42:3. +*66:24. **I will cover the heaven.** ſ102, Ge +2:24. Destroy the empire. Ezk 30:3, 18. Ex 10:21-23. Is *13:9-11. 34:4. Je 13:16. Jl 2:2, 31. **make the stars.** Overwhelm the dependent states. But compare the similar imagery used to describe the time of distress immediately following the great tribulation. Is √13:9, 10. Je √2:31. √3:15. Am 5:18-20. *8:9. Zp 1:15. Mt √24:29. Mk 13:24. Lk 21:25. 2 P 3:10, 12. Re *6:12, 13. **dark.** Pr +*20:20. **the sun.** The king. **the moon.** The queen, or some state less than the kingdom. Re 8:12.

8. **All.** ſ102, Ge +2:24. **bright lights of heaven.** Heb. lights of the light in heaven. Ge 1:14♀. **dark.** Heb. them dark. Pr +*20:20. **set darkness upon.** Involve the whole land in desolation and woe.

9. **vex.** Heb. proke to anger, or grief. Re 11:18. 18:10-15. **when.** Ezk 29:12. 30:23, 26. Je 25:15-25.

10. **amazed.** Ezk 27:35. Dt 29:24. 1 K 9:8. **my sword.** Dt 32:41. **horribly afraid.** Jsh *2:11. **and they.** Ezk 26:16. 30:9. Ex 15:14-16. Je 51:9. Zc 11:2. Re 18:10. **life.** Heb. nephesh, Ge +44:30. **in the day.** Ezk 27:27.

11. **The sword.** Ezk 26:7. 30:4, 22-25. Je *27:6. 43:10. 46:13, 24-26.

12. **the mighty.** Ezk 31:11. **the terrible.** Ezk 28:7. 30:11. 31:12. Dt 28:49, 50. Hab 1:6, 7. **they shall.** Ezk 29:19. Is 25:2, 3.

13. **destroy.** Ezk 29:8. 30:12. **neither.** ver. 2. Ezk 29:11. 34:18.

14. **and cause.** The neighboring countries shall be in a state of quietness, like a river that smoothly glides along, having no longer a political crocodile to foul their waters, or to disturb their peace. Ezk 34:18. Jb 41:1.

15. **destitute of that whereof.** Heb. desolate from the fulness thereof. Ezk 29:12, 19, 20. Ps 24:1. 107:34. **then.** Ezk 6:7. 30:26. Ex 7:5. *14:4, 18. Ps *9:16. 83:17, 18.

16. **the lamentation.** ver. 2. Ezk 26:17. 2 S 1:17. 3:33, 34. 2 Ch *35:25. Je 9:17, 18. **the daughters.** Jg *11:40.

17. **in the twelfth year.** ver. 1. Ezk 1:2. **the fifteenth.** That is, of the twelfth month, just a fortnight (for fourteen nights, or two weeks) after the preceding prophecy.

18. **wail.** ver. 2, 16. Ezk 21:6, 7. Is 16:9. Mi 1:8. Lk 19:41. Ro 12:15. **cast them down.** That is, predict that they shall be cast down. Ezk 20:25n. 43:3. Je 1:10. Ho 6:5. **the daughters.** The cities and colonies of the celebrated nations afterwards enumerated. Nu +21:25mg. **unto the.** ver. 21, 24, etc. Ezk 26:20. +31:14. Ps 30:9. 63:9. Is *14:15. **nether.** Dt +32:22 (✳S#8482h). **with them.** Ge 6:5. **pit.** Heb. bor, Ge +37:20.

19. **Whom dost.** Ezk 27:3, 4. 28:12-17. 31:2, 18. **go down.** Is √14:9-15. **with the uncircumcised.** ver. 21, 24, 29, 30. Ezk +*28:10. 1 S 17:26, 36. Je *9:25, 26.

20. **fall.** ver. 23-26, 29, 30. Ezk 29:8-12. **slain by.** ſ53, 2 S +1:19. **she is delivered to the sword.** or, the sword is laid. **draw her.** Ps 28:3. Pr 24:11. Je 22:19.

21. **The strong.** Pharaoh is here represented as descending into the regions of the dead, whither many mighty warriors and potentates had gone before him, who welcome him to their dreary mansion. The bold imagery of eastern poetry abounds in these descrip-

tions: yet they imply the general belief, that when the body is cast into the grave, the soul enters an invisible state, where it retains its consciousness and capacities (Scott). ver. +√27n. 1 S 28:12n. **shall speak.** ?ſ155D, Ge +4:10. Ezk 31:15, 16. Is *14:10, 16. Lk 16:24. **out of.** Is 1:31. √14:9, 10. +*30:33. +*66:24. Lk √16:23, 24. **hell.** Heb. sheol, Ge +37:35. **gone down.** ver. +*19, 24, 25. Nu +*16:30-34n. Ps +*9:17. +*55:15. Pr +*14:32.

22. **Asshur is there.** ver. 24, 26, 29, 30. Ezk 31:3, etc. Ge 10:11. Nu 24:24. 2 K 19:35. Ps 83:8-10, Assur. Is +*30:33. *37:36-38. Na 1:7-12. 3:1, etc. Re *19:20. *20:10. **graves.** Heb. qeber, Ge +23:4.

23. **graves.** The niches in the sides of the subterranean burying places. Heb. qeber, Ge +23:4. Ezk 26:20. Is √14:15. **pit.** Heb. bor, Ge +37:20. **grave.** Heb. qeburah, Ge +35:20. **which caused.** ver. 24-27, 32. Ezk 26:17, 20. Is √14:16. 51:12, 13. **terror.** or, dismaying. or, downfall. ver. 24, 25, 26, 27, 30, 32. Ezk 26:17. Je 48:39. 49:37. **the land of the living.** Ezk +*26:20. Jb 28:13. Ps 27:13. 116:9. 142:5. Is 38:11. Je 11:19.

24. **Elam.** Ge *10:22. 14:1. 1 Ch 1:17. Je 25:25. *49:34-39. Da 8:2. **grave.** Heb. qeburah, Ge +35:20. **which are.** ver. 18, 21. Ezk 26:20. **which caused.** ver. 23. **borne their shame.** ver. 25, 30. Ezk +*16:52, 54. 34:29. 36:6, 7, 15. 39:26. 44:13. Je 3:24, 25. Hab 2:16. **pit.** Heb. bor, Ge +37:20.

25. **set her.** Ps 139:8. Re 2:22. **a bed.** A cell, or bier, in the sepulchral vault, in which the corpse was deposited. 2 S 4:7. 2 K 6:12. Jb 7:13. **all of them uncircumcised.** See on ver. 19, 21. Ezk +*28:10. 44:7, 9. 2 S 1:20. 1 Ch 10:4. Ac 7:51. **though their terror.** Mt +*10:28. Lk *12:4, 5. **land of.** Ezk +26:20. **pit.** Heb. bor, Ge +37:20.

26. **Meshech.** Supposed to be the Moschi, a people between Iberia (Spain) and Armenia (ancient country now divided between Turkey, Soviet Russia, and Iran. See Minni, Je +51:27), from whom, probably, the Muscovites (ancient Russians) are descended. Ezk *27:13. √38:2, 3. √39:1. Ge 10:2, 12. 1 Ch 1:5. Ps 120:5. **Tubal.** Probably the Tibarenians, a people of Pontus, west of the Moschians (an ancient people of Asia, south of the Caucasus, who are mentioned in classical writers with that of the Tibareni, two tribes generally identified with Meshech and Tubal). Ge +10:2. **graves.** Heb. qeber, Ge +23:4. **all of them uncircumcised.** ver. 19, 20, 24. **caused their terror.** ver. 23, 27, 32.

27. **shall not lie with.** ver. 21. Jb 3:13-15. Is √14:18, 19. **to hell.** Heb. sheol, Ge +37:35. That is, to the grave; and are buried in their armor, with their weapons lying by their sides, as was a very ancient practice in various nations. Sir J. Chardin, in a MS. note on this place, observes, "In Mingrelia they always sleep with their swords under their heads, and their other arms by their sides; and they inter them with their arms placed in the same manner." This practice seems to have arisen from the belief that they attended them into a future state of existence. Virgil (Aen. l. vi. 52) describes his heroes thus in the Elysian fields: "These pleasing cares the heroes felt alive, For chariots, studs, and arms, in death survive" (Pitt). Theologically the issue here is, does sheol ever represent the literal grave, or does it always represent the world of the unseen dead? Through an incomplete induction of Scripture evidence, some have mistakenly asserted that bodies

are never placed in *sheol*, only in *qeber* (the grave). This passage appears to have been left unaccounted for, for here not only bodies but weapons are so placed. However, this is elevated Hebrew poetry, and the unusual use of *sheol* found here is not generally sustained elsewhere, but see the references. The context shows that this is not a theological description of the destinies of the saved or unsaved dead, but a description of the terror of military defeat, and the dishonor of being left unburied (ver. 19, 21). Those who would press this passage into service as a prooftext to prove that there is no conscious existence after death, and that *sheol* is an exact synonym for the *grave*, must not object if the reference at ver. 21 to the mighty speaking "out of the midst of hell" is taken equally literally by others to show that Scripture does indeed teach the conscious existence of the dead, the eternal conscious punishment of the wicked or unsaved dead, as taught clearly elsewhere (See on Ezk +*18:4n, 20n). There is a progress of doctrine to be seen in Scripture; although Moses was learned in all the wisdom of the Egyptians (Ac 7:22), which people certainly believed in a conscious afterlife, Moses did not write a full account of the nature of the intermediate state. No doubt these matters were left unrevealed in part, because of the dreadful distortions of the truth found in the false religions of Israel's idolatrous neighbors. Rather, we are left with these matters relatively unrevealed (Dt 29:29) until "life and immortality" was brought to light at the appearing of our Savior Jesus Christ (2 T 1:10). Jesus spoke more about hell than any other person in the New Testament, and warned us unmistakably that its punishment is conscious torment (Mk 9:43-46. Lk 16:24), and lasts forever (Mt +*25:46). **with.** T#1005‡, 1006‡. Ps 16:10. Am *9:2. **their weapons of war.** Heb. weapons of their war. Is 54:17. 2 C 10:4. **but their iniquities.** Ezk +*18:20n. Jb 20:11. Ps 49:14. 92:7, 9. 109:18. Pr +*14:32. Jn +*8:24.

28. **thou shalt be broken.** Je 25:15, 16, 18-26. Da 2:34, 35.

29. **Edom.** Ezk ch. 25, 35. Ge 25:30. 36:1, etc. Is ch. 34. 63:1-6. Je 49:7-22. La 4:21, 22. Am 1:11, 12. Ob 1, 2, etc. Ml 1:3, 4. **laid.** Heb. given, *or* put. ver. 23. Ezk 31:14. 35:12. **pit.** Heb. *bor*, Ge +37:20.

30. **the princes.** The kings of Media, Armenia, and other nations north of Chaldea, or of the Syrians and others north of Judah, with "all the Zidonians," kings of Zidon, Tyre, and other cities of Phoenicia. Ezk *38:6, 15. *39:2. Je *1:14. 4:6. **the Zidonians.** Ezk *28:21-23. Ge *10:15. 1 K *5:6. Je 25:22. **and bear.** ver. 24, 25. **pit.** Heb. *bor*, Ge +37:20.

31. **Pharaoh shall.** Pharaoh, who said he was a *god*, shall be found among the dead. Ezk +*28:9. **shall be comforted.** Pharaoh shall console himself, when he sees all these mighty nations and proud conquerors in the same condition as himself. This is spoken according to the common sentiments of mankind, who are better satisfied to suffer with a multitude than alone; though it can be no comfort to those who have perished in their sins, to find multitudes as miserable as themselves (Lk 16:24), Scott. Ezk 14:22. 31:16. La 2:13.

32. **I have caused.** ver. +*27. Ge 35:5. Jb 31:23. Je 25:15, 29-33. Zp 3:6-8. 2 C 5:11. He 10:31. Re 6:15-17.

EZEKIEL 33

The prophet is instructed in the duties of his office, as the watchman of Israel, 1-9; commanded to state the rule by which God dealt with them, and the equity of his conduct, 10-20; informed of the destruction of Jerusalem; and ordered to expose the vain hopes and crimes of those who remained in the land, 21-29; and shown the hypocrisy and covetousness of those, who came to hear the word of God from him, 30-33.

2. **speak.** ver. 17, 30. Ezk 3:11, 27. **When I bring the sword upon a land.** Heb. A land when I bring a sword upon her. Ezk 6:3. 11:8. 14:17, 21. 21:9-16. Le 26:25. Je 12:12. 15:2, 3. 25:31. 47:6, 7. Zc 13:7. **set.** ver. 7. 2 S 18:24-27. 2 K 9:17-20. Is 21:6-9. 56:9, 10. 62:6. Je 51:12. Ho 9:8.

3. **blow the trumpet.** ver. 8, 9. Ne 4:18, 20. Is *58:1. Je 4:5. 6:1. 51:27. Ho 8:1. Jl 2:1. Am +*3:6. 1 C 14:8.

4. **whosoever heareth.** Heb. he that hearing heareth. 2 Ch 25:16. Pr *29:1. Je *6:17, +*19. 42:20-22. Zc 1:2-4. Ja *1:22. **his blood.** ver. 5, 9. Ezk *18:13. Le 20:9, 11, etc. 2 S 1:16. 2 K 2:37. Ac 18:6. *20:26, 27. **head.** ʃ171Q12, Jg +5:30.

5. **heard.** Ps 95:7. He *2:1-3. **trumpet.** Am +*3:6. **his blood.** Is 51:2. Jn 8:39. **But.** Ex 9:19-21. 2 K 6:10. Ac *2:37-41. Col *1:28. 1 T √4:6, 16. He 11:7. **soul.** Heb. *nephesh*, Ge +12:13.

6. **and blow.** Is 56:10, 11. Am +*3:6. 1 C 14:8. **person.** Heb. *nephesh*, Jsh +10:28. **he is.** ver. 8, 9. Ezk +*18:20n, 24. Pr +*14:32. Jn +*8:21-24. **his blood.** Ezk √3:18-20. 34:10. Ge +*9:5. 42:22. 2 S 4:11.

7. **I have.** Ezk √3:17-21. SS 3:3. 5:7. Is 62:6. Je 6:27. 31:6. Mi 7:4. Ep *4:11. He √13:17. **thou shalt.** Ezk 2:7, 8. 1 K 22:14, 16-28. 2 Ch 19:10. Je 1:17. +*23:28n. 26:2. Ac *5:20. √20:20, 26, 27. 1 C 11:23. +*15:3. Col 1:28, 29. 1 Th 4:1, 2. **soul.** Heb. *nephesh*, Ge +12:13.

8. **O wicked.** ver. 14. Ezk *18:4n, 10-13, 18, 20n. Ge +*2:17. 3:4. Pr 11:21. Ec *8:13. Is 3:11. Je 8:13. **surely.** ʃ147B, Ge +2:16. **if thou.** Ezk 13:9, 10. Je 8:11, 12. 14:13-16. **that wicked.** ver. 6. Nu 27:3. Ac √20:26, 27.

9. **if thou.** Ezk 3:19, 21. Ps *40:9, 10. Mt +*24:4, 25. Ac 13:40. 18:5, 6. 28:23-28. Ga *5:19-23. *6:7, 8. Ep *5:3-6. Ph +*3:18, 19. 1 Th 4:3-8. 5:14. Re +*1:5. **if he.** Pr 15:10. *29:1. Lk +*12:47. Jn +*8:24. Ac √13:46. He √2:3. 12:25. **thou hast.** Ac *20:26. 2 C 2:15-17. **soul.** Heb. *nephesh*, Ge +12:13.

10. **If our.** The impenitent Jews seem to have charged the prophet's messages with inconsistency: for whilst he warned them to repent, and assured the penitent of forgiveness, he also predicted that the people "would pine away in their transgressions." The prediction, however, merely implied that God foresaw that the people in general would be impenitent, though some individuals would repent and be pardoned. Ezk 24:23. Le 26:39. **pine away.** Ezk 4:17. Le 26:39‼Ρ. **how.** Ezk 37:11. Ps 130:7. Is *49:14. 51:20. Je 2:25.

11. **As I live.** Ezk 5:11. *14:16-18. 16:48. Nu 14:21, 28. Dt +32:40. Is 49:18. Je 22:24. 46:18. Zp 2:9. Ro *14:11. **I have.** Ezk *18:23, 32. 2 S 14:14. La *3:33. Ho 11:8. Lk *15:20-32. 1 T +√2:4. 2 P +√3:9. **no pleasure.** Je 27:13. Jn 5:40. **but that.** Lk *15:7. **turn ye.** ʃ84, Ge +6:17. Ezk *14:6. *18:30, 31. Le √26:39-42. Pr *1:23. *8:36. Is 44:22. √55:6, 7. Je *3:12, 22.

31:18-20. Da *9:13. Ho 14:1. Ac +*3:19. 26:20. **why.** ⌐85L, Ge +27:45.

12. say. ver. 2. **The righteousness.** ver. 18. Ezk 3:20, 21. *18:24-26. 2 S *24:10-15. **as for.** ver. 19. Ezk *18:21, 27-32. 1 K 8:48-50. 2 Ch +√7:14. Mt 21:28-31. Ro *3:25. **neither.** 1 J *2:1.

13. if. Ge +4:7. Je +7:5. 2 P +*1:10. **he trust.** Ezk *3:20. *18:24. Lk *18:9-14. Ro *10:3. Ph 3:9. He +*10:38. 2 P √2:20-22. 1 J √2:19. **to his own righteousness.** Is √64:6. Ro *10:3. He *6:4-6. *10:26, 29. 2 P √1:9. **he shall die.** Ezk √18:4n, 24. Ro √6:23.

14. Thou shalt. ver. 8. Ezk 3:18, 19. 18:27. Is 3:11. Je 18:7, 8. Lk *13:3-5. **surely.** ⌐147B, Ge +2:16. **if.** Je +7:5. 1 C +*15:2. **he turn.** Pr √28:13. Is √55:7. Je 4:1. Ho 14:1. Ac +*3:19. **and do.** Mt √7:21. Jn +√13:17. He +*5:9. **that which is lawful and right.** Heb. judgment and justice. Ezk *18:5mg, 21, 27. Ps +*15:1-5. Je +*22:3. Mi +√6:8. Ml +*3:5. Mt *9:13. 1 C +*6:9-11. Ga *5:19-23. He √6:9-12. Ja *1:26, 27. *3:17. √4:17. 2 P √1:5-11. 1 J √2:3, 29. *5:17.

15. restore. "The sin is not forgiven, unless that which is taken away be restored," says Augustine. Ezk *18:7, 12, 16. Ex *22:26, 27⌐⌐. Le 6:2, 4, 5⌐⌐. Dt 24:6, 10-13, 17⌐⌐. Jb 22:6. 24:3, 9. Am 2:8. **give again.** ⌐41, Ge +10:1. Ex *22:1-4. Le 6:2-5. Nu 5:6-8. Lk √19:8, 9. Ep √4:28. **walk.** Ezk 20:11, 13, 21. Le *18:5. Ps 119:93. Lk 1:6. Col +*1:10. **statutes of life.** Le *18:5. Ro √3:20. 7:10, *12, 16, *22. Ga √2:16, 21. *3:24. **he shall.** Ezk 18:27, 28. Le 18:5⌐⌐. Ro *2:7. Re *22:12-14. **shall not.** ⌐144D, Ge +40:23.

16. None of his sins. Ezk +*18:22. Ps 79:8. Is *1:18. *43:25. *44:22. Mi √7:18, 19. Ro 4:7. 5:16, 21. He 8:12. 1 J *2:1-3. Since the unsaved will go to hell to suffer eternal punishment (Ezk +*18:4n, 20n; Mt +25:46), while the saved upon death go immediately to be with Christ (2 C +5:8. Ph +1:23); since the unsaved will experience eternal torment (Lk 16:24), while the saved experience eternal life (Jn 11:25, 26. Re +*14:13), there is no middle ground (Jn √3:36). The sins of the saved person "shall not be mentioned unto him" (Ezk +*18:22), for Christ died for our sins (2 C √5:15, 17, 21), forever purged our sins by his shed blood (Ep 1:7. Re 1:5) by the forever complete and perfect sacrifice of himself just once (He 10:10-12) on the cross (1 P 2:24). In Christ we are a new creature (2 C *5:17), justified by faith (Ro 5:1), no longer under condemnation (Jn 3:18. 5:24. Ro 8:1), possessing the righteousness of Christ (Ph 3:9), ready to be presented faultless before God (Ju 24), on the basis of our placing faith in his finished work for us (Ep 2:8-10).

17. the children. ver. 20. Ezk +*18:4n, 20n, 25, 29. Jb 35:2. 40:8. Mt 25:24-26. Lk 19:21, 22. **The way.** Ezr *9:13. Ps *50:21. **their way.** Is √55:8, 9. **not equal.** ⌐23, Ezk +18:25.

18. righteous turneth from. ver. 12, 13. Ezk *18:26, 27. 2 Ch *24:2, 17, 18, 24, 25. He +*10:38, 39. 2 P √2:20-22.

19. But if. ver. +√14. Je +7:5. **turn from.** Ezk 18:27, 28. 2 Ch +√7:14. *33:1, 2, 12, 13.

20. Yet. T#272. ver. 17. Ezk *18:25, 29. Ge +*18:25. Pr +14:9 (T#706). 19:3. Mt 25:24, 25. Lk +19:14 (T#695). Ro 3:7, 8. 9:9-19, +20 (T#273), 21. **I will judge.** Ezk *18:30. Dt *32:4, 5. Ps *50:6. 62:12. Ec 12:14. Zp 3:5. Mt *16:27. Jn *5:29. 2 C √5:10. He 12:23. Re √20:12-15. *22:12.

21. in the twelfth. This was on Wednesday, January 25, A.M. 3416 or 3417. According to the date here given, this escaped Jew did not come to the prophet, with intelligence of Jerusalem being smitten, until about eighteen months after the event; but instead of the "*twelfth year,*" eight MSS. and the Syriac read the *eleventh.* Ezk 1:2. **one that.** Ezk 24:26, 27. **The city.** This was the very message which God had promised the prophet, Ezk 24:26. 2 K 24:4, etc. 25:2, 4. 2 Ch 36:17, etc. Je 39:2-8. 52:4-14.

22. the hand. ⌐22A14.8L, 1 K +18:46. Ezk 1:3. 3:22. 37:1. 40:1. **and my.** Ezk 3:26, 27. ♣*24:26, 27. 29:21.

24. they that. The small remnant which continued in the land under Gedaliah, after the desolation of Jerusalem, flattered themselves, notwithstanding all of their other crimes, that they should inherit the whole land. ver. 27. Ezk 5:3, 4. 34:2. Je 39:10. 40:7-10. 52:6. **wastes.** ver. 27. Ezk 36:4. **the land of Israel.** Ezk 11:17. **Abraham was one.** Heb. *echad,* Dt +6:4n. Is *51:2. **he inherited the land.** Ac ◐+√7:5. **but we.** Mi 3:11. Mt 3:9. Lk *3:8. Jn *8:33, 39. Ro 4:12. 9:7. 1 Th *5:3. **is given us.** Nu ch. 34. Dt *34:3, 4. Jsh ch. 13-16, 18, 19.

25. Ye eat. Ge *9:4. Le +*3:17n. 7:26, 27. √17:10-14. √19:26)⌐⌐. Dt 12:16, 23-25. 1 S 14:32-34. Ac *15:20, 21, 29. 21:25. **lift up.** Ezk 18:6, 12, 15. Dt 4:19. Ps 24:4. Je 44:15-19. **idols.** Ezk +30:13. **and shed.** Ezk *9:9. 22:6, 9, 27. **shall ye.** ⌐76, Ge +13:6. Je 7:9, 10.

26. Ye stand. Ge 18:8, 22. 27:40. Mi 2:1, 2. Zp 3:3. **work abomination.** Ezk 18:12. Le 18:26-30. 20:13. 1 K 11:5-7. 1 P 4:3. Re +*21:8, 27. **ye defile.** Ezk 18:6, 11, 15. 22:9-11. Ex +*20:14. Je 5:8, 9. *23:10. Ja *4:4. **shall ye possess.** ⌐76, Ge +13:6. Le 18:25, 28. 20:22. Dt 4:25, 26. 29:18-23. Jsh 23:15, 16. 1 S 2:30. Ps 50:16-20. 94:20, 21. Is *1:19, 20. Mt +*5:5.

27. surely. ver. 24. Ezk 5:12-17. 6:11-14. Je 15:2-4. 42:22. 44:12. **will I give.** Ezk 39:4. Dt 32:24, 25. Re *6:8. **to be devoured.** Heb. to devour him. **in the caves.** Ge +19:30. Jg 6:2. 1 S 13:6. 22:1. 23:14. 24:3. Je 41:9.

28. I will lay. Ezk 6:14. 12:20. 15:8. 36:34, 35. 2 Ch 36:21. Is 6:11. Je 9:11. 16:16. 25:11. *44:2, 6, 22. Mi 7:13. Zc 7:13, 14. **most desolate.** Heb. desolation and desolation. ver. 29. Ezk 6:14. 35:3mg, 7mg. **and the pomp.** Ezk 7:24. 24:21. 30:6, 7. **and the mountains.** Ezk 6:2-6. 36:4.

29. shall. Ezk 6:7. 7:27. 23:49. 25:11. Ex 14:18. Ps *9:16. 83:17, 18. **because.** Ezk 6:11. 8:6-15. 22:2-15, 25-31. 36:17, 18. 2 K 17:9-18. 2 Ch *36:14-17. Je 5:1-9, 25-31. Mi 6:9-12. Zp 3:1-4.

30. the children. Je 11:18, 19. 18:18. **against thee.** *or,* of thee. 2 K 6:12. Ec +*10:20. Lk *12:3. **Come.** Is √29:13. 58:2. Je *23:35. 42:1-6, 20. Mt *15:8. 22:16, 17.

31. as the people cometh. Heb. according to the coming of the people. Ezk 8:1. 14:1. 20:1, etc. Lk +*10:39. Ac *10:33. **they sit before thee as my people.** *or,* my people sit before thee. Mt *15:7, 8. *23:27, 28. **and they hear.** Je 6:16, 17, +*19. 43:1-7. 44:16. Pr *23:12. Mt √7:24-27. Lk +*6:48, 49. *8:21. +*11:28. Ja *1:22-24. 1 J *3:17, 18. **will not do.** Lk +*6:46. Ja +*1:22. **with their mouth.** Ps *78:36, 37. Is √29:13. Ja √2:14-16. 1 J *3:17, 18. **show much love.** Heb. make loves, *or,* jests. Is *28:13. Je *23:33-38. Mt +*12:36.

Lk √16:14. Ep √5:4. 1 J √3:18. **their heart**. 2 S +24:45mg. Hab +*2:9. Mt 6:24. *13:22. 19:22. Lk √12:15-21. Ep +*5:5. Col *3:5. 1 T √6:9, 10. **their covetousness**. Ezk +*16:49. Ps +*10:3. Pr +*11:24. Ac *5:2. 1 T +*6:5.

32. **of one**. Mk 4:16, 17. 6:20. Jn 5:35. **a pleasant voice**. Heb. a song of loves. Ezk 31:3mg. **play well**. 1 S 16:17. Ps 33:3. Is 23:16. **they hear**. Is +*6:9. Jb +*37:2. Je +*29:19. Lk +*8:18. +*11:28. **do them not**. 2 S +24:45mg. Mt √7:21, 26, 27. Lk +√6:46.

33. **when**. 1 S 3:19, 20. Je 28:9. Jn *8:28. **it will come**. Mt *24:35. **shall**. Ezk *2:5. 2 K 5:8. Is 41:23. Lk 10:11. Jn √14:29.

EZEKIEL 34

The shepherds of Israel are sharply rebuked and severely threatened, 1-10. The Lord promises to be the Shepherd of his scattered flock, and to feed and tend them in his pastures and fold, 11-16; to punish the powerful oppressors among the Jews, and to rescue the oppressed, 17-22. Figurative predictions of Christ and his kingdom, 23-31.

2. **the shepherds**. The *shepherds* of Israel, signify their kings and princes, priests and prophets; the *flock*, the whole of the people; the *fat* and *wool*, the tithes and offerings, taxes and imposts: these they exacted with great rigor, and even oppressed and destroyed the people to enrich themselves; but they bestowed no pains to provide for the welfare of the state, or for the souls of those entrusted to them. They knew nothing about their flock: it might be diseased, infirm, bruised, maimed, strayed, or lost, for they watched not over them. Ezk 33:24. Je 2:8. 3:15. 10:21. 12:10. Jn *10:1, 2, 12. **Woe**. ver. 8-10. Ezk 13:19. Je 23:1. Mi *3:1-3, 11, 12. Zp 3:3, 4. Zc 11:17. Mt +*24:45-51. Lk +*12:42-46. 20:46, 47. Ro 16:18. 2 P *2:3. ✗110. Maledictio; or, Imprecation B940. Expression of feeling by way of malediction or execration. For other instances of this figure see Dt 28:16. Ru 1:16. 1 S 3:17. Ps 109:6-19. Is 3:11. Je 48:46. Mt 11:21. 2 T +*4:14. **feed themselves**. Is 56:11. Zc 11:5, 16, 17. **feed the flocks**. 2 S 5:2. Ps 78:71, 72. Is 40:11. Jn *21:15-17. Ac *20:26, 29. 1 P *5:2-4.

3. **eat**. Le *3:14-17. 1 S 2:15-17. Is *56:11, 12. Zc *11:5, 16. **ye kill**. Ezk 19:3, 6. 22:25-28. 33:25, 26. 1 K 21:13-16. 2 K 21:16. Is 1:10, 15. Je 2:30. 22:17. La 4:13. Mi 3:1-3. Zp 3:3.

4. **diseased**. ver. 16. Is 56:10. Je +*8:22. Zc 11:15, 16. Mt *9:36. He 12:12. **neither**. ✗129. Paradiastole; or, Neithers and Nors B238. The repetition of the disjunctives *neither* and *nor*, or *either* and *or*. For other instances of this figure see Lk 18:29. Jn 1:13. Ro 8:35. 1 C 3:21, 22. 2 Th 2:2. **sought**. Mt 10:6. 18:12, 13. Lk 15:4-6. **but with**. Ex 1:13, 14⁹℘. Le 25:46, 53℘℘. Je 22:13. Mt 21:35. 24:49. 2 C 1:24. Ja +*5:1-6. 1 P *5:2, 3. Re 13:14-17. 17:5, 6.

5. **they were**. ver. 6. Ezk 33:21, 28. 1 K *22:17. 2 Ch 18:16. Je 23:2. 50:6, 17. Zc 13:7. Mt *9:36. **because there is no shepherd**. *or*, without a shepherd, and so ver. 8. Nu *27:15-17. Zc 10:2, 3. **and they became**. ver. 8. Is 56:9. Je 12:9-12. Jn *10:12. Ac 20:29-31.

6. **wandered**. Ezk 7:16. Je 13:16. 40:11, 12. Mt 18:12. He 11:37, 38. 1 P *2:25. **my flock**. Jn *10:16. **scattered**. Mt 26:31. **face**. Ge +1:2. **and none**. Ps 142:1. Je 5:1.

7. **ye shepherds**. ver. 9. Ps 82:1-7. Is 1:10. Je 13:13, 18. 22:2, 3. Mi 3:8, 9. Ml 2:1. Mt 23:13-36. Lk 11:39, etc.

8. **prey**. ver. 5, 6, 31. **the shepherds**. ver. 2, 3, 10, 18. Ac 20:33. 1 C 9:15. 2 P 2:13. Ju 12.

9. **O ye shepherds**. ver. 7.

10. **I am**. Ezk 5:8. 13:8. 21:3. 35:3. Je 21:13. *23:1, 2. 50:31. Na 2:13. Zc 10:3. 1 P 3:12. **and I will**. Ezk *3:18, 20. *33:6-8. Je 13:18-20. Ro *14:10. 2 C *5:10. He √13:17. **and cause**. 1 S 2:29-36. Je 39:6. 52:9-11, 24-27. **neither shall**. ver. 2, 8. **for I will**. ver. 22. Ps *23:5. 72:12-14. 102:19, 20.

11. **I, even I**. ✗84, Ge +6:17. Ezk 5:8. 6:3. Ge 6:17. Le 26:28. Dt 32:39. Is 45:12. 48:15. 51:12. Ho 5:14. **search**. Ps *23:1-3. 80:1. 119:176. Is 40:10, 11. 56:8. Je 23:3. 31:8. Mt 13:11, 12. Lk +√19:10. Jn √10:16, 27-29.

12. **As a shepherd seeketh out**. Heb. According to the shepherd's seeking of, etc. 1 S 17:34, 35. Lk 15:4-6. Jn 10:11, 12. **all places**. Ezk *28:25. 36:24. 37:21, 22. Dt +30:3n. Je *23:3, 4. **in the cloudy**. Ezk +*30:3. Ge +9:13. Is 50:10. Je 13:16. Jl 2:1-3. Am 5:18-20. Zp 1:15. Ac 2:19-21.

13. **I will bring**. T#378. ver. 23-29. Ezk 11:17. 20:40-42. 28:25, 26. 36:1-15, 24, 33-36. 37:1-3, 11-24, +*25 (T#949), 26-28. 38:8. *39:24-29. Dt 30:1-6. Ps 106:47. Is √11:11-16. 27:6, 13. 49:22, 23. 65:9, 10. 66:19, 20. Je 3:17, 18. 16:14-16. *23:3, 4, 8. 30:3, 18. 31:8. 32:37. 46:27, 28. Ho 1:10, 11. *3:4, 5. 14:5-7. Am √9:14, 15. Mi 2:12, 13. *4:6, 7. Zp 3:19, 20. Zc *10:6-10. Lk *21:24. **and feed**. Ezk 36:18-25. Mi 7:14, 15. **rivers**. 2 S +22:16.

14. **feed them**. ver. 27. Ps *23:1, 2. 34:8-10. Is 25:6. 30:23, 24. 40:11. Je 31:12-14, 25. Jn *10:9. Re 7:16, 17. **there shall**. Je 33:12, 13.

15. **feed**. Ps *23:2. Je *23:4. **I will cause**. Ps *23:2. SS 1:7, 8. Is 11:6, 7. 27:10. 65:9, 10. Je 3:15. 31:2. Ho 2:18. Zp 3:13. Jn *21:15.

16. **seek that**. ver. 4, 11. Is *40:11. *61:1-3. Mi *4:6, 7. Mt 11:28. 15:24. *18:11-14. Mk *2:17. Lk *5:31, 32. *15:4-7. +*19:10. 22:31, 32. **and bring**. Jn +*10:16. **but I**. Ezk 39:18. Dt 32:15. Is 5:17. *10:16. Je 50:11. Am 4:1-3. **I will feed**. Is *49:26. Je 9:15. *10:24. 23:15. Mi 7:14.

17. **as for**. ✗63B, Ge +2:10. **I judge**. ver. 20-22. Ezk 20:37, 38. Zc *10:3. Mt √25:31-33. **cattle and cattle**. Heb. small cattle of lambs and kids. ✗84, Ge +6:17. Ex 12:3mg,n. **he goats**. Heb. great he goats. Ezk 39:18mg. Is 1:11mg.

18. **a small**. Ezk 16:20, 47. Ge 30:15. Nu 16:9, 13. 2 S 7:19. Is 7:13. **to have**. ver. 2, 3. Mi 2:2. 3 J 9, 10. **tread**. Ezk 32:2. Mt 15:6-9. 23:13. Lk 11:52. **deep waters**. Ezk 32:14. **foul**. Ezk 32:2. Nu ◐19:17. Ro 6:4. **with**. Is 1:12.

20. **Behold**. ver. 10, 17. Ps 22:12-16. Mt 25:31-46. **even I**. ✗84, Ge +6:17. **fat cattle**. Is 10:16. Am 4:1.

21. **ye have**. ver. 3-5. Da 8:3-10. Zc 11:5, 16, 17. **pushed**. Lk 13:14-16.

22. **will I**. ver. 10. Ps 72:12-14. Je 23:2, 3. Zc 11:7-9. **and I**. ver. 17.

23. **I will**. Ec 12:11. Is *40:11. Je 23:4-6. Mi *5:2-5. Zc 13:7. Jn √10:11, 14. He *13:20. 1 P *2:25. *5:4. **shall feed**. Is 30:20, 21. *40:11. Je 3:15. 23:3, 4. **my servant David**. ✗121A5, Ge +9:27. *David* king of Israel had been dead upwards of 400 years; and from that time till now there never has been a ruler of any kind

in the Jewish nation of the name of David. By *David*, then, we must understand the *Messiah*, as the Jews themselves acknowledge, so called because descended from him, and also as being the *well beloved, o agapatos*, Son of the Father, as the name imports, and in whom all the promises to David were fulfilled. See the references. For a contrasting viewpoint which holds that David, resurrected, will reign over Israel in Jerusalem, see Ho 3:5n. ver. 24. Ezk 37:24, 25. 1 K 11:32, 34. 14:8. Is 11:1. +*55:3, 4. Je √30:9. Ho *3:5. Lk *1:32, 33. Re 22:16.

24. **I the Lord will.** ver. 30, 31. Ezk 36:28. 37:23, 27. 39:22. Ex 29:45, 46. Is 43:2, 3. Je 31:1, 33. 32:38. Zc 13:9. Re 21:3. **a prince.** Ezk 37:22. Jsh 5:13-15. Ps 2:6. Is +*9:6, 7. 55:4. Je *23:5, 6. 33:15-17. Mi +*5:2. Mt 28:18. Lk 1:31-33. Ac 5:31. 1 C 15:25. Ep 1:21, 22. Ph *2:9-11. He +*2:9, 10. Re 19:13-16.

25. **I will make.** Ezk *37:26. Is +*55:3. Je *31:31-33. Zc 6:13. He *13:20. **and will.** Le *26:6. Jb 5:22. Is √11:6-9. *35:9. Ho *2:18-23. **and they.** ver. 28. Ps 4:8. Je *23:6. 33:16. **wilderness.** Ps 65:12.

26. **make them.** Ge +*12:2. *22:18. Is √19:24. 49:6. 53:11. Zc *8:13, 23. Ep *2:13-15. **my hill.** Ezk 20:40. Ps *2:6. 68:16. 132:14-16. 133:3. Is *2:2-4. *56:7. Mi *4:1, 2. **I will cause.** Le 26:4. **showers.** Dt 28:12. Ps 68:9. Is 32:15, 20. 44:3. Zc 10:1. Ml √3:10.

27. **the tree.** Ezk 47:12. Le *26:4. Ps *85:12. *92:12-14. Is *4:2. 35:1, 2. 61:3. Je *31:12. Jn *15:5-8. **the earth.** Ezk 35:14. *36:30. Le +*26:4. Ps 67:6. 85:12. Ro +*8:18-23. **safe in their land.** Ezk 28:26. 38:8, ●11. Is +*11:11. Je +*23:6. Am √9:14, 15. **know that.** Ezk 33:29. 39:28. He +*8:10, 11. **when I.** ver. 10. Le *26:13. Is *9:4. √10:27. √14:2, 3. 52:2, 3. Je *2:20. √30:8. Ro +*11:25. **the bands of.** Is 58:6. **served.** Je 25:14. 27:7.

28. **they shall.** It is evident that this prophecy could at most have only a typical accomplishment in the return from captivity under Zerubabel, and in their subsequent prosperity; but the restoration from the Jews from their present captivity, and the consequent peace and prosperity of the church and the world, fully answer to this energetic language. In the clearer light on prophecy available to us nearly two centuries since the preceding words of this note were written, we should modify it to say "the consequent peace and prosperity of Israel and the world during the millennial reign of Christ fully answer to this energetic language." ver. 8. Ezk 36:4, 15. Is +*11:11. Am √9:11-15. **neither.** ver. 25, 29. Je *30:10. 46:27. **dwell safely.** Ezk *39:26. Je 32:37. **none shall.** Zp 3:13.

29. **I will.** Is 4:2. +*11:1, etc. 53:2. Je +*23:5. 33:15. Zc 3:8. 6:12. **of renown.** *or,* for renown. Ps 72:17. Is +*9:6. **consumed.** Heb. taken away. ver. 26, 27. Ezk 36:29. Is 49:9, 10. Re 7:16. **neither.** Ezk 36:3-6, 15. Re 21:3, 4.

30. **they know.** ver. 24. Ezk 16:62. *37:27. Ps 46:7, 11. Is 8:9, 10. Mt 1:23. 28:20.

31. **ye my.** Ezk 36:38. Ps 77:20. 78:52. 80:1. 95:7. 100:3. Is 40:11. Mi 7:14. Lk *12:32. Jn *10:11, 16, 26-30. 20:15-17. Ac +*20:28. 1 P 5:2, 3. **I am your God.** ver. 24. Ex 29:46. Jn +*20:28.

EZEKIEL 35

A prophecy and judgment against the Edomites of mount Seir for their hatred of Israel, and insulting over their distress, 1-15.

1. **word of the Lord came.** Ezk 21:1. 22:1. 34:1. 2 P +*1:21.

2. **set.** Ezk 6:2. 20:46. 21:2. 25:2. Is 50:7. Ep 6:19. **mount.** Ezk 25:8. Ge 32:3. 36:8, 9. Dt *2:5. Jsh 24:4. 2 Ch 20:10, 22, 23. 25:11-14. **and prophesy.** Ezk 25:12-14. 32:29. Ps 83:3-18. Is ch. 34. *63:1-6. Je *9:25, 26. 49:7-22. La 4:21, 22. Am 1:11, 12. Ob 1, 10, etc.

3. **I am.** Ezk 5:8. 21:3. 29:3, 10. Je 21:13. Na 2:13. 3:5. **and I will stretch.** Ezk 6:14. Je 6:12. 15:6. 51:25. **most desolate.** Heb. desolation and desolation. ver. 7mg. Ezk 5:15. 33:28mg.

4. **lay.** ver. 9. Ezk 6:6. Is *34:5. Je 49:7, 8. Jl 3:19. Ml 1:3, 4. **thou shalt know.** ver. 9, 12. Ezk 6:7. Ex 9:14. 14:4.

5. **thou hast had.** ver. 12. Ezk 25:12. Ge 25:22, 23. 27:26, 28, 29, 41, 42. Ps *137:7. Am *1:11, 12. Ob *10-16. **perpetual hatred.** *or,* hatred of old. Heb. *olam*, Ge +9:12. Ezk 25:15. **shed the blood of.** Heb. poured out. Je 18:21mg. **force.** Heb. hands. Je 18:21. **in the.** Ezk 21:25, 29. Ps 137:7. Da *9:24. Ob 11.

6. **I will.** Ps 109:16. Is 63:2-6. Ob 15. Mt *7:2. Re 16:5-7. 18:6, 24. 19:2, 3. **since.** Ps *109:17.

7. **most desolate.** Heb. desolation and desolation. ver. 3mg, 9. Ezk 33:28mg. **passeth.** Ezk 29:11. Jg 5:6, 7. 2 Ch 15:5, 6.

8. **fill his mountains.** Ezk 31:12. 32:4, 5. 39:4, 5. Is 34:2-7.

9. **I will make.** After being subdued by Nebuchadnezzar, about five years after the destruction of Jerusalem, many of the Edomites, during the Babylonian captivity, being driven from their ancient habitation by the Nabatheans, seized upon the southwestern part of Judea (Strabo, l. xvi); but afterwards they were conquered by Hyrcanus, and reduced to the necessity of embracing the Jewish religion (Josephus, Ant. l. xiii. c. 9. sec. 1); and at last became either incorporated with that nation, or swallowed up and lost among the Nabathean Arabs, so that the very name was abolished and disused about the end of the first century after Christ. Their country is now barren; and their cities, even Bozra and Petra, totally demolished and in ruins (See Prideaux's *Connection*, an. 129, Newton on the Prophecies, Dissert. iii., and Burckhardt's *Trav. in Syria*, etc.). 2 K 14:7n. Je 49:16n. **perpetual.** Heb. *olam*, Ge +9:12. ver. 4. Ezk 25:13. Je 49:17, 18. Zp 2:9. Ml *1:3, 4. **and ye.** Ezk 6:7. 7:4, 9. 36:11.

10. **thou hast.** Ezk 36:5. Le 25:23. Nu 35:34. Ps *83:4-12. Je 49:1. Ob 13. **whereas.** *or,* though. Ezk *36:2, 5. *48:35. Ps 48:1-3. 76:1. 132:13, 14. Is 12:6. 31:9. Zp 3:15-17. Zc 2:5.

11. **I will even.** Ps 137:7. Am 1:11. Mt *7:2. Ja *2:13. **and I.** Ps *9:16. 83:17, 18.

12. **And thou.** ver. 9. Ezk 6:7. **I have heard.** Ps 94:9, 10. **they are given.** Ezk 36:2. Ps 83:12. **consume.** Heb. devour. ver. 10. Ezk 39:4mg.

13. **with.** 1 S *2:3. Ch 32:15, 19. Is 10:13-19. 36:20. 37:10, 23, 29. Da 11:36. Ml 3:13. 2 P 2:18. Ju 15, 16. Re *13:5, 6. **boasted.** Heb. magnified. Je 48:26, 42. **have multiplied.** Jb 34:37. 35:16. Ps 73:8, 9. Ec 10:14mg. **I have.** ver. 12. Ex 16:12. Nu 14:27. 2 K 19:28. Je 29:23.

14. **whole earth rejoiceth.** Ezk +*34:27. Is 14:7, 8. 35:1, 2, 6, 7. *65:20-25. Ro 8:20-22. **I will.** Is *65:13-15. Je ●48:47n. Ml *1:3, 4.

15. **didst rejoice at.** Ezk 36:2-5. Ps *137:7. Pr +*17:5. La 4:21. Ob 12, 15. **shalt.** ver. 3, 4. **Idumea.**

Ezk 36:5. Is 34:5, 6. Mk 3:8. **and they**. ver. 4, 9. Ezk 39:6, 7. Ps *9:16. La 4:21, 22.

EZEKIEL 36

The insults and blasphemies of the heathen over Israel's desolations rebuked, with threatenings against them, 1-7. Promises of abundant and permanent blessings to the mountains of Israel, 8-15. God had cast out Israel for their sins; and he promises to restore them, not for their deservings, but for the honor of his own name, 16-24. Promises of abundant spiritual blessings, and of great temporal prosperity, accompanied by the deepest self-abasement and prayers of those who received them, 25-38.

1. **the mountains**. Ezk 6:2, 3. 33:28. 34:14. 37:22. Ps *125:2. **hear**. ver. 4, 8. Ezk 20:47. 37:4. Je 22:29.

2. **Because**. ver. 5. Ezk 25:3. 26:2. Ps *40:15. **hath said**. ✳122, Ex +15:9. **even**. Dt 32:13. Ps 78:69. Is 58:14. Hab 3:19. **ancient**. Heb. *olam*, Jb +22:15. **high places**. Ge 49:26. Dt 33:15. **our's**. Ezk 35:10. Je 49:1.

3. **Because**. Heb. Because for because. Ezk 13:10. Le 26:43. **they have made**. Je ch. 39, 41, 52. La ch. 1-5. **swallowed**. Jb 5:5. Ps 35:25. 56:1, 2. 57:3. 61:1. Pr 1:12. Ec 10:12. Je 51:34. La 2:2, 5, 16. **and ye**. Dt 28:37. 1 K 9:7, 8. Ps 44:13, 14. 79:10. Je 18:16. 24:9. 33:24. La 2:15. Da 9:16. **taken up in the lips of talkers**. *or*, made to come upon the lip of the tongue. **and are**. Jb 30:1-10. Ps 35:15, 16. 69:12. Mt 27:39-44. 1 C 4:13.

4. **ye mountains**. ✳38G, Dt +32:1. **Thus saith**. ✳112, Is +24:3. **to the mountains**. ver. 1, 6. Dt 11:11. Mi 6:2. **rivers**. *or*, bottoms, *or*, dales. Ezk +*31:12. 2 S 22:16. **desolate**. ver. 33-35. Ezk 6:14. 33:24, 27. 2 Ch *36:17-21. Is 6:11. 24:1-12. **a prey**. Ezk 34:28. Ps 79:4. Is 64:10, 11. Je 25:9-13. 29:10.

5. **Surely**. Ezk 38:19. Dt *4:24✝℗. Is 66:15, 16. Zp 3:8. Zc 1:15. **against the**. ver. 3. Je 25:9, 15-29. Zp 2:8-10. **against all**. Ezk 25:8-14. ch. 35. Ps *137:7. Is 34:5. 63:1-6. Je 49:7-22. La 4:21. Am 1:11, 12. Ob 1, etc. Ml 1:2-4. **appointed**. Ezk 35:10-12. Ps 83:4-12. Je 49:1. **with the**. Ezk 35:15. Pr *17:5. 24:17, 18. Ob 12. Mi 7:8. **with despiteful**. Ezk 25:12, 15. Am 1:11. **minds**. Heb. *nephesh*, Ge +23:8.

6. **the land of Israel**. Ezk +11:17. **the mountains**. ver. 4, 5, 15. Ezk 34:29. Ps 74:10, 18, 23. *123:3, 4.

7. **I have lifted**. ✳22A14.8K, Ex +6:8. Ezk 20:5, 15. Ge 14:22. Ex 6:8✝℗. Nu 14:30✝℗. Dt 32:40✝℗. Da 12:7. Re 10:5, 6. **the heathen**. Ezk ch. 25-35. Je 25:9, 15-29. ch. 47-51. La *4:22. Am ch. 1. Zp ch. 2.

8. **O mountains**. ✳38G, Dt +32:1. **ye shall**. Ezk *34:26-29. Ps 67:6. 85:12. Is 4:2. 27:6. 30:23. Ho 2:21-23. Am √9:13-15. **for**. The Edomites, and other enemies of the Jews, who thought they would soon be in possession of the whole land of Judea, might be assured that the predicted seventy years of the captivity were wearing away, and the time would soon arrive when the Jews would repossess and cultivate their own land, and eat its fruits. **at hand**. Ezk 12:25. Ph 4:5. He 10:37. Ja 5:8, 9.

9. **I am for you**. Le *26:42. Dt *11:11. Ps 46:11. Ro √8:31. **I will turn**. Ps 99:8. Ho 2:21-23. Jl 3:18. Am √9:14. Hg 2:19. Zc 8:12. Ml *3:10, 11.

10. **I will**. ver. 37. Is 27:6. 47:17-23. Je 30:19. 31:27, 28. 33:12. Zc 8:3-6. **the wastes**. ver. 33. Is 51:3. 52:9. 58:12. 61:4. Je 31:10-14. Am √9:14, 15.

11. **I will multiply**. Je 31:27. 33:12. **and I will settle**. The circumstances of the Jews were never so prosperous after the captivity as they had been before; hence this prophecy must refer to their preservation from idolatry, and their adherence to the worship of God; and especially of the coming of the promised Savior. These predictions refer also to a future return of the Jews to their own land, when converted to Christ; and then indeed the Lord "will do better" unto them and their land, than at their beginnings. Je 30:18. 31:38-40. Ho 2:22, 23. Ob 19-21. Mi 7:14, 15. **will do better**. ver. 35. Is 30:26. +*54:7-10. +*65:17. Je 23:5-8. 31:17. Jl 3:18-21. Am √9:15. Hg 2:6-9. Zc 8:11-15. √10:6. He +*8:8-13. 11:40. **and ye**. Ezk 35:9. 37:6, 13. Is 52:4-6. Ho 2:20. 1 J *5:20.

12. **I will cause**. The prophet is still personifying the mountains, valleys, and wastes of Judea. **they shall**. Je 32:15, 44. Ob 17-21. **no more**. ver. 13. Ezk 5:17. 14:15. Ge 42:36. Nu 13:32. Je 15:7.

13. **thou land devourest**. Nu 13:32✝℗. 2 K *17:25, 26.

14. **no more**. Ezk 37:25-28. Is 35:9. 60:21. Am √9:15. **bereave**. *or*, cause to fall.

15. **men**. ver. 6. Ezk 34:29. Is 54:4. 60:14. Mi 7:8-10. Zp 3:19, 20. **thou bear**. Ps 89:50. Zp 2:8.

17. **they defiled**. Le 15:19✝℗. *18:24-28, 30✝℗. Nu 35:33, 34✝℗. Ps 106:37, 38. Is 24:5. Je *2:7. 3:1, 2, 9. 16:18. Mi 2:10. **as the**. Ezk 22:10. Le 15:19✝℗, etc. 18:19✝℗. Is √64:6.

18. **I poured**. Ezk 7:8. 14:19. 21:31. 2 Ch 34:21, 25. Is 42:25. Je 7:20. 44:6. La 2:4. 4:11. Na 1:6. Re 14:10. 16:1, etc. **for the**. Ezk 16:36-38. 23:37. Nu *35:33. 2 K 24:3, 4. **idols**. ver. 25. 2 K +23:24.

19. **I scattered**. Ezk 5:12. 22:15. Le 26:33✝℗. Dt 28:64✝℗. Am 9:9. **according to their way**. Ezk 7:3, 8. 18:30. 22:31. 39:24. Ro *2:6. Re *20:12-15.

20. **they profaned**. The Jews, when thus scattered, appeared to them an abject and wretched company of people. They were recognized as worshippers of Jehovah wherever they went; but they were looked upon as a viler and more worthless race than any of the idolaters among whom they were driven. Many would ascribe their wickedness to the tendency of their religion, which they abhorred, and not to their acting inconsistently with it; and regard their miseries, not as the punishment of their sins, but as proofs of God's inability to protect them. This profanation of his holy name, Jehovah was determined to wipe away, by showing mercy to them. ver. 23. Is 52:5. Le *18:21. 19:12✝℗. Am 2:7. Ro ♭2:24. **These**. Ex 32:11-13. Nu 14:15, 16. Dt *28:63. Jsh 7:9. 2 K 18:30, 35. 19:10-12. Je 33:24. Da 3:15.

21. **I had pity**. Ezk 20:9, 14, 22. Dt 32:26, 27. Ps 74:18. Is 37:35. 48:9. **profaned among**. Ro 2:24.

22. **not for your sakes**. ver. 32. Dt 7:7, 8✝℗. 9:5-7✝℗. Ps 106:8. 115:1, 2. T 3:5.

23. **sanctify**. Ezk 20:41. 38:22, 23. Nu 20:12, 13. Dt *28:58. Ps 46:10. Is 5:16. *48:11. +52:5. Ro 2:24. 1 P +*3:15. **and the heathen**. Ezk 39:28. Ex 15:4-16. Ps 102:13-16. 126:1-3. Da 2:47. 3:28, 29. 4:2, 3, 34-37. 6:26, 27. **when I shall**. Ezk 20:41. 28:22. *37:28. 38:23. 1 P *2:9. **in you**. ✳159. Repetitio; or, Repetition B263: repetition of the same word or words irregularly in the same passage. Here (ver. 23-29) the words "you" and "your" are very frequently thus repeated, giving great emphasis to the whole of this precious promise

for Israel in the latter day. The use of this figure strongly forbids the interpretation of this passage to any but Israel (ver. 22, 32). For other instances of this figure see Jn 14:3. 16:12-15. Ga 4:9. 1 Th 5:1, 3. 2 T 3:14, 15. Re 8:7-12. **their.** *or*, your. Ezk 28:25. 38:16.

24. **take you from.** Ezk 11:17. +*34:13. 37:21, 25. 39:27, 28. Le 25:23. Dt *30:3-5)𝒫. Ps 107:2, 3. Is √11:11-16. 27:12, 13. 43:5, 6. Je 23:3-8. 30:3, 18. 31:8. 32:37. 50:17-20. Ho 1:11. Am √9:14, 15. Ro +*11:25, 26.

25. **Then.** Ex 17:8. Ml 3:4, 16. Mt 25:1. 1 Th 4:17. Note the importance of "then," as pointing in context to the *time* to which this prophecy applies; notice likewise the "when" of Ezk +*34:27, and the "afterward" of Jl 2:28. A disregard for the time element indicated in these prophecies has led to much misapplication of Scripture. **will I sprinkle.** Le *14:5-7. Nu 8:7. *19:13-20. Ps *51:7. Is *44:3. *52:15. Jn +*3:5. Ac +1:5. T √3:5, 6. He *9:13, 14, 19. +√10:22. 1 J *5:6. **water.** ∫22K4, Je +2:13. **filthiness.** ver. 17, 29. Ezk *37:23. Ps *51:2. Pr *30:12. Is 4:4. Je *33:8. Zc *13:1. Ac +*22:16. 1 C *6:11. 2 C *7:1. Ep *5:26, 27. T *2:14. He *9:14. 1 J √1:7. Re +*1:5. *7:14. **from all your idols.** Is *2:18-20. 17:7, 8. Je 3:22, 23. Ho 14:3, 8. Zc 13:2. **cleanse.** ∫22C24, Ps +51:2.

26. **new heart.** ∫52A1. Correspondence: simple alternation B367. Simple alternation, consisting of four members: two series with two members each. The *first* corresponds with the *third*, and the *second* with the *fourth*. Here, "heart" and "spirit" are repeated. Examples cited by EWB in B include Jsh 9:22-25. Pr 1:8-19. Is 32:5-7. Je 17:5-8. He 1:11. This figure occurs frequently, and may involve subject matter rather than words. Examples are cited in B and the margins of the Companion Bible, and will not be marked here. T#799. Ezk 11:19, 20. Dt *30:6. Ps *51:10. 110:3. Je 24:7. 31:18, *33. *32:39. 50:4, 5. Jn *3:3-5. 2 C *3:18. √5:17. Ga 6:15. Ep √2:10. 2 T *1:9. T *3:5. Re 21:5. **the spirit.** Heb. *ruach*, Ge +41:38. **stony.** Ezk *11:19, 20. Zc *7:12. Mt *13:5, 20, 21. Mk *4:16, 17. 2 C 3:3.

27. **I will.** Ezk 37:14. 39:29. Pr 1:23. Is 44:3, 4. 59:21. Jl *2:28, 29. Zc √12:10. Lk *11:13. Ro √8:9, 14-16. 1 C *3:16. *6:19. Ga √5:5, 22, 23. Ep +*1:13, 14. 2 Th √2:13. T √3:3-6. 1 P 1:2, 22. 1 J *3:24. **spirit.** Heb. *ruach*, Ge +41:38. **and cause you.** Ezk *37:24. Je +*31:33. Ga 5:16. Col 2:6. Ph √2:12, 13. T √2:11-14. He *13:21. 1 J *1:6, 7. 2 J 6. **my statutes.** Ex 12:24, 43. 30:21. Dt +4:1)𝒫. He 9:1. **my judgments.** Ex 21:1. Dt +4:1)𝒫. 5:1. 6:1. 12:1. Ml 4:4.

28. **dwell in the land.** ver. *10. Ezk 28:25. 37:25. 39:28. Ge *13:14-17. Am √9:15. **be my people.** Ezk 11:20. 37:23, 27. Le 26:12)𝒫. SS 6:3. Je 30:22, 32. 31:33. 32:38. Ho 1:10. Zc 13:9. Mt 22:32. 2 C √6:16-18. 7:1. He +*8:10. +*11:16. Re 21:3, 7.

29. **save.** ver. +*25. Je 33:8. Ho 14:2, 4, 8. Jl 3:21. Mi 7:19. Zc 13:1. Mt +*1:21. Ro 6:14. *11:26. T *2:14. 1 J √1:7-9. **call for.** ver. 8, 9. Ezk +*34:27, 28. Ps 105:6. Ho 2:21-23. Mt √6:33. **lay no famine.** Ezk 34:29.

30. **I will.** Ezk +*34:27. Hg 2:19. **reproach.** Dt 29:23-28)𝒫. Jl 2:17, 26.

31. **shall ye.** Ezk 6:9. 16:61-63. 20:43. Le 26:39. Ezr 9:6, etc. Ne 9:1-3, 26-35. Je 31:18-20. Da *9:4-20. **evil.** Is +45:7. **shall lothe yourselves.** Jb 42:6. Is 6:5. +*64:6. Zc √12:10, 11. Lk *18:13. Ro *6:21. 2 C √7:10, 11.

32. **not for your.** T#342. ver. 22. Dt 9:5. Da 9:18, 19. Mt +8:8 (T#663). Ac +20:24 (T#586). 1 C +4:7 (T#668). 2 T √1:9. T √3:3-6. **be ashamed.** Ezk 16:63. Ezr 9:6. Ro √6:21. 1 P √4:2, 3.

33. **In the day.** ∫171T2, Ge +2:17. **cleansed you.** Dt 9:4, 6. Mi *7:18. **cause you to dwell.** Zc 8:7, 8. **wastes.** ver. 10. Is 58:12. Je 32:43. 33:10. 50:19, 20. Am √9:14, 15.

34. **shall be tilled.** La *3:31, 32. **whereas it lay desolate.** Ezk 6:14. Dt 29:23-28. 2 Ch 36:21. Je 25:9-11.

35. **they shall.** Ps 58:11. 64:9. 126:2. Je 33:9. **like the garden of Eden.** Ezk 28:13. 37:13. Ge *2:8, 9)𝒫. 13:10. Is *51:3. Jl 2:3.

36. **the heathen.** Ne 4:6-9. **shall know.** Ezk 17:24. 34:30. 37:28. 39:27-29. Mi 7:15-17. **I the Lord have.** Ezk 22:14. 24:14. 37:14. Nu *23:19. Ho 14:4-9. Mt √24:35. 2 C *1:20.

37. **I will yet.** Ezk 14:3. 20:3, 31. Ps 10:17. 102:17. Is √55:6, 7. Je *29:11-13. 50:4, 5. Zc √10:6, 7. 13:9. Mt *7:7, 8. Ph *4:6. He √4:16. 10:21, 22. Ja *4:2, 3. 1 J √5:14, 15. **I will increase.** ver. 10. Ps *81:10.

38. **holy flock.** Heb. flock of holy things. Is 66:20. Ro *12:1. 15:16. Ph 2:17. **as the flock.** Ex 23:17. 34:23. Dt 16:16. 2 Ch 7:8. 30:21-27. 35:7, etc. Ps 23:1, 2. 77:20. 80:1. 95:7. Zc 8:19-23. Lk *12:32. Jn *10:14. Ac 2:5-11. **solemn feasts.** Ge +17:21h. Le *23:2n. **the waste.** ver. 33-35. Ezk 34:31. Je 30:19. 31:27, 28. Jn √10:16. Re 7:4-9.

EZEKIEL 37

By a vision of the resurrection of dry bones, the restoration of Judah and Israel from their hopeless condition is prefigured and predicted, 1-14. The reunion of Judah and Israel is predicted, by the uniting of two sticks in the prophet's hand, 15-22. The blessings of their union under Christ their king, 23-28.

1. **The hand.** In this vision, the *dry bones* aptly represent the ruined and desperate state of both Israel and Judah; and the *revivification* of these bones signifies their restoration to their own land after their captivity, and also their recovery from their present long dispersion. Although this is the genuine scope of the vision, yet the doctrine of a general resurrection of the dead may justly be inferred from it; for "a simile of the resurrection," says Jerome, after Tertullian and others, "would never have been used to signify the restoration of the people of Israel, unless such a future resurrection had been believed and known; because no one attempts to confirm uncertain things by things which have no existence." Ezk 1:3. *3:14, 22. 8:1. 33:22. 40:1. 2 P *1:21. Re 1:10. **carried.** Ezk *8:3. 11:24. 1 K 18:12. 2 K 2:16. Lk *4:1. Ac 8:39. 2 C 12:1-4. **in the spirit.** Heb. *ruach*, Is +48:16. Ezk 3:12. ∫121A4. Metonymy of the Cause B543. The *Spirit* is put for special revelations and visions communicated by Him. For other instances of this figure see 2 Th 2:2. 1 J 4:1-3. Re 1:10. 4:2. 17:3. 21:10. **the valley.** ver. 2. Ezk 3:22h, 23h (plain). ◖17:22-24. Am 1:5. Zc 12:11. 14:4, 5. **full of bones.** ver. 11. Ps *141:7. Da +*12:2. 1 C *15:22. Ep 2:1.

2. **pass by them.** Ne 2:12-16. Ps ◖48:12-14. Lk 19:41-44. **valley.** *or*, champaign. Dt 11:30. **they were.** ver. 11. Ps 32:4. 141:7. Ep 2:1.

3. **can.** Je 30:10-17. Jn *6:5, 6. Ro *11:15. **O Lord God.** Dt *32:39. 1 S *2:6. Je *32:17, 27. Jn *5:21.

√11:25, 26. Ac 26:8. Ro *4:17. 2 C *1:9, 10. He 11:19.

4. Prophesy. ver. 11, 15, 16. Nu 20:8. 1 K +13:2n. +*17:20-22. Mt 21:21. Lk *7:14. Jn 2:5. *11:43. **O ye.** Ezk 36:1. Is +*26:19n. 42:18. Je 22:29. Mi 6:2. Jn √5:25, 28, 29. Ac 17:30. **hear.** Ps 119:25, 50. Jn √5:24. He *4:12.

5. I will. ver. 9, 10, 14. Ge +*2:7n. Ps 104:29, 30. Jn 20:22. Ro 8:2. Ep 2:5. **breath.** Heb. *ruach*, Ge +6:17. ver. 6, 8, 9, 10, 14. Ge 7:15. Jn 6:63.

6. I will. ver. 8-10. **sinews.** 2 K *5:14. Je 30:17. 1 C 15:35, 38. **put.** Ge +*2:7ⁿℙ. **breath.** Heb. *ruach*, Ge +6:17. **ye shall know.** ver. 14. Ezk 6:7, 13. 7:4, 9. 11:10, 12. 20:38. 28:22-26. 32:15. +*34:27. 35:9, 12, 15. 38:23. 39:6, 22, 28. Dt 29:6. 1 K 20:28. Is 49:23. Jl *2:27. 3:17.

7. I prophesied as. Je 13:5-7. 26:8. Ac 4:19. 5:20-29. **there.** 1 K 19:11-13. Ac *2:2, 37. 16:26-29. **bones came together.** Ezr 2:1. Je 50:4.

8. the sinews and. Is 66:14. **skin covered.** Ne 10:29. **breath.** Heb. *ruach*, Ge +6:17. Ge +*2:7n. Mt 23:13-28.

9. Prophesy unto. Jn 5:25, 28, 29. **wind.** *or*, breath. Heb. *ruach*, Nu +16:22. Am 4:13mg. **Come.** ver. 5, 14. SS 4:16. Jn 3:8. Ac 2:2. **four winds.** Da 7:2. 11:4. Re 7:1. **breath.** Heb. *ruach*, Ge +6:17.

10. the breath. Heb. *ruach*, Ge +6:17. Ps *104:30. Pr *1:23. Re *11:11. 20:4, 5. **and stood.** Is 51:17. 52:1, 2. Lk 7:14, 15. Jn 11:43, 44. Re *11:11. **great army.** Ps +*149:6-9. Is 60:8, 9.

11. whole house. ver. 16, 19. Ezk 36:10. 39:25. 1 K 18:31, 32. Is √11:12, 13. Je 31:1. 33:24-26. Ho 1:11. Ro 11:26. 2 C 5:14. Ep 2:1. **Our bones.** ver. 1-8. Nu 17:6, 12, 13. Ps *77:7-9. 102:3. 141:7. Is 40:27. Je 2:25. La 2:21, 22. 3:4. **hope is lost.** Ezk 33:10. Is *49:14. Ro ❂+*11:1, 2. **cut off.** 2 Ch 36:14-21. La 3:54. Ho 1:6, 9.

12. Therefore. Jb 35:14, 15. **I will open.** This is a pointed allusion to the resurrection; under which figure Isaiah (Is +*26:19n) also describes the restoration of the house of Israel, when he says, "thy dead men shall live;" at which time their *bones* are said to *flourish* (Is *66:14), or to be restored to their former strength and vigor; and, in like manner, St. Paul (Ro *11:15) expresses their conversion by "life from the dead." In the land of their captivity, they seemed as absolutely deprived of their country as persons committed to the grave are cut off from the land of the living; but when Cyrus issued his proclamation, Jehovah, as it were, opened their graves, and when he stirred up their spirits to embrace the proffered liberty, he put his Spirit within them, that they might live; and their re-establishment in their own land evinced the truth of God in the prediction, and his power in its accomplishment. ver. 21. Dt 32:39. Ps 17:15. 49:14, 15. Is 25:6, 9. +*26:19n. 66:14. Da +*12:2. Ho 6:2. 13:14. 1 Th √4:16. Re 20:13. **graves.** Heb. *qeber*, Ge +23:4. **come up out.** Ps *71:20. Is 26:19n. 66:10-14. Ho 6:1-3. √13:14. Lk 15:24. Jn 5:24-29. Ro 8:10, 11. *11:15. 1 C +√15:45. Ep 2:4, 5. Re 11:11. *20:4-6, 11-15. **and bring.** ver. 25. Ezk 28:25. +*34:13. 36:24. Ezr 1:2. Am √9:14, 15. **land of Israel.** Ezk +11:17.

13. ye shall know. ver. 6. Ezk 16:62. Ps 126:2, 3. **when.** Ezk +36:25n. Ro *1:4. 8:11. 2 C *4:14. Re *11:11.

14. shall put. ver. 9. Ezk 11:19. 18:31. 36:27. 39:29. Is 32:15. Jl *2:28, 29. Zc *12:10. Ac 2:16, 17. Ro 8:2,

11. I C +√15:45. **T** √3:5, 6. **spirit.** Heb. *ruach*, Is +48:16. **I the Lord.** ver. 6. Ezk 5:13, 17. 17:24. 22:14. 36:36, 38.

16. take thee. Nu *17:2, 3. **stick.** lit. wood. ♫121D8, Ge +40:19. **For Judah.** Ge 49:8-12. 1 Ch 5:2. 2 Ch 10:17. 11:11-17. 15:9. 30:11-18. Zc √10:6. **For Joseph.** Ge 49:22-26. 1 K 11:26. 12:16-20. 1 Ch √5:1. 2 Ch 10:19. Is 11:13. Je 31:6. Ho 5:3, 5.

17. join them. ver. 22-24. Is *11:13. Je 50:4. Ho 1:11. Zp 3:9.

18. Wilt. Ezk 12:9. 17:12. 20:49. 24:19. Mt 24:3.

19. Behold. ver. 16, 17. 1 Ch 9:1-3. Zc √10:6. Ep 2:13, 14. Col 3:11. **be one.** ver. +22.

20. in thine. Ezk 12:3. Nu 17:6-9. Ho 12:10.

21. I will take. Ezk +*34:13. 36:24. 39:25. Dt *30:3, 4. Is √11:11-13. 27:12, 13. 43:6. 49:12. Je 16:15. 23:3, 8. 29:14. 30:3, 10, 18. 31:8-10. 32:37. 33:7, 11. 50:19. Am √9:14, 15. Ob 17-21. Mi 7:11, 12.

22. I will make. Is √11:12, 13. Je *3:18. 32:39. *50:4. Ho *1:11. Zc √10:6. Ep 2:19-22. **the mountains.** Ezk 6:2. 17:22. 20:40. 34:13. 36:1, 36. 40:2. 43:12. **and one king.** It is evident that the grand union of Israel and Judah here predicted, and their government under one king, and that king to be David, must still be future; for, politically speaking, they never had a *king* from that day to this, far less a king or prince of that name (See on Ezk 34:23. Je 30:1). ver. 24. Ezk 34:23, 24. Ge +*49:10. Ps *2:6, 12. 72:1, 8. Is +*9:6, 7. Je *23:5, 6. 30:21. 33:14-17, 26. Ho 3:4, 5. Lk 1:32, 33. Jn *10:16. 12:13. Re 11:15. **no more two.** Ezk 35:10.

23. Neither shall they defile. Ezk *14:11. 20:43. 36:25, 29, 31. 39:7. 43:7, 8. Is 2:18. Je 3:17. Ho 14:8. Zc 13:1, 2. 14:21. **idols.** 2 K +23:24. **detestable things.** Ezk +16:17mg. Is +*66:17n. **transgressions.** Ezk 14:11. 18:22, 28, 30, 31. 21:24. 33:10, 12. 39:24. Is 53:5, 8. **but.** Ezk 20:41. 28:25. 36:24, 29. Le 20:7, 8. Mi 7:14, 18-20. **will cleanse.** Ezk 36:25. Je 50:20. Ep 5:26, 27. He 9:13, 14. 1 J √1:7, 9. **so shall.** ver. 27. Ezk 36:28. 39:22. Ge *17:7, 8. Ps 68:20, 35. Je 31:1, 33. 32:38, 39. Ho 1:10. Zc 13:9. 2 C *6:16. Re 21:3, 4, 7.

24. David. ver. 22n, 25. Is +*55:3, 4. Je 23:5. 30:9. Ho 3:5. Lk +*1:32. **my servant.** Ezk 34:23, 24. 1 K 11:32. 14:8. **one shepherd.** ver. 22n. Ezk 34:23, 24. Ps 78:71, 72. 80:1. Ec 12:11. Is *40:11. Mi +*5:2, 4. Zc *13:7. Jn √10:11, 14-16. Ep 4:4-6. He √13:20. 1 P *5:4. **they shall.** Ezk 36:27. Dt *30:6. Je 31:33. 32:39. 1 C 11:2. Ep √2:10. Ph √2:12, 13. T √2:11-13. √3:3-8. 1 J √2:6. **judgments.** Ezk +33:14mg. **and do.** Ezk ❂+*33:31.

25. they shall dwell in. T#949. ver. 21. Ezk 16:60, 61. 20:34, 35, 37, 38, 40. 28:25. 34:+13 (T#378), 23, 24, 28, 29. 36:11, 24-26, 28, 33. 37:26. Je 30:3, 9, 10. 31:1, 4, 10, 17, 24, 31-33, 38. 32:41. 33:7-9, 15, 16, 24-26. 50:4, 5, 19, 20. Ho 2:14, 15, 19. 3:4, 5. Jl 3:1, 2, 17, 20. Am √9:14, 15. Ob 17, 21. Mi 2:12, 13. 5:3, 4, 7, 13. 7:14, 17. Zp 3:9. Zc *2:10, 12. 10:√6, 8, 9. 12:6, 10. Lk *21:24. Ro 11:+√2, 12, 15, 23-33. 2 C 3:15, 16. **shall dwell.** ♫113, Nu +9:20. **even they.** Is +*60:21. 66:22. Jl *3:20. Am √9:15. Zp 3:14, 15. Zc 14:11. **children' children.** Ac +*2:39. **for ever.** Heb. *olam*, Ex +*12:24. **my servant.** 2 S 3:18. **David.** ver. 22n, +24. Is +*9:6, 7. Je *23:5. √30:9. Da *2:44, 45. *7:13, 14, 18. Ho *3:5. Zc 6:12, 13. Lk +*1:32, 33. Jn *12:34. He 7:2, 21. **for ever.** Heb. *olam*, Ex +*12:24.

26. **I will make.** Ezk 34:25. Ge *17:7. 2 S 23:5. Ps *89:3, 4. Is +*55:3. 59:20, 21. Je +*32:40. Ho 2:18-23. Jn *14:27. He *13:20, 21. **everlasting.** Heb. *olam*, Ge +9:16. +17:7. Is 44:7. **covenant.** Said of the Noahic covenant, Ge +*9:16; Abrahamic, Ge +17:7; Davidic, Is +*55:3; and the New covenant, Je 32:40. He 12:24. √13:20. **multiply.** Ezk 36:10, 37. Is 27:6. 49:21. Je 30:19. 31:27. Ho 1:10, 11. Zc 8:4, 5. He 6:14. **set my sanctuary.** ver. 28. Ezk 11:16. 40:2n. 43:7. 45:1, etc. 48:8, 10, 21. Le 26:11, 12. 1 K 8:20, 21. Ps 68:18. Is 2:2. 60:13n. Jl 2:1. Mi 4:1, 2. Hg 2:7. Zc *1:16. 2:5. √6:12, 13. Jn 1:14. 2 C 6:16. Re *21:3. **in the midst.** Ho 11:9. Jl 2:27. Re 21:3. **for evermore.** Heb. *olam*, Ps +18:50.

27. **tabernacle.** Le 26:11)𝒫. Is 60:13n. Am √9:11. Zc √6:12, 13. Jn 1:14. Col 2:9, 10. Re *21:3, 22. **I will.** ver. 23. Ezk 11:20. 14:11. 36:28. Le 26:12)𝒫. Ho 2:23. 2 C)6:16.

28. **the heathen.** Ezk 36:23, 36. 38:23. 39:7, 23. Ps *46:10, 11. 79:10. 102:15. 126:2. Zc *14:9. Ro 11:15. **sanctify.** Ezk 20:12. Ex 31:13. Le 20:8. 21:8. Jn 17:17-19. 1 C 1:30. Ep *5:26. 1 Th *5:23. **when.** Ezk +34:27. 36:25n. **my sanctuary.** ver. +*26. Is 60:13n. Zc √6:12, 13. Re 21:3. **in the midst.** ver. +26. Ezk 43:9. Zp 3:5, 15, 17. **for evermore.** Heb. *olam*, Ps +18:50.

EZEKIEL 38

A prophecy of the formidable preparations of Gog and Magog, with their allies, to invade the land of Israel in the latter days, 1-17; and of the glorious power of God to be displayed in their destruction, 18-23.

1. **the word.** Ezk 37:15.

2. **Son.** ver. 14. Ezk 2:1. 39:1, 17. **set.** Ezk 6:2. 20:46. 25:2. 35:2, 3. **Gog.** i.e. *mountain*, in reference to the Caucasus mountains, chief seat of the Scythian people. Rather, "Gog (the prince) of the land of Magog, the prince of Rosh, Meshech, and Tubal." By *Magog* is most probably meant the Scythians or Tartars, called so by the Arabian and Syrian writers, and especially the Turks, who were originally natives of Tartary (inhabiting parts of Russia and central and western Siberia); and by *Rosh*, the Russians, descendants of the ancient inhabitants on the river Araxes or Rosh. Josephus concurs in identifying Magog with the Scythians (Ant. i. vi. 1). But compare "Og" (Dt 3:1-13). 1 Ch +5:4. Re 20:8, 9. **Magog.** Jerome identifies Magog as the "Scythian nations, fierce and innumerable, who live beyond the Caucasus and the Lake Maeotis, and near the Caspian Sea, and spread out even onward to India." Ge 10:2. 1 Ch 1:5. Compare "Agag," Nu 24:7. **the chief prince of.** or, prince of the chief of. Rather, prince of Rosh. The meaning is that Magog is the head of the three great Scythian tribes, of which "Rosh" is the first. Gesenius identifies Rosh with Russia. A P. Stanley remarks "This early Biblical notice of so great an empire is doubly interesting from its being a solitary instance. No other name of any modern nation occurs in the Scriptures, and the obliteration of it by the A.V. is one of the many remarkable variations of our version from the meaning of the sacred text of the Old Testament" (Smith's *Dictionary of the Bible*, vol. iv. p. 2752, 2753). ver. 2, 3. Ezk 39:1. Ge +46:21. **Meshech.** Ezk 27:13. 32:26n. Ge +10:2. 1 Ch 1:5, 17. Ps 120:5. Is 66:19. **Tubal.** Ezk 27:13. 32:26n. Ge +10:2. 1 Ch 1:5. Is 66:19.

3. **I am against.** Ezk 13:8. 29:3. 35:3. 39:1, 2, etc.

4. **I will.** Here, God brings forth Gog against Israel, but in Re 20:7, 8, Satan brings Gog forth, showing these are different events. Additional evidence includes these events are not identical includes (1) the event in Re 20:7, 8, is clearly post-millennial, while these events are premillennial (Ezk 38:16n); (2) Here, Gog is from the north of Israel (ver. 6), whereas in Re 20:7, 8, Gog is brought from the four quarters of the earth. 2 S 24:1. 1 Ch 21:1. **turn thee.** Ezk *29:4. 39:2. 2 K *19:28. Is 37:29. +*59:19mg. **back.** or, lead thee away enticingly. Is 47:10 (perverted). Je 50:6. **put hooks.** Ezk 29:4. Is 30:28. 37:29. **bring thee forth.** Zc √12:1-8. Mt 24:14-30. Re 16:14. 17:14. 19:17-21. **all thine army.** ∫121N2, Ge +34:29. ver. 15. Da 11:40. Re 9:16. **horses.** ver. 15. Ps 20:7. Pr 21:31. Da 11:40. Ro 16:20. **all of them clothed.** Ezk 23:12. **company.** or, gathered host. Ezk 16:40. **bucklers.** Ezk 23:24. **handling.** 1 Ch 12:8. 2 Ch 25:5. Je 46:9.

5. **Persia.** Now Iran. Ezk 27:10. Da 2:32, 39. 5:28-31. 8:20. **Ethiopia.** Ezk 30:4, 5, 9. Ge 2:13. 10:6-8. 2 K +19:9. Ps 68:31. Je 46:9. Da 11:43. Zp 2:12. 3:10. **Libya.** or, Phut. Ezk 27:10. 30:5mg. Ge *10:6. 1 Ch 1:8. Je 46:9. Da 11:43. Na +*3:9, Put.

6. **Gomer.** The people descended from Gomer, a son of Japheth (Ge 10:2, 3), who are supposed to have lived on the north side of the Black sea. By some identified with the German race (C. L. Feinburg, on Ezekiel, states "The former (Gomer) are the hordes of the Cimmerians, tribes that settled along the Danube and Rhine and later formed the Germanic people," p. 221), but by most with the Celtic in Denmark, Britain, Scotland (Gael), Ireland, and Wales (Cymry). Ge *10:2. 1 Ch 1:5. **his bands.** ver. 9, 22. Ezk 12:14. 39:4. **Togarmah.** Descendants of Gomer, the son of Japheth, supposed to have settled in the northern part of Armenia (Ezk 32:26n. *Minni*, Je 51:27). Ezk *27:14. Ge 10:3. 1 Ch 1:6. Da 11:40. **of the north.** Contrast Re 20:8, where Gog comes from the four quarters of the earth, thus a worldwide gathering of enemies against Jerusalem, whereas here Gog is from the north, showing these are two different events (see ver. 4n, 16n). ver. 15. Ezk 32:30. 39:2. Ps 48:2. 107:3. Is √43:6. Je +*1:14. 3:18. 23:8. 31:8. Zc +*2:6.

7. **Be thou prepared.** 2 Ch 25:8. Ps 2:1-4. Pr +*21:30. Is *8:9, 10. 37:22. 54:17. Je *46:3-5, 14-16. 51:12. Jl *3:9-12. Am *4:12. Zc 14:2, 3. **and prepare.** Je 46:14.

8. **After many days.** ver. 16. Is 24:22. Ho 3:3-5. Hab 2:3. Mt +*25:12. Pointing to a then, and yet future time, when Israel shall have been recently "gathered," and before the Restoration is perfected (CB). ver. 12. Ho √3:5. Zp *2:1. **thou shalt be visited.** Ex +*20:5n. Is 24:22. 29:6. Je +11:22mg. 32:5. La 4:22. **in the latter years.** ver 14, *16, 18. Ezk 39:8, 11. Ge 49:1. Nu 24:14. Dt 4:30. 31:29. Is 2:2. Je 23:20. 30:24. 48:47. 49:39. Da 2:28. 10:14. Ho 3:5. Mi 4:1. **into the land.** ver. 12. Ezk +*34:13. 36:24, etc. 37:21, +*25, etc. 39:27-29. Is √11:11, 12, etc. 66:8. Je √30:3, 7, 18. 32:37. Am √9:14, 15. **the sword.** Is 1:20. Ho 11:6. **gathered.** ver. 12. Ezk 20:34. 28:25. +*34:13. 36:24. 37:21. Is *11:12. 54:7. 56:8. Je 23:3. 29:14. Zp 3:19, 20. **out of many people.** Not true of the Babylonian captivity, but a reference to worldwide dispersion, such as took place since the destruction of Jerusalem in A.D. 70. ver. 12. Is √11:11n. *43:6. Je 31:8. Mt

24:31. Lk 21:24. **the mountains.** Ezk +*34:13. 36:1-8. 37:22. **always waste.** Thus much longer than the seventy years of Babylonian captivity. Ezk 5:14. Is ◖61:4. Je 2:15. 22:5. **it is brought.** 1 P 2:9. **and they shall.** ver. 11. Ezk 28:26. 34:25-28. Je 23:6. 33:16. Da 9:27. **safely.** or, confidently. lit. "leaningly." ver. 11, 14. *S#983h. Ezk 28:26mg, 26. 30:9 (careless). 34:25, 27, 28. 38:8, 11mg, 14. 39:6mg, 26. Ge 34:25 (boldly). Le 25:18 (in safety), 19. 26:5. Dt 12:10. 33:12, 28. Jg 8:11 (secure). 18:7 (careless). 1 S 12:11. 1 K 4:25mg. Jb 11:18. 24:23. Ps *4:8. *16:9mg. 78:53. Pr *1:33. 3:23, 29. 10:9. Is 14:30. 32:17 (assurance). 47:8 (carelessly). Je *23:6. 32:27. 33:16. 49:31 (without care). Ho 2:18. Mi 2:8 (securely). Zp 2:15 (carelessly). Zc 14:11.

9. **shalt ascend.** Ezk 13:11. Is 21:1, 2. 25:4. 28:2. Da *11:40. **and come.** Is 10:3. **like.** ver. 16. Je *4:6-13. Jl 2:2. **storm.** ver. 22. Ezk 13:11. Is ◖4:6. 25:4. 28:2. 30:30. 32:19. **cloud.** Ezk 30:3. 34:12. Is ◖4:5. 25:4, 5. Je 4:13. **all thy.** Is 8:9, 10.

10. **that at.** Ps 83:3, 4. 139:2. Pr 19:21. Is 10:7. Mk *7:21. Jn 13:2. Ac *5:3, 9. 8:22. 1 C 4:5. **come into.** ↗171J1, 2 K +12:4. **think an evil thought.** or, conceive a mischievous purpose. Ps 36:4. Pr 6:14, 18. 12:2. Je +6:19. Da 11:44, 45. Mi 2:1. Re 17:13.

11. **go up.** Ex 15:9. Ps 10:9. Pr *1:11-16. Is 37:24, 25. Je 49:31. Ro 3:15. Re 20:7-9. **unwalled villages.** Dt 3:5. Est 9:19. Zc 2:4. **go to.** Jg 18:7, 27. Je 49:31, 32. Zc 2:4, 5. **safely.** or, confidently. ver. +*8. Ezk 28:26mg. 39:6mg. 1 K 4:25mg. Ps *16:9mg. Pr 3:29, 30. **without walls.** Is 26:1. Je *49:31. Zc 2:4.

12. **take a spoil, and to take a prey.** Heb. spoil the spoil, and to prey the prey. ↗147D, Ge +1:29. Ezk 29:19mg. Ps 83:4. Pr 1:13. Is 10:6. ◖17:12-14. Je 30:16. **to turn.** Is 1:24, 25. Am 1:8. Zc 13:7. **the desolate.** ver. 8. Ezk 36:33-35. Je 32:43, 44. 33:12, 13. Zc 1:12, 17. **and upon.** ver. 8. Zc 10:8-10. **the people.** Ezk 39:13. **gathered out.** ver. 8. **which have gotten.** Note the motive of the invasion: to plunder newly established Israel's great wealth. Is 60:5-9. *61:6. Je *49:31. **cattle and goods.** ver. 13. Ge 31:18. **midst.** Heb. navel. Ezk 5:5. Dt 32:8. Jg *9:37mg. Is 2:2. Zc 2:8.

13. **Sheba.** Ezk 27:12, 15, 20, 22, 23, 25. 1 K +10:1. A very fertile country in Arabia, adjoining the Red Sea, the eastern part of modern Yemen, the kingdom of the Sabeans (Jb 1:15). **Dedan.** A country in the Arabian peninsula, not far from the Edomites. Ezk 25:13. 27:15, 20. Ge +10:7. Is 21:13. Je 25:23. 49:8. **the merchants.** Ezk 27:12, 25. **of Tarshish.** Ezk 27:12. Ge +10:4. 2 Ch +9:21n. 20:36, 37. Ps 72:10. Is 66:19. Jon 1:3. **with all.** Ezk 19:3-6. 32:2. Nu ◖23:24. Ps 57:4. Is ◖11:6. Je 50:17. 51:38. Mi ◖5:8. Na 2:11-13. Zc 11:3. **Art thou come.** 1 P *5:8.

14. **in that day.** ver. 19. Ezk 29:21. Is +*2:11. 4:1, 2. 10:20, 27. 12:1, 4. 27:1, 12, 13. 52:6. Zc 2:11. 3:10. 9:16. 12:6, 9, 11. 13:1, 2. 14:4, 6, 8, 9, 13, 20, 21. **my people.** Dt +*32:43. Compare verse 16, "my land." **dwelleth.** ver. 8, 11. Je *23:6. Zc 2:5, 8. **shalt.** Ezk 37:28.

15. **thou shalt come.** Ezk *39:2. Da +*9:26. *11:40, 44. Hab +*3:16. **thy place.** ver. 6. Ezk 39:2. Is 14:31. Je 1:14. 6:22. 46:20, 24. Da *11:◖40, *44. **north parts.** Young renders "sides of the north;" Leeser, "farthest ends of the north;" Darby, "uttermost north;" F.W. Grant, "farthest north." ver. 6. Ezk 39:2. Da 11:44.

Young notes for "sides," lit. "thighs." ver. 6. Ezk 32:23. Ps 48:2. Is 14:13. **riding upon horses.** ver. 4. Ezk 23:6. 26:7, 10. Is 31:1, 3. Ho 1:7. Jl ◖1:6. Hab 1:8. **and many.** ver. 4, 6. Jl 3:2. Zp 3:8. Zc 12:2-4. 14:2, 3. Re *16:14, 16. 20:8. **a mighty army.** Jl 2:1-20. Re 6:4.

16. **shalt come up against.** Mi √5:6. **as a cloud.** ver. 9. **it shall be.** Though it is not generally agreed what people or transactions are here predicted, yet it seems evident that the prophecy is not yet accomplished. Nothing occurred in the wars of Cambyses, or Antiochus Epiphanes with the Jews, that answers to it; and the expression here used—*in the latter days*— plainly implies, that there should be a succession of many ages between the publication of the prediction and its accomplishment. It is therefore supposed, with much probability, that its fulfillment will be posterior to the conversion of the Jews and their restoration to their own land; and that the Turks, Tartars, or Scythians, from the northern parts of Asia, perhaps uniting with the inhabitants of some more southern regions, will make war upon the Jews, and be cut off in the manner here predicted.

Since the preceding note was written nearly two centuries have passed, and it seems possible that the fulfillment of this prophecy must take place after the regathering of the Jews to their own land, since they are now in their own land, but before the final and complete restoration (Is √11:11n). It is most probable that these events take place before the millennium, and are not those of Re 20:8. While some would identify these events with Re 20:8, there is nothing to recommend the identification except the name "Gog and Magog," all other attendant circumstances being totally different (see ver. 4n). Perhaps these events may take place before the Great Tribulation of Je 30:7. It is unlikely that the Jews could be burying the remains of the huge armies described here at any time during the tribulation. If the Millennium immediately follows the seven year tribulation period, this would argue for a pretribulation placement of these events, for there is no record or likelihood of this activity (which will take seven years, Ezk 39:9) taking place during the Millennium. The destruction of Russia and her allies by Israel may leave a power vacuum in the Middle East and lead to a one world government, perhaps headed at some point by the Antichrist. An agreement with Israel may allow it to exist in peace until the agreement is broken, and the events of the Great Tribulation take place, followed by the Second Advent of Christ, and the establishment of his millennial kingdom.

Students of Scripture greatly differ in the fine points of prophetic interpretation, and there is particular disagreement at this time in placing the rapture of the church. It appears that of the three positions—pretribulation, midtribulation, and posttribulation, the pretribulation rapture position holds a slight edge in probability because its proponents generally are more consistent in their interpretation of the Olivet discourse in Matthew chapter 24, and parallel passages in Mark and Luke. It is possible, but not certain, that these events of Ezk ch. 38 and 39 will precede the rapture of the church. They could take place during the time period between the rapture and the onset of the seven year Great Tribulation.

As to the three positions held regarding the millennium, the premillenial, postmillennial, or amillennial positions, only the premillennial position appears to agree with consistent Bible interpretation in taking into account the requirements for the fulfillment of prophecies connected with the Abrahamic, Davidic, and New covenants in their connection with the literal re-establishment of natural Israel in Palestine, and the setting up of the theocratic kingdom of Christ on the throne of David to rule over the nation Israel and the world from the capital city Jerusalem during his millennial reign, Is +*11:11n. ver. 8. Dt 31:29. Is 2:2. Da 2:28. 10:14. Ho 3:5. Mi 4:1. 1 T 4:1. 2 T 3:1. **the latter days.** ver. +*8. Je 49:39. Da 2:28. **I will bring thee.** Ex +*9:16. Dt +*2:30. 1 S +*18:10n. Is +*45:7. Am +*3:6. Ep +*1:11. **my land.** Le +*25:23n. Dt 32:43. Ps 10:16. 85:1. Is 14:2, 25. Je 2:7. Ho 9:3. Jl 1:6. 3:2. Zc 9:16. Compare "my people," ver. 14, and "my mountains," ver. 21. **heathen may know.** ver. 23. Ezk 35:11. 36:23. 37:28. 39:6, 7, 21. Ex 14:4. 1 S 17:45-47. 2 K 19:19. Ps *9:16. 83:17, 18. Da 3:24-29. 4:32-37. 6:15-27. Mi 7:15-17. Hab 3:2. Mt 6:9, 10. **when I.** ver. 23. Ezk 20:41. 28:22, 25. 36:23. 39:27. Ge +*12:3. Nu 27:14. Dt 32:51. Ps +*122:6. Is 5:16.

17. **Art thou he.** Je 6:22, 23. 2 Th 2:3, 7. **whom.** ver. 10, 11, 16. Nu 24:17-24. Ps 2:1-3. 110:5, 6. Is 10:20-27. 11:4. 14:24-27. 27:1. 29:1-8. 34:1-6. *63:1-6. 66:15, 16. Je 30:1-11. Da 2:44, 45. *11:40-45. Jl 2:20. 3:9-17, 19. Mi 5:3-15. Zp 1:14. 3:8. Zc √12:2-9. √14:1-3. **by.** Heb. by the hands of. 1 K +16:12mg. 2 Ch 29:25mg. 2 Ch 34:14mg,n. Je 37:2mg. 50:1mg. **years.** Is 63:4.

18. **same time.** ✔171T2, Ge +2:17. **land of Israel.** Ezk 11:17. **that my fury.** Ezk 5:13, 15. 14:19-21. 36:5, 6. Dt 32:22. Ps 18:7, 8. 89:46. Is 59:18. 63:3-6. Da *8:25. Na 1:2. He 12:29. **my face.** Is 11:4. 2 Th √2:8. Re 2:16. 19:15, 21.

19. **in my.** Ezk 36:5, 6. 39:25. Dt 29:20. Ps 78:21. Is 42:13. Jl 2:18. Zp 1:18. 3:8. Zc 1:14. 8:2. **fire of my wrath.** Ps 89:46. Zp 1:18. Ml 4:1. **Surely.** Is 2:19, 21. 24:18. 30:32. Jl 3:16. Hg 2:6, 7, 21, 22. He 12:26. Re 6:12. 11:13. 16:18, 20.

20. **the fishes.** Je 4:23-26. Ho 4:3. Na 1:4-6. Zc 14:4, 5. Re 6:12, 13. **the fowls.** Ho 4:3. **face.** Ge +1:2. **shall shake.** Ps 18:7-15. Is 5:25. Je 4:24. **at my presence.** Ps 68:2, 8. 97:5. 114:7. Is 2:10-21. 64:1-3. Je 4:26. **the mountains.** Ps 68:8. Is 5:25. 64:3. Je 4:24. Na 1:5. Hab 3:6, 10. **steep places.** or, towers, or stairs. SS 2:14. Is 30:25. Na 1:6. 2 C 10:4.

21. **I will.** Ezk 14:17. Ps 105:16. **a sword.** Is 66:16. Je 25:29. **my mountains.** Is 14:25. 49:11. 65:9. **every.** Jg *7:22. 1 S 14:20. 2 Ch 20:23. Hg 2:22. Zc *14:12, 13. Re *6:3-8.

22. **I will plead.** Ezk 17:20. Is 66:16. Je 25:31. Zc 14:12-15. **with pestilence.** Ezk 5:12, 17. 6:11, 12. 7:15. 12:16. 14:19, 21. 24:16n. 28:23. 33:27. Le 26:25. Nu 14:12. 16:46-49. Dt +28:21. 2 S 24:13. 1 K 8:37. 1 Ch 21:12, 14. 2 Ch 6:28. +*7:13, 14. 20:9. Je 14:12. 21:6. 24:10. 27:8, 13. 28:8. 29:17, 18. 32:24, 36. 38:2. 34:17. 42:17, 22. 44:13. Am 4:10. Hab 3:5. Zc 14:12. Mt 24:7. Lk 21:11. Re 6:8. **and with blood.** Ezk 5:17. 14:19. 28:23. 32:6. Nu 23:24. 2 S 1:22. Is 34:3, 7. 49:26. Je 25:27. Re 8:7. 14:20. 16:6. **an overflowing rain.** Ezk 13:11. Ge 19:24. Ex 9:22-25. Jsh 10:11. Ps *11:6. 18:12-14. 77:16-18. Is 28:17. 29:6. 30:30-33. Mt 7:27. Re 16:21. **great hailstones.** Ezk 13:11, 13. Jsh

*10:11. Ps 148:8. Is 28:2. 30:30. 32:19. Re 8:7. 11:19. *16:21. **fire.** Ezk 39:6. Is 29:6. 30:30. 2 P +*3:7. Re 8:7, 8. **brimstone.** Ge 19:24. Dt 29:23. Jb 18:15. Ps +*11:6. Is +*30:33. 34:9. Lk 17:29. Re 14:10. *19:20. +*21:8.

23. **magnify.** Ezk 36:23. **sanctify myself.** ver. +*16. Ezk 20:41. 28:22. 36:23. *37:28. Le 22:32. Nu 20:12. Is 8:13. **and I.** ver. 16. Ezk 37:28. 39:7, 13, 27. Ex 7:5, 17. 8:10, 22. 9:14-16. Ps *9:16. Da 11:40-45. 12:1. Zp 1:7mg. Ro 9:17, 22. Re 15:3, 4. 19:1-6. **they shall know.** Ezk 6:10. Ps *9:16.

EZEKIEL 39

God will glorify himself in the terrible destruction of Gog and Magog, 1-7. The multitude of weapons burned by Israel, 8-10. The burial of Gog and his multitude in Hamon-gog, 11-16. The birds and beasts invited to feed on the slain, 17-20. The heathen shall see God's judgments, and the reasons for which he punished Israel, 21-24; whom he will gather again with everlasting favor, 25-29.

1. **son.** Ezk 38:2, 3. **Behold.** Ezk 35:3. *38:3. Na 2:13. 3:5. **the chief prince of Meshech and Tubal.** Or, "prince of Rosh, Meshech, and Tubal." See on Ezk 38:2.

2. **I will.** It is probable that none of the invaders will escape: but perhaps the inhabitants of Magog in general are meant. The immense army of Gog, led forth against Israel, will almost empty his land; and the subsequent judgment upon those that remain at home, will reduce them to a sixth of the whole. Ezk 38:4. Ps 40:14. 68:2. Is 37:29. **turn thee back.** Is +*59:19mg. Jl √2:20. **leave but the sixth part of thee.** or, strike thee with six plagues; or, draw thee back with a hook of six teeth, as Ezk 38:4. 45:13. **and will cause.** Ezk 38:15. Da 11:40. **to come up.** Ezk *38:15. Hab +*3:16. **north parts.** Heb. sides of the north. Ezk +38:6. **the mountains.** ver. 4, 17. Ezk 6:2. *38:8, 21.

3. **I will smite.** Ezk 30:21-24. Ps 11:2. 37:14. *46:9. 58:7. *76:3-5. Je 21:4, 5. Ho 1:5. *2:18.

4. **fall.** ver. 17-20. Ezk 38:21. Ps *9:3-10. Is *14:25-27. 34:4. **all thy bands.** Ezk 38:6. **I will.** Ezk *29:5. 32:4, 5. 33:27. Is 34:2-8. Je 15:3. Re *19:17-21. **ravenous birds.** Is 46:11. **sort.** Heb. wing. Ezk 5:3mg. Ge 7:14. Is +24:16mg. **beasts.** ver. 17. Ezk 33:27. Re *6:8. **to be devoured.** Heb. to devour. Ezk 35:12mg.

5. **open field.** Heb. face of the field. Ezk 29:5mg. 32:4. Je 8:2. 22:19. **for I have spoken.** Ezk 17:24. Nu *23:19. Is √55:11.

6. **I will send a fire.** Some terrible judgment will destroy the countries whence the army of Gog was led forth, about the same time that the army itself shall be cut off. Ezk 28:18. 30:8, 16. *38:19-22. 1 K 18:24, 38. 2 K 1:10. Ps *11:6. Is *66:14-16. Am 1:4, 7, 10. Na 1:6. Zc 14:12. He 12:28, 29. Re *20:9. **Magog.** Ezk 38:2. **carelessly.** or, confidently. Ezk +*38:8h, 11mg. Jg 18:7. **in the isles.** Ezk 26:15, 18. 27:3, 6. *38:6, 13. Ps 72:10. Is 42:4, 10. ●49:1. ●60:9. *66:19. Je 25:22. Zp 2:11. **they shall know.** Ezk 6:7.

7. **will I.** ver. 22. Ezk *38:16, 23. Is 52:6. **and I will.** Ezk 20:9, 14, 39. 36:20, 21, 36. Ex +*20:7. Le 18:21. **the heathen.** Ezk *38:16, 23. Ps 83:16, 18. **the Holy One.** Is 12:6. 43:3, 14. 45:11. 55:5. 60:9, 14.

8. **it is come.** The prophet, seeing in vision the

accomplishment of the prediction, speaks of it as already come and done. Ezk 7:2-10. 21:7. Is 33:10-12. Re 16:17. 21:6. **it is done.** Re +*10:7n. **this.** Ezk +*38:17. Jl 2:11, 31. Zp 1:14. 2 P *3:8. Ju 6. Re 6:17. 10:7.

9. **shall go.** Ps 111:2, 3. Is +*66:24. Ml 1:5. **and shall.** ✻121S4, 2 K +4:29. ver. 10. Jsh 11:6. Ps *46:9. Zc 9:10. **set on fire.** The language here employed seems to intimate that the army of Gog will be cut off by miracle, as that of Sennacherib; for the people are described as going forth, not to fight and conquer, but merely to gather the spoil, and to destroy the weapons of war, as no longer of use. **handstaves.** *or,* javelins. **and they.** When the immense number and destruction of the invaders are considered, and also the little fuel comparatively which is necessary in warm climates, we may easily conceive of this being literally fulfilled. **burn them with fire.** *or,* make a fire of them. Is 44:15. **the weapons.** ver. 10. Ps 140:7. **the shields.** Ezk 23:24.

10. **shall spoil.** Ex 3:22. 12:36. Jg 6:1, 6. 7:19-25. 2 Ch 14:9-15. ch. 20. Is 9:4. 10:24-34. *14:2. 33:1. Mi 5:8. Hab 2:8. Zp 2:9, 10. Mt *7:2. Ro +*11:25. Re 13:10. 18:6.

11. **the valley.** Probably the valley near the sea of Gennesareth, as the Targum renders, and so called because it was the great road by which the merchants and traders from Syria and other Eastern countries went into Egypt. Perhaps what is now called the plains of *Haouran,* south of Damascus. **graves.** Heb. *qeber,* Ge 23:4. Ps *49:14. Is 34:1-3. **on the east.** Ezk 47:18. Nu 34:11. Lk 5:1. Jn 6:1. **noses.** or, *mouths.* **Hamongog.** *that is,* The multitude of Gog. Nu 11:34mg. Je +10:13mg.

12. **cleanse.** ver. 14, 16. Nu 19:16. Dt *21:23.

13. **shall bury.** Ps 53:5. Is +*66:24. **a renown.** Ezk 34:29. Dt 26:19. Ps *149:6-9. Je 33:9. Zp 3:19, 20. 1 P 1:7. **the day.** ver. 21, 22. Ezk 28:22. Ps 126:2, 3.

14. **they shall.** Nu 19:11-19. **continual employment.** Heb. continuance. Is +*58:11. **to cleanse.** ver. 12. **seven months.** ver. 12.

15. **bone.** Nu 19:11. **set.** Heb. build. Ezk 4:2. Lk 11:44. **a sign.** ✻S#6725h. 2 K 23:17h (title). Je +31:21h (waymarks). **in the valley.** ver. 11. **Hamon-gog.** i.e. *the multitude of Gog,* ✻S#1996h. ver. 11.

16. **Hamonah.** that is, The *multitude.* ✻S#1997h. **cleanse.** ver. 12. Nu 35:33.

17. **Speak.** Ge 31:54. 1 S 9:13. 16:3. Is 56:9. Je 12:9. Zp 1:7. Re √19:17, 18. **every feathered fowl.** Heb. the fowl of every wing. ver. 4. Is *18:6. **Assemble.** Je 12:9. **to my.** ver. 4. 1 S 17:46. Is 11:4. 18:6. *34:6. Je *46:10. Zp *1:7. 2 Th *1:7-9. **sacrifice.** *or,* slaughter. **may eat.** Ezk 44:15. Is 3:11-17.

18. **eat.** Ezk 29:5. 34:8. Re *19:17, 18, 21. **goats.** Heb. great goats. Ezk 34:17mg. **of bullocks.** Ps 68:30. Is 34:7. Je 50:11, *27. *51:40. **fatlings.** Dt 32:14. Ps *22:12. Am 4:1. **of Bashan.** Ge 49:16, 17. Nu +21:33. Dt 33:22. Jsh 12:4n. 1 K 4:13.

19. **eat fat till ye be full.** Is 23:18.

20. **be filled.** Ezk 38:4. Ps *76:5, 6. Hg 2:22. Re 19:18.

21. **I will set.** Ezk 36:23. 38:16, 23. Ex 9:16. 14:4. Is *26:11. *37:20. Ml *1:11. **my glory.** ver. 13. Ps *102:15. Is 11:10mg. *59:19. *60:1-3. *66:18. **my judgment.** Ezk 28:25, 26. Ps 9:16. Is √26:9. 42:1-4. Mi 5:15. **and my hand.** ✻22A14.7, Ex +9:3. Ex 7:4. 8:19.

1 S 5:7, 11. 6:9. Ps *10:16. 32:4. Mi *4:11-13.

22. **know.** ver. 7, 28. Ezk 28:26. 34:27-31. Ps *9:16. ch 46. 59:13. Is 12:4-6. Je 24:7. 31:34. Ho +*8:2. 13:4. Jl 2:27. 3:17. Jn *17:3. 1 J *5:20. **and forward.** Ezk 43:27. 1 S 18:9. Is 18:2, 7.

23. **the heathen.** Ezk 36:18-23, 36. 2 Ch 7:21, 22. Je 22:8, 9. 40:2, 3. La 1:8. 2:15-17. **into captivity.** Dt 28:15-68. **for their iniquity.** T#486. Ge +6:13 (T#566). Ex +22:20 (T#362). +35:2 (T#643). Le 26:14-39. +*32:23 (T#733). Dt 4:25-27. 28:15-25, 33, 37-48, 58-63, 66, 67. 2 Ch 24:20-24. Ne 9:25-30. Jb +27:13 (T#490). Ps +12:5 (T#523). +34:16 (T#303). +37:9 (T#87). +58:11 (T#630). Je 25:8-14. 44:6-11. Zc +10:11 (T#381). **hid I.** ver. 29. Ezk ◗22:26. Dt *31:17, 18. 32:20. Ps 10:1. 30:7. Is *1:15. 8:17. ◗28:15. ◗53:3. +*54:8. 57:17. √59:2. 64:7. Je 33:5. **gave them.** Le 26:25. Dt 32:30. Jg 2:14. 3:8. Ps 106:41. Is 42:24.

24. **According.** Ezk 36:19. Le 26:24. 2 K 17:7, etc. Ezr 9:7. Ps 78:55-64. Is 1:20. 3:11. *59:2, 17, 18. Je 2:17, 19. 4:18. 5:25. Da 9:5-10. **face.** ✻22A4, Ge +19:13.

25. **Now.** After the destruction of Gog; i.e. after the "gathering" but before the final "Restoration," and therefore before the Millennium (CB). Ezk 38:2n. **will I.** The return of a few Jews from Babylon, and their continuance, increase, partial reformation, and prosperity, till the days of Christ, followed by their present long continued dispersion under the frown of God, and destitute of his Spirit, could in no degree answer to these predictions. Hence we must conclude, that some future events, exactly suitable to them, shall yet take place relative to the nation of Israel. Ezk +*34:13. 36:21, 24. +*37:25. Is 27:12, 13. 56:8. Je 3:18. 23:3. *30:3, 10, 18. 31:3. 32:37. Am √9:14, 15. Ro 11:26-31. **bring again.** Ezk 16:53. 20:34. Dt *30:3. Jb *42:10. Ps 14:7. Je 32:44. Jl 3:1-8. **the whole.** Ezk 20:40. 37:21, 22. Je 30:3. 31:1. Ho *1:11. Ro √11:26, 27. **and will.** Ezk 36:4-6, 21-23. Jl 2:18. Zc 1:14. 8:2.

26. **they have borne.** Ezk 16:52, 57, *58, 63. 32:24, 25, 30. Ps 99:8. Je 3:24, 25. 30:11. Da 9:16. **when they.** Ezk +38:8. Le 26:5, 6. Dt 28:47, 48. 32:14, 15. 1 K 4:25. Mi 4:4. **none made.** Ezk 34:28. Le 26:6. Is 17:2. Je 7:33.

27. **I have.** ver. 25. Ezk 28:25, 26. Is 27:6, 7. **and am.** ver. 13. Ezk 20:41. 36:23, 24. *38:16, 23. Le 10:3. Is 5:16.

28. **shall they.** ver. 22. Ezk 34:30. Ho 2:20. **which caused them.** Heb. by my causing of them, etc. ver. 23. **but I have.** Note the time element signaled by "but" here, in contrast with "when" in the following references: Ezk ◗28:25. ◗32:7. ◗34:27. ◗35:11. ◗36:23. ◗*37:13, 28. Compare "then" at Ezk 36:25n. Is 59:19n. **have left none.** Dt 30:3, 4. Ne 1:8-10. Ps 147:2. Is *27:12. Am √9:9. Mt √24:31. Ro 9:6-8. +*11:1-7.

29. **hide.** ver. 23-25. Ezk 37:26, 27. Is 45:17. +*54:8-10. **for.** Ezk 36:25-27. 37:14. Is 32:15. 44:3-5. 59:20, 21. Jl √2:28. Zc *12:10. Ac *2:17, 18, 33. 1 J *3:24. **spirit.** Heb. *ruach,* Ge +41:38.

EZEKIEL 40

EZEKIEL's vision of the model of a city; and of an angel, with a line and reed, measuring the temple, 1-5. A description of the east gate of the outer court, 6-19; of the north gate, 20-23; and of the south gate,

24-26; of the south gate of the inner court, 27-31; of the east gate, 32-34; and of the north gate, 35-38. The eight tables for sacrifice, 39-43. The chambers for the singers and for the priests, 44-47. The porch and pillars of the temple, 48, 49.

1. **In the five.** On Tuesday, April 20, A.M. 3430. B.C. 574. Ezk 1:2. 8:1. 29:17. 32:1, 17. **after.** Ezk 33:21. 2 K ch. 25. Je ch. 39, 52. **selfsame.** Ge +*7:13n. Ex 12:41. **hand.** Ezk 1:3. 3:14, 22. 11:24. 37:1. Re 1:10.

2. **the visions.** There can be little doubt, that the grand outlines of the description of the temple, in the following extraordinary vision, were taken from that of Solomon's, with all the additions made to it in after ages; and we may suppose that Zerubbabel and the other Jews had respect to it, as far as circumstances would permit, in rebuilding the temple after the captivity. There are, however, many circumstances which conclusively show, that something infinitely superior to either the first or second temple was intended; and that the external description must be considered as a figure and emblem of spiritual blessings. Probably the more immediate accomplishment of the prophecy will be subsequent to the conversion and restoration of the Jews, the destruction of Gog and Magog, and the pouring out of the Spirit, mentioned at the close of the last chapter, and continue through the thousand years, during which Satan will be chained up in the bottomless pit (Re 20:1-6). The explicit details of the temple construction recorded in the vision argue for a literal fulfillment (Is 60:13n). It appears from Zc 6:12, 13, that the builder of this Millennial Temple will be Messiah himself. Ezk 1:1. 8:3. Da 7:1, 7. Ac 2:17. 16:9. 2 C 12:1-7. **land of Israel.** Ezk +27:17. **a very.** Ezk 17:22, 23. Is 2:2, 3. Da 2:34, 35. Mi 4:1. Re 21:10. **by.** *or*, upon. **as the.** Ezk 48:30-35. Ga 4:26. Re *21:2, 10-23. **frame.** 1 Ch 28:12, 19. **on the south.** Ps 48:2. Is 14:13.

3. **whose.** Ezk 1:7, 27. Da *10:5, 6. Re 1:15. **with.** Ezk 47:3. Is 8:20. 28:17. Zc 2:1, 2. Re *11:1. *21:15.

4. **behold.** Ezk 2:7, 8. 3:17. 43:10, 11. 44:5. Mt 10:27. 13:9, 51, 52. **shall show thee.** Re 1:1, 19. **declare all.** Is 21:10. Je 26:2. Ac *4:20. *20:27. 22:14, 15. 1 C 11:23. 1 J 1:1, 3.

5. **a wall.** Ezk 42:20. Ps 125:2. Is 26:1. 60:18. Zc 2:5. Re 21:12. **by the cubit.** Ezk 43:13. Dt 3:11. **hand breadth.** ♪79, Ge +21:16. ver. 43. Ex 25:25. 37:12. **so he.** Ezk 42:20. Re 21:16.

6. **unto.** ver. 20. Ezk 8:16. 11:1. 43:1. 44:1. 46:1, 12. 1 Ch 9:18, 24. Ne 3:29. Je 19:2. **which looketh.** Heb. whose face *was* the way. Ezk 43:1. Re 7:2. **stairs.** ver. 26. 1 K 6:8. **threshold.** Ezk 10:18. 43:8. 46:2. 47:1. Ps 84:10mg. **one reed.** ver. 5, 7.

7. **little chamber.** Ezk 42:5. 1 K 6:5-10. 1 Ch 9:26. 23:28. 2 Ch 3:9. 31:11. Ezr 8:29. Je 35:4.

9. **the posts.** Ezk 45:19.

10. **the little.** ver. 7. **they three.** The entrance into the outer court seems to have been through a porch with doors at both ends; and on each side of this porch were three small chambers, or rooms, for the use of the porters, a reed square in size, with a passage of five cubits between them. The common *cubit*, termed the "cubit of a man" (Dt 3:11), was about 18 inches; but the cubit used by the angel was, as we learn from Ezk 43:13, "a cubit and a hand breadth," or about three inches more than the common cubit. Hence the

measuring *reed*, which was "six cubits long, by the cubit and the hand breadth," ver. 5, must have been about 10 1/2 feet. 1 K 6:5, 6.

12. **space.** Heb. limit, *or*, bound. **six cubits.** ver. 5, 7. 1 K 6:10.

13. **the gate.** The whole arch of the east gate, measured from the southern extremity of the opposite room, was 25 cubits; including the dimensions of the two rooms, or twelve cubits, ver. 7; the spaces before the rooms or two cubits, ver. 12; and the breadth of the entrance, ten cubits, ver. 11; making in all 24 cubits, leaving one cubit for the thickness of the walls.

14. **the court.** Ezk 8:7. 42:1. Ex 27:9. 35:17. Le 6:16. 1 Ch 28:6. Ps 100:4. Is 62:9.

15. **the face of the gate.** This was the whole length of the porch, from the outward front (Ezk 41:21, 25), to the inner side which looks into the first court (ver. 17); including the thickness of the walls (ver. 6), chambers (ver. 7), and spaces between them.

16. **narrow.** Heb. closed. Ezk 41:16, 26. 1 K *6:4. Ps 58:4. Pr 17:28. 1 C 13:12. **the little.** ver. 7, 12. **arches.** *or*, galleries, *or* porches. ver. 21, 22, 25, 30. Ezk 41:15. 42:3. Jn 5:2. **inward.** *or*, within. 1 K 6:30. 2 Ch 29:16. **palm trees.** Ezk 41:18. 1 K 6:29, 32, 35. 2 Ch 3:5. Ps 92:12. Re 7:9.

17. **the outward.** Ezk 10:5. 42:1. 46:21. Re *11:2. **they were.** 1 K 6:5. 1 Ch 9:26. 23:28. 2 Ch 31:11. **thirty.** Ezk 42:4. 45:5. **pavement.** 2 S 12:31. Je 43:9n-11. Mt 25:32.

19. **he measured.** 1 Ch 28:11, 12. **unto the.** ver. 23, 27. Ezk 46:1, 2. **without.** *or*, from without. **pavement.** Jn 19:13.

20. **the gate.** ver. 6. **that looked.** Heb. whose face *was.* ver. 6mg.

21. **the little.** ver. 7, 10-16, 29, 30, 36, 37. **arches.** *or*, galleries, *or* porches. ver. 16, 26, 30-34. **after.** ver. 8, 10, 13, 15, 25, 29.

22. **palm trees.** ver. 16, 31, 37. 1 K *6:29, 32, 35. 7:36. 2 Ch 3:5. Re 7:9. **and they.** ver. 6, 26, 31, 34, 37, 49. He 6:1. **seven steps.** 1 K 6:8. **before them.** Or, "suitable to them," that is, to the arches of the east gate. The north gate into the outward court, and every thing belonging to it, were exactly the same as the east gate.

23. **the gate of.** That is, the gate of the inner court was opposite, and exactly answered to the gate of the outward court, both on the north and east side; and between the gates of the outward and inner court was a space of an hundred cubits. ver. 19, 27, 28, 44. **and he.** Ex 27:9-18. 38:9-12.

24. **and behold.** ver. 6, 20, 35. Ezk 46:9. **and he.** ver. 21, 28, 29, 33, 35, 36. **according.** That is, according to the measures of the eastern and northern gates. There does not appear to have been any gates on the *west*, though the courts seem to have extended to the western wall.

25. **windows.** ver. 16, 22, 29. Jn 12:46. 1 C 13:12. 2 P 1:19. **the length.** ver. 21, 33.

26. **seven.** ver. 6, 22. 2 P 3:18. **palm trees.** ver. 16, 22. Ps 92:12, 13. SS 7:7, 8.

27. **in the.** ver. 23, 32. **and he.** ver. 19, 23, 47.

28. **he brought.** As the outward court inclosed the inner, the prophet was led from the south gate of the outward court to the south gate of the inner, which was opposite it, and so into the inner court itself. **according.** ver. 32, 35.

29. **the little**. The entrance into the inner court seems to have been through a portico, exactly like that at each gate of the outward court; but the ascent was by eight steps, instead of seven. ver. 7, 10, 12. 1 Ch 28:11, 12. 2 Ch 31:11. Ne 13:5, 9. Je 35:2-4. 36:10. **and there**. ver. 16, 22, 25.

30. **the arches**. These are supposed to have been built over the spaces which separated the little chambers, or porters' lodges. **five and**. ver. 21, 25, 29, 29, 33, 36. **five cubits**. Instead of five cubits, it seems evident, from the parallel places, that we should read *twenty-five*: the word *esrim* appears to have been lost out of the text. **broad**. Heb. breadth.

31. **and palm**. ver. 26, 34. **eight**. ver. 22, 26, 34, 37.

32. **into the**. ver. 28-31, 35.

33. **it was**. ver. 21, 25, 36.

34. **palm trees**. That is, probably, the capital of each pillar was ornamented with sculpture, representing leaves or branches of the palm tree. **eight steps**. ver. 6, 22, 26, 31, 34, 37, 49.

35. **to the**. ver. 27, 32. Ezk 44:4. 47:2. **measured**. The north gate, as well as the east, was built in the same manner, and of the same dimensions, as the south gate. See the parallel passages.

36. **little**. ver. 21, 29, 36.

37. **the posts**. ver. 31, 34. **the utter court**. That is, "the *outer* court," as the word *utter* primarily denotes.

38. **the chambers**. ver. 12. Ezk 41:10, 11. 1 K 6:8. **where**. This place, where the legs and entrails of the sacrifices, especially of the burnt offerings, were washed, was just within the portico of the north entrance to the inner court, or court of the priests. An allusion to this is most probably made by the inspired apostle when writing his Epistle to the Hebrews, at the 10th chapter and 22nd verse. "Let us draw near with a true heart in full assurance of faith, having our hearts sprinkled from an evil conscience, and our bodies washed with pure water." Le *1:9. 8:21. 2 Ch 4:6. He +*10:22. **burnt offering**. Le +*23:12. Is +56:7. Je 33:18n.

39. **tables on that**. Ezk 41:22. 44:16. Ml 1:7, 12. Lk 22:30. 1 C 10:16-21. **the burnt offering**. Le *1:3, etc. +*23:12. Is +56:7. Je 33:18n. **the sin offering**. Le 4:2, 3, 13, etc. +*23:19. Is 53:5, 10. 2 C 5:21. **the trespass offering**. Le +5:6n, etc. 6:6. 7:1, 2.

40. **at the side**. Two tables were on each side, as you come into the porch of the gate; and two on each side of the inner part of the gate that looked towards the altar; in all eight tables, on which they slew and cut up the victims. It does not appear that any such tables were used either in the tabernacle or temple; and this seems to intimate the introduction of a new and more spiritual dispensation. See the references on ver. 38, 39. Ezk 41:22. **as one goeth up**. *or*, at the step. ver. 35. **north gate**. Le 1:11.

42. **of hewn stone**. Ex 20:25. La 3:9. Am 5:11. **instruments**. Ex 38:3.

43. **within**. These were probably for hanging up the victims in order to flay them. **hooks**. *or*, end-irons. *or*, the two hearth-stones. **upon**. Le 1:6, 8, 12. 8:20.

44. **the inner**. ver. 23, 27. **chambers**. ver. 7, 10, 29. 1 Ch *6:31, 32. 16:41-43. 25:1, etc. Ep 5:19. Col *3:16.

45. **chamber**. The word *chamber* probably here de-

notes a row of chambers, of which there seems to have been three: one for the singers; one for the priests who in their courses took charge of the sacred vessels and treasures; and one for the priests who attended on the altar and sacrifices. **whose**. Ezk 8:5. **the keepers**. Le 8:35. Nu *3:27, 28, 32, 38. 18:5. 1 Ch 6:49. *9:23. 2 Ch 13:11. Ps *134:1. Ml 2:4-7. 1 T 6:20. Re 1:6. **charge**. *or*, ward, *or*, ordinance, and so ver. 46. Ezk 44:8mg. 1 Ch 9:23. Ml +3:14mg.

46. **the keepers**. Ezk 44:15. Le 6:12, 13. Nu 18:5. **these**. Ezk 43:19. *44:15, 16. 48:11. 1 K *2:35. 1 Ch 29:22. **which come**. Le 10:3. Nu 16:5, 40. Ep 2:13.

47. **measured**. Ezk 43:13-16. **court**. This was the inner court, or court of the priests, which was of the same dimensions with each division of the outer court; and the altar stood directly before the porch of the temple. **an hundred cubits long**. ver. 19, 23, 27. **foursquare**. Ezk 48:20. Re 21:16.

48. **the porch**. The length of the porch was twenty cubits, the same as the breadth of the temple, and the breadth eleven cubits, *that is*, one cubit more than in Solomon's temple. Two bivalve, or folding doors, each leaf of them being three cubits wide, seem to have formed the entrance; which, with five cubits, perhaps of brick or stone work, on each side, called "the post of the porch," amount to sixteen cubits; and the other four cubits may be supposed to have been the distance from these posts to the outside of the walls of the temple. 1 K *6:3. 2 Ch 3:4.

49. **the steps**. This was a flight of steps which led from the inner court to the temple. ver. 31, 34, 37. **pillars**. 1 K *7:15-21. 2 Ch 3:15, 17. Je 52:17-23. Re 3:12.

EZEKIEL 41

The posts, doors, walls, chambers, foundations, dimensions, divisions, and ornaments, of the temple itself, 1-26.

1. **he brought**. See on Ezk 40:2, 3, 17. **to the temple**. 1 K *6:2. Zc √6:12, 13. Ep 2:20-22. 1 P 2:5. Re 3:12. 11:1, 2. 21:3, 15. **and measured**. Ex 26:15, etc. **the posts**. These were probably a sort of door-case on each side of the entrance; and the *tabernacle* perhaps was a kind of covering to the door, of the same dimensions.

2. **the door**. *or*, the entrance. This was the door out of the porch into the sanctuary, which seems to have been wider than that from the court to the porch. Ex 26:36. 36:37. 1 K 6:31-35. 2 Ch 3:7. 29:7. Jn *10:7, 9. **the length**. 1 K 6:2, 17. 2 Ch 3:3. **the breadth**. 1 K 6:3.

3. **two cubits**. This was the thickness of the partition wall between the sanctuary (ver. 2) and holy of holies (ver. 4); the breadth of the wall on each side of the gate being seven cubits, and the entrance into holy place six cubits in width.

4. **twenty cubits**. 1 K *6:20. 2 Ch *3:8. Re 21:16. **This**. Ex *26:33, 34. He 9:3-8. **most holy**. The Holy of Holies. ver. 21, 23. Ezk 44:13. 45:3. 1 K 6:16.

5. **side chamber**. ver. 6, 7. Ezk 42:3-14. 1 K *6:5, 6.

6. **one over another**. Heb. side chamber over side chamber. **thirty in order**. *or*, three and thirty times, *or* feet. We find by Josephus (Ant. l. viii. c. 3. sec. 2), that around Solomon's temple were chambers *three* stories high, each story consisting of *thirty* chambers;

which are supposed to have been on the north, south, and east sides of the temple. **and they.** 1 K 6:6, 10. **have hold.** Heb. be holden. 1 P 1:5. **but.** That is, the beams or supporters of the chambers were not let into the main wall of the temple; but rested on projections of the outer wall, which became a cubit narrower at every story, leaving a ledge of one cubit, to support the beams. Ne 13:4, 5.

7. **there was,** etc. Heb. *it was* made broader, and went round. 1 K *6:8. Mt 13:32. He 6:1. **an enlarging.** In the same proportion in which the thickness of the wall decreased, the chambers increased, so that the middle story was one cubit larger, and the upper story two cubits larger, than the lower rooms; and a winding staircase, which widened in the same manner as the rooms, ascended from the bottom to the top. **increased.** Ps 84:7.

8. **a full.** Ezk 40:5. 2 Ch 3:3. Re 21:16.

9. **was five.** ver. 5. **that which.** This appears to have been a walk, or gallery of communication between the chambers, five cubits broad, into which the doors opened. ver. 11. Ezk 42:1, 4.

10. **the chambers.** As the word rendered *chambers* is different from that used before, it is supposed there was another row of buildings, parallel with the side-chambers, with a passage of twenty cubits between.

11. **and the breadth.** ver. 9. Ezk 42:4.

12. **separate.** ver. 13-15. Ezk 42:1, 10, 13. Re 21:27. 22:14, 15. **the wall.** This appears to have been a building erected at the west end of the temple.

13. **he measured.** These verses (ver. 13-15) seem to intimate, that all the buildings of the temple occupied an area of 100 square cubits.

15. **galleries.** *or,* several walks, *or,* walks with pillars. ver. 16. Ezk 42:3, 5. SS 1:17. 7:5. Zc 3:7. **an hundred.** Ezk 40:47. **with the inner.** ver. 17. Ezk 42:15.

16. **door posts.** or, thresholds. Ezk 40:6, 7. **narrow.** ver. 26. Ezk *40:16, 25. 1 K *6:4. 1 C 13:12. **cieled with wood.** Heb. cieling of wood. 1 K 6:15. 2 Ch 3:5. Hg 1:4. **from the ground up to the windows.** *or,* the ground unto the windows. **covered.** Probably either by the jutting out of the main wall of the temple; or by lattice work, or curtains, or by both. 1 K 6:18.

17. **To that.** That is, the windows were placed above the height of the door, at the east end of the temple, and thus continued, at the same height, and at measured distances, along both sides of the holy place, to the wall of the inner sanctuary, in which there were no windows. **measure.** Heb. measures. Ezk 42:15.

18. **with cherubims.** 1 K *6:29-32. 7:36. 2 Ch 3:7. **palm trees.** Ezk 40:16, 22. Re 7:9. **and every.** Ezk 1:10. 10:14, 21. Re 4:7-9.

19. **the face.** Ezk 1:6, 10. 10:14.

20. **cherubims.** 2 Ch 3:7.

21. **posts.** Heb. post. Ezk 40:14. 1 S 1:9. 1 K 6:33mg.

22. **altar.** This must signify the altar of incense; which, both in the tabernacle and Solomon's temple, was covered with plates of gold. It is very remarkable, that in this temple described by Ezekiel, there is not the least mention of gold or silver, though there was such a profusion of these metals in the former; which may probably imply, that a glory of a more spiritual nature was intended under these emblems. Ex *30:1-3. 1 K *6:20, 22. 7:48. 2 Ch 4:19. Re 8:3. **This is.** This is probably an intimation, that under the New Testament dispensation a table would be substituted

for an altar, in the ordinance of the Lord's Supper. Ezk 23:41. 44:16. Ex 25:28-30. Le 24:6. Pr 9:2. SS 1:12. Ml *1:7, 12. 1 C 10:21. Re *3:20. **before.** Ex *30:8.

23. **the temple.** 1 K 6:31-35. 2 Ch 4:22.

24. **the doors.** 1 K 6:31-35. **two leaves.** Ezk 40:48.

25. **cherubims.** See on ver. 16-20.

26. **narrow windows.** See on ver. 16. Ezk 40:16.

EZEKIEL 42

The chambers within the wall of the court for the priests, 1-12. The use thereof, 13, 14. The dimensions of the ground, on which all these buildings stood, 15-20.

1. **he brought.** Ezk 40:2, 3, 24. 41:1. **the utter court.** Ezk 40:20. Re 11:2. **chamber.** This seems to denote a row of chambers in three stories; which appear to have been situated in the inner court (here called the outer court in reference to the temple, ver. 13, 14), just before the separate place, at the entrance from the north. ver. 4. Ezk 41:9, 12-15.

2. **Before.** Perhaps this means that the north door was 100 cubits from the entrance into the court; and that the doorway, or portico, was 50 cubits in length; or, that it faced one of the cloisters, the length of which was 100 cubits, and its breadth 50, which was the proportion of all the cloisters.

3. **Over.** One side of these buildings looked upon the void space about the temple of twenty cubits, and the other toward the pavement belonging to the outer court. **the twenty.** Ezk 41:10. **the pavement.** Ezk 40:17, 18. 2 Ch 7:3. **gallery against.** Ezk 41:15, 16. SS 1:17. 7:5.

4. **before.** There seems to have been two rows of these chambers, and a walk between of ten cubits in width; with an entrance into it from the chambers, of one cubit in width. 1 K 6:5, 6. **a walk.** ver. 11. **a way.** Mt 7:14. Lk 13:24.

5. **were higher than these.** *or,* did eat of these. Ezk 41:7. **than the lower, and than the middlemost of the building.** *or, and* the building *consisted* of the lower and middlemost. ver. 6.

6. **three stories.** Ezk 41:6. 1 K 6:8.

8. **the length.** Ezk 41:15. **before.** Passing from the north to the south side of the temple (ver. 11, 12), the prophet was shown that the space of ground, which was before the temple on the east, measured 100 cubits.

9. **from under.** *or,* from the place of. Ezk 46:19. **the entry.** *or,* he that brought me. Ezk 44:5. 46:19. **as one goeth.** *or,* as he came. 1 K 6:8-10.

10. **the thickness.** Rather, "the *breadth* of the wall," that is, the breadth of ground which it enclosed. Ezk *41:12. **over against.** These south chambers were exactly like those on the north. ver. 1, 13. Ezk 41:13-15.

11. **the way.** ver. 2-8.

12. **was a door.** ver. 9.

13. **they be holy.** Ex 29:31. Le 6:14-16, 26)₽. 7:6. 10:13, 14, 17. 24:9)₽. Nu 18:9. **approach.** Ezk 40:46. Le 10:3. Nu 16:5, 40. 18:7. Dt 21:5. **the most holy.** Le 2:3, 10)₽. 6:14, 17, 25, 29. 7:1, 6. 10:13, 17. 14:13. 21:22. Nu 1:9, 10. 18:9, 10. 18:9, 10. Ne 13:5. **meat offering.** Le +*23:13. **sin offering.** Le +*23:19. **trespass offering.** Le +5:6n.

14. **they not go.** Ezk 44:19. Ex 28:40-43. 29:4-9.

Le 8:7, 13, 33-35. Lk 9:62. **and shall put**. Le *16:3, 4, 23. Is 61:10. Zc 3:4, 5. Ro 3:22. *13:14. Ga *3:27. 1 P *5:5.

15. **measuring**. Ezk 41:2-5, 15. **gate**. Ezk 40:6, etc.

16. **side**. Heb. wind. ver. 17-20. Ezk 37:5. **the measuring reed**. Estimating the reed at 10 1/2 feet, 500 reeds will be nearly equal to a mile; so that from this statement we find the temple, with its outbuildings, was built on a square, nearly an English mile on each side, and four miles in circumference. This not only far exceeds the size of Solomon's temple, or that after the captivity, which was only 500 cubits, or a furlong, on each side, and exactly half a mile in circuit; but is nearly equal to the whole extent of Jerusalem itself, which, when greatest, was but 33 furlongs in circumference, somewhat less than 4 1/4 miles. Some take the LXX. reading of "cubit" for "reed" in order to accommodate the measures given here to those given for Solomon's temple, but the LXX. is unsupported by the Hebrew text. Some suggest that this points figuratively and mystically of the spiritual temple, the church under the gospel, and its spiritual glory, for the original temple mount is not large enough to contain the area described. But it may be that the literal dimensions are correct, that the area described merely encloses the entire temple grounds. Perhaps the geographical changes prophesied elsewhere (Ps *48:2. Is 35:7. Zc √14:4, 10) will render the area designated suitable for such a large temple compound. Ezk 40:3. Zc 2:1. Re 11:1, 2.

20. **it had**. Ezk 40:5. SS 2:9. Is 25:1. 26:1. 60:18. Mi 7:11. Zc 2:5. **five hundred**. Ezk *45:2. 48:20. Re 21:12-17. **a separation**. Ezk 22:26. 44:23. 48:15. Le 10:10. Lk 16:26. 2 C *6:17. Re 21:10-27.

EZEKIEL 43

The glory of God returns to the temple, 1-5. He promises to preserve the people from those sins which had deprived them of his presence, 6-9. He commands the prophet to show them the pattern of the house, etc., for their instruction, 10-12. The measures for the altar for burnt offerings, 13-17. Rules for consecrating it, and the priests, 18-27.

1. **the gate that**. Ezk 40:6. 42:15. 44:1. 46:1.

2. **the glory**. Ezk 1:28. 3:23. 9:3. 10:18, 19. Is 6:3. Jn 12:41. **came**. Ezk ◑√11:23. **and his voice**. Ezk 1:24. Re 1:15. *14:2. 19:1, 6. **the earth**. Ezk *10:4. Is *60:1-3. Hab 2:14. 3:3. Re 18:1. 21:23.

3. **according to the appearance**. Ezk 1:4-28. *8:4. 9:3. 10:1-22. 11:22, 23. **I came**. ſ108A3, Is +6:10. **to destroy the city**. *or*, to *prophesy* that the city should be destroyed. Ezk *9:1, 5. 32:18. Je 1:10. Re 11:3-6. **the river**. Ezk 1:3. 3:23.

4. **the glory**. Though the personal presence of Immanuel in the second temple rendered it more glorious than that of Solomon (Hg 2:5-9), yet this part of the vision rather relates to the times predicted in the whole of this description—those which shall succeed the conversion of the Jews, and their restoration to their own land. **came**. Ezk 10:18, 19. 40:6. 42:15. 44:1, 2. 46:1.

5. **the spirit**. Heb. *ruach*, Is +48:16. Ezk *3:12-14. 8:3. 11:24. 37:1. 40:2. 1 K 18:12. 2 K 2:16. Mt *4:1. Ac *8:39. **and brought**. SS 1:4. 2 C 12:2-4. **inner court**. Ezk 8:16. **the glory**. Ezk 44:4. Ex *40:34, 35.

1 K *8:10, 11. 2 Ch 5:14. Is 6:3. Hg *2:7-9. Re ◑*21:22, 23.

6. **I heard**. Ezk 1:26-28. Le 1:1. Is 66:6. Re 16:1. **the man**. Ezk 40:3.

7. **the place of my throne**. Ezk 1:26. 10:1. Ps 47:8. 99:1. Is *6:1. Je 3:17. 14:21. 17:12. Ac *7:48, 49. Re 22:3. **and the place**. 1 Ch 28:2. Ps 99:5. Is 60:13. *66:1. Mt 5:34, 35. **where I will dwell**. ver. 9. Ezk 37:26-28. 48:35. Ex 29:45)ᷟℛ. Ps 68:18. 132:14. Jl 3:17. Mt *28:20. Jn *1:14. *14:23. 2 C *6:16. Re 21:2, 3. **in the midst**. Ps 46:5. **for ever**. Heb. *olam*, Ex +*12:24. Ge +9:12. **no more defile**. Ezk 20:39. 23:38, 39. *39:7. Ho 14:8. Zc 13:2. 14:20, 21. **whoredom**. ver. 9. Ezk 16:15-17, 25, 26. Je 3:1-5. Ho 4:13, 14. 9:1. Ja 4:4. **by the carcasses**. ver. 9. Le 26:30)ℛ. 2 Ch 34:5n. Je 16:18. **high places**. Ezk 16:16. 20:29. 36:2. 2 K +21:3. Je 32:35. Mi 1:5.

8. **setting**. Ezk 5:11. 8:3-16. 23:39. 44:7. 2 K 16:10, 14, 15. *21:4-7. 23:11, 12. 2 Ch 33:4, 7. **by my thresholds**. Is 6:4. **their post**. Is +*66:17n. **my posts**. Ezk 41:21. 46:2. **and the wall between me and them**. *or*, for *there was but* a wall between me and them. Is 59:2. **defiled my holy name**. Ezk 23:39. **abominations**. Ezk 23:26. Le 26:30. 1 K 12:28. Ml 2:11.

9. **Now let**. Rather, "Now shall they put away their whoredom and the carcasses of their kings far from me, and I will dwell in the midst of them for ever." It is a prediction and a promise, not an exhortation. Ezk +*18:30, 31. Ho 2:2. Col 3:5-9. **the carcasses**. ver. 7. Ezk 37:23. Le 26:30. Je 16:18. **and I**. ver. 7. Ezk 37:26-28. 2 C √6:16-18. **for ever**. Heb. *olam*, Ex +*12:24.

10. **show**. Ezk 40:4. Ex 25:40. 1 Ch 28:11, 19. **that they**. ver. 11. Ezk 16:61, 63. 31:31, 32. Ro 6:21. **pattern**. *or*, sum, *or* number.

11. **show them**. Ezk ch. 40-42. 44:5, 6. He 8:5. **all the ordinances**. 1 C 11:2. **and do**. Ezk 11:20. 36:27. Mt *28:20. Jn +*13:17.

12. **Upon**. Ezk 40:2. 42:20. Ps 93:5. Is 2:2, 3. Jl 3:17. Mi 4:1, 2. Zc 14:20, 21. Re 21:27.

13. **the measures**. Ex 27:1-8. 2 Ch 4:1. **The cubit**. Ezk *40:5. 41:8. **bottom**. Heb. bosom. ver. 14, 17. **edge**. Heb. lip. Ezk 3:5, 6. 36:3. +47:7mg. Ex 26:4. Jg +7:22mg.

14. **the lower settle**. These *settles* were *ledges* by which the altar was narrowed towards the top; and the whole of it may be thus computed:

HEIGHT: Base (ver. 13), 1 cubit; To first ledge (ver. 14), 1 cubit; to upper ledge (ver. 14), 4 cubits; To hearth (ver. 15), 4 cubits; In all, 10 cubits.

BREADTH: Upper ledge (ver. 17), 14 cubits; For higher ledge (ver. 14), 2 cubits; For lower ledge (ver. 14), 2 cubits; For base (ver. 13), 2 cubits; In all, 20 cubits.

Hence, the upper part of the altar was only twelve cubits square (ver. 16), the upper settle, or ledge, being in all fourteen cubits (ver. 17), deducting two cubits from its dimension. Though this altar was the same in height and breadth with that of Solomon, yet it differed materially from it in having settles or ledges; on which the priests walked round the altar, to officiate in offering sacrifices.

15. **the altar**. Heb. Harel, that is, the *mountain of God*. Probably so called in opposition to the idolatrous *high places*. **the altar**. Heb. Ariel, that is, the *lion of God*. Rather, "the hearth of God," from the

Arabic *irat*, or *iryat*, a hearth, and *ail*, God. Is 29:1mg, 2, 7. **four horns.** Ex 27:2. Le 9:9. 1 K 2:28. Ps 118:27.

16. **twelve cubits.** Ex ☾20:26. *27:1, 2. 2 Ch 4:1. Ezr 3:3. **square.** Ex 38:1, 2.

17. **and the border.** Ex 25:25. 30:3. 1 K 18:32. **his stairs.** Rather, "its ascents," *maalothehoo*, probably an inclined plane; for the law ordained that the priest should not ascend by *stairs*. Ex 20:26. **look toward.** Ex 8:16. 40:6. 1 K 6:8. Ne 9:4.

18. **to offer.** Ezk 45:18, 19. Ex 40:29. Le 1:5-17. 8:8-21. 16:19. He 9:21-23. 10:4-12. 12:24. **to sprinkle.** Ezk 10:2. Le *1:5)℘. 2 Ch 34:4. Jb 2:12. Is 28:5. Ho 7:9.

19. **the priests the Levites.** Ezk 40:46. *44:15. 48:11. Dt 17:9. Jsh 3:3. 8:33. 1 S 2:35, 36. 1 K *2:27, 35. 2 Ch 30:27. Ne 11:20. Is 61:6. 66:21, 22. Je 33:18-22. 1 P 2:5, 9. **which approach.** Nu 16:5, 40. 18:5. **a young.** Ezk 45:18, 19. Ex 29:10, 11. Le 4:3, etc. 8:14, 15. 2 C *5:21. He 7:27. **sin offering.** Ex 29:14)℘. Le +*23:19.

20. **take.** ver. 15. Ex *29:12, 36. Le 4:25, 30, 34. 8:15. 9:9. **and on the four.** ver. 16, 17. **thus shalt.** ver. 22, 26. Ezk 45:18, 19. Le 16:19. He 9:21-23.

21. **burn.** Ex *29:14. Le *4:12, 21. 8:17. He *13:11, 12.

22. **a kid.** ver. 25. Ex 29:15-18. Le *4:27, 28, 30. 8:18-21. Is *53:6, 10. 1 P 1:19. **and they.** ver. 20, 26.

24. **offer them.** Le 1:3-6. **cast salt.** Le *2:13. Nu 18:19. 2 Ch 13:5. Mt *5:13. Mk *9:49, 50. Col *4:6. **burnt offering.** Le 6:9. +*23:12.

25. **Seven days.** Ex 29:35-37. Le 8:33. **sin offering.** Le +*23:19.

26. **Seven days.** Ex 29:35, 36. **they shall.** Le *8:33, 34. **consecrate themselves.** Heb. fill their hands. Ex +28:41mg. 29:24. 32:29mg.

27. **that upon.** Le *9:1-6, 23, 24. **make.** Ro 15:16. Ph 2:17. He *13:15. **burnt offerings.** Le +*23:12. **peace offerings.** *or*, thank offerings. Le +*23:19. Je +33:11. **I will accept.** Ezk 20:40, 41. Le 22:27)℘. Dt 33:11)℘. Jb 42:8. Ho 8:13. Ro *12:1. Ep 1:6. Col 1:20, 21. 1 P *2:5.

EZEKIEL 44

The east gate assigned to the prince alone, 1-3. The people reproved for admitting strangers to pollute the sanctuary, 4-9. Idolatrous priests to be excluded from their office, 10-14. The sons of Zadok, who had adhered to the worship of God, accepted in it, 15, 16. Ordinances for the priests, 17-31.

1. **the outward.** So called in opposition to the temple itself, which was the inner sanctuary. Ezk 40:6, 17. 42:14. 2 Ch 4:9. 20:5. 33:5. Ac 21:28-30. **looketh.** Ezk 43:1, 4. 46:1.

2. **because.** Ezk 43:2-4. Ex 24:10. Is 6:1-5.

3. **for.** Ezk 34:23, 24. 37:24, 25. 46:2, 8. 2 Ch 23:13. 34:31. **the prince.** It is probable that the *prince* mentioned here and elsewhere, does not mean the Messiah, but the ruler of the Jewish nation for the time being. For it is not only directed where he should sit in the temple, and eat his portion of the sacrifices, and when and how he should go out; but it is also ordered (Ezk 45:22), that at the passover he shall offer a bullock, a sin offering for himself and the people; and to guard

him against any temptation of oppressing the people, he had a provision of land allotted to him (Ezk 45:8), out of which he is to give an inheritance for his sons (Ezk 46:18). These appear plainly to be political rules for common princes, and for a succession of them; but as no such rules were observed under the second temple, the fulfillment of it must still be future. Ezk 34:24. 37:25. Zc √6:12, 13. **to eat.** Ge 31:54. Ex 24:9-11. Dt 12:7, 17, 18. Is 23:18. 62:9. 1 C 10:18, etc. Re *3:20. **he shall enter.** Ezk 40:9. 46:2, 8-10.

4. **the way.** Ezk 40:20, 40. **the glory.** Ezk 3:23. 10:4, 18, 19. 11:22, 23. 43:4, 5. Is 6:3, 4. Hg 2:7. Ml 3:1. **and I fell.** Ezk 1:28. 43:3. Ge 17:3. Nu 16:42-45. Ps 89:7. Re 1:17.

5. **mark well.** Heb. set thine heart. Ezk 40:4. Ex 9:21mg. Dt 32:46. 1 Ch 22:19. 2 Ch 11:16. Pr 24:32mg. Da 10:12. He *8:5. **concerning.** Ezk 43:10, 11. Dt 12:32. Mt *28:20. **and mark well.** Ps 119:4. **the entering.** Ps 96:8, 9. Ac 8:37.

6. **thou shalt say.** Ezk 2:5-8. 3:9, 26, 27. Is 6:1, 9. Jn 12:41. Ro 10:21. **rebellious.** Heb. rebellion, put for rebellious people. *ſ*121N1, Ge +31:54. **let it suffice.** Ezk 45:9. 1 P 4:3.

7. **ye have brought.** ver. 9. Ezk 7:20. 22:26. 43:7, 8. Le 22:25. Ac 21:28. **strangers.** Heb. children of a stranger. ver. 9. Ex +12:43 (*S#5236h). Ps 18:44mg. Is *56:6, 7. Je 8:19. Da 11:39. Ml 2:11. **uncircumcised in heart.** The introduction of uncircumcised persons to eat of the peace offerings and oblations, would have been a gross violation of the Mosaic law; but, as there was no law to exclude "the uncircumcised of *heart*," who were circumcised and ritually clean, this seems to point out a new and different constitution. Le 26:41)℘. Dt 10:16)℘. 30:6. Je 4:4. 9:25, 26. Ac 7:51. Ro 2:28, 29. Col *2:11-13. **in flesh.** *ſ*88, Ge +17:11. **when.** Le 3:16. 21:6, 8, 17, 21. 22:25. Ml 1:7, 12-14. Jn *6:52-58. **the fat.** Le 3:13-17)℘. 17:11. **broken.** Ge 17:14. Le 26:15. Dt 31:16, 20. Is 24:5. Je 11:10. 31:32. He 8:9.

8. **ye have not.** Le *22:2, etc. Nu 18:3-5. Ne 13:4-9. Ac 7:53. 1 T 6:13, 14. 2 T 4:1. **set keepers.** 1 K 12:31. 13:33, 34. 2 K 17:32. **charge.** *or*, ward, *or* ordinance, and so ver. 14, 16. Ezk 40:45mg, 46. 48:11mg. 1 Ch 23:32. Ezr 8:24-30. Ml +3:14mg.

9. **Thus saith.** Ezk 31:10, 15. 43:18. 45:9, 18. 46:1, 16. 47:13. **No stranger.** ver. 7. Nu *16:9, 39, 40. Ps 50:16. 93:5. Da 11:39. Jl 3:17. Zc 14:21. Mk √16:16. Jn √3:3-5. T 1:5-9. **flesh.** *ſ*88, Ge +17:11.

10. **the Levites.** ver. 15. Ezk 22:26. 48:11. 2 K 23:8, 9. 2 Ch 29:4, 5. *36:14. Ne 9:34. Je 23:11. Zp 3:4. 1 T 5:22. **idols.** 2 K +23:24. **bear.** Ge 4:13. Le 19:8. Nu 5:31. Ps 38:4. Is 53:11.

11. **they shall be.** As few, if any, of those who, before the captivity, had been guilty in these respects, lived to witness the restoration of the temple service; and as it does not appear that their descendants were thus degraded for the idolatry of their ancestors; it is probable that a thorough reformation of the whole church, or the prevalence of pure religion among the converted Jews, is here predicted. **having charge.** ver. 14. Ezk 40:45. 1 Ch 26:1, etc. **ministering to the house.** 2 Ch *29:4, 5. **shall slay.** 2 Ch 29:34. 30:17. 35:10, 11. **and they.** ver. 15. Nu 16:9. 18:6. Dt 10:8)℘.

12. **they ministered.** 1 S 2:29, 30. 2 K 16:10-16. Is 9:16. Ho 4:6. 5:1. Ml 2:8, 9. **caused the house of Israel to fall into iniquity.** Heb. were for a stumblingblock

of iniquity unto, etc. Ezk *14:3, 4. Is *9:16. Ml *2:8. **therefore**. Ezk 20:6, 15, 23, 28. Dt 32:40-42. Ps 106:26. Am 8:7. Re 10:5, 6. **and they shall**. ver. 10, 13.

13. **they shall not**. ver. ❶15. Nu 18:3. 2 K 23:9. 1 C=3:12-15. **bear**. Ezk 32:30. 36:7.

14. **keepers**. Nu 18:4. 1 Ch 23:28-32. 2 Ch *29:34.

15. **the sons**. Ezk 40:46. 43:19. 48:11. 1 S *2:35. 1 K 2:35. 1 Ch 29:22. 1 T 3:3-10. 2 T 2:2. Re 2:1, 8, 12, 18. 3:1, 7, 14, 22. **when**. ver. 10. **come near**. ver. ❶13. 1 C=3:12-15. **they shall stand**. Dt 10:8. Zc 3:1-7. **the fat**. ver. 7. Le 3:16, 17. **the blood**. Le 17:5, 6.

16. **They shall enter**. He=10:19. Re 1:6. **to my table**. To place the *showbread* there. It is observable, that the table in the sanctuary is mentioned rather than the altar of incense; perhaps intimating the change in the external institutions of Divine worship which should take place before the accomplishment of this prophecy. It is not easy to determine, whether any external regulations, with respect to Divine ordinances, answerable to these predictions, will be made among the converted Jews, when reinstated in their own land, or not. But a consistent adherence to the rule of literal interpretation would favor such a view. Ezk 41:22. Ml 1:7, 12. 1 C=10:21. **keep**. Nu *18:1, 5, 7, 8. Dt 10:8. 33:8-10. 1 Ch 23:28, 32.

17. **they shall**. Ex 28:29, 40, 42, 43◗℘. 39:27-29. Le 16:4. Re 4:4. 19:8.

18. **bonnets**. Ezk 24:17. Ex 28:40, 41. 39:28◗℘. Is 61:10. 1 C 11:4-10. **linen breeches**. Ex 28:42, 43. 1 C 14:40. **with anything that causeth sweat**. *or*, in sweating *places*. Heb. in, *or* with sweat. ∫121G, Ge +31:1. By Metonymy of the Effect, "sweat" is put for the garments which cause it.

19. **they shall put**. Ezk 42:13, 14. Le 6:10, 11. **sanctify**. Ezk 46:20. Ex 29:37. 30:29. Le 6:27. Mt 23:17-19. 1 C 3:5, 6.

20. **shave**. Le *21:5◗℘, etc. Dt 14:1. **nor suffer**. Nu 6:5. 1 C 11:14.

21. **drink wine**. Le *10:9◗℘. Lk 1:15. 1 T 3:8. 5:23. T 1:7, 8.

22. **Neither**. This was prohibited only to the high priest under the law; but is here extended to all the priests, perhaps to intimate the superior sanctity of the times to which it refers. **a widow**. Le *21:7, 13, 14◗℘. Dt 25:5. 1 T 3:2, 4, 5, 11, 12. T 1:6. **put away**. Heb. thrust forth. Dt 24:1-4. **that had a priest before**. Heb. from a priest.

23. **shall teach**. Ezk 22:26. Le 10:10, 11◗℘. Dt 33:10. Ho 4:6. Mi 3:9-11. Zp 3:4. Hg 2:11-13. Ml *2:6-9. Ga=6:6. 1 T=4:11, 12. 2 T 2:24, 25. T 1:9-11.

24. **in controversy**. This seems to intimate, that controversies, in the period predicted, will be generally decided by arbitration, according to the law of God; and not by litigations before human tribunals, according to the laws of man. Dt *17:8-13◗℘. 1 Ch 23:4. 2 Ch 19:8-10. Ezr 2:63. **they shall keep**. 1 T 3:15. **in all**. Le ch. 23. Nu ch. 28, 29. Ne ch. 8. **hallow my sabbaths**. Ezk 22:36. Le 19:30◗℘. Is +*58:13n, 14.

25. **come at no dead person**. Le *21:1-6◗℘. 22:4. Mt 8:21, 22. Lk 9:59, 60. 2 C 5:16. 1 Th 4:13-15.

26. **And after**. Nu 6:10◗℘, etc. *19:11-13. He 9:13, 14.

27. **unto the inner**. ver. 17. **he shall offer**. Le *4:3, etc. 8:14, etc. Nu 6:9-11. He 7:26-28. **sin offering**. Le +*23:19.

28. **for an inheritance**. Col =3:24. **I am their inheritance**. Ezk 45:4. 48:9-11. Nu *18:20◗℘. Dt 10:9◗℘. 18:1, 2◗℘. Jsh *13:14, 33. Ro=8:17. Ep=1:11. 1 P=1:4. 5:2-4. **no possession**. Ac =4:32. 1 C=7:30. 2 C =6:10. **possession**. SS 2:16.

29. **eat**. Le 2:3, 10. *6:14-18, 26, 29. 7:6. Nu 18:9-11. 1 C 9:13, 14. He 13:10. **meat offering**. Le +*23:13. **sin offering**. Le +*23:19. **trespass offering**. Le +*5:6n. **dedicated**. *or*, devoted. Le *27:21, 28, compared with Nu *18:14◗℘. 1 C=3:21-23.

30. **first**. *or*, chief. Ezk 20:40. 48:14. Ex 13:2◗℘, 12, 13. *22:29, 30◗℘. Nu 3:13◗℘. 18:12, 13◗℘. **all the firstfruits**. Ex 13:2, 12, 22:29. 23:19. Le +*23:10. Nu 3:13. 15:19-21. 18:12-18, 27-30. Dt 18:4. 2 Ch 31:4-6, 10. Ne 10:35-37. Ja *1:18. **oblation**. or, heave offering. Ezk 20:40. 45:6, 7, 13, 16. 48:8-10, 12, 18, 20, 21. Ex 29:27n. Ezr +8:25. Ne +10:37. **first of your dough**. Nu 15:20◗℘. **that he may**. Dt 26:10-15. Pr *3:9, 10. Ml *3:10, 11.

31. **priest shall not**. Ex *22:31. Le 17:15. *22:8◗℘. Dt 14:21. Ro 14:20, 21. 1 C 8:13.

EZEKIEL 45

The holy oblation for the land, for the sanctuary, and for the priests and Levites, 1-6. The portions of the prince and the people, 7, 8. Ordinances of justice to be observed by them, 9-12. Oblations to be presented in the beginning of the year, at the passover, and in the feast of tabernacles, 13-25.

1. **shall divide by lot**. Heb. cause the land to fall by lot. Ezk *47:21, 22. 48:29. Ge ❶24:44n. Nu *26:55, 56. 34:13. Jsh 13:6. +14:2n. Ps 16:5, 6. **ye shall offer**. ver. 2-7. Ezk +44:30. 48:8-23. Ex 29:27n. Le 25:23. Ezr +8:25. Pr *3:9, 10. **an holy portion**. Heb. holiness. Zc 14:20, 21. **the length**. That our translators rightly added the word *reeds*, is evident from the length and breadth of the sanctuary being exactly the same as before (compare ver. 2 with Ezk 42:16-19). Estimating the reed at 3 1/2 yards, this holy oblation would constitute a square of nearly fifty miles on every side. From the north side a portion of nearly twenty miles in width, and nearly fifty in length, was appointed for the priests; and in the midst of this portion, the area of the sanctuary, about a mile square, to be enclosed by a wall (ver. 1, 2). Next to this, on the south, was the Levites' portion, of the same dimensions as that of the priests (ver. 5); and south of this was the portion for the city, of the same length as those of the priests and Levites, but only half the width (ver. 6). These three formed the square of 25,000 reeds, or nearly fifty miles; and that set apart for the prince, the breadth of which is not mentioned, extended in length from north to south, along the east and west sides of the square. As Canaan would not admit of so large a portion for the sanctuary, etc., this was no doubt intended to intimate the large extent of the church in the glorious times predicted. Contrary to the last statement of the preceding note, it is possible to take these predictions literally since Israel will then possess all of the land originally promised to Abraham, and certain geographical changes will doubtless make a literal fulfillment of the prophecy entirely possible (See note on Ezk +42:16). **five and twenty thousand**. Ezk 48:8.

2. **five hundred in length**. Ezk *42:16-20. **suburbs**. *or*, void places.

3. **and in it.** Ezk 48:8, 10.

4. **holy portion.** ver. 1. Ezk 44:28. 48:11. **which.** Ezk 40:45. 43:19. 44:13, 14. Nu 16:5. **a place for their houses.** 2 K 23:11. 1 Ch 26:12, 13. **holy place for.** Ezk 48:10.

5. **the five.** Ezk *48:10, 13, 20. **the ministers.** 1 C 9:13, 14. **for a possession.** Ezk 40:17. 1 Ch 9:26-33. Ne 10:38, 39.

6. **the city.** Ezk *48:15-18, 30-35. **whole house.** Ezk 48:19.

7. **for the prince.** Ezk 34:24. 37:24. 46:16-18. *48:21. Ps *2:8, 9. Is +*9:5, 6. Lk +*1:32, 33.

8. **and my princes.** In the predicted period, not only shall the ministers and worshipers of God be liberally provided for, but the princes will be both able and willing to defray the expenses of government, without oppressing their subjects, and will rule over them with equity and clemency, as the vicegerents of God; while the people will submit to them conscientiously, and live in peace, prosperity, and holiness. These things deem to be represented in language taken from the customs of the times in which the prophet wrote. Tithes are not mentioned in any part of the vision, which shows that the ritual Mosaic law will not be in force. Ezk 19:3-7. *22:27. *46:18. 2 K 15:19, 20. Pr 28:16. Is *11:3-5. 32:1, 2. 60:17, 18. Je 22:17. *23:5. Mi 3:1-4. Zp 3:13. Ja 2:6. +*5:1-6. Re 19:11-16. **according.** Jsh 11:23.

9. **Thus saith.** Ezk +44:9. **Let it.** Ezk 44:6. 1 P 4:3. **princes of.** Dt 17:14-20. **remove.** Ne 5:10. Ps 82:2-5. Is 1:17. Je *22:3. Zc 8:16. Lk 3:14. **execute.** Ezk 43:14-16. **take away.** Ne 5:1-13. 1 C 6:7, 8. **exactions.** Heb. expulsions. Jb 20:19. 22:9. 24:2-12. Mi 2:1, 2, 9.

10. **just balances.** Le *19:35, 36♪℘. Pr *11:1. 16:11. 20:10. 21:3. Am 8:4-6. Mi 6:10, 11. **just ephah.** Dt 25:13-15. Pr 20:10.

11. **ephah.** The *ephah* was a dry measure, and the *bath* a liquid measure, containing about seven gallons, four pints, or three pecks, three pints; and the *homer* about seventy-five gallons, five pints. Le +*27:16n. Is 5:10. **the measure.** Ex +5:8.

12. **the shekel.** Ex *30:13♪℘. Le *27:25♪℘. Nu *3:47♪℘. **twenty shekels.** That is, 20+25+15=60; for the *maneh* as a weight was equal to sixty shekels, though as a coin it was only equal to fifty, weighing about two pounds six ounces; and reckoning the shekel at 2*s*. 6*d*. being in value 6*l*. 4*s*.

13. **the oblation.** Ezk +44:30. **give the sixth.** Ezk 39:2.

14. **ordinance of oil.** ver. 25. Nu 28:5. **the tenth.** ver. 11. **the cor.** 1 K +4:22mg.

15. **lamb.** *or,* kid. Ezk 34:17mg. Ex 12:3mg,n. **out of the fat pastures.** or, well-watered land. Ge 13:10. Pr *3:9, 10. Ml 1:8, 14. **meat offering.** Le +*23:13. **burnt offering.** Le +*23:12. **peace offerings.** or, thank offerings. ver. 17. **to make.** Le 1:4♪℘. 6:30. Da *9:24. Ro 5:10. 2 C √5:19-21. Ep 2:16. Col 1:21. He 2:17. 9:22, 23.

16. **the people.** Ex 30:14, 15. 2 Ch 29:31. **shall give this.** Heb. shall be for. **for.** *or,* with. Is 16:1.

17. **the prince's.** The *prince* is never mentioned in the ritual appointments of Moses, but here he is required to provide the oblations; and the variations in the Mosaic law, in the number of the several sacrifices, and the proportion of the meat offering to each,

being ten times as much as the law prescribed, with several other circumstances, seem more like enacting a new law, than enforcing that of Moses. These variations may intimate a change in the external constitution of the church; and it is probable that they are to be understood emblamatically (but see notes on ver. 1, and Ezk 44:16n; Je 33:18n). Ezk 40:38. 46:4-12. 2 S 6:19. 1 K 8:63, 64. 1 Ch 16:2, 3. 29:3-9. 2 Ch 5:6. 7:4, 5. 8:12, 13. 30:24. 31:3. 35:7, 8. Ezr 1:5. 6:8, 9. Ps 68:18. Jn 1:16. Ro 11:35, 36. Ep 5:2. **burnt offerings.** Le +*23:12. **meat offerings.** Le +*23:13. **drink offerings.** Ex 29:40. Le +*23:13. **in the feasts.** Ge +17:21h. Le *23:2n. Nu ch. 28, 29. Is 66:23. **new moons.** ver. 18. Ezk 46:1, 3, 6. Nu 28:11. 2 Ch +2:4. **the sabbaths.** Is +*58:13n, 14. **he shall prepare.** ver. 22-24. Le 14:19. Nu 6:16, 17. Ps 22:15-26, 29. Jn 6:51-57. 1 C 5:7, 8. He 13:10. 1 P *2:24. +*3:18. **sin offering.** Le +*23:19. **meat offering.** Le +*23:13. **burnt offering.** Le +*23:12. **peace offerings.** *or,* thank offerings. Ezk 43:27mg. Le 7:15. +*23:19. Je +*33:11. Col *3:17. He *13:15. **make reconciliation.** 2 Ch 29:20-24.

18. **In the first month.** This seems to enjoin, not a mere dedication, but an annual purification of the sanctuary; of which there is nothing said in the Mosaic law. Ex 12:2. Nu 28:11-15. Mt *6:33. **bullock.** Ex 29:1-14♪℘. **without blemish.** Le 22:20. He √7:26. √9:14. 1 P *1:19. **and cleanse.** Ezk 43:22, 26. Le 8:1-13. *16:16, 33. He *9:22-25. *10:3, 4, 19-22.

19. **and upon the four corners.** Ezk *43:14, 20. Le 16:18-20. **the settle.** Ezk 43:14.

20. **every one.** Le *4:27-30. Ps *19:12. Ro 16:18, 19. He 5:2. **that is simple.** Who wants understanding to conduct himself properly. √108K54, Pr +1:4. Ps *19:7. Pr 19:25. **so shall.** ver. 15, 18. Le 16:20.

21. **ye shall.** Ex ch. 12. Le *23:5-8. Nu *9:2-14. *28:16-25. Dt 16:1-8. 1 C 5:7, 8. **passover.** Ex 12:18♪℘. Le +*23:5. **unleavened bread.** Le +*23:6.

22. **the prince.** Mt *20:28. 26:26-28. **bullock.** Le *4:14. 2 C √5:21.

23. **seven days.** Le *23:8. **a burnt.** Nu *28:15-31. 29:5, 11-38. **seven bullocks.** Nu 23:1, 2. Jb 42:8. He 10:8-12.

24. **he shall prepare.** Ezk 46:5-7. Nu 28:12-15, 20, 21.

25. **In the seventh.** The prince shall do at the *feast of tabernacles* (Le +*23:34) the same thing he was desired to do on the *passover*. Le 23:33-43. Nu *29:12-38. Dt *16:13-15. 2 Ch 5:3. 7:8-10. Ezr 3:4, 5. Ne 8:14-18. Zc 14:16-19. Jn 7:2, 37-39. **sin offering.** Le +*23:19. **burnt offering.** Le +*23:12. **meat offering.** Le +*23:13. **according to the oil.** ver. +14. Le 5:11. Nu 18:12. Dt 12:17.

EZEKIEL 46

Ordinances for the prince in his worship, 1-8, and for the people, 9-15. Rules for the prince's disposal of his inheritance, 16-18. The places for boiling or baking the oblations, 19-24.

1. **Thus saith.** Whether the rules for public worship here laid down were designed to be observed in those things wherein they differed from the law of Moses, in the ministrations of the second temple, is not certain. In the latter history of the Jewish church, the law of Moses *only* was followed, except in the corruption of following the traditions of the fathers. **The gate.** The

prophet had before observed that the east gate of the *outer* court was shut, and was told that it must only be opened for the prince; and now he is informed that the gate of the *inner* court on the east was also shut, and is to be opened only on the sabbath and new moons, till the evening. **shall be shut**. Ezk 44:1, 2. **six working**. Ge 3:19. Ex +*20:9. Lk 13:14. **on the sabbath**. Ezk 45:17. Le 23:3n. 2 Ch 23:31. Is +*58:13n, 14. *66:23. He *4:9, 10. **new moon**. 1 Ch 23:31. 2 Ch +2:4. Ps 81:3, 4.

2. **the porch**. Jn 10:1-3. **by the post**. ver. 8. Ezk 44:3. 2 Ch 23:13. 34:31. **the priests**. Col 1:28. **prepare**. Or, "offer," as the word *asah* frequently denotes. The whole of this seems to intimate the constant, reverential, and exemplary attendance of kings on the pure ordinances of religion, in the approaching flourishing days of the church. Or rather, of Israel during the Millennial reign of Christ. **his**. Ezk 45:16, 17, 20, 22. **burnt offering**. Le +*23:12. **peace offerings**. Le +*23:19. **he shall worship**. 1 K 8:22, 23. 1 Ch 17:16. 29:10-12. 2 Ch 6:13. 29:29. Mt 26:39. He 5:7, 8. **but the gate**. ver. 12.

3. **people of the land**. Ezk 45:16. Is 66:23. Lk 1:10. Jn 10:9. He +*10:19-22.

4. **the burnt**. The proportions of the burnt offerings, and also of the meat and drink offerings, are very different here from those prescribed in the Mosaic law. The meat offering, under the law, was only three tenths of an epha to a bullock, two tenths for a ram, and one tenth for a lamb, with the fourth part of a hin of oil. Ezk 45:17. Nu 28:9, 10.

5. **the meat**. ver. 7, 11, 12. Ezk 45:24, 29. Nu 28:12. **as he shall be able to give**. Heb. the gift of his hand. Le 14:21. Nu 6:21. 9:10. Dt 16:17.

8. **he shall go**. ver. 2. Ezk 44:1-3. Col 1:18.

9. **when the people**. This may intimate, that every thing should be regulated, in divine worship, so as to prevent disorder and interruption, and also that men should go forward and make progress in religion, and not turn their backs upon God. 1 C 14:40. **come before**. Ex 23:14-17. 34:23. Dt 16:16. Ps 84:7. Ml 4:4. **solemn feasts**. Ge +17:21h. Le *23:2n. **he that entereth**. Ezk 1:12, 17. Ph 3:13, 14. He 10:38. 2 P 2:20, 21.

10. **the prince in the midst**. 2 S 6:14-19. 1 Ch 29:20, 22. 2 Ch 6:2-4. 7:4, 5. 20:27, 28. 29:28, 29. 34:30, 31. Ne 8:8, 9. Ps 42:4. 122:1-4. Mt √18:20. *28:20. He 3:6. 4:14-16. Re 2:1. **when they go in**. Ex 23:14-17. Dt 16:16. **go forth**. 2 S 5:24. Jn +*10:4.

11. **in the feasts**. Le ch. *23. Nu ch. 15, 28, 29. Dt ch. 16. **the meat**. ver. 5, 7.

12. **a voluntary**. Le +1:3. 23:38. Nu 29:39. 1 K 3:4. 1 Ch 29:21. 2 Ch 5:6. 7:5-7. 29:31. Ezr 1:4. 3:5. 6:17. Ps *40:7, 8. Ro *12:1. Ep 5:2. **burnt offering**. Le +*23:12. **peace offerings**. Le +*23:19. **one**. ♪63A1, Ge +14:20. i.e. the gate keeper. **open him**. ver. 1, 2, 8. Ezk 44:3. **as he did**. Ezk 45:17.

13. **Thou shalt daily**. It is observable, that there is nothing said about the *evening* sacrifice, or the additional lamb, morning and evening, on the sabbath, which makes an important difference between this and the old laws; and is probably an intimation of that change in the external forms of religion which the coming of the Messiah should introduce. Ex 29:38-42𝓟. Nu 28:3-8, 10𝓟. Da 8:11-13. Jn 1:29. 1 P 1:19, 20. Re 13:8. **of the first year**. Heb. a son of his year. Ex

12:5. Le 12:6mg. **every morning**. Heb. morning by morning. 2 S +13:4mg. Ps 92:2. Is 50:4.

14. **every morning**. ver. +13. **the sixth**. Nu 28:5. **perpetual**. Heb. *olam*, Ge +9:12.

15. **every morning**. ver. +13. **a continual**. Ex 29:38. Nu 28:3-8. He *7:27. *9:26. 10:1-10.

16. **If the prince**. Ge 25:5, 6. Nu 27:1-11. 36:7. 2 Ch 21:3. Ps 37:18. Mt 25:34. Lk 10:42. Jn 8:35, 36. Ro 8:15-17, 29-32. Ga 4:7.

17. **to the year**. That is, to the year of *Jubilee*, called the *year of liberty*, because there was then a general release: all servants had their liberty; and all alienated estates returned to their former owners. Le +*25:10𝓟. Mt 25:14-29. Lk 19:25, 26. Ga 4:30, 31. This shows that this prophecy will, and must yet, be literally fulfilled (CB).

18. **the prince**. Ezk 45:8. 1 K 21:4-7, 16. Ps 72:2-4. 78:72. Is 11:3, 4. 32:1, 2. Je *23:5, 6. **thrust**. Ezk 22:27. 1 K 21:19. Mi 1:1, 2. 3:1-3. **inheritance out**. Ps 68:18. Jn √10:28. Ep 4:8. **my people**. Ezk 34:3-6, 21.

19. **the entry**. This entry was at the west side of the north gate of the inner court (see Ezk 44:4, 5). Ezk 40:44-46. 42:9. **a place**. This place was at the west corners of the inner court, or court of the priests; where they prepared the most holy things, the trespass and sin offering, which none but the priests might eat; that they might not "bear them out into the utter court, to sanctify the people," that is, by touching them incapacitate them from discharging their ordinary occupations.

20. **boil the trespass offering**. Ezk 44:29. Le +5:6n. Nu 18:9. 1 S *2:13-15. 2 Ch *35:13. **sin offering**. Le +*23:19. **bake the meat offering**. Le 2:4-7. ch. 7. +*23:13. **to sanctify**. See on Ezk 44:19.

21. **in every corner of the court there was a court**. Heb. a court in a corner of a court; and a court in a corner of a court.

22. **courts**. These courts in the corners of the outer court, or court of the people, appear to have been a kind of uncovered apartments, surrounded with little chambers for the cooks, and used for dressing the peace offerings of the people. On these their families and friends feasted; and portions were sent to the poor, the widow, and the orphan; and thus the spirit of devotion preserved the spirit of mercy, charity, and benevolence, in the land. **joined**. or, made with chimneys. **corners**. Heb. cornered.

24. **where the ministers**. ver. 20. 1 Ch 23:27-29. Mt +*24:45. Jn 21:15-17. 1 P 5:2.

EZEKIEL 47

The prophet is shown waters springing from under the threshold of the temple, growing wider and deeper, and at length becoming an impassable river, which healed the desert, and the dead sea; abounded with fish; and had on each bank fruit trees filled with new fruit every month, the leaves of which served for medicine, 1-12. The borders of the land appointed, as to be divided among Israelites and sojourners, 13-23.

1. **the door**. Ezk 41:2, 23-26. **waters issued**. Solomon's temple and the second temple were doubtless well supplied with water, probably conveyed there by means of pipes; but *these* waters flowed *from* the temple, not as a common sewer, but as a fertilizing

river. A fountain producing abundance of water was not in the temple, and could not be there on the top of such a hill; and consequently these waters, as well as those spoken of by *Joel* and *Zechariah*, must be understood figuratively and typically. These waters doubtless were an emblem of the "gospel preached with the Holy Ghost sent down from heaven;" and their gradual rise beautifully represents its progress, from small beginnings to an immensely large increase; and the latter part of the representation may relate to the times when it shall fill the earth, and produce the most extensive and important effects on the state of mankind in every nation. The preceding note of nearly two centuries ago fails, however, to maintain a consistently literal interpretation. Surely there is no reason why, with the changes geologically and geographically predicted for these times (Ezk +*42:16n. 45:1n. Ps 46:2, 3. Zc 14:4, 10), and the supernatural character of the period predicted with the presence of the Messiah reigning from Jerusalem, that these predictions should not be literally fulfilled. Just as there is no justification for spiritualizing or allegorizing away the literal meaning and fulfillment of the predictions regarding the destruction of Jerusalem and the second advent of Christ, so there is no justification for disbelieving in the literal fulfillment of the predictions here. See note below, and on Ezk +46:2n. Ps √46:4. Is 30:25. 55:1. Je 2:13. Jl √3:18. Zc *13:1. √14:8. Jn 7:37-39. Re 22:1, 17. **came down**. or, were coming down. Is 12:3. 44:3. Jl 3:18. Zc 14:8. Re 22:1. **from under**. Referring to the perennial source which has supplied the fountain of Gihon (CB). ver. 12. 2 K +*18:17n. *20:20. 2 Ch 32:3-5. Ne 2:14. Is 2:3. Is *22:11.

2. **northward**. Ezk 44:2, 4. **there ran**. Lk 24:47. Jn 4:22.

3. **the man**. Ezk *40:3. Zc 2:1. Re 11:1. 21:15. **waters were to the ancles**. Heb. waters of the ancles. Lk 24:49. Ac 2:4, 33. 10:45, 46. 11:16-18.

4. **the waters were to the knees**. Ac 8:4. 19:10-20. Ro 15:19. Col 1:6.

5. **waters to swim in**. Heb. waters of swimming. Is 11:9. Da 2:34, 35. Hab 2:14. Mt 13:31, 32. Jn 7:37-39. Re 7:9. 11:15. 20:2-4. 22:1.

6. **hast thou**. Ezk 8:17. 40:4. 44:5. Je 1:11-13. Zc 4:2. 5:2. Mt 13:51.

7. **at the**. Is 44:18, 19. 43:19. Jl 3:18. **bank**. Heb. lip. Jg +7:22mg. 1 K 9:26. 2 K 2:13mg. **many**. ver. 12. Ge 2:9, 10. Nu 24:6. Ps 1:3. Je 17:8. Re 22:2.

8. **east country**. Jsh 22:11. **and go down**. Is 35:1, 7. 41:17-19. 43:20. 44:3-5. 49:9, 10. Je 31:9. **desert**. or, plain. Heb. Arabah. Dt *3:17. 4:49. Jsh *3:16. Je 5:6mg. **the sea**. This was the Dead sea, or sea of Sodom, east of Jerusalem, in which it is said no living creature is found; or, at least, from its extreme saltness, it does not abound with fish like other seas. The healing of these waters denotes the calling of the Gentiles. Or, more literally, the freshening of its waters newly supplied by the fountain issuing forth from the temple. **the waters**. 2 K *2:19-22. Is *11:6-9. Ml 1:11. Mt 13:15.

9. **that every**. Jn √3:16. 11:26. **thing**. Heb. *nephesh*, soul, Ge +2:19. Le 11:10. **which moveth**. Ge 1:20. **rivers**. Heb. two rivers. Ps 78:16. **shall live**. Is 12:3. Jn *4:10, 14. 5:25. 6:63. 11:25. *14:6, 19. Ro 8:2. 1 C 15:45. Ep 2:1-5. **a very great**. Is 49:12. 60:3-10. Zc 2:11. 8:21-23. Ac 2:41, 47. 4:4. 5:14. 6:7. 21:20g.

for they. Ex +*15:26. Ps +*103:3. Is 30:26.

10. **fishers**. Typifying apostles and preachers of the gospel. Mt 4:19. 13:47-50. Mk 1:17. Lk 5:4-10. Jn 21:3-11. **En-gedi**. 2 Ch 20:2. **Eneglaim**. i.e. *spring of two heifers*, *S#5882h, only here. **the fish**. Great quantities of all kinds of fish usually caught in the Mediterranean. Typifying genuine converts of all nations, kindreds, and people. **the great sea**. ver. 15. Ezk 48:28. Nu *34:6. Jsh 23:4. Ps 104:25. **exceeding**. Is 49:12, 20.

11. **the miry places**. Typifying those who reject, neglect, or pervert the gospel. **shall not be healed, they shall be**. or, and *that which* shall not be healed, shall be, etc. He +*6:4-8. +*10:26-31. 2 P √2:19-22. Re +*21:8. *22:11, 15. **given**. Dt 29:23. Jg 9:45. Ps 107:34. Je 17:6. Mk 9:48, 49.

12. **by the river**. ver. 7. Ps 92:12. Is 60:21. *61:3. **grow**. Heb. come up. Is 53:2. **trees for meat**. Typically, probably believers, "trees of righteousness," who still bring forth "fruit unto holiness," and "whose end is eternal life." Yet even these details must not be denied a literal fulfillment. Ge 2:9. Re 2:7. **whose**. Jb 8:16. Ps +*1:3. Je +*17:8. **new**. or, principal. **their waters**. SS 4:12. 7:12, 13. **medicine**. or, bruises and sores. Is *1:6. Je +*8:22. Re *22:2, 14.

13. **This shall**. Nu 34:2-12. **Joseph**. Ezk 48:4-6. Ge 48:5, 21, 22⅋. 49:26. 1 Ch +*5:1. Je 3:18. 31:1. **shall have**. √63C, Ge +25:32.

14. **lifted up mine hand**. or, swore. Ezk 20:5, 6, 15, 23, 28, √42. 36:7. Ge *22:16, 17. Nu 14:28. Ps 106:26. He *6:13. Certainly here is the key to the whole question of interpretation: the fulfillment of these predictions is based upon God's own oath and covenant with Abraham, Isaac, and David in their respective covenants (See notes and references on Ezk +36:25n). **to give**. Ezk √20:42. Ge *12:7⅋. +*13:15. *15:7. 17:8. 26:3. +*28:13. 50:24⅋. Nu 14:16, 30. **fall**. Ezk 48:29. Pr 16:33.

15. **And this**. ver. 17-20. **Hethlon**. i.e. *hiding place*, *S#2855h. Ezk 48:1. **Zedad**. Nu *34:8, 9.

16. **Hamath**. Nu 13:21. 34:8. 1 K 8:65. Am 6:14. Zc 9:2. **Berothah**. i.e. *place of wells; cypress-like*, *S#1268h. 2 S 8:8, Berothai. **Sibraim**. i.e. *double hope*, *S#5453h, only here. **Damascus**. Ge 14:15. 1 Ch 18:5. Ac 9:2. **Hazar-hatticon**. or, the middle village. *S#2694h. **Hauran**. i.e. *cavernous; very white*, *S#2362h. ver. 18. The district of *Auranitis*, now *Haouran*, S.W. of Damascus.

17. **the border from**. The Holy Land, as here described, extended from about 31 degrees to 35 degrees N. lat. and from 34 degrees to 37 degrees E. long.; being bounded on the north by a line drawn from the Mediterranean to Hamath; on the east by Damascus, Hauran, Gilead, and the land of Israel east of Jordan, unto the south of the Dead sea; on the south by Tamar and Kadesh, unto the river of Rhinocorura; and on the west by the Mediterranean sea, from the same point, northward, "till a man come over against Hamath;" and its length from north to south would be about 280 miles, and its breadth about 150 miles. The boundaries of the land are nearly the same as were marked out by Moses; except, that it does not appear, whether any part, or what part, of the country east of Jordan, is included within the eastern boundary. The ten tribes, as well as Judah and Benjamin, are to be admitted to a full share in this inheritance, which seems to imply that a future restoration to the promised

land is predicted (Scott). **Hazar-enan.** Ezk 48:1. Nu 34:9.

18. **east side.** Nu 34:10-12. **from.** Heb. from between. 2 K 16:14. **from Gilead.** Ge 31:23, 47, Galead. Nu 32:1. Jg 10:8. **land of Israel.** Ezk +27:17. **Jordan.** Ge 13:10. Jb 40:23.

19. **south side.** Nu 34:3-5. **Tamar.** Ezk 48:28. **strife.** or, Meribah. Nu *20:13)𝒫. Dt 32:51. 33:8. Ps 81:7. **river.** or, valley. Nu 34:5. Jsh 12:3. **southward.** or, toward Teman. Jsh 12:3mg.

20. **west side.** Nu 34:6. **Hamath.** 1 Ch 13:5.

21. **divide this land.** Nu 34:13-15.

22. **ye shall divide.** ver. 13, 14. Ezk 45:1. 48:29. Jsh +14:2n. **and to the.** Is *56:3-8. Jn +*10:16. Ac 2:5-10. 11:18. Ep 2:12, 13, 19-22. *3:6. Re *7:9, 10. **strangers.** ver. 23. Ezk 14:7. 22:7, 29. Ge +23:4 (✱S#1616h). Ex 12:48mg. Zc 7:10. Ml 3:5. **born in.** Ex 12:19, 48, 49. Le 16:29. **they shall have.** Ac 15:9. Ro 10:12. Ga 3:28, 29. Col 3:11.

23. **the stranger.** ver. +22. Dt 10:19. Zc 7:10. Ml 3:5.

EZEKIEL 48

The portions allotted to Dan, Asher, Naphtali, Manasseh, Ephraim, Reuben, and Judah, 1-7. The allotments for the sanctuary, the priests, Levites, city, and prince, 8-22. The portions of Benjamin, Simeon, Issachar, Zebulun, and Gad, 23-29. The plan of the city, its gates, dimensions, and name, 30-35.

1. **the names.** Ex 1:1-5. Nu 1:5-15. 13:4-15. Re 7:4-8. **From.** Ezk 47:15-17. Nu 34:7-9. **a portion.** Heb. one *portion.* **Dan.** Ge 30:3-6. Jsh *19:40-47. Jg 18:26-29. 2 S 24:2. 1 K 12:28, 29. 1 Ch 7:12n. Mt 20:15, 16.

2. **Asher.** Ge 30:12, +13. Dt +*33:24n. Jsh *19:24-31.

3. **Naphtali.** Ge 30:7, 8. Jsh *19:32-39.

4. **by the border.** In this division of the Holy Land, a portion is laid out for each of the twelve tribes directly across the country, from east to west; and deducting the square of 25,000 reeds, or nearly fifty miles on each side, between Judah and Benjamin, for the priests, Levites, city, and temple, with the inheritance of the prince to the east and west (see on Ezk 45:1) from 280 miles, the length of the country from north to south, there will remain for each tribe a portion of less than twenty miles in width, and 150 in length. This division of the land entirely differs from that which was made in the days of Joshua, in which the tribes were not only differently placed, but confused and intermixed; while here distinct lots are assigned to each of the twelve tribes, in a regular mathematical form. *Literally* such a division never took place in the past, but will take place as described in the future Messianic kingdom reign of Christ during the Millennium. **Manasseh.** Ge 30:22-24. 41:51. 48:5, 14-20. Nu 32:39-42. Jsh 13:29-31. *17:1-11.

5. **Ephraim.** Jsh ch. 16. 17:8-10, 14-18.

6. **Reuben.** Ge 29:32. 49:3, 4. Nu 32:33, 37, 38. Jsh 13:15-21.

7. **Judah.** Ge 29:35. Jsh ch. 15. 19:9.

8. **the offering.** Ezk +44:30. 45:1-6. Ex 29:27n. **the sanctuary.** ver. 35. Is 12:6. 33:20-22. Zc 2:11, 12. 2 C *6:16. Ep 2:20-22. Col 2:9. Re 21:3, 22. 22:3.

9. **the oblation.** ver. +8, 10, 21. Ezk +44:30.

10. **for the priests.** Ezk 44:15, 28. 45:4. Nu 35:1-9. Jsh ch. 21. Mt 10:10. 1 C 9:13, 14. **toward the east.** Nu 3:38. **and the sanctuary.** ver. 8.

11. **It shall be for the priests that are sanctified.** or, The sanctified *portion shall be* for the priests. **the sons.** Ezk 40:46. 43:19. 44:15, 16. **charge.** or, ward, or ordinance. Ezk 40:45mg. 44:8mg. Zc 3:7mg. Ml +3:14mg. Mt +*24:45, 46. 2 T 4:7, 8. 1 P 5:4. Re 2:10. **as the Levites.** Ezk 44:10.

12. **a thing.** Ezk 45:4. Le 27:21.

13. **Levites.** Nu 1:53. Jsh 21:1. **five and twenty thousand in.** Ezk 45:3, 5. Dt 12:19. Lk 10:7.

14. **they shall.** Ex 22:29. Le 25:32-34. 27:10, 28, 33. Nu 18:12-14. **for.** ver. 12. Le 23:20. 27:9, 32. Ml 3:8-10.

15. **a profane.** Ezk 22:26. 42:20. 44:23. 45:6. **for the city.** The holy oblation of 25,000 reeds, or near fifty square miles, was divided into three parts from north to south (see on Ezk 45:1): a portion on the north of 10,000 reeds in width, and 25,000 in length, for the priests, in the midst of which was the sanctuary or temple, surrounded by a wall 500 reeds square (ver. 9, 10. see on Ezk 42:15); next to this another portion of the same dimensions for the Levites (ver. 13, 14); and on the south another portion of the same length, but only 5000 reeds in breadth, for the city (ver. 15). The city was situated in the midst of this portion, being 4500 reeds, or about nine miles square (see on ver. 30), having a suburb of 250 reeds, or about half a mile on each side (ver. 17), leaving 10,000 reeds or nearly ten miles, on the east side, and the same on the west side, for the profit of those who serve the city out of all the tribes (ver. 18, 19). On the east and west sides of this square of 25,000 reeds, is the portion of the prince; each of which, estimating the breadth of the land at 150 miles, would form a square of fifty miles. Thus the whole plan of the division of the country, laying out of the city, temple, and all its appendages, is perfectly regular and uniform; and would therefore convey to the minds of the Jews the most complete idea they were capable of conceiving of the most perfect church, commonwealth, city, temple, and conveniences, on the largest and grandest scale for the Divine worship; and it doubtless ultimately points out the land of Immanuel, the city of the New Jerusalem, and his temple, the Christian church, the house of the living God. 1 T 3:15. Re 21:16.

18. **that serve.** Jsh 9:27. Ezr 2:43-58. Ne 7:46-62.

19. **shall serve.** Ezk *45:6. 1 K 4:7-23. Ne ch. 11.

20. **foursquare.** Ezk 40:47. He 12:27. Re 21:16.

21. **the residue.** ver. 22. Ezk 34:23, 24. 37:24. 45:7, 8. Ho 1:11. **and westward.** ver. 8-10.

23. **Benjamin.** ver. 1-7. Ge 35:16-19. Jsh 18:21-28. **a portion.** Heb. one *portion.* ver. 1.

24. **Simeon.** Ge 29:33. 49:5-7. Jsh *19:1-9.

25. **Issachar.** Ge 30:14-18. Jsh *19:17-23.

26. **Zebulun.** Ge 30:19, 20. Jsh *19:10-16.

27. **Gad.** Ge 30:10, 11. Nu 32:33-36. Jsh 13:24-28.

28. **from Tamar.** Ezk 47:19. 2 Ch 20:2. **strife in Kadesh.** Heb. Meribah-kadesh. Nu 20:1, 13. Ps 106:32. **the river.** or, brook (of Egypt). Ezk 47:19. Ge 15:18. Nu 34:5. Jsh 13:3. Is 27:12. **the great sea.** Ezk 47:15, 19, 20. Nu 34:5. Jsh 15:12.

29. **the land.** Ezk 47:13-22. Nu 34:2, 13. Jsh ch. 13-21. **divide by lot.** Jsh +14:2n. Pr 16:33.

30. **the goings.** ver. 16, 32-35. Re 21:16. **four.** It

is certainly most obvious to interpret these measures, not of *cubits*, but of the *measuring reed* which the prophet's conductor had in his hand (see on Ezk 45:1n); according to which, the city would be about thirty-six miles in circumference, and nine miles on each side of the square; which was nearly nine times larger than the greatest extent to which ancient Jerusalem ever attained (See on ver. 15, and Ezk 42:16). Young notes that the number is not to be read as 504,000 but 4,500. Young calls attention here to Is 37:36, where "a hundred and eighty and five thousand" (185,000)

should be read "a hundred, and eighty, and five thousand," or 5,180.

31. **the gates.** Is 26:1, 2. 54:12. 60:11. Re *21:12, 13, 21, 25.

35. **and the name.** Ge *22:14. Je *33:16. Zc 14:21. **The Lord.** Heb. *Jehovah shammah.* i.e. *The Lord is there.* Signifying the personal presence of Messiah who will reign visibly in Israel (Is +*9:6, 7. Lk +*1:32, 33. Re 11:15. 20:4-10). Ex +*15:26. *17:15. Jg *6:24. Ps 46:5. 48:3, 14. 68:18. 77:13. 132:14. Is *12:6. 14:32. *24:23. Je 3:17. Jl 3:21. Zc *2:10. Re *21:3. *22:3.

DANIEL

DANIEL 1

Jehoiakim, with part of the sacred vessels, is carried captive, 1, 2. Nebuchadnezzar commits Daniel, and certain young Jews, to the master of the eunuchs, to be instructed in the Chaldee learning; allotting them a daily portion, and changing their names, 3-7. They refuse to eat of the king's meat; and, being permitted to live on pulse and water, they improve in vigor and comeliness, 8-16. God confers on them knowledge and wisdom; so that, being far superior to the wise men of Babylon, they are preferred by the king, 17-21.

1. **the third year of.** 2 K *24:1, 2, 13. 2 Ch 36:5-7. **Babylon.** i.e. *confusion,* S#894h, 2 K +17:24.

2. Cir. A.M. 3398. B.C. 606. **the Lord gave.** Da 2:37, 38. 5:18. Dt 28:49-52. 32:30. Jg 2:14. 3:8. 4:2. 2 K 24:3. Ps 106:41, 42. Is 42:24. **with part.** Da 2:42. 5:2. 2 K 24:13. 2 Ch *36:7, 10. Je 27:19, 20. **Shinar.** Note the reference to the Pentateuch. Other references to the Pentateuch in Daniel are at ver. 5. Da 2:28. 8:11. 9:4, 11, 13, 15, 16, 17. 11:30. See related note (Is +*1:2). Ge +10:10▶℘. 11:2▶℘. 14:1, 9▶℘. Jsh 7:21h. Is *11:11. Zc 5:11. **and he.** Da 5:2, 3. Jg 16:23, 24. 1 S 5:2. 31:9, 10. Ezr 1:7. Je 51:44. Hab 1:16.

3. **Ashpenaz.** i.e. *nose of a horse,* *S#828h. **the master.** 2 K 18:17. Je 39:3. **eunuchs.** ver. 18. Ge +37:36mg. 2 K +8:6mg. **certain of the children.** Foretold 2 K 20:17, 18. Is *39:7. Je 41:1. **the princes.** Est 1:3. 6:9.

4. **Children.** The word *yeladim,* rendered *children,* is frequently used for *lads,* or *young men* (see Ge 21:8, 14-16), *neaniskous,* as the LXX. render; and Daniel must have been at this time at least seventeen or eighteen years of age. *S#3206h. Rendered "children" at Da 1:10, 13, 15, 17. Ge 30:26. 33:1, 2, 5, 5, 6, 7, 13, 14. Ex 1:17, 18. 2:6. 21:4. 1 S *1:2. A K √2:23n, 24h. Ezr 10:1. Ne 12:43. Jb 21:11. Is 2:6. 8:18. 29:23. 57:4, 5. La *4:10. Ho 1:2. Rendered otherwise at Ge 4:23 (young man). 21:8 (child), √14n, 15, 16. 32:22 (sons). 37:30 (child). 42:22. 44:20. Ex 2:3 (child), 6, 7, 8, 9, 9, 10. 21:22 (fruit). Ru 1:5 (sons). 4:16 (child). 2 S 6:23 (child). 12:15, 18, 18, 18, 18, 19, 19, 21, 21, 22, 22. 1 K 3:25. *12:8 (young men), 10, 14. 14:12 (child). 17:21, 21, 22, 23. 2 K 4:1 (sons), 18 (child), 26, 34, 34. 2 Ch 10:8 (young men), 10, 14. Jb 38:41 (young ones). 39:3. Ec 4:13 (child), 15. Is *9:6. 11:7 (young ones). Je 31:20 (child). Jl 3:3 (boy). Zc 8:5 (boys). **in whom.** Le 21:18-21. 24:19, 20. Jg 8:18. 2 S 14:25. Ac 7:20. Ep 5:27. **and skilful.** Rather, as Houbigant renders, "apt to understand wisdom, to acquire knowl-

edge, and to attain science;" for it was not a knowledge of the sciences, but merely a capacity to learn them, that was required. Da 2:20, 21. 5:11. Ec 7:19. Mt 2:1. Ac 7:22. **ability.** See on ver. 17-20. Pr 22:29. **the tongue.** Dt 28:49. **Chaldeans.** Da 2:2, 4. 9:1. Je 22:25. Ezk 23:23.

5. **a daily.** Athenaeus says the kings of Persia were accustomed to order for their courtiers the food left at their tables. 1 K 4:22, 23. 2 K 25:30. Mt *6:11. Lk *11:3. **provision.** 1 K 8:59mg. Ne 11:23mg. Je 52:34mg. **which he drank.** Heb. of his drink. **stand.** ver. 19. Ge 41:46▶℘. 1 S 16:22. 1 K 10:8. 2 Ch 9:7. Je 15:19. Lk 1:19. +*21:36.

6. **Daniel.** Da 2:17. Ezk 14:14, 20. 28:3. Mt 24:15. Mk 13:14.

7. **the prince.** ver. 3, 10, 11. **gave names.** Da 4:8. 5:12. Ge 41:45. 2 K 23:34. *24:17. **Belteshazzar.** i.e. *Bel's prince* or *superior; lord of the straitened's treasure,* *S#1095h. Da 10:1. Also *S#1096h. Da 2:26. 4:8, 9, 18, 19, 19, 19. 5:12. **Hananiah.** Da 2:49. 3:12-30. **Shadrach.** i.e. *rejoicing in the way; little friend of the king,* *S#7714h. Also *S#7715h. Da 2:49. 3:12, 13, 14, 16, 19, 20, 22, 23, 26, 26, 28, 29, 30. **Meshach.** i.e. *agile, expeditious; waters of quiet,* *S#4335h. Also *S#4336h. Da 2:49. 3:12, 13, 14, 16, 19, 20, 22, 23, 26, 26, 28, 29, 30. **Abednego.** i.e. *servant of light* or *the sun,* *S#5664h. Also *S#5665h. Da 2:49. 3:12, 13, 14, 16, 19, 20, 22, 23, 26, 26, 28, 29, 30.

8. **Daniel.** i.e. *judge of God, my God is judge; divine judgment,* *S#1840h. Da 1:6, 7, 8, 9, 10, 11, 11, 17, 19, 21. 2:19. 8:1, 15, 27. 9:2, 22. 10:1, 2, 7, 11, 12. 12:4, 5, 9. 1 Ch 3:1. Ezr 8:2. Ne 10:6. Ezk *14:14, 20. 28:3. (1) The second son of David by Abigail the Carmelitess, 1 Ch 3:1. He is called Chileab in 2 S 3:3. (2) A priest of the family of Ithamar, the son of Aaron, who went up from Babylon with Ezra, Ezr 8:2; Ne 10:6. (3) The last of the greater prophets, author of the book of Daniel, called Belteshazzar by the Chaldeans. **purposed.** Ru *1:17, 18. 1 K 5:5. Ps *119:106, 115. Pr 23:7. Ac *11:23. 1 C *7:37. 2 C *9:7. **heart.** Pr 16:1. **defile.** Heathen nations not only ate unclean beasts, which were forbidden by the Jewish law, but even the clean animals that were eaten were first offered as victims to their gods, and part of the wine was poured out as a libation on their altars. Hence Athenaeus (l. iv. c. 10) calls the beasts served up at the tables of the Persian kings, *ieria, victims.* Daniel was therefore resolved not to defile himself with their viands; yet he did not rudely refuse what was intended as a kindness, but mildly and modestly requested the

proper officers to indulge him in this respect. Ex 34:15. Le 3:17. 7:26. 11:45-47. 17:10-14. 19:26. Dt 32:38. Ps 106:28. *141:4. Ezk *4:13, 14. Ho 9:3, 4. Ac *10:14-16. 15:29. Ro *14:15-17. 1 C 8:7-10. *10:18-21, 28-31. 1 T 5:22. **king's meat.** Ezk 4:13. Ho 9:3. **wine.** Jg 13:4.

9. **God had brought.** T#266. Ge 32:28. 39:21. Ex 3:21. 1 K 8:50. Ezr 7:27, 28. Ne 1:11. 2:4. Ps 4:3. *75:6, 7. *106:46. Pr +*16:7. Ac 7:9, 10.

10. **I fear.** Pr 29:25. Jn 12:42, 43. **why.** ʃ85L, Ge +27:45. **worse liking.** Heb. sadder. Ge 40:6. Mt 6:16-18. Lk 24:17. **sort.** *or,* term, *or* continuance. **endanger.** Da 5:19.

11. **Melzar.** *or,* the steward. i.e. *chief butler,* S#4453h. ver. 16.

12. **Prove.** Re 2:10. **pulse to eat.** Heb. of pulse that we may eat, etc. *Pulse, zeroim,* denotes all leguminous plants, which are not reaped, but *pulled* or *plucked;* which, however wholesome, was not naturally calculated to render them fatter in flesh than the others. ver. 16. Ge 1:29, 30. Dt 8:3. Ro 14:2.

13. **our countenances.** La 4:7.

15. **their.** Ex 23:25. Dt 28:1-14. 2 K 4:42-44. Ps 37:16. Pr 10:22. Hg 1:6, 9. Ml 2:2. Mt 4:4. Mk 6:41, 42. **appeared.** 1 S 16:12. Ps 45:2.

16. **Melzar.** ver. 11mg. **took away.** Le 11:4-23. Ezk 4:14. Ac 10:14.

17. **God.** Da 2:21, 23. 1 K 3:12, 28. 4:29-31. 2 Ch 1:10, 12. Jb 32:8. Ps +*119:98-100. Pr 2:6. Ec 2:26. Is 28:26. Lk 21:15. Ac 6:10. 7:10. Col 1:9. Ja +*1:5, 17. **knowledge.** Ac 7:22. **Daniel had understanding.** *or,* he made Daniel understand. Da 4:9, 10. 5:11, 12, 14. 10:1. Ge *41:8-15. Nu 12:6. 2 Ch 26:5. Ezk 28:3. 1 C 12:7-11.

18. **eunuchs.** ver. 3. Ge +37:36mg. 2 K +8:6mg.

19. A.M. 3401. B.C. 603. **communed.** 1 K 10:2. **therefore.** See on ver. 5. Da 2:49. Ge 41:46. 1 K 17:1. Pr 22:29. Je 15:19.

20. **in all.** 1 S 18:30. 1 K 4:29-34. 10:1-3, 23, 24. Ps +*119:99. Lk 21:15. **wisdom and understanding.** Heb. wisdom of understanding. **ten.** Ge 31:7. Nu 14:22. Ne 4:12. Jb 19:3. **the magicians.** Da 2:2-11, 21-23. 4:7, 8, etc. 5:7, 8, 11, 12, 17. Ge 41:8. Ex 7:11, 12, 22. 8:7, 19. Is 19:3. 47:12-14. 2 T 3:8, 9.

21. **Daniel continued.** Da *6:28. *10:1. Ex 25:30. 27:20. 28:29, 30, 38. 29:38, 42. 30:8. Ezk 39:14. "He lived to see that glorious time of the return of his people from the Babylonian captivity, though he did not die then. So *till* is used Ps 110:1. 112:8."

DANIEL 2

Nebuchadnezzar, perplexed with a dream which he had forgotten, with menaces and promises requires his wise men to make it known to him, with the interpretation, 1-9. They acknowledge their inability, and are sentenced to die, 10-13. Daniel obtains respite, joins in prayer with his friends, has the dream revealed to him, and blesses God, 14-23. He stays the decree, and is brought before the king, 24-30. The dream and its interpretation, 31-45. The king honors Daniel, and confesses that his God is pre-eminent above all gods, 46, 47. Daniel and his friends are greatly preferred, 48, 49.

1. **in.** Da 1:1-5. 2 Ch 36:5-7. **the second.** That is, the *second* according to the Babylonian computation,

but the *fourth* according to that of the Jews, who reckon from the time he was associated with his father. 2 K 23:36. 24:12. See on Je 25:1. **Nebuchadnezzar.** ver. 3. Da 4:5. Ge 40:5-8. 41:1, etc. Jb *33:15-17. **his spirit.** Heb. *ruach,* Ps +106:33. ʃ121A10, Ge +26:35. ver. 3. **and his.** Da 6:18. Est 6:1.

2. **commanded.** See on Da 1:20. 4:6. 5:7. Ge 41:8. Ex 7:11. 22:18. Dt +*18:10-12. Is 8:19. 19:3. 47:12, 13. Ml +*3:5. **magicians.** *S#2748h. Da 1:20. 2:2. Ge 41:8, 24. Ex 8:11, 22. 8:7, 18, 19. 9:11, 11. For *S#2749h, see ver. 10. **astrologers.** Da 1:20. 2:10, 27. 4:7. 5:7, 11, 15. Is 47:13n. **sorcerers.** Is +47:12. Ml +*3:5. **the Chaldeans.** ver. 4, 5, 10. Da 1:4.

3. **I have dreamed.** ver. 1. Ge 40:8. 41:15. **spirit.** Heb. *ruach,* Ps +106:33. ʃ121A10, Ge +26:35. Da 4:5. Ge 41:8.

4. **in.** Ge 31:47. Ezr 4:7. Is 36:11. Je 10:11. **Syriack.** *S#762h. 2 K 18:26. Ezr 4:7, 7. Is 36:11. *Aramith,* "Aramean," the language of *Aram* or Syria; a general term comprehending both the *Chaldee* and *Syriac,* the latter merely differing from the former as a dialect, and being written in a different character. With the following words the Chaldee part of Daniel commences; and is continued to the end of the seventh chapter. **O king.** Da 3:9. 4:19. 5:10. 6:6, 21. 1 S 10:24. 1 K 1:25, 31. Ne 2:3. Mt 21:9. Mk 11:9, 10. **live.** 2 S 16:16mg. **for ever.** Chal. *alam,* Ex +*12:24. **tell.** Da 4:7. 5:8. Ge 41:8. Is 44:25.

5. **ye shall.** This was unreasonable, arbitrary, and tyrannical in the extreme; but, in the course of God's providence, it was overruled to serve the most important purpose. Da 3:29. 1 S 15:33. Ps 50:22. 58:7. **cut in pieces.** Chal. made pieces. **made.** Dt 13:16. Jsh 6:26. 2 K 10:27. Ezr *6:11.

6. **ye shall.** ver. 48. Da 5:7, 16, 29. Nu 22:7, 17, 37. 24:11. **rewards.** *or,* fee. Da 5:17mg.

7. **Let.** ver. 4, 9. Ec 10:4.

8. **gain.** Chal. buy. ver. 9. Est 3:7. Ep *5:16. Col *4:5.

9. **there is.** Da 3:15. Est 4:11. **for.** 1 K 22:6, 22. Pr 12:19. Is 44:25. Ezk 13:6, 17, 19. 2 C 2:17. **lying.** Zc 10:2. **the time.** ver. 21. Da 5:28, 31. 7:25. **I shall know.** Is *41:22-24, 28, 29.

10. **magician.** *S#2749h. Da 2:10, 27. 4:7, 9. 5:11. **Chaldean.** i.e. *inhabitant of Chaldea,* *S#3779h. See Da 5:30. Also see Da 2:5, 10. 3:8. 4:7. 5:7, 11.

11. **and there.** This was their decision: and when the living and true God, who indeed condescends to dwell with men, and who alone could reveal the dream and the secrets contained in it, actually made it known to Daniel, he evinced the infinite difference between Jehovah and his prophets, and the idols and magicians of Babylon. ver. 27, 28. Da 5:11. Ge 41:39. Ex 8:19. Mt 19:26. **except.** Is *44:24, 25. **whose.** Ex 29:45. Nu 35:34. 1 K 8:27. 2 Ch 6:18. Ps 68:18. 113:5, 6. 132:14. Is 8:18. +*57:15. 66:1, 2. Jl 3:21. Jn +*1:1-3, 14. 14:17, 23. 2 C *6:16. Re 21:3.

12. **For this cause.** Da 3:13. *5:19. Jb 5:2. Ps 76:10. Pr 16:14. 19:12. 20:2. 27:3, 4. 29:22. Mt 2:16. 5:22.

13. **the decree.** Da 6:9-15. Est 3:12-15. Ps 94:20. Pr 28:15-17. Is 10:1. **and they.** Da 1:19, 20. 6:12. Je 36:26.

14. **answered.** Chal. returned. Da 3:16. **with.** 2 S 20:16-22. Ec 9:13-18. **Arioch.** Ge 14:1. **captain of the king's guard.** *or,* chief marshal. Chal. chief of the executioners, *or* slaughtermen. Ge 37:36mg. 39:1. 40:3.

2 K 25:8. Je 39:9mg. 52:12mg, 14.

15. **hasty.** Hab 1:6. **made.** ver. 9.

16. **and desired.** ver. 9-11. Da 1:18, 19. He 11:1.

17. **Hananiah.** Da 1:7, 11. 3:12.

18. **they would.** Da 3:17. 1 S 17:37. Est 4:15-17. Ps 50:15. 91:15. Pr √3:5, 6. Is 37:4. Je √33:3. Mt 18:12, √19. Ac 4:24-31. 12:4, 5. Ro 15:30, 31. 2 T 4:17, 18. **mercies.** ✸96F2, Ge +4:10. Ex 34:5, 6. Pr 18:10. Ph 4:6, 7. **of the God of heaven.** Chal. from before God. **concerning this secret.** T#1677. ver. 18, 19, 27, 28, 29, 30, 47. 4:9. Am *3:7. **Daniel and his fellows should not perish.** or, they should not destroy Daniel, etc. Ge *18:28. Ml 3:18. 2 P 2:9.

19. **was.** ver. 22, 27-29. Da 4:9. 2 K 6:8-12. Ps 25:14. Am *3:7. 1 C 2:9, 10. **in.** Da 7:7. Nu *12:6. Jb 4:13. 33:15, 16. Mt 2:12, 13.

20. **answered and said.** Dt 1:41. **Blessed.** Ge 14:20. 1 K 8:56. 1 Ch 29:10, 20. 2 Ch 20:21. Ps 41:13. 50:23. 72:18, 19. 103:1, 2. 113:2. *115:18. 145:1, 2. Chal. *alam* doubled, Ps +41:13. Da 7:18. 1 Ch 16:36. 29:10. Ne 9:5. Je 7:7. 25:5. **for wisdom.** ver. 21-23. 1 Ch 29:11, 12. Jb 12:13, 16-22. Ps 62:11. 147:5. Pr 8:14. Je *32:18, 19. Mt *6:13. Ju *24, *25. Re *5:12, 13.

21. **he changeth.** ver. 9. Da 7:25. 11:6. 1 Ch 29:30. Est 1:13. Jb 34:24-29. Ps 31:14, 15. Ec 3:1-8. Je *27:5-7. **he removeth.** Da 4:17, 32. 1 S 2:7, 8. Jb *12:18. Ps *75:6, 7. 113:7, 8. Pr 8:15, 16. Lk 1:51, 52. Ac 13:21, 22. Re 19:16. **he giveth.** Ex 31:3, 6. 1 K 3:8-12, 28. 4:29. 10:24. 1 Ch 22:12. 2 Ch 1:10-12. Pr 2:6, 7. Lk 21:15. 1 C *1:30. Ja +*1:5, 17. *3:15-17.

22. **revealeth.** ver. 11, 28, 29. Ge 37:5-9. 41:16, 25-28. Jb *12:22. Ps *25:14. Is 41:22, 24, 26. 42:9. Am 4:13. Mt 11:25. 13:13. Ro 16:25, 26. 1 C 2:9-11. Ep 3:5. Col 1:25-27. **he knoweth.** Jb 26:6. Ps *139:11, 12. Je 23:24. Lk 12:2, 3. Jn 21:17. 1 C 4:5. He *4:13. **the darkness.** Jb 38:19. **and the.** Da 5:11, 14. Ps 36:9. 104:2. Jn 1:9. 8:12. 12:45, 46. 1 T 6:16. Ja 1:17. 1 J *1:5.

23. **thank.** 1 Ch 29:13. Ps 50:14. 103:1-4. Is 12:1. Mt 11:25. Lk 10:21. Jn 11:41. **O thou.** Ge 32:9-11. Ex 3:15. 1 K 8:57. 18:36. 1 Ch 29:10. 2 Ch 20:6. **who hast.** See on ver. 20, 21. Pr 8:14. 21:22. 24:5. Ec 7:19. 9:16, 18. **and hast.** ver. 18, 29, 30. Ge *18:17. Ps *25:14. Je *29:11, 12. Am +*3:7. Jn 15:15. Re 1:1. 5:5.

24. **Arioch.** ver. 15. **Destroy.** See on ver. 12, 13. Ac 27:24.

25. **brought.** Pr 24:11, 12. Ec 9:10. **I have.** Chal. That I have. **captives of Judah.** Chal. children of the captivity of Judah. Da 1:6. 6:13. Ne 7:6. Je *29:1. 1 C 1:27, 28.

26. **Daniel.** Da 1:7. 4:8, 19. 5:12. **Art.** ver. 3-7. Da 4:18. 5:16. Ge 41:15. 1 S 17:33.

27. **cannot.** See on ver. 2, 10, 11. Da 5:7, 8. Jb 5:12, 13. Is 19:3. 44:25. 47:12-14.

28. **a God.** Ps 115:3. Mt *6:9. Ja *1:17. **that revealeth.** See on ver. 18, 47. Ge *40:8. 41:16. Is 41:22, 23. Am 4:13. **maketh known.** Chal. hath made known. **in the latter.** Da 10:14. Ge 49:1𝒫. Nu 24:14𝒫. Dt +*4:30𝒫. 31:29𝒫. Is 2:2. Je 30:24. 48:47. Ezk +*38:8, 16. Ho 3:5. Mi 4:1. 2 T 3:1. He 1:1. 2 P 3:3.

29. **came into thy mind.** Chal. came up. Je 3:16mg. Ezk 38:10. **he that.** ver. 22, 28, 47. Am *4:13.

30. **this secret.** Ge *41:16. Ac *3:12. 1 C 15:8-12. **but.** ver. 17, 18, 49. Is 43:3, 4. 45:4. Mt +*24:22. Mk 13:20. Ro √8:28. 1 C 3:21-23. 2 C 4:15. **their sakes**

---

that shall make known the interpretation to the king. or, the intent that the interpretation may be made known to the king. **and.** ver. 47.

31. **sawest.** Chal. wast seeing. **a great image.** Jb 4:13-16. **stood.** ✸155E2, La +3:1. **and the form.** Da 7:3-17. Mt 4:8. Lk 4:5. **terrible.** Is 13:11. 25:3-5. Ezk 28:7. Hab 1:7.

32. **head.** ver. 37, 38. Da 4:22, 30. 7:4. Is 14:4. Je 51:7. Re 17:4. **breast.** ver. 39. Da 7:5. 8:3, 4. 11:2. **belly.** ver. 39. Da 7:6. 8:5-8. 11:3, etc. **thighs.** or, sides.

33. **legs of iron.** ver. 40-43. Da 7:7, 8, 19-26.

34. **a stone.** ver. 44, 45. Da *7:13, 14, 27. Ps *118:22. Is *28:16. Zc 12:3. Mt *16:18. Mt *21:42, 44. Ac *4:11. 1 P *2:4, 6-8. Re 11:15. **was cut.** Da *8:25. Jb 34:20. La 4:6. Zc *4:6. Jn 1:13. 2 C 5:1. He 9:24. **without hands.** or, which *was* not in hands. ver. 45mg. Da 8:25. Jb 34:20. La 4:6. Ac 7:48. 17:24, 25. 19:26. 2 C 5:1. Ep 2:11. Col 2:11. He 9:11, 24. **which smote.** Ps *2:8-12. *110:5, 6. +*149:6-9. Is 60:12. Zc 12:3. Re 17:14. 19:11-21. **and brake.** Da 8:25. Ps *2:9. Is 8:9, 14, 15. 30:14. Re *2:27.

35. **like the chaff.** Ps *1:4, 5. Is 17:13, 14. 41:15, 16. Ho *13:3. Mi 4:13. **no place.** Jb 6:17. Re *37:10, 36. 103:16. Re 12:8. 20:11. **became.** Ps *2:2, 3. Ps *89:25, 27. Mi 4:1, 2. **and filled.** Ps *2:8. 22:27. 46:9. 66:4. 67:1, 2. *72:8, 16-19. 80:9, 10. 86:9. Is 11:9. Zc *9:10. √14:8, 9. 1 C *15:25. Re *11:15. *20:2, 3.

36. **we will tell.** ✸96D4, Ge +29:27. ver. 23, 24.

37. **a king of kings.** ✸147H, Ge +9:25. 1 K 4:24. Ezr 7:12. Is 10:8. 47:5. Je *27:6, 7. Ezk *26:7. Ho 8:10. Re +*1:5. 17:14. **the God of heaven.** Da 4:25, 32. 5:18. 2 Ch 36:23. Ezr 1:2. Pr 8:15. Je 28:14. Re 19:16. **power.** Da 4:3, 34. 1 Ch 29:11, 12. Ps 62:11. Mt *6:13. Jn 19:11. Re 4:11. 5:12, 13. **and glory.** Is 13:19.

38. **the beasts.** Da 4:21, 22. Ps 50:10, 11. Je 27:5-7. 28:14. Ezk 26:7. **Thou art.** The Chaldean monarchy, over which Nebuchadnezzar was the only king of note; in whose time it extended over Chaldea, Assyria, Arabia, Syria, Egypt, and Libya: the head of gold represented its immense riches. See on ver. 32. Da 4:20-22. 7:4. **gold.** ✸45, Is +40:31.

39. **another kingdom.** The empire of the Medes and Persians, whose union was denoted by the breast and two arms of silver; and which was established on the ruins of that of the Chaldeans on the capture of Babylon by Cyrus, B.C. 538. ver. 32. Da *5:25-31. *7:5. *8:3, 4, 20. 11:2. 2 Ch *36:20, 22, 23. Ezr 1:2. Is 13:17. 21:2. 44:28. 45:1-5. Je 51:11. **another third.** The empire of the Macedonians, or "brazen-coated Greeks," aptly denoted by the belly and thighs of brass, founded by Alexander the Great, who terminated the Persian monarchy by the overthrow of Darius Codomanus at Arbela, B.C. 331. ver. 32. Da *7:6, 7, 23. *8:5, etc., 21, 22. 10:20. *11:1-4, etc. Jl 3:6. Zc 6:3-6. 9:13. Re 13:1, 2. 17:3, 16, 17.

40. **the fourth.** The Roman empire, which comprised nearly the whole world. ver. 33. Da *7:7, 19-26. 8:24, 25. +*9:26, 27. 11:36-45. Lk *2:1. 3:1. Mt 17:24-27. 22:17-21. Jn *11:48. 19:12. Ac 16:37, 38. 22:25-28. 25:9-11. **forasmuch.** Da 7:7. Je 15:12. Am 1:3.

41. **the feet.** See on ver. 33-35. Da 7:7, 8, 20-24. Lk 21:24. Re 12:3. 13:1-18. 17:12-17.

42. **the toes.** Da 7:24. Re 13:1. **broken.** or, brittle.

43. **one to another**. Chal. this with this. **even**. The Roman empire became weakened by a mixture of barbarous nations, by the incursions of whom it was torn asunder about the fourth century after Christ, and at length divided into ten kingdoms, answering to the ten toes of the image. The ten toes represent ten yet future kings. They cannot represent ten barbarous tribes which overthrew the Roman empire, because Da 7:24 specifies they must come from inside the empire, whereas the barbarous tribes came from outside the old Roman empire. Da 7:7, 8, 23, 24. Re 13:1, etc. 17:12-17.

44. **in the days**. Chal. in their days. ver. 41, +43n. **these kings**. The days of the ten yet future kings. Re 17:12-18. **God of heaven**. See on ver. 28, 37. **set up a kingdom**. Da *4:3, 34. *7:13, 14, 27. Ge +*49:10. Ps *2:6-12. 22:28. 72:1, etc. 89:3, 4, 19-36. *110:1-4. Is +*9:6, 7. *11:2-9. *24:23. Ob 21. Mi *4:7. Zc √14:9. Mt 3:2, 3. *25:31-46. 28:18. Lk +*1:32, 33. Jn ◐18:36, 37. 1 C +*15:24-28. Ep 1:20-22. 2 Th √1:7-10. Ju 14, 15. Re *11:15. √20:1-10. **which shall never**. Da 4:3, 34. *6:26. √7:13, 14, 27. Ps 145:13. Ezk 37:25. Mi 4:7. Lk +*1:32, 33. Jn 12:34. He 12:28. Re *11:15. **be destroyed**. Zc ◐14:3. He ◐19:11-19. **kingdom**. Chal. kingdom thereof. **not be left**. Da 7:18. Jl 3:17. Am +*9:15. Mi 4:1-3, 7. Ac +*1:6. 3:19-21. 15:16, 17. **break in pieces**. Da 8:25. Ps *2:9. 21:8, 9. Is *60:12. Mi *4:3. 1 C √15:24, 25. Re 2:27. 19:15-20. **and consume**. Lk 20:18. **for ever**. Ge +9:12. Ex +*12:24. 1 C 15:24, 25. Re *20:3.

45. **thou sawest**. ver. 34, 35. Is 28:16. Zc 12:3. Mt 21:24. **without hands**. *or*, which *was* not in hands. ver. 34mg. Lk 17:20. 2 C *10:4, 5. **the great God**. ✱22I2, Ex +15:16. Dt 10:17. 2 S 7:22. 1 Ch 16:25. Ne 4:14. 9:32. Jb 36:26. Ps 48:1. 96:4. 135:5. 145:3. Je 32:18, 19. Ml 1:11. Re 19:17. **made known**. Ge 41:28, 32. Mt *24:35. Re √1:19. *4:1. **hereafter**. Chal. after this. **sure**. Nu *23:19.

46. **fell**. 2 S 14:22. Mt +*8:2. Lk 17:16. Ac +*10:25. √14:11-18. 28:6. Re 11:16. +√19:10. +√22:8, 9. **and commanded**. Ac 14:13. **and sweet**. Le 26:31. Ezr 6:10.

47. **a God of gods**. ✱147H, Ge +9:25. Da 11:36. Dt 10:17. Jsh 22:22. Ps 136:2. **a Lord**. See on ver. 37. Da *4:17, 32, 34, 35. Jb 12:19. Ps *2:10, 11. 72:11. 82:1. Pr 8:15, 16. 1 T 6:15. Re +*1:5. 17:14. 19:16. **a revealer**. See on ver. 19, 28. Da 4:8, 9. Ge 41:39. Am +*3:7.

48. **a great**. ver. 6. Da 2:6. 5:16. Ge 41:39-43. Nu 22:16, 17. 24:11. 1 S 17:25. 25:2. 2 S 19:32. 2 K 5:1. Jb 1:3. Je 5:5. **ruler**. Da 5:29. 6:1, 2. **and chief**. Da 4:9. *5:11. **governors**. Da 3:2, 3, 27. 6:7.

49. **he set**. ver. 17. Da 1:17. *3:12-30. Pr 28:12. **sat**. Est 2:19, 21. 3:2. Je 39:3. Am 5:15.

DANIEL 3

Nebuchadnezzar sets up a golden image, and commands all his ministers of state, and officers, when they hear all kinds of music, to fall down and worship it, on pain of being cast into a fiery furnace, 1-6. His orders are almost universally complied with, 7. Shadrach, Meshach, and Abednego, are accused of disobedience, 8-12. The king vehemently threatens them, if they persist in refusal, defying any God to deliver them; but they answer calmly and resolutely, 13-18. They are cast into the furnace, the flame of which

kills those who threw them in, 19-23. The king is astonished, at seeing them walk unhurt in the fire, with "a fourth like to the Son of God," 24, 25. They come forth; and all the immense company see that the fire has not touched them, 26, 27. Nebuchadnezzar blesses God, and decrees severe punishment on those who spake against him, 28, 29. The subsequent promotion of the three Jews, 30.

1. A.M. 3424. B.C. 580. **made**. Da 2:31, 32. 5:23. Ex 20:23. 32:2-4, 31. Nu 33:52. Dt 7:25. Jg 8:26, 27. 1 K 12:28. 2 K 19:17, 18. Ps *115:4-8. *135:15-18. Is 2:20. 30:22. 40:19, etc. 46:6. Je 10:9. 16:20. Ezk 7:20. +√16:17. *23:14. Ho 8:4. Hab 2:19. Ac 17:29. 19:26. Re 9:20. **threescore**. Note the number *six* in conjunction with the height and breadth of this image, and *six* musical instruments named in ver. 5, etc. Ge 1:26-31 (man created on the sixth day). Ex 20:9 (six days of the week allotted for secular work). Nu 11:5 (six foods of Egypt). Dt ◐8:8 (seven foods of Canaan). 1 S *17:4, 7 (note the six pieces of armor, and the weight of his spear's head, 600 shekels). 2 S 21:20. 2 K 18:32 (six foods). Ho 2:5 (six things sought), ◐8, 9 (seven things given by God). Ezk 40:5 (six handbreadths to a cubit). ◐41:8 (great cubit of seven hand breadths). Mt 27:45. Re √13:18. Other instructive examples of the number *six* include six steps in Lot's downfall: (1) lifted up his eyes, Ge 13:10; (2) he chose, Ge 13:11; (3) journeyed east, Ge 13:11; (4) dwelt, Ge 13:12; (5) pitched his tent toward Sodom, Ge 13:12; (6) dwelt in Sodom, Ge 19:1, etc. Six earthquakes mentioned in Scripture: (1) Ex 19:18. (2) 1 K 19:11. (3) Am 1:1. Zc 14:5. (4) Mt 27:54. (5) Mt 28:2. (6) Ac 16:26. Sixfold opposition to the work of God seen in the opposition to Nehemiah: (1) grief, Ne 2:10. (2) laughter, Ne 2:19. (3) wrath, indignation, mocking, Ne 4:1-4. (4) fighting and open opposition, Ne 4:7, 8. (5) conference, Ne 6:1, 2. (6) false friends, Ne 6:10-14. Six principal words are used for "man" in the Bible, four Hebrew, and two Greek: (1) Adam, S#120h, Ge 1:26. (2) Ish, S#376h, Zc 6:12. (3) Enosh, S#582h, Ps 8:4a. Jb 25:6n. (4) Geber, S#1397h, Zc 13:7. (5) Anthropos, S#444g, Mt 4:4. (6) Aner, S#435g, Mt 7:24. In Matthew's account of the temptation of Jesus by the devil (Mt 4:1-11), the word "devil" occurs four times (Mt 4:1, 5, 8, 11), "tempter" one time (Mt 4:3), and "satan" once (Mt 4:10), making *six* in all (Mt 4:1-11). In Luke's account of the temptation (Lk 4:1-13), "devil" occurs five times (Lk 4:2, 3, 5, 6, 13), and "satan" once (Lk 4:8), making *six* in all (Lk 4:1-13). Jesus was charged *six* times with having a devil: (1) Mt 12:24. Mk 3:22. (2) Jn 7:20. (3) Jn 8:48. (4) Jn 8:52. (5) Jn 10:20. (6) Lk 11:15. Nathaniel West in *The Thousand Years* states, regarding the symbolism of the number *six*: "Prophetic Numbers are indeed symbolical. No one denies this. We know that the sacred 7 is so, and lies at the basis of the Sacred Calendar of the Jews, and also the Civil Calendar of the Christians. It points to the 'Rest,' the 'Sabbath' of God. It symbolizes that Rest to which all believers come, even now, first in their souls by faith; a Rest to which they shall yet come, soul and body together, and the 'sign' of both which is the 7th day rest of the Christian Sabbath, now. The 6 is no less symbolical, just because literal. It is a secular number grounded in the 6 days' work of creation which preceded the 7th of rest, the 6 days commanded of God for man's toil, but in which the

unbelieving and ungodly, still secular in soul, and pressed with worldly care, abide without a Sabbath. They remember not the 7th to keep it holy. They have no peace, no rest. Their souls have never ceased from their work, as God did from His. The 6 can never give the 7. The World can never bring, or give, God's rest. If the Kingdom of God and His Christ has 7 as its holy signature, the Kingdom of Satan and Antichrist has 6 as its signature; an earthly kingdom, carnal, restless, and unsabbatized; the rule of worldly-minded men, without a sign of sanctity, or covenant between themselves and God; a Godless, Christless kingdom, and a Godless, Christless nation, wherever found. It is the atheist's mark. It is the apostate's sign. It is the seal of anti-Christianity, in league with civil power; the 10-horned 'Beast,' who would blot the *Heptad* from the Calendar and put the *Decade* there, profane the 7 and consecrate the 6 and 10. We see the symbolism of it in Daniel 3:1, where the Golden Image of the Babylonian King was reared upon the plains of Dura, '66 cubits high.'—It means negation; no God, no Sabbath, no religion, save the world's religion; no Rest for man or beast; no heaven; no hope; no immortality" (pp. 99, 100). Is +*58:13n, 14. **in the plain**. Ge 11:2. **Dura**. i.e. *circle or dwelling*, *S#1757h, only here. **in the province**. ver. 30. Da 2:48. Est 1:1.

2. **sent**. Ex 32:4-6. Nu 25:2. Jg 16:23. 1 K 12:32. Pr 29:12. Re 17:2. **rulers of**. Est 1:1.

3. **the princes**. *Achashdarpenaya*, rendered *lieutenants* in Est 3:12, etc., probably *chief satraps* or *viceroys*, from the Persian *achash*, great, eminent, and *sitrab*, a satrap. Ps ch. 82. Ac 19:34, 35. Ro 1:21-28. 3:11. 1 C 1:24-26. Re 13:13-16. 17:13, 17. **the governors**. *Signaya*, in Persian, *shagnah*, deputies or lieutenants. ver. 3, 27. Da 2:48. 6:7. **captains**. *Pacawatha*, governors of provinces. Ne 5:14, 18. See Est 3:13. Hg 1:14. **the judges**. *Adargazraya*, chief judges, or senators, from *adar*, great, and Chald. *gezar*, to judge, decree. **the treasurers**. *Gedavraya*, written *gizzavraya*, Ezr 7:21, *treasurers*, from the Persian *gunjvar*. **the counsellors**. *Dethavraya*, counsellors, judges, from *dath*, in Persian, *dad*, law, and *var*, possessor or guardian. **the sheriffs**. *Tiphtaya*, probably the same as the Arabic *Mufti*, or head officer of law.

4. **aloud**. Chal. with might. Da 4:14. Pr 9:13-15. Is 40:9. *58:1. Re 18:2. **it is commanded**. Chal. they command. Ho 5:11. Mi 6:16. **O people**. Da *4:1. 6:25. Est 8:9.

5. **the cornet**. *Karna*, the *horn*. See on ver. 10, 15. **flute**. *Mashrokeetha*, in Syriac, *mashrookeetha*, the *pipe* or *flute*, as Theodotion renders. **dulcimer**. *or*, singing. Chal. symphony. ver. 10, 15. Lk 15:25. **worship**. Ex 34:14.

6. **falleth**. ver. 11, 15. Ex +*20:5. Is 44:17. Mt +*4:9. Re *13:15-17. **the same**. Da 2:5, 12, 13. Mk 6:27. **hour**. or, moment. ver. 15. Da 4:19, 33. 5:5. **a burning**. Ge 19:28. Je *29:22. Ezk 22:18-22. Mt 13:42, 50. Re 9:2. 14:11.

7. **when**. See on ver. 10. **all the people**. ʃ94, Je +4:2. Je 51:7. Ac 14:16. 1 J 5:19. Re 12:9. 13:3, 8, 14. 17:8. 19:20. **worshipped**. Ex 34:17. Is 2:8, 9.

8. **and accused**. Da 6:12, 13. Ezr 4:12-16. Est 3:6, 9. Ac 16:20-22. 17:6-8. 28:22. 1 P 4:3, 4.

9. **king**. ver. 4, 5. **O king**. See on Da 2:4. 5:10. 6:6, 21. Ro 13:7. **for ever**. Chal. *alam*, Ex +*12:24.

10. **hast made**. ver. 4-7. Da 6:12. Ex 1:16, 22. Est

3:12-14. Ps 94:20. Ec 3:16. Is 10:1. Jn 11:57. Re 13:16, 17. **the cornet**. Ex *15:20, 21. 32:18, 19. 1 Ch 15:16, 28. 16:5, 6. 25:1-6. 2 Ch 29:25. Ps 81:1-3. 92:1-3. 149:3, 4. 150:3-6. Am 6:5.

12. **certain**. Da *2:49. 6:13. 1 S 18:7-11. Est 3:8. Pr 27:4. Ec 4:4. **not regarded thee**. Chal. set no regard upon thee. Da 6:13. Ac *5:28. 17:7.

13. **in his**. ver. 19. Da 2:12. Ge 4:5. 1 S 20:30-33. Est 3:5, 6. Pr 17:12. 27:3. 29:22. Lk 6:11. **Then**. Mt 10:18. Mk 13:9. Lk 21:12. Ac *5:25-27. 24:24.

14. **Is it**. ʃ85, Ge +3:9. **true**. *or*, of purpose. Ex 21:13, 14. **my gods**. ver. 1. Da 4:8. Is 46:1. Je 50:2.

15. **ye hear**. See on ver. 10. **harp**. *Kaithros*, in Arabic, *kitharat*, Greek *kithara*, the *guitar*. 1 Ch ●13:8n. **sackbut**. *Sabbecha, sambuka, sambuke*, a kind of harp. **psaltery**. *Pesanter, psaltarion*, a stringed instrument struck with a plectrum; probably similar to what is called a *psalterium* in Egypt, which Hasselquist (*Travels*, p. 84) describes as a large oblique triangle, with two bottoms two inches from each other, and about twenty catguts of different sizes. **dulcimer**. *Soomphanya*, probably the same as the *pipe*. **ye fall**. Lk 4:7, 8. **have made**. ʃ37A, Ex +32:32. **well**. ʃ63D2, Ge +30:27. ʃ63F, Ge +33:10. ver. 17. Ge 30:27. Ex 32:32. Lk 13:9. **and who**. ver. 28, 29. Da 6:16, 20. Ex +*5:2. 2 K *18:35. 2 Ch 32:15-17. Is 36:20. 37:23. Mt *27:43.

16. **answered and said**. Dt 1:41. **we are**. Mt *10:19. Mk 13:11. Lk 12:11. 21:14, 15. Ac 4:8-12, 19. 5:29. 6:15. 24:10-13. Ph *4:6, 7. 1 P *5:7.

17. **our God**. Da 4:35. 6:20-22, 27. Ge 17:1. 18:14. 1 S 17:37, 46. Jb 5:19. 34:29. Ps 27:1, 2. 62:1-6. 73:20. 115:3. 121:5-7. Pr 18:10, 11. Is 12:2. 26:3, 4. 54:14. Lk 1:37. Ac 20:24. 21:13. 27:20-25. Ro √8:31. He *7:25. *11:1. **will deliver**. Is ●+57:1. 2 T 4:17.

18. **But if not**. Ge ●28:20. Est *4:16. Jb *13:15. Is 45:11n. Mt 6:10. 26:39, 42. Lk 11:2. 22:42. Ac 21:14. 1 J 5:14. **be it**. Jb *13:15. Pr 28:1. Is *51:12, 13. Je 26:12-15. Mt √10:28, 32, 33, 39. 16:25. Lk 12:3-9. Ac 4:10-13, 19. *5:29-32. 7:51-60. He 11:33, 34. Re 2:10, 11. *12:11. **will not serve**. Ex +*20:3-5. Le 19:4. Jsh 24:15. 1 K 19:14, 18. 1 C +*12:3. +√15:58.

19. **was Nebuchadnezzar**. See on ver. 13. Pr 16:14. 19:12. 21:24. Is 51:33. Lk 12:4, 5. Ac 5:33. 7:54. **full**. Chal. filled. **the form**. Da 5:6. Ge 4:5, 6. 31:2. **he spake**. Ex 15:9, 10. 1 K 20:10, 11. 2 K 19:27, 28. Ps 76:10. Pr 16:14. 27:3, 4. **one seven times**. Da 6:24. Le 26:18, 21, 24, 28. **than**. 1 K 18:33-35. Mt 27:63-66.

20. **most mighty men**. Chal. mighty of strength. **to bind**. See on ver. 15. Ac 12:4-7. 16:23, 25.

21. **in their**. Herodotus (l. i. c. 195) says the Babylonish dress was a linen tunic, another of woollen, a white short cloak, and a turban. **coats**. *or*, mantles. **hats**. *or*, turbans.

22. **commandment**. Chal. word. **urgent**. Ex 12:33. **flame**. *or*, spark. **slew**. Da 6:24. Ps *9:15. 10:14. Pr 11:8. 21:18. Zc 12:2, 3. Mt 27:5. Ac 12:19.

23. **fell**. Da 6:16, 17. Ps 34:19. 66:11, 12. 124:1-5. Je 38:6. La 3:52-54. 2 C 1:8-10. 4:17. 1 P 4:12, 13.

24. **astonied**. Da 5:6. Ac 5:23-25. 9:6. 12:13. **counsellors**. *or*, governors. See on ver. 2, 3. **O king**. ver. 9, 10, 17. Da 4:22, 27. 5:18. 6:7, 22. 1 S 17:55. Ac 26:13, 27.

25. **walking**. See on Is *43:2. **the midst**. Zp 3:15. Mt *18:20. **the fire**. Zc 2:5. **they have no hurt**. Chal.

there is no hurt in them. Ps 91:3-9. Mk 16:18. Ac 28:5, 6. 1 P 3:13. **the fourth.** Ac 12:6, 7. **the Son of God.** √108H11, √24L, Ge +6:2. Or, as *bar elahin* may be rendered, "a son of the gods," i.e. a Divine person, or angel. A Divine, most beautiful, and glorious countenance; either of a mere angel, or rather of Jesus Christ, the Angel of the covenant (Ml 3:1), who did sometimes appear in the Old Testament before his incarnation (Matthew Poole). These pre-incarnate appearances, called theophanies (Ge +*12:7), were appearances of the Angel of Jehovah, which a careful study of the occurrences proves to be Jehovah himself (See on ver. +*28. Ge +*19:24n). ver. 18, +28. Jb +*1:6. *38:7. Ps *34:7. Pr 30:4. Mt *27:54. Lk +*1:35. Jn 1:34. 19:7, 8. Ro *1:4.

26. **mouth.** Chal. door. **ye servants.** ver. 17. Da 2:47. 6:20. Ezr 5:11. Ac 16:17. 27:23. Ga 1:10. Re 19:5. **the most.** Ge 14:18. **come forth.** Jsh 3:17. 4:10, 16-18. Is 28:16. 52:12. Ac 16:37.

27. **the princes.** See on ver. 2, 3. 1 S 17:46, 47. 2 K 19:19. Ps 83:18. 96:7-9. Is 26:11. Ac 2:6-12. 26:26. **upon.** Is 43:2. He *11:34. **nor was.** This miraculous manifestation of Divine power was witnessed by the court and the nation, and was felt as a just punishment on the transgressors, and a signal display of mercy to Shadrach, Meshach, and Abednego, which should operate on all believers to similar acts of faith and confidence in the Lord. Mt *10:30. Lk 21:17, 18. Ac 27:34.

28. **Blessed.** See on Da 2:47. 4:34. 6:26. Ge 9:26. Ezr 1:3. 7:23-28. Ps *76:10. *138:7. **hath sent.** ver. 25. Da 6:22, 23. Ge 19:15, 16. Nu 20:16. 2 Ch 32:21. Ps 34:7, 8. 103:20. Is 37:36. Mt 18:10. Ac 5:19. 12:7-11. He 1:14. **his angel.** ver. 25. Ge +*12:7. +16:13. +17:1. 18:10, 13, 17, 20, etc. +*19:24n. 21:17. 22:11, 15. Ex 3:2. 23:23. 33:2. Jsh 5:13-15. Jg 6:11, 20. 13:3, 6, 9. Pr 8:31. Zc *1:12, 13. Jn *8:56, 58. Ac 7:30, 32, 33, 38. 12:6, 7. **delivered.** ver. 17. Ps *91:1-3. **that trusted.** Da *6:23. 1 Ch 5:20. 2 Ch +*20:20. Ps 22:4, 5. 33:18, 21. *34:8, 22. *62:8. *84:11, 12. *118:8, 9. 146:5, 6. 147:11. Is √26:3, 4. Je *17:7, 8. 2 C 1:9, 10. Ep 1:12, 13. 1 P 1:21. **and have.** Ezr 6:11. Ac 4:19. **yielded.** Ro *12:1. 14:7, 8. Ph 1:20. He 11:37. Re √12:11. **serve.** See on ver. 16-18. Ex +*20:5. Mt √4:10.

29. **Therefore.** Da 6:26, 27. **I make a decree.** Chal. a decree is made by me. **amiss.** Chal. error. 2 S 6:7mg. **the God.** See on ver. 15, 17, 28. **cut in pieces.** Chal. made pieces. See on Da 2:5mg. **because.** Da 6:27. Dt 32:31. Ps 3:8. 76:10. *89:8. *113:5.

30. **the king.** Da *5:19. 1 S *2:30. Ps +√91:14. Jn *12:26. Ro √8:31. **promoted.** Chal. made to prosper. Ps +*1:3.

DANIEL 4

Nebuchadnezzar proclaims to all nations the dealings "of the most high God" with him, adding benevolent salutations and admiring praises, 1-3. He states that he had a dream which the magicians could not interpret, 4-7; and that he related it to Daniel, 8-18; who interpreted it, 19-27. The dream is fulfilled, in Nebuchadnezzar's loss of dignity, reason, and almost the human form, for a season, 28-33; but, being restored, he humbly and fervently adores and praises God, 34-37.

1. **Nebuchadnezzar.** This is a regular *decree,* and one of the most ancient extant; and no doubt contains the exact words of Nebuchadnezzar, copied out by Daniel from the state papers of Babylon, and preserved in the original language. **unto all.** Da 3:4, 29. 7:14. Est 3:12. 8:9. Zc 8:23. Ac 2:6. **Peace.** Da 6:25, 27. 1 Ch 12:18. Ezr 4:17. 5:7. Ro 1:7. Ep 1:2. 1 T 1:2. 1 P 1:2.

2. **I thought it good.** Chal. It was seemly before me. Jsh 7:19. Ps *51:14. 71:18. *77:13, 14. 78:12-16, 43-55. *89:1, 2. 92:1, 2. 105:1, 2. 106:2. 107:8. 111:2. **that.** Da 3:26. Ps 66:16. Ac 22:3-16. 26:9-16.

3. **great.** T#274. ver. 34. Da 2:44. 6:27. 7:18. Ex 15:11. Dt 4:32-34. Jb *5:8, 9. Ps 71:19, 20. 72:18. 77:11-14, 19. 86:10. 92:5. 104:24. 105:27. Is 25:1. 28:29. Ro *11:33. He 2:4. **his kingdom.** ver. 17, 34, 35. Da 2:44. 6:26. +*7:14, 27. Ps 66:7. *145:13. Is +*9:7. Je 10:10. Lk +*1:32, 33. 1 T 1:17. He +*1:8. Re *11:15. **everlasting.** Chal. *alam,* Ge +17:7. Ps 10:16. *90:1, 2. 103:19. Mi 4:7. Lk +*1:32, 33. **his dominion.** Ps +*145:13. **is from.** Jb 25:2. 1 P 4:11.

4. **I Nebuchadnezzar.** After he had successfully finished his wars in Syria, Egypt, etc., and the immense improvements and buildings at Babylon, and in the enjoyment of uninterrupted peace and prosperity in his palace. **was.** Ps 30:6, 7. Is 47:7, 8. 56:12. Je 48:11. Ezk 28:2-5, 17. 29:3. Zp 1:12. Lk *12:19, 20. 1 Th *5:2, 3.

5. **a dream.** See on Da 2:1. 5:5, 6, 10. 7:28. Ge *20:3. 31:11, 24. 41:1. Jg 7:13-15. Jb 7:13, 14. *33:15-17. **and the thoughts.** Da 2:28, 29.

6. **to bring.** See on Da 2:2. Ge 41:7, 8. Is 8:19. 47:12-14.

7. **Then came.** Da 2:1, 2. 1 S 6:2. Ezk +*21:21. **but.** Da 2:7. Ge *41:8. Is *44:25. Je 27:9, 10. 2 T 3:8, 9.

8. **Belteshazzar.** Da 1:7. 5:12. Is 46:1. Je 50:2. **according to.** Is 46:1. Je 50:2. 51:44. **and in.** See on ver. 9, 18. Da 2:11. 5:11, 14. Nu 11:17, etc. Is 63:11. **spirit.** Ge +41:38.

9. **master.** See on Da 1:20. 2:48. 5:11. **the spirit.** ver. 8. Ge +*41:38. 1 S 4:8. Is *63:11. 2 P √1:21. **no secret.** ver. 5. Da 2:3. Ge 11:6-8. Is 33:18. 54:14. Ezk 28:3. **tell.** ver. 18. Da 2:4, 5. Ge 40:9-19. 41:15, etc. Jg 7:13-15.

10. **saw.** Chal. was seeing. **a tree.** This represented his exceedingly prosperous condition, the height of his exaltation, the extent of his dominions and renown, the splendor of his kingdom, the multitude of his subjects who received protection from him, and the peace and plenty they enjoyed. ver. 20-26. Ps *37:35, 36. Is 10:33, 34. Je *12:2. Ezk *31:3-18.

11. **reached.** ver. 21, 22. Ge 11:4. Dt 9:1. Mt 11:23.

12. **the beasts.** Je 27:6, 7. Ezk 17:23. 31:6. **shadow.** La 4:20. **the fowls.** Mt 13:32. Lk 13:19.

13. **in the visions.** ver. 5, 10. Da 7:1. **a watcher.** Either a holy angel, or a divine person, called a *watcher,* as watching over the affairs of men. ver. 17, 23. Ps *103:20. **an holy.** Da 8:13. Dt 33:2. Ps 89:7. Zc 14:5. Mt 25:31. Mk 1:24. Lk 4:34. Ju 14. Re 14:10.

14. **aloud.** Chal. with might. Da 3:4. Re 10:3. 18:2. **Hew.** ver. 23. Da 5:20. Mt *3:10. 7:19. Lk 3:9. *13:7-9. **let.** ver. 12. Je 51:6, 9. Ezk 31:12, 13.

15. **leave.** See on ver. 25-27. Jb 14:7-9. Is *14:4, 12-17. Ezk 29:14, 15.

16. **Let his.** Here a transition is made from the tree to Nebuchadnezzar, whom it represented; the tree being lost sight of, a person came in its stead. This

person having lost the heart, or disposition of a man, and conceiving himself a beast, should act as such, and herd among them. **be changed.** See on ver. 32, 33. Is 6:10. Hab 1:11. Mk 5:4, 5. Lk 8:27-29. **seven times.** That is, seven years, a *time* in the prophetic language denoting a *year.* ver. 23, 25, 31. Da 7:25. 11:13. 12:7. Re 12:14.

17. **by the decree.** ver. 13, 24. 1 K *22:19, 20. 1 T *5:21. **the demand.** Ge 24:47h. Jg 4:20h. 1 P 3:21g. **the holy.** See on ver. 8, 9, 13. Jb 1:6. Is 6:3, 8. Re 4:8. **that the living.** Ps *9:16. 83:17, 18. Ezk 25:17. **the most High.** ver. 25, 32-35. Da 2:21. 5:18-21. Je 27:5-7. **giveth.** T#245. 1 K 19:15. 2 K 8:12. Ps 75:6, 7. Ezk 20:24-26. Ho 13:11. Jn *19:11. **the basest.** ver. 25. Da 11:21. Ex 9:16. 1 S 2:8. 1 K 21:25. 2 K 21:6, etc. 2 Ch 28:22. Ps 12:8. 113:7, 8. Ezk 7:24. 1 C 1:28.

18. **forasmuch.** ver. 7. Da 2:7. 5:8, 15. Ge 41:8, 15. Is 19:3. 47:12-14. **but.** See on ver. 8, 9. Da 2:26-28. 1 K 14:2, 3. Am +*3:7. **spirit.** Ge +41:38.

19. **Daniel.** ver. 8. Da 1:7. 2:26. 5:12. **was astonied.** He saw the design of the dream; and felt acutely for his prince and benefactor. Accordingly he expresses himself with the greatest delicacy and kindly feeling. ver. 9. Da 7:28. 8:27. 10:16, 17. Je 4:19. Hab 3:10. **for one hour.** 2 C 7:8. Ga 2:5. **let not.** ver. 4, 5. 1 S 3:17. **My lord.** ver. 24. Da 10:16. Ge 31:35. 32:4, 5, 18. Ex 32:32. 1 S 1:15. 24:8. 26:15. 2 S 18:31. 1 K 18:7. **the dream.** 1 S 25:26. See on 2 S 18:32. Je +*29:4, 7.

20. **The tree.** See on ver. 10-12. Ezk 31:3, 16.

21. **Whose leaves.** ver. 12. **under which.** Da *2:38. **the fowls.** ver. 12. Ezk 17:23. 31:6. Mt 13:32.

22. **thou.** See on Da 2:37, 38. 2 S 12:7. Mt 14:4. **thy greatness.** Da 5:18-23. Ge 11:4. 28:12. 2 Ch 28:9. Ps 36:5. 108:4. Je *27:4, 6-8. Re 18:5.

23. **saw.** See on ver. 13-17. **and let his.** ver. 15. Da 5:21.

24. **the decree.** See on ver. 17. Jb 20:29mg. Ps *2:7. 148:6. Is 14:24-27. 23:9. 46:10, 11. **come.** Jb 1:12-19. 40:11, 12. Ps 107:40.

25. **drive.** See on ver. 32, 33. Da 5:21, etc. Jb 30:3-8. Mk 5:3, 4. **and thy dwelling.** All the circumstances of Nebuchadnezzar's case, says Dr. Mead (*Medica Sacra,* ch. vii), agree so well with hypochontriasis, that to me it appears evident the Almighty God brought this dreadful distemper upon him, and under its influence he ran wild into the fields: then fancying himself transformed into an ox, he fed on grass, after the manner of cattle; and through neglect of himself, his hair and nails grew to an excessive length, so that the latter became thick and crooked, resembling birds' claws. Virgil (Ecl. vi. 48), says of the daughters of Praetus, who are related to have been mad, *Implerunt falsis mugitibus agros,* "With mimic lowings they filled the fields." **to eat.** Ps 106:20. **till.** See on ver. 17, 32, 34, 35. Da 2:21. 5:21. Ps 75:7. +*83:18. Je *27:5. Jn 19:11.

26. **to leave.** ver. 15. Jb *14:7-9. **the heavens.** ʃ121J20, Ps +73:9. Metonymy of the Subject B580. "Heaven" is put for God who dwells there. Mt 5:34. 21:25. Lk 15:18, 21.

27. **let.** Ge 41:33-37. Ps 119:46. Ac 24:25. 2 C 5:11. **break off.** Ge 27:40. Ex 32:2, 3, 24. Jb 34:31, 32. Ps 136:24h. Pr 16:6. √28:13. Is √55:6, 7. Ezk 18:21, 27-32. Mt 3:8. Ac *8:22. 26:20. Ja *4:8-10. 1 P 4:8. **by**

showing mercy. T#526. Le 18:9, 10. 25:35. Dt *15:10, 11. Jb +6:14 (T#7). Ps *41:1-3. Pr +21:13 (T#687). Is 58:5-7, 10-12. Ezk *18:7. Mt *25:35. Lk 3:11. 11:41. 16:9. Ac 10:2-4. Ga 5:6, 13, 22. Ep 4:28. Ja 1:27. 2:1-9. 1 J *3:17. **the poor.** Ezk +*16:49. **if it.** Da 7:12. 1 K *21:29. Jl 2:14. Jon 3:9. Zp 2:2, 3. **lengthening of thy tranquillity.** *or,* healing of thine error.

28. **All this came.** Da 5:21-23. Nu *23:19. Pr 10:24. Zc 1:6. Mt *24:35.

29. **end.** Ge 6:3. Ec √8:11. 1 P 3:20. 2 P √3:9, 10, 15. Re 2:21. **in.** *or,* upon.

30. **Is not.** Da *5:20. Ps 73:8. *75:4, 5. Pr *16:18. Hab 1:15, 16. 2:4, 5. Lk *12:19, 20. 14:11. 1 P 5:5. **great.** Ge 10:10. 11:2-9. Re 16:19. 17:5. 18:10, 21. **that.** 1 Ch 29:12-14. 2 Ch 2:5, 6. Is 10:8-15. 37:24, 25. Ezk 28:2-5. 29:3. **and for.** Da 5:18, 19. Est 1:4. Ps 49:20. 104:1. 145:5-12. 1 C *10:31. Re 21:24-26.

31. **the word.** Da 5:4, 5. Ex 15:9, 10. Jb 20:23. Lk 12:20. Ac *12:22, 23. 1 Th *5:3. **fell.** ver. 24, 34. Mt 3:17. Jn 12:28. Ac 9:3-5. Re 16:7. **The kingdom.** Da 5:28. 1 S 13:14. 15:23. Ezk *31:10, 11.

32. **they shall drive.** See on ver. 14-16, 25, 26. Da 5:21. Jb 30:5-7. **until.** See on ver. 17, 25. Ex 8:10. 9:14, 29. Jsh 4:24. Jb 12:18-21. Ps *9:16. Pr 8:15, 16. Is 37:20. 45:3. Je 27:5.

33. **same.** Da 5:5. Jb 20:5. Is 30:13, 14. 1 Th *5:2. **fulfilled.** Nu *23:19. **and he was.** See on ver. 25, 32.

34. A.M. 3441. B.C. 563. **at the end.** ver. 16, 26, 32. **lifted.** ʃ144A12, Ge +22:13. Ps 121:1. 123:1. 130:1, 2. Jon 2:2-4. Lk *15:18. *18:13. **understanding returned.** Lk 15:17. 2 T +*1:7. **I blessed.** 1 Ch *29:10, 11. Jb 1:21. Ps 50:14. 103:1-4. 107:8, 15, 22, 31. Is 24:15. La *3:19-23. **the most High.** ver. 17, 32. Ps +*7:17. La 3:38. **praised.** Ps *71:8. Je *33:11. He +*13:15. **honored.** Ps *71:8. 96:6. 104:1. 145:5. Jn *5:23. 1 T +*1:17. **him.** Da 12:7. Ps 90:2. 102:24. 146:10. Je 10:10. Jn 5:26. 1 T 1:17. 6:16. Re 4:10. 10:6. **for ever.** Chal. *alam,* Ex +*12:24. **whose dominion.** See on ver. 3. Da *2:44. +*7:14. Ps 10:16. *145:13. Is +*9:6, 7. Je 10:10. Mi *4:7. Lk +*1:33. Re *11:15. **everlasting.** Chal. *alam,* Ge +17:7. **is from.** Ps 90:1. +*102:28.

35. **all.** Jb 34:14, 15, 19-24. Is *40:15-17, 22-24. **and he.** 1 S 3:18. Jb 23:13. *34:29. Ps 33:9-11. *115:3. *135:6. Is 14:24-27. 46:10, 11. Mt 11:25, 26. Ac 4:28. Ep +*1:11. Ph *2:10, 11. **the inhabitants.** Ps 33:8, 14. 49:1. Is √26:9. **none.** Jb 9:4, 13. 34:29. 40:9-12. 42:2. Pr +*21:30. Is 43:13. Ac 5:39. 9:5. 11:17. 1 C 10:22. **What.** Jb *9:12. 33:12, 13. 40:2. Is *45:9-11. Ro 9:19, 20. 11:33-36. 1 C 2:16.

36. **my reason.** Every thing was fulfilled that was exhibited in the dream and its interpretation; and God so ordered it in his providence, that Nebuchadnezzar's counsellors and lords sought for him and gladly reinstated him in his kingdom. It is confidently believed that he was a true convert, and died in the faith of the God of Israel. ver. 34. **mine.** ver. 15, 16, 32. 2 Ch 33:12, 13. **added.** 1 S *2:30. Jb 13:12. *42:12. Ps *103:2-5, 8-10. Pr *22:4. Mt √6:33. 2 C 4:17.

37. **I Nebuchadnezzar.** ver. 3, 34. Da 5:4, 23. Ex 18:11. 1 P 2:9, 10. **the King.** Da 5:23. Mt 11:25. Ac 17:24. **all.** Dt 32:4. 1 S 2:3. Ps 33:4, 5. 99:4. 119:75. 145:17, 18. Is 5:16. Re *4:11. *15:3. *16:7. 19:1, 2. **those that walk.** ver. 30, 31. Da 5:20-24. Ex 18:11. 2 Ch 33:11, 12, 19. Jb 40:11, 12. Ezk 16:56, 63. Ja 4:6, 7. 1 P 5:5, 6.

DANIEL 5

Belshazzar feasts with his lords, etc. they drink wine out of the sacred vessels of God, and join in praising their idols, 1-4. A hand is seen writing on the wall; and the astrologers being unable to read what was written, the king and his nobles are exceedingly terrified, 5-9. Daniel, by means of the queen, is brought in, 10-16. He rejects the king's proffered reward; and sharply reproves his pride, idolatry, and impiety, 17-24. He explains the handwriting, as denouncing the immediate death of the king, and the translation of his kingdom to the Medes and Persians, 25-28. The promised honors are ordered him, 29. That very night Belshazzar is slain, and Darius the Mede takes the kingdom, 30, 31.

1. **Belshazzar**. i.e. *the splendor of brightness; lord of whose treasure,* ✻S#1113h. ver. 1, 2, 9, 22, 29, 30. Da 7:1. **made**. Ge 40:20. Est *1:2, 3, 7, 8. Is 21:4, 5. 22:12-14. Je 51:39, 57. Na 1:10. Mk 6:21, 22. **feast**. ✻171I8, Ge +3:19. **lords**. Da 4:36.

2. **Belshazzar**. *Belshazzar* is said by Josephus (Ant. l. x. c. 11) to be the same as *Naboandelus*, the *Nabonadius* of Ptolemy, and the *Labynetus* of Herodotus (l. i.). He reigned seven years, during which time he was engaged in unsuccessful wars with the Medes and Persians; and at this very time was besieged by Cyrus. Modern authorities identify Belshazzar as the eldest son of Nabonidus, and served as coregent while his father was away from the capital. This explains "third ruler" in ver. 29, and agrees with Je *27:7. **tasted the wine**. ✻108H7, Pr +31:4. Pr +*20:1. *23:29-32. 31:4. Hab *2:5. **the golden**. Da 1:2. 2 K 24:13. 25:15. 2 Ch 36:10, 18. Ezr 1:7-11. Je 27:16-22. 52:19. **father**. *or*, grandfather. ver. 11, 13, 18. 2 S 9:7. 1 K +*15:10n. 2 K 8:25-27. 14:3. 15:1, 2, 11-13. 2 Ch 11:20. 15:16. 34:1, 2. Je √27:7. Ro 9:10. There is no word in Chaldee or Hebrew for "grandfather." The word "father" is used by the figure of speech Synecdoche of the Species (✻171G2, Ge +13:8), whereby one relationship is put for, and includes others. **taken out**. Chal. brought forth. Ezr 1:7. **wives**. Ge +4:19. **concubines**. 1 Ch +2:48. **might**. ver. 4, 23.

3. **golden vessels**. Da 1:2. 2 K 25:15. 2 Ch *36:10. Je *52:19.

4. **praised**. ver. 23. See on Da 4:37. Jg 16:23, 24. Is 42:8. Ho 2:8-13. Re *9:20, 21. **of gold**. Da 3:1-7, 8, etc. Ps *115:4-8. 135:15-18. Is 40:19, 20. 42:17. 46:6, 7. Je 10:4-9. Hab 2:19. Ac 17:29. 19:24-28. Re *9:20.

5. **the same hour**. Da 3:6. 4:19, 31, 33. Jb 20:5. Ps 78:30, 31. Pr *29:1. Lk *12:19, 20. 1 Th *5:2, 3. **wrote**. ver. 8, 15, 24-28. Col 2:14. Re 20:12-15.

6. **the king's**. See on ver. 9. Da 2:1. 3:19. Jb 15:20-27. 20:19-27. Ps 73:18-20. Is 21:2-4. **countenance**. Chal. brightnesses. ver. 9. **was changed**. Chal. changed it. **and his thoughts**. ver. 10. See on Da 4:5, 19. 7:28. **so that**. Ps 69:23. Is 13:7, 8. 21:3, 4. **joints**. *or*, girdles. Is 5:27. ✻✻45:1. Chal. bindings, *or* knots. **and his knees**. Is 35:3. Ezk 7:17. 21:7. Na *2:10. He 12:12.

7. **aloud**. Chal. with might. Da 4:14mg. **to bring**. See on Da *2:2. 4:6. Ge *41:8. Is *44:25, 26. +*47:13. **be clothed**. ver. 16, 29. Da 2:6. Ge 41:42-44. Nu 22:7, 17. 24:11. 1 S 17:25. **scarlet**. *or*, purple. **a chain**. Pr 1:9. SS 1:10. Ezk 16:11. **the third**. Da 2:48. 6:2, 3. Est 3:1. 10:2, 3.

8. **but**. Because, probably, it was written in the ancient Hebrew or Samaritan character. See on Da 2:27. 4:7. Ge 41:8. Is 47:9, 12-15.

9. **greatly**. ver. 6. Da *2:1. Jb 18:11-14. Ps 18:14. Ac 22:6, 9. Re 6:15. **countenance**. Chal. brightnesses. ver. 6mg. Da 10:8. **changed**. Ps 48:6. Is 13:6-8. 21:2-4. Je 6:24. 30:6. Mt 2:3.

10. **the queen**. This was probably *Nitocris*, the queen-mother, widow of Evil-merodach, son of Nebuchadnezzar, and father of Belshazzar. **O king**. See on Da 2:4. 3:9. 6:6, 21. 1 K 1:31. **live**. 2 S 16:16mg. **for ever**. Chal. *alam*, Ex +*12:24. **let not**. Ge 35:17, 18. 1 S 4:20-22. Jb 13:4. 21:34.

11. **a man**. See on Da 2:47. 4:8, 9, 18. Ge 41:11-15. **spirit**. Chal. *ruach*, Ge +41:38. **father**. *or*, grandfather. See on ver. *2. **light**. Da 2:11. 2 S 14:17. Ac 12:22. 14:11. Re 3:9. **Nebuchadnezzar**. Nebuchadnezzar was certainly the *grandfather* of Belshazzar; but the term *father* in Hebrew and Chaldee is frequently used to denote a *progenitor*, or *ancestor*, however remote. 1 K +*15:10n. **father**. *or*, grandfather. ✻171G, Ge +13:8. **king**. ✻84, Ge +6:17. ver. *2mg. **father**. ✻84, Ge +6:17. **master**. See on Da *2:48. *4:8, 9. Ac 16:16.

12. **an excellent**. ver. 14. Da *6:3. Ps 16:3. Pr 12:26. 17:27. Col 1:29. **spirit**. Chal. *ruach*, Ge +41:38. ✻121A3, Nu +11:17. Ps 78:8. 2 C +*12:18. **interpreting of**. *or*, of an interpreter of, etc. **dissolving**. *or*, of a dissolver. **doubts**. Chal. knots. ver. 16. 1 K 10:1-3. 2 Ch 9:1, 2. **whom**. Da 1:7. 4:8, 19.

13. **Art thou**. Though Daniel was one of the chief ministers of state, who did "the king's business" in the palace (Da 8:27), yet Belshazzar seems to have known nothing of him. This shows that he was a weak and vicious prince, who minded pleasure more than business, according to the character given him by historians. He appears to have left the care of public affairs to his mother, Nitocris, a lady celebrated for her wisdom, who evidently knew Daniel well, and probably constantly employed him in the government of the kingdom. ver. 11. Da 1:21. 2:48. 8:1, 27. **the children**. Da 1:6. 2:25. 6:13. 2 K 24:11-15. Ezr 4:1. 6:16, 19, 20. 10:7, 16. **father**. *or*, grandfather. See on ver. +*2, 11, 18. **Jewry**. i.e. *land of Judea,* ✚S#3061h, so rendered only here. Lk 23:5. Jn 7:1, 3, Judea.

14. **that the spirit**. Chal. *ruach*, Ge +41:38. See on ver. 11, 12.

15. **And now**. ver. 7, 8. See on Da 2:3-11. Is 29:10-12. 47:12, 13.

16. **make**. Chal. interpret. Ge 40:8. **thou shalt**. See on ver. 7. Ac 8:18.

17. **Let**. Daniel, on this occasion, behaved in a very different manner to Belshazzar, than he had formerly done to Nebuchadnezzar. Belshazzar had that very night insulted the God of heaven in the most daring manner; and the venerable prophet, as His delegate, denounced sentence against him. ver. 29. Ge 14:23. Ex *23:8. 2 K 3:13. 5:16, 26. Ac 8:20. **rewards**. *or*, fee. Da 2:6mg. **I will read**. Ps 119:46.

18. **O thou**. Da 3:17, 18. 4:22. 6:22. Ac 26:13, 19. **the most high God**. Da 2:37, 38. 4:17, 22-25, 32. Dt 32:8. Ps +*7:17. 9:2. 47:2. 92:8. La 3:35, 38. Ac 7:48. **father**. ✻171G, Ge +13:8.

19. **that he**. Da 3:4. *4:17, 22. Je 25:9, etc. √27:5-7. Hab 2:5. Ro 13:1. **whom he would he slew**. ſ132G, Ge +3:19. Da 2:12, 13. 3:6, 20, 21, 29. Pr 16:14. Jn *19:11.

20. **when**. Da 4:30-33, 37. Ex 9:17. 18:11. 2 S *22:28. Jb 15:25-27. 40:11, 12. Pr *16:5, 18. Is 14:12-17. Lk 1:51, 52. 18:14. **mind**. Chal. *ruach*, Ge +26:35. ſ121A10, Ge +26:35. **hardened**. 1 S 6:6. 2 K 17:14. 2 Ch 36:13. Jb *9:4. Je 19:15. He +*3:13. **in pride**. *or*, to deal proudly. **deposed**. Chal. made to come down. Is 47:1. Je 13:18. 48:18. Ezk 30:6.

21. **he was driven**. See on Da *4:25, 32, 33. Jb 30:3-7. **his heart was made like**. *or*, he made his heart equal, etc. **till**. See on Da *4:17, 25, 32, 35, 37. Ex 9:14-16. Ps 83:17, 18. Ezk 17:24.

22. **thou**. ver. 18. Ps 119:46. Mt 14:4. Ac 4:8-13. **his son**. ſ171G, Ge +13:8. He was, strictly speaking, "his grandson"; but the term *son* is frequently used to denote filiation at any distance. ver. *2mg. 1 K +15:10n. **hast**. Ex 10:3. 1 S *6:6. 2 Ch *33:22, 23. 36:12. Is 26:10, 11. Mt 21:32. Ac 5:29-33. 1 P 5:5, 6. **though**. Pr *29:1. Lk +*12:47. Jn +*13:17. Ja *4:6, 17.

23. **lifted**. ver. 3, 4. 2 K 14:10. Ps *14:1. Pr *18:12. 28:14. Is 2:12. *10:33. 33:10. 37:23. Je 50:29. Ezk 28:2, 5, 17. 31:10. Hab 2:4. 1 T 3:6. Re 13:5, 6. **the Lord**. See on Da 4:37. Ge 14:19. Ps 115:16. **and they**. See on ver. 2-4. 1 S 5:1-9. **hast praised**. Jg 16:23. **which**. Ps *115:4-8. 135:15-17. Is 37:19. 46:6, 7. Hab 2:18, 19. 1 C +*8:4. **in whose**. Ge *2:7. Jb *12:10. *34:14, 15. Ps 104:29. +*146:4. Is *42:5. Ac *17:25, 28, 29. **breath**. Chal. *nishma*, same as Heb. *neshamah*, Ge +*2:7. **and whose**. Jb *31:4. Ps *139:3. Pr 20:24. Je *10:23. He *4:13. **hast thou**. Ro *1:21-23. Ro √3:23.

24. **Then was**. See on ver. 5.

25. **And this**. ſ3, Ge +49:10. **MENE**. i.e. *who is numbered*, ❋S#4484h. ver. 26. Ezr 7:25 (set). Compare ❋S#4483h: Da 2:24 (ordained), 49 (set). 3:12. Had these words been written in the Chaldean character, every one who knew the alphabet of the language could at least have *read* them: they are pure Chaldee, and literally denote "He is numbered, he is numbered; he is weighed; they are divided." **TEKEL**. i.e. *be weighed*, ❋S#8625h. ver. 27. **UPHARSIN**. i.e. *divided*, ❋S#6537h. ver. 28.

26. **God**. Da 9:2. Jb +*14:14. Is ch. 13, 14. 21:1-10. ch. 47. Je 25:11, 12. √27:7. ch. 50, 51. Ac 15:18.

27. **Thou art weighed**. 1 S *2:3. Jb *31:6. Ps *62:9. Je 6:30. Ezk 22:18-20. **art found wanting**. Mt 22:11, 12. Ro √3:23. 1 C 3:13.

28. **PERES**. Peres, *he was divided*, ❋S#6537h. ver. 25. Pronounced *paras*, denotes *Persians*, who seem evidently referred to. **Thy**. ver. 31. Da *6:28. 7:5. *8:3, 4, 20. 9:1. Ezr 1:2. Is 13:17. 21:2. 45:1, 2. **Medes**. Is *21:2. **Persians**. ❋S#6540h. Da 5:28. 6:8, 12, 15. Ezr 4:24. 6:14.

29. **they clothed**. See on ver. 7, 16.

30. **In that night**. ver. 1, 2. Ps 76:5. Is *21:4-9. 47:9. Je *51:11, 28-32, 39-42, 56, 57.

31. **Darius**. This was *Cyaxares*, son of Astyages, king of Media, and maternal uncle to Cyrus, who allowed him the title of his conquests, as long as he lived. Da 6:1. *9:1. **Median**. i.e. *one from Media*, ❋S#4077h. **took**. Da 7:18. Ps 75:7. **being**. Chal. *he as the son of*, etc. **about**. *or*, now.

DANIEL 6

Daniel is highly preferred by Darius, and envied by his courtiers, who can find no occasion against him except concerning his religion, 1-5. Darius is prevailed on to sign a decree prohibiting everyone, during thirty days, to present any petition to either God or man, except to the king; under pain of being cast into the den of lions, 6-9. Daniel prays three times a day to God as usual; is accused before Darius; the execution of the sentence is urgently demanded; and Daniel is cast into the den of lions, 10-17. The king shows much grief: but Daniel is miraculously preserved; and his accusers are devoured by the lions, 18-24. Darius commands all his subjects to fear before the almighty God, whom Daniel serves, 25-27. Daniel's subsequent prosperity, 28.

1. **Darius**. Da 5:31. 8:3, 4. 1 P *2:14. **an**. Ex +*18:21, 22. Est 1:1.

2. **of**. Da 2:48, 49. 5:16, 29. 1 S *2:30. Pr 3:16. **that**. Mt 18:23. Lk 16:2. **and the**. Ezr 4:22. Est 7:4. Pr 26:6. Lk 19:13, etc. 1 C 4:2.

3. **was preferred**. Da 2:46-48. 4:18. 5:11, 12. 22:29. **an**. Da 5:12, 14. 9:23. Ge 41:38-41. Ne 7:2. Pr 3:3, 4. 17:27. Ec 2:13. **spirit**. Heb. *ruach*, Ge +41:8. ſ121A3, Nu +11:17. **thought**. Intended to make him *grand vizier* or *emiru'l umra*. Daniel had now been employed full sixty-five years as prime minister under the kings of Babylon; and was justly entitled, from his acknowledged wisdom, to this preference.

4. Cir. A.M. 3467. B.C. 537. **sought**. Da 3:8. Ge 43:18. Jg 14:4. Ps 37:12, 13, 32, 33. 109:3. Pr 29:27. Ec *4:4. Je 18:18, 23. 20:10. Mt 26:4. 27:18. Lk 20:20. 22:2. 1 P *2:20. **but**. 1 S 18:14. 19:4, 5. 22:14. Lk 23:14, 15. Jn 19:4. 2 C 11:12. Ph 2:15. 1 T 5:14. T 2:8. 1 P 2:12. 3:16. 4:14-16. **find none**. Ne 5:9. Jb *1:1. Ps 59:4. Ezk *14:14. Jn 19:6. T 2:8. **faithful**. Lk +*16:10, 12. 1 C *4:2. He 3:5.

5. **We shall**. 1 S 24:17. Est 3:8. Is +*54:17. Jn 19:6, 7. Ac 24:13-16, 20, 21.

6. **assembled together**. *or*, came tumultuously. ver. 11. Ps 56:6. 62:3. 64:2-6. Mt 27:23-25. Lk 23:23-25. Ac 22:22, 23. **King**. ver. 21. Da 2:4. 3:9. 5:10. Ne 2:3. Pr 26:28. Ac 24:2, 3. **live**. 2 S 16:16mg. **for ever**. Chal. *alam*, Ex +*12:24.

7. **All**. See on ver. 2, 3. Da 3:2, 27. **captains**. Da 3:2, 27. Ezr 5:3. Ne 2:7. Est 3:12. Hg 1:1, 14. 2:2, 21. Ml 1:8. **have consulted**. Ps *2:2. 59:3. 62:4. 83:1-3. 94:20, 21. Mi 6:5. Mt 12:14. 26:4. Mk 15:1. Jn 12:10. Ac 4:5-7, 26-28. **decree**. *or*, interdict. **save of thee**. Ps *12:2, 3. 62:3, 4. Pr *26:23-26, 28. **he shall**. Da 3:6, 11. Ps 10:9. Na 2:12.

8. **establish**. Est 3:12. 8:10. Is 10:1. **according**. ver. 12, 15. Est *1:19. *8:8. **altereth not**. Chal. passeth not. Mt *24:35.

9. **signed**. Ps 62:9, 10. 118:9. 146:3. Pr 6:2. *7:21-23. Ec *9:12. Is 2:22.

10. **when Daniel knew**. Ex 1:17, 19-21. Mt 2:13, 14. Lk +*14:26. Ac √4:17-19. +*5:29. **his windows**. 1 K 8:30, 38, 44, *47-50. 2 Ch 6:38. Ps *5:7. Jon 2:4. He +*4:16. **his chamber**. T#1182. Ac 9:39, 40. **toward Jerusalem**. T#1258. 1 K 8:30. Ps 5:7. 28:2. +*122:6. *138:2. Jon 2:4. **he kneeled**. T#1259. 1 K 8:54. 19:18. 2 K 1:13. 2 Ch 6:13. Ezr 9:5. Ps +*95:6. Mt 17:14, 15. Mk 1:40. 10:17. Lk 5:8. 22:41. Ac *7:60. 9:40. 20:36, 37. 21:4, 5. Ep 3:14. **three times**. T#1171. ver. 13.

Ps +*55:17. 86:3mg. 119:164. Lk 18:7. 21:36. Ac 1:14. 2:1, 2, 15. *3:1. 6:4. 10:2, 4, *9, 31. 12:5, 16, 17. Ro +*12:11, 12. Ep 6:18. Ph 4:6. Col 4:2. 1 Th *5:17. 2 T 1:3. **gave thanks.** Ps 34:1. Ph *4:6, 7. Col 3:17. 1 Th *5:17, 18. He *13:15. **as he did aforetime.** He saw what was designed, but he knew whom he served; and therefore, as a public and eminent person, he determined to set a decided example of his religion, without fearing what man could do to him. T#1253. Ne 6:11. Ps 11:1, 2. Mt +*10:28-33. Lk 12:4-9. Ac √4:18, 19, 29. √5:20, 29, 40-42. *20:24. Ph 1:14, 20. Re *2:10, 13. +*12:11.

11. **assembled.** See on ver. 6. Ps 10:9. 37:32, 33.

12. **they.** See on Da 3:8-12. Ac 16:19, 24. 24:2-9. **the den.** It is probable that these lions were kept for the purpose of devouring certain criminals, whom the laws might consign to that kind of death. **The thing.** ver. 8. Est 1:19.

13. **That Daniel.** Da 1:6. 2:25. *5:13. **regardeth not.** Da 3:12. Est 3:8. Ac +*5:29. *17:7.

14. **was sore.** The king now clearly perceived for what purpose the decree had been solicited; and was exceedingly displeased with himself that he had suffered himself to be so deluded. See on Da 3:13. Mt 27:17-24. Mk *6:26. Lk 23:13-21. Jn 19:7-12. **and he.** He strove during the whole day, by every means, to evade or annul the edict; but the foolish constitution of his government did not allow him to pardon any person who had broken one of the decrees, however arbitrary and unreasonable. 2 S 3:28, 29.

15. **Know.** ver. 8, 12. Est 8:8. Ps √94:20, 21.

16. **the king.** 2 S 3:39. Pr 29:25. Je 26:14. 38:5. Mt 14:8-10. 27:23-26. Mk 6:25-28. 15:14, 15. Jn 19:12-16. Ac 24:27. 25:9, 11. Ro 13:3. **Thy God.** ver. 20. Da 3:15, 17, 28. Dt *32:31. Jb *5:19. Ps 37:39, 40. 91:14-16. 118:8, 9. Is 43:2. Ac 27:23, 24.

17. **a stone.** All this precaution served the purposes of Divine Providence. There could be no trick or collusion here: if Daniel be preserved, it must be by the power of Jehovah the God of Israel. La *3:53. Mt *27:60-66. Ac 12:4. 16:23, 24.

18. **and passed.** 2 S 12:16, 17. 19:24. 1 K 21:27. Jb 21:12. Ps 137:2. Pr 18:14. Ec 2:8. Is 24:8, 9. Am 6:4-6. Jon 3:3-9. Re 18:22. **instruments.** *or,* table. **and.** Da 2:1. Est 6:1. Ps 77:4.

19. **arose very early.** Mt 28:1. Mk +*1:35. 16:2. 2 C 2:13. 1 Th 3:5.

20. **is.** See on ver. 16, 27. Da 3:15, 17, 28, 29. **servest.** 1 Ch 16:11. Ps 71:14-18. 73:23. 119:112. 146:2. Pr 23:17, 18. Ho 12:6. Lk *18:1. Ac 6:4. Ro 2:7. Col 4:2. 1 Th *5:17, 18. Ja 1:25. **able.** Da *3:17. Ge 18:14. Nu 11:23. 14:15, 16. Je +*32:17. Mk *4:40. Lk 1:37. 2 C 1:10. 2 T 1:12. *4:16-18. He *7:25. Ju *24.

21. **O king.** See on ver. 6. Da 2:4. Ne 2:3. **live.** 2 S 16:16mg. **for ever.** Chal. *alam,* Ex +*12:24.

22. **My God.** ver. 20. 2 S 22:7. Ps 31:14. 38:21. *46:1. 118:28. Mi 7:7. Mt 27:46. Jn 20:17, 28. **hath sent.** Da +*3:28. Nu 20:16. 2 Ch 32:21. Ps 34:7. Is *63:9. Ac 12:11. 27:23. He *1:14. **hath shut.** 1 S 17:37. Ps 91:11-13. 2 T 4:17. He 11:33. **not hurt.** Is *43:2. **forasmuch.** ver. 23. Ps 18:19-24. 26:6. *84:11. Is 3:10. Ac 24:16. 2 C 1:12. 1 P *4:19. 1 J *3:19-21. **and also.** Ge 40:15. 1 S 24:9-11. 26:18. Ps 7:1-4. Ac 25:8-11.

23. **was.** ver. 14, 18. Ex 18:9. 1 K 5:7. 2 Ch 2:11. 12. **because.** Da 3:25, 27, 28. 1 Ch 5:20. 2 Ch +*20:20.

Ps +√9:10. *37:40. 118:8, 9. 146:3-6. Pr 18:10. Is √26:3. Mt 9:28-30. 17:20. Mk 9:23. Lk *7:50. 17:5, 6. Jn *11:40. He √11:33.

24. **and they brought.** Dt √19:18-20. Jg 1:7. Est *7:10. *9:25. Ps *7:15-17. Pr *11:8. **them.** This savage act accorded with the customs of those times; contrary to the Divine law which enacted that "the fathers should not be put to death for the children, nor the children for the fathers" (Dt 24:16). Dt +*24:16. Jsh *7:24, 25. 2 K *14:6. Est *9:10. Ps *9:16. 10:15. Pr *26:27. Ro 12:19. **the lions.** Da *3:22. Ps *54:5. Is 38:13.

25. **king.** Da *4:1. Ezr 1:1, 2. Est 3:12. 8:9. **Peace.** Ezr 4:17. 1 P 1:2. 2 P 1:2. Ju 2.

26. **make.** Da *3:29. Ezr 6:8-12. 7:12, 13. **tremble.** Ps *2:11. *99:1-3. 119:120. Is 66:2. Je 10:10. Lk 12:5. He 12:29. **for.** Da 4:34. Dt 5:26. Ru 1:16. 1 S 17:26, 36. Ezr 1:3. Ho 1:10. Ac *17:25. Ro 9:26. 1 Th *1:9. Re 4:10. 5:14. **the living.** Ps 42:2. **and stedfast.** Ps 93:1, 2. 146:10. Ml +*3:6. He *6:17, 18. Ja √1:17. **for ever.** Chal. *alam,* Ex +*12:24. **and his kingdom.** See on Da *2:44. 4:3, 34. 7:14, 27. Ps *10:16. 29:10. 145:12, 13. Is +*9:7. Mt *6:13. Lk +*1:33. Re *11:15. **not be destroyed.** Ps 10:16.

27. **delivereth.** Jb 36:15. Ps 18:48, 50. 32:7. 35:17. 97:10. Lk 1:74, 75. 2 C 1:8-10. 2 T *4:17, 18. **and he.** Da 4:2, 3, 34. Je 32:19, 20. Mk 16:17, 18. Ac 4:30. He 2:4. **power.** Chal. hand.

28. **and in.** Da 1:21. 2 Ch 36:22, 23. Ezr 1:1, 2. Is 44:28. 45:1. **Persian.** i.e. *inhabitant of Persia,* ✽S#6543h, only here.

DANIEL 7

Daniel has a vision of four great beasts arising out of the sea; the fourth having ten horns; among which a little horn comes up, 1-8; and of Messiah's kingdom, 9-14. An angel interprets the vision, of four kingdoms which would succeed each other: and shows the nature of the fourth kingdom, with the mischiefs done by the little horn, and the destruction of that kingdom, to make way for the kingdom of God, 11-28.

1. Cir. A.M. 3449. B.C. 555. **Belshazzar.** Da 5:1, 22, 30. 8:1. Je √27:7. **Daniel.** Da *2:1, 28, 29. 4:5. Nu *12:5, 6. Jb *33:14-17. Je 23:28. Jl *2:28. Am +*3:7. Ac 2:17, 18. **had.** Chal. saw. **a dream.** Ge +20:3. **visions.** ver. 7, 13, 15. Ge 15:1. 46:2. Jb 4:13. Ezk 1:1. 2 C 12:1. **he wrote.** Is 8:1. 30:8. Hab 2:2. Ro +*15:4. Re +*1:19. 10:4. **matters.** *or,* words.

2. **the four winds.** Da 8:8. 11:4. Ezk 37:9. Zc 2:6. Re 7:1. **the great sea.** ver. 17. Nu 34:6. Ps √65:7. 93:3, 4. Hab 3:8. Is 17:12, 13. 27:1. 57:20. Re 13:1. 17:15. 21:1.

3. **four.** Four *kingdoms* (ver. 17), called *beasts,* from their tyranny and oppression, emerging successively from the wars and commotions of the world. Da 2:32, 33, 37-40. Zc 6:1-8. **beasts.** ver. 4-8, 17. Ps 74:13, 14. 76:4. Is 27:1. 51:9. Ezk 19:3-8. 29:3. 32:2. Re *13:1, 2.

4. **The first.** Da ❁2:37, 38. **like a lion.** Dt 28:49, 50. 2 S 1:23. Is *5:26-29. Je *4:7, 13. 25:38. 48:40. 49:19. 50:17, 44. **eagle's wings.** Dt *28:49. Je 4:13. *48:40. 49:22. La 4:19. Ezk *17:3. Hab *1:6-8. Mt 24:28. **the wings.** Da 4:31-33. Je 50:30-32. **and it.** *or,* where with it, etc. **lifted.** Da 4:30. 5:18-23. Is 14:13-17. Je 25:9-26. Hab 2:5-10. **and a.** Da 4:32, 36, 37. Jb 25:6. Ps 9:20. Ezk 28:2, 9.

5. **another**. Da *2:39. *8:3. 2 K 2:24. Pr 17:12. Ho 13:8. **a bear**. 1 S 17:34-36. 2 S 17:8. Pr 28:15. Is 13:17, 18. Ho 13:8. Am 5:19. **itself on one side**. *or*, one dominion. Da *5:28, 31. *8:3, 4, 20. 11:2. Ezr 1:2. **three ribs**. Representing the conquest by Persia of Babylon, Lydia, and Egypt. **Arise**. 2 Ch 36:20. Is 13:17, 18. 21:2. 56:9. Je 50:21-32. Ezk 39:17-20.

6. **and lo**. Da *2:39. *8:5-7, 20, 21. 10:20. *11:3, etc. Ho 13:7. Re 13:2. **another**. The Greek empire, founded by Alexander the great. **like a leopard**. SS 4:8. Je 5:6. 13:23. Ho 13:7. Hab 1:8. **which had**. Da 8:5. **four wings**. ver. 4. Ezk 17:3. **four heads**. "Heads" represent leadership, hence, reference is to the four divisions into which the empire was divided by Alexander's generals. Da 8:8, 22. 11:3, 4, etc. **dominion was given**. Da 2:39.

7. **I saw**. See on ver. 2, 13. **a fourth**. The Roman empire, which succeeded and destroyed the Grecian, was exceedingly powerful, and became mistress of the world. See on ver. 19, 23. Da *2:40. 8:10. 2 S 22:43. Re *13:1-10. **and stamped**. Re 6:16, 17. 14:19. 16:1. 19:15-21. **and it had ten**. See on ver. 24. Da *2:41, 42, 44. Re 12:3. *13:1. √17:7, 12. The ten horns, seen as contemporaneous, not successive to each other, represent ten kings (ver. 24) at some time yet future, among whom one will arise, uprooting three in the process, who will then rule over all.

8. **another**. See on ver. 20-25. Da *8:9-12. Re *13:5-8, 11-13. **eyes like**. Da 8:23-25. Zc 11:17. Re 9:7. **a mouth speaking great**. See on ver. 25. Da 8:11. √11:36. 1 S 2:3. Ps *12:3. 2 Th √2:4. 2 T 3:2. 2 P 2:18. Ju 16. Re √13:1, 5-8.

9. **till**. See on Da 2:34, 35, 44, 45. 1 K *22:19. 1 C +*15:24, 25. Re *4:2, 3. 19:18-21. *20:1-4. **were cast down**. rather, were set in place. 2 S 12:30, 31. Ps 9:7. Je +43:11. Mt 25:31-33. Re 4:2. **the Ancient**. ver. 13, 22. Ps *90:2. 102:24, 25. Is +*9:6. Mi +*5:2. Hab 1:12. **of days**. √22D4B. Anthropomorphism B893. Circumstances are attributed to God as to time: days. For other instances of this figure see Mi 5:2mg. He 13:8. 2 P 3:18g. **did sit**. Ps 9:5. 29:10. Is 28:6. **whose garment**. Ps 45:8. 104:2. Mt 17:2. Mk 9:3. Ph 3:9. 1 T *6:16. 1 J 1:5. Re *1:13, 14. **was white**. Is 1:18. Mt 28:3. Re 3:5. 4:4. 19:8, 11. **his throne**. Is *6:1-3. Ac 2:30, 33. 2 Th *1:7, 8. 2 P 3:7-10. **and his wheels**. Ps 104:3, 4. Ezk *1:13-21. 10:2-7, 9-13. **burning fire**. Ex 3:2. 19:18. Dt 4:24. 9:3. Ps 18:8. 50:3. Ezk 1:4. He 12:29. Re 4:5.

10. **fiery**. Ps 50:3. 97:2, 3. Is 30:27, 33. 66:15, 16. Na 1:5, 6. 2 P +*3:7. **thousand thousands**. Dt 33:2. 1 K 22:19. Jb 25:3. Ps *68:17. Zc 14:5. Mt 16:27. *25:31. He *12:22. Ju *14. Re *5:11. **stood before**. Da +1:5. Zc 3:4. Lk +21:36. **the judgment**. ver. 22, 26. Ps *9:4, 7. 96:11-13. Ml *3:16-18. Re 11:18. *20:11-15. **the books**. √22D5K1B. Anthropomorphism B894. A Book of Judgment is attributed to God. For another instance of this figure see Re 20:12. Da 12:1. Ex +32:32. Is 65:6. Lk 10:20. Re *20:12.

11. **the voice**. See on ver. 8, 25. 2 P 2:18. Ju 16. Re 13:5, 6. 20:4, 12. **even**. ver. 26. Da 8:25. 11:45. Ps 7:6. 2 Th √2:8. Re 18:8. √19:20. √20:10. **his body**. Mt +*24:28. Lk +*17:37. **the burning flame**. Ps *11:6. *50:3. *97:3. Is +*30:33. 2 Th √1:7-10. √2:8. 2 P +*3:7, 10, 12. Re *20:7-9.

12. **the rest**. ver. 4-6. Da 8:7. Jn 12:20. Ac 2:9. **taken away**. Da 2:34, 35. **their lives were prolonged**.

Chal. a prolonging in life was given them. Da 2:44, 45. **a season and time**. Da +2:21.

13. **I saw**. T#968‡. Jn 1:2 (T#969‡). Ac 7:55, 56. Re 7:10. **one like**. Ps +*8:4, 5. Is +*9:6, 7. Ezk 1:26. Mt 13:41. *24:30. 25:31. 26:64. Mk 13:26. 14:61, 62. Lk 21:27, 36. Jn *3:13. *5:27. 12:34. Ac 7:56. Ph 2:6-8. He 2:14. Re √1:7, 13, 18. 14:14. **Son of man**. "His title '*the* Son of man' expresses his visible state, formerly in His humiliation, hereafter in His exaltation" (Fausset, on Daniel 7:13, Comm. vol. 4, p. 421). T#1914. Ps +*8:4, 5. √80:17. Mt 8:20. 9:6. 10:23. 11:19. 16:♣*13, +*27n, 28. 19:28. 24:30. 25:31. 26:64. Jn 1:51. +*3:13. 5:25, 27. Ac *7:56. 2 T 4:1n. He 2:7. Re 1:13. *14:14. **the clouds of heaven**. Ge +9:13. Mt √24:30. √26:64. Mk 13:26. Ac √1:9-11. Re √1:7. **the Ancient**. ver. 9, 22. **and they**. Ps 47:5. 68:17, 18. Je 49:19. Ep 1:20, 21. 1 T *6:16. He *9:24.

14. **given**. ver. 27. Ps *2:6-8. *8:6. *110:1, 2. Mt *11:27. √28:18. Lk 10:22. *19:11, 12n, 15. Jn *3:35. 5:22-27. 1 C *15:27. Ep *1:20-22. Ph √2:9-11. He *1:3, 4. 1 P 3:22. Re 3:21. **that all**. Da 3:4, 7, 29. Ps 72:17. Is 60:12. Ph ♣2:9, 11. Re *11:15. 17:14. **an everlasting**. Chal. *alam*, Ge +17:7. Ge +9:12. Is +*9:7. Lk +√♣1:32, 33. Re √11:15. **dominion**. ver. 18, 27. Da 2:35, 44. 4:3. 6:26. Ps +*45:6. 145:13. 146:10. Is +*9:7. Ob +*21. Mi 4:7. Lk +*1:33. Jn *12:34. 1 C +*15:24-28. He +*1:8. +*12:28n. Re 20:1-6. **his kingdom**. Da 2:44, 45. Ps *2:6. Is +*9:6, 7. *11:3-5. Mi 4:1-7. 5:2-5. Zc 14:9, 16, 17. Lk +*1:32, 33. 2 T √4:1.

15. **was grieved**. ver. *28. Da *8:27. *10:8, 16. Je 15:17, 18. 17:16. Hab 3:16. Lk *19:41-44. Ro *9:2, 3. Re 10:9-11. **in my spirit**. Jb +*14:22. Pr 20:27. Ec +*12:7. Mt +*10:28. Mk 2:8. 1 C 2:11. 2 C 5:8. Ph 1:21-24. He 12:23. Ja 2:26. 1 P √3:4. Re 6:9-11. **body**. Chal. sheath. Ge +*2:7. 1 Ch 21:27. Jb +*14:22. Is +*10:18mg. 2 P *1:14. **the visions**. See on Da *2:1, 3. *4:5. Ge *40:7, 8. 41:8.

16. **one**. ver. 10. Da 8:13-16. 10:5, 6, 11, 12. 12:5, 6. Ge 40:8. Zc 1:8-11. 2:3. 3:7. Re 5:5. 7:13, 14.

17. **great**. ver. 3, 4. Da *2:37-40. 8:4, 19-22. Nu 34:6. **arise out**. See on ver. 3. Ps 17:14. Jn 18:36. Re 13:1, 11.

18. **the saints**. ver. 22, 27. Da 4:13, 23. Ps 45:16. +*149:9. Is 60:12-14. Zc 13:8, 9. 1 Th *3:13. 2 T 2:11, 12. Re 2:26, 27. 3:21. 5:10. 20:4. **most High**. Chal. high ones, *that is*, things, *or* places. ver. 22, 25. Jn +*14:2. Ep 1:3. *2:4-7. 6:12. Plural of majesty or excellence (√96F2, Ge +4:10). Singular form used at Da 3:26. 4:2, 17, 24. Reference here must be to a person, not place or thing, for ver. 27 speaks of "the most High, whose kingdom." Ps +*7:17. 78:17, 35, 56. 83:18. Mk 5:7. Lk 1:76. 8:28. Ac 7:48. 16:17. Ro 9:5. 1 C 10:9. **shall take**. or, receive. Chal. *kebal*, to take from another (CB). ver. 22, √27. Da 2:6. 5:31. Ps +*149:6-9. Mt 11:12. 25:34. 2 T *4:8. Re 20:4. **possess the kingdom**. Is 11:19. *26:9. Mt ♦4:8, 9. 25:34. Lk 12:32. 13:28, 29. 14:15. 17:20, 21. 21:31. *22:16, 18, √29, 30. 2 C ♦4:4. Ep ♦2:2. 2 T *2:11, 12. He 12:28, 29. 1 P ♦5:8. Re √2:26, 27. 5:10. ♦12:9. *20:2, 3. **for**. Chal. *ad*, Ps +9:18. **ever and ever**. Chal. *alam* doubled, Da +2:20. Ps +41:13. Je 7:7. 25:5.

19. **the fourth**. See on ver. 7. Da 2:40-43. **the others**. Chal. those.

20. **the ten horns**. The ten kingdoms into which the western Roman empire was divided; which were primarily, according to Machiavel and Bp. Lloyd, (1)

The Huns in Hungary, A.D. 356. (2) The Ostrogoths in Maesia, 377. (3) The Visigoths in Pannonia, 378. (4) The Sueves and Alans in Gascoigne and Spain, 407. (5) The Vandals in Africa, 407. (6) The Franks in France, 407. (7) The Burgundians in Burgundy, 407. (8) The Heruli and Turingi in Italy, 476. (9) The Saxons and Angles in Britain, 476. (10) The Lombards, first upon the Danube, 526, and afterwards in Italy. Though the ten kingdoms differed from these in later periods, and were sometimes more or less, yet they were still known by that name. Prophetic interpretation and application has largely changed in viewpoint since the preceding note was written nearly two centuries ago. Since these kings are yet future (See notes on ver. 7 and on Ezk 38:16), the preceding identification may not be valid. Since the tribes did not exist at the same time and place, and are tribes, not personal kings, and since more than ten such tribes have been identified, their identification with the ten kings of Daniel is doubtful. Furthermore, ver. 24 states they were or are to be "out of this kingdom," that is, from within the kingdom, whereas the barbarian tribes were all from outside the Roman empire. Likewise, attempts to identify the ten kings with the nations of the European Common Market are not likely to be valid, for the extent of the European Common Market does not sufficiently include the eastern portion of the ancient Roman empire (The ancient Roman empire included a part of southern Europe, western Asia, and northern Africa), which is also in view in the prophetic Scriptures. If these ten kingdoms are to come into being after the events of Ezk ch. 38, 39, perhaps upon the establishment of a one-world government, then identification with the situation of today would be invalid. If the ten kings are to be identified with the ten toes of the image in Da 2:41, 42, 44, then they must be future, for the ten kings have not as yet been given their power (Re 17:12). See on ver. 8, 11, 23. Da *8:9-11. **mouth**. ver. 8. Da *11:37. Re *13:5, 6. **whose look**. ver. 25. Da 11:36, 37.

21. **the same horn**. ver. 25. Da 8:12, 24. 9:26, 27. *11:31-35. 12:7. Re *11:7-9. 12:3, 4, 13-17. √13:5-7, etc. 17:6, 14. 19:19. **prevailed against**. Da 8:10, 24. Zc 13:8, 9. 14:1, 2. Re √13:7-10, 16, 17. *14:12.

22. **the Ancient**. See on ver. 9-11. Da 8:25. 2 Th √2:8. Re 11:11-18. 14:8-20. 19:11-21. 20:9-15. **came**. ver. 9, 13, 14. Dt 30:3. Zc 14:5. Mt 24:29-31. Ep ◑+1:10. T 2:13. **judgment**. ver. 10, 18, 26. Ps +*149:9. Is 63:4. Mt *19:28. Lk *22:29, 30. 1 C *6:2, 3. Re *1:6. 3:21. 5:10. 11:2. 19:20. *20:4. **saints possessed**. ver. +*18. Da +*2:44, 45. Ge 9:12. Ps √49:14. Is +*9:7. Lk 22:30. 1 C 6:2-4. 2 T 2:12. Re 1:5, 6. 5:10. 11:15. 22:4, 5.

23. **the fourth**. See on ver. 7, 17. Da 2:40. Lk 2:1. Jn 11:48.

24. **the ten horns**. ver. 20n. Re 12:3. *13:1, 2. 17:3, √12, 13, 16-18. **another shall rise**. This evidently points out the papal supremacy, in every respect *diverse* from the former, which from small beginnings thrust itself up among the ten kingdoms, till at length it successively eradicated three of them—the kingdom of the Heruli, of the Ostrogoths, and of the Lombards. Others, seeing these events as yet future, interpret this of the Antichrist. That it does not apply to the Pope of Rome is quite certain, for (1) the pope never uprooted three kings to establish himself; (2) the "little horn" follows,

not precedes, the breakup of Rome; (3) the pope has never been a "king" in a sense parallel to that of the other "ten horns"; (4) the "little horn," if identical with the Antichrist, cannot be the pope, for the Antichrist must come from one of the four divisions of the Grecian Empire (Da 8:8, 9, 21-23): Greece, Turkey, Syria, Egypt; as the last king of the north is the king of Syria (Da 11:36-43), and is the Antichrist, Antichrist must be from Syria: but no pope has or will likely come from there. See on ver. 8, 20n. Da 8:9-12. 11:36. 2 Th 2:3-10. 1 T 4:1-3.

25. **he shall speak**. In assuming infallibility, professing to forgive sins, and to open and shut heaven, thundering out bulls and anathemas, excommunicating princes, absolving subjects from their allegiance, and exacting obedience to his decrees in open violation of reason and Scripture. ver. 8, 20. Da *8:11, 24, 25. *11:28, 30, 31, 36, 37. Is *37:23. 2 Th √2:4. Re √13:5, 6, 11. **great words**. ver. 8, 11. **the most High**. Da 4:17. **shall wear out**. By wars, crusades, massacres, injustice, seizure of property, persecution, etc. Dt 8:4. Jsh 9:4, 5. Je *30:4-7. Mt *24:15-22. Re +*6:9, 10. 11:7-10. 12:6, 14. *13:7-10. 14:12. 16:6. *17:6. *18:24. **the saints**. ver. 18, 22. **and think**. Appointing feasts and fasts, canonizing saints, perhaps changing the Sabbath, etc. Da 2:21. 11:31, 36-38. 12:11. 2 Th *2:4. 1 T 4:1-3. Re *13:15-17. **change times and laws**. Ge 1:14. 17:21. 18:14. **until**. Re 17:14. **a time**. That is, three years and a half, or, reckoning thirty days to a month, 1260 days, equal to the same number of years in prophetic language; which, dated from the decree of Phocas constituting him the supreme head of the church, A.D. 606, will terminate 1866. But in Da 4:16, a "time" is equivalent to a year, thus the period must be three and one half *years*, corresponding to what is said in Da 12:7, 11, 12 and Re 13:5 (where forty-two months is equal to three and one half years). Compare this time with that of Da 9:26, 27, where at the middle of the seven years, or three and one half years, the covenant is broken by the Antichrist, and see the same length of time expressed in Re 12:6, 14. Da 4:25, 32. 8:14. *12:7, 11, 12. Nu ◑14:34. Re ◑90:4. Ezk ◑4:5. 2 P ◑3:8. Re *11:2, 3. *12:6, 14. 13:5, 7.

26. **the judgment shall sit**. See on ver. 10, 11, +*22. 2 Th *2:8. Re 11:13. 20:10, 11. **his dominion**. ver. 24, 25. **to consume and**. Da *2:44. Is *60:12. Re 11:15. 19:20. **unto the end**. Da 8:17-19. *9:26. 11:40. 12:4, 9, 13. Mt *24:14.

27. **the kingdom and**. See on ver. 14, 18, 22. Ps +*149:5-9. Is 49:23-26. 54:3. 60:11-16. Zp 3:19, 20. Zc 14:9. Re *20:4. **whose kingdom**. Da 2:44. 4:34. Ps √145:10-13. Is +*9:7. Lk +*1:33. Jn 12:34. Ac 2:34-36. Ph 2:9. **shall be given**. ver. +*18. Re *2:26, 27. *3:21. **and all**. Ps *2:6-12. 22:27, 28. 72:11. 86:9. Is 60:12. Ob 21. Re *11:15. **dominions**. *or*, rulers. Re 17:14. 19:16. **serve and obey**. 2 T 2:12. Re 5:10. 20:6. **him**. or, them. Same grammatical antecedent as "whose," taken by some to be "the most High," by others to be the "people of the saints." Perhaps the latter view is preferable. Dt 28:1-14. Is 65:17-25. Zc 14:2-4. Re 19:11-21.

28. **the end**. Da 8:17, 19. 11:27. 12:9, 13. **my cogitations**. See on ver. 15. Da 8:27. 10:8, 16. **but**. Ge 37:10. Mk 9:10. Lk *2:19, 51. 9:44. Here ends the portion of Daniel written in Chaldee. The remainder of the book is written in Hebrew.

DANIEL 8

Daniel has a vision of a ram, and a he-goat that overcame the ram, 1-7. The horn of the goat is broken, and four horns come up in its stead, 8. A little horn springs from one of them, and becomes exceedingly great, and does much mischief, 9-12. The two thousand three hundred days of the suspension of the daily sacrifice, 13, 14. Gabriel shows Daniel that this vision related to the kingdom of the Medes and Persians as conquered by the Macedonians and to a power that would thence arise, and extensively, and for a long time, prevail against the saints, 15-25. The certainty and remote futurity of the events; and Daniel's grief, astonishment, and sickness, 26, 27.

1. Cir. A.M. 3451. B.C. 553. **the third**. See on Da *7:1. **me Daniel**. ver. 15. Da 7:15, 28. 9:2. 10:2, 7. 11:4.

2. **I saw in**. ver. 3. See on Da 7:2, 15. Nu 12:6. He 1:1. **Shushan**. i.e. *lily; joyfulness,* ❋S#7800h. Ne 1:1. Est *1:2, 5. 2:3, 5, 8. 3:15, 15. 4:8, 16. 7:16. 8:14, 15. 9:6, 11, 12, 13, 14, 15, 15, 18. **the palace**. 1 Ch 29:1. **province**. Ge 10:22. 14:1. Is 11:11. 21:2. Je 25:25. 49:34-39. Ezk 32:24. **I saw**. Ezk 8:3. **the river**. ver. 3, 6. Je 17:8. **Ulai**. i.e. *muddy water; senseless; my leader,* ❋S#195h. ver. 16.

3. **I lifted**. ✓144A12, Ge +22:13. Da 10:5. Nu 24:2. Jsh 5:13. 1 Ch 21:16. Zc 1:18. 2:1. 5:1, 5, 9. 6:1. a **ram**. The Medo-Persian empire, of which a ram was the ensign; and a ram's head with horns, one higher than the other, is still to be seen on the ruins of Persepolis. ver. 20. Da 2:39. 7:5. 2 Ch 36:20. **one**. Media was the more ancient kingdom; but Persia, after Cyrus, was the most considerable. Da 5:31. 6:28. Ezr 1:2. 4:5. Est 1:3. Is 13:17. 21:2. 44:28. Je 51:11. **the other**. Heb. the second. Ge 4:19.

4. **pushing**. Da 2:39. 5:30, 31. *7:5. 11:2. Is 45:1-5. Je ch. 50, 51. Ezk 34:21. **neither**. ver. 7. Jb 10:7. Ps 7:2. 50:22. Mi 5:8. **but**. Da 5:19. 11:3, 16, 36. Is 10:13, 14.

5. **an he goat**. ver. 21. Da 2:32, 39. 7:6. **the face**. Ge 1:2. **touched not the ground**. *or,* none touched *him* in the earth. **a notable horn**. Heb. an horn of sight. Alexander the Great. ver. 8, 21. Da 11:3.

6. **to the**. See on ver. 3.

7. **moved**. Da 11:11. **and there was no**. Le 26:37. Jsh 8:20. **but**. See on Da 7:7. **there was none**. See on ver. 4.

8. **waxed**. Dt 31:20. Est 9:4. Je 5:27. Ezk 16:7. **when**. Da 4:31. 5:20. 2 Ch 26:16. Ps 82:6, 7. Ezk 28:9. **the great**. ver. 22. Da *7:6. 11:4. **toward**. Da 2:39. 7:2. Mt 24:31. Mk 13:27. Re 7:1.

9. **came**. ver. 23, 24. Da *7:8, 20-26. 11:21, 25, etc. **the pleasant**. Da *11:16, 41, 45. Ps *48:2. 106:24mg. Je *3:19. Ezk *20:6, 15. Zc *7:14.

10. **to the host**. *or,* against the host. ver. 24, 25. Da 11:28, 30, 33-36. *12:3. Ge 15:5. 22:17. Ex 12:41. Is 14:13. Je 33:22. Mt *24:29. Re 1:20. *12:4. **host and**. ✓93A, Ge +1:26. By Hendiadys, "starry host," only one thing, not two. **and stamped**. ver. 7. Da 7:7, 21, 25.

11. **he magnified**. ver. 25. Da 5:23. 7:25. *11:36. 2 K 19:22, 23. 2 Ch 32:15-22. Is 14:13, 14. 37:23, 29. Je 48:26, 42. Jl ✓2:20mg. Zp 2:8, 10. 2 Th ✓2:4. Re ✓13:5-7. **to**. *or,* against. Ps *2:1-3. **the prince**. ver.

25. Da 11:36. Jsh *5:14, 15. He 2:10. Re 17:14. 19:13-16. **by him**. *or,* from him. **the daily**. ver. 12, 13. Da 9:27. 11:31. 12:11. Ex 29:38-42)℘. Nu 28:3)℘. 1 Ch 16:40. 2 Ch 29:7. Is +*58:11 (continually). Ezk 46:14. **and the place**. See on Da *9:26, 27. Ex 15:17. 1 K 8:13, 39, 43. Lk *21:5, 6, 24.

12. **an host was given him against the daily sacrifice**. *or,* the host was given over for the transgression against the daily *sacrifice.* Da *11:31-35. *12:11. Re 13:7. **and it cast**. Ps 119:43, 142. Is 59:14. 2 Th ✓2:10-12. **and it practiced**. ver. 4. Da 11:28, 36. 1 S 23:9. Jb 12:6. Je 12:1, 2. Re ✓13:11-17.

13. **one saint**. Da 4:13. See on 7:16. *12:5, 6. Dt *33:2. Jb 5:1. 15:15. Ps 89:5, 7. Zc 1:9-12, 19. 2:3, 4. *14:5. 1 Th *3:13. 1 P *1:12. Ju *14. **that certain saint**. *or,* the numberer of secrets, *or,* the wonderful numberer. Heb. *Palmoni.* Jg *13:18mg,n. Ru 4:1. Ps 12:6. 87:6. 138:2. 139:6. *147:4. Is +*9:6. *40:12, 26. Mt *10:29, 30. *11:27. Lk *10:22. Jn *1:18. **How**. Da *12:6. Ps *74:9, 10. 79:5. Is *6:11. Re 6:10. **the vision**. See on ver. 11, 12. **daily**. ver. 11. **and the**. Da *9:27. *11:31. *12:11. Mt *24:15. Mk *13:14. Lk *21:20. **of desolation**. *or,* making desolate. Da 9:27. 11:31. 12:11. Mt *24:15. **the host**. Nu 4:23, 30, 35, 39, 43. 8:24, 25. **to be trodden**. ver. 10. Da *7:23. Is *63:18. Lk +*21:24. He *10:29. Re *11:2.

14. **Unto**. Da *7:25. 9:27. 12:7, 11. Re 11:2, 3. 12:14. 13:5. **two thousand and three hundred**. That is, 2300 years, which, reckoned from the time Alexander invaded Asia, B.C. 334, will be A.D. 1966. Of course, the preceding note assumes that each day corresponds to a year (Nu 14:34. Ps 90:4. Ezk 4:5. 2 P 3:8), an interesting but apparently a mistaken identification here. Adventists used this text to predict the coming of Christ in 1843 or 1844 (calculating 2300 years from the start of the seventy weeks of Da 9:24, in 457 B.C.) which did not materialize, so subsequently was reinterpreted of Christ entering the holy of holies of the heavenly sanctuary to cleanse it, an interpretation at variance with ver. 13 above, for the heavenly sanctuary can hardly be "trodden." No doubt the reference is to 2300 literal days, probably a time period occurring in the time of Antiochus Epiphanes who reigned from 175 to 164 B.C., who prefigures the future Antichrist. Some interpret this 2300 days of the future Antichrist, noting that the time falls short 110 days of the three and one half years elsewhere mentioned in that connection (Da 9:27). In support of this view, note the correspondences among these several visions listed in the note on ver. 17. **days**. Heb. evening, morning. ver. +26. Ge *1:5. **then**. Is 1:27. Ro 11:26, 27. 1 P 1:12. Re 11:15. **sanctuary**. The land of Israel is called a sanctuary (Ex 15:17. Ps 78:54), and its literal cleansing is described as taking place in the last times upon the overthrow of Antichrist's forces assembled against Israel (Ezk 39:12-15). Ex 15:17. Ps 78:54. Ezk *37:27, 28. **cleansed**. Heb. justified. Da *9:24. Le 8:10. =16:20. Is 45:25. Ezk *39:12-15. Ga 3:8. He 9:23. 10:10-13.

15. **I Daniel**. See on Da 7:28. **sought**. Da 7:16-19. 12:8. Mt 13:36. 24:15. Mk 4:12. 13:14. 1 P 1:10, 11. Re *13:18. **as**. Da 10:5, 16. Jsh 5:14. Is +*9:6. Ezk *1:26-28. Mt 24:30. Re 1:13.

16. **I heard**. Da 10:11, 12. Ac 9:7. 10:13. Re 1:12. **between**. ver. 2. Da 12:5-7. **Gabriel**. i.e. *man of God,* ❋S#1403h. Da *9:21h, 22. Lk *1:19, 26. **make**. Da

9:22, 23. 10:14, 21. 12:7, 8. Zc 1:9. 2:4. He 1:14. 1 P 1:10, 11. Re 22:16.

17. **I was.** Da 10:7, 8, 16. Ge 17:3. Ezk 1:28. Mt 17:8. Mk 9:4, 5. Re 1:17. 19:9, 10. 22:8. **Understand.** ver. 15. Da 9:23. 10:11. **O son of man.** Da +7:13. Ps +8:4. See on Ezk 2:1. 6:2. 8:15. Mt 8:20. **at the time of the end.** ver. 19. Da *7:26. +*9:26, 27. 11:35, 36, *40. *12:4, 9, 13. Je +*30:7. Hab 2:3. Mt *24:14. It is possible that the visions of Daniel ch. 7-12 are synchronous, and all relate to the same "time of the end," as the preceding references show. Common threads through the several visions appear to be the "little horn," Da +8:9; the "daily sacrifice" taken away, Da +8:11; specific time periods (Da 7:25, 1260 days; Da 8:14, 2300 days; Da 9:27, midst of the week or 1260 days; Da 12:7, 11, 12, 1260, 1290, and 1335 days); sanctuary cleansed and anointing of the Holy of Holies, Da 8:14 and 9:24; and a common "end" or "time of the end," in the references above.

18. **I was.** ver. 17, 27. Da 10:8, 9. Ge 2:21. 15:12. 1 S 26:12. Jb 4:13. 33:15. Pr 19:15. Is 29:10. Lk *9:32. 22:45. Ac 20:9. **on my face.** Ezk 1:28. 2:1, 2. **he touched.** Da 10:10, 16, 18. Ge 15:12. Jb 4:13. Ezk 2:2. Zc 4:1. Ac 26:6. Re *1:17. **set me upright.** Heb. made me stand upon my standing.

19. **I will.** See on ver. 15-17. Re 1:1. **what shall be.** Mt *24:3-44. **the last end.** ver. +*17n, 23, 24. Da +*9:26, 27. 11:27, 35, 36. 12:*4, 7, 8. Hab *2:3. Re 10:7. 11:18. 15:1. 17:17. **indignation.** Is 10:5, 6. Je +*30:7. Mi 7:9. Re 14:10. *S#2195h: Da 8:19. 11:36. Ps 38:3 (anger). 69:24. 78:49 (indignation). 102:10. Is 10:5, 25. 13:5. 26:20. 30:27. Je 10:10. 15:17. 50:25. La 2:6. Ezk 21:31. 22:24, 31. Ho 7:16 (rage). Na 1:6. Hab 3:12. Zp 3:8. **time appointed.** Ge +17:21h. **the end shall be.** Mt 24:6, 13, 14, 15. Lk 21:24.

20. **The ram.** See on ver. 3. Da 11:1, 2. **Media and.** Da 5:28, 31. Ezr 1:2.

21. **the rough.** See on ver. 5-7. Da 10:20. 11:2. **Grecia.** i.e. *supple; clay; unstable; effervescing,* *S#3120h. Da 10:20. 11:2. Ge +10:2, Javan. **the great.** See on ver. 8. Da *11:3.

22. **being broken.** After Alexander's death, in the prime of life and in the height of his conquests, his brother and two sons were all murdered; and the kingdom was divided among four of his generals: (1) Seleucus, who had Syria and Babylon; (2) Lysimachus, who had Asia Minor; (3) Ptolemy, who had Egypt; and (4) Cassander, who had Greece, etc. **whereas.** ver. 3. Da *11:4.

23. **in the latter time.** Da 10:14. Nu 24:24. Ezk +*38:8, 16. 1 T 4:1. 2 T 3:1. 1 J 2:18. 4:3. **when.** Ge 15:16. Mt 23:32. 1 Th 2:16. **come.** Heb. accomplished. Da 9:24. **to the full.** Re 14:15, 18. 18:5. **a king.** The Roman empire, which reduced Judea to a province, burnt the city and temple, and scattered the Jews to the four winds of heaven. Others interpret this king of Antiochus as its primary reference, who portrayed in type the future Antichrist, to whom this must ultimately refer. See on ver. 9-12. Da *7:8, 11, 20, 25. **fierce countenance.** Dt 28:50. Re 17:13, 17. 19:19. **and understanding.** ver. 25. Da 11:21, 24. 2 Th √2:9-11. Re *13:11-14. 17:13. *19:20. **dark sentences.** Nu +12:8. **shall stand.** ver. 6.

24. **not by his own power.** ver. 22. 2 Th √2:9, 10. Re √13:2-9. *17:12, 13, 17. **shall prosper.** See on ver. 12. Da 11:36. **shall destroy.** ver. 10, 12. Da 7:8, 23,

*25. 11:31-36. Zc 13:8, 9. 14:1, 2. Re 13:10. 16:6. 17:6. 19:2. **holy people.** Heb. people of the holy ones. Da 7:18, 22, +*25. Is 63:18. Re 14:12.

25. **through his policy.** See on ver. 23, 24. Da 7:8. 11:21-25, 32, 33. Pr *29:12. **craft.** 2 Th √2:9, 10. Re *13:12-14. 16:13, 14. **magnify.** ver. 11. Da 7:8, *25. 11:36, 37. Je 48:26. 2 Th √2:4. Re *13:5, 6. **peace.** *or,* prosperity. Da 11:21. Ps 122:7. Zc 7:7. 1 Th √5:3. **stand up.** See on ver. 11. Da 11:36. Re 17:14. 19:16. **against the Prince.** ♪147H, Ge +9:25. Against Jesus of Nazareth, the true Messiah; for it was by the authority of the Romans that He was condemned and crucified; and his followers were persecuted with the most unrelenting cruelty, first by the Roman emperors, and then by the Roman pontiffs. The future Antichrist will set himself directly against Jesus Christ (Re 19:19). 1 T 6:15. Re 1:5. *17:14. 19:16. **but he.** Da 2:34, 35, 44, 45. 7:26. 11:45. Jb 34:20. Ps 92:7. Is 10:12. 14:25. 31:8. La 4:6. Mi 5:5-7. Na 1:11. Zp 2:13. Zc 10:11. Ac 12:23. 2 Th √1:7-9. Re *19:19-21. **broken without hand.** Da *2:34, 45. Is *11:4. 2 Th *2:8.

26. **the vision of.** See on ver. 11-15. Da 10:1. **wherefore shut.** Da 12:4, 9. Is +*8:16. Ezk *12:27. 2 Th 2:6-10. Re 10:4. *22:10. **for it.** It is now 2387 years since Daniel had this vision; and the utter desolation of the sanctuary has continued 1764 years; and no doubt the end of the 2300 years is not far distant (this internal evidence points to 1834 when this note was written, or, using the dates in the *Comprehensive Bible,* 2379 and 1756, it was in 1826 that this note was prepared from Scott who wrote it in 1820; thus, the *Comprehensive Bible* was prepared six years after Scott, and the *Treasury* was prepared some eight years after the *Comprehensive Bible*). See note on ver. 14, where the end of the 2300 years was thought to be A.D. 1966, but during that year the only event of prophetic significance, the "Six Day War" in Israel, whereby Israel regained control of all of Jerusalem, perhaps fulfilling Lk 21:24, does not seem to have any immediate relationship to the prophecies here. Da 10:1, 14. Is 24:22. Ho 3:3, 4. **days.** ver. 14. Da 12:11, 12. Ezk *12:27. Re 9:15. 11:3. 12:6.

27. **fainted.** See on ver. 7. Da *7:28. 10:8, 16. Hab +*3:16. **and did.** ver. 2. Da 2:48, 49. 5:14. *6:2, 3. 1 S 3:15. **but.** See on ver. 15-17.

DANIEL 9

Daniel, being assured that the end of the captivity was near, fasts; humbles himself in confessing his sins and those of this people; and earnestly prays for the restoration of Jerusalem, 1-19. Gabriel is sent to inform him, that the city, being rebuilt, shall continue for sixty-nine weeks of years; after which the Messiah will be cut off, but not for himself, and the city and sanctuary will be destroyed, 20-26. Antichrist confirms a covenant for one week, but in the midst of the week terminates the temple sacrifices, desecrates the temple with his abominations, desolating judgments overwhelm the city and nation, and the judgment determined upon the desolator is rendered, 27.

1. A.M. 3466. B.C. 538. **Darius.** Da *1:21. *5:31. *6:1, 28. 11:1. **Ahasuerus.** This was the *Astyages* of the heathen historians; as we learn from Tobit 14:15, where the taking of Nineveh is ascribed to Nebuchadnezzar and *Assuerus,* who were the same with Nabopol-

lasar and *Astyages*. which. *or*, in which he, etc.

2. **understood by books.** T#258. Da 8:15, 16. Ps *119:24, 99, 100. +126:5 (T#431). Je 29:1. Mt *24:15. Mk ◐+*12:24. 13:14. Jn +*5:39. Ac *8:34. 18:9-11. Ro *10:17. 1 T √4:13. 2 T *2:15. √3:15-17. 1 P *1:10-12. 2 P √1:19-21. Re *1:3. **to Jeremiah.** 2 Ch *36:21. Je √25:11, 12. *27:7. √29:10. Zc 7:5. **desolations of.** Ps 74:3-7. 79:1, 2. Is 6:11, 12. 24:10-12. *64:10. Je *7:34. 25:18. *26:6, 18. La 1:1. Mi *3:12.

3. **I set.** Da +*6:10. Ne *1:4, etc. Ps 102:13-17. Je √29:10-13. √33:3. Ezk 36:37. Ja *5:16-18. **by prayer and.** Ph *4:6. **with fasting.** Da 10:2, 3. Jg 20:26n. 2 Ch +√7:14. Ezr 8:21. 9:5. 10:6. Ne 1:4. 9:1. Est 4:1-3, 16. Ps 35:13. 69:10, 11. Is 22:12. Jl 1:13. 2:12. Jon 3:6-9. Mt +4:2 (T#193). +6:16 (T#192). Lk 2:37. Ac 10:30. Ja *4:8-10. **and sackcloth.** T#1276. 2 K 19:1. Ne 9:1-3. Ps 35:13. Jl 1:13. Jon 3:8. **and ashes.** T#1222. Jon 3:5-9.

4. **made.** ver. 5-12. Le 26:40-42)℘. 1 K *8:47-49. 2 Ch +√7:14. Ne 9:2, 3. Ps *32:5. Pr √28:13. Je 3:13. 1 J √1:8-10. **the great.** Ex +*20:6)℘. 34:6, 7. Nu 14:18, 19)℘. Dt 5:10. 7:9)℘. 1 K 8:23. Ne 1:5. 9:32. Je 32:17-19. Mi *7:18-20. Na 1:2-7. Lk 1:72. Ro √8:28. Ja 1:12. *2:5. 1 J 5:2, 3. **the covenant.** T#1131. Dt *7:9. Ne 1:5. 9:32. Ps 74:20. 106:44, 45. Je 14:21. **and mercy.** Ex +*20:6)℘. 34:6, 7)℘.

5. **We.** 1 J √1:8. **have sinned.** ♪12, Ps +1:1. ver. 15. 1 K √8:47-50. 2 Ch 6:37-39. Ezr 9:6. Ne *1:6-8. *9:33, 34. Ps *106:6. Is √64:5-7. Je 3:25. *14:7. **departing.** Ps 18:21. 119:102. Is 59:13. Ezk 6:9. Ho 1:2. Ml *3:7. He +*3:12.

6. **have we.** ver. 10. 2 K 17:13, 14. 2 Ch 33:10. √36:15, 16. Is 30:10, 11. Je 6:16, 17. 7:13, 25, 26. 25:3-7. 26:5. 29:19. 32:32, 33. 44:4, 5, 16. Zc 1:4-6. 7:8-12. Mt 21:34-40. 23:37. Lk 20:10-12. Ac 7:51, 52. 13:27. 1 Th 2:15, 16. **which spake.** Ex 4:16. 7:1. Dt 33:1. He *1:1. **our kings.** Ezr 9:7. Ne 9:32, 34.

7. **righteousness.** ver. 8, 14. Dt 32:4. Ezr 9:13. Ne *9:33, 34. Ps *19:9. 51:4, 14. 119:137. *145:17. Je 12:1. Lk 23:40, 41. **belongeth unto thee.** *or*, thou *hast*, etc. **unto us.** Ezr 9:6, 7. Ps 44:15. Is 45:16, 17. Je 2:26, 27. 3:25. Ezk 16:63. 36:31. Ro *6:21. **all Israel.** ver. 11. 1 K 12:17. Ezr 2:70. 7:13. 10:5. **near.** Dt *4:27. 2 K 17:6, 7. Is *11:11. Je 24:9. Am 9:9. Ac 2:5-11. **whither.** Le 26:33, 34.

8. **to us.** See on ver. 6, 7. **because.** Je 14:20. La 1:7, 8, 18. 3:42. *5:16.

9. **To the Lord.** From God's *goodness* flow His *mercies*; and from His *mercies*, *forgiveness*. ver. 7. Ex 34:6, 7. Nu 14:18, 19. Ne *9:17, 31. Ps 62:12. *86:5, 15. *130:4, 7. 145:8, 9. Is √55:7. 63:7. La 3:22, 23. Jon +4:2. Mi *7:18, 19. Ep 1:6-8. 2:4-7. **though.** See on ver. 5. Ne *9:18, 19, 26-28. Ps 106:43-45. Je 14:7. Ezk 20:8, 9, 13, 14.

10. **which.** See on ver. 6. 2 K 17:13. 18:12. Ezr 9:10, 11. Ne 9:13-17. He 1:1.

11. **all.** ver. 7. 2 K 17:18-23. Is 1:4-6. Je 8:5-10. 9:26. Ezk 22:26-31. **the curse.** Le *26:14)℘, etc. Dt 27:15-26. *28:15)℘, etc. 29:20)℘, etc. 30:17-19)℘. 31:17, 18)℘. 32:19-42. Zc +*5:3. **Moses the servant.** 1 Ch 6:49. 2 Ch 24:9. Ne 10:29.

12. **confirmed.** 2 K 17:13. Is 44:26. La 2:17. Ezk 13:6. Zc 1:6. Mt +*5:18. Ro 15:8. **our judges.** 1 K 3:9. Jb 12:17. Ps *2:10. 148:11. Pr 8:16. **bringing upon.** Am +*3:6. **evil.** Is +*45:7. **for under.** The destruction of Jerusalem by the Romans, and the condition of the

Jews during almost eighteen centuries, have far more exceeded all the miseries of the capture of Jerusalem by the Chaldeans, and in the Babylonish captivity, than those miseries exceeded the judgments inflicted on other nations; for the guilt of crucifying the Messiah, and rejecting his gospel, was immensely more atrocious than all their other transgressions. La 1:12. *2:13. 4:6. Ezk *5:9. Jl 2:2. Am √3:2. Mt 24:21. Mk 13:19. Lk 21:22.

13. **As it is written.** Thus every succeeding part of the Sacred Writings attests and proves the divine authority of the preceding. The *history* relates the fulfillment of former *predictions*; and then new prophecies are added, which future events accomplish, and thus demonstrate their inspiration to the latest ages. See on ver. 11. Le 26:14)℘, etc. Dt *28:15)℘, etc. Is +*42:9. La 2:15-17. Jn +*10:35. *13:19. +*14:29. *16:4. **law of Moses.** Ex +*24:4. yet. Je √36:24. **made we not our prayer before.** Heb. intreated we not the face of, etc. Ex 32:11. Jb 11:19. 36:13. Is 9:13. Je *2:30. *5:3. +26:19mg. Ho 7:7, 10, 14. **that.** Ps +√9:10. **we might turn.** Dt 29:4. Ps 85:4. 119:18, 27, 73. Is 64:7. Je 31:18. 44:27. La 5:21. Lk 24:45. Jn 6:45. *8:32. Ep 4:21. **and understand.** Ps +119:27 (T#1736). Ep 1:17, 18. Ja +*1:5.

14. **watched.** Je *31:28. *44:27. **the Lord.** See on ver. 7. Ne 9:33. Ps 51:14. **for.** ver. 10.

15. **hast brought.** Ex 6:1, 6)℘. 12:41)℘. 14:18)℘. ch. 15. 32:11)℘. 1 K 8:51. Ne 1:10. Ps +119:132 (T#1139). Je 32:20-23. 2 C 1:10. **hast gotten.** Ex 9:16. 14:18. Ne 9:10. Ps 106:8. Is 55:13. Je 32:10. **gotten thee renown.** Heb. made thee a name. Ex 14:18. 1 Ch 17:21. Ne 9:10. Is 63:12, 14. Je 32:20. **we have sinned.** See on ver. 5. Lk *15:18, 19, 21. *18:13.

16. **according to.** T#1128. 1 S *12:7. Ne 9:8. Ps 31:1. 44:4. *71:2. 143:1, 11. Mi 6:4, 5. 2 Th 1:6. 1 J √1:9. **be turned.** T#1522. Ps 85:4, 5. Jon 3:8, 9. Hab 3:2. **thy holy.** See on ver. 20. Ps 87:1-3. Jl 3:17. Zc 8:3. **for the.** Ex +*20:5)℘. Le 26:39, 40. Ps 106:6, etc. Ezk 18:4n, 20n. Mt 23:31, 32. Lk 11:47-51. **Jerusalem.** 1 K 9:7-9. Ps 44:13, 14. 79:4. Is 64:9-11. Je 24:9. 29:18. La 1:8, 9. *2:15, 16. **a reproach.** Pr *14:34. Je 24:9. 29:18. 42:18. 44:8, 12. Ezk 5:14, 15. 22:4.

17. **cause.** Nu *6:23-26)℘. Ps 4:6. *67:1. *80:1, 3, 7, 19. 119:135. +*122:6-9. *137:5, 6. Re 21:23. **face.** ♪22A4, Ge +19:13. **thy sanctuary.** La 5:18. **for.** See on ver. 19. Jn 16:24. 2 C 1:20.

18. **incline.** 1 K 8:29. 2 K 19:16. Ps 17:6, 7. Is 37:17. 63:15-19. 64:12. **behold.** Ex 3:7. Ps *80:14-19. **which is called by thy name.** Heb. whereupon thy name is called. Je 7:10. +14:9mg. *15:16. 25:29. 1 C 1:2. **for we.** ver. 5. Da 2:17, 18. Mt 18:19, 20. **present.** Heb. cause to fall. Je 36:7mg. 37:20mg. **for our righteousnesses.** Is √64:6. Je 14:7. Ezk 36:32. **great mercies.** 1 Ch *21:13. Is *54:7. Lk 18:13.

19. **O Lord, forgive.** Le *26:40-42. Nu 14:19. Dt *30:1-3. 1 K 8:30-39. 2 Ch 6:21, 25-30, 39. Am 7:2. Lk 11:8. **do.** ♪108B, Ps +37:5. "To do" is an idiom for to bring to pass, do a very great deal, do all. **defer.** Ps 44:23-26. 74:9-11. 79:5. 85:5, 6. 102:13, 14. Is 64:9-12. **thine.** Ps 79:8-10. 102:15, 16. 115:1, 2. Je 14:7, 20, 21. Ezk 20:9, 14, 22. 36:22. 39:25. Ep 1:6, 12. 3:10. **for thy.** See on ver. 18. Ps *79:6, 9, 10. Is 63:16-19. Je +14:9mg. *15:16mg. 25:29.

20. **whiles.** Da +*10:12. Ps √32:5. *65:2, 3. *86:5-7. 145:18. Is 58:9. +*65:24. Ac 4:31. 10:30, 31. **confess-**

ing my. See on ver. 4. Ec +*7:20. Is 6:5. Ro √3:23. Ja 3:2. 1 J √1:8-10. for. See on ver. 16. Ps 137:5, 6. Is 56:7. 62:6, 7. Zc 8:3. Re 21:2, 10.

21. speaking. Ps 69:13. *91:15. *145:18, 19. Is +*65:24. the man Gabriel. Da 8:16. 10:16. Lk *1:19, 26. to fly. Ps 103:20. 104:4. Is 6:2. Ezk 1:11, 14. He 1:7. swiftly. Heb. with weariness, or flight. ʃ102, Ge +2:24. touched. Da 8:18. 10:10, 16, 18. Is 6:6, 7. Ac 12:7. He 1:14. about the time. 2 S 24:15. 1 K *18:29, 36-39. Ezr 9:5. Mt 27:46. Ac 3:1. 10:3, 9. evening. Ezr 9:5. Mt +14:23. oblation. Le +*23:13, the meat or meal offering, gift or donation offering (CB).

22. he informed. See on ver. 24-27. Da *8:16. *10:11, 12, 19, 21. Zc 1:9, 14. 6:4, 5. Re 4:1. give thee skill and understanding. Heb. make thee skilful of understanding.

23. at the beginning. Da 10:12. Ps 69:13. Ezk √14:14n. commandment. Heb. word. for. Da 10:11, 19. Lk 1:28. greatly beloved. Heb. a man of desires. ʃ121R5, Ge +27:15. SS 7:10. Ezk 24:16. 26:12mg. understand. Mt *24:15.

24. Seventy weeks. That is, seventy weeks of years, or 490 years, which reckoned from the seventh year of Artaxerxes, coinciding with the 4256th year of the Julian period, and in the month Nisan, in which Ezra was commissioned to restore the Jewish state and polity (Ezr 7:9-26), will bring us to the month Nisan of the 4746th year of the same period, or A.D. 33, the very month and year in which our Lord suffered, and completed the work of our salvation. Sir Robert Anderson has since given a detailed calculation regarding the seventy weeks, a period which begins March 14, B.C. 445, and for the sixty-ninth week, ends Sunday, April 6, A.D. 32, the day of the triumphal entry of Jesus into Jerusalem (Lk 19:28-40) in fulfillment of Zc 9:9 (Anderson, The Coming Prince, pp. vi., 128). As to the seventieth week, it is yet future. "A careful study of the Angel's words (Da 9:24) will show that not so much as one of them has been thus accomplished" (Anderson, p. 79). Le 25:8. Nu 14:34. Ezk 4:6. Ac +*1:6, 7. Ro +*11:25. holy city. Is 48:2. Zc 8:3. finish. or, restrain. Ge 8:2. 23:6. Ex 36:6. Is 66:7-14. Ezk 36:24-30. Ro *11:25-29. the transgression. Is +*60:21n. Mt 1:21. 1 J 3:8. and to. La 4:22. Col 2:14. He 9:26. 10:14. make and end of. or, seal up. 1 K 21:8. Jb 14:17. Ezk 28:12. to make. Le 8:15. 2 Ch 29:24. Is 53:10. Ro 5:10. 2 C 5:18-20. Col 1:20, 21. He 2:17. reconciliation. lit. "to cover over" (Ge 6:14), or "scrape out," that is, erase; as in Ex 29:36. It means to do away with a charge against a person by means of bloodshedding, or otherwise (e.g. by intercession, Ex 32:30), so as to secure his reception into Divine favor. Zc √13:1. ✱S#3722h: Ge 6:14 (pitch). 32:20 (appease). Ex 29:33, 36, 37. 30:10, 15, 16. 32:30. Le 1:4. 4:20, 26, 31, 35. 5:6, 10, 13, 16, 18. 6:7, 30. 7:7. 8:15, 34. 9:7. 10:17. 12:7, 8. 14:18, 19, 20, 21, 29, 31, 53. 15:15, 30. 16:6, 10, 11, 16, 17, 18, 20, 24, 27, 32, 33, 34. 17:11. 19:22. 23:28. Nu 5:8. 6:11. 8:12, 19, 21. 15:25, 28. 16:46, 47. 25:13. 28:22, 30. 29:5. 31:50. √35:33 (cleansed). Dt 21:8. √32:43 (be merciful). 1 S 3:14. 2 S 21:3. 1 Ch 6:49. 2 Ch 29:24. 30:18. Ne 10:33. Ps 65:3. 78:38 (forgave). 79:9. Pr 16:6 (purged), 14 (pacify). Is 6:7. 22:14. √27:9. 28:18 (disannulled). 47:11 (mg, expiate). Je 18:23 (forgive). Ezk 16:63 (am pacified). 43:20 (purge), 26. 45:15, 17, 20 (reconcile). Girdlestone (O.T. Synonyms, ch. 12, sec. 1) remarks

"...purgation is not the moral change, but the removal either of guilt or of the punishment that follows from guilt." The removal of the punishment of Israel is yet future, and was not fulfilled at the crucifixion. Ps +*130:8. to bring in. Is 51:6, 8. *53:10, 11. 56:1. Je *23:5, 6. Ro 3:21, 22, 25. 1 C 1:30. 2 C √5:21. Ph 3:9. He *9:12-14. 2 P 1:1. Re 14:6. everlasting. Heb. olam plural, Ps +61:4. righteousness. Is √1:26. to seal up. Is 11:9. Je +*31:31-40. Mt 11:13. Lk +*24:25-27, 44, 45. Jn 19:28-30. Ro *11:25-29. "In what sense were vision and prophet sealed up at the death of Christ, considering that the greatest of all visions was yet to be given (The Revelation), and the days were still to come when the words of the prophets were to be fulfilled (Lk 21:22)?" (Anderson, p. 79). prophecy. Heb. prophet. Ac 3:22. 1 C 13:8-10. and to anoint. Da +*8:14. Ps *2:6. +*45:7. Is +*61:1-3. Ezk √43:7, 26, 27. Zc √6:12, 13. Lk +*1:35. +*4:18-21. Jn 1:41. *2:13-22. *3:34. Ac *4:27. *10:38. He +*1:8, 9. 9:11. "And whatever meaning is to be put upon 'anointing the most holy,' it is clear that Calvary was not the accomplishment of it. All these words point to the practical benefits to be conferred in a practical way upon the people, at the second advent of Christ" (Anderson, p. 79). Tregelles (on Daniel, p. 99) states "...the expression does not in a single case in any other passage apply to any person, but always to the most holy place of the tabernacle or temple, or else to things such as sacrifices which were 'most holy.'" Da +*8:13, 14. Ex 26:33. 29:37. 30:25-31. 40:9-16. Le 8:10. Is +*56:7. 60:13n. Je 33:18n. Ezk 20:40, 41. +*37:26-28. 40:2n, 38. 43:12. Zc 14:16, 17. the most holy. or, saint of saints. T#1916. Mk 1:24. Lk +*1:35. Ac *3:14. He +√4:15. +*7:26. Re +*3:7.

25. and understand. See on ver. 23. Mt 13:23. 24:15. Mk 13:14. Ac 8:30. from the going forth. Ezr 4:24. 6:1-15. 7:1, 8, 11-26. Ne *2:1-8. 3:1. restore and to build Jerusalem. or, build again Jerusalem: as 2 S 15:25. Ps 71:10. unto the Messiah. i.e. the anointed. ʃ22D5L, Ps +45:7. T#1884. Ge +*49:10. Ps 2:3, 6. 110:4. Zc 6:13. Mk +*✱1:15. Mt 2:1, 2. Lk *2:25, 26. ✱*3:15. Jn *1:41. √4:25, 26. ✱S#4899h: Da 9:25, 26. Le 4:3, 5, 16 (anointed). 6:22. 1 S 2:10, 35. 12:3, 5. 16:6. 24:6, 6. 24:6, 6, 10. 26:9, 11, 16, 23. 2 S 1:14, 16, 21. 19:21. 22:51. 23:1. 1 Ch 16:22. 2 Ch 6:42. Ps *2:2. 18:50. 20:6. 28:8. 84:9. 89:38, 51. 105:15. 132:10, 17. Is 45:1. La 4:20. Hab 3:13. the Prince. Da 8:11, 25. 1 S +9:16 (✱S#5057h). 2 S *7:25-29. 1 Ch +5:2mg. Ps *89:3, 4. Is +*9:6. +*55:3, 4. Mi +*5:2. Mt 25:34. 27:37. Lk *2:4. Ac 3:14, 15. *5:30, 31. Re +*1:5. 19:16. seven weeks. The seventy weeks are here divided into three periods. (1) Seven weeks, or 49 years, for the restoration of Jerusalem. (2) Sixty-two weeks, or 434 years, from that time to the announcement of the Messiah by John the Baptist. Note however the more precise identification of Sir Robert Anderson given above at ver. 24. (3) One week, or seven years, for the ministry of John and of Christ himself to the crucifixion. Note however, that it is better to take this seven-year period as yet future, as the notes and references to verse 24 conclusively show. There seems no adequate basis to bring in the ministry of John the Baptist for this calculation, and no evidence that his ministry added to that of Christ total exactly seven years. One might wrongly but more plausibly suggest the seven years includes the continued offer

of the Gospel to the Jewish nation after Pentecost until, clearly rejected by Israel, the apostle declared, "lo, we turn to the Gentiles" (Ac 13:46); such a view would be mistaken, however, for the apostles continued to bring the message "to the Jew first" (Ro 1:16) throughout the book of Acts even after this incident (Ac 14:1. 17:1, 10, 17. 18:4, 7, 19. 19:8. 28:23, 29-31). This week or period of seven years is best taken as the future time of the Great Tribulation during which Antichrist will be revealed. **be built again.** Heb. return and be builded. **wall.** *or,* breach, *or,* ditch. *S#2742h. Jb 41:30 (sharp pointed things). Ps 68:13 (gold). Pr 3:14. 8:10, 19. 16:16. Is 28:27 (threshing instrument). 41:15 (sharp). Jl 3:14, 14 (decision). Am 1:3 (threshing instrument). Zc 9:3 (fine gold). This word is from the same root word as *S#2742h, rendered "diligent" (Pr *10:4. 12:24, 27. 13:4. 21:5); *S#2757h, rendered "cheeses" and "harrows" (1 S 17:18. 2 S 12:31. 1 Ch 20:3), from root word *S#2782h, rendered "determined" (Da 9:26, 27. 11:36. Jb 14:5), "decreed" (Is 10:22); "moved" (Jsh 10:21. Ex 11:7); "bestir" (2 S 5:24); "maimed" (Le 22:22). Perhaps a common thread of meaning underlying these several words and renderings would be to move within confines, to be pressed or beaten into place. **even in.** Ne 4:8, 16-18. Ep 5:16. **troublous times.** Heb. strait of times. Ne *4:8, 16-18. 6:15. 9:36, 37.

26. **And after.** Lk +2:10. Jn +5:39. Ro +1:4. **Messiah.** ♪22D5L, Ps +45:7. Ps 22:15. 89:44, 45. Is *53:8. Mk *9:12. Lk *24:25-27, 45-47. Jn 11:51, 52. 12:32-34. 2 C √5:21. Ga 3:13. 1 P 2:21, 24. *3:18. **cut off.** Ge 9:11. Ex 12:15. 30:33, 38. Le 7:20. 18:29. 20:17. Dt 20:20. Ps 37:9, 34. Pr 2:22. Is 44:14h. Je 10:3h. 11:19. Ac 2:22, 23. **but not.** *or,* and shall have nothing. Scott cites Lowth, who notes "The vulgar Latin render the words to this sense, 'The people that deny him, shall be no longer his' Da 11:17h," and Rabbi Croll, "He shall have no successor." As of the risen Messiah's kingdom there shall be no end, so he has no successor. Ge 5:24. 42:36. Ps *22:6, 7. Is *53:4-6, 8n, 12. Je 31:15. Zc 13:7. Mt ✱20:28. 26:56. Mk 14:50. Jn *1:11. +*14:30. **for himself.** T#1976. Is 50:6. *53:4-6, 12. Mt ✱20:28. Jn *10:11, 18. 1 C +*15:3. 1 P ✱*2:24. Re +*1:5, 6. **and the people,** etc. *or,* and the Jews they shall be no more his *people.* Da 11:17. Ho 1:9. **and the people.** *or,* and the prince's (Messiah's, ver. 25) future people. The Romans, who under Titus, after the expiration of the 70 weeks, destroyed the temple and city, and dispersed the Jews. Rather, after the sixty-nine weeks, for the Angel specifically states, after having already discussed the first seven weeks, that this takes place after the additional sixty-two weeks. **the prince that shall come.** Da 7:8, 20, 21, 24-26. 8:9-12, 23-25. 11:36-45. Hab +*3:16. This is a reference to the future Antichrist, not to the Messiah or to the Roman Titus. **shall destroy.** The subject of this verb is "people," not "prince," therefore the following references must not be taken to relate to Titus, for Titus is not mentioned in Scripture, though the destruction of the city and the temple which his forces wrought, of course, is. **shall destroy the city and.** Mt 21:41. *22:2, 7. *23:38. +*24:2, 3. Mk 13:2. Lk *19:41-44. 21:6, √12-24. Ac 6:13, 14. **and the end.** Mt *24:6-14. Mk 13:7. Lk √21:12-24. **with a flood.** Da *11:10, 22. Is *8:7, 8. Je 46:7, 8. Am 8:8. 9:5. Na 1:8. **the war.** Mt *24:6, 7, 14. Lk *21:20, 24. **desolations are determined.** *or,* it shall be cut off by desolations. **desolations.**

Mt 23:38. **are determined.** ver. 25 (wall, or, ditch). 11:36. Jb 14:5. Is 10:22. There is an unannounced interval of time between this last and the following statements. For other instances of unannounced prophetic time intervals see Is +61:2n.

27. **And he.** Amillenarians favor taking "Messiah" as the antecedent for this pronoun, and would perhaps favor the following original *Treasury* references: Is *42:6. *53:11. +*55:3. Je +*31:31-34. +*32:40-42. Ezk √16:60-63. Mt 26:28. Ro *5:15, 19. √15:8, 9. Ga 3:13-17. He *6:13-18. 8:8-13. *9:15-20, 28. 10:16-18. *13:20, 21. Premillennialists take the grammatical reference to be to the "prince that shall come," a view favored because that grammatical reference is nearer, and because what is now said further in this verse does not "fit" the Messiah, but the Antichrist. ver. 26. Da 7:8, 23, 24. 8:23-25. 11:36-45. 1 J 2:18. **the covenant.** *or,* a covenant. Da √11:21-24. Is 28:18. Je 19:7. By no means should this covenant be understood to be made by the Messiah! For one thing, it is in the wrong time frame, the seventieth week of Daniel's prophecy. For another, Christ did not make any seven-year covenants which he then proceeded to break after three and one half years! This is the seven-year covenant made by Antichrist with the Jewish nation, which the Antichrist breaks in the middle of the tribulation. **for one week.** This is Daniel's seventieth week, a time period of seven years which is yet future, as careful consideration of events described in its connection will show. Ge 29:27. Re 11:7. **cause the sacrifice.** Mt 27:51. He 10:4-22. Amillenarians would probably favor the preceding original *Treasury* references, suggesting that Christ's death on the cross put an end to sacrifices and offerings, for He truly was the completion of all the Old Testament types, whose one sacrifice forever put away sin. More consistent with the immediate context however, which places this event during the future seventieth week, is the premillennial view which holds this to be a reference to the Antichrist forbidding the Jews the right to have sacrifices in their temple, much as did Antiochus in former times (see on Da 8:11). Da 7:25. 8:11, 12, 13. 11:31. 12:11. Mt *24:15. 2 Th 2:4. Re 11:3. 12:6, 14. 13:1, 5, 6. **for the overspreading of abominations he shall make it desolate.** *or,* with the abominable armies. *or,* upon the battlements shall be the idols of the desolator. Da 8:13. 12:11. Is 8:8. Mt √24:15. Mk 13:14. Lk 21:20. **abominations.** The plural here (in contrast to the singular form at Da 11:31) may be a plural of importance, the same in its emphasis as what has elsewhere been called the plural of majesty (♪96F2, Ge +4:10). The reference is probably to the desecrating influence upon the temple and land of Israel brought by the placement of some terrible "abomination," image or idol, in the temple, for this word frequently refers to God's abhorrence of pagan idols and idolatry. Da 11:31. *12:11. 2 K 23:13. Is 10:22, 23. 28:22. 44:19. *66:3. +*66:17n. Lk 21:24. Ro 11:26. Re 13:14, 15. 14:9-11. 19:20. 20:4. **make it.** That is, the Jewish temple. Da 8:9-14. 11:45. 12:1, 7, 11. Mt √24:15. 2 Th √2:4. Re 11:1, 2. 13:6, 14, 15. **until the consumation.** The end of the seventieth week, so also the end of the Great Tribulation, and of many other prophetic events which culminate at that time. Is 10:22, 23. +*28:22. Je 4:27. 5:10, 18. 30:11. 46:28. Ezk 11:13. Jl 3:1, 2, 9-16. Na 1:8, 9. Zc 14:1-3. Mt 24:29-31. 25:31-46. Ro 11:25-29. Re 16:19. **that deter-**

mined. Da 11:36. Le 26:14, etc. Dt 4:26-28. 28:15, etc. 29:18, etc. 30:17, 18. 31:28, 29. 32:19, etc. Jb *14:5. Ps 69:22-28. Pr 16:4, 5. Is *10:22, 23. *28:18-22. *66:5, 6. Lk 2:34. Ro 11:26. 1 Th 2:15, 16. 2 Th √2:3-12. **shall be poured.** Re 16:1-4, 8, 10, 12, 17. **upon the desolate.** or, upon the desolator. Da 7:11, 25, 26. 8:25. 11:45. Is 11:4. 2 Th 1:7-10. √2:3-12. Ju 14, 15. Re 19:20. 20:10.

DANIEL 10

Daniel, after long mourning and fasting, has a vision, the glory of which overpowers him, 1-9. An angel comforts and strengthens him; and telling him of the opposition of the prince of Persia, the assistance he had from Michael, and the coming of the prince of Grecia, promises him further information, 10-21.

1. A.M. 3470. B.C. 534. **Cyrus.** Da 1:21. *6:28. 2 Ch 36:22, 23. Ezr 1:1, 2, 7, 8. 3:7. 4:3, 5. 5:13-17. 6:3, 14. Is 49:28. 45:1. **whose.** Da 1:7. 4:8. 5:12. **and the.** Da 8:26. 11:2. Ge 41:32. Lk 1:20. Re *19:9. 21:5. 22:6. **but.** ver. 14. Da 12:4, 9. **time appointed.** Heb. *tzaba.* Generally rendered "host" or "army." Here, "warfare" or "conflict." Da 8:10, 11, 12. Jb 10:17. Is 40:2. **long.** Heb. great. **and he.** Da 1:17. 2:21. 5:17. *8:16. 9:22, 23. Ep *1:18. *3:17-19. **understood.** ∫24A, Ge +32:24.

2. **I Daniel.** Ezr 9:4, 5. Ne 1:4. Ps 42:9. 43:2. 137:1-5. Is 66:10. Je 9:1. Mt 9:15. Ro 9:2, 3. Ja 4:9, 10. Re 11:5. **three full weeks.** Heb. weeks of days. T#1763. Da ◑+*9:24-27.

3. **I ate.** Da 6:18. Is 24:6-11. 1 C 9:27. **pleasant bread.** Heb. bread of desires. ver. 11mg. Da 11:8mg. Jb 33:20mg. Je +25:34mg. Ezk +26:12mg. Am 5:11mg. Na 2:9mg. **neither did.** 2 S 12:20. *14:2. 19:24. Ps 104:15. Pr 27:9. Mt ◑*6:17.

4. **as.** Da 8:2. Ezk 1:3. **Hiddekel.** Ge *2:14.

5. **and behold.** Da 12:6, 7. Jsh 5:13. Zc 1:8. Re 1:13-15. **a certain man.** Heb. one man. **clothed.** Da 12:6, 7. Ezk 9:2. **loins.** Is 11:5. Ep 6:14. Re 1:13-15. *15:6, 7. **Uphaz.** Je *10:9.

6. **like the beryl.** Ex 28:20. Ezk 1:16. 10:9. Re 21:20. **his face.** Ezk 1:14. Mt 17:2. Lk 9:29. Re *1:13-17. *19:12. **his arms.** Ezk 1:7. Re 1:15. 10:1. **like the voice.** Ezk 1:24. Re 10:3, 4.

7. **alone.** 2 K +*6:17. Ac *9:7. 22:9. **but.** Ezk 12:18. He 12:21. **so.** Ge 3:10. Is 2:10. Je *23:24.

8. **I was.** Ge 32:24. Ex 3:3. Jn 16:32. 2 C *12:2, 3. **and there.** See on Da 7:28. 8:27. Hab 3:16. Mt *17:6. Mk 9:6. Re 1:17. **comeliness.** or, vigor. Jb *42:5, 6. Is *6:5. **turned.** Ge 32:25, 31. 2 C 12:7.

9. **deep sleep.** Da +*8:18. Ge 2:21. 15:12. Jb 4:13. 33:15. SS 5:2. Lk 9:32. 22:45. Re *1:17. **on my face.** Ezk 3:23, 24.

10. **an hand.** ver. 16, 18. Da 8:18. 9:21. Je *1:9. Re *1:17. **set.** Heb. moved. Am 9:9mg.

11. **a man.** See on Da 9:23. Ezk √14:14n, 20. Jn 13:23. 21:20. **greatly beloved.** Heb. of desires. ∫121R5, Ge +27:15. ver. +3mg. Ps *45:11. SS *7:10. **understand.** See on Da 8:16, 17. 9:22, 23. **upright.** Heb. upon thy standing. Ac +*26:16. **I stood.** Jb 4:14-16. 37:1. Mk 16:8. Ac 9:6.

12. **Fear not.** ver. 19. Ps +*34:4. Is 35:4. *41:10, 14. Mt 28:5, 10. Mk 16:6. Lk 1:13, 30. 2:10. 24:38. Ac 18:9, 10. 27:24. 2 T +*1:7. Re *1:17. **from.** Daniel, as Bp. Newton observes, was now very far advanced

in years; for the third year of Cyrus was the 73rd of his captivity; and being a youth when carried captive, he cannot be supposed to have been less than ninety. Old as he was, "he set his heart to understand" the former revelations which had been made to him, and particularly the vision of the ram and he-goat, as may be collected from the sequel; and for this purpose he prayed and fasted three weeks. His fasting and prayers had the desired effect, for an angel was sent to unfold to him those mysteries; and whoever would excel in divine knowledge, must imitate Daniel, and habituate himself to study, temperance, and devotion. ver. 2, 3. Da 9:3, 4, *20-23. Ps +13:1 (T#1784). Is *58:9. +*65:24. Ac *10:4, 30, 31. Ep +*6:12. **chasten.** Da *9:3, 4, 20-23. Le 16:29, 31. Nu 29:7. Jg 20:26n. 2 Ch +√7:14. Ps √69:10. **thy words were heard.** T#545. Da 9:21-23. Ge 18:32. 32:28. Ex 32:11, 14. Nu 11:2. 14:19, 20. Dt 9:14, 18-20. 26:7, 8. 1 S 1:27. *12:18. 1 K 17:22. *18:37, 38. 2 K 6:18. 19:20. 20:5, 6, 11. 1 Ch 4:10. Ps 18:6. 34:4, 5, 6, 10. 34:15, 17. *50:15. *65:2. 66:19, 20. *84:11. 86:5. *91:15. 106:23. 118:5. +126:5 (T#431). *145:18, 19. Is 45:19. +*65:24. Je *15:1. √33:3. Ezk 14:14. Ho 12:4. Jl 2:32. Mt +5:14 (T#670). *7:7-11. Lk 18:7, 8. Ac 12:5, 7. 1 T +*2:1-3, 8. Ja *4:3, 8. *5:16-18. 1 P *3:12. Re 8:3, 4. **and I.** ver. 11. Da *9:20-22. Ac *10:3-5, 30, 31. 1 T +*2:1, 2.

13. **the prince.** ver. 20. Ezr 4:4-6, 24. Is 24:21. Je 46:25. Zc 3:1, 2. Mt 4:8. 1 C 8:5. 10:20. 2 C 4:4. Ep √6:12. 1 Th 2:18. **Michael.** ver. 21. Da *12:1. Ju *9. Re *12:7. **one.** or, the first. Col *2:10. 1 P 3:22.

14. **in the latter days.** See on Da 2:28. Ge *49:1)℘. Nu 24:14)℘. Dt *4:30℘. 31:21)℘. Is 2:2. Ezk +*38:8, 16. Ho 3:5. Mi *4:1. 1 T 4:1. 2 T *3:1. 1 P 1:5. 2 P 3:3. Ju 18. **the vision.** ver. 1. Da *8:26. *12:4, 9. Hab *2:3. He *2:3.

15. **I set.** See on ver. 9. Da 8:18. Ezk 24:27. 33:22. Lk 1:20. **became dumb.** Ps 39:2, 9.

16. **like.** ver. 5, 6, 18. Da 8:15. 9:21. Ezk 1:26. Ph 2:7, 8. Re 1:13. **touched.** ver. 10. Is 6:7. Je 1:9. Ezk 3:27. 33:22. Lk 1:64. **opened.** ∫108H6A, Jg +11:35. 21:15. **my lord.** ver. 17. Da 12:8. Ex 4:10, 13. Jsh 5:14. Jg 6:13, 15. 13:8. Jn +√20:28. **my sorrows.** T#1390. ver. 8, 9. Da 7:15, 28. 8:17, 27. 2 S 22:5-8. Ps +69:29 (T#1704). Ec 1:18.

17. **the servant of this my lord.** or, this servant of my lord. Mt 22:43, 44. Mk 12:36. **talk.** Ge 32:30. Ex 24:10, 11. 33:20. Jg 6:22. 13:21-23. Is 6:1-5. Jn *1:18. **straightway.** See on ver. 8. **breath.** Heb. *neshamah,* Ge +2:7.

18. **again.** See on ver. 10, 16. Da 8:18. **he touched.** Is 6:6-8. **he strengthened.** 1 S 23:15. Jb 16:5. 23:6. Ps 27:14. Is 35:3, 4. Lk 22:32, 43. Ac 18:23. 2 C √12:9, 10. Ep *3:16. Ph *4:13. Col *1:11.

19. **O man.** ver. 11. Da 9:23. Jn 11:3, 5, 36. 15:9-14. 19:26. 21:20. **beloved.** ∫121R5, Ge +27:15. **fear not.** See on ver. *12. Jg 6:23. Is *41:10, 14. 43:1, 2. Lk 24:36-38. Jn *14:27. 16:33. Re 1:17. **be strong.** Jsh 1:6, 7, 9. Is 35:4. Hg 2:4. Zc 8:9, 13. 1 C 16:13. Ep 6:10. 2 T 2:1. **Let.** 1 S 3:9, 10. **be strong.** ∫84, Ge +6:17. **thou hast.** See on ver. 18. Ps 138:3. 2 C *12:9.

20. **knowest thou wherefore.** Nu 24:12, 14. Jsh *5:13-15. **to fight.** See on ver. 13. Is 37:36. Ac 12:23. Ep +*6:12. **the prince of Grecia.** Da 7:6. 8:5-8, 21. 11:2-4.

21. **I will**. Da 8:26. ch. 11, 12. Is 41:22, 23. 43:8, 9. Am +*3:7. Ac 15:15-18. **show thee**. 1 S 9:27. +*23:16. Ml *2:7. Lk 24:27. Jn +*5:39. 2 T +*3:15. **scripture of truth**. Pr +*22:21. Ec 12:10. Jn √17:17. Ja 1:18. **holdeth**. Heb. strengtheneth himself. ver. 19. 1 Ch +11:10mg. **Michael**. ver. 13. Da +*9:25. +*12:1. Ju *9. Re *12:7.

DANIEL 11

A prediction of the Persian empire being overthrown by the Grecian, and the Grecian divided into four parts, 1-4. A prophecy of leagues and conflicts between the kings of the south and of the north, 5-20. The exploits of one of the latter princes, 21-29, who, being checked in his progress by the ships of Chittim, shall turn his fury against the Holy Land, 30-35. An impious tyranny set up in the last days by the last king of the north, Antichrist, 36-39. Events that shall take place in the latter times involving the dominion, success, and destruction of powers hostile to the people of God, 40-45.

1. **in the**. See on Da *5:31. *9:1. **Mede**. i.e. *measure*, ✳S#4075h, only here. **to confirm**. Da 10:18, 19. Ac +*14:22.

2. **will I**. Da 8:26. 10:1, 21. Pr 22:21. Am +*3:7. Jn √10:35. 18:37, 38. Re 21:5. **three**. These were, Cambyses, son of Cyrus; Smerdia the Magian impostor, and Darius Hystaspes. Ezr 4:5, 6. **the fourth**. Xerxes, son of Darius, of whom Justin (l. ii. c. 10) says, that "there was so great an abundance of riches in his kingdom, that when rivers were dried up by his army, yet his wealth remained unexhausted." **far richer**. Ps 73:6, 7. **stir**. Herodotus (l. vii. c. 60) says the army of Xerxes consisted of 5,283,220 men, besides the Carthaginians, consisting of 300,000 men, and 200 ships. ver. 25. Da 2:32, 39. *7:5. *8:4. **through his riches**. Ezr 4:4-7, 23, 24.

3. **a mighty**. Alexander the Great, whose kingdom after his death, as we have seen (Da 7:6n), was divided into four parts. Da *7:6. *8:5-9, 21. **rule**. √147D, Ge +1:29. **do**. ver. 16, 36. Da 4:35. 5:19. 8:4, etc. Ep +*1:11. He 2:4. Ja 1:18.

4. **he shall stand**. Jb 20:5-7. Ps 37:35, 36. 49:6-12. 73:17-20. Lk *12:20. **and shall be**. Da 7:6. 8:8, 22. Ps 39:6. Ec 2:18, 19. 4:8. Mt 12:25. **be plucked**. Da 7:8. Je 12:15, 17. 18:7. 31:40. 45:4.

5. **the king**. Ptolemy Lagus, king of Egypt, Cyrene, etc. ver. 8, 9, 11, 14, 25, 40. Is 19:1, etc. **south**. √171.O.7. Synecdoche of the Whole B639. The *south* is put for Egypt, with respect to Palestine. For another instance of this figure see Je 13:19. **and one**. ver. 3, 4. **he shall**. Seleucus Nicator, who had Syria, etc., to which he added Macedonia and Thrace.

6. **the end of years**. ver. 13mg. 2 Ch 18:2mg. Ezk +*38:8, 9, 16. **join themselves**. Heb. associate themselves. ver. 23. 2 Ch 20:35. **for the king's**. After many wars between Ptolemy Philadelphus, king of Egypt, and Antiochus Theos, king of Syria, they agreed to make peace, on condition that the latter should put away his wife Laodice, and her sons, and marry Berenice, Ptolemy's daughter. **king**. ver. 7, 13, 15, 40. **an agreement**. Heb. rights. Ps 17:2. **retain**. Jb 38:15. Ps 10:5. Ezk 30:21. Zc 11:16, 17. **she shall be**. Antiochus recalled Laodice, who, fearing another change, caused him to be poisoned, and Berenice and her son to be

murdered, and set her son Callinicus on the throne. **he that begat her**. *or*, whom she brought forth. **he that strengthened**. Her father Ptolemy, who died a few years before.

7. **out of**. Jb 14:7. Is 9:14. 11:1. Je 12:2. Ml 4:1. **one stand**. Ptolemy Euergetes, who, to avenge his sister's death, marched with a great army against Callinicus, took all Asia from Mount Taurus to India, and returned to Egypt with an immense booty. ver. 20. Ps 49:10-13. 109:8. Lk *12:20. **in his estate**. *or*, in his place, *or*, office. ver. 20, 21, 38. Pr 28:2. **and shall prevail**. Ps 55:23. Ezk 17:18.

8. **carry captives**. lit. shall bring into captivity. Is 49:25mg. **their gods**. Ge 31:30. Ex 12:12. Nu 33:4. Dt 12:3. Jg 18:24. Is 37:19. 46:1, 2. Je 43:12, 13. 46:25. Ho 8:6. 10:5, 6. **their precious vessels**. Heb. vessels of their desire. Da 1:2, 3. +10:3mg. Is 2:16mg. Je +25:34mg. Ho 13:15mg. Na 2:9mg. **he shall continue**. Callinicus died an exile, and Euergetes survived him four or five years.

10. **his sons**. Seleucus Cerannus and Antiochus the Great, sons of Callinicus. But the former being poisoned, the latter was proclaimed king, retook Seleucia and Syria, and then, after a truce, returned and overcame the Egyptian forces. **be stirred up**. *or*, war. **overflow**. ver. 22, 40. Da +*9:26. Is 8:7, 8. Je 46:7, 8. 51:42. **then shall he return, and be stirred up**. *or*, then shall he be stirred up again. Da 9:25. **to his**. ver. 7, 39. Is 25:12.

11. **king of the south**. ver. 5, 9. **moved**. ver. 44. Da 8:7. Ps 76:10. **the multitude**. ver. 10. Da 2:38. 1 K 20:13, 28. Ps 33:16, 17. Ec 9:11, 12. Je 27:6.

12. **his heart**. Da 5:19, 20, 23. 8:25. Dt 8:14. 2 K 14:10. 2 Ch 25:19. 26:16. 32:25. Pr 16:18. Is 10:7-12. Ezk 28:2, 5, 17. Hab 2:4-6. Ac 12:22, 23. 1 T 3:6. 1 P 5:5. **not be**. 1 P 5:5.

13. **the king**. See on ver. 6, 7. **certainly**. √147B, Ge +2:16. **after certain years**. Heb. at the end of times, *even* years. ver. 6. Da 4:16. 12:7.

14. **robbers of thy people**. Heb. children of robbers. or, destroyers. lit. "breakers forth." 1 K 12:15n. Ps 17:4. Ezk 18:10mg. **exalt themselves**. Ac 4:25-28. Re 17:17. **to establish**. Ac 13:27. **but they shall fall**. Thus it is that the book of Daniel was understood in this time, and some of the Jews undertook to fulfill the prophecy, but failed. It never works for men to try to help God out, as in the case of Rebekah, Ge 27:8, etc. This shows the impossibility of men to endeavor to fulfill prophecy, even when they appear to find themselves in the right circumstances to do so. Equally impossible is it for men or Satan to thwart the fulfillment of prophecy. Is 41:4, √22, √23. 26. 43:9, *13. 44:7. 45:21. 46:10. 48:14.

15. **cast up**. Je 5:10. 6:6. 33:4. 52:4. Ezk 17:17. **most fenced cities**. Heb. city of munitions. After fourteen years, Ptolemy Philopater having been succeeded by Ptolemy Epiphanes, then a minor, Antiochus raised a greater army than before, and having defeated his best troops under Scopas, recovered possession of Caelo-Syria and Palestine, with all their fortified cities. **shall not**. See on ver. 6. Da 8:7. Jsh +*1:5. Pr +*21:30, 31. **his chosen people**. Heb. the people of his choices. Ex 15:4.

16. **shall do**. See on ver. 3, 36. Da 8:4, 7. **glorious land**. *or*, goodly land. ver. 41mg, 45mg. Da *8:9. Is 8:8. Heb. land of ornament. Je +3:19mg.

17. **He shall also**. Being assisted by the Jews, he purposed to subdue Egypt; but, entering into treaty with Ptolemy, he gave him his daughter Cleopatra in marriage, thinking to engage her to betray the interests of her husband; but in which he was deceived. **set his face**. ver. 19. 2 K 12:17. 2 Ch 20:3. Pr +*19:21. Ezk 4:3, 7. 25:2. Lk 9:51. **upright ones**. *or*, much uprightness, *or*, equal conditions. Nu ◐23:10. Jb ◐1:1, 18. Ps ◐11:7. Pr *16:13. **daughter of women**. A reference to Cleopatra's beauty and prominence. **corrupting her**. Heb. to corrupt. 1 S 18:21. **not stand**. Est +*1:12. **neither**. Da +*9:26. Ps 56:9. Ezk 17:17. Mt 12:30. Lk 11:23. Ro √8:31.

18. **he turn**. He subdued most of the maritime places and isles of the Mediterranean; but, being driven from Europe by the Roman consuls, he took refuge in Antioch; and, in order to raise the tribute they imposed upon him, he attempted to rob the temple of Elymais, and was there slain. **the isles**. Ge 10:4, 5. Je 2:10. 31:10. Ezk 27:6. Zp 2:11. **for his own behalf**. Heb. for him. **the reproach**. Heb. his reproach. **he shall cause**. Nu +*32:23. Jg 1:7. Est 7:10. Pr *26:27. Ho 12:14. Mt *7:2.

19. **but**. From the preceding verses in this chapter let us learn: (1) That God, in his providence, sets up one and pulls down another, as he pleases, Da 4:17, 25. (2) That this world is full of wars and fightings, which result from the indulgence of the lusts of men, Ja 4:1. (3) That all the changes and revolutions of states were plainly and perfectly foreseen by the God of heaven, Is 45:21. (4) That no word of God can fall to the ground, but what he has declared shall infallibly come to pass, Pr +*21:30, 31. Jn +*10:35. For the elucidation of the historical parts of Scripture, it is advantageous to notice the writings of heathen authors: light is thus thrown on many passages of Holy Writ, by showing the accomplishment of the prophecies therein contained, or customs elucidated, which, in the course of years, or in our more northern latitude, would be to us inexplicable. We have therefore reason to bless God for human learning, by which many have done great service to the readers of His blessed word. **not be found**. Jb *20:8. Ps 27:2. *37:36. Je 46:6. Ezk 26:21.

20. **estate**. *or*, place. ver. 7, 21mg. **a raiser of taxes in the**. Heb. one that causeth an exactor to pass over the, etc. Seleucus Philopater, who levied on his subjects the tribute imposed on his father, and was poisoned by his treasurer Heliodorus. Dt 15:2, 3. 2 K 23:35. **glory of the kingdom**. ver. 16, 41. The historical fulfillment as this pertained to Palestine is to be found in 2 Maccabees, ch. 3. **anger**. Heb. angers. Pr 30:33.

21. **estate**. *or*, place. ver. 7, 20. **shall stand**. Da 7:8. 8:9, 23, 25. **a vile person**. Antiochus Epiphanes, called also *Epimanes*, or madman, for his despicable conduct. 1 S 3:13. Ps 12:8. 15:4. Is 32:5, 6. Na 1:14. **peaceably**. Da 8:25. Ezk 16:49. **by flatteries**. ver. 32, 34. Jg 9:1-20. 2 S 15:2-6. Ps 55:21. Pr 29:5.

22. **with**. ver. 10. Da +*9:26. Is 8:7, 8. Am 8:8. 9:5. Na 1:8. Re 12:15, 16. **also**. Da 8:10, 11, 25.

23. **work deceitfully**. Da *8:25. Ge 34:13. Ps 52:2. Pr 11:18. Ezk 17:13-19. Ro 1:29. 2 C 11:13. 2 Th √2:9, 10.

24. **peaceably**. ver. 21. Da 8:25. **even upon the fattest**. *or*, into the peaceable and fat, etc. Ge 27:28, 39. **he shall scatter**. Jg *9:4. Pr 17:8. 19:6. ◐22:16.

forecast his devices. Heb. think his thoughts. Da 7:25. Pr 23:7. Ezk 38:10. Mt 9:4.

25. **stir up**. ver. 2, 10. Pr 15:18. 28:25. **courage**. lit. heart. **the south with**. Antiochus defeated the army of Ptolemy Philometor, and in the next campaign made himself master of all Egypt, except Alexandria. While they had frequent conferences at the same table, they spoke lies to each other; and the former returned to Syria laden with riches.

26. **that feed**. 2 S 4:2-12. 2 K 8:14, 15. 10:6-9. Ps 41:9. Mi 7:5, 6. Mt 26:23. Mk 14:20. Jn 13:18, 26. **the portion**. Da 1:5, 8. **overflow**. ver. 10, 22.

27. **hearts**. Heb. their hearts. **shall be to do mischief**. 2 S 13:26-28. Ps 12:2. 52:1, 2. 58:2. 64:6. Pr 12:20. 23:6-8. 26:23-26. **speak lies**. Ps 62:9. Je 9:3-5. 41:1-3. **but**. See on Pr *19:21. Ezk 17:9, 10, 15. **for yet**. ver. 29, 35, 40. Da 8:19. 10:1. 12:9. Hab 2:3. Ac *1:7. *17:31. 1 Th *5:1. **time appointed**. ver. 29, 35. Ge +17:21h.

28. **the holy covenant**. The Jews having rejoiced at a report of his death, Antiochus took Jerusalem, and slew 40,000 of the inhabitants, and polluted the temple. For the historical fulfillment see 1 Maccabees 1:15, 19-24. See on ver. 22, 30-32. Da 8:24. Ac 3:25.

29. **time appointed**. ver. 27, 35. Da +*8:19. 10:1. Ge +17:21h. Is 14:31. Ac 17:26. Ga 4:2. **as the former**. ver. 23, 25.

30. **the ships of Chittim**. Antiochus was compelled to retire from Egypt by Roman ambassadors. Edward J. Young states "the reference appears to be to the Roman ships of Popilius Laenas which, according to Livy (45:10; also Polybius 29:1) sailed to Egypt in order to prevent Syria from taking that country (*Daniel*, p. 244). Ge 10:4. Nu *24:24)𝒫. 1 Ch 1:7, Kittim. Is 23:1, 12. Je *2:10. Ezk 27:6. **and have indignation**. See on ver. 28. Da 7:25. Re 12:12, 13, 17. **against the holy covenant**. ver. 28. Da +*9:27. **have intelligence**. Ne 6:12-14. Mt 24:10. **forsake the holy covenant**. These were apostate Jews who already had forsaken the Mosaic rites. ver. 28. 1 C +*12:3. He +*10:26, 29.

31. **arms**. Da 8:24, 25. Re 17:12-14. **they shall pollute**. See on Da 8:11. 12:11. La 1:10. 2:7. Is 66:17n. Ezk 7:20, 21. 9:7. 24:21, 22. **shall take**. See on Da 8:12, 13, 26. +*9:27. Ho 3:4. **daily sacrifice**. Da +8:11. +*9:27n. 12:11. Antiochus made practicing the Mosaic ritual illegal (Josephus, Ant. vii. 5, 4). **place the abomination**. Antiochus caused a Grecian god, an altar to Jupiter, to be set up in place of the brazen altar, thus defiling the Temple with its image. Da 8:13. +*9:27. 12:11. Mt *24:15. Mk 13:14. Lk *21:20. **maketh desolate**. *or*, astonisheth. Da 8:13. Ac 13:40, 41.

32. **shall he**. Pr 19:5. 26:28. **corrupt**. *or*, cause to dissemble. 1 C +*12:3. 2 Th √2:9-12. Re √13:12-15. **by flatteries**. Pr 20:19. 28:23. 29:5. 1 Th 2:5. Ep *6:10-18. Re 13:8. 14:12. **the people**. 1 Ch +*28:9. Ps +√9:10. 46:1. Je 31:34. Jn √17:3. 2 C 4:3-6. 1 J +*2:3, 4. *5:20. **shall be strong**. Mi 5:7-9. 7:15-17. Zc 9:13-16. 10:3-6, 12. 12:3-7. 14:1-4. Ml 4:2, 3. 2 T +*2:1-3. He *10:32, 33. 1 P *1:5. 1 J √5:4. Re 6:11. 7:9, 10. √12:7-11.

33. **understand among the people**. Notice here that it is not the professionally trained theologians and clergy, but the ordinary people of God, those believers taught in the word who understand doctrine, who will be used to instruct, direct, and encourage the faith of other weaker believers during the time of tribulation and persecution. This proves (1) the perspicuity of

Scripture, (2) the right of private judgment, (3) the validity and efficacy of informal Bible study and teaching, (4) the value of house fellowships and ongoing small group one-another ministry (1 P 4:10). This was fulfilled in the time of Antiochus by the Hasidaeans (1 Maccabees 2:42, 43), but as this whole prophecy is typical of what shall be in the time of the Antichrist, how richly suggestive this passage is concerning how believers will need to associate and teach informally in those difficult times of future tribulation. Da *12:3, 4, 10. 2 Ch +15:3. 35:3n. Ps +102:18. Pr +*8:9. *18:1n. Is +√8:16, 20n. *30:20. *32:3, 4. Je +*23:28n. Zc 8:20-23. Ml +*2:7. Mt +*13:11, 51, 52. +√24:45, 46. 28:20. Lk +*24:44-47. Jn +6:14. Ac 4:2-4. *11:26. 14:21. +*18:2, 26. Ro 16:3, +*5. 1 C 16:19. He *5:12-14. 2 P √1:20n. 2 J +*10. **shall instruct.** Da *12:3. 1 T +*4:16. 2 T *2:24, 25. **shall fall.** Mi *7:8. Zc √12:8mg. Mt *10:21. 20:23. +*24:9. Jn *16:2. Ac 12:2, 3. 1 C 4:9. 2 T *1:12. √3:12. *4:6. He 11:34-37. Re *1:9. √2:10, 13. √6:9. 7:14. √12:11. √13:7-10. *17:6.

34. **shall fall.** ver. 14, 19, +*33. Pr 24:17. **they shall be.** Re 12:2-6, 13-17. 13:1-4. **but many.** Da 7:21. Mt 24:11, 12. Re 13:7. **cleave.** Je +*23:28n. Ezk +*33:32. Mt √7:15. Ac *20:29, 30. Ro *16:18. 2 C √11:13-15. Ga *2:4. Ep *4:14. 1 T √4:1, 2. 2 T *3:1-7. √4:3. T 1:11. 2 P √2:1-3, 18, 19. 1 J √2:18, 19. √4:1, 5. 2 J √7-10. Ju +*3, 4. Re 2:20. √13:11-14.

35. **some.** ver. 33. Da 8:10. 12:10. Mt 16:17, 23. 26:56, 69-75. Lk *22:31. Jn 20:25. Ac 13:13. *15:37-39. 1 C √10:12. 2 Th √2:3. 2 T √4:10. He +*10:38. 2 P *2:20, 21. √3:17. **to try.** Da 12:10. Dt 8:2, 3, 16. 2 Ch 32:31. Pr 17:3. Zc √13:9. Ml *3:2-4. *4:1-3. Ja *1:2, 3. 1 P √1:6, 7. Re *2:10. **them.** *or,* by them. **make them white.** 2 P *3:14. Ju √24. Re *7:9, 13, 14. **even.** ver. 29, 40. Da +*8:17, 19. +*9:27. 10:1. 12:4, 11. Hab *2:3. Mt 24:13. Re 13:10. 14:15. 17:17. **time appointed.** ver. 27, 29. Ge +17:21h. There is an unannounced time gap between the preceding prophecy and that of the following section, just as there was between Da 9:26, 27. For other instances of an unannounced prophetic time gap between adjacent statements of prophecy, see Is 61:2n. While some interpreters take the following verses to be a continued description of Antiochus Epiphanes, careful attention to the statements of the prophecy show that they apply more accurately, if not exclusively, to the future Antichrist. Note that the original notes of the *Treasury* retained below reflect the older view that the prophecy regards the Romans, Constantine, and finally the bishop of Rome. The correspondences or parallels drawn between these various individuals, Antiochus and Antichrist may be valid as types to portray the nature of the coming Antichrist.

36. **the king.** ver. 27. Da *7:8, 24. +*8:23. +*9:26. **do according to his will.** See on ver. 3, 16. Da 7:25. 8:4. Is 13:13, 14. Jn 5:30. 6:38. Re 13:7. 17:13. **and he.** The preceding verses (from ver. 31) relate to the Romans, who not only destroyed the city and temple of Jerusalem, and crucified the Messiah, but during almost 300 years sought by every means to extirpate Christianity. The conversion of Constantine, though it stopped the rage of persecution, gave but little help to true religion. The power first exercised by the emperors, in calling and influencing ecclesiastical councils, gradually passed into the hands of the clergy; and the bishop and the church of Rome at last carried it to

an enormous length, magnifying themselves above every god. **exalt.** See on Da 7:8, 20, 25. 8:11, 25. Is 14:13. 2 Th √2:3, 4. Re √13:5, 6. 17:3. **speak.** See on Da +*8:11, 24, 25. Re √13:6. **the God of gods.** Da *2:47. Dt 10:17. Jsh 22:22. Ps 136:2. **till the indignation.** Da *7:20-25. +*8:19. 12:7, 11-13. Ps 92:7. Is +*26:20. Re 11:2, 3. 12:14. √13:5. √14:10. **for that determined.** Da *4:35. +*9:26, 27. Nu *23:19. Jb 23:13, 14. Ps 33:10, 11. Pr +*19:21. Is √46:10, 11. Ac *4:28. Re *10:7. *17:17.

37. **Neither shall.** Jn 5:43. **the desire of women.** √121R5, Ge +27:15. Ge 3:16. Dt 5:21. 21:11. 1 S 9:20. 2 S 1:26. SS 7:10. Je 7:18. 44:17. Ezk *8:14. 24:16. 1 T *4:3. **nor regard any god.** Ge 3:5. Is +*14:13. 2 Th √2:4.

38. **But in his estate.** *or,* But in his stead. Heb. But as for the almighty God, in his seat he shall honor, yea, he shall honor a god whom, etc. 1 T *4:1, 2. **forces.** ver. 7, 10, 19, 31, 39. Is ◑+60:5. *or,* munitions. Heb. *Mauzzim, or,* gods protectors. Saints and angels, who were invoked as intercessors and *protectors,* had miracles ascribed to them, their relics worshipped, and their shrines and images adorned with costly offerings. But the reference may be to the Antichrist's giving military might the place that religion holds in normal men's thinking. **a god.** Re 13:12-17. 17:1-5. 18:12. **honor with.** Re 9:20, 21. **pleasant things.** Heb. things desired. ver. +*8mg. Is 44:9mg. Jl 3:5mg.

39. **most strong holds.** Heb. fortresses of munitions. **strange.** Ex 12:43 (*S#5236h). Ezk 44:7, 9. Ml 2:11. **rule over.** Re *13:15. **gain.** Heb. a price. Dt 23:18. 2 S 24:24. Pr 1:13, 14. La 5:4mg. Re 18:9-13.

40. **at the time of the end.** See on ver. 35. Da +*8:17, 19. +*9:27. 12:4, 9. **the king of the south.** The Saracens. The king of the south is the king of Egypt. See on ver. 5, 6. Ezk 38:14-18. **the king of the north.** The king of the north is the king of Syria. The king of the north is not Russia, for tidings out of the north will trouble him, and if he were the king of Russia, there would be no king farther to the north than he (ver. 44). Since Antichrist is the king of the north, it seems quite clear here that Antichrist must come from Syria. Mi 5:5n. **shall come.** Da 9:26. Hab +*3:16. **like a whirlwind.** Is 5:28. *21:1. 66:15. Je 4:13. Hab *3:14. Zc *9:13, 14. **with horsemen.** Ezk *38:3-6, 15. Re *9:16. *16:12. **overflow.** See on ver. 10, 22.

41. **enter.** See on ver. 45. Ezk 38:8-13. **glorious land.** *or,* goodly land. ver. +16mg. Heb. land of delight, *or* ornament. Da +8:9. **escape.** Da 12:1. Thus the rule of Antichrist is not absolutely universal. **even.** Is *11:13-15. Je 9:26. 48:47. 49:6. **Moab.** Is √16:4.

42. **stretch forth.** Heb. send forth. Ex 9:15. **land of Egypt.** Ezk 29:14, 15. Zc 10:10, 11. 14:17, 18. Re 11:8.

43. **the Libyans.** See on Je 46:9, 10. Ezk √38:5, 6. **at his steps.** Jg 4:10. Ezk 11:8mg.

44. **tidings.** Je 51:31. **east.** ver. 11, 30. Ezk 38:9-12. Re 9:16. 16:12. 17:13. 19:19-21. **make away many.** Re 13:7.

45. **he shall.** Zc 13:8, 9. 14:2. **between.** Jl 2:20. Zc 14:8. **in the.** ver. 16, 41. Da 8:9. Ps *48:2. Is 2:2. 14:13. Mi 4:2. 2 Th √2:4. **glorious holy mountain.** *or,* goodly. Heb. mountain of delight of holiness. ver. 41mg. **he shall come.** Da 2:35. 7:26. √8:25. Ezk *38:22, 23. *39:2. Jl 3:2, 12. 2 Th √2:8. Re √13:10. 14:14-20.

*16:14. *19:19-21. 20:2, 9. **none shall help him**. Is *11:4. 24:21, 22. Zc 12:1-9. *14:1-3, 12, 13. 2 Th *2:8. Re *19:20.

DANIEL 12

Michael will deliver the people of God out of the extreme trouble of the Great Tribulation, 1. The resurrection of the dead, and the happiness of the righteous, 2, 3. Daniel is ordered to shut up these words, till a time when they would be better understood, 4. The duration and end of these predicted events, 5-12. The prophet is bidden to go, and enter his rest in peace, 13.

1. **at that time**. See on Da 11:35. **Michael**. i.e. *who is like unto God?*, ❋S#4317h. (1) The father of Sethur the spy, from Asher, Nu 13:13. (2) A man of Gad, 1 Ch 5:13. (3) descendant of the man of Gad, 1 Ch 5:14. (4) A Levite of the family of Gershom, 1 Ch 6:40. (5) A chief man of Issachar, 1 Ch 7:3. (6) A descendant of Benjamin, 1 Ch 8:16. (7) A captain of Manasseh who joined David at Ziklag, 1 Ch 12:20. (8) The father of Omri, 1 Ch 27:18. (9) A son of King Jehoshaphat, 2 Ch 21:2. (10) The father of Zebadiah, Ezr 8:8. (11) The angel who is called by Daniel the prince of the people of Judah, Da *10:13, 21. 12:1. Also, the archangel mentioned in Ju *9, and the leader of the hosts of the angels, Re *12:7-9. **stand up**. He x10:12. Ju +9 (T#1013‡). **the great prince**. Da +*9:25. 10:21. Is +*9:7. Ezk 34:24. 37:24. Ep 1:21. Re +*1:5. 17:14. 19:11-16. **time of trouble**. Da 8:24, 25. +*9:12, 26. Is +*26:20, 21. Je +√30:7. Mt √24:21. Mk 13:19. Lk *21:23, 24. Re *16:17-21. **thy people**. Is *11:11, etc. 27:12, 13. Je +*30:7. Ezk *37:21-28. *39:25-29. Ho *3:4, 5. Jl *3:16-21. Am √9:11-15. Ob *17-21. Zc *12:3-10. Ro *11:5, 6, 15, 26. **written**. ♪22C43, Ex +31:18. Ex +*32:32, 33◗℘. Ps *56:8. *69:28. Is 4:3. Ezk 13:9. Lk *10:20. Ph 4:3. Re √3:5. √13:8. √20:12, 13, 15. **book**. ♪22D5K1A, Ex +32:32.

2. **many**. *♪171F, Is +53:12. Jb +*19:25-27. Is +*26:19. Ezk +*37:1-4, 12. Ho +*13:14. Mt *22:29-32. Lk ◗2:34. Jn √11:23-26. 1 C +*15:20-22, 51-54. 1 Th √4:14, +√16n. Re √20:4-6, 12. **that sleep**. This is not "soul sleep," for the very next words state "in the dust of the earth," and therefore is a reference to the body (1 C √15:35), not the soul. 2 K +*24:6n. Jb *7:21. +*14:21. Ps 6:5. +*13:3. Ec +*9:5. Mt *9:24. +*27:52. Jn *11:11. Ac 7:60. √13:36n. 1 C +*11:30. 15:6, 18, 20, 51. 1 Th √4:13-18. *5:10. Ja √2:26. He ◗+*12:23. 2 P 3:4. **the dust**. Ge +*2:7. +*3:19. Jb 7:21. Ps 22:15. +*146:4. Ec +*3:19-21. **shall awake**. This also is spoken in reference to the physical body, not the soul or spirit, for the only kind of resurrection known to Scripture is bodily resurrection. Jb +*19:25, 26. Is +*26:19n. +43:10n. Mt +*27:52. Jn +*2:19, 21. +*5:28, 29. Re +*14:13. **some to everlasting life**. Heb. *olam*, Ge +17:7. Ps *49:14, 15. Ezk *37:11-14. Mt √25:46. Jn √5:28, 29. Ac *24:15. 26:8. 1 C *15:20, 23, 51, 52. 1 Th *4:16. He 11:35. **and some**. +*26:19n, 21. 27:6. 1 C 15:23. Re √20:5. **shame**. ♪144B, Dt +33:19. **everlasting**. Heb. *olam*, Ge +17:7. **contempt**. T#573-7. Jb 22:15, 16, 19. Ps 2:4, 5. 52:1, 5, 6. 59:7, 8. Pr 1:26, 27. 3:34. Is +*66:24. Je +20:11 (T#513). Lk +*13:28. Ro 9:21. 2 Th √1:7-10.

3. **they that be**. Da 11:+*33, 35. Pr +*11:30. Mt +*24:45. 1 C 3:10. 2 T √3:15-17. 2 P 3:15. Re 20:4-

6. **wise**. *or*, teachers. 2 Ch 30:22. Pr 16:23. Ac *13:1. Ep *4:11. 1 T +*4:16. He +*5:12. **shine**. Pr *4:18. Mt *13:43. *19:28. 1 C *15:40-42. 1 Th *2:19, 20. Re 1:20. **turn many**. Pr *10:21. 11:25, √30. Je *23:22. Ml *2:6. Lk *1:16, 17. Jn *4:36. Ro *1:16, 17. Ph *2:16, 17. Ja *5:19, 20. **as the stars**. Nu *24:17. **for ever**. Heb. *olam*, Ps +21:4 (✤S#5769h). **and ever**. Heb. *ad*, Ps +9:18 (❋S#5703h).

4. **shut**. Da 8:26. Re *10:4. 22:10. **to the**. ver. 9. Da 8:17. 10:1. 11:40. Re 5:1-5. **many**. Da *11:33. Is 11:9. 29:18, 19. 30:26. 32:3. Zc 14:6-10. Mt *24:14. Ro 10:18. Re 14:6, 7. **to and fro**. 2 Ch 16:9. Je 5:1. Ezk 22:30. Am 8:12. The Hebrew word underlying "to and fro" (S#7751h) differs from another related Hebrew word only by the difference of "s" being read "sh." This word is defined by Gesenius "go" or "rove about," p. 1001b, and "go eagerly, quickly, to and fro," p. 1002a. If read "sh," the word would be S#7750h, for which Gesenius gives "swerve, fall away, ...apostatize," "those falling away to falsehood (Ps 40:5)," p. 962a. Thus, one reading might support the usual view that there would be increased travel in the latter days. The alternative reading would suggest that apostasy would be rampant. **knowledge**. An alternate reading suggests "calamities" or "wickedness" shall be increased, a reading supported by the LXX. The difference arises from the very slight difference between the Hebrew letters for "d" and "r," *daleth* and *resh*, which are often confused, in Hebrew a change from *hadda'ath* to *hara'oth*, as discussed in the CB margin. If "knowledge" is the correct reading, the reference might be either to the "knowledge explosion" of our day, or perhaps an increase of knowledge about Biblical prophecy. If the alternative readings "apostatize" and "wickedness" are correct, this passage becomes strikingly similar to the New Testament prophecies of Paul (2 Th √2:3, 7. 1 T 4:1. 2 T 3:1-5). T#941. ver. 10. 1 Ch +*12:32. Pr +*4:18. Is *11:9. *25:6, 7. *29:18, 24. 35:6-8. 41:18, 19. 52:7, 8. *54:13. Je ◗+8:7. Mt +*24:45. 2 P *3:18.

5. **other two**. Da 10:5, 6, 10, 16. **bank**. Heb. lip. Jg +7:22mg. **of the river**. Da *10:4.

6. **one said**. Da 8:16. Zc 1:12, 13. Ep 3:10. 1 P 1:12. **man**. See on Da *10:5, 6. Ezk 9:2. Re 15:6. 19:14. **upon**. *or*, from above. Re 10:2-5. **How long**. Da *8:13. Ps 74:9. Re 6:10.

7. **he held**. Ge 14:22. Dt *32:40◗℘. Re *10:5-7. **liveth**. Da 4:34. Jb 27:2. Je 4:2. **for ever**. Heb. *olam*, Ex +*12:24. **that it**. ver. 11, 12. Da +*7:25. 8:14. 11:13. Re *11:2, 3, 15. *12:6, 14. 13:5. **a time**. That is, 1260 years, to be reckoned from the time the "saints were delivered into the hand" of "the little horn." As noted at Da 8:14, there is no basis here to take "days" and arbitrarily make them "years." Rather, these are the literal days of the last three and a half years of the Great Tribulation, Daniel's Seventieth Week. Da +*8:19. Ge +17:21h. **and half**. *or*, a part. **and when**. Lk 21:14. Re 10:7. 11:7-15. **the holy**. See on Da 8:24. Dt 7:6. 26:19. Is 62:12. 1 P *2:9. **be finished**. Lk *21:24.

8. **but**. Lk 18:34. Jn 12:16. Ac √1:7. 1 P *1:11. **what**. See on ver. 6. Da 10:14.

9. **Go**. ver. 13. **closed**. ver. 4. Da 8:26. Is +*8:16. *29:11. Re *10:4.

10. **shall be**. Da *11:35. Ps *51:7. Is *1:18. Ezk *36:25. Zc *13:9. 1 C 6:11. 2 C 7:1. T *2:14. He 12:10. 1 P 1:7, 22. Re 3:18. *7:13, 14. 19:8, 14. **but the wicked**.

1 S 24:13. Ec +1:15. Is √32:6, 7. Ezk 47:11. Ho +*14:9. Ro 11:8-10. 2 Th √2:10-12. Re 9:20, 21. 16:11. 22:11. **but the wise.** ver. 3. Da +*11:33, 35. Ps 107:43. Pr 1:5. 2:1-5. Mk 4:11. Lk +*24:45. Jn +*7:17. 8:47. 18:37. 1 C √2:10-16. 1 Jn *5:20. **shall understand.** 1 Ch +*12:32. Je ◐+8:7. 1 J *2:18-22.

11. **the time.** Da *8:11, 12, 26. 11:31. **the abomination.** Heb. to set up the abomination, etc. Probably Mohammedanism, which sprang up in power the same year as the papal, A.D. 606; and 1290 years from that time will be A.D. 1896, and 1335 years, A.D. 1941. But as noted at ver. 7, and at Da 8:14, there is no basis for taking "days" as years. Rather, these literal days point to a time thirty days after the end of the Great Tribulation not expressly identified in Scripture as to their significance. Some suggest that it relates to time necessary for Christ to judge the nations before the Millennium, in Mt 25:31-46. **daily sacrifice.** Da +*8:11, 13. +*9:27. +*11:31. **abomination.** Da +*9:27. +*11:31. Mt *24:15. Mk 13:14. Re 11:2. **maketh desolate.** or, astonisheth. Da 7:25. 2 Th *2:4. **a thousand.** Da 1:12. 7:25. 8:14. Re 11:2. 12:6. 13:5.

12. **Blessed.** Ps +*1:1. Mt *10:22. Ro 11:15. Re 20:4. **waiteth.** Ps *37:9. 130:5-8. Is *30:18. Mt *24:13.

Mk 13:13. 1 C +*15:58. He *10:36. Re *2:26. **thousand three hundred and.** The precise event at which this period terminates is not identified in Scripture, but it may refer to the actual beginning of the Millennium, when Christ invites the sheep nations to inherit the kingdom prepared for them, Mt 25:34. The forty-five days beyond the preceding period of ver. 11 may provide time to set up the covenanted boundaries of Israel (Ge 15:18. Is +26:15. Je +7:7. +33:21n. Ac +*7:5. He *11:13, 39), and provide time for the complete return of all Jews worldwide to Israel (Is 27:12. 43:6. Je 31:8. Ezk 34:12. √39:28. Am *9:9), and setting up the machinery of Millenial rule (Da +*7:18, 22. Ps +*149:9. Is *2:2-4. √26:9. Mt *19:28. Lk *22:29, 30. 1 C √6:2, 3. Re 5:10. 11:15). Ro 11:15. Re 20:4.

13. **go.** ver. 9. **for thou.** or, and thou, etc. **shalt rest.** ver. 3. Is *57:1, 2. Zc 3:7. Mt *19:28. Lk *22:29, 30. 2 C √5:1. 2 Th √1:7. 2 T *4:7, 8. Re √14:13. **stand.** Ps +*1:5. Lk +√21:36. Ju *14, *15. A reference to standing or rising in resurrection. ver. 2. Jb √19:25. Ps *16:11. *17:15. Is +*26:19n. Ac +24:15. **in thy lot.** Jg 1:3. Ps +16:5, 6. 105:11. 125:3. Jn *14:2. Col *1:12. 1 P √1:4. **at the end.** 2 T *1:12. He +*11:13.

HOSEA

HOSEA 1

An account of the prophet, and of the times when he lived, 1. At God's command, and to expose the idolatry of Israel, he takes a wife of whoredoms; and calls his children, by names expressive of the judgments which were coming on his people, 2-9. The increase and restoration of Judah and Israel, under one Head is predicted, 10, 11.

1. **word.** Je 1:2, 4. Ezk 1:3. Jl 1:1. Jon 1:1. Zc 1:1. Jn *10:35. 2 P *1:21. **Hosea.** i.e. *deliverer,* ✳S#1954h. Ho 1:1, 2, 2. 2 K +15:30. Ro 9:25, Osee. **in the days.** Is 1:1. Mi 1:1. **Uzziah.** 2 K 14:16-20. 15:1, 2, 32. ch. 16, 18. 2 Ch ch. 26-32.

2. **beginning.** Mk 1:1. **by.** Nu 12:6, 8. Hab 2:1. Zc 1:9. **Go.** Ho 3:1. See on Is 20:2, 3. Je 13:1-11. Ezk ch. 4, 5. **a wife.** That is, says Abp. Newcome, a wife from among the Israelites, who were a people remarkable for spiritual fornication, or idolatry. Others think that the prophet's wife bore a good character when he married her, and afterwards became "a wife of whoredoms," and brought her children under the suspicion of being "children of whoredoms." **whoredoms.** Ho 4:12, 12. 5:3, 4. 6:10. 7:4. 2 K 9:22. 2 Ch 21:13. Je 3:2. Ezk *16:17-35. 20:30. 23:3, 7, 43. Na 3:4. **children.** ⨍63E2, 1 S +13:8. The sense, as we see from verses 3, 6, and 8, must be "and (beget) children," etc. Ho 2:4. 2 P 2:14mg. **for the land.** lit. earth. ⨍171.O.4. Synecdoche of the Whole B638. The *earth* is put for the land of Judea. For other instances of this figure see Ho 4:1. Jl 1:2. Note the reference to the Pentateuch. Other references to the Pentateuch in Hosea are found at Ho 1:10. 2:12, 13, 15, 18, 19, 20. 3:1, 3, 4. 4:4, 8, 10, 13, 14. 5:6, 10, 11. 6:3, 5, 9. 7:10. 8:1, 12, 13, 14. 9:7, 10, 12, 17. 10:2, 7, 8, 10, 12. 11:1, 8. 12:3, 4, 7, 12. 13:5, 6, 8, 15. 14:3, 9. See related note (Is 1:2). Ex 34:15, 16▸𝒫. Le 17:7▸𝒫.

20:5▸𝒫. Nu 15:39▸𝒫. Dt *31:16▸𝒫. 2 Ch 21:13. Ps *73:27. 106:39. Je 2:13. 3:1-4, 9. Ezk 6:9. ch. *16, *23. Ja *4:4. Re 17:1, 2, 5. **departing.** Ho 4:10. 7:8. 8:11, 14. 10:1. 12:14. 13:9.

3. **he went.** Is 8:1-3. **Diblaim.** i.e. *double fig cake,* ✳S#1691h.

4. **Call.** ver. 6, 9. Is +*7:14. +*9:6. Mt +*1:21. Lk 1:13, 31, 63. Jn 1:42. **Jezreel.** That is, *God will disperse,* as seed is when sown; probably intimating also the speedy dispersion of Israel by Shalmaneser. **little while.** Ho 10:14. **and I.** 2 K 9:24, 25. 10:7, 8, 10, 11, 17, 29-31. *15:8, 10-12. **avenge.** Heb. visit. Ho 2:13. 9:7. Je +9:25mg. 23:2. **blood.** ⨍171I11, Dt +19:12. **will cause.** 2 K 15:29. 17:6, etc. ✱18:9-12. 1 Ch 5:25, 26. Je 3:8. Ezk 23:10, 31.

5. **at that day.** 2 K 17:6. 18:11. **I will.** Ho 2:18. Ps 37:15. 46:9. Je 49:34, 35. 51:56. **in the valley.** Jsh 17:16. Jg 6:33.

6. **Lo-ruhamah.** ⨍32, Ge +31:21. *that is,* Not having obtained mercy. i.e. *the uncompassionate,* ✳S#3819h. ver. 6, 8. Ho 2:23. Ro ▸9:25. 1 P ▸2:10. **for.** 2 K *17:6, 23, etc. Is 27:11. **no more have.** Heb. not add any more to have. **but I will utterly take them away.** or, that I should altogether pardon them. See on Ho 9:15-17. Ge 18:24. Ex 23:21. Is 2:9.

7. **I will.** Ho 11:12. 2 K 19:35. Is *7:5-8. ch. 36. *37:35, 36. **will save.** Is +*7:14. +*12:2. 49:6. Je +*23:5, 6. Zc 2:6-11. 4:6. 9:9, 10. Mt +*1:21-23. T *3:4-6. **by the Lord.** 2 K 19:35. Is 11:4. Da +3:25n, +28. 2 Th 2:8. **their God.** Ne +*9:6. Ps 102:24. Ec 12:14. Je 23:5. Zc *13:7. T *2:13. **not save.** 1 S 17:39. Is 31:1. Zc 4:6. 2 C 10:4. **by bow.** Ps 33:16. 44:3-6.

8. **weaned.** 1 S +1:22n.

9. **Call.** Ho 3:4. Ro ◐+*11:1, 25. **Lo-ammi.** that is, *Not my people.* ver. 10. Ho 2:23. Is +*54:7. Je 15:1. 23:39. La 5:22. Ezk 11:19, 20. Da +9:26. 1 P 2:10.

10. **the number.** T#375. Ge 12:7. 13:16. 22:17⸰𝒫. 26:4. 32:12⸰𝒫. Ex 6:4. 32:13. Nu 23:10. Is 27:6. 48:19. 60:22. 65:23. Ezk 37:26. Ro 9:27, 28. He 11:12. **the sand.** ℐ102B, ℐ138B, Ge +13:16. Ge 22:17. Je 33:22. **cannot be measured.** Nu 23:10⸰𝒫. **and it.** See on Ro ⸰9:25, 26. **in the.** or, instead of that. **it was said.** Ho 2:23. Is 43:6. *49:17-22. *54:1-3. 60:4, etc. 65:1. 66:20. 1 P ⸰2:9, 10. **Ye are the sons.** Is 63:16. 64:8. Jn √1:12. Ro √8:14-17. *9:24-26. 2 C *6:18. Ga 4:6, 7. 1 J √3:1, 2. **living God.** 1 Th *1:9.

11. **Then shall.** This seems to refer to the future conversion and restoration of the Jews and Israelites, under one head, Jesus Christ; so that there shall be one flock and one shepherd. **the children of Judah.** Ho 3:5. Is √11:12, 13. Je *3:18, 19. *23:5-8. 30:3. 31:1-9. 33:15-26. 50:4, 5, 19. Ezk 16:60-63. 34:23, 24. *37:16-25. Mi 2:12, 13. Zc *10:6-9. Ro *11:25, 26. **one.** Heb. *echad*, Dt +6:4. **head.** Ho 3:5. Is 26:13. Je 23:5, 6. 30:9, 21. Ezk *34:23. *37:24. Ep *1:22, 23. *5:23. **for.** An allusion to the word *Jezreel*. God who *sowed* them among the nations in his wrath, shall *reap* and *gather* them in His mercy: see Ho 2:22, 23. Ps 22:27-30. 110:3. Is +*54:7. Je *24:6. 31:28. *32:41. Am √9:15. Zc √10:6. Ro 11:15. **day.** ℐ121P4, Dt +4:32.

HOSEA 2

Israel is convicted of aggravated idolatry and base ingratitude, and threatened with heavy judgments, 1-13. God allures them with promises of reconciliation, and of many blessings to them, and to others, by their means, 14-23.

1. **unto.** See on Ho 1:9-11. **Ammi.** that is, *My people.* ✽S#5971h. Ex 19:5, 6. Je 31:33. 32:38. Ezk 11:20. 36:28. 37:27. Zc *13:9. **Ruhamah.** that is, *Having obtained mercy.* ✽S#7355h. ver. 23. Ro 11:30, 31. 2 C 4:1. 1 T 1:13. 1 P 2:10.

2. **Plead with.** Is *58:1. Je 2:2. 19:3. Ezk 20:4. 23:45. Mt 23:37-39. Ac 7:51-53. 2 C 5:16. **mother.** ℐ155E4, 2 S +20:19. **she is not.** ℐ155E3, Is +32:9. Is 50:1. Je 3:6-8. **let her.** Ho 1:2. Je 3:1, 9, 13. Ezk √16:20, 25. *23:43. **whoredoms.** Ex +34:15.

3. **I strip.** ver. 10. Is 47:3. Je *13:22, 26. Ezk 16:37-39. 23:26-29. Re 17:16. **was born.** Ezk 16:4-8, 22. **as.** Is 32:13, 14. 33:9. 64:10. Je 2:31. 4:26. 12:10. 22:6. Ezk 19:13. 20:35, 36. **a dry.** Je 2:6. 17:6. 51:43. **and slay.** Ex 17:3. Jg 15:18. Am *8:11-13.

4. **I will not.** Ho 1:6. Is 27:11. Je *13:14. 16:5. Ezk √5:11. 8:18. 9:10. Zc 1:12. Ro 9:18. 11:22. Ja *2:13. **they be.** They are all idolaters; and have been consecrated to idols, whose marks they bear. **children of.** Ho 1:2. 2 K 9:22. Is 57:3. Jn 8:41.

5. **their mother.** ver. 2. Ho 3:1. 4:5, 12-15. Is 1:21. 50:1. Je 2:20, *25. *3:1, 6-9. Ezk 16:15, 16, 28, etc. 23:5-11. Re 2:20-23. 17:1-5. **hath done.** Ho 9:10. Ezr 9:6, 7. Je 2:26, 27. 11:13. Da *9:5-8. **I will.** ver. 13. Ho 8:9. Is 57:7, 8. Je 3:1-3. Ezk 23:16, 17, 40-44. **lovers.** or, my Baals, or lords. Je 44:17, 18. Ezk 23:5. **give.** ver. 8, 12. Jg 16:23. Je 44:17, 18. **and my water.** ℐ174, Ge +18:27. **drink.** Heb. drinks.

6. **I will.** Ge +*6:13 (T#566). Jb *3:23. *19:8. Pr *13:15. La *3:7-9. Lk 15:14-16. 19:43. **make a wall.** Heb. wall a wall. ℐ147D. Polyptoton, Ge +1:29. Ezk 13:5mg.

7. **she shall follow.** Ho 5:13. 2 Ch 28:20-22. Is 30:2, 3, 16. 31:1-3. Je *2:28, 36, 37. 30:12-15. Ezk 20:32.

23:22. **I will go.** Ho *5:15. *6:1, 2. 14:1. Ps 116:7. Je *3:22-25. *31:9, 18. 50:4, 5. La 3:40-42. Lk *15:17-20. **first.** 1 Ch 8:9n. Je 2:2. *3:1. *31:32. Ezk *16:8. 23:4. **for.** Ho 13:6. Dt 6:10-12. 8:17, 18. 32:13-15. Ne 9:25, 26. Je 14:22. Da 4:17, 25, 32. 5:21.

8. **she.** Is 1:3. Hab 1:16. Ac 17:23-25. Ro 1:28. **her corn.** ver. 5. Ho 10:1. Jg 9:27. Je 7:18. 44:17, 18. Ezk *16:16-19. Da 5:3, 4, 23. Lk 15:13. 16:1, 2. **wine.** Heb. new wine. Ho 4:11. Is 24:7-9. **season.** Ge +17:21h. **which they prepared for Baal.** or, *wherewith* they made Baal. Ho 8:4. 13:2. Ex 32:2-4. Jg 17:1-5. Is 46:6.

9. **will I.** Da 11:13. Jl 2:14. Ml 1:4. 3:18. **take.** ver. 3. Is 3:18-26. 17:10, 11. Ezk 16:27, 39. 23:26. Zp 1:13. Hg 1:6-11. 2:16, 17. **recover.** or, take away. or, rescue. Ge 31:16.

10. **now.** ver. 3. Is 3:17. Je 13:22, 26. Ezk 16:36, 37. 23:29. Lk 12:2, 3. 1 C 4:5. **lewdness.** Heb. folly, or, villainy. ✽S#5040h, only here. Hebrew root word is S*5036h, rendered "fool" at Ps 14:1, "vile person" at Is 32:5, 6. **and none shall.** Ho 5:13, 14. 13:7, 8. Ps 50:22. Pr 11:21. Mi 5:8.

11. **cause.** Ho 9:1-5. Is 24:7-11. Je 7:34. 16:9. 25:10. Ezk 26:13. Na 1:10. Re 18:22, 23. **her feast.** 1 K 12:32. Is 1:13, 14. Am 5:21. *8:3, 5, 9, 10. **new moons.** 2 K *4:23. 2 Ch +2:4. **sabbaths.** Is +*58:13n. **solemn feasts.** Ge +17:21h. Le *23:2n.

12. **destroy.** Heb. make desolate. Je 22:6. ✤S#8074h. Le 26:31, 32. Jb 16:7. Ps 79:7 (laid waste). Je 10:25. Ezk 14:8 (make him; lit. make him desolate). 30:12 (waste), 14. 32:10 (amazed). **These.** ver. 5. Ho 9:1. **rewards.** or, my hire, or fee. Dt 23:18⸰𝒫. **I will.** Ps *80:12, 13. Is *5:5, 6. 7:23. 29:17. 32:13-15. Je 26:18. Mi 3:12.

13. **I will visit.** Ho 9:7, 9. Ex 32:34⸰𝒫. Je 23:2. **the days.** Ho 9:10. 13:1. Jg 2:11-13. 3:7. 10:6. 1 K 16:31, 32. *18:18, etc. 2 K 1:2. 10:28. 21:3. **she burned.** Ho 11:2. Je 7:9. 11:13. 18:15. **she decked.** Ezk *23:40-42. **earrings.** or, ring. A reference to a nose ring. Ge 24:22. 35:4. **jewels.** lit. "smooth thing." Pr 25:12. **she went.** ver. 5, 7. Je 2:23-25. **forgat.** Dt 6:12. 8:11-14. 32:18. Jg 3:7. 1 S 12:9. Jb 8:13. Ps 78:11. 106:13, 21. Is 17:10. Je 2:32. Ezk 22:12. 23:35. There is an unannounced time gap between the prophecies of this and the next verse. For other unannounced prophetic time gaps, see +61:2n.

14. **Therefore.** Is *30:18. Je 16:14. **I will.** SS 1:4. Jn 6:44. 12:32. **and bring.** ver. 3. Is 11:16. Je 2:2. Ezk 20:10, √35, 36. Re 12:6, 14. **into the wilderness.** Ho 9:10. 11:1. 12:10, 14. 13:4. Ps +*74:14. Is 4:5. 9:16. *32:16. 43:16. 48:21. 50:2. 51:10. Je 2:6. 7:22, etc. 9:3, etc. 14:14. 23:7. *31:2. 34:13. Ezk 20:5, etc. Am 2:10. 3:1. Mi 6:4. *7:15. Hg 2:6. **and speak.** Is 35:3, 4. 40:1, 2. 49:13, etc. 51:3, etc. Je 3:12-24. 30:18-22. 31:1-37. 32:36-41. 33:6-26. Ezk √20:35, 36. 34:22-31. 36:8, etc. 37:11-28. 39:25-29. Am √9:11-15. Mi *7:14-20. Zp 3:9-20. Zc 1:12-17. 8:19-23. Ro *11:26, 27. **comfortably.** or, friendly. Heb. to her heart. Ge +34:3mg. Jg 19:3mg. Is *40:2mg.

15. **I will.** ver. 12. Le 26:40-45. Dt *30:3-5. Ne 1:8, 9. Is 65:21. Je 32:15. Ezk 28:26. Am √9:14. **from thence.** Nu 16:13, 14⸰𝒫. Is +*51:11. **the valley.** Ex +17:14. Jsh ⸰7:26. Is +65:10. **for a door.** La 3:21. Ezk *37:11-14. Zc 9:12. Jn √10:9. Ac 14:27. **of hope.** An allusion to the contrasting meaning of Achor (trouble). **she shall sing.** Ex *15:1-21⸰𝒫. Nu 21:17. Ps 30:5mg.

*106:12n. Is 12:5, 6. *24:16. +*35:10. +*51:11. Je *31:7, 12. Zp *3:7, 12, 14, 15. Zc +*2:10. **as in the days.** Ho *11:1. Je *2:2. Ezk *16:8, 22, 60. **and as in the day.** Ezk 20:36. Mi +*7:15. **when she came up.** Ex 1:10꞉ꟿ. 4:22. 12:38꞉ꟿ. 13:18꞉ꟿ.

16. **Ishi.** that is, *My husband.* *S#376h. ver. 7. Is 54:5. Je 3:14. Jn 3:29. 2 C 11:2. Ep *5:25-27. Re 19:7. **Baali.** that is, *My lord.* *S#1180h.

17. **I will.** Ex √23:13꞉ꟿ. Jsh *23:7. Ps √16:4. Is 2:18. Ezk 6:6. 36:25, 26. 37:23. Zc 13:2. **and they.** Je 10:11. Zc *13:2.

18. **in that day.** Is 2:11, 17. 26:1. Ps +*118:24. Zc 2:11. 14:4, 9. **will I.** Jb *5:23. Ps 91:1-13. Is *11:6-9. +*65:25. Ezk *34:25. Jl *2:22. Ro √8:19-21. **I will break.** Ps *46:9. Is *2:4. Ezk √39:9, 10. Mi 4:3. Zc *9:10. **and will.** Le 25:18, 19꞉ꟿ. *26:5, 6꞉ꟿ. Dt 12:10꞉ꟿ. 33:12, 28꞉ꟿ. Ps 23:2. Je *23:6. 30:10. 33:16. Ezk *34:25, 28. Mi 4:4. Zc 3:10.

19. **And I will.** Ps 36:5-7. Is 54:5. *62:3-5. Je 3:14, 15. Jn *3:29. Ro 7:4. 2 C 11:2. Ep *5:25-27. Re 19:7-9. 21:2, 9, 10. **betroth.** Ex 22:16꞉ꟿ. Dt 20:7꞉ꟿ. 22:23, 25, 27, 28꞉ꟿ. 28:30꞉ꟿ. 2 S 3:14. **for ever.** Heb. *olam*, Ex +*12:24. Is √51:22. +*54:8-10. Je +*31:31-37. +*32:38-41. Ezk +*37:25-28. *39:29. Jl *3:20. **in righteousness.** Ps *85:10. +*130:8. Is 45:23-25. 54:14. +60:21. Je 4:2. Ro *3:25, 26. Ep *1:7, 8. *5:23-27. **in mercies.** Is +*55:3.

20. **thou shalt know the Lord.** Ex 6:7꞉ꟿ. Is ❶1:3. 11:9. 54:13. Je *9:24. *24:7. +*31:33, 34. Ezk *38:23. Mt √11:27. Lk *10:22. ❶19:42, 44. Jn *6:45. +√8:55. √17:3. 2 C *4:6. Ph *3:8. Col +√1:10. 2 T √1:12. He +*8:11. 1 J √4:6. *5:20.

21. **I will hear, saith.** Is +*65:24. Zc 8:12. √13:9. Mt √6:33. Ro √8:32. 1 C 3:21-23.

22. **the earth.** ꓩ16, Ge +1:27. ꓩ50. Climax; or, gradation B256: repeated Anadiplosis, relating to *words*, where by the *last* word of one sentence is repeated as the *first* word of the next. For other instances of this figure see Jl 1:3, 4. Jn 1:1, 2. 1:4, 5. Ro 5:3, 4, 5. 8:29, 30. 10:14, 15. Ja 1:3, 4. 1:14, 15. 2 P 1:5-7. **shall hear.** ꓩ155D, Ge +4:10. Ps *67:6. Zc *8:12. **and they.** Ho *1:4, 11.

23. **I will sow.** Ps 72:16. Is *61:9. Je 31:27. Zc 10:9. Ac 8:1-4. Ja 1:1. 1 P 1:1, 2. **and I will have mercy.** ver. 1mg. Ho 1:❶*6, 7. Ps 68:20. Is +*55:3. Mi 7:19. Zc √1:16. √10:6. Ro ꟷ9:25. *11:30-32. 1 P 2:9, 10. **not obtained mercy.** Ho 1:6, +9. **and I will say.** Ho *1:10. Zc 2:11. √13:9. Ro *9:25, 26. **they shall say.** Ho 1:11. Zc *13:9. Ro 9:26. 1 P *2:10. **Thou art my God.** Ho 8:2. Dt 26:17-19. Ps 22:27. 68:31. 118:28. SS 2:16. Is 44:5. Je 16:19. 32:38. Zc 8:22, 23. √13:9. *14:9, 16. Ml 1:11. Jn +*20:20. Ro 3:29. 15:9-11. 1 Th *1:9, 10. Re 21:3, 4.

HOSEA 3

The Lord's intended future kindness to Israel, notwithstanding their wickedness, illustrated by the emblem of Hosea's conduct towards his adulterous wife, 1-3. The desolation of Israel before their restoration, 4, 5.

1. **Go yet.** Ho 1:2, 3. **friend.** Je 3:1, 20mg. Mt 26:50. **according.** Ho 11:8. Dt 7:6, 7. Jg 10:16. 2 K 13:23. Ne 9:18, 19, 31. Ps 106:43-46. Je 3:1-4, 12-14. 31:20. Mi *7:18-20. Zc √1:16. Lk 1:54, 55. **look to other gods.** Dt 31:18, 20꞉ꟿ. Ps 123:2. Is 17:7, 8. 45:22. Mi 7:7.

love flagons. Ho 4:11. 7:5. 9:1, 2. Ex 32:6. Jg 9:27. Am 2:8. 6:6. 1 C 10:7, 21. 1 P 4:3. **wine.** Heb. grapes. Ge 40:10. 49:11.

2. **I bought.** Ge 31:41. 34:12. Ex 22:17. 1 S 18:25. **fifteen shekels.** Ex 21:7, 32. Le 27:4. **an homer.** Le 27:16. Is 5:10. Ezk 45:11. **half homer.** Heb. *lethech*.

3. **Thou shalt abide.** ver. +*4. Dt *21:13꞉ꟿ. Je √30:22-24. √31:1-9. **not play.** Je *2:20. Ja *4:4. **be for thee.** Ex 6:7.

4. **many days.** ver. 3. Dt *28:59. Mi +*3:6. Mt +*25:19. Ac +*1:6. Ro 11:25. **and without.** ꓩ18, Dt +28:4. **a king.** Ho *10:3. Ge +*49:10. Je 15:4, 5. Mi 4:9. Jn *19:15. **prince.** Ho 8:4. **without a sacrifice.** 2 Ch 15:2. Da +*8:11-13. +*9:27. +*12:11. Mt +*24:1, 2. Lk *21:24. Ac 6:13, 14. He *10:26. **an image.** Heb. a standing, *or* statue, *or* pillar. Ex 23:24. +*34:13. 2 K +*17:10. Is *19:19, 20. **ephod.** Ex 28:4꞉ꟿ. Le 8:7. Jg 8:27. 17:5. 1 S 2:18. 14:3. 21:9. 22:18. 23:6, 9. 28:6. 30:7. 2 S 6:14. Ezr 2:63. 7:65. **without teraphim.** Ge 31:19mg, 34, 35꞉ꟿ. Jg 17:5. 18:17-24. 2 K 23:24mg. Ezk 20:32. 21:21mg. Mi 5:11-14. Zc 13:2.

5. **Afterward.** ver. 4. Ho 6:2. Is 24:22. Ezk +*38:8n, 16. Hab 2:3. **return.** Ho 2:7. *5:4, 15. *6:1. 7:10. 11:5. 12:6. 14:1-3. Je 3:22, 23. *31:6-10. Ezk +*34:16. **seek the Lord.** Ho 5:6, 15. 2 Ch +√7:14. Is *27:12, 13. Je *50:4, 5. **and David their king.** This clearly requires David's resurrection, and agrees with other statements affirming the resurrection of Abraham, Isaac, and Jacob (Mt +*8:11). 1 K 12:16. Is +*55:3, 4. Je +*30:9. +*33:17. Ezk √34:23, 24. +*37:22-25. Am *9:11. Mi *2:13n Ac *15:16-18. **shall fear.** Ho *10:11. Ps 130:3, 4. Is 60:6. Je 33:9. Ezk 16:63. Ro 2:4. **his goodness.** Ho 14:2 (graciously). Ex 18:9. 33:19꞉ꟿ. Nu 10:32. 2 S 7:28. 1 K 8:66. 1 Ch 17:26. 2 Ch 7:10. Ne 9:25, 35. Is 63:7. Je 31:12. 33:9. Zc 9:17. **in the latter days.** Ge 49:1꞉ꟿ. Nu 24:14꞉ꟿ. Dt *4:30꞉ꟿ. 31:29꞉ꟿ. Is *2:2. Je 30:24. Ezk +*38:8, 16. Da 2:28. 10:14. Mi *4:1. Ro +*11:25.

HOSEA 4

God denounces judgments on Israel, for their aggravated impieties and iniquities, 1-5. He exposes the ignorance and wickedness of the priests, and profligacy of the people, he will leave their wives and daughters to commit lewdness, without present punishment, 12-14. He warns Judah, not to imitate Israel's crimes, which are still further reproved, 15-19.

1. **Cir. A.M. 3224. B.C. 780. Hear.** 1 K 22:19. Is 1:10. 28:14. 34:1. 66:5. Je 2:4. 7:2. 9:20. 19:3. 34:4. Am 7:16. Re 2:11, 29. **for.** Ho 12:2. Is *1:18. 3:13, 14. 5:3. 34:8. Je 25:31. Mi 6:2. **controversy.** A judicial inquiry and cause (CB). Ho *12:2. Is *1:18. 3:13, 14. Je 25:31. *30:31. Mi 6:2. **land.** ꓩ171.O.4, Ho +1:2. **no truth.** Is *59:13-15. Je 6:13. 7:3-6. Mi 7:2-5. **nor knowledge.** ver *6. Ho 2:20. √5:4. Je 4:22, 28. 5:4. ❶*9:24. Jn +*8:55. Ro *1:21, 28. 1 C 15:34. 1 J √2:3, 4. 4:7, 8.

2. **swearing.** Is 24:5. 48:1. 59:2-8, 12-15. Je 5:1, 2, 7-9, 26, 27. 6:7. 7:6-10. 9:2-8. 23:10-14. Ezk 22:2-13, 25-30. Mi 2:1-3. 3:2, 9-12. 6:10-12. 7:2-4. Zp 3:1-5. Zc +*5:3, 4. 7:9-11. **blood.** Heb. bloods. Ho 12:14mg. Ge +4:10mg. 2 K +*9:26mg. **toucheth.** Ho 5:2. 6:9. La 4:13-15. Mt 23:35-37. Ac 7:52. 1 Th 2:15. Re 17:6.

3. **the land.** Is 24:4-12. Je 4:27, 28. *12:4. Jl 1:10-13. Am 1:2. *5:16. 8:8-10. Na 1:4. **mourn.** ꓩ155D,

Ge +4:10. **with the beasts.** Je 4:25. 12:4. Ezk 38:20. Zp *1:3.

4. **let.** ver. 17. Am 5:13. 6:10. Mt 7:3-6. **as.** Nu 16:1, etc.)ℙ. Dt *17:12)ℙ. Je 18:18. Ro *2:8. *10:21.

5. **in the day.** Je 6:4, 5. 15:8. **and the prophet.** Ho 9:7, 8. Is 9:13-17. Je *6:4, 5, 12-15. 8:10-12. 14:15, 16. *15:8. 23:9. Ezk 13:9-16. 14:8-10. Mi 3:5-7. Zc 11:8. 13:2. **destroy.** Heb. cut off. **thy.** Ho 2:2. Is 50:1. Je 15:8. 50:12. Ezk 16:44, 45. Ga 4:26.

6. **My people.** ver. 12. Is 1:3. *3:12. 5:13. Je *4:22. 8:7. **destroyed.** Heb. cut off. **for lack of.** ver. *1. Ho *6:6. 2 Ch 15:3. Jb *36:12. Pr *19:2. *29:18. Is *5:13. *27:11. 45:20. Je 5:3, 4, 21. Mt +*15:14. 2 C 4:3-6. **because.** 1 S 2:12. Pr *1:30-32. Is *28:7. 56:10-12. Je 2:8. *8:8, 9. Ml *2:7, 8. Mt 23:16-26. **rejected.** Ho 8:12. Je 6:10, 19. **I will also reject.** Zc 11:8, 9, 15-17. Ml 2:1-3, 9. Mt *21:41-45. Mk 12:8, 9. Lk 20:16-18. **seeing.** Ho 8:14. *13:6. 2 K 17:16-20. Ps 119:61, 139. Is 17:10. Mt *15:3-6. **forgotten.** ♪121C2B, Is +44:21. **I will also.** Ho 1:6. 1 S 2:28-36. *3:12-15. **forget.** ♪22C4, Ps +13:1.

7. **they were.** ver. 10. Ho 5:1. 6:9. *13:6, 14. Dt 32:15. Ezr 9:7. **therefore.** ♪63K, Ge +37:13. 1 S *2:30. Je 2:26, 27. Ml *2:9. Ph *3:19. **their glory.** ♪182, Ge +18:27.

8. **eat.** Le 6:26. 7:6, 7. or, sin offering. i.e. those sin offerings which should have been wholly burnt, and not eaten (CB). Le 6:26, 30)ℙ. +*23:19. Nu *18:9. **sin.** √♪121L5, Ge +4:7. "Sin" is put for "sin offering." **set their heart on their iniquity.** Heb. lift up their soul to their iniquity. 1 S 2:29. Ps *24:4. 25:1. Is 56:11. Ezk 14:3, 7. Mi 3:11. Ml 1:10. Ro 16:18. T 1:11. 2 P 2:3. **heart.** Heb. *nephesh*, soul, Ex +23:9.

9. **like people.** Is 9:14-16. *24:2. Je *5:31. 8:10-12. 23:11, 12. Ezk *14:10n. 22:26-31. Mt +*15:14. **punish.** Heb. visit upon. Ho 1:4mg. Ex +*20:5)ℙ. 32:34)ℙ. Je +9:25mg. **reward them.** Heb. cause to return. Ps 109:17, 18. Pr 5:22. 17:13. Is 3:10, 11. Zc 1:6.

10. **they shall eat.** Le *26:26)ℙ. Pr 13:25. Is 65:13-16. Mi *6:14. Hg *1:6. Ml 2:1-3. **they shall commit.** ver. 14. Ho 9:11-17. **left off.** 1 Ch +*28:9. 2 Ch 24:17, 18. Ps 36:3. 125:5. Je 34:15, 16. Ezk 18:24, 26. Zp 1:6. Lk +*8:13. 1 C +*15:2. 2 P √2:20-22. **to take heed.** Lk +*8:18. +*10:28. +*11:28. He *2:1. 2 P +*1:5-11, 19.

11. **take.** ver. 12. Pr *6:32. +*20:1. *23:27-35. Ec *7:7. Is *5:12. *28:7. Lk *21:34. Ro *13:11-14. **heart.** ♪121I1, Ge +3:7.

12. **ask.** Nu 27:21. Jg 18:5. Je 2:27. 10:8. Ezk 21:21. Hab *2:19. **stocks.** Idols made of wood (CB). Is *45:20. Je *2:27. **their staff.** Referring to divination by rods (CB). Ezk 21:21. **for.** Ho 5:4. Is 44:18-20. Mi 2:11. 2 Th √2:9-11. **spirit.** Heb. *ruach*, Ge +41:8. **to err.** or, go astray, wander. Ge 20:13. 2 Ch 33:9. Ps 95:10. Pr +*10:17. 14:22. +*19:27. Is *3:12. 9:16. 19:14. 21:4mg. *28:7. 30:28. √35:8. √53:6. *63:17. Je 23:13, √32. 42:20mg. 50:6. Am *2:4. Mi 3:5. Mt *22:29. Mk +*12:24, 27. He 3:10. Ja 1:16. +*5:19. **gone.** Ho 9:1. Le 17:7. 20:5. Nu 15:39. Dt 31:16. 2 Ch 21:13. Ps 73:27. Je 3:1-3. √5:7. Ezk ch. *16, *23. **from under.** Nu 5:19, 29. Ezk 23:5.

13. **sacrifice.** Dt 12:2)ℙ. Is 1:29. 57:5, 7. Je 3:6, 13. Ezk 6:13. 16:16, 25. 20:28, 29. **therefore.** 2 S 12:10-12. Jb 31:9, 10. Am 7:17. Ro *1:23-28.

14. **I will not.** or, Shall I not, etc. **punish.** ver. 17. Is 1:5. He 12:8. **for.** 1 C *6:16. **are separated.**

Ju *19. **and they.** 1 K 14:23, 24. 15:12. 2 K 23:7. **harlots.** Ge 38:21, 22)ℙ. Dt 23:17)ℙ. **therefore.** ver. 1, 5, 6. Ho 14:9. Pr +*28:5. Is 44:18-20. 56:11. Da 12:10. Jn 8:43. Ro 3:11. Ep 4:18. **fall.** or, be punished. Pr 10:10mg.

15. **play the harlot.** ver. 12. Je 3:6-10. Ezk 23:4-8. yet. Ho 11:12. 2 K 17:18, 19. Je 3:10, 11. Lk +*12:47, 48. Ep +*5:11. **Gilgal.** Ho 9:15. 12:11. Jg 3:19. 1 S 7:16. 10:8. 11:14, 15. Am *4:4. *5:5. **Beth-aven.** i.e. *house of naught*, put for Bethel, the house of God, now profaned by Jeroboam (CB). ♪146, Ge +10:10. Ho 5:8. 10:5, 8. 1 K 12:28, 29. 13:1. 2 K 10:29. 17:6-23. Je ✶48:13. Am 3:14. 7:13. **nor.** Is 48:1. Je *5:2. Ezk 20:39. Am 6:10. 8:14. Zp 1:5, 6.

16. **slideth.** Ho 11:7. 1 S 15:11. Je *3:6, 8, 11, 12. 5:6. 7:24. *8:5. 14:7. Ps *125:5. Zc 7:11mg. He +*3:12. **as a lamb.** Le 26:33. Is 7:21-25. 22:18.

17. **Ephraim.** Ho 11:2. 12:1. 13:2. **let.** ver. 4. Ps 81:12. Mt +*15:14. Re +*22:11.

18. **drink.** Dt 32:32, 33. Is *1:21, 22. Je 2:21. **sour.** Heb. gone. ♪121G, Ge +31:1. Ml 3:7. **committed.** ver. 2, 10. 2 K 17:7-17. **her.** Ex 23:8. Dt *16:19. 1 S 8:3. 12:3, 4. Pr 30:15, 16. Am 5:12. Mi *3:11. 7:3. **rulers.** Heb. shields. Ps 47:9. ♪121N2. Metonymy of the Adjunct, Ge +34:29. **Give ye.** ♪118. Metallage; or, A Changing Over B681. A different subject of thought substituted for the original subject. By the figure Metallage the fact of continual whoredom (or idolatrous worship) is changed to the new thought of the rulers loving to continually command "Give ye (sacrifices)," with contempt for the sacrifices Jehovah commanded. Ho 8:13.

19. **wind.** Ho 13:15. Is 57:13. Je 4:11, 12. 51:1. Zc 5:9-11. **and.** Ho 10:6. Is 1:29. 42:17. Je *2:26, 27, 36, 37. 3:24, 25. 17:13.

HOSEA 5

The judgments of God are denounced against the priests, people, and princes, both of Israel and Judah, for their manifold sins, 1-14. An intimation is given of mercy on their repentance, 15.

1. **O priests.** Ho 4:1, 6, 7. 6:9. Ml 1:6. 2:1. **O house.** Ho 7:3-5. 1 K 14:7-16. 21:18-22. 2 Ch 21:12-15. Je 13:18. 22:1, etc. Am 7:9. Mi 3:1, 9. **for.** Ho 9:11-17. 10:15. 13:8. **ye have.** Ho 9:8. Mi 7:2. Hab 1:15-17. **Tabor.** Jg 4:6. Je 46:18.

2. **the revolters.** Ho 6:9. 9:15. Je 6:28. **profound.** Ps 64:3-6. 140:1-5. Is *29:15. Je 11:18, 19. 18:18. Lk 22:2-5. Ac 23:12-15. **though.** or, and, etc. **a rebuker.** lit. a correction. Ho 6:5. Is 1:5. Je 5:3. 25:3-7. Am 4:6-12. Zp 3:1, 2. He 3:19.

3. **know.** ♪121C2A2, Ge +39:6. Am √3:2. He *4:13. Re 3:15. **Ephraim.** ver. 9, 11, 13. Ho 6:4. 8:11. 12:1. 13:1. Ge 48:19, 20. Dt 33:17. Is 7:5, 8, 9, 17. **not hid.** ♪144D, Ge +40:23. **thou.** Ho 4:17, 18. 1 K 12:26-33. 14:14-16. Ezk 23:5.

4. **They will not frame their doings.** lit. They will not give. Or, Their doings will not suffer *them*. Ps 36:1-4. 78:8. Jn √3:19, 20. 2 Th √2:11, 12. **for.** Ho 4:12. Je 50:38. **and.** Ho 4:1. 1 S 2:12. Ps +√9:10. Je 9:6, 24. 22:15, 16. 24:7. Jn +*8:55. 16:3. 1 J √2:3, 4.

5. **the pride.** Ho 7:10. Pr 30:13. Is *3:9. 9:9, 10. 28:1-3. Am 8:7. **testify.** Is 44:9. 59:12. Je 14:7. Mt 23:31. Lk 19:22. **fall in.** Ho 4:5. 14:1. Pr 11:5, 21. 14:32. 24:16. Je 3:3. Am 5:2. **Judah.** ver. 14. Ho 8:14.

2 K 17:19, 20. Ezk 23:31-35. Am 2:4, 5.

6. **go.** Ex 10:9, 24-26)✓. Pr 15:8. 21:27. Je 7:4. Mi 6:6, 7. **to seek.** Dt 4:29)✓. **not find.** Pr *1:28. Is *1:11-15. 66:3. Je 11:11. La 3:44. Ezk 8:18. Am 5:21-23. Mi 3:4. Jn *7:34. **he.** SS 5:6. Lk 5:16. **withdrawn.** Ho 9:12. Ge +6:3.

7. **dealt.** Ho 6:7. Is 48:8. 59:13. Je *3:20. 5:11. Ml 2:11. **begotten.** Ne 13:23, 24. Ps 144:7, 11. Ml 2:11-15. **a month.** 2 K *15:13. Ezk 12:28. Zc 11:8.

8. **Blow.** Ho 8:1. Je 4:5. 6:1. Jl 2:1, 15. **Gibeah.** Ho 9:9. 10:9. Jg 19:12-15. 20:4-6. 1 S 15:34. 2 S 21:6. Is *10:29. **Ramah.** 1 S 7:17. 8:4. 15:34. Is 10:29. **Beth-aven.** Ho *4:15. 10:5, 8. Jsh 7:2. 1 K 12:29. **after.** Jg 5:14. 20:40.

9. **Ephraim.** ver. 12, 14. Ho 8:8. 9:11-17. 11:5, 6. 13:1-3, 15, 16. Jb 12:14. Is 28:1-4. Am 3:14, 15. 7:9, 17. **have.** Is 46:10. 48:3, 5. Am +*3:7. Zc 1:6. Jn 16:4.

10. **princes.** ver. 5. **like.** ✓160B, Ge +25:31. **remove.** Dt *19:14)✓. 27:17. 1 K 15:16-22. 2 K 16:7-9. 2 Ch 28:16-22. Jb 24:2. Pr 17:14. *22:28. *23:10. Is 5:8. Mi 2:2. **like.** ✓160B, Ge +25:31. Ps 32:6. 88:17. 93:3, 4. Pr 17:14. Mt 7:27. Lk 6:49.

11. **oppressed.** Dt *28:33)✓. 2 K 15:16-20, 29. Am *5:11, 12. **he willingly.** or, willfully. 1 K *12:26-33. 2 K 10:29-31. Ps +*119:63. Mi *6:16. Ac 5:29. Ro 6:13. He +*10:26.

12. **as a moth.** Jb 13:28. Is 50:9. 51:8. **rottenness.** or, a worm. Pr 12:4. Jon 4:7. Hab +*3:16. Mk ✓9:44-48.

13. **his wound.** Je 30:12, 14. Mi 1:9. **went.** Ho 7:11. 10:6. 12:1. 2 K *15:19, 29. 16:7. 2 Ch 28:16-18. **to king Jareb.** i.e. contender, ✱S#3377h. Ho 5:13. 10:6. or, to the king of Jareb; or, to the king that should plead. **yet.** 2 Ch 28:20, 21. Is *1:6. Je *30:12, 15.

14. **as a lion.** Ho 13:7, 8. Jb 10:16. Ps 7:2. La 3:10. Am 3:4-8. **will tear.** Ps 7:2. *50:22. Mi 5:8. **none.** Dt 28:31. Jb 10:7. Is 5:29. Am 2:14.

15. **return.** ✓22C20. Anthropomorphism B888. Human actions are attributed to God: returning. ver. 6. Ex 25:21, 22. 1 K 8:10-13. Ps 132:14. Is 26:21. Ezk 8:6. 10:4. 11:23. Mi 1:3. **my place.** ✓22D3B. Anthropomorphism B892. A place is attributed to God. Is 18:4. **till.** Ho *8:2. 14:1-3. Le +*26:40-42)✓. Dt *4:29-31. *30:1-3. 1 K 8:47, 48. 2 Ch 6:36, 37. +✓7:14. Ne 1:8, 9. Jb 33:27. Is 64:5-9. Je 3:13. ✓29:12-14. *31:18-20. Ezk 6:9. *20:43. 36:31. Da 9:4-12. **acknowledge their offense.** lit. be guilty. Ho 4:15. 6:1. 14:1-3. Ezk 39:23-29. Hab 1:11. Zc 12:10, 11. **seek my face.** Ho 3:5. Dt +*4:29)✓. Je ✓29:13. Zc 8:21, 22. **in their affliction.** Dt +*4:30. Jg 4:3. 6:6, 7. 10:10-16. 2 Ch 33:12, 13. Jb 27:8-10. Ps *50:15. 78:34. 83:16. 119:67. Pr 1:27, 28. 8:17. Is ✓26:9, 16. 64:9-12. Je ✓2:27. Ezk 20:44. Zp ✓2:1-3. Lk *13:25. **seek me early.** Ho 5:6. Jb 7:21. 8:5. 24:5. Ps 63:1. *78:34. Pr 1:28. 7:15. 8:17. 11:27. 13:24. Is 65:24. Zc 12:9, 10. *13:9.

HOSEA 6

Exhortations to repent and hope in God, 1-3. A lamentation over those who had sinned after conviction, 4. Reproofs of obstinate sinners, and threatenings against them, 5-11.

1. **let us return.** T#869. Ho ✓5:15. ✓14:1. Dt 4:30, 31. 30:2, 3, 8. 1 S 14:36. 1 Ch +*28:9. 2 Ch 15:2. Jb *33:27, 28. Ps 73:28. 145:18. Is *2:3-5. ✓55:7. 58:2.

Je 3:22. 50:4, 5. La 3:40, 41. Zp +*2:1-3. Zc 1:3. Ml 2:7. 3:7. Jn *14:6. Ac +✓3:19-21. Ep 3:12. **he hath torn.** Ho 5:12-14. 13:7-9. Dt *32:39. 1 S *2:6. Jb *5:18. 34:29. Ps 30:7-11. Is *29:13. 30:22. Je 30:12-17. 33:5, 6. La 3:32, 33. Ezk 7:9. **will heal.** Ex +15:26. Je 30:17. **will bind.** ✓22C29, Jb +5:18. Ep 2:13-18.

2. **after two days.** Ps 30:4, 5. +*102:13, 16. 1 C +*15:4, 20. **revive us.** Ho +*13:14. Ezr 9:8. Ps 71:20. +*80:18. 85:6. Is +*26:19n, 20. Hab *3:2. **the third day.** 2 K 20:5. Ps ✓90:4. +*118:24. Is ✓24:22n. Lk 13:32?. 2 P *3:8. Re 11:11. **raise us up.** Ezk *37:11-13. Da +*12:2. Am *9:11, 14, 15. Lk *2:25. Ac +*1:6. +*3:19-21. **we shall live.** Ge 17:18. Ps 61:7. Jn *14:19. Ro 14:8. **in his sight.** Ho 7:2. Jb 19:26. Is 24:23. Mt 19:28. 23:39. Lk 21:36. Jn 1:51n. 1 J 3:2.

3. **we know.** Ho *2:20. Is 54:13. Je 24:7. +*31:34. Mi 4:2. Jn ✓17:3. **if.** Pr *2:1-5, 9. Mt *13:11, 12. Jn ✓7:17. ✓8:12, 31, 32. Ac +*3:19-21. ✓17:11, 12. Ph *3:13-15. He *3:14. **follow on.** Pr *23:12. Da +*11:33. Mt 24:13. Lk 8:11-15. 22:31, 32. Jn *8:31. 15:9, 10. Ac *11:23. *14:22. Ro 2:7-9. Ga 4:11. 5:7. 6:9. Col +*1:10. 1 Th 3:5. 2 P *3:18. **his going forth.** 2 S *23:4. Ps 19:4-10. Pr +*4:18. Mi +*5:2. Ml *4:2. Lk *1:78, 79. Jn ✓16:28. 2 P ✓1:19. Re *22:16. **prepared.** or, sure, or fixed. Ge ✓41:32mg. Dt 13:14 (certain). 2 S 7:16, 26 (established). Ps 51:10mg. 57:7mg. 93:2. Pr *4:18 (perfect). Is 2:2. Mi 4:1. **as the morning.** Ho +14:5. Ge +*8:22. 2 S *23:3-5. Ps 30:5. 49:14. 90:14. 110:3. Je +*31:35, 36. +*33:25, 26. 2 P 1:19. **unto us.** Ps *72:6. Zc *9:9. Mi +*5:2. **as the rain.** Ho *10:12. *14:5. Dt *32:2. Jb 29:23. Ps 65:9. 72:6. Is 5:6. *32:15. *44:3. Ezk *36:25. Jl *2:23, 24. Mi *5:7. Zc *10:1. **former rain.** or, as the latter rain sprinkling the earth. Dt 11:14h)✓. 1 Ch 10:3 (archers). 2 Ch 35:23 (archers). Pr 26:18 (casteth). Je 5:24.

4. **what.** ✓85I, Ge +18:2. Da 11:8. Is 5:3, 4. Je 3:19. 5:7, 9, 23. 9:7. Mt *23:37, 38. Lk *13:7-9. 19:41, 42. **what shall.** ✓36. Aporia; or, Doubt B929. An expression of feeling by way of doubt. The speaker expresses himself as though he were at a loss as to what course to pursue. For other instances of this figure see Ho 11:8. Mt 21:25, 26. Lk 16:3. **for.** Jg 2:18, 19. Ps 78:34-37. 106:12, 13. Je 3:10. 34:15, 16. Mt 13:21. 2 P ✓2:20-23. **goodness.** or, mercy, or, kindness. **as a.** Ho 13:3. **it goeth away.** Mk +*4:17. Lk +*8:13.

5. **have I.** 1 S 13:13. 15:22, 23. 1 K 14:6-12. 17:1. 18:17, 18. 2 K 1:16. 2 Ch 21:12-17. Is *58:1. Je 1:10, 18. *5:14. 13:13, 14. ✓23:29. Ezk 3:9, 10. 43:3. Ac 7:31-44. **I have.** 1 K 19:17. Is 11:4. Je 23:29. 2 C ✓10:5, 6. He ✓4:12. Re 1:16. *2:16. 19:15, 21. **by.** ✓121I2, Ge +2:17. **and thy judgments are as.** or, that thy judgments might be as, etc. Ho 14:9. Ge +*18:25. Dt 33:2)✓. Je 34:10, 11. Ps 37:6. 119:120. Zp 3:5. Ro *2:5. Ep 6:17. 1 P 2:7.

6. **I desired mercy.** 1 S *15:22. Ps 50:8, 9. Pr *21:3. Ec 5:1. Is 1:11-17. 58:6-10. Je 7:22, 23. Da 4:27. Am 5:21-24. Mi +*6:6-8. Mt +*5:7.)9:13.)12:7. +*23:23. Mk *12:33. **not sacrifice.** Ps 50:8, 9. Pr 21:3. Is *1:11. **the knowledge of God.** Ho 4:1. 1 Ch +*28:9. Jb 22:21. Je *9:23, 24. 22:16. Col +*1:10. 1 J +✓2:3. 3:6. **burnt offerings.** Le +*23:12.

7. **men.** or, Adam. Ge *3:6, 11. Jb 31:33. Ps 49:12. 82:7. **transgressed.** Ho 8:1. 2 K 17:15. 18:12. Is 24:5. Je 31:32. Ezk *16:59-61. 20:37. He 8:9. **the covenant.** Ge 2:16, 17. Jsh 24:1, 25. Is ◑+*42:6. Ro 5:12, 19. 1 C 15:22, ◑+*45, 47. Ga 3:10. 1 Th 5:9. **they dwelt.**

Ho 5:7. Is 24:16. 48:8. Je 3:7-11, 20. 5:11. 9:6.

8. Gilead. Ho *12:11. Jsh 21:38. 1 K 17:1. **polluted with blood.** *or,* cunning for blood. Ho 5:1, 2. 2 S 3:27. 20:8-10. 1 K 2:5. Ps 10:8, 9. 59:2, 3. Is 59:6, 7. Je 11:19. Mi 7:2. Mt 26:15, 16. Ac 23:12-15. 25:3.

9. as troops. Ho 7:1. Ezr 8:31. Jb 1:15-17. 12:6. 24:2-17. Pr 1:11-19. **so.** Ho 5:1, 2. Je 11:9. Ezk *22:25, 27. Mi 3:9-11. Zp 3:3, 4. Mk 14:1. Lk 22:2-6. Jn 11:47-53. Ac 4:24-28. **company.** Is +*47:12 (❋S#2267h). **by consent.** Heb. with *one* shoulder, *or* to Shechem. 1 K 12:25. Zp 3:9mg. **lewdness.** *or,* enormity. ❋S#2154h. Le 18:17 (wickedness)◑𝒫. 19:29◑𝒫. 20:14, 14◑𝒫. Jg 20:6. Jb 17:11 (purposes). 31:11 (heinous crime). Ps 26:10 (mischief). 119:150. Pr 10:23. 21:27mg. *24:9 (thought). Is 32:7. Je 13:27. Ezk 16:27, 43, 58. 22:+*9, 11. 23:21, 27, 29, 35, 44, *48, 48, 49. 24:13.

10. I have seen. Je 2:12, 13. *5:30, 31. 18:13. 23:14. **there.** See on Ho 4:11, 17. 5:3, 4. 1 K 12:28-30. 15:30. 2 K 17:7-23. Je 3:6-11. Ezk 23:5-11.

11. harvest for thee. Ho 8:7. 10:12, 13. Pr 22:8. Is √17:5-8. Je 51:33. Jl *3:12, 13. Mi *4:12. Mt +*13:30, 39. Lk 3:17. Ga *6:7, 8. Re *14:14-20. **when.** Ps +*102:16, 22. **I returned the captivity.** Jb *42:10. Ps *126:1, 4. +*147:2. Je *29:14. Ezk *20:34, 41. 39:25. Am +*9:14. Zp 2:7. *3:20. Ac +*1:6.

HOSEA 7

Heavy charges of atrocious crimes brought against the kings, nobles, and people of Israel, 1-10. Awful denunciations of the wrath of God against them, 11-16.

1. I would. Je 51:9. Mt 23:37. Lk 13:34. 19:42. **the iniquity.** Ho 4:17. 6:8-10. 8:9. 11:12. 12:14. 13:1, 2, 16. Is 28:1-3. Mi 6:16. **wickedness.** Heb. evils. Ho 8:5. 10:5. Ezk 16:46, 51. 23:4. Am 8:14. **they commit.** Ho 5:1. 6:10. 11:12. 12:1, 7. Is 59:12-15. Je 9:2-6. Mi 7:3-7. **the troop.** See on Ho 6:9. **spoileth.** Heb. strippeth. Is 32:11.

2. consider not in. Heb. say not to. Dt 32:29. Ps 50:22. Is 1:3. 5:12. 44:19. 57:1. **I remember.** Ho 9:9. Ps 25:7. *90:8. Je 14:10. 17:1. Am 8:7. Lk 12:2, 3. 1 C 4:5. Re 20:12, 13. **their own.** Nu +*32:23. Jb 20:11-29. Ps *9:16. Pr *5:22. Is 26:16. Je 2:19. 4:18. **have beset.** He *12:1. **are before.** Jb 34:21. Ps 90:8. Pr 5:21. Je 16:17. 32:19. He *4:13.

3. They make. Ho 5:11. 1 K 22:6, 13. Pr 17:4. ◑20:26. 28:4. *29:12. Je 5:31. 9:2. 28:1-4. 37:19. Am 7:10-13. Mi 6:16. 7:3. Ro *1:32. 1 J 4:5.

4. are all. ◤171A, Ex +9:6. **adulterers.** See on Ho 4:2, 12. Je 5:7, 8. *9:2. Ja *4:4. **as an oven.** See on ver. 6, 7. **who ceaseth,** etc. *or,* the raiser will cease. **raising.** *or,* waking. Ps 73:20.

5. the day. Ge 40:20. Da 5:1-4. Mt 14:6. Mk 6:21, 22. **made.** Pr +*20:1. Is *5:11, 12, 22, 23. 28:1, 7, 8. Hab *2:15, 16. Ep +*5:18. 1 P 4:3, 4. **bottles of wine.** *or,* heat through wine. S#2534h. Ezk 3:14. **he stretched.** 1 K 13:4. **with scorners.** Ps +*1:1. 69:12. Pr 13:20. 23:29-35. Da 5:4, 23.

6. they. ver. 4, 7. 1 S 19:11-15. 2 S 13:28, 29. Ps 10:8, 9. Pr 4:16. Mi *2:1. **made ready.** *or,* applied. Is 41:21mg. Ezk 9:1.

7. devoured. Ho 8:4. 1 K 15:28. 16:9-11, 18, 22. 2 K 9:24, 33. 10:7, 14. 15:10, 14, 25, 30. **there.** ver. 10, 14. Ho *5:15. Jb 36:13. Is 9:13. 43:22. *64:7. Je +*10:25. Ezk 22:30. Da 9:13.

8. he hath. Ho 5:7, 13. 9:3. Ezr 9:1, 2, 12. Ne 13:23-25. Ps *106:34, 35. Je +*10:2. Ezk 23:4-11. Ml 2:11. **a cake.** Ho 8:2-4. 1 K 18:21. Zp 1:5. Mt *6:24. Re √3:15, 16.

9. Strangers. ◤95, Ps +7:13. **devoured.** Ho *8:7. 2 K 13:3-7, 22. 15:19, 29. Pr *23:35. Is *42:22-25. 57:1, 11. **here and there.** Heb. sprinkled. Ezk 36:25h. **knoweth it not.** Jg 16:20.

10. the pride. See on Ho 5:5. Je 3:3. **and they.** ver. 7. Ho 6:1. Dt 4:29◑𝒫. Pr 27:22. Is 9:13. Je 8:5, 6. 25:5-7. 35:15-17. Am 4:6-13. Zc 1:4. **nor.** Ps 10:4. 14:2. 53:2. Je *3:10. Ro 3:11.

11. a silly. Ho *11:11. **without.** Ho 4:11. Pr 6:32mg. 15:32mg. 17:16. **heart.** ◤121I1, Ge +3:7. **they call.** Ho 5:13. 8:8, 9. 9:3. 12:1. 14:3. 2 K 15:19. 17:3, 4. Is 30:1-6. 31:1-3. Je 2:18, 36. Ezk 23:4-8.

12. I will spread. Jb 19:6. Je 16:16. Ezk *12:13. 17:20. 32:3. Mt +*13:47. **I will bring.** Ec 9:12. **as their.** Le 26:14, etc., 28◑𝒫. Dt 27:14-26◑𝒫. 28:15, etc. 29:22-28. 31:16-29. 32:15-43. 2 K 17:13-18. Je 44:4. Re *3:19. **congregation.** Ex +*12:3◑𝒫.

13. Woe. Ho 9:12. Is *31:1. La 5:16. Ezk 16:23. Mt *23:13-29. Re 8:13. **have fled.** T#694. Ho 11:2. Ge 3:8. Jb 11:12. 21:14, 15. 22:17. Ps 139:7-9. Je 2:5, 13. Jon 1:3, 10. **destruction.** Heb. a spoil. Ho 9:6mg. Ezk 45:9. Am 3:10mg. Hab 1:3. **transgressed.** Ho 14:9. **though.** Dt 7:8◑𝒫. 9:26◑𝒫. 15:15◑𝒫. 21:8◑𝒫. 24:18◑𝒫. Ne 1:10. Ps 106:10. 107:2, 3. Is 41:14. 43:1-3. 63:8-10. Mi *6:4. 1 P 1:18, 19. **spoken.** ver. 3. Ho 11:12. Is 59:13. Je 18:11, 12. 42:20. 44:17, 18. Ezk *18:2, 25. Ml *3:13-15. 1 J *1:10.

14. they have not. Jb 35:9, 10. Ps *78:34-37. Is +*29:13. Je *3:10. Zc *7:5. **when.** Is 52:5. 65:14. Am 8:3. Ja 5:1. **assemble.** Ho 3:1. Ex 32:6. Jg 9:27. Is *58:5. Am 2:8. Mi 2:11. Ro 16:18. Ph +*3:19. Ja *4:3. **corn.** ◤121D4, Ge +27:28. **and.** ◤174, Ge +18:27. **wine.** ◤121D13, Ge +27:28. **rebel against.** *or,* apostatized from. Ps 101:4. Pr 5:7. +*22:6. Je 17:5. ◐32:40. Da 9:5, 11.

15. I have. 2 K 13:5, 23. 14:25-27. Ps 18:34. 106:43-45. 144:1. **bound.** *or,* chastened. ver. 12. Jb 5:17. Ps 94:12, 13. Pr 3:11, 12. He *12:5-11. Re *3:19. **imagine.** Ps *2:1. 62:3. Pr +*21:30. Je +*17:9. Na *1:9, 11. Ac 4:25. Ro 1:21. 2 C √10:5.

16. return. Ho 6:4. 8:14. *11:7. Ps 78:37. Je 3:10. Lk +√8:13. 11:24-26. **most High.** Ho 11:7. **like.** Ps *78:57. **the rage.** ver. 13. Ps 12:4. 52:2. 57:4. 73:9. Is 3:8. Je 18:18. Mt +*12:36, 37. Ja 3:5-8. 2 P 2:8. Re 13:5, 6. **this.** Ho 8:13. 9:3, 6. Ezk 23:32. 36:20. **land of Egypt.** Ho 9:3, 6. Is 30:3, 5.

HOSEA 8

Reproofs of Israel's idolatry, hypocrisy, rebellion, and folly; and denunciations of deserved punishment, in which Judah also is joined, 1-14.

1. the trumpet. Ho 5:8. Is 18:3. *58:1. Je 4:5. 6:1. 51:27. Ezk 7:14. 33:3-6. Jl 2:1, 15. Am +*3:6. Zp 1:16. Zc 9:14. 1 C 15:52. **thy mouth.** Heb. the roof of thy mouth. Jb 6:30mg. +31:30mg. Ps 119:103mg. **He shall come.** ◤63B, Ge +25:28. Dt 28:49◑𝒫. **as.** Dt *28:49◑𝒫. Je 4:13. 48:40. Hab 1:8. Mt 24:28. **the house.** ◤121.O, Ge +28:22. Ho 9:15. 2 K 18:17. Am 8:3. 9:1. Zc 11:1. Ep 2:19-22. He 3:6. 1 P 2:5. *4:17. **transgressed.** Ho 6:7. Is 24:5. Je 31:32. Ezk 16:59. He 8:8-13. **my covenant.** Dt 4:13◑𝒫.

2. **shall cry.** Ho +*5:15. 7:13, 14. Dt √4:29-31.
2 K 10:16, 29. 2 Ch *15:10-15. 20:21, 22. Jb *8:5-7.
22:23-30. Ps +*50:15. *78:34-37. Is 48:1, 2. +*65:24.
Je 7:4. 36:7. Jl *2:15-19, 32. Mi 3:11. Zc *12:10. √13:9.
Mt +*7:21-23. 25:11, 12. Lk *13:25-27. T *1:16. 1 J
*2:4. **we know thee.** Is 29:13. Ezk √39:22. Jl 2:17,
27. Zc √13:9. Mt *7:22. 15:8. Jn +*8:54, 55.

3. **cast.** Ps 36:3. 81:10, 11. Am 1:11. 1 T 5:12. **good.**
or, the Gracious One (CB). Ho 3:5. 14:2. **the enemy.**
Le 26:36. Dt 28:25. La 3:66. 4:19.

4. **set.** Ho 7:7. 1 K 12:16-20. 2 K 15:10-30, *Shallum,
Menahem, Pekahiah.* **I knew it not.** Ps *1:6. Mt √7:23.
25:12. Mk +√13:32. Lk 13:25, 27. Jn 10:14. 1 C *8:3.
Ga 4:9. **of.** Ho 2:8. 13:2. 1 K 12:28. 16:31. **that they.**
Ho 13:9. 1 K 13:34. Je 44:7, 8. Ezk 18:31.

5. **calf.** ver. 6. Ho 10:5. 1 K *12:28, 29. Ps 106:19.
Is 14:20. 45:20. Ac 7:41. **mine.** Dt 32:22. 2 K 17:16-
18, 21-23. **how.** Pr 1:22. Je 4:14. *13:27. **will it be.**
√63BA, Ps +21:11. i.e. how long ere they are able
to practice innocency?

6. **from.** Ps 106:19, 20. **the workman.** Ps 115:4-8.
135:15-18. Is 44:9-20. Je 10:3-9, 14, 15. Hab 2:18-20.
Ac 17:29. 19:26. **the calf.** Ho 10:2, 5, 6. Je 43:12, 13.
50:2. **shall.** 2 K 23:15, 19. 2 Ch 31:1. 34:6, 7.

7. **sown.** Ho 10:12, 13. Nu +*32:23. Jb 4:8. Pr 22:8.
Ec 5:16. Ga √6:7, 8. **it hath.** Is 17:11. Je 12:13. **stalk.**
or, standing corn. Ex 22:6. **the strangers.** Ho 7:9.
Dt 28:33. Jg 6:3-6. 2 K 13:3-7. 15:19, 29.

8. **swallowed.** 2 K 17:1-6. 18:11. Je 50:17. 51:34.
La 2:2, 5, 16. Ezk 36:3. **among.** Le 26:33. Dt 28:25,
64. **a vessel.** Is 30:14. Je 22:28. 48:38. 51:34. Ro *9:22.
2 T *2:20, 21.

9. **they.** Ho 5:13. 7:11. 2 K 15:19. Ezk 23:5-9. **a
wild.** Jb *39:5-8. Is 1:3. Je 2:24. **hath.** Ho 2:5-7, 10-
13. 12:1. 2 Ch 28:20, 21. Is 30:6. Ezk 16:33, 34. **lovers.**
Heb. loves. Pr 7:18.

10. **now.** Ho 10:10. Ezk 16:37. 23:9, 10, 22-26, 46,
47. **sorrow a little.** or, begin to sorrow in a little while,
as Hg 2:6. **for.** 2 K 14:26. 15:19, 20. 17:3. 1 Ch 5:26.
the king. Is 10:8. 36:13. Ezk 26:7. Da 2:37.

11. **Ephraim.** Ho 4:17. Ps 106:15. **many.** Ho 10:1,
2, 8. 12:11. Is 10:10, 11. **altars.** Dt 4:28. Je 16:13.

12. **written.** Ex 17:14)𝒫. 24:4, 7)𝒫. 34:27)𝒫. Nu
33:1, 2)𝒫. Dt *4:6-8)𝒫. Ne *9:13, 14. Ps √119:18.
147:19, 20. Pr *22:20, 21. Ezk *20:11, 12. Ro *3:1,
2. *7:12. **but.** Ho *4:6. 2 K 17:15, 16. Ne *9:26. Ps
50:17. Is *30:9. Je *6:16, 17, +*19. 8:8, 9. *44:16.
Mk +*7:9.

13. **They sacrifice,** etc. or, In the sacrifices of mine
offerings, they sacrifice flesh and eat it. Je 7:21-23.
Zc 7:6. **but.** Ho 5:6. 9:4. 12:11. 1 S *15:22, 23. Pr
*21:27. Is *1:11, 15. 66:3. Je 14:10-12. Am 5:22. 1 C
11:20, 29. **now will.** Ho 9:9. Ex +*20:5. 32:34. Am
8:7. Re 16:19. **they shall.** Ho 2:15. 7:16. 9:3, 6. 11:5.
Dt *28:68)𝒫.

14. **forgotten.** Ho 13:6. Dt 32:18)𝒫. Ps 106:21. Is
17:10. Je 2:32. 3:21. 23:27. **Maker.** Ps *100:3. Is 29:23.
43:21. *64:8. Ep √2:10. **and buildeth.** 1 K 12:31, 32.
16:31, 32. 2 Ch 23:17. 24:7. **and Judah.** 2 Ch 26:10.
27:4. Is 22:8-11. **I will send.** 2 K 18:13. Is 42:13, 25.
Je 17:27. Am 1:4, 10, 12, 14. 2:5. **his cities.** 2 K 18:13.

HOSEA 9

*Israel is sentenced to distress and captivity for their
aggravated sins, but especially their idolatry, 1-17.*

1. **Rejoice.** Ho 10:5. Is 17:11. 22:12. La 4:21. Ezk
21:10. Am 6:6, 7, 13. 8:10. Ja 4:16. 5:1. **as.** Ezk 16:47,
48. 20:32. Am 3:2. **gone.** See on Ho 4:12. 5:4, 7. **thou
hast loved.** Ho 2:12. Je 44:17. **reward.** Dt 23:18
(hire))𝒫. **upon.** or, in, etc.

2. **floor.** Ho 2:9, 12. Ge +*50:10. Dt +*16:13mg.
Is 24:7-12. Jl 1:3-7, 9-13. Am 4:6-9. 5:11. Mi 6:13-16.
Hg 1:9. 2:16, 17. **winepress.** or, winefat. **fail.** lit. lie.
√155C, Le +19:23. Ge 18:15. Le 6:2.

3. **shall not dwell.** Le 18:28. 20:22-24. Dt 4:26, 27.
28:63. Jsh 23:15. 1 K 9:7. Mi 2:10. Zc 7:14. **the Lord's
land.** Le +25:23n. Dt +*32:43. Je 2:7. 16:18. Ezk
+*38:16. Jl 2:18. Zc 2:12. Ml 3:12. **but.** ver. 6. Ho
8:13. 11:5. Dt 28:68. Is 11:15, 16. "Not into Egypt
itself, but into another bondage as bad as that." **and.**
Ezk *4:13. Da +*1:8. Ac 10:14. **in Assyria.** Ho 11:11.
2 K *17:6.

4. **shall not.** Ho 3:4. Jl 1:13. 2:14. **offerings.** √63E1,
Le +4:2. **neither.** Ho 8:13. Is *1:11-15. 57:6. 66:3.
Je 6:20. Am 4:4, 5. 5:22. Ml 1:9, 10. **pleasing.** √22C16,
Ps +104:32. **bread.** √171I8. Synecdoche of the Species,
Ge +3:19, bread put for all kinds of food. **of mourners.**
√108H4, Is +58:7. Nu 19:11, 14)𝒫. Dt 26:14)𝒫. Ne
8:9-12. Ezk 24:17n, 22. Ml 2:13. **their bread.** √171I8,
Ge +3:19. Ex 40:23. Le +*17:11. 21:6, 8, 17, 21.
Nu 4:7. *28:2. Am 8:11, 12. Jn 6:51. **soul.** Heb. *neph-
esh,* Ge +12:13.

5. **What.** Is 10:3. Je 5:31. **in.** Ho 2:11. Jl 1:13. **solemn.** Ge +17:21h.

6. **they.** Dt 28:63, 64. 1 S 13:6. 2 K 13:7. **destruction.**
Heb. spoil. Ho 7:13mg. **Egypt.** ver. 3. Ho 7:16. 8:13.
11:11. Is 11:11. 27:12. Zc 10:10, 11. **shall gather them
up.** That is, shall rake them out for manure, or for
burning; not for burial in their own land; this would
be *asaph,* but here it is *kabaz* (CB). Je 8:2. Ezk 29:5.
Memphis. i.e. *gate of the blessed,* ＊S#4644h, only
here. **the pleasant places for their silver, nettles.** or,
their silver shall be desired, the nettle shall, etc. Heb.
the desire of. ver. 16mg. Da 10:3mg. **nettles.** Ho 10:8.
Ps 107:34. Pr 24:31. Is 5:6. 7:23. 32:13. 34:13. **tabernacles.** Ex +27:21n. Or, "tents," "tents" being put by
the Figure of Speech Metonymy of Adjunct (√121.O,
Ge +28:22) for the place where their tents were formerly pitched.

7. **days of visitation.** Ex 32:34)𝒫. Is 10:3. *34:8.
Je +*8:12. 10:15. 11:23. 45:21. Ezk 7:2-7. 12:22-28.
Am 8:2. Mi 7:4. Zp 1:14-18. Lk 19:44. 21:22. Re 16:19.
days of recompence. ＊S#7966h. Is *34:8. Mi 7:3 (reward). **Israel.** Is 26:11. Ezk 25:17. 38:23. **the prophet.**
ver. 8. Je 6:14. 8:11. 23:16, 17. La 2:14. Ezk *13:3,
10. Mi 2:11. Zp *3:4. Zc 11:15-17. **spiritual man.** Heb.
man of the spirit. Heb. *ruach,* Is +48:16. **mad.** 2 K
9:11. Je 29:26. Mk 3:21. Ac 26:24, 25. 2 C 5:13. **the
multitude.** Ezk 14:9, 10. 2 Th √2:10-12.

8. **watchman.** SS 3:3. Is 21:6-11. 62:6. Je 6:17. 31:6.
Ezk +*3:17, 18. 33:7. Mi 7:4. He 13:17. **with.** 1 K
17:1. 18:1, 36-39. 22:28. 2 K 2:14, 21. 3:15-20. 4:1-7,
33-37, 41, 43. 5:14, 27. 6:17, 18. 7:2, 19. 13:21. **but.**
Ho 5:1. 1 K 18:19. 22:6, 11, 22, 23. Je 6:14. 14:13.
La 2:14. 4:13, 14. **in the.** or, against the. Jn 15:24.
Ro 8:7.

9. **deeply.** Is 24:5. 31:6. **days.** √171T2B, Ps +102:11.
Gibeah. Ho 10:9. Jg *19:22-30. ch. 20, 21. This implies
a common knowledge of the history in Judges, and
argues for the existence of the Pentateuch and other
writings in Hosea's time as we know them still today.

Ex +*24:4. 2 K 14:6n. 22:8n. **therefore**. Ho 8:13.

10. **found**. Ho 11:1. Ex 19:4-6. Dt 32:10. Je 2:2, 3. 31:2. **grapes**. Ho 2:15. Nu 13:23, 24. Is 28:4. Mi 7:1. **fig tree**. Mt 21:19. **but**. Nu 25:3)℘, etc. Dt 4:3)℘. Ps *106:28. **Baal-peor**. Nu 25:3)℘. Dt 4:3)℘. Ps 106:28. **separated**. Ho 4:14. Jg 6:32. 1 K 16:31. Je 11:13. Ro 6:21. **that shame**. ♪121G, Ge +31:1. A reference to the Asherah and its worship. Is +*66:17n. Je 3:24. 11:13. **and their**. Nu 15:39. Dt 32:17. Ps 81:12. Je 5:31. Ezk 20:8. Am 4:5. **were according**. or, became abominable like that which they loved. Je +*2:2. 2 C ◐3:18. **as they loved**. or, to their love. ♪121R4, Je +2:33. i.e. to their idols, which were the objects of their love.

11. **their**. Ge *41:52. *48:16-20. 49:22. Dt 33:17. Jb 18:5, 18, 19. **from the birth**. Ps 58:8. 71:6. Ec 6:3. Am 1:13. **from the womb**. ver. 14. Dt 28:18, 57. Ps 139:14-16. Lk 23:29. **conception**. Ge 3:16h. Ru 4:13h. Je 1:5.

12. **yet**. ver. 13, 16. Le 26:22)℘. Dt *28:32, 41, 62)℘. 32:25. Jb *27:14. Je 15:7. 16:3, 4. La 2:20. **not**. Nu 26:65. Jg 4:16. **woe**. Ho 5:6. 7:13. Dt √31:17. 1 S 16:14. *28:15, 16. 2 K 17:18, 23. **depart**. Ho 5:6. Ge +6:3.

13. **as**. Ezk ch. 26-28. **shall**. ver. 16. Ho 10:14. 13:8, 16. 2 K 15:16. Je 9:21. Am 7:17.

14. **what**. ver. 13, 16. Mt 24:19. Mk 13:17. Lk 21:23. *23:29. 1 C 7:26. **wilt**. ♪37D. Aposiopesis; or, Sudden Silence B154: in inquiry and deprecation. For other instances of this figure see Jn 6:62. Ac 23:9. **give them**. ♪61. Ejaculatio; or, Ejaculation B479: parenthetic addition by way of wish or prayer. For another instance of this figure see Ro 3:4. **a miscarrying womb**. Heb. a womb that casteth the fruit. Jb 21:10. Je 50:9.

15. **is in**. Ho 4:15. 12:11. Jsh 4:19-24. 5:2-9. 10:43. 1 S 7:16. *13:4-15. *15:12-33. Am 4:4. 5:5. Mi 6:5. **I hated**. Le 26:30. Ezk 23:18. Zc 11:8. **I will drive**. ver. 3, 17. Ho 1:6, 9. 3:4. 1 K 9:7-9. 2 K 17:17-20. Ps 78:60. Je 3:8. 11:15. 33:24-26. Am 5:27. **house**. ♪121.O, Ge +28:22. **all**. Ho 5:1, 2. Is 1:23. Je 5:5. Ezk 22:27. Mi 3:11. Zp 3:3. Ac 4:5-7, 27. 5:21. **revolters**. or, apostates. lit. "turners aside." *S#5637h. Ho 4:16. Dt 21:18 (stubborn), 20. Ne 9:29 (withdrew). Ps 66:7 (rebellious). 68:6, 18. 78:8 (stubborn). Pr 7:11. Is *1:23. 30:1. 65:2. Je 5:23. 6:28. Zc 7:11 (away).

16. **their root**. ver. 11-13. Jb 18:16. Is 5:24. 40:24. Ml 4:1. **the beloved fruit**. Heb. the desires. ♪121R5, Ge +27:15. ver. 6mg. Ps +113:9. +127:3. Ezk 24:21.

17. **My God**. 2 Ch 18:13. Ne 5:19. Ps 31:14. Is 7:13. Mi 7:7. Jn +*20:17, 28. Ph *4:19. **cast them away**. Ho 1:9. Is +*54:7. Je 23:39. La 5:22. **because**. Ho 7:13. 1 K 14:15, 16. 2 K 17:14-20. 2 Ch *36:16. Ps 81:11-13. Pr *29:1. Is 48:18. Je 25:3, 4. 26:4-6. 35:15-17. Zc 1:4. 7:11-14. Ac 3:23. **not hearken**. Je +29:19. **wanderers**. T#377. Dt *28:64, 65)℘. 32:36. 2 K 17:6, 18-20, 23. Am 8:2. 9:9. Jn 7:35. Ja 1:1.

HOSEA 10

Reproofs of Israel's manifold sins, denunciations of terrible judgments, and exhortations to repentance, 1-15.

1. **Cir. A.M. 3264. B.C. 740. Israel is**. Is *5:1-7. Ezk 15:1-5. Na *2:2. Jn *15:1-6. **an empty vine**. or, a vine emptying the fruit which it giveth. Jg 9:8-13. 2 K 4:39. **fruit**. ♪147E, Is +24:16. T#160. Ho 13:15.

Jb +21:15 (T#689). Is 1:5. Col 3:5. 1 J 5:17. **unto himself**. Pr *13:7. Zc 7:5, 6. Lk 12:21. Ro 14:7, 8. 2 C 5:16. Ph 2:21. **to the multitude**. Ho 2:8. 8:4, 11. 12:8, 11. 13:2, 6. 13:2, 6. Je 2:28. **images**. Heb. statues, or standing images. Ex +34:13. Le 26:1. 1 K 14:23mg. 2 K +17:10. Is +*66:17n.

2. **Their heart is divided**. or, He hath divided their heart. Ho 7:8. 1 K 18:21. 2 K 17:32, 33, 41. Is 44:18. Zp 1:5. Mt √6:24. Lk 16:13. 2 Th √2:11, 12. Ja *1:8. *4:4. 1 J *2:15. Re 3:15, 16. **found faulty**. or, held guilty. Ho 9:17. **he shall**. Ex 23:24)℘. 34:13)℘. Dt 7:5)℘. 12:3)℘. **break down**. Heb. behead. ver. 5-8. Ho 8:5, 6. 1 S 5:4. Je 43:13. Mi 5:13. Zc 13:2.

3. **We have**. ver. 7, 15. Ho 3:4. 11:5. 13:11. Ge +*49:10. Mi 4:9. Jn *19:15.

4. **swearing**. Ho 6:7. 2 K 17:3, 4. Ezk 17:13-19. Ro 1:31. 2 T 3:3. **thus**. Dt 29:18)℘. 32:32, 33)℘. Is 5:7. 59:13-15. Am 5:7. 6:12. Ac 8:23. He +*12:15. Re 8:10, 11.

5. **Samaria**. ver. 7. Ho 7:1. 8:5, 6. 13:16. **the calves**. Ho 8:5, 6. 13:2. Dt 9:21. 1 K *12:28-32. 2 K 10:29. 17:16. 2 Ch 11:15. 13:8. **Beth-aven**. ♪146, Ge +10:10. Ho *4:15. 5:8. Jsh 7:2. **for the people**. Jg 18:24. Re 18:11-19. **the priests**. or, Chemarim. 2 K 23:5mg. Zp +1:4. Priests of Baal, or black ones, from *kamar*, to be black, from the black dress (or cassocks) worn by them (CB). **rejoiced**. lit. leaped, or exulted. 1 K 18:26. **for the glory**. Ho 9:11. 1 S √4:21, 22. Ac 19:27.

6. **carried**. Ho 8:6. Is 46:1, 2. Je 43:12, 13. Da 11:8. **present**. Ho 5:13. 2 K 17:3. **receive**. Ho 4:19. Is 1:29. 44:9-11. 45:16. Je 2:26, 27, 36, 37. 3:24, 25. 48:13. Ezk 36:31, 32. **ashamed**. Ho 11:6. Jb 18:7. Is 30:3. Je 7:24. Mi 6:16.

7. **Samaria**. 1 K 21:1. 2 K 1:3. **king**. ver. 3, 15. 2 K 15:30. 17:4. **the water**. Heb. the face of the waters. ♪144A1, Ge +11:8. Ge +1:2)℘. 7:18)℘. Jb 24:18. Ju 13.

8. **high places**. ver. 5. Ho 4:15. 5:8. **the sin**. Dt 9:21. 1 K 12:28-30. 13:34. 14:16. Am 8:14. Mi 1:5, 13. **the thorn**. Ho *9:6. Ge 3:18)℘. Ex 22:6. Is 32:13. 34:13. **their altars**. 1 K 13:2. 2 K 23:15. 2 Ch 31:1. 34:5-7. **they shall**. Is *2:19. Lk *)23:30. Re *)6:16. *9:6. **mountains**. Ge 49:22, 26. Jg 4:5.

9. **from**. Ho 9:9. Jg √19:22-30. *20:5, 13, 14. **the battle**. Jg 20:17-48. **did not**. Ge 6:5. *8:21. Zp 3:6, 7. Mt 23:31, 32.

10. **in my desire**. Dt *28:63)℘. Is 1:24. Je 15:6. Ezk 5:13. 16:42. **and the**. Ho 8:1, 10. Je 16:16. 21:4. Ezk 16:37. 23:9, 10, 46, 47. Mi 4:10-13. Zc *14:2, 3. Mt *22:7. **they**, etc. or, I shall bind them for their two transgressions, or, in their two habitations. Scholars are very much divided in their renderings and interpretations of this clause. The Companion Bible margin suggests "they being joined (or yoked) (in cohabitation. Put for idolatries) together in committing idolatry." **two**. Pusey suggests (*Minor Prophets*, p. 104) the two transgressions may designate the two calves of Bethel and Dan, or the twofold guilt of fornication, spiritual, and in the body; the breach of both tables of God's law. Others suggest unfaithfulness towards Jehovah and devotedness to idols; Keil suggests (*Minor Prophets*, vol i, p. 133) apostasy from Jehovah and the royal house of David. Ho 3:5. 1 K 12:26-33. 5:20. Je 2:13. **furrows**. S#5869h, Ge +24:13. Ho 2:10 (sight).

11. **an heifer**. Ho 4:16. Je 50:11. Mi 4:13. **and**

loveth. Ho 2:5. 3:1. 9:1. Dt *25:4. Ro 16:18. but. Ho 11:4. her fair neck. Heb. the beauty of her neck. Judah. 2 Ch 28:5-8. Is 28:24.

12. Sow. Ho 8:7. Ps +*126:5, 6. Pr *11:18. 18:21. Ec 11:6. Is 32:20. Ja *3:18. reap. Ga √6:7-9. break. Je *4:3, 4. time. Dt 4:29⸖𝒫. Ps *105:4. Is 31:1. √55:6. Je √29:12-14. 50:4, 5. Am 5:4, 6, 8, 14, 15. Zp *2:1-3. Lk *13:24, 25. 2 C *6:2. He 3:7. rain. Ho *6:3. Dt 32:2⸖𝒫. Ps 72:6. Is 5:6. 30:23. *44:3. 45:8. Ezk *34:26. Ac *2:18. 1 C 3:6, 7. The form of the Hebrew word used here is more often rendered "teach" than "rain." S#3384h: Ex 15:25 (showed). Dt 17:10 (inform), 11 (teach). 24:8. 33:10. Jg 13:8. 1 S 20:20 (shoot). 2 S 11:20 (shoot). 1 K 8:36. 2 K 13:17 (shot). 17:27. 19:32 (shoot). 2 Ch 6:27. 35:23 (shot). Jb 8:10. 12:7, 8. *27:11. Ps *25:8, 12. +*32:8. 45:4. 64:4, 7 (shoot). Pr 4:4. Is √2:3. *28:9, 26. 37:33 (shoot). Ezk 44:23. Mi 3:11. √4:2. Hab 2:19. Another form of the same Hebrew word is used at Ho 6:3, and rendered "former rain." Girdlestone (Synonyms, ch. 17, sec. 2) states this verb "signifies to project, and hence to point out or teach."

13. plowed. Ho 8:7. Jg 14:18. Jb 4:8. Pr 22:8. Ga √6:7, 8. eaten. Pr 1:31. 12:19. 18:20, 21. 19:5. didst. Ps 52:7. 62:10. in the. Ps 33:16. Ec 9:11.

14. shall a. Ho 13:16. Is 22:1-4. 33:14. Am 3:8, 9. 9:5. and all. 2 K 17:6. 18:9, 10. Is 17:3. Je 48:41. Mi +*5:11. Na 3:12. Hab 1:10. as. 2 K 18:33, 34. 19:11-13. Shalman. i.e. peaceable; he spoiled them; their peace offering, *S#8020h. Beth-arbel. i.e. house of the ambush of God, *S#1009h. the mother. Ho 13:16. Ge 32:11. Is 13:16-18. Je 13:14. Na 3:10.

15. shall Bethel. ver. 5. Am 7:9-17. your great wickedness. Heb. the evil of your evil. √147H, Ge +9:25. Ro *7:13. in a morning. ver. 3, 7. Is 16:14. the king. 2 K 17:4, 23.

HOSEA 11

Israel's ingratitude for his benefits, 1-4. His judgments on them, 5-7. Intimations of mercy, 8-11. Judah's fidelity, contrasted with Israel's treachery, 12.

1. Israel. Ho 2:15. Dt 7:7, 8. Je *2:2. Ezk *16:6, 22. Ml 1:2. called. Ex 4:22, 23⸖𝒫. Mt ⸖2:15. An illustration of the "law of double reference." See 2 S 7:12-16; Dt 18:15 w Ac 3:22, 23. Is 25:8n. Je ch. 50, 51 w Re 18:0-21; Ge 3:15. Mt +*16:23 ("law of double reference"). out of Egypt. T#1891. Mt +*✱2:14, 15.

2. they called. ver. 7. Dt 29:2-4. 1 S 8:7-9. 2 K 17:13-15. 2 Ch *36:15, 16. Ne 9:30. Is 30:9-11. Je 35:13. 44:16, 17. Zc 1:4-6. 7:11, 12. Lk 13:34. Jn √3:19-21. Ac 7:51, 52. 2 C 2:15, 16. they sacrificed. Ho 2:13. 13:1, 2. Jg 2:13. 3:7. 10:6. 1 K 16:31, 32. 18:19. 2 K 17:16. burned. 1 K 12:33. Is 65:7. Je 18:15. 44:15.

3. taught. Ex 19:4. Nu 11:11, 12. Dt *1:31⸖𝒫. 8:2. *32:10-12⸖𝒫. Is *46:3. +*63:9. Ac 13:18. I healed. Ho 2:8. 7:1. 14:4. Ex *15:26⸖𝒫. +*23:25. Is 1:2. 30:26. Je +8:22. 30:17.

4. drew. Ps 73:28. 116:15. SS 1:4. Is +*63:9. Je 30:21. 31:32. Mt 11:29. Jn +*6:44. *12:32. 2 C 5:14. of a man. 2 S 7:14. I was. Le *26:13. take off. Heb. lift up. Ge 14:22. Is *30:28. and I laid. Ho 2:8. Ps 78:23-25. 105:40. Jn 6:32-58.

5. shall not. Ho 7:16. 8:13. 9:3, 6. but. Ho 5:13. 10:6. 2 K 15:19, 29. 17:3-6. 18:11. Is 8:6-8. Am 5:27. "They became tributaries to Salmanasser." because.

Ho *6:1. 2 K 17:13, 14. 18:12. Je 8:4-6. Am 4:6, 8-10. Zc 1:4-6.

6. the sword. Ho 10:14. 13:16. Le 26:31, 33. Dt 28:52. 32:25. Je 5:17. Mi 5:11. consume. Ps 80:11-16. Is 9:14. 18:5. 27:10, 11. Ezk 15:2-7. 20:47. Ml 4:1. because. Ho 10:6. Ps *106:39, 43. Is 30:1.

7. are bent. Ho 4:16. 14:4. Ps 78:57, 58. Pr 14:14. Je 3:6, 8, 11. 8:5. 14:7. they called. ver. 2. Ho 7:16. Ex 2:23. 3:7. Jg 10:16. 2 K *13:23. 2 Ch 30:1-11. Ps 30:5. 78:38. 81:11. 103:11. 106:43-45. Je 31:20. La 3:22. Am 5:4-6, 14, 15. Mi 7:18, 19. Lk 15:20. none at all would exalt him. Heb. together they exalted not.

8. How shall I give. √22, Ge +3:9. √85I, Ge +18:12. √36, Ho +6:4. Ho 6:4. Je 9:7. La 3:33. Mt 23:37. Lk 19:41, 42. Admah. Ge 14:2, 8⸖𝒫. *19:24, 25. Dt *29:23⸖𝒫. Is 1:9, 10. Je 49:18. 50:40. Am 4:11. Zp 2:9. 2 P 2:6. Ju *7. Re 11:8. 18:18. Zeboim. Dt 29:23. Mine. Dt *32:36. Jg 10:16. 2 S 24:16. 2 K 13:23. Ps 106:45. Is *63:15. Je 3:12. *31:20. Am 7:3, 6. heart. √141, Is +22:4. La *1:20. within. √121G1, Is +63:15. repentings. √22B, Ge +6:6.

9. not execute. Ho 14:4. Ex 32:10-14. Dt 32:26, 27. Ps 78:38. Is 27:4-8. 48:9. Je 30:11. 31:1-3. Ezk 20:8, 9, 13, 14, 21-23. return. 1 S 26:8. 2 S 20:10. for. Nu *23:19⸖𝒫. Is √55:8, 9. Mi *7:18-20. Ml +*3:6. Ro +*11:28, 29. not man. √144D, Ge +40:23. Is +*57:15. the Holy One. Is 12:6. Ezk 37:27, 28. Zp 3:15-17. in the midst. Ex 33:5⸖𝒫.

10. walk. Is 2:5. 49:10. Je 2:2. 7:6, 9. 31:9. Mi 4:5. Zc 10:12. Jn *8:12. Ro *8:1. 2 P *2:10. he shall roar like. √22F1, Is +42:13. Is 31:4. 42:13. Je 25:30. Jl 3:16. Am 1:2. 3:4, 8. shall tremble. Jb 37:1. Ps *2:11. 119:120. Is 64:2. Je 5:22. 33:9. Hab +*3:16. Ac 24:25. west. Is 11:11. Zc *8:7.

11. out. Ho *3:5. 9:3-6. Is √11:11. Zc 10:10. as a dove. Ho 7:11. Is *60:8. and I. Je 31:12. 32:37. Ezk *28:25, 26. 36:33, 34. *37:21, 25. Am √9:14, 15. Ob 17.

12. compasseth. Ho 7:16. 12:1, 7. Ps 78:36. Is 29:13. 39:8. 44:20. 59:3, 4. Mi 6:12. with deceit. Is 29:13. Ezk +*33:31. Mt 15:8, 9. Mk 7:6, 7. Judah. Ho 4:15. 2 K 18:4-7. 2 Ch 13:10-12. ch. 29-32. ruleth. Ge 32:28. 1 C *6:2. Re *1:6. *3:21. *5:10. saints. or, most holy. Jsh 24:19. Ps +*149:9. Pr 30:3.

HOSEA 12

Ephraim and Judah are reproved, 1, 2. The conduct of the nation exposed, by comparison with that of their pious ancestor Jacob, whom God especially favored, and a call to repentance, 3-6. Ephraim's crimes and ingratitude provoke God to punish him, 7-14.

1. feedeth. Ho 8:7. Jb 15:2. Je 22:22. east wind. Ho 13:15. Ge +*41:6. Ezk +27:26. Jon 4:8. Hab 1:9. he daily. Ho 11:12. and they. Ho *5:13. 7:11. 2 K 15:19. *17:4-6. Is 30:6, 7. oil is carried. Ho 5:13. 2 K 17:4. Is 30:2-7. 57:9.

2. a controversy. Ho 4:1. Je 25:31. Mi 6:2. and will. 2 K 17:19, 20. Is 8:7, 8. 10:6. Je 3:8-11. Ezk 23:11, etc., 31, 32. punish. Heb. visit upon. Ho 2:13. 4:9mg. 8:13. 9:9. Ex +32:34. Is 10:12. 24:21mg. Je +9:25mg. according to his doings. Is 3:11. 59:18. Mt 16:27. Ro 2:6. Ga *6:7.

3. took. Ge *25:22, 26⸖𝒫. Ro 9:11-13. had, etc. Heb. was a prince, or, behaved himself princely. Ge 32:24-28⸖𝒫. Ja 5:16-18.

4. **power.** T#1377. Ge 32:28. **angel.** ver. 5. Ge 32:29, 30. 48:15, 16. Ex 3:2-5. Is *63:9. Ml 3:1. Ac 7:30-35. **wept.** ♪106, Ge +31:7. **made.** Ge 32:9-12. He *5:7. **found.** Ge *28:11-19♪℘. *35:9, 11, 12, 15. **spake.** Ps 66:6. 1 Th *4:17. He 6:13-18.

5. **Even.** Ge 28:16. 32:30. 35:7. **is his memorial.** Ex *3:14, 15♪℘. Ps 135:13. Is 42:8.

6. **turn.** Ho *14:1. Pr *1:23. Is 31:6. √55:6, 7. Je 3:14-22. La 3:39-41. Jl 2:13. Zc 1:3. Ac +*2:38. 26:20. **keep.** Ho 4:1. Pr 21:3. Is *1:16, 17. 58:6-11. Je 22:15, 16. Am 5:24. Mi +*6:8. Zc 7:9, 10. 8:16, 17. Ja 1:27. *2:13. **wait.** Ge 49:18♪℘. Ps 27:14. *37:7. 123:2. 130:5-7. Is 8:17. 25:9. 26:8. √30:18. 32:2. 40:31. La *3:25, 26. Hab 2:3. Zp 3:8. Mk 15:43. Lk 2:25. 23:51. **continually.** 1 K 10:8. 1 Ch +16:11.

7. **a merchant.** or, Canaan. Ezk 16:3. Zc 14:21. Jn 2:16. **the balances.** Le 19:35, 36♪℘. Pr 11:1. 16:11. Am *8:4-6. Mi 6:10, 11. 1 T *6:9, 10. **he loveth.** Le 6:2♪℘. 19:13♪℘. Is 3:5. Ezk 22:29. Am 2:7. 3:9, 10. 4:1. 5:11, 12. Mi 2:1, 2. 3:1-3. 7:2, 3. Ml +*3:5. Mt *23:14. Ja +*5:4. **oppress.** or, deceive. 1 S 12:3.

8. **Yet.** Jb 31:24, 25. Ps 49:6. 52:7. 62:10. Zc 11:5. Lk *12:19, 20. 16:13, 14. 1 T 6:5, 17. Re *3:17. **I have.** Dt 8:17. Is 10:13, 14. Hab 1:16. 2:5, 6. **in all,** etc. or, all my labors suffice me not; *he shall have punishment of iniquity in whom is sin.* **they.** Pr 30:12, 20. Je 2:23, 35. Ml 2:17. 3:13. Lk 10:29. 16:15. **that.** Heb. which.

9. **I that.** Ho 13:4. Ex 20:2. Le 19:36. 26:13. Nu 15:41. Ps 81:10. Mi 6:4. **yet.** Ge 25:27. 2 S 7:2. 11:11. Je 35:7. He 11:9-13. **as in.** Le +*23:40-43♪℘. Ezr 3:4. Ne *8:15-17. Zc *14:16-19. Jn *7:2. **tabernacles.** Le +*23:34, 39n, 42. Lk *=9:27, 33. **solemn feast.** Ge +17:21h. Le *23:2n.

10. **have also.** 1 K 13:1, etc. 14:7-16. 17:1, etc. 18:21-40. 19:10. 2 K *17:13. Ne 9:30. Je *25:4. Am 7:14, 15. He 1:1. 2 P *1:21. **multiplied.** Nu 12:6. Jl *2:28. Ac 2:17, 18. 2 C 12:1, 7. **used.** Ho 1:2-5. 3:1. Is *5:1-7. 20:2-5. Je 13:1-14. 19:1, 10, 11. Ezk ch. 4, 5, 15. 20:49. 23:2, etc. **ministry.** Heb. hand. 1 K +16:12mg.

11. **iniquity.** Ho 6:8. 1 K 17:1. **surely.** Je 10:8, 15. Jon +*2:8. **they sacrifice.** Ho 4:15. 9:15. Am 4:4. 5:5. **their altars.** Ho 8:11. 10:1. 2 K 17:9-11. Je 2:20, 28.

12. **Jacob.** Ge 27:43. 28:5♪℘. 29:1. Dt 26:5♪℘. **Israel.** Ge 32:27, 28. **served.** Ge 29:18-28♪℘. 31:41. **kept sheep.** Ge 30:31♪℘.

13. **by a prophet.** ♪171E12, Ge +14:22. ♪32, Ge +31:21. Ho 13:4, 5. Ex 12:50, 51♪℘. 13:3♪℘. Nu 12:6-8♪℘. Dt *18:15. 1 S 12:8. Ps 77:20. Is 63:11, 12. Am 2:11, 12. Mi 6:4. Ac 3:22, 23. 7:35-37. **and by.** Jn 6:32.

14. **provoked.** 1 K 12:25—13:5. 2 K 17:7-18. Ezk *23:2-10. **most bitterly.** Heb. with bitternesses. Je 6:26. **therefore.** 2 S 1:16. 1 K 2:33, 34. Ezk 18:13. 24:7, 8. 33:5. **blood.** Heb. bloods. Ho 4:2mg. Ge 4:10mg. 2 K +*9:26mg. **and his.** Ho 7:16. Dt *28:37♪℘. 1 S 2:30. Da 11:18.

HOSEA 13

The glory of Ephraim was about to end in dreadful judgments, for his idolatry and ingratitude to God, 1-8. Promises of mercy, and redemption from the grave, 9-14. The terrible desolation of Samaria foretold, 15, 16.

1. **Ephraim.** 1 S 15:17. Pr 18:12. Is 66:2. Lk 14:11. **spake.** Jsh 4:14. Jb 29:21-25. **trembling.** Je 49:24. **exalted.** Nu 2:18-21. 10:22. 13:8, 16. 27:16-23. Jsh 3:7. 1 K 12:25. Lk 14:11. **offended.** Ho 11:2. 1 K 16:29-33. 18:18, 19. 2 K 17:16-18. **died.** Ge 2:17. Ro *5:12. 2 C 5:14.

2. **now.** Nu 32:14. 2 Ch 28:13. 33:23. Is 1:5. 30:1. Ro 2:5. 2 T 3:13. **molten images.** 1 K 12:28. 2 Ch +24:3. **sin more and more.** Heb. add to sin. Jg 10:6. Is 7:10mg. **have made.** Ho 2:8. 8:4. 10:1. Ps 115:4-8. Is 46:6, 7. Je 10:4. Hab 2:18, 19. **according.** Ho 10:6. 11:6. Ps 135:17, 18. Is 44:17-20. 45:20. 46:8. Je 10:8. Ro 1:22-25, 31. 1 C *2:14. 2 C *4:3, 4. Ep 4:17, 18. **the men that sacrifice.** 1 K 12:26-33. or, the sacrifices of men. Le +18:21. Dt +18:10. Jsh 15:8n. 2 K 17:17. +21:6. 23:10. Ezk 20:26. Mi 6:7. **kiss.** 1 S 10:1. 1 K 19:18. Ps *2:12. Ro 11:4.

3. **as the morning cloud.** Ho 6:4. **as the chaff.** Ps +*1:4. 68:2. 83:12-17. Is 17:13. 41:15, 16. Da *2:35.

4. **I am.** Ho 12:9. Ex *20:2. Ps 81:9, 10. Is *43:3, 10, 11. 44:6-8. *45:21. Ju 21. **for.** Is 43:11-13. 45:21, 22. Ac √4:12.

5. **know.** Ex 2:25. Ps *1:6. 31:7. 142:3. Am √3:2. Na 1:7. 1 C 8:3. Ga 4:9. **in the wilderness.** Dt *2:7♪℘. 8:15♪℘. 32:10♪℘. Je 2:2, 6. **great drought.** Heb. droughts. Ps 63:1.

6. **According to.** Ho 10:1. Dt *8:12-14. 32:13-15. Ne *9:25, 26, 35. Je 2:31. **therefore.** Ho 8:4. Dt 6:10-12. 8:12-14♪℘. *32:15, 18♪℘. Ps *10:4. Is 17:10. Je *2:32.

7. **I will be.** Ho 5:14. Is 42:13. Je *5:6. La 3:10. Am 1:2. 3:4, 8.

8. **as a bear.** 2 S 17:8. Pr *17:12. Am 9:1-3. **wild beast.** Heb. beast of the field. Ho 2:12, 18. Le 26:22♪℘. Ps 80:13. Is 5:29. 56:9. Je 12:9.

9. **thou.** Ho *14:1. Dt 32:5♪℘. 2 K 17:7-17. Ps 103:4. Pr 6:32. 8:36. Is 3:9, 11. Je 2:17, 19. 4:18. 5:25. Ml 1:9. **but.** ver. 4. Dt 33:26. Ps 33:20. 46:1. 121:1, 2. 146:5. Ep 1:3-5. T *3:3-7. **is thine help.** Heb. in thy help.

10. **I will be their king.** or, Where is thy king? "King Hosea being then in prison, 2 K 17:4." Ps 10:16. 44:4. 47:6, 7. 74:12. 89:18. 149:2. Is 33:22. 43:15. Je *8:19. Zc √14:9. Jn 1:49. **where.** ver. 4. Ho 10:3. Dt 32:37-39. Je 2:28. **thy judges.** Ho 8:4. Jg 2:16-18. 1 S ♪8:5, 6, 19, 20. 12:11, 12. 1 K 12:20.

11. **I gave thee a king.** Ho 10:3. 1 S *♪8:7-9. ♪10:19. 12:13. *♪15:22, 23. *♪16:1. 31:1-7. 1 K 12:15, 16, 26-32. 14:7-16. 2 K 17:1-4. Pr 28:2.

12. **iniquity of Ephraim.** Dt 32:34, 35. Jb *14:17. 21:19. Ps *32:3, 5. Ro *2:5. **bound up.** Dt 32:32, 35♪℘.

13. **sorrows.** Ps 48:6. Is *13:8. 21:3. Je 4:31. 13:21. 22:23. 30:6, +*7. 49:24. Mi 4:9, 10. Mt +*24:8. 1 Th *5:3. **an unwise son.** Pr +*22:3. Ac 24:25. **for he.** 2 K 19:3. Is 26:17, 18. 37:3. 66:8, 9. Ac *16:29-34. 2 C *6:2. He 3:7, 8. **stay.** 2 K 4:6. **long.** Heb. a time. **the breaking forth.** 2 K 19:3.

14. **I will ransom.** The Hebrew word underlying "ransom" (S#6299h) "especially refers to the deliverance from *bondage*" (Girdlestone, *Synonyms*, ch. xi., sec. 1). To redeem by power in virtue of the legal right (CB). Ho 6:2. Ex 13:13, 15. Jb √19:25-27. 33:24. Ps +*16:10. 30:3. 31:5. 49:7, 8, 15. 71:20. 86:13. 130:7, +*8. Is *25:8. 29:22. Ezk *37:11-14. Ro 11:15. **them from.** Ezk +16:49, *55, 60. Ac 3:21. Ju ◗*7. **power.** Heb. hand. **of the grave.** Heb. *sheol,* Ge +37:35.

Ezk *37:12. T#1002‡: Ac 2:31, 32. Re 1:18. **redeem**. S#1350h. To redeem by purchase by assertion of the kinship right (CB). Ge 48:16. Ex 6:6. 15:13. Nu 5:8. Ru 2:20mg. 3:9mg, 13 (kinsman). 4:4, 6, 14mg. 1 K 16:11. Jb √19:25. Is 35:9. 41:14. 43:1, 14. 44:6, 22-24. 47:4. 48:17. 49:7, 26. 51:10. 52:3. *59:20. 62:12. 63:4. Je 31:11. 32:7, 8. He 2:14, 15. **O death**. ♪38G, Dt +32:1. Is +*26:19. 1 C 15:21, 22, +*)55. 2 C *5:4. Ph *3:21. 1 Th √4:14-17. Re *20:13, 14. 21:4. **O grave**. ♪38G, Dt +32:1. **repentance shall be hid**. Nu *23:19. 1 S 15:29. Je 15:6. Ml +*3:6. Ro √11:29. Ja √1:17. **mine eyes**. ♪22A6, Ps +11:4.

15. **Though**. Ho 10:1. **he be fruitful**. Ge *41:52. *48:19. *49:22. Dt *33:17. **an east wind**. Ho 4:19. +12:1. Ge ◑+*41:6. Ps *1:4. Is 17:13. 41:16. Je *4:11, 12. ◑18:17. Ezk ◑17:10. ◑19:12. **his spring**. Ho 9:11-16. Dt 33:28♪ℙ. Jb 18:16-19. Ps 109:13. Pr 5:18. Is 14:21, 22. **fountain**. Heb. *mayan*, Ge +7:11. Pr 5:16. **pleasant vessels**. Heb. vessels of desire. Da +11:8mg. Na 2:9mg.

16. **Samaria**. "Fulfilled 2 K 17:6, 18." 2 K 8:12. 15:16. 18:9-11. Is 7:8, 9. 8:4. 17:3. Am 3:9-15. 4:1-3. 6:1-8. 9:1-4. Mi *1:4-6. 6:16. **rebelled**. or, been bitter. ✛S#4784h. Nu 20:24. 27:14. Dt 21:√18, +*21 (✛S#4784h). 1 S 12:15. 1 K *13:21, 26. Ps 5:10. 105:28. Is 1:20. 50:5. *63:10. Je 4:17. La 1:18, 20. 3:42. **their infants**. Ho 10:14, 15. 2 K 8:12. 15:16. Ps 137:8, 9. Is 13:16. Am 1:13. Na 3:10. **ripped up**. 2 K 8:12. 15:16. Am 1:13.

HOSEA 14

Encouraging calls to repentance, and counsels respecting it, 1-3. Promises of peculiar blessings to Israel, 4-8. These things worthy of particular attention, 9.

1. **return**. Ho 5:15. *6:1-3. *8:2. 12:6. Dt *30:1-3. 1 S 7:3, 4. 2 Ch 30:6-9. Is √55:6, 7. Je 3:12-14. 4:1. Jl *2:12, 13. Zc 1:3, 4. Ac 26:18-20. **thou**. Ho *13:9. Je 2:19. La 5:16. Ezk 28:14-16.

2. **Take with you words**. Ho *8:2. Le *26:40. 1 K *8:33. Jb *34:31, 32. Pr √28:13. Jl 2:17. Mt *6:9-13. Lk *11:2-4. *15:18. √18:13. 1 J √1:9. **say**. ♪122, Ex +15:9. Ps *60:1. Is 30:19. **Take away**. 2 S *12:13. *24:10. Jb 7:21. Ps *51:2-10. Is 6:7. 44:22. Ezk *36:25, 26. Mi *7:19. Zc *3:4. +√13:9. Jn *1:29. Ro 11:27. T *2:14. He 10:4. 1 J *1:7. *3:5. **receive**, etc. or, give good. Mt *7:11. Lk *11:13. 15:21-24. Ep *1:6, 7. *2:7, 8. 2 T √1:9. **graciously**. or, O Gracious One. Ho 3:5. 8:3. Eminent Jewish commentators take this as a title of the Messiah (CB). **render**. Ps 66:13, 14. 116:14, 18. Jon 2:9. **the calves**. ♪46A, Le +26:30. ♪117, Ge +19:8. Metalepsis, "calves" are but by *Metonymy* (of Subject) for sacrifices, and then, by another *Metonymy*, these sacrifices are put for the confession and praises rendered (B610). ♪121J6, Ps 23:5. The word "calves" means *oxen*; i.e., the animals used in sacrifice. Thus we have two *Metonymies*. First, *oxen* are put (by Metonymy of the Subject) for the *sacrifices* offered; and

then *the lips* are put (by Metonymy of the Cause) for the *confession* made by them. So that the verse really should read: "So shall we offer our sacrifices of confession and prayer"; being exactly what is expressed in Ps 51:17 and He 13:15. Ps 51:17. **lips**. ♪121BD, Dt +17:6. Ps *69:30, 31. 116:17. 141:2. Ro √10:9, 10. He *)13:15. 1 P *2:5, 9.

3. **Asshur**. Ho 5:13. 7:11. 8:9. 12:1. 2 Ch 16:7. Ps 146:3. Je 31:18, etc. **we will not**. Dt 17:16)ℙ. Ps 20:7, 8. *33:17. Is 30:2, 16. 31:3. 36:8. **neither**. ver. 8. Ho *2:17. Is 1:29. 2:20. 27:9. Ezk *36:25. 37:23. 43:7-9. Mi 5:10-14. Zc 13:2. **for**. Ex 22:22-24. Ps *10:14. *68:5. 146:9. Pr 23:10, 11. Jn 14:18mg.

4. **heal their backsliding**. T#791. Ho 11:7. Ex +*15:26. Is *43:25. *48:9, 11. 57:18. 59:2. Je *3:12, 22. 5:6. *8:22. 14:7. 17:14. 33:6. Mt 9:12, 13. 1 J √1:9. **I will love**. Dt 7:7, 8. Zp 3:17. Ro *3:24. Ep *1:6, 7. √2:4-9. 2 T √1:9. T 3:4-7. **for**. Nu 25:4, 11. Ps 78:38. Is *12:1. 2 C *5:19-21.

5. **as the dew**. Ho 6:4. 13:3. Dt 32:2. 2 S 23:4. Jb 29:19. Ps *72:6. 133:3. Pr *19:12. Is 18:4. +*26:19n. 44:3. Mi 5:7. **he shall**. Ho 6:3. SS *2:1, 2, 16. 4:5. Mt 6:28, 29. Lk 12:27. **grow**. or, blossom. Is *27:6. **cast**. Heb. strike. 2 K 19:30. Ps 72:16. 92:12. Is *27:6. 35:2. Ezk 17:22-24. Ep 3:17. **roots**. Jb 29:19.

6. **branches**. Ps 80:9-11. Ezk 17:5-8. 31:3-10. Da 4:10-15. Mt 13:31, 32. Jn *15:1, etc. Ro 11:16-24. **spread**. Heb. go. 2 Ch 26:8mg. **and his beauty**. Ps 52:8. 128:3. **his smell**. Ge 27:27. SS 4:11-15. 2 C *2:14, 15. Ph *4:18.

7. **that dwell**. Ps *91:1. SS 2:3. Is 32:1, 2. **revive**. Ho 6:2. Ps 85:6. 138:7. Is 61:11. Jn 11:25. 12:24. 1 C 15:36-38. **grow**. or, blossom. ver. 5mg. SS 6:11. Zc 8:12. **scent**. or, memorial. Ho 12:5. **wine**. SS 1:2, 3.

8. **shall say**. ♪63BA, Ge +26:7. **What have**. ♪85H, Jg +11:12. ver. 2, 3. Jb 34:32. Ac 19:18-20. 2 C *6:16. 1 Th *1:9. 1 P 1:14-16. 4:3, 4. **with idols**. Ps 96:5. *97:7. Is *2:6, 8, 18, 20, 22. *17:7, 8. Zc 10:2. Jn *5:43. Re 9:20. **I have heard**. Jb 33:27. Je 31:18-20. Lk 10:39. *15:20. Jn *1:47, 48. 2 C 3:18. **I am**. Is 41:19. 55:13. 60:13. From me. Is *45:24. Jn 1:16. *15:1-8. Ga *5:22, 23. Ep 5:9. Ph 1:11. 2:13. 4:13. Ja √1:17.

9. **Who**. ♪85D, Ps +25:12. **wise**. Ps *107:43. Pr *1:5, 6. 4:18. Je *9:12. Da +*11:33. +*12:10. Mt *13:11, 12. Lk 1:17. Jn √8:47. *18:37. **prudent**. Pr +*22:3. **for the ways**. Ps *25:10. **are right**. Ho 6:5. Ge +*18:25. Dt 32:4♪ℙ. Jb 26:14. 34:10-12, 18, 19. 36:23. Ps 18:30. *19:7, 8. 77:19. 119:75, 128. 145:17. Pr 10:29. Ezk 18:25. 33:17-20. Da 4:37. Zp 3:5. Ro 7:12. **the just shall walk**. ♪108B. Idiom B827. "To walk" is used for proceeding happily and prosperously. Jb 17:9. Ps 84:5, 7. Pr *10:29. Is 8:13-15. Mt 11:19. Lk 1:17. **but**. Ex *14:20. 1 S 5:11. Ps 119:165. Pr +*4:19. *10:29. 11:5. 15:9. Da +*12:10. Mi 2:7. Na 3:3. Mt *21:44. Lk *2:34. 4:28, 29. 5:8. 7:23. Jn √3:19, 20. 8:9. 9:39. 15:24. Ro 9:32, 33. 1 C 1:23, 24. 2 C 2:15, 16. *7:10. 2 Th √2:9-12. 1 P *2:6-8.

JOEL

JOEL 1

The prophet describes the entire destruction of the fruits of the earth, by drought and noxious insects, 1-7. He calls on the people to lament over their calamities, with prayer and fasting, 8-17. He cries to God for them, and represents the very beasts as joining in his supplications, 18-20.

1. A.M. 3204. B.C. 800. **word**. Je 1:2. Ezk 1:3. Ho 1:1. Ac 1:16. 2 P √1:21. **to**. Ac 2:16. **Pethuel**. i.e. *man of God*, *S#6602h, only here.

2. **Hear**. Dt *32:1. Ps *49:1. Is 34:1. Je 5:21. Ho 5:1. Am 3:1. 4:1. 5:1. Mi 1:2. 3:1, 9. Mt 13:9. Re 2:7. **ye old**. Jb 8:8. 12:12. 15:10. 21:7. **land**. lit. earth. ♪171.O.4, Ho +1:2. **Hath**. ♪85C, Ge +18:14. Jl 2:2. Dt 4:32-35. Is 7:17. Je √30:7. Da +*12:1. Mt *24:21.

3. **Tell ye your children**. Note the reference to the Pentateuch. Other references to the Pentateuch in Joel are at ver. 4, 9, 13, 16. Jl 2:1, 3, 11, 13, 16, 17, 18, 20, 26. 3:1. See related note (Is +*1:2). Ex 10:1, 2. 13:14. Dt 4:9)♃. 6:6, 7)♃. 11:19)♃. Jsh 4:6, 7, 21, 22. Ps 44:1. 71:18. *78:3-8. 145:4. Is 38:19. **children**. ♪50, Ho +2:21.

4. **That which the palmerworm hath left**. Heb. The residue of the palmerworm. Jl 2:25. Am 4:9. The learned Bochart, and others, are of opinion that the four Hebrew words, *gazam, yelek, arbeh, chasil,* respectively rendered *palmerworm, locust, cankerworm,* and *caterpillar,* denote four different species of locusts. See on Ex 10:4. **the locust eaten**. ♪155B, Ge +9:5. Ex 10:12-15. Dt *28:38, 42)♃. 1 K 8:37. 2 Ch 6:28. 7:13. Ps 78:46. 105:34. Je *46:23. Am 7:1. Re 9:3-7. **locust**. ♪50, Ho +2:21. **the cankerworm eaten**. ♪50, Ho +2:21. Na 3:15-17. **the caterpillar**. Is 33:4. Je 51:14, 27.

5. **Awake**. Is 24:7-11. Am 6:3-7. Lk *21:34-37. Ro *13:11-14. **weep**. ver. 11, 13. Je 4:8. Ezk 30:2. Ja 5:1. **for**. Is *32:10-12. Lk *16:19, 23-25.

6. **nation**. Jl 2:2-11, √20, 25. Pr 30:25-27. **my land**. Dt +*32:43. Ps 107:34. Is 8:8. 32:13. Ho 9:3. **whose**. Pr 30:14. Re *9:7-10. **teeth**. ♪155B, Ge +9:5.

7. **laid my vine**. ver. 12. Ex 10:15. Ps *80:8, 13, 14. 105:33. Is *5:1-6. 24:7. 27:2. Je 8:13. Ho 2:12. 10:1. Hab 3:17. **barked my fig tree**. Heb. *laid* my fig tree for a barking. Ho 9:10. Mt 21:19. Lk 13:6, 7.

8. **Lament**. ver. 13-15. Jl 2:12-14. Is *22:12. 24:7-12. 32:11. ◑*62:5. Je 9:17-19. Ja 4:8, 9. 5:1. **the husband**. Pr 2:17. Je 3:4. Ml 2:15.

9. **meat offering**. ver. 13, 16. Jl 2:14. Ex *29:40, 42. Le +*23:13)♃. Ho 9:4. **drink offering**. Ex 29:40)♃. Le +*23:13)♃. Nu 15:3-10)♃. **the priests**. Jl 2:17. La 1:4, 16. **the Lord's**. Ex 28:1. 2 Ch 13:10. Is 61:6. **ministers**. Nu 3:6)♃.

10. **field**. ver. 17-20. Le 26:20. Is 24:3, 4. Je 12:4, 11. 14:2-6. Ho 4:3. **mourneth**. ♪155D, Ge +4:10. **the new wine**. ver. 5, 12. Jl 2:19, 24. Is *24:7, 11. Je 48:33. Ho 9:2. Hg 1:11. **dried up**. *or,* ashamed. ver. 11. Je 2:26. **languisheth**. ♪155C, Le +19:23. Is 16:8.

11. **ashamed**. ver. 10mg. Je *14:3, 4. Ro 5:5. **because**. Is 17:11. Je 9:12.

12. **The vine**. Dr. Shaw (*Travels*, p. 187) observes, that in Barbary, in the month of June, the locusts are no sooner hatched than they collect themselves into compact bodies, each a "furlong or more square; and marching directly after they are come to life, make their way towards the sea and let nothing escape them, eating up every thing that is green or juicy; not only the lesser vegetables, but the *vine* likewise, the *fig tree*, the *pomegranate*, the *palm*, and the *apple tree*, even all the trees of the field." ver. 10. Hab 3:17, 18. **the pomegranate**. Nu 13:23. Ps 92:12. SS 2:3. 4:13. 7:7-9. **joy**. ver. 16. Ps *4:7. Is 9:3. *16:10. 24:11. Je 48:33. Ho 9:1, 2.

13. **Gird**. ver. 8, 9. Jl 2:17. Je *4:8. 9:10. Ezk 7:18. **ye ministers**. Ex 30:20)♃. 1 C 9:13. He 7:13, 14. **lie**. 2 S *12:16. 1 K 21:27. Jon 3:5-8. **sackcloth**. ♪121S3U, Jb +16:15. Da +9:3. **ye ministers**. Is 61:6. 1 C 4:1. 2 C 3:6. 6:4. 11:23. **for**. ver. 9. Le 2:8-10. Nu 29:6. **meat offering**. Le +*23:13. **drink offering**. Le +*23:13.

14. **Sanctify**. Jl 2:15, 16. 2 Ch *20:3, 4. **solemn assembly**. *or,* day of restraint. Jl 2:15. Le +*23:36)♃. Nu 29:35)♃. Dt 16:8)♃. 2 K 10:20. 2 Ch 7:9. Ne 8:18. Is 1:13. Am 5:21mg. **the elders**. Dt 29:10, 11. Jsh +20:4. 2 Ch 20:13. Ne 9:2, 3. **cry**. Jon 3:8.

15. **Alas**. Jg +*6:22. **for the day**. ♪121P4, Dt +4:32. Jl 2:2. Je +*30:7. Am 5:16-18. **the day of the Lord**. Jl 2:1. Ps 37:13. Is +2:12. *13:6-9. Je +*30:7. 46:10. Ezk 7:2-12. 12:22-28. 30:3. Am *5:18. Zp 1:14-18. Lk *19:41-44. Ja 5:9. Re *6:17.

16. **Is not**. ♪85B, Ge +13:9. **the meat**. ver. 5-9, 13. Am 4:6, 7. **joy**. Dt *12:6, 7, 11, 12)♃. 16:10-15)♃. Ps 43:4. 105:3. Is 62:8, 9.

17. **seed**. Heb. grains. **rotten**. ♪24B, Ge +23:16.

18. **the beasts groan**. ver. 20. 1 K 18:5. Je 12:4. 14:5, 6. Ho *4:3. Ro √8:22. **the herds**. ♪63I1C2B, Jb +21:17. Supply ellipsis, "(how are) the herds."

19. **to thee**. Ps +*50:15. 91:15. Mi 7:7. Hab 3:17, 18. Lk *18:1, 7. Ph √4:6, 7. **the fire**. Jl 2:3. Je *9:10. Am 7:4. **pastures**. *or,* habitations. Jl 2:22. Ps 65:12.

20. **cry**. Jb *38:41. Ps *104:21, +27. 145:15. 147:9. **the rivers**. Jl 3:18. 2 S 22:16. 1 K 17:7. 18:5. Ezk +*31:12. **dried up**. Is *5:13. Am *4:8.

JOEL 2

A figurative description of the locusts, as a mighty army, sent forth to ravage the land, 1-11. Earnest calls to public fasting, prayer, and repentance, 12-17. Promises of manifold blessings, 13-27. Predictions of the pouring out of the Spirit, under the gospel; and of subsequent events, 28-32.

1. **Blow**. ver. 15. Nu *10:3, 9. Je 4:5. Ho 8:1. **trumpet**. *or,* cornet. Le +*23:24. 1 Ch 15:28. Ho 5:8. **and sound**. Nu 10:5-7, 9)♃. Ezk 33:3, 6. Am +*3:6. Zp 1:16. **in my**. Jl 3:17. Ps 87:1. Da 9:16, 20. Zp 3:11. Zc 8:3. **holy mountain**. or, mountain of my sanctuary. Is 60:13n. Ezk +*37:26. 40:2n. Zc *1:16. √6:12, 13. **let**. Ezr 9:3, 4. Ps 119:120. Is 66:2, 5. Da 9:22. 10:7, 10. Da 6:26. Ph 2:12. **for the day of the Lord**. ver. 11, 31. Is +*2:12. +*13:6. Ezk 7:5-7, 10, 12. 12:23. Ho 1:15. Am +*5:18. 8:2. Ob 15. Zp *1:14, 15. Ml

*4:1. 1 C +*3:13. 1 Th +*5:2. Ja 5:9. 1 P 4:7.

2. **A day of darkness.** "The quantity of these insects," says Volney (*Travels*, vol. i. p. 188), a French author, "is incredible to all who have not themselves witnessed their astonishing numbers; *the whole earth is covered* with them for the space of several leagues. The *noise* they make in brousing on the trees and herbage may be heard at a great distance, and resembles that of an army in secret. Wherever their myriads spread, the verdure of the country disappears; trees and plants, stripped of their leaves and reduced to their naked boughs and stems, cause the dreary image of *winter* to succeed in an instant to the rich scenery of *spring*. When these clouds of locusts take their flight, to surmount any obstacles or to traverse more rapidly a desert soil, the *heavens* may literally be said to be *obscured* by them." ver. 10, 31. Jl 3:14, 15. Ex 20:21. Ps 97:2. Pr +20:20. Is *5:30. *8:22. Je 13:16. Ezk *32:7, 8. Am *5:18-20. Zp +*1:14, 15. He 12:18. Ju 13. **clouds.** Ge +9:13. Ezk +*30:3. 34:12. **as the morning.** Am 4:13. or, blackness, or darkness. Heb. *shahar.* A homonym with two meanings: (1) to be *black* or *dark* (Jb 30:30). Hence put for seeking in the early morning while yet dark (Ps 78:34. 63:1. Pr 1:28. Is 26:9. Ho 5:15); (2) *dawn* or *morning* (Ge 19:15. 32:24, 26. Jsh 6:15. Ho *6:3. 10:15). **a great.** ver. 5, 11, 25. Jl 1:6. **there hath not been.** Jl 1:2, 3. Ex 10:6, 14. Da +*12:1. Mk *13:19. **ever.** Heb. *olam*, Ps +5:11. **many generations.** Heb. generation and generation. Dt 32:7mg. Ps 10:6mg.

3. **fire.** Jl 1:19, 20. Ps 50:3. Am 7:4. **devoureth before.** Is 24:6, 10. Re 9:16. **the land.** Ge 2:8)*P*. 13:10)*P*. Is 51:3. Ezk 28:13. 31:8, 9. 36:35. **and behind.** Jl 1:4-7. Ex 10:5, 15. Je 5:17. Zc *7:14. **desolate wilderness.** Jl 3:19. Ps 107:34mg.

4. **as the appearance.** Hab 1:8. Re *9:7.

5. **the noise.** Na 2:3, 4. 3:2, 3. Re *9:9. **like the noise of a.** Is 5:24. 30:30. Mt 3:12. **a strong people.** Not locusts. The symbol must not be confused with what is symbolized (CB). ver. 2.

6. **all.** Ps 119:83. Is 13:8. Je 8:21. *30:6. La 4:8. Na 2:10. **blackness.** Heb. pot.

7. **They shall run.** In their progress, says Dr. Shaw, "they kept their ranks like men of war; climbing over every tree or wall that was in their way. Nay, they *entered into our very houses* and bedchambers, like *so many thieves*. Every effort of the inhabitants to stop them was unavailing; the trenches they had dug were quickly filled up, and the fires they had kindled extinguished, by infinite swarms succeeding each other." 2 S 1:23. 2:18, 19. Ps 19:5. Is 5:26-29. **climb.** ver. 9. 2 S 5:8. Je 5:10. **they shall march.** Pr *30:27.

8. **sword.** or, dart. 2 Ch 23:10. 32:5mg. Ne 4:17, 23. Jb 33:18. 36:12. SS 4:13.

9. **enter.** Ex 10:6. Je 9:21. Jn *10:1. **windows.** Is 24:10. Je *9:21. **like a thief.** A thief is a man (not an insect); so are these (CB). Mt 24:43, 44. Lk 12:39. 1 Th *5:2. 2 P *3:10.

10. **earth.** Ps 18:7. 114:7. Na 1:5. Mt 27:51. Re 6:12. 20:11. **the heavens.** Is 34:4. **the sun.** ver. 2, 31. Jl 3:15. Is *13:10. 34:4. Je 4:23. Ezk 32:7. Am 5:8. Mt √24:29. Mk 13:24, 25. Lk 21:25, 26. Ac 2:20. Re 6:12. 8:12. **dark.** Pr +20:20.

11. **utter.** Jl 3:16. 2 S 22:14, 15. Ps 46:6. Is 7:18. 13:4. 42:13. Je *25:30. Am 1:2. **his army.** ver. 25. **he is.** Je 50:34. Re 18:8. **the day of the Lord.** ver. +*1,

31. Je +*30:7. Am 5:18, 20. Zp √1:14, 15. Re *6:17. **who.** Nu *24:23)*P*. Je *10:10. Na 1:6. Zp 1:14. Ml *3:2. Re 6:17.

12. **now.** Ac √17:30. 2 C *6:2. **turn.** Dt *4:29, 30. 1 S 7:3. 1 K *8:47-49. 2 Ch 6:38, 39. *7:13, +√14. Is √55:6, 7. Je *4:1. 29:12, 13. La 3:40, 41. Ho *5:15. *6:1. 12:6. *14:1, 2. Zc 1:3, 4. Ac 26:20. **with all your heart.** Dt +6:5)*P*. 2 K +*20:3. 1 Ch 12:38n. Ps *95:7, 8. **with fasting.** ver. 15. Jg +20:26n. 1 S 7:6. 2 Ch *20:3, 4. Ne 9:1, 2. Is 22:12. Jon 3:5-8. Zc 7:3, 5. *12:10-14. Ja *4:8, 9. **with mourning.** T#1264. Ne 1:4. Ps 35:13, 14. 55:1, 2. 88:9. Da 10:12. Zc 12:10.

13. **rend.** ♪162B, 2 Ch +*31:8. Here the word "rend" is used only once, but with two significations: in the former sentence it is used figuratively; in the latter literally—the heart not being rent in the same sense in which garments are rent. 2 K 22:19. Ps *34:18. *51:17. 147:3. Is *57:15. 66:2. Ezk *9:4. Mt +*5:3, 4. **not your garments.** Ge 37:29, 34)*P*. Nu 14:19. 2 S 1:11. 1 K 21:27. 2 K 5:7. 6:30. 22:11. Jb 1:20. Is 58:5. Mt *6:16-18. 1 T *4:8. **he is gracious.** Ex *34:6, 7)*P*. Nu 14:18)*P*. 2 Ch 30:9. Ne 9:17, 31. Ps 86:5, 15. 103:8. 145:7-9. Jon *4:2. Mi *7:18. Ro *2:4. *5:20, 21. Ep *2:4. **and merciful.** Jon +4:2. **slow.** Ne 9:17. Ps 103:8. Na 1:3. Ja *1:19, 20. 2 P +*3:9. **and repenteth.** ♪22B, Ge +6:6. Dt 32:36. Ps 106:45. Je 18:7, 8. Am 7:2-6. Jon 4:2. 2 C 12:10.

14. **Who.** Ex 32:30. Jsh 14:12. 1 S 6:5. 2 S *12:22. 2 K 19:4. Am *5:15. Jon 1:6. √3:9. Zp 2:3. 2 T 2:25. **repent.** ♪22B, Ge +6:6. **and leave.** Is *65:8. Hg *2:19. 2 C 9:5-11mg. even. Jl 1:9, 13, 16. **meat offering.** Le +*23:13. **drink offering.** Le +*23:13.

15. **Blow.** ver. 1. Nu *10:3, 7. **sanctify a fast.** T#892. ver. +12. Jl 1:14. 1 K 21:9, 12. 2 K 10:20. Je 36:9.

16. **sanctify.** Ex *19:10, 14, 15, 22)*P*. Jsh 7:13. 1 S 16:5. 2 Ch 29:5, 23, 24. 30:17, 19. 35:6. Jb 1:5. **assemble.** Jl 1:14. Dt 29:10, 11. 2 Ch *20:13. Jon 3:7, 8. **gather the children.** Dt +*29:11n. Ne +*12:43. Is 54:13. Mt 14:21. 15:38. 19:13-15. Lk 18:15. Mk 9:36, 37. **let.** Zc 12:11-14. Mt 9:15. 1 C *7:5. **closet.** Ps 19:5. Is 4:5.

17. **the priests.** Jl 1:9, 13. **between.** 1 K *6:3. 2 Ch 8:12. Ezk *8:16. Mt *23:35. **and let.** Ho 14:2. **Spare.** Ex 32:11-13)*P*. 34:9. Dt *9:16-29)*P*. Ne 13:22. Ps 118:25. Is 37:20. 64:9-12. Da 9:18, 19. Am 7:2, 5. Ml 1:9. **and give.** Ps 44:10-14. 74:10, 18-23. 79:4. 89:41, 51. Ezk 36:4-7. **thine heritage.** Dt 32:9)*P*. **that.** Ne 9:36, 37. Is 63:17-19. **rule over them.** or, use a byword against them. Dt 28:37. 1 K 9:7. 2 Ch 7:20. Ps 44:14. **wherefore.** Nu 14:14-16. Dt 9:26-29)*P*. 32:27. Ps *42:10. 79:10. 115:2. Ezk 20:9. *39:22. Mi *7:10. Mt 27:43.

18. **Then.** ver. 12, 17, 28n. Ezk 36:25n. 39:28n. Ho 5:15. **be jealous.** ♪22B, Ex +20:5. Is 42:13. Zc *1:14. 8:2. **his land.** Le +*25:23n. Dt +*32:43)*P*. Ezk +*38:16. Ho 9:3. **and pity.** ♪22B. Anthropomorphism B883. *Pity* is attributed to God. Dt *32:16, 36, 43. Jg 10:16. Ps 103:13, 17. Is *60:10. 63:9, 15. Je 31:20. La 3:22. Ezk 36:21. Ho 11:8, 9. Lk *15:20. Ja 5:11. **his people.** Dt +*32:43. Ezk *38:14.

19. **will answer.** Is +*65:24. **I will send.** ver. 24. Jl 1:10. Is 62:8, 9. 65:21-24. Ezk *36:29. Ho *2:15, 22. Am *9:13, 14. Hg 2:16-19. Zc *9:17. Ml *3:10-12. **be satisfied.** ver. 26. Ps *81:13, 16. Mt √6:33. **and I.** Ezk 34:29. 36:15. 39:29. Zp 3:19, 20.

20. **remove.** ver. 2-11. Jl 1:4-6. Ex *10:19. Is

+*59:19. Ezk 39:2-4. **the northern army.** Je *1:14, 15. Da +*11:40-45. Ezk *38:6, 15. *39:2. Re 9:3-11, 13-19. **will drive him.** Is 59:19. **the east sea.** The East sea is the Dead Sea, once the fertile vale of Siddim (Ge 14:3), in which sea were formerly Sodom and Gomorrah, Admah and Zeboim, until God overthrew them. The Dead Sea is called the salt sea in Scripture. Ge 14:13. Nu 34:3, 12. Dt 3:17. 4:49. Jsh 3:16. 12:3. 15:25. 18:19. 2 K 14:25. Ezk 47:7, 8, 18. Zc *14:8. **the utmost sea.** or, western. The *utmost sea* is rather the *hinder sea*, that is, that which is behind one who is looking toward the East, the name in Hebrew from "fronting you," a reference to the Mediterranean (Pusey, *Minor Prophets*, p. 187). Dt *11:24)‣℘. 34:2)‣℘. Zc 14:8. **his stink.** Is +*66:24. Ezk √39:12-16. **because.** 2 K 8:13. **he.** The invader, the antichrist or beast of Da ch. 7 and 8 (CB). **done.** Heb. magnified to do. Ps +126:2mg, 3. Je 48:26. Da +*8:11, 25. +*11:36. 2 Th √2:4. Re √13:5-7.

21. **Fear not.** Ge 15:1. Is 41:10. 54:4. Je 30:9, 10. Zp 3:16, 17. Zc 8:15. **O land.** ⨍38G, Dt +32:1. **be glad.** Ps 65:12, 13. 96:11, 12. 98:8. Is 35:1, 2. 44:23. 55:12, 13. Ho +2:15, 21, 22. **for the Lord.** ver. 20. Dt 4:32. 1 S 12:16, 24. Ps 71:19. +*126:1-3. Je √33:3.
22. **Be not afraid.** Jl 1:18-20. Ps 36:6. 104:11-14, 27-29. 145:15, 16. 147:8, 9. Is √11:6-9. *30:23, 24. √65:25. Ezk *34:25. Ho +*2:18. Jon 4:11. Ro √8:19-21. **ye beasts.** ⨍38F, Ps +148:7. **for the pastures.** Jl 1:19. Ps 65:12. Is 51:3. **for the tree.** Le 26:4, 5. Ps *67:6. 107:35-38. Ezk 34:26, 27. 36:8, 30, 35. Ho 14:5-7. Am √9:14, 15. Hg 2:16-20. Zc √8:12. Ml 3:10-12. **yield.** Ge ◖*4:12. Ro *8:19-23. 1 C 3:7. Re √22:3. **strength.** Strength is here put for abundance, ⨍121N2. Metonymy of the Adjunct, Ge +34:29.
23. **Be glad.** Is *65:18. **ye children of Zion.** Ps 149:2. La 4:2. Zc 9:13. Ga 4:26, 27. **rejoice.** Ps 28:7. 32:11. 33:1. 95:1-3. 104:34. Is 12:2-6. 41:16. *61:10. Ho +2:15. Hab 3:17, 18. Zp 3:14-17. Zc +*2:10. √9:9. *10:7. Lk 1:46, 47. Ph 3:1, 3. *4:4. **the former rain.** *or*, a teacher of righteousness. ver. 28, 29. Dt 32:2. Jb 33:23. Ps 72:6, 7. Is 30:21, 23. Da +*11:33. Ho 10:12n. Ep √4:8-11. **moderately.** Heb. according to righteousness. or, in due measure. Le 26:4)‣℘. Dt 11:14)‣℘. 28:12)‣℘. **he will.** Le *26:4. Dt +11:14. 28:12. Pr 16:15. Je 3:3. 5:24. Ho +*6:3. Zc *10:1. Ja √5:7, 8. **in the first.** Pusey (*Minor Prophets*, p. 191) states, "This would belong only to the latter rain, which falls about the first month, Nisan, or our April, *the former rain* falling about 6 months earlier, at their seed time (Ho 6:3)." Ge 8:13. Nu 9:5. Ezk 29:17. 45:18, 21. Am 4:7. or, as at the first. Is √1:26. Ho +2:15. Ml 3:4.
24. **the floors.** Jl 3:13, 18. Ge +50:10. Le 26:10. Dt +*16:13mg. Pr *3:9, 10. Am *9:13. Ml √3:10. **the fats.** Jl 3:13. Is 5:2.
25. **I will restore.** Jb 42:10mg. Pr *22:4. Is 54:4. √61:7. Ezk 18:22n. Mt +*19:28. Ac +*3:19, 21. Ro *8:19-23. **the years.** Jb *42:10. Ps *31:15. +*90:12. +*91:16. Is ◖+*38:10. √61:7. **that the locusts.** ver. 2-11. Jl 1:4-7. Zc √10:6. **my great army.** ⨍103. Figure of speech Hypocatastisis, Ge +3:13. Here the symbol, and what is symbolized, are joined together, and the army of men (ver. 11, 20) is implied by the Figure *Hypocatastasis* (CB).
26. **ye shall eat.** Le *26:5, 26)‣℘. Dt 6:11, 12. 8:10. Ne 9:25. Ps *22:26. 103:5. Pr 13:25. SS 5:1. Is 55:2. 62:8, 9. Mi 6:14. Zc 9:15, 17. 1 T 6:17. **and praise.**

Le 19:24)‣℘. Dt 12:7, 12, 18)‣℘. 16:11)‣℘. 26:10, 11)‣℘. 1 T 4:3-5. **that he.** ver. 20, 21. Ge 33:11. Ps 13:6. 72:18. 116:7. *126:2, 3. Is 25:1. **my people.** ⨍76, Ge +13:6. Dt +*32:43. **never be ashamed.** Ps 25:2, 3. *37:19. Is √29:22, 23. *45:17. 49:23. *54:4. Zp *3:11. Ro 5:5. 9:33. 10:11. 1 J 2:28.
27. **ye shall know.** ver. 17. Jl *3:17. Le *26:11-13)‣℘. Dt 23:14)‣℘. Ps *9:16. Ezk +*39:22. Ho 8:2. **in the midst.** Jl *3:17. Le 26:11, 12. Dt 23:14. Ps *46:5. 68:18. Is +*12:6. Ezk √37:26-28. Zp √3:5, 15, 17. Zc 2:5. 2 C 6:16. Re 21:3. **that I am the Lord.** Is *45:5, 6, 18, 21, 22. 52:6. *53:6. Ezk +*39:22, 28. **my people.** ⨍76, Ge +13:6. Dt +*32:43. **shall never be ashamed.** ver. 26. 1 P 2:6.
28. **And it shall.** Zc 13:4. Ac ▸2:17-21. **afterward.** Note carefully this time indicator. Had Israel responded to their Messiah at the first advent, or had they responded to the preaching of the apostles recorded in Acts (Ac 3:18-26), the "times of refreshing" would have immediately been ushered in (Ac +*3:19, 21), and the subsequent elements of this prophecy would then have come to pass. The context shows the promise is primarily to natural Israel (thus the command to go to the Jew first, Ac +*1:8. Ro +*1:16), to whom the apostles offered it, and will come to pass "afterwards," that is, after the events just predicted in the preceding passage: the full restoration (ver. 25) of Israel to their land, with God himself dwelling in their midst (ver. 27), upon their repentance and earnest calling upon Him (ver. 13). Since the church has never replaced natural Israel in the plan of God, because of the irrevocable promise of the "sure mercies of David" made exclusively to natural Israel (Is +*55:3), both the application and ultimate fulfillment of this prophecy are reserved until after the second advent of Christ, when the blessings of this promise will be made available to "all flesh" through Israel as the spiritual center of the earth (Ge 12:3. Mi 4:1, 2. Zc 8:3, 22, 23). ver. +*18. Is +*32:15. Ezk 36:25n. **that I.** Pr *1:23. Is *32:15. *44:3. Ezk *39:29. Zc *12:10. Jn *7:39. Ac √2:16-18. 1 C *12:8. Ep *4:8, 11. **pour out.** ⨍22C38, Ps +79:6. ⨍22K4, Je +2:13. **spirit.** Heb. *ruach*, Ge +41:38. **upon all.** √⨍171B, Ge +24:10. **flesh.** Is *40:5. √49:6. Zc √12:10. Lk *3:6. Ac √2:2-4, 33, 39. 10:44-47. 11:15-18. 15:7, 8. **your daughters.** Is *54:13. Hab *2:14. Ac 21:9. Ga 3:28. He +*8:11. 1 J *2:20. **shall prophesy.** Ex +15:20n. Nu 11:16, 17, 29. Ac *21:9. 1 C 11:5, 13. **dream.** Ge 37:5-10. Nu 12:6. Je √23:28n.
29. **upon the servants and.** 1 C 7:21. √12:13. Ga *3:28. Col *3:11. **pour out.** ⨍22C38, Ps +79:6. ⨍22K4, Je +2:13. **spirit.** Ge +41:38.
30. **show wonders in the heavens.** Mt √24:29. Mk 13:24. Lk *21:11, 25, 26. Ac *2:19, 20. Re √6:12-17. **pillars of smoke.** Ge 19:28. Jsh 8:20. Jg 20:38, 40. SS 3:6. Re *18:9, 18.
31. **The sun shall.** ver. 10. Jl 3:1, 15. Is 13:9, 10. 34:4, 5. Zc 14:6. Mt √24:29. 27:45. Mk 13:24, 25. Lk 21:25. Re *6:12, 13. **the moon into.** Re 6:12. **before.** Ml 4:5. **the great and terrible.** ver. 11. Zp +*1:14. Ml *4:1, 5. **day of the Lord.** ver. +*1, +*11.
32. **whosoever shall call.** Ps +*50:15. Is √55:6, 7. Je √33:3. Zc √13:9. Ac ▸2:21. Ro √10:11-14. 1 C 1:2. **delivered.** Is 57:1. Lk +√21:36. Ro ▸10:13. 1 Th 4:17. **for in mount Zion.** Is 46:13. *59:20, 21. Ob *17, 21. Zc √14:1-5. Jn 4:22. Ro √11:26. He *12:22. **shall be deliverance.** Na *1:2. Lk +*21:36. 1 Th +*1:9, 10.

*5:9. **and in the remnant.** Is 1:9. 10:22. √11:11, 16. Je 31:7. Mi *4:6, 7. 5:3, 7, 8. Jn +*10:16. Ac 2:39. 15:17. Ro √8:28-30. *9:27. +*11:5, 7, 23. **shall call.** Ro √9:24. 2 Th +*2:13, 14. 2 T +*1:9.

JOEL 3

Prophecies of divine judgments to be executed upon the enemies of God's people, 1-15; and of the subsequent peace, prosperity, security, and purity of Israel, 16-21.

1. **in those days.** Jl 2:29. Da +*12:1. Zp 3:19, 20. **when.** Jl +2:25. Dt *30:3♪℘. 2 Ch 6:37, 38. Jb *42:10. Ps 14:7. 85:1. *126:1, 4. Is √11:11, etc. Je 16:15. *23:3-8. 29:14. *30:3, 18. Ezk *16:53. *37:21, 22. *38:14-18. *39:25, 28, 29. Am √9:14.

2. **also gather.** Zp *3:8. Zc +*12:2. √14:2-4. Re 16:14, 16. 19:19-21. 20:8. **the valley of Jehoshaphat.** ver. 12. 2 Ch=20:21-26. Ezk *39:11. Zc *14:4. **will plead.** Is *66:16. Je 25:31. Ezk *38:22. Am 1:11. Ob 10-16. Zc 12:3, 4. Re 11:18. 16:6. 18:20, 21. **My people.** Dt +*32:43. Ho 2:23. Mt 25:31-46. **My heritage.** Dt 32:9♪℘. **Israel.** Ezk √37:22. **and parted my land.** Je 12:14. 49:1. Ezk 25:8. 35:10. Zp 2:8-10.

3. **They have.** Ob 16. Na 3:11. **cast lots.** Jsh +14:2n. 2 Ch 28:8, 9. Am 2:6. Ob *11. Na *3:10. Re 18:13.

4. **and what.** Jg 11:12. 2 Ch 21:16. 28:17, 18. Ac 9:4. **O Tyre.** Am *1:6-10, 12-14. Zc 9:2-8. **Palestine.** i.e. *land of wanderers,* ✱S#6429h. Ex 15:14. Ps 60:8. 83:7. 87:4. 108:9. Is 14:29, 31. **will ye.** Ezk *25:12-17. **swiftly.** Dt 32:35. Is 34:8. 59:18. Je 51:6. Lk 18:7. 2 Th 1:6. He 10:30.

5. **ye.** 2 K 12:18. 16:8. 18:15, 16. 24:13. 25:13-17. Je 50:28. 51:11. Da 5:2, 3. **into.** 1 S 5:2-5. **pleasant.** Heb. desirable. Is 44:9mg. Da +10:3mg. 11:+8mg, 38mg.

6. **children of.** ♪144A3, Ge +11:5. **have ye.** ver. 3, 8. Dt 28:32, 68. Ezk +*27:13. **Grecians.** Heb. sons of the Grecians.

7. **I will raise.** Is 11:12. *43:5, 6. *49:12. Je *23:8. 30:10, 11, 16. 31:8. 32:37. Ezk +*34:12, 13. +*36:24. +*38:8. Zc *10:6-10. **and will.** ver. 4. Ge +*6:13 (T#566). Jg 1:7. 1 S 15:33. Est 7:10. Mt *7:2. Ro +*12:19. 2 Th +*1:6, 7. Ja *2:13. Re 13:10. 16:6, 7. 19:2.

8. **I will.** Dt 32:30. Jg 2:14. 4:2, 9. **your sons and.** Is 14:1, 2. 60:14. **Sabeans.** i.e. *they who come; go about; busybodies,* ✱S#7615h, only here. Ge 10:7. Jb *1:15. Ezk *23:42. **far off.** Je 6:20.

9. **Proclaim.** Ps 96:10. Is 34:1. Je 31:10. 50:2. **Prepare.** Heb. Sanctify. Ezk 21:21, 22. Re *16:14. **wake.** Is *8:9, 10. Je *46:3, 4. Ezk *38:7.

10. **your plowshares.** Is ◑*2:4. Ho *2:18. Mi ◑*4:3. Lk +*22:36. **pruning hooks.** or, scythes. **let.** 2 Ch 25:8. Is 45:24. Zc 12:8. 2 C *12:9.

11. **Assemble.** ver. 2. Ezk *38:9-18. Mi *4:12. Zp +*3:8. Zc *14:2, 3. Re *16:14-16. *19:19, 20. 20:8, 9. **cause,** etc. or, the Lord shall bring down thy mighty ones. Ps *103:20. Is 10:34. *13:3. 37:36. Mt *13:41. 2 Th √1:7. Re *19:14. **to come down.** Ps +*149:9. Ho +*11:12. Zc +*14:5. Ju *14, *15. Re *17:14.

12. **valley.** ver. 2, 14. 2 Ch 20:26. Ezk 39:11. Zc *14:4, 5. **and come up.** Ps *2:8, 9. 7:6. 76:8, 9. *96:13. 98:9. *110:5, 6. Is *2:4. *3:13. Ezk +*30:3. Mi *4:3. Re 19:11. **Jehoshaphat.** *Jehoshaphat* denotes *the judgment of the Lord*; and is probably a descriptive name of the same place which St. John calls *Armageddon.* **there will I sit.** ver. 2. 2 S 12:30, 31. Je +43:11. Mt √25:31-46.

13. **the sickle.** Dt 16:9. Je 50:16. Mk 4:29. Re 14:15, 16, 18. **the harvest.** ♪121P10, Dt +24:19. Je *51:33. Ho *6:11. Mt *13:39. **for the press.** Jl 2:24. Is *63:3. La 1:15. Re *14:17-20. **for their.** Ge 13:13. 15:16. 18:20. Da *8:23. Mt *23:32.

14. **multitudes.** ver. 2. Is 34:2-8. 63:1-7. Ezk *38:8-23. *39:8-20. Re 16:14-16. *19:17-21. **decision.** or, concision. Ph 3:2. or, threshing. 2 K 13:7. Is 41:15. **for the day of the Lord.** Jl 2:1. Ps 37:13. 2 P 3:7.

15. **The sun.** Jl +*2:10, 31. Is 5:30. 13:10. 34:4. Zc 14:6. Mt √24:29. Lk 21:25, 26. Re *6:12, 13.

16. **roar.** ♪22F1, Is +42:13. Jl 2:11. Is *42:13. Je *25:30, 31. Ezk *38:18-22. Ho 11:10. Am 1:2. 3:8. **heavens and earth.** Jl 2:10. Ezk *38:19, 20. Hg +*2:6. He +*12:26, 27. Re 11:13, 19. 16:18. **shall shake.** Is 2:19, 21. He +*12:26. **hope.** Heb. place of repair, or, harbor. Ps 18:2. ch. 46. 61:3. 91:1, 2. *146:5. Pr 18:10. Is 33:16, 21. 51:5, 6, 16. Je *14:8. *17:7. **and the strength.** 1 S 15:29. Ps 29:11. Zc *10:6, 12. 12:5-8.

17. **shall ye know.** ver. 21. Jl 2:27. Ps 9:11. 76:2. Is 12:6. Ezk 6:7. 48:35. Mi √4:7. Zp *3:14-16. **dwelling in Zion.** Ps *2:6. +*102:16. **my holy mountain.** Da *11:45. Ob 16. Zc *8:3. **Jerusalem.** Is 4:3. Je 31:23. Ezk 43:12. Ob 17. Zc 14:20. **holy.** Heb. holiness. **there.** Is 35:8. *52:1. Na *1:15. Zc *14:21. Re *21:27.

18. **in that day.** Ps +*118:24. **the mountains.** Jb 29:6. Is *55:12, 13. Am *9:13, 14. **and all.** Is 30:25. 35:6. 41:17, 18. **rivers.** Jl 1:20. 2 S 22:16. Is *41:18, 19. 43:19. Ezk +*31:12. **flow.** Heb. go. Zc *14:8. **and a fountain.** Heb. *mayan,* Ge +7:11. Ps *46:4. Ezk *47:1-12. Zc *14:8. Re *22:1, 2, 17. **of the house.** Ezk *47:1. **the valley.** Nu *25:1. Mi 6:5. **Shittim.** Nu *25:1. 33:49♪℘. Jsh 2:1. Mi *6:5.

19. **Egypt.** Is 11:15. *19:1, etc. Zc 10:10, 11. 14:18, 19. **Edom.** Is 34:1, etc. 63:1-6. Je *49:17. La 4:21. Ezk ch. 25, 35. Am *1:11, 12. Ob 1, 10, etc. Ml 1:3, 4. **for the violence.** Ps 137:7. Je 51:35. Ob 10-16. Hab 2:8. 2 Th 1:6. **against.** ♪181E, Ge +3:24. **innocent blood.** Dt 19:10♪℘. 27:25♪℘.

20. **Judah.** Is 33:20. Ezk +*37:25. Am √9:15. **dwell.** or, abide. or, remain, be established. S#3427h. ver. 12 (sit). Ps 9:7 (endure). 29:10 (sitteth). Is 13:20 (inhabited). Je 50:13, 39, 40. La 5:19 (remainest). Ho 3:3, 4. **for ever.** Heb. *olam,* Ex +*12:24.

21. **will cleanse.** Nu ◑*35:23. Is *4:4. Ezk 36:25, 29. Mt 27:25. **cleansed.** or, cleared. Ex ◑34:7. Nu 14:18. If the text should read *nakam* instead of *nakah, avenge* instead of *clear,* this would be a vivid reference to the Pentateuch (CB). Dt 32:42, 43♪℘. 2 K 9:7. Re 6:10, 11. **for the Lord.** or, even I the Lord that. ver. 17. Ps 87:3. Ezk *48:35. Re 21:3.

AMOS

AMOS 1

Some account of the prophet, and of the time when he prophesied, 1, 2. The judgments of God on Syria, 3-5; Philistia, 6-8; Tyre, 9, 10; Edom, 11, 12; and Ammon, 13-15.

1. **The words**. Je 1:1. 7:27. **Amos**. i.e. *to lade, to burden*, *S#5986h. Am 7:8, 10, 11, 12, 14. 8:2. **who**. Am *7:14. Ex 3:1. 1 K 19:19. Ps 78:70-72. Mt 4:18, 19. 1 C 1:27. **Tekoa**. 2 S 14:2. 2 Ch 11:6. 20:20. Je 6:1. **he saw**. Is 1:1. Mi 1:1. **in the**. 2 K 14:21. 15:1, 2, Azariah. 2 Ch ch. 26. Ho 1:1. Mt 1:8, 9, Ozias. **and in**. Am 7:9-11. 2 K 14:23-29. **the earthquake**. *106, Ge +31:20. Zc *14:5.

2. **The Lord**. Am 3:7, 8. Pr 20:2. Is 42:13. Je *25:30. Ho 13:8. Jl 2:11. *3:16. **roar**. *22F1, Is +42:13. **the habitations**. Am 4:7, 8. Is *33:9. Je 12:4. 14:2. Jl 1:9-13, 16-18. **mourn**. *155D, Ge +4:10. **Carmel**. 1 S 25:2. Is 33:9. *35:2. Je 50:19. Na 1:4.

3. **For three**. Hebrew idiom to express several, or many (CB). ver. 6, 9, 11, 13. Am 2:1, 4, 6. Jb 5:19. 19:3. 33:29mg. Pr 6:16. 30:15, 18, 21, 29. Ec 11:2. **Damascus**. Is 7:8. *8:4. √17:1. Je 49:23-27. Zc 9:1. **and four**. *or*, yea, for four. **turn away the punishment thereof**. *or*, convert it, *or*, let it be quiet, *and so* ver. 6, 9, etc. **because**. 1 K 19:17. 2 K 8:12. 10:32, 33. 13:3, 7. Is 41:15. **threshed Gilead**. 2 K *13:7. Jl 3:14. **with**. *103. Hypocatastasis, Ge +3:13.

4. **I will**. ver. 7, 10, 12, 14. Am 2:2, 5. Jg 9:19, 20, 57. Je 17:27. *49:27. 50:32. Ezk 30:8. 39:6. Ho 8:14. **Hazael**. 1 K 19:15. 2 K 8:7-15. 10:32, 33. 13:3. **palaces**. or, fortresses. ver. 7, 10, 12, 14. Am 2:2, 5. 3:9, 9, 10, 11. 6:8. **Ben-hadad**. 1 K 20:1, etc. 2 K 6:24. *13:3, 25. 2 Ch 16:2.

5. **break**. Dt 3:5. 1 K 4:13. Is 43:14mg. Je 50:36mg. 51:30. La 2:9. Na 3:13. **the plain of Aven**. *or*, Bikathaven. Probably *Heliopolis*, now *Baalbek*, situated between Libanus and Antilibanus, 56 miles N.W. of Damascus, according to Antoninus, and celebrated for its temple of the sun. Ho 4:15. 5:8. 10:5, 8. **the house of Eden**. *or*, Beth-eden. Probably the village of *Eden*, in Mount Lebanon, marks the site of this place. It is delightfully situated by the side of a most rich and cultivated valley, contains about 400 or 500 families, and is, according to modern authorities, about 20 miles S.E. of Tripoli, and five miles from the cedars. 2 K *19:12. Is 37:12. Ezk 27:23. **the people**. Am 9:7. 2 K 16:9. Is 22:6.

6. **three**. ver. 3, 9, 11. **Gaza**. 1 S 6:17. 2 Ch 28:18. Is √14:28-31. Je *47:4, 5. Ezk *25:15, 16. Zp *2:4-7. Zc 9:5. Ac 8:26. **carried**, etc. *or*, carried them away with an entire captivity. Ch 21:16, 17. 28:17mg. Je 13:19. 47:1. Jl 3:6. **to Edom**. ver. 9, 11. Ezk 35:5. Ob 11.

7. **I will**. Dt 32:35, 41-43. Ps 75:7, 8. 94:1-5. Zp 2:4. Ro *12:19. **a fire**. ver. 4. 2 K 18:8. 2 Ch 26:6. Je 25:18-20. *47:1. Zc 9:5-7. **wall**. *171S5, Ge +14:7. By Synecdoche of the Part, "wall" is put for the whole city enclosed by it. ver. 10, 14.

8. **I will cut**. Is 20:1. Je 47:5. Ezk 25:16. **from Ashkelon**. 1 S 6:17. Zc *9:5, 6. **turn**. Ps 81:14. Is 1:25.

Zc 13:7. **hand**. *22A14.8G, Is +1:25. **and the**. Is 14:29-31. Je 47:4, 5. Ezk 25:16. Zp 2:4-7.

9. **Tyrus**. Is. ch. 23. Je 47:1-7. Ezk ch. *26-28. Jl 3:4-8. Zc 9:2-4. **because**. ver. 6, 11. **brotherly covenant**. Heb. covenant of brethren. 2 S 5:11. 1 K 5:1-11. 9:11-14. 2 Ch 2:8-16.

10. **send a fire**. ver. 4, 7, etc. Ezk 26:12. Zc 9:4. **wall**. *171S5, Ge +14:7. ver. *7.

11. **Edom**. Is 21:11, 12. ch. *34. 63:1-7. Je √49:7-22. La 4:21. Ezk *25:12-14. 32:29. ch. 35. Ob 1, etc. Ml 1:4. **because**. Ge 27:40, 41)𝒫. Nu √20:14-21. Dt 2:4-8. √23:7. 2 Ch 28:17. Ps 83:3-8. 137:7. La 4:21, 22. Ezk 25:12. 35:5, 6, 11. Jl *3:19. Ob 10-14. Ml *1:2. Note reference to the Pentateuch. Other references are at ver. 14. Am 2:4, 7, 8, 9, 10, 11. 3:1, 2, 9, 14. 4:1, 2, 4, 5, 7, 9, 10, 11, 13. 5:4, 7, 12, 17, 21, 22. 6:1, 2, 12, 14. 7:3, 16. 8:5, 7, 10. 9:4, 6, 7, 13, 14, 15. See related note (Is +*1:2). **his brother**. Ge 25:24-26)𝒫. **did cast off all pity**. Heb. corrupted his compassions. **tear**. 2 Ch 28:17. **perpetually**. Heb. *ad*, Ps +9:18 (*S#5703h). **kept his wrath**. Ps *83:4, 6. 85:5. *137:7. Ec 7:9. Is 57:16. Mi *7:18. Ep 4:26, 27. 5:1. **for ever**. Heb. *netsach*, Jb +4:20 (*S#5331h).

12. **Teman**. Ge *36:11, 15. Jb 2:11. Je 49:7, 20. Ob 9, 10. Hab 3:3. **Bozrah**. Ge *36:31, 33. Is *34:6. √63:1. Je *49:13, 22.

13. **the children**. Dt 2:19. 1 S 11:1. Je √49:1-6. Ezk 21:28. *25:2-7. Zp *2:8-11. **and for**. Dt 23:3, 4. Jg 10:7-9. 11:15-28. 1 S 11:1, 2. 2 S 10:1-8. 2 K 24:2. 2 Ch 20:1, 10. Ne 2:19. 4:7, etc. Ps 83:7. **because**. 2 K 8:12. 15:16. Ho 10:14. *13:16. **ripped up the women with child**. *or*, divided the mountains. **enlarge**. Is 5:8. Je 49:1. Ezk 35:10. Hab 2:5, 6.

14. **kindle**. Je 17:27. **wall**. *171S5, Ge +14:7. ver. *7. **Rabbah**. Dt 3:11)𝒫. 2 S 11:1. *12:26, 27. Je *49:2. Ezk *25:5. **with shouting**. Am 2:2. Jb 39:25. Is 9:5. **with a**. Ps 83:15. Is 30:30. Da 11:40. Zc 7:14.

15. **their king**. Je *49:3.

AMOS 2

The judgment of God against Moab, for his impotent revenge on the dead king of Edom, 1-3; on Judah, for his contempt of God's law, 4, 5; and on Israel, for idolatry, iniquity, and ingratitude, 6-16.

1. **For three**. ver. 4, 6. Am 1:3, 6, 9, 11, 13. Nu ch. 20-25. Dt 23:4, 5. Ps 83:4-7. Mi 6:5. **of Moab**. Is 11:14. ch. 15, 16. 25:10. Je ch. 48. Ezk *25:8-10. *Zp 2:8, 9. **because**. 2 K 3:9, 26, 27. Pr 15:3. **burned**. *106, Ge +31:7.

2. **Kirioth**. i.e. *cities*, *S#7152h. Jsh 15:25. Je *48:24, 41. **with tumult**. Am 1:14. Is 9:5. Je 48:34.

3. **cut off**. Nu +*24:17, 18. Je *48:7, 25.

4. **For**. Dt 31:16-18. 32:15-27. **Judah**. Am 3:2. 2 K 17:19. Je *9:25, 26. Ho *5:12, 13. 6:11. 12:2. **because**. Le *26:14, 15, 43)𝒫. Jg 2:17-20. 2 S 12:9, 10. 2 K 22:11-17. 2 Ch *36:14-17. Ne 1:7. 9:26, 29, 30. Is 5:24, 25. Je 8:9. Ezk ch. *16. *20:13, 16, 24. 22:8. 23:11, etc. Da *9:5-12. Ac *7:51. *13:40, 41. 1 Th *4:8. **and their lies**. 2 K 17:15. Ps 40:4. Is 9:15, 16. 28:15. 44:20. Je 16:19, 20. *23:13-15, 25-32. 28:15,

16. Ezk 13:6-16, 22. 22:28. Hab 2:18. Ro *1:25. **after.** Jg 2:11-17. 10:6. 2 Ch 30:7. Je 8:2. 9:14. Ezk 20:13, 16, 18, 24, 30. 1 P 1:18.

5. **I will.** Je √17:27. 21:10. 37:8-10. 39:8. 52:13. Ho *8:14.

6. **Thus saith.** Amos, says Abp. Newcome, first prophesies against the Syrians, Philistines, Tyrians, Edomites, Ammonites, and Moabites, who dwelt in the neighborhood of the twelve tribes, and had occasionally become their enemies and persecutors. Having thus taught his countrymen that the providence of God extended to other nations, he briefly mentions the idolatrous practices and consequent destruction of Judah, and then passes on to his proper subject, which was to exhort and reprove the kingdom of Israel, and to denounce against it the Divine judgments. **For three.** Am 6:3-7. 2 K 17:7-18. 18:12. Ezk 23:5-9. Ho 4:1, 2, 11-14. 7:7-10. 8:4-6. 13:2, 3. Mi 6:10-16. **because they sold.** Am 5:11, 12. 8:4-6. Le 25:39)𝒫. Dt 15:12)𝒫. 2 K 4:1. Ne 5:5. Is 5:22, 23. 29:21. Jl 3:3, 6. Mi 3:2, 3. **and the poor.** Ex *23:6-8. Ezk +*16:49. **a pair of shoes.** Ru 4:7.

7. **pant.** Am 4:1. 1 K 21:4. Pr 28:21. Mi 2:2, 9. 7:2, 3. Hab 2:6. Zp 3:3. Ja 2:6. A Hebrew homonym meaning (1) to grasp or long for (Jb 7:2. 36:20. Ps 119:131. Ec 1:5. Je 2:24. 14:6); (2) to crush (like *shuph* in Ge 3:15). Rendered "swallow up" in Am 8:4. Jb 5:5. Ps 56:1, 2. 57:3. Ezk 36:3. So here it means "crush." Render: "crush the head of the poor ones in the dust of the earth" (CB). **turn aside.** Am +*5:12. Is *10:2. **way of the meek.** Mt +*5:5. Ja +*2:5. +*5:4, 6. **man and his father.** This was done in the Canaanite idolatry, with the women of the temples (CB). Le 18:8, 15. Ezk *22:11. 1 C *5:1. **go in.** Ge +29:30. 38:2, 9, 16. **maid.** *or,* young woman. Ge +*24:14 (❋S#5291h). **to profane.** Le 18:21)𝒫. +*19:8. 20:3)𝒫. 2 S 12:14. Is 48:11. Ezk 20:9, 14. 36:20-23. Ml 1:12. Ro 2:24. 1 C 5:1.

8. **laid.** Ex +*22:26, 27)𝒫. Dt 24:12-17)𝒫. Ezk 18:7, 12. **by every altar.** Am 6:4. Is 57:7. Ezk 23:41. 1 C *8:10. 10:7, 21. **they drink.** Am 6:6. Jg 9:27. Ho 4:8. **the condemned.** *or,* such as have fined, *or* mulcted.

9. **yet destroyed I.** Ge *15:16. Ex 3:8. 34:11. Nu *21:24)𝒫. Dt 2:24-34)𝒫. Jsh 3:10. 24:8-12. Jg 11:21-23. Ne 9:22-24. Ps 135:10-12. 136:17-22. **whose height.** Nu 13:28, 29, 32, *33)𝒫. Dt 1:28. 2:10, 11. 3:11. 9:1-3. **I destroyed.** Jsh 11:21, 22. 2 S 23:16-22. Jb *18:16. Is *5:24. Ml *4:1.

10. **I brought.** Ex *12:51)𝒫. Dt 4:47)𝒫. Ne 9:8-12. Ps 105:42, 43. 136:10, 11. Je 32:20, 21. Ezk 20:10. Mi 6:4. **and led.** Nu 14:34. Dt *2:7)𝒫. *8:2-4)𝒫. Ne 9:21. Ps 95:10. Ac 7:42. 13:18. **to possess.** Nu 14:31-35. Dt 1:20, 21, 39.

11. **I raised.** 1 S 3:20. 19:20. 1 K 17:1. 18:4. 19:16. 20:13, 35, 41. 22:8. 2 K 2:2-5. 6:1. 17:13. 2 Ch *36:15. Je +*7:25. 2 P √1:20, 21. **Nazarites.** Nu *6:2)𝒫. Jg 13:4-7. La 4:7. Lk 1:3-17. **Is it not.** √85B, Ge +13:9. Is 5:3, 4. Je 2:5, 31. Mi 6:3, 4.

12. **ye gave.** T#466-4. Ex 32:21-23. **wine.** Nu 6:3. **and commanded.** Am *7:12, 13. Is *30:10, 11. Je *11:21. 26:11. Mi 2:6. Mt 21:34-38. Ac 4:18. 5:28. 7:51. 1 Th 2:15, 16.

13. **Behold.** Ps 78:40. Is *1:14. 7:13. *43:24. Ezk 6:9. 16:43. Ml 2:17. **I am pressed**, etc. *or,* I will press your place, as a cart full of sheaves presseth.

14. **the flight.** Am 9:1-3. Jb 11:20mg. Ec *9:11. Is

*30:16, 17. Je *9:23. *46:6. **the strong.** Ps 33:16. **himself.** Heb. his soul, *or* life. Heb. *nephesh,* Nu +23:10.

15. **neither.** Ps *33:16, 17. **himself.** Heb. his soul, *or* life. Heb. *nephesh,* Nu +23:10.

16. **courageous.** Heb. strong of his heart. Je 48:41. **shall flee.** Jg 4:17. 2 K 7:8, etc. Mk 14:52.

AMOS 3

God expostulates with Israel and Judah, and warns them of approaching judgments, 1-8. He calls the Philistines and Egyptians to behold the punishment of Samaria and the ten tribes for their sins, 9-15.

1. **Hear.** 2 Ch 20:15. Is 46:3. 48:12. Ho 4:1. 5:1. Mi 3:1. Re 2:29. **against the whole family.** Je *8:3. 31:1. 33:24-29. Ezk 37:16, etc. Mi 2:3. **which.** Am 2:10. Ex 12:51)𝒫.

2. **only.** Ex 19:5, 6. Dt *7:6)𝒫. *10:15. 26:18. 32:9. Ps *147:19, 20. Is *63:19. **known.** √121C2A2, Ge +39:6. **all.** Ge 10:32. Je 1:15. 10:25. Na 3:4. Zc 14:17, 18. Ac 17:26. **therefore.** Ezk *9:6. 20:36-38. Da 9:12. Mt +*11:20-24. Lk +*12:47, 48. Ro *2:9. 1 P +*4:17. **punish.** Heb. visit upon. Ex 32:34)𝒫. Je 9:25mg. +11:22mg. 13:21mg. Ho 2:13. 8:13. 9:9.

3. **Can two walk.** Ge 5:22. 6:9. 17:1. Le 23:17n. Ps +*119:63. 2 C +*6:14-16.

4. **a lion.** ver. 8. Am 1:2. Ps 104:21. Je 2:15. Ho 11:10. **cry.** Heb. give forth his voice. **den.** Ps 104:22.

5. **a bird fall.** Ec 9:12. Je 31:28. Ezk 12:13. Da 9:14.

6. **a trumpet.** Je *4:5. 6:1. Ezk *33:3. Ho 5:8. Zp 1:16. **and the people.** Je *5:22. *10:7. 2 C *5:11. **be afraid.** *or,* run together. **shall there.** That is, Shall there be any *evil,* or calamity (not *moral* evil), inflicted on a wicked city, which does not proceed from me, as the effect of my wrath? These animated interrogatives were intended to convince the people that they had cause for alarm, as their monstrous iniquities called down the vengeance of God to punish them with these calamities. Ge *50:20. Is *14:24-27. +*45:7. Ac *2:23. *4:28. **be evil.** Am 5:13. 2 S *17:14. Jb +*2:10. +*9:22. Ps 141:5. Is +√45:7. **the Lord hath not done it?** *or,* and shall not the Lord do *somewhat?* 1 K 11:14. Ps 94:7, 9, 10. Is 9:13. Mi 6:9. Mt 18:7. 1 C 2:8. 1 T 1:13, 16. **done it.** √108A4, Ge +31:7. Ex +*4:21. Le 14:34n. Nu 16:41n. Dt +*2:30. Jsh 6:21n. 10:40n. Jg 9:23n. 14:4n. 21:15n. Ru +*1:13. 1 S +18:10n. 2 S 12:11n. 24:1n. 1 K 12:15n. 2 K +*6:33. Is 6:10n. Je *4:10n. ☽+*29:11. Ezk 14:9n. 20:25n. +38:16. Ep +*1:11. Re +*17:17.

7. **Surely.** Jb 31:18. Mi 6:4. **will do.** Ex 12:12. Nu 5:30. 33:4. Dt 10:18. 33:21. **but he revealeth.** Ge *6:13. √18:17. 20:7. Ex *33:13. Nu 12:7, 8. Dt +*29:29. 1 K 22:19-23. 2 K 3:17-20. 6:12. 22:13, 20. Ps √25:14mg. *103:7. Da 2:10, 11, +*19. 8:15, 16. +*9:22-27. +*10:21. *11:2. Mt *13:11. Lk 2:*26, 29, 36, 37. Jn √15:15. Re 1:1, 19. 4:1. ch. 6-20.

8. **lion.** ver. 4. Am 1:2. Re 5:5. *10:3. **who can.** Am 2:12. 7:12-17. Jb 32:18, 19. Je 20:9. Ac *4:20. +*5:20, 29. 1 C *9:16. **the Lord.** √95, Ps +7:13.

9. **Publish.** 2 S 1:20. Je 2:10, 11. 31:7-9. 46:14. 50:2. **Ashdod.** Am 1:8. 1 S 5:1. **the mountains.** Am 4:1. 6:1. Je 31:5. Ezk 36:8. 37:22. **and behold.** Dt 29:24-28. Je 22:8, 9. **oppressed.** *or,* oppressions. Am 4:1. 8:6. Le +*19:13)𝒫. Dt +*24:14)𝒫. Jb 35:9. Ec 4:1.

10. **know not to do.** Ps 14:4. Je *4:22. 5:4. 2 P

3:5. **right**. ❋S#5228h. 2 S 15:3. Pr +*8:9 (plain). 24:26. Is 26:10 (uprightness). 30:10 (right things). 57:2 (uprightness). 59:14 (equity). **who store**. Hab *2:8-11. Zp 1:9. Zc 5:3, 4. Ja +*5:3, 4. **robbery**. or, spoil. Ho 7:13mg.

11. **An adversary**. Am 6:14. 2 K 15:19, 29. *17:3-6. *18:9-11. Is 7:17, etc. 8:7, 8. 10:5, 6, 9-11. Ho 11:5, 6. **there shall be**. or, shall come. ✻63B, Ge +25:28. **and thy**. ver. 10, 15. Am 2:5. 6:8. 2 Ch 36:19.

12. **As the**. 1 S 17:34-37. Is 31:4. **taketh**. Heb. delivereth. **so shall**. Am 9:2, 3. 1 K 20:30. 22:25. Is 8:4. √17:1-6. Ro +*11:4, 5. 1 P +*4:17, 18. **in Damascus in a couch**. or, on the bed's feet. or, in the corner of a couch. ✻63I1A, Ex +12:4. 1 K 20:34. 2 K 16:9.

13. **and testify**. Dt 8:19. 30:18, 19. 2 K 17:13, 15. 2 Ch 24:19. Ac 2:40. 18:5, 6. 20:21. Ep 4:17. 1 Th 4:6. **the Lord God**. Am 5:27. Jsh 22:22. Is 1:24. Re ▶15:3. **the God of hosts**. Ja +5:4.

14. **in the**. Ex 32:34▶℘. **visit the transgressions of Israel upon him**. or, punish Israel for his transgressions. ver. +2mg. **I will**. Am 9:1. 1 K 13:2-5. 2 K 23:15. 2 Ch 31:1. 34:6, 7. Je *48:13. Ho *10:5-8, 14, 15. Mi 1:6, 7.

15. **the winter house**. Je 36:22. **the summer house**. Jg 3:20. **the houses**. 1 K 22:39. Ps 45:8. **the great**. ver. 11. Am 6:11. Is 5:9.

AMOS 4

The prosperous Israelites are reproved and threatened for oppression and idolatry, 1-5. Their incorrigibleness under previous visitations, 6-11. They are warned to prepare to meet God, who is about to execute vengeance upon them, 12, 13.

1. **ye kine**. By the "kine of Bashan," some understand the proud, luxurious matrons of Israel; but it is probable that the prophet speaks catachrestically, and means the wealthy, effeminate, and profligate rulers and nobles of Samaria. Nu +21:33. Dt 32:14, 15. Jsh 12:4n. 1 K 4:13. Ps *22:12. Je 50:11, 27. Ezk *39:18. Na 1:4. **the mountain**. Am 6:1. 1 K 16:24. **which oppress**. Am 2:6, 7. 3:9, 10. 5:11. 8:4-6. Ex +*22:21-25. Le +*19:13▶℘. Dt +*15:9-11. +*24:14▶℘. 1 S 12:3, 4. Ps +*12:5. 140:12. Pr *22:22, 23. 23:10, 11. Ec 4:1. 5:8. Is *1:17-24. 5:8. 58:6. Je 5:26-29. 6:6. 7:6. Ezk +*16:49. 22:7, 12, 27, 29. Mi 2:1-3. 3:1-3. Zc 7:10, 11. Ml +*3:5. Ja +*5:1-6. **crush**. Dt 28:33. Jb *20:19mg. Je 51:34. **Bring**. Am 2:8. Is *56:11, 12. Jl 3:3.

2. **hath sworn**. Am 6:8. Ge 22:16▶℘. See on Ps *89:35. He 6:13. **with hooks**. 2 Ch 33:11. Jb 40:24. 41:2. Is 37:29. Je *16:16. Ezk 29:4, 5. Hab *1:15, 16. **posterity**. or, remnant of you. Ezk 23:25.

3. **ye shall go**. 2 K 25:4. Ezk *12:5, 12. **before her**. Jsh 6:5, 20. **them into the palace**. or, away the things of the palace. 2 K 7:7, 8, 15. Is 2:20. 31:7. Zp 1:18. Mt 16:26.

4. **Come**. ✻60A, Ge +3:22. ✻83, 1 K +22:15. A bitter irony and sarcasm, addressed to the idolatrous Israelites. Am 3:14. 5:5. Ec 11:9. Ezk *20:39. Ho 4:15. 9:15. 12:11. Jl 3:9-12. Mt *23:32. 26:45. Mk 14:41. **Bethel**. 1 K 12:29. **at Gilgal**. Am 5:5. Ho *4:15. 9:15. 12:11. **and bring**. Nu 28:3, 4. Le 7:13. **sacrifices**. A reference to burnt offerings. Le +*23:12. Ho *6:6. **every morning**. Nu 28:4. **and your tithes**. Dt 14:28, 29. 26:12. **three years**. Heb. three *years* of days.

✻171T2C, Ge +24:55. Nu 28:3▶℘. Dt *14:28▶℘. Je +28:3mg.

5. **offer a sacrifice**. Heb. offer by burning. Le *7:12, 13▶℘. +*23:17▶℘. Ps 56:12. Je 17:26. +*33:11. He *13:15. **with leaven**. Leavened bread might be eaten by the offerer, but not consumed on the altar (Le 2:11, 12). Leaven is mentioned five times in Exodus; four in Leviticus; one in Deuteronomy; *and not elsewhere*. The Mosaic law was well known (Ex +24:4. 2 K 14:6n. 2 K 22:8n. Ho 9:9n). There was no "historic growth" of the Pentateuch (CB). Ex 12:15. 13:3, 7. 23:18. 34:25. Le ❶*2:11▶℘. 6:17. 7:13. ❶23:17. Dt 16:3. **proclaim**. Le 22:18-21. Dt 12:6, 7. Mt 6:2. **free offerings**. Le *22:18, 21▶℘. +*23:38. Dt *12:6, 17▶℘. **for**. Ps 81:12. Mt 15:9, 13, 14. 23:23. Ro 1:28. 2 Th √2:10-12. **this liketh you**. Heb. so ye love. ✻60A, Ge +3:22. Ho 9:1, 10.

6. **cleanness of teeth**. From *want of food*, occasioned by severe famine. ✻121S3D. Metonymy of the Adjunct B606. "Cleanness of teeth" put for famine. **and want**. Le 26:26. Dt 28:38. 1 K 17:1. 18:2. 2 K 4:38. 6:25-29. 8:1. Ezk 16:27. **yet**. ✻8, Ps +118:1. See on ver. 8, 9. 2 Ch 28:22. Is 1:5. 9:13. *26:11. Je *5:3. 8:5-7. Ho √5:15. √6:1. 7:14-16. Jl 2:12-14. Hg *2:17. Zc 1:3-6. Re 2:21. 9:20, 21. 16:10, 11.

7. **I have**. Le 26:18-21, 23, 24, 27, 28. Dt 28:23, 24▶℘. 1 K *8:35, 36. 2 Ch +√7:13, 14. Is 5:6. Je 3:3. 5:24, 25. 14:4, 22. Ezk *22:23, 24. Hg 1:10, 11. Zc 10:1. 14:17. Ml +*3:10. Ja 5:17. Re 11:6. **when**. Jl 2:23. Jn 4:35. **and I**. Ex 8:22. 9:4, 26. 10:23. Jg 6:37-40. 1 C 4:7. **and the**. See on Jl 1:10-18.

8. **two**. 1 K 18:5. Is 41:17, 18. Je 14:3. **but**. Ezk 4:16. Mi 6:14. Hg 1:6. **yet**. ✻8, Ps +118:1. See on ver. 6, 9-11. Je 23:14. Ho 7:10.

9. **with**. Dt *28:22▶℘. 1 K 8:37. 2 Ch 6:28. Hg 2:17. **when**, etc. or, the multitude of your gardens, etc., did the palmworm, etc. **the palmworm**. Am 7:1, 2. Dt 28:42. Jl *1:4. *2:25. **yet**. ✻8, Ps +118:1. See on ver. 6, 8. Jb 36:8-13. Is *1:5. 42:24, 25. Je 5:3.

10. **pestilence**. Ex 9:3-6. 12:29, 30. +*15:26. Le 26:16, 25▶℘. Dt 7:15. *28:21, 22, 27, 60. Ps *78:49, 50. **after the manner**. or, in the way. Ex 9:3, 6▶℘. 12:29▶℘. Dt 28:27▶℘. Ps 78:50. Is 10:24, 26. **your young**. Le 26:25. 2 K *8:12. 10:32. Je 6:11. 11:22. 18:21. 48:15. **and have taken away your horses**. Heb. with the captivity of your horses. Nu 31:26mg. 2 K 13:3-7. Is 49:25mg. **the stink**. Am 8:3. Dt 28:26. Je 8:1, 2. 9:22. 15:3. 16:4. Jl *2:20. **yet**. ✻8, Ps +118:1. See on ver. 6. Ex 8:19. 9:12, 17, 34, 35. 10:3, 27. 14:4.

11. **as God**. Ge 19:24, 25▶℘. Dt 29:23▶℘. Is 1:9. 13:19. Je 49:18. 50:40. Ho 11:8. 2 P 2:6. Ju *7. **as a firebrand**. Zc *3:2. 1 C +*3:15. Ju +*23. **yet**. ✻8, Ps +118:1. See on ver. 6. Je 6:28-30. Ezk 22:17-22. 24:13. Re 9:20.

12. **thus**. See on ver. 2, 3. Am 2:14, 15. 9:1-4. Ps 10:17. **prepare**. Am 5:4-15. 2 K *20:1. Ps *98:9. Pr 16:1. Is 47:3. Ezk 13:5. 22:30. Ho *10:8. 13:8. Zc +*14:5. Mt 5:25. *24:44-51. *25:1-13. Mk *13:32-37. Lk 12:35, 36. ❶47. 14:31, 32. +*21:34-36. 1 Th *5:2-4. Ja *4:1-10. Ju 14. Re 3:3. 19:7.

13. **he that**. This is a most powerful description of the majesty of Jehovah, the God of hosts. Jb 38:4-11. Ps 65:6. Is *40:12. 42:5. Zc *12:1. **and createth**. Heb. *bara*, Ge 1:1. Ps 135:7. 147:18. Is +45:18 (❋S#1254h). Je 10:13. 51:16. Some modern critics allege that this

word was not used before the time of Jeremiah; but it is used, besides the Pentateuch, in Ps 51:10. 89:12, 47. 102:18. 104:30. 148:5. Ec 12:1; and in Isaiah frequently (CB). **wind.** *or*, spirit. Pr 30:4. Ec 3:21. Ezk 37:9mg. Jn √3:8. **and declareth.** Ps 7:9. *139:2. Je +*17:10. Da 2:28. Mt 9:4. Lk 7:39, 40. Jn +*2:25. **that maketh.** Am *5:8. 8:9. Ex 10:22. 14:20. Is 5:30. Je 13:16. **darkness.** Pr +20:20. **and treadeth.** Dt 32:13)𝒫. 33:29)𝒫. Mi *1:3. Hab 3:19. **The Lord.** Am 3:13. 5:8. 6:8. 9:6. Is *47:4. 48:2. Je *10:16. 51:19. **is his name.** Ex +*6:3n. 15:3)𝒫. Ps +68:4. +*83:18.

AMOS 5

A lamentation over Israel, 1-3. Exhortations to seek God, with promises, instructions, and rebukes, 4-15. The judgments of God on the scornful and presumptuous, 16-20. God rejects the hypocritical services of Israel, and sentences them to captivity, 21-27.

1. **Hear.** Am 3:1. 4:1. **I take.** ver. 16. Je *7:29. 9:10, 17, 20. Ezk 19:1, 14. 26:17. 27:2, 27-32. 28:12. 32:2, 16. Mi 2:4.

2. **virgin.** √155E5, Nu +21:25. Ge +24:16 (*S#1330h). Is 37:22. 47:1. Je 14:17. 18:13. 31:4. 46:11. La 2:13. **is fallen.** 2 K 15:29. 17:6. Is 3:8. Ho 14:1. **she shall.** Is 14:21. 24:20. 43:17. Je 51:64. **she is.** Je 4:20. **none.** Am 7:2-5. 9:11. Is 51:17, 18. Je 2:27, 28. 30:12-14. La 1:16-19. Ezk 16:36, 37. Ho 6:2.

3. **The city.** Dt 4:27. *28:62. Is 1:9. 10:22. *30:17. Ezk 12:16. Ro 9:27. **by a thousand.** Dt 32:30)𝒫.

4. **Seek ye me.** ver. 6. Dt 12:5)𝒫. *30:1-8. 1 Ch +*28:9. 2 Ch *15:2. 20:3. 34:3. Ps +√9:10. 14:2. 27:8. Is 9:13. √55:6, 7. Je 10:21. √29:12, 13. La 3:25, 26. Ho *10:12. Zp 1:6. 2:3. Mt 7:8. **and.** Ps 22:26. 69:32. 105:3, 4. Is +*55:3. **shall live.** Le 18:5)𝒫. Dt 30:19)𝒫. Ne 9:29. Is +*26:19. 38:16. +*55:3. Ezk 3:21. 18:19. 20:11. 33:19. 37:3, 5, 6, 14. Ho 6:2. Hab 2:4. Lk 10:28. Ro 1:17. 10:5. Ga 3:12. He 10:38.

5. **seek not.** Am 4:4. Ho 4:15. 9:15. 10:14, 15. 12:11. **Beer-sheba.** Am 8:14. Ge 21:33. *26:23, 25. 46:1. **Gilgal.** √140, Ge +4:25. There is a *paronomasia* here, both on the letters and words: *haggilgal galoh yigleh oovaith el yiheyeh leawen,* "Gilgal shall surely go into captivity, and Bethel (the house of God) shall come to nought," or Aven, i.e. Beth-aven, the house of iniquity. Literally, The Roller, rolling, shall roll away: i.e. *be utterly removed.* **and Beth-el.** Am 7:17. Le 26:30-32. Dt 28:41. Ho 4:15. 10:8, 15. **come.** Jb 8:22. Ps 33:10. Is 8:10. 29:20. 1 C 1:28. 2:6. Re 18:17.

6. **Seek.** ver. 4. Ezk 33:11. **lest.** Ex 22:6. **the house.** Am 6:6. Ge 48:8-20. Jsh 18:5. Jg 1:22, 23. 2 S 19:20. 1 K 11:28. Ezk 37:19. Zc √10:6. **there.** Is 1:31. Je 4:4. 7:20. Ezk 20:47, 48. Mk √9:43-48.

7. **turn.** ver. 11, 12. Am *6:12. Dt 29:18)𝒫. Is 1:23. 5:7. 10:1. 59:13, 14. Ho 10:4. Hab 1:12-14. **leave.** Ps *36:3. 125:5. Ezk 3:20. *18:24. 33:12, 13, 18. Zp 1:6.

8. **the seven stars.** Jb *9:9. *38:31, 32. Is 13:10. **shadow of death.** Jb 3:5. 10:21, 22. 12:22. 16:16. 24:17. 28:3. 34:22. 38:17. Ps +*23:4. 44:19. 107:10, 14. Is *9:2. Je 2:6. *13:16. Mt 4:16. Lk 1:79. **into the morning.** Jb 38:12, 13. **maketh.** Am 4:13. 8:9. Ex 10:21-23. 14:24-28. Ps 104:20. 105:28. Is 59:10. Je 13:16. **that calleth.** Am *9:6. Ge 7:11-20. 1 K 18:44, 45. Jb 37:13. 38:34. Is 48:13. 2 P 3:5, 6. **face.** √144A1, Ge +11:8. **The Lord.** Am 4:13.

9. **strengtheneth.** 2 K 13:17, 25. Je 37:10. Mt 11:12.

Lk +*1:52. He 11:34. **against the strong.** Am 2:14. Jb 5:3. Is 29:5. **spoiled.** Heb. spoil. Am 3:10mg. Ho 7:13mg. **come against.** Mi +*5:8-11.

10. **hate.** Am 7:10-17. 1 K 18:17. 21:20. 22:8. 2 Ch 24:20-22. 25:16. 36:16. Pr 9:7, 8. Is *29:21. Je 20:7-10. Jn 7:7. 15:19, 22-24. Re 11:10. **in the gate.** √171S7B, Ge +14:7. ver. *12. Ge +14:7. **abhor.** Je 17:16, 17. Jn 3:20. 8:45-47.

11. **treading.** Am 4:1. Is 5:7, 8. 59:13, 14. Mi 2:2. 3:1-3. Ja 2:6. Re 11:8-10. **ye have built.** Dt *28:30, 38, 39)𝒫. Is 65:21, 22. Mi *6:15. Zp *1:13. Hg √1:6. **pleasant vineyards.** Heb. vineyards of desire. √121R5, Ge +27:15. Jb 33:20mg. Is 32:12mg. Je +25:34mg. Ezk +26:12mg.

12. **I know.** Dt 31:21. Is 66:18. Je 29:23. He 4:12, 13. **manifold.** 2 K 17:7-17. Ne ◑9:27. Is 47:9. **mighty.** Ps ◑89:19. Is 63:1. Je 50:34. Re *18:5. **they afflict.** Am 2:6, 7, 26. Ac 3:13, 14. 7:52. Ja +*5:4, 6. **take.** 1 S 8:3. Ps 26:9, 10. Is 1:23. 33:15. Mi 3:11. 7:3. **bribe.** *or*, ransom. Ex 30:12. Nu 35:31, 32)𝒫. Pr 6:35. 13:8. 21:18. Is 43:3. **and they turn aside.** Am 2:7. Ex 23:6)𝒫. Dt 16:19)𝒫. 24:17)𝒫. Is 10:2. 29:21. La 3:34, 35. Ezk +*16:49. Ml +*3:5. **the poor.** Ezk +*16:49. **in the gate.** ver. 10. Ge +14:7. Dt 16:18. Ru 4:1. Jb 29:7, etc. 31:21. Pr 22:22.

13. **the prudent.** Pr +*22:3. **keep silence.** Am *6:10. Jb 24:4. Pr ◑11:10. 28:12, 28. 29:2. Ec 3:7. Is 36:21. Je *8:14. Ho 4:4. Mi 7:5-7. Mt 27:12-14. **an evil.** Ec 9:12. Is 37:3. Mi 2:3. Hab +*3:16. Zp +*2:2, 3. Ep *5:15, 16. *6:13. 2 T *3:1.

14. **Seek.** Ps 34:12-16. Pr 11:27. Is 1:16, 17. 55:2. Mi +*6:8. Mt √6:33. Ro 2:7-9. **and so.** Am 3:3. Ge 39:2, 3, 23. Ex 3:12. Le *26:12. Jsh *1:9. 1 K *6:13. 1 Ch 28:20. 2 Ch 15:2. Ps 46:11. Is 8:10. Mt 1:23. 28:20. Ph *4:8, 9. 2 T 4:22. **as.** Nu 16:3. Is 48:1, 2. Je 7:3, 4. Mi *3:11.

15. **Hate the evil.** Ps *34:14. 36:4. *37:27. *97:10. 119:104. 139:21, 22. Is *1:16, 17. Ro 7:15, 16, 22. 8:7. *12:9. 1 Th 5:21, 22. 3 J 11. **love the good.** Mi +*6:8. Ph 4:8. **establish.** ver. 10, 24. Am 6:12. 2 Ch 19:6-11. Ps 82:2-4. Je 7:5-7. **in the gate.** √171S7B, Ge +14:7. **it may.** Ex 32:30. 2 S 16:12. 1 K 20:31. 2 K 19:4. Jl *2:14. Jon *3:9. Zp +*2:3. **the remnant.** ver. 6. 2 K 13:7. 14:26, 27. 15:29. Je 31:7. Mi 2:12. 5:3, 7, 8. **Joseph.** √171R, Ex +12:40. "Joseph" is put for the ten tribes or the kingdom of Israel.

16. **the Lord.** ver. 27. Am 3:13. **saith thus.** √121S4, 2 K +4:29. **Wailing.** Am 8:10. Is 15:2-5, 8. 22:12. Je 4:31. 9:10, 18-20. Jl 1:8, 11, 14. Mi 1:8. 2:4. Re 18:10, 15, 16, 19. **streets.** lit. open places. Heb. *rechob*, *S#7339h. This word signifies a courtyard or *square*. It is applied to the broad open space adjacent to the gate of a town, where public business was transacted (Dt 13:16); to the court before the temple (Ezr 10:9) or before a palace (Est 4:6). When the word is used of a *street*, it often more properly refers to the idea of *publicity* rather than of width (Ge 19:2. Jg 19:15. 2 S 21:12). Ge 19:2. Dt 13:16. Jg 19:15, 17, 20. 2 S 21:12. 2 Ch 29:4. 32:6. Ezr 10:9. Ne 8:1, 3, 16. Est 4:6. 6:9, 11. Jb 29:7. Ps 55:11. *144:14. Pr 1:20n. 5:16. 7:12. 22:13. 26:13. SS 3:2 (broad ways). Is 15:3. 59:14. Je 5:1 (broad places). 9:21. 48:38. 49:26. 50:30. La 2:11, 12. 4:18. Ezk 16:24, 31. Da 9:25. Na 2:4 (broad ways). Zc 8:4, 5. **highways.** Heb. *chuts*, S#2351h. Properly, "out of doors." The term applies generally to what is *outside* the residence (Pr 7:12, without),

and to other places than streets, as to a pasture-ground (Jb 5:10mg) or inheritance "in the land" (Jb 18:17). Broad and narrow streets are distinguished under the terms *rechob* and *chuts* in the following passages, though the point is frequently lost in the A.V. by rendering the latter term "abroad" or "without": Pr 5:16. 7:12. 22:13. Je 5:1. 9:21. Na 2:4. The same distinction is expressed by the terms *rechob* and *shuk* (S#7784h, Pr +7:8) in SS 3:2. In the light of these distinctions in Hebrew it is interesting to consider the New Testament expressions "highways and hedges" (Mt 22:9. Lk *14:23) and the "narrow" and "broad" way (Mt *7:13, 14). The familiar expression "highways and byways" does not occur as such in Scripture; the only reference to "byways" is in Jg 5:6 in the A.V. **such.** 2 Ch 35:25. Ec 12:5. Je *9:17-19. Mt 9:23. Mk 5:38.

17. **in.** Is 16:10. 32:10-12. Je 48:33. Ho 9:1, 2. **I will.** Ex 12:12, 23)𝒫. Jl 3:17. Na 1:12, 15. Zc 9:8. **pass through.** ⨍22C22, Ex +12:12.

18. **that desire the day.** Is *5:19. 28:15-22. Jb 36:20. Je √17:16. Ezk 12:22, 27. Ml *3:1, 2. 2 P √3:4. **the day of the Lord is.** Is +2:12. 5:30. 9:19. +13:6. 24:11, 12. Je +*30:7. Da +*12:1. Jl 1:15. *2:1, 2, 10, 31. Zp 1:14, 15. Ml *4:1. 1 Th +*5:2, 3. 2 P √3:10.

19. **As if.** They should go from one evil to another. Am 9:1, 2. 1 K 20:29, 30. Jb *20:24, 25. Is *24:17, 18. Je 15:2, 3. 48:43, 44. Ac 28:4. **a bear.** The Syrian bear is fiercer than a lion (CB). 2 K 2:24. La 3:10. Da 7:5.

20. **Shall not.** ⨍85B, Ge +13:9. **darkness.** Jb 3:4-6. 10:21, 22. Is 13:10. Ezk 34:12. Na 1:8. Mt 22:13. Ju 13. Re 16:10. **not light.** ⨍144D, Ge +40:23.

21. **hate.** Pr 15:8. *21:27. 28:9. Is *1:11-16. 66:3. Je *6:20. 7:21-23. Ho 8:13. Mt 23:14. **feast days.** Le 23:2n. Dt 16:16. **I will not.** Ge 8:21. Le *26:31)𝒫. 1 S *15:22. Ezk *20:41. Ep *5:2. Ph 4:18. **smell in your solemn assemblies.** *or,* smell your holy days. Le 23:36)𝒫. Nu 29:35)𝒫. Dt 16:8)𝒫. Jl 1:14mg.

22. **offer.** Ps 50:8-13. Is *66:3. Mi *6:6, 7. **burnt offerings.** Le +*23:12. **meat offerings.** Le +*23:13. **I will not accept.** Le 1:4)𝒫. Ml 1:7. **peace offerings.** Le +*23:19. *or,* thank offerings. Am 4:4, 5. Le 7:12-15. Ps 50:14, 23. 107:21, 22. 116:17. Je +*33:11. **viols.** *or,* lutes. *S#5035h. Am 6:5. 1 S 10:5 (psaltery). 2 S 6:5. 1 K 10:12. 1 Ch *13:8. 15:16, 20, 28. 16:5. 25:1, 6. 2 Ch 5:12. 9:11. 20:28. 29:25. Ne 12:27. Ps 33:2. 57:8. 71:22. 81:2. 92:3. 108:2. 144:9. 150:3. Is 5:12 (viol). 14:11. 22:24mg,n.

23. **the noise.** Am 6:5. 8:3, 10. 1 Ch 25:1, 7. Is 5:12.

24. **let.** ver. 7, 14, 15. Jb 29:12-17. Pr 21:3. Is *1:17. Ho *6:6. Mi +*6:8. Mk 12:32-34. **run down.** Heb. roll on. A reference to Gilgal. **mighty.** *or,* inexhaustible. **stream.** Heb. *nahal,* a wady, or intermittent stream; not *nahar,* a constant-flowing river (CB), S#5158h. A *brook* or summer watercourse, the Arabic *wady,* signifying both the stream and the torrent-bed or valley (translated very variously in the A.V., "brook," "valley," "river," "stream," etc.): Le 11:9, 10 (rivers). Nu +13:23 (brook, mg. valley). 34:5 (river). Jg +16:4 (valley, mg. brook). Is +*27:12 (stream). For *nahar,* a perennial river, see S#5104h, Ezk +32:2, and 2 K +5:12n.

25. **Have ye offered.** Le 17:7. Dt *32:17-19. Jsh 5:5-7. *24:14. Ne 9:18, 21. Is 43:23, 24. Je 7:22, 23. Ezk *20:8, 16, 23, 24. Ho 9:9, 10. Zc 7:5. Ac *)7:42,

43. **unto me.** Le 17:7)𝒫. Dt 32:17)𝒫. Ps 106:37. 1 C 10:7.

26. **the tabernacle of your Moloch.** *or,* Siccuth your king. Le +*18:21. 20:2-5. 1 K 11:33. 2 K *23:5, 11, 12, 13, Milcom. "Siccuth" is a reference to the Babylonian name of the planet Saturn. **Moloch.** ⨍106, Ge +31:7. i.e. *a king; rule,* S#4432h. Le +18:21, Molech. The Massoretic Hebrew pointing vocalizes this word as *bosheth,* denoting "shame" or "detestable thing." **Chiun.** i.e. *image, pillar* (as set up); statue; *Raiphan* or Saturn, *S#3594h. or, Kaiwan* your star god. *Chiun,* in Arabic *kaiwan,* most probably denotes *Saturn;* rendered by the LXX. *Raiphan,* and in Ac 7:43, "Remphan," probably the same as the Coptic *Rephan* (See Kircher, *Lingua Aegypt.* restit. p. 49). Ac *7:43.

27. **beyond.** Am 3:12. 2 K 15:29. 16:9. *17:6. Is 8:4. Ac *7:43. **whose.** Am 4:13.

AMOS 6

Woes denounced on the self-indulgent and self-confident Jews and Israelites, 1-6. Predictions of terrible calamities, 7-14.

1. **to them.** Jg 18:7. Is 32:9-11. 33:14. Je 48:11. 49:31. Lk *6:24, 25. *12:17-20. Ja 5:5. 1 P 5:7. **at ease.** *or,* secure. Is 22:12, 13. Je 7:4. +*48:10. Zp *1:12. Re *3:17. **and trust.** Am 4:1. 8:14. 1 K 16:24. **named.** Ex 19:5, 6. Nu 1:17. La 1:1. **chief.** *or,* firstfruits. Ex *19:5)𝒫. Dt *28:13. Ja 1:18.

2. **Pass.** Je 2:10, 11. Na 3:8. **Calneh.** Ge 10:10. 10:9, Calno. Ezk 27:23, Canneh. **from thence.** ⨍107, Ge +10:5. **Hamath.** Ge 10:18)𝒫. Nu 34:7, 8)𝒫. 2 K 17:24, 30. 18:34. 19:13. **Gath.** 1 S 5:8. 17:4, 23. 2 Ch 26:6. **better.** Is 10:9-11. 36:18, 19. 37:12, 13. Ezk 31:2, 3. Na *3:8.

3. **put far away.** Am 5:18. *9:10. Ec 8:11. Is 47:7. 56:12. Ezk *12:22, 27. Mt 24:48. 1 Th *5:3. 2 P 3:4. Re 18:7. **the evil day.** Am +*3:6. 5:13. 9:10. **and cause.** ver. 12. Am 5:12. Ps 94:20. **seat.** *or,* habitation.

4. **lie.** Is 5:11, 12. 22:13. Lk 16:19. Ro 13:13, 14. Ja 5:5. **beds.** Either sofas to recline on at table, or beds to sleep on; which among the ancients, were ornamented with ivory inlaid. **stretch themselves upon their couches.** *or,* abound with superfluities. 1 S 25:36-38. Ps 73:7. Lk 12:19, 20.

5. **chant.** *or,* quaver. **to the.** Ge 31:27. Jb 21:11, 12. Ec 2:8. Is 5:12. 1 P 4:3. Re 18:22. **like.** Am 5:23. 8:3. 1 Ch 23:5.

6. **drink.** This probably refers to the costliness and magnificence of the drinking vessels, as well as to the quantity drank. **wine in bowls.** *or,* in bowls of wine. 1 K +7:40. Ho 3:1. 1 T 5:23. **chief.** Mt 26:7-9. Jn 12:3. **but.** Ge *37:25-28. 42:21, 22. Est 3:15. Ro 12:15. 1 C 12:26. **not grieved.** La=1:12. **affliction.** *or,* breach. 2 K 15:29. 17:3-6. Is 30:26. 51:19mg. Je 6:14mg. +*30:7. **Joseph.** ⨍171R, Ex +12:40.

7. **shall they.** Am 5:5, 27. 7:11. Dt 28:41. Lk *21:24. **and the.** 1 K 20:16-20. Est 5:8, 12-14. 7:1, 2, 8-10. Is 21:4. Da 5:4-6. Na 1:10.

8. **sworn.** Am 4:2. *8:7. Ge 22:16)𝒫. Je 51:14. He *6:13-17. **himself.** Heb. *nephesh,* Ge +27:31. ⨍22A1, Le +26:11n. Is 42:1. Je 9:9. He 10:38. **I abhor.** Heb. *taab.* A homonym, with two meanings. Here, to abhor. In Ps 119:20, 40, 174, to desire or long for (CB). Le 26:11. Ps 78:59. 106:40. Zc 11:8. **the excellency.** ⨍11, Ge +2:23. Am 8:7. Ps *47:4. Ezk *24:21. **and hate.**

Am 3:11. La 2:5. **therefore**. Mi 1:6-9. **all that is therein**. Heb. the fulness thereof. Ps 24:1. 50:12.

9. **if**. Am 5:3. 1 S 2:33. Est 5:11. 9:10. Jb 1:2, 19. 20:28. Ps 109:13. Is 14:21.

10. **And a**. Abp. Newcome says that this obscure verse seems to describe the effects of the famine and pestilence during the siege of Samaria. **uncle**. ⨍171G2. Figure of Speech Synecdoche of the Species, where one relationship is put for and includes others. Here "uncle" is put for any relative. For other instances of this figure, see Ge +13:8. **that burneth**. Am 8:3. Jsh ●7:25. 1 S *31:12. 2 K 23:16. 2 Ch 16:14. 21:19. Je 16:6. 34:5. **bring out the bones**. Jb 7:15mg. 19:20. 2 Ch ●34:5n. **Hold**. Am 5:13. Nu 17:12, 13. 2 K 6:33. Ezk 24:21-23. **for**. Je 44:26. Ezk 20:39. **we may not make**. or, they will not make, or, have not made. That is, *call upon, or invoke*. Is 26:13. 49:1. 62:6.

11. **the Lord**. Am 3:6, 7. 9:1, 9. Ps 105:16, 31, 34. Is 10:5, 6. 13:3. 46:10, 11. √55:11. Ezk 29:18-20. Na 1:14. **he will**. ver. 8. Am 3:15. 2 K 25:9. Ho 13:16. Zc 14:2. Lk *19:44. **breaches**. or, droppings. Ec 10:18.

12. **horses**. Is 48:4. Je 5:3. 6:29, 30. Zc 7:11, 12. **for**. Am 5:7, 11, 12. 1 K 21:7-13. Ps 94:20, 21. Is 59:13, 14. Ho 10:4, 13. Mi 7:3. Hab 1:3, 4. Ac *7:51, 52. **hemlock**. Dt 29:18 (wormwood)◗⅌.

13. **which**. Ex 32:18, 19. Jg 9:19, 20, 27. 16:23-25. 1 S 4:5. Jb 31:25, 29. Ec 11:9. Is 8:6. Je 9:23. 50:11. Jon 4:6. Hab 1:15, 16. Zp 3:11. Lk *12:19, 20. Jn *16:20. Ja *4:16. Re 11:10. **nought**. ⨍111, Ge +18:27. **Have**. 2 K 13:25. 14:12-14, 25. 2 Ch 28:6-8. Is 7:1, 4. 17:3, 4. 28:14, 15. Da 4:30.

14. **I will**. Dt 28:49◗⅌. 2 K 15:29. 17:6. Is 7:20. 8:4-8. 10:5, 6. Je *5:15-17. Ho 10:5, 6. **from the entering**. Nu *34:8. 1 K 8:65. Ezk *47:15-17. **Hemath**. Ezk 48:1. **unto**. 2 K 14:25. **river**. or, valley. Am +5:24n. Ge 26:17. Jsh 13:3. 15:47. **the wilderness**. or, Arabah. Dt 1:1◗⅌. +11:30. Jb 24:5. 39:6. Is 33:9. 35:1, 6. *40:3. 41:19. 51:3. Je 2:6. 5:6. 17:6. 50:12. 51:43. Ezk 47:8. Zc 14:10.

AMOS 7

The judgments of grasshoppers and of fire are averted by the prayer of Amos, 1-6. By a wall and a plumbline is shown the strict justice of God in Israel's punishment, 7-9. Amaziah, the priest, accuses Amos to Jeroboam, and forbids him to prophesy at Bethel, 10-13. Amos shows how God had called him to prophesy, and predicts the ruin of Amaziah and his family, 14-17.

1. **showed**. ver. 4, 7. Am 8:1. Je 1:11-16. 24:1. Ezk 11:25. Zc 1:20. **he**. Am *4:9. Ex 10:12-16. Is 33:4. Jl 1:4. 2:25. Na 3:15-17. **grasshoppers**. or, green worms. *Govai*, in Arabic *gabee*, "locusts," probably in their caterpillar state, in which they are most destructive. This is supposed to have been an emblem of the first invasion of the Assyrians. **mowings**. Or rather, feedings or grazings, as the people of the East make no hay. This was probably in the month of March, which is the only time of the year that the Arabs to this day feed their horses with grass. **the king's mowings**. 1 K 4:7. 18:5.

2. **when**. Ex 10:15. Re 9:4. **O Lord**. ver. 5. Ex 32:11, 12. 34:9. Nu 14:17-19. Je 14:7, 20, 21. Da 9:19. Ja 5:15, 16. **by whom shall Jacob arise**. or, who of (or, for) Jacob shall stand? ver. 5. Is *51:19. Ezk 9:8.

11:13. **for**. Ps 12:1. 44:22-26. Is 37:4. Je 42:2. Zc 4:10.

3. **repented**. ⨍22B, Ge +6:6. ver. 3, 6. Dt *32:36◗⅌. 1 Ch 21:15. Ps 106:45. Ho 11:8. Jl 2:14. Jon *3:10. Ja √5:16.

4. **showed**. ver. 1, 7. Re 4:1. **called**. This is supposed to denote the invasion of Tiglathpileser, which threatened entire destruction. Am 1:4, 7. 4:11. 5:6. Ex 9:23, 24. Le 10:2. Nu 16:35. Is 27:4. 66:15, 16. Je 4:4. 21:12. Jl 2:30. Mi 1:4. Na 1:6. He 1:7. **a part**. Mi 2:4.

5. **cease**. ver. 2. Ps 85:4. Is 10:25. **for**. ver. 2, 3. Is 1:9. Je 30:19.

6. **repented**. ⨍22B, Ge +6:6. Jg 2:18. 10:16. Ps 90:13. 135:14. Je 26:19. Jon 4:2.

7. **a wall**. 2 S 8:2. 2 K 21:13. Is 28:17. 34:11. La 2:8. Ezk 40:3. Zc 2:1, 2. Re 11:1. 21:15.

8. **Amos**. Je 1:11-13. Zc 5:2. **A plumbline**. This was an emblem of strict justice; and intimated that God would now visit them according to their iniquities. 2 K *21:12, 13. Is *28:17. 34:11. La 2:8. Da *5:27. **I will set**. La 2:8. **I will not**. Am *8:2. Je 15:6. Ezk 7:2-9. Mi *7:18. Na 1:8, 9.

9. **the high places**. Am 3:14. 5:5. Ge *26:23-25, Beer-sheba. 46:1. Le 26:30, 31. 2 K +21:3. **Isaac**. ⨍121A5, ⨍121T3, Ge +9:27. Ps 105:9, 10. Je 33:26. **sanctuaries**. Le 26:31. Is 16:12. Ezk 21:2. **Israel**. ⨍121A5, ⨍121T3, Ge +9:27. **I will**. "Fulfilled, 2 K *15:8-10."

10. **the priest**. 1 K 12:31, 32. 13:33. 2 K 14:23, 24. 2 Ch 13:8, 9. Je 20:1-3. 29:26, 27. Mt 21:23. This was truly a lying prophet; there was not one word of truth in his message to Jeroboam. **of Bethel**. Am 3:14. 4:4. 5:5, 6. **hath conspired**. 1 K 18:17. Je 26:8-11. 37:13-15. 38:4. Lk 23:2. Ac 5:28. *24:5. **against thee**. 1 K 12:26-33. **in the midst**. or, openly. ver. 8. Da 6:10. Ep +*5:11. **not able**. Ge 37:8. Je 18:18. Ac 7:54.

11. **thus**. Je 26:9. 28:10, 11. Ac 6:14. **Jeroboam shall die**. This charge was not true. Note what Amaziah omitted to repeat (CB). ver. ●9. Ps 56:5. Mt 26:61. Ac 17:6, 7. 24:5. **sword**. lit. mouth of the sword. ⨍144A2, Ge +34:26. **and Israel**. Am 6:7, 8. 2 K 17:6.

12. **O thou**. 1 S *9:9. 2 Ch 16:10. Is 30:10. **go**. Am 2:12. Mt 8:34. Lk 8:37, 38. 13:31. Ac 16:39. **eat**. 1 S 2:36. Is 56:11. Ezk 13:19. Ml 1:10. Ro 16:18. 1 C 2:14. 1 P 5:2.

13. **prophesy**. Am *2:12. Ac *4:17, 18. *5:28, 40. **for**. 1 K 12:29, 32. 13:1. **chapel**. or, sanctuary. ver. 9. **king's court**. Heb. house of the kingdom. Da 4:30.

14. **neither**. 1 K 20:35. 2 K 2:3, 5, 7. 4:38. 6:1. 2 Ch 16:7. 19:2. 20:34. **an herdman**. Am 1:1. Zc *13:5. 1 C 1:27. **a gatherer**. Rather, as *bolais* is rendered by the LXX. and Vulgate, *knidzon, vellicans*, "a scraping," or a scraper of sycamores; for the fruit does not ripen till it is rubbed with iron combs. **sycamore fruit**. or, wild figs. 1 K 10:27. 1 Ch 27:28. 2 Ch 1:15. 9:27. Ps 78:47. Is 9:10.

15. **the Lord took me**. Ex 3:1-10. Jg 6:11 1 S 2:18, 35, 36. 9:16. 2 S *7:8. 1 K √11:28mg. *19:19. Ne 1:11. Ps *78:70-72. Da 1:19. Mt 4:18, 19. 9:9. Ac 9:3. Ro +*12:11. Ph 3:5, 6. 1 T 1:13. **as I followed**. Ge +*24:27. Heb. from behind. Ps 78:71mg. Je +17:16mg. **Go**. Je 1:7. Ezk 2:3, 4. Lk 24:46-48. Ac +*1:8. *4:20. √5:20, 29-32.

16. **hear**. 1 S 15:16. 1 K 22:19. Je 28:15-17. **Prophesy not**. ver. 13. Is 30:10. Mi 2:6. **Israel**. ⨍121A5, ⨍121T3, Ge +9:27. **and drop**. Dt *32:2◗⅌. Ezk 20:46. 21:2. Mi 2:6mg. **Isaac**. ⨍121A5, ⨍121T3, Ge +9:27.

17. **Thy wife**. Is 13:16. Je 20:6. 28:12, 16. 29:21, 25, 31, 32. La 5:11. Ho 4:13, 14. Zc *14:2. **thy land**. Ps 78:55. **die**. 2 K *17:6. Ezk 4:13. Ho 9:3. **divided by line**. ✸121B, Jsh +17:14. 2 S 8:2. Ps 60:6. Mi 2:5. Zc 2:1. **and Israel**. ver. 11. Le 26:33-39. 2 K 15:29. 17:6, 23. Je 36:27-32.

AMOS 8

The vision of a basket of summer fruit, signifying the near approach of Israel's end, 1-3. Severe reproofs that their oppression of the poor shall cause their joy to be turned into mourning, and bring on heavy judgments and the end of their prosperity in the land, 4-10. A famine of the word of God prophetically threatened, 11-14.

1. **showed unto me**. Am 7:1, 4, 7. **summer fruit**. ✸121P9, Is +16:9. ver. 2. 2 S 16:2. Je 40:12.

2. **Amos**. Am 7:8. Je 1:11-14. Ezk 8:6, 12, 17. Zc 1:18-21. 5:2, 5, 6. **A basket**. Dt 26:1-4. 2 S 16:1, 2. Is 28:4. Je 24:1-3. 40:10. Mi 7:1. **The end**. There is here not only an allusion to the nature of the summer fruit, which must be eaten as soon as gathered, but also a paronomasia upon the words *kayitz*, "summer fruit," and *ketz*, "an end." Je 1:12. 5:31. La √4:18. Ezk 7:2, 3, 7, 10. 12:23. 29:8. Re *14:15, 18. **I will not**. Am 7:8. **pass by**. That is, forgive them. Am 7:8.

3. **the songs**. ✸121N1, Ge +31:54. By Metonymy of the Adjunct, "songs" are put for singers: "And the singers of the temple shall howl in that day." ver. 10. Am 5:23. Ho 10:5, 6. Jl 1:5, 11, 13. Zc 11:1-3. **shall be howlings**. Heb. shall howl. Je 47:2. **many**. Am 4:10. Is 37:36. Je 9:21, 22. Na 3:3. **they shall**. Am 6:9, 10. Je 22:18, 19. **with silence**. Heb. be silent. Am 6:10. Le 10:3. Ps 37:7mg. 39:9.

4. **Hear**. Am *7:16. 1 K 22:19. Is 1:10. 28:14. Je 5:21. 28:15. **swallow**. Am 2:6, 7. 5:11, 12. Jb 5:5. Ps +*12:5. *14:4. 56:1. 140:12. Pr *30:14. Is 32:6, 7. 42:14. Mt 23:14. Ja 5:6. **the needy**. Pr 14:31. **the poor**. Ex 22:25. Pr 14:21. Ezk +*16:49.

5. **When**. Nu *10:10. *28:11, etc. 2 K *4:23. Ps *81:3, 4. Is *1:13, 14. Col *2:16. **new moon**. *or*, month. Nu 10:10✸. 2 Ch +2:4. **be gone**. Ml 1:13. **and the sabbath**. Ex +*20:8-10✸. Ne *13:15-21. Is +*58:13n, 14. Je 17:27n. Mt 15:8. Ro 8:6, 7. **set forth**. Heb. open. ✸121.O, Ge +28:22. Ge 44:11. **making**. Le *19:36. Dt 25:13-16. 1 Ch 23:29n. Pr *11:1. *16:11. 20:10, 23. Is 1:22. Ezk 45:10-12. Mi *6:10-12. **falsifying the balances by deceit**. Heb. perverting the balances of deceit. Ho *12:7. Hab +*2:9mg.

6. **buy the poor**. ver. 4. Am +*2:6. Ex *21:2. Le *25:39-42. Ne *5:1-5, 8. Jl 3:3, 6. **pair of shoes**. Am 2:6. Ru 4:7. **and sell**. That is, sell the refuse of the wheat as though it were good wheat.

7. **sworn**. Am 6:8. Dt 33:26-29. Ps 47:4. 68:34. Lk 2:32. **the excellency of Jacob**. Am 4:2, 6:8. Ex 15:7✸. 1 S 15:29. Ho 5:5. 7:10. **I will**. Ex 17:16. 1 S 15:2, 3. Ps 10:11. Is 43:25. Je 17:1. +*31:34. Ho 7:2. 8:13. 9:9. He *8:12. *10:17. **never**. Jb 4:20 (✸S#5331h). **forget**. ✸22C4, Ps +13:1.

8. **the land**. It is supposed that an earthquake is here intended; the rising and falling of the ground, with a wave-like motion, and its leaving its proper place and bounds, in consequence of an earthquake, being justly and beautifully compared to the swelling, overflowing, and subsiding of the Nile. Ps 18:7. 60:2,

3. 114:3-7. Is 5:25. 24:19, 20. Je 4:24-26. Mi 1:3-5. Na 1:5, 6. Hab 3:5-8. Hg 2:6, 7. **every one mourn**. ver. 10. Am *9:5. Je *4:28. 12:4. Ho *4:3. 10:5. Mt √24:30. **rise**. Am 9:5. Is 8:7, 8. Je 46:8. Da +*9:26.

9. **I will cause**. This is supposed to refer to an eclipse; and Abp. Usher has shown that about eleven years after Amos prophesied there were two great eclipses of the sun, one at the feast of tabernacles, and the other some time before the passover. Am 4:13. 5:8. Jb 5:14. Is *13:10. 29:9, 10. *59:9, 10. Je *15:9. Jl *2:2. 3:15. Mi √3:6. Mt *24:29. Re 6:12. 8:12. and **I**. T#1975. Ex 10:21-23. Mt ✸27:45. Mk 15:33. Lk 23:44.

10. **I will turn**. See on ver. 3. Am 5:23. 6:4-7. Dt 16:14. 1 S 25:36-38. 2 S 13:28-31. Jb 20:23. Is 21:3, 4. 22:12-14. Da 5:4-6. Ho 2:11. Na 1:10. **your feasts**. Ex 12:14✸. 23:15, 16✸. Le +*23:2n. **sackcloth**. ✸121S3U, Jb +16:15. Ge +*37:34. Is *15:2, 3. Je *48:37. La 2:10. Ezk *7:18. *27:30, 31. Da +9:3. **and baldness**. Is 3:24. **as the mourning**. Je *6:26. Zc √12:10. Lk 7:12, 13. **a bitter**. Jb 3:5mg.

11. **but**. Ge=41:56. 1 S *3:1. 28:6, 15. 2 Ch 15:3. Ps +*74:9. Pr *29:18. Is 5:6. 30:20, 21. La 2:9. Ezk *7:26. Mi √3:6. Mt *9:36. Lk 15:14. Jn *6:35. Ep 2:12. 1 T 6:5. Re 3:17.

12. **shall run**. Pr 14:6. Da +*12:4. Mt *11:25-27. 12:30. *24:23-26. Jn *7:34. Ro 9:31-33. 11:7-10. 2 T *3:6, 7.

13. **the fair**. Dt 32:25. Ps 63:1. 144:12-15. Is *40:30. 41:17-20. Je 48:18. La 1:18. 2:10, 21. Ho *2:3. Zc 9:17. **virgins**. Ge +24:16 (✸S#1330h).

14. **swear**. Ho 4:15. Zp 1:5. **sin**. Dt 9:21. 1 K *12:28, 29, 32. 13:32-34. 14:16. 16:24. 2 K *10:16, 29. Ho 8:5, 6. 10:5. 13:2, 16. **Thy god**. Ex *32:4, 5. **manner**. Heb. way. Ac 9:2. 18:25, 26. 19:9, 23. 24:14. **Beersheba**. See on Am 5:5. **shall fall**. Dt 33:11. 2 Ch *36:16. Ps 36:12. 140:10. Pr *29:1. Is 43:17. Je 25:27. 51:64.

AMOS 9

The certainty of the judgments being inflicted on Israel, 1-7. A remnant would be preserved, 8-10. A prediction of Christ, the blessings of the kingdom, and the restoration of Israel, 11-15.

1. **I saw**. 2 Ch 18:18. Is 6:1. Ezk 1:28. Jn *1:18, 32. Ac 26:13. Re 1:17. **upon**. Am 3:14. Ezk 9:2. 10:4. **the altar**. Am 7:13. 1 K 13:1. The altar of burnt offerings (CB, p. 1231). Ex 29:12, 13, 16, 44. 35:16. 38:1. 40:10, 29. Called the brasen altar: Ex 38:30. 39:39. Called the altar that is by the door of the tabernacle: Le 1:5. 4:7, 18. The altar of the Lord: Le 17:6. Dt 12:27. Jsh 22:29. New Testament allusions to the altar of burnt offerings: Mt 5:23. 23:18, 35. Lk 11:51. 1 C 9:13. 10:18. He 7:13. 13:10. **Smite**. Is 6:3, 4. Ezk 9:5. Zc 11:1, 2. **lintel**. *or*, chapiter, *or* knop. **posts**. 1 K 6:33, 35. **cut them**. *or*, wound them. Jg 16:29, 30. Jb 6:9. Is 38:12. Jl 2:8. **in the head**. Ps *68:21. Is 9:14. Hab 3:13. **shall not flee**. Am *2:14, 15. Is 24:17, 18. 30:16. Je 48:44. **not be delivered**. Am *6:1. Pr √11:4.

2. **Though**. All these energetic expressions were intended to show the utter impossibility of escape from the threatened judgments. **they dig**. Jb 26:6. Ps √139:7-10. Is 2:19. Je 23:24. Ezk 8:8. 12:5, 7. **into**. Ge *42:38. *44:29, 31. Nu √16:30, 33. Ps √9:17. Ezk +*32:27n. Mt *5:29, 30. +*10:28. Lk *12:5. **hell**. Heb. *sheol*, Ge +37:35. The contrast in this verse between *hell* and *heaven* shows that the unseen world, and not *the*

grave, is here meant (Scott). This use of *sheol* shows it is a place, and that existence there is conscious, otherwise the statement would be nonsensical. Amos is not postulating that one could dig into a place of non-existence or annihilation, he is setting forth what is in fact impossible—digging into sheol—as though it were possible, to cut off all avenues of possible escape from God's threatened judgment. In this sentence both hell and heaven are regarded as inaccessible to mortal men, but if men could hide in hell, the living among the dead, even there they could not escape God's predicted judgment, for God would reach them. Ge √37:35. Dt 32:22. 2 S √12:23. Ps +*16:8-11. 49:14. 86:13. 141:7. Pr 9:18. **climb.** Jb *20:6, 7. Is √14:13-16. Je 49:16. *51:53. Ezk √28:13-16. Ob *4. Lk 10:18. **heaven.** *ƒ*45, Is +40:3.

3. **hide.** Jb 34:22. Je 23:23, 24. **hid.** Ps *139:9-11. Je 16:16. **my sight.** *ƒ*22A6, Ps +11:4. **the serpent.** Is 27:1.

4. **go.** Le *26:33, 36-39*)ℙ*. Dt *28:64, 65. Ezk *5:2, 12. Zc 13:8, 9. **command the sword.** Le 26:33*)ℙ*. Dt 28:25*)ℙ*. **set.** Le 17:10*)ℙ*. 20:5*)ℙ*. Dt *28:62, 63. 2 Ch 16:9. Ps *34:15, 16. Je 24:6. 39:12. 44:11. **for evil.** Am +*3:6. Is +*45:7. Je *21:10. **not for good.** Je *44:11, 27.

5. **toucheth.** Ps 46:6. 144:5. Is 64:1, 2. Mi *1:3, 4. Na 1:5, 6. Hab 3:10. Re 20:11. **and all.** Am 8:8. Je 12:4. Ho 4:3. **shall rise.** Ps 32:6. 93:3, 4. Is 8:7, 8. Mt 7:27.

6. **buildeth.** Ps *104:3, 13. **stories.** *or*, spheres. Heb. ascensions. *Maaloth*, "upper chambers," which in eastern houses are the principal apartments. Perhaps there is a reference here to the various *systems* which God has created in illimitable space, transcending each other as the planets do in our system. *❋S#4609h. Ex 20:26 (steps). 1 K 10:19, 20. 2 K 9:13 (stairs). 20:9 (degrees), 10, 11 (degrees, dial). 1 Ch 17:17 (high degree). 2 Ch 9:18, 19. Ezr 7:9 (to go up; mg, the going up). Ne 3:15. 12:37. Ps 120:t. 121:t. 122:t. 123:t. 124:t. 125:t. 127:t. 128:t. 131:t. 132:t. 133:t. 134:t. Is 38:8. Ezk 11:5 (things that come into). 40:6, 22, 26, 31, 34, 37, 49. 43:17. **in the heaven.** Is 48:13. **troop.** *or*, bundle. Ge 2:1. *Aguddah* probably is the same as the Arabic *ijad*, "an arch, vault," and may here denote the vault of heaven, or atmosphere, which God "hath founded, or established, upon, or over, *al*, the earth," and into which "he calleth the waters of the sea, and poureth them out upon the face of the earth." **calleth.** Am *5:8. Ge 7:11-19. Je 5:22. **face.** Ge +1:2. **The Lord.** Am *4:13. Ex 3:14, 15. **is his name.** Ex +*6:3n. +15:3*)ℙ*.

7. **ye not as.** Je 9:25, 26. 13:23. **Have not.** Am 2:10. Ex 12:51. Is 43:3. Ho 12:13. **brought up Israel.** Ex 13:3, 9, 14, 16*)ℙ*. 33:1*)ℙ*. Dt 5:15*)ℙ*. 6:21*)ℙ*. **the Philistines.** Dt 2:23. Je 47:4. **the Syrians.** Am 1:5. 2 K 16:9. **Caphtor.** or, Crete. Dt 2:23*)ℙ*. **Kir.** i.e. *a wall, fortress*, ❋S#7024h. Am 1:5. 2 K 16:9. Is 15:1. 22:6. A city from which the Syrians came forth to settle in the country north of Palestine. Its location is unknown. Tiglath-pileser sent the captive Syrians to it after the conquest of Damascus.

8. **the eyes.** ver. 4. Ps 11:4-6. Pr 5:21. 15:3. Je 44:27. **and I.** Ge 6:7. 7:4. Dt 6:15. 1 K 13:34. Ho 1:6. 9:11-17. 13:15, 16. **saving.** Dt 4:31. Is 10:21, 22. 27:7, 8. Je 5:10. √30:11. +√31:35, 36. +√33:24-26. Jl

2:32. Ob 16, 17. Ro +*11:1-7, 28, 29. **not utterly destroy.** 1 S +12:22. Is +√41:9. +60:10. Je +*4:27. Zc √10:6. Ro +√11:1, 2.

9. **and I.** Le 26:33. Dt 28:64. **sift.** Heb. cause to move. *ƒ*22C33. Anthropomorphism B890. Human actions are attributed to God: sifting. Lk 22:31, 32. **among all.** Le 26:33. Ja 1:1. **like as.** Is 27:8. **yet shall not.** Ge 19:22. 2 K 10:23. Ezk +*9:6. √39:28. Zc *10:9. *13:8, 9. Ml *3:6. Lk 22:31. Re 7:3. **grain.** Heb. stone.

10. **the sinners.** Is 33:14. Ezk 20:38. 34:16, 17. Zp 3:11-13. Zc 13:8, 9. Ml 3:2-5. 4:1. Mt 3:10-12. 13:41, 42, 49, 50. **The evil.** Am 6:1, 3. Ps 10:11. Ec √8:11. Is 5:19. *28:14, 15. 56:12. Je 18:13. Ml 3:15. Mt *24:50.

11. **that day.** Ac ▶15:15-17. 2 Th +*1:10. **raise.** 2 S *7:13. 1 K *11:38, 39. Ps +*102:13, 16. +*147:2. Is +*9:6, 7. √11:1-10. Je +*23:5, 6. 30:9. 33:14-16, 20-26. Ezk 17:24. 34:23, 24. *37:24, 25. Ho √3:5. Mi +*5:2. Lk +*1:31-33, 69, 70. Ac 2:30-36. +*15:16. **the tabernacle.** 2 S *7:13. Is *16:5. Ezk 21:25-27. 37:27. La 2:6. Ac +*15:16. **of David.** Ac +❋*13:23. +*15:16. **is fallen.** Ps *80:16. Mt 23:38. Lk 13:35. **close.** Heb. hedge, *or* wall. Jb 1:10. Ps 80:12. 89:40. Is 5:5. **as in.** Ps 143:5. Is *63:11. Je 46:26. La *5:21. Ezk √36:11. Mi *7:14. **of old.** Heb. *olam*, Ge +6:4.

12. **possess.** Is 11:14. 14:1, 2. Jl 3:8. Ob *18-21. **Edom.** Ge 27:29, 37, 40. Nu *24:17, 18. 2 S 8:14. Ps 60:8. Ml 1:4. **which are called by my name.** Heb. upon whom my name is called. Dt 28:10. 2 S 12:28mg. 1 K 8:43mg. Is 43:7. 63:19. 65:1. Je 7:10mg. +14:9mg. +*15:16mg. Da 9:18, 19. Ac ▶15:17. Ja 2:7.

13. **plowman.** Le *26:5*)ℙ*. Ezk 36:35. Ho 2:21-23. Jn 4:35. **shall overtake.** Is 29:17. *35:1-9. +*51:3. 55:12, 13. 60:13-17. *65:25. Je 31:5, 6. Ezk *34:26, 27. *36:8, 29, 30, 35. Ho 2:21. Jl 3:18. **the reaper.** Ps *144:13-15. Jn *4:36. **soweth.** Heb. draweth forth. **the mountains.** Is 35:1, 2. 55:13. Jl *3:18, 20. **sweet wine.** *or*, new wine. **the hills.** ver. 5. Jg 5:5. Ps 97:5. Na 1:5. **melt.** *ƒ*102, Ge +2:24.

14. **I will bring.** Am ◖5:11. Dt *30:5*)ℙ*. Ps *53:6. Is √11:11. Je *30:3, 18. *31:23, +*36. +*33:26. Ezk 16:53. +*28:25. +*34:13. 36:24. *39:25. Jl *3:1, 2. Zp 2:7. √3:20. Zc √8:7, 8. Ro +√11:1. **build.** Is *61:4. +*65:21, 22. Je *30:18. *31:38-40. Ezk +*36:10, 33-36. *37:25-28. Zc +*1:17. **and inhabit.** Ho 11:11. **plant.** Am 5:11. Is *62:8, 9. Ezk *28:26. Ho 2:21-23. Jl 2:23. 3:18. Zp *1:13. Zc *8:12. **and drink.** Zc 9:17.

15. **I will plant.** Le 25:18, 19*)ℙ*. 26:5*)ℙ*. Zc *8:8. **their land.** Ge 13:15*)ℙ*. *17:8. Dt +*32:43. 1 K +*4:21n. Is +*60:21n. Je +*7:7. 24:6. *32:41. Ezk 28:25. +*34:28. 36:24, 28. *37:12, 21, 25. *38:8. Jl √3:20, 21. Mi *4:4. Zc 3:9. **they shall.** As the Jews, after their return from Babylon, were driven from their land by the Romans, this can only refer to their future conversion and restoration, and to the security and peace of the church. The preceding note, written nearly two centuries ago, need only change the last words "the church" to "Israel" to be fully correct, for this prophecy pertains to natural Israel, not the New Testament church. **no more be pulled up.** Is +√11:11n. 32:18. 33:20. *51:22. √60:21n. Je *7:7. +*23:8. 24:6. *31:40. *32:41mg. Ezk 34:28. √36:11. 37:23-27. Ho +*2:19. Jl *3:20. Mi 4:4. Zp √3:15. Zc +√9:8. +*14:11. **which I have given them.** Nu 32:7, 9*)ℙ*. Dt 3:18*)ℙ*. 26:15*)ℙ*. 28:52*)ℙ*. Jsh 2:9, 14. 18:3. 23:13, 15. 2 Ch +*20:7. Je √25:5. Ezk √28:25.

OBADIAH

OBADIAH

A prediction of the ruin of Edom for his pride, and his malice against the descendants of his brother Jacob, 1-16. Promises of glorious times, in the latter ages, 17-21.

1. A.M. 3417. B.C. 587. **Obadiah**. i.e. *servant of Jehovah*, *S#5662h. 1 Ch 3:21. 7:3. 8:38. 9:16, 44. 12:9. 2 Ch *17:7. Ezr 8:9. Ne 10:5. 12:25. Ob 1. Also *S#5662h: 1 K 18:3, 3, 4, 5, 6, 7, 16. 1 Ch 27:19. 2 Ch 34:12. (1) The head of a family which apparently descended from David, 1 Ch 3:21. (2) A descendant of Tola, the son of Issachar, 1 Ch 7:3. (3) A son of Azel, a Benjamite, 1 Ch 8:38; 9:44. (4) A Levite, the son of Shemaiah, 1 Ch 9:16. (5) A Gadite who joined David in Ziklag, 1 Ch 12:9. (6) The governor of the house of Ahab, king of Israel. He hid and fed many of the Lord's prophets during the persecution of Jezebel. 1 K 18:3-16. (7) One of the princes of Judah who taught the people the law in the reign of Jehoshaphat, 2 Ch *17:7. Young notes (*Concise Critical Comments*, p. 596), "The vision of Obadiah was delivered according to most critics about B.C. 585, in the reign of Jehoiakim, but its position in the Jewish Canon points to a much earlier date, and Obadiah is conjectured to have been the prince of that name commissioned by Jehoshaphat (2 Ch 17:7), to teach in Judah, B.C. 913." (8) The father of Ishmaiah, 1 Ch 27:19. (9) A Levite overseer of repairs of the house of the Lord in the time of Josiah, 2 Ch 34:12. (10) A son of Jehiel, Ezr 8:9. (11) A priest who sealed the covenant made by Nehemiah, Ne 10:5. (12) A porter for the sanctuary, Ne 12:25. (13) Obadiah, the fourth of the minor prophets, lived after the destruction of Jerusalem, B.C. 588, but nothing more is known about him, Ob 1. But see on (7) above. **concerning**. Ps *137:7. Is *21:11, 12. ch. *34. 63:1-6. Je *9:25, 26. 25:17, 21. 49:7-22. La 4:21, 22. Ezk 25:12-14. 35:3, etc. Jl 3:19. Am 1:11, 12. Ml 1:3, 4. **We**. Je 49:14, 15. 51:46. Mt *24:6. Mk 13:7. **rumor**. lit. hearing. ∫121R1, Le +13:55. **from the Lord**. Am +*3:6. **and an**. Is 18:2, 3. 30:4. **Arise**. Je 6:4, 5. 50:9-15. 51:27, 28. Mi 2:13.

2. **made thee small**. Nu 24:18. 1 S 2:7, 8. 2 K *14:7. Jb 34:25-29. Ps 107:39, 40. Is 23:9. Je ▸49:15. Ezk 29:15. Mi 7:10. Ml *1:3. Lk 1:51, 52.

3. **pride**. Jb *20:5-7. Pr *16:18. 18:12. 29:23. Is 10:14-16. *14:13. 16:6. Je 48:29, 30. *49:16. Ezk +*16:49. Ml 1:4. **thou that dwellest**. Jerome observes, that all the southern parts of Palestine, from Eleutheropolis to Petra and Elath, were full of caverns, hewn out of the rocks, and that the people had subteraneous dwellings similar to ovens. The whole of Idumea was very mountainous, and these caverns are the *clefts of the rock* here referred to; in which they thought themselves safe, and no power brought against them could dislodge them from their fastnesses. **clefts**. Heb. *chaga-vim*, chasms. *S#2288h. SS 2:14. Je *49:16n. **rock**. Heb. *sela*, a cliff or abrupt and elevated rock. Here without the Hebrew article, as Is 16:1. With the article, applied as a proper name to *Petra*, 2 K √14:7n. 2 Ch 25:12. Possibly Jg 1:36. Certain descriptive terms are

used exclusively in connection with *Sela*: (1) *Chagavim*, in this verse, "clefts." (2) *Seiph*, a cleft. S#5553h. Jg 15:8, 11. Is 2:21. 57:5. (3) *Tsechiach*, a *bald* spot, as the summit of a rock exposed to the drying sun. *S#6706h. Ne 4:13. Ezk 24:7, 8. *26:4, 14. (4) *Nekik*, a *cranny* or fissure. *S#5357h. Is 7:19. Je 13:4. 16:16. (5) *Shen*, a *tooth* or sharp edge or end of a crag. S#8127h. 1 S 14:4, 5. Jb 39:28. Used as a proper name, 1 S 7:12 (Shen). **whose habitation**. Ps 60:9. Hab *2:9. **saith in his heart**. Is √14:13-15. *47:7, 8. Je 49:4. Re 18:7, 8.

4. **Though**. ∫102C, Mt +5:29. **exalt**. Jb 20:6, 7. 39:27, 28. Je *49:16. Hab *2:9. **set thy nest**. Note the reference to the Pentateuch. See also ver. 5, 10, where reference is also made to the Pentateuch. See related note (Is +*1:2). Nu 24:21▸𝒫. Hab 2:9. **among**. Ps 139:8. Is 14:12-15. Je 51:53. Am *9:2.

5. **if robbers**. Je ▸49:9. **how**. 2 S 1:19. Is 14:12. Je 50:23. La 1:1. Zp 2:15. Re 18:10. **would**. ∫85B, Ge +13:9. **if the grape gatherers**. Dt 24:21▸𝒫. Is +*17:6. 24:13. Je 6:9. ▸49:9. Mi 7:1. **some grapes**. or, gleanings. Jg 8:2. Is *17:6.

6. **are the**. Ps 139:1. Is 10:13, 14. 45:3. Je *49:10. 50:37. Mt *6:19, 20. **how are his**. Da 2:22.

7. **the men of**. The Chaldeans, whose agents they became in persecuting the Jews. Ps 55:12, 13. 83:5-8. Je 4:30. 30:14. La 1:19. Ezk 23:22-25. Re 17:12-17. **men that were at peace with thee**. Heb. men of thy peace. Ps 41:9mg. Je 20:10mg. 38:22mg. **they that eat thy bread**. Heb. the men of thy bread. Ps 41:9. Jn 13:18. **there is**. ver. 8. Is 19:11-14. 27:11. Je *49:7. Ho 13:13. **in him**. or, of it.

8. **Shall I**. ∫85B, Ge +13:9. **in that day**. ver. 15, 16. Is 63:1-6. Je 49:13. **even**. Jb *5:12-14. Ps 33:10. Is 19:3, 13, 14. 29:14. 1 C 1:19, 20. *3:19, 20.

9. **thy**. Ps *76:5, 6. Is 19:16, 17. Je 49:22. 50:36, 37. Am 2:16. Na 3:13. **O**. Ge 36:11. Jb 2:11. Je 49:7, 20. Ezk 25:13. Am *1:12. **every**. Is 34:5-8. 63:1-3. **mount**. ver. 21. Dt 2:5.

10. **violence**. Ge *27:11, 41-44▸𝒫. 32:6-8. Nu 20:14-21. Dt 23:7▸𝒫. Ps 83:5-9. *137:7. La 4:21. Ezk 25:12. *35:5, 6, 12-15. Jl *3:19. Am √1:11. **shame**. Ps 69:7. 89:45. 109:29. 132:18. Je 3:25. 51:51. Ezk 7:18. Mi 7:10. **and**. Je 49:13, 17-20. Ezk 25:13, 14. 35:6, 7, 9, 15. Ml 1:3, 4. **for ever**. Heb. *olam*, Ex +*12:24.

11. **in the day that the**. 2 K 24:10-16. 25:11. Je 52:28-30. **captive his forces**. or, his substance. ∫121N2. Metonymy of the Adjunct, Ge +34:29. ver. 13mg. Is *60:5mg. Ro 11:25. **cast**. Jl 3:3. Na 3:10. **even**. Ps 50:18. *137:7. Je 39:4, 5.

12. **thou**, etc. or, do not behold, etc. **looked**. Ps 22:17. 37:13. 54:7. 59:10. 92:11. Mi 4:11. 7:8-10. Mt 27:40-43. **the day**. ∫121P4, Dt +4:32. **rejoiced**. Jb 31:29. Ps *137:7. Pr +*17:5. +*24:17, 18. La 4:21. Ezk 25:6, 7. 35:15. Mi 7:8. Mt 5:44. Lk 19:41. **thou have**. 1 S 2:3. Ps 31:18. **spoken proudly**. Heb. magnified thy mouth. Ps 35:21. Is 37:24. 57:4. Ezk 35:13. Ja 3:5. 2 P 2:18. Ju 16. Re 13:5.

13. **looked**. 2 S 16:12. Ps 22:17. Zc 1:15. **substance**. or, forces. ver. 11mg.

14. **neither shouldest.** Am 1:6, 9. **delivered up.** *or,* shut up. Ps 31:8. **in the day.** ver. 12. Ge 35:3. Is 37:3. Je +*30:7.

15. **the day of the Lord.** Ps *37:12, 13. *110:5, 6. Is 2:11, 17. 10:25. Je *9:25, 26. 25:15-29. 49:12. La 4:21, 22. Ezk +*30:3. Jl *3:11-14. Mi 5:15. Zc 14:14-18. 1 P *4:17. **all the heathen.** Ezk +*30:3. Mi 5:15. Zc 14:2. Re 13:+*3, *7, 8, *16, 17. **as thou hast done.** Ge +*12:3. Jg *1:7. Ps 137:8. Ezk 35:15. Jl 3:7, 8. Hab 2:8. Mt *7:2. √25:31-46. Ja *2:13.

16. **as ye.** Ps 75:8, 9. Is 49:25, 26. 51:22, 23. Je 25:15, 16, 27-29. 49:12. Jl 3:17. 1 P *4:17. **so shall.** Je *30:16. Ezk 25:12-14. Mt *7:2. Ja *2:13. **swallow down.** *or,* sup up. Jb 6:3. Is +42:14mg. Hab 1:9. **and they shall be.** Is 8:9, 10. 26:14. 29:7, 8. La 4:21, 22. Ezk 35:14, 15.

17. **upon.** Is +*24:23. 46:13. Jl +*2:32. **shall be.** Je *46:28. Jl *2:32. 3:16. Am 9:8. Ro +*11:26. **deliverance.** *or,* they that escape. Ps *71:2. *83:3. +*94:13. Is 16:1-5. +*26:20. 57:1. Je 44:14, 28. Ezk 7:16. Jl 2:32. Zp +*2:3. Lk +*21:36. **there shall be holiness.** *or,* it shall be holy. Is 1:26, 27. 4:3, 4. +√60:21. Jl *3:17. Zc 8:3. 14:20, 21. Re 21:27. **shall possess.** Nu 24:18, 19. Ps *69:35. Is *14:1, 2. +*26:15. Jl *3:19-21. Am √9:11-15. Mi *4:11-13. Ac +*7:5.

18. **shall be a fire.** Dt 4:24. Jb *31:3. Is *10:17, 18. 31:9. Mi 5:8. Zc *12:6. He *12:29. **the house of Joseph.** 2 S 19:20. Ezk 37:16, 19. Am 5:15. 6:6. **for**

stubble. Ps 83:6-15. Is 5:24. 47:14. Jl 2:5. Na 1:10. 1 C 3:12. **there shall not be.** ver. 9, 10, 16. **any remaining.** ver. 14. Nu 24:19. Is 63:1-6. Je 49:7-22.

19. **the south.** Nu 24:18, 19. Jsh 15:21. Ps *60:6-12. Is +*30:6. Je 32:44. Am *9:12. Mi *7:8-10. Ml *1:4, 5. **the plain.** Jsh 13:2, 3. 15:33, 45, 46. Jg 1:18, 19. Is 11:13, 14. Ezk 25:16. Am 1:8. Zp *2:4-7. Zc *9:5-7. **Philistines.** Ge +10:14. **the fields of Ephraim.** 2 K 17:24. Ezr 4:2, 7-10, 17. Ps 69:35. Je 31:4-6. Ezk 36:6-12, 28. +*37:21-25. 47:13-21. 48:1-9. **Benjamin.** Jsh 13:25, 31. 18:21-28. 1 Ch 5:26. Je 49:1. Am *1:13. Mi 7:14.

20. **the captivity of this.** Je 3:18. 33:26. Ezk 34:12, 13. Ho 1:10, 11. Am √9:14, 15. Zc √10:6-10. **Zarephath.** 1 K *17:9, 10. Lk 4:26, Sarepta. **Sepharad.** *i.e. drawn apart; end of wandering; end of spreading out; boundary, limit,* *S#5614h. **which is in Sepharad, shall possess.** *or,* shall possess that which is in Sepharad, they shall possess. Je 13:19. 32:44. *33:13.

21. **saviors.** Jg 2:16. 3:9, 15. 2 K 13:5. Is 19:20. Da +*12:3. Ho +*11:12. Jl +*2:32. +*3:11. Mi *5:4-9. Zc 9:11-17. 10:5-12. 1 T +*4:16. Ja +*5:20. **shall come.** Is 63:1. Mi *4:7. **to judge.** Ps +*149:5-9. Da 7:27. Lk √22:30. 1 C +*6:2, 3. Re 19:11-13. +*20:4. **and the kingdom.** Ps *2:6-9. *22:28. 102:15. Is +*9:6, 7. Da *2:35, 44. 7:14, 27. Zc +*14:9. Mt *6:10, 13. Lk *1:32, 33. 1 C +*15:24, 25, 28. Re *11:15. *19:6, 16.

JONAH

JONAH 1

God commands Jonah to go and prophesy against Nineveh, 1, 2. Fleeing from the service, he attempts to sail to Tarshish; but is overtaken by a tempest, and discovered by lot, 3-10. The mariners reluctantly cast him into the sea; the storm abates, and they sacrifice to Jehovah, 11-16. Jonah is swallowed by a great fish; and continues in its belly three days, 17.

1. A.M. 3142. B.C. 862. **the word of the Lord.** Jon 2:10. 3:1, 3. 4:4, 9, 10. Dt 18:18, 19. Jn 7:16. 8:28, 46, 47. 12:49. 14:10, 24. 17:8. 2 P +*1:21. **Jonah.** i.e. *a dove,* *S#3124h. Jon 1:1, 3, 5, 7, 15, 17, 17. 2:1, 10. 3:1, 4. 4:1, 5, 6, 6, 8, 9. 2 K √14:25. Mt √12:39-41. *16:4. Lk *11:29, 30, 32, Jonas.

2. **Nineveh.** Jon 3:2, 3. 4:11. Ge 10:11, 12. 2 K 19:36. Na 1:1. ch. 2, 3. Zp 2:13-15. **cry.** Jon 3:2, 4. Jg 7:3, 20. Is *58:1. Je 1:7-10. Ezk 2:7, 8. 3:5-9. Jl 3:9. Am 4:5. Mi 3:8. Mt 10:18. **for.** Note the reference to the Pentateuch. Other references to the Pentateuch in Jonah are at ver. 9. Jon 4:2, 8. See related note (Is +*1:2). Ge *18:20, 21㏒. Ezr 9:6. Ja +*5:4. Re 18:5.

3. **to flee.** Jon 4:2. Ex 4:13, 14. 1 K 19:3, 9. Je 20:7-9. Ezk 3:14. Lk 9:62. Ac 15:38. 26:19. 1 C 9:16. **Tarshish.** Ge +10:4. **from the presence.** ſ22A4, Ge +19:13. Ge 3:8. 4:16. Nu 35:34. Jb 1:12. 2:7. Ps 139:7-12. Pr 27:8. 2 Th 1:9. **Joppa.** Jsh 19:46. 2 Ch 2:16. Ezr 3:7. Ac 9:36. **going.** lit. coming. ſ171J14. Synecdoche of the Species B633. Verbs having a special meaning are used in a more general sense. "To come" is used of going as well as coming. For other instances of this figure see Mk 16:2. Jn 6:17. 11:29. Ac 28:14.

Re 6:1, 3, 5, 7. **Tarshish.** As Jonah embarked at *Joppa,* a seaport on the Mediterranean, it was probably either *Tarsus* in Cilicia, or rather *Tartessus* in Spain, to which he intended to flee. When we reflect how such a message would be received in the streets of London at this day, we shall not wonder at the prophet's reluctance to announce the destruction of the proud and idolatrous Nineveh. 1 K *10:22. 2 Ch +9:21n. 20:36, 37. Is 2:16. 23:1, 6, 10. 60:9. Je 10:9. Ezk 27:12, 25.

4. **the Lord.** Ex 10:13, 19. 14:21. 15:10. Nu 11:31. Ps *48:7. *107:24-31. 135:7. Am 4:13. Mt 8:24-27. Ac 27:13-20. **send out.** Heb. cast forth. **like.** Heb. thought.

5. **mariners.** lit. salt men. Ezk 27:9, 27, 29. **cried.** ver. 6, 14, 16. Ex 2:23. 1 K 18:26. Is 44:17-20. 45:20. Je 2:28. Ho 7:14. **every man.** Mi 4:5. **and cast.** Jb *2:4. Ac *27:18, 19, 38. Ph 3:7, 8. **wares.** or, tackling. lit. "vessels, instruments." Ge 24:53. **the sides.** lit. "thighs." ſ96F3, Ge +8:4. Ge 49:13. 1 S 24:3. Ezk 32:23. Am 6:10. **ship.** The deck, or covered part. Hebrew root *saphan,* to cover. Dt 33:21mg. 1 K 6:9. 7:3, 7. Je 22:14. Hg 1:4. **and was.** Jg 16:19. Mt 25:5. 26:40, 41, 43, 45. Lk 22:45, 46.

6. **shipmaster.** lit. chief of the rope. Heb. *rab hachobel. rab,* captain or head. 2 K 25:8. Est 1:8. Da 1:3. *chobel.* Ezk 27:8, 27, 28, 29 (pilot). **What.** Is 3:15. Ezk 18:2. Ac *21:13. Ro *13:11. Ep *5:14. **O sleeper.** Ps 13:3. Lk 22:46. 1 Th 5:6. **arise.** Ps *78:34. *107:6, 12, 13, 18-20, 28, 29. Je *2:27, 28. Mk *4:37-41. **if.** Jon *3:9. 2 S 12:22. Est *4:16. Jl 2:14. Am *5:15. **call upon.** T#1690. ver. 13-15. Ps 107:23-30. Mk 4:37-39.

7. **every.** Jg 7:13, 14. Is 41:6, 7. **and let.** Jsh 7:14-18. +14:2n. Jg 20:9, 10. 1 S 10:20, 21. 14:41, 42. Est

3:7. Ps 22:18. Pr +*16:33. Mt 27:35. Ac *1:23-26. 13:19. **for.** Jsh 7:10-13. 22:16-20. 1 S 14:38, 39. Jb 10:2. **evil.** Is +*45:7. Am +*3:6. **and the.** Nu +*32:23. Jsh 7:18. 1 C 4:5.

8. **Tell.** Jsh *7:19. 1 S *14:43. Ja +*5:16. **What is thine.** Ge 47:3. 1 S 30:13.

9. **I am.** Ge 14:13. 39:14. 40:15. Ex 3:18. Ph 3:5. **and I.** 2 K 17:25, 28, 32-35. Jb 1:9. Ps 146:5, 6. Ho 3:5. Ac 27:23. Re 15:4. **the Lord.** *or,* Jehovah. **the God of heaven.** 2 Ch 36:23. Ezr 1:2. 5:11, 12. 6:9, 10. 7:12, 13, 21, 23. Ne 1:4, 5. 2:4, 20. Ps 136:26. Da 2:18, 19, 44. Re 11:13. 16:11. **which.** Ge 1:1, 10乃P. Ne 9:6. Ps 95:5, 6. 146:5, 6. Ac 14:15. 17:23-25.

10. **were.** Jsh 2:11. 1 S *15:22, 23. 1 K 13:20-22. Jn 19:8. **exceedingly afraid.** Heb. afraid, with great fear. ♪147D, Ge +1:29. Da 5:6-9. **Why.** Jsh 7:25. 2 S 24:3. **he fled.** ver. 3. Jb 27:22.

11. **What.** 1 S 6:2, 3. 2 S 21:1-6. 24:11-13. Mi 6:6, 7. **calm unto us.** Heb. silent from us. ver. 12. Ps +37:7mg. Pr 26:20mg. **wrought, and was tempestuous.** *or,* grew more and more tempestuous. Heb. went and was, etc.

12. **Take.** 2 S 24:17. Jn 11:50. **for I know.** Jsh 7:12, 20, 21. 1 Ch 21:17. Ec 9:18. Ac 27:24. **for my sake.** Ps *32:5. *51:3, 4. Je 3:13. 14:20.

13. **Nevertheless the.** There was great humanity and tender feeling in these men. They were probably affected deeply with the candid confession, the disinterested, submissive conduct of the disobedient prophet, and were unwilling to cast him into the deep, until they found that every effort to save themselves was in vain. **rowed.** Heb. digged. Am 9:2. **but.** Jb 34:29. Pr +*21:30.

14. **they cried.** ver. 5, 16. Ps 107:28. Is 26:16. **let us not.** T#1465. Jon 1:4-6. Ge 4:13-15. 20:3, 7. 21:14-16. 32:9-12. Ex 10:16, 17. 20:18, 19. 32:10-12. Nu 11:1, 2. 14:15, 16, 19, 20. 16:20-22, 43-45. 20:2-6. 21:6, 7. Jg 15:18. 2 S 12:13-16. 1 K 8:37-39. 2 K 1:13, 14. 1 Ch 21:16, 17. 18:30, 31. Is *38:1-5. La 2:19. 3:52-58. Da 2:17, 18. Mt 8:23-25. 14:28-30. 26:39. Mk 4:38, 39. 5:22, 23. Lk 4:38, 39. 7:2-5. 8:41, 42. Jn 4:46, 47. Ja 5:14, 15. 1 J *5:16, 17. **life.** Heb. *nephesh,* soul, Ge +44:30. **lay not.** Ge 9:6. Dt *21:8. Ac 28:4. **for thou hast done.** Ps *115:3. 135:6. Da *4:34, 35. Mt 11:26. Ep 1:9, +*11.

15. **they.** Jsh 7:24-26. 2 S 21:8, 9. Ps 39:9. **took up.** Ge 47:30. Ex 28:12, 29. **and the.** Ps *89:9. 93:3, 4. *107:29. Mt *8:26. Lk *8:24. **ceased.** Heb. stood. Ge 19:17.

16. **feared.** ver. 10. Is √26:9. Da *4:34-37. 6:26. Mk *4:41. Ac 5:11. **offered,** etc. Heb. sacrificed a sacrifice unto the Lord, and vowed vows. Ge 8:20. Jg 13:16. 2 K 5:17. Ps *76:11. 107:22. Is 60:5-7. **made vows.** Ge 28:20. Le +*23:38. Ps 50:14. 66:13-16. 116:14. Ec *5:4.

17. **the Lord.** Jon 4:6. Ge 1:21. Ps 104:25, 26. Hab 3:2. **prepared.** or, appointed, or assigned. Jon 4:6, 7, 8. From Hebrew *manah,* to number. Hence, to appoint, as in Jb 7:3. Da 1:5, 10, 11, and Chaldea **menah,** Da 5:25, 26. Never means to create (CB). **great fish.** Mt 12:40, Greek, *ketos,* any large marine monster; whence *cetaceae,* the mammalian order of fish. **in.** Mt √12:39, 40. *16:4. Lk *11:30. **belly.** Heb. bowels. Jon 2:1. **for three days and.** ♪108H12, 1 S +30:12. Jsh 5:11n. 1 S 30:12n. 1 K 16:8n.

JONAH 2

Jonah's prayer in the fish's belly, and his thanksgiving and vows, 1-9. His marvellous deliverance, 10.

1. **prayed.** T#1190. 2 Ch 33:11-13. Ps +*50:15. 91:15. Is 26:16. Ho *5:15. *6:1-3. Ja 5:13. **out.** Jb 13:15. Ps 130:1, 2. La 3:53-56. Ac 16:24, 25.

2. **I cried.** Jon 1:2, 6, 14. Ge 32:7-12. 24-28. 1 S 30:6. Ps 4:1. 18:4-6. 22:24. 34:6. *65:2. *120:1. *130:1. 142:1-3. Lk 22:44. He *5:7. **by reason of mine.** *or,* out of mine. 1 S 1:16. **he heard.** Ps 65:2. Is 45:19. **out.** Ps 18:5, 6. 61:2. 86:13. 88:1-7. 116:3. Mt √12:38-41. **hell.** *or,* the grave. Heb. *sheol,* Ge +*37:35n. Dt +32:22. Jb 26:6. Ps +*9:17. +*16:10. *139:7, 8. Is +*14:9, 11. Ezk +*32:27n. Am +*9:2n. Hab 2:5. Mt √12:40. Ac *2:27, 31. **and thou heardest.** ♪90, Ps +17:1. Ps 34:6. 65:2.

3. **thou.** Jon 1:12-16. Ps 69:1, 2, 14, 15. *88:5-8. La 3:54. **deep.** or, shady place. Jb 41:31. Ps 68:22. 69:2, 15. 107:24. **midst.** Heb. heart. Pr 23:34. **the floods.** or, tides. lit. "river." ♪96F1, Ge +3:8. Ge 2:10, 13. 2 K 5:12n. Ezk +32:2. **all thy billows.** lit. "heaps." ♪90, Ps +17:1. Ge 31:46, 47, 48, 51, 52. Jsh 7:26. 8:29. Ps *42:7.

4. **I said.** Ps *31:22. 77:1-7. Is 38:10-14, 17. 49:14. Ezk 37:11. **out.** 1 K 9:7. Je 7:15. 15:1. **yet will.** Ps 42:5, 11. *43:5. **toward.** 1 K *8:38, 39, 42, 48. 2 Ch 6:38. Ps 5:7. Da +*6:10.

5. **waters compassed.** Ge 7:18. Ps 40:2. *69:1, 2. La 3:54. **soul.** Heb. *nephesh,* Ge +12:13. **the depth.** T#1205. ✻S#8415h. Ge 1:2 (deep). 7:11. 8:2. 49:25. Ex 15:5, 8. Dt 8:7. 33:13. Jb 28:14. 38:16, 30. 41:32. Ps 33:7. 36:6. 42:7. *71:20. 77:16. 78:15. 104:6. 106:9. 107:26. 135:6. 148:7. Pr 3:20. 8:24, 27, 28. Is 51:10. 63:13. Ezk 26:19. 31:4, 15. Am 7:4. Hab 3:10.

6. **bottoms.** Heb. cuttings off. ✻S#7095h. 1 K 6:25 (cut down). 7:37 (size). **mountains.** Dt 32:22. Ps 65:6. 104:6, 8. Is 40:12. Hab 3:6, 10. **the earth.** Jb 38:4-11. Pr 8:25-29. **yet.** Ps +*16:10. Is 38:17. Ac *13:33-37. **her bars.** Je 51:30. La 2:9. Am 1:5. Na 3:13. **for ever.** Heb. *olam,* Ex +*12:24. **corruption.** *or,* the pit. Jb +*9:31 (✻S#7845h). 33:24, 28. Ps 9:15. 30:3, 9. 55:23. 143:7. Is *38:17.

7. **my soul.** Heb. *nephesh,* Ge +34:3. ♪121A7, Ge +9:5. Ps 22:14. 27:13. 107:5. 119:81-83. He 12:3. **fainted.** T#1329. Jon 4:8. Ps 27:13. 77:3. 84:2. 107:4-6. 142:3h (overwhelmed). Je 14:2. La *2:12h (swooned). **I remembered.** ♪121C2B, Is +44:21. By Metonymy of the Cause, the verb "remember" is used of a strong desire or wish for the thing mentioned or remembered. Here, Jonah desired the Lord, and called upon Him. 1 S 30:6. Ps 20:7. 42:5, 11. 43:5. 77:10, 11. 143:5. Is 50:10. La 3:21-26. 2 C 1:9, 10. **my prayer.** 2 Ch 30:27. Ps *18:6. *66:19. Is +*65:24. Re 5:8. 8:3, 4. **holy.** ver. 4. Ps 5:7. 11:4. 65:4. Mi 1:2. Hab *2:20.

8. **observe.** 1 S 12:21. 2 K *17:15. Ps 31:6. Je 2:13. 10:+*2, 8, 14, 15. 16:19. Hab *2:18-20. **lying vanities.** or, vanities of emptiness. Ps *31:6. Je +*8:19. +14:22. *16:19. 1 C *8:4. **forsake.** Je 17:13. **mercy.** Heb. *hesed.* A homonym, with two meanings: (1) lovingkindness, as in Ge 24:12. 2 S 7:15. 1 Ch 19:2. 2 Ch 6:14. Ps 103:4, 8, 11, 17. (2) correction, or chastisement, Le 20:17 (a wicked thing bringing down punishment). Jb 37:13 (mercy, or chastisement, synonymous with "correction" in preceding clause, mg. *rod*). Pr 25:10 (put to shame, i.e. by correction).

9. **I will sacrifice**. Ge 35:3. Le 7:12. +*23:19. Nu 15:3, 8. Ps *50:14, 23. 66:13-15. 107:22. 116:17, 18. Pr 7:14. Je +*33:11. Ho *14:2. Ro *12:1. He *13:15. **I will pay**. Le +*23:38. Dt 23:18. 2 S 15:7. Jb 22:27. Pr 7:14. Ec *5:4, 5. **Salvation**. ♪74, Jg +5:31. Ps 3:8. 37:39, 40. 68:20. Is *43:11. 45:17. Ho *13:4. Jn 4:22. Ac √4:12. Re 7:10.

10. **spake**. Jon 1:17. Ge 1:3, 7, 9, 11, 14. Ps *8:6-9. *33:9. 105:31, 34. Is 50:2. Mt 8:8, 9, 26, 27.

JONAH 3

Jonah, at God's renewed command, goes to Nineveh, and denounces its destruction, 1-4. The Ninevites excited by the king, believe, fast, pray, reform, and trust in God's mercy, 5-9. The Lord repents him of the evil, 10.

1. **the word**. Jon 1:1. Lk 10:30. **the second time**. Ge +22:15. *41:32. Jn 21:15-17.

2. **Nineveh**. *Nineveh*, the capital of Assyria, was situated on the eastern bank of the river Tigris, opposite the present Mosul, about 280 miles north of Babylon, and 400 miles N.E. of Damascus, in lat. 36 degrees 20 minutes N. long. 73 degrees 10 minutes E. It was not only a very ancient (Ge 10:11), but also a very great city. Strabo (l. xvi) says that it was much larger than Babylon, the circuit of which he estimates at 385 furlongs; and according to Diodorus Siculus (l. ii), it was an oblong parallelogram, extending 150 furlongs in length, 90 in breadth, and 480 in circumference, i.e. about 20 miles long, 12 broad, and 60 in compass. This agrees with the account given here of its being "an exceeding great city of three days' journey," i.e. *in circuit*; for 20 miles a day was the common computation for a pedestrian (See Herodotus, l. v. c. 35). It was surrounded by large walls 100 feet high, so broad that three chariots could drive abreast on them, and defended by 1500 towers 200 feet in height. See Notes on Nahum (Na 2:6n, 10n. 3:1n, 18n). ver. 3. Jon *1:2. 1 S *15:22, 23. Zp 2:13-15. **preach**. Je 1:17. 15:19-21. Ezk 2:7. 3:17. Mt 3:8. Jn 5:14.

3. **arose**. Ge 22:3. Mt 21:28, 29. 2 T 4:11. **Nineveh was**. Na 2:8, 9. **an exceeding great city**. Heb. a city great of God. So Ge +*23:6mg. 30:8mg. Jb 1:16mg. Ps 36:6mg. 80:10mg. ♪24L. Antimeria, Ge +6:2.

4. **Yet**. ver. 10. Dt 18:22. 2 K 20:1, 6. Is *38:1. Je 18:7-10. **forty**. The number *forty* in Scripture is often associated with testing, probation, or chastisement of man, or, in the government of God, with the penalty and judgment of man's sin. Ge 7:12. 18:28, 29. 50:3. Ex 16:35. 24:18. Nu 13:25. 14:34. Dt 9:18, 25. 25:3. 29:5. Jsh 5:6. 14:7. Jg 3:11. 5:31. 8:28. 13:1. 1 S 4:18. 17:16. 2 S 5:4. 15:7. 1 K 2:11. 11:42. 19:8. 2 K 12:1. Ps 95:10. Ezk 4:6. 29:11-13. Mt 4:2. Ac 1:3. 7:30, 36, 42. 13:18, 21. He 3:9, 17.

5. **believed**. Ex 9:18-21. Ob +*21. Mt *12:41. Lk *11:32. Ac 27:25. He 11:1, 7. **and proclaimed**. 2 Ch 20:3. Ezr 8:21. Je 36:9. Jl 1:14. 2:12-17. **from**. Je 31:34. 42:1, 8. Ac 8:10. **greatest**. ♪96E2, 1 S +17:14. Heterosis of Degree, the Positive for the Superlative, "From their great one (i.e., the greatest one among them) to their small (i.e. smallest) one."

6. **word**. Je 13:18. **and he arose**. Ps *2:10-12. Ja 1:9, 10. 4:6-10. **and covered**. Est 4:1-4. Jb 2:8. *42:6. Je 6:26. La 3:29. Da *9:3. Mi 1:10. Mt 11:21. Lk 10:13.

7. **proclaimed**. T#1272. ver. 5. 2 Ch *20:3. Ezr

8:21. Jl *2:15, 16. **published**. Heb. said. **nobles**. Heb. great men. 2 K 10:11. **herd**. Jl 1:18. Ro +*8:20-22.

8. **and beast**. T#1262. ver. 7. Jon 4:11. **sackcloth**. Ge +37:34. Da +9:3. **cry mightily**. T#1263. Jon 1:6, 14. Ps 130:1, 2. **let**. Is *1:16-19. √55:6, 7. √58:6. Ezk √18:21-24, 27, 30-32. *33:11. Da *4:27. Mt 3:8. Ac +*3:19. 26:20. **the violence**. Is 59:6.

9. **Who can tell**. Jon 1:6. 2 S 12:22. Ps 106:45. Ezk *18:21-23. Jl *2:13, 14. Am *5:15. Lk *15:18-20. **if**. ♪63K, Ge +37:13. Here it is not necessary to put the word "if" in italics. The Hebrew idiom means *who knoweth?* in the sense of *no one knows whether, or no one knows but that* (see Ps 90:11. Ec *2:19. 3:21. 6:12. 8:1. Jl 2:14). The A.V. renders Ec 2:19 "who knoweth whether" (without italics). 2 Ch 34:19-21. Is 39:5, 8. EWB (B123) cites Ralph Venning (*Orthodox Paradoxes*, 1650-1660 A.D.) who beautifully expresses the theology of this and similar passages in the following lines:

But stay! Is God like one of us? Can He,
When He hath said it, alter His decree?
Denounced judgment God doth oft prevent,
But neither changeth counsel nor intent;
The voice of heaven doth seldom threat perdition,
But with express or an implied condition:
So that, if Nineveh return from ill,
God turns his hand: He doth not turn His will.

10. **God saw**. 1 K 21:27-29. Jb 33:27, 28. Je 31:18-20. Lk 11:32. 15:20. **and God repented**. T#608. Jon 4:2. Ge +6:6. Je *18:7-10. 26:2, 3, 13, 19. Ezk 33:14, 15. Jl 2:13. Am *7:3, 6.

JONAH 4

Jonah, displeased at the mercy of God to Nineveh, peevishly expostulates, and prays for death, 1-3. God gently reproves him, 4. He leaves the city; is shadowed by a gourd, which withers; he manifests great impatience and rebellion; but is shown, by his concern about the gourd, the propriety of God's mercy to Nineveh, 5-11.

1. **it displeased Jonah**. ver. 4, 9. 2 K 14:25-27. Je 20:7, 8. Mt 20:15. Lk 7:39. 15:28. Ac 13:46. Ja 4:5, 6. **he was very angry**. T#1308. ver. 8-11. Ja *1:19, 20.

2. **he prayed**. 1 K *19:4. Je 20:7. **I fled**. Jon *1:3. Lk *10:29. **Tarshish**. Ge +10:4. **thou art**. Ex *34:6, 7♪₱. Nu *14:18, 19₱. Ps *78:38. *86:5, 15. 103:8. *145:8. Ho 11:8, 9. Jl *2:13, 14. Mi *7:18. **God**. Heb. *El*, Ex +15:2. **and merciful**. T#233. Ex 34:6, 7. Nu 14:18. Dt 4:31. +33:9 (T#672). Jb +36:7 (T#585). Ps 25:6. 36:7. *86:5. 100:5. *103:8-10. 106:44, 45. 116:5. 119:64. *138:8. +145:9 (T#228). Da *9:9. Jl *2:13. Lk +√6:35, 36. Jn √6:37. Ep *2:4-7. Ja +5:11 (T#225). **slow to anger**. Jn *3:36. **and of**. Jon 3:10. Ex 32:14. Ps 90:13. Je *18:8. Am 7:3, 6. **and repentest**. Is 55:9. Ezk 18:25, 27.

3. **take**. Nu 11:15. 20:3. 1 K √19:4. Jb *3:20, 21. 6:8, 9. Je *20:14-18. Ph *1:21-25. **life**. Heb. *nephesh*, soul, Ge +44:30. **for**. ver. 8. Jb 7:15, 16. Ec 7:1. 1 C 9:15.

4. **Doest thou well to be angry?** *or*, Art thou greatly angry? ver. 9. Nu 20:11, 12, 24. Ps √37:8. 106:32, 33. Ec *7:8, 9. Mi 6:3. Mt 20:15. Ep √4:26. T *1:7. Ja √1:19, 20.

5. **Jonah**. Jon 1:5. 1 K 19:9, 13. Is 57:17. Je 20:9.

till. Ge √19:27, 28. Je 17:15, 16. Lk *19:41-44. Perhaps Jonah still hoped that God would destroy Nineveh, for if He did not, Nineveh could be used as His rod against Israel in the future, no doubt the cause of Jonah's grave concern over Nineveh being spared.

6. **the Lord.** Jon 1:17. Ps *103:10-14. **gourd.** *or,* palmerist. Heb. *Kikajon.* Probably the *palma Christi,* called *kiki,* or *kouki,* by the Egyptians, and *Elkheroa* by the Arabs, from which castor oil is extracted. It is as large as the olive tree, has leaves like those of a vine, sometimes as broad as the brim of a hat, and is of very quick growth. **So Jonah.** Est 5:9. Pr 23:5. Is 39:2. Am 6:13. Lk 10:20. 1 C 7:30. **was exceeding glad.** Heb. rejoiced with great joy.

7. **God prepared.** Jb 1:21. Ps 30:6, 7. 102:10. He *12:5-7. **a worm.** Dt 28:39. **it withered.** Ps 90:5, 6. Is 40:6-8. Jl 1:12.

8. **that God prepared.** ver. 6, 7. Jon 1:4, 17. Ezk 19:12. He *12:9, 10. Re *3:19. **vehement.** *or,* silent. *or,* cutting. *S#2759h, only here. From Hebrew root S#2790h; 2 S 19:10mg. Jb 1:14 (plowing). Zp 3:17mg. **east wind.** Ge +41:6. Ex 10:13, 19⯑. **and the sun.** Ps 121:6. SS 1:6. Is 49:10. Re 7:16. **and wished.** ver. 3. Le 10:3. 1 S 3:18. 2 S 15:25, 26. Jb 2:10. Ps 39:9. **in himself.** Heb. *nephesh,* Ex +15:9.

9. **Doest thou well to be angry.** *or,* Art thou greatly angry. ver. 4. **I do well to be angry.** *or,* I am greatly angry. Ge 4:5-14. Jb 18:4. 40:4, 5. Ja *3:8-10. **even.** Jg 16:16. Jb 5:2. Mt 26:38. 2 C *7:10. Re 9:6.

10. **had pity on.** *or,* spared. lit. "hast hastened upon." ver. 11. Ge 45:20mg. Ps 72:13. Ezk 16:5. **neither madest it grow.** *or,* nourished it. lit. "make great." Ge 12:2. **came up in a night.** Heb. was the son of the night. ♪108B, 1 S +20:31. Ge 17:12mg.

11. **And.** ♪85B, Ge +13:9. **should.** ver. 1. Is *1:18. Mt 18:33. Lk 15:28-32. **Nineveh.** Jon 1:2. 3:2, 3. Na 3:8. **that great city.** God's great concern and compassion for the city is revealed in the book of Jonah, and confirmed by the following reference passages, which show Christ's manner of sending his disciples into the city, his own ministry to cities and single individuals within cities, and his great compassion for Jerusalem. Evangelism began from a city, Jerusalem. Missionary activity began when missionaries were commissioned and sent forth from the church in the city of Antioch. Paul spent quality time teaching God's word in various cities, establishing adult men as permanent leaders and elders who would remain in the churches to continue the teaching after Paul went on to other places (compare Paul's own instructions to Timothy in this regard, 1 T +*4:16; 2 T +*2:2). Paul furnished converts a carefully balanced and sequenced spiritual diet, preserved most fully for us in the structure and sequence of the book of Romans. Paul first emphasized doctrine (Ro ch. 1-8), so believers would get the right perspective upon their own condition in the light of God's character (Mt ◐+*25:24n), essential motivation for Christian service. Paul next concentrated on prophecy, so believers would have a correct perspective on where God is leading in his total plan (Ro ch. 9-11), and how he is absolutely committed to keeping his covenants and fulfilling his promises (Ro 11:29. 15:8). After thorough doctrinal and prophetic teaching, believers were ready for instruction in the practical application of spiritual truth (Ro ch. 12-16), what Scripture calls the "meat of the word" (He 5:14). The structure of Romans constitutes a plan for in-depth discipleship, an investment in the lives of individuals, where the person who is thoroughly taught in the word teaches everything he knows to those he is discipling. Such instruction must not only be substantial in content, but must focus on teaching the disciple to be an independent, self-motivated student of Scripture, who knows how to feed upon, rightly interpret and apply the word of God (Da 11:33n. Ro 14:12. 2 P 1:20n). The goal in disciple-making is to teach oneself out of a job. Independence, not dependence, is the desired outcome of instruction. We must invest quality time with each person being discipled, and must not abandon new disciples after six months of instruction! Rather, we must continue to invest our life in their training for as long as they continue to desire spiritual growth, and for as long as the Lord enables us to be spiritually profitable to them, until they are equipped and are successful in discipling others. Greater attention needs to be paid to the need for worldwide urban evangelism. But a truly effective missionary thrust must be supported by a strong home base consisting of churches that are thoroughly taught and practiced in the principles and doctrines of God's word (2 T +/3:15-17). The pastor's ministry must concentrate on systematically teaching the Bible. His goal must be to develop stable spiritual leadership in the congregation. To be more effective, churches need to be prepared to do unusual and unconventional ministry (something Jonah was not attitudinally and spiritually prepared for), to reach people where they are, at the times they are available. A teaching ministry conducted by means of home Bible studies is one method to reach people presently outside of the church (2 J +*10). See related notes (1 Th 3:5n. He 3:13n. 6:9n). Jon 1:2. 3:2, 3. Ps 48:2. Ezk 48:35. Zc 8:3. Mt 7:6. *9:35-38. *10:11-14, 23. 11:1. 23:37. Lk *13:6-10. Jn *4:4, 5. Ac +*1:8. 13:1-3. *14:3, 28. 18:1. 19:1, √8-10, 20, 21. 20:2, 3, √31. 28:11, 14. He 12:22. **are.** Heb. *yesh,* Pr 8:21. **sixscore.** It is generally calculated that the young children of any place are a fifth of the inhabitants, and consequently the whole population of Nineveh would amount to above 600,000; which is very inferior to that of London and Paris, though they occupy not one quarter of the ground. In eastern cities there are large vacant spaces for gardens and pasturages, so that there might be very "much cattle." **that cannot.** Dt 1:39. **discern.** ♪121S3Z. Metonymy of the Adjunct B608. Not discerning the right hand from the left is put for extreme youth. **and also.** Ps *36:6. 104:14, 27, 28. *145:8, 9, 15, 16. **much cattle.** Jon 3:2, 7.

MICAH

The time when Micah prophesied, 1. Judgments denounced against Samaria and Jerusalem for their sins, 2-7. A lamentation over the terror and distress occasioned by the Assyrian invasion, 8-16.

1. A.M. 3254. B.C. 750. **Micah**. i.e. *who is like Jehovah?* ver. 14, 15. *S#4318h. Jg 17:5, 8, 9, 10, 12, 12, 13. 18:2, 3, 4, 13, 15, 18, 22, 22, 23, 26, 27, 31. 1 Ch 5:5. 8:34, 35. 9:40, 41. 23:20. 24:24, 24, 25. 2 Ch 18:14. 34:20. Je √26:18. (1) An Ephraimite who, having fallen into idolatry, hired a Levite to be his priest. His idols were stolen from him by the Danites, Jg 17:5, etc. (2) The sixth of the minor prophets, a native of Moresheth-gath, west of Jerusalem, in Gath. Thus Micah is one of several prophets who did come out of Galilee (Jn ◐7:52). He was a contemporary of Isaiah, and prophesied during the reigns of Jotham, Ahaz, and Hezekiah, B.C. 750-698. (3) Micah, a Reubenite, 1 Ch 5:5. (4) The son of Merib-baal, 1 Ch 8:34, 35. Called **Micha** in 2 S 9:12. (5) A Levite of the family of Asaph. 1 Ch 9:15. He is called Micha in Ne 11:17, 22, and Michaiah in Ne 12:35. (6) A Levite of the family of Kohath, 1 Ch 23:20, called Michah in 1 Ch 24:24, 25. (7) The father of Abdon, 2 Ch 34:20, and called Michaiah in 2 K 22:12. **Jotham**. 2 Ch ch. 27-32. Is 1:1. Ho 1:1. **which**. Is 1:1. Am 1:1. Ob 1. Na 1:1. Hab 1:1. **concerning**. ver. 5. Ho 4:15. 5:5-14. 6:10, 11. 8:14. 12:1, 2. Am 2:4-8. 3:1, 2. 6:1.

2. **all ye people**. Heb. ye people all of them. **hearken**. Mi 3:1, 9. 6:1, 2. Dt 32:1)℗. 1 K *22:28. Ps 49:1, 2. *50:1, 4. Is *1:2. Je *22:29. Mk 7:14-16. Re 2:7, 11, 17, 29. 3:6, 13, 22. Note the reference to the Pentateuch. Other references to the Pentateuch in Micah are at ver. 3. Mi 2:1, 2, 4, 5, 7, 10. 3:4, 6, 11. 4:1, 8, 13. 5:2, 4, 6, 8, 10, 12. 6:2, 4, 7, 10, 11, 13, 14, 15, 16. 7:3, 6, 14, 15, 17, 18. See related note (Is +*1:2). **all that therein is**. Heb. the fulness thereof. Ps 24:1. 50:12. Je 47:2mg. Am 6:8mg. **let**. Ge *31:50, 51)℗. Ps 50:7. Je 29:23. Ml 2:14. +*3:5. **the Lord from**. Ps 11:4. 28:2. Jon 2:7. Hab √2:20.

3. **cometh**. Is *26:21. 64:1, 2. Ezk 3:12. Ho *5:14, 15. **his place**. √22D3A, 1 K +8:39. Ps *115:3. **and tread**. Dt 33:29)℗. Jb 40:12. Is 2:10-19. 25:10. 63:3, 4. Am *4:13. **the high**. Dt 32:13)℗. 33:29. Is *58:14. Hab 3:19.

4. **the mountains**. √121J7B, Je +3:23. Dt 32:22. Jg *5:4, 5. 2 K ch. 17, 25. 1 Ch 12:15. Ps 68:2. *97:5. Is *64:1-3. Am 9:5. Na 1:5, 6. Hab 3:6, 10. 2 P *3:10-12. Re *20:11. **the valleys**. Zc *14:4. **as wax**. Ps 68:2. **a steep place**. Heb. a descent. Jsh 7:5.

5. **the transgression of Jacob**. 2 K 17:7-23. 2 Ch *36:14-16. Is 50:1, 2. 59:1-15. Je 2:17, 19. 4:18. 5:25. 6:19. La 5:16. 1 Th 2:15, 16. **is it**. 1 K 13:32. Ho 7:1. 8:5, 6. Am 6:1. 8:14. **Samaria**. √121G, Ge +31:1. **high places**. 1 K 12:31. 14:23. 2 K +21:3. Ezk 6:6. **they**. 2 K *16:3, 4, 10-12. 2 Ch 28:2-4, 23-25. **Jerusalem**. √121G, Ge +31:1.

6. **I will make**. Mi 3:12. 2 K 19:25. Is 25:2, 12. Je 9:11. 51:37. Ho 13:16. **and I will pour**. Je 51:25. La 4:1. Ezk 13:14. Hab 3:13. Mt *24:2.

7. **all the graven images**. Ex 20:4)℗. Le 26:30. 2 K 23:14, 15. 2 Ch 31:1. 34:+3, 6, 7. Is 2:18. 27:9. Ho 8:6. 10:5, 6. **the hires**. The technical Pentateuchal word for a harlot's hire, to which idolatry is compared (CB). Dt 23:18)℗. Je 44:17, 18. Ho *2:5, 8, 12. 8:9, 10. 9:1. **for**. Dt 23:18. Jl 3:3. Re 18:3, 9, 12, 13.

8. **I will wail**. Is 16:9. 21:3. 22:4. Je 4:19. 9:1, 10, 19. 48:36-39. **I will go**. Is 20:2-4. **naked**. √171N, Ge +8:13. **a wailing**. Jb 30:29. Ps *102:6. **owls**. Heb. daughters of the owl. Jb +30:29. Is 13:21mg.

9. **her wound is incurable**. *or, she is* grievously sick of her wounds. Is *1:5, 6. Je *10:19. *15:18. *30:11-15. **it**. 2 K *18:9-13. Is 8:7, 8. **he**. ver. 12. 2 Ch *32:1, etc. Is 10:28-32. 37:22-36. **the gate**. Ge +22:17. Ob 11, 13.

10. **Declare**. 2 S *1:20. Am 5:13. 6:10. **Gath**. Jsh 11:22. **Aphrah**. i.e., dust. S#1036h. Jsh 18:23, Ophrah. **roll**. Jb 2:8. Je *6:26. La 3:29.

11. **Pass**. Is 16:2. Je 48:6, 9. **thou inhabitant of Saphir**. i.e. *fair; beautiful*, *S#8208h. *or*, thou that dwellest fairly. Heb. inhabitress. Is 12:6mg. Je 10:17mg. **having**. ver. 8. Is 20:4. 47:2, 3. Je *13:22. Ezk 16:37. Na 3:5. **Zaanan**. *or*, the country of flocks. *S#6630h. **Beth-ezel**. *or*, a place near. *S#1018h.

12. **Maroth**. i.e. *bitterness, bitter fountains*, *S#4796h. Ru 1:20. **waited carefully**. *or*, was grieved. 1 S 4:13. Jb 30:25. Is 59:9-11. Je 8:15. 14:19. **but**. ver. 9. Is +*45:7. Am +*3:6.

13. **Lachish**. Jsh *15:20, 39. 2 K 14:19. *18:13, 14, 17. 19:8. 2 Ch 11:9. 32:9. Is 37:8. **bind**. Ge 19:17. 1 K +18:44mg. Is 10:31. Je 4:29. **she**. Ex 32:21. 1 K 13:33, 34. 14:16. 16:31. Re 2:14, 20. 18:1-5. **for**. 2 K 8:18. 16:3, 4. Je 3:8. Ezk 23:11.

14. **give**. 2 S 8:2. 2 K 16:8. 18:14-16. 2 Ch 16:1-3. Is 30:6. **to**. *or*, for. Moresheth-gath. i.e. *possession of Gath*, *S#4182h. **houses**. Ps 62:9. 118:8, 9. 146:3, 4. **Achzib**. *that is*, a lie. Jsh 15:44. 19:29. Jg 1:31.

15. **will**. Is 7:17, etc. 10:5, 6. Je 49:1. **Mareshah**. Jsh 15:44. **he**, etc. *or*, the glory of Israel shall come to, etc. 1 S *22:1. Is *5:13. 10:3. **Adullam**. Jsh *15:35. 2 S *23:13. 2 Ch 11:7.

16. **Make thee bald**. √121S3V. Metonymy of the Adjunct B607. The sign put for the thing signified in connected words and phrases: "making bald" is put for grieving. For another instance of this figure see Is 3:24. Dt 14:1. Jb *1:20. Is *3:24. *15:2. *22:12. Je 6:26. *7:29. 16:6. 47:5. 48:37. Am 8:10. **thy delicate**. Dt 28:56, 57. Is 3:16, etc. La 4:5-8. **for**. Dt 28:41. 2 K 17:6. Is 39:6, 7.

God's judgment against oppression, 1-3. A lamentation for the removal of his people, 4-6. Reproofs of the people's injustice, avarice, opposition to the prophets, and attachment to false prophets, with lamentations and denunciations of judgment upon them, 1-11. Predictions of the restoration and regathering of Israel to Christ, and of his victories and kingdom, 12, 13.

1. Cir. A.M. 3274. B.C. 730. **devise iniquity**. Est

3:8, 9. 5:14. 9:25. Ps 7:14-16. 140:1-8. Pr 6:12-19. 12:2.
Is 32:7. 59:3-8. Je 18:18. Ezk 11:2. Na 1:11. Lk 20:19,
20. 22:2-6. Ac 23:12. Ro 1:30. **work evil.** Ps 36:4. Pr
4:16. **upon their beds.** Ps *4:4. **when.** Ho *7:6, 7.
Mt 27:1, 2. Mk 15:1. Ac 23:15. **because.** Ge 31:29)𝒫.
Dt 28:32. Ne 5:5. Pr 3:27. Ec 4:1. Jn 19:11. **is.** Heb.
yesh, Pr 8:21.

2. **they covet fields.** Ex 20:17. Le 6:4)𝒫. Dt 5:21)𝒫.
1 K 21:2-19. Jb 31:38, 39. Is *5:8. Je 22:17. Am *8:4-
6. Hab 2:5-9. 1 T *6:10. **so they.** Mi 3:9. Ex +*22:21-
24. 2 K 9:26. Ne *5:1-5, 11. Jb 24:2-12. Ezk 18:12,
13. 22:12, 27, 29. Am *8:4-6. Ml +*3:5. **oppress.** *or*,
defraud. Le +*19:13)𝒫. 1 S 12:3, 4. Ml +*3:5. Mk
*10:19. 1 Th +*4:6.

3. **this family.** Je *8:3. Am 3:1, 2. **do.** ver. 1. Je
18:11. 34:17. La 2:17. Ja *2:13. **devise an evil.** Is
+*45:7. Am +*3:6. **from which.** Am 2:14-16. √9:1-4.
Zp 1:17, 18. **necks.** Je 27:12. La 1:14. 5:5. Ro 16:4.
go haughtily. Is 2:11, 12. 3:16. 5:19. 28:14-18. Je 13:15-
17. 36:23. 43:2. Da 4:37. 5:20-23. **for.** Am *5:13. Ep
+*5:16. *6:13.

4. **shall.** Nu 23:+7n, 18)𝒫. 24:3, 15, 20, 23)𝒫. Jb
27:1. 29:1. Is 14:4. Ezk 16:44. Hab 2:6. Mk 12:12.
and lament. 2 S 1:17. 2 Ch 35:25. Je 9:10, 17-21.
14:17, 18. Jl 1:8, 13. Am 5:1, 17. **a doleful lamentation.**
Heb. a lamentation of lamentations. √147D, Ge +1:29.
√147H, Ge +9:25. La ch. 1-5. Ezk 2:10. **and say.**
√56, Is +14:16. **We be.** Dt 28:29. Is 6:11. 24:3. Je
*9:19. 25:9-11. Zp 1:2. **he hath changed.** ver. 10. Mi
1:15. 2 K 17:23, 24. 2 Ch 36:20, 21. Is 63:17, 18.
Heb. *mur*, changed for the worse. ✳S#4171h. Le 27:10,
33. Ps √15:4. 46:2 (removed). 106:20. Je 2:11. 48:11.
Ezk 48:14 (exchange). Ho 4:7. Note that the Hebrew
word *halaph* frequently means to change for the better
(Le +27:10, ✚S#2498h). **how hath.** √48, Ps +2:4. **turning away he.** *or*, instead of restoring, he, etc.

5. **cast.** Nu 26:55, 56)𝒫. Dt 32:8, 9. Jsh +14:2n.
18:4-6, 10. Ps +*16:6. Ho 9:3. **cord.** √121B, Jsh
+17:14. **the congregation.** Dt 23:2, 3, 8. Ne 7:61-65.

6. **Prophesy ye,** etc. *or*, Prophesy not *as* they prophesy. Heb. Drop, etc. Is *30:10. Je 5:31. *11:21.
26:8, 9, 20-23. Ezk 20:46. 21:2. Am *2:12. *7:13-16.
Ac *4:17-19. *5:28, 29, 40-42. 7:51, 52. 1 Th *2:15,
16. **they shall not prophesy.** Ps 74:9. Ezk 3:26. Am
8:11-13. **that they.** Je 6:14, 15. 8:11, 12.

7. **named.** Mi 3:9. Is *48:1, 2. *58:1. Je 2:4. Mt
*3:8-10. Jn 8:39, 40. Ro *2:28, 29. *9:6-13. 2 T *3:5.
is. Nu *11:23)𝒫. Is 50:2. *59:1, 2. Zc √4:6. 2 C 6:12.
spirit. Heb. *ruach*, Is +48:16. **straitened.** *or*, shortened. Jb +21:4mg. **do not my words.** Jb *23:12. Ps
*19:7-11. 119:70, 71, 92, 93, √99-103. Pr +*8:8, 9. Is
34:16. Je +*15:16. Jn +*5:39. Ro 7:13. 2 T +*3:15,
16. **walketh.** Ps +*1:1. 15:2. *84:11. Pr 2:7. 10:9, 29.
14:2. *28:18. Ho 14:9. Col +*1:10. 1 Th *4:1. **uprightly.**
Heb. upright. Pr 21:27. T *1:15.

8. **of late.** Heb. yesterday. Ps 90:4. **risen.** 2 Ch
28:5-8. Is 9:21. **with the garment.** Heb. over against
a garment. Lk 10:30. **that pass by.** Lk 10:30-37. **securely.** 2 S 20:19. 2 Ch 28:8. Ps 55:20, 21. 120:6, 7.
Pr 3:29, 30.

9. **women.** *or*, wives. Ge 4:19. **cast.** ver. 2. Mt
*23:14. Mk 12:40. Lk 20:47. **from their children.** 1 S
26:19. Jl 3:6. **my glory.** Ps 72:19. Ezk 39:21. Hab
2:14. Zc 2:5. 2 C *3:18. 4:6. **for ever.** Heb. *olam*, Ex
+*12:24.

10. **and depart.** Dt 4:26. 30:18. Jsh 23:15, 16. 1 K

9:7. 2 K 15:29. 17:6. 2 Ch 7:20. 36:20, 21. **for this.**
Dt 12:9)𝒫. Ps 95:11. He *4:1-9. **because.** Le *18:24-
28)𝒫. 20:22-26. Ps 106:38. Je *3:2. **it shall destroy.**
Le 18:28)𝒫. 20:22)𝒫. 26:38)𝒫. Je *9:19. 10:18. Ezk
*36:12-14.

11. **a man.** 1 K 13:18. 22:21-23. 2 Ch 18:19-22. Is
9:15. Je 14:14. *23:14, 25, 32. 27:14, 15. 28:2, 3, 15.
29:21-23. Ezk *13:3-14, 22. 22:28. 2 C √11:13-15.
2 Th √2:8-10. 2 P *2:1-3. 1 J *4:1. Re 16:13, 14. **walking
in the spirit and falsehood do lie.** *or*, walk with the
wind and lie falsely. **spirit.** Heb. *ruach*, Ge +41:8.
and. √93A, Ge +1:26. By Hendiadys, a false and lying
spirit. **saying.** √122, Ex +15:9. **I will.** Mi 3:5, 11.
1 K 22:6. Je 6:13, 14. 8:10, 11. 23:17. Ro 16:18. Ph
*3:19. 2 P *2:13-19. **he shall.** Is 30:10, 11. Je 5:31.
2 Th √2:11.

12. **surely assemble.** Mi 4:6, 7. Is √11:11, 12. *14:1.
27:12, 13. Je 3:18. 31:8. Ezk 37:21, 22. Ho 1:11. Ro
*11:26. **I will put.** Mi 7:14. Je 23:3. *31:10. Ezk 34:11,
12, 22, 31. **Bozrah.** Ge 36:33. Is 34:6. Am 1:12. **they.**
Je 31:7-9. Ezk *36:37. Zc *8:22, 23. 9:14, 15. √10:6-
8.

13. **breaker.** Ex 19:22, 24. 2 S 5:20. 1 Ch 14:11.
15:13. Is 42:7, 13-16. 45:1, 2. 49:9, 24, 25. 51:9, 10.
55:4. *57:14. 59:16-19. *62:10. Je 51:20-24. Da *2:34,
35, 44. Ho 13:14. Zc 12:8. 1 C 15:21-26. He *2:14,
15. **they have.** Zc *10:5-7, 12. 12:3-8. **their king.** Note
"their king" (David) mentioned separately from "the
Lord on the head of them." At Ho 3:5n, note the
separate mention of "the Lord their God" and "David
their king," followed by mention of "fear the Lord
and his goodness." This may indicate that David himself
will rule literally in Jerusalem concurrently as Christ
the Messiah rules from Jerusalem over the whole earth.
Compare Is 52:12, "the Lord will go before you," and
"the God of Israel will be your rereward." Is 49:10.
*51:12. 52:8, 12. Je *23:5, 6. Ezk *20:33-44. 34:23,
24. Ho *1:11. +*3:5n. Zp +*3:15. Zc 2:10-13. 9:14,
15. 14:3-5. Mt +*23:39. Jn √10:27-30. He +*2:9, 10.
6:20. Re 7:17. 17:14. 19:13-17. **and the Lord.** Mi *4:7.
Is *52:12. Ho *3:5.

MICAH 3

*MICAH reproves the princes for their cruelty, and
the prophets for their falsehoods and selfishness, 1-7.
He declares himself inspired, emboldened, and authorized by the Spirit of God, to protest against the sins
and presumption of the princes, priests, and prophets;
and to denounce the desolations of the city and temple,
8-12.*

1. Cir. A.M. 3294. B.C. 710. **Hear.** ver. 9, 10. Is
1:10. Je 13:15-18. 22:2, 3. Ho 5:1. Am 4:1. **Is it.** Dt
1:13-17. 16:18. +*17:18-20. 2 Ch 19:5-10. Ps 14:4.
82:1-5. Je 5:4, 5. 1 C 6:5.

2. **hate.** 1 K 21:20. 22:6-8. Am 5:10-14. Lk 19:14.
Jn 7:7. 15:18, 19, 23, 24. Ac 7:51, 52. Ro 12:9. 2 T
3:3. **love.** 2 Ch 19:2. Ps 15:4. 139:21, 22. Pr 28:4. Jn
18:40. Ro 1:32. **pluck.** Ps 53:4. Is 3:15. Ezk *22:27.
34:3. Am 8:4-6. Zp *3:3. Zc 11:4, 5.

3. **eat.** Ps *14:4. **and chop.** Ezk 11:3, 6, 7.

4. **Then.** Mi 2:3, 4. Je 5:31. **cry.** Ps 18:41. +*66:18.
Pr *1:28. 28:9. Is *1:15. Je 2:27, 28. *11:11. Ezk *8:18.
Zc 7:13. Mt 7:22, 23. Lk 13:25, 26. Jn +*9:31. Ja
*2:13. 1 P *3:12. **not hear.** Ps +*66:18. **he will even.**

Dt 31:17, 18⊁ℛ. 32:19, 20⊁ℛ. Is 59:1-15. Je 33:5. **as.** T#1805. Is 3:11. Am 8:4-6, *11, 12. Zc 7:9-13. Ro *2:8, 9.

5. **concerning.** ver. 11. Is 9:15, 16. Je 14:14, 15. 23:9-17, 27, 32. 28:15-17. 29:21-23. Ezk *13:10-16. 22:25-29. Ml 2:8. Mt +*15:14. **make my people err.** Is +*8:16, 20n. Ezk 13:19, 22. 14:10n. Ho 4:9. Mt +*15:14. *23:13, 15. Mk √12:24, 27. Ac *20:29, 30. Ep 4:14. 1 T ◐+*4:16. **that bite.** Mi 2:11. Is *56:9-12. Je *8:11. Ezk *13:10, 18, 19. Zc 9:7. Mt *7:15. Ro 16:18.

6. **night.** Ps *74:9. Is +√8:20-22. Je *13:16. Ezk *13:22, 23. Zc *13:2-4. **that ye shall not have a vision.** Heb. a vision. Am +*8:11. **that ye shall not divine.** Heb. from divining. Dt +*18:10, 14⊁ℛ. Nu 22:7⊁ℛ. 23:23⊁ℛ. **the sun.** Is *29:10. *59:10. Je 15:9. Ho +*3:4. Am *8:9, 10.

7. **the seers.** Ex 8:18, 19. 9:11. 1 S *9:9. Is *44:24, 25. 47:12-14. Da 2:9-11. Zc *13:4. 2 T 3:8, 9. **cover.** Le 13:45. Ezk 24:17, 22. **lips.** Heb. upper lip. Le 13:45. Ezk 24:17mg, 22. **no answer.** 1 S 14:37. 28:6, 15. Ps +*74:9. Am +*8:11.

8. **I am.** Jb 32:18. Is 11:2, 3. *58:1. Je 1:18. 6:11. 15:19-21. 20:9. Ezk 3:14. Mt 7:29. Mk 3:17. Ac 4:8-12, 19, 20. 7:54-57. 13:9-12. 18:5, 6, 9-11. 1 C 2:4, 12, 13. **power.** Lk *24:49. 2 T +*1:7. **spirit.** Heb. *ruach,* Is +48:16. **to declare.** Is *58:1. Ezk 16:2. 20:4. 22:2. 43:10. Mt *3:7-12. Ac 7:51, 52.

9. **I pray.** ver. 1. Ex 3:16. Ho 5:1. **that.** Le 26:15. Dt 27:19. Ps 58:1, 2. Pr 17:15. Is 1:23. Je 5:28.

10. **build up Zion.** Je +*22:13-17. Ezk 22:25-28. Hab *2:9-12. Zp 3:3. Mt 27:25. Mk *12:40. Jn 11:50. **blood.** Heb. bloods. 2 K +*9:26mg.

11. **heads.** Mi 7:3. Nu 16:15. 1 S 8:3. 12:3, 4. Is 1:23. Ezk 22:12, 27. Ho 4:18. Zp 3:3. **judge for reward.** Ex 23:8⊁ℛ. Dt 10:17⊁ℛ. *16:19⊁ℛ. *27:25⊁ℛ. Ml 2:9. **and the priests.** Je 6:13. 8:10. Ml 1:10. 1 T 3:3. T 1:11. 1 P 5:2. **and the prophets.** ver. 5. Is 56:11. Ac 8:18-20. 2 P 2:1-3, 14, 15. Ju 11. **yet.** 1 S 4:3-6. Is *48:2. Je *7:4, 8-12. Ezk +*33:31. Mt *3:9. Ro *2:17, etc. **and say.** Heb. saying. ♪122, Ex +15:9. Ge 3:12. **none evil can come.** Je *23:17. Ezk 12:27. Am 6:3. *9:10. 2 P *3:3, 4.

12. **Zion.** Mi 1:6. Ps *79:1. 107:34. Je *26:18. Mt *24:2. Ac 6:13, 14. **heaps.** Mi 1:6. **the mountain.** Mi 4:1, 2. Is 2:2, 3.

MICAH 4

A prediction of the establishment, enlargement, peace, and prosperity of Israel in the latter days, 1-8. Assurances that Zion's troubles should end happily, and her enemies be destroyed, 9-13.

1. **in the last days.** Ge *49:1⊁ℛ. Nu 24:14. Is *2:1-3. Je 48:47. Ezk +*38:8, 16. Da *2:28. 8:17. *10:14. *12:13. Ho +*3:5. Mt *24:6, 14. Jn 6:39, 40. Ac *2:16, 17. 2 T 3:1. He *1:2. Ja *5:3. 1 P 1:5, ◐20. 2 P *3:3. 1 J 2:18. Ju 18. **the mountain.** Mi 3:12. Ps 24:3. 68:15, 16. Is *2:2-4. *11:9. +*66:20. Ezk *17:22-24. 28:16. 40:2. Da *2:35, 44. 7:14, 18, 22, 27. Zc √8:3. Re *11:15. +*20:4. 21:1, etc. **house of the Lord.** 2 S *7:13, 16. Is +*2:2. 60:13n. Ezk 40:2n. Am +*9:11. Acts *15:16. **top of the mountains.** Is *2:2. 25:6, 7. 41:15. Ezk 17:23. **and people.** Ge +*49:10. Ps 22:27. 68:29-32. 72:7-11, 16-19. 86:9. *110:3. Is *11:10. 27:13. 43:6. *49:6, 19-23. 54:2. *60:3-14. *66:18-23. Je 3:17. 16:19. Zp 3:9,

10. Zc 2:11. 14:16-21. Ml 1:11. Acts *15:17. Ro +*11:25, 26. Re *15:4.

2. **shall come.** SS 1:4. **and say.** Is *2:3. Je 31:6. 50:4, 5. Zc *8:20-23. **and he.** Dt 6:1. Ps *25:8, 9, 12. Is 54:13. Mt *11:25-30. Jn 6:45. *7:17. Ac 10:32, 33. 13:42. Ja *1:19-25. **for the law.** Ps *110:2. Is √26:9. *42:1-4. *51:4, 5. Ho +*6:3. Zc +*14:8, 9. Mt *28:19, 20. Mk √16:15, 16, 20. Lk *24:47. Ac +*1:8. *13:46, 47. Ro *10:12-18. 15:19. **the word.** T#1919. Ge 15:1-4. 1 S 3:1-21. 2 S 7:4. 1 K 17:8-24. Ps 33:6. Is *40:8. Je 25:3. Jn ✱*1:1-14. +*3:34. Lk 1:2. He *4:12. 11:3. 1 P *1:23. 2 P 3:5. Re 19:13.

3. **he shall judge.** 1 S 2:10. Ps 2:5, 9. *72:8, 11, 17. 82:8. 96:13. 98:9. *110:5, 6. Is 11:3-5. 51:5. Mt +*25:31, 32. Jn *5:22, 23, 27-29. 16:8-11. Ac √17:31. Re *19:11. **and rebuke.** Mi 5:15. 7:16, 17. Ps *2:5-12. 68:30, 31. *110:1, 2, 5, 6. Is 25:3. 60:12. Da *2:44. Jl 3:2, 9-16. Zc 12:3-6. 14:3, 12-19. Re 19:17-21. 20:8, 9. **they shall.** Ps 46:9. Is *2:4. 11:6-9. Ho 2:18. Jl *3:10. Zc *9:10. **pruninghooks.** *or,* scythes. Is 2:4mg. Jl 3:10mg. **neither.** Ps *72:7. Is +*9:7. 60:17, 18. +*65:25. He *7:2.

4. **But.** The connection of this prophecy with the close of the preceding chapter shows that the establishment of the nation of Israel back in their original land is intended, though we perceive a long span of centuries during which the abrogation of the Mosaic dispensation, and the destruction of Jerusalem by the Romans, and the dispersion of the Jews to the ends of the earth has occurred in the interim. The grand accomplishment of these predictions to literal, natural Israel must clearly still be future. **they.** 1 K 4:25. Is 36:16. Zc *3:10. **none shall.** Le *26:6. Is √54:14. Je *23:5, 6. *30:10. Ezk √34:25, 28. *38:11. √39:26. **for.** 2 S +1:3. Ps +24:10. Is 1:20. 40:5. 44:6. 58:14. Je +6:6.

5. **all.** 2 K 17:29, 34. Je 2:10, 11. **name of.** Jon 1:5, 6. **and we.** Ge *17:1. Ps 71:16. Is 2:5. Zc 10:12. Col +*2:6. *3:17. **the name.** Ex +*3:14, 15. Ps *20:7. 48:14. 145:1, 2. Is *26:13. **for ever.** Heb. 'olam,' Ps +21:4. **and ever.** Heb. 'ad,' Ps +9:18.

6. **In that day.** ver. 1. Je 33:14. **will I assemble.** Mi 2:12. Ps 38:17. Is *35:3-6. Je 31:8. Ezk *34:13-17. Zp *3:19. He 12:12, 13. **will gather.** Ps 147:2. Is 56:8. Je 3:18. 30:17, 18. Ezk *34:12, +*13. 36:24. 37:21, 22, +*25. 39:25-29. Lk *19:10. Jn *10:16.

7. **I will.** Mi *2:12. *5:3, 7, 8. *7:18. Is 6:13. 10:21, 22. √11:11-16. 49:21-23. 60:22. 66:8. Ho 1:10. Zc 9:13-17. *10:5-12. Ro *11:5, 6, 25-27. **cast far off.** Is +*41:9. Zc √10:6. **the Lord shall reign.** Ps *2:6. Is +*9:6, 7. +*24:23. Je +√23:5. Da +*7:14, 27. Jl *3:17. Lk *1:33. Re *11:15. **in mount Zion.** Mi ◐3:12. Ps *2:6. +*102:16. Is 4:3, 4. +*24:23. +*51:11. +*52:8. *60:14, 15. 62:1-4. 65:19. **for ever.** Heb. 'olam,' Ex +*12:24.

8. **O tower.** The Targumist applies these words to the Messiah: "But thou, O Messiah, who art hidden because of the sins of the congregation of Zion, the kingdom shall come unto thee." 2 K +5:24mg. Ps 48:12, 13. Is 5:2. Mt 21:33. Mk 12:1. **the flock.** *or,* Edar. Ge 35:21⊁ℛ. **the strong.** 2 S 5:7. Is 10:32. Zc 9:12. **the daughter.** Zp 3:10, 14. Zc *9:9. **the first.** Nu 24:19. Ps 18:43. Je *3:17. Da 2:44. 7:18. Ob +*21. Zp √3:20. Zc *9:10. 12:6-9. Lk *24:47. Ep 1:21. Re 22:5.

9. **why.** Je 4:21. 8:19. +*30:6, 7. **is there.** Is 3:1-7. La 4:20. Ho +*3:4. *10:3. *13:10, 11. **for pangs.** Is 13:8. 21:3. 26:17. 42:14. Je 6:24. 22:23. +*30:6.

50:43. Ho 13:13. Mt +*24:8.

10. **and labor.** Is 66:7-9. Ho 13:13. Jn 16:20-22. **go forth out.** 2 K 20:18. 25:4. 2 Ch 33:11. 36:20. Ho 1:10. 2:14. Zc √14:2. Re +*12:14. **Babylon.** Am 5:25-27. Ac 7:42, 43. **there shalt.** Mi 7:8-13. Ezr 1:1, 2. Is 45:13. 48:20. 52:9-12. Zc 2:7-9. **redeem.** Ps 106:10. Je 15:21.

11. **many.** Is 5:25-30. 8:7, 8. 33:3. Ps 21:11. Je 52:4. La *2:15, 16. Jl 3:2, etc. Zc *12:3. **gathered against.** Zp +*3:8. Re +*16:16. **Let her.** Nu 35:33. Ezk 25:3. 26:2. 36:2. Ob 12. **let our.** Mi 7:10. Ob 12.

12. **they know not.** Is ●94:11. Is √55:8. Je 29:11. Ro *11:33, 34. **he shall gather.** Is √17:5-8. 21:10. Jl 3:12, 13. Zp +*3:8. Zc *14:1-3. Mt +*13:30, 39. Lk 3:17. 17:34-37. Re 14:14-20. +*16:16. **floor.** Ge +50:10. Dt +*16:13mg. Mt *3:12.

13. **and thresh.** Is *41:15, 16. Je 51:33. Ho 10:11. Hab +*3:12. **thine horn.** Am 6:13. hoofs. Dt 25:4❀. *33:25. Is 5:28. **thou shalt beat.** Mi *5:8-15. Je *51:19, 20. Da *2:44. Zc 9:13-15. 10:3-5. 12:6. Ml +*4:3. Jn +*18:36. Re *2:26, 27. **I will consecrate.** Le 27:28❀. Jsh 6:19, 24. 2 S 8:10, 11. Ps 68:29. 72:10. Is 18:7. *23:18. *60:5-9. +*61:6. Zc *14:14. Ro +*11:25. 15:25-28. 1 C 16:2. Re 21:24-26. **their substance.** Ob +11mg. Zc 14:20, 21. **the Lord of.** Ps 97:5. Zc 4:14. 6:5.

MICAH 5

A prophecy of the birth and kingdom of Christ; and of his powerful protection of his people, 1-6; of the increase, purity, and peace of Israel, and the ruin of its enemies, 7-15.

1. **gather.** Dt 28:49. 2 K 24:2. Is 8:9, 10. 10:6. Je 4:7. 25:9. Jl 3:9-11. Hab 1:6-10. +*3:16. **he hath.** Dt 28:51-57. 2 K √25:1-3, 21. Ezk 21:21, 22. 24:2. Lk 19:43, 44. **they.** Jb 16:10. La 3:30. Mt 5:39. 26:67. 27:30. Jn 18:22. 19:3. Ac 23:2. 2 C 11:20. **judge.** 1 S 8:5, 6. 1 K 22:24. Ps 7:8, 11. 9:4, 13. +*50:6. *94:2. 96:13. Is 33:22. La 3:30. 4:20. 5:8, 12. Am 2:3. **rod.** Mi 7:14. Mt=27:30. **upon the cheek.** T#1949. Mt ✹*26:67. ✹27:30. Lk *22:64.

2. **But thou.** Mt ❫2:6. Jn ❫7:42. **Bethlehem.** T#1887. Mt ✹2:1, 6. Lk ✹2:4-6. Jn 7:42. He 7:14. **Ephratah.** Ge 35:19. 48:7, Ephrath. Jsh 12:9n. Ru 4:11. 1 S 17:12. 1 Ch 2:50, 51, 54. 4:4. Ps 132:6. **little.** 1 C 1:27-29. **among.** 1 S 10:19. 23:23. **thousands.** Ex 18:+21, 25❫❀. Dt 1:15. Jsh 22:21. Jg 6:15. 12:6mg,n. 15:15n. 1 S 6:19n. 8:12. 10:19. 17:18. 23:23. 1 K 20:30n. 1 Ch 12:20. **of Judah.** 1 Ch +5:2. Ps ●+60:7. Mt ✹2:6. He ✹7:14. Re ✹5:5. **yet.** Is 11:1. 53:2. Ezk 17:22-24. Am *9:11. Lk 2:4-7. 1 C 1:27, 28. **come forth.** Zc ●*9:9. 1 Th=4:16. **that is.** Ge +*49:10. 1 Ch 5:2. Is +*9:6, 7. Je +*23:5, 6. Ezk 34:23, 24. 37:22-25. Zc *9:9. Mt 28:18. Lk *1:31-33. 23:2, 38. Jn 19:14-22. Re 19:16. **ruler.** Je 30:9. Ac=7:35. **whose.** Ps *90:2. 102:25-27. Pr *8:22, 23. Jn +*1:1-3. √8:58. Col *1:17. He +*13:8. 1 J *1:1, 2. Re *1:11-18. 2:8. 21:6. **of old.** Heb. *kedem,* ✚S#6924h. Always used of the past; rendered (1) ever, Pr 8:23. (2) eternal, Dt 33:27. (3) everlasting, Hab √1:12. (4) old, Ne 12:46. Ps 44:1. 55:19. 68:33. 74:2. 77:5, 11. 78:2. 119:152. 143:5. Je 46:26. La 1:7. 2:17. Mi 7:20. (5) ancient, Dt 33:15. 2 K 19:25. Is 19:11. 23:7. 37:26. 45:21. 46:10. 51:9. (6) past, Jb 29:2. (7) aforetime, Je 30:20. (8) before, Ps 139:5. Pr 8:22. **from.** T#76-3. Ps 72:17. Pr 8:22-24. Jn +*1:1, 2. +*8:35, 58. *17:5. 1 J *1:1, 2. Re +*1:8,

17. **everlasting.** *or,* the days of eternity. Heb. *olam,* Ge +17:7. ♪22D4B, Da +7:9. Mi 7:14. Ps √90:2. 93:2. Pr *8:22, 23. Jn *1:1, 2. √6:54n.

3. **Therefore.** Mi 7:13. Ho 2:9, 14. **give them up.** Mi 6:14. 1 K 14:16. 2 Ch 30:7. Is 49:1-23. Ho 11:8. Zc 13:7-9. Mt √21:43. **until the time.** Ps +*102:13, 16. Ho 3:4, 5. +*5:15. 6:2. Mt *19:28. +*23:39. Lk +*21:24. Ac +*3:19. Ro +*11:25. **she which travaileth.** Mi *4:10. Ge +*3:15. Is +*7:14. +*66:7, 8. Mt ✹1:21, 23. +*24:8. Jn *16:21, 22. Re *12:1, 2. **brought forth.** Mt √19:28. **then the remnant.** Mi 4:7. Is *10:20, 21. 11:11. Je 31:1, 7-9. Ro 9:27, 28. 11:4-6. **his brethren.** Mt 12:50. 25:40. Ro 8:29. He *2:11, 12.

4. **And he.** Ge 49:24❫❀. Ps 80:1. Je 31:10. Ezk *34:23. **stand.** Mi 7:14. Ps 23:1, 2. Is 40:10, 11. 49:9, 10. Ezk 34:22-24. Jn √10:27-30. **feed.** *or,* rule. Mi 7:14. Ps *2:8. Is 40:11. 49:10. Mt 2:6mg. **in the majesty.** Ex 23:21. 1 Ch 29:11, 12. Ps 45:3-6. 72:19. 93:1. 145:12. Mt 25:31. Jn *5:22-29. 10:38. 14:9-11. Re 1:13-18. **name.** ♪121T1, Dt +28:58. ♪144A4A, Is +30:27. the **Lord.** Jn 20:17. Ep 1:3. **shall abide.** Mi 4:4 (sit). Ezk 34:25, *28 (dwell). 38:8. Jl +3:20mg. Am 9:14 (inhabit). Mt 16:18. 1 P 1:5. Ju 1. **shall he be great.** Ps 22:27. *72:8, 17. 98:3. Is 49:5, 7. *52:10, 13. Zc *9:10. Lk *1:32. Re *11:15.

5. **this.** Ps *72:7. Is +*9:6, 7. *14:3-5, 25. Zc *9:10. Lk 2:14. Jn 14:27. 16:33. Ep *2:14-17. Col √1:20, 21. **when the Assyrian.** This is a title of the Antichrist, who will come from the same general geographical territory (Da 11:40n). Is +*7:14, 20. 8:7-10. √10:12, 24. 14:25. *30:31. √31:8, 9. 37:31-36. 65:8, 9. Je 33:15-26. **tread in our palaces.** Da +*9:27. 11:40-45. Mt +*24:15. 2 Th *2:3, 4. Re 11:1, 2. **then shall we.** Is 44:28. 59:19. Zc 1:18-21. 9:13-16. 10:3-6. 12:6-9. Re 17:14. 19:14, 15. **seven.** Ge +21:28, 31. Jb 5:19. Pr 6:16. 30:18, 29. Ec 11:2. Am 1:3, 6. **shepherds.** Pusey remarks "The *shepherds* are manifestly inferior, spiritual, shepherds, acting under the One Shepherd, by His authority, and He in them" (*Minor Prophets,* vol. ii. p. 75). Da +*11:33. 1 P *5:1-4. **eight.** As *seven* is the symbol of a sacred whole, so *eight,* when united with it, is something beyond it (Pusey). The spiritual significance of the number *eight* often includes the thought of a new beginning (for the first day of the week is the eighth day, a new beginning), resurrection, and regeneration. There are eight cases of individual resurrection from the dead apart from that of Christ: (1) 1 K 17:17-22. (2) 2 K 4:32-37. (3) 2 K 13:20, 21. (4) Lk 7:11-15. (5) Mk 5:35-42. Lk 8:49-55. (6) Jn 11:1-45. (7) Ac 9:36-41. (8) Ac 20:9-12. Noah is called the "eighth person" (2 P 2:5), and eight persons were saved in the ark (1 P 3:20). Circumcision was performed on the eighth day (Ge 17:12), foreshadowing the "circumcision of Christ" connected with the new creation or regeneration of the individual (Col 2:11). The feast of Tabernacles (Le +*23:34, 39n, 42) lasted eight days (Le 23:36). It will be the principal feast during the Millennium (Ezk 45:18-25. Zc *14:16-19). Ec 11:2. **principal men.** Heb. princes of men. Probably a reference to civil power or authority. Jsh 13:21. Ps 83:12. Ezk 32:30.

6. **they.** Is 10:12. 14:2. 30:31. 31:8, 9. 33:1. Na 2:11-13. 3:1-3. **waste.** Heb. eat up. lit. feed on. Nu 14:9. Je 6:3. Ac 10:13. **the land of Nimrod.** Ge 10:8-11mg❫❀. 1 Ch 1:10. **in the entrances thereof.** *or,* with her own naked swords. or, passes. Na 3:13. **thus shall he deliver.**

Is *14:25. Ezk *39:2. Mt 24:30, 31. Lk √1:71, 74. Ro +*11:26. **the Assyrian.** 2 K 15:29. 17:3-5. 18:9-15. 19:32-35. 2 Ch 33:11. Is 10:5-12. **when he cometh.** Ezk √39:16.

7. **the remnant.** ver. 3, 8. Ezk 14:22. Jl 2:32. Am 5:15. Zp 3:13. Ro 11:5, 6. **as a dew.** Dt 32:2)℘. Jg 6:36-40. Ps 72:6. √110:3. 133:3. Is 32:13-17. 44:3-5. *66:19. Ezk 47:1-12. Ho +*6:3. 14:5. Zc 14:8. Mt 28:19. Ac 9:15. 11:15-18. 13:46-48. Ro 11:12-15. 15:19, 20. 1 C 3:6. **as the showers.** Dt 32:2. Ps 65:10. Zc 10:1. **tarrieth not.** Is *55:10, 11. Je 14:22. Ac 16:9, 10. Ro 9:30. 10:20.

8. **among the Gentiles.** Mi +*4:7. *7:16. Zp 3:15, 20. **as a lion.** Mi 4:13. Nu 23:24)℘. 24:9)℘. Ps *2:8-12. *110:5, 6. Is +*31:4. *41:15, 16. Ob *18, 19. Zc *9:15. *10:5. 12:3-6. Mt *10:14, 15. Ac 18:6. 2 C 2:15-17. **sheep.** or, goats. Ex 12:21. **treadeth down.** Mi 4:13. Ml +*4:3. **and none.** Ps 50:22. Ho 5:14. He *2:3. 12:25.

9. **hand.** Ps 21:8, 9. 106:26. Is 1:25. 11:14. 14:2-4. √26:11. 33:10. 37:36. Lk +*19:27. 1 C √15:25. Re +*19:13-21. *20:8, 9.

10. **in that day.** Mi 4:1, 6. Is +*2:11. **that I.** Ps 20:7, 8. 33:16, 17. *147:10, 11. Je 3:23. Ho 1:7. 14:3. Hg √2:22. Zc *4:6. *9:10. **will cut.** This seems to refer to those happy times when the Jews shall be converted and restored to their own land; and all their enemies being destroyed, shall have no further need of cavalry or fenced cities. ver. 9. Dt 17:16)℘. Is 2:7. 31:1. Zc 9:10.

11. **I will cut.** √18, Dt +28:4. ver. 14. Dt 29:23. Is 1:7. 6:11. **and throw.** Is 2:12-17. La 2:2. Ezk 38:11. Ho 10:14. Am *5:9. Zc 2:4, 5. *4:6.

12. **cut off.** Is 2:6-8, 18, 20. +*8:19, 20. 27:9. Zc 13:2-4. Re 19:20. 22:15. **witchcrafts.** or, sorceries. Ex 22:18)℘. Le 19:26)℘. 20:27. Dt +*18:10)℘. 2 K 9:22. 2 Ch +33:6. Is 47:9, 12. Na 3:4. Ga 5:20. Re 22:15. **soothsayers.** i.e. users of secret or occult arts (CB). Dt +*18:10. 2 K 17:17. +*21:6 (❋S#6049h, observed times). Is +2:6.

13. **graven images.** Mi 1:7. 2 Ch +34:3. Is 17:7, 8. Ezk 6:9. 36:25. 37:23. Ho 2:16, 17. 14:3, 8. Na 1:14. **cut off.** Zc 13:2. **standing images.** or, statues. Probably Asherahs. ver. 14. Ex 23:24)℘. +34:13)℘. Dt 7:5)℘. 2 K +17:10. Ho 3:4. 10:2. **no more worship.** Is 2:8, 18. Ezk 6:9. Zc *13:2. **the work.** Ps 115:4. 135:15. Is 2:8.

14. **groves.** Ex +34:13)℘. Dt 7:5)℘. 12:3)℘. Jg 3:7. 1 K 14:23. 2 K +*17:10. 21:3n. 23:6. Is 17:8. 27:9. +*66:17n. Je 17:2. **cities.** or, enemies. ver. 11.

15. **execute vengeance.** ver. 8. Ps +*58:10. +*149:7-9. Is 1:24. 65:12. Ezk 25:17. Jl *3:12. Na 1:2. 2 Th √1:8.

MICAH 6

The Lord has a controversy with his people for their great ingratitude, 1-5. The vain attempts of alarmed sinners to obtain his favor, contrasted with his reasonable requirements and service, 6-8. His voice against the city should be attended to, 9. Reproofs of Israel's iniquity, injustice, and idolatry; with awful threatenings, 10-16.

1. **ye.** Mi 1:2. 1 S 15:16. Je 13:15. Am 3:1. He 3:7, 8. **Arise.** The manner of raising attention, says Abp. Newcome, in ver. 1, 2, by calling a man to urge

his plea in the face of all nature, and on the inanimate creation to hear the expostulation of Jehovah with his people, is truly awakening and magnificent. The words of Jehovah follow in ver. 3-5; and God's mercies having been set before the people, one of them is introduced in a beautiful manner, asking what his duty is towards so gracious a God, ver. 6, 7. The answer follows in the words of the prophet, ver. 8. **contend.** Dt 4:26. 32:1. Ps 50:1, 4. Is 1:2. Je 22:29. Ezk 36:1, 8. Lk *19:40. **before.** or, with. Mi 1:4. Is 2:12-14. **let.** Ezk 37:4.

2. **Hear ye.** Dt 32:1)℘. **O mountains.** √38G, Dt +32:1. **foundations.** Dt 32:22. 2 S 22:8, 16. Ps 104:5. Pr 8:29. Je 31:37. **a controversy.** Is *1:18. 5:3, 4. *43:26. Je 2:9, 29-35. 25:31. Ezk 20:35, 36. Ho √4:1. *12:2.

3. **O my.** ver. 5. Ps 50:7. 81:8, 13. **what.** Je *2:5, 31. **wherein.** Is *43:22, 23. **testify.** Ps 51:4. Ro 3:4, 5, 19.

4. **I brought.** Ex *12:51)℘. 14:30, 31)℘. 20:2)℘. Dt 4:20, 34)℘. 5:6. 9:26. Ne 9:9-11. Ps *77:20. 78:51-53. 106:7-10. 136:10, 11. Is *63:9-12. Je 32:21. Ezk 20:5-9. Am 2:10. Ac 7:36. **and redeemed.** Ex 6:6)℘. 13:13-16)℘. Dt 7:8. 15:15. 24:18. 2 S 7:23. **house of servants.** Ex 13:3mg, 14)℘. 20:2)℘. Dt 5:6)℘. 6:12)℘. 7:8)℘. **Moses.** Ex *15:20, 21)℘. Nu 12:1, 4, 10, 15)℘. 20:1)℘. 26:59)℘. **Miriam.** Dt 24:9)℘. 1 Ch 6:3.

5. **remember now.** Nu 22:5)℘. 23:7)℘. 24:10, 11)℘. 25:1)℘. 31:16)℘. Dt 8:2, 18. 9:7. 16:3. *23:4, 5)℘. Ps 103:1, 2. 111:4. Ep 2:11. **Balak.** Nu ch. 22-25. 31:16. Dt 23:4, 5. Jsh *24:9, 10. Jg 11:25. Re 2:14. **Balaam.** Nu 31:8. Jsh 24:9, 10. Ne 13:2. 2 P 2:15. Ju 11. Re 2:14. **Shittim.** Nu 22:41. 23:13, 14, 27, 28. 25:1. 33:49. Jsh 4:19. 5:9, 10. 10:42, 43. **know the righteousness.** Jg 5:11mg. Ps 36:10. 71:15, 16, 19. 143:11. Ro 3:25, 26. 1 J √1:9.

6. **Wherewith.** √85I, Ge +18:12. 2 S 21:3. Mt 19:16. Lk 10:25. Jn 6:28. Ac 2:37. √16:30. Ro *10:2, 3. **bow.** Ps 22:29. 95:6. Ep 3:14. **the high.** Ge 14:18-22. Da 3:26. 4:9. 5:18, 21. Mk 5:7. Ac 16:17. **with.** Le 1:3, etc. Nu 23:1-4, 14, 15, 29, 30. He 10:4-10. **burnt offerings.** Le +*23:12. **of a year old.** Heb. sons of a year. Ex 12:5mg. Le 9:3)℘. 23:12.

7. **pleased.** 1 S √15:22. Ps 50:8-13. *51:16. Is *1:11-15. 40:16. Je 7:21, 22. Ho 6:6. Am 5:22. **ten thousands.** √102, Ge +2:24. **rivers.** Jb 29:6. **shall I give.** Le +18:21. Dt +18:10. Jsh 15:8n. Jg 11:31, 39. 2 K 3:27. 16:3. +21:6. 23:10. Je +*7:31. 19:5. Ezk 16:20, 21. 23:37. Ho +13:2mg. **body.** Heb. belly. Ps 132:11mg. Phm 12. **for the sin.** Ps *49:7, 8. **soul.** Heb. nephesh, Ge +27:31.

8. **O man.** Ro *9:20. 1 C 7:16. Ja *2:20. **what is good.** 1 S *12:23, 24. Ne 9:13. Ps *73:28. Ec 6:12. La *3:26, 27. Am 5:15. Lk +*6:35. *10:42. Ro 7:16. 2 Th 2:16, 17. **require of thee.** √168, Is +1:11. Dt *10:12, 13. Ps √15:2-5. Is 33:15-17. 58:6, 7. Je 9:24. 22:3. Ezk √18:5-9. Zc 8:16. Mt 19:17. Jn √3:7. Ro *3:23, 24. √6:23. Ep √2:8-10. T √3:5-8. 1 J +√2:3, 4. √3:23, 24. √5:11-13. **to do justly.** T#1324. Ge +*18:19. Le +*19:15. 1 S √15:22. Ps √82:3. *112:5mg. 119:121. Pr *21:3. Ec *12:13. Is *1:16-19. 56:1. *58:6-11. Je *7:3-6. 22:15. 23:5. Ezk 45:9. Ho *6:6. *12:6. Am 5:24. Zp 2:3. 3:5. Zc *7:9, 10. Mt *3:8-10. Mk 12:30-34. Lk *11:42. +√16:10. Ro 13:7. Col +*4:1. T *2:11, 12. Ja *1:27. 2 P 1:5-8. **love mercy.** T#1373. Ps 37:26. 112:4, 9. Pr 3:3. 11:17. Is 57:1, 2. Zc 7:9. Mt +*5:7. √18:32-35. Lk +*6:36. Ep √4:32. Col 3:12, 13. 1 P

*3:8, 9. **walk humbly.** Heb. humble *thyself* to walk. Ge +*5:22. Le 26:41. 2 Ch +*7:14. 30:11. *32:26. 33:12, 13, 19, 23. 34:27. Is +*57:15. *66:2. Ezk 16:63. Da *4:37. Mt +*5:3. Lk 14:10. *18:13-17. 22:26. Ro *10:1-3. √12:3. Ph +*2:3. Ja √4:6-10. 1 P *5:5, 6.

9. **Lord's.** Mi 3:12. Is 24:10-12. 27:10. 32:13, 14. 40:6-8. 66:6. Je 19:11-13. 26:6, 18, 20. 37:8-10. Ho 13:16. Am 2:5. 3:8-15. 6:1. Jon 3:4. Zp 3:2. **city.** ∫121J19, 1 S +22:19. **and.** 2 K 22:11-20. Ps 107:43. Pr 22:3. Is 26:11. Ho *14:9. **the man of wisdom shall see thy name.** *or,* thy name shall see that which is wisdom. Ex 34:5-7. Ps 9:+√10, 16. 48:10. 83:18. Is 30:27. **hear.** 2 S 21:1. Jb 5:6-8, 17. 10:2. Is 9:13. 10:5, 6. Je 14:18-22. La 3:39-42. Jl 2:11-18. Am 4:6-12. Jon 3:5-10. Hg *1:5-7. He *12:5. Re *3:19.

10. **Are,** etc. *or, Is there* yet unto every man an house of the wicked, etc. **yet.** ∫19, Dt +22:1. **the treasures.** Jsh *7:1. 2 K 5:23, 24. Pr 10:2. 21:6. Je 5:26, 27. Am 3:10. Hab 2:5-11. Zp 1:9. Zc +*5:3, 4. Ja +*5:1-4. **the house.** Pr *3:33. **and.** Le *19:35, 36. Dt 25:13-16. Pr 11:1. 20:10, 23. Ezk 45:9-12. Ho 12:7, 8. Am *8:5, 6. Lk √6:38. **scant measure.** Heb. measure of leanness. **abominable.** Nu 23:7, 8)℘. Pr 22:14.

11. **count them pure.** *or,* be pure. Pr +*17:15. *24:24. **the wicked balances.** Dt 25:13-16)℘. Ho 12:7. **the bag.** Pr 16:11.

12. **the rich.** Mi 2:1, 2. 3:1-3, 9-11. 7:2-6. Is 1:23. 5:7. Je 5:5, 6, 26-29. 6:6, 7. Ezk 22:6-13, 25-29. Ho 4:1, 2. Am 5:11, 12. 6:1-3. Zp 3:3. **spoken.** Is *32:7. 59:3-15. Je √9:2-6, 8. Ho 7:1, 13. Ro 3:13. 1 C *6:8. **deceitful.** Je 9:5. 17:9. Ho 12:7. Ac *5:2. Ro 3:13.

13. **I make.** Le *26:16)℘. Dt 28:21, 22. Jb 33:19-22. Ps *107:17, 18. Is *1:5, 6. Je 14:18. Ac 12:23. 1 C +*11:30. **sick.** 1 K +22:34mg. **in making.** La 1:13. 3:11. Ho 5:9. 13:16.

14. **eat.** Le *26:26)℘. Is *9:20. 65:13. Ezk 4:16, 17. Ho √4:10. Hg √1:6. 2:16. **and thou.** Dt 32:22-25. Is 3:6-8. 24:17-20. Je 48:44. Ezk 5:12. Am 2:14-16. 9:1-4.

15. **shalt sow.** Le 26:20. Dt *28:38-40)℘. Is 62:8, 9. 65:21, 22. Je 12:13. Jl 1:10-12. Am *5:11. Zp 1:13. Hg √1:6.

16. **the statutes.** Le 20:8. 2 K 17:34. Je 10:3. **of Omri are kept.** *or,* he doth much keep the, etc. 1 K *16:25-32. Ho *5:4, 11. **the works.** 1 K 16:30-33. 18:4. *21:25, 26. 2 K 16:3. 21:3. Is 9:16. Re 2:20. **the house of Ahab.** 1 K 16:30, etc. 21:25, 26. 2 K 21:3. **ye walk.** Ps +*1:1. Je 7:24. **that.** 1 K 9:8. 2 Ch *29:8, 9. 34:25. Je 18:15, 16. *19:8. 24:8, 9. 29:18. Ezk 8:17, 18. **desolation.** *or,* astonishment. Dt 28:37)℘. **therefore.** Ps 44:13, 14. Is 25:8. Je *51:51. La *5:1. Ezk 39:26. Da 9:16.

MICAH 7

The prophet complains of the decrease of godly men, and the iniquity of his people; yet encourages himself to trust in God, 1-7. Israel expects victory over her insulting foes, and deliverance from her afflictions, with renewed consolations and prosperity, 8-13. Prayers and predictions of glorious times, 14-17; with an exulting view of the unequalled mercy and truth of God towards his people, 18-20.

1. **Woe.** Ps 120:5. Is 6:5. 24:16. Je 4:31. 15:10. 45:3. **when they have gathered the summer fruits.** Heb. the gatherings of summer. ∫121P9, Is +16:9. Am 8:1.

as the grapegleanings. Jg 8:2. Is 17:6. 24:13. **my soul.** Heb. *nephesh,* Nu +11:6. **desired.** Is 28:4. Ho 9:10. Mk 11:13.

2. **good.** *or,* godly, *or,* merciful. Mi 6:8. Ps +43:1mg. 86:2mg. 145:17mg. Is 57:1. **is perished.** Ps *12:1. *14:1-3. Is 57:1. Je √5:1. Mt +*7:14. Ro 3:10-18. **they all.** Pr 1:11. 12:6. Is 59:7. Je 5:16. **hunt.** 1 S 24:11. 26:20. Ps 57:6. Je 5:26. 16:16. La 4:18. Hab 1:15-17.

3. **do evil.** Pr 4:16, 17. Je 3:5. Ezk 22:6. Ep *4:19. **the prince.** Mi 3:11. Is 1:23. Je 8:10. Ezk 22:27. Ho 4:18. Am 5:12. Mt 26:15. **the judge.** Mi 3:11. **asketh.** *or,* judgeth. ∫63E2, 1 S +13:8. **the great.** 1 K 21:9-14. **for a reward.** Dt *16:19)℘. **his mischievous desire.** Heb. the mischief of his soul. Heb. *nephesh,* Ex +15:9. **wrap.** Is 26:21. Lk 12:1, 2. 1 C 4:5.

4. **as a brier.** 2 S 23:6, 7. Is 9:18. 55:13. Ezk 2:6. He √6:8. **the day.** ∫121P4, Dt +4:32. Is *22:5. Ezk 12:23, 24. Ho 9:7, 8. Am 8:2. **thy visitation.** Is 10:3. Je +*8:12. 10:15. **now.** Is 22:5. Na *1:10. Lk *21:25.

5. **Trust ye not in.** ∫138C, Ge +22:14. Jb 6:14, 15. Ps 118:8, 9. Je *9:4, 5. Mt *10:16. **keep the doors.** ∫142, Ge +20:16. Jg 16:5-20. Ps *141:3. Ec *10:20. Mt *10:36. **her.** ∫142, Ge +20:16.

6. **son.** Ge *9:22-24. 49:4. 2 S 15:10-12. 16:11, 21-23. Pr +*15:20. *30:11, 17. Ezk *22:7. Ml ◐+*4:6. Mt *10:21, 35,)36. Lk *)12:53. *21:16. 2 T *3:2, 3. **dishonoreth.** Ex 20:12)℘. Dt 5:16)℘. **a man's.** ∫138C, Ge +22:14. Ps *41:9. *55:12-14. Je 12:6. 20:10. Ob *7. Mt *)10:36. 26:23, 49, 50. Jn *13:18.

7. **I will look.** Ps *5:3. 34:5, 6. 55:16, 17. 109:4. 142:4, 5. Is 8:17. *45:22. Hab 3:17-19. Lk 6:11, 12. He +*9:28. **wait.** Ge 49:18. Ps 25:5. 27:12-14. *37:7. 40:1-3. 62:1-8. Is *12:2. *25:9. La 3:25, 26. Hab 2:1. Lk 2:25-32. **my salvation.** Is +*25:9. He +*9:28. **my God.** Ps *4:2, 3. *17:6. *20:1. 38:15. +*50:15. 65:2. 1 J √5:14, 15.

8. **Rejoice.** Jb 31:29. Ps 13:4-6. 35:15, 16, 19, 24-26. 38:16. Pr 24:17, 18. Je 50:11. La 4:21, 22. Ezk 25:6. 35:15. Ob 12. Is 8:20. Na 1:10. Re 11:10-12. **when I fall.** T#1331. Ps √37:24. 41:10-12. Pr *24:16. Da 11:33. Zc √12:8mg. Ro 11:11. 14:4. Ju √24. **I shall arise.** Jb 13:15. Ps 112:4. **when I sit.** Ps 107:10-15. 112:4. Is 9:2. 49:9. *50:10. Mt 4:16. Lk 1:78, 79. **darkness.** Pr +20:20. Lk *22:53. Jn 12:27. Col 1:12, 13. **the Lord.** Ps *27:1. *84:11. 97:11. 112:4. Is 2:5. 50:10. *60:1-3, 19, 20. Ml *4:2. Jn *8:12. Ac 26:18. 2 C 4:6. Re 21:23. 22:5.

9. **I will bear.** Le 26:41. 1 S 3:18. 2 S 16:11, 12. 24:17. Jb 34:31, 32. Je 10:19. La 1:18. *3:39-42. Lk *15:18, 19. He *12:6, 7. **indignation.** ∫121C1C, Ps +79:6. **until.** 1 S 24:15. 25:39. 26:10. Ps 7:6. 35:1. 43:1. Je 50:17-20, 33, *34. 51:35, 36. Hab *3:2. Re 6:10, 11. 18:20. **and execute judgment.** Ps 7:8. *37:6. Is 50:7-9. **he will.** Jb 23:10. Ps 17:15. *37:6. Ml 3:18. 1 C 4:5. 2 Th 1:5-10. 2 T 4:8.

10. **Then,** etc. *or,* And thou wilt see her that is mine enemy, and cover her with shame. **she that.** Ps 137:8, 9. Is 47:5-9. Je 50:33, 34. 51:8-10, 24. Na ch. 2, 3. Re 17:1-7. **shame.** Ps *35:26. 109:29. Je 51:51. Ezk 7:18. Ob 10. **her.** ∫155E3, Is +32:9. **Where.** Ps *42:3, 10. 79:10. 115:2. Is 37:10, 11. Da 3:15. Jl 2:17. Mt 27:43. **mine eyes.** Mi *4:11. Ps 58:10. Ml 1:5. Re 18:20. **now shall.** 2 S *22:43. 2 K 9:33-37. Ps 18:42. Is 25:10-12. 26:5, 6. 41:15, 16. 51:22, 23. 63:2, 3. Zc *10:5. Ml 4:3. **trodden down.** Heb. for a treading down.

11. **the day.** Ne 2:17. 3:1, etc. 4:3, 6. Ps +*102:13, 14, 16. Da +*9:25. Am √9:11-15. Ac 15:16. **shall the decree.** Heb. *chok*, prescribed limit or boundary. Ezr 4:12-24. Ne 2:8. Jb 26:10. 38:10. Pr 8:29. Is 24:5. Je 5:22. **far removed.** Is 9:4.

12. **In that day.** √18, Dt +28:4. **also.** Mi +5:5. Is *11:11, 16. 19:23-25. *27:12, 13. +*43:6. 49:12. 60:4-9. *66:19, 20. Je 3:18. 23:3. 31:8. Ezk 37:21, 22. 39:27, 28. Ho 11:11. Zc 10:10. **and from.** *or,* even to. √18, Dt +28:4. This verse may be rendered, "In that day they (people) shall come to thee from Assyria and the fenced cities; and from the fortress (probably *Pelusium* at the entrance of Egypt), even to the river (Euphrates)," etc. The expressions employed in this prophecy appear to be too strong for the events which transpired after the Babylonian captivity; and seem to refer to the future restoration of Israel, after their land has lain desolate for ages. **the fortified cities.** Is 19:6. 37:25. **the river.** √171E12, Ge +14:22. √32, Ge +31:21. Ge 31:21. Ex 23:31. Dt *11:24. 2 Ch +9:26. Is +*27:12.

13. **Notwithstanding the land shall be.** *or,* After that the land hath been. Le 26:33-39)𝔓. Is 6:11-13. 24:3-8. Je 25:11. Da +*9:26, 27. Lk *21:20-24. **for the fruit.** Mi 3:12. Jb 4:8. Pr 1:31. 5:22. 31:31. Is 3:10, 11. Je *17:10. 21:14. 32:19. Ga √6:7, 8.

14. **Feed.** *or,* Rule. Mi +*5:4mg. Ps *23:1-4. 28:9. +*45:6. 95:7. 100:3. *110:2. Is 40:11. 49:10. Je *50:19. Mt 2:6mg. Jn √10:27-30. **with thy rod.** Ps +*23:4. 110:2. **which dwell.** Ex 33:16. Nu 23:9)𝔓. Dt 33:28)𝔓. Je 49:31. Jn 17:16. **in the midst.** Is 35:2. 37:24. 65:10. Je 50:19, 20. Ezk +*34:13, 14. Zp 3:13. **Bashan.** Nu +21:33. Jsh 12:4n. Ps 22:12. **as in.** Ps 77:5-11. 143:5. La 1:7. 5:21. Am *9:11. Ml 3:4. **of old.** Heb. *olam,* Ge +6:4.

15. **according to the days.** Citing this passage, Peters notes "The restoration of the entire Jewish nation will take at least forty years" (*Theocratic Kingdom,* vol. 2, Proposition 113, Observation 6, footnote 6, p. 91). Mi +6:4. Ex 12:51)𝔓. Ps 68:22. *78:12, etc. Is 11:16. 51:9. 63:11-15. Je √23:7, 8. Ezk √20:36n. Ho 2:15. Re +*12:6, 14. **I will show.** Mi 2:12, 13. Ex 34:10)𝔓. Is 11:15, 16. 19:20. 27:12. Zc *14:4. Jn +*1:51. 14:12.

16. **nations.** Mi +*5:8. Ps 126:2. +*149:5-9. Is

26:11. *60:6-10. 66:18. Ezk *38:23. *39:17-21. Zc *8:20-23. 9:13-16. 12:9. Re 11:18. **their might.** Mi 4:8. Zc 12:6. 14:12-21. **lay their hand.** √121S3N, Jg +18:19. Jb *21:5. 29:9, 10. *40:4. Is 52:15. Ro *3:19.

17. **lick the dust.** Ge +*3:14, 15. Ps 72:9. Is 49:23. 60:14. +*65:25. La 3:29. Re *3:9. **move.** 1 S 14:11. Ps 18:45. Je 16:16. **worms.** *or,* creeping things. Dt 32:24)𝔓. **they shall be afraid.** Ex 15:14-16. Jsh 2:9-11. 9:24. Ps 9:20. Is 2:10, 11, 19-21. *26:11. 64:2. Je 33:9. Zc 14:5. Re 6:15-17. 18:9, 10.

18. **a God.** Heb. *El,* Ex +15:2. Ex *15:11)𝔓. Dt 33:26. 1 K *8:23. Ps 35:10. 71:19. 89:6, 8. 113:5, 6. Is 40:18, 25. *46:8, 9. **that pardoneth.** Ex *33:18, 19. *34:6, +7)𝔓. Nu 14:18, 19. Ne *9:17. Ps 65:3. *86:5, 15. *103:2, 3. 130:4, 7, 8. Is *1:18. *43:25. *44:22. √55:7. Je *31:34. 33:8. 50:20. Da *9:9. Jon 4:2. Lk *24:47. Jn *1:29. Ac *13:38, 39. **passeth.** Nu 23:21. Ezk 33:11. Am *7:8. *8:2. **the remnant.** ver. *14. Mi 2:12. *4:7. *5:3, 7, 8. Jl *2:32. Ro *11:4-7. He *8:9-12. **his.** √96D3, Ge +49:4. **he retaineth.** Ps *77:6-10. 85:4, 5. *103:9. Is 57:10, 16. Je *3:5, 12. La *3:31, 32. Zp 3:17. **for ever.** Heb. *ad,* Ps +9:18. **he delighteth.** Is 62:5. 65:19. Je *32:41. Ezk *33:11. Zp 3:17. Lk *15:5-7, 9, 10, 23, 24, 32. Ep *2:4, 5. Ja *2:13. **in mercy.** Ps *57:10. *86:5, 15. Is √54:7, 8. Ezk 33:11. Da 9:9. Zc √10:6.

19. **turn.** Dt *30:3, 6. 32:36. Ezr 9:8, 9. Ps 80:14. *90:13, 14. Is 63:15-17. Je 31:20. La *3:32. Ho 14:4. Zc *1:3. Ac +*3:19-21. **have compassion.** Je *12:15. 31:20. La *3:32. Ezk 36:25-27. **subdue.** Dt *30:6. 1 Ch 17:10. Ps 103:12. +*130:8. Is 38:17. +*60:21. Ezk *11:19, 20. *36:25-27. Da +*9:24. Ro √6:14, 17-22. 7:23-25. 8:2, 3, 13. T *2:14. Ja 4:5, 6. 1 J *3:8. **cast.** Ps 32:1. *103:12. Is *38:17. *43:25. Je *31:34. *33:8. √50:20. Da +*9:24.

20. **wilt perform.** Ge √12:2, 3. *17:7, 8. *22:16-18. 26:3, 4. 28:13, 14. Ps *105:8-10. Je +*33:25, 26. Ml 3:6. Lk *1:54, 55,)72-74. Ac 3:25, 26. +*7:5. Ro *11:26-31. He *6:13-18. **mercy to Abraham.** T#117. 2 Ch +*20:7. Mt *8:11. Lk 13:28, 29. Ac +*7:5. Ro +*4:13. Ga 3:9, 14-18, *29. **sworn unto.** Ge 50:24)𝔓. Ps 105:9, 10, 42. Is +√55:3. Ac +*7:5n. Ro +*15:8. He *6:16-18. **from the days.** Je 46:26. **of old.** Heb. *kedem,* Mi +5:2.

NAHUM

NAHUM 1

The subject of the prophecy, and the writer of it, 1. The majesty and terrible effects of God's indignation, 2-6. His love to his people and severity to his enemies, 7, 8. The prophet foretells the ruin of the Assyrian king and his army, and the rejoicing of the Jews, 9-15.

1. Cir. A.M. 3291. B.C. 713. **burden.** √121L4, Is +22:1. Is 13:1. 14:28. 15:1. 21:1. 22:1. 23:1. Je 23:33-37. Zc 9:1. **Nineveh.** Ge *10:11. Jon *3:3, 4. 4:11. Zp 2:13. **Nahum.** i.e. *comforted,* ✳S#5151h. **Elkoshite.** i.e. *God my bow,* i.e. *defense; of the gathered of God,* ✳S#512h. A dweller in Elkosh, which Jerome says was a village of Galilee (Jn ⚫7:52). Others think it was in the territory of Simeon.

2. **God is jealous, and the Lord revengeth.** *or,* The

Lord *is* a jealous God, and a revenger. Ex *20:5-7)𝔓. *34:14. Dt *4:24)𝔓. Jsh *24:19. Is 42:13. Ezk 38:18, 19. 39:25. Jl 2:18. Zc 1:14. 8:2. Note the reference to the Pentateuch. Other references to the Pentateuch in Nahum are at ver. 3, 4, 12, 13, 15. Na 3:4, 18. See related note (Is +*1:2). **revengeth.** √22B, Ex +15:7. Dt *32:35, 42. Ps 94:1. Is *59:17, 18. 65:6, 7. Ro +*12:19. 13:4. He *10:30. **is furious.** Heb. that hath fury. lit. "lord of wrath." Le 26:28. Jb 20:23. Is 51:17, 20. 59:18. 63:3-6. 66:15. Je 4:4. 25:15. 36:7. La 4:11. Ezk 5:13. 6:12. 8:18. 36:6. Mi 5:15. Zc 8:2. Jn +*3:36. **reserveth.** Dt 32:34, 35, 41-43. Je 3:5. Mi +*7:18. Ro 2:5, 6. 2 P *2:9. Ju *13. **wrath.** √63A2, 2 S +6:6. **for his enemies.** 1 Th +*5:9.

3. **slow.** Ex 34:6, 7)𝔓. Ne *9:17. Ps *103:8. 145:8. Pr ⚫14:17. Jl 2:13. Jon *4:2. Ja 1:19. **great.** Jb 9:4. Ps 62:11. 66:3. 147:5. Ep 1:19, 20. **and will not.** Ex

34:7)ℙ. Nu 14:18)ℙ. Jb 10:14, 15. **his way.** Ex 19:16-18. Dt 5:22-24. 1 K 19:11-13. Jb 38:1. Ps *18:7-15. 50:3. *97:2-5. 104:3. Is 19:1. 66:15. Da 7:13. Hab 3:5-15. Zc 9:14. Mt 26:64. Re *1:7. **the clouds.** Ge +9:13.

4. **rebuketh.** Ex 14:21, 22, 27-29)ℙ. Jb 38:11. Ps *18:15. 104:7. *106:9. 114:3, 5. Is *50:2, 3. 51:10. Am +*5:8. Mt *8:26. **and drieth.** Jsh 3:13-15. 4:23. Ps 74:15. Is 19:5-10. 44:27. Ezk 30:12. **Bashan.** Nu +21:33. Jsh 12:4n. Is *33:9. Am 1:2. **Carmel.** Mi 7:14. **flower.** ʃ155C, Le +19:23.

5. **mountains.** 2 S 22:8. Ps 29:5, 6. *68:8. *97:4, 5. 114:4, 6. Is 2:12-14. Je 4:24. Mi 1:3, 4. Hab 3:10. Mt 27:51. 28:2. Re 20:11. **the hills.** Jg 5:5. Ps 46:6. 97:5. Is 64:1, 2. Mi 1:4. **the earth.** 2 P √3:7-12.

6. **can stand.** Jb 9:4. Ps *2:12. 76:7. 90:11. Is 27:4. Je *10:10. Ml 3:2. Re 6:17. **indignation.** Is +66:14. **abide.** Heb. stand up. Je *10:10. 51:64. Ml *3:2. **his fury.** ver. 2. Dt 32:22, 23. Is 10:16, 17. La 2:4. 4:11. Ezk 30:16, 17. Re *16:1, 8, 9.

7. **Lord is good.** Ex +*34:6. Dt *4:31. 1 Ch *16:34. Ezr 3:11. Ps *25:8. 100:5. 136:1, etc. √145:6-10. Je +*29:11. *33:11. La 3:25. Ro +*11:22. 1 J *4:8-10. **strong hold.** *or*, strength. Jg 6:26mg. Ps 18:1, 2. 27:5. *46:1. 62:6-8. 71:3. *84:11. 91:1, 2. 144:1, 2. Pr 18:10. Is 25:4. 26:1-4. 32:2. **in the day.** Ps 20:1. +*50:15. 59:16. 77:2. 86:7. 91:15. Is 37:3, 4. Je +*30:7. Hab +*3:16. **and he knoweth.** Ps *1:6. Mt *7:23. Jn √10:27. Ga 4:9. 2 T √2:19. **that trust.** 2 S *22:31. 1 Ch 5:20. 2 Ch 16:8, 9. 32:8, 11, 21. Ps +√9:10. *84:12. Je *17:7, 8. Da 3:28. *6:23. Mt 27:43. 2 T 1:12mg.

8. **with.** Is 8:7, 8. 28:17. Ezk 13:13. Da +*9:26. 11:10, 22, 40. Am 8:8. 9:5, 6. Mt 7:27. 2 P 3:6, 7. **utter end.** Ps *1:6. **the place.** ver. 1. Na 2:8. Zp 2:13-15. **darkness.** Jb 30:15. Pr *4:19. Is 8:22. Je 13:16. Mt 8:12.

9. **imagine against.** ver. 11. Ps *2:1-4. 21:11. 33:10. +*140:2. Pr +*21:30. Is 8:9, 10. Ezk *38:10, 11. Ho +*7:15. Ac *4:25-28. 2 C *10:5. **he will make.** 1 S 3:12. 26:8. 2 S 20:10. Ezk 20:17. Zp *2:13-15. **affliction.** ver. 7. **not rise up.** ver. Mg. Ps 16:25. Je 51:64. Zp √3:15. **second time.** Is +√11:11n.

10. **while they be.** 2 S 23:6, 7. Mi 7:4. 1 Th 5:2, 3. **thorns.** Is 10:17. 27:4. **drunken.** Na 3:11. 1 S 25:36-38. 2 S 13:28. Je 51:39, 57. **they shall.** Ps 68:2. Is 9:18. 10:17-19. 27:4. Ml *4:1.

11. **one.** ver. 9. 2 K 18:13, 14, 30. 19:22-25. 2 Ch 32:15-19. Is 10:7-15. Da *7:8, 21. *8:9, 23-25. **wicked counsellor.** Heb. counsellor of Belial. Dt +15:9. Jg +19:22. 1 S 2:12. 2 S 20:1. 2 K 18:+13, +17, *26-28. 2 Ch 13:7. Ps 120:2. 123:3.

12. **Though,** etc. *or*, *If they would have been* at peace, so *should they have been* many, and so should they have been shorn, and he should have passed away. **yet.** 2 K *19:35, 37. Is 10:32-34. 14:24-27. 17:14. 30:28-33. 31:8, 9. 37:36. **cut down.** Heb. shorn. Is 7:20. **pass.** ver. 15. Ex 12:12)ℙ. Is 8:8. Da 11:10. **I will.** Ps *30:5. 103:9. *125:3. Is 30:19. 51:22. √54:8, 11. 60:18-20. Jl 2:19. Re 7:16.

13. **will I.** Ge 27:40)ℙ. Is 9:4. *10:5, 12, 27. 14:25. Je 2:20. Mi 5:5, 6. **will burst.** Ps 107:14. Je 5:5. *30:8. 14. **given.** Ps 71:3. Is *14:24. 33:13. **that.** Ps 109:13. Pr 10:7. Is 14:20-22. **out.** Ex 12:12. Le 26:30. 2 K √19:37. Is 19:1. 46:1, 2. Je 50:2. **cut off.** Ezk 31:3. **graven image.** 2 Ch +34:3. **molten image.** 2 Ch +34:3. **I will make.** Na 3:4-6. 2 K 19:37. 2 Ch 32:21. **grave.**

Heb. *qeber*, Ge +23:4. **for.** 1 S 3:13. Is 37:37, 38. Da *11:21.

15. **upon.** Is *18:3. *40:9, 10. +)52:7. Lk 2:10, 14. Ac 10:36. Ro *10:15. **bringeth good tidings.** Is 41:27. **that publisheth.** Ps +*68:11. Is +*27:6. **keep.** Heb. feast. ʃ147D, Ge +1:29. Dt 16:16)ℙ. 23:21)ℙ. **perform.** Ps 107:8, 15, 21, 22. 116:12-14, 17, 18. Is 19:21. **vows.** Le +*23:38. **the wicked.** Heb. Belial. ver. 11mg, 12. 1 S +30:22. **no more.** Is *37:36-38. 52:1. Jl 3:17. Zc 14:21. **he is.** ver. 14. Is 29:7, 8.

NAHUM 2

Predictions of the siege and taking of Nineveh; the ruin of the Assyrian empire; the captivity of the princes and people; the plundering and destruction of the city, and the extinction of the royal family; for their oppression, cruelty, and tyranny, 1-13.

1. **He that dasheth in pieces.** *or*, The disperser, *or*, hammer. Ps 68:2. Pr 25:18. Is 14:6. Je 23:29. 25:9. 50:23. 51:20-23. Ezk 9:2mg. Mi 2:13. **keep.** Na 3:14, 15. 2 Ch 25:8. Je 46:3-10. 51:11, 12. Jl 3:9-11. **make thy.** Jb 40:7. Je 1:17. **fortify.** Pr 24:5.

2. **hath turned away.** Ps 80:9. Is 5:5, 6. *10:5-12. Je 12:10. 25:29. **excellency of Jacob, as the excellency.** *or*, the pride of Jacob as the pride. Je 13:9. Zp 3:11. **for.** Ge 49:22, 23. Ps *80:12-15. Je 49:9. Ho *10:1.

3. **mighty men.** 2 S 23:8. 1 K 1:8, 10. **made red.** Is 63:1-3. Zc 1:8. 6:2. Re 6:4. 12:3. **valiant men.** Jg 3:29. +6:12. 1 S 18:17. 31:12. 2 S 11:16. **in scarlet.** *or*, dyed scarlet. Je 22:14. Ezk 23:14. **flaming.** *or*, fiery. ʃ102, Ge +2:24. **preparation.** Je 46:14. Ezk 7:14. 38:7. **the fir trees.** ʃ121D1. Metonymy of the Cause, 2 S +6:5. Fir trees put for fir spears, the weapon being named from the wood of which it is made (Pusey, vol. ii. p. 143). Is 14:8. Ho 14:8. Zc 11:2.

4. **chariots.** This is not a prediction of the modern automobile and traffic jams! Na 3:2, 3. Is 37:24. 66:15. Je 4:13. Ezk 26:10. Da 11:40. **rage.** 2 K 9:20. Je 46:9. **streets.** Heb. *chuts*, Am 5:16n (✙S#2351h, highways), outside, or narrow streets. **justle.** Is 33:4. Jl 2:9. **broad ways.** Heb. *rechob*, Am 5:16n (✳S#7339h, streets), public square or broad streets. **they shall seem.** Heb. their show. **like torches.** lit. "with the fire of steels," possibly a reference to a scythed chariot (See Pusey, vol. ii. p. 127, 142), or the steel covering of the chariots, Jsh 17:16 (Keil, *Minor Prophets*, vol. ii. p. 20).

5. **He.** Na +3:18. Mi +5:5, 6. **recount.** Is 21:5. Je 50:29. 51:27, 28. **worthies.** *or*, gallants. Na 3:18. Jg 5:13. 2 Ch 23:20. **they shall stumble.** Na 3:3. Is *5:26, 27. Je 46:12. **make haste.** Hab 1:6-10. **defence.** *or*, covering, *or* coverer.

6. **gates.** Is 45:1, 2. **dissolved.** *or*, molten. Jsh 2:9. 2 P *3:10, 11.

7. **Huzzab.** *or*, that which was established; *or*, there was a stand made. i.e. *established; beautifully beaming*, ✳S#5324h. **led away captive.** *or*, discovered. La 4:22mg. **doves.** Is *38:14. *59:11. Lk 23:27, 48. **tabering.** Taber means to beat as a taber or tabret. Ex +*15:20. 1 S 10:5.

8. **Nineveh.** Jon *3:3. *4:11. **of old.** *or*, from the days *that* she *hath been.* Ge 10:11. **like.** Je 51:13. Re 17:1, 15. **Stand.** Na 3:17. Is 13:14. 47:13. 48:20. Je 50:16. 51:30. **look back.** *or*, cause *them* to turn.

9. **ye.** Is 33:1, 4. Je 51:56. **for there is none end of the store.** *or*, and *their* infinite store, etc. ver. 12,

13. **pleasant furniture**. Heb. vessels of desire. 2 Ch 36:10mg. Je +25:34mg. Ezk 26:12mg. Da +11:8mg.

10. **She is**. Nineveh was taken and utterly ruined by Assuerus, or Cyaxares, king of Media, and Nabuchodonosor, or Nabopolassar, king of Babylon, B.C. 606, or 612. Diodorus, who with others ascribes the taking of it to Arbaces the Mede and Belesis the Babylonian, says that he "dispersed the citizens in the villages, levelled the city with the ground, transferred the gold and silver, of which there were many talents, to Ecbatana the metropolis of the Medes; and thus subverted the empire of the Assyrians." **empty**. Na 3:7. Ge 1:2. Is 13:19-22. 14:23. 24:1. 34:10-15. Je *4:23-26. 51:62. Zp 2:13-15. 3:6. Re 18:21-23. **the heart**. Jsh 2:11. Ps 22:14. Is 13:7, 8. **the knees**. Da 5:6. **and much**. Is 21:3. Je *30:6. **and the faces**. Jl ⁴2:6.

11. **Where is**. 2 K *18:34. Ps *37:10, 35, 36. **the dwelling**. Na 3:1. Jb 4:10, 11. Is 5:29. Je 2:15. 4:7. 50:17, 44. Ezk 19:2-8. Zp 3:3. **lions**. ∫173, Ge +27:44. **none**. Ge 49:9. Is 31:4.

12. **The lion**. Jb 4:10, 11. Je 4:7. Da 7:4. **and filled**. Ps 17:12. Is 10:6-14. Je 51:34.

13. **I am**. Na 3:5. Je 21:13. 50:31. 51:25. Ezk 5:8. 26:3. 28:22. *29:3, 10. 35:3. 38:3. *39:1. **I will burn**. Jsh 11:9. 2 K 19:23. Ps 46:9. Is +*30:31-33. **and the sword**. Is 31:8, 9. 37:36-38. **I will cut**. Na 3:1, 12. Is 33:1-4. 49:24, 25. **the voice**. 2 K *18:17, 19, 27-35. *19:9, 23. 2 Ch 32:9-16, 19.

NAHUM 3

Heavy charges and denunciations against Nineveh, 1-7. The desolation of No in Egypt, a warning to Nineveh to expect similar destruction, 8-10. Further predictions of her ruin, and of the inefficacy of all methods to prevent it, 11-19.

1. **Woe to**. Na 24:2. Ezk 22:2, 3. 24:6-9. Jon *1:2. Hab *2:12. Zp 3:1-3. **bloody city**. Heb. city of bloods. 2 K +9:26mg. Ezk 22:2, 3. 24:6, 9. Hab 2:12. **full**. Na 2:12. Is 17:14. 42:24. Ho 4:2.

2. **noise**. Na 2:3, 4. Jg 5:22. Jb 39:22-25. Is 9:5. Je 27:4-8. 47:3. Hab *1:6-10.

3. **bright sword and the glittering spear**. Heb. flame of the sword, and lightning of the spear. Na 2:4. Ge *3:24. Jb +41:21. Is 13:8mg. Hab 3:11. **and there**. Is 37:36. Je *33:5. Ezk 31:3-13. 39:4.

4. **Because**. Pr 14:34. Ezk 23:7, 11, 12. **harlot**. ∫155E3, Is +32:9. Re 17:2. **the mistress**. Ex 22:18⁹𝒫. Dt +*18:10⁹𝒫. Is 23:15-17. 47:*9, 12, 13. Re 17:1-5. 18:2, 3, 9, 23. **witchcrafts**. Mi *5:12. **that selleth nations**. To rob them of liberty and bring them into slavery, to make them tributary (Keil, vol. ii. p. 31). Dt 32:30. Jg 2:14. 3:8. 2 K *16:10. **families**. A reference to smaller peoples or tribes (Keil). Je 25:9. Ezk 20:32.

5. **I am**. See on Na 2:13. Nu +√32:23. Ezk 23:25. **I will discover**. Na 2:13. Is *3:17mg. Ezk 16:37. 23:29. Mi 1:11. Hab 2:16. **skirts**. Ex 28:33, 34. 39:24. **I will show**. Is 47:2, 3. Je 13:22, 26. Ezk 16:37. **thy shame**. Je 13:26.

6. **I will cast**. Jb 9:31. 30:19. Ps 38:5-7. La 3:16. Ml 2:3. 1 C 4:13. **make**. Na 1:14. Jb 30:8. Ml 2:9. **will set**. 1 K 9:7, 8. Is *14:16-19. Je 51:37. Zp 2:15. 1 C 4:9. He 10:33. Ju *7.

7. **that all**. Nu 16:34. Je 51:9. Re 18:10. **Nineveh**. Na 2:9, 10. Je 51:41-43. Re 18:16-19. **who**. Is 51:19. Je 15:5. La 2:13.

8. **thou**. Ezk 31:2, 3. Am *6:2. **populous No**. *or*, nourishing No. Heb. No-amon. i.e. *temple, portion*, ✻S#4996h. Je *46:25mg, 26. Ezk *30:14-16. **the rivers**. ✚S#2975h. Heb. *yeorim*, properly a *canal*, specifically a branch of the Nile (Ex 7:19. 8:5. 2 K 19:24. Jb 28:10. Ps 78:44. Is 7:18. 19:6, 7. 33:21. 37:25. Ezk 29:3, 4, 5, 10. 30:12) or the Nile itself (Ge 41:1, 2, 3, 17. Ex 1:22. 2:3, 5. 4:9. 7:15, 17, 18, 20, 21, 24, 25. 8:3, 9, 11. 17:5. Is 23:3, 10. Je 46:7, 8. Ezk 29:3, 9. Am 8:8. 9:5. Zc 10:11), and in Daniel it refers to the river Ulai (Da 12:5, 6, 7). **that had**. Is 19:5-10. **the sea**. Jb 41:31. Is 18:2. 19:5.

9. **Ethiopia**. Is *20:5. Je 46:9. Da 11:43. **infinite**. lit. and there is no end. ver. 3. Na 2:9. Is 2:7. **Put**. i.e. *extension; afflicted*, ✻S#6316h. Ge 10:6, Phut. 1 Ch 1:8. Je 46:9mg. Ezk 27:10. 30:5mg. 38:5mg. **Lubim**. i.e. *dwellers in a thirsty land*, ✻S#3864h. 2 Ch 12:3. 16:8. Da 11:43. **thy helpers**. Heb. in thy help.

10. **she carried**. Ps 33:16, 17. Is 19:4. *20:4. **went into captivity**. Dt 28:41⁹𝒫. Is *20:4. **her young**. 2 K 8:12. Ps 137:9. Is 13:16. Ho 13:16. Am 1:13. **at**. La 2:19. 4:1. **cast lots**. Jsh +*14:2n. Jl 3:3. Ob 11.

11. **Thou also**. Diodorus relates, that while the Assyrian army were feasting for their former victories, those about Arbaces being informed of their negligence and drunkenness, fell upon them unexpectedly, slew many, and drove the rest into the city. **shalt be drunken**. Na 1:10. Ps *11:6. *75:8. Is 29:9. 49:26. 63:6. Je *25:15-17, 27. 51:57. Re *14:10. **thou shalt be hid**. Keil cites Calvin, "Thou wilt vanish away as if thou hadst never been; the Hebrews frequently using the expression being hidden for being reduced to nothing." Na 1:8. 2:12. 1 S 13:6. 14:11. Is 2:10, 19. Ho 10:8. Am 9:3. Ob √16. Mi 7:17. Lk 23:30. Re 6:15-17. **thou also**. Na 2:1. Je 4:5. 8:14. **seek strength**. Ep 6:10, 11.

12. **thy strong holds**. Hab 1:10. Re 6:13.

13. **thy people**. Is 19:16. Je 50:37. 51:30. **the gates**. Na 2:6. Ps 107:16. Is 45:1, 2. **thy bars**. Ps 147:13. Je 51:30.

14. **Draw**. ∫60A, Ge +3:22. ∫96B, Nu +24:21. 2 Ch 32:3, 4, 11. Is 22:9-11. 37:25. **fortify**. Na 2:1. Is *8:9, 10. Je 46:3, 4, 9. Jl 3:9-11. **brickkiln**. or, the brickwork. Heb. *malben*, fortifications or walls built with bricks. 2 S +12:31. Je *43:9n.

15. **shall the**. ver. 13. Na 2:13. Zp 2:13. **it**. Jl *1:4. 2:25. **make thyself many as the locusts**. Ex *10:13-15.

16. **above**. ∫102B, ∫138B, Ge +13:16. Ge 15:5. 22:17. Ne 9:23. Je 33:22. **spoileth**. *or*, spreadeth himself. Ho 7:1.

17. **Thy crowned**. Re *9:7. **thy captains**. Je 51:27. **great grasshoppers**. Am 7:1. **not known**. Ps *37:10, 35, 36. 92:7. Ob *16.

18. **Thy shepherds**. That is, the rulers and tributary princes, who, as Herodotus informs us, deserted Nineveh in the day of her distress, and came not to her succor. Diodorus also says, that when the enemy shut up the king in the city, many nations revolted; each going over to the besiegers for the sake of their liberty; that the king dispatched messengers to all his subjects, requiring power from them to succor him, and that he thought himself able to endure the siege, and remained in expectation of armies which were to be raised throughout his empire, relying on the oracle, that the city would not be taken till the river became its enemy. See on Na 2:6n. Ex 15:16. Ps *76:5, 6. Is 56:9, 10.

Je 51:39, 57. **O king**. Je 50:18. Ezk 31:3, etc. 32:22, 23. Mi 5:5, 6. **nobles**. *or*, valiant ones. Is 47:1. Je 14:3. Re 6:15. **shall dwell**. Ge 3:19. **thy people**. 1 K 22:17. Is 13:14. **no man gathereth**. Dt 30:4♪𝓟.

19. **There is no**. Je 30:13-15. 46:11. *50:18. Ezk 30:21, 22. Mi 1:9. Zp 2:13-15. **healing**. Heb. wrinkling.

Le 13:6. **thy bruise**. Ps 60:2. La 2:11. **thy wound**. Ps 64:7. Mi 1:9. **is grievous**. Je 10:19. 14:17. 30:12. **the bruit**. i.e. noise or rumor. Je 10:22. **shall clap**. Jb 27:23. Ps 47:1. Is *14:8, etc. 55:12. La 2:15. Ezk 25:6. 31:3. Re 18:20. **upon**. Na 2:11, 12. Is 10:6-14. 37:18. Re 13:7. 17:2. 18:2, 3.

HABAKKUK

HABAKKUK 1

The prophet complains that violence and contention prevailed among his people, 1-4. The Lord shows him the vengeance to be inflicted by the Chaldeans, 5-11. He adores God, and laments the treachery and cruelty of prosperous sinners, 12-17.

1. A.M. 3404. B.C. 600. **burden**. ♪121L4, Is +22:1. Is 22:1. Na 1:1. **Habakkuk**. i.e. *embracing continually*, *S#2265h. Hab 3:1.

2. **how**. Ps *6:3. *13:1, 2. 74:9, 10. 94:3. Re 6:10. **cry**. Dt +*24:15. Jb 19:7. Ps 18:6, 41. 22:24. Je 20:8. **and thou wilt not save**. Ps 22:1, 2. Je 14:9. La 3:8.

3. **show me iniquity**. Ps 12:1, 2. 55:9-11. 73:3-9. 120:5, 6. Ec 4:1. 5:8. Je 9:2-6. Ezk 2:6. Mi 7:1-4. Mt 10:16. 2 P 2:8. **for spoiling**. Hab 2:17. Ho 7:13. **violence**. Mi 6:12. **strife and**. 1 K 19:10. Je 15:10. 20:14.

4. **the law**. Ps 11:3. 119:126. Pr √28:4. Ec √8:11. Mk *7:9. Ro 3:31. **slacked**. *S#6313h. Ge 45:26 (fainted). Ps 38:8 (feeble). 77:2 (ceased). See also *S#6314h. La 2:18 (rest). **never**. Jb +4:20 (*S#5331h). **for the wicked**. 1 K 21:13. Jb 21:7. Ps 22:12, 16. 58:1, 2. 59:2, 4. 82:1-5. 94:3, 20, 21. Pr *17:4. √29:12. Is 1:21-23. 59:2-8, 13-15. Je 5:27-29. *12:1, 6. 26:8, 21-23. 37:14-16. 38:4-6. Ezk 22:25-30. Ho 10:4. Am 5:7, 12. Mi 2:1, 2. 3:1-3. 7:2-4. Mt 23:34-36. 26:59-66. 27:1, 2, 25, 26. Ac 7:52, 59. 23:12-14. Ja 2:6, 7. **wrong**. *or*, wrested. Ex +*23:2, 6. Dt *16:19. Jb 19:7. Ec +*5:8. Is 29:21. Ezk 9:9mg. Mi 3:9. **judgment**. Le +*19:15, 35. Pr *17:15. *28:5. Mi +*6:8. Mt +*23:23. Jn +*7:24. Ja +*5:4, 6.

5. **Behold**. ♪12, Ps +1:1. Ac ▶13:41. **ye among**. Dt 4:27. Je 9:25, 26. 25:14-29. **and regard**. Is *29:14. La 4:12. Da 9:12. Ac *13:40, 41. **for**. Is 28:21, 22. Je 5:12, 13. 18:18. Ezk 12:22-28. Zp 1:12, 18.

6. **I raise**. Note the reference to the Pentateuch. Other references to the Pentateuch in Habakkuk are at ver. 8. Hab 2:6, 9, 10, 14. 3:3, 8, 10, 19. See related note (Is +*1:2). Dt *28:49-52▶𝓟. 2 K 24:2. 2 Ch ✱36:6, 17. Is 5:26, 27. 23:13. 39:6, 7. Je 1:15, 16. 4:6, 7. *5:15. 6:22, 23. 21:4. 25:9. **breadth**. Heb. breadths.

7. **their judgment**, etc. *or*, from them shall proceed the judgment of these and the captivity of these. Je 39:5-9. 52:9-11, 25-27. Da 5:19, 27.

8. **horses**. Dt 28:49. Is 5:26-28. **fierce**. Heb. sharp. Pr 27:17. **evening**. Je 5:6. Zp 3:3. **they**. Dt 28:49, 50▶𝓟. Je 4:13. La 4:19. Ezk 17:3, 12. Ho *8:1. Mt *24:28. Lk *17:37.

9. **for**. ver. 6. Hab 2:5-13. Dt 28:51, 52. Je 4:7. 5:15-17. 25:9. **their faces shall sup up as the east**. *or*, the supping up of their faces, as, etc. *or*, their faces shall look toward the east. Heb. the opposition of their faces shall be toward the east. Jb 39:24. Is 27:8. Je 4:11, 12. Ezk 17:10. 19:12. Ho 13:15. **they shall gather**. Hab 2:5. Ge 41:49. Jg 7:12. Jb 29:18.

Ps 139:18. Je 15:8. 33:22. Ho 1:10. Ro 9:27. **as the sand**. ♪102B, ♪138B, Ge +13:16.

10. **scoff**. 2 K 24:12. 25:6, 7. 2 Ch 36:6, 10. **they shall deride**. Is 14:16. Je 32:24. 33:4. 52:4-7.

11. **shall his**. Da 4:30-34. **mind**. Heb. *ruach*, Ge +26:35. ♪121A10, Ge +26:35. **change**. Da +*9:27. **imputing**. Da 5:3, 4, 20. √11:36, 38.

12. **thou not**. Dt 33:27. Ps √90:2. 93:2. 102:27. Is 40:28. +*57:15. La 5:19. Mi +*5:2. 1 T 1:17. 6:16. He 1:10-12. +*13:8. Re +*1:8, 11. **mine**. Is 43:15. 49:7. Ac 3:14. **we**. Hab 3:2. Ps √102:28. 118:17. Is 27:6-9. Je 4:27. 5:18. 30:11. +√33:24-26. 46:28. Ezk 37:11-14. Am +*9:8, 9. Mt +*22:32. **we**. ♪182, Ge +18:22. **shall not die**. 1 C 15:53, 54. 1 T 6:16. **thou hast ordained**. 2 K 19:25. Ps 17:13. Is 10:5-7. 37:26. Je 25:9, etc. Ezk 30:25. **mighty God**. Heb. Rock. Dt 32:4, 15, 18, 30, 31. 1 S 2:2. 2 S 23:3. Ps 18:1, 2, 31, 46. 19:14. **established**. Heb. founded. Ps 8:2mg. **for**. Is 27:9, 10. Je 30:11. 31:18-20. 46:28. He 12:5, 6.

13. **Thou art**. ♪169, Je +12:1. **of purer eyes than**. Jb *15:15. Ps *5:4, 5. *11:4-7. *34:15, 16. Ja √1:13. 1 P *1:15, 16. **evil**. Is +*45:7. **canst not**. Ps √5:4. Is 43:25. Ro 3:26. **iniquity**. *or*, grievance. ver. 3. Is 10:1. **wherefore lookest**. Ps *10:1, 2, 15. *73:3, Je *12:1, 2. 2 P 3:9. **deal**. Is 21:2. *33:1. **holdest**. Est *4:14. Ps *35:22. *50:3, 21. 83:1. Pr *31:8, 9. Is 64:12. 1 C 2:8. Ep *5:11-13. 1 T 1:13, 16. Ja √4:17. 2 P √3:9. **the wicked**. ver. *3, *4. 2 S 4:11. 1 K *2:32. Ps *37:12-15, 32, 33. 56:1, 2. Ac *2:23. *3:13-15. 2 Th *2:8.

14. **creeping**. *or*, moving. Ge 9:3. **no ruler**. Pr 6:7.

15. **take**. Je *16:16. Ezk 29:4, 5. Am *4:2. Mt 17:27. **they catch**. Ps 10:9. Lk 5:5-10. Jn 21:6-11. **drag**. *or*, flue-net. ver. 16. Is 19:8. Mt 13:47. **therefore**. Je 50:11. La 2:15, 16. Ezk 25:6. 26:2. 35:15. Re 11:10.

16. **they**. ver. 15. Dt *8:17, 18. Is 2:8. *10:13-15. *37:24, 25. Ezk 28:3-5. 29:3. Da 4:30. 5:23. **plenteous**. *or*, dainty. Heb. fat. Ge 41:2, 4, 5, 7.

17. **and**. ver. 9, 10. Hab 2:5-8, 17. Is 14:16, 17. Je 25:9-26. ch. 46-49, 52. Ezk ch. 25-30.

HABAKKUK 2

The prophet, waiting earnestly for an answer, is ordered to write his vision, which would certainly be fulfilled, 1-3. The proud are not upright; but "the just by faith shall live," 4. The judgment of the Chaldeans for insatiableness, 5-8; for covetousness, 9-11; for cruelty, 12-14; for drunkenness, 15; for treachery, 16; and idolatry, 18, 19. A call to the whole earth to keep silence before God, 20.

1. **stand**. Ps 73:16, 17. Is *21:6, 8, 11, 12. **tower**. Heb. fenced place. 2 S 18:24. 2 K 9:17. 17:9. Is 21:5. 62:6. **and will watch**. Hab 1:12-17. Nu 9:8. Jb +*37:2. Ps 5:3. *85:8. Mi 7:7. **unto me**. *or*, in me. 2 C 13:3. Ga 1:16. **what I shall answer**. Is *50:4. **when I am**

reproved. *or*, when I am argued with. Heb. upon my reproof, *or*, arguing. Jb 23:5-7. 31:35, 37. Je 12:1.

2. **Write.** Dt *27:8)𝒫. 31:19, 22. Is 8:1. *30:8. Je *36:2-4, 27-32. Da +*12:4. Re *1:18, 19. +*14:13. *19:9. *21:5-8. **make it plain.** Nu 35:32n. Dt +27:8. Pr +*8:9. Is 35:8. Je 31:21. Jn *16:28, 29. 1 C *14:19. 2 C *3:12. **upon tables.** Boxwood tables smeared with wax (CB). Lk 1:63. **may run.** Heb. *ruz*, to run as a messenger (Jb 9:25. Je 23:21. 51:31. Zc 2:4); *or*, to flee for refuge (Ps 18:10. Hg 1:9).

3. **the vision.** Je 27:7. Da *8:19. +*9:24-27. +*10:1, 14. *11:27, 35. *12:9. Ac *1:7. √17:26. Ga 4:2. 2 Th √2:6-8. Re *22:10. **is.** *or*, is deferred. ᶠ63l2, Jsh +3:3. **appointed time.** Ge +17:21h. Mi +*5:3. **but.** Ex *12:41. Ps *102:13. Je *25:12, etc. He *10:36, 37. **wait.** 2 K *6:33. Ps *27:14. *130:5, 6. Is √30:18. La *3:25, 26. Mi *7:7. Lk 2:25. Ja *5:7, 8. **it will surely.** Is √55:11. Lk *18:7, 8. 2 P 2:3. √3:9. **not tarry.** ᶠ144D, Ge +40:23. He 10:37.

4. **his.** Jb *40:11, 12. Da *4:30, 37. *5:20-23. Lk *18:14. 2 Th +√2:4. 1 P *5:5. **soul.** Heb. *nephesh*, Ge +34:3. **but the just.** Is 30:15. Jn √3:36. Ro √l:17. Ga *2:16. ▷3:11, 12. He *▷10:38. 1 J √5:10-13. **by his faith.** Ge 12:15h (faithfully).

5. **Yea also.** *or*, How much more. Dt 31:27. 1 S 14:30. 23:3. 2 S 4:11. 16:11. Jb 15:16. Pr 15:11. 19:7. 21:27. Ezk 14:21. **he transgresseth.** Pr +*20:1. *23:29-33. *31:4, 5. Is *5:11, 12, 22, 23. 21:5. Je *51:39. Da 5:1-4, 23. Na 1:9, 10. Re 17:6. **by wine.** ᶠ121G, Ge +31:1. Heb. *yayin*, S#3196h. From the root *yayan*, to *ferment*, is used of every sort of wine, and includes fermented wine of all kinds. The following passages show certainly that *yayin* was fermented, and was intoxicating: Ge *9:21. 14:18. 1 S √25:36, 37. Is *28:1. Je *23:9. *Yayin* was also used for sacred purposes and for blessing, as in the following passages: Ge 49:12. Ec 9:7. Am 9:13. The Nazarite, at the expiration of his vow, drank *yayin*. Nu 6:13-20. It was used at the Feasts of Jehovah (Dt 14:24-26), and was poured out as a drink offering to Jehovah (Ex 29:40. Le 23:13. Nu 15:5), (*CB*, Ap. 27.I., p. 29). **a proud man.** ver. *4. Ps +*119:21. *138:6. Pr 30:13, 14. Is *2:11, 12, 17. 14:13-16. 16:6. Je 50:29. Ezk 28:17. Da *5:20-23. 8:25. 11:36, 37. 2 Th 2:4. Ja *4:6. **keepeth.** 2 K 14:10. 1 Th *4:11. **who enlargeth.** Is 5:8. *10:7-13. **desire.** Heb. *nephesh*, Ex +15:9. **as hell.** Heb. *sheol*, Ge +*37:35. ᶠ102B, Ge +13:16. Pr *27:20. 30:15, 16. Ec *5:10. Is *5:14. **as death.** ᶠ102B, Ge +13:16. **gathereth.** ver. 8-10. Is *14:16, 17. Je 25:9, 17-29. Re 20:8.

6. **take.** Nu 23:7, 18. Is 14:4-19. Je 29:22. 50:13. Ezk 32:21. Mi 2:4. **parable.** Nu 23:7n. **proverb.** Nu +12:8. Ps 78:2. **say.** ᶠ138C, Ge +22:14. **Woe to him.** *or*, Ho, he. ver. 9, 12, 15, 19. **that increaseth.** Hab 1:9, 10, 15. Jb 20:15-29. 22:6-10. Pr 22:16. Je *17:11. +*48:10. 51:34, 35. Ezk +*16:49. 28:4, 5, 8. Am +*8:5. Ja +*5:1-4. **how.** Ps 94:3. Lk *12:20. 1 C 7:29-31. 1 P 4:7. **ladeth.** ver. 13. Is 44:20. 55:2. **thick clay.** *or*, pledges. ✽S#5671h, only here. From ✽S#5670h. Dt 15:6 (lend), 6 (borrow), 8 (surely, lit. lending), 8 (lend)◁𝒫. 24:10 (fetch)◁𝒫. Jl 2:7 (break).

7. **they.** Pr *29:1. Is 13:1-5, 16-18. 21:2-9. 41:25. 45:1-3. 46:11. 47:11. 48:14, 15. Je 50:21-32. 51:11, 27, 28, 57. Da 5:25-31. Na 1:9, 10. 1 Th *5:3. Re 18:10, 17. **bite.** Ec 10:8. Je 8:17.

8. **thou.** ver. 10, 17. Is *33:1, 4. Je *25:12, 14.

27:7. 30:16. 50:10, 37. 51:13, 44, 48, 55, 56. Zc 2:8, 9. Re *13:10. **blood.** Heb. bloods. ver. 12, 17. 2 K +9:26mg. **the violence.** Ps 137:8. Is 47:6. Je 50:11, 17, 18, 28, 33, 34. 51:8, 11, 24, 34, 35. Jl 3:19. Mi 4:11-13. Zc 1:15. 2:8. 12:2-4. 14:12. Re 6:10. 18:20-24.

9. **that coveteth an evil covetousness.** *or*, that gaineth an evil gain. Ge 13:10-13. 19:26-38. Dt √7:25, 26. Jsh 7:21-26. 1 K 21:2-4, 19-24. 2 K 5:20-27. Jb 20:19-28. Pr 1:19. 15:27. Je 6:13. 8:10. +*22:13-19. Ezk 14:3. *22:27. +*33:31. Am +√8:5. Mi 2:2. Zc 5:1-4. Lk *12:15. Ac 1:17-25. Ju 11. **set his nest.** Nu 24:21)𝒫. Jb 39:27. Ps 10:3-6. 49:11. 52:7. Pr 18:11, 12. Is 28:15. 47:7-9. Je *49:16. Ob *4. Lk 12:19. **on high.** Ge 11:4. Is 14:13. **delivered from.** Pr *11:28. +*21:30. Is *14:24-27. *28:15. 47:8. Je 5:12. 21:13. 49:4. Am +*9:1-4, 10. Ob 3. Ro 2:3. 1 Th *5:3. He 2:3. 2 P 2:18-20. Re 6:15-17. *18:7. **power of evil.** Heb. palm of the hand. Keil renders, "hand of calamity." Is +*45:7. 49:16.

10. **consulted.** 2 K 9:26. 10:7, 8. Is 14:20-22. Je 22:30. 36:31. Na 1:14. Mt 27:25. **sinned.** Nu 16:38)𝒫. 1 K 2:23. Pr 1:18. 8:36. Is 33:11. **soul.** Heb. *nephesh*, Ge +12:13.

11. **cry out.** Ge +*4:10. Dt +*24:15. Jsh 24:27. Jb 31:38-40. Je +*10:25. Lk *19:40. He 12:24. Ja +*5:3, 4. Re *6:10. **beam.** *or*, piece, *or*, fastening. **answer it.** *or*, witness against it.

12. **Woe to him.** Ge *4:11-17. Jsh *6:26. 1 K *16:34. Je +*22:13-17. Ezk *24:9. Da *4:27-31. Mi *3:10. Na 3:1. Jn *11:47-50. Re 17:6. **blood.** Heb. bloods. ver. 8. 2 K +9:26mg.

13. **is it not.** Ge *11:6-9. 2 S 15:31. Jb *5:13, 14. Ps *39:6. *127:1, 2. Pr +*21:30. Is 41:5-8. *50:11. √55:2. Je *51:58, 64. Ml *1:4. **Lord of hosts.** Ex 15:26n. 1 S +1:3. Ps +24:10. **people.** Heb. *am*, S#5971h. ver. 5, 8, 10. Hab 3:13, 16. Ge 33:15 (folk). Often used of Israel as God's people (Ex 33:13), distinct from heathen (Ps 18:43). **people.** Heb. *leom*, S#3816h. Ge 25:23 (people, meaning races). 27:29 (nations). Ps 2:1. 47:3. Pr 14:34. 24:24. Je ▷51:58 (folk). **weary themselves.** Is 47:13. **for very vanity.** *or*, in vain. Is ◐*65:23. Je *▷51:58.

14. **the earth.** Nu *14:21)𝒫. Ps 22:27. 67:1, 2. *72:19. 86:9. 98:1-3. Is *6:3. *▷11:9. Zc +*14:8, 9. Re *11:15. *15:4. **shall be filled.** Is +*27:6. +*66:19. **with the knowledge of the glory.** *or*, by knowing the glory. Is 60:1-3, 11-22. *66:18, 19. Ezk *28:22. *39:13, 21. He 8:11.

15. **unto him.** T#367. Ge 4:9-11. √19:32-35. Ex 21:28-30. Dt 32:33-35. 2 S 11:13. 13:26-28. 2 K 21:9-12. Je 25:15. 51:7. Ml +2:10 (T#685). Jn √3:19. Re 17:2, 6. 18:3. **that puttest.** Ho *7:5. **bottle.** Heb. *chemeth*, ✽S#2573h. Ge 21:14, 15, 19. So called from its usual rancidity, a leathern or skin bottle for holding water or strong drink. **makest him drunken.** ᶠ96B, Ge +8:5. Ge 9:22)𝒫. Pr +*20:1. Is *5:11, 13. **that thou.** Ge *9:22. Ex 32:25. Ezk 22:10. 23:14, 16, 18, 20. **nakedness.** Is +*20:4.

16. **with shame for glory.** *or*, more with shame than with glory. Pr 3:35. Is 47:3. Ho 4:7. Ph *3:19. **drink.** Ps 75:8. Is 49:26. 51:21-23. Je 25:26, 27. *51:57. Re 18:6. **and let.** Is *20:4. *47:3. Na *3:5, 6. Re *17:16. **the cup.** Je *25:27-29. **shameful spewing.** Is 28:7, 8. Ho 7:5.

17. **the violence.** Zc 11:1. **because.** ver. 8. Ps 55:23. 137:8. Pr 28:17. Re 10:20-24. **blood.** ver. 8mg. 2 K

+9:26mg. **of the city**. Je 50:28, 33, 34. 51:24, 34-37.

18. **profiteth**. Is 37:38. 42:17. *44:9, 10. 45:16, 20. 46:1, 2, 6-8. Je 2:27, 28. 10:3-5. 50:2. Ro 6:21. **a teacher of lies**. Is *28:15. Je 10:8, 14, 15. Jon +2:8. Zc *10:2. Mt +*15:14. +*23:13, 15. Ro *1:23-25. Ep *4:14. 2 Th √2:9-11. 1 T *4:1, 2. 2 T 3:13. 2 J +*9-11. Ju +*3. Re √13:11-15. *19:20. **that the**. Ps *115:4-8. 135:15-18. Is 1:31. 44:14-20. **maker of his work**. Heb. *fashioner of his fashion*. **dumb**. Je +*2:5. 14:14. 1 C *12:2.

19. **that**. 1 K √18:26-29. Ps 97:7. Is 44:17. Je 51:47. Da 3:7, 18, 29. 5:23. Jon 1:5. **it is**. Ps *115:4-8. Is 40:19. 46:6. Je 10:4, 9. Da 3:1. Ac *17:29. Re 17:4. **and there**. Ps *135:17. Je 10:14. Re *13:15. **breath**. Heb. *ruach*, spirit, Ge +6:17.

20. **the Lord**. Ps *11:4. *115:3. 132:13, 14. Is *6:1. *66:1, 6. Jon *2:4, 7. Ep *2:21, 22. **holy temple**. Mi 1:2. **let all the earth keep silence before him**. 1 Ch 13:7n, 10. Jb 37:14. 40:4. Ps 4:4. +37:7mg. *46:10. 76:8, 9. *89:7. Is *41:1. +*58:13n. Je 8:14. Zp *1:7. Zc *2:13.

HABAKKUK 3

The prophet prays that God would revive his work, and have mercy on his people, 1, 2. He commemorates the displays made of Jehovah's glory in his ancient works for Israel, as encouraging hope of future deliverance, 3-15. He shows how deeply he was affected by the prospect of the approaching judgments; but resolves to rejoice in God when all other comforts failed, 16-19.

1. **prayer**. Ps 86:t. 90:t. **upon Shigionoth**. *or*, according to variable songs, *or* tunes, *called in Hebrew, Shigionoth. i.e. wanderings*, ✱S#7692h. Ps 7:t.

2. **I have**. ver. 16. Hab 1:5-10. Ex 9:20, 21. 2 Ch 34:27, 28. Jb 4:12-21. Ps 119:120. Is 66:2. Je 36:21-24. Da 8:17. He 11:7. 12:21. Re *15:4. **speech**. Heb. *report, or hearing*. ♪147D, Ge +1:29. ♪121R1, Le +13:55. Is *53:1. Ro √10:16, 17. **afraid**. T#1303. Ex 14:31. Am *3:8. **O Lord**. Ezr 9:8. Ps 85:6. 90:13-17. 138:7, 8. Is 51:9-11. 63:15-19. 64:1-4. Ho 6:2, 3. Jn 10:10. Ph 1:6. **revive**. *or*, preserve alive. Ps 85:5-7. +119:25 (quicken). Is 63:15, 17. Ho 5:6. 6:2. **thy work**. Is +*60:21. in the midst. ♪144A6, Ge +45:6. Je 25:11, 12. 52:31-34. Da *9:2, +*27. **midst**. ♪16, Ge +1:27. **make known**. Is 64:1, 2. Ezk +*38:16. +*39:7. in wrath. Ex 32:10-12. Nu 14:10-23. 16:46, 47. 2 S 24:10-17. Ps 6:1, 2. 38:1. 78:38. Is 54:8. +*61:2. Je 10:24. 29:10. La 3:32. Na *1:2. Zp *1:15. Zc 1:12. 1 Th +*1:10. **remember mercy**. Dt +*32:43. Ps 85:1, 5, +*7. Is +*26:20. √54:7, 8, 10. Mi *7:18, 20. Zp +*2:3. Zc √10:6. Lk 1:72, 78. +*21:36.

3. **God came**. Dt +*33:2. Jg *5:4, 5. Ps *68:7, 8. Is 63:1-5. *64:3. **from**. Ge 36:11. Je 49:7. Am +*1:12. Ob 9. **Teman**. *or*, the south. Jsh 12:3mg. **Paran**. Ge 21:21. Nu 10:12. 12:16. 13:26. Dt *33:2♪♪. 1 S 25:1. **Selah**. ver. 9, 13. Ps 3:2, 4, 8. 4:2, 4. 7:5. +*9:16 (✱S#5542h). **His glory**. Ex 19:16-20. 20:18. 24:15-17. Dt 5:24. Ps 68:17. 114:3-7. Mt +*24:30. **and the earth**. Is 6:3. 2 C 3:7-11. Re 5:13, 14. **his praise**. Is √12:5. Ho +*2:15. Zc +*2:10.

4. **brightness**. Ex 13:21. 14:20. Ne 9:12. Ps 18:12. 104:2. Is 60:19, 20. Mt 17:2. 2 Th +*2:8. 1 T √6:16. Re 1:13, 17. 21:23, 24. 22:5. **light**. ♪121N2, Ge +34:29. **horns coming out of his hand**. *or*, bright beams out

---

of his side. Ge 19:11. Ps ◐31:8. 37:24. Is *62:3. *66:14. Da *12:3. **the hiding**. Jb 26:14. Ps +*83:3. Pr 18:10. Is 49:2. **his power**. Ps +*149:9.

5. **went**. Ex 12:29, 30. Ex 23:27. Nu 14:12. 16:46-49. Ps 68:1, 2. 78:50, 51. Je *25:30-33. Na *1:2, 3. Re 19:19-21. **and**. Ps 18:7-13. **burning coals**. *or*, burning diseases. Dt 32:24. Ps +*11:6mg. 18:8. 76:3. 78:48. *140:10. Zc 14:5, *12, 15, 18.

6. **and measured**. Ex 15:17. 23:31. Nu ch. 34. Dt +*32:8. Jb 42:2. Is *40:12. Ac +*17:26. **and drove**. Jsh 10:42. 11:18-23. Ne 9:22-24. Ps 135:8-12. Re 19:17, 18. **the everlasting**. Heb. *ad*, Ps +9:18 (✱S#5703h). **mountains**. ver. 10. Ge *49:26. Dt *33:15. Jg 5:5. Ps 68:16. 114:4-7. Is 64:1-3. Na *1:5. Zc +*14:4, 5, 10. **perpetual**. Heb. *olam*, Ge +9:12. **his ways**. Ps √90:2. 103:17. Is 51:6, 8. Mi +*5:2. Mt *24:35. Lk 1:50. He +*13:8. **everlasting**. Heb. *olam*, Ge +17:7.

7. **saw the**. Ex 15:14-16. Nu 22:3, 4. Jsh 2:10. 9:24. **Cushan**. *or*, Ethiopia. i.e. *blackness*, ✱S#3572h, only here. Ge 10:6, 7. **in affliction**. *or*, under affliction, *or* vanity. ✛S#205h. Hab 1:3 (iniquity). Nu 23:21 (iniquity). Dt 26:14 (mourning). Jb 4:8 (iniquity). 15:35 (vanity; mg, iniquity). Ps 5:5 (iniquity). 10:7 (vanity). 36:4mg. √66:18 (iniquity). Pr 11:7 (unjust). 12:21 (evil). 17:4 (false). 22:8 (vanity). Is 1:13mg. 10:1 (unrighteous). 55:7mg. 58:9. 59:7. 66:3 (an idol). Je 4:14 (vain), 15 (affliction). Ezk 11:2 (mischief). +30:17 (Aven). Ho 9:4 (mourners). Am 5:5 (nought). Mi 2:1 (iniquity). Zc 10:2 (vanity). **curtains**. ♪121D3, 2 S +7:2. **Midian**. Ge 25:1-4. Nu 31:2, etc. Ps 83:5-10.

8. **Was**. ♪85E, Ge +17:17. **the Lord**. Ex 14:21, 22. Jsh 3:16, 17. Ps *114:3, 5. Is 50:2. Na 1:4. Mk 4:39. Re 16:12. **the rivers**. Is 8:7, 8. Je 46:7, 8. 47:2. **against the sea**. Ps √65:7. 89:9. 93:3, 4. Is 5:30. *51:42. Da 7:2. Na 1:4. Re 13:1. 21:1. **ride**. ver. 15. Dt *33:26, 27♪♪. Ps 18:10. 45:4. *68:4, 17. *104:3. Is 19:1. Re 6:2. 19:11, 14. **thy chariots**. Ps +*68:17. **of salvation**. *or, were* salvation.

9. **bow**. Dt 32:23. Ps 7:12, 13. 35:1-3. 45:4, 5. Is 51:9, 10. 52:10. La 2:4. **according**. Ge +*15:18-21. +*17:7, 8. +*22:16-18. 26:3, 4. 28:13, 14. Ps 77:8. 105:8-11. Is 41:2-4. Zc *9:11-17. Lk 1:72-75. Ac +*26:6, 7. He *6:13-18. **Selah**. ver. 3, 13. Ps +*9:16. 143:6. **Thou**. Ex 17:6. Nu 20:11. Ps 78:15, 16. 105:41. 1 C 10:4. **the earth with rivers**. *or*, the rivers of the earth. Ps *74:15. *78:15, 16. *105:41.

10. **mountains**. ver. 6. Ex *19:16-18♪♪. Jg 5:4, 5. Ps 68:7, 8. 77:18. 97:4, 5. 114:4, 6. Is 64:1, 2. Je 4:24. Mi 1:4. Na 1:5. Mt 27:51. Re 6:14. 20:11. **trembled**. Ps 60:2. Re 6:15, 16. **the overflowing**. Ex 14:22-28. Jsh 3:15, 16. 4:18, 23, 24. Ne 9:11. Ps 18:15. 66:6. 74:13-15. 77:16-19. 114:3-8. 136:13-15. Is 11:15, 16. 63:11-13. He 11:29. Re 16:12. **the deep**. Ge +1:2. Ex 14:22♪♪. Ps 42:7. 65:13. *93:2-5. 96:11-13. 98:7, 8. Is 43:20. *55:12.

11. **sun**. Is 24:23. Jl 3:15. Mt 24:29. **stood still**. Jsh √10:12, 13. Is 28:21. 38:8. **habitation**. Nu 19:4. **at the light of thine arrows they went**. *or*, thine arrows walked in the light. ♪22D5C, Ps +18:14. Jsh 10:11. Ps *18:12-14. 77:17, 18. +110:4mg. 144:5, 6. **spear**. ♪22D5E. Anthropomorphism B893. *A spear is attributed to God.*

12. **didst march**. Dt +*33:2. Nu 21:23-25. Jsh ch. 6-12. Ne 9:22-24. Ps 44:1-3. 78:55. Is *63:1-6. Ac 13:19. 2 Th √1:7-10. Re *19:11-16. **thresh**. Jg 5:4. Ps 18:42. 68:7. Is 41:2. Je *51:33. Am 1:3. Mi *4:12, 13.

13. **wentest**. Ex 14:13, 14. 15:1, 2. Ps 68:7, 19-23.

for the salvation. Is 35:4, 10. salvation with. Ps *77:20. 89:19-21. 99:6. 105:15, 26. Is *63:11, 12. He +*9:28. Re 12:10. thine anointed. Ps *105:15. +*149:6-9. Ro +*8:19. Re *2:26, 27. thou woundedst. ♪22C40, Ps +110:6. Ex 12:29, 30. Jsh 10:11, 24, 42. 11:8, 12. Ps 18:37-45. *68:21. 74:13, 14. √110:6. Re 19:19-21. the head. Ps *83:2. discovering. Heb. making naked. Ps +137:7mg. the foundation. Ml 4:1. unto the neck. 2 Th +*2:8.

14. the head. Ex 11:4-7. 12:12, 13, 29, 30. 14:17, 18. Ps 78:50, 51. 83:9-11. they. Ex 14:5-9. 15:9, 10. Ps 83:2-8. 118:10-12. Ac 4:27, 28. came out. Heb. were tempestuous. Da 11:40. Jon 1:11, 13. Zc 9:14. their. Ex 1:10-16, 22. Ps 10:8. 64:2-7.

15. walk through. ver. 8. Ps *68:17. *77:19. *89:23-25. heap. or, mud. Ge 11:3 (morter). Ex 8:14 (heaps). Nu +*11:32 (✳S#2563h). Jb 4:19 (clay). 30:19 (mire).

16. I heard. ver. 2. Hab *1:5-11. my belly. Ps *119:120. Je 4:19. *23:9. Ezk 3:14. Da 8:27. 10:8. rottenness. Jb 13:28. Pr 12:4. *14:30. Ho 5:12. I trembled. Is +*66:2. that I might rest. Ps 91:15. *94:12, 13. Is +*26:20, 21. *57:1. Je *15:10, 11. *31:2. *45:3-5. Ezk *9:4-6. Zp +*2:3. Lk +*21:36. 1 Th +*5:9. 2 Th √1:6-10. Re +*11:18. the day of trouble. Je +*30:7. Da +*12:1. when he cometh. Is 10:12. Ezk 38:15. 39:2.

Da +*9:26. +*11:40, 44. Mi √5:5, 6. Zc 14:3, 13. 2 Th *1:8. ◐*2:9. up unto. Jg 20:23. 2 S 5:19. the people. Is 26:11. 44:7. he will. Hab 1:6. Dt 28:49-52. 2 K 24:1, 2. Je 25:9-11. invade them. or, cut them in pieces. Ge 49:19. Zc 12:9. with his troops. Is 59:19. Da 11:25. Zc 12:8.

17. the fig tree. Dt 28:15-18, 30-41. Je 14:2-8. Jl 1:10-13, 16-18. Am 4:6-10. Hg 2:16, 17. shall not. Lk 21:25, 26. fail. Heb. lie. ♪155C, Le +19:23. Le 6:2, 3.

18. Yet. Hab *2:4. Jb +*13:15. Lk 13:2-5. Jn 9:2, 3. Ro 8:35-39. 2 C *5:7. He 10:34. *11:1. 12:4. I will rejoice. Dt 12:18. 1 S 2:1. Jb 13:15. Ps *4:7. 33:1. 46:1-5. 85:6. 97:12. 104:34. 118:15. 149:2. Is *41:16. *61:10. Zc 10:7. Lk *1:46, 47. Ro 5:2, 3. Ph √4:4. Ja 1:2, 9, 10. 1 P 1:8. 4:12, 13. the God. Ex 15:2. Ps 18:46. 24:5. 25:5. 27:1, 9. 68:19. 118:14. Is *12:2. 17:10. Mi 7:7. Lk 2:30. He +*9:28.

19. my strength. Ps 18:1, 32. *27:1. 46:1. *84:11. Is *12:2. 45:24. Zc 10:12. 2 C √12:9, 10. Ep 3:16. Ph √4:13. Col 1:11. like. 2 S 1:23. *22:34. 1 Ch 12:8. Ps 18:33. to walk. Dt *32:13▶𝒫. *33:29▶𝒫. Is 58:14. Am 4:13. Mi 1:3. high places. Is 33:16mg. stringed instruments. Heb. Neginoth, Ps ch. 4, 6, 54, 55, 67, 76, titles. Ps *150:4.

ZEPHANIAH

ZEPHANIAH 1

The time when Zephaniah prophesied, 1. Denunciations of wrath against Judah and Jerusalem, for idolatry and apostacy, 2-6. Predictions of terrible judgments, coming on men of different orders and descriptions, which could by no means be avoided, 7-18.

1. A.M. 3374. B.C. 630. word of the Lord. Ezk 1:3. Ho 1:1. 2 T √3:16. 2 P √1:19. Zephaniah. i.e. *protected; Jehovah hides; treasured up of Jehovah,* ✳S#6846h. 2 K 25:18. 1 Ch 6:36. Je 21:1. 29:25, 29. 37:3. 52:24. Zc 6:10, 14. (1) The priest whom the captain of the king of Babylon took to Riblah, 2 K 25:18. Je 21:1. (2) An ancestor of the prophet Samuel, 1 Ch 6:36. (3) A priest, the father of Joshiah and Hen, Zc 6:10, 14. (4) The ninth of the minor prophets, lived in the days of Josiah, a contemporary of Jeremiah, and uttered his prophecies between B.C. 620 and 609. Cushi. i.e. *blackness; the Ethiopian,* ✳S#3569h. 2 S 18:21, 21, 22, 23, 31, 31, 32, 32. Je 36:14. (1) A man sent by Joab to tell David the issue of the battle with Absalom, 2 S 18:21, 23. (2) The great-grandfather of Jehudi, Je 36:14. (3) Father of Zephaniah the prophet, Zp 1:1. Gedaliah. 1 Ch +25:3. Amariah. Ezr +7:3. Hizkiah. i.e. *strength of God; my strength is Jehovah,* ✳S#2396h. in the days. 2 K ch. 22, 23. 2 Ch ch. 34, 35. Je 1:2. 25:3.

2. I will, etc. Heb. By taking away I will make an end. utterly. 2 K 22:16, 17. 2 Ch 36:21. Is 6:11. Je 6:8, 9. 24:8-10. 34:22. 36:29. Ezk 33:27-29. Mi 7:13. all. Jb 42:2. Ps 8:6. Is 44:24. land. Heb. face of the land. Ge 4:14. 6:1. 7:23. Ex 33:16. Nu 12:3. Dt 7:6. 14:2. 2 S 14:7mg. Is 23:17. Je 25:26. 28:16. Ezk 38:20. Am *9:8.

3. consume man. Je *4:23-26. *12:4. Ho 4:3. consume the. ♪18, Dt +28:4. stumbling blocks. or, idols.

Is 3:6. 27:9. Ezk 7:19. +*14:3-7. 44:12. Ho 14:3, 8. Mi *5:11-14. Zc √13:2. Mt 13:41. Re 2:14. cut off man. Ezk 14:13-21. 15:6-8.

4. stretch. ♪22A14.8A, Ex +7:5. Ex 15:12. 2 K 21:13. *23:8. Is 14:26, 27. I will cut off. This probably refers in the first instance to the reformation which Josiah effected, and also to the final extirpation of the devotees of Baal, with the priests of the tribe of Levi who united with them in their worship, by the Chaldeans. the remnant of Baal. "Fulfilled, 2 K 23:4, 5. 2 Ch 34:4." the Chemarims. i.e. *mourning; changed ones; blackness, sadness; one who goes about in black, in mourning, an ascetic, a priest,* ✳S#3649h. 2 K 23:5mg. Ho √10:5mg.

5. worship the host of heaven. Note the reference to the Pentateuch. Other references to the Pentateuch in Zephaniah are at ver. 6, 8, 13, 17. Zp 2:3, 7, 9, 11. 3:4, 5, 7, 13, 15, 16, 17, 19, 20. See related note (Is +*1:2). Dt 4:19▶𝒫. 17:3▶𝒫. See on 2 K 23:12. Je 19:13. 32:29. and them. 1 K 18:21. 2 K 17:33, 41. Mt +*6:24. and that swear. Dt 10:20. Is 48:1. Je 4:2. *5:2. Ho 4:15. by the Lord. or, to the Lord. Is 44:5. 45:23. Ro 14:11. swear by. Jsh 23:7. Malcham. 1 K *11:33, Milcom. Am 5:26, Moloch.

6. turned. 1 S 15:11. Ps 36:3. 125:5. Is *1:4. Je 2:13, 17. 3:10. *15:6. Ezk 3:20. Ho 4:15, 16. 11:7. He 10:38, 39. 2 P 2:18-22. from the Lord. Ho 1:2. and those. Ps 10:4. 14:2, 3. Is 43:22. Ho 7:7. Ro 3:11. He *2:3. not sought. Dt 4:29▶𝒫. 1 Ch +*28:9. He ◐√11:6.

7. Hold thy peace. 1 S 2:9, 10. Jb 40:4, 5. Ps 46:10. 76:8, 9. Is 6:5. Am 6:10. Hab +*2:20. Zc *2:13. Ro 3:19. 9:20. for the day of the Lord. ver. 14. Is +*2:12. +*13:6. Ezk 7:7, 10. +*30:3. Jl +*2:1, 2, 11, 31. Am √5:18-20. Ml *4:1. Ph *4:5. 2 P √3:10-12. for the Lord. Is 34:6. Je *46:10. Ezk *39:17-20. Re *19:17,

18. **he hath.** Pr 9:1-6. Ezk *39:17-21. Mt 22:4. 24:27, *28. Lk *14:16, 17. *17:34-37. Re *19:17, 18, 21. **bid.** Heb. sanctified, or prepared. 1 S 16:5. 20:26. Lk *14:17. Col 1:12.

8. **the day.** Is +*2:12. 13:6. **sacrifice.** ver. +7. **punish.** Heb. visit upon. Ex 32:34ℙ. Is 10:12mg. 24:21mg. Je +9:25mg. **the princes.** 2 K 23:30-34. 24:12, 13. 25:6, 7, 19-21. Is 39:7. Je 22:11-19, 24-30. 39:6, 7. **king's children.** 1 K 22:26. 2 K 11:2. Je 36:26. *39:6. **strange.** Dt 22:5. 2 K 10:22. Is 3:18-24. Mt=22:11.

9. **those.** Or, "that leap over the threshold," by which is probably meant the *Philistines*, who after the time that Dagon fell before the ark and was broken on the threshold, leaped over it when entering his temple. **leap.** ♪142, Ge +20:16. 1 S 5:5. 2 S 22:30. 1 K ❰x18:26. Ps 18:29. SS 2:8. Is 35:6. **which fill.** 1 S 2:15, 16. 2 K 5:20-27. Ne 5:15. Pr *29:12. Ac 16:19.

10. **in that day.** ver. 7, 15. Je 39:2. **the noise.** ♪144, Ge +3:8. Is 22:4, 5. 59:11. *66:6. Je 4:19-21, 31. Am 8:3. **the fish gate.** 2 Ch *33:14. Ne 3:3. **the second.** 2 K 22:14mg. 2 Ch 34:22mg. Ne 11:9. **from the hills.** 2 S 5:7, 9. 2 Ch 3:1.

11. **Howl.** Je 4:8. 25:34. Ezk 21:12. Jl 1:5, 13. Zc 11:2, 3. Ja *5:1. **Maktesh.** i.e. a mortar, hollow place, ✳S#4389h. A place in or near Jerusalem, inhabited by silver merchants. It may have been a quarter of Jerusalem devoted to minting operations. It may have been the "Phoenician quarter" of the city where foreign merchants resided. Others think it is a valley, so named here for its mortar-like shape. Some Jewish authorities think it is a reference to the Kedron valley. **all the merchant.** Ne 3:31, 32. Ho √12:7, 8. Jn *2:16. Re *18:11-18. **that bear silver.** Pr +*11:4. Ezk √7:19. Ja *5:1. Re *18:11.

12. **that I.** Je 16:16, 17. Am 9:1-3. Ob 6. Lk 15:8. 19:10. **search.** Ps 7:9. 26:2. Je 11:20. *17:10. 20:12. Re *2:23. **with candles.** Ps 119:104. Pr 6:23. 20:27. Lk 15:8. Ph 2:15. 2 P 1:19. **the men.** Je *48:11. Am +*6:1. Re 2:23. **settled.** Heb. curded, or thickened. Ex 15:8. Jb 10:10. Zc 14:6mg. **on their lees.** Ps 55:19. Je *48:11. **The Lord will not do.** Jb 21:15. 22:12-14. Ps 10:4, 5, *11-13. 14:1. *94:7. Is 5:19. ❰*41:23. Je 10:5. Ezk +*8:12. *9:9. Ml *2:17. *3:14, 15. 2 P √3:4.

13. **their goods.** ver. 9. Is 6:11. 24:1-3. Je 4:7, 20. 5:17. 9:11, 19. 12:10-13. Ezk 7:19, 21. 22:31. Mi 3:12. **build.** Dt *28:30, 39, 51ℙ. Is 5:8, 9. ❰*65:21, 22. Am 5:11. ❰+*9:14. Mi 6:15. **wine.** Hab 2:5n.

14. **the great day of the Lord.** ver. 7. Is +*2:12. +*13:6. 22:5. Je +*30:7. Ezk +*30:3. Jl +*2:1, 11, 31. Am +*5:18. Ml 4:5. Ac 2:20. 1 C +*3:13. 1 Th +*5:2. 2 P +*3:10. Re 6:17. **it is near.** ♪84, Ge +6:17. Ezk 7:6, 7, 12. 12:23. Am 8:2. Ro *13:12. Ph 4:5. He *10:37. Ja 5:9. 2 P 2:3. **hasteth greatly.** He *10:37. Re *22:30. **even the voice.** ver. 10. Is 22:4, 5. 66:6. Je 25:36. Jl 2:11. 3:16. 1 Th √4:16. He 12:26. **the mighty man.** Is 15:4. 33:7. Je 48:41. Re √6:15-17.

15. **day of wrath.** ♪173, Ge +27:44. ver. +18. Zp +*2:2, 3. Is 22:5. Je +*30:7. Am √5:18-20. Na *1:2. Ml 4:1. Lk *21:22, 23. Ro *2:5. 1 Th +*1:10. 2 P √3:7. Re √6:17. **a day.** ♪113, Nu +9:20. **trouble and distress.** Jb 15:24. Je +*30:7. Da +*12:1. Jl *2:11. Ml 3:2. Lk *21:25, 26. **wasteness and desolation.** Jb 30:3. 38:27. **a day of darkness.** Jb 3:4-8. Jl *2:+2, 11. Am 8:9. Mt +8:12. +*24:29. **clouds.** Ge +9:13. Ezk +*34:12. **thick darkness.** Ex +10:22. Dt +4:11. Pr #+20:20. Mk 13:24, 25.

16. **day of the trumpet.** Is 59:10. Je *4:19, 20. 6:1. 8:16. Ho 5:8. 8:1. Am 2:2. +*3:6. Hab *1:6-10. 3:6. 1 Th +*4:16n. Re +*11:18, 19. **and alarm.** ♪93A, Ge +1:26. i.e. of the trumpet, yes—and an alarming trumpet too. **and against.** Ps 48:12, 13. Is 2:12-15. 32:14. **high towers.** Heb. corners. ♪171S2, Ge +14:7. By Synecdoche of the Part, "corner" is put for **tower,** which was usually placed at the corner. 2 Ch 26:15.

17. **distress.** Dt 28:52, 53. **they shall walk.** Dt *28:28, 29ℙ. Ps 79:3. Is 29:10. *59:9, 10. La 4:14. Mt +*15:14. Jn 9:40, 41. Ro 11:7, 25. 2 C +*4:4. 2 P *1:9. 1 J 2:11. Re 3:17. **because.** Is 24:5, 6. 50:1. 59:12-15. Je 2:17, 19. 4:18. La 1:8, 14, 18. 4:13-15. 5:16, 17. Ezk 22:25-31. Da 9:5, etc. Mi 3:9-12. 7:13. **and their blood.** 2 K 9:33-37. Ps 79:2, 3. 83:10. Je *9:21, 22. 15:3. *16:4-6. 18:21. La 2:21. 4:14. Am 4:10. **as dust.** ♪138B, Ge +13:16.

18. **their silver.** ver. +*11. Ps 49:6-9. 52:5-7. Pr +*11:4. 18:11. Is 2:20, 21. Je 9:23, 24. Ezk +*7:19. Mt *16:26. Lk √12:19-21. *16:22, 23. **in the day.** ver. +*15. Jb +*21:30. **but.** Zp 3:8. Le 26:33-35. Dt 29:20-28. 31:17. Is 24:1-12. Je 4:26-29. 7:20, 34. 9:11. **the fire.** Zp *3:8. Nu +25:11. Dt 32:21-25. 1 K 14:22. Ps 78:58. 79:5. Ezk 8:3-5. 16:38. 36:5, 6. 1 C 10:22. **jealousy.** Ex +20:5. **he shall.** ver. 2, 3. Is 1:24.

ZEPHANIAH 2

An exhortation to seek God, without delay, in hope of preservation in the day of his anger, 1-3. Prophecies against the Philistines, 4-7; Moabites, Ammonites, 8-11; Ethiopians, 12; and Assyrians, 13-15.

1. **Gather.** Ex 5:7, 12. Nu 15:32, 33. 1 K 17:10, 12. **gather together.** 2 Ch 20:4. Ne 8:1. 9:1. Est 4:16. Jl √1:14. *2:12-18. Mt *18:20. **O nation.** Is *1:4-6, 10-15. Je 12:7-9. Zc 11:8. **desired.** or, desirous. or, longing. ♪24C, 2 K +18:21. i.e. not desirable. or better, incapable of shame. A reference to Israel's initial restoration to Palestine without a Messianic longing before the Great Tribulation mentioned in ver. 2. Ge 31:30. Dt 9:24. Jb 14:15. Ps 84:3. Is 26:8, 9. Ac +√3:19-21.

2. **Before the decree.** Zp 3:8. 2 K 22:16, 17. 23:26, 27. Ezk 12:25. Mt +*24:35. 2 P √3:4-10. **as the chaff.** Jb 21:18. Ps *1:4. Is *17:13. 41:15, 16. Ho 13:3. **before the fierce.** Zp +*1:18. 2 K 23:26. 2 Ch *36:16, 17. Ps *2:12. 50:22. Je 23:20. La 4:11. Na 1:6. Ml 4:1, 2. Lk 13:24-28. **before the day of.** Ps 95:7, 8.

3. **Seek ye.** Dt 4:29ℙ. Ps 45:4. *105:4. Is √55:6, 7. Je 3:13, 14. 4:1, 2. +*29:12, 13. Ho 7:10. 10:12. Am *5:4-6, 14, 15. Mt *7:7, 8. **all ye meek.** 2 Ch 34:27, 28. Ps 22:26. *25:8, 9. 76:9. *149:4. Is 11:4. 61:1. Je 22:15, 16. Zc 8:19. Mt +*5:5. Ja *1:21, 22. 1 P 3:4. **judgment.** or, ordinances. Is 58:2. Je 8:7. **seek righteousness.** Ph 3:13, 14. 1 Th 4:1, 10. 1 P 1:22. 2 P +*3:18. **seek meekness.** T#1372. 2 Ch +*7:14 (T#1366). Ps √25:9. 1 T +*2:8. **it may.** Ge +*18:25, 32. 2 S *12:22. Je 5:1-3. Jl *2:13, 14. Am +*5:15. Jon 3:9. Mt +*7:14. Hid. Ge 7:15, 16. Ex 12:27. Ps 27:5. 31:20. 32:6, 7. 57:1. +*83:3. 91:1. +*94:13. Pr 14:26. *18:10mg. Is +*26:20, 21. *51:16. Je 39:18. 45:5. Hab +*3:16. Ml 3:16-18. Lk +√21:36. Col *3:2-4. 1 Th +*1:10. Re +*3:10. Heb. satar, ✚S#5641h, Niphal, Future: Ge 4:14. 31:49 (absent). 1 S 20:24. Jb 13:20. Ps 55:12. 86:46. Pr 28:28. Je 23:24. Ho 13:14. Am 9:3. For this passage (Zp 2:3), Gesenius specifically notes, "i.e. escape (the Lord's) judgment" (p. 711b),

under the second definition, "be hid, concealed, especially figurative of escaping God's notice, Ge 4:14." Note that the Kal, Future form of this word is used at Pr 22:3.

4. **Gaza.** Je 25:20. ch. 47. Ezk 25:15-17. Am *1:6-8. Zc *9:5-7. **Ashkelon.** Je 47:5. **Ashdod.** Ac 8:40, Azotus. **at the noon day.** During the noon day siesta (CB). Ps 91:6. Je 6:4. 15:8.

5. **Cherethites.** Je 47:7. Ezk *25:16, Cherethims. **the word.** Am 3:1. 5:1. Zc 1:6. Mk 12:12. **O Canaan.** Jsh 13:3. Jg 3:3. Zc *14:21.

6. **the sea.** ver. 14, 15. Is 17:2. Ezk 25:5.

7. **the coast.** Is 14:29-32. Ob 19. Zc 9:6, 7. Ac 8:26, 40. **the remnant.** ver. 9. Is √11:11, 14. *37:31. Je 31:7. Mi 2:12. +*4:7. +*5:3-8. Hg 1:12. 2:2. Ro 11:5. **Ashkelon.** Zc 9:6. **for.** or, when, etc. **shall visit.** Ge 50:24╻𝒫. Ex 3:16╻𝒫. 4:31. Lk 1:68. 7:16. **turn.** Zp *3:20. Ps 85:1. *126:1-4. Is 14:1. Je 3:18. 23:3. √29:14. 30:3, 18, 19. 33:7. Ezk 39:25. Am √9:14, 15. Mi 4:10.

8. **heard.** Je *48:27-29. Ezk *25:8-11. **the revilings.** Ps 83:4-7. Je *49:1. Ezk *25:3-7. 36:2. Am 1:13. **magnified.** Da +8:11.

9. **as I.** Nu 14:21. Is 49:18. Je 46:18. Ro 14:11. **Surely.** Is 11:14. ch. 15, 16. 25:10. Je ch. 48. 49:1-7. Ezk 25:1, etc. Am 1:13-15. 2:1-3. **as Gomorrah.** ver. 14. Ge *19:24, 25╻𝒫. Dt *29:23. Is *13:19, 20. Je *49:18. 50:40. **nettles.** 𝒥173, Ge +27:44. Dt 29:23╻𝒫. Jb 30:7. Is *34:9-13. **perpetual.** Heb. olam, Ge +9:12. Je *25:12. **the residue.** ver. 7. Zp 3:13. Jl *3:19, 20. Mi +*5:7, 8.

10. **for.** ver. 8. Pr *11:2. *16:18. *18:12. Is *16:6. Je 48:29. Da 4:37. 5:20-23. Ob 3. 1 P 5:5. **and magnified.** Ex 9:17. 10:3. Is 10:12-15. 37:22-29. Ezk 38:14-18. Da +8:11.

11. **for.** Dt 32:38. Ho 2:17. Zc 13:2. **famish.** Heb. make lean. Is 17:4. **and men.** Ps *2:8-12. 22:27-30. 72:8-11, 17. 86:9. 97:6-8. ch. 117. 138:4. Is *2:2-4. *11:9, 10. Mi 4:1-3. Zc 2:11. *8:20-23. 14:9-21. Ml *1:11. Jn 4:21-23. 1 T *2:8. Re *11:15. **isles of the heathen.** Ge *10:5╻𝒫. Is 24:14-16. 42:4, 10. 49:1.

12. **Ethiopians.** Ge 10:6, 7. Is 18:1, etc. *20:4, 5. 43:3. Je 46:9, 10. Ezk *30:4-9. **my.** Ps 17:13. Is 10:5. 13:5. Je 47:6, 7. 51:20-23.

13. **he will.** Ps 83:8, 9. Is √10:12, 16. 11:11. Ezk 31:3, etc. **stretch.** 𝒥22A14.8A, Ex +7:5. **north.** 𝒥171.O.9, Je +13:20. **will make.** Na *1:1. 2:10, 11. 3:7, 15, 18, 19. Zc 10:10, 11.

14. **flocks.** ver. 6. Is *13:19-22. *34:11-17. Re *18:2. **all.** 𝒥171B, Ge +24:10. **cormorant.** or, pelican. Ps 102:6. **upper lintels.** or, knops, or chapiters. Am 9:1. **for he shall uncover.** or, when he hath uncovered. Is 22:6mg. **the cedar.** Je 22:14.

15. **the rejoicing.** Is 10:12-14. 22:2. 47:7. Re 18:7-10. **I am.** Is *47:8. Ezk 28:2, 9. 29:3. Re *18:7. **how is.** Is 14:4, 5. La 1:1. 2:1. Re 18:10-19. **every.** 1 K 9:7, 8. Jb 27:23. Ps 52:6, 7. La 2:15. Ezk *27:36. Na *3:19. Mt 27:39.

ZEPHANIAH 3

Sharp rebukes of Jerusalem, for divers aggravated sins of idolatry, oppression, disobedience, failure to draw near to God, harboring false prophets, wresting the law, and failure to receive instruction from the judgment rendered to the heathen nations, 1-7. Gracious promises to the people of God; an exhortation to wait for the restoration of Israel, 8-13. An exhortation to rejoice for their salvation by God, their deliverance from captivity and dispersion, their glorious return to the land of Israel, and their new status among the people of the earth, 14-20.

1. **her that is filthy.** or, gluttonous. Heb. craw. Le 1:16. Ezk +*16:49. **polluted.** Je *2:23. **the oppressing city.** Dt +*24:14. Is *1:21. 5:7. 30:12. 59:13. Je 6:6. 22:17. Ezk +*16:49. 22:7, 29. Am 3:9. 4:1. Mi 2:2. Zc 7:10. Ml +*3:5.

2. **obeyed not.** Dt +*28:15, etc. Ne *9:26. Je *7:23-28. *22:21. Zc *7:11-14. **she received not.** 1 S +*25:17. Is 1:5. Je *2:30. *5:3. Ezk 24:13. He *12:5. **correction.** or, instruction. Ps *50:17. Pr √1:7. *3:11. 5:12. Je *32:33. 35:13, 17. Jn √3:18, 19. 2 T √3:16. **trusted not.** Ps +√9:10. 78:22. Is *30:1-3. *31:1. Je *17:5, 6. **drew not near.** Ps *10:4. Is 29:13. 43:22. He +*10:22. Ja +*4:8.

3. **princes.** Jb 4:8-11. Ps 10:8-10. Pr √28:15. Is 1:23. Je 22:17. Ezk *22:6, 25-27. Mi 3:1-4, *9-11. **evening.** Je 5:6. Hab 1:8.

4. **light.** Is 9:15. 56:10-12. Je 5:31. 6:13, 14. 8:10. 14:13-15. √23:9-17, 25-27, 32. 27:14, 15. La 2:14. Ezk 13:3-16. Ho 9:7. Mi 2:11. 3:5, 6. Mt *7:15. 2 C √11:13-15. Ep *4:14. 2 P *2:1-3. 1 J *4:1. Re *19:20. **her priests.** 1 S 2:12-17, 22. Ezk *22:26. 44:7, 8. Ho 4:6-8. Ml 2:8. **polluted.** Le 19:8╻𝒫. 21:23╻𝒫. 22:15╻𝒫. Nu 18:32╻𝒫. **done violence.** Je 2:8. Ezk *22:26mg.

5. **just.** Dt *32:4. Ps 99:3, 4. 145:17. Ec 3:16, 17. Is 45:21. Hab √1:13. Zc 9:9. Ro 3:26. 1 P 1:17. **in the midst.** ver. 15, 17. Nu 5:3╻𝒫. Dt 7:21╻𝒫. 23:14. Is 12:6. Ezk 48:35. Mi 3:11. Zc 2:5. **he will.** Ge +*18:25. Jb 8:3. 34:10, 17-19. Ro *1:18. Ja *1:13. **every morning.** Heb. morning by morning. 2 S +13:4mg. Ps +*101:8. Is 28:19. 33:2. 50:4. Je 21:12. La 3:23. **bring.** Ps *37:6. Is 42:3, 4. Mi 7:9. Lk *12:2. Ro +*2:5. 1 C 4:5. **but.** Je *3:3. *6:15. 8:12.

6. **cut.** Is ch. 10, 15, 16, 19. 37:11-13, 24-26, 36. Je 25:9-11, 18-26. Na ch. 2, 3. 1 C 10:6, 11. **towers.** or, corners. 𝒥171S2, Ge +14:7. Zp 1:16. 2 K 14:13. 2 Ch 26:9, 15. Je 31:38.

7. **Surely.** ver. 2. Is 5:4. 63:8. Je *8:6. 36:3. Lk *19:42-44. 2 P √3:9. **so their dwelling.** Je *5:1. 7:7. *17:25-27. 25:5. 38:17. **howsoever.** 2 Ch 28:6-8. 32:1, 2. 33:11. 36:3-10. **they rose early.** Mi *2:1, 2. **corrupted.** Ge 6:12╻𝒫. Dt 4:16. Ho 9:9.

8. **Therefore wait.** Ps *27:14. *37:7, 34. 62:1, 5. 123:2. 130:5, 6. Pr 20:22. Is +*30:18. La 3:25, 26. Ho 12:6. Mi 7:7. Ja *5:7, 8. **until the day.** Ml +*4:5. **rise up.** Jb 19:25h (stand). Ps +*12:5. 78:65, 66. *82:8. +*102:13. Is 42:13, 14. 59:16-18. **to the prey.** Zp +*2:2. Ge 49:27. Is 33:23. *49:24, 25. *60:5mg. *61:6. Ezk *39:10, 21. Mi *4:12, 13. Zc 14:14. Mt 24:28. Lk 17:37. Ro +*11:25n. Ja *5:3. **gather the nations.** Ezk *38:14-23. Jl *3:2, 9-16. Mi *4:11-13. Zc *12:3. *14:2, 3. Mt +*25:32. Re +*16:14, 16. 19:17-19. **to pour.** Je +*10:25. **for all the earth.** Zp +*1:18. Dt 32:21, 22. SS 8:6. Ezk 36:5, 6. *38:19. 2 P *3:10. **the fire.** Zp 1:18. Dt 4:24╻𝒫. Ps *79:5. Is +*24:6. Na *1:2. Ml +√4:1. 2 P +√3:7. **my jealousy.** Zp 1:18. Ezk +*38:19.

9. **will I turn.** Ne ◑*13:24. Is *19:18. Je *31:23. Mt +*12:35. Ep *4:29. Col *4:6. **pure.** ✱S#1305h. 2 S 22:27. 1 Ch 7:40 (choice). 9:22 (chosen). 16:41 (chosen). Ne 5:18. Jb *33:3 (clearly). Ec 3:18 (manifest). Is 49:2 (polished). 52:11 (clean). Je 4:11 (cleanse).

51:11mg. Ezk 20:38 (purge). Da 11:35 (purge). 12:10 (purified). **language.** Heb. lip. Ge +*11:1mg. Jg +7:22mg. Is ◑6:5. 19:18mg. **that.** 1 K 8:41-43. Ps 22:27. 86:9, 10. 113:3. Je 16:19. Hab 2:14. Zc 2:11. *8:20-23. +*14:9. Ac 2:4, etc. Ro 15:6-11. Re *11:15. **to serve.** Re 7:14, 15. **with one.** Je *31:34. *32:39. **consent.** Heb. shoulder. Ho 6:9mg.

10. **beyond.** Ps 68:31. 72:8-11. Is √11:11. *18:1, 7, etc. 27:12, 13. 49:20-23. *60:4-12. *66:18-21. Ml 1:11. Ac 8:27. 24:17. Ro 11:11, 12. 15:16. 1 P 1:1.

11. **shalt thou.** ver. 19, 20. Ps 49:5. Is 45:17. 54:4. 61:7. 65:13, 14. Je *31:19. Jl 2:26, 27. Ro *6:21. 9:33. 1 P 2:6. **that rejoice.** Nu 16:3. Is 13:3. 48:1, 2. Je 7:4, 9-12. Ezk 7:20-24. 24:21. Mi 3:11. Ml *4:1. Mt 3:9. Ro 2:17. **because of my holy.** *or,* in my holy. Ps *48:2, 3. 87:1, 2. Is 11:9. Da 9:16, 20.

12. **leave.** Is 14:32. 61:1-3. Zc *11:11. 13:8, 9. Mt +*5:3. 11:5. 1 C 1:27, 28. Ja *2:5. **they shall trust.** Ps 37:40. Is 50:10. Na 1:7. Mt 12:21. Ro 15:12. Ep *1:12, 13. 1 P *1:21. **in the name.** Ps +√9:10. 20:1.

13. **remnant.** Zp 2:7. Is 6:13. *10:20-22. Mi *4:7. Ro +*11:4-7. **not do iniquity.** Ps +*130:8. Is *11:6-9. *35:8. +*60:21. 65:20. Je *31:33. 32:40. Ezk +*36:25-27. Jl 3:17, 21. Zc 14:20, 21. Mt *13:41. 1 J *3:2, 9, 10. *5:18. **nor speak lies.** Is *63:8. Jn 1:47. Col *3:9. Re *14:5. +*21:8, 27. **they shall feed.** Le 26:5, 6⁝𝒫. Ps *23:2. Is 65:10. Je *23:4. Ezk *34:13-15, 23-28. Mi *4:4. 5:4, 5. 7:14. Re *7:15-17. **and none.** Le √26:6. Ps +*34:4. Is *17:2. *54:14. Je *30:10. *46:27. Ezk *34:28. *39:26. Mi *4:4. 2 T +*1:7. He +*13:6. 1 P *3:14.

14. **Sing.** T#88. Dt +32:43 (T#237). Is 24:13-16. Ho +*2:15. Zc +*2:10. Lk +23:41 (T#571). **shout.** Ezr 3:11-13. Ne 12:43. Ps 14:7. 47:5-7. 81:1-3. 95:1, 2. 100:1, 2. 126:2, 3. Is *12:6. 24:14-16. 35:2. 40:9. 42:10-12. 51:11. *54:1. 65:13, 14, 18, 19. Je 30:19. 31:13. 33:11. Zc *2:10, 11. *9:9, 10, 15-17. Mt 21:9. Lk 2:10-14. Re 19:1-6. **O daughter of Jerusalem.** Mi 4:8.

15. **hath taken.** Ge 30:23. Ps 85:3. Is 25:8. 40:1, 2. 51:22. Mi *7:18-20. Zc 1:14-16. 8:13-15. √10:6, 7. **he hath.** Is ch. 13, 14. Je ch. 50, 51. Mi *4:6, 7. 7:10, 16, 17. Hab 2:8, 17. Zc 2:8, 9. 12:3. Ro 8:33,

34. Re 12:10. **the king.** Is 33:22. Ezk 37:24, 25. Zc *9:9. Jn 1:49. *12:15. 19:19. Re 19:16. **in the midst.** ver. 5, 17. Dt 7:21⁝𝒫. Is *12:6. Ezk 37:26-28. 48:35. Da 3:25. Jl 3:20, 21. Zc 2:5, 10. Re 7:15. 21:3, 4. **thou.** Ps *91:10. Is 35:10. 51:22. 60:18. 65:19. Je *31:40. Ezk 39:29. Jl 3:17. Am √9:15. Zc 14:11.

16. **be said.** Is *35:3, 4. 40:9. √41:10, 13, 14. 43:1, 2. 44:2. 54:4. Je 46:27, 28. Hg 2:4, 5. Zc 8:15. Jn 12:15. He *12:12. **Fear thou not.** Dt 7:21⁝𝒫. **slack.** *or,* faint. Is 13:7. 2 C 4:1. Ga √6:9. Ep 3:13. He 12:3-5. Re 2:3.

17. **in the midst.** ver. 5, 15. Ps +*102:13, 16. Zc 14:3, 5. **is mighty.** Ge *17:1. 18:14. Dt 10:17⁝𝒫. Jsh 4:24. Ps 24:8-10. 89:19. Is +*9:6. *12:2, 6. 63:1, 12. He √7:25. **will rejoice.** ʃ22B, Ps +104:21. Nu 14:8. Dt *30:9⁝𝒫. Ps 147:11. *149:4. Is ◑61:10. *62:4, 5. *65:19. Je √32:41, 42. Lk *15:5, 6, 23, 24, 32. Jn 15:11. **with joy.** Ps 147:11. **he will.** Ge 1:31. 2:2. Is 18:4. Jn 13:1. **rest.** Heb. be silent. Ps 37:7mg. **joy over.** Ps 149:4. Pr 11:20. **with singing.** Is +*51:11.

18. **gather.** ver. 20. Dt *30:3, 4⁝𝒫. Je *23:3. 31:8, 9. Ezk +*34:13. 36:24. +*37:25. Ho 1:11. Ro +*11:25, 26. **sorrowful.** Ps *42:2-4, 10. 43:3. 63:1, 2. 84:1, 2. 137:3-6. La *1:4, 7. *2:6, 7. Ho 9:5. **solemn assembly.** Ge +17:21h. Ex 27:21n. Le *23:2n. **the reproach of it was a burden.** Heb. the burden upon it *was* reproach.

19. **I will undo.** ver. 15. Is 25:9-12. 26:11. 41:11-16. 43:14-17. 49:25, 26. 51:22, 23. 66:14-16. Je 30:16. 46:28. 51:35, 36. Ezk *39:17-22. Jl 3:2-9. Mi 7:10. Na 1:11-14. Zc 2:8, 9. 12:3, 4. 14:2, 3. Re 19:17-21. 20:9. **and I will save.** Je 31:8. Ezk *34:16. Mi *4:6, 7. He 12:13. **and I will.** Dt 26:19⁝𝒫. Is *60:14. 61:7. √62:7. Je 33:9. Ezk 39:26. **get them praise.** Heb. set them for a praise. Ps 78:43mg. **where they have been put to shame.** Heb. of their shame.

20. **bring you.** Ezk +*34:13. +*37:25. **in the time.** Ps +*102:13, 16. **gather.** Ps +*147:2. Is √11:11, 12. *27:12, 13. *56:8. Ezk *28:25, 26. *34:16. *37:21. 39:28. Am √9:9, 14, 15. **for I will.** ver. 19. Dt 26:19⁝𝒫. Is 25:8. 60:15, 18. 61:9. 62:7, 12. Mi *4:8. Ml 3:12. Re 5:13. **I turn.** Zp 2:7. Dt *30:3. Ps 35:6. Je 29:14. Ezk 16:53. Ho *6:11. Jl 3:1.

HAGGAI

HAGGAI 1

The time when Haggai prophesied, 1. He reproves the delay of the Jews in building the temple; and exhorts them to proceed, 2-11. They obey, and receive encouragement from God, 12-15.

1. **second.** Hg 2:1, 10, 20. Ezr *4:5, 24. 5:1, 2. Zc 1:1, 7. **the king.** Da 11:2. **the sixth.** *Elul,* the sixth month of the ecclesiastical year, answering to a part of *September.* **first day of the month.** 2 Ch +2:4. **by.** Heb. by the hand of. The Hebrew idiom for God speaking "by the prophets" (CB). Note the reference to the Pentateuch. Other references to the Pentateuch in Haggai are at ver. 6, 8. Hg 2:5, 11, 12, 13, 17. See related note (Is +*1:2). Ex 4:13. 9:35⁝𝒫. 35:29⁝𝒫. Le 8:36⁝𝒫. 10:11⁝𝒫. 26:46⁝𝒫. Nu 4:37, 45⁝𝒫. 9:23⁝𝒫. 10:13⁝𝒫. 15:23⁝𝒫. 16:40⁝𝒫. 27:23⁝𝒫. 36:13⁝𝒫. Jsh 14:2. 20:2. 21:2, 8. 22:9. Jg 3:4. 2 S 12:25. 1 K 8:53, 56.

12:15. 14:18. 15:29. 16:7, +*12mg. 17:16. 2 K 14:25. 1 Ch 11:3mg. 25:2mg. 29:8. 2 Ch 10:15. 23:18mg. *29:25mg. 33:8. √34:14mg,n. Ezr 6:14. 9:11mg. Ne 8:14mg. 9:14. 10:29mg. Est 1:12mg. Ps 63:10mg. 77:2mg. Is 20:2mg. Je +*37:2mg. 50:1mg. Ezk 38:17mg. Ho 12:10mg. **Haggai.** i.e. *festive, feast, or festival; exaltation or festival of the Lord,* ✱S#2292h. Hg 1:1, 3, 12, 13. 2:1, 10, 13, 14, 20. Ezr 5:1, 2. 6:14. **unto Zerubbabel.** i.e. *sown in Babylon,* ✱S#2216h. Hg 1:1, 12, 14. 2:2, 4, 21, 23. 1 Ch 3:19, 19. Ezr 2:2. 3:2, 8. 4:2, 3. 5:2. Ne 7:7. 12:1, 47. Zc *4:6, 7, 9, 10. Mt 1:12, 13, Zorobabel. Lk 3:27. **son of.** ʃ171G2. Figure of speech Synecdoche of Genus, Ge +13:8. Son is here put for grandson. 1 K 15:10n. 1 Ch 3:19n. 6:20n. 7:6n. Ezr 5:1n. 7:1n. **Shealtiel.** i.e. *asked for from God,* ✱S#7597h. Hg 1:1. 2:23. 1 Ch 3:17, Salathiel. Ezr 3:2, 8. Ne 12:1. Also Hg 1:12, 14. 2:2. Mt 1:12, Salathiel. Lk 3:27. **governor.** *or,* captain. Ezr 1:8. 2:63.

Ne 5:14. 8:9. **Joshua**. Hg 1:12, 14. 2:2, 4. Ezr 2:2. 3:8. 5:2. Ne 12:1, 10. Zc 3:1, 3, 8, 9. 6:11. **Josedech**. i.e. *Jehovah is righteous*. *S#3087h. Hg 1:1, 12, 14. 2:2, 4. 1 Ch 6:14, 15, Jehozadak. Zc 6:11.

2. **the Lord of hosts**. Ex 15:26n. Ps +24:10. **This**. Nu 13:31. Ezr *4:4, 5, 23, 24. 5:1, 2. Ne 4:10. Pr 22:13. 26:13-16. 29:25. Ec 9:10. 11:4. SS 5:2, 3. **The time**. Ps 1:3. **be built**. Ezr 3:2.

3. **by Haggai**. Ezr *5:1. Zc 1:1.

4. **Is it time**. Je 33:10, 12. **to dwell**. 2 S *7:2. Ezr 2:70. Ps *132:3-5. Mt √6:33. Ph *2:21. **cieled**. or, panelled. Used of the lining of an arched roof. 1 K 6:9. 7:3, 7. Je 22:14. **and this house**. Ps 74:7. 102:14. Je 26:6, 18. 52:13. La 2:7. 4:1. Ezk 24:21. Da +*9:17, 18, 26, 27. Mi 3:12. Mt +*24:1, 2.

5. **thus**. ver. 7. Hg 2:15-18. La 3:40. Ezk 18:28. Lk 15:17. 2 C √13:5. Ga *6:4. **Consider your ways**. Heb. Set your heart on your ways. ver. 7. Hg 2:15, 18. Ex 7:23. 9:21mg. Jb 1:8. 2:3. Ps 48:13mg. Pr +6:6. 24:32mg. Is 41:22. 44:19mg. Ezk 40:4. Da 6:14. 10:12. 1 C *11:31.

6. **have sown**. ver. 9. Hg 2:16. Le *26:20. Dt *28:38-40)𝒫. 2 S 21:1. Ps 107:34. Is 5:10. Je 14:4. Ho *4:10. 8:7. Jl 1:10-13. Am 4:6-9. Mi *6:14, 15. Zc 8:10. Ml 2:2. 3:9-11. **eat**. Le *26:26)𝒫. 1 K 17:12. Jb 20:22. Je 44:18. Ezk 4:16, 17. Mi 6:14. **earneth wages**. or, is hiring himself out. lit. "making himself sweet." Zc 8:10. **with holes**. Heb. pierced through. Jb 20:28. Zc 5:4. 1 T +*6:17.

7. **Consider**. See on ver. 5. 1 S *2:30. Ps 119:59, 60. Pr +6:6. +*14:12, 13. Is 28:10. Da 10:12. 2 C *13:5. Ph 3:1.

8. **to**. 2 Ch 2:8-10. Ezr 3:7. 6:4. Zc 11:1, 2. **and build**. See on ver. 2-4. Jon 3:1, 2. Mt 3:8, 9. **and I will take pleasure**. Hg 2:7, 9. 1 K *8:29. *9:3. 2 Ch 7:16. Ps 87:2, 3. 133:13, 14. Zp *3:17. **I will be glorified**. Hg 2:7. Ex 29:43. Le 10:3)𝒫. Ps 132:13, 14. Is 60:7, 13. 66:11. Jn 13:31, 32.

9. **Ye looked**. They had used all proper means in the cultivation of their lands, and had "sown much;" but when they rationally entertained the most sanguine expectations of a large increase, they were strangely disappointed; and even what they had brought home was unaccountably wasted, as if the Lord had "blown upon it," and driven it away! And the reason was, because they neglected the temple, and left it in ruins, whilst they eagerly employed themselves in building and decorating their own houses; therefore they were visited by drought and famine, and by various diseases on man and beast. See on ver. 6. Hg 2:16, 17. Is 17:10, 11. Ml 3:8-11. **blow upon it**. *or*, blow it away. 2 S 22:16. 2 K 19:7. Is 40:7. Ml 2:2. **Why**. Jb 10:2. Ps 77:5-10. **Because**. See on ver. 4. Jsh 7:10-15. 2 S 21:1. Mt 10:37, 38. 1 C +*11:30-32. Re 2:4. 3:19. **unto his own**. Ph *2:21.

10. **the heaven**. Le *26:19)𝒫. Dt *28:23, 24)𝒫. 1 K *8:35. 17:1. Je 14:1-6. Ho 2:9. Jl 1:18-20.

11. **And**. ∫148, Ge +8:22. **I called**. Dt 28:22mg. 1 K 17:1. 2 K 8:1. Jb 34:29. Je *14:3, 4. La 1:21. Am 5:8. 7:4. 9:6. **new wine**. Heb. *tirosh*, Ge +*27:28. **upon all**. Hg *2:17.

12. **spirit**. Heb. *ruach*, Ge +41:8. 1 Ch 5:26. 2 Ch 21:16. 36:22. Ezr 1:1. Je 51:11. **Zerubbabel**. ver. 14. Ezr *5:2. Is √55:10, 11. Col 1:6. 1 Th 1:5, 6. √2:13, 14. **sent him**. Je 43:1. **fear**. Ge 22:12. Ps 112:1. Pr *1:7. Ec 12:13. Is 50:10. Ac 9:31. He 12:28.

13. **the Lord's**. Jg 2:1mg. Is 42:19. 44:26. Ezk 3:17. Ml *2:7. 3:1. 2 C 5:20. **I am with you**. Hg 2:4. 2 Ch 15:2. 20:17. 32:8. Ps 46:7, 11. Is 8:8-10. *41:10. 43:2. Je 15:20. 20:11. 30:11. Mt 1:23. *18:20. *28:20. Ac 18:9, 10. Ro √8:31. 2 C √12:9. 2 T *4:17, 22.

14. **stirred up**. 1 Ch 5:26. 2 Ch 36:22. Ezr 1:1, 5. 7:27, 28. Ps *110:3. 1 C 12:4-11. 2 C 8:16. He *13:21. **the spirit**. Heb. *ruach*, Ge +41:8. ∫121A10, Ge +26:35. Put by the figure of speech Metonymy of Adjunct for the state of mind and feeling. 1 Ch 5:26. 2 Ch 21:16. 36:22. Ezr 1:1. Je 51:11. **governor of**. ver. 1. Hg 2:21. **and they**. Hg 2:4. Ezr *5:2, 8. Ne 4:6. 1 C √15:58. Ph *2:12, 13.

15. **the four and**. ver. 1. Hg 2:1, 10, *18, 20.

HAGGAI 2

The prophet encourages the Jews, by assuring them that this temple, though far inferior to the former in magnificence, would be rendered more glorious by the presence of the Messiah, 1-9. By the law concerning things holy and unclean, he shows that their sins had deprived them of God's blessings, which from that time he would vouchsafe them, 10-19. He predicts the prosperity of Christ's kingdom, under that of Zerubbabel, his ancestor and type, 20-23.

1. **the seventh**. ver. 10, 20. Hg 1:15. **the prophet**. Heb. the hand of the prophet, etc. Hg +*1:1mg. 2 P *1:21.

2. **Zerubbabel**. Mt 1:12. Lk 3:27. **governor**. Hg 1:14. Ezr 1:8. 2:63. Ne 8:9. **Josedech**. 1 Ch 6:15.

3. **is left**. Ezr *3:12. Zc 4:9, 10. **this house**. The Temple is regarded as one throughout. Actually three temples are alluded to: that of Solomon; the second under Zerubbabel; and the future millennial sanctuary of Ezekiel (ver. 7). **first**. 1 K 5:15-17. 6:7, 15, 18, 20-22, 30, 35. 7:48-51. 1 Ch *22:5. **glory**. Ezk 7:20. Lk 21:5, 6.

4. **now**. Dt 31:23. Jsh 1:6, 9. Jg 6:14. 1 Ch 22:13. 28:20. Is 35:3, 4. Zc *8:9. 1 C 16:13. Ep *6:10. 2 T 2:1. **saith the Lord**. Is *43:1. **and work**. Zc 6:15. *8:9, 13. **with you**. Hg 1:13. Ex 3:12. Jsh *1:7, 8. Jg 2:18. 1 S 16:18. 2 S 5:10. Mk 16:20. Ac 7:9. 2 T *4:17.

5. **According to**. Ex *29:45, 46)𝒫. 33:12-14. 34:8, 10. **the word**. Dt *28:1-42. Ps 105:8. **I covenanted**. Ps √89:34. *111:5. Ml +*3:6. **when ye came**. Ex 12:51)𝒫. **so**. Nu 11:25-29. Ne *9:20, 30. Ps 51:11, 12. Is *63:11-14. Zc *4:6. Jn *14:16, 17. **spirit**. Heb. *ruach*, Ge +41:38. Ne *9:20. Is 63:10, 11. Zc √4:6. **fear**. Jsh 8:1. 2 Ch 20:17. Is *41:10, 13. Zc 8:13, 15. Mt 28:5. Lk *12:32. Ac 27:24. Re 1:17.

6. **Yet**. ver. 21, 22. He 12:26-28. **once**. or, first. Hg 1:1. 2:1. Heb. *echad*, one of several. Dt +*6:4. There had been shakings before; but this one would be extreme and final (CB). He)12:26, 27. Greek *hapax*, once for all: i.e. *first, before the fulfillment of the promise given in the clause which follows* (CB). **a little while**. Ps *37:10. Is 10:25. 29:17. Je 51:33. He *10:37. **and I will shake**. A pleonasm for "I will shake the heavens and the earth and all nations" (Peters, *Theocratic Kingdom*, vol. 2, p. 497). Ps 46:3. 77:18. Is √13:13. *24:18-20. 34:4. 64:1, 2. Je *4:23-26. 10:10. Ezk 38:20. Jl *2:30-32. *3:16. Mt √24:29, 30. Mk 13:24-26. Lk *21:25-27. Ac 2:19, 20. He +*12:26. Re 6:12-17. 8:5-12. 11:19. 16:2-21. **the heavens**. "Heavens" put for political heights and glory, forms of government, etc.,

as explained in ver. 21, 22. Is 13:10-13. 14:12-15. 34:4, 5. 51:16n. Je 4:23-25. Ezk 32:7. Jl 2:10. **and the earth.** "Earth" is put for the multitude of the people, their strength and power, whereby the heavens are supported. Ge 6:11. Re 12:16.

7. **I will shake.** Ezk 21:27. Da *2:44, 45. 7:20-25. Jl *3:9-16. Lk *21:10, 11. He +*12:26. Re *6:12-17. **all nations.** *∫171A, Ex +9:6. i.e. people in all nations. Is 24:21, 22. Da 12:1. **and the desire.** ∫121R5, Ge +27:15. Ge +*3:15. *22:18. +*49:10. 1 S 9:20. 2 Ch 21:20. Zc *9:9, 10. Lk 2:*10, *11, 27, 29, 30, 46. Ro 15:9-15. Ga *3:8. **all nations.** *∫171A, Ex +9:6. i.e. *many in all nations.* **shall come.** Ge +*49:10. Da *7:14, 18, 27. Ml 3:1. He 10:37. **I will fill.** Ex *40:34, 35. 1 K 8:11. 2 Ch +*5:13, 14. Ps 80:1. Ml *3:1. Lk *19:47. 20:1. 21:38. Jn *1:14. *2:13-17. 7:37-39. *10:23-38. Col *2:9. **this house.** As this is mentioned after the great shaking, this must refer to the future millennial temple of Ezekiel (Is 60:13n. Ezk +*37:26. 40:2n. Jl 2:1. Zc *1:16. √6:12, 13). Ml 3:1. Mt ✳21:12. Lk ✳2:27, 32. **glory.** This "glory" is connected with the final peace (ver. *9. Is 9:6. 60:18). The second Temple was connected with "grace," not "glory," and was followed by wars, not peace (Mt 10:34. 24:6-8. Lk 12:51), CB. Ps 24:7-10. +*102:16. Is 60:1. Ezk *43:5.

8. **The silver.** 1 K 6:20-35. 1 Ch *29:12-16. Ps 24:1. 50:10-12. Is 2:7. 60:13, 17. 61:6.

9. **glory.** ver. +*7n. Ps 24:7-10. Ezk 43:5. Lk *2:14. Jn *1:14. 2 C *3:9, 10. 1 T *3:16. 1 Th 2:19, 20. He *1:1-3. 12:28. Ja *2:1. **latter house.** Ezk 43:2, 4, 5. 44:4. Ml 3:1. Mt ✳21:12. Lk ✳2:27, 32. **saith.** Whoever compares the description of the temple of Solomon, in the first book of Kings, with the most splendid accounts of the second temple, however adorned with costly stones and other magnificent decorations in after ages, must perceive that the former, being wholly overlaid with pure gold, was incomparably more glorious than the latter in its greatest magnificence; and the Jews themselves allow that the ark of the covenant, fire from heaven, the Urim and Thummim, the anointing oil, the Shechinah, or visible glory, and the spirit of prophecy, which distinguished the former temple, were wanting in this. In nothing, in fact, could the second temple excel the first in glory, except in the personal presence of "the Desire of all nations," He who is "the glory of the Lord," and the true temple, "in whom dwells all the fulness of the Godhead bodily," and who was the true Shechinah, of which that of Solomon's temple was merely a type. And if it be admitted that the presence of the promised Messiah was intended, then it will follow that "Jesus of Nazareth" was He; for the second temple, in which as the "Prince of peace" he preached peace and reconciliation with God, has been utterly destroyed for upwards of seventeen hundred years. **give.** Ps *85:8, 9. Is +*9:6, 7. *54:4, 10, 13. 57:18-21. Mi *5:5. Lk *2:14. Jn √14:27. Ac 10:36. Ep *2:14-17. Ph *4:7. Col *1:19-21. **peace.** Is +*9:6. Mi +*5:5. Zc √9:9, 10.

10. **the four and.** ver. 1, 20. Hg 1:1, 15. **by.** Hg +*1:1mg.

11. **Ask now.** Le *10:10, 11)℘. Dt *17:11)℘. *21:5. *33:10)℘. Is +√8:20n. Ezk 44:10-12, 23, 24. Ml *2:7. Mt *8:4. T *1:9.

12. **If one bear.** Ex 29:37. Le 6:27, 29. 7:6. Ezk 44:19. Mt *23:19. **holy flesh.** Je 11:15. **skirt.** lit. *wing.* Ru 3:9. **wine.** Heb. *yayin,* Hab 2:5n. **No.** Le 6:27)℘.

13. **If one.** Le 7:19. Nu 5:2, 3. 9:6-10. *19:11-22. Ezk 44:25. **body.** Heb. *nephesh,* soul, Le +19:28. **unclean.** Le *22:4, 6)℘.

14. **So is this people.** Hg 1:4-11. Pr 15:8. 21:4, 27. 28:9. Is *1:11-15. T *1:15. Ju *23. **and that.** Ezr 3:2, 3. **unclean.** Is 6:5. √64:6. Ro *14:20. T *1:15.

15. **consider.** ver. 18. Hg 1:5, 7. Ps 107:43. Is 5:12. Ho 14:9. Ml 3:8-11. Ro 6:21. 1 C 11:31. **from before.** Ezr 3:10. 4:24. **stone was laid.** Is 28:16. Mk 4:19. 1 P 2:6, 7.

16. **when one came to an.** Hg 1:6, 9-11. Pr *3:9, 10. Is 9:20. Zc 8:10-12. Ml 2:2. Mk 4:20. **press.** Is 63:3.

17. **with blasting.** Hg 1:9. Ge 41:6, 23, 27. Dt *28:22)℘. 1 K 8:37. 2 Ch 6:28. Is 37:27. Am 4:9. **with hail.** Ex 9:18-29. Is 28:2. **in all.** Hg 1:11. Ps 78:46. Is 62:8. Je 3:24. **yet.** 2 Ch 28:22. Jb 36:13. Is *9:13. 42:25. Je *5:3. 6:16, 17. 8:4-7. Ho 7:9, 10. Am 4:8-11. Zc 1:2-4. 7:9-13. Re 2:21. 9:20, 21.

18. **Consider.** ver. 15. Dt 32:29. Lk 15:17-20. **even.** Hg 1:14, 15. Ezr 5:1, 2. Zc *8:9, 12. He 11:10.

19. **as yet.** Hab 3:17, 18. **from this day.** Ge 26:12. Le 26:3, etc. Dt 15:10. *28:2-15. Ps *84:10-12. 128:1-5. *133:3. Pr *3:9, 10. Zc 8:11-15. Ml √3:10. Mt √6:33. 1 C *6:14-18. **I will bless.** Ge 22:17, 18. Is *1:19. Ro 11:26. 1 T *4:8.

20. **in the four.** ver. 10.

21. **Zerubbabel.** Hg 1:1, 14. 1 Ch 3:19. Ezr 2:2. 5:2. Zc *4:6-10. **I will shake.** ver. 6, 7. Ps 46:6. Ezk 26:15. 38:19, 20. Jl 3:16. He 12:26, 27. 2 P *3:10, 12. Re 16:17-19. **the heavens and the earth.** ver. 6. Ge 1:1. Ex 20:11. 31:17. 39:10. 31:28. 2 K 19:15. 2 Ch 2:12. Is 37:16. Je 23:24. 32:17.

22. **overthrow.** Is 60:12. Ezk 21:27. +*38:8, 9, 21. Da *2:34, 35, 44, 45. *7:25-27. *8:25. +*11:40. *12:1. Mi +*5:8, 15. Zp 3:8. Zc 10:11. 12:2-5. 14:3. Mt +*24:7. Re *11:15. *17:14. **and I will overthrow the chariots.** Ex 14:17, 28. 15:4, 19. Ps 46:9. 76:6. Ezk *39:20. Mi *5:10. Zc *4:6. *9:10. **every.** Jg 7:22. 1 S 14:16. 2 Ch 20:22, 23. Is *9:19. 19:2. 43:16, 17.

23. **O Zerubbabel.** It seems evident that the Messiah is here described under the name of Zerubbabel, as elsewhere under that of David (Ezk 34:23n), whose kingdom, after these mighty convulsions, should supersede all others. **my servant.** 2 S 7:12, 16. Ps ch. 63. Is *42:1. Zc 4:7-10. **and will.** Ge 41:42. Est 3:10. SS 8:6. Je 22:24. Zc 4:7-10. 6:13. Jn 6:27. 2 T *2:19. **signet.** ∫22D5N, Je 22:24. **for.** Is *42:1. +*43:10n. 49:1-3. Zc *4:6-14. Mt *12:17, 18. Lk 3:23, 27. ◐23:35. Jn 7:42. 1 P *2:4-6. Re 19:16. **chosen thee.** Dt +10:15. 1 K 8:16. 11:34. Ps *33:12. Is +*9:6, 7. Mt 11:27. 22:14. 24:22, 24, 31. Lk 18:7. Ro *8:28-30, 33. 11:28. Col 3:12. 1 Th 5:9. T 1:1. 1 P 1:1, 2. 2:8, 9. Re 17:14.

ZECHARIAH

ZECHARIAH 1

The prophet expostulates with the Jews, and exhorts them to repentance, 1-6. His vision of horses and their riders, 7-11. Comfortable promises to Jerusalem, 12-17. A vision of four horns and four carpenters, 18-21.

1. A.M. 3484. B.C. 520. **the eighth.** ver. 7. Zc 7:1. Ezr *4:24. 6:15. Hg 1:1, 15. 2:1, 10, 20. **Zechariah.** i.e. *remembered of Jehovah*, S#2148h. Zc 1:1, 7. 7:1, 8. Ezr *5:1. 6:14. Also 2 K 14:29. 15:11. 18:2. 1 Ch 9:21, 37. 15:20. 16:5. 2 Ch 17:7. 24:20. 34:12. Ezr 8:3, 11, 16. 10:26. Ne 8:4. 11:4, 5, 12. 12:16, 35, 41. Also 2 K 15:8. 1 Ch 5:7. 15:18, 24. 24:25. 26:2, 11, 14. 27:21. 2 Ch 20:14. 21:2. 26:5. 29:1, 13. 35:8. Is 8:2. Mt √23:35. Lk *11:51. Twenty-seven other individuals with this name are mentioned in the Bible: Seven Levites: (1) 1 Ch 9:21; 26:2, 14. (2) 1 Ch 15:18, 20; 16:5. (3) 1 Ch 24:25. (4) 1 Ch 26:11. (5) 2 Ch 20:14. (6) 2 Ch 29:13. (7) 2 Ch 34:12. Four priests: (8) 2 Ch 35:8. (9) Ne 11:12. (10) Ne 12:16. (11) Ne 12:35, 41. (12) The son of Jehoiada the high-priest. He was stoned to death at the command of King Joash, 2 Ch 24:20, 21. (13, 14) Two chief men who returned from Babylon with Ezra, Ezr 8:3; 8:11, 16. (15) The father of Iddo, 1 Ch 27:21. (16) The son of Jeberechiah, Is 8:2. (17) A chief of Reuben, 1 Ch 5:7. (18) A Benjamite, 1 Ch 9:37, called Zacher in 1 Ch 8:31. (19) A priest, 1 Ch 15:24. (20) A prince of Judah, 2 Ch 17:7. (21) A son of Jehoshaphat, 2 Ch 21:2. (22) A man who lived in the time of Uzziah, 2 Ch 26:5. (23) One who took a foreign wife, Ezr 10:26. (24) A prince who stood beside Ezra while he read the law, Ne 8:4. (25, 26) Two descendants of Pharez, Ne 11:4; 11:5. (27) Father of Abi, 2 Ch 29:1; see 2 K 18:2. (28) Zechariah, the eleventh of the twelve minor prophets and a priest, was born in Babylon of priestly descent, and returned to Jerusalem with Zerubbabel and the high-priest Joshua, Ezr 5:1; 6:14; Zc 1:1, 7; 7:1, 8. He prophesied B.C. 520-518. **Iddo.** Ezr +5:1. *6:14. Ne 12:4, 16.

2. **Lord.** 2 K 22:16, 17, 19. 23:26. 2 Ch *36:13-20. Ezr 9:6, 7, 13. Ne 9:26, 27. Ps *60:1. 79:5, 6. Je 44:6. La 1:12-15. 2:3-5. 3:42-45. 5:7. Ezk *5:11-13. *22:18, 31. Da 9:11, 12. Zp 2:1-3. Mt 23:30-32. Ac 7:52. **sore displeased.** Heb. with displeasure. √147D, Ge +1:29. ver. 14, 15. Zc 8:2.

3. **Turn.** Dt *4:30, 31. *30:2-10. 1 K 8:47, 48. 2 Ch 15:4. 30:6-9. Ne 9:28. Is 31:6. √55:6, 7. Je 3:12-14, 22. 4:1. *25:5. 35:15. La 3:39-41. Ezk 33:11. Ho 6:1. 14:1. Jl 2:12. Ml 3:7. Lk 15:18-20. Ac +*3:19. Ja *4:8-10. **and.** Je 12:15. 29:12-14. *31:18-20. La 5:21. Ho 14:4. Mi +*7:19, 20. Lk 15:21, 22. Ac +√3:19-21.

4. **as.** 2 Ch 29:6-10. 30:7. 34:21. Ezr 9:7. Ne 9:16. Ps 78:8. 106:6, 7. Ezk 18:14-17. 1 P 1:18. **unto.** Zc 7:11-13. 2 Ch 24:19-22. √36:15, 16. Ne 9:26, 30. Is 30:9-11. Je 6:16, 17. *7:25. 13:16-18. 17:19-23. 25:3-7. *35:15. 36:2, 3, etc. 44:4, 5. Ezk 3:7-9. Mi 2:6. Ac 7:51, 52. 1 Th 2:15, 16. **Turn.** ver. 3. Is *1:16-19. 31:6. Je 3:12. 7:3-7. 18:11. Ezk 18:30-32. 33:11. Ho √14:1, 2. Am 5:13-15, 24. Ml *3:7. Mt 3:8-10. Ac

+*3:19. 26:20. **but.** Je 11:6-8. 13:9, 10. 26:5. 36:23, 24. 44:16.

5. **Your fathers.** √73. Epimone; or, Lingering B401. Repetition, not of words, but of sense or thought, in order to dwell upon for the sake of impressing. The figure extends to include ver. 3-6. For other instances of this figure see Mt 7:21-23. 12:31, 32. 15:18-20. Mk 7:20-23. Jn 21:15-17. Col 2:14, 15. **where are they.** Jb 14:10-12. Ps 90:10. Ec 1:4. 9:1-3. 12:5, +*7. Is √64:6. La 5:7. Ac 13:36. He 7:23, 24. +*9:27. 2 P 3:2-4. **for ever.** Heb. *olam*, Ex +*12:24.

6. **my words.** Is 55:1. **did.** Nu *23:19. +*32:23. 2 Ch 36:17-21. Is 44:26. Je 26:15. 44:28. La 2:17. Ezk 12:25-28. Da *9:7, 11, 12. Am *4:6. Mt √24:35. **take hold of.** *or*, overtake. Dt +*28:15, 45. Je 42:16. Am 9:10. 1 Th 5:4. **they returned.** Jb 6:29. Ml 3:18. **Like.** La *1:18. 2:17. 4:11, 12. Ezk 37:11. **thought.** Nu 33:56. Je 23:20. **according to our ways.** Dt 28:20. Is 3:8-11. Je 4:4. 18:8-11. Ezk 20:43. Ho 9:15. Ro 2:6-11.

7. A.M. 3485. B.C. 519. **the eleventh.** ver. 1. **Sebat.** i.e. *smite thou; tribe*, *S#7627h, only here. *Sebat* is the Chaldee name of the eleventh month of the ecclesiastical year, but the fifth of the civil year, answering to part of *January* and *February*. **Berechiah.** i.e. *blessed of Jehovah*, *S#1296h. ver. 1. 1 Ch 3:20. 9:16. 15:23. Ne 3:4, 30. 6:18. (1) A grandson of Pedaiah, 1 Ch 3:20. (2) Father of Asaph, a chief singer, 1 Ch 15:17; called Berachia in 1 Ch 6:39. (3) A Levite near Jerusalem, 1 Ch 9:16. (4) A doorkeeper for the ark of the covenant in the Tabernacle, 1 Ch 15:23. (5) An Ephraimite who opposed bringing captives from Judah as bondmen into Samaria, 2 Ch 28:12. (6) Father of Meshullam, Ne 3:4, 30; 6:18. (7) Father of Zechariah the prophet, Zc 1:1, 7.

8. **by night.** Ge 20:3. 1 K 3:5. Jb 4:13. Da 2:19. 7:2, 13. **behold.** Zc 13:7. Jsh 5:13. Ps 45:3, 4. Is 63:1-4. **riding.** Zc 6:2-7. Re *6:2, 4, 5, 8. 19:11, 14, 19-21. **among.** SS 2:16. 6:2. Is 41:19. 55:13. +*57:15. Re 2:1. **speckled.** *or*, bay. Zc 6:6, 7.

9. **what.** ver. 19. Zc 4:4, 11. 6:4. Da 7:16. 8:15. Re 7:13, 14. **the angel.** ver. 11, 12, 13, 14, 19. Zc 2:3. 4:1, 5. 5:5, 10. 6:4, 5. Ge 31:11. Da 8:16. 9:22, 23. 10:11-14. Re 17:1, 7. 19:9, 10. 22:8-16.

10. **the man.** ver. 8, 11. Zc 13:7. Ge 32:24-31. Ho 12:3-5. **These.** ver. 11. Zc 4:10. 6:5-8. Jb *1:6, 7. *2:1, 2. Ps *34:7. *68:17. 103:20, 21. Ezk 1:5-14. He *1:14. 1 P *5:8. Re 12:7-12.

11. **they answered.** ver. 8, 10. Ps 68:17. *103:20, 21. Mt 6:10. 13:41, 49. 24:30, 31. 25:31. 2 Th *1:7. Re 1:1. **We.** Zc 6:7. Da 10:20. Re *16:13, 14. **is.** ver. 15. 1 Th *5:3.

12. **the angel.** ver. 8, 10, 11. Ex 23:20-23. Is 63:9. He *7:25. **how long.** Zc 7:9. Ps 74:10. 79:5. +*102:13. Is 14:1. 49:13. 64:9-12. Re 6:10. **thou hast.** Zc 7:5. 2 Ch 36:21. Je √25:11, 12. *29:10. Da *9:2.

13. **with good.** ver. 14-16. Zc 2:4-12. 8:2-8, 19. Is 40:1, 2. Je 29:10. 30:10-22. 31:3, etc. Am √9:11-15. Zp *3:14-20. **comfortable words.** ver. 17. Ps +*102:13. Is *40:1, 2.

14. **the angel.** ver. 9, 13. Zc 2:3, 4. 4:1. **Cry.** ver. 17. Is 40:1, 6. **I am.** Zc *8:2, 3. Ex *34:14. Is +*9:7.

37:32. 42:13. 59:17. 63:15. Ho 11:8. Jl *2:18. Na *1:2. jealous. ✻147D, Ge +1:29. ✻22B, Ex +20:5.

15. sore displeased. ✻147D, Ge +1:29. ver. 2, 11. Is 47:7-9. Je 48:11-13. Re 18:7, 8. at ease. Is 32:9, 11. Am *6:1. for. Is 54:8. He 12:6, 7. displeased. ✻22B. Anthropomorphism B883. *Displeasure* is attributed to God. and. Ps *69:26. 83:2-5. 137:7. Is 10:5-7. *47:6. Je 51:24, 34, 35. Ezk *25:3-7, 12-17. *26:2, 3. 29:6, 7. 35:3-9. 36:4, 5. Am 1:3-6, 9-13. Ob *10-16. the affliction. Is +*45:7. 47:11. Je 44:11.

16. I am. Zc 2:10, 11. 8:3. Is *12:1. √54:8-10. Je 31:22-25. 33:10-12. Ezk 37:24-28. 39:25-29. 48:35. Ho +*5:15. my house. Zc 4:9. √6:12, 13. Ezr 6:14, 15. Is 44:26-28. 60:13n. Ezk 40:2n. Hg 1:14. and. Zc 2:1, 2. Ne *6:15, 16. Jb 38:5. Is 34:11. Je 31:39, 40. Ezk *40:1-3. 47:3. Da +*9:25.

17. My cities. Ne 11:3, 20. Ps 69:35. Is 44:26. 61:4-6. Je 31:23, 24. 32:43, 44. 33:13. Ezk 36:10, 11, 33. Am √9:14. Ob 20. prosperity. Heb. good. the Lord shall. Is 40:1, 2. 49:13. *51:3, 12. 52:9. 54:8. 66:13. Je 31:13, 14. Zp *3:15-17. Mt 23:37. choose. Zc 2:12. 3:2. 2 Ch 6:6. Ps √132:13, 14. Is *14:1. +*41:8, 9. Ro *11:28, 29. Ep 1:4.

18. lifted. ✻144A12, Ge +22:13. Zc 2:1. 5:1, 5, 9. Jsh 5:13. Da 8:3. four horns. ver. 21. 2 K 15:29. 17:1-6. 18:9-12. 22:11. ch. 24, 25. Ps 75:4, 5. Da 2:37-43. 7:3-8. 8:3-14. 11:28-35.

19. What. ver. 9, 21. Zc 2:2. 4:11-14. Re 7:13, 14. scattered. ver. 21. Zc 8:14. 2 K 24:2, 10. 25:8-10. Ezr 4:1, 4, 7. 5:3. Je 50:17, 18. Da 12:7. Hab 3:14. 20. four. Zc 9:12-16. 10:3-5. 12:2-6. Dt 33:25. Jg 2:16, 18. 1 S 12:11. Ne 9:27. Is 54:15-17. Ob +*21. Mi +*5:5, 6, 8, 9.

21. These are the. ver. 19. Da 12:7. fray. That is, to *terrify*, or *affright*, from the French *effrayer*. Zp 3:13. which. Ps 75:4, 5. Is *43:14. Je *50:8, 9. La 2:17. Ezk 25:1, etc.

ZECHARIAH 2

The prophet has a vision of One who came to measure Jerusalem; and an assurance of its flourishing state under God's protection, 1-5. The people are warned to leave Babylon, before the impending judgments were executed, 6-9. A call on Zion to rejoice in the presence of God, and the increase of the church; and on all flesh to be silent before him, 10-13.

1. lifted. ✻144A12, Ge +22:13. Zc 1:18. a man. Zc 1:16. Ezk *40:3, 5. 47:4. Re *11:1. *21:15, 16.

2. Whither. Zc 5:10. Jn 16:5. To. Je 31:39. Ezk 45:6. 48:15-17, 30-35. Re 11:1. 21:15-17.

3. the angel. Zc 1:9, 13, 14, 19. 4:1, 5. 5:5. and another. Zc 1:8, 10, 11. He *1:14.

4. young. Je 1:6. Da 1:17. 1 T 4:12. Jerusalem. We learn from Josephus (Bel. l. v. c. 4.2), that Jerusalem actually overflowed with inhabitants, and gradually extended itself beyond its walls, and that Herod Agrippa fortified the new part, called Bezetha. Zc 1:17. 8:4, 5. 12:6. 14:10, 11. Is 33:20. 44:26. 54:2. Je 30:18, 19. *31:24, 27, 38-40. 33:10-13. Ezk *36:10, 11. 38:11. Mi 7:11, 12.

5. a wall. Zc 9:8. Ex *14:19-24. Ps 46:7-11. *48:3, 12-14. Is 4:5. 12:6. *26:1, 2. 33:21. *60:18, 19. Da 3:25. Zp 3:15. the glory. Zc +*6:13. Ex +*13:21, 22. 2 Ch +*5:13. Ps 3:3. *68:18. Is 4:5, 6. *40:5. 60:19. Ezk 43:1-7. Hg 2:7-9. Mt +*24:30. +*25:31. Lk 2:32.

2 P +*1:17. Re *21:10, 11, 23. *22:3-5. in the midst. ✻144A6, Ge +45:6. Ps *46:5. Ezk *48:35. Jl *3:21.

6. ho. Ru 4:1. Is *55:1. and flee. ver. 7. Ge 19:17. Is 48:20. 52:11, 12. Je 1:14. 3:18. 31:8. 50:8. 51:6, 45, 50. 2 C *6:16, 17. Re 18:4. land of the north. Je +*1:14. 6:22. 10:22. Ezk +*38:6. spread. Note the reference to the Pentateuch. Other references to the Pentateuch in Zechariah are at ver. 8, 10, 12. Zc 3:5, 6, 7. 4:2. 5:3, 4. 6:14. 7:3, 10, 14. 8:3, 6, 12, 13. 9:11. 10:1, 10, 12. 11:12. 12:1. 13:2, 3. 14:11, 16, 18, 21. See related note (Is +*1:2). Dt 4:37✻⅋. *28:64✻⅋. Ps 68:14. Je 15:4. 31:10. Ezk 5:12. 11:16. 12:14, 15. *17:21. Am 9:9.

7. Deliver. Ge 19:17. Nu 16:26, 34. Is *48:20. *52:11. Je 50:8. *51:6, 45. Ac *2:40. 2 C +*6:17, 18. Re *18:4. that. Is 52:2. Mi 4:10. daughter. The Babylonians were vanquished by the Persians, formerly their servants, under Darius Hystaspes, who took Babylon after a siege of twelve months, demolished its walls, and put 300,000 of the inhabitants to death.

8. After. ver. 4, 5. Zc 1:15, 16. Is 11:10. 60:15. Jl 2:28n. Mt *24:29, 30. the glory. ver. 5. Zc +√6:13. Ps +*102:16. Is *11:10. 60:7-14. *61:1-3. Mt +*24:30. Jn 17:4. 2 Th +√1:7-10. 1 P +√1:11. sent. ver. 9, 11. Is 48:15, 16. Ml 3:1. Jn 14:23, 24, 26. 15:21-23. 17:18. 1 J 4:9, 10, 14. the nations. 2 K 24:2. Is *52:10. Je 50:17, 18. 51:34, 35. Ezk 25:6, 7, 12, 15. 26:2. 35:5. Jl 3:2-8. Am 1:3-5, 9, 11, 13. Ob 10-16. Mi 4:11. 5:6. 7:10. Hab 2:8, 17. Zp 2:8. which spoiled. Is *17:12-14. Ezk +*38:12. 2 Th *1:6. for. Ge 20:6. Ps 105:13-15. Ac 9:4. 2 Th √1:6. toucheth. ✻108B, Ge +26:29. the apple. Dt *32:10✻⅋. Ps *17:8. Mt 25:40, 45. his eye. ✻182, Ge +18:22. ✻22A5, 2 S +16:22.

9. I will. Is 10:32. 11:15. 13:2. 19:16. and they. Is 14:2. 33:1, 23. Je 27:7. Ezk 39:10. Hab 2:8, 17. Zp 2:9. and ye. ver. 8. Zc 4:9. 6:15. Je *28:7-9. Ezk 33:33. Jn +*13:19. *16:4.

10. Sing. Zc 12:10. 14:9. Ps 47:2. 102:16. Is *12:6. *24:14, 16. +*35:10. +*51:11. Ho +2:15. Jl 2:23. Hab *3:3. and rejoice. Zc *9:9. Ps 47:1-9. 98:1-3. Is *12:6. 35:10. 40:9. 42:10. 51:11. *52:9, 10. *54:1. *61:10. 65:18, 19. 66:14. Je 30:19. 31:12. 33:11. Zp *3:14, 15. Ph √4:4. lo. Zc 4:5. Ps 40:7. Is 40:9-11. Ml *3:1. I come. Hg +*2:7. I will dwell. Zc *8:3. Ex 25:8. 29:45, 46✻⅋. Le *26:11, 12✻⅋. Nu 5:3. Ps 68:18. Ezk *37:27. 43:9. Jl 3:17, 21. Zp 3:17. Mt *28:20. Jn *1:14. *14:23. 2 C *6:15, 16. Re 2:1. 21:3. midst. ✻144A6, Ge +45:6.

11. many nations. Zc *8:20-23. Ex *12:49✻⅋. Nu 9:14✻⅋. Ps *22:27-30. 68:29-31. *72:8-11, 17. *102:21, 22. Is *2:2-5. *11:9, 10. 19:24, 25. 42:1-4. 45:14. *49:6, 7, 22, 23. 52:10. 54:2, 3. *60:3-5, +*11, etc. 66:19, 20. Je *3:17. 16:19. Ml 1:11. Lk 2:32. Ac 28:28. 1 P 2:9, 10. Re *11:15. in that day. Zc 3:10. my people. Ex 12:49. midst. ✻144A6, Ge +45:6. thou. ver. 9. Ezk 33:33. Jn 17:21, 23, 25.

12. inherit. Ex 19:5, 6. *34:9. Dt 9:29. *32:9✻⅋. Ps +*82:8. +*94:14. 135:4. Is √19:25. Je 10:16. 51:19. holy land. Zc 7:14. Da 11:41. Ho 9:3. Ml 3:12. choose Jerusalem again. Zc √1:16, 17. Ps 101:8. Is +*11:11n. +*24:23. +√41:9. 52:9, 10. *62:6, 7. 66:13. Am +*9:11. Ac 15:16.

13. Be silent. Ps 46:10. Hab +*2:20. Zp *1:7. Ro 3:19. 9:20. for he. Ps 68:5. 78:65. Is +*26:20, 21. 42:13-15. 51:9. 57:5. Zp 3:8. his holy habitation. Heb. the habitation of his holiness. Dt *26:15✻⅋. 2 Ch 30:27mg. Ps 11:4. 68:5. Is +*57:15. 63:15. Je 25:30.

ZECHARIAH 3

A vision of Joshua standing before the angel in filthy garments, and resisted by Satan: but the angel orders him change of raiment and a fair mitre, and gives him encouraging promises, 1-7. A prophecy of the branch, and the stone on which were seven eyes; with further promises, 8-10.

1. **he.** Zc 1:9, 13, 19. 2:3. **Joshua.** ver. 8. Zc 6:11. Ezr 5:2. Hg 1:1, 12. 2:4. **standing.** ✓121S2, Ge +21:6. Dt 10:8. 18:5. 1 S 6:20. 2 Ch 29:11. Ps 106:23. Is 15:19. Ezk 41:11, 15. Lk +*21:36. **the angel.** Ge 48:16. Ex 3:2-6. 23:20, 21. Ho 12:4, 5. Ml 3:1. Ac 7:30-38. **Satan. that is,** an adversary. Nu 22:22, 23. 1 Ch 21:1. Jb *1:6-12. *2:1-8. Ps *109:6mg. Lk *22:31. Ep *6:11, 12. 1 P 5:8. Re 12:9, 10. **at his right hand.** Jb 30:12. Ps 109:6. **resist him.** Heb. be his adversary. Ge +*3:15. Nu 22:32mg. 1 S 29:4. 2 S 19:22. 1 K 5:4. 11:14, 23, 25.

2. **the Lord said.** Ps 109:31. Lk 22:32. Ro 16:20. 1 J *3:8. **The Lord rebuke.** Da +*12:1. Mk 1:25. Lk 4:35. 9:42. Ju *9. Re 12:9, 10. **chosen.** Zc 1:17. 2:12. 2 Ch 6:6. Jn 13:18. Ro ✓8:33. Re 17:14. **a brand.** Am *4:11. Ro *11:4, 5. Ju *23.

3. **was clothed.** 2 Ch 30:18-20. Ezr 9:15. Pr 30:12. Is 4:4. ✓64:6. Da 9:18. Mt 22:11-13. Re 3:17. 7:13, 14. 19:8.

4. **those.** ver. 1, 7. Dt 1:38. 1 S 16:21. 1 K 10:8. 22:19. Is 6:2, 3. Lk 1:19. Re 5:11. **Take.** Is 43:25. Ezk 36:25. Ga 3:27, 28. Ph 3:7-9. Re 7:14. **I have.** 2 S 12:13. Ps *32:1, 2. 51:9. Is 6:5-7. Jn 1:29. Ro ✓6:23. He 8:12. **from thee.** 2 S 12:13. 24:10. Jn 7:21. **and I will.** Is *61:3, 10. Lk 15:22. Ro 3:22. *13:14. 1 C 6:11. 2 C ✓5:21. Ga *3:27. Ph *3:9. Col *3:10, 11. Re *19:7, 8.

5. **Let them set.** Ex *29:5, 6▶𝒫. **fair.** Zc *6:11. Ex *28:2-4. 29:6. Le *8:6-9. He 2:8, 9. *4:14-16. 5:1-6. Re 4:4, 10. 5:8-14. **mitre.** or, turban. Ex 28:37.

6. **the angel of.** ver. 1. Ge 22:15, 16. 28:13-17. 48:15, 16. Ex 23:20, 21. Is 63:9. Ho 12:4. Ac 7:35-38. **protested.** Ge 43:3▶𝒫. Dt 8:19▶𝒫. Je 11:7.

7. **If.** Je +7:5. Jn 15:7, 14. **wilt walk.** Col +*1:10. 1 Th 4:1. 1 J +*2:3, 6. **if thou wilt keep.** Ge 26:5. Le 8:35▶𝒫. 10:3. 1 K 2:3. 1 Ch 23:32. Ezk 44:8, 15, 16. 48:11. Ml *2:7. 1 T 6:13, 14. 2 T 4:1, 2. **charge.** or, ordinance. Le 18:30. Ps 109:8mg. Ezk 48:11mg. Ml +3:14mg. **judge.** Dt 17:8-13▶𝒫. 1 S 2:28-30. Je 15:19-21. Ml 2:5-7. Mt +*19:28. Lk +*22:30. 1 C +*6:2, 3. Re *3:21. **I will.** Zc 1:8-11. 4:14. 6:5. Ex 33:21. Jsh 20:4. Is 56:5. Lk 20:35, 36. Jn +*14:2. He 12:22, 23. Re 5:9-14. **places.** Heb. walks. Ep *1:3. Re 3:4, 5. **these that.** 1 K 22:19. Ps 103:21. Mt 18:10. 1 T 5:21.

8. **for.** Ps 71:7. Is 8:18. 20:3. 1 C 4:9-13. **wondered at.** Heb. of wonder, or sign, as Ezk 12:11. 24:24. Is 8:18. 20:3. 1 C 4:9. **my.** Is *42:1. 49:3, 5. *52:13. *53:11. Ezk 34:23, 24. 37:24. Mt *12:18. Ph *2:6-8. **the BRANCH.** ✓22H1A, Is +4:2. Zc *6:12. Ps 80:15. Is 4:2. *11:1, 10. 53:2. Je +*23:5, 6. *33:15. Ezk 17:22-24. 34:29. Lk 1:78mg.

9. **the stone.** ✓22L2, Is +8:14. Zc 4:7. Ps ✓118:22. Is 8:14, 15. *28:16. Da 2:34, 44. Mt *16:18. *21:42-44. Ac 4:11. Ro 9:33. Ep *2:20-22. 1 P *2:4-8. **I have laid.** Hg 2:23. **upon.** or, fixed upon. Dt 11:12. 1 K 9:3. Ezr 5:5. **seven.** Zc *4:10. Ge +21:28, 31. Re 5:6. **eyes.** 2 Ch *16:9. Mk 6:20. Lk 20:20. Re *5:6. **I will**

engrave. Ex 28:11, 21, 36. Jn 6:27. 2 C 1:22. 3:3. 2 T *2:19. **remove.** Zc *13:1. Is 53:4, etc. +*60:21. Je +*31:34. *50:20. Ezk 37:23. Da +*9:24-27. Mi +*7:18, 19. Jn ✓1:29. Ep 2:16, 17. Col 1:20, 21. 1 T 2:5, 6. He 7:27. *9:25, 26. 10:10-18. 1 J ✓2:2. **that land.** Dt +*32:43. Is 60:21. Je 3:18. +7:7. Am +*9:15. **in one day.** Zc *12:10, 11. Ge 27:45. 1 S 2:34. 1 K 20:29. 2 Ch 28:6. Is 9:14. 10:17. 47:9. *66:5-9. He *7:27. *9:12, 26, 28. *10:10, 12, 14.

10. **In that day.** Zc 2:11. Is *2:4. Ho +*2:18. Hg 2:9. **shall.** 1 K 4:25. Is 36:16. Ho 2:18. Mi *4:4. Jn 1:45-48.

ZECHARIAH 4

A vision of a golden candlestick, with seven lamps, supplied with oil, through pipes, from two olive trees, 1-3; explained to mean the effectual assistance, which God would afford Zerobbabel and Joshua in finishing the temple, 4-10. The two olive trees are the two anointed ones, 11-14.

1. **the angel.** Zc 1:9, 13, 19. 2:3. 3:6, 7. **waked.** 1 K 19:5-7. Je 31:26. Da *8:18. *10:8-10. Lk 9:32. 22:45, 46.

2. **What.** Zc 5:2. Je 1:11-13. **a candlestick.** Ex *25:31-38)𝒫. 37:17-24. 40:24, 25. 1 K 7:49, 50. 1 Ch 28:15. 2 Ch 4:7, 20-22. 13:11. Is 62:1, 2. Je 52:19. Mt 5:14-16. Re *1:12, 20. 2:1. **a bowl.** Heb. her bowl. 1 K 7:50. **seven.** Ex 25:37)𝒫. Re *4:5. **seven pipes to the seven lamps.** or, seven several pipes to the lamps, etc. ver. 12. Re 11:3-12.

3. **olive trees.** ver. 11, 12, 14. Ex 27:20, 21. Jg 9:9. Ro 11:17, 24. Re 11:4.

4. **What.** ver. 12-14. Zc 1:9, 19. 5:6. 6:4. Da 7:16-19. 12:8. Mt 13:36. Re 7:13, 14.

5. **Knowest.** ver. 13. Mk 4:13. **No.** Ge 41:16. Ps 139:6. Da 2:30. 1 C 2:12-15.

6. **Not.** Zc 9:13-15. Nu 27:16. 2 Ch *14:11. Is *11:2-4. *30:1. 32:15. *63:10-14. Ezk 37:11-14. Ho *1:7. Hg *2:2-5. 1 C *2:4, 5. 2 C *10:4, 5. 1 P 1:12. **Not by.** 1 S 17:39. Is 31:1. Ho *1:7. 2 C *10:4. **might.** or, army. Ge 34:29. 47:6. Ex 14:4, 9. Dt 33:11. Ru 3:11. 1 S 2:4. 17:20. 2 Ch *32:7, 8. Jb 20:21. Ps *20:6-8. *33:16, 20, 21. *44:3-7. 84:7. Pr 12:4. Ec 10:10. **power.** Dt 8:18. Jg 16:5. Is 37:3. 44:12. Mi *3:8. Lk *4:14. Ac +*1:8. 4:33. 1 C *2:4. Ep *3:16. 1 Th *1:5. 2 T +*1:7. **spirit.** Heb. ruach, Is +48:16. Ge 6:3. Ps *51:11, 12.

7. **O great.** Zc 14:4, 5. Ps 114:4, 6. Is 40:3, 4. 41:15. 64:1-3. Je *51:25. Da 2:34, 35. Mi 1:4. 4:1. Na 1:5, 6. Hab 3:6. Hg 2:6-9, 21-23. Mt *17:20. *21:21. Mk *11:23. Lk 3:5. Re 16:20. **become a plain.** Is *40:4. 42:16. **headstone.** ver. 9. Ps 24:7-10. *118:22. Is 28:16. Mt 21:42. Mk 12:10. Lk 20:17. Jn 19:30. 20:17. Ac 4:11. Ep *2:20. 4:8. 1 P 2:7. **shoutings.** Ezr *3:11-13. *6:15-17. Jb 38:6, 7. Re 5:9-13. 19:1-6. **Grace.** Je 33:11. Ro 11:6. Ep 1:6, 7. 2:4-8.

8. **have.** Ezr 3:8-13. 5:2, 16. **his hands.** Zc ✓6:12, 13. Ezr *6:14, 15. Mt *16:18. He *12:2. **and.** Zc 2:8, 9, 11. 6:15. Is *48:16. Je *28:7-9. Jn 3:17. 5:36, 37. 8:16-18. 17:21.

10. **despised.** Ezr 3:12, 13. Ne 4:2-4. Jb 8:7. Pr +*4:18. Da *2:34, 35. Ho +*6:3. Hg 2:3. Mt *13:31-33. 1 C ✓1:28, 29. **for they,** etc. or, since the seven eyes of the Lord shall rejoice. Is 66:11, 14. Lk 15:5-10, 32. **and shall.** Am 7:7, 8. **plummet.** Heb. stone

of tin. ♪121D7, Ex +7:19. **those**. Zc 3:9. Re 8:2. **they are**. Zc 1:10, 11. 2 Ch √16:9. Pr *15:3. Ezk 1:15-20. Re 5:6.

11. **What**. ver. 3. Re 11:4.

12. **What be**. Mt 20:23. Re 11:4. **through**. Heb. by the hand of. Hg +*1:1mg. **empty**, etc. *or*, empty out of themselves *oil into* the gold. **the golden**. Heb. the gold.

13. **Knowest**. ver. 5. He *5:11, 12.

14. **These**. Zc 6:13. Ex 29:7. 40:15. Le 8:12. 1 S 10:1. 16:1, 12, 13. Ps *2:6mg. 89:20. 110:4. Is 61:1-3. Da +*9:24-26. Hg 1:1, 12. He +*1:8, 9. 7:1, 2. Re *11:3, 4. **anointed ones**. Heb. sons of oil. Is 5:1mg. 21:10mg. **that**. Zc 3:1-7. 6:5. Dt 10:8. 1 K 17:1. Je 49:19. Lk 1:19. Re 11:3-13. **the Lord**. Zc 6:5. 14:9. Jsh 3:11, 13. Ps 8:1, 6, 9. 97:5. Is 54:5. Mi 4:13.

ZECHARIAH 5

Visions of a large flying roll, signifying the judgments about to be executed on the wicked, the curse upon thieves and false swearers, 1-4; and of an ephah, with a woman sitting in it, covered with a talent of lead, and carried to be stationed in the land of Shinar; signifying the durable miseries of the Jews, when they should have filled up their measure of iniquity, 5-11.

1. **lifted**. ♪144A12, Ge +22:13. **roll**. ver. 2. Is 8:1. Je 36:1-6, 20-24, 27-32. Ezk *2:9, 10. Re 5:1, etc. 10:2, 8-11.

2. **What**. Zc 4:2. Je 1:11-14. Am 7:8. **flying**. Zp 1:14. 2 P 2:3. **the length**. Ge 6:11-13. Re 18:5.

3. **the curse**. Le 26:14)♥, etc. Nu 22:6. Dt 11:28, 29. √27:15-26. +*28:15)♥, etc. *29:19-28. Ps 109:17-20. √119:21. Pr +*3:33. √26:2. Is *24:5, 6. 43:28. Je 26:6. +*29:19. Da +*9:11. Ml *3:9. 4:6. Mt +*25:41. Ga +*3:10-13. He *6:6-8. Re +*21:8. *22:○3, 15. **the face**. Ml 4:6. Lk *21:35. **every one**, etc. *or*, every one of this *people* that stealeth, holdeth *himself* guiltless, as it *doth*. **stealeth**. ♪171K1, Dt +19:5. By Synecdoche of the Species, "stealing" and "swearing"—two of the commonest kinds of sin—are put for other kinds. Ex +*20:15. Pr 29:24. 30:9. Je 7:9. Ho 4:2. Ml √3:8-10. 1 C +*6:7-10. Ep √4:28. Ja +*5:4. **sweareth**. ver. 4. Zc 8:17. Le *19:12)♥. Ec 9:2. Is 48:1. Je 5:2. 23:10. Ezk 17:13-16. Ml +*3:5. Mt √5:33-37. *23:16-22. 1 T *1:9, 10. Ja √5:12. **shall be cut off**. or, hath been let off, or declared innocent, or goeth unpunished. Nu 5:31. Ps 19:12, 13. Je 2:35. 49:12.

4. **the house**. Pr +*3:33. **the thief**. Ex 21:16. 22:1-4, 10, 12. Le 6:2-5. Dt 24:7. Pr 6:30, 31. Ezk 18:10, 13. Mt 27:38, 44. 1 C +*6:10. Ep *4:28. T 2:10. 1 P 4:15. **him that**. ver. 3. Zc 8:17. Le 19:12. Ml +*3:5. **and it shall remain**. Ex +*20:5. Le 14:34-45. Dt 7:26. Jb 18:15. 20:26. Pr +√3:33. Hab 2:9-11. Ja *5:2, 3. **shall consume it**. Le 14:45)♥.

5. **the angel**. Zc 1:9, 14, 19. 2:3. 4:5. **Lift**. ♪144A12, Ge +22:13. ver. 1.

6. **This is an ephah**. "The meaning of this vision," says Abp. Newcome, "seems to be, that the Babylonish captivity had happened on account of the wickedness of the Jews, and that a like dispersion would befall them if they relapsed into like crimes." The woman who sat in the ephah was an emblem of the Jewish nation; the casting of the weight of lead on the mouth of the ephah seems to mean the condemnation of the Jews, after they had filled up the measure of their

iniquities by crucifying the Messiah; the "two women, with wings like a stork, and the wind in their wings," seem emblematical of the Roman armies and the rapidity of their conquests; and their lifting up of the ephah and carrying it through the air, to build it a house in Shinar or Babylon, where it was fixed on its own basis, represents the taking of Jerusalem, the dispersion of the Jews, and the long continuance of that calamity, as a just punishment of their unbelief. Ezk 45:10, 11. Am 8:5.

7. **talent**. *or*, weighty piece. Is 13:1. 15:1. 22:11. **is a woman**. Je 3:1, 2. Ezk ch. 16, 23. Ho ch. 1-3. Mt *13:33. Re 2:20. 17:1, *5, etc., 18.

8. **This is wickedness**. Ge 15:16. Mt 12:43-45. 23:32. 1 Th 2:16. 2 Th √2:7-12. **the weight**. ver. 7. Ps 38:4. Pr *5:22. La 1:14. Am 9:1-4. He 17:15, 16. *18:21.

9. **lifted**. ♪144A12, Ge +22:13. **for**. Dt 28:49. Da +*9:26, 27. Ho 8:1. Mt 24:28. **wings of a stork**. Le 11:19. Dt 14:18.

10. **Whither**. Perhaps the departure of the woman in the ephah represents an aspect of the cleansing of the land (Je 7:11. Ezk 39:12. Jn 2:16) of the union of evil commercialism and apostate religion.

11. **To**. Dt 28:59. Je 29:28. Ho 3:4. Lk *21:24. **the land of Shinar**. Ge +10:10)♥. 11:2)♥. 14:1, 9)♥. Jsh 7:21. Is *11:11. Da 1:2. 1 T 4:1-5. 1 J 4:1-6. Re 3:14-22. 9:1-21. 16:13-16, 19. 18:1-5, 21-24.

ZECHARIAH 6

A vision of four chariots, with horses of different colors, 1-8. By crowns, put on Joshua's head, and then preserved in the temple, the Branch, as the Messiah, as Priest and King, as building the temple, and as executing the counsel of peace, is prefigured and predicted, 9-15.

1. **I turned**. Zc 5:1. **lifted**. ♪144A12, Ge +22:13. **four**. Zc 1:18, 19. Da 2:38-40. 7:3-7. 8:22. **and the**. 1 S 2:8. Jb 34:29. Ps 33:11. 36:6. Pr +*21:30. Is *14:26, 27. 43:13. 46:10, 11. Da 4:15, 35. Ac 4:28. Ep +*1:11. 3:11. **brass**. Dt 8:9.

2. **red**. Zc *1:8. Re *6:2-5. 12:3. 17:3. **black**. ver. 6. Re 6:5, 6.

3. **white**. Re *6:2. 19:11. 20:11. **grisled**. ver. 6, 7. Zc 1:8. Ge 31:10, 12. Da 2:33, 40, 41. Re 6:8. **bay**. *or*, strong.

4. **unto**. Zc 1:9, 19-21. 5:5, 6, 10. He *1:14.

5. **These**. Zc 1:10, 11. 2 K *6:15-17. Ps *68:17. *104:3, 4. Ezk 1:5, etc. 10:9-19. 11:22. Da 7:10. He 1:7, 14. Re 7:1-3. 9:14, 15. 14:6, etc. **spirits**. *or*, winds. 1 K 19:11. Ps 148:8. Da 7:2. *10:13, 20, 21. **go**. Zc 4:10. 1 K *22:19-22. 2 Ch 18:18, 19. Jb 1:6. 2:1, 2. Da 7:10. Mt 18:10. Lk 1:19. 1 P *5:8. Re 9:2, 3, 9. **the Lord**. Zc 4:14. Is 54:5.

6. **the north**. Je 1:14, 15. 4:6. 6:1. 25:9. 46:10. 51:48. Ezk 1:4. **go forth after**. Da 7:5, 6. 11:3, 4. **toward**. Da 11:5, 6, 9, 40.

7. **the bay**. Zc 1:10. Ge 13:17. 2 Ch 16:9. Jb 1:6, 7. 2:1, 2. Da 7:7, 19, 24.

8. **cried he upon**. *or*, called to, or appealed to. Jg 4:10, 13. Jon 3:7. **quieted**. Zc 1:15. Jg *8:3. 15:7. Jb 15:13. *34:29. Ec 10:4. Is 1:24. 18:3, 4. *32:17. 42:13-15. 48:14. 51:22, 23. Je 51:48, 49. Ezk 5:13. 16:42, 63. Re 18:21, 22. **spirit**. Heb. *ruach*, Is +48:16.

9. **the word**. Zc 1:1. 7:1. 8:1.

10. **captivity**. 2 K 24:15, 16. Ezr 1:11. 2:1. Ne 7:6.

Est 2:6. Je 28:6. Ezk 1:1. **which**. Ezr 7:14-16. 8:26-30. Is 66:20. Ac 24:17. Ro 15:25, 26. **the son**. ver. 14.

11. **make**. Zc *3:5. Ex *28:36-38. *29:6. 39:30. Le 8:9. Ps 21:3. SS 3:11. He 2:9. Re 19:12. **Joshua**. Zc 3:1. Hg 1:1, 14. 2:4.

12. **Behold**. Zc 13:7. Is 32:1, 2. Mi *5:5. Mk 15:39. Jn 19:5. Ac 13:38. √17:31. He 7:4, 24. 8:3. 10:12. **whose**. Zc *3:8. Ps *80:15-17. Is 4:2. *11:1. *53:2. Je *23:5. 33:15. Ezk *34:29. Lk 1:31-35, 78mg. Jn 1:45. Ac *13:22, 23. Re 22:16. **grow up out of his place**. *or*, branch up from under him. **he shall build**. ♪90, 91 +17:1. Zc *1:16. 4:6-9. 8:9. Ps 127:1. Is 2:2. *28:16. Mt *16:18. 26:61. Mk 14:58. 15:29. Jn +*2:19-21. 1 C *3:9-11, 16, 17. *6:19. 2 C *6:16. Ep *2:20-22. He 3:3, 4. 1 P 2:4, 5. **the temple**. Zc *1:16. Is 56:7. 60:13n. Ezk +*37:26. 40:2n. Jl 2:1. Hg 2:7.

13. **and**. ♪148, Ge +8:22. **bear the glory**. Zc +*2:5, 8. Ps 21:5. 45:3, 4. 72:17-19. Is +*9:6. 11:10. *22:24. 49:5, 6. Je +*23:6. Da +*7:13, 14. Hg *2:7-9. Mt *16:27. *24:30. *25:31. Lk √24:26. Jn 13:31, 32. 17:1-5. Ep 1:20-23. Ph √2:5-11. He 1:3. 2:7-9. *3:3. 1 P √1:11. 3:22. Re 3:21. 5:9-13. 19:11-16. **a priest**. See on ver. 11. Ge 14:18. Ps *110:4. He 3:1. 4:14-16. 6:20. 7:1, 24, 25, etc. 10:12, 13. **counsel of peace**. Ac 4:14. Ps *85:9-11. Is 54:10. Da +*9:25-27. Mi +*5:4, 5. Ac 10:36-43. Ro *5:1. 2 C *5:19, 20. Ep 2:13-18. Col 2:18-20. He 7:1-3.

14. **Helem**. i.e. *hammer; strength, smiter*, ✱S#2494h. ver. 10. See ✱S#1987h, 1 Ch 7:35, Helem. (1) An Israelite descended from Asher, 1 Ch 7:35. (2) The head of a family of the Jews who dwelt in Jerusalem when Darius gave permission to rebuild the Temple, Zc 6:14. Same as Heldai, Number 2, 1 Ch 27:15. **Hen**. i.e. *gracious gift*, ✱S#2581h. **a memorial**. Ex 12:14♪𝒫. *28:12, 29. Nu 16:40. 31:54. Jsh 4:7. 1 S *2:30. Mt 26:13. Mk 14:9. Ac 10:4. 1 C 11:23-26.

15. **And they**. Is *2:2, 3. *60:5-7. Mi *4:1, 2. **far off**. Ac +*2:39. **come and build**. Is 56:6-8. *57:19. *60:10. 1 C *3:10-15. Ep *2:13-22. 1 P 2:4, 5. **and ye**. ver. 12. Zc 2:8-11. 4:8, 9. Jn 17:20, 21. **And this**. Zc 3:7. Is 3:10. 58:10-14. Ro 16:26. 2 P √1:5-10. **if**. Ge +4:7. Je +7:5. 26:3. **diligently obey**. Zc 3:7. Ex *15:26. Dt +*28:1, 2. Is +*58:10-14. Je *7:23. Mt 3:1, 2. 4:17. √7:21-23. Lk +*6:46. +*11:28. Jn +*13:17. Ac *2:38. +*3:19. Ro √16:25-27. He +*5:9. +*11:6. 1 J +*2:3. 3:21, 24. Re *22:14.

ZECHARIAH 7

The Jews inquire concerning the observance of certain appointed fasts, 1-3. The prophet reproves them for not regarding God in their fasting, etc. 4-7. He warns them not to copy the obstinacy and rebellion of their fathers, and exhorts them to practice justice and mercy, 8-14.

1. **the fourth**. Zc 1:1. Ezr 6:14, 15. Hg 2:10, 20. Chisleu. i.e. *confidence*, ✱S#3691h. Answering to part of *November* and part of *December*. Ne 1:1.

2. **they**. ♪63A1, Ge +14:20. Zc 6:10. Ezr 6:10. 7:15-23. 8:28, etc. Is 60:7. **Sherezer**. i.e. *prince of fire, he beheld treasure; Asur protect the king*, ✱S#8272h. 2 K 19:37. Is 37:38. Zc 7:2. (1) One of the sons of Sennacherib, king of Assyria, 2 K 19:37 (Sharezer). (2) A Jew mentioned in Zc 7:2. **Regemmelech**. i.e. *royal friend; stoning of the king*, ✱S#7278h. **pray be-**fore the Lord. Heb. intreat the face of the Lord. Zc *8:21. Ex 32:11mg. 1 S 13:12. 1 K *8:28-30. 13:6. Je 26:19mg.

3. **speak**. Dt *17:9-11♪𝒫. 33:10♪𝒫. Ezk 44:23, 24. Ho 4:6. Hg 2:11. Ml *2:7. **Should**. ver. 5. Ne 8:9-11. 9:1-3. Ec 3:4. Is 22:12, 13. Jl 2:17. Mt 9:15. Ja *4:8-10. **fifth**. This was a fast for the burning of the temple, as that of the seventh month was for the death of Gedaliah; and seeing that the city and temple were in part rebuilt, they wished to know whether they should continue the observance of them. Zc 8:19. 2 K *25:8, 9. Je 52:12-14. **should I**. Is 58:3. Ml 3:14. **separating**. Zc 12:12-14. 1 C 7:5.

5. **When**. Is 58:5. **seventh**. Zc 8:19. 2 K 25:23, 25. Je 40:8. 41:1-4, 15-18. **seventy**. From the eleventh year of Zedekiah to the fourth of Darius Hystaspes are just seventy years. See on ver. 3. Zc 1:12. Je 25:11. **did**. ver. 6. Is 1:11, 12. *58:4-6. Ho *7:14. Mt 5:16-18. 6:2, 5, 16. 23:5. Ro 14:6-9, 17, 18. 1 C *10:31. 2 C *5:15. Col 3:23.

6. **did not ye eat for**. *or, be* not ye they that did eat for, etc. Dt 12:7. 14:26. 1 S +*16:7. 1 Ch 29:22. Je +*17:9, 10. Ho 8:13. 9:4. 1 C √10:31. *11:20, 21, 26-29. Col *3:17.

7. **Should ye not hear the words**. *or, Are* not *these* the words, etc. Is +*55:3, 6, 7. **cried**. Zc 1:3-6. Is *1:16-20. Je 7:5, 23. 36:2, 3. Ezk 18:30-32. Da *9:6-14. Ho 14:1-3. Am 5:14, 15. Mi +*6:6-8. Zp 2:1-3. **former**. Heb. the hand of the former. ver. 12mg. Hg +*1:1mg. **the south**. Heb. *Negeb*. Dt 34:3. Is +30:6. Je 17:26. 32:44. 33:13. **the plain**. Heb. *Shephelah*, ✱S#8219h. Low country, specifically the maritime plain, rendered "vale" (Dt 1:7. Jsh 10:40. 1 K 10:27. 2 Ch 1:15. Je 33:13); "valley" (Jsh 9:1. 11:2, 16. 12:8. 15:33. Jg 1:9. Je 32:44); "plain" (Je 17:26. Ob 19. Zc 7:7); "low plains" (1 Ch 27:28. 2 Ch 9:27); "low country" (2 Ch 26:10. 28:18).

9. **saying**. See on ver. 7. Zc 8:16, 17. Le +*19:15, 35-37. Dt 10:18, 19. +*15:7-14. 16:18-20. Ps 82:2-4. Pr *21:3. Is *58:6-10. Je 7:5-7, 23. Ezk 45:9. Ho 10:12, 13. Am 5:24. Mi +*6:8. Mt *23:23. Lk *11:42. Ja *2:13-17. **Execute true judgment**. Heb. Judge judgment of truth. ♪147D, Ge +1:29. Je 21:12mg. Jn 7:+*24, 51. **show mercy**. Mi +*6:8. Mt 23:23. Ja *1:27.

10. **oppress not**. Ex *22:21-24♪𝒫. 23:9. Dt +*24:14-18♪𝒫. 27:19. Ps 72:4. Pr *22:22, 23. 23:10, 11. Is *1:16, 17, 23. Je 5:28. 22:15-17. Ezk 22:7, 12, 29. Am 4:1. 5:11, 12. Mi 2:1-3. 3:1-4. Zp 3:1-3. Ml +*3:5. Mt 23:14. 1 C +*6:10. Ja +*5:4. **the widow**. Dt 14:29. 24:19-21. 26:12, 13. **fatherless**. Dt 10:17, 18. Ps 10:14. 68:5. 82:3. **stranger**. Ge 23:4 (✱S#1616h). Ex 12:48mg. Ezk 47:+22, 23. Ml 3:5. **poor**. Dt +*24:14. Ps +*12:5. Ezk +*16:49. **imagine evil**. Zc 8:17. Ps 21:11. *36:4. 140:2. Pr 3:29. 6:18. *23:7. Je 11:19, 20. 18:18. Mi *2:1. Mk +*7:21-23. Ja √1:14, 15. 1 J *3:15.

11. **refused to hearken**. ♪12, Ps +1:1. Zc 1:4. Ex 10:3. Dt +*28:15. 1 S +√25:17. 2 K 17:13-15. 2 Ch 33:10. Ne *9:17, 26, 29. Pr *1:●5, 24-32. ●2:2. Is *1:19, 20. Je 6:16, 17. *7:24. 13:10. 26:5, 6. +*29:19. 35:15. 36:31. *44:16. Ezk 3:7. Ho 4:16. Da 9:5. Zp 3:2. Ac 7:51. He 12:25. **pulled away the shoulder**. Heb. gave a backsliding shoulder. Dt *10:16. Ne 9:29. Je 8:5. Ho 4:16. +*9:15. He +*10:38, 39. **stopped**. Heb. made heavy. Ps 58:4, 5. Is 6:10. Ac 7:57.

12. **their hearts**. Ne 9:29. Jb 9:4. Is 48:4. Je 5:3. *7:23-26. Ezk 2:4. 3:7-9. *11:19. *36:26. **lest**. Ne *9:29,

30. Ps 50:17. Is 6:10. Mt 13:15. Mk 4:12. Lk 8:12. Jn √3:19, 20. Ac 28:27. 2 Th √2:10-12. **Lord of hosts.** Je +6:6. **sent.** Ne *9:30. Ac *7:51, 52. 1 P *1:11, 12. 2 P √1:21. **spirit.** Heb. *ruach,* Is +48:16. **by the former.** Heb. by the hand of the former. √121BB, Ezr +9:11. ver. 7mg. Hg +*1:1mg. **therefore.** 2 Ch *36:16. Je 26:19. Da +*9:11, 12. 1 Th 2:15, 16.

13. **as he cried.** Ps 81:8-12. Pr *1:24-28. Is 50:2. Je 6:16, 17. Lk 13:34, 35. 19:42-44. **so.** Pr 21:13. 28:9. Is *1:15. Je 11:11. 14:12. Ezk 14:3. 20:3. Mi 3:4. Mt 25:11, 12. Lk 13:25. Ja 4:3. **I would not hear.** Jb 27:9. Ps +*66:18. Mi 3:4. Jn +*9:31.

14. **scattered.** Zc 2:6. 9:14. Le 26:33. Dt *4:27. *28:33, 64. Ps 58:9. Is 17:13. 21:1. 66:15. Je 4:11, 12. 23:19. 25:32, 33. 30:23. 36:19. Ezk *36:19. Am 1:14. Na 1:3. Hab 3:14. **whom.** Dt 28:33, 49. Je 5:15. **the land.** Le *26:22\P. 2 Ch 36:21. Je 52:30. Da 9:16-18. Zp 3:6. **the pleasant land.** Heb. the land of desire. Zc 2:12. Ps *48:2. Je +3:19mg. Ezk *20:15. Da *8:9. Ho 9:3. Ml 3:12.

ZECHARIAH 8

Promises, that Jerusalem shall be replenished with inhabitants, and be prosperous, 1-8. The people are encouraged to build the temple, by the assurance of manifold blessings, 9-15. Exhortations to truth, justice, and piety, that their mournful fasts might be turned into cheerful feasts, 16-19. A prediction of the conversion of many nations, by the example and endeavors of pious Jews, 20-23.

2. **I was jealous.** Zc 1:14-16. Ex +*20:5. Ps 78:58, 59. Is 42:13, 14. 59:17. 63:4-6, 15. Ezk 36:5, 6. La 4:11, 12. Jl 2:18. Na *1:2, 6.

3. **I am.** Zc 1:16. Je 30:10, 11. **dwell.** Zc 2:10, 11. Ex 29:45\P. Is *12:6. La 4:22. Ezk *48:35. Jl *2:17. *3:17, 21. Jn *1:14. *14:23. 2 C 6:16. Ep *2:21, 22. Col *2:9. Re 21:3. **a city.** Zc 14:20, 21. Is *1:21, 26. 60:14. Je √31:23. 33:16. Ezk *48:35. **the mountain.** Is 2:2, 3. **the holy.** Is 11:9. *65:25. 66:20. Ezk 40:2. Mi *4:1. Re 21:10, 27.

4. **There.** 1 S 2:31. Jb 5:26. 42:17. Is √65:20-22. La 2:20, 21, etc. Ic 5:11-15. He 12:22. **streets.** broad or open places. S#7339h, Am 5:16n. **very age.** Heb. multitude of days. Jb 32:7. Ec 11:1.

5. **playing.** Zc 2:4. Ps 128:3, 4. 144:12-15. Je 30:19, 20. *31:27. 33:11. La 2:11, 19. Mt 11:16, 17.

6. **marvellous.** *or,* hard, *or* difficult. 2 S 13:2. **should.** √85C, Ge +18:14. Ge *18:14\P. Nu 11:22, 23. 2 K 7:2. Ps 90:4. Is *55:8-11. Je 32:17, 27. Lk 1:20, 37. *18:27. Ro *4:20, 21. 6:19-21.

7. **I will save.** Ps 107:2, 3. Is √11:11-16. 27:12, 13. *43:5, 6. 49:12. 59:19. 66:19, 20. Je 31:8. Ezk *37:19-25. Ho 11:10, 11. Am √9:14, 15. Ml 1:11. Ro 11:25-27. **east country.** Ps 50:1. 113:3. Is 43:5. 59:19. Ml 1:11. **west country.** Heb. country of the going down of the sun. This passage, in its full import, seems to refer to the future restoration of the Jews from their present long dispersion, in which many have settled in the western parts of the world. Dt 11:30. Ps 50:1. 113:3. Ml 1:11.

8. **and they shall dwell.** Je 3:17, 18. 23:8. 32:41. Ezk 37:25. Jl 3:20. Am √9:14, 15. Ob *17-21. Zp *3:14-20. **they shall be my.** Zc 13:9. Le 26:12. Je *4:2. *30:22. 31:1, 33. 32:38, 39. Ezk 11:20. 36:28. 37:27. Ho *2:19-23. 2 C 6:16-18. Re 21:3, 7. **in truth.** Je 4:2.

9. **Let.** ver. 13, 18. Jsh 1:6, 8. 1 Ch 22:13. 28:20. Is 35:4. Hg *2:4, etc. Ep *6:10. 2 T 2:1. **the prophets.** Ezr *5:1, 2. Hg *1:1, 12. 2:21. **foundation.** Hg 2:18.

10. **before.** Hg *1:6-11. 2:16-18. **there was no hire for man.** or, the hire of man became nothing, etc. **neither.** Jg 5:6, 7, 11. 2 Ch 15:5-7. Je 16:16. **for.** Is 19:2. Am +*3:6. 9:4. Mt 10:34-36.

11. **But now.** ver. 8, 9. Ps 103:9. Is 11:13. 12:1. Hg 2:19. Ml 3:9-11. **former days.** 1 K 4:20.

12. **the seed.** √12, Ps +1:1. Ge 26:12. Le 26:4, 5. Dt 28:3-12\P. Ps *67:6, 7. Pr *3:9, 10. Is 30:23. Ezk *34:26, 27. 36:30. Ho *2:21-23. Jl *2:22. Am √9:13-15. Hg *2:19. **prosperous.** Heb. of peace. Ps *72:3. Ja 3:18. **ground shall give.** Le 26:4, 20\P. Dt 11:17\P. Ps ◐78:46. *85:12. **the heavens.** Ge 27:28. Dt 32:2. 33:13, 28. 1 K 17:1. Pr 19:12. Ho 14:5. Hg 1:10. **the remnant.** ver. 6. Mi 4:6, 7. 1 C 3:21. **to possess.** Is 61:7. Ezk 36:12. Ob 17-20. Mt √6:33.

13. **a curse.** Dt 28:37. 29:23-28. 1 K 9:7, 8. 2 Ch 7:20-22. Ps 44:13, 14, 16. 79:4. Is 43:28. 65:15, 16. Je 24:9. 25:18. 26:6. 29:18. *42:18. 44:12, 22. La 2:15, 16. 4:15. Ezk 5:15. Da +*9:11. **O house.** Zc 1:19. 9:13. √10:6. 2 K 17:18-20. Is 9:20, 21. Je 32:30-32. 33:24. Ezk 37:11, 16-19. **ye shall.** The consideration that all nations who now worship the true God, and receive the Sacred Scriptures as His word, have derived the whole of their divine knowledge, under God, from Jewish prophets, apostles, and teachers, and that the Savior "in whom all nations shall be blessed," sprang from that favored race, emphatically explains what is meant by "ye shall be a blessing." The full accomplishment of this prediction, however, is probably reserved for the future restoration of the Jews. ver. 20-23. Zc 10:6-9. Ge *12:2, 3\P. 26:4. Ru 4:11, 12. Ps 72:17. Is *19:24, 25. Mi 5:7. Zp *3:20. Hg 2:19. Ga 3:14, 28, 29. **fear not.** ver. 9. Is 35:3, 4. 41:10-16. *43:5. 1 C 16:13. **be strong.** ver. +9.

14. **As.** Zc 1:6. Ps 33:11. Is 14:24. Je *31:28. **I repented not.** 2 Ch *36:16. Je 4:28. 15:1-6. 20:16. Ezk 24:14. Ja *1:17.

15. **have.** Nu 23:19. Je 29:11-14. 32:42. Ezk *39:25-29. Mi 4:10-13. *7:18-20. **fear.** ver. 13. Is 43:1, 2. Zp 3:16, 17. Lk 12:32.

16. **are.** Dt 10:12, 13. 11:7, 8. Is *1:16, 17. Mi +*6:8. Lk 3:8-14. Ep 4:17. 1 P 1:13-16. **Speak.** ver. 19. Zc 7:9. Le 19:11. Ps 15:2. Pr 12:17, 19. Je 9:3-5. Ho 4:1, 2. Mi 6:12. Ep \4:25. 1 Th 4:6. Re 21:8. **execute the judgment of truth and peace.** Heb. judge truth and the judgment of peace. Zc 7:9mg. Is +*9:7. 11:3-9. *32:17. Am 5:15, 24. Mt +*5:9. Jn +*7:24. **gates.** √171S7B, Ge +14:7.

17. **let.** Zc 7:10. Pr *3:29. 6:14. Je 4:14. Mi 2:1-3. Mt 5:28. 12:35. 15:19. Ep *4:25. **evil.** Is +*45:7. **love no false oath.** √175B, Ge +21:6. Zc +*5:3, 4. Le 6:3\P. 19:12\P. Je 4:2. Ml +*3:5. **things.** Ps 5:5, 6. 10:3. Pr *6:16-19. *8:13. Je *44:4. Hab 1:13.

19. **the fourth.** 2 K 25:3, 4. Je 39:2. *52:6, 7. **the fifth.** Zc 7:3. Je *52:12-15. **the seventh.** Zc 7:5. 2 K *25:25. Je 41:1-3. **the tenth.** Je *52:4. Ezk 24:1, 2. **joy.** Est 8:17. 9:22. Ps 30:11. Is 12:1. *35:10. 51:11. Je 31:12, 13. **feasts.** Heb. solemn, *or,* set times. Ge +17:21h. Le *23:2n. 2 K 4:16mg. **therefore.** ver. 16. Lk 1:74, 75. T *2:11, 12. Re 22:15.

20. **there.** Zc 2:11. 14:16, 17. 1 K 8:41, 43. 2 Ch 6:32, 33. Ps 22:27. 67:1-4. 72:17. 89:9. ch. 117. 138:4, 5. Is *2:2, 3. 11:10. 49:6, 22, 23. *60:3-12. 66:18-20.

Je 16:19. Ho 1:10. 2:23. Am 9:12. Mi *4:1, 2. Ml 1:11. Mt +*8:11. Jn 12:20, 21. Ac 8:27. 15:14-18. Ro 15:9-12. Re 11:15.

21. **saying.** ♪56, Is +14:16. **Let.** Ps ch. 122. **speedily.** *or,* continually. Heb. going. ♪147B, Ge +2:16. Ho 6:3. Is *2:3. Jon 1:11mg. Mi *4:2. **pray before the Lord.** Heb. intreat the face of the Lord. Zc 7:2mg. **I will.** Ps 103:22. 146:1, 2.

22. **many people.** Is 25:7. 55:5. 56:7. 60:3, etc. *66:23. Je 4:2. Mi 4:3. Hg 2:7. Ga 3:8. Re *15:4. 21:24. **to pray.** Mk 11:17.

23. **ten men.** Ge 31:7, 41. Nu 14:22. Jb 19:3. Ec 11:2. Mi +*5:5. Mt 18:21, 22. **out.** Is 66:18. Ac 2:9-11. Re 7:9, 10. 14:6, 7. **take.** 1 S 15:27, 28. Is 3:6. 4:1. Lk 8:44. Ac 19:12. **We will.** Nu 10:29-32. Ru 1:16, 17. 2 S 15:19-22. 2 K 2:6. 1 Ch 12:18. Is *55:5. *60:3. Ac +*13:47, 48. **we have.** Ge 30:27. Nu 14:14-16. Dt 4:6, 7. Jsh 2:9-13. 1 K 8:42, 43. 1 C 14:25.

ZECHARIAH 9

Predictions of judgments on the Syrians, Tyrians, and Philistines; with intimations of mercy to a remnant, and promises of protection to the Jews, 1-8; of Christ's coming to Jerusalem, riding on an ass's colt; and of the nature, extent, and benefits of his kingdom, and of the blood of his covenant, 9-11; of the victories obtained by the sons of Zion against the forces of Antichrist; their privileges, and their joy in the goodness and beauty of the Lord, 12-17.

1. Cir. A.M. 3494. B.C. 510. **burden.** That is, "The burden of the word of the Lord shall fall and rest on the land of Hadrach (probably Caelo-Syria) and Damascus;" which was fulfilled by Alexander, who seized on immense treasures in that city. Is 13:1. Je 23:33-38. Ml 1:1. **Hadrach.** i.e. *spherical, round,* ✱S#2317h. **Damascus.** Ge 14:15. Is 7:8, 9. 17:1-3. Je *49:23-27. Am 1:3-5. 3:12. 3:12. **the rest.** Zc 5:4. Is 9:8, etc. **when.** Zc *8:20-23. 2 Ch *20:12. Ps 25:15. 123:1, 2. 145:15. Is 17:7, 8. 45:20-22. 52:10. Je 16:19. *32:19, 20. Mt +*24:30. Re +*1:7. **the eyes.** ♪142, Ge +20:16. **of.** ♪181E, Ge +3:24.

2. **Hamath.** That is, Hamath and Tyre, which border upon Hadrach and Damascus, "shall share their burden"; which was accomplished when Alexander conquered Tyre, Syria, and Phoenicia. Nu 13:21. 2 K 23:33. 25:21. Je 49:23. Am 6:14. **Tyrus.** Is ch. 23. Ezk ch. 26-28. Jl 3:4-8. Am 1:9, 10. **Zidon.** 1 K 17:9. Ezk 28:21-26. Ob 20. **it be very wise.** Ezk 28:3-5, 12.

3. **build.** Jsh 19:29. 2 S 24:7. **heaped.** 1 K 10:27. Jb 22:24. 27:16. Is 23:8. Ezk 27:33. 28:4, 5. **as the dust.** ♪102B, ♪138B, Ge +13:16. **fine gold.** Pr 3:14.

4. **the Lord.** Pr 10:2. 11:4. Is 23:1-7. Ezk 28:16. Jl 3:8. **he will.** Ezk 26:17. 27:26-36. 28:2, 8. **shall.** Ezk 28:18. Am 1:10.

5. **Ashkelon.** Is 14:29-31. Je 47:1, 4-7. Ezk 25:15-17. Zp 2:4-7. Ac 8:26. **Gaza.** Am *1:6-8. Zp 2:4. **and be.** Je 51:8, 9. Ezk 26:15-21. Re 18:9-11, 15-17. **for.** Is 20:5, 6. Ro 5:5. Ph 1:20.

6. **a bastard.** Dt 23:2. Ec 2:18-21. 6:2. Is 2:12-17. 23:9. 28:1. Da *4:37. Am 1:8. Zp 2:10. He 12:8. 1 P 5:5. **Ashdod.** Ne 13:23-25. Zp 2:7. **Philistines.** Je 47:1, etc.

7. **I will.** 1 S 17:34-36. Ps 3:7. 58:6. Am 3:12. **blood.** Heb. bloods. Ge +4:10mg. 2 K +9:26mg. Ho 4:2mg.

out of his mouth. Ps 16:4. Ezk 33:25. **abominations.** 2 K 23:24. 1 Ch 15:8mg. Is 66:3. Je 4:1. 7:30. Da +*9:27. 11:31. 12:11. Ho 9:10. **from between his teeth.** Ps 58:6. Am 3:12. **he that remaineth.** Pusey (*Minor Prophets,* vol ii. p. 399, 400) states "better, 'And he too shall remain over to our God.' Of the Philistines too, as of Israel, *a remnant shall be saved.* After this visitation their idolatry should cease; God speaks of the Philistine nation as one man; He would wring his idol-sacrifices and idol-enjoyments from him; he should exist as a nation, but as God's." Compare the predictions of the Millennial restoration of the site of Sodom (Ezk 16:53n, 55), and of Moab, etc., (Je 48:47n). Zc *8:23. Jg 1:21. Is *11:12-14. 19:23-25. Je 48:47. 49:6, 39. Ezk 12:57-61. **a governor.** Zc 12:5, 6. Is 49:22, 23. 60:14-16. Je 13:21. Mi +*5:2. Ga 3:28. **a Jebusite.** 2 S 24:16-23. 1 K *9:20, 21. 1 Ch 11:4-6. 21:15-30. 22:1. Is 11:14.

8. **I will.** Zc 2:5. 12:8. Ge 32:1, 2. Ps *34:7. 46:1-5. 125:1, 2. Is 4:5. 26:1. 31:5. 33:20-22. 52:12. Jl +*3:16, 17. Re 20:9. **mine house.** ♪121.O. Metonymy of the Adjunct, Ge +28:22. "House" put by Metonymy for the land and people among whom God dwells in his Temple at Jerusalem. Je 12:7. Ho 8:1. 9:15. **because of him that passeth by.** 2 K 23:29. 24:1. Je 46:2, 13. Da 11:6, 7, 10-16, 27-29, √40-45. **no oppressor.** Zc *14:11. Ps *72:4. Is *52:1. √54:14. *60:18. Je 31:12. Ezk *28:24, 25. 39:29. Am √9:15. Re *20:1-3. **for now.** Zc *4:10. Ex 3:7, 9. 2 S 16:12. 2 Ch *16:9. Ac 7:34.

9. **Rejoice.** Zc 2:10. Ps 97:6-8. Is *12:6. 40:9. 52:9, 10. 62:11. Zp 3:14, 15. **daughter.** ♪155E5, Nu +21:25. **behold.** Ps *2:6. 45:1. *110:1-4. Is +*9:6, 7. 32:1, 2. Je +*23:5, 6. *30:9. Mt 21:4, 5. Mk 11:9, 10. Lk *19:37, 38. Jn *1:49. 12:13-15. 19:15. **thy King.** Mt ✱21:1-5. **cometh unto.** Mi ◐+5:2. Mt ▶21:5. Jn ▶12:15. 1 Th=5:2, 3. 2 Th=2:8. **he is just.** T#1917. 2 S 23:3. Ps 34:19, 21. +*45:6, 7. 85:9-12. Is 41:2. *45:21. *53:11. Je *23:5. Mt *1:21. 27:19-24. Lk 1:17. 23:47. Jn 7:18. Ac ✱3:14. 7:52. 22:14. Ro *3:24-26. Ja 5:6. 1 P 2:22. 1 J *2:1, 29. **having salvation.** *or,* saving himself. i.e. *showing himself a Savior.* Ps 33:16. Is 63:5. **lowly.** Ps 22:24. Is 53:4, 7. Mt 11:29. 21:5-7. Mk 11:7. Lk 19:30-35. Jn 12:14-16. **riding upon.** T#1912. Jg 5:10. 10:4. 12:14. 2 S 13:29. 16:2. 17:23. 18:9. 19:26. 1 K 1:33, 38, 44. ◐10:25-29. 13:13, 23, 27. Ec 10:7. Je 17:25. 22:19. Jn ✱12:12-16. **the foal.** Mt 21:1, 2. There is an unannounced time gap between this prophecy and that which is contained in the next verse. For other instances of unannounced prophetic time gaps, see Is 61:2n.

10. **I will.** Ho *1:7. +*2:18. Mi *5:10, 11. Hg 2:22. 2 C *10:4, 5. **cut off.** Zc 14:12-15. Is 63:1-6. Jl 2:2-11, 20. 3:2, 9-16. Re 19:11-21. **the battle.** Zc 10:4, 5. **he shall speak peace.** Ps *46:9. 47:3. 72:3, 7, 17. 85:8. Is +*9:6, 7. 11:10. 49:6. 57:18, 19. Mi 4:2-4. +*5:5. Ac 10:36. Ro 15:9-13. 2 C 5:18, 20. Ep *2:13-17. Col *1:20, 21. **unto the heathen.** Zc 14:16-21. Is *2:2-4. 11:4-12. 35:1-8. *65:20-25. Lk 1:32, 33. Re 20:1-10. **his dominion.** Ps *2:8-12. ▶72:8-11. 98:1-3. Is +*9:6, 7. 60:12. Mi *5:4. Re *11:15. **from the river.** Ge 15:18. Ex 23:31. Dt 11:24. 1 K 4:21. Is +*27:12.

11. **As for thee.** Dt 5:31. 2 S 13:13. 2 Ch 7:17. Da 2:29. **by the blood of thy covenant.** *or,* whose covenant *is* by blood. Ex 24:5-8)℗. Mt 26:28. Mk 14:24. Lk 22:20. 1 C 11:25. He 9:10-26. 10:29. 13:20. **I have.** Ps 69:33. 102:19-21. 107:10-16. Is 42:7, 22. 49:9. 51:14.

53:12. 61:1. Lk 4:18. Ac 26:17, 18. Col 1:13, 14. **out of.** Ge 37:24)𝒫. Jb *33:24. Ps 30:3. *40:2. Is *38:17. *51:14. Je 38:6. Lk 16:24. Re 20:3. **pit.** Heb. *bor,* Ge +37:20.

12. **Turn you.** Is +*26:20, 21. 52:2. Je 31:6. 50:4, 5, 28. 51:10. Jl 3:16. Mi 4:8. Na 1:7. He *6:18. **strong hold.** Heb. *bizzaron,* only here. A safe because inaccessible place (CB). 2 K 14:7n. Je 49:16n. Ezk 35:9n. Ob +*3. **prisoners of hope.** Ps 119:49. Is *42:7. *49:9. *61:1. **even.** Is 38:18. 49:9. Je 31:17. La 3:21, 22. Ezk 37:11. Ho +*2:15. **I will render double.** ✸121L9, Ge +43:12. i.e. a prosperity and blessing double what was possessed before. The firstborn's share (CB). Jb +*42:10. Pr 1:23. Is +*40:2. +*61:7.

13. **When.** Zc 12:8. **bent Judah.** Zc 1:21. 10:3-7. 12:2-8. Mi +*5:4-9. Re 17:14. **and raised up.** Ps +*149:2-9. La 4:2. Am 2:11. Ob +*21. **against thy.** Da +*8:21-25. +*11:32-24. Jl *3:6-8. Mi 4:2, 3. Mk 16:15-20. Ro 15:16-20. 1 C 1:21-28. 2 C 10:3-5. 2 T 4:7. **O Greece.** i.e. *hot and active,* ✸S#3120h. Ge 10:+2 (Javan), 4. Is 66:19. Ezk 27:13. Da 8:21. 11:2. Jl 2:6. **made thee.** Zc 12:8. Ps 18:32-35. 45:3. 144:1. *149:6. Is 41:15, 16. 49:2. Ep 6:17. He +*4:12. Re 1:16. 2:12. 19:15, 21.

14. **seen over them.** Zc 2:5. 12:8. √14:1-5. Ex 14:24, 25. Jsh 10:11-14, 42. Is √31:5. *63:1-6. Jl 2:11. Mt 28:20. Ac 4:10, 11. Ro 15:19. 2 Th √1:7-10. He 2:4. Ju *14, *15. Re *11:15. 19:11-21. **his arrow.** ✸22D5B, Dt +32:23. Ps 18:14. 45:3-5. 77:17, 18. 144:5, 6. Is 30:30. Re 6:2. **as the lightning.** Mt +*24:27. **blow the trumpet.** Jsh 6:4, 5. Is 18:3. *27:13. Jl *2:1, 15. Mt +*24:31. 2 C 10:4, 5. 1 Th *4:16. Re 10:7. *11:15. **whirlwinds.** Is 21:1. +*66:15.

15. **defend them.** Zc *12:8. Is √31:5. *37:35. **they shall devour.** Zc 10:5. 12:6. *14:14. Mi *5:8. Re 19:13-21. **subdue.** 1 S 17:45-51. 1 C 1:18, 25. **with sling stones.** or, with the stones of the sling. Jb 41:28, 29. 1 S 17:49. +*25:29. **shall drink.** ver. 17. Zc 10:7. Ps 78:65. SS 1:4. 5:1. 7:9. Is 55:1. Ac 2:13-18. Ep +*5:18. **wine.** Heb. *yayin,* Hab 2:5n. **filled like bowls.** or, fill both the bowls, etc. Zc 14:20. Ex 27:3. 38:3. Nu 4:14. 1 K +7:40. Je 52:18. Am *6:6. **the corners.** Ex 27:2. Le 1:5, 11. 4:7, 18, 25. **the altar.** Dt 12:27. Am +9:1.

16. **shall save.** Ps 100:3. Is 40:10, 11. Je 23:3, 4. Ezk 34:22-26, 31. Mi 5:4, 5. 7:14. Lk 12:32. Jn √10:27-30. 1 P 5:2-4. **as the flock.** Jn *10:11. **as the stones.** Is 62:3. Hg 2:23. Ml *3:17. **lifted.** Zc *8:23. Is 10:18. *11:10-12. 60:3, 14. Zp 3:20.

17. **how great is his goodness.** Ps *23:6. *31:19. *33:5. 36:7-9. 86:5, 15. 145:7, 8. Is 63:7, 15. Jn √3:16. Ro √5:8, 20, 21. Ep *1:7, 8. 2:4, 5. 3:18, 19. T 3:4-7. 1 J *4:8-11. **how great is his beauty.** Ex 15:11. Ps 45:2. 50:2. 90:17. SS 2:3, 4. 5:10-16. Is 33:17. Jn *1:14. 2 C 4:4-6. Re *5:12-14. **corn.** Is 62:8, 9. 65:13, 14. Ezk 36:29. Ho 2:21, 22. Jl 2:26. 3:18. Am 8:11-14. *9:13, 14. Ep *5:18, 19. **cheerful.** or, grow, or speak. SS 7:9. **new wine.** Heb. *tirosh,* Ge +27:28. **maids.** Ge +24:16 (✸S#1330h).

ZECHARIAH 10

An exhortation to seek and expect rain, and other blessings from God; as the distresses of the people had arisen from idols, false teachers, and corrupt rulers, 1-3. Messiah represented by the cornerstone, tent peg, and battle bow, 4. Promises to the Jews of triumph over enemies, 5; extraordinary assistance, reflected in deliverance from world-wide dispersion, restoration to the land of Israel, and growth in number, 6-11; their ultimate spiritual restoration to the Lord, 12.

1. **Ask ye.** Ezk 36:37. Mt *7:7, 8. Jn *16:23, 24. Ja *5:16-18. **rain in.** Dt *11:13. 28:23, 24. 1 K 17:1. 18:41-45. Is 5:6. 30:23. Je 14:22. Ezk 34:26. Am 4:7. Ml 3:10. **the time.** Dt *11:14)𝒫. Jb 29:23. Pr 16:15. Ho +*6:3. Jl +*2:23, 24. Ja *5:7. **latter rain.** Je 3:3. 5:24, 25. **bright clouds.** or, lightnings. Jb 36:27-31. 37:1-6. Je 10:13. 51:16. **and give.** Ps 65:9-13. 72:6. 104:13, 14. Is 44:3-5. Ezk 34:26. Ho 10:12. Mi 5:7. 1 C 3:6, 7.

2. **the idols.** Heb. the *teraphims.* Ge +31:19mg. Jg *17:5. 18:14. Is 44:9, 10. 46:5-7. Je 10:8-14. 14:22. Ezk 21:21mg. Ho 3:4. Hab *2:18. **the diviners.** Is +44:25. Je *23:25-27. 27:9. 29:8, 21, 22. La 2:14. Ezk 13:6-16, 22, 23. 21:29. Mi 3:6-11. **false dreams.** Je +*23:28n. √29:8. **they comfort.** Jb 13:4. 21:34. Je 6:14. 8:11. 14:13, 14. 23:17. 28:4-6, 15. 37:19. **therefore.** Je 13:17-20. 50:17. 51:23. Mi 2:12. **a flock.** Is 14:9. Je 51:40. **troubled, because there.** or, answered that there. Nu 27:17. 1 K *22:17. Ezk *34:5, 8. Mt *9:36. Mk 6:34.

3. **anger.** Zc 11:5-8, 17. Is 56:9-12. Je 10:21. 23:1, 2. 50:6. Ezk *34:2, 7, 10, etc. **and I.** Ezk *34:16, 17, 20, 21. Mt *25:31-33, 41. **punished.** Heb. visited upon. Is 10:12mg. 24:21mg. Je +11:22mg. 25:12mg. Zp 1:8mg. **visited.** Ex 4:31. Ru 1:6. Zp 2:7. Lk 1:68, 78. 1 P 2:12. **as.** Pr 21:31. SS *1:9.

4. **of him came forth.** Zc 1:20, 21. 9:13-16. 12:6-8. Nu 24:17. Is 41:14-16. 49:2. 54:16. Je 1:18, 19. *30:21. Mi +*5:5-8. Mt 9:38. 2 C √10:4, 5. Ep *4:8-11. *6:10-17. 2 T 2:4, 5. He *7:14. Re 17:14. 19:13-15. **the corner.** 1 S 14:38mg. Is 19:13mg. *28:16. Mt *21:42. Ep *2:20. **the nail.** Ezr 9:8. Is √22:23-25. **the battle bow.** ✸17I11, Ps +44:6. Zc 9:8, 10. Ge 49:24. Re *6:2.

5. **as mighty.** Zc 9:13. 12:8. 1 S 16:18. 2 S 23:8. Ps 45:3. *76:1-4. Lk 24:19. Ac 7:22. 18:24. 2 C 10:4. **tread.** Ps *18:42. Is 10:6. 25:10. *63:6. Mi 7:10. Mt 4:3. **streets.** Am +5:16n (✤S#2351h). **because.** Zc 14:3, 13, 14. Dt 20:1. Jsh 10:14, 42. Is 8:9, 10. 41:12, 13. *42:13. Jl 3:12-17. Mt 28:20. Ro 8:31-37. 2 T 4:7, 17. Re 19:13-15. **and the riders on horses shall be confounded.** or, they shall make the riders on horses ashamed. Zc 12:4. Ps 20:7, 8. 33:16, 17. Ezk 38:15. 39:18-20. Hg 2:22. Re 19:17, 18.

6. **I will strengthen.** ver. 12. Ps 89:21, 22. Is 41:10. Ezk 37:16. Ob +*18-21. Mi 4:6, 7, 18. *5:8, 9. 7:16, 17. Zp 3:19, 20. **I will save.** Zc 8:7, 8. Je 3:18. +*23:6-8. 31:1, 31. 33:24-26. 46:27, 28. 50:4, 5. Ezk 39:25. Ho 1:11. Ro 11:25, 26. **bring them.** Ezk *37:19-22. **for I have mercy.** Is 14:1. Je 31:20. +*33:26. Ho 1:7. 2:23. 14:4-8. Mi +*7:18-20. Na *1:7. Ro 11:32. **as though.** Zc 8:11. Is *30:26. 49:17-21. +*54:7-10. 60:14-17. *61:7. Je 30:18-20. Ezk +*36:11. Jl +*2:25. Zp *3:15. Ro 11:15. **for I am.** Zc *13:9. Is 41:17-20. *65:23, 24. Je *33:2, 3. Ezk *36:37.

7. **and their.** Zc 9:15, 17. Ge 43:34. Ps 104:15. Pr 31:6, 7. Ac 2:13-18. Ep +*5:18, 19. **yea.** Ge +*18:19. Ps 90:16. 102:28. Is 38:19. Je 32:39. Ac 2:39. 13:33. **their heart.** 1 S 2:1. Ps 13:5. 28:7. Is 66:14. Hab 3:18. Zp 3:14. Lk 1:47. Jn 16:22. Ac 2:26. Ph 4:4. 1 P 1:8. **as through.** Ps 104:15. **wine.** Heb. *yayin,* Hab 2:5n.

8. **hiss.** ✸22C6, Is +5:26. Is 5:26. 7:18. 11:11, 12. 27:12, 13. +*55:1-3. Mt *11:28. Re 22:17. **gather.** Ezk

+20:34. 22:20. **for.** Zc 9:11. Ex *15:13. Ps 106:10. *107:1-3. Is 44:22. 47:4. 51:11. 52:1-3. Je 31:10, 11. 1 T 2:4-6. Re 14:3, 4. **and they.** Ex *1:7. 1 K 4:20. Is *49:19-22. Je 30:19, 20. 33:22. Ezk *36:10, 11, 37, 38. Ho 1:10.

9. **sow.** Est 8:17. Je *31:27. Da ch. 3-6. Ho +*2:23. Am +*9:9. Mi *5:7. Ac 8:1, 4. 11:19-21. ch. 13, 14, etc. Ro 11:11-15. **remember.** Dt *30:1-4)ℙ. 1 K 8:47, 48. Ne 1:9. Je 51:50. Ezk 6:9. **live.** Is 65:9, 23. Ac *2:38, 39. 3:25, 26. 13:32, 33. Ro 11:16, 17, 24.

10. **bring them again.** Dt *30:3, 5)ℙ. **out of the.** Zc 8:7. Is √11:11-16. 19:23-25. 27:12, 13. Ho *11:11. Mi *7:11, 12. **into.** Je 22:6. Ezk 47:18-21. Ob 20. Mi 7:14. **place.** Is *49:19-21. 54:2, 3. 60:22.

11. **he shall.** Ps 66:10-12. Is *11:15, 16. 42:15, 16. *43:2. **with affliction.** T#381. Zc 12:2, 3, 6, 9. 13:8, 9. 14:1-3, 12-16, 20. Ge +6:13 (T#566). Ps +37:9 (T#87). +58:11 (T#630). 124:1-5. Is 11:14. +24:4 (T#86). Je *30:7, 11. Ezk 20:33-37. 38:8-12, 16, 21, 22. +39:23 (T#486). Jl *3:1, 2, 12, 17. Mi √4:11-13. **smite.** Ex 14:21, 22, 27, 28. Jsh 3:15-17. 2 K 2:8, 14. Ps 77:16-20. 114:3, 5. Is 11:15, 16. Re 16:12. **deeps of the river.** Na +3:8n. **the pride.** Ezr 6:22. Is *10:24-27. *14:25. *30:31. Mi +*5:5, 6. **the scepter.** Ezk 29:14-16. *30:13, 20, 21. 31:1, etc. 32:1, etc.

12. **I will.** ver. 6. Zc 12:5. Ps 68:34, 35. Is 41:10. 45:24. Ep *6:10. Ph √4:13. 2 T 2:1. **walk.** Ge *5:24)ℙ. 6:9)ℙ. 17:1)ℙ. 24:40. Is 2:5. Mi *4:5. +*6:8. Col *2:6. 3:17. 1 Th 2:12. 4:1. 1 J 1:6, 7.

ZECHARIAH 11

The destruction of Jerusalem, the temple, and the Jewish rulers, 1-3. Under the type of Zechariah is shown Christ's care of his flock, and the people's hatred of him, 4-7. The rejection of the nation, for ingratitude and contempt of Christ, is denoted, by his breaking the two staves, called Beauty and Bands, 8-14. The emblem and curse of a foolish, or "idol shepherd," 15-17.

1. **O Lebanon.** ♪38G, Dt +32:1. Zc 10:10. Je 22:6, 7, 23. Hab 2:8, 17. Hg 1:8. **that.** Zc 14:1, 2. Dt 32:22. Mt *24:1, 2. Lk 19:41-44. *21:23, 24.

2. **Howl.** Is *2:12-17. 10:33, 34. 14:8. Ezk 17:3, 22-24. 31:2, 3, 17, 18. Am 6:1, 2. Na 3:8, etc. Lk 23:31. **fir tree.** ♪38G, Dt +32:1. **mighty.** *or,* gallants. **for.** Is 32:15-19. Ezk 20:46-48. **forest of the vintage.** *or,* defenced forest. Je +33:3mg.

3. **a voice.** ver. 8, 15-17. Je *25:34-36. Jl 1:13. Am 8:8. Zp 1:10, 11. Mt +*15:14. *23:13-33. Ja *5:1-6. **for their.** 1 S 4:21, 22. Is 65:15. Je 7:4, 11-14. 26:6. Ezk 24:21-25. Ho 1:9, 10. 10:5. Zp 3:11. Mt 3:7-10. 21:43-45. Ac 6:11-14. 22:21, 22. Ro 11:7-12. **a voice.** Ps 22:21. Je 2:30. Ezk *19:3-6. Zp 3:3. Mt 23:31-38. Ac 7:52. **for the pride.** Je +*12:5. *49:19. 50:44.

4. **Lord.** Zc 14:5. Is 49:4, 5. Jn 20:17. Ep 1:3. **Feed.** ver. 7. Is 40:9-11. Ezk 31:23, 24. Mi *5:4. Mt 15:24. 23:37. Lk 19:41-44. Jn 21:15-17. Ro *8:36. 15:8. 1 C 15:31, 32.

5. **possessors.** Je 23:1, 2. Ezk 22:25-27. 34:2, 3, 10. Mi 3:1-3, 9-12. Mt 23:14. Jn 16:2. **hold.** Je *2:3. *50:7. **sell.** Ge 37:26-28. 2 K 4:1. Ne 5:8. Mt 21:12, 13. 2 P 2:3. Re 18:13. **Blessed.** Dt *29:19-21. Ho *12:8. 1 T +*6:5-10. **I am rich.** Ps +*62:10. 1 T +*6:9. Re √3:17. **and their.** Ezk 34:4, 6, 18, 19, 21. Jn *10:1, 12, 13.

6. **no more pity.** ver. 5. Is 27:11. +54:7. Ezk 8:18.

9:10. Ho 1:6. Mt 18:33-35. *22:7. *23:35-38. Lk *19:43, 44. *21:22-24. 1 Th *2:16. He √10:26-31. Ja *2:13. **deliver.** Heb. make to be found. ver. 9, 14. Zc 8:10. Is 3:5. 9:19-21. Je 13:14. Mi 7:2-7. Hg 2:22. Mt 10:21, 34-36. 24:10. Lk 12:52, 53. 21:16, 17. **into the hand.** Da +*9:26, 27. Mt *22:7. Jn 19:15. **they shall.** Ml 4:6. **and out.** Ps 50:22. Is *2:19. Ezk *9:5. Ho 2:10. Mi *5:8. 6:14. He *2:3. *10:26, 27.

7. **I will.** ver. 4, 11. Zc 13:8, 9. **even you, O poor.** *or, verily* the poor. Is 11:4. 61:1. Je 5:4, 5. Zp *3:12. Mt 11:5. Mk 12:37. 1 C *1:26. Ja *2:5. **staves.** ver. 10, 14. Le 27:32. 1 S 17:40, 43. Ps 23:4. **one.** Ps ch. 133. Ezk 37:16-23. Jn 17:21-23. **Bands.** *or,* Binders. Jn *10:16. Ep *2:13-16. **I fed.** Ps *23:1. Is 40:11. Jn *10:11. 14:16. He *13:20. 1 P *5:4.

8. **in.** Ho 5:7. Mt *23:34-36. *24:50, 51. **and my.** Le 26:11, 30, 44. Dt 32:19. Ps 5:5. 78:59. 106:40. Je 12:8. 14:21. Ho 9:15. He 10:38. **soul.** Heb. *nephesh,* Ge +34:3. **lothed them.** Heb. was straitened for them. Is 49:7. Lk 12:50. 19:14. Jn 7:7. 15:18, 23-25. **soul.** Heb. *nephesh,* Ge +34:3.

9. **I will.** Je 23:33, 39. Mt 13:10, 11. *23:38, 39. Jn *8:21, 24. 12:35. Ac 13:46, 47. 28:26-28. **that that dieth.** Ps 69:22-28. Je 15:2, 3. 43:11. Mt +*15:14. 21:19. Re +*22:11. **and let.** Dt 28:53-56. Is 9:19-21. Je 19:9. Ezk 5:10. **another.** Heb. his fellow, *or,* neighbor.

10. **Beauty.** ver. 7. Ps 50:2. 90:17. Ezk 7:20-22. *24:21. Da +*9:26. Lk *21:5, 6, 32. Ac 6:13, 14. Ro 9:3-5. **that.** Nu 14:34. 1 S 2:30. Ps 89:39. Je 14:21. 31:31, 32. Ezk 16:59-61. Ho 1:9. Ga 3:16-18. He 7:17-22. 8:8-13.

11. **broken.** Is 53:5, 10. **so,** etc. *or,* the poor of the flock, etc., certainly knew. **poor.** ver. 7. Ps 69:33. 72:12-14. Is 14:32. Zp 3:12. Lk 7:22. *19:48. Ja *2:5, 6. **that waited upon.** *or,* were watching me. 1 S 1:12. 19:11. Ps 59:t. Is 8:17. 26:8, 9. 40:31. Lk 3:25, 26. Mi 7:7. Lk 2:25, 38. *23:48, 51. Ac 1:21, 22. **knew.** ver. 6. Le 26:38, etc. Dt 28:49, etc. 31:21, 29. 32:21-42. Lk 24:49-53. Jn *6:68, 69. Ro 11:7, etc. Ja *5:1-6.

12. **ye think good.** Heb. *it be* good in your eyes. 1 K 21:2mg. 2 Ch 30:4mg. **give.** Mt 26:15. Jn 13:2, 27-30. **So.** Ge 37:28. Ex *21:32)ℙ. Mt ✱26:15. Mk 14:10, 11. Lk 22:3-6. **thirty pieces.** T#1928. Mt ✱26:14, 15.

13. **Cast it.** ♪60A, Ge +3:22. T#1929. Note how specific this amazing prophecy is: the money obtained was to (1) be cast down to the potter; (2) be silver; (3) be precisely thirty pieces; (4) be thrown down, (5) in the house of the Lord. Ge 21:15. 2 Ch 24:10. Is 54:7-10. Mt ✱27:3-10, 12. Ac 1:18, 19. **the potter.** Je 18:2. Mt ✱27:7. **a goodly price.** ♪27, Ge +3:22. Is 53:2, 3. Ac 4:11.

14. **I cut.** ver. 9. Ge +*49:10. Is 9:21. 11:13. Ezk *37:16-20. Mt 24:10. Jn *11:49, 51, 52. Ac 23:7-10. Ga 5:15. Ja 3:14, 16. 4:1-3. **Bands.** *or,* Binders. ver. 7.

15. **foolish shepherd.** Ps 14:1. Is 56:10-12. Je 2:26, 27. La 2:14. Ezk 13:3. Da +*7:24-26. +*9:27. Mt +*15:14. 23:17. *24:15. Lk 11:40. Jn √5:43. 2 Th √2:4-8, 10-12. Re *13:1-10.

16. **which.** Je 23:2, 22. Ezk 34:2-6, 16. Mt *7:15, 16. *23:2-4, 13-29. Lk 12:45, 46. Jn 10:12, 13. **cut off.** *or,* hidden. ver. 8, 9. Ps +*83:3, 4. Da 11:41. Zp +*2:3. Re +*12:6, 14. **neither.** Ge 33:13. 1 S 17:34, 35. Is 40:11. **feed.** *or,* bear. Am 7:10. Ac *20:28-30.

but. Ge 31:38. Is *56:11. Ezk 34:10, 21. Jn *10:1.

17. **Woe**. 1 K 13:30. Is 1:4. 17:12. 28:1. Je 22:18. 23:1. Ezk 13:3. 34:2. Am 5:18. Hab 2:6. Mt *23:13, 16. Lk 11:42-52. 2 Th √2:8-10. Re 19:20. 20:10. **idol shepherd**. Jb 13:4. Is 9:15. 44:10. Je *23:32. 1 C *8:4. 10:19, 20. **that leaveth**. Jn *10:12, 13. **the sword**. Is 6:9, 10. 29:10. 42:19, 20. Je 50:35-37. Ho 4:5-7. Am 8:9, 10. Mi 3:6, 7. Jn 9:39. 12:40. Ro 11:7. Re *13:10-12. **his arm**. 1 S 2:31. 1 K 13:4. Ezk 30:22-24. **utterly darkened**. Ge 27:1. Dt 34:7. Jb 17:7.

ZECHARIAH 12

Jerusalem shall be made a cup of trembling, and a burdensome stone, to all her enemies, 1-5. The Jews shall be marvelously strengthened, sanctified, and prospered, 6-8. "In that day," the pouring out of the Spirit of grace shall cause them to look, with deep repentance, on him whom they had pierced, 9-14.

1. Cir. A.M. 3594. B.C. 500. **burden**. Zc 9:1. Is 14:28. 15:1. 17:1. La 2:14. Ezk 12:10. Na 1:1. Ml 1:1. **for Israel**. Is 51:22, 23. Je 30:10, 16. 50:34. Ezk 36:5-7. Jl 3:19-21. Ob 16, 17. **which stretcheth**. The omnipotence of Jehovah is the guarantee that His word will be carried out (CB). Jb 26:7. Ps 102:25, 26. *104:2-4. 136:5, 6. Is 40:12, 22. 42:5. 44:24. 45:12, 18. 48:13. 51:13. Je 10:12. 51:15. He 1:10-12. **and layeth**. Ps 24:2. 102:25. 104:2-5. Am 4:8, 13. **formeth**. F. W. Grant notes "Thus, along with the formation of the heavens and the earth, as of equal importance with these (the body being moreover passed over in the matter) there is put by the inspired writer this formation of the spirit of man. And this is the complete upsetting of the materialistic theory. The spirit of man is *formed* within him. It is a separate entity then in each individual man, not (like the breath of life) a common principle shared by all" (*Facts and Theories as to a Future State*, ch. iv. p. 48). Ge +*2:7》𝒫. Nu 16:22》𝒫. *27:16n. Jb 12:10. +*14:22. 27:3. +*34:14. Ps 51:10. +*146:4. Ec +*12:7. Is 42:5. 43:7. 44:24. *57:16. Je 38:16. Ezk +*18:4n, +*20n. Da 5:23. Am 4:13mg. Ac 17:25, 28. 1 C √2:11. He +*12:9, 23. **spirit**. Heb. *ruach*, Nu +16:22.

2. **a cup**. Ps 75:8. Is √51:17, 22, 23. Je *25:15, 17. 49:12. 51:7. La 4:21. Hab 2:16. Re 14:10. 16:19. 18:6, 20, 24. **trembling**. *or*, slumber. Je 51:57. *or*, poison. Je 8:14mg. **when they**, etc. *or*, and also against Judah *shall he be*, which shall be in siege against Jerusalem. Zc √14:2, 3, 14. Jl *3:2. Mi *5:5, 6. Hab +*3:16.

3. **in that day**. ver. 4, 6, 8, 9, 11. Zc 2:8, 9. 10:3-5. 13:1, 2, 4. 14:2, 3, 4, 6, 8, 9, 13, 20, 21. Is 60:12. *66:14-16. Ezk ch. *38, *39. Jl 3:8-16. Ob 18. Mi 5:8, 15. 7:15-17. Hab 2:17. +*3:16. Zp 3:19. Hg 2:22. **will I make**. Is *49:16. **a burdensome stone**. Da *2:34, 35, 44, 45. Mt *21:44. Lk 20:18. **shall be cut**. Ge +*12:3. **though all**. Zc √14:2, 3. Mi *4:11-13. Re 16:14. 17:12-14. 19:19-21. 20:8, 9. **be gathered**. Zp +*3:8. Re +*16:16.

4. **that day**. ver. +*3. Is 24:21. **I will smite**. Zc 10:5. 14:15. Dt 28:28. 2 K 6:14, 18. Ps *76:5-7. Ezk +*38:3, 4. 39:20. **I will open**. Zc +*9:8. 1 K 8:29. 2 Ch *6:20, 40. +*7:14, 15. Ne 1:6. Ps 32:8. √33:18. Is 37:17. Je 24:6. Da 9:18. Ho +*5:15. Lk 22:61. Ac *17:30.

5. **the governors**. ver. 6. Jg 5:9. Is 1:10, 23, 26. 29:10. 32:1. 60:17. Je 30:21. 33:26. Ezk 45:8, 9. **The**

inhabitants, etc. *or*, *There is* strength to me, *and to* the inhabitants, etc. Zc √10:6, 12. Ps *3:6. 18:32, 39. 20:6, 7. *27:3. *46:1, 5. 68:34, 35. 118:10-14. 144:1. Is 28:6. 41:10-16. Jl +*3:16. 2 C *12:9, 10.

6. **like an hearth**. Is 10:16, 17. Je 5:14. Ob *18. Re 20:9. **like a torch**. Ps *11:6. *97:3. **they shall devour**. Zc *9:15. Ps *46:6, 7. +*149:6-9. Is *41:15, 16. Da *2:34, 35, 44, 45. Mi +*4:13. +*5:5-8. Re 19:19, 20. **on the right**. Is 9:20. 54:3. 2 C 6:7. **Jerusalem shall**. Zc 1:16. 2:4, 12. 8:3-5. *14:10, 11. Ne ch. 11. Je 30:18. *31:38-40. Ezk 48:30-35.

7. **save the tents of Judah**. These would be the inhabitants dwelling outside of the protective walls of Jerusalem, needing and receiving divine protection first. Zc *4:6. 11:11. Is 2:11-17. 23:9. Je *9:23, 24. Mt 11:25, 26. Lk 1:51-53. 10:21. Jn 7:47-49. Ro 3:27. 1 C 1:26-31. 2 C 4:7-12. Ja *2:5. 4:6. **do not magnify**. Jb 19:5. Ps 35:26. 38:16. 55:12.

8. **defend**. Zc +*2:5. +*9:8, 15, 16. *14:3. Is 63:1-6. Jl 2:11. +*3:16, 17. 2 Th √1:7-10. Ju *14, 15. Re 11:19-21. **he that is**. Zc 9:13. Is +*30:19, 26. Je +*30:19-22. Ezk +*34:23, 24. Jl *3:9, 10. Mi 5:8. 7:16. He 11:34. **feeble**. *or*, abject. Heb. fallen. Is 49:7. 53:3. Je 27:10. Da *11:33, 34. Mi +*7:8. **shall be as David**. 1 S *17:32-51. Is +*40:29. **the house of David**. Ps *2:6, 7. +*45:6, 7. *110:1, 2. Is +*7:13, 14. +*9:6, 7. Je +*23:5, 6. √33:15, 16. Ezk +*37:24-26. Ho *1:7. +*3:5. Mi +*5:2-4. Mt *1:23. Jn 17:21-23. Ro 1:3, 4. *9:5. 1 T *3:16. Re 22:13, 16. **as the angel**. Zc 3:1, 2. Ge 22:15-17. 48:15, 16. Ex 23:20, 21. Jsh *5:13, 14. 2 S *14:17-20. Is +*63:9. Da +3:25n, 28. Ho 12:3-5. Ml 3:1. Ac 7:30-35.

9. **I will seek**. ver. 2-6. Zc 9:13. Is *54:17. Ezk *39:2-5. Jl *3:2, 14, 16. Hg *2:22. **all the nations**. Zc *14:2. **come against**. Ge 34:27. Pr 28:22.

10. **I will pour**. 𝒻22C38, Ps +79:6. 𝒻22K4, Je +2:13. Pr *1:23. Is 32:15. 44:3, 4. 59:19-21. Ezk *39:29. Jl *2:28, 29. Ac 2:17, 33. 10:45. 11:15. T *3:5, 6. **the house**. ver. 7. **the spirit**. Heb. *ruach*, Ge +41:38. Ps *51:12. **of grace**. Is +*30:18, 19. He +*10:29. **of supplications**. T#842. Zc √13:9. Ps 10:17. +*122:6. Is +*30:19. +*65:24. Je 3:21. *31:9. *50:4. Ho +*5:15. *8:2. Ro 8:15, *26, 27. 2 C *7:10. Ga 4:6. Ep +*6:18. Ju *20. **and they shall**. That this relates to the crucifixion of Jesus of Nazareth, and to his being pierced by the soldier's spear, we have the authority of the inspired apostle John for affirming; and this application agrees with the opinion of some of the ancient Jews, who interpret it of Messiah the son of David, as Moses Hadarson, on Ge ch. 28, though Jarchi and Abarbanel refer it to the death of Messiah the son of Joseph, whom they say was to be the suffering Messiah, while the former is to be the triumphant Messiah. Ps 22:16, 17. Jn *1:29. 19:34-37. He *12:2. Re +*1:7. **look upon me**. *or*, look unto me. 𝒻108B, Ge +21:16. Zc 2:10. 14:9. Ge 15:5. 19:17, 26. Ex 33:8. Nu *21:9. Is *45:22. Ezk *20:35. Ho *5:15. Mt 23:39. 》24:30. Lk 23:35. Jn *3:14, 15. 》19:37. 2 C √3:16. *5:21. **whom they have**. T#1950. Zc 13:7. Jn ✳19:34-37. Re ✳+*1:7. **pierced**. Zc 13:3. Ps *22:16. Is *53:5. Je +37:10mg (✳S#1856h). Jn ✳19:34, 》37. Re ✳1:7. **they shall mourn**. Ge=45:3. Ex 11:6. =12:29, 30. Je 6:26. Am 5:17. *8:10. Mt +*24:30. 26:75. Ac *2:37. 2 C √7:9-11.

11. **as the mourning**. 2 K *23:29, 30. 2 Ch √35:20-25. **Hadadrimmon**. i.e. *sound of the pomegranate*, ✳S#1910h. **valley of Megiddon**. i.e. *rendezvous,*

❋S#4023h. Jsh 12:21. +17:11. Jg 1:27. 5:19. 1 K 4:12. 9:15. 2 K 9:27. 23:29, 30. 1 Ch 7:29. 2 Ch 35:22. Re *16:16.

12. **the land.** Je 3:21. 4:28. 31:18. Mt +*24:30. Re +*1:7. **every family apart.** Heb. families, families. Ex 12:30. Ezk 24:23. **the family of the house of David apart.** Je 13:18. Jon 3:5, 6. **and their wives apart.** Zc 7:3. Jl 2:16. 1 C 7:5. **Nathan.** 2 S *5:13, 14. 7:2-4. 12:1. Lk *3:31.

13. **Levi.** Ex 6:16-26. Nu ch. 3, 4. Ml 2:4-9. **apart.** Mt ◑26:3, 4. Jn 18:35. **Shimei.** or, Simeon, as LXX. Heb. S#8097h, Nu +3:21, Shimites. Compare ❋S#8096h, 2 S +16:5. 2 S 16:5. 1 K 1:8. 1 Ch 3:19. 4:27. 6:17. 23:7, 10. 2 Ch 29:14.

14. **and their wives apart.** ver. 12. Pr 9:12. Mt +*5:4.

ZECHARIAH 13

The fountain to be opened for the cleansing of Jerusalem, 1. The extirpation of idolatry and false prophets, 2-6. The sufferings of Christ, the scattering of his sheep, the destruction of unbelievers, and the saving of a remnant through severe trials, 7-9.

1. **In that day.** Zc 12:3, 8, 11. **a fountain.** Zc 14:8. Jb 9:30, 31. Ps *51:2, 7. Is *1:16-18. Ezk +*36:25. Jn *1:29. *19:34, 35. 1 C 6:11. Ep *5:25-27. T *3:5-7. He *9:13, 14. *10:10, 14. 1 J √1:7. 5:6. 1 P *1:18, 19. Re +*1:5, 6. 7:13, 14. **the house of David.** Zc 12:7, 10. **and to.** Lk *24:47. Ac +*1:8. Ro +*1:16. **uncleanness.** Heb. separation for uncleanness. Le 15:2, etc. Nu 19:9-22. Ezk 36:17, 29. *37:23.

2. **I will cut off.** Ex 23:13⅃𝒫. Dt 12:3. Jsh 23:7. Ps *16:4. Is *2:18, 20. Ezk 30:13. 36:25. 37:23. Ho *2:16, 17. 14:8. Mi +*5:12-14. Zp 1:3, 4. 2:11. **the names.** Ex +*23:13. Ps +*16:4. Ho 2:17. **cause.** 1 K 22:22. Je 8:10-12. 23:14, 15. 29:23. Ezk 13:12-16, 23. 14:9. Mi 2:11. Mt 7:15. 24:24. 2 C √11:13-15. 2 P *2:1-3, 15-19. 1 J 4:1, 2. Re 19:20. **unclean.** Mt *12:43. Lk 11:20. Re 16:13, 14. 18:2. 20:1-3. **spirit.** Heb. *ruach*, Jg +9:23.

3. **and his father and.** Ex 32:27, 28. Dt *13:6-11⅃𝒫. 18:20⅃𝒫. 33:9. Mt 10:37. Lk 14:26. 2 C 5:16. **thrust.** Zc 12:10. Je +*37:10 (❋S#1856h).

4. **come to pass.** Jl 2:28. **the prophets.** Je 2:26. Mi *3:6, 7. **wear.** 2 K 1:8. Is 20:2. Mt 3:4. 11:8, 9. Mk 1:6. Re 11:3. **rough garment.** Heb. garment of hair. Ge 27:16. 2 K 1:8. **to deceive.** Heb. to lie. Is 59:13.

5. **I am no.** Am *7:14. Ac 19:17-20.

6. **What.** 1 K 18:28. 20:35-41. Re 13:16, 17. 14:11. **I was.** Ps 22:16. Pr 27:5, 6. Jn 18:35. 19:14-16. **my friends.** Mk 3:21. Jn *1:11.

7. **O sword.** ⅃22D5D, Dt +32:41. Dt 32:41, 42. Is 27:1. Je 47:6. Ezk 21:4, 5, 9, 10, 28. **my shepherd.** Zc 11:4, 7. Ps=106:23. Is *40:11. Ezk +*34:23, 24. 37:24. Mi +*5:2, 4. Jn √10:10-18. He *13:20. 1 P *5:4. **the man.** Is +*9:6. Je +*23:5, 6. Ho 12:3-5. Mt *1:23. 11:27. Jn +*1:1, 2. +*5:17, 18, 23. +*8:58. +*10:30, 38. 14:1, 9-11, 23. 16:15. 17:21-23. 1 C √15:47. Ph +*2:6. Col +*1:15-19. 1 T +*2:5. He +*1:6-12. Re +*1:8, 11, 17. 2:23. 21:6. 22:13-16. **my fellow.** or, my equal. Is 6:1-3. Jn +*5:18. Ph √2:6. or, neighbor. Le 6:2. 18:20. 19:15, 17. 25:14, 15, 17. **the Lord.** Ne +*9:6. Ho *1:7. Ml 3:1. **of hosts.** Je +6:6. **smite.** T#1921. Is +*53:4-10. Da +*9:24-26. Mt ❋◑26:31. Mk ▶14:27. Jn *1:29. √3:14-17. *10:11, 14-18. Ac 2:23.

4:26-28. Ro *3:24-26. *4:25. 5:6-10. *8:32. 2 C √5:21. Ga *3:13. Col 1:19, 20. He 10:5-10. 1 P 1:18-20. *2:24, 25. *3:18. 1 J 2:2. 4:9, 10. Re 13:8. **the sheep.** T#1930. Mt ❋26:31, 56. Mk ❋14:27, 50. Jn 16:32. **I will turn.** Zc 11:7, 11. Ps 81:15. Is 1:25. Ezk 38:12. Am 1:9. Mt 10:17, 18, 42. *18:10, 11, 14, 34, 35. 24:9. Lk *12:32. 17:2. Jn 15:18, 20. 18:8, 9. **hand.** ⅃22A14.8G, Is +1:25. **little ones.** Je 49:20. Lk 12:32.

8. **two.** Zc 11:6-9. Dt 28:49-68. Is 65:12-15. 66:4-6, 24. Ezk 5:2-4, 12. Da +*9:27. Ml 3:1, 2, +*5. 4:1-3. Mt 3:10-12. 21:43, 44. *22:7. *23:35-37. *24:21. Lk *19:41-44. 20:16-18. *21:20-24. 23:28-30. 1 Th 2:15, 16. Re 8:7-12. 16:19. **die.** Ge +49:33 (❋S#1478h). **but the third.** Zc 14:1, 2. Is 6:13. *10:20-22. Je 30:11. Jl 2:31, 32. Am +*9:8, 9. Mt *24:22. Mk 13:20. Ro 9:27-29. +*11:1-5.

9. **bring the third.** Ps 66:10-12. Is *10:20-22. 43:2. Da +*11:35. 1 C *3:11-13. 1 P 4:12. **fire.** T#1337. 1 P *4:12. **refine.** Jb 23:10. Pr 17:3. Is 48:10. Ml 3:2, 3. Ja 1:12. 1 P *1:5-9. **try them.** ⅃22C31, Ps +17:3. T#1416. Ps 66:10. Is 1:25. *48:10. Ezk *22:19-22. Da +*12:10. Mt +26:41 (T#1414). **they shall call.** Zc +*12:10. Ps +*50:15. 91:15. Is 58:9. +*65:23, 24. Je 29:11, 12. Ho +*5:15. *6:1-3. *8:2. *14:2. Jl *2:32. Ac 2:21. Ro *10:12-14. **I will hear.** Zc √10:6. Ps 34:15-19. 91:15. Is +*65:24. Ho *2:21-23. **It is my people.** Zc *8:8. Le 26:12, 44, 45⅃𝒫. Dt 26:17-19. Ps 144:15. Is 44:1-6. Je *30:22. 31:33. 32:38. Ezk *11:20. 36:28. *37:27. Ho +*2:23. Mt 22:29-32. He 8:10. Re 21:3, 4, 7. **they shall say.** Ezk *37:27, 28.

ZECHARIAH 14

It is predicted that Jerusalem shall be taken and spoiled by many and cruel enemies, 1, 2. In Jerusalem's most hopeless hour, the Lord himself fights against the attacking nations, 3. The second advent of Messiah accompanied by physical changes in the geography of the Holy Land, 4. The Messiah accompanied upon his return with all his saints, 5. The day of the Lord accompanied by signs in the sun and moon, 6, 7. Living waters shall flow forth from Jerusalem, 8. The Lord shall be king over the whole earth, 9. Jerusalem is rebuilt and replenished, 10, 11. The plague of all who have fought against her, 12, 13. The wealth of the nations will fall to Israel, 14. The plague extends to the animal creation, 15. Israel shall be the spiritual center of the world, 16. The judgment upon nations which fail to worship the Lord and keep the Feast of Tabernacles at Jerusalem as required during the Millennium, 17-20. The holiness of Israel in the latter days, 20, 21.

1. **the day of the Lord.** Is +*2:12. *13:6, 9, 13. Je +*30:7, 8. Jl 2:31. 3:14. Am *5:18-20. Ml 4:5. Ac 2:20. 1 Th 5:2. 2 P 3:7, 8, 10, 12. Re 16:14.

2. **gather all nations.** Dt 28:9, etc. Ps 79:1. Is 5:26. +*59:19. Je *30:7, 8. 34:1. Ezk +*38:14-17. Da 2:40-43. 8:13. Jl *3:2, 11. Ob 15. Mt *22:7. Lk 2:1. 2 Th 2:8. Re 11:7. 13:7. 16:12-14. 17:14. **against.** Ps *83:4. Is *29:3-7. **the city.** Mt 23:37, 38. *24:15, 16. Mk 13:14, 19. Lk 19:43, 44. *21:20-24. **the houses.** Is 13:16. La 1:10. 5:11, 12. Am 7:17. Mt *24:19-21. **women ravished.** La *5:11. **go forth into.** Mi √4:10. **the residue.** Lk *21:24. **shall not.** Zc 13:8, 9. Is 65:6-9, 18. Mt 24:22. Ro 9:27-29. Ga 4:26, 27.

3. **and fight.** ver. 12, 13. Zc 2:8, 9. *10:4, 5. 12:2-

6, +*8, 9. Ps *46:5, 8, 9. 83:9-17. Is 10:24, 25. 14:25. 29:7, 8. 30:26-32. 31:4-9. √34:1-4. *63:1-6. 66:15, 16. Da *2:34, 35, 44, 45. Jl *3:2, 9-17. Zp 3:19. Hg 2:21, 22. Re 6:4-17. 8:7-13. **as when.** Ex 15:1-6. Jsh 10:42. 2 Ch 20:15. **fought.** Jsh 10:14. **battle.** 2 S 17:11.

4. **his feet.** ver. 7. Is *52:7. Ezk *11:23. *43:2. Ac √1:11, 12. **cleave.** Zc *4:7. Ps 46:2, 3. Is 64:1, 2. Ezk *38:19, 20. +*42:16n. 45:1n. *47:1n. Mi 1:3, 4. Na 1:5, 6. Hab 3:6. Mk 11:23. **a very.** ver. 10. Jl *3:12-14. **half of the.** Ezk 47:1-12.

5. **the mountains.** *or,* my mountains. **for the,** etc. *or,* when he shall touch the valley of the mountains to the place he separated. **ye shall flee.** Nu 16:34. Am *2:14-16. Re 11:13. 16:18-21. **ye fled.** ✗106, Ge +31:7. Is 29:6. Am *1:1. **the Lord.** Ps 96:13. 97:4-6. 98:9. Is 64:1-3. 66:15, 16. Da *7:9-14, 21-27. Mt 16:27. *24:3, 27-31. 25:31. Mk 13:26, 27. Lk 21:27. 2 Th √2:8. Ju *14, *15. Re 6:16, 17. 20:4, 11. **Azal.** i.e. *proximity, he has reserved,* ✱S#682h, only here. **the Lord.** Ex 15:26. **God shall come.** Da +*7:22. **and all.** Dt *33:2. Ps +*149:9. Is √24:23. Ho +*11:12. Jl 3:11. Ro √8:19. 1 Th *3:13. 2 Th √1:7-10. Ju *14. **the saints.** Jb 5:1. Ps 89:5, 7. Is *13:3. Da 4:13. 8:13. Mt *16:27. +*24:30, 31. +*25:31. Ju *14.

6. **that the.** "That is, it shall not be clear in some places, and dark in other places of the world." Is 5:30. *13:10. Jl 2:30, 31. *3:15. Mt +*24:29. Re *6:12. **not.** Ps 97:10, 11. 112:4. Pr +*4:18, 19. Is 50:10. 60:1-3. Ho *6:3. Lk 1:78, 79. Jn 1:5. 12:46. Ep *5:8-14. Col 1:12. 2 P √1:19. Re 11:3, 15. **clear.** Heb. precious. Ps +37:20mg. **dark.** Heb. thickness. Zp 1:12.

7. **it shall be one day.** *or,* the day shall be one. Ps 118:24. Re 21:23. 22:5. **which.** Ps 37:18. Mt +*24:36. Mk +*13:32. Ac +*1:7. 15:18. 17:26, 31. 1 Th *5:2. **at evening.** Is +*9:7. 11:9. √30:26. *60:19, 20. Da +*12:4. Ho 3:5. 1 C 2:9. Re *11:15. 14:6. 20:2-4. 21:23. 22:5.

8. **in that day.** Jl *3:18. **living waters.** ✗22K4, Je +2:13. Ezk √47:1-12. Jl *3:18. Lk 24:47. Jn *4:10, 14. *7:38. Re *22:1, 2, 17. **the former.** *or,* eastern. Jl 2:20. **hinder sea.** Jl +2:20n. **in summer.** Is 35:7. 41:17, 18. 49:10. 58:11. Re 7:16, 17.

9. **the Lord.** Zc *8:20-23. Ge +*49:10. 1 S 2:10. Ps *2:6-8. 22:27-31. 47:2-9. 67:4. 72:8-11, 17. 86:9. Is *2:2-4. √24:23. 45:22-25. 49:6, 7. 52:10. 54:5. 60:12-14. Ezk 48:35. Da *2:44, 45. 7:27. Am 9:12. Mi 4:1-3. 5:4. Zp 3:9. Ml *1:11. Re *11:15. **shall be king.** Zc 2:10. 12:10. Ps *18:43. 45:6. 47:2, 7. 59:13. 102:16. Is 12:6. Je 23:5, 6. Ob +*21. Zp 3:14, 15. **all the earth.** Zc 4:14. 6:5. Ps 72:8. Re *11:15. **one Lord.** Zc 13:7. Mk +*12:32. 1 C √2:8. √15:47. Ep *4:5, 6. Ja *2:8. **and his name one.** Dt +*6:4. Je *23:6. Mt *1:23. +√28:19. Ep *3:14, 15.

10. **the land shall be.** ver. 4. Zc *4:6, 7. Ps 46:2, 3. Is 29:17. *40:3-5. Ezk +*42:16n. 45:1n. 47:1n. Hab 3:6. Lk 3:4-6. **turned.** *or,* compassed. Ge 19:4. **plain.** Heb. *arabah,* Am +*6:14. Dt +11:30. **from Geba.** Jsh 21:17. 1 K 15:22. Is 10:29. **Rimmon.** Jsh 15:32. Jg 20:45, 47. 21:13. 1 Ch 4:32. 6:77. **lifted up.** Ps 48:2. 68:15. Is *2:2. **inhabited.** *or,* shall abide. Zc 2:4. 12:6. Je 30:18. **from Benjamin's.** 2 Ch 25:23. Ne *3:1. 8:16. *12:39. Je 20:2. *31:38-40. 37:13. 38:7. **corner gate.** 2 Ch 26:9. **the tower.** Je *31:38. **Hananeel.** i.e. *graciously given of God,* ✱S#2606h. Ne 3:1. 12:39. Je 31:38.

11. **no more utter destruction.** or, curse. Nu 21:3.

Is *11:6-9, 11, 12. 60:18. Je +*31:40. Ezk +*37:26. Jl *3:17, 20. Am +*9:15. Ml 4:6. Ro 8:18-25. Re 21:4. *22:3. **shall be safely inhabited.** or, shall abide. Zc 2:4. 8:4, 8. +*12:6. Le 26:5)✗. Is *26:1, 2. 66:22. Je +*23:5, 6. 30:10. 33:15, 16. Ezk 28:26. +*34:22-29.

12. **the plague wherewith.** ver. 3. Zc 12:9. Ps *110:5, 6. Is ch. 34. *66:15, 16, 24. Ezk *38:18-22. *39:4-6, 17-20. Jl *3:1, 2. Mi 4:11-13. 5:8, 9. 7:16, 17. Re ch. 16. 19:17-21. **Their flesh.** Le 26:18, 21, 24, 28. Dt 28:59. 2 Ch 21:15, 18, 19. Ps 90:11. Ac 12:23. Re 9:5, 6. 16:10, 11, 21. 17:16. 18:6-8. **their tongue.** Lk 16:24. **consume.** Dt 4:24. 9:3. He 12:29.

13. **a great.** Zc 12:4. Jg *7:22. 1 S *14:15-23. 2 Ch *20:22-24. Ezk +*38:21-23. Re 17:12-17. **his hand.** Jg 7:22. Hg *2:21, 22.

14. **Judah also shall.** *or,* thou also, O Judah, shalt, etc. Zc 10:4, 5. 12:5-7. **at.** *or,* against. ver. 3. Jg 9:45. 1 S 23:1. 2 S 12:27. "Against" is an inappropriate translation here, though supported by the Targum and the Vulgate, and followed by Luther and Calvin. The LXX. and the Syriac render properly "at" or "in," followed by Koehler, Hengstenberg, Keil, Pusey, and most competent modern Hebrew scholars. The correct rendering, following the Hebrew idiom, must be "in" or "at." The same idiom occurs at Ex 17:8, "at Rephidim;" Jg 5:19, "fought...in Taanach;" 2 Ch 35:22, "in the valley of Megiddo." Pusey explains (*Minor Prophets,* vol. ii. p. 454), "...when used of people, it always means 'fight against,' yet, of place, it as often, means 'fight in.' " "Against" is inappropriate here because it is not in accordance with this text or its context to suggest that Judah is to fight against Jerusalem; rather, Judah is fighting with Jerusalem against all nations gathered against her. **and the.** 2 K 7:6-18. 2 Ch 14:13-15. 20:25-27. Is 23:18. Ezk *39:9, 10, 17, etc. **wealth.** Is +*60:5. +*61:6. Mi 4:13.

15. **so shall.** ver. 12. Jsh 7:24, 25. Ro 8:20-22.

16. **that every.** Zc *8:20-23. 9:7. Is 60:6-9. 66:18-21, *23. Jl 2:32. Ac 15:17. Ro 9:23, 24. 11:5, 16, 26. Re 11:13, 15-17. **go up.** Ps 86:9. Is 66:18-20. **the King.** ver. 17. Ps 24:7-10. Is 6:5. Je 46:18. 48:15. 51:57. Ml 1:14. Lk 19:38. Jn 1:49. Ph √2:9-11. Re 19:16. **the Lord of hosts.** Je +6:6. **keep the feast.** ver. 18, 19. Le +*23:33-36, 43)✗. Nu 29:12-38. Dt 16:13-16)✗. 31:10-13. 2 Ch 7:8-10. 8:13. Ezr 3:4. Ne *8:14-18. Ho *12:9. Mt +*17:4. Jn 7:2, 37-39.

17. **that.** Ps *2:8-12. *110:5, 6. Is 45:23. *60:12. Je 10:25. Ro 14:10, 11. **all.** Ge 10:32. +*12:3. 28:14. Am 3:2. Ac *17:26, 27. **even.** Dt 11:17. 28:23, 24. 1 K 8:35. 17:1. 2 Ch 6:26. 7:13. Is 5:6. Je 14:4, 22. Am 4:7, 8. Ja 5:17. Re 11:6.

18. **And if.** Dt 16:13, 17. Ps 126:1-3. **that have no.** Heb. upon whom *there is* not. Dt 11:10, 11)✗. **rain.** ✗63I1D, Nu +26:4. "And if the family of Egypt go not up, and come not, not upon them (shall be no rain); there shall be the plague," because Egypt has no rain, as it is, and is therefore thus excepted here (B101). **feast of.** Le +*23:34. **tabernacles.** Le +*23:42.

19. **punishment.** *or,* sin. ✗121C1E, Ge +19:15. Jn 3:19.

20. **shall there.** Pr 21:3, 4. Is *23:18. Jl *3:17. Ob *17. Zp 2:11. Ml 1:11. Lk 11:41. Ac 10:15, 28. 11:9. 15:9. Ro 14:17, 18. Col 3:17, 22-24. T 1:15, 16. 1 P 4:11. **bells.** or, bridles. Ex 28:33-35. **HOLINESS.** Ex 28:36)✗. 39:30)✗. Le 8:9. Ps 110:3. Is *4:3. *35:8. Je *31:40. 1 C 3:16, 17. 1 P 2:5, 9. Re 1:6. 5:10. 20:6.

*21:27. **and the**. Le 6:28. 1 S 2:14. Ezk 46:20-24. **the bowls**. Zc 9:15. Ex 25:29. 37:16. Nu 4:7, 14. 7:13, 19, 84, 85. 1 K +7:40. 2 Ch 4:8mg.

21. **every**. Zc 7:6. Dt 12:7, 12. Ne 8:10. Ro 14:6, 7. 1 C *10:31. 1 T 4:3-5. **no more**. Is 4:3. 35:8. Ezk 44:9. Ho 12:7mg. Jl 3:17. Mt 21:12, 13. Mk 11:15-17. Jn *2:15, 16. 1 C +*6:9-11. Re 18:11-15. 21:27. 22:15. **Canaanite**. This is the word which, divided into two in Zc 11:7, 11, is rendered "the poor of the flock." As one word it means merchant, or trafficker; but it is also used as typical of what is unclean (CB). Zp 1:11. Mt 21:12. **in the house**. Ep *2:19-22. 1 T 3:15. He 3:6. 1 P *4:17. The predictions contained in this chapter seem to relate to events which gradually extend from the death of Christ to the glorious days of the Millennium: —the destruction of Jerusalem by the Romans, whose armies were composed of many nations, which was "the day of the Lord," in which he came

"to destroy those who would not that he should reign over them," ver. 1, 2; the subversion of the Roman empire, after being the executioners of the Divine vengeance on the Jews, by God's stirring up of the barbarous nations to invade them, ver. 3; the effusion of Divine knowledge from Jerusalem, by the promulgation of the Gospel, ver. 4-9; the rebuilding and replenishing of Jerusalem, ver. 10, 11; the destruction of the nations who shall fight against her, ver. 12-15; the conversion of the remnant of those nations to the Lord, ver. 16-19; and the peace and purity of the universal church in the latter days, ver. 20, 21. The preceding note, written nearly two centuries ago, goes astray in a number of points in the presentation and interpretation of prophecy, but is retained as an example of the view of prophecy held at that time. A more correct view may be learned by consulting the chapter headnotes and the references.

MALACHI

MALACHI 1

The love of God to Israel contrasted with his hatred of Edom, 1-5. God reproves the Jews, especially the priests, for ingratitude, and contempt of him and his ordinances; and foretells the calling of the Gentiles, 6-14.

1. Cir. A.M. 3684. B.C. 420. **burden**. ♪121L4, Is +22:1. Is 13:1. Hab 1:1. Zc 9:1. 12:1. **by**. Heb. by the hand of. Hg +*1:1mg. 2:1mg. **Malachi**. i.e. *my messenger or worker, messenger of the Lord,* ❋S#4401h.

2. **I have**. The prophet shows in these verses (ver. 2-5) how much Jacob and the Israelites were favored by Jehovah, more than Esau and the Edomites. Through every period of the history of Jacob's posterity, they could not deny that God had remarkably appeared on their behalf; but he had rendered the heritage of Esau's descendants, by wars and various other means, barren and waste forever. Note the reference to the Pentateuch. Other references to the Pentateuch in Malachi are at ver. 6, 7, 8, 13. Ml 2:2, 5, 15. 3:5, 6, 10, 16, 17. 4:4. See related note (Is +*1:2). Dt *7:6-8♪. *10:15♪. 32:8-14. 33:3♪. Is 41:8, 9. 43:4. Je 31:3. Ro *11:28, 29. **Wherein**. ver. 6, 7. Ml *2:17. *3:7, 8, 13, 14. Je 2:5, 31. Lk 10:29. **yet I**. Ge *25:23. 27:27-30, 33. *28:3, 4, 10-17. *32:28-30. *48:4. Ro *9:10-▶13. **Jacob**. ♪121T3, ♪121A5, Ge +9:27. Figure of speech Metonymy of Adjunct, whereby "Jacob" is put for his posterity.

3. **Esau**. ♪121T3, ♪121A5, Ge +9:27. Figure of speech Metonymy of Adjunct, whereby "Esau" is put for his posterity. Note that this verse, quoted in Romans 9:13, is often misapplied. The statement given here in Malachi regarding God's love for Jacob and hatred of Esau was given long after they were born, and applies not to them personally, but to their posterity, as the their histories in Scripture abundantly show (Ezk +35:5, 9n). **hated**. Ge 29:30, 31. Dt 21:15, 16. Mt *10:37. Lk *14:26. **laid**. Is 34:9-12. Je *49:16-18. Ezk 25:13, 14. 35:3, 4, 7, 9, 14, 15. Jl *3:19. Ob *10, 18, 19, etc. **the dragons**. Is *13:21, 22. 34:13, 14. 35:7. Je 9:11. 10:22. 49:33. 51:37.

4. **but**. Is 9:9, 10. Ja 4:13-16. **Lord of hosts**. Je +6:6. **They shall build**. Jb 9:4. 12:14. 34:29. Ps *127:1. Pr +*21:30. Is 10:4, 15, 16. La 3:37. Ezk *35:2-4, 7, 9, 14, 15. Ob 1, 10, 16-18. Mt 12:30. **The border**. Je 31:17. Ezk 11:10. Am 6:2. **The people**. ver. 3. Ps 137:7. Is 11:14. 34:5, 10. 63:1-6. La 4:21, 22. Ezk 25:14. 35:9. **indignation**. Is +66:14. **for ever**. Heb. *olam,* Ex +*12:24.

5. **your**. Dt 4:3. 11:7. Jsh 24:7. 1 S 12:16. 2 Ch 29:8. Lk 10:23, 24. **The Lord**. Ps *35:26, 27. 58:10, 11. 83:17, 18. Ezk 38:16, 23. 39:21, 22. **from**. *or,* upon. Heb. from upon.

6. **son**. Ex +*20:12♪♪. Le 19:3. Dt 5:16. Pr 30:11, 17. Ho *11:1. Mt 15:4, 6. 19:19. Mk 7:10. 10:19. Lk 18:20. Ep *6:2. **a servant**. Ps *123:2. Is *41:8. 1 T 6:1, 2. T 2:9, 10. 1 P 2:17-19. **if then**. From this verse to Ml 2:9, the prophet reproves the priests and people for sacrificing the refuse of beasts; and denounces punishment against the former for not teaching the poeple their duty in this respect. Ex 4:22, 23. Is 1:2. 64:8. Je 31:9. Mt 6:9, 14, 15. Lk 6:36, 46. 1 P 1:17. **a father**. Ml 2:10. Dt 32:6. Is 63:16. **and if**. Mt +*7:21. Lk +*6:46. Jn +*13:13-17. **unto you**. ♪14, Is +5:3. **O priests**. Ml 2:8. 1 S 2:28-30. Je 5:30, 31. 23:11. Ezk 22:26. Ho 4:6. 5:1. **And ye**. Ml 2:14-17. 3:7, 8, 13, 14. Je 2:21, 22. Ho 12:8. Lk 10:29.

7. **Ye offer**, etc. *or,* Bring unto my, etc. **polluted**. T#1806. Le 2:11. 21:6. Dt 15:21♪♪. **bread**. ♪17118, Ge +3:19. **The table**. ver. 12. 1 S 2:15-17. Ezk 41:22. 1 C 10:21. *11:20-22, 27-32.

8. **if ye offer the blind**. ver. 14. Le *22:19-25♪♪. Dt *15:21♪♪. **for sacrifice**. Heb. to sacrifice. **or accept**. ver. 10, 13. Jb *42:8. Ps 20:3. Je 14:10. Ho 8:13. **thy governor**. Ne 5:14, 15.

9. **I**. ♪60A, Ge +3:22. **beseech**. 2 Ch 30:27. Jb *42:8. Je 27:18. Ho *13:9. Jl 1:13, 14. 2:17. Zc 3:1-5. Jn +*9:31. He *7:26, 27. **God**. Heb. the face of God. Ex +32:11mg. Je +26:19mg. La 2:19. Zc 7:2mg. Heb. *El,* Ex +*15:2. **be gracious**. Jb 33:24. Zc +*12:10. **by your means**. Heb. from your hand. 1 K +10:29mg. **will he**. Ac 19:15, 16. Ro 2:11. 1 P 1:17.

10. **Who**. Instead of *mi,* "who," one MS. (30K) with the LXX. reads *ki,* "surely," which is adopted by Houbi-

gant and Abp. Newcome, who renders, "Surely the doors shall be closed against you, neither shall ye kindle the fire of my altar in vain." **even.** 1 S 2:36. Jb 1:9-11. Is 56:11, 12. Je 6:13. 8:10. Mi 3:11. Jn 10:12. Ph 2:21. 1 P 5:2. **neither.** 1 C 9:13. **I have.** Is *1:11-15. Je *6:20. Am *5:21-24. He +*10:38. **an offering.** Heb. *minchah*, meal offering, Le +*23:13.

11. **from.** As the preceding verse was a prediction of the abolition of the Levitical priesthood, so this is a prophecy of the conversion of the Gentiles, and the spiritual priesthood of the Gospel times. As none but priests of Aaron's race might burn incense before Jehovah, a total change of the external administration of the sacred ordinances is evidently predicted. Ps 50:1. *113:3. Is 45:6. *59:19. +*60:3, 5. Zc 8:7. **my name.** ver. 14. Ps 22:27-31. 67:2. 72:11-17. 98:1-3. Is 11:9, 10. 45:22, 23. 49:6, 7, 22, 23. 54:1-3, 5. 60:1-11, 16, etc. +*66:19, 20. Am *9:12. Mi *5:4. Zp 3:9. Zc *8:20-23. Mt *6:9, 10. *28:19. Ac 10:45. 15:7-9, 17, 18. Ep *3:1-3, 5-8. Re *11:15. *15:4. **great among.** Zc +*14:9. **and in every.** Is *24:14-16. 42:10-12. *60:23. Zp 2:11. Jn *4:21-23. Ac 10:30-35. Ro 15:9-11, 16. 1 T *2:8. Re 8:3. **incense.** Ps 141:2. Is 60:6. Lk 1:10. Ro *12:1. Ph *4:18. He 13:15, 16. Re 5:8mg. *8:3, 4. **pure offering.** Jn *4:21, 23. **for my name.** Is +*66:19, 20.

12. **ye have.** ver. 6-8. Ml 2:8. 2 S 12:14. Ezk 36:21-23. Am 2:7. Ro 2:24. **The table.** ver. 7, 13. Nu 11:4-8. Da *5:3, 4.

13. **Behold.** 1 S 2:29. Is 43:22. Am 8:5. Mi 6:3. Mk 14:4, 5, 37, 38. **weariness.** Dt 20:8. Is 40:30, 31. Ro ◐2:7. 1 C ◐/15:58. Ga ◐*6:9. 2 Th ◐*3:13. He ◐*6:12. **and ye have snuffed at it.** *or*, whereas ye might have blown it away. ✦182, Ge +18:22. **torn.** ver. 7, 8. Le 22:8, 19-23. Dt 15:21. Ezk 4:14. 44:31. **should I accept.** Ml 2:13. Le 22:20✦𝒫. Is 1:12. 57:6. Je 7:9-11, 21-24. Am 5:21-23. Zc 7:5, 6. Mt 6:1, 2, 5, 16.

14. **cursed.** Ml +*3:9. Ge 27:12. Jsh 7:11, 12. Pr +*3:33. Je *48:10. Mt +*24:51. Lk 12:1, 2, 46. Ac ✦5:1-10. Re +*21:8. **which hath in his flock.** *or*, in whose flock is. Ec *5:4, 5. Mk 12:41-44. 14:8. 2 C 8:12. **for I.** ver. 8, 11. Dt 28:58. Ps *47:2. 48:2. 95:3. Is +*57:15. Je 10:10. Da *4:37. Zc +*14:9. Mt 5:35. 1 T *6:15. **great.** ✦22I2, Ex +15:16. **my name.** Ps 68:35. 76:12. Da 9:4. He 12:29. Re *15:4.

MALACHI 2

The priests are sharply reproved, for profaning the covenant made with their fathers, and neglecting their duty, 1-9; and both the priests and people for marrying strange wives, 10-12; and treacherously divorcing their former wives, 13-16; and for impiety and presumption, 17.

1. **O ye priests.** Ml 1:6. Je 13:13. La 4:13. Ho 5:1.

2. **If.** Ge +4:7. Je +7:5. 2 P +1:10. **ye will not hear.** Le *26:14✦𝒫, etc. Dt +*28:15✦𝒫, etc. 30:17, 18. Ps 81:11, 12. Is 30:8-13. Je 6:16-20. 13:17. 25:4-9. +*29:19. 34:17. Ezk 3:7. Zc 1:3-6. 7:11-14. **if ye will not lay.** Is 42:25. 47:7. 57:11. **to give.** Jsh 7:19. Je 13:16. Lk 17:18. Ro *1:+21, 24, 27. 1 P 4:11. Re 14:7. 16:9. **my name.** Ps +*9:10. **Lord of hosts.** Je +6:6. **send a curse.** Ge *3:17-19. Dt *28:20✦𝒫. Ho 6:1. **curse your blessings.** Dt √28:2, 16-18, 53-57✦𝒫. Ps 69:22. 109:7-15. Da +*9:11. Ho 4:7-10. 9:11-14. Hg 1:6, 9. 2:16, 17. Lk 23:28-30. **I have cursed.** By

sending them unfruitful seasons. Ml +*3:9. Dt +*28:20. Is +*45:7. Am +*3:6. Hg 1:11. Ac 12:23. Ro 1:27.

3. **I will.** Jl 1:17. **corrupt.** *or*, reprove. Ml 3:11. Ezr 10:18. Ps 106:9. Is 17:13. Je *29:27. **spread.** Heb. scatter. ver. 9. 1 S 2:29, 30. 1 K *14:10. 2 K 9:36, 37. Jb 20:7. Ps 83:10. Je 8:2. Na 3:6. Lk 14:35. 1 C 4:13. **feasts.** ✦121P7, Ex +23:18. **one shall take you away with it.** *or*, it shall take you away to it.

4. **ye.** 1 K 22:25. Is 26:11. Je 28:9. Ezk 33:33. 38:23. Lk 10:11. **that my covenant.** Is 1:24-28. 27:9. Ezk 20:38-41. 44:9-16. Mt 3:12. Jn 15:2. He=8:6.

5. **covenant.** Nu 3:45. 8:15. 16:9, 10. 18:8-24. *25:10-13✦𝒫. Dt *33:8-10✦𝒫. Ps 106:30, 31. Ezk 34:25. 37:26. 44:15, 16. **life and peace.** Ro=8:6. **I gave.** Ex 32:26-29. Dt 33:8-11. **the fear.** He=12:28.

6. **law of truth.** Ps 37:30. ◐106:13. 119:142. Je *23:22. Ezk 44:23, 24. Da +*10:21. Ho 4:6. Mt 22:16. Mk 12:14. Lk 20:21. Ep 4:15. 2 T 2:15, 16. T 1:7-9. Re 14:5. **iniquity.** 1 P=2:1. **he walked.** Ge *5:21-24. 6:9. 17:1. Lk 1:6. **with me.** 1 J=1:3. **turn many.** Je 23:22. Da +*12:3. Lk 1:16, 17. Ac=26:17, 18. 1 Th 1:9, 10. Ja +*5:19, 20.

7. **the priest's.** Le *10:11✦𝒫. Dt *17:8-11✦𝒫. 21:5. *24:8. 33:10✦𝒫. 2 Ch +15:3. 17:8, 9. 30:22. 35:3n. Ezr +*7:10. Ne √8:2-8. Je 15:19. 18:18. Da ◐+*11:33n. Hg *2:11-13. 2 T *2:24, 25. **knowledge.** Mk +*12:24. Ro=15:14. 1 T +*4:16. T=2:1. **the messenger.** Ml 3:1. Is 42:19. 44:26. Hg 1:13. Jn 13:20. 20:21. Ac 16:17. 2 C=5:20. Ga 4:14. 1 Th 4:8. **Lord of hosts.** Je +6:6.

8. **ye are.** Ps 18:21. 119:102. Is 30:11. 59:13. Je 17:5, 13. Ezk 44:10. Da 9:5, 6. He 3:12. **ye have caused.** ver. 9. 1 S 2:17, 24, 30. Is 9:16. Je 18:15. 23:11-15. Mt *15:2-5. Lk *11:45, 46. Ro 2:19-24. 14:21. **stumble at.** *or*, fall in. Mt +*15:14. *18:6, 7. **ye have corrupted.** ver. 5, 10. Le 21:15. Ne 13:29. Ezk 22:26. *44:10. Zp 3:4.

9. **made.** ver. 3. 1 S *2:17, 30. Pr 10:7. Da +*12:2, 3. Mi +*3:6, 7. **before.** 1 K 22:28. Je 28:15, 16. 29:20-22, 31, 32. Ezk 13:12-16, 21. Mk 7:13, 14. Lk 20:45-57. **but.** ver. 8. Mt 5:21, 22, 27, 28, 33-37, 43, 44. 19:17, 18. 23:16-24. Mk 7:8-13. Lk 10:29. 11:42. Ro 7:7-10. **have been partial in.** *or*, lifted up the face against. Heb. accepted faces. Dt 1:17mg. Jb 13:8. Mi 3:11. Ga 2:6. Ja *2:4. 2 P *3:16.

10. **Have we.** ✦138C, Ge +22:14. **all.** Ml 1:6. Jsh 24:3. Is 51:2. *63:16. 64:8. Ezk 33:24. Mt 3:9. Lk 1:73. 3:8. Jn *8:33, 39, 41, 53, 56. Ac 7:2. Ro 4:1. 9:10. 1 C 8:6. Ep 4:6. He +*12:9. **father.** Dt 32:6. Ps 103:13. Is 63:16. 64:8. Je 3:4, 19. 31:9. **hath not.** Jb *31:15. Ps 100:3. Is 43:1, 7, 15. 44:2. Jn 8:41. Ac *17:25-29. **one.** Mk +*12:32. Ac *17:26. Ep *4:6. T#960‡. Dt *6:4. Ps 83:18. Mk 10:18. Ro 3:29, 30. Jn 4:24. 1 C +√8:6. **God.** Heb. *El*, Ex +15:2. **created.** ✦S#1254h. Ge 1:1, 27. 2:3. 5:2. 6:7. Dt *4:32. Ps 89:12, 47. Is 4:5. 41:20. 43:7. 45:8, 12, *18. 54:16, 16. Je 31:22. The Hebrew word *bara* is only used of the acts of God, and generally refers to the creation of something new (Je 31:22). The word thus allows for the concept of God's creation of the universe from nothing. Here it refers to the unity of mankind because they share a common Creator. **why.** T#685. ver. 11, 14, 15. Jb +36:6 (T#631). Ec +3:22 (T#634). +9:9 (T#635). Je 9:4, 5. Mi 7:2-6. Mt 7:12. 10:21. 22:16, 37-40. Lk +10:33 (T#414). +11:52 (T#633). +12:57 (T#632). Ac 7:26. 1 C 6:6-8. Ga 5:14 (T#413). Ep 4:25. 1 Th

+3:12 (T#412). 4:6. **by profaning.** ver. 8, 11. Ex 34:10-16. Jsh 23:12-16. Ezr 9:11-14. 10:2, 3. Ne √13:29.

11. **Judah hath.** Je 3:7, 8, 20. 5:11. **and an.** Le 18:24-30. Je 7:10. Ezk 18:13. 22:11. Re +*21:8. **profaned.** Ex 19:5, 6. Le 20:26. Da 7:3-6. 14:2. 33:26-29. Ps 106:28, 34-39. Je 2:3, 7, 8, 21, 22. **loved.** or, ought to love. **and hath.** Ge 6:1, 2. Jg 3:6. 1 K 11:1-8. Ezr *9:1, 2, 12. *10:2. Ne *13:23-29. Ho *6:7. 2 C *6:14-18. **the daughter.** That is, a woman addicted to the worship of a strange god. The prophet here censures intermarriages with women of the surrounding idolatrous nations; and also divorces, which seem to have been multiplied for the purpose of contracting these prohibited marriages. **strange.** Ex 12:43 (*S#5236h). Da 11:39. **god.** Heb. *El*, Ex +15:2.

12. **cut off.** Le 18:29. 20:3. Nu 15:30, 31. Jsh 23:12, 13. 1 S 2:31-34. Ho 4:9. 1 C +*11:30. He *13:17. **the master and the scholar.** or, him that waketh, and him that answereth. Girdlestone states "It is the teacher's business to awaken thought in the heart of the pupil, and it is the scholar's business to answer to the test to which his understanding is put" (*O. T. Synonyms*, ch. 18, sec. 6). 1 Ch 25:8. Ezr 10:18, 19. Ne *13:28, 29. Ps 134:1. Is 9:14-16. 24:1, 2. Ezk 14:10. Ho 4:4, 5. Mt +*15:14. 2 T 3:13. Re 19:20. **out of.** Nu 24:5. Zc 12:7. **and him.** ver. 10. Ge 4:3-5. 1 S 3:14. 15:22, 23. Is 61:8. 66:3. Am 5:22. **an offering.** Heb. *minchah*, a meal offering, Le +*23:13.

13. **covering.** Dt 15:9. 1 S 1:9, 10. 2 S 13:19, 20. Ps 78:34-37. Ec 4:1. **tears.** Ps 39:12. Je 11:11. **crying out.** Dt +*24:15. A reference to the tears, weeping, and crying out of the wronged wives and children (CB). **insomuch.** Dt 26:14. Ezr 10:9-14. Ne 8:9-12. Pr 15:8. 21:27. Is *1:11-15. Je 6:20.

14. **Wherefore.** √6311A, Ex +12:4. Supply by ellipsis, from ver. 13, "does He not regard our offering." Ml 1:6, 7. 3:8. Pr 30:20. Is 58:3. Je 8:12. **the Lord.** Ml +*3:5. Ge 31:50. Jg 11:10. 1 S 12:5. Je 42:5. Mi 1:2. **the wife.** ver. 15. Pr *5:18, 19. Ec 9:9. Is 54:6. 1 C *7:10, 11. **thy companion.** Ge 2:18. Pr 2:17. SS 1:15mg. Ezk 16:8.

15. **did.** Ge +*1:27. +*2:20-24. Mt *19:4-6. Mk 10:6-8. 1 C 7:2. **make one.** Ge 2:24𝒫. Dt +*6:4. **residue.** or, excellency. **the spirit.** Heb. *ruach*, Is +48:16. Ge +*2:7. Jb +*27:3. Ec +*12:7. Jn 20:22. **wherefore one.** Is 51:2. Ezk 33:24. That he. Ge 24:3-7, 44. 26:34, 35. 27:46. 28:2-4. Dt 7:4. Ezr 9:2. Ne 13:24. Je 2:21. 1 C √7:14. Ep √6:4. 1 T 3:4, 5, 11, 12. T 1:6. **godly seed.** Heb. seed of God. Ge 6:2. Ps 25:13. Pr 11:21. 20:7. Ho *1:10. Ac *3:25. 1 C 7:14. 2 C *6:18. **take heed.** ver. 14. Pr +*4:23. 6:25. 7:25. Mt *5:28, 29. *15:19. 1 C 7:2-5. Ep 5:28, 33. He 12:15. Ja √1:14, 15. 1 P 3:7. **spirit.** Heb. *ruach*, Ge +106:33. **treacherously.** or, unfaithfully. Ge 2:24. Pr 5:18. Ec 9:9. Mk 10:7. 1 C 7:11. Ep *5:25. 1 P √3:7. **the wife.** Ge +4:19.

16. **the Lord.** Dt 24:1-4. Is 50:1. Mt *5:31, 32. √19:3-9. Mk 10:2-12. Lk 16:18. **that he hateth putting away.** or, if he hate *her*, put *her* away. Heb. to put away. Pusey remarks, concerning the alternate rendering, that it "seems to enjoin what Malachi reproves these for, their cruelty to their wives, as also it gives an unbounded license of divorce" (*Minor Prophets*, vol. ii. p. 484). The reading ought to be rejected. Dt 24:1𝒫. **covereth.** Le 13:47-58. Ps 73:6. 109:18, 29. Pr √28:13. Is 28:20. 30:1. 59:6. Mi 7:2, 3. Re ◐*7:14.

17. **wearied the Lord.** Ps 95:9, 10. Is 1:14. 7:13. *43:24. Je 15:6. Ezk 16:43. Am 2:13. Ep +*4:30. **Wherein.** ver. 14. Ml 1:6, 7. *3:8. **When ye say.** Ps +*50:16, 17. **Every one.** Ml 3:13-15. Jb 34:5-9, 17, 36. 36:17. Ps 73:3-15. Mt 11:18, 19. **Where.** Ex 17:7. Dt 32:4. 1 S 2:3. Ps 10:11-13. Ec √8:11. Is 5:18, 19. +*30:18. Ezk 8:12. 9:9. Zp 1:12. 2 P *3:3, 4.

MALACHI 3

A prediction of the Messiah's forerunner; and of the Messiah himself, in the first advent, 1. The second advent of Messiah to cleanse and purge Israel, 2, 3. Israel will be restored, 4. The wicked will be judged for sorcery, adultery, false oaths, and the oppression of workers in their wages; justice will be rendered to the poor, 5, 6. The people are warned to repent, especially of their sacrilege and proud blasphemy, 7-15. A blessing is promised to such as feared God and spake together of him, when the righteous shall be separated from the wicked, 16-18.

1. **Behold.** Mt ▸11:10. **I will.** Ml *2:7. *4:5. Mt *11:10, 11. Mk *1:▸2, 3. Lk *▸1:76. *▸7:26-28. Jn *1:6, 7. **send my messenger.** T#1893. Ml *4:5, 6. Mt +√11:14. 17:9-13. Mk 9:13. Lk 1:15-17, 76, 77. 7:37. **and he.** Ml *40:3-5. 62:10. Mt *3:1-3. *17:10-13. Lk *1:16, 17. *3:3-6. Jn *1:15-23, 33, 34. *3:28-30. Ac *13:24, 25. *19:4. **and.** Ps *110:1. Is +*7:14. +*9:6. Hg *2:7-9. Lk *2:11, 21-32, 38, 46. *7:19, 20. *19:47. Jn *2:14-16. **the Lord.** Ex 23:20▸𝒫. 33:14, 16▸𝒫. Ne +*9:6. Ps 110:1. Zc 13:7. Mt 22:41-45. Ac 2:34-36. **suddenly come.** T#1882. Ge +*49:10. Lk ✱2:1, 2, 7. **to his temple.** T#1883. Hg *2:7, 9. Mt *21:12. Lk ✱2:27, 32. **even the messenger.** Ge 48:15, 16. Ex *23:20. Is +*63:9. Ho 12:3-5. Ac *7:38. He 8:6. *9:15. *12:24. **of the covenant.** Is +*42:6. 49:8. 1 C +*15:45. T √1:2. He +*13:20. 1 P √1:20. **he shall come.** Hg *2:7. Lk 10:1. **the Lord of hosts.** Je +6:6. There is an unannounced gap of time between the close of this verse and what is predicted in the next. For other instances of such prophetic time gaps see Is +61:2n.

2. **who may abide.** √85K, Ge +3:9. Ml *4:1. Jl 2:11. Am *5:18-20. Mt *3:7-12. *21:31-44. *23:13-35. *25:10. Lk *2:34. *3:9, 17. *7:23. *11:37-47, 52-54. +*21:36. Jn 6:42-44. *8:41-48, 55. *9:39-41. *15:22-24. Ac 7:52-54. Ro *9:31-33. 11:5-10. He *10:28, 29. *12:25. 1 P *2:7, 8. 2 P *3:10. Re *1:6, 7. *6:17. **who shall stand.** √85K, Ge +3:9. Ps *1:5. **for.** Is 4:4. Zc +*13:9. Mt *3:10-12. 1 C √3:13-15. Re 2:23. **like fullers.'** Ps 2:7. Is *1:18. Je *2:22. Mk *9:3. Re +*1:5. *7:14. *19:8. **sope.** Jb 9:30. Je 2:22. Mk 9:3.

3. **sit.** √22C12. Anthropomorphism B888. Human actions are attributed to God: *sitting*. For another instance of this figure see Ps 2:4. Ps 66:10. Pr 17:3. 25:4. Is 1:25. 48:10. Je 6:28-30. Ezk 22:18-22. Da *12:10. Zc +*13:9. Lk 3:16. Ep *5:26, 27. T *2:14. He 12:10. 1 P 1:7. 4:12, 13. Re 3:18. **a refiner.** Jb 23:10. Ps 66:10. **purify.** √22C31, Ps +17:3. Is 1:25mg. Ezk 22:19. Zc *13:9. 1 P *4:17. **the sons.** Ml 1:6-10. 2:1-8. Is 61:6. 66:19-21. Je 33:18, 22. Ezk 44:15, 16. Re 1:6. 5:10. **purge.** Ps 51:7. Is *4:4. Mt 3:12. 2 T=2:20, 21. **as gold and.** 2 T=2:20, 21. 1 P=1:7. **that they.** Le 6:28. Pr 25:4. 2 C 4:10, 11. **an offering.** Ml 1:11. Le +*23:13. Ps 4:5. 50:14, 23. 69:30, 31. 107:21, 22. 116:17. 141:1, 2. Ho 14:2. Jn *4:23, 24. Ro *12:1.

15:16. 1 C 2:2. Ep 1:6, 7. Ph 2:17. 4:18. 2 T 4:6. He *13:15, 16. 1 P=2:5, 9.

4. **the offering.** Ps *51:19. Is 1:26, 27. 56:7. Je *30:18-20. *31:23, 24. Ezk 20:40, 41. 43:26, 27. Zc 8:3. *14:20, 21. Jn *4:24. **as in.** 1 Ch 15:26. 16:1-3. 21:26. 29:20-22. 2 Ch 1:6. 7:1-3, 10-12. 8:12-14. 29:31-36. 30:21-27. 31:20, 21. Je 2:2, 3. **of old.** Heb. *olam*, Ge +6:4. former. *or*, ancient. 1 S +24:13 (✻S#6931h).

5. **I will come near.** Ml *2:17. Ex +32:34. Ps *50:3-6. +*96:13. *98:9. Ezk 34:20-22. Lk *18:7, 8. He *10:30, 31. Ja *5:8, 9. Ju *14, *15. Re 2:14, 20-23. 18:21, 23, 24. **a swift.** Ml 2:14. Ps *50:7. 81:8. Je *29:23. Mi 1:2. Mt *23:14-35. **the sorcerers.** Ex 22:18)𝒫. Le *20:6, 10, 27. Je *7:9, 10. Ezk 22:6-12. 1 C +*6:9, 10. Ga *5:19-21. Re +*21:8. *22:15. ✻S#3784h: Ex 7:11. 22:18 (witch). Dt +*18:10 (witch). 2 Ch 33:6 (witchcraft). Da 2:2. **adulterers.** Ex +*20:14)𝒫. Le 20:10)𝒫. Dt +*5:18, 21. Je *7:9. Ezk *22:11. He +*13:4. **false swearers.** Le 6:3-5)𝒫. 19:12)𝒫. Dt +*5:11, 20. Je *7:9. Zc +*5:3, 4. 8:17. Re +*21:8. **against those.** Ex *22:21-24. Le +*19:13. Dt +*24:14, 15, 17. 27:19. Ps +*12:5. Pr *22:22, 23. *23:10, 11. Je *22:13-17. Ezk +*16:49. *22:7. Mi 2:2. Ja +*5:4, 12. **oppress.** *or*, defraud. Ex 22:21)𝒫. Dt +*24:14)𝒫. 1 Th +*4:6. **the widow.** Is +1:17. Ezk 22:7. Zc *7:10. Mt *23:14. Mk 12:40. **fatherless.** Ge +11:28. Ex 22:22)𝒫. Dt +*10:18. 14:29)𝒫. 16:11, 14)𝒫. 24:17)𝒫. **stranger.** Ge 23:4 (✻S#1616h). Ex 12:48mg. Zc 7:10. Mt +25:35. **fear not.** Ge 20:11. 42:18. Ex *1:17. *18:21. Ne 5:15. Jb +*21:14, 15. Ps *36:1. Pr *8:13. *16:6. Is 1:2. Je +*10:25. √22:13, 16. Lk 18:4. 23:40. Ro 3:18.

6. **I am.** Ge 15:7, 18. 22:16. Ex 3:14, 15. Ne 9:7, 8. Is 41:13. 42:5-8. 43:11, 12. 44:6. 45:5-8. Je 32:27. Ho 11:9. **I change not.** God the Father is immutable (Ps 33:11. Mt ◑12:32. +*28:19n. He 6:17. ◑13:8). Nu *23:19)𝒫. 1 S 15:29. Ps 102:26. Is +*31:2. 59:1. Ho 13:14. Ro +*11:29. He 1:12. *6:18. +*13:8. Ja √1:17. Re +*1:8. 22:13. **therefore.** Ps 78:38, 57. 103:17. 105:7-10. Is 40:28-31. La 3:22, 23. Ro 5:10. √8:28-32. 11:28, 29. Ph *1:6. 2 Th √2:13, 14. **not consumed.** Le +*26:42. Ps √89:34. Is +*41:8, 9. +√54:7-10. +√55:3. Je +*33:20, 21n. La √3:22. Ezk 16:60. Zc √10:6.

7. **from the.** Ex 32:9-14. Dt 9:7-21. 31:20, 27-29. Ne 9:16, 17, 26, 28-30. Ps 78:8-10. Ezk 20:8, 13, 21, 28. Lk 11:48-51. Ac *7:51, 52. **Return unto me.** Le 26:40-42. Dt *4:29-31. *30:1-4. 1 K 8:47-49. Ne 1:8, 9. Is √55:6, 7. Je 3:12-14, 22. Ezk 18:30-32. Ho 14:1. Zc *1:3. Ja *4:8. **Wherein.** ver. 13. Ml 1:6. Is 65:2. Mt 23:27. Lk 15:16. Ro 7:9. 10:3, 21.

8. **Will.** ♪85K, Ge +3:9. **a man.** Ps 29:2. Pr *3:9, 10. Mt 22:21. Mk 12:17. Lk 20:25. Ro 13:7. **rob.** ver. 9. Pr 22:22. **In tithes.** Ml 1:8, 13. Ge +*14:20. Le 5:15, 16. 27:2-34)𝒫. Nu 18:21-32)𝒫. Dt 12:17)𝒫, etc. 14:22-29)𝒫. Jsh 7:11. Ne 10:37-40. *13:4-14. Ps 119:126. Mt +*23:23. Ro 2:22. **and offerings.** Ex 29:27n. Dt 18:3. Ezr +8:25. Ezk 44:30. 1 C 9:13.

9. **are.** ♪63K, Ge +37:13. **cursed with a curse.** Ml 2:2. Dt √28:15-19. Jsh 7:12, 13. 22:20. Pr +*3:33. +*26:2. Is 43:28. Da +*9:11. Hg 1:6-11. 2:14-17. Zc +*5:3. Ga √3:13.

10. **all the tithes.** Christians are often urged to tithe based upon a mistaken appeal to this Old Testament text, which is wrested out of its rightful context, when applied to such a purpose. Grounds for New Testament tithing must be placed on a different basis (Mt 23:23n). The storehouse is clearly the temple, not the church. The tithe constituted the Jewish income tax to support their national government, which was a theocracy. Reading further in the context (Ml 3:12), the time of application is particularly related to the yet future restoration of Israel (Is +*11:11n), not to the present church age. See related notes (Ge 14:20n. Mt 6:2n. *23:23n. Lk 11:41n, 42n. 2 C 8:12n). 2 Ch 31:4-10. Ne 10:33-39. Pr *3:9, 10. **into the storehouse.** The storehouse was part of the Jewish temple, and was used to store food grains for the Levites. Taken in context this passage lends no support whatsoever to the mistaken doctrine of "storehouse tithing," whereby Christians have been directed to restrict all their financial giving to their own denomination or local church, or as a variation, church members have been directed to pay the tithe to the local church, and restrict giving to outside organizations to amounts over and above the church tithe. 1 Ch 26:20. 2 Ch 31:11-19. Ne *10:38. 12:44, 47. 13:5, 10-13. **meat.** lit. prey. ♪171110, Ps +111:5mg. **and prove.** 1 K 17:13-16. Ps 37:3. Hg 2:19. Mt √6:33. 2 C √9:6-8. **open.** ♪22C30, Ps +78:23. Ge 7:11)𝒫. 8:2)𝒫. =41:56. Dt *28:12. 2 K 7:2, 19. Je 3:3. 5:24, 25. Am 4:7. Zc 10:1. Lk +*6:38. **of heaven.** Is 64:1. **pour you out.** Heb. empty out. Ec 11:3. Heb. *rook*, ✻S#7324h: Hiphil, Preterite: Le 26:33 (draw out). Ezk 28:7. 30:11. Ml 3:10. Hiphil, Infinitive: Is 32:6 (make empty). Hiphil, Future: Ge 14:14 (armed. mg, led forth). Ex 15:9 (draw). Ps 18:42 (cast). Ec 11:3 (empty). Je 48:12. Ezk 5:2, 12. 12:14. Hab 1:17. Hiphil, Participle: Ge 42:35 (emptied). Zc 4:12. Hophal, Preterite: Je 48:11. Hophal, Future: SS 1:3 (poured forth). **a blessing.** 1 K 10:13. Ps *37:4. Hg 2:18, 19. Ep *3:20. **that there.** Ex *36:6. Le 26:10. 2 Ch +*31:10. Lk 5:6, 7. 12:16, 17. Jn 21:6-11.

11. **rebuke.** Jl 2:20. Am 4:9. 7:1-3. Hg 2:17. **the devourer.** Jl 1:4. Am 4:9. **destroy.** Heb. corrupt. Je 11:19. Ezk 16:47. Da 8:24, 25. 9:26. **neither.** Dt 11:14. Is *65:18, 19, 21. Je 8:13. Jl 1:7, 12. 2:22. Mi 4:4. Hab 3:17. Zc 3:10. 8:12.

12. **all.** Dt 4:6, 7. 2 Ch 32:23. Ps 72:17. Is 61:9. Je 33:9. Zp 3:19, 20. Zc *8:23. Lk 1:48. **a delightsome.** Dt 8:7-10. 11:12. Is 62:4. Ezk 20:15. Da 8:9. 11:41. Ho 9:3. Zc 2:12. 7:14mg.

13. **Your.** Ml *2:17. Ex 5:2. 2 Ch 32:14-19. Jb 34:7, 8. Ps 10:11. Is 5:19. 28:14, 15. 37:23. 2 Th √2:4. **What.** ver. 8. Ml 1:6-8. 2:14, 17. Jb 40:8. Je 8:12. Ro 9:20.

14. **It is.** Jb +*21:14, 15. *22:17. 34:9. 35:3. Ps 73:8-13. Is 58:3. Zp *1:12. **ordinance.** Heb. observation. Le 18:30. 22:9. 2 K 11:5, 6, 7 (watch). Ezk 40:45mg. 44:8mg. 48:11mg. Hab 2:1 (watch). Zc 3:7mg. **and that.** Is 58:3. Jl 2:12. Zc 7:3-6. Ja 4:9. **mournfully.** Heb. in black. Is 50:3.

15. **we call.** Ml 4:1. Est 5:10-14. Ps 10:3, 4. 49:18, 19. *73:3, 12-17. Da 4:30, 31, 37. 5:20-28. Ac 12:21-23. 1 P 5:5. **yea.** Ml 2:17. Jb 12:6. 21:7-15, 30. Pr 12:12. Ec 9:1, 2. Je 12:1, 2. Hab 1:13-17. **set.** Heb. built. Jb 22:23. Je 12:16. **they that tempt.** Nu 14:22, 23. Dt 6:16. Ps 78:18, 41, 56. 95:9. 106:14. Mt 4:6, 7. Ac 5:9. 1 C 10:9. He 3:9.

16. **that feared.** ver. 5. Ml 4:2. Ge 22:12. 1 K 18:3, 4, 12, 13. Jb +*28:28. Ps 33:18. *66:16. *111:10. 112:1. *147:11. Is *50:10. Je ◑8:6. Ac *9:31. *10:2. Re *15:4. **spake often.** Dt 6:6-8. 1 S 9:27. 23:16-18. Est 4:5-17.

Ps 16:3. *66:16. 73:15-17. +*119:63. Pr 13:20. 18:24. Ezk *9:4. Da 2:17, 18. +*11:33. Lk 2:38. *24:14-31. Jn 1:40-47. 12:20-22. Ac 1:13. 2:1. 4:23-30. Ro *12:13. 2 C +*7:2. Ep √5:19. 1 Th 5:11, 14. He +*3:12, 13. √10:24, 25. √12:15. 1 P *4:9, 10. 3 J 8-10. **one to another.** Ro +*12:5. **the Lord hearkened.** 2 S 7:1-4. 2 Ch 6:7, 8. Ps *139:4. Mt √18:19, 20. Ac 4:31-33. **a book.** ♪22D5K1A, Ex +32:32. Est 2:23. 6:1. Jb 19:23-25. Ps *56:8. 139:16. Is *65:6. Da *7:10. Mt √12:35-37. Re *13:8. *20:12. **of remembrance.** Ex 28:29♪℗. Nu 10:10♪℗. **feared the Lord.** Ps *145:19. **that thought.** Ps 5:1. √10:4. *19:14. *20:7. *37:4. *94:19. 104:33, 34. 139:17, 18. Is √26:3mg, 8. He *4:12, 13. **his name.** Ps +√9:10.

17. **they shall.** SS 2:16. Je *31:33. 32:38, 39. Ezk 16:8. 36:27, 28. Zc +*13:9. Jn √10:27-30. *17:6, 9, 10, 24. Ro +*11:1. 1 C 3:22, 23. 6:20. 15:23. Ga 5:24. 2 Th √1:7-10. He *12:16. Is +*2:11. Ezk +*38:14. Mt *7:22. 2 Th +*1:10. **jewels.** *or*, special treasures. Ex *19:5♪℗. Dt 7:6♪℗. 14:2♪℗. 26:17, 18♪℗. 1 Ch 29:3. Ps *135:4. Pr 31:10. Ec 2:8. Is *62:3, 4. T *2:14. 1 P *2:9. **and I.** Ne 13:22. Ps *103:8-13. Is 26:20, 21. Je 31:20. Zp 2:2. Mt 25:34. Ro 8:32. 2 C 6:18. 1 J 3:1-3. **son.** Ml 1:6. 1 P 1:13-16.

18. **shall.** ver. 14, 15. Ml 1:4. Jb 6:29. 17:10. Je *12:15. Jl 2:14. Zc 1:6. **discern.** T#462. Ge +*18:25. Jb +2:3 (T#645). Ps *58:10, 11. 94:13. +*149:7, 9. Is *3:10, 11. Je 15:19, 20. Ezk *44:23, 24. Da +*12:1-3. Mt +*10:15n. 13:43, 48-50. +*25:46. +28:19 (T#458). Ro 2:5, 6. 2 Th *1:5-10. Re *20:12. **righteous.** T#648. Ps 37:16, 17. **between him.** Jsh √24:15. Da 3:17-26. Jn *12:26. Ac *16:17. *27:23. Ro *1:9. *6:16-22. 1 Th *1:9.

MALACHI 4

The judgments awaiting the impenitent and unbelieving Jews, and the benefits to be enjoyed by believers, at the "rising of the Sun of righteousness," 1-3. The people are charged to regard and exhorted to study the law of Moses, 4; and John the Baptist is predicted under the name of Elijah, 5, 6.

1. **the day.** ver. 5. Ml *3:2. Ezk 7:10. Jl +*2:1, 31. Zp 1:14-16. Zc 14:1, 2. Lk 19:43, 44. 21:20-24. 2 P +*3:7-12. **shall burn.** Ps √21:9, 10. +*50:2, 3. 97:3. Is 1:31. 4:4. *10:16-18. √24:6. 26:11. 29:6. *31:9. √66:15. Ezk 22:21, 31. 36:5. *38:19. Ob 18. Na 1:5, 6. Zp *1:18. 3:8. Mt *3:12. 2 Th √1:8. **and all the proud.** Ml 3:15, 18. Ex 15:7. Ps *1:4-6. *119:+*21, 119. Is 2:12-17. 5:24. 24:4. 40:24. 41:2. 47:14. Na 1:10. Lk 1:51, 53. Re 1:7. **burn them up.** Dt 4:24. Ps √21:9, 10. √24:6. +*30:30-33. Mt *13:30, 40, 42, 49, 50. Jn *15:6. 2 P +√3:7. **that it.** Jb 18:16. Am 2:9. **neither root nor.** Hab 3:13.

2. **that fear.** Ml +*3:16. Ps *85:9. Is 50:10. 66:1,

2. Lk 1:50. Ac 13:26. Re 11:18. **the Sun.** Ge 1:16. Dt 4:31. Jg *5:31. 2 S *23:4. Ps 67:1. *84:11. Pr +*4:18. Is 9:2. 30:26. 49:6. *60:1-3, 19, 20. Ho *6:3. Mt 4:15, 16. *13:43. Lk 1:78. 2:32. Jn 1:4, 8, 14. 8:12. 9:4. 12:35, 36, 40. Ac 13:47. 26:18. Ep 5:8-14. 2 P √1:19. 1 J 2:8. Re 2:28. 22:16. **arise.** ♪105. Hypotyposis; or, Word Picture B445. The visible representation of objects or actions by words. For other instances of this figure see Dt 28:1-14. 28:15-45. 28:49-68. Ps ch. 22. 37:35. 45:2. ch. 59. 78:65, 66. 92:12-14. Is 1:6-9. 1:11-15. 5:26-30. 34:1. 44:9-17. 46:6, 7. 53:2. Je 4:19-31. La 4:4-8. Col 2:14, 15. Re 19:11-16. **healing.** Ps 103:3. 147:3. Is 53:5. 57:18, 19. Je 17:14. 33:6. Ezk 47:12. Ho 6:1. 14:4. Mt 11:5. Re 22:2. **wings.** Ru 2:12. Mt 23:37. **ye shall.** Ps *92:12-14. Is 49:9, 10. 55:12, 13. *66:14. Je 31:9-14. Ho 14:5-7. Jn 15:2-5. 2 Th 1:3. 2 P +*3:18.

3. **tread down.** Ge +*3:15. Jsh 10:24, 25. 2 S 22:43. Jb 40:12. Ps 18:40-42. +*58:10. 91:13. 101:8. +*149:7, 9. Pr 2:21. 11:31. Is 17:14. 25:10. 26:6. 41:11, 12, 15. 63:3-6. Ezk 38:17-22. 39:6-16. Da 7:18, 27. Mi 4:13. 5:8. *7:10, 15, 16. Zc 9:13-16. *10:5. Jn +*18:36. Ro *16:20. Re 11:15. 14:20. 19:19, 20. **ashes.** Ezk 28:18. **in the day.** Ml 3:17. Ezk +*30:3.

4. **the law.** Ex +*20:3-17♪℗, etc. Dt 4:5, 6. Ps *147:19, 20. Is +*8:20. 42:21. Mt 5:17-20. 19:16-22. 22:36-40. Mk 12:28-34. Lk 10:25-28. 16:29-31. Jn +*5:39-47. Ro 3:31. 13:1-10. Ga 5:13, 14, 24, 25. Ja 2:9-13. **Moses my servant.** Nu 12:7♪℗. **in Horeb.** Dt *4:10♪℗. **with the statutes.** Ex ch. 21-23. Le ch. 1. Dt 4:1♪℗. Ps 147:19.

5. **I will send.** Ml 3:1. Is +*40:3. Mt √11:13, 14. *17:9-13. 27:47-49. Mk 9:11-13. Lk 1:17. 7:26-28. 9:30. Jn ◑√1:21, 25. **Elijah the prophet.** 2 Ch 21:12. Mt 17:3. Re 11:3-12. **before the coming.** Is 66:7. Jl 2:31. Hab +*3:16. Zp 2:2. 3:8. Mt ◑24:29. Ac 2:20. **great and dreadful.** ver. 1. Is +*2:12. +*13:6. Je +*30:7. Ezk 30:3. Da 12:1. Jl *2:31. Am +*5:18. Ac 2:19, 20. Re 6:17. **day of the Lord.** 1 C +*3:13. 2 Th +*1:10. Re 1:10n.

6. **turn.** Lk *1:16, ▶17, 76. **fathers to the children.** Ml 2:13n. Ge +*18:19. Ex +*13:8. Dt +*6:20. 2 S +6:20. 1 Ch +*28:9. Jb +*1:5. Ps √78:3, 5-8. +*101:2 (T#492). Pr +*19:18. +*22:6. Is 28:9. 38:19. 2 C 12:14. Ep √6:4. Col √3:21. 1 T 3:4. +*5:8. 2 T +*3:14-17. **children to their fathers.** Ex +*20:12. Le 19:3. Dt *27:16. Ps 34:11. Pr *1:8. 6:20. 7:1. 10:1. ◑+*15:20. 17:6. *20:11, 20. *23:22. *30:17. Ec 12:1. Is 45:10. Ezk 20:18. ◑*22:7. Mi ◑*7:6. Mt *15:4. Mk *7:10. Ep √6:1-3. Ph +*2:12. Col √3:20. 1 T *5:4. **lest.** Is 61:2. Da +*9:26, 27. Zc 11:6. 13:8. 14:2. Mt *22:7. 23:35-38. 24:27-30. Mk 13:14-26. Lk 19:41-44. 21:22-27. **and smite.** Dt 29:19, etc. Is +*24:6. 43:28. 65:15. Da +*9:11. Zc +*5:3. 14:12. Mk 11:21. Ga *3:10. He 6:8. 10:26-31. Re 22:3, 20, 21.

THE NEW TREASURY
OF SCRIPTURE
KNOWLEDGE

NEW TESTAMENT

MATTHEW

The geneology of Christ in the line of Joseph, from Abraham and David, 1-17. His miraculous conception, by the Holy Ghost, of the virgin Mary: and the doubts of Joseph, to whom she was espoused, removed by an angel; who directs him to take her home, and to call the Son born of her, Jesus, 18-21. This is shown to accord with the prediction of Isaiah, 22, 23. Joseph obeys, and Jesus is born, 24, 25.

1. A.M. 4000. B.C. 5. **generation**. Ge 2:4. 5:1. 37:2. Is 53:8. Lk 3:23-38. Ro *9:5. **Christ**. Mt 27:17. Col ◐4:11. **the son**. ♪171G, Ge +13:8. **of David**. Mt 9:27. *12:23. 15:22. 20:30. 21:9. 22:42-45. 2 S 7:13, 16. Ps 89:36. *132:11. Is +*9:6, 7. *11:1. Je +*23:5. 33:15-17, 26. Am 9:11. Zc 12:8. Lk *1:31, 32, 69, 70. Jn *7:42. Ac 2:30. +*13:22, 23. Ro *1:3, 4. 2 T 2:8. Re *22:16. **the son**. ♪171G, Ge +13:8. **of Abraham**. Ge +*12:3. +*♣22:18. 26:3-5. 28:13, 14. Lk +*3:34. Ro 4:13. Ga √3:16. He *2:16.

2. **Abraham**. Ge *21:2-5. Jsh 24:2, 3. 1 Ch 1:28. Is 51:2. Lk +*3:34. Ac 7:8. Ro 9:7-9. He 11:11, 17, 18. **begat Isaac**. Ge +*♣17:19. ♣*21:12. **Isaac begat**. Ge *25:26. Jsh 24:4. 1 Ch 1:34. Is 41:8. Ml 1:2, 3. Ro 9:10-13. **Jacob**. i.e. *supplanter*, ✻S#2384g. Mt 1:2, 2, 15, 16. 8:11. 22:32. Mk 12:26. Lk 1:33. 3:34. 13:28. 20:37. Jn 4:5, 6, 12. Ac 3:13. 7:8, 12, 14, 15, 32, 46. Ro 9:13. 11:26. For ✻S#3290h, see Ge +25:26. **Jacob begat**. Ge *29:32-35. 30:5-20. 35:16-19. 46:8, etc. 49:8-12. Ex 1:2-5. Nu +*♣24:17. 1 Ch 2:1, etc. 5:1, 2. Lk 1:33. 3:23, 33, *34. Ac 7:8. He *7:14. Re 7:5, Juda. **Judas**. Ge +*♣49:10. 1 Ch +*♣5:2. Ps +*♣60:7. He *7:14.

3. **Judas**. Ge *38:27, 29, 30. 46:12, Judah, Pharez, Zarah. Nu 26:20, 21. 1 Ch 2:3, 4, Zerah. 9:4. **Phares**. i.e. *divisions*, ✻S#5329g. Mt 1:3. Lk 3:33. For ✻S#6557h, see Ge +46:12, Pharez. **Zara**. i.e. *a rising; clearness*, ✻S#2196g. For ✻S#2226h, see Ge +38:30, Zarah. **Thamar**. i.e. *a palm tree*, ✻S#2283g. For ✻S#8559h, see Ge +38:6, Tamar. Ge 38:6, 11, 24-26, Tamar. 1 Ch *2:4. **and Phares**. Ge 46:12. Nu 26:21. Ru *4:12, 18. 1 Ch 2:5. 4:1, Hezron. Lk +3:33. **Aram**. i.e. *exalted*, ✻S#689g. Lk 3:33. For ✻S#7410h, see Jb +32:2, Ram. Ru 4:19. 1 Ch 2:9, Ram.

4. **Aminadab**. Ru 4:19, 20. 1 Ch 2:10-12, Amminadab. **Naasson**. i.e. *serpent, enchanter*, ✻S#3476g. Lk 3:32. For ✻S#5177h, see 1 Ch +2:10, Nahshon. Nu 1:7. 2:3. 7:12, 17. 10:14, Nahshon.

5. **Salmon**. Ru 4:21. 1 Ch 2:11, 12, Salma, Boaz. **Booz**. ✻S#1003g. Mt 1:5. Lk 3:32. For ✻S#1162h, see Ru +2:1, Boaz. **Rachab**. i.e. *breadth*, ✻S#4477g. See also ✻S#4460h: He +11:31, Rahab. Ja 2:25. For ✻S#7343h, see Jsh +2:1, Rahab. Jsh 2:1, etc. 6:22-25. He 11:31. Ja 2:25, Rahab. **Booz**. Ru 1:4, 16, 17, 22. ch. 2-4. **Ruth**. i.e. *satisfied*, ✻S#4503g. For ✻S#7327h, see Ru +1:4, Ruth. Obed. Ru *4:13, 21, 22. **Obed begat**. Lk 3:32. **Jesse**. i.e. *substance*, ✻S#2421g. Mt 1:5, 6. Lk 3:32. Ac 13:22. Ro 15:12. For ✻S#3448h, see 1 Ch +2:12, Jesse.

6. **Jesse**. Ru 4:22. 1 S 16:1, 11-13. 17:12, 58. 20:30, 31. 22:8. 2 S 23:1. 1 Ch 2:15. Ps 72:20. Is ♣11:1, 10.

Lk 3:23, 32. Ac 13:22, 23. **David**. i.e. *beloved*, ✻S#1138g. Mt 1:1, 6, 17, 17, 20. 9:27. 12:3, 23. 15:22. 20:30, 31. 21:9, 15. 22:42, 43, 45. Mk 2:25. 10:47, 48. 11:10. 12:35, 36, 37. Lk 1:27, 32, 69. 2:4, 4, 11. 3:31. 6:3. 18:38, 39. 20:41, 42, 44. Jn 7:42, 42. Ac 1:16. 2:25, 29, 34. 4:25. 7:45. 13:22, 22, 34, 36. 15:16. Ro 1:3. 4:6. 11:9. 2 T 2:8. He 4:7. 11:32. Re 3:7. 5:5. 22:16. For ✻S#1732h, see 1 S +16:19, David. **Solomon**. i.e. *peaceableness*, ✻S#4672g. Mt 1:6, 7. 6:29. 12:42. Lk 11:31. 12:27. Jn 10:23. Ac 3:11. 5:12. 7:47. For ✻S#8010h, see 2 S +5:14, Solomon. 2 S *12:24, 25. 1 Ch 3:5. 14:4. 28:5. **her**. 2 S 11:3, 26, 27. 1 K 1:11-17, 28-31. 15:5. Ro 8:3. **Urias**. i.e. *flame of Jehovah*, ✻S#3774g. For ✻S#223h, see 2 S +11:3, Uriah. 2 S 23:39. 1 Ch 11:41, Uriah.

7. **Roboam**. i.e. *enlargement of the people*, ✻S#4497g. For ✻S#7346h, see 1 K +14:21, Rehoboam. 1 K 11:43. 12:1, etc. 1 Ch 3:10. 2 Ch 9:31. 13:7, Rehoboam. **Abia**. i.e. *worshipper of Jehovah*, ✻S#7g. Mt 1:7. Lk 1:5. For ✻S#29h, see 1 S +8:2, Abiah, and 1 Ch +3:10, Abia. 1 K 14:31, Abijah. 2 Ch 12:1, Abijah. **Asa**. i.e. *curing*, ✻S#760g. Mt 1:7, 8. For ✻S#609h, see 1 Ch 9:16, Asa. 1 K 15:8-23. 2 Ch ch. 14-16.

8. **Josaphat**. i.e. *Jehovah is judge*, ✻S#2498g. For ✻S#3092h, see 2 S +8:16, Jehoshaphat. 1 K 15:24. 22:2, etc. 2 Ch 3:1. 2 Ch ch. 17-20, Jehoshaphat. **Joram**. i.e. *height; Jehovah has exalted*, ✻S#2496g. For ✻S#3141h, see 1 Ch +26:25, Joram. 1 K 22:50. 2 K 8:16, Jehoram. 1 Ch 3:11. 2 Ch 21:1. **begat**. A comparison with Old Testament history shows Matthew compressed his genealogy at this point, omitting Ahaziah (2 K *8:25), Joash (2 K 11:2), Amaziah (2 K 14:1), who belong between Joram (2 K 8:24) and Uzziah (2 Ch 26:1). 1 K +*15:10n. **Ozias**. i.e. *strength of God*, ✻S#3604g. Mt 1:8, 9. For ✻S#5818h, see 2 Ch +26:1, Uzziah. 2 K 14:21. 15:1-6, Azariah.

9. **Joatham**. i.e. *Jehovah is perfect; God showed himself wholly*, ✻S#2488g. For ✻S#3147h, see Jg +9:5, Jotham. 2 K 15:7, 32-38. 1 Ch 3:11-13. 2 Ch 26:21. ch. 27, Jotham. **Achaz**. i.e. *possessor*, ✻S#881g. For ✻S#271h, see 1 Ch +8:35, Ahaz. 2 K 15:38. 16:1, etc. 2 Ch 27:9. 28:1, etc. Is 7:1-13, Ahaz. **Ezekias**. i.e. *strength of God*, ✻S#1478g. Mt 1:9, 10. For ✻S#2396h, see 2 K +16:20, Hezekiah. ch. 18-20. 2 Ch 28:27. ch. 29-32. Is ch. 36-39, Hezekiah.

10. **Manasses**. i.e. *forgetfulness*, ✻S#3128g. Mt 1:10. Re 7:6. For ✻S#4519h, see Ge +41:51, Manasseh. 2 K *20:21. *21:1-18. 24:3, 4. 1 Ch 3:13-15. 2 Ch 32:33. 33:1-19, Manasseh. **Amon**. i.e. *son or foster-child*, ✻S#300g. For ✻S#526h, see Ne +7:59, Amon. 2 K 21:19-26. 2 Ch 33:20-24. **Josias**. i.e. *sustained of Jehovah*, ✻S#2502g. Mt 1:10, 11. For ✻S#2977h, see 1 K +13:2, Josiah. 2 K 21:26. ch. 22. 23:1-30. 2 Ch 33:25. ch. 34, 35. Je 1:2, 3, Josiah.

11. **Josias**. "Some read, Josias begat Jakim, and Jakim begat Jechonias." **Jechonias**. i.e. *whom God establishes*, ✻S#2423g. Mt 1:11, 12. For ✻S#3204h, see Je +24:1, Jeconiah. 2 K 23:31-37. ch. 24. 1 Ch 3:15-17. 2 Ch 36:1, etc. Je 22:10-28, √30n. **about**. 2 K 24:14-

16. 25:11. 2 Ch 36:10, 20. Je 27:20. 39:9. 52:11-15, 28-30. Da 1:2.

12. **Jechonias.** 2 K 25:27, Jehoiachin. 1 Ch 3:17, 19, etc., Jeconiah. Je 22:24, 28, Coniah. **Salathiel.** i.e. *the loan of God*, ⁕S#4528g. Mt 1:12, 12. Lk 3:27. For ⁕S#7597h, see Hg +1:1, Shealtiel. **and.** Ezr 3:2. 5:2. Ne 12:1. Hg 1:1, 12, 14. 2:2, 23, Shealtiel, Zerubbabel. Lk 3:27. **Zorobabel.** i.e. *born at Babylon; dispelling of human illusions*, ⁕S#2216g. Mt 1:12, 13. Lk 3:27. For ⁕S#2216h, see Hg +1:1, Zerubbabel.

13. **Abiud.** i.e. *the honor of a father*, ⁕S#10g. For ⁕S#31h, see 1 Ch +8:3, Abihud. **Azor.** i.e. *helpful*, ⁕S#107g. Mt 1:13, 14. Compare ⁕S#5809h, Je +28:1, Azur.

14. **Sadoc.** i.e. *righteous*, ⁕S#4524g. For ⁕S#6659h, see 2 S +8:17, Zadok. **Achim.** i.e. *judicious*, ⁕S#885g. Compare ⁕S#3137h, 1 Ch +4:22, Jokim. **Eliud.** i.e. *God of majesty*, ⁕S#1664g. Mt 1:14, 15.

15. **Eleazar.** i.e. *God has helped*, ⁕S#1648g. For ⁕S#499h, see Ex +6:23, Eleazar. **Matthan.** i.e. *a gift*, ⁕S#3157g. For ⁕S#4977h, see 2 K +11:18, Mattan.

16. **Joseph.** i.e. *to progress; he shall add*, ⁕S#2501g. Mt 1:16, 18, 19, 20, 24. 2:13, 19. Lk 1:27. 2:4, 16, 33, 43. √3:23. 4:22. Jn 1:45. 6:42. For ⁕S#3130h, see Ge +30:24, Joseph. **Mary.** i.e. *myrrh of the sea*, ⁕S#3137g. (1) The mother of Jesus. Mt 1:16, 18, 20. 2:11. 13:55. Mk 6:3. Lk 1:27, 30, 34, 38, 39, 41, 46, 56. 2:5, 16, 19, 34. Ac 1:14. (2) Mary Magdalene. Mt 27:56a, 61a. 28:1a. Mk 15:40a, 47a. 16:1a. Lk 8:2. 24:10a. Jn 19:25b. 20:1, 11, 16, 18. (3) Mary, sister of Martha. Lk 10:39, 42. Jn 11:1, 2, 19, 20, 28, 31, 32, 45. 12:3. (4) Mary, mother of James. Mt 27:56b, 61b. 28:1b. Mk 15:40b, 47b. 16:1b, 9. Jn 19:25a. (5) Mary, mother of John. Ac 12:12. (6) Mary, of Rome. Ro 16:6. For ⁕S#4813h, see Ex +15:20, Miriam. **of whom.** The Greek reference is to Mary, not Joseph (compare verse +*11, especially Je 22:30). Mk +*6:3. Lk 1:31-35. 2:7, 10, 11. **Jesus.** i.e. *Savior*, S#2424g. For ⁕S#3091h, see Ex +17:9, Joshua. **who.** Mt 27:17, 22. Jn 4:25.

17. **So all.** ℐ166. Symperasma; or, Concluding Summary B468: addition of conclusion by way of a brief summary. For other instances of this figure see Jn 20:30. He 11:39. **Christ.** ver. 18. Mt 2:4. 11:2. 16:16, 20. 22:42. 23:10. 24:5, 23. 26:63. Mk 8:29. 9:41. 12:35. 13:21. 14:61. 15:32. Lk 3:15. 4:41. 9:20. 20:41. 22:67. 23:35, 39. 24:26, 46. Jn 1:20, 25, ◐41mg. 3:28. 4:◐25, 29. 7:26, 27, 31, 41, 42. 10:24. 11:27. 12:34. *20:31.

18. **the birth.** Lk 1:27, etc. **espoused.** Ge 24:53. Jg *14:8. Lk *1:26, 27. Jn 3:29. **before.** Mt 26:34g, 75g. Ge *29:26-28. Ex 1:19. Jg *14:8. Is 7:+✱14, 16. Mk 14:30g, 72g. Lk 2:26g. 3:23. 22:34g, 61g. Jn 4:49g. 8:◐41, *58g. 14:9g. Ac 2:20g. 7:2g. 25:16g. Ga √4:4. **came together.** Ge 6:4. 38:18. Dt *20:7n. Ru +4:13. 1 C 7:5. **of the Holy Ghost.** Ge 1:2. +*3:15. Jb 14:4. 15:14. Ps 104:30. Lk 1:25, +*35. Ga √4:4, 5. He *7:26. 10:5. Used here without the Greek articles (*pneuma hagion*), as at Mt 1:18, 20. 3:11. Mk 1:8. Lk 1:15, 35, 41, 67. 2:25. 3:16. 4:1a. 11:13. Jn 1:33b. 7:39b. 20:22. Ac 1:2, 5, 8. 2:4a. 4:8, 31*. 6:3, 5. 7:55. 8:15, 17, 19. 9:17. 10:38, 45n. 11:16, 24. 13:9, 52. 19:2, 2, 6. Ro 5:5. 9:1. 14:17. 15:13, 16. 1 C 2:13*. 6:19◐. 12:3b. 2 C 6:6. 1 Th 1:5, 6. 2 T 1:14. T 3:5. He 2:4. 6:4. 1 P 1:12. 2 P 1:21. Ju 20. Alford (in his *Greek Testament*, vol. 1, p. 6) notes that the reference is to the Holy Spirit, for it is well known usage to omit

the articles after certain prepositions or when a word or expression came to bear a technical conventional meaning, as if it were a proper name. The *Companion Bible* suggests, however, that without the articles the expression refers to the gift given by the Holy Spirit, rather than to the Holy Spirit himself, the gift usually being specified in the context.

19. **Joseph.** ver. 20. **her husband.** Le 19:20. Dt 22:23, 24. **a just.** Ge 6:9. Ps 112:4, 5. Mk 6:20. Lk 2:25. Ac 10:22. **a public.** Ge 38:24. Le 20:10. Dt 22:21-24. Jn 8:4, 5. **was minded.** Dt 24:1-4. Mk 10:4.

20. **while.** Ps 25:8, 9. 94:19. 119:125. 143:8. Pr √3:5, 6. 12:5. Is √26:3mg. 30:21. **the angel.** Jg 13:3, 8, 9. Lk 1:10-13, 19, 26, etc. 2:8-14. **in a dream.** Mt 2:13, 19, 22. Ge 31:11. Nu 12:6. Jb 4:13-16. 33:15-17. Jl 2:28. **Joseph.** Is 7:2, 13. Je 33:26. Lk 2:4. **fear not.** Mt 28:5. Ge 46:3. Dt *22:21. 1 K 17:13. Is 51:7. Je 40:9. Lk 1:30. **for that.** ver. 18. Je 31:22. ℐ96G4. Heterosis of Gender B534. the neuter is put for the masculine or feminine. For other instances of this figure see Mt 18:11. Lk 1:35. Jn 1:46. 3:6n. He 7:7. 1 J 1:1. 5:4, 8n. **conceived.** Gr. begotten. S#1080g. Mt 1:2 (begat). 2:1 (born). 19:12. 26:24. Mk 14:21. Lk 1:13 (bear). Jn 1:13 (born). 3:3-8. 8:41. Ac 13:33. 1 C 4:15. Phm 10. He 1:5. 5:5. 11:12 (sprang), 23. 1 J 2:29. 3:9. 4:7. 5:1, 4, 18.

21. **she.** Ge 17:19, 21. 18:10. Jg 13:3. 2 K 4:16, 17. Lk 1:13, 35, 36. Ga √4:4, 5. **thou.** Lk 1:31. 2:21. **name.** ℐ144A4, Ge +4:26. **JESUS.** that is, *Savior*, Heb. Nu 13:16. 14:6. Ne 8:17. Hg 1:1. Zc 3:1. Lk 1:31. **for he shall save.** Ps 130:7, +*8. Is *12:1, 2. 45:21, 22. Je *23:6. 33:16. Ezk 36:25-29. Da +*9:24. Zc +*9:9. Mt *18:11. Lk +*19:10. Jn √1:29. √3:16. *12:47. Ac 3:26. √4:12. *5:30, 31. *13:23, 38, 39. 2 C *5:19. Ep *5:25-27. Col *1:20-23. 1 T *1:15. √4:10. T √2:14. He √7:25. 1 J √1:7. √2:1, 2. 3:5. Re +*1:5, 6. *7:14. **from their.** Mt *20:28. Ac 3:26. +*10:43. Ro *8:32. 2 C √5:21. Ga 1:3, 4. Ep *5:2. Col *1:14. 1 T +*2:6. T *2:14. 1 P *3:18. **sins.** Le +5:6.

22. **that.** Mt 2:15, 23. 5:17. 8:17. 12:17. 13:35. 21:4. 1 K 8:15, 24. Ezr 1:1. Lk 21:22. 24:44. Jn +*10:35. 12:38-40. 15:25. 17:12. 18:9. 19:24, 28, 36, 37. Ac 3:18. 13:27-29. Re 17:17.

23. **Behold.** ℐ92A. Gnome; or, Quotation B784. The citation of a well-known saying without giving the author's name, where the sense originally intended is preserved, though the words may vary. For other instances of this figure see Mt 2:6. 11:10. 12:18. 13:14, 15. 21:5, 16, 42. 22:44. 26:31. 27:35. Lk 4:18. Jn 19:37. Ac 3:22, 23. 13:33. 15:16, 17. Ro 14:11. 15:3, 12. Ep 4:8. He 1:8, 9, 10-13. 5:6. 7:17, 21. 10:5, 6. 1 P 2:6. **a virgin.** Is +*✱✱7:14. +*9:6. 11:1. ⁕S#3933g. Mt 1:23. 25:1, 7, 11. Lk *1:27, 27. Ac 21:9. 1 C 7:25, 28, 34, 36, 37. 2 C 11:2. Re 14:4. **they shall call his name.** or, his name shall be called. ℐ144A4, Ge +4:26. **Emmanuel.** Is +*7:14. 8:8, Immanuel. **interpreted.** ℐ95, Ps +7:13. **God with us.** Mt *28:20. Ps 46:7, 11. Is *7:14. 8:8-10. +*9:6, 7. +*12:2. 43:10, 11. *44:6. Mi +*5:2. Lk 1:32, 33. Jn √1:1, 14. Ac 18:9, 10. +*20:28. Ro 1:3, 4. √9:5. 2 C *5:19. Ph 2:5, 6. Col +√1:15, 16. √2:9. 1 T √3:16. 2 T 4:17, 22. He 1:3, +√8. 2 P √1:1. 1 J 3:16.

24. **did as.** Ge 6:22. 7:5. 22:2, 3. Ex 40:16, 19, 25, 27, 32. 2 K 5:11-14. Jn 2:5-8. +*15:14. He *11:7, 8, 24-31. Ja 2:21-26.

25. **knew.** Ge +4:1. **till.** ver. +18. Mk +*6:3. Lk

2:7. **she had.** Ex 13:2. 22:29. Lk 2:7. Ro 8:29. **and he.** Lk 2:21. **firstborn.** Ex 13:2. Lk *2:7, 21.

MATTHEW 2

Wise men from the east, guided by a star, come to Jerusalem, inquiring for "him, who was born King of the Jews," 1, 2. Herod, being alarmed, learns that Christ should be born at Bethlehem, and sends the wise men thither, 3-8. The star guides them to Jesus, whom they honor and worship; and, being warned by God, they return home another way, 9-12. Joseph is directed to go, with the child and his mother, into Egypt, 13-15. Herod murders the children at and near Bethlehem, 16-18. After Herod's death, Joseph returns from Egypt, with Jesus and Mary, and goes to dwell at Nazareth in Galilee, 19-23.

1. A.M. 4001. B.C. 4. "Fourth year before the account called *Anno Domini.*" **Jesus.** Mt 1:25. Lk 2:4-7. **Bethlehem.** i.e. *house of bread,* ✳S#965g. ver. *5, 6, 8, 16. 1 S 16:1. Mi +*5:2. Lk *2:4, 11, 15. Jn *7:42. For ✳S#1035h, see Jsh +19:15. **of Judaea.** Jsh 19:15. He 7:14. **the days.** ♪171T2B, Ps +102:11. **Herod.** i.e. *mount of pride,* ✳S#2264g. Mt 2:1, 3, 7, 12, 13, 15, 16, 19, 22. 14:1, 3, 6. Mk 6:14, 16, 17, 18, 20, 21, 22. 8:15. Lk 1:5. 3:1, 19, 19. 8:3. 9:7, 9. 13:31. 23:7, 8, 11, 12, 15. Ac 4:27. 12:1, 6, 11, 19, 20, 21. 13:1. 23:35. (1) Herod the Great, Mt 2:1-18. (2) Herod Antipas, Mk 6:16, 22. Lk 3:1. 13:32. 23:7-12. (3) Archelaus, Mt 2:22. (4) Philip, Lk 3:1. See Mk 6:22. (5) Herod Philip. Mk 6:17. (6) Herod Agrippa I, Ac 12:1-19. (7) Herod Agrippa II, Ac 26:28. This was Herod the Great, for an account of whom see the Connection of the Old and New Testaments in the Comprehensive Bible. ver. 3, 19. Ge +*49:10. Da +*9:24, 25. Hg *2:6-9. **there came.** Ps ✳72:10. **wise men.** Mt *12:42. Ezr 7:9. Est 1:13. Je 39:3, 13. Da 2:12, 48. 4:6. **from the east.** ♪171.O.6, 1 K +4:30. Ge 10:30. 25:6. Nu 23:7. 1 K *4:30. Jb 1:3. Ps 72:9-12. Is 11:10. 60:1, etc. **to.** Lk 2:22. **Jerusalem.** i.e. *foundation of peace,* ✳S#2414g. Mt 2:1, 3. 3:5. 4:25. 5:35. 15:1. 16:21. 20:17, 18. 21:1, 10. Mk 3:8, 22. 7:1. 10:32, 33. 11:11, 15, 27. 15:41. Lk 2:22, 42. 18:31. 19:28. 23:7. Jn 1:19. 2:13, 23. 4:20, 21, 45. 5:1, 2. 10:22. 11:18, 55. 12:12. Ac 1:4. 8:1, 14. 11:2, 22, 27. 13:13. 18:21. 20:16. 21:17. 25:1, 7, 9, 15, 24. 26:4, 10, 20. 28:17. Ga 1:17, 18. 2:1. See also ✳S#2419g, Mk +11:1. For ✳S#3389h, see Jsh +10:1.

2. **born.** Mt 21:5. Ps *2:6. Is +*9:6, 7. 32:1, 2. Je +*23:5. 30:9. Zc +*9:9. Lk *1:32, 33. *2:11. *19:38. *23:3, 38. Jn *1:49. *12:13. *18:37. 19:12-15, 19. **King.** Mt 27:11, 37. Je 23:5. **his star.** Nu +*24:17. Is *60:3. Lk 1:78, 79. 2 P √1:19. Re 2:28. *22:16. **are come.** Ge +*49:10. **worship.** ver. 10, 11. Ps *45:11. Jn √5:23. *9:38. +√20:28. He √1:6.

3. **he.** Mt 8:29. 23:37. 1 K 18:17, 18. Lk ◐2:25, 38. Jn 11:47, 48. Ac 4:2, 24-27. 5:24-28. 16:20, 21. 17:6, 7.

4. **the chief.** Mt 21:15, 23. 26:3, 47. 27:1. 1 Ch 24:4, etc. 2 Ch 36:14. Ezr 10:5. Ne 12:7. Ps *2:2. Lk 1:5. Jn 7:32. 18:3. **scribes.** Mt 7:29. 13:52. 2 Ch 23:8. 34:13, 15. Ezr *7:6, 11, 12. Je 8:8. Mk 8:31. Lk 20:19. 23:10. Jn 8:3. Ac 4:5. 6:12. 23:9. **he demanded.** Ml +*2:7. Jn 3:10. **should be.** ♪96C6. Heterosis of Tenses B521: the present put for the future, to show that something will certainly come to pass, and is spoken

of as though it were already present. For instances of this figure see Mt 3:10. 5:46. 11:3. 17:11. 26:2, 29. Mk 9:31. Lk 13:32. 17:21n. Jn 12:26, 31, 34. Ac (1:6). Ro *8:30. 1 C 15:2, 12, (35), 42-44. (16:5). 2 C *5:1. Ep 1:3. Col 1:13n. He 12:28n. 2 P 3:11, 12. Re (11:5).

5. **they said.** Jn +*6:14. **In Bethlehem.** Ge 35:19. Jsh 19:15. Ru 1:1, 19. 2:4. 4:11. 1 S 16:1. Mi +*5:2. Jn 7:42.

6. **And thou.** ♪92A, Mt 1:23. ♪92D1, ver. 15. **Bethlehem.** ver. 1. Mi +*5:2. Jn *7:42. **the land.** ♪171.O.5. Synecdoche of the Whole B638: the land is put for city. **of Judah.** 1 Ch +✳5:2. Mi +✳5:2. He 7:14. Re 5:5. ♪92F2. Gnome; or, Quotation B794: where the words are changed by an inference and explanation. Here, we have "land of Judah" instead of Ephrathah, which was its ancient name (see Ge 35:16, 19. 48:7), as being better understood by Herod. Instead of the positive "art little," we have the negative, "art in no wise least," because, though little in the time of Micah, yet now, after the birth of the Messiah, it could no longer be so called, in view of the event which had given the city true greatness. Instead of "thousands," we have by Metonymy, properly translated, "princes," because Messiah was the Prince of princes. Instead of "be ruler," we have "be shepherd of" (A.V. rule, margin *feed*). This explanation brings in the next verse but one in Micah, "He shall stand and feed." Finally, the words of the prophet, "unto me," are omitted, because the emphasis is now on the *fact* rather than the *purpose* (though both were true); and hence the *reason* is given in the word "for," and the fact is added in the words, "my people" (B794). For other instances of this figure see Ac 7:43. Ro 9:27, 29, 33. Ep 4:8. **art not.** ♪175B, Ge +21:16. **princes.** ♪121K3. Metonymy of the Subject B583: "princes" are put for the *thousands* whom they led. Jg 6:15mg. 1 S 10:19. Mi +*5:2. **a Governor.** Mt 28:18. Ge +*17:6. +*49:10. Nu +*24:19. 1 Ch +*5:2. Ps *2:1-6. Is +*9:6, 7. Ep 1:22. Col *1:18. He 7:5. Re *2:27. *11:15. **rule.** *or,* feed. 2 S 5:2. 7:7. Ps 78:71, 72. Is *40:11. Je *23:4-6. Ezk *34:23-25. *37:24-26. Mi 5:4. Jn 21:16. Re +*2:27. 7:17. 12:5. 19:15. **Israel.** i.e. *prince with God,* ✳S#2474g. Mt 2:6, 20, 21. 8:10. 9:33. 10:6, 23. 15:24, 31. 19:28. 27:9, 42. Mk 12:29. 15:32. Lk 1:16, 54, 68, 80. 2:25, 32, 34. 4:25, 27. 7:9. 22:30. 24:21. Jn 1:31, 49. 3:10. 12:13. Ac 1:6. 2:36. 4:8, 10, 27. 5:21, 31. 7:23, 37, 42. 9:15. 10:36. 13:17, 23, 24. 28:20. Ro 9:6, 27, 27, 31. 10:1, 19, 21. 11:2, 7, 25, 26. 1 C 10:18. 2 C 3:7, 13. Ga 6:16. Ep 2:12. Ph 3:5. He 8:8, 10. 11:22. Re 2:14. 7:4. 21:12. For S#3478h, see Ge +32:28.

7. **when he.** Mt 26:3-5. Ex 1:10. 1 S 18:21. Ps 10:9, 10. 55:21. 64:4-6. 83:3, 4. Is 7:5-7. Ezk 38:10, 11. Re 12:1-5, 15.

8. **Go.** 1 S 23:22, 23. 2 S 17:14. 1 K 19:2. Jb 5:12, 13. Ps 33:10, 11. Pr +*21:30. La 3:37. 1 C *3:19, 20. **that.** Mt 26:48, 49. 2 S 15:7-12. 2 K 10:18, 19. Ezr 4:1, 2. Ps *12:2, 3. 55:11-15. Pr 26:24, 25. Je 41:5-7. Lk 20:20, 21.

9. **the star.** ver. 2. Ps *25:12. Pr *2:1-6. 8:17. 2 P √1:19.

10. **the star.** ♪63I1D, Nu 26:4. By ellipsis, supply (standing over where the young child was). **they rejoiced.** ♪147D, Ge +1:29. Dt 32:43. Ps 67:4. 105:3. Lk 2:10, 11, 20. Ac 13:46-48. Ro 15:9-13.

11. **they saw.** Lk 2:16, 26-32, 38. **worshipped.** ver.

*2. Mt +*4:9, 10. +8:2. +*14:33. Ps *2:12. 95:6. Is ★49:7. Jn √5:22, 23. Ac *10:25, 26. He *1:6. Re +*19:10. +*22:8-10. **treasures.** ƒ121.O, Ge +28:22. **presented.** *or,* offered. Ge 43:11. 1 S 9:7. 10:27. 1 K 10:2, 10, 25. 2 Ch 32:23. Ps 45:12. 68:29. ★72:10, 15. 76:11. Is 18:7. ★60:6. **gold.** Ps 72:15. Is 60:6. **frank-incense.** Ex 30:23, 34. Le 2:1, 2. 6:15. Nu 7:14, 86. Ps *45:8. SS 4:6, 14. Is 60:6. Ml 1:11. Re 5:8mg. 18:13. **myrrh.** Ex 30:23. Est 2:12. Ps *45:8. Pr 7:17. SS 1:13. 3:6. 4:6, 14. 5:1, 5, 13. Mk 15:23. Jn 19:39.

12. **warned.** ver. 22. Lk 2:26. **in a dream.** ver. 13, 19, 22. Mt 1:20. 27:19. Ge 20:6, 7. 31:11, 24. Nu 12:6. 1 K 3:5. Jb 33:15-17. Da 2:19. **they departed.** Ex *1:17. Ac *4:19. +*5:29. 1 C 3:19.

13. **the angel.** ver. 19. Mt 1:20. Ac 5:19. 10:7, 22. 12:11. He 1:13, 14. **appeareth.** ƒ96C5. Heterosis of Tenses B520: the present put for the past. For other instances of this figure see Ac 9:26. Ga 2:14. He 2:16mg. 7:3, 8. **Arise.** Mt 10:23. Pr +*22:3. Re 12:6, 14. **Egypt.** i.e. *tribulation,* ❋S#125g. Mt 2:13, 14, 15, 19. Ac 2:10. 7:9, 10, 10, 11, 12, 15, 17, 34, 34, 36, 39, 40. 13:17. He 3:16. 8:9. 11:26, 27. Ju 5. Re 11:8. **be thou there.** Ex 1:17, 19-21. Da *6:10. Ac 5:29. **until.** ver. 19, 20. Jsh 3:13, 17. 4:10, 18. Da 3:25, 26. Ac 16:36. **for.** ver. 16. Ex 1:22. 2:2, 3. Jb 33:15, 17. Ac 7:19. Re 12:4. **destroy.** Ex=1:22. Gr. *apollumi,* ❋S#622g. Rendered (1) destroy: Mt 2:13. √10:28. 12:14. 21:41. 22:7. 27:20. Mk 1:24. 3:6. 9:22. 11:18. 12:9. Lk 4:34. 6:9. 9:56. 17:27, 29. 19:47. 20:16. Jn 10:10. Ro 14:15. 1 C 1:19. 10:9, 10. 2 C 4:9. Ja 4:12. Ju 5. (2) lose: Mt 10:39, 39, 42. 16:25, 25. Mk 8:35, 35. 9:41. Lk 9:24, 24, 25. 15:4, 8, 9. 17:33, 33. Jn 6:39. 12:25. 17:12. 18:9. 2 J 8. (3) be lost: Mt √18:11. Lk 15:4b, 6. √19:10. 2 C 4:3. (4) lost: Mt 10:6. 15:24. Lk *15:24, 32. Jn 6:12. (5) perish: Mt 5:29, 30. 8:25. 9:17. 18:14. 26:52. Mk 4:38. Lk 5:37. 8:24. 11:51. 13:3, 5, 33. 15:17. 21:18. Jn 3:15, 16. 6:27. 10:28. 11:50. Ac 5:37. Ro 2:12. 1 C 1:18. 8:11. 15:18. 2 C 2:15. 2 Th 2:10. He 1:11. Ja 1:11. 1 P *1:7. 2 P *3:6, 9. Ju 11. (6) be marred: Mk 2:22. (7) die: Jn 18:14.

14. **he took.** ver. 20, 21. Mt 1:24. Ac 26:19. **into Egypt.** Ge=37:28.

15. **until.** ver. 19. Ac 12:1-4, 23, 24. **that.** ver. 17, 23. Mt 1:22. 4:14, 15. 8:17. 12:16-18. 21:4. 26:54, 56. 27:35. Lk 24:44. Jn 19:28, 36. Ac 1:16. **Out.** Ge=37:36. Ex 4:22, 23. Nu 24:8. Ho ★11:1. He=11:27. ƒ92C. Gnome; or, Quotation B786: where the sense is accommodated, being quite different from that which was first intended, and the sense is accommodated by analogy to quite a different event or circumstance. For other instances of this figure see Mt 2:17, 18. 8:17. 13:35. 15:8, 9. 27:9, 10. Ac 13:40, 41. Ro 9:27, 28. 9:29. 10:6-8. 1 C 1:19, 20. 10:6, 11. Re 1:7, 17. 11:4. ƒ92D1. Gnome; or, Quotation B790: where the words are from the Hebrew. Here, the quotation of Ho 11:1 agrees with the Hebrew, not the Septuagint (LXX). For other instances of this figure see Mt 12:18-21. ƒ92D2. Gnome; or, Quotation B790: where the words are from the LXX, see Lk 4:18 for an example.

16. **when.** Ge 39:14, 17. Nu 22:29. 24:10. Jg 16:10. Jb 12:4. **was exceeding.** Pr 27:3, 4. Da 3:13, 19, 20. **and slew.** Ge 49:7. 2 K 8:12. Pr 28:15, 17. Is +*26:20, 21. 59:7. Ho 10:14. Re 17:6. **according.** ver. 7.

17. **fulfilled.** ver. 15. Je ★31:15. **Jeremy.** i.e. *exalted of the Lord,* ❋S#2408g. Mt 2:17. 16:14. 27:9. For S#3414h, see Je +1:1.

18. **Rama.** i.e. *height,* ❋S#4471g. For ❋S#7414h, see Je +31:15, Ramah. Jsh +*18:25. Jg 4:5. 19:13. 1 S 22:6. 1 K 15:17, 21. 2 Ch 16:1. Ezr 2:26. Ne 7:30. 11:33. Is 10:29. Je 31:15. 40:1. Ho 5:8. ƒ92C, ver. +15. **a voice.** Je ★31:15. **lamentation.** Je 4:31. 9:17-21. Ezk 2:10. Re 8:13. **Rachel.** i.e. *a ewe,* ❋S#4478g. For ❋S#7354g, see Ge +29:28. Ge 35:16-20. 48:7. 1 S 10:2. Je ★31:15. **would.** Ge 37:30, 33-35. 42:36. Jb 14:10. **are not.** Ge 37:30. 42:13, 36. Je 10:20. La 5:7.

19. **Herod.** Ps 76:10. Is 51:12. Da 8:25. 11:45. **an angel.** ver. 13. Mt 1:20. Ps 139:7. Je 30:10. Ezk 11:16.

20. **Arise.** ver. 13. Pr +*3:5, 6. for. Ex=4:19. 1 K 11:21, 40. 12:1-3. **they.** ƒ96F3, Ge +8:4. **child's.** Mt +√10:28. 26:38. Ge +12:13. Mk 3:4. 14:34. Lk 6:9. 17:33. Jn 12:25. Ac 3:23. Ro 11:3. He 10:39. Ja *5:20. Re √6:9. 8:9. *12:11. 16:3. **life.** Gr. *psuche* or *psyche,* ❋S#5590g. This Greek word occurs 105 times in the New Testament, and its uses and occurrences may be classified as follows: (1) ƒ121A7. Metonymy of the Cause, "soul" put for "life," which is the effect of it. The natural life of the body, Mt 2:20. 6:25, 25. 10:39, 39. 16:25, 25. 20:28. Mk 3:4. 8:35, 35. 10:45. Lk 6:9. 9:56. 12:22, 23. 14:26. 17:33a. Jn 10:11, 15, 17. 12:25a, 25b. 13:37, 38. 15:13. Ac 15:26. 20:10, 24. 27:10, 22. Ro 11:3. 16:4. Ph 2:30. 1 J 3:16, 16. Re 8:9. 12:11. Rendered "soul," Mt 16:26, 26. Mk 8:36, 37. Lk 12:20. 1 Th 2:8. (2) The immaterial, invisible part of man: Mt √10:28. Ac 2:27, 31. 1 Th 5:23. He 4:12. (3) The disembodied man (2 C 5:3, 4. 12:2): Re 6:9. 20:4. (4) The seat of personality: Lk 9:24, 24. He 6:19. 10:39. (5) ƒ121A9A. Metonymy of Cause. The seat of perception, feeling, desire: Mt 11:29. Lk 1:46. 2:35. Ac 14:2 (mind), 22. 15:24. (6) ƒ121A9B. Metonymy of Cause. The seat of will and purpose: Mt 22:37. Mk 12:30, 33. Lk 10:27. Ac 4:32. Ep 6:6. Ph 1:27. Col 3:23. He 12:3. (7) The seat of appetite: Re 18:14. (8) ƒ121A8. Metonymy of Cause, soul put for person. ƒ171Q1A. Synecdoche of the Part, an integral part of man (individually) is put for the whole person. Used of persons or individuals: Ac 2:41, 43. 3:23. 7:14. 27:37. Ro 2:9. 13:1. Ja *5:20. 1 P 3:20. 2 P 2:14. Re 18:13. (9) ƒ171Q2. Synecdoche of the Part. The expression "my soul," "his soul," etc., becomes by Synecdoche the idiom for *me, myself, himself,* etc. Used to emphasize the personal pronoun (a) in the first person: Mt 12:18. 26:38. Mk 14:34. Lk 12:19, 19. Jn 10:24 (us). 12:27. 2 C 1:23. He 10:38 (soul); (b) in the second person: 2 C 12:15mg. He 13:17. Ja 1:21. 1 P 1:9, 22. 2:25; (c) in the third person: 1 P 4:19. 2 P 2:8. (10) ƒ171Q3. Synecdoche of the Part. "Soul" (Gr. *psyche*) is also used of animals. An animate creature, human or other: 1 C 15:45. Re 16:3. (11) The "inward man," seat of the new life: Lk 21:19. 1 P 2:11. 3 J 2. Compare the classification of the corresponding Old Testament term *nephesh* at Ge 2:7n.

21. **he arose.** Ge 6:22. He 11:8.

22. **Archelaus.** i.e. *ruling the people,* ❋S#745g. **he was.** Ge 19:17-21. 1 S 16:2. Ac 9:13, 14. **being.** ver. 12. Mt 1:20. Ps 48:14. 73:24. 107:6, 7. 121:8. Is 30:21. 48:17, 18. **into.** Mt 3:13. Lk 2:39. Jn 7:41, 42, 52. **Galilee.** i.e. *circuit,* ❋S#1056g. Mt 2:22. 3:13. 4:12, 15, 18, 23, 25. 15:29. 17:22. 19:1. 21:11. 26:32. 27:55. 28:7, 10, 16. Mk 1:9, 14, 16, 28, 39. 3:7. 6:21. 7:31. 9:30. 14:28. 15:41. 16:7. Lk 1:26. 2:4, 39. 3:1. 4:14, 31, 44. 5:17. 8:26. 17:11. 23:5, 6, 49, 55. 24:6. Jn 1:43. 2:1, 11. 4:3, 43, 46, 47, 54. 6:1. 7:1, 9, 41, 52,

52. 12:21. 21:2. Ac 9:31. 10:37. 13:31. For *S#1551h, see Jsh +20:7.

23. **Nazareth**. Mt 4:13. 21:11. Mk 1:9, 24. Lk 1:26. 2:4, *39, 51. 4:16, 34. 18:37. Jn *1:45, 46. 18:5, 7. 19:19. Ac 2:22. 10:38. **spoken**. ♪106. Ge +31:7. **He shall**. Mt 26:71. Nu 6:13. Jg 13:5. 1 S 1:11. Ps 69:9, 10. Is 11:1. 53:1, 2. Am 2:10-12. Jn 1:45, 46. Ac 24:5. **Nazarene**. i.e. *kept, guarded, preserved; a flower*, *S#3480g. Mt 2:23. 26:71. Mk 10:47. Lk 18:37. 24:19. Jn 18:5, 7. 19:19. Ac 2:22. 3:6. 4:10. 6:14. 22:8. 24:5. 26:9.

MATTHEW 3

JOHN the Baptist's preaching and manner of life; and the prophecy fulfilled in him, 1-4. Multitudes resort to him, and are baptized, 5, 6. His bold and solemn address to the Pharisees and Sadducees, 7-10. His testimony concerning Christ, 11, 12. Jesus is baptized; the Holy Spirit descends on him; and the Father, by a voice from heaven, declares him to be his beloved Son, 13-17.

1. **those**. Lk *3:1, 2. **John**. Mt 11:11. 14:2, etc. 16:14. 17:12, 13. 21:25-27, 32. Mk *1:4, 15. 6:16-29. Lk 1:13-17, 76. 3:2-20. Jn *1:6-8, 15-36. 3:27-36. Ac 1:22. 13:24, 25. 19:3, 4. **John**. Lk 1:13. Jn 1:6, 7. **Baptist**. Gr. *baptistees*, *S#910g. Mt 3:1. 11:11, 12. 14:2, 8. 16:14. 17:13. Mk 6:24, 25. 8:28. Lk 7:20, 28, 33. 9:19. **preaching**. Is 40:3-6. Mk *1:7. Lk 1:17. **the wilderness**. Mt 4:1. *11:7. Jsh 14:10. 15:61, 62. Jg 1:16. Lk 7:24.

2. **Repent**. Mt 4:17. 11:20. 12:41. 21:29-32. 1 K 8:47. Jb 42:6. Ezk *18:30-32. 33:11. Ml *4:5, 6. Mk 1:4, 15. *6:12. Lk 1:16, 17. 3:3. +*13:3, 5. *15:7, 10. 16:30. √24:47. Ac +*2:38. +*3:19. 11:18. *17:30. 20:21. *26:20. 2 C √7:10. 2 T +2:25. He 6:1. 2 P √3:9. Re 2:5, 21. **kingdom of**. Mt +*4:17. 5:3, 10, 19, 20. √6:10, 33. *10:7. 11:11, 12. +*13:11, 24, 31, 33, 44, 45, 47, 52. 18:1-4, 23. 20:1. 22:2. +*23:13. 25:1, 14. Da +*2:44. Mk ◐+1:15. Lk 6:20. 9:2. *10:9-11. +*17:20, 21. Jn *3:3-5. Ro *14:17. Col *1:13n. **heaven**. ♪121J20, Ps +73:9. **at hand**. Mt +*4:17. +*10:7. ◐+*21:43.

3. **by**. Is *♪40:3. Mk 1:3. Lk 3:3-6. Jn 1:23. **Esaias**. i.e. *salvation of Jehovah*, *S#2268g. Mt 3:3. 4:14. 8:17. 12:17. 13:14. 15:7. Mk 7:6. Lk 3:4. 4:17. Jn 1:23. 12:38, 39, 41. Ac 8:28, 30. 28:25. Ro 9:27, 29. 10:16, 20. 15:12. For *S#3470h, see Is +1:1, Isaiah. **The voice**. Jn 1:23. **Prepare**. Ps 68:4. Is ♪40:3. *57:14, 15. Ml *3:1. Lk 1:17, 76. 3:4. **the Lord**. Ne +*9:6. Is ♪40:3, Jehovah. Jn *8:24. 1 C *12:3.

4. **John had**. ♪154. Prosopographia; or, Description of Persons B446. For other instances of this figure see Is 63:1-6. Ezk 16:4-26. **his raiment**. Mt 11:8. 2 K *1:8. Is 20:2. Zc 13:4. Ml 4:5. Mk *1:6. Lk *1:17, 76. 7:25. He 11:37. Re 11:3. **girdle**. ♪63G, Ge +50:23. Supply by ellipsis, (was bound). **and his**. Mt 11:18. Le *11:22. Lk 7:33. **wild**. Dt 32:13. 1 S 14:25-27. Ps 81:16.

5. **went out**. Mt 4:25. 11:7-12. Mk *1:5. Lk *3:7. 16:16. Jn 3:23. 5:35. **Jerusalem**. ♪121J14, Ge +47:15. **and all**. ♪171A, Ex +9:6. 2 Ch 29:36. **Judea**. ♪121J14, Ge +47:15. **all the**. ♪171L1, Nu +16:3. **region**. Ge 13:10, 11. 1 K 7:46. 2 Ch 4:17. **round about**. Mt 19:1. **Jordan**. i.e. *the descender*, *S#2446g. Mt 3:5, 6, 13. 4:15, 25. 19:1. Mk 1:5n, 9. 3:8. 10:1. Lk 3:3. 4:1. Jn 1:28. 3:26. 10:40.

6. **were**. ver. 11, 13-16. Ezk *36:25. Mk *1:8, 9. Lk *3:16. Jn *1:25-28, 31-33. *3:5, 23-25. 4:2. Ac +*1:5. +*2:38-41. 8:13, 23. 9:17, 18. *10:36-38. 11:16. 19:4, 5, 18. +*22:16. Ro √6:3, 4, 11. 1 C √1:14-17. 6:11. *7:19. *10:2. Ga *3:26, 27. Ep *4:5. 5:25, 26. Col *2:12. T *3:5, 6. He 6:2. 9:10g. 1 P 3:21. **baptized**. Gr. *baptizo*, *S#907g. Mt 3:6. 11:1, 1, 13, 14, 16. 20:22, 23, 23. 28:19. Mk 1:4, 5, 8, 8, 9. 6:14 (Baptist). +*7:4n. 10:38, 38, 39, 39. *16:16. Lk 3:7, 12, 16, 16, 21, 21. 7:29, *30. √11:38. 12:50. Jn 1:25, 26, 28, 31, 33, 33. 3:22, 23, 23, 26. 4:1, 2. 10:40. Ac 1:5, 5. +*2:38, 41. 8:12, 13, 16, 36, 38. 9:18. 10:47, 48. 11:16, 16. 16:15, 33. 18:8. 19:3, 4, 5. +*22:16. Ro √6:3, 3. 1 C 1:13, √14, 15, √16, √17. *10:2. √12:13. +*15:29, 29. Ga *3:27. **in Jordan**. 2 K *5:14. Mk +*1:9n. **confessing**. Le 16:21. 26:40. Nu 5:7. Jsh *7:19. Jb *33:27, 28. Ps √32:5. Pr √28:13. Da 9:4. Mk +1:5. Lk *15:18-21. Ac +*19:18. Ja √5:16. 1 J √1:9.

7. **the Pharisees**. i.e. *separatist, expounders; self-righteousness*, *S#5330g. Mt 5:20. 9:11, 14, 34. 12:2, 14, 24, 38. 15:1, 12. 16:1, 6, 11, 12. 19:3. 21:45. 22:15, 34, 41. 23:2, 13, 14, 15, 23, 25, 26, 27, 29. 27:62. Mk 2:16, 18, 18, 24. 3:6. √7:1, 3, 5. 8:11, 15. 10:2. 12:13. Lk 5:17, 21, 30, 33. 6:2, 7. *7:30, 36, 36, 37, 39. 11:37, 38, 39, 42, 43, 44, 53. 12:1. 13:31. 14:1, 3. 15:2. 16:14. 17:20. 18:10, 11. 19:39. Jn 1:24. 3:1. 4:1. 7:32, 32, 45, 47, 48. 8:3, 13. 9:13, 15, 16, 40. 11:46, 47, 57. 12:19, 42. 18:3. Ac 5:34. 15:5. 23:6, 6, 7, 8, 9. 26:5. Ph 3:5. **Sadducees**. i.e. *just, justified; the righteous*, *S#4523g. Mt 3:7. 16:1, 6, 11, 12. 22:23, 34. Mk 12:18. Lk 20:27. Ac 4:1. 5:17. 23:6, 7, 8. **baptism**. Gr. *baptisma*, *S#908g. Mt 3:7. 20:22, 23. 21:25. Mk 1:4. 10:38, 39. 11:30. Lk 3:3. 7:29. 12:50. 20:4. Ac 1:22. 10:37. 13:24. 18:25. 19:3, 4. Ro √6:4. Ep √4:5. Col √2:12. 1 P *3:21. **O generation**. Mt *12:34. +*23:33. Ge +*3:15. Ps 58:3-6. Is 57:3, 4. 59:5. Lk 3:7-9. Jn √8:44. 1 J 3:10. Re 12:9, 10. **of vipers**. Ps 58:4. 140:3. **who**. Je 6:10. 51:6. Ezk *3:18-21. *33:3-7. Ac 20:31. Ro 1:18. He *11:7. **flee**. Ro +*5:9. Ep 5:6. Col 3:6. 1 Th +*1:10. 2 Th 1:9, 10. He *6:18. Re 6:16, 17. **wrath to come**. Jn +*3:36. 1 Th +*1:10.

8. **forth**. Mt 21:28-30, 32. Is *1:16, 17. √55:7. Lk *3:8, 10-14. Ac 26:20. Ro 2:4-7. 2 C √7:10, 11. 2 P 1:4-8. **fruits**. Mt 21:25. Lk *7:30. Ga √5:22, 23. Ep 5:9. Ph *1:11. **meet**, etc. *or*, answerable to amendment of life. Je 7:3-7. √26:13. 36:3. Jon 3:10. Ac *26:20. **for**. ♪181E, Ge +3:24.

9. **think**. Gr. *dokeo*, *S#1380g. Trench notes that this word "expresses the subjective mental estimate or opinion about a matter which men form" (*Synonyms of the New Testament*, p. 304). Bullinger (*Critical Lexicon and Concordance*, p. 788, 789) gives the definition "to seem, to appear, to have the appearance; *then*, to seem to one's self, be of opinion, to hold for, believe; to form an estimate *or* opinion, *which may be right*, (Jn √5:39n; Ac 15:28; 1 C 4:9; 7:40n) *but which may be wrong*, (Mt 6:7; Mk 6:49; Jn 16:2)," to which latter set of references Trench adds Ac 27:13. The distribution and renderings of this word are as follows: Rendered (1) think: Mt 3:9. 6:7. 17:25. 18:12. 21:28. 22:17, 42. 24:44. 26:53, 66. Lk 10:36. 12:40. 13:4. 19:11. Jn 5:*39n, 45. 11:13, 56. 13:29. 16:2. Ac 12:9. 26:9. 1 C 4:9. 7:40. 8:2. *10:12. 12:23. 14:37. 2 C 11:16. 12:19. Ga 6:3. Ph 3:4. Ja 4:5. (2) seem: Lk 8:18. Ac 17:18. 25:27. 1 C 3:18. 11:16. 12:22. 2 C 10:9. Ga 2:6, 6, 9.

He *4:1. 12:11. Ja *1:26. (3) suppose: Mk 6:49. Lk 12:51. 13:2. 24:37. Jn 20:15. Ac 27:13. He 10:29. (4) seem good: Lk 1:3. Ac 15:25, 28. (5) please: Ac 15:22, 34. (6) be accounted: Mk 10:42. Lk 22:24. (7) trow: Lk 17:9. (8) be of reputation: Ga 2:2. (9) own pleasure: He 12:10. **not.** ✓152B, Is +49:14. **say within.** Mk 7:21. Lk 3:8. 5:22. 7:39. 12:17. **We.** Ezk 33:24. Lk 16:24. Jn *8:33, 39, 40, 53. Ac 13:26. Ro ✓2:28, 29. *4:1, 11-16. *9:6-8. Ga 4:22-31. **God.** Mt +*8:11, 12. Lk 19:40. Ac 15:14. Ro 4:17. 1 C 1:27, 28. Ga 3:27-29. Ep 2:12, 13. **these stones.** Mt 4:3. 7:9. Lk 19:40. **children.** ✓134. Parechesis; or, Foreign Paronomasia B322. The Hebrew words which underlie the Greek exhibit paronomasia. Here, "stones" (Hebrew *abanim*) and "children" (Hebrew *banim*) exhibit this figure. For other instances of this figure see Mt 10:30. 11:17, 29. Mk (8):32). Lk 7:41, 42. Jn 1:5. (10:1). Ro 13:8. 15:4. 1 C 1:23, 24. 2 C 11:17.

10. **now.** Is 5:7. Ml 3:1-3. 4:1. Ac ✓17:30, 31. He 3:1-3. 10:28-31. 12:25. **the axe.** ✓103, Ge +3:13. Dt *20:20. Lk 3:9. 23:31. **the trees.** ✓7, Allegory or repeated Hypocatastasis, Ga +4:24. **therefore.** Ps *1:3. 92:13, 14. Is 61:3. Je 17:8. Jn *15:2. 1 P *4:17. **good fruit.** Mt 7:16-20. **is hewn.** ✓96C6, Mt +2:4. Mt 7:19. 21:19. Ps 80:15, 16. Is 5:2-7. 27:11. Ezk 15:2-7. Lk *13:6-9. Jn *15:6. He *6:8. 1 P 4:17, 18. **and cast.** Je 11:16. Jn +*15:6.

11. **baptize.** ver. 6. Mk 1:4, 8. Lk 3:3, 16. Jn 1:26, *33. Ac +*1:5. 11:16. 13:24. 19:4. **with.** ✓108D. Idiom B835: idiomatic use of prepositions. The Hebrew has fewer prepositions than Greek. The Hebrew *beth* primarily means *in*, but also means *by, among, at, upon*, and *with*. It is a great mistake, therefore, always to translate *en in*, as is too frequently done in the New Testament. It must be taken with all the shades and breadth of meaning which the Hebrew *beth* has. For other instances of this idiom see Mt 7:2, 6. Mk 3:22. Lk 11:20. 22:49. Re 1:5. 5:9. **water.** Mk *1:8. Lk *3:16. Jn *1:33. Ac +*1:5. 2:33. *11:16. **unto.** Gr. *eis*. Note that the force and meaning of this preposition here is not "in order that," as is argued by some for the same preposition used in the same connection but rendered "for" at Ac +*2:38, "*for* the remission of sins," but is "because of." John did not urge his hearers to be baptized in order to repent, but to be baptized because of their repentance, which is the exact reverse. This preposition may also equally well be understood here to have the force of "as a sign or profession of," and has this force at Mt 28:19. 1 C 1:13. 10:2. **repentance.** ver. 2, 8. Ac 13:24. 19:4. **but.** Lk 1:17. Jn 1:15, 26, 27, 30, 34. 3:23-36. Ac 13:25. **whose.** Mk 1:7. Lk 7:6, 7. Ac 13:25. Ep 3:8. 1 P 5:5. **shoes.** ✓138B, Ge +13:16. **he shall.** Is *4:4. *44:3. 59:20, 21. Zc +*13:9. Ml 3:2-4. Mk 1:8. Lk *3:16. Jn 1:33. Ac +*1:5. *2:2-4. 11:15, 16. 1 C ✓12:13. Ga *3:27, 28. **with.** Jn *3:5. Ac 2:4. 1 C ✓12:13. **Ghost.** Gr. *pneuma*, Mt +1:18n. Jn *7:39. Ac *1:5. 11:15, 16. 1 C ✓12:13. **and.** ✓93A, Ge +1:26. with Holy Spirit and fire: i.e. with Holy Spirit, yes— and burning purifying spirit too. Not two things, but one thing: Judgment! **fire.** Dt 4:24. Ps +*149:9. Is 1:27. ✓4:4. 10:17. *62:1. Am 1:4. 5:6. Zc 12:6. Ml ✓3:2, 3. *4:1. Lk 12:49. Ac 2:3. 1 C +*6:2. He 12:29. 2 P +✓3:7. Re 2:26, 27. 14:18.

12. **fan.** ✓103, Ge +3:13. ✓22C44, Je +15:7. Is 30:24. 41:16. Je 4:11. 15:7. 51:2. Lk 3:17. 22:31. **he will throughly.** Mt 13:41, 49, 50. Ml 3:2, 3. 4:1. Jn

15:2. **and gather.** Mt +*13:30, 40, 43. Am *9:9. 2 Th *2:1. **wheat.** ✓7, Allegory by continued Hypocatastasis, Ga 4:24. **but.** Jb 21:18. Ps *1:4. *35:5. Is *5:24. *17:13. +*24:6. Ho 13:3. Ml 3:18. *4:1. Lk *3:17. 2 P 3:7. **with unquenchable.** Is 1:31. 34:10. +*66:24. Je 7:20. 17:27. Ezk 20:47, 48. Mk ✓9:43-48. **fire.** Mt 13:30, 41, 42. +*25:41, 46. Is 5:24. 10:16, 17. 66:15, 16. Mk 9:48. 2 Th *1:8. He 10:27. Re 14:10, 11. 20:9, 10, 14, 15.

13. **from Galilee.** Mt 2:22. Mk *1:9. Lk *3:21. **to Jordan.** lit. upon (Gr. *epi*) Jordan. Dale notes that this construction places Jesus upon the bank of the Jordan where he was baptized (*Christic Baptism*, p. 145). See related note on the preposition *epi* at Ac 2:38. Compare notes on Mk 1:4, 5, 9. **baptized.** T#35. He 7:11-14.

14. **John.** Lk 1:43. Jn 13:6-8. **I have.** Jn 1:16. 3:3-7. Ac *1:5-8. Ro ✓3:23, 25. Ga 3:22, 27-29. 4:6. Ep 2:3-5. Re 7:9-17.

15. **Suffer.** Jn *13:7-9. **for thus.** Ps *40:7, 8. Is *42:21. Lk *1:6. Jn *4:34. *8:29. 9:4. *13:15. *15:10. Ph *2:7, 8. He *7:26. 1 P 2:21-24. 1 J *2:6. **to fulfill.** Mt *5:17. 8:4. *17:24-27. Lk 2:39, 41, 42. 17:14. Nu ✓8:5-7 w He 7:13, 14.

16. **Jesus.** Mk 1:10. **when.** Lk 3:23. **up.** Mk 1:10. **out of.** Gr. *apo*, lit. from. ver. 7. Ge 17:22, LXX. SS 3:6, LXX. 6:5, 6 (4, 5, LXX). Lk 2:4. Re 7:2. **lo.** Ezk 1:1. Lk *3:21. Jn 1:51. Ac 7:56. **and he saw.** Mt 12:18. Ps ✱45:7. Is ✱*11:2. *42:1. 59:21. ✱*61:1. Lk *3:22. 4:18, 21. Jn *1:31-34. *3:34. Ac *10:38. Col 1:18, 19. 1 J 5:6, 8. **the Spirit.** Gr. *pneuma*. The Holy Spirit himself (commonly called the Third Person of the Trinity), symbolized by the bodily form of a dove. Mt 1:20. 4:1. 10:20. 12:28, 31, 32. 22:43. 28:19. Mk 1:10, 12. 3:29. 12:36. 13:11. Lk 2:26, 27. 3:22. 4:1b, 14. 10:21. 12:10. Jn 1:32, 33a. 3:6a, 8, 8, 34. 6:63a. 14:17, 26. 15:26. 16:13. Ac 1:16. 2:4b, 33, 38. 5:3, 9. 7:51. 9:31●. 10:45n. 11:28. 13:2, 4. 15:28. 16:6, 7. 20:23, 28. 21:4. 28:25. Ro 8:16a, 26, 26, 27. 15:16, 19, 30. 1 C 2:10, 10, 11b, 14. 3:16. 6:11. 12:3a, 4, 7, 8, 9, 11, 13a. 2 C 13:14●. Ga 3:14. 5:22. 6:8b. Ep 2:18. 3:5, 16. 4:3, 4, 30. 5:9, 18. 6:17, 18. 2 Th 2:13. 1 T 4:1a. He 3:7. 9:8, 14. 10:15, 29. 1 P 1:2, 11, 22. 3:18. 4:14. 1 J 4:2a. 5:6, 6, 7, 8. Re 1:10. 2:7, 11, 17, 29. 3:6, 13, 22. 4:2. 14:13. 17:3. 21:10. 22:17. For the other uses of *pneuma*, see Mt +*8:16n.

17. **lo.** Jn 5:37. 12:28-30. Re 14:2. **a voice.** Mk 1:11. **This.** Mt 12:18. 17:5. Ps *2:7. Is *42:1, 21. Mk 1:11. 9:7. Lk 3:22. 9:35. Ga 4:4, 5. Ep *1:6. Col *1:13. 2 P *1:17. 1 J 5:9. **my beloved.** ✓24.O, Ge +9:5. Ge=37:3. **Son.** Mt +*14:33. Mk 14:61, 62. Jn ✓3:16. 17:24. Ep 1:4. 1 J *4:15. 5:5. Note all three persons of the Trinity. Mt +✓28:19. Ge +*1:26. Is 6:8. +*42:1n. 48:12, 16. Ro *15:30. 1 C 12:4-6. 2 C ✓13:14. Ep 2:18. 4:4-6. 5:18-20. He 9:14. 1 P 1:2. Ju 20, 21. **am.** ✓96C4. Heterosis of Tenses B520: the aorist for the present, thus put for a past action or state continued up to the present time. For other instances of this figure see Mt 23:2. Mk 1:11. 16:19. Lk 1:47. 3:22. 15:16. Jn 1:12. 11:56. 15:6. 1 J 4:8. **well pleased.** T#57. Ps 40:7, 8. Jn 4:34. 5:30. 6:38. 8:29, 49. 17:4.

MATTHEW 4

Christ, being led by the Spirit into the wilderness, fasts forty days; is tempted by the devil; overcomes him by the word of God, and is ministered to by angels, 1-11. He dwells at Capernaum, and fulfills a prophecy of Isaiah, by preaching in Galilee, 12-17. He calls Peter, Andrew, James, and John, to follow him, 18-22. He teaches in the synagogues, and heals the diseased; so that, his fame being spread abroad, he is followed by great multitudes, 23-25.

1. **was.** Mk *1:12, 13, etc. Lk *4:1, etc. Ro 8:14. **of the spirit.** Gr. *pneuma*, Mt +3:16. 1 K 18:12. 2 K 2:16. Ezk 3:12, 14. 8:3. 11:1, 24. 40:2. 43:5. Ac 8:39. **into.** Mk 1:12. Lk 4:1. **the wilderness.** Mt 3:1. **to.** Ge +*3:15. Jn +*14:30. He 2:18. 4:15, 16. **tempted.** He *2:18. +*4:15. Ja √1:13. **devil.** i.e. *accuser, adversary,* *S#1228g. Gr. *diabolos*. Mt 4:1, 5, 8, 11. 13:39. 25:41. Lk 4:2, 3, 5, 6, 13. 8:12. Jn 6:70. 8:44. 13:2. Ac 10:38. 13:10. Ep 4:27. 6:11. 1 T 3:6, 7, 11 (slanderers). 2 T 2:26. 3:3 (false accusers). T 2:3 (false accusers). He 2:14. Ja 4:7. 1 P 5:8. 1 J 3:8, 8, 8, 10. Ju 9. Re 2:10. 12:9, 12. 20:2, 10.

2. **fasted.** T#193. Ex 24:18. *34:28. Dt 9:9, 18, 25. 18:18. 1 K *19:8. Ezr 8:21-23. Da +*9:3. Jon 3:5-10. Lk 2:36, 37. *4:2. Ac 10:30. 13:2, 3. 14:23. 2 C 6:5. 11:27, 28. **forty.** Ex ◑=34:28. Jon 3:4n. Mk 1:13. Lk 4:2. **he was.** Mt 21:18. Mk 11:12. Jn 4:6, 7. 19:28. He 2:14-17.

3. **the tempter.** ✓24B, Ge +23:16. T#14. Mt 10:1. +*13:38, 39. Ge 3:1-7. 1 Ch 21:1. Jb 1:9-12. 2:4-7. Is 27:1. Mk 5:9. Lk 11:15. 22:31, 32. Jn √8:44. +*14:30. 2 C *4:4. Ep 2:2. 6:12. 1 Th 3:5. 1 P *5:8. Re 2:10. 9:10, 11. 12:9-11. **If.** ✓184A, 1 C +15:2. First class condition, which assumes the condition to be true. By the use of "if," Satan was not calling into question whether in fact Jesus is the Son of God; rather, he thereby assumes this to be true. Mt 3:17. 27:40. Lk 4:3, 9. **Son of God.** ver. 6. Mt +*14:33. **command.** Ge 3:1-5. 25:29-34. Ex 16:3. Nu 11:4-6. Ps 78:17-20. He 12:16, 17. **bread.** Mt 7:9. Lk 11:11.

4. **It is written.** T#1034. ver. 6, 7, 10. Mk 12:10. Lk 4:4, 8, 12. Jn 7:42. Ro +*15:4. Ep *6:17. **Man.** Dt *)8:3. Lk 4:4. Jn 4:34. 6:49-51. **bread.** ✓171, Ge +3:19. Mt 6:11. +*24:45. **but.** Mt 14:16-21. Ex 16:8, 15, 35. 23:15. 1 K 17:12-16. 2 K 4:42-44. 7:1, 2. Hg 2:16-19. Ml 3:9-11. Mk 6:38-44. 8:4-9. Jn 6:5, etc., 31, etc., 63. **by.** T#1047. Dt 8:3. That is, as Dr. Campbell renders, "by every thing which God is pleased to appoint;" for *rama*, which generally signifies a *word*, is, by a Hebraism, here taken for a *thing*, like *davar*, in Hebrew. **every word.** Dt 32:47. Jsh +*1:8. Ps *17:4. √119:11. 1 S=21:9. Jb +*23:12. Je +*15:16. Jn +*5:39. *6:63. 1 C 3:15. Ep *6:17. He √4:12. 1 P 4:18. Re 19:15.

5. **taketh.** ✓63H, Ge +12:15. Lk 4:9. Jn 19:11. **the holy.** Mt 5:35. 27:53. Ne *11:1, 18. Ps 46:4. 48:1. Is 48:2. 52:1. Da 9:16, 24. Re 11:2. 21:2. 22:19. **on.** 2 Ch 3:4.

6. **saith.** T#17-3. Ge 3:4, 5. Jb 1:9-11. Ga +*1:8n. 2 Th +2:13 (T#257). 1 T 4:1-3. **If thou.** ✓184A, 1 C +15:2. **Son of God.** ver. 3. Mt +*14:33. Mk *14:61, 62. **for.** ver. 4. 2 C *11:14. 2 P +*3:16. **He shall.** Ps)91:11. Lk 4:9-12. He 1:14. **lest.** Jb 1:10. 5:23. Ps 34:7, 20. 37:24. Pr 3:23.

7. **It.** ver. 4, 10. Mt 21:16, 42. 22:31, 32. Is +*8:20. **Thou.** ✓92F3. Gnome; or, Quotation B796: where the words are changed in *number*. In Dt 6:16 it is: "Ye shall not tempt." If the command is given to all in general, then surely it applies to each individual in

particular: and so the Lord applied it in reply to the Tempter. For other instances of this figure see Ro 4:7. 10:15. **shalt not.** Ex 17:2, 7. Nu 14:22. Dt)6:16. Ps 78:18, 41, 56. 95:9. 106:14. Pr +*22:3. Ml 3:15. Ac 5:9. 1 C 10:9. He 3:9. **tempt.** Is 7:12. Lk 10:25.

8. **the devil.** ver. 5. Lk 4:5-7. **mountain.** Mt 5:1. **and showeth.** Mt 16:26. Est 1:4. 5:11. Ps 49:16, 17. Da *4:30. Lk 4:5. 2 C 4:18. Ep 2:2. He 11:24-26. 1 P 1:24. 1 J √2:15, 16. Re *11:15. **all the kingdoms.** Ps *2:8. **world.** Gr. *kosmos*, *S#2889g. Rendered (1) world: Mt 4:8. 5:14. 13:35, 38. 16:26. 18:7. 24:21. 25:34. 26:13. Mk 8:36. 14:9. 16:15. Lk 9:25. 11:50. 12:30. Jn 1:9, 10, 10, 10, 29. 3:16, 17, 17, 17, 19. 4:42. 6:14, 33, 51. 7:4, 7. 8:12, 23, 23, 26. 9:5, 5, 39. 10:36. 11:9, 27. 12:19, 25, 31, 31, 46, 47, 47. 13:1, 1. 14:17, 19, 22, 27, 30, 31. 15:18, 19, 19, 19, 19, 19. 16:8, 11, 20, 21, 28, 28, 33, 33. 17:5, 6, 9, 11, 11, 12, 13, 14, 14, 14, 15, 16, 16, 18, 21, 23, 24, 25. 18:20, 36, 36, 37. 21:25. Ac 17:24. Ro 1:8, 20. 3:6, 19. 4:13. 5:12, 13. 11:12, 15. 1 C 1:20, 21, 27, 27, 28. 2:12. 3:19, 22. 4:9, 13. 5:10, 10. 6:2, 2. 7:31, 31, 33, 34. 8:4. 11:32. 14:10. 2 C 1:12. 5:19. 7:10. Ga 4:3. 6:14, 14. Ep 1:4. 2:2, 12. Ph 2:15. Col 1:6. 2:8, 20, 20. 1 T 1:15. 3:16. 6:7. He 4:3. 9:26. 10:5. 11:7, 38. Ja 1:27. 2:5. 3:6, 4. 4. 1 P 1:20. 5:9. 2 P 1:4. 2:5, 5, 20. 3:6. 1 J 2:2, 15, 15, 15, 16, 16, 17. 3:1, 13, 17. 4:1, 3, 4, 5, 5, 5, 9, 14, 17. 5:4, 4, 5, 19. 2 J 7. Re 11:15. 13:8. 17:8. (2) adorning: 1 P 3:3.

9. **All.** Mt 26:15. Ps *2:8. Jn 13:3. **I give.** 1 S 2:7, 8. Ps 72:11. 113:7, 8. Pr 8:15. Je 27:5, 6. Da 2:37, 38. 4:32. 5:18, 19, 26-28. Lk 22:53. Jn 12:31. 14:30. 16:11. 1 J 5:19. Re 13:2. 19:16. **if.** ✓184C. Hypothetical Propositions; or, Conditional ("if") Sentences: Third Condition; or, contingency with idea of realization. The more probable future condition, undetermined, but with prospect of determination, indicating an expected result based on the present general or particular circumstances. For other instances of this third class of conditional sentence see Mt 5:13, 19, 20, 23, 32, 46, 47. 6:14, 15, 22, 23. 7:9, 12. 8:2, 31. 9:21. 10:13. 12:11, 28, 29. 15:14. 16:19, 25, 26. 17:20. 18:3, 12, 13, 15, 16, 17, 19, 35. 21:3, 21, 22, 24, 25, 26. 22:24. 24:26, 28, 48. 26:35. 28:14. Mk 1:40. 3:24, 25. 4:26. 5:28. 7:11. 8:3, 36. 9:43, 45, 47, 50. 10:12. 11:3, 31, 32. 12:19. 14:21, 31. 16:18. Lk 4:7. 5:12. 6:33. 9:13. 10:6. 11:12. 12:45. 13:3, 5, 9. 14:34. 15:8. 17:3, 4. 19:31. 20:5, 6, 28. 22:68. Jn 3:2, 3, 5, 12, 27. 5:31, 43. 6:51, 62, 65. 7:17, 37, 51. 8:16, 24, 31, 36, 51, 52, 54, 55. 9:22, 31. 10:9. 11:9, 10, 40, 48, 57. 12:24, 26, 32, 47. 13:8, 17, 35. 14:3, 14, 15, 23. 15:4, 6, 7, 10, 14. 16:7. 19:12. 20:23. 21:22, 23, 25. Ac 5:38. 9:2. 13:41. 26:5. Ro 2:25, 26. 7:2, 3, 20. 9:27. 10:9. 11:22, 23, 24. 12:20. 13:4. 14:8, 23. 15:24. 1 C 4:15, 19. 5:11. 6:4. 7:11, 28, 36, 39, 40. 8:8, 10. 9:16. 10:28. 11:14, 15. 12:15, 16. 13:1, 2. 14:5, 6, 7, 9, 11, 14, 23, 24, 28, 30. 16:4, 7, 10. 2 C 5:1. 9:4. Ga 1:8. 5:2. 6:1. Ph 3:11, 12. Col 3:13. 4:10. 1 Th 5:10. 1 T 1:8. 2:15. 3:15. 2 T 2:5, 21. He 3:6, 7, 14, 15. 4:7. 6:3. 10:38. 12:20. 13:23. Ja 2:2, 14, 15, 16, 17. 4:15. 1 P 3:13. 1 J 1:6, 7, 8, 9, 10. 2:1, 3, 15, 24, 29. 3:20, 21. 4:12, 20. 5:14, 16. 3 J 10. Re 3:3, 20, 21. 11:5. 22:18, 19. For the other classes of the conditional sentence, see for the First Condition, ✓184A, 1 C +15:2; for the Second Condition, ✓184B, Lk +7:39; ✓184B, Mt +11:21; ✓184B, Mt +23:30; for the Fourth Condition, ✓184D1, Lk +22:67; ✓184D2, Lk +1:62. **fall down.**

Da 3:5. Lk 4:7mg. **and worship.** 1 C 10:20, 21. 2 C 4:4. 1 T 3:6. 1 P 5:8, 9. Re +*19:10. +*22:8, 9.

10. **Then saith.** He=11:24, 25. **Get.** *J*34, Ps +50:16. Mt 16:23. Ja 4:7. 1 P 5:9. **Satan.** *Satanas* 1 Ch 21:1. Jb 1:6, 12. 2:1. Ps 109:6. Zc 3:1, 2. Gr. *Satanas,* i.e. *an adversary,* *S#4567g. Mt 4:10. 12:26. 16:23. Mk 1:13. 3:23, 26. 4:15. 8:33. Lk 4:8. 10:18. 11:18. 13:16. 22:3, 31. Jn 13:27. Ac 5:3. 26:18. Ro 16:20. 1 C 5:5. 7:5. 2 C *2:11. *11:14. 1 Th 2:18. 2 Th 2:9. 1 T 1:20. 5:15. Re 2:9, 13, 13, 24. 3:9. 12:9. 20:2, 7. See *S#4566g, 2 C 12:7. For *S#7854h, see Jb 1:6, Satan. **Thou shalt.** Dt)6:13, 14. 10:20. Jsh 24:14. 1 S 7:3. Lk 4:8. **worship.** T#744. Mt ❍+*14:33. Ex +*20:2, 3, *5. *34:14. Dt 11:16. Ps +22:28 (T#280). 96:4, 5, 8, 9. Ec +12:13 (T#295). Lk 4:8. Ac 14:15. Col +2:18 (T#80). Re +*19:10. +*22:8, 9. **and him only.** *J*92E. Gnome; or, Quotation B791: where the words are varied by omission, addition, or transposition. Here, the words are varied by addition, for the words "and him only shalt thou serve" are not quoted from Deuteronomy, but added by our Lord. For other instances of this figure see Mt 4:15, 16. 5:31. 12:18-21. 19:5. 22:24. Lk 4:8. Ro 11:3, 4. 1 C 2:9. 14:21. 1 P 1:24, 25. **shalt thou.** T#241. Mt 22:37, 38. Ex 20:2. Dt 10:20. 13:4. 1 S 7:3. 1 Ch 29:11. Ps +22:28 (T#280).

11. **the devil.** Lk *4:13. 22:53. Jn 14:30. 2 C 4:4. Ep 6:12. **behold.** ver. 6. Mt 26:53. 28:2-5. 1 K 19:5. Mk *1:13. Lk *22:43. Jn 12:29. 1 T 3:16. He *1:6, 14. Re 5:11, 12.

12. **when.** Mt 14:3. Mk *1:14. 6:17. Lk *3:19, 20. *4:14, 31. Jn 3:24. 4:43, 54. Ac 10:37. **cast.** *or*, delivered up. Mt 10:17, 19. **into Galilee.** Is *9:1, 2. Lk 4:14.

13. **leaving.** Mt 16:4. Lk *4:30, 31. **Nazareth.** i.e. *guarded,* *S#3478g. Mt 2:23. 4:13. 21:11. Mk 1:9. Lk 1:26. 2:4, 39, 51. 4:16. Jn 1:45, 46. Ac 10:38. **came and dwelt.** Mt 9:1. Mk 1:21. Lk 4:31. Jn 2:12. **Capernaum.** i.e. *village of comfort,* *S#2584g. Mt 4:13. 8:5. 11:23. 17:24. Mk 1:21. 2:1. 9:33. Lk 4:23, 31. 7:1. 10:15. Jn 2:12. 4:46. 6:17, 24, 59. **upon the sea coast.** ver. 18. Mt 8:24. Jn 6:1. **Zabulon.** i.e. *abiding.* Jsh 19:10-16, Zebulun. *S#2194g. Mt 4:13, 15. Re 7:8. **Nephthalim.** i.e. *my wrestlings.* Jsh 19:32-39, Naphtali. *S#3508g. Mt 4:13, 15. Re 7:6.

14. **it.** Mt 1:22. 2:15, 23. 8:17. 12:17-21. 26:54, 56. Lk 22:37. 24:44. Jn 15:25. 19:28, 36, 37. **Esaias.** Mk 1:2. **saying.** Is 9:1, 2.

15. **The land.** *J*92E, Mt +4:10. Is)9:1, 2. **Galilee.** Jsh 20:7. 21:32. 1 K *9:11. 2 K 15:29. Is *9:1, 2.

16. **which sat.** *J*171J12, Is +42:7. **in darkness.** Mt 6:23. Ps 107:10-14. Is +9:2. *42:6, 7. 60:1-3. Mi 7:8. Lk *1:78, 79. *2:32. Jn *3:19. *8:12. Ep 5:8, 14. 1 P *2:9. **region and.** *J*93A, Ge +1:26. "In a region and shadow of death." This does not denote two places, but one: in a region, yes—in death's dark region too, as is clear from Is 9:1, 2. **shadow.** Jb 3:5. 10:21, 22. 12:22. 16:16. 24:17. 28:3. 34:22. 38:17. Ps *23:4. 44:19. 107:10, 14. Is 9:2. Je 2:6. 13:16. Am 5:8.

17. **that.** Mk *1:14. **began.** Ac 1:22. 10:37. **Repent.** Mt 3:2. 9:13. *10:7. Mk *1:15. Lk 5:32. 9:2. 10:11-14. 15:7, 10. 24:47. Ac +*2:38. +*3:19. 11:18. √17:30. 20:21. 26:20. 2 T *2:25, 26. He 6:1. **kingdom of heaven.** Mt *3:2. 5:3, 10, 19, 20. 7:21. 8:11. 10:7. *11:11, 12. 13:11, ❍19, 24, 31, 33, 44, 45, 47, 52. 16:19. 18:1, 3, 4, 23. 19:12, 14, 23. 20:1. 22:2. 23:13. 25:1. Mk ❍+1:15. **at hand.** Mt 3:2. √10:7. 12:28 ❍+*21:43. Is 56:1. Mk 1:14, 15. Lk 11:20.

18. **walking.** Mk 1:16-18. Lk 5:2. **sea.** Mt 15:29. Nu 34:11. Dt 3:17, Chinnereth. Lk 5:1, lake of Gennesaret. Mk 7:31. Jn 6:1. 21:1, sea of Tiberias. **two.** Mt 10:2. Lk 6:14. Jn *1:40-42. 6:8. **Simon.** i.e. *a hearing; obeying,* *S#4613g. Mt 4:18. 10:2, 4. 13:55. 16:16, 17. 17:25. 26:6. 27:32. Mk 1:16, 29, 30, 36. 3:16, 18. 6:3. 14:3, 37. 15:21. Lk 4:38. 5:3, 4, 5, 8, 10. 6:14, 15. 7:40, 43, 44. 22:31, 31. 23:26. 24:34. Jn 1:40, 41, 42. 6:8, 68, 71. 12:4. 13:2, 6, 9, 24, 26, 36. 18:10, 15, 25. 20:2, 6. 21:2, 3, 7, 11, 15, 16, 17. Ac 1:13. 8:9, 13, 18, 24. 9:43. 10:5, 6, 17, 18, 32, 32. 11:13. (1) A sorcerer who practiced magic arts and deceived the people of Samaria, Ac 8:9, 13, 18, 24. (2) A name often applied to the apostle Peter, Mt 4:18. Mk 1:16. Lk 4:38. Jn 1:40. Ac 10:5. 2 P 1:1. (3) Simon the Canaanite, Mt 10:4. Mk 3:18. Lk 6:15, called Simon Zelotes in Ac 1:13, one of the twelve apostles. (4) One of the brethren of our Lord, Mt +*13:55. Mk +*6:3. (5) A Pharisee in whose house Jesus' feet were washed with tears and anointed with ointment, Lk 7:36-40. (6) A leper in Bethany, Mt 26:6. Mk 14:3. (7) The father of Judas Iscariot, Jn 6:71. 12:4. (8) Simon the Cyrenian, who was compelled to bear the cross of Jesus on the way to Golgotha, Mt 27:32. Mk 15:21. Lk 23:26. (9) Simon the tanner at Joppa, with whom Peter lodged, Ac 9:43. 10:6. **called Peter.** Mt 10:2. Jn 1:42. **Andrew.** i.e. *manly,* *S#406g. Mt 4:18. 10:2. Mk 1:16, 29. 3:18. 13:3. Lk 6:14. Jn 1:40, 44. 6:8. 12:22. Ac 1:13. **casting.** Mt 13:47. Ge +*24:27. Ezk 47:10. Am *7:15. **for.** Ex 3:1, 10. Jg 6:11, 12. 1 K 19:19-21. Ps 78:70-72. Am 7:14, 15. 1 C *1:27-29.

19. **Follow.** Mt 8:22. 9:9. *16:24. 19:21. Mk *2:14. Lk 5:27. 9:59. Jn 1:43. *12:26. 21:22. **I will.** Ezk 47:9, 10. Mk 1:17, 18. Lk *5:10, 11. 1 C 9:20-22. 2 C 12:16. **fishers.** Mt *13:47. Je 16:16.

20. **they.** ver. 22. Mt 10:37, 38. 19:27. 1 K 19:21. Ps 110:3. *119:60. Mk *10:28-31. Lk 18:28-30. Ga 1:16. Ph *3:7, 8. **their nets.** Jn 21:6. **and followed.** Mk *10:37, 38.

21. **other.** Mt *10:2. 17:1. 20:20, 21. *26:37. Mk 1:19, 20, 29. *3:17. *5:37. 10:35. Lk *5:10, 11. 9:54. Jn 21:2. Ac 12:2. **mending.** Lk 5:2.

22. **immediately left.** ver. 20. Mt 10:37. 19:27. Dt 33:9, 10. Mk 1:20. 10:28. Lk *5:11. 9:59, 60. 14:26, 33. 18:28. 2 C 5:16.

23. **Jesus.** Mt 9:35. Mk 6:6. Jn 7:1. Ac *10:38. **all Galilee.** Is *9:1, 2. **teaching.** Mt 12:9. 13:54. Ps 74:8. Mk 1:21, 39. 3:1. 6:2. Lk 4:15, 16, 31, 33, 44. 6:6. 13:10. Jn 6:59. *18:20. Ac 9:20. 13:14, etc. 18:4. **preaching.** T#65. Mt 7:28, 29. 9:35. 13:54. Mk *1:14, 15. Lk 4:43. Jn 7:14, 15, *46. **the gospel.** Mt 13:19. *24:14. Mk 1:14. Lk 4:17, 18. *8:1. 20:4. Ro 10:15. **of.** *J*181E, Ge +3:24. **the kingdom.** Da *2:44. Mt *24:14. **healing.** Mt 8:16, 17. 9:35. 10:1, 7, 8. 11:5. 15:30, 31. Ps 103:3. Mk 1:32-34. 3:10. Lk 4:40, 41. 5:17. 6:17. 7:22. 9:11. 10:9. Ac 5:15, 16. *10:38. **all.** √*171B, Ge +24:10. **and all.** *J*108B. Idiom B825. "All" is an idiom signifying "some of every kind." For another instance of this idiom see Ac 10:12. **among the people.** Ac 5:12. 6:8.

24. **his fame.** lit. hearing. *J*121R1, Le +13:55. Mt 9:26, 31. 14:1. Jsh 6:27. 1 K 4:31. 10:1. 1 Ch 14:17. Mk 1:28. Lk *4:14, 37. 5:15. **Syria.** 2 S 8:6. Mk 7:26. Lk 2:2. Ac 15:23, 41. **all sick.** ver. 23. Mt 8:14, 15. 9:35. 14:35. Ex +*15:26. **taken.** Lk 4:38. **torments.** Mt 8:6. **possessed.** Mt 8:16, 28, 33. 9:32. 12:22. 15:22. 17:18. Mk 1:32. 5:2-18. Lk 4:33-35. 8:27-37. Jn 10:21.

Ac *10:38. lunatic. Mt 17:15. those that. Mt 8:6, 13. 9:2-8. Mk 2:3-5, 9, 10. Lk 5:24. Ac 8:7. 9:33. He 12:12.

25. followed. Mt 5:1. 8:1. 12:15. 15:30. 19:2. Mk *3:7, 8. 6:2. Lk 6:17, 19. from Galilee. Mt 19:1. Mk 3:7, 8. Lk 6:17. Decapolis. i.e. *ten cities,* ✳S#1179g. Mt 4:25. Mk 5:20. 7:31.

MATTHEW 5

Christ's sermon on the mount, 1, 2. Christ shows who are blessed, 3-12. His disciples, as "the salt of the earth and the light of the world," and as resembling "a city set on a hill" and a candle in a room, must be right examples in good works, 13-16. He came not to destroy, but to fulfill and establish the law, 17-20. The sixth commandment, vindicated from corrupt glosses, and spiritually expounded and enforced, 21-26; and the seventh, 27-32; and the third, 33-37. Exhortations, to suffer wrong patiently, 38-42; to love our enemies, 43-47; and to aim at perfection, 48.

1. seeing. Mt 4:25. 13:2. Mk 4:1. he went. Mt 15:29. Mk 3:13, 20. Lk 6:12, 17. Jn *6:2, 3. into a mountain. Mt 4:8. 14:23. 15:29. 17:1. 21:1. 28:16. Mk 6:46. 9:2. Lk 9:28. Jn 6:15. was set. Lk 4:20. his. Mt 4:18-22. 10:2-4. Lk 6:13-16.

2. he opened. ℐ108H6A, Jg +11:35. Mt 13:35. Jb 3:1. 33:2. Ps *78:1, 2. Pr 8:6. 31:8, 9. Da 10:16. Lk 1:64. 6:20, etc. Ac 8:35. 10:34. 18:14. 2 C 6:11. Ep *6:19.

3. Blessed. ver. *4-11. *11:6. *13:16. *24:46. Ps +*1:1. *2:12. *32:1, 2. *41:1. *84:12. *112:1. *119:1, 2. *128:1. 146:5. Pr *8:32. Is +*30:18. Lk *6:20, 21, etc. *11:28. Jn *20:29. Ro *4:6-9. Ja *1:12. Re 1:3. *19:9. 20:6. *22:14. the poor. T#933. Mt *11:25. *18:1-3. Le *26:4, 41, 42. Dt *8:2. 2 Ch +√7:14. 33:12, 19, 23. *34:27. Jb *42:6. Ps *34:18. *51:17. 147:3. Pr *16:19. *29:23. Ec 7:3, *8. Is +*57:15. *61:1. *66:2. Je 31:18-20. Da *5:21, 22. Mi +*6:8. Lk *4:18. *6:20. *18:14. 1 C 1:28, 29. 2 C *6:10. Ja *1:10. *2:5. *4:9, 10. Re 3:17. in spirit. ℐ121A2, Metonymy of the Cause, Ps +51:10. "Spirit" (Gr. *pneuma*) put for character as being in itself invisible, and manifested only in one's actions. Lk 9:55. Ro 8:15, 15. 1 C 4:21. Ga 6:1. 1 T 4:12. 2 T √1:7. 1 P 3:4. Re 19:10. For additional examples of this figure of speech see ℐ121A2, Mt +26:41. For the other uses of *pneuma,* see Mt +*8:16n. for theirs. Mt 3:2. +*8:11. Mk *10:14. Lk 12:32. Ja *2:5. kingdom of heaven. Mt 4:17.

4. Blessed. ℐ18, Dt +28:4. that mourn. ℐ101, Dt +32:42. In the Beatitudes, the participle is put out of its usual place, and made to begin the sentences instead of ending them: thus calling attention to the emphasis placed upon it (B694). Ps 6:1-9. 13:1-5. 30:7-11. 32:3-7. 40:1-3. 69:29, 30. 116:3-7. *126:5, 6. Ec *7:3, 4. Is *12:1. 25:8. 30:19. 35:10. 38:14-19. 51:11, 12. 57:17, 18. *61:2, 3. 66:10. Je 31:9-12, 16, 17. Ezk 7:16. *9:4. Zc *12:10-14. 13:1. Lk *6:21, 25. 7:38, 50. 16:25. Jn *16:20-22. 2 C √1:3-7. 6:10. √7:9, 10. Ja 1:12. 4:9. comforted. Re *7:14-17. *21:4.

5. the meek. T#438, 931. Mt *11:29. *21:5. Nu *12:3. Ps 22:26. √25:9. *37:11. *69:32mg. 76:8, +*9. *147:6. *149:4. Pr 14:29. *15:1, 18. *16:32. 19:11. *20:3. Ec 7:8. Is *11:4. *29:19. *61:1. Am 2:7. Zp +*2:3. Lk 18:9-14. Ga *5:23. Ep *4:2. Col *3:12. 1 T *6:11. 2 T *2:25. T *3:2. Ja *1:21. *3:13. 1 P *3:3,

4, 15. inherit the earth. Ge +*22:17. Ps *25:13. 27:13. √37:9, 11, 22, 29, 34. +*106:4, 5. 115:16-18. Pr 2:21, 22. 10:30. 11:31. 12:7. Is 11:9. 26:6. 45:18. 54:17. +*55:3. 57:13. +*60:21n. +*66:22. Da +*7:14, 18. Ac +*7:5. Ro *4:13. He +*11:16. Re √5:10.

6. are. Ps *42:1, 2. *63:1, 2. 84:2. *107:9. Is *26:9. Am *8:11-13. Lk *1:53. 6:21, 25. Jn 6:27. hunger. T#883. Jb *23:12. Ps 81:10. 119:103. Is 49:10. 55:1, 2. *65:13. Je *15:16. Am +*8:11. Lk *1:53. 6:21. Jn *6:35. Re 21:6. 22:17. thirst. Ps *42:2. 63:1. Is *26:9. 44:3. Jn *7:37, 38. Re 22:17. for they. Ps 4:6, 7. 17:14, 15. 63:5. 65:4. 81:10. 107:9. 145:19. SS 5:1. Is 25:6. 41:17, 18. 44:3. 49:9, 10. +*55:1-3. 65:13. 66:11, 12. Jn *4:14. 6:48-58. 7:37, 38. Re 7:16, 17.

7. merciful. T#527, 918. Mt *6:14, 15. 18:33-35. 25:34-36. Dt 24:12, 13, +*14. 2 S 22:26. Jb 31:16-22. Ps +*12:5. *18:25. 37:26. *41:1-4. +58:11 (T#630). 112:4, 5, 9. Pr 3:3, 4. *11:17. 14:21. *19:17. 22:9. Is 57:1, 2. *58:6-12. Ezk +*16:49. Da *4:27. Mi +*6:8. Mk 11:25, 26. Lk *6:35, 36, +38 (T#408). Ga √6:9, 10. Ep √4:32. 5:1, 2. Col 3:12. T +1:8 (T#354). He +13:3 (T#686). Ja *2:13. 3:17. for they. Mt 7:2. 25:35. Pr 11:24-26. Ho 1:6. 2:1mg, 23. Ro 11:30, 31. 1 C 7:25. 2 C 4:1. 1 T 1:13, 16. 2 T 1:16-18. He 4:16. *6:10. Ja *2:13. 1 P 2:10.

8. pure. T#921. Mt 23:25-28. 1 Ch 29:17-19. Ps 15:2. *18:26. *24:3, 4. +*51:6, 10. 73:1. Pr 22:11. Ezk 18:5, 6, 9. 36:25-27. Ac √15:9. *24:16. 2 C *7:1. 1 T 1:5. 3:9. +*4:12. 2 T *2:21, 22. T *1:15. He *9:14. *10:22. Ja ◐1:8. 3:17. 4:8. 1 P √1:22. in heart. 1 K +*8:18. Pr +*4:23. 22:11. for they. Ge 32:30. Jb *19:26, 27. Ps 11:7. *15:1. +*17:15. 42:2. 140:13. 1 C 13:12. He √12:14. 1 J *3:2, 3. Re *22:4.

9. peacemakers. T#913. Ge *13:8. 1 Ch 12:17, 18. Ps *34:12-14. 120:6, 7. +*122:6-8. Pr 12:20. +*16:7. Ac 7:26. Ro √12:18. 14:1-7, 17-19. 1 C 6:6-8. 2 C 5:20. *13:11. Ga 5:22. Ep 4:1-3. Ph 2:1-3, *14. 4:2. Col 3:13-15. 1 Th 5:23. 2 T 2:22-24. He √12:14. Ja 1:19, 20. *3:16-18. 1 P 3:10, 11. for. ver. 45, 48. Ps 82:6, 7. Lk +*6:35. 20:36. Ro 8:14. Ep 5:1, 2. Ph *2:15, 16. 1 P 1:14-16.

10. persecuted. T#934. Mt 10:23, 39. 19:29. Ps 37:12, 13. 69:7, 9. Is *51:7, 8. Mk 10:30. Lk 6:22, 23. 21:12, 13. Jn 15:20, 21. Ac 5:40, 41. 8:1. 9:4. Ro *8:17, 35-39. 1 C 4:9-13. 2 C 4:8-12, √17. Ph 1:28, 29. 2 T *2:12. √3:11, 12. He *10:34, 35. Ja 1:2-5. 5:11. 1 P *3:13, 14, 17. *4:12-16. 1 J 3:12. Re *2:10. for. ver. 3. Mt +4:17. 2 Th *1:4-7. Ja *1:12.

11. when. Mt 10:25. 27:39. Ps +√9:10. 35:11. *37:40. 55:22. 69:7, 9. *118:6. Pr *29:25. Is *51:7, 8. *63:9. 66:5. Je *1:19. Zc 2:8. Lk *6:22, 26. 7:33, 34. *21:18, 19. Jn 9:28. Ro *8:35: 2 C 12:10. Ga 4:29. Ph *1:28, 29. He 11:26. 12:3. +*13:5, 6. 1 P *2:23. men. ℐ63A1, Ge +14:20. falsely. Gr. lying. Lk 3:14. 2 T 3:3. 1 P *3:16. *4:14. for my sake. Mt 10:18, 22, 39. 19:29. 24:9. Ps 44:22. Mk 4:17. 8:35. 13:9, 13. Lk *6:22. 9:24. 21:12, 17. Jn 15:21. Ac 9:16. Ro 8:36. 1 C 4:10. 2 C 4:11. Re 2:3.

12. Rejoice. Lk 6:23. Ac *5:41. 13:52. *16:25. Ro *5:3. 2 C √4:17. 6:10. 7:4. *12:10. Ph 1:29. *2:17, 18. Col 1:11, 24. 1 Th 1:6. He *10:34. Ja *1:2. 1 P 1:6. *4:13. for great. Mt 6:1, 2, 4, 5, 16. *10:41, 42. 16:27. *25:21, 23. Ge 15:1. Ru 2:12. Ps 19:11. 58:11. Pr 11:18. Is 3:10. Da +*12:3. Mk +*10:30. Lk 6:23, 35. ◐+*12:47, 48. +*14:14. +*18:30. 1 C 3:8, 12-15. 2 C √4:17. 9:6. Ph 3:14. Col 3:24. 1 T +*4:8. He

*11:6, 26. Ja +*1:12. 2 P +*1:11. Re *11:18. 22:12.
in heaven. Mk +*10:21. He 10:34-37. 1 P +*1:4n.
for so persecuted. Mt 21:34-38. 23:31-37. 1 K 18:4,
13. 19:2, 10, 14. 21:20. 22:8, 26, 27. 2 K 1:9. 2 Ch
16:10. 24:20-22. *36:16. Ne *9:26. Je 2:30. 26:8, 9,
21-23. 43:2, 3. Lk 6:23. 11:47-51. 13:34. Ac *7:51,
52. 1 Th 2:15. Ja *5:10.

13. **Ye**. ∫138C, Ge +22:14. **are**. ∫119, Ge +49:9.
the salt. Le *2:13. Ep *4:29. Col *4:6. **earth**. ∫121J17,
Ge +6:11. **but if**. ∫7, Allegory as continued Metaphor,
Ga +4:24. ∫184C, Mt +4:9. Mk *9:49, 50. Lk *14:34,
35. He *6:4-6. 2 P *2:20, 21.

14. **Ye**. ∫138C, Ge +22:14. **the light**. T#670. Ps
119:105. Pr +*4:18. Je 5:1. Ezk 22:29, 30. Da +10:12
(T#545). Lk 2:32. Jn 1:4, 9. 5:35. 8:12, 29. 9:5. *12:35,
36. Ro 2:19, 20. 15:21. 2 C 6:14. Ep *5:8-14. Ph 2:15.
1 Th *5:5. 1 J 1:5. Re 1:20. 2:1. **world**. Gr. *kosmos*,
Mt +4:8. **A city**. Ge 11:4-8. Ps 48:2. Re 21:14, etc.
set on a hill. Jsh 20:7n.

15. **Neither**. ∫138C, Ge +22:14. **do**. Mk 4:21, 22.
Lk 8:16, 17. 11:33. **candle**. Pr 31:18. **put it under**.
Mt +6:2n. +*25:27, 29. Lk *19:23. **a bushel**. "A measure containing about a pint less than a peck." **but
on**. He 9:2. Re 1:12. **it giveth**. Ex 25:37. Nu 8:2. 1 C
*12:7.

16. **your light**. Pr +*4:18. 31:18. Is 58:8. *60:1-3.
Ro 13:11-14. Ep *5:8. Ph *2:15, 16. 1 Th 2:12. 5:6-8.
1 P *2:9. 1 J 1:5-7. **that they**. Mt 6:1-5, 16. 23:5. Ac
9:36. Ep 2:10. 1 T 2:10. 5:10, 25. 6:18. T 2:7, 14.
3:1, 7, 8, 14. Phm 6. He 10:24. 1 P 2:12. 3:1, 16.
see. Ge +30:27. 39:3. Ps 34:2. Ja +*1:22. *2:18, 20.
and glorify. Mt 9:8. *15:31. Is 61:3. Jn *15:8. 1 C
14:25. 2 C 9:13. Ga 1:24. Ph *1:11. 2 Th 1:10-12.
1 P *2:12. 4:11, 14. **your Father**. ver. 45, 48. Mt *6:9.
23:9. Lk 11:2.

17. **Think not**. Mt 10:34. *22:29. **to destroy**.
❋S#2647g. Mt 5:17, 17. 24:2 (thrown down). 26:61.
27:40. Mk 13:2 (thrown down). 14:58. 15:29. Lk 9:12
(lodge). 19:7 (be guest). 21:6 (thrown down). Ac 5:38
(come to nought), 39 (overthrow). 6:14. Ro 14:20.
2 C 5:1 (dissolved). Ga 2:18. Compare ❋S#360g, Ph
+1:23n. **the law**. Mt 7:12. Lk 16:16, 17. Jn 8:5. Ac
6:13. 18:13. 21:28. Ro *3:21, 31. 10:4. Ga *3:17-24.
but to fulfill. Mt +3:15. 8:4. 17:24-27. Ps *40:6-8. Is
42:21. Lk 2:39, 41, 42. 17:14. Jn 1:17. Ro *8:4. *10:4.
Ga 4:4, 5. Ph *3:3. Col √2:16, 17. He *10:3-12.

18. **verily**. ver. 26. Mt 6:2, 5, 16. 8:10. 10:15, 23,
42. 11:11. 13:17. 16:28. 17:20. 18:3, 13, 18. 19:23,
28. 21:21, 31. 23:36. 24:2, 34, 47. 25:12, 40, 45. 26:13,
14. Mk 3:28. 6:11. 8:12. 9:1, 41. 10:15, 29. 11:23.
12:43. 13:30. 14:9, 18, 25, 30. Lk 4:24. 11:51. 12:37.
13:35. 18:17, 29. 21:32. 23:43. Jn 1:51. 3:3, 5, 11.
5:19, 24, 25. 6:26, 32, 47, 53. 8:34, 51, 58. 10:1, 7.
12:24. 13:16, 20, 21, 38. 14:12. 16:20, 23. 21:18.
heaven. Mt *24:35. Ps 102:26. Is *51:6. Lk *16:17.
21:33. He 1:11, 12. 2 P 3:10-13. Re 20:11. **one jot**.
Jn +*10:35. **no wise**. ∫158. Repeated Negation; or,
Many No's B340. The repetition of divers negatives,
a form of Synonymia, the synonyms being negatives
of different kinds heaped together for a special purpose.
Here, to express the certainty of Divine Truth. EWB
notes that in Scripture, whenever man uses this strong
asseveration, the result always contradicted what was
denied (Mt 16:22. 26:35. Jn 13:8. 20:25), but when
our Lord used this emphatic negative, He always made
it good. For other instances of this figure see Mt 5:20,

26. 13:14. 16:22, 28. 18:3, 39. 22:29. 24:34, 35. 26:29,
35. Mk 14:25. Lk 1:15. 6:37. 10:19. 18:7, 30. 21:18.
22:18, 34, 67, 68. Jn 3:18. 4:14, 48. *6:35, 37. 8:12,
51. 10:5, √28. *11:26. 13:8, 38. 20:25. Ac 28:26. Ro
4:8. 1 Th 4:15. 5:3. He 8:12. 10:17. *13:5. 1 P 2:6.
2 P 1:10. Re 3:12. **pass**. Ps 119:89, 90, 152. Is 40:8.
1 P 1:25. **fulfilled**. T#42. Mt 24:35. Is +42:21 (T#284).
Lk 16:17. 24:44. Jn √1035. Ac 1:16. 3:18.

19. **Whosoever**. Gr. *os ean*, conditional conjunction
introducing a third class condition. ∫184C, Mt +4:9.
shall break. Dt 27:26. Ps 119:6, 128. Mk 7:11. Lk
11:42. 1 C *3:12-15. Ga 3:10-13. Ja √2:10, 11. **these**.
Mt *23:23. Dt 12:32. Lk 11:42. **least**. ∫96E2, 1 S 17:14.
shall teach. Mt 15:3-6. 23:16-22. Ml 2:8, 9. Ro 3:8.
6:1, 15. 1 T 6:3, 4. Re 2:14, 15, 20. **be called**. Mt
+*16:27. **the least**. Mt 11:11. 18:1-4. 1 S *2:30. ∫172.
Synoeceiosis; or, Cohabitation B294. The repetition
of the same word in the same sentence with an extended
meaning. In the former place, the allusion is to the
distinction which the Pharisees made between different
commandments (just as Rome has since made the distinction between "venial" and "mortal" sins). There
is no such distinction (Ja 2:10), and therefore, when
in the latter place Christ says "he shall be called the
least," he means that he will not be there at all, for
there will be no such distinction there. There is no
least in either case. For other instances of this figure
see Mt 18:1, 4. 19:16, 17. Jn 6:28, 29. Ac 26:28, 29.
shall do. Mt *7:24-27. 28:20. Dt +*26:16, 18. Lk *8:21.
10:25, 26. Jn +*13:17. Ac 1:1. Ro 13:8-10. Ga 5:14-
24. Ph 3:17, 18. 4:8, 9. 1 Th 2:10-12. 4:1-7. 1 T 4:11,
12. 6:11. T 2:8-10. 3:8. Ja √1:22. Re *22:14. **and teach**.
T#396. Pr 27:9. Da +*11:33n. Ro 12:7. 1 Th +5:11
(T#110). 1 T +*4:16. 2 T +*2:2. **great**. Mt 19:28.
20:26. Da +*12:3. Lk 1:15. 9:48. 22:24-26. 1 P 5:4.
kingdom of heaven. Mt 4:17.

20. **except**. ∫184C, Mt +4:9. **your righteousness**.
Jb 27:6. Ph √3:9. **exceed**. T#308. ver. +48 (T#285).
Mt *23:2-5, 23-28. Lk *11:39, 40, 42, 44. 12:1. 16:14,
15. 18:10-14. 20:46, 47. Ro 6:15. 9:30-32. *10:2, 3.
2 C 5:17. +7:1 (T#501). Ph 3:9. **scribes and Pharisees**.
Mt 16:12. **ye shall**. Mt 3:10. 7:21. 18:3. Mk 10:15,
25. Lk 18:17, 24, 25. Jn √3:3-5. He *12:14. Re 21:27.
in no case. ∫158, ver. +18. **enter**. T#560. Mt +*7:21-
23. 10:33. +12:31n, 32n. +*13:30, 49. *18:3. 25:10-
12, 31, +32 (T#387), 33. Ps *95:11. Pr +16:4 (T#256).
Lk +9:24 (T#554). +12:10 (T#562). +16:26 (T#390).
1 C √6:9, 10. Ga 5:19-21. Ep *5:5, 6. He √12:14. Ja
+1:15 (T#287). Re *21:27.

21. **it**. ver. 27, 31, 33, 38, 43. 2 S 20:18. Jb 8:8-
10. Jn 12:34. Ac 15:21. Ga 4:21. **by them**. *or*, to them.
Thou. Mt 19:18. Ge *9:5, 6. Ex +*20:13. Le 24:21.
Dt)5:17. Mk 10:19. Lk 18:20. Ro 13:9. Ja 2:11. **and**.
Ex 21:12-14. Nu *35:12, 16-21, 30-34. Dt 21:7-9. 1 K
2:5, 6, 31, 32. **the judgment**. Dt 16:18. 17:9. 2 Ch
19:5, 6.

22. **I say**. ver. 28, 34, 44. Mt 3:17. 17:5. Dt 18:18,
19. Ac 3:20-23. 7:37. He 5:9. 12:25. **That**. Ge 4:5, 6.
37:4, 8. 1 S 17:27, 28. 18:8, 9. 20:30-33. 22:12, etc.
1 K 21:4. 2 Ch 16:10. Est 3:5, 6. Ps *37:8. Da 2:12,
13. 3:13, 19. Ep *4:26, 27, 31. Col 3:8. Ja 1:19. **whosoever**. ∫18, Dt +28:4. **his brother**. ver. 23, 24, 47.
Mt 18:21, 35. Dt 15:11. Ne 5:8. Ob 10, 12. Ro 12:10.
1 C 6:6. 1 Th 4:6. 1 J 2:9. √3:10, 14, 15. 4:20, 21.
5:16. **without a cause**. Ps 7:4. 25:3. 35:19. 69:4. 109:3.
La 3:52. Jn 15:25. Ro 12:18. 13:4. Ep 4:26. **be**. ver.

21. the judgment. An inferior court of judicature, in every city, consisting of 23 members, which punished criminals by strangling or beheading. **whosoever.** Mt 11:18, 19. 12:24, 37. 1 S 20:30. 2 S 16:7. Jn 7:20. 8:48. Ac 17:18. 1 C 6:10. Ep *4:31, 32. T 3:2. 1 P 2:23. 3:9. Ju 9. **Raca.** that is, *vain fellow.* i.e. *vain; empty, worthless,* ✻S#4469g, only here. Compare S#7386h, Ne +5:13. 2 S 6:20. Ja 2:20. ♪171K1, Dt +19:5. **in danger.** Gr. *enokos,* liable or obnoxious to, from *enekomai,* to bind, oblige. Pr 13:3. Ja 3:2-12. **the council.** The *Sanhedrin, sunedrion,* composed of 72 elders, who alone punished by stoning. Mt 10:17. 26:59. Mk 14:55. 15:1. Jn 11:47. Ac 4:15. 5:27. **fool.** Ps 14:1. 49:10. 53:1. 92:6. Pr 14:16. 18:6. Je 17:11. or, *Moreh,* a Hebrew expression of condemnation. Nu 20:10h. **in danger.** Lk +9:24. **hell.** Gr. *gehenna,* ✻S#1067g. Mt 5:22, 29, 30. Mt √10:28. 18:9. 23:15, 33. Mk 9:43, 45, 47. Lk √12:5. Ja 3:6. See Jsh +*15:8n. For ✻S#86g, *hades,* see Mt +11:23. 2 P ◑2:4. **fire.** Mt 18:8. +*25:41. Dt +*32:22. Ps 88:11. Is +*66:24. Lk +*16:23, 24. Re 20:14. +*21:8.

23. if. ♪184C, Mt +4:9. Mt 6:15. Mk 11:25. **thou.** Mt *8:4. 23:18, 19. Dt *16:16, 17. 1 S 15:22. Is 1:10-17. Ho 6:6. Am 5:21-24. **gift.** ♪63H, Ge +12:15. Supply by ellipsis (relative: of a combined word, where the omitted word is contained in another word, the one combining the two significations), "(even thy sacrifice) to the altar." An offering was the only gift that could be brought to an altar. **to the altar.** The brazen altar, before the porch of the Temple (Wordsworth, *Greek Testament),* the altar of burnt offering. Mt 23:18, 35. Ex *27:1, 2. 1 K 9:25. 2 K 16:14, 15. 2 Ch 7:7. 15:8. 29:18. 33:16. 35:16. Ezr 3:2, 3. Ne 10:34. Am +*9:1. Lk 11:51. 1 C 9:13. 10:18. He 7:13. 13:10. **rememberest.** Ge 41:9. 42:21, 22. 50:15-17. Le 6:2-6. 1 K 2:44. La 3:20. Ezk 16:63. Lk 19:8. 1 C √11:28. **ought against.** Mk 11:25. Re 2:4, 14, 20.

24. there. Mt 18:15-17. Jb +*42:8. Pr 25:9. Mk 9:50. Ro *12:17, 18. 1 C 6:7, 8. 1 T +*2:8. Ja 3:13-18. 5:16. 1 P 3:7, 8. **be reconciled.** 1 S 29:4. 1 C 7:11. **and then.** Mt *23:23. 1 C √11:28.

25. agree with. Ge 32:3-8, 13-22. 33:3-11. 1 S 25:17-35. Pr 6:1-5. 25:8. Lk *12:58, 59. 14:31, 32. **thine adversary.** Lk *12:58. 18:3. **whiles.** Jb *22:21. Ps 32:6. Is √55:6, 7. Lk 13:24, 25. 2 C *6:2. He 3:7, 13. 12:17. **and the judge.** 1 K 22:26, 27. **officer.** Mt 26:58.

26. Thou. Mt 18:34. 25:41, 46. Lk 12:59. 16:26. 2 Th √1:9. Ja *2:13. **by no means.** ♪158, ver. +18. **hast paid.** Gr. *apodidomi,* ✻S#591g. Rendered (1) pay: Mt 5:26. 18:25a, 26, 28, 29, 30, 34. Lk 7:42. 12:59. (2) give: Mt 12:36. 20:8. Lk 16:2. Ac 4:33. 19:40. 2 T 4:8. He 13:17. 1 P 4:5. Re 22:12. (3) render: Mt 21:41. 22:21. Mk 12:17. Lk 20:25. Ro 2:6. 13:7. 1 C 7:3. 1 Th 5:15. 1 P 3:9. (4) reward: Mt 6:4, 6, 18. 16:27. 2 T 4:14. Re 18:6, 6. (5) sell: Ac 5:8. 7:9. He 12:16. (6) yield: He 12:11. Re 22:2. (7) Mt 5:33, perform. 18:25b, payment. 27:58, deliver. Lk 4:20, give again. Lk 9:42, deliver again. 10:35, repay. 19:8, restore. Ro 12:17, recompense. 1 T 5:4 (with S#287g), requite. **uttermost farthing.** Mk 12:42.

27. Thou. Mt 19:18. Ex +*♪20:14. Le 18:20. 20:10. Dt 5:18. 22:22-24. Pr 6:32. Mk 10:19. Lk 18:20. Ro 13:9. 1 C +*6:9. He +*13:4.

28. I say. ver. 22, 39. Mt 7:28, 29. **That.** Ge 34:2. *39:7, etc. Ex *20:17. 2 S *11:2. Jb 24:15. √31:1, 9. Ps +*101:3. *119:37. Pr *6:25. Is 33:15. Ja √1:14, 15.

2 P 2:14. 1 J *2:16. **looketh.** Ezk +23:16. **to lust.** Gr. *epithumeo,* ✻S#1937g. Mt 5:28. 13:17 (desired). Lk 15:16 (would fain). 16:21 (desiring). 17:22. 22:15. Ac 20:33 (coveted). Ro √7:7. √13:9. 1 C 10:6 (lusted). Ga 5:17. 1 T 3:1 (desireth). He 6:11. Ja 4:2 (lust). 1 P 1:12 (desire). Re 9:6. Compare related noun, *epithumia,* ✻S#1939g, 1 Th +4:5. **hath.** Ps 119:96. Ro *7:7, 8, 14. **heart.** Mt 12:35. Pr +*4:23. Je +*6:19. Mk +*7:21.

29. if. ♪184A, 1 C 15:2. Mt 18:8, 9. Mk *9:43-48. **right eye.** ♪103, Ge +3:13. Ex 29:20. 1 S 11:2. Zc 11:17. **offend thee.** or, do cause thee to offend. Mt 15:12. 17:27. ♪96A1. Heterosis of Verbs B512: intransitive for transitive. For other instances of this figure see Mt 5:45. 1 C 2:2. 3:6. 13:12. 2 C 2:14. (9:8). Ga 4:9. Ep (1:8). 2 T 2:19. **pluck.** Mt 19:12. Ezk 23:34. Ro 6:6. √8:13. 1 C *9:27. Ga *5:24. Col √3:5. 1 P 4:1-3. ♪102C. Hyperbole B428. In hypotheses, impossible in themselves, but are used to express the greatness of the subject spoken of. It is perfectly clear that Christ does not wish us to mutilate our bodies: so this must be an hyperbolical or emphatic exhortation to avoid and remove everything and anything that causes us to stumble. For other instances of this figure see Mt 5:30. 1 K 20:10. Ps 139:8-10. Pr 27:22. Ob 4. Mk 8:36. *9:45, 47. Lk 9:25. 10:4. Jn *21:25. Ro 9:3. 1 C 4:15. 13:1-3. Ga 1:8. Ju 23. See related figure, ♪102, Ge +7:19. **for.** Mt 16:26. Pr 5:8-14. Mk 8:36. Lk 9:24, 25. **hell.** Gr. *gehenna,* ver. +22.

30. if. ♪184A, 1 C +15:2. **right hand.** ♪103, Ge +3:13. **offend.** Mt 11:6. 13:21. 16:23. 18:6, 7. 26:31. Lk 17:2. Ro 9:33. 14:20, 21. 1 C 8:13. Ga 5:11. 1 P 2:8. **cut it off.** Every one must immediately see, says Bp. Porteus, that the eye to be plucked out is the eye of concupiscence, and the hand to be cut off is the hand of violence and vengeance; that is, these passions are to be checked and subdued, let the conflict cost us what it may. Ezk 23:34. Mk 9:43, 44. **cast.** Mt 22:13. +*25:30. Lk +*12:5.

31. Whosoever. ♪92E, Mt +4:10. Divorces were carried to a scandalous and criminal excess among the Jews; the school of Hillel permitting a man to put away his wife, if he saw a woman handsomer than her, or if she displeased in her manners, or even in dressing his victuals! Mt 19:3n, 7, 9n. Dt ▶24:1-4. Is 50:1. Je 3:1, 8. Mk *10:2-9.

32. I say. ver. 28. Lk 9:30, 35. **whosoever.** Mt *19:8, 9. Ml 2:14-16. Mk 10:5-12. Lk 16:18. Ro 7:3. 1 C 7:4, 10, 11. **fornication.** Gr. *porneia,* ✻S#4202g. Mt 15:19. *19:9. Mk 7:21. Jn 8:41. Ac 15:20, 29. 21:25. Ro 1:29. 1 C 5:1, 1. 6:13, 18. 7:2. 2 C 12:21. Ga 5:19. Ep 5:3. Col 3:5. 1 Th 4:3. Re 2:21. 9:21. 14:8. 17:2, 4. 18:3. 19:2. **and whosoever.** ♪184C, Mt +4:9.

33. it hath. Mt 23:16. **Thou.** Ex *20:7. Le *19:12. Nu √30:2, etc. Dt 5:11. 23:23. Jg +*11:35. Ps 50:14. 76:11. Ec 5:4-6. Na 1:15. 1 T 1:10. **shalt perform.** Nu 30:2. Dt ▶23:21. Jb 22:27. Ps 22:25. 50:14. 66:13, 14. 116:14, 18. Ec 5:4. Na 1:15.

34. Swear. Dt ◐10:20. 23:21-23. Ec 9:2. Ja *5:12. **not at all.** ♪171C, Ex +20:10. **heaven.** Mt *23:16-22. Is +*57:15. ▶66:1. Ac 7:49. Re 4:2. **throne.** ♪22D3C1, Ps +11:4.

35. the earth. Ps 99:5. Is ▶66:1. **footstool.** ♪22D3D1, Is +66:1. 1 Ch 28:2. La 2:1. **the city.** Mt 4:5. 2 Ch 6:6. Ps ▶48:2. 87:2. Ml 1:14. Re 21:2, 10. **great King.** Ps 95:3.

36. **shalt.** Mt 23:16-21. **because.** Mt 6:27. 10:30. Lk 12:25.

37. **let.** 2 C 1:17-20. Col *4:6. Ja 5:12. **yea.** ♪84, Ge +6:17. **nay.** ♪84, Ge +6:17. **whatsoever.** Mt 12:36, 37. Pr 10:19. **cometh.** Mt 13:19. 15:19. Jn √8:44. Ep 4:25. Col 3:9. Ja 5:12. **evil.** ver. 39. Mt 6:13. 12:35. Lk 6:45.

38. **An eye.** Ex ▶21:22-27. Le ▶24:19, 20. Dt 19:19, 21.

39. **That.** Le *19:18. 1 S 24:*4n-6, 10-15. 25:31-34. *26:8-10. Jb 31:29-31. Pr √20:22. 24:29. Lk √‖6:29n. Ro √12:17-19. 1 C *6:7. 1 Th 5:15. He 12:4. Ja *5:6. 1 P 3:9. **resist not.** Mt 26:52. Ge *26:22. Pr ◑+*19:25. Lk ◑+√22:36. Jn *18:11, 36. Ro +*12:19. **evil.** Dt 19:19. 1 C 5:13. **whosoever.** Mt 26:67. 1 K 22:24. Jb 16:10. Is *50:6. La *3:30. Mi 5:1. Mk 14:65. Lk 6:29. 22:+*36, 64. Jn ◑*18:20-23. 19:3. Ac 16:37. 23:1-3. Ro 12:17. 1 P *2:20-23.

40. **will sue.** T#716. Pr 19:11. Lk *6:29. 1 C *6:1, 6, 7. **thy cloak.** Mt 24:18. Mk 13:16.

41. **compel.** Mt 27:32. Mk 15:21. Lk 23:26.

42. **Give to him.** Mt 10:8. 25:◑8, ◑9, 35-40. 26:11. Dt *15:7-14. Jb 31:16-20. Ps *37:21, 25, 26. 112:5-9. Pr *3:27, 28. 11:24, 25. √19:17. 21:26. Ec 11:1, 2, 6. Is 58:6-12. Da 4:27. Lk 3:11. *6:30-36, +*38. 11:41. 12:33. 14:12-14. Ac ◑18:20. √20:35. Ro 12:20. 2 C 9:6-15. Ga +*6:10. 1 T 6:17-19. He +*6:10. +*13:16. Ja 1:27. *2:15, 16. 1 J *3:16-18. **from him.** Dt +*15:8. **turn not.** Le 25:35. Dt *15:8, 10.

43. **Thou.** Mt 19:19. 22:39, 40. Le ▶19:18. Mk 12:31-34. Lk 10:27-29. Ro 13:8-10. Ga 5:13, 14. Ja 2:8. **and hate.** Ex 17:14-16. Dt 23:6. *25:17, 19. 1 S 24:19. Ezr 9:12. Ps 41:10. 139:21, 22.

44. **Love your enemies.** Ex 23:4, 5. Le 19:18. 2 K 6:22. 2 Ch 28:9-15. Ps *7:4. 35:13, 14. Pr 25:21, 22. Lk 6:27, 28, 34, 35. *23:34. Ac *7:60. Ro √12:14, 20, 21. 1 C *4:12, 13. 13:4-8. 1 Th 5:15. 1 P *2:23. √3:9. **do good.** 1 S *24:17, 18. Ga 6:10. **pray for.** T#1473. Ps 35:13, 14. Je 29:7. Lk *6:27, 28. 23:33, 34. Ac 7:59, 60. 2 T 4:◑+*14, 16. 1 P 3:9. **persecute.** T#1639. Je 29:7. 1 C *4:12.

45. **ye.** ver. *9. Lk +*6:35. Jn *13:35. Ep *5:1. Ph 2:15. 1 J *3:9, 10. **your Father.** ver. 16, 48. Mt *6:9. 23:9. **for he maketh.** T#1261. Mt 6:26, 28-30. Dt 10:18. Jb *2:10. 25:3. Ps 104:14, 21, 27, 28. *145:9. Lk +*6:35. Ac *14:17. 17:26. **rise.** ♪96A1, ver. 29. **the evil and.** Jb +*9:22n. Ec +*9:2. Am +√3:6. **and sendeth.** Le 26:4. Jb *2:10. Is √55:9-11. La 3:38. Ac 14:17.

46. **if.** ♪184C, Mt +4:9. Mt 6:1. Lk 6:32-35. 1 P *2:19-23. **publicans.** Mt 9:10, 11. 11:19. 18:17. 21:31, 32. Lk 15:1. 18:13. 19:2, 7.

47. **if.** ♪184C, Mt +4:9. **salute.** ♪121S2, Ge +21:6. Mt 10:12. Lk *6:32. 10:4, 5. **your brethren.** ver. 22. **what.** ver. 20. 1 P 2:20. **do not even.** Mt 6:7, 32. Je +*10:2. 3 J 7.

48. **perfect.** T#285. Mt 19:21. 22:37-39. Ge 6:9. *17:1. Le *11:44. *19:2. *20:26. Dt *▶18:13. 1 K 8:61. Jb *1:1, 8. 2:3. 9:20, 21. Ps 37:+*18n, 37. 119:1mg. Pr +21:3 (T#629). 23:17. Ec ◑7:16. 2p 3:13. Lk 6:36, *40. Jn 17:23. 1 C 2:6. *10:31. 2 C +*7:1 (T#501). *13:9, 11. Ph √3:12-15. Col 1:28. *4:12. He *13:21. Ja *1:4. √3:2. 1 P *1:15, 16. *5:10. 2 P *3:11, 12. 1 J 3:2. Ju 21. **even.** ver. 16, 45. Ep 3:1. √4:32. 5:1, 2. 1 J 3:3.

MATTHEW 6

Cautions and rules about almsgiving, 1-4, and prayer, 5-8. The Lord's prayer, 9-13. Those who seek forgiveness must forgive, 14, 15. Cautions and rules about fasting, 16-18. Treasure to be laid up in heaven, 19-21. The single eye, 21-23. God and Mammon cannot both be served, 24. Solicitude about worldly things, being vain, needless, and injurious, should be shunned; and "the kingdom of God and his righteousness" sought in the first place, 25-34.

1. **heed.** Mt 16:6. Mk 8:15. Lk 11:35. 12:1, 15. He *2:1. **ye do.** 1 J 2:29. **alms.** *or*, righteousness. ♪121C1B, Ge +20:13. ♪171K1, Dt +19:5. Dt 24:13. Ps 112:9. Da 4:27. 2 C 9:9, 10. **to be seen.** T#483. ver. 5, 16. Mt 5:16. 23:5, 15, 28-30. 2 K 10:16, 31. Ezk +*33:31. Zc 7:5, 6. 13:4. Lk +16:15 (T#703). Jn *5:44. *12:43. Ga 6:12, 13. **otherwise.** ver. 4, 6. Mt 5:46. 10:41, 42. 16:27. 25:40. 1 C 9:17, 18. He *6:10. 11:26. 2 J 8. **of your.** *or*, with your. ver. 9, 26, 32. Mt 5:16, 48. 23:9.

2. **when.** Ge 47:29. Jb 31:16-20. Ps 37:21. 112:9. Pr 19:17. Ec 11:2. Is 58:7, 10-12. Lk 11:41. 12:33. Jn 13:29. Ac 9:36. 10:2, 4, 31. 11:29. 24:17. Ro √12:8. 1 C 13:3. 2 C 9:6-15. Ga 2:10. Ep 4:28. 1 T 6:18. Phm 7. He *13:16. Ja 2:15, 16. 1 P 4:11. 1 J 3:17-19. **do not sound a trumpet.** *or*, cause not a trumpet to be sounded. Pr 20:6. Ho 8:1. **as the hypocrites.** ver. 5, 16. Mt 7:5. 15:7. 16:3. 22:18. 23:13-29. 24:51. Is 9:17. 10:6. Mk 7:6. Lk 6:42. 12:1, 56. 13:15. **in the synagogues.** ver. 5. Mt 23:6. Mk 12:39. Lk 11:43. 20:46. **glory.** 1 S 15:30. Lk *16:15. Jn 5:41, 44. 7:18. 1 Th 2:6. **Verily.** ver. 5, 16. Mt +*5:18. **I say.** Note Christ's effective use of incongruity and contrast to evoke humor. Pr 17:22. For other instances of humor see Mt 6:5, 16, 26, 34. 7:1-4, 6, 16. 8:22. 11:16-19. 12:27. **They have.** ♪8, Ps +118:1. ver. +*5, 16. Ps 17:14. Lk *6:24. Ph 4:18. Phm 15.

3. **But when.** Mt 10:42. 19:21. 25:35, 37-40. Lk 6:38. 14:12-14. Ro 12:8. **doest alms.** ver. 2. Ps *112:9. **let not.** ♪138C, Ge +22:14. Giving is to be done without ostentation (ver. 2), and with virtual secrecy. Certainly within the church, giving is to be kept confidential, and no church officer is to reveal to anyone—even the pastor, what any individual has given. For further insights into the Biblical standards of giving, see Mt 8:4. 9:30. 12:19. +23:23n. Mk 1:44. Jn 7:4. **know.** ♪155A, Ge +31:35. **right hand.** Ge +48:13. Dt 15:7. Ps 104:28. 145:16. Pr 3:27. 31:20. Ezk 21:21n. Ac 3:7.

4. **alms.** T#916. ver. 1. Ac 10:2, 4, 31. **seeth.** ver. 6, 18. 2 K 17:9. 1 Ch +*28:9. Ps 17:3. 44:21. 139:1-3, 12. Je +*17:10. 23:24. He *4:13. Re *2:23. **reward.** Mt 10:42. *25:34-40. 1 S *2:30. Lk 8:17. 14:14. 1 C 4:5. He +*6:10. Ju *24.

5. **when.** Mt 7:7, 8. 9:38. 21:22. Ps 5:2. +*55:17. Pr 15:8. Is √55:6, 7. Je √29:12. Da +*6:10. *9:4, etc. Lk *18:1. Jn √16:24. Ep √6:18. Col 4:2, 3. 1 Th √5:17. Ja *5:15, 16. **prayest.** ♪171K1, Dt +19:5. **not be as.** T#1255. ver. 2. Mt 23:14. Jb 27:8-10. Is *1:15. Mk 12:40. Lk 18:10, 11. 20:47. **for.** Mt 23:6. Mk 12:38. Lk 11:43. **love.** ♪121C2C1, Ps +11:5. **seen of men.** ver. 1, 16. Mt 23:5. **Verily.** ver. 2. Pr 16:5. Lk 14:12-14. Ja 4:6. **They have.** ♪8, Ps +118:1. T#565. ver. +2. Jb 12:6. 21:7-15. Ps 17:14. +42:10 (T#511). 73:3-7, 12. 92:7. +103:10 (T#552). Je 12:1, 2. Ezk 18:4n. Lk 6:24-26. *16:25. 2 Th 1:4-8.

6. **enter.** T#881. Mt +*14:23. 26:36-39. Ge 32:24-29. 2 K 4:33. Is ‹26:20. Jn 1:48. Ac 9:40. 10:9, 30. **closet.** or, inner chamber. Mt 24:26. Ge 43:30. 1 K 20:30mg. 2 K 4:10. Lk 12:3. **shut thy door.** ver. 1, 18. 2 K *4:33. Is +*26:20. **pray.** Ps 34:15. Is +*65:24. Jn 20:17. Ro 8:5. Ep 3:14. **which is in secret.** T#1278. Mt 14:23. 26:36-39. Ge 32:24-26. 2 K 4:32, 33. Is *26:20. Jn 1:48. Ac 9:40. 10:9, 10. **shall reward.** ver. 4, 18. Mt +5:26 (❋S#591g).

7. **use not.** 1 K *18:26-29. Ec 5:2, 3, 7. Ac 19:34. **vain repetitions.** T#1274. Mt 26:39, 42, 44. 1 K ◐8:26-54. Da 9:18, 19. **the heathen.** ver. 32. Mt 5:47. 18:17. Je +*10:2. 3 J 7. **they think.** 1 K 18:26, 29. **much speaking.** Pr 10:19. Ec *5:2. Is 1:15mg.

8. **Be not.** Mt 23:3. 2 K 17:15. Je +*10:2. **your Father.** T#1145. ver. 9, 32. Ps 38:9. 69:17-19. Is 63:15, 16. 64:7, 8. Lk 12:30. Jn *16:23-27. Ph *4:6. **before.** Is +*65:24. Da *2:21-23. Mk *11:24.

9. **this manner.** Lk 11:1, 2. **Our.** ver. 1, 6, 14. Mt 5:16, 45, 48. *7:11. 10:29. *26:29, 42. Dt 32:6. 1 Ch ?29:10. Ps 68:5. Is 63:16. *64:8. Lk *15:18, 19, 21. Jn *14:6, 13. 16;23. *20:17. Ro 1:7. *8:15, 16. Ga 1:1. *4:6. 1 T *2:5. 1 P 1:17. **Father.** Jn 4:23. 16:23. Ep 4:6. 1 J *3:1. **which art.** Mt *7:21. *23:9. 2 Ch 20:6. Jb *22:12. Ps 2:4. 11:4. 102:19. *115:3. *123:1. Is 40:22. +*57:15. 66:1. Ac 7:55, 56. 1 T +*6:16. **Hallowed.** ƒ108B, Je +12:3. Le 10:3. Nu 20:12. 2 S 7:26. 1 K 8:43. 1 Ch 17:24. Ne *9:5. Ps 72:18, 19. *111:9. 103:20-22. *113:2, 3. Is *6:3. *8:13. +*29:23. 37:20. +57:15. Ezk 20:41. 28:22. *36:23. +*38:16, 23. Hab *2:14. Zc 14:9. Ml *1:11, 14. Lk *1:49. 2:14. 11:2. 1 T *6:16. 1 P +*3:15. Re 4:11. +*5:12. **thy name.** ƒ144A4, Ge +4:26. Ex +*6:3n. Le 18:21. 20:3. 21:6. +22:32. 1 S 18:30. Ps 5:11. 7:17. +√9:10. 102:15. 113:1-3. Is +29.23. Ml 1:11, 12. Jn *17:6.

10. **Thy kingdom.** T#1531. ver. *33. Mt 3:2. 4:17. 16:28. +*26:29. Ps *2:6-12. *145:11, 13. Is +*2:2-4. Je +*23:5, 6. Da +*2:44. +*7:13, 14, 27. Zc +*9:9. Mk 1:15. *11:10. Lk 12:29-31. 19:11, 38. Col *1:13. Re *11:15. *12:10. 19:6. √20:4, 6. **come.** The kingdom is future and not present. Mt 7:22. 19:28. √25:34. 26:29. Ps +*82:8. Mk 14:25. 15:43. Lk 12:32. +*17:20, 21. 19:11. 22:18, 29, 30. 23:42. Ac +*1:6n. 1 Th 2:12. 2 Th *3:5. 2 T +*4:1n. **Thy will.** T#1384. Mt *7:21. 12:50. √26:39, 42, 44. Jg *10:15. 2 S 15:25, 26. Ne 9:33. Jb *1:20, 21. 15:14, 15. 40:3, 4. Ps *31:14, 15. 38:12-14. 39:9. +*40:8. 42:7-11. 44:22. 57:1. 77:9-12. 131:1, 2. 141:5. Je *42:5, 6. Mk *3:35. Lk √22:42. Jn 4:34. √6:40. √7:17. Ac 13:22. 21:14. 22:14. Ro +*12:2. Ep *6:6. Col 1:9. 1 Th *4:3. 5:18. He 10:7, 36. *13:21. 1 P 2:15. 4:2. **in earth.** Mt +*5:5. Dt +*11:21. **as it is.** Mt 28:18. Ne 9:6. Ps *103:19-21. Da *4:35. Lk *2:14. He *1:14.

11. **Give us.** ver. 26. Mt *4:4. *7:7. Ex 16:16-35. Jb √23:12. Ps 33:18, 19. *34:10. Pr *30:8, 9. Is 33:16. Lk 11:3. Jn 6:31, etc. 2 Th 3:12. 1 T *6:8. **daily.** Mt 4:4. 24:45. 2 K 25:30. Is +58:11. Je 37:21. **bread.** ƒ171I8, Ge +3:19. T#1497. Mt 7:9-11. Ge *28:20, 21. Nu 11:18, 19. Jb 38:41. Ps 78:27-29. +*145:15, 16. Pr *30:8, 9. Is 33:16. La 1:11. 2:11, 12. 5:6-9. Jn 4:34.

12. **forgive us.** T#1498. Ge 50:17. Ex 10:16, 17. 32:30-32. 34:6-9. Nu 14:17-19. Dt 9:16-20, 23-29. Jg 10:7-10. 2 S *24:10. 1 K 8:30, 34, 39, 50. 1 Ch 21:1, 7, 8. 2 Ch 6:19-21, 26, 27, 28-30, 36-39. 30:18-20. Jb 7:21. Ps 25:17, 18. *32:1, 2. *51:1-9, 14. 65:3. 79:8,

9. +*103:3, 8-12. *130:1-7. Is *1:18. *30:18-20. *43:25, 26. 54:8, 9. √55:6, 7. Je 31:34. Da 9:17-19. Ho *14:1, 2. Am 7:2, 3. Mi +*7:18, 19. Lk 7:48. ‖11:4. *18:13. 22:61, 62. 23:33, 34, 42, 43. Ac *8:22-24. *13:38. Ep *1:7. Col √2:13. Ja *5:14, 15. 1 J √1:7-9. *2:1, 2. *5:16. **debts.** Mt 18:21-27, 34. Lk *7:40-48. 11:4. **as we.** ver. 14, 15. Mt *18:21, 22, 28-35. Dt √15:7-11. Ne 5:12, 13. Mk 11:25, 26. Lk *6:37. *17:3-5. Ep √4:32. Col *3:13. **forgive our.** T#539. Mk 11:25, 26. Lk 23:34. Ep +√4:32 (T#203). **debtors.** Mt 18:24. Lk 11:4. 13:4mg.

13. **lead.** ƒ111, Ge +18:27. ƒ121I2, Ge +2:17. √ƒ108A4, Ge +31:7. Mt *26:41. Ge *22:1. Dt *8:2, 16. 1 Ch +*4:10. Ps *141:4. Pr *30:8, 9. Mk 14:38. Lk √11:4n. 22:31-46. 1 C √10:13. 2 C √12:7-9. He 11:36, 37. Ja ◐1:2. 1 P 5:8. 2 P *2:9. Re 2:10. +*3:10. **temptation.** T#1721. Mt 26:41. Ps 28:3. 40:1, 2. Jn *17:15. **deliver us.** T#1478. 1 Ch +*4:10. 6:28-30. 20:5-13. Ps +39:8 (T#1699). 40:11-13. *121:7, 8. 140:1, 2. Je 15:21. Lk +√21:36. Jn √17:15. Ro 15:31. 2 C *12:7-9. Ga 1:4. 1 Th +*1:10. 2 Th 3:1-3. 2 T *4:17, 18. He *2:14, 15. 1 J *3:8. *5:18, 19. Re 7:14-17. *21:4. **from evil.** Ro 12:9. 1 Th 5:22. or, the evil one. Mt 13:19. ƒ108J. Idiom B854: involving changes of usage of words in the Greek language. "Evil" (Gr. *poneeros*) is defined by Aristotle as being only weak, but this is not the meaning in either the LXX or the New Testament, where its prevailing meaning is active harmfulness and mischievousness. EWB gives the following references, which are not here otherwise cross-referenced or marked for this figure: Mt 5:11, 39. 6:19-24. 7:11. 12:45. 20:15. 22:18. Mk 12:15. Lk 11:13, 26. 20:23. **For thine.** ver. *10. Ex 15:18. 1 Ch +*29:11, 12. Ps 10:16. 47:2, 7. *145:10-13. Da *4:25, 34, 35. 7:18. 1 T 1:17. *6:15-17. Re 5:13. 19:1. **is the kingdom.** ƒ94, Hendiatris; or, Three for One: three words used, but one thing meant, Je +4:2. i.e. powerful, glorious kingdom. Ps +*22:28. *145:11, 13. Re +*11:15. **the power.** T#1130. Dt 3:24, 25. 9:28, 29. 2 Ch *14:11. 20:6, 7. Ne 9:32. Ps 79:11. 83:18. 86:9, 10. 106:8. Je 32:17. **the glory.** T#1126. Ex 32:11, 12. Nu 14:13-15. Dt 9:28. Jsh 7:7-9. 1 K 8:59, 60. 2 K 19:17-19. 1 Ch 16:35. Ps 67:2. +*79:9 (T#538). 102:15. 109:27. 115:2. √145:11. Is 37:20. 64:1, 2. Je 14:21. Da 9:17, 19. Jl 2:17. Zc √2:8. +√6:13. Jn +*14:13 (T#1123). 1 P +√1:11. **for ever.** lit. unto the ages, as in Lk 1:33. Ro 1:25. 9:5. 11:36. 16:27. 2 C 11:31. He √13:8. Greek *aion,* ❋S#165g, rendered (1) ever: Mt 6:13. 21:19. Mk 11:14. Lk 1:33, 55. Jn 6:51, 58. 8:35, 35. 12:34. 14:16. Ro 1:25. 9:5. 11:36. 16:27. 2 C 9:9. Ga 1:5, 5. He √13:8. 6:20. 7:17, 21, 24. 13:8, 21, 21. 1 P 1:23, 25. 4:11, 11. 5:11, 11. 2 P 2:17. 3:18. 1 J 2:17. 2 J 2. Ju 13. Re 1:6, 6. 4:9, 9, 10, 10. 5:13, 13, 14. 7:12, 12. 10:6, 6. 11:15, 15. 14:11, 11. 15:7, 7. 19:3, 3. 20:10, 10. 22:5, 5. For the various usages, see Ga 1:5 (unto the ages of the ages); Mt 21:19 (unto the age); Mt 12:32 (this age); Mt 6:13 (unto the ages); Mt 13:39 (end of the age); Lk 1:70 (from the age). **Amen.** Mt √28:20. Nu 5:22. Dt 27:15, etc. 1 K *1:36. 1 Ch 16:36. Ps 41:13. 72:19. 89:52. 106:48. Je 28:6. 1 C 14:16. 2 C 1:20. Re 1:18. *3:14. 19:4. 22:20.

14. **if.** ƒ184C, Mt +4:9. Mt 16:24, 26. Ge +4:7. Je +7:5. Lk 14:26, 33, 34. Jn 8:√31, 36, 39, 42, 46, 51. 7:17. 14:15, 23. *15:6, 10. 2 P +*1:10. **ye forgive.** ver. 12. Mt 7:2. 18:21-35. Pr 21:13. Mk *11:25, 26.

Ep √4:32. Col *3:12, 13. Ja *2:13. 1 J 3:10.

15. **But if.** ℐ184C, Mt +4:9. Mt 5:23. 18:35. Ja *2:13.

16. **when ye fast.** ℐ171K1, Dt +19:5. T#192. ver. 17, 18. Mt 9:14, 15. 2 S 12:16, 21. Ezr *8:23. Ne *1:4. Est 4:16. Ps *35:13. 69:10. 109:24. Is *58:5-9. Da +*9:3. Jl +*1:14. +*2:12, 13. Zc 7:5. Lk 2:37. Ac 10:30. 13:2, 3. 14:23. 1 C 7:5. 2 C 6:5. 11:27. **be not.** ver. 2, 5. 1 K 21:27. Is 58:3-5. Zc 7:3-5. Ml 3:14. Mk 2:18. Lk 18:12. **sad countenance.** Lk 24:17. **disfigure.** 2 S 15:30. Est 6:12. **appear unto men.** ver. 1, 5. Mt 23:5. **They have.** ℐ8, Ps +118:1. ver. 2, 5. Lk 6:24. Ph 4:18. Phm 15.

17. **anoint.** Ex +28:41. Ru 3:3. 2 S 12:20. 14:2. Ec 9:8. Is 1:6. Da 10:2, 3. Zc 7:5. Mk 6:13. Lk ●7:46. 10:34. Ja 5:14. **wash.** Gr. *nipto*, *S#3538g. Mt 15:2. Mk 7:3. Jn 9:7, 7, 11, 11, 15. 13:5, 6, 8, 8, 10, 12, 14, 14. 1 T 5:10.

18. **appear not.** T#893. ver. 2. 2 C 5:9. 10:18. Col *3:22-24. 1 P 2:13. **in secret.** 2 K 17:9. **shall reward.** ver. 4, 6. Ro +*2:6, 7. 1 P 1:7.

19. **Lay not.** Mt 19:21. Ge 45:20. Jb 31:24, 25. Ps *39:6. *62:10. Pr 11:4. 16:6. √23:4, 5. Ec 2:26. 5:10-14. Je +*45:5. Zp 1:18. Lk 12:√15, 21, 33, 34. *18:22, 24, 25. Jn *6:27. Ph *4:5. Col *3:1-3. 1 T √6:8-10, 17-19. He *10:34. +*13:5. Ja +*5:1-3. 1 J √2:15, 16. **treasures.** ℐ132F, Jg +10:17. **moth and rust.** Ja 5:2, 3. **thieves break through.** Mt 24:43. Ex 22:2. Jb 24:16. Je 2:34. Ezk 12:5. Lk 12:39.

20. **lay up.** ℐ70, Ex +16:35. Mt *19:21. Pr *19:17. *30:25. Is 33:6. Lk *12:33. +*16:9. 18:22. Ph *3:20. +*4:17. 1 T 6:17, √19. He 10:34. *11:26. Ja +*2:5. 1 P √1:4. 5:4. Re *2:9. **treasures.** ℐ22D5.O, Dt +28:12. Mt 10:40-42. Mk 10:21. Lk 14:14. 16:9. 1 C 13:13. Ph 4:8, +*17. Col 3:23, 24. 1 T +*4:8. Re +*11:18. **in heaven.** 2 T +*4:1, 18. He +*11:16. 1 P +*1:4. **where neither.** T#341. Mt 22:30. 25:46. Is 60:20. 1 C +*15:50. 1 P +*1:4, 5.

21. **For.** ℐ138C, Ge +22:14. **where.** Is 33:6. Lk 12:34. 1 C 7:32-34. 2 C 4:17, 18. Col √3:2. **there.** Mt 12:34, 35. Pr +*4:23. Je 4:14. 22:17. +*45:5. Ac 8:21. Ro 7:5-7. Ph *3:19, 20. Col 1:5. √3:1-3. He +*3:12. 1 J *2:15-17. **heart.** ℐ12I11, Ge +3:7.

22. **light of.** Lk *11:34-36. **if therefore.** ℐ184C, Mt +4:9. **single.** Ac 2:46. 2 C 11:3. Ep 6:5. Col 3:22.

23. **But if.** ℐ184A, 1 C +15:2. **thine eye.** Mt 20:15. Dt 15:9. 28:54, 56. Pr 23:6. 28:22. Is 44:18-20. Mk 7:22. Ep 4:18. *5:8. 1 J 2:11. **If.** ℐ184C, Mt +4:9. Mt 23:16, etc. Jb *38:15. Pr 26:12. Is 5:20, 21. +√8:20n. Je 4:22. 8:8, 9. Lk 8:10. Jn 9:39-41. Ro 1:22. 2:17-23. 1 C 1:18-20. √2:14. 3:18, 19. Ga 3:1. Re 3:17, 18. **the light.** Mt +*15:14. *23:15. 24:24. Jb 10:22. Pr +*16:25. Is *5:20. Ezk 14:10n. Jn +*9:41. 1 C +*3:18. Ga √6:3. Ep +*4:14. 2 T 3:6, 7, 13. 2 P 2:18. 2 J *9, *10. **be darkness.** ℐ125, Jb +22:6. Pr +*4:19. Is +9:2. **how great.** Pr *20:20. Is +*8:20. *17:14.

24. **No.** ℐ138C, Ge +22:14. **can serve.** ℐ132G, Ge +3:19. Mt +*4:10. Jsh √24:15, 19, 20. 1 S 7:3. 1 K *18:21. 2 K *17:33, 34, 41. Ezk 20:39. Zp 1:5. Lk 16:13. Ro *6:16-22. Ga 1:10. 2 T 4:10. Ja √4:4. 1 J √2:15, 16. **two masters.** Mt 12:30. **hate.** ℐ121C2C2, Ge +29:31. **the one.** Ge 29:30, 31. Pr 13:24. Ml 1:2. Lk 14:26. 16:13. Ro +9:13. **hold to.** T 1:9. **the other.** Mt +11:3g. **Ye cannot.** ℐ95, Ps +7:13. Ga *1:10. Ja *4:4. 1 J *2:15. **mammon.** Lk √16:9, 11, 13. 1 T √6:9, 10, 17.

25. **I say.** Mt 5:22, 28. Lk 12:4, 5, 8, 9, 22. **Take

no thought. Mt +*13:22. 1 S 9:5. 10:2. Ps *55:22. Mk 4:19. 13:11. Lk 8:14. *10:40-42. 12:11, 22, 25, 26, 29, 30. 1 C 7:32-34. +*12:25. Ph 2:20. √4:6. 1 T 6:8. 2 T +*1:7. 2:4. He +*13:5, 6. 1 P √5:7. Rather, "Be not anxiously careful." From a Greek word meaning "anxious, *or*, distracting care" which divides or distracts the mind. Gr. *merimnao*, *S#3309g. Rendered (1) take thought: Mt 6:25, 27, 28, 31, 34, 34. 10:19. Lk 12:11, 22, 25, 26. (2) care: 1 C 7:32, 33, 34, 34. Ph 2:20. (3) be careful: Lk 10:41. Ph 4:6. (4) have care: 1 C 12:25. **Is not.** Lk 12:23. Ro +*8:32. **life.** Gr. *psyche*, ℐ121A7, Mt +2:20. ℐ121A7, Ge +9:5. Note the close association in this verse of the *psyche* or soul with the mention of the body. Sometimes Scripture mentions body and soul, sometimes body and spirit. Mt +*10:28. Ge +2:7n. Ec ●12:7 w 1 C 5:3, 5. **than raiment.** ℐ63D2, Ge +30:27. Supply ellipsis, "(and if God grants the greater, how much more the less)." T#754. ver. 30-32.

26. **the fowls.** Mt 10:29-31. Ge 1:29-31. Jb 12:7-9. 35:11. *38:41. Ps 104:11, 12, 27, 28. 145:15, 16. *147:8, 9. Lk 12:6, 7, 24, etc. Ac 10:12. **of.** ℐ181E, Ge +3:24. **barns.** Lk 12:18. **your heavenly.** ver. 32. Mt 7:9-11. Lk 12:32. **Are ye not.** Mt √10:31. √12:12.

27. **by taking thought.** ver. 25n. Ps 5:36. Ps 39:5, 6. Ec 3:14. Lk 12:25, 26. 1 C 12:18. **stature.** Rather, "age," as *eelikia* also denotes (see Jn 9:21); and the word *peekus*, "cubit," like its Hebrew counterpart, *tephachoth*, "handbreadths" (Ps 139:5) and English "span," is used to denote any short duration. Lk 2:52.

28. **why.** ver. 25, 31. Mt 10:10. Lk 3:11. 22:35, 36. **the lilies.** Ho 14:5. Lk 12:27. **of.** ℐ181E, Ge +3:24.

29. **even Solomon.** 1 K 10:5-7. 2 Ch 9:4-6, 20-22. 1 T 2:9, 10. 1 P 3:2-5. **one of these.** Mt 18:10. 25:40, 45. Lk 15:7, 10.

30. **Wherefore.** ℐ77, Ex +3:19. **if God.** ℐ184A, 1 C +15:2. **clothe.** Ps 90:5, 6. 92:7. 103:15, 16. Is *40:6-8. Lk 12:28. Ja 1:10, 11. 1 P 1:24. **O ye.** Mt 8:26. 14:31. 16:8. 17:17, 20. Mk 4:40. 9:19. Lk 9:41. 17:6. Jn 20:27. He +*3:12, 13.

31. **take no thought.** ver. 25n. Ph *4:6. 1 P *5:7. **What shall we eat.** Mt 4:4. 15:33. Le 25:20-22. 2 Ch 25:9. Ps *34:9, 10. *37:3, 25. 55:22. 78:18-31. Lk *12:29. 1 P *5:7.

32. **after.** Mt 5:46, 47. 20:25, 26. Ps 17:14. Lk 12:30. Ep 4:17. 1 Th 4:5. **seek.** ℐ108B. Idiom B827. "To seek" is an idiom indicating that the Gentiles seek after, put in the first place, and are over-anxious, with excessive solicitude, for the things just mentioned in ver. 31. For another instance of this idiom see Lk 12:30. **for your.** ver. 8. Ps *84:11. 103:13. Lk *11:11-13. 12:30. 1 C 3:22.

33. **seek ye.** Mt +*5:6, 20. 1 K 3:11-13. 17:13. 2 Ch 1:7-12. 31:20, 21. Pr *2:1-9. 3:9, 10. Hg 1:2-11. 2:16-19. Lk 12:31. Jn 6:27. **first.** Mt 7:5. 23:26. **the kingdom.** ver. 10. Mt 3:2. +4:17. +*13:44-46. Ac 20:25. 28:31. Ro *14:17. Col 1:13, 14. 2 Th 1:5. 2 P 1:11. **his righteousness.** Mt 5:6, ●20. 22:36-39. Is 45:24. Je 23:6. Mi +*6:8. Lk 1:6. Ro 1:17. 3:21, 22. *10:3. 14:17. 1 C *1:30. 2 C √5:21. Ph √3:9. 2 P 1:1. **and all.** Mt 19:29. Le 25:20, 21. Dt=33:11. Ps 34:9, 10. *37:3, 4, 18, 19, 25. *84:11, 12. Mk +*10:29, 30. Lk 18:29, 30. Ro √8:31, 32. 1 C 3:22. 1 T *4:8. 1 P 3:9. **shall be added.** Mt *5:6. 1 S *2:30. 1 K *3:11-14. Lk 10:42.

34. **Take.** ℐ138C, Ge +22:14. **no thought.** ver. 11,

25n. Ex 16:18-20. La 3:23. **for the morrow.** ſ24E, Ge +30:33. Dt 33:25. 1 K 17:4-6, 14-16. 2 K 7:1, 2. Pr +*22:3. Lk 11:3. 14:28-30. He +*13:5, 6. **Sufficient.** ſ138C, Ge +22:14. Jn *14:27. 16:33. Ac 14:22. 1 Th 3:3, 4. Ja *4:13, 14.

MATTHEW 7

Cautions against rash judgment, 1-5. Things holy are not to be cast to dogs, 6. Encouragements to prayer, 7-11. The rule of doing as we would be done to, 12. The strait gate and narrow way, and the wide gate and broad way, 13, 14. A warning against false prophets, who may be known by their fruits, 15-20. No gifts or miracles will avail the workers of iniquity at the day of judgment, 21-23. The parable of the house built upon the rock, 24, 25; and that on the sand, 26, 27. Christ concludes, and the people are astonished at his doctrine, 28, 29.

1. **Judge not.** ver. 5. Is 66:5. Ezk 16:52-56. Lk 6:37. *7:43. Jn +*7:24. Ro *2:1, 2. *14:3, 4, 10-13. 1 C *2:15. *4:3-5. 10:15. Ja 3:1. 4:11, 12. 5:9. **that ye.** Mt 6:14. 18:23-35. 1 C √11:31. 2 C *5:10. *13:5. Ja *2:13. 3:1.

2. **For with.** ſ138C, Ge +22:14. Jg 1:7. Ps 18:25, 26. 137:7, 8. Je 51:24. Ob 15. Mk 4:24. Lk +*6:38. Ro 2:1, 3. 14:10. 2 C 9:6. 2 Th 1:6, 7. Ja *2:13. *4:11, 12. Re 18:6. **and with.** ſ138B, Ge +13:16. ſ108D, Mt +3:11. Mt +6:2. Le 24:19. Jg 1:7. 1 S 15:33. Mk 4:24. Lk 6:37.

3. **why.** Lk 6:41, 42. 18:11. **mote.** ſ103, Ge +3:13. **but.** 2 S 12:5, 6. 2 Ch 28:9, 10. Ps 50:16-21. Jn *8:7-9. Ga *6:1. **beam.** ſ103, Ge +3:13.

4. **Or how.** ſ7, Allegory as continued Hypocatastasis, Ga +4:24. **mote.** ſ138B, Ge +13:16.

5. **Thou hypocrite.** Mt 6:2. 22:18. 23:14, etc. Lk 12:56. 13:15. **first.** ſ138C, Ge +22:14. T#615. Mt 6:33. 23:26. Ps +*51:9-13. Lk 4:23. 6:42. Ac 19:15. Ro 2:21-23.

6. **Give not.** T#436. Mt +6:2. 7:9, 10. 10:5, 11. *15:26. 2 Ch 19:2. Ps *39:1. Pr *9:7, 8. *13:1. *14:7. +16:4 (T#256). *23:9. Je 7:16. Lk 19:20. 1 C 14:38. 1 J *5:16. **that.** Mt *10:14, 15. *15:26. Pr *9:7, 8. *23:9. *26:11. Lk +12:10 (T#562). Ac *13:45-47. Ph 3:2. He *6:6. *10:29. 2 P *2:22. **dogs.** ſ132G, Ge +3:19. ſ103, Ge +3:13. Mt 15:26. Ps 22:16. 1 K 22:38. 2 K 9:10, 36. Is 56:10, 11. 66:3. Ph 3:2. 2 P √2:2. Re 22:15. **neither cast.** 1 S 25:+√17, *25. Pr 11:22. 14:7. +16:22. +*22:3. 23:9. 29:9. **pearls.** Mt +*13:46. **before swine.** ſ103, Ge +3:13. 2 P √2:22. **under.** ſ108D, Mt +3:11. **turn.** Mt 22:5, 6. *24:10. 2 C *11:26. 2 T *4:14, 15. **and rend.** Mk 9:18.

7. **Ask.** T#1223. ver. 11. Mt +*18:19. *21:22. Ge 32:26. 1 K 3:5. Ps 10:17. +*50:15. 86:5. 145:18, 19. Is √55:6, 7. Je √29:12, 13. √33:3. Mk √11:24. Lk √11:9, 10, 13. *18:1. Jn 4:10. *14:13, 14. *15:7, 16. √16:23, 24, 26, 27. Ro *8:26, 27. He +*4:16. Ja +*1:5, 6, 17. √4:2. *5:15, 16, 18. 1 J *3:21, 22. √5:14, 15. Re 3:17, 18. **seek.** Mt √6:33. 1 Ch +*28:9. 2 Ch 15:2. Ps 10:4. *27:8. 32:6. 69:32. 70:4. 105:3, 4. 119:2. Pr *8:17. SS 3:2. Is √55:6. Je √29:13. Am 5:4. Ro 2:7. 3:11. He √11:6. **knock.** T#1367. Lk 12:36. 13:25. Re √3:20.

8. **For every one.** Mt 15:22-28. 2 Ch 33:1, 2, 19. Ps 81:10, 16. Jon 2:2. 3:8-10. Lk 23:42, 43. Ac 9:11. Ja *4:3.

9. **what man.** Lk *11:11-13. **if.** ſ184C, Mt +4:9. **a stone.** Mt 4:3. Lk 4:3.

10. **a serpent.** Je 29:11. Lk 6:35. Ja 1:17.

11. **If.** ſ184A, 1 C +15:2. **being evil.** Mt 12:34. Ge *6:5. *8:21. Jb 15:14, 16. Je √17:9. Ro *3:9-19, 23. Ga 3:22. Ep *2:1-3. T 3:3. **know.** ſ121C2A3, Is +53:11. **how much.** Ex 34:6, 7. 2 S 7:19. Ps *86:5, 15. 103:11-13. Is *49:15. √55:8, 9. Ho 11:8, 9. Mi *7:18. Ml 1:6. Lk 3:21. *11:11, etc. Jn √3:16. Ro √5:8-10. √8:32. Ep 2:4, 5. 1 J *3:1. 4:10. **your Father.** Mt 23:9. **good things.** T#1541. Ps *34:10. *84:11, 12. 85:12. Je +*29:11. 33:14. Ho 14:2mg. Lk 2:10, 11. *11:13. 2 C *9:8-15. T *3:4-7.

12. **Therefore.** ſ138B, Ge +13:16. **all.** Pr 18:24. 24:29. Lk *6:31. **whatsoever.** ſ184C, Mt +4:9. **do ye.** T *3:2. **for this.** Mt 5:17. 11:13. *22:39, 40. Le *19:18. Is *1:17, 18. Je 7:5, 6. Ezk 18:7, 8, 21. Am 5:14, 15. Mi +*6:8. Zc *7:7-10. 8:16, 17. Ml +*3:5. Mk 12:29-34. Lk 16:16. Ro √13:8-10. Ga *5:13, 14. 1 T 1:5. Ja √2:10-13.

13. **Enter.** 1 Ch +*28:9. **at the.** Mt *3:2, 8. *18:2, 3. *23:13. Pr *9:6. Is *55:7. Ezk *18:27-32. Mk 10:24. Lk *9:23. *13:24, 25. *14:33. Jn √10:7, 9. √14:6. Ac *2:38-40. +*3:19. *14:22. 2 C *6:17. Ga *5:24. **strait.** ſ101, Dt +32:42. Here the adjective (in Greek) is placed before the noun to call attention to its narrowness. So with the adjectives "wide" and "broad," which are both to be emphasized (B694). **for wide.** Ge 6:5, 12. Ps 14:2, 3. Is 1:9. Ro 3:9-19. 2 C *4:4. Ep *2:2, 3. 1 J 5:19. Re 12:9. 13:8. 20:3. **gate.** ſ171S7B, Ge +14:7. **that leadeth.** Mt *25:41, 46. Pr 7:27. *14:12. *16:25. Ro 9:22. Ph 3:19. 2 Th √1:8, 9. 1 P 4:17, 18. Re 20:15. **destruction.** Gr. *apoleia*, ✸S#684g. lit. the destruction. Mt 26:28 (waste). Mk 14:4. Jn 17:12 (lit. the perdition). Ac 8:20 (perish. lit. be to destruction). 25:16 (die. lit. to destruction). Ro *9:22. Ph 1:28 (perdition). 3:19. 2 Th 2:3 (lit. the perdition). 1 T 6:9. He 10:39. 2 P 2:1 (damnable. lit. heresies of *perdition*), 1 (destruction), 2 (pernicious), 3 (damnation). 3:7, 16. Re 17:8, 11. W. J. Eerdman establishes that "destruction" is equivalent to "abaddon," the lowest pit of Sheol, the "deep" or the "abyss" (*The Unseen World: A Concordance with Notes*, p. 22). Jb 26:6 (✸S#11h). Re 9:11mg.

14. **Because.** *or*, How. **gate.** ſ171S7B, Ge +14:7. **narrow.** Mt *16:24, 25. Pr 4:26, 27. 8:20. Is 30:21. *35:8. 57:14. Je 6:16. Mk 8:34. Jn 15:18-20. 16:2, 33. Ac *14:22. 1 Th 3:2-5. **the way.** Mt 18:8. Ps *16:11. Jn √14:6. **which leadeth.** Ro *8:13. **life.** Gr. *dzoe*, ✸S#2222g. Rendered (1) life: Mt 7:14. 18:8, 9. 19:16, 17, 29. 25:46. Mk 9:43, 45. 10:17, 30. Lk 1:75. 10:25. 12:15. 18:18, 30. Jn 1:4, 4. 3:15, 16, 36, 36. 4:14, 36. 5:24, 24, 26, 26, 29, 39, 40. 6:27, 33, 35, 40, 47, 48, 51, 53, 54, 63, 68. 8:12. 10:10, 28. 11:25. 12:25, 50. 14:6. 17:2, 3. 20:31. Ac 2:28. 3:15. 5:20. 8:33. 11:18. 13:46, 48. 17:25. Ro 2:7. 5:10, 17, 18, 21. 6:4, 22, 23. 7:10. 8:2, 6, 38. 11:15. 1 C 3:22. 15:19. 2 C 2:16. 16. 4:10, 11, 12. 5:4. Ga 6:8. Ep 4:18. Ph 1:20. 2:16. 4:3. Col 3:3, 4. 1 T 1:16. 4:8. 6:12, 19. 2 T 1:1, 10. T 1:2. 3:7. He 7:3, 16. Ja 1:12. 4:14. 1 P 3:7, 10. 2 P 1:3. 1 J 1:1, 2, 2. 2:25. 3:14, 15. 5:11, 11, 12, 12, 13, 16, 20. Ju 21. Re 2:7, 10. 3:5. 11:11. 13:8. 17:8. 20:12, 15. 21:6, 27. 22:1, 2, 14, 17, 19. (2) lifetime: Lk 16:25. **and few.** T#669. Mt *18:19, 20. √20:16. 22:14. 25:1-12. Ge 6:11, 12. 7:1. 18:32. Nu 14:23, 24. Is 1:5-9. *24:16. Je √5:1. Ezk 22:17, 18, *30. +*33:31. Ml

+*3:16. Mk 10:24, 25. Lk 9:26. √12:32. √13:23-30. √18:8. Jn 1:11. *3:18, 36. 5:40. 10:1, 7, 9. *14:6. Ac *4:12. 14:22. 28:22. Ro 9:27-29, 32. 11:4-6, 14. *12:2. 1 C 1:26. +*6:9, 10. Ga 5:21. Ep 2:2, 3. 2 T 1:15. 3:5. T 1:16. He 6:11, 12. 10:39. Ja *2:13. 4:17. 1 P *3:20, 21. *4:18. 2 P +*1:10. 1 J *2:3, 4. Re *3:4. ◐7:9. +20:4 (T#440).

15. **Beware.** Mt 10:17. 16:6, 11. Pr +*14:15. Mk 12:38. Lk 12:15. Ac 13:40. Ph 3:2. Col 2:8. 2 P *3:17. **false prophets.** T#474. Mt *24:4, 5, 11, 24, 25. Dt *13:1-3. Jb +:7 (T#15). Ps +5:9 (T#702). +12:3 (T#198). Is 9:15, 16. Je 6:14. 14:14-16. √23:13-16. 28:15-17. 29:21, 32. Ezk 13:10, 16, 18, 22. *14:10n. Mi 3:5-7, 11. Mk 13:22, 23. Lk 6:26. Ac *13:6. √20:29, 30. 1 T 4:1. T 1:10, 11. 2 P *2:1-3. 1 J *4:1. Re 2:2. 16:13. 19:20. 20:10. **which.** Zc 13:4. Mk 12:38-40. Ro +*16:17, 18. 2 C √11:13-15. Ga 2:4. Ep √4:14. 5:6. Col *2:8. 1 T *4:1-3. 2 T *3:5-9, 13. 4:3. 2 P 2:1-3, 18, 19. Ju 4. Re 13:11-17. **are ravening.** Is 56:10, 11. Ezk +22:25n, 27. Mi 3:5. Zp 3:3, 4. Jn 10:12. Ac 20:29-31. Re 17:6.

16. **Ye.** √138C, Ge +22:14. **shall.** ver. 20. Mt +6:2n. 12:33. Lk 6:37, 44. Ga 5:19-22. Ja 2:18. 2 P 2:10-18. Ju 10-19. **know.** Gr. *epiginosko,* Mt +11:27. **Do.** √85C, Ge +18:14. Lk *6:43-45. Ac 10:47n. Ja 3:12. **thorns.** He 6:8.

17. **every.** Ps *1:3. 92:13, 14. Is 5:3-5. 61:3. Je 11:19. 17:8. Lk *6:45. *13:6-9. Ro *6:22. Ga √5:22-24. Ep 5:9. Ph 1:11. Col +*1:10. Ja *3:17, 18. **but.** Mt 12:33-35. Ga *5:19-21. Ju 12.

18. **cannot.** Lk 6:43. Ro 8:7, 8. Ga 5:17. 1 J *3:9, 10. **neither can.** Jb *14:4. Je *13:23. Mt 12:33.

19. **bringeth.** Mt 3:10. 21:19, 20. Is 5:5-7. 27:11. Ezk 15:2-7. Lk 3:9. *13:6-9. Jn √15:2-6. He *6:8. Ju 12. **cast into.** Jn *15:6.

20. **by their fruits.** ver. 16. Ac 5:38. **know.** Gr. *epiginosko,* Mt +11:27.

21. **Not every.** √73, Zc +1:5. **saith.** Mt *25:11, 12. Ho +*8:2, 3. Lk √6:46. *13:25. Ac 19:13, etc. Ro *2:13. 1 C +*12:3. T *1:16. Ja *1:22. 2:20-26. **Lord, Lord.** √84, Ge +22:11. √108C5, Mt +23:7. Mt 25:11. Lk +*6:46. **shall enter.** Mt *18:3. 19:24. *21:31. 25:11, 12, 21. Is 48:1, 2. Mk 9:47. *10:23, 24. Lk 18:25. Jn *3:5. Ac *14:22. He 4:6. **kingdom of heaven.** Mt +4:17. **that doeth.** ver. 24-27. Mt 5:19. 6:10. 12:50. 21:29-31. 26:42. Mk 3:35. Lk +*11:28. 22:42. Jn 4:23, 34. 6:38, 40. √7:17. √9:31. +*13:17. Ro 2:13. √12:2. Ep *2:10. 6:6. Col *4:12. 1 Th 4:3. 5:18. T 3:8. He 10:7, 9. *13:21. Ja +*1:22. 1 P *2:15. 4:2. 1 J *3:21-24. Re 22:14. **the will.** 1 S +*16:7. Ps 75:6, 7. Jn 6:38. *7:17. Ep √6:6. 1 Th *4:3. **my Father.** Mt *10:32, 33. 12:50. 15:13. 16:17. *18:10, 14, 19, 35. *26:39, 42. Jn 5:17, 18. √10:29, 30. *14:7. *15:23. Re 2:27. *3:5. **in heaven.** Mt 6:9.

22. **Many.** ver. 13. Mt 25:11, 12. Lk 10:20. 13:25-27. **to me.** See on ver. 21. Mt 24:36. Is *2:11, 17. Ml *3:17, 18. Lk 10:12. 1 Th *5:4. 2 Th *1:10. 2 T 1:12, 18. *4:8. **in that day.** Ml *3:17. Ac +*17:31. 2 Th +*1:10. **Lord.** ver. 21. Mt 25:11. Ac 19:13. 1 C ◐12:3. **Lord.** √84, Ge +22:11. **have we.** √85B, Ge +13:9. Mt 10:5-8. Nu *24:4. *31:8. 1 K 22:11, etc. Je *23:13, etc. Lk *13:26. Jn *11:51. Ac *19:13-15. 1 C *13:1, 2. He √6:4-6. **prophesied.** Je ▶14:14. 27:15. **thy name.** √16, Ge +1:27. **cast out.** Mt 12:27. Mk 9:38.

23. **I never knew.** √22, Ge +3:9. T#21. Mt 10:33.

15:13. *25:12. 1 S +*16:7. Ps *1:6. ◐31:7. 37:18. 101:4. 144:3. Ho 8:4. 13:5. Am 3:2. Mk 4:16, 17. Jn 6:70. √10:14, 27, +28 (T#515), 29, 30. 17:12. Ro +8:34 (T#516). 2 C +1:22 (T#517). *13:5. 2 T *2:19. 2 P ◐+*2:20. 1 J *2:19. **depart.** Mt +*13:41. +*25:41. Ps 5:5. *◐6:8. +*50:16. 75:6, 7. 119:115. 139:19. Hab *1:13. Lk *13:25, 27. Re *22:15. **work iniquity.** Ps 5:5. 92:7, 9. 94:4. 101:8. 125:5.

24. **whosoever heareth.** ver. 7, 8, 13, 14. Mt 5:3, etc., 28-32. 6:14, 15, 19, etc. 12:50. Lk *6:47-49. +*11:28. Jn +*13:17. *14:15, 22-24. 15:10, 14. Ro *2:6-9. Ga *5:6, 7. √6:7, 8. Ja *1:21-27. *2:17-26. 1 J √2:3. *3:22-24. 5:3-5. Re 22:14, 15. **and doeth.** T#1075. ver. 21. Lk +*11:28. Ja +*1:22. **liken.** √160A, Ps +1:3. **a wise.** Mt 25:2. Jb 28:28. Ps *111:10. *119:99, 130. Pr 10:8. 14:8. Ja *3:13-18. **which.** 1 C 3:10, 11.

25. **And.** √148, Ge +8:22. **the rain.** Ezk 13:11, etc. Ml 3:3. Ac *14:22. 1 C *3:13-15. Ja *1:12. 1 P 1:7. **for it.** Mt *16:18. Ps *92:13-15. 125:1, 2. Ep *3:17. Col *2:7. 1 P 1:5. 1 J √2:19.

26. **doeth them not.** 1 S *2:30. Pr 14:1. Je *8:9. Lk *6:49. Ja *2:20. **likened.** √160A, Ps +1:3. **foolish.** Ezk 13:10-14.

27. **the rain.** Mt 12:43-45. +*13:19-22. Ezk 13:10-16. 1 C *3:13. He *10:26-31. 2 P √2:20-22. **and great.** Am 6:11.

28. **came to pass.** √144A11, Ge +38:11. Mt 11:1. 13:53. 19:1. 26:1. Lk 7:1. **people were astonished.** Mt *13:54. 22:33. Ps 45:2. Mk 1:22, 27. 6:2. 11:18. Lk 4:22, 32, 36. *19:48. Jn *7:15, 46. Ac *13:12. **doctrine.** √108B, Mk +4:2.

29. **having.** Mt *5:20, 28, 32, 44. *21:23-27. *28:18. Dt *18:18, 19. Ec 8:4. Is *50:4. Je *23:28, 29. Mi 3:8. Mk 1:22. Lk *21:15. Jn 7:46. Ac 3:22, 23. 6:10. He √4:12, 13. **and not.** Mt *15:1-9. *23:2-6, 15-24. Mk 7:5-13. Lk 20:8, *46, *47.

MATTHEW 8

Christ cleanses a leper, 1-4; heals a Centurion's servant, and predicts the calling of the Gentiles and rejection of the Jews, 5-13; heals Peter's wife's mother, 14, 15, and many others, fulfilling a prophecy of Isaiah, 16, 17; shows in what spirit he ought to be followed, 18-22; calms the tempestuous sea by his word, 23-27; and casts out devils from two possessed men, suffering them to go into the swine, 28-32. The Gergesenes desire him to leave them, 33, 34.

1. **come.** Mt 5:1. **great.** ver. 18. Mt 4:25. 12:15. 15:30. 19:2. 20:29. Mk 3:7. Lk 5:15. 14:25-27.

2. **behold.** Mk 1:40, etc. Lk 5:12. **a leper.** Mt 10:8. 26:6. Le 13:44-46. Nu 5:2, 3. 12:10, ◐=13. Dt 24:8, 9. 2 S 3:39. 2 K 5:1, 27. 7:3, 4. 15:5. 2 Ch 26:19-21. Lk 4:27. +7:22. 17:12-19. **worshipped.** Mt *2:2, 8, 11. *4:9. 9:18. +*14:33. 15:25. 18:26. 20:20. *28:9, 17. Jsh +*5:14. Mk *1:40. *5:6, 7. 15:19. Lk *5:12. 24:52. Jn *9:38. Ac 10:25. 1 C *14:25. He *1:6. Re +*5:12. *19:10. *22:8, 9. **if.** √184C, Mt +4:9. Mt *9:◐18, 28, 29. *13:58. ◐15:25. ◐18:26. ◐28:9. Mk *9:22-24.

3. **And Jesus.** ver. 28-34. Mt 9:1-8, 18-26, 20-22, 27-31, 32-35. 12:9-13, 22. 15:21-28. 17:14-18. 20:29-34. 26:51. Mk 1:40-45. 6:53-56. Lk 5:12-14. 13:10-17. 14:2-6. Jn 4:46-54. 5:1-15. 9:1-39. 11:17-46. **put.** 2 K 5:11. **I will.** Ge 1:3. Ps 33:9. Mk 1:41. 4:39. 5:41. 7:34. 9:25. Lk 5:13. 7:14. Jn 5:21. 11:43. 15:24. **immedi-**

ately. Mt 11:4, 5. 2 K 5:14. Lk 17:14, 15. **leprosy.** ſ100, Ge +10:9. ſ121N2, Ge +34:29. Le 13:44.

4. **See.** Mt 6:1. 9:30. *12:16-19. 16:20. 17:9. Mk 1:43, 44. 5:43. 7:36. Lk *5:14. Jn 5:41. 7:8, 18. 8:50. **show.** Mt 3:15. +*5:17. Le 13:2, etc. *14:2, etc. Is *42:21. Lk 17:14. **Moses.** i.e. *drawn out of the water,* ***S#3475g.** Mt 17:3, 4. 19:7, 8. 22:24. Mk 1:44. 7:10. 10:3, 4. 12:19. Lk 5:14. 9:30. 20:28, 37. Jn 1:45. 3:14. 5:45, 46. 6:32. 7:19, 22. 8:5. 9:29. Ac 3:22. 6:11. 7:20, 22, 29, 31, 32, 40, 44. 15:21. 26:22. Ro 9:15. 10:5, 19. 1 C 10:2. 2 C 3:13, 15. He 3:2, 3, 5. 7:14. 8:5. 11:23, 24. 12:21. Also ***S#3475g.** Mt 23:2. Mk 9:4, 5. 12:26. Lk 2:22. 9:33. 16:29, 31. 24:27, 44. Jn 1:17. 7:22, 23. 9:28. Ac 13:39. 21:21. 28:23. Ro 5:14. 1 C 9:9. 2 C 3:7. He 3:16. 10:28. Ju 9. Re 15:3. Also ***S#3475g.** Ac 6:14. 7:35, 37. 15:1, 5. 2 T 3:8. He 9:19. For S#4872h, see Ex +2:10. **for.** Mt 10:18. 2 K 5:7, 8. Mk 1:44. 6:11. 13:9. Lk 5:14. 21:13. Jn 10:37, 38.

5. **entered.** Mt 4:13. 9:1. 11:23. Mk 2:1. Lk 7:1. **a centurion.** This was a Roman military title; and therefore this officer may be concluded to have been a Gentile (See fuller particulars under Mk 15:39). Mt 27:54. Mk 15:39. Lk 7:2, etc. Ac 10:1, etc. 22:25. 23:17, 23. 27:13, 31, 43.

6. **my.** Jb 31:13, 14. Ac 10:7. Col 3:11. 4:1. 1 T 6:2. Phm 16. **servant.** Gr. *pais.* ſ46C. Catachresis; or, Incongruity B677. One word is changed for another only remotely connected with it; of one word, where the Greek receives its real meaning by permutation from the Hebrew, or some other language, or foreign usage. *Pais,* "a child," is used of "a servant," from the Hebrew *nahar,* which has both meanings. For another instance of this figure involving this term see Ac 4:27. For other instances of this figure involving various other terms see Mt 24:29. 28:1. Lk 1:37. 16:17. Ac 10:22. 13:34. Ro 14:11. 1 C 2:6. 15:54. 2 C 6:12. Ga 2:21. 1 Th 4:4. He 11:31. 1 P 3:14. Re 2:7. 14:8. **palsy.** T#1632. Mt 4:24. 9:2. Mk 2:3, etc. Ac 8:7. 9:33.

7. **I will.** Mt 9:18, 19. Mk 5:23, 24. Lk 7:6.

8. **not worthy.** T#663. Mt 3:11, 14. 15:26, 27. *25:37-39. Ge *32:10. Jb 13:23. Ps 10:17. 26:2. *51:3. 115:1. *139:23, 24. Lk 5:8. 7:6, 7. 15:19, 21. +18:14 (T#537). Jn 1:27. 13:6-8. Ro 7:24. 1 C 15:9, 10. Ep 3:8. 1 J +1:8 (T#507). **but speak.** T#1584. ver. 3. Nu 20:8. Ps 33:9. 107:20. Mk 1:25-27. Lk 7:7.

9. **Go.** Jb 38:34, 35. Ps 107:25-29. 119:91. 148:8. Je 47:6, 7. Ezk 14:17-21. Mk 4:39-41. Lk 4:35, 36, 39. 7:8. **Do.** Ep 6:5, 6. Col 3:22. T 2:9. **it.** ſ63D2, Ge +30:27. Supply by ellipsis of a latter clause, called *Anantapodoton,* i.e., without *apodosis,* "(how much more art Thou, who art God, able to command, or to speak the word only that my servant may recover)."

10. **he marvelled.** ſ176, Nu +24:5. Mk ●6:6. Lk 7:9. **I have.** Mt 15:28. Lk 5:20. 7:50.

11. **That many.** ſ88, Ge +15:15. Mt 19:30. 21:41. *24:31. Ge +*12:3. +*22:18. *28:14. +*49:10. Ps *22:27. 98:3. Is *2:2, 3. *11:10. 49:6. 52:10. 60:1-6. Je 16:19. Da *2:44. Mi 4:1, 2. Zc *8:20-23. Ml *1:11. Mk 10:31. Lk *13:28-30. 14:23, 24. Ac 10:45. *11:18. *14:27. 15:9. Ro 10:12. 11:30-36. *15:9, etc. Ga 3:28, 29. Ep 2:11-14. *3:6. Col *3:11. Re 7:9. **east and west.** Is 11:14. 45:6. 59:19. **shall sit.** *Anaklithasontai,* "shall recline," i.e. at table; referring to the recumbent posture used by the easterns at their meals. Mt ●19:28.

Lk 12:37. *13:29. 14:15. 16:22. *22:30. Re *3:20, 21. 19:9. **with Abraham.** Mt 22:32. Mi +*7:20. Mk 12:26. 13:28. 20:37. Ac 3:13. 7:32. Ro *15:8. **and Jacob.** Is +*29:23. **in.** Mt 3:2. Je 3:18, 19. Lk *13:28. Ac *14:22. 1 C +*6:9. 15:50. 2 Th 1:5. **the kingdom.** Mt +4:17. Ps 2:8. **of heaven.** Mt 5:11, 12. 2 T +*4:18n. He 11:13, +*16n. 1 P *1:4n.

12. **the children.** ſ121Q1, Je +28:5. Mt *3:9, 10. *7:22, 23. *21:43. Ac *3:25. Ro *9:4, 5. **be cast.** Mt 3:10. +*13:30, 41, 42, 50. *21:43. 22:12, 13. 24:51. *25:30. Lk *13:28. 17:30-37. 2 P *2:4, 17. Ju *13. **outer darkness.** T#573-5. Mt 22:13. 25:30. Je 13:16. Zp 1:15. 2 P 2:17. Ju 13. **weeping and.** Mt 13:42, 50. 24:51. Lk 13:28. Re ●21:4.

13. **centurion.** Lk *7:1-10. **Go.** ver. 4. Ec *9:7. Mk 7:29. Jn *4:50. **and as.** Mt *9:29, 30. *15:28. *17:20. Mk *9:23. **And his.** Jn *4:52, 53. **selfsame hour.** Mt *9:22. Ps *107:20. Jn 4:53.

14. **into.** ver. 20. Mt 17:25. Mk 1:29-31. Lk 4:38, 39. **wife's.** Mk 1:30. 1 C *9:5. 1 T 3:2. 4:3. He 13:4.

15. **touched.** ver. 3. Mt 9:20, 29. 14:36. 20:34. 2 K 13:21. Is 6:7. Mk 1:41. Lk 8:54. Ac 19:11-13. **and ministered.** Lk 4:38, 39. Jn 12:1-3.

16. **the even.** Mk 1:32-34. Lk *4:40, 41. **they brought.** Mt 4:24. 9:2. Mk 2:3. Ac 5:15. **and he.** Mt 12:22. Mk 1:25-27, 34. 5:8. 9:25. Ac 19:13-16. **spirits.** 1 S 18:10. Gr. *pneuma,* **✢S#4151g.** Here used of demons or evil spirits, as at Mt 10:1. 12:43, 45. Mk 1:23, 26, 27. 3:11, 30. 5:2, 8, 13. 6:7. 7:25. 9:17, 20, 25, 25. Lk 4:33, 36. 6:18. 7:21. 8:2, 29. 9:39, 42. 10:20. 11:24, 26. 13:11. Ac 5:16. 8:7. 16:16, 18. 19:12, 13, 15, 16. 2 C 11:4. Ep 2:2. 6:12mg. 2 Th 2:2. 1 T 4:1b. 1 J 4:1, 1, 3, 6b. Re 16:13, 14. 18:2. The word *pneuma,* spirit, is used of (1) God, Jn 4:24a. (2) Christ, 1 C 6:17. (3) The Holy Spirit, Mt +3:16. (4) ſ121A1. The operations of the Holy Spirit, Lk +1:17. (5) ſ121A2. The New Nature, Ro +8:1. (6) ſ121A3. Psychological uses: 1) the principle of life, of which death is described as giving up or commending to God the *spirit,* Mt +27:50. 2) the distinctive, self-conscious, inner life of man: 1 C +2:11. 3) "life" in the physiological sense, but drawing rather to the meaning of "soul," Lk +8:55. (7) ſ121A2. *Spirit* is put for character, as being in itself invisible and manifested in one's actions, Mt +5:3. (8) ſ121A2. By Metonymy, *spirit* is put for what is invisible, etc. Mt +26:41n. (9) ſ171Q1B. By Synecdoche, *spirit,* an integral part of man individually, is put for the whole man, Mk +2:8. (10) Adverbial use, whereby *spirit* implies essence, or whatever is spoken of as possessed or done, as being so in the highest degree, Ac +18:25. (11) *Spirit* is used of angels or spirit-beings, Lk +24:37. (12) *Spirit* is used of demons or evil spirits, Mt +8:16. (13) *Spirit* is used of neutral beings, 1 J +4:2b,n. (14) *Spirit* is used of the resurrection body, Ro +1:4. (15) ſ121A1. *Spirit* in the phrase *pneuma hagion,* Holy Spirit, without the Greek articles, is put for the various gifts of the Spirit, "power from on high," Mt +1:18n. Compare the classification of the corresponding Old Testament Hebrew word, *ruach,* Ge +*6:3n. **and healed.** Mt 14:14. Ex 15:26.

17. **it might.** Mt 1:22. 2:15, 23. **Himself.** ſ92C, Mt +2:15. Is ✓53:4. *63:9. He ✓4:15. 1 P *2:24. **bare.** ſ121C1E, Ge +19:15. **sicknesses.** Ex +23:25. Ac 10:38.

18. **saw.** ver. 1. Mk 1:35-38. Lk 4:42, 43. Jn 6:15. **great multitudes.** Ps 2:8. **unto.** Mt 14:22. Mk *4:35. 5:21. 6:45. 8:13. Lk *8:22.

19. **a certain.** ſ108E1. Idiom B836. Idiomatic use of numerals. According to Hebrew idiom, the numeral "one" is used instead of the ordinary pronoun. For other instances of this idiom see Mt 9:18. 16:14. 18:24, 28. 21:19mg. 26:69. Mk 10:17. 12:42. Lk 5:12, 17. Jn 6:9. 7:21. 20:7. Re 8:13. **scribe.** Ezr 7:6. Mk 12:32-34. Lk *9:57, 58. 1 C 1:20. **I will.** Jsh 1:16. 2 S 15:15. Ps 2:8. Lk 14:25-27, 33. 22:33, 34. Jn 13:36-38. Re 14:4.

20. **have nests.** Ps 84:3. 104:17. Mt 6:26. 10:29, 31. **the Son of man.** Mt 9:6. 10:23. 11:19. 12:8, 32, 40. 13:37, 41. 16:13, +*27n, 28. 17:9, 12, 22. 18:11. *19:28. 20:18, 28. 24:27, 30, 37, 39, 44. 25:31. 26:2, 24, 45, 64. Ps *80:17. Mk +2:10. Lk 2:7, 12, 16. +5:24. 8:3. Jn +1:51. **hath not.** T#58. Mt 16:24. Ps +*40:17. 69:29. 109:22. Is *53:2, 3. Ro 15:2, 3. 1 C 4:11. 2 C *8:9. Ph 2:7, 8. He 12:2.

21. **another.** Mt +11:3. Lk *9:59-62. **suffer.** Mt 19:29. Le 21:11, 12. Nu 6:6, 7. Dt 33:9, 10. 1 K 19:20, 21. Hg 1:2. 2 C 5:16.

22. **Follow.** Mt 4:18-22. 9:9. Jn 1:43. **and let.** Mt +6:2n. Je 16:5. Lk 9:60. 15:32. Ep *2:1, 5. 5:14. Col 2:13. 1 T *5:6. **their dead.** ſ145, Jg +11:40.

23. **entered into a ship.** Mt 9:1. Mk *4:36. Lk *8:22.

24. **there.** T#1287. Ps 107:23-27. Is 54:11. Jon *1:4-6, 13-16. Mk 4:37, 38. Ac 27:14, etc. 2 C 11:25, 26. **but.** Lk *8:23. Jn 6:17, 18. 11:5, 6, 15.

25. **and awoke.** Ps 10:1. 44:22, 23. Is 51:9, 10. Mk *4:38, 39. Lk 8:24. **save.** 2 Ch 14:11. 20:12. Jon 1:6. **perish.** Gr. *apollumi,* Mt +*2:13. T#1637. Ps 80:14-16. Jon 1:6, 14. Mk 4:38.

26. **Why.** Mt 6:30. *14:30, 31. 16:8. Ex 14:13. Is 30:7, 15. *41:10-14. Mk *4:40. Lk *8:25. Ro *4:20. **fearful.** Ps +*34:4. 46:1-3. Is √43:2. Jn *14:27. 2 T +*1:7. Re +*21:8. **and rebuked.** ver. 27. Mt 14:32. Jb 38:8-11. Ps *65:7. *89:8, 9. 93:3, 4. 104:6-9. *107:28-30. 114:3-7. Pr 8:28, 29. Is *50:2-4. 63:12. Na 1:4. Hab 3:8. Mk *4:39, 41. *6:48-51. Lk *8:24, 25. Re 10:2.

27. **the men marvelled.** Mt 9:33. 14:33. 15:31. Mk 1:27. *4:41. 6:51. 7:37. Lk *8:25. Jn 9:32. **What manner.** God the Son is unequalled, there is none like him. Ex =14:21. Is ◐*40:13, 14. Je ◐+*10:6. Mt +*28:19n. Ph 2:5-11. He *1:1-12. **that even.** God the Son is sovereign. Mt 28:18, +*19n. Lk 5:9. Jn 5:21.

28. **when.** Mk 5:1, etc. Lk 8:26, etc. Ac 10:38. **Gergesenes.** i.e. *those come from pilgrimage,* *S#1086g, only here. Some are of the opinion that *Gergasa* was the country of the ancient *Girgashites;* but it is more probable that *Gergesenes* was introduced by Origen upon mere conjecture; as before him most copies seem to have read *Gadarenes,* agreeably to the Parallel Passages and the ancient Syriac version. *Gadara,* says Josephus (Bell. l. iv. c. 24), was the metropolis of Perea, or the region beyond Jordan; and he also observes that it was sixty furlongs, or about eight miles from Tiberias. It is therefore rightly placed opposite Tiberias, at the southeast end of the lake. Pliny (l. v. c. 18) says it was called *Hippodion,* was one of the cities of Decapolis, and had the river Hieromax, or Jarmouk, flowing before it. It was of heathen jurisdiction; whence perhaps it was destroyed by the Jews; but was rebuilt by Pompey, and joined to the province of Syria (Josephus, Ant. l. xiv. c. 8). Augustus afterwards gave it to Herod (Ant. l. xv. c. 11), on whose death it was again annexed to Syria. It is now called *Om Keis:* its

ruins are in a very mutilated state, and when visited by Burckhardt it had not a single inhabitant. The remains of the sepulchral caverns in which the demoniacs abode are still to be seen (*Travels in Syria,* etc., pp. 270-273). Ge 10:16. 15:21. Dt 7:1. **there met.** Mt 5:1-20. Lk 8:26-39. **two.** Mk 5:2. Lk 8:27. **possessed.** Mt 4:24. **coming.** Mk 5:2-5. Lk 8:27, 29. **tombs.** *S#3419g. Mt 8:28. 23:29. 27:52, 53, 60, 60. 28:8. Mk 5:2, 3. 6:29. 15:46, 46. 16:2, 3, 5, 8. Lk 11:44, 47, 48. 23:55. 24:2, 9, 12, 22, 24. Jn 5:28. 11:17, 31, 38. 12:17. 19:41, 42. 20:1, 2, 3, 4, 6, 8, 11, 11. Ac 13:29. **so.** Jg 5:6.

29. **cried out.** Mk 1:23, 24, 26, ◐+*34. Lk 4:33, 41. Ac 8:7. **What have.** ſ85H, Jg +11:12. ſ108H8, 2 S +16:10. Jg 11:12. 2 S 16:10. 19:22. 1 K 17:18. 2 K 3:13. 2 Ch 35:21. Jl 3:4. Mk *1:24. *5:7. Lk *4:34. *8:28-31. Jn *2:4. **thou Son of God.** Mt *4:3, 6. 14:33. Mk *3:11. Lk *4:41. Ac *16:17. Ja *2:19. **torment.** Mt *25:41. Jb *21:30. Mk *5:6-10. Lk +*16:24. Ja 2:19. 2 P *2:4. Ju *6. Re *20:10. **before the time.** Jb 21:30. Re 12:12.

30. **an herd.** Le 11:7. Dt *14:8. Is 65:3, 4. 66:3. Mk 5:11. Lk 8:32. 15:15, 16.

31. **devils besought.** Mk 5:7, 12. Lk 8:30-33. Re 12:12. 20:1, 2. **If.** ſ184C, Mt +4:9. **suffer us.** T#1718. Jb 1:12. 2:6.

32. **Go.** ſ96B, Nu +24:21. 1 K 22:22. Jb 1:10-12. 2:3-6. Ac 2:23. 4:28. Re 20:7. **the whole.** Jb 1:13-19. 2:7, 8. Mk 5:13. Lk 8:33.

33. **they that.** Mk 5:14-16. Lk 8:34-36. Ac 19:15-17.

34. **whole.** ſ171A, Ex +9:6. **they besought.** ver. 29. Dt 5:25. 1 S 16:4. 2 S 6:9. 1 K 17:18. 18:17. Jb +*21:14. 22:17. Ho *9:12. Mk ◐1:37. 5:17, 18. Lk 4:29, ◐42. 5:8. *8:28, 37-39. 9:53. Jn ◐4:40. Ac 16:39.

MATTHEW 9

Jesus returning to Capernaum, 1, heals one sick of palsy, 2-8; calls Matthew from the receipt of custom, 9; justifies himself for eating with publicans and sinners, 10-13; and his disciples for not fasting like the Pharisees, 14-17; is entreated by a ruler to heal his daughter, 18, 19; heals a woman of an inveterate issue of blood, 20-22; raises the ruler's daughter, 23-26; gives sight to two blind men, 27-31; and casts a devil out of a dumb man, 32. The people wonder, but the Pharisees ascribe it to the prince of the devils, 33, 34. Jesus compassionates the multitudes, and preaches to them; and charges his disciples to pray, that laborers might be sent forth into the harvest, 35-38.

1. **he.** Mt 7:6. 8:18, 23. Mk *5:21. Lk 8:37. Re 22:11. **his.** Mt 4:13. Mk 2:1.

2. **they brought.** Mt 4:24. 8:16. Mk 1:32. 2:1-3. Lk 5:18, 19. Ac 5:15, 16. 19:12. **sick.** Mt +4:24. **on a bed.** Mk 2:4. 6:55. Lk 5:18. **seeing their faith.** ver. 22, 29. Mt 8:10, 13. 15:28. 17:20. Mk 2:4, 5. 9:23. 10:52. Lk 5:19, 20. 7:9, 50. 17:19. 18:42. Jn +*2:25. Ac 3:16. 14:9. Ja *1:6, 7. 2:18. 5:15. **Son.** ver. 22. Mk 5:34. Jn 21:5. Lk +15:31. **good cheer.** ver. 22. Ps √32:1, 2. Ec 9:7. Is *40:1, 2. 44:22. Je 31:33, 34. Lk 5:20. 7:47-50. Jn +16:33. Ac 13:38, 39. Ro 4:6-8. *5:11. Col 1:12-14. **thy sins.** Rather, "thy sins *are* forgiven thee;" the words being an affirmation, not a prayer or wish. The word *be,* however, was used by our translators in the indicative plural for *are.* As the palsy is frequently produced by intemperance, it is probable,

from our Lord's gracious declaration, that it was the case in the present instance. Lk +7:48. Jn 5:14. Ja 5:15.

3. **certain**. Mt 7:29. Mk *2:6, 7. 7:21. Lk 5:21. 7:39, 49. **said within**. Lk +16:3. **This**. Mt 26:65. Le 24:16. Mk 14:64. Lk 7:49. Jn +*10:33-36. Ac 6:11-13.

4. **knowing**. T#76-7. Mt +*11:27. 12:25. 16:7, 8. +*28:19n. 1 K 8:39. Ps *44:21. *139:2. Mk *2:8. 8:16, 17. 12:15. Lk 5:22. 6:8. 7:40. 9:46, 47. 10:22. 11:17. Jn +*2:24, 25. 6:61, 64. 10:15. 16:19, 30. 21:17. Col 2:3. He *4:12, +13 (T#219). Re *2:23. **Wherefore**. Mt 15:19. Je +*17:9, 10. Ezk 38:10. Mk 7:21. Ac 5:3, 4, 9. 8:20-22.

5. **whether**. Mk 2:9-12. Lk 5:23-25. **Arise**. Is 35:5, 6. Jn 5:8-14, 17, 18. Ac 3:6-11, 16. 4:9, 10. 9:34. 14:8-11.

6. **the Son of man**. Mt +8:20. 12:8. Mk 2:28. Lk 6:5. Jn 5:27. **hath power**. Mt 28:18. **to forgive**. Is 43:25. Mi *7:18. Mk 2:7, 10. Lk 5:21. Jn 5:21-23. 10:28. 17:2. 20:21-23. Ac 5:31. 7:59, 60. 2 C 2:10. 5:20. Ep √4:32. Col 3:13. **then**. ∫81, Ge +15:13. **Arise**. ver. 5. Lk 13:11-13. Jn +5:8. Ac 9:34.

8. **they marvelled**. Mt 12:23. 15:31. Mk *2:12. 7:37. Lk 2:20. *5:26. 7:16. 23:47. Ac 2:43. 4:21. 11:18. 21:20. **glorified**. Mt 5:16. 15:31. Lk 5:25. 13:13. 17:15. 23:47. Ac 4:21. Ga 1:24. **such power**. Mk 2:1-12. **men**. ∫96F3, Ge +8:4.

9. **named**. Mt 21:31, 32. Mk 2:14, etc. Lk *5:27, 28, Levi. 15:1, 2. 19:2-10. **Matthew**. i.e. *gift of God*, ✳S#3156g. Mt 9:9. 10:3. Mk 3:18. Lk 6:15. Ac 1:13. **sitting**. Ge +*24:27. Am 7:15. **Follow**. Mt 4:18-22. 1 K 19:19-21. Jn +1:43. Ga 1:16.

10. **came to pass**. ∫144A11, Ge +38:1. **sat**. Mt +11:19. Mk *2:15, 16, etc. Lk 5:29, etc. **many**. Mt 5:46, 47. Jn +*9:31. 1 T 1:13-16.

11. **they said**. Mk 2:16. 9:14-16. **Why**. ver. 14. Mt *11:19. 15:2. 21:23. Is +*65:5n. Mk 2:24. Lk *5:29, 30. 6:2. 15:1, 2. 19:7. 1 C 5:9-11. Ga 2:15. He 5:2. 2 J 10. **your Master**. Mt +22:24. **with**. Lk❍11:37. ❍14:1.

12. **They that be whole**. ∫138C, Ge +22:14. Ps 6:2. 41:4. 147:3. Je 17:14. 30:17. 33:6. Ho 14:4. Mk 2:17. Lk 5:31. 8:43. 9:11. 18:11-13. Ro 7:9-24. Re 3:17, 18. **are sick**. Ro *3:9.

13. **go**. Mt 12:3, 5, 7. 19:4. 21:42. 22:31, 32. Mk 12:26. Lk 10:26. Jn 10:34. **what that meaneth**. Mt *12:7. Lk +24:27. **I will**. Mt +*23:23. 1 S *15:22. Pr √21:3. Ec 5:1. Is *1:11. Ho ⏁6:6. Mi +*6:6-8. Mk 12:33. He *13:16. **for**. ∫150. Proecthesis; or, Justification B465: addition of conclusion by way of justification. It is a conclusion by way of adding a justifying reason for what has been said. For another instance of this figure see Mt 12:12. **I am**. Mt 5:17. 10:34, 35. +*18:11. 20:28. Mk 1:38. *2:17. *10:45. Lk *5:32. 9:56. 12:49, 51. 13:7. +*19:10. Jn 5:43. 6:38, 42. 9:39. 10:10. 12:27, 46, 47. 18:37. **to call**. Mt 18:11-13. Mk 2:17. Lk 5:32. 15:3-10. +*19:10. Ro 3:10-24. 1 C +*6:9-11. 1 T 1:13-16. **righteous**. ∫121Q1, Je 28:5. **but sinners**. Mt 3:2, 8. 4:17. 11:20, 21. 21:28-32. Is √55:6, 7. Lk √15:7. *24:47. Ac +*2:38. +*3:19. 5:31. 11:18. *17:30, 31. 20:21. 26:18-20. Ro 2:4-6. 1 T *1:15. 2 T +*2:25, 26. 2 P √3:9.

14. **the disciples**. Mt *11:2. 14:12. Lk 7:18. *11:1. Jn 1:35. *3:25. *4:1. Ac 18:25. 19:3. **Why**. ver. +*11. Mt 6:16. 11:18, 19. Pr 20:6. Mk 2:18-22. Lk *5:33-39. 18:9-12. **but thy**. ver. 10. Mk 2:15. Lk 6:30.

15. **Can**. Mt 25:1-10. Jg 14:11, etc. Ps 45:14, 15.

Jn *3:29. Re 19:9. 21:2. **the children**. ∫108B, 1 S +20:31. Mt 8:12. 13:38. Mk 2:19. Lk 5:34. +10:6. **but**. ∫7, Allegory by continued Hypocatastasis, Ga +4:24. **days will come**. Mt +26:11. Lk +17:22. **when**. Lk 24:13-21. Jn 16:6, 20-22. Ac 1:9, 10. **and then**. Is 22:12. Jn 16:20. Ac 3:1-3. 14:23. 1 C 7:5. 2 C 11:27.

16. **No man**. ∫138C, Ge +22:14. Jn 1:17. **new cloth**. *or*, raw, *or* unwrought cloth. **old garment**. ∫7, Allegory as continued Hypocatastasis, Ga +4:24. **for**. Ge 33:14. Ps 125:3. Is 40:11. Jn *16:12. 1 C *3:1, 2. 13:13.

17. **old**. Ge 21:14. Jsh 9:4. Jb 32:19. Ps 119:83. Lk *5:39. **perish**. Gr. *apollumi*, Mt +2:13.

18. **behold**. Mk *5:22, etc. Lk *8:41, etc. **a certain**. ∫108E1, Mt +8:19. **ruler**. Mk 5:22. Lk 8:41, 49. 13:14. 18:18. Ac 13:15. **worshipped**. Mt +8:2. +*14:33. 15:25. 17:14. 20:20. 28:17. Mk 5:22. Lk 17:15, 16. Ac 10:25, 26. Re +*5:12. **My daughter**. ver. 24. Mk 5:23. Lk 7:2. 8:42, 49. Jn 4:47-49. **but come**. T#1450. Mt 8:8, 9. 1 K 17:19-22. 2 K 4:27-35. 5:11. Jn 11:21, 22, 25, 32. **lay thy hand**. T#1578. Mk 6:5. 7:32. 8:23, 25. 16:18. Lk 4:40. 13:13. Ac +6:6. 9:12. 28:8.

19. **arose**. Mt 8:7. Jn 4:34. Ac *10:38. Ga *6:9, 10.

20. **behold**. Mk *5:25-34. Lk 8:43-48. **an issue**. Le 15:25, etc. **touched**. Mt 14:36. Mk +3:10. 5:28. 6:56. 8:22. Ac 5:15. 19:12. **hem**. Mt 14:36. 23:5. Nu 15:38, 39. Dt 22:12. Mk +5:27. 6:56. Lk 8:44.

21. **If**. ∫184C, Mt +4:9. Mk 5:26-33. Lk 8:45-47. Ac 19:12. **touch**. Mk 3:10. **be whole**. Ps 42:11. 67:2. Mk +10:52.

22. **turned**. Lk +22:61. **Daughter**. ver. +*2. Mk 5:34. Lk *8:48. **thy faith**. ver. 29. Mk 10:52. Lk 7:50. 17:19. 18:42. Ac 14:9. He 4:2. **from**. Mt 8:13. 15:28. 17:18. Jn 4:53. Ac 16:18.

23. **into**. ver. 18, 19. Mk 5:35-38. Lk 8:49-51. **the minstrels**. Mt 11:17. Ge 23:2. 1 S 25:1. 2 S 19:35. 2 Ch *35:25. Ezr 2:65. Ne 7:67. Ec 12:5. Je *9:17-20. 16:6. Ezk 24:17. Am 5:16. Mk 5:38-40. Lk 7:32. Ac 9:39. Re 18:22.

24. **give**. 1 K 17:18-24. Ac 9:40. 20:10. **the maid**. Ac 20:10. **not dead**. Ho 13:14. Jn 11:4, 11-13, 25. **but sleepeth**. Da 12:2n. Jn 11:4, 11, 25. **And**. Mt 27:39-43. Ps 22:6, 7. Is 49:7. 53:3.

25. **the people**. 1 K 17:19, 20. 2 K 4:32-36. Ac 9:40, 41. **and took**. Mt 8:15. Mk +1:31. 5:41. 8:23. 9:27. Lk 8:54.

26. **the fame hereof**. *or*, this fame. ver. 31. Mt 4:24. 14:1, 2. Mk 1:45. 6:14. Ac 26:26.

27. **two**. Mt 11:5. 12:22. 20:30-34. Mk 8:22, 23. 10:46. Lk 7:21. Jn 9:1, etc. **Thou son**. ∫171G, Ge +13:8. **of David**. Mt +1:1. 12:23. 15:22. 20:30, 31. 21:9, 15. 22:41-45. Mk 10:47, 48. 11:10. 12:35-37. Lk 18:38, 39. 20:41. Jn *7:42. Ro 1:3. √9:5. **have mercy**. Mt 15:22. 17:15. 20:30, 31. Mk 9:22. 10:47, 48. Lk 16:24. 17:13. 18:38, 39.

28. **come**. Mt 8:14. 13:36. **Believe**. ver. 22. Mt 8:2. 9:28. 13:58. Mk 1:40. 9:23, 24. Jn 4:48-50. 9:35. 11:26, 40. **am able**. Is 42:6, 7.

29. **touched**. Mt 20:34. Mk +1:41. 8:25. Jn 9:6, 7. **According**. ver. +2. Mt 8:6, 7, 13. 15:28. Mk 10:52. Ph 4:19. Ja *1:6, 7.

30. **their**. 2 K 6:17. Ps 146:8. Is 35:5. 42:7. 52:13. Jn 9:7-26. **straitly**. Mt +8:4. 12:16. 17:9. Mk 1:43. 5:43. 14:5. Lk 5:14. 8:56. Jn 11:33, 38g. **no man know**. Mt 12:16, 17, 19. Jn 7:8.

31. **spread**. ver. 26. Mt 4:24. 28:15. Mk 1:44, 45. 7:36.

32. **a dumb**. Mt 12:22, 23. Mk 7:32-37. 9:17-27. Lk 11:14. **possessed**. Mt +4:24.

33. **And when**. It seems evident that this man was dumb, not from any natural defect, but from the power of an evil spirit; for when the evil spirit was expelled, he was immediately capable of speaking. The spectators were justly surprised at these multiplied and astonishing miracles; for in one afternoon our Lord had raised the daughter of Jairus from the dead, healed a woman with an issue of blood, restored two blind men to sight, and cured this dumb demoniac; and all this in Capernaum. **the dumb**. ♪121E1, Ge +25:23. Mt 15:30, 31. Ex 4:11, 12. Is 35:6. Mk 7:32-37. Lk 11:14. **marvelled**. Mt 8:27. 15:31. Mk 1:27. Jn 9:32. **It**. 2 K 5:8. Ps 76:1. Je 32:20. Lk 7:9. Jn +15:24.

34. **Pharisees said**. Mt 12:23, 24. Mk +3:22. Lk 11:15. Jn 3:20. **he casteth**. Mt 12:24. Mk ◖1:24. **the prince**. Mt +12:24.

35. **Jesus went**. Mt 4:+23, 24. 11:1, 5. Mk 1:32-39. *6:+6, 56. Lk 4:43, 44. *13:22. Ac 2:22. *10:38. **the kingdom**. Mt +13:19. **healing every sickness**. Mt 4:23. 10:1.

36. **when**. Mt 14:14. 15:32. Mk 6:34. He +*4:15. 5:2. **moved**. ♪22A18, Is +63:15. **with compassion**. Mt 14:14. 15:32. 20:34. Mk 1:41. 6:34. 8:2. 9:22. Lk 7:13. 15:20. **fainted**, etc. *or*, were tired and lay down. Is 32:18. Je 50:6mg. Lk +7:6g. **scattered**. Mt 15:24. 1 P 2:25. **as sheep**. ♪160A, Ps +1:3. Mt *10:6. 15:24. Nu ▶27:17. 1 K 22:17. 2 Ch 18:16. Is 56:9-11. Je 50:6, 17. Ezk 34:3-6. Zc 10:2. 11:16. 13:7, 8. Jn 10:11.

37. **The harvest**. Mt 28:19. Mk 16:15. Lk *10:2. 24:47. Jn *4:35, 36. Ac 16:9, 10. 18:10. **but**. Ps 68:11. 1 C 3:9. 2 C 6:1. Ph 2:19-21. Col 4:11. 1 Th 5:12, 13. 1 T 5:17.

38. **Pray**. Lk 6:12, 13. Ac 13:2. 2 Th *3:1. **the Lord**. Mt 10:1-3. Jn 20:21. Ep *4:11. **that**. Ps *68:11, 18. Je *3:15. Mi 5:7. Mk 1:12. Lk 10:1, 2. Jn 10:4g. Ac 8:4. 1 C 12:28.

MATTHEW 10

Christ sends out twelve apostles, with power to work miracles, 1. Their names, 2-4. They must not go to Gentiles or Samaritans, but to Israel, 5, 6. He instructs them, both as to their preaching and conduct, 7-15. He forewarns them of persecutions, and suggests motives of comfort and constancy, 16-39. He promises blessings to those who should receive them, 40-42.

1. **called**. Mt 19:28. 26:20, 47. Mk 3:13, 14. 6:7, etc. Lk 6:13. Jn 6:70. Re 12:1. 21:12-14. **he gave**. Mt 6:13. 28:18, 19. Mk *3:15. 16:17, 18. Lk 9:1, etc. 10:19. 21:15. 24:49. Jn 3:27, 35. 17:2. 20:21-23. Ac +*1:8. 3:15, 16. 19:15. **power**. T#100. Mt 7:29. Mk 16:19. 18:18, 19. Jn 20:23. Ac 8:17-19. 15:28, 29. 2 C 12:12. Ja +5:15 (T#189). **against**. *or*, over. ♪181E, Ge +3:24. Mk 6:7. Jn 17:2. Ro 9:21. **spirits**. Gr. *pneuma*, Mt +8:16. **to heal**. Ac *9:34.

2. **apostles**. Lk 6:13. 9:10. 11:49. 22:14. Ac 1:26. Ep 4:11. He 3:1. Re 18:20. **Simon**. Mt 4:18. 16:16-18. Mk 1:16, 17. 3:16. Lk 6:14. Jn 1:40-42. Ac 1:13. 1 P 1:1. 2 P 1:1. **Andrew**. Mk 1:29. 3:18. 13:3. Jn 6:8. 12:22. **James**. i.e. *supplanter*, *S#2385g. ver. 3. Mt 4:21. 13:55. 17:1. 20:20. 26:37. 27:56. Mk 1:19, 29. 3:17, 18. 5:37. 6:3. 9:2. 10:35, 41. 13:3. 14:33. 15:40. 16:1. Lk 5:10. 6:14, 15, 16. 8:51. 9:28, 54. 24:10. Jn 21:2. Ac 1:13, 13, 13. 12:2, 17. 15:13. 21:18. 1 C

15:7. Ga 1:19. 2:9, 12. Ja 1:1. Ju 1. (1) James the Elder was a son of Zebedee and Salome, brother of John the Evangelist, probably a cousin of Jesus, and one of the three favorite apostles. His apostolic labors were confined to Jerusalem and Judea, and in A.D. 44 he was beheaded by order of King Herod Agrippa, thus becoming the first martyr among the apostles. Ac 12:2. (2) James the Less, or the Little, was a son of Alpheus and Mary, Mk 15:40; Mt 10:3; Ac 1:13, and was also one of the twelve apostles. (3) James, "the brother of the Lord," Ga 1:19; compare Mt 13:55; Mk +*6:3, or simply James, Ac 12:17; 15:13, is identified by some with James the Less and regarded as a cousin of Jesus, while others distinguish between the two and take the designation "the brother of the Lord" in the strict sense of the words. He stood at the head of the Church in Jerusalem after the dispersion of the disciples and the departure of Peter, Ac 12:17, and he presided at the Apostolical Council in Jerusalem, A.D. 50. **John**. Lk 22:8. Jn 13:23. 20:2. 21:20, 24. Ac 3:1. 1 J 1:3, 4. 2 J 1. 3 J 1. Re 1:1, 9. 22:8.

3. **Philip**. Mk 3:18. Lk 6:14. Jn 1:43-46. 6:5-7. 12:21, 22. 14:9. **Bartholomew**. i.e. *son that suspends the waters; a furrow*, *S#918g. Mk 3:18. Lk 6:14. Ac 1:13. **Thomas**. Lk 6:15. Jn 11:16. 20:24-29. 21:2. **Matthew**. Mt 9:9. Mk 2:14. Lk 5:27, Levi. 6:15. Ac 1:13. **publican**. ♪11, Ge +2:23. **James**. Mt 27:56. Mk 3:18. Lk 6:15, 16. Ac 1:13. 12:17. 15:13. 21:18. Ga 1:19. 2:9. Ja 1:1. **Alphaeus**. i.e. *produce, gain*, *S#256g. Mk 2:14. 3:18. Lk 6:15. Ac 1:13. **Lebbeus**. i.e. *courageous*, *S#3002g, only here. Mk 3:18. Lk 6:16, Judas the brother of James. Jn 14:22, Judas, not Iscariot. Ac 1:13. Ju 1. **Thaddaeus**. i.e. *that praises or confesses*, *S#2280g. Mk 3:18.

4. **Simon**. Mk 3:18. Lk 6:15, Simon Zelotes. Ac 1:13. **Canaanite**. i.e. *zealous, acquired*, *S#2581g. Mk 3:18. **and Judas**. Mt 26:14, 47. 27:3. Mk 3:19. 14:10, 43. Lk 6:16. 22:3, 47. Jn 6:71. 13:2, 26-30. 18:2-5. Ac 1:16-20, 25. **Iscariot**. i.e. *man of murder, he will be hired*, *S#2469g. Mt 10:4. 26:14. Jsh 15:25n. Mk 3:19. 14:10. Lk 6:16. 22:3. Jn 6:71. 12:4. 13:2, 26. 14:22.

5. **sent**. Mt 22:3. Lk 9:2. 10:1. Jn *20:21. **Go not**. Mt 4:15. √15:24. Jn 7:35. Ac 10:45-48. 11:1-18. 22:21-23. Ro 15:8, 9. 1 C 10:32. Ga ◖*3:28. 1 Th 2:16. 1 Th 4:2n. 2 T 2:15n. **the way**. Ac 11:19. **of the Samaritans**. i.e. *guardianship, prison*, *S#4541g. 2 K 17:24, etc. Ezr 4:10. Lk *9:52-54. 10:33. 17:16. Jn *4:5, 9, 20, 22-24, 39, 40. 8:48. Ac +*1:8. 8:1, 5, etc., 25.

6. **go**. Mt *15:24-26. Lk *24:47. Ac 3:26. *13:46. 18:6. 26:20. *28:25-28. Ro 11:11-15. *15:8. **lost**. Gr. *apollumi*, Mt +2:13. Mt *9:36. 15:24. *18:11, 12. Ps *119:176. Is √53:6. Je *50:6, 17. Ezk 34:5, 6, 8, *16. Lk *15:3-10. 1 P *2:25.

7. **As ye go**. Mt 3:1. **preach**. Mt 4:17. 11:1. Is *58:1. 61:1. Jon 3:2. Mk *6:12. Lk 9:60. *16:16. Ac 4:2. **kingdom of heaven**. Mt 3:2. +4:17. 11:11, 12. 21:31, 43. 23:13. Mk ◖+1:15. Lk 9:2, 6. 10:9-11. Ac 20:25. 28:31. **at hand**. Mt 3:2. 4:17. ◖+*21:43. Is 56:1. Lk 21:31.

8. **Heal**. ver. 1. Mt 11:5. Mk 16:18. Lk *10:9. Ac 4:9, 10, 30. 5:12-15. **freely ye**. Mt 5:42. 2 K 5:15, 16, 20-27. Is 55:1. Lk 3:11. 6:38. 12:33. Jn 15:25g. Ac 3:6. *8:18-23. *20:33-35. Ro 3:24. 2 C 8:7, 9. 9:8. 11:7g. Ga 2:21g. Re 21:6. 22:17. **freely give**. T#406. ver. +*42. Mt 5:42. 6:1-4. 25:34-36, 40-46. Le +25:35 (T#526). Pr 21:13. 22:9. 28:27. Ec 11:1, 2. Lk 3:11. +*11:41. 12:33, 34. 16:9, 11, 13, 14. Ac 20:35. Ro

12:8, 10, 20. 2 C 8:7. 9:6. Ga *6:9, 10. Ep 4:28. 1 Th +3:12 (T#406). 1 T 6:17-19. He 13:16. 1 J 3:17.

9. Provide. *or*, Get. **neither.** Mk 6:8. Lk 9:3. 10:4. *22:35. 1 C 9:7, etc. **gold.** /121D5, Ge +23:9.

10. scrip. 1 S 9:7. *17:40. Mk 6:8. Lk 22:35, 36. **two.** Lk *3:11. 2 T 4:13. **staves.** Gr. a staff. **for the.** /138C, Ge +22:14. Le +*19:13. Nu 18:31. Dt +*24:15. Lk *10:7, etc. 1 C *9:4-14. Ga *6:6, 7. 1 T *)5:17, 18. 2 T 2:6.

11. enquire. Ge 19:1-3. Jg 19:16-21. 1 K 17:9, etc. Jb 31:32. Lk 10:38-42. 19:7. Ac 16:15. 18:1-3. 3 J 7, 8. **worthy.** Mt 8:8. 22:8. Ac 16:15. **and there.** Mk 6:10. Lk 9:4. √10:7, 8. Ac 16:15. 1 T *5:13.

12. salute it. Jg 19:20. 1 S 25:6. 1 Ch 12:18. Lk *10:5, 6. Ac 10:36. 2 C 5:20. 3 J 14.

13. And if. /184C, Mt +4:9. **worthy.** Ps 35:13. Is 45:23. Lk 10:6. 2 C 2:16. **let your.** Ac 10:36. 2 C 5:18. **return.** Ps 35:13.

14. whosoever. ver. 40, 41. Mt 18:5. Mk 6:11. 9:37. Lk 9:5, 48. 10:10, 11. Jn 13:20. 2 C +*7:2. 1 Th *4:8. 3 J +*9. **shake.** /138B, Ge +13:16. Mt +*7:6. Ne 5:13. Ac *13:51. *18:6. 20:26, 27.

15. verily. Mt 5:18. 24:34, 35. **It.** Mt 11:22-24. Ezk 16:48-56. Mk 6:11. Lk 10:11, 12. Jn 15:22-24. **more tolerable.** Mt 11:23, 24. La 4:6. Ezk +*16:49. Mk 6:11. Lk +*12:48. Ro *2:12, 16. **the land.** Ge 18:20. 19:28. **Sodom.** i.e. *burning, fettered,* ❋S#4670g. Mt 10:15. 11:23, 24. Mk 6:11. Lk 10:12. 17:29. Ro 9:29. 2 P 2:6. Ju 7. Re 11:8. **Gomorrha.** i.e. *bondage,* ❋S#1116g. Ro 9:29. 2 P 2:6. Ju 7. **in the day of judgment.** That Scripture does not teach a single day of general judgment for all should be clear to anyone who will carefully compare the passages to see who is being judged, who is doing the judging, the basis upon which the judgment is rendered, when the judgment is said to take place, where the judgment takes place, and what the results of the judgment are said to be. In the study of Scripture, it is most important not only to compare things that are alike in some way (as judgment), but to note also the points of difference. Similarity and likeness do not establish identity when there are differences to be accounted for! Several judgments mentioned in Scripture include (1) the judgment of sin at the cross, Jn +12:31; (2) the believer's judgment of himself, 1 C +11:32; (3) the judgment seat of Christ, 2 C +5:10; (4) the judgment of the righteous living and dead at his appearing, 2 T +*4:1n; (5) the judgment of Israel, Ezk +20:35; (6) judgment of the nations, Mt 25:32; (7) the extended period of judgment and rule over his kingdom, 2 T +*4:1n; (8) judgment of angels, 2 P +2:4; (9) the great white throne judgment, Re +20:11. To confuse these judgments by merging them into one is to wrongly divide the Scripture. Mt √12:36. 13:40-42. *25:31-33, 46. Ps 96:13. Ec 11:9. Jn 5:22. 12:48. Ac 10:42. √17:31. 24:25. Ro √14:10. 1 C 3:10. 2 C √5:10. 2 T *4:1, 8. He √9:27. 2 P √2:9. √3:7. 1 J 4:17. Ju 6, 14, 15. Re *11:18. √20:12, 13.

16. I send. ver. 5. Jn 17:18. **as sheep.** Lk 10:3. Jn 10:12. Ac 20:29. Ro *16:19. **wise.** T#457. Mt 25:2. Ge 3:1, 13. Ne 6:3. Pr +31:4 (T#369). Je +23:2 (T#463). Ezk *2:8. Lk 21:15. Ac 6:4. *20:28-31. Ro 2:21. *16:19. 1 C 9:25-27. *14:20. 2 C 11:3, 14. Ep *5:15-17. Ph 2:15. Col 1:9. *4:5. 1 Th 2:10. 1 T *4:12-16. 6:20, 21. 2 T 1:13. 2:3, 4, 22, 23. 4:5, 7. T 2:7, 8. **harmless.** *or*, simple. T#660. Mt +11:29 (T#62). Pr +16:7 (T#737). Ro 16:18, 19. 1 C 4:12. 13:4, 7.

14:20. 2 C *1:12. 8:20. 11:3. Ga 5:22, 23. +6:1 (T#437). Ph *2:15. 1 Th 2:10. 5:22. He 10:34. +12:14 (T#499). Ja 5:6. **doves.** Le=1:14. Is 38:14. 59:11. Ho 7:11.

17. beware. Mi 7:5. Mk 13:9, 12. Jn 15:19. 17:14. Ac 14:5, 6. 17:14. 23:12-22. 2 C 11:24-26. Ph *3:2. 2 Th *3:2. 2 T 4:15. **deliver you.** Mt *24:9, 10. Mk 13:9, 11. Lk 12:11, 12. 21:12, 13. Jn 16:2. Ac 4:6, etc. 5:26, etc. *14:5. 23:1, etc. **councils.** Mt 5:22. 26:59. Jn 11:47. **scourge.** Mt 20:19. 23:34. Dt 25:2, 3. Mk 13:9. Lk 21:12. Ac *5:40. 22:19. 26:11. 2 C *11:23-25. He 11:36.

18. And. /77, Ex +3:19. **be.** Ps 2:1-6. Ac 5:25-27. *12:1-4. 16:19. 23:33, 34. ch. 24-26. 2 T 4:16, 17. Ja 2:6. **for my sake.** ver. 22, 39. Ac *9:15, 16. **for a testimony.** Mt 8:4. Mk 13:9. Lk 21:12, 13. Ph *1:13. 2 T 1:8. Re 1:9. 6:9. 11:7.

19. when. Mk *13:11-13. Lk *12:11. *21:14, 15. **take.** Mt 6:25, 31, 34. Ph *4:6. Ja +*1:5. **it shall.** Ex *4:12, 15. Nu 23:5. Dt 18:18. 2 S 23:2. Is 50:4. Je 1:7-9. Da 3:16-18. Jn 14:26. 15:26. Ac 4:8-14. 5:29-33. 6:10. 13:9. 26:2, etc. 1 C 2:4. 15:10. 2 C 13:3. 1 Th 2:13. 2 T 4:17. He 1:1. 2 P *1:21.

20. but. 2 S 23:2. Mk 12:36. Lk 11:13. 21:15. Ac 2:4. 4:8. 6:10. 7:55, 56. 28:25. 1 P 1:12. 2 P *1:21. **Spirit.** Gr. *pneuma,* Mt +3:16. Jn *14:16, 26. **your Father.** Mt 6:32. Lk 12:30-32. **which speaketh.** Je 1:2, 9. 2:1. 25:3, 4. 26:12, 15. Ezk 1:3. Da 2:19. Mi 3:8.

21. the brother shall. ver. 34-36. Mt 24:10. Mi *7:5, 6. Zc 13:3. Mk 13:12, 13. Lk 12:51-53. *21:16, 17. **the children.** 2 S 16:11. 17:1-4. Jb 19:19.

22. shall be hated. Mt 24:9. Is *66:5, 6. Mk 13:13. Lk *6:22, 23. 21:17. Jn 7:7. *15:18, 19, 21. 17:14. 1 J *3:13. **of all.** /171A, Ex +9:6. **for.** ver. 39. Mt 5:11. Jn 15:21. Ac 9:16. 2 C 4:11. Re 2:3. **but he.** /138C, Ge +22:14. Mt √24:13. Da 12:12, 13. Mk 13:13. Lk 8:15. Ro *2:7. Ga *6:9. He 3:14. 6:11. 10:36. Ja *1:12. Ju *20, 21. Re 2:7, 10, 17, 26. 3:21. **endureth.** 1 C 1:8. 2 C 1:13. Ga *6:9. He √3:6, 14. Re *2:10. **the end.** Gr. *telos,* ❋S#5056g. Mt 17:25. 24:6, 13, 14. 26:58. Mk 3:26. 13:7, 13. Lk 1:33. 18:5 (continual coming. lit. unto the end). 21:9. 22:37. Jn 13:1. Ro 6:21, 22. 10:4. 13:7 (custom), 7. 1 C 1:8. 10:11 (ends). 15:24. 2 C 1:13. 3:13. 11:15. Ph 3:19. 1 Th 2:16 (uttermost). 1 T 1:5. He 3:6, 14. 6:8, 11. 7:3. Ja 5:11. 1 P 1:9. 3:8 (Finally). 4:7, 17. Re 1:8 (ending). 2:26. 21:6. 22:13. Contrast ❋S#4930g, *sunteleia,* Mt +24:3.

23. when. Mt 2:13. 4:12. 12:14, 15. 23:34. Lk 4:29-31. Jn *7:1. 10:39-42. *11:53, 54. Ac 8:1. 9:24, 25. 13:50, 51. 14:6, 7, 19, 20. 17:10, 14. 20:1. **flee.** Mt *12:14, 15. Pr +*22:3. *27:12. Ac *8:1. *9:23-25, 30. *14:5-7. *17:10, 14. *20:1. **another.** Gr. *allos,* S#243g. Another quantitatively, of the same kind, in contrast to *heteros* (S#2087g, Mt +11:3), which means another qualitatively, of a different kind. Vine notes that the two words are used interchangably only in 1 C 1:16 and 6:1; 12:8-10; 14:17, 19, where the difference, though present, is not so readily discernible (*Expository Dictionary*, vol. 1, p. 60). The distinction is maintained and particularly asserted by Paul in Ga 1:6, 7. Rendered (1) other or others: Mt 4:21. 5:39. 12:13. 13:8. 20:3, 6. 21:8, 36, 41. 22:4. 25:16, 17, 20a, 22. 27:42, 61. 28:1. Mk 3:5. 4:8, 36. 6:15, 15. 7:4, 8. 8:28b. 11:8. 12:5b, 9, 31, 32. 15:31, 41. Lk 5:29. 6:10, 29. 9:8, 19b. 20:16. 23:35. Jn 4:38. 6:22, 23. 7:12, 41a. 9:9b, 16. 10:16, 21. 12:29. 15:24. 18:16, 34. 19:18, 32. 20:2, 3, 4, 8, 25, 30. 21:2, 8, 25. Ac 4:12. 15:2. 1 C 1:16.

3:11. 9:2, 12, 27. 14:19, 29. 2 C 1:13. 8:13. 11:8. Ph 3:4. 1 Th 2:6. He 11:35. Ja 5:12. Re 2:24. 17:10. (2) another: Mt 2:12. 8:9. 10:23. 13:24, 31, 33. 19:9. 21:33. 26:71. Mk 10:11, 12. 12:4, 5a. 14:19, 58. Lk 7:8, 19, 20. 22:59. Jn 4:37b. 5:7, 32, 43. *14:16. 18:15. 21:18. Ac 2:12b. 19:32b. 21:34b. 1 C 3:10. 10:29. 12:8, 9, 10, 10, 10. 14:30. 15:39b, 39c, 39d, 41b, 41c. 2 C 11:4. Ga *1:7. He 4:8. Re 6:4. 7:2. 8:3. 10:1. 12:3. 13:11. 14:6, 8, 15, 17, 18. 15:1. 16:7. 18:1, 4. 20:12. (3) some: Mt 13:5, 7. 16:14. Mk 4:5, 7. 8:28a. Lk 9:19a. Jn 7:41b. 9:9a. Ac 19:32a. 21:34a. (4) one: Jn 4:37a. Ac 2:12a. 1 C 15:39a, 41a. (5) miscellaneous: more, Mt 25:20b. otherwise, Ga 5:10. **have gone over.** *or,* end, *or,* finish. ∫63BB, 1 S +16:11. Literally, "Ye will not have finished *going over* the cities," etc., referring to verses 6 and 7. **till.** Mt *16:28. *▪17:1-13. *21:1-11. +*23:39. *24:1, 2, 21, 27, 30, 34, 48. 25:13. 26:64. Is 2:1-4. +*45:17. Ezk 39:25. Mk 9:1. 13:26. Lk 9:27. 18:8. 21:27. Ro +*11:26. **Son of man.** ∫144A3, Ge +11:5. Mt 8:20. *16:28n.

24. **The disciple.** ∫138C, Ge +22:14. 2 S 11:11. Lk 6:40. Jn *3:30. *13:16. *15:20, 21. He *12:2-4. **master.** Mt 22:24.

25. **It is.** ∫138B, Ge +13:16. **If they.** ∫184A, 1 C +15:2. Mt 9:34. 12:24. Mk *3:22. Lk 11:15. Jn 7:20. *8:48, 52. 10:20. Ac 26:24. **Beelzebub.** *or,* Beelzebul. i.e. *lord of the flies; dung god,* *S#954g. Mt 10:25. 12:24, 27. 2 K *1:2, 3, 6. Mk 3:22. Lk 11:15, 18, 19.

26. **Fear.** ver. 28. Pr 28:1. 29:25. Is 8:12. 41:10, 14. 43:1, 2. 51:7, 8, 12, 13. Je 1:8, 17, 18. Ezk 2:6. Ac 4:13, 19. 1 P 3:14. **for.** Is 45:19. 48:16. Mk 4:22. Lk 8:17. 12:2, 3. 24:47. Jn 18:20. Ac +*1:8. 1 C *4:5. 1 T 5:25. **nothing covered.** ∫171C, Ex +20:10. **revealed.** Ec *12:14.

27. **I tell.** Mt 13:1-17, 34, 35. Lk 8:10. Jn 16:1, 13, 25, 29. 2 C 3:12. **in the ear.** Lk 10:23. **that preach.** Pr 1:20-23. 8:1-5. Ac 5:20, 28. 17:17. **housetops.** Lk 5:19.

28. **And fear not.** ver. 26. Ps 56:4. Is √8:12-14. *51:7, 12, 13. Je *1:8, 17. Ezk 2:6. 3:9. Da *3:10-18. Lk *12:4, 5. Ac *20:23, 24. *21:13. Ro *8:35-39. 2 T *4:6-8. He 7:25. 11:35. 1 P 3:14. Re *2:10. **body.** Mt +6:25. **not able.** Mt *22:31, 32. Mk 12:26, 27. Lk *12:4, 5. Ac 7:59. 2 C 4:18. **kill.** Ge ●*37:21. **soul.** Gr. *psyche,* Mt +2:20. The immaterial, invisible, eternally conscious part of man, as in Ac 2:27, 31. 1 Th *5:23. He *4:12. For the other uses of *psyche,* see Mt +2:20n. It is evident that *soul* cannot mean here the "future life" or "opportunity for future life." The word *psyche* is never used when the future, eternal life is spoken of. Rather, a different word, *zoe* (Lk +10:25g), is used. It is equally clear that the *soul* here can not mean the physical life in the body or the body itself, for that *can* be killed by man, whereas here the soul *cannot* be killed. It is of no use to argue that in other passages the soul can be killed, for in such passages *soul* is used to mean *person,* without specific reference to the immaterial, invisible, eternally conscious part of man, which is what is in view here. Mt +6:25. Ge 35:18. Jb +*14:22. Ps +*16:10. 22:26. Ec +*12:7. **fear him.** Jb 37:24. Ps *34:7. 119:120. Pr *14:26, 27. 28:1. 29:25. Ec 5:7. *8:12, 13. +12:13. Is *41:10. *66:2. Je 5:22. Ac *4:19. He *10:31. *12:28, 29. 1 P *1:17. **able.** Mt *25:46. Mk *9:43-48. Lk *16:22-26. Jn *5:29. 2 Th √1:8-10. Ja 4:12. Re *20:10-15. **destroy.** Gr. *apollumi,* Mt +2:13. This Greek word never means annihi-

late, but rather means to render unsuitable for the use originally intended. A "lost" coin is not annihilated; neither are the "lost sheep of the house of Israel," nor those Jesus came to seek and to save (Mt 18:11). In this very chapter (Mt 10:39), the loss or gain of *psyche* is spoken of as occurring in this present life, an impossibility if *apollumi* means annihilation. Note the order of statement in Luke 12:5. Follow carefully Paul's logic in 1 C 15:16-18, and note that "perished" in verse 18 is *apollumi,* the same word as here. Paul argues that if Christ has not truly been raised from the dead, then those that are asleep in Christ are perished; since Christ is raised from the dead, the dead in Christ are not perished. Nor are the dead who are not in Christ annihilated, for they shall yet be resurrected and judged (John 5:28, 29). To suggest that all persons who have died are non-existent until the resurrection, but are kept "alive" in God's memory, has not a shred of Biblical evidence to support it, and is contrary to Biblical teaching, for then upon resurrection it would not be the same person (note Christ's own emphatic statement of his personal bodily resurrection identity, Lk 24:39), but a reconstituted copy of the person. Since only bodies are resurrected, not spirits or souls, the whole materialist viewpoint is fallacious in positing a break in the continuity of conscious existence of the person. The materialist viewpoint was held even more consistently by the Sadducees, a viewpoint utterly demolished by our Lord's answer to them in Mt 22:23-32. ver. 6g. Mt 9:17. Jb 19:10. Ho 13:9, 10. Lk +9:24. **both.** Is +*10:18. Lk 12:5. **soul.** Gr. *psyche,* Mt +2:20. **hell.** Gr. *gehenna,* Mt +5:22. Mt +5:29. 1 S 28:19. Ps 139:8. Is +*66:24.

29. **two.** Lk *12:6, 7. **farthing.** "In value a halfpenny farthing, as being the tenth of the Roman penny. See Mt 18:28." **and one.** Mt *6:26. Jb 38:41. Ps *50:11. +*104:27-30. **shall not.** ∫108E2. Idiom B836. Sometimes, following Hebrew idiom, the negative is joined with the verb instead of the predicate: "one of them shall not fall," instead of the Greek idiom, "not one of them shall fall." For another instance of this figure see Lk (12:6). **without.** Is 36:10.

30. **the very hairs.** ∫138B, Ge +13:16. ∫134, Mt +3:9. "Hairs" and "numbered" in Hebrew have a similar sound, *mene, manyan,* the figure of speech Parechesis. Mt 5:36. 1 S 14:45. 2 S 14:11. 1 K 1:52. Da 3:27. Lk 12:7. *21:18. Ac 27:34. **numbered.** Jb 14:16. *31:4. Ps +*40:17.

31. **Fear ye not.** Lk 1:13. **more value.** Mt 6:26. 12:11, 12. Ps +*8:5. Lk 12:24. 13:15, 16. 1 C 9:9, 10.

32. **confess.** ∫108B. Idiom B828. "To confess" is used of abiding in the faith, and walking according to truth. For other instances of this idiom see Ro *10:9, 10. 1 J 4:15. lit. confess in me. Vincent states "The idea is that of confessing Christ out of a state of oneness with him. 'Abide in me, and being in me, confess me.' It implies identification of the confessor with the confessed, and thus takes confession out of the category of mere formal or verbal acknowledgment. 'Not every one that *saith* unto me, Lord! Lord! shall enter into the kingdom of heaven.' The true confessor of Christ is one whose faith rests in him. Observe that this gives great force to the corresponding clause, in which Christ places himself in a similar relation with those whom he confesses" (*Word Pictures in the New Testament,*

vol. 1, p. 61). Lk ◐/12:9. Jn √17:23. Ro 8:1n. **me before men.** T#866. Ge=40:14. Ps *119:46. Lk *12:8, 9. Jn *1:49. √6:68, 69. *9:22, 25, 33. √11:27. Ac *4:7-12. *5:29-32, 42. 9:29. Ro √10:9, 10. 1 T *6:12, 13. 2 T 1:8. 4:2. He 10:35. 1 J *4:15. Re 1:9. *2:13. 20:4. **him will I.** Mt *25:34. 1 S *2:30. Ml *3:17. Lk *12:8. Re *3:5. **confess.** Gr. *homologeo,* ✻S#3670g. Rendered (1) confess: Mt 10:32, 32. Lk 12:8, 8. Jn 1:20, 20. 9:22. 12:42. Ac 23:8. 24:14. Ro 10:9. He 11:13. 1 J 1:9. 4:2, 3, 15. 2 J 7. (2) profess: Mt 7:23. 1 T 6:12. T 1:16. (3) promise: Mt 14:7. (4) give thanks: He 13:15. (5) confession is made: Ro 10:10. See for the related term *exomologeomai,* ✻S#1843g, Mk +1:5. **before my.** Mt +*7:21. Mk +*13:32. Jn *5:30. +*14:28. Ro *8:34. 1 C *11:3. +*15:28. 1 T *2:5. He *7:25. 9:24. 1 J 2:1.

33. **deny me.** Gr. *arneomai,* S#720g, Lk +12:9. Mt 26:70-75. Mk *8:38. Lk *9:26. *12:9. 2 T *2:12, 13. 2 P *2:1. 1 J *2:23. **deny before.** Gr. *arneomai,* S#720g, Lk +12:9. lit. disown. To disown, reject, or repudiate one in the face of former relationship or better knowledge (See Cremer, *Lexicon,* p. 111). Mt √7:23. *25:12. Lk √12:9. *13:25.

34. **Think not.** Mt 5:17. Lk 12:51-53. **that I.** Je 15:10. Lk *12:49-53. Jn *7:40-52. Ac 13:45-50. *14:2, 4. *28:24, 25. **but a sword.** ♪121B, Ex +5:3. "Sword" is put for war or slaughter by Metonymy of the cause. The object of his coming was peace, but the *effect* of it was war (B548). Ps 18:34. Lk +*22:36. Re 6:4.

35. **to set.** ver. *21. Mt *24:10. Ezk 22:7. Mi *7:5, 6. Mk *13:12. Lk *21:16.

36. **man's foes.** Mt 10:21. 24:10. Ge +*3:15. *4:8-10. *37:17-28. 1 S *17:28. 2 S 15:12. *16:11. Jb *19:13-19. Ps 27:10. *41:9. 55:12, 13. 69:8. Je *9:4. 12:6. 20:9, 10. Mi *⸍7:6. Mk 13:12. Lk 21:16. +24:27. Jn 13:18. 1 J *3:11, 12.

37. **that loveth father.** Mt *22:37. Ge 12:4. Ex 12:38. Dt *33:9. Ne 13:3. Is 51:2. Lk √14:26, 33. Jn √5:23. *21:15-17. 2 C *5:14, 15. Ph *3:7-9. **or mother.** 1 K 15:13. **not worthy.** ver. 38. Mt *22:8. Lk *20:35. +*21:36. Col +*1:10. 2 Th *1:5-7. Re *3:4.

38. **taketh not.** Mt *16:24, 25. *27:32. Mk *8:34. *10:21. 15:21. Lk *9:23, 24. *14:27, 33. 23:26. Jn 19:17. 2 T *3:10, 12. **followeth after.** Mt 9:9. Jn 8:12. 12:26. 21:19. **not worthy.** ver. +*37. Lk √9:62.

39. **findeth his.** Mt 10:21. 24:10. Mk *8:35, 36. Lk 9:24. *17:33. Jn *12:25. Ac *20:24. Ro *8:17. Ph *1:20, 21. 2 T *4:6-8. Re *2:10. √12:11. **life.** Gr. *psyche,* ♪121A7, Mt +2:20. ♪121A7, Ge +9:5. **lose.** Gr. *apollumi,* Mt +2:13. **loseth.** Gr. *apollumi,* Mt 2:13. **life.** Gr. *psyche,* ♪121A7, Mt +2:20. ♪121A7, Ge +9:5. **for my sake.** ver. 18, 22. Mk 13:9.

40. **He that.** ver. 20. Mt 18:5. 25:40, 45. Lk 9:48. *10:16. Jn *13:20. *20:21. 2 C 5:20. Ga 4:14. 1 Th *4:8. **and he that receiveth.** ♪16, Ge +1:27. ♪113, Nu +9:20. Jn √5:23. *12:44-49. Ph *2:10, 11. 1 J 2:22, 23. 2 J *9. **that sent.** Jn 4:34.

41. **that receiveth a prophet.** Ge 20:7. 1 K 17:9-15, 20-24. *18:3, 4. 2 K 4:8-10, 16, 17, 32-37. Ac 16:15. Ro 16:1-4, 23. 2 T *1:16-18. He *6:10. 3 J *5-8. **receive.** ♪113, Nu +9:20. **a righteous man's.** Mt 6:1, 4, 6, 18. *16:27. *25:34-40. Is 3:10. Lk 14:13, 14. 1 C 9:17. 2 Th 1:6, 7. 2 J 8. **reward.** Mt 5:12.

42. **shall give.** T#915. ver. +*8. Mt *25:34-36, 40. Dt *15:10. Ps *37:25, 26. *41:1-3. 112:5, 6, 9. Pr *11:24, 25, 27. *14:21. *19:17. *22:9. 28:8, 27. Ec 11:1, 2. Is

32:8. 58:7, 8, 10, 11. Mk *10:21. Lk √6:38. 11:41. *12:33. *14:13, 14. *16:9. 2 C *8:12. √9:6-8, 10. 1 T *6:17-19. He *13:16. **one.** Mt 8:5, 6. 18:3-6, 10, 14. 25:40. Zc 13:7. Mk 9:41, 42. Lk 17:2. 1 C 8:10-13. **little ones.** Mt 18:10. 1 C 3:1. **a cup.** Mt 25:37, 40. Mk *9:41. 12:42, 43. 14:7, 8. 2 C √8:12. **name of a disciple.** Mt *18:3, 5. **he shall.** Pr 24:14. Lk *6:35. √14:14. 2 C 9:6-15. Ph *4:15-19. He *6:10. 2 J *8. **lose.** Gr. *apollumi,* Mt +2:13. **his reward.** Mt +*5:12.

MATTHEW 11

Jesus continues to preach in the cities, 1. John the Baptist sends his disciples to inquire of him, whether he is the Messiah, or whether another were to be expected; whom Jesus refers to the miracles wrought by him, 2-6. His testimony to John, 7-15. The perverseness of the people concerning both John and Jesus illustrated, 16-19. He upbraids the impenitency of those who had witnessed most of his mighty works; and denounces woes against Chorazin, Bethsaida, and Capernaum, 20-24. He adores the wise and holy sovereignty of the Father, in revealing his truth; and declares his own personal and mediatorial power and majesty, 25-27. He invites and instructs the weary to come unto him for rest, 28-30.

1. **came to pass.** ♪144A11, Ge +38:1. Mt 7:28. 13:53. 19:1. 26:1. **commanding.** Mt 28:20. Jn 15:10, 14. Ac 1:2. 10:42. 1 Th 4:2. 2 Th 3:6, 10. 1 T 6:14. **he departed.** Mt 4:23. 9:35. 12:9. Is 61:1-3. Mk 1:38, 39. Lk 4:15-21. 8:1. Ac *10:38.

2. **when.** Lk 7:18-23. **in the prison.** Mt 4:12. *14:3, 4. Mk 6:17, 18. Lk 3:19, 20. Jn 3:24. **he sent.** Mt 9:14. Jn 3:25-28. 4:1. Ac 19:1-3.

3. **Art thou he.** Mt 2:2-6. Ge +*3:15. +*12:3. *22:18. +*49:10. Nu +*24:17. Dt *18:15-18. Ps *2:6-12. *110:1-5. Is +*7:14. +*9:6, 7. Je +*23:5, 6. Ezk *34:23, 24. Da +*9:24-26. Ho 3:5. Jl +*2:28-32. Am 9:11, 12. Ob +*21. Mi +*5:2. Zp *3:14-17. Hg 2:7. Zc +*9:9. Ml *3:1. *4:2. Jn 4:21. 7:31, 41, 42. **that should.** ♪96C6, Mt +2:4. **come.** ♪24B, Ge 23:16. ♪108B. Idiom B827. "To come," where the simple verb is used for all that pertains to Christ's advent. For other instances of this idiom see 1 J 4:2, 3; 5:6. See Mt 3:11. 21:5, 9. 23:39. Nu 24:19. Ps *40:7. *118:26. Is *35:4. Ezk 21:27. Da 7:13. +*9:26. Hg *2:7. Zc +*9:9. Mk 1:7. 11:9. Lk 3:16. 18:8. 19:38. Jn 1:9. 3:31. *4:25, 26, 29. *6:14. *11:27. 12:13. Ro 5:14. He 10:37. **look for.** Lk 3:15. **another.** Gr. *heteros,* ✻S#2087g. Vine notes that "*Allos* expresses a numerical difference and denotes another of the same sort; *heteros* expresses a qualitative difference and denotes another of a different sort" (*Expository Dictionary,* vol. 1, p. 60). Rendered (1) another: Mt 8:21. 11:3. Mk 16:12. Lk 6:6. 9:56, 59, 61. 14:19, 20, 31. 16:7, 18. 19:20. 20:11. 22:58. Jn 19:37. Ac 1:20. 7:18. 12:17. 17:7. Ro 2:1, 21. 7:3, 3, 4, 23. 13:8. 1 C 3:4. 4:6. 6:1. 10:24. 12:9, 10. 15:40b. 2 C 11:4, 4. Ga 1:6. 6:4. He 7:11, 13, 15. Ja 2:25. 4:12. (2) other: Mt 6:24, 24. 12:45. 15:30. 16:14. Lk 4:43, 5:7. 7:41. 8:3, 8. 10:1. 11:16, 26. 16:13, 13. 17:34, 35, 36. 18:10. 23:32, 40. Ac 2:4, 13, 40. 4:12. 8:34. 15:35. 17:34. 23:6. 27:1. Ro 8:3. 13:9. 1 C 8:4. 10:29. 14:17, 21. 2 C 8:8. Ga 1:19. Ep 3:5. Ph 2:4. 2 T 2:2. He 11:36. (3) other thing: Lk 3:18. 22:65. 1 T 1:10. (4) some: Lk 8:6, 7. (5) next day: Ac 20:15. 27:3. (6) miscellaneous renderings: be

altered, Lk 9:29. another Psalm, Ac 13:35. else, Ac 17:21. another matter, Ac 19:39. one, 1 C 15:40a. another place, He 5:6. strange, Ju 7. For *allos*, *S#243g, see Mt +10:23.

4. **Go and show.** Jn 2:23. *5:36.

5. **blind.** ♪11, Ge +2:23. Mt 9:30. Ps 146:8. Is 29:18. *♪35:4-6. *42:6, 7, ♪18. 61:1. Lk *4:18. *7:21, 22. Jn 2:23. 3:2. 5:36. 10:25, 38. 14:11, 12. Ac 2:22. 4:9, 10. **the lame.** Mt 15:30, 31. 21:14. Is ♪35:6. Ac 3:2-8. 14:8-10. **the lepers.** Mt 8:1-4. 10:8. 26:6. 2 K 5:7, 14. Mk 1:42. Lk 5:12, 13. 17:12. **the deaf.** Is ♪29:18, 19. ♪42:18. 43:8. Mk 7:35, 37. 9:25. **the dead.** Mt 9:24, 25. Is ♪26:19n. Mk 5:21-24, 35-43. Lk 7:14-16, 22. 8:40-42, 49-56. Jn √11:43, 44. **the poor.** Mt +*5:3. Ps 22:26. 72:12, 13. Is 61:1-3. 66:2. Je 52:16. Zc 11:7. Lk *4:18. 6:20. Ja *2:5. **gospel preached.** Is ♪61:1. 1 C 1:26.

6. **blessed.** Mt 5:3-12. Ps 1:1, 2. 32:1, 2. 119:1. Lk 11:27, 28. **whosoever.** Mt *13:55-57. 15:12-14. 17:27. 18:7. *21:44. *24:10. *26:31. Is *8:14, 15. Mk 6:3. Lk *2:34. 4:23-29. Jn 6:60, 61, 66. 7:41, 42. Ro *9:32, 33. 1 C *1:22-24. √2:14. Ga 5:11. 1 P *2:7, 8. **shall.** lit. may. ♪96B. Heterosis of Moods B513: subjunctive for indicative. For other instances of this figure see Jn 15:8. 1 C 6:4. Ja 4:13, 15.

7. **Jesus.** Lk 7:24-30. **What.** ♪85D, Ps +25:12. Mt *3:1-3, 5. 21:25. Mk 1:3-5. Lk 1:80. 3:3-7. 8:18. Jn 1:38. 5:35. **A reed.** Ge 49:4. 1 K 14:15. 2 K 18:21. Is 36:6. Ezk 29:6, 7. 2 C 1:17, 18. Ep +*4:14. Ja 1:6.

8. **what went.** ♪18, Dt +28:4. ♪85D, Ps +25:12. **A man.** Mt 3:4. 2 K 1:8. Is 20:2. Zc 13:4. Mk 1:6. 1 C 4:11. 2 C 11:27. Re 11:3. **wear soft.** 1 K 10:5. 2 Ch 9:4.

9. **what.** ♪85D, Ps +25:12. **A prophet.** ver. 13, 14. Mt *14:5. 17:12, 13. *21:24-26. Mk 6:20. 9:11-13. 11:32. Lk *1:15-17, 76. 20:6. **yea.** ♪69B, Pr +6:16.

10. **this is he.** Ps +*83:18. Lk +*1:76. **of whom.** Mt *3:3. Is *40:3. 57:14. Ml *♪3:1. 4:5. Mk 1:2, 4. Lk 1:17, 76. 7:26, 27. +*24:27. Jn 1:23. **Behold.** ♪92A, Mt +1:23.

11. **born.** ♪142, Ge +20:16. Jb 14:1, 4. 15:14. 25:4. Ps 51:5. Ga 4:4. Ep 2:3. **a greater.** Mt 3:11. 1 S *2:30. Lk 1:15. *7:28. Jn *5:35. **risen.** Lk 7:16. Jn 7:52. Ac 13:22. **he that.** Mt 5:19. Is 30:26. Zc 12:8. Lk 9:48. Jn 1:15, 27. 3:30. 1 C 6:4. 15:9. Ep 3:8. **kingdom of heaven.** Mt 4:17. **greater.** Since John was clearly a divinely inspired man, which is not true of any of us in this day, we must take care not to injudiciously apply this statement to ourselves. It does not mean that we are now greater than John the Baptist. Rather, this refers to the kingdom Christ will establish at the Second Advent, when we will be greater than John the Baptist was in Jesus' day. No doubt John the Baptist will, in that future time, be greater than ourselves (See Peters, *Theocratic Kingdom*, vol. 1, pp. 253, 254). Mt *13:16, 17, 43. Ps *16:11. 68:13. 89:15-17. *91:11. Is 35:10. Da *12:3. Ml 3:17. Jn *7:39. *10:41. Ro +*8:19. 16:25, 26. Col 1:26, 27. 2 T 1:10. He 11:40. 1 P 1:10. 4:13.

12. **from.** Mt 21:23-32. Lk 7:29, 30. *13:24. 16:16. Jn *6:27. Ep 6:11-13. Ph 2:12. **kingdom of heaven.** Mt 4:17. **suffereth violence, and the violent take.** or, is gotten by force, and they that thrust men take, etc. Je 13:22mg. Lk 16:16g. **take it by force.** Pr 12:24. +13:4. 14:23. Is +*60:8, 11. Da 7:18. Am 5:9. Lk 5:1. 13:24. *16:16n. Jn 6:15.

13. **all the prophets.** Mt +*5:17, 18. Ml 4:6. Lk *24:27, 44. Jn 5:46, 47. Ac 3:22-24. 10:43. 13:27. Ro 3:21. **and the law.** Lk *16:16. He 10:1. **until John.** Dt *18:18. Jn *1:29, 45.

14. **if.** ♪185C. Emphatic Concession. Grammatically this is a concessive clause; Burton (*Moods and Tenses*, p. 114, sec. 282) gives Lk 6:32, 33, 34; Jn 8:55, etc., as parallel examples of this grammatical structure, where the sense is simply "and if." Dana and Mantey (*Manual Grammar*, p. 292, sec. 278) cite this text under "Emphatic Concession," with the explanation "This type of clause expresses concession with the added thought that the supposed assumption has no likelihood of fulfillment," furnishing Ga 1:8 as an additional example. Robertson (*Grammar*, p. 1026) follows Burton, giving the additional examples of Mk 16:18 and Re 11:5, but in the same paragraph does state "With *kai ei* the supposition is considered improbable." For other instances of this construction see Jn 8:16. 1 C 4:7. 7:11. **ye will.** Ezk 2:5. 3:10, 11. Jn 16:12. 1 C 3:2. **receive.** Pr 4:10. Zc 1:6. Lk 8:13g. Ac 8:14g. 11:1g. 13:48. +*17:11. 1 C 2:14g. 2 C 8:17g. 1 Th 1:6g. √2:13g. 2 Th √2:10g. Ja *1:21g. **this.** Mt *17:10-13. Ml 4:5. Mk 9:11-13. Lk 1:17. Jn 1:21-23. Re *20:4. **Elias.** i.e. *Greek form of Elijah*, *S#2243g. Mt 11:14. 16:14. 17:3, 4, 10, 11, 12. 27:47, 49. Mk 6:15. 8:28. 9:4, 5, 11, 12, 13. 15:35, 36. Lk 1:17. 4:25, 26. 9:8, 19, 30, 33, 54. Jn 1:21-23, 25. Ro 11:2. Ja 5:17. For *S#452h, see 1 K +17:1. ♪32, Antonomasia. Bengel notes "The absence of the article shows an *antonomasia*. That is, not this is literally *Elias*, but is like him in office; is the *Elias* of the New Testament... John is called Elias on account of the office of forerunner, which he had in common with the Tishbite" (*Word Studies*, vol. 1, p. 168). For other instances of this figure see Ge +31:21. This text does not furnish any material which supports reincarnation, for the Bible does not contain the concept of reincarnation, but everywhere teaches bodily resurrection (Jb +7:9. +16:22. Is 43:10n. Da +*12:2. He +*9:27) of the righteous and unrighteous (Jn 5:28, 29), separated by the millennium (Re 20:5, 11-15). The Bible clearly teaches death is followed by the judgment (He +*9:27), not reincarnation. There is no second opportunity after this life to choose eternal life (Mt 12:32. Ec 1:15. Da +*12:10. Jn √3:36. 1 C 15:16-23. 2 C *5:11. 6:2. He 6:4-6. +*9:27. Re *22:11). Mt 17:10-13. Ml 4:5. Mk 9:11-13. Lk 1:17. Jn ◐√1:21. **which was.** Mt 17:9-13. Ml *3:1. *4:5, 6. Mk 9:13. Lk 1:15-17, 76, 77. 7:37.

15. **He that.** ♪74, Jg +5:31. **hath ears.** Mt 13:9, 43. Mk 4:9, 23. 7:16. Ezk 3:27. Lk 8:8. 14:35. Re 2:7, 11, 17, 29. 3:6, 13, 22. 13:9. **to hear.** ♪147A, Ge +50:24.

16. **whereunto.** La 2:13. Mk 4:30. Lk 13:18, 20. **this.** Mt 12:34. 23:36. 24:34. **It is.** Lk 7:31-35. **markets.** Je 5:1. Lk 11:43. **fellows.** Mt +20:13g.

17. **We.** Is 28:9-13. 1 C 9:19-23. **piped.** Mt 9:15, 23. 1 K 1:40. Is 30:29. Je 9:17-20. 31:4. Lk 15:25. **ye have not.** Pr 29:9. **danced.** ♪134, Mt +3:9. The figure *Parachesis* is seen by the Syriac, referring to which the Lord doubtless used. There we see a beautiful example of *Paronomasia*, for the word "danced" would be *rakedton*, and the word "lamented" would be *arkedton*. ♪139. Paromoeosis; or, Like-Sounding Inflections B178. The repetition of inflections similar in sound. Here, the Greek words underlying the English "danced" and "lamented" end with the same inflection,

"sasthe." The language of Syria, which Christ probably used, would have been *rakedtoon* and *arkedtoon*, words similar in sound from the same root, differing only in the conjugation. For other instances of this figure see Jn 1:5. (10:1). 1 C 1:23, 24. **mourned.** 2 S 1:17. Lk 8:52. **lamented.** Mt 24:30. Je 5:3. Na 2:7. Lk 8:52. 23:27.

18. **John.** Mt 3:4. Je 15:17. 16:8, 9. Da 10:3. Mk 1:6. 1 C 9:27. **came.** *ʃ*18, Dt +28:4. **neither.** *ʃ*63A2, 2 S +6:6. By ellipsis (absolute: of accusative), supply "John came neither eating (with others) nor drinking (strong drink)" or "John came (declining invitations) to eat and drink" (B12). **eating.** *ʃ*108B, Pr +31:4. **nor drinking.** Lk *1:15. **He.** Mt 10:25. 2 K 9:11. Je 29:26. Ho 9:7. Jn 7:20. 8:48. 10:20. Ac 26:24.

19. **Son of man.** Mt 8:20. **came.** Lk *5:29, 30. 7:34, 36. 14:1. Jn *2:2. 12:2, etc. Ro 15:2. **eating and.** *ʃ*108B, Pr +31:4. Mt *9:10. Lk 7:36. 14:1. Jn *2:2. *12:2. **a friend.** *ʃ*60B, Ge +20:16. *S5384g. Lk 7:6, 34. 11:5, 5, 6, 8. 12:4. 14:10, 12. 15:6, 9, 29. 16:9. 21:16. 23:12. Jn 3:29. 11:11. 15:13, 14, 15. 19:12. Ac 10:24. 19:31. 27:3. Ja 2:23. 4:4. 3 J 14. **publicans.** Mt 5:46. 18:17. 21:31, 32. Lk +3:12. **and sinners.** Mt 9:10, 11. Mk 2:15, 16. Lk 5:30. 7:34. 15:1, 2. 19:7. **But wisdom.** *ʃ*88, Ge +15:15. Ps 92:5, 6. Pr 8:1-36. *17:24. Lk 11:49. 1 C 1:24-29. Ep 3:8-10. Re 5:11-14. 7:12. is **justified.** Ps +*51:4. Lk *7:29, 35. Ro *3:4. *11:33. 1 C √2:14, 15. **her children.** Pr 8:32. Lk 7:35. 10:6. +*16:8.

20. **began.** Lk 10:13-15. **upbraid.** Ps 81:11-13. Is 1:2-5. Mi 6:1-5. Mk 9:19. 16:14. Ja +*1:5. **wherein.** Jn 20:30. **because.** Mt 12:41. 21:28-32. Je 8:6. Lk 5:32. Ac *17:30. 2 T +*2:25, 26. Re 2:21. 9:20, 21. 16:9, 11.

21. **Woe.** *ʃ*110, Ezk +34:2. Mt 18:7. 23:13-29. 26:24. Je 13:27. Lk 10:12-15. 11:42-52. Ju 11. **Chorazin.** *ʃ*121J19, 1 S +22:19. i.e. *woody places*, *S#5523g. Lk 10:13. **Bethsaida.** Mk 6:45. 8:22. Lk *9:10. Jn 1:44. 12:21. **for if.** ver. 23n. Mt 12:41, 42. Ezk 3:6, 7. Lk 11:31, 32. Ac 13:44-48. 28:25-28. *ʃ*184B. Hypothetical Propositions; or, conditional ("if") sentences: the Second Condition; or, contrary to fact or impossible, dealing with past time. For other instances of the Second Condition see Mt 12:7. Mk 13:20. Lk 12:39. Jn 11:21, 32. 14:7, 28. 18:30. Ro 9:29. 1 C 2:8. 1 J √2:19. **mighty works.** Is +*9:6. 10:21. 49:26. 60:16. Je 32:18. Lk 9:43. Ep 1:21. Re 7:10, 12. **Tyre.** i.e. *to distress*, *S#5184g. Mt 11:21, 22. 15:21. Mk 3:8. 7:24, 31. Lk 6:17. 10:13, 14. Ac 21:3, 7. For *S#6865h, see 1 K +7:13. **and.** ver. +22. Mt 15:21. Je 25:22. 47:4. Ezk 28:2-24. Am 1:9, 10. Mk 3:8. 7:24, 31. Lk 6:17. 10:13, 14. Ac 12:20. **Sidon.** i.e. *hunting, fishery*, *S#4605g. Mt 11:21, 22. 15:21. Mk 3:8. 7:24, 31. Lk 4:26. 6:17. 10:13, 14. Ac 27:3. For *S#6721h, see Ge +10:19. **repented.** Jb 42:6. Jon 3:5-10. **sackcloth.** Ge +*37:34. 1 K 20:31. Da +9:3. Re 11:3. **ashes.** Est 4:1. Jon 3:6.

22. **more tolerable.** ver. 24. Mt 10:15. *23:14. Ps 86:13. Lk 10:14. +*12:47, 48. He *2:3. 6:4-8. *10:26-31. **Tyre.** Is ch. 23. Je 25:22. 27:3. Ezk ch. 26-28. 29:18. Am 1:9, 10. Zc 9:2, 3. **the day.** Mt +*10:15n. 12:36, 41, 42. 23:33. Lk 10:12, 14. 11:31, 32. Jn *3:17-19. *5:29. 12:31. 16:8. Ac √17:31. 24:25. 1 C 3:13. 1 T 5:24. He +*9:27. 2 P *2:4, 9. 3:7. 1 J 4:17. Ju 6. Re 14:7.

23. **Capernaum.** *ʃ*121J19, 1 S +22:19. Mt *4:13.

8:5. 17:24. Lk 4:23. Jn 4:46, etc. **which art.** Ge 11:4. Dt 1:28. Is *14:13-15. La 2:1. Ezk 28:12-19. 31:16, 17. Ob 4. Lk 14:11. 2 P 2:4-9. **exalted.** *ʃ*102, Ge +2:24. **brought down.** Is 14:15. La 2:1. Ezk 26:20. 31:14, 16, 17. 32:18, 24. **hell.** Gr. *hades*, *S#86g. Mt 11:23. 16:18. Lk 10:15. +*16:23. Ac 2:27, 31. 1 C 15:55mg. Re 1:18. 6:8. 20:13, 14. **for if.** *ʃ*184B, ver. +21. A statement such as this argues strongly against absolute predestination, for our Lord himself states that had Sodom witnessed his mighty works, it would not have been destroyed, for it would have repented (ver. 21). Thus things could and would turn out in a different manner if different choices had been made. Clearly the will and decision of individual men is involved in the ultimate issue of events. Our Lord argues that this is one basis and reason for there being degrees of punishment in eternity (ver. 24. Ezk 18:*4n, 20n. Lk +*12:47, 48). ver. 14 w Ml 4:5. Mt 23:39. 1 S 13:13, 14. 2 K 13:19. Ps 81:13, 14. 1 S +*30:15. Je 23:22. 51:9. Ezk √3:6. Da 3:18. Jl 2:28n. Lk 4:23. *13:34. 19:42. **in Sodom.** Mt 10:15. Ge 13:13. 19:24, 25. Ezk +*16:48-50. Lk 10:12. 17:29. Ro 9:29. 2 P 2:6. Ju √7. Re 11:8. **done in thee.** Lk 4:23.

24. **more tolerable.** ver. 14. Mt +*10:15n. La 4:6. Ezk +*16:49. Mk 6:11. Lk *10:12. +*12:47, 48. He *2:3. +*10:26-29. Ju √7. **land of Sodom.** ver. 23. Ge 18:20. 19:28. **day of judgment.** T#383, ver. +*22. Mt +*10:15n. Ps 50:3-6. Ac *17:31. 24:25. Ro 14:10, 11. 2 C 5:10. 2 T 4:1. He +*9:27. 2 P 3:7. Ju 6. Re √20:12.

25. **At that time.** *ʃ*49, Jn +10:22. **Jesus.** Lk 10:21, etc. **answered and.** *ʃ*171J11, Jb +3:1. *ʃ*108H1. Idiom B837. "Answered and said" was used by Hebrew idiom of whatever kind of speech is in question, whether denoting "*prayed* and said," "*asked* and said," "*addressed* and said," etc. Other instances of this idiom may be seen at Mk √11:14 and Mk 12:35. Mt 17:4. 22:1. 24:2. 28:5. Mk 11:14. Ac 3:12. **said.** Mk 1:35. **I thank.** 1 Ch 29:13. Da 2:23. Lk *10:21. Jn 11:41. Ro 6:17. 14:11. 15:9. 2 Th *2:13, 14. **Lord.** Ge 14:19, 22. Dt 10:14, 15. 2 K 19:15. Is 66:1. Da 4:35. Ac 17:24. **because.** Mt 13:11-16. Is 5:21. 29:10-14, 18, 19. Mk 4:10-12. Jn 7:48, 49. 9:39-41. 12:38-40. Ro 11:8-10. 1 C 1:18-29. *2:6-8. 3:18-20. 2 C 3:14. 4:3-6. **hast hid.** √*ʃ*108A4, Ge +31:7. 2 C 3:14. *4:3, 4. **the wise.** Jb 37:24. Is 5:21. 29:14. Ro 1:22. 1 C *1:18-27. *3:18. **and hast revealed.** Mt *13:11. *16:17. +*18:3, 4. 21:16. 1 S 2:18. 3:4-21. Ps *8:2. *19:7. 25:9, 12. Pr +*8:9. Is +√8:20n. 61:1. Je 1:5-8. Mk 10:14-16. Lk 8:10. 1 C *1:26, 27. **unto babes.** Lk 9:47. 1 C 14:20. 1 P 2:2.

26. **for so.** Jb *33:13. Ps +*115:3. Is 46:10. Ro +*9:18. *11:33-36. 1 C 1:21. Ep 1:9, +*11. 3:11. 2 T *1:9. **seemed good.** Mt 18:14. Lk 12:32. Ga 1:15. He 13:21.

27. **are.** Mt 28:18. Jn *3:35. *5:21-29. *13:3. √17:2. 1 C *15:25-27. Ep *1:20-23. Ph 2:10, 11. He *1:2. *2:8-10. 1 P 3:22. Re 2:27. **no man.** 1 S=6:19. Lk *10:22. Jn *1:18. ◐2:25. 6:46. *10:15. Col=2:18. **knoweth.** Gr. *epiginosko*, *S#1921g. Rendered (1) know: Mt 7:16, 20. 11:27, 27. 17:12. Mk 5:30. 6:33, 54. Lk 1:4. 7:37. 23:7. 24:16, 31. Ac 3:10. 9:30. 12:14. 19:34. 22:24, 29. 25:10. 27:39. 28:1. Ro 1:32. 1 C 13:12, 12. 2 C 13:5. Col 1:6. 1 T 4:3. 2 P 2:21, 21. (2) acknowledge: 1 C 14:37. 16:18. 2 C 1:13, 13, 14. (3) perceive: Mk 2:8. Lk 1:22. 5:22. (4) take knowledge of: Ac 4:13.

24:8. (5) have knowledge of: Mt 14:35. (6) know well: 2 C 6:9. As a strengthened form of *ginosko, epiginosko* has the sense of know well or thoroughly, not merely to be acquainted with, knowledge "which has a powerful influence on the one who possesses it" (EWB, *Foundations of Dispensational Truth*, p. 120fn). Compare *oida*, Jn 8:55n. **but the Father.** Mt 24:36. **neither.** Jn *1:18. 6:46. 7:29. 8:19. 10:15. *14:6-9. 17:2, 3, *6, 25, 26. 1 J 2:23. *5:19, 20. 2 J 9. **whomsoever.** Mt 22:14. Dt +10:15. Mk 4:11. Jn 17:9, 26. Ac +*13:48. 2 T +*2:25.

28. **Come.** Mt 12:20. Ge=45:18, 19. Ex 3:10. 2 Ch 10:4. Is *45:22-25. *53:2, 3. +*55:1-3. Jn 5:40. √6:37. 7:37. 10:27, 28. Re *22:17. **all.** Mt *23:4. Ge 3:17-19. Ex=2:11. =5:5. Jb *5:7. *14:1. Ps 32:4. *38:4. *90:7-10. Ec 1:8, 14. *2:22, 23. *4:8. Is *1:4. *61:3. *66:2. Mi +*6:6-8. Lk 11:46. Ac 13:39. *15:10. Ro *7:22-25. Ga *5:1. **and I.** ver. *29. Ru 2:12. Ps 94:13. *116:7. Is 11:10. 14:3. *28:12. *48:17, 18. Je *6:16. 31:25. Lk 10:42. 2 Th 1:7. He *4:1.

29. **my yoke.** Mt 7:24. *17:5. Nu=7:9. Je ●9:5. 31:18. La 3:27. Ho 11:4. Jn *13:17. *14:21-24. *15:10-14. Ac 15:10. 1 C 9:21. 2 C *10:5. Ga 5:1. 1 Th 4:2. 2 Th *1:8. He *5:9. **and learn.** T#887. ver. *27. Mt 23:8. *28:20. Lk *6:46-48. *8:35. *10:39-42. Jn *13:15. Ac *3:22, 23. 7:37. Ep *4:20, 21. Ph *2:5. 1 J *2:6. **for I am.** T#62. Mt +5:5. +10:16 (T#660). *12:19, 20. *21:5. Nu 12:3. Ps 131:1. Is *42:1-4. 50:6. 53:7. Zc +*9:9. Mk 15:4, 5. Lk 9:51-56. 23:34. 2 C *10:1. Ph *2:+3 (T#482), 7, 8. Ja +1:4 (T#498). 1 P *2:20-23. **meek.** ſ134, Mt +3:9. The words "meek" and "rest" in the Syriac exhibit paronomasia, "I am *neech* and *v'eneechkon*" (B322). Nu=12:3. **and ye.** ver. *28. Ps *116:7. Is *28:12. Je *●6:16. Lk +*24:27. He *4:3-11. **find rest.** Ps *119:165. Is ●48:22. Ro ●7:23. Ph *4:7. 2 T *1:7. **souls.** Gr. *psyche*, ſ121A9A. Metonymy of Cause. Lk 1:46. 2:35. Ac 14:2, 22. 15:24. Here the *psyche* may be regarded as the seat of perception, feeling, desire. Ps 84:2. 139:14. Is 26:9. For the other uses of *psyche*, see Mt +2:20n. For other instances of ſ121A9, see Ge +23:8.

30. **my yoke.** Pr *3:13, 17. Mi +*6:8. Ac 15:10, 28. Ga 5:*1, 13, 18. 1 P *2:24. 1 J *5:3. **burden.** Mt ●23:4. Ps ●*38:4. Lk ●11:46. Jn 16:33. Ac 27:10g. Ro *7:23-25. *10:3, 4. 2 C *1:4, 5. *4:17. *12:9, 10. Ga 6:5. Ph *4:13.

MATTHEW 12

The disciples pluck ears of corn to eat, on the sabbath, 1. Christ vindicates them from the charge of breaking the sabbath, 2-8; heals the withered hand of one in the synagogue; and shows it lawful to do good on the sabbath, 9-13. The Pharisees seek to kill him; he withdraws, yet works miracles, and so fulfills a prophecy of Isaiah, 14-21. He casts out a devil from a dumb and blind man, 22, 23; confutes the charge of the Pharisees, of casting out devils by Beelzebub, 24-30; and shows the sin against the Holy Ghost to be unpardonable, and that every idle word must be accounted for, 31-37. He rebukes those who sought a sign, and will give none but that of Jonah, 38-40. The Ninevites, and the queen of the south, will condemn that generation, 41, 42. By a parable he shows their awful state, 43-45. His disciples are his most endeared relations, 46-50.

1. **At that time.** Mt 11:25. **went.** Mk 2:23-28. Lk 6:1-5. **to pluck.** Dt *23:25.

2. **Behold.** ver. 10. Ex 20:9-11. 23:12. 31:15-17. 35:2. Nu 15:32-36. Is +√58:13n, 14. Mk 3:2-5. Lk 6:6-11. 13:10-13, +*14n, 15-17. 14:3. 23:56. Jn 5:9-11, 16, 17. 7:21-24. 9:14-16. Col √2:16.

3. **Have ye not read.** ver. 5. Mt 19:4. 21:16. 22:31. Mk 12:10, 26. Lk 6:3. 10:26. **what David.** 1 S *21:3-6. Mk 2:25, 26.

4. **the showbread.** Ex *25:30. 40:23. Le *24:5-9. 1 K 7:48. 1 Ch 9:32. 23:29. 2 Ch 4:19. Ne 10:33. He 9:2. **but only.** Ex 29:32, 33. Le 8:31. 24:9.

5. **on the sabbath.** Nu *28:9, 10. 1 Ch 9:32. Lk 10:26. Jn 7:22, 23. **profane.** ſ46A, Le +26:30. Ne 13:17. Ezk 24:21.

6. **in this place.** ver. 8, 41, 42. Mt 23:17-21. 2 Ch 6:18. Hg 2:7-9. Ml 3:1. Jn *2:19-21. Ep *2:20-22. Col √2:9. 1 P 2:4, 5.

7. **if.** ſ184B, Mt +11:21. Mt *9:13. 22:29. Ac 13:27. **what this.** Lk +*24:27. **I will.** That is, I desire, or require mercy, or acts of humanity, rather than sacrifice. Mt 23:23. 1 S *15:22. Pr *21:3. Ec 5:1. Is *1:11-17. Ho ▶6:6. Mi +*6:6-8. Mk 12:33. He *13:16. **and not.** ſ96E1, Ps +118:8. i.e. rather than. **condemned.** Jb 32:3. Ps 94:21. 109:31. Pr 17:15. Ja 5:6.

8. **the Son of man.** Mt 8:20. **is Lord.** Mt 9:6. Mk 2:10, 28. 9:4-7. Lk 5:24. 6:5. Jn 5:17-23. 1 C 9:21. 16:2. Re 1:10. **the sabbath day.** Mt +*5:17, 18. Ge *2:3. Ex *16:22, 23, 29, 30. +*20:8-11. 23:12. 31:13-17. 34:21. 35:1-3. Le 19:3, 30. 23:3. 24:7, 8. Nu *15:32, 36. 28:9, 10. Dt +*5:12-15. Ne *9:14. *10:31. *13:15-22. Is 56:2, 6, 7. +√58:13n, 14. Je √17:21, 22, 24, 25, 27n. Ezk 12:12, 20. 22:8, 26. *46:1, 3. Mk *1:21. *2:27, 28. Lk +*4:16. 6:1-9. 13:10-13, +*14n, 15-17. 14:1-6. *23:56. Jn +*5:17, 18. 7:21-23. 9:14-16. √20:19, 26. Ac 13:14, 15, 44. *16:13. +*17:2. *18:4. √20:7. 1 C √16:2. He √4:4, 9. Re 1:10.

9. **he went.** Mk 3:1-5. Lk 6:6-11.

10. **which.** 1 K 13:4-6. Zc 11:17. Jn 5:3. **Is it lawful.** Mt 19:3. 22:17, 18. Lk 13:10-14. 14:3-6. 20:22. Jn 5:10. 9:16. **that.** Ex 23:4, 5. Dt 22:4. Is 32:6. 59:4, 13. Lk 6:6, 7. 11:54. 20:20. 23:2, 14. Jn 8:6.

11. **What man.** This was an *argumentum ad hominem*. The Jews held that such things were lawful on the sabbath day, and our Savior very properly appealed to their canons in vindication of his intention to heal the distressed man. Lk 13:15-17. 14:5. **and if.** ſ184C, Mt +4:9. Ex 23:4, 5. Dt 22:4.

12. **is a man better.** Mt 6:26. 10:31. Lk 12:24. **Wherefore.** ſ150, Mt +9:13. **it is lawful.** Mk 3:4. Lk 6:9. 14:3. Jn 5:16, 17.

13. **Stretch forth.** 1 K ●13:4. **and it.** Lk 13:13. Ac 3:7, 8.

14. **the Pharisees.** Mt 21:46. Mk *3:6. Lk *6:11. Jn 5:18. 7:1, 19. 10:39. 11:53, 57. **went out.** ver. 9. Mt 27:1. **held a council.** or, took counsel. Mt 22:15. 26:4. 27:1, 7. 28:12. Mk 15:1. Jn 11:53. 12:10. **destroy.** Gr. *apollumi*, Mt +2:13.

15. **he withdrew.** Mt *10:23. 14:13. Pr +*22:3. Is ✦42:2. Lk 6:12. Jn 7:1, 6, 8, 30. 8:20. 10:39-42. 11:54. **great multitudes followed.** Mt 4:24, 25. 19:2. Mk 3:7-12. 6:56. Lk 6:17-19. Jn 9:4. Ga 6:9. 1 P 2:21. **healed them all.** Mt +*4:23. +*8:16. 14:14. 15:30. Ps +*103:3. Mk 1:34. 3:10. Lk 4:40, 41. 5:17. 7:22. 9:11. 10:9. Ac 5:15, 16. *10:38.

16. **charged them.** Mt 8:4. 9:30. 16:20. 17:9. Mk

1:25, 34. 3:12. 7:36. 8:30. Lk 4:41. 5:14, 15. 9:21.

17. it might. Mt 8:17. 13:35. 21:4. Is 41:22, 23. 42:9. 44:26. Lk 21:22. 24:44. Jn 10:35. 12:38. 19:28. Ac 13:27. **saying.** Is 42:1-4.

18. Behold. ♪92A, Mt +1:23. ♪92D1, Mt +2:15. ♪92E, Mt +4:10. This prophecy is expressly referred to the Messiah by the Targumist, who renders, "Behold my servant the Messiah," etc. *ha audi mesheecha*; and it was amply fulfilled in the gentle, lowly, condescending, and beneficent nature of Christ's miracles and personal ministry, his perseverance in the midst of opposition, without engaging in contentious disputation, and his kind and tender dealing with weak and tempted believers. Is ▶42:1-3. Lk +*24:27. **my servant.** Ps=105:26. Is 41:8. 43:10. 49:5, 6. 52:13. 53:11. Ezk 34:24. Zc 3:8. Ac 3:26. 4:27, 30. Ph *2:6, 7. He *5:5. **whom I have chosen.** Ps 89:19. Is 49:1-3. Lk *9:35. 23:35. 1 P *2:4. **my beloved.** Mt *3:17. 17:5. Mk 1:11. 9:7. Lk *9:35. Ep 1:6. Col 1:1, 13mg. 2 P 1:17. **my soul.** ♪22A1, Le +26:11n. Gr. *psyche.* ♪171Q2. Figure of speech Synecdoche of the Part. The expression "my soul," "his soul," etc. becomes by Synecdoche the idiom for *me, myself, himself*, etc. *Psyche* is used to emphasize the personal pronoun in the first person, as at Mt 26:38. Mk 14:34. Lk 12:19, 19. Jn 10:24 (us). 12:27. 2 C 1:23. He 10:38 (soul). For the other uses of *psyche* see Mt +2:20n. For other instances of ♪171Q2, see Nu +23:10. **well pleased.** Is *53:11. **I will put.** Mt 3:16. Is *11:2. 59:20, 21. *61:1-3. Lk 3:22. *4:18. Jn 1:32-34. *3:34. Ac *10:38. Col *2:9. **spirit.** Gr. *pneuma*, ♪121A, Lk +1:17n. **and he shall.** Is +*2:4. 32:15, 16. *49:6. *60:2, 3. 62:2. Je 16:19. Lk 2:31, 32. Ac 11:18. 13:46-48. 14:27. 26:17, 18. Ro *15:9-12. Ep 2:11-13. 3:5-8.

19. not strive. Mt +*11:29. Is ✱▶42:2. Zc +*9:9. Lk 17:20. Jn 18:36-38. 2 C 10:1. 2 T 2:24, 25.

20. bruised. Mt +*11:28. 2 K 18:21. Ps 51:17. 147:3. Is 36:6. 40:11. ✱▶42:3. +*57:15. 58:5. +*61:1-3. La 3:31-34. Ezk 34:16. Lk *4:18. 2 C 2:7. 2 T *2:24. He 12:12, 13. **not quench.** Is 43:17. **till he.** Ps 98:1-3. Is 42:3, 4. Ro 15:17-19. 2 C 2:14. 10:3-5. Re 6:2. 19:11-21. **judgment.** Zc *9:9. **unto victory.** Jn *18:36. 1 C *15:54.

21. in his name. Ps *98:1-3. Is 11:10. *42:4. Lk +*24:27. Ro *15:12, 13. Ep 1:12, 13. Col 1:27.

22. Then was. Mt 9:32. Mk *3:11. Lk 9:1. 11:14. **possessed.** Mt 4:24. **he healed.** Mk 7:35-37. 9:17-26. **blind.** Ps 51:15. Is 29:18. 32:3, 4. 35:5, 6. Ac 26:18. **and saw.** Lk 7:21.

23. the people. Mt 9:33. 15:30, 31. **were amazed.** Lk 2:47. **Is not.** Mt 9:27. 15:22. 21:9. 22:42, 43. Is *11:1. Jn 4:29. 7:26, 31, 40-42. **son.** ♪171G, Ge +13:8.

24. when. Mt 9:34. Mk 3:22. Lk 11:15. **Pharisees heard.** Mt 9:34. Mk ●1:24. 3:22. **Beelzebub.** Gr. Beelzebul, and so ver. 27. Mt 10:25. 2 K 1:2, 3, 6. Mk 3:22. Lk 11:15, 18, 19. **the prince.** Mt 9:34. Jn 12:31. 14:30. 16:11. Ep 2:2.

25. Jesus knew their thoughts. Mt 9:4. Ps 139:2. Je +*17:10. Am 4:13. Mk 2:8. 3:24. Lk 11:17. Jn +*2:24, 25. 21:17. 1 C +*2:11. He +*4:13. Re *2:23. **Every kingdom.** ♪138B, Ge +13:16. Is 9:21. 19:2, 3. Mk 3:23-26. Lk 11:17, 18. Ga 5:15. Re 16:19. 17:16, 17. **divided.** T#114. Ac +*4:32 (T#111). Ro 16:17, 18. 1 C 1:11-13. 3:3, 4. 12:24-27. Ga 5:15. 1 J 3:14, 15. 4:20. Ju 18, 19.

26. And if. ♪184A, 1 C +15:2. Mk *3:23, 25, 26.

Lk *11:18. **Satan.** 1 C 5:5. **how.** ♪85C, Ge +18:14. **his.** Jn 12:31. 14:30. 16:11. 2 C *4:4. Col 1:13. 1 J 5:19g. Re 9:11. 12:9. 16:10. 20:2, 3.

27. if I. ♪184A, 1 C +15:2. **by.** Mt +*6:2n. 10:25. 15:5, 14, 26. 16:18, 23. 18:28. 19:24. 23:3, 5, 13, 24, 25, 27. 24:28. 24:43. Mk 4:21. Lk 5:39. 11:8. 16:1-9. 18:5. 22:25. Ga 5:17. 1 J *4:4. **Beelzebub.** ver. 24. Lk 11:19. **by whom.** Mt √7:22. 1 S 16:23. Mk 9:38, 39. Lk 9:49, 50. 11:19. Ac *19:13-16. **your children.** 1 K 20:35. 2 K 2:3. 4:1, 38. 5:22. 6:1. 9:1. **they.** ver. 41, 42. Lk 19:22. Ro 3:19.

28. if. ♪184C, Mt +4:9. **I cast.** ver. 18. Mt 10:7, 8. Mk 16:17. Lk √11:20. Ac +*10:38. 1 J √3:8. **Spirit.** Gr. *pneuma*, Mt +3:16. **kingdom of God.** Mt *3:2. *6:33. *19:24. *21:31, 43. Is +*9:6, 7. Da *2:44. +*7:14. Mk +1:15. *11:10. Lk +*1:32, 33. +4:43. 9:2. 10:11. *11:20. 16:16. +√17:20, 21. Jn +3:3. Ac +*1:3, 6. Ro *14:17. Col +*1:13. He +*12:28. **is come.** Ge 6:13. Is 60:1. He 12:22. **unto you.** Jn *5:36.

29. how can. Is *49:24-26. *53:12. Mk 3:27. Lk *11:21, 22. 1 J √3:8. 4:4. Re 12:7-10. 20:1-3, 7-9. **except.** ♪184C, Mt +4:9. **bind the strong man.** He 2:14, 15. Re √20:2. **and then.** Jn *16:11.

30. not with me. Mt *6:24. Ex =32:26. Jsh 5:13. √24:15. 1 Ch 12:17, 18. Mk *9:40. Lk *9:50. *11:23. Jn 8:34, 44. *15:23. Ro 6:16. 1 C 10:17. 2 C *6:15, 16. 2 P 2:19. 1 J √2:19. 3:8. Re √3:15, 16. **is against.** T#487. 1 K *18:21. Mk ●9:40. Jn 3:17. Ga *1:9. Re *3:15. **gathereth.** Ge +*49:10. Ho 1:11. Jn *11:52.

31. All manner of sin. Is *1:18. √55:7. Ezk 33:11. Mk 3:28-30. Jn √6:37. Ac 13:38, 39. 1 T *1:13-15. He *6:4-6, etc. +*10:26, 29. 1 J √1:9. √2:1, 2. **and blasphemy.** *Blasphemy, blasphemia*, either from *blaptein tain phaman*, to hurt or blast the reputation, or from *ballein tais phamais*, to smite with words, or reports, when applied to men denotes injurious speaking, or calumny, and when used in reference to God signifies speaking impiously of his nature, attributes, and works. **but the blasphemy.** What the Holy Spirit did to prove the divinity of Christ's person and mission, the Pharisees turned into an argument to show that Christ was an impostor, and actuated by Satanic agency. Thus their sin consisted in the unreasonable and absurd rejection of the Son of God as the Savior of men, in opposition to the plain and unanswerable testimony of the Holy Spirit. This sin against the Holy Spirit is a rejection of the truth as it is revealed in the Divine Word, especially of that truth as it respects Christ and His salvation—this in disregard of many favorable opportunities to know the truth as it is in Christ and His Word—with severe and bitter feelings of aversion and hatred, peculiarly provoked by any distinct reference to the Holy Spirit and His work in either the inspired Word, or the Divine Savior whom it His office to honor (James Morgan, *The Scripture Testimony to the Holy Spirit*, pp. 144, 147). Le 24:16. Mk 3:28-30. Lk 12:10. Ac *5:3. 7:51. 1 J +*5:16. **shall be.** ♪96C9, Ge +2:10. **Ghost.** Gr. *pneuma*, Mt +3:16. **shall not be forgiven.** The sin against the Holy Ghost is unpardonable because of its own nature: it consists in the rejection of the way of salvation by Christ, in opposition to the fullest evidence, and the only evidence that shall ever be given (He 2:3). The sin against the Holy Spirit consists in continued impenitence and unbelief (He √10:26-29). It is not an act, but a habit. It is the calm, determined, and persevering rejection of Jesus

Christ, as the Savior of men, in opposition to all the testimony of His word and Spirit. Consequently in its nature it is incapable of forgiveness. No one who is afraid of having committed this sin has done so; for its very nature is to have no fear on that account. It is committed and continued in delightedly and knowingly, where it is committed at all. Fear is incompatible with its nature. Yet we need to be on our guard against this sin, lest we be betrayed into it. The progress of sin is rapid and dangerous. We need to be watchful against both the sins of the life and the sins of the heart. Apostasy may be nearer to any of us than we imagine (Ro 11:20. He +*3:12. 1 J 3:24). Cherish a sense of dependence on both the teaching and support of the Spirit. Through Him cleave unto Christ and ye shall be safe (See Morgan, *The Scripture Testimony to the Holy Spirit*, pp. 148-151).

32. whosoever. Mt 11:19. 13:55. Lk 7:34. *12:10. *23:34. Jn *7:12, 52. 9:24. Ac *3:14, 15, 19. 26:9-11. 1 T 1:13, 15. **the Son of man.** Mt 8:20. **it shall be forgiven.** Lk 23:34. Ac *8:18, 19, 22. 1 T *1:12, 13. **but whosoever.** Jn 7:39. He √6:4-6. √10:26-29. **speaketh against.** ſ73, Zc +1:5. That the Holy Spirit can be the subject of blasphemy (by attributing his miraculous works to Satan) proves him to be as much a person as the Son; and it proves him to be divine, because it shows that he may be sinned against, and so sinned against that the blasphemer shall not be forgiven. A person he must be, or he could not be blasphemed: a divine person he must be to constitute this blasphemy a sin against him in the proper sense, and of so malignant a kind as to place it beyond the reach of mercy (Watson, *Theological Institutes*, vol. i. p. 629, cited in McClintock and Strong, vol. iv. p. 309, article "Holy Ghost"). "These passages (Mt 12:31, 32. Mk 3:28, 29. Lk 12:10) at least imply beyond cavil the personality of the Holy Spirit, for sin and blasphemy can only be committed against persons" (T. Rees, *International Standard Bible Encyclopedia*, vol. 1, p. 486, article "Blasphemy"). Ge ◑+1:2. Lk +*3:22n. Jn 14:26. 16:13, 14. Ac 8:29, 39. 13:2. 15:28. 16:7. 20:28. 28:25. Ro 8:27. 1 C 2:10, 11. 12:8, 11. Ep 4:30. **Holy Ghost.** Mt +3:16. Jn 7:39. **it shall not.** ſ175B, Ge +21:16. God the Holy Spirit is immutable (Mt +*28:19n). Jb 36:13. Mk 3:29. Lk +12:10. 16:23-26. **in this.** Mk 10:30. Lk 16:8. Jn +√6:54n. Ep *1:21. **world.** Gr. *aion*, Mt +6:13. lit. "this age," as in Mt 13:22. Mk 4:19. Lk 16:8. 20:34. Jn +√6:54n. Ro 12:2. 1 C 1:20. 2:6, 8. 3:18. 2 C 4:4. Ep 1:21. 2:2. 6:12. 1 T 6:17. **the world to come.** Ezk 33:16n. Mk +*10:30. Jn +√6:54n. Ep *1:21. He 6:5. +*9:27.

33. make the tree good. Mt *23:26. Ezk *18:31. Am 5:15. Lk 11:39, 40. Ep *4:23, 24. Ja *4:8. **and his fruit good.** Mt 3:8-10. *7:16-20. Lk 3:9. *6:43, 44. Jn *15:4-7. Ja 3:12.

34. generation. Mt 3:7. *23:33. Ge 3:15. Lk 3:7. Jn √8:44. 1 J 3:10. **of vipers.** Ps 58:4. 140:3. **how.** Mt 7:11. 13:14, 15. 1 S 24:13. Jb *14:4. Ps 10:6, 7. *52:2-5. 53:1. 64:3-5. 120:2-4. 140:2, 3. Is *32:6. 59:4, 14. Je 7:2-5. Ro *3:10-14. Ja 3:5-8. **for out.** ſ138C, Ge +22:14. Mt 13:52. *15:18, 19. Mk 7:20-23. Lk 6:45. Jn 8:43. 12:39. Ro 8:7. Ep √4:29. **heart.** Pr +*4:23. Je +*17:9. **mouth speaketh.** Ps *37:30, 31. Pr 10:20, 21. *15:4, 23, 28. *16:23, 24. Col √4:6.

35. good man. Mt 5:37. *13:52. Ps *37:30, 31. Pr *10:20, 21. *12:6, 17-19. *15:4, 23, 28. *16:21-23.

*25:11, 12. Ep √4:29. Col √3:16. √4:6. **treasure.** ſ121.O, Ge +28:22. **and an.** ver. *34.

36. every. Ec *12:14. Ro *2:16. Ep *5:4-6, 11. Ju *14, 15. Re *20:12. **idle word. Rama argon,** i.e. *aergon*, from *a*, privative, and *ergon*, work, a word that produces no good effect, and is not calculated to produce any. ✻S#692g. Mt 12:36. 20:3, 6, 6. 1 T 5:13, 13. T 1:12 (slow). 2 P 1:8 (barren). "Discourse," says Dr. Doddridge, "tending to innocent mirth, to exhilarate the spirits, is not *idle discourse*; as the time spent in necessary recreation is not *idle time*." Ezk +*33:31. Ep *4:29, 31. Col *4:5, 6. **give account.** Mt √16:27. Ec 12:14. Ro *14:12. 1 P 4:5. ſ108B. Idiom B828. "To give account" means not simply to render a mere account, but to suffer the consequences of unrighteousness. For another instance of this idiom see 1 P 4:5. **day of judgment.** Mt +*10:15n. Ac √17:31.

37. For by. Mt 5:22. Pr *13:3. Ja *3:2-12. **justified.** Lk *19:22. Ro √10:10. Ja *2:21-25. **and by.** 1 T *5:13.

38. Master. Mt 22:24. **see a sign.** Mt *16:1-4. Mk *8:11, 12. Lk *11:16, 29. 23:8. Jn *2:18. *4:48. *6:30. 1 C *1:22.

39. wicked. ver. 45. Mt 16:4. Mk 8:38. Lk 11:29. **adulterous.** Mt 17:17. Nu 15:39. Ps 73:27. 106:39. Is *57:3. Ezk *16:26. 23:27. Ho *1:2. Mk 8:38. Ja √4:4. Re 2:20-22. **generation.** Mt 17:17. +*24:34. Mk 9:19. Lk 9:41. Ac 2:40. **no sign.** Mt 16:4. Lk 11:29, 30. **Jonas.** i.e. *dove*, ✻S#2495g. ver. 40, 41. Mt 16:4. Lk 11:29, 30, 32, 32. For ✻S#3124h, see Jon +1:1, Jonah.

40. For as. ſ92B. Gnome; or, Quotation B786. Where the original sense is modified in the quotation or reference. In this reference to Jon 1:17, the words are used with a new and different application. For other instances of this figure see Jn 3:14, 15. 19:36. Ep 5:31, 32. **Jonas.** Jon ▶1:17. 2:1. Lk 11:30. +*24:27. **three days.** ſ108H12, 1 S +30:12. **so shall.** Mt 16:21. 17:23. 27:40, 63, 64. Mk 8:31. Jn 2:19. **Son of man.** Mt 8:20. **three days and three nights.** This is an idiom which, like the shorter expression, "three days," can refer to any part of three days. Had Christ been in the tomb for a full three days, or 72 hours, it could not be said of him that he arose on the third day, but the fourth, contrary to the repeated statements of Scripture (Mt 16:21. 17:23. 20:19. Lk 24:7, 21, 46. 1 C +*15:4). It is clear that the expression "after three days" was not understood by the Jews to be a reference to a fourth day, as is clear from Mt √27:63, 64. Compare Mt 16:21 w Mk 8:31. Mk 10:34 w Lk 9:22. The chronology provided in Luke 23:50—24:3 is unanswerable: there is only the time from late Friday afternoon when "the sabbath drew on" (Mt 27:62. Lk 23:54), "the day before the sabbath" (Mk 15:42) when Jesus was buried (Lk 23:54), the sabbath on which the women rested (Lk 23:56), and early Sunday morning when the women went to the tomb (Lk 24:1). The two disciples on the road to Emmaus state specifically "and beside all this, today is the third day since these things were done" (Lk 24:21). Thus "three days and three nights" is an idiom (ſ108H12, Figure of Speech Idiom, 1 S +30:12n), perfectly understood as such by the Jews of that day (Mt √27:63, 64. Jn 2:19), the figure of speech ſ171T8, Synecdoche of the Part, where a part of a day is taken for a whole day, Jsh 5:11n. 1 S *30:12n. 1 K 16:8n. Est 4:16 w 5:1. **in the heart.** ſ144A7, Ex +15:8. Dt 4:11mg. Ps +*16:10. *63:9. Is 14:9. Jon

*2:1-6. Lk *16:23. 23:43. Jn √2:19-23. Ep *4:9. Re *6:9, 10.

41. **men.** Mt 11:20-24. Jon 1:2. Lk 10:12-15. *11:32. **of Nineveh.** Ge 10:+11, 12. 2 K 19:36. Is 37:37. Jon 1:2. *3:2-7. 4:11. Na 1:1. 2:8. 3:7. Zp 2:13. Lk 11:32. **rise.** ver. 42. Is 54:17. Je 3:11. Ezk 16:51, 52. Ro 2:27. He 11:7. **rise in judgment.** ver. 32. Mt +*10:15n. Ob +*21. Lk +*10:14. **this generation.** ver. 39, 45. Mt 16:4. 17:17. 23:36. **condemn it.** Je 3:11. Ro 2:27. **because.** Jon 3:5-10. **at.** Gr. *eis.* Used here in the sense of "because of," Ac +*2:38n, or "on the basis of." Mt +*26:28n. Mk +*1:4n. **behold.** ver. 6, 42. Jn 3:31. 4:12. √8:53-58. He √1:2, 3. 3:5, 6.

42. **queen.** 1 K 10:1, etc. 2 Ch 9:1, etc. Lk 11:31, etc. Ac 8:27, 28. **the judgment.** ver. 41. Mt +*10:15n. **shall condemn it.** ver. 41. Jn 3:19. **she came from.** Ps 2:8. 72:8. Zc 9:10. **to hear the wisdom.** 1 K 3:9, 12, 28. 4:29, 34. 5:12. 10:4, 7, 24. 2 Ch 1:7-12. 9:22. 1 C 1:22. **behold.** ver. 6, 41. Mt 3:17. 17:5. Is +*7:14. +*9:6, 7. *11:1-3. Jn *1:14, 18. 1 C *1:24. Ph √2:6, 7. Col √2:3, 9. 1 T *3:16. He √1:2-4.

43. **When.** ſ7, Allegory by continued Hypocatastasis, Ga +4:24. This is an *Allegory.* It is to be interpreted of the Jewish nation, as verse 45 declares. By application also it teaches the unclean spirit's going out of his own accord, and not being "cast out" (verse 28, 29). When he is "cast out," he never returns; but when he "goes out," he comes back; and finds only a "reformed character," instead of the Holy Spirit indwelling in the one who is born again (B750). Had there been no reality in demoniacal possessions, as some have supposed, our Lord would scarcely have appealed to a case of this kind here, to point out the real state of the Jewish people, and their approaching desolation. Had this been only a vulgar error, of the nonsense of which the learned scribes and wise Pharisees must have been convinced, the case, not being in point, because not true, must have been treated with contempt by the very people for whose conviction it was designed. **the unclean.** Mk 3:30. Lk 11:24. Ac 8:13. **spirit.** Gr. *pneuma,* Mt +8:16. **gone out.** Ro ◐8:11. 1 C ◐6:19, 20. **he walketh.** Jb *1:7. 2:2. 1 P *5:8. **dry places.** Ps 63:1. Is 13:21. 35:6, 7. 41:18. Je 2:6. Ezk 47:8-12. Am +*8:11-13. Re 18:2. **seeking rest.** Mt 8:29. Mk 5:7-13. Lk 8:28-32.

44. **my house.** ver. 29. Lk 11:21, 22. Jn 13:27. Ep 2:2. 1 J 4:4. **he findeth.** Mt 13:20-22. Ps 81:11, 12. Ho 7:6. Jn 12:6. 13:2. Ac 5:1-3. 8:18-23. 1 C 11:19. 2 Th √2:9-12. 1 T 6:4, 5, 9, 10. 1 J √2:19. Ju 4, 5. Re 13:3, 4, 8, 9.

45. **seven.** ver. 24. Mk 5:9. 16:9. Ep 6:12. **spirits.** Gr. *pneuma,* Mt +8:16. **more wicked.** ver. 39. Mt 23:15. Lk 7:21. **they enter.** Jn √13:27. **dwell there.** It is clear that God is a Spirit (Jn 4:24), yet He is a person. Satan is a spirit being, and he is a person. Evil spirits are likewise persons. To suggest that the Holy Spirit is not a person is to accord less to Him than is granted of angels, Satan, and wicked spirits. To suggest that a person cannot be said to indwell another person is contrary to the express language of Scripture: if Satan could "enter into" Judas (Lk 22:3) and "fill the heart" of Ananias (Ac 5:3), why cannot the Holy Spirit, as a Divine person, indwell believers? Ro 8:11. 1 C 6:19, 20. **and the last.** Mt 27:64. Lk 11:26. Jn *5:14. He √6:4-8. +*10:26-31, 39. 2 P √2:14-22. 1 J +*5:16, 17. Ju 10-13. **Even so.** And so it was;

for they became worse and worse, as if totally abandoned to diabolical influence, till the besom of destruction swept them away. Mt 21:38-44. 23:32-39. 24:34. Lk 11:49-51. 19:41-44. Jn 15:22-24. Ro 11:8-10. 1 Th 2:15, 16.

46. **yet talked.** Mk *3:21, 31-35. Lk *8:10, 19-21. **his mother.** Mt +*1:16. **his brethren.** Mt +*13:55. Mk +*6:3. Jn 2:12. *7:3, 5, 10. Ac 1:14. 1 C *9:5. Ga *1:19.

48. **Who is.** Mt 10:37. Dt 33:9. Mk 3:32, 33. Lk 2:49, 52. Jn 2:3, 4. 2 C 5:16.

49. **his disciples.** Mt 28:7. Mk 3:34. Jn 17:8, 9, 20. 20:17-20.

50. **shall do.** Mt √7:20, 21. 17:5. Mk 3:35. Lk +*8:21. 11:27, 28. Jn 6:29, 40. +*13:17. +*15:14. Ac 3:22, 23. √16:30, 31. *17:30. 26:20. Ga *5:6. 6:15. Col 3:11. He +*5:9. Ja +*1:21, 22. 1 P 4:2. 1 J 2:17. √3:23, 24. Re 22:14. **the will.** Mt *6:10. Ro √12:2. 1 Th *4:3. **the same.** Mt 25:40, 45. 28:10. Ps 22:22. Jn 20:17. Ro *8:29. He *2:11-17. **and sister.** SS 4:9, 10, 12. 5:1, 2. 1 C *9:5. 2 C 11:2. Ep *5:25-27. **and mother.** Jn 19:26, 27. 1 T 5:2.

MATTHEW 13

The parable of the sower, 1-9. The reason why Jesus taught by parables, 10-17. The parable explained, 18-23. The parable of the tares, 24-30; of the grain of mustard seed, 31, 32; of the leaven, 33. The scripture fulfilled in Christ's teaching by parables, 34, 35. That of the tares explained, 36-43. The parable of the hid treasure, 44; of the Pearl of great price, 45, 46; of the net cast into the sea, 47-50; and of the householder, 51, 52. Christ's countrymen are offended in him; his remark on it, and subsequent conduct, 53-58.

1. **house.** Mt 23:38. **sat.** Mk 2:13. *4:1. **sea.** Da 7:1, 2. Mk 4:1. Re 13:1. 17:15.

2. **great.** Mt 4:25. 15:30. Ge +*49:10. Lk *8:4-8. **so.** Mk 4:1. Lk 5:3. **a ship.** *To ploion,* "the ship," or "boat;" which Mr. Wakefield supposes was a particular vessel kept on the lake for the use of Christ and his disciples. **and sat.** Lk 4:20.

3. **in.** ver. 10-13, 34, 35, 53. Mt 22:1. 24:32. Jg 9:8-20. 2 S 12:1-7. Ps 49:4. 78:2. Is 5:1-7. Ezk 17:2. 20:49. 24:3, etc. Mi 2:4. Hab 2:6. Mk 3:23. *4:2, 13, 33. 12:1, 12. Lk *8:10. 12:41. 15:3, etc. Jn 16:25mg. **parables.** A parable, *parabola,* from *para,* near, and *ballo,* I cast, or put, has been justly defined to be a comparison or similitude, in which one thing is compared with another, especially spiritual things with natural, by which means those spiritual things are better understood, and make a deeper impression on a honest and attentive mind. In a parable, a resemblance in the principal incidents is all that is required; smaller matters being considered as a sort of drapery. Maimonides, in *Morch Nevochim,* gives an excellent rule on this head: "Fix it as a principle to attach yourself to the grand object of the parable, without attempting to make a particular application of all the circumstances and terms which it comprehends." **a sower.** Is 55:10. Am 9:13. Mk *4:2-9. Lk *8:5-8.

4. **the way.** ver. 18, 19.

5. **stony places.** ver. *20. Ezk 11:19. 36:26. Am 6:12. Zc *7:12. **of earth.** ſ29, Ex +19:6. i.e. "no deep earth."

6. **when.** ver. *21. Is *49:10. Ja *1:11, 12. Re 7:16.

because. Mt *7:26, 27. Lk 8:13. Ep *3:17. Col *1:23.
*2:7. **they withered.** Jn 15:6.

7. **among thorns.** ver. *22. Ge 3:18. Je *4:3, 4.
Mk 4:18, 19.

8. **good.** ver. 23. Lk *8:15. Ro 7:18. **some an hundredfold.** ver. 23. Mt *19:29. Ge +*26:12. Mk
+*10:30. Jn *15:8. Ga 5:22, 23. Ph 1:11.

9. **hath ears.** ver. *16. Mt 11:15. Dt 29:4. Ps 40:6.
Mk 4:9, 23. 7:14-16. Re 2:7, 11, 17, 29. 3:6, 13, 22.
13:8, 9. **to hear.** ✓147A, Ge +50:24.

10. **Why.** Mk 4:10, 33, 34.

11. **Because.** Mt *11:25, 26. 16:17. 19:11. Ps *25:8,
9, 14. Is 29:10. *35:8. Mk *4:11. Lk 8:10. *10:39-42.
Jn *7:17. Ac *16:14. ✓17:11, 12. 1 C *2:9, 10, 14.
4:7. Col 1:27. Ja *1:5, 16-18. 1 J *2:20, 27. **given.**
2 T +*2:25. **mysteries.** Ro +*16:25. 1 C 2:7. 4:1. 13:2.
*15:51. Ep 1:9, 18. *3:3-9. 5:32. 6:19. Col *1:26, 27.
2:2. 1 T *3:9, 16. **kingdom of heaven.** Mt +4:17. *16:19.
not given. ✓✓108A4, Ge +31:7. Mt 11:27. Mk 4:11,
12. Lk 8:10. 10:22. Jn ✓6:44, 45, 65.

12. **For whosoever hath.** ✓138C, Ge +22:14. Mt
*19:29. 25:29. Mk +*4:24, 25. 10:29, 30. Lk +*8:18.
*9:26. +*12:48. 18:29, 30. *19:24-26. Jn *15:2-5. Ja
4:6. **from him shall be taken.** Mt *21:43. Is *5:4-7.
Mk *12:9. Lk 10:42. *12:20, 21. 16:2, 25. 2 J 8. Re
2:5. *3:15, 16.

13. **because.** ver. 16. Dt 29:3, 4. Is 42:18-20. 44:18.
Je 5:21. Ezk 12:2. Mk 8:17, 18. Jn *3:19, 20. *9:39-
41. Ro 11:8. 2 C *3:14. *4:3, 4. **seeing.** ✓147B, Ge
+2:16. **see not.** Ac 28:26, 27. **hearing.** ✓147B, Ge
+2:16. **neither do.** ver. 19. Jn 6:36. *7:16, 17. *8:43.
2 C 10:12mg.

14. **fulfilled.** Mt 1:22. Mk 1:2. **the prophecy.** Is
*6:9, 10. Ezk *12:2. Mk 4:12. Lk 8:10. +24:27. Jn
12:39, 40. Ac 28:25-27. Ro *11:8-10. 2 C *3:14, 15.
By hearing. ✓92A, Mt +1:23. ✓92F5. Gnome; or, Quotation B797: where the words are changed in mood
or tense. Here the indicative mood is put by Heterosis
of the verb for the imperative found in Isaiah. **not.**
✓158, Mt +5:18.

15. **heart.** Ps 119:70. He +*3:13. **is waxed.** ✓108A3,
Is +6:10. Dt 32:15. **ears.** Zc 7:11. Jn *8:43, 44. Ac
7:57. 2 T 4:4. He *5:11. **their eyes.** Is 29:10-12. *44:20.
Jn 5:40. 9:39, 41. 2 Th *2:10, 11. **should understand.**
Je ◑5:21. Ac 7:51, 52. Ro *10:10. **and should be.** Lk
22:32. Ac *3:19. 2 T *2:25, 26. He 6:4-6. **and I.** Is
57:18. Je 3:22. *17:14. 33:6. Ho 14:4. Ml *4:2. Mk
*4:12. Re 22:2.

16. **blessed are your.** Mt +*5:3-11. 16:17. Lk 2:29,
30. *10:23, 24. Jn 8:56. *20:29. Ac *26:18. 1 C 6:11.
2 C *4:6. Ep *1:17, 18. He 6:9. 10:39. **eyes.** ✓171Q15.
Synecdoche of the Part B647. The *eye* is put for the
man himself, in respect to his vision, mental or physical.
For other instances of this figure see Lk 10:23. 1 C
2:9.

17. **That many.** Lk *10:24. Jn 8:56. Ep 3:5, 6. He
*11:13, 39, 40. 1 P *1:10-12.

18. **Hear ye.** ver. 11, 12. Mk *4:14, etc. Lk 8:11-
15.

19. **heareth.** ver. 13, 14. **the word.** Mt 4:23. 24:14.
Lk *8:11, etc. 9:2. 10:9. Ac 1:3. *28:31. Ep 3:8. **the
kingdom.** ver. 38. Mt 4:23. 8:12. 9:35. 24:14. Lk 12:32.
Ac 20:25. 28:23. Ro 14:17. **and understandeth it not.**
Jb 34:32. Ps 25:9. Pr 1:7, 20-22. *2:1-6. 17:16. 18:1,
2. Mk *9:32. Jn ✓3:19, 20. 8:43. 18:38. Ac 17:32. 18:15.
*24:25, 26. 25:19, 20. 26:31, 32. Ro 1:28. 2:8. 1 C

✓2:14. 8:2. 2 C ✓4:2-4. 2 Th *2:12. He *2:1. 5:11, 12.
2 P *3:16. 1 J *5:20. **the wicked one.** ver. 38. Mt
5:37. 6:13. Mk *4:15. Lk *8:12. Jn 17:15. Ep 6:16.
2 Th 3:3. 1 J *2:13, 14. 3:12. 5:18, 19. **This.** ver. *4.

20. **received.** ver. 5, 6. **anon.** 1 S 11:13-15. 2 Ch
24:2, 6, 14. Ps 78:34-37. 106:12, 13. Is *58:2. Ezk
+*33:31, 32. Mk *4:16, 17. 6:20. Jn 5:35. Ac 8:13.
*26:28. Ga 3:1. 4:14, 15. *5:7.

21. **root in himself.** ver. *6. Mt 7:22, 23, 26, 27.
Jb 19:28. Pr *12:3, 12. Lk +✓8:13. Jn 6:26, *61-65,
70, 71. *15:5-7. Ac 8:21-23. Ga 5:6. 6:15. Ep *3:17.
Col +*1:23. +*2:7. He 4:2. 2 P ✓1:8, 9. 1 J ✓2:19,
20. **dureth for a while.** Mt 10:22. 24:13. Jb *27:8-10.
Ps 36:3. Ho *6:4. Lk +✓8:13. Ro *2:7. 1 C +*15:2.
Ga 5:7. Ph *1:6. 2 T *1:15. He +*3:12-14. 1 P *1:5.
for when tribulation. Mt *5:10-12. *10:37-39. 16:24-
26. Mk 4:17. 8:34-36. *13:12, 13. Lk *9:23-25. 14:26-
33. 21:12-18. Jn *12:25, 26. Ac *14:22. 2 C 4:18. Ga
1:6. 6:12. 2 T 4:10. He *10:34-39. Ja 1:2. Re 2:13. **is
offended.** ver. 57. Mt *11:6. 15:12. 24:9, 10. 26:31,
33. 2 T 1:15.

22. **seed.** ver. 7. Mk 4:18. Lk *8:14. 18:24. 2 T
4:10. **among the thorns.** Je *4:3. **the care.** T#741.
Mt 6:24, 25. *19:16-24. Ge 13:10-13. Jsh *7:20, 21.
2 K *5:20-27. Ps +26:4 (T#122). Je *4:3. Mk +4:19
(T#625). *10:23-25. Lk 12:✓15, 21, 29, 30. *14:16-24.
*21:34. Ac 5:1-11. 8:18. 2 C 11:28g. Ga 1:4. Ph 3:18,
19. 1 T ✓6:9, 10. 2 T 4:10. 2 P 2:14, 15. 1 J ✓2:15,
16. Ju 11. **world.** Gr. *aion*, Mt +6:13. ver. 38, 39,
40. 2 T ✓4:10. ✓121P2. Metonymy of the Adjunct B593.
"Age" (*aion*), a period of time, is put for what takes
place in it. For other instances of this figure see Lk
16:8. Ro 12:2. 2 C 4:4. Ep 2:2. 6:12. 2 T 4:10. He
1:2. 11:3. **the deceitfulness.** Mt 19:23. Ps 52:7. *62:10.
Pr 11:28. 23:5. Ec 4:8. 5:10, 11, 13, 14. Zc ✓11:5.
Mk *4:19. *10:21-23. Lk 18:24, 25. 2 Th 2:10. 1 T
✓6:9, 17. He +*3:13. Re ✓3:17. **choke the word.** Lk
*8:14. 2 T 4:10. Ju 12. **becometh unfruitful.** Lk 13:6-
9. Jn 15:2-6. 2 P ◑*1:8.

23. **that received.** ver. 8. Mk *4:20. Lk +*8:15.
good. Pr *1:5, 6. *2:2-6. Ezk *18:31. 36:26. Mk 10:15.
Jn *1:11-13. *8:47. *10:26, 27. 17:7, 8. Ac 16:14. ✓17:11.
2 Th ✓2:10, 13, 14. He *4:2. 8:10. Ja +*1:21, 22. 1 P
*2:1, 2. 1 J 5:20. **heareth.** ✓93B, Is +66:11. The figure
Hendiadys is disguised in the A.V. through the separation of the two words: "He that was sown upon the
good ground, this is he who *hears* and *understands*
the word." The person who heareth and understandeth
is one. One act is meant, and not two. All hear, but
this one heareth, yes—and understandeth it too (B671).
the word. Jb +*37:2. Pr 2:10, 11. ✓4:7. Mk +*4:24.
Lk +*8:18. +*11:28. Jn ✓5:24. Ac +*17:11. Ro ✓10:17.
Ga *3:2. 1 Th ✓2:13. **and understandeth.** ver. 19. Lk
*24:45. Jn *8:43. Ac *8:30, 31. 1 C ✓2:14. Ja 1:21,
22, 25. 2 P *3:16. 1 J 5:20. **beareth fruit.** Mt *3:8,
10. 12:33. Ps ✓1:1-3. 92:13-15. Ho 14:8. Lk 6:43, 44.
*13:9. Jn ✓15:1-8, 16. Ga ✓5:22, 23. Ph 1:11. 4:✓8,
17. Col 1:6, +✓10. He 6:7. 13:15, 16. 2 P +*1:5-8.
some an hundredfold. ver. 8. Mt *19:29. 25:14-29.
Ge +*26:12. Mk +*10:30. 1 C 15:41. 2 C 8:1, 2.
9:6, 10. 1 Th *4:1. 2 P *1:5-8. *3:18.

24. **put.** Mt 21:33. Jg 14:12, 13. Is *28:10, 13. Ezk
17:2. **The kingdom.** ver. 33, 44, 45, 47. Mt 3:2. 20:1.
22:2. 25:1. Mk 4:30. Lk 13:18, 20. **good seed.** ver.
19, 37. Mt 4:23. Col 1:5. 1 P *1:23. 1 J 3:9.

25. **men slept.** Mt *25:5. Is 56:9, 10. Mk 13:37.

Ac *20:29-31. Ro *13:11, 12. Ga 2:4. Ep *5:13-16. 1 Th *5:5-7. 2 Th 2:7. 2 T *4:3-5. He *12:15. 2 P 2:1. 1 J 2:18. 2 J +*9-11. Ju *4. Re 2:14, 15, 20. **his enemy.** ver. *39. Ge +*3:15. 2 C √2:11. √11:13-15. 1 P √5:8. Re 12:9. 13:14. **sowed.** Dt 22:9. **tares.** ver. *38. Ac *20:29, 30. 2 C √11:13-15. Ga 1:7-9. **among.** ƒ144A6, Ge +45:6.

26. **But when.** Mk *4:26-29.

27. **the servants.** 1 C 3:5-9. 12:28, 29. 16:10. 2 C 5:18-20. 6:1, 4. Ep 4:11, 12. **whence.** Ro +*16:17. 1 C 1:11-13. 15:12, etc. Ga 3:1-3. Ja 3:15, 16. *4:4. **tares.** *Zizania*, doubtless denotes darnel, the *lolium temulentum* of the naturalists, a noxious weed which bears a strong resemblance to wheat. "It is well known," says Mr. Forskal, "to the people of Aleppo. It grows among corn. If the seeds remain mixed with the meal, they occasion dizziness to those who eat of the bread. The reapers do not separate the plant; but, after the threshing, they reject the seeds by means of a van or sieve." Other travelers say, that, in some parts of Syria, it is drawn up by the hand in the harvest.

28. **Wilt.** Mt +*15:14. Lk 9:49-54. 1 C 5:3-7. 2 C *2:6-11. 1 Th 5:14. Ju 22, 23.

29. **Nay.** 1 C 4:5.

30. **Let both.** ver. *39. Mt *3:12. 22:10-14. 25:6-13, *32. Ml *3:18. 1 C 4:5. 5:5-13. Ph 3:18, 19. 2 Th 3:6. **grow together.** 1 S 25:29. **the harvest.** ver. +*39. Is √17:5-8. Ho √6:11. Jl *3:13. 1 C 15:20, 23. Re √14:14-20. **to the reapers.** ver. *39-43. 1 T 5:4. **Gather ye.** ver. *41. Mt *8:12. Mi +*4:11-13. Lk 17:30-37. **first the tares.** Mt 15:13. 24:40, 41. Is 8:12. Re 3:17. *18:7. **and bind.** 1 S 25:29. **to burn.** ver. 40. Mt +*25:41. Is +*24:6. *27:10, 11. Ezk 15:4-7. Ml +*4:1. Jn +*15:6. 2 P +*3:7. **but gather.** Mt *3:12. Is *27:12. +*43:6. Je 31:8. Ezk *34:12. *37:12. +*38:8n. *39:28. Am 9:9. Lk 3:17. 1 Th ◐4:16, 17. **wheat.** Mt 3:12. Lk *3:17. Jn 12:24.

31. **put.** ver. 24. Lk *19:11. *20:9. **The kingdom.** Mt 4:17. Mk *4:30-32. Lk 13:18, 19. **a grain.** ƒ138B, Ge +13:16. Ac 1:15. **of mustard seed.** Mt *17:20. Mk 4:31. Lk 13:19. *17:6.

32. **the least.** ƒ138B, Ge +13:16. Ps 72:16-19. Is +*2:2-4. Ezk 47:1-5. Da +*2:34, 35, 44, 45. Mi 4:1-3. Zc *4:10. +*8:20-23. *14:7-10. Ac 1:15. 21:20g. Ro 15:18, 19. Re 11:15. ƒ96E4. Heterosis of Degree B527: the comparative for the superlative. For other instances of this figure see Mt 18:1. Jn 10:29. 1 C 13:13. 15:19. **seeds.** ƒ63I1D, Nu +26:4. By ellipsis (repetition: of preceding connected words), supply to read "Which indeed is the least of all seeds (which a man takes and sows in a field);" from verse 31; i.e., not the least, absolutely, but relatively, as to those seeds which are usually sown in the field. **becometh a tree.** Jg 9:14, 15. Ezk 17:22, 23. 31:3-6. Da *4:10-12, 20-22. **the birds of the air.** ver. 4, 19. Mt 8:20. Ge=15:11. +40:19. Dt 28:26. Ps 104:12. Ezk *17:23, 24. *31:6. Da 4:12, 21. Re 2:20. √18:12.

33. **Another.** Lk 13:20, 21. **like unto leaven.** Leaven is always characterized as evil, the "leaven of malice and wickedness," the ferment of the lust of the flesh— the human will in revolt from God (F.W. Grant, *Numerical Bible*, vol. 1, p. 283, 284). It is inconceivable how the Jewish audience, well schooled in the Biblical use of this term, could take this term to mean otherwise without a direct word of explanation from the Savior. Mt 16:11, 12. Ex 12:15. 34:25. Le 2:◐4, *11. √7:13.

+23:17n. Ezk ◐46:11. Am +4:5n. Mk *8:15. Lk *12:1. *13:21. *21:1. 1 C √5:6-8. 2 C 7:1. Ga *5:7-9. 2 Th=2:4. **a woman.** 2 C 11:2. Ep 5:24. 1 T 2:11, 12. Ep 5:24. Re *2:20. *17:1-6. **and hid.** ver. 25. Mt ◐*11:27. 2 C ◐*4:2. Ep *4:14. *5:11. **three.** Ge 18:6. Jg 6:19. 1 S 1:24. **measures.** Gr. "A measure containing about a peck and a half, wanting a little more than a pint." **meal.** 1 K 17:14-16. Jn 6:32-35. 2 J=9. **till.** Jb 17:9. Pr +*4:18. Ho *6:3. Jn 15:2. 16:12, 13. Ph *1:6, 9. *2:13-15. 1 Th *5:23, 24. 2 P *3:18. **the whole.** Ml 1:7. Ro 11:16. 1 C 5:6. 10:17. √15:33. 1 Th ◐5:23. **was leavened.** 1 C 5:6. Ga 5:9. Some understand leaven here to be representing the gospel, and its success and good influence in the world until the end of the age. Others understand leaven to be a type of evil, and here represents the spread of evil until the end of the age. This latter view appears to be more consistent with the prophecies and typology of Scripture. Practically every other mention of leaven in Scripture connects it with evil. Why would Jesus radically change the symbolism here without explanation? Furthermore, the fact that the leaven was *hid*, and at that by a *woman*, is taken as further evidence by some interpreters that leaven here represents a sinister influence. Others argue, in turn, that the "leaven" and the "hiding" and the "woman" are merely the backdrop to the parable, and each individual detail must not be overly pressed into service in an interpretation (see note on ver. 3), when the purpose of the detail is simply to lend coloring to the story. But perhaps this is an example among interpreters of avoiding the implications of Scripture, of skirting the clear teaching of a text by arbitrarily invoking, when convenient, a principle which allows them to gloss over the specific terms of Scripture.

34. **these things.** ver. *13. Mk *4:33, 34. Jn 16:25mg, 29mg.

35. **it might be.** ver. *14. Mt 21:4, 5. **I will.** ƒ92C, Mt +2:15. **open.** ƒ108H6A, Jg +11:35. Mt 5:2. Ps ⊁78:2. **in parables.** Nu 21:27. **I will utter.** Ps 49:4. Is 42:9. Am *3:7. Lk *10:24. Ro *16:25, 26. 1 C 2:7. Ep *3:5, 9. Col 1:25, 26. 2 T *1:9, 10. T 1:2, 3. He 1:1. 1 P *1:11, 12. **from.** Mt 25:34. Lk 11:50. Jn 17:24. Ac +*15:18. He 4:3. 9:26. 1 P *1:20, 21. Re 13:8. 17:8. **world.** Gr. *kosmos*, Mt +4:8.

36. **Jesus sent.** Mt 14:22. 15:39. Mk 6:45. 8:9. **multitudes.** ver. 2. Lk 10:23, 24. **went into the house.** ver. *1. Mt 9:28. Ps=73:16, 17. Mk *4:34. **Declare.** ver. *11. Mt 15:15, 16. Mk 4:13, 33, 34. 7:17. Jn *16:17-20.

37. **He.** ver. *24, *27. Mk 4:14. Jn *4:36, 37. **that soweth.** Ac 8:1. **good seed.** Ps 22:30. Is 53:10. Ho 2:23. Mk 16:15, 20. Lk 24:47. Ro 10:18. Col 1:6. Ja 1:18. **is the Son of man.** ver. +*41. Mt 10:40. *16:13-16. Lk *10:16. Jn *13:20. 20:21. Ac +*1:8. Ro 15:18. 1 C *3:5-7. He 1:1. *2:3.

38. **field.** Mt 24:14. *28:18-20. Ge=37:15. Le=27:16. Mk *16:15-20. Lk 24:47. Ro 10:18. 16:26. Col *1:6. Re 14:6. **is.** ƒ119, Ge +49:9. **world.** Gr. *kosmos*, Mt +4:8. **the good seed.** Ps 22:30. Is 53:10. Ho 2:23. Zc 10:8, 9. Jn *1:12, 13. 12:24. Ro *8:17. Ja *1:18. 2:5. 1 P +*1:23. 1 J 3:2, 9. **are.** ƒ119, Ge +49:9. **children of the kingdom.** ƒ108B, 1 S 20:31. T#653. ver. 43. Mt +*8:12. Mk 2:19. 1 J 3:10. **tares are.** T#690. Mt 23:33. Ps +2:2 (T#68). +5:9 (T#165, 702). 36:1. +42:10 (T#511). 53:1-3. 55:9-11. 73:6-9. Pr +5:22

(T#166). Is +24:5 (T#86). Ho 4:2. Jn 7:7. 8:44. 15:24, 25. +17:14 (T#740). Ac 7:51. 13:10. Ro 1:30. *3:13-18. *8:7. **the children of the wicked one.** ver. *19. Mt 23:15, 33. Ge +*3:15. Jg +19:22. Jn 6:12. √8:44. Ac *13:10. Ph 3:18, 19. 1 J *3:8, 10, 12.

39. **enemy.** ver. *25, *28. 2 C *2:17. √11:3, 13-15. Ep *2:2. *6:11, 12. 2 Th √2:8-11. 1 P *5:8. Re 12:9. 13:14. 19:20. *20:2, 3, 7-10. **the harvest.** ver. +*30, *49. Is √17:5-8. 18:5-7. Ho √6:11. Jl *3:13. Re *14:15-19. **end of the.** ver. 40, 49. Mt +√24:3. 28:20. Da 12:13. He 9:26. **world.** Gr. *aion*, Mt +6:13. lit. "end of the age," ver. 40, 49. Mt *24:3. 28:20. He 9:26. **reapers.** Mt *25:31. Da 7:10. 2 Th √1:7-10. Ju *14. Re 14:15.

40. **the tares.** ver. *30. **are gathered.** Mt 24:39. Is √24:22. Mi √4:11-13. **and burned.** ver. 30, 42, 49, 50. Mt *3:12. +*25:46. Is +*24:6. Ml 3:18. +*4:1. Jn *15:6. 2 P +*3:7. **fire.** 1 C ◐3:13, 15. **end of this.** ver. 39. **world.** Gr. *aion*, Mt +6:13.

41. **Son of man.** Mt +8:20. +*16:27n. **send forth his angels.** Mt +*24:31. Ps +*68:17. 103:20, 21. Is *13:3. Da 7:10. Jl *3:11. Mk 13:27. He *1:6, 7, 14. Re 5:11, 12. **and they.** ver. 49. Mt *18:7. Ps *35:5, 6. Ro *16:17, 18. 2 P 2:1, 2. **gather out.** ver. +*30. Mt *8:12. +*25:31. Lk 17:26-37. **things that offend.** *or*, scandals. Mt 15:12. 16:23. 18:7. Zp *1:3. Lk 17:1. Ro 9:33. **and them.** Mt +*7:22, 23. +*25:41. Lk 13:26, 27. Ac *17:31. Ro *2:8, 9, 16. 2 Th √1:7, 8. 2 P *2:1, 2. Re *21:27. **do iniquity.** 1 J 3:4.

42. **shall cast.** ver. *50. Mt *3:12. +*25:41. Ps *21:9. Is +*30:33. +*66:24. Je 29:22. Ezk 23:25. Da 3:6, 15-17, 21, 22. Mk √9:43-49. Lk +*16:23, 24. Re 9:2. *14:10. *19:20. *20:10, 14, 15. +*21:8. **wailing.** ver. *50. Mt *8:12. *22:13. Lk *13:28.

43. **Then shall.** Mt *25:34, 46. Jg *5:31. Pr +*4:18. Da +√12:3. Ml *3:18. 1 C 15:24, 41-54, *58. Col *3:4. 1 J *3:2. Re 21:3-5, 22, 23. **the righteous.** Ml 4:2. 2 Th 1:10. **shine forth.** Is 24:23. Da +*12:3. in **the kingdom.** ver. 38. Mt +*25:34. *26:29. Lk 12:32. +*22:29, 30. Ja +*2:5. **Who hath ears.** ver. +9. Mt +11:15. **to hear.** √147A, Ge +50:24.

44. **kingdom of heaven.** √121J20. Figure of speech Metonymy of the Subject. Heaven is put for God who dwells there. For other instances of this figure see Ps +73:9. 2 T +*4:18n. **like.** Mt *6:21. ◐*25:18. Jn 3:21. Ps 19:10. Pr *2:2-5. *16:16. 17:16. 18:1. Jn *6:35. Ro +*15:4. 1 C *2:9, 10. Col *2:3. *3:3, 4, 16. **treasure.** Ex=19:5. Dt 4:20. 32:8. Ps 135:4. Ro=1:16. **hid.** Dt 26:1-5. 32:10. Is *51:1, 2. **in a field.** ver. 38. Dt 32:8-10. Jn 15:19. 17:6, 9, 11-13, 14, 15, 16. **hath found.** Mt 15:24. Jn 1:11. **he hideth.** Dt *32:28, 29. **for joy.** Mt *19:21, 27, 29. Lk *14:33. *18:23, 24. *19:6-8. Ac *2:44-47. *4:32-35. Ph *3:7-9. He 10:34. *11:24-26. *12:2. **selleth all.** ver. 46. Mt 25:9. Ps 22:1. Is 53:4-10. Lk 14:33. Jn 11:51, 52. Ro √8:32. 2 C *8:9. Ep 5:25. Ph 2:7. 3:7, 8. **buyeth.** Pr 23:23. Is 55:1. 2 P 2:1. Re *3:18.

45. **like.** Mt 16:26. 22:5. Pr *3:13-18. 8:10, 11, 18-20. Re 3:18. **seeking.** Jb *28:18. Ps 4:6, 7. 39:6, 7. Ec 2:2-12. *12:8, 13. Lk +*19:10. Jn *15:16. Ac 15:14. Ep 2:17.

46. **one pearl.** Mt +7:6. Jb 28:18. Pr 2:4. *3:13-15. √4:7. 8:11. 20:15. 31:10. Is *33:6. La 4:7. Ml 3:17mg. Lk +10:42. 1 C 3:21-23. Ga 3:28. Ep *3:8. 5:27. Col *2:3. 2 Th=1:10. 1 T 2:9. 1 J √5:11, 12. Re 17:4. 21:21. **went.** ver. 44. Mk *10:28-31. Lk 18:28-30. Ac 20:24.

Ga *6:14. **sold all.** Mt 19:21, 29. Lk 14:33. Ro *8:32. 2 C *8:9. **bought it.** Is 55:1. 1 C *6:20. 1 P *1:18, 19.

47. **a net.** Mt *4:19. Jb 19:6. Ezk 12:13. *32:3. Ho *7:12. Hab 1:15. Mk 1:16, 17. Lk *5:10. Jn 21:6. **the sea.** Ge 1:20-23. Re *17:15. **and gathered.** ver. *26-30, 38. Mt *22:9, 10. 25:1-4. Lk 14:21-23. Jn *15:2-6. Ac 5:1-10. 8:18-22. *20:30. 1 C 5:1-6. *10:1-12. *11:19. 2 C √11:13-15, 26. 12:20, 21. Ga *2:4. 2 T *3:2-5. 4:3, 4. T 1:9-11. 2 P 2:1-3, 13-22. 1 J *2:18, 19. *4:1-6. Ju 4, 5. Re *3:1, 15-17. **every kind.** Mt 22:10. 25:1, 2. Jn 6:70. 1 C 3:10. 2 C 12:20, 21.

48. **was full.** Jn 21:6, *11. **drew to shore.** Jn *21:11. **gathered the good.** ver. 30, 40-43. Mt *3:12. 25:31-46. Is *27:12, 13. Je *16:16. Ezk *34:12. Am 9:9. Jn *17:12. 21:11. **cast the bad.** Mt 15:13, 14. 22:12, 13. Le 11:9. Ezk *20:38. Ro 16:17. 1 C *10:4, 5.

49. **world.** Gr. *aion*, Mt +6:13. **the angels.** ver. *39. Mt +*24:31. **and sever.** ver. 41. *25:5-12, 19-33. 2 Th √1:7-10. Re *20:12-15. **from among.** √144A6, Ge +45:6. √108H3. Idiom B838: involving idiomatic phrases. "Out of the way" (*ek mesou*) is a Greek idiom which always implies decisive action, either of the person's own will or of force on the part of others. For other instances of this idiom see Is 52:11. 57:1. Ac 17:33. 23:10. 1 C 5:2. 2 C 6:17. Col 2:14. 2 Th 2:7.

50. **cast.** ver. *42. **furnace of fire.** ver. 42. Mt +*25:41. Mk *9:42-48. Re *19:20. **wailing.** ver. 42. Mt 8:12. 24:50, 51. Lk 13:27, 28. Re *14:10, 11. *16:10, 11.

51. **Have ye understood.** ver. *11, *19. Mt 15:17. *16:11. 24:15. Mk 4:34. 7:14, 18. *8:17, 18. Lk *9:44, 45. Jn ◐10:6. 13:12. 16:29. Ac √8:30, 31. 1 J 5:20.

52. **every scribe.** Mt *23:34. Ezr *7:6, 10, 21. Da +*11:33. Lk 11:49. 1 C 12:7. 2 C *3:4-6. Col 1:7. 1 T 3:6, 15, 16. +*4:13-16. 2 T *3:16, 17. T *1:9. 2:6, 7. **instructed unto the kingdom.** Mt 11:11. *28:19. Da +*11:33. +*12:3. Ac 14:21. **householder.** Ro=12:7. 1 T=3:2. =4:11, 13, 16. 2 T=2:24. He=5:12. 13:17. Ja=3:1. **which bringeth.** Mt *12:35. +*24:45. Pr 10:20, 21. *11:30. 15:7. 16:20-24. 18:4. *22:17, 18. Ec 12:9-11. Je *15:16. Da +*11:33. Jn +*5:39. Ac √17:11. 2 C *4:5-7. 6:10. Ep 3:4, 8. Col *3:16. **treasure.** √121.O, Ge +28:22. 1 Ch=9:26. **things new.** SS 7:13. Jn *13:34. Ep 3:3-5. He 5:12-14. 1 J *2:7, 8. **and old.** √174, Ge +18:27.

53. **came to pass.** √144A11, Ge +38:1. Mt 7:28. 11:1. 19:1. 26:1. **finished.** √63BB, 1 S 16:11. Supply by ellipsis, "(speaking) these parables." **he departed.** Mk *4:33-35.

54. **when.** Mt 2:23. Mk *6:1, 2. Lk *4:16-30. Jn *1:11. **his own country.** Mt 2:23. Lk 4:23. **he taught.** Mt 4:23. 26:55. Ps *22:22. *40:9, 10. Ac 13:46. 28:17-29. **they were astonished.** Mt 7:28. **Whence hath.** Mt *21:23. Mk *11:28. Jn *7:15, 16. Ac *4:13. **wisdom.** Ac=7:22. **mighty works.** Mt 7:22. 11:20, 21, 23. 14:2. Mk 6:14.

55. **the carpenter's.** Ps *22:6. Is *49:7. *53:2, 3. Mk +*6:3. Lk 3:23. 4:22. Jn 1:45, 46. *6:42. 7:41, 42, 48, 52. 9:29. **is not his.** Mt +*1:18-20. Lk 1:27. 2:5-7. **and his brethren.** Mt *12:46, 48. *27:56. Ps √69:8. Mk +*6:3. 15:40, *47. 16:1. Lk 24:10. Jn *19:25. **James.** Ga *1:19. **Joses.** i.e. *increaser, whom Jehovah helps*, ✳S#2500g. Mt 27:56. Mk 6:3. 15:40, 47. Lk 3:29. Ac 4:36. (1) One of the brothers of our Lord; (2) Joses, Ac 4:36, also called Barnabas.

56. **Whence then hath**. Jn 7:15, 52.

57. **they were offended**. ver. 21. Mt *11:6. 15:12. Is *8:14. *49:7. *53:3. Mk 6:3. Lk *2:34, 35. 7:23. Jn 6:42, 61. 1 C *1:23-28. 1 P 2:7, 8. **A prophet**. ♪138C, Ge +22:14. 2 K 5:8. Is 53:3. Je 11:21. 12:6. Mk *6:14. Lk 4:24. Jn 4:44. 7:5. Ac *3:22, 23. 7:37-39, 51, 52. **own country**. Jn 7:41, 42. **own house**. Mk 3:19, 21. Jn 7:3, 5.

58. **he did not many**. Mk *6:5, 6. Lk 4:25-29. Ro 11:20. He *3:12-19. *4:6-11. **because**. Mt 17:20. Mk 9:23.

MATTHEW 14

Herod supposes Jesus to be John the Baptist risen from the dead, 1, 2. An account of John's imprisonment and death, through the resentment of Herod, Herodias, and her daughter, 3-12. Jesus departs to a desert place, and miraculously feeds the multitudes, 13-21. He retires to a mountain to pray, having sent the disciples away in a ship, 22-24. He comes to them walking on the sea, 25-27. Peter obtains leave to come on the water, begins to sink, and is preserved, and rebuked, 28-31. Jesus enters the ship, the storm ceases, and the disciples worship him as the Son of God, 32, 33. Landing at Gennesaret, he heals all the sick, who touch the hem of his garment, 34-36.

1. **Herod**. This was Herod Antipas, the son of Herod the Great, by Malthace, and tetrarch of Galilee and Peraea, which produced a revenue of 200 talents a year (Josephus, Ant. l. xvii. c. 13, sec. 4). He married the daughter of Aretas, king of Arabia, whom he divorced in order to marry Herodias, the wife of his brother Philip, who was still living. Aretas, to revenge the affront which Herod had offered his daughter, declared war against him, and vanquished him after an obstinate engagement. This defeat, Josephus assures us (Ant. l. xviii. c. 7), the Jews considered as a punishment for the death of John the Baptist. Having gone to Rome to solicit the title of king, he was accused by Agrippa of carrying on a correspondence with Artabanus king of Parthia, against the Romans, and was banished by the emperor Caius to Lyons, and thence to Spain, where he and Herodias died in exile. Mk *6:14-16. 8:15. Lk *9:7-9. 13:31, 32. 23:8-12, 15. Ac 4:27. **Tetrarch**. Lk 3:1. **the fame**. Mt 4:24. ♪108B. Idiom B830. lit. hearing. "Hearing" is used, not merely of the act of hearing, but of what is heard: a narration, report, fame. This is a kind of Metonymy. ♪121C2D5. Metonomy of the Cause B557. To hear or "hearing" is used of *fame*, the effect of hearing or being heard. For another instance of this idiom see Jn 12:38. **of**. ♪181E, Ge +3:24.

2. **servants**. Mt 8:6. **This**. Mt 11:11. 16:14. Mk *6:15, 16. 8:28. Jn 10:41. **mighty works**. Mt 13:54. **do show forth themselves in him**. *or*, are wrought by him. 1 C 12:6, 11. Ga 2:8. 3:5. Ep 1:+*11, 20. 2:2. Ph 2:13.

3. **Herod**. Mt 4:12. Mk *6:17. Lk *3:19, 20. Jn 3:23, 24. **bound**. ♪96C3. Heterosis of Tenses B520. The Aorist for the past. The Aorist, or indefinite past tense, is used to denote an action definitely past and completed some time ago. Here, "had bound." For another instance of this figure see Jn 18:24. **in prison**. Mt 11:2. Jn 3:24. **Herodias'**. i.e. *heroic; the glory of the skin*, *S#2266g. ver. 6. Mk 6:17, 19, 22. Lk 3:19. This

infamous woman was the daughter of Aristobulus and Berenice, and grand-daughter of Herod the Great. **his**. Lk 3:1. **Philip's**. Herod Philip, son of Herod and Great and Mariamne.

4. **not lawful**. Mt 22:24. Ge 38:8. Dt 25:5, 6. 1 K 21:19. 2 Ch 26:18, 19. Pr 28:1. Is +*8:20n. Mk *6:18. 12:19. Lk 20:28. Ac 24:24, 25. **to have her**. Le *18:6, 16. *20:21. 2 S 12:7.

5. **when**. Mk *6:19, 20. 14:1, 2. Ac 4:21. 5:26. **he feared**. Mt 21:26, 46. **because**. Mt 11:9. 21:26, 32. Mk 11:30-32. Lk 20:6. **as**. ♪160, Ge +25:31.

6. **birthday**. Ge 40:20. Est 1:2-9. 2:18. Da 5:1-4. Ho 7:5, 6. Mk 6:21-23. **the daughter**. Mt 22:24. **danced**. Est 1:10-12. **before them**. Gr. in the midst. Jn 8:3. Ac 4:7.

7. **he promised**. Est 5:3, 6. 7:2. **with an oath**. ver. +*9. Nu +*30:2n. Jg +*11:30, 31n. Ezk ◐17:18n. Ac +*23:12.

8. **being**. 2 Ch 22:2, 3. Mk 6:24. **Give**. 1 K 18:4, 13. 19:2. 2 K 11:1. Pr 1:16. 29:10. **head**. Jg +7:25. **a charger**. Nu 7:13, 19, 84, 85. Ezr 1:9.

9. **the king**. ver. 1. Mk 6:14. **sorry**. ♪121Q2. Metonymy of the Adjunct B598. The appearance of a thing, or an opinion about it, is put for the thing itself: in verbs. Here, the king appeared to be sorry. For another instance of this figure see Mk 6:48. Compare this figure in nouns, ♪121Q1, Je 28:5; in connected words or sentences, ♪121Q3, 2 S 22:8. ver. 5. Mt 27:17-26. Da 6:14-16. Mk 6:20, 26. Lk 13:32. Jn 19:8, 12-16. Ac 24:23-27. 25:3-9. **the oath's**. ver. +*7. Nu 30:5-8. Jg *11:30, 31, 39. 21:1, 7-23. 1 S 14:24, 28, 39-45. 25:22, 32-34. 28:10. 2 K 6:31-33. Ec *5:2. Ezk 17:18n.

10. **and beheaded**. Mt 17:12. 21:35, 36. 22:3-6. 23:34-36. 2 Ch 36:16. Je 2:30. Mk 6:27-29. 9:13. Lk 9:9. Re 11:7. **the prison**. Josephus (Ant. l. xviii. c. 2) informs us that John the Baptist was imprisoned and beheaded by Herod in the strong castle of Machaerus, which he describes as situated about 60 stadia east of Jordan, not far from where the river discharges itself into the Dead sea.

11. **head**. Jg +7:25. **and given**. Ge 49:7. Pr 27:4. 29:10. Je 22:17. Ezk 16:3, 4. 19:2, 3. 35:6. Re 16:6. 17:6. **the damsel**. This was Salome, the daughter of Herodias by her uncle and husband Philip. Nicephorus (l. i. c. 20) and Metaphrastes relate, that she accompanied her mother Herodias and Herod in their banishment; and when passing over a river that was frozen, the ice broke, and she sunk up to her neck, and the ice uniting, she suffered the same punishment she had caused to be inflicted on John the Baptist. If true, this was certainly a wonderful providence; but it must be confessed that it appears contrary to the account of Josephus, who says, that she first married Philip the Tetrarch, and then Herod the king of Chalcis, by whom she had three sons (Ant. l. xviii. c. 7).

12. **his disciples**. Mt 9:14. **took**. Mt 27:58-61. Ac 8:2. **told Jesus**. Jn 12:22.

13. **Jesus heard**. ver. 1, 2. Mt 10:23. 12:15. Mk 6:30-33. Lk 9:10-17. Jn 6:1-13. **he departed**. Mt *10:23. 12:15. 15:21. Pr +*22:3.

14. **moved**. ♪22A18, Is +63:15. **compassion**. T#60. Mt *9:35, 36. 15:32, etc. *23:37. Jb +36:7 (T#585). Ps +119:68 (T#224). +145:9 (T#228). Mk *6:34. 8:1, 2. 9:22. Lk 7:13. 19:41, +42 (T#372). Jn +1:12 (T#584). 11:33-35. 13:34. 15:9. Ac *10:38. +20:24 (T#586). Ro 5:6-8. 8:37. Ep 5:2. He 2:17. +*4:15.

5:2. Ja +5:11 (T#225). 1 J +2:12 (T#583). Re +22:17 (T#370). **he healed.** Lk *9:11.

15. **his.** Mk 6:35, 36. Lk 9:12. **send.** ver. 22. Mt 15:23. Mk 8:3.

16. **they.** 2 K 4:42-44. Jb 31:16, 17. Pr 11:24. Ec 11:2. Lk 3:11. Jn 6:5-7. 13:29. 2 C 8:2, 3. 9:7, 8.

17. **We have.** Mt 15:33, 34. Nu 11:21-23. Ps 78:19, 20. Mk 6:37, 38. 8:4, 5. Lk 9:13. Jn 6:5-9. **five.** Mt 16:9. Mk 8:19. **loaves.** Jn 6:9.

18. **Bring them.** Mt 17:17. 21:2. Nu 11:23. 1 K 17:10-16. 2 K 4:1-7, 42-44. Mk *6:37, 38. Jn *6:8, 9.

19. **he commanded.** Mt 15:35. Mk 6:39, 40. 8:6. Lk 9:14, 15. Jn 6:10. **looking.** 2 Ch 6:13. Ps 123:1, 2. Mk 6:41. 7:34. Lk 9:16. Jn 11:41. 17:1. Ac 7:55. **he blessed.** Mt ⬤+15:36. *26:26. Mk 6:41. 8:7. 14:22. Lk 9:16. +*24:30. 1 C 10:16. **and brake.** ⨍108H4, Is +58:7.

20. **were.** Mt 5:6. 15:33. Ex 16:8, 12. Le 26:26. 1 K 17:12-16. 2 K 4:43, 44. Pr 13:25. Ezk 4:14-16. Hg 1:6. Lk 1:53. 9:17. Jn 6:7, 11. **and they took.** Mt 15:37, 38. 16:8-10. 2 K 4:1-7. Mk 6:42-44. 8:8, 9, 16-21. Jn 6:12-14. **that remained.** 2 Ch=31:9, 10. Lk 15:17. Ph 4:18.

21. **about.** Jn 6:10. Ac 4:4, 34. 2 C 9:8-11. Ph *4:19. **women.** Ne +*12:43. **and children.** Mt 15:38. Dt +*29:11n. Ne +*12:43. Is 54:13. Lk +*18:15.

22. **And straightway.** Mk 6:45-51. Jn 6:15-21. **Jesus.** Mk 6:45. **constrained.** Lk 14:23. **a ship.** Mt 15:39. **other side.** Mt 8:18. **while.** Mt 13:36. 15:39. **sent.** ver. 15.

23. **he went.** Mt 6:6. 26:36. Mk 6:46. Lk 6:12. 9:28. Ac 6:4. **into a mountain.** T#1200. Mt 5:1. Ex 3:12. 19:17. 32:1, 11. 2 S 15:30, 31. 1 K 18:42-44. 19:11-13. 2 K 1:9-15. Lk 6:12, 13. 9:28-31. **apart.** T#531. Mt 6:6. Ps +1:2 (T#665). Mk +*1:35. Lk 5:16. 9:18. **to pray.** T#64. Mt 26:36, 39, 42, 44. Ps 21:2. Mk 1:35. 6:46. Lk 5:16. 6:12. 9:18, 28, 29. 11:1. Jn 11:41, 42. 14:15, 16. 17:1. Ro +8:34 (T#516). He 5:7-9. **the evening.** T#1161. Ge 24:11, 12. 1 K 18:36. 1 Ch 23:30. Ezr 9:5. Ps *55:17. Da 9:21. Mk 13:35. **he was.** Jn 6:15-17. **alone.** T#1218. Ge 32:24. Mk +*1:35. Lk 5:16. 6:12. *9:18.

24. **tossed.** Mt 8:24. Is 54:11. Mk 6:48. Jn 6:18.

25. **the fourth watch.** The Jews at this time divided the night into *four* watches: the first was from six o'clock in the evening till nine (Mk 13:35, even), the second from nine till twelve (Mk 13:35, midnight), the third from twelve till three (Mk 13:35, cockcrowing. Lk 12:38), and the fourth from three till six (Mt 14:25. Mk 6:48. 13:35, morning); so that it probably began to be daylight before our Lord came to his disciples. However, H. B. Swete states "The Lord reached the boat about 3 a.m." (*Comm. on Mark,* p. 137). Note that all four watches are named at Mk 13:35. For the Jewish division of daytime into twelve hours, see Jn 11:9n. Mt 24:43. Mk 13:35. Lk 12:38. **walking on the sea.** This suspension of the laws of gravitation was a proper manifestation of omnipotence. Jb 9:8. Ps 93:3, 4. 104:3. Mk 6:48. Jn 6:19. Re 10:2, 5, 8.

26. **they were.** 1 S 28:12-14. Jb 4:14-16. Da 10:6-12. Mk 6:49, 50. Lk 1:11, 12. 24:5, 37, 45. Ac 12:15. Re 1:17. **It is.** Lk +4:30. 24:16, 39. Jn ⬤+20:14. **a spirit.** or, apparition. lit. a phantom. ✱S#5326g. Mk 6:49.

27. **Be of good cheer.** Mt 9:2. Jn 16:33. Ac 23:11. **it is I.** Is 41:4, 10, 14. 51:12. Lk 24:38, 39. Jn 6:20.

14:1-3. Re 1:17, 18. **be not afraid.** Mt 17:7. Dt 31:6. Jsh 10:25. 1 Ch 22:13. 28:20. Ps +*34:4. *46:1, 2. Is 41:13. 43:1, 2. Jn 14:1. 16:33. Ph 4:13. 2 T +*1:7.

28. **if.** ⨍184A, 1 C +15:2. **bid.** T#1571. Mt 19:27. 26:33-35. Mk 14:31. Lk 22:31-34, 49, 50. Jn 6:68. 13:36-38. Ro 12:3.

29. **he walked.** Mt 17:20. 21:21. Mk 9:23. 11:22, 23. Lk 17:6. Jn 21:7. Ac 3:16. Ro 4:19. Ph 4:13.

30. **when he saw.** Mt 26:69-75. 2 K 6:15. Ps 93:3, 4. Is *43:2. Mk 14:38, 66-72. Lk 22:54-61. Jn 18:25-27. 2 T 4:16, 17. **boisterous.** *or,* strong. **afraid.** Ge +19:30. **sink.** ✱S#2670g. Mt 18:6 (drowned). **Lord.** Mt 8:24-26. Ps 3:7. 69:1, 2. 107:27-30. 116:3, 4. La 3:54-57. Jon 2:2-7. Lk 8:24. 2 C 12:7-10.

31. **stretched.** Ps *138:7. Is 63:12. La *3:57. Mk 1:31, 41. 5:41. Ac 4:30. **and caught.** Ge 22:14. Dt 32:36. Mk 16:7. Lk 22:31, 32. 24:34. 1 P 1:5. Ju *24. **O thou.** Mt 6:30. 8:26. 16:8. 17:20. Mk 4:40. 16:14. Lk 24:25. **wherefore.** Ge +19:30. **doubt.** Mt 21:21. 28:17. Mk 11:23. Ro 4:18-20. 1 T 2:8. Ja *1:6-8.

32. **come.** Ps 107:29, 30. Mk 4:41. 6:51. Jn 6:21.

33. **they that.** ver. 22, 29. Mk 6:51, 52. **worshipped.** Mt 2:11. 8:2. 9:18. *15:25. 20:20. *28:9, 17. Lk ⬤14:10. 24:52. Jn √5:23. 9:38. +√20:28. Ph 2:10, 11. He +*1:6. Re +*5:11-13. **Of a truth.** Jn 6:14. **the Son of God.** Mt 3:17. 4:3, 6. 8:29. *16:16. *17:5. 26:63. 27:40, 43, +*54n. Ps *2:7. Da *3:25. Mk 1:1. 3:11. *14:61. *15:39. Lk +*1:35. *4:41. *8:28. Jn *1:34, 49. 5:25. *6:68, 69. *9:35-38. 10:36. *11:27. 17:1. *19:7. 20:31. Ac √8:37n. 9:20. Ro *1:4. 2 C 1:19. He 1:2. 4:14. 1 J 4:15. 5:5. Re 2:18.

34. **when.** Mk 6:53-56. Jn 6:24, 25. **the land of Gennesaret.** i.e. *garden of the prince,* ✱S#1082g. Mk 6:53. Lk 5:1. *Gennesaret* was a fertile district, in which were situated the cities of Tiberias and Capernaum, extending along the western shore of the lake to which it gave name, about thirty stadia, or nearly four miles, in length, and twenty stadia, or two miles and a half, in breadth, according to Josephus (Bel. l. iii. c. 10, sec. 8). Lk 5:1.

35. **had knowledge.** Mk *6:54-56. **they sent.** Mt 4:24, 25. Mk 1:28-34. 2:1, etc. 3:8-10. 6:55. **all that were diseased.** Mt 4:24. 8:16.

36. **besought him.** Ps +*103:3. Je 17:14. *33:6. **only.** Mt *9:20, 21. Mk 3:10. 6:56. Lk *6:19. 8:47. Ac 5:15. *19:11, 12. **hem.** Mt 23:5. Ex 28:33, etc. Nu 15:38, 39. **perfectly.** Mk 10:52. Jn 6:37. 7:23. Ac 3:16. 4:9, 10, 14-16.

MATTHEW 15

Jesus reproves the Scribes and Pharisees, for setting their traditions above God's commandments; and exposes their hypocrisy, 1-9. He warns the people against their doctrine, and shows the source and nature of defilement, 10-20. He tries the faith, and heals the daughter, of a woman of Canaan, 21-28; heals great numbers at the sea of Galilee, 29-31; and again feeds the multitude by miracle, 32-39.

1. **came.** Mk 7:1-23. **scribes.** Mt 5:20. 23:2, 15, etc. Lk 5:30. Ac 23:9. **which.** Mk 3:22. Lk 5:17, 21.

2. **Why.** Mt 9:11. **transgress.** Mk *7:2, 5. Ga 1:14. Col *2:8, 20-23. 1 P 1:18. **tradition.** "Tradition," in Latin *traditio,* from *trado,* I deliver, hand down, exactly agreeing with the original *paradosis,* from *paradidomi,* I "deliver," "transmit." Among the Jews it signi-

fies what is called the *oral law*, which they say has been successively handed down from Moses, through every generation, to Judah the Holy, who compiled and digested it into the *Mishneh*, to explain which the two Gemaras, or Talmuds, called the Jerusalem and Babylonish, were composed. Of the estimation in which these were held by the Jews, the following may serve as an example: "The words of the Scribes are lovely beyond the words of the law, for the words of the law are weighty and light, but the words of the Scribes are all weighty." ver. 3, 6. Dt *4:2. +*12:32. Pr +*30:6. Ga 1:14. Col 2:8. Re +*22:18, 19. **the elders**. He 11:2. **for they**. Lk 11:38. **bread**. *171I8, Ge +3:19.

3. **Why**. Mt *7:3-5. Mk 7:6-8, 13. Col *2:8, 23. T *1:14. **tradition**. ver. +2. Mk √7:9.

4. **God**. Mt 4:10. 5:17-19. Is +*8:20n. Ro 3:31. **Honor**. Mt 19:19. Ge 9:20-27. 22:6-10. 31:35. 45:9-11. 47:12. Ex +*)20:12. Le 19:3. Dt)5:16. 27:16. Jg √11:36. 1 S 2:12. 3:9. 8:3. 2 S 15:10. 1 K *1:5, 6. 2:19. Est 2:20. Pr 1:8. 3:1, 2. 10:1. 13:1. *15:5. 17:25. 19:13, 26. 23:22. √28:24. Je 35:5-10, 16-19. Ezk 22:7. Mi 7:6. Ml 1:6. Mk 7:10. 10:19. Lk *2:51. 18:20. Ep √6:1, 2. Col *3:20. 1 T √5:4, 8. 2 T *3:1, 2. **He that**. Ex)21:15, 17. Le 20:9. Dt 21:18-21. √27:16. Pr *20:20. *30:11, 17.

5. **ye say**. Mt 23:16-18. Am 7:15-17. Mk √7:10-13. Ac 4:19. 5:29. **Whosoever**. *184B, Mt +23:30. **It is**. Ge 28:22. Le 27:9, etc. Pr 20:25. Mk 7:11, 12. **a gift**. Mt 23:18. **thou mightest**. Is +*58:7. Mk *7:12.

6. **honor**. 1 T √5:3, 4, 8, 16. *108B. Idiom B830. "Honor" has a wide range of meaning in Hebrew, and is used of nourishment, maintenance. For other instances of this idiom see 1 C 12:26. 1 T 5:3, 17. 1 P 3:7. **Thus**. Ps 119:126, 127, 139. Je 8:8, 9. Ho 4:6. Ml 2:7-9. Mk 7:13. Ro 3:31. **commandment of God**. Lk 5:1. Jn +*10:35. Ro 9:6. Re 1:2. **none effect**. Ro 2:23. Ga 3:17g. **tradition**. ver. 2.

7. **hypocrites**. Mt 6:2. 7:5. 23:23-29. **well**. Is)29:13. Mk 7:6. Ac 28:25-27.

8. **this people**. *92C, Mt +2:15. Lk +*24:27. **draweth**. Is)29:13. Ezk +*33:31. Jn 1:47. 1 P 3:10. **lips**. T#1261. Ps +*50:16, 17. Is 29:13. *58:1-3. Je 12:2. Ezk +*33:31. Mk 7:5-7. Ro 8:26. 2 T *3:5. T 1:16. Re 3:1. **but**. Pr *23:26. Je 12:2. Ac *8:21. He +*3:12.

9. **in vain**. Ex 20:7. Le 26:16, 20. 1 S 12:21. 25:21. Ps 39:6. 73:13. Ec *5:2-7. Is 1:13-15. 58:1-3. Ml 3:14. Mk 7:7. 1 C 15:2. Ja 1:26. 2:20. **worship**. Jn 4:24. **teaching**. Dt +*12:32. Pr +*30:5, 6. Is √29:13. Col *2:18-22. 1 T 1:4. 4:1-3, 6, 7. T 1:14. He 13:9. Re 22:18.

10. **he called**. 1 K 22:28. Mk 7:14, 16. Lk 20:45-47. **understand**. Mt +*13:19. 24:15. Is 6:9. +*55:3. Lk 24:45. Ep 1:17, 18. Col 1:9. Ja +*1:5.

11. **that which goeth**. Mk 7:15. Lk 11:38-41. Ac 10:14, 15. 11:8, 9. 21:28. Ro 14:14, 17, 20. 1 T √4:4, 5. T √1:15. He 9:13. 13:9. Re 21:27. **but**. ver. 18-20. Mt √12:34-37. Ps 10:7. 12:2. 52:2-4. 58:3, 4. Is 37:23. 59:3-5, 13-15. Je 9:3-6. Ro 3:13, 14. Ja √3:5-8. 2 P 2:18.

12. **Knowest**. Mt 17:27. 1 K 22:13, 14. 1 C 10:32, 33. 2 C 6:3. Ga 2:5. Ja 3:17. **offended**. Mt 11:6. 13:21, 41, 57. 24:10. 26:31, 33. Mk 6:3. Jn 16:1g. Ro 14:21g. 2 C 11:29g.

13. **Every plant**. *103, Ge +3:13. Mt 13:40, 41. Ps 92:13. Is +*60:21. 61:3. Jn *15:2, 6. 1 C √3:9, 12-

15. **which my**. Mt 7:21. **hath not**. Mt +*13:38-41. **planted**. Ps 1:3. **rooted up**. Ju 12.

14. **Let them alone**. T#477. Mt 7:15. 24:4. 2 Ch +19:2 (T#112). Ps +*119:63. Pr *19:27. Is 65:5n. Ho 4:17. Mk *4:24. Lk 21:8. Ro *16:17, 18. 1 C 5:11-13. +11:19 (T#176). 15:53. Ga *1:7-9. Ep +4:27 (T#18). +*5:11. Ph 3:2, 3. 1 T +*6:5 (T#177). 2 T 2:19. 3:5. 2 Th 3:6, 14, 15. T 3:10. Ja +5:20 (T#175). 2 J √10, 11. Ju +*3. **they**. Mt 23:16-24. Is *3:12. *9:16. 42:19. 56:10. Je 5:31. 50:6. Ezk 3:18. Ml +*2:7, 8. Lk *6:39. **And if**. *138C, Ge +22:14. *184C, Mt +4:9. Je 5:31. 6:15. 8:12. Ezk √14:9, 10. Mi 3:6, 7. Ro 2:19. 2 P 2:1, 17. Re 19:20. 22:15. **both**. T#478. Mt 23:13, 15. Is *9:16. Ezk √14:10. **fall into**. Mt +6:2n.

15. **Declare**. Mt 13:36. Mk 4:34. 7:17. Jn 16:29.

16. **Are ye also**. ver. 10. Mt 13:51. 16:9, 11. Is 28:9, 10. Mk 6:52. 7:18. 8:17, 18. 9:32. Lk 9:45. 18:34. 24:45. **He *5:12. without understanding**. Ro 1:21, 31. 10:19.

17. **that**. Mk 7:19, 20. Lk 6:45. 1 C 6:13. Col 2:21, 22. Ja 3:6. **and is**. 2 K 10:27.

18. **those things**. *73, Zc +1:5. ver. 11. Mt *12:34, 35. 1 S 24:13. Ps 36:3. Pr 6:12. 10:32. 15:2, 28. Lk 19:22. Ep +*4:29. Ja 3:6-10. Re 13:5, 6. **heart**. 1 K +*8:18. **defile**. ver. 11. Pr *10:19. 15:28. 1 C *3:17. Ja √3:6.

19. **out**. Mt 12:34. Ge *6:5. *8:21. Ps 58:3. Pr +*4:23. *6:14. 22:15. 24:9. Ec *9:3. Je +*17:9, 10. Mk √7:21-23. Ro 1:21. 3:10-19. 7:18. *8:7, 8. Ga √5:19-21. Ep *2:1-3. T *3:2-6. **evil thoughts**. Mt 9:4. Ps 56:5. 119:113. Is √55:7. 59:7. Je 4:14. Ac *8:22. Ja √1:13-15. 2:4. **murders**. 1 J √3:15. **adulteries**. Ex 20:15, 16. Mt 5:28. 1 C +*6:9, 18. **blasphemies**. Ep 4:31.

20. **which**. 1 C *3:16, 17. √6:9-11, 18-20. Ep *5:3-6. Re +*21:8, 27. **but**. ver. 2. Mt 23:25, 26. Mk √7:2-5. Lk 11:38-40.

21. **and departed**. Mt 12:15. 14:13. Mk 7:24-30. **Tyre**. Mt 10:5, 6. 11:21-23. Ge 49:13. Jsh 11:8. 13:6. 19:28, 29. Jg 1:31.

22. **a woman**. Mt 3:8, 9. Ps 45:12. Ezk 3:6. Mk 7:26. **Canaan**. i.e. *humiliation, to be low*, ✱S#5478g, only here. Mk 7:26. Ge 10:15, 19. Jg 1:30-33. Ac 7:11. 13:19. **Have**. Mt 9:27. 17:15. Ps 4:1. 6:2. Lk 17:13. 18:13. **son**. *171G, Ge +13:8. Mt 1:1. 20:30, 31. 22:42-45. Lk 18:38, 39. Jn 7:41, 42. **my**. Mt 17:15. Mk 7:25. 9:17-22. **vexed**. Mt 4:24.

23. **he answered**. Ge 42:7. Dt 8:2. Ps 28:1. La 3:8. **her not**. *1. Accismus; or, Apparent Refusal B962. ver. 26. Mt ?21:29. **Send**. T#1581. Mt 14:15. Mk 10:47, 48.

24. **said**. *60C, Ge +19:2. **I am not**. Mt 9:36. *10:5, 6. Is √53:6. Je 50:6, 7. Ezk 34:5, 6, 16, 23. Lk *15:4-6. Ac 3:25, 26. *13:46. Ro *15:8. 1 P *2:25. **lost**. Gr. *apollumi*, Mt +2:13. **sheep of**. Ps *79:13. 95:7. Je 50:6. Ezk 34:6. Ac *3:25, 26. Ro 9:4.

25. **came**. Mt 20:31. Ge *32:26. Ho 12:4. Lk √11:8-10. *18:1, etc. Ja *1:3. **worshipped**. Mt +*8:2. +*14:33. Re +5:12. **Lord**. Mk 9:22, 24. **help me**. T#1554. Ps 22:19. 30:10. 35:1, 2. 40:13. 70:1. 79:9.

26. **It**. *60C, Ge +19:2. **is not**. *1, ver. 23. Mt +6:2n. +*7:6. Ex 4:22. Mk 7:27, 28. Lk 16:1-9. Ac 22:21, 22. Ro 9:4. Ga 2:15. Ep 2:12. Ph 3:2. Re 22:15. **bread**. *171I8, Ge +3:19. **dogs**. *√103, Ge +3:13. *111, Ge +18:27. *Tois kunariois*, "to the little dogs," lap dogs, etc. the diminutive of *kuon*, "a dog." The Jews, while they boasted of being the children of God,

gave the name of "dogs" to the heathen, for their idolatry, etc. Mt +*7:6. 2 S 3:8. Ps 22:16. Pr 26:11. Re 22:15.

27. **Truth.** Mt 8:8. Ge 32:10. Jb 40:4, 5. 42:2-6. Ps 51:4, 5. Ezk 16:63. Da 9:18. Lk 7:6, 7. 15:18, 19. 18:13. 23:40-42. Ro 3:4, 19. 1 C 15:8, 9. 1 T 1:13-15. **yet.** ♪30. Antistrophe; or, Retort B965. A turning of the words of a speaker against himself. For another instance of this figure see 2 C 11:22. Mt *5:45. Lk *16:21. Ro 3:29. 10:12. Ep 3:8, 19.

28. **Jesus.** Jb 13:15. 23:10. La 3:32. **O woman.** ♪59, Ge +28:16. Our Lord's purpose being now answered, he openly commended her faith, and assured her that her daughter was healed. Mk 14:8. **great.** Mt 8:10. 9:2. 14:31. 1 S *2:30. Lk 17:5. Ro 4:19, 20. 2 Th 1:3. **be it.** Mt 8:13. *9:29, 30. Jb *13:15. Ps 145:19. Mk 5:34. *7:29, 30. 9:23, 24. Lk 7:9, 50. 18:42, 43. Jn 4:50-53. Ro *10:12. **very hour.** Mt 9:22. 17:18. Jn 4:52, 53.

29. **and came.** Mk 7:31. **unto.** Mt 4:18. Jsh 12:3, Chinneroth. Is 9:1. Mk 1:16. Lk 5:1, lake of Gennesaret. Jn 6:1, 23. 21:1, Tiberias. **went.** Mt 5:1. 13:2.

30. **great.** Mt 4:23-25. 8:1. **lame.** 11:4, 5. 14:35, 36. 21:14. Ps +*103:3. Is *35:5, 6. Mk 1:32-34. 6:54-56. Lk 6:17-19. 7:21, 22. Ac 2:22. 5:15, 16. 19:11, 12. **maimed.** ver. 31. Mt 18:8. Mk 9:43.

31. **the dumb.** Mt 9:33. Mk *7:37. **the maimed.** Mt 18:8. Mk 9:43. Lk 14:13, 21. **the lame.** Mt 21:14. Ac 3:2-11. 14:8-10. **the blind.** Lk 7:21. **they glorified.** Mt *5:16. 9:8. Ps 50:15, 23. Mk 2:12. Lk 2:20. 5:25, 26. 7:16. 13:13. 17:15-18. 18:43. 23:47. Jn 9:24. Ac 4:21. 11:18. **God.** Ge 32:28. 33:20mg. Ex 24:10. Is 29:23. Lk 1:68. Ac 13:17.

32. **Jesus.** Mt 9:36. 14:14. 20:34. Mk *8:1, 2. 9:22. Lk 7:13. **I have.** He +*4:15. **compassion.** ♪22A18, Is +63:15. **three.** Mt 12:40. 27:63. Ac 27:33. **and have.** Mt 6:32, 33. Lk 12:29, 30. **lest.** 1 S 14:28-31. 30:11, 12. Mk 8:3.

33. **Whence.** Nu 11:21, 22. 2 K 4:42-44. Mk 6:37. 8:4, 5. Jn 6:5-7. **to fill.** Mt 14:15. Lk 9:13. Jn 6:8, 9.

34. **How.** Mt 16:9, 10. **few.** Lk 24:41, 42. Jn 21:9, 10.

35. **to sit.** Mt 14:19, etc. Mk 6:39, 40. Lk 9:14-16. Jn 6:10.

36. **and gave thanks.** Mt ◐+14:19. 26:27. Mk 8:6. 14:23. Lk *22:17, 19. ◐+√24:30. Jn *6:11, 23. Ac 27:35. Ro 14:6. 1 C √10:30, 31. 11:24. 14:16, 17. **and brake.** ♪108H4, Is +58:7. **gave to.** Mt 14:19.

37. **all.** ver. 33. Mt 14:20, 21. 2 K 4:42-44. Ps 107:9. Lk 1:53. **seven.** Mt 16:9, 10. Mk 8:8, 9, 19-21.

38. **four thousand men.** Mt ◐14:21. *16:9, 10. **women.** Ne +*12:43. **and children.** Mt 14:21. Dt +*29:11n. Ne +*12:43. Is 54:13.

39. **he sent.** Mt 14:22. Mk 8:10. **Magdala.** i.e. *magnificent,* ✻S#3093g, only here. Jsh 19:38n. Mk 8:10. 15:40.

MATTHEW 16

Jesus rebukes the hypocrisy of the Pharisees and Sadducees, who required a sign from heaven; and refuses to give any but the sign of Jonas, 1-4. He warns the disciples against the leaven of the Pharisees and Sadducees, explains his meaning, and reproves the disciples for unbelief and want of understanding, 5-12. The opinions of the people concerning him, 13, 14.

Peter's confession of Christ commended, 15-17. The foundation of the church, and the power of the keys, 18-20. Jesus foretells his death and resurrection, and rebukes Peter for dissuading him from suffering, 21-23. He shows that his disciples must deny themselves, and suffer, in prospect of a future reward, 24-27. The speedy establishment of his kingdom, 28.

1. **Pharisees.** Mt 5:20. 9:11. 12:14. 15:1. 22:15, 34. 23:2. 27:62. **Sadducees.** ver. 6, 11, 12. Mt 3:7, 8. 22:23. Mk 12:18. Lk 20:27. Ac 4:1. 5:17. 23:6-8. **tempting.** Mt 19:3. 22:18, 35. Mk *8:11. 10:2. 12:15. Lk 10:25. 11:16, 53, 54. 20:23. Jn 6:6. *8:6. *12:37. **a sign.** Mt *11:3-5. *12:38, 39. Mk 8:11-13. Lk 11:16, 29, 30. 12:54-56. +*21:11. Jn 6:30, 31. Ac 2:22. 1 C 1:22.

2. **When.** Lk 12:54-56. **weather.** Ge +9:14.

3. **lowring.** ✻S#4768g. Mk 10:22 (was sad). **O ye.** Mt 7:5. 15:7. 22:18. 23:13. Lk 11:44. 12:56. 13:15. **the signs.** Mt 3:1-3. 4:23. 11:5. 12:28. Ge +*49:10. 1 Ch +*12:32. Is *35:4-6. Da +*9:24. Lk *19:44.

4. **wicked.** Mt +*12:39, 40. Mk *8:12, 38. Ac 2:40. **but.** Jon 1:17. Lk 11:29, 30. **And he.** Mt 4:13. +*15:14. 21:17. Ge 6:3. Ho 4:17. 9:12. Mk 5:17, 18. Ac 18:6.

5. **were come.** Mt 15:39. Mk *8:13, 14.

6. **Take heed.** Lk 12:15. **beware.** ver. 11. Lk 12:1. Ac 5:35g. 1 Th √5:21. 1 J 4:1. **the leaven.** ♪103, Ge +3:13. ver. 12. Mt 13:33n. Ex 12:15-19. Le *2:11. Mk 8:15. Lk 12:1. 13:20, 21. 1 C *5:6-8. Ga *5:9. 2 T 2:16, 17. **the Pharisees.** ver. 1.

7. **they reasoned.** ver. 8. Mk 8:16-18. 9:10. 21:25. Lk 3:15. 9:46. **It is.** ♪63D1. Ellipsis B51: when a whole clause is omitted in a connected passage; when the first member of a clause is omitted. Here, supply by ellipsis "And they reasoned among themselves, saying (Jesus spoke thus, ver. 6), because we have taken no bread." For other instances of this figure see Mt 25:27n. Mk 3:30. Lk 9:13. Jn 5:7. 2 Th *2:3. For additional instances of this figure which occur as the unexpressed protasis ("if" clause) of an apodosis ("then" clause) in hypothetical propositions of the fourth condition (to express mere assumption with a remote idea of realization), see ♪184D2, Lk +1:62. **because.** Mt 15:16-18. Ac 10:14.

8. **when.** Mt 26:10. Jn +*2:24, 25. 16:30. He *4:13. Re *2:23. **O ye.** Mt 6:30. 8:26. 14:31. 17:20. Mk 6:52. 8:17. 16:14. Lk 17:6.

9. **ye not.** Mt 15:16, 17. Mk 7:18. Lk 24:25-27. Re 3:19. **the five loaves.** Mt 14:17-21. Mk 6:38-44. Lk 9:13-17. Jn 6:9-13. **baskets.** Mt 14:20. Mk 6:43. 8:19. Lk 9:17. Jn 6:13.

10. **Neither the seven.** Mt 15:34-38. Mk 8:5-9, 17-21. **baskets.** Mt 15:37. Mk 8:8, 20. Ac 9:25.

11. **How is it.** Mk 4:40. 8:21. Lk 12:56. Jn 8:43. **beware.** ver. 6. **leaven.** ver. 6. Mt +13:33n. **Sadducees.** ver. 1.

12. **Then understood.** Mt 17:13. **beware.** ver. 6. Lk 12:1. **of bread.** Jn 6:27. **but.** Mt 15:4-9. 23:13, etc. Ac *23:8. **the doctrine.** Mt 5:20. 23:3. 1 C 5:6, 7. Ga 5:9.

13. **When.** Mk 8:27-29. Lk 9:18-20. **came.** Mt 15:21. Ac *10:38. **Caesarea Philippi.** S#2542g and S#5375g. Mt 16:13. Mk 8:27. *Caesarea Philippi* was anciently called *Paneas,* from the mountain of Panium, or Hermon, at the foot of which it was situated, near the springs of Jordan; but Philip the tetrarch, the son of Herod the Great, having rebuilt it, gave it the name of Caesarea in honor of Tiberius, the reigning emperor,

and added his own name to it, to distinguish it from another Caesarea on the coast of the Mediterranean. It was afterwards named *Neronias* by the young Agrippa, in honor of *Nero*; and, in the time of William of Tyre, it was called *Belinas*. It was, according to Josephus, a day's journey from Sidon, and 120 stadia from the lake of Phiala; and, according to Abulfeda, a journey of a day and a half from Damascus. Many have confounded it with *Dan*, or *Leshem*; but Eusebius and Jerome expressly affirm that Dan was four miles from Paneas, on the road to Tyre. It is now called *Banias*, and is described, by Seetzen, as a hamlet of about twenty miserable huts, inhabited by Mohammedans; but Burckhardt says it contains about 150 houses, inhabited by Turks, Greeks, etc. **Whom**. Mk 8:27. Lk *9:18, etc. Jn 6:68, 69. **I the**. Mt 8:20. 9:6. 12:8, 32, 40. 13:37, 41. 25:31. Da *7:13. Mk 8:38. 10:45. Jn 1:51. 3:14. 5:27. 12:34. Ac 7:56. He 2:14-18. **Son**. *144A3, Ge +11:5.

14. **Some**. *108E1, Mt +8:19. **John**. Mt *14:2. Mk 6:14. 8:28. Lk 9:7. **Elias**. Mt 17:10. Ml *4:5. Mk 6:15. 9:11. Lk 9:8, 18, 19. Jn 1:21. 7:12, 40, 41. 9:17. **Jeremias**. *S#2408g. Mt 2:17. 27:9. For *S#3414h, see Je +1:1. **one of the prophets**. Mt 21:11. Jn 6:14.

15. **But**. Mt 13:11. Mk *8:29. Lk *9:20.

16. **Simon Peter**. Jn 1:40, 42. 6:68, 69. **Thou**. ver. 20. Mt 1:1. 11:2. *14:33. *26:63, 64, 68. *27:54. Ps *2:7. Mk *14:61, 62. Lk 2:26. 4:41. 9:20. 22:67. 23:2. Jn *1:41, 49. 4:25, 26. √6:69. 10:24, 25. *11:27. *20:31. Ac 4:27. *8:37. 9:20. 18:5. Ro 1:4. He 1:2-5. 1 J *4:15. 5:5, 20. **Christ**. i.e. *anointed, consecrated*, S#5547g. Mt 1:17. 2:4. 11:2. 16:16. 22:42. 23:8, 10. 26:63, 68. Mk *8:29. 9:41. 12:35. 14:61. 15:32. Lk 2:11, 26. 4:41, 41. *9:20. 20:41. 22:67. 23:2, 35, 39. 24:26, 46. Jn 1:20, 25, 41. 3:28. 4:25, 29, 42. 6:69. 7:26, 27, 31, 41, 41, 42. 9:22. 10:24. *11:27. 12:34. **the son**. Mt 14:33. 1 J 4:15. 5:5. **the living God**. Mt 26:63. Dt 5:26. Jsh 3:10. 1 S 17:26. 2 K 19:4, 16. Ps *42:2. 84:2. Is 37:4, 17. Je *10:10. 23:36. Da *6:20, 26. Ho 1:10. Jn 6:57. Ac 14:15. Ro 9:26. 14:11. 2 C 3:3. 6:16. 1 Th 1:9. 1 T 3:15. 4:10. He +*3:12. 9:14. 10:31. 12:22. 1 P 1:23. Re 4:9, 10. 7:2. 10:6. 15:7.

17. **Blessed**. Mt 5:3-11. 13:16, 17. Lk 10:23, 24. 22:32. Jn *20:29. Ro √10:9, 10. 1 P 1:3-5. 5:1. **Simon**. Jn 1:42. 21:15-17. **Bar-jona**. i.e. *son of Jonas or Jonah*, *S#920g, only here. Mt 10:3. Mk 10:46. Ac 13:6. **for**. Ga 1:11, 12, 16. **flesh and blood**. Lk ◑+*24:39. Jn *1:13. 1 C *15:50. Ga 1:16. Ep 6:12. He 2:14. *171Q11. Synecdoche of the Part B644. "Flesh and blood" is put for the *human* nature as distinct from the Divine nature: or for the body of man as animal, mortal, and corruptible. Here, this emphasis denotes "no human being revealed this unto thee." For other instances of this figure see 1 C 15:50. Ga 1:16. Ep 6:12. He 2:14. **but**. Mt *11:25-27. Is *54:13. Lk 10:21, 22. Jn √6:44, 45. 17:6-8. 1 C 1:28, 29. 2:9-12. Ga *1:15, 16. Ep *1:17, 18. √2:8-10. 3:5, 18, 19. Col 1:26, 27. 1 J 4:15. 5:20. **my Father**. Jn 6:45. 1 C +*12:3. 1 J *5:1, 5. **in heaven**. Mt 7:11, 21.

18. **thou**. Mt 10:2. Jn √1:42. Ga *2:9. **Peter**. Gr. *Petros*. i.e. *a stone, a piece of rock*, *S#4074g. Mt 4:18. 8:14. 10:2. 14:28, 29. 15:15. 16:16, 18, 22, 23. 17:1, 4, 24, 26. 18:21. 19:27. 26:33, 35, 37, 40, 58, 69, 73, 75. Mk 3:16. 5:37. 8:29, 32, 33. 9:2, 5. 10:28. 11:21. 13:3. 14:29, 33, 37, 54, 66, 67, 70, 72. 16:7. Lk 5:8. 6:14. 8:45, 51. 9:20, 28, 32, 33. 12:41. 18:28.

22:8, 34, 54, 55, 58, 60, 61, 61, 62. 24:12. Jn 1:40, 44. 6:8, 68. 13:6, 8, 9, 24, 36, 37. 18:10, 11, 15, 16, 16, 17, 18, 25, 26, 27. 20:2, 3, 4, 6. 21:2, 3, 7, 11, 15, 17, 20, 21. Ac 1:13, 15. 2:14, 37, 38. 3:1, 3, 4, 6, 11, 12. 4:8, 13, 19. 5:3, 8, 9, 15, 29. 8:14, 20. 9:32, 34, 38, 39, 40, 40. 10:5, 9, 13, 14, 17, 18, 19, 21, 23, 25, 26, 32, 34, 44, 45, 46. 11:2, 4, 7, 13. 12:3, 5, 6, 7, 11, 13, 14, 14, 16, 18. 15:7. Ga 1:18. 2:7, 8, 11, 14. 1 P 1:1. 2 P 1:1. This important incident recorded most fully here in Matthew does not seem to be understood by the apostles as giving any primacy or special authority to Peter, for just a short time later they are arguing about who should be greatest in the Kingdom (Mt 18:1n. 20:21-24). **upon**. Is 28:16. 1 C 3:10, 11. Ep 2:19-22. Re 21:14. **rock**. *22L3, Dt +32:31. *135, Ps +68:28. Gr. *Petra*. What is the "rock" upon which Christ will build His church? Greek grammar is against "rock" referring to Peter, for "Peter" is masculine gender, while "rock" is neuter gender. Some counter, however, that such nice distinctions in the Greek were not made in the Aramaic, the language which Jesus actually spoke. The fact that there are such nice distinctions in the Greek at numerous points as seen by the figure of speech Paronomasia (*140, Ge +4:25), as at Mt 21:41; 22:3; 24:7; shows that Matthew was originally written in Greek, and is not a translation from the Aramaic. No less an authority than Nigel Turner cites this very distinction (Petros, petra) as evidence that Jesus on this occasion spoke in Greek, not Aramaic (*Grammatical Insights*, p. 181; *Grammar of N.T. Greek*, vol. iv. p. 38), and that Matthew's gospel was originally written in Greek, and is not a translation from the Aramaic. The "rock" may be the truth of Peter's confession, the faith which underlies the confession, or it may be a reference to Christ himself. The latter view seems to be favored by the reference passages. Mt *7:24-27. Is 28:16. 1 C 3:9-11. √10:4. Ep *2:20-22. Col 1:18. 1 P 2:4-6. Re 21:14. **I will build**. This verb is first person singular, future tense, active voice, indicative mood. Since the tense of this verb is future, some understand the founding of Christ's church as future to this time of his speaking. If this is the correct understanding, then the church of the New Testament is distinct from the church of the Old Testament. Others, however, believe that the church is one in both Testaments, though in the Old Testament the church is national, in the New Testament it is universal. In support of the latter view, the church in Mt 18:17 is spoken of as already existing, not future. Various titles and expressions in the New Testament show the church to be in both Testaments (Ac 7:38; Ro 11:17-21; 1 C 3:16, 17; 2 C 6:16; Ep 2:11-16, 21; Ga 4:26; He 12:22). Zc +*6:12, 13. 1 C 3:9. Ga √2:9. He 3:3, 4. 1 P 2:4, 5. **my**. Mt 18:17. Ac 2:47. 8:1. Ep 3:10. √5:25-27, 32. Col √1:18. 1 T 3:5, 15. **and the gates**. *171S7B, Ge +14:7. Ge 22:17. 2 S 18:4. Jb 38:17. Ps 9:13. 69:12. 107:18. 127:5. Pr 24:7. SS 8:6. Is 28:6. 38:10. 1 C +*15:55mg. **hell**. Gr. *hades*, Mt +11:23. **shall not**. Ps 125:1, 2. Is 28:16. 54:17. Jn √5:24. √10:27-30. 11:25, 26. Ac *5:39. Ro √8:33-39. 1 C +*15:55. He 12:28. Re 1:18. *11:15. *20:6. *21:1-4.

19. **give**. Ac 2:14, etc. 10:34, etc. 15:7. **the keys**. Is 22:22. Lk +*11:52. Ac 2:14, 41. 10:5, 6, 44, 45. 15:√7, 28. 1 C *5:3-5. 2 C *5:18, 20. 2 P 1:20. Re ◑1:18. 3:7. 9:1. 20:1-3. Perhaps the use of the "keys"

is seen in Peter's "binding" (Ac 5:3-10. 8:20-23) and "loosing" (Ac 2:38-42, opening the door to the Jews. Ac 10:45, opening the door to the Gentiles). **kingdom of heaven.** Mt 4:17. **and whatsoever.** ♪184C, Mt +4:9. Mt √18:18n. Ml √3:18. Jn √20:23. 1 C 5:4, 5. 2 C 2:10. 1 Th 4:8. Re 11:6. **thou.** ♪121I1, Ge +3:7. **shalt bind.** ♪121I2, Ge +2:17. ♪121S3A. Metonymy of the Adjunct B606. The sign is put for the thing signified in connected words and phrases: "to bind and loose" is put for exercising of authority. For another instance of this figure see Mt *18:18. Gr. *dasas*, second person singular, first aorist active, subjunctive mood. **shall be.** Gr. *estai*, third person singular, future middle indicative. **bound.** Gr. *dedemenon*, present passive participle, nominative singular neuter. **whatsoever.** ♪184C, Mt +4:9. **thou shalt loose.** Gr. *lusas*, second person singular, first aorist active subjunctive. Ac +*3:19. *10:43. Ga *5:1. 1 J √1:9. **shall be loosed.** Gr. *lelumenon*, perfect passive participle, nominative singular neuter. In the Greek text some very fine shades of meaning are preserved which are not generally translated into the English versions. "Shall be loosed" is a rare construction in Greek called the "future passive periphrastic perfect indicative" (Robertson, *Word Pictures*, vol. 1, p. 149, on Mt 18:18), which more literally may be rendered "shall have been already loosed in heaven." The special point of using this tense is to show that the apostles would by their teaching and preaching "bind" and "loose" by the message of Christ what had already been bound and loosed in heaven, for Christ's words were not his own, but those of the Father who sent him (Jn 5:19, 30. 6:38. 8:26, 42. √12:49. √14:10. 17:8, 14). See the fuller explanation at Mt 18:18n.

20. charged. Mt 8:4. *12:16-19. 17:9. Is *52:13. Mk 5:43. 8:30. 9:9. Lk 9:21, 36. Jn 2:4. Ac 15:24g. He 12:20g. **Jesus.** ver. 16. Jn 1:41, 45. *20:31. Ac 2:36. 1 J 2:22. 5:1.

21. From that time. Mt 4:17. **began.** Mt 17:12, 22, 23. 20:17-19, 28. 26:2. Mk 8:31. 9:12, 30-32. 10:32-34. Lk 9:22, 31, 44, 45. 13:33. 18:31-34. *24:6-8, 26, 27, 46. 1 C +*15:3, 4. **chief priests.** Mt 26:47. 27:12. 1 Ch 24:1-19. Ne 12:7. **and be.** Mt 27:63. Jn 2:19-21. Ac 2:23-32. **the third day.** Mt +*12:40n. 20:19. 27:63, 64. Lk 18:33. 24:7, √21, 46. Jn 2:19. Ac 10:40. 1 C +*15:4.

22. began. ver. 16, 17. 26:51-53. Mk 8:32. Jn 13:6-8. **Be it far from thee.** Gr. Pity thyself. *♪63A1, Ge +14:20. Supply by ellipsis (absolute: of the nominative), "(God be) merciful to Thee, Lord!" 2 S 20:20. 23:17. 1 K 22:13. 1 Ch *11:19. Ac 21:11-13.

23. he turned. Lk 22:61. **and said.** An example of "double reference." Ge 3:15. Is 7:14, 15. 14:12-14. 25:8n. Je 29:10-14. Ezk 28:11-17. Ho +11:1. Mk 5:7-16. Lk 4:33-35. **Get thee.** ♪34, Ps +50:16. Mt *4:10. Ge *3:1-6, 17. Mk *8:33. Lk 4:8. 2 C √11:14, 15. **Satan.** 2 S 19:22. 1 Ch *21:1. Zc *3:1, 2. Jn 6:70. Ac *5:3. 1 C 5:5. Re 2:9. **thou art.** Mt 13:41. 18:7. Is *8:14. Ro *14:13, 21. **thou savorist.** Mk 8:33. Ro *8:5-8. 1 C *2:14, 15. Ph 2:5. *3:19. Col *3:2.

24. If. ♪184A, 1 C +15:2. Mt *10:38. Mk 8:34. *10:21. Lk *9:23-27. *14:25-27. Ac *14:22. Col 1:24. 1 Th 3:3. 2 T *3:12. He *11:24-26. **come after.** Mt 10:24, 25. 1 C +*11:1. He *13:12, 13. **deny himself.** 2 T 2:12, 13. **and take.** Mt 10:38, 39. 27:32. Mk 15:21. Lk 23:26. Jn 19:17. 1 P *4:1, 2. **follow me.** Jn *8:12.

25. whosoever. ♪184C, Mt +4:9. ♪125, Jb +22:6. **will save.** ♪121C2C2, Ge +29:31. Mt *10:39. Est 4:14, 16. Mk *8:35. Lk 14:33. 17:33. Jn *12:25. Ac *20:23, 24. Re *12:11. **life.** Gr. *psyche*, ♪121A7, Mt +2:20. ♪121A7, Ge +9:5. **life.** Gr. *psyche*, ♪121A7, Mt +2:20. ♪121A7, Ge +9:5. **for my sake.** Mk 13:9. **shall find it.** Re 2:10.

26. for what. Mt *5:29. Jb 2:4. Zp *1:18. Mk 8:36. Lk *9:25. **if he.** ♪184C, Mt +4:9. **gain.** Mt *4:8, 9. 18:1-5. 23:12. Jb *27:8. Mk 10:35-45. Lk *12:20. 16:25. 22:24-30. Jn 13:3-17. 1 J *2:16. **world.** Gr. *kosmos*, Mt 4:8. **and lose.** Gr. *dzemoo*, ✳S#2210g. Rendered (1) lose: Mt 16:26. Mk 8:36. (2) suffer loss: 1 C 3:15. Ph 3:8. (3) be cast away: Lk 9:25. (4) receive damage: 2 C 7:9. **soul.** Gr. *psyche*, ♪121A7, Mt +2:20. T#984‡ . Ge 19:17. *35:18. Jg *9:17. Lk 9:24. **or what shall.** Ps *49:7, 8. Mk 8:37. **soul.** Gr. *psyche*, ♪121A7, Mt +2:20.

27. the Son of man. ♪144A3, Ge +11:5. The title "Son of man" designates Christ's human nature, as the title "Son of God" denotes his divine nature (Ac 8:37n). The use of "Son of man" here in reference to his second coming in glory shows unmistakably that this coming is personal, physical, and visible. Peters notes that this title serves particularly to identify Jesus Christ as the Messiah in fulfillment of the Davidic Covenant, noting "it is the peculiar, distinctive, predicted name of the Messiah given to Him in virtue of His covenanted relationship to the Kingdom" (*Theocratic Kingdom*, vol. 1, p. 566). Mt +*8:20. +*19:28. +*24:30. *25:31-34, 46. *26:64. Ps √80:17. Da +√7:13. Mk 1:2n. *8:38. *13:26. *14:62. Lk *9:26. 21:27. 22:69. Jn 1:51n. 3:13n. *5:27. 13:31. Ac +*1:11. *7:56. 1 Th 1:10. 2 Th 1:10. 1 J √4:2n. 2 J √7n. Re +*1:7. **shall come.** Mt 24:44. 26:64. Lk 12:40. 17:30. Jn 1:51. Ac +*1:11. **the glory.** Mt *24:30. *25:31. Ps +*102:16. Is *2:19, 21. 35:2. *40:5. 60:1, 2, 19. 62:2. Zc *6:13. Mk 8:38. Lk 9:26. Jn +*17:5. Col 3:4. **with his angels.** Mt 13:41, 49. 25:31. Dt 33:2. Da *7:10. Zc *14:5. 1 Th 4:16. 2 Th *1:7-10. Ju *14. **and then.** Mt 10:+*15n, 26. *41, *42. +*12:36. Ec *12:14. Lk 8:17. 12:2, 3. √14:14. Jn 5:29. Ro 2:16. 2 T *4:8. He +√9:27, 28. Re √11:18. *22:12. **shall reward.** Mt 5:12, +26g. 6:4, 6, 18. Ps 62:12. Pr 24:12. Ec ❍*9:5. Il:9. 12:14. Is 3:10, 11. √40:10. Je *17:10. 32:19. Ezk 7:27. Lk *14:14. Jn 5:29. Ac 10:42. Ro *2:6. 14:12. 1 C 3:8. 2 C *5:10. Ep *6:8. Col 3:24, 25. 1 T +*4:8. He +√9:27. 1 P 1:17. Re 2:10, 23. *3:21. √11:18. 20:12. 22:12-15. **every man.** Jn 5:28. **according to.** T#556. Mt 5:19. Jb 34:11. Ps +33:5 (T#232). *62:12. Pr 24:12. Is *3:10, 11. Je *17:10. 32:19. Lk 19:16-19. Ro +2:11 (T#231). 14:12. 2 C √5:10. Ga *6:7, 8. 1 P *1:17. Re *2:23. 22:12.

28. There. Mk *9:1. Lk *9:27. **not.** ♪158, Mt +5:18. **taste.** Lk 2:26. Jn *8:51, 52. He *2:9. **till.** Mt +*23:39. **see.** This appears to refer to the mediatorial kingdom which our Lord was about to set up, by the destruction of the Jewish nation and polity, and the diffusion of the gospel throughout the world. The preceding original *Comprehensive Bible* note reflects a mistaken prophetic position still held by some Amillenarian interpreters, answered directly by Peters (*Theocratic Kingdom*, vol. 2, Proposition 153, Observation 4, Note 4, p. 562), who states "who urge the destruction of Jerusalem (which John only survived) as the fulfillment (of Mt 16:27, 28). How this can be reconciled with a coming *in glory*, with a coming of *the Son of Man* (i.e. in His humanity), etc., we are not informed. More than this: this coming is specifically predicted, over against all such assertions, to be one, not for *the destruction* of Jerusalem but for *its salvation*, as e.g. Ps 102:16, "when the Lord shall build up Zion, He shall appear in His glory," with which compare Micah 3:12 in connection with following chapter; Zc ch. 14; Am 9:11, etc." In context, however, the experiences on the mount of transfiguration reported in chapter 17 may be the fulfillment of this prophecy. Peters also notes in connection with the transfiguration, that "the glorified condition of Christ, Moses, and Elias thus indicates...the futurity of the Kingdom.—a Kingdom not to be realized at the First Advent in humiliation, not during the absence of the Bridegroom, but at the Second Advent, when He and His saints come 'in glory.' " The transfiguration furnished "an earnest, actual reception of glory," and served as "a most direct proof that the covenant and prophets would *yet be fulfilled*." The transfiguration reveals the relationships of those who will be with Christ in his future eternal earthly kingdom. Peter, James, and John, represent unglorified, mortal men living on the earth, who personally witness and rejoice in the manifested glory of the Messiah. Jesus is personally present in this kingdom in His state of glory, as are Moses and Elias, who also appeared "in glory." Moses and Elias are purposely chosen as a correct exhibition of the two parties, forming one class, who shall appear in glory with Christ: (1) the dead saints, and (2) the living saints translated. Peters notes that the transfiguration "stands forth, pre-eminently, as a Divine confirmation of the Theocratic Kingship of Jesus, of the glory of His saints, and of the happiness of the nations who shall witness it—a fact so striking and corroborative of the ultimate Redemption of saints and of the race, that Peter seizes upon it as *a grand proof* that Jesus shall come unto so great Salvation" (*Theocratic Kingdom*, vol. 2, p. 561). Others see in this a reference to the experience of Pentecost of Acts ch. 2, for Christ promised "I will come to you" in the person of the Holy Spirit (Jn 14:18. Re 3:20). However, the parallel passages make it clear that this is a reference to the second advent of Christ, in full agreement with the position taken by Peters, noted above. Mt √10:23. 23:36. *24:3, 27-31, 34, 42, 44. *25:31. *26:64. Mk 1:15. *13:26, 30. Lk *18:8. *21:27, 28, 31, 32. **Son of man**. ∫144A3, Ge +11:5. Mt 8:20. **coming**. Mt +*24:30. *26:64. Da 7:13, 14. Lk *23:42. 2 P √1:16-18. Re 1:7. **in his kingdom**. Mt 20:21. *25:31, +*34. Da 7:14. Mk 9:1. Lk 9:27. 23:42. Ac *1:3, 6n. Col *1:13n. 2 T +*4:1n. 2 P 1:11. 3:4, 13. Re *11:15.

MATTHEW 17

The transfiguration of Christ, who discourses with Moses and Elias before Peter, James, and John, 1-8. He charges them not to make it known; and instructs them concerning the coming of Elias, 9-13. He casts out an evil spirit, and reproves the unbelief of the people and of his disciples, 14-21. He foretells his death and resurrection, 22, 23; and pays tribute with money obtained by miracle, 24-27.

1. **after**. Mk 9:2-8. Lk 9:28-36. **six days**. St. Luke, taking in both the day of the preceding discourse and that of the transfiguration, as well as the *six* intermedi-

ate ones, says it was *eight* days after. Lk *9:28. **Peter**. Mt 4:21. *26:37. Mk *5:37, 38. 9:2. 13:3. Lk 8:51. 9:28. 2 C 13:1. **an high**. Dt 3:25. 2 P 1:18.

2. **transfigured**. Lk *9:29. Ro *12:2. 2 C 3:18g. Ph 2:6, 7g. **his face**. Mt 28:3. Ex=34:29-35. Jn 1:14. 17:24. Ac 26:13-15. 2 C 3:7. Re 1:13-17. 10:1. 19:12, 13. 20:11. **raiment**. Mt 28:3. Ps 104:2. Da 7:9. Mk *9:3. Re 1:14.

3. **behold**. Mk 9:4. Lk *9:30, 31. **appeared**. Hence we see that they who on earth have been faithful to Christ, though they be dead, yet live in him, and retain their *personal identity*, and will hereafter have the *same* bodies, as on earth, but *glorified*. Perhaps also the Holy Spirit thus intimates the doctrine of *mutual recognition* in a *future* state of glory (Wordsworth, *Greek Testament*, vol. 1, p. 61). Ge 37:35n. 1 S 28:12. 2 S 12:23. Lk +*16:23. 1 C 2:9. +*13:12. **Moses**. Mt 11:13, 14. Dt 18:18. *34:5, 6, 10. Lk 24:27, 44. Jn 1:17. 5:45-47. 2 C 3:7-11. Ph *1:23. He 3:1-6. **Elias**. ver. 10-13. 1 K 17:1. 18:36-40. 2 K *2:11-14. Ml 4:5, Elijah. Lk 1:17. 9:33. 16:16.

4. **answered**. Mk *9:5, 6. Lk 9:33. **it is**. Ex 33:18, 19. Ps 4:6. 16:11. 63:1-5. Is 33:17. Zc 9:17. Jn 14:8, 9. 17:24. Ph 1:23. 1 J 3:2. Re 21:23. 22:3-5. **if thou wilt**. ∫184A, 1 C +15:2. The use of the first class condition in this hypothetical proposition shows this was a foregone conclusion with Peter. Ac 18:14. 2 C 11:1. **tabernacles**. Le +=23:34, 42. Ne 8:15.

5. **bright cloud**. Mt +*24:30. Ex 24:15, 16. 33:9. *40:34, 35. 1 K 8:10-12. 2 Ch +*5:12. Ps 18:10, 11. Lk 9:34. Ac 1:9. 2 P 1:17. Re 1:7. **a voice**. Ex 19:19. Dt 4:11, 12. 5:22. Jb 38:1. Ps 81:7. Jn 5:37. 12:28-30. Ac 9:3-6. **out of**. ∫22D3J5, Ex +13:21. **This**. Mt 3:17. Mk 1:11. 9:7. Lk 3:22. 9:35. Jn √3:16, 35. √5:20-23. Ep *1:6. Col 1:13mg. He *1:1, 2. *2:1-3. 2 P √1:16, 17. **in whom**. Mt 12:18. Ex=33:17. Is 42:1, 21. Jn 15:9, 10. **well pleased**. Is=41:8. **hear**. ∫74, Jg +5:31. Dt *18:15, 18, 19. Jn *1:18. Ac *3:22, 23. 7:37. He *1:1, 2. *2:1-3. *5:9. 12:25, 26.

6. **heard**. 2 P *1:18. **they fell**. Ge 17:3, 17. Le 9:24. Jsh 5:14. Jg 13:20, 22. 1 Ch 21:16. Ezk 1:28. 3:23. 43:3. 44:4. Da 8:17. 10:7-9, 16, 17. Ac 9:4. 22:7. 26:14. Re 1:17. **afraid**. Mt 14:27. Ge +19:30. Mk 6:50. Lk 24:37. Re 1:17.

7. **touched**. Da 8:18. 9:21. 10:10, 18. Re *1:17. **Arise**. Lk 24:5. Ac 9:6. **afraid**. Ge +19:30.

8. **lifted**. ∫144A12, Ge +22:13. **they saw**. Ge=45:1. Mk 9:8. Lk 9:36. Ac 12:10, 11.

9. **Jesus**. Mt 16:20. Mk 8:30. *9:9, 10. Lk 8:56. 9:21, 22, 36. **Tell**. Mt 8:4. 12:16. **the vision**. Lk 24:23. Ac 7:31g. **until**. ver. 23. Mt 16:21. Lk 18:33, 34. 24:46, 47. **Son of man**. Mt 8:20.

10. **Why**. ver. 3, 4. Mt 11:14. 27:47-49. Ml 4:5, 6. Mk 9:11. Jn 1:21, 25. **Elias**. Ml ⏵4:5. Mt 11:14. 16:14.

11. **shall**. ∫96C6, Mt +2:4. **and restore**. ∫108A1, Ex +8:18. Is 11:11n. Ml *4:6. Mk *9:12. Lk 1:16, 17. 3:3-14. Ac +*1:6. +*3:21.

12. **and they**. Mt 11:9-15. 21:23-25, 32. Mk 9:12, 13. 11:30-32. Lk 7:33. Jn 1:11. 5:32-36. Ac 13:24-28. **knew**. Gr. *epiginosko*, Mt +11:27. **but**. Mt 11:2. *14:3-10. Mk 6:14-28. Lk 3:19, 20. Ac 7:52. **Likewise**. ver. 22, 23. Mt 16:21. Is 53:3, etc. Lk 9:21-25. 17:25. Ac 2:23. 3:14, 15. 4:10.

13. **understood**. Mt 16:12. **he spake**. Mt 11:14.

14. **when**. Mk 9:14-28. Lk 9:37-42. **kneeling**. Mk 1:40. 10:17. Ac 10:25, 26.

15. **have**. Mt 9:27. 15:22. Mk 5:22, 23. 9:22. Lk

9:38-42. Jn 4:46, 47. **for.** Mt 4:24. Mk 9:17, 18, 20-22. **lunatic.** T#1613. *Selaniadzetai,* from *selana,* the "moon," one who was affected with his disorder at the change and full of the moon. This is the case in some kinds of madness and epilepsy. This youth was no doubt epileptic; but it was evidently either produced or taken advantage of by a demon or evil spirit. Mt 4:24. **for oftimes.** Mt 8:31, 32. Jb 1:10-19. 2:7. Mk 5:4, 5.

16. **and they.** ver. 19, 20. Mt 10:1. 2 K 4:29-31. Mk 6:7. Lk 9:1, 40. 10:17. Ac 3:16. 19:15, 16.

17. **O faithless.** ✗59, Ge +28:16. Mt 6:30. 8:26. +*12:39. 13:58. 16:8. Dt 32:20. Ps 78:8. Mk 9:19. 16:14. Lk 9:41. 24:25. Jn 20:27. He 3:16-19. **and perverse.** Dt 32:5, 20. Ac 2:40. 20:30. Ph 2:15. **generation.** Mt +24:34. **how long shall I be.** ✗59, Ge +28:16. Ex 10:3. 16:28. Nu 14:11, 27. Ps 95:10. Pr 1:22. 6:9. Je 4:14. Jn 8:25. 14:9. Ac 13:18. **how long.** ✗85K, Ge +3:9. ✗85Q, Ps +2:1. **suffer you.** Ac 18:14. 2 C 11:1, 4, 19, 20. Ep 4:2. Col 3:13. 2 T 4:3g.

18. **rebuked.** Mt 8:26. 12:22. Zc 3:2. Mk 1:25, 34. 5:8. 9:25-27. Lk 4:35, 36, 39, 41. 8:29. 9:42. Ac 16:18. 19:13-15. Ju 9. **from.** Mt 8:13. 9:22. 15:28. Jn 4:52, 53.

19. **Then came.** Mk 4:10. 9:28. **Why could.** Mt ❶10:1.

20. **Because.** ver. 17. Mt 9:2. 13:58. 14:30, 31. Jn 11:40. He 3:19. **little faith.** Mt 6:30. **If.** ✗184C, Mt +4:9. Mt *21:21, 22. Mk *11:23. Lk 17:6. 1 C 12:9. 13:2. **faith.** That is, as Bp. Pearce well remarks, a thriving and increasing faith, like a grain of mustard seed, which, from being the least of seeds, becomes the greatest of all herbs. **a grain.** Mt 13:31. Mk 4:31. Lk 13:19. **grain.** ✗138B, Ge +13:16. **this mountain.** ver. 1, 9. Mk *11:22-24. 1 C 13:2. **nothing.** Jb 42:2. Mk 9:23. Lk 1:37. 18:27.

21. **this.** Mt 12:45. **but.** Mk 9:29. Lk 2:37. Ac 13:2, 3. 14:23. 1 C 7:5. **by prayer.** Gr. *proseukee,* ✳S#4335g; Rendered (1) prayer: Mt 17:21. 21:13, 22. Mk 9:29. 11:17. Lk 6:12. 19:46. 22:45. Ac 1:14. 2:42. 3:1. 6:4. 10:4, 31. 12:5. 16:13, 16. Ro 1:9. 12:12. 15:30. 1 C 7:5. Ep 1:16. 6:18. Ph 4:6. Col 4:2, 12. 1 Th 1:2. 1 T 2:1. 5:5. Phm 1:4, 22. 1 P 3:7. 4:7. Re 5:8. 8:3, 4. (2) pray earnestly: Ja 5:17. T#1817. 1 K *17:20, 21. 2 Ch +✗7:14. Ezk 36:37. Da *9:3. Ep 6:18. **and fasting.** T#1243. Dt 9:18. Jg 20:26. 1 S 7:5, 6. 2 S 12:15-23. 1 K 21:27. 2 Ch *20:3, 4. Ezr *8:21-23. Ne 9:1-3. Ps 35:13. 69:10. 109:24-26. Is 58:3-11. Je 14:12. Da *9:3. 10:2, 3. Jl 1:14. *2:12. Jon *3:5-9. Mk 9:28, 29. Lk 2:37. 5:33, 34. Ac 10:30, 31. 13:2, 3. 14:23. 1 C *7:5. 2 C 11:27.

22. **The Son.** Mt 16:21. 20:17, 18. Mk 8:31. *9:30-32. 10:33, 34. Lk 9:22, 43-45. 18:31-34. 24:6, 7, 26, 46. Ac *2:23. **betrayed.** Mt 24:10. 26:16, 46. Ac 7:52. 1 C 11:23.

23. **they shall.** Ps 22:15, 22, etc. Is 53:7, 10-12. Da 9:26. Zc 13:7. **the third.** Mt 16:21. Ps +*16:10. Jn +*2:19. Ac 2:23-31. 1 C +*15:3, 4. **And they were.** Jn 16:6, 20-22.

24. **when.** Mk 9:33. **Capernaum.** Mt 4:13. **tribute.** "Gr. didrachma, in value fifteen pence." Ge 24:22. Ex 30:13. 38:26. 2 K 12:4. 2 Ch 24:6. Ne *10:32, 33. This *tribute* seems to have been the half shekel which every male among the Jews paid yearly for the support of the temple, and which was continued by them, wherever dispersed, till after the time of Vespasian

(See Josephus, Bel. l. vii. c. 6). **Doth not.** Mt +*5:17. **master.** Mt 22:24. **pay.** Jn +4:8n.

25. **Yes.** Mt 3:15. 22:21. Ro 13:6, 7. **prevented.** Jn +*2:25. **What thinkest.** Mt 18:12. 21:28. **custom.** Ro 13:7. **tribute.** Mt 22:17, 19. Mk 12:14. **of their.** 1 S 17:25.

26. **strangers.** Is 49:23. 60:10, 16, 17. **the children.** Mt 21:43. Is *60:5. *61:6. Ezk 30:3. Mi 4:13. Zc *14:14. Jn 2:16. 14:2. Ro 11:25.

27. **lest.** T#459. Mt *15:12-14. Mk +12:12 (T#67). Ro *14:21. 15:1-3. 1 C *8:9, 13. *9:19-22. ✓10:32, 33. 11:1. 2 C ✓6:3, 4. 1 Th ✓5:22. 2 T 2:24. T 2:7, 8. 1 P +3:8 (T#135). **offend.** Mt 5:29, 30. 13:41. 15:12. 18:6, 8, 9. Mk 9:42, 43, 45, 47. Lk 17:2. Jn 6:61. 1 C 8:13g. **and take.** Ge 1:28. 1 K 17:4. Ps 8:8. Jon 1:17. 2:10. He 2:7, 8. **a piece of money.** "*or,* a stater, half an ounce of silver, value 2s. 6d., after 5s. the ounce." **that take.** 2 C *8:9. Ja *2:5.

MATTHEW 18

Jesus teaches humility by the emblem of a little child, 1-4. He inculcates attention to his "little ones," and watchfulness against stumbling others, or falling ourselves, 5-10. He illustrates his care of his people, by the parable of a lost sheep, 11-14; shows how to act towards an offending brother, 15-17; assures the apostles that what they bind or loose shall be bound or loosed in heaven, 18; gives special promises to those who unite in prayer, or meet in his name, 19, 20; and enforces the constant forgiveness of injuries, by a parable of a king, and his dealings with a servant, who was deeply indebted to him; yet was not influenced by his readiness to forgive him, to forgive his fellow servant, 21-35.

1. **the same.** Mt 17:24. Mk 9:33-37. **Who.** Mt 20:20-28. 23:11. Mk 9:34. 10:35-45. Lk 9:46-48. 22:24-27. Ro 12:10. Ph 2:3. That such a controversy as this could repeatedly occur shows both the humanity of the apostles, and most forcibly, that Peter was not understood by the rest of the apostles to have the primacy among them, for they obviously did not so understand our Lord's words to Peter in Mt 16:18, 19. **greatest.** ✗96E4, Mt +13:32. **in.** Mt 3:2. 5:19, 20. 7:21. Mk 10:14, 15. **kingdom of heaven.** Mt 4:17. Ac +1:6.

2. **a little child.** Mt 11:25. 19:13, 14. 1 K 3:7. Je 1:7. Mk *9:36, 37, 42. 10:13-16. Lk *9:47, 48. 10:21. 17:2. +*18:15, 16.

3. **Verily.** Mt 5:18. 6:2, 5, 16. Jn 1:51. *3:3. **Except.** ✗184C, Mt +4:9. Mt *13:15. Ps +*19:7. *51:10-13. 119:59. *131:2. Is 6:10. ✓55:7. Je 31:18, 19. Ezk *18:27. +*33:11. Da +*12:3. Mk *4:12. Lk *22:32. Jn ✓6:44. Ac 3:+*19, 26. 11:21. 26:18, 20. *28:27. Ja +*5:19, 20. **and become.** Mt 11:25. 19:14. Ps 131:2. Mk *10:14, 15. Lk *18:16, 17. 1 C 14:20. 1 Th 2:7. 1 P *2:2. **shall not.** Ps 7:11, 12. Jn 3:36. **enter.** Mt *5:20. *19:23. Lk *13:24. Jn *3:3, 5. Ac *14:22. Ga 6:15. 2 P *1:11.

4. **humble.** Mt +*5:3. 11:29. 20:27. 23:11, 12. Ps 9:12. 131:1, 2. 138:6. Pr 3:34. 16:19. 18:12. 22:4. 29:23. Is +*57:15. Mi +*6:8. Lk 14:11. 18:14. Jn *13:14, 15. Ep 4:1, 2. Ph ✓2:3-9. Col 3:12. Ja *4:10. 1 P *5:5. **greatest.** ✗172, Mt +5:19. ver. 1. Mt 20:26, 27. Mk 10:43. Lk 4:48.

5. **receive.** Mt *10:40-42. *25:40, 45. Mk 9:41. Lk *9:48. 17:1, 2. **in my name.** ver. 20. Mt 24:5. Mk 9:37, 39. 13:6. Lk 1:59. 9:48, 49. 21:8. 24:47. Ac

4:17, 18. 5:28, 40. **receiveth.** Mk 9:37. Jn 13:20. Ga 4:14.

6. **offend.** ver. 8. Mt 17:27. Jsh 22:25. Ps 105:15. Ezk 14:10n. Zc 2:8. Mk 9:42. Lk 17:1, 2. Ac 9:5. Ro 14:13-15, 21. 15:1-3. 1 C *8:9-13. 10:32, 33. 2 Th 1:6-9. **little.** ver. 2, 10, 14. Zc 13:7. Lk 17:2. **better for.** Mk 14:21. **that a.** This mode of punishment appears to have obtained in Syria as well as in Greece, especially in cases of parricide. That it was customary in Greece we learn from Suidas, in *uperbolon lithon,* and the scholiast on the *Equites* of Aristophanes: *Otan gar kateponton tinas, baros apo ton traxalon ekremon,* "When a person was drowned, they hung a weight about his neck." **drowned.** *S#2670g, *katapontizomai.* Mt +14:30 (sink).

7. **unto.** Ge 13:7. 1 S 2:17, 22-25. 2 S 12:14. Lk 17:1. Ro 2:23, 24. 1 T 5:14, 15. 6:1. T 2:5, 8. 2 P 2:2. **world.** Gr. *kosmos,* Mt +4:8. **offences.** Mt 13:41. **for.** Am +*3:6. Mk 13:7. Ac 1:16. 1 C 2:8. √11:19. 2 Th 2:3-12. 1 T 1:13, 16. 4:1-3. *5:14. *6:1. 2 T 3:1-5. 4:3, 4. Ju 4. **that offences come.** Ac 20:30. Ro 14:13. **but woe.** Mt 13:41, 42. 23:13, etc. 26:24. Jn 17:12. Ac 1:18-20. 2 P 2:3, 15-17. Ju 11-13. Re 2:14, 15, 20-23. 19:20, 21.

8. **if.** √184A, 1 C +15:2. Mt *5:29, 30. 14:3, 4. Dt 13:6-8. Mk √9:43-48. Lk 14:26, 27, 33. 18:22, 23. Ro *8:13. 1 C *9:27. Col *3:5. **and cast.** Is 2:20, 21. 30:22. Ezk 18:31. Ro 13:12. Ph 3:8, 9. **enter into life.** Mt +*7:13. 19:16, 17. Mk 9:43, 45. Jn √5:24. **maimed.** Mt 15:30, 31. 19:12. **rather than.** √96E1, Ps +118:8. **everlasting.** Gr. *aionios,* *S#166g. Rendered (1) "eternal": Mt 19:16. 25:46b. Mk 3:29. 10:17, 30. Lk 10:25. 18:18. Jn 3:15. 4:36. 5:39. 6:54n, 68. 10:28. 12:25. 17:2, 3. Ac 13:48. Ro 2:7. 5:21. 6:23. 2 C 4:17, 18. 5:1. 1 T 6:12, 19. 2 T 2:10. T 1:2a. 3:7. He 5:9. 6:2. 9:12, 14, 15. 1 P 5:10. 1 J 1:2. 2:25. 3:15. 5:11, 13, 20. Ju 7, 21. (2) "everlasting": Mt 18:8. 19:29. 25:41, 46a. Lk 16:9. 18:30. Jn 3:16, 36. 4:14. 5:24. 6:27, 40, 47. 12:50. Ac 13:46. Ro 6:22. 16:26. Ga 6:8. 2 Th 1:9. 2:16. 1 T 1:16. 6:16. He 13:20. 2 P 1:11. Re 14:6. (3) with S#5450g, "the world began": 2 T 1:9. T 1:2b. (4) with S#5450g, "since the world began": Ro 16:25. (5) "for ever": Phm 15. **fire.** Mt 25:41, 46. Is 33:14. Mk 9:48, 49. Lk +*16:24. 2 Th √1:8, 9. Re 14:10. 20:15. +*21:8.

9. **if.** √184A, 1 C +15:2. **thine eye.** Mt 5:29. Jb *31:1. **to enter.** Mt 19:17, 23, 24. Ac 14:22. He 4:11. Re 21:27. **rather.** Mt 16:26. Lk 9:24, 25. **hell.** Gr. *gehenna,* Mt +5:22. T#996‡. Mt 23:13-15. Is 66:22-24. Mk 9:43-47. Lk +12:5 (T#995‡).

10. **heed.** ver. 6, 14. Mt 12:20. Ps 15:4. Zc 4:10. Lk 10:16. Ac *9:5. Ro *14:1-3, 10, 13-15, 21. 15:1. 1 C 8:8-13. 9:22. 11:22. 16:11. 2 C 10:1, 10. Ga 4:13, 14. 6:1. 1 Th 4:8. 1 T 4:12. **despise not.** T#673. Pr 3:34. 9:12. 12:5. 14:21. 15:20. *19:29. 22:10. 29:8. **one.** Mt 6:29. 25:40, 45. Lk 15:7, 10. **little ones.** ver. 2, 6, 14. Mt 10:42. Zc 13:7. **in heaven.** Lk 1:19. **their angels.** Mt 1:20. 2:13, 19. 24:31. Ge 32:1, 2. 2 K 6:16, 17. Ps *34:7. *91:11. Da 10:13, 20. 12:1. Zc +*3:7. Lk 16:22. Ac 5:19. 10:3. 12:7-11, 23. 27:23. Col 2:18. 1 T 5:21. He *1:14. Re 1:20. **behold.** 2 S 14:28. 1 K 22:19. 2 K 25:19mg. Est 1:14. Ps 17:15. Zc *2:8. +*3:7. Lk 1:19. Ac 2:28. Re 22:4. **face.** √22A4, Ge +19:13. **my Father.** ver. 14, 19, 35. Mt +*7:21.

11. **is come to.** Mt *9:12, +13. 10:6. 15:24. Lk *9:56. 15:24, 32. +*19:10. Jn √3:17. *10:10. 12:47. Ga 3:13.

Ep 2:1, 4, 5. 1 T *1:15. **that.** √96G4, Mt +1:20. **lost.** Gr. *apollumi,* Mt +2:13.

12. **How.** Mt 17:25. 21:28. 22:42. 1 C 10:15. **if.** √184C, Mt +4:9. Mt 12:11. Ps 119:176. Is √53:6. Je 50:6. Ezk 34:16, 28. Lk 15:4-7. Jn 10:11-18. 1 P 2:25. **goeth into.** 1 K 22:17. Ezk 34:6, 12. **and seeketh.** ver. 11. Ps 119:176. Ezk *34:4, 11, 12, 16. Lk +*19:10. **gone astray.** Is √53:6.

13. **if.** √184C, Mt +4:9. **he rejoiceth.** Ps 147:11. Is 53:11. 62:5. Je 32:37-41. Mi *7:18. Zp 3:17. Lk 15:5-10, 23, 24. Jn 4:34-36. Ja *2:13.

14. **not the will.** Mt 11:26. Ezk *18:32. Lk 12:32. Jn *6:39, 40. √10:27-30. 17:12. Ro √8:28-39. Ep 1:5-7. 1 T +*2:4. 1 P *1:3-5. 2 P +*3:9. **your.** Mt 5:16. *6:9, 32. 23:9. **one.** √111, Ge +18:27. Is *40:11. Zc 13:7. Jn *21:15. 1 C 8:11-13. 2 T 2:10. He 12:13. 2 P √3:9. **perish.** Gr. *apollumi,* Mt +2:13.

15. **if thy brother.** √184C, Mt +4:9. ver. *35. Mt 5:23, 24. Le 6:2-7. Lk *17:3, 4. 1 C *6:6-8. *8:12. 2 C 7:12. Col *3:13. 1 Th *4:6. **go and tell.** Le +*19:17. Jsh 22:13. Ps *141:5. Pr 15:23. *25:9, 10. 27:5, 6. Ep +*5:11. 2 Th 3:15. T 3:10. **thou hast gained.** Pr *11:30. Ro *12:21. 1 C 9:19-22. Ga *6:1. Col *3:13. Ja *5:16, 19, 20. 1 P *3:1.

16. **But if.** √184C, Mt +4:9. **take with.** Nu 16:25. Jsh 22:13. **that in.** Mt ◐26:60. Nu 35:30. Dt *17:6. *)19:15. 1 K 21:13. Jn 8:17. 2 C *13:1. 1 T *5:19. He 10:28. 1 J 5:7, 8. Re 11:3. **mouth.** √121B, Dt +17:6.

17. **And if.** √184C, Mt +4:9. **tell it unto the church.** i.e. the particular congregation to which he belongs. Our Lord's hearers would understand him to mean the particular synagogue of which the parties were members (William Webster and William Wilkinson, *Greek Testament,* vol. 1, p. 90). Jsh 22:16. Ac *6:1-3. *15:6, 7. 1 C *5:4, 5. *6:1-4, 6, 7. 2 C *2:6, 7. 3 J 9, 10. **neglect to hear.** 1 S +*25:17. **let him be.** Ro +*16:17, 18. 1 C *5:3-5, 9-13. 2 Th √3:6, 14, 15. 1 T +*6:5. T *3:10, 11. 2 J √9-11. **an heathen.** Mt *6:7. Ezr 6:21. Ezk 11:12. Lk ◐7:6. Jn 7:49. 2 C *6:14-17. Ep *4:17-19. *5:11, 12. **a publican.** Mt *5:46. *11:19. *21:31, 32. Lk *15:1. *18:11. *19:2, 3.

18. **Whatsoever.** Mt √16:19. Je 18:23. Jn √20:23. Ac 15:23-31. 1 C 5:4, 5. 2 C *2:10. Re 3:7, 8. **ye.** √12I1I, Ge +3:7. **shall bind.** √121I2, Ge +2:17. √121S3A, Mt +16:19. Gr. *dasate,* 2 person plural, 1 aorist active subjunctive. **shall be.** Gr. *estai,* 3 person singular, future middle indicative. **bound.** Gr. *dedemena,* perfect passive participle, nominative plural neuter. The same unusual form is found in Matthew 16:19. Burton (*New Testament Moods and Tenses,* section 94, p. 45) also gives Lk 12:52 and He 2:13 as instances of what he terms the "periphrastic Future Perfect." It may be more literally rendered "shall (or must) already have been bound." **ye shall loose.** Gr. *lusate,* 2 person plural, 1 aorist active subjunctive. **shall be.** Gr. *estai,* 3 person singular, future middle indicative. **loosed.** Gr. *lelumena,* perfect passive participle, nominative plural neuter. More literally this may be rendered "shall (or must) already have been loosed." In the Greek text important distinctions in tenses are made here, so that the participles may be more literally rendered as indicated. The sense is that the apostles were to loose and bind what already had been permanently loosed (permitted) and bound (forbidden) in heaven; thus the apostles carried out their teaching in accordance with what was already taught by Christ,

as the mandate of heaven; heaven did not merely ratify the earthly decisions of the apostles.

19. Again. Bengel (*Word Studies*, vol. 1, p. 229) identifies this as *epitasis*, introducing an emphatic addition. *ſ*77, Ex +3:19. Mt 19:24. Ga 5:3. **That if.** *ſ*184C, Mt +4:9. Mt 5:24. *21:22. Mk √11:24. Jn √15:7, 16. Ac 1:14. 2:1, 2. *4:24-31. 6:4. *12:5, 12, 16, 17. Ep *6:18-20. Ph 1:19. Phm 22. Ja *5:14-16. 1 J 3:22. √5:14-16. Re 11:4-6. **two.** Dt 17:6. **agree.** T#1305. Ac 8:15, 17. 1 C ●7:5. He 13:18. 1 P 3:7, 8. *S#4856g. Mt 18:19. 20:2, 13. Lk 5:36. Ac 5:9. 15:15. Gr. *sumphoneo*, lit. to sound together, i.e., to be in accord, primarily of musical instruments, is used in the N.T. of the agreement (a) of persons concerning a matter, Mt 18:19. 20:2, 13. Ac 5:9. (b) of the writers of Scripture, Ac 15:15. (c) of things that are said to be congruous in their nature, Lk 5:36 (W. E. Vine, *Expository Dictionary*, vol. 1, p. 43). Note related words at 2 C 6:15 (concord, *sumphonesis*) and Lk 15:25 (music, *sumphonia*); Ac 28:25 (they agreed not, *asumphonos*). **any thing.** Mt *21:22. Jn *14:14. Ro +*8:32. Ep +*3:20. Ph +*4:19. 1 J √5:14, 15. **shall ask.** Lk +√11:9. +*18:1. Ja +*1:5, 6. 4:2. **it shall.** Mt +*7:7. Jn 14:13, 14. 16:23, 24. 1 J *3:22. √5:14. **my Father.** ver. 10, 35. Mt 7:21.

20. where two. ver. 19. 1 S 9:27. Da *3:25. +*11:33. Ml +*3:16. 1 C 5:4. Phm +*2. **or three.** Ec 4:12. 1 Th 1:1. **gathered.** Ge +*49:10. Dt +*12:5. Jn 20:19. Ac 4:30, 31. *11:26. *18:26. *20:7, 8. 1 C ●1:10-13. 5:4. 11:20. +*16:19. He +*10:25. Ja *5:16. **in my name.** ver. +5. **there.** Mt 28:20. Ex *20:24. Zc 2:5. Jn +*8:58. 12:26. 14:23. *20:19, 20, 26. Ro 8:9, 10. 1 C 5:3. 2 C *13:5. Ga 2:20. Ep 3:16-19. Col 2:5. Re 1:11-13. 2:1. 21:3. **in the midst.** God the Son is omnipresent. T#76-6. Mt +*28:19n, 20. Nu=1:50. 1 K ●+8:27. 1 Ch=9:27. Ps *145:18. Pr +15:3 (T#220). Jn 3:13. Jn 20:19, 26. Ep 1:23. Col 1:27.

21. brother sin against. ver. 15. **till.** ver. 15. Lk *17:3, 4. Ep √4:32. Col *3:13. **seven times.** Ps +119:164n. Pr 24:16. Lk 17:4.

22. I say not. Jn 16:26. **but.** Mt 6:11, *12, *14, *15. Ge 4:24. Is √55:7mg. Mi *7:19. Mk *11:25, 26. Ro *12:21. Ep 4:26, 31, √32. 5:1. Col *3:8, 13. 1 T 2:8. **seventy times seven.** Wordsworth notes "The number *seven* in Holy Scripture is used to signify completeness (Lk 23:56. 24:1n); and the multiplication of 70x7 here signifies that there is to be no stint or limit to the spirit of forgiveness. The number *seventy-seven* is used to express the fulness of *retribution* for Lamech (Ge 4:24). And for bringing in of *forgiveness* of sins into the world there are *seventy-seven* generations from Adam to Christ (Lk 3:23-38. *Hilary* and *Augustine*). But here the number is *seventy times seven*, the number of years from the rebuilding of the wall of Jerusalem unto Christ, who brought in the forgiveness of sins (Da 9:24)" (*Greek Testament*, vol. 1, p. 66).

23. is the kingdom. Mt 3:2. 13:24, 31, 33, 44, 45, 47, 52. 25:1, 14. **which.** Mt 25:19-30. Lk 16:1, 2. 19:12-27. Ro 14:12. 1 C 4:5. 2 C 5:10, 11.

24. one. *ſ*108E1, Mt +8:19. **owed.** Lk 7:41, 42. 13:4mg. 16:5, 7. **ten thousand.** *Murion talanton*, a myriad of talents, the highest number known in Greek arithmetical notation. According to Prideaux, the Roman talent was equal to 216*l*.; ten thousand of which would amount to 2,160,000*l*. If the Jewish talent of silver be designed, which is estimated by the same

learned writer at 450*l*., this sum amounts to 4,500,000*l*.; but if the gold talent is meant, which is equal to 7200*l*., then the amount is 72,000,000*l*. A talent is about $1000 in American money (A. T. Robertson, *Word Pictures*, vol. 1, p. 150). This immense sum represents our *boundless* obligations to God, and our utter incapacity, as sinners infinitely indebted to Divine justice, of paying one mite out of the talent. 1 Ch 29:7. Ezr 9:6. Est 3:9. Ps 38:4. 40:12. 130:3, 4. **talents.** "A talent is 750 ounces of silver, which after five shillings the ounce is 187*l*. 10s." Mt 25:15.

25. had not. Lk 7:42. **commanded.** Ex 21:2. Le 25:39. Dt 15:12. Is 50:1. Je 34:14. **and children.** 2 K 4:1. Ne 5:5, 8.

26. worshipped him. *or*, besought him. Mt +8:2. Ac 10:25. Re 3:9. **have.** ver. 29. Lk 7:43. Ro *10:3.

27. moved. Jg 10:16. Ne 9:17. Ps 78:38. 86:5, 15. 145:8. Ho 11:8. **forgave.** Lk 7:42.

28. the same. Mt +6:2n. **one.** *ſ*108E1, Mt +8:19. **an hundred.** Rather, "a hundred denarii," as our *penny* does not convey one *seventh* of the meaning. This would amount to about 3*l*. 2s. 6d. English; which was not one six hundred thousandth part of the 10,000 talents, even calculating them as Roman talents. About $20 in American money (A. T. Robertson, *Word Pictures*, p. 151, citing Goodspeed). **pence.** "The Roman penny is the eighth part of an ounce, which after five shillings the ounce is sevenpence halfpenny." Mt 20:2, 9, 10, 13. 22:19. Mk 6:37. 12:15. 14:5. Lk 7:41. 10:35. 20:24. Jn 6:7. 12:5. Re 6:6. **and took.** Dt 15:2. Ne 5:7, 10, 11. 10:31. Is 58:3. Ezk 45:9.

29. Have. ver. 26. Mt 6:12. Phm 18, 19.

30. but. 1 K 21:27-29. 22:27.

31. they. Ps 119:136, 158. Je 9:1. Mk 3:5. Lk *19:41. Ro 9:1-3. *12:15. 2 C 11:21. He 13:3. **and came.** Ge 37:2. 2 K +*5:13. Lk 14:21. Ep +*5:11. He *13:17.

32. O thou. Mt 25:26. Lk 19:22. Ro 3:19.

33. even as I. Mt *5:44, 45. +*6:12. Lk +*6:35, 36. Ep √4:32. 5:1, 2. Col 3:13. 1 J 4:11.

34. was wroth. Jb 22:4-11. Ps 18:25, 26. Pr √21:13. Ezk 25:12-14. Lk *6:38. Ja *2:13. **and delivered.** ver. 30. Mt 5:25, 26. Lk 12:58, 59. 2 Th √1:8, 9. Re 14:10, 11.

35. my. ver. 10, 19. Mt 7:21. **do.** Mt *6:12, 14, 15. 7:1, 2. Pr *21:13. Mk 11:26. Lk +*6:37, 38. Ja *2:13. **if.** *ſ*184C, Mt +4:9. **from.** Le +*19:18. Pr 21:2. Je 3:10. Zc 7:12. Lk 16:15. Ro 6:17. Ep √4:32. Ja 3:14. 4:8. 1 P 1:22. Re 2:23.

MATTHEW 19

Jesus journeys towards Judea, and heals the sick, 1, 2; answers the Pharisees concerning divorces, and his disciples on the expediency of marriage, 3-12; receives little children, 13-15; discourses with a rich young man concerning eternal life, and detects his love of wealth more than of God, 16-22; shows the difficulty of a rich man's salvation, 23-26; and makes gracious promises to those who renounce worldly objects for his sake, 27-30.

1. came to pass. *ſ*144A11, Ge +38:1. Mt 7:28. 11:1. 13:53. 26:1. **that when.** Mk 10:1. Jn 10:40. **he departed.** This was our Lord's final departure from Galilee, previous to his crucifixion; but he appears to have taken in a large compass in his journey, and passed through the districts east of Jordan. Some learned men, however, are of opinion, that instead of "beyond Jordan," we should render, "by the side of Jordan," as *peran*, especially with the genitive, sometimes signifies. Mt 17:24. **into the coasts**. Mt 4:25. Lk 9:51. 17:11. Jn 10:40. 11:7. **Judaea**. i.e. *land of Juda*, *S#2449g. Rendered (1) Judaea: Mt 2:1, 5, 22. 3:1, 5. 4:25. 19:1. 24:16. Mk 1:5. 3:7. 10:1. 13:14. Lk 1:5, 65. 2:4. 3:1. 5:17. 6:17. 7:17. 21:21. Jn 3:22. 4:3, 47, 54. 7:3. 11:7. Ac 1:8. 2:9. 8:1. 9:31. 10:37. 11:1, 29. 12:19. 15:1. 21:10. 26:20. 28:21. Ro 15:31. 2 C 1:16. Ga 1:22. 1 Th 2:14. (2) Jewry: Lk 23:5. Jn 7:1. For S#3063h, "Judah," see Ge +35:23. **beyond Jordan**. Mt 3:5, +6, 13. 4:25. Mk 3:8. 10:1. Lk 3:2, 3. Jn *1:28. *3:26. *10:40.

2. **great multitudes**. Mt 4:23-25. 9:35, 36. 12:15. 14:35, 36. 15:30, 31. Mk 1:34. 6:55, 56.

3. **The Pharisees**. Lk 17:20. Jn 8:3. **tempting**. Mt 16:1. 22:16-18, 35-38. Mk 10:2. 12:13-15. Lk 11:53, 54. Jn 8:6. He 3:9. **Is it**. Mt 5:31, 32. Ml 2:14-16. **put away**. *Apolusai*, S#630g. To dismiss a wife by releasing her from the bond of marriage. Mt 1:19. 5:31, 32. Mk 10:2, 4, 11. Lk 16:18. Also used of putting away a husband, Mk 10:12. **for every cause**. In context Jesus answered this question with a firm "no," but gives an exception in verse 9, "except it be for fornication." When divorce is based on fornication (the word is used in a non-technical sense, so it includes adultery), the divorce is justified. Nevertheless, divorce was often obtained on other grounds, and the question remains, is the divorced but truly innocent party permitted to remarry? Remarriage is clearly permitted in Scripture (a) if the first husband or wife has died (Ro 7:2); (b) if the Christian mate is divorced by an unbelieving mate for faith in Christ, or the unbelieving mate otherwise deserts the marriage, 1 C 7:15; (c) if the divorced person is the innocent victim of the divorce action of a licentious partner (Mt 5:28-30) who obtains a divorce to marry another woman; under Mosaic law, if the dismissed party were guilty of adultery, such a person was to be stoned (Dt 22:21), and there would be no basis for granting a bill of divorcement in accordance with Dt 24:1-4! Such innocently divorced persons are permitted the right to remarriage (1 C 7:28, "But and if thou marry, thou hast not sinned"). Remarriage in such cases does not disqualify from church office; the text in 1 T 3:2, "A bishop must be the husband of one wife," is a reference to polygamy (having more than one wife at the same time), not divorce and remarriage, or remarriage after the death of a spouse.

4. **Have**. Mt 12:3. 21:16, 42. 22:31. Mk 2:25. 12:10, 26. Lk 6:3. 10:26. **that**. Ge ᐅ1:27. 2:18, 21-23. 5:2. Ml 2:15.

5. **said**. Ge ᐅ2:21-24. Ps 45:10. Mk 10:5-9. Ep 5:31. **shall a man**. Ge 2:18. Pr 18:22. 1 C 7:2. He +*13:4. **leave**. ♪102, Ge +2:24. **cleave**. *Proskollathasetai*, "shall be *cemented* to his wife," as the Hebrew *davak* implies; a beautiful metaphor, forcibly intimating that nothing but death can separate them. Ge 34:3. Dt 4:4. 10:20. 11:22. 1 S 18:1. 2 S 1:26. 1 K 11:2. Ps 63:8. Ro 12:9. Ep *5:33. 1 P *3:7. **wife**. Ge +2:18. +4:19. **and they twain**. ♪92E, Mt +4:10. Ge ᐅ2:24. 1 C *6:16. 7:2, 4. **one**. Dt +*6:4. Ml *2:15. **flesh**. ♪171Q6, Ge +6:12.

6. **God**. Pr 2:17. Ml 2:14. Mk 10:9. Ro 7:2. 1 C 7:10-14. Ep 5:28. He 13:4. **hath joined**. *Sunedzeuxen*, "hath yoked together," as oxen in the plow, where

each must pull equally in order to bring it on. Among the ancients, they put a *yoke* upon the necks of a new married couple, or *chains* on their arms, to show that they were to be *one*, closely united, and pulling equally together in all the concerns of life. Mk 10:9.

7. **Why**. Mt *5:31. Dt √24:1-4. Je 3:1. Mk 10:4. **writing of divorcement**. Is 50:1. Je 3:8. **and to**. Mt 1:19. Ml 2:16.

8. **Moses**. Ex +*24:4. **because**. Ps 95:8. Zc *7:12. Ml 2:13, 14. Mk *10:5. **hardness**. Dt 10:16. Mk 3:5. 6:52. 16:14. He 3:8. **suffered**. Mt 3:15. 8:31. 1 C 7:6. **but**. Ge √2:24. 7:7. Je 6:16.

9. **Whosoever**. Mt 5:32. Mk 10:11, 12. Lk 16:18. 1 C *7:10-13, 39. **put away**. Mt 5:32. Mk 10:12. **shall**. ♪184C, Mt +4:9. **except**. The fact that this exception to the "no divorce" law is only recorded in Matthew does not diminish its authority, for there are no textual grounds for disputing its place here. Mark and Luke record the general rule; Matthew, in giving the fuller account, records the exception. To diminish or discount the authority of a Scripture statement because only mentioned once, or by one author, is as surely taking "away from the words of the book of this prophecy" (Re 22:19) as excising them in any other manner from the text would be. Likewise, diminishing the authority of a text because it occurs in an "admittedly obscure book of symbolism," as the book of Revelation is alleged to be, in an effort to discredit the teaching of the millennium, and two resurrections separated by the thousand years, falls under the same stern condemnation, and no one should so place themselves as mishandling and wresting the Scriptures to avoid the very texts of Scripture which serve to correct their mistaken viewpoint (2 C 4:2. 2 P 1:20n. *3:16). This is not to deny the validity of the hermeneutical rule that the obscure is to be interpreted in the light of the clear, not the clear by the obscure: but it is to caution against the arbitrary declaration of a text as obscure, when its teaching in context is very clear, in order to justify our dismissal of the text because it contradicts our position. While it is true that we must interpret Scripture harmoniously, and must not take one text in opposition to all the rest of Scripture teaching when it results in a contradiction, in this case what is asserted is an "exception," the very word used here, and an exception is not a contradiction. 2 Ch 21:11. Je 3:8. Ezk 16:8, 15, 29. 1 C 5:1. **doth**. Ge 12:18, 19. 20:3. Je 3:1. Ro 7:2, 3. 1 C 7:4, 11, 39.

10. **If the case**. ♪184A, 1 C +15:2. Ge *2:18. Pr *5:15-19. *18:22. *19:13, 14. *21:9, 19. 1 C *7:1, 2, 8, 26-28, 32-35, 39, 40. 1 T 4:3. *5:11-15. **the man**. ♪171E5. Synecdoche of the Genus B621. "Man" is put for "husband."

11. **All men cannot**. 1 C *7:2, 7, 9, 17, 35. **save they**. Mt 20:23. **given**. Mt 13:11.

12. **which were made**. Le 21:20. Dt 23:1n. 2 K 20:18. Is *39:7. *56:3-5. **which have**. 1 C *7:1, 32-38. *9:5, 15. He +*13:4. **to receive**. ♪147A, Ge +50:24.

13. **little children**. T#1452. ver. +*14. Mt 18:2-5. Ge 48:1, 9-20. 1 S 1:24. Ps 115:14, 15. Je 32:39. Mk *10:13. Lk 9:47. +√18:15. Ac +*2:39. 1 C +*7:14. **his**. ♪63A3. Ellipsis (Absolute: of the pronoun) B18. For other instances of this figure see Mt 21:7. Mk 5:23. 6:5. 8:25. Lk 24:40. Jn 11:41. Ac 13:3. 19:6. Ro 2:18. (6:3, 4). Ep (3:17, 18). 1 T 6:1. He (4:15). **hands on them**. Ge 48:14-16. **and the**. Mt 16:22. 20:31. Mk

10:48. Lk 9:49, 50, 54, 55. 18:39.

14. Suffer. Ge 17:+*7, 8, 24-26. 21:4. Jg 13:7. 1 S 1:11, 22, 24. 2:18. Mk 10:14, 15. Lk 18:16, etc. **little children.** Mt 11:25. *18:3-5. *21:16. Ge +*17:7. Jl '+*2:16. Lk +*18:15. Ac +*2:39. 1 C √7:14. 1 P *2:1, 2. **forbid them not.** Mk 9:39. Lk 9:50. **for.** Mt *11:25. +*18:3. 1 C 14:20. 1 P 2:1, 2.

15. he laid. Is 40:11. Mk 10:16. 1 C +*7:14. 2 T +*3:15.

16. one came. Mk 10:17. Lk 18:18. **Good Master.** √156, Jn +3:2. Jn 7:12. **what.** Lk 10:25. Jn 6:27-29. Ac √16:30. **shall I do.** Hab *2:4. Ro 3:28. 9:30, 31. 10:5. Ga 3:11, 12. **have.** ver. 29. 1 J √5:13. **eternal.** Gr. *aionios*, Mt +18:8. ver. 29. Mt +*25:46. Da +*12:2. Lk 10:25. Jn *3:15, 36. 4:14. +*5:39. *6:40, 47, 54, 68. √10:28. 12:25. √17:2, 3. √20:31. Ac 13:46, 48. Ro *2:7. 5:21. √6:22, 23. 1 T 1:16. 6:12, 19. T 1:2. √3:5-7. He 9:12, 15. 1 J 1:2. 2:25. √5:11-13, 20. Ju *21.

17. there. 1 S 2:2. Ps 52:1. 145:7-9. Ja 1:17. 1 J 4:8-10, 16. **good.** √172, Mt +5:19. **but one.** Mk 12:29. Ro 16:27. **but if.** √184A, 1 C +15:2. Le 18:5. Ne 9:29. Ezk 20:11-13, 21. Lk 10:26-28. Ro 2:13. 10:5. Ga 3:11-13. **commandments.** √63A4, 1 K +3:22. Supply ellipsis, (of God).

18. Which. Mk 10:19. Ga 3:10. Ja √2:10, 11. **Thou shalt do.** Mt 5:21-28. Ge +*9:5, 6. Ex +*❭20:13. Dt +*❭5:17. Mk 10:19. Lk 18:20. Ro 13:9. 1 J √3:15. **not commit adultery.** Mt *5:27. Ex ❭20:14. Le 18:20. Dt ❭5:18. 22:22. Pr 6:32. Ro 13:9. 1 C +*6:9. He +*13:4. **not steal.** Ex ❭20:15. Le 19:11. Dt ❭5:19. Ro 13:9. Ep √4:28. **not bear false witness.** Ex ❭20:16. 23:1. Dt ❭5:20. 19:16-20. Pr 19:5, 9. 21:28. 24:28. 25:18.

19. Honor. Mt 15:4-6. Ex +*❭20:12. Le 19:3. Dt +*❭5:16. Pr +*30:17. Je 35:18, 19. Ml 4:6. Mk 7:10. Ep √6:1, 2. **love thy neighbor.** Mt 5:43. 22:39. Le +*❭19:18. Mk 12:31. Lk 10:27. Ro 13:9. Ga 5:14. Ja 2:8. **as thyself.** Le +*19:18. Lk 6:31. Ep 5:29.

20. All. Mk 10:20. Lk 15:7, 29. 18:11, 12, 21. Jn 8:7. Ro √3:19-23. 7:9. Ga *3:24. Ph *3:6. **from.** Ezk 4:14. **what.** Mk 10:21. Lk 18:22.

21. If. √184A, 1 C +15:2. Mt 5:19, 20, 48. *6:24. *16:26. Ge 6:9. 17:1. Jb 1:1. Ps 37:37. Lk 6:40. Ph 3:12-15. **go.** Mt 6:19, 20. Mk 10:21. Lk 12:33. 14:33. 16:9. 18:22. ◐√19:8. Ac 2:44, 45. 4:32-35. 1 T √6:17-19. He 10:34. **give to the poor.** Mt 5:42. Le 25:35. Dt 15:7. Ps 41:1. Pr 3:27, 28. 22:9. 25:21. 31:20. Ezk +*16:49. 18:5-9. Mk 9:41. Lk 3:11. 1 C 13:3. 2 C 8:9. 9:6. 1 T 5:8, 16. 1 T 6:17, 18. He 6:10. Ja 2:15, 16. 1 J 3:17, 18. **treasure in heaven.** √22D5.O, Dt +28:12. Mt √6:19, 20. Mk +*10:21. Lk *12:33, 34. He *10:34. **come.** ver. 28. Mt 4:19. 8:22. 9:9. 16:24. Mk 2:14. 8:31. 10:21. Lk 5:27. 9:23. 18:22. Jn 1:43. *10:27. *12:26.

22. But when. Ps 62:10. Ezk +√33:31. **he went.** Mt 13:22. 14:9. Jg 18:23, 24. Da 6:14-17. Mk 6:26. 10:22. Lk 18:23. Jn 19:12-16. **for.** Mt 6:24. 16:26. Ex ◐*20:17. Ps 17:14. Ezk +*33:31. Ep *5:5. Col *3:5.

23. That. Mt +*13:22. Dt 6:10-12. 8:10-18. Jb 31:24, 25. Ps 49:6, 7, 16-19. Pr *11:28. 30:8, 9. Mk 10:23, 25. Lk 12:15-21. 16:13, 14, 19-28. 18:24. 1 C 1:26. 1 T √6:9, 10. Ja 1:9-11. 2:6. +*5:1-4. **rich.** Mk +4:19. **enter.** Mt 5:20. 18:3. 21:31. Jn +*3:3, 5. Ac *14:22. 1 C +*6:9, 10.

24. It is easier. √138B, Ge +13:16. So in the *Koran* (Surat vii. 37), "The impious, who in his arrogance

shall accuse our doctrine of falsity, shall find the gates of heaven shut; nor shall he enter *till a camel shall pass through the eye of a needle.*" It was a common mode of expression among the Jews to declare anything that was rare or difficult (See Lightfoot). ver. 26. Mt 23:24. Je 13:23. Mk *10:24, 25. Lk 18:25. Jn 5:44. **camel.** Mt 23:24. **rich man.** ver. 22, 23. 1 T +*6:5, 9, 17-19. **kingdom of God.** Mt +12:28.

25. Who. Mt 24:22. Mk 13:20. Lk 13:23, 24. Ro *10:13. 11:5-7.

26. beheld them. Mk 3:5, 34. 10:21, 23, 27. Lk 6:10. 20:17. 22:61. Jn 1:42. **with men.** 2 K 7:2. Lk *18:27. **but.** Ge *18:14. Nu 11:23. Jb *42:2. Ps 3:8. 62:11. +115:3. Je *32:17, 27. Zc 8:6. Mk *10:27. *11.23. 14:36. Lk *1:37. *18:27. He 6:6.

27. we have forsaken. Mt 4:20-22. 9:9. Dt 33:9. Mk 1:17-20. 2:14. 10:28. Lk 5:11, 27, 28. 14:33. 18:28. Ph 3:8. **what.** Mt 20:10-12. Lk 15:29. 1 C 1:29. 4:7. '

28. in the regeneration. Ps +*71:20. Is +*26:19n. 54:1. 65:17. +*66:7-9, 22. Ho +*2:18. Jl *2:25. Mi +*5:3, 4. Zc √10:6. Lk 13:28. Jn 3:7. Ac +√3:19, 21. +*13:33. Ro *8:19-23. 1 Th +*4:16. T 3:5g. 2 P *3:13. Re 21:5. **when.** Mt *16:27. 25:31. Lk 9:26. 2 Th √1:7-10. Re *20:11-15. **Son of man.** Mt 8:20. **shall sit.** Mt +*25:31. He 8:1. 12:2. **the throne.** √22D3C2, Ps +45:6. Ps 132:11, 12. Ezk=37:24. Ac 2:30. Re 3:21. **ye shall.** √171M, Ge +6:12. Mt 20:21. Lk *22:28-30. 1 C 6:2, 3. 2 T 2:12. Re *2:26, 27. 3:21. **judging.** Mt +*10:15n. 1 C +*6:2, 3. Re 20:11, 12. **the twelve.** Ex 15:27. 24:4. 28:21. Le 24:5. Jsh 3:12. 1 K 18:31. Ezr 6:17. Ac +√26:6, 7. Ja 1:1. Re √7:4-8. 12:1. 21:12-14. 22:2. **Israel.** Ge=13:15. Ro 4:13. Ga=3:16.

29. every. Mt 16:25. Mk ‖10:29, 30. Lk ‖18:29, 30. 1 C 2:9. **forsaken.** Dt=33:9. **or brethren.** Mt 8:21, 22. 10:37, 38. Lk 14:26, 33. 2 C 5:16. Ph *3:8, 9. **for my.** Mt 5:11. 10:22. Mk *10:29. 13:9. Lk 6:22. 18:29. 21:12. Jn 15:19. Ac 9:16. 1 P 4:14. 3 J 7. **shall receive.** Mt 13:12. Mk +*‖10:30. Ro √8:18. 2 C √4:17. 2 T *2:12. 1 P *4:13. **an hundredfold.** Mt +*13:8, 23. Ge +*26:12. Mk +*10:30. **inherit.** ver. 16. Mt 25:34, 46. Mk 10:17. Lk 10:25. 18:18. T 3:7. **everlasting.** Gr. *aionios*, Mt +18:8. **life.** ver. 16.

30. first shall be last. Mt +*8:11, 12. 20:16. 21:31, 32. Mk 10:31. Lk *7:29, 30. 13:30. *18:9, 13, 14. Ro 5:20, 21. *9:30-33. Ga 5:7. He 4:1.

MATTHEW 20

Jesus speaks a parable of laborers sent at different hours into a vineyard, and applies it, 1-16. He foretells his own death and resurrection, 17-19; rejects the request of the mother of James and John in behalf of her sons; and represses the indignation and ambition of the other apostles, 20-28; and gives sight to two blind men, 29-34.

1. the kingdom. This parable was intended to illustrate the equity of God's dealings, even when "the first are placed last, and the last first." Mt 3:2. 13:24, 31, 33, 44, 45, 47. 22:2. 25:1, 14. **a man.** Mt 9:37, 38. 21:33-43. SS 8:11, 12. Is 5:1, 2. Jn 15:1. **early.** If the work day was twelve hours long, and ended at 6 P.M., the householder must have sought his workers some time before 6 A.M. Mt 23:37. Ec *9:10. SS 8:11, 12. Je 25:3, 4. **laborers.** Mk 13:34. 1 C √15:58. He 13:21. 2 P √1:5-10. **vineyard.** Mt 21:28, 33.

2. he had. ver. 13. Ex 19:5, 6. Dt 5:27-30. **a penny.**

"The Roman penny is the eighth part of an ounce, which after five shillings the ounce is seven pence halfpenny." ver. 9, 10, 13. Mt 18:28mg. 22:19mg. Mk 12:15. Lk 10:35. Re 6:6. **he sent.** 1 S 2:18, 26. 3:1, 21. 16:11, 12. 1 K 3:6-11. 18:12. 2 Ch 34:3. Ec 12:1. Lk 1:15. 2 T +*3:15.

3. **the third hour.** Our 9 A.M. Mk 15:25. Jn √11:9n. Ac 2:15. ◐23:23. **standing.** ver. 6, 7. Mt 11:16, 17. Pr 19:15. Ezk +*16:49. Ac 17:17-21. 1 T *5:13. He *6:12. **idle.** Mt +*12:36. Je +*48:10. **marketplace.** Mt 11:16, 17. Ge +*14:7. 2 K 7:1n. Je 5:1. Am +*5:16n. Lk 11:43.

4. **Go.** Mt 9:9. 21:23-31. Lk 19:7-10. Ro 6:16-22. 1 C 6:11. 1 T 1:12, 13. T 3:8. 1 P 1:13. 4:2, 3. **and whatsoever.** Col 4:1.

5. **sixth hour.** Our 12 noon. Mt 15:33, 34. 27:45. Lk 23:44-46. Jn 1:39. 4:6. +*11:9n. ◐19:14. Ac 3:1. 10:3, 9. **and ninth hour.** Our 3 P.M. Mt 27:45, 46. Mk 15:33, 34. Lk 23:44. Jn +*11:9n. Ac 3:1. 10:3, 30. **and did.** Ge 12:1-4. Jsh 24:2, 3. 2 Ch 33:12-19. He 11:24-26.

6. **the eleventh hour.** Our 5 P.M. ver. 9. Ec *9:10. Lk 23:40-43. Jn 9:4. +*11:9n. 1 C 15:8. **Why.** Pr 19:15. Ezk +*16:49. Ac *17:21. He 6:12.

7. **Because.** Ac 14:16. *17:30, 31. Ro 10:14-17. 16:25. Ep 2:11, 12. 3:5, 6. Col 1:26. **Go.** Mt 22:9, 10. Ec 9:10. Lk 14:21-23. Jn 9:4. **and.** Ep √6:8. He √6:10.

8. **when.** Mt 13:39, 40. 25:19, 31. Ro 2:6-10. 2 C 5:10. He 9:28. Re 20:11, 12. **even.** Our 6 P.M., the start of the first watch (Mt 14:25n. Mk 13:35). Jn *9:4. **unto.** Ge 15:2. 39:4-6. 43:19. Lk 10:7. 12:42. 16:1, 2. 1 C 4:1, 2. T 1:7. 1 P 4:10. **steward.** Lk 8:3. Ga 4:2. **their hire.** Le +*19:13. Dt +*24:15. Ml +*3:5. Ja +*5:4.

9. **were hired.** or, were called. Only the first group (ver. 2) were hired by agreement for a particular wage. Those called to the vineyard agreed to be paid at the pleasure of the master of the vineyard. **eleventh hour.** Our 5 P.M. ver. 6. Jn +*11:9n. **they received.** ver. 2, 6, 7. Lk 23:40-43. Ro 4:3-6. 5:20, 21. Ep 1:6-8. 2:8-10. 1 T 1:14-16.

10. **they supposed.** Ezk 18:2-4. **likewise received.** ver. 2, 13. Ge +*18:25. Lk +*6:35.

11. **they murmured.** Is *29:24. 58:13. La 3:39. Lk 5:30. 15:2, 28-30. 19:7. Ac 11:2, 3. 13:45. 22:21, 22. 1 Th 2:16. Ju +*16. **against.** Mk 14:14. Lk *12:39.

12. **wrought but one hour.** or, continued one hour only. They had worked from 5 to 6 P.M. **equal.** Lk 14:10, 11. Ro 3:22-24, 30. Ep √3:6. **borne.** Is 58:2, 3. Zc 7:3-5. Ml 1:13. 3:14. Lk 15:29, 30. 18:11, 12. Ro 3:27. 9:30-32. 10:1-3. 11:5, 6. 1 C 4:11. 2 C 11:23-28. **heat.** or, hot wind. Ge 31:40. +*41:6. Is 49:10. Ezk 17:10. Jon 4:8. Lk 12:55. Ja 1:11.

13. **Friend.** Gr. *hetairos*, ✶S#2083g. A term of kindly address, to be distinguished from *philos* (✶S#5384g, Mt +11:19), a term of endearment (Vine, *Expository Dictionary*, vol. 2, p. 132). Mt 11:16. 22:12. 26:50. **I do.** ver. +10. Ge +*18:25. Dt +*32:4. Jb 34:8-12, 17, 18. 35:2. 40:8. Ps 92:15. Ro *9:14, 15, 20. **no wrong.** At first reading it would appear that the householder was unfair for paying those who worked but one hour a whole day's wage, and paid the same amount to those who faithfully worked the entire twelve hour day, the point of their protest. But the householder was not unfair to them—he paid them

precisely what they had agreed to work for, and a good daily wage at that. He was fair to them, and generous to the rest. He gave the rest according to their need, not their effort, for they were called, not hired, and the later workers had entrusted their wage to his fairness, not having bargained for a set sum. 1 C √15:58. Ga +*6:9. He √6:10.

14. **thine.** Mt 6:2, 6, 16. 2 K 10:16, 30, 31. Ezk 29:18-20. Lk 15:31. 16:25. Ro 3:4, 19. **I will.** Jn 17:2.

15. **Is it not.** Mt 11:25. Ex 33:19. Dt 7:6-8. 1 Ch 28:4, 5. Je 27:5-7. Jn 17:2. Ro 9:15-24. 11:5, 6. 1 C 4:7. Ep 1:5. 2:1, 5. Ja *1:18. **to do.** Ps +*115:3. Is +46:10. Ro +9:18. Ep +*1:11. **Is thine.** Mt +*6:23. Dt 15:9. 28:54. Pr 23:6. 28:22. Mk √7:22. Ga 3:1. Ja 5:9. **because.** Jon 4:1-4. Ac 13:45.

16. **the last.** Mt +*8:11, 12. 19:30. *21:31. Mk 10:31. Lk 7:47. 13:28-30. 15:7. 17:17, 18. Jn 12:19-22. Ro 5:20. 9:30, 31. **for.** ♩74, Jg +5:31. Mt +*7:13. 11:28. 22:14. Mk 16:15. Lk 14:24. Jn *5:40. √6:37. 7:37. Ro *8:30. 1 Th √2:13. 2 Th *2:13, 14. Ja 1:23-25. 2 P +*1:10. Re 19:9. 22:17. **but few.** Mt +√7:14. **chosen.** Ac +*13:48. Ep *1:4. Re *17:14.

17. **Jesus.** Mk 10:32-34. Lk 18:31-34. Jn 12:12. **took.** Mt 13:11. 16:13. Ge 18:17. Jn 15:15. Ac 10:41.

18. **go up.** Mk 10:32, 33. 15:41. Lk 2:4, 42. 18:31. 19:28. Jn 2:13. Ac 18:22. **and the.** Mt 16:21. 17:22, 23. 26:2. Ps 2:1-3. 22:1, etc. 69:1, etc. Is ch. *53. Da +*9:24-27. Ac 2:23. 4:27, 28. **betrayed.** Mt 27:2. Jn 18:30, 31. Ac 2:23. 3:13. 4:27. 21:11. **they.** Mt 26:66. 27:1. Mk 14:64, 65. Lk 22:71. Jn 19:7.

19. **shall deliver.** Mt 27:2, etc. Mk 15:1, 16, etc. Lk 23:1, etc. Jn 18:28, etc., *35. Ac 3:13-16. 1 C +*15:3-7. **to mock.** Mt 26:67, 68. 27:27-31. Ps 22:7, 8. 35:16. Is *53:3. Mk 14:65. 15:16-20, 29-31. Lk 22:63. 23:11. Jn 19:1-4. **to crucify.** Mt 26:2. 27:26. Lk 24:7. Jn 12:32, 33. 18:32. **the third.** Mt +*12:40n. 16:21. 17:23. Is +*26:19. Ho 6:2. Mk 9:31. 10:34. Lk 9:22. 24:46. 1 C 15:4.

20. **came.** Mk 10:35-45. **the mother.** Mt 4:21. 27:56. Mk 15:40, Salome. Jn *19:25. **Zebedee's.** Mk 10:35. **worshipping.** Mt 2:11. 8:2. +*14:33. 15:25. 28:17.

21. **What.** ver. 32. 1 K 3:5. Est 5:3. Mk 6:22. 10:36, 51. Lk 18:41. Jn 15:7. **Grant.** Mt 18:1. √19:28. Je 45:5. Mk 10:37. Lk 22:24. Ro 12:10. Ph +*2:3. Re *3:21. **the one.** Mt ◐27:38. 1 K 2:19. Ps 45:9. 110:1. Mk 16:19. Ro 8:34. Col *3:1. **in thy kingdom.** Mt 16:28. *25:31, 34. Lk +*17:20, 21. √19:11. 23:42. √24:21. Jn 18:36. Ac +√1:6.

22. **Ye know not.** Mk 10:38. Lk 9:33. 23:34. Ro 8:26. Ja 4:3. **the cup.** Mt *26:39, 42. Ps *11:6. 75:3. Is *51:17, 22. Je 25:15, etc. 49:12. Mk 14:36. Lk 22:42. Jn 18:11. **baptized with.** Mk 10:39. Lk 12:50. **We are able.** Mt 26:35, 56. Pr *16:18.

23. **Ye.** Mt *16:24. Zc 4:12. Jn 17:14. Ac *12:2. Ro *8:17. 2 C *1:7. Ph 3:10. Col 1:24. 2 T *2:11, 12. √3:12. Re 1:9. 11:14. **but to sit.** Rather, "to sit on my right hand, and on my left, is not mine to give, except to them for whom it is prepared of my Father." Mt 25:31-40. Lk 19:11-27. Jn 5:22, 27. Ph 3:14. 2 P +*1:11. **not mine.** Lk ◐+*22:29. 1 C +*11:3. +*15:28. **it shall.** ♩63K, Ge +37:13. or, supply by ellipsis, (it is already given). **for whom.** Mt *25:34. Mk 10:40. Jn 14:2. 17:24. 1 C √2:9. He +*11:16.

24. **they.** Mt 21:15. 26:8. Pr 13:10. Mk 10:41. Lk 13:14. 22:23-25. 1 C 13:4. Ph 2:3. Ja 3:14-18. 4:1, 5, 6. 1 P *5:5.

25. **called**. Mt +*11:29. 18:3, 4. Jn 13:12-17. **the princes**. Mk 10:42. Lk 22:25-27. **exercise dominion**. Gr. *katakurieuousin*, rule imperiously, lord it over, or tyrannize over, from *kata*, intensitive, or denoting "ill," and *kurieuo*, "to rule," from *kurios*, a lord. Da 2:12, 13, 37-45. 3:2-7, 15, 19-22. 5:19. 1 P 5:3. **great**. Mk 6:21. **exercise authority**. Gr. *katexousiaxousin*, "exercise arbitrary power" or "authority," from *kata*, and *exousiadzo*, "to exercise authority." This was true of all the governments in our Lord's time, both in the east and in the west.

26. **it**. Mt *23:8-12. Mk *9:35. 10:43-45. Lk 9:48. 14:7-11. 18:14. *22:25, 26. Jn 18:36. 2 C 1:24. 10:4-10. Ph +*2:3. 1 P √5:3. 3 J 9, 10. Re 13:11-17. 17:6. **minister**. Gr. *diakonos*, a deacon, properly, a servant at table. Mt 22:13. 25:44. 27:55. Ex 24:13. Ac *13:5n. 1 C 3:5. 2 T 1:18. Phm 13. He *1:14. 1 P 4:11.

27. **whosoever will be**. Mt *18:4. 22:3. Mk 9:33-35. *10:44. Lk 22:26. Ac 20:34, 35. Ro 1:14. 1 C *9:19-23. 2 C 4:5. *11:5, 23-27. 12:15. **let him**. Ro 12:10. Ph +*2:3. He +*13:17. 1 P +*5:5.

28. **Son of man**. Mt 8:20. **came**. T#1868. Mt +9:13. Mk 10:45. Lk +*19:10. 22:27. Jn *13:4-17. 2 C *8:9. Ph √2:4-8. He *5:8. **and to give**. Jb *33:24. Ps *49:7. Is 44:22. *53:5, 8, 10, 11. Ezk 37:23. Da +*9:24-26. Jn *10:15. *11:50-52. Ro *3:24-26. 4:25. 2 C 5:15, 21. Ga 1:4. 2:20. +*3:13. 4:4, 5. Ep +*1:7. *5:2. Col 1:14. 1 T *2:6. T √2:14. He *2:9. *9:28. 1 P *1:18, 19. √2:24. √3:18. Re +*1:5. *5:8, 9. **life**. Gr. *psyche*, √121A7, Mt +2:20. √121A7, Ge +9:5. **a ransom**. Ex +=12:13. Mk 10:45g. **for many**. √√171F, Is +53:12. Mt +*26:28n. Is *53:*4-6, 11, 12. Mk *14:24. Jn ◑+1:9. *11:51, 52. Ro 5:15-19. 2 C ◑√5:15. He 2:10. *9:28. 2 P +*3:9. 1 J √2:2. Re 5:9. 7:9.

29. **as they departed**. Mt 9:27-31. Mk 10:46-52. Lk 18:35-43. 19:1. **Jericho**. i.e. *constant fragrance*, ✱S#2410g. Nu +22:1 (✱S#3405h). Mk 10:46. Lk 10:30. 18:35. 19:1. He 11:30.

30. **two**. Mt 9:27-31. 12:22. 21:14. Ps 146:8. Is 29:18. 35:5, 6. 42:16, 18. 59:10. +*61:1, 2. Mk 10:46. Lk +*4:18. 7:21. Jn 9:1, etc. **way side**. T#1214. Mk 10:46-52. **Have mercy**. Mt 9:27. 12:23. 15:22. 17:15. Lk 16:24. 17:13. **Son of David**. √171G, Ge +13:8. Mt 1:1. 21:9. 22:42. Ac 2:30. Ro +*1:3, 4.

31. **rebuked**. Mt 15:23. 19:13. Lk 18:15. **but they cried**. Mt +*7:7, 8. Ge *32:25-29. Lk √11:8-10. *18:1, etc., 39. Col 4:2. 1 Th +*5:17. **son**. √171G, Ge +13:8.

32. **What**. ver. 21. Ezk 36:37. Mk 10:36. Ac 10:29. Ph *4:6.

33. **Lord**. Ps √119:18. Ep 1:17-19.

34. **Jesus**. Mt 9:36. 14:14. 15:32. Ps 145:8. Lk 7:13. Jn 11:33-35. He 2:17. +*4:15, 16. 1 P 3:8. **touched their eyes**. Mt 9:29. Mk 7:33. Lk 22:51. Jn 9:6, 7. **received sight**. Lk 7:21. **and they**. Mt 8:15. Ps 119:67, 71. Lk *18:43. Ac *26:18.

MATTHEW 21

Jesus enters Jerusalem on an ass's colt, amidst the acclamations of the multitudes, 1-11. He drives the buyers and sellers out of the temple; heals the blind and lame; and answers the objections of the priests, 12-16. He causes the barren fig tree to wither; and shows the disciples the power of faith and prayer, 17-22. He silences those who demand by what authority he acted, 23-27; and exposes the wickedness, and pre-

dicts the doom, of the priests and rulers, by a parable of two sons, 28-32, and by that of a vineyard let out to husbandmen, 33-46.

1. **when**. Mk 11:1. Lk 18:31. 19:28, 29. Jn 12:12-15. **Bethphage**. i.e. *green fig house*, ✱S#967g. Mt 21:1. Mk 11:1. Lk 19:29. **Bethphage** was a village on the declivity of Mount Olivet, and somewhat nearer to Jerusalem than Bethany. **the mount**. Mt *24:3. 26:30. 2 S 15:30. Ne 8:15. Ezk 11:23. Zc +*14:4. Mk 11:1. 13:3. 14:26. Lk 19:29, 37. 21:37. 22:39. Jn 8:1. Ac *1:12. **two disciples**. Mk 14:13.

2. **Go into**. Mt 26:18. Mk 11:2, 3. 14:13-16. Lk 19:30-32. Jn 2:5-8. **loose them**. 1 S 8:16.

3. **if**. √184C, Mt +4:9. **The Lord**. √171E12, Ge +14:22. 1 Ch 29:14-16. Ps *24:1. 50:10, 11. Hg 2:8, 9. Lk 7:13. Jn 3:35. 17:2. Ac 17:25. 2 C *8:9. **straightway**. 1 S 10:26. 1 K 17:9. Ezk 1:1, 5. 7:27. 2 C 8:1, 2, 16. Ja 1:17.

4. **this**. Mt 1:22. 26:56. Jn 19:36, 37. **saying**. Zc 9:9. Jn 12:15.

5. **Tell ye**. √92A, Mt +1:23. Zc)9:9. Notice that Zc 9:9 is quoted, but not Zc 9:10. Compare the similar break in quotation of prophecy made by Jesus at Lk 4:19, 20. **Behold**. √92G, Lk +4:18. Lk +*24:27. **the daughter**. Ps 9:14. Is 1:8. 10:32. 12:6. 37:22. 40:9. *62:11. La 1:6. Zp 3:14, 15. Zc 2:10. Mk 11:4, etc. **thy King**. Mt 2:2, 6. Ge +*49:10. Nu +*24:19. Ps *2:6-12. 45:1, etc. 72:1, etc. *110:1-4. Is +*9:6, 7. 32:1. Je +*23:5, 6. Ezk 34:24. 37:24. Da 2:44, 45. +*7:13, 14. Ho +*3:5. Mi +*5:2. Zc +*6:12, 13.)9:9. Lk 1:32. 19:38. Jn *1:49. 19:15-22. **meek**. Mt +*11:29. 12:19, 20. 2 C 10:1. Ph 2:3-5. **sitting**. Dt 17:16. Jg +5:10. 12:14. 2 S 16:2. 1 K 1:33. 10:26. Ho 1:7. Mi 5:10, 11. Zc *9:10.

6. **and did**. Ge 6:22. 12:4. Ex 39:43. 40:16. 1 S 15:11. Mk 11:4. Lk 19:32-34. Jn +*15:14.

7. **brought**. Mk 11:4-8. Lk 19:32-35. **put**. 2 K 9:13. **him**. √63A3, Mt +19:13.

8. **spread**. 2 K 9:13. **others**. Le 23:40. Jn 12:13.

9. **Hosanna**. ver. 15. 2 S 14:4. Ps *118:24-26. Je 31:7. Mk 11:9, 10. **son of David**. √171G, Ge +13:8. ver. 15. Mt 1:1. 20:30. 22:42. **Blessed**. Mt 23:39. Ps)118:26. Ezk 34:23, 24. Lk 13:35. 19:37, 38. Jn 12:13-15. **in the highest**. Ps 148:1. Lk 2:14.

10. **And when**. Mk 11:11. **all**. Mt 2:3. Ru 1:19. 1 S 16:4. Jn 12:16-19. Ac 21:30. **Who**. SS 3:6. Is 63:1. Lk 5:21. 7:49. 9:9. 20:2. Jn 2:18. Ac 9:5.

11. **This**. Mt 16:13, 14. Dt 18:15-19. Lk 7:16. Jn 7:40. 9:17. Ac 3:22, 23. 7:37. **the prophet**. ver. 46. Mk 6:15. Lk 7:16, 39. 9:8, 19. 13:33. 24:19. Jn 1:21. 4:19. 6:14. 7:40. 9:17. Ac 3:22. **of Nazareth**. Mt *2:23. Mk 1:24. Jn 1:45, 46. 6:14.

12. **went**. Ml 3:1, 2. Mk 11:11. **and cast**. Mk 11:15. Lk *19:45, 46. Jn 2:14-17. **the temple**. Hg ✱2:7, 9. Ml ✱3:1. Lk 2:27, 32. **moneychangers**. Ex 30:13. Dt 14:24-26. **doves**. Le 1:14. 5:7, 11. 12:6, 8. 14:22, 30. 15:14, 29. Lk 2:24.

13. **It is**. Mt 2:5. Lk +*24:27. Jn 15:25. **My**. Ps 93:5. Is)56:7. **house of prayer**. 1 K 8:29, 30, 41-43. 2 Ch 6:40. **but ye**. √92G, Lk +4:18. **den of theives**. √102, Ge +2:24. Je)7:11. Ezk 7:22. Mk 11:17. Lk 19:46.

14. **the blind**. Mt 9:35. 11:4, 5. 15:30, 31. Is 35:5, 6. Lk 7:21. Ac 3:1-9. 10:38.

15. **when**. ver. 23. Mt 26:3, 59. 27:1, 20. Is 26:11. Mk 11:18. Lk 19:39, 40. 20:1. 22:2, 66. Jn 11:47-49,

57. 12:19. **wonderful.** Is 9:6. 28:29. Ac 2:22. **Hosanna.** ver. 9. Mt 22:42. Jn 7:42. **the son of David.** ✗171G, Ge +13:8. ver. 9. **they were.** Mt 20:24. 26:8. Jon 4:1. Lk 13:14.

16. **Hearest.** Lk *19:39, 40. Jn *11:47, 48. Ac *4:16-18. **have.** ver. 42. Mt 12:3, 5. 19:4. 22:31. Mk 2:25. 12:10. **Out.** ✗92A, Mt +1:23. Mt *11:25. Ps *✗8:2. **babes.** Mt +*11:25. Lk 9:47. 1 C 1:27. **and sucklings.** ✗174, Ge +18:27.

17. **he left.** Mt 16:4. Je 6:8. Ho 9:12. Mk 3:7. Lk 8:37, 38. **went out.** Mk 11:19. Lk 21:37. **Bethany.** *Bethany* was a village to the east of the mount of Olives, on the road to Jericho; fifteen stadia (Jn 11:18), or nearly two miles, as Jerome states, from Jerusalem. This village is now small and poor, and the cultivation of the soil around it is much neglected; but it is a pleasant, romantic spot, shaded by the mount of Olives, and abounding in vines and long grass. It consists of from thirty to forty dwellings, inhabited by about 600 Mohammedans, for whose use there is a neat little mosque standing on an eminence. Here they show the ruins of a sort of castle as the house of Lazarus, and a grotto as his tomb; and the house of Simon the leper, of Mary Magdalene and of Martha, and the identical tree which our Lord cursed, are among the monkish curiosities of the place. Mk 11:1, 11, 12, 19. 14:3. Lk *10:38. 19:29. 24:50. Jn 11:1, +*18. 12:1-3. **lodged there.** Lk 21:37.

18. **in.** Mk 11:12, 13. **he hungered.** Mt 4:2. 12:1. Lk 4:2. Jn 4:6, 7. 19:28. He +*4:15.

19. **a fig tree.** Gr. one fig tree. ✗108E1, Mt +8:19. Mt 8:19. 26:69. Je √8:13. **and found.** Is *5:4, 5. Mi *7:1. Mk 11:13. Lk 3:9. *13:6-9. 19:41-44. Jn *15:2, 6. 2 T 3:5. T 1:16. **Let.** Mk 11:14. Lk 19:42-44. He 6:7, 8. 2 P 2:20-22. Re 22:11. **for ever.** Gr. *aion*, Mt +6:13. lit. "unto the age," as in Mk 3:29. 11:14. Lk 1:55. Jn 4:14. 6:51, 58. 8:35, 51, 52. 10:28. 11:26. 12:34. 13:8. 14:16. 1 C 8:13. 2 C 9:9. He 5:6. 6:20. 7:17, 21, 28. 1 P 1:23, 25. 1 J 2:17. 2 J 2. Ju 13. **the fig tree.** Ju 12.

20. **How.** ✗85E, Ge +17:17. Is 40:6-8. Mk *11:20, 21. Ja 1:10, 11.

21. **If ye have.** ✗184B, Mt +23:30. Mt *17:20. Mk *11:22, 23. 16:17. Lk *17:6, 7. Jn *15:7, 16. 16:24. Ro 4:19, 20. 1 C 13:2. Ja 1:6. **and doubt not.** Mk 11:23. Ac 10:20. Ro *4:20. 14:23. Ja 1:6. 2:4. 3:17. Ju 9g, 22g. **also if.** ✗184C, Mt +4:9. **say.** ✗138B, Ge +13:16. **this mountain.** ver. 1. **Be thou removed.** Mt 8:12.

22. **all things.** T#1433. Mt *7:7, 11. +*18:19. Ps 57:2, 3. Je +*33:3. Mk √11:24. Lk √11:8-10. Jn *14:13. 15:7. √16:24. Ro +*8:32. Ep *3:20. Ja √5:16. 1 J *3:22. √5:14, 15. **whatsoever.** ✗184C, Mt +4:9. **receive.** ✗63C, Ge +25:32. Supply by ellipsis (absolute: brachylogia), "(if it be His will)," Ja 5:14, 15; 1 J 5:14, 15. This is the one abiding condition of all real prayer, and the *Ellipsis* must be thus supplied wherever it is found (B48).

23. **when.** Mk 11:27, 28. Lk 19:47, 48. 20:1, 2. **the chief priests.** 1 Ch 24:1, etc. Mk 11:18. Lk 20:1-8. **as he was teaching.** Mt 26:55. Ac 5:42. 15:35. **By what.** Mt 9:11. √22:42-46. Ex 2:14. Jn 1:25. Ac 4:7. 7:27.

24. **I also.** Mt 10:16. Pr 26:4, 5. Lk 6:9. 1 C 3:19. Col 4:6. **one thing.** lit. word. *Grk. logos.* ✗108B, Lk +1:2. **if ye.** ✗184C, Mt +4:9.

25. **baptism of John.** Mt 3:1, etc. 11:7-15. 17:12,

13. Mk 1:1-11. 11:27-33. Lk 1:11-17, 67-80. 3:2-20. 7:28-35. Jn 1:6, 15, 25-34. 3:26-36. **Whence.** ✗21, Jg +14:18. Mt 13:54. **from heaven.** ✗121J20, Ps +73:9. Da 4:26. Lk 15:18, 21. Jn 3:27. **from men.** Ac 5:38, 39. **reasoned.** Mt 16:7. Mk 8:16. Lk 3:15mg. 20:14. **If.** ✗36, Ho +6:4. ✗184C, Mt +4:9. **Why.** ver. 32. Mt 3:7, 8. Lk √7:30. 20:5. Jn √3:18. 5:33-36, 44-47. 10:25, 26. 12:37-43. 1 J 3:20.

26. **But if.** ✗36, Ho +6:4. ✗184C, Mt +4:9. **we fear.** ver. 46. Mt 14:5. Is 57:11. Mk 11:32. 12:12. Lk *20:6, 19. 22:2. Jn 9:22. Ac 5:26. **for all.** ✗171A, Ex +9:6. Mt 11:9. Mk *6:20. Lk 7:29. Jn *5:35. 10:41, 42.

27. **We cannot tell.** Mt +*15:14. 16:3. 23:16, etc. Is 6:10. 28:9. 29:10-12. 42:19, 20. 56:10, 11. Je 8:7-9. Ml 2:6-9. Lk 20:7, 8. Jn 9:30, 40, 41. Ro 1:18-22, 28. 2 C *4:3, 4. 2 Th 2:9, 10.

28. **what.** Mt 17:25. 18:12. 22:17. Lk 13:4. 1 C 10:15. **A certain.** Lk 15:11-32. **Son.** Lk 15:31g. **go work.** Mt 20:5-7. Ps 40:1. Mk 13:34. Lk 12:37. 19:13. Jn 9:4. 1 C √15:58. **in my vineyard.** ver. 33. Mt 20:1.

29. **I will not.** ✗1, Mt +15:23. ver. 31. 1 S +*15:23. Je 44:16. Ep 4:17-19. **he repented.** ver. 32. Mt 3:2-8. 27:3. 2 Ch 33:10-19. Is *1:16-19. √55:6, 7. Ezk 18:28-32. Da 4:34-37. Jon 3:2, 8-10. Lk 15:17, 18. Ac 26:20. 1 C 6:11. 2 C 7:8, 10. Ep 2:1-13. He 7:21.

30. **I go.** Mt *23:3. Ezk +√33:31. Ro *2:17-25. T 1:16. **went not.** 1 S +*15:22, 23.

31. **did.** Mt +*7:21. 12:50. Ezk 33:11. Lk 15:10. Ac *17:30. 2 P √3:9. **The first.** 2 S 12:5-7. Jb 15:6. Lk 7:40-42. 19:22. Ro 3:19. **Verily.** Mt 5:18. 6:5. 18:3. **the publicans.** Mt 9:9. 11:19. 20:16. Lk 7:29, *37-50. 15:1, 2. *18:13, 14. 19:9, 10. Ro 5:20. 9:30-33. 1 T 1:13-16. **go into.** Mt +*7:21. **the kingdom of God.** ver. 43. Mt +12:28. **before you.** ver. 32. Mt 19:30.

32. **came.** Mt 3:1-8. Is 35:8. Je 6:16. Lk 3:8-13. 2 P 2:21. **way of righteousness.** Mt *3:8-12, 15. Pr 8:20. 12:28. 17:23. 2 P 2:21. **believed him not.** ver. 25. Mt 11:18. Lk √7:29, 30. Jn 5:33-36. Ac 13:25-29. **the publicans.** ver. 31. Mt 11:19. Lk 3:12, 13. 7:29, 37, etc. **repented not.** Ps 81:11, 12. Je 5:1. 17:23-27. Zc 7:11, 12. Jn 5:37-40. 2 T 2:25. He +*3:12. *6:6-8. Re *2:21.

33. **Hear.** In this parable, in its primary sense, the householder denotes the Supreme Being; the family, the Jewish nation; the vineyard, Jerusalem; the fence, the Divine protection; the winepress, the law and sacrificial rites; the tower, the temple; and the husbandmen, the priests and doctors of the law. Mt +*13:18. 1 K 22:19. Is 1:10. Je 19:3. Ho 4:1. **There.** ver. 28. Dt 32:32, 33. Ps 80:8-16. SS 8:11, 12. Is *✗5:1-4. 27:2-6. Je *2:21. Ezk 15:1-6. 19:10-14. Ho 10:1. Jl 1:7. Mk 12:1. Lk 20:9-19. Jn 15:1. **hedged it.** Is 5:2. **let it out.** SS 8:11, 12. **husbandmen.** Mt 23:2. Dt 1:15-17. 16:18. 17:9-12. 33:8-10. Ml 2:4-9. **went.** Mt 25:14, 15. Mk 13:34. 19:12. **far country.** Mt ◐+√25:19. Lk 15:13.

34. **he sent.** 2 K 17:13, 14, etc. 2 Ch *36:15, 16. Ne 9:29, 30. Je *25:3-7. 35:15. Zc 1:3-6. 7:9-13. Mk 12:2-5. Lk 20:10-19. **that.** SS *8:11, 12. Is 5:4.

35. **took his servants.** Mt 5:12. 22:6. 23:31-37. 1 K 18:4, 13. 19:2, 10. *22:24-27. 2 K 6:31. 21:16. 2 Ch 16:10. 24:19, 21, 22. *36:15, 16. Ne *9:26. Je 2:30. 25:3-7. 26:21-24. *37:15. 38:6. 44:4. Lk 13:33, 34. Ac *7:52. 2 C 11:24-26. 1 Th *2:15, 16. He 11:36, 37. Re 6:9. **beat one.** 2 Ch *36:16. Je *20:2. Ac 5:40. 2 C 11:24, 25. He *11:36, 37. **killed another.** Mt 22:6. 1 Th 2:15. He 11:37. **stoned another.** Mt 23:37.

2 Ch 24:21. Jn 10:31-33. Ac 7:59. 14:5, 19. He 11:37.
36. **other servants.** Mt 22:4. Mk 12:5.
37. **last.** Mt 3:17. Mk *12:6. Lk *20:13. Jn 1:18,
34. √3:16, 35, 36. He *1:1, 2. **They.** Is 5:4. Je 36:3.
Zp 3:7. Lk 18:2g.
38. **This.** Mt 2:13-16. 26:3, 4. *27:1, 2. Ge 37:18-
20. Ps *2:2-8. Mk 12:7, 8. Lk 20:14. Jn 1:11. 11:47-
53. Ac 4:27, 28. 5:24-28. Ro 8:17. He *1:2. **let us
kill.** Ge 37:20. 1 K 21:19.
39. **caught.** Mt 26:50, 57. Mk 14:46-53. Lk *22:52-
54. Jn 18:12, 24. Ac *2:23. 4:25-27. **cast.** Mk 12:8.
He 13:11-13. **slew.** Ac 2:23. 3:14, 15. 4:10. 5:30. 7:52.
Ja 5:6.
40. **cometh.** Mt 24:50. 25:19. 2 S 12:5, 6. **what.** Je
17:27. Mk 12:9. Lk 20:15, 16. He 10:29.
41. **They say.** Our Lord here causes them to pass
that sentence of destruction upon themselves which
was literally executed about forty years afterwards by
the Roman armies. **He will.** Mt 3:12. *22:6, 7. *23:35-
38. *24:21, 22. Le 26:14, etc. Dt 28:59-68. Ps *2:4,
5, 9. Is 5:5-7. Da 9:26. Zc 11:8-10. 12:12. 13:8. 14:2,
3. Ml 4:1-6. Lk 17:32-37. 19:41-44. *21:22-24. 1 Th
*2:16. He 2:3. 12:25. **miserably.** Mt 22:7. Lk 19:27.
Ro *2:8, 9. 2 C +*5:11. 2 Th √1:8, 9. **destroy.** Gr.
apollumi, Mt +2:13. **and will let out.** ver. +*43. Mt
+*8:11, 12. Is 49:5-7. +*65:15. +*66:19-21. Mk 12:9.
Lk 13:28, 29. 14:23, 24. 20:16. *21:24. Ac *13:46-48.
15:7. 18:6. 28:28. Ro ch. *9-11. 15:9-18. **fruits.** ver.
34, *43. **in their seasons.** Mt +*24:45.
42. **Did.** ver. +*16. **in the scriptures.** Mt +*22:29.
26:54, 56. Mk +*12:24. Lk 4:21. 24:27, 32, 45. Jn
2:22. +√5:39. Ac +*17:2, 11. 18:24, 28. Ro 1:2. √15:4.
16:26. 1 C +*15:3, 4. 2 T +*3:15. 2 P 3:16. **The
stone.** √92A, Mt +1:23. √22L1, Ps +118:22. Ge=49:24.
Ps ⟩118:22, 23. Is *28:16. Zc 3:8, 9. Mk 8:31. 12:10,
11. Lk 20:17, 18. Ac *4:11. Ro 9:33. Ep *2:20. 1 P
*2:4-8. **builders rejected.** Lk 22:2. Jn *7:48, 49. **head
of the corner.** Jb 38:6. Je 51:26. Zc 4:7. Col *1:18.
the Lord's doing. Ne 6:16. Ep 1:22, 23. 2:20. He 5:4,
5. **and it is.** Hab 1:5. Ac 13:40, 41. Ep 3:3-9.
43. **The kingdom of God.** ver. 31. Mt +*8:11, 12.
+12:28. Is 28:2. Jl 2:28n. Lk 10:10, 11. +*17:20n,
21. Jn *3:3, 5. 1 C √15:50n. Col +*1:13. **shall be taken.**
ver. 41. Mt √22:8. 1 K ○√11:39. Je 22:5. Ho 3:4. Mi
√5:3. Lk 14:24. Jn ●11:48. Ac 13:46. **from you.** Mt
*8:11, 12. 22:1-14. Lk *13:28. 14:15-24. *17:22. 19:11-
27, 41-44. +*21:31. **and given.** Is +*65:13. Da √7:27.
Lk +*12:32. Ro 4:13, 24. 8:17, 18. 1 C 15:50n. Ep
1:11n. Re 11:18. **a nation.** Ex +*19:5, 6. Dt 32:21.
Is *26:2. +*54:1. Jn +*10:16. 2 Th 2:1. 1 P √2:9. Re
1:5, 6. √5:9, 10. √20:6. **bringing forth.** ver. 41. Mt
*3:10. +*24:45. Le +*26:40-42. Is *5:4, 7. Ho +*3:5.
*5:15. Lk +21:36. Ac +*3:19-21. Ro *14:17. 1 C 13:2.
Ep *5:9. Col +√1:10.
44. **whosoever.** √92A, Mt +1:23. **whosoever.** Ps 2:12. Is
*⟩8:14, 15. *60:12. Zc 12:3. Lk 2:34. *20:18. Ro 9:32,
33. 1 C *1:23. 2 C 4:3, 4. 1 P 2:8. **but.** Mt 26:24.
27:25. Ps 2:9. 21:8, 9. *110:5, 6. Da *2:34, 35, 44,
45. Zc *12:3. Jn 19:11. 1 Th 2:16. He 2:2, 3. **it will
grind.** Is 17:13. 60:12. Je +*31:10. Am +*9:9.
45. **they.** Mt +*13:12-14. Mk 12:12. Lk 11:45.
20:19.
46. **But when.** Mt 26:4. Mk 11:18. 14:1. Lk 19:47,
48. 22:2. Jn 7:25, 30, 44. **they sought.** Mt 12:14. 2 S
12:7-13. Pr 9:7-9. 15:12. Is 29:1. Jn 7:1, 7. 11:50. **they
feared.** ver. 11, 26. Mt 14:5. Mk 11:32. Ac 5:26. **be-**

cause. ver. 11, 26. Mk 12:37. Lk *7:16, 39. Jn *6:14.
*7:40, 41. Ac 2:22.

MATTHEW 22

*Jesus speaks the parable of the marriage-supper,
and the wedding garment, 1-14. Jesus answers the
Pharisees and Herodians about paying tribute to Caesar, 15-22; the Sadducees about the resurrection and
future state, 23-33; and a lawyer concerning the chief
commandment in the law, 34-40; and inquires how
the Messiah could be David's Son, and yet his Lord,
41-46.*

1. **answered.** Mt 11:25. **and spake.** Mt 9:15-17.
12:43-45. 13:3-11. 20:1-16. 21:28-46. Mk 4:33, 34. Lk
8:10. 14:16.
2. **kingdom.** Mt 13:24, 31-33, 44-47. 25:1, 14. **which.**
Mt 25:1-13. Ps 45:10-16. Lk 14:16-24. Jn 3:29, etc.
2 C 11:2. Ep 5:24-32. Re *19:7-9.
3. **sent.** Mt *3:2. 10:6, 7. Est 6:14. Ps 68:11. Pr
9:1-3, 5. Is 55:1, 2. Je 25:4. 35:15. Mk 6:7-12. Lk
3:3. *9:1-6. 14:15-17. Re 22:17. **to call.** Lk 14:17. **that
were bidden.** 1 S 9:13. Zp 1:7. **and they would not.**
√111, Ge +18:27. Mt √23:37. Ps 81:10-12. Pr 1:24-
32. Is 30:15. Je 6:16, 17. Ho 11:2, 7. Lk 13:34. 15:28.
19:27. Jn √5:40. Ac 13:45. Ro 10:21. He 12:25.
4. **other.** Mt 21:36. Lk 10:1-16. 24:46, 47. Ac +*1:8.
11:19, 20. 13:46. 28:17, etc. **Behold.** Pr *9:1, 2. SS
5:1. Is *25:6. *55:1. Jn *6:50-57. Ro *8:32. 1 C 5:7,
8. **my dinner.** Jn 21:12g. **my oxen.** Pr 9:2. **and all.**
ver. 8. Ge=43:16. Ne 9:17. Ps 86:5. Lk 14:17. **come.**
ver. 3.
5. **they.** Ge *19:14. *25:34. Ps *106:24, 25. Pr *1:7,
24, 25. Ac *2:13. *24:25. Ro *2:4. He √2:3. **one.** Mt
*13:22. *24:38, 39. Lk *14:18-20. *17:26-32. Ro *8:6.
1 T *6:9, 10. 2 T *3:4. 1 J *2:15, 16.
6. **the remnant.** Mt 5:10-12. 10:12-18, 22-25. 21:35-
39. 23:34-37. Jn 15:19, 20. 16:2, 3. Ac 4:1-3. *5:40,
41. 7:51-57. 8:1. 1 Th 2:14, 15. **entreated them spitefully.** Lk 11:45g. .18:32. Ac 14:5. 1 C *11:24. 1 Th
2:2. **and slew.** Mt 21:35. Ac 7:58. 12:2. He *11:37,
38.
7. **he was wroth.** Mt 21:40, 41. Da +*9:26. Zc *14:1,
2. Lk *19:27, 42-44. +*21:21-24. 1 Th *2:16. He √2:3.
1 P *4:17, 18. **his armies.** Dt 28:49, etc. Is *10:5-7.
13:2-5. Je 51:20-23. Jl 2:11, 25. 3:2. Lk *19:27. **destroyed.** Gr. *apollumi*, Mt +2:13.
8. **The wedding.** ver. 4. **but they.** Jn 1:11. **not worthy.** Mt *10:11-13, 37, 38. +*21:43. Mi *5:3. Lk √20:35.
+*21:36. Ac √13:46. Col +*1:10. 2 Th √1:5. Re *3:4.
22:14.
9. **Go ye.** Pr 1:20-23. 8:1-5. 9:4-6. Is *55:1-3, 6, 7.
Mk *16:15, 16. Lk 14:21-24. 24:47. Ac 13:47. Ep 3:8.
Re *22:17. **into the highways.** Ezk 21:21. Ob 14. **as
many.** Lk 14:21. **bid.** Mt 11:28. Ro 10:21.
10. **and gathered.** Mt +*13:47. **both bad and good.**
ver. 11, 12. Mt +*13:30, 38, 47, 48. 25:1, 2. Lk +*6:35.
1 C +*6:9-11. 2 C 12:21. 2 P +*3:9. 1 J √2:19. Re
2:14, 15, 20-23. **and the.** Mt 25:10. Re 5:9. 7:9. 19:6-
9.
11. **when.** Mt 3:12. 13:30. 25:31, 32. Zp 1:12. 1 C
*4:5. He +*4:12, 13. Re *2:23. **which had not.** 2 K
10:22. Ps 45:13, 14. Is 52:1. *61:3, 10. 64:6. Je 11:15.
Zp=1:8. Zc 3:3, 4. Lk 15:22. Ro *3:22. √13:14. 2 C
5:3. Ga √3:27. Ep 4:24. Col *3:10-12. He +*12:14.
Re *3:4, 5, 18. 16:15. √19:8. 22:14.

12. **Friend.** Mt 20:13. 26:50. Jn +*15:14. **how.** Mt *5:20. √7:22, 23. Ac *5:2-11. *8:20-23. 1 C *4:5. **And he was.** 1 S 2:9. Jb 5:16. Ps 107:42. Je 2:23, 26. Lk 4:35g. Ro 3:19. T 3:11.

13. **servants.** Mt 20:26. 1 C 3:5. **Bind.** Mt 12:29. 13:30. Is 52:1. Da 3:20. Jn 21:18. Ac 21:11. Re 21:27. **outer darkness.** Mt +*8:12. +*25:30. 2 Th *1:9. 2 P 2:4, 17. Ju *6, *13. **there.** Mt +*13:42, 49, 50. +*24:51. Ps *37:12. 112:10. Lk 13:28. Ac 7:54.

14. **For.** √74, Jg +5:31. **many are called.** Mt +*7:13, 14. *20:16. Lk *13:23, 24. Re 17:14. **few are chosen.** Mt +√7:14. *11:27. *24:22, 24, 31. Dt +10:15. Lk 18:7. Re 17:14.

15. **went.** Ps 2:2. Mk 12:13-17. Lk 20:20-26. **took counsel.** Mt 12:14. **how.** Ps 41:6. 56:5-7. 57:6. 59:3. Is 29:21. Je 18:18. 20:10. Lk 11:53, 54. He 12:3.

16. **they sent.** The profound malice of the Pharisees appears here in their choice of companions, their affected praise, and the artful and difficult questions they proposed. Lk *20:20. **their disciples.** Mk 2:18. **the Herodians.** i.e. *partisans of Herod*, ✽S#2265g. Mt 16:11, 12. Mk 3:6g. 8:15. 12:13g. Lk 23:7. **Master.** ver. 24, 26. Mt 26:18, 49. Mk 10:17. Lk 7:40. **we know.** √60D, Ge +37:19. Ps 5:9. 12:2. 55:21. Pr 29:5. Is 59:13-15. Je 9:3-5. Ezk +*33:30, 31. Jn 3:2. **true.** Ml 2:6. Jn 7:18. √14:6. 18:37. 2 C 2:17. 4:2. 1 J *5:20. **the way.** Mk 1:3. 12:14. Lk 1:76. 3:4. 20:21. Jn 1:23. Ac 9:2. 13:10. 18:25, 26. Ro 11:33. He 3:10. Re 15:3. **in truth.** Jn 17:19. **neither.** Le +*19:15. Dt 33:9. 1 K 22:14. Jb 32:21, 22. Mi 3:9-12. Ml 2:9. Mk 12:14. Lk 20:21. Ac 10:34. 2 C 5:16. Ga 1:10. 2:6. 1 Th 2:4. Ja 2:1, 9. 3:17.

17. **What.** Je 42:2, 3, 20. Ac 28:22. **Is.** Dt *17:14, 15. Ezr 4:13. 7:24. Ne 5:4. 9:37. Ac 5:37. Ro 13:6, 7. **tribute.** Mt 17:25. Lk 23:2. Ro 13:6, 7. **Caesar.** Lk 2:1. 3:1. 23:2. Jn 19:12-15. Ac 17:7. 25:8.

18. **perceived.** Mk 2:8. Lk 5:22. 9:47. 20:23. Jn +*2:25. Re *2:23. **Why.** ver. 35. Mt 16:1-4. 19:3. Mk 12:15. Lk 10:25. Jn 8:6. Ac 5:9. **hypocrites.** Mt 6:2.

19. **a penny.** "In value sevenpence halfpenny." Mt *18:28mg. 20:2mg. Re 6:6.

20. **Whose.** √22, Ge +3:9. **superscription.** *or*, inscription. Lk 20:24.

21. **Render.** Mt 17:25-27. Pr 24:21. Lk 23:2. Ro *13:7. 1 P *2:17. **are Caesar's.** This conclusion is drawn from their own maxims and premises. They held that "wherever the money of any king is current, there the inhabitants acknowledge that king for their lord" (Maimonides on Gezelah, c. 5). Now, by admitting that this was Caesar's coin, and by consenting to receive it as the current coin of their country, they in fact acknowledged their subjection to his government, and of course their obligation to pay the tribute demanded of them. This answer was full of consummate wisdom, and it completely defeated the insidious designs of his enemies. He avoided rendering himself odious to the Jewish people by opposing their notions of liberty, or appearing to pay court to the emperor, without exposing himself to the charge of sedition and disaffection to the Roman government. Pr +*22:3. Is √52:13. **and unto God.** ver. 37. Mt *4:10. Da +*3:16-18. +*6:10, 11, 20-23. Ml 1:6-8. 3:8-10. Ac +*4:19. +*5:29. 1 T 2:2. 1 P 2:13-17.

22. **they marvelled.** ver. 33, 46. Mt *10:16. Pr +*21:30. 26:4, 5. Mk 5:20. Lk *20:25, 26. 21:15. Jn 7:15. Ac 6:10. Col *4:6. **and left.** Mk 12:12.

23. **same.** Mk 12:18, etc. Lk 20:27, etc. **the Sadducees.** ver. 34. Mt 3:7. 16:1, 6, 11, 12. Mk 12:18. Lk 20:27. Ac 4:1. 5:17. 23:6-8. **which say.** Ac 4:2. *23:8. *26:8. 1 C *15:12-14. 2 T 2:18.

24. **Master.** √171E12, Ge +14:22. ver. 16, 36. Mt *7:21. 8:19. 9:11. 10:24, 25. 12:38. 17:24. 19:16. 23:8. 26:18. Mk 4:38. Lk *6:46. 7:40. Jn 1:38. **Moses said.** Ex +*24:4. Mk 12:26. Lk 16:29. 20:37. Jn 1:45. 5:45, 46. 7:23. Ac 3:22. 15:21. Ro 9:15. 10:5, 19. 2 C 3:15. **If a man.** √92E, Mt +4:10. √184C, Mt +4:9. Ge +*38:8, 9, 11. Dt *25:5-10. Ru 1:11-13. 3:9. Mk 12:19. Lk 20:28.

25. **there were.** Mk 12:19-23. Lk 20:29-33. He +*9:27.

26. **seventh.** *or*, seven.

29. **do err.** Mk √12:24, 27. **not knowing.** T#1055. Mt 5:18. Jb *19:25-27. Ps +*16:9-11. *17:15. *49:14, 15. *73:25, 26. Is *25:8. +*26:19n. *57:1, 2. Da +*12:2, 3. Ho *13:14. Lk √16:29-31. +*24:44-47. Jn +√5:39. ⦿+6:14. 7:49. *20:9. Ac 13:27. Ro +*15:4. 1 C 15:34. **the scriptures.** Mt 21:42. **nor the power.** Ge *18:14. Je *32:17. Lk *1:37. Ac *26:8. 1 C 6:14. Ep 1:19. Ph *3:21.

30. **in the resurrection.** Mt 24:38. Is +*54:1. Mk *12:24, 25. Lk √20:34-36. Jn *5:28, 29. 1 C *7:29-31. 1 J *3:1, 2. **as the angels.** Mt *13:43. *18:10. Ps ⦿+*8:5n. *103:20. Zc *3:7. Lk +*20:36. He *2:7, 9. 1 J *3:2. Re *5:9-11. *19:10.

31. **the resurrection.** Ps +*49:15. Is *25:8. +*26:19n. Da +*12:2. Ho +*13:14. Lk 14:14. Jn *5:28, 29. 6:39. 11:23-26. 12:24. *14:19. Ac 17:18. √24:14, 15. Ro 8:11, 23. 1 C *6:14. 15:23-56. 2 C *4:14. Col *3:4. 1 Th *4:14, 16. 2 T +*1:10. 1 P *1:3. **have ye not read.** Mt 9:13. 12:3, 5. 19:4. 21:16, 42.

32. **I am.** Ex 3:ᴵ6, 15, 16. Ac 7:32. He 11:16. **God of Abraham.** Mt +*8:11. Lk 16:22. Ac 3:13. **God is.** Mk 12:26, 27. Lk *20:37, 38. **the dead.** Mt +*10:28. Mk 12:27. Lk *9:30. √20:37. Ac 2:36. Ro *14:9. 1 C 15:18, 29n. Ph 3:20, 21. He +*11:16. 20:13. **the living.** He 12:9, 23. Re 6:9, 10.

33. **they were astonished.** ver. 22. Mt *7:28, 29. Mk 6:2. 12:17. Lk 2:47. 4:22. 20:39, 40. Jn 7:46.

34. **when.** Mk 12:28-33. Lk 10:25-28. **Sadducees.** ver. 23. **they.** Mt 12:14. 25:3-5. Is 41:5-7. Jn 11:47-50. Ac *5:24-28. 19:23-28. 21:28-30.

35. **a lawyer.** Lk 5:17. *7:30. 10:25-28. 11:45, 46, 52. 14:3. Ac 5:34. 1 T 1:7. T 3:13. **tempting.** ver. 18. Mk 10:2. Jn 8:6.

36. **Master.** ver. +*24. **which is.** Mt *5:19, 20. 15:6. 23:23, 24. Ho 8:12. Mk *12:28-33. Lk 11:42. **in the law.** Mt 12:5. Lk *10:25, 26. Jn 1:45. 8:5, 17. 10:34. 15:25.

37. **thou shalt love.** T#409. Dt +*ᴵ6:5. 10:12. 30:6. 2 K 23:25. Ps +145:9. Mk *12:29, 30, 33. Lk 10:27. Ro 8:7. He 10:16, 17. 1 J *5:2-5. Ju +21 (T#288). **with all.** √77, Ex +3:19. Dt 4:29. *10:12. 11:13. 13:3. 26:16. 30:2, 6, 10. Jsh 22:5. 1 K 2:4. 8:48. 2 K 23:3, 25. 2 Ch 6:38. 15:12. 34:31. Je 32:41. **thy heart.** 2 K +*20:3. 1 Ch 12:38n. **soul.** Gr. *psyche*. √121A9B. Metonymy of the Cause. Here *psyche* is used for the seat of will and purpose, as at Mk 12:30, 33. Lk 10:27. Ac 4:32. Ep 6:6. Ph 1:27. Col 3:23. He 12:3. For the other uses of *psyche*, see Mt +2:20n. For other instances of √121A9, see Ge +23:8. Nu 21:4. Dt 11:13.

39. **the second.** 1 J 4:21. **Thou shalt love.** Mt 19:19. Le +*ᴵ19:18. Mk 12:31. Lk 10:27, 28. Jn *13:34, 35.

15:12, 13, 17. Ro 12:9, 10. *13:8-10. 1 C ch. *13.
14:1. Ga *5:14. Ep 1:15. *5:2. Ph 1:9. Col 1:3, 4.
1 Th *3:12, 13. 2 Th 1:3. 1 T *1:5. 6:11. 2 T 2:22. He
13:1. Ja 2:8. 1 P 2:17. *4:8. 1 J 2:9, 10. *3:10, 11,
14-19, 23. *4:7, 8, 11, 20, 21. **neighbor.** Lk *10:29-
37. Ro *15:2. Ga 6:10. **as thyself.** 2 C ❶10:12. Ga
5:22. Ep *5:29. Ph ❶*2:4.

40. **On these two.** Mt 7:12. Mk 12:31. Jn 1:17. Ro
3:19-21. √13:9. 1 T 1:5. Ja √2:8. 1 J 4:7-11, 19-21. **all.**
Mt 7:12. Ga 5:14. **law and.** Lk 16:16.

41. **the Pharisees.** ver. 15, 34. Mk 13:35-37. Lk
20:41-44. **were gathered.** ver. 34.

42. **What.** Mt 2:4-6. 14:33. 16:13-17. Jn 1:49. 6:68,
69. +√20:28. Ph *2:9-11. 3:7-10. Col 3:11. 1 P 2:4-7.
Re 5:12-14. **Christ.** Mt 1:1, 17. **son.** ♪171G, Ge +13:8.
The Son. Mt 1:1. 21:9. Is +*7:13, 14. +*9:6, 7. *11:1-
4. Je +*23:5, 6. Ezk *34:23, 24. Am *9:11. Lk 1:69,
70. Jn 7:41, 42. Ac 13:22, 23.

43. **David.** Ac 4:25. **in spirit.** Gr. *pneuma,* Mt
+3:16. 2 S 23:2. Mk 12:36. Lk 2:26, 27. Ac 1:16. 2:30,
31. He 3:7. 2 P +*1:21. Re 1:10. 4:2.

44. **The Lord.** This passage is expressly referred
to the Messiah by several of the Jews. Rabbi Joden
(in Midrash Tillim on Ps 18:35) says, "In the world
to come, the Holy Blessed God shall cause the king
Messiah to sit at his right hand, as it is written, The
Lord said to my Lord," etc. So Rabbi Moses Hadarson,
in Bereshith Rabba on Ge 18:1; and Saadias Gaon on
Da 7:13, says "This is Messiah our righteousness, as
it is written, The Lord said to my Lord," etc. Ps *❶110:1.
Ac 2:30, 34, 35. 1 C 15:25. He 1:3, 13. 10:12, 13.
12:2. **my Lord.** Jn +√20:28. 1 C 1:2. Ph *3:8. **right
hand.** Mt 20:21, 23. 1 K 2:19. Ps 45:9. Mk 10:37, 40.
Ac *7:56. Ro √8:34. He *10:12, 13. √12:2. 1 P *3:22.
till. Ge +*3:15. Ps *2:8, 9. 21:9. Is *63:1-6. Lk *19:27.
1 C +*15:25, 28. Re 19:19-21. 20:1-3, 11-15. **thy footstool.** Jsh 10:24. 1 K 5:3.

45. **If.** ♪184A, 1 C +15:2. **how.** ♪22, Ge +3:9. Jn
+*8:58. Ro *1:3, 4. √9:5. Ph *2:6-8. 1 T *3:16. He
*2:14. Re *22:16.

46. **no.** Mt 21:27. Jb 32:15, 16. Is 50:2-9. Lk 13:17.
*14:6. Jn 8:7-9. Ac 4:14. **neither.** Mk 12:34. Lk 20:40.

MATTHEW 23

*Jesus exhorts the people to regard the scriptural
instructions of the Scribes and Pharisees; but not to
follow their bad examples and especially not to imitate
their ambition, 1-12. He denounces divers woes on
them, for their blindness, hypocrisy, and iniquity, 13-
33. He predicts the destruction of Jerusalem, and the
calamities of the Jews for their atrocious crimes, 34-
39.*

1. **to the multitude.** Mt 15:10, etc. Mk 7:14. Lk
11:43. 12:1, 57. 20:45, 46.

2. **The scribes.** Ezr 7:6, 10, 11, 25. Ne √8:4-8. Ml
+*2:7. Mk 12:38. Lk *20:45, 46. **sit.** ♪96C4, Mt +3:17.
♪121S1, Ge +49:10. Metonymy of the Adjunct,
whereby the sign is put for the thing signified, "sit"
is put for public teaching (Mt 26:55. Lk 4:20. Jn 8:2.
Ac 22:3), or for judgment (Ex 18:13. Jg 5:10. Ps 29:10.
110:1. Mt 27:19). Dt 17:10, 11. Ja 9:28, 29. Ac 22:3.
Moses'. ♪121S1, Ge +49:10. "Moses" is put for the
Law and precepts and authority of Moses. **seat.** ♪121S1,
Ge +49:10. "Seat" is put for right, authority, or rule
(B604).

3. **whatsoever.** Mt 15:2-9. Ex 18:19, 20, 23. Dt 4:5.
5:27. 17:9-12. 2 Ch 30:12. Is +*8:20. Ac 5:29. Ro *2:21,
23. 13:1. 1 C 14:34n. **but do not.** Mt *5:20. Ml 2:7,
8. **for.** Mt *21:30. Ps 50:16-20. Ro 2:19-24. 1 C *9:27.
2 T 3:5. T 1:16.

4. **they bind.** ver. 23. Mt +*11:28-30. Lk 11:46.
Ac *15:5, 10, 28. Ga *6:13. Re *2:24, 25.

5. **all.** Mt *6:1-16. 2 K 10:16. Lk 16:15. 20:47. 21:1.
Jn 5:44. 7:18. 12:43. Ph 1:15. 2:3. 2 Th 2:4. **they make.**
Ex 13:9. Dt 6:8. 11:18. Pr 3:3. 6:21-23. **the borders.**
Mt 9:20. Nu *15:38, 39. Dt 22:12.

6. **love the uppermost.** Mt 20:21. Pr 25:6, 7. Mk
12:38, 39. Lk 11:43, etc. 14:7-11. 20:46, 47. Ro 12:10.
Ja 2:1-4. 3 J 9.

7. **markets.** Mt 11:16. 20:3. 6:56. 7:4. Lk 7:32. Ac
16:19. 17:17. **Rabbi.** i.e. *my master,* ✱S#4461g. Rendered (1) Master: Mt 26:25, 49. Mk 9:5. 11:21. 14:45,
45. Jn 4:31. 9:2. 11:8. (2) Rabbi: Jn 1:38, 49. 3:2, 26.
6:25. (3) rabbi: Mt 23:7, 7, 8. Compare ✱S#4462g:
Mk 10:51. Jn ❶20:16. **Rabbi.** ♪108C5. Idiom B834.
The duplication of the noun follows a Hebrew manner
of idiomatic degree of comparison of emphasizing adjectives, and making them superlative. Here, "Rabbi,
Rabbi," means most excellent Rabbi; similarly, "Lord,
Lord," means most gracious Lord; "peace, peace," signifies *perfect peace.* Compare the figure *Epizeuxis,*
♪84, Ge +6:17. For other instances of this figure see
Mt 7:21. Mk 14:45.

8. **be.** ver. 10. 2 C *1:24. 4:5. Ja *3:1. 1 P *5:3.
one. Mt 10:25. 11:29. 17:5. 22:24. 26:49. Jn *13:13,
14. Ro 14:9, 10. 1 C 1:12, 13. 3:3-5. **all.** Lk 22:32. Jn
21:23. Ep *3:14, 15. Col 1:1, 2. Phm 16. Re 1:9. 19:10.
22:9.

9. **call.** 2 K 2:12. 6:21. 13:14. Jb *32:21, 22. Ac
22:1. 1 C 1:12, 13. 3:4. 4:15. 1 T 5:1, 2. He 12:9. **for
one.** Mk 12:29. **your father.** Mt 5:16, 45, 48. 6:1, 8,
9, 14, 26, 32. 7:11. 18:14. Ml 1:6. Mk 11:25. Lk 11:13.
Ro 8:14-17. 2 C 6:18. 1 J 3:1.

10. **neither be.** Mi +*6:8. Lk 14:10. 22:26. Ro *12:3.
Ph *2:3. Ja *4:10. 1 P *5:5. **masters.** ver. 8. **for one
is.** Lk 5:5. 8:24, 45. 9:33, 49. 17:13.

11. **he that is greatest.** Mt *20:26, 27. Mk 10:43,
44. Lk 22:26, 27. Jn 13:1-9, 14, 15. Ro +*12:3. 1 C
9:19. 2 C 4:5. 11:23. Ga 5:13. Ph *2:+*3, 5-8.

12. **whosoever.** ♪138B, Ge +13:16. **shall exalt.** Pr
17:19. 25:6, 7, 27. Is 14:13, 14. Ob 4. Mk 10:37. Lk
14:11. 18:14. Ja 4:6. 1 P *5:5. **shall be abased.** 2 S
22:28. Jb 40:12. Ps 18:27. 101:5. Pr 15:25. *16:18.
*29:23. Is 2:12. Je *50:32. Ezk 21:26. 31:14. Da 4:37.
Ml 4:1. Lk 1:51, 52. 10:15. **shall humble.** Mt +*5:3.
*18:4. Jb 22:29. Ps 138:6. Pr *15:33. *16:19. 18:12.
Is +*57:15. Ro +*12:3. 2 C +*1:24. Ph +*2:3. 1 P
*5:3. **shall be exalted.** Mt +*19:28. Jb 5:11. Ps
+*91:14. Is 33:16. *58:14. Da +*12:3. Hab 3:19. Mk
+*10:30. Lk +*14:14. *19:17. 1 C *6:2. 1 T +*4:8.
2 T +*4:8. Ja +*2:5. *4:10. 1 P 5:6. Re +*3:21. +*5:10.
*11:12, 18.

13. **woe.** ver. 14, 15, 27, 29. Mt +6:2n. Is 5:8-22.
9:14, 15. 10:1. 33:14. Hab 2:6-17. Zc 11:17. Lk 11:43,
44, +*52. **hypocrites.** ver. 23, 25, 27, 29. Mt 6:2.
Lk 12:1. **for ye shut.** Mt 16:19. 21:31, 32. Lk +*11:52.
Jn 7:46-52. √9:22, 24, 34. Ac *4:5, 17, 18. 5:28, 40.
8:1. 13:8. 1 Th *2:15, 16. 2 T 3:8. 4:15. Re 3:7. **kingdom
of heaven.** Mt 4:17. **neither go in.** Mt *5:20. 21:31.
Lk *7:30. **neither suffer.** Mi +3:5.

14. **for ye devour.** Josephus says (Ant. l. xvii. c.

3) that this sect pretended to a more exact knowledge of the law, on which account women were subject to them, as pretending to be dear to God. Ex +*22:22-24. Jb 22:9. 24:21. 31:16-20. Zc *7:10. Ml +*3:5. Mk 12:40. Lk 11:39. 16:14. 20:47. 2 T 3:6. T 1:10, 11. Ja *1:27. 2 P 2:14, 15. **for a pretence.** Mt *6:5. Ezk *33:30-33. **long prayer.** That these were long we learn from *Bab. Berachoth*, fol. 32, where we are told that the very religious prayed *nine hours a day.* Mt *6:7. Ec +*5:2. Mk 12:40. **therefore.** ver. 33. Mt +*11:22, 24n. Lk +*12:48. Ja 3:1. 2 P 2:3.

15. **for.** Ga *4:17. *6:12. **to make.** Mt *6:23. Lk 11:52. **proselyte.** Est *8:17. Ac 2:10. 6:5. *13:43. **ye make.** Mt 6:23. Ezk *13:19, 22. Mi *3:5. Jn *8:44. Ac *13:10. 14:2, 19. 17:5, 6, 13. Ep 2:3. **the child.** Mt 13:38. Dt +15:9. Jg +*19:22. Lk ◐10:6. Jn 17:12. 2 Th 2:3. **hell.** Gr. *gehenna*, Mt +5:22.

16. **ye blind.** ver. 17, 19, 24, 26. Mt +*15:14. Is 56:10, 11. Ml *2:8. Lk 4:18. 6:39. Jn 9:39-41. Ro 2:19. 2 P 1:9. Re 3:17. **Whosoever shall swear.** Mt 5:33, 34. Ja 5:12. **by the temple.** ver. 21, 35. Mt 26:61. 27:5, 40, 51. Mk 14:58. 15:29, 38. Lk 1:9, 21, 22. 23:45. Jn 2:19-21. 2 Th 2:4. Re 3:12. **it is.** Mt 15:5, 6. Mk 7:10-13. **he is.** Ga 5:3.

17. **Ye fools.** Mt 5:22. 25:2. Ps 94:8. **and blind.** ver. 16. **or.** ver. 19. Ex 30:26-29. Nu 16:38, 39.

18. **swear by the altar.** Mt *5:34, 35. Ex √29:37. **guilty.** *or*, debtor. ver. 15. **the gift.** Mt 5:23, 24. 8:4. 15:5. Lk 21:1, 4. He 5:1. 8:4. *or*, bound.

19. **or.** Ex 29:37. 30:29.

21. **the temple.** ver. 16. **and by him.** Ex 15:17. 1 K 8:13, 27. 2 Ch 6:2. 7:2. Ps 26:8. 132:13, 14. Ep 2:22. Col 2:9.

22. **by heaven.** Mt 21:25. **by the throne.** Mt 5:34. Ps *11:4. Is *66:1. Ac *7:49. **by him.** Re 4:2, 3.

23. **hypocrites.** ver. 13. **for.** Lk *‖11:42. **pay tithe.** Ge +*14:20n. 1 C +*9:13, 14. ◐+*16:2. Gr. *apodekatoo,* ✱S#586g: Mt 23:23. Lk 11:42. 18:12. He 7:5. **anise.** Gr. *anathon*, dill. *Dill* is a species of plant of the pentandria digynia class, growing native in Spain and Portugal. The root is fusiform and long; stems, erect-groved, jointed, branched, and about two feet in height; leaves, doubly pinnated, sweet and odorous; flowers, flat, terminal umbels; corolla, five ovate, concave, yellow petals, with apexes inflected; germen, like that of fennel; seeds, scarcely the length of a carraway seed, but broader and flatter, of a brown color, aromatic, sweetish odor, and warmish, pungent taste. *Cummin* is a plant of the same class as dill: it rises eight or ten inches on a slender, round, procumbent, branching stem; leaves, a dark green, narrow, linear, and pointed; flowers, purple, in numerous four-rayed umbels; corolla, five unequal petals, inflected, and notched at the apex; seeds, oblong, striated, of a brown color, strong, heavy odor, and warm, bitterish taste. Is 28:25, 27. **the weightier.** Mt *9:13. *12:7. *22:37-40. 1 S *15:22. Pr *21:3. Je *22:15, 16. Ho +*6:6. Mi +√6:8. Mk *12:31. Ga *5:22, 23. **judgment.** Ps 33:5. Je 5:1. Mi +*6:8. Hab +*1:4. Zc *7:9. **mercy.** Mt 9:13. 12:7. *25:43. Ps 109:16. Pr *21:13. Ezk *34:4. Ho +*6:6. Zc 7:9. 11:16. Lk 16:20, 21. Ja +*4:17. 1 J *3:17. **and faith.** *or*, stedfastness. 1 Ch +*28:9. 2 Ch +*20:20. Lk +*8:13. 18:8g. Ac 3:16g. 15:9g. Ro 3:25g. 4:9g, 14g, 19g, 20g. 5:2g. 10:8g, √17g. 11:20g. 12:6g. 1 C +*15:2, 58. Ga 6:9. Ep 2:8g. Col +*1:23. +*2:7. 1 T 1:19b,g. He +*3:12-14. *6:10, 11. √11:6,

39g. 12:15. 2 P √1:5-10. √3:17. **these ought.** Mt *5:19, 20. Le *27:30. Nu 18:21. Dt 14:22-29. Notice that Jesus does not condemn tithing, he approves it. What he condemned was the neglect of the weightier matters of the law. Those who believe the practice of tithing is obligatory for New Testament Christians argue that (1) unless the reasons for a law no longer obtain, the law continues in force, where there is no explicit repeal of the law; (2) what passed away of the Old Testament economy was the symbolical and figurative, of which the tithe is neither, but a duty issuing from the moral law, which is of perpetual force; (3) since the law did not become obsolete, there is no reason to expect in the New Testament a formal re-enactment of the law. "Similarly there is no formal re-enactment of the Sabbath law; but Christians recognize the law respecting the seventh of time, and by a parity of reasoning should recognize the law respecting the tenth of substance" (Richard Duke, cited by Henry Lansdell in *The Tithe in Scripture*, footnote, p. 140). Like the sabbath, the tithe is a pre-Mosaic institution, part of the original system of worship established by God, and practiced by the Patriarchs. This being the case, neither tithing nor sabbath observance need be considered abrogated by virtue of Christ fulfilling the law of Moses (Jn 1:17. Ro 6:14. 10:4. Ep 2:15. Col 2:14). Lk ◐11:41n, 42n.

24. **blind guides.** ver. 16. Mt +*15:14. **Which strain.** ʃ138B, Ge +13:16. Mt +6:2n. *7:4. 15:2-6. 19:24. √27:6-8. Lk *6:7-10. Jn √18:28, 40. **camel.** Mt 19:24. Le 11:4. Mk 10:25. Lk 18:25.

25. **for.** Mt *15:19, 20. Mk 7:4, etc. Lk 11:39, 40. T 1:15. **the cup.** Mk 7:4. **full.** Is 28:7, 8. **extortion.** Lk 16:14. 20:47. **and excess.** 1 C 7:5.

26. **cleanse.** Mt 12:33. Is √55:7. Je 4:14. 13:27. Ezk 18:31. Lk 6:45. 2 C 7:1. He *10:22. Ja 4:8. **first.** Mt *6:33. 7:5.

27. **like.** Is 58:1, 2. Lk *11:44. Ac 23:3. **sepulchres.** Nu 19:16. **are within.** Ps ◐45:13. *51:10. **bones.** 2 K +23:14. **all uncleanness.** 2 K 23:16. Ezk 39:14, 15. Ep 5:3.

28. **ye also.** ver. 5. 1 S +*16:7. Ps 51:6. Je +*17:9, 10. Lk 16:15. He +*4:12, 13. **outwardly appear.** Ps ◐45:13. **but.** Mt 12:34, 35. 15:19, 20. Mk √7:21-23.

29. **ye build.** ʃ63J1, Ge +13:9. Lk 11:47, 48. Ac 2:29. **garnish.** ʃ63J1, Ge +13:9.

30. **If we had.** ʃ184B. Hypothetical Propositions: Second Condition, contrary to fact or impossible, unclassified. Here, "If we were, which is not the case." For other instances of this construction see Mt 5:13. 6:1. 15:5. 21:21. 24:43. *25:27. 26:24. Mk 9:42. 12:49. 13:22. 14:21. Lk 17:6. 19:23, 42. Jn 4:10. 8:19, 39. 14:2. 15:24. 18:36. 19:11. Ac 18:14. 24:19. 26:32. Ro 7:7. 1 C √12:19. Ga 2:17. 4:15. He 4:8. 7:11. 8:4, 7. 9:26. 10:2. Compare ʃ184B, Lk +*7:39. ʃ184B, Mt +11:21. **the blood.** ver. 34, 35. Mt 21:35, 36. 2 Ch 36:15, 16. Je 2:30.

31. **witnesses.** Jsh 24:22. Jb 15:5, 6. Ps 64:8. Lk 19:22. **children.** T#169. Pr 27:19. Ec 1:15. +7:20 (T#163). Da +*12:10. Re +*22:11. **which killed.** Lk *11:48. Ac *7:51, 52. 1 Th *2:15, 16.

32. **Fill.** ʃ83, 1 K 22:15. Christ was not inciting to murders and martyrdoms; but, using the figure *Epitrope*, He granted their position, and ironically told them to act accordingly (B972). **the measure.** Ge 15:16. Nu 32:14. Da 8:23. Zc 5:6-11. 1 Th 2:15, 16. **your fathers.** Jg 2:19. Je 16:12. 2 T 3:13.

33. **serpents**. T#652. Mt 3:7. 12:34. 21:34, 35. Ge +*3:15. Ps 58:3-5. Is 57:3, 4. Lk 3:7. Jn +*8:44. ◐10:14. Ac 20:29. 2 C 11:3. Re 12:9. **vipers**. Ps 58:4. 140:3. **how**. ver. 14. He *2:3. 10:29. 12:25. **the damnation**. Mt +*10:15n. Lk 10:14. **hell**. Gr. *gehenna*, Mt +5:22.

34. **I send**. Mt 10:16. *28:19, 20. Lk 11:49. *24:47. Jn *20:21. Ac +*1:8. 1 C 12:3-11. Ep *4:8-12. **prophets**. Ac 11:27. *13:1. *15:32. 1 C 12:28. Re 11:10. **and wise**. Pr *11:30. 1 C 2:6. *3:10. Col *1:28. **scribes**. Mt +*13:52. **ye shall kill**. Mt 10:16, 17. 21:35. 24:9. Mk 13:12. Lk 21:16. Jn 16:2. Ac *7:51, 52, 58, 59. 9:1, 2. 12:2. 14:19. 22:19, 20. 1 Th 2:16. He 11:37. **scourge**. Mt 10:17. Mk 13:9. Lk 12:11. 21:12. Ac *5:40. 22:19. 26:11. 2 C *11:23-25. **persecute**. Mt 10:23. Ac 8:1. 14:5, 6. 17:13, 14.

35. **upon**. Mt *27:25. Ge +*9:5, 6. Nu 35:33. Dt 21:7, 8. 2 K 21:16. 24:4. Is 26:21. Je 2:30, 34. 26:15, 23. La 4:13, 14. Re *18:24. **righteous blood**. Mt 27:4. Ps 94:21. Jl 3:19. Jon 1:14. **the blood**. ✓171l11, Dt +19:12. Lk 11:51. He 12:24. 1 J 3:12. Ju 11. **righteous Abel**. ✸S#6g: Mt 23:35. Lk 11:51. He 11:4. 12:24. For ✸S#1893h, see Ge +4:2. Ge 4:8. He *11:4. 12:24. 1 J *3:11, 12. **unto**. 2 Ch *24:20-22. Zc 1:1. Lk 11:51. **Zacharias**. ✓106, Ge +31:7. **Barachias**. i.e. *blessing of the Lord*, ✸S#914g, only here. For ✸S#1296h, see Zc +1:7. **the temple**. ver. 16. 1 K 6:2. **the altar**. Ex 40:6, 29. 2 K 16:14. Ezk 40:47.

36. **All these**. Mt 16:28. *24:34. Ezk *12:21-28. Mk 9:1. *13:30, 31. Lk 9:27. *21:32, 33. **this generation**. Mt +*24:34. Je +7:29.

37. **O Jerusalem**. ✓121J19, 1 S +22:19. Je 4:14. 6:8. Lk 13:34. 19:41-44. Re 11:8. **Jerusalem**. ✓84, Ge +6:17. Ge +22:11. **thou**. ver. 30. Mt 5:12. *21:35, 36. *22:6. 2 Ch 24:21, 22. Ne +*9:26. Je *2:30. 26:23. Mk 12:3-6. Lk 13:33. 20:11-14. Ac 7:51, 52. 1 Th 2:15. Re 11:7. 17:6. **how often**. ✓85M, La +1:1. Mt 26:55. 2 Ch *36:15, 16. Ps *81:8-14. Je *6:16, 17. 11:7, 8. *25:3-7. 35:15. *42:9-13. 44:4. Zc 1:4. Lk 4:44. **would I**. ✓124, Dt +5:29. **gathered**. Mt 24:31. Ps 106:47. 107:3. 147:2. Pr 1:24. Mk 13:27. **thy children**. Lk 23:28. **even**. Dt *32:11, 12. Ru 2:12. Ps *17:8. 36:7. 57:1. 61:4. 63:7. *91:4. Is 31:5. Ml 4:2. **wings**. ✓22G2, Ps +91:4. **and ye**. Mt 22:3. Pr *1:24-31. Is *30:15. 50:2. Je *6:17. Ho 11:2, 7. Lk 14:17-20. 15:28. 19:14-44. Jn 1:5, 10, 11. ✓5:40.

38. **your house**. Mt 24:2. 1 K *9:7, 8. 2 Ch 7:20, 21. Ps 69:24, 25. Pr +*17:13. Is 64:10-12. Je *7:9-15. ✓12:7. ✓22:5. Ezk ✓10:18, 19. ✓11:23. Da +*9:26. Zc 11:1, 2, 6. 14:1, 2. Mk 13:14. Lk 13:35. *19:43, 44. *21:6, 20, 24. Ac 6:13, 14. **desolate**. Le 26:31. Ps ╮69:25. Mi 3:12. ◐4:1.

39. **Ye shall not**. Ho *3:4. Lk 2:26-30. *10:22, 23. ‖13:35. *17:22. Jn *8:21, 24, 56. 14:9, *19. **till**. Mt 10:23. +*16:28n. 24:34. 1 S +12:22. Is +*52:8. +60:10. 62:4. +*65:24. Je +*4:27. Ho *3:4, 5. +*5:15. 6:1. Mi +*2:13. Zc ✓9:14. ✓10:6. Ml +*3:6. Jn +*21:22, 23. Ac +✓3:19-21. Ro +*11:25, 26. 2 C *3:15, 16. **ye shall say**. Ps ╮118:26. Is *30:19. Ho 8:2. 14:2. Jl 2:17. Zc *13:9. **Blessed**. Mt *21:9. Ps *╮118:26. Is 40:9-11. Zc 12:10. Mk 11:9, 10. Lk 19:38. Ro +*11:25, 26. 2 C 3:14-18.

MATTHEW 24

Christ foretells the destruction of the temple, 1, 2; and the preceding signs and attendant calamities, inter- mixing *counsels and warnings, 3-28; also the subsequent revolutions and miseries, in figurative language, which may be understood of the end of the world, 29-31. By the parable of a fig-tree, he shows the certainty of the prediction, 32-35. No man knows the day or hour, which shall come suddenly, 36-41. All ought to watch, as vigilant servants who expect their master, 42-51.*

1. **went out**. Mt 21:17. Lk ✓21:1, 27, 28, 37. **departed**. Mt 21:23. 23:39. Je 6:8. Ezk 8:6. 10:17-19. 11:22, 23. Ho 9:12. Ac *13:46. He 10:26, 27. **show**. Mk *13:1, 2. Lk *21:5, 6. Jn 2:20.

2. **said**. Mt 24:34. **There**. Josephus (Bell. l. vii. c. 1) says that "Caesar gave orders that they should now demolish the whole city and temple, except the three towers Phaselus, Hippicus, and Mariamne, and a part of the western wall; but all the rest was laid so completely even with the ground, by those who dug it up from the foundation, that there was nothing left to make those who came thither believe it had ever been inhabited." 2 S 17:13. 1 K *9:7, 8. Ps 79:1. Is 64:11. Je *7:4. *26:18. Ezk 7:20-22. Da +*9:26, 27. Mi 1:6. 3:12. Lk ✓19:44. 2 P 3:11.

3. **he sat**. Mt 21:1. Mk *13:3, 4. **the disciples**. Mt 13:10, 11, 36. 15:12. 17:19. **privately**. Mk 4:34. **Tell**. Da +*12:6-8. Lk *21:7. Jn *21:21, 22. Ac +*1:6, 7. 1 Th 5:1, etc. **when shall**. Lk 17:20-27. *21:12-24. **and what shall**. ver. ✓4-26, ✓37-39. **the sign**. ver. 30, 32, 33, 43. **coming**. Gr. *parousia*, ✸S#3952g. Rendered (1) coming: Mt 24:3, 27, 37, 39. 1 C 15:23. 16:17. 2 C 7:6, 7. Ph 1:26. 1 Th 2:19. 3:13. 4:15. 5:23. 2 Th 2:1, 8, 9. Ja 5:7, 8. 2 P 1:16. 3:4, 12. 1 J 2:28. (2) presence: 2 C 10:10. Ph 2:12. Thayer defines this word in reference to this passage: "In the N.T. esp. of *the advent*, i.e. the future, visible, *return* from heaven of Jesus, the Messiah, to raise the dead, hold the last judgment, and set up formally and gloriously the kingdom of God" (*Lexicon*, p. 490b, definition 2). This is certainly not a reference to some imagined "invisible presence" commencing in 1914. No invisibility is implied or required elsewhere when this word is used: 1 C 16:17. 2 C 7:6. ✓10:10. Ph 1:26. 2:12. The coming of Christ is clearly taught to be literal, visible, and bodily. Mt +*16:27n, 28. +*24:30. Da +*7:13n. Zc ✓9:14. +*12:10. Mk 1:2n. Jn +*1:51n. Ac ✓1:11. 2 T +*4:1n. T *2:13. Re ✓1:7. **and of**. ver. ✓27-31, ✓40-51. Mt ✓25:1-46. **the end**. Gr. *sunteleia*, ✸S#4930g. The joining of two ages, the consumation or completion of the various parts of a scheme. Vine states "The word does not denote a termination, but the heading up of events to the appointed climax" (*Dictionary*, vol. 2, p. 27). Mt +*13:39, 40, 49. 28:20. He 9:26. **world**. Gr. *aion*, Mt +6:13. Jn +*6:54n.

4. **Take heed**. Je *29:8. Mk 13:5, 6, 9, 22, 23, 33. Lk 21:8. 2 C ✓11:13-15. Ep +*4:14. 5:6. Col 2:8, 18. 2 Th ✓2:3. 2 P 2:1-3. 1 J 3:7. *4:1.

5. **many shall come**. ver. 11, 24. Je ✓14:14. 23:21, 25. 27:15. Jn ✓5:43. Ac ✓5:36, 37. 8:9, 10. 1 J 2:18. Re ✓13:8. **in my name**. Mt 18:5. Lk 9:48. **Christ**. ver. 23. Mt 1:17. **deceive many**. ver. 11, 24.

6. **ye shall hear**. Je 4:19-22. 6:22-24. 8:15, 16. 47:6, 7. Ezk *7:24-26. 14:17-21. 21:9-15, 28. Da ch. *11. Mk 13:7, 8. Lk 21:9. Re 6:2-4. **rumors**. lit. hearing. ✓121R1, Le +13:55. **see**. Ps ✓27:1-3. ✓46:1-3. *112:7. Is 8:12-14. *12:2. 26:*3, *4, 20, 21. Hab +*3:16-18. Lk 21:19. Jn *14:1, 27. 2 Th *2:2. 1 P 3:14, 15. **must**.

Mt *26:54. Lk 13:33. 22:37. Ac *27:24-26. Re 1:1. **but**. ver. 14. Da +*9:24-27. 1 P 4:7.

7. **nation shall**. 2 Ch *15:6. Is 5:25. 9:19-21. 19:2. Ezk 21:27. Hg 2:21, 22. Zc *14:2, 3, 13. He 12:27. Re 6:4. **kingdom against**. Is 19:2. Je 51:46. Hg 2:22. Zc 14:13. **famines**. Is *24:19-23. Ezk 14:21. Jl +*2:30, 31. Zc +*14:4. Lk 21:11, 25, 26. Ac 2:19, 20. *11:28. Re 6:5, 6, 8. **earthquakes**. Is 2:19, 21. 5:25. 13:13. 24:20. 29:6. Jl 3:16. Hg *2:6, 7, 21. Lk 21:11. Ro 8:20-23. He +*12:26. Re 6:12.

8. **beginning**. Le *26:18-29. Dt +*28:59. Is 9:12, 17, 21. 10:4. 1 Th *5:3. 1 P 4:17, 18. **sorrows**. lit. "birth pangs." ver. 15-21. Ps 48:6. Is 13:8. 21:3. 26:17. 42:14. *66:7, 8. Je 4:31. 6:24. 13:21. 22:23. *30:4-7. 49:24. 50:43. Da 7:21. *8:9-14, 23-26. *9:27. 11:40-45. *12:1, 7. Ho 13:13. Mi 4:9, 10. *5:3. Zc 12:10—14:21. Mk *‖13:8. Jn 16:21. Ac 2:24g. Ro 8:22. 11:25-27. Ga 4:19, 27g. 1 Th 5:3g. Re 12:2g.

9. **shall they**. Mt 5:11. 10:17, 21, 22. *22:6. 23:34. Mk 13:9-13. Lk 11:49. 21:12, 16, 17. Jn *15:19, 20. 16:2. Ac 4:2, 3. *5:40, 41. *7:59. 12:1, 2, etc. 21:31, 32. 22:19-22. 28:22. 1 Th 2:14-16. 1 P *4:16. Re *2:10, 13. +*6:9-11. *7:14. **to be afflicted**. ver. 21, 29. Re 2:10. **shall kill**. Mt +*23:34. Jn 16:2. **be hated**. Mt 10:22. Ps 44:22. Lk 6:22. Jn *15:18-21. 17:14. Re 11:9, 10. **all**. *ℐ171A, Ex +9:6. **for my**. Jn 15:21.

10. **And then**. 2 T 3:1. **shall many**. Mt *11:6. *13:21, 57. 15:12. *26:31-34. Mk 4:17. Jn 6:60, 61, 66, 67. 2 T 1:15. 4:10, 16. **betray**. Mt +*10:21, 35, 36. 26:21-24. Mi *7:5, 6. Mk 13:12. Lk 12:53. *21:16.

11. **false prophets**. ver. 5, 24. Mt *7:15. Mk 13:22. Ac √20:29, 30. 1 T 4:1, 2. 2 P *2:1. 1 J 2:18, 26. *4:1. 2 J *7. Ju 4. Re 13:11. 19:20. **deceive many**. ver. 5, 24. 2 Th √2:10, 11.

12. **because**. Lk 18:7. Ja 4:1-4. 5:1-6. **iniquity**. 2 Th 2:6-8. **the love**. 2 Th √2:10. 2 T 3:1-5. Re *2:4, 5, 10. *3:15, 16. **shall wax cold**. 2 Th 2:3, 4.

13. **shall endure**. ver. 6. Mt *10:22. Pr 16:17. Da 12:12, 13. Mk *4:16, 17. *13:13. Lk +*8:13, 15. Jn +*8:31. +*15:6. Ro *2:7. √11:22. 1 C *1:8. 9:27. √10:12. √15:58. Ga √6:9. Ep √4:30. He *3:6, 14. √6:4-6. *10:36, 39. Ja 1:12. 1 P 1:23. 1 J *2:27. Ju *24. Re *2:10, 26. 3:5. **unto the**. Ro 5:10. 6:14. √8:30. 1 C 1:8. 2 C 1:13. Ga +*6:9. Col +*1:21-23. 1 Th *5:23, 24. 2 Th 3:3. 2 T 4:6, 8. He √3:6, 14. *6:11. 1 P *1:5. 1 J √2:19. Ju 1. Re *2:26. **end**. Gr. *telos*, ✱S#5056g, Mt +10:22. The actual *end* of anything. Here, of life or the age. Compare "end" (Gr. *sunteleia*, ver. +*3). **shall be saved**. This verse has absolutely no bearing on the absolute eternal security of the salvation possessed now by every individual believer in Christ (Jn √10:28, 29. Ro √8:30-39. Ep 1:13. √4:30. 2 T √1:12. *2:19. 1 J √5:13. Ju *24), for it is in the context of prophecy respecting the final deliverance of Jews at the end of the great tribulation (Zc +*13:9), who are delivered upon their final repentance (Is 11:11n) and turning to God out of desperate straits when seemingly all hope is gone, by the "deliverer out of Zion" (Ro +*11:26). Jb *17:9. Ps √37:24, 28. *138:8. Pr +*4:18. Je 32:40. Lk 12:32. 22:32. Jn √5:24. *6:39, 51. 11:26. 14:19. *17:12, 24. Ro *8:38, 39. Ph *1:6. 2 T √1:12. √4:18. He √7:25. 9:28n. *10:14. 1 J *2:17.

14. **this gospel**. Mt *4:23. 9:35. 10:7. Ac *20:25. 1 C +*1:17. **of**. ℐ181E, Ge +3:24. **the kingdom**. Mt 13:19. 21:43. +*25:34. Ps 102:22. Zc √14:9. Ac +*1:6n. 28:31. 1 C +*15:50n. Ep +*1:11n. Col +*1:13n. 2 T

+*4:1n, 18n. 1 P 1:4n. Re +*5:10n. √11:15. **shall be**. T#89. Mt *28:19. Ps +*68:11. Is +*27:6. ◐+*66:19. Mk 14:9. *16:15, 16. Lk 24:47. Ac +*1:8. Ro 10:18. *15:18-21. *16:25, 26. Col *1:6, 23. 1 T +*2:6. Re 11:3. √14:6, 7. **in all**. Mk 16:15. Lk 2:1. 4:5. Ac 11:28. Ro 1:8. 10:18. 1 P 1:1, 2. Re *3:10. 12:9. 16:14. **the world**. Gr. *oikoumene*, ✱S#3625g. Lk 2:1. 4:5. 21:26 (earth). Ac 11:28. 17:6, 31. 19:27. 24:5. Ro 10:18. He 1:6. 2:5. Re 3:10. 12:9. 16:14. Not the same as ver. 3 (world, lit. age, Mt +13:39, *aion*) or ver. 21 (world, *kosmos*, Mt +4:8). **for a witness**. Mt 8:4. Ac +*1:8. **unto all nations**. Mt 25:32. **and then**. ver. *3, *6. Mt 10:23. Ezk 7:5-7, 10.

15. **When ye**. Da +*9:27n. 11:40-45. 12:1, 7. Mk *13:14. Lk *19:43. *21:20. 2 Th 2:4. Re 11:1, 2. **abomination of desolation**. Da 8:13. +*⊁9:25-27. 11:45. *⊁12:11. Re 13:14-17. **by**. Da +*9:27. 11:31. *12:11. Lk +*24:27. **by Daniel**. Da +*9:27. 2 Th *2:3, 4. **the holy place**. Da +*9:27. Mk 13:14. Jn 11:48. Ac 6:13, 14. 21:28. 2 Th 2:4. Ezk 40:4. Da +*9:22, 23, 25. *10:12-14. He *2:1. Re *1:3. 3:22.

16. **Then**. Da 9:27. 11:41. **let them**. Ge *19:15-17. Ex *9:20, 21. Pr +*22:3. Je 6:1. 37:11, 12. Lk *21:21, 22. He 11:7. **in Judea**. Notice the frequently specific Jewish references in this discourse. See ver. 13 (endurance to the end is necessary for the faithful remnant of Jews in the tribulation: Da 12:12, 13. Zc √13:9; "shall be saved" is a reference to the deliverance prophesied for the Jews in the tribulation period: Jl +*2:31, 32. Ro +*11:26). ver. 14 (worldwide preaching of the gospel of the kingdom for a witness to all nations will be accomplished by Jewish evangelists during the tribulation period, Is +*27:6); ver. 15 (holy place, or temple); ver. 20 (flight on the sabbath day); ver. 21 (great tribulation, specifically pertaining to the Jews, as a time of "Jacob's trouble," Je +*30:7. Da +*12:1); ver. 28 (the carcass, possible reference to the great number of dead bodies in the holy land after the battle described in Ezk ch. 38, 39. Note especially Ezk 39:4); ver. 31 (angels gathering his elect from every land: not the rapture of the Church, for Christ comes alone at the rapture, 1 Th 4:16; this corresponds to the supernatural return of the Jews to their land at the final restoration of Israel, predicted in such texts as Is 27:12. 43:6. Je 31:8. Ezk 34:12. 38:8n. Am 9:9). Failure to notice that these references are Jewish has led many interpreters to apply to the Church what belongs to Israel, and has led to a woeful misunderstanding of Bible prophecy. It is on this point that the correctness of a prophetic system of interpretation stands or falls when measured against the total teaching of scripture (Ezk 38:16n). **flee**. Pr +*22:3. Is +*16:3, 4. Re √12:6, 14. **mountains**. Ps 60:8-12. Is *16:1-5. +*26:20, 21. 63:1-6. Ezk 20:35-38. Ho 2:14, 20-23. Zc 14:5.

17. **which**. Mt *6:25. Jb 2:4. Pr 6:4, 5. Mk *13:15, 16. Lk *17:31-33. **the housetop**. Mt *10:27. Dt *22:8. Is 22:1. Lk 5:19. **not come**. Lk 9:59-62.

18. **let him**. Lk 17:23. **his clothes**. Mt 5:40.

19. **woe unto them**. Dt +*28:53-56. 2 S 4:4. 2 K 15:16. La *4:3, 4, 10. Ho *13:16. Mk *13:17, 18. Lk *21:23. *23:28-30. 1 C 7:26.

20. **But pray**. ℐ164, 1 S +17:7. ℐ121S4, 2 K +4:29. **neither**. T#641. Ex *16:23-30. +*20:8-12. 23:12. 31:13-17. 34:21. 35:3. Le 23:3. 26:2. Dt 5:12-15. Is +*58:13n, 14. Je 17:21, 22, √27n. Lk *23:56. Ac *1:12. Col ◐√2:16.

21. **great tribulation.** Dt +*4:30. Ps 69:22-28. Is *65:12-16. *66:15, 16. Je +*30:7. Da +*9:26. +*⟩12:1. Jl 1:2. *2:2. Zc 11:8, 9. *14:2, 3. Ml *4:1. Mk *13:19. Lk 19:43, 44. +*21:23, 24. 1 Th *2:16. 2 Th 1:4-7. He *10:26-29. Re ❶+*3:10. +*6:17. +*7:14. **was not.** Ex 10:14. Jl √2:2. Re 16:18. **world.** Gr. *kosmos,* Mt +4:8.

22. **except.** Mk *13:20. **those days.** Lk 21:22. **shortened.** 1 C 7:29. **no flesh.** Lk 3:6. **but for.** Is 6:13. 44:1. *45:4. +*65:8, 9, 22. Zc 13:8, 9. √14:2, 3. Lk 18:7. Ac +*13:48. Ro *9:11. *11:25-31. 2 T 2:10. **elect's sake.** The use of the term "elect" here has prompted some interpreters to apply this prophecy to the Church of the New Testament. But the term is used both of (1) Israel: Is √45:4. 65:8, 9, +*22. Mk 13:22, 27. Ro 11:28. 1 P 1:2, and (2) the Church, Christians, or believers of this age: Jn *15:16. Ro 8:33. Ep 1:4. 2:10. Col 3:12. 2 Th 2:13. T 1:1. 2 J +*1. The term "elect" is also used of (3) angels, 1 T 5:21, and (4) Christ, Is 42:1. 1 P 2:6. In the context of this Olivet prophecy, it is probably best to take "elect" as a reference to Israel, particularly the believing remnant which is saved by the Deliverer at the second advent of Christ (Ro 11:26), in harmony with the rest of the Jewish imagery in this chapter (see ver. 16n). Lk +*18:7. Ac +*13:48 (T#254). Ep +*1:4 (T#255). 2 T +*2:10. **be shortened.** Re 12:12.

23. **Then if.** ⨍184C, Mt +4:9. ver. 5, 22. Dt *13:1-3. Mk *13:21. Lk *17:23, 24. *21:8. Jn *5:43. **Christ.** ver. 5. Mt 1:17. 2 C √11:13-15.

24. **there.** ver. *5, *11. 2 P *2:1-3. *3:17. **false Christs.** 1 J 2:18. **false prophets.** ver. 11. Ho 2:17. Zc *13:2. 2 Th √2:9-11. **and shall.** Dt 13:1-3. Ac 8:9. 2 Th √2:9-11. Re *13:13, 14. 16:14. *19:20. **great.** Da 8:24. 2 Th 2:9, 10. **signs and wonders.** Dt 13:1-3. Jn 4:48. 2 Th *2:9-12. **insomuch.** Jn *6:37, 39. √10:28-30. Ro √8:28-39. 2 T *2:19. 1 P 1:5. 1 J 5:18. Re *12:9-11. *13:7, 8, 14. **if.** ⨍184B, Mt +23:30. This is the second class condition, indicating contrary to fact or impossible. Webster and Wilkinson note, "This denotes a moral impossibility; by which is meant that high degree of improbability which leaves no room for doubt; as when it is alleged, He 6:18, 'in which it was impossible for God to lie." Free will is not incompatible with the moral necessity for offences coming, nor with the moral impossibility of the elect being deceived" (*Greek Testament,* vol. 1, p. 119). Mk *13:22. Ac 20:16. Ro 12:18. Ga 4:15. **were possible.** Mt 18:14. Jn √10:28, 29. Ro √8:28-30. 2 T *2:19. **deceive.** ver. 5, 11. 1 C 6:9. Ep 5:6. 2 Th 2:3. 2 T 3:13. 2 P *3:17. 1 J 4:1. **the very elect.** ver. 22.

25. **I have told you before.** Is *44:7, 8. 46:10, 11. 48:5, 6. Lk 21:13. Jn 13:19. 14:29. 16:1, 4. 2 P *3:17.

26. **Wherefore.** Our Lord not only foretells the appearance of these impostors, but also the *manner* and *circumstance* of their conduct. Accordingly Josephus (Ant. l. xx. c. 7. Bell. l. ii. c. 13) says that many impostors persuaded the people to follow them to the *desert,* promising them *signs* and *wonders* done by the providence of God (See also Ac *21:38). One persuaded the people to go up into the *temple,* which being set on fire by the Romans, 6000 perished in the flames. **if.** ⨍184C, Mt +4:9. **they shall say.** ver. 5, 23. Lk ❶12:20. **he is in the desert.** Mt 3:1. Dt ❶+*33:2. Is √40:3. Lk 3:2, 3. Ac *21:38. Re ❶+*12:6, 14. **go not.** Mt ❶11:7-9. **secret chambers.** ver. 3n. Is +*26:20.

Mt 6:6. Lk 12:3, 24. **believe it not.** ver. 23. Ep +*4:14. 1 J *4:1. 1 P *3:15. 2 P *1:16.

27. **as the lightning.** Jb 37:3. 38:35. Is *30:30. Ezk 1:14. Zc *9:14. Lk *17:24, etc. 1 Th ❶5:1-3. **the coming.** Gr. *parousia,* ver. +*3n. 37, 39. Mt +*16:27n, 28. Ml *3:2. *4:5. 1 Th ❶4:14-18. 2 Th *2:8. Ja *5:8. 2 P *3:4. **Son of man.** Mt 8:20.

28. **For.** ⨍74, Jg +5:31. **wheresoever.** ⨍184C, Mt +4:9. Dt +*28:49. Jb 39:27-30. Je 16:16. Ho 8:1. Am 9:1-4. Hab 1:8. Lk *17:37. **the carcass.** 1 S √17:46. Is +*66:24. Ezk √39:4, 11-16. Mk 6:29. Lk +√‖17:37n. **the eagles.** Dt +*28:49. 1 S √17:44, 46. Hab 1:8. Lk +√17:37n. Jn 11:48. **be gathered.** Pr 30:17. Ezk √39:17. Ho 8:1. Re *19:17, 18.

29. **Immediately after.** ver. *8. Da *7:11, 12. Mk *13:24, 25. **the tribulation.** ver. +*21. **shall the sun.** Is *13:10. +*24:23. 34:4. Je *4:23-28. Ezk 32:7, 8. Jl *2:10, 30, 31. *3:15. Am 5:20. 8:9. Zp *1:14, 15. Zc 14:6. Lk *21:25, 26. Ac *2:19, 20. Re *6:12-17. 8:12. **darkened.** Pr +20:20. **and.** ⨍148, Ge +8:22. **the stars.** Is 14:12. 34:4. Re 6:13. **shall fall.** Is 2:12. **the powers.** ⨍46C, Mt 8:6. Here, *dunameis, powers,* means really *armies,* from the Hebrew *chayeel* which has both meanings (B678). Jb 26:11. Hg +*2:6, 7. Lk 21:26. He *12:26. 2 P *3:10.

30. **And.** ⨍148, Ge +8:22. **shall appear.** Da +*⟩7:13. Lk *21:28. **the sign.** ver. *3. Da *7:13. Mk 13:4. Re *1:7. **the Son of man.** Mt +8:20. +*16:27n. Da ⟩7:13. **and then shall all.** Ge +*12:3. 28:14. **mourn.** Mt +11:17. Zc *12:10, 12. Re √1:7. 6:15-17. **shall see.** ver. 3n. Mt *16:27n, 28. +*23:39. *26:64. Mk *13:26. 14:62-64. Lk *21:27. 22:69. Ac *1:11. 2 Th *1:7, 8. Re √1:7. **coming.** ver. ❶3g. Mt +*16:28g. Ps 98:9. Da 7:13. Zc +*14:4, 5. Lk 18:8. Jn 14:3. 16:22. Ac +*3:19-21. 1 C 1:7. 4:5. 11:26. 15:23. Ph 3:20, 21. Col 3:4. 1 Th 1:10. 2:19. 3:13. 4:14-17. *5:2-4, 23. 2 Th 1:7. 3:5. 4:5. 1 T 6:14. 2 T 4:1, 8. T *2:13. He *9:28. 10:37. Ja *5:8, 9. 1 P 1:7, 13. 5:4. 2 P *3:3, 4, 9-12. 1 J 2:28. 3:2. Ju 14, 15. Re 2:25. 16:15. 22:12, 20. **the clouds.** Mt +*17:5. 26:64. Ge +9:13. Ex +*13:21. 24:15. 2 K 2:11. 2 Ch +√5:13. Ps +68:17. 104:3. Is 19:1. Da 7:13. Mk 13:26. 14:62. Ac 1:9. 1 Th 4:17. **with power.** Is 24:21-23. Da 7:21, 22. Mk 9:1. 14:62. Lk 21:27. Ro +*11:26. 2 Th *1:9. 2 P *1:16. **and.** ⨍93A, Ge +1:26. By Hendiadys, great and glorious power. **great glory.** Mt *16:27. +*25:31. Ex 24:16. Ps +*102:16. Zc +*2:5. *6:13. Mk *8:38. Jn +*1:14. 2 Th *1:9. 2:8. 2 P 1:17, 18.

31. **And.** ⨍148, Ge +8:22. **he.** Mt *28:18. Mk 16:15, 16. Lk 24:47. Ac 26:19, 20. **shall send.** Ps 50:4, 5. Mk 13:27. 1 Th ❶4:16-18. **his angels.** Mt +*13:41, 49. *25:31. Dt 30:4. Mk 8:38. 2 Th √1:7. Re 1:20. 2:1. *14:6-9. **with.** Nu 10:1-10. Ps *81:3. Is *27:13. 1 C *15:52. 1 Th *4:16. **a great sound of a trumpet.** *or,* a trumpet and a great voice. ⨍93A, Ge +1:26. **sound.** Le=23:23-25. 1 Th 4:16. **trumpet.** Le +*23:24. *25:9. 1 S 13:3. 2 S 2:28. Is √18:3. *27:13. Zc +*9:14. 1 C 15:51, 52. 1 Th 4:16. Re 11:15. **gather.** There appear to be several "gatherings" mentioned in scripture: (1) the gathering of Israel to the land of Palestine in unbelief, Zp +*2:1. (2) the gathering of the confederation of nations against Israel in the tribulation, Zp +*3:8. (3) the gathering of the wicked for destruction at the end of the tribulation, Is +*24:22. (4) the supernatural worldwide and complete regathering of Israel at the end of the great tribulation, Mt 24:31. Is 27:12. 43:6.

Ezk 34:12. 39:28. (5) the gathering of the nations for judgment at the end of the tribulation, Mt 25:32. (6) the gathering of believers in the rapture before the tribulation, Ezk +*17:23. Hab +*3:16. Zp +*2:3. 2 Th 2:1. It is necessary not only to observe similarities, but to note differences, when comparing things which, though they have the same name (as "gathering") are really seen to be different as to time, place, and the persons involved. See note on Mt 10:15n. We must not lump all raptures, all gatherings, all trumpets, all resurrections, all elect, and all judgments into one, when Scripture clearly teaches there are several of each of these which must be distinguished. Mt +*23:37. 25:32. Ps +*147:2. Is *11:12. +*27:12. 49:18. 60:4, 9. Je *29:14. Ezk +*34:12. 37:12. +*39:28. Am 9:9. Zc *14:5. Mk 13:27. Jn 11:52. Ep *1:10. 2 Th *2:1. **his elect**. ver. 22. Ne +*1:9. Ezk √39:28. **from**. Ps 22:27. 67:7. Is 13:5. 42:10. +*43:6. *45:22. Je +*31:8. Ezk +*38:8n. *39:28. Zc *9:10. Ro *10:18. **the four winds**. ſ121.O, Ge +28:22. Je 49:36. Ezk 37:9. Da 7:2. 8:8. 11:4. Zc 2:6. Re 7:1. **end of heaven**. ſ121Q3, 2 S +22:8. Dt 4:32. 30:4. Ps 19:6.

32. **a parable**. Mk *13:28, 29. Lk *21:29, 30. **When**. Mk 11:13.

33. **when**. ver. *3, *15. **know**. Ezk *7:2, etc. Lk 21:31. Ep 5:16. 1 Th ●5:1-5. He *10:37. Ja 5:8, 9. 1 P *4:7. Re 1:3. **it**. *or*, he. **at the doors**. Ja 5:9. Re 3:20.

34. **This generation**. This may be understood as a reference not to a length of time, as the period of a man's life, but to a class of persons, as, the generation of the wicked (J. N. Darby, *Collected Writings*, Vol. 11, Prophetic No. 4, "Brief Remarks on the work of Rev. David Brown," p. 372, citing Dt 32:5, 20). Mt 11:16. *12:+*39, 41, 42, 45. *16:28. *23:36. Nu *32:13. Dt √32:5, 20. Ps 22:30. 24:6. Mk 8:12. *13:30, 31. Lk 7:31. 11:30-32, 50, 51. 17:25. 21:32, 33. 1 P 2:9. **not pass**. ſ158, Mt +5:18. Ps +*102:28. **till**. Mt +*16:28n. +*23:39. Lk *9:27.

35. **Heaven**. Mt *5:18. Ps ●+*89:37. 102:26. Is 34:4. *)51:6. 54:10. Je *31:35, 36. ●+*33:25. Lk 16:17. He 1:11, 12. 12:27. 2 P *3:7-13. Re 6:14. 20:11. 21:1. **my words**. Nu +*23:19. Ps *19:7. √89:34. √119:89, 152. Pr +*30:5. Is √40:8. √55:11. T *1:2. 1 P *1:23, 25. Re 3:14. **not**. ſ158, Mt +5:18.

36. **of that day**. 2 Th +*1:10. **knoweth no**. ver. +*42, *44. Mt *25:13. Zc 14:7. Mk +√||13:32. Ac *1:7. 1 Th *5:1, 2. 2 P *3:10. Re 3:3. *16:15. **my Father**. Mt +*10:32. Jn +*14:28.

37. **days of Noe**. Ge 6:11-13. 7:7. Jb *22:15-17. Am *6:3-6. Lk *17:26, 27. 1 Th 5:3. He *11:7. 1 P 3:20, 21. 2 P 2:5. 3:5, 6. **so shall**. ver. 27. **the coming**. Gr. *parousia*, ver. +*3n.

38. **they were eating**. Ge *6:2. 1 S 25:36-38. *30:16, 17. Is *22:12-14. Ezk +*16:49, 50. Am 6:3-6. Lk *12:19, 45. *14:18-20. 17:26-28. +*21:34, 35. Ro *13:13, 14. 1 C 7:29-31. **marrying**. Mt 22:30. **Noe entered**. Ge 7:13-24.

39. **knew not**. Mt 13:13-15. Jg 20:34. Pr 23:35. *24:12. 29:7. Is 1:3. 42:25. 44:18, 19. Lk *19:44. Jn *3:20. Ac 13:41. Ro *1:28. 1 Th 5:3. 2 P *3:5. **the coming**. Gr. *parousia*, ver. +*3n. 2 Th 2:8.

40. **the one**. Mt +*13:30, 40. 2 Ch 33:12-24. Lk *17:34-37. 23:39-43. 1 C *4:7. 2 P 2:5, 7-9. **taken**. Mt 24:31. Ps √37:9-11. √101:5, 6. Pr 14:32. Is ●57:1. 1 Th ●4:17. 2 Th ●2:1. Re 14:14-16.

41. **Two**. The *mulon* was a *hand-mill* composed of two stones; "the uppermost of which is turned round by a small handle of wood or iron iron that is placed in the rim. When this stone is large, or expedition required, a second person is called to assist; and as it is usual for *women* alone to be concerned in this employment, who seat themselves over against each other with the millstone between them, we may see not only the propriety of the expression, Ex 11:5," but the force of this (Dr. Shaw, p. 231). **grinding**. Jg 16:21. Jb 31:10. Ec 12:3. **at the mill**. Ex 11:5. Is 47:2. **taken**. The "taking" here and in ver. +40, is not the rapture of the church, but the gathering out of all things that offend described in the parable of the wheat and tares (and thus parallel to the destruction of the wicked that were "taken" in the flood of Noah, ver. 39), Mt +*13:30, 40. Lk *17:34n, 37n. **and the other**. Mt 21:44. Ex 14:20. 1 S 5:11. Ho 14:9. 1 P 2:6-8. **left**. Is 24:6. Lk 18:8. 1 Th 4:15n, 17.

42. **Watch**. ver. 44. Mt *25:13. *26:38-41. Ps 127:1. Pr *8:34. Mk *13:33-37. 14:34-38. Lk *12:35-40. 18:1. +√21:36. Ac 20:31. Ro 13:11. 1 C 16:13. Ep +*6:18. Col *4:2. 1 Th 5:6. 2 T 4:5. He *13:17. 1 P *4:7. *5:8. Re 3:2, 3. 16:15. **for**. ver. *36, *44. Mk 13:33-35. **ye know not**. The passages which speak of the time as *unknown* must be in reference to the rapture (ver. 36, 44. Mt 25:13), for the timing of the Second Advent will be *known* in that day to students of Scripture (Da +*9:27. 12:7. 1 Th 5:1, 2. Re 12:6, 14. 13:5), for the length of the tribulation is precisely known, as well as the event which marks its beginning. **your Lord**. Jn 13:13.

43. **But know**. Lk 12:39-46. **if**. ſ184B, Mt +23:30. **goodman**. Mt 20:11. Pr 7:19. **had**. Lk 12:39. 1 Th *5:2-6. 2 P *3:10, 11. **in what watch**. Mk 13:35. **the thief**. 1 Th 5:2, 4. 2 P 3:10. Re 3:3. 16:15. **have watched**. ver. 42. **would not**. Ex *22:2, 3. **broken**. Mt 6:19.

44. **be ye also ready**. ver. 42. Mt *25:10, 13. Mk 13:35-37. Lk 12:40. Ph 4:5. 1 Th 5:6. T 3:1. Ja 5:9. 2 P 3:12. Re 19:7. 22:14. **Son of man**. Mt 8:20. **cometh**. ver. +*3n. Mt *16:27n. Lk 17:30. 18:8.

45. **Who then is**. ſ121I1, Ge +3:7. Lk 12:41-43. *16:10-12. *19:17. Ac +*20:28. 1 C 4:1, 2. 1 T 1:12. 2 T √2:2. He 3:5. 1 P 4:10, 11. Re 2:13. **faithful**. Mt +*13:52. +*25:21. Ge +*18:19. 2 K 12:15. Ps 101:2, *6. Je +*23:28n. Ezk ●√13:7. 1 C +*4:2. Col +*1:7. 2 T +*2:2. He *3:5. 1 P 4:10. **wise**. Mt 25:2. Da +*11:33n. √12:3. Col 1:28. **servant**. Mt +*10:24, 25. +*20:27. +*23:11. Mk 13:34. Ro *12:3. Ph *2:3. **ruler**. Mt *25:21. Ps +*149:9. 2 C ●√1:24. 1 T *3:5. *5:17. 2 T 2:12. He *13:7, 17, 24. 1 P 5:1-3. Re 2:27. **household**. Ro +16:5. Ga 6:10. Ep 2:19. He 3:5, 6. **to give**. Mt +*13:52. √25:35-40. Pr 31:15. Ezk 34:2. Jn 21:15-17. Ac +*20:28. 1 C *3:1, 2. Ep +*4:11-13. 1 P 5:1-3. **meat**. Mt 4:4. 6:11. 2 K 25:29. Jb 36:31. Ps +104:27. 145:15. Pr +27:27. 31:15. Je √3:15. Da +*11:33. 1 C 3:2. **due season**. Mt +*21:41, 43. Ge *17:21 (✥S#4150h). Le 23:2n. Nu 28:2n. 2 K 25:30. 1 Ch +*12:32. Ps *104:27. Ec 10:17. Je ●*8:7. Da *12:4, 7, 9, 10. Lk +*12:42. 2 T *4:2. He +*3:13. +*4:16.

46. **Blessed**. Mt *25:34. Lk 12:37, 43. Ph *1:21-23. 2 T *4:6-8. 1 P *5:4. 2 P 1:13-15. 1 J *3:17. Re 2:19. *16:15. **find so doing**. 2 Ch=35:15.

47. **ruler over**. Mt *25:21, 23. Ps +*149:5-9. Pr 14:11, 19. Da +*12:3. Lk 12:37, 44. 19:17. *22:28-

30. Jn *12:26. 2 T *2:12. 1 P *5:4. Re 1:6. *2:26. *3:21. *21:7.

48. **if.** ✓184C, Mt +4:9. Mt *18:32. *25:26. Lk *19:22. **say.** Dt 9:4. *15:9. 2 K 5:26. Is *32:6. Mk ✓7:21. Lk +*12:45. Jn *13:2. Ac *5:3. *8:22. **delayeth.** Mt 25:5. Ex 9:4. *15:9. 2 K 5:26. Is *32:6. Mk ✓7:21. Lk +*12:45. Jn *13:2. Ac *5:3. *8:22. **delayeth.** Mt 25:5. Ex=32:1. Ec +*8:11. Ezk ✓12:22, 27. Hab 2:3. He 10:36, 37. 2 P *3:3-5. Re ❍22:7, 12, 20.

49. **to smite.** Is *66:5. 2 C +*1:24. 11:20. 1 P +*5:3. 3 J 9, 10. Re *13:7. 16:6. 17:6. 19:2. **and to.** Mt 7:15. 1 S 2:13-16, 29. Is *56:12. Ezk 34:3. Mi 3:5. Ro *16:18. Ph *3:19. T 1:11, 12. 2 P 2:13, 14. Ju *12. **drink.** Jn 2:10. 1 Th 5:7.

50. **come.** ver. *42-44. Mt *25:19. Pr *29:1. Lk 20:16. 1 Th *5:2, 3. Re *3:3.·**in a day.** Mt 25:13. 2 P 3:12.

51. **cut him asunder.** or, cut him off. 2 S 12:31. 1 Ch 20:3. Am 1:3. He 11:37. **and appoint.** Jb *20:29. Ps *11:6. Is *33:14. Lk *12:46. **portion.** 1 C ❍9:23. **hypocrites.** Mt 6:2. 7:21-27. 25:3, 11, 12. Lk ❍12:46. Jn ❍*10:28, 29. 2 P 2:20-22. **there shall.** Mt +*8:12. 22:13. 25:30. Is *65:14. Lk *13:28. Re ❍14:3.

MATTHEW 25

The parable of the wise and foolish virgins, 1-13. That of the talents committed to servants of different characters, 14-30; and a most solemn representation of the day of judgment, and of its infinitely important proceedings and consequences, 31-46.

1. **Then.** Mt 24:42-51. Lk +*21:34-36. **the kingdom.** Mt 3:2. 4:17. +*13:24, 31, 38, 44, 47. *20:1. *22:2. Da *2:44. **ten.** Ps 45:14. SS 1:3. 5:8, 16. 6:1, 8, 9. Lk 19:13. 1 C 11:2. Re 14:4. **which.** Mt *5:16. Lk *12:35, 36. Ph *2:15, 16. **lamps.** Jn 18:3. Ac 20:8. Re 4:5. 8:10. **went.** 2 T 4:8. T 2:13. 2 P 1:13-15. 3:12, 13. **the bridegroom.** Mt *9:15. 22:2. Ps 45:9-11. Is *54:5. 62:4, 5. Ho 2:19. Mk 2:19, 20. Lk 5:34, 35. Jn *3:29. 2 C 11:2. Ep *5:25-33. Ja 4:4. Re *19:7. *21:2, 9.

2. **And five.** Mt *7:24-27. *13:19-23, 38-43, *47, 48. *22:10, 11. Je 24:2. 1 C 10:1-5. 1 J *2:19. Ju *5. **foolish.** Mt 7:26. 23:17. 1 C 4:10. **wise.** Mt 7:24. +*10:16. +*24:45. Ge 41:39. Lk +*16:8. 1 C 4:10.

3. **foolish.** Mt *23:25, 26. Is 48:1, 2. 58:2. Ezk +*33:31. Ro 8:9. 2 T *3:5. He +*12:15. Re *3:1, 15, 16.

4. **oil.** Ps +*45:7. Zc 4:2, 3. Jn 1:15, 16. *3:34. Ro *8:9. 2 C *1:22. Ga 5:22, 23. 1 J *2:20, 27. Ju 19.

5. **tarried.** ver. +*19. +*24:48. Hab 2:3. Lk 12:45. *20:9. He *10:36, 37. 2 P *3:4-9. Re 2:25. **they.** Mt 26:40, 43. SS 3:1. 5:2. Is 5:27. Jon 1:5, 6. Mk 13:35, 37. 14:37, 38. Lk *18:8. Ro *13:11, 12. Ep *5:14. 1 Th *5:6-8. 1 P *5:8.

6. **at midnight.** Mt *24:44. Ex=11:4, 6. Mk *13:33-37. Lk 12:20, 38-40, 46. 1 Th *5:1-3. Re 16:15. **a cry.** Mt *24:31. Jn *5:28, 29. 1 C 15:52. 1 Th +*4:16. 2 P 3:10. **Behold.** ver. *31. Ps *50:3-6. 96:13. 98:9. 2 Th ✓1:7-10. Ju *14, *15. **go.** ver. 1. Is *25:9. Am 4:12. Ml *3:1, 2. Re 19:7-9.

7. **Then all.** Lk 12:35. Ro *13:12. 2 P *3:14. Re *2:4, 5. *3:2, 19, 20.

8. **Give us.** Mt 3:9. ❍*5:42. Lk 16:24. Ac 8:24. Re *3:9. **for.** Mt +*13:20, 21. +*24:13. Jb 8:13, 14. *18:5. 21:17. Pr +*4:18, 19. +*13:9. 20:20. Lk +*8:18.

*12:35. Col *1:23. He +*3:14. Re 2:10. **gone out.** or, going out. He 4:1.

9. **Not so.** ✓63C, Ge +25:32. Mt ❍*5:42. **lest.** Ps *49:7-9. Je 15:1. Ezk *14:14-16, 20. 18:20. **but.** Is *55:1-3, 6, 7. Ac 8:22. Re *3:17, 18. **buy for yourselves.** Mt 13:44.

10. **the bridegroom.** ver. 6. Re *1:7. 22:12, 20. **ready.** ver. *20-23. Mt *24:44. Am 8:12, 13. Lk *12:36, 37. *13:24, 25. Col 1:12. 2 T *4:8. 1 P 1:13. **with him.** Is 40:10. **to the marriage.** ✓121.O, Ge +28:22. By Metonymy of the Adjunct, "marriage" is put for the place where the marriage was to be celebrated. Mt 22:2. Re 19:7, 9. **door was shut.** Ge *7:16. Nu 14:28-34. Ps *95:11. Lk *13:25. He 3:18, 19. Re *22:11.

11. **saying.** Mt +*7:21-23. He *12:16, 17.

12. **I know you not.** ✓22C2, Ge +3:9. Mt ✓7:23. *10:33. Ps *1:6. 5:5. 6:8. +*50:16. Hab *1:13. Lk *13:25-30. Jn *9:31. ✓10:14, 27. 1 C 8:3. Ga 4:9. 2 T ✓2:19.

13. **Watch.** Mt 24:42-44. Mk 13:33-37. Lk +*21:34-36. Ac *20:31. 1 C 16:13. 1 Th *5:6. 2 T *4:5. 1 P *4:7. *5:8. Re 16:15. **know neither.** T#385. Mt *24:37-39, 50. Ec +9:12 (T#149). Mk 13:32-36. Lk 17:24, 28-30. +*21:35, 36. Ac +*1:7.

14. **as.** Mt *21:33. Mk *13:34. Lk 17:22. *19:12, 13. *20:9. **far country.** ver. +*19. Mt 21:33. 26:11. Lk 15:13. **and delivered.** Lk 16:1-12. Ro 12:6-8. 1 C 3:5. *4:1, 2. *12:4, 7-29. Ep *4:11, 12. 1 P *4:9-11.

15. **talents.** "A talent is 187l. 10s." Mt 18:24n. Lk +*12:48. *19:13, 14. **to every.** Ro *12:6. 1 C 4:2. 12:7, 11, 29. 2 C 6:1. Ep 4:7. 2 T 1:6. 1 P 4:10. 2 P 1:8.

16. **went.** 2 S 7:1-3. 1 Ch 13:1-3. ch. 22-26. 28:2, etc. 29:1-17. 2 Ch 1:9, 10. *15:8-15. *17:3-9. 19:4-10. *31:20, 21. 33:15, 16. ch. 34, 35. Ne 5:14-19. Is 23:18. 49:23. 60:5-16. Ac 13:36. Ro *15:18, 19. 1 C *9:16-23. 15:10. 1 T *6:17, 18. 2 T 2:6. *4:5-8. Phm 6, 7. 3 J 5-8. **made.** ✓121C, Ge +12:5.

17. **he also.** Ge +*18:19. 2 S 19:32. 1 K 18:3, 4. 2 K 4:8-10. Jb 29:11-17. *31:16-22. Pr *3:9, 10. Ec 11:1-6. Mk 14:3-8. Ac 9:36-39. 10:2. 11:29, 30. 2 C *8:12. 9:11-14. Ga ✓6:9, 10. Ep *5:16. Col 4:17. 1 T 5:10. 2 T 1:16-18. He ✓6:10, 11. 1 P 4:10.

18. **and hid.** Pr *18:9. 26:13-16. Hg 1:2-4. Ml 1:10. Lk 19:20. He *6:12. 2 P *1:8.

19. **a long.** ver. 5, 14. Mt 9:15. 21:33. *24:48. Dt *28:59. Ps 102:13, 16. Is 32:10. La 5:20, 21. Ezk +*38:8. Mk 13:31-37. Lk 5:35. 13:35. 17:22. *19:12. ✓20:9. Jn 7:33-36. 8:21-24. 12:35. 13:33. 16:5-7, 16-22. 17:11-13. **cometh.** Mt 24:50. Lk 20:16. **reckoneth.** Mt +*10:15n. 18:23, 24. Lk 16:1, 2, 19, etc. Ro *14:7-12. 1 C *3:12-15. 2 C *5:10. Ja 3:1.

20. **behold.** Lk 19:16, 17. Ac *20:24. 1 C *15:10. Col 1:29. 2 T 4:1-3. Ja *2:18.

21. **Well done.** 2 Ch *31:20, 21. Lk *16:10. Ro 2:29. 1 C *4:5. 2 C 5:9. 10:18. 1 P 1:7. **faithful servant.** ver. 23. Mt +*24:45. 2 K 12:15. **a few things.** Lk ✓16:10. 1 C +*4:2. 1 T 3:13. **I will.** ver. 34-40, 46. 10:40-42. +*24:47. Pr 12:24. Lk 12:44. *22:28-30. Re 2:10, +*26-28. *3:21. *21:7. **enter.** ver. 23. Ne 8:10. Ps *16:10, 11. Jn 12:26. 14:3. 15:11. 17:24. Ro 8:17. Ph 1:23. 2 T 2:12. He *12:2. 1 P *1:8. 2 P ✓1:11. Re *7:17. **joy.** ✓121.O, Ge +28:22. i.e. By Metonymy of the Adjunct, whereby the contents are placed for what contains them, and what is placed, for the place where

it is located, "joy" is put for the place where the lord manifested his joy.

22. I have. Lk *19:18, 19. Ro 12:6-8. 2 C 8:1-3, 7, 8, *12.

23. Well. ver. 21. Mk *12:41-44. *14:8, 9. **been faithful.** T#923. ver. 29. Mt +*13:12. **joy.** ✓121.O, Ge +28:22.

24. he which. Our Lord placed the example of negligence in him to whom the *least* was committed, probably to "intimate," says Doddridge, "that we are accountable for the *smallest* advantage with which we are entrusted; but it cannot imply that they who have received *much* will ordinarily pass their account *best*; for it is too plain, in fact, that most of those whose dignity, wealth, and genius give them the greatest opportunities of service, seem to forget that they have any Master in heaven to serve, or any future reckoning to expect; and many render themselves much more criminal than this wicked and slothful servant who hid his talent in the earth." **and said.** Ezk +33:20. **Lord.** Mt *7:21. Lk *6:46. **I knew.** Notice that a wrong conception of who God is will make it impossible to render proper service to Him (Ps +✓9:10). Mt *20:12. 1 S 25:3. Jb ◐+*1:22. +*2:10. 21:14, 15. Pr +✓19:3. Is +✓29:24. 58:3. Je 2:31. 44:16-18. Ezk 18:+*25-29. Ml 1:12, 13. 3:14, 15. Lk *15:29. *19:20-22. Ro 8:7. 9:+*14, 20. **reaping where.** 2 C ◐8:12. **gathering.** Is 18:5.

25. I was afraid. Ge +*19:30. 2 S 6:9, 10. Ps +✓9:10. Pr 26:13. Is *57:11. Ro *8:15. 2 T *1:6, 7. Re +*21:8. **and went.** ver. 18. **thou hast.** Mt 20:14.

26. Thou wicked. Mt *18:32. Jb *15:5, 6. **and slothful.** Pr 19:15. 20:4. Ec +*10:18. Je +*48:10. Ro +*12:11. He *6:12.

27. oughtest. This statement should forever settle the question as to the lawfulness of charging, earning, and receiving interest: the servant was told that he should have invested the money, so that the lord would have received his own with interest. The Israelites were not allowed to charge interest on money lent to their brethren (Dt 23:19, 20; Is +*24:2), for in the Old Testament law provision was carefully made that no person, if the law were faithfully followed, would ever be reduced to penury. Unjust interest charges would quickly reduce the needy to poverty (Ne 5:1-13). Christ here commends productivity and the prudent investment of resources, and censures indolence. Lk *19:22, 23. Ro 3:19. Ju *15. **should.** ✓184B, Mt +23:30. "Conclusion of a condition of the second class (determined as unfulfilled). The condition is not expressed, but it is implied. 'If you had done that' " (A. T. Robertson, *Word Pictures*, vol. 1, p. 200). For additional instances of the ellipsis of the first member of a clause, see ✓63D1, Mt +16:7. **with usury.** Dt 23:19, 20. Is +*24:2.

28. Take therefore. Lk *10:42. *19:24.

29. unto. Mt *13:12. Mk 4:25. Lk +*8:18. +*12:48. *16:9-12. 19:25, 26. Jn 1:16. *15:2. **shall be taken.** Mt *21:41. La 2:6. Ho 2:9. Lk *10:42. *12:19-21. 16:1-3, *20-25. Jn 11:48. Re *2:5.

30. cast. Mt *3:10. *5:13. Je 15:1, 2. Ezk 15:2-5. Lk 14:34, 35. Jn *15:6. T *3:14. He *6:7, 8. Re *3:15, 16. **unprofitable servant.** Lk ✓17:10. **outer darkness.** Mt +*8:12. *13:42, 50. 22:13. *24:51. Lk *13:28. 2 P *2:17. Ju *13. Re +*21:8.

31. Son of man. ver. 6. Mt 8:20. +*16:27n. 19:28.

26:64. Da *7:13, 14. Zc *14:5. Mk *8:38. 14:62. Lk 9:26. 22:69. Jn 1:51. *5:27-29. Ac +*1:11. 1 Th ✓4:16. 2 Th ✓1:7, 8. He +*1:8. Ju *14. Re +*1:7. **shall come.** Mt +*24:30. Re +*1:7. **in his glory.** Mt *16:27. +*24:30. Lk *9:26. Jn +*1:14. Col +*3:4. **angels with him.** Zc +*)14:5. Lk 12:8. Ju *14. **then.** Mt *19:28. Ps 9:7. Re *3:21. *20:11. **sit upon.** Jl 3:12. **the throne.** 2 S 12:30. Zc 6:13. Lk +*1:32. Ac +*2:30. Re +*3:21. **of his glory.** Ps *102:15, 16. Zc *6:13. Col +*3:4. 1 Th 2:12.

32. before. Mt +*10:15n. Ps 96:13. 98:9. Ac ✓17:30, 31. Ro *2:12, 16. *14:10-12. 2 C ✓5:10. Re ✓20:12-15. **gathered.** Mt +*24:31n. 2 S 12:31. Is 34:8-12. Jl *3:2, 11, 12. Zp +*3:8. **all nations.** Mt 24:14. 28:19, 20. Jl +*3:12. Ro 14:10. 16:26. **he shall separate.** T#387. Mt *3:12. +5:20 (T#560). +*13:30, 42, 43, 49. 22:11-13. Ge 30:33. 2 S 12:31. Ps 1:5. 50:3-5. Je +*43:11. Ezk *20:38. 34:17-22. Ml *3:18. Lk 16:26. 1 C *4:5. **as.** Ps 78:52. Jn 10:14, 27.

33. the sheep. Ps *79:13. 95:7. 100:3. Jn ✓10:26-28. 21:15-17. **his right.** Ge +48:13, 14, 17-19. Ps 45:9. *110:1. Ec *10:2. Mk *16:19. Ac 2:34, 35. Ep *1:20. He *1:3.

34. the King. ver. 40. Mt 21:5. 22:11-13. 27:37. 1 S 12:12. Ps 2:6. 24:7-10. Is 6:5. +*9:7. *32:1, 2. 33:17, 22. Je 10:10. +*23:5, 6. Ezk *37:24, 25. Da +*9:25. Zp 3:15. Zc 9:9, 10. Lk *1:31-33. 19:38. Jn 1:49. 12:13. *19:15, 19-22. Re 17:14. *19:16. **right hand.** 1 K 2:19. Ps 45:9. 110:1. **Come.** ver. 21, 23, 41. Mt *5:3-12. Ge +*12:2, 3. Dt 11:23-28. Ps 37:22. 115:13-15. Is 65:23. Lk *11:28. Ac *3:26. Ga *3:13, 14. Ep 1:3. 1 Th 2:12. 1 P 1:3. **inherit.** Mt 19:29. Zc 2:12. Lk *12:32. Ac 20:32. Ro *4:13. *8:17. 1 C +*6:9. Ga 5:21. Ep +✓1:11n. 5:5. Col +✓3:24. 2 T 2:12. *4:1n, 8. T 3:7. He 1:14. 6:12, 17. 12:28. Ja *2:5. 1 P +*1:4n, 5, 9. *3:9. Re *5:10. 21:7. **the kingdom.** Mt +*13:43. +*16:28. +✓24:14. Lk 12:32. 22:29. 2 T +*4:1n. He +*12:28. Ja 2:5. 2 P +*1:11. **prepared.** Mt 20:23. Mk 10:40. Jn *14:2, 3. 1 C *2:9. He *11:16. **from.** Mt +*13:35. Ac *15:18. Ep *1:4-6. 2 T 1:9. 1 P 1:19, 20. Re 13:8. **world.** Gr. *kosmos*, Mt +4:8.

35. I was an hungered. ver. 40. Mt *10:40-42. 26:11. Dt *15:7-11. Jb 29:13-16. 31:16-21. Ps 112:5-10. Pr *3:9, 10. *11:24, 25. 14:21, 31. *19:17. 22:9. Ec 11:1, 2. Is *58:7-11. Ezk 18:7, 16. Da 4:27. Mi +*6:8. Mk *14:7. Lk 11:41. *14:12-14. Jn 13:29. Ac *4:32. *9:36-39. 10:31. 11:29. 2 C 8:1-4, 7-9. *9:7-14. Ga *6:10. Ep 4:28. 1 T *6:17-19. Phm 7. He *6:10. 13:16. Ja *1:27. *2:15, 16. 1 P 4:9, 10. 1 J *3:16-19. **thirsty.** ver. 42. Pr *25:21. Ro *12:20. **gave me drink.** Mt +*10:42. **I was a stranger.** T#715. ver. 43. Ge *18:2-8. *19:1-3. 23:4 (✱S#1616h). Ex 12:48mg. 22:21. 23:9. Le 19:10, 33, 34. Dt 1:16. 10:18, 19. +26:11. Jsh +20:9. Jg 19:20, 21. Jb *31:32. Ml +*3:5. Ac *16:15. Ro *12:13. 16:23. 1 T *5:10. T 1:8 (T#354). He *13:1-3. 1 P 4:9. 3 J 5-8.

36. Naked. ✓171N, Ge +8:13. Jb 31:19, 20. Lk 3:11. Jn 21:7. Ja *2:14-16. **clothed.** 2 Ch 28:15. Pr 31:20. **was sick.** ver. 43. Ps 41:6-8. Ezk *34:4. Lk 10:33, 34. Ac *20:35. 28:8, 9. Ja *1:27. *5:14, 15. **I was in prison.** Ph 4:10-14. 2 T *1:16-18. He *10:34. *13:3.

37. saying. ✓56, Is +14:16. **when.** Mt *6:3. 1 Ch 29:14. Pr 15:33. Is ✓64:6. 1 C 15:10. 1 P *5:5, 6.

40. the King. ver. 34. Pr 25:6, 7. **Inasmuch.** Mt +*10:42. 2 S 9:1, 7. Pr 14:31. *19:17. Mk *9:41. Jn 19:26, 27. 21:15-17. 1 C 16:21, 22. 2 C 4:5. *5:14,

15. *8:7-9. Ga *5:6, 13, 22. 1 Th 4:9, 10. 1 P *1:22. 1 J *3:14-19. *4:7-12, 20, 21. 5:1, 2. **unto one.** Mt 6:29. 18:10. Lk 15:7, 10. **the least.** Mt +*10:42. *12:49, 50. *18:5, 6, 10. 28:10. Mk *3:34, 35. Jn 20:17. Ro 8:29. 1 C 12:26, 27. He 2:11-15. *6:10. **ye have done it unto me.** Mt 27:55. Ge=40:14. Nu=3:6. Ac *9:4, 5. 1 C *12:26, 27. Ep 5:30. He *6:10.

41. **them.** ver. *33. **Depart.** Mt +*7:23. Ps 6:8. +*9:17. 119:115. 139:19. Lk 13:27. **ye cursed.** Dt √27:15-26. +*28:15, 16, etc. Ps +*119:21. Pr +*3:33. Je *17:5. Zc +*5:3. Ga +*3:10-13. He *6:8. **everlasting.** Gr. *aionios*, Mt +18:8. ver. *46. Mt *3:12. +*13:40, 42, 50. 18:8. Is +*33:14. +*66:24. Mk √9:43-48. Lk +*16:24. 2 Th √1:8, 9. Ju *7. Re √14:10, 11. √20:10-15. **fire.** Re √19:20. **prepared for.** Mt 8:29. Ja 2:19. Re 14:11. 20:10. **the devil.** Jn √8:44. Ro 9:22, 23. 2 P *2:4. 1 J 3:10. Ju *6. Re *12:7-9. **his angels.** 2 C 12:7. 2 P 2:4. Ju 6.

42. **I was an hungered.** ver. 35. Mt 10:37, 38. 12:30. Jb 22:7. Am 6:6. Jn √5:23. √8:42-44. 14:21. 1 C 16:22. 2 Th *1:8. Ja 2:15-24. 1 J 3:14-17. 4:20.

43. **stranger.** Dt *27:19. Je 7:6. He √13:2. **took me not in.** Dt 23:4. Jg 19:15. 1 S 25:10. Lk 2:7. 9:53. **naked.** ſ171N, Ge +8:13. **clothed me not.** Ps +*12:5. Ezk +*16:49. Ja 2:15, 16. 1 J 3:17. **visited me not.** Mt 8:15. 27:55. Ps 109:16. Pr 21:13. Ezk 34:4. Zc 11:16. Lk 8:3. 16:20, 21. Ja 4:17.

44. **when.** ver. 24-27. Mt +*7:22. 1 S 15:13-15, 20, 21. Je 2:23, 35. Ml 1:6. *2:17. 3:13. Lk 10:29.

45. **Inasmuch.** ver. 40. Ge +*12:3. Nu 24:9. Ps 105:15. Pr *14:31. 17:5. 21:13. Zc +*2:8. Jn 15:18, 19. Ac √9:4, 5. 1 J 3:12-20. 5:1-3. **did it not.** Lk 10:16. Ac 9:5. 1 C 8:12. Ja +*4:17.

46. **everlasting.** Gr. *aionios*, Mt +18:8. **punishment.** T#567. ver. *41. Mt +*13:30, 38, 40, 42. 26:24. 1 Ch +*28:9 (T#555). Jb +8:13 (T#573-1). +27:8 (T#572). Da +*12:2. Mk 3:29. *9:43, 44, 46, 48, 49. 14:21. Lk 3:17. +9:24 (T#554). +*16:26 (T#390). Jn *3:36. *5:29. Ac 24:15. Ro *2:5-9. 11:22. 2 C √5:11. +6:2 (T#553). Ph 3:18, 19. 2 Th √1:7-9. He 10:31. Ja +1:15 (T#287). Ju 6, 7, 13. Re √14:9-11. √20:10, 15. +*21:8. **the righteous.** Mt +*13:43. 19:16. Ps +*16:10, 11. Ro 5:19, 21. **into life.** T#864. Lk *20:36. Jn √3:15, 16, 36. 4:14. 6:47, 51, 54. √10:27, 28. *11:25, 26. Ro 2:7. √6:23. Ga 6:8. T 1:2. 1 J 2:25. √5:11-13. Ju *21. **eternal.** Gr. *aionios*, Mt +18:8.

MATTHEW 26

Jesus foretells his crucifixion after two days, 1, 2. The chief priests conspire against him, 3-5. A woman pours precious ointment on his head: the disciples censure, but Jesus commends her, 6-13. Judas bargains with the chief priests to betray him, 14-16. Jesus eats the passover, and marks out the traitor, 17-25. He institutes the Lord's supper, 26-29; and foretells that all his apostles would forsake him, and Peter deny him, 30-35. His agony and prayer in the garden, 36-46. He is betrayed and apprehended, 47-50. A disciple cuts off the high priest's servant's ear; but Jesus forbids all resistance, 51-56. He is arraigned before Caiaphas, falsely accused, condemned, and treated with insult and indignity, 57-68. Peter thrice denies him, with peculiar aggravations; but going out he weeps bitterly, 69-75.

1. **came to pass.** ſ144A11, Ge +38:1. **when.** Mt 7:28. 11:1. 13:53. 19:1.

2. **know.** Mk 14:1, 2. Lk 22:1, 2, 15. Jn 13:1. **the feast.** Ex 12:11-14. 34:25. Jn 2:13. 6:4. 11:55. 12:1. **passover.** Le +*23:5. **Son of man.** Mt 8:20. **betrayed.** ver. 24, 25. Mt 17:22. 20:18, 19. 27:4. Lk 24:6, 7. Jn 13:2. 18:2.

3. **assembled.** Mt 21:45, 46. Ps *2:1, 2. 56:6. 64:4-6. 94:20, 21. Je 11:19. 18:18-20. Jn 11:47-53, 57. Ac *4:25-28. **the palace.** ver. 58, 69. Je 17:27. Mk 14:54, 66. 15:16. Lk 11:21. 22:55. Jn 18:15. Re 11:2. **Caiaphas.** i.e. *searcher, depression,* ✻S#2533g. Mt 26:3, 57. Lk 3:2. Jn 11:49. 18:13, 14, 24, 28. Ac 4:6. This was *Joseph,* surnamed *Caiaphas,* who succeeded Simon son of Camith in the high-priesthood, about A.D. 25. He married the daughter of Annas, who had also been the high priest. About two years after our Lord's death, he was deposed by Vitellius-governor of Syria; and unable to bear his disgrace, and perhaps the stings of conscience for the murder of Christ, he killed himself about A.D. 35. See Josephus, Ant. l. xviii. c. 2-4. Jn 11:49. 18:13, 14, 24. Ac 4:5, 6.

4. **consulted.** Mt 21:46. Ps 2:2. Jn 11:53. **by.** Mt 23:33. Ge 3:1. Ac 7:19. 13:10. 2 C 11:3.

5. **Not.** Ps 76:10. Pr 19:21. +*21:30. Is 46:10. La 3:37. Mk 14:2, 12, 27. Lk 22:7. Jn 18:28. Ac 4:28. **day.** ſ63B, Ge +25:28. **lest.** Mt 14:5. *21:26, 46. 27:24. Lk 20:6. 22:6.

6. **in Bethany.** Mt *21:17. Mk 11:12. Jn 11:1, 2. 12:1, 2. **Simon.** Mk 14:3. **leper.** ſ11, Ge +2:23.

7. **came.** Jn 12:2, 3. **very.** Ex 30:23-33. Ps 133:2. Ec 9:8. 10:1. SS 1:3. Is 57:9. Lk 7:37, 38, 46. **ointment.** Ex +=30:1. 1 Ch +=9:30. SS +=1:12. Jn 12:3. **poured.** Gr. *katacheo,* ✻S#2708g. Mk 14:3.

8. **they.** Mt 20:24. 21:15. 1 S 17:28, 29. Ec 4:4. Mk 14:4. Lk 13:14. Jn 12:4-6. **To.** Ex 5:17. Am 8:5. Hg 1:2-4. Ml 1:7-10, 13.

9. **this ointment.** Jsh 7:20, 21. 1 S 15:9, 21. 2 K 5:20. Mk 14:5. Jn 12:5, 6. 13:29. 2 P 2:15. **sold.** ſ121C1H, Dt +28:33.

10. **understood.** Mt 16:8. **Why.** Jb 13:7. Mk 14:6. Lk 7:44-50. 11:7. Ga 1:7. 5:12. 6:17. **a good.** Ne 2:18. 2 C 9:8. Ep √2:10. Col +*1:10. 2 Th 2:17. 1 T 3:1. 5:10. 2 T 2:21. T 1:16. 2:14. 3:1, 8, 14. He 13:21. 1 P 2:12.

11. **ye have.** Mt *25:34-40, 42-45. Dt *15:11. Mk *14:7. Jn *12:8. Ga *2:10. 1 J *3:17. **the poor.** Ex +23:3. **but.** Mt *18:20. *25:14. *28:20. Jn *13:33. 14:19. *16:5, 28. *17:11. Ac +*3:21. **ye have not.** Mt 9:15. Mk 2:20. Lk 5:35. Jn 7:33. 12:35. ✻13:33. *14:19. *16:5, 16-19, 28. **always.** Gr. *pantote,* ✻S#3842g. Rendered (1) always: Mt 26:11, 11. Mk 14:7, 7. Lk 18:1. Jn 8:29. 11:42. 12:8, 8. 18:20b. Ro 1:9. 1 C 1:4. 15:58. 2 C 2:14. 4:10. 5:6. 9:8. Ga 4:18. Ep 5:20. Ph 1:4, 20. 2:12. Col 1:3. 4:12. 1 Th 1:2. 3:6. 2 Th 1:3, 11. Phm 4. (2) ever: Lk 15:31. Jn 18:20a. 1 Th 4:17. 5:15. 2 T 3:7. He 7:25. (3) alway: Jn 7:6. Ph 4:4. Col 4:6. 1 Th 2:16. 2 Th 2:13. (4) evermore: Jn 6:34. 1 Th 5:16.

12. **For in that.** 2 Ch 16:14. Mk *14:8. 16:1. Lk 23:56. 24:1. Jn 12:7. 19:39, 40.

13. **Wheresoever.** Mt 24:14. 28:19. Ps 98:2, 3. Is 52:10. Mk 13:10. 16:15. Lk 24:47. Ro 10:18. 15:19. Col 1:6, 23. 1 T 2:6. Re 14:6. **this gospel.** Ac 20:24. Ep 1:13. 6:15. **world.** Gr. *kosmos,* Mt +4:8. **there.** 1 S *2:30. Ps *112:6. Pr *10:7. Mk 14:9. 2 C 10:18. He *6:10. **memorial.** Ac 10:4.

14. **one**. Mk 14:10. Lk *22:3-6. Jn *13:2, 27, 30. **Judas**. ver. 25, 47. Mt 10:4. 27:3. Mk 3:19. Lk 6:16. Jn 6:70, 71. 12:4. 18:2. Ac *1:16, 17, 25. **Iscariot**. Jsh 15:25. Je 48:24, 41.

15. **What**. Ge 38:16. Jg 16:5. 17:10. 18:19, 20. Is 56:11. Lk *22:5, 6. Jn 11:57. 1 T 3:3. √6:9, 10. 2 P 2:3, 14, 15. **covenanted with**. or, weighed unto him. Ge 23:16. Je 32:9. **thirty**. Probably *shekels* or *staters*, as some read, which reckoning the shekel at 3*s.*, with Prideaux, would amount to about 4*l.* 10*s.*, the price for the meanest slave! (See Ex 21:32.) Mt 27:3-5, 9. Ge=37:26-28. Zc ✱11:12, 13. Ac 1:18.

16. **he**. Mk 14:11. Lk 22:6. **to betray**. Mt 20:18, 19.

17. **the first**. Ex *12:6, 18-20. 13:6-8. Le 23:5, 6. Nu 28:16, 17. Dt 16:1-4. Mk 14:12. Lk *22:7. **unleavened**. Le +*23:6. **Where**. Mt 3:15. 17:24, 25. Lk 22:8, 9. **the passover**. ✱121P8, Ex +12:21. Ac 12:3, 4.

18. **Go**. Mk *14:13-16. Lk 22:10-13. **The Master**. ver. 49. Mt 21:3. 22:24. 23:8, 10. Mk 5:35. Jn 11:28. 20:16. **My time**. ver. 2, 45. Lk 22:53. Jn 7:6, 8, 30. 8:20. 12:23. 13:1. 17:1. **keep the passover**. Mt 3:15. He 11:28.

19. **the disciples**. Mt 21:6. Jn 2:5. 15:14. **and they**. Ex 12:4-8. 2 Ch 35:10, 11. **passover**. Le +*23:5. Dt *16:6.

20. **when**. Mk 14:17-21. Lk *22:14-16. Jn 13:21. **he**. Ex 12:11. SS 1:12.

21. **Verily**. ver. 2, 14-16. Ps 55:12-14. Lk *22:21, 22. Jn 6:70, 71. *13:18-21. Ac *1:16. He *4:13. Re *2:23.

22. **exceeding sorrowful**. ver. 38. Mk 14:19, 20. Lk 22:23. Jn 13:22-25. 21:17.

23. **He that**. Ru 2:14. Ps *41:9. Mk *14:20. Lk 22:21. Jn *13:18, 26-28. **dippeth**. Gr. *embapto*, ✱S#1686g. Mk 14:20g. Jn 13:26g.

24. **Son of man goeth**. ✱96C7. Heterosis of Tenses B522: the present for the Paulo post futurum, denoting something which will soon be past. Here, *goeth* denotes "will soon be gone" or "given over." For other instances of this figure see Mt 26:28, 45. Mk 14:24, 41. Lk 22:19, 22, (37). 24:49. Jn (13:3). (14:3, 18, 19). (17:11). 20:17. 1 C 11:24. 2 T 4:6. **written**. ver. *54, *56. Ge +*3:15. Ps ch. *22. *69:1-21. Is *50:5, 6. ch. *53. Da +*9:26. Zc *12:10. *13:7. Mk *9:12. Lk 18:31. *22:22. *24:25-27, 44, 46. Jn 7:33. 8:21, **22**. 14:12. 16:28. *19:24, 28, 36, 37. Ac *2:23. 4:28. *13:27-29. *17:2, 3. *26:22, 23. *28:23. 1 C +*15:3. 1 P *1:10, 11. **but**. Mt *18:7. *27:3-5. Ps *55:15, 23. 109:6-19. Ob 7. Mi 7:6. Mk *14:21. Lk 17:1. 22:22. Jn *17:12. Ac *1:16-20. **good for**. He 4:3. Jb 3:1-19. Je 20:14-18. Jn *17:12. **if he**. ✱184B, Mt +23:30.

25. **Judas**. ver. 14. 2 K 5:25. Pr 30:20. **Master**. ver. 49. Jn 1:38. **Thou hast said**. ✱108H13. Idiom B847. "Thou sayest" is not an idiom which conveys a simple affirmation or consent, but means "*thou* (and not I) hast said it," denoting "those are your words, not mine." ver. 64. Mt +*27:11n. Lk 22:70. Jn 18:37.

26. **as**. Mk 14:22-25. Lk *22:18-20. 2 C √11:23-25. **Jesus**. Lk 24:30. 1 C 11:23-25. **blessed it**. "Many Greek copies have *gave thanks.*" Mt 14:19. Mk 6:41. Lk +√24:30. Jn +*6:11. **and brake**. ✱108H4, Is +58:7. Ac 2:46. 20:7. 1 C *10:16, 17. **Take**. Mk 14:22. Jn 6:33-35, 47-58. 1 C 11:26-29. **this**. Ezk 5:4, 5. Lk 22:20. Jn 6:53. 1 C 10:4, 16. Ga 4:24, 25. **is**. ✱119, Ge +49:9. **my body**. Jn 6:51.

27. **he took**. Mk 14:23, 24. Lk 22:20. **gave thanks**. Mt 15:36. **Drink**. Ps 116:13. SS 5:1. 7:9. Is 25:6. 55:1. Mk *14:23. 1 C 10:16. 11:28. **ye all**. Ex 12:47. Lk *22:17.

28. **For this**. Mk 14:24. **my**. Ex *24:7, 8. Le +*17:11. Je 31:31. Zc 9:11. Mk 14:24. Lk 22:19. 1 C 11:25. He 9:14-22. 10:4-14, 29. *13:20. **blood**. Ex 12:13. +24:8. Ac *20:28. Ep 1:7. Col 1:14. Re +*1:5. 5:9. **the new**. Ex ◐19:5. Je 31:31. Mk 14:24. Lk 22:20. 1 C 11:25. 2 C 3:6. He 9:14-18. **testament**. He 9:15. **is**. ✱96C7, ver. +24. **shed for**. Mt 1:21. Mk 10:45. Jn 10:11. 11:50-53. Ro *8:32-34. Ep 5:25-27. He 2:17. 3:1. 9:28. **many**. *✱171F, Is +53:12. Notice that when "many" is used in a contrast (as with *one*, or one person, Christ), it clearly means *all* (Ro √5:12, 15, 19). Mt +*20:28. Jn +*1:9. Ro √5:12, 15, ◐+*18, 19. Ep *1:7. Col *1:14, 20. He *9:22, 28. 1 J *2:2. Re *7:9, 14. **for**. Gr. *eis*. While this is a verbal parallel to Mk 1:4 and Ac 2:38, the preposition *eis* varies in its meaning in different contexts. Here it clearly expresses purpose, telling us Christ shed his blood for the purpose of the remission of our sins. Robertson states "But it by no means follows that the same idea is expressed by *eis aphesin* (for remission) in Mk 1:4 and Ac 2:38 (cf. Mt 10:41)," though in the abstract that may be true. It remains a matter for the interpreter to decide" (A. T. Robertson, *A Grammar of the Greek New Testament*, p. 595). The preposition *eis* in a number of other passages (Mt 10:41. √12:41. Mk +*1:4n. Ac +*2:38n) is better understood to mean the ground or basis (of repentance, remission, etc.). Mk 1:4mg. Lk 1:77mg. **remission**. Ro 3:25. He √9:22. **sins**. Le +=5:6.

29. **I will**. Ps 4:7. 104:15. Is 24:9-11. Mk 14:25. Lk 22:15-18. **not**. ✱158, Mt +5:18. **fruit**. ✱142, Ge +20:16. **until**. Mt *6:10. *7:21, 22. *18:20. 19:28. 28:20. Ps 40:3. SS 5:1. Is 53:11. Zp 3:17. Zc 9:17. Mk *14:25. Lk *14:15. 15:5, 6, 23-25, 32. *22:18, 29, 30. Jn 15:11. *16:22. 17:13. Ac +*1:6. *10:41. He *12:2. Re 5:8-10. 14:3. 19:9. **when**. ✱96C6, Mt +2:4. **drink it**. Is *25:6. Zc *10:7. **with you**. Mt +*13:43. 16:28. +*19:28. +*25:34. Is 25:6, 34. Lk +*12:32. +*22:18, 29, 30. Jn +*14:3. Re *3:20. 7:17. **Father's kingdom**. Lk +*22:29, 30. Jn +*14:2. 2 P *1:11. Re *11:15.

30. **when**. Ps 81:1-4. Mk 14:26. Ep 5:19, 20. Col *3:16, 17. **hymn**. *or*, psalm. **they went**. Ex 12:22. Lk 21:37. 22:39. Jn 14:31. 18:1-4. **mount of Olives**. Mt 21:1.

31. **All**. ver. 56. Mt 11:6. 15:12. 24:9, 10. Mk 14:27, 28. Lk 22:31, 32. Jn *16:32. **I will**. ✱92A, Mt +1:23. Is *53:10. Zc ▶13:7. **and the**. Jb 6:15-22. 19:13-16. Ps 38:11. 69:20. 88:18. La 1:19. Ezk 34:5, 6.

32. **I am**. Mt 16:21. 20:19. 27:63, 64. Mk 9:9, 10. Lk 18:33, 34. **I will**. Mt *28:6, 7, 10, 16, 17. Mk 14:28. *16:7. Jn 21:1, etc. 1 C 15:6.

33. **Though**. ✱184A, 1 C +15:2. ✱185A, Lk +11:8. Mt *23:12. Mk 14:29. Lk 22:31, 33. Jn 13:36-38. 21:15. **yet**. Ps 17:5. 119:116, 117. Pr 16:18, 19. 20:6. 28:25, 26. Je +*17:9. Ro 12:10. Ph +*2:3. 1 P 5:5, 6.

34. **Jesus said**. Lk *22:31-34. Jn 13:38. **That**. ver. 75. Mk 14:30, 31. Lk 22:34. Jn 13:38.

35. **Peter said**. Lk 22:33. Jn *13:36, 37. **Though**. ✱184C, Mt +4:9. Mt 20:22, 23. Pr *28:14, 26. 29:23. Je +*17:9. Mk *14:31. Jn 11:16. Ro 11:20. 1 C √10:12. Ph *2:12. 1 P 1:17. **not**. ✱158, Mt +5:18. **Likewise**. Mt 20:24. Ex 19:8.

36. **a place.** Mk 14:32-35. Lk 22:39-46. Jn 18:1, etc. **Gethsemane.** i.e. *press for olives, oil press,* *S#1068g. Mt 26:36. Mk 14:32. Compare *S#1660h, *gath,* Jg +6:11 and S#8081h, *shemen,* Ge +20:18. *Gethsemane* was a garden at the foot of the mount of Olives, beyond the brook Cedron; an even plat of ground, says Maundrell, not above fifty-seven yards square, where are shown some old olive trees, supposed to identify the spot to which our Lord was wont to resort. Ex +=29:40. **while.** ver. 39, 42. Ps 22:1, 2. 69:1-3, 13-15. He 5:7.

37. **Peter.** Mt 4:18, 21. 17:1. 20:20. Mk 5:37. **sorrowful.** Ps 42:5, 6. 43:5. Mk 14:33, 34. Lk 22:44. Jn *12:27. Ph 2:26.

38. **My soul.** Gr. *psyche,* ✍171Q2. Synecdoche of the Part, Mt +12:18. **sorrowful.** T#1407. Jb 6:2-4. Ps *69:20. 88:1-7, 14-16. *116:3. Is *53:3, 10. Lk 18:23. Ro √8:32. 2 C √5:21. Ga +*3:13. 1 P *2:24. *3:18. **unto death.** 2 K 20:1. 2 Ch 32:24. Is 38:1. Jon 4:9. **tarry.** ver. 40. Mt 25:13. 1 P 4:7. **and watch.** ver. 41. Mt 24:42.

39. **he went.** Lk *22:41, 42, 44. **and fell.** T#1241. Ge 17:3. Nu 14:5. 16:22, 44, 45. 20:6. Dt 9:18. Jsh 7:6. 1 Ch 21:16. Ezk 1:28. 9:8. 11:13. Lk 5:12. 17:16. Ac 10:25. Re 4:10. 5:8, 14. 7:11, 12. 19:4, 10. **and prayed.** Mk 1:35. *14:35, 36. Lk 22:41, 42. He *5:7. **O my Father.** ver. 42. Mt 11:25. Mk 14:36. Lk 10:21. 22:42. 23:34, 46. Jn 11:41. 12:27, 28. 17:1, 5, 11, 21, 24, 25. **if.** ✍184A, 1 C +15:2. Mt 24:24. Mk 13:22. **let this.** T#1459. Mt 20:22. Lk 22:41, 42. Jn 18:11. **cup.** Mt 20:22. Lk 12:50. He 2:10. **pass from.** Ex 12:23, LXX, **not as I will.** ver. 42. Mt 6:10. 2 S 15:26. Jn *5:30. *6:38. 12:28. *14:31. Ro 15:1-3. Ph *2:8.

40. **and findeth.** ver. 43. Mt 25:5. SS 5:2. Mk 13:36. 14:37. Lk 9:32. 22:45. **What.** ver. 35. Jg 9:38. 1 S 26:15, 16. 1 K 20:11. **watch.** Mt 24:42.

41. **Watch.** T#724. Mt 6:13. +*24:42. *25:13. Pr *1:10. Mk *13:33-37. 14:38. Lk +12:37 (T#738). +*21:36. 22:40, 46. 1 C 16:13. Ep +*18). √6:18. 1 P 4:7. *5:8. Re 16:15. **enter.** Mt 6:13. Pr 4:14, 15. Lk 8:13. 11:4. 1 C √10:13. 2 P *2:9. Re +*3:10. **temptation.** T#1414. Ge 32:24-26. Ex 17:3, 4. Jb 1:20-22. 23:8-10. 34:31, 32. Ps 57:1-3. La 3:53-57. Da 6:10. Zc 13:9. Lk *22:31, 32. 2 C *12:7, 8. Ep *6:16-18. He *4:15, 16. 1 P *5:8-10. **the spirit.** Gr. *pneuma.* ✍121A2. Metonymy of the Cause. "Spirit" put for that which is invisible as opposed to the flesh, whether in reference to the *will, mind,* what is spiritual in contrast with what is outward and corporate, or in reference to supernatural judgment. Mk 14:38. Ac 17:16. 18:5. 1 C 5:4. 2 C +*12:18. Ph 1:27. 2:1. 2 Th 2:8. "Spirit" is also put for living or life-giving food, Jn 6:63b; for the gospel, 2 C 3:6; for the reason, 1 C 2:12a. For additional instances of this figure of speech, see ✍121A2, Ps +51:10. For the other uses of *pneuma* see Mt +*8:16n. **is willing.** Ps 119:4, 5, 24, 25, 32, 35-37, 115, 117, 173, 174. Is +*26:8, 9. Ro 7:18-25. 8:3. 1 C 9:27. Ga 5:16, 17, 24. Ph 3:12-14. **but the flesh.** ✍78, Ph 4:10. Ps *103:14.

42. **the second.** ver. 39. Ge +*22:15. Ps 22:1, 2. 69:1-3, 17, 18. 88:1, 2. Mk 14:39, 40. He +*4:15. *5:7, 8. **O my Father.** ver. 39. Mt 6:10. Ro 5:19. **if.** ✍184A, 1 C +15:2.

43. **for.** Pr 23:34. Jon 1:6. Lk 9:32. Ac 20:9. Ro 13:1. 1 Th 5:6-8.

44. **prayed.** Mt ◑+*6:7. Da 9:17-19. Lk *18:1.

2 C √12:8. **third time.** 1 S +*23:4. **saying the same.** ver. 39, 42.

45. **Sleep on.** That is, as it is well paraphrased by Euthymius, "Since you have thus far failed to watch, sleep on the rest of the time, and take your rest, *if you can.*" 1 K 18:27. Ec 11:9. **the hour.** ver. 2, 14, 15, 18. Mk 14:41, 42. Lk 22:53. Jn 12:23, 27. 13:1. 17:1. **Son of man.** Mt 8:20. **is betrayed.** ✍96C7, ver. +24. Mt 17:22. 20:18. Mk 9:31. 10:33. Lk 9:44. 18:32.

46. **let us be going.** 1 S 17:48. Lk 9:51. 12:50. 22:15. Jn 14:31. Ac 21:13.

47. **lo.** ver. 14, 55. Mk 14:43. Lk 22:47, 48. Jn *18:1-8. Ac *1:16.

48. **Whomsoever.** 2 S 3:27. 20:9, 10. Ps 28:3. 55:20, 21. **hold.** Mk 14:44.

49. **Hail.** Mt 27:29, 30. Mk 15:18. Jn 19:3. **master.** ver. 25. Jn 1:38. **kissed him.** *Katephilasen,* he kissed him affectionately, eagerly, or repeatedly, from *kata, intensive,* and *phileo,* to kiss, still pretending the most affectionate attachment to our Lord. Ge 27:26. 1 S 10:1. 2 S 20:9. Pr 27:6. Mk 14:45, 46. Lk 7:38, 45. 15:20. Ac 20:37. 1 Th 5:26.

50. **Friend.** ✍57. Diasyrmos; or, Raillery B937. An expression of feeling by way of tearing away disguise. For another instance of this figure see Jn 7:4. Rather, "*Companion* (*etaire*), against whom (*eph'o,* the reading of all the best MSS.) art thou come?" Mt +*20:13n. 22:12. 2 S 16:17. Ps 41:9. *55:12-14. Lk 22:48. Jn 13:27. **his ear.** Lk 22:50.

51. **one of them.** ver. 35. Mk 14:47. Lk 9:55. 22:36-38, 49-51. Jn 18:10, 11, 36. 2 C 10:4. **his sword.** Lk +*22:36, 38.

52. **Put up.** T#736. Mt 5:39. Ge 49:5-7. Ex *20:13. Le *19:18. Nu +32:23 (T#733). Jb +27:13 (T#490). Ps *5:6. +58:11 (T#630). Pr 17:14. 18:6. *20:22. +21:7 (T#489). *24:29. 26:17. 30:33. Ezk +22:29 (T#488). 25:12-14. *35:5, 6. Ho 4:2, 3. Am *1:11. Hab 2:12. Lk *3:14. 18:20. ◑+√22:36. Jn +18:11. Ro *12:17, 19. 1 C 4:11, 12. 2 C *10:4. 1 Th *5:14, 15. Ja 2:11. 3:16. *4:1, 12. 1 P *2:21-23. 3:9. Re 13:10. **they.** Mt *23:34-36. Ge *9:6. 1 S 15:33. Ps 55:23. Ezk 35:5, 6. Re 11:18. 13:10. 16:6. **take the sword.** ✍108H5. Idiom B842. "To take the sword" is used for rashly usurping magisterial power instead of giving obedience and subjection to God. **perish.** Gr. *apollumi,* Mt +2:13.

53. **Thinkest thou. I cannot.** Jn 10:18. **I cannot.** Mt +*11:23n. **my Father.** Jn 5:17. **and he.** Mt *4:11. 25:31. 2 K √6:17. Ps +*68:17. Da *7:10. Jl *2:11. Lk 22:43. Jn 18:36. 2 Th 1:7. Ju 14. **twelve.** Mt 10:1, 2. **legions.** A "legion," *legeon,* from the Latin *legio,* from *lego,* to collect, or choose, was a particular division or battalion of the Roman army, which at different times contained different numbers. In the time of our Savior it probably consisted of 6200 foot and 300 horse, twelve of which would amount to 78,000 men. Mk 5:9, 15. Lk 8:30.

54. **But how then.** ver. 24. Mt 1:22. Ps ch. 22, 69. Is ch. 53. Da +*9:24-26. Zc 13:7. Lk 24:25, 26, 44-46. Jn +*10:35. Ac 1:16. **the scriptures.** ver. 56. Mt 21:42. **that thus.** ver. 31, 56. Ps 88:8, 18. Is 53:7-10. Lk 13:33. Jn *18:11.

55. **Are ye come.** Mk 14:48-50. Lk *22:52, 53. **a thief.** Mt 21:13. Mk 11:17. Lk 10:30. 19:46. Jn 18:40. **I sat.** Mk 12:35. Lk 2:46. 4:20. 21:37, 38. Jn 8:2. 18:20, 21. **with you.** Ac 26:26. 2 P 1:16. **teaching.** Mt 4:23. 9:35. 13:54. 21:23. Mk 1:21. 11:17. 12:35. Lk 19:47. 20:1. 21:37. Jn 7:14, 28. 8:20. 10:23. 18:20.

56. **that**. ver. 54. Mt 1:22. Ge +*3:15. Is 44:26. La 4:20. Da +*9:24, 26. Zc ♣13:7. Jn 6:45. Ac 1:16. 2:23. **Then**. ver. 31. Ps 88:8, 18. Is 63:3. Mk 14:50-52. Jn 16:32. *18:8, 9, 15, 16. 2 T 4:16.

57. **they that**. Ps 56:5, 6. Mk 14:53, 54. Lk 22:54, 55. Jn 11:49. *18:12-14, 24. **away to**. Ac 16:40. **Caiaphas**. ver. +*3.

58. **afar off**. Pr 29:25. **palace**. ver. 3, 57. **and went**. Jn 18:15, 16, 25. **and sat**. Ps +*1:1. **the servants**. Mt 5:25. Mk 14:54, 65. Jn 7:32, 45, 46. 18:3, 12, 22. 19:6. Ac 5:22, 26.

59. **all**. ♪171L2. Synecdoche of the Whole B636. The *whole* is put for every part of it with "every" and "all." Here, "all" denotes "the whole council." For other instances of this figure see Mk 1:33. 14:55. Ac 2:47. 7:10. 15:22. Ph 1:13. **council**. Mt 5:22. **sought**. Dt 19:16-21. 1 K 21:8-13. Ps *27:12. *35:11, 12. 94:20, 21. Pr 25:18. Mk *14:55, 56. Ac 6:11-13. 24:1-13.

60. **found none**. Da 6:4, 5. T 2:8. 1 P 3:16. **At**. Dt 19:15. Mk 14:57-59. **though many**. Ps 27:12. 35:11. **found they none**. He *7:26. 1 P *2:22. **came two**. Mt 18:16. Dt *17:6. 19:15.

61. **This**. ver. 71. Mt 12:24. Ge 19:9. 1 K 22:27. 2 K 9:11. Ps 22:6, 7. Is 49:7. 53:3. Lk 23:2. Jn 9:29. Ac 6:14. 17:18. 18:13. 22:22. **I am**. The words of our Lord were widely different from this statement of them; so that the testimony of these witnesses was *false*, though it had the semblance of truth. Mt 27:40. Je 26:8-11, 16-19. Mk 15:29. Jn +*2:19-21. Ac 6:13. **destroy**. Mt 27:40. **the temple**. Mt 23:16, 35. 27:5. **three days**. Mt 16:21. ◐27:63. Mk *14:58, 59. Jn +*2:19.

62. **Answerest**. Mt 27:12-14. Mk 14:60. Lk 23:9. Jn 18:19-24. 19:9-11.

63. **Jesus**. Mt 27:12, 14. Ps 38:12-14. Is *53:7. Da 3:16. Mk 14:61. 15:3-5. Lk 23:9. Jn 19:9. Ac 8:32-35. 1 P 2:23. **I adjure**. Le 5:1. *19:12. Nu 5:19-21. 1 S 3:17, 18. 14:24, 26, 28. 1 K *22:16. 2 Ch 18:15. Pr 29:24. Mk 5:7. **living God**. Mt 16:16. **that**. Mk 14:61. Lk 22:66-71. Jn 8:25. 10:24. 18:37. **the Christ**. Mt 1:17. 16:16. 22:42-45. 27:40, 43, 54. Ps *2:6, 7. Is +*9:6, 7. Jn 1:34, 49. √3:16-18. √5:18-25. 6:69. 10:30, 36. 19:7. √20:31. 1 J √5:11-13. **the Son of God**. Mt 14:33. 27:54n.

64. **Thou**. ♪108H13, ver. +25. ver. 25. Mt *27:11n. Mk 14:62. Lk 22:70. Jn 18:37. **Hereafter**. Mt +*16:27n. +*24:30. +*25:31. Da +*7:13. Lk *21:27. 25:31. Jn 1:50, 51. Ac +*1:11. Ro 14:10. 1 Th *4:16. Re +*1:7. 20:11. **see**. Mt +*16:27n. +*24:3n, 30. Ac +*1:11. Re +*1:7. **Son of man**. Mt 8:20. +*16:27n. Da ⏏7:13, 14. **sitting**. Ps *110:1. Mk 16:19. He *1:3. **the right hand**. ♪22A15C, Ps +110:1. Ps *110:1. Lk *22:69. Ac 7:55, 56. He *1:3. *12:2. **coming**. Mt +*24:30. Jn 14:3. 1 Th ◐4:16. Re √1:7. **clouds**. Ge +9:13. 2 Ch +5:13.

65. **the high priest**. Le 21:10. 2 K 18:37. 19:1-3. Je 36:24. Mk 14:63, 64. **rent his clothes**. i.e. great robe of office. ♪96F2, Ge +4:10. Ge 37:29. Le *10:6. *21:10. Nu 14:6. 2 S 1:11. 3:31. Jb 1:20. Ac 14:14. He. Mk 9:3. 1 K 21:10-13. Lk 5:21. Mk 2:7. Lk 5:21. **blasphemy**. Le *24:16. Jn √10:33, 36. *19:7.

66. **He**. Le 24:11-16. 1 K 21:10, 13. Jn 10:33. 19:7. Ac 7:52. 13:27, 28. Ja 5:6. **guilty**. or, worthy, or liable to. Mk 3:29g.

67. **did**. Mt 27:30. Nu 12:14. Dt 25:9. Jb 30:9-11. Is 50:6. 52:14. 53:3. Mk 10:34. 14:65. 15:19. 1 C 4:13. He *12:2. **buffeted him**. *ekolaphisan,* "smote him with

their fists," as Theophylact interprets. **and others**. Mt 5:39. 1 K 22:24. Je 20:2. La 3:30, 45. Lk 22:63. Jn 18:22. *19:3. Ac 23:2, 3. 2 C 11:20, 21. **smote him**. *Errapisan,* "smote him on the cheek with the open hand," as Suidas renders. They offered him every indignity, in all its various and vexatious forms. Mt 5:39. 27:29, 30. Jb 16:10. Ps 69:20. Is *50:6. Lk *22:64. Ac *23:2, 3. He 5:7, 8. **the palms of their hands**. *or,* rods. Mi 5:1.

68. **Prophesy**. Mt 27:39-44. Ge 37:19, 20. Jg 16:25. Mk 14:65. Lk 7:39. 22:63-65. **thou**. Mt 27:28, 29. Mk 15:18, 19. Jn 19:2, 3, 14, 15. 1 P 2:4-8. **Christ**. ver. 63. **Who is**. Lk 7:39.

69. **Peter**. ver. 58. 1 K 19:9, 13. Ps +*1:1. Mk *14:66-68. Lk *22:55-57. Jn *18:16, 17, 25. 2 P 2:7-9. **and a**. ♪108E1, Mt +8:19. **Jesus**. ver. 71. Mt 2:22, 23. 21:11. Jn 1:46. 7:41, 52. Ac 5:37.

70. **he denied**. ver. 34, 35, 40-43, 51, 56, 58. Ps 119:115-117. Pr 28:26. 29:23, 25. Is 57:11. Je +*17:9. Ro 11:20. 1 C 10:12. Re +*21:8.

71. **when**. Mk 14:68, 69. Lk 22:58. Jn 18:25-27. **the porch**. Lk 16:20. Ac 10:17. 12:13, 14. 14:13. Re 21:12, 13, 15, 21, 25. 22:14. **This**. ver. 61. **with Jesus**. Ac 4:13. **of Nazareth**. Mk 1:24.

72. **with**. Mt 5:34-36. Ex 20:7. Is 48:1. Zc +*5:3, 4. 8:17. Ml +*3:5. Ac +*5:3, 4. **I do not**. ver. 74. Lk 22:34.

73. **they that stood by**. Lk 22:59. Jn 18:26. **Surely**. Lk 22:59, 60. Jn 18:26, 27. **for**. Jg *12:6n. 2 K 8:21n. Ne 13:24. Mk *14:70. Ac 2:6, 7. **speech**. Jn 4:42g. 8:43g.

74. **began**. Mt 27:25. Jg 17:2. 21:18. 1 S 14:24-28. Mk 14:71. Ac 23:12-14. Ro 9:3. 1 C 16:22. **saying**. Mt +*10:28, 32, 33. Jn √21:15-17. Re *3:19. **And**. Mk 14:30, 68, 72. Lk 22:60. Jn 18:27.

75. **remembered**. ver. 34. Lk 22:61, 62. Jn 13:38. **deny**. Mt 10:28. Pr 29:25. Ac 3:13, 14. **And he**. Mt 27:3-5. Lk 22:31-34. Ro 7:18-20. 1 C 4:7. Ga 6:1. 1 P 1:5. **wept bitterly**. Ps *51:17. Is 22:4. Je 9:1. Mi 1:8. Jn 21:17. 2 C √7:9, 10.

MATTHEW 27

Jesus is delivered bound to Pilate, 1, 2. Judas, in remorse, restores the silver, and hangs himself, 3-5. The priests fulfill the scripture, in disposing of the money, 6-10. Christ is silent before Pilate, 11-14, who proposes to release him, according to the custom of the feast, 15-18. Pilate's wife, alarmed by a dream, warns him to desist, 19. He washes his hands, to clear himself; and, being urged by the people, with imprecations on themselves and their children, he releases Barabbas, and delivers Jesus to be crucified, 20-26. He is mocked, and crowned with thorns by the soldiers, 27-31; crucified between two thieves, 32-38; and reviled by the people and rulers, 39-44. The land is darkened, 45; Jesus calling on God expires, 46-50. The veil of the temple is rent, the earth quakes, the tombs burst open, and the centurion confesses him, as "the Son of God," 51-54. Certain women witness these scenes, 55, 56. Joseph of Arimathea asks his body and buries it, 57-61. His tomb is sealed by the chief priests, and a watch placed at it, 62-66.

1. **the morning**. Jg 16:2. 1 S 19:11. Pr +*4:16-18. Mi 2:1. Lk 22:66. Ac 5:21. **all**. Mt 23:13. 26:3, 4. Ps *2:2. Mk 15:1. Lk 23:1, 2. Jn 18:28. Ac 4:24-28. **took**

counsel. Mt 12:14. 22:15. 28:12. Ge=37:18. Jn 11:53.

2. **bound.** Ge 22:9. =39:20. Jn 18:12, 24. Ac 9:2. 12:6. 21:33. 22:25, 29. 24:27. 28:20. 2 T 2:9. He 13:3. **they led.** Lk *23:1. Jn *18:28. **delivered.** Mt 20:19. Lk 18:32, 33. 20:20. Ac 3:13. **Pontius Pilate.** Pilate. i.e. *close pressed*, ✳S#4091g. Mt 27:2, 13, 17, 22, 24, 58, 58, 62, 65. Mk 15:1, 2, 4, 5, 9, 12, 14, 15, 43, 44. Lk 3:1. 13:1. 23:1, 3, 4, 6, 11, 12, 13, 20, 24, 52. Jn 18:29, 31, 33, 35, 37, 38. 19:1, 4, 6, 8, 10, 12, 13, 15, 19, 21, 22, 31, 38, 38. Ac 3:13. 4:27. 13:28. 1 T 6:13. *Pontius Pilate* governed Judea ten years under the emperor Tiberias, from his 13th to his 23rd year, A.D. 26 to 36; (Josephus, Ant. l. i. c. 5) but, having exercised great cruelties against the Samaritans, they complained to Vitellius, governor of Syria, who sent Marcellus, one of his friends, to superintend Judea, and ordered Pilate to Rome, to give an account of his conduct to Tiberius (Ant. l. xviii. c. 5). The emperor was dead before he arrived; but it is an ancient tradition that he was banished to Vienne in Dauphiny, where he was reduced to such extremity that he killed himself with his own sword two years after (Eusebius, l. ii. c. 7. Oros. l. vii. c. 5. Ado, Chron. Aetat. 7). Lk 3:1. 13:1. Ac 3:13. 4:27. 1 T 6:13. **the governor.** ver. 11, 14, 15, 21, 27. Ac 23:24.

3. **Judas.** Mt 26:14-16, 47-50. Mk 14:10, 11, 43-46. Lk 22:2-6, 47, 48. Jn 13:2, 27. 18:3. **repented.** Mt 21:29. Jb 20:5, 15-29. 2 C √7:10. **thirty pieces.** Mt 26:15.

4. **I have sinned.** Ge 42:21, 22. Ex 9:27. *10:16, 17. 12:31. Nu +22:34. 1 S 15:24, 30. 1 K 21:27. Jb *20:5. Ro 3:19. **the innocent.** ver. 19, 23, 24, 54. 2 K 24:4. Je 26:15. Jon 1:14. Lk 23:22, 41, 47. Jn 19:7. Ac 13:28. He 7:26. 1 P 1:19. **blood.** √171Q10, Ps +94:21. **What.** ver. 25. Ac 18:15-17. 1 T 4:2. T 1:16. 1 J 3:12. Re 11:10. **see.** ver. 24. 1 S 28:16-20. Jb 13:4. 16:2. Lk 16:25, 26. Ac 18:15.

5. **cast down.** Pr +12:25. **the temple.** ver. 40, 51. Lk 1:9. **and departed.** Jg 9:54. 1 S 31:4, 5. 2 S +*17:23. 1 K 16:18. Jb 2:9. 7:15. Ps 55:23. Ac *1:18, 19.

6. **It is not.** Mt *23:24. Lk 6:7-9. Jn 18:28. **to put.** Dt 23:18. Is 61:8. **the treasury.** Mk 7:11. 12:41, 43. Lk 21:1. Jn 8:20. **because.** The Jews considered it was strictly forbidden by the Divine law to bring any filthy or iniquitous gain into the temple. For this reason they now refused to allow this money to be placed in the chest of the temple, amongst the former contributions for its repairs. In this they were right enough, but by the very act of refusing this money, they proved themselves to be gross perverters of *the spirit* of God's requirements: they saw not that it was much less lawful for them, who had hired Judas to this sordid action, to be employed in the service of the temple. Those that "bear the vessels of the Lord," ought to be holy. Thus our Lord's words, "Ye blind guides! ye strain at a gnat, and swallow a camel."

7. **potter's.** Zc ✳11:13.

8. **that.** Ac 1:19. **unto.** Mt 28:15. Dt 34:6. Jsh +4:9. Jg 1:26. 2 Ch 5:9.

9. **fulfilled.** Mt 1:22. Lk +24:27. **spoken.** √106, Ge +31:7. **by.** Mt 24:15. **Jeremy.** The words here quoted are not found in *Jeremiah*, but in *Zechariah*; and a variety of conjectures have been formed, in order to reconcile the discrepancy. The most probable opinion seems to be, that the *name* of the prophet was originally omitted by the Evangelist, and that the name of *Jere-*

miah was added by some subsequent copyist. It is *omitted* in two MSS. of the twelfth century, in the Syriac, later Persic, two of the Itala, and in some other Latin copies; and what renders it highly probable that the original reading was *dia tou prophatou, by the prophet*, is, that St. Matthew frequently omits the name of the prophet in his quotations. See Mt 1:22. 2:5, 15. 13:35. 21:4. This omission is approved of by Bengel, Dr. A. Clarke, and Horne. Nevertheless, the reading "Jeremy" is firmly established, being supported by numerous significant early manuscript witnesses, as well as later ones, and must be accepted as the correct reading (see a modern listing and brief discussion of this evidence in Bruce M. Metzger, *A Textual Commentary on the Greek New Testament*, p. 66). It is possible, as noted in the *Companion Bible* margin, and its Appendix 161, to understand that this prophecy was *spoken* by Jeremiah, not written, and to take the apparent citation of Zc 11:12, 13, as a parenthetical statement within words otherwise attributed to Jeremiah. More likely, this is a composite quotation from Zc 11:13, Je 18:18, and 32:6, etc., and the prophecy is referred to Jeremiah as the more prominent of the two. In Mark 1:2, etc., the composite quotation from Isaiah and Malachi is similarly referred to Isaiah (see A.T. Robertson, *Word Pictures*, vol. 1, p. 224). For other instances of composite quotations see (1) Mt 21:5. Is 62:11 w Zc 9:9. (2) Mt 21:13. Is 56:7 w Je 7:11; (3) Mk 1:2, 3. Ml 3:1 w Is 40:3. (4) Lk 3:4, 5. Ml 3:1 w Is 40:3. (5) Lk 4:18. Is 61:1, 2 w Is 58:6. (6) Ac 1:20. Ps 69:25 w 109:8. (7) Ro 3:10-12. Ec 7:20 w Ps 14:2, 3 w 53:2, 3. (8) Ro 3:13-18. Ps 5:9 w Is 59:7, 8 w Ps 36:1. (9) Ro 9:33. Is 28:16 w 8:14. (10) Ro 11:26, 27. Is 59:20, 21 w 27:9. (11) 1 C 15:54-56. Is 25:8 w Ho 13:14. (12) 2 C 6:16. Le 26:11, 12 w Ezk 37:27. (13) Ga 3:8. Ge 12:3 w 18:18. (14) 1 P 2:7, 8. Ps 118:22 w Is 8:14. **And they.** √92C, Mt +2:15. Je 32:6-9. Zc ▶11:12, 13. **thirty.** Mt 26:15. Ex 21:32. Le 27:2-7. **pieces of silver.** Ge=37:28. Zc ▶11:13. **of the children of Israel did value.** *or*, bought of the children of Israel.

10. **the potter's field.** Je 18:2.

11. **Jesus stood.** Mt 10:18, 25. Mk 15:2. Lk 23:3. Jn 18:33-36. **governor.** ver. 2. **King of the Jews.** ver. 29, 37, 42. Mt 2:2. Mk 15:2, 9, 12, 18, 26, 32. Lk 23:3, 37, 38. Jn *18:33, 39. 19:3, 14, 15, 19, 21. **Thou sayest.** √108H13, Mt +26:25. By his answer, A.T. Robertson suggests (*Word Pictures*, vol. 1, p. 225), Jesus confesses that he is the king of the Jews. The *Companion Bible* margin identifies this as a Hebraism. But Nigel Turner states that the presence of the pronoun in Greek makes the statement emphatic: *You* have said. Jesus is non-committal, and in essence is suggesting, "Are you putting these words in my mouth? Are you making the claim for me that I am the Messiah? Jesus did not publicly announce his Messiahship before the crucifixion to his enemies. His answer means, "You are saying this, not me." This form of expression is found at Mt 26:25, 64. 27:11. Mk 15:2. Lk 23:3. There is some manuscript evidence that supports this construction as being the correct reading at Mk 14:62 also (see Nigel Turner's discussion in his *Grammatical Insights*, pp. 72-75). Mt *26:25, 64. Mk 14:62. Lk 22:70. Jn 18:37. 1 T 6:13.

12. **answered nothing.** ver. 14. Mt +26:63. 2 K 18:36. Ps 38:13, 14. 39:1. Ec 3:7. Is ✳53:7. Mk 15:3-

5. Jn 19:9-11. Ac 8:32. 1 P 2:23.

13. **Hearest.** Mt 26:62. Jn 18:35. *19:10. Ac 22:24.

14. **never a word.** Is ✷53:7. **marvelled.** Ps 71:7. Is 8:18. Zc 3:8. 1 C 4:9.

15. **feast.** Mt 26:5. Mk 15:6, 8. Lk *23:16, 17. Jn *18:38, 39. Ac 24:27. 25:9.

16. **a notable.** Mk *15:7. Lk *23:18, 19, 25. Jn 18:40. Ac 3:14. Ro 1:32. 16:7g. **Barabbas.** i.e. *son of his father*, ✷S#912g. Mt 27:16, 17, 20, 21, 26. Mk 15:7, 11, 15. Lk 23:18. Jn *18:40.

17. **Whom.** ver. 21. Jsh √24:15. 1 K 18:21. **or Jesus.** ver. 22. Mt 1:1. Mk 15:9-12. Jn 19:15.

18. **he.** Ge 37:11. 1 S 18:7-11. Ps 106:16. Pr 27:4. Ec 4:4. Is 26:11. Mk 15:10. Ac 5:17. *7:9. 13:45. Ja 4:5. **envy.** Or, "malice," *phthonos*, probably from *phthino*, to decay, wither, pine away, according to that of Solomon, Pr 14:3. Ge=37:11. Jn *11:47, 48. 12:19. 1 J *3:12.

19. **judgment seat.** Jn 19:13. Ac 12:21. 18:12, 16, 17. 25:6, 10, 17. **his wife.** Ge 20:3-6. 31:24, 29. Jb 33:14-17. Pr *29:1. **Have.** ſ65. Enthymema; or, Omission of Premise B168. The conclusion is stated and one or both of the premises omitted. Here the fire, and feeling, and urgency of Pilate's wife is all the more forcible, in that she does not stop to formulate a tame, cold argument, but she omits the major premise; which is greatly emphasized by being left for Pilate to supply. The complete Syllogism would have been: (1) It is very wicked to punish a just or innocent man. (2) Jesus is a just man. (3) Have therefore nothing to do with punishing him. The conclusion thus contains the proof of each of the premises on which it rests. Thus is emphasized one of the four testimonies borne to the innocence of the Lord Jesus by Gentiles at the time of His condemnation: (1) Pilate's wife, Mt 27:19. (2) Pilate himself, Mt 27:24. (3) The dying malefactor, Lk 23:41. (4) The Centurion, Lk 23:47. For other unmarked instances of this figure see Lk *5:21n. Ro 4:1, 2. 6:17. 7:6. 8:1. 1 C 11:6. 15:19. Ga 3:18, 21. 2 Th ◐3:10n. He 12:8. 1 J 5:1. **nothing to do.** Jg +11:12. 2 Ch *35:21. Jn +2:4. **that just.** ver. 4, 24. Is 53:11. Zc +*9:9. Lk 23:41, 47. 1 P 2:22. 1 J *2:1. **in a dream.** Mt 2:12. Jb *33:14-16.

20. **persuaded.** Mk 15:11. Ac 14:18, 19. 19:23-29. **should.** Lk 23:18-20. Jn 18:40. 19:15, 16. Ac 3:14, 15. **destroy.** Gr. *apollumi*, Mt 2:13.

21. **release unto.** Lk 23:18. Jn 18:40. Ac *3:14.

22. **What.** ver. 17. Jb 31:31. Ps 22:8, 9. Is 49:7. 53:2, 3. Zc 11:8. Mk 14:55. 15:12-14. Lk 23:20-24. Jn 19:14, 15. Ac 13:28.

23. **Why.** Ge 37:18, 19. 1 S 19:3-15. 20:31-33. 22:14-19. **what evil.** Lk 23:41. Jn *8:46. **But.** Mt 21:38, 39. Ac 7:57. 17:5-7. 21:28-31. 22:22, 23. 23:10, 12-15.

24. **a tumult.** Mt 26:5. **and washed.** Gr. *aponipto*, ✷S#633g, only here. Ex 30:19-21. Dt *21:6, 7. Jb 9:30, 31. Ps 26:6. 73:13. Je 2:27, 35. **innocent of.** Ge=37:22. Ac 20:26. **just.** ver. 4, 9, 19, 54. Lk 23:4. Jn 19:4. Ac 3:14. 2 C *5:21. 1 P *2:22. *3:18. 1 J *2:1. **blood.** ſ171I11, Dt +19:12. **see ye.** ver. 4.

25. **His blood.** Mt 21:44. 23:30-37. *24:21. Ge 4:10. =42:22. Nu *35:33. Dt 19:10, 13. ◐*21:8. Jsh 2:19. 2 S 1:16. 3:28, 29. 1 K 2:32. 2 K 24:3, 4. Ps 109:12-19. Is *59:3, 4. Je 2:34. Ezk 22:2-4. 24:7-9. Mi *3:12. Lk 11:50. Ac *5:28. 7:52. 18:6. 1 Th *2:15, 16. He 10:28-30. **on us.** ſ171Q12, Jg +5:30. **on our children.**

Ex +*20:5. Dt 5:9. La *5:7. Ezk 18:4n, 14, etc., 20n. Ac ◐+*2:39.

26. **released.** Mk 15:15. Lk 23:25. **scourged.** This of itself was a severe punishment, the flesh being generally *cut* by the whips used for this purpose. Mt 20:19. Is ✷50:6. 53:5. Mk 10:34. Lk 18:32, 33. *23:16, 24, 25. Jn 19:1, 16. 1 P 2:24.

27. **common hall.** or, governor's house. Mk *15:16. Jn 18:28, 33. 19:8, 9. Ac 23:35g. Ph *1:13. **band.** Jn 18:3. Ac 10:1. 21:31. 27:1.

28. **stripped.** Ge=37:23. Mk *15:17. Lk 23:11. Jn 19:2-5. **a scarlet robe.** St. Mark calls it a "purple robe;" but by *porphura* is denoted whatever is of a dazzling red; and the words *kokkikon*, "scarlet," and *porphura*, "purple," are not unfrequently interchanged. Lk 23:11. Re 17:4. 18:12, 16.

29. **platted.** Mt 20:19. Ps 35:15, 16. 69:7, 19, 20. Is 49:7. 53:3. Je 20:7. He 12:2, 3. **bowed the knee.** Mk 1:40. **mocked him.** ver. 31, 41. Mt 20:19. Lk 22:63. **Hail.** ſ60D, Ge +37:19. ver. 37. Mt 26:49. Mk 15:18. Lk 23:36, 37. Jn 19:3. **King.** ver. 11.

30. **they spit.** Mt 26:67. Jb 30:8-10. Is 49:7. ✷50:6. 52:14. 53:3, 7. Mi 5:1. Mk 14:65. 15:19. Lk 18:32, 33. **smote.** Mi ✷5:1.

31. **had mocked.** ver. 29. **and led.** Mt 20:19. 21:39. Nu 15:35. 1 K 21:10, 13. Is 53:7. Jn 19:16, 27. Ac 7:58. He *13:11, 12.

32. **as.** Mt 21:39. Le 4:3, 12, 21. Nu 15:35, 36. 1 K 21:10, 13. Ac 7:58. He 13:11, 12. **they found.** Mt 16:24. Mk 15:21. Lk 23:26. **Cyrene.** Ac 2:10. 6:9. 11:20. 13:1. **compelled.** Mt 5:41.

33. **Golgotha.** i.e. *place of a skull*, ✷S#1115g. Mk 15:22g. Lk 23:27-33. Jn *19:17g.

34. **gave.** ver. 48. Ps *69:21. Mk *15:23. Jn 19:28-30. **vinegar.** St. Mark says, "wine mingled with myrrh;" but as the *sour wine* used by the Roman soldiers and common people was termed *oinos*, "wine," and *oxos*, "vinegar" (*vin aigre*, French), is *sour wine*; and as *xola*, *gall*, is applied to bitters of any kind, it is not difficult to reconcile the two accounts. Ps ✷❭69:21. **with gall.** Ps *69:21. Je 23:15. Mk 15:23. Lk 23:36. Ac 8:23.

35. **they crucified.** Ps 22:16. Jn 20:20, 25, 27. Ac 4:10. Ga *3:13. Ph *2:8. Col *1:20. 1 P *2:24. **parted.** ſ92A, Mt +1:23. Ps ✷❭22:18. Mk 15:24, etc. Lk 23:34. Jn *19:23, 24. **that it.** Ps 22:18.

36. **sitting down.** ver. 54. Ge=37:25. Mk 15:39, 44. **they watched.** ver. 54. Ps *22:17.

37. **his accusation.** Mk 15:26. Lk *23:38. Jn *19:19-22. Ac 25:18, 27. **king.** Ps *2:6. Is +*9:7. 32:1. Je *23:5. Ezk *37:24. Zc *9:9.

38. **two thieves.** ver. 44. Is *53:12. Mk *15:27, 28. Lk *22:37. 23:32, 33, 39-43. Jn 18:40. *19:18, 31-35. **one on.** Mt 20:21. Mk 10:37.

39. **reviled.** Ps *22:6, ❭7, 17. *31:11-13. *35:15-21. *69:7-12, 20. 109:2, 25. La *1:12. 2:15-17. Mk *15:29, 30. Lk 22:65. *23:35-39. Ja 2:7g. 1 P *2:22-24. **wagging.** 2 K 19:21. Jb 16:4. Ps *109:25. Is 37:22. Je 18:16. La 2:15.

40. **saying.** Ge 37:19, 20. Re 11:10. **that destroyest.** Mt *26:61. Lk 14:29, 30. Jn +*2:19-22. **temple.** ver. 5, 51. Lk 1:9. **If.** ſ184A, 1 C 15:2. ſ60D, Ge +37:19. ver. 43, *54. Mt *4:3, 6. 14:33. *26:63, 64. **come.** Mt *16:4. Mk *16:31.

41. **mocking.** Jb 13:9. Ps ✷22:7, 8, 12, 13. 35:16. Is 28:22. *49:7. Zc 11:8. Mk *15:31, 32. Lk 4:23. *18:32. 22:52. *23:35, 39.

42. **saved others.** *f*60D, Ge +37:19. Mk *5:41. Lk 7:14. Jn *9:24. 11:43, 47. Ac *4:14. **himself he cannot.** Mt √26:53, 54. Jn √10:18. **If.** *f*184A, 1 C +15:2. **the King.** ver. *37. Mt *2:2. Lk *19:38. *23:35, 37. Jn *1:49. 12:13. **let him.** Mt 12:38. Lk 11:16. **we will believe.** Jn 4:48.

43. **trusted.** *f*60D, Ge +37:19. Ps *3:2. 14:6. *)22:8. 37:5. 42:10. 71:11. Pr 16:3. Is 36:15, 18. 37:10. **deliver him.** Ps 91:14. **if he will have him.** Or, "if he delight in him." *f*184A, 1 C +15:2. Ps)18:19. 41:11. **I am.** ver. 40. Jn √3:16, 17. √5:17-25. +*10:30, 36. *19:7. **Son of God.** Ex 4:22. Ps 89:26, 27. 2 S 7:14. 1 Ch 22:10. Lk 3:38. Jn *1:12, 13. Ro 8:14, 17. Ph 2:14, 15.

44. **thieves.** ver. 38. Jb 30:7-9. Ps 35:15. Mk *15:32. Lk *23:39-43.

45. **from.** Mk 15:25, 33, 34. Lk 23:44, 45. Jn 19:14. **sixth hour.** Our 12 noon. Mt +20:5. Jn +*11:9n. **darkness.** That this general darkness was wholly preternatural is evident from this, that it happened at the *passover*, which was celebrated only at the *full moon*, a time in which it was impossible for the sun to be eclipsed, natural eclipses happening only at the time of the new moon. Pr +*20:20. Is 50:3. Am 8:9. Re 8:12. 9:2. **ninth hour.** Our 3 p.m. Mt +20:5. 1 K 18:29. Jn +*11:9n. Ac 3:1.

46. **ninth hour.** Our 3 p.m. ver. +45. **Jesus.** Mk 15:34. Lk 23:46. Jn 19:28-30. He *5:7. **cried.** T#1185. Lk 23:33, 34, 42, 46. **Eli.** i.e. *my God,* *S#2241g, only here. Ps)22:1. 71:11. Is 53:10. La 1:12. **Eli.** *f*84, Ge +22:11. **sabachthani.** i.e. *hast thou forsaken me?* *S#4518g. Mt 27:46. Mk 15:34. **My.** *f*59, Ge +28:16. **why hast.** 2 C 13:4. **forsaken.** Ps *)22:1. Hab √1:13. 2 C 5:21.

47. **This.** Mt 11:14. Ml 4:5. Mk 15:35, 36.

48. **and filled.** ver. 34. Ps 69:21. Lk 23:36. Jn *19:29, 30. **vinegar.** Ru 2:14.

49. **let us.** ver. 43.

50. **when.** Mk 15:37. Lk *23:46. Jn *19:30. **yielded.** Mt +*20:28. Ge +*25:8, 17. 35:29. 49:33. Jb 3:11. 10:18. 11:20. 13:19. 14:10. Ps 22:14, 15. 31:5. Is *53:9-12. Je 15:9. La 1:19. Da 9:26. Lk ◐8:55n. Jn 10:11, 15, √18. Ac 5:5, 10. 7:59. 12:23. Ro 6:8-11. He 2:14. 9:14. **ghost.** or, spirit. Gr. *pneuma*, *f*121A3, Metonymy of the Cause. The "spirit" put for: (1) "spirit" as the principle of life, of which death is described as (a) giving or commending to God of the "spirit": Mt 27:50. Mk 15:39. Lk 23:46. Jn 19:30. Ac 7:59. (b) of departed persons as Ac 23:8. He 12:9, 23. (2) the distinctive, self-conscious inner life of man, as in 1 C √2:11. Lk 1:80. 2:40. 1 C √2:11. 5:3, 5. 6:20. 7:34. 1 Th 5:23. He 4:12. Ja 4:5. (3) "life" in the physiological sense, but drawing rather to the meaning of "soul" (John Laidlaw, *The Biblical Doctrine of Man*, p. 132) as in Lk 8:55. Ja 2:26. Re 11:11. 13:15. For other examples of the use of this figure of speech see *f*121A3, Nu +11:17. For the other uses of *pneuma*, see Mt +*8:16n.

51. **the veil.** Ex *26:31-37. 40:21. Le 16:2, 12-15. 21:23. 2 Ch 3:14. Is 25:7. Mk *15:38. Lk *23:45. Ep *2:13-18. He *6:19, 20. *9:7, 8. *10:19-22. **temple.** ver. 5, 40. Lk 1:9. **the earth did quake.** ver. 54. Mt 28:2. Ex 19:18. Jg 5:4. 2 S 22:8. Ps 18:7, 15. 77:18. Is 29:6. Je *10:10. Mi 1:3, 4. Na 1:3-5. Hab 3:10, 13. He 12:25-27. Re 11:13, 19.

52. **And.** *f*107, Ge +10:5. **graves.** Mt +8:28 (*S#3419g). **many.** Is 25:8. +*26:19n. Ho +*13:14.

Jn *5:25-29. 1 C 15:20. **bodies.** Mt 28:6. Da +*12:2n. Jn +*2:19, 21, 22. **the saints.** Da 7:18, 22. Ac 9:32. **which slept.** Da +*12:2n. Jn 11:11-13. Ac 7:60. 13:36. 1 C 7:39. 11:30. 15:6, 18, 20, 51. 1 Th 4:13-15. 5:10. 2 P 3:4. **arose.** Mt 28:6.

53. **graves.** Mt +8:28 (*S#3419g). **after his.** Ac *26:23. 1 C *15:20. **holy.** Mt 4:5. Ne 11:1. Is 48:2. Da +*9:24. Re 11:2. 21:2. 22:19.

54. **the centurion.** ver. 36. Mt 8:5. Ac 10:1. 21:32. 23:17, 23. 27:1, 43. **watching.** ver. 36. **saw.** ver. 51. Mk 15:39. Lk 23:47, etc. **feared.** 2 K 1:13, 14. Ac *2:37. *16:29, 30. Re 11:13. **Truly.** ver. 40, 43. Mt 14:33. 26:63. Da 3:25. Lk 22:70. *23:47. Jn 19:7. Ro 1:4. **the Son of God.** Since they were Romans that said this, some think it evident that they meant to say that he was not only an *innocent,* but altogether a *just* man, as in Lk 23:47. But in fact that expression is explained by this; for, as Jesus was crucified by the Jews for saying that he was "the Son of God;" so if he were a righteous man, and unjustly condemned, he must be "the Son of God." Some render, "a son of a god," that is, according to the pagan notions, a *hero,* or *demi-god,* such as Hercules, Bacchus, etc. But in this, and in some other places, the article is omitted before *uios, son,* when it is used in the highest sense; and Bishop Middleton, on the Greek article, has shown, that *theou uios,* son of God, and *uios tou theou,* "the son of God," are used without any exact discrimination. "The centurion," as he observes, "could not fail to know the alleged blasphemy for which our Savior suffered; and had he intended, in heathen phraseology, to express his admiration of our Savior's conduct, he would not have called our Savior *theou uios.*" For the same grammatical construction: "son of God," where "son" occurs without the article *before* an expressed verb: ver. 40, 54. Mt 4:3, 6. 14:33. Mk 15:39. Lk 4:3, 9. Jn 10:36. This is known more technically as the anarthrous predicate preceding the verb. "Son of God" occurs with the article following the verb: Mt 16:16. 26:63. Mk 3:11. Lk 4:41. 22:70. Jn 1:49. 11:27. 20:31. Ac 9:20. 1 J 4:15. 5:5. This is technically termed the arthrous predicate following the verb. A rule has been formulated by E. C. Colwell for this grammatical construction as follows: "A definite predicate nominative has the article when it follows the verb; it does not have the article when it precedes the verb" (*Journal of Biblical Literature* LII, 1933, p. 13; cited in Robert H. Countess, *The Jehovah's Witness' New Testament,* pp. 48, 49. See Nigel Turner, *Grammar,* vol. 3, p. 183). See the note on Jn 1:1 for the bearing on translation and doctrine of this grammatical construction. It must be carefully noted that the absence of the Greek article before a predicate noun occurring before the verb does not of itself make the noun indefinite or qualitative. The absence of the Greek article is sometimes occasioned by the fact that the noun or phrase has become a formal expression much like a proper name. Sometimes the Greek article is used to point out which noun is the subject of the expressed verb in a predicate nominative construction, to make the statement non-reversible (as in 1 J 4:16, "God is love," but not "love is God"). When both the subject and predicate nominative have the article, they are spoken of as identical and interchangeable (Mt 13:38, field, world; Jn 1:4, life, light; 11:25, the resurrection, the life; 1 C 15:56, the sting, the sin;

1 J 3:4, sin, transgression; Re 1:8, Alpha, Omega. See A. T. Robertson, *A Grammar of the Greek New Testament*, pp. 768, 769, where he cites the additional examples Mt 5:13. 6:22. 16:16. 19:17. 24:45. 26:26, 28. 27:11. Mk 1:11. 6:3. 12:7. 13:11. Jn 1:21. 3:10. 6:14, 50, 63. 8:12. 9:8. 10:7, 11. 14:6, 21. Ac 4:11. 8:10. 9:21. 21:28. 1 C 11:3. 2 C 3:17. Ep 2:14. Ph 3:3. Re 1:17. 3:17). The absence of the article, therefore, is no sure proof, in and of itself, that the noun must be indefinite or qualitative. Sometimes the article is introduced to point back to a previous mention of the same subject in either a near or remote context. This element of Greek style involves not using the article at the first mention of a subject, but using the article for each succeeding reference to the same subject. An example of the anaphoric use of the article in a near context is Galatians 3:23, where Paul literally says "before the coming of *the faith*," *teen pistin*, in reference to faith defined in ver. 22. "Faith" is articular in Galatians 3:25, for it refers to verse 22. James 2:14 affords another instance, where it is literally, "Can the faith save," the article referring to the kind just specified earlier in the verse, a faith which does not produce works. An example involving a more remote context is references to the "dragon" in Revelation. In Re 12:3, the Greek lacks an article when referring to "a great red dragon," but every subsequent mention has the article, showing that the dragon of chapter 20 and chapter 12 are identical. This grammatical feature is called the *anaphoric* use of the article. Perhaps there is in some contexts an interweaving of several of these factors taken together. An example of this may be seen in the absence or non-use of the Greek article in connection with the "holy spirit" or "Holy Spirit," where it is difficult to determine whether the reference is to the Person or his gifts. The first mention in a narrative would not usually have the article, but for doctrinal emphasis to show that the Person, not the gift is meant, the article is sometimes used (Ac *5:3. 7:51. 10:19. 11:12, 15, 28. *13:2. 15:8. 16:32. 21:11. These examples are discussed by Nigel Turner, *Grammatical Insights into the New Testament*, pp. 17-22).

55. **many**. Lk 23:27, 28, 48, 49. Jn 19:25-27. **women**. T#196. Pr 31:20, 26-28. Mk 12:43, 44. Lk 24:1, 10. **afar off**. Ps 38:11. Lk 23:49. **ministering**. Mt *25:40, 44. Nu=3:6. Lk *8:2, 3. He +*6:10.

56. **Mary Magdalene**. ver. 61. Mt 15:39. 28:1. Mk 15:40, 41, 47. 16:1, 9. Lk *8:2. 24:10. Jn 20:1, 18. **Mary the**. Mk 15:47. 16:1. Jn 19:25. **James**. Mt *13:55. Mk 15:40. 16:1. Lk 6:15. **the mother**. Mt 20:20, 21.

57. **there**. Mk *15:42, 43. Lk *23:50, 51. Jn 19:38-42. **rich man**. Is ✱53:9. **Arimathea**. i.e. *a high place*, ✱S#707g. Mt 27:57. Jsh +*18:25. 1 S 1:1. 7:17. Mk 15:43. Lk 23:51. Jn 19:38. Jsh +*18:25.

58. **and begged**. Mk *15:44-46. Lk 23:52, 53. Jn 19:38.

59. **wrapped**. Mk *15:46. Jn *19:39, 40. 20:5.

60. **in his**. Is 53:9. **new tomb**. Jn *19:41, 42. **hewn**. 2 Ch 16:14. Is 22:16. **rolled**. Ge 29:3, 8, 10. **a great**. ver. 66. Mt 28:2. Mk 16:3, 4. Lk 24:2. Jn 11:38. 20:1.

61. **Mary Magdalene**. ver. 56. **the other**. Mt 10:23n. **Mary**. ver. 56. Mt 28:1. **sitting over against**. Mk *15:47.

62. **the day**. Mt 26:17. Mk 15:42. Lk *23:54-56. Jn 19:14, 31, 42. **preparation**. ʃ142, Ge +20:16. **the chief priests**. ver. 1, 2. Ps *2:1-6. Ac 4:27, 28.

63. **that deceiver**. Lk 23:2. Jn 7:12, 47. 2 C 6:8.

After three days. ʃ108H12, 1 S +30:12. ver. *64. Mt *12:40n. 16:21. 17:23. 20:19. 26:61. 28:6. 1 S 30:12n. Mk 8:31. 10:34. Lk 9:22. 18:33. 24:6, 7. Jn +*2:19. 1 C ◐+√15:4.

64. **until the third day**. ver. 63. Mt +*12:40n. Lk √9:22. **and steal**. Mt *28:13. **so the last**. Mt *12:45. 2 S 13:16. Lk 11:26.

65. **have a watch**. ver. 66. Mt 28:11. **make**. Mt 28:11-15. Ps 76:10. Pr +*21:30. Ju ◐=9.

66. **and made**. Every thing was here done which human policy and prudence could, to prevent a resurrection, which these very precautions had the most direct tendency to authenticate and establish. **sealing**. Da *6:17. 2 T 2:19. Re 20:3. **the stone**. ver. 60. Mt 28:2. **setting a watch**. ver. 65.

MATTHEW 28

Early on the first day of the week, the women go to the sepulcre, 1. An earthquake, and an angel rolling away the stone, terrify the guard, 2-4. The angel declares the resurrection of Jesus to the women, and orders them to tell the disciples, 5-8. Jesus himself appears to them, 9, 10. The priests hire the soldiers to say, that the disciples had stolen the body while they slept, 11-15. Jesus appears to the disciples in Galilee, 16, 17. He sends them to preach the gospel, and baptize all nations; and promises his presence with his church to the end of the world, 18-20.

1. **end of the sabbath**. ʃ171T3. Synecdoche of the Part B655: the sabbath is sometimes put for the full week. For other instances of this figure see Lk *18:12. Ac *13:42mg. 1 C *16:1. The Hebrew word *Schabbath*, from which our English word is derived, signifies *rest*, and is applied to all solemn festivals, equally with that one day of every week devoted in the worship of God.— Ezk 20:21, "they polluted my *sabbaths*." Three evangelists say, the transaction recorded in this verse, occurred upon the first day in the week, early in the morning, about sun-rising, and John says, while it was yet dark. *Opse sabbaton* does not signify "in the evening of the *sabbath*," but "*sabbaths*." Hence, the great feast having been concluded, the term "end of the sabbaths" denotes the time very clearly. Again, it may be observed that the Jews, speaking of their passover, sometimes speak according to their *civil computation*, wherein they measured their days from sun-rising to sun-rising. Sometimes according to their *sacred computation*, which was from *sun-set to sun-set*. This reconciles Nu 28:18, which seems to make the fourteenth day of the first month, the first day of unleavened bread. Mk *16:1, 2. Lk 23:56. *24:1, 22. Jn *20:1, etc. **began to dawn**. Lk 23:54. **first**. ʃ46C, Mt 8:6. Gr. *mia*, "one," is the Greek cardinal numeral, but it is used here for the ordinal, *first*, like the Hebrew *echad*, which has both meanings (See Ge 1:5, etc. Mk 16:9. Dt 6:4). **Mary Magdalene**. Mt 27:56, 61. **the other Mary**. Mt 27:56, 61.

2. **was**. *or*, had been. **earthquake**. Mt 27:51-53. Ac 16:26. Re +11:19. **angel of**. Mt 16:3-5. Lk 2:9. *24:2-5. Jn *20:1, 12, 13. 1 T 3:16. He *1:14. 1 P 1:12. **rolled**. Mt 27:60, 66. Ge 29:10. Mk *16:4, 5.

3. **countenance**. Mt 17:2. Ps 104:4. Ezk 1:4-14. Da 1:15. 10:5, 6. Re 1:14-16. 10:1. 18:1. **his raiment**. Mt 17:2. Da 7:9. Mk 9:3. 16:5. Lk 9:29. Ac 1:10. Re 3:4, 5.

4. **the**. ver. 11. Mt 27:65, 66. **shake**. Jb 4:14. Ps 48:6. Da 10:7. Ac 9:3-7. 16:29. Re 1:17.

5. **answered**. Mt 11:25. **Fear**. Is 35:4. 41:10, 14. Da 10:12, 19. Mk 16:6. Lk 1:12, 13, 30. He 1:14. Re 1:17, 18. **ye seek**. Ps 105:3, 4. Lk *24:5. Jn 20:13-15. He 1:14. **which was**. Mt 27:35.

6. **risen**. Mt +*27:52. Jn +*2:21, 22. **as he said**. Mt +*12:40n. *16:21. *17:9, 23. *20:19. *26:31, 32. *27:63. Mk *8:31. Lk 24:6-8, 23, *44. Jn +*2:19. *10:17. **Come**. Mk *16:6. Lk 24:12. Jn *20:4-9. **the Lord**. Lk 7:13. Jn 4:1.

7. **go**. ver. 10. Mk *16:7, 8, 10, 13. Lk 24:*9, *10, 22-24, 34. Jn 20:17, 18. **he goeth**. ver. *16, *17. Mt *26:32. Mk 14:28. Lk *24:6. Jn *21:1, etc. 1 C +*15:4, 6. **to**. Mt *24:25. Is *44:8. 45:21. Jn *14:29. 16:4.

8. **with**. Ezr *3:12, 13. Ps 2:11. Mk *16:8. Lk 24:36-41. Jn *16:20, 22. 20:20, 21.

9. **as**. Is 64:5. Mk *16:9, 10. Jn *20:14-16. **All hail**. Lk 1:28. Jn 20:19. 2 C 13:11g. **and held**. 2 K 4:27. SS 3:3, 4. Lk *7:38. 10:39. Jn *12:3. ◐*20:17. Re 3:9. **worshipped**. ver. *17. Mt +8:2. +*14:33. Lk *24:52. Jn +√20:28. Re +*5:11-14.

10. **Be not afraid**. ver. 5. Mt 14:27. Ge 45:4. 50:19. Lk 24:36-38. Jn 6:20. **go tell**. ver. 7. Jg 10:16. Ps 103:8-13. Mk 16:7. Jn 20:18. **my brethren**. Mt *12:48-50. 25:40, 45. Ps *22:22. Mk 3:33-35. Jn 20:17. 21:23. Ro *8:29. He √2:11-18. **go into**. ver. 7.

11. **some**. ver. 4. Mt 27:65, 66.

12. **assembled with**. Mt 26:3, 4. 27:1, 2, 62-64. Ps *2:1-7. Jn 11:47, 48. 12:10, 11. Ac 4:5-22. 5:33, 34, 40. **taken counsel**. Mt 12:14.

13. **and stole**. Mt *27:64.

14. **And if**. ƒ184C, Mt +4:9. **governor's**. Mt 27:2. **we**. Ac 12:19, 20.

15. **they took**. Mt 26:15. 1 T 6:10. **reported**. Mt 9:31. Mk 1:45. **until**. Mt 27:8. Jsh +4:9.

16. **the eleven**. Mk 16:14. Jn 6:70. Ac 1:13-26. 1 C 15:15. **went**. ver. 7, 10. Mt 26:32. **into a mountain**. Mt 5:1. Mk +6:2.

17. **when**. Mt 16:28. **worshipped**. ver. *9. Mt 8:2. +*14:33. Ps 2:12. *45:11. Jn √5:23. Re +*5:12. **but some**. 1 C *15:6. **doubted**. Mt 14:31. Mk *16:11. Lk *24:11, 37, 41. Jn *20:25.

18. **All power**. Mt 9:6. *11:27. 16:28. Jb 23:6. 25:2. 2 Ch 20:6. Ps *2:6-9. 62:11. 78:38. 89:19, 27. 110:1-3. Is +*9:6, 7. Da +*7:13, 14. Lk *1:32, 33. ◐4:6. 10:22. 22:29. Jn *3:35. √5:22-27. 13:3. 17:2, 5. Ac 2:36. *10:36. Ro *14:9. 1 C 15:27. Ep *1:10, 20-22. Ph √2:9-11. Col *1:16-19. *2:9, 10. He *1:2. *2:8. 1 P *3:22. Re *11:15, 17. 17:14. *19:13, 15, 16. **is given**. Gr. was given. Mt *17:5. **in heaven and**. Mt 6:10. Lk 2:14. 11:2.

19. **Go ye therefore**. Ps 22:27, 28. 98:2, 3. Is 42:1-4. 49:6. 52:10. 66:18, 19. Mk +*16:15, 16. Lk 24:47, 48. Ac +*1:8. 13:46, 47. 28:28. Ro 10:18. Col +*1:23. **and teach**. T#458. Mt +4:23 (T#65). Dt 33:10. Jsh +1:8 (T#48). Ne *8:8. Ps +36:9 (T#279). Ec 12:9. Je 1:17. √23:28. 26:2. Ezk 2:7. *3:10, 11. Ml +3:18 (T#462). Ac 5:42. *20:18, 20, 26-28. 1 C +1:17 (T#430). 4:1, 2. 9:16. 2 C *2:17. *4:1, 2. Ga 1:10. 1 Th *2:3-5. 2 T √2:15. *4:1-5. T 2:1. 1 P *4:11. Ju +3 (T#188). *or*, make disciples, *or* Christians, of all nations. Mt +*13:52. Ac *14:21mg. **all nations**. Mt 24:14. Mk 11:17. 16:15. Lk *24:47. Ro *1:5. **baptizing them**. The fact that this is a command to the eleven (ver. 16)

disciples to baptize individuals proves that the baptism spoken of here is ritual baptism with water, not the real baptism by the Holy Spirit, for real baptism cannot be accomplished by means of human administrators (Ac +*2:38n). F. G. Hibbard argues: (1) The apostles were never commissioned to baptize with the Holy Ghost: this is accomplished directly by Christ (Jn 1:33. Ac 2:17). "Indeed, we recollect of but one individual in apostolic times that imbibed the dangerous error that any being but God could baptize with the Holy Spirit: This person was Simon Magus. Ac 8:18" (Hibbard, *Christian Baptism*, Part 2, p. 159). (2) The commission of the apostles to baptize would naturally have been understood by them of water baptism, unless special instruction had been given them to the contrary (pp. 160, 161). (3) The apostles did understand their commission as referring to water baptism, as is most clearly shown by their subsequent practice (Ac 8:36, 38. 10:47. 19:1-6). "Here, then, we are brought to a direct issue, and one of the following conclusions is irresistibly forced upon us; that either the apostles erred, and acted, not only *without* divine authority, but *against* that authority in a matter so vital as that which involved the spirituality and uncorruptness of the religion of Jesus; or, water baptism is a divinely instituted rite of the Christian religion. But if it be a divine institution, the duty of submission thereto needs no further argument. The proof is complete" (F. G. Hibbard, *Christian Baptism*, Part 2, p. 162). This, then, is an example of a verse respecting baptism which does not mention the element water, yet most certainly has reference to water baptism. Notice also that the command for baptizing is co-extensive with the command to go, and to teach. This proves the perpetuity of the ordinance: as long as men are to go, and to teach the gospel, just so long are they also to baptize. In this passage the ordinance of ritual water baptism is instituted by Christ himself after his resurrection without any hint of its temporary obligation. If he intended baptism to be temporary, he could not have associated baptism with other parts of ministerial duty intended to be of perpetual force. Were ritual water baptism only applicable to Jewish believers as a temporary and exclusively Jewish ordinance, applicable only to the pre-gospel dispensation as some ultra-dispensationalists teach, we must certainly have expected a clear word limiting the ordinance of the same or equal authority as these words establishing the ordinance, but this we do not find. This text clearly teaches the contrary, for the disciples were commanded to teach "all nations, baptizing them." Since all nations are to be baptized, it is absurd to insist that the command is exclusively Jewish. Contrary to the assertion that only Jewish believers were baptized in Acts, or that all baptisms were conducted by Jewish Christians, Cornelius was most certainly a Gentile, and he was water baptized (Ac 10:48) after receiving the Holy Spirit. It is not certain that the Ethiopian eunuch was a Jew (Ac 8:27), and it is most certain that the Philippian jailor was a Gentile, a Roman, in charge of the prison (Ac 16:27, 35, 36). Paul in his ministry was accompanied by Gentile converts who assisted in his work. These assistants most certainly conducted the majority of the ritual water baptisms that occurred under the ministry of Paul, for Paul asserts to the Corinthians that he had baptized none of them save Crispus and Gaius, the household of Stephanus, and he did not recall if he had baptized any others—yet there were enough baptized believers who received ritual water baptism under the ministry of Paul to form one of three contending parties at Corinth (1 C 1:12). Certainly when Paul writes "every one of you saith, I am of Paul" he does not mean to limit "every one of you" (1 C 1:12) to Crispus, Gaius, and the household of Stephanus. This proves, then, that others were baptized during Paul's ministry besides the very few he personally baptized. We are not explicitly told just who performed the ritual water baptisms under Paul's ministry, but as it is certain that Paul enjoyed the assistance of a number of non-Jewish fellowlaborers, there is no reason to suppose that they were not employed at times in this service. Who baptized Lydia (Ac 16:14n, 15n)? If she was not baptized by Paul, she must have been baptized by one of the brethren who accompanied Paul at this time (Ac 16:40n), among whom were Silas, Luke, and Timothy. Nothing is said of the family background of Silas, but his name suggests that he may have been a Hellenistic Jew, and from Acts 16:37 we know he was a Roman citizen. Both Luke and Titus were companions and fellowlaborers of Paul, and both were Gentile Christians. Considering the fact that Titus is directly stated to have been an uncircumcised Gentile (Ga 2:3), was sent by Paul to Corinth (2 C 8:6, 16. 12:18), who accompanied Paul and Barnabas at the time of the Jerusalem Council (Ac 15:2), and most probably was converted through the instrumentality of Paul himself (T 1:4), there is no reason to believe that Titus and other Gentile brethren were not entrusted with the performance of ritual water baptisms and other duties associated with founding, administrating, and establishing the new churches. T#37. Jn 3:22. Ac +*2:38, 39, 41. 8:12-16, 36-38. 9:18. 10:47, 48. 16:14, 15, 33. 19:3-5. +*22:16. 1 C 1:13-16. 15:29. 1 P 3:21. **in.** Ac 8:16. Ga 3:27. **the name.** T#970‡. Mt +*3:16, 17. Ge +*1:26. Nu *6:24-27. Is +*42:1n. 48:16. Zc +*14:9. Jn +1:2 (T#969‡). √15:26. 16:15. Ro 8:9. √15:30. 1 C *12:4-6. 2 C √13:14. Ga *4:6. Ep 2:18. 4:4-6. 2 Th 3:5. 1 P 1:2. 1 J 5:7. Ju 20, 21. Re 1:4-6. 4:8. **the Father.** Mt 24:36. **Holy Ghost.** Mt +3:16g. Careful study of Scripture demonstrates that all three (and only these three, and no others)—Father, Son, and Holy Spirit—are the persons of the Godhead, who are associated on an equality of being, and possess the attributes and prerogatives of Deity: The Father, Son, and Holy Ghost are each (1) called God: Ex 20:1, 2. Jn +*20:28. Ac +*5:3, 4. (2) called Lord: Ro 10:12. Lk 2:11. 2 C 3:17. (3) everlasting: Ro 16:26. Re 22:13. He 9:14. (4) called holy: Re 4:8 w 15:4. Ac 3:14. 1 J 2:20. (5) called true: Jn 7:28. Re 3:7. 1 J 5:6. (6) omnipresent: Je 23:24. Ep 1:23. Ps 139:7. (7) almighty: Ge 17:1. Re +*1:8. Ro 15:19. (8) powerful: Je 32:17. He 1:3. Lk 1:35. They each (9) give strength: Is 40:28, 29. Ph *4:13. Ep 3:16. (10) create: Ge 1:1. Jn 1:2, 3. Jb 33:4. Each is (11) omniscient: Ac 15:18. Jn 21:17. 1 C 2:10, 11. They each (12) sanctify: Ju 1. He 2:11.

1 P 1:2. (13) give eternal life: Ro 6:23. Jn 10:28. Ga 6:8. (14) are life: Dt 30:20. Col 3:4. Ro 8:10. (15) teach: Is 48:17. Lk 21:15. Jn 14:26. (16) impart knowledge: Is 54:13. Ga 1:12. 1 J 2:20. (17) raise the dead: Jn 5:21a. Jn 5:21b. 1 P 3:18. (18) raised Christ bodily from the dead: 1 C 6:14. Jn 2:19. 1 P 3:18. (19) comfort: 2 C 1:3. Ph 2:1, 2. Jn 15:26. (20) distribute spiritual gifts: Ja 1:17. Ep 4:8. 1 C 12:11. (21) divinely inspire God's prophets and spokesmen: He 1:1. 2 C 13:3. Mk 13:11. (22) send pastors: Je 3:15. Mt 10:5. Ac 13:2. (23) send gifted servants: Je 26:5. Ep 4:11. Ac 20:28. (24) may be tempted: Dt 6:16. 1 C 10:9. Ac 5:9. (25) indwell believers: 2 C 6:16. Ep 3:17. 1 C 3:16. (26) indwell individual believers: Ep 2:22. Col √1:27. 1 C *6:19. (27) fellowship with believers: 1 J 1:3a. 1 J 1:3b. Ph 2:1. (28) work in us: He 13:20, 21. Col 1:28, 29. 1 C 12:11. They each are (29) omnipotent: Is 40:12. He 2:14. Ac 10:38. (30) sovereign: Ep +*1:11. Mt 8:27. 1 C 12:11. (31) immutable: Ml +*3:6. He 13:8. Mt 12:32. Possess the attribute of (32) immensity: Je 23:24. Jn 3:13. Ps 139:7. The members of the Trinity are further said to share the attributes of (33) truth: Ex 34:6. Jn 14:6. 1 J 5:6. (34) benevolence: Ro 2:4. Ep 5:25. Ne 9:20. (35) wisdom: Jb 12:13. Col 2:3. Is 11:2. (36) invisibility: 1 T 6:16. Col 1:27. Lk 24:39. (37) incomprehensibility: Ro 11:33. Ep 3:8, 19. 1 C 2:10, 11, 14. (38) being unequaled: Je 10:6. Mt 8:27. Is 40:13, 14. (39) justice: Ge 18:25. Ac 3:14. Jn 16:8. (40) goodness: Mk 10:18. Jn 10:11. Ps 143:10. (41) love: 1 J 4:16. Ep 5:2. Ro 5:5. (42) mercy: Ep 2:4. Ju 21. Ga ?5:22, 23. (43) grace: Ps 84:11. 2 C 8:9. He 10:29. (44) faithfulness: Ps 36:5. He 2:17. Ep ?4:30. Several divine attributes are incommunicable: they belong to God exclusively, and cannot be communicated, delegated, or given to a created being. These include eternity (3), omnipresence (6), omniscience (11), sovereignty (30), immutability (31), and immensity (32). Since only God can possess the incommunicable attributes, yet Scripture ascribes them to Jesus and to the Holy Spirit, all three persons must be God. There is no other explanation which properly agrees with all the statements of Scripture.

20. **Teaching them.** Mt *7:24-27. Dt *5:32. 12:32. Je 26:2. Ac *2:42. 14:3. *20:20, 21, 27. 1 C 11:2, 23. 14:37. Ep *4:11-17, 20, etc. Col *1:28. 1 Th *4:1, 2. 2 Th 3:6-12. 1 T *6:1-4. T 2:1-10. 1 P 2:10-19. 2 P *1:5-11. 3:2. 1 J 2:3, 4. 3:19-24. Re 22:14. **to observe.** Dt=33:9. Jn +*14:15. Ro 15:18, 19. **all things.** Je 26:2. **commanded.** Ac 1:2. 1 C 11:2. 14:37. 2 Th 3:6. 1 J +√2:3n. **with you.** Mt +*1:23. √18:20. Ge *39:2, 3, 21. Ex 3:12. Jsh 1:5. 1 Ch=28:21. Ps 46:7, 11. Is 8:8-10. *41:10. Mk *16:20. Jn 12:26. *14:3, 18-23. 17:24. Ac *18:9, 10. Ph 4:13. 2 T *4:17. He +*13:5, 6. Re 22:21. **alway.** lit. all the days. Lk 1:75. **unto.** Mt *13:39, 40, 49. +*24:3. Dt 1:31. Ps 77:20. **end.** Gr. *suntelia*, *S#4930g, Mt 24:3n. **world.** Gr. *aion*, Mt +6:13. lit. end of the age, as in Mt +*13:39. Jn +√6:54n. **Amen.** Mt *6:13. 1 K *1:36. 1 Ch 16:36. Ps 72:19. Re 1:18. 22:20.

MARK

The gospel is introduced by John the Baptist's minis-
try, 1-8. The baptism and temptation of Christ, 9-13.
John being imprisoned, Jesus preaches in Galilee, and
calls Simon and Andrew, James and John, to follow
him, 14-20. He casts out an unclean spirit, 21-28; heals
Peter's wife's mother, and many sick persons, 29-34;
retires very early in the morning for prayer; preaches
in the synagogues of Galilee; and cleanses a leper,
35-45.

1. **beginning.** Lk 1:2, 3. 2:10, 11. Ac 1:1, 2. **gospel.**
Mk √16:15, 16. Is 52:7. Mt 4:23. 24:14. Lk 2:10, 11.
24:47. Jn √3:16. Ac 20:24. Ro √1:16, 17. 2:16. 10:8.
16:25. 1 C 1:18. +*15:1-4. 2 C 3:8, 9. 4:3, 4, 6. 5:18,
19. Ga √1:8. Ep 1:13. 3:4. 6:15, 19. 1 Th 2:9. 2 T
*1:10. 1 P :1:25. Re 14:6. **Christ.** Jn √20:31. Ro *1:1-
4. 1 J *1:1-3. √5:11, 12. **son.** Ps *2:7. Mt 3:17. +*14:33.
+*16:16. 17:5. Lk +*1:35. Jn *1:14, 34, 49. √3:16.
*6:69. √20:31. Ro 1:3, 4. *8:3, 32. He *1:1, 2.

2. **written.** Ps 40:7. Mt 2:5. 26:24, 31. Lk 1:70.
18:31. **in.** Several MSS. have, "by Isaiah the prophet."
See the parallel texts, and note on composite quotations
at Mt 27:9n. **prophets.** √171E13, Ge +46:7. **Behold.**
√92G, Lk +4:18. Ml ▶3:1. Ne +*9:6. Ps 110:1. Is 40:3.
Mt 11:10. Lk *1:15-17, 76. *7:27, 28. Ac 2:34-36. **before
thy face.** Use of "face" denotes a real, visible presence
(Peters, *Theocratic Kingdom*, vol. 2, p. 351). As the
quoted prediction is as fully applicable to the Second
Advent as it is to the first, this proves Christ's Second
Coming will be literal, personal, and visible. Ezk
*20:35. Mt 11:10. +*16:27n. 18:10. +*24:3n, 30. Lk
1:76. 2:31. 7:27. Jn +*1:51n. Ac +*1:11. 1 C *13:12.
1 J *3:2. Re +*1:7.

3. **voice.** Mt ▶40:3-5. Mt *3:3. Lk 3:4-6. Jn *1:15,
19-34. 3:28-36. **Prepare.** Lk 1:76.

4. **did baptize.** Mt *3:1, 2, 6, 11. Lk *3:2, 3. Jn
*3:23. Ac 10:37. 13:24, 25. *19:3, 4. **in the wilderness.**
It is unnecessary to suppose that in such a location
conditions were suited to immersion, or that there
was sufficient water for immersion. Note the phrase
"in the wilderness." This is a phrase designating geo-
graphic locality, not the element into which baptism
took place. The same is true for baptism "in Jordan"
(ver. 9n), "in Aenon" (see Jn 3:23). **of.** √181E, Ge
+3:24. **repentance.** Lk √13:3. Ac +*3:19. **for.** *or*, unto.
Gr. *eis*. Sometimes the preposition *eis* expresses purpose (Mt *26:28n. 1 C 2:7, for our glory), sometimes
the ground or basis (as here, Mt 10:41. √12:41. Ac
2:38n), sometimes the notion of sphere or influence
(1 C 10:2n), sometimes motion toward without entering
in (Mt 17:27, to the sea. 18:29, at his feet. Mk 11:1,
"nigh to Jerusalem," but still two miles away. Lk 10:30,
"to Jericho," but he never got there. Jn 20:4, "came
first to the sepulchre," etc.), and sometimes motion
into or within (Jn 20:6n). Here, *eis* means "with reference to," in the sense that "baptism was on the basis
of the repentance and confession of sin" (A. T. Robertson, *Word Pictures*, vol. 1, pp. 253, 254). Robertson
notes "Certainly John did not mean that the baptism
was the means of obtaining the forgiveness of their

sins or necessary to the remission of sins" (p. 253).
Mt ◐10:41. ◐26:28n. Ac +*2:38n. **remission.** Mt
*26:28. Lk *1:77. Ac *10:43. 13:38, 39. +*22:16. Ro
*3:25. Ep *1:7. He √9:22.

5. **there.** Mt 3:5, 6. 4:25. **Judea.** √121J19, 1 S
+22:19. **baptized.** Jn 1:28. 3:23. **in the river.** J. Ditzler
points out that the river Jordan flows from the mountains to where it empties into the Dead Sea, down a
steep of 3,000 feet. The direct length of the Jordan
to the Dead Sea is sixty miles, by its windings it is
two hundred miles. The water from the melting snow
capped mountains is very cold, and falls fifteen feet
to the mile (counting the windings), or sixty feet to
the mile (as the crow flies). The fall of the Mississippi
is a little over *five inches* to the mile, yet it runs from
three to five miles an hour, much as it winds. The
Jordan is so rapid a stream that even the best swimmer
can not bathe in it without endangering his life. In
the neighborhood of Jericho (there is where John baptized) the bathers are compelled to tie themselves together with ropes, to prevent their being swept away
by the rapidity of the current. John the Baptist could
not have baptised in the river under such conditions.
The cold water would alone make this impossible. The
tumultuous rush of the dangerous current would make
it impossible to immerse the great numbers John baptized, for "while a man could take another and dip
him by being very careful, it is not possible that one
man could immerse great numbers in such a rapid
stream, for the physical labor, the certainty of many
being swept away from his hold and drowning, forbid.
In a few minutes the limbs would become so numb
in such a cold stream as to make the action of the
lower limbs impossible" (J. Ditzler, *Baptism*, p. 40).
Baptism in the river itself being out of the question,
the expression "in the river" used here ought to be
understood in the same sense of designating locality
that "in Jordan" does in ver. 9. Jsh 3:15n. **confessing.**
Gr. *exomologeomai*, ✱S#1843g. Rendered (1) confess:
Mt 3:6. Mk 1:5. Ac 19:18. Ro 14:11. 15:9. Ph 2:11.
Ja 5:16n. Re 3:5. (2) thank: Mt 11:25. Lk 10:21. (3)
promise: Lk 22:6. See for *homologeo*, ✱S#3670g, Mt
+10:32. Le 26:40-42. Jsh 7:19. Ps √32:5. Pr √28:13.
Ac 2:38. +*19:18. 1 J √1:8-10.

6. **clothed.** 2 K *1:8. Zc 13:4. Mt 3:4. **eat.** Le *11:22.

7. **There cometh.** Mt *3:11, 14. Lk *3:16. 7:6, 7.
Jn 1:27. *3:28-31. Ac *13:25. **latchet.** √138B, Ge
+13:16. Ge 14:23. Is 5:27.·Lk 3:16. Jn 1:27.

8. **have.** Mt *3:11. **with water.** Mt *3:11. Ac +*1:5.
he shall. ver. 10. Pr 1:23. Is 32:15. *44:3. Ezk 36:25-
27. 39:29. Jl *2:28, 29. Jn 1:33. Ac +*1:5. 2:4, 16,
17, 33. 10:45. *11:15, 16. 19:4-6. 1 C √12:13. T *3:5,
6. **Holy Ghost.** Gr. *pneumati hagio*, Mt +1:18n.

9. **came to pass.** Mt 3:13-
15. Is *42:21. Lk *3:21. **in Jordan.** This is an idiom
meaning "in the region of the Jordan," a reference to
the locality, not the element. The same idiom occurs
in ver. 4, "in the wilderness;" Jn 1:28, "in Bethabara;"
Jn 3:23, "in Aenon;" and all have reference to the
geographical locality, not to the element water. Jn
10:40.

10. **coming**. Mt 3:16. Jn 1:31-34. **out**. Mt +3:16. **opened**. *or*, cloven, *or* rent. Is 64:1. **the Spirit**. Gr. *pneuma*, Mt +3:16. Is *11:2, 3. 42:1. **like a dove**. Lk *3:22. Jn *1:32.

11. **there**. Mt 3:17. Is *64:1. Jn 5:37. 12:28-30. 2 P 1:17, 18. **Thou**. Mk 9:7. Ps *2:7. Is 42:1. Mt *17:5. Lk 9:35. Jn 1:34. √3:16, 35, 36. √5:20-23. *6:69. Ro *1:4. Col *1:13. **am**. ♪96C4, Mt +3:17.

12. **the spirit**. Gr. *pneuma*, Mt +3:16. Mt *4:1, etc. Lk *4:1, etc. **driveth**. Or, "sendeth him forth," *ekballei auton*. The expression does not necessarily imply any violence; but seems to intimate the energy of that impulse on our Lord, by which he was inwardly constrained to retire from society.

13. **forty**. Ex 24:18. 34:28. Dt 9:11, 18, 25. 1 K 19:8. **tempted**. He *2:17, 18. +*4:15. **and the**. 1 K 19:5-7. Mt 4:11. 26:53. 1 T 3:16. **ministered**. Mt 4:11. He *1:14.

14. A.M. 4031. A.D. 27. **after**. Mt 4:12. 11:2. 14:2. Lk *3:20. Jn 3:22-24. **preaching**. Is *61:1-3. Mt 4:23. 9:35. *24:14. Lk *4:17-19, 43, 44. 8:1. Ac 20:25. 28:23. Ep 2:17.

15. **The time**. Da 2:44. ✷9:22-27. Lk 3:15. ◑21:8. Jn 7:8. Ro +5:6. Ga *4:4. Ep *1:10. **kingdom of God**. Mk 4:11, 26, 30. 9:1, 47. *10:14, 15, 23-25. *12:34. √14:25. 15:43. Mt 3:2. ◑+4:17. 10:7. +*12:28. 16:28. Lk +4:43. 10:9, 11. 11:20. 16:16. +*17:21. √19:11. 21:31. Jn +3:3. Ac +1:3. **at hand**. Mt 4:17. 10:7. ◑+*21:43. **repent**. Mt 4:17. 11:20. 21:31, 32. Lk +5:32. +√13:3, 5. 15:7, 10. 24:47. Ac +*2:36-38. 5:31. 20:21. 2 T +*2:25, 26. **believe**. Mk *16:16. Ge √15:6. 2 Ch +*20:20. Ac √16:30, 31. 19:4. 20:21. Ro 4:24. 16:26. Ga 3:6. He 6:1. **the gospel**. Ro 1:9. 1 C √15:1-4. 2 C 8:18. 10:14. Ga 3:8. 1 Th 3:2.

16. **as he**. Mt 4:18, etc. Lk 5:1, 4, etc. **Simon**. Mk 3:16, 18. Mt 10:2. Lk 6:14. Jn 1:40-42. 6:8. 12:22. Ac 1:13.

17. **Come**. 1 C 1:26-29. **fishers**. ♪103, Ge +3:13. Ezk 47:10. Mt 4:19, 20. Lk *5:10. Ac *2:38-41.

18. **forsook**. Mk 10:28-31. Mt 19:27-30. Lk 5:11. *14:33. 18:28-30. Ph 3:8.

19. **James**. Mk 3:17. 5:37. 9:2. 10:35. 14:33. Mt 4:21. Ac 1:13. 12:2.

20. **they left**. Mk 10:29. Dt 33:9. 1 K 19:20. Mt 4:21, 22. 8:21, 22. 10:37. Lk 14:26. 2 C 5:16.

21. **they went**. Mt 4:13. Lk 4:31. 10:15. **Capernaum**. *Capernaum* was a city of Galilee (Lk 4:31), situated on the confines of Zebulun and Naphtali (Mt 4:13), on the western border of the lake of Tiberias (Jn 6:59), and in the land of Gennasereth (Mk 6:53. Mt 14:34), where Josephus (Bell. l. iii. c. 10. Sec. 8), places a spring of excellent water called *Capernaum*. Dr. Lightfoot places it between Tiberias and Tarichea, about two miles from the former; and Dr. Richardson, in passing through the plain of Gennasereth, was told by the natives that the ruins of *Capernaum* were quite near. The Arab station and ruins mentioned by Mr. Buckingham, said to have been formerly called *Capharnaoom*, situated on the edge of the lake, from nine to twelve miles N.N.E. of Tiberias, bearing the name of *Talhewn*, or as Burckhardt writes it, *Tel Houm*, appear too far north for its site. Mt *4:13. Lk 4:31-37. **he entered**. ver. 39. Mt 6:2. Mt 4:23. Lk 4:16. 13:10. Ac 13:14, etc. 17:2. 18:4.

22. **they were**. Je *23:29. Mt *7:28, 29. 13:54. Lk 4:32. 21:15. Jn *7:46. Ac 6:10. 9:21, 22. 2 C 4:2. He

*4:12, 13. **as the**. Mk 7:3-13. Mt 23:16-24.

23. **a man**. ver. 34. Mk 5:2. 7:25. 9:25. Mt 12:43. Lk *4:33-37. **spirit**. Gr. *pneuma*, Mt +8:16.

24. **Saying**. Mk 3:11, ◑22. 5:7. Ps +*50:16. Mt 8:29. Lk 4:41. 8:28. Ac 16:17. 19:15. **Let**. Mk 5:7. Ex 14:12. Mt 8:29. Lk 8:28, 37. Ja *2:19. **what**. ♪85H, Jg +11:12. ♪108H8, 2 S +16:10. **Jesus of Nazareth**. Mk 10:47. 14:67. Mt +2:23. 26:71. Lk 4:34. 18:37. 24:19. Jn 18:5, 7. 19:19. Ac 2:22. **destroy**. Gr. *apollumi*, Mt +2:13. Da +*9:24. Mt +*8:29. 1 J 3:8. **the Holy One**. Ps 16:10. *89:18, 19. Da 9:24. Lk +*1:35. 4:34. Jn 6:69. Ac 2:27. 3:14. *4:27, 30. He 7:26. 1 J 2:20. Re 3:7.

25. **rebuked**. ver. 34. Mk 3:11, 12. 9:25. 2 Ch ◑+*19:2. Ps +*50:16. Lk *4:35, 41. Ac 16:17, 18. **Hold**. ver. 34. Ps +*50:16.

26. **spirit**. Gr. *pneuma*, Mt +8:16. **torn**. Mk 9:20, 26. Lk 9:39, 42. 11:22. **came out**. Ex ◑=2:12.

27. **all amazed**. ver. 22. Mk 4:41. 7:37. Mt 8:27. 9:33. 12:22, 23. 15:31. Lk 8:25. **new doctrine**. "new" is *kainos*, and in this use has a negative connotation. Trench says "*kainos* may express only the novel and strange, as contrasted, and that unfavorably, with the known and the familiar" (*Synonyms*, p. 221). Ac 17:19. He 13:9. **for**. Lk *4:36. 9:1. 10:17-20. **spirits**. Gr. *pneuma*, Mt +8:16.

28. **his fame**. ver. 45. Mi 5:4. Mt 4:24. 9:31. Lk 4:14, 37.

29. **entered**. Mt 8:14, 15. Lk 4:38, 39. 9:58.

30. **wife's**. 1 C 9:5. **lay sick**. Mt 8:14. Lk 4:38. **they tell**. Mk 5:23. Jn 11:3. Ja 5:14, 15.

31. **by the hand**. ver. +*41. Mk 5:41. Ac 9:41. **ministered**. Mk 15:41. Ps 103:1-3. 116:12. Mt +*27:55. Lk 8:2, 3.

32. **at even**. ver. 21. Mk 3:2. Mt *8:16, 17. Lk *4:40.

33. **all**. ♪171A, Ex +9:6. ♪171L2, Mt +26:59. ver. 5. **the city**. ♪121J19, 1 S +22:19. ver. 21. Ge +19:4. Ac 13:44.

34. **suffered not**. ver. 25. Mk +*3:12. Ps +*50:16. Lk 4:41. Ac *16:16-18. **speak, because they**. *or*, say that they.

35. **morning**. Mk 6:48. +13:35. 16:2. Ge +19:27. 28:18. Jg 6:38. 9:33. 2 S 23:4. 2 K 3:22. Jb 1:5. Ps +*5:3. 130:6. Is 26:9. Lk 24:1. Jn 20:1. **rising up**. Mk 6:46-48. Ps 5:3. 109:4. Lk *4:42. 6:12. 22:39-46. Jn 4:34. 6:15. Ep *6:18. Ph 2:5. He *5:7. **before day**. T#1160. 1 S 1:19. Ps 63:1. 78:34. Is *26:9. **went out**. Lk *6:12. **solitary place**. T#1207. Ps 107:4-7. Mt *14:23. Lk *5:16. 9:18. **there prayed**. Mk 6:46. Ps 109:4. Mt *11:25. 26:39. Lk 3:21. 10:21. 11:1. 22:32. 23:34, 46. Jn *11:41. 17:9. He 5:7.

37. **All**. ver. 5. Zc 11:11. Jn 3:26. 11:48. 12:19.

38. **Let**. Lk *4:43. **for**. Is *61:1-3. Lk *2:49. *4:18-21. Jn *9:4, 5. *16:28. *17:4, 6, 8.

39. **preached**. ver. 21. Mt *4:23. Lk 4:43, 44. **Galilee**. *Galilee* was a province of Palistine, being bounded, says Josephus (Bel. l. iii. c. 2), on the west by Ptolemais and Mount Carmel; on the south by the country of Samaria and Scythopolis, on the river Jordan; on the east by the cantons of Hippos, Gadara, and Gaulon; and on the north by the confines of the Tyrians. It was divided into Lower and Upper Galilee: *Upper Galilee*, so called from its being mountainous, was termed *Galilee of the Gentiles* (Mt 4:15), because inhabited, says Strabo (l. xvi.), by Egyptians, Arabians, and

Phoenicians, and comprehended the tribes of Asher and Naphtali; the *Lower Galilee* contained the tribes of Zebulun and Issachar, and was sometimes termed the Great Field. It was, says Josephus (Bel. l. ii. c. 9), very populous and rich, containing 204 cities and towns. **and cast.** Mk 7:30. Ge +*3:15. Lk 4:41.

40. **there.** Mt 8:2-4. Lk 5:12-14. **a leper.** Le ch. 13, 14. Nu 12:10-15. Dt 24:8, 9. 2 S 3:29. 2 K 5:5, etc., 27. 7:3. 15:5. Mt 11:5. Lk 17:12-19. **beseeching.** T#1600. Nu 12:10-13. Mt 8:2, 3. Lk 5:12. 17:12, 13. **kneeling.** Mk 10:17. 2 Ch 6:13. Mt 17:14. Lk 22:41. Ac +*7:60. Ep 3:14. **if thou.** ſ184C, Mt +4:9. Mk 9:22, 23. Ge *18:14. 2 K 5:7.

41. **moved.** ſ22A18, Is +63:15. Mk 6:34. Mt 9:36. Lk 7:12, 13. He 2:17. +*4:15. **and touched.** ver. 31. Mk 3:10. 5:23, 27, 41. 6:5. 7:33. 8:22, 23, 25. 9:27. 10:13, 16. **I will.** Mk 4:39. 5:41, 42. Ge 1:3. Ps *33:9. He *1:3.

42. **immediately.** ver. 31. Mk 5:29. Ps 33:9. Mt 15:28. Jn 4:50-53. 15:3.

43. **straitly charged.** Mk 3:12. 5:43. 7:36. Mt 9:30. Lk 8:56.

44. **say nothing.** Mt 12:16, 17, 19. Jn 8:20. **show.** Le 4:2-32. ◖13:49. *14:2-4, 10. Mt 23:2, 3. Lk 5:14. 17:14. **for a testimony.** Is *42:21. Mk +*6:11. Ro *15:4. 1 C 10:11.

45. **and began.** Mk *7:36. Ps 77:11. Mt 9:31. Lk *5:15. T 1:10. **blaze abroad.** Mt 9:31. 28:15. **could.** Mk 2:1, 2, 13. **the city.** 2 C 11:26. **they came.** Mk 2:2, 13. 3:7. Lk 5:17. Jn 6:2.

MARK 2

Jesus heals a paralytic, and shows his authority on earth to forgive sins, 1-12. He calls Matthew; and answers those who blamed him for eating with publicans and sinners, 13-17. He vindicates his disciples, when blamed for not fasting frequently, and accused of breaking the sabbath, 18-28.

1. **again.** Mk 1:45. Mt *9:1. Lk 5:18. **and it.** Mk 7:24. Lk 18:35-38. Jn 4:47. Ac 2:6.

2. **straightway.** ver. 13. Mk 1:33, 37, 45. 4:1, 2. Lk 5:17. 12:1. **and he.** Mk 1:14. 6:34. Ps 40:9. Mt 5:2. Lk 8:1, 11. Ac 8:25. 11:19. 14:25. 16:6. Ro 10:8. He *2:3. 2 T *4:2.

3. **bringing.** Mt 9:1, 2, etc. Lk 5:18, etc.

4. **they uncovered.** Dt 22:8. Lk *5:19. Ga 4:15. **let down.** ſ96C5, Mt +2:13.

5. **saw.** Ge 22:12. Jn +*2:25. Ac *11:23. 14:9. Ep √2:8. 1 Th 1:3, 4. Ja *1:6, 7. 2:18-22. **he said.** ver. 9, 10. Is *53:11. Mt 9:2. Lk 5:20. 7:47-50. Ac 5:31. 2 C 2:10. Col 3:13. **Son.** The Jews believed that not only death but all disease was the consequence of sin. "There is no death without sin, nor any chastisement without iniquity" (Shabbath, c. 5. fol. 55. l.); and that "no diseased person could be healed of his disease till his sins were blotted out" (Nedarim, fol. 41.1). Our Lord, therefore, as usual, appeals to their received opinions, and asserts his high dignity, by first forgiving the sins, and then healing the body of the paralytic. Mk 5:34. Mt 9:22. Lk 8:48. **sins.** Jb *14:4. 33:17-26. Ps √32:1-5. 90:7-9. +*103:3. Is 38:17. *43:25. Da *9:9. Mi +*7:18. Jn 5:14. 1 C +*11:30. Ja 5:15.

6. **and reasoning.** Mk 8:17. Mt 16:7, 8. Lk 5:21, 22. 2 C 10:5mg.

7. **speak.** Mk 14:64. Mt 9:3. 26:65. Jn 10:33, 36.

who can. Jb 14:4. Ps 130:4. Is 43:25. Da 9:9. Mi +*7:18. Lk 5:21. 7:49. Jn 20:20-23. **but God.** Lk 18:19. Jn ◖20:21.

8. **when.** 1 Ch 29:17. Mt 9:4. Lk 5:22. 6:8. 7:39, 40. Jn +*2:24, 25. 6:64. 21:17. He *4:13. Re *2:23. **perceived.** Gr. *epiginosko*, Mt +11:27. **in his.** In the following texts, "spirit" refers to the sentient element in man, that by which he perceives, reflects, feels, and desires (Vine, *Dictionary*, vol. 4, p. 62): Mk 8:12. Ge 26:35. +*41:8. Da *7:15. Jn 13:21. Ac 17:16. 20:22. 1 C +*2:11. 2 C 7:1. 1 P 3:4. **spirit.** Gr. *pneuma*. ſ171Q1B. Figure of speech Synecdoche of the Part, where a part is put for the whole. Here, an integral part of man (individually) is put for the whole man, *pneuma* is put for one's self. Mk 8:12. Lk 1:47. Jn 11:33. 13:21. 1 C 14:14. 16:18. 2 C 2:13. 7:1, 13. Ga 6:18. Ph 4:23. 2 T 4:22. Phm 25. For other instances of this figure compare ſ171Q1A, Ge +12:5. For the other uses of *pneuma* see Mt +*8:16n. **Why.** Mk 7:21. Ps *139:2. Pr 15:26. 24:9. Is √55:7. Ezk 38:10. Lk 24:38. Ac *5:3. *8:22. **your hearts.** 1 S √16:7. 1 Ch *29:17.

9. **is it.** Mt 9:5. Lk 5:22-25. **Thy sins.** ver. 5.

10. **Son of man.** ver. 28. Mk 8:31, 38. 9:9, 12, 31. 10:33, 45. 13:26. 14:21, 41, *62. Da +*7:13, 14. Mt +8:20. 16:13. Lk +5:24. Jn +1:51. **hath power.** ver. 28. Mt 12:8. 28:18. Lk 6:5. Jn 5:20-27. **to forgive.** Mt 9:6-8. Ac *5:31. 1 T 1:13-16.

11. **Arise.** Mk 1:41. Jn 5:8-10. 6:63.

12. **insomuch.** Mk 1:27. Mt 9:8. 12:23. Lk 7:16. **glorified.** Mt 15:31. Lk 5:26. 13:13. 17:15. Ac 4:21. **We never.** Mt *9:8, 33. Jn 7:31. 9:32.

13. **by.** Mt 9:9. 13:1. **and all.** ver. 2. Mk 3:7, 8, 20, 21. 4:1. Pr 1:20-22. Lk *19:48. *21:38.

14. **he saw.** Mk 3:18. Mt *9:9. Lk *5:27. **Alpheus.** Mk 3:18. Lk 6:15. Ac 1:13. **receipt of custom.** or, place where the custom was received. **Follow me.** Mk 1:17-20. Mt 4:19-22.

15. **came to pass.** ſ144A11, Ge +38:1. **as Jesus sat.** Mt 9:10, 11. 21:31, 32. Lk *5:29, 30. 6:17. 15:1.

16. **How.** ver. 7. Is +*65:5n. Lk 15:2, etc. *18:11. 19:7, 10. 1 C 2:15. He 12:3. **publicans.** Mt 18:17.

17. **They that are whole.** Mk 7:20-23. Mt *9:12, 13. Lk 5:31, 32. 15:7, 29. √16:15. Jn 9:34, 40, 41. **I came.** Is +*1:18. √55:7. Mt *18:11. Lk 15:10. +*19:10. Ac 20:21. 26:20. Ro √5:6-8, 20, 21. 1 C +*6:9-11. 1 T *1:15, 16. T *2:14. *3:3-7.

18. **disciples of John.** Mt 9:14-17. 11:2. 14:12. Lk 5:33-39. 7:18. 11:1. Jn 1:35. 3:25. 4:1. Ac 18:25. 19:3. **Why.** Mk 7:5. Mt *6:16, 18. 23:5. Lk *18:12. Ro *10:3. **fast.** Lk *18:12. **fast not.** ver. 15. Mt 9:10. Lk 5:30.

19. **Can.** Ge 29:22. Jg 14:10, 11. Ps 45:14. SS 6:8. Mt 25:1-10.

20. **the bridegroom.** Ps 45:11. SS 1:4. 3:11. Is 54:5. 62:5. Jn 3:29. 2 C 11:2. Re *19:7. 21:9. **be taken.** Zc *13:7. Mt 26:31. Jn 7:33, 34. 12:8. 13:33. 16:7, 28. 17:11, 13. Ac 1:9. +*3:21. **and.** Ac *13:2, 3. *14:23. 1 C *7:5. 2 C 6:5. 11:27.

21. **seweth.** Ps 103:13-15. Is 57:16. Jn *16:12. 1 C √10:13. **new.** or, raw, or, unwrought. Mt 9:16.

22. **bottles.** Jsh 9:4, 13. Jb 32:19. Ps 119:80, 83. Mt 9:17. Lk 5:37, 38. **marred.** Gr. *apollumi*, Mt +2:13. **new.** "New" wine is *neos*; "new" skins is *kainos*. The two Greek words for "new," while generally synonymous, may be distinguished here: *neos* is new in the sense of brand new, new as opposed to old, referring

to age; *kainos* is new in quality or condition, the sense of fresh, not yet used, but with no reference to age— the new wineskins conceivably could have remained unused for a long time. Perhaps this distinction holds at 2 P 3:13, where "new" heavens and a "new" earth may be understood as new in quality, not in time, for Scripture elsewhere states that the "earth abideth forever" (Ec +*1:4). For *neos*, *S#3501g: rendered (1) new: Mt 9:17, 17. Mk 2:22, 22, 22. Lk 5:37, 37, 38, 39. 1 C 5:7. He 12:24. (2) new man: Col 3:10. (3) young woman: T 2:4. For *kainos*, *S#2537g: Mt 9:17. 13:52. 26:28, 29. 27:60. Mk 1:27. 2:21, 22. 14:24, 25. 16:17. Lk 5:36, 36, 38. 22:20. Jn 13:34. 19:41. Ac 17:19, 21. 1 C 11:25. 2 C 3:6. 5:17, 17. Ga 6:15. Ep 2:15. 4:24. He 8:8, 13. 9:15. 2 P 3:13, 13. 1 J 2:7, 8. 2 J 5. Re 2:17. 3:12, 12. 5:9. 14:3. 21:1, 1, 2, 5. Examination of all the above-listed occurrences will show that no passage contradicts the distinction suggested. Some scholars, contrary to the distinctions maintained by Trench (*N.T. Synonyms*, pp. 219-225) and Cremer (*Biblico-Theological Lexicon of New Testament Greek*, pp. 321, 740), suggest no such neat difference can be maintained (See Roy A. Harrisville, *The Concept of Newness in the New Testament*; J. H. Moulton and G. Milligan, *The Vocabulary of the Greek Testament*, p. 314, 315).

23. **that**. Mt 12:1-8. Lk 6:1-5. **to pluck**. Dt *23:24, 25.

24. **why**. ver. 7, 16. Mt 7:3-5. 15:2, 3. 23:23, 24. He 12:3. **that**. Ex 20:10. 31:15. 35:2, 3. Nu 15:32-36. Ne 13:15-22. Is 56:2, 4, 6. +*58:13n. Je √17:20-27.

25. **Have**. Mk 12:10, 26. Mt 19:4. 21:16, 42. 22:31. Lk 10:26. **what**. 1 S *21:3-6.

26. **Abiathar**. It appears from the passage referred to here, that *Ahimelech* was then high priest at Nob; and from other passages, that *Abiathar* was his son. Various conjectures have been formed in order to solve this difficulty; and some, instead of untying, have *cut* the knot, by pronouncing it an interpolation. The most probable opinion seems to be, that both father and son had two names (for other examples of persons having two names see 2 Ch 34:20n. Ne 7:24n. 11:6n, 11n), the father being also called Abiathar; and this appears almost certain from 2 S 8:17. 1 Ch 18:16, where *Ahimelech* seems evidently termed *Abiathar*, while *Abiathar* is called *Ahimelech* or *Abimelech* (Compare 1 K 2:26, 27). 1 S 14:3, Ahiah. 1 S 21:1. 22:9, 11, 20-22. 23:6, 9. 2 S 8:17. 15:24, 29, 35. 20:25. 1 K 1:7. 2:22, 26, 27. 4:4. **did eat**. 1 S ⟩21:6. **which is not lawful**. Ex 25:30. *29:32, 33. Le 24:5-9. Mt 12:2-7.

27. **The sabbath**. *25, Ge +4:4. Ex *23:12. Dt 5:14. Ne 9:13, 14. Is +*58:13n. Ezk 20:12, 20. Lk *6:9. Jn 7:23. 1 C 3:21, 22. 2 C 4:15. Col √2:16. **and**. "And" is omitted in most Greek texts. *41, Ge +10:1.

28. **Son**. *144A3, Ge +11:5. Mt 16:27n. **is Lord also of**. Mk 3:4. Mt 12:8. Lk 6:5. *13:15, 16. *14:5, 6. Jn *5:9-11, 16, 17. *9:5-11, 13, 14, 16. 20:19, 26. Ep 1:22. Re *1:10.

MARK 3

Jesus restores a man's withered hand in the synagogue, on the sabbath, 1-5. The Pharisees conspire his death: he retires, is followed by multitudes, and heals many, 6-12. He chooses twelve apostles, 13-19. His friends look upon him as beside himself, 20, 21.

He confutes the blasphemous absurdity of the scribes, who ascribe his casting out devils to the power of Beelzebub, 22-30. Those who do the will of God are regarded as his nearest relations, 31-35.

1. **he entered**. Mk 1:21, 23, 29. Mt 12:9-14. Lk 6:6-11. **withered**. 1 K 13:4, 6. Zc 11:17. Jn 5:3.

2. **they watched**. Ps *37:32. Is 29:20, 21. Je *20:10. Da 6:4. Lk 6:7. 11:53, 54. 14:1. 20:20. Jn 9:16. Ac 9:24. Ga 4:10g. **that**. Lk 11:54. 20:20. Jn *8:6.

3. **he saith**. Is 42:4. Da +*6:10. Lk 6:8. Jn 9:4. 1 C √15:58. Ga √6:9. Ph 1:14, 28-30. 1 P 4:1. **Stand forth**. *or*, Arise, stand forth in the midst. Lk 6:8.

4. **Is it lawful**. *96E1, Ps +118:8. Heterosis of Degree, the positive for the comparative. i.e. more lawful to do good than to do evil. The evil His enemies did on the sabbath was in watching Him (B526) with malicious intent. Mk 2:27, 28. Ho +*6:6. Mt 12:10-12. Lk 6:9. 13:13-17. 14:1-5. Jn 5:16, 17. **sabbath**. T#639. Mk 2:23-28. +6:2 (T#640). Mt 12:1-5, 11-13. 24:20. Lk 6:1-10. 13:11-17. Jn 5:8-10, 16, 17. **life**. Gr. *psyche*, *121A7, Mt +2:20. *121A7, Ge +9:5. **But**. Mk 9:34. Lk 14:6.

5. **looked**. ver. 34. Mk 5:32. 10:21, 23. 11:11. **with anger**. *141, Is +22:4. With *anger* at their desperate malice and wickedness, and with *commiseration* for the calamities which they would thereby bring on themselves. Ex=11:8. Mt 5:22. Lk 6:10. 13:15. Ep 4:26. Re *6:16, 17. **grieved**. Ge 6:6. Jg 10:16. Ne 13:8. Ps 95:10. Is 63:9, +*10. Lk 19:40-44. Ac 7:51. Ep +*4:30. 1 Th *5:19. He 3:10, 17. **hardness**. *or*, blindness. Mk +6:52. 16:14. Is *6:9, 10. 42:18-20. 44:18-20. Mt 13:14, 15. Ro 11:7-10, 25. 2 C 3:14. Ep 4:18. **Stretch**. 1 K 13:4, 6. Mt 12:13. Lk 6:10. 17:14. Jn 5:8, 9. 9:7. He 5:9.

6. **Pharisees**. Ps 109:3, 4. Mt 12:14. +21:46. Lk *6:11. 20:19, 20. 22:2. Jn 5:18. 7:1, 19. 11:53. **went forth**. ver. 1. **took counsel**. Mk 15:1. Mt 22:15. 27:1. 28:12. **Herodians**. Mk 8:15. 12:13. Mt 22:16. Lk 23:7. **how**. Jn 7:30. **destroy**. Gr. *apollumi*, Mt +2:13.

7. **Jesus**. Mt 10:23. 12:15. Lk *6:12. Jn 10:39-41. 11:53, 54. Ac 14:5, 6. 17:10, 14. **withdrew**. Pr +*22:3. Is 42:2. **and a**. Mk 1:45. Mt 4:25. Lk *6:17. **Galilee**. Mk 1:39. 10:1. Jsh 20:7. 21:32. Mt 4:25. Lk 23:5. Jn 7:41, 52.

8. **from Jerusalem**. Lk 6:17. **Idumea**. i.e. *earthy*, *S#2401g, only here. For *S#123h, see Is +34:5. Ezk 35:15. 36:5. Ml 1:2-4, Edom. **beyond Jordan**. Mk +10:1. Nu 32:33-38. Jsh 13:8; etc. Mt 4:25. **Tyre**. Mk 7:24, 31. Jsh 19:28, 29. Ps 45:12. 87:4. Is ch. 23. Ezk ch. 26-28. Mt 11:21.

9. **small ship**. Mk 4:1. 6:32, 45. 8:10. Lk 5:3. **because**. Mk 5:30, 31. Jn 6:15. **throng him**. Mk 5:24, 31.

10. **healed many**. Mk 1:34. Mt 12:15. 14:14. **pressed**. *or*, rushed. **touch**. Mk 5:27, 28. 6:56. Mt 9:20, 21. 14:36. Lk 6:19. Ac 5:15. 19:11, 12. **as many**. Mk 5:29, 34. Ge 12:17. Nu 11:33. Lk 7:2, 21. Ac 22:24g. He 11:36g. 12:6.

11. **unclean**. ver. +*30. Mk 1:23, 24, 26, 34. 5:5, 6. Mt 8:31. Lk *4:41. Ac 16:17. 19:13-17. Ja *2:19. **fell down**. Lk 8:28. **and cried**. Mk +*1:24. 5:7. **the Son**. Mk 1:1. Mt 4:3, 6. 8:29. *14:33. Lk 8:28.

12. **straitly charged**. Mk 1:25, 34. Mt 12:16. Ac 16:18. **should not**. Mk +*1:24. 7:36. Ps *50:16. Mt 9:30. 12:16. 17:9. Lk 5:14, 15. Jn 8:20.

13. **he goeth**. Mt *10:1, etc. Lk 6:12-16. **whom he**

would. Dt=18:5. =21:5. 1 Ch=15:2. =16:41. 2 Ch=29:11. Jn 13:18. 15:16, 19. Ac 9:15. Ep 1:4. 1 P 2:9.

14. he ordained. T#450. Jn 15:16. Ac 1:24, 25. 13:2, 3. 14:23. Ga 1:1, 15-20. 1 T +5:22 (T#401). 2 T *2:2. T 1:15. **twelve.** Dt=1:23. **be with.** 1 Ch 4:23. **and.** Lk 9:1-6. 10:1-11. 24:47. Ac +*1:8.

15. have power. Mt 10:1. Lk *9:1. 10:19. 12:12. Ac 4:33. 6:10. **to heal.** Mk 16:18. Mt 10:1. Lk *9:6. Ac 3:7. 5:16. 9:34. 14:10. 16:18. 19:12. 28:8. 1 C 12:9. **cast out devils.** Mk 6:7. ◐9:38. 16:17. Mt 12:43-45. Lk 10:17. Ac 5:16. 8:7. 19:13-16.

16. Simon. Mk 1:16. Mt +*16:16-18. Jn *1:42. 1 C 1:12. 3:22. 9:5. Ga 2:7-9, Cephas. 2 P 1:1.

17. James. Mk 1:19, 20. 5:37. 9:2. 10:35. 14:33. Jn 21:2, 20-25. Ac 12:1. **he surnamed.** Is 58:1. Je 23:29. He *4:12. Re 10:11. **Boanerges.** i.e. *commotion; sons of thunder,* ❋S#993g, only here. **which is.** Mt +6:2n. Lk 9:54. **sons of thunder.** Lk 10:6. Ac 4:36.

18. Andrew. Jn 1:40. 6:8. 12:21, 22. Ac 1:13. **Philip.** Jn 1:43-45. 6:5-7. 14:8, 9. **Bartholomew.** Mt 10:3. Lk 6:14. Ac 1:13. **Matthew.** Mk 2:14. Mt 9:9. Lk 5:27-29, Levi. 6:15. **Thomas.** Jn 11:16. √20:24-29. 21:2. Ac 1:13. **James.** Mk +*6:3. Mt 10:3. +*13:55. Lk 6:15. Ac 15:13. 21:18. 1 C 9:5. 15:7. Ga 1:19. 2:9. Ja 1:1. **Alpheus.** Mk 2:14. **Thaddeus.** Mt 10:3. Lk 6:16. Jn 14:22. Ac 1:13, Judas the brother of James. Ju 1. **Simon.** Mt 10:4. Lk 6:15. Ac 1:13, Simon Zelotes. **Canaanite.** *Kananitas,* so called, not from being a native of Canaan, *Xanaan,* which would have been *Xananaos,* but from the Hebrew *kana,* to be zealous, whence he is called in Greek *Zelotes,* or the *Zealot,* from *dzalo-o,* to be zealous.

19. Judas. Mt 26:14-16, 47. 27:3-5. Jn 6:64, 71, 72. 12:4-6. 13:2, 26-30. Ac 1:16-25. **Iscariot.** Jsh 15:25. Je 48:24, 41. **into an house.** *or,* home. Mk 2:1. 7:17. 9:28.

20. so that. ver. 9. Mk *6:31. Lk 6:17. Jn 4:31-34.

21. And. ver. 21-35. ♪148, Ge +8:22. **when.** Some render, "And they who were with him (in the house, ver. 19), hearing (the noise) went out to restrain (*auton,* i.e. *oxlon,* the multitude), for they said, It (the mob) is mad." This, however, is contrary to all the versions; and appears an unnatural construction. **friends.** *or,* kinsmen. ver. 31. Jn *7:3-10. **He is beside.** 2 K 9:11. Je 29:26. Ho 9:7. Jn *10:20. Ac 26:24. 2 C 5:13. 2 T +*1:7.

22. which. Mk 7:1. Mt 15:1. Lk 5:17. **said.** Mk ◐+*1:24. **He hath.** Ps 22:6. Mt 9:34. 10:25. *12:24. Lk *11:15. Jn *7:20. 8:48, 52. 10:22. **by.** ♪108D, Mt +3:11.

23. in parables. Ps 49:4. Mt 13:34, 35. **How.** Mt *12:25-30. Lk 11:17-23.

24. And. ♪148, Ge +8:22. ♪138B, Ge +13:16. **if.** ♪184C, Mt +4:9. **divided against.** Jg 9:23, etc. 12:1-6. 2 S 20:1, 6. 1 K 12:16, etc. Is 9:20, 21. 19:2, 3. Ezk 37:22. Zc 11:14. Jn 17:21. 1 C 1:10-13. Ep 4:3-6.

25. And. ♪138B, Ge +13:16. **if.** ♪184C, Mt +4:9. **a house.** Ge 13:7, 8. 37:4. Ps 133:1. Ga 5:15. Ja 3:16.

26. if. ♪184A, 1 C +15:2. **be divided.** Lk 4:6. 2 C 11:13, 14. Ep 6:12. **hath an end.** Lk 22:37.

27. can enter. Ge +*3:15. Is *27:1. *49:24-26. 53:12. 61:1. Mt 12:29. Lk 10:17-20. *11:21-23. Jn *12:31. Ro 16:20. Ep √6:10-13. Col *2:15. He *2:14. 1 J √3:8. 4:4. Re 12:7-9. *20:1-3.

28. Verily. Mk 8:12. 9:1, 41. 10:15, 29. 11:23. 12:43.

13:30. 14:9, 18, 25, 30. Mt +5:18. Lk +4:24. Jn +1:51. **All sins.** Is +*1:18. Mt +*12:31n, 32n. Lk *12:10. Ac 8:18, 19, 22. 13:38, 39. He *6:4-8. √10:26-31. 1 J √1:9. +*5:16. **sons.** ♪144A3, Ge +11:5. Ep 3:5. **and blasphemies.** Le 24:16.

29. blaspheme against. Ac 7:51. He 10:29. **Ghost.** Gr. *pneuma,* Mt +3:16. **hath never.** Gr. *aion,* Mt +6:13. Lk +12:10. **but is.** Mk 12:40. Mt +*25:46. 2 Th √1:9. Ju *7, *13. **in danger.** Mk 14:64. Mt 5:21, 22. 26:66. 1 C 11:27. He 2:15. Ja 2:10. **eternal.** Gr. *aionios,* Mt 18:8.

30. Because. ♪63D1, Mt +16:7. Here the first clause is ommitted: "(Jesus said this unto them), because they said, He hath an unclean spirit." **they said.** ver. 22. Jn 10:20. **unclean.** ver. 11. Mk 1:23, 26, 27. 5:2, 8, 13. 6:7. 7:25. 9:25. Mt 10:1. 12:43. Lk 4:33, 36. 6:18. 8:29. 9:42. 11:24. Ac 5:16. 8:7. Re 16:13. 18:2. **spirit.** Gr. *pneuma,* Mt +8:16.

31. There came. Mt 12:46-48. Lk 8:19-21. **his brethren.** These are certainly his literal half-brothers, of which Scripture names four. Jesus also had at least three half-sisters (Mt 13:56 uses "all," not "both," indicating more than two). "Brethren" here mentioned in such close connection with Mary, Christ's mother, certainly points to their being his natural brothers, not cousins. Sons of another woman would not be following Mary around. While Jesus is Mary's *firstborn* son, this does not indicate she had no other children, for if that were the case, the word would have been *monogenes,* only begotten son (as in Lk 7:12. 8:42. 9:38), not "firstborn" (*protokos,* Mt 1:25. Lk 2:7. Ro 8:29. Col +*1:15n, 18. He 1:6. 11:28. 12:23. Re 1:5). The term *firstborn* does not imply that there are no others, for Christ is the firstborn from the dead (Re 1:5) that he may bring many sons into glory (He 2:10) by resurrection (1 C 15:20-23). It was foretold in prophecy that Jesus would have brothers, and his mother would have other children, Ps √69:8, 9. If his "brethren" were merely cousins, the term "sungenes," used of kin, kinsmen, and kinsfolk (Mk 6:4. Lk 1:36, 58. 2:44. 14:12. 21:16. 18:26. Ac 10:24. Ro 9:3. 16:7, 11, 21), and cousin (Lk 1:36, 58) was available to indicate this, but was not used. Note that "brethren" is distinguished from "kinsmen" at Lk 14:12 and Lk 21:16. Mk +*6:3. Mt +*13:55. Jn 2:12. 7:3, 5, 10. Ac 1:14. 1 C 9:5. Ga 1:19. **his mother.** Mt +1:16.

32. thy mother. Mt 1:16. **thy brethren.** ver. +*31n. Mk +*6:3. Jn 7:3. **seek for thee.** ver. 21. Lk 4:42. 8:19. 19:3. Jn 6:24. 12:21.

33. Who is. Dt 33:9. Mt 12:48. Lk 2:49. Jn 2:4. 2 C 5:16. **or my brethren.** ver. 21. Mk +*6:3. Jn *7:3-5.

34. looked. ver. +5. **Behold.** Ps 22:22. SS 4:9, 10. 5:1, 2. Mt 12:49, 50. 25:40-45. 28:10. Lk *11:27, 28. Jn 20:17. Ro 8:29. He 2:11, 12.

35. whosoever. Mt *12:50. Jn +*15:14. Ro 8:29. He 2:11. 1 J 2:17. **shall do.** Mt +*7:21. Lk +*11:28. Ja +*1:25. 1 J √3:22, 23. **the will of God.** Mt 12:50. Lk 8:21. Jn +*7:17. 1 Th 4:3. 1 J *2:17. **the same is my.** Ro 8:29. He 2:11.

MARK 4

The parable of the sower, 1-9. Why Christ taught by parables, 10-13. The interpretation of the parable, 14-20. Knowledge is given in order to be communicated,

21, 22. A call to hear with attention, 23-25. The parable of the seed sown, imperceptibly growing up, and ripening for harvest, 26-29. Parable of the grain of mustard seed, 30-32. Christ teaches only by parables, which he expounds to his disciples, 33, 34. He stills a tempest by his word, 35-41.

1. **he began**. Mk 2:13. Mt +*13:1, 2, etc. Lk 8:4, etc. **so that**. Lk 5:1-3.

2. **by parables**. ver. 11, 34. Mk 3:23. Ps 49:4. 78:2. Mt +*13:3, 10, 34, 35. **in his**. Mk 12:38. Mt 7:28. Jn √7:16, 17. 18:19. **doctrine**. ♪108B. Idiom B826. "Doctrine" means the thing taught; but it is used idiomatically and by Metonymy for the discourse in which it is taught. It has to do with the style and manner as well as the thing taught. For other instances of this figure see Mk 11:18. 12:38. Mt 7:28. Ac 2:42. 1 C 14:26.

3. **Hearken**. ver. 9, 23. Mk 7:14, 16. Dt *4:1. Ps *34:11. 45:10. Pr 7:24. 8:32. Is 46:3, 12. 55:1, 2. Ac 2:14. He *2:1-3. Ja *2:5. Re 2:7, 11, 29. **there**. ver. 14, 26-29. Ec 11:6. Is 28:23-26. Mt +*13:3, 24-26. Lk 8:5-8. Jn 4:35-38. 1 C 3:6-9.

4. **the fowls**. ver. 15. Ge 15:11. Mt +*13:4, 19. Lk 8:5, 12.

5. **stony ground**. ver. 16, 17. Ezk 11:19. 36:26. Ho 10:12. Am 6:12. Mt +*13:5, 6, 20, 21. Lk 8:6, +*13.

6. **the sun**. SS 1:6. Is 25:4. Jon 4:8. Ja 1:11. Re 7:16. **no root**. Ps +*1:3, 4. 92:13-15. Je +*17:5-8. Ep 3:17. Col +*2:7. 2 Th 2:10. Ju 12.

7. **fell among thorns**. ver. 18, 19. Ge *3:17, 18. Je 4:3. Mt 13:7, 22. Lk 8:7, 14. 12:15. 21:34. 1 T √6:9, 10. 1 J √2:15, 16.

8. **fell on good**. ver. 20. Is *58:1. Je √23:29. Mt +*13:8, 23. Lk *8:8, 15. Jn √1:12, 13. √3:19-21. √7:17. 15:5. Ac √17:11. Col *1:6. He *4:1, 2. Ja √1:19-22. 1 P *2:1-3. **an hundred**. Mk ◐+*10:30. Ge +*26:12. Jn *15:5. Ph *1:11.

9. **hath ears**. See on ver. 3, 23, √24. Mk 7:14, 16. Ezk 3:27. 12:2. Mt *11:15. +*13:9. 15:10. Lk +*8:18. Re *3:6, 13, 22. **hear**. ♪147A, Ge +50:24.

10. **when he was alone**. ver. 34. Mk 7:17. Pr +*13:20. Mt +*13:10, etc., 36. Lk *8:9, etc. **asked of him**. Pr √4:7.

11. **Unto you**. Mt *11:25. +*13:11, 12, 16. 16:17. Lk 8:10. *10:21-24. 1 C *2:10. 4:7. 2 C 4:6. Ep 1:9. *2:4-10. T *3:3-7. Ja 1:16-18. 1 J 5:20. **them**. 1 C *1:18. *5:12, 13. Col √4:5. 1 Th 4:12. 1 T 3:7. **all these**. Mt 13:13.

12. **That seeing**. ♪147B, Ge +2:16. Rather, as *hina* frequently denotes, "So that seeing they see, and do not perceive, and hearing they hear, and do not understand," etc. The expression appears to be proverbial; and relates to those who *might* see what they now overlook through inattention and folly. See the parallel texts. Dt *29:2, 4. Is ◐6:9, 10. 44:18. Je 5:21. Mt +*13:14, 15. Lk 8:10. Jn *12:37-41. Ac 28:25-27. Ro 11:8-10. **lest**. Jn *5:40. *6:36, 37. 2 C *3:15. **be converted**. Je +*31:18-20. Ezk *18:27-32. Ac +*3:19. 2 T √2:25. He *6:6.

13. **Know**. Mk 7:17, 18. Mt +*13:51, 52. 15:15-17. 16:8, 9. Lk *8:11. 24:25. 1 C 3:1, 2. He √5:11-14. Re *3:19.

14. **sower**. T#428. See on ver. 3. Ps +*19:7 (T#47). Pr *6:23. Ec 11:6. Is 32:20. Mt +*13:19, 37. 20:1. Lk *8:11. *10:2. Jn *4:35, 36. 1 C *3:8, 9. **the word**. Mk 2:2. Col *1:5, 6. 1 P +*1:23-25.

15. **these**. See on ver. 4. Ge 19:14. Is *53:1. Mt 22:25. Lk √8:12. 14:18, 19. Ac 17:18-20, 32. 18:14-17. 25:19, 20. 26:31, 32. He *2:1. 12:16. **Satan**. Jb 1:6-12. Zc 3:1. Mt +*13:19. Ac +*5:3. 2 C √2:11. √4:3, 4. 2 Th *2:9. 1 P *5:8. Re *12:9. *20:2, 3, 7, 10.

16. **stony ground**. Mk *6:20. 10:17-22. Ezk +*33:31, 32. Mt 8:19, 20. +*13:20, 21. Lk +*8:13. Jn 5:35. Ac *8:13, 18-21. 24:25, 26. 26:28.

17. **have no root**. ver. 5, 6. Jb 19:28. 27:8-10. Ezk +*33:31, 32. Mt 12:31. Lk 6:49. 12:10. Jn 6:66. +*8:31. *15:2-7. Ep +*4:14. 2 T +*1:15. +*2:17, 18. *4:10. 1 J √2:19. **endure**. Mt ◐10:22. 24:13n. Lk +*8:13. **but for a time**. Ho *6:4. Lk +*8:13. Jn *5:35. Ac *26:28. 1 C +*15:2. 2 C 4:18. Ga 1:6. 5:7. Col +*1:23. 2 P +*1:10. **when affliction**. Mt 11:6. +*13:21. +*24:9, 10. 1 C √10:12, 13. Ga 6:12. 1 Th √3:3-5. 2 T *4:16. He √10:29. Ja 1:2. Re *2:10, 13. **are offended**. Mt 11:6.

18. **sown among thorns**. See on ver. 7. Je 4:3. Mt +*13:22. Lk *8:14.

19. **the cares**. Mk *10:21-23. Ps *39:6. *127:2. Ec 1:13. 2:26. 8:16. Mt √6:25, 31. +*13:22. Lk 8:14. 10:40, 41. 12:17-21, 29, 30. 14:18-20. √21:34. 2 C 11:28g. Ph √4:6. 2 T +*4:10. 1 P √5:7. **of this**. Mt +*12:32. Jn +*6:54n. **world**. Gr. *aion*, Mt +6:13. lit. "age." ♪121P2, Mt +13:22. 2 T 4:10. **the deceitfulness of riches**. T#625. Mk *10:23. Ge 13:10-13. Dt 8:11-14. 32:13-15. 2 Ch 26:3, 5, 15, 16. Ps 30:6. *52:7. 55:19. *62:10. 92:7. Pr 1:32. *23:+4 (T#626), +5 (T#627). 28:20. 30:8, 9. Ec *4:8. √5:10-16. Je 22:21. Ezk +*16:49, 50. 28:5. Mt +13:22 (T#741). *19:23, 24. Ac 5:1-11. 2 Th 2:10. 1 T √6:9, 10, 17, +18 (T#406). **the lusts**. 1 Th +*4:5g. 1 P 4:2, 3. 1 J √2:15-17. **unfruitful**. Is 5:2, 4. Mt 3:10. +*13:22. +*25:24n. Lk *13:6. *19:20. Jn *15:2. He *6:7, 8. 2 P √1:8. Ju *12.

20. **which**. See on ver. 8. Mt +*13:23. Lk *8:15. Jn *15:4, 5. Ro 7:4. Ga √5:22, 23. Ph *1:11. Col +*1:10. 1 Th *4:1. Ja +*1:21, 22. 2 P *1:8. **an hundred**. ver. 8. Mk ◐+*10:30. Ge +*26:12.

21. **Is a candle**. ♪85C, Ge +18:14. Is 60:1-3. Mt *5:15, 16. +6:2n. Lk *8:16. 11:33. Ac 10:47n. 1 C 12:7. Ep 5:3-15. Ph 2:15, 16. **bushel**. "The word in the original signifieth a less measure, as Mt 5:15mg."

22. **nothing hid**. Ps 40:9, 10. 78:2-4. Ec 12:14. Mt *10:26, 27. Lk *8:17. 12:2, 3. Ac 4:20. 20:27. Ro *2:16. 1 C √4:5. 1 T *5:25. 1 J *1:1-3.

23. **have ears**. See on ver. 9, +*24. Mt 11:15. Re 2:7, 11, 17, 29. **hear**. ♪147A, Ge +50:24.

24. **Take heed**. Pr +*19:27. Je 17:21. Ezk 14:10n. Mt +*15:14. Lk +*8:18. Ac √17:11. He *2:1. 1 J *4:1. 1 P 2:2. 2 P 2:1-3. **what ye hear**. Mk 8:15. Ps +*119:63. Pr +*19:27. 20:12. Is +*8:20n. 65:5n. Ezk +*14:10n. Mt 16:12. Lk ◐+*8:18. 1 T 1:4. +*4:16. 2 T 4:3. 1 J 4:1. 2 J 9-11. Ju +*3. **with what measure**. Le 24:19. Jg +*1:7. 1 S 15:33. Mt 7:2. Lk +*6:37, 38. 2 C √9:6. **that hear**. Mk *9:7. Is +*55:3. Jn *5:25. √10:16, 27.

25. **he that hath**. Mk 10:29, 30. Mt +*13:12. *21:43. *25:28, 29. Lk +*8:18. *16:9-12. *19:24-26. Jn *15:2. Ja 4:6. **from him**. Mk 6:11. Je *5:25. Lk 16:2. 20:16. Re 2:5.

26. **So is**. Mt 3:2. 4:17. +*13:11, 31, 33. Lk *13:18. **as if**. ver. 3, 4, 14, etc. Pr 11:18. Ec 11:4, 6. Is 28:24-26. 32:20. Mt +*13:3, 24. Lk *8:5, 11. Jn *4:36-38. 12:24. 1 C +*3:6-9. Ja 3:18. 1 P *1:23-25.

27. **night and day.** Mk 5:5. La 2:18. Lk 2:37. 18:7.
Ac 9:24. 20:31. 26:7. 1 Th 2:9. 3:10. 2 Th 3:8. 1 T
5:5. 2 T 1:3. **should spring.** Is 61:11. **and grow.** Ec
8:17. 11:5. Jn 3:7, 8. 1 C 15:37, 38. 2 Th 1:3. 2 P
√3:18.

28. **the earth.** Ge 1:11, 12. 2:4, 5, 9. 4:11, 12. Is
*61:11. 1 C *3:7, 9. **fruit.** Ge 1:12. Jn +*15:16. **first.**
ver. 31, 32. Ps +*1:3. 92:13, 14. Pr +*4:18. Ec 3:1,
11. Ho +*6:3. Ph *1:6, 9-11. Col +√1:10. 1 Th 3:12,
13. **blade.** Mt 13:26.

29. **brought forth.** *or*, ripe. Jb 5:26. 2 T 4:7, 8. **he
putteth.** Is 57:1, 2. Jl *▶3:13. Mt +*13:30, 39-43. Re
*14:13-17.

30. **Whereunto.** Is *40:18. La 2:13. Mt 11:16. Lk
13:18, 20, 21. 1 C *3:1, 2. **we.** ✦96D4, Ge +29:27.

31. **like.** Mt +*13:31-33. Lk 13:18, 19. **mustard
seed.** Mustard, *sinapi*, is a well-known plant of the
tetradynamia siliquosa class, distinguished by its yellow
cruciform flowers, with expanding calyx, and its pods
smooth, square, and close to the stem. Its seed was
probably the smallest known to the Jews; and though
its ordinary height does not exceed four feet, yet a
species grows to the height of from three to five cubits,
with a tapering, ligneous stalk, and spreading branches.
is less than. Ge 22:17, 18. Ps 72:16-19. Is 2:2, 3. +*9:7.
49:6, 7. *53:2, 12. 54:1-3. 60:22. Ezk 17:22-24. Da
*2:34, 35, 44, 45. Am +*9:11-15. Mi 4:1, 2. Zc 2:11.
*8:20-23. 12:8. 14:6-9. Ml 1:11. Mt 13:32n. Ac 2:41.
4:4. 5:14. 19:20. 21:20. Re 11:15. 20:1-6.

32. **it groweth.** Da ▶4:9. **and becometh.** Pr +*4:18.
Is 11:9. Ac 2:41. 4:4. 5:14. *19:20. *21:20. **shooteth.**
Ps 80:9-11. Ezk 31:3-10. Da 4:10-14, 20-22. **fowls.** Ezk
▶17:23. *31:6. Da ▶4:12. **lodge.** Ps 91:1. SS 2:3. Is 32:2.
La 4:20. Mi 4:1.

33. **with many.** Mt +*13:34, 35. **as they.** Jn √16:12.
1 C 3:1, 2. He √5:11-14.

34. **when.** ver. 10, 11. Mk 7:17-23. Mt +*13:36,
etc. 15:15, etc. Lk 8:9, etc. 24:27, 44-46.

35. **the same.** Mt 8:23. Lk 8:22. **Let.** Mk 5:21. 6:45.
8:13. Mt 8:18. 14:22. Jn 6:1, 17, 25.

36. **even.** ver. 1. Mk 3:9.

37. **there arose.** Mt *8:23, 24. Lk *8:22, 23. **great
storm.** Jb 1:12, 19. Ps 107:23-31. Jon 1:4. Ac 27:14-
20, 41. 2 C 11:25.

38. **in the.** Ps *4:8. Jn 4:6. He 2:17. +*4:15. **and
they.** 1 K 18:27-29. Jb 8:5, 6. Ps 44:23, 24. Is 51:9,
10. Mt 8:25. Lk 8:24. **Master.** Mk 5:35. 9:17, 38. 10:17,
20, 35. 12:14, 19, 32. 13:1. 14:14. Mt 22:24. Lk 7:40.
Jn 1:38. **carest.** Ge +*19:30. Ps 10:1, 2. 22:1, 2. 77:1-
10. Is 40:27, 28. 49:14-16. 54:6-8. 63:15. 64:12. La
3:8. Jon 1:6. 1 P *5:7. **perish.** Gr. *apollumi*, Mt +2:13.

39. **he arose.** Ex 14:16, 22, 28, 29. Jb 38:11. Ps
29:10. 93:3, 4. 104:7-9. 107:29. 148:8. Pr 8:29. Je 5:22.
rebuked. Mk 9:25. Ps 106:9. Ec *8:4. Na 1:4. Lk 4:39.
be still. Mk 1:25g. **the wind.** Ps 89:9. La 3:31. **great
calm.** Mk 6:51. Jb 38:11. Ps 65:7. 89:9. 93:4. Mt 14:32.

40. **Why.** Ps 46:1-3. Is 42:3. 43:2. Mt 8:26. 14:31.
Lk 8:25. Jn 6:19, 20. **fearful.** Ps +*34:4. Jn *14:27.
2 T +*1:7. Re *21:8. **no faith.** Mt *6:30. 16:8.

41. **feared.** ✦147D, Ge +1:29. Mk 5:33. 1 S 12:18-
20, 24. Ps *33:8. *89:7. Jon *1:9, 10, 14-16. Ml 2:5.
Lk 5:26. He 12:28. Re 15:4. **What manner.** T#77.
Mk 1:27. 7:37. +16:20 (T#43). Jb 38:11. Mt 8:3,
27. 14:32, 33. Lk 4:35, 36. 8:25. Jn 2:23. 5:36. 7:31.
10:37, 38. 11:42-45, 47, 48. √20:30, 31. **that even.**
Lk 5:9.

MARK 5

*Jesus casts out a legion of devils; and suffers them
to enter and destroy a herd of swine, 1-13. The owners
entreat him to depart; and the man, who had been
possessed, desires to be with him; but is sent to declare
what Jesus had done for him, 14-20. Jairus entreats
Christ to heal his daughter, 21-24. By the way, he
heals a woman of an inveterate issue of blood, 25-34.
He raises Jairus's daughter to life, 35-43.*

1. **came over.** Mk 4:35. Mt *8:28-34. Lk *8:26, etc.
Gadarenes. i.e. *fortified*, ✱S#1046g. Lk 8:26, 37.

2. **out.** Is 65:4. Lk *8:27. **the tombs.** ✦115, 2 K
+19:7. **a man.** St. Matthew gives a brief account of
two demoniacs who were dispossessed on this occasion;
but Mark and Luke omit the mention of one (who
was perhaps not so remarkable). That these wretched
men were not merely mad, as some suppose, but really
possessed of evil spirits, appears clearly from the language employed, as well as from the narrative itself.
St. Matthew expressly affirms that they were "possessed with devils," or demoniacs, *daimonidzomenoi*;
St. Mark says he had "an unclean spirit," i.e. *a fallen
spirit*; and St. Luke asserts, that he "had devils (or
demons) a long time," and was called *Legion*, "because
many devils were entered into him." With supernatural
strength the demons burst asunder the chains and fetters with which he was bound; they address Christ
as the "Son of the most high God;" they beseech him
to suffer them to enter into the swine; and when he
had given them leave, they *"went out* and *entered*
into the swine," etc. **with.** ver. 8. Mk 1:23, 26. 3:30.
7:25. Lk 9:42. **spirit.** Gr. *pneuma*, Mt +8:16.

3. **dwelling.** Mk 9:18-22. Is 65:4. Da 4:32, 33. Lk
*8:29.

4. **tame.** Ja 3:7, 8.

5. **tombs.** Gr. *mnema*, ✱S#3418g. Mk 5:5. Lk 8:27.
23:53 (sepulchre). 24:1. Ac 2:29. Re 11:9 (graves). **crying.** 1 K 18:26. Jb 2:7, 8. Jn *8:44.

6. **he ran.** Ps 66:3mg. 72:9. Lk 4:41. Ac 16:17. Ja
*2:19. **worshipped.** Mt +8:2.

7. **What.** ✦85H, Jg +11:12. Mk +*1:24. 1 K *17:18.
Ho 14:8. Mt 8:29. Lk 4:34. **Jesus.** Ph *2:10. **Son.** Mk
3:11. 14:61. Mt 16:16. Jn √20:31. Ac *8:37. 16:17. **most
high God.** Mk 11:10. Ge +14:18. Nu 24:16. Ps 57:2.
78:17, 35, 56. 83:18. Is 14:14. 57:15. Da 3:26. 4:24,
32. 5:18, 21. 7:18, 22, 25, 27. Mi 6:6. Lk 1:32, 76.
6:35. 8:28. Ac 7:48. 16:17. Ro *9:5. 1 C 10:9. 1 Th
3:13. He 7:1. **I adjure.** 1 K 22:16. Mt 26:63. Ac 19:13.
1 Th 5:27mg. **that.** Ge +*3:15. Mt 8:29. Lk 8:28. Ro
16:20. He *2:14. Ja 2:19. 2 P *2:4. 1 J √3:8. Ju *6.
Re 12:12. *20:1-3.

8. **Come out.** Mk 1:25. 9:25, 26. Ac 16:18. **spirit.**
Gr. *pneuma*, Mt +8:16.

9. **What is.** Lk 8:30. 11:21-26. **Legion.** i.e. *a division
of the Roman army*, ✱S#3003g. Mk 5:9, 15. Lk 8:30.
Mt 26:53. **we are many.** Mt *12:45.

10. **he besought.** ver. 13. Mk 3:22. Lk *8:31.

11. **herd.** Le 11:7, 8. Dt *14:8. Is 65:4. 66:3. Mt
8:30. Lk 8:32.

12. **all the devils.** Jb 1:10-12. 2:5. Lk 4:41. 22:31,
32. 2 C 2:11. 1 P *5:8. **besought.** Ro +1:4. **Send us.**
Demons are persons, for only persons can beseech
and speak of themselves as *we* and *us*. Ac +*5:32.
Ro +*1:4.

13. **gave them leave.** Some have seen a moral prob-

lem here: how could Jesus permit this destruction of the property of an innocent party? The objection against the action or inaction of Jesus is of no more force than the objection to the providence of God generally, for many things are permitted of God, such as the destruction of property and life by natural phenomenon (earthquakes, floods, tornadoes, pestilence), and this is no unanswerable objection to the goodness of God. Rather, our moral sensibilities ought to be outraged that the owners of the herd did not respond in repentance and faith at the miracle wrought in the lives of the demoniacs, but the owners rather desired Christ to leave the vicinity. 1 K 22:22. Jb 1:12. *2:6. Am +*3:6. Mt 8:32. Col *2:9. 1 P 3:22. Re 13:5-7. 20:7. **spirits.** Gr. *pneuma*, Mt +8:16. **the herd.** Jn *8:44. Re 9:11.

14. **they that fed.** Mt 8:33. Lk 8:34.

15. **him that.** ver. 4. Is 49:24, 25. Mt 9:33. 12:29. Lk 8:35, 36. 10:39. Col 1:13. **right mind.** 1 C *6:11. 2 T +*1:7. **and they.** 1 S 6:20, 21. 16:4. 1 Ch 13:12. 15:13. Jb 13:11. Ps 14:5. 2 T +*1:7.

16. **swine.** These swine were in all probability Jewish property, and kept and used in express violation of the law of God; and, therefore, their destruction was no more than a proper manifestation of the *justice* of God.

17. **pray him to depart.** T#1574. ver. 7. Mk 1:24. Ge 26:16. Dt 5:25. 1 K 17:18. Jb +*21:14, 15. Mt 8:34. Lk 5:8, 9. 8:37. Ac 16:39. 2 C √2:14.

18. **prayed.** ver. 7, 17. Ps 116:12. Lk 8:38, 39. 17:15-17. 23:42, 43. Ph 1:23, 24. **be with.** Lk 9:61, 62. Ph *1:23.

19. **Go home.** Ge +16:9. Ps 66:16. Is 38:9-20. Da 4:1-3, 37. 6:25-27. Jon 2:1, etc. Jn 4:29. Ac 22:1-21. 26:4-29. **tell them.** Ps 107:2. Lk 12:8, 9. Jn *1:41. Ac 4:19, 20. 2 T 1:8. 1 P *3:15.

20. **began to publish.** Ps 51:12, 13. 66:16. Is 38:9, 19. Jn 1:40-42. **Decapolis.** Mk 7:31. Mt 4:25.

21. **passed over.** Mt 9:1. Lk 8:40. **people gathered.** Lk 8:40.

22. **there.** Mt *9:18, 19. Lk *8:41, 42. **rulers.** Lk 13:14. Ac 13:15. 18:8, 17. **Jairus.** i.e. *running water*, **☀S#2383g.** Lk 8:41. See +*S#2971h, Nu +32:41, Jair. **he fell.** ver. 33. Mt 2:11. Lk 5:8. 8:28. Ac 10:25, 26. Re 22:8.

23. **besought.** T#1447. Mk 7:25-27. 9:17-24. 2 S 12:15-23. Ps +*50:15. 107:18. Mt 15:22-28. 17:14-18. Lk 4:38. 7:2, 3, 12. Jn 4:46-50. 11:3. **of death.** T#1332. Ge 4:13, 14. 19:19, 20. *32:9-11. Ex 10:17. 20:19. Nu 21:6, 7. 1 S 12:19. 2 S *12:15, 16. 22:5-7. 2 K 1:13, 14. 20:1-6. 1 Ch *21:16, 17. Ps *39:11-13. 55:4-6. 88:1-13. *107:17-19. 116:3, 4. 142:1-7. 143:7-9. La 2:19. Da 2:17-19. Jon 1:13, 14. 3:5. Mt 8:24, 25. 14:29, 30. 26:38, 39. Lk 7:2, 3. 8:41, 42. **I pray.** √63IID, Nu +26::4. Here the A.V. adds: "I pray thee," but it is better to repeat the verb from the beginning of the verse, and then we may take the other words literally:— "*I beseech thee earnestly* that having come thou wouldest lay on her thy hands" (B101). **lay thy hands.** √63A3, Mt +19:13. Mk 6:5, 6, 13. 16:18. 2 K 5:11. Mt 8:3. Lk 4:40. 13:13. Ac 28:8. Ja *5:14, 15.

24. **went.** Lk 7:6. Ac *10:38. **and thronged.** ver. 31. Mk 3:9, 10, 20. Lk 8:42, 45. 12:1. 19:3.

25. **a certain.** Mt 9:20-22. Lk 8:43, 44. **an issue.** Le 15:19, 20, 25-27. **twelve.** Lk 13:11. Jn 5:5, 6. Ac 4:22. 9:33, 34.

26. **had suffered.** No person will wonder at this account when he considers the therapeutics of the Jewish physicians, in reference to diseases of this kind (for an account of which, see Drs. Lightfoot and Clarke): from some of their nostrums, she could not have been *bettered*; from others, she must have been made *worse*; from all, she must have *suffered many things*; and from the *persons* employed, the *expense* of the medicaments, and the *number of years* she was afflicted, it is perfectly credible that she had spent *all she had*. She was, therefore, a fit patient for the Great Physician. Jb 13:4. Je 8:22. 30:12, 13. 51:8. **spent all.** Ge=47:18. Lk 15:14. 21:4. **nothing.** Ps *108:12.

27. **touched.** Mk 6:56. 2 K 13:21. Mt 14:36. Ac 5:15. 19:12.

28. **be whole.** or, saved. ver. 23, 34. Mk 10:52.

29. **straightway.** Ex +*15:26. Jb 33:24, 25. Ps 30:2. +*103:3. 107:20. 147:3. **fountain.** Le 20:18. **felt.** lit. knew. √121C2A3, Is +53:11. **plague.** ver. 34. Mk 3:10. 1 K 8:37. Lk 7:21.

30. **knowing.** Gr. *epiginosko*, Mt +11:27. **virtue.** Lk *6:19. 8:46. 1 P 2:9mg.

31. **Thou seest.** Lk 8:45. 9:12.

32. **he looked.** Mk 3:5.

33. **the woman.** Mk 4:41. Lk 1:12, 29. 8:47. **fearing.** √141, Is +22:4. Ge +19:30. **and told.** Ps 30:2. 66:16. 103:2-5. 116:12-14.

34. **Daughter.** Mt 9:2, 22. Lk 8:48. **thy faith.** Mk *9:23, 24. 10:52. Mt *9:2, 28, 29. ◑13:58. *15:28. 21:22. Lk *7:50. 8:48. 17:19. 18:42. Jn *4:50, 51. Ac *3:16. *14:8-10. **go.** 1 S 1:17. 20:42. 2 K 5:19. Ec 9:7.

35. **there came.** Lk *8:49. **ruler.** √121K1, Dt +9:1. **house certain.** ver. 38. Ro 16:10, 11. 1 C 1:11. **Thy daughter.** Jn 5:25. 11:25. **why.** Lk 7:6, 7. Jn 11:21, 32, 39. **the Master.** Mk 10:17. Mt 26:18. Jn 11:28.

36. **heard.** Ge +18:10. **only believe.** ver. 34. Mk 9:23. 2 Ch +*20:20. Mt 9:28, 29. +*17:20. Lk 8:50. Jn 4:48-50. *11:40. Ro 4:18-24.

37. **he suffered no.** Lk 8:51. Ac 9:40. **save.** Mk 9:2. 14:33. 2 C 13:1.

38. **and seeth.** Je 9:17-20. Mt 9:23, 24. 11:17. Lk 8:52, 53. Ac 9:39.

39. **not dead.** Da +*12:2. Jn *11:11-13. Ac 20:10. 1 C +*11:30. 1 Th 4:13, 14. 5:10.

40. **they laughed.** Ge 19:14. Ne 2:19. Jb 12:4. Ps 22:7. 123:3, 4. Lk 16:14. Ac 17:32. **when.** Mk 7:33. 8:23. 1 K 17:19. 2 K 4:33. Mt +*7:6. 9:24, 25. Lk 8:53, 54. Ac 9:40. **he taketh.** He took just so many as prudence required, and as were sufficient to prove the reality of the cure; to have permitted the presence of more, might have savored of ostentation. **damsel.** √180B, Mk +13:26.

41. **took.** Mk 1:31. Ac 9:40, 41. **Talitha cumi.** ☀S#5008g, only here. This is pure Syriac, the same as in the Syriac version, the proper translation of which is given by the evangelist. Compare ☀S#2924h, *taleh*, 1 S 7:9 (lamb). Is 65:25 (lamb). **interpreted.** √95, Ps +7:13. ☀S#3177g, *methermeeneuomai*. Mk 15:22, 34. Mt 1:23. Jn 1:41. Ac 4:36. 13:8. Compare the related words ☀S#1329g, *diermeeneuo*, Lk +24:27; ☀S#2058g, *hermeenia*, 1 C +12:10; ☀S#2059g, *hermeenuo*, Jn +1:38. **Damsel.** Mk 1:41. Ge 1:3. Ps *33:9. Lk 7:14, 15. 8:54, 55. Jn *5:28, 29. *11:43, 44. Ro 4:17. Ph *3:21.

42. **damsel.** √180B, Mk +13:26. **astonished.** Mk

1:27. 4:41. 6:51. 7:37. Ac 3:10-13.

43. **he charged.** Mk 1:43. 3:12. 7:36. Is 52:13. Mt 8:4. 9:30. *12:16-18. 17:9. Lk 5:14. 8:56. Jn 5:41. 7:8. **and commanded.** This was to show that she had not only returned to life, but was also restored to perfect health; and to intimate, that though raised to life by *extraordinary* power, she must be continued in existence, as before, by the use of *ordinary* means. The advice of a heathen, on another subject, is quite applicable: *Nec Deus intersit, nisi dignus vindice nodus inciderit.* "When the miraculous power of God is necessary, let it be resorted to; when not necessary, let the ordinary means be used" (Horace). To act otherwise would be to tempt God. **given.** Lk 24:30, 42, 43. Ac 10:41.

MARK 6

Jesus preaches and is despised in his own country, 1-6. He sends out the apostles to preach, with power over unclean spirits, 7-13. The opinions of Herod and others concerning Christ, 14-16. Herod imprisons and beheads John the Baptist, at the instigation of Herodias, 17-29. The apostles return to Jesus, 30-33. He teaches, and miraculously feeds, the multitudes, 34-44. He walks on the sea to his disciples, 45-52. They land at Gennesaret, and he heals the sick, who only touched the hem of his garment, 53-56.

1. **and come.** Mt 13:54-58. Lk *4:16-30. **own country.** Mt 2:23. Lk 4:23.

2. **sabbath.** T#640. Mk +3:4 (T#639). Le 19:30. Ps 84:1-10. 132:7. Is +*58:13. 66:23. Ezk 46:3. Lk *4:16, 31. 13:10, +*14n. Ac 13:14-16, 42, 44. 15:21. 17:2. 18:4. 1 C 16:2. He 10:25. **he began.** Mk 1:21, 22, 39. Mt 4:23. Lk 4:15, 16, 31, 32. 6:6. 13:10. Ac 13:14. **astonished.** Mt 7:28. **From.** Mk 11:28. Mt 21:23. Jn 6:42. 7:*15, 52. Ac 4:13, 14. **wisdom.** Ac=7:22. **hands.** ♪144A5, Ge +9:5.

3. **this.** Mt +*13:55, 56. Lk *4:22. Jn 6:42. **carpenter.** Is 49:7. *♣53:2, 3. 1 P 2:4. Mary. Mt 1:16. Jn *6:42. **the brother of.** Mk +*3:31n. Ps +*69:8. Mt 1:18, *25. +*13:55. Lk 2:7. Ac 1:14. **James.** Mk 15:40. Mt 12:46. 1 C 9:4. Ga *1:19. **Juda.** Jn 14:22. Ju 1. **Simon.** Mk 3:18. Ac 1:13. **offended.** Is *53:3. Mt *11:6. +*13:57. 15:12. Lk 2:34. 4:23-29. 7:23. Jn 6:60, 61. 1 C 1:23.

4. **A prophet.** Je 11:21. 12:6. Mt 13:57. Lk *4:24. Jn 4:44. 7:5. **own country.** Jn 7:41, 42. **own house.** Mk 3:19, 20. Jn 7:3.

5. **he could.** Mk 9:23. Ge 19:22. 32:25. Is 59:1, 2. Mt *13:58. He 4:2. **laid his hands.** ♪63A3, Mt +19:13. Mk 5:23.

6. **marvelled.** Mk 5:20. Is 59:16. Je 2:11. Mt ◐8:10. Lk 7:9. Jn 9:30. **their unbelief.** Mt *17:20. **And he went.** Mt 4:23. *9:35. 11:1. Lk *4:31, 44. 8:1. 13:22. Ac *10:38.

7. **the twelve.** Mk 3:13, 14. 9:35. Mt 10:1, etc. Lk 6:13-16. 9:1-6. 10:3, etc. 22:35. **to send.** Jn 17:18. **by two.** Mk 11:1. 14:13. Ex 4:14, 15. Ec 4:9, 10. Re 11:3. **and two.** ♪108E4. Idiom B836. In Hebrew the numeral is repeated or doubled to express distribution. Here, "He sent them two two" (i.e. two and two together): i.e. in pairs. Compare the Greek idiom in Lk 10:1 and 9:14. In Mark 6:40 both the Hebrew and Greek idioms are used. For other instances of this figure see Mk 6:39, 40. 2 C 4:16. **and gave.** ♪15G, Ge +35:3. **power.** Mk 16:17. Mt *10:9. Lk 10:17-20. **over.** ♪181E,

Ge +3:24. **unclean.** Mk 3:30. **spirits.** Gr. *pneuma,* Mt +8:16.

8. **take.** Mt *10:9, 10. Lk *10:4. *22:35. **save.** St. Matthew says that they were to take "neither two coats, neither shoes, nor yet staves;" but this precept plainly means, "Go just as you are; take no other coat, shoes, or staff than what you already have." **scrip.** 1 S 17:40. Mt 10:10. Lk 22:35, 36. **money.** *"The word signifieth* a piece of brass money, in value something less than a farthing, Mt 10:9: but here it is taken in general for money." Mk 12:41. Mt 10:9, 10. Lk 9:3.

9. **be shod.** Mt 10:10. Ac 12:8. Ep *6:15. **sandals.** The *sandal* consisted only of a *sole,* fastened about the foot and ankle with straps. Ac 12:8. **not put on.** ♪15E. Anacoluthon; or, Non-sequence B724. Anacoluthon is a breaking off the sequence of thought. The construction suddenly changes, as from *indirect* to the *direct* form of speech. Here, "But being shod with sandals; and put not on two coats." For other instances of this figure see Lk 5:14. Jn 5:44. Ac 1:4. 17:3. **two coats.** Mk 14:63g. Lk 3:11.

10. **there abide.** Mt *10:11-13. Lk 9:4. *10:7, 8. Ac 16:15. 17:5-7. 1 T *5:13.

11. **whosoever.** ♪15C. Anacoluthon B721. The construction suddenly changes by a change of persons, or from participles to finite verbs, or from singular to plural, and *vice versa.* Here, some authorities read "whatsoever place" for "whosoever," constituting this an anacoluthon. For other instances of this figure see Mk 13:26. Lk 11:11. 1 C 7:13. 2 C 5:6, 8. Ga 6:1. Ep 1:20. Col 1:26. **shall not.** Ne 5:13. Mt 10:14. Lk 9:5. *10:10, 11. Ac *13:50, 51. *18:6. **shake.** ♪138B, Ge +13:16. **for a testimony.** Mk 1:44. Mt 10:18. 24:14. Lk 9:5. 2 Th ◐1:10. Ja 5:3. **more tolerable.** Ezk +*16:48-51. Mt +*10:15. 11:20-24. Lk 10:12-15. +*12:48. Jn 15:22-24. Ro *2:12, 16. He 6:4-8. *10:26-31. 2 P 2:6. Ju *7. **and.** Gr. or. **in the day.** Mt 12:36. Ro 2:5, 16. 2 P 2:9. 3:7. 1 J 4:17.

12. **went out.** Lk 9:6. **preached.** Mk 1:3, 15. Ezk 18:30. Mt 3:2, 8. 4:17. 9:13. 11:20. Lk 11:32. +*13:3, 5. 15:7, 10. 24:47. Ac +*2:38. +*3:19. 11:18. 20:21. 26:20. 2 C √7:9, 10. 2 T +*2:25, 26.

13. **cast.** See on ver. 7. Mt 10:7, 8. Lk 10:17. **anointed.** Jn 9:6, 7. 1 C 12:9. Ja *5:14, 15. 1 J 2:20.

14. **king Herod.** ver. 22, 26, 27. Mt 14:1, 2. Lk 3:1. *9:7-9. 13:31. 23:7-12. **of him.** or, of these mighty works. ♪63A4, 1 K +3:22. **his name.** Mk 1:28, 45. 2 Ch 26:8, 15. Mt 9:31. 1 Th 1:8. **John the Baptist.** ♪24B, Ge +23:16. Mk 8:28. Mt 16:14. **risen from the dead.** Mt +*11:14n. +27:52. **mighty works.** Mt +*13:54. **show forth.** 1 C 12:6, 11. Ga 2:8. 3:5. Ep 1:11, 20. 2:2. Ph 2:13.

15. **it is Elias.** Mk *8:28. 9:12, 13. 15:35, 36. Ml 4:5, Elijah. Mt *16:14. 17:10, 11. Lk 1:17. 9:8, 19. Jn *1:21, 25. **a prophet.** Mt 21:11. Lk 7:16, 39. Jn 6:14. 7:40. 9:17. Ac 3:22, 23.

16. **It is.** Ge 4:10, 11. Ps 53:5. Mt 14:2. 27:4. Lk 9:9. Re 11:10-13.

17. **A.M.** 4032. **A.D.** 28. **Herod.** Mt 4:12. 11:2. 14:3, etc. Lk 3:19, 20. Jn 3:24. **Philip's.** Lk 3:1.

18. **It is.** Le *18:16. *20:21. 1 K 22:14. Ezk 3:18, 19. Mt +*14:3, 4. Ac 20:26, 27. 24:24-26.

19. **Herodias.** Ge 39:17-20. 1 K 21:20. **a quarrel.** or, an inward grudge. Ge 49:23g. Ec 7:9. Lk 11:53g. Ep 4:26, 27.

20. **feared.** Mk 11:18. Ex 11:3. 1 S 18:14. 1 K 21:20.

2 K 3:12, 13. 6:21. 13:14. 2 Ch 24:2, 15-22. 26:5. Ezk 2:5-7. Da 4:18, 27. 5:17. Mt 14:5. 21:26. Lk 8:37. Ac 24:25. **observed him**. *or*, kept him, *or* saved him. 1 S 19:11. Ps *37:32. Zc 3:9. Lk 9:7. 20:20. **and heard**. Mk 4:16. Ps 106:12, 13. Ezk +*33:31, 32. Jn *5:35. **gladly**. Mk 4:16. 12:37. Mt +*13:20.

21. **when**. Ge 27:41. 2 S 13:23-29. Est 3:7. Ps 37:12, 13. Ac 12:2-4. **his birthday**. Ge 40:20. Est 1:3-7. 2:18. Pr 31:4, 5. Da 5:1-4. Ho 7:5. 1 P 4:3. Re 11:10. **made a supper**. 1 K 3:15. Est 1:3. 2:18. **to his lords**. Re 6:15. **high captains**. Mk 10:42. Ac 21:31. Re 18:23. **chief**. Lk 19:47. Ac 13:50. 17:4. 25:2. 28:7, 17. **Galilee**. Lk 3:1.

22. **the daughter**. Est 1:10-12. Is 3:16, etc. Da 5:2. Mt 14:6.

23. **he**. 1 S 28:10. 2 K 6:31. Mt 5:34-37. 14:7. **Whatsoever**. Est *5:3, 6. 7:2. Pr 6:2. Mt 4:9.

24. **said**. Ge 27:8-11. 2 Ch 22:3, 4. Ezk 19:2, 3. Mt 14:8. **The head**. Jb 31:31. Ps 27:2. 37:12, 14. Pr 27:3, 4. Ac 23:12, 13.

25. **with haste**. Pr 1:16. Ro 3:15. **a charger**. Nu 7:13, 19, etc.

26. **was exceeding**. Mt 14:9. 27:3-5, 24, 25. Lk 18:23g. **his oath**'s. ver. 23. Jg +*11:30, 31n, 35. **their sakes**. Is 8:13.

27. **the king**. Mt 14:10, 11. **an executioner**. *or*, one of his guard. *Spekoulator*, in Latin, *speculator*, from *speculor*, to look about, spy, properly denotes a sentinel; and as these sentinels kept guard at the palaces of kings, and the residences of Roman governors, so they were employed in other offices besides guarding, and usually performed that of executioners (See Josephus, Ant. l. xvii. c. 7). As, however, we learn from Josephus (Ant. l. xviii. c. 5. sec. 1, 2), that Herod was at this very time engaged in war with Aretas, king of Arabia, in consequence of Herod's having divorced his daughter in order to marry Herodias, his brother Philip's wife; and as this event occurred at an entertainment given at the castle of Machaerus, while his army was on its march against his father-in-law; we are furnished with an additional reason why a *speculator*, or sentinel, should have been employed as an executioner; and are thus enabled to discover such a latent and undesigned coincidence as clearly evinces the truth of the evangelical narrative. See Bishop Marsh, *Lectures*, P. v. pp. 78-82, and Horne's *Introduction*, vol. I, pp. 101, 102 (page 94 of the seventh edition of 1834). See related notes on undesigned coincidence at Ac +*12:12n.

29. **his disciples**. Mt 9:14. **they came**. 1 K 13:29, 30. 2 Ch 24:16. Mt 14:12. 27:57-60. Ac 8:2.

30. **the apostles**. Mt 10:2. Lk 6:13. 9:10. 17:5. 22:14. 24:10. Jn 13:16. Ac 1:2. **gathered**. ver. 7, etc. Lk 9:10. 10:17. **and told**. Lk 14:21. Jn 15:15. Ac 14:27. **both**. Ac 1:1. 20:18-21. 1 T 4:12-16. T 2:6, 7. 1 P 5:2, 3.

31. **Come**. Mk 1:45. 3:7, 20. Mt 14:13. Jn *6:1, 2. **apart**. Ex +3:1. Pr +*18:1. Mt 14:23. 15:29. 17:1. 20:17. Lk 9:10. 22:41. Ga 1:17, 18. Re 1:9. **and rest**. Ge 18:4. Ex 16:23. 23:12. Dt 33:12. Jb 11:19. Ps +*127:2. Ec ◐+*2:23. Mt 8:18, 24. *11:29.

32. **they departed**. Mt 14:13. **privately**. Ge 32:24. Ex +=3:1. Ps 55:7. Je 9:2. Mt 28:16. Lk 5:16. Ga 1:17, 18.

33. **knew**. Gr. *epiginosko*, Mt +11:27. ver. 54, 55. Mt 15:29-31. Jn 6:2. Ja 1:19.

34. **saw**. Mt *14:14. 15:32. Lk *9:11. Ro 15:2, 3.

He 2:17. +*4:15. **moved**. ⨍22A18, Is +63:15. **because**. Nu ▶27:17. 1 K *22:17. 2 Ch 18:16. Je 50:6, 17. Ezk ▶34:5. Zc 10:2. Mt 9:36. 10:6. Jn 10:11. **and he**. Is 61:1-3.

35. **when the day**. Mt 14:15, etc. Lk 9:12, etc. Jn *6:5, etc. **far spent**. Jg 19:8mg, 9mg, 11. Je 6:4. Lk 24:29.

36. **Send them away**. ver. 45. Mk 3:21. 5:31. Mt 15:23. 16:22.

37. **Give**. Mk 8:2, 3. 2 K 4:42-44. Mt 14:16. 15:32. Lk 9:13. Jn 6:4-10. **Shall**. ⨍85E, Ge +17:17. Nu *11:13, 21-23. 2 K *4:43. 7:2. Mt 15:33. Jn 6:7. **pennyworth**. "The Roman penny is sevenpence half-penny; as Mt 18:28mg." Mk 12:15. 14:5. Mt 20:2n, 13n.

38. **Five**. Mk 8:5, 19. Mt 14:17, 18. 15:34. 16:9. Lk 9:13. Jn 6:9.

39. **all sit down**. 1 K 10:5. Est 1:5, 6. Mt 15:35. 1 C 14:33, 40. **by companies**. ⨍108E4, ver. +7.

40. **in ranks**. ⨍108E4, ver. 7. **by hundreds**. It is generally supposed that they were so arranged as to be a hundred in rank, or depth, and fifty in front, or file; which would make the number just five thousand, and will reconcile this account with St. Luke's, who only speaks of their sitting down by **fifties**. Lk 9:14, 15.

41. **looked up**. Mk 7:34. Mt +*14:19. Lk 9:16. Jn 11:41. 17:1. **blessed**. T#1439. Mk 8:6, 7. 14:22. Dt 8:10. 1 S 9:13. Mt +*14:19. 15:36. 26:26. Lk 9:16. +*24:30. Jn 6:11, 23. Ac 27:35. Ro 14:6. 1 C √10:31. 14:16. Col *3:17. 1 T *4:4, 5.

42. **all did eat**. Mk 8:8, 9. Dt 8:3. 2 K 4:42-44. Ps 145:15, 16. Mt 14:20, 21. 15:37, 38. Lk 9:17. Jn 6:12, 13.

43. **twelve baskets**. Mk 8:19, 20. Mt 16:9g.

45. **straightway**. Mt 14:22-32. Jn 6:15-17, etc. **constrained**. Mt 8:18. Lk 14:23. **the ship**. ver. 32, 51. Mk 3:9. **unto Bethsaida**. i.e. *house of provision, house of hunting*, *S#966g. Mk 6:45. 8:22. Mt 11:21. Lk 9:10. 10:13. Jn 1:44. 12:21. See *S#6719h, *tsayad*, Je 16:16, hunters. *or*, over against Bethsaida. *Bethsaida*, according to Josephus, was situated on the sea of Gennesareth, in the lower Gaulonitis (consequently on the east of the lake, as Pliny states, l. v. c. 15), and at the beginning of the mountainous country (Bel. l. ii. c. 13. l. iv. c. 27); and it was raised from a village to the honor of the emperor's daughter (Ant. l. xviii. c. 3). Some learned men, however, are of opinion that the *Bethsaida* mentioned in the gospels was a different place; and that it was situated on the western shore of the sea of Tiberias, in Galilee, near Chorazin and Capernaum, with which it is associated (Mt 11:21, 23. Jn 12:21); and Bishop Pococke mentions the ruins of a town or large village in the plain of Huttin, about two miles west of the lake, still bearing the name of *Baitsida*, which he thinks occupies its site. Mk 8:22. Mt 11:21. Lk 9:10. 10:13. Jn 6:17. **he sent**. ver. 36.

46. **had sent**. Lk 9:61g. 14:33g. Ac 18:18, 21. 2 C 2:13. **he departed**. Mk +*1:35. Mt 6:6. *14:23. Lk 5:16. 6:12. 1 P 2:21. **mountain**. Mt 5:1. 28:16.

47. **when even**. Mk +*13:35. Mt 14:23. Jn *6:16, 17.

48. **he saw**. Is 54:11. Jon 1:13. Mt 14:24. **the fourth watch**. ⨍49, Jn +10:22. Our 3 a.m. to 6 a.m. Mk 13:35, morning. Ex 14:24. 1 S 11:11. Mt +*14:25n. Lk 12:38. **he cometh**. Jb 9:8. Ps 93:4. 104:3. **would have**. ⨍121Q2, Mt +14:9. Ge 19:2. 32:26. Lk 24:28.

49. **they saw**. Ge +21:19. Jb 9:8. Lk ◑+*24:16. **supposed**. Jb 4:14-16. Mt 14:25, 26. Lk 24:37.

50. **were troubled**. Lk 24:37. **good cheer**. Dt 31:6. Jsh 10:25. 1 Ch 22:13. 28:20. Jn 16:33. **it is I**. Is 43:2. Mt *14:27. Lk 24:38-41. Jn 6:19, 20. 20:19, 20. **be not afraid**. Is 41:13. 43:1. Mt 17:7.

51. **the ship**. ver. 32, 45. Mk 3:9. **wind ceased**. Mk 4:39. Ps 93:3, 4. 107:28-30. Mt 8:26, 27. *14:28-32. Lk 8:24, 25. Jn *6:21. **and they**. Mk 1:27. 2:12. 4:41. 5:42. 7:37.

52. **they**. Mk 7:18. 8:17, 18, 21. 9:32. Mt 16:9-11. Lk 24:25. **their**. Mk 3:5. 16:14. Is 63:17. **hardened**. Mk 8:17. Jn 12:40. Ro 11:7. 2 C 3:14.

53. **the land**. Mt 14:34-36. Lk 5:1. Jn 6:24.

54. **knew**. Gr. *epiginosko*, Mt +11:27. ver. 33. Ps +√9:10. Ph *3:10.

55. **ran through**. Mk 2:1-3. 3:7-11. Mt 4:24. **in beds**. Mk 2:4. Mt 9:2. Lk 5:18. **sick**. Mt 4:24. 8:16.

56. **they laid**. Ac 5:15. **in the streets**. T#1208. Mk 7:4. SS 3:2. Am +5:16n. Mt 6:5. Lk 11:43. **touch**. Mk 3:10. 5:27, 28. 2 K 13:21. Mt 14:36. Lk 6:19. 8:47. 22:51. Ac 5:15. 19:12. **the border**. T#1726. Nu 15:38, 39. Dt 22:12. Mt 9:20. 14:34-36. Lk 8:44. **him**. *or*, it. **made whole**. Mk 10:52.

MARK 7

The Pharisees find fault with the disciples for eating with unwashen hands; and Jesus shows that their traditions "make void the law of God," 1-13. He teaches the source and nature of defilement, 14-23; heals the daughter of a Syrophenician woman, 24-30; and a man who was deaf, and had an impediment in his speech, 31-37.

1. **the Pharisees**. Mk 3:22. Mt 15:1. Lk 5:17. 11:53, 54. Ph *3:5, 7.

2. **defiled**. *or*, common. ver. 5. Ac 10:14, 15, 28. 11:8. Ro 14:14mg. He 10:29g. Re 21:27g. **they found**. Da 6:4, 5. Mt 7:3-5. 23:23-25.

3. **For**. ∫136, Is +60:12. **wash**. Gr. *nipto*, ✻S#3538g. Mt 6:17. 15:2. Jn 9:7, 7, 11, 15. 13:5, 6, 8, 8, 10, 12, 14. 1 T 5:10. For ✻S#3068g, *louo*, see Jn +13:10. For ✻S#3067g, *loutron*, see Ep +5:26. For ✻S#4150g, *pluno*, see Re +7:14. For ✻S#628g, *apolouo*, see Ac +22:16. For ✻S#633g, *aponipto*, see Mt 27:24. For ✻S#637g, *apopluno*, see Lk 5:2. For ✻S#1026g, *breko*, see Lk +7:38. **oft**. *or*, diligently. Gr. *pugma*, ✻S#4435g, only here. With the fist. ∫24I, Is +21:7. Up to the elbow. Theophlact. *Pugma, the fist*; which Dr. Lightfoot illustrates by a tradition from the Talmudical tracts, that when they washed their hands they washed the fist up to the *joint of the arm*. The Jews laid great stress on these *washings*, or *baptisms, baptismous*, considering eating with unwashen hands no ordinary crime, and feigning that an evil spirit, called *Shibta*, has a right to sit on the food of him who thus eats, and render it hurtful. **the tradition**. ver. 7-10, 13. Dt 4:2. 12:32. Pr +*30:6. Mt 15:2-6. Ga 1:14. Col 2:8, 21-23. 1 P 1:18. Re √22:18, 19. **the elders**. He 11:2.

4. **the market**. Mk 6:56. Lk 11:43. **except**. Jb 9:30, 31. Ps 26:6. Is 1:16. Je 4:14. Mt 27:24. Lk √11:38, 39. Jn √2:6. 3:25. He *9:10. Ja 4:8. 1 J 1:7. **wash**. Gr. *baptizo*, S#907g, Mt +*3:6. T#31. Ex 29:4. Le 8:5, 6. Nu 8:5-7. Dt +23:11. Lk √11:38. He 6:2. 9:10. lit. baptize. Lk √11:38g. This clearly shows that among the Jews, ceremonial washings for cleansing were called "baptisms," and involved applying water to the object, not the immersion of the object or person in water (Ac 1:5n), for notice the inclusion of their beds or couches in the ceremony, which no doubt was accomplished by sprinkling. After every return from the market, and before every instance of eating or drinking, they could scarcely be supposed to have practiced *immersion*! This usage of the word *baptizo* proves that the word does not mean exclusively to immerse. Dr. Robert H. Countess has conclusively shown, reviewing carefully the works of James W. Dale, that (1) Dale's work stands up under careful scrutiny in the light of developments in the study of linguistics and lexicography which have occurred since his writing, studies which do not diminish but enhance the validity of Dale's findings; (2) Dale has established that *baptizo* is a word having not just a single or univocal meaning, but it is a word which is used with multiple meanings: (I) Primary use: (A) Intusposition, with influence. As the word "intusposition" is in no English dictionary which I can find—not even the unabridged thirteen volume *Oxford English Dictionary* or its recent (1987) *Supplement*, I have attempted to produce the following definition by a careful study of Dale (See Dale, *Classic Baptism*, pp. 126, 127, and index entry, p. 366): i.e. placement and continuance entirely within a fluid, such that an object baptized is completely invested by the baptizing element, whatever it may be, involving consequent, though only indirectly expressed, full influence, influence which varies according to object and element. (B) Intusposition for influence; (C) Influence with rhetorical figure; (D) Intusposition without influence. (II) Secondary use: (A) Controlling influence without intusposition in fact or by figure; (B) Controlling influence with or without intusposition: (1) Stupefaction; (2) Drunkenness; (3) Purification; (4) Class of persons thoroughly imbued. Dr. Countess illustrates, with the examples furnished by Dale's volumes, each of these uses of *baptizo* from the Greek classics, the Septuagint, the New Testament, and the Church Fathers. (3) Alexander Carson argued that *baptizo* had but one meaning, stating "My position is, that it always signifies to dip; never expressing anything but mode" (*Baptism: Its Mode and Subjects*, p. 55). Carson boldly states a self-evident canon, "A word that applies to two modes can designate neither" (*Baptism*, p. 90). For Carson's view this is a fatal admission. Dr. Countess observes, "Carson's self-contradiction continues to follow him wherever he goes, because he asserted that "It not only signifies to dip or immerse..." Since *dipping* is a clearly observable, univocal modal activity, and since *immersing* is not, Carson has unwittingly impaled his univocal definition upon two different (equivocal) horns of a dilemma" (Robert H. Countess, *Development of an Instructional Model for Teaching Christian Baptism in the Military Chapel Environment*, unpublished MS., page 10 of Chapter 6). Dr. Countess informs me that his MS. is to be published probably by Presbyterian and Reformed Publishing Company, publishers of his other book, *The Jehovah's Witnesses' New Testament*, which I have cited in a note on Mt 27:54. Carson's statement, "Baptizo in the whole history of the Greek language has but one (meaning). It not only signifies to dip or immerse, but it never has any other meaning" is from page 19 of his work on baptism.

Even without Dale's elaborate classification scheme for the multiple meanings of *baptizo*, Carson's own statement betrays the equivocal use of the term, and invalidates Carson's whole argument. **washing.** Gr. *baptismos*, lit. baptizing. *S#909g. Mk 7:4, 8. He 6:2. 9:10. **cups.** Mt 23:25. Lk 11:39. **pots.** "Gr. Sextarious; about a pint and a half." **tables.** *or*, beds. Gr. *klinee*, *S#2825g. Mk 4:21. 7:4, 30. Mt 9:2, 6. Lk 5:18. 8:16. 17:34. Ac 5:15. Re 2:22.

5. **the Pharisees and.** Mk 2:16-18. Mt 15:2. Ac 21:21, 24. Ro 4:12. 2 Th 3:6, 11. **tradition.** ver. 3. Col *2:8. **but eat.** Lk √11:38. **unwashen.** ver. 2.

6. **Well.** Is ▶29:13. Mt *15:7-9. Lk +24:27. Ac 28:25. **Esaias.** Mk 1:2. **hypocrites.** Mt 6:2. 23:13-15. Lk 11:39-44. **honoreth.** Is *▶29:13. Ezk +*33:31. Ho 8:2, 3. Jn 5:42. 8:41, 42, 54, 55. 15:24. 2 T 3:5. T 1:16. Ja 2:14-17. **their heart.** 1 S +*16:7. Pr 23:26.

7. **in vain.** 1 S 12:21. Ml 3:14. Mt *6:7. *15:9. 1 C √15:14, 58. T *3:9. Ja *1:26. *2:20. **worship.** Dt 4:24. Na 1:2. Lk ◑+14:10. Jn 4:24. Ac 16:14. 18:7, 13. 19:27. Ro 1:25. Ph *3:3. **teaching.** Is +*8:20n. Je *23:21, 22, 29. 1 P 1:18. **doctrines.** Col 2:22. T 1:14. **the commandments.** Dt *12:32. Je *23:21, 22, 29. Col *2:22. 1 T *4:1-3. Re *14:11, 12. *22:18.

8. **laying.** Is 1:12. **commandment.** 1 C 7:19. He 12:17. 14:12. **the traditions.** ver. 3, 4.

9. **Full.** 2 K 16:10-16. Is 24:5. 29:13. Je 44:16, 17. Da 7:25. 11:36. Mt 15:3-6. 2 Th 2:4. **well.** ✓60A, Ge +3:22. **reject.** *or*, frustrate. ver. 13. Ps 119:126. Je +*8:9. Lk *7:30. Ro 3:31. Ga 2:21. 3:15g. He 10:28g.

10. **Honor.** Mk 10:19. Ge 45:9-11. Ex +*▶20:12. Le 19:3. Dt +*▶5:16. 27:16. Je 35:18, 19. Zch 22:7. Mi 7:6. Ml 1:6. Mt 15:4. 19:19. Lk 18:20. Ep +*6:2. 1 T 5:4. **Whoso.** Ex ▶21:17. Le 20:9. Dt 27:16. Pr 20:20. 30:11, *17. Mt 15:4.

11. **But.** Mt *5:19. **If.** ✓184C, Mt +4:9. **It is Corban.** i.e. *offering,* *S#2878g. Mk 7:11. Mt 27:6. Hebrew S#7133h, *corban, offering,* as at Le 1:2. Nu 5:15. Ezk 20:28. 40:43. Rather, "Let it be a *corban,*" a formula common among the Jews on such occasions; by which the Pharisees released a child from supporting his parents; and even deemed it sacrilege if he afterwards gave any thing for their use. See Lightfoot. Le 1:2n. 2:1. 7:13. *19:5n. Mt 15:5. 23:18. 27:6. 1 T √5:4-8. **whatsoever.** ✓184C, Mt +4:.

12. **no more.** Is +*58:7. **to do ought.** 1 T *5:4.

13. **the word.** ver. 9. Is +*8:20n. Je 8:8, 9. Ho 8:12. Mt 5:17-20. 15:6. T 1:14. **of God.** Lk 5:1. Jn √10:35. Ro 9:6. Re 1:2. **none effect.** T#1103. Ro 2:23. Ga 3:17. **tradition.** Lk 12:1. **such.** Ezk 18:14. Ga 5:21.

14. **when.** 1 K 18:21. 22:28. Ps 49:1, 2. 94:8. Mt 15:10. Lk 12:1, 54-57. 20:45-47. **Hearken.** ✓66, Ge +9:13. **and understand.** ver. 18. Pr 8:5. Is 6:9. Mt 13:51. 15:16. Ac 8:30.

15. **There.** Though it is very true, says Dr. Doddridge, that a man may bring guilt upon himself by eating to excess, and a Jew, by eating what was forbidden by the Mosaic law; yet still the pollution would arise from the wickedness of the heart, and be just proportionable to it, which is all our Lord asserts. **nothing.** ver. 18-20. Le 11:42-47. Ac *10:14-16, 28. 11:8-10. 15:20, 21. 21:28. Ro 14:17. 1 C 10:25. 1 T √4:3-5. T √1:15. He 9:10, 13. 13:9. Re 21:27. **but.** ver. 20-23. Pr √4:23. Mt 12:34, 35. 15:16-20.

16. **If.** ✓184A, 1 C +15:2. **have ears.** Mk 4:9, 23. Mt 11:15. 13:9, 43. Lk 8:8. 14:35. Re 2:7, 11, 17, 29.

3:6, 13, 22. **hear.** ✓147A, Ge +50:24.

17. **when he was entered.** Mk 3:19. 4:10, 34. 9:28. **disciples asked.** Mt 13:10, 36. 15:15.

18. **without understanding.** ver. 14. Mk 4:13. 8:17, 18. Is 28:9, 10. Je 5:4, 5. Mt 15:16, 17. 16:11. Lk *24:25. Jn 3:10. Ro 1:21, 31. 10:19. 1 C 3:2. He *5:11, 12. **defile.** ver. 15.

19. **entereth not.** Mt 15:17. 1 C 6:13. Col *2:21, 22. **purging all meats.** Lk 11:41. Ac 10:14, 15. 11:9. Ro *14:17. Ga 2:12. Col *2:16-23. 1 T √4:3. T *1:15. He 9:10. 13:9.

20. **That which.** ✓73, Zc +1:5. ver. 15. Ps 41:6. Ho 7:6. Mi 2:1. Mt *12:34-37. 15:11. Ep *4:29. Ja √1:14, 15. *3:6. 4:1.

21. **From within.** Mt 12:34. *15:19. **out of the heart.** Ge *6:5. *8:21. Jb *14:4. 15:14-16. 25:4. Ps 14:1, 3. 53:1, 3. 58:2, 3. Pr +*4:23. Ec 9:3. Je 4:14. +*17:9. Mt *15:19. *23:25-28. Lk 16:15. Jn *3:19. Ac *5:4. *8:22. Ro 1:21. 7:5, 8. 8:7, 8. 1 C √2:14. Ga *5:19-21. Ep 4:17-19. 5:8. T 1:15. 3:3. Ja √1:14, 15. 4:1-3. 1 P 4:2, 3. **evil thoughts.** Dt 15:9. Ps 56:5. Pr 15:26. 23:7. 24:9. Is 59:7. Je 4:14. +*6:19. Ezk *38:10. Mt 9:4. Ja 2:4. **adulteries.** ✓41, Ge +10:1. Ex +*20:14. **fornications.** 1 C +*6:9, 18. **murders.** Ex +*20:13.

22. **thefts.** Ex +*20:15. Ep *4:28. **covetousness.** Gr. covetousnesses. Ps +*10:3. *S#4124g: Lk √12:15. Ro 1:29. 2 C 9:5. Ep 4:19 (greediness). 5:3. Col √3:5. 1 Th *2:5. 2 P 2:3, 14. Compare *S#4123g: 1 C 5:10, 11. *6:10. Ep 5:5. **wickedness.** Gr. wickednesses. *S#4189g. Mt 22:18. Lk 11:39. Ac 3:26. Ro 1:29. 1 C 5:8. Ep 6:12. **deceit.** Pr 11:18. 12:17. 24:28. 26:24-28. Mt 19:18. 2 C 4:1, 2. Ep 5:6. Col 2:8. 1 P 2:1, 2. 3:10. *S#1388g: Mk 14:1 (craft). Mt 26:4 (subtilty). Jn 1:47 (guile). Ac 13:10. Ro 1:29. 2 C 12:16 (guile). 1 Th 2:3. 1 P 2:1, 22. 3:10. Re 14:5. Compare *S#1389g, 2 C 4:2 (handling deceitfully). **lasciviousness.** *S#766g. Ro 13:13 (wantonness). 2 C 12:21. Ga 5:19. Ep 4:19. 1 P 4:3. 2 P 2:7 (filthy), 18. Ju 4. **an evil eye.** ✓46B, Ex +5:21. Here the *Catachresis* is only in appearance, as "an evil eye" is put by Metonymy for *envy,* which does proceed out of the heart (B677). Dt *15:9. +*28:54, 56. 1 S 18:8, 9. Ps +37:1 (T#174). Pr 23:6. 28:22. Mt 6:23. 20:15. 2 P ◑2:14. **blasphemy.** *S#988g. Mk 2:7. 3:28. 7:22. 14:64. Mt 12:31, 31. 15:19. 26:65. Lk 5:21. Jn 10:33. Ep 4:31 (evil speaking). Col 3:8. 1 T 6:4 (railings). Ju 9 (railing). Re 2:9. 13:1, 5, 6. 17:3. **pride.** 2 Ch 32:25, 26, 31. Ps *10:4. +*119:21. Ob 3, 4. 2 C *10:5. 1 P +*5:5. **foolishness.** Pr 12:23. 22:15. 24:9. 27:22. Ec 7:25. 2 C 11:1, 17, 21. Ep 5:17. 1 P *2:15.

23. **All these.** 1 C +*6:9, 10. **evil things.** Lk 1:79. Ga 5:19. **defile.** ver. 15, 18, 23. 1 C 3:17. T *1:15. Ju 8.

24. **from.** Mt 15:21, etc. **Tyre.** Mk 3:8. Ge 10:15, 19. 49:13. Jsh 19:28, 29. Is 23:1-4, 12. Ezk 28:2, 21, 22. **and would.** Mk 2:1. 3:7. +*6:31, 32. Is 42:2. Mt 9:28. 1 T 5:25. **could not.** SS 1:3, 12. Jn 12:3.

25. **a certain woman.** Mt 15:22. whose. Mk 9:17-23. **spirit.** Gr. *pneuma,* Mt +8:16. **at.** Mk 1:40. 5:22, 23, 33. Lk 17:16. Ac 10:25, 26. Re 22:8, 9.

26. **Greek.** *or,* Gentile. i.e. *non-Jewish,* *S#1674g. Used here and at Ac 17:12. Is 49:12. Ro *1:16. 1 C 12:13. Ga 3:28. Col 3:11. **a Syrophenician.** i.e. *exalted palm, purple,* *S#4949g, only here. Mt 4:24. 15:22. Ac 21:2, 3.

27. **Let.** Mt +*7:6. +*10:5, 6. 15:23-28. Ac 22:21,

22. Ro +*15:8. Ep 2:12. **first be filled.** Ac 3:26. Ro +*1:16. 3:29. **not meet.** Mt 10:6. **cast it.** Mt +*7:6.

28. **yet.** Ps 145:16. Is 45:22. 49:6. Mt +*5:45. Lk 7:6-8. 15:30-32. Ac 11:17, 18. Ro 3:29. 10:12. 15:8, 9. Ep 2:12-14. 3:8. **crumbs.** Lk 16:21.

29. **For this.** Is +*57:15, 16. 66:2. Mt +*5:3. 8:9-13. 1 J √3:8. **go thy way.** Mt 8:13. Jn 4:50.

30. **she was.** Jn 4:50-52. **she found.** 1 J √3:8.

31. **from.** ver. 24. Mt *15:29, etc. **Decapolis.** Mk 5:20. Mt 4:25.

32. **bring.** Mt 9:32, 33. Lk 11:14. **deaf.** Is 35:5, 6. **put his hand.** Mk 5:23.

33. **took him aside.** Mk +*5:40. *8:23. 1 K 17:19-22. 2 K 4:4-6, 33, 34. Jn *9:6, 7. **and put.** This was clearly a *symbolical* action (2 K +13:17n); for these remedies evidently could not, by their natural efficacy, avail to produce so wonderful an effect. As the ears of the deaf appear closed, he applies his fingers to intimate that he would open them; and as the tongue of the dumb seems to be tied, or to cleave to the palate, he touches it, to intimate he would give loose and free motion to it. He accommodated himself to the weakness of those who might not indeed doubt his power, but fancy some external sign was requisite to healing. It was also thus made manifest, that this salutiferous (i.e. curative) power came from Himself, and that He who by one word, *ephphatha*, had healed the man, must be Divine. **he spit.** Jn 9:6. **touched.** Mk 1:41.

34. **looking.** Mk *6:41. Jn *11:41. *17:1. **he sighed.** √141, Is +22:4. Mk *8:12. Ps +12:5. Is *53:3. Ezk 21:6, 7. Lk *19:41. Jn *11:33, 35, 38. He +*4:15. **Ephphatha.** i.e. *opened,* *S#2188g, 'only here. Mk 5:41. 15:34. **Be opened.** Mk 1:41. Lk 7:14. 18:42. Jn 11:43. Ac 9:34, 40.

35. **straightway.** Mk 2:12. Ps *33:9. Is 32:3, 4. 35:5, 6. Mt 11:5.

36. **he charged.** Mk 1:44, 45. 3:12. 5:43. 8:26. Is *42:2.

37. **were.** Mk 1:27. 2:12. 4:41. 5:42. 6:51. Ps 139:14. Ac 2:7-12. 3:10-13. 14:11. **He hath done.** Ge 1:31. 2 S 3:36. Ps 39:9. 98:1. Is 12:5. 38:15. Ezk 14:23. Lk 13:17. 23:41. Jn 13:7. **he maketh.** Ex 4:10, 11.

MARK 8

Jesus miraculously feeds the multitudes, 1-9; refuses the Pharisees a sign, 10-13; warns the disciples against their leaven, and that of Herod; and reproves them for dullness of understanding, 14-21; gives sight to a blind man at Bethsaida, 22-26; approves Peter's confession, predicts his own sufferings, and rebukes Peter for objecting to them, 27-33; and teaches self-denial and a willingness to suffer for his sake, 34-38.

1. **the multitude.** Mt 15:32, etc.

2. **compassion.** Mk 1:41. 5:19. 6:34. 9:22. Ps 103:13. 145:8, 15. Mi 7:19. Mt 9:36. 14:14. 20:34. Lk 7:13. 15:20. He 2:17. +*4:15. 5:2. **and have.** Mt 4:2-4. 6:32, 33. Jn 4:6-8, 30-34.

3. **if.** √184C, Mt +4:9. **they will faint.** Jg 8:4-6. 1 S 14:28-31. 30:10-12. Ps 103:14. Is 40:31.

4. **From.** Mk 6:36, 37, 52. Nu 11:21-23. 2 K 4:42-44. 7:2. Ps 78:19, 20. Mt 15:33. Jn 6:7-9.

5. **asked.** Mk 11:13. Jn ◑+*2:25. 11:34. **How.** Mk 6:38. Mt 14:15-17. 15:34. Lk 9:13.

6. **to sit.** Mk 6:39, 40. Mt 14:18, 19. 15:35, 36. Lk 9:14, 15. 12:37. Jn 2:5. 6:10. **gave thanks.** Mk 6:41-44. 1 S 9:13. Mt 15:36. 26:26. Lk +*24:30. Jn 6:11, 23. Ro 14:6. 1 C √10:30, 31. Col *3:17. 1 T *4:3-5. **brake.** √108H4, Is +58:7. **before the people.** 2 K *4:43.

7. **fishes.** Lk 24:41, 42. Jn 21:5, 8, 9. **he blessed.** Mk 6:41. Mt 14:19.

8. **and were.** This was another incontestable miracle—four thousand men, besides women and children (Mt 15:28), fed with seven loaves (or rather *cakes*) and a few small fishes! Here there must have been a manifest *creation* of substance—for they all ate, and were filled. ver. 19, 20. Dt *8:10. Ps 107:8, 9. 132:15. 145:16. Mt 16:10. Lk 1:53. Jn 6:11-13, 27, 32-35, 47-58. Re 7:16, 17. **they took.** 1 K 17:14-16. 2 K 4:2-7, 42-44.

10. **straightway.** Mt *15:39. **Dalmanutha.** i.e. *leanness,* *S#1148g, only here. *Dalmanutha* is supposed to have been a town east of the sea of Gennesareth, in the district of *Magdala,* and not far from the city of that name.

11. **Pharisees.** Mk 2:16. 7:1, 2. Mt 12:38. 16:1-4. 19:3. 21:23. 22:15, 18, 23, 34, 35. Lk 11:53, 54. Jn 7:48. **seeking.** Lk *11:16. 12:54-57. Jn *4:48. *6:30. 1 C 1:22, 23. **a sign.** Dt 13:1. 18:18. **tempting.** Mk 12:15. Ex 17:2, 7. Dt 6:16. Ml 3:15. Lk 10:25. Ac 5:9. 1 C 10:9.

12. **he sighed.** Mk *3:5. 7:34. 9:19. Is *53:3. Lk 19:41. Jn 11:33-38. **spirit.** Gr. *pneuma,* √171Q1B, Mk +2:8n. **Why.** Mk 6:6. Lk *16:29-31. 22:67-70. Jn 12:37-43. **There.** Mt 12:39, 40. *16:4. Lk 11:29, 30.

13. **he left.** Ps 81:12. Je 23:33. Ho 4:17. 9:12. Zc 11:8, 9. Mt +*7:6. +*15:14. Lk 8:37. Jn 8:21. 12:36. Ac 13:45, 46. 18:6.

14. **had forgotten.** Mt *16:5.

15. **he charged.** Nu 27:19-23. 1 Ch +*28:9, 10, 20. 1 T 5:21. 6:13. 2 T 2:14. **Take.** Pr +*19:27. Mt 16:6, 11, 12. Lk 12:1, 2, 15. **the leaven of the.** √103, Ge +3:13. By the figure *Hypocatastasis* the word "doctrine" is implied. Ex 12:18-20. Le 2:11. 1 C *5:6-8. **of Herod.** Mk 12:13. Mt 16:6. 22:15-18.

16. **reasoned.** Mt 16:7, 8. Lk 9:46. 20:5.

17. **knew.** Mk 2:8. Jn +*2:24, 25. 16:30. 21:17. He √4:12, 13. Re *2:23. **perceive.** Mk 3:5. *6:52. 16:14. Is ▶6:9, 10. 63:17. Mt 15:17. 16:8, 9. Lk *24:45. He √5:11, 12.

18. **see.** Mk 4:12. Dt 29:4. Ps 69:23. 115:5-8. Is 6:9, 10. 42:18-20. 44:18. Je ▶5:21. Ezk ▶12:2. Mt 13:14, 15. Jn 12:40. Ac 28:26, 27. Ro 11:8. **do.** 2 P 1:12.

19. **brake.** √108H4, Is +58:7. **the five.** Mk 6:38-44. Mt 14:17-21. Lk 9:12-17. Jn 6:5-13.

20. **the seven.** √32, Ge +31:21. ver. 1-9. Mt 15:34-38.

21. **How.** ver. 12, 17. Mk 6:52. 9:19. Ps 94:8. Mt *16:11, 12. Jn 14:9. 1 C 6:5. 15:34.

22. **Bethsaida.** Mk 6:45. Mt 11:21. Lk 9:10. 10:13. Jn 1:44. 12:21. **they bring.** Mk 2:3. *6:55, 56. **to touch.** T#1585. Mk 1:41. 5:27-29. Mt 8:3, 15. 9:29.

23. **he took.** Mk 7:33. **by the.** Is 51:18. Je 31:32. Ac 9:8. He 8:9. **out.** Mk 7:33. Is 42:2. **spit.** Jn *9:6, 7. Re 3:18. **put his hands.** Mk 5:23.

24. **I see.** Jg 9:36. Is 29:18. 32:3. 1 C 13:9-12.

25. **his.** √63A3, Mt +19:13. **and saw.** Pr +*4:18. Mt 13:12. Lk 7:21. Ph 1:6. 1 P *2:9. 2 P *3:18.

26. **Neither.** ver. 23. Mk 5:43. 7:36. Mt 8:4. 9:30. 12:16.

27. **the towns.** Mt 16:13, etc. **and by.** Lk 9:18, 19, etc. **Whom.** Mt 16:13. Lk 9:18-21. Jn 6:68, 69.

28. John. Mk 6:14-16. Mt *14:2. 16:14. Lk 9:7-9. **Elias.** Mk 9:11-13. Ml *4:5, Elijah. Jn *1:21.

29. But. Mk 4:11. Mt *16:15. Lk 9:20. 1 P 2:7. **Thou.** Mt √16:16. Jn 1:41, 49. 4:42. √6:69. 11:27. Ac 8:37. 9:20. 1 J 4:15. 5:1.

30. he charged. ver. 26. Mk 7:36. 9:9. Mt 16:20. Lk 9:21.

31. he began. Mk 9:31, 32. 10:33, 34. Mt 16:21. 17:22, 23. 20:17-19. Lk 9:22. 18:31-34. 24:6, 7, 26, 44. **rejected.** Mk 12:10. 1 S 8:7. 10:19. Ps 118:22. Is *53:3. Mt 21:42. Lk 17:25. Jn 12:48. Ac 3:13-15. 7:35, 51, 52. **and after.** Ho 6:2. Jon 1:17. Mt +*12:40n. Jn +*2:19. 1 C +*15:4.

32. openly. Jn 16:25, 29. **Peter.** Mk 4:38. Mt *16:22. Lk 9:21. 10:40. Jn 13:6-8.

33. turned. Mk 3:5, 34. Lk 22:61. **and looked.** ♪149. Pragmatographia; or, Description of Actions B452. For other instances of this figure see Ac 6:15. 7:55, 56. **he rebuked.** Le +*19:17. 2 S 19:22. Ps *141:5. Pr *9:8, 9. Mt *16:23. Lk 9:55. 1 T *5:20. T *1:13. Re *3:19. **Get.** Ge 3:4-6. Jb 2:10. Mt *4:10. Lk 4:8. 1 C 5:5. **savorest.** Mt 6:31, 32. Ro *8:5-8. 1 C √2:14. Ph 3:19g. Ja *3:15-18. 1 P 4:1, 2. 1 J √2:15, 16.

34. called. Mk 7:14. Lk 9:23. 20:45. **Whosoever.** Mk √9:43-48. Mt 5:29, 30. 7:13, 14. 16:24. Lk 13:24. *14:27, 33. Ro 15:1-3. 1 C 8:13. 9:19. Ph *3:7, 8. T *2:12. **take.** Mk 10:21. Mt *10:38. 27:32. Jn 19:17. Ac *14:22. Ro 6:6. √8:17, 18. 1 C 4:9-13. *15:31. 2 C √4:17. Ga √2:20. *5:24. *6:14. Ph √3:10. Col 1:24. 3:5. 2 T 3:11. 1 P *4:1, 13. Re *2:10. **follow.** Nu 14:24. 1 K 14:8. Lk 14:26. 18:22. Jn √10:27. 13:36, 37. 21:19, 20. He *13:13. 2 P 1:14. 1 J *3:16.

35. will save. Est 4:11-16. Je 26:20-24. Mt 10:39. 16:25. Lk 9:24. 17:33. Jn *12:25, 26. Ac 20:24. 21:13. 2 T 2:11-13. 4:6-8. He 11:35. Re 2:10, 11. *7:14-17. *12:11. **life.** Gr. *psyche*, ♪121A7, Mt +2:20. ♪121A7, Ge +9:5. **lose.** Gr. *apollumi*, Mt +2:13. **lose.** Gr. *apollumi*, Mt +2:13. **life.** Gr. *psyche*, ♪121A7, Mt +2:20. ♪121A7, Ge +9:5. **for.** Mt 5:10-12. 10:22. 19:29. Lk 6:22, 23. Jn 15:20, 21. Ac 9:16. 1 C 9:23. 2 C 12:10. 2 T 1:8. 1 P 4:12-16.

36. what. Jb 2:4. Ps 49:17-19. 73:18-20. Mt 4:8-10. 16:26. Lk 9:25. *12:19, 20. *16:19-23. Ph 3:7-9. Re 18:7, 8. **profit.** Jb 22:2. Ml 3:14. Ro 6:21. He 11:24-26. Ja 1:9-11. **if he.** ♪184C, Mt +4:9. ♪102C, Mt +5:29. **world.** Gr. *kosmos*, Mt +4:8. **lose.** Mt +16:26 (✱S#2210g). **soul.** Gr. *psyche*, ♪121A7, Mt +2:20.

37. Or what. Ps *49:7, 8. 1 P *1:18, 19. **soul.** Gr. *psyche*, ♪121A7, Mt +2:20.

38. ashamed. Mt *10:32, 33. Ps *119:46. Lk 9:26. *12:8, 9. Ac 5:41. Ro +*1:16. Ga *6:14. 2 T *1:8, 12, 16. √2:12, 13. He 11:26. 12:2, 3. 13:13. 1 J 2:23. **adulterous.** Mt +*12:39. 16:4. Ja *4:4. **the Son.** Mk 14:62. Da +*7:13. Mt +*16:27n, 28. +*24:30. +*25:31. 26:64. Jn *1:14. 5:27. 12:34. **when.** Dt +*33:2. Ps√102:16. Da *7:10. Zc +*14:5. Mt +*13:41. Jn 1:51. 2 Th √1:7, 8. Ju *14, *15.

MARK 9

The transfiguration of Christ, 1-10. He shows that John the Baptist is "Elias who was to come," 11-13. He casts out a dumb and deaf spirit, having rebuked the company, and the disciples, for their unbelief, 14-29. He foretells his own death and resurrection, 30-32; reproves the ambition of the disciples, 33-37; forbids

them to hinder one, who cast out devils in his name, though he followed not with them, 38-41; shows the guilt of offending weak believers, 42; and warns his hearers to part with all occasions of sin however valued; showing the eternal doom of the wicked, especially of apostates, in most awful language, 43-50.

1. That. Mt +*16:28n. Lk 9:27. **taste.** Lk 2:26. Jn 8:51, 52. He 2:9. **the kingdom.** Mt +*24:30. *25:31. Lk 22:18, 30. Jn *21:23. Ac 1:6, 7.

2. after. Mt 17:1, etc. Lk 9:28, etc. **Peter.** Mk 5:37. 14:33. 2 C 13:1. **an high.** Ex 24:13. 1 K 18:42, 43. Mt 14:13. Lk 6:12. **apart.** Mk 5:37. Mt 26:37. **transfigured.** Mk 16:12. Ex 34:29-35. Is 33:17. 53:2. Mt *17:2. Lk 9:29. Jn *1:14. Ro *12:2. 2 C 3:7-10. Ph *2:6-8. 3:21. 2 P *1:16-18. Re 1:13-17. 20:11.

3. his raiment. Ps 104:1, 2. Da *7:9. Mt *28:3. Ac 10:30. Re 1:14. **exceeding.** Ps 51:7. 68:14. Is *1:18. Re 7:9, 14. 19:8. **no.** Ml 3:2, 3.

4. appeared. Mt 11:13. 17:3, 4. Lk 9:19, 30, 31. 24:27, 44. Jn +*5:39, 45-47. Ac 3:21-24. 1 P 1:10-12. Re 19:10. **Elias.** Moses was the founder of the Jewish polity, and Elias the most zealous reformer and prophet of the Jewish church; and their presence implied that the ministry of Christ was attested by the law and the prophets. 2 K 2:11, 12, Elijah. **Moses.** Dt *34:5, 6.

5. it is. Ex 33:17-23. Ps 63:2, 3. 84:10. Jn 14:8, 9, 21-23. Ph +*1:23. 1 J *3:2. Re 22:3, 4. **tabernacles.** Le +=23:42.

6. wist not. Mk 16:5-8. Da 10:15-19. Re 1:17. **afraid.** Mt 17:6, 7.

7. a cloud. Ex 40:34. 1 K 8:10-12. 2 Ch +*5:13. Ps 97:2. Da +*7:13. Mt 17:5-7. 26:64. Lk 9:34-36. Ac 1:9. Re +*1:7. **This is.** Mk 1:11. Ps *2:7. Mt 3:17. 26:63. 27:43, 54. Lk 3:22. Jn 1:34, 49. 3:16-18. 5:18, 22-25, 37. 6:69. 9:35. 15:26. 19:7. √20:31. Ac *8:37. Ro *1:4. 2 P 1:17. 1 J 4:9, 10. 5:11, 12, 20. **hear.** Ex 23:21, 22. Dt *18:15-19. Ac 3:22, 23. 7:37. He *2:1. 12:25, 26.

8. suddenly. Lk 9:36. 24:31. Ac 8:39, 40. 10:16.

9. he charged. Mk 5:43. 8:29, 30. Mt 12:19. 17:9. **till.** ver. 30, 31. Mk 8:31. 10:32-34. Mt +*12:40. 16:21. 27:63. Lk 24:46.

10. they. Ge 37:11. Lk 2:50, 51. 24:7, 8. Jn 16:17-19. **what.** ver. 32. Mt 16:22. Lk 18:33, 34. *24:25-27. Jn +*2:19-22. *12:16, 33, 34. 16:17, 29, 30. Ac 17:18.

11. Why say. ver. 4. Ml 3:1. *4:5. Mt 11:14. 17:10, 11.

12. Elias. Ml ▸4:5. **restoreth.** Mk 1:2-8. Is 40:3-5. Ml 4:6. Mt 3:1, etc. 11:2-18. Lk *1:16, 17, 76. *3:2-9. Jn 1:6-36. 3:27, etc. Ac +*1:6. +*3:21. **he must.** Ps ch. 22. 69:1, etc. Is ch. 53. Da +*9:24-26. Zc +*13:7. **set.** Ps *22:6, 7. 69:12. 74:22. Is *49:7. 50:6. 52:14. *53:1-3. Da +*9:26. Zc 11:13. +*13:7. Lk *23:11, 39. Ac 4:11. Ph *2:7, 8.

13. Elias. Mt +*11:14n. 17:12, 13. Lk 1:17. **and they.** Mk 6:14-28. Mt *14:3-11. Lk *3:19, 20. Ac 7:52.

14. when. Mt 17:14, etc. Lk 9:37. **the scribes.** Mk 2:6. 11:28. 12:14. Lk 11:53, 54. He 12:3.

15. were. ver. 2, 3. Ex 34:30. **greatly amazed.** It is probable that our Lord's face shone with rays of glory, as the face of Moses did when he descended from Mount Sinai; for no other adequate reason for the people's surprise can be assigned. Mk 10:32. 14:33. 16:5, 6. **running to.** Ex ◑=34:3.

16. **What.** Mk 8:11. Lk 5:30-32. **with them.** *or*, among yourselves.

17. **Master.** ver. 38. Mk 4:38. **I have brought.** Mk 5:23. 7:26. 10:13. Mt 17:15. Lk 9:38. Jn 4:47. **a dumb.** ⨍121E1, Ge +25:23. ver. 25. Mt 12:22. Lk 11:14. **spirit.** Gr. *pneuma*, Mt +8:16.

18. **teareth him.** *or*, dasheth him. ver. 26. Mt 7:6. 15:22. Lk 9:39. **he foameth.** As these symptoms accord very much with those of epileptic persons, some have ventured to assert that it was no real possession; but the evangelist expressly affirms that he had "a dumb spirit," which tare him, that our Lord charged him to "*come out* of him," etc. ver. 20. Ju 13. **gnasheth.** Jb 16:9. Ps 112:10. Mt 8:12. Ac 7:54. **and they.** ver. 28, 29. Mk ◖6:7. 11:23. 2 K 4:29-31. Mt ◖10:1. 17:16, 19-21. Lk 9:◖1, 40. 10:17.

19. **O faithless.** Mk 16:14. Nu 14:11, 22, 27. 32:13, 14. Dt *32:5, 20. Ps 78:6-8, 22. 106:21-25. Mt 12:39. 17:17. Lk 9:41. 24:25. Jn 12:27. *20:27. He 3:10-12. **generation.** Mt +*12:39. **how long.** Jn 8:25. 14:9. **suffer you.** Ac 18:14. 2 C 11:1, 4, 19, 20. Ep 4:2. Col 3:13. 2 T 4:3.

20. **the spirit.** Gr. *pneuma*, Mt +8:16. ver. 18, 26. Mk 1:26. 5:3-5. Jb 1:10, etc. 2:6-8. Lk 4:35. 8:29. 9:42. Jn *8:44. 1 P *5:8.

21. **How.** Mk 5:25. Jb 5:7. 14:1. Ps 51:5. Lk 8:43. 13:16. Jn 5:5, 6. 9:1, 20, 21. Ac 3:2. 4:22. 9:33. 14:8.

22. **destroy.** Gr. *apollumi*, Mt +2:13. **if.** ⨍184A, 1 C +15:2. Mk 1:40-42. Mt 8:2, 8, 9. 9:28. 14:31. **have.** Mk 5:19. 7:26. Mt 9:36. 15:22-28. 20:34. Lk 7:13.

23. **If.** ⨍184A, 1 C +15:2. Mk *11:23. 2 Ch +*20:20. Mt *17:20. 21:21, 22. Lk 17:6. Jn 4:48-50. *11:40. Ac 14:9. 2 Th 1:11. He √11:6. **all things.** √⨍171A, Ex +9:6. i.e. all things comprehended in the promise. Not all things indiscriminately. Faith always has respect to what is said or promised (B615). Mk 10:27.

24. **with.** 2 S 16:12mg. 2 K 20:5. Ps 39:12. 126:5. Je 14:17. Lk 7:38, 44. Ac 20:19, 31. 2 C 2:4. 2 T 1:4. He *5:7. 12:17. **help.** ⨍69A. Epanorthosis; or, Correction B909. A recalling what has been said, in order to correct it as by an afterthought: where the retraction is absolute. Here, the father has said "Lord, I believe; (but, remembering his weakness, the speaker immediately corrects this great profession of faith, and says) help thou mine unbelief." For other instances of this figure see Jn 12:27 and Ro 14:4. T#1735. Lk √17:5. Ro +*10:17. Ga 3:2, 5. Ep *2:8. Ph 1:29. 2 Th 1:3, 11. He *11:6. *12:2.

25. **he rebuked.** Mk 1:25-27. 5:7, 8. Zc 3:2. Mt 8:26. 17:18. Lk 4:35, 39, 41. *9:42, 43. Ac *10:38. 1 J *3:8. Ju 9. **foul.** or, unclean. Mk +3:30. **spirit.** Gr. *pneuma*, Mt +8:16. **Thou.** If this had been only a natural disease, as some have contended, could our Lord with any propriety have thus addressed *it*? If the demoniacal possession had been false, or merely a vulgar error, would our Lord, the Revealer of truth, have thus established falsehood, sanctioned error, or encouraged deception, by teaching men to ascribe effects to the malice and power of evil spirits, which they had no agency in producing? Impossible! Such conduct is utterly unworthy the sacred character of the Redeemer. Is 35:5, 6. Mt 9:32, 33. 12:22. Lk 11:14. **dumb.** ⨍121E1, Ge +25:23. **spirit.** Gr. *pneuma*, Mt +8:16. **I charge.** Lk 8:29. Ac 16:18.

26. **cried.** ver. 18, 20. Mk 1:26. Ex 5:23. Re 12:12.

27. **took him.** Mk 1:31, 41. 5:41. 8:23. Is 41:13. Ac 3:7. 9:41.

28. **asked.** Mk 4:10, 34. Mt 13:10, 36. 15:15. **Why.** Mt *17:19, 20.

29. **This.** Mt 12:45. Lk 11:26. **by prayer.** T#1468. Mk 5:2-8. 1 K 17:20-22. 2 K 4:33, 34. Mt 15:21-28. 17:21. Ac 9:40, 41. 2 C 12:8. Ep *6:18. Ja *5:15. **fasting.** Jg 20:26n. 2 Ch +*7:14. Da +*9:3. Lk 2:37. Ac 14:23. 1 C 9:27. 2 C 6:5. 11:27.

30. **through.** Mt 27:22, 23. Jn 7:1-9. **he.** ver. 9. Mk +*6:31, 32.

31. **The Son.** ver. 12. Mk 2:10. 8:31. Mt 16:21. 17:12. 20:18, 19, 28. 21:38, 39. 26:2. Lk 9:44. 18:31-33. *19:44. 24:26, 44-46. Jn +*2:19. 3:14. √10:18. Ac 2:23, 24. 4:27, 28. 2 T *2:12. **delivered.** ⨍96C6, Mt +2:4. **the third day.** Mk 8:31. Ho 6:2. Mt +*12:40n.

32. **they.** ver. 10. Mk 6:52. Mt 13:19. 17:13. Lk 2:50. 9:45. 18:34. 24:25, 26, 45. Jn 8:27, 28. 10:6. 12:16. 14:5-9. 16:17-19. **were.** Mk 7:18. 8:17, 18, 33. 16:14. Jn 4:27. 16:19.

33. **he came.** Mt 17:24. **What.** Mk 2:8. Ps 139:1-4. Jn +*2:25. 21:17. He *4:13. Re *2:23.

34. **they had.** Mt *18:1, etc. *20:21-24. Lk *9:46-48. *22:24, etc. Ro 12:10. Ph 2:3-7. 1 P 5:3. 3 J 9.

35. **the twelve.** Mk 4:10. 6:7. 10:32. 11:11. 14:10, 17, 20, 43. Lk 8:1. 9:1, 12. 18:31. 22:3, 47. Jn 6:67, 70, 71. 20:24. Ac 6:2. 1 C 15:5. **If.** ⨍184A, 1 C +15:2. Mk *10:42-45. Pr *13:10. Je 45:5. Mt *20:25-28. 23:11, 12. Lk 14:10, 11. 18:14. 22:26. Ja 4:6. **and servant.** Gr. *diakonos*, ✱S#1249g. Mk 10:43. Mt 20:26. 22:13. 23:11. Jn 2:5, 9. 12:26. Ro 13:4, 4. 15:8. 16:1. 1 C 3:5. 2 C 3:6. 6:4. 11:15, 23. Ga 2:17. Ep 3:7. 6:21. Ph 1:1 (deacons). Col 1:7, 23, 25. 4:7. 1 Th 3:2. 1 T 3:8, 12. 4:6. **of all.** Mk 10:43-45. Jn 13:12-15. Ro 15:1-3. 1 C 9:19-22. 10:24, 32, 33. 2 C *8:9. Ga *6:9, 10. Ep 6:5-8. Ph *2:3, 4.

36. **took a child.** ver. 42. Mk 10:16. Mt *18:2, 6. 19:14, 15. 21:16. Lk *9:48. 10:21. 17:2. 18:16. **taken him.** Mk 10:16. Mt 18:2. Lk 9:48.

37. **receive one.** Mt 10:40-42. 18:3-5, 10. 25:40. Lk 9:48. **in my name.** ver. 39. Mk 13:6. Mt 18:5. 24:5. Lk 1:59. 9:48, 49. 21:8. 24:47. Ac 4:17, 18. 5:28, 40. **receive me.** Lk 10:16. Jn √5:23. √10:30. 12:44, 45. 14:21-23. 1 Th 4:8.

38. **Master.** Nu *11:26-29. Lk 9:49, 50. 11:19. **casting out.** Mk 16:17. Mt 7:22. 12:27. Lk 10:17. Ac 3:6. 16:18. 19:13. **we forbad.** Mk 10:14. Mt 19:14. Lk 9:50. 18:15.

39. **Forbid.** Mk *10:13, 14. Mt +*13:28, 29. Ph *1:18. **there.** Mt *7:22, 23. Ac *19:13-16. 1 C *9:27. *13:1, 2. **lightly.** 1 C √12:3.

40. **he that.** Mt 6:24. *12:30. Lk *9:50. *11:23. 2 C 6:15, 16.

41. **whosoever.** See on Mt *10:42. *25:35, 40. 1 C *13:3. He *6:10. **because.** Jn 19:25-27. Ro *8:9. 14:15. 1 C 3:23. *15:23. 2 C 10:7. Ga *3:29. *5:24. 1 P 4:14. **lose.** Gr. *apollumi*, Mt +2:13.

42. **offend.** Is 9:16. Mt 17:27. *18:6, 10. Lk *17:1, 2. Ro 14:13, 15, 21. 16:17. 1 C 8:10-13. 10:32, 33. 2 C 6:3. Ph 1:10. 1 T 5:14, 15. 2 P 2:2. **little ones.** ver. 36. Zc +*13:7. **it is better.** Mk 14:21. Mt 25:45, 46. Ac 9:4. 26:11-14. 2 Th 1:6-9. Re 6:9, 10. 16:6, 7. **that a.** ⨍184B, Mt +23:30.

43. **if.** ⨍184C, Mt +4:9. Dt *13:6-8. Mt *5:29, 30. *18:8, 9. Ro *8:13. 1 C *9:27. Ga *5:24. Col *3:5. T *2:12. He *12:1. 1 P *2:1. **offend thee.** *or*, cause thee

to offend: and so ver. *45, *47. **enter into**. ver. 45. Mt +*7:14. 18:8, 9. 19:17. Jn 5:24. **maimed**. Mt 15:30, 31. Lk *14:13, 21. **hell**. Gr. *gehenna*, Mt +5:22. **quenched**. ver. 48. Mt 3:12. +*25:41. Lk 3:17.

44. **their**. ver. *46, *48. Is +*⟩66:24. Mt +*25:41. Lk +*24:27. **the fire**. Is +*33:14. Mt *3:12. +*25:41, 46. 2 Th √1:9. Re *14:10, 11. *20:10, 15. +*21:8.

45. **And if**. ʄ184C, Mt +4:9. **thy foot**. ver. *43, *44. Mt 18:8. **cut**. ʄ102C, Mt +5:29. **hell**. Gr. *gehenna*, Mt +5:22.

46. **Where**. ʄ8, Ps +118:1. **their worm**. Lk *16:24-26.

47. **And if**. ʄ184C, Mt +4:9. **thine**. Ge *3:6. Jb *31:1. Ps *119:37. Mt *5:28, 29. *10:37-39. Lk 14:26. Ro *8:13. Ga 4:15. Ph 3:7, 8. **offend thee**. *or*, cause thee to offend. ver. 43mg. **pluck**. ʄ102C, Mt +5:29. **hell**. Gr. *gehenna*, Mt +5:22.

48. **Where**. ʄ8, Ps +118:1. **their worm**. ver. *44, *46. Jb +*14:22. Is +*66:24. **the fire**. ver. 43. Lk *16:24.

49. **every one**. Whitby supposes this to mean, "Every wicked man shall be seasoned with fire itself, so as to be inconsumable, and shall endure for ever to be tormented; and therefore may be said to be *salted with fire*, in allusion to that property of salt, which is to preserve things from corruption." Beza and Gilpin would read, "Every Christian is purified by the difficult and fiery trials of life, in the same manner as (*kai* for *hos*, as in Mk 10:12. Jn 14:20) every sacrifice with salt." Lightfoot and Doddridge, "He that is a true sacrifice to God shall be seasoned with the salt of grace to the incorruption of glory; and every victim to Divine justice shall be salted with fire to endure for ever." 2 C 2:16. **salted**. In this world ye may look for offences. Ye are to expect severe trials and temptations; but these are exercises of your Christian virtues, and are designed to make you to be acceptable sacrifices to God. The word rendered *shall be salted* appears to be used for the same reason as the word rendered *fire*, on account of its double sense. In the Old Testament the Hebrew word *malah, to salt*, is used (1) for cleansing, seasoning, and preserving (Le 2:13), and there spoken of sacrifices (compare Ezk 43:24). And so it is here appropriately applied to the fire of God's Spirit and of earthly trials, which are designed by God to season men, and render them acceptable sacrifices to Him; (2) *salt* is also used for what is perpetually barren and bituminous, and its effect on the earth is described by burning (Dt 29:23. Jb 39:6. Ps 107:34. Je 17:6. Ezk 47:11. Captive cities were sown with salt (Jg 9:45). The word *malah* is specially applied to the *Dead Sea*, which is called the Sea of Salt (Ge 14:3. Nu 34:12). Lot's wife became a *pillar of salt* (*melah*, Ge 19:26), a monument of an unbelieving soul. Our Lord's meaning therefore is, If men will not be *seasoned* by the refining fire of God's Spirit, and of this world's trials, they will be salted with the fire of Tophet, "the fire and brimstone" (Re 20:10), the Dead Sea, or Salt Sea, of Gehenna, the Lake of Fire (Re 21:8), *that* fire which has the property of *salt*, in that it does not consume but *preserve* its victims—even for evermore. Hence the ungodly are often spoken of as *burnt sacrifices* to God's justice, which is compared to fire (He 12:29. Is 66:15, 16. Je 12:3. 46:10. Ezk 21:9, 10. 39:6). St. John the Baptist said of Christ, He shall baptize you with the Holy Ghost and with *fire* (Mt 3:11). Note

Peter's reference to the *fiery trial* which is to try us (1 P 4:12), and the trial of our faith *with fire* (1 P 1:7. Compare Jb 23:10. Ps 66:10. Pr 17:3. Is 48:10. Je 23:29. Zc 13:9). Hence the sense of this passage is, that men are to be baptized in this world with the Holy Ghost and *fire*, that is, with the purifying flame of love and zeal, cleansing and smelting away the dross of worldly and carnal affections, and with the sanctifying illuminations of the Holy Ghost; and they are also tried in this world in the *furnace of suffering*, in order that they may be presented a living and holy sacrifice acceptable to God, as of a sweetsmelling savour (Ro 12:1. 2 C 2:15. Ep 5:2. 1 P 2:5). And if this is not the result of God's grace, and of the temporary fire of the trials of this life, they will be reserved for God's severe and righteous judgment, for everlasting fire, in the world to come (Wordsworth, *Greek Testament*, vol. 1, p. 136). 2 C 2:16. He 12:29. **with fire**. 1 C 3:13. 1 P 4:12. **and every sacrifice**. Le *2:13. Ezk *43:24. 1 C *3:15.

50. **Salt**. ʄ138C, Ge +22:14. **is good**. Jb *6:6. Mt *5:13. Lk *14:34, 35. **but if**. ʄ184C, Mt +4:9. **Have salt**. On account of the cleansing and purifying effect of salt, the Levitical sacrifices were to be seasoned with it (Le 2:13. Ezk 43:24); an emblem of that purity which is necessary to make a sacrifice acceptable to God. This spiritual salt is to be preserved in the heart, and to season the life and conversation (Col 4:6), so that nothing that is *corrupt* may proceed from the mouth (Ep 4:29); and so the disciples of Christ may be the salt of the earth (Wordsworth, *Greek Testament*, vol. 1, p. 136). Ezk +*24:10. 43:24. Da +*11:33n. Ep *4:29. Col *4:6. He +*3:12, 13. **have peace**. Ps *34:14. *133:1. Jn *13:34, 35. *15:17, 18. Ro *12:18. *14:17-19. 2 C *13:11. Ga *5:14, 15, 22. Ep *4:2-6, 31, 32. Ph *1:27. *2:1-3. Col 3:12, 13. 1 Th 5:13. 2 T *2:22. He √12:14. Ja *1:20. *3:14-18. 1 P *3:8, 9.

MARK 10

Jesus teaches in Judea, 1; answers the Pharisees concerning divorce, 2-12; receives and blesses young children, 13-16; instructs and proves the rich young man; shows the danger of affluence; and makes gracious promises to those who forsake worldly objects for his sake, 17-31. He again predicts his own death and resurrection; reproves the ambition of James and John, and the other apostles, 32-45; and gives sight to blind Bartimeus, 46-52.

1. A.M. 4033. A.D. 29. **he arose**. Mt 19:1, etc. **by**. Mk +3:8. Mt ◑3:5. 4:25. 19:1. Lk ◑3:3. Jn 1:28. 3:26. *10:40. *11:7. **resort**. Ps 71:3. Jn 10:41. **as he was wont**. Lk +*4:16. 22:39. **he taught**. Ec 12:9. Je 32:33. Jn 18:20.

2. **the Pharisees**. Mk 8:15. Mt 9:34. 15:12. 23:13. Lk 5:30. 6:7. 7:30. 11:39, 53, 54. 16:14. Jn 7:32, 48. 11:47, 57. **Is it**. Ml 2:16. Mt 5:31, 32. +*19:3. 1 C 7:10, 11. **tempting**. Mk 8:11. Mt 16:1. 22:35. Jn 8:6. 1 C 10:9.

3. **What**. Is +*8:20n. Lk 10:25, 26. Jn +*5:39. Ga 4:21. **Moses**. Ex +*24:4.

4. **Moses suffer**. Dt ⟩24:1-4. Is 50:1. Je 3:1. Mt 1:19. 5:31, 32. 19:7.

5. **For**. Dt 9:6. 31:27. Ne 9:16, 17, 26. Mt 19:8. Ac 7:51. He 3:7-10.

6. **the beginning**. Ge 1:1. 2 P 3:4. **God**. Ge ⟩1:27.

*2:20-23. *5:2. Ml 2:14-16. Mt 19:4.

7. **this cause.** Ge ⟩2:24. Ps 45:10. Mt 19:5, 6. Ep 5:31.

8. **one flesh.** 1 C 6:16. Ep 5:28.

9. **hath joined.** Ro 7:1-3. 1 C 7:10-13.

10. **in the house.** See on Mk 4:10. 9:28, 33.

11. **Whosoever.** Mt 5:31, 32. +*19:9n. Lk 16:18. Ro 7:3. 1 C 7:4, 10, 11. He 13:4.

12. **And if.** ♪184C, Mt +4:9. **a woman.** That a woman among the Jews *could*, in some cases, divorce her husband, appears from *Bereshith Rabba*, 18., and *Ketuvoth*, 7.9, cited by Wetstein; and it appears from Josephus, that it was done by some women of distinguished rank. They probably learnt this of the Romans, among whom it was practiced in the most scandalous manner (see Juvenal, Sat. vi. v. 222-230). Our Lord might judge it seasonable thus to check its progress; and St. Mark, writing to the Gentile Christians, would deem it very suitable to them. Mk 6:17. 1 C 7:11, 13. **she committeth.** Ge 2:24. Ps 45:10. Mt 19:5, 6. 1 C 6:16. Ep 5:31.

13. **they.** Mt *19:13-15. Lk *18:15, 16. **disciples.** ver. 48. Mk 9:38. Ex 10:9-11. Dt 31:12, 13. Jl 2:16.

14. **he was.** Mk 3:5. 8:33. Lk 9:54-56. Ep 4:26. **displeased.** ♪141, Is +22:4. **Suffer.** Ge +*17:7, 10-14. Nu 14:31. Dt 4:37. 29:11, 12. 1 S 1:11, 22, 27, 28. Ps 78:4. 115:14, 15. Is 65:23. Je 32:39, 40. Lk 18:15, 16. Ac +*2:39. 3:25. Ro 11:16, 28. 1 C +*7:14n. 2 T 1:5. 3:15. **for.** Ps 131:1, 2. Mt 18:4, 10. 19:14. 1 C *14:20. 1 P √2:2. Re 14:5.

15. **Whosoever.** Mt *18:3-5. Lk 18:17. Jn 3:3-6.

16. **he took.** Ge 48:14-16. Dt 28:3. Is *40:11. Lk 2:28-34. 24:50, 51. Jn 21:15-17.

17. **when.** Mt 19:16, etc. Lk 18:18, etc. **one.** ♪108E1, Mt +8:19. **running.** T#1275. Mk 9:25. Mt 28:8. Jn 20:2-4. **kneeled.** Mk 1:40. Da 6:10. Mt 17:14. **Good.** Mk 12:14. Jn 3:2. 7:12. **what shall.** T#1476. Jn 6:28. Ac 2:37. 9:6. √16:30, 31. Ro 10:2-4, *9, *10. T √3:5-7. **inherit.** Mt 19:16, 29. 25:34. Lk 10:25. 18:18. T 3:7. **eternal.** Gr. *aionios*, Mt +18:8. 25:46. Lk 10:25. Jn 4:14. +*5:39. 6:27, 40. Ac *13:46, 48. Ro 2:7. √6:23. 1 J 2:25. √5:11-13.

18. **Why.** Mt 19:17. Lk 18:19. Jn 5:41-44. Ro 3:12. **none good but one.** God the Father possesses the attribute of essential goodness (Mt +*28:19n), as does God the Son (Jn 10:11), and God the Holy Spirit (Ps 143:10). By this statement Jesus did not deny his own goodness, but claimed it was a proof of his deity. Ex +√34:6. Ps 33:5. Ro 2:4. +*11:22. 16:27. Ep 2:7. 2 Th *1:11. 1 T ◑√6:16n. T 3:4. Re *15:4. **that is.** 1 S 2:2. Ps 36:7, 8. *86:5. *119:68. Ja *1:17. 1 J 4:8, 16.

19. **knowest.** Mk 12:28-34. Is +*8:20. Mt 5:17-20. 19:17-19. Lk 10:26-28. 18:20. Ro 3:20. Ga 4:21. **commit.** Ex 20:12-17. Dt 5:16-24. Ro *13:9. Ga 5:14. Ja *2:11. **adultery.** Ex ⟩20:14. **kill.** Ex ⟩20:13. **false.** Ex ⟩20:16. Ep 4:25. **Defraud.** Le +*⟩19:13. Mi 2:2. Ml +*3:5. 1 C 6:7-9. 1 Th +*4:6. **honor.** Ex ⟩20:12. Mt 19:19. Ep *6:2.

20. **all these.** Is 58:2. Ezk 5:14. +*33:31, 32. Ml 3:8. Mt *19:20. Lk 10:29. 18:11, 12. Ro √3:20, 23. 7:9. Ph 3:6. 2 T 3:5. **from my youth.** Ezk 4:14.

21. **beholding.** ♪93B, Is +66:11. i.e. lovingly beheld. **loved.** ♪141, Is +22:4. Ge 34:19. Is 63:8-10. Lk 19:41. 2 C 12:15. **One thing.** Ps 27:4. Ec 3:19. Lk +*10:42. 18:22. Jn 9:25. Ph 3:13. Ja *2:10. 2 P 3:8. Re 2:4, 14, 20. **sell.** Pr 23:23. Mt 13:44-46. 19:21. Lk

*12:33. Ac *2:44, 45. 4:34-37. **give.** Is *58:7. Mt +*19:21. Lk *14:13, 14. **treasure.** ♪22D5.O, Dt +28:12. Mt +*5:12. √6:19-21. *16:26. Lk +*14:14. +*16:9. Ph 3:20. Col *1:5. 1 T √6:17-19. 2 T *4:8. He 10:34-37. *11:16. 1 P +*1:4n, 5. Re *11:18. **take.** Mk 8:34. Mt 16:24. Lk 9:23. Jn 12:26. 16:33. Ro 8:17, 18. 2 T 3:12.

22. **sad.** Mk 6:20, 26. Ezk +*33:31. Mt 19:22. 27:3, 24-26. Lk 18:23. 2 C *7:10. 2 T 4:10. **for.** Ge 13:5-11. Dt 6:10-12. 8:11-14. Jb 21:7-15. Ps *62:10. Ezk +*33:31. Mt 13:22. Lk √12:15. Ep 5:5. 1 T √6:9, 10. 1 J √2:15, 16.

23. **looked.** Mk 3:5. 5:32. **How hardly.** Mt *19:23-26. Lk *18:24. 1 C 1:26. Ja *2:5. *4:4. **have riches.** Mt +*13:22. 1 T +*6:9. **enter.** ver. 15. Mt 18:3. Jn *3:5. 2 P 1:11.

24. **astonished.** Mt 19:25. Lk 18:26, 27. Jn 6:60. **Children.** Jn 13:33. 21:5. Ga 4:19. 1 J *2:1. 4:4. 5:21. **how hard.** Mt +*7:14. **trust.** Jb 31:24, 25. Ps 17:14. 49:6, 7. *52:7. *62:10. Pr 11:28. 18:11. 23:5. Je 9:23. Ezk 28:4, 5. Hab 2:9. Zp 1:18. Lk 12:16-21. 16:14. 1 T *6:17. Ja +*5:1-3. Re 3:17.

25. **It is.** ♪138B, Ge +13:16. **easier.** Je 13:23. Mt 7:3-5. 19:24, 25. 23:24. Lk 18:25.

26. **out.** Mk 6:51. 7:37. 2 C 11:23. **Who.** Lk +*13:23. 18:26. Ac √16:31. Ro √10:9-13.

27. **With men.** Ge *18:13, 14. Nu 11:21-23. 2 K 7:2. Zc 8:6. Mt *19:26. Lk *18:27. **for.** Jb *42:2. Je *32:17, 27. Lk *1:37. *18:27. Ph *3:21. He *7:25. 11:19. **all things.** Mk 9:23. *14:36. Ge ⟩18:14.

28. **Lo.** Mk 1:16-20. Mt *19:27-30. Lk 14:33. 18:28-30. Ac *14:22. Ph 3:7-9. **followed.** Mt *19:28.

29. **There.** Ge +*12:1-3. 45:20. Dt 33:9-11. Lk 22:28-30. He 11:24-26. **for.** Mk 8:35. Mt 5:10, 11. 10:18. 1 C 9:23. Re 2:3.

30. **shall receive.** T#415. Mt +5:7 (T#527). ‖19:29. Ps +58:11 (T#630). Lk +6:38 (T#408). **an hundredfold.** Ge +*26:12. 2 Ch *25:9. Jb 42:10. Ps 84:11. Pr *3:9, 10. 16:16. Is 40:2. 61:7. Ml 3:10. Mt 13:+*8, 23, 44-46. *‖19:29. Lk 18:30. 2 C 6:10. 9:8-11. Ph 3:8. 2 Th 2:16. 1 T 6:6. 1 J 3:1. Re 2:9. 3:18. **now in this time.** Mt √6:33. Lk *‖18:30. Ro 3:26. 8:18. 1 T +√4:8. He 9:9. 1 J 5:13. **house.** Mt 19:29. Lk 18:29. **brethren.** Mk 3:35. **with persecutions.** Mt *5:11, 12. Jn *15:20. 16:22, 23. Ac 5:41. +*14:22. 16:25. Ro 5:3. 8:35. 2 C 12:10. Ph *1:29. 2 Th 1:4. 2 T √3:11, 12. He 12:6. Ja 1:2-4, 12. 5:11. 1 P *1:6. 4:12-16. *5:10. **world.** Gr. *aion*, Mt +6:13. **to come.** Mt 12:32. Lk 18:30. 20:35. Ep 1:21. 2:7. He 6:5. **eternal.** Gr. *aionios*, Mt +18:8. ver. 17. Jn 10:23. Ro √6:23. 1 J 2:25. √5:11-13.

31. **But many.** Mt +*8:11, 12. 19:30. √20:16. *21:31, 43. Lk *7:29, 30, 40-47. *13:30. 18:11-14. Ac 13:46-48. Ro 9:30-33.

32. **they were in.** Mt 20:17, etc. Lk 18:31, etc. **they were amazed.** This probably refers to a sort of indefinable awe which the apostles began to feel for Jesus, which the mighty miracles he wrought, and the air of majesty and authority he now assumed, were calculated to inspire. Zc 3:8. Lk 9:51. Jn 11:8, 16. **And he.** Mk 4:34. Mt 11:25. 13:11. Lk 10:23, 24.

33. **we go.** Ac 20:22. **and the Son.** Mk 8:31. 9:31. Mt 16:21. 17:22, 23. 20:17-19. Lk 9:22. *18:31-33. 24:6, 7. **condemn.** Mk 14:64. Mt 26:66. Ac 13:27. Ja 5:6. **deliver.** Mk 15:1. Mt 27:2. Lk 23:1, 2, 21. Jn 18:28. 19:11. Ac 3:13, 14.

34. **mock.** Mk 14:65. 15:17-20, 29-31. Ps 22:6-8, 13. Is *53:3. Mt 27:27-44. Lk 22:63-65. 23:11, 35-39. Jn 19:2, 3. **spit.** Mk 14:65. Jb 30:10. Is 50:6. Mt 26:67. **third day.** Ps *16:10. Ho 6:2. Jon 1:17. 2:10. Mt +*12:39, 40. 1 C +*15:4.

35. **James.** St. Matthew says that this request was made by *Salome* their mother; but though she made the request as *from herself*, yet it is evident that they had set her upon the business; and therefore Jesus, knowing *whence* it came, immediately addressed the sons. Mk 1:19, 20. 5:37. 9:2. 14:33. **come.** Mt *20:20-28. **we would.** lit. we desire. ✓108B, 1 T +6:9. 2 S 14:4-11. 1 K 2:16, 20.

36. **What.** ver. 51. 1 K 3:5, etc. Jn 15:7.

37. **may sit.** T#1583. Mk 16:19. 1 K 22:19. Ps 45:9. 110:1. Mt +*19:28. +*20:21. **in.** Mk 8:38. Mt 25:31. Lk 24:26. 1 P 1:11.

38. **Ye know not.** 1 K 2:22. Je 45:5. Mt 20:21, 22. Ro 8:26. Ja 4:3. **drink of the.** Mk 14:36. Ps 75:8. Is 51:22. Je 25:15. Mt 26:39. Lk 22:42. Jn 18:11. **baptized with the.** Lk 12:50.

39. **We can.** Mk 14:31. Pr 16:18. Mt 26:35, 56. Jn 13:37. **Ye shall.** Mk 14:36. Mt 10:25. 16:24. Jn 15:20. 17:14. Ac *12:2. Col 1:24. Re *1:9.

40. **to sit.** Mt 20:23. 25:34. Jn 17:2, 24. He +*11:16. **not mine.** Mt 20:23. 1 C +*15:28. **for whom.** Mt 19:11. Ro *8:17. Col 1:5. **prepared.** Mt *25:34. Jn +*14:2. 17:24. 1 C *2:9. 2 C 5:2. Ph 3:20. 2 T 4:8. T *2:13. He 10:34-37. +*11:16. 1 J *3:2, 3. Re 21:2.

41. **they.** Mk 9:33-36. Pr 13:10. Mt 20:24. Lk 22:24. Ro 12:10. Ph +*2:3. Ja *4:5, 6.

42. **Ye know.** Mt 20:25. Lk 22:25. 1 P 5:3. **are accounted.** *or,* think good.

43. **But.** Mt 20:26. **so.** Jn 18:36. Ro *12:2. **whosoever.** Mk *9:35. Mt 20:26, 27. 23:8-12. Lk *9:48. 14:11. 18:14. Jn 13:13-18. 1 C 9:19-23. Ga 5:13. 1 P *5:5, 6.

44. **And whosoever.** Mt 20:27. **of all.** ✓77, Ex +3:19.

45. **came.** Mt *11:29. *20:28. Lk +*19:10. *22:26, 27. Jn *13:14. Ph *2:5-8. He *5:8. **and to give.** Mk 14:22. Is *53:10-12. Da +*9:24, 26. Jn 10:18. 11:51, 52. 2 C *5:21. Ga *3:13. 1 T √2:4-6. T *2:14. 1 P 1:19. **life.** Gr. *psyche,* ✓121A7, Mt +2:20. ✓121A7, Ge +9:5. **ransom.** Mt 20:28g. 1 T *2:6. **for many.** Mt +*26:28n. He 9:28.

46. **they came.** Mt 20:29, etc. Lk 18:35, etc. **as he went.** St. Luke says that this took place "as he was come nigh unto Jericho," and afterwards records an event which took place in that city. But the words *en to engidzein auton eis Ieriko,* may be rendered "When he was nigh Jericho," which is equally true of him who is gone a little way from it, as of him who is come near it; and as it is probable that Jesus stayed some days in the neighborhood, this might occur as he went out of the city during that time, and he might afterwards re-enter it. **blind Bartimeus.** i.e. *son of one esteemed; son of one unclean,* *S#924g. St. Matthew mentions *two* blind men who received their sight on this occasion; but Bartimeus was probably the more remarkable of the two, and therefore mentioned by name. **Timeus.** i.e. *highly prized; polluted,* *S#5090g. **begging.** Lk 16:20, 22. Jn 9:8. Ac 3:2, 3.

47. **Jesus.** Mt 2:23. 21:11. 26:71. Lk 4:16. 18:36, 37. Jn 1:46. 7:41, 52. 19:19. Ac 6:14. **thou.** Is +*9:6, 7. *11:1. Je +*23:5, 6. Mt *1:1. 9:27. 12:23. 15:22. 20:30. 21:9. 22:42-45. Ac +*13:22, 23. Ro *1:3, 4. Re *22:16.

48. **many.** Mk 5:35. Mt 19:13. 20:31. Lk 18:39. **but.** Mk 7:26-29. Ge 32:24-28. Je +*29:13. Mt 15:23-28. Lk 11:5-10. 18:1, etc. Ep *6:18. He *5:7. **have.** Ps 62:12.

49. **stood.** Ps 86:15. 145:8. Mt 20:32-34. Lk 18:40. He 2:17. +*4:15. **Be.** Jn 11:28. **rise.** Pr 6:9. SS 2:10. Is 60:1. Lk 22:46. Jn 5:8. Ep 5:14.

50. **casting away.** T#1233. Ph 3:7-9. He 12:1.

51. **What.** ver. 36. 2 Ch 1:7. Mt 6:8. 7:7, 8. Lk 18:41-43. Ph *4:6. **Lord.** Dt 4:7. Ph 4:5.

52. **thy faith.** Mk 5:34. Mt 9:22, 28-30. 15:28. Lk 7:50. 8:48. **made thee whole.** *or,* saved thee. **he received.** Mk 8:25. Ps 33:9. 146:8. Is 29:18, 19. 35:5. 42:16-18. Mt 11:5. 12:22. 21:14. Jn 9:5-7, 32, 39. Ac *26:18. **followed.** Mk 1:31. Lk 8:2, 3. **in the way.** Ge +*24:27. Ac 26:13.

<h2 style="text-align:center">MARK 11</h2>

Jesus enters Jerusalem, riding on an ass, amidst the acclamations of the multitude, 1-11. He curses a barren fig tree, 12-14; and drives the traders from the temple, 15-19. From the fig tree being dried up, he shows his disciples the power of faith, and directs them how to pray, 20-26. He silences the priests and scribes, who questioned his authority, 27-33.

1. **when.** Mt 21:1, etc. Lk 19:29, etc. Jn 12:14, etc. **Jerusalem.** *S#2419g. Mk 11:1. Mt 23:37, 37. Lk 2:25, 38, 41, 43, 45. 4:9. 5:17. 6:17. 9:31, 51, 53. 10:30. 13:4, 22, 33, 34, 34. 17:11. 19:11. 21:20, 24. 23:28. 24:13, 18, 33, 47, 49, 52. Ac 1:8, 12, 12, 19. 2:5, 14. 4:6, 16. 5:16, 28. 6:7. 8:25, 26, 27. 9:2, 13, 21, 26, 28. 10:39. 12:25. 13:27, 31. 15:2, 4. 16:4. 19:21. 20:22. 21:4, 11, 12, 13, 15, 31. 22:5, 17, 18. 23:11. 24:11. 25:3, 20. Ro 15:19, 25, 26, 31. 1 C 16:3. Ga 4:25, 26. He 12:22. Re 3:12. 21:2, 10. See also *S#2414g, Mt +2:1. **Bethphage.** i.e. *place of early figs; the drain of the valley,* Mt +21:1. **Bethany.** i.e. *house of humiliation, affliction, singing, or grace,* Jn +11:18. **mount of Olives.** Mk 13:3. 14:26. 2 S 15:30. Ne 8:15. Ezk 11:23. Zc +*14:4. Mt +*24:3. 26:30. Lk 19:29, 37. 21:37. 22:39. Jn 8:1. Ac *1:12. **he.** See on Mk 6:7. 14:13.

2. **Go your way.** Mt 21:2, 3. Lk 19:30, 31. **whereon never.** Nu 19:2. Dt 21:3. Jg 15:13. 16:11. 1 S 6:7. Ps =8:6. +*104:30. Lk ||19:30. 23:53. Jn 19:41. **loose him.** 1 S 8:16.

3. **if.** ✓184C, Mt +4:9. **the Lord.** Mk 12:35-37. Ps 24:1. Mt 7:21. Lk 7:13. Ac +√10:36. 17:25. 1 C 8:5, 6. +*12:3. 16:22. 2 C *8:9. Ga *1:19. He 2:7-9. **and straightway.** Mk 14:15. 1 Ch 29:12-18. Ps 110:3. Ac 1:24.

4. **and found.** Mt 21:6, 7. 26:19. Lk 19:32-34. Jn 2:5. He 11:8. **without.** Je 17:27. 49:27. **where.** ✓143, Ge +19:2.

5. **What do ye.** Ep +*5:11.

6. **had commanded.** Mt 4:20. 7:24. 9:9. 21:6. 26:19. Lk 5:5. 6:47. Jn 2:7. 11:29. 14:21. 21:6.

7. **the colt.** Zc +*9:9. Mt 21:4, 5. Lk 19:35. **and cast.** 2 K 9:13. Mt 21:7, 8. Lk 19:36. Jn 12:12-16.

8. **spread.** 2 K 9:13. **cut.** Le 23:40.

9. **Hosanna.** 2 S 14:4. Ps 118:25, 26. Je 31:7. Mt 21:9. 23:39. Lk 19:37, 38. Jn 12:13. 19:15. **Blessed.** Ps ▸118:26. Ezk 34:23, 24. Mt 23:39. Lk 13:35. Jn 12:13. **that cometh.** Is 62:11.

10. **the kingdom.** Is +*9:6, 7. Je 33:15-17, 26. Ezk

34:23, 24. 37:24, 25. Ho 3:5. Am 9:11, 12. Lk +*1:31-33. **our father David.** Ac 2:29. **in the highest.** Ps *148:1. Lk 2:14. *19:38-40. Jn *12:12-15.

11. **Jesus.** Ml *3:1. Mt *21:10-16. Lk 19:41-45. **when.** Ezk 8:9. Zp 1:12. **he went.** Mt 21:17. Lk 21:37, 38. Jn 8:1, 2.

12. **on.** Mt 21:18, etc. **he was.** Mt 4:2. Lk 4:2. Jn 4:6, 7, 31-33. 19:28. He 2:17. +*4:15.

13. **seeing.** Mt 21:19. Lk *13:6-9. **a fig tree.** The *fig tree, sukea,* is a genus of the polygamia triaecia class of plants, seldom rising above twelve feet, but sending off from the bottom many spreading branches. The leaves are of a dark green color, nearly a span long, smooth, and irregularly divided into from three to five deep rounded lobes; and the fruit grows on short and thick stalks, of a purplish color, and contains a soft, sweet, and fragrant pulp, intermixed with numerous small seeds. **if.** ♪184A, 1 C +15:2. Mk 8:5. Jn 11:34. **haply.** Ru 2:3. 1 S 6:9. Lk 10:31. 12:6, 7. **might find.** Jn 15:8. **he found.** Is 5:7. **for.** Dr. Campbell observes, that the declaration, "for the time of (*ripe,* Ed.) figs was not yet," is not the reason why our Lord did not find any fruit on the tree, because the fig is of that class of vegetables in which the fruit is formed in its immature state before the leaves are seen. But as the fruit is of a pulpy nature, the broad, thick leaves come out in profusion to protect it from the rays of the sun during the time it is ripening. If the words, "for the time," etc. however, are read as a parenthesis, they then become a reason why Jesus Christ should look for fruit, because the season for gathering not having fully come, it would remove all suspicion that the fruit had been gathered: while the presence of the leaves incontestably proved the advance of the tree to the state in which fruit is found. **yet.** ♪63K, Ge +37:13. The Passover did not occur at the proper fig-season; but figs remained on the trees (dried) right through the winter. These, which could generally be found were called *pag.* The name is preserved in the word Bethphage (house of figs). At the time of the Passover, such figs might well have been looked for. The Lord went to see "if consequently he might find anything thereon." It was "if consequently," because "it was not the proper season of figs" (*suka:* not *olunthoi,* as the others were called, and for which he sought). We must also remember that in the East all fruit trees were enclosed in gardens, and had an owner. This tree, though, by the roadside (Mt 21:19) must have been enclosed, and as it grew over the wall, passers by might partake of the fruit (Dt 23:24). But the owner had probably shaken the fruit off, or gathered it himself, and hence deserved the judgment which came upon him (see Le 19:9, 10. 23:22. Dt 24:19-21). This is one of the two miracles of destruction wrought by Jesus: and we know that in the other case the owners of the swine were justly punished (B124).

14. **answered and said.** ♪171J11, Jb +3:1. ♪108H1, Mt +11:25. Mk 9:5. 10:24. 12:35. 14:48. 1 S 14:28. Mt 11:25. Lk 13:14. 14:3. 22:51. Jn 2:18. 5:17. 10:32. Ac 3:12. **No.** ver. 20, 21. Is 5:5, 6. Mt 3:10. 7:19. 12:33-35. 21:19, 20, 33, 44. Jn 15:6. He 6:4-8. 10:26-31. 2 P 2:20-22. Re 22:11. **ever.** Gr. *aion,* Mt +6:13.

15. **and Jesus.** Mt 21:12-16. Lk 19:45, 46. Jn 2:13-17. **the tables.** Dt 14:25, 26. **moneychangers.** Ex 30:13. **doves.** Le 1:14. 5:7. 12:8. 14:22. Lk 2:24.

16. **would not suffer.** Mk 7:29. Jn 5:27. **vessel**

through. Ex 3:5. 1 T 3:15. **the temple.** Hab +2:20.

17. **Is it.** 1 K 8:41-48. Is ♪56:7. 60:7. Zc *8:22. Lk 19:46. +24:27. **of all nations the house of prayer.** or, an house of prayer for all nations. **a den.** Je ♪7:11. Ho 12:7. Mt 21:13. Lk 19:46. Jn 2:16.

18. **and sought.** Mk 3:6. 12:12. 14:1, 2. Is 49:7. Mt *21:15, 38, 39, 45, 46. 26:3, 4. Lk 19:47. Jn 11:53-57. **destroy.** Gr. *apollumi,* Mt +2:13. **feared.** ver. 32. Mk 6:20. 1 K 18:17, 18. 21:20. 22:8, 18. Mt 21:46. Ac 24:25. Re 11:5-10. **astonished.** Mk 1:22. Mt 7:28. Lk *4:32. Jn 7:46. **doctrine.** ♪108B, Mk +4:2.

19. **when even.** ver. 11. Lk *21:37. Jn *12:36.

20. **they saw.** St. Matthew informs us that this tree grew by the *wayside,* and was therefore not *private,* but *public* property; so that the destruction of it really injured no one. Our Lord was pleased to make use of this miracle to prefigure the speedy ruin of the Jewish nation, on account of its unfruitfulness under greater advantages than any other people enjoyed at that day; and, like all the rest of his miracles, it was done with a gracious intention—to alarm his countrymen, and induce them to repent. See on ver. 14. Jb 18:16, 17. 20:5-7. Is 5:4. 40:24. Mt 13:6. 15:13. 21:19, 20. Jn 15:6. He 6:8. Ju 12.

21. **cursedst.** Pr +*3:33. Zc +*5:3, 4. Mt +*25:41. 1 C *16:22.

22. **Have.** T#1330. ver. 24. Mk *9:23, 24. 10:46-52. 2 Ch +*20:20. Ps 6:8, 9. 17:6. 18:3. 20:6. 22:9, 10. *37:4-7. 55:16. *56:9-11. 60:12. *62:8. 71:1-5. *73:28. *86:6, 7. 121:1, 2. Is 7:9. Mi *7:7-9. Hab √3:17, 18. Mt *8:10, 13. 9:28-30. 15:21-28. *17:19-21. *21:21, 22. Jn *14:1. *15:7. T 1:1. He *4:16. 10:21, 22. √11:6. Ja *1:5-7. *5:14, 15. 1 J √5:14, 15. **faith in God.** or, the faith of God. ♪181E, Ge +3:24. Ac 3:16. Ro 3:22. Ga 2:20. 3:22. Ep 3:12. Ph 3:9. Col *2:12.

23. **whosoever.** Mt *17:20. *21:21, 22. Lk 17:6. 1 C 13:2. **this mountain.** ♪171K1, Dt +19:5. Zc 4:7. **Be thou removed.** This appears to have been a proverbial form of speech, to signify the *removing* or *conquering* great difficulties. A *rooter up of mountains* was a common epithet applied to any Rabbin who was an eminent and learned man. Ps 46:2. 1 C 13:2. Re 8:8. **and shall.** Mt 14:31. Ro *4:18-25. He 11:17-19. Ja +*1:5, 6. **not doubt.** 2 K 7:2. Mt 21:21. Ac 10:20. Ro *4:20, 21. 14:23. Ja *1:6. 2:4. Ju 9, 22. **but shall believe.** Mk 9:23. 16:17. Jn 14:12. **shall have.** Mt 19:26. **whatsoever.** Ps *37:4. Jn *14:13. *15:7.

24. **What things.** Mt *7:7-11. √18:19. *21:22. Lk √11:9-13. *18:1-8. Jn *14:13. 15:7. *16:23-27. Ja *1:5, 6. *5:15-18. 1 J *3:22. √5:14, 15. **ye desire.** Col 1:9. **believe.** T#1312. Mk 5:36. 9:23. Ex 4:30, 31. Ps 116:10. 119:66. Jon 3:5. Mt *8:13. *9:28, 29. *21:21, 22. Jn *4:49, 50. 6:68, 69. 11:22. Ro 10:14. He *11:6. 1 J √5:14, 15. **receive.** or, have received. Is +*65:24. Mt 6:8.

25. **stand.** T#544. Ex 9:29. 1 K 8:22. 1 Ch ◑+17:16 (T#1283). 2 Ch 6:13. Zc 3:1. Mt 26:39. Lk 18:11, +13. 22:41, 42. Ac 20:36. Re 11:4. **forgive.** T#920, 1144, 1338. Pr *20:22. 25:21, 22. Mt *5:44, 45. *6:12, 14, 15. 18:23-35. Lk *6:35, 37. 11:4. Ro 12:20. Ep √4:32. Col *3:13. Ja *2:13. 1 P 3:9. **if.** ♪184A, 1 C +15:2. **have ought against.** Mt 5:23. 6:15. Col 3:13. Re 2:4, 14, 20. **your Father.** Mt 23:9.

26. **But if.** ♪184A, 1 C +15:2. Mt *6:15. *18:28, 34, 35. Ro 1:31. Ja 2:13.

27. **as he.** Ml 3:1. Mt 21:23-27. Lk 20:1-8. Jn 10:23.

18:20. **the chief**. Mk 14:1. Ps *2:1-5. Ac 4:5-8, 27, 28.

28. **By what**. Mk 6:2. Ex 2:14. Nu 16:3, 13. Mt 9:11. *21:23. Jn 1:25. 7:52. Ac 4:7. 7:27, 28, 38, 39, 51.

29. **I will**. Is 52:13. Mt *21:24. Lk 20:3-8. **question**. *or*, thing.

30. **baptism of John**. Mk 1:1-11. 9:13. Mt ch. 3. Lk 3:1-20. Jn 1:6-8, 15-36. 3:25-36. **from heaven**. Da 4:26. Lk 15:18, 21. Jn 3:27. **from men**. Ac 5:38, 39. Ga 1:10-12.

31. **they reasoned**. Mk 8:16. Mt 16:7. Lk 20:14. **If**. ♪184C, Mt +4:9. **Why**. Mt 11:7-14. 21:25-27, 31, 32. Lk *7:30. Jn 1:15, 29, 34, 36. 3:29-36.

32. **But if**. ♪184C, Mt +4:9. **men**. ♪63D2, Ge +30:27. Supply by ellipsis "(it will not be wise)" or "(what will happen to us), for..." ♪15D. Anacoluthon; or, Non-sequence B723. A breaking off the sequence of thought. Sometimes the construction is broken off altogether, and is not completed at all. Here, the reasonings of the rulers are broken off, and the sense must be supplied by *Ellipsis*. For other instances of this figure see Ro 5:12. 1 T 1:3, 4. **they**. Mk *6:20. 12:12. Mt *14:5. 21:46. Lk 20:19. 22:2. Ac 5:26. **for**. Mt *3:5, 6. 11:9. 21:31, 32. Lk 7:26-29. 20:6-8. Jn 5:35. 10:41.

33. **We**. Is 1:3. 6:9, 10. 29:9-14. 42:19, 20. 56:10. Je 8:7-9. Ho 4:6. Ml 2:7, 8. Mt +*15:14. *23:16-26. Jn 3:10. Ro 1:18-22, 28. 2 C 3:15. ✓4:3, 4. 2 Th ✓2:10-12. **Neither**. Jb *5:13. Pr 26:4, 5. Mt +*7:6. 16:4. 21:27. Lk 10:21, 22. 20:7, 8. 22:66-69. Jn 9:27.

MARK 12

The parable of the vineyard let out to wicked husbandmen, 1-12. Jesus answers the Pharisees and Herodians about paying tribute to Caesar, 13-17; the Sadducees, concerning the resurrection, 18-27; and a Scribe, concerning the first commandment in the law, 28-34. He demands of the Scribes, whose Son the Messiah was to be, 35-37; warns the people against the ostentation and hypocrisy of the Scribes, 38-40; and commends a poor widow, who had cast two mites into the treasury, 41-44.

1. **he began**. Mk 4:2, 11-13, 33, 34. Ezk 20:49. Mt 13:10-15, 34, 35. 21:28-33. 22:1-14. Lk 8:10. 22:9. **A certain**. Mt 21:33-40. Lk 20:9-15. **planted**. Dt 32:32, 33. Ps 80:8-16. Is *5:1-4. 27:2-6. Je 2:21. Ezk 15:1-6. 19:10-14. Ho 10:1. Jl 1:7. Mt 21:28. Lk *13:6-9. Jn 15:1-8. Ro 11:17-24. **and set**. Ne 9:13, 14. Ps 78:68, 69. 147:19, 20. Ezk 20:11, 12, 18-20. Ac 7:38, 46, 47. Ro 3:1, 2. 9:4, 5. **and digged**. Jl 3:13. **and let**. SS *8:11, 12. Is 7:23. **and went**. Mk 13:34. Mt 25:14. Lk 15:13. 19:12.

2. **at**. Ps +*1:3. Mt 21:34. Lk 20:10. **he sent**. Je 26:5. **a servant**. Jg 6:8-10. 2 K 17:13. 2 Ch *36:15. Ezr 9:11. Je 25:4, 5. 35:15. 44:4. Mi 7:1. Zc 1:3-6. 7:7. Lk +*12:48. Jn *15:1-8. He *1:1.

3. **they**. 1 K 18:4, 13. 19:10, 14. 22:27. 2 K 6:31. 21:16. 2 Ch 16:10. 24:19-21. *36:16. Ne *9:26. Je 2:30. 20:2. 26:20-24. 29:26. 37:15, 16. 38:4-6. 44:4. Mt 5:12. 22:6. 23:34-37. Lk 11:47-51. 13:33, 34. Ac *7:52, 59. 2 C 11:24-26. 1 Th 2:15. He 11:36, 37. **and sent**. Je 44:4, 5, 16. Da 9:10, 11. Zc 7:9-13. Lk 20:10-12.

5. **and him**. Mk 9:13. Ne 9:30. Je 7:25, etc. Mt 5:12. 21:35, 36. 22:6. 23:37. Lk 6:22, 23, 26.

6. **one**. Ps *2:7, 8. Mt +*1:23. 11:27. 26:63. Jn 1:14, 18, 34, 49. ✓3:16-18. Ro *8:3. 1 J *4:9. ✓5:11, 12. **his**. Mk 1:11. 9:7. Ge 22:2, 12. 37:3, 11-13. 44:20. Is 42:1. Mt 3:17. 17:5. Lk 3:22. 9:35. Jn 3:35. He 1:1, 2. **They**. Ps 2:12. Jn ✓5:23. He 1:6. Re 5:9-13.

7. **This**. ver. 12. Ge +*3:15. 37:20. 1 K 21:19. Ps 2:2, 3. 22:12-15. Is 49:7. 53:7, 8. Mt 2:3-13, 16. Jn 1:11. 11:47-50. Ac 2:23. 5:28. 7:52. 13:27, 28. Ro 8:17. He 1:2.

8. **killed**. Mt 21:35. Ac *2:23. *7:52. 1 Th *2:15. **cast**. Mt 21:33, 39. Lk 20:15. He 13:11-13.

9. **shall**. Mt 21:40, 41. Lk 19:27. **he will**. Le 26:15-18, 23, 24, 27, 28. Dt 4:26, 27. +*28:15, etc., 61. Jsh 23:15. 2 S 12:5, 6. Pr 1:24-31. Is *5:5-7. Da +*9:26, 27. Zc *13:7-9. Mt 3:9-12. 12:45. *22:7. 23:34-38. 24:50. 25:19. Lk 19:27, 41-44. 20:15, 16. **destroy**. Gr. *apollumi*, Mt +2:13. **and will**. Is 29:17. 32:15, 16. 65:15. Je 17:3. Ml 1:11. Mt +*8:11-13. 21:43. Lk 20:16. Ac 13:46-48. 18:6. *28:23-28. Ro 9:30-33. 10:20, 21. 11:1, etc.

10. **have**. ver. 26. Mk 2:25. 13:14. Mt 12:3. 19:4. 21:16. 22:31. Lk 6:3. **The stone**. Ps *♪118:22, 23. Is 28:16. Mt 21:42. Lk 20:17, 18. Ac 4:11, 12. Ro 9:33. Ep *2:20-22. Col *1:18. 1 P *2:7, 8.

11. **This was**. Nu 23:23. Hab 1:5. Ac 2:12, 32-36. 3:12-16. 13:40, 41. Ep 3:8-11. Col 1:27. 1 T *3:16.

12. **feared**. Mk 11:18, 32. Mt *21:26, 45, 46. Lk 20:6, 19. Jn *7:19, 25, 30, 44. **people**. T#67. Mt 21:8, 9. Mk 11:8-10. Lk 4:14, 15. 5:15. Jn 6:15. *11:47, 48. *12:19. **knew**. 2 S 12:7, etc. 1 K 20:38-41. 21:17-27.

13. **they send**. Ps 38:12. 56:5, 6. 140:5. Is 29:21. Je 18:18. Mt *22:15, 16. Lk 11:54. *20:20, etc. **Herodians**. Mk *3:6. *8:15. Mt *16:6.

14. **Master**. Mk 14:45. Ps 12:2-4. 55:21. 120:2. Pr 26:23-26. Je 42:2, 3, 20. **we know**. Jn 7:18. 2 C 2:2, 17. 4:2. 5:11. 1 Th 2:4. **carest**. Dt 33:9, 10. 2 Ch 18:13. Is 50:7-9. Je 15:19-21. Ezk 2:6, 7. Mi 3:8. 2 C 5:16. Ga 1:10. 2:6, 11-14. **for thou**. Ex 23:2-6. Dt 16:19. 2 Ch 19:7. **Is it**. Ezr 4:12, 13. Ne 9:37. Mt 17:25-27. 22:17. Lk 20:22. 23:2. Ro 13:6, 7.

15. **knowing**. Mt 22:18. Lk 20:23. Jn +*2:24, 25. 21:17. He ✓4:13. Re *2:23. **Why tempt**. Mk 10:2. Ex 17:2. Mt 22:18. Lk +*1:35. 20:23. 22:28. Jn 8:6. Ac 5:9. 1 C 10:9. **a penny**. "Valuing of our money, sevenpence halfpenny, as Mt 18:28mg."

16. **image**. Mt 22:19-22. Lk 20:24-26. 2 T 2:19. Re 3:12.

17. **Render**. Pr 24:21. Mt 17:25-27. Ro *13:7. 1 P *2:13, 17. **and to**. ver. 30. Pr 23:26. Ec *5:4, 5. Da 3:16. +*6:10. Ml 1:6. Ac +*4:19, 20. +*5:29. Ro 6:13. 12:1. 1 C *6:19, 20. 2 C ✓5:14, 15. **And they**. Jb 5:12, 13. Mt 22:22, 33, 46. 1 C 14:24, 25.

18. **come**. Mt *22:23, etc. Lk 20:27, etc. **say**. Ac 4:1, 2. *23:6-9. 1 C *15:13-18. 2 T 2:18.

19. **If**. ♪184C, Mt +4:9. Ge 38:8. Dt *25:5-10. Ru 4:5. **that**. Ru 1:11, 13. **his brother**. Dt ▶25:5.

20. **were seven**. Mt 22:25-28. Lk 20:29-33.

24. **Do ye**. As the five books of Moses were the only Scriptures which the Sadducees admitted as Divine, our Lord confutes them by an appeal to these books, and proves that they were ignorant of those very writings which they professed to hold sacred. He not only rectified their opinions, but so explained the doctrine as to overthrow the erroneous decision of the Pharisees, that if two brothers married one

woman, she should be restored at the resurrection to the *first* (Zohar in Gen. fol. 48. Yalkut Rubeni, Col. 134.1. and 178.2). Is +*8:20n. Je 8:7-9. Ho 6:6. 8:12. Mt *22:29. Jn +*5:39. 20:9. Ac +*17:11. Ro √15:4. 2 T √3:15-17. **not.** ∫85B, Ge +13:9. In Negative Affirmation. **err.** Jb *6:24. Pr +*19:27. Is 9:16. **because.** Jb *19:25-27. Ps +*9:10n. Is 25:8. +*26:19n. Ezk *37:1-14. Da +*12:2. Ho 6:2. *13:14. **know not.** Here, the "not" is *mee*, which denies subjectively, and implies not merely negative ignorance, but positive unwillingness to know the Scriptures. See Mt 22:29. 1 Ch=28:19. Jb 24:16. Is +*8:20n. Jn +*5:39, 46. 20:9. 1 C 15:34. **the scriptures.** Mt +21:42. 1 Th *2:13. 2 T +√3:15-17. **neither.** Mk 10:27. Ge *18:14. Je +*32:17. Lk 1:37. 1 C 6:14. Ep 1:19, 20. Ph *3:21.

25. **shall rise.** Da +*12:2. 1 C *15:42, 49, 52. **neither marry.** Mt 22:30. 24:38. Lk 17:27. *20:34-36. 1 C 15:42-54. He 12:22, 23. 1 J 3:2. **as the angels.** Ps ◐+*8:5. Lk 20:36. He 2:7, 9.

26. **have.** ver. 10. Mt 21:16. 22:31, 32. **in the book.** ver. 19. Ex 3:2-6, 16. Lk 20:37. Ac 1:20. 7:30-32. Ro 11:2mg. **of Moses.** Ex +*24:4. **I am.** Ge +*17:7, 8. 26:24. +*28:13. 31:42. 32:9. 33:20mg. Ex ◐3:6. Is 41:8-10. Ac 7:32. **of Abraham.** Mt *8:11. Lk 16:22. Ac 3:13.

27. **is not.** Ro 4:17. 14:9. He 11:13-16. **ye.** ver. 24. Pr +*19:27. He 3:10.

28. **one.** Mt *22:34-40. **Which.** Mt 5:19. 19:18. +*23:23. Lk 11:42.

29. **hear.** ver. 32, 33. Dt +*◐6:4. 10:12. 30:6. Pr 23:26. Mt 10:37. Lk 10:27. 1 T 1:5. **is one.** Mt 19:17. 23:9. Jn 5:44. 17:3. Ro 3:30. 1 C *8:4, 6. Ga 3:20. Ep 4:6. 1 T 1:17. +*2:5. Ja *2:19. 4:12. Ju 25.

30. **shalt love.** Dt ◐6:5. Mt 22:37-40. 1 J *5:3. **with all.** Dt 4:29. 10:12. 11:13. 13:3. 26:16. 30:2, 6, 10. Jsh 22:5. 1 K 2:4. 8:48. 2 K *23:3, 25. 2 Ch 6:38. 15:12. 34:31. Je 32:41. **heart.** ∫173, Ge +27:44. **soul.** Gr. *psyche*, ∫121A9B, Mt +22:37. **this is.** ∫99. Homoeoteleuton; or, Like Endings B176. The repetition of the same letters or syllables at the end of successive words. For another instance of this figure see 1 P 1:3, 4.

31. **Thou.** Le +*◐19:18. Mt 7:12. 19:18, 19. 22:39. Lk 10:27, 36, 37. Ro *13:8, 9. 1 C *13:4-8. Ga *5:14. Ja *2:8-13. 1 J *3:17-19. 4:7, 8, *11, 21. **greater.** Mt +*23:23.

32. **Master.** ver. 14, 19. Mk 4:38. **one God.** ver. 29. Dt 4:35, 39. 5:7. +*◐6:4. Is 44:8. *45:5, 6, 14, 18, 21, 22. 46:9. Je 10:10-12. **none other.** Dt ◐4:35, 39. 1 S 2:2. 2 S 22:32. Ps 18:31. Is 43:3, 10, 11. *44:6, 8. 45:5, 18, 22. *46:9. Zc √14:9. Ml *2:10. Jn *17:3. Ro 16:27. 1 C +*8:4, 6. Ep *4:5, 6. 1 T +*2:5.

33. **the understanding.** Dt 4:6. Lk 2:47. Ro 1:21, 31. 1 C 1:19. Col 1:9. 2:2. 2 T 2:7. **soul.** Gr. *psyche*, ∫121A9B, Mt +22:37. **to love.** Dt ◐6:5. **neighbor as.** Le ◐19:18. **is more.** 1 S +*◐15:22. Ps 50:8-15, 23. +*51:16, 17. Pr 15:8. *21:3. Is *1:11-17. 58:5-7. Je 7:21-23. Ho *6:6. Am 5:21-24. Mi +*6:6-8. Mt 9:13. 12:7. 1 C *13:1-3. **whole burnt.** Ps 40:6. He 10:6, 8.

34. **Thou.** Mt 12:20. Ro 3:20. 7:9. Ga 2:19, 20. **the kingdom.** Mk +1:15. **And no.** Jb 32:15, 16. Mt 22:46. Lk 14:6. 20:40. Ro 3:19. Col *4:6. T 1:9-11.

35. **answered and said.** ∫108H1, Mt +11:25. Mk 11:14. **while.** Mk 11:27. Lk 19:47. 20:1. 21:37. Jn 18:20. **in the temple.** Mt 26:55. **How.** Mt *22:41, 42. Lk 20:41-44. Jn *7:42. **son.** ∫171G, Ge +13:8.

36. **David.** Ac 2:34, 35. 4:25. **by.** 2 S *23:2. Ne 9:30. Mt *22:43-45. Lk 10:21. Ac 1:16. 28:25. 1 C 12:3. 2 T √3:16. He 3:7, 8. 4:7. 1 P 1:11. 2 P √1:21. **Ghost.** Gr. *pneuma*, Mt +3:16. **The Lord.** Ps *◐110:1. Ac 2:34-36. 1 C 15:25. He 1:13. 10:12, 13. **Sit.** Mk 10:37, 40. 1 K 2:19. Ps 45:9. Mt 20:21, 23. **till.** 1 C +*15:28. **thy footstool.** Jsh 10:24. 1 K 5:3. Is 66:1. Ac 7:49.

37. **David.** ver. 36. **and whence.** Mt *1:23. Ro *1:3, 4. √9:5. 1 T *3:16. Re *22:16. **And the.** Mt *11:5, 25. 21:46. Lk *19:48. *21:38. Jn *7:46-49. 12:9, 12. Ja *2:5. **heard.** Mk 6:20. Lk *5:1. 15:1. 1 C 1:26.

38. **said.** Mk 4:2. **doctrine.** ∫108B, Mk +4:2. ∫24H, Jg +16:23. By Antimereia of the noun, whereby a noun is put for a verb, the noun "doctrine" is put instead of the verb, "during his teaching" or "while he taught" (B496). **Beware.** Ezk 22:25. Mt 10:17. 23:1-7, 14. Lk 20:45-47. **which.** Mt 6:5. Lk 11:43. 14:7-11. 3 J 9. **love.** ∫108B, 1 T +6:9. **and.** ∫15G, Ge +35:3. **marketplaces.** Mk 6:56. 7:4. Mt 11:16. 20:3. Lk 7:32. Ac 16:19. 17:17.

39. **chief seats.** Lk *11:43. Ja 2:2, 3. **uppermost rooms.** Lk 14:7, 8.

40. **devour.** Ezk *22:25. Mi 2:2. 3:1-4, *11. Zp *3:4. Ml +*3:5. Mt 23:14n. Lk 11:39. 16:14. 20:47. 2 T 3:6. **widows'.** Ja 1:27. **long.** Mt *6:5, 7. +*23:14n. **greater.** Dt +*32:22. Ps *86:13. Mt 11:22-24. 23:33. Lk +*12:47, 48. Ja 3:1.

41. **sat.** Mt 27:6. Lk 21:1-4, etc. **against the treasury.** ∫143, Ge +19:2. ver. 43. Mt 27:6. Jn 8:20. **cast.** 2 K *12:9. 2 Ch *24:8, 10. **money.** "A piece of brass money, see Mt 10:9." Mk 6:8. **the treasury.** 2 K 12:9.

42. **a certain.** ∫108E1, Mt +8:19. Mt 8:19. **two mites.** "It is the seventh part of one piece of that brass money." Lk 12:59. **farthing.** Mt 5:26.

43. **Verily.** Mk 3:28. **That.** Ex 35:21-29. Jg 19:20. Ps 34:9. Mt 10:42. Ac 11:29. 2 C 8:2, √12. √9:6-8.

44. **cast in of.** Mk *14:8. 1 Ch *29:2-17. 2 Ch *24:10-14. *31:5-10. 35:7, 8. Ezr *2:68, 69. Ne *7:70-72. 2 C *8:2, 3. Ph *4:10-17. **but she.** 1 K *17:12. Lk 4:26. 6:38. *19:8, 9. **all her.** Dt *24:6. Lk *8:43. *15:12, 30. *21:2-4. 1 J *3:17. **living.** ∫121F, Ge +49:6.

MARK 13

Christ predicts the destruction of the temple, and of Jerusalem, 1, 2; and shows what signs and calamities should go before that catastrophe, 3-23, and what should happen at the time of his coming, 24-27. The parable of the fig tree, showing the near and certain approach of these events, 28-31. No man knows the day or hour; therefore all ought to watch and pray, and be ready, 32-37.

1. **as he.** Mt +*24:1, etc. Lk 21:5, etc. **out.** Ezk 7:20-22. 8:6. 10:4, 19. 11:22, 23. Ml 3:1, 2.

2. **answering.** ∫108H1, Mt +11:25. **there.** 2 S 17:13. 1 K 9:7, 8. 2 Ch 7:20, 21. Je 26:18. Mi 1:6. 3:12. Mt +*24:2. Lk *19:41-44. 21:6. Ac 6:14. Re 11:2.

3. **as.** Mt +√24:3. **Peter.** Mk 1:16-19. 5:37. 9:2. 10:35. 14:33. Mt 10:2. 17:1. Jn 1:40, 41. **privately.** Mk 4:34. Mt 13:10, 36.

4. **when shall.** Da *12:6, 8. Mt +√24:3. Lk *21:7. Jn 21:21, 22. Ac +*1:6n, 7n. 1 Th *5:1, 2, 4.

5. **Take.** ver. 9, 23, 33. Je *29:8. Mt +*24:4, 5. Lk 21:8. 1 C 15:33. Ep *5:6. Col 2:8. 1 Th 2:3. 2 Th *2:3. 1 J 3:7. 4:1. Re 20:7, 8.

6. **many.** ver. 21, 22. Je 14:14. 23:21-25. 27:15. Mt

+*24:23, 24. Jn *5:43. 1 J 2:18. 4:1. **in my name.** Mk 9:37, 39. Lk 9:48. **I am.** Jn +*8:24. **and shall.** ver. 22. Mt +*24:5, 11, 23, 24. Ac 5:36-39.

7. **when.** Ps 27:3. 46:1-3. 112:7. Pr 3:25. Is 8:12. Je 4:19-21. 51:46. Mt +*24:6, 7. Lk 21:9-11. Jn 14:1, 27. **rumors.** lit. hearing. ſ121R1, Le +13:55. **not troubled.** 2 Th 2:2. **must.** 2 S 14:14. Da ▶2:28. Mt 18:7. Lk 13:33. Ac 17:3. **come to pass.** Re 1:1. **the end.** Mt +*24:14. 1 P 4:7. **not yet.** Mt +*24:6, ◑14. 2 Th *2:2, 3, 7, 8.

8. **nation shall.** 2 Ch 15:6. Is ▶19:2. Je 25:32. Hg 2:22. Zc 14:13. Re 6:4. **kingdom against.** Is 19:2. **earthquakes.** Re 6:12. **famines.** Ac *11:28. Re 6:8. **these.** Mt +*24:8. **sorrows.** "The word in the original importeth the pains of a woman in travail." Ps 48:6. Is 37:3. Je 4:31. 6:24. 13:21. 22:23. 49:24. 50:43. Mi 4:9, 10. Mt +*24:8. Jn 16:21. Ac 2:24. Ro 8:22. 1 Th 5:3.

9. **take.** ver. 5. Mt 10:17, 18. *23:34-37. +*24:9, 10. Lk 21:16-18. Jn 15:20. 16:2. Ac 4:1-21. 5:17-40. 6:11-15. +*7:54-60. 8:1-3. 9:1, 2, 13, 14, 16. 12:1-3. 16:20-24. 21:11, 31-40. 22:19, 20. 23:1, 2. 24:1, etc. ch. 25, 26. 1 C 4:9-13. 2 C 11:23-27. Ga 6:1. Ph 1:29. 2 Th 1:5. 2 J 8. Re 1:9. *2:10, 13. *6:9-11. **councils.** *Sunedria*, "Sanhedrins," the grand national council, and smaller courts of judicature in each city: see on Mt 5:22. For the fulfilment of these predictions, see Note on Mt ch. 24. Ac 4:15. **synagogues.** Mt 23:34. **before rulers.** Ac 17:6. 18:12. 24:1. 25:6. **and kings.** Ac 25:23. 27:24. 2 T 4:16, 17. **for my sake.** Mk 8:35. 10:29. Mt 5:11. 10:18, 29, 39. 16:25. +*24:9. Lk 6:22. 9:24. 18:29. 21:12. **for a testimony.** Mk 1:44. 6:11. Mt 8:4. 10:18. Lk 9:5. *21:13.

10. **the gospel.** Mk 14:9. *16:15. Mt +*24:14. 28:18, 19. Ro 1:8. *10:18. 15:19. *16:25, 26. Col *1:6, 23. Re 14:6.

11. **and deliver.** ver. 9. Mt 10:17, 21. Ac 3:13. **take no thought.** Ex 4:10-12. Je 1:6-9. Da 3:16-18. Mt 6:25. 10:19, 20. Lk 12:11, 12. *21:14, 15. Ac *2:4. *4:8, etc., 31. 6:10, 15. 7:55. **shall be given.** Nu 23:5. Dt 18:18. Is 50:4. Jn 3:27. Ep 6:19, 20. Ja +*1:5. **for it.** Lk 21:15. Ac 4:8. 6:10. 13:9. 1 C 15:10. 2 C 13:3. 1 Th 2:13. He 1:1. **but.** 2 S 23:2. 1 C 2:13. Ep 3:5. 1 P 1:12. **Ghost.** Gr. *pneuma*, Mt +3:16.

12. **shall betray.** Ezk 38:21. Mi ▶7:4-6. Mt 10:21, 35, 36. +*24:10, 12. Lk 12:52, 53. 21:16. **children.** Mi ▶7:6. **put to death.** Mt 23:34. Lk 11:49. Jn 16:2.

13. **ye.** Mt +*5:11, 12. +*24:9. Dt ◑11:12. 2 Ch 16:9. Lk *6:22, 23. *21:17-19. Jn *15:18, 19. 17:14. 1 J *3:13. **for my.** ver. 9. Jn 15:21. **but.** Da +*12:12, 13. Mt 10:22. +*24:13. Ro +*2:7. Ga *6:9. He 3:14. 10:36, 39. Ja 1:12. Re *2:10. +*3:10. **unto the end.** 1 C 1:8. 2 C 1:13. Ga *6:9. He 3:6, 14. 6:11. Re 2:26.

14. **the abomination.** Da +*8:13. +*9:27. 11:31. +*▶12:11. Mt +*24:15, etc. Lk 21:20-22. **spoken.** Lk +*24:27. **where.** La 1:10. Ezk 44:9. **let him.** Da +*9:22, 23, 25-27. Mt +*13:51. Ac 8:30, 31. 1 C 14:7, 8, 20. Re 1:3. 13:18. **then.** Lk *21:20-24. **flee.** Ge 17:17, 19.

15. **let him.** Ge 19:15-17, 22, 26. Jb 2:4. Pr 6:4, 5. +*22:3. Mt +*24:16-18. Lk 17:31-33. Ac 27:18, 19, 38. Ph 3:7, 8. He 11:7. **housetop.** Lk 5:19.

16. **his garment.** Mk 10:50. Mt 5:40.

17. **woe to them.** Dt 28:56, 57. La 2:19, 20. 4:3, 4, 10. Ho 9:14. 13:16. Mt +*24:19-21. Lk 21:23. *23:29. 1 C 7:26.

19. **in those.** ver. 24. Dt 28:59. 29:22-28. Is 65:12-

15. La 1:12. 2:13. 4:6. Da 9:12, +*26. +*▶12:1. Jl *2:2. Mt +*24:21. Lk *21:22-24. **such as.** Jl +*2:2. Re *16:18. **from the beginning.** Mk 10:6. Dt 4:32. **God created.** Ge 1:1.

20. **except.** ſ184B, Mt +11:21. **no flesh.** Lk 3:6. **for the elect's.** ver. 22, 27. Is 1:9. 6:13. 65:8, 9. Zc 13:8, 9. Mt 22:14. +*24:22n. Lk 18:7. Ro 11:5-7, 23, 24, 28-32. Re 7:14. **hath chosen.** Dt +*10:15. Jn 13:18. 15:16, 19. Ep 1:4. 2 Th *2:13. 2 T *1:9. Ja *2:5. Re 13:8. 17:8.

21. **if any.** ſ184C, Mt +4:9. ver. 6. Dt 13:1-3. Mt +*24:5, 23-25. Lk *17:23, 24. *21:8. Jn 5:43. **here is.** Mt 24:26-28. **Christ.** Mt 1:17.

22. **false Christs.** 1 J *2:18. **false prophets.** Dt ▶13:1-5. Mt 7:15. 1 T 4:1, 2. 2 P 2:1. **shall show.** Dt 13:1-3. Ac 8:9. 2 Th √2:9-11. Re 13:13, 14. 16:14. 19:20. **signs.** Jn 4:48. **to seduce.** ver. 6. **if it were possible.** ſ184B, Mt +23:30. ver. *6. Mt +*24:24. Jn √10:27-29. 2 Th *2:8-14. 2 T *2:19. 1 J *2:19, 26, 27. Re *13:8, 13, 14. 17:8. **the elect.** ver. 20. Mt 24:22n.

23. **take.** ver. 5, 9, 33. Mt *7:15. Lk 21:8, 34. 2 P 3:17. **behold.** Is 44:7, 8. Mt +*24:25. Jn +*13:19. 14:29. 16:1-4. 2 P *3:17.

24. **in those days.** Is ▶13:10. 24:20-23. Je 4:23-25, 28. Ezk 32:7. Da 7:10. 12:1. Jl 2:30, 31. Am 5:20. Zp 1:14-18. Mt +*24:29, etc. Lk 21:25-27. Ac 2:19, 20. 2 P 3:10, 12. Re 6:12-14. 20:11. **after.** Mt +*24:29. **that tribulation.** ver. 19. Je +*30:7. **the sun shall.** Is 13:10. 24:23. Je 4:23, 24. Ezk 32:7. Jl *2:10, 31. *3:15. Am 5:20. 8:9. Zp *1:14, 15. Zc 14:6. Lk *21:25-28. Ac 2:20. Re 6:12. 8:12. **darkened.** Pr +20:20.

25. **the stars.** Is 14:12. *34:4. 2 P 3:10. Re 6:13. **the powers.** Jb 26:11. Is ▶34:4. Hg 2:6, 7. Lk 21:26. He 12:26.

26. **they.** ſ15C, Anacoluthon, Mk +6:11. Note the shift from the grammatical "second person" of the preceding context (ver. 14 "ye," 21 "you," 23 "ye") to the "third person" *they* of this verse. This marks a corresponding shift in time from what could have applied to the disciples and Christians of the first century fulfilled in part at the fall of Jerusalem to events which are to occur long after at the end of the age. **shall see.** Mt *16:27n. Re +*1:7. **Son of man.** Mk 2:10. Da ▶7:13. Mt +*16:27n. **coming.** Mk 8:38. *14:62. Da *7:9-14. Mt 16:17, +*27n. +*24:30. +*25:31. 26:64. Ac +*1:11. 1 Th *4:16. 2 Th √1:7-10. Re +*1:7. **clouds.** Ge +9:13. 2 Ch +5:13. **great.** ſ180B. Zeugma (Mesozeugma; or, Middle-yoke) B134. The *Zeugma* is so called when the verb or adjective occurs in the middle of the sentence. Here in the Greek the adjective "great" is put between the two nouns, thus: "Power, great, and glory," and it applies to both in a peculiar manner. This *Zeugma* calls our attention to the fact that the power will be great and the glory will be great: and this more effectually emphasizes the greatness of both, than if it had been stated in so many words. For other instances of this figure see Mk 5:40, 42. Lk 1:64. **power.** Mk 9:1. Mt +*25:31. 26:64. **and glory.** Ps 68:17. Ac 7:55.

27. **shall he send.** Mt +*13:41, 49. +*24:31. Lk 16:22. Re 7:1-3. 15:6, 7. **shall gather.** Ge +*49:10. Dt ▶30:4. Zc 2:6. Mt 23:37. +*24:31n. *25:31, 32. Jn +*10:16. 11:52. 1 Th 4:14-17. 2 Th 2:1. Re 7:5-9. **his elect.** ver. 20, 22. Is 65:9. Mt +*24:22n, 24, 31. Lk 18:7. Ro 8:33. Ep *1:4. Col 3:12. 2 T 2:10. 1 P 1:2. **four winds.** Je 49:36. Ezk 37:9. Da 7:2. 8:8. 11:4. Zc

2:6. Mt 12:42. Re 7:1. **from the uttermost**. Dt 30:4. Ac 1:8. **to the uttermost**. Dt 4:32. 30:4. Ps 19:6.

28. **learn a parable**. Mt +*24:32, 33. Lk 21:29-31. **When her branch**. Mk 11:13.

29. **know**. Ezk 7:10-12. 12:25-28. He 10:25-37. Ja 5:9. 1 P 4:17, 18. **at the doors**. Ja 5:9. Re 3:20.

30. **Verily**. Mk 3:28. **this generation**. Mt +*16:28n. *23:36, 38. +*24:34. Lk 11:50, 51. 21:32.

31. **Heaven**. Ps ◐+*89:37. 102:25-27. Is 34:4. 51:6. Je ◐+*33:25. Mt +*5:18. +*24:35. Lk *16:17. He *1:10-12. 12:27. 2 P *3:10-12. Re 20:11. 21:1. **my words**. Nu *23:19. Jsh 23:14, 15. Ps *19:7. 119:89, 152. Is √40:8. Zc 1:6. Lk 21:33. 2 T 2:13. T 1:2. 1 P *1:23, 25.

32. **of that day**. ver. 26, 27. Mt +*24:36-42. *25:6, 13, 19. Jn *14:11. Ac *1:7. 1 Th *5:2. 2 P *3:10. Re *3:3. **knoweth**. "To preclude the curiosity of men," says Dr. Hammond, "and to engage their vigilance, Christ is pleased to tell them, that no dispensation of God, either by man (as Daniel), or by angels, or, which is the highest, by the Son of man, had ordered us thus to know the seasons; this being no part of the prophetic office, or within the commission of Christ himself." Dt +*29:29. Mt 25:13. Jn ◐13:7. 16:12. Ro ◐*13:11. 1 C 13:12. Ep ◐3:5. 1 Th *5:1, 2, 4. **neither the Son**. T#70. Is 42:6. Mt 11:27. +14:23 (T#64), 33. ‖24:36. +*28:19. Lk 10:22. Jn *3:35. √5:19-23, 25, 26, 30. 6:+38 (T#72), 57. 8:28, 29. ◐+*10:30. 14:10. 20:17. Ac 1:4. 1 C +√15:28. 2 C 13:4. Ph 2:6, 7. Re *1:1. **but the Father**. Ho ◐+√8:4. Zc 14:7. Mt ◐+*10:32. Jn ◐*5:20. +*14:28. Ac *1:7.

33. **Take ye heed**. ver. 5, 23, 35-37. Mk 14:37, 38. Mt +*24:42-44. *25:13. 26:40, 41. Lk *12:40. *21:34-36. Ro *13:11, 12, 14. 1 C 16:13. Ep *6:18. 1 Th *5:5-8. He √12:15. 1 P 4:7. *5:8. Re 3:2. 16:15. **watch and pray**. Mk 14:38. Ne 4:9. Ps 127:1. Pr 8:34. Mt 24:42. 25:13. 26:41. Lk 12:37. 18:1. +√21:36. Ac 20:31. 1 C 16:13. Ep *6:18. Col *4:2. 1 Th 5:6. He 13:17. 1 P *5:8. Re 3:2, 3. 16:15. **ye know not**. ver. 32. Ro ◐*13:11.

34. **as a**. Mt +*24:45. +*25:14-30. Lk *12:36-38. 19:12-17. **far journey**. Mk 12:1. Mt 21:33. ◐+*25:19. **left his house**. He 3:6. **gave authority**. Mt +*16:19. +*18:18. Ac +*20:28. He *13:17. 1 P *5:3, 5. **his servants**. Mk +*9:35. Da +*11:33n. 1 C *4:1, 2. **and to every man**. Nu =4:19. Mt ◐+*24:45. Ro *12:4-8. 13:6. 1 C 3:5-10. 12:4-31. √15:58. Col 3:24. 4:1. **his work**. Ps 62:12. Lk *19:13. **and commanded**. Ezk 3:17-21. 33:2-9. Mt +*24:45-47. Lk 12:36-40. Ac 20:29-31. **the porter**. 1 Ch=9:22, 19. Ps 84:10. Ezk 44:11. Mt *16:19. Lk 12:36. Jn 10:3. Re 3:7. **to watch**. ver. 33, 37.

35. **Watch**. √66, Ge +9:3. ver. 33. Mt +*24:42, 44. Lk +√21:36. **when**. Mt 24:43. **at even**. Mk 1:32. 11:11, 19. Note Jesus names all four watches of the night here (Mt +*14:25n). *Even*, the first watch, was our 6 p.m. to 9 p.m. Mt 20:8. *Midnight*, the second watch, was our 9 p.m. to 12 midnight. Mt 25:6. Lk +12:38. *Cockcrowing*, the third watch, was our 12 midnight to 3 a.m. Lk 12:38. *Morning*, the fourth watch, was our 3 a.m. to 6 a.m. Mk 1:35. *6:48. Ps 130:6. Mt 14:25n. **midnight**. Jg 7:19. 16:3. Ps 119:62. Is 59:10. Lk 11:5. Ac 16:25. 20:7. **cockcrowing**. Mk 14:30, 68, 72. Jg 7:19. **morning**. Mk 6:48. Ex 14:24.

36. **coming suddenly**. Mt 24:44. 1 Th 5:1-6. **he find**. Mk 14:37, 40. Pr 6:9-11. 24:33, 34. SS 3:1. 5:2. Is

56:10. Mt +*24:48-51. *25:5. 26:40. Lk 21:34. 22:45. Ro 13:11-14. Ep 5:14. 1 Th 5:6, 7.

37. **I say**. ver. 33, 35. Lk *12:41-46.

MARK 14

The chief priests and scribes conspire to put Jesus to death, 1, 2. A woman pours precious ointment on his head: with the circumstances attending her conduct, 3-9. Judas bargains with the chief priests to betray him, 10, 11. The disciples by the direction of Jesus prepare the passover, 12-16. He eats it with them, and points out the traitor, 17-21. He institutes the Lord's supper, 22-25. He foretells that all the disciples would forsake him, and that Peter would deny him, 26-31. His agony and prayer in the garden, and his warnings to the disciples, 32-42. He is betrayed, apprehended, and forsaken, 43-52. He is arraigned before Caiaphas, condemned, and treated with cruel indignity, 53-65. Peter thrice denies him, but repents, 66-72.

1. **two**. Mt 26:2. Lk *22:1, 2. Jn *11:53-57. 13:1. **the passover**. Ex *12:6-20. Le +*23:5. Nu 28:16-25. Dt 16:1-8. Jn 6:4. **unleavened bread**. Ex 23:15. 34:18. Le +*23:6. Dt 16:16. 2 Ch 8:13. 30:13, 21. 35:17. Ezr 6:22. **chief**. Ps *2:1-5. Jn 11:47. Ac 4:25-28. **sought**. Mk 12:12. Jn 11:53. **by craft**. Ps 52:3. 62:4, 9. 64:2-6. Mt 26:4.

2. **Not**. Pr *19:21. +*21:30. La 3:37. Mt *26:5. **day**. √63B, Ge +25:28. **lest**. Mk *11:18, 32. Mt 27:24. Lk 20:6. 22:6mg. Jn 7:40. 12:19.

3. **being**. Mt 26:6, 7. Jn 11:2. 12:1-3. **of ointment**. SS 4:13, 14. 5:5. Lk *7:37, 38. **spikenard**. or, pure nard, *or* liquid nard.

4. **there**. Ec 4:4. Mt 26:8, 9. Jn 12:4, 5. **Why**. Ex 5:4-8. Ml 1:12, 13.

5. **pence**. See Mt 18:28mg. Jn 6:7. **have been given**. Jn 12:5, 6. 13:29. Ep 4:28. **And they**. Ex 16:7, 8. Dt 1:27. Ps 106:25. Mt 20:11. Lk 15:2. Jn 6:43. 1 C 10:10. Ph 2:14. Ju 16.

6. **Let**. Jb *42:7, 8. Is 54:17. 2 C 10:18. **a good**. Mt 26:10. Jn 10:32, 33. Ac 9:36. 2 C 9:8. Ep *2:10. Col +*1:10. 2 Th 2:17. 1 T 5:10. 6:18. 2 T 2:21. 3:17. T 2:7, 14. √3:8, 14. He 10:24. 13:21. 1 P 2:12.

7. **ye have**. Dt *▶15:11. Mt 25:35-45. 26:11. Jn 12:7, 8. 2 C 9:13, 14. Phm 7. Ja 2:14-16. 1 J 3:16-19. **the poor**. Ex +*23:3. **ye may do**. 2 C *9:7. Ga *6:10. **but**. Mk 2:20. Mt 9:15. Jn 7:33. 12:35. 13:33. 14:19. 16:5, 16-19, 28. 17:11. Ac +*3:21.

8. **hath done**. "It appears to me more probable," says Dr. Doddridge, "that Matthew and Mark should have introduced this story out of its place—that Lazarus, if he made this feast (which is not expressly said by John), should have made use of Simon's house, as more convenient—and that Mary should have poured this ointment on Christ's head and body, as well as on his feet,—than that, within the compass of four days, Christ should have been twice anointed with so costly a perfume; and that the same fault should be found with the action, and the same value set upon the ointment, and the same words used in defense of the woman, and all this in the presence of many of the same persons; all which improbable particulars must be admitted, if the stories be considered as different." The rebuke which Judas received from Christ at this unction determined him in his resolution to

betray his Master; and therefore Christ's rebuke, and Judas' revenge, are united, as cause and effect, by Matthew and Mark. Compare Lk 7:45n. 1 Ch 28:2, 3. 29:1-17. 2 Ch 31:20, 21. 34:19-33. Ps *110:3. 2 C 8:1-3, 12. **what she could.** Mk 12:43. Mt 15:28. Lk 21:3. **she is.** Mk 15:42-47. 16:1. Lk 23:53-56. 24:1-3. Jn 12:7. 19:32-42. **to the burying.** Mt *26:12. Re 12:11.

9. **Wheresoever.** Mk 16:15. Mt *26:12, 13. **this gospel.** Mk 13:10. Mt 24:14. Ac 20:24. Ep 1:13. 6:15. **world.** Gr. *kosmos*, Mt +4:8. **a memorial.** Nu 31:54. Ps 112:6-9. Zc 6:14. Ac 10:4.

10. **Judas.** Mt *26:14-16. Lk *22:3-6. Jn 13:2, 30. **Iscariot.** Jsh 15:25n. Je 48:24, 41. **one.** Ps 41:9. 55:12-14. Mt 10:4. Jn 6:70, 71. **the twelve.** Mk 9:35. **went unto.** Mt 20:18, 19. **to betray.** Jn 13:2.

11. **they heard.** Jn 11:57. **they were.** Ho 7:3. Lk 22:5. **and promised.** 1 K 21:20. 2 K 5:26. Pr 1:10-16. 28:21, 22. Mt 26:15. 1 T *6:10. 2 P *2:14, 15. Ju 11. **he sought.** Lk *22:5, 6. **conveniently.** 2 T 4:2g.

12. **the first.** Ex *12:6, 8, 18. 13:3. Le 23:5, 6. Nu 28:16-18. Dt 16:1-4. Mt *26:17. Lk *22:7. **killed.** *or*, sacrificed. Dt *16:6, 7. Ac 14:13, 18. 1 C *5:7, 8. 10:20. **the passover.** ♪121P8, Ex +12:21. Le +*23:5. Ac 12:3, 4. **Where.** Mt *3:15. Lk 22:8, 9. Ga *4:4.

13. **two.** Mk 11:2. Mt 21:2. Lk 19:29. *22:8. **Go.** Mk 11:2, 3. Mt 8:9. *26:18, 19. Lk 19:30-33. *22:10-13. Jn 2:5. +*15:14. He *4:13. *5:9.

14. **The Master.** Mk 4:38. 10:17. 11:3. Mt 23:8. Jn 11:28. 13:13. **guestchamber.** Lk 2:7g. 22:11. **where I.** Re *3:20. **passover.** ♪121P8, Ex +12:21. ver. +12.

15. **he will.** 2 Ch 6:30. Ps *110:3. Pr 16:1. 21:1, 2. Jn +*2:24, 25. 21:17. 2 T *2:19. He *4:13. **upper.** Lk 22:12. Ac 1:13. 20:8.

16. **and found.** Lk 19:32. 22:13, 35. Jn 16:4.

17. **in the evening.** Mt 26:20. Lk *22:14.

18. **as they sat.** Ex 12:11. Mt 26:21. **Verily.** ver. 9, 25. Mk +3:28. Mt +*5:18. Lk +4:24. Jn +1:51. **One.** Ps ▸41:9. 55:13, 14. Lk *22:21. Jn 6:70, 71. *13:21. **eateth with me.** Ru 2:14. Jn 13:18, 26.

19. **and to.** Mt *26:22. Lk *22:21-23. Jn *13:22. **one by one.** Jn 8:9. **and another said.** Mt *26:25.

20. **It is.** ver. 43. Mt 26:47. Lk 22:47. Jn 6:71. **the twelve.** ver. 10. **dippeth.** ver. 18. Ru 2:14. Ps 41:9. Mt *26:23. Jn 13:26.

21. **Son of man.** Mk 2:10. **goeth.** ver. 49. Ge +*3:15. Ps 22:1, etc. 69:1, etc. Is 52:14. ch. 53. Da *9:24, 26. Zc 13:7. Mt 26:24, 54, 56. Lk 22:22. 24:26, 27, 44. Jn 7:33. 8:21, 22. 14:12. 16:28. 19:28, 36, 37. Ac 2:23. 4:27, 28. 13:27-29. **as it is written.** ver. 49. Mk 9:12. Lk 18:31. 24:25-27, 46. Ac +*17:2, 3. 26:22, 23. 1 C +*15:3. 1 P 1:10, 11. **but.** Ps 55:15. 109:6-20. Mt 18:7. 27:3-5. Lk 17:1. 22:22. Ac 1:16-20, 25. **by whom.** Ob *7. Mi *7:6. **good were.** Mt 18:6, 7. 26:24, 25. Mk 9:42. Jn 17:12. **if.** ♪184B, Mt +23:30. **never been born.** Jb 3:1-19. Je 20:14-18.

22. **as.** Mt 26:26-29. Lk *22:19, 20. 1 C 10:16, 17. *11:23-29. **took bread.** Jn 6:35. **and blessed.** Mk 6:41. Lk +*24:30. Jn 6:23. **brake.** ♪108H4, Is +58:7. **Take.** Jn 6:48-58. **this is.** ♪119, Ge +49:9. That is, this *represents* my body, the substantive verb, whether expressed or understood, being often equivalent to *signifies* or *represents* (See Ex 12:11. Da 7:24. Mt 13:38, 39. Lk 8:9. 15:26. 18:36. Jn 7:36. 10:6. Ac 10:17. Re 1:20. 5:6, 8. 11:4. 17:12, 18. 19:8). ver. 24. Ge 41:26, 27. Zc 5:7, 8. Lk 22:20. 1 C 10:4, 16. Ga 4:25. **my body.** Jn 6:51, 53.

23. **when.** ver. 22. Mt 15:36. Lk 22:17. Ro 14:6. 1 C 10:16. **and they all.** Mt *26:27.

24. **This is.** ♪119, Ge +49:9. Ex ▸24:8. Zc ▸9:11. Mt 26:28. Jn 6:53. 1 C *10:16. 11:25. He 9:15-23. 10:29. 13:20, 21. **new.** Je 31:31. Lk *22:20. 1 C 11:25. 2 C 3:6. **which.** Mk 10:45. Re 5:8-10. 7:9-17. **is shed.** ♪96C7, Mt +26:24. **for many.** Mt 20:28. 26:28n.

25. **I will.** Ps 104:15. Mt 26:29. Lk *22:16-18, 29, 30. **no more.** ♪158, Mt +5:18. **until.** Mt +*26:29. Lk 22:18. Ac ◐*10:41. **new.** Jl 3:18. Am +*9:13, 14. Zc 9:17. **in the kingdom.** Mk +1:15. Is *25:6. Mt +*8:11. Lk *14:15. √22:18, 30. Jn *16:22. Re *7:17. 19:9.

26. **sung.** Ps 47:6, 7. Ac 16:25. 1 C 14:15. Ep *5:18-20. Col *3:16. Ja 5:13. Re 5:9. **hymn.** *or*, psalm. This was probably Ps ch. 113-118, which the Jews term the great *Hallel*, or *praise*, and always sing at the paschal festivity. **they went.** Mt 26:30. Lk 22:39. Jn 18:1-4.

27. **All.** Mt 26:31. Lk 22:31, 32. Jn *16:1, 32. 2 T 4:16. **offended.** Mt 15:12. **for it is written.** Lk +24:27. **I will smite.** Zc ▸13:7.

28. **after.** Mk 16:7. Mt 16:21. 26:32. *28:7, 10, 16. Jn *21:1, 4. 1 C +*15:4-6.

29. **Although.** ♪185A, Lk +11:8. Pr *28:14, 26. Je +*17:9. Mt 26:33-35. Lk 22:33, 34. Jn 13:36-38. 21:15. 1 C *10:12.

30. **That.** The conjunction *hoti* makes "this day" a part of what He said. We have the same construction in Lk 4:21; 19:9, but not in Mt 21:28; Lk 22:34; +23:43 (CB). **this day.** Ge 1:5, 8, 13, 19, 23. Lk ◐+23:43. **before.** ver. 66-72. Mt 26:69-75. Lk 22:54-62. Jn 18:17, 25-27. 1 C 10:12. **crow twice.** Samuel J. Andrews notes "That Mark should say, 'Before the cock crow twice thou shalt deny me thrice,' while the other Evangelists say, 'Before the cock crow thou shalt deny me thrice,' makes no real discrepancy. The latter speak generally of the cock-crowing as a period of time within which the three denials should take place; Mark more accurately says, that during this period the cock should not crow twice ere the denials were made" (*The Life of Our Lord*, p. 496). Webster and Wilkinson note that the expression "second crowing" "shows the accuracy of S. Mark, on the supposition that he wrote for the use of Christians at Rome. The Western world generally reckoned two cockcrowings, one at about 3 a.m. ("cockcrowing," Mk 13:35), the other at the dawn of day. This last was the only one reckoned in the East (*Greek Testament*, vol. 1, p. 221). Stuart Custer notes the fact that Matthew and Luke do not mention the cock's crowing twice is simply a case of their providing general information, whereas Mark, as the disciple of Peter, having been told the particulars more precisely, gives the more detailed account, incidentally proving the independent testimony of the four evangelists (*Does Inspiration Demand Inerrancy?*, p. 107). John W. Haley remarks, "The four evangelists agree as to the *number* of the denials; but Matthew, Luke, and John represent them as occurring before the crowing of the cock; Mark as occurring before the cock should crow 'twice.'" Haley further states, "Alford, Whitby, and many commentators note that cocks are accustomed to crow twice,—at or near midnight, and not far from day-break. Inasmuch as *few persons hear* the *first* crowing, the term generally denotes the *second*. All the evangelists refer to this latter; but Mark

with greater precision designates it as the 'second crowing.' It seems probable that no one of the evangelists has mentioned *all* the denials by Peter during that sorrowful night. As the accusation was caught up, reiterated, and flung in his face by one and another of the servants and the guard, the terror-stricken man, in his agitation and in his anxiety to clear himself, *would be likely to repeat the denial a considerable number of times, and in every variety of phrase.* And, meanwhile, he would naturally be shifting about from place to place. This hypothesis accounts for the difficulty as to the *persons* who accosted him, and the *places* where he was when the denials were uttered" (*An Examination of the Alleged Discrepancies of the Bible*, pp. 424, 425). A careful reading of the four accounts lends support to the possibility that Jesus in Mk 14:30 predicted two series of three denials, three denials before each of two cockcrowings: (1) The first series of three. First denial: Jn 18:17, place, the door (*thura*) without; time, entering; the questioner, the porteress (*thuroros*). Second denial: Mt 26:70; Mk 14:68, place, the hall (*aule*); time, sitting; questioner, a certain maid. Lk 22:56-58 combines the same place and time, with the same maid, and another (*heteros*, masculine). Third denial: Mt 26:71, place, the gateway or porch (*pulon*). Time, an interval of an hour. Jn 18:25, 26 combines the same place and time, with another maid and bystanders, one of them being a relative of Malchus. A cock crew: Mk 14:68. Jn 18:27. (2) The second series of three. First denial: Mk 14:63, place, beneath the hall; time, shortly after; questioner, the maid again. Second denial: Mt 26:73; Mk 14:70, place, the gate (*pulon*); time, shortly after; questioners, the bystanders. Third denial: Lk 22:59, 60, place, the midst of the hall (*aule*, ver. 55); time, an hour after (ver. 59); questioner, a certain one (masculine). A cock crew: (Mt 26:74. Mk 14:72. Lk 22:61). We thus have a combined record in which there remains no difficulty, while each word retains its own true grammatical sense (*Companion Bible*, Appendix 160, pp. 183, 184. Compare Johnston M. Cheney, *The Life of Christ in Stereo*, Appendix III, pp. 222-224). George W. DeHoff cites Bishop Horne as stating "Pertness and ignorance may ask a question in three lines which it will cost learning and ingenuity thirty pages to answer; and when this is done, the same question shall be triumphantly asked again the next year, as if nothing had ever been written on the subject" (*Alleged Bible Contradictions Explained*, p. 39). DeHoff provides in his initial chapters and introduction valuable discussion of the sources, causes, value and proper manner of solving alleged discrepancies, noting "Frequently several possible solutions of a difficulty are given. It is not claimed that these are the only possible solutions, nor, indeed, the correct ones" (p. 10). Clearly, that an alleged difficulty *can* be reasonably explained by reverent scholarship is sufficient to remove the difficulty. One overly magnified (by infidelity) alleged source of difficulties is the multiplicity of various readings in the original manuscripts of the Bible. DeHoff cites Dr. Bently, who said "The real text of the sacred writers does not now (since the originals have been so long lost) lie in any single manuscript or edition, but is dispersed in them all. 'Tis competently exact indeed, even in the worst manuscript now extant; nor is one article of faith or moral precept either perverted or lost in them, choose

as awkwardly as you can, choose the worst by design, out of the whole lump of readings" and "Make your thirty thousand (variations) as many more, if numbers of copies can ever reach that sum; all the better to a knowing and serious reader, who is thereby more richly furnished to select what he sees genuine. But even put them into the hands of a knave or a fool, and yet with the most sinistrous and absurd choice, he shall not extinguish the light of any one chapter, nor disguise Christianity but that every feature of it will be the same" (pp. 48, 49). ver. 68, 72. Mt 26:34, 75. Lk 22:34, 60. Jn ◐√13:38. 18:27.

31. **he spake.** 2 K 8:13. Jb 40:4, 5. Ps 30:6. Pr 16:18. 28:26. 29:23. Je 10:23. +*17:9. Jn *13:36-38. **If.** ∫184C, Mt +4:9. **Likewise.** Ex 19:8. Dt 5:27-29.

32. **they came.** Mt 26:36, etc. Lk *22:39. Jn *18:1, etc. **while.** ver. 36, 39. Ps 18:5, 6. 22:1, 2. 88:1-3. 109:4.

33. **Peter.** Mk 1:16-19. *5:37, 38. 9:2. Mt 17:1. **and began.** Ps 38:11. 69:1-3. 88:14-16. Is *53:10. Mt *26:37, 38. Lk 22:44. He *5:7.

34. **My soul.** Gr. *psyche*, ∫171Q2, Mt +12:18. Ps ▶42:5, 6. 43:5. Is *53:3, 4, 12. La 1:12. Jn *12:27. **exceeding sorrowful.** Mk 6:26. Mt 26:38. Lk 18:23. **unto death.** 2 K 20:1. 2 Ch 32:24. Is 38:1. Jon 4:9. **and watch.** ver. 37, 38. Mk 13:35-37. Mt +*24:42. Ep *6:18, 19. 1 P 4:7. 5:8.

35. **went forward.** Lk 22:41, 42. **and fell.** Ge 17:3. Dt 9:18. 1 Ch 21:15, 16. 2 Ch 7:3. Mt 26:39. Lk 17:15, 16. Ac 10:25, 26. He *5:7. Re 4:10. 5:14. **the hour.** ∫121P5. Metonymy of the Adjunct B595. "Hour" is put for what is done at the time. Here, "hour" is put for the *suffering* to take place at this time. For another instance of this figure see Jn 12:27. **if.** ∫184A, 1 C +15:2. **might pass.** ver. 41. Lk 22:53. Jn 2:4. 12:23, 27. 13:1. 16:4. 17:1.

36. **Abba.** i.e. *father*, ✱S#5g. Mt +*6:9. Ro *8:15g, 16. Ga *4:6g. **Father.** Mt 11:25. *26:39, 42. Lk 10:21. 22:42. 23:34, 46. Jn 11:41. 12:27, 28. 17:1, 5, 11, 21, 24, 25. **all.** Mk 10:27. Ge +*18:14. Jb +*42:2. Je +*32:27. Mt 19:26. 2 T 2:13. T *1:2. He *5:7. *6:18. **take.** Lk 22:41, 42. **this cup.** Mk 10:38. Mt 20:22. **nevertheless.** Ps *40:8. Mt 6:10. 26:42. Jn 4:34. *5:30. *6:38, 39. 12:27. 18:11. Ph *2:8. He *5:7, 8.

37. **and findeth.** ver. 40, 41. Mk 13:36. Lk 9:31, 32. 22:45, 46. **Simon.** ver. 29-31. 2 S 16:17. Jon 1:6. Mt 25:5. 26:40. 1 Th 5:6-8. **couldest.** Je √12:5. He 12:3. **watch.** Mt +*24:42.

38. **Watch.** T#1427. ver. 34. Mk 13:33-37. Ne 4:9. Ps 102:7. 119:147. 130:6. *141:2, 3. Mt 24:42. 25:13. 26:40, 41. Lk +*21:36. *22:40, 46. 1 C 16:13. Ep *6:18. Col *4:2, 3. 1 P *4:7. *5:8. Re 3:2, 3, 10. **enter into.** Mt +*6:13. **The spirit.** Gr. *pneuma*, ∫121A2, Mt +26:41n. Ro 7:18-25. Ga 5:17. Ph 2:12. **the flesh.** He 5:2.

39. **he went.** Mt 6:7. 26:42-44. Lk 18:1. *22:43, 44. 2 C 12:8. **the same.** ver. 36.

40. **eyes were heavy.** Lk 9:32. **neither.** Mk 9:6, 33, 34. Ge 44:16. Lk 9:33. Ro 3:19.

41. **third time.** 2 C 12:8. **Sleep.** Mk 7:9. Jg 10:14. 1 K 18:27. 22:15. 2 K 3:13. Ec 11:9. Ezk 20:39. Mt 26:45, 46. **it is enough.** Lk +*22:38. **the hour.** ver. 35. Jn 7:30. 8:20. 12:23, 27. 13:1. 17:1. **Son of man.** Mk 2:10. **is betrayed.** ∫96C7, Mt +26:24. ver. 10, 18. Mk 9:31. 10:33, 34. Mt 17:22. 20:18. 26:2. Lk 9:44. 18:32. Jn 13:2. Ac 7:52.

42. **Rise up.** Mt 26:46. Jn *13:1. 14:31. *18:1, 2.
43. **while.** Mt 26:47. Lk *22:47, 48. Jn *18:3-9. Ac 1:16. **and with.** Ps *2:1, 2. 3:1, 2. 22:11-13.
44. **a token.** Ex 12:13. Jsh 2:12. Ph 1:28. 2 Th 3:17. **Whomsoever.** 2 S 20:9, 10. Ps 55:20, 21. Pr 27:6. Mt 26:48-50. **and lead.** 1 S 23:22, 23. Ac 16:23.
45. **Master.** Mk 12:14. Is 1:3. Ml 1:6. Mt 23:8-10. Lk 6:46. Jn 1:38. 13:13, 14. 20:16. **master.** ſ108C5, Mt +23:7. **and kissed him.** Mt *26:49, 50. Lk 7:38, 45. 15:20. *22:48. Ac 20:37.
46. **they laid.** Jg 16:21. La 4:20. Mt *26:50. Jn 18:12. Ac 2:23.
47. **one of them.** Mt *26:51-54. Lk 22:49-51. Jn *18:10, 11. **sword.** Lk +*22:38.
48. **answered and said.** Mk 11:14. **Are ye.** 1 S 24:14, 15. 26:18. Mt *26:55. Lk *22:52, 53. **a thief.** Mk 11:17. Mt 21:13. Lk 10:30. 19:46. Jn 18:40.
49. **was daily.** Mk 11:15-18, 27. 12:35. Mt 21:23, etc. Lk 19:47, 48. 20:1, 2. 21:37, 38. Jn 7:28-30, 37. 8:2, 12. 10:23. 18:20. **in the temple.** Lk 2:46. Jn *18:20. **teaching.** Mk 1:21. 11:17. 12:35. Mt 4:23. 9:35. 13:54. 21:23. Lk 19:47. 20:1. 21:37. Jn 7:14, 28. 8:20. 10:23. 18:20. **but.** ſ63C, Ge +25:32. By ellipsis add, (this is done that). **the scriptures.** Ps ch. *22, *69. Is ch. *53. Da 9:24-26. Zc *13:7. Mt √26:54, 56. Lk 22:37. 24:25-27, 44, 45. **must be.** Mt √26:54. Lk *22:37. *24:44. Ac *1:16. **fulfilled.** Mt 1:22.
50. **they all forsook.** ver. 27. Jb *19:13, 14. Ps *38:11. *88:7, 8, 18. Is 63:3. Jn *16:32. *18:8, 9. 2 T 4:16.
51. **there followed.** "Though this incident," observes Dr. Campell, "recorded by Mark, may not appear of great moment, it is, in my opinion, one of those circumstances we call *picturesque*, which, though in a manner unconnected with the story, enliven the narrative, and add to its credibility. It must have been late in the night, when, as has been very probably conjectured, some young man, whose house lay near the garden, being roused out of sleep by the noise of the soldiers and armed retinue passing by, got up, stimulated by curiosity, wrapt himself (as Casauron supposes) in the cloth in which he had been sleeping, and ran after them." Could it be that this account is of Mark himself, who would have been a young man at this time? The incident is not repeated in the other gospels, and it could be just such a detail which Mark could supply about himself. **linen cloth.** Mk 15:46. Jg 14:12. Pr 31:24.
52. **he left.** Mk 13:14-16. Ge 39:12. Jb 2:4.
53. **they led.** Is 53:7. Mt *26:57, etc. Lk 22:54, etc. Jn *18:13, 14, 24. **and with.** Mk 15:1. Mt 26:3. Ac 4:5, 6.
54. **Peter.** ver. 29-31, 38. 1 S 13:7. Mt *26:58. **even.** ver. 68. Jn 18:15, 16. **the palace.** ver. 66. Mt 26:3. **and he.** 1 K 19:9, 13. Pr 28:14. Mt 6:13. Lk *22:55, 56. Jn 18:18, 25. 1 C 10:12. **the servants.** ver. 65. Mt 5:25. Jn 7:32, 45, 46. 18:3, 12, 22. 19:6. Ac 5:22, 26. **and warmed.** ver. 67. Is 44:16. Je 36:22. Lk 22:44. Jn 18:18. **fire.** ſ121N2, Ge +34:29.
55. **all.** *ſ171L2, Mt +26:59. **the council.** Mt 5:22. **sought.** 1 K 21:10, 13. Ps 27:12. 35:11. Mt *26:59, 60. Ac 6:11-13. 24:1-13. **and found.** Da 6:4. 1 P 3:16-18.
56. **false witness.** Ps *27:12. *35:11. **agreed not.** ver. 59. Dt 17:6. 19:15.
57. **and bare.** Mk 15:29. Je 26:8, 9, 18. Mt *26:60,

61. *27:40. Jn +*2:18-21. Ac 6:13, 14.
58. **heard him say.** Ac 6:14. **I will.** Mk *15:29. Mt *27:40. Jn +*2:19. **this temple.** Mk 15:29, 38. Mt 23:16. **with hands.** Ac 7:48. 17:24. Ep 2:11. He 9:11, 24. **three days.** Mt 16:21. Jn 2:19. **made without hands.** Da *2:34, 45. Ac 7:48. 17:24. 2 C *5:1. Col 2:11. He *9:11, 24.
59. **neither.** ver. 56.
60. **Answerest thou nothing.** Mk 15:3-5. Mt 26:62, 63. Jn 19:9, 10.
61. **he held his peace.** Mk 15:4, 5. Ps 39:1, 2, 9. Is *53:7. Mt +*26:63. 27:12-14. Jn 19:9. Ac 8:32, 33. 1 P *2:23. **Art thou.** Mk 15:2. Mt 11:3-5. +*16:16. 26:63, 64. Lk *22:66-70. Jn 10:24. 18:37. **the Christ.** Mt 1:17. **the Son.** Ps *2:7. 119:12. Is +*9:6, 7. Mt 3:17. 8:29. +*14:33. Jn 1:34, 49-51. 5:18-25. 10:30, 31, 36. 19:7. **the Blessed.** Lk 1:68. Ro 1:25. *9:5. 2 C 1:3. 11:31. Ep 1:3. 1 T 1:11. 6:15. 1 P 1:3.
62. **I am.** Mk 15:2. Mt 26:64. +27:11n. Lk *22:70. 23:3. Jn ◐+8:24n. **ye shall see.** Mt +*16:27n. +*24:30. Lk *21:27. **the Son of man.** Mk 2:10. Da 🜨7:13, 14. The passage of Daniel, to which our Lord refers, was always considered by the Jews as a description of the Messiah. In *Zohar*, in *Gen.* fol. 85, col. 338, it is said, referring to this prophecy, "This is the King Messiah." Our Savior, therefore, now in his lowest state of humiliation, asserted his claims as the Messiah, who shall appear in the clouds of heaven, as the judge of the world. Mk *13:26. 16:19. Ps *110:1. Da +*7:13, 14. Mt +*24:30. Lk 22:69. Ac 1:9-11. 2 Th √1:7-10. He 1:3. 8:1. 10:12, 13. 12:2. Re +*1:7. 20:11. **sitting.** Ps 🜨110:1, 2. **right hand.** Mt +*26:64. Lk *22:69. Ac 7:56. **coming.** Da 7:13. Re +*1:7. **the clouds.** Ge +9:13. 2 Ch +5:13. Mt +*25:30. Re +*1:7.
63. **rent his clothes.** Ge 37:29. Le 10:6. 21:10. Nu 14:6. 2 S 1:11. 3:31. Jb 1:20. Is 36:22. 37:1. Je 36:23, 24. Ac 14:13, 14.
64. **heard the blasphemy.** Mk 2:7. Le 24:16. 1 K 21:9-13. Mt 9:3. 26:65, 66. Lk 5:21. 22:71. Jn 5:18. 8:58, 59. √10:31-33, 36. *19:7. **all condemned.** Lk 23:50, 51. **guilty.** Mk 3:29g. **of death.** Le *24:16.
65. **began to spit.** Mk 10:34. 15:19. Nu 12:14. Jb 30:10. Is ✱50:6. Mt *26:67, 68. *27:30. Lk 22:63, 64. He *12:2. **cover his face.** Est *7:8. Jb 9:24. Is 53:3. **the servants.** ver. 54. **strike him.** Is 52:14. *53:3. Mi *5:1. Mt 5:39. Jn 18:22. 19:3. Ac 23:2.
66. **as Peter.** ver. 54. Mt *26:58, 69, 70. Lk *22:55-57. **the palace.** ver. 54. Mt 26:3. **one of the maids.** Jn *18:15-18.
67. **Jesus.** Mk 10:47. Mt 2:23. 21:11. Jn 1:45-49. 19:19. Ac *10:38. **of Nazareth.** Mk 1:24.
68. **he denied.** ver. 29-31. Jn 13:36-38. 2 T 2:12, 13. **know not.** Ju 10. **neither.** Pr 29:25. Mt +*10:28, 33. **he went.** Mt 26:71, 72. **and the.** ver. 30, 72.
69. **a maid.** *H paidiskee*, "the maid," and not the one mentioned in ver. 66, but *allee*, another, as St. Matthew states (Mt 26:71), she who was the *janitrix*, or doorkeeper, Jn 18:17. **and began.** ver. 38. Lk 22:58. Jn 18:25. Ga 6:1.
70. **a little after.** Mt 26:73, 74. Lk 22:58-60. Jn 18:26, 27. **for thou art.** Jg 12:6. Ac 2:7. **and thy speech.** *H lalia sou*, "Thy dialect," or mode of speech. From various examples produced by Lightfoot, and Schoetgen, it appears that the Galileans used a very corrupt dialect and pronunciation; interchanging the gutterals, and other letters, and so blending or dividing words

as to render them unintelligible, or convey a contrary sense. Thus when a Galilean would have asked, "whose is this lamb," he pronounced the first word so confusedly that it could not be known whether he meant *chamor*, "an ass," *chamar*, "wine," *amar*, "wool," or *immar*, "a lamb." A certain woman intending to say to a judge, "My lord, I had a picture which they stole; and it was so great, that if you had been placed in it, your feet would not have touched the ground," so spoiled it by her pronunciation, that her words meant, "Sir slave, I had a beam, and they stole thee away; and it was so great, that if they had hung thee on it, thy feet would not have touched the ground." Jg 12:6n. 2 K 8:21n. 1 Ch 6:36n. Ne 13:24. Mt 26:73. Ac 2:6, 7.

71. **he began.** 2 K 8:12-15. 10:32. Je +*17:9. 1 C 10:12.

72. **the second.** ver. *30, *68. Mt *26:34, 74. **Peter.** 2 S *24:10. Ps 119:59, 60. Je *31:18-20. Ezk *16:63. *36:31. Lk *15:17-19. *22:60, 61. **deny me.** Ac 3:13, 14. **when he thought thereon, he wept.** *or*, he wept abundantly, *or* he began to weep. Ezk 7:16. Mt *26:75. Lk *22:62. 2 C √7:10.

MARK 15

Jesus is bound, and delivered up unto Pilate; and when accused before him, and interrogated by him, he continues silent, 1-5. Pilate, induced by the priests and people, releases Barabbas, and delivers Jesus to be crucified, 6-15. The soldiers crown him with thorns, and cruelly mock him; and then lead him away to the place of crucifixion, 16-24. He is crucified between two thieves, and reviled by the people and the priests, 25-32. The sun is darkened; and Jesus, calling on God, expires, 33-37. The veil of the temple is rent; and the centurion confesses him to be "the Son of God," 38, 39. Certain women are spectators of his crucifixion, 40, 41. Joseph of Arimathea asks Pilate for the body, which having obtained he honorably inters, 42-47.

1. **straightway.** Ps *2:2. Mt 27:1, 2. Lk 22:66. Ac 4:5, 6, 25-28. **a consultation.** Mk 3:6. Ps 71:10. **and delivered.** Mk 10:33, 34. Mt 20:18, 19. Lk 18:32, 33. 23:1, 2, etc. Jn *18:28, etc. Ac *2:23. *3:13. 4:26. **Pilate.** Lk 3:1. 13:1. Ac 3:13. 4:27. 1 T 6:13.

2. **Art thou.** Mt 2:2. 27:11. Lk 23:3. Jn *18:33-37. 19:19-22. 1 T 6:13. **King of the Jews.** ver. 9, 12, 18, 26, ◐+32. Mt 2:2. 27:29, 37. Lk 23:37, 38. Jn 18:33, 39. 19:3, 19, 21. **Thou sayest.** Mt +27:11n. Lk 22:70.

3. **the chief.** Mt 27:12. Lk *23:2-5. Jn 18:29-31. 19:6, 7, 12. **but.** ver. 5. Mk 14:60, 61. Is *53:7. **answered nothing.** Mt +*26:63.

4. **Answerest.** Mt 26:62. 27:13. Jn *19:10.

5. **Jesus.** Is *53:7. Jn 19:9, 10. **answered nothing.** Mt +*26:63. **Pilate.** Ps *71:7. Is 8:18. Zc 3:8. Mt 27:14. 1 C 4:9.

6. **at the feast.** Mt 26:2, 5. 27:15. Lk *23:16, 17. Jn *18:39, 40. Ac 24:27. 25:9.

7. **Barabbas.** Mt 27:16. Lk 23:18, 19, 25. Jn *18:40. **made insurrection.** Ac 5:36, 37. **committed murder.** Ac 3:14.

8. **him to do.** √63BC, Ge +9:20. **ever.** ✻S#104g. Gr. *aei*, rendered (1) alway: 2 C 4:11. 6:10. T 1:12. He 3:10. (2) always: Ac 7:51. 1 P 3:15. 2 P 1:12. (3) ever: Mk 15:8.

9. **Will.** Mt *27:17-21. Jn 18:39. 19:4, 5, 14-16. Ac

3:13-15. **King of the Jews.** ver. +2.

10. **for envy.** Ge 4:4-6. =37:11. 1 S 18:8, 9. Ps=106:16. Pr *27:4. Ec 4:4. Mt 27:18. Jn 11:47, 48. 12:19. Ac 13:45. T 3:3. Ja 3:14-16. 4:5. 1 J 3:12.

11. **chief priests.** Ho 5:1. Mt 27:20. Jn *18:40. Ac *3:14.

12. **What.** Mt 27:22, 23. Lk 23:20-24. Jn 19:14-16. **whom.** ver. 1, 2. Mk 11:9-11. Ps *2:6, 7. Is +*9:6, 7. Je +*23:5, 6. Zc *9:9. Mt *2:2-4. 21:5. Lk 23:2. Jn ◐19:15. Ac 5:31.

13. **And they.** √161. Simultaneum; or, Insertion B714. A parenthetic insertion between the record of two simultaneous events. For another instance of this figure see Re 16:15. **Crucify him.** Ac 13:28.

14. **Why.** Is 53:9. Mt 27:4, 19, 24, 54. Lk 23:4, 14, 15, 21, 22, 41, 47. Jn 18:38. 19:6. He 7:26. 1 P 1:19. **And they.** √161, ver. +13. Ps 69:4. Is *53:3. Mt 27:23-25. Lk 23:23, 24. Jn 19:12-15. Ac 7:54-57. 19:34. 22:22, 23. **what evil.** Lk 23:41. Jn +*8:46. **Crucify.** Ge=37:20.

15. **willing.** Pr 29:25. Is *57:11. Mt 27:26. Lk *23:24, 25. Jn *19:1, 16. Ac 24:27. 25:9. Ga 1:10. **when.** Mk 10:34. Ps 129:3. Is 50:6. 53:5. Mt 20:19. 27:26. Lk 18:33. 23:16. Jn 19:1. 1 P 2:24.

16. **the soldiers.** Mt 27:27. **Pretorium.** *Praitorion*, in Latin, *praetorium*, was properly the tent or house of the *praetor*, a military, and sometimes a civil officer. This was a magnificent edifice in the upper part of the city, which had been formerly Herod's palace, and from which there was an approach to the citadel of Antonia, which adjoined the temple (Josephus, Ant. l. xv. c. 9. sec. 3. Bell. l. i. c. 21. sec. 1. l. v. c. 4. sec. 3). Mt 27:27. Jn 18:28, 33. 19:9. Ac 23:35. Ph 1:13. **band.** Jn 18:3, 12. Ac 10:1. 21:31. 27:1.

17. **clothed.** Mt *27:28-30. Lk 23:11. Jn 19:2-5. **purple.** Re 17:4. 18:12, 16.

18. **Hail.** ver. 29-32. Ge 37:10, 20. Mt 27:42, 43. Lk 23:36, 37. Jn 19:14, 15. **King of the Jews.** ver. +2.

19. **they smote.** Mk 9:12. 10:34. 14:65. Jb 13:9. 30:8-12. Ps 22:6, 7. 35:15-17. 69:12, 19, 20. Is 49:7. 50:6. 52:14. 53:3-5. Mi 5:1. Mt 20:18, 19. Lk 18:32, 33. 22:63. 23:11, 36. He 12:2, 3. 13:13. **spit upon.** Mk 14:65. **and bowing.** Ge 41:43. 43:28. 1 K 19:18. Est 3:2-5. Is 45:23. Ro 11:4. 14:10, 11. Ph 2:10. **worshipped.** Mt +*8:2.

20. **mocked him.** Mk 10:34. Mt 20:19. 27:41. Lk 18:32. 22:63. **and led.** Is 53:7. Mt 27:31. Jn 19:16.

21. **they compel.** Mt 5:41. 27:32. Lk 23:26. Jn ◐19:17. **a Cyrenian.** i.e. *belonging to Cyrene* (i.e. *wall; coldness; hitting*), ✻S#2956g. Mt 27:32. Lk 23:26. Ac 2:10. 6:9. 11:20. 13:1. **Alexander.** i.e. *man defender; helper of men*, ✻S#223g. Ac 4:6. 19:33, 33. 1 T 1:20. 2 T 4:14. (1) Son of Simon the Cyrenian, who was compelled to carry the cross of Jesus, Mk 15:21. (2) A leading man in Jerusalem when Peter and John were apprehended, Ac 4:6. (3) A Jewish convert who was with Paul when a tumult was raised by the Ephesians, Ac 19:33. Perhaps the same as Number 1. (4) A convert who afterward apostatized, 1 T 1:20. (5) A man who hindered the work of Paul, 2 T 4:14. Perhaps the same as Number 4. **and Rufus.** i.e. *red*, ✻S#4504g. Ro 16:13. **to bear.** Lk 14:27. Jn 19:17-20.

22. **Golgotha.** Mt 27:33, etc. Lk *23:27-33, Calvary. Jn 19:17, etc. **interpreted.** √95, Ps +7:13. Mk +5:41.

23. **they.** Ps 69:21. Mt 27:34. Lk 23:36. Jn *19:28-

30. **myrrh.** Mt 2:11. *27:34. Jn 19:39. **but.** Mk 14:25. Mt +*26:29. Lk 22:18.

24. **crucified.** Dt 21:23. Ps 22:16, 17. Is 53:4-8. Ac 5:30. 2 C √5:21. Ga *3:13. 1 P *2:24. **they parted.** Ps ≀22:18. Mt *27:35, 36. Lk *23:34. Jn *19:23, 24.

25. **third hour.** Our 9 a.m. Mt 20:3. Jn +*11:9n. Ac 2:15. **and they.** ver. 33. Mt 27:45. Lk 23:44. Jn 19:14. Ac 2:15.

26. **the superscription.** Dt 23:5. Ps 76:10. Pr 21:1. Is 10:7. 46:10. **his accusation.** Lk 23:2. Jn 19:12. Ac 25:18, 27. **was written.** Ac 17:23. **THE KING OF THE JEWS.** ver. +2. Ps *2:6. Zc *9:9. Mt 2:2. *27:37. Lk *23:37, 38. Jn *19:18-22.

27. **with him.** Mt 27:38. Lk 23:32, 33. Jn 19:18. **two thieves.** Is 53:12. Jn 18:40. **one on.** Mk 10:37. Mt 20:21.

28. **fulfilled.** Is ✦≀53:12. Lk *22:37. 2 C *5:21. He *12:2.

29. **passed by.** La *1:12. **railed.** Ps ≀22:7, 8, 12-14. *35:15-21. *69:7, 19, 20, 26. 109:25. La √1:12. 2:15. Mt 27:39, 40. Lk 22:65. 23:39. Ja 2:7. **wagging.** 2 K 19:21. Jb 16:4. Ps ≀109:25. Is 37:22. Je 18:16. La 2:15. **Ah.** Ps 35:21, 25. 40:15. **thou that.** ∫60D, Ge +37:19. **destroyest.** ∫24B, Ge +23:16. Mk *14:58. Ge 37:19, 20. Mt 26:61. Jn +*2:18-22. **the temple.** ver. 38. Lk 1:9.

31. **also.** Ps *2:1-4. 22:16, 17. Mt 27:41-43. Lk *23:35-37. **He.** Lk 4:23. *7:14, 15. 23:39. Jn *11:43, 44, 47-52. 12:23, 24. 1 P 3:17, 18. **himself.** Mt 26:53, 54. Jn *10:18.

32. **Christ.** Mk +*14:61, 62. Mt +1:17. Jn 20:25-29. **King of Israel.** ver. ❶+2. Is 44:6. Zp +*3:15. Zc *9:9. Mt 27:42. Lk +*23:2. Jn +*1:49. 12:13. 19:12-15. Ac 17:7. that. Ge=37:20. Ro 3:3. 2 T 2:18. **see and believe.** Lk *16:31. Jn 4:48. 6:30. 20:8, 29. 2 C ❶*5:7. **And.** Mt *27:44. Lk *23:39-43.

33. **when.** ver. 25. Mt 27:45. Lk 23:44, 45. **sixth hour.** Our 12 noon. Mt +20:5. Jn +*11:9n. **darkness.** Ps 105:28. Is 50:3, 4. Am 8:9, 10. **ninth hour.** 1 K 18:29. Ac 3:1.

34. **at.** Da 9:21. Lk 23:46. Ac 10:3. **Eloi.** ∫84, Ge +22:11. i.e. *my God,* ✱S#1682g, only here. Ps ≀22:1. Mt 27:46. He *5:7. **interpreted.** ∫95, Ps +7:13. Mk +5:41. **My God.** ∫59, Ge +28:16. Or, "My God, my God, to what (*eis ti, sort of persons,* understood) hast thou left me." So also the Syriac version, which Dr. A. Clarke is inclined to adopt; though he observes, "Whatever may be thought of the above mode of interpretation, one thing is certain, that the words could not be used by our Lord in the sense in which they are generally understood. This is sufficiently evident; for he well knew why he was come unto that hour, nor could he be forsaken of God, in whom dwelt all the fulness of the Godhead bodily. The Deity, however, might constrain so much of its consolatory support, as to leave the human nature fully sensible of all its sufferings; so that the consolations might not take off any part of the keen edge of his passion: and this was necessary to make his sufferings meritorious." **why.** Ps 27:9. *42:9. 71:11. Is 41:17. La 1:12. 5:20. 2 C 13:4.

35. **he.** ver. 23. Mk 9:11-13. Ps *69:21. Mt 17:11-13. 27:47-49. Lk 23:36. Jn *19:28-30.

36. **and filled.** ver. 23. Ru 2:14. Ps ≀69:21. Lk 23:36. Jn 19:28-30.

37. **Jesus cried.** Ps 31:5. Mt 27:50. Lk *23:46. Jn

*19:30. **gave up.** ver. 39g. Ge +*25:8n, 17. 35:29. 49:33. Jb 3:11. 10:18. 11:20. 13:19. 14:10. Je 15:9. La 1:19. Lk 23:46g. Jn *10:18. Ac 5:5, 10. 7:59. 12:23.

38. **the veil.** Ex *26:31-34. 40:20, 21. Le 16:2, etc. 2 Ch 3:8-14. Mt *27:51-53. Lk *23:45. Ep *2:13-16. He 4:14-16. 6:19. *9:3-12. *10:19-23. **temple.** ver. 29. Lk 1:9.

39. **the centurion.** The centurion was a military captain, and commander of a century, or 100 men. In order to have a proper notion of his office, it may be desirable to explain the construction and array of the Roman legion. Each legion was divided into ten cohorts, each cohort into three maniples, and each maniple into two centuries—so that there were thirty maniples, and sixty centuries in a legion, which, if the century had always, as the word imports, consisted of 100 soldiers, would have formed a combined phalanx of 6000 men. The number in a legion, however, varied at different periods; in the time of Polybius it was 4200. The order of battle was that of three lines—the *hastati,* or spearmen, occupied the front; the *principes,* the second line; the *triarii* (also called *pilani,* from their weapon, the *pilam*), the third. The centurions were appointed by the tribunes, and generally selected from the common soldiers according to their merit; although the office was sometimes obtained for money, or through the favor of the consuls. Their badge was a vine rod, or sapling. ver. 44. Mt 8:5-10. Ac 10:1, 2. 27:1-3, 43. **ghost.** Gr. *pneuma,* ∫121A3, Mt +27:50. **he said.** Mt 27:43, 54. Lk *23:47, 48. **the Son of God.** Da ❶3:25. Mt +14:33. +√27:54n.

40. **women.** Ps *38:11. Mt 27:55, 56. Lk *23:49. Jn *19:25-27. **Mary Magdalene.** ver. 47. Mk 16:1, 9. Mt 27:56, 61. 28:1. Lk *8:2, 3. 24:10. Jn 19:25. 20:1, 11-18. **Mary the.** ver. 47. Mk 16:1. Mt +*13:55. 27:55, 61. Jn 19:25. 1 C 9:5. Ga 1:19. Ja 1:1. **James.** Lk 6:15. **the less.** Lk 19:3. **Salome.** i.e. *peaceable,* ✱S#4539g. Mk 16:1g. Mt 27:56. (1) A woman who followed Jesus from Galilee and witnessed his crucifixion "afar off," Mk 15:40; 16:1. She was the wife of Zebedee and the mother of the apostles James and John. (2) "The daughter of Herodias." She danced before Herod, and asked for the head of John the Baptist, Mt 14:6-8; Mk 6:22-25. She is not named in the New Testament, but is mentioned by Josephus, an ancient Jewish historian.

41. **ministered.** Mt 25:44. 27:56. Lk 8:2, 3. **came up.** Lk 2:4.

42. **now when.** Mt *27:57, 62. Lk *23:50-54. Jn *19:38. **the preparation.** Mt 27:62.

43. **an honorable.** Mk 10:23-27. Lk 23:50. Ac 13:50. 17:12. **waited for.** Mk 14:25. Mt 6:10. 7:21, 22. *19:28. 26:29. Lk *2:25, 38. 11:2. 22:18, 29, 30. 23:51. +*24:21. Ac +*1:6. **kingdom of God.** Mk +1:15. **and went.** Mk 14:54, 66, etc. Mt 19:30. 20:16. Ac 4:8-13. Ph 1:14.

44. **marvelled.** Jn 19:31-37. **if.** ∫184A, 1 C +15:2. **centurion.** ver. 39.

45. **he gave.** Mt 27:58. Jn 19:38.

46. **fine linen.** Mk 14:51. **and took.** Mt 27:59, 60. Lk *23:53. Jn *19:38-42. **and laid.** Is *53:9. **hewn.** 2 Ch 16:14. Is *22:16. **and rolled.** Mk 16:3, 4. Ge 29:3, 8, 10. Mt 27:60. 28:2. Jn 11:38.

47. **Mary Magdalene.** ver. 40. Mk 16:1. Mt 27:61. 28:1. Lk *23:55, 56. 24:1, 2.

MARK 16

An angel informs the women that Jesus is risen, 1-8. He appears to Mary Magdalene, 9-11; to two disciples going into the country, 12, 13; and to the eleven; whom he upbraids for their unbelief, and commissions to preach the gospel to all the world, 14-18. He ascends into heaven, 19. The gospel is every where preached, and confirmed by miracles, 20.

1. **when.** Mk 15:42. Mt 28:1, etc. Lk 23:54, 56. 24:1, etc. Jn 19:31. 20:1, etc. **sabbath was past.** Mk 1:32. **Mary Magdalene.** Mk 15:40, 47. Lk 24:10. Jn 19:25. **sweet.** Mk 14:3, 8. 2 Ch 16:14. Lk 23:56. Jn *19:40. **anoint.** Mk 14:8. Jn 11:2. 12:3.

2. **very early.** Mr. West supposes that the women made two different visits to the sepulchre, and, in consequence of that, two distinct reports to the disciples; that Mary Magdalene, with the other Mary and Salome, set out not only early, but *very early* in the morning, *lian proi,* i.e. before the time appointed to meet Joanna and the other women there (Lk 24:10). This interpretation, which is adopted by several eminent writers, is very probable, and reconciles the apparent discrepancy in the evangelists. Mt 28:1. Lk *24:1. Jn *20:1. **the first day.** ver. 9. **came.** ✓171J14, Jon +1:3. i.e. went.

3. **Who.** Mk 15:46, 47. Mt 27:60-66.

4. **they saw.** Mt *28:2-4. Lk 24:2. Jn 20:1. **rolled.** Ge 29:10. Mt 28:2. **very great.** Mt 27:60.

5. **entering.** Lk *24:3. Jn 20:8. **a young.** This appears to have been a different angel from that mentioned by St. Matthew. The latter sat in the porch of the tomb, and had assumed a terrible appearance to overawe the guard (Mt 28:1); but this appeared as a young man, within the sepulchre, in the inner apartment. The two angels spoken of by St. John (Jn 20:11) appeared some time after these; but whether they were the same or different cannot be ascertained; nor whether the angels which manifested themselves to the second party of women, recorded by St. Luke (Lk 24:4), were the same or different. Da 10:5, 6. Mt 28:3. Lk 24:4, 5. Jn *20:11, 12. **clothed.** Mk 9:3. Da 7:9. Jn 20:12. Ac 1:10. **white garment.** Mt 28:3. Re 6:11. 7:9. **and they.** Mk 6:49, 50. Ge +19:30. Da 8:17. 10:7-9, 12. Lk 1:12, 29, 30.

6. **Be not.** Ge +19:30. Mt 14:26, 27. 28:4, 5. Re 1:17, 18. **Ye seek.** Ps 105:3, 4. Pr 8:17. **Jesus.** Jn 19:19, 20. Ac 2:22, 23. 4:10. 10:38-40. **which.** *41, Ge +10:1. **was crucified.** Mk 15:24. **he is risen.** Mk 9:9, 10. 10:34. Ps 71:20. Mt +*12:40n. 28:6, 7. Lk 24:4-8, 20-27, 46. Jn +*2:19-22. 1 C +*15:3-7. **they laid.** Mk 15:46.

7. **tell.** Mk 14:50, 66-72. Mt *28:7. 2 C 2:7. **into Galilee.** Mk *14:28. Mt 28:10, 16. **there.** Mk 14:28. Mt *26:32. 28:10, 16, 17. Jn 21:1. Ac 13:31. 1 C 15:5.

8. **they went.** Mt *28:8. Lk *24:9-11, 22-24. **for they trembled.** ver. 5, 6. Lk 24:37. **neither.** 2 K 4:29. Lk 10:4. **were afraid.** Mk 9:6.

9. **the first day.** T#644. Ps 118:24. Mt 28:1, 8, 9. Jn 20:19. Ac *20:7. 1 C *16:2. Re +*1:10. **he appeared.** Mk 15:40, 47. Mt 28:9. Lk 24:10. Jn *20:14-18. **Magdalene.** i.e. *of Magdala; magnificent,* ✱S#3094g. Mk 15:40, 47. 16:1, 9. Mt 27:56, 61. 28:1. Lk 8:2. 24:10. Jn 19:25. 20:1, 18. Compare ✱S#3093, Mt 15:39. **out.** Lk 8:2.

10. **she went.** Mt 28:10. Lk *24:10. Jn *20:18. **as.** Mk 14:72. Mt 9:15. 25:75. Lk 24:17. Jn *16:6, 20-22.

mourned. Lk 6:25. Ja 4:9. Re 18:11, 15, 19.

11. **believed not.** ver. 13, 14, 16. Mk 9:19. Ex 6:9. Jb 9:16. Lk *24:11, 23-35.

12. **he appeared.** ver. 14. Lk *24:13-32. Jn 21:1, 14. **another form.** J. A. Alexander states Luke gives the cause, "their eyes were holden," while Mark gives the effect, they perceived him in "another form" (Commentary on Mark, pp. 439, 449). Ge ◖27:16. Lk 9:29g. +*24:13, 16. **unto two.** Lk ✓24:13-31.

13. **they went.** Lk *24:33-35. **neither.** Lk *16:31. Jn *20:8, 25.

14. **he appeared.** ver. 12. **unto the eleven.** Lk *24:36-43. Jn *20:19, 20, 36. 1 C *15:5-8. **at meat.** *or,* together. **and upbraided.** Mk 7:18. *8:17, 18. Mt 6:30. 8:26. *11:20. 14:31. 15:16, 17. *16:8-11. *17:20. Lk 22:32. *24:25, 38, 39. Jn 20:27. Re *3:19. **unbelief.** Nu *14:11. Ps 95:8-11. Lk 24:41. He 3:7, 8, 15-19. **hardness.** Mk 3:5. 10:5. Mt 19:8. He 3:8. **believed not.** ver. 11, 13.

15. **Go.** T#480. 2 K +16:3 (T#359). Ps 9:17. 74:20. Mt ◖*10:5, 6. +*28:19, 20. Lk +10:1 (T#448). *14:21-23. *24:47, 48. Jn *15:16. .*20:21. Ro *2:12. *10:14, 15. 1 J *4:14. **into all.** Mk *13:10. Ps *22:27. *67:1, 2. *96:3. 98:3. Is *42:10-12. *45:22. *49:6. 52:10. *60:1-3. Lk *2:10, 11, 31, 32. Ac +*1:8. Ro 10:18. *16:26. Ep 2:17. Col *1:6, 23. Re *14:6. **world.** Gr. *kosmos,* Mt +4:8. **to every.** Ro 8:22. Col *1:23. **creature.** *171E2. Synecdoche of the Genus B620. Words of a wider meaning are used in a narrower sense: the universal for the particular, but of the same kind. Here, "creature" is put for "man." For other instances of this figure see Col 1:23. 1 P 2:13.

16. **that believeth and.** Mk 1:15. Lk 7:50. 8:12. Jn ✓1:12, 13. ✓3:15, 16, 18, 36. ✓5:24. 6:29, 35, 40. 7:37, 38. *11:25, 26. 12:46. ✓20:31. Ac *10:43. *13:38, 39. ✓16:30-32. Ro 3:6. *4:5, 24. ✓10:9. He 10:38, 39. 1 P 1:21. *3:21. 1 J ✓5:10-13. **is baptized.** T#36, 894. Mt +*28:19. Jn *3:3, 5. Ac +*2:38, 41. *8:36-39. 10:48. 13:24. +*22:16. Ro ✓6:3, 4. *10:9-14. 1 C ✓12:13. Ga ✓3:27. Col ✓2:12. 1 P *3:20, 21. **shall be saved.** Ac ✓16:31. Ro ✓10:9. Ep ✓2:8. T 3:5. 1 P 3:21. **but he.** Jn ✓3:18, 19, 36. +*8:24. *12:47, 48. Ac 13:46. 2 C 4:3, 4. 2 Th ✓1:8. ✓2:8, 12. Re *20:15. +*21:8. **believeth not.** ver. 11. Lk 24:11, 41. Ac 28:24. Ro 3:3. 2 Th 2:12. 2 T 2:13. 1 P 2:7. **shall be damned.** For each positive requirement for salvation, there is in Scripture a negative statement threatening loss of salvation if the requirement is not satisfied. That is, belief as a requirement for salvation is stated positively and negatively (Ac 16:31 w Jn 3:18); repentance is spoken of positively and negatively (Ac 17:30 w Lk 13:3). Although baptism is enjoined as a command, it is nowhere stated in the negative (i.e. "he that is not baptised is lost," or the equivalent), as all positive, essential requirements for salvation are. This passage comes closest to being such a negative statement, but it lacks the negative clause pertaining to baptism. Nor can such a clause be "supplied" as though its omission were a mere ellipsis, for in so essential a matter, we dare not add to what is expressly written (Pr ✓30:6. Re ✓22:18, 19). Therefore, the physical rite of water baptism cannot be shown from Scripture to be necessary to salvation. Mk 16:16 is not a command statement, nor is it in the subjunctive mood of a conditional clause, which would have to read "If one believes and is baptized he shall be saved." If it were so worded here

or anywhere, then baptism would be a necessary condition with which one must comply in order to be saved. But Mark 16:16 is a mere declaration that the baptized believer shall be saved. Had the Bible said "He that is baptized, and takes the Lord's Supper, and pays tithes and offerings, and forsakes not the assembling of himself with other believers, and cares for widows and orphans, shall be saved," it would have been a declarative statement of general Bible truth. But that is not the same as saying "If a person does all these things he shall be saved." What one receives when he believes, he does not lose when he is baptized. Nowhere in the New Testament is baptism made a command or a condition essential to salvation. It never occurs as such in the imperative mood in a command statement, or in the subjunctive mood in a conditional clause, with the promise that by subscribing to such one shall receive salvation. There are four, perhaps five, conditions or terms of salvation, all of which are stated both positively and negatively: (1) one must hear the Word of God: positive, Ro 10:17. Jn 5:24. negative, Ac 3:23. (2) one must be convicted by the Holy Spirit: positively, Jn 6:44. 16:8-11. negatively, Ro 8:9. (3) repentance is a means by which one receives salvation: positively, Ac 11:18. *17:30, 31. 2 P *3:9. negatively, Lk +*13:3. 2 C 7:10. (4) belief in or on Jesus Christ as personal Savior and Lord: positively, Ac 10:43. *15:9. 16:31. Ro 1:16. Ga *3:26. Ep *2:8, 9. 1 J √5:1, 11-13. negatively, Jn 3:18. 8:24. (5) confession of Christ as Lord before men: positively, Ro √10:9, 10. negatively, Mt 10:32, 33. As with repentance, confession is not regarded in Scripture as an act which is separate from belief; it is concomitant. If not, then one who is dumb cannot be saved; nor could a person isolated from society be saved through the reading of the Word. All four or five conditions or terms of salvation are stated both positively and negatively; baptism is not one of these. Just as the verb "baptize" is never used in the entire New Testament in the subjunctive mode in a promise of salvation, neither is the noun "baptism" used in the instrumental, means, or agency case of prepositions so as to offer salvation, justification, or the new birth by or through baptism. In stating the conditions of salvation, Scripture does teach that (1) one receives a pure heart by faith in Christ, Ac 15:9; (2) one is justified by faith, Ro 5:1. Ac 13:39; (3) one is saved by grace through faith, Ep 2:8, 9; (4) one is said to be a child of God by faith in Christ Jesus (Ga 3:26. Ep 3:17), but one is never said to receive a pure heart, be justified, be saved, or to be a child of God by or through baptism (some of the preceding information I first learned when I heard Albert Garner debate in Gainesville, Florida, in 1974. Much of the information is also in his book, *Defense of the Faith*, Part 2, Chapter 2, "The Baptismal Regeneration Heresy," especially pp. 238-241, "Objections Answered, Mark 16:16"). The one word *believe* represents all a sinner can do and all a sinner must do to be saved. Hearing, conviction of the Holy Spirit, repentance, confession of sin, confession of Christ before others, are all con-

comitants of—things that accompany—true belief, not so many discrete requirements for salvation. A study of what the New Testament says regarding Abraham's faith (Ro 4:3-5, 10, 11, 24. Ga 3:6. He 11:17-19. Ja 2:21) will show that Abraham was declared righteous (Ge 15:6) chronologically before any act of obedience on his part, before the institution of circumcision, before the sacrifice of Isaac, and of course well before the establishment of the Mosaic law. This teaches us that no ordinance, no act of obedience, no obedience to law, and no "act of faith" precedes the imputation of righteousness—simply believing God.

17. **these signs.** Mk 11:23. Jn 14:12. **shall follow.** Lk 1:3g. **In my name.** Mk 6:13. 9:38. Lk *10:17. Ac *5:16. *8:7. *16:18. *19:12-16. **they.** ♪41, Ge +10:1. **shall speak.** Ac *2:4-11, 33. 10:46. *19:6. 1 C √12:10, 28, 30. *13:1, 8. 14:2, 5-27, 39. **tongues.** ♪121BC. Metonymy of the Cause B546. "Tongue" is put for the language peculiar to any people or nation: other *tongues* put for other *languages*. For other instances of this figure see Ac 2:4. 1 C 14:18.

18. **shall take.** Ge +*3:15. Ps 91:13. Lk *10:19. Ac *28:3-6. Ro 16:20. **if.** ♪184C, Mt +4:9. It is fully asserted here, that the *apostles* of our Lord should not lose their life by poison, and there is neither record nor tradition to disprove it. But it is worthy of remark, that Mohammed, who styled himself *the apostle of God*, lost his life by poison; and, had he been a true prophet, or a true apostle of God, he would not have fallen into the snare. 2 K 4:39-41. **they shall lay hands.** T#400. Mk 5:23. 6:5. Lk 4:40. Ac 3:6-8, 12, 16. 4:10, 22, 30. *5:15, 16. 8:17-19. *9:12, 17, 18, 34, 40-42. 19:12. *28:8, 9. 1 C 12:9. Ja √5:14, 15.

19. **after.** Mt 28:18-20. Lk 24:44-50. Jn 21:15, 22. Ac 1:2, 3. **he was received.** 2 K 2:11. Lk 9:51. *24:50, 51. Jn 6:62. 13:1. 16:28. 17:4, 5, 13. 20:17. Ac *1:2, 3, 9-11. 2:33. +*3:21. Ep 1:20-22. *4:8-11. 1 T 3:16. He 4:14. 6:20. 7:26. 9:24. 10:12, 13, 19-22. 1 P *3:22. **and sat.** ♪96C4, Mt +3:17. Ps *110:1. Mt 22:44. 26:64. Ac *7:55, 56. 1 C *15:24, 25. He 1:3. *8:1. *10:12. *12:2. 1 P *3:22. Re +*3:21. **right hand.** ♪22A15C, Ps +110:1. Ro *8:34. Ep 1:20. Col 3:1.

20. **they went.** Ac ch. 2-28. **every where.** ♪171D. Synecdoche of the Genus B619. Words denoting universality do not always affirm it of particulars. Here, "every where" signifies everywhere where they went; in every kind of place; or everywhere where they were able to go. For other instances of this figure see Lk 18:1. 24:53. Ac 28:22. 1 C 4:17. See related figures listed at Ge 24:10n. Ge +7:19n. 1 K √18:10. **the Lord.** Ac 4:30. 5:12. 8:4-6. 14:3, 8-10. Ro 15:19. 1 C 2:4, 5. 3:6-9. 2 C 6:1. He *2:3, 4. **working with.** 1 Ch=28:21. Mt 18:20. **confirming.** T#43. Mk +4:41 (T#77). Ac 4:4, 5. 14:31. 19:9. 1 K 18:38, 39. Jn 3:1, 2. Ac 8:6. 14:3. He 2:4. **the word.** Mk 2:2. 4:14, 20, 33. Mt 13:19-23. Lk 1:2. 8:11-15. Ac *8:4. Ja *1:21-23. 1 J 2:7. **with signs.** Ac 2:43. *4:29, 30. *5:12. 6:8. *8:6. *14:3. 15:12. 19:11. Ro 15:19. 1 C *2:4, 5. 2 C 12:12. He *2:3, 4. **following.** 1 T 5:10, 24. 1 P 2:21g.

LUKE

The preface, and dedication to Theophilus, 1-4. An account of Zacharias and Elisabeth, 5-7. The angel Gabriel appears to Zacharias in the temple, and promises him a son in his old age, who would be singularly eminent and useful, 8-17. He is chastised for unbelief, by being struck dumb, 18-23. Elisabeth conceives, and hides herself, 24, 25. The angel appears to the virgin Mary; and assures her that she should become the mother of the Messiah, the King of Israel, by the power of the Holy Spirit, 26-33. Her humble faith and acquiescence, 34-38. She visits Elisabeth, and is saluted by her: she prophesies, and praises God, 39-56. The birth, circumcision, and naming of John the Baptist, 57-63. Zacharias, restored to the use of speech, prophetically praises God, 64-79. The manner in which John spent his youth, 80.

1. A.M. 3998. B.C. 6. **those.** Jn √20:31. Ac *1:1-3. 1 T *3:16. 2 P 1:16-19. **most surely.** *Peplarophoramenon,* the passive participle of *plarophoreo,* from *plarasphora,* "full measure;" and is applied to a ship fully laden, to a tree in full bearing, etc. Hence it implies that fulness of evidence by which any fact is supported, and also that confidence, or feeling of assent, by which facts so supported are believed. Ac 3:18. Ro 4:21. 14:5. Col 2:2. 4:12. 1 Th 1:5. 2 T 4:5, 17. He 6:11. 10:22.

2. **delivered.** 1 C 11:2, 23. 15:3. **which.** Lk 24:48. Mk 1:1. Jn *15:27. 16:4. Ac *1:3, 8, 21, 22. 4:20. *10:39-41. 11:15. He *2:3. 1 P 5:1. 1 J *1:1-3. **eyewitnesses.** Ac 4:20. 1 P 5:1. 2 P √1:16. 1 J 1:1, 3. **and ministers.** Ac *26:16. Ro *15:16. 1 C *4:1. Ep *3:7, 8. 4:11, 12. Col 1:23-25. **the word.** Mk 4:14. √108B. Idiom B832. "Word" in the New Testament follows the Hebrew idiom, and signifies not merely *a word,* but *speech,* which is the outcome of words. For other instances of this idiom see Mt 21:24. Ac 6:2. 10:29, 44. 19:38. 1 C 15:2.

3. **seemed.** Ac 15:19, 25, 28. 1 C 7:40. 16:12. **having.** Mk 16:17. Ac *1:1-3. 1 T 4:6. 2 T 3:10. **from the very first.** Ac 26:5. **in order.** ver. 1. Ps 40:5. 50:21. Ec 12:9. Ac *11:4. 18:23. **most.** Ac 1:1. 23:26. 24:3. 26:25g. **Theophilus.** i.e. *God-given,* ✻S#2321g. Ac 1:1.

4. **mightest know.** Gr. *epiginosko,* Mt +11:27. Jn √20:31. **the certainty.** 1 P +*3:15. 2 P √1:15, 16. **instructed.** Ac 18:25. 21:21, 24. Ro 2:18. 1 C 14:19. Ga 6:6g.

5. **Herod.** Mt 2:1. **Judea.** Lk 4:44. **Zacharias.** i.e. *remembered of Jah,* ✻S#2197g. Lk 1:5, 12, 13, 18, 21, 40, 59, 67. 3:2. 11:51. Mt 23:35. For ✻S#2148h, see Zc +1:1. **of the course.** ver. 8. 1 Ch *24:10, 19. 2 Ch *8:14. Ne 12:4, 17, Abijah. **Elizabeth.** i.e. *oath of God,* ✻S#1665g. Lk 1:5, 7, 13, 24, 36, 40, 41, 41, 57. For ✻S#472h, see Ex +6:23.

6. **righteous.** Lk *2:25. 16:15. *23:50. Ge 6:9. *7:1. *17:1. Jb *1:1, 8. 9:2. Mt 23:35. Mk 6:20. Ac 4:19. 8:21. *10:22. Ro *3:9-25. *8:4. Ph *3:6-9. T 3:3-7. **walking.** Ge 17:1. Dt 28:9. 1 K *9:4. 2 K +*20:3. Ps *119:1, 6. Ac 9:31. 23:1. *24:16. 1 C 11:2. 2 C 1:12. Ph 3:6. Col +*1:10. T 2:11-14. 1 J 2:3, 29. 3:7. **blame-**

less. Jn +*17:6. Ph *2:15. 3:6. Col 1:22. 1 Th 2:10. 3:13. *5:23. 2 P √3:14.

7. **they had.** Ge 15:2, 3. 16:1, 2. 25:21. 30:1, 2. Jg 13:2, 3. 1 S 1:2, 5-8. **no child.** Ge +*11:30. **barren.** ver. 36. Ge +*11:30. **well stricken.** ver. 18. Lk 2:36. Ge 17:17. *18:11. 1 K 1:1. 2 K 4:14-16. Ro 4:19, 20. He 11:11, 12.

8. **he executed.** Ex 28:1, 41. 29:1, 9, 44. 30:30. Nu 18:7. 1 Ch 24:2, 19. 2 Ch 11:14. **in.** ver. 5. 1 Ch 24:19. 2 Ch 8:14. *31:2, 19. Ezr 6:18.

9. **his lot.** Ex *30:7, 8. 37:25-29. Nu 16:40. 1 S 2:28. 1 Ch 6:49. 23:13. 2 Ch 26:16-18. 29:11. He *9:6, 7. **burn incense.** Ex 30:1-6. **the temple.** ver. 21, 22. Lk 11:51. Mt 23:16, 35. 27:5, 40, 51. He 9:2, 3. Re 11:2, 19.

10. **praying without.** Le *16:17. Ps *141:2. He 4:14-16. 9:24. Re *8:3, 4. **incense.** T#1256. Nu 16:44-46. Ps 141:2. Re 5:8. *8:3, 4.

11. **appeared.** ver. 19, 28. Lk 2:9, 10. Jg *13:3, 9. Ac 5:19. *10:3, 4. He *1:14. **right side.** Ac 7:55, 56. **altar of incense.** Ex 30:1-6, 10. 37:25-29. 39:38. 40:5, 26, 27. Le 4:3, 7, 13, 18. 16:13, 18. Nu 4:11. 1 S 2:28. 1 K 6:20, 22. 1 Ch 6:4, 9. 28:18. 2 Ch 4:19. 13:11. 26:16. 29:18. Ps 141:2. Is 6:6. Ml 1:11. Re 5:8. 6:9. *8:3, 4. 9:13. 11:1. 14:18. 16:7.

12. **he was troubled.** ver. 29. Lk 2:9, 10. 9:34. Jg *6:22. +*13:22. Jb 4:14, 15. Da *10:7, 8, 17. Mk 16:5. Ac 10:4. 19:17. Re *1:17. **fear.** Ge +*19:30.

13. **the angel.** ver. 11. **Fear not.** ver. 30. Lk 2:10. 5:10. 8:50. 12:7, 32. 24:36-40. Ge 15:1. +*19:30. Jsh 8:1. Jg *6:23. Is 43:1, 5. 44:2. Je 46:27, 28. Da *10:12. Mt 28:5. Mk *16:6. **thy prayer.** T#1445. Ge 15:2-5. *25:20, 21. *30:22, 23. 1 S *1:9-11, 20-23. Ps 118:21. Ac +*10:4, 31. **and thy.** Ge 17:10. *18:14. Jg 13:3-5. 1 S 2:21. 2 K 4:16, 17. Ps +*113:9. +*127:3-5. **thou.** ver. 60-63. Lk *2:21. Ge 17:19. Is 8:3. Ho 1:4, 6, 9, 10. Mt *1:21. **name.** √144A4, Ge +4:26. **John.** i.e. *grace; dove,* ✻S#2491g. Lk 1:13, 60, 63. 3:2, 15, 16, 20. 5:33. 7:18, 19, 20, 22, 24, 24, 28, 29, 33. 9:7, 9, 19. 11:1. 16:16. 20:4, 6. Mt 3:1, 4, 13, 14. 4:12. 9:14. 11:2, 4, 7, 11, 12, 13, 18. 14:2, 3, 4, 8, 10. 16:14. 17:13. 21:25, 26, 32. Mk 1:4, 6, 9, 14. 2:18, 18. 6:14, 16, 17, 18, 20, 24, 25. 8:28. 11:30, 32. Jn 1:6, 15, 19, 26, 28, 29, 32, 35, 40. 3:23, 24, 25, 27. 4:1. 5:33, 36. 10:40, 41, 41. Ac 1:5, 22. 10:37. 11:16. 13:24, 25. 18:25. 19:3, 4. (1) A relation of Annas the high priest, Ac 4:6. (2) The Hebrew name of the evangelist Mark, Ac 12:25; 13:5, 13; 15:37. (3) John the Baptist, Mt 3:1. (4) John the apostle and evangelist, Mt 4:21. 10:2. 17:1. Mk 1:19, 29. 3:17. 5:37. 9:2, 38. 10:35, 41. 13:3. 14:33. Lk 5:10. 6:14. 8:51. 9:28, 49, 54. 22:8. Ac 1:13. 3:1, 3, 4, 11. 4:13, 19. 8:14. 12:2, 12. Ga 2:9. Re 1:1, 4, 9. 21:2. 22:8. Compare Johanan, 2 K +25:23.

14. **have joy.** ver. 58. Ge *21:6, 7. Pr 15:20. 23:15, 16, *24, 25.

15. **he shall.** ver. 32. Je 1:5. Ga 1:15. **great.** Lk *7:28. Ge 12:2. 48:19. Jsh 3:7. 4:14. 1 Ch *17:8. *29:12. Mt *11:9-19. Jn *5:35. **shall drink neither.** √158, Mt +5:18. Lk *7:33. Nu *6:2-4. Jg *13:4-7, 14. Mt 11:18. Ep +*5:18. **filled.** ver. 41, 67. Zc 9:15. Ac *2:4, 14-18. *11:24. Ep √5:18. **Ghost.** Gr. *pneuma,* Mt +1:18n.

even. Ps 22:9. Is 49:1, 5. Je *1:5. Ga 1:15.

16. **many**. ✓92G, Lk +4:18. ver. *76. Is *40:3-5. 49:6. Da +*12:3. Ml *3:1. Mt *3:1-6. *21:32. **children of Israel**. Ac 5:21.

17. **go before**. ver. 16, 76. Is *40:3-5. Ml *3:1. Jn 1:13, 23-30, 34. 3:28. **in the**. Ml *4:5, 6. Mt ✓11:14n. 17:11, 12. Mk 9:11-13. Jn 1:21-24. Re 20:4. **spirit**. ✓121A3, Nu +11:17. Gr. *pneuma*, ✓121A1. Metonymy of the Cause: where the cause is put for the effect, the person for the action. Here, the Spirit is put for the gifts and operations produced by the Spirit, the special divine endowment of mighty spiritual power from on high by the operation of the Holy Spirit of God. Lk 4:18. Mt 12:18. Jn 3:5, 6b. 4:23, 24b. 7:39. Ac 2:17, 18. 5:32. 6:10. 10:44, 47. 11:15. 15:8. 1 C 2:4. 7:40. 12:13b. 14:2, 12, 32. 2 C 1:22. 3:3. 4:13. 5:5. Ga 5:5. Ep 1:13, 17. Ph 1:19. 1 Th 4:8. 5:19. 1 J 4:13. Re 22:6. For the other uses of *pneuma* see Mt +*8:16n. For additional instances of the figure ✓121A1, see Jn +3:34. **and**. ✓93A, Ge +1:26. By Hendiadys, *powerful spirit*. **power**. 1 K 17:1. *18:18, 21. *21:20. 2 K 1:4-6, 16, Elijah. Mt 3:4, 7-12. *11:14n. 14:4. 17:11. **turn**. Lk 3:7-14. Is 63:16. Ml *✝4:6. **and the**. ✓66I2, Jsh +3:3. Supply by ellipsis (of repetition: from succeeding clause), "and the (hearts of the) disobedient." **disobedient**. Is 29:24. Mt 21:29-32. Ro *10:21. 1 C +*6:9-11. **to**. *or*, by. **the wisdom**. Pr *4:7. Da +*11:33n. +*12:3. Ho +*14:9. Ep 1:8. 2 T ✓3:15. Ja 3:17. **of the just**. Ge 6:9. Ps 111:10. Jn 1:29. Ac *3:14. Col 2:3. **to make**. ✓41, Ge +10:1. Lk 7:27. 1 S 7:5. 1 Ch 29:18. 2 Ch 29:36. Ps 10:17. 78:8. 111:10. Am *4:12. Ml 3:1. Mt 11:10. Mk 1:2. Jn *1:29. Ac 10:33. Ro 9:23. Col 1:12. 2 T 2:21. 1 P *9:2. 2 P 3:11-14. 1 J 2:28. **prepared**. Lk 2:31. 2 Ch 29:36.

18. **the angel**. ver. 11. **Whereby**. ver. *34. Ge *15:8. *17:17. *18:12. Jg *6:17, 36-40. 2 K 20:8. Is *38:22. **for**. ver. *7. Nu 11:21-23. 2 K *7:2. Ro *4:17, 19-21. T 2:2.

19. **I am**. ver. 26. Da *8:16. *9:21-23. Mt 18:10. He *1:14. **Gabriel**. i.e. *strength of God*, *S#1043g. Lk 1:19, 26. For *S#1403h, see Da +8:16. **that stand**. 1 K 17:1. 18:15. 2 K 3:14. 5:16. Est 1:14. Jb 1:6. Is 63:9. Mt 18:10. **and to**. Lk 2:10.

20. **thou shalt**. ver. 22, 62, 63. Ex 4:11. Ezk 3:26. 24:27. **dumb**. *Siopon*, "silent;" for in this case, though there was no natural imperfection or debility of the organs of speech, as in *dumbness*, yet *thou shalt not be able to speak*. This was at once a proof of the severity and mercy of God: of severity, in condemning him to nine months' silence for his unbelief; of mercy, in rendering his punishment temporary, and the means of making others rejoice in the events predicted. **because**. ver. 45. Ge *18:10-15. Nu 20:12. 2 K 7:2, 19, 20. Is 7:9. Mk 9:19. 16:14. Re 3:19. **which**. Ro 3:3. 2 T 2:13. T *1:2. He *6:18.

21. **waited**. ver. 10. Nu 6:23-27. **the temple**. ver. 9.

22. **perceived**. Gr. *epiginosko*, Mt +11:27. **he beckoned**. ver. 62. Jn 13:24. Ac 12:17. 19:33. 21:40.

23. **came to pass**. ✓144A11, Ge +38:1. **the days**. ver. 8. 2 K 11:5-7. 1 Ch 9:25. 2 Ch 23:8. **ministration**. Ac 13:2. Ph 2:17. He 1:7. 8:6. 9:21. 10:11.

25. **hath**. ver. 13. Ge 21:1, 2. 25:21. 30:22. 1 S 1:19, 20. 2:21, 22. He 11:11. **to take**. Ge *30:23. 1 S 1:6. Ps +*113:9. Is 4:1. 54:1-4.

26. **the sixth**. ver. 24. **the angel**. ver. 19. **a city**.

Lk 2:4. Mt 2:23. Jn 1:45, 46. 7:41, 42.

27. **a virgin**. Lk 2:4, 5. Ge +*3:15. Is +*7:14. Je 31:22. Mt *1:16, 18, 21, 23. **Joseph**. Lk 2:4, 16. 3:23. 4:22. Mt ch. 1, 2. 13:55. Jn 1:45. 6:42. **house of David**. Lk 2:4. Mt 1:16, 20. **Mary**. Mt +*1:16.

28. **Hail**. Da 9:21-23. 10:19. **highly favored**. *or*, graciously accepted, *or* much graced. ver. 30. Ps 45:2. Da 9:23. Ho 14:2. Ep 1:6. **the Lord**. Jg *6:12. Is 43:5. Je 1:8, 19. Ac 18:10. **blessed**. ver. 42. Lk 11:27, 28. Jg *5:24. Pr 31:29-31. Mt 12:48-50.

29. **she was**. ver. 12. Mk 6:49, 50. 16:5, 6. Ac 10:4. **and cast**. ver. 66. Lk 2:19, 51. **what**. Jg 6:13-15. 1 S 9:20, 21. Ac 10:4, 17.

30. **Fear not**. ver. 13. Lk 12:32. Is 41:10, 14. 43:1-4. 44:2. Mt 28:5. Ac 18:9, 10. 27:24. Ro +*8:31, 32. He *13:6. **found favor**. ✓171J4, Ge +6:8. Ge 6:8. Ac 7:46. He 4:16.

31. **And**. ✓148, Ge +8:22. **thou**. ver. 27. Is +*7:14. Mt +*1:23. Ga ✓4:4. **and shalt**. ver. 13. Lk *2:21. Mt *1:21, 25. 1 T *3:16.

32. **shall be great**. ver. 15. Lk 3:16. Mi *5:4. Mt 3:11. 12:42. Ph *2:9-11. **and**. ✓148, Ge +8:22. **shall be called**. Mt 16:16. 27:54. Jn 1:34. **the Son**. ✓171G, Ge +13:8. ver. 35. Mt 14:33. Mk 5:7. 14:16. Jn 6:69. Ac 16:17. Ro *1:4. He 1:2-8. **the Highest**. ver. 35, 76. Lk 6:35. Mk 5:7. Ac 7:48. **shall give**. ver. 69. Lk ✓19:12, 15. 2 S *7:11-13, 16. Ps 89:4. +*132:11. Is +*9:6, 7. *11:1, 10. *16:5. Je +*23:5, 6. +*30:9. 33:15-17. Ezk 17:22-24. *34:23, 24. +*37:24, 25. Da ✓7:14. Ho +*3:5. Am +*9:11-15. Mt 28:18. Jn ✓3:35, 36. *5:21-29. 12:34. Ac 2:30, 36. 15:16. Ep *1:20-23. He *1:1-8. Re 3:7. **the throne**. Ac +*2:30. He ●10:12, 13. Re +*3:21. **David**. Is +*55:3. Mt 1:1. Ac +*13:23. Re *22:16.

33. **he shall reign**. Ps *45:6. *89:35-37. Is +*24:23. Da *2:44. *7:13, 14, 27. Ob +*21. Mi *4:7. 1 C *15:24, 25. He +*1:8. Re *11:15. *20:4-6. *22:3-5. **the house**. Ps 118:26. Mt ●23:37, 38. Lk ●13:35. Jn ●1:11, 12. Ro 9:6. Ga 3:29. 6:16. Ph 3:3. **of Jacob**. Lk 3:23, *34. Le *26:42, 44. Nu +✝24:17. Dt *32:9. Ps 59:13. ✓135:4, 12, 21. Is *49:5, 6. 62:1, 2. Ezk *34:11-13. Ob +*17. Zc *2:12. Mt 1:2. Ac ●2:36. **for ever**. Gr. *aion*, Mt +6:13. Ge +*9:12. 2 S *7:16. Is *9:7. Da +*7:14. Ep 2:7. 3:21. He 1:8. 2 P 1:11. Re ✓11:15. **of his kingdom**. Da *2:44. *7:14, 18, 27. Mi 4:7. Jn 12:34. 1 C ●✓15:24-28. 2 T +*4:1n. He +*1:8. Re *11:15. **no end**. T#91. Ps +*45:6, 7. *145:13. Da ✓7:14. Mi ✓4:7. 1 C ●✓15:25n. 1 T 1:17. 2 T +*4:18n. He 12:28. 1 P 4:11. 2 P *1:11. Re 1:6. ✓11:15. 22:3, 5.

34. **How shall**. Jg 13:8-12. Ac 9:6. **know not**. Ge 19:8. Nu 31:17. Jg 11:39.

35. **The Holy**. ver. 27, 31. Mt *1:20. **Ghost**. Gr. *pneuma*, Mt +1:18n. **the power**. Lk 5:17. **the Highest**. ✓121K6. Metonymy of the Subject B583. God is put for the power manifested by Him. ver. 32. **overshadow**. ✓22L8, Ps +121:5. 1 K 8:12. **that**. ✓96G4, Mt +1:20. **holy thing**. Jb 14:4. 15:16. 25:4. Ps ●51:5. ●58:3. Mk 1:12, 13. +12:15. *15:23. Jn *8:46. *14:30. Ac 3:14. Ro *1:3, 4. 5:12. 10:5. 2 C ✓5:21. Ep 2:3. He 2:17, 18. +*4:15. *7:26-28. Ja *1:17. 1 P *2:22. 1 J 1:5. 2:16. 3:5. **the Son of God**. T#71. ver. 32. Lk *4:34. Ps *2:7. Mt +*14:33. ●*26:63, 64. +*27:54n. Mk *1:1, 24. Jn *1:14, 18, 34, 49. 6:69. ✓20:31. Ac *8:37n. Ro *1:3, 4. Ga *2:20. He 1:5, 6.

36. **thy cousin**. ver. 24-26. **conceived**. Ge +*29:31. **barren**. ver. 7. Ge +*11:30.

37. **with**. Lk *18:27. Ge *18:14. Nu *11:23. Jb +*42:2. Je *32:17, 27. Zc 8:6. Mt *19:26. Mk *10:27. Ro *4:20, 21. Ph *3:21. **nothing**. ⨍108E3, Ps +103:2. ⨍46C, Mt 8:6. Here, Gr. *rheema*, "word" or "saying," is used for "thing," the Hebrew *davar* having both meanings.

38. **Behold**. 2 S 7:25-29. Ps 116:16. Ro 4:20, 21. **be**. 1 S *3:18. Ps 119:38. **angel departed**. Jg 6:21. Ac 12:10.

39. **into**. ver. 65. Jsh 10:40. 15:48-59. 20:7. 21:9-11. **city**. This was most probably *Hebron*, a city of the priests, and situated in the hill country of Judea (Jsh 11:21. 21:11, 13), about 25 miles south of Jerusalem, and nearly 100 from Nazareth. Such was the intense desire of Mary's mind to visit and communicate with her relative Elizabeth, that she scrupled not to undertake this long journey to effect her purpose.

41. **came to pass**. ⨍144A11, Ge +38:1. **the babe**. ver. 15, 44. Ge 25:22. Ps 22:10. **filled**. ver. 15, 67. Lk 4:1. Ac 2:4. 4:8. 6:3. 7:55. Ep *5:18. Re 1:10. **Ghost**. Gr. *pneuma*, Mt +1:18n.

42. **Blessed art**. ver. 28, 48. Lk +*11:28. Jg 5:24. **among**. ⨍108C1, Pr +30:30. **blessed is**. Lk 19:38. Ge *22:18. Dt 28:4. Ps 21:6. *45:2. 72:17-19. Ac 2:26-28. Ro *9:5. He *12:2. **the fruit**. Ge 30:2. Ps +*127:3. La 2:20.

43. **whence**. Lk 7:7. Ru 2:10. 1 S 25:41. Mt 3:14. Jn 13:5-8. Ph +*2:3. **my Lord**. Lk 2:11. 20:42-44. Ps 110:1. Jn *13:13. +*20:28. Ph *3:8.

44. **the babe**. ver. 41. **leaped**. ver. 41. Lk 6:23. **for joy**. Scripture says much that bears upon the issue of abortion. (1) Note that Scripture here attributes emotion to an unborn child. (2) The fetus is formed by God, Jb 31:15mg. Je 1:5. (3) God planned the life before it took form, Je 1:5. (4) God delivers new life from the womb, Ps 71:6. Ga 1:15, 16. (5) Note the despondent wish for spontaneous abortion during a period of depression, Je 20:17. (6) An untimely birth preferable to living and dying in disrepute, Ec 6:3. (7) The majesty and marvel of life, Ps 139:14-16. (8) Life is sacred and precious, Ge 9:6. (9) Jesus warned not to offend one of these little ones, Mt 18:6. (10) Christ's concern and care seen in his blessing little ones, Lk 18:15-17. (11) Children are given by God, Ge 33:5. 48:9. Jsh 24:3. Ps +*113:9. +*127:3. Is 8:18. (12) Christ esteemed children highly, Mt 19:14. (13) Maternal love is normal, Ge 21:16. Ex 2:3. Logically, abortion does violence to maternal love. (14) If a woman injures a man's secret parts, her hand was to be cut off, Dt 25:11. If a man injured a pregnant woman, and (a) caused premature birth, but infant and mother otherwise were uninjured, he shall be punished by fine, Ex 21:22; (b) if the mother or child are injured or die, a corresponding severity of punishment, including the death penalty, was prescribed, Ex 21:23-25. Thus abortion, even accidentally induced, required the death penalty. (15) The supreme value of the individual utterly argues against any possible contrary justification for an abortion, Mt 10:31. 16:26. Mk 8:36, 37. Lk 12:7. (16) If God was utterly opposed to, and displeased with the religious sacrifice of children to Molech (2 K +21:6), the burning of which had never been commanded, authorized, or even entered into God's mind (Je 7:31), how much more must God be displeased with the destruction of the helpless unborn in the name of granting women the right to choice

over their own bodies. (17) God sets great value on a child. Our response to a child is our response to God, Mt 18:1-6. Ja 1:27. (18) Conception, development in the womb, and birth are mentioned together at Ho 9:11. God has his hand in each of these stages of development, as the references show. Thus, it is unscriptural to suggest that the unborn child is not yet a person. (19) The unborn child responds to external stimuli, can hear, for the "babe leaped in her womb," Lk 1:41, 44. (20) Abortion constitutes injustice to the weak and helpless, and places one under God's curse, not his blessing, Dt 27:17, 19. (21) We are not to despise one of these little ones, Mt 18:10. (22) The virgin birth and incarnation began at the moment of the miraculous conception by the Holy Spirit in Mary's womb, Lk 1:35. Is 49:1. (23) The fact that the word "abortion" does not occur in the Bible (but see Jb 3:16) has no bearing upon the issue. "Cannabalism" is not mentioned by that term in the Bible either, and so for a host of other concepts such as millennium, rapture, trinity, infant baptism, believer's baptism, using musical instruments in New Testament worship. There is no express command or example for New Testament believers to tithe. There is no express command to worship God on Sunday, or to observe Sunday as the Sabbath. There is no express command or example in the New Testament of the baptism of adult believers that come from Christian homes. There appears to be no express command or incontrovertible example of the precise mode (i.e. immersion, pouring, or sprinkling) of Christian baptism in the New Testament. Neither is there command or example authorizing women to receive the sacrament of the Lord's supper. There is no express example or command authorizing the taking of the Lord's *supper* in the morning! The virgin birth is not mentioned in the Gospel of Mark. Repentance is not mentioned in the Gospel of John. The Gospel of John says nothing about Christ having cast out devils. We must use extreme caution whenever we base an argument on the alleged silence of Scripture (see 1 Ch 16:42n). Though abortion is not mentioned by name in Scripture, a prayerful and submissive, careful examination of the passages adduced above should lead to the firm conviction that abortion is not in harmony with the will of God at any time, for any reason. Yet, should a woman seek and obtain an abortion, this does not constitute the committing of the unforgivable sin (Mt 12:31n). God in his mercy is able to forgive even this sin, and welcome the truly repentant sinner to his fold (Jn 6:37. 2 C 7:10).

45. **blessed**. ver. *20, 48. Lk 11:27, *28. 1 Ch +*20:20. Jn *11:40. √20:29n. **that believed: for there**. **or**, which believed that there, etc. Ac 27:25.

46. **My soul**. Gr. *psyche*, ⨍121A9A, Mt +11:29. ⨍132A, Ge +4:23. ⨍121A8, Ps +16:10. Ge +41:8. 1 S *2:1. Ps *34:2, 3. 35:9. *103:1, 2. Is 24:15, 16. 45:25. 61:10. Hab *3:17, 18. Mk 12:30. Ro 5:11. 1 C *1:31. 2 C 2:14. Ph *3:3. 4:4. He 6:19. Ja 1:21. 1 P *1:8. **magnify**. Ps *34:3. *69:30. Ac 10:46.

47. **spirit**. Gr. *pneuma*, ⨍171Q1B, Mk +2:8n. **rejoiced**. ⨍96C4, Mt +3:17. 1 S *2:1. Ps 35:9. Is 61:10. Hab *3:18. Ac 16:34. **God**. Lk *2:11. Ps *14:7. 106:21. Is +*12:2, 3. *25:9. *43:11. *45:21, 22. Zp 3:14-17. Zc *9:9. 1 T *1:1. 2:3. 4:10. 2 T +*1:9. T 1:3. *2:10, √13. *3:4-6. Ju 25.

48. **regarded**. Lk 9:38. 1 S 1:11. 2:8. 2 S 7:8, 18,

19. 16:12. Ps 25:18. *102:17. 113:7, 8. 136:23. *138:6. Is *66:2. 1 C *1:26-28. Ja *2:5, 6. **of his.** ‍✎29, Ex +19:6. i.e. humiliated handmaiden. **all generations.** ver. 28, 42, 45. Lk *11:27. Ge 30:13. Ps 72:17. Ml 3:12.

49. **he.** Ge *17:1. Ps 24:8. *89:8, 19. Is 1:24. 63:1. Je 10:6. 20:11. Zp 3:17. **hath.** Ps 71:19-21. *126:2, 3. Mk 5:19. Ep *3:20. **and holy.** Ex *15:11. Dt 28:58. 1 S 2:2. Ps 99:3, 9. *111:9. Is *6:3. +*57:15. Mt +*6:9. Re 4:8. *15:4.

50. **his mercy.** Ge +*17:7. Ex +*20:6. +*34:6, 7. Dt 5:10. *7:9. Ps 31:19. *33:18. *85:9. 89:1, 2. *100:5. *103:11, 17, 18. 115:13. 118:4. 145:19. *147:11. Ml +*3:16-18. Re 19:5. **that fear him.** Jb +*28:28. Ro *11:22. 1 P *1:17.

51. **showed.** Ex 15:6, 7, 12, 13. Dt 4:34. Ps 63:5. *89:10, 13. *98:1. 118:15, 16. Is *40:10. 51:9. *52:10. 63:12. Re 18:8. **arm.** ‍✎22A12, Ex +15:16. **he hath scattered.** Ge +*10:32. *11:8. Ex 15:9-11. 18:11. 1 S *2:3, 4, 9, 10. Jb 40:9-12. Ps *2:1-6. *33:10. 89:10. Is *8:10. 10:12-19. Je 48:29, 30. Da *4:37. 5:22-28. Ja 4:6, 10. 1 P *5:5. **the proud.** Ps +*119:21. Mk 7:22. Ro 1:30. 2 T 3:2. Ja 4:6. 1 P *5:5. **the imagination.** Ge *6:5. *8:21. Dt *29:19, 20. Jb *5:12. Ro *1:21. 2 C √10:5.

52. **He hath.** ‍✎138B, Ge +13:16. Rather, "He hath taken away (or snatched, *katheile*) the mighty from their throne;" which is well expressed by Seneca (Hercul. Oetaeus, p. 301), "Who bestoweth kingdoms on the wretched, and plucketh them away from the noble" or exalted. **put down.** Lk 14:11. *18:14. 1 S *2:4, 6-8. Jb 5:11-13. 12:19. 34:24-28. Ps 75:7. 107:40, 41. *113:6-8. 147:6. Ec 4:14. Ezk 17:14, 24. 21:26. Da *4:30. Am 9:11. Mk +*6:3. Ja *1:9, 10. *4:10. **the mighty.** Ac 8:27g. **and exalted.** Lk 6:25. 16:25. Ge 45:26. Ps 78:70, 71. Am 5:9. Mk 10:31. **low degree.** Mt +*5:3-5. 1 C *1:26-29. Ph +*2:3. Ja +*2:5. 1 P *5:6.

53. **He hath.** ‍✎138B, Ge +13:16. **filled.** Lk *6:21. 1 S *2:5. Ps *34:10. *107:8, 9. 146:7. Is 25:6. *65:13, 14. Je 31:25. Ezk *34:29. Mt +*5:6. Jn *6:11-13, 35. Ja *2:5. Re *7:16, 17. **the rich.** Lk 6:24. 12:16-21. *16:19-25. *18:11-14, 24, 25. 1 C 1:26. 4:8. Ja 2:6. *5:1-6. Re 3:17, 18. **sent empty.** Lk *6:24. 18:10-14. 20:11. Jb 22:9. Mt +*6:5.

54. **He hath.** ver. 70-75. Ps *98:3. Is +√41:8, 9. *44:21. 46:3, 4. 49:14-16. +√54:6-10. 63:7-16. Je *31:3, 20. +√33:24-26. Mi *7:20. Zp 3:14-20. Zc 9:9-11. Ro *11:26-29. He 2:16. **servant Israel.** Is *41:8, 9. 42:1. 44:1, 2, 21. 45:4. 49:3. **remembrance.** ver. 72, 73. Ps 98:3. Mi *7:20. **his mercy.** Zc √10:6.

55. **he spake.** Ge +*12:3. *17:19. +*22:18. 26:4. 28:14. Ps 105:6-10. 132:11-17. Ro *11:28, 29. Ga *3:16, 17, 29. **to Abraham.** ‍✎29, Ex +19:6. Here, *the fathers* is in the Accusative because more general; while Abraham, etc., is in the Dative, because more personal. **his seed.** Ge 17:7. 18:18. 22:17. **for ever.** Gr. *aion.* Ge 9:12. Mt +6:13.

57. **full time.** ver. 13. Lk 2:6, 7. Ge 21:2, 3. Nu 23:19.

58. **her neighbors.** ver. 25. Ru 4:14-17. Ps +*113:9. **showed great mercy.** Ge 19:19. **they rejoiced.** ver. 14. Ge 21:6. Is 66:9, 10. Ro *12:15. 1 C 12:26.

59. **eighth day.** Lk 2:21. Ge *17:12. 21:3, 4. Le *12:3. Ac 7:8. Ph 3:5.

60. **Not.** ver. 13, 63. 2 S 12:25. Is 8:3. Mt 1:25.

62. **made signs.** ver. 22. **how he.** ‍✎184D2. Hypothetical Propositions; or, Conditional ("if") Sentences: Fourth Condition; or, mere assumption with remote idea of realization, involving the apodosis ("then" clause, or conclusion). For other instances of this construction see Lk 6:11. 9:46. 18:36. Ac 5:24. *8:31. 10:17. 17:18. 26:29.

63. **writing table.** Pr 3:3. Is 8:1. 30:8. Je 17:1. Hab 2:2. **His name.** ver. 13, 60.

64. **his mouth.** ver. 20. Ex 4:15, 16. Ps 51:15. Je 1:9. Ezk 3:27. 29:21. 33:22. Mt 9:33. Mk 7:32-37. **opened.** ‍✎108H6A, Jg +11:35. **and he.** Ps 30:7-12. 118:18, 19. Is 12:1. Da 4:34-37. **spake.** ‍✎180B, Mk +13:26. **and praised.** Lk 2:28. 24:53.

65. **fear.** Lk 5:26. 7:16. Ac 2:43. 5:5, 11. 19:17. Re 11:11. **sayings.** *or,* things. **hill country.** ver. 39. Jsh 10:6, 40.

66. **laid.** Lk 2:19, 51. 9:44. Ge 37:11. Ps 119:11. **And the.** ver. 80. Lk 2:40. Ge *39:2. Jg 13:24, 25. 1 S 2:18. 16:18. 1 K 18:46. Ps *80:17. 89:21. Ac 4:28, 30. 11:21. 13:11.

67. **filled.** ver. 15, 41. Nu 11:25. 2 S 23:2. Jl *2:28. 2 P *1:21. **Ghost.** Gr. *pneuma.* Mt +1:18n.

68. **Blessed.** Ge 9:26. 14:20. 1 K 1:48. 8:15. 1 Ch 29:10, 20. Ezr 7:27. Ps 41:13. 72:17-19. 89:52. 106:48. 150:6. Ep 1:3. 1 P 1:3. **God of Israel.** Mt 15:31. he. Lk 7:16. 19:44. Ex 3:16, 17. 4:31. Ps 111:9. Ep *1:7. **visited.** Lk 7:16. 19:44. Ex 4:31. Ps 8:4. Ac 15:14. He 2:6. **and redeemed.** ver. 71. Lk 2:38. 21:28. 24:21. Ps 19:14. 111:9. 130:7, 8. Is 43:1. 59:20. Ac 7:35. Ro 3:24. He 9:12.

69. **raised up.** Jg 3:9, 15. **an horn.** 1 S *2:10. 2 S 22:3. Ps 18:2. *132:17, 18. Ezk *29:21. **in the house.** 2 S 7:26. 1 K 11:13. Ps 89:3, 20, etc. Is +*9:6, 7. *11:1-9. Je +*23:5, 6. 33:15-26. Ezk 34:23, 24. 37:24, 25. Am *9:11. Mk 11:10. Ro 1:2, 3. Re 22:16. **David.** ver. 32. Ac +*13:23.

70. **spake.** 2 S 23:2. Je +*23:5, 6. 30:10. Mk 12:36. Ac 28:25. Ro 1:2. He *1:1. 3:7. 2 P √1:21. Re 19:10. **which.** Lk *24:26, 27, 44. Ge +*3:15. +*12:3. +*49:10. Da +*9:24-27. Ac 3:21-24. 1 P 1:12. 2 P 3:2. **world.** Gr. *aion.* Mt +6:13. lit. "from the age", as in Jn 9:32. Ac 3:21. 15:18. Col 1:26.

71. **we.** ver. 74. Ex 18:10. Dt *33:29. Ps 18:17. 106:10, 47. Is *14:1-3. 44:24-26. √51:22, 23. 54:7-17. +*59:19, 20. Je 23:6. 30:9-11. 32:37. Ezk 28:26. 34:25, 28. +*38:8n. Jl *2:20. Zp *3:15-20. Zc 9:9, 10, 14. +*12:8. Ac +√3:19-21. Ro +*11:26. 1 J *3:8. **hand.** ‍✎144A5, Ge +9:5.

72. **perform.** ver. 54, 55. Ge +*12:3. *17:7. +*22:18. 26:4. 28:14. Ps *98:3. Ezk *16:60. Mi *7:20. Ac *3:25, 26. Ro 11:28. He 6:13-18. **the mercy.** Dt +*32:43. Is 49:10. +√55:3. Mi *7:20. **and.** ver. 54, 55. Ge 17:4-9. Le *26:42, 44. Ps *105:8-10. 106:45. 111:5. Ezk 16:8, 60. Ga 3:15-17. **covenant.** Le *26:42, 44. Mi *7:20. Ro 9:4. √15:8.

73. **The oath.** Ge +*12:3. *17:4. +*22:16, 17. 24:7. 26:3. Ex *2:24. Dt 7:8, 12. Ps 105:9. Je 11:5. He *6:14, 16, 17. **father.** ‍✎171G, Ge +13:8.

74. **that we.** ver. 71. Is 35:9, 10. 45:17. 54:13, 14. 65:21-25. Ezk 34:25-28. +*39:28, 29. Jl +*3:17. Zp *3:15-17. Zc *9:8-10. Ml 4:1-3. Ro *5:1. *6:18, 22. *8:15. 2 T +*1:7. He *2:15. *9:14. Re 2:10. **might serve.** Dt 28:47. Ne 8:10. Ps 100:2. **without fear.** T#1493. Jb 9:34, 35. Ps +*34:4. 64:1. Zp 3:15.

75. **In holiness.** Dt 6:2. Ps 105:44, 45. Je 31:33,

34. +*32:39, 40. Ezk 36:24-27. Mt 1:21. Ro √12:1, 2. 2 C *7:1. Ep *1:4. √2:10. *4:24. Ph *1:10, 11, 27. √4:8. Col +*1:10. 1 Th 2:10. *4:1-3, 7. 2 Th *2:13. 2 T +*1:9. T 1:8. *2:11-14. *3:8. He √12:14. 1 P *1:14-16. *2:24. 2 P √1:4-8. 1 J √2:6, 15-17. *3:3, 6, 7. **before him.** Nu=8:22. Ac *24:16. **all the days.** Je 32:39. Mt 28:20.

76. **shalt be.** Lk 7:26, 28. 20:6. Mt 11:9. 14:5. 21:26. Mk 11:32. **Highest.** ver. 32, 35. Lk 6:35. 8:28. Ps +78:17, 35, 56. +83:18. 87:5. Da 7:18. Mk 5:7. Ac 7:48. 16:17. Ro *9:5. 1 C 10:5. 1 Th 3:13. **thou shalt.** ver. 16, 17. Lk 3:4-6. 7:27. Dt 31:3. Is *40:3-5. Ml *3:1. *4:5. Mt 3:3, 11. *11:10. Mk 1:2, 3. Jn 1:23, 27. 3:28. Ac 13:24, 25. **the Lord.** Jn *10:30. 1 C √2:8. +*12:3. Ph *2:11. **his ways.** Lk 20:21.

77. **give.** Lk *3:3, 6. Je *31:34. Mk 1:3, 4. Jn 1:7-9, 15-17, 29, 34. 3:27-36. Ac 19:4. **knowledge.** ƒ121C2A3, Is +53:11. **by.** *or,* for. **the remission.** Lk 7:47-50. Mk 1:4. Ac +*2:38. +*3:19. *5:31. *10:43. *13:38, 39. Ro *3:25. *4:6-8. Ep *1:7.

78. **tender.** *or,* bowels of the. ƒ22A18, Is +63:15. Ps 25:6mg. Is 63:7, 15. Jn √3:16. Ep 2:4, 5. Ph 1:8. 2:1. Col 3:12. 1 J *3:17. *4:9, 10. **dayspring.** *or,* sunrising, *or* branch. ƒ121N1, Ge +31:54. Nu *24:17. Is *11:1. 60:1. Zc 3:8. 6:12. Ml *4:2. Ep 5:14. 2 P *1:19. Re 22:16. **from on high.** Lk 24:49. Is 32:15. **hath visited.** ver. 68.

79. **give light.** Lk 2:32. Is *9:2. *42:7, 16. 49:6, 9. *60:1-3. Mt *4:16. Jn *1:4, 9. *8:12. 9:5. 12:46. Ac *26:18. 2 C *4:6. Ep *5:8, 14. 1 Th 5:4, 5. 1 J *1:5-7. **darkness.** Lk 5:31, 32. Is +9:2. Col *1:13. 1 P *2:9. **shadow of death.** Jb 3:5. 10:22. Ps *23:4. 44:19. 107:10, 14. Je 2:6. **to guide.** Ps 25:8-10, 12, 13. +*32:8. 85:10-13. Pr 3:17. 8:20. Is 48:17, 18, 22. 57:19-21. 59:8. Je 6:16. Mt √11:28, 29. Ro 3:17. 1 Th 3:11mg. 2 Th 3:5. **peace.** Lk 2:14. Ps *85:10. Is *32:17, 18. *54:13. *55:12. 59:8. Ac *10:36.

80. **the child.** ver. 15. Lk 2:40, 52. Jg 13:24, 25. 1 S 3:19, 20. **waxed strong.** Ep *3:16. **spirit.** Gr. *pneuma.* ƒ121A3, Mt +27:50. ƒ121A3, Nu +11:17. **and was.** Mt 3:1. 11:7. Mk 1:3, 4. **the deserts.** Lk 3:2. 5:16. **his showing.** Lk 10:1. Jn 1:31.

LUKE 2

Joseph and Mary go to Bethlehem, to be enrolled there, according to the decree of Augustus, 1-5. Jesus is there born and laid in a manger, 6, 7. An angel makes this known to shepherds; and the heavenly host praise God in their hearing, 8-14. The shepherds, finding it to be as the angel had said, report these transactions, and glorify God, 15-20. Jesus is circumcised, 21; and presented at the temple, with the accustomed sacrifice of the poor, for the purifying of Mary, 22-24. Simeon's prophecy concerning him, 25-35; and that of Anna, 36-38. He grows, and increases in wisdom, 39, 40. At twelve years of age he goes with his parents to Jerusalem, and hears and asks questions of the doctors in the temple, 41-50. He returns to Nazareth, and is subject to his parents, 51, 52.

1. **came to pass.** ƒ144A11, Ge +38:1. **in those days.** ver. 2, 7. Ge ❋49:10. Ml ❋3:1. **decree.** Ac 17:7. **Caesar.** Lk 3:1. 20:22. Ac 11:28. 25:11, 21. Ph 4:22. **Augustus.** i.e. *majestic,* ❋S#828g, only here. **all.** Mt *24:14. Mk *14:9. *16:15. Ac *11:28. *19:27. Ro 1:8. **all.** ƒ171A, Ex +9:6. **world.** lit. "habitable world." Gr. *oikoumene,*

Mt +24:14. ƒ171.O.2, Is +13:11. **taxed.** *or,* enrolled. Ac 5:37.

2. **taxing.** Ac 5:37. **Cyrenius.** i.e. *spearman, warrior,* ❋S#2958g, only here. **governor.** Lk 3:1. Ac *13:7. 18:12. 23:26. 26:30. **Syria.** Ac 15:23.

3. **all went.** ƒ171A, Ex +9:6. Ro *13:7. **every one.** ver. 4.

4. **Joseph.** Lk *1:26, 27. *3:23. **went up.** ver. 42. Lk 18:31. 19:28. Mt 20:17, 18. Mk 10:32, 33. 15:41. Jn 2:13. Ac 18:22. **from Galilee.** Lk 1:26. **city of Nazareth.** ver. 39, 51. Lk 4:16. Mt 2:23. Jn 1:46. **into Judea.** Lk 23:5. **unto.** ver. 11. Ge 35:19. 48:7. Ru 1:19. 2:4. 4:11, 17, 21, 22. 1 S 16:1, 4. *17:12, 58. 20:6. 2 S 5:7, 9. 1 Ch 11:5, 7. Mi +*5:2. Mt *2:1-6. Jn 7:42. **Bethlehem.** ver. 15. Mt 2:1. **he was.** Lk 1:27. *3:23-31. Mt *1:1-17, 20. **lineage.** Ac 3:25. Ep 3:15. **of David.** Ac +*13:23.

5. **taxed.** ƒ96A3. Heterosis of Voice B512: middle for passive. lit. to enroll himself. For another instance of this figure see 1 C 10:2. **Mary.** Dt *22:22-27. Mt *1:18, 19.

6. A.M. 4000. B.C. 4. **so.** ƒ144A11, Ge +38:1. Ps 33:11. Pr 19:21. Mi +*5:2. **while.** Mt 2:1. **the days.** Lk 1:57. Re 12:1-5.

7. **she.** Is +*7:14. Mt *1:25. Ga *4:4. **firstborn.** Mk +3:31n. +*6:3. Col +*1:15n. He 1:6. **and wrapped.** ver. 11, 12. Jb 38:9. Ps 22:6. Is *53:2, 3. Mt *8:20. +*13:55. Jn *1:14. 2 C √8:9. **manger.** ver. 16. **no room.** Jn ◐14:3. **the inn.** Lk 10:34. 22:11. Ge 42:27. 43:21. Ex 4:24. Mk 14:14.

8. **there were.** Ge 35:21. Mi 4:8. **abiding.** Ge 31:39, 40. Ex *3:1, 2. 1 S 17:34, 35. Ps *78:70, 71. Ezk 34:8. Jn *10:8-12. **watch over their flock by night.** *or,* the night watches.

9. **lo.** Lk 1:11, 28. Jg 6:11, 12. Mt *1:20. Ac 27:23. 1 T *3:16. **the angel.** Lk 1:11. Mt 28:2. Ac 5:19. **came upon.** or, stood by. ver. 38. Lk 20:1. 24:4. Ac 12:7. 23:11. **and the glory.** Lk 9:31, 32. Ex 16:7, 10. *24:16, 17. 40:34, 35. Le 9:6, 23. Nu 14:10. 16:19, 42. 20:6. 1 K 8:11. Is *6:3. 35:2. 40:5. 60:1. Ezk 3:23. Jn *12:41. Ac *7:55. 2 C *3:18. *4:6. Re 18:1. **and they.** Lk *1:12. Is *6:4, 5. Ac 22:6-9. 26:13, 14. He 12:21. Re 20:11.

10. **the angel.** Lk 24:4-7. **Fear not.** Lk *1:13, 30. Da 10:11, 12, 19. Mt 28:5. Re 1:17, 18. **I bring.** Lk 1:19. 8:1. Is *40:9. 41:27. *52:7. *61:1. Ac 13:32. Ro 10:15. **good tidings.** Ac 10:43. Ro 1:4. **great joy.** Lk 15:7. Ac 8:8. Ro *5:11. 1 P *1:8. **to all.** ver. 31, 32. Lk *24:47. Ge +*12:3. Ps 67:1, 2. 98:2, 3. Is 49:6. 52:10. Da +*9:26. Zc 9:9. Mt *28:18, 19. Mk 1:15. *16:15. Jn 11:50. Ro 15:9-12. Ep *3:8. Col *1:23.

11. **unto.** Lk 1:69. Is +*9:6. Mt *1:21. Ga *4:4, 5. 2 T 1:9, 10. T *2:10-14. *3:4-7. 1 J *4:14. **in the city.** See on ver. *4. Mt 1:21. **is born.** Mt 2:2. **city of.** ƒ142, Ge +20:16. **a Savior.** ƒ11, Ge +2:23. Mt 1:21. Jn 4:42. Ac 5:31. 13:23. Ph 3:20. 2 T 1:10. **which is.** ver. *26. Lk 1:43. 20:41, 42. Ge +*3:15. +*49:10. Ps *2:2. Da +*9:24-26. Mt 1:16. *16:16. Jn +*1:41, 45. *6:69. 7:25-27, 41. √20:31. Ac *2:36. *17:3. 1 J *5:1. **Christ.** Lk 3:15. 23:2. La 4:20. Mt 1:16. 16:16, 20. Jn 11:27. **the Lord.** Lk 1:43. *19:31. 20:42-44. Ac *2:36. 10:36. Ro *14:9. 1 C +*2:8. *8:6. *12:3. *15:47. 2 C *4:5. Ph *2:11. *3:8. Col *2:6. Re *19:16.

12. **a sign.** Ex 3:12. 1 S 2:34. 10:2-7. 2 K 19:29. 20:8, 9. Ps 22:6. Is +*7:11, 14. *53:1, 2. **wrapped.** ver. 7.

13. **a multitude.** Ge 28:12. 32:1, 2. 1 K 22:19.

2 Ch 18:18. Jb 38:7. Ps 68:17. *103:20, 21. 148:2. Is *6:2, 3. Ezk 3:12. Da *7:10. Lk 15:10. Ep 3:10. He *1:14. 1 P 1:12. Re *5:11, 12. **heavenly host**. Ac ●7:42.

14. **Glory**. Lk 19:38. Ps 69:34, 35. 85:9-12. 96:11-13. Is *44:23. *49:13. Jn 17:4. Ep *1:6. *3:20, 21. Ph 2:11. Re *5:13. **to**. √63, Ge +2:10. **in the highest**. Lk 10:21. Ps 148:1. Mt 6:10. 21:9. 28:18. Ac 7:49. Ep 3:15. Ph 2:10. Col 1:16, 20. Re 5:13. **on earth**. √31, Is +1:21. *26:9. Mt 6:10. Jn 17:4. **peace**. Lk 1:79. Ps 29:11. 85:10. 119:165. Is +*9:6, 7. *57:19. Je 14:13. +*23:5, 6. Mi 5:5. Hg 2:9. Zc *6:12, 13. Jn *14:27. Ac 10:36. Ro 1:7. *5:1. 2 C 5:18-20. Ep *2:14-18. Ph √4:7. Col *1:20. He *13:20, 21. **good will**. Gr. *eudokia*. Lk 3:22. Ps 106:4. Mt 3:17 (*eudokessa*, well pleased). 12:18. 17:5. Mk 1:11. Jn √3:16. Ep *2:4, 7. 2 Th 2:●12, 16. T 3:4-7. He ●10:6, 8, 38. 2 P 1:17. 1 J *4:9, 10. **toward**. Lk 3:22. 12:32. Ep 1:5, 9. Ph 2:13.

15. **into**. Lk 24:51. 2 K 2:1, 11. 1 P 3:22. **shepherds**. Gr. men the shepherds. Is +40:13mg. **Let**. ver. 4. Ex 3:3. Ps 111:2. Mt 2:1, 2, 9-11. 12:42. Jn 20:1-10.

16. **with**. Lk 1:39. Ec 9:10. **found**. See on ver. 7, 12. Lk 19:32. 22:13.

17. **made known**. ver. 38. Lk 8:39. Ps 40:9, 10. 66:16. 71:17, 18. Ml *3:16. Jn 1:41-46. 4:28, 29. Ac 4:20. 1 J 1:3. **the saying**. ver. 10-12.

18. **wondered**. ver. 33, 47. Lk 1:65, 66. 4:36. 5:9, 10. Is 8:18.

19. **Mary kept**. ver. 51. Lk 1:66. 9:43, 44. Ge *37:11. 1 S 21:12. Ps *119:11. Pr 4:4. Ho +*14:9.

20. **glorifying**. Lk 18:43. 19:37, 38. 1 Ch 29:10-12. Ps 72:17-19. 106:48. 107:8, 15, 21. Is 29:19. Mt 9:8. Ac 2:46, 47. 11:18.

21. **eight**. Lk 1:59. Ge *17:12. Le *12:3. Mt 3:15. Ro √15:8. Ga *4:4, 5. Ph *2:8. **child**. √63D2, Ge +30:27. Supply by ellipsis (then they circumcised him). **his name was**. √144A4, Ge +4:26. Lk 1:31. Mt *1:21, 25. Ac √4:12. **before**. Mt 1:21, 25.

22. **her purification**. See on Le *12:2-6. **according**. ver. 21, 27. Ga 4:4. **law of Moses**. Jn 7:23. **present**. 1 S 1:22, 24.

23. **law of the Lord**. ver. 24, 39. Ex 13:9. 2 Ch 31:3. Ro 7:22. **Every**. Ex *13:2, 12-15. *22:29. *34:19. Nu *3:13. 8:16, 17. 18:15. **openeth**. √142, Ge +20:16. **holy**. Lk +*1:35.

24. **law of**. ver. 23. **A pair**. One was for a burnt offering (Le +*23:12), and the other for a sin offering (Le +*23:19). The rich were required to bring a *lamb*; but the poor and middling classes were required to bring either *two turtle doves*, or *two young pigeons*. This is a proof of the comparative poverty of Joseph and Mary; and shows that this event occurred before the offering of the Magi, which would have enabled them to offer a lamb. Le 1:14. 5:7. ▶12:2, *6-8. 2 C √8:9.

25. **just**. Lk 1:6. Ge +*6:9. Jb *1:1, 8. Da 6:22, 23. Mi +*6:8. Ac 10:2, 22. 24:16. T 2:11-14. **devout**. Ac 2:5. 8:2. 22:12. He 5:7. 12:28. **waiting for**. ver. 38. Lk 23:51. Ge 49:18. Is *25:9. 40:1. *49:23. Mk √15:43. 1 Th 1:10. **consolation**. Lk *6:24. Is *40:1. 49:13. *51:3, 11, 12. 52:9, 10. 57:18. Ho 6:2, 3. Jn 11:24, 25. 1 C 14:3g. 2 Th *2:16. **of Israel**. Ac 26:6, 7. 28:20. **Holy**. Lk 1:41, 67. Nu 11:25, 29. 2 P *1:21. **Ghost**. Gr. *pneuma*. Mt +1:18n.

26. **revealed**. Ps *25:14. Am +*3:7. Mt 2:12, 22. Ac 10:22. 11:26. Ro 7:3. He 8:5. 11:7. 12:25. **Ghost**.

Gr. *pneuma*. Mt +3:16. **see death**. *Idein ton thanaton*, to "see death," is a Hebraism for to *die*, exactly corresponding to the expression found in Ps 89:48. Lk 9:27. Ps 89:48. Jn 8:51. Ac 2:27. He 11:5. **the Lord's**. Lk *9:20. 23:35. 1 S 24:6. Ps *2:2, 6. Is *61:1. Da +*9:24-26. Jn 1:41. 4:29. √20:31. Ac 2:36. 9:20. *10:38. 17:3. He +*1:8, 9. **Christ**. Lk 3:15. Mk 8:29.

27. **by**. Lk 4:1. Mt 4:1. Ac 8:29. 10:19. 11:12. 16:7. Re *1:10. 17:3. **Spirit**. Gr. *pneuma*. Mt +3:16. **the parents**. ver. 33, 41, 43, 48, 51. Lk 3:23. **to**. See on ver. 22.

28. **took**. Mk 9:36. 10:16. **and**. ver. 13, 14, 20. Lk 1:46, 64, 68. 24:53. Ps 32:11. 33:1. 105:1-3. 135:19, 20.

29. **Lord**. Ac 4:24. 2 P 2:1. Ju 4. Re 6:10. **servant**. Ja 1:1. **depart**. Ge +*15:15. =*46:30. Ph +*1:23. **in peace**. Ps *37:37. Is +*57:1, 2. Re +*14:13. **according**. ver. 26.

30. **mine eyes have**. See on ver. 10, 11. Lk *3:6. Ge *49:18. 2 S 23:1-5. Is 40:5. 49:6. *52:10. Ac 4:10-12. **thy salvation**. √121E1, Ge +25:23. Gr. *to soterion*, not the usual *soteria*. Used of Jehovah Himself (not merely of salvation as such). Lk 3:6. Ps 27:1. *85:7. =132:16. Is 62:11.

31. **prepared**. Lk 1:17. 24:47. Ps 96:1-3. 97:6-8. 98:2, 3. Is 42:1-4, 10-12. 45:21-25. 62:1, 2.

32. **light**. Is *9:2. *42:6, 7. *49:6. 52:10. 60:1-3, 19. *61:1-3. Mt *4:16. Jn *8:12. Ac 13:47, 48. 26:23. *28:28. Ro √15:8, 9. **to lighten**. Is *25:7. 60:2. **the Gentiles**. Ps *98:2. **and the glory**. Ps 85:9. Is 4:2. 45:25. 46:13. *60:19. Je 2:11. Hg ✱2:7, 9. Zc 2:5. Jn +*1:14. 1 C 1:31. Re 21:23. **thy people**. ver. 10. Dt +*32:43.

33. **Joseph and**. ver. 27, 48. Lk 1:65, 66. Is 8:18.

34. **blessed**. Ge 14:19. 47:7. Ex 39:43. Le 9:22, 23. He 7:1, 7. **is set**. Is *8:14, 15. Ho +*14:9. Mt *21:44. Jn 3:20. 9:29. Ro *9:32, 33. 1 C 1:23. 2 C *2:15, 16. Ph 1:16. 1 Th 3:3g. 1 P 2:7. **the fall**. √22L2, Is +8:14. Is *8:14. Mt 21:44. Jn 9:39. 1 C *1:23, 24. 2 C 2:16. 1 P *2:7-9. **and rising**. Da +*12:2. Ac 2:36-41. 3:15-19. 6:7. 9:1-20. **of many**. Da +▶12:2. 1 Th +*4:16n. **for a sign**. Ps 22:6-8. 69:9-12. Is 8:18. Mt 11:19. 26:65-67. 27:40-45, 63. Jn 5:18. 8:48-52. 9:24-28. Ac 4:26, 27. 13:45. 17:6, 7. 24:5. √28:22. 1 C 1:23. He 12:1-3. 1 P 4:14.

35. **a sword**. Ps 42:10. Jn 19:25. **soul**. Gr. *psyche*. √121A9A, Mt +11:29. **that the thoughts**. Lk 5:22. 6:8. 9:46, 47. 16:14, 15. 24:38. Dt 8:2. Jg 5:15, 16. Mt 12:24-35. Jn 8:42-47. *9:16. 15:22-24. Ac 8:21-23. 1 C *11:19. 1 J √2:19.

36. **Anna**. i.e. *gracious*, ✱S#451g, only here. For ✱S#2584h, see 1 S +1:2, Hannah. **a prophetess**. Ex +*15:20n. Jg 4:4. 2 K 22:14. 2 Ch 34:22. Ne 6:14. Is 8:3. Ac *2:17, 18. 21:9. 1 C 12:1. Re 2:20. **Phanuel**. i.e. *face of God*, ✱S#5323g, only here. For ✱S#6439h, see 1 Ch +4:4, Penuel. **Aser**. i.e. *happy*, ✱S#768g. Lk 2:36. Re 7:6. For ✱S#836h, see Ge +30:13, Asher. Jsh 19:24. **she**. Lk 1:7, 18. Jb 5:26. Ps 92:14.

37. **widow**. 1 T *5:3, 5. **which**. Ex 38:8. 1 S 2:22. Ps 23:6. 27:4. 84:4, 10. 92:13. 135:1, 2. Re 3:12. **departed not**. Lk 24:53. Ex 33:11. Pr 8:34. Am +*3:7. Re 7:15. **but served**. Ps 22:2. Ac *26:7. Ph 3:3. 1 T 5:5. He 9:9. 10:2. 12:28. Re 7:15. **fastings**. Lk 5:33. Mt 6:16-18. Ac 13:2. 14:23. 2 C 6:5. 11:27. **prayers**. 1 Th +*5:17. **night and day**. Mk 4:27.

38. **coming**. ver. 9, 27. Lk 20:1g. **gave thanks**. ver.

28-32. Lk 1:46, etc., 64, etc. Is 52:9. 2 C 9:15. Ep 1:3. **looked**. ver. 25. Lk 23:51. *24:21. Is 40:1. Mk *15:43. 1 C *1:7. T √2:13. He √9:28. **redemption**. Lk 1:68. Is 52:9. **Jerusalem**. *or*, Israel.

39. **performed**. ver. 21-24. Lk 1:6. Dt 12:32. Mt 3:15. Ga *4:4, 5. **they returned**. ver. 4. Mt 2:22, 23. **Nazareth**. *Nazareth, now Nassara*, was a small town of Zebulun, in Lower Galilee, according to Eusebius, fifteen miles east of Legio, near mount Tabor, and, according to D'Arvieux, about eight leagues, or according to Maundrell, seven hours, or about twenty miles, S.E. of Acre. It is one of the principal towns of the pashalic of Acre, containing a population of about 3000 souls, of whom 500 are Turks, the remainder being Christians. It is delightfully situated on elevated ground, in a valley, encompassed by mountains. ver. 4, 51. Mt 2:23.

40. **the child**. ver. 52. Jg 13:24. 1 S 2:18, 26. 3:19. Ps 22:9, 10. Is *53:1, 2. **grew**. Lk 1:80. Ex=2:1, 2. Ac 7:20. He 11:23. **strong**. Lk 1:80. Ep *6:10. 2 T 2:1. **spirit**. Gr. *pneuma*. ∫121A3, Mt +27:50. **filled**. ver. 47, 52. Is *11:1-5. Col 2:2, 3. **wisdom**. ver. 52. Lk 3:2. **the grace**. Ps *45:2. Jn *1:14. Ac 4:33. **upon him**. Is 40:5.

41. A.M. 4012. A.D. 8. **his parents**. ver. 27. **went**. Ex *23:14-17. 34:23. Dt 12:5-7, 11, 18. 16:1-8, 16. 1 S *1:3, 21. **the feast**. Ex 12:14. 23:15. Le +*23:5. Nu 28:16. Dt *16:1, 16. Jn *2:13. 6:4. 11:55. 13:1.

42. **went up**. ver. 4. Jn 11:55.

43. **fulfilled**. 2 Ch 30:21-23. 35:17. **the days**. Ex 12:15, 16. Le 23:6-8. Dt 16:3.

44. **in**. Ps 42:4. 122:1-4. Is 2:3. **acquaintance**. Lk 23:49.

46. **after three**. ver. 44, 45. 1 K 12:5, 12. Mt +12:40n. 16:21. 27:63, 64. **temple**. ∫171.O.11. Synecdoche of the Whole B639. The temple is put for certain of the parts comprehended in it. For another instance of this figure see Jn 18:20. **sitting**. Mt 26:55. **the doctors**. Lk 5:17. Jn 3:10. Ac 5:34. **both**. Is 49:1, 2. 50:4.

47. **were astonished**. Lk *4:22, 32. Ps 119:99. Mt *7:28. Mk 1:22. Jn *7:14, 15, 46. Ac 2:7. **his understanding**. Ge=41:39. Is *50:4. Mk 12:33.

48. **Son**. Lk 15:31. **thy father**. ∫121Q1, Je +28:5. ver. 27, 49. **sorrowing**. Lk 16:24, 25. Ac 20:38g. Ro 9:2. 1 T 6:10g.

49. **I must**. Lk 13:33. **my**. ver. 48. Ps *40:8. Ml 3:1, 2. Mt *10:37. 21:12. Jn *2:16, 17. *4:34. 5:17. 6:38. 8:29. *9:4. 14:2. **business**. 1 S 21:8. Jn 9:4. 17:4. 19:30. 1 C 3:12.

50. **understood not**. Lk 9:45. *18:34. *24:25. Mk *9:32. Jn *10:6.

51. **came**. ver. 39. **Nazareth**. ver. 4. **and was subject**. Ge ◐+16:9. Mt 3:15. *15:4. Mk +*6:3. Ep 5:21. +√6:1, 2. Ph *2:5, 7, 8. 1 T +*3:4. 1 P *2:21. **kept**. ver. 19. Lk 1:66. Ge=37:11. Da 7:28.

52. **Jesus**. ver. *40. Lk *1:80. 1 S *2:26. **increased**. Ex=2:1, 2. 2 S 5:10. Ac 7:20. He 11:23. **stature**. *or*, age. Lk 12:25. 19:3. Ps 39:5. Mt 6:27. Jn 9:21, 23. Ep 4:13. He 11:11. **and in favor**. ver. 40. Ge=39:4, 6. 1 S=2:26. Pr *3:3, 4. Ac 7:9, 10. 24:16. Ro *14:17, 18. **and man**. ∫174, Ge +18:27.

LUKE 3

The time when John the Baptist entered on his ministry, 1, 2. His preaching and exhortations, 3-14. His testimony to Jesus, 15-18. He is put in prison by Herod, 19, 20. Christ is baptized and receives testimony from heaven, 21, 22. His genealogy is traced back to Adam, 23-38.

1. A.M. 4030. A.D. 26. **Tiberius**. i.e. *watching, from the Tiber*, ✳S#5086g. **Caesar**. Lk 2:1. Lk 20:22. **Pontius**. i.e. *bridged; of the sea*, ✳S#4194g. Mt 27:2. Ac 4:27. 1 T 6:13. **Pilate**. Lk 23:1-4, 24, 25. Ge +*49:10. Mt 27:2. Ac 4:27. 23:26. 24:27. 26:30. **governor**. Lk 2:2. **Herod**. ver. 19. Lk 8:3. 9:7, 9. 13:31. 23:6-11. Mk 6:14. 8:15. Ac 4:27. **tetrarch**. i.e. *ruler of the fourth part of a realm*, ✳S#5075g. Also ✳S#5076g: Mt *14:1. Lk 3:19. 9:7. Ac 13:1. **his**. Mt 14:3. Mk 6:17. **Iturea**. i.e. *encircled*, ✳S#2484g. *Iturea* was a province of Syria east of Jordan, now called *Djedour*, according to Burckhardt, and comprising all the flat country south of Djebel Kessoue as far as Nowa, east of Djebel el Sheikh, or mount Hermon, and west of the Hadj road. **Trachonitis**. i.e. *rocky region; cruel*, ✳S#5139g. *Trachonitis*, according to Strabo and Ptolemy, comprehended all the uneven country on the east of Auranitis, now Haouran, from near Damascus to Bozra, now called *El Ledja* and *Djebel Haouran*. **Lysanias**. i.e. *grief dispelling*, ✳S#3078g. **Abilene**. i.e. *the father of mourning*, ✳S#9g. *Abilene* was a district in the valley of Lebanon, so called from *Abila* its chief town, eighteen miles N. of Damascus, according to Antoninus.

2. **Annas**. i.e. *one who answers*, ✳S#452g. Jn *11:49-51. 18:13g, 14, 24g. Ac 4:6g. **and Caiaphas**. Mt 26:3. Jn 18:13, 24. Ac 4:6. **high priests**. Je *52:24. 24:11. 1 K 12:22. Je 1:2. 2:1. Ezk 1:3. Ho 1:1, 2. Jon 1:1. Mi 1:1. Zp 1:1. **came**. Lk 1:80. 2:40. **unto John**. Lk 1:13. Jn 1:6, 7. **in**. Lk 1:80. 7:24. Jsh 15:61. Jg 1:16. 1 S 23:19. Is 40:3. Mt 3:1. 11:7. Mk 1:3. Jn 1:23.

3. **the country**. Mt *3:5, 6. Mk 1:4, 5. Jn 1:28. 3:26. **preaching**. Mt 3:6, 11. Mk 1:4. Jn 1:31-33. Ac 13:24. 19:4. +*22:16. **baptism**. Gr. *baptisma*, Mt +3:7. **of repentance**. Ac +*3:19. 5:31. **for the remission**. Lk 1:77. 24:47. Mt ◐3:11n. Ac +*2:38. +*22:16.

4. **The voice**. Is ▶40:3-5. Mt 3:3. Mk 1:3. Jn *1:23. **Prepare**. Lk 1:16, 17, 76-79. Is 57:14. 62:10. Ml 4:6. Jn 1:7, 26-36. 3:28-36.

5. **valley**. Lk 1:51-53. Is 2:11-17. 35:6-8. ▶40:4. 49:11. 61:1-3. Ezk 17:24. Ja 1:9-11. **and the crooked**. Is 42:16. 45:2. He 12:12, 13.

6. **all flesh**. ∫171E1, Ge +6:12. Lk *2:10, 11, 30-32. *24:47. Ps *98:2, 3. 136:25. Is ▶40:5. 49:6. *52:10. Je 45:5. Mt +24:22. Mk 13:20. *16:15, 16. Jn 17:2. Ac 2:17. Ro 3:20. *10:12, 18. 1 C 1:29. Ga 2:16. T 2:11. 1 P 1:24. **the salvation**. ∫121E1, Ge +25:23. Lk 1:69, 71, 77. 2:30. Ac 28:28.

7. **O generation**. Ge +*3:15. Ps 58:4, 5. Is 59:5. Mt *3:7-10. *23:33. Jn *8:44. Ac 13:10. 1 J *3:8-10. **to flee**. Ro *1:18. *2:8, 9. 1 Th +*1:10. He 6:18. Re *6:16.

8. **fruits**. Is *1:16-18. Ezk 18:27-31. Ac 26:20. 2 C √7:10, 11. Ga *5:22-24. Ph 1:11. He 6:7, 8. **worthy of**. *or*, meet for. **We have Abraham**. Lk 13:28, 29. 16:23-31. Is 48:1, 2. Je 7:4-10. Mt 3:9. Jn *8:33, 39. Ro 4:16. *9:6, 7. **of these**. Lk 19:40. Jsh 4:3-8. Mt +*8:11, 12. 21:43. Ga *3:28, 29. *6:15.

9. **the axe**. Lk *13:7, 9. 23:29-31. Is 10:33, 34. Ezk 15:2-4. 31:18. Da 4:14, 23. Mt *3:10. 7:19. Jn +*15:2, 6. He 10:28, 29. 12:29. Re +*21:8.

10. **What shall.** T#1689. ver. *8, 11-14. Lk 18:18-23. Ac *2:37. *9:6. *16:28-31. 22:10.

11. **He that hath.** 2 C √8:13-15. **two coats.** ✓171K2, Ex +23:4. By Synecdoche of the Species, one kind of vestment is put for any kind. Lk 9:3. 11:41. 18:22. 19:8. Is 58:7-11. Ezk *18:7. Da 4:27. Mt 10:10. 25:40. Mk 6:9. 14:5-8, 63g. Jn 13:29. Ac 10:2, 4, 31. 2 C 8:3-14. Ep *4:28. 1 T 6:18. He *6:10. Ja 1:27. *2:15-26. 1 J *3:17. 4:20. **impart.** Lk 18:22. Mt 5:42. *10:8. Lk +*6:38. *12:33. Ac *20:35. 1 Th 2:8.

12. **came also.** Lk *7:29, 30. 15:1, 2. 18:13, 14. Mt 21:31, 32. **publicans.** Lk 5:27, 29. 7:29. 18:10, 11, 13. 19:2. Mt 11:19. **what shall.** ver. 10.

13. **Exact.** Lk *19:8. Ps 18:23. Pr *28:13. Is *1:16, 17. √55:6, 7. Ezk 18:21, 22, 27, 28. Mi +*6:8. Mt *7:12. 1 C *6:10. Ep *4:28. T √2:11, 12. He *12:1.

14. **the soldiers.** The evangelist does not say *stratiotai, soldiers,* but *strateuomenoi,* men actually *under arms,* or marching to battle. Now, as we learn from Josephus that Herod was at this time engaged in war with Aretas, a king of Arabia, Michaelis concludes, that these military men were a part of Herod's army, then on its march from Galilee, which must of necessity have passed through the country where John was baptizing (See on Mark 6:27). Mt *8:5, 6, 10. Ac *10:1, 2, 7. 1 C √7:20. 2 T *2:4. **And what shall we do.** Observe that neither John, Christ (Lk +22:36), nor Paul (1 C 7:20) required that for spiritual reasons soldiers should leave the military service, or that individuals should avoid political or military service because of their faith, contrary to many who so teach today, but without clear Biblical warrant (Pr 30:6. Is 8:20. Mk 7:9). 1 Ch +*12:32n. Ac 10:7. **Do violence to no man.** or, Put no man in fear. Le 19:11. Jb 24:9. Ro 13:9, 10. Ph 2:15. **accuse.** ✓108J, Ge +43:18. Lk 19:8. Ex +*20:16. *23:1. Le *19:11. T 2:3. Re 12:10. **and be content.** Mt 20:10-15. Ph √4:11. 1 T *6:8-10. He 13:5, 6. **wages.** or, allowance. 1 C 9:7. 2 C 11:8.

15. **expectation.** or, suspense. Mk +*1:15. Jn +*6:14. 10:24. **mused.** or, reasoned, or debated. Jn 1:19, etc. 3:28, 29. **whether.** Jn 1:19, 20. **the Christ.** Lk 2:11, 26. 20:41. 23:35, 39. 24:26, 46. Ac 2:31. 8:5. 17:3. 26:23. Mt 1:17. Mk 8:29. Jn 1:20. Ac 18:5.

16. **I indeed.** Mt *3:11. Mk 1:7, 8. Jn 1:26, 33. Ac +*1:5. 11:16. 13:24, 25. 19:4, 5. **with water.** Is *44:3, 4. Jl *2:28, 29. Ac +*1:5. 10:47. **mightier.** Mk 1:7, 8. **cometh.** Jn 1:15, 27. *3:30, 31. Ac 7:33. 13:25. **latchet.** ✓138B, Ge +13:16. Is 5:27. Jn 1:27. **he shall.** Pr 1:23. Is 32:15. 44:3, 4. Ezk 36:25. Jl *2:28, 29. Jn 7:38. Ac 2:33. 10:44. 11:15. 1 C √12:13. **with.** Jn *1:33. Ac +*1:5. *11:15, 16. 1 C *6:11. **Ghost.** Gr. *pneuma.* Mt +1:18n. **and with fire.** Lk 12:49. Is 4:4. Zc 13:9. Ml 3:2, 3. Ac *2:3, 4, 17, 18.

17. **fan.** ✓22C44, Je +15:7. Is 30:24. Je 15:7. Mt 3:12. **gather the wheat.** Lk 22:31. Am 9:9. Mi 4:12. Mt +*13:30. 2 Th *2:1. **but the chaff.** Ps +*1:4. 21:9, 10. *35:5. Ml *4:1. Mt +*3:12. Mk *9:43-49. 1 J *2:19. **he will burn.** Is +*24:6. Mt +*13:30. 2 P +*3:7. **unquenchable.** Is 34:10. +*66:24. Je 7:20. Ezk 20:47, 48. Mt +*25:46. Mk √9:43, 45, 46, 48.

18. **many other things.** Jn *1:15, 29, 34. *3:29-36. 20:30. 21:25. Ac 2:40.

19. **But Herod.** Pr 9:7, 8. 15:12. Mt 11:2. 14:3, 4. Mk *6:17, 18.

20. **Added yet this.** Lk 13:31-34. 2 K 21:16. 24:4. 2 Ch 24:17-22. *36:16. Ne +*9:26. Je 2:30. Mt 21:35-41. 22:6, 7. 23:31-33. 1 Th *2:15, 16. Re 16:6. **prison.** ✓151, Ge +1:28.

21. **that.** Mt 3:13-15. Mk 1:9. Jn 1:32, etc. **baptized, and praying.** T#1225. Lk 9:28, 29. Mk *1:35. Jn 12:27, 28. Ac +*22:16. **the heaven.** Mt *3:16, 17. Mk 1:10, 11. Jn 1:32-34.

22. **Ghost.** Gr. *pneuma.* Mt +3:16. T#345. Mt 12:32n. +*28:19n. Jn 14:16. 2 C 13:14. Ep 2:18. +*4:30. 1 P 1:2. 1 J 5:7. The Holy Spirit is a person, for (1) designations proper to personality are given him. Jn 16:14, the masculine pronoun in Greek is used, in violation of Greek grammar, to emphasize He is a person. Some of the best manuscripts employ the masculine pronoun at Ep 1:14, see Tischendorf's 8th edition. (2) The title "comforter," "paraclete," cannot be taken as an abstract influence, as is evident in its use in reference to Christ in 1 J 2:1, where it is rendered "advocate." (3) The Holy Spirit is mentioned in the immediate connection with other persons, and in such a way as to imply his own personality. Mt 28:19. Jn 16:14. 17:4. Ac 15:28. 2 C 13:14. 1 P 1:1, 2. Ju 21. (4) The Holy Spirit does things only a person can do. Ge 1:2. 6:3. Lk 12:12. Jn 3:8. 14:26. 15:26. 16:8. Ac 2:4. 8:29. 13:2. 16:6, 7. 20:28. Ro 8:11, 26. 15:19. 1 C *2:10, 11. 12:8-11. Ga 4:6. 2 P 1:21. (5) He is affected as a person by the acts of others. That which can be resisted, grieved, vexed, or blasphemed, must be a person, for only a person can perceive insult and be offended. The blasphemy against the Holy Ghost (Mt +*12:31n, 32n) cannot be merely blasphemy against a power or attribute of God, since in that case blasphemy against God would be a less crime than blasphemy against his power. That against which the unpardonable sin can be committed must be a person. Is 63:10. Mt 12:31. Ac 5:3, 4, 9. 7:51. Ro 8:26, 27. 15:30. Ep +√4:30. (6) References to the Holy Spirit as a person distinct from the Father and the Son cannot be explained as personification, for the personification is maintained consistently throughout Scripture, whether in prose or poetry. To suppose that the "Holy Spirit" is merely a reference to the influence or power of God, or some other attribute, will result in meaningless tautology when the terms which are wrongly held to be equivalents to the Holy Spirit are substituted in the text: Ac 10:38, "God anointed him (Jesus) with the Holy Spirit and with power"; does this mean anointed him with power and with power? So for Ro 15:13, 19. 1 C 2:4. Such a notion is contradicted by all those passages where the Holy Spirit is distinguished from his own gifts: Lk 1:35. 4:14. Ro 8:26. 1 C 12:4, 8, 11. **descended.** Jn 1:32. **bodily.** *S#4984g. Lk 3:22. 1 T 4:8. **shape.** *S#1491g. Lk 3:22. 9:29 (fashion). Jn 5:37. 2 C 5:7 (sight). 1 Th 5:22 (appearance). **a voice.** T#1781. Ex 19:17-19. 1 K 19:13. Mt 3:17. Mk 1:11. **from heaven.** Lk 11:13. Mt 7:11. Jn *12:27, 28. **Thou art.** Lk *9:34, 35. Ps *2:7. Is *42:1. Mt 12:18. 17:5. 27:43. Col 1:13. 1 P 2:4. 2 P *1:17, 18. 1 J 5:9. **beloved Son.** Mk 9:7. Jn 15:26. 17:24. Ro 1:4. Ep 1:6. **am.** ✓96C4, Mt +3:17.

23. **began to be.** Mt 3:16. 4:17. Ac 1:1, 2. **thirty.** Ge=41:46. Nu *4:3, 35, 39, 43, 47. **being.** Lk 2:27. 4:22. Mt +*13:55. Mk +*6:3. Jn 1:45. *6:42. **which.** The real father of *Joseph* was *Jacob* (Mt 1:16); but having married the daughter of *Heli,* and being perhaps adopted by him, he was called his son, and as such was entereed in the public registers; *Mary* not being

mentioned, because the Hebrews never permitted the name of a woman to enter their genealogical tables, but inserted her husband as the son of him who was, in reality, but his father-in-law. Hence it appears that St. Matthew, who wrote principally for the Jews, traces the pedigree of Jesus Christ from Abraham, through whom the promise was given to the Jews, to David, and from David, through the line of Solomon, to Jacob the father of Joseph, the reputed or legal father of Christ; and that St. Luke, who wrote for the Gentiles, extends his genealogy upwards from Heli the father of Mary, through the line of Nathan, to David, and from David to Abraham, and from Abraham to Adam, who was the immediate "son of God" by creation, and to whom the promise of the Savior was given in behalf of himself and all his posterity. The two branches of descent from David, by Solomon and Nathan, being thus united in the persons of Mary and Joseph, Jesus the son of Mary reunited in himself all the blood, privileges, and rights, of the whole family of David, in consequence of which he is emphatically called "the Son of David." **Heli.** i.e. *ascending,* ✸S#2242g. Compare ✸S#5941h, 1 S +1:3, Eli.

24. **Matthat.** i.e. *gift,* ✸S#3158g. Lk 3:24, 29. **Levi.** i.e. *to adhere,* ✸S#3017g. Lk 3:24, 29. **Melchi.** i.e. *the Lord is king,* ✸S#3197g. Lk 3:24, 28. Two ancestors of Joseph, the husband of Mary. **Janna.** i.e. *answering,* ✸S#2388g.

25. **Amos.** i.e. *a burden,* ✸S#301g. **Naum.** i.e. *ease,* ✸S#3486g. For ✸S#5151h, see Na +1:1. **Esli.** i.e. *reserved,* ✸S#2069g. **Nagge.** i.e. *clearness,* ✸S#3477g.

26. **Maath.** i.e. *fearing,* ✸S#3092g. **Mattathias.** i.e. *gift of Jehovah,* ✸S#3161g. Lk 3:25, 26. For ✸S#4993h, see Ezr 10:43, Mattithiah. **Semei.** i.e. *obeys,* ✸S#4584g. For ✸S#8096h, see 2 S +16:5, Shimei.

27. **Joanna.** i.e. *Jehovah is gracious giver,* ✸S#2490g. **Rhesa.** i.e. *will; course,* ✸S#4488g. **son of Zorobabel.** Mt *1:12. **Salathiel.** 1 Ch 3:17. Ezr 3:2. **Neri.** i.e. *light of God,* ✸S#3518g.

28. **Addi.** i.e. *my witness,* ✸S#78g. **Cosam.** i.e. *diviner,* ✸S#2973g. **Elmodam.** i.e. *God of measure,* ✸S#1678g. **Er.** i.e. *watch,* ✸S#2262g.

29. **Jose.** i.e. *a savior,* ✸S#2499g. **Eliezer.** i.e. *God of help,* ✸S#1663g. **Jorim.** i.e. *the height,* ✸S#2497g. 30. **Simeon.** i.e. *hearkening,* ✸S#4826g. Lk 2:25, 34. 3:30. Ac 13:1. 15:14. 2 P 1:1. Re 7:7. **Juda.** i.e. *praise; confession,* ✸S#2455g. **Jonan.** i.e. *pigeon,* ✸S#2494g. **Eliakim.** i.e. *my God arises,* ✸S#1662g. Mt 1:13.

31. **Melea.** i.e. *filling,* ✸S#3190g. **Menan.** i.e. *enchanted; soothsayer,* ✸S#3104g. **Mattatha.** i.e. *gift of the Lord,* ✸S#3160g. **of Nathan.** i.e. *a giver,* ✸S#3481g. For ✸S#5416h, see 2 Ch +9:29. 2 S *5:14. 1 Ch 3:5. 14:4. Zc 12:12.

32. **was the son of Jesse.** Ru 4:18-22. 1 S 16:1. 17:12, 58. 20:31. 1 K 12:16. 1 Ch 2:10-15. Ps 72:20. Is +*✸11:1, 2. Mt +*1:6. Ac 13:22, 23. **which was the son of Obed.** i.e. *serving,* ✸S#5601g. Mt 1:5. For ✸S#5744h, see Ru +4:17. Nu 1:7. 2:3. 7:12. 1 Ch 2:11, 12, Nahshon, Salma, Boaz. **Salmon.** i.e. *he that rewards; clothing,* ✸S#4533g. Mt 1:4, 5. For ✸S#8012h, see Ru 4:21. 1 Ch 2:51, 54. **Naasson.** Ex 6:23. Nu 1:7. 2:3. 7:12, 17. 10:14. Mt 1:4.

33. **Aminadab.** i.e. *noble nation,* ✸S#284g. Mt 1:4. For ✸S#5992h, see 1 Ch +15:11. Ru 4:19, 20. 1 Ch 2:9, 10. Aminadab, Ram, Hezron. Mt 1:3, 4. **Esrom.**

i.e. *dart of joy,* ✸S#2074g. Mt 1:3. For ✸S#2696h, see Ge +46:9, 12. Nu 26:20, 21, Hezron. **Phares.** Ge 38:29. Ru 4:12. 1 Ch 2:4, 5. 9:4, Pharez. **of Juda.** Ge 29:35. 49:8, Judah. Mt 1:2, Judas.

34. **of Jacob.** Lk 1:33. Ge 29:35. Nu +✸24:17. Mt 1:2. **which was the son of Isaac.** Ge +*✸17:19. 21:3, *✸12. 25:26. ✸26:2-5. 1 Ch 1:34. Mt 1:2. Ac 7:8. Ro 9:6-8. He *11:17-19. **Abraham.** i.e. *faithfulness; father of a great multitude,* ✸S#11g. ver. 8, 8. Lk 1:55, 73. 13:16, 28. 16:22, 23, 24, 25, 29, 30. 19:9. 20:37. Mt 1:1, 2, 17. 3:9, 9. 8:11. 22:32. Mk 12:26. Jn 8:33, 37, 39, 39, 40, 52, 53, 56, 57, 58. Ac 3:13, 25. 7:2, 16, 17, 32. 13:26. Ro 4:1, 2, 3, 9, 12, 13, 16. 9:7. 11:1. 2 C 11:22. Ga 3:6, 7, 8, 9, 14, 16, 18, 29. 4:22. He 2:16. 6:13. 7:1, 2, 4, 5, 6, 9. 11:8, 17. Ja 2:21, 23. 1 P 3:6. For ✸S#85h, see Ge +17:5. Ge +*12:3. 21:3. +*✸22:18. 26:4. 28:14. Mt 1:1. Lk 1:54, 55. Jn *11:51, 52. Ac 3:25. Ro 4:13. Ga 3:8, *16. **Thara.** i.e. *late,* ✸S#2291g. For ✸S#8646h, see Ge +11:26, Terah. Ge 11:24-32. Jsh 24:2. 1 Ch 1:24-28, Terah, Nahor, Reu, Serug, Peleg, Eber, Shelah. **Nachor.** i.e. *snoring,* ✸S#3493g. For ✸S#5152h, see Ge +11:22, Nahor.

35. **Saruch.** i.e. *a branch; intertwined,* ✸S#4562g. For ✸S#8286h, see Ge +11:20, Serug. Ge 11:18-21, Serug, Reu. **Ragau.** i.e. *fellowship,* ✸S#4466g. For ✸S#7466h, see Ge +11:18, Reu. **Phalec.** i.e. *to cut,* ✸S#5317g. For ✸S#6389h, see Ge +10:25, Peleg. Ge 10:25, Peleg. **Heber.** i.e. *companion,* ✸S#1443g. For ✸S#5677h, Ge +10:24. Ge 11:16, 17, Eber. **Sala.** i.e. *branch,* ✸S#4527g. For ✸S#7974h, see Ge +10:24, Salah. Ge 11:12-15.

36. **Cainan.** i.e. *fixed,* ✸S#2536g. ver. 37. This Cainan is not found in the Hebrew text of any of the genealogies, but only in the Septuagint; from which, probably the evangelist transcribed the register, as sufficiently exact for his purpose, and as more generally suited to command attention (See on Ge 11:12). It may here be remarked, that though some of the same names occur here, from Nathan downwards, as in Joseph's genealogy, yet there appears no sufficient evidence that the same persons were intended, different persons often bearing the same name. **Arphaxad.** i.e. *one that heals,* ✸S#742g. For ✸S#775h, see Ge +10:22. **Sem.** i.e. *fame,* ✸S#4590g. For ✸S#8035h, see Ge +5:32. Ge 7:13. 9:18, 26, 27. 10:21, 22. 11:10, etc. 1 Ch 1:17, Shem. **Noe.** i.e. *consolation,* ✸S#3575g. Lk 17:26, 27. Mt 24:37, 38. He 11:7. 1 P 3:20. 2 P 2:5. For ✸S#5146h, see Ge +5:29, Noah. Ge 5:29, 30. 6:8-10, 22. 7:1, 23. 8:1. 9:1. Ezk 14:14. He 11:7. 1 P 3:20. 2 P 2:5, Noah. **Lamech.** i.e. *wild man,* ✸S#2984g. For ✸S#3929h, see Ge +4:18.

37. **Mathusala.** i.e. *man of a dart,* ✸S#3103g. For ✸S#4968h, see Ge +5:21. Ge 5:6-28. 1 Ch 1:1-3, Methusaleh, Mahalaleel. **Enoch.** i.e. *dedicated,* ✸S#1802g. Lk 3:37. He 11:5. Ju 14. For ✸S#2585h, see Ge +5:21. **Jared.** i.e. *descended,* ✸S#2391g. For ✸S#3382h, see Ge +5:15. **Maleleel.** i.e. *praise of God,* ✸S#4111h, see Ge +5:12, Mahalaleel. **Cainan.** i.e. *fixed,* ✸S#2536g. ver. 36n. For ✸S#7018h, see Ge +5:9.

38. **Enos.** i.e. *a mortal,* ✸S#1800g. For ✸S#583h, see Ge +4:26. **Seth.** i.e. *appointed,* ✸S#4589g. For ✸S#8352h, see Ge +4:25. **which was the son of Adam.** i.e. *red earth, earthy,* ✸S#76g. Ro 5:14, 14. 1 C 15:22, 45, 45. 1 T 2:13, 14. Ju 14. For ✸S#120h, see Ge

+2:19. Ge 4:25, 26. 5:3. **of God**. Ge 1:26, 27. 2:7. 5:1, 2. Is 64:8. Ac 17:26-29. 1 C 15:45, 47. He 12:9.

LUKE 4

Jesus fasts forty days, being tempted by the devil, and overcomes all his temptations, 1-13. He preaches in Galilee with great renown, 14, 15. He goes to Nazareth: and while his words excite admiration, the citizens are so offended, that they seek to kill him; but he avoids them by miracle, 16-30. He casts out an unclean spirit, 31-37; heals Peter's wife's mother, 38, 39; and works many other miracles, 40, 41. He preaches through the cities of Galilee, 42-44.

1. A.M. 4031. A.D. 27. **Jesus**. Mt 4:1, etc. **full**. ver. 14, 18. Lk 3:22. Is *11:2-4. *61:1. Mt 3:16. Jn 1:32. *3:34. Ac 1:2. *10:38. **Ghost**. Gr. *pneuma*, Mt +1:18n. **and was led**. Lk *2:27. 1 K *18:12. Ezk *3:14. Mt *4:1. Mk *1:12, etc. Ac *8:39. Ro 8:14. **Spirit**. Gr. *pneuma*, Mt +3:16. **the wilderness**. *63H, Ge +12:15. 1 K 19:4. Mk 1:13.

2. **forty**. Ex 24:18. *34:28. Dt *9:9, 18, 25. 1 K *19:8. Mt *4:2. Mk 1:13. **tempted**. Ge +*3:15. 1 S 17:16. He 2:18. **he did**. Est 4:16. Jon 3:7. **he afterward**. Mt 4:2. 21:18. Jn 4:6. He +*4:15.

3. **If thou be**. *184A, 1 C +15:2. Lk 3:22. Mt 4:3.

4. **It**. ver. 8, 10. Is +*8:20. Jn √10:34, 35. Ep *6:17. **That**. Lk 22:35. Ex 23:25. Dt)8:3. Jb +*23:12. Je +*15:16. 49:11. Mt 4:4. 6:25, 26, 31. **word of God**. Ep *6:17.

5. **And**. *107, Ge +10:5. **taking**. Mt *4:8, 9. 1 C 7:31. Ep 2:2. 6:12. 1 J √2:15, 16. **world**. Gr. *oikoumene*, Mt +24:14. **in a moment**. Jb 20:5. Ps 73:19. 1 C 15:52. 2 C 4:17.

6. **All**. Jn *8:44. 2 C 11:14. Re 12:9. 20:2, 3. **and the**. Est 5:11. Is 5:14. 23:9. 1 P 1:24. **and to**. Jn *12:31. +*14:30. Ep 2:2. Re *13:2, 7.

7. **If thou**. *184C, Mt +4:9. **worship me**. *or*, fall down before me. Lk 8:28. 17:16. Ex +34:14. Ps 72:11. Is 45:14. 46:6. Mt 2:11. Re 4:10. 5:8. 22:8.

8. **Get**. Mt *4:10. 16:23. Ja 4:7. 1 P 5:9. **for**. ver. 4. Ex 34:14. Dt *6:13. 10:20. Mt *4:10. Ep *6:17. Re 19:10. 22:9. **and him**. *92E, Mt +4:10. **only**. 1 S 7:3. 2 K 19:15. Ps 83:18. Is 2:11.

9. **And**. *107, Ge +10:5. **brought**. Jb 2:6. Mt 4:5. **on**. 2 Ch 3:4. **If**. *184A, 1 C +15:2. ver. 3. Mt 4:6. 8:29. Ro 1:4.

10. **It is written**. ver. 3, 8. 2 C 11:14. Ep *6:17. He. Ps)91:11, 12. He 1:14.

11. **And in**. Ps)91:12.

12. **Thou**. Dt *6:16. Ps 95:9. 106:14. Ml 3:15. Mt 4:7. 1 C 10:9. He 3:8, 9.

13. **devil had ended**. Mt 4:11. Jn +*14:30. He 2:17, 18. +*4:15. Ja √4:7. **for a season**. Lk *22:53. Ac 13:11.

14. **returned**. Mt 4:12. Mk 1:14. Jn 4:43. Ac *10:36, 37. **in**. ver. 1. Ac 1:8. **Spirit**. Gr. *pneuma*, Mt +3:16. **and there**. ver. 37. Mt 4:23-25. Mk 1:28.

15. **he**. ver. 16. Lk 13:10. Mt 4:23. 9:35. 13:54. Mk 1:39. **being**. Is 55:5. Mt 9:8. Mk 1:27, 45. Jn *4:45.

16. **to**. Lk 1:26, 27. 2:39, 51. Mt *2:23. *13:54. Mk 6:1. **as his custom was**. ver. 15. Lk 2:42. *22:39. Mk *10:1. Jn 18:20. Ac +*17:1, 2. **went into**. ver. 31. Ps *22:22. *40:9, 10. Mt 4:23, Mk 6:2. **and stood**. Ac 13:14-16. 17:2. **to read**. Ac 13:15, 27. *15:21. 2 C 3:15. Col 4:16. 1 Th 5:27.

17. **the book**. Lk 3:4. 20:42. Ac 7:42. 13:15, 27.

he had. Anaptuksas, "unrolled the book;" the Sacred Writings being anciently (as they are still in the synagogues) written on skins of parchment, and rolled on two rollers, beginning on each end, so that in reading from right to left, they rolled off with the left hand while they rolled on with the right. **the place**. Is)61:1, 2. Lk +24:27.

18. **The**. *92A, Mt +1:23. *92D2. Gnome; or, Quotation B790. Where the words are cited from the Septuagint. Here, from Is 61:1, 2. David McCalman Turpie, in his *The Old Testament in the New*, shows in Table D "the quotations of the New Testament which differ from the original Hebrew text, but agree with the Septuagint Version" (p. xi, 87). (1) passages which agree with the LXX and have the same order, but differ from the Hebrew in the rendering of a word or words: Mt 4:7; 13:14, 15; Lk 4:12; Ac 2:25-28; 8:32, 33; 28:26, 27; Ro 4:7, 8; 10:18; 1 C 9:9; 15:32; Ga 4:27; He 2:13. (2) passages which agree with and have the same order as the LXX, differ from the Hebrew by the omission of a word or words: Ac 7:35. (3) passages which agree with the LXX, but differ from the Hebrew by the rendering and omission of a word or words: Ro 15:12; He 11:21. (4) passages which agree with the LXX, but differ from the Hebrew by the addition of a word or words: Mt 21:42; Mk 12:10, 11; Lk 20:17; Jn 12:38; Ro 10:16; 12:20; 15:10, 21; 1 C 6:16; He 13:6; 1 P 2:7. (5) passages which agree with the LXX, but differ from the Hebrew by the rendering and addition of a word or words: Ro 4:3; 9:29; Ja 2:23. (6) passages which agree with the LXX, but having a slightly different order, differ from the Hebrew by the rendering and omission of a word or words: Ro 11:34; 1 T 5:18. (7) passages which agree with the LXX, but having a slightly different order, differ from the Hebrew, by the rendering and addition of a word or words: Ro 10:20, 21; Ga 3:6. (8) passages which agree with the LXX, but differ from the Hebrew by the rendering, the omission and the addition of a word or words: He 10:37, 38. (9) passages which agree with the LXX, differ from the Hebrew by the rendering and omission of a clause or clauses: He 2:6-8; 10:5-7; Ja 4:5. **Spirit**. Gr. *pneuma*, *121A1, Lk +1:17. Ps 45:7. Is *11:2-5. 42:1-4. 48:16. 50:4. 59:21. Mt 12:18. Mk 1:10. Ac 1:2. *10:38. **anointed**. Ps 2:2, 6mg. +*45:7. Da *9:24. Jn 1:41mg. Ac 4:27. *10:38. **to preach**. Lk 6:20. 7:22. Is 29:19. *66:2. Zp 3:12. Zc 11:11. Mt +*5:3. 11:5. Ja *2:5. **hath sent**. Is *61:2. Lk 1:78. Jn *3:34. Col *2:9. **to heal**. 2 Ch 34:27. Ps 34:18. 51:17. *147:3. Is +*57:15. 66:2. Ezk +*9:4. **to preach deliverance**. Ps 102:20. 107:10-16. 146:7. Is 42:7. 45:13. 49:9, 24, 25. 52:2, 3. Zc 9:11, 12. Mt *4:16. +*11:28. Jn *8:36. Col 1:13. 2 T *2:26. **and recovering**. Ps *146:8. Is 29:18, 19. 32:3. 35:5. 42:16-18. 60:1, 2. Ml 4:2. Mt 4:16. 9:27-30. *11:5. Jn 9:39-41. 12:46. Ac *26:18. Ep 5:8-14. 1 Th 5:5, 6. 1 P 2:9. 1 J 2:8-10. **sight**. Ge +3:7. **to set**. Notice that our Lord here cites Is)58:6 with his reading from Is 61:1, 2, thus forming a composite quotation (Mt +*27:9n). This gives us insight into the fact that our Lord himself compared Scripture with Scripture in expounding its meaning (Lk +*24:27, 44, 45. Jn +*5:39. Ac +*17:11). *92G. Gnome: Composite Quotations B799, where several citations are amalgamated. For other instances of this figure see Mt 21:5, 13. Mk 1:2, 3. Lk 1:16, 17. Ac 1:20. Ro 3:10-18. 9:33. 11:8, 26, 27. 1 C 15:54, 55. 2 C 6:16. Ga 3:8. He

9:19, 20. 1 P 2:7. **at liberty.** Ro *6:13, 14, 18. **bruised.** Ge +*3:15. Is *42:3. Mt 12:20.

19. **To preach.** Lk *19:42. +24:27. Le √25:8-13, 50-54. Nu 36:4. Is 49:8. 61:2. 63:4. 2 C *6:1, 2. **acceptable.** Ps 69:13.

20. **and he.** ver. 17. Mt 20:26-28. **closed the book.** Our Lord ended his reading at Is 61:2, in the middle of the sentence. His stopping point is most instructive, for the rest of the prophecy pertains to what will transpire at the second advent. Thus, between clauses of the same sentence is an unannounced time interval. For other unannounced prophetic time intervals, see Is 61:2n. Compare Mt 21:4, 5, w Zc 9:9 but not Zc 9:10. **and sat.** Lk 5:3. Mt 5:1, 2. 13:1, 2. 26:55. Mk 4:1. Jn 8:2. Ac *13:14-16. 16:13. **And the.** Lk 19:48. Ac 3:4, 12.

21. **This day.** Lk 10:23, 24. Mt 13:14. Jn 4:25, 26. +*5:39. Ac 2:16-18, 29-33. 3:18. **this scripture.** Mt 21:42. Mk 12:10. Jn 2:22. Ac 1:16. 8:32, 35. Ro 4:3. 9:17. 10:11. 11:2. Ga 3:8, 22. 4:30. 1 T 5:18. 2 T 3:16. Ja 2:8, 23. 4:5. 1 P 2:6. 2 P 1:20. **fulfilled.** Mt 1:22.

22. **wondered.** Mt 13:54, 55. Mk 6:2, 3. Jn 6:42. **the gracious.** Lk *2:47. 21:15. Ps *45:2, 4. Pr 10:32. 16:21. 25:11. Ec 12:10, 11. SS 5:16. Is *50:4. Mt *13:54. Mk 6:2. Jn *1:14. √7:46. Ac 6:10. T 2:8. **proceeded.** Re 19:21. **Is not.** Mt 13:55, 56. Mk +*6:3. Jn *6:42. **Joseph's son.** Lk 2:27. 3:23.

23. **proverb.** ♪138A, Ge +10:9. **Physician.** Lk 6:42. 23:39. Mt 27:42. Mk 15:31. Ro 2:21, 22. **whatsoever.** Mt *4:13, 23. +*11:23, etc. Mk 2:1-12. Jn 2:12. 4:48. **do.** Jn 2:3, 4. 4:28. 7:3, 4. Ro 11:34, 35. 2 C 5:16. **thy country.** ver. 16. Mt 13:54. Mk 6:1.

24. **Verily.** Lk 12:37. 18:17, 29. 21:32. 23:43. Mt +*5:18. Mk +3:28. Jn +1:51. **No prophet.** Mt 10:36. *13:57. Mk 6:4, 5. Jn *4:41, 44. Ac 22:3, 18-22. **is accepted.** Dt 33:24. Ac 10:35.

25. **many.** Lk 10:21. Is 55:8. Mt 20:15. Mk 7:26-29. Ro 9:15, 20. Ep 1:9, 11. **when the.** 1 K *17:1. *18:1, 2, Elijah. Ja *5:17. Re 11:6. **three years and six months.** Wordsworth notes that "This term of three years and a half appears under that name as a type of suffering and persecution in Holy Writ. The famine in the days of Elias, when the Church of God was persecuted by Ahab and Jezebel, lasted for three years and a half (Lk 4:25). The times in which the ancient Church underwent persecution under Antiochus Epiphanes, was three years and a half (Josephus, B.J.v.9). The earthly ministry of the great head of the church, during which He endured rebuke and contradiction from the corrupt and degenerate teachers of his own people, lasted, it is probable, for three years and a half" (*Greek Testament*, vol. 4, p. 221). This period, equal to 1260 days or 42 months, represents "a chronological period of suffering" (Wordsworth, p. 34, on James 5:17).

26. **save.** 1 K 17:9, etc., Zarephath. Ob *20. **Sarepta.** i.e. *she hath refined*, *S#4558g. For *S#6886h, see 1 K +17:9. Sarepta, a city of Phoenicia, on the coast of the Mediterranean, is called Zarphand by the Arabian geographer Sherif Ibn Idris, who places it twenty miles N. of Tyre, and ten S. of Sidon; but its real distance from Tyre is about fifteen miles, the whole distance from that city to Sidon being only twenty-five miles. Maundrell states, that the place shown him for this city, called Sarphan, consisted of only a few houses, on the tops of the mountains, within about

half a mile of the sea; between which there were ruins of considerable extent. **Sidon.** Ac 12:20. **unto.** 1 K 17:12. **widow.** Mk 12:42.

27. **many lepers.** 2 K 7:3. **Eliseus.** i.e. *God of my salvation*, *S#477h, see 1 K +19:16, Elisha. 1 K 19:19-21. **saving.** Mt 12:4. Jn 17:12. Ro +*9:15. **Naaman.** i.e. *pleasantness*, *S#3497g. For *S#5283h, see Ge +46:21. 2 K ch. *5. Jb 21:22. 33:13. 36:23. Da 4:35.

28. **were.** Lk 6:11. 11:53, 54. 2 Ch 16:10. 24:20, 21. Je 37:15, 16. 38:6. Ac 5:33. 7:54. 13:46, 50. 22:21-23. 1 Th 2:15, 16.

29. **and thrust out.** Le 24:14. Nu 15:35. Jsh 7:24, 25. 1 K 21:13. Mt 8:34. Jn 8:37, 40, 59. 15:24, 25. Ac 7:57, 58. 16:23, 24. 21:28-32. **brow.** *or*, edge. **that.** 2 Ch 25:12. Ps 37:14, 32, 33.

30. **passing through.** Lk +*24:16. Jg 18:20n. Pr +*22:3. Is +*53:2. Je 37:12. Mt 26:48. Mk 14:44. Jn *8:59. *10:39. 18:6, 7. Ac 12:18. **the midst.** Ge +27:16. went his way. Ps 18:29. *37:32, 33. Jn 7:30.

31. **came.** Mt 4:13. Mk 1:21. **taught.** ver. 15, 16. Mt 4:23. 10:23. Ac 13:50-52. 14:1, 2, 6, 7, 19-21. 17:1-3, 10, 11, 16, 17. 18:4. 20:1, 2, 23, 24. **on the sabbath.** Mk 6:2.

32. **astonished.** ver. 36. Je 23:28, 29. Mt *7:28, 29. Mk 1:22. Jn 6:63. 1 C 2:4, 5. 14:24, 25. 2 C 4:2. 10:4, 5. 1 Th 1:5. T *2:15. He √4:12, 13.

33. **in the synagogue.** Mk 1:23. **unclean.** Mt +*3:30. **spirit.** Gr. *pneuma*, Mt +8:16. **cried out.** Mt 8:29.

34. **Let us alone.** *or*, Away. Lk 8:37. Ac 16:39. **what have.** ♪85H, Jg +11:12. ♪108H8, 2 S +16:10. ver. 41. Lk 8:28. Mt 8:29. Mk +*1:24, 34. 5:7. Ja *2:19. **of Nazareth.** Lk 18:37. 24:19. Mt +2:23. 26:71. Mk 1:24. 10:47. 14:67. Jn 18:5, 7. 19:19. Ac 2:22. **art thou come.** Ge +*3:15. Mt +*8:29. He *2:14. 1 J √3:8. Re 20:2. **destroy.** Gr. *apollumi*, Mt +2:13. **I know thee.** Mk 1:34. Ac 19:15. Ja 2:19. **the Holy One.** Lk +*1:35. Ps +*16:10. 89:18, 19. Da +*9:24. Mk 1:24. Jn 6:69. Ac 2:27. 3:14. 4:27. He 7:26. 1 J 2:20. Re 3:7.

35. **Jesus.** ver. 39, 41. Ps +*50:16. Zc 3:2. Mt 8:4, 26. 17:18. Mk 3:11, 12. Ac 16:17, 18. **Hold thy peace.** Mt 22:12. Mk 1:25. 4:39. **thrown.** Lk 9:39, 42. 11:22. Mk 1:26. 9:26. Re 12:12.

36. **they were.** ver. 32. Lk 8:25. Mt 8:27. 9:33. 12:22, 23. Mk 1:27. 4:41. 7:37. **What.** ver. 32. Lk 10:17-20. Mk 16:17-20. Ac 19:12-16. **and power.** Lk 5:17. **unclean.** ver. 33. Mk +*3:30. **spirits.** Gr. *pneuma*, Mt +8:16. **they come.** 1 P 3:22.

37. **the fame.** *Eekos*, the "sound;" a very elegant metaphor, says Dr. Adam Clarke. The people are represented as struck with astonishment, and the sound goes out through all the coasts; in allusion to the propagation of sound by a smart stroke upon any substance. ver. 14. Is 52:13. Mt 4:23-25. 9:26. Mk 1:28, 45. 6:14.

38. **he.** Mt *8:14, 15. Mk 1:29-31. 1 C *9:5. **arose.** ♪63H, Ge +12:15. **taken with.** Mt 4:25. **they besought.** Lk 7:3, 4. Mt 15:23. Jn 11:3, 22. Ja *5:14, 15.

39. **stood over.** Lk 20:1g. **and rebuked.** ver. 35. Lk 8:24. 9:42. Mt 8:26. 17:18. Mk 4:39. 9:25. **and ministered.** Lk 8:2, 3. 10:40. Ps 116:12. Jn 12:2. 2 C √5:14, 15.

40. **when.** Mt 8:16, 17. Mk 1:32-34. **laid his hands.** Lk 7:21-23. Jb 5:18. Mt 4:23, 24. 11:5. 14:13, 14. Mk 3:10. 5:23. 6:5, 55, 56. Ac 5:15. 19:12.

41. **crying out.** ver. 33-35. Mk 1:25, 26, 34. 3:11.

5:12. **Thou art**. Mt 8:29. 26:63. Jn +*5:39. √20:31. Ac +10:43. 16:17, 18. Ja *2:19. **Son of God**. Lk 8:28. Mt +14:33. Mk +1:24. Ro +1:4. **rebuking**. ver. 35. Mt 12:16. **suffered them not**. Ps +*50:16. Mk +*1:34. +*3:12. **speak**, etc. *or*, say that they knew him to be Christ. Mt 1:17. 12:15, 17. Mk 8:29. Jn 7:30.

42. **when**. Lk 6:12. Mk +*1:35. Jn 4:34. **into a desert place**. Lk 5:16. **and the**. Mt 14:13, 14. Mk *1:37, 45. 6:33, 34. Jn 6:24. **and stayed**. Lk 8:37, 38. 24:29. Jn 4:40. Ro 1:18g. 2 Th 2:6mg.

43. **I must**. Lk 13:33. Mk 1:14, 15, 38, 39. Jn 9:4. Ac *10:38. 2 T 4:2. **kingdom of God**. Lk 6:20. 7:28. 8:1, 10. 9:2, 11, 27, 60, 62. 10:9, 11. 11:20. 12:31. 13:18, 20, 28, 29. 14:15. 16:16. 17:20, 21. 18:16, 17, 24, 25, 29. 19:11. 21:31. 22:16, 18. 23:51. Mt +12:28. Mk +1:15. Jn +3:3. **therefore am I sent**. ver. 18. Lk 9:48. 10:16. Is 42:1-4. 48:16. 61:1-3. Jn 4:34. 6:38-40. 20:21.

44. **he**. ver. 15. Mt 4:23. Mk 1:39. **Galilee**. Many of the Jewish traditions, in accordance with Is 9:1, 2, assert that Galilee was the place where the Messiah should first appear. Thus also Is 2:19, "When he shall arise to smite terribly the earth," is expounded in the book *Zohar*, as referring to the Messiah: "When he shall arise, and shall be revealed in the land of Galilee." Lk 23:5. Jn 3:22. 5:1.

LUKE 5

Jesus teaches the people from Simon's ship, 1-3; who, by his direction and power, takes a large draught of fishes, 4-7. Simon, James, and John, follow him, 8-11. He cleanses a leper, 12-15; withdraws for prayer, 16; heals a paralytic, and silences the objections of the scribes and Pharisees against his forgiving sins, 17-26; calls Levi, and justifies his own eating with publicans and sinners, 27-32; and vindicates his disciples for not fasting, at present, after the manner of the Pharisees, and John's disciples, but foretells that they will fast after his ascension, 33-35. The parable of the old bottles and worn garments, 36-39.

1. **it**. Lk 8:45. 12:1. Mt 4:18, etc. 11:12. Mk 1:16, etc. 3:9. 5:24. **came to pass**. √144A11, Ge +38:1. **to hear**. Lk +*8:18, 21. Mk 2:13. 4:1. Jn *5:24. 12:48. 14:23. Ac 8:25. 13:26. 14:3. 15:7. 1 C 1:18. Ep 1:13. Ph 2:16. Col 1:25. 3:16. 2 T 2:15. Ja *1:19, 21-25. **the word of God**. Lk 8:11, 21. 11:28. Mt 15:6. Mk 4:14-20. 7:13. Jn +10:35. Ac 4:31. 6:2, 7. 8:14. 11:1. 12:24. 13:5, 7, 46, 48. 16:32. 17:13. 18:11. Ro +9:6. √10:17. 1 Th √2:13. Re 1:2. **the lake**. Lk 8:22, 23, 33. Nu 34:11, Chinnereth. Dt 3:17. Jsh 12:3, Chinneroth. 13:27. Mt +4:18. 14:34. Mk 6:53.

2. **the fishermen**. This account of the calling of Peter and Andrew, James and John, will be found, as Dr. Townson observes, on a near inspection to tally marvellously with the preceding ones of Matthew and Mark; and is one of the evidences, that the Evangelists vary only in the number or choice of circumstances, and write from the same idea of the fact which they lay before us. Though St. Matthew and Mark do not exactly tell us that St. Peter was in the vessel when he was called by Christ, they signify as much in saying that he was casting a net into the sea; and though only St. Luke informs us that James and John assisted Peter in landing the fish, yet it is implied, for Mark says, that when Christ had gone a little further, he saw them mending their nets, which had been torn by the weight of fish hauled on shore. **washing**. Gr. *apopluno*, *S#637g, only here. Mt 4:21. Mk 1:19.

3. **which**. Mt 4:18. Jn 1:41, 42. **he sat**. Lk +4:20. Mt 5:1. 13:1, 2. Mk 4:1, 2. Jn 8:2.

4. **Launch**. Mt 17:27. Jn 21:6.

5. **Master**. Lk 8:24, 45. 9:33, 49. 17:13g. **we**. Ps 127:1, 2. Ezk 37:11, 12. Jn 21:3. **nevertheless**. Lk 6:46-48. 2 K 5:10-14. Ezk 37:4-7. Jn 2:5. 15:14.

6. **they enclosed**. 2 K 4:3-7. Ec 11:6. Jn 21:6-11. Ac 2:41. 4:4. 1 C √15:58. Ga *6:9.

7. **partners**. Jb 41:6. 2 C 6:1. **that they should**. Ex 23:5. Pr 18:24. Ac 11:25, 26. Ro 16:2-4. Ga 6:2. Ph 4:3. **sink**. Gr. *bathizo*. *S#1036g. 1 T 6:9 (drown).

8. **he fell down**. ver. 12. Lk +8:28. 2 S=6:9. Mt 2:11. Jn 11:32. Ac 10:25, 26. Re 1:17. 22:8, 9. **Depart**. Ex *20:19. Jg *13:22. 1 S *6:20. 2 S *6:9. 1 K *17:18. 1 Ch 13:12. Da 10:16, 17. Mt +8:34. 17:6. **I am**. Jb 40:4. *42:5, 6. Is *6:5. Da 10:16. Mt 8:8.

9. **he**. Lk 4:32, 36. +8:25. Ps 8:6, 8. Mk 9:6. **draught of the fishes**. *29, Ex +19:6. i.e. captured fishes. Mt +*13:47.

10. **James**. Lk 6:14. Mt 4:21. 20:20. **partners**. ver. 7. 2 C 3:5, 6. 8:23. **Fear not**. ver. 26. Lk +1:13. **from**. Ezk 47:9, 10. Mt 4:19. 13:47. Mk 1:17. Ac 2:4. **catch**. 2 T 2:26mg.

11. **they forsook all**. Lk *18:28-30. Mt 4:20. 10:37. 19:27. Mk *1:18-25. √10:21, 28-30. Ph *3:7, 8. **and followed**. Nu +*32:11, 12. Dt 13:4. 1 K *14:8. +*18:21. Ps *68:3. Jn *8:12. √10:27. *12:26. Ep 5:1. Re *14:4.

12. **a certain**. *108E1, Mt +8:19. **a man**. Mt 8:2-4. Mk 1:40-45. **full**. Lk 17:12. Ex 4:6. Le ch. 13, 14. Nu 12:10-12. Dt 24:8. 2 K 5:1, 27. 7:3. 2 Ch 26:19, 20. Mt 26:6. **leprosy**. Lk +7:22. **fell**. ver. 8. Lk +17:16. Le 9:24. Jsh 5:14. 1 K 18:39. 1 Ch 21:16. **besought**. Lk 17:13. Ps +*50:15. 91:15. Mk 5:23. **if**. *184C, Mt +4:9. Ge +*18:14. Mt 8:8, 9. 9:28. Mk 9:22-24. He *7:25.

13. **touched**. Lk 22:51. Mt 8:3, 15. +9:29. Mk 1:31. +5:23. 7:33. 8:22. **I will**. Ge 1:3, 9. Ps 33:9. 2 K 5:10, 14. Ezk 36:25-27, 29. Ho 14:4. Mt 9:29, 30. **immediately**. Lk 4:39. 8:54, 55. Jn 4:50-53.

14. **he charged**. Mt 8:4. 9:30. +12:16. 17:9. Mk 1:34. 5:43. 7:36. 8:26. **but go**. *15E, Mk +6:9. **and show**. Lk +17:14. Le 13:2. **and offer**. Le 13:49. *14:4, 10, 21, 22. Mt 10:18. 24:14. Mk 1:44. 6:11. Ja 5:3.

15. **so**. Pr 15:33. Mk 1:45. 1 T 5:25. **went**. Mt 4:23-25. 9:26. Mk 1:28, 45. **great multitudes**. Lk 6:17. 12:1. 14:25. Mt 4:25. 15:30, 31. Mk +1:34. 2:1, 2. 3:7. Jn 6:2.

16. **withdrew**. Lk 6:12. 9:28. Mt *14:23. Mk +*1:35, 36. 6:46. Jn 6:15. **wilderness**. T#1216. Lk 1:80. 8:29. Ge 21:14-16. Ex 14:10, 11. Nu 21:5-7. 1 K 19:4. Ps 107:4-6. Mk 1:45.

17. **it came**. Lk 8:22. 20:1. **a certain**. *108E1, Mt +8:19. **teaching**. Lk +9:11. **that there**. ver. 21, 30. Lk *7:30. 11:52-54. 15:2. Jn 3:21. **doctors of**. Lk 2:46. Mt 22:35. Ac 5:34. 1 T 1:7g. **Jerusalem**. Mt 15:1. Mk 3:22. 7:1. **power**. Lk 1:35. 4:36. 6:19. 8:46. 24:49. Mt 11:5. Mk 16:18. Ac 4:30. 6:8. *10:38. 19:11, 12.

18. **men brought**. Mt 9:2-8. Mk 2:3-12. Jn 5:5, 6. Ac 9:33. **in a bed**. Mk 6:55.

19. **not find**. Lk 8:20. **they went**. Mk 2:4. **housetop**. Lk 12:3. 17:31. Dt 22:8. 1 S 9:25, 26. 2 S 11:2. 16:22.

Ne 8:16. Is 15:3. Je 19:13. 48:38. Mt 10:27. 24:17. Ac 10:9. **through.** Mk 2:4.

20. **he saw.** Lk 7:9, 50. 17:19. 18:42. Ge 22:12. Mt 8:10, 13. 9:22, 29. 15:28. 17:20. Mk 9:23. 10:52. Jn +*2:25. Ac 3:16. 11:23. 14:9. Ep *2:8. Ja 2:18. 5:15. **Man.** Lk +12:14. **thy sins.** Lk +7:48. Ps 90:7, 8. 107:17, 18. Is 38:17. Mt 9:2. Mk 2:5. Jn 5:14. 2 C 2:10. Col 3:13. Ja *5:14, 15.

21. **scribes.** ver. 17. Lk 7:49. Mk 2:6, 7. **began to reason.** Lk 3:8. 13:25, 26. 14:9. **Who.** ♪65, Mt +27:19. Gordon H. Clark notes (*Logic*, p. 4) this is the figure *enthymeme*, the conclusion ("Jesus is a blasphemer") of an argument in which one or both of the premises are unstated or taken for granted. The unstated premises are (1) anyone who can really forgive sins is God (implied in the rhetorical question); (2) Jesus is only a man and is not God (unstated). Therefore, claiming to be God, he is a blasphemer. The argument is valid in form, involving no fallacy, but the second premise is false, rendering the conclusion untrue. Lk 7:49. Jn 5:12. **blasphemies.** Le *24:16. 1 K 21:10-14. Mt 9:3. 26:65. Mk 14:64. Jn √10:33, 36. Ac 6:11-13. **Who can.** Ex 34:6, 7. Jb 14:4. Ps *32:5. 35:5. 51:4. 86:5. +*103:3. 130:4. Is *1:18. *43:25. 44:22. Da 9:9, 19. Mi 7:19. Mk *2:7. Ro 8:33. **but God.** Lk 18:19. Jn +*20:28.

22. **perceived.** Gr. *epiginosko,* Mt +11:27. Lk 6:8. 1 Ch +*28:9. Ps *139:2. Pr 15:26. Is 66:18. Ezk +*11:5. 38:10. Mt 9:4. 12:25. Jn +*2:24, 25. He √4:12, 13. Re *2:23. **their thoughts.** Lk +2:35. **What.** Lk 24:38. Mk 8:17. Ac *5:3.

23. **is easier.** Mt 9:5. Mk 2:9. **and walk.** Is 35:6. Jn 5:8.

24. **Son of man.** Lk 6:5, 22. 7:34. 9:22, 26, 44, 56, 58. 11:30. 12:8, 10, 40. 17:22, 24, 26, 30. 18:8, 31. 19:10. 21:27, 36. 22:22, 48, 69. 24:7. Da 7:13. Mt +8:20. 12:8. 16:13. 25:31. 26:64. Mk 2:+10, 28. Jn +1:51. 3:13. 5:27. Re 1:13. **power.** Is 53:11. Mt 9:6. 28:18. Jn 5:8, 12, 22, 23. 17:2. 20:22, 23. Ac 5:31. **I say.** ver. 13. Lk 7:14. 8:54. Jn 11:43. Ac 3:6-8. 9:34, 40. 14:10. **Arise.** Jn +5:8. **and take.** Jn 5:8-12.

25. **immediately.** ver. 13. Lk 8:44, 55. 18:43. Ge 1:3. Ps *33:9. **glorifying.** Lk +13:13. 17:15-18. 18:43. Ps 50:23. 103:1-3. 107:20-22. Mt +9:8. Jn 9:24.

26. **and they.** Lk 1:65. 7:16. 9:43. 13:17. 18:43. Mt 9:8. 12:23. Mk 2:12. Ac 4:21. Ga 1:24. **and were.** ver. 8. Lk 1:65. 7:16. 8:25, 35, 37. Je 33:9. Ho 3:5. Mt 9:8. 28:8. Mk 4:41. 5:15. Ac +2:43. 5:11-13.

27. **saw a publican.** Lk +3:12. **named Levi.** Mt 9:9, etc. 10:3, Matthew. Mk 2:13, 14. 3:18. 6:15. Ac 1:13. **Follow me.** Lk 18:22. Mt 4:19-21. 8:22. Jn 1:43. 12:26. 21:19-22.

28. **left all.** ver. 11. Lk 9:59-62. 14:33. 1 K 19:19-21. Ps *110:3. Mt 19:22-27. **and followed.** Lk 9:23. Mt 4:19.

29. **made.** Lk 7:34. 14:1, 13. Mt 10:32, 33. 11:19. Jn 1:41. 4:28, 29. 12:2. **and there.** Lk *15:1. Mt 9:10. Mk 2:15. 1 C 5:9-11. 10:27.

30. **their scribes and.** ver. 17, 21. Lk *7:29, 30, 34, 39. 15:1, 2. 18:11. 19:7. Is +*65:5n. Mt 21:28-32. Mk 2:16. *7:3. Ac +23:9. **murmured.** Mt 23:13. **publicans.** Lk 7:34. 15:1, 2. Mt +11:19.

31. **They that.** Je 8:22. Mt 9:12, 13. Mk 2:17. Re *3:17, 18. **but they.** Jn 1:12. Ro 3:10, 23. 6:23. 1 T *1:15. Re √3:20.

32. **came not.** Lk 4:18, 19. 9:56. *15:7, 10. *18:10-14. +*19:10. 24:47. Is √55:6, 7. +*57:15. Mt 18:11.

Jn 9:39. Ac +*2:38. *3:19, 26. *5:31. √17:30. 20:21. *26:18-20. 1 C +*6:9-11. 1 T *1:15, 16. 2 T *2:25, 26. 2 P +√3:9. **but sinners.** Jsh 6:25. **to repentance.** Lk +*13:3, 5. 15:7, 10. 24:47. Pr √28:13. Mt 4:17. 11:20. Mk +*1:15. Ac 5:31.

33. **Why.** Mt *18:12. Is *58:3-6. Zc 7:6. Mt *6:16. 9:14-17. Mk 2:18-22. **disciples of John.** Mt 11:2. 14:12. Jn 1:35. 3:25. 4:1. Ac 18:25. 19:3. **fast often.** T#1169. Lk 2:37. 18:1, 12. **and make.** Lk 11:1. 20:47. Pr 28:9. Is 1:15. Mt 6:5, 6. 23:14. Mk 12:40. Ac 9:11. Ro 10:2, 3. 1 T 2:1. **but.** ver. 30. Lk 7:34, 35.

34. **the children.** ♪108B, 1 S +20:31. Lk +10:6. Jg 14:10, 11. Ps 45:14. SS 2:6, 7. 3:10, 11. 5:8. 6:1. Mt 25:1-10. Re 19:7-9. **bridegroom.** Ps 45:10-16. Is 54:5. 62:5. Zp 3:17. Mt 22:2. +25:1. Jn *3:29. 2 C 11:2. Ep *5:25-27. **is with them.** Jn 16:16.

35. **the days.** Lk +17:22. **when.** Lk 24:17-21. Da +*9:26. Zc 13:7. Mt +26:11. Jn 12:8. 13:33. 14:3, 4. 16:4-7, 16-22, 28. 17:11-13. Ac 1:9. 3:21. **then shall they fast.** Is 22:12. Mt 6:17, 18. Jn 16:20. Ac *13:2, 3. 14:23. 1 C *7:5. 2 C 11:27.

36. **a parable.** Mk 4:33. Jn 16:12. **No man.** Mt 9:16, 17. Mk 2:21, 22. Jn 1:17. **if.** ♪184A, 1 C +15:2. **agreeth.** Le 19:19. Dt 22:11. 2 C 6:16.

37. **old bottles.** Ge 21:14. Jsh 9:4, 13. Jb 32:19. Ps 119:83. **perish.** Gr. *apollumi,* Mt +2:13.

38. **new wine.** Ezk 36:26. 2 C *5:17. Ga 2:4, 12-14. 4:9-11. 5:1-6. 6:13, 14. Ph 3:5-7. Col 2:19-23. 1 T 4:8. He 8:8-13. 13:9, 10. Re 21:5.

39. **desireth.** Mt +6:2n. **The old is.** Je 6:16. Mk 7:7-13. Ro 4:11, 12. 7:6. 2 C 3:6. He 11:1, 2, 39.

LUKE 6

Jesus vindicates his disciples from the charge of breaking the sabbath, 1-5. He shows it lawful to do good on the sabbath; and restores a withered hand, 6-10. His enemies are filled with madness, 11. He spends the night in prayer, 12; appoints the twelve apostles, 13-16; heals divers diseased persons, 17-19; pronounces blessings and woes, 20-26; and teaches love to enemies, meekness, liberality, mercy, and candor, 27-38. He shows, by parables, that knowledge is indispensably needful in teachers, and holiness in reformers, 39-42. The tree is known by his fruit, 43-25. The parable of the wise and the foolish builders, 46-49.

1. **the second.** Ex 12:15, 16. Le 23:7, 10, 11, 15. Dt 16:9. **that.** Mt 12:1, etc. Mk 2:23, etc. **and his.** Dt *23:25.

2. **Why.** ver. 7-9. Lk 5:33. Mt 12:2. 15:2. +*23:23, 24. Mk 2:24. Jn 5:9-11, 16. 9:14-16. **not.** Ex 20:10. 31:15. 35:2. Nu 15:32-35. Is +*58:13n.

3. **Have.** Mt 12:3, 5. 19:4. 21:16, 42. 22:31. Mk 2:25. 12:10, 26. **what.** 1 S *21:3-6. Mt 12:3, 4. Mk 2:25, 26.

4. **which.** Le *24:5-9.

5. **Son.** ♪144A3, Ge +11:5. Mt 16:27n. **Lord also of.** Mt 12:5-8. Mk *2:27, 28. 9:7. Re 1:10. **sabbath.** Lk 13:14n.

6. **it came.** Mt 12:9-14. Mk 3:1-6. **he entered.** Lk 4:16, 31. *13:10, 13, 14. 14:3. Mt 4:23. Mk 3:1. Jn *9:16. **there.** 1 K 13:4. Zc 11:17. Jn 5:3.

7. **watched.** Lk 13:14. 14:1-6. Ps 37:32, 33. 38:12. Is 29:21. Je 20:10. Mk 3:2. Jn 5:10-16. 9:16, 26-29. **would.** ♪96C9, Ge +2:10. **on the sabbath.** Lk 13:14n. **that.** Lk 11:53, 54. 20:20. Mt 26:59, 60.

8. **But**. Lk 5:22. 7:40. 1 Ch +*28:9. 29:17. Jb *42:2. Ps 44:21. Jn +*2:25. 21:17. He *4:13. Re *2:23. **Rise**. Is 42:4. Jn 9:4. Ac 20:24. 26:26. Ph 1:28. 1 P 4:1. **stand forth**. Mk 3:3.

9. **Is it lawful**. Lk 14:3. Mt *12:11-13. Mk 3:4. Jn *7:19-24. **to save**. Lk 9:56. **life**. Gr. *psyche*, ✓121A7, Mt +2:20. ✓✓171Q1, Ge +12:5. ✓121A7, Ge +9:5. **destroy**. Gr. *apollumi*, Mt +2:13.

10. **looking**. Mk 3:5. **Stretch**. Ex 4:6, 7. 1 K 13:6. Ps 107:20. Jn 5:8.

11. **they**. Lk 4:28. Ps 2:1, 2. Ec 9:3. Ac 5:33. 7:54. 26:11. **communed**. Mt 12:14, 15. 21:45, 46. Mk 3:6. Jn 7:1. 11:47, 48. Ac 4:15, 16. 5:33, 34. **what**. ✓184D2, Lk +1:62.

12. **that**. Lk 5:16. Ps 55:15-17. 109:3, 4. Da +*6:10. Mt *6:6. Mk +*1:35. 14:34-36. He *5:7. **into a mountain**. Lk 22:39. **continued all night**. T#1759. Ge 32:24-26. 1 S 15:10, 11. 2 S 12:16. Ps 22:2. Jl 1:13. Mt *14:23-25. Mk 6:46. Col 4:2. **in prayer**. Ps 5:3, 109:4. Mk +*1:35. He *5:7.

13. **when**. Lk 9:1, 2. Mt 9:36-38. *10:1-4. Mk 3:13-19. 6:7. **twelve**. Lk 22:30. Mt 19:28. Re 12:1. 21:14. **apostles**. Lk 11:49. 2 C *5:20. Ep *2:20. 4:11. He 3:1. 2 P 3:2. Re 18:20.

14. **Simon**. Lk 5:8. Jn *1:40-42. 21:15-20. Ac 1:13. 2 P 1:1. **Andrew**. Mt 4:18. Jn 6:8. **James**. Lk 5:10. Mt 4:21. Mk 1:19, 29. 5:37. 9:2. 14:33. Jn 21:20-24. Ac 12:2. **Philip**. Mt 10:3. Jn 1:45, 46. 6:5. 14:8, 9. Ac 1:13.

15. **Matthew**. Lk 5:27, Levi. Mt 9:9. **Thomas**. Jn 11:16. *20:24-29. **James**. Ac 15:13. Ga 1:19. 2:9. Ja 1:1. **Alpheus**. Mt 10:3. Mk 2:14. 3:18. Ac 1:13. **Simon**. Mt *10:4. Mk 3:18, Simon the Canaanite. Ac 1:13. **Zelotes**. i.e. *zealous, jealous*, *S#2208g. Ac 1:13.

16. **Judas**. i.e. *praised, confession*, S#2455g. (1) Judah, the patriarch, Mt 1:2, 3. (2) Judas, the betrayer of Christ, surnamed "Iscariot," which probably means *Ish Kerioth*, "the man from Kerioth," a town of Judah, Jsh 15:25n. Mt 10:4. 26:14, 15, 25, 47. 27:3-10. Mk 3:19. 14:10, 43. Lk 6:16. 22:3, 47, 48. Jn 6:71. 12:4. 13:2, 26, 29. 18:2, 3, 5. Ac 1:16, 25. (3) The one called Juda in Mk 6:3. See Mt 13:55. (4) One of the apostles, Lk 6:16, Jn 14:22, and a brother of James, Ju 1. Called Lebbaeus in Mt 10:3, Thaddaeus in Mk 3:18, and Jude in Ju 1. (5) Judas of Galilee, the leader of an insurrection against the Roman enrolment under Augustus, successful at first, but finally defeated, Ac 5:37. (6) Judas, in whose house Paul found shelter in Damascus during his blindness, Ac 9:11-17. (7) Judas, surnamed Barsabas, who, together with Paul, Barnabas, and Silas, was chosen to carry the decisions of the Council of Jerusalem, to Antioch, Ac 15:22-33. **the brother**. Mt 10:3, Lebbeus, Thaddeus. Mk 3:18, Thaddeus. Jn 14:22. Ju *1. **Judas Iscariot**. Mt 26:14-16. 27:3-5. Jn *6:70, 71. Ac 1:16-20, 25. **the traitor**. Ps 41:9. 1 J *2:19.

17. **and a**. Mt 4:23-25. 12:15. Mk 3:7, etc. **the sea**. Mt 11:21. 15:21. Mk 3:8. 7:24-31. **which**. Lk 5:15. Mt 14:14. **to be**. Ps 103:3. 107:17-20.

18. **vexed**. Mt 15:22. 17:15. Ac 5:16. **unclean**. Mk +3:30. **spirits**. Gr. *pneuma*, Mt +8:16.

19. **sought**. Nu 21:8, 9. 2 K 13:21. Mt 9:20, 21. *14:36. Mk 3:10. 6:56. 8:22. Jn 3:14, 15. Ac 5:15, 16. 19:12. **for**. Lk 8:45, 46. Mk *5:30. 1 P 2:9g.

20. **he lifted**. ✓144A12, Ge +22:13. Lk 16:23. 18:13. Mt *5:2, etc. 12:49, 50. 17:8. Mk 3:34, 35. Jn 4:35.

6:5. 11:41. 17:1. **Blessed**. ver. 24. Lk 4:18. 16:25. 1 S 2:8. Ps 37:16. 113:7, 8. Pr 16:19. 19:1. Is 29:19. +*57:15, 16. 61:1. *66:2. Zp 3:12. Zc 11:11. Mt *11:5. Jn 7:48, 49. 1 C *1:26-29. 2 C 6:10. 8:2, 9. 1 Th 1:6. Ja 1:9, 10. +*2:5, 6. Re 2:9. **poor**. Ps 9:12, 18. 10:2, 9, 12. +*12:5. 40:17. 69:29. 72:2, 4, 12, 13. 82:3, 4. 86:1. 109:22. 113:7. **for**. Lk 12:32. 13:28. 14:15. Mt +*5:3, 10. Ac 14:22. 1 C 3:21-23. 2 Th 1:5. Ja 1:12.

21. **ye that hunger**. ver. 25. Lk *1:53. Ps 42:1, 2. 132:15. 143:6. Is *55:1, 2. Mt +*5:6. 1 C *4:11. 2 C 11:27. 12:10. **for ye shall be filled**. Ps *17:15. 63:1-5. 65:4. *107:9. Is 25:6. 44:3, 4. 49:9, 10. *65:13. 66:10. Je 31:14, 25. Mt +*5:6. Jn 4:10. *6:35. 7:37, 38. Re *7:14, 16, 17. **ye that weep**. ver. 25. Ps 6:6-8. 42:3. 119:136. ✓126:5, 6. Ec 7:2, 3. Is 25:8. 30:19. 57:17, 18. +*61:1-3. Je 9:1. 13:17. 31:9, 13, 18-20. Ezk 7:16. +*9:4. Mt +*5:4. Jn 11:35. *16:20, 21. Ro 9:1-3. 2 C *1:4-6. *6:10. *7:10, 11. Ja *1:2-4, 12. 4:9. 1 P 1:6-8. Re *21:3, 4. **ye shall laugh**. ✓121S2, Ge +21:6. Ge 17:17 Ps 28:7. 30:11, 12. 126:1, 2. Is +*12:1, 2. 65:14.

22. **when men**. Mt *5:10-12. 10:22. Mk *10:29, 30. 13:9-13. Jn 7:7. 15:18-20. *17:14. 2 C 11:23-26. Ph 1:28-30. 1 Th 2:2, 14, 15. 2 T 3:11, 12. 1 P *2:19, 20. *3:14. 4:12-16. **separate**. T#935. Lk 20:15. 2 Ch=13:9. Is +*65:5n. *66:5. Jn 9:22-28, 34. 12:42. 16:2. Ac 22:22. 24:5. **reproach**. Ps 69:7, 9. Is 66:5. He 11:26. 1 P *4:14. **cast out**. Dt 22:19. Jn 9:34. **for**. Lk 21:17. Mt 10:18, 22, 39. Jn *15:21. Ac 9:16. 1 C 4:10, 11.

23. **Rejoice**. Mt +*5:12. Ac *5:41. 13:52. Ro *5:3. 2 C 6:10. 7:4. 12:10. Ph 1:29. 2:17. Col 1:11, 24. 1 Th 1:6. He 10:34. 13:13. Ja *1:2, 3. 1 P 1:6. *4:13. **leap**. Lk 1:41, 44. 2 S 6:16. Is 35:6. Ac 3:8. 14:10. **your reward**. ver. 35. Mt +*5:12. 6:1, 2. Ro ✓8:18. 2 C ✓4:17. 2 Th 1:5-7. 2 T 2:12. 4:7, 8. He 11:6, 26. 1 P 4:13. Re 2:7, 10, 11, 17, 26. 3:5, 12. 21:7. **for in**. 1 K 18:4. *19:2, 10, 14. 21:20. 22:8, 27. 2 K 6:31. 2 Ch 16:10. 24:20, 21. *36:16. Ne +*9:26. Je 2:30. 26:8, 20, 23. Mt 21:35, 36. 23:31-37. Ac *7:51, 52. 1 Th *2:14, 15. He *11:32-39.

24. **woe**. Lk *12:15-21. 18:23-25. Jb 21:7-15. Ps 49:6, 7, 16-19. 73:3-12. Pr 1:32. Je 5:4-6. *22:21. Am 4:1-3. *6:1-6. Hg 2:9. 1 T 6:17. Ja 2:6. *5:1-6. Re 18:6-8. **have received**. Lk *16:19-25. Mt *6:2, +*5, 16.

25. **full**. Dt 6:11, 12. 1 S 2:5. Pr 30:9. Is 28:7. 65:13. Ezk +*16:49. Ph 4:12, 13. Re 3:17. **shall hunger**. Is 8:21. 9:20. 65:13. **laugh**. ✓121S2, Ge +21:6. Lk 8:53. 16:14, 15. Jb ✓20:5. Ps 22:6, 7. Pr ✓14:13. Ec *2:2. *7:3, 6. Ep 5:4. Ja 4:9. **mourn**. Lk *12:20. 13:28. Jb 20:5-7. 21:11-13. Ps 49:19. Is 21:3, 4. 24:7-12. Da 5:4-6. Am 8:10. Na 1:10. Mt 22:11-13. 1 Th 5:3. Re 18:7-11.

26. **when**. Je *45:5. Mi 2:11. Jn 7:7. *15:19. Ro 16:18. 2 Th 2:8-12. Ja ✓4:4. 2 P 2:18, 19. 1 J 4:5, 6. Re 13:3, 4. **so**. 1 K 22:6-8, 13, 14, 24-28. Is 30:10. Je *5:31. 2 P 2:1-3.

27. **unto**. Lk 8:8, 15, 18. Mk 4:24. **Love**. ver. 35. Lk 23:34. Ex *23:4, 5. Jb 31:29-31. Ps 7:4. Pr 24:17. *25:2, 21, 22. Mt *5:43-45. Ac 7:60. Ro *12:17-21. 1 Th 5:15. 1 P 3:9. **do**. ver. 22. Ac *10:38. Ga 6:10. 3 J 11.

28. **Bless**. Lk *23:34. Mt *5:44. Ac *7:60. Ro ✓12:14. 1 C 4:12. Ja 3:10. 1 P *3:9. **pray for**. Lk 23:34. Ac 7:60. 1 C 4:12. 2 T 4:16. 1 P 3:9. **despitefully**. Ezk 25:15. 36:5. Ac 14:5. 1 P 3:16.

29. **unto him.** Pr ❶+*19:25. Mt +*5:39. Ro *12:17. 1 P *2:19-23. **smiteth.** While Jesus and the rest of Scripture certainly teaches us not to retaliate against those who have wronged us, that is not the lesson here. Jesus is not recommending for His followers an absolute policy of non-resistance. To properly understand and apply this text, it is necessary to remember the political conditions which existed in Israel at the time Jesus spoke these words. He is recommending to his hearers what was the most prudent response possible to the authority of Rome. They were to avoid bringing unnecessary suffering upon themselves, by cooperating with this foreign power in all matters which did not compromise their faith and obedience to God and his word. Jesus is hardly teaching Christians to let everyone else in the world walk all over them. He was encouraging them to make the best of a bad situation, where they could not hope to gain by resisting the occupying power. Lk 22:❶+*36, *64. 1 Ch +*12:32n. 2 Ch 18:23. Pr +*22:3. Is 50:6. La 3:30. Mi 5:1. Mt 26:67. Mk 14:65. Jn 18:22. 19:3. Ac 23:2. 1 C 4:11. 2 C 11:20. **and him.** 2 S 19:30. Mt 5:40, 41. 1 C *6:7. He 10:34. **cloak.** Mt 24:18. Mk 13:16. **coat.** The coat, kiton, was a tunic or undergarment, over which the Jews and other nations threw a cloak or gown, imation, when they went abroad or were not at work.

30. **Give.** This must be understood in the light of the historical situation then prevailing in Israel under Roman rule. It is not a universal command for all Christians to give away everything they own to anyone who happens to ask for it. Bertrand Russel (*Why I Am Not a Christian*, under the heading "The Character of Christ," p. 15) and other skeptics have taken related but similar passages (Mt 5:42. 19:21) out of context and asserted that they never met a Christian who obeyed this commandment of Christ. The writings of skeptics are full of such nonsense. Such assertions on their part serve more to show their willful ignorance than any defect in the teaching of Christ. ver. 38. Lk 11:41. 12:33. 18:22. Dt √15:7-10. Ps *37:21, 26. 41:1. *112:5, 9. Pr 3:27, 28. 11:24, 25. *19:17. 21:26. 22:9. Ezk 11:1, 2. Is 58:7-10. Ec 18:16. Mt *5:42, etc. ❶*25:8, 9. Ac *20:35. 2 C *8:9. *9:6-14. Ep *4:28. 1 J *3:17. **and him.** Ex 22:26, 27. Ne 5:1-19. Mt 6:12. 18:27-30, 35.

31. **as ye would.** ∫138B, Ge +13:16. Pr 18:24. 24:29. Mt √7:12. 22:39. Ga 5:14. Ja 2:8-16.

32. **if.** ∫184A, 1 C +15:2. Mt 5:46, 47. **what.** ver. 33, 34. 1 P 2:19, 20.

33. **And if.** ∫184C, Mt +4:9. Mt 5:47. **what thank.** ver. 32. Lk 17:9, 10.

34. **if ye lend.** ∫184C, Mt +4:9. ver. 35. Lk 14:12-14. Dt *15:8-11. Ps *37:26. Pr 19:17. Mt 5:42.

35. **love.** ver. *27-31. Le *25:35-37. Ps *37:26. *112:5. Pr *19:17. *22:9. Ro √5:8-10. 2 C √8:9. **do good.** Mi +*6:8. Ro 12:20, 21. Ga +*6:10. He 6:9, 10. Ja 1:27. 2:15, 16. T 3:8. 1 J 3:17. **and lend.** The *New World Translation* adds in brackets "lend (without interest)." ver. +30. Dt *15:7-11. Ps 37:26. 112:5. Pr 19:17. **hoping for nothing.** or, without expecting any return (NEB); or, never despairing (RV, ASV); hoping for nothing back (Rotherham); or, not losing hope of anything (i.e. not thinking any sacrifice useless); or, despairing of no man (RVmg). ver. 33. Dt 23:19, 20. Ps 15:5. Pr 1:19. 15:27. *22:16. 28:22. Is +*24:2. 1 T

3:3, 8. +*6:5. **your reward.** 1 T +*4:8. Re 11:18. **great.** Lk +*12:48. **and ye.** Mt +*5:44, 45. Jn 13:35. 15:8. 1 J *3:10-14. 4:7-11. **the Highest.** Lk 1:32, 35, 76. Mk 5:7. Ac 7:48. **for he is kind.** Ge *18:25. Dt 20:20. 2 Ch 15:7. Ps 34:8. 68:18. 112:4. +*145:9. Is +27:4. Mt +*5:45. 10:42. Ac *14:17. 17:25, +*30. 1 T 6:17.

36. **merciful.** ver. +*35. Is +27:4. Jon +4:2. Mt +*5:7, 48. Ep √4:31, 32. 5:1, 2. Ja 3:17. 1 P *1:15, 16. **is merciful.** Ps 112:4. 2 C 1:3. Col 3:12. Ja 5:11.

37. **Judge not.** ver. 41, 44. Is +*65:5n. Mt +6:2n. +*7:1. Jn ❶+*7:24. Ro *2:1, 2. *14:3, 4, 10-16. 1 C *4:3-5. ❶*5:3. Ja 4:11, 12. 5:9. **shall not.** ∫158, Mt +5:18. **condemn not.** Jb 15:6. Pr *17:15. 30:10. Mk 3:2. Ro 2:1. +*14:4, 22. **not be condemned.** Is 50:9. Jn 3:18. 5:24. Ro 8:1, 34. 14:22. 1 J 3:21. **forgive.** Lk 17:3, 4. Mt +*5:7. *6:14, 15. 18:35. Mk *11:25, 26. 1 C √13:4-7. Ep √4:32. Col *3:13.

38. **Give.** Lk 3:11. 12:33. Mt 5:42. 6:1-4, 23. 10:8. ❶*25:8, 9. **and it.** T#408. ver. 30. Lk +18:28 (T#674). Dt 15:10. 2 Ch *31:10. Ezr 7:27, 28. Jb 31:16-20. √42:11, 12. Ps *37:3, 25, 26. +58:11 (T#630). 112:5, 6. Pr *3:9, 10. 10:22. *11:24-26. *13:7. *19:17. 22:9. Ec 11:1, 2. Is 32:8. Ml *3:9-12. Mt +5:7 (T#527). 10:42. Mk +10:30 (T#415). Ac *20:35. 2 C 8:14, 15. *9:6-8. Ph 4:17-19. **bosom.** Ps 79:12. Pr 6:27. Is 65:6, 7. Je 32:18. **with.** Le 24:19. Dt 19:16-21. Jg 1:7. 1 S 15:33. Est 7:10. 9:25. Ps 18:25, 26. 41:1, 2. Mt *7:2. Mk 4:24. Ja *2:13. Re 16:5, 6.

39. **Can.** Pr +*19:27. Is *9:16. 56:10. Mt +*15:14. 23:16-26. Mk +*4:24. Ro 2:19. 1 T 6:3-5. 2 T 3:13. **shall.** Je 6:15. 8:12. 14:15, 16. Mi 3:6, 7. Zc 11:15-17. Mt 23:33.

40. **The disciple.** ∫138B, Ge +13:16. Lk 22:27. Mt *10:24, 25. Jn *13:16. *15:20. He 12:3. **master.** Mt 22:24. **that is perfect shall be as his master.** *or*, shall be perfected as his master. Mt 23:15. 1 C 1:10. 2 C 3:18. 13:11. Ph ❶+*3:12. 2 T 3:17. He *13:21. 1 P *5:10. 1 J 3:2.

41. **why.** Mt *7:3-5. Ro 2:1, 21-24. **but.** 2 S 12:5-7. 20:9, 10, 20, 21. 1 K 2:32. 1 Ch 21:6. Ps 36:2. Je +*17:9. Ezk 18:28. Jn 8:7, 40-44. Ja 1:24.

42. **hypocrite.** Lk 13:15. Mt 23:13-15. Ac 8:21. 13:10. **cast.** Lk 22:32. Ps 50:16-21. 51:9-13. Pr 18:17. Mt 26:75. Ac +*2:38. 9:9-20. Ro *2:1, 21, etc. 2 C 5:18. 1 Th 2:10-12. Phm 10, 11. **first.** Mt 6:33. 23:26. **see.** Mt 6:22, 23. 2 T 2:21. 2 P 1:9. Re 3:17, 18.

43. **good tree.** Ps 92:12-14. Is 5:4. 61:3. Je 2:21. Mt 3:10. 7:16-20. *12:33.

44. **For of.** Ga 5:19-23. T *2:11-13. Ja 3:12. Ju 12. **grapes.** Gr. a grape.

45. **good man.** Ps 37:30, 31. 40:8-10. 71:15-18. Pr 10:20, 21. 12:18. 15:23. 22:17, 18. Mt +*12:35. Jn 7:38. *15:1, 5. Ep 4:29. 5:3, 4, 19. Col *4:6. **treasure.** Mt +*13:52. 2 C 4:6, 7. Ep 3:8. Col *3:16. He 8:10. **and an evil.** Ps 12:2-4. 41:6, 7. 52:2-4. 59:7, 12. 64:3-8. 140:5. Is *32:6. Je 9:2-5. Mt 15:18, 19. Mk 7:20-23. Jn 8:43. 12:39. Ac +*5:3. *8:19-23. Ro 3:13, 14. 8:7. Ja 3:5-8. Ju 15. **for.** Mt +*12:34-37.

46. **why call.** Lk *13:25-27. Ml *1:6. Mt √7:21-23. *25:11, 12, 24, 44. Jn *13:13-17. Ga *6:7. 1 P 3:6. **Lord, Lord.** ∫84, Ge +22:11. Mt √7:21. **and do not.** Ezr ❶+*7:10. Ezk +*33:31, 32. Jn ❶+*13:17. Ja +*1:22.

47. **cometh.** Lk 14:26. Is +*55:3. Mt √11:28. Jn √5:40. √6:35, 37, 44, 45. 1 P 2:4. **heareth.** Mt 7:24,

25. 17:5. Jn 8:52. 9:27, 28. +*10:27. **doeth them.** Lk +*8:8, 13. +*11:28. Mt 11:29, 30. 12:50. Jn +*13:17. *14:15, 21-24. *15:9-14. Ro 2:7-10. He *5:9. Ja *1:22-25. √4:17. 2 P +*1:10. 1 J 2:29. 3:7. Re 22:14.

48. **and laid.** Pr 10:25. Is 28:16. Mt 7:25, 26. 1 C 3:10-12. Ep *2:20. 2 T *2:19. **digged deep.** lit. dug and deepened. √93B, Is +66:11. By Hendiadys, dug very deep, till he reached the rock itself. **rock.** Dt 32:15, 18, 31. 1 S 2:2. 2 S 22:2, 32, 47. 23:3. Ps 95:1. Is 26:4. 1 P 2:4-6. **the flood.** 2 S 22:5. Ps 32:6. 93:3, 4. 125:1, 2. Is 59:19. Na 1:8. Jn 16:33. Ac +*14:22. Ro √8:35-38. 1 C √3:13-15. √15:55-58. 2 P 3:10-14. 1 J 2:28. Re 6:14-17. 20:11-15. **could not.** 2 P +*1:10. Ju +*24. **for.** Ps 46:1-3. *62:2.

49. **that heareth.** ver. 46. Lk *8:5-7. 19:14, 27. Je 44:16, 17. Ezk +*33:31. Mt 21:29, 30. 23:3. Jn 15:2. Ja *1:22-26. 2:17-26. 2 P *1:5-9. 1 J +*2:3, 4. **built.** Ezk 13:10-14. **against.** Mt +*13:20-22. +*24:10. Ac *20:29. 26:11. 1 Th 3:5. **immediately.** Pr 28:18. Ho 4:14. Mt 12:43-45. Mk 4:17. 1 J √2:19. **the ruin.** Lk 10:12-16. 11:24-26. +*12:47. Am 6:11. He +*10:26-29. 2 P +*2:20-22.

LUKE 7

Jesus commends the faith, and heals the servant of a centurion, 1-10. He raises a widow's son at Nain, 11-17. He sends back the messengers of John the Baptist, with an account of his miracles, 18-23; bears testimony to John, 24-30; and exposes the perverseness of the people, respecting both John and himself, 31-35. He is entertained by a Pharisee, 36. A woman of previous bad character washes and anoints his feet, 37-39. He justifies to the Pharisee his conduct towards her by a parable, and shows that she loved much, and that her many sins were pardoned, 40-50.

1. **when.** Mt 7:28, 29. **he entered.** Mt 8:5-13.

2. **centurion's.** Lk 23:47. Mt +*27:54n. Ac +*10:1, 2. 22:26. 23:17. 27:1, 3, 43. **who.** Ge 24:2-14, 27, 35-49. 35:8. 39:4-6. 2 K 5:2, 3. Jb 31:15. Pr 29:21. Ac 10:7. Col 3:22-25. 4:1. **was sick.** Lk 8:42. Mt *8:6. Jn 4:46, 47. 11:2, 3.

3. **beseeching.** Lk 8:41. 9:38. Mt 8:5. Jn 4:47. Phm 10.

4. **worthy.** ver. 6, 7. Lk 20:35. Mt 10:11, 13, 37, 38. Ga *5:6. Re 3:4.

5. **he loveth.** 1 K 5:1. 2 Ch 2:11, 12. Ga 5:6. 1 J 3:14. 5:1-3. **and.** 1 Ch 29:3, etc. Ezr 7:27, 28. 1 J 3:18, 19.

6. **Jesus.** Mt 20:28. Mk 5:24. Ac *10:38. **trouble.** Lk 8:49. **for.** ver. 4. Lk 5:8. 15:19-21. Ge 32:10. Pr 29:23. Mt 3:11. 15:26, 27. Ja 4:6, 10. **not worthy.** Jn ◐7:49. 1 C *13:4. Ro 12:3. Ph 2:3, 4. **enter.** Lk ◐14:1. Mt ◐18:17. Ac 10:28.

7. **worthy.** ver. 6. 1 C *13:4. **but.** Lk 4:36. 5:13. Ex 15:26. Dt 32:39. 1 S 2:6. Ps 33:9. 107:20. Mt 8:16. Mk 1:27. **servant.** T#1694.

8. **under.** Ac 22:25, 26. 23:17, 23, 26. 24:23. 25:26. **one.** Gr. this man. **and he goeth.** Ac 10:7, 8. Col 3:22. 1 T 6:1, 2.

9. **he marvelled.** Mt 8:10. 15:28. **not in.** Ps 147:19, 20. Mt 9:33. Ro 3:1-3. 9:4, 5.

10. **found.** Mt 8:13. 15:28. Mk 9:23. Jn 4:50-53.

11. **And.** √148, Ge +8:22. **he went.** Ac *10:38. **Nain.** i.e. *beautiful*, *S#3484g, only here. Compare Heb. *naah*, *S#4999h, Ps +23:2 (pastures).

12. **the only.** Gr. *monogenes*, *S#3439g. Lk 8:42. 9:38. Ge 22:2, +12. Jg 11:34. 2 S 14:7. 1 K 17:9, 12, 18, 23. 2 K 4:16, 20. Ps 25:16, LXX. Je 6:26. Am 8:10. Zc 12:10. Jn 1:14, 18. 3:16n, 18. He 11:17. 1 J 4:9. **and.** √148, Ge +8:22. **a widow.** Jb 29:13. Ac 9:39, 41. 1 T 5:4, 5. Ja 1:27. **and much.** Lk 8:52. Jn 11:19. Ac 11:24, 26. 19:26.

13. **And.** √148, Ge +8:22. **the Lord.** ver. 19. Lk 10:1, 39. 11:39. 12:42. 13:15. 17:5, 6. 18:6. 19:8, 31, 34. 22:61. 24:3, 34. Mk 16:19. Jn 4:1. **had compassion.** Jg 10:16. Ps 86:5, 15. 103:13. Is *63:9. Je 31:20. La 3:32, 33. Mt +9:36. Mk 1:41. 8:2. Jn 11:33-35. He 2:17. +*4:15. **Weep not.** Lk 8:52. Je 31:15, 16. Jn 20:13, 15. 1 C 7:30. 1 Th 4:13.

14. **And.** √148, Ge +8:22. **bier.** *or,* coffin. 2 S 3:31. **Young.** Lk 8:54, 55. 1 K 17:21. Jb 14:12, 14. Ps 33:9. Is +*26:19n. Ezk 37:3-10. Jn 5:21, 25, 28, 29. 11:25, 43, 44. Ac 9:40, 41. Ro 4:17. Ep 5:14. **Arise.** ver. 22. Lk *8:54. Mt 10:8. 11:5. 27:42. Mk 5:41. Jn *11:43. Ac *9:40.

15. **And.** √148, Ge +8:22. **sat up.** Ac 9:40. **he delivered.** Lk 9:42. 1 K 17:23, 24. 2 K *4:32-37. 13:21. Jn 19:27. Ac 9:41. Col 4:1. He 11:35.

16. **And.** √148, Ge +8:22. **a fear.** Lk 1:65. 5:8, 26. 8:37. Je 33:9. Mt 28:8. Ac 5:5, 11-13. **they glorified God.** Lk 2:20. 13:13. 23:47. Mt 5:16. 9:8. 15:31. Mk 2:12. Ac 2:43. 4:21. 11:18. 21:20. Ga 1:24. **a great prophet.** ver. 39. Lk 9:19. 24:19. Dt 18:15. Mt 21:11. Jn 1:21, 25. 4:19. 6:14. 7:40, 41. 9:17. Ac 3:22, 23. 7:37. **is risen.** Mt 11:11. Jn 7:52. Ac 13:22. **God hath visited.** Lk *1:68. 19:44. Ge +*49:10. Ex 4:31. Ps 65:9. 106:4, 5. Zc 9:9. Jn *3:2.

17. **And.** √148, Ge +8:22. **this rumor.** Lk 4:14. Mt 4:24. 9:31. Mk 1:28. 6:14.

18. **And.** √148, Ge +8:22. **disciples of John.** See on Mt 11:2-6. Jn 3:26.

19. **John.** When we remember the Baptist's solemn testimony to Christ, the sign from heaven, and the miraculous impulse which made him acknowledge Jesus the Messiah, we shall be constrained to think that he sent to Christ, not for his own satisfaction, but for that of his disciples. It could be, however, that John had grown despondent, having been imprisoned by Herod. **two.** Lk 10:1. Jsh 2:1. Mk 6:7. Ac 10:7, 8. Re 11:3. **Art thou.** Lk 18:8. **that cometh.** Lk 3:16. Ge +*3:15. 22:18. +*49:10. Dt 18:15-18. Ps 40:7. *110:1-4. 118:26. Is +*7:14. +*9:6, 7. 11:1. 40:10, 11. 59:20, 21. Je +*23:5, 6. Da 7:13. +*9:24-26. Mi +*5:2. Hg 2:7. Zc *9:9. Ml 3:1-3. 4:2. Mt 3:11. Mk 1:7. Jn 4:25. +*6:14. 11:27. Ro 5:14. He 10:37. **or look we.** Lk 3:15.

20. **Art thou he.** ver. +*19.

21. **he cured.** Mk 1:34. **plagues.** 1 K 8:37. Ps 90:7-9. Mk 3:10. 5:29, 34. Ac 22:24. 1 C 11:30-32. He 11:36. 12:6. Ja *5:14, 15. **evil spirits.** *Pneumata ponara,* are here clearly distinguished from bodily disorders. Gr. *pneuma,* Mt +8:16. Lk 8:2. 11:26. Mt 12:45. Ac 19:12-16. **gave sight.** √24A, Ge +32:24. Lk 18:42. Mt 9:30. 12:22. 15:31. 20:34. 21:14. Mk 8:25. Jn 9:7.

22. **Go.** Jn 1:46. 2:23. 5:36. **how that.** ver. 21. Lk 18:35-43. Jb 29:15. Ps 146:8. Is *29:18, 19. 32:3, 4. *35:5, 6. *42:6, 7, 16. +*61:1-3. Je 31:8. Mt 9:28-30. +*11:5. 21:14. Jn *3:2. 9:30-33. Ac *26:18. **the lame.** Is 35:6. Mt 15:30, 31. Ac 3:2-8. 8:7. 14:8-10. **the lepers.** See on Lk 5:12-15. 17:12-19. Mt 8:2. 10:8. 26:6. Mk

1:42. **the deaf.** Is 43:8. Mk 7:32-37. **the dead are.** See on ver. 14, 15. Lk 8:53-55. Is ▸26:19n. **to the poor.** Lk +*4:18. 6:20. Is *60:1-3. 61:1. Zp 3:12. Mt +*5:3. Ja *2:5.

23. **blessed.** Lk 2:34. Ps 118:22. Is *8:14, 15. Mt 11:6. *13:57, 58. 15:12. 17:27. *21:42. 24:10. 26:31. Mk 6:3. Jn *6:60-66. Ac 4:11. Ro *9:32, 33. 1 C *1:21-28. √2:14. 1 P *2:7, 8.

24. **What.** See on Mt 11:7, 8. **wilderness.** Lk 1:80. 3:2. Mt *3:1-5. Mk 1:4, 5. Jn 1:23. **A reed.** Ge 49:4. 1 K 14:15. 2 K 18:21. Is 36:6. Ezk 29:6, 7. 2 C 1:17-20. Ep √4:14. Ja 1:6-8. 2 P 2:17. 3:17.

25. **A man.** 2 K 1:8. Is 59:17. Mt *3:4. Mk 1:6. 1 P 3:3, 4. **are in.** 2 S 19:35. 1 K 10:5. 2 Ch 9:4. Est 1:3, 11. 4:2. 5:1. 8:15. Mt 6:29.

26. **A prophet.** Lk *1:76. 20:6. Mt 14:5. 21:26. Mk 6:20. 11:32. **and.** Lk 16:16. See on Mt 11:9-14. Jn 3:26, etc. 5:35.

27. **This is he.** Mk 1:2, 4. **written.** Lk +*24:27. **Behold.** Lk 1:15-17, 76. Ne +9:6. Is 40:3. 57:14. Ml ▸3:1. 4:5, 6. Jn 1:23. Col 1:16.

28. **Among.** Lk *1:14, 15. 3:16. **born.** √142, Ge +20:16. **of women.** Jb 14:1. 15:14. 25:4. Ga *4:4. **not a greater.** Lk 1:15. Mt +*11:11, 14n. Jn *5:35. **but.** Lk 9:48. 10:23, 24. Mt *11:11. *13:16, 17. Jn 7:39. *10:41. Ep 3:8, 9. Col *1:25-27. He 11:39, 40. 1 P √1:10-12. **kingdom of God.** Lk 4:43.

29. **all the people.** Lk 20:6. **the publicans.** Lk 3:12. *18:13. Mt 21:32. **justified God.** √121I2, Ge +2:17. ver. 35. Jg 1:7. Ps +*51:4, 5. Ro 3:4-6. 10:3. Re 15:3. 16:5. **being baptized.** Lk *3:12. Mt *3:5, 6. 21:31, 32. **baptism of John.** Ac 18:25. 19:3.

30. **Pharisees and.** ver. ◑16, 33. Mt 21:25, 32. 23:13. Mk 11:31. **lawyers.** Mt 22:35. **rejected.** *or*, frustrated. Lk *13:34. *20:6. Dt 18:15, 19. Je *8:8. Mt *21:32. Mk *7:9. Ro *10:21. 2 C *6:1. Ga *2:21. 3:15. He 10:28. **the counsel.** Ps *33:11. 107:11. Pr √1:25. *19:21. Ac 2:23. 13:36. √20:27. Ep +*1:11. 1 T +*2:4. He 6:17. **against.** *or*, within. **being not baptized.** Lk 20:5. Mt 3:5-12. √21:25. Mk √11:30, 31.

31. **Whereunto.** Lk 13:18, 20. La 2:13. Mt 11:16, etc. Mk 4:30. **liken.** ver. *25. Mt 11:16-19.

32. **are like.** Pr 17:16. Is 28:9-13. 29:11, 12. Je 5:3-5. See on Mt ‖11:16-19. **children.** Zc 8:5. **the marketplace.** Lk 11:43. Mt +11:16. **have piped.** Pr 29:9. **have mourned.** Lk 8:52.

33. **came neither.** Lk 1:15. Je 16:8-10. Da 10:3. Mt *3:4. *11:18. Mk 1:6. **eating.** √108B, Pr +31:4. **nor drinking wine.** Lk *1:15. **He.** Mt 10:25. Jn 7:20. 8:48, 52. 10:20. Ac 2:13.

34. **Son of man.** Lk 5:24. Mt 8:20. 16:27n. Mk 2:10. Jn 1:51. **eating.** √108B, Pr +31:4. ver. 36. Lk 5:29. 11:37. 14:1. Mt *9:10. Jn *2:2. 12:2. **a friend.** Lk 15:2. 19:7. Mt 9:11. **publicans and.** Lk 3:12. 5:30. 15:1. Mt 9:10, 11. 21:31, 32. Mk 2:15, 16.

35. **wisdom.** √88, Ge +15:15. Lk 11:49. Ro *11:33. **is justified.** √121I2, Ge +2:17. ver. 29. Ps *92:5, 6. *107:43. Pr 8:32-36. 17:16. Ho +*14:9. Mt ‖11:19. Ro *3:4. 1 C √2:14, 15. **her children.** Lk 10:6. *16:8. Pr 8:32. Jn *3:33. Ro *1:16. 1 C *1:21.

36. **one.** Mt 26:6, etc. Mk 14:3, etc. Jn 11:2, etc. **And he.** ver. 16. Lk 11:37. 14:1. **sat down.** ver. 34. Jn ◑4:6.

37. **which.** ver. 34, 39. Lk *5:30, 32. 18:13. 19:7. Mt 21:31. Jn *9:24, 31. Ro √5:8. 1 T *1:9, 15. 1 P 4:18. **a sinner.** Lk 15:7. Mt 21:32. **knew.** Gr. *epi-*

ginosko, Mt +11:27. **an alabaster.** Mt 26:7. Mk 14:3. Jn 11:2. 12:2, 3.

38. **And.** √148, Ge +8:22. **stood at his feet.** In taking their meals, the eastern people reclined (not sat, as in ver. 37) on a couch, leaning on the left elbow, with their heads towards the table, or triclinium, and their naked feet (the sandals being previously taken off) turned the contrary way, so as to be easily accessible to those who came behind the couch, where the servants were waiting. **weeping.** Lk 6:21. 22:62. Jg 2:4, 5. Ezr 10:1. Ps 6:6-8. 38:18. 51:17. +*126:5, 6. Is *61:3. Je 31:9, 18-20. Jl 2:12. Zc 12:10. Mt +*5:4. 2 C √7:10, 11. Ja 4:9. **wash.** ver. 44. Ge 18:4. Jn 13:4, 5. Gr. *brecho*, ⚹S#1026g. Rendered (1) wash: Lk 7:38, 44. (2) rain: Lk 17:29. Ja 5:17, 17. Re 11:6. (3) send rain: Mt 5:45. **did wipe.** ver. 44. Jn 11:2. 12:3. **and kissed.** ver. 45. Lk 15:20. Mt 26:49. Mk 14:45. Ac 20:37. **and anointed.** ver. 45, 46. Ec 9:8. SS 1:3. Is 57:9.

39. **spake within.** Lk 3:8. 12:17. 16:3. 18:4. 2 K 5:20. Pr 23:7. Mk 2:6, 7. 7:21. **This man.** ver. 16. Lk 15:2. Jn 7:12, 40, 41, 47-52. 9:24. **if he were.** √184B.· Hypothetical Propositions; or, Conditional ("if") Sentences: Second Condition; or, Contrary to Fact or Impossible. The premise is assumed to be contrary to fact, stated as if it were untrue or unreal, although in actual fact it may be true, dealing with present time. For other instances of this grammatical construction see Jn 5:46. 8:42. 9:33, 41. 15:19, 22. 18:36. 1 C 11:31. Ga 1:10. 3:21. He 4:8. 11:15. **a prophet.** ver. 16. Mt 21:11. Jn 4:19. **would.** ver. 37. Lk 15:2, 28-30. 18:9-11. 22:64. Is +*65:5n. Mt 9:12, 13. 20:16. 21:28-31.

40. **answering.** Lk 5:22, 31. *6:8. Mt 17:25. Jn +*2:24, 25. 16:19, 30. **Master.** Lk 8:49. 9:38. 10:25. 11:45. 12:13. 18:18. 19:39. 20:21, 28, 39. 21:7. 22:11. Mt 22:24. Mk 4:38. Jn 1:38. **say on.** Lk 18:18. 20:20, 21. Ezk +*33:31. Ml 1:6. Mt *7:22. 26:49. Jn 3:2. 13:13.

41. **a certain.** Lk 11:4. 13:4mg. Is 50:1. Mt 6:12. *18:23-25. **debtors.** Lk 16:5. **the one.** ver. 47. Ro 5:20. 1 T 1:15, 16. **owed.** √134, Mt +3:9. In the Greek (as in the English) the words "owe" and "love" are very different: but to a Hebrew, the two words would immediately be, in the mind, *achab* and *chab*, constituting this Parechesis or foreign paronomasia. **pence.** See Mt 18:25mg. **the other.** Lk +*12:48. Nu 27:3. Je 3:11. Jn 15:22-24. Ro 3:23. 1 J √1:8-10.

42. **when.** Ps 49:7, 8. Mt 18:25, 26, 34. Ro √5:6. Ga 3:10. **nothing to pay.** Ge=47:18. Ep √2:8, 9. 2 T √1:9. **he frankly forgave.** Ps *32:1-5. +*51:1-3. +*103:3. Is 43:25. 44:22. Je 31:33, 34. Da 9:18, 19. Ho *14:4. Mi *7:18-20. Mt 6:12. Ac 13:38, 39. Ro *3:24. 4:5-8. 8:32g. 11:6. 2 C 2:7, 10. 12:13. Ep *1:7. √4:32. Col *2:13. *3:13. **love.** √134, Mt +3:9. See ver. 41n.

43. **I.** ver. 47. 1 C 15:9, 10. 2 C √5:14, 15. 1 T *1:13-16. **he.** √63C, Ge +25:32. By ellipsis, supply (will love him most). **Thou.** Lk *10:28. Ps 116:16-18. Mk 12:34. **rightly judged.** Mt ◑7:1. Jn *7:24. 1 C 2:15. 10:15.

44. **he turned.** ver. 9, 38n. Lk 22:61. **Seest.** ver. 37-39. **thou gavest me no water.** √64, Ps +1:1. Ge *18:4. *19:2. 24:32. Jg *19:21. 1 S 25:41. Jn √13:5. 1 T *5:10. Ja *2:6. **for my feet.** lit. "Water upon my feet thou didst not give." Samuel J. Baird notes "The preposition *epi* with the accusative, means *upon*, with the idea of previous or present motion,—to wit (in

this place), of the water, poured and flowing upon the feet" (*A Bible History of Baptism*, p. 125). Ex 30:19n, 21n. 2 K *3:11n. SS +5:3. Is 44:3. **but she.** ✓164, 1 S +17:7. **and wiped.** ver. 38.

45. **gavest me no kiss.** Ge 29:11. 33:4. Ex 18:7. 2 S *15:5. *19:39. 20:9. Mt *26:48, 49. Ro 16:16. 1 C 16:20. 2 C 13:12. 1 Th 5:26. 1 P 5:14. **this woman.** Many have supposed that this person was Mary Magdalene, and Mary the sister of Lazarus. But there is no indication in the gospel history, that Mary Magdalene was the sister of Lazarus; but on the contrary, it would appear that they were perfectly distinct persons, the sister of Lazarus residing at Bethany, while Mary Magdalene appears to have resided at Magdala, east of Jordan, a distance of nearly ninety miles. Add to this, that our Savior seems to have been now in or near Nain, not at Bethany; and the woman appears from the recital to have been previously unknown to him. Mk ◑14:8n. **to kiss.** ver. 38.

46. **with oil.** Ru 3:3. 2 S 14:2. Ps *23:5. 92:10. 104:15. 141:5. Ec 9:8. Da 10:3. Am 6:6. Mi 6:15. Mt 6:17.

47. **Her sins.** ver. 42. Lk 5:20, 21. Ex 34:6, 7. **which are many.** ver. 37, 39. Is *1:18. ✓55:7. Ezk 16:63. 36:29-32. Mi *7:19. Ac 5:31. Ro ✓5:20. 1 C +*6:9-11. 1 T *1:14, 15. 1 J *1:7. **are forgiven.** Mk *2:7-10. **she loved much.** ver. 43. Mt 10:37. Jn *21:15-17. 2 C *5:14. Ga 5:6. Ep 6:24. Ph 1:9. 1 J 3:18. *4:10, 19. 5:3. **little is forgiven.** Breaking even one commandment makes us guilty of all (Ja 2:10). All our righteousnesses are as filthy rags (Is 64:6). We all have come short of the glory of God (Ro 3:23). Since all are sinners, we are all equally guilty before God. Being "forgiven little" must be a reference to our perception of guilt forgiven, not the actual quantity of guilt involved. In another sense, of course, just as there are degrees of reward in heaven, and degrees of punishment in hell based on differing degrees of guilt (Lk +*12:48), so here there is expressed degrees of difference of love to God based upon the amount forgiven. Notice in particular, however, the cause/effect relationship stated (Ps +✓9:10), and its bearing upon how to increase our love for God! We will increase our love to God as we increase our consciousness of the enormity of our sin. Ps 5:4. Is +*57:15. ✓64:6. Hab 1:13. Ro *3:10, 19, 23. Ga *3:22. Ja *2:10. **loveth little.** A wrong concept of sin leads to a wrong conception of our guiltiness before God, and a mistaken notion of the nature of God's provision for sin, Jesus the lamb of God, and the payment provided for sin in the substitutionary blood atonement, and to a wrong conception of God himself (Ps +✓9:10. Mt 25:26n) and His plan of salvation. Jn 3:30. Jn +*14:15. Ro *5:8. 7:13, 18. 10:3. 2 C *5:13-15. Ep 3:8. 2 J +*2:3-5. *4:19.

48. **Thy sins.** Lk 5:20. Mt 9:2. Mk *2:5. Jn 20:23. Ac 2:38. Ja 5:15. 1 J 2:12.

49. **Who is this.** Lk 5:20, 21. Mt 9:3. Mk *2:7.

50. **Thy faith.** ver. 9, 47. Lk 8:12, +*18, 42, 48. 18:42. Hab +*2:4. Mt 9:22. Mk *5:34. 10:52. Ac *3:16. Ro ✓10:17. Ep ✓2:8-10. 1 T 1:14. Ja 2:14-26. **go.** Lk 8:48. Ec 9:7. Mk 5:34. **in peace.** Ex 4:18. Jg 18:6. 1 S 1:17. 20:13, 42. 2 K 5:19. Ac 15:33. Ro *5:1, 2.

LUKE 8

Our Lord preaches, attended by his apostles, and by some women who ministered to him, 1-3. The para-

ble of the sower with its interpretation, 4-15; and that of the lighted candle, 16-18. Christ's obedient disciples are his most beloved relations, 19-21. He calms a violent tempest, 22-25; and casts out the legion, 26-39. He heals the woman who had an issue of blood and raises Jairus's daughter, 40-56.

1. **that.** Lk 4:43, 44. Mt 4:23. 9:35. 11:1. Mk 1:39. Ac *10:38. **the glad.** Lk *2:10, 11. +*4:18. Is +*61:1-3. Mt +*13:19. Ac 13:32. Ro 10:15. **the kingdom.** Mt 3:2. Ro 14:17. Col 1:13. **and the.** Lk 6:14-16. Mt 10:2-4. Mk 3:16-19.

2. **certain women.** Lk 23:27, 49, 55. Mt *27:55, 56. Mk 15:40, 41. *16:1. Jn *19:25. Ac 1:14. **spirits.** Gr. *pneuma*, Mt +8:16. Lk 7:21. **Mary.** Lk 24:10. Mt 27:56, 61. 28:1. Mk 15:40, 47. *16:1, 9. Jn 19:25. 20:1, 18. **Magdalene.** Lk 7:45n. Mt 15:39. **out.** ver. 30. Mk 16:9.

3. **Joanna.** i.e. *whom Jehovah has graciously given,* ✱S#2489g. Lk 24:10. (1) An ancestor of Christ, Lk 3:27, S#2490g. (2) A female disciple, the wife of Chuza, Lk 8:3. 24:10. **Chuza.** i.e. *prophet,* ✱S#5529g. **Herod's.** Lk 9:7-9. Jn 4:46-53g. Ac 13:1. Ph 4:22. **Susanna.** i.e. *lily,* ✱S#4677g. **which ministered.** Lk 7:37, 38. 2 K 4:10. Pr 31:20. Mt 27:55, 56. Mk 14:3. Ac 21:9. Ro 16:1-3, 6, 12. 1 T 5:10. **of their substance.** Lk 21:2-4. Ex 35:25. 1 Ch 29:14. Pr 31:20. Is 23:18. Mt 2:11. 25:40. 26:11. Jn 12:3. Ac 9:36-39. 2 C ✓8:9. Ph +*4:17. 1 T *5:10.

4. **when much.** Mt 13:2-13, 18-23. Mk 4:1-20.

5. **sower.** ver. 11. Mt +*13:3, 4, 18, 19, 24-26, 37. Mk 4:2-4, 15, 26-29. **fell.** ver. 12. He *2:1. Ja 1:23, 24. **it.** Ps 119:118. Mt 5:13. **and the.** Ge 15:11.

6. **a rock.** ver. 13. Je 5:3. Ezk 11:19. 36:26. Am 6:12. Mt +*13:5, 6, 20, 21. Mk 4:5, 6, 16, 17. Ro 2:4, 5. He 3:7, 8, 15.

7. **thorns.** ver. 14. Lk 21:34. Ge 3:18. Je 4:3. Mt +*13:7, 22. Mk 4:7, 18, 19. He 6:7, 8.

8. **other.** ver. *15. Mt +*13:8, 23. Mk *4:8, 20. Jn *1:12, 13. *3:3-5. Ep ✓2:10. Col +*1:10. **an hundredfold.** Ge +*26:12. Mt +*13:8, 23. *19:29. Mk +*10:30. **He that.** Pr 1:20-23. 8:1. *20:12. Je *13:15. *25:4. Mt *11:15. *13:9. Mk 4:23. Re *2:7, 11. **to hear.** ✓147A, Ge +50:24.

9. **What.** Ho +*6:3. Mt +*13:10, 18, 36. 15:15. Mk 4:10, 34. 7:17, 18. Jn 15:15.

10. **Unto.** Lk 10:21-24. Ps *25:14. Am +*3:7. Mt *11:25. +*13:11, 12. *16:17. Mk 4:11, 12. Ro *16:25, 26. 1 C *2:7-11. 12:11. Ep 3:3-9. Col *1:26-28. 2:2. 1 T *3:16. 1 P 1:10-12. **that seeing.** ✓147B, Ge +2:16. Dt 29:4. Is *❭6:9, 10. 29:14. 44:18. Je 5:21. Mt +*13:14-17. Jn *12:40. Ac 28:26, 27. Ro 11:7-10. 1 C ✓2:14.

11. **The seed.** Is +*8:20. Mt +*13:19. Mk 4:14, etc. 1 C *3:6, 7, 9-12. Col *1:5, 6. Ja *1:21. 1 P +*1:23-25.

12. **by the wayside.** ver. 5. Pr 1:24-26, 29. Mt +*13:19. Mk 4:15. Ja 1:23, 24. **then cometh.** Pr 4:5. Is 65:11. Mt +*13:19. Mk 4:15. 2 Th 2:9-14. He *2:1. Re 12:9. **believe.** Mk *16:16. Ac 14:9. 15:11. ✓16:31. Ro ✓10:9. Ep ✓2:8.

13. **receive.** Ps 106:12-14. Is *58:2. Ezk +*33:22. Mt +*13:20, 21. Mk 4:16, 17. 6:20. 10:15. Jn 5:35. Ga 3:1, 4. 4:15-20. Ja 1:21. **with joy.** Ps 106:12, 13. Is 58:2. Ezk +*33:31, 32. Mk 6:20. Jn 5:35. **and these.** Jb 19:28. Pr 12:3, 12. Ep 3:17. Col 2:7. Ju 12. **for a while believe.** Lk 22:31, 32. Dt +*29:18. 30:17. Ps 106:12. Ho +*4:10. 6:4. Jn +*2:23-25. *6:66. ✓8:30-

32. 12:42, 43. 15:2, 6. Ac 8:13-23. 1 C 13:2. +*15:2. Ga *1:6. +*4:11. *5:7. Col +*1:23. 1 Th +*3:5. 1 T +*1:19. 2 T *2:18, 19. He *10:39. Ja 2:26. 2 P *2:20, 22. 1 J √2:19. **in time.** Pr 24:10. Je +*12:5. Ja 1:2. **fall away.** Ezk +*33:18. 1 C +*15:2. 2 Th 2:3. 1 T 4:1. +*6:10. He +*3:12. +*10:38.

14. **are.** ƒ119, Ge +49:9. **and are choked.** ver. 7. Lk 16:13. Mt 6:24, 25. +*‖13:22. Mk +*‖4:19. 1 T √6:9, 10, 17. 2 T +*4:10, 16. 1 J √2:15-17. **cares.** Lk 17:26-30. *21:34. **riches.** Lk 18:24, 25. **pleasures.** Gr. *heedonee*, *S#2237g. T 3:3. Ja 4:1, 3. 2 P 2:13. **this life.** Mk ◑+*4:19. **and bring.** Lk *13:6-9. Jn *15:6. **no fruit.** 2 P +*1:8. Ju 12. **to perfection.** Pr 11:30. He 6:1, 9.

15. **in an honest and.** Lk 6:45. Dt 30:6. 2 K +*20:3. 1 Ch 12:38n. Ps +*51:10. Je 31:33. 32:39. Ezk 36:26, 27. Ro 7:18. Ep √2:8. He *4:2. Ja 1:16-19. 1 P *2:1, 2. **heard.** ƒ108B. Idiom B828. "To hear" is used of understanding and obeying. For another instance of this idiom see Jn 8:47. **the word.** Mt +*13:23. Jn +*8:31. Ac +*17:11. **keep.** Lk +*11:28. Jb +*23:11, 12. Ps +*1:1-3. *119:11, 127-129. Pr 3:1. Je +*15:16. Jn 14:15, 21-24. 15:10. Ro 1:18g. *2:7. 1 C 7:19. He *2:1. +*3:14. Ja +*1:22-25. 1 J √2:3. **bring forth fruit.** Ho 14:8. Jn 15:5, 16. Ro 6:22. 7:4. Ga 5:22-26. Ph 1:11. Col +*1:6, 10. **with patience.** Lk 21:19. Mt +*24:13. Ro 2:7. Ph *3:13-15. He +*6:11, 12. *10:36. *12:1. Ja 1:4. 5:7, 8, 11.

16. **when.** Lk 11:33. Mt *5:14-16. Mk 4:21, 22. Ac *26:18. Ph *2:15, 16. Re 1:20. 2:1. 11:4.

17. **nothing is secret.** Lk 12:2, 3. Ec 12:14. Mt 10:26, 27. 1 C *4:5. 1 T 5:25.

18. **Take heed.** Lk 9:44. Dt 32:46, 47. Pr 2:2-5. Je 17:21. Mk +*4:23, 24. 13:14. Ac 10:33. √17:11. He *2:1. Ja *1:19-25. 1 P *2:1, 2. **how ye hear.** Lk √11:28. Dt *28:1, 2, ◑+*15. Jb +*37:2. Pr √4:20-22. 23:19. Je ◑+*29:19. Mk ◑+*4:24. Ja +*1:25. **for whosoever hath.** Lk 19:26. Mt +*13:12. 25:29. Mk 4:25. +*10:29, 30. Jn *15:2. Ja *4:6. **from him.** Lk 12:20, 21. 16:2-4, 19-25. *19:24, 26. Mt *7:22, 23. 1 C 13:1-3. **seemeth to have.** *or*, thinketh that he hath. Pr +*14:12. Ro +*12:3. 1 C *3:18. 8:2. 14:37. Ph 3:4. Ja 1:26.

19. **Then came.** Mt *12:46-50. Mk +*3:21, 31-35.

20. **thy brethren.** Mt +*13:55, 56. Mk +*6:3. Jn 7:3-6. Ac 1:14. 1 C 9:5. Ga 1:19.

21. **My mother.** Lk 11:27, 28. Mt *12:49, 50. 25:40, 45. 28:10. Jn +*15:14, 15. 20:17. 2 C *5:16. 6:18. He *2:11-13. **which hear.** ver. 15. Mt *7:21-26. 17:5. Jn 6:28, 29. 13:17. Ja 1:22. 1 J 2:29. *3:22, 23. 3 J 11. **and do it.** T#1093. Lk +*11:28. Ps 119:67. Mt +*5:19. +*7:21. Jn *14:21. +*15:14. 17:6. Ga *5:6. Ja +*1:22, 25.

22. **that.** Mk 8:18, 23-27. Mk 4:35-41. Jn 6:1. **Let.** Mt 14:22. Mk 5:21. 6:45. 8:13.

23. **he fell.** Ps 44:23. Is 51:9, 10. He +*4:15. **came.** Ps 93:3, 4. 107:23-30. 124:2-4. 148:8. Is 54:11. Ac 27:14-20.

24. **Master.** Ps 69:1, 2. 116:3, 4. 142:4, 5. La 3:54-56. Jon 2:2-6. Mt 14:30. 2 C 1:9, 10. **perish.** Gr. *apollumi*, Mt +2:13. **he arose.** Ps 65:7. 104:6-9. 107:25-29. Is 50:2. Je 5:22. Na 1:4. **and rebuked.** As the agitation of the sea was merely the effect of the wind, it was necessary to remove the cause of the commotion before the effect would cease. But who, by simply saying, Peace, be still (Mk 8:39), could do this but God? One word of our Lord can change the face of

nature, and calm the troubled ocean, as well as restore peace to the disconsolate soul.

25. **Where.** Lk 12:28. Is *43:2. Mt 6:30. *8:26. 14:31. *17:20. Mk 4:40, 41. Jn 11:40. **being afraid.** Ge 1:9, 10. Jsh 10:12-14. Jb 38:8-10. Pr 8:29. 30:4.

26. **Gadarenes.** Mt 8:28, etc., Gergesenes. Mk 5:1, etc.

27. **met.** Mk *5:2-5. **and ware.** 1 S 19:24. **but.** Nu 19:16. Is 65:4.

28. **he cried.** Lk 4:33-36. Mt 8:29. Mk 1:24-27. 5:6-8. Ac 16:16-18. **What have.** ƒ85H, Jg +11:12. ver. 37, 38. Mk +*1:24. Ac 19:15. Ja *2:19. **most high.** Lk 1:76. Ps +*78:17, 35, 56. +*83:18. Da 7:18. Mt 11:10. Mk 5:7. Ac 7:48. 16:17. Ro *9:5. 1 C 10:9. 1 Th 3:13. **I beseech.** Is 27:1. Ja *2:19. 2 P *2:4. 1 J √3:8. Ju *6. Re 20:1-3, 10. **torment.** Mt +*8:29.

29. **commanded.** Mk 5:8. Ac 19:12-16. **unclean.** Mk 3:30. **spirit.** Gr. *pneuma*, Mt +8:16. **caught.** Lk 9:39, 42. Mk 5:3-5. 9:20-26. 2 T 2:25, 26.

30. **Legion.** Mt 26:53. Mk 5:9. **many.** ver. 2. Mt 8:29. Mk 16:9.

31. **they besought.** T#1582. ver. 28. Jb 1:11. 2:5. Mk *5:10. Ph 2:10, 11. **not command.** Mk 5:10. **the deep.** "The abyss," says Dr. Doddridge, "the prison in which many of these fallen spirits are detained; and to which some, who may, like these, have been permitted for a while to range at large, are sometimes by Divine justice and power remanded." *S#12g. Mt +*25:41. Ro 10:7g. Re 9:1, 2, 11g. 11:7g. 17:8g. 19:20. *20:1-3g, 14, 15.

32. **there an.** Le 11:7. Is 65:4. 66:3. Mt 8:30-33. Mk 5:11-13. **besought.** Jb 1:10. Ps 62:11. Jn 19:11. 1 J 4:4. **he suffered.** 1 K 22:22. Jb 1:12. 2:6. Re 20:7.

33. **Then.** By this was fully evinced the sovereign power of our Lord, and the reality of diabolical agency; "for," says Dr. Doddridge, "it was self-evident that a herd of swine could not be confederates in any fraud: their death, therefore, in this instructive circumstance, was ten thousand times a greater blessing to mankind than if they had been slain for food, as was intended." **the herd.** Jn 8:44. 1 P 5:8. Re 9:11.

34. **they fled.** Mt 8:33. 28:11. Mk 5:14. Ac 19:16, 17.

35. **and found.** Is 49:24, 25. 53:12. He *2:14, 15. 1 J *3:8. **sitting.** Lk 2:46. 10:39. Mk 5:15. Ac 22:3. **clothed.** ver. 27. Lk 15:17. **in his.** Ps +*51:10. **right mind.** Lk 15:17. Col 1:13. 2 T +√1:7.

37. **besought.** ver. 28. Lk 5:8. Dt 5:25. 1 S 6:20. 2 S 6:8, 9. 1 K 17:18. Jb 21:14, 15. Mt 8:34. Mk 5:17. Ac 16:39. **and he went.** Lk 9:5, 56. 10:10, 11, 16. 1 S 18:14. Mk 6:20. Ac 24:25.

38. **besought.** ver. 28, 37. Dt 10:20, 21. Ps 27:4. 32:7. 116:12, 16. Mk 5:18. Ph 1:23. **saying.** Ex 12:25-27. 13:8, 9, 14-16. Ps 71:17, 18. 78:3-6. 107:21, 22, 31, 32. 111:2-4. 145:3-12. Is 63:7-13. Mk 5:19, 20. Ac 9:13-16. Ga 1:23, 24. 1 T 1:13-16.

39. **Return.** 1 T 5:8. **and published.** Lk 17:15-18. Dt 10:21. Ps *66:16. 126:2, 3. Da 4:1-3, 34-37. Mk 1:45. Jn 4:29.

40. **that.** Mt 9:1. Mk 5:21. **the people.** Lk 5:1. 19:6, 37, 38, 48. Mk 6:20. 12:37. Jn 5:35. **waiting.** Pr 8:34. Ac 10:33.

41. **there.** Mt 9:18-25. Mk 5:22, etc. **a ruler.** Lk 13:14. Ac 13:15. 18:8, 17. **and he fell.** Lk 5:8. 17:16. Re 5:8. **and besought.** Mt 8:7, 8. Mk 5:23. Jn 4:46-49. 11:21. Ac 9:38.

42. one. Lk 7:12. Ge 44:20-22. Jb 1:18, 19. Zc +*12:10. **and she.** Jb 4:20. Ps 90:5-8. 103:15, 16. Ec 6:12. Ezk 24:16, 25. Ro *5:12. **But.** ver. 45. Mk 5:24.

43. having. Le 15:25, etc. Mt 9:20-22. Mk 5:25. **twelve.** ver. 27. Lk 13:11, 16. Mk 9:21. Jn 5:5, 6. 9:1, 21. Ac 3:2. 4:22. 14:8-10. **had spent all.** Lk 15:14. 2 Ch 16:12. Ps 108:12. Is 2:22. +*55:1-3. Mk 5:26. 9:18, 22. **neither.** Jb 13:4.

44. behind. Lk 7:38. **touched.** Dt 22:12. Mt *9:21. Mk 5:27, 28. 6:56. Ac 5:15. 19:12. **immediately.** Lk 13:13. Ex +*15:26. Ml 4:2. Mt 8:3. 20:34. Lk 13:13.

45. Who. ♪22C2, Ge +3:9. "Not that he was ignorant who had touched him," says Epiphanius (Anacorat. sec. 38, cited by Bulkley), "but that he might not be himself the divulger of the miracle, and that the woman, hearing the question, and drawing near, might testify the singular benefit she had received, and that, in consequence of her declaration, she might presently hear from His lips, that her faith had saved her; and that by this means, others might be excited to come and be healed of their disorders." **the multitude.** Lk *6:19. 9:13. Mk 5:30-32.

46. for. Lk *6:19. 1 P 2:9mg.

47. when. Ps 38:9. Ho 5:3. **she came.** 1 S 16:4. Ps 2:11. Is 66:2. Ho 13:1. Hab 3:16. Mt 28:8. Mk 5:33. Ac 16:29. 1 C 2:3. 2 C 7:15. Ph *2:12. He 12:28. **she declared.** Lk 17:15, 16. Ps 66:16. **touched him.** Mt 14:36. Mk 6:56.

48. Daughter. Mt 9:2, 22. 12:20. 2 C 6:18. **thy faith.** Lk +*7:50. 17:19. 18:42. Mt 8:13. Mk 5:34. Ac 14:9. He 4:2. **go.** Ex 4:18. 1 S 1:17. 2 K 5:19.

49. he. ver. 41-43. Mt 9:23-26. Mk 5:35.

50. believe. ver. 48. Is 50:10. Mk 5:36. 9:23. √11:22-24. Jn 11:25, 40. Ro 4:17, 20.

51. he suffered. 1 K 17:19-23. 2 K 4:4-6, 34-36. Is 42:2. Mt 6:5, 6. Mk +*5:40. Ac 9:40. **save.** Lk 6:14. 9:28. Mk 5:37-40. *9:2. *14:33.

52. all. Ge 23:2. 37:34, 35. 2 S 18:33. Je 9:17-21. Ezk 24:17. Zc +*12:10. **she.** Mk 5:38, 39. Jn 11:4, 11-13.

53. laughed. Lk 16:14. Jb 12:4. 17:2. Ps 22:7. Is +*53:3. **knowing.** Mk 15:44, 45. Jn 11:39. 19:33-35.

54. he put. ver. 51. Mk 5:40. **took.** Je 31:32. Mt 9:25. Mk 1:31. 5:41. 8:23. 9:27. **Maid.** Lk *7:14, 15. Jn 5:21, 28, 29. *11:43. Ac 9:40. Ro 4:17.

55. her spirit. Gr. *pneuma*, ♪121A3, Mt +*27:50n. This expression, thus used of one who had been dead, strongly implies, that at death the soul not only exists separately, but returns and is reunited to the body, when it is raised from the dead. 1 K √17:21-23. Ec +*12:7. Jn *11:44. Ac 7:59. 1 C 5:5. Ja 2:26. **came again.** Ge 45:27. Jg 15:19. 1 S 30:12. **and he.** Lk 24:41-43. Mk 5:43. Jn 11:44.

56. were astonished. Lk 2:47. Ac 2:7, 12. **he charged.** Lk 5:14. Mt *8:4. 9:30. Mk 5:42, 43.

LUKE 9

Jesus sends forth the twelve apostles, 1-6. Herod desires to see him, 7-9. The apostles return; Jesus retires with them, but the multitudes follow him, 10, 11. He feeds them by miracle, 12-17. The different opinions concerning him and Peter's confession, 18-21. He foretells his death, and warns his disciples to prepare for self-denial and sufferings, 22-27. His transfiguration, 28-36: he heals a demoniac, 37-42; again foretells his

death, 43-45; checks the ambitious disputes of his disciples, 46-48; will not allow them to forbid any who "cast out devils in his name," 49, 50; reproves the fiery zeal of James and John against the Samaritans who would not receive them, 51-56; and answers some who were not disposed to follow him unreservedly and immediately, 57-62.

1. he. Lk *6:13-16. Mt 10:2-5. Mk *3:13-19. 6:13-17. **gave.** Lk 10:19. Mt *10:1. 16:19. Mk *6:7. 16:17, 18. Jn 14:12. Ac +*1:8. 3:16. 4:30. 9:34.

2. to preach. Lk *10:1, 9, 11. 16:16. Mt 3:2. *10:7, 8. 13:19. 24:14. Mk 1:14, 15. *6:12. 16:15. He 2:3, 4.

3. Take. Lk *10:4, etc. 12:22. 22:35. Ps 37:3. Mt 10:9, 10. Mk *6:8, 9. 2 T 2:4. **neither have.** ♪96B, Ex +20:8. **two.** Lk 3:11. 5:29. 12:28. Mk 14:63g.

4. whatsoever house. Lk *10:5-8. Mt *10:11. Mk *6:10. Ac 16:15. **there abide.** 1 T 5:13.

5. whosoever. ver. 48. Lk 10:10-12, 16. Mt *10:14, 15. Mk 6:11. 9:37. Ac *13:50, 51. *18:6. **shake.** ♪138B, Ge +13:16. ver. 53-56. Ne 5:13. **a testimony.** Lk 5:14. Mt 10:18. Mk 1:44. **against them.** 2 Th 1:10. Ja 5:3.

6. preaching the gospel. ver. 1, 2. Mk *6:12, 13. 16:20. Ac 4:30. 5:15.

7. A.M. 4036. **A.D.** 32. **Herod.** Jb 18:11, 12. Ps 73:19. Mt 14:1-12. Mk 6:14-28. **Tetrarch.** A "tetrarch," *tetrarkees*, from *tetras*, "four," and *arkee*, "government," properly signifies a *prince*, or ruler over a quarter of any region; and had its origin from Galatia, which was governed by four princes. In the New Testament, however, it denotes a prince, or king, who reigns over the fourth part of a former kingdom. By Herod's will his kingdom was thus divided among his sons: Archelaus had one-half, consisting of Idumea, Judea, and Samaria; Herod Antipas, one-fourth, consisting of Galilee and Perea; and Philip the remaining fourth, consisting of Batanea, Trachonitis, and Auranitis. **he was perplexed.** Lk 21:25. Is 22:5. Mi 7:4. Ac 2:12. 5:24. 10:17.

8. of some. ver. 19. Mt 17:10. Mk 6:15. 8:28. Jn 1:21. **Elias had appeared.** Ml 4:5. **prophets.** Lk 7:16. Mt 4:3. 14:2. 21:8, 11. Jn 1:45. 3:2. +*6:14. 9:17.

9. John. ver. 7. **And he.** Lk 13:31, 32. *23:8.

10. the apostles. Lk 10:17. Zc 1:10, 11. Mk 6:30. He 13:17. **he took.** Mt *14:13. Mk 2:7. +*6:31, 32. **Bethsaida.** Mt 11:21. Mk 6:45. Jn 1:44.

11. And. Jn 6:5-14. **when.** Mt 14:14. Mk 6:33, 34. Ro 10:14, 17. **and he.** Is 61:1. Jn 4:34. √6:37. Ro 15:3. 2 T 4:2. **the kingdom.** Lk 8:1, 10. Mt 21:31, 43. Ac 28:31. **healed.** Lk 1:53. 5:31. He *4:16.

12. when. Mt 14:15, etc. Mk 6:35, 36, etc. Jn 6:1, 5, etc. **wear away.** Lk 24:29. Jg 19:8, 9, 11. Je 6:4. **Send.** Mt 15:23, 32. **and lodge.** Lk 19:7. **for.** Ps 78:19, 20. Ezk 34:25. Ho 13:5. **get victuals.** Ps 34:10. 1 T 4:8.

13. Give. 2 K 4:42, 43. Mt 14:16, 17. Mk 6:37, 38. Jn 6:5-9. **have.** Nu 11:21-23. Pr 11:24, 25. **except.** ♪184C, Mt +4:9. ♪63D1, Mt +16:7. There is something wanting here, which may be thus supplied: "We have no more than five loaves and two fishes; (therefore we are not able to give to them to eat) except we should go and buy meat for all this people" (B52).

14. Make. Mk 6:39, 40. 8:6. 1 C 14:40.

16. and looking. 2 Ch 6:13. Ps 121:1, 2. 123:1, 2. Mt 14:19. Mk 7:34. Jn 11:41. 17:1. Ac 7:55. **he blessed.** Lk +√24:30. 1 S 9:13. Mt +14:19. +15:36.

17. eat. Ps 37:16. Pr 13:25. Mt 14:20, 21. 15:37,

38. Mk 6:42-44. 8:8, 9. **were.** Ps 107:9. **and there.** 2 K 4:44. Mt 16:9, 10. Mk 8:19, 20. Jn 6:11-13. Ph 4:18, 19.

18. **as.** Lk 11:1. 22:39-41. Mt 26:36. **Whom.** Mt 16:13, 14. Mk 8:27-30. Jn 6:68, 69.

19. **John.** See on ver. 7, 8. Ml 4:5. Mt *14:2. Mk 6:14. Jn 1:21, 25. **Elias.** ver. 8. Mt 17:10. Mk 6:15. 9:11. Jn 1:21. **old.** Mt 21:11. Mk 6:15. Jn +*6:14. 7:40. 9:17.

20. **whom.** Mt 5:47. 16:15. 22:42. **The Christ of God.** Lk 22:67. 23:35. Mt 1:17. √16:16, 17. 26:63. Mk 8:29. 14:61. Jn *1:41, 49. 4:29, 42. *6:69. 7:41. *11:27. √20:31. Ac 3:18. 4:26. *8:37. 9:22. 17:3. 1 J 5:1. Re 11:15. 12:10.

21. **straitly charged.** Mt 16:20. 17:9. Mk 8:31.

22. **Son of man.** ver. 26, 44, 58. Lk +5:24. 18:31. **must suffer.** ver. 44. Lk 18:31-34. 24:7, +*26. Ge +*3:15. Ps ch. 22, 69. Is ch. 53. Da 9:26. Zc 13:7. Mt 16:21. 17:12, 22, 23. Mk 8:31. 9:30, 31. 10:33, 34. Ac 4:25-28. 13:27-29. 1 C 15:4. 1 P √1:11. **be rejected.** Lk 17:25. 20:17. Mt 21:42. Mk 12:10. **the third day.** Lk 18:33. 24:7, 21, 46. Mt +*12:40n. 16:21. 17:23. 20:19. 27:64. Mk 8:31. Jn +*2:19. Ac 10:40. 1 C +*15:4.

23. **If.** ſ184A, 1 C +15:2. Lk *14:26, 27. Mt *10:38, 39. *16:22-25. Mk *8:34-38. Jn *8:31. *12:25, 26. Ro *8:13. Col *3:5. 2 T *3:12. **deny.** 2 T 2:12, 13. T *2:12. **take up.** Ac *14:22. Col 1:24. 1 P 4:13. **daily.** Ro 8:36. 1 C *15:30, 31. **follow me.** Jn *8:12.

24. **will save.** Lk *17:33. Jn 12:25. Ac *20:23, 24. He *11:35. Re 2:10. *12:11. **life.** ſ121A7, Ge +9:5. Gr. *psyche,* here used for the seat of personality, as in He 6:19. 10:39. For the other uses of psyche, see Mt +2:20n. Is 53:10 w 1 T 2:6. **lose.** Gr. *apollumi,* Mt +2:13. T#554. Lk 12:4, 5. √13:23, 24. Mt *5:22. +√10:28. 16:25, 26. 18:8. Mk *9:43-48. 2 T *2:11, 12. He 4:1. 1 P 4:17, 18. Re +2:11 (T#563). **his life.** ſ121A7, Ge +9:5.

25. **what.** Lk 4:5-7. *12:19-21. *16:24, 25. Ps *49:6-8. Mt 16:26. Mk 8:36. *9:43-48. Ac 1:18, 25. 2 P 2:15-17. Re 18:7, 8. **if he.** ſ102C, Mt +5:29. **world.** Gr. *kosmos,* Mt +4:8. **lose.** Gr. *apollumi,* Mt +2:13. **himself.** Or, as in the parallel passage, *tan psukeen autou,* "his soul," or life. **be cast away.** Mt 13:48, 50. +16:26 (*S#2210g). Mk 8:36. 1 C 3:15. *9:27. 2 C *7:9. Ph 3:8g.

26. **whosoever.** Lk *12:8, 9. Ps 22:6-8. Is *53:3. Mt *10:32, 33. Mk 8:38. Jn 5:44. 12:43. Ro √1:16. 2 C 12:10. Ga 6:14. 2 T √1:8, 12, 16. *2:12. He 11:16, 26. 13:13. 1 P 4:14-16. Re 3:5. **of him.** Lk 13:25-27. Mt *7:22, 23. 1 C 3:15. 2 P 1:11. 1 J 2:28. Re +*21:8. **when he cometh.** Dt 33:2. Da 7:10, 13. Zc *14:5. Mt 16:27. +*24:30, 31. +*25:31. 26:64. Jn 1:51. Ac +*1:11. 2 Th 1:8-10. ◐4:16. Ju 14. Re +*1:7. 20:11. **his own glory.** Lk 24:26. Mt 19:28. 25:31. Mk 10:37. Jn 17:24. **his Father's.** Ac 1:4. **holy angels.** Zc +*14:5. Mt 13:41. 16:27. Mk 8:38. Ac 10:22. Re 14:10.

27. **I tell.** Mt *16:28. Mk 9:1. Jn *14:2. 16:7. **some.** Jn 21:22, 23. **taste.** Lk 2:26. Jn 8:51, 52, 59. He 2:9. **till.** ver. 28-35. Lk 21:31, 32. Mt 10:23. 16:28—17:8. 23:36. *24:34. Mk 1:15. 9:1-8. 13:30. 2 P *1:16-18. **see.** Lk 22:18. Mt *24:14, 15, 30. Mk 14:25. **the kingdom.** Lk +4:43. Ho=12:9.

28. **about.** Mt *17:1, etc. Mk *9:2, etc. **eight.** Le=23:39. Mt 17:1n. **sayings.** *or,* things. **he took.** Lk 8:51. Mt 26:37-39. Mk 14:33-36. 2 C 13:1. **into.** ver.

18. Lk 6:12. Ps 109:4. Mk +*1:35. 6:46. He *5:7.

29. **the fashion.** Ex 34:29-35. Ps 104:2. Is 33:17. *53:2. Da 7:9. Mt *‖17:2. 28:3. Mk 9:2, 3. Jn *1:14. Ac 6:15. Ph 3:7, 8. 2 P *1:16-18. Re 1:13-16. 20:11. **altered.** Mk 16:12g.

30. **two men.** Mt *22:32. **with him.** Ph *1:23. **which.** Lk 24:27, 44. Mt *17:3, 4. Mk 9:4-6. Jn 1:17. Ro √3:21-23. 2 C 3:7-11. He 3:3-6. **Elias.** ver. 19. Lk 1:17. Ja 5:17, 18.

31. **appeared.** 2 C *3:18. Ph 3:21. Col 3:4. 1 P 5:10. **spake.** ver. 22. Lk 13:32-34. Jn 1:29. 1 C 1:23, 24. 1 P 1:11, 12. Re 5:6-12. 7:14. **decease.** lit. exodus. Dt ◐=3:25-27. 2 P 1:15.

32. **were heavy.** Lk 22:45, 46. Da 8:18. 10:9. Mt 26:40-43. Mk 14:40. **saw his glory.** Ex *33:18-23. Is *60:1-3, 19. +*66:18. Jn *1:14. 17:24. 2 P √1:16. 1 J *3:2. Re 22:4, 5.

33. **it is.** Ps 4:6, 7. 27:4. 63:2-5. 73:28. Jn 14:8, 9. 2 C 4:6. **and let.** Mt 17:4. Mk 9:5, 6. **tabernacles.** Le +=23:34, 42. Ne 8:15. **not knowing.** Mt 20:22. Mk *9:6. 10:38. 14:40.

34. **a cloud.** Ex 14:19, 20. 24:15, 16. 33:9. 40:34-38. 2 Ch +*5:13. Ps 18:9-11. Is 19:1. Mt *17:5-7. Mk 9:7, 8. 2 P 1:17. **and they.** Jg 6:22. 13:22. Da 10:8. Re 1:17.

35. **a voice.** Lk *3:22. Jn 12:28. 2 P *1:17, 18. **out of the cloud.** ver. +*34. **This.** Lk *3:22. Mt 3:17. Jn √3:16, 35, 36. 2 P *1:17, 18. **hear.** Dt *18:15, 18, 19. Is +*55:3, 4. Jn 5:22-24. Ac *3:22, 23. He √2:3. 3:7, 8, 15. +*5:9. 12:25, 26.

36. **found.** ſ171J5, 1 S +13:15. **And they.** Ec 3:7. Mt 8:4. 12:16. *17:9. Mk 9:9, 10.

37. **on the next day.** Mt *17:14-21. Mk 9:14-29.

38. **beseech.** T#1313. Ne +1:5. **look.** Lk 7:12. 8:41, 42. Mt 15:22. Jn 4:47. **for.** Ge 44:20. Zc +*12:10.

39. **lo.** Lk 4:35. 8:29. Mt *17:15. Mk 5:4, 5. 9:20, 26. Jn *8:44. 1 P *5:8. Re 9:11. **spirit.** Gr. *pneuma,* Mt +8:16.

40. **and they.** ver. 1. Lk 10:17-19. 2 K 4:31. Mt *17:20, 21. Ac 19:13-16.

41. **O faithless.** Lk 8:25. Dt 32:20. Ps 78:8. Mk 9:19. Jn *20:27. He 3:19. 4:2, 11. **perverse.** Dt 32:5. Ps 78:8. Mt 3:7. 12:39, 45. 16:4. 23:36. Ac 2:40. 20:30. Ph 2:15. **generation.** Mt +*12:39. **how long.** Ex 10:3. 16:28. Nu 14:11, 27. Je 4:14. Mt 17:17. Jn 14:9. **and suffer.** Ac 13:18. 18:14. Ro 2:4. 2 C 11:1, 4, 19, 20. Ep 4:2. Col 3:13. 2 T 4:3g. He 3:9-11. **Bring.** 2 K 5:8. Mt 11:28. Mk 10:14, 49. He *7:25.

42. **the devil.** ver. 39. Mk 1:26, 27. 9:20, 26, 27. Re 12:12. **spirit.** Gr. *pneuma,* Mt +8:16. **and delivered.** Lk 7:15. 1 K 17:23. 2 K 4:36, 37. Ac 9:41.

43. **amazed.** Lk 4:36. 5:9, 26. 8:25. Ps 139:14. Zc 8:6. Mk 6:51. Ac 3:10-13. **mighty.** Is +*9:6. +*10:21. 49:26. 60:16. Je 32:18. Mt 11:21. Ep 1:21. Re 7:10, 12.

44. **these.** Lk 1:66. 2:19, 51. Is 32:9, 10. Jn 16:4. 1 Th 3:3, 4. He *2:1. 12:2-5. **for.** ver. 22. Lk *18:31. 24:6, 7, 44. Mt 16:21. 17:22, 23. 20:18, 19. 21:38, 39. 26:2. Mk 8:31. 9:31. Jn +*2:19-22. 19:11. Ac *2:23. 3:13-15. 4:27, 28. into. 2 S 24:14.

45. **understood not.** ver. 46. Lk 2:50. 18:34. 24:25, 26. Mt 13:19. 16:22. 17:13. Mk 6:52. 8:16-18, 32, 33. 9:10, 32. Jn 8:27, 28. 10:6. 12:16, 34. 14:5. 16:17, 18. 2 C *3:14-16. **was hid.** Lk 18:34. 24:16.

46. **arose a reasoning.** Lk 14:7-11. *22:24-27. Mt 18:1, etc. 20:20-22. 23:6, 7. Mk 9:33-37. Ro +*12:3,

10. Ga 5:20, 21, 25, 26. Ph +*2:3, 14. 3 J 9. **should.** ◟184D2, Lk +1:62.

47. **perceiving.** Lk 5:22. 7:39, 40. Ps 139:2, 23. Je +*17:10. Jn +*2:25. 16:30. 21:17. He ✓4:13. Re *2:23. **took.** Mt +*18:2-4. 19:13-15. Mk 10:14, 15. 1 C 14:20. 1 P *2:1, 2. **a child.** Lk 10:21. 17:2. 18:16. Mt 11:25. 18:6. 19:13-15. 21:16. Mk 9:42. 10:13-16. 1 C +*7:14.

48. **Whosoever shall receive this.** Lk 10:16. Mt 10:40-42. +*18:5, 6, 10, 14. 25:40, 45. Mk 9:37. Jn 12:44, 45. 13:20. 14:21. 1 Th 4:8. **in my name.** ver. 49. Lk 1:59. 21:8. 24:47. Mt 18:5. 24:5. Mk 9:37, 39. 13:6. Ac 4:17, 18. 5:28, 40. **he that is least.** Lk 7:28. 14:11. 22:30. Pr 18:12. Mt +*19:28. *23:11, 12. Ph +*2:3. 1 P 5:3, 4, 6. Re 3:21. 21:14.

49. **we saw.** Nu *11:27-29. Mk 9:38-40. 10:13, 14. Ac 4:18, 19. 5:28. 1 Th 2:16. 3 J 9, 10. **casting out.** Lk 10:17. Mt 7:22. 12:27. Mk 16:17. Ac 3:6. 16:18. 19:13. **we forbad.** Nu 11:28. Mt 19:14.

50. **Forbid him not.** Jsh 9:14. Pr *3:5, 6. Mt *13:28-30. 17:24-26. Lk 15:28. Ac 11:2. 2 C 2:7, 10. Ph *1:15-18. **for.** Lk *11:23. *16:13. Mt 6:24. *12:30. Mk *9:40, 41. 1 C +*12:3. 2 C 6:15, 16.

51. **received up.** Lk 24:51. 2 K 2:1-3, 11. Mk 16:19. Jn 6:62. 13:1. 16:5, 28. 17:11. Ac 1:2, 9. Ep 1:20. *4:8-11. 1 T *3:16. He 6:20. *12:2. 1 P 3:22. **he stedfastly.** Lk 12:50. Is 50:5-9. Ac 20:22-24. 21:11-14. Ph 3:14. 1 P 4:1. **set his face.** Ge 31:21. 2 K 8:11. 12:17. Is *50:7. Je 21:10. 42:15. 44:12. Ezk 6:2. 13:17. 20:46. 21:2. 25:2. 28:21. 29:2. 35:2. 38:2. Da 11:17. **to go.** Lk 13:22. 17:11. 18:31. 19:11, 28. Mk 10:32.

52. **sent.** Lk 7:27. 10:1. Ml 3:1. **and they.** Mt 10:5. **the Samaritans.** Lk 10:33. 17:16. 2 K 17:24-33. Ezr 4:1-5. Jn 8:48. **make ready.** ◟63A2, 2 S +6:6. i.e. to prepare a reception for him.

53. **did not receive him.** ver. 48. Jn 4:9, 40-42.

54. **wilt thou.** 2 S 21:2. 2 K 10:16, 31. Ja 1:19, 20. 3:14-18. **fire.** 2 K *1:10-14. Ps +*104:4. Mk 3:17. Ac 4:29, 30. Re 13:13.

55. **and rebuked.** 1 S 24:4-7. 26:8-11. 2 S 19:22. Jb 31:29-31. Pr 9:8. Mt 16:23. Re 3:19. ◟80. Epitimesis; or, Reprimand B930. An expression of feeling by way of censure, reproof, or reproach. For other instances of this figure see Lk 24:25. Ro 9:20. **Ye know.** Nu 20:10-12. Jb 2:10. 26:4. 34:4-9. 35:2-4. 42:6. Je +*17:9. Mt 26:33, 41, 51. Jn 16:9. Ac 23:3-5. 26:9-11. Ro *12:14, 19. Ja *1:19, 20. *3:10, 16, 17. 1 P *3:9. **spirit.** Gr. *pneuma*, ◟121A2, Mt +5:3n. Nu 14:24.

56. **the Son.** Lk +*19:10. Mt 18:11. 20:28. Jn *3:17. 10:10. 12:47. 1 T *1:15. **destroy.** Gr. *apollumi*, Mt +2:13. **lives.** Gr. *psyche*, ◟121A7, Mt +2:20. ◟121A7, Ge +9:5. **but to save.** Jn *12:47. **And.** Lk 6:27-31. 22:51. 23:34. Mt 5:39. Ro 12:21. 1 P 2:21-23.

57. **a certain.** Ex 19:8. Mt 8:19, 20. Jn 13:37.

58. **Jesus.** Lk 14:26-33. 18:22, 23. Jsh 24:19-22. Jn 6:60-66. **Foxes.** Ps 84:3. 2 C ✓8:9. Ja *2:5. **hath not.** Ge=37:15. 1 C 4:11.

59. **Follow me.** Mt 4:19-22. 9:9. 16:24. **suffer.** 1 K 19:20. Hg 1:2. Mt ✓6:33. *8:21, 22.

60. **Jesus said.** Mt +6:2n. **Let.** Lk 15:32. Je 16:5. Mt 8:22. Ep *2:1, 5. 1 T 5:6. Re 3:1. **the dead.** Jn 5:25. Ro 6:18. **but.** Jn 21:15-17. 1 C 9:16. 2 C 5:16-18. 2 T 2:3, 4. 4:2, 5.

61. **but.** Lk 14:18-20, 26. Dt 33:9. 1 K *19:20. Ec 9:10. Mt 10:37, 38. Mk ◖5:18, 19. **bid them.** Is +*38:1. Mk 6:46g.

62. **No.** ◟138C, Ge +22:14. Lk *17:31, 32. Ps 45:10.

*78:8, 9. Mt +*13:20, 21. Jn 6:66. Ac 15:37, 38. Ph 3:13. 2 T 4:10. He 6:1. 10:38. Ja 1:6-8. 2 P *2:20-22. **having put.** ◟7, Allegory by continued Hypocatastasis, Ga +4:24. Lk 10:2. **looking back.** Lk +*8:13. Ge *19:17. Ex 2:12. Pr *4:25. He ✓10:38, 39. **is fit.** Lk 14:35. He 6:7. **for.** Gr. *eis.* Ac +2:38n. Col 1:13. **the kingdom.** Lk +*17:20, 21. Mt 8:11, 12. Jn 18:36. Re 11:15.

LUKE 10

Jesus sends out seventy disciples, to work miracles and preach: and pronounce a woe against Chorazin, Bethsaida, and Capernaum, 1-16. The seventy return with joy at their success; and Christ instructs them in what they should rejoice, 17-20. He adores the Father, for revealing his gospel to the simple only; and declares his own personal and mediatorial authority and glory, 21, 22; and the happiness of his disciples, 23, 24. A lawyer inquires what he must do to inherit eternal life; and Jesus refers him to the law of God, 25-28; and shows him by the example of a good Samaritan, who is his neighbor, 29-37. He commends Mary's attention to his doctrine, and reproves Martha, who was "cumbered about much serving," 38-42.

1. **these.** Mt 10:1, etc. Mk 6:7, etc. **appointed.** T#448. Is 62:6. Ml *2:7. Ac *20:24, 28. 26:16-18. Ro *12:6-8. 1 C 1:1. *12:7-11. 2 C 5:18. Col 4:17. 1 T 1:12. T 1:3. **other seventy.** Rather, seventy others, as Dr. Campbell renders; for the expression other seventy implies that there were seventy sent before, which was not the case: it seems to refer to the twelve apostles whom our Lord had previously chosen. Ex 24:1, 9. Nu=11:16, 24-26. **two and.** Ec 4:9-12. Ac 13:2-4. Re 11:3-10. **whither.** Lk 1:17, 76. 3:4-6. 9:52. Ml 3:1.

2. **The harvest.** Mt *9:37, 38. Jn *4:35-38. 1 C 3:6-9. **the laborers.** Mt 20:1. Mk 13:34. 1 C 15:10. 2 C 6:1. Ph 2:25, 30. Col 1:29. 4:12. 1 Th 2:9. 5:12. 1 T 4:10, 15, 16. 5:17, 18. 2 T 2:3-6. 4:5. Phm 1. **are few.** 1 K 18:22. 22:6-8. Is 56:9-12. Ezk 34:2-6. Zc 11:5, 17. Mt 9:36. Ac 16:9, 10. Ph 2:21. Re 11:2, 3. **pray.** 2 Th 3:1. **the Lord.** Lk 9:1. Nu 11:17, 29. Ps 68:11. Je 3:15. Mk 16:15, 20. Ac 8:4. 11:19. 13:2, 4. +*20:28. 22:21. 26:15-18. 1 C 12:28. Ep 4:7-12. 1 T 1:12-14. He 3:6. Re 2:1. **send forth.** Mk 1:12. Jn 10:4.

3. **Go.** Jn 15:16. **I send.** Ps 22:12-16, 21. Ezk 2:3-6. Mt *10:16, 22. Jn 15:20. 16:2. 17:18. Ac 9:2, 16. **wolves.** Zp 3:3. Mt 7:15. Jn 10:12. Ac *20:29.

4. **neither.** Lk 9:3, etc. 22:35. Mt 10:9, 10. Mk 6:8, 9. **and salute.** ◟108B, 2 K +4:29. ◟102C, Mt +5:29. Lk 9:59, 60. Ge 24:33, 56. 1 S 21:8. 2 K *4:24, 29. Pr 4:25.

5. **into whatsoever.** Lk 19:9. **Peace be.** Jg 19:20. 1 S 25:6. 1 Ch 12:18. Is 57:19. Mt *10:12, 13. Ac 10:36. 2 C 5:18-20. Ep 2:17. **return.** Ps 35:13.

6. **And if.** ◟184C, Mt +4:9. **the Son.** Lk 5:34. 7:35. 16:8. 20:34, 36. 1 S 20:31. 25:17. 2 S 7:10. 12:5. Ps 89:22. Is +*9:6. Mt 23:15. Mk 2:19. 3:17. Jn 12:36. 17:12. Ac 3:25. 4:36. Ep 2:2, 3. 5:6, 8. Col 3:6. 1 Th 5:5. 2 Th 2:3. 3:16. Ja 3:18. 1 P 1:14g. 2 P 2:14. **if.** ◟184A, 1 C +15:2. **it shall.** Ps 35:13. Is 45:23. 2 C 2:15, 16.

7. **in.** Lk 9:4. Mt 10:11. Mk *6:10. Ac *16:15, 34, 40. **for the laborer.** Ge +*29:15. Dt 12:12, 18, 19. Ps 90:17. *128:2. Pr 14:23. 22:29. Ec 2:24. Mt *10:10. 1 C *9:4-15. Ga *6:6. Ph *4:17, 18. 1 T *◖5:17, 18.

2 T 2:6. 3 J 5-8. **his hire**. Le +*19:13. Nu 18:31. Dt +*24:15. Je +*22:13. 1 C *9:4, 7-14. **Go not**. Mt *10:11. 1 T *5:13.

8. **receive you**. ver. 10. Lk 9:48. Mt 10:40. Jn 13:20. **eat**. Ge 43:31, 32. 1 S 28:22-25. 2 S 12:20, 21. 2 K 6:22, 23. 1 C 10:27.

9. **heal**. Lk 9:2. Mt 10:8. Mk 6:13. Ac 28:7-10. **The kingdom**. ver. 11. Lk +4:43. +*17:20, 21. Da 2:44. Mt *3:2. *4:17. +*10:7. Mk +1:15. 4:30. Jn *3:3, 5. Ac 28:28, 31.

10. **go**. Lk 9:5. Mt 10:14. Ac 13:51. 18:6.

11. **the very dust**. Ne 5:13. Ac *13:51. *18:6. **notwithstanding**. ver. 9. Dt 30:11-14. Ac 13:26, 40, 46. Ro 10:8, 21. He 1:3.

12. **more tolerable**. Lk +*12:47, 48. La *4:6. Ezk +*16:48-50. Mt +*10:15. 11:24. Mk 6:11. Jn 15:22, 24. He *2:2, 3. *10:28, 29. **in that day**. Lk 21:34. Mt 7:22. Ac *17:31. 1 C 3:13. 2 Th 1:10. 2 T 1:12. 4:8. **for Sodom**. Mt 10:15. 11:23, 24. Ro 9:29. 2 P 2:6. Ju 7. Re 11:8.

13. **unto**. Mt 11:20-22. **Bethaida**. Lk 9:10. Mt 11:21. Mk 6:45. 8:22. Jn 1:44. 5:2. 12:21. **for if**. ſ184A, 1 C +15:2. Lk 11:31, 32. Ezk *3:6, 7. Mt +*11:23n. 12:41, 42. Jn *9:41. Ac 28:25-28. Ro 9:29-33. 11:8-11. 1 T 4:2. Ja *4:17. **Tyre**. Is ch. 23. Je 25:22. 47:4. Ezk ch. 26-28. Am 1:9, 10. **which**. Lk 9:10-17. Mk 8:22-26. **repented**. Jb 42:6. Is 61:3. Da 9:3. Jon 3:5, 6. Re 11:3.

14. **more tolerable**. ver. 12. Lk +*12:47, 48. Am 3:2. Mt 11:24. Jn *3:19. 15:22-25. Ro 2:1, 27. **at the judgment**. Lk 11:31, 32. Mt +*10:15n. 12:36, 41, 42. 23:33. Jn 5:29. 12:31. 16:8. Ac *17:31. 24:25. 1 T 5:24. He +*9:27. 2 P 2:4, 9. 3:7. 1 J 4:17. Ju 6. Re 14:7.

15. **Capernaum**. Lk 4:23, 31. 7:1, 2. Mt 4:13. **which**. Ge 11:4. Dt 1:28. Is ▸14:13-15. Je 51:53. Ezk 28:12-14. Am 9:2, 3. Ob 4. Mt 11:23. **thrust**. Lk 13:28. Is 5:14. 14:15. La 2:1. Ezk 26:20. 31:14, 16-18. 32:18, 20, 24, 27. Mt +*10:28. 2 P *2:4. **hell**. Gr. *hades*, Mt +11:23.

16. **heareth you**. Lk 9:48. Mt 10:40. *18:5. Mk 9:37. Jn *12:44, 48. 13:20. 1 Th 4:8. **despiseth you**. Ex *16:7, 8. Nu 14:2, 11. *16:11. 1 S 8:7. Mt 25:45. Jn 12:48. Ac *5:4. 1 Th *4:8. **despiseth him**. Ml *1:6. Jn √5:22, 23. 1 Th *4:8.

17. **returned**. ver. *1-9. Lk 9:1. Ro 16:20. **even**. Mk 16:17. **through thy name**. Jn 14:13.

18. **I beheld Satan**. Jn *12:31. 16:11. Ep *2:2. *6:12. Col 2:15. He *2:14. 1 J *3:8. Re 9:1. *12:7-9. 20:2. **fall from**. Is 14:12. Re 12:9, 12. *20:3, 10.

19. **I give**. Ge +*3:15. Ps *91:13. Is 11:8. Ezk 2:6. Mk 16:18. Ac *28:5. Ro *16:20. **serpents and**. Lk 11:12. Dt 8:15. Re 9:3. **the enemy**. Mt 13:25, 28, 39. 1 P 5:8. **and nothing**. ſ158. Mt +5:18. Lk 21:17, 18. Is 11:8, 9. Jn √10:28, 29. Ro *8:28, 31-39. He +*13:5, 6. Re 11:5. **hurt**. ſ121C2D4. Metonymy of the Cause in verbs of operation B557. "To hurt" or "to injure" is put for the hurt or injury done. For another instance of this figure see Ro 8:31.

20. **in this**. Mt *7:22, 23. 10:1. 26:24. 27:5. 1 C *13:2, 3. **spirits**. Gr. *pneuma*, Mt +8:16. **your names**. Ex 32:32, 33. Ps *69:28. 87:6. Is *4:3. *56:5. Je 17:13. Ezk 13:9. Da *12:1. Ph *4:3. He *12:23. Re *3:5. *13:8. 17:8. √20:12, 15. *21:27. **written**. Ex +32:32. Ezr=2:62, 63. **in heaven**. Je ●17:13. Ph 3:20.

21. **Jesus rejoiced**. Lk 15:5, 9. Is 53:11. 62:5. Zp 3:17. **spirit**. Gr. *pneuma*, Mt +3:16. ſ108B. Figure

of speech Idiom B832. "Spirit" (Gr. *pneuma*) is used to denote the greatest degree of any mental quality, or whatever is spoken of as possessed or done, as being so in the highest degree. Here, "rejoiced in spirit" means rejoiced exceedingly. For other instances of this figure see Ac +*18:25n. 19:21. 20:22. Ro 1:9. **I thank**. Mt 11:25, 26. Jn 11:41, 42. 17:24-26. Ro 14:11g. 15:9g. Re 7:12. **Father**. Lk 22:42. **Lord**. Ps 24:1. Is 66:1. Ac 17:24. **thou hast hid**. Lk 8:10. Jb 5:12-14. 37:24. Is 29:14. Mt 13:11. 18:3. Mk 4:11. Jn 9:39. Ro 1:22. 1 C *1:19-26. 2:6-8. 3:18-20. 2 C 3:14. *4:3, 4. Col 2:2, 3. **revealed**. Lk 8:10. Ps 8:2. *19:7. 25:14. Pr +*8:9. Is 29:18, 19. 35:8. Mt 11:25. *13:11-16. *16:17. 21:16. Mk 10:15. 1 C 1:27-29. 2:6, 7. Ja 1:5. 1 P 2:1, 2. **unto babes**. Lk 9:47. Mt *18:3, 4. 1 C 14:20. **even so**. Je 11:5. Ep 1:5, +*11. **seemed good**. Lk 12:32. Mt 18:14. Ga 1:15. He 13:21.

22. **All things**. "Many ancient copies add, And turning to his disciples he said." Mt 11:27. *28:18. Jn *3:35. *5:22-27. 13:3. *17:2, 10. 1 C *15:24. Ep *1:21, 22. Ph *2:9-11. He 2:8. **and no**. Jn *1:18. √6:44-46. 7:29. 8:19. 10:15. *14:6-9. 17:5, 25, 26. 2 C 4:6. 1 J *5:20. 2 J 9. **to whom**. Jn 17:6, 9, 26.

23. **he turned**. Lk 22:61. **Blessed**. Mt *13:16, 17. 16:17. **eyes**. ſ171Q15, Mt +13:16.

24. **many**. Jn *8:56. Ep *3:5, 6. He *2:1. *11:13, 39. 1 P *1:10, 11.

25. **a certain**. Lk 7:30. 11:45, 46. Mt 22:35. **tempted him**. Lk 4:12. *11:16, 54. Mt 4:7. 16:1. 19:3. 22:18, 35. Mk 8:11. 10:2. 12:15. Jn 6:6. 1 C 10:9. **Master**. Lk 7:40. 18:18. **what shall**. Lk 18:18. Mt 19:16. Mk 10:17-19. 12:28-32. Jn 6:28. Ac √16:30, 31. **to inherit**. Mt 19:16, +*29. Ga 3:18. **eternal**. Gr. *aionios*, Mt +18:8. **life**. Gr. *zoe*, S#2222g. Rendered (1) life: Lk 1:75. 10:25. 12:15. 18:18, 30. Mt 7:14. 18:8, 9. 19:16, 17, 29. 25:46. Mk 9:43, 45. 10:17, 30. Jn 1:4, 3. 3:15, 16, 36, 36. 4:14, 36. 5:24, 24, 26, 26, 29, 39, 40. 6:27, 33, 35, 40, 47, 48, 51, 53, 54, 63, 68. 8:12. 10:10, 28. 11:25. 12:25, 50. 14:6. 17:2, 3. 20:31. Ac 2:28. 3:15. 5:20. 8:33. 11:18. 13:46, 48. 17:25. Ro 2:7. 5:10, 17, 18, 21. 6:4, 22, 23. 7:10. 8:2, 6, 10, 38. 11:15. 1 C 3:22. 15:19. 2 C 2:16, 16. 4:10, 11, 12. 5:4. Ga 6:8. Ep 4:18. Ph 1:20. 2:16. 4:3. Col 3:3, 4. 1 T 1:16. 4:8. 6:12, 19. 2 T 1:1, 10. T 1:2. 3:7. He 7:3, 16. Ja 1:12. 4:14. 1 P 3:7, 10. 2 P 1:3. 1 J 1:1, 2, 2. 2:25. 3:14, 15. 5:11, 11, 12, 13, 16, 20. Ju 21. Re 2:7, 10. 3:5. 11:11. 13:8. 17:8. 20:12, 15. 21:6, 27. 22:1, 2, 14, 17, 19. (2) lifetime, Lk 16:25. See the note on Mt +*10:28.

26. **What is written**. Is +*8:20n. Mt 5:19. Ro 3:19. 4:14-16. 10:5. Ga 3:12, 13, 21, 22. **in the law**. Mt 12:5. 22:36. Jn 1:45. 8:5, 17. 10:34. 15:25.

27. **Thou**. Dt ▸6:5. *10:12. *30:6. 2 K 23:25. Mt 22:37-40. Mk 12:30, 31, 33, 34. He 8:10. **with all**. Dt 4:29. 10:12. 11:13. 13:3. 26:16. 30:2, 6, 10. Jsh 22:5. 1 K 2:4. 8:48. 2 K 23:3, 25. 2 Ch 6:38. 15:12. 34:31. Je 32:41. **heart**. ſ173, Ge +27:44. 2 K +*20:3. 1 Ch 12:38n. **and**. ſ148, Ge +8:22. **soul**. Gr. *psyche*, ſ121A9B, Mt +22:37. **and thy**. Le +*▸19:18. Mt 19:19. Ro *13:9. Ga *5:13, 14. Ja *2:8. 1 J 3:18.

28. **Thou hast**. Lk 7:43. Mk 12:34. **this do**. ſ96B, Nu +24:21. Ge 4:7. Le +*▸18:5. Ne 9:29. Ps +*19:11. Ezk *20:11, 13, 21. Mt *19:17. Ro 2:13. √3:19-22. *7:10, 18. *10:4, 5. Ga *3:12, 13, 21, 22. Ja *3:2.

29. **willing**. Lk *16:15. 18:9-11. Le 19:34. Jb 32:2. Ro 4:2. *10:3. Ga 3:11. Ja 2:24. **justify**. ſ121I2, Ge

+2:17. **And.** ver. 36. Mt 5:43, 44. **neighbor.** ✓24D. Antimereia of the Adverb B494: adverb for noun. lit. "And who is near to me": i.e., my neighbor. Mt 22:39. Ro 13:10. For another instance of this figure see Jn 1:27.

30. **went down.** Jon 1:3. Lk ◐18:31. ◐19:28. **from Jerusalem.** The whole way from Jericho to Jerusalem, says Josephus (Bel. l. iv. c. 8. sec. 2), is desert and rocky; and nothing can be more savage than the present aspect of these wild and gloomy solitudes; which have been so noted as the haunts of the most desperate bandits, as to obtain, in the time of Jerome, the appellation of the field of blood. Here, says Mr. Buckingham, pillage, wounds, and death, would be accompanied with double terror, from the frightful aspect of every thing around; here the unfeeling act of passing by a fellow creature in distress, strikes one with horror, as an act more than inhuman; and here too, the compassion of the good Samaritan is doubly virtuous, from the purity of the motive which must have led to it, in a spot where no eyes were fixed upon him, and from the bravery which was necessary to admit of a man's exposing himself, by such delay, to the risk of a similar fate. **Jericho.** Lk 18:35. 19:1. Mt 20:29. Mk 10:46. He 11:30. **fell among.** Je 3:2. **stripped him.** Mi 3:8. **wounded.** Ps 88:4, 5. Je 51:52. La 2:12. Ezk 30:24.

31. **by chance.** According to Vine (*Expository Dictionary of New Testament Words*) the word signifies concurrence of events, rather than chance. That God sees the fall of every sparrow, and knows the number of hairs on our heads (Mt 10:29, 30), shows Jesus taught divine providence, not chance, accounts for all that happens. Ge ◐+*24:44n. Ru 2:3mg. 2 S 1:6. Ec 9:11. **priest.** Nu 8:19. Je 5:31. Ho 5:1. 6:9. Ml 1:10. Jn 1:19. **he passed.** Jb 6:14-21. Ps 38:10, 11. 69:20. 142:4. Pr 21:13. 24:11, 12. Ml 2:7-9. Ja *2:13-16. 1 J *3:16-18.

32. **Levite.** i.e. *joined, cleaving to,* ✱S#3019g. Jn 1:19. Ac 4:36. **and looked.** Ps 109:25. Pr 27:10. Ac 18:17. 2 T 3:2.

33. **Samaritan.** Lk *9:52, 53. 17:16-18. Pr 27:10. Je 38:7-13. 39:16-18. Mt 10:5. Jn 4:9. 8:48. **came.** Le 14:3. He 13:13. **had compassion.** T#414. Lk 7:13. 15:20. Ex 2:6. 32:31-33. 1 S 24:16-18. 1 K 8:50. Jb 1:9, 21. 13:15. *29:12, 13. Da 3:16-18. *6:10. Mt 9:36. 14:14. 15:32. 18:33. 20:34. Mk 1:41. 6:34. 8:2. 9:22. Ac 2:44, 45. 4:32-35. Ro 9:1-3. 2 C *8:9. 12:14. He 11:24-26.

34. **went.** ver. 34. Ex 23:4, 5. Pr 24:17, 18. 25:21, 22. Mt *5:43-45. Ro 12:20, 21. 1 Th 5:15. **bound.** Ps 147:3. Is 1:5, 6. Mk 14:8. **pouring.** Gr. *epicheo,* ✱S#2022g, only here. **oil.** Dt 28:40. Ps 23:5. Is 1:6. Mk 6:13. Ja 5:14. Re 3:18. **and wine.** Jg 19:19. Pr 17:22. 1 T 5:23. **his own.** 1 K 1:33. **an inn.** Lk 2:7. Ge 42:27. Ex 4:24. **took care.** Ac 18:26.

35. **two pence.** See Mt 18:28mg. 20:2mg. **the host.** Ro 16:23. **Take care.** Le 19:18. Mt 19:19. Mk 12:31. Phm 18. Ja 2:8. **whatsoever.** Lk 14:13, 14. Pr 19:17. **come again.** Lk 19:15g.

36. **thinkest.** Lk 7:42. Mt 17:25. 21:28-31. 22:42. **was.** ver. 29.

37. **He that.** Pr *14:21. Ho *6:6. Mi +*6:8. Mt *20:28. +*23:23. 2 C ✓8:9. Ep 3:18, 19. *5:2. He 2:9-15. Re +*1:5. **Go.** Lk +*6:32-36. Mt *5:44. Jn *13:15-17. 1 P *2:21. 1 J *3:16-18, 23, 24. *4:10, 11.

38. **a certain.** Jn *11:1-5, 19, 20. 12:1-3. **Martha.** i.e. *who becomes bitter; she was rebellious; lady,* ✱S#3136g. Lk 10:38, 40, 41. Jn 11:1, 5, 19, 20, 21, 24, 30, 39. 12:2. **received.** Lk 8:2, 3. 19:6. Jn 1:38, 39. Ac *16:15. 17:7. Ro +*15:7. Ja 2:25. 2 J *10.

39. **sat at.** Lk 2:46. 8:35. Dt 33:3. Pr 8:34. SS 2:3. Jn 11:20, 29, 32. 12:3. Ac 22:3. 1 C 7:32, etc. **the Lord's.** Lk 7:13. **feet.** Lk 7:37, 38. 8:35. Mt 15:30. Mk 5:22, 23. 7:25. Jn 11:32. Re 1:17. **and heard his word.** Ho 14:8. Mt +*13:23.

40. **cumbered.** Lk 12:29. Jn 6:27. 1 C *7:35. **much serving.** Jn 12:2. **came to.** Lk 20:1. **dost.** Nu +*11:1. Mt 14:15. 16:22. Mk 3:21. 4:38. **my sister.** Lk 9:55. Jon 4:1-4. **serve alone.** Mt 8:15. Jn *12:2. **bid her.** T#1557.

41. **Martha.** ✓84, Ge +22:11. **thou art.** Lk 8:14. *21:34. Mk *4:19. 1 C *7:32-35. Ph *4:6. **careful.** Lk 12:11. Mt 6:25. **many.** Ec 6:11. Mt *6:25-34.

42. **one thing.** Lk *18:22. Ps *27:4. *73:25, 28. Ec 3:19. Mk 10:21. Jn 9:25. Ph 3:13. 2 P 3:8. **needful.** Ec 12:13. Mt ✓6:33. *16:26. Mk *8:36. Jn *6:27. ✓17:3. 1 C *13:3. Ga *5:6. Col *2:10, etc. 1 J ✓5:11, 12. **chosen.** Dt *30:19. Jsh ✓24:15, 22. Ru 2:12. Ps *17:15. 119:30, 111, 173. Mt 11:28. **good.** Ps 16:5, 6. 73:26. *119:57, 72, 162. 142:5. La 3:24. **which.** Lk +*8:18. *12:20, 33. 16:2, *25. Mt +*5:6. Mk 14:9. Jn *4:14. ✓5:24. ✓10:27, 28. Ro *8:35-39. Ph *1:6. Col *3:3, 4. 1 P *1:4, 5.

LUKE 11

Jesus teaches his disciples to pray, and encourages earnestness and importunity by two illustrations, 1-13. He casts out a devil, and exposes the absurdity and malice of those who ascribed the miracle to the power of Beelzebub, 14-26. He shows the blessedness of true piety above all external privileges, and warns the impenitent Jews, 27-36. Dining with a Pharisee, he exposes the ignorance, hypocrisy, and wickedness of the Scribes and Pharisees, 37-52; who eagerly endeavor to ensnare and accuse him, 53, 54.

1. **that.** Lk *6:12. 9:18, 28. *22:39-45. Mt *14:23. Mk +*1:35. He 5:7. **teach.** T#1647. Jb *37:19. Ps 10:17. 19:14. Zc 12:10. Ro *8:26, 27. Ep 2:18. 6:18. Ja *4:2, 3. Ju *20. **as John.** Lk 5:33. **his disciples.** Mt 9:14.

2. **When.** Ec 5:2. Ho *14:2. Mt *6:6-8. **Our.** Is 63:16. Mt *6:9, etc. Ro 1:7. *8:15. 1 C 1:3. 2 C 1:2. Ga 1:4. Ep 1:2. Ph 1:2. 4:20. Col 1:2. 1 Th 1:1, 3. 3:11-13. 2 Th 1:1, 2. 2:16. **which.** 2 Ch 20:6. Ps *11:4. Ec *5:2. Da 2:28. Mt 5:16. 10:32. **Hallowed.** Lk 1:49. Le 10:3. 22:32. Nu 20:12. 1 K 8:43. 2 K 19:19. Ps *57:11. 72:18, 19. 108:5. Is 8:13. 29:23. Ezk 20:41. 28:22. 36:23. 38:16, 23. Hab 2:14. 1 P *3:15. Re *15:4. **thy name.** ✓144A4, Ge +4:26. Le 18:21. 20:3. 21:6. +*22:32. Ps 5:11. +✓9:10. Ml *1:11, 12. Jn 17:6. **Thy kingdom.** Lk 10:9-11. Is +*2:2-5. Da *2:44. *7:18, 27. Mt 3:2. +4:17. ✓6:33. +*26:29. Mk +1:15. Ro *14:17. Re *11:15. 19:6. *20:4. **Thy will.** T#1538. Lk 22:41, 42. Jg 10:15. 2 S 15:25, 26. Ps *103:20. Is 6:2, 3. Mt +*6:10. 26:39, 42. Mk 14:35, 36, 39. Ac *21:14.

3. **Give.** Ex 16:15-22. Jb +*23:12. Pr *30:8. Is 33:16. Mt 6:11, 34. Jn *6:27-33. **day by day.** *or,* for the day. Ne=11:23. Ac *17:11. 2 C 4:16.

4. **forgive us.** Lk 7:48. Ge 50:17. Ex 32:32. Nu 14:19. 1 K 8:34, 36. Ps 25:11, 18. *32:1-5. +*51:1-3. *130:3,

4. **Is** 43:25, 26. **Da** 9:19. **Ho** *14:2. **Mt** +*6:12. 1 J
√1:8-10. **our sins.** Mt 6:12. **for we.** Mt +*6:14, 15.
18:35. Mk *11:25, 26. Ep √4:31, 32. Col 3:13. Ja *2:13.
lead. ♪111, Ge +18:27. Lk 8:13. 22:40, 46. Je +*29:11.
Mt 6:13. *26:41. Mk 14:38. 1 C √10:13. 2 C 12:7, 8.
Ja 1:2. Re 2:10. +*3:10. There is no suggestion intended here that God might "lead us into temptation."
The balanced sentence employs a contrast, where the
first member ("lead us not into temptation") is employed solely to emphasize the last member ("but deliver us from evil"). For other instances of this construction, see Jn 20:27. Ro 12:21. 1 C 10:24. 2 C 3:6. Ep
5:17, 18. Ph 2:4. Col 3:2. **but deliver.** Ge 48:16. Ps
*121:7. Jn *17:15. 2 Th *3:3. 2 T *4:18.

5. **Which of you.** Lk 18:1-8. **at midnight.** Mk 13:35.

6. **in his journey.** *or*, out of his way. **have nothing.**
Ex 4:2. Ps 62:5. Jn 6:9. 2 C 12:9.

7. **Trouble.** Lk 7:6. Mt 26:10. Mk 14:6. Ga 6:17.
the door. Lk 13:25. Mt 25:10. **I cannot.** SS +5:3.

8. **Though.** ♪185A. Concessive Clauses: Logical
Concession. The concession is assumed to be a fact.
For other instances of this construction see Lk 18:4.
Mt 26:33. Mk 14:29. 2 C 4:16. 7:8, 12. 11:6. 12:11.
Ph 2:17. Col 2:5. He 6:9. **because of his importunity.**
Lk *18:1-8. 22:44. Ge 18:32. *32:26. Ex √17:11. Dt
9:18. Is √62:6, 7. Mt *15:22-28. Jn 4:49. Ac 12:5. Ro
15:30. 2 C 12:8. Col 2:1. *4:12. Ja *5:16, 17. **give
him.** Ps 37:3, 4. Ro *8:32. 2 C 8:9. 9:8. Ph *4:19. Ja
4:2, 3. 2 P 1:3.

9. **I say.** Lk 13:24. Mt 6:29. 21:31. Mk 13:37. Re
2:24. **Ask.** 1 K 3:5. Ps +*50:15. *118:5. Je √33:3. Zc
10:1. Mt √7:7, 8. √18:19. *21:22. Mk +*11:24. Jn 4:10.
+*14:13. √15:7, 16. √16:23, 24. Ro 12:12. 2 C √12:8,
9. Ep 6:18. Col 4:2. He *4:16. Ja +*1:5, 6. +*4:2,
3. +*5:15, 16. 1 J *3:22. √5:14, 15. **it shall be given
you.** Ps 84:11. 91:15. Pr 10:24. *15:29. Jn 15:7. Ac
*10:4. 2 C 1:20. 1 P *3:12. 1 J 3:22. **seek.** Lk 13:24.
Dt 4:27, 29. 1 Ch +*28:9. 2 Ch 15:2. Ps +*9:10.
27:4, 8, 9. 32:6. +*34:4, 10. 105:3, 4. Pr 2:4. 8:17.
SS 3:1-4. 5:6. Is 45:19. √55:6, 7. Je √29:12, 13. La
+*3:25. Da *9:3. Am 5:4-6. Jn 1:45-49. Ac 10:4-6.
Ro *2:7. He √11:6. **ye shall find.** 2 Ch +*7:14. Jb
22:27. 33:26. Ps 10:17. 145:18, 19. Pr 2:5. Je 29:13,
14. 33:3. **knock.** ver. +*8. Lk 12:36. 13:25. 1 S +*23:4.
2 K=13:18, 19. Ps +*40:17. Is 45:11. *62:6, 7. Ac
12:5-17. Re *3:20. **be opened.** Ps +*34:15. 143:8. Pr
3:5, 6. 15:8. Is +*65:24. Jn 1:38, 39. Ac 5:19. 12:10.
2 C 6:2. Col *4:3.

10. **every one.** Lk 18:1. Ps 31:22. La 3:8, 18, 54-
58. Jon 2:2-8. Ja 4:3. 5:11. **seeketh.** Je √29:13. **knocketh.**
ver. +*8. Lk 12:36. 13:25.

11. **a son.** Is 49:15. Mt 7:9, 10. **ask bread.** Lk 4:3.
Mt 4:3. **father.** Ps 103:13. **will he.** ♪15C, Mk +6:11.
or if. ♪184A, 1 C +15:2.

12. **if.** ♪184C, Mt +4:9. **offer.** Gr. give. **a scorpion.**
Lk 10:19. Ezk 2:6. Re 9:3, 10.

13. **If ye.** ♪184A, 1 C +15:2. Lk 18:6, 7. **being
evil.** Ge *6:5, 6. *8:21. Jb 15:14-16. Ps *51:5. Je +*17:9.
Mt 7:11. *12:34. Jn 3:5, 6. Ro √3:23. *7:18. T 3:3.
know. Is 49:15. Mt 7:11. He 12:9, 10. **how.** Mt 6:30.
Ro 5:9, 10, 17. *8:32. 2 C 3:9-11. **your.** Mt +23:9.
heavenly. ver. 2. Lk 15:30-32. Mt *5:16, 45. 6:14,
32. **give the.** T#350. Lk *3:21. Pr +*1:23. Is 44:3,
4. Ezk *36:26, 27, 37. Jl +*2:28. Mt 7:11. Jn *4:10.
*7:37-39. *14:16, 17. Ac *1:4, 5, 14. 2:38. *4:31. 8:15.
2 C 1:21, 22. Ga 4:6. Ep *3:14-19. He *12:9, 10. Ja

*1:13, 17. **Spirit.** Gr. *pneuma*, Mt +1:18n. ♪121A1,
Jn +3:34.

14. **casting out.** Mt 9:32, 33. 12:22, 23. Mk 7:32-
37. **dumb.** ♪121E1, Ge +25:23. The evil spirit was
not dumb, but produced or was the source of the dumbness. This is an instance of Metonymy of the Effect,
where the effect is put for the person producing the
effect, or for the author of it. Mt 12:22. Mk 9:17, 25.
people wondered. Mk +5:20.

15. **He.** Mt 9:34. 12:24-30. Mk 3:22-30. Jn 7:20.
8:48, 52. 10:20. **Beelzebub.** Gr. Beelzebul, and so ver.
18, 19. 2 K *1:2, 3, 6. Mt 10:25. 12:24, 27. Mk 3:22.
the chief. Mt 9:34. Jn 12:31. +*14:30. 16:11. Ep 2:2.

16. **tempting him.** Mt 12:38, 39. 16:1-4. Mk *8:11,
12. Jn 6:30. 8:6. 1 C *1:22. **a sign.** Lk 21:11.

17. **knowing.** Mt 9:4. 12:25. Mk *3:23-26. Jn
+*2:25. Re *2:23. **Every.** ♪138B, Ge +13:16. 2 Ch
10:16-19. 13:16, 17. Is 9:20, 21. 19:2, 3. Mt 12:25.

18. **If.** ♪184A, 1 C +15:2. **Satan.** Mt 12:26. 1 C
5:5. **ye say.** ver. 15. Mt 12:31-34. Ja 3:5-8.

19. **if.** ♪184A, 1 C +15:2. **by whom.** Lk 9:49. 1 S
16:23. Mt +6:2n. 7:22. 12:27, 28. Mk 9:38. Ac 19:13.
your sons. ♪14, Is +5:3. 1 K 20:35. 2 K 2:3. 4:1, 38.
5:22. 6:1. 9:1. **shall.** ver. 31, 32. Lk 19:22. Jb 15:6.
Mt 12:41, 42. Ro 3:19.

20. **if I.** ♪184A, 1 C +15:2. Ac *10:38. 1 J *3:8.
with. ♪108D, Mt +3:11. **the finger.** ♪22A16, Ex +8:19.
Ex=8:19. 31:18. Dt 9:10. Ps 8:3. Mt *12:28. **no doubt.**
Lk 17:21. Mt 19:24. 21:31, 43. **the kingdom.** For the
destruction of the kingdom of Satan plainly implies
the setting up of the kingdom of God. The reasoning
of the Pharisees (ver. 17, and Mt 12:24, 25), was not
expressed, and Jesus, *knowing their thoughts*, gave
ample proof of his *omniscience.* This, with our Lord's
masterly confutation of their reasonings, by a conclusion drawn from their own premises, one would have
supposed might have humbled and convinced those
men; but the most conclusive reasoning, and the most
astonishing miracles, were lost upon a people who were
obstinately determined to disbelieve every thing that
was good relative to Jesus of Nazareth. Lk +4:43. 10:9,
11. Da *2:44. Mt 3:2. Mk 1:15. Ac 20:25. 28:23-28.
2 Th 1:5. **is come.** Lk 16:16. +*17:20, 21. Mt 4:17. 11:12.
12:28. ◐√21:43. Mk 1:14, 15.

21. **a strong man.** Pr 11:16. See on Mt 12:29. Mk
3:27. **his palace.** Mt 26:3.

22. **when a stronger.** Ge +*3:15. Is 27:1. 49:24,
25. 53:12. 63:1-4. Col 2:15. 1 J *3:8. 4:4. Re *20:1-3.
overcome. Mt 12:29. Jn 16:33. Col *2:15. **his armor.**
Ep *6:11, 13. **divideth.** Is *53:12.

23. **not with me.** Lk *9:50. 18:17. Ex=32:26. Mt
*12:30. Mk 9:40. Jn 11:52. He=13:13. Re *3:15, 16.

24. **the unclean.** Mt 12:43-45. Mk +3:30. **spirit.**
Gr. *pneuma*, Mt +8:16. **he walketh.** Jb 1:7. 2:2. 1 P
*5:8. **dry places.** Lk 8:29. Jg 6:37-40. Ps 63:1. Is 13:21.
35:1, 2, 7. 41:17-19. 44:3. Je 2:6. Ezk 47:8-11. Ep
*2:2. Re 18:2. **seeking rest.** Pr 4:16. Is 48:22. 57:20,
21. **I will.** Mk 5:10. 9:25.

25. **he findeth.** 2 Ch 24:17-22. Ps 36:3. 81:11, 12.
125:5. Mt 12:44, 45. 2 Th 2:9-12. 2 P 2:10-19. Ju 8-
13.

26. **spirits.** Gr. *pneuma*, Mt +8:16. Lk 7:21. **more
wicked.** Mt 23:15. **last state.** Zp 1:6. Mt *12:45. 27:64.
Jn √5:14. He *6:4-8. √10:26-31. 2 P √2:20-22. 1 J 5:16.
Ju 12, 13.

27. **certain woman.** Lk 12:13. **lifted.** ♪144A12, Ge

+22:13. Lk +6:20. 17:13. Jg 21:2. 1 S 11:4. Ac 2:14. 4:24. 14:11. 22:22. **Blessed.** Lk *1:28, 42, 48. 1 K 10:8. 2 Ch 9:7.

28. **Yea rather.** Lk 6:47, 48. +*8:21. Ps +*1:1-3. 112:1. *119:1-6. 128:1. Is 48:17, 18. Mt *7:21-25. *12:48-50. Jn +*13:17. Ja +*1:21-25. 1 J *3:21-24. Re 1:3. 22:7, 14. **blessed.** T#1100. Ja 1:25. **that hear.** Lk +*8:18. Jb +*37:2. Mk +*4:24. **the word of God.** Lk +5:1. Ac +*17:11. 1 Th √2:13. **and keep.** Lk √6:46. Le 19:37. 22:31. Nu 15:40. Dt *4:40. +*26:16. Ps 119:105. Mt √7:21. Jn +*13:17. Ro 2:13. 2 T +*3:15-17. Ja √1:22.

29. **when.** Lk 12:1. 14:25, 26. **This is.** ver. 50. 9:41. Is 57:3, 4. Mt 3:7. 23:34-36. Mk *8:38. Jn *8:44. Ac 7:51, 52. **generation.** Mt +*12:39. **they seek.** Mt 12:38, 39. 16:1-4. Mk 8:11, 12. Jn 2:18. 6:30. 1 C 1:22.

30. **as Jonas.** Lk 24:46, 47. Jon *1:17. 2:10. 3:2, etc. Mt +*12:40. **Ninevites.** i.e. inhabitants of Nineveh. ✺S#3536g. Lk 11:30. Mt 12:41. **Son of man.** Lk +5:24. Mt +8:20. Mk +2:10. Jn +1:51.

31. **queen.** 1 K *10:1, 2, etc. 2 Ch 9:1. Mt 12:42. **rise.** Lk 10:13-15. Is 54:17. Je 3:11. Mt 11:20-24. Ro 2:27. He 11:7. **the judgment.** Lk 10:14. **and condemn.** Je 3:11. Ezk 16:51, 52. Ro 2:27. He 11:7. **uttermost parts.** Ps 2:8. 72:8. Zc 9:10. **to hear.** 1 C 1:22. **the wisdom.** 1 K 4:29-34. 5:12. 10:23, 24. 2 Ch 1:7-12. 9:22. **a greater.** ver. 32. Lk 3:22. 9:35. Is +*9:6, 7. Mt 12:6. Col *1:15-19.

32. **men.** Jon 3:5-10. **of Nineveh.** i.e. *agreeable,* ✺S#3535g. only here. For ✺S#5210h, Ge +10:12. Ge +10:11. **in the judgment.** Ob +*21. Mt +*10:15n. **they repented.** Jon *3:5. **a greater.** ver. 31. Jon 1:2, 3. 4:1-4, 9. Mt 12:6. He 7:26.

33. **when.** Lk 8:16, 17. Mt *5:14, 15. Mk 4:21, 22. **a candle.** Pr 20:27. **a bushel.** See Mt 5:15mg. **may see.** Mt *5:16. 10:27. Jn 11:9. 12:46. Ph *2:15, 16.

34. **light of.** Ps √119:18. Mt +*6:22, 23. Mk *8:18. Ac *26:18. Ep *1:17, 18. **single.** Ac *2:46. 2 C 1:12. *11:3. Ep +6:5. Col *3:22. **but.** Ge *19:11. Dt 15:9. 28:54, 56. 2 K *6:15-20. Ps *81:12. Pr 23:6. *28:22. Is *6:10. *29:10. 42:19, 20. *44:18. Je 5:21. Mt 20:15. Mk *4:12. *7:22. Ac 13:11. Ro 11:8-10. 1 C √2:14. 2 C *4:4. Ga 3:1. 2 Th *2:9-12.

35. **Take heed.** Pr *16:25. 20:27. 26:12. Is *5:20, 21. Je 8:8, 9. Mt +*6:23. Jn 7:48, 49. 9:39-41. Ro 1:22. 2:19-23. 1 C 1:19-21. *3:18-20. Ja 3:13-17. 2 P 1:9. 2:18, 19. Re 3:17.

36. **If.** ƒ184A, 1 C +15:2. **no part dark.** Jb 11:15. SS 4:7. Je +*10:2. Mt +*6:23. Ac *20:26. *24:16. 1 C 5:6. 2 C +*6:17. 7:1. Ep +*5:8, 11, 27. 1 Th 4:4. +*5:22, 23. 2 T 2:21. 1 P 3:16. 2 P *3:14. **the whole.** Ps *119:97-105. Pr *1:5. 2:1-11. 4:18, 19. 6:23. 20:27. Is +*8:20n. 42:16. Ho +*6:3. Mt 13:11, 12, 52. Mk 4:24, 25. 2 C 4:6. Ep +*4:14. Col *3:16. 2 T √3:15-17. He *5:14. Ja *1:25. 2 P √3:18. **the bright shining of a candle.** Gr. a candle by its bright shining. Mt 5:16.

37. **a certain Pharisee.** Lk 7:36. 14:1. 1 C 9:19-23. **to dine.** Gr. to breakfast. Lk 14:1. Jn 21:12, 15g.

38. **he marvelled.** Mt 15:2, 3. Mk *7:2-5. Jn 3:25. **washed.** Gr. *baptizo,* Mk +*7:3n.

39. **the Lord.** Lk 7:13. **Now.** Lk 20:47. Mt *23:25, 26. Ga 1:14. 2 T 3:5. T 1:15, 16. **the cup.** Mk 7:4. **but.** Lk 16:15. Ge *6:5. 2 Ch 25:2. 31:20, 21. Pr 26:25. 30:12. Je 4:14. Mt *12:33-35. *15:19, 20. Jn 12:6. 13:2.

Ac *5:3. *8:21-23. Ja 4:8. **ravening.** Lk 16:14. Ps 22:13. Ezk 22:25, 27. Zp 3:3. Mt 7:15.

40. **fools.** Lk *12:20. 24:25. Ps *14:1. 75:4, 5. 94:8, 9. Pr 1:22. 8:5. Je 5:21. Mt 23:17, 26. 1 C 15:36. Ep 5:17. **did.** Ge +*1:26. +*2:7. Nu 16:22. Ps 33:15. 94:9, 10. Zc 12:1. He 12:9.

41. **rather.** Lk 12:33. 14:12-14. 16:9. 18:22. 19:8. Dt *15:8-10. Jb 31:16-20. Ps 41:1. 112:9. Pr 14:31. 19:17. Ec 11:1, 2. Is *58:6-11. Da *4:27. Mt 5:42. 6:1-4. 25:34-40. 26:11. Ac 9:36-39. 10:31, 32. 11:29. 24:17. 2 C 8:7-9, 12. 9:6-15. Ep *4:28. He +*6:10. 13:16. Ja 1:27. 2:14-16. 1 J *3:16, 17. **give alms.** ƒ121C1B, Ge +20:13. Mt 6:1. **of such things as ye have.** *or,* as you are able. This is clearly the central principle underlying the New Testament standard of giving. The stress in the New Testament is upon giving as God has prospered (1 C 16:2), according to one's ability (Ac 11:29), with willingness and cheerfulness, not legalistic obligation (2 C 8:12. 9:7). We are to first take care of the needs of our own family (1 T +*5:8), and remain debt-free (Ro 13:8), though this is interpreted by some not as a stricture upon such debts as mortgages, but refers to our obligation to remain current in payments on debt. Such evidence as the New Testament furnishes shows that giving was not based on the tithe system, but on voluntary gifts and offerings for the support of those by whom they were taught (Ga 6:6. 1 T 5:17. He 13:16), in the giving of alms (Ac 9:36), and in the support of poorer brethren in the faith (Ro 12:8. 2 C 8:14. Ga 6:10). See further on ver. 42 and Mt ◐23:23n. Le 5:7. 14:30. 27:8. Dt *16:17. Ezr 2:69. Ne 5:8. Ac *11:29. 2 C *8:12. **all things.** ƒ60A, Ge +3:22. ƒ27A, Ge +3:22. Mt 15:10-20. Mk 7:14, 15, 18-23. Ac 10:15. Ro 14:14-18. 2 C *7:1. 1 T *4:4, 5. T √1:15. Ja 4:8.

42. **woe.** Mt 23:13, +*23n, 27. **for ye tithe.** Tithing is not taught in the New Testament as an obligation for the Christian under grace. It is popular, though probably not scriptural, to suggest that the Christian under grace should do more than the minimum required under law—forgetting that the Jews were obligated to pay more than one tithe, perhaps as many as three, which involved payments amounting to about one quarter of their income or more. Thus the application of the concept of "tithe" to the Christian, based upon the pattern set forth in the Old Testament, would appear to be an oversimplification of the evidence, and a misapplication of Old Testament principles. The Jewish tithes constituted their civil income tax during the theocracy. To mandate Christians of today to pay, in addition to income tax, a tithe to the church on either their gross or net earnings, is to lay upon them a burden too grievous to be borne, and is contrary to the very spirit of Christ's teaching in the parallel text (Mt +*23:4). Because we are not under law, but under grace, Christian giving must not be made a matter of legalistic obligation, lest we fall into the error of Galatianism. Paul's statement in Colossians 2:16-23 would appear to forever forbid the legalistic application of the Old Testament laws and rituals to the New Testament believer. The basis of appeal to New Testament believers under grace was in prospect of their eternal reward, what Jesus called "laying up treasure in heaven" (Mt 6:19-21. Ph +*4:17). The apostles never censured believers for their failure to pay tithes, and never commanded them to pay tithes to the New Testa-

ment church. Such a command to Jewish believers would have conflicted with their continuing obligation, while the Temple yet stood, to pay tithes to Israel. If they stopped paying tithes to the Temple, they could scarcely worship there in good standing. Would Jewish Christians be under obligation to pay tithes to both the Jewish and Christian church? Lk 18:12. Dt 14:22. Mt ☉+*23:23n. Col 2:16n. **and all.** √ſ171B, Ge +24:10. i.e. herb of every (tithable) kind. **and pass over.** Dt 10:12, 13. 1 S *15:22. Pr 21:3. Is *1:10-17. 58:2-6. Je 7:2-10, 21, 22. Mi +*6:8. Ml 1:6. 2:17. Jn 5:42. T *2:11, 12. 1 J 4:20, 21. **judgment.** Ps 33:5. Je 5:1. Mi +√6:8. Zc +*7:9. **the love of God.** 1 J 3:17. **these ought.** 1 S +*15:22. Mt 5:19. **and not.** Le *27:30-33. 2 Ch 31:5-10. Ne 10:37, 38. Ec 7:18. Ml 3:8-10.

43. **for.** Lk 14:7-11. 20:46. Pr 16:18. Mt 23:6, 7. Mk 12:38, 39. Ro 12:10. Ph +*2:3. Ja 2:2-4. 3 J 9. **love.** ſ121C2C1, Ps +11:5. **markets.** Lk 7:32. Mt 11:16. 20:3. Mk 6:56. 7:4. Ac 16:19. 17:17.

44. **for.** Nu 19:16. Ps *5:9. Ho 9:8. Mt *23:27, 28. Ac 23:3. **graves.** Mt +8:28 (✱S#3419g). **not aware.** Nu 19:16. Ep 5:3.

45. **lawyers.** ver. 46, 52. Mt +22:35. **thou reproachest.** Lk 18:32g. 1 K 22:8. Je 6:10. 20:8. Am 7:10-13. Jn 7:7, 48, 49. 9:40, 41. Ac 14:5g.

46. **Woe.** Is *10:1. Mt 23:2-4. Mk *7:7, 8. Ga *6:13. **lawyers.** ver. 45, 52. Mt 22:35. **lade.** Mt 11:28-30. Ac *15:10. **with burdens.** Mt 11:30. **grievous.** Pr 27:3. **ye yourselves.** Is 58:6.

47. **for.** Mt *23:29-33. Ac *7:51, 52. 1 Th 2:15, 16. **ye build.** Their guilt did not lie in building and adorning the tombs of the prophets, considered simply in itself, but in their hypocrisy, in giving this testimony of respect to the prophets whilst they were actuated by the spirit, and followed the example of their persecutors and murderers.

48. **Truly.** As in your conduct you imitate your fathers, truly ye bear witness to them; and in effect approve the works of your fathers: for one would imagine that you erected these monuments, not so much in honor of the prophets, as of the persecutors by whom they were so wickedly destroyed (Doddridge). Mt *23:31. **ye bear.** Jsh 24:22. Jb 15:6. Ps 64:8. Ezk 18:19. **allow.** Ro 1:32. **your fathers.** Ac 7:51, 52. **for.** 2 Ch *36:16. Mt 21:35-38. He 11:35-38. Ja 5:10.

49. **the wisdom.** Probably by the *wisdom of God* we are to understand the "logos," or *word of God*, that is, our Lord himself; this being a dignified and oriental mode of expression for *I say*, as it is in the parallel passage. Lk 7:35. Pr 1:2, etc., 20. 8:1-12, 22, 23, 30. 9:1-3. Mt 11:19. 1 C *1:24, 30. Col 2:3. **I will send.** Lk 24:47. 2 Ch +*24:19. 36:15, 16. Mt *23:34. Ac +*1:8. Ep 4:11. Re 16:6. **prophets.** 1 C 12:28. Re 18:20. **and some.** Lk 21:16, 17. Mt 21:35. 22:6. Jn 16:2. Ac 7:57-60. 8:1, 3. 9:1, 2. 12:1, 2. 22:1, 2, 4, 5, 20. 26:10, 11. 2 C 11:24, 25. **slay and.** Mt 5:12. 1 Th 2:15.

50. **the blood.** Ge *9:5, 6. Nu 35:33. 2 K 24:4. Ps 9:12. Is 26:21. Re 18:20-24. **all the prophets.** Ac 10:43. **the foundation.** Mt +*13:35. **world.** Gr. *kosmos*, Mt +4:8. **may.** Ex 20:5. Je 7:29. 51:56. **required of.** Ge 9:5. 42:22. 2 S 4:11. 1 K 2:32. 2 Ch 24:22. Ps 9:12. *10:13. Ezk 3:18. 33:6, 8. **this generation.** Lk 21:22.

51. **the blood of Abel.** Ge 4:8-11. He 11:4. 12:24. 1 J 3:12. Ju 11. **Zacharias.** 2 Ch *24:20-22. Zc 1:1. Mt *23:35. **perished.** Gr. *apollumi*, Mt +2:13. **the**

altar. Ex 40:6, 29. 2 K 16:14. Ezk 40:47. **the temple.** lit. house. ſ171E4A. Synecdoche of the Genus B620. "house" is put for temple. For another instance of this figure see Ac 7:47. 2 Ch 35:5. **It shall.** Ex +*20:5. Je 7:28. 51:56.

52. **for.** Lk 19:39, 40. Ml *2:7. Mt *23:13. Mk *7:13. Jn *7:42-52. *9:24-34. Ac *4:17, 18. *5:40. **taken away.** Je 18:15. Ezk 22:26. Ml 2:7, 8. Mt 23:15. **key.** ſ121S1, Ge +49:10. i.e. the means or power of entering into, or the right of attaining knowledge B604. Ps *119:97-105. 1 Ch=9:27. Is +*8:20n. Je *23:28-30. Ml *2:7, 8. Mt 16:19. **of knowledge.** T#633. 1 Ch +*12:32. Jb +21:14 (T#363). Ps +*49:20. Pr 4:13. +8:10 (T#391). 23:23. Je +*8:7. Da *12:4, 9, 10. Ro 2:20. **ye enter not.** Lk *7:30. Mt 5:20. 21:31. **were entering.** Lk 14:23. **hindered.** *or*, forbad. Ne 4:8. 1 Th 2:18.

53. **to urge.** Ge 49:23. Ps 22:12, 13. Is 9:12. Mk 6:19. **to speak.** Lk 20:20, 27. Je 18:18. 20:10. 1 C 13:5.

54. **Laying wait.** Lk *20:20. Dt 19:11. Is 29:21. La 4:19. Mt 12:10. Mk 3:2. Jn 8:6. Ac 23:21. **seeking.** Ps 37:32, 33. 56:5, 6. Mt 22:15, 18, 35. Mk *12:13.

LUKE 12

Jesus warns his disciples against hypocrisy, and the fear of man in confessing him. He shows the danger of blasphemy against the Holy Ghost and teaches dependence on him, 1-12. He refuses to act as judge in temporal things, and warns his disciples against covetousness, by the parable of a rich man suddenly torn by death from all his purposed and expected enjoyments, 13-21. He cautions them against anxious cares and exhorts them to seek spiritual blessings, 22-34, and to be always ready for the coming of their Lord, 35-40. He instructs and warns his ministers by the parable of a faithful, and of a wicked steward, 41-48. He predicts the divisions which his gospel would occasion, 49-53; reproves those who knew not the signs of the times, 54-56; and counsels the people to seek reconciliation to God without delay, 57-59.

1. **mean time.** Ac 26:12g. **when.** Lk 11:29. **an innumerable.** Lk 5:1, 15. 6:17. Ps 3:6. Ac 21:20g. 1 C 4:15. **trode.** 2 K 7:17. **first.** 1 C 15:3. Ja 3:17. **Beware.** Mt *16:6-12. Mk 8:15, etc. Ac 5:35. **the leaven.** Lk 13:20, 21. Mt +*13:33n. 1 C *5:6-8. Ga 5:9. **which.** ver. 56. Lk 11:44. Jb 20:5. 27:8. 36:13. Is 33:14. Mt +6:2. 23:28. Mk 12:15. Ga 2:13g. 1 T 4:2. Ja 3:17. 1 P 2:1.

2. **nothing covered.** Lk 8:17. Ec 12:14. Is 45:19. 48:16. Mt 10:26. Mk 4:22. Jn *15:15. *18:20. Ro 2:16. 1 C *4:5. 2 C *5:10. 1 T 5:25. Re 20:11, 12.

3. **whatsoever.** Jb 24:14, 15. Ec 10:12, 13, +*20. Ezk 33:30. Mt 12:36. Jn 14, 15. **in closets.** Ge 43:30. Jg 16:9. 1 K 20:30. 22:25. 2 K 9:2. 2 Ch 18:24. Mt +*6:6. 24:26. **proclaimed.** The houses in Judea being flat-roofed, with a balustrade round about, were used for the purpose of taking the air, sleeping, and prayer, and, it seems, for announcing things in the most public manner. So among the Turks, a crier announces the hours of public worship from the minaret or tower of the mosque. **housetops.** Lk 5:19. 17:31. Dt 22:8. 1 S 9:25, 26. 2 S 11:2. 16:22. Ne 8:16. Is 15:3. Je 48:38. Mt 10:27. 24:17. Ac 10:9.

4. **my friends.** SS 5:1, 16. Is 41:8. Jn 15:14, 15. Ja 2:23. **Be not afraid.** ſ66, Ge +9:3. Ps +*34:4. Pr

*29:25. Is 8:12, 13. *51:7-13. Je *1:8, 17. 26:14, 15.
Ezk 2:6. 3:9. Da 3:16, 17. Mt +√10:28n. Ac 4:13. 20:24.
Ph 1:28. 2 T +*1:7. He +*13:6. 1 P *3:14. Re
2:10.

5. **forewarn**. Mk 13:23. 1 Th 4:6. **Fear him**. ♪66,
Ge +9:3. Jb 37:24. Pr 14:26. Ec +*12:13. Je 5:22.
10:7. He 10:31. Re 14:7. 15:4. **after he hath killed**.
If hell is merely the grave, then what is the meaning
of the statement God "hath power to cast into hell"?
Clearly this passage is not affirming God's power to
cast bodies into graves, but is stating his power to
cast into hell (gehenna) *after* he hath *killed*. From
the parallel passage (Mt 10:28) it is clear that "killed"
has reference to the body, not the soul. "Casting into
gehenna" must then refer to the soul or spirit, not
the body, and proves that life and consciousness continue after the physical death of the body, otherwise
what is there to fear? That body and soul are together
in hell (Mt 10:28) proves that the resurrection is viewed
as already in that case taken place, in order that they
may be there together. Ja 4:12. **power**. Ps 9:17. Mt
+√10:28n. 25:41, 46. 2 P 2:4. Re 20:14. **hell**. Gr. *gehenna*, Mt +5:22. T#995‡. Mt +*10:28. Re +20:15
(T#997‡).

6. **five**. See Mt 10:29mg. **and not one**. ver. 24, 27.
Jb 38:41. Ps 50:10, 11. 113:5, 6. 145:15, 16. 147:9.
forgotten. ♪22C4, Ps +13:1.

7. **the very hairs**. Lk 21:18. 1 S 14:45. 2 S 14:11.
1 K 1:52. Da 3:27. Mt 10:30. Ac 27:34. **Fear not**.
ver. 32. Lk 1:13. Ps +*34:4. 2 T +*1:7. **ye are**. ver.
24. Jb 35:11. Ps 8:6. Is 43:3, 4. Mt 6:26. 10:31. 12:12.
1 C 9:9, 10.

8. **Whosoever**. 1 S *2:30. Ps *119:46. Mt +*10:32,
33. Ro √10:9, 10. 2 T 2:12. He 10:35. 1 J 2:23. Re
2:10, 13. 3:4, 5. **him shall**. Ml 3:17. **Son of man**. Lk
+5:24. **confess before**. Lk 15:10. Mt 10:32, 33. 25:31-
34. 1 T 5:21. Ju *24, *25. Re 3:5. **angels**. Lk 16:22.

9. **he**. Lk *9:26. Mt 10:33. Mk 8:38. Ac 3:13, 14.
2 T 2:12. 2 P 2:1. 1 J *2:23. Re *3:8, 10, 12. **that
denieth**. Gr. *arneomai*, ✱S#720g. Rendered (1) deny:
Mt 10:33, 33n. 26:70, 72. Mk 14:68, 70. Lk 8:45. 12:9.
22:57. Jn 1:20. 18:25, 27. Ac 3:13, 14. 4:16. 1 T 5:8.
2 T 2:12, 12, 13. 3:5. T 1:16. 2:12. 2 P 2:1. 1 J 2:22,
22, 23. Ju 4. Re 2:13. 3:8. (2) refuse: Ac 7:35. He
11:24. **shall**. Lk 13:25-27. Mt √7:23. 25:12, 31, 41.
1 J 2:23, 28. **be denied**. Gr. *aparneomai*, ✱S#533g. lit.
utterly denied. Mt 16:24. 26:34, 35, 75. Mk 8:34. 14:30,
31, 72. Lk 9:23. 12:9. 22:34, 61. **before the angels**.
ver. 8.

10. **whosoever shall**. Lk 23:34. Le 24:16. Mt
+*12:31n, 32n. Mk *3:28, 29. 1 T 1:13. He *6:4-8.
+*10:26-31. 1 J *5:16. **against**. Lk 7:34. Mt 11:19.
Jn 7:12. 9:24. **Son of man**. Lk +5:24. **shall be forgiven**.
1 T *1:12, 13. **Ghost**. Gr. *pneuma*, Mt +3:16. Is
+*63:10. **shall not**. T#562. Mt +*12:31n, 32n. Mk
3:28, 29. He 3:7-11. +√10:26-29. 1 J +*5:16.

11. **when they**. Lk 21:12-14. Mt *10:17-20. 23:34.
Mk 13:9-11. Ac 4:5-7. 5:27-32. 6:9-15. **magistrates**.
Lk 20:20. T 3:1. **and powers**. Ro 13:1. **no thought**.
ver. 22. Lk 21:14. Mt 6:25. **shall answer**. Ac 19:33.

12. **shall teach**. Lk *21:15. Ex 4:11, 12. Mt *10:19,
20. Mk *13:11. Jn 14:26. 15:26. Ac 4:8. *6:8, 10. 7:2,
etc., 55. ch. 26. 2 T *4:17.

13. **And one**. Lk 11:27. **Master**. T#1471. Lk 6:45.
Ps 17:14. Ezk +*33:31. Ac 8:18, 19. 1 T 6:5.

14. **Man**. Lk 5:20. 22:58, 60. Mi +*6:8. Ro 2:1, 3.

9:20. **who made**. Ex 2:14. Jn ◐5:27. 6:15. 8:11. *18:35,
36. Ac=7:27.

15. **Take heed**. Lk 8:14. 16:14. 21:34. Jsh 7:21. Jb
31:24, 25. Ps +*10:3. 62:10. 119:36, 37. Pr 23:4, 5.
28:16. Je 6:13. 22:17, 18. Mi 2:2. Hab 2:9. Mt +*13:22.
Mk 7:22. 1 C 5:10, 11. 6:10. Ep 5:3-5. Col 3:5. 1 T
√6:6-11. 2 T 3:2. He +*13:5. 2 P 2:3, 14. **for**. ver.
22. Jb 2:4. Ps *37:16. Pr *15:16. 16:16. Ec 4:6-8. 5:10-
16. Mt 6:25, 26. 1 T *6:6-8. **abundance**. Pr 23:4.

16. **The ground**. Ge +*26:12-14. 41:47-49. Jb 12:6.
Ps *49:16-20. 73:3, 12. Ho 2:8. Mt +*5:45. Ac 14:17.
Ja +*5:1-3.

17. **What**. ver. 22, 29. Lk 10:25. 16:3. Ac 2:37.
√16:30. **shall**. ver. 33. Lk 3:11. 11:41. 14:13, 14. 16:9.
18:22. 19:17. Ec 5:10. 11:2. Is 58:7. Mt 5:42. Ro *12:13.
2 C 9:6-15. 1 T +*6:17, 18. 1 J *3:16, 17.

18. **This will**. ver. 21. Lk 16:4, 6. Ps 17:14. Ja 3:15.
4:15. **barns**. ver. 24. Mt 6:26.

19. **soul**. Gr. *psyche*, ♪171Q2, Mt +12:18. ♪171Q,
Nu +23:10. Ps 103:+*1, 2. 104:1. 146:1. Is 42:1. **Soul**.
Gr. *psyche*, ♪171Q2, Mt +12:18. The absurdity of the
assertion of some, that "soul" invariably means
"breath," or "life," can be seen by the use of "soul"
here. Dt 6:11, 12. *8:12-14. Jb 31:24, 25. Ps *49:5-
13, 18. *52:5-7. 62:10. Pr 18:11. 23:5. Is 5:8. Ho 12:8.
Hab 1:16. Mt *6:19-21. 1 T *6:17. Ja +*5:1-3. **much
goods**. Dt *8:17. **for many**. Jb *14:1. Pr *27:1. Ja *4:13-
15. **take**. Lk *16:19. *21:34. Jb 21:11-13. Ec 2:24. *11:9.
Is 5:11, 12. 22:13, 14. Am 6:3-6. 1 C *15:32. Ph *3:19.
1 T 5:6. 2 T *3:4. Ja *5:5. 1 P 4:3. Re 18:7. **be merry**.
Lk 15:23.

20. **God**. Lk *16:22, 23. Ex 16:9, 10. 1 S 25:36-
38. 2 S 13:28, 29. 1 K 16:9, 10. Jb *20:20-23. *27:8.
Ps 73:19, 20. 78:30, 31. Da *5:1-6, 25-30. Na 1:10.
Mt *24:48-51. 1 Th *5:3. **Thou fool**. Lk 11:40. Je
+*17:11. Mt 16:26. Ja *4:14. **this night**. Ps 102:24.
Pr *10:27. Ec +*7:17. Is +*38:10. Je 17:11. 1 C 11:30.
thy soul shall be required of thee. *or*, do they require
thy soul. Jb *27:8. **soul**. Gr. *psyche*, ♪121A7, Mt +2:20.
then. Est 5:11. 8:1, 2. Jb *27:16, 17. Ps *39:6. *49:6-
10, 16-19. √52:5-7. Pr *11:4. 28:8. Ec 2:18-22. *4:8.
5:14-16. Je *17:11. Da 5:28. 1 T *6:7.

21. **he**. ver. *33. Lk *6:24. Ps *52:7. Ho 10:1. Hab
*2:9. Mt √6:19-21. Ro *2:5. 1 T *6:19. Ja +*5:1-3.
rich. Lk *16:11. 2 C *6:10. 1 T √6:17-19. Ja +*2:5.
Re *2:9.

22. **Take**. ver. 11, 25, 26, 29. Lk 10:41. 1 S 9:5.
10:2. Ps *55:22. Mt 6:25, 27, 28, 31, 34. 10:19. 13:22.
Mk 13:11. 1 C 7:32-34. 12:25. Ph 2:20. √4:6. 1 T
◐+*5:8. He +*13:5. 1 P *5:7. **life**. Gr. *psyche*, ♪121A7,
Mt +2:20. ♪121A7, Ge +9:5. Lk 9:24. 14:26. Le 17:11.
2 S 14:7. Est 8:11.

23. **life**. Gr. *psyche*, 121A7, Mt +2:20. ♪121A7,
Ge +9:5. **is more**. Ge 19:17. Jb 1:12. 2:4, 6. Pr 13:8.
Ac 27:18, 19, 38.

24. **the ravens**. The raven is a species of the corvus
or crow tribe, of the order Picae, known by its large
size, its plumage being of a bluish black, and tail round-
ish at the end. It was probably selected by our Lord
as being unclean. 1 K 17:1-6. Jb 12:7-9. 38:41. Ps
145:15, 16. 147:9. Mt 6:26. **God feedeth**. Ro √8:32.
1 T 5:8. **how**. ver. 7, 30-32. Jb 35:11. Mt 10:31.

25. **taking thought**. ver. +22. Mt 5:36. 6:27. **stature**.
Lk 2:52. 19:3. Ps 39:5.

26. **If**. ♪184A, 1 C +15:2. **not able**. Je +*12:5. **why**.
ver. 29. Ps 39:6. Ec 7:13. 1 P *5:7.

27. **the lilies.** ver. 24. Ho 14:5. Mt 6:28-30. Ja 1:10, 11. **that.** 1 K 10:1-13. 2 Ch 9:1-12. **not arrayed.** Jn 13:4. **like one.** Lk 15:7, 10. Mt 18:10. 25:40, 45.

28. **If.** ⌐184A, 1 C +15:2. **which.** Is 40:6, 7. 1 P 1:24. **how much more.** Ps *23:1. *34:9, 10. *37:25. *84:11. Is *33:15, 16. Ro √8:32. Ph *4:19. He +*13:5. **O ye.** Lk 8:25. 17:6. Mt 8:26. 14:31. 16:8. 17:17, 20.

29. **seek.** ver. 22. Lk 10:7, 8. 22:35. Mt 6:31. **neither,** etc. *or*, live not in careful suspense. Ja 1:6.

30. **all.** Mt 5:47. 6:32. Ep 4:17. 1 Th 4:5. 1 P 4:2-4. **the nations.** Mt 6:7, 8. **world.** Gr. *kosmos*, Mt +4:8. **seek.** ⌐108B, Mt +6:22. **your.** ver. 32. Mt 6:1, 8, 32. 10:20. 18:14. Jn 20:17.

31. **rather seek.** Lk 10:42. 1 K *3:11-13. Ps *34:9, 10. *37:3, 19, 25. *84:11. Is 33:15, 16. Mt 5:6, 20. √6:33. Jn *6:27. Ro *8:31, 32. 14:17. 1 C 12:31. 1 T *4:8. He +*13:5. **the kingdom.** Lk +4:43. 11:2. Mt 6:10. **be added.** 1 K 3:11-14. Ps *37:4, 25. Mk +*10:29, 30. 1 T 4:8. 1 P 3:9.

32. **Fear not.** ver. 7. Lk 1:13. Is 41:10, 13, 14. 43:5. 44:2. **little flock.** Ps 23:1. SS 1:7, 8. Is *40:11. 41:14mg. 53:6. Ezk 36:38. Zc +*13:7. Mt 7:+*14 (T#669), 15. 18:12-14. 20:16. 26:31. Jn *10:16, 26-30. 21:15-17. Ac *20:28, 29. 1 P 5:2, 3. T#959‡: Re 5:9, +10 (T#973‡). *x7:3, 4. *x14:1, 3. T#972‡: Jn 14:2, 3. Ga +6:16 (T#974‡). Col 1:5. He 12:22, 23. 1 P *1:3, 4. **it is.** Lk 2:14. 10:21. Mt *11:25-27. Ep 1:5-9. Ph *2:13. 2 Th 1:11. **good pleasure.** Mt 18:14. **to give.** Clearly, this kingdom is future, and in harmony with other scripture is strictly earthly, in fulfillment of covenant and prophecy. The reward is predetermined before it is received, and is received at the second advent of Christ on earth. Lk 3:11. +*6:38. Mt 5:42. *10:8. ◑*21:43. Mk 10:40. Ac *20:35. 2 C 5:2. Ph 3:20. Col 1:5. 2 T 4:8. T 2:13. He 10:34-37. 1 P √1:4, 5, 7. 1 J 3:2, 3. Re 21:2. **the kingdom.** Lk 6:20. *13:29. √22:28-30. Je 3:19. Mt +*5:5. +*8:11. +*13:19, 43. 25:34. Jn +*14:2. 18:36. Ro 5:17. *6:23. *8:28-32. 1 C 6:2. Ep 1:+*11, 18. 1 Th 2:12. 2 Th 1:5. 2 T *4:1. He 12:28. Ja +*2:5. 1 P 1:3-5. 2 P √1:10, 11. Re 1:6. 2:26-28. 3:21. *20:4. 22:5.

33. **Sell.** Lk 18:22. Mt *19:21. Ac *2:45. 4:34, 35. 1 C 7:30. 2 C 8:2. **give alms.** Lk 11:41. **provide.** Lk 16:9. Hg 1:6. Mt 6:19-21. Je 12:6. 1 T *6:17-19. Ja +*5:1-3. **a treasure.** ⌐22D5.O, Dt +28:12. ver. 21. Mt *6:20. 1 P √1:4. **faileth not.** Lk 16:9. **neither moth.** Ja 5:2, 3.

34. **where.** Mt 6:21. 1 C 7:32-34. 2 C 4:17, 18. Ph 3:20. Col 1:5. *3:1-3. 1 J √2:15-17.

35. **your loins.** 1 K 18:46. 2 K 4:29. 9:1. Jb 38:3. 40:7. Pr 31:17. Is 5:27. 11:5. Je 1:17. Jn 21:7, 18. Ac 12:8. Ep *6:14. 1 P 1:13. **be girded.** Lk 17:8. Ex *12:11. Ps 18:32n. Je +1:17. Mt *3:20. 2 T *2:4. 1 P *1:13. **your lights.** Mt *5:16. *25:1, 4-10. Ph 2:15.

36. **men.** Lk 2:25-30. Ge 49:18. Is 64:4. La 3:25, 26. Mt 24:42-44. Mk 13:34-37. Ja 5:7, 8. 2 P 1:13-15. Ju 20, 21. **that wait.** Lk 23:51. Ps 40:1. Ph 3:20. 1 Th 1:10. 2 P 3:12. **return.** Gr. *analusee*. A. B. Bruce notes "the figure is taken from sailors making the return voyage to the port whence they had sailed" (*Expositor's Greek Testament*, vol. 1, p. 560). M. R. Vincent states "The verb means, originally, to unloose: so of vessels, to unloose their moorings and go to sea. Of departing generally. This is its sense in the only other passage where it occurs, Philippians 1:23, "having a desire to depart, or break up; the metaphor being drawn from

breaking up an encampment." Compare departure (*analuseos*), 2 T 4:6. The rendering *return* is a kind of inference from this: when he shall leave the wedding and return" (*Word Studies in the New Testament*, vol. 1, p. 370). The TDNT notes "In the NT its predominant meaning is 'to leave.' It is used euphemistically for death in kindly concealment of its terror, i.e., 'to depart' (Ph 1:23). 'analusis' accordingly means 'leaving,' 'departing' (2 T 4:6). The special sense of 'to return' occurs at Lk 12:36, though here, too, 'analusee' might mean leaving, with the thought of return only in the ensuing 'when he cometh and knocketh.'" In a footnote further reference is made to Wisdom 2:1; 2 Maccabees 8:25; 12:7, with the added comment "It is not clear how 'analuo' could come to mean 'to return'; perhaps it has something to do with the unyoking of draught animals" (vol. 4, p. 337). Mt 22:1, etc. 25:1, etc. Ph 1:23n. 2 T 4:6. **when.** SS 5:5, 6. **and knocketh.** Lk 11:10. 13:25. Re *3:20. **open.** 1 Ch=9:19, 22. Mk 13:34.

37. **Blessed.** ver. 43. Lk +√21:36. Mt +√24:45-47. 25:20-23. Ph 1:21, 23. 2 T 4:7, 8. 1 P *5:1-4. 2 P √1:11. √3:14. Re +*14:13. **watching.** T#738. Lk +√21:36. Mt +15:14 (T#477). +26:41 (T#724). Mk *13:33-37. 1 C *10:12. 16:13. Ep +4:27 (T#18). *5:15, 16. *6:10. 1 Th 5:6. 1 T 6:12. 2 T 2:3. 4:5. 1 P 4:7. **verily.** Lk 4:24. 18:17, 29. 21:32. 23:43. Mt +5:18. Mk +3:28. Jn +1:51. **that.** Is 62:5. Je 32:41. Zp 3:17. Jn 12:26. 13:4, 5. 1 C 2:9. Re 3:21. *7:17. 14:3, 4. 19:9. **gird himself.** ver. 35. Lk 17:8. **sit down.** Lk 22:27. **and serve.** Mt 21:28.

38. **And if.** ⌐184C, Mt +4:9. **shall come.** Mt 25:6. 1 Th 5:4, 5. **second watch.** Our nine o'clock till midnight. Ex 14:24. Jg 7:19. Mt +*14:25n. Mk 13:35. **third watch.** Our midnight to 3 a.m. Mk 13:35, cockcrowing.

39. **this know.** Mt +6:2n. +*‖24:43, 44. **if.** ⌐184B, Mt +11:21. **the thief.** 1 Th *5:2-4. 2 P *3:8-10. Re *3:3. *16:15. **broken through.** Ex 22:2. Jb 24:16. Je 2:34. Ezk 12:5. Mt 6:19, 20. 24:43.

40. **ready.** ver. 47. Lk +*21:34-36. Mt 24:42, 44. 25:10, *13. Mk 13:33-36. Ro 13:11, 14. 1 Th 5:6. 2 P 3:12-14. Re 19:7. **Son of man.** Lk +5:24. **cometh.** Lk 21:27. Mt +*16:27n. **when ye think not.** Lk +*21:34, 36. Mk +*13:32, 33.

41. **Lord.** Mk 13:37. 14:37, 38. 1 P 4:7. 5:8. **unto all.** ver. 47, 48. Mk 13:37.

42. **the Lord.** Lk 7:13. **Who then is.** Lk 19:15-19. Mt +√24:45, 46. *25:20-23. 1 C *4:1, 2. T 1:7. **faithful.** Ge +*18:19. Ps 101:2, *6. Is +*32:20. Je +*23:28n. Mt +√‖24:45. +*25:21. **wise.** Gr. *phronimos*, ✱S#5429g. Lk 12:42. 16:8. Mt 7:24. 10:16. *24:45. +25:2, 4, 8, 9. Ro 11:25. 12:16. 1 C 4:10. 10:15. 2 C 11:19. Thayer gives the meaning "prudent, denotes primarily one who has quick and correct perceptions, hence 'discreet,' 'circumspect'" (p. 582b), "mindful of one's interests" (p. 658b). Da +*11:33n. √12:3. **steward.** Lk 16:1-12. Mt 20:8. 1 C 4:1, 2. 1 P 4:10. **ruler.** 1 T 3:15. 5:17. He 3:5. 13:7, 17. **to give.** Je 23:4. Ezk 34:3. Mt +*13:52. Jn *21:15-17. Ac +*20:28. 1 P*5:1-4. **portion.** 2 Ch=31:14-16. Ne=13:13. Pr 31:15. **in due season.** Ge +17:21 (✚S#4150h). Le 23:2n. Nu 28:2n. Pr 15:23. Ec 10:17. Is 50:4. Mt +√24:45. 2 T 4:2.

43. **Blessed.** Jn *13:17. Re 16:15. **whom.** ver. 37. **so doing.** Mt *5:16. Jn *15:8. Ac *10:38. T √3:8.

44. **that he will.** Lk 19:17-19. √22:29, 30. Ps

+*149:6-9. Da +*12:2, 3. Mt +*24:47. *25:21, 23. Re *3:21.

45. and if. ✓184C, Mt +4:9. Ezk 12:22, 27, 28. Mt 24:48-50. 2 P 2:3, 4. **his heart.** Mt +*5:8. **delayeth.** Ec ✓8:11. Hab *2:3. Mt 25:5. He *10:37. 2 P ✓3:4, 9. **and shall.** ✓148, Ge +8:22. He *12:14. 2 P *3:14. **to beat.** Is 65:5. Je 20:2. Ezk 34:3, 4. Mt 22:6. 2 C 11:20. 3 J 9, 10. Re 13:7-10, 15-17. 16:6. 17:5, 6. 18:24. **to eat.** Is 56:10-12. Ezk 34:8. Jn 2:10. Ro 16:18. Ph 3:18, 19. 2 P 2:13, 19. Ju 12, 13. Re 18:7, 8. **be drunken.** Ec 10:17. 1 Th 5:7.

46. lord. ver. 19, 20, 40. 2 P 3:12, *14. Re 16:15. **and.** ✓148, Ge +8:22. **cut him in sunder.** or, cut him off. 2 S 12:31. 1 Ch 20:3. Ps 37:9. 94:14. Is +*33:14. Am 1:3. Mt +*24:51. 2 Th *2:8, 12. He 6:8. 11:37. 2 P 2:1-3. Ju 4, 13. Re 6:16. **and will appoint.** Jb 20:29. Ps 11:5. Mt *7:22, 23. +*13:41, 42, 49, 50. **portion with.** Ro +*2:12. Re *21:8. **the unbelievers.** Mt *24:51.

47. knew. Lk 10:12-15. Nu 15:30, 31. 2 Ch 33:9. Mt 11:22-24. Jn 9:41. 12:48. 15:22-24. 19:11. Ac ✓17:30. *22:14. 2 C 2:15, 16. Ja ✓4:17. 2 P ✓2:21. **prepared not.** "The antithesis in this passage," observes Bp. Jebb (*Sacred Literature*, p. 201), "has prodigious moral depth: he who sins against knowledge, though his sins were only sins of *omission*, shall be beaten with *many stripes*; but he who sins *without knowledge*, though his sins were sins of *commission*, shall be beaten with only *few stripes*. Mere negligence against the light of conscience, shall be severely punished, while an offense, in itself comparatively heinous, if committed ignorantly, and without light, shall be mildly dealt with." The passage teaches degrees of punishment in the future life, and shows that those who have never heard the gospel will receive less a penalty than those who rejected its light. But both classes of servants will have their portion with the unbelievers (ver. 47), and whether they sinned "in the law" or "without law," shall perish without law (Ro 2:12). For the absolute justice of God (Ge +*18:25) to be effected, life after death, and conscious punishment of unbelievers is necessary (See Ezk 18:4n, 20n). ver. 40. Am ◑+*4:12. He +*9:27. **shall.** Dt 25:2, 3. **with many.** Mk 12:40. Re 18:6, 7.

48. knew not. Le *5:17. Nu *15:29, 30. Dt 11:2. Ac ✓17:30. Ro 1:19, 20. ✓2:12-16. 1 T 1:13. **few stripes.** Lk 10:12. Ps +*86:13. La *4:6. Jon *4:11. Mt +*10:15n. +*11:22. 23:14. Ac *17:30. Ro +*2:12. 1 T *1:13. He ✓10:29. **For.** ✓138C, Ge +22:14. Lk 16:2, 10-12. Ge 39:8, etc. Mt +*13:12. 25:14-29. Jn 15:22. 1 C 9:17, 18. 1 T 1:11, 13. 6:20. T 1:3. Ja 3:1g.

49. am come. ver. 51-53. Lk +*19:10. **send fire.** Lk +*3:16. Is *10:17. 11:4. Jl +*2:30, 31. Ml 3:2, 3. 4:1. Mt *3:10-12. 10:34-36. 2 P ◑3:7, 10-12. **and what.** Lk 11:53, 54. 13:31-33. 19:39, 40. Jn 9:4. 11:8-10. 12:17-19. **if it.** ✓184B, Mt +23:30. **kindled.** Ps 78:21. Ml 3:2.

50. I have. Mt *20:17-22. Mk 10:32-38. **and how.** Ps *40:8. Jn 4:34. 7:6-8, 10. 10:39-41. 12:27, 28. 18:11. *19:30. Ac 20:22. **straitened.** or, pained. Ac 18:5. 2 C 5:14. Ph 1:23. **till.** Jn 12:27. 19:28, 30.

51. give peace. ver. 49. Zc 11:7, 8, 10, 11, 14. Mt *10:34-36. 24:7-10. **Nay.** Re 6:4. **division.** Lk ◑11:17. Jn *7:12, 43. 9:16. 10:19. ◑17:23. 1 C ◑1:10.

52. there shall be. Ps 41:9. Mi 7:5, 6. Jn 7:41-43. 9:16. 10:19-21. 15:18-21. 16:2. Ac 13:43-46. 14:1-4. 28:24. **house divided.** Jsh 23:12. 2 P 2:21.

53. son against the father. Lk +24:27. Ezk 22:7. Mi ▶7:6. Zc 13:2-6. Mt 10:21, 22. 24:10.

54. When. Ge +9:14. 1 K 18:44, 45. Mt 16:2, etc. **cloud.** Ge +9:13. 1 K 18:43, 44.

55. when ye see. Ge +9:14. Jb 37:17. **will be heat.** Ge 31:40. Is 49:10. Ezk 17:10. Jon 4:8. Mt 20:12. Ja 1:11.

56. hypocrites. Mt +6:2. **ye can discern.** Ge +9:14. 1 Ch +*12:32. Mt 11:25. 16:3. 24:32, 33. **face.** Ge +1:2. **not discern this time.** Lk 19:42-44. Ge +*49:10. 1 Ch ◑+*12:32. Ps *32:6. +*74:9. Da +*9:24-26. Is *35:4-6. *55:6. Hg 2:7. Ml 3:1. 4:2. Mt 3:1-3. Ac 3:24-26. Ga *4:4.

57. why even. Dt 32:29. Mt 15:10-14. 21:31, 32. Ac 2:40. 13:26-38. 1 C 11:14. **of yourselves.** T#420. Lk 21:30. Jb 32:8. Ps +102:18 (T#49). Pr 18:1n. Is +*8:20n. Je *23:28n. Da +*11:33n. Jn +*6:14. ◑7:49. Ro +1:19 (T#206). 1 P 1:20n. 1 J 2:27. **judge ye.** T#632. Jn +✓5:39. +*7:24. Ac 4:19. +✓17:11 (T#1121). 1 C 10:29. 11:13. 1 Th *5:21. 1 J *4:1.

58. thou goest. ver. 13, 14. Pr 25:8, 9. Mt *5:23-26. **thine adversary.** Lk 18:3. Mt 5:25. 1 P 5:8. **give diligence.** Lk 14:31, 32. Ge 32:3-28. 1 S 25:18-35. Jb 22:21. 23:7. Ps 32:6. Pr 6:1-5. Is ✓55:6. 2 C *6:2. He 3:7-13. **the judge.** Lk 13:24-28. Jb 36:17, 18. Ps 50:22. **into.** Mt 18:30. 1 P 3:19. Re 20:7.

59. thou shalt. Lk 16:26. Mt 18:34, 35. 25:41, 46. 2 Th 1:3. **mite.** Lk 21:2. See Mk 12:42mg.

LUKE 13

Jesus shows that calamities are no proof of peculiar guilt; and exhorts his hearers to repent, if they would escape impending ruin, 1-5. The parable of a barren fig tree, which was to be cut down, 6-9. Jesus heals a woman who had been long bowed down and silences the objection of the hypocritical ruler of the synagogue, 10-17; He compares the kingdom of God to a grain of mustard seed, 18, 19, and to leaven, 20, 21. Being asked whether few should be saved, he warns the people to "strive to enter in at the strait gate," before it was finally shut, 22-30. He will not be diverted from his course by the threatenings of Herod, 31-33. He predicts, and laments over, the approaching desolations of Jerusalem, 34, 35.

1. the Galileans. i.e. *a circuit, rolling, revolution,* ✱S#1057g. ver. 2. Lk 22:59. 23:6. Mt 26:69. Mk 14:70. Jn 4:45. Ac 1:11. 2:7. 5:37. The *Galileans* are frequently mentioned by Josephus as the most turbulent and seditious people, being upon all occasions ready to disturb the Roman authority. It is uncertain to what event our Lord refers; but it is probable that they were the followers of Judas Gaulonitis, who opposed paying tribute to Caesar and submitting to the Roman government. A party of them coming to Jerusalem during one of the great festivals, and presenting their oblations in the court of the temple, Pilate treacherously sent a company of soldiers, who slew them, and "mingled their blood with their sacrifices" (Josephus, Ant. l. xviii). Ac 5:37. **Pilate.** Lk 23:1. **mingled.** La 2:20. Ezk 9:5-7. 1 P 4:17, 18.

2. Suppose. ver. 4. Jb 4:7. 8:20. 22:5-16. Jn ✓9:2. Ac *28:4.

3. Nay. Despite this direct denial by our Lord, many still wrongly suppose that sickness and misfortune always result from God's punishment of personal sin, a belief nowhere supported by the teaching of Scripture, confounding as it does misfortune and sickness with God's chastening of his children or sons (He 12:5, etc.). Nu +*32:23. Jb +*9:22n. Jn √9:3. **I tell.** ƒ8, Ps +118:1. **except.** ƒ184C, Mt +4:9. **ye repent.** T#606. ver. 5. Lk 5:32. 15:7, 10. 24:47. 2 Ch +*7:14 (T#607). Ezk 14:6. *18:30. Mt 3:1, 2, 10-12. 4:17. 11:20. Mk +*1:15. 6:12. Ac *2:38-40. +*3:19 (T#601). 5:31. *8:22. √11:18. √17:30. *20:21. 26:20. Ja +4:10 (T#357). Re *2:5, 21, 22. **ye shall.** Lk 19:42-44. 21:22-24. 23:28-30. Mt 12:45. 22:7. 23:35-38. 24:21-29. **perish.** Gr. *apollumi*, Mt +2:13.

4. **in Siloam.** Ne 3:15. Is 8:6. Jn 9:7, 11. **fell.** 1 K 20:30. Jb 1:19. **sinners.** *or*, debtors. Lk 7:41, 42. 11:4. Mt 6:12. 18:24.

5. **I tell.** ƒ8, Ps +118:1. **except.** ƒ184C, Mt +4:9. **ye repent.** ver. +*3. Is 28:10-13. Ezk 18:30. **perish.** Gr. *apollumi*, Mt +2:13.

6. **fig tree.** Ps *80:8-13. Is *5:1-4. Je 2:21. Ho 9:10. Jl 1:7. Mt *21:19, 20. Mk 11:12-14. **and he came.** Lk 20:10-14. Mt 21:34-40. Jn +*15:16. Ga 5:22. Ph 4:17.

7. **Then said.** ƒ56, Is +14:16. **three years.** Le 19:23. 25:21. Ro 2:4, 5. **cut it down.** Lk 3:9. +*12:46. Ex 32:10. Da 4:14. Mt *3:10. 7:19. Jn +*15:2, 6. Ro 11:20-23. 2 P 2:9, 17. 3:7, 9. **why.** Ex 32:10. Mt 3:9.

8. **Lord, let.** Ex 32:11-13, 30-32. *34:6, 9. Nu 14:11-20. Jsh 7:7-9. Ps 106:23. Je 14:7-9, 13, etc. 15:1. 18:20. Jl 2:17. Ro *2:4. 10:1. 11:14. 2 P 3:√9, 15.

9. **And if.** ƒ184C, Mt +4:9. Lk 19:42. Ex 32:32. Ezr 9:13-15. Is 5:5-7. Da 3:15. **well.** ƒ63D2, Ge +30:27. ƒ63F, Ge +33:10. ƒ37A, Ex +32:32. **if not.** ƒ184C, Mt +4:9. Ezr 9:14, 15. Ps 69:22-28. Da 9:5-8. Jn *15:2. 1 Th 2:15. He *6:8. Re *15:3, 4. 16:5-7.

10. **was teaching.** Lk 4:15, 16, 44. Mt 4:23. Mk 6:2.

11. **a spirit.** Gr. *pneuma*, Mt +8:16. ver. 16. Lk 8:2. Jb 2:7. Ps 6:2. Mt 9:32, 33. Ac 16:16. 1 J 4:6. **infirmity.** ƒ121E1, Ge +25:33. **eighteen.** Lk 8:27, 43. Mk 9:21. Jn 5:5, 6. 9:19-21. Ac 3:2. 4:22. 14:8-10. **bowed.** Ps 38:6. 42:5mg. 145:14. 146:8. **in no wise.** He 7:25g.

12. **Woman.** Lk 6:8-10. Ps 107:20. Is 65:1. Mt 8:16. **loosed.** ver. 16. Jl 3:10.

13. **he laid.** Lk 4:40. Mk 5:23. 6:5. 8:25. 16:18. Ac 9:17. **and immediately.** Lk 17:14-17. 18:43. Ps 103:1-5. 107:20-22. 116:16, 17. **made straight.** Le 26:13. **glorified.** Lk 5:25, 26. 7:16. 17:15. 18:43. 23:47. Mt 9:8.

14. **the ruler.** Lk 8:41. Mk 5:22. Ac 13:15. 18:8, 17. **answered.** Mk 11:14. **with indignation.** Lk 6:11. Mt 20:24. 21:15. 26:8. Mk 10:14, 41. 14:4. Jn 5:15, 16. Ro 10:2. 2 C 7:11g. **because.** Jn 5:15, 16. Ro 10:2. **healed on the sabbath.** Christ's doctrine and spirit regarding the Sabbath are recorded in the eleven or so occasions where it is mentioned in the following parallel passages: Lk 4:16-22, 31-37, 38-41. 6:1-5. *14:3. Mt 12:2, 9-21. Mk 6:1-6. Jn 5:5, etc. 7:21, etc. 9:16. From these narratives we "find (1) That our Lord always honored and kept the Sabbath; (2) That He performed miracles of healing upon it, only when important occasions arose, and in order to confirm His doctrine, and ensure faith in His messiahship; (3) That these acts were never in violation, but entirely in accordance with the Mosaic law; (4) That they were especially designed to relieve the institution from the oppressive traditions of the Scribes and Pharisees; (5) That no objections were taken against them at first, and that

the cavils afterwards raised were only pretences to cover their hatred to His divine mission; (6) That our Lord's defences of Himself and His disciples proceeded on what had ever been the real import of the fourth commandment, though misunderstood; and assumed that the Sabbath itself was of perpetual obligation; (7) That all this is confirmed by our Lord's caution concerning the flight of his disciples at the destruction of Jerusalem, Mt 24:20; and (8) By the conduct and doctrines of his inspired apostles at the first promulgation of the gospel—then it will be admitted that our Savior, so far from relaxing the fourth commandment, or abrogating the essential law of the Sabbath, vindicated it, established it, and left it in more than its original authority and glory" (Daniel Wilson, *The Lord's Day*, p. 70). Wilson argues "That nothing is abrogated under the Christian dispensation with respect to the Sabbath, but those temporary and figurative enactments which constituted the peculiarities of the Jewish age" (p. 80, 81). Wilson believes that the distinguishing promise of the New Covenant is the promise to write God's laws into our minds, and upon our hearts (He 8:10), taking "my laws" to be a reference to the decalogue. This is compared to 2 C 3:3, where Paul mentions "tables of stone" (taken to be the two tables of the ten commandments) and "fleshy tables of the heart." Wilson argues that in the transfer of these tables of the law to our hearts by the Holy Spirit, not one of the commandments is lost in the transfer (pp. 85-87). Ps 119:128. Is +*58:13n. Ro 7:22. 1 J 5:3. Yet, though Wilson alludes (on p. 83) to Col 2:14-17, he really skirts this one text which, above all others, seems clearly to remove the Sabbath commandment as an obligation to Christians, with the mere assertion that "nothing but the ceremonies and shadows connected with it are dispersed; the substance still remaining" (p. 84). Ac 15:10. Ro 14:1, 5. 1 C 9:20. Ga 4:7-11. 5:1. **There are six.** Ex +*20:9. 23:12. 34:12. 35:2. Le 23:3. Dt 5:13. Ezk 20:12. 46:1. **and not.** Lk 6:7. 14:3-6. Mt *12:10-12. Mk 3:2-6. Jn *5:16. 9:14-16.

15. **The Lord.** Lk 7:13. **Thou hypocrite.** Lk 6:42. 12:1. Jb 34:30. Pr 11:9. Is 29:20. Mt 6:2. 7:5. 15:7, 14. 23:13, 28. Ac *8:20-23. 13:9, 10. **doth not.** Lk *14:5. Mt 12:11. Jn *7:21-24.

16. **being.** Lk 3:8. 16:24. *19:9. Mt 15:24. Ac 13:26. Ro 4:12-16. **daughter.** ƒ171G, Ge +13:8. **whom.** ver. 11. Jb 2:6, 7. Jn *8:44. 2 T *2:26. **Satan hath bound.** ver. 11. Mt 4:10. Ac √10:38. 1 C 5:5. 2 C 12:7. **be loosed.** ver. 12. Mk 2:27. 7:35.

17. **all his.** Lk 14:6. 20:40. Ps 40:14. 109:29. 132:18. Is *45:24. 2 T 3:9. 1 P *3:16. **and all.** Lk 19:37-40, 48. Ex 15:11. Ps 111:3. Is 4:2. Mk 12:37. Jn 12:17, 18. Ac 3:9-11. 4:21. **rejoiced.** Lk 5:26. 18:43. Ps 98:1. Is 12:5. Mk 7:37. **glorious things.** Ex 34:10. Dt 10:21. Jb 5:9. 9:10.

18. **Then said.** Mt 13:31, 32. Mk 4:30-32. **Unto.** ver. 20. Lk 7:31. La 2:13. Mt 11:16. +*13:31. Mk 4:30. **the kingdom.** Lk +*4:43. +*17:21. Mk 4:26, 30, etc.

19. **like.** Lk 17:6. Mt +*13:31, 32. *17:20. Mk 4:31, 32. **cast.** SS 4:12, 16. 5:1. 6:2. 8:13. Is 58:11. 61:11. Je 31:12. **and it.** Ps 72:16, 17. Is +*2:2, 3. +*9:7. 49:20-25. 51:2, 3. 53:1, 10-12. 54:1-3. 60:15-22. Ezk 17:22-24. 47:1-12. Da 2:34, 35, 44, 45. Mi 4:1, 2. Zc 2:11. *8:20-23. 14:7-9. Ac 2:41. 4:4. *15:14-18. 21:20g. Ro 15:19. Re *11:15. **and the fowls.** Ps 104:12. Ezk

17:23. 31:6. Da ▶4:12, 21. Mt 8:20. +*‖13:32.

20. And again. Mt ‖13:33. **Whereunto.** ver. 18. Mt 11:16. **the kingdom.** ver. 18. Lk +*4:43.

21. like leaven. Lk 12:1. See Mt +*13:33mg,n. **three measures.** Ge 18:6. Jg 6:19. 1 S 1:24. **till.** Jb 17:9. Ps 92:13, 14. Pr +*4:18. Ho +*6:3. Jn *4:14. 15:2. 1 C *5:6. 10:5. Ga 5:9. Ph 1:6, 9-11. 1 Th ◑*5:23, 24. Ja 1:21.

22. through. Lk 4:43, 44. 8:1. Mt 9:35. 11:1. Mk 6:6. Ac *10:38. **journeying.** ver. 33. Lk 9:51. 17:11. 18:31. 19:11, 28. SS 7:1. Is +*2:2. 60:5. Mk 10:32-34. Ep 6:15.

23. are there few. Mt +√7:14. 19:25. *20:16. 22:14. Re ◑7:9. **that be saved.** Ac 2:47. 1 C 1:18. 2 C 2:15. **And.** Lk 12:13-15. 21:7, 8. Mt +*24:3-5. Mk 13:4, 5. Jn 21:21, 22. Ac +*1:7, 8.

24. Strive. T#750. Lk *9:23. *14:33. +√21:36. Ge 32:25, 26. Mt 11:12. Mk 10:24. Jn *6:15, 27. Ac *14:22. 1 C 9:24-27. Ep *6:12-18. Ph *2:12, 13. Col 1:29. *4:12. 1 T 4:10. *6:12. 2 T *4:7. He 4:11. 12:4. 1 P 4:7. 2 P √1:10. Ju +*3. **the strait.** Mt +*7:13, 14. **for many.** Pr *1:24-28. 14:6. 21:25. Ec 10:15. Is *1:15. 58:2-4. Ezk +*33:31. Mk 6:18-20. Jn *7:34. 8:21. 13:33. Ro *9:31-33. 10:3. **shall not.** Lk +*9:24. Pr 1:27. 2 C +*6:1, 2. He *12:17. Re 6:16.

25. once. Ps *32:6. Is √55:6. 2 C *6:1, 2. He *3:7, 8, 15. 12:17. **risen up.** He ◑10:12. **hath shut.** T#1796. Lk 19:42. Ge 7:16. Mt *25:10. Re +*22:11. **begin.** ver. 25. Lk 3:8. 5:21. 14:9. **to knock.** Lk *11:10. 12:36. **Lord.** Lk 6:46. Mt *7:21, 22. 25:11, 12. **Lord.** ♪84, Ge +22:11. **I know.** ♪22C2, Ge +3:9. ver. 27. Lk 12:9. Mt √7:23. 10:33. +*25:41.

26. begin. ver. +25. **We.** Ge 31:54. Ex 18:12. 24:11. Is 58:2. 2 T 3:5. T 1:16. **taught in.** Is 42:2. Mt 12:19.

27. I tell. ver. 25. Ps +*1:6. Mt √7:22, 23. 25:12, 41. 1 C 8:3. Ga 4:9. 2 T +*2:19. **know.** ♪22C2, Ge +3:9. **depart.** Ps *5:4-6. ▶6:8. 28:3. 101:8. 119:115. 125:5. 139:19. Ho 9:12. Mt √7:23. +*25:41. **workers of.** Ps 92:7, 9. 94:4. 101:8. 125:5. Mt +*13:41.

28. weeping. Ps *112:10. Mt +*8:11, 12. +*13:42, 50. 22:13. *24:51. *25:30. **when.** Lk *16:23. Mt +*8:11. **shall see.** T#573-4. Lk 16:23. Is +*66:24. Da +*12:2. Mt +25:32 (T#387). Jn 7:34. Re *14:10. **Abraham.** Lk 20:37. Mt +*8:11. +*19:28. 22:32. Mk 12:23. Ac 3:13. 7:32. **all the prophets.** Ac +*10:43. Re +*11:18. **in the kingdom.** Lk +4:43. 14:15. *23:42, 43. 2 Th *1:5. 2 P *1:11. **you.** Lk 10:15. Re +*21:8. *22:15.

29. they shall come. Ge 28:14. Ps *107:3. Is *43:5, 6. 45:6. 49:6, 12. 54:2, 3. ▶59:19. 66:18-20. Je 3:18. Ml ▶1:11. Mt 19:30. Mk 10:31. 13:27. Ac 28:28. Ep 3:6-8. Col 1:6, 23. Re 7:9, 10. **from the east.** 1 Ch 9:24. Ps 107:3. **sit down.** Lk 14:15. 22:30. Re 19:9. **the kingdom.** Lk +4:43.

30. there are last. Mt *3:9, 10. +*8:11, 12. 19:30. 20:16. *21:28-31. Mk 10:31. Ep *3:6. **there are first.** Lk 7:30. Mt *21:31, 32. Ro *9:30, 31.

31. Get. Ne 6:9-14. Ps 11:1, 2. Pr +*22:3. Je +*36:19. Am 7:12, 13. **depart hence.** Mt 19:1. Mk 10:1. **for Herod.** Lk 3:1.

32. Go ye. ♪62. Eleutheria; or, Candor B932. An expression of feeling by way of bold freedom of speech in reprehension. For other instances of this figure see Jn 8:44. 1 J 3:10. **that fox.** ♪103, Hypocatastasis, Ge +3:13. This was probably Herod Antipas, tetrarch of Galilee, who is described by Josephus as a crafty and incestuous prince, with which the character given him

by our Lord, and the narratives of the evangelists, exactly coincide. Lk 3:19, 20. 9:7-9. 23:8-11. Ezk 13:4. Mi 3:1-3. Zp 3:3. Mk 6:26-28. **I cast.** Lk 7:22. 9:7. Mk 6:14. Jn 10:32. 11:8-10. **the third day.** Ho ?*6:2. Mt +*12:40n. **I shall be.** ♪96C6, Mt +2:4. Jn 17:4, 5. 19:28, 30g. He +*2:10. *5:9. 7:28.

33. I must. Lk 2:49. 4:43. 9:22. 17:25. 19:5. 21:9. 22:37. 24:7, 26, 44. Mt 24:6. Mk 13:7. Jn 3:14. 4:34. 9:4. 11:9, 54. 12:35. Ac 3:21. *10:38. 17:3. 1 C 15:25. **the day.** ♪63BC, Ge +9:20. **following.** Ac 20:15g. 21:26g. **for.** ♪60A, Ge +3:22. Lk 9:53. Mt 20:18. Ac 13:27. **a prophet.** Mt 21:11. **perish.** Gr. *apollumi*, Mt +2:13. **out of Jerusalem.** ver. 22.

34. Jerusalem. Lk 19:41, 42. Mt 23:37-39. **Jerusalem.** ♪84, Ge +22:11. **killest.** ver. 33. 2 Ch 24:21, 22. *36:15, 16. Ne +*9:26. Je *2:30. 26:23. La 4:13. Mt 5:12. 21:35, 36. 22:6. Ac 7:52, 59. 8:1. 1 Th 2:15. Re 11:8. **and stonest.** Mt 21:35. **how often.** Dt 5:29. 32:29. Ps 81:10, 13. Is 48:17-19. 50:2. Mt 26:55. **would I have.** Je 51:9. **gathered.** Ps 106:47. 107:3. 147:2. Pr 1:24. Mt 24:31. Mk 13:27. **thy.** Lk 19:44. 23:28. Ps 149:2. La 1:16. Jl 2:23. Ga 4:25, 26. **as.** Dt *32:11, 12. Ru 2:12. Ps 17:8. 36:7. 57:1. 61:4. 63:7. 91:4. Is 31:5. Ml 4:2. **and ye.** Lk 15:28. Ne 9:30. Ps 81:11. Pr 1:24-30. Is 30:15. Je 6:16. 7:23, 24. 35:14. 44:4-6. Ho 11:2, 7. Zc 1:4. Mt 22:3. Jn *1:5, 10, 11. *5:40. Ac 3:14, 15.

35. your house. Lk 11:51. 21:5, 6, 24. Le *26:31, 32. 1 K 9:7, 8. Ps *69:25, 26. Is 1:7, 8. *5:5, 6. 64:10, 11. Je ▶12:7. ▶22:5. Ezk 10:18, 19. 11:23. Da +*9:26, 27. Mi *3:12. Zc 11:1, 2. 14:2. Mt +*23:38. Jn ◑+*14:2. Ac 6:13, 14. **Ye shall not.** Ho +*3:4, 5. Mt +*23:39. Jn 7:34-36. 8:22-24. 12:35, 36. 14:19-23. **until.** Mt +*23:39. **Blessed.** Lk 19:38-40. Ps ▶118:26. Is 40:9-11. 52:7. Zc +*12:10. Mt 21:9. Mk 11:9, 10. Jn 12:13. Ro √10:9-15. 2 C 3:15-18.

LUKE 14

Jesus, on the sabbath, heals a man who had the dropsy and justifies himself in so doing, 1-6. By parables he teaches humility, 7-11; and hospitality to the poor, 12-14. The parable of the great supper, 15-24. The necessity of self denial and renouncing the world, in order to be the disciples of Christ, inculcated, 25-33. The worthlessness of salt which has lost its savor, 34, 35.

1. went into. Lk 7:34-36. 11:37. 13:31. 1 C 9:19-22. **chief.** Jn 3:1. 7:50. 19:39. Ac 5:34. **to eat.** Lk 7:34. Mt 11:19. Jn 2:2. 12:2. **bread.** ♪171I8, Ge +3:19. **they watched.** Lk 6:7. 11:53, 54. 17:20g. 20:20. Ps *37:32. 41:6. 62:4. 64:5, 6. Pr 23:7. Is *29:20, 21. Je 20:10, 11. Mk 3:2.

3. answering. Mk 11:14. **the lawyers.** Lk 11:44, 45. Mt 22:35. **Is it lawful.** Lk 6:9. *13:14-16. Mt 12:10, 12. Mk 3:4. Jn 5:16, 17. 7:23.

4. they held their peace. Mt 21:25-27. 22:46. Ac 11:18.

5. Which of. ♪85A, Ps +56:13. Lk 13:15. Ex 23:4, 5. Dt *22:4. Mt 12:11, 12. **a pit.** Gr. *phrear*, ✱S#5421g. Lk 14:5. Jn 4:11 (well), 12. Re 9:1 (pit), 2, 2. For the Hebrew equivalent see Ge 16:14 (✱S#875h).

6. could not answer. Lk 13:17. 20:26, 40. 21:15. Mt 22:46. Mk 3:4. 12:34. Ac 6:10.

7. put. Jg 14:12. Pr 8:1. Ezk 17:2. Mt 13:34. **they.** Lk 11:43. 20:46. Mt 23:6. Mk 12:38, 39. Ac 8:18, 19.

Ro +*12:3. Ph +*2:3. 3 J 9.

8. **When**. That there were among the Jews of these times many disputes about seats at banquets, we learn both from Josephus and the Rabbins; nor were these matters unattended to by the Greeks and Romans. Similar admonitions to this of our Lord, also occur in the Rabbinical writers. Rabbi Akiba said, Go two or three seats lower than the place that belongs to thee, and sit there till they say unto thee, Go up higher; but do not take the uppermost seat, lest they say unto thee, Come down: for it is better they should say unto thee, Go up, go up, than they should say, Go down, go down. See Schoetgen, *Horae Hebraicae et Talmudicae*. Pr *25:6, 7. Ph +*2:3.

9. **and thou**. Est 6:6-12. Pr 3:35. 11:2. 16:18. *25:6, 7. Ezk 28:2-10. Da 4:30-34. **begin**. Lk 3:8. 5:21. 13:25, 26.

10. **go**. 1 S 15:17. Pr 15:33. 25:6, 7. **room**. 1 S 9:22. **Friend**. Pr 25:7. **then**. Is 60:14. Re 3:9. **have worship**. Ge 37:7, 9. 42:6. Ex 18:7. 1 K 1:23. 18:7. 1 Ch *29:20. Ps 45:11. Is 49:23. Da 2:46. Mt +*8:2. ◐+*14:33. 18:26. Mk ◐7:7. Jn ◐4:23, 24. Ac 10:25.

11. **For**. ✶138B, Ge +13:16. **whosoever**. Lk 1:51, 52. 10:15. *18:14. 1 S 15:17. 2 S 22:28. Jb 5:11. *22:29. 40:10-12. Ps *18:27. +*119:21. 138:6. Pr 15:33. *18:12. *29:23. Is 2:11, 17. +*57:15. Ezk 21:26. Mt 18:4. 23:12. Ja 4:6, 10. 1 P *5:5, 6. Ju 10.

12. **to him**. ver. 1. **When**. Lk 1:53. Pr 14:20. 22:16. Ja 2:1-6. **a dinner**. Jn 21:12g. **and a recompense**. Lk 6:32-36. Zc 7:5-7. Mt 5:46. 6:1-4, 16-18.

13. **a feast**. Lk 5:29. **call**. ver. 21. Lk 11:41. Dt 14:29. 16:11, 14. 26:12, 13. 2 S 6:19. 2 Ch 30:24. Ne *8:10, 12. Est 9:22. Jb 29:13, 15, 16. 31:16-20. Pr 3:9, 10. 14:31. 31:6, 7. Is 58:7, 10. Mt 14:14-21. 15:32-39. 22:10. *25:35. Ac 2:44, 45. 4:34, 35. 9:39. Ro 12:13-16. 1 T 3:2. 5:10. T 1:8. Phm 7. He 13:2. 1 J 3:17. **the poor**. ver. 21. Ps 41:1. Pr 14:21. 19:17. 28:27. Mt 19:21. Ga 2:10. **the maimed**. ✶41, Ge +10:1. The figure of speech Asyndeton bids us to pass quickly over these details to note the emphatic climax, "and thou shalt be blessed," ver. 14. Note the use of the opposite figure of speech in ver. 21.

14. **be blessed**. Jb *42:10. Pr *11:25. 2 C 5:10. Re √20:6. **they cannot**. Lk *6:35. Mt 5:46. **be recompensed**. Ru 2:12. Pr *11:18. *19:17. Mt +*5:12. *6:4. *10:41, 42. *16:27. *25:34-40. Mk *10:21. Ro 2:6, 16. *14:10. 1 C *3:11-15. *4:5. Ga 6:9, 10. Ep 6:8. Ph +*4:17-19. 1 T +*4:8. *6:17-19. He 9:15. *10:35. *11:6. Re √11:18. **at**. Is 3:10, 11. *40:10. 62:11. Mt *16:27. Ro 2:16. 14:10. 1 C 3:8, 13. 15:23. 2 C 5:10. Col *3:24. 1 Th 4:16, 17. 2 Th +*1:10. 2 T +*4:1n. Re 22:12. **the resurrection**. Lk 20:35, 36. Da +*12:2, 3. Mt +*10:15n. Jn *5:29. Ac *24:15. Ro 8:11, 23. 1 C 3:8, 13. He √11:35. Re +*11:18. 22:12. **of the just**. Lk √20:35, 36. Jn 6:39, 40, 44, 54. 11:24. Ac *24:15. 1 C 6:14. 15:22-24, 52. Ph +*3:11. 1 Th +*4:16n. Re *20:4, 5.

15. **Blessed**. Lk 12:37. 13:29. 22:16, 30. Mt +*8:11. 25:10. Jn 6:27, etc. Re *19:9. **the kingdom**. Lk +4:43.

16. **Then said**. ✶128. Parabola; or, Parable: i.e. Continued Simile B751. Comparison by continued resemblance. For other instances of this figure see Mt ch. 13. 25:1-12. Lk ch. 15, 16. **A certain**. Pr 9:1, 2. Is *25:6, 7. Je 31:12-14. Zc 10:7. Mt *22:2-14. **bade**. SS 5:1. Is *55:1-7. Mk 16:15, 16. Re 3:20. 22:17.

17. **his**. Lk *3:4-6. *9:1-5. *10:1, etc. Est 6:14. Pr

*9:1-5. Mt *3:1, etc. *10:1, etc. Ac *2:38, 39. 3:24-26. *13:26, 38, 39. **bidden**. Zp 1:7. **Come**. SS 2:4. Is *55:1, 2. Mt *11:27-29. *22:3, 4. Jn *7:37. 2 C *5:18-21. *6:1. He 3:15. Re 19:9. 22:17.

18. **all**. Lk 20:4, 5. Is 28:12, 13. 29:11, 12. Je 5:4, 5. 6:10, 16, 17. Mt 22:5, 6. *23:37. Jn *1:11. *5:40. Ac 13:45, 46. 18:5, 6. 28:25-27. **consent**. ✶63A4, 1 K +3:22. **make excuse**. Ex 3:11, 13. 4:1, 10, 13. SS +*5:3. **I have**. Lk 8:14. 17:26-31. 18:24. Dt 20:5, 6. Mt 24:38, 39. 1 T √6:9, 10. 2 T 4:4, 10. He 12:16. 1 J √2:15, 16.

20. **have married**. ver. 26-28. Lk 18:29, 30. Dt 20:7. 24:5. 1 C *7:29-31, 33.

21. **and showed**. Lk 9:10. 1 S 25:12. Mt 15:12. 18:31. Mk 6:30. He 13:17. **being**. ver. 24. Ps 2:12. Mt 22:7, 8. He 2:3. 12:25, 26. Re 15:1, etc. 19:15. **Go**. Lk 24:47. Pr 1:20-25. 8:2-4. 9:3, 4. Je 5:1. Zc 11:7, 11. Mt 21:28-31. Jn 4:39-42. 7:47-49. 9:39. Ac 8:4-7. Ja *2:5. Re *22:17. **the poor**. Those whom no one would think of inviting, but who would welcome the invitation (Lk 15:1); "the poor" who could not afford to buy "a piece of ground" (ver. 18) or "five yoke of oxen" (ver. 19). ver. 13. Lk 7:22, 23. 1 S 2:8. Ps 113:7, 8. Mt *11:5, 28. 22:9, 10. Mk 12:37. **and the maimed**. ✶148, Ge +8:22. The figure of speech Polysyndeton (Many Ands) directs us to pause and consider each of these four classes, which are in direct contrast to the four classes which made excuses in the intervening parable. The maimed are those who would be most unlikely to be able to say, "I have married a wife" (ver. 20). Note the remarkable use of the opposite figure Asyndeton (No Ands) in ver. 13 with the same four words. **and the halt**. ver. 13g (lame). Those who could not "go" to use the oxen, or to "prove them," at the plough, ver. 19. Ps 38:7. Is 33:23. *35:6. **and the blind**. Those who could not say, "I must needs go and see" the piece of land which I have bought, ver. 18 (See B209).

22. **it is**. Ac ch. 1-9. **and yet**. Ge 24:23. Ps 103:6. 130:7. Jn +*14:2. Ep 3:8. Col 2:9. 1 T 2:5, 6. 1 J 2:2. Re 7:4-9.

23. **Go**. Ps 98:3. Pr 1:21. Is 11:10. 19:24, 25. *27:13. *49:5, 6. 66:19, 20. Zc *14:8, 9. Ml 1:11. Mt *21:43. *22:9, 10. +*28:19, 20. Mk *16:15. Ac *9:15. *10:44-48. 11:18-21. *13:47, 48. 18:6. 22:21, 22. *26:18-20. 28:28. Ro *1:16. 10:18. *15:9-12. Ep *2:11-22. Col *1:23. **compel**. Lk 24:29. Ge *19:2, 3. =43:16. Ps 110:3. Mt 14:22. Mk 6:45. Ac *16:15. Ro *11:13, 14. 1 C *9:19-23. 2 C *5:11, 20. *6:1. Col *1:28. 2 T *4:2. **to come in**. Lk 11:52.

24. **That none**. Pr *1:24-32. Mt *21:43. 22:8. 23:38, 39. Jn √3:19, 36. *8:21, 24. Ac *3:46. 13:46. Ro ◐+*11:1. He *12:25, 26.

25. **there went**. Lk 12:1. Jn 6:24-27. **he turned**. Lk 22:61.

26. **If any**. ✶184A, 1 C +15:2. ver. 33. Dt *13:6-8. *33:8, 9. Ps *73:25, 26. Mt *‖10:37. 19:29. Ph *3:8. **hate**. ✶102, Ge +2:24. ✶121C2C2, Ge +29:31. Lk 5:28. 16:13. 21:16. Ge *29:30, 31. Dt 21:15n. =33:9. Jb *7:15, 16. Ec 2:17-19. Ml 1:2, 3. Mt 6:24. ‖10:37. Jn *12:25. Ro +*9:13. **yea**. Lk *9:23. Ac *20:24. Re √12:11. **life**. Gr. *psyche*, ✶121A7, Mt +2:20. ✶121A7, Ge +9:5. Lk 9:24. 12:23.

27. **doth**. Lk 9:23-25. Mt *10:38. 16:24-26. Mk 8:34-37. 10:21. 15:21. Jn 19:17. 2 T √3:12. **cannot**. Mt 13:21. Ac 14:22. 2 T 1:12.

28. **intending**. Ge *11:4-9. Pr *24:27. **sitteth**. Ps

+*112:5. Pr +*22:3. **first**. ver. 31. Lk 12:33. 16:8-10. Pr *6:8. 13:16. +*22:3. *24:27. Mt 16:25, 26. 2 C 6:2. He 2:3. **counteth**. ver. *33. Jsh *24:19-24. Mt 8:20. 10:22. *20:22, 23. Ac *21:13. 1 Th +*3:4, 5. 2 P 1:13, 14. **to finish**. Mt +*13:20, 21.

30. **began to build**. Mt 7:27. 27:3-8. Ac 1:18, 19. 1 C 3:11-14. He 6:4-8, √11. 10:38. 2 P 2:19-22. 2 J 8.

31. **make war**. 2 S +*11:1n. 1 K 20:11. 2 K 18:20-22. Pr 20:18. 25:8. Ac 17:18g. **first**. ver. 28. Pr 13:16. **consulteth**. 2 K 14:10.

32. **great way**. Dt 20:11-15. **ambassage**. Jsh 9:4. **and desireth**. Lk 12:58. Jsh *9:6. 1 K 20:31-34. 2 K 10:4, 5. Jb 40:9. Mt 5:25. Ac 12:20. Ja 4:6-10.

33. **whosoever**. ver. 26. Lk 5:11, 28. 18:22, 23, 28-30. Ac 5:1-5. 8:19-22. Ph *3:7, 8. 2 T 4:10. He 11:26. 1 J √2:15, 16. **forsaketh**. Lk 9:61. Mt 10:37. Mk 6:46. 8:35. Ac 18:18, 21. 2 C 2:13g. Ph 3:6-8.

34. **Salt**. Common salt, or muriat of soda, consists of soda in combination with muriatic acid, and is for the most part an artificial preparation from sea water, though found in some countries in a solid and massive state. See particularly Le *2:13. **but if**. √184C, Mt +4:9. Mt *5:13. Mk *9:49, 50. Col *4:6. He *2:4-8.

35. **but**. Jn *15:6. **He**. Lk *8:8. *9:44. Mt *11:15. *13:9, 43. Re *2:7, 11, 17, 29. **to hear**. √147A, Ge +50:24.

LUKE 15

The Pharisees murmur at Christ for receiving sinners, 1, 2. The parable of the lost sheep, 2-7; that of the lost piece of silver, 8-10; and that of the prodigal son and his elder brother, 11-32.

1. **drew near**. Lk 5:29-32. 7:29. 13:30. Ex 33:21. Dt 5:31. Ezk 18:27, 28. Mt 9:10-13. 21:28-31. Ro *5:20. 1 T *1:15. **all**. *√171A, Ex +9:6. **publicans**. Lk 5:29, 30. 7:34. Mt 11:19. **to hear**. Mk 12:37.

2. **Pharisees and scribes murmured**. ver. 29, 30. Lk 5:30. 7:34, 39. 19:7. Ex 16:2, 7, 8. 17:3. Nu 14:2. Jsh 9:18. 1 C 5:9-11. **This man**. √60B, Ge +20:16. Lk 7:39. **receiveth sinners**. Ro 16:2. Ph 2:29. **eateth with**. Lk 5:30. Mt 9:11. Mk 2:16. Ac 11:3. 1 C √5:9-11. Ga 2:12.

4. **man**. Lk 13:15. Mt *12:11. *18:12. Ro 2:1. **having**. 1 K 22:17. Ps *119:176. Is *53:6. Je 50:6. Ezk 34:8, 11, 12, 16, 31. Mt 18:12, 13. Jn *10:11, 15, 16, 26-28. 1 P *2:25. **lose**. Gr. *apollumi*, Mt +2:13. **wilderness**. Ex 3:1. 1 S 17:28. **lost**. Gr. *apollumi*, Mt +2:13. **go after**. Lk +*19:10. Ge=37:17. Ezk 34:4, 11, 12, 16. **until**. Ga *6:1. 1 T √4:13-16. 2 T +*2:12. He +*3:13, 14. Ja +*5:19. 1 J 5:16. Ju 23.

5. **when**. Lk 19:9. 23:43. Is 62:12. Jn 4:34, 35. Ac 9:1-16. Ro 10:20, 21. Ep 2:3-6. T 3:3-7. **he layeth**. Is 40:10, 11. 46:3, 4. 49:22. 60:4. *63:9. 66:12. Mi *5:4. Ep 1:19, 20. √2:10. 3:7. 1 Th 1:5. 2 T 2:26. 1 P 1:5. **rejoicing**. ver. 23, 24, 32. Is *53:10, 11. 62:5. Je 32:41, 42. Ezk 18:23. *33:11. Mi +*7:18. Zp 3:17. Jn 15:11. He *12:2.

6. **his friends**. ver. 7, 10, 24. Lk 2:13, 14. Is 66:10, 11. Jn 3:29. +*15:14. Ac +*11:23. 15:3. Ph 1:4. 2:17. 4:1. 1 Th 2:19. 3:7-9. **Rejoice**. Ps 22:22. Mt *18:13. Ju 24. **for**. Ps 119:176. 1 P *2:10, 25. **lost**. Gr. *apollumi*, Mt +2:13. ver. 4.

7. **joy**. ver. 10, 32. Lk 2:10. *5:32. Mt *18:13, 14. **one sinner**. ver. 10. Lk 7:37. Ezk *33:11. Mt 6:29. 18:10. 25:40, 45. **that repenteth**. ver. 10. Lk 5:32.

+*13:3, 5. **just**. Lk 5:32. 16:15. 18:11, 12. Pr 30:12. Mt 9:13. **just**. √12:1l2, Ge +2:17. **which**. ver. 29. Lk *16:15. *18:9-11. Pr 30:12. Ro 7:9. Ph *3:6, 7, 9.

8. **pieces**. " 'Drachma,' here translated *a piece of silver*, is the eighth of an ounce, which cometh to 7 1/2 d., and is equal to the Roman penny. Mt 18:28." Dt 22:15. **if**. √184C, Mt +4:9. **lose**. Gr. *apollumi*, Mt +2:13. **and seek**. Lk +*19:10. Ezk 34:12. Jn 10:16. 11:52. Ep 2:17. **till**. ver. 4.

9. **Rejoice**. ver. 6, 7. **neighbors**. Ru 4:17. **lost**. Gr. *apollumi*, Mt +2:13.

10. **there**. Lk 2:10-14. Ezk 18:23, 32. *33:11. Mt *18:10, 11. 28:5-7. Ac 5:19, 20. 10:3-5. He *1:14. Re *5:11-14. **the angels**. Lk 12:8. **one**. Lk 7:47. 13:5. 2 Ch 33:13-19. Mt *18:14. Ac 11:18. 2 C √7:10. Phm 15. **repenteth**. Lk +*13:3.

11. **A certain man**. Mt 21:23-31.

12. **give**. Dt 21:16, 17. Ps 16:5, 6. 17:14. **And he**. Mk 12:44. **living**. √121F, Ge +49:6.

13. **and took**. 2 Ch 33:1-10. Jb 21:13-15. 22:17, 18. Ps 10:4-6. 73:27. Pr 27:8. Is 1:4. 30:11. Je 2:5, 13, 17-19, 31. Mi 6:3. Mt 21:33. Ep *2:11-13, 17. **wasted**. ver. 30. Lk 16:1, 19. Jb 20:14, 15. Pr 5:8-14. 6:26. 18:9. 21:17, 20. 23:19-22. 28:7. 29:3. Ec 11:9, 10. Is 22:13. 56:12. Am 6:3-7. Ro 13:13, 14. 1 P 4:3, 4. 2 P 2:13. **riotous living**. Ep 5:18. T 1:6. 1 P 4:4. **be in want**. 2 C 11:9. Ph 4:12.

14. **spent all**. Lk 8:43. Ge=47:18. Pr *21:20. **arose**. 2 Ch 33:11. Pr 21:20. Ezk *16:27. Ho 2:9-14. Am *8:9-12. **famine**. Ge=41:56, 57. Ru 1:1. Ps 105:16. Is 55:2. Am +*8:11, 12.

15. **he went**. ver. 13. Ex 10:3. 2 Ch 28:22. Is 1:5. 9:10-13. 57:17. Je 5:3. 8:4-6. 31:18, 19. 2 T 2:25, 26. Re 2:21, 22. **joined himself**. 2 Ch 20:36. **to feed**. Lk 8:32-34. Ezk 16:52, 63. Na 3:6. Ml 2:9. Ro 1:24-26. 6:22. 1 C *6:9-11. Ep 2:2, 3. 4:17-19. 5:11, 12. Col 3:5-7. T 3:3.

16. **he would**. Lk 16:21. Pr 23:21. Is 44:20. 55:2. La 4:5. Ho 12:1. Ro 6:19-21. **have filled**. √96C4, Mt +3:17. **husks**. Ex ◐16:31. Pr *27:7. **that**. Ps 73:22. no. Ps 142:4. Is 57:3. Jon 2:2-8.

17. **when**. Lk 8:35. 16:23. 1 K 8:47. 2 Ch 6:37. Ps 73:20. Ec *9:3. Je 31:19. Ezk 18:28. Ac 2:37. *16:29, 30. 26:11-19. Ep 2:4, 5. 5:14. T 3:4-6. Ja 1:16-18. **came to himself**. Lk *8:35. Ac 12:11. 2 T +√1:7. **How**. ver. 18, 19. La 1:7. **hired servants**. Le 25:50. Jb 7:1. **and to spare**. 2 Ch=31:9, 10. Mt 14:20. Ph 4:18. **perish**. Gr. *apollumi*, Mt +2:13. **with hunger**. Le=22:4, 6, 7. 1 J=1:6, 7.

18. **will arise**. 1 K 20:30, 31. 2 K 7:3, 4. 2 Ch 33:12, 13, 19. Ps *32:5. 116:3-7. Je 31:6-9. 50:4, 5. La 3:18-22, 29, 40. Ho 2:6, 7. 14:1-3. Jon 2:4. 3:9. **will say**. Ho +*14:2. **Father**. Lk 11:2. Is 63:16. Je *3:19. 31:20. Mt +*6:9, 14. 7:11. **I have**. Lk 18:13. Ex 10:16. Le 26:40, 41. 1 K 8:47, 48. Ne 1:6. Jb 33:27, 28. 36:8-10. Ps 25:11. 32:3-5. 51:3-5. Pr +*28:13. Is √55:7. Je 3:12, 13. Mt 3:6. 1 J √1:8-10. **against**. ver. 21. Da 4:26. Mt 21:25. Jn 3:27. **heaven**. √121J20, Ps +73:9. Ex 9:22. Mt 14:19.

19. **no**. Lk 5:8. 7:6, 7. Ge 32:10. Jb 42:6. 1 C 15:9. 1 T 1:13-16. **make**. Ge 48:20. Jsh 9:24, 25. Ps *84:10. Is 41:15. Mt 15:26, 27. Ja *4:8-10. 1 P 5:6. **hired servants**. Le=22:10. Jn 15:15.

20. **And**. √148, Ge +8:22. **he arose**. Is √55:7. **But**. Dt *30:2-4. Jb 33:27, 28. Ps 86:5, 15. *103:8-13. Is 49:15. √55:6-9. 57:18. Je 31:20. Ezk 16:6-8. Ho 11:8.

Mi +*7:18, 19. Ac *2:39. Ep *2:13, 17. **had compassion.** Ho +*11:8. Mk 8:2. **and fell.** Ge 33:4. 45:14, 15. 46:29. Ac 20:37. **and kissed.** Lk 7:38, 45. Ge 29:13. 31:55. 2 S 14:33. Mt 26:49. Mk 14:45. Ac 20:37.

21. **said.** ♪56, Is +14:16. **Father.** ver. 18, 19. Le 26:40. Ps *32:5. *51:4. *130:3, 4. Je 3:13. Ezk 16:63. Ro *2:4. **against.** Ps *51:4. 143:2. 1 C 8:12. **son.** ♪37C, Ge +25:22.

22. **the best.** Ps 45:13. 132:9, 16. Is 61:10. Ezk 16:9-13. Zc 3:3-5. Mt 22:11, 12. Ro 3:22. *13:14. Ga 3:27. Ep 4:22-24. Re 3:4, 5, 18. 6:11. 7:9, 13, 14. 19:8. **and.** ♪148, Ge +8:22. **a ring.** Ge 38:18, 25. 41:42. Est 3:10. 8:2. Ro 8:15. Ga 4:5, 6. Ep 1:13, 14. Ja 2:2. Re 2:17. **and shoes.** Dt 33:25. Ps 18:33. SS 7:1. Ezk 16:10. Ep *6:15.

23. **And.** ♪148, Ge +8:22. **the fatted.** Ge 18:7. 1 S 28:24. Ps 63:5. Pr 9:2. Is 25:6. 65:13, 14. Mt 22:2, etc. **eat.** Ru 1:22. 2 Ch 30:21. **be merry.** ver. 24, 29, 30. Lk 12:19. 16:19. Re 11:10.

24. **this.** ver. 32. Mk 8:22. Jn 5:21, 24, 25. 11:25. Ro *6:11, 13, 21. 8:2. 11:15. 2 C √5:14, 15. Ep √2:1, 5. *5:14. Col 2:13. 1 T 5:6. Ju 12. Re *3:1. **he.** ver. 4, 8. Lk +*19:10. Ge 45:28. Je 31:15-17. Ezk 34:4, 16. Mt 18:11-13. **lost.** Gr. *apollumi*, Mt +2:13. **they.** ver. 7, 9, 10, 23. Ge=43:34. Ec 9:7. 10:19. Is 35:10. 66:11. Je 31:12-14. Ro *12:15. 1 C 12:26.

25. **his elder son.** ver. 11, 12. **he heard music.** Lk 7:32. Ex 15:20. 2 S 6:14. Ps 30:11. 126:1. 149:3. 150:4. Ec 3:4. Je 31:4, 13.

27. **Thy brother.** ver. 30. Ac 9:17. 22:13. Phm 16. **and thy.** ver. 23. **he hath received.** Ro 11:28, 31.

28. **he was angry.** ver. 2. Lk 5:30. 7:39. 1 S 17:28. 18:8. Is 65:5. 66:5. Jon 4:1-3. Mt 20:11. Ac *13:45, 50. 14:2, 19. 22:21, 22. Ro 10:19. 1 Th 2:16. **would not.** Lk 9:50. Ac 11:3. 2 C *2:7, 10. **therefore.** Lk 13:34. 24:47. Ge 4:5-7. Jon 4:4, 9. 2 C 5:20.

29. **Lo.** Lk √17:10. *18:9, 11, 12, 20, 21. 1 S 15:13, 14. Is 58:2, 3. 65:5. Zc 7:3. Mt 20:12. Ro 3:20, 27. 7:9. 10:3. Ph 3:4-6. 1 J √1:8-10. Re 3:17. **neither transgressed.** ♪121I2, Ge +2:17. **yet.** ver. 7. Lk 19:21. Ml 1:12, 13. 3:14. Re 2:17. **make merry.** ver. 23.

30. **this.** ver. 32. Lk 18:11. Ex 32:7, 11. **devoured.** ver. 13, 22, 23. Pr 29:3. **thy living.** ver. 12. Mk 12:44.

31. **Son.** Lk 2:48. 16:25. 19:22, 23. Mt 9:2. 11:19. 20:13-16. 21:28. Mk 2:5. 7:27, 28. 10:24. Ro *9:4, 5. 11:1, 35. Ep 6:1. Col 3:20. 1 T 1:18. 2 T 2:1. **thou art.** Jn 8:35. **and all.** ver. 12.

32. **was meet.** Lk 7:34. Ps 51:8. Is *35:10. Ho 14:9. Jon 4:10, 11. Ac *11:18. Ro 3:4, 19. 15:9-13. **make merry.** ver. 23. **for this.** ver. 24. Ep 2:1-10. **was dead.** ver. 24. Ep 5:14. 1 T 5:6. Re 3:1, 2. **lost.** Gr. *apollumi*, Mt +2:13.

LUKE 16

The parable of the prudent response of the business manager to the unjust accusations of his wealthy employer, and the instructions deduced from it, 1-13. Jesus reproves the hypocrisy of the Pharisees who deride him, and speaks of the introduction of the gospel, 14-18. The account of the rich man and Lazarus, 19-31.

1. **a certain.** Mt 18:23, 24. 25:14, etc. **a steward.** Lk 8:3. *12:42. Ge 15:2. 43:19. 1 Ch 28:1. 1 C 4:1, 2. T 1:7. 1 P 4:10. **rich man.** Ja *2:6-9. +*5:1-6. **ac-**

cused. Gr. *diaballo*, ✳S#1225g, only here. The word means to bring charges with hostile intent against someone, whether falsely and slanderously or justly, but maliciously and insidiously. The word expresses "giving currency to a damaging insinuation" (Thayer, *Lexicon*, p. 340a). Here it is most probable that the charges were false and slanderous, and it is not the steward but the rich employer who is unjust. The employer's injustice involves malicious gossip to spread an unfounded and slanderous accusation of unfaithfulness, which is used as a pretext for justifying his dismissal of his accountant. This graphic portrayal shows our Lord's sensitivity to labor/management problems, and his firm stance for justice. Le +*19:15. Pr 17:4, 15. +*18:13. Jn +*7:24, 51. Ja *2:6-9. **wasted.** ver. 19. Lk 15:13, 30. 19:20. Pr 18:9. Ho 2:8. Ja 4:3.

2. **How.** Ge 3:9-11. 4:9, 10. 18:20, 21. 1 S 2:23, 24. 1 C 1:11. 1 T 5:24. **give.** Lk 12:42. Ec 11:9, 10. 12:14. Mt 12:36. 25:19. Ro 14:12. 1 C 4:2, 5. 2 C 5:10. 1 P ●*3:15. 4:5, 10. 1 T 4:14. Re 20:12. **stewardship.** ver. 3, 4. 1 C 9:17. 1 T 1:4g. **for.** Lk *12:20. 19:21-26.

3. **said.** Lk 7:39. 18:4. Est 6:6. Mt 9:3. **What shall.** ♪36, Ho +6:4. Lk 12:17. Is 10:3. Je 5:31. Ho 9:5. Ac 9:6. **I cannot.** Pr 13:4. 15:19. 18:9. 19:15. 21:25, 26. 24:30-34. 26:13-16. 27:23-27. 29:21. 2 Th 3:11. **to beg.** Lk *16:20, 22. Jb 15:23. Ps 109:10. Pr 20:4. Mk 10:46. Jn 9:8. Ac 3:2.

4. **resolved.** Pr 30:9. Je 4:22. Ja 3:15. **put out.** Ac 13:22g.

5. **his.** Lk 7:41, 42. Mt 18:24.

6. **measures.** "The word *Batos* in the original containeth nine gallons three quarts. See Ezk 45:10-14." **Take.** ver. 9, 12. T 2:10.

7. **An hundred.** Lk 20:9, 10, 12. SS 8:11, 12. **measures.** "The word here interpreted a *measure*, in the original containeth about fourteen bushels and a pottle. Gr." 1 K 4:22mg. Ezr 7:22mg. Ezk 45:14.

8. **unjust.** "Unjust" may be taken here as descriptive not of the steward, but of the money with which he dealt, for money often serves unrighteous motives and purposes, so that the term has reference to what we might call an accountant or business manager today. ver. 9, 10. Lk 18:6. Mt 6:24. Ac 1:18g. 1 T 6:10. Ja 1:25, "forgetful hearer," involves a similar idiom (Robertson, *Word Pictures*, vol. 2, p. 217). **done.** ver. 4. Ge 3:1. Ex 1:10. 2 S 13:3. 2 K 10:19. Pr 6:6-8. **wisely.** Pr +*22:3. Mt 25:2. **children of this.** Lk 10:6. 20:34. Ps *17:14. Mt 13:38. Jn 8:23. 1 C 3:18, 19. Ga 1:4. Ph 3:19. **world.** Gr. *aion*, Mt +6:13. lit. "this age," Mt +12:32. ♪121P2, Mt +13:22. **in their generation.** Ps 49:10-19. Mt 17:26. **wiser.** Mt +*11:19. **children of light.** T#655. Is 42:18. Jn *12:35, 36. Ep *5:8. 1 Th *5:5-8. 2 Th ●2:3. 1 P 2:9. 1 J 3:10.

9. **I say.** Mt +6:2n. 15:26. Mk 7:27. **Make.** Lk *11:41. 12:33. *14:14. Pr 10:2. 11:4. *19:17. Ec *11:1. Is *58:7, 8. Ezk 7:19. Da 4:27. Mt √6:19, 20. *19:21. *25:35-40. Ac *10:4, 31. 2 C 9:12-15. 1 T √6:17-19. 2 T 1:16-18. **of the.** ver. 11, 13. Mt 6:24. **mammon.** or, riches. ver. 11, 13. Pr *23:5. Mt 6:24. 1 T *6:9, 10, 17. **of unrighteousness.** ver. 8. Pr 22:16. Je 17:11. Mk 10:24. **when.** Ps *73:26. Ec 12:3-7. Is *57:16. **receive you.** Lk 6:38. 15:20-24. Ps +*126:6. Ec 11:1. Da +*12:3. 1 Th +*2:19, 20. He 10:34. 2 P +*1:10. **into.** 2 C *4:17, 18. *5:1. 1 T *6:18, 19. Ju *21. **everlasting.** Gr. *aionios*, Mt +18:8. Da +*12:3. He +*10:34.

habitations. Lk *12:33. Mt *19:21. Jn +*14:2. 2 C 5:1.

10. faithful in. T#1866. ver. 11, 12. Lk 19:17. 1 K +*12:7n. 2 K 12:15. 2 Ch 31:12. Je +*12:5. +*48:10. Mt *25:21, 23. 1 C 4:2. *11:31. Ep +*1:1. Ph +*2:12. He 3:2. 3 J 5. he that is unjust. 1 K +*12:10n. Ps +*12:5. Pr *29:12. Ec +*5:8. Ezk +*16:49. Mi ❶+*6:8. Ml +*3:5. Mt ❶+*23:23. Jn +*7:24, 51. 12:6. 13:2, 27.

11. If. ⌐184A, 1 C +15:2. in. ver. 9. mammon. or, riches. ver. 9mg. Mt 6:24. commit. Jn 2:24g. true. ⌐101, Dt +32:42. Lk 12:33. 18:22. Pr 8:18, 19. Ep *3:8. Ja *2:5. Re 3:18.

12. if. ⌐184A, 1 C +15:2. been faithful. Da 6:4. in that. Lk 19:13-26. 1 Ch *29:14-16. Jb 1:21. Ezk 16:16-21. Ho 2:8, 9. Mt √25:14-29. that which is your. Lk 10:42. Col 3:3, 4. 1 P √1:4, 5.

13. servant. Ac 10:7. Ro 14:4. 1 P 2:18. can serve. ver. 9, 11. Lk 9:50. 11:23. Jsh √24:15. Mt 4:10. ‖6:24. Ro 6:16-22. 8:5-8. Ga *1:10. 2 T +*4:10. Ja *4:4. 1 J *2:15, 16. hate. Lk +*14:26. Ro +*9:13. Ye cannot. ⌐95, Ps +7:13. serve God. ver. 9. Ja 1:1. and mammon. ver. 9, 11. Mt 6:24.

14. who. Lk 11:39. 12:15. 20:47. Is 56:11. Je 6:13. 8:10. Ezk 22:25-29. +*33:31. Mt 23:14. covetous. Ps +*10:3. Mt 23:25. 1 T 6:10. 2 T 3:2. He 13:5. derided. Lk 8:53. 23:35. Ps 22:7. 35:15, 16. 119:51. Is *53:3. Je 20:7, 8. Ezk +*33:31. Ga 6:7. He 11:36. 12:2, 3.

15. Ye are. T#703. Lk 18:9-12. 2 K 10:16. Ps +10:2 (T#549). 39:6. Pr 3:35. +16:5 (T#550). 20:6. Hab 2:16. Mt 6:5, 16. 23:5-7. 2 C 10:12. Ph +*2:3 (T#482). 3:19. justify yourselves. ⌐121I2, Ge +2:17. Lk 10:29. 11:39. 18:11, 14, 21. 20:20, 47. Pr 20:6. Mt 6:2, 5, 16. 23:5, 25-27. Ro 3:20. Ja 2:21-25. before men. Mt 6:2, 5, 16. 23:5, 7. God knoweth. 1 S +*16:7. 1 Ch +*28:9. 29:17. 2 Ch 6:30. Jb 10:4. Ps 7:9. 138:6. 139:1, 2. Pr 21:2. Je +*17:10. Mt *23:25. Jn +*2:25. 21:17. Ac 1:28. 15:8. Ro 8:27. 1 C *4:5. Re 2:23. for that. 1 S *2:30. Ps 10:3. 49:13, 18. Pr 16:5. Is 1:10-14. Am 5:21, 22. Ml 3:15. 1 P 3:4. 5:5. is abomination. ⌐121R7, Ge +43:11. Pr 6:16, 17. 8:13.

16. Law. ver. 29, 31. Lk +*24:27, 44. Mt 5:17. 7:12. 11:9-14. 22:40. Jn 1:45. 6:45. 7:23. Ac 3:18, 24, 25. Ac 10:43. 13:15. 24:14. 26:22. 28:23. Ro 3:21. were until. Mt *11:13. Col *2:17. the kingdom of God. Lk +4:43. 9:2. 10:9, 11. +*17:20. Mt 3:2. 4:17. 10:7. Mk 1:14, +15. and every. Lk *7:26-29. 15:1. Mt 21:32. Mk 1:45. Jn 11:48. *12:19. presseth into it. Mt √11:11, 12. This text, with Mt 11:12, is best understood as meaning that the generality of men pressed against or resisted the kingdom of God, which accords well with Lk +*7:30. Mt *23:13. Jn √1:11. *12:37. Ro 11:8, 11, 12.

17. it. Lk 21:33. Ps 102:25-27. Is 51:6. Mt +*5:18. 2 P 3:10. Re 20:11. 21:1, 4. than. Is √40:8. Ro 3:31. 1 P 1:25. to fail. ⌐46C, Mt 8:6. Here, Gr. piptein, to fall or fail, is used for not to be fulfilled, or to be of no effect. The Hebrew has both meanings. See Jsh 23:14; Est 6:10 (B678). 1 S 3:19. Ro 9:6. 1 C 13:8g.

18. putteth away. T#427. Ge 2:23, 24. Ml *2:15, 16. Mt *5:32. +*19:3-9n. Mk *10:2-12. Ro *7:2, 3. 1 C *7:4, 10-12.

19. There was. ver. 1. rich. Lk *12:16-21. *18:24, 25. 1 T *6:17-19. Ja +*5:1-5. clothed. ver. 1. Lk 15:13. Jb *21:11-15. Ps *73:3-7. Ezk +*16:49. Am *6:4-6. Re 17:4. 18:7, 16. purple. Jg 8:26. Est 8:15. Pr 31:22.

Ezk 16:13. *27:7. Mk *15:17, 20. Re 18:12, 16. fine linen. Ex 26:1, 31, 36. 28:6, 15. 36:8, 35. 39:3, 8. Ezk 16:10. 27:7. fared sumptuously. Lk 15:23. Ja 5:5.

20. a certain. Lk *18:35-43. 1 S *2:8. Ja *1:9. *2:5. Lazarus. Jn 11:1, 2, 14, 43. 12:1, 2, 9, 10, 17. was laid. Ac *3:2. his gate. Mt 26:71g. full. ver. *21. Dt +*28:35. Jb *2:7, 8. Ps *34:19. 38:7, 8. 73:14. Is *1:6. Je *8:22.

21. desiring. Lk 15:16. 1 C *4:11. 2 C *11:27. crumbs. Mt *15:27. Mk *7:28. Jn *6:12. moreover. Ro 7:7g. 8:37g.

22. that. Jb *3:13-19. Is *57:1, 2. Re *14:13. was carried. Ps *91:11, 12. Mt +*13:38-43. *24:31. Ep 4:8. He *2:14. the angels. Lk 12:8. 15:10. 2 K *6:17. Ps *34:7. Mt *18:10. Ac 12:15. He *1:13, 14. Abraham's. Mt +*8:11. Jn 13:23. 21:20. the rich. Lk *12:20. Jb *21:13, 30-32. Ps *49:6-12, 16-19. 73:18-20. Pr 14:32. Mk 8:36, 37. Ja 1:11. 1 P *2:24. died. Jb 4:21. 27:19. Ps ❶+*146:4. and was buried. 2 K 9:34, 35. Jb 4:21. 21:13. *27:19. Ec 8:10. Is 14:18. 22:16.

23. in hell. Gr. hades. Mt +11:23. T#1194. Ps +*9:17. +*16:10. ❶49:15. +*55:15. *86:13. Pr 5:5. 7:27. 9:18. 15:24. Is 14:+*9, 15. 50:11. +*66:24. Da *12:2. Mt 5:22, 29. 11:23. +*12:40. 18:9. 23:33. +*25:41, 46. Ac 2:27. 1 C 15:55mg. 2 P 2:4. Re 20:13, 14. in torments. T#1292. ver. 28. Lk 8:28. Mt *8:29. Ja *2:19. Re *14:10, 11. 20:10. seeth. Lk 13:28, 29. Is ❶+*63:16. +*66:24. Mt +*17:3n. Re 14:10. Abraham. Lk *13:28. Mt +*8:11, 12. in his. Lk 23:43. Jn 13:23. 2 C *5:6-8. Ph +*1:23.

24. Father Abraham. ver. 30. Lk 3:8. 19:9. Mt 3:9. Jn 8:33-39, 53-56. Ro 4:12. 9:7, 8. have mercy. Lk 17:13. 1 S 28:16. Is 27:11. Ja *2:13. send Lazarus. T#1598. ver. 27. dip. Gr. bapto. *S#911g. Lk 16:24. Jn 13:26. Re 19:13. For related words see Mk +*7:4n. in water. Is 41:17, 18. 65:13, 14. Jn 4:10, 14. 7:37. Re 7:16, 17. 22:1. and cool. Zc 14:12. Ja 3:6. for. Is +*66:24. Mt +*25:41. Mk *9:43-49. 2 Th *1:8. Re 14:10, 11. 19:20. 20:15. tormented. T#573-8. Lk 2:48g. Is +*33:14. Mt +*8:29. flame. T#343. Ps +9:17 (T#561). 21:9. Is +*30:33. +*33:14. +*66:24. 2 Th 1:8. Re 9:2. 20:10. +*21:8.

25. Son. ver. 24. Lk 15:31. remember. T#573-2. ver. 23. Pr 5:11-14. Je 8:20. La 1:7. Da 5:22, 23, 30. Mk 9:46. Ro +3:19 (T#128). 2 C +1:12 (T#131). receivedst. Lk *6:24. Jb 21:13. 36:11, 12. thy good. Lk 6:24. Jb *21:13, 14. 22:18. Ps *17:14. 37:35, 36. 49:11, 17. 73:7, 12-20. Ro 8:7. Ph 3:19. 1 J √2:15, 16. likewise. ver. 20. Jn 16:33. Ac *14:22. 1 Th 3:3, 4. He 11:25, 26. Re *7:14-17. but now. T#525, 1802. 1 S 2:8. Pr +16:5 (T#550). Je +20:11 (T#513). is comforted. Re +*14:13. and thou. Mt 19:23.

26. between. 1 S 25:36. Ps 49:14. Ezk 28:24. Ml 3:18. 2 Th 1:4-10. Ja 1:11, 12. 5:1-7. cannot. T#390. Lk 13:26, 27. Jb +27:8 (T#572). Is *38:18. Mt +25:46 (T#567). 2 C +6:2 (T#553). He +*9:27. Re +*22:11, 12. they pass. Lk 12:59. Ps 50:22. Mt 25:46. Jn √3:36. 2 Th 1:9. Re 20:10. 22:11.

28. testify. Ac 2:40. 8:25. 10:42. 18:5. 20:21, 23, 24. 23:11. 28:23. 1 Th 4:6. lest. T#1335. Ge 4:13, 14. Ex 10:16, 17. 32:10-12. Jg 10:9, 10. 1 S 12:19. 2 K 1:13, 14. Ps *49:12, 13. Jon 1:14. 3:6-9. Ac 8:22-24.

29. They have. ver. 16. Is +√8:20n. *34:16. Ml 4:2-4. Jn +*5:39-45. Ac 15:21. √17:11, 12. 2 T √3:15-17. 2 P √1:19-21. Moses. ver. 31. Lk +*24:27. Ex

+*24:4. Jn *5:46. Ac 26:22. 28:23. ſ121A6. Metonymy of the Cause B544. The writer is put for his writing or book. For other instances of this figure see Lk 24:27. Ac 15:21. 21:21. 2 C 3:15. **the prophets.** Ac *10:43. **let them hear.** Jn 5:45-47. Ga 4:21.

30. **father.** ver. 24. **but if.** ſ184A, 1 C +15:2. **repent.** Lk +*13:3, 5. Re *16:9-11.

31. **If they.** ſ184A, 1 C +15:2. From this answer of Abraham we learn that the Sacred Writings contain such proofs of a divine origin, that though all the dead were to rise, the proofs could not be more evident, nor the conviction greater; and that to escape eternal perdition, and obtain eternal glory, a man is to receive the testimonies of God, and to walk according to their dictates. T#433. Ps +*19:7 (T#47). Je +*23:28, 29. 2 C *10:4, 5. He *4:12. **hear not Moses.** T#1021. ver. 29. Jn *5:46. Ro √15:4, 8. 2 T √3:15-17. **and the prophets.** Ac 13:40, 41. **neither.** Ex +*9:30. Jn *5:47. *11:43-53. 12:10, 11. 2 C *4:3. **be persuaded.** Ge 9:27mg. Ac *19:8. *26:28. *28:23. 2 C *5:11. **rose from.** Mt √28:11-15. Jn √12:10, 11. Ac 4:10, 17.

LUKE 17

Jesus teaches his disciples, carefully to avoid giving offences, 1, 2; and to forgive one another, 3, 4. Being asked by the apostles to increase their faith, he shows the power of faith, 5, 6; and man's best obedience has no merit with God, 7-10. He cleanses ten lepers; of whom one only, and he a Samaritan, returns to give thanks to God, 11-19. The spiritual nature of the kingdom of God, 20-22. The manner in which it was about to be established, with the ruin of all who neglected it, 23-37.

1. **It is.** Mt 16:23. 18:7. Ac 20:30. Ro 14:13, 20, 21. 16:17. 1 C 8:13. 10:32. √11:19. 2 Th 2:10-12. 1 T 4:1, 2. 1 P √2:8. Re 2:14, 20. 13:14, etc. **offenses.** Mt +*13:41. 17:27. **but woe.** Lk 22:22. Mt 26:24. Mk 9:42. 14:21.

2. **better.** Mt 18:6. 26:24. Mk *9:42. 1 C 9:15. 2 P 2:1-3. **that a.** lit. if a. ſ184A, 1 C +15:2. **one.** Is 40:11. Zc 13:7. Mt 18:3-5, 10, 14. Jn 21:15. 1 C 8:11, 12. 9:22. **little ones.** Lk +9:47. ◑+18:15. 1 J 2:12, 13.

3. **heed.** Lk *21:34. Ex 34:12. Dt 4:*9, 15, 23. 2 Ch *19:6, 7. Ac 5:35. Ep 5:15. He *12:15. 2 J *8. **If.** ſ184C, Mt +4:9. Mt *18:15-17, 21, 22. **rebuke.** Le +*19:17. Ps *141:5. Pr *9:8, 9. +*17:10. *27:5, 6. Ga *2:11-14. 2 Th 3:15. 1 T +*5:19, 20. 2 T 4:2. T 3:10. Ja *5:19, 20.

4. **if.** ſ184C, Mt +4:9. Mt *18:21, 22, 35. 1 C *13:4-7. Ep √4:31, 32. Col 3:12, 13. **seven times.** Ps +*119:164n. Pr 24:16. Mt 6:21. **turn again.** Lk +22:32. **I repent.** Mt *5:44. *6:12, 14, 15. *18:16, 17. Ro +*12:20, 21. 2 Th 3:13, 14.

5. **the apostles.** Lk 9:10. Mk 6:30. **the Lord.** Lk 7:13. **Increase.** T#1484. Ps +*138:3. Mk √9:24. 2 C *12:8-10. Ph √4:13. 2 Th *1:3. He *12:2. 1 P 1:22, 23. 2 P √3:18. **faith.** T#1483. Lk 22:31, 32. Mt 17:20. Mk √9:23, 24. *11:23. Ac 6:8. 11:24. Ro *4:20, 21. ◑*10:17. Ep *2:8. 6:23. 1 Th *3:10.

6. **If.** ſ184A, 1 C +15:2. Mt *17:20, 21. 21:21. Mk 9:23. 11:22, 23. 1 C 13:2. **as a grain.** Lk 13:19. Mt 13:31, 32. **ye might.** ſ184B, Mt +23:30. **sycamine tree.** The *sukaminos, sycamine,* is probably the same as the *shekem,* or *sycamore,* of the ancients (for a description of which see 1 Ch 27:28n), and must not be confounded

with our sycamore, which is the *acer majus,* or greater maple. Dr. Shaw (*Travels,* p. 435) says it is one of the most common timber trees of the Holy Land: and that, from having a large and more extensive root than other trees, it is alluded to as the most difficult to be rooted up. It must, however, be observed, that the Syriac, Arabic, and Latin, render it the *morus,* or mulberry tree, for which Hiller, Celsius, and other learned men, contend. Lk 19:4. 2 S ◑5:23n. 1 Ch ◑14:15n. 27:28n. 2 Ch 1:15. 9:27. Ps 78:47. Am 7:14. **it should.** ſ184E. Hypothetical Propositions; or, Conditional ("if") Sentences: mixed conditions. Here, the protasis ("if" clause) is a First Class Condition, determined as fulfilled. The apodosis ("then" clause, expressing result) is Second Class, determined as unfulfilled. For other instances of this grammatical structure involving mixed conditions see Jn 8:39. Jn 13:17. Ac 5:38, 39. 8:31. 24:19. 1 C 7:28. 9:11.

7. **which of you.** Lk 13:15. 14:5. Mt 12:11.

8. **Make.** Ge 43:16. 2 S 12:20. **and gird.** Lk 12:35, 37. Ex 28:39. Ps 18:32n. Is 22:21. Jn 13:4.

9. **Doth.** ſ136, Is +60:12. **the things.** Lk 3:13. Ac 23:31. **trow.** ſ111, Ge +18:27.

10. **when ye shall.** 1 Ch 29:14-16. Jb 10:15. 22:2, 3. 35:6, 7. 41:11. Ps *16:2, 3. 35:6, 7. Pr 9:12. Is 6:5. 64:6. Je ◑+*48:10. Ezk ◑+*16:49. Mt 25:◑+*26, 30, 37-40. Ro 3:12. 11:35. 1 C *9:16, 17. 15:9, 10. Ph *3:8, 9. Phm 11. 1 P 5:5, 6. **We are.** Jb 10:15. Ro +*12:3. Ph +*2:3. **unprofitable.** Ps *143:2. Is √64:6. Ro *3:27. 1 C *4:7. **have done.** T#1865. 1 C *10:12. 1 P *4:18. **our duty.** 1 C ◑√15:58.

11. **as he went.** Lk 9:51, 52. 13:22. 18:31. 19:11, 28. **passed through.** 1 K *16:24. Mt 19:1. Jn √4:4. **midst.** ſ144A6, Ge +45:6.

12. **lepers.** Lk 7:22. **which stood.** Lk 5:12. 18:13. Le *13:45, 46. Nu 5:2, 3. 12:14, 15. 2 K 5:27. 7:3. 15:5. 2 Ch 26:20, 21. La 4:15.

13. **lifted.** ſ144A12, Ge +22:13. Lk 11:27. Jg 21:2. 1 S 11:4. Ac 2:14. 4:24. 14:11. 22:22. **Master.** Lk 5:5. **have.** Lk 16:24. 18:38, 39. Mt 9:27. 15:22. 17:15. 20:30, 31. Mk 9:22. 10:47, 48.

14. **Go show.** Lk 5:14. Le *13:1, 2, etc., ▶49. *14:2, etc. Mt 3:15. 5:17. *8:4. Mk 1:44. **as.** 2 K 5:14. Is *65:24. Mt 8:3. Jn *2:5. 4:50-53. 9:7. 11:40.

15. **one of them.** ver. 17, 18. 2 Ch 32:24-26. Ps 30:1, 2, 11, 12. 103:1-4. 107:20-22. 116:12-15. 118:18, 19. Is 38:19-22. Jn 5:14. 9:38. **glorified God.** Lk 7:16. 13:13.

16. **fell.** Lk 5:8. 8:28. Ge 17:3. Nu 16:22. Mt 2:11. 26:39. Mk 5:33. Jn √5:23. Ac 10:25, 26. 1 C 14:25. Re 4:10. 5:14. 19:4, 5, 10. **and he.** Lk 9:52-56. 10:32-35. Mt 10:5. Jn 4:9, 21, 22, 39-42. 8:48. Ac +*1:8. 8:5, etc.

17. **ten.** ver. 12. **but.** Ge 3:9. Ps 106:13. Jn 8:7-10. Ro 1:21.

18. **not found.** 2 Ch 32:25. **to give.** Ps 29:1, 2. 50:23. 106:13. Is 42:12. Jn 9:24. Re 14:7. **save.** 2 K 17:24. Is 61:5. Mt +*8:10, 11. 15:24-28. 19:30. 20:16. 1 J 5:20.

19. **thy faith.** Lk 7:50. 8:48. 18:42. Mt 9:22. Mk 5:34. 10:52.

20. **when the.** Lk 10:11. 16:16. +*19:11, 12n. +*21:31. Mt +*23:39. Mk +*13:32. Ac +*1:6, 7. **kingdom of God.** Lk +*4:43. 11:20. +√21:31. +*22:29, 30. Da 2:34, 35, 44, 45. 7:14, 27. Mt 11:12. *12:28. +√21:43. Jn +*18:36. Re 11:15. **cometh not.** Lk 12:39.

14:1g. ◑+*21:31. Mt 25:13. Jn 18:36. 1 Th 5:2, 3. 2T +*4:1. **observation**. *or*, outward show. Gr. *paratarasis*, peculiar to Luke, and employed (as also *tarasis*) to denote medical observation of disease (see William K. Hobart, *Medical Language of Luke*, p. 153). There is no basis for understanding this word to mean "outward show." While the kindred term *parateerein* often in the New Testament occurs in a context implying hostility (Mk 3:2. Lk 6:7. 14:1. 20:20. Ac 9:24. Ga 4:10), yet the word itself does not possess this connotation, but "was employed in medical language to express close observation of the symptoms of an illness—the constitution of a patient, etc." (Hobart, p. 153). Robertson gives "watching either assiduously like the physician at the bedside or insidiously with evil intent" (*Word Pictures*, vol. 2, on Luke 6:7, p. 81). In context, Jesus is answering the question as to *when* the kingdom of God would come. The point Jesus makes here is that the *time* of the appearance of his kingdom cannot be discerned by watching for signs of its approach. The advent of the kingdom is as sudden and unexpected as the Second Coming of Christ, and is postponed until then. Only God knows the precise timing of these events (Mk +*13:32. Ac +*1:6, 7). ver. 23, 24. Lk 12:31, 32. 16:16n. Da 2:44. Zc *4:6. Jn *18:36. Ro *14:17. 1 C 4:20. Col 1:13. He 12:22, 23. Re 1:9.

21. **Lo here**. ver. 23. Lk 21:8. Mt *24:23-28. Mk *13:21-23. **the kingdom**. Lk +*21:31. +*22:29, 30. Mt +√21:43. Jn +*18:36. Ro *14:17. Col 1:27. **is**. ⨍96C6, Mt +2:4. Heterosis of Tenses, whereby the Present is put for the Future, to show that something will certainly come to pass, and is spoken of as though it were already present. Compare for this figure Mt 26:2; 1 C 15:42-44. **within you**. *or*, among you. Lk 10:9-11. √11:20. Mt *12:28. Mk +1:15. Jn *1:26. 12:35. This passage, especially the marginal reading "among you," has been the subject of much controversy. Those who favor the marginal reading argue that Christ could scarcely have said of the Pharisees he was addressing that the kingdom of God was *within* them. But Robertson cites authority for suggesting that there is no clear instance where *entos* means *among*. The only other N.T. occurrence of the word at Mt 23:26 necessarily requires the meaning "within" ("the inside of the cup"). Robertson comments "What Jesus says to the Pharisees is that they, as others, are to look for the kingdom of God within themselves, not in outward displays and supernatural manifestations. It is not a localized display 'Here' or 'There.' It is in this sense that in Luke 11:20 Jesus spoke of the kingdom of God as 'come upon you,' speaking to the Pharisees" (*Word Pictures*, vol. 2, p. 229). Lk √11:20. Mt 12:28. Jn 1:26. 12:35. More consistently with the teaching of Scripture, Peters states: "Surely He did not mean that the Pharisees who addressed Him and *to whom* He spoke, had the Kingdom *within them* individually, personally. The phrase 'within you' is susceptible of an easy and consistent solution" (*Theocratic Kingdom*, vol. 2, Proposition 110, Observation 2, p. 41). The kingdom is covenanted to the Jewish nation; it is an elect nation; the kingdom belonged so exclusively to them that the public ministry of John the Baptist, Jesus and the disciples, was confined to that nation. The kingdom was tendered to the Jewish nation; on its refusal (through its representative men) to repent, the kingdom is postponed, and those who are to receive it as an inheritance with Christ

are grafted into that elect nation. These considerations show at once *how* this kingdom was "*within*" them. It was truly "*within*" the nation, it being the elect nation (Peters, *Theocratic Kingdom*, vol. 2, p. 42).

22. **days**. ⨍121P4, Dt +4:32. **will come**. Lk 19:43. *21:6. 23:29. Mk 2:20. Jn 4:21. **when**. Lk *5:35. *13:35. Mt *9:15. 25:19, 24. Jn *7:33-36. *8:21-24. *12:35. √13:33. *16:5-7, 16-22. *17:11-13. **to see**. Am 5:18. Jn 8:56. **days of**. ver. +*24. 1 C 1:8. 2 C 1:14. Ph *1:6. 1 Th 5:2. **shall not**. Mt 25:14, +*19.

23. **See here**. ver. 21. Lk √21:8. Mt +*24:23-26. Mk *13:21-23.

24. **as the lightning**. Jb 37:3, 4. Ezk 1:14. Zc 9:14. Mt *24:27. **in his day**. Ml 3:1, 2. 4:1, 2. Mt +*24:30. +*25:31. 26:64. 1 C 1:8. 1 Th 5:2. 2 Th 2:2, 8. Ja *5:8. 2 P *3:10.

25. **must he suffer**. Lk 9:22. 13:33. *18:31, 33. 24:25, 26, 46. Mt *16:21. 17:22, 23. 20:18, 19. Mk 8:31. 9:31. 10:33. **be rejected**. 1 S 8:7. 10:19. Is +*53:3. Mt *21:42. Mk 12:10. Jn *1:11. 12:38. 1 P *2:4.

26. **as it was**. Ge 6:5. 7:7-23, Noah. Jb 22:15-18. Mt *24:37-39. 1 Th 5:3. He 11:7. 1 P 3:19, 20. 2 P 2:5. 3:5, 6. **the days**. ⨍121P4, Dt +4:32. **the days of the Son**. ver. 22, 24. Lk 18:8. 1 C 1:8.

27. **did eat**. Lk *12:19, 20. *16:19-23. Dt 6:10-12. 8:12-14. 1 S 25:36-38. Jb 21:9-13. Is 21:4. 22:12-14. Mt 24:38, 39. 1 Th *5:1-3. **they drank**. ⨍41, Ge +10:1. **in marriage**. Lk 20:35. Mt 22:30. Mk 12:25. **until the day**. Ge 7:7. **the flood came**. Ge 7:17-24. **destroyed**. Gr. *apollumi*, Mt +2:13.

28. **days of Lot**. i.e. *protection*, ✱S#3091g. ver. 29, 32. 2 P 2:7. For ✱S#3876h, see Ge +11:27. Ge 13:13. 18:20, 21. 19:4-15. Ezk +*16:49, 50. Ja +*5:1-5. **they drank**. ⨍41, Ge +10:1.

29. **same day**. Ge 19:16-25. Dt 29:23-25. Is 1:9. 13:19. Je 20:16. 50:40. La 4:6. Ho 11:8. Am 4:11. Zp 2:9. Mt 11:23, 24. 2 P 2:6. Ju +*7. Re 11:8. **rained fire**. Ge 19:24. 2 Th √1:8. 2 P √3:7. **Sodom**. Lk +10:12. **destroyed**. Gr. *apollumi*, Mt +2:13.

30. **in the day**. ver. 24. Lk 21:22, 27, 34-36. Mt 16:27. +*24:3, 27-31, 44. 26:64. Mk 13:26. 1 C 1:7. 2 Th 1:7. 1 P 1:7, 13. 4:13. Re *1:7. **is revealed**. 2 Th +*1:7.

31. **he which**. Lk 21:21. Mt 24:17, 18. Mk 13:15, 16. **the housetop**. The flat-roofed eastern houses have stairs on the outside, by which a person may ascend and descend without coming into the house; and in walled cities they usually form continued terraces, from one end of the city to the other, terminating at the gates; so that one may pass along the tops of the houses and escape out of the city without coming down into the street. Lk 5:19. Jb 2:4. Je 45:5. Mt 6:25. 16:26. *24:17-21. Mk 13:14-16. Ph *3:7, 8. **not return**. Ge 19:26.

32. **Remember**. ⨍89. Exemplum; or, Example B467. Addition of conclusion by way of example. Ge *19:17, 26. 1 C 10:6-12. He +*10:38, 39. 2 P √2:18-22.

33. **shall seek**. Lk *9:24, 25. Mt 10:39. 16:25. Mk *8:35-37. Jn *12:25. Re 2:10. **to save**. Ac 20:28. Ep 1:14. 1 Th 5:9. 2 Th 2:14. 1 T 3:13. He 10:39. 1 P 2:9. **life**. Gr. *psyche*, ⨍121A7, Mt +2:20. ⨍121A7, Ge +9:5. **lose**. Gr. *apollumi*, Mt +2:13. **life**. Gr. *psyche*, ⨍121A7B, Mt +2:20. ⨍121A7, Ge +9:5. **preserve it**. Ac 7:19. 1 T 6:13. 2 T *4:6-8.

34. **I tell you**. Lk 13:3, 5, 24. Is 42:9. Mt *24:25.

Mk 13:23. Jn 14:29. **in that night.** Mt *24:40, 41. **two.** Ps 26:9. 28:3. Je 45:5. Ezk *9:4-6. Ml *3:16-18. Ro 11:4-7. 1 Th x4:16, 17. 2 P 2:9. **one shall be taken.** This is not the rapture, but the second advent, for here those that are taken are destroyed (Mt 24:41n). Mi √4:12. Mt *8:12. +*13:30, 41.

35. **Two women.** Mt √24:41n. **grinding.** Ex 11:5. Jg 16:21. Jb 31:10. Ec 12:3. Is 47:2. **taken.** ver. +*34n. Mt *8:12. +*13:30, 41.

36. **Two men.** "This verse is wanting in most of the Greek copies." Mt 24:40. **taken.** ver. +*34n. Mt *8:12. +*13:30, 41.

37. **Wheresoever.** ♪138C, Ge +22:14. Jb 39:29, 30. Is +√66:24. Ezk 39:4, 5, 11, 12-18. Da +*9:26, 27. Jl 3:2, 9-16. Am 9:1-4. Zp +*3:8. Zc 13:8, 9. 14:2. Mt 24:28. Jn x11:48. Ro 2:8, 9, 16. 1 Th 2:16. Re *16:14-16. 19:17-21. **the body.** Ezk √39:11-15. Da √7:11. Mt +*‖24:28. Re 19:18. Whatever interpretation and application is made here of the term "body," must consistently apply equally to the term "carcass" used in Mt +*‖24:28. To suggest the body is that of Christ, or believers, or the nation Israel, does not harmonize with Scripture. Rather, suggesting that "body" and "carcass" refer to the defeated armies gathered against Jerusalem at the end of the tribulation described in Ezk 39:17-21, seems to fit precisely, and is no doubt the event Christ is alluding to, reinforced by the mention of "eagles" directly in this connection, for the "feathered fowl" are invited to feast upon the carnage after that great battle (Ezk 39:17). To suggest that eagles here represent the Romans is not supported by the context, for the Romans are not otherwise alluded to in this passage, and the fall of Jerusalem in A.D. 70 is not the subject of this prophecy, for here these events take place at the second advent, when "the Son of man shall be revealed" (ver. 30). Neither is it necessary to regard the eagles as being angels, nor is it necessary to suggest that they are the saints (the position taken by Peters, *Theocratic Kingdom*, vol. 2, p. 320). They are literal eagles, birds of prey, gathered to feast literally upon the dead bodies left after the great battle of Ezk 39:4-6. Peters sees here the translation or rapture of the saints, which my notes (on ver. 34 and Mt 24:41) conclusively show to be a mistaken view. Peters further errs here when he takes the question "*Where, Lord*" to mean "i.e. when shall this be witnessed or made known" (vol. 2, p. 320, 321). But the question is not *when*, but *where*, and Peters' next statement that "the evidence of such a removal *will be openly shown when these very ones* shall be gathered together at the overthrow of Antichrist" (p. 321), citing Zc 14, Re 19, Jl 3, in "his efforts *to crush the Jews at Jerusalem*," in a "mighty confederation against the truth" (Peters, *Theocratic Kingdom*, vol. 2, p. 105), is correct in placing these events at Jerusalem, but incorrect in taking this to be the translation of the saints. "In comparing prophecy it is distinctly announced that he shall unite nations and armies into an expedition into Palestine and a siege against Jerusalem, Dan 11, last part and 12:1; Is 14:24-27; Jl 3; Zc 14; Re 14:20; Re 16:16; Ezk 38:8-19, and that he is to be destroyed by a revelation of Christ in Palestine, Ezk 38:21-23; 2 Th 2:8; Re 19:11-20, etc." (Peters, vol. 2, p. 105). This passage therefore answers the question *where*, not *when*, for Christ already informed them as to *when* these events would take place (ver.

30, at his advent). The eagles are not the saints, and there is not a reference here to the rapture or translation of the saints, for the rapture or translation of the saints logically must be prior to Christ's revelation in power and glory *with* his saints (Ps +*149:5-9. Zc +*14:5). **the eagles.** Dt ◐28:49. Ezk *39:27-30. Pr 30:17. Is ◐+*40:31. Ezk √39:17-21. Ho ◐8:1. Hab 1:8. Mt +*‖24:28. Re ◐4:7. *19:17-21. **be gathered together.** 1 S √17:44, 46. Ezk √39:4, 17.

LUKE 18

The parable of the unjust judge and the importunate widow, showing that men should pray without fainting, 1-8. That of the Pharisee and the publican, 9-14. Jesus receives and blesses little children, showing that his disciples should be like them, 15-17. He detects the covetousness of a young ruler; shows the dangers of riches; and promises great rewards to those, who forsake things present for his sake, 18-30. He foretells his own sufferings, death, and resurrection, 31-34. He opens the eyes of a blind man, 35-43.

1. **ought always.** ♪171D, Mk +16:20. T#1151. Lk 11:5-8. +*21:36. Ge 32:9-12, 24-26. 1 S +7:8 (T#1367). Jb 27:8-10. Ps 55:16, 17. 65:2. 86:3mg. +*102:17. 142:5-7. Is √62:6, 7. Je +*10:25. √29:12, 13. Ac 10:2. Ro *12:12. Ep *6:18. Ph √4:6. Col *4:2, 12. 1 Th √5:17. **to pray.** T#530. Jb 42:8. Pr *4:6. Is 55:6. Ezk 36:37. Mt 5:44. *6:9-13. +14:23 (T#64). 26:41. Ep *6:18. Col *4:2. 1 Th 3:10. *5:17, 18. 1 T 2:1-3, 8. He 4:15, 16. Ja *5:13, 16. 1 P *4:7. **and not to faint.** Ps 27:13. Jon 2:7. 2 C 4:1, 16. Ga √6:9. Ep 3:13. 2 Th 3:13. He 12:3-5.

2. **city.** Gr. certain city. Is 1:10. Ezk 16:26, 46. 20:7. Re 11:8. **which.** ver. 4. Ex 18:21, 22. 2 Ch *19:3-9. Jb 29:7-17. Ps 82:1-4. Is √10:1, 2. Je 22:16, 17. Ezk 22:6-8. Mi *3:1-3. Ro 3:14-18. 2 C 8:21. **regarded.** ver. 4. Lk 20:13. Pr 29:7. Is 33:8. Mt 21:37. Mk 12:6. He 12:9.

3. **a widow.** Dt 27:19. 2 S 14:5, etc. Jb 22:9. 29:13. Is *1:17, 21-23. =54:4, 5. Je 5:28. Re 18:7. **Avenge.** ver. 7, 8. Ps 79:1-3, 5. 54:5. 55:9. 143:12. Is 63:15. Ro +*6:10. 13:3, 4. **adversary.** Lk 12:58.

4. **he said.** Lk 12:17. 16:3. He *4:12, 13. **Though.** ♪185A, Lk +11:8. **fear not.** Ex +*9:30. **nor regard.** Lk 11:8.

5. **because.** Lk 11:8. Jg 16:16. 2 S 13:24-27. **continual coming.** Is 62:7. **weary.** ♪102, Ge +2:24. ver. 39. Mt 15:23. Mk 10:47, 48. 1 C 9:27.

6. **the Lord.** Lk 7:13. **unjust judge.** lit. judge of unrighteousness. Lk 16:8, 9. Ja 2:4.

7. **shall not.** ♪158, Mt +5:18. Lk *11:13. Mt *7:11. 15:22-28. Mk 7:24-30. 2 P √3:9. **avenge.** T#1436. Jg 16:27-30. 1 S *24:11-15. *26:10, 11. Ps *9:8, 18. 10:15-18. *54:1-7. +*58:10. Is *63:4. Je +*10:25. 20:11-13. 2 Th *1:6. Re +*6:10. 18:20. **elect.** Dt +*10:15. Mt +*24:22n, 23, 24, 31. Mk 13:20. Ro *8:28-30, 33. 11:28. Col 3:12. 1 Th 1:4. 5:9. 2 T +*2:10. T 1:1. 1 P 1:1, 2. 2:8, 9. 2 P +*1:10. Re 17:14. **which cry.** Lk *2:37. Ex +*22:23. Dt +*24:15. Ps *9:12. 22:2. *88:1. 1 Th *3:10. 1 T *5:5. 2 T *1:3. Re *7:15. **day and night.** Ps 32:4. 42:3. La 2:18. Mk ◐4:27. ◐5:5. Ac 9:24. Re 4:8. 7:15. 12:10. 14:11. 20:10. **though.** Ps 13:1, 2. Hab 2:3. He *10:35-37. Ja 5:7. 2 P √3:9.

8. **he will avenge.** Ps 46:5. 143:7-9. Ro +*12:19. 2 P 2:3. +*3:7-9. Re 6:10. 19:2. **speedily.** Hab 2:3. He

*10:37. Re 1:1. **when.** Lk 7:19. Mt 11:3. *24:9-13, 24, 44. 25:5. 1 Th *5:1-3. He 10:23-26. Ja *5:1-8. **Son of man.** Lk +5:24. Mt +*16:27n. **cometh.** Mt +16:28. +*24:◑3g, 30. **find.** Lk 17:26-30. Dt *32:20. Je *5:1. Ezk *22:30. +*33:31. Mt +*7:14. 24:12, 22, 38, 39. 1 Th 4:15, 17. **faith.** or, the faith. Lk 17:5. 1 T +*1:19. Ju +*3. Re 2:19. 13:10. 14:12. **on the earth.** Re +*5:10n. +*6:10g.

9. **which trusted.** ver. 14. Lk 10:29. 15:29. *16:15. Pr *30:12. Is +*65:5n. 66:5. Mt 5:20. Jn 9:28, 34. Ro 7:9. 9:31, 32. 10:3. Ph 3:4-6. **in themselves.** Lk 11:22. 2 C 1:9. He 2:13. **that they were righteous.** or, as being righteous. Pr 30:12. Is +*65:5n. Jn 7:48, 49. **and despised.** ver. 11. Lk 7:39. 15:2, 30. 19:7. 23:11. Is +*65:5n. Jn 7:47-49. 8:48. Ac 4:11. 22:21, 22. Ro 14:3, 10. 3 J *9.

10. **Two men.** Lk 1:53. **into.** ver. 14. Lk 1:9, 10. 19:46. 1 K 8:30. 10:5. 2 K 20:5, 8. 2 Ch 9:4. Jn 7:14. Ac 3:1. 10:9. **a Pharisee.** Lk +*7:29, 30. Mt 21:31, 32. Ac 23:6-8. 26:5. Ph 3:5. **a publican.** Lk 3:12.

11. **stood and.** ♪86, Is +3:16. ver. 13. 1 S 1:26. 1 K 8:14, 22. 2 Ch 6:12. Ps 134:1. 135:2. Mt 6:5. Mk 11:25. Ac 27:21. **God.** Is *1:15. *58:2, 3. Je 2:23, 35. Ezk +*33:31. Mi 3:11. 1 C 4:7, 8. 15:9, 10. 1 T 1:12-16. Re *3:17, 18. **as.** Lk 20:47. Is +*65:5n. Mt 3:7-10. 19:18-20. Ga 3:10. Ph 3:6. Ja 2:9-12. **extortioners.** Lk 11:39. Mt 23:25. 1 C 5:10, 11. 6:10.

12. **fast.** T#194. Lk 5:33. +*17:10. Nu 23:4. 1 S 15:13. 2 K 10:16. Jb +21:15 (T#689). Ps +106:13 (T#411). Is *1:15. 58:2-5. Zc 7:5, 6. Mt 6:1, 5, 16. 9:14. 15:7-9. Mk 2:18. Ro 3:27. *10:1-3. 1 C 1:29. 2 C +7:10 (T#609). Ga 1:14. +4:17 (T#623). Ep 2:9. 1 T 4:8. 2 T +3:5 (T#191). **week.** lit. sabbath. ♪171T3, Mt +28:1. **I give.** Lk 11:42. Le 27:30-33. Nu 18:24. Ml 3:8. Mt +*23:23, 24. **tithes of all.** T#1290. Lk +*11:41n, 42n. Ge 28:22. Dt *14:22, 23. 2 Ch 31:5. Ml 3:10. Mt 23:2, 3, +*23n. Mk 12:42.

13. **standing.** ♪86, Is +3:16. T#1284. ver. 11. Ge 24:12-14. Ex 33:10. 1 K 8:14, 22, 55. 2 K *23:3. 1 Ch ◑+17:16 (T#1283). 2 Ch 20:9, 13, 19. Ne 9:4, 5. Mk 11:25. **afar off.** Lk 5:8. 7:6, 7. 17:12. 23:49. Ezr 9:6. Jb 42:6. Ps 40:12. Is 6:5. Ezk 16:63. Da 9:7-9. Ac 2:37. **not lift.** Jb 22:29mg. **his eyes.** Lk 6:20. Ps *40:12. Jn 6:5. 17:1. **but smote.** T#1230. Lk 23:48. Je 31:18, 19. Mt 11:17. 2 C 7:11. **God.** Ps 25:7, 11. 41:4. +*51:1-3. 86:15, 16. 119:41. 130:3, 4, 7. Da *9:5, 9-11, 18, 19. He √4:16. 8:12. **merciful.** Ezr 9:6, 7. Ps +*4:1. 25:11. 40:12. 41:4. 51:1-17. 79:9. Ezk 16:63. Da 9:8, 19. He *2:17. 1 J *2:2. 4:10. **a sinner.** T#1387. Lk 15:18-21. 23:40-43. Ex 10:16, 17. 34:8, 9. Jg *10:10. 2 Ch 33:12, 13, 19, 23. Ps 51:1-9. 106:6. Is 1:18. *55:6, 7. 64:5, 6. Jon 3:4, 5. Mt 9:13. Mk +11:25 (T#1338). Ac 8:22. Ro *5:8, 20, 21. 1 T *1:15. 1 J √1:8-10.

14. **went.** Lk 5:24, 25. 7:47-50. 1 S 1:18. Ec 9:7. **justified.** Lk 7:35. 10:29. 16:15. Jb 9:20. 25:4. 33:32. Ps 143:2. Is 45:25. 50:8. 53:11. Hab √2:4. Ro *3:20. *4:5. *5:1, 9. 8:33. Ga 2:16. Ja 2:21-25. **rather than.** ♪63H, Ge +12:15. ♪96E1, Ps +118:1. T#1809. **for every.** Lk 1:52. 14:11. Ex 18:11. Jb 22:29. 40:9-13. Ps 138:6. Pr 3:34. 15:33. 16:18, 19. 18:12. 29:23. Is 2:11-17. +*57:15. Da 4:37. Hab 2:4. Mt +*5:3. 18:4. 23:12. Ja *4:6, 10. 1 P *5:5, 6. **he that humbleth.** T#537. Lk 14:11. Jg +10:15 (T#356). 2 Ch +√7:14. 33:12, 13. Ps *9:12. Pr +*28:13 (T#124). *29:23. Mt +8:8 (T#663). Ph 2:5-11. Ja *4:6, +10 (T#357). 1 P *5:5, 6.

15. **they brought.** 1 S 1:24. Mt 19:13-15. Mk 10:13-16. **infants.** Dt +*29:11n. Ne +*12:43. Jl +*2:16. 1 C +*7:14n. ✻S#1025g: Lk 1:41, 44 (babe). 2:12, 16. Ac 7:19 (children). 2 T +*3:15 (child). 1 P √2:2 (babes). **they rebuked.** ver. 39. Lk 9:49, 50, 54. Mt 20:31. Mk 10:48.

16. **Suffer.** Ge 17:10-14. 21:4. Dt 29:11. 31:12. 2 Ch 20:13. Je 32:39. Mt *18:3, 4. Ac +*2:39. 1 C +*7:14. **little children.** Lk 9:47. 1 C +*7:14n. **forbid them not.** Lk 9:50. Mk 9:39. **for.** Mt 18:3, 4. 1 C *14:20. 1 P √2:2. **the kingdom.** Lk +4:43.

17. **Verily.** ver. 29. Lk 4:24. 12:37. 21:32. 23:43. Mt +*5:18. Mk +3:28. Jn +1:51. **Whosoever.** Ps *131:1, 2. Mk *10:15, 16. Jn 3:3, 5. 1 P 1:14. **receive.** Lk +*8:13. Jn √1:12. Ja √1:21. **as.** Mt 18:3.

18. **a certain.** Mt 9:18. ‖19:16, etc. Mk ‖10:17, etc. Jn 3:1. **Good Master.** Lk 6:46. 7:40. Ezk +*33:31. Ml *1:6. Jn 7:12. 13:13-15. **what.** Lk 10:25. Jn 6:28. Ac *2:37. √16:30. **inherit.** ver. 30. Mt 19:16, 29. **eternal.** Gr. *aionios*, Mt +18:8. Ro *6:22, 23. 1 J √5:11-13.

19. **Why callest.** Lk +*1:35. 11:13. Jb 14:4. 15:14-16. 25:4. 1 T *3:16. He *7:26. Ja *1:17. 1 J *3:5. **good.** Hab 1:12. Mk 2:7. Jn *10:14. Ac 2:27. 3:14. **none is.** Ge +*6:5. Ro √3:23. **save one.** 1 S *2:2. Ps 89:6. *119:68. Ro 16:27. Re 15:4.

20. **knowest.** Lk 10:26-28. Is +*8:20. Mt 19:17-19. Mk 10:18, 19. Ro √3:20. 7:7-11. **Do not commit.** Ex 20:12-17. Dt 5:16-21. Ro 13:9. Ga √3:10-13. Ep +*6:2. Col 3:20. Ja √2:8-11. **adultery.** Ex +*♭20:14. Le 18:20. Dt ♭5:18. 22:22. Pr 6:32. Mt 5:27. Ro 13:9. 1 C +*6:9. He +*13:4. **kill.** Ge +*9:5, 6. Ex +*♭20:13. Dt ♭5:17. Mt 5:21. Ro 13:9. 1 J √3:15. **steal.** Ex +*♭20:15. Le *19:11. Dt ♭5:19. Ro 13:9. Ep √4:28. **bear false witness.** Ex +*♭20:16. 23:1. Dt ♭5:20. 19:16-20. Pr 19:5, 9. 21:28. 24:28. 25:18. **Honor thy.** Ex +*♭20:12. Le 19:3. Dt ♭5:16. Je 35:18, 19. Mt 15:4. Mk 7:10. Ep +*6:2. Col *3:20.

21. **All these.** ver. 11, 12. Lk 15:7, 29. √17:10. Mt √5:20. 19:20, 21. Mk 10:20, 21. Ro *10:2, 3. Ph *3:6. **from.** Ezk 4:14.

22. **Yet lackest.** T 1:5. 3:13. **one thing.** Lk +*10:42. Ps 27:4. Ph 3:13. Ja √2:10. 2 P 3:8. **sell.** Lk *12:33. *16:9. Mt 6:19, 20. Ac 2:44, 45. 4:34-37. 1 T √6:17-19. **treasure.** ♪22D5.O, Dt +28:12. **in heaven.** Mt √6:19, 20. **and come.** Lk 9:23, 57-62. Mt 19:21, 27, 28. **follow me.** Jn 1:43. Ph *3:6-9.

23. **when he heard.** Ezk +*33:31. **he was very sorrowful.** Jg 18:23, 24. Mt 19:22. 26:38. Mk 6:26. 10:22. 14:34. **very rich.** Lk +*8:14. √12:15. ◑*19:8. *21:34. Jb 31:24, 25. Ps *62:10. Mt 6:24. Mt +*13:22. *16:26. Ep √5:5. Ph *3:8. Col √3:5. 1 J √2:15, 16.

24. **he was.** Mk 6:26. 2 C √7:9, 10. **How hardly.** Dt 6:10-12. 8:11-17. Ps 10:3, 4. 73:5-12. Pr *11:28. 18:11. 30:9. Je 2:31. 5:5. Mt +*13:22. 19:23-25. Mk *10:23-27. 1 C 1:26, 27. 1 T √6:9, 10. Ja *2:5-7. +*5:1-6. **the kingdom.** Lk +4:43.

25. **For.** ♪138B, Ge +13:16. **easier.** Mk 10:25. **a camel.** Some would render *a cable*; but it may justly be doubted whether *kameelos* ever was so translated before, for the word for a cable, as the scholiast on Aristophanes (Vesp. 1130) expressly affirms, is written *kamilos*, not with an *eta*, but with an *iota*. This is the reading of a few MSS. but it evidently appears to be a gloss. It was a common mode of expression among the Jews. Hence Rabbi Shesheth said to Rabbi Amram,

who had advanced an absurdity, "Perhaps thou art one of the Pambidithians, who can make an elephant pass through the eye of a needle." Mt 23:24.

26. **Who.** Lk 13:23.

27. **The things.** Lk *1:37. Ge +*18:14. Jb *42:2. Je +*32:17, 27. Da *4:35. Zc 8:6. Mt *19:26. Mk 10:27. 14:36. Ep *1:19, 20. 2:4-10. He 6:6.

28. **Lo.** Lk *5:11. Mt 4:19-22. 9:9. 19:27. Mk 10:28. Ph 3:7-9. **left all.** T#674. Lk 5:11, 28. 14:33. Ge 22:10, 12. Jg +10:15 (T#356). Mt 4:20, 22. 10:37-39. 16:24-26. *19:29. Mk 1:18, 20. 8:34-37. +*10:28-30. Lk *14:26, 27, 33.

29. **Verily.** Lk 4:24. **There.** Lk 14:26-28, 33. Dt *33:8, 9, 11. Mt 10:37-39. 19:28-30. Mk +*10:29-31. **or.** ʃ129, Ezk +34:4. **for the kingdom.** Mt 19:29. Mk 10:29.

30. **Who.** Mk +*10:30. **not.** ʃ158, Mt +5:18. **manifold more.** Lk 12:31, 32. 2 Ch 25:9. Jb +*42:10. Ps 37:16. 63:4, 5. 84:10-12. 119:72, 103, 111, 127, 162. Is 40:2. 61:7. Ro *6:21-23. Ph *4:7. 1 T *4:8. 6:6. He +*13:5, 6. Re *2:10, 17. 3:21. **present time.** Ge ◑+*6:13 (T#566). Mt √6:33. +*12:32. Mk +*‖10:30. Ro 3:26. 8:18. 1 T +*4:8. He 9:9. **world.** Gr. *aion*, Mt +6:13. Lk 20:35. Mt +*12:32. Ep 1:21. 2:7. 2 T *4:8. He 6:5. **everlasting.** Gr. *aionios*, Mt +18:8. ver. 18. Mt 19:16.

31. **the twelve.** Mk 9:35. **Behold.** Lk 9:22. 24:6, 7. Mt 16:21. 17:22, 23. *20:17-19. Mk 8:31. 9:30, 31. *10:32-34. **we go.** Lk 9:51. 13:22. 17:11. 19:11, 28. **up to.** Lk 2:4. **and.** Lk 21:22. 24:44-46. Ps ch. 22, 69. Is ch. 53. Da +*9:26. Zc 13:7. Mt 1:22. 26:24. Jn 6:45. **Son of man.** Mt +5:24.

32. **delivered.** Lk 23:11, 12. Mt *27:2. Mk 15:1. Jn 18:28, 30, 32, 35. Ac 3:13, 14. **unto the Gentiles.** Mt 27:2. Jn 18:30, 31. Ac 2:23. 3:13. 4:27. 21:11. **mocked.** Lk 22:63-65. 23:11, 35. Ps *22:6, 7. *69:21. Is *50:6. 52:14. 53:3. Mi 5:1. Mt 26:67. 27:26-31. Mk 14:65. 15:17-20. Jn 18:22. 19:1-5. **spitefully.** Ac 14:5. **and spitted on.** Mt *26:67. Mk 14:65. 15:19.

33. **scourge.** Is *50:6. Mt 27:26. Jn *19:1. **and put.** Mk 8:31. **third day.** Lk 9:22. 24:7, 21-23. Ps +*16:10. Mt +*12:40n. 27:63, 64. Ac *2:29-32. 1 C +*15:3, 4.

34. **understood none.** Lk 2:50. *9:45. 24:25, 45. Ps 139:6. Mk 9:32. Jn 10:6. 12:16. 16:1-19. 1 C 2:10, 11. **was hid.** Lk 2:50. 9:45. 24:16. **neither knew.** ʃ144D, Ge +40:23.

35. **as.** Mt 20:29, 30. Mk 10:46, 47. **Jericho.** Lk 10:30. **begging.** Lk 16:20, 21. 1 S 2:8. Jn 9:8. Ac 3:2.

36. **he.** Lk 15:26. Mt 21:10, 11. **what it.** ʃ184D2, Lk +1:62.

37. **they.** Mk 2:1-3. Jn 12:35, 36. 2 C 6:2. **Jesus.** Lk 2:51. Mt 2:23. Jn 1:45. 19:19. Ac 2:22. 4:10. **of Nazareth.** Mk 1:24.

38. **Jesus.** Ps 62:12. Is +*9:6, 7. 11:1. Je +*23:5, 6. Mt 1:1. 9:27. 12:23. 15:22. 21:9, 15. 22:42-45. Ro 1:3. Re 22:16. **son.** ʃ171G, Ge +13:8. **have mercy.** Lk 17:13.

39. **rebuked.** ver. 15. Lk 8:49. 11:52. 19:39. Mt 19:13. **but.** Lk 11:8-10. 18:1. Ge 32:26-28. Ps 141:1. Je 29:12, 13. Mt *7:7. 26:40-44. 2 C *12:8. **son.** ʃ171G, Ge +13:8.

40. **stood.** Mt 20:31-34. Mk 10:48-52.

41. **What.** 1 K 3:5, etc. Mt *7:7. 20:21, 22. Mk 10:36. Ro 8:25. Ph √4:6.

42. **Receive.** Lk 7:21. Ps 33:9. 107:20. Mt 8:3. 15:28.

thy faith. Lk 7:50. 8:48. 17:19. Mt 9:22. Mk 5:34. **hath saved.** Lk 7:3. 8:36, 48, 50. Mk 10:52. Jn 11:12. Ac 4:9. Ja 5:15.

43. **immediately.** Lk 5:25. 8:44, 55. **he.** Ps 30:2. 146:8. Is 29:18, 19. 35:5. 42:16. 43:8. Mt 9:28-30. 11:5. 21:14. Jn 9:5-7, 39, 40. Ac 26:18. **followed.** Lk 4:39. 5:26. 17:15-18. Ps 103:1-3. 107:8, 15, 21, 22, 31, 32. Is 43:7, 8, 21. Ac 4:21. 11:18. Ga 1:24. 2 Th 1:10-12. 1 P *2:9. **glorifying.** Lk 7:16. 13:13. *17:15. **all the people.** Lk 5:26. 19:37. **gave praise.** Lk 13:17. 17:18. Ro 4:20. Re 4:9.

LUKE 19

The conversion of Zaccheus the publican, 1-10. The parable of a nobleman going to receive a kingdom, and entrusting money to his servants; with the account required of them; and the punishment of his enemies, 11-27. Jesus enters Jerusalem riding on an ass, amidst the acclamations of the multitude, 28-38. He answers the objections of the Pharisees, 39, 40; weeps over the city, and predicts its destruction, 41-44; drives the traders from the temple, 45, 46; and teaches daily there, while the rulers seek to kill him, 47, 48.

1. **entered.** Lk 18:35. Mt 20:29. Mk 10:46. **Jericho.** Lk 10:30. Jsh 2:1. 6:1, etc., 26. 1 K 16:34. 2 K 2:18-22.

2. **Zacchaeus.** i.e. *just, pure,* ✻S#2195g. ver. 5, 8. **the chief.** *Arkitelonees,* rather, "a chief publican," or tax gatherer. Probably *Zaccheus,* who appears from his name to have been a Jew, farmed the revenue of the district around Jericho, having others under him, who either rented of him smaller portions, or were employed as servants to collect the taxes. Lk 3:12. **and he.** Lk 18:24-27. 2 Ch 17:5, 6. **was rich.** 1 T *6:17.

3. **he sought.** Lk 9:7-9. 23:8. Jn 1:38. 12:21. **because.** Lk 12:25. **stature.** Lk 2:52.

4. **climbed.** Lk 5:19. **a sycamore.** Lk +17:6n. 1 K 10:27. 1 Ch 27:28n. 2 Ch 1:15. 9:27. Is 9:10. Am 7:14.

5. **he looked.** Ps 139:1-3. Ezk 16:6. Jn 1:48. 4:7-10. **Zaccheus.** Ec 9:10. 2 C +*6:1, 2. **for.** ver. 10. Ge 18:3-5. 19:1-3. Ps 101:2, 3. Jn *10:3. 14:23. Ep 3:17. He *13:2. Re √3:20. **I must.** Lk 13:33. **abide.** Jn 1:38, 40. Ac 16:15.

6. **he.** Lk 2:16. Ge 18:6, 7. Ps 119:59, 60. Ga 1:15, 16. **received.** Lk 10:38. **joyfully.** Lk 5:29. Is 64:5. Ac 2:41. 16:15, 34.

7. **they all murmured.** Lk 5:30. 7:34, 39. 15:2. 18:9-14. Mt 9:4, 11-13. 21:28-31. **guest.** Lk 9:12.

8. **the Lord.** Lk 7:13. **Behold.** Lk 3:8-13. 11:41. 12:33. *16:9. 18:22, 23. Ps 41:1. Mt 3:8. Ac 2:44-46. 4:34, 35. 2 C 8:7, 8. 1 T √6:17, 18. Ja 1:10, 11. **the half.** Mk 12:44. **I give.** Lk 18:22. **and if.** ʃ184A, 1 C +15:2. Assuming the actual fact, no doubt being thrown on it. Not a mere possible case (CB). **by false.** Lk 3:14. Ex 20:16. **accusation.** ʃ108J, Ge +43:18. **I restore.** Ex *22:1-4, 7. Le 5:16. 6:1-6. Nu *5:7. 1 S 12:3. 2 S 12:6. 1 K 20:34. 2 K 8:6. Ne *5:6-13. Pr *6:31. Ezk +*33:15n. Mt 5:23, 24, +26g. Ep +*4:28.

9. **unto him.** Rather, as Elsner renders *pros auton,* "concerning him;" for our Lord speaks of him in the third person. **This day.** Lk 2:30. 13:30. Jn 4:38-42. Ac √16:30-32. 1 C +*6:9-11. 2 C +*6:2. 1 P 2:10. **salvation come.** Jn 4:26. 9:37. Ac *16:31. 1 T *6:19. **house.** ʃ121J4, Ge +7:1. **forsomuch.** Lk 3:8. 13:16.

16:24, 25, 27, 30. Jn 8:33. Ac 3:25. Ro *4:11, 12, 16. Ga *3:7, 14, 29. **son.** ⌐171G, Ge +13:8.

10. **Son of man.** Lk +5:24. **come to.** Lk *5:31, 32. 15:4-7, 9, 32. Ge=37:16. Je 31:20. Ezk *34:11, 16. Mi *7:19. Mt *1:21. *5:17. +*9:12, 13. *10:6. 15:24. +*18:11. *20:28. Mk 2:17. *10:45. Jn 5:14. *10:10. Ro *5:6. 1 T *1:13-16. He *7:25. 1 J *3:8. *4:9-14. **to save.** Is *53:11. Mt 1:21. **lost.** Gr. *apollumi*, Mt +2:13. Ps 119:176. Mt +*10:28.

11. **was nigh.** ver. 28. Lk 9:51. 13:22. 17:11. 18:31. **to Jerusalem.** Is +*24:23. **they thought.** Lk +*17:20. +*24:21. Mk 1:15. Ac +*1:6, 7. 2 Th *2:1-3. **kingdom of God.** Lk +4:43. +*22:29, 30. Mt +*21:43. Jn +*18:36. **immediately appear.** Lk +√21:31.

12. **A certain.** Mt 25:14-30. Mk 13:34-37. **a far country.** Lk 20:9. 24:51. Mt 21:38. +√25:19. Mk 12:1. 16:19. Ac 1:9, 10. **to receive.** This statement in parable must not be taken to teach that the kingdom is in the third heaven, or that it is received in the third heaven, for prophecy is clear that the public investiture of the kingdom made by the Father to Christ takes place *on earth* (Da √7:13, 14), and that the kingdom promised by prophecy and covenant is earthly (Ep +*1:11n. 2 T +*4:18n). ver. 15. Mt 28:18. Da +*7:14. Lk +*1:32. Jn 18:37. 1 C *15:25. Ep 1:20-23. Ph 2:9-11. He 12:28n. 1 P 3:22. Re 11:15, 18. **a kingdom.** Da *2:44. Mt 25:34. Lk *22:29, 30. 2 T +*4:1. **and to return.** Mt 16:27. 19:28. 24:30. 25:31. Ac +*1:11. √17:31. He *9:28. Re +*1:7.

13. **his ten.** Mt 25:2, 14. Jn 12:26. Ga 1:10. Ja 1:1. 2 P 1:1. **delivered.** Mt 25:15. Ro 12:6-8. 1 C 12:7-11, 28, 29. 1 P *4:9-11. **pounds.** "*Mina*, here translated a *pound*, is 12 1/2 oz. which, according to 5*s* the ounce, is 3*l*. 2*s*. 6*d*." **Occupy.** Ezk 27:15, 21mg, 27. Da 8:27. Mt 25:16. **till I come.** Jn 21:22, 23. 1 C 11:26.

14. **his citizens.** ver. *27. 1 S *8:7. Ps *2:1-3. 35:19. 69:4. Is 49:7. Zc 11:8. Jn *1:11. *15:18, 23-25. *19:14, 15. Ac *3:14, 15. 4:27, 28. *7:51, 52. **We will not.** T#695. ver. 27. Ge=37:8. Nu 16:12. 1 K +11:4 (T#23). Jb *21:14. 27:22. Ps 12:4 (T#705). +14:1 (T#22). *30:11. Je +*6:16. Ezk +33:20 (T#272). Mt +*23:37. Jn +*5:40. Ro 1:28. 2 P +*3:5 (T#707).

15. **was returned.** Lk 10:35. **having received.** ver. 12. Ps *2:4-6. Da √7:14. Lk +*1:32. 1 C ◐√15:24. **money.** Gr. silver, and so ver. 23. **that he.** Lk +*12:48. *16:2, etc. Mt 18:23, etc. 25:19. Ro 14:10-12. 1 C 4:1-5.

16. **Lord.** 1 Ch 29:14-16. 1 C 4:7. 15:10. Col 1:28, 29. 2 T 4:7, 8. Ja 2:18-26.

17. **Well.** Ge 39:4. 1 S *2:30. Mt 25:21. Ro 2:29. 1 C *4:5. 2 T 2:10. 1 P 1:7. 5:4. Re 20:12. **been faithful.** Lk √16:10. 22:30. Da +*12:3. Mt *25:21. 1 C 4:2. 15:41. 1 T 3:13. Re *2:26-29. **authority.** ver. 19. Lk 12:44. Ps +*49:14. Mt ◐20:25. 24:47. Ep ◐6:9. Ja ◐5:6. Re +*5:10.

18. **thy pound.** Mt +*13:23. Mk 4:20. 2 C 8:12. **hath gained.** ver. 16. 1 C 4:7. 15:10.

19. **Be.** ver. 17. Lk 12:44. Is 3:10. Mt 24:47. 1 C 3:8. 15:41, 42, √58. 2 C 9:6. 2 J 8.

20. **Lord.** ver. *13. Lk *3:9. *6:46. Pr *26:13-16. Mt *25:24. Ja √4:17. **napkin.** lit. sweatrag for wiping perspiration from face. Mt +6:2n. 7:15. Lk 10:21. 13:32. 14:8-11, 16-24. 18:11, 12. 22:25. Jn 11:44. 20:7. Ac 19:12g.

21. **I feared.** Ex 20:19, 20. 1 S 12:20. Ps +√9:10. 18:23, 26. Mt 25:+*24n, 25. Ro 8:15. 2 T +√1:7. Ja

*2:19. 1 J *4:18. Re +*21:8. **because.** 1 S 6:19-21. 2 S 6:9-11. Jb 21:14, 15. Ezk 18:25-29. Ml *3:14, 15. Ro 8:7. Ju 15. **austere.** 1 S 25:3. **thou takest.** Lk 21:3. Mk 12:43, 44. 2 C 8:12. 9:7.

22. **Out.** 2 S 1:16. Jb 9:20. *15:5, 6. Mt *12:37. 22:12. Ro *3:19. **wicked servant.** Mt 18:32. **Thou knewest.** Mt 25:+*24n, 26, 27.

23. **Wherefore.** Ro 2:4, 5. **bank.** Mt 21:12. **might.** ⌐184B, Mt +23:30. **required.** Lk 3:13. **mine own.** Mt 25:27. **usury.** Ex 22:25-27. Dt 23:19, 20. Is +*24:2. Mt *25:27n.

24. **that stood by.** 1 K 10:8. 2 Ch 9:7. Est 4:5. **Take.** Lk *12:20. 16:2. Mt *21:43. **and give.** ver. 16. Lk *8:18. Ac *13:46.

25. **Lord.** Lk 16:2. 2 S 7:19. Is √55:8, 9.

26. **That unto.** Lk +*8:18. +*12:48. 18:29, 30. Mt +*13:12. 19:29. 25:28, 29. Mk 4:25. +*10:29, 30. Jn *15:1-3. Ja 4:6. **and from.** That is, the *poor man*, who possesses but *little*. Lk 16:3. 1 S *2:30. 15:28. 2 S 7:15. Ps 109:8. Ezk 44:12-16. Mt 21:43. Ac 1:20. 2 J 8. Re 2:3. 3:11.

27. **mine enemies.** ver. 14, 42-44. Lk 21:22, 24. Nu 14:36, 37. 16:30-35. Ps 2:3-5, 9. 21:8, 9. 69:22-28. Is 66:6, 14. Na 1:2, 8. Mt 21:37-41. *22:7. 23:34-36. 1 C *15:25. 1 Th *2:15, 16. He 10:13. Re 19:11-21. **would not.** ver. +*14. Nu 16:12. Jb *21:14. Ro +*9:20. **and slay.** Lk 20:16. 1 S 15:33. Mt *21:41. 22:7. Mk 12:9.

28. **he went.** Lk 9:51. 12:50. 18:31. Jsh 3:11. Ps *40:6-8. Mk 10:32-34. Jn +*10:4. 18:11. He *12:2. 1 P 4:1. **ascending.** ver. 11. Lk 2:4. 9:51. 10:30. 13:22. 17:11. 18:31.

29. **when.** Zc 9:9. Mt 21:1, etc. Mk 11:1, etc. Jn 12:12-16. **Bethany.** ver. 37. Lk 24:50. Mt 21:17. 26:6. Mk 11:1, 11, 12. 14:3. Jn 11:1, 18. 12:1. **Mount of Olives.** ver. 37. Lk 21:37. 22:39. 2 S 15:30. Ne 8:15. Ezk 11:23. Zc 14:4. Mt 21:1. +*24:3. 26:30. Mk 11:1. 13:3. 14:26. Jn 8:1. Ac 1:12. **sent two.** Lk 22:8. Mk 14:13.

30. **Go ye.** ver. 32. Lk 22:8-13. 1 S 10:2-9. Jn 14:29. **whereon yet.** Lk 23:53. Nu 19:2. Dt 21:3. Jg 15:13. 16:11. 1 S 6:7. Ps=8:6. +*104:30. Mk ‖11:2. Jn 19:41. **loose him.** 1 S 8:16.

31. **And if.** ⌐184C, Mt +4:9. **the Lord.** Lk +7:13. Ps 24:1. 50:10-12. Mt *21:2, 3. Mk 11:3-6. Ac 10:36. **hath need.** ver. 34. Ps 50:10.

32. **went.** Lk 5:5. 6:47. Jn 2:5, 7. **as he had said.** Lk 21:33. 22:13. 1 K 8:56. Ps 93:5. 111:7. Ezk 12:25. Da 9:12. Mt 5:18. 17:27. Ro 4:16.

33. **the owners.** Mk 11:5.

34. **The Lord hath need.** Zc 9:9. Mk 11:6. Jn 10:35. 12:16. 2 C √8:9.

35. **they cast.** 2 K 9:13. Mt 21:7, 8. Mk 11:7, 8. Jn *12:14, 15. Ga 4:15, 16. **they set.** Zc *9:9.

36. **as he went.** Mt 21:8. **they spread.** 2 K 9:13.

37. **at the descent.** ver. 29. Mk 13:3. 14:26. **the mount.** ver. 29. **the whole.** Lk 7:16. 18:43. Ex 15:1, etc. Jg 5:1, etc. 2 S 6:2-6. 1 K 8:55, 56. 1 Ch 15:28. 16:4, etc. 2 Ch 29:28-30, 36. Ezr 3:10-13. Ps 106:12, 13. Jn 12:12, 13. **for all.** Jn 12:17, 18.

38. **Blessed.** Lk 13:35. Ps 72:17-19. ▶118:22-26. Ezk 34:23, 24. Zc *9:9. Mt 21:9. 23:39. Mk *11:9, 10. Jn 12:12, 13. **the King.** Mt 25:34. **peace.** Lk *2:10-14. Ps 148:1. Ro *5:1. Ep *2:14-18. Col *1:20. **glory.** Ep 1:6, 12. 3:10, 21. 1 T +*1:17. 1 P 1:12. He 5:9-14. 19:1-6.

39. And some. Mt *21:15, 16. **Master.** Lk 7:40. **rebuke.** Is 26:11. Mt +*23:13. Jn 11:47, 48. 12:10, 19. Ac 4:1, 2, 16-18. Ja 4:5.

40. if these. ℐ184A, 1 C +15:2. **the stones.** Ps 96:11. 98:7-9. 114:1-8. Is *55:12. Hab 2:11. Mt 3:9. 21:15, 16. 27:45, 51-54. 2 P 2:6.

41. beheld the city. Lk 13:34, 35. 23:28-31. Mt *23:37-39. Ac 17:16. **and wept.** ℐ141, Is +22:4. Ge=42:24. 2 K 8:11. Ps 119:53, *136, 158. 126:6. Je 9:1. 13:17. 17:16. Ho 11:8. Mk 3:4. Jn *11:35. Ac *20:31. Ro 9:2, 3. Ph 3:18. He 5:7.

42. If. ℐ184B, Mt +23:30. Second class condition, determined as unfulfilled. This form of expressing a wish is used where the desire cannot be, or has not been, realized (Webster and Wilkinson, *Greek Testament*). T#372. Lk 13:9. Dt *5:29. *32:29. Ps 47:7. 81:13-15. 107:43. +119:68 (T#224). +145:9 (T#228). Is *48:18. Je 5:3. Ezk 18:31, 32. *33:11. Jon +4:2 (T#233). **in this.** ver. 44. Ps 32:6. 95:7, 8. Is √55:6. Jn *12:35, 36. 2 C *6:1, 2. **thy day.** ℐ121P4, Dt +4:32. **the things.** Lk 1:77-79. 2:10-14. 10:5, 6. Ac 10:36. 13:46. He 3:7, 13, 15. +*10:26-29. 12:24-26. **peace.** ℐ37C, Ge +25:22. **but now.** Is *6:9, 10. 29:10-14. 44:18. Mt *13:14, 15. Jn 12:38-41. Ac 28:25-27. Ro 11:7-10. 2 C 3:14-16. 4:3, 4. 2 Th √2:9-12.

43. the days. Lk 17:22. +*21:20-24. 23:29. Dt *28:49-58. Ps 37:12, 13. Da +*9:26, 27. Mt *22:7. 23:37-39. Mk 13:14-20. 1 Th *2:15, 16. **cast.** Or, "cast a *bank*" or *rampart, karax.* This was literally fulfilled when Jerusalem was besieged by Titus; who surrounded it with a wall of circumvallation in three days, though not less than 39 furlongs in circumference; and when this was effected, the Jews were so enclosed on every side, that no person could escape from the city, and no provision could be brought in. 2 K 19:32. Ec 9:14. Is 29:1-4. 37:33. Je 6:3-6. Ezk 4:2. 21:22. 26:8. Hab 1:10. **and compass.** Lk 21:20. Je 4:17. 6:3.

44. lay. ℐ63H, Ge +12:15. Lk 21:6. 1 K 9:7, 8. 2 K 8:12. Ps 137:9. Is 13:16, 18. Ho 10:14. 13:16. Mi *3:12. Na 3:10. **thy children.** Lk 13:34, 35. Mt 23:37, 38. **leave.** Lk 21:6. 2 S 17:13. Mi 1:6. Mt *24:2. Mk 13:2. **because.** ver. 42. Lk 1:68, 78. La 1:8. Da *9:24. Jn √3:18-21. 1 P 2:12. **time of.** Lk *12:56. Je +*8:12. Mt 16:3. **visitation.** Lk *1:68, 69, 77-79. Ge 50:24. Jb 29:2. Je 6:6. 1 P 2:12.

45. went. Mt 21:12, 13. Mk *11:15-17. Jn *2:13-17. **sold.** Dt 14:25, 26.

46. It is written. Ps 93:5. Is ⸥56:7. Je *7:11. Ezk 43:12. Ho 12:7. Mt 23:14. Lk +*24:27. **house of prayer.** 1 K 8:29, 30, 41-43. 2 Ch 6:40. **den of thieves.** Je ⸥7:11. Ezk 7:22. Mt 21:13. Mk 11:17.

47. taught. Lk 20:1. 21:37, 38. Mt 21:23. 26:55. Mk 11:27, etc. Jn 18:20. **the chief priests.** Mt *21:15. 26:3, 4. Mk *11:18. 12:12. 14:1. Jn 7:19, 44. 8:37-40. 10:39. 11:53-57. **the chief.** Mk 6:21. **sought.** Lk 20:19. Mt 21:46. **destroy.** Gr. *apollumi*, Mt +2:13.

48. could. Lk 20:19, 20. 22:2-4. Mt 22:15, 16. **the people.** Mt *7:28, 29. **were very attentive to hear him.** *or*, hanged on him. lit. "they hung upon him hearing," which is beautifully expressive of their earnest attention, and high gratification. Ne 8:3. Mk *12:37. Jn *7:46-49. Ac 16:14.

LUKE 20

Jesus answers those who demand by what authority he acts, 1-8; speaks the parable of the vineyard let out to wicked husbandmen, 9-18; shows that tribute should be paid to Caesar, 19-26; confutes the Sadducees, concerning the resurrection of the dead; and puts all his adversaries to silence, 27-40; inquires how Christ was both David's Son, and David's Lord, 41-44; and warns the people against the ambitious and hypocritical Scribes, 45-47.

1. that. Lk 19:47, 48. Mk 11:27. Jn 18:20. **taught.** Ac 5:42. 15:35. **the chief.** 1 Ch ch. 24. **came upon.** Lk 2:9, 48. 4:39. 10:40. 21:34. 24:4. Ac 4:1. 6:12. 10:17. 11:11. 12:7. 17:5. 22:13, 20. 23:11, 27. 28:2.

2. Tell. Lk 19:35-40, 45, 46. Mt 21:23-27. Mk 11:28-33. Jn *7:15. **who.** Ex 2:14. Jn 2:18. 5:22-27. Ac 4:7-10. 7:27, 35-39, 51.

3. I will. Lk 22:68. Mt 15:2, 3. Col 4:6.

4. baptism. Lk 7:28-35. Mt 11:7-19. 17:11, 12. 21:25-32. Jn 1:6, 19-28. **from.** Lk 15:18. Da 4:25, 26.

5. If. ℐ184C, Mt +4:9. **Why.** Lk *7:30. Jn 1:15-18, 30, 34. *3:26, 36. 5:33-35. Ac 13:25.

6. if. ℐ184C, Mt +4:9. **all.** Mt 21:26, 46. 26:5. Mk 12:12. Ac 5:26. **for.** Lk 1:76. 7:26-29. Mt *14:5. 21:26. Jn 10:41.

7. that. Is *6:9, 10. 26:11. 29:9-12, 14. 41:28. 42:19, 20. 44:18. Je 8:7-9. Zc 11:15, 17. Ml 2:7-9. Jn √3:19, 20. 9:39. 2 Th 2:10-12. 2 T 3:8, 9. 2 P 3:3.

8. Neither tell. Lk 22:68. Jb 5:12, 13. Pr 26:4, 5. Mt +*15:14. 16:4. 21:27. Mk 11:33.

9. this. Mt 21:33, etc. Mk 12:1, etc. **planted.** Dt 32:32, 33. Ps 80:8-14. Is *⸥5:1-7. 27:2-6. Je *2:21. Ezk 15:1-6. 19:10-14. Ho 10:1. Jl 1:7. Mt 21:28. Jn 15:1-8. 1 C 3:6-9. **and let.** SS 8:11, 12. **husbandmen.** Dt 1:15-18. 16:18. 17:8-15. **went.** Lk 15:13. 19:12. Mt 25:14, 15. Mk 13:34. **for.** ℐ63H, Ge +12:15. **long time.** Dt *28:59. Ho *3:4, 5. Mt +√25:19.

10. the season. Ps +*1:3. Je 5:24. Mt 21:34-36. Mk 12:2-5. **sent.** Jg 6:8-10. 2 K 17:13. 2 Ch *36:15, 16. Ne 9:30. Je 25:3-7. 26:2-6. 35:15. 44:4, 5. Ho 6:4-6. Zc 1:3-6. 7:9-13. Jn √15:16. Ro 7:4. **beat.** Lk 11:47-50. 13:34. 1 K 18:13. 22:24-27. 2 K 6:31. 21:16. 2 Ch 16:10. 24:19-21. 26:15, 16. Ne *9:26. Je 2:30. 20:2. 26:20-24. 29:26, 27. 37:15, 16. 38:4-6. 44:4. Mt 5:12. 22:6. 23:34, 37. Ac *7:52. 2 C 11:24-26. 1 Th *2:15. He *11:36, 37.

11. sent another. Mt 22:4. **entreated.** Mt 23:30-37. Ac 5:41. 7:52. 1 Th 2:2. He 11:36, 37. **and sent.** Lk 1:53. Ge 31:42. Dt 15:13. 1 S 6:3. Jb 22:9. Ho 10:1.

12. wounded. Lk 10:34. Ac 19:16g. **cast.** Lk 13:33, 34. 1 K 22:24-27. 2 Ch 24:19-22. Ne 9:26. Ac 7:52. 1 Th 2:15. He 11:36, 37.

13. What. Is 5:4. Ho 6:4. 11:8. **I will send.** Lk 9:35. Ge=37:13. Mt 3:17. 17:5. Jn 1:34. √3:16, 17, 35, 36. Ro 8:3. Ga *4:4. 1 J 4:9-15. **my beloved son.** Mt 3:17. Mk 12:6. **it may.** Je 36:3, 7. **reverence.** Lk 18:2.

14. reasoned. ver. 5. Mt 16:7. 21:25. **the heir.** Ps *2:1-6, 8. 89:27. Mt 2:2-16. Jn 1:11. Ro 8:17. He *1:2. **let.** ver. 19. Lk 19:47. 22:2. Ge 37:18-20. 1 K 21:19. Mt 27:21-25. Jn 11:47-50. Ac 2:23. 3:15.

15. they. He 13:12. **cast him out.** 2 Ch=13:9. **What.** Mt 21:37-40. Mk 12:6-9.

16. come. 2 S 12:5, 6. Mt 24:50. 25:19. **destroy.** Gr. *apollumi*, Mt +2:13. Lk 19:27. Ps 2:8, 9. 21:8-10. Mt 21:41. *22:7. Ac *13:46. **shall give.** Ne 9:36, 37. Mt 8:11, 12. 21:43. Mk 12:9. Ac *13:46. 18:6. 28:28. **to others.** Jn *10:16. **God forbid.** Ro 3:4, 6, 31. 6:2, 15. 7:7, 13. 11:1, 11. 1 C 6:15. Ga 2:17. 3:21. 6:14.

17. beheld. Lk 19:41. 22:61. 2 K 8:11. Mt 19:26.

Mk 3:5. 10:23. **What**. Lk 22:37. 24:44. Jn 15:25. **The stone**. Ps ▶118:22. Is *28:16. Zc 3:9. Mt *21:42. Mk 8:31. 12:10. Ac 4:11. Ep 2:20. 1 P *2:7, 8. **the head**. Jb 38:6. Je 51:26. Zc 4:7.

18. **shall fall**. This is an allusion to the Jewish mode of stoning. "The place of stoning was twice as high as a man. From the top of this one of the witnesses struck the culprit on the loins, and felled him to the ground: if he died of this, well; if not, the other witness threw a stone upon this heart," etc. Our Lord seems to refer not only to the dreadful crushing of the Jews by the Romans, but also to their general dispersion to the present day. Lk 2:34. Is *8:14, 15. Da *2:34, 35, 44, 45. Zc 12:3. Mt 21:44. Ro 9:32, 33. 1 C 1:23, 24. 1 Th 2:16. 1 P 2:8. **grind**. Is 17:13. Je 31:10. Am 9:9.

19. **the same**. ver. 14. Lk 19:47, 48. Mt 21:45, 46. 26:3, 4. Mk 12:12. **they feared**. Lk 22:2. Mt 14:5. 21:11, 26. Mk 11:32. Ac 5:26.

20. **they watched**. 1 S 19:11. Ps *37:32, 33. 38:12. Is 29:20, 21. Je 11:19. 18:18. 20:10. Zc 3:9. Mt 22:15, 18. Mk 6:20. 12:13, 15. **feign**. 2 S 14:2. 1 K 14:2-6. Ps 66:3. 81:15mg. 2 P 2:3. **take hold**. ver. 26. Lk 11:54. Ps 56:5. Mk 3:2. **they might deliver**. Mt 27:2. Jn 18:28-32. **power and**. Lk 12:11. 1 C 15:24. **the governor**. Mt 27:2, 11. 28:14. Ac 23:24.

21. **Master**. Ps 12:2. 55:21. Je 42:2, 3. Mt 22:16. 26:49, 50. Mk 12:14. Jn 3:2. **sayest**. 2 C 2:17. Ga 1:10. 1 Th 2:4, 5. **acceptest**. 2 Ch 19:7. Jb 34:19. Ac 10:34, 35. Ga 2:6. **the way**. Lk 1:76. 3:4. Ps 27:11. Mt 3:3. 22:16. Mk 1:3. 12:14. Jn 1:23. Ac 9:2. 13:10. 18:25, 26. Ro 11:33. He 3:10. Re 15:3. **truly**. *or*, of a truth.

22. **lawful**. Dt 17:15. Ezr 4:13, 19-22. 9:7. Ne 5:4. 9:37. Mt 22:17-21. Mk 12:14-17. Ac 5:37. **give tribute**. Lk 23:2. Mt 17:25. Ro +*13:6. **unto Caesar**. Lk 2:1. 3:1. 23:2. Jn 19:12, 15. Ac 17:7.

23. **he perceived**. Lk 5:22. 6:8. 11:17. Jn +*2:24, 25. 1 C 3:19. He *4:13. **craftiness**. 1 C 3:19. 2 C 4:2. 11:3. 12:16. Ep 4:14. **Why**. ver. 20. Lk 11:16, 53, 54. Ps 95:9. Mt 16:1. 22:18. 1 C 10:9.

24. **a penny**. See Mt 18:28mg. 20:2. **image**. The image was the head of the emperor: the superscription his titles. Julius Caesar was the first who caused his image to be struck on the Roman coin; and Tiberius was the emperor at this time. This therefore was a denarius of Caesar, and consequently this was respecting the tribute required by the Roman government. **Caesar's**. ver. 22. Lk 2:1. 3:1. 23:2. Ac 11:28. 25:8-12. 26:32. Ph 4:22.

25. **Render**. Pr 24:21. Mt *17:27. 22:21. Mk 12:17. Ro *13:6, 7. 1 P *2:13-17. **unto God**. Pr 23:26. Ac +*4:19, 20. +*5:29. 1 C *6:20. 10:31. 1 T 2:2. 1 P 4:11.

26. **they could**. ver. 20, 39, 40. Jb 5:12, 13. Pr +*21:30. 26:4, 5. 2 T 3:8, 9. **and they marvelled**. Lk 13:17. Mt 22:12, 22, 34. Mk 5:20. Jn 7:15. Ro 3:19. T 1:11.

27. **the Sadducees**. Mt 3:7. 16:1, 6, 11, 12. 22:23, etc. Mk 12:18, etc. Ac 4:1, 2. 5:17. 23:6-8. 1 C 15:12. 2 T 2:17, 18. **which deny**. Ac 4:1, 2. 23:8. 1 C 15:12.

28. **Master**. ver. 21, 39. Lk 7:40. **Moses wrote**. ver. 37. Lk 16:29. Ge 38:8, 11, 26. Dt ▶25:5-10. Ru 1:11, 12. 3:9. Jn 1:45. 5:45, 46. 7:23. Ac 3:22. 15:21. Ro 9:15. 10:5, 19. 2 C 3:15. **If**. ᵴ184C, Mt +4:9.

29. **and died**. Le 20:20. Je 22:30.

32. **died**. Jg 2:10. Ec 1:4. 9:5. He +*9:27.

33. **in the resurrection**. Mt 22:24-28. Mk 12:19-23.

34. **The children**. Lk 10:6. 16:8. **world**. Gr. *aion*, Mt +6:13. **marry**. Lk 17:27. 1 C 7:2, etc. Ep 5:31. He +*13:4.

35. **accounted worthy**. Lk +√21:36. Mt 22:8. Ac 5:41. 2 Th 1:5, 11. Re 3:4. **to obtain**. Da +*12:2, 3. Jn *5:29. Ac 24:15. He *11:35. **that**. Jn +√6:54n. **world**. Gr. *aion*, Mt +6:13. Lk 18:30. Is 64:5. Mk +*10:30. **the resurrection**. lit. the resurrection that out of dead ones, or the resurrection, that one out of or from among dead ones (Peters, *Theocratic Kingdom*, vol. 2, p. 299). Lk +*14:14. **from**. Gr. *ek*, a preposition which in this construction signifies *out of, from, from among*, and when used before a genitive signifies *a whole* from which *a part* is taken, as at Ac 3:23; 19:33; 1 C 5:13; He 5:1 (See Peters, *Theocratic Kingdom*, vol. 2, p. 298). Ac 4:2. Ph +*3:11. 1 P 1:3. **neither**. Lk 17:27. Is +*54:1. Mt +*22:29. 24:38. Mk +*12:24.

36. **Neither can**. Is *25:8. Ho *13:14. Jn 11:25. Ro 6:9. 1 C 15:26, 42, *53-55. Ph 3:21. 1 Th 4:13-17. Re *20:6. +*21:4. 22:2-5. **they are**. Ge 1:26. Ps 82:6. Zc 3:7. Mt √22:30. Mk *12:25. 1 C *15:49, 52. Re 5:6-14. 7:9-12. 22:9. **equal unto**. Ps ◐+*8:5. 1 C ◐+*6:3. **the children of God**. Ro *8:17-23. 1 C 15:52. Ga *3:26. 1 J *3:1, 2. **being the children**. Lk +10:6. **of the resurrection**. Lk +*14:14. Is +*26:19. *54:1. Ro 8:23.

37. **even Moses**. ver. 28. Ex ▶3:2-6. Dt 33:16. Ac 7:30-32. **when**. There is a remarkable passage in Josephus (De Maccab. c. 16), which proves that the best informed among the Jews believed in the immateriality and immortality of the soul, and the souls of righteous men were in the presence of God in a state of happiness. "They who lose their lives for the sake of God, *live* unto God, as do Abraham, Isaac, and Jacob, and the rest of the patriarchs." Not less remarkable is a passage in *Shemoth Rabba* (fol. 159.1), "Why doth Moses say (Ex 32:13), Remember Abraham, Isaac, and Jacob? R. Abin saith, The Lord said unto Moses, I look for ten men from thee, as I looked for that number in Sodom. Find me out ten righteous persons among the people, and I will not destroy thy people. Then saith Moses, Behold, here am I, and Aaron, Eleazar and Ithamar, Phinehas, and Caleb, and Joshua; but, saith God, there are but seven: where are the other three? When Moses knew not what to do, he saith, O Eternal God, *do those live who are dead?* Yes, saith God. Then saith Moses, If those that are dead do live, remember Abraham, Isaac, and Jacob." Ge +*17:7. +*28:13, 21. 32:9. Mt 22:31-33. Mk 12:26, 27. Ro 11:2. **he calleth**. Ex ▶3:15. Ac 7:32. **the God**. Lk 16:22. Mt +*8:11. Ac 3:13.

38. **For he**. Mt +*22:32. **a God**. Ps 16:5-11. 22:23-26. 23:4. 145:1, 2. He 11:16. **for all**. Jn 6:57. 11:25, 26. 14:19. Ro 6:10, 11, 22, 23. *14:7-9. 2 C *5:15. 6:16. 13:4. Ga 2:19. Col 3:3, 4. 1 Th 5:10. He 9:14. 1 P 4:2. Re 7:15-17. 22:1.

39. **thou**. Mt 22:34-40. Mk 12:28-34. Ac 23:9.

40. **durst not ask**. Lk 14:6. Pr 26:5. Mt 22:46. Mk 12:34.

41. **How**. Mt 22:41, 42. Mk 12:35, etc. **Christ**. Lk 3:15. 18:38, 39. Is +*9:6, 7. *11:1, 2. Je +*23:5, 6. 33:15, 16, 21. Mt 1:1. Jn 7:42. Ac 2:30. Ro *1:3, 4. Re 22:16. **David's son**. Mt 1:1.

42. **himself**. Lk 24:44. 2 S 23:1, 2. Mt 22:43. Mk 12:36, 37. Ac 1:20. 13:33-35. He 3:7. **The Lord**. Ps *▶110:1. Mt 22:44, 45. Ac 2:30, 34, 35. 4:25. 1 C *15:25.

He 1:13. 10:12, 13. **Sit thou.** 1 K 2:19. Ps 45:9. Mt 20:21, 23. Mk 10:37, 40.

43. **thine enemies.** Lk 19:27. Ps 2:1-9. 21:8-12. 72:9. 109:4-20. 110:5, 6. Re 19:14-21. **thy footstool.** Jsh 10:24. 1 K 5:3. Is 66:1. Ac 7:49.

44. **how.** Lk 1:31-35. 2:11. Is +*7:14. Mt +*1:23. Ro *1:3, 4. *9:5. Ga *4:4. 1 T 3:16. Re 22:16.

45. **in the audience.** Ezk 22:25. Mt 15:10. 23:1. Mk 8:34. 12:38. 1 T *5:20.

46. **Beware.** Lk 12:1. Mt 16:6. Mk 8:15. 2 T 4:15. **which desire.** Lk 11:43. 14:7. Pr 29:23. Mt *23:5-7. Mk 12:38, 39. Ro 12:10. Ph +*2:3-5. 3 J 9. **love greetings.** Lk 11:43. **the markets.** Lk 7:32. Mt 11:16. 20:3. Mk 6:56. 7:4. Ac 16:19. 17:17. **chief rooms.** Lk 14:7, 8.

47. **devour.** Lk 11:39. 16:14. Ex +*22:22-24. Is 10:2. Je 7:6-10. Ezk 22:7. Am +*2:7. 8:4-6. Mi 2:2, 8, 9. 3:2, 3. Mt 23:14. Mk 12:40. 2 C 11:20. 2 T 3:6. **for a show.** Lk 12:1. Ezk +*33:31. Mt 6:5, 7. 23:26-28. 1 Th 2:5. 2 T 3:2-5. T 1:16. **the same.** Lk *10:12-14. +*12:47, 48. Mt +*11:22-24. Ja 3:1.

LUKE 21

Christ prefers the widow's two mites to the large offerings of the rich, 1-4. He foretells the destruction of the temple, 5, 6; the signs and calamities which would precede and accompany it, giving suitable exhortations and promises, 7-19; and the destruction and continued desolations of Jerusalem, 20-24. The signs of his coming, 25-33. He exhorts to watchfulness and prayer, 34-36. He daily preaches at the temple, and retires at night to the mount of Olives, 37, 38.

1. **and saw.** Mk 7:11-13. *12:41-44. **casting.** 2 K *12:9. 2 Ch 24:10. **the treasury.** Jsh 6:19, 24. 1 K 14:26. 2 K 24:13. 2 Ch 36:18. Ne 13:13. Mt 27:6. Jn 8:20.

2. **mites.** Lk 12:59. See Mk 12:42mg.

3. **Of.** Lk 4:25. 9:27. 12:44. Ac 4:27. 10:34. **more than.** Lk 11:41mg. Ex 35:21-29. Jg 19:20. Ps 34:9. Mk 12:43, 44. 14:8, 9. 2 C √8:2, 3, 12. √9:6, 7.

4. **offerings.** ʃ121.O, Ge +28:22. **of.** ʃ181E, Ge +3:24. Ep ●2:8. **of her penury.** Ph 4:11. **all the living.** Lk 8:43. 15:12, 30. Dt 16:16. 1 Ch 21:24. Ac *2:44, 45. 4:34. 1 J 3:17.

5. **as some spake.** Mt 24:1, etc. Mk 13:1, etc. Jn 2:20. **how.** ʃ143, Ge +19:2.

6. **As for.** ʃ15A. Anacoluthon; or, Non-sequence B720. Sometimes the accusative stands alone at the beginning of a sentence. For other instances of this figure see Ac 10:36. Ro (8:3). **days will come.** Lk 17:22. **there shall not.** Lk *19:44, etc. 1 K 9:7-9. 2 Ch 7:20-22. Is 64:10, 11. Je 7:11-14. 26:6, 9, 18. La 2:6-8. 4:1. 5:18. Ezk 7:20-22. Da +*9:26, 27. Mi *3:12. Zc 11:1. 14:2. Mt *24:2. Mk 13:2. Ac 6:13, 14.

7. **Master.** Lk 7:40. **when.** ver. 32. Da 12:6, 8. Mt +*24:3. Mk 13:3, 4. Jn 21:21, 22. Ac +*1:6, 7. **what.** ver. 20, 21, 27, 28. Mt 24:15, 16. Mk 13:14.

8. **Take heed.** Je 29:8. Mt +*24:4, 5, 11, 23-25. Mk 13:5, 6, 9, 21-23, 33. 2 C √11:13-15. Ep 5:6. Col 2:8. 2 Th *2:3, 9-11. 2 T 3:13. 1 J 3:7. 4:1. 2 J 7. Re 12:9. **for many.** Such were Simon Magus (Ac 8:9, 10); Dositheus the Samaritan (Origin, Cont. Cels. i. 1); Theudas, when Fadus was procurator (Josephus, Ant. l. xx. c. 4. sec. 1); and numerous impostors who arose when Felix was procurator, who "were apprehended

and killed every day" (Josephus, Ant. l. xx. c. 7. sec. 5). Je 14:14. 23:21, 25. 27:15. Mt 24:23, 24. Mk 13:21, 22. Jn *5:43. Ac 5:36, 37. 8:9, 10. 1 J *2:18. **in my name.** Lk 9:48. **I am.** Jn +*8:24. **and the time.** *or*, and, The time. Mt 3:2. 4:17. Mk 1:15. Re 1:3.

9. **when.** ver. 18, 19. Ps 27:1-3. 46:1, 2. 112:7. Pr *3:25, 26. Is 8:12. 51:12, 13. Je 4:19, 20. Mt +*24:6-8. Mk 13:7, 8. **commotions.** 1 C 14:33. 2 C 6:5. 12:20. Ja 3:16. **terrified.** Lk 24:37. **must.** Lk 13:33. **come to pass.** Da ♭2:28. Re 1:1. **but.** ver. 8, 28. **the end.** Je *4:27. Mt *24:14. 1 P 4:7.

10. **Nation shall.** This portended the dissensions, insurrections, and mutual slaughter of the Jews, the open wars of different tetrarchies, and the civil wars in Italy between Otho and Vitellius (Josephus, Ant. l. xx. Bel. l. ii.). 2 Ch 15:5, 6. Is ♭19:2. Hg 2:21, 22. Zc 14:2, 3, 13. Mk 13:8. Ac 2:19, 20. 11:28. He 12:27. Re 6:2-12.

11. **earthquakes.** Re 6:12. **famines.** Ac *11:28. Re 6:8. **pestilences.** Le 26:25. Nu 14:12. Dt 28:21. Je 14:12. 21:6. 27:13. Ezk 5:12. 6:11. 7:15. Mt *24:7. **fearful sights.** Is 19:17. **and great signs.** Josephus, in the preface to his history of the Jewish wars, relates, that a star hung over the city like a sword, and a comet continued a whole year; that the people being at the feast of unleavened bread, at the ninth hour of the night, a great light shone around the altar of the temple, and continued an hour; that a cow led to sacrifice brought forth a lamb; that just before sunset chariots and armies were seen all over the country fighting in the clouds, and besieging cities, etc. ver. 25-27. Lk 11:16. Mt 16:1. *24:29, 30. Mk 8:11. Re 12:1, 3. 13:13. 15:1.

12. **before.** Lk 11:49-51. Mt *10:16-25. 22:6. *23:34-36. +*24:9, 10. Mk *13:9-13. Jn *15:20. *16:2, 3. Ac 4:3-7. 5:17-19, 40. *6:12-15. *7:57-60. 8:3. *9:4. 12:1-4. *16:22-26. 21:30, 31. 22:30. 24:1, etc. 25:1, 2, 11, 12, 22-25. 26:2, etc. 1 Th *2:15, 16. 1 P *4:12-14. Re *2:10. **they shall.** Lk 12:11, 12. Mt 10:17-22. **persecute.** Jn *15:20. 16:2, 3. Re 2:10. **synagogues.** Ac 22:19. 26:11. **prisons.** Ac 4:3. 5:18. 8:3. 12:4. 16:24. 24:27. 2 C 11:23. **being brought.** Ac 16:19. **before kings.** Ac 25:23. 27:24. 2 T 4:16, 17. **rulers.** Ac 17:6. 18:12. 24:1. 25:6. **for my.** 1 P 2:13.

13. **shall turn.** Ph 1:13, 14, 19, *28. 1 Th 3:3, 4. 2 Th *1:5.

14. **Settle.** Lk 9:44. *12:11, 12. Mt *10:19, 20. **meditate.** Mk *13:11.

15. **I will.** Lk *12:12. *24:45. Ex *4:11, 12. Pr 2:6. Je *1:9. Mt 10:19. Mk 13:11. Ac 2:4. *4:8-13, 31-33. Ep 6:19. Col 4:3, 4. Ja +*1:5. **and.** ʃ93A, Ge +1:26. i.e. a mouth (*Metonymy*, for speech), and wisdom, by Hendiadys wisdom of speech. **wisdom.** 1 S 18:30. Da 1:20. Ja 1:5. **which.** Ac *6:10. 24:25. *26:28. 2 T 4:16, 17. **to gainsay.** Lk 14:6. 20:40. Mt 22:46. Mk 12:34. Ac 4:14.

16. **ye shall.** Je *9:4. *12:6. Mi *7:5, 6. Mt *10:21. Mk *13:12. **parents.** Lk 12:53. 14:26, 33. Mt 10:35. **and some.** Lk 11:49. Mt 23:34. Jn 16:2. Ac *7:59. 12:2. *26:10, 11. Re 2:13. +*6:9. √12:11.

17. **be hated.** Lk *6:22. Mt *10:22. *24:9. Mk 13:13. Jn 7:7. *15:19. *17:14. 1 J 3:12. **for.** Lk *6:22. Mt +*5:11. Jn *15:20, 21. Ac 9:16. 2 C 4:5, 11. 12:10. Ph *1:29. 1 P *4:14. Re *2:3.

18. **not.** ʃ158, Mt +5:18. **an hair.** ʃ138B, Ge +13:16. Lk 10:19. *12:7. 1 S *14:45. 25:29. 2 S 14:11.

Da 3:27. Mt *10:30. Jn *10:28. Ac *27:34. **perish.** Gr. *apollumi,* Mt +2:13.

19. patience. Lk *8:15. Ps 27:13, 14. *37:7. 40:1. Mt 10:22. 24:13. Ro *2:7. √5:3. 8:25. 15:+*4, 5. 1 C √10:13. 1 Th 1:3. 2 Th 3:5. He *6:11, 12, 15. √10:36. Ja *1:3, 4. 5:7-11. Re *1:9. 2:2, 3. +*3:10. 13:10. 14:12. **possess.** Lk 9:24. He 10:34. **souls.** Gr. *psyche,* used here of the "inward man," seat of the new life, as in 1 P 2:11. 3 J 2. ⌐121A9C, Figure of speech Metonymy of the Cause, "soul" put for the inward man, one of its manifestations as the seat of the new life. For the other uses of *psyche,* see Mt +2:20n. For other instances of ⌐121A9C, see Ge +23:8 and Mt +11:29. T#985‡: Mt +*10:28.

20. when ye shall see. ver. *7. Lk *19:43. Da +*9:27. Mt +*24:15. Mk *13:14.

21. flee. Accordingly, when Cestius Gallus came against Jerusalem, and unexpectedly raised the siege, Josephus (Bel. l. ii. c. 19) states that many of the noble Jews departed out of the city, as out of a sinking ship; and when Vespasian afterwards drew towards it, a great multitude fled to the mountains. And we learn from Eusebius (*Hist. Eccles.* l. iii. c. 5) and Epiphanius (*Adver. Nazar.* l. i. tom. 2), that at this juncture, all who believed in Christ left Jerusalem, and removed to Pella, and other places beyond Jordan; and so escaped the general shipwreck of their country, that we do not read of one who perished in Jerusalem. Lk *17:31-33. Ge *19:17, 19, 26. Ex *9:20, 21. Pr +*22:3. Mt +*24:16-18. Mk 13:15, 16. **and let them.** Nu 16:26. Je *6:1. 35:11. 37:12, 13. Re 18:4. **depart out.** Je *37:12. **the countries.** Lk 17:31. Mt 24:18. Mk 13:16. Jn 4:33. Ja 5:4.

22. the days. Dt 32:35. Is 34:8. 63:4. Je 5:29. Ho 9:7. **of vengeance.** Lk 18:7, 8. Ps +*58:10. Is *34:8. +*61:2. Je 51:6. Ho ▶9:7. Ro *2:5. 2 P *2:9. +*3:7. **all.** Lk 4:21. 18:31. 22:37. 24:44. Le *26:14-33. Dt 28:15-68. 29:19-28. 32:34, *43. Ps 69:22-28. +*149:7-9. Is 65:12-16. Da +*9:26, 27. Zc 11:1, etc. *14:1, 2. Ml 4:1. Mt +1:22. Mk *13:19, 20. Jn 13:18. Ac 1:16. 3:18. 13:27. Re 17:17.

23. woe. Lk *23:29. Dt *28:56, 57. La *4:10. Ho *9:12-17. *13:16. Mt 24:19. Mk 13:17. 1 C 7:26. **great distress.** Lk *19:27, 43, 44. Mt *21:41, 44. 1 Th 2:16. He +*10:26-31. Ja 5:1. 1 P *4:17, 18. **the land.** ver. 25, 35. **and wrath.** 1 Th *2:16.

24. shall fall. Those who perished in the siege were 1,100,000, besides vast numbers who were slain at other times and places; and nearly 100,000 more were taken and sold for slaves; and their nation has been dispersed in all countries for upwards of 1700 years, while their city has been trodden under foot of the Romans, Saracens, Mamalukes, Franks, and Turks, who possess it to this day. In 1948 Israel became a nation, and in 1967, after the "Six Day War," once again possessed Jerusalem, an event which may have prophetic significance in the light of this passage. Je *29:18. **edge.** lit. mouth. ⌐144A2, Ge +34:26. Ge 34:26. Jsh 6:21. 8:24. 10:28. He 11:34. **led.** Le 26:33. Dt 4:27. *28:64-68. Ne 1:8. Ps 44:11. Je 9:16. Ezk 12:15. 20:23. 22:15. Zc 7:14. **Jerusalem.** Ps 79:1. Is 5:5. *63:3, 18. La 1:15. Da 8:10, 13. Re *11:2. **trodden down.** Ps 79:1. Is ▶63:18. Da 8:10. Zc 12:3. **until.** Is 66:12, 19. Ezk +*34:13. Da +*9:27. 12:7. Ml 1:11. Ro +√11:25. **times of.** Ezk +*30:3.

25. signs. ver. 11. Is 13:10, 13, 14. 24:23. Je 4:23.

Ezk *32:7, 8. Jl +*2:30, 31. 3:15. Am 5:20. *8:9, 10. Zp 1:15. Hg 2:6, 21. Mt +*24:29. 27:45. Mk 13:24-26. 15:33. Ac *2:19, 20. He 12:26. 2 P *3:10-12. Re *6:12-14. 8:12. 20:11. **stars.** Is 14:12. 34:4. Re 6:13. **upon the earth.** ver. 23, 35. Da +*12:1. **distress.** Lk 12:50. 19:43. Zp +*1:15. 2 C 2:4. **with perplexity.** Lk 8:45. Is 22:4, 5. Mi 7:4. **the sea.** Ps 46:3. ▶65:7. 88:7. 93:3, 4. Is *5:30. 28:2, 15, 18. 29:6. 30:30. 51:15. Ezk 38:22. Hab 3:8-10.

26. hearts failing. Ge 42:28. Le 26:36. Dt 28:32-34, 65-67. Ps ◑*112:7. Pr ◑*1:33. He 10:26, 27. **for looking.** Ac 12:11. **earth.** Gr. *oikoumene,* Mt +24:14. **for the powers.** Mt 24:29. Mk 13:25. 2 P 3:10-12. **of heaven.** Ps 33:6. Is ▶34:4. 40:26.

27. see. Da *7:10, 13. Mt +*24:30. *26:64. Mk 13:26. Ac *1:9-11. Re +*1:7. *14:14. **coming.** Lk 12:40. Da ▶7:13. Mk 14:62. 1 Th 4:16. 2 Th 2:8. **with power.** Mt *16:27, 28. 25:31. Mk 9:1. Re 19:11-16. **great glory.** Ps +*102:16.

28. And when. 2 Th +*1:7. **look up.** Lk 13:11. Ps 98:5-9. Is +*12:1-3. *25:8, 9. 30:19. 60:1, 2. Zc *9:14. 12:8. Jn 8:7, 10. Ac *7:55. He +*9:28. **lift up.** ⌐121S3E2. Metonymy of the Adjunct B606. The sign is put for the thing signified in connected words and phrases. To lift up the head is put for lifting up the soul, or taking courage, or rejoicing. For other instances of this figure see Jg +8:28. Lk 13:11. Jb 10:15. Ps *3:3. 34:5. *121:1. 123:1. Is 40:26. Da 4:34. Jn 8:7, 10. 11:41. 17:1. Ac *1:10. *7:55. 1 C *1:7. **for your.** Lk +*18:7. Pr 23:18. Is +√59:19, 20. Jn 16:16, 19, 20, 22. Ac *3:20. Ro +*11:26. 1 Th 1:10. **redemption.** Lk 1:68. Ro *3:24. *8:19, 23. Ep 1:14. +*4:30. Col *1:14. **draweth nigh.** Ps √25:14. Da +*11:33n. Am +*3:7. Ml √4:5, 6. Mt 25:6. Ro 13:11. 1 Th 5:4. Re 16:15.

29. Behold. Mt 24:32-35. Mk 13:28-30.

30. of your own selves. Lk +*12:57. Mt 16:3.

31. when. Lk 12:51-57. Mt 16:1-4. 23:39. Ezk 32:7. 34:27. +*39:28n. Lk 17:22. **these things.** ver. 7, 17, 20, 22, √24, √25-27. Mt √24:33. **the kingdom of God.** Lk +4:43. 17:20, 21. *19:11. Mk +1:15. 2 T +*4:1. **nigh at hand.** ver. +*28. Mt ◑+*10:7. +*21:43. √24:33. He 10:37. Ja 5:9. 1 P 4:7.

32. Verily. Lk 4:24. 12:37. 18:17, 29. 23:43. Mt +5:18. Mk +3:28. Jn +1:51. **This generation.** Lk 9:27. 11:50, 51. Mt 16:28. 23:36. +*‖24:34. Mk 13:30.

33. Heaven. Lk 16:17. Ps ◑*89:37. *102:25, 26. Ec ◑+*1:4. Is *34:4. *51:6. Je +*33:25. Mt +*5:18. +*24:35. Mk 13:31. He 1:11, 12. 12:27. 1 P 1:25. 2 P *3:7-14. Re 20:11. 21:1. **my words.** Nu 23:19. Ps 119:89, 152. Is √40:8. 1 P 1:23, 25.

34. take. ver. 8. Lk 17:3. Mk 13:9. Ac 5:35. He *12:15. 2 P *3:14. **lest.** Ro *13:13. 1 Th *5:6-8. 1 P *4:7. **your hearts.** ⌐171Q20, Ge +31:20. Lk *12:45. Le 10:9, 10. Pr 21:4, 5. Is *28:7, 8. *56:10-12. Ho 4:11, 12. Ac 14:17. Ro *13:11-13. 1 Th *5:6-8. Ja 5:5. 1 P *4:3-7. **surfeiting.** Dt *29:19, 20. 1 S 25:36. Is 28:1-3. 1 C *5:11. *6:10. Ga *5:20, 21. **drunkenness.** Ro 13:13. 1 C +*6:10. Ga +*5:21. 1 Th 5:7. **cares.** Lk *8:14. *10:41. Mt +*13:22. Mk *4:19. 1 C 6:3, 4. Ph √4:6. **that day.** Lk 10:12. *12:40, 46. Ps 35:8. Mt *24:39-50. Mk 13:35-37. 1 Th *5:2-4. 2 P *3:10, 14. Re 3:3. **come upon.** Lk 20:1g. 1 Th *5:3.

35. as a snare. Ps 11:6. 69:22. *73:19, 20. Ec *9:12. Is ▶24:17, 18. Je 48:43, 44. Ro 11:9. 1 Th *5:2, 3. 1 T *6:9. Re *3:3. *16:15. **all them.** ⌐142, Ge +20:16.

dwell. Lk 17:37. Ge 7:4. Je 25:29. Ac 17:26. **the face.** ƒ144A1, Ge +11:8. Ge +1:2. **of the whole earth.** Or, "of this whole land"; the land of Judea, on which these heavy judgments were to fall.

36. **Watch.** Lk *12:37-40. Ps 127:1. Pr *8:34. Mt +*24:42. *25:13. 26:41. Mk *13:33, 37. 14:34-38. Ac 20:31. 1 C 16:13. 1 Th 5:6. 2 T 4:5. He *13:17. 1 P 4:7. 5:8. Re 3:2, 3. *16:15. **pray always.** Lk *18:1. Jb 27:10. Ps 40:1. Ac 10:2. Ep *6:18, 19. Col *4:2. 1 Th +*5:17. **accounted worthy.** Lk *20:35. Zp +*2:3. Mt *10:37. 21:28. Col +√1:10. 2 Th √1:5, 11. 2 T *4:8. T *2:13. He *9:28. or, prevail. Lk 23:23. Ho 12:4. Ja 5:16. **to escape.** Ge 19:29. Ps 32:6, 7. 37:38-40. *71:2. *83:3. +*94:13. Pr 3:25, 26. +*11:8. 14:26. Is 4:2. *16:1-5. +*26:20. +*57:1. Je 11:11. 15:21. 44:14. Jl +*2:32. Ob +*17mg. Hab +*3:16. Zp +*2:3. Ml *3:17. Mt +*6:13. Ro 2:3. 1 Th +*1:10. 5:3. He 2:3. Re +*3:10. **stand.** Ezr 9:15. Ps +*1:5. 76:7. Pr +*22:29n. Je 15:19. 35:19. 40:10. Da +*1:5. 7:10. +*12:13. Ml *3:2. Ep 6:13, 14. 1 Th *2:19. 1 J 2:28. Ju *24. Re 6:17. **before.** Is *24:23. Ho 6:2. **Son of man.** Lk +5:24.

37. **the day time.** Or, "every day," *tas heemeras;* which probably refers to the four last days of his life. He taught all day in the temple, and withdrew every evening, and lodged in Bethany, a town on the eastern declivity of the Mount of Olives. Lk *22:39. Mt 21:17. 26:55. Mk 11:12. Jn 12:1. **teaching in.** Jn *8:2. **at night.** Mt 21:17. Mk 11:19. **abode.** Mt 21:17. **mount.** Lk 19:37. 22:39. Zc 14:4. Mt 21:1. 26:30. Jn *8:1. 18:2. Ac 1:12.

38. **all the people.** Jn 8:1, 2. **came.** ƒ63H, Ge +12:15. **to hear.** Lk *19:48.

LUKE 22

The priests and scribes determine to put Jesus to death, 1, 2. Judas bargains to betray him, 3-6. Two apostles prepare the passover, and Jesus eats it with the twelve, 7-18. He institutes the Lord's supper, 19, 20; points out the traitor, 21-23; checks the ambition of the disciples, and promises them an honorable station in his kingdom, 24-30. He shows Peter that Satan desired to sift him and his brethren; but that his faith should not fail, though he would thrice deny him, 31-34, and instructs his disciples about their approaching dangers, 35-38. His agony and prayer in the garden, and his warnings to the apostles, 39-46. He is betrayed and apprehended, 47-49; he heals him whose ear Peter cut off, 50-53; and is led to the high priest, 54. Peter thrice denies him, but bitterly repents, 55-62. Jesus is mocked, insulted, and condemned, 63-71.

1. **the feast.** Ex 12:6-23. Le 23:5, 6. Mt 26:2. Mk 14:1, 2, 12. Jn 11:55-57. 1 C *5:7, 8. **unleavened.** Lk 2:41. Ex 23:15. 34:18. Le +*23:6. Dt 16:16. 2 Ch 8:13. 30:13, 21. 35:17. Ezr 6:22. **Passover.** Le +*23:5. Jn 6:4.

2. **the chief priests.** Lk 19:47, 48. 20:19. Ps *2:1-5. Mt 21:38, 45, 46. 26:3-5. Jn 11:47-53, 57. Ac 4:27. **they feared.** Lk 19:48. 20:19. 21:38. Ac 5:26.

3. **entered.** Mt 26:14. Mk 14:10, etc. Jn 6:70, 71. 12:6. 13:2, 27, 30. Ac *5:3. 1 C 5:5. **Judas.** Lk 6:16. Mt 27:3. Jn 6:71. 12:4. Ac 1:16. **Iscariot.** Jsh 15:25n. Je 48:24, 41. **being.** ver. 21. Lk 6:16. Ps *41:9. 55:12-14. Mt 26:23. Mk +9:35. 14:18-20. Jn *13:18, 26.

4. **went.** Mt *26:14. Mk 14:10, 11. **captains.** These were not military officers, but presidents of the temple.

Among the priests who were in waiting in the temple, says Bp. Pearce, some were appointed *phulakes,* for a *guard* to the temple; and over these were *strateegoi, commanding officers:* both sorts are mentioned by Josephus (Bel. l. vi. c. 5. sec. 3). ver. 52. 1 Ch 9:11, etc. Ne 11:11. Ac 4:1. 5:24, 26.

5. **were glad.** Jn ◑20:29. **and covenanted.** Zc *11:12, 13. Mt *26:15, 16. 27:3-5. Ac 1:18. 8:20. 1 T √6:9, 10. 2 P 2:3, 15. Ju 11.

6. **betray.** Mt 20:18, 19. **in the absence of the multitude.** *or,* without tumult. Mt 26:5. Mk 14:2. Ac 24:18.

7. **the day of.** ver. 1. Ex 12:6, 18. Mt 26:17. Mk 14:12. **unleavened bread.** Ex 12:18. Le +*23:5. Nu 28:16. 1 C 5:7.

8. **he sent.** Mk 14:13-16. **Go.** Lk 1:6. Mt 3:15. Ga *4:4, 5. **prepare.** Jn 14:3. **passover.** ƒ121P8, Ex +12:21. Le +*23:5. Ac 12:3, 4.

10. **Behold.** Lk 19:29, etc. 1 S 10:2-7. Mt *26:18, 19. Jn 16:4. Ac 8:26-29.

11. **The Master.** Lk 7:40. 19:31, 34. Mt 21:3. 23:8. Jn 11:28. **Where is.** Lk 2:7. 19:5. Re *3:20. **passover.** ƒ121P8, Ex +12:21.

12. **he.** Jn +*2:25. 21:17. Ac 16:14, 15. **a large.** Mk 14:15. Ac 1:13. 20:8.

13. **they went.** Lk 21:33. Jn 2:5. 11:40. He 11:8. **as he had said.** Lk 19:32.

14. **when.** Ps *23:5. 116:13. Je 16:7. Mt 26:20. Mk 14:17. **the hour.** Ec 3:1. Jn 17:1. Ga *4:4. **sat down.** ver. ◑69. Ex *12:6, 11. **apostles.** Mk 6:30.

15. **With desire I have desired.** *or,* I have heartily desired. ƒ147D, Ge +1:29. Lk 12:50. SS 7:10. Jn 4:34. 13:1. 17:1. **desired.** ƒ108C8. Idiom B835. Idiomatic degrees of comparison: verb and cognate noun. A verb can be exalted to a superlative degree, as well as an adjective, by using with it a cognate noun. For other instances of this idiom see Jn 3:29. Ac 4:17. 5:28. **passover.** ƒ121P8, Ex +12:21. He ◑=11:28.

16. **I will not.** ver. 18-20. **until.** ver. 30. Lk 12:37. *14:15. Jn 6:27, 50-58. Ac *10:40, 41. 1 C *5:7, 8. He 10:1-10. Re *19:9. **the kingdom.** Lk +4:43.

17. **took.** Ps *23:5. 116:13. Je 16:7. Mt 26:27. Mk 14:23. **cup.** ƒ121J13, Je +49:12. **gave thanks.** ver. 19. Lk 9:16. +*24:30. Dt 8:10. 1 S 9:13. Mt 15:36. Jn 6:11. Ro 14:6. 1 T *4:4, 5.

18. **I will not.** ƒ158, Mt +5:18. ver. 16. Mt 26:29. Mk 14:25. 15:23. **the fruit.** Jg 9:13. Ps 104:15. Pr 31:6, 7. SS 5:1. Is 24:9-11. 25:6. 55:1. Zc 9:15, 17. Ep +*5:18, 19. **until.** Lk 9:27. 21:31. Da 2:44. Mt 16:18. +*26:29. Mk 9:1. Ac +*1:6. 2:30-36. Col 1:13. **kingdom of God.** Mk 15:43.

19. **he took.** Mt *26:26-28. Mk 14:22-24. 1 C 10:16. *11:23-29. **gave thanks.** ver. 17. Lk +*24:30. Mt 15:36. Jn 6:11, 23. Ac 27:35. 1 Th 5:18. **brake.** ƒ108H4, Is +58:7. **is my.** ver. 20. Ge 41:26, 27. Ezk 37:11. Da 2:38. 4:22-24. Zc 5:7, 8. 1 C 10:4. Ga 4:25. **body.** 1 C 10:16. **given.** ƒ96C7, Mt +26:24. That the ancient Jews, in celebrating the passover, had in view the sufferings of the Messiah, is evident from *Pesachim,* fol. 119, quoted by Schoetgen; where, among the five things said to be contained in the *Great Hallel,* or the hymn composed of several Psalms sung after the paschal supper, one is, the sufferings of the Messiah, for which they refer to Ps 116:9. Jn 6:51. 1 C 11:24, 25. Ga 1:4. Ep 5:2. T 2:14. 1 P 2:24. **this do.** Ps 78:4-6. 111:4. SS 1:4. 1 C 11:24. **remembrance.** Ex 12:14. 1 C 11:24, 25. He 10:3. 1 C 4:17. 2 T 1:6.

20. **the cup.** ♪121J13, Je +49:12. ver. 17. **This.** Ex=)24:8. Zc 9:11. Mt 26:28. Mk 14:24. 1 C 10:16-21. 11:25. He 8:6-13. 9:17-23. 12:24. 13:20. **the new.** Je *31:31. 2 C 3:6. *9:15, 18-22. **testament.** He 10:29. 13:20. **for you.** Mt 26:28. Mk 14:24.

21. **the hand.** Jb 19:19. Ps *41:9. Mi 7:5, 6. Mt *26:21-23. Mk 14:18-20. Jn *13:18, 19, 21, 26. **is.** ♪63, Ge +2:10.

22. **truly.** Lk 24:25-27, 46. Ge +*3:15. Ps ch. 22, 69. Is ch. 53. Da +*9:24-26. Zc 13:7. Mt 26:24, 53, 54. Mk 14:21. Ac 2:23. 4:25-28. 13:27, 28. 26:22, 23. 1 C +*15:3, 4. 1 P *1:11. **Son of man.** Lk +5:24. **goeth.** ♪96C7, Mt +26:24. Jn 7:33. 8:21, 22. 14:12. 16:28. **determined.** Ac *2:23. *4:28. 10:42. 17:26, 31. Ro 1:4. Re *13:8. **but.** Ps 55:12-15. 69:22-28. 109:6-15. Ob 7. Mi 7:6. Mt 27:5. Jn 17:12. Ac 1:16-25. 2 P 2:3. **woe unto.** Lk 17:1. Mt 18:7.

23. **inquire.** Mt 26:22. Mk 14:19. Jn *13:22-25. **should do.** 2 S ●15:15. Jn ●2:5.

24. **a strife.** Lk *9:46-48. Mt *20:20-24. Mk 9:34, 50. 10:37-41. Ro 12:10. 1 C *3:3. *13:4. Ph +*2:3-5. Ja 4:5, 6. 1 P *5:5, 6.

25. **The kings.** Mt 20:25-28. Mk 10:41-45. **lordship.** Ro 14:9. 2 C *1:24. 1 T 6:15. 1 P 5:3. **benefactors.** Mt +6:2n.

26. **ye shall not.** Lk 9:48. Mt 18:3-5. 23:8-12. Ro 12:2. 1 P 5:3. 3 J 9, 10. **is greatest.** Ro +*12:3. 1 P *5:3. **the younger.** 1 P 5:5. **is chief.** Mt 2:6. Ac 7:10. 14:12. 15:22. He 13:7, 17, 24. **doth serve.** Mt *20:26, 27. Mk 10:43, 44. Jn 13:14. Ga *5:13. 6:2, 10. He *13:17, 24.

27. **is greater.** Lk *12:37. 17:7-9. Mt *20:28. Jn *13:5-16. 2 C √8:9. Ph *2:7, 8. **but I am.** T#61. Ge=40:4. Ps +145:9 (T#228). Mt 9:11, 12. 19:14, 15. 20:27, 28. Mk *10:45. Jn *13:5, 13, 14. 2 C √8:9. Ph *2:5-8. He 2:11, 12, 16.

28. **continued.** Ru 1:16. 2 K 2:2. Mt *19:28, 29. *24:13. Jn *6:67, 68. √8:31. 13:1. Ac 1:25. Ro 16:4. 2 T 1:16. **my temptations.** Lk 4:2. Mt 4:1. He *2:18. +*4:15. Ja 1:2.

29. **I appoint.** Lk +*12:32n. *19:17. Mt +*24:47. *25:34. 28:18. Jn 17:18. Ac 14:22. 1 C *9:25. 2 C *1:7. 1 Th ●+*2:12. 2 T *2:12. Ja *2:5. 1 P *5:4. Re 1:6. 21:14. **a kingdom.** Lk +*12:32. +*13:28, 29. Ezk 37:21, 22. Da 7:18, 27. Mi 4:6-8. *7:20. Mt +*5:5. +*8:11. 16:27. 25:34. Mk 11:10. Ro 5:17. 2 Th *1:5. **as my Father hath appointed unto me.** Lk *1:32. 19:15. Ps *2:8. Is 49:5-12. Da +*7:13, 14. Ph *2:9-11.

30. **eat.** ver. *16:18. Lk *12:37. *13:29. *14:15. 2 S 9:9, 10. 19:28. Mt +*8:11. Re *19:9. **my table.** Ps +*23:5. Is 25:6. Ezk 39:17-22. Re 19:17, 18. **my kingdom.** Mt 13:41. 1 C +*15:24n. 2 T 4:1. 2 P *1:11. **and sit.** Ps *49:14. Mt +*19:28. Ro 5:17. 1 C *6:2, 3. Re 1:6. *2:26, 27. *3:21. 4:4g. *20:4. **judging.** 1 C 6:2. **twelve tribes.** Ac 26:7. Ja 1:1. Re 21:12.

31. **Simon.** Lk 10:41. Ac 9:4. **Simon.** ♪84, Ge +22:11. **Satan.** Jb *1:8-11. 2:3-6. Zc 3:1. 1 C 5:5. 2 C 2:11. 1 P *5:8, 9. Re 12:10. **hath desired.** Jb 1:8mg. **to have you.** Mt 26:31, 56. Mk 14:27, 50. **sift.** Am 9:9. **as wheat.** Lk 3:17. Is 41:16. Je 15:7. Mt 3:12. Jn 16:32.

32. **I have prayed for.** T#1720. Is *53:12. Zc 3:2-4. Mk +*1:35. Jn 14:19. *17:9-11, 15-21. Ro 5:9, 10. √8:32-34. He √7:25. √9:24. 1 P 1:5. 1 J √2:1, 2. **thy faith.** T#1485. Lk +*8:13. +*17:5. 2 T 2:18. T 1:1. He *12:15. 2 P 1:1. 1 J *2:19. **and when.** ver. 61,

62. Mt 18:3. 26:75. Mk 14:72. 16:7. Ac +*3:19. **converted.** Lk 1:16, 17. 17:4. Ps *19:7. 23:3. *51:13. Mt 13:15. 18:3. Mk 4:12. Jn 14:19. *21:17. Ac +*3:19. 28:27. Ja 5:19. 1 P 5:8, 10. **strengthen.** Ps *32:3-6. *51:12, 13. Jn 21:15-17. 2 C 1:4-6. Ga 6:2. 1 Th 3:2. 1 T 1:13-16. He 10:25. 12:12, 13. 1 P 1:13. 5:8-10. 2 P √1:10-12. 3:14, 17, 18.

33. **I am.** 2 K 8:12, 13. Pr √28:26. Je 10:23. +*17:9. Mt 20:22. 26:33-35, 40, 41. Mk 14:29, 31, 37, 38. Jn 13:36, 37. Ac 20:23, 24. 21:13. 1 C √10:12. **prison.** Ac 12:4. **death.** Jn 21:19.

34. **the cock.** Mt 26:34, 74. Mk 14:30, 71, 72. Jn 13:38. 18:27. **shall not.** ♪158, Mt +5:18.

35. **When.** Lk *9:3. *10:4. Mt 10:9, 10. Mk 6:8, 9. **scrip.** 1 S 17:40. Mt 10:10. Mk 6:8. **lacked.** Lk 12:29-31. Ge 48:15. Dt 8:2, 3, 16. 1 K 4:27. Ne 9:21. Ps *23:1. 34:9, 10. 37:3. Mt √6:31-33.

36. **But now.** ♪121S4, 2 K +4:29. T#1861. Lk 9:3. 10:3. Pr 17:3. Is 48:10. Mt 10:22-25. Jn 15:20. 16:33. 17:15. 1 Th 2:14, 15. 3:4. 1 P 4:1. **scrip.** ver. +35. **no sword.** ♪63I2, Jsh +3:3. ver. 38. Nu *31:3. Jg 3:2. 1 Ch +*5:22. Ne *4:13. Ps 18:34. Pr +*20:18. Mt ●+*5:39. 10:34. Jn ●18:11, 36. Ac 22:25-29. 23:23.

37. **this.** ver. 22. Lk 18:31. *21:22. *24:25, 26, 44-46. Mt 1:22. 26:54-56. Jn *10:35. 19:28-30. Ac 1:16. 13:27-29. **must.** Lk 13:33. **And he.** Lk 23:32. Is ♭53:12. Mk 15:27, 28. 2 C √5:21. Ga 3:13. **for the things.** Jn 17:4. 19:30. **an end.** Mk 3:26.

38. **two swords.** ver. +*36, 49. Mt 26:51. Mk 14:47. **It.** Dt 3:26. Mt 26:52-54. Mk 14:41. Jn *18:36. 2 C 10:3, 4. Ep *6:10-18. 1 Th 5:8. 1 P 5:9.

39. **he came.** Mt 26:30, 36-38. Mk 14:26, 32-34. Jn *18:1, 2. **as he was wont.** Lk 1:9. 2:42. *4:16. 21:37. Mk 10:1. 11:11, 19. 13:3. Jn 18:2. He 5:7. **mount of Olives.** Lk 19:29.

40. **the place.** Jn 18:2. **Pray.** ver. 46. Lk 11:4. 1 Ch 4:10. Ps 17:5. 19:13. 119:116, 117, 133. Pr 30:8, 9. Mt 6:13. 26:41. Mk 14:38. 2 C 12:7-10. Ep *6:18, 19. 1 P 4:7. *5:8, 9. Re +*3:10. **enter not.** Lk 11:4. Mt 6:13.

41. **withdrawn.** Ac 21:1g. **stone's cast.** ♪79, Ge +21:16. **and kneeled.** Mt *26:39. Mk 14:35. Ac 7:60.

42. **Father.** Lk 10:21. 23:34, 46. Mt 11:25. 26:39, 42, 44. Mk 14:36. Jn 11:41. 12:27, 28. 17:1, 5, 11, 21, 24, 25. He 5:7. **if thou.** ♪184A, 1 C +15:2. **willing, remove.** Gr. willing to remove. **cup.** ver. 17-20. Is 51:17, 22. Je 25:15. Mt 20:22. Jn 18:11. **not.** Ps 40:8. Mt 6:10. Jn 4:34. *5:30. *6:38. He 10:7-10.

43. **an angel.** T#1766. Lk 1:11-13. 4:10, 11. Ge 21:17. Nu 20:16. Jg 6:11. 13:9. 1 K 19:5-8. 2 Ch 32:20, 21. Ps 91:11, 12. Da 9:20-23. 10:2-6, 12. Zc 1:9. Mt *4:6, 11. 26:53. Jn 12:29. Ac 10:1-4, 30, 31. 12:5-9. 1 T 3:16. He *1:6, 14. **strengthening.** ver. 32. Dt 3:28. Jb 4:3, 4. Is 35:3, 4. Da 10:16-19. 11:1. Ac 18:23. He 2:17.

44. **being.** Ge 32:24-28. Ps 22:1, 2, 12-21. 40:1-3. 69:14-18. 88:1-18. 130:1, 2. 143:6, 7. La 1:12. 3:53-56. Jon 2:2, 3. Jn √12:27. 2 C √5:21. He *5:7, 8. **agony.** T#1304. Ps ✱22:14, 15. **prayed more earnestly.** Ac 12:5mg. **his.** Is 53:10. La 1:12. Ro 8:32. **as.** ♪160B, Ge +25:31. **great drops.** T#1285. Dr. Mead observes from Galen, "Cases sometimes happen, in which, through *mental pressure*, the pores may be so dilated that the blood may issue from them, so that there may be a bloody sweat;" and Bp. Pearce gives an instance from Thaunus, of an Italian gentleman being

so distressed through the fear of death, that his body was covered with a bloody sweat. Our Lord was in the bloom of life, and in perfect health, and it is evident the fear of death could have no place in his mind; and consequently this must have been produced by a preternatural cause. William K. Hobart observes, "The medical language employed affords internal evidence of the authenticity of verses 43, 44 of Luke xxii., which are omitted in some MSS. (*Medical Language of Luke*, p. 85). Hobart notes that there is in Luke's account, whether parallel with the other synoptic gospels or not, "a class of words running through the Gospel of St. Luke which does not occur in other New Testament writings, but which is in common use in Greek medical language," even apart from those portions which record the miracles of healing (p. 85).

45. sleeping. Mt *26:40, 43. Mk 13:36. *14:37, 40, 41. **for sorrow.** Hobart notes this expression as a medical term employed exclusively in Luke's account, for only Luke assigns a cause for their sleepiness. The other evangelists merely say "their eyes were heavy," but Luke states that it arose from anxiety. It is evident that their condition was owing to their anxiety for their Lord, coupled with the want of their usual rest (*Medical Language*, p. 84).

46. Why sleep ye. ver. 40. Lk +*21:34-36. Pr 6:4-11. Jon 1:6. **rise.** Pr 6:9. SS 2:10. Is 60:1. Mt *26:41. Mk 10:49. Jn 5:8. Ep 5:14.

47. while. Mt 26:45-47. Mk 14:41-43. Jn *18:2-9. **Judas.** ver. 3-6. Mt 26:14-16, 47. Mk 14:10, 43. Ac *1:16-18.

48. betrayest. 2 S 20:9, 10. Ps 41:9. 55:21. Pr +*26:23. 27:6. Mt 26:48-50. Mk 14:44-46. **Son of man.** Lk +5:24.

49. shall. lit. If we shall. *J*108G. Idiom B837: idiomatic forms of question. The Hebrew may idiomatically begin a question with "if," but Greek idiom never uses "if" in this sense to ask a question. Here, therefore, the Hebrew idiom is followed. **with the sword.** *J*108D, Mt +3:11. ver. 38.

50. smote a servant. Mt 26:51-54. Mk 14:47. Jn *18:10, 11. Ro 12:19. 2 C 10:4.

51. answered and. Mk 11:14. **Suffer.** Jn 17:12. 18:8, 9. **And he.** Mk 1:41. Ro 12:21. 2 C 10:1. 1 P 2:21-23.

52. Jesus. Mt 26:55. Mk 14:48, 49. **captains.** ver. 4. 2 K 11:15. Jn 18:12. Ac 5:26. **a thief.** Lk 10:30. 19:46. Mt 21:13. Mk 11:17. Jn 18:40.

53. I was. Lk 21:37, 38. Mt 21:12-15, 23, 45, 46. Jn 7:25, 26, 30, 45. **in the temple.** Lk 2:46. Jn 8:2. 18:20. **but.** Jg 16:21-30. Jb 20:5. Jn 12:27. 16:20-22. **your hour.** Jb *20:5. Mk 14:35, 41. Jn 8:44. 12:27. 16:4. **the power.** Lk 4:6, 13. Jn 13:30. +*14:30. Ac 26:18. 2 C 4:3-6. Ep 6:12. Col 1:13. Re 12:9-12. *20:10. **darkness.** Ge +1:2. Mi 7:8. Ac 26:18. Ep 6:12. Col 1:13. 1 Th 5:5.

54. took. Our blessed Lord before his death passed another examination. One was before the Jewish Sanhedrin, whose proper province it was to try such as were accused as false prophets or blasphemers. This was a kind of ecclesiastical court. The other, with which the next chapter opens, was before Pilate, the Roman governor of Judea at that time; he principally took cognizance of criminal things, such especially as concerned the peace of the country, considered as part of the Roman empire. Mt *26:57, 58. Mk 14:53, 54. Jn *18:12-17, 24. **And Peter.** ver. 33, 34. 2 Ch 32:31.

55. had. ver. 44. Mt 26:69. Mk 14:66. Jn 18:17, 18. **the hall.** Mt 26:3. **Peter sat.** Ps +*1:1. 26:4, 5. 28:3. Pr 9:6. 13:20. 1 C 15:33. 2 C 6:15-17.

56. a certain maid. Mt 26:69. Mk 14:6, 17, 66-68. Jn 18:17. **earnestly looked.** Lk 4:20. Ac 3:4g.

57. he denied. ver. 33, 34. Lk 12:9. Mt 10:33. 26:70. Jn 18:25, 27. Ac 3:13, 14, 19. 1 C *10:12. 2 T 2:10-12. 1 J √1:9.

58. another. A *maid* challenged Peter in the second instance, according to Matthew and Mark; yet here it is said *heteros, another* (man) and he also answers to a *man*. But *heteros*, as Wetstein shows, may be, and is in innumerable instances applied to a *female*; and Matthew says, "she said to them that were there," and Mark, "she began to say to them that stood by." So that the maid gave the information to those around her, and some *man* charged Peter with it. Probably several joined in the accusation, though he answered to an individual, for St. John says, "*They* said unto him," etc. Mt 26:71, 72. Mk 14:69, 70. Jn 18:25. **Man.** ver. 60. Lk 12:14.

59. confidently. Mt *26:73, 74. Mk 14:69, 70. Jn 18:26, 27. Ac 12:15.

60. Man. ver. 58. Lk 12:14. **the cock.** ver. 34. Mt 26:74, 75. Mk 14:71, 72. Jn 18:27.

61. turned. Lk 7:9, 13, 44. 9:55. 10:23, 41. 14:25. 23:28. Mt 9:22. 16:23. Mk 5:30. 8:33. Jn 1:38. **looked.** Lk 20:17. 1 K 8:29. Ne 1:6. Jb 33:27. Is *57:15-18. Je 31:18-20. Ho 11:8. Zc 12:4. Mk 10:21. Ac 5:31. **And Peter.** Ezk 16:63. 36:31, 32. Ac 11:16. 20:35. Ep 2:11. Re 2:5. **the word.** Jn=15:3. **Before.** ver. 34. Mt 26:34, 75. Jn 13:38. **deny.** Ac 3:13, 14.

62. and wept. Ps 38:18. *126:5, 6. 130:1-4. 143:1-4. Is 22:4. Je 9:1. 31:18. Ezk 7:16. Mi 1:8. Zc *12:10. Mt +*5:4. 26:75. Mk 14:72. 1 C 10:12. 2 C √7:9-11.

63. the men. Mt 26:59-68. Mk 14:55-65. Jn 18:22. **mocked.** Lk 18:32. 23:11, 36. Jb 16:9, 10. 30:9-14. Ps 22:6, 7, 13. 35:15, 16, 25. 69:7-12. Is 49:7. 50:6, 7. 52:14. 53:3. Mi 5:1. Mt 20:19. 27:28-31, 39-44. Mk 10:34. 15:16-20, 27-32. He *12:2, 3. 1 P 2:23.

64. blindfolded. Jg 16:21, 25. **struck him.** Mt +*26:67. **Prophesy.** Lk 7:39.

65. blasphemously. Lk 12:10. Mt +*12:31n, 32n. 27:39g. Ac 26:11. 1 T 1:13, 14.

66. as soon. Mt 27:1. Mk 15:1. Jn 18:24, 28. **elders.** Ps *2:1-3. Ac *4:25-28. 22:5. **council.** Ac 4:15. 5:21, 27, 34, 41. 6:12, 15. 22:5g, 30. 23:1, 6, 15, 20, 28. 24:20.

67. Art thou. lit. If thou art. *J*184A, 1 C 15:2. Mt 11:3-5. 26:63, etc. Mk 14:61, etc. Jn 10:24. **the Christ.** Mt 1:17. **If I tell.** *J*184D1. Hypothetical Propositions; or, Conditional ("if") Sentences: Fourth Condition; or, Mere Assumption with Remote Idea of Realization, involving the Protasis ("if," or conditional clause). For other instances of this construction see Ac 17:11, 27. 20:16. 24:19. 25:20. 27:12, 39. 1 C 14:10. 15:37. 1 P *3:14, 17. **ye will not.** *J*158, Mt +5:18. Lk 16:31. Jn +*5:39-47. 8:43-45. 9:27, 28. 10:25, 26. 12:37-43.

68. if I also. *J*184C, Mt +4:9. Lk 20:3-7, 41-44. Je 38:15. **will not.** *J*158, Mt +5:18.

69. shall. Mt 26:64. Mk *14:62. **Son of man.** Lk +5:24. **sit on.** Ps *}110:1. Da +*}7:13, 14. Mt 22:44. 26:64. Mk 14:62. 16:19. Ac 2:34-36. 7:55, 56. Ro 8:34. Ep 1:20-23. 4:8-10. Col 3:1. He 1:3. 8:1. *12:2. 1 P 3:22. Re 3:21. 22:1. **the power.** Ac 8:10.

70. the Son of God. Lk 4:41. Ps 2:7, 12. Mt 3:17.

+14:33. 27:43, 54. Jn 1:34, 49. 10:30, 36. 19:7. **Ye say**. Lk ◑*23:3. Mt 26:25, 64. ◑+*27:11n. Mk 14:62. 15:2. Jn 18:37.

71. **What need**. Mt 26:65, 66. Mk 14:63, 64.

LUKE 23

Jesus is accused before Pilate, who sends him to Herod, 1-7. He is silent before Herod, who mocks him and sends him back, 8-11. Pilate and Herod are made friends, 12. Pilate, convinced of the innocence of Jesus, is yet prevailed on by clamor to give him up to crucifixion, and to release Barabbas, 13-25. Jesus is led away, Simon of Cyrene bearing his cross, 26. To the women and others who bewailed him, he predicts the calamities coming on the Jews, 27-31. He is crucified between two thieves, and prays for his murderers, 32-34. The people, rulers, priests, and soldiers, and one of the thieves, scoff at him, 35-38. The other thief rebukes his companion, and confesses Christ, who promises that he shall "that day be with him in paradise," 39-43. The land is darkened, the veil of the temple rent, and Jesus, commending his spirit into the hand of his Father, expires, 44-46. The centurion confesses him; and the people with his acquaintance retire, smiting their breasts at what they had seen, 47-49. Joseph of Arimathea asks for the body and buries it, 50-54. The women prepare spices; but rest on the sabbath, according to the commandment, 55, 56.

1. **whole multitude**. Lk 22:66. Mt 27:1, 2, 11, etc. Mk 15:1, etc. Jn 18:28, etc. **Pilate**. Lk 3:1. 13:1. Ac 3:13. 4:27. 1 T 6:13.

2. **they**. Zc 11:8. Mk 15:3-5. Jn 18:30. **perverting**. ver. 5, 14. 1 K 18:17. Je 38:4. Am 7:10. Ac 16:20, 21. 17:6, 7. 24:5. **forbidding**. Lk 20:20-25. 1 K 21:10-13. Ps 35:11. 62:4. 64:3-6. Je 20:10. 37:13-15. Mt *17:27. *22:15, 17, 21. 26:59, 60. Mk 12:13, 14, 17. 14:55, 56. Ac 24:13. 1 P 3:16-18. **Caesar**. Lk 2:1. 3:1. Mt 22:17. **that**. Lk 22:69, 70. Mt 26:63, 64. Mk 14:61, 62. Jn *6:15. +*18:36. 19:12. Ac 17:7. **is Christ**. Mt *15:32. Jn 4:25, 26. **a king**. Ps +*2:2, 6mg. Mk *15:32. Jn +*1:49. Ac *17:7.

3. **Pilate**. Mt 27:11. Mk 15:2. Jn *18:33-37. 1 T *6:13. **the King**. ver. 38. Lk *1:32, 33. 19:38-40. Mk 15:18, 32. Jn 1:49. √18:36, 37. 19:3, 19-21. **he answered**. 1 T 6:13. **Thou sayest it**. This was the most solemn mode of affirmation used by the Jews. When the inhabitants of Zippor, inquired whether Rabbi Judah were dead, the son of Kaphra answered, "Ye say" (*Berachoth Hier.* cited by Wagensell in Sota, p. 1001. *apud* Schoetgen, *Hor.* Heb. vol. i. p. 225). But contrast the evidence presented in the note on Mt +*27:11n. Lk 22:70.

4. **I find**. ver. 14, 15, 22. Mt 27:19, 24. Mk 15:14. Jn +*8:46. 18:38. 19:4-6. He 7:26. 1 P 1:19. *2:22. 3:18.

5. **they**. ver. 23. Lk 11:53. Ps 22:12, 13, 16. 57:4. 69:4. Mt 27:24. Jn 19:15. Ac 5:33. 7:54, 57. 23:10. **all Jewry**. Lk 1:5. 2:4. 4:44. 7:17. Ac 1:8. 2:9. 8:1. 10:37. 11:1, 29. **beginning**. Lk 4:14, 15. Mt 4:12-16, 23. Mk 1:14. Jn 1:43. 2:11. 7:41, 52. Ac 10:37.

6. **a Galilean**. Lk 13:1. Ac 5:37.

7. **knew**. Gr. *epiginosko*, Mt +11:27. **Herod's**. Lk 3:1. 13:31.

8. **for**. Lk 9:7-9. 19:3. Mt 14:1. Mk 6:14. Jn 12:21. **and he**. Lk 4:23. 2 K 5:3-6, 11. Mt 12:38. Ac 8:19.

9. **but**. Lk 13:32. Ps 38:13, 14. 39:1, 2, 9. Is *53:7.

Mt +*7:6. 27:14. Ac 8:32. 1 P 2:23. **answered him**. Mt +*26:63.

10. **and vehemently**. ver. 2, 5, 14, 15. Lk 11:53. Ac 18:28g. 24:5.

11. **Herod**. Ac 4:27, 28. **set**. Lk 18:9. 22:64, 65. Ps 22:6. 69:19, 20. Is 49:7. *53:3. Mt 27:27-30. Mk 9:12. 15:16-20. Ga 4:14. **mocked**. Lk 22:63. **arrayed**. Mt 27:28. Mk 15:17. Jn 19:5. **gorgeous**. Ja 2:2g.

12. **Pilate and**. Ps 2:2. 83:4-6. Mt 16:1. Ac 4:27. Re 17:13, 14.

13. **And Pilate**. Mt 27:21-23. Mk 15:14. Jn 18:38. 19:4. **the rulers**. Lk 24:20.

14. **as one**. ver. 1, 2, 5. **having examined**. Ac 3:13. 12:19. **have found**. ver. 4. Da 6:4. Mt 27:4, 19, 24, 54. Ac 13:28. He 7:26.

15. **nothing**. Rather, "nothing worthy of death is committed by him;" *pepragmenon auto* being put for *pepragmenon up' autou*, or *pepraken autos*, "he hath done nothing." **worthy**. Lk 12:48. Dt 19:6. 21:22. 1 S 26:16. 1 K 2:26. Je 26:11, 16. Ac 23:29. 25:11, 25. 26:31. Ro 1:32.

16. **chastise**. ver. 22. Is *53:5. Mt 27:26. Mk 15:15. Jn 19:1-4. Ac 5:40, 41.

17. **of necessity**. Mt 27:15. Mk 15:6. Jn 18:39.

18. **they**. Mt *27:16-23. Mk 15:7-14. Jn 18:40. Ac *3:14. **Away**. Dt 17:7. 19:19. Jn 19:15. Ac 21:36. 22:22.

19. **sedition**. ver. 2-5. **for murder**. Ac 3:14.

20. **willing**. Mt 14:8, 9. 27:19. Mk 15:15. Jn 19:12.

21. **But**. Ac 3:13. **they cried**. Ac 12:22. 21:34. 22:24. Crucify. ver. 23. Mt 27:22-25. Mk 15:13, 14. Jn 19:15. **crucify**. √84, Ge +6:17.

22. **Why**. ver. 14, 20. 1 P 1:19. 3:18. **what evil**. ver. 41. Jn 8:46. **found no**. ver. 14, 15. **I will**. ver. 16.

23. **instant**. ver. 5. Ps 22:12, 13. 57:4. Zc 11:8. **prevailed**. Lk 21:36. Mt *27:24, 25.

24. **Pilate**. Mt 27:26. Mk 15:15. Jn 19:1, 16, 17. **gave sentence**. *or*, assented. Ex +*23:2. Pr *17:15. **it should be**. Ex +*23:2.

25. **for sedition and**. ver. 2, 5, 19. Mk 15:7. Jn 18:40. **whom**. ver. 18. 1 S 12:13. Mk 15:6. Ac 3:14. **but**. Mt 27:26. Mk 15:15. Jn 19:16.

26. **they laid**. Mt 27:32, etc. Mk 15:21, etc. Jn 19:16, 17. **a Cyrenian**. Ac 2:10. 6:6, 9. 11:20. 13:1. **that**. Lk 9:23. 14:27.

27. **and of**. ver. 55. Lk 8:2. Mt 27:55, 56. Mk 15:40. **bewailed**. Lk 8:52.

28. **turning**. Lk 22:61. **daughters**. SS 1:5. 2:7. 3:5, 10, 11. 5:8, 16. 8:4. **your children**. Mt 23:37.

29. **the days**. Our Lord here refers to the destruction of Jerusalem, and the final desolation of the Jewish state; an evil associated with so many miseries, that sterility, which had otherwise been considered an approbrium, was accounted a circumstance most felicitous. No history can furnish us with a parallel to the calamities and miseries of the Jews; raping and murder, famine and pestilence, within; fire and sword, and all the terrors of war, without. Our Savior himself wept at the foresight of these calamities; and it is almost impossible for persons of any humanity to read the relation of them in Josephus without weeping also. He might justly affirm, "if the misfortunes of all, from the beginning of the world, were compared with those of the Jews, they would appear much inferior in the comparison" (Proem. sec. 4). Lk 17:22. 19:43. *21:23, 24. Mt 24:19. Mk 13:17-19. **Blessed**. Lk 1:24, 25. Dt

28:53-57. Ho 9:12-16. 13:16.

30. **begin to say.** Pr 1:24-33. Is *2:19. Ho ▶10:8. Re √6:16. √9:6.

31. **For.** ſ138B, Ge +13:16. **if.** ſ184A, 1 C +15:2. **in a green tree.** ſ22H1C, Is +4:2. Ps 1:3. Pr 11:31. Je 25:29. Ezk 15:2-7. *20:47, 48. 21:3, 4. Da +*9:26. Mt 3:12. Jn *15:6. He *6:8. 1 P *4:17, 18. Ju 12. **what shall.** Je +*12:5. Ml *4:1. Mt *3:10. **the dry.** A. T. Robertson notes (*Word Pictures,* vol. 2, p. 284) that green wood, being hard to burn, is a symbol of the innocent; dry wood, which catches fire easily, is the symbol of guilt. The application of this proverb is what will Jerusalem do, if they are so bold as to crucify the Messiah, at the time of its judgment from God?

32. **two other.** Lk 22:37. Ge=40:2, 3. Is *53:9, 12. Mt 20:21. 27:38. Mk 10:37. *15:27, 28. Jn 19:18. He *12:2.

33. **when.** Mt 27:33, 34. Mk 15:22, 23. Jn 19:17, 18. He 13:12, 13. **Calvary.** or, the place of a skull. ✱S#2898g. Mt 27:33 (skull). Mk 15:22. Jn 19:17. **they crucified.** Lk 24:7. Dt 21:23. Ps 22:16. Zc *12:10. Mt 20:19. 26:2. Mk 10:33, 34. Jn 3:14. 12:33, 34. 18:32. Ac 2:23. 5:30. 13:29. Ga *3:13. 1 P 2:24.

34. **Then said.** 2 Ch ◐24:22. Ac 3:17. 7:60. 2 T 4:16. **Father.** ver. *46, 47, 48. Lk 6:27, 28. 22:42. Ge 50:17. Ps 106:16-23. Mt *5:44. Mk 1:35. Ac 7:60. Ro 12:14. 1 C *4:12, 13. 1 P 2:20-23. 3:9. **forgive.** T#1630. Is ✱53:12. Mt *5:44. Ac *7:59, 60. **they know not.** Lk +*12:47, 48. Mk 10:38. Jn 15:22-24. 19:11. Ac *3:17. *13:27. 1 C √2:8. 1 T 1:13. **And they.** Ps ▶22:18, 19. Mt 27:35, 36. Mk 15:24. Jn *19:23, 24.

35. **the people.** Ps *22:12, 13, 17. Zc *12:10. Mt 27:38-43. Mk 15:29-32. **the rulers.** Lk 24:20. **derided.** Lk 16:14. Ge 37:19, 20. Ps 4:2. ▶22:7. 35:15, 19-25. 69:7-12, 26. 71:11. Is 49:7. 53:3. La 3:14. Ga 6:7. **He saved.** Lk 4:23. *7:14, 15. Jn *3:16. *11:43. **let him.** Mt 26:53, 54. Jn 10:18. **if he be.** ſ184A, 1 C +15:2. Lk 4:3, 9. **Christ.** Lk 9:20. 22:67-70. Ps *22:6-8. Is *42:1. Mt 1:17. 3:17. 12:18. 1 P 2:4. **the chosen.** Lk 9:35. 1 K 8:16. Ps 89:3, 19. Is 42:1. 49:7. Mt 12:18. 1 P 2:4.

36. **mocked him.** ver. 11. Lk 22:63. Ps *69:21. Mt 27:29, 30, 34, 48. Mk 15:19, 20, 36. Jn *19:28-30. **vinegar.** Ps 69:21. Mt 27:48. Mk 15:36. Jn 19:29.

37. **If thou be.** ſ184A, 1 C +15:2. ver. 35. **king of the Jews.** ver. 3. Mt 27:11.

38. **a superscription.** ver. 3. Mt 27:11, *37. Mk 15:18, *26, 32. Jn 19:3, *19-22. **Latin.** i.e. *of Rome's strength,* ✱S#4513g, only here. **This is.** Jn 14:1. **the king.** ver. 3. Mt 27:11.

39. **one of the malefactors.** Lk 17:34-36. Mt *27:44. Mk *15:32. **railed on him.** Mt 27:39. **if.** ſ184A, 1 C +15:2. **save thyself and.** ver. 35, 37.

40. **rebuked.** Le +*19:17. Ep +*5:11. **Dost.** Lk +*12:5. Ps 36:1. Re 15:4. **fear God.** Pr 1:7. Ro 3:18. **seeing.** 2 Ch 28:22. Je 5:3. Re 16:11.

41. **we indeed.** Lk 15:18, 19. Le 26:40, 41. Jsh 7:19, 20. 2 Ch 33:12. Ezr 9:13. Ne 9:3. Da 9:14. Ja 4:7. 1 J √1:8, 9. **due reward.** T#571. Ge=41:9, 12. Ex 15:1, 6, 7. Dt +32:43 (T#237). Ps 28:4, 5. 94:1, 2. Zp +3:14 (T#88). Re *6:9, 10. 15:3, 4. 18:20. 19:1-7. **but.** ver. 47. Lk 22:69, 70. Mt 27:4, 19, 24, 54. 1 P 1:19. **done nothing.** ver. 22. Jn +*8:46. **amiss.** Ac 25:5. 28:6.

42. **Lord.** Lk 18:13. Ps 106:4, 5. Jn +√20:28. Ac √16:31. 20:21. Ro √10:9-14. 1 C *6:10, 11. 1 P 2:6, 7. 1 J 5:1, √11-13. **remember.** T#1670. Lk *12:8. Ge

40:14. Jg 16:28. Ne *5:19. 13:14, 22, 29-31. Jb 7:7, 8. *10:9, 12. Ps 13:1, 2. 42:9. 74:2. √106:4, 5. 132:1. Je 15:15. La 5:1, 2. Mt *10:32. Ro √10:9, 10. He 6:10. **when.** Lk 14:14. +*21:31. 22:18. Ps *49:14. 90:14. +*102:16. 143:8. Mt +*23:39. +*26:29. Ac +*1:3, 6. +*3:19-21. 1 P +*1:11. **comest into.** Lk 19:12n. Mt +*16:27n, 28. **thy kingdom.** Lk +*17:20, 21. +√21:31. +*22:29, 30. 24:26. Ps *2:6. Is +*9:6, 7. *53:10-12. Da +*7:13, 14. Mt +√21:43. Jn +*1:49. +*18:36. 2 T +*4:1n, 18n. 1 P 1:11. 2 P +*1:11.

43. **Verily.** Lk 4:24. 12:37. 18:17, 29. 21:32. Mt +*5:18. Mk +3:28. Jn +1:51. **To day.** Jesus "promises him immediate and conscious fellowship after death with Christ in Paradise which is a Persian word and is used here not for any supposed intermediate state, but the very bliss of heaven itself" (Robertson, *Word Pictures,* vol. 2, pp. 286, 287). "A common method of dealing with this text is by altering the punctuation. They would have us read the words, 'Verily I say unto thee *today:* thou shalt be with me in Paradise.' But the order of the words in the sentence is all against them. With the emphasis they give it, *seemeron* 'today' should precede the verb. As compare in the Greek, Mt 16:3; Mk 14:30; Lk 19:5, 9; Ac 13:33; He 3:7, 15. But, beside this, the Lord is answering a prayer in which a *time* wherein the thief sought to be remembered was expressed. He had said, 'Lord, remember me *when* Thou comest in Thy kingdom.' The Lord says virtually, 'You shall not wait for that: *today* you shall be with Me.' This is the simple, intelligible reason for the specification of time: 'Today,' not when I come merely, 'shalt thou be with me in Paradise'" (F. W. Grant, *Facts and Theories as to a Future State,* p. 148). Dt +*4:26. Je 42:21. **shalt thou.** Lk 15:4, 5, 20-24. +*19:10. Ge=40:13. Jb 33:27-30. Ps *32:5. +*50:15. Is *1:18, 19. *53:11. √55:6-9. +*65:24. Mi *7:18. Mt 20:15, 16. Ro *5:20, 21. 1 T *1:15, 16. He √7:25. **with me.** Zc *3:2. Jn +*14:3. 17:24. 2 C +*5:8. Ph +*1:23. **in paradise.** "This Persian word was used for an enclosed park or pleasure ground (so Xenophon). The word occurs in two other passages in the N.T. (2 C 12:4; Re 2:7), in both of which the reference is plainly to heaven" (Robertson, *Word Pictures,* vol. 2, p. 287). Lk 16:22. Ge 2:8. Ne 2:8. Ec 2:5. SS 4:12, 13. Is 51:3. Ac 2:31. 2 C √12:2, 4g. Ep 4:9. Re *2:7g. +*14:13.

44. **sixth hour.** Our 12 noon. Mt +*20:5. 27:45. Mk 15:33. Jn +*11:9n. 19:14. **there.** Ex 10:21-23. Ps 105:28. Jl +*2:31. Am 5:18. 8:9. Hab 3:8-11. Ac 2:20. **earth.** or, land. **ninth hour.** Our 3 p.m. 1 K 18:29. Ps +141:2. Mt +20:5. 27:45, 46. Jn +*11:9n. Ac 3:1. 10:3, 30. "The *hour* of the Lord's death was foretold in the daily offering of the incense and the evening sacrifice; the *day* was foretold in the Passover (Le=23:11. 1 C +*15:4), and the *year* in Daniel's prophecy, Da 9:25, 26" (Ada Habershone, *Outline Studies of the Tabernacle,* pp. 41, 42).

45. **and the veil.** Ex 26:31. Le 16:12-16. 2 Ch 3:14. Mt *27:51-53. Mk 15:38. Ep *2:14-18. He 6:19. 9:3-8. 10:19-22. **temple.** Lk 1:9.

46. **cried.** Mt *27:46-49. Mk 15:34-36. Jn *19:30. **Father.** ver. 34. Lk 22:42. Ps ▶31:5. Jn *10:18. Ac *7:59. 1 P *2:23. **commend.** ſ96C9, Ge +2:10. T#1709. 2 T 1:12. 1 P 4:19. **spirit.** Gr. *pneuma,* ſ121A3, Mt +27:50. Ec +*3:21. +*9:5. +*12:7. Ac *7:59. +*23:8, 9. He *12:23. 1 P 3:19. **having.** Mt 27:50,

etc. Mk 15:37, etc. Jn 19:30. **gave up**. Jn *10:18. **Ghost**. *S#1606g. Lk 23:46. Mk 15:37, 39. The word used in Luke for His dying is, as in Mark, "He expired"—"breathed out." It is the simple reality of death as man endures it, quite different from the terms used in Matthew (Mt 27:50) and John (Jn 19:30). It is passive endurance; in the others activity of will, though in surrender. Here, as true Man, He dies like other men; committing His spirit to His Father, His work accomplished (F. W. Grant, *Numerical Bible*, vol. 5, p. 464). Ge +*25:8n, 17. 35:29. 49:33. 2 K ❍+*24:6n. Jb 3:11. 10:18. 11:20. 13:19. 14:10. Je 15:9. La 1:19. Ac 5:5, 10. 12:23.

47. **centurion**. Lk 7:2, 6. Mt +8:5. **he glorified God**. ver. 41. Lk +7:16. Mt √27:54n. Mk *15:39. Jn 19:7. **righteous man**. Mt 27:19, 24.

48. **smote**. Lk 18:13. Je 31:19. Mt 11:17. Ac 2:37.

49. **acquaintance**. Lk 2:44. Jb 19:13. Ps 38:11. 88:8, 18. 142:4. **the women**. ver. 27, 55. Lk 8:2. Mt 27:55, 56, 61. Mk 15:40, 41, 47. Jn 19:21-27. Ac 1:14. **afar off**. Lk 18:13. Ps *38:11. 88:8.

50. **there**. Mt 27:57, 58. Mk 15:42-45. Jn 19:38. **a counsellor**. Mk 15:43. **a good**. Lk 2:25. Ac 10:2, 22. 11:24.

51. **had not**. Ge 37:21, 22. 42:21, 22. Ex +*23:2. Pr √1:10. Is 8:12. Mk ❍14:64. **Arimathea**. 1 S 1:1. **waited for**. ver. 42. Lk 2:25, 38. Ge 49:18. Mk *15:43. **the kingdom of God**. Lk +4:43.

52. **went unto Pilate**. Jn *19:38-42.

53. **and wrapped**. Is *53:9. Mt 27:59, 60. Mk 15:46. **hewn in stone**. 2 Ch 16:14. Is 22:16. **wherein**. Lk 19:30. Mk 11:2. Jn 19:41.

54. **the preparation**. Mt 27:62. Jn 19:14, 31, 42. **drew on**. lit. began to dawn. Mt 28:1.

55. **the women**. ver. 49. Lk 8:2. Mt 27:61. Mk 15:47. **beheld the sepulchre**. This testimony of Luke, corroborated by Mark, effectively demolishes the notion of some unbelievers that the women went to the wrong tomb on the resurrection morning. Mk 15:47.

56. **prepared**. Lk 24:1. 2 Ch 16:14. Mk 16:1. Jn 19:39. **rested**. Ex 12:16. +*20:8-10. 31:14. 35:2, 3. Le 19:3, 30. 23:8. Dt 5:14. Is +*58:13n, 14. Je *17:24, 25, 27n.

LUKE 24

Two angels inform the women at the sepulchre, that Jesus is risen, 1-7. They report it to the others, but are not believed, 8-11. Peter goes to the sepulchre, 12. Jesus appears, as a stranger, to two disciples when going to Emmaus; converses with them, explains the scriptures, and then discovers himself, but disappears, 13-32. They return, and report it to the eleven, who inform them that Jesus had appeared to Simon, 33-35. He joins the company; shows them his hands and his side, and eats with them, 36-43. He reminds them of his words concerning his suffering and resurrection, "opens their understandings," interprets the scriptures, and commissions them to preach his gospel to the nations, beginning at Jerusalem, 44-48. He promises the Holy Spirit, leads them forth to Bethany, blesses them, and ascends into heaven, 49-51. They worship him with joy, and praise God at the temple continually, 52, 53.

1. **upon**. Mt *28:1-8. Mk *16:1, 2. Jn *20:1, 2. **first day**. "The *first* day of the week is the day after the *Sabbath*, or Seventh Day, and is therefore the *Eighth*

Day. Indeed, as the number *Seven* is the *Sabbatical* number, or number of *Rest*, in Holy Scripture, so *Eight* may be called the *Dominical*. *Seven* is expressive of *rest* in Christ; *Eight* is expressive of *Resurrection* to *new life* and *glory* in Him. In accordance with this principle, the *Eighth* Day was the Day of *Circumcision* (cp. Lk 1:59. Ph 3:5),—the type of Christian Baptism,— the Sacrament of *Resurrection*,—in which we *rise* from the death of sin to newness of Life in Him. Our Lord received the name Jesus on the *eighth* day (Lk 2:21); He as our *Jesus, Joshua, Savior*, brings us to the heavenly Canaan,—to the glory of the Resurrection. The Name *Jesus, Savior*, given to Him on the *Eighth Day*, makes in the *universal* language (Greek) the number *eight* in hundreds, tens, and units,—888. The great Day of the Feast of Tabernacles—the type of His Incarnation—was the *Eighth* (John 7:37). And in His Sermon on the Mount He pronounces *eight Beatitudes* describing the way that leads to the fruition of heavenly glory. Hence we also find, that the *Transfiguration*—which was a figure and a glimpse of the future glory of the bodies of the Saints after the Resurrection—is mentioned as having taken place *eight* days after our Lord had said, "There be some standing here which shall not taste of death till they see the kingdom of God" (Lk 9:27)" (Wordsworth, *Greek Testament*, vol. 1, p. 252). Ac 20:7. 1 C 16:2. Re 1:10. **they came**. ver. 10. Lk 8:2, 3. 23:55, 56. Mt 27:55, 56. Mk 15:40. **bringing**. To embalm the body of our Lord; which shows that they had no hope of his resurrection on the third day. Joseph Nicodemus and Joseph of Arimathea had done this before the body was laid in the tomb; but on account of the approach of the sabbath, it was probably hastily and imperfectly performed; and hence a second embalming would be deemed necessary, for which purpose the spices now brought by the women were intended. Lk 23:56. **spices**. Mk 16:1.

2. **they found**. Mt 27:60-66. *28:2. Mk 15:46, 47. 16:3, 4. Jn 20:1, 2. **the stone**. Mt 27:60. Mk 15:46. Jn 11:38. 20:1. **rolled away**. Ge 29:3, 8, 10.

3. **they entered in**. ver. 23. Mk *16:5. Jn *20:6, 7. **the Lord Jesus**. Lk 7:13. Mk 16:19.

4. **much perplexed**. Ga 4:20. **two**. Mary Magdalene and the other Mary saw only one angel in white, sitting on the stone which he had rolled from the door of the sepulchre; but the women here mentioned saw no angel till they had entered the sepulchre, when two appeared to them in "garments shining like lightning," as the word imports. This, and several other variations, show there were two distinct companies of women, who went successively to the tomb on the morning of the resurrection; which renders the whole account clear and consistent (See Note on Mk 16:2). Mt 28:2. Mk 16:5, 6. Jn *20:12. **men**. Lk 2:9. Ac 1:10. 10:30. **stood by**. Ge 18:2. Mt 28:2-6. Mk 16:5. Jn 20:11, 12. Ac 1:10.

5. **they**. ver. 37. Lk 1:12, 13, 29. Da 8:17, 18. 10:7-12, 16-19. Mt 28:3-5. Mk 16:5, 6. Ac 10:3, 4. 24:25. Re 11:13. **the living**. or, him that liveth. Is ▶8:19. Jn 6:57. He 7:8. Re 1:17, 18. 2:8.

6. **is risen**. Ps ✱16:10. **remember**. ver. 44-46. Lk 9:22, 44. 18:31-33. Mt +*12:40n. 16:21. *17:22, 23. 20:18, 19. 27:63. 28:6. Mk 8:31. 9:9, 10, 31, 32. 10:33, 34.

7. **Saying**. ver. 6. Lk 9:22, 44. **Son of man**. Lk +5:24. **must be delivered**. ver. 26, 44. Lk 13:33. **be**

crucified. Mt 20:19. **third day**. ver. 46. Lk 9:22.

8. **they remembered**. Jn *2:19-22. 12:16. 14:26. 16:4.

9. **returned from**. ver. 22-24. Mt *28:7, 8. Mk 16:7, 8, 10. **and told**. Jn 20:18.

10. **Mary Magdalene**. Lk *8:2, 3. Mk 15:40, 41. 16:9-11. Jn 20:11-18. **Joanna**. Lk 8:2, 3. **Mary**. Mt 27:56. Mk 15:40, 41.

11. **idle tales**. ver. 25. Ge 19:14. 2 K 7:2. Jb 9:16. Ps 126:1. Ac 12:9, 15. **believed them not**. Ge=45:26. Mk 16:11, 16.

12. **arose Peter**. Jn *20:3-10. **stooping down**. Jn 20:5, 6. **linen clothes**. Jn 19:40. 20:5-7. **departed**. Jn 20:10.

13. **two**. ver. 18. Mk *16:12n, 13. **Emmaus**. *Emmaus* was situated, according to the testimony both of St. Luke and Josephus (Bel. l. vii. c. 27), sixty furlongs from Jerusalem, that is, about seven miles and a half. It has generally been confounded with *Emmaus*, a city of Judah, afterwards called *Nicopolis*; but Reland has satisfactorily shown that they were distinct places; the latter, according to the old Itinerary of Palestine, being situated 10 miles from Lydda, and 22 miles from Jerusalem. D'Arvieux (vol. vii. p. 259) states, that going from Jerusalem to Rama, he took the right from the high road to Rama, at some little distance from Jerusalem, and "travelled a good league over rocks and flint stones, to the end of the valley of terebinthine trees," until he reached *Emmaus*; which "seems, by the ruins which surround it, to have been formerly larger than it was in our Savior's time. The Christians, while masters of the Holy Land, re-established it a little, and built several churches. Emmaus was not worth the trouble of having come out of the way to see it."

14. **they talked together**. Lk 6:45. Dt 6:7. Ml +*3:16. Ac 20:11g. 24:26.

15. **Jesus**. ver. 36. Ge=45:15. Mt *18:20. Jn 14:18, 19.

16. **eyes were holden**. ver. ◑+*31. Lk 9:45. 18:34. Ge +*3:7. +*19:11. 21:19. Nu 22:31. 2 K 6:18-20. 1 Ch 21:16. Mk 16:12. Jn *20:14. *21:4. Ac 26:18. **that**. Ge ◑+*27:16. **should not**. That Jesus was unrecognized is perfectly understandable. I myself did not recognize my own father when I went to the airport to pick him up, though I had seen him just days before, and had to have it announced over the public address system where I was waiting to meet him—and I had walked right by where he was seated, and did not see him, nor did he see me. I saw my next door neighbor several times in the grocery store just yesterday, and did not recognize her until she started to talk to my wife. We often fail to recognize what we do not expect to see. Furthermore, Jesus evidently was not of such a singular appearance as to be instantly recognizable, as Peter apparently was (Lk 22:56), for the chief priests and scribes required Judas to identify him in the crowd. Even before his resurrection Jesus was unrecognized, on occasion, for he apparently was able to lose himself in the crowd, and so escape threatened destruction. Isaiah distinctly predicts that his appearance would not be remarkable. Therefore, it is not necessary to assume, as some do, that Christ "materialized" and "dematerialized" his body in order to be seen by men, and assumed different forms to different people after the resurrection, as though he did not have his own permanent resurrected and glorified body. Luke re-

ports Christ emphatically declaring, ver. 39, in language which could not be stronger, that He himself was there before them in his own physical body. Lk +*4:30. Is +*53:2. Mt 26:48. Mk *14:44. *16:12n. **know**. Gr. *epiginosko*, Mt +11:27.

17. **and are sad**. Ge=40:7. Ezk *9:4-6. Mt 6:16. Jn 16:6, 20-22.

18. **Cleopas**. i.e. *the whole glory; famed of all*, ✱S#2810g, only here. Jn 19:25.

19. **Concerning**. Lk 7:16. Mt 21:11. Jn 3:2. 4:19. +*6:14. 7:40-42, 52. Ac *2:22. *10:38. **of Nazareth**. Mk 1:24. **a prophet**. Mt 21:11. **mighty**. Ac 7:22. 18:24. **in deed**. Ac 2:22.

20. **chief priests**. Lk 22:66-71. 23:1-5. Mt 27:1, 2, 20. Mk 15:1. Ac 2:23. 3:13-15. 4:8-10, 27, 28. 5:30, 31. 13:27-29. 1 Th 2:15. **our rulers**. Lk 18:18. 23:13, 35. Mt 9:18. Jn 3:1. 7:26, 48. 12:42. Ac 3:17. 4:5, 8. 13:27. 1 C 2:8.

21. **we trusted**. Lk 2:38. Mt √20:21. Mk +*15:43. Ac √1:6. **redeemed Israel**. Lk *1:68. Ps +*130:8. Is +*59:20. Ac +*1:6. Ro +*11:26. 1 P 1:18, 19. Re 5:9. **the third day**. √108H12, 1 S +30:12. Lk 9:22. Mt +*12:40n.

22. **and certain women**. ver. 9-11. Mt 28:7, 8. Mk 16:9, 10. Jn 20:1, 2, 18. **early at**. ver. 1.

23. **found not his body**. ver. 3. **vision of angels**. ver. 4, 5, 9.

24. **went**. ver. 12. Jn 20:1-10.

25. **he said**. √80, Lk +9:55. **O fools**. Rather, *inconsiderate* men, *anoeetoi*, justly termed such, because they had not attended to the description of the Messiah by the prophets, nor to *His* teaching and miracles, as proofs that He alone was the person described. Mk 7:18. *8:17, 18. 9:19. *16:14. Ga 3:1, 3. He 5:11, 12. **slow of heart**. Lk 9:45.

26. **suffered**. ver. 7, 44, *46. Lk 18:31-33. Ps ch. 22, 69. Is ch. 53. Zc *13:7. Mt 26:54. Jn 11:49-52. 12:24, 32. Ac 3:18. +*17:3. 1 C +*15:3, 4. He *2:8-10. 9:22, 23. 12:2. 1 P 1:3, +√11. **his glory**. Zc +√6:13. Lk 9:26. 1 C 15:17. 1 P +√1:11.

27. **beginning**. √180A, Ge +4:20. ver. *44. Ge +*3:15. 12:3. 18:18. *22:18. *26:4. 28:14. +*49:10. Ex 12:3-28, 43-51. Le ch. =16. Nu 20:11. 21:6-9. 24:17. Dt *18:15. Jn +*5:39, 45-47. Ac 3:22. 7:37. 8:35. 28:23. **at Moses**. √121A6, Lk +16:29. Lk 16:16. Jn 1:45. 3:14. +*5:39, 45-47. Ac 3:22. 7:2-53. 8:35. 13:27. 28:23. **and all**. ver. 25. 2 S 7:12-16. Ps *16:9, 10. 132:11. Is +*7:14. +*9:6, 7. *40:10, 11. *50:6. 52:13, 14. ch. *53. 61:1. Je +*23:5, 6. *33:14, 15. Ezk *34:23. *37:25. Da 7:13, 14. +*9:24-26. Jon 1:17. 3:5. Mi +*5:2-4. 7:20. Zc 6:12. *9:9. 12:10. *13:7. Ml *3:1-3. 4:2. Jn *1:45. Ac *3:24. *10:43. 13:27-30. 28:23. Re *19:10. **the prophets**. Christ's actual citations from the prophets given in the gospels are: (1) Mt 9:13 w Ho 6:6. (2) Mt 10:35, 36 w Mi 7:6. (3) Mt 11:10 w Ml 3:1. (4) Mt 11:28-30 w Je 6:16. (5) Mt 12:7 w Ho 6:6. (6) Mt 12:18 w Is 42:1-3. (7) Mt 12:21 w Is 42:4. (8) Mt 12:39-42 w Jon 1:17. (9) Mt 13:14 w Is 6:9, 10. (10) Mt 15:8 w Is 29:13. (11) Mt 21:5 w Zc 9:9. (12) Mt 21:13 w Je 7:11. (13) Mt 24:15 w Da 9:27. (14) Mt 27:9 w Zc 11:13. (15) Mk 7:6 w Is 29:13. (16) Mk 9:44 w Is 66:24. (17) Mk 11:17 w Is 56:7. (18) Mk 13:14 w Da 9:27. (19) Mk 14:27 w Zc 13:7. (20) Lk 4:18 w Is 61:1, 2 and 58:6. (21) Lk 7:27 w Ml 3:1. (22) Lk 12:53 w Mi 7:6. (23) Lk 19:46 w Is 56:7 and Je 7:11. (24) Jn 6:45 w Is 54:13. **expounded**. T#1015. Ac 17:2, 3.

❋S#1329g, *diermeeneuo*. Ac 9:36 (by interpretation). 1 C 12:30 (interpret). 14:5, 13, 27. See ❋S#1328g, 1 C 14:28 (interpreter). For related words, see Mk +*5:41. **all the scriptures.** ver. 32, 45. Mt 21:42. **concerning himself.** "Jesus found himself in the Old Testament, a thing that some modern scholars do not seem able to do" (A. T. Robertson, *Word Pictures*, vol. 2, p. 294). Jn +*5:39.

28. **whither they went.** ver. 13. **he made.** That is, he was directing his steps as if to go onwards; and so he doubtless would, had he not been withheld by their friendly importunities. There is not the smallest ground for founding a charge of *dissimulation* against our Savior, or affording any encouragement to dissimulation in others. Ge 19:2. 32:26. 42:7. 1 S ◐*16:2n. Mk 6:48.

29. **constrained.** Lk 14:23. Ge 19:2, 3. *32:26. 2 K 4:8. Ac 16:15. **Abide.** T#1569. Jn 4:40, 41. He *13:2. **far spent.** Lk 9:12. Jg 19:9, 11. Je 6:4.

30. **he took.** ver. 35. Mt 15:36. Mk 8:6. **and blessed.** T#1270. Lk 9:16. 22:17, 19. Dt +8:10 (T#1240). Jsh 9:14. 1 S 9:13. Mt +14:19. ◐+15:36. *26:26. Mk 6:41. 8:7. 14:22. Jn 6:11, 23. Ac 27:35. Ro 14:6. 1 C *10:16, 30. 11:24. 14:16. Col *3:17. 1 T √4:3-5. **and brake.** √108H4, Is +58:7.

31. **their eyes.** ver. *16. Jn *20:13-16. **opened.** ver. ◐+*16, 45. Lk +*4:18. Ge +*3:7. +*21:19. Nu 22:31. 2 K 6:17-20. 1 Ch 21:16. Ps *119:18. Jn 9:39. 20:16. 21:7. Ac 9:17, 18. 26:18. 2 C *4:4, 6. Ep *1:18. **knew.** Gr. *epiginosko*, Mt +11:27. i.e. fully recognized him. Ge=45:1. **vanished out of their sight.** *or*, ceased to be seen of them. Lk *4:30. Jn *8:59. 10:39.

32. **Did.** Jb 32:18, 19. Ps 39:3. *104:34. Pr 27:9, 17. Is *50:4. Je +*15:16. *20:9. *23:29. Jn *6:63. He √4:12. **while he talked.** Ge ◐3:10. Ps 45:2. Jn 7:46. **opened.** ver. *45. Ge=41:56. Ac +*17:2, 3. *28:23. **the scriptures.** ver. 27, 45. Mt 21:42.

33. **and found.** Mk 16:13. Jn *20:19-26. **and them.** Ac 1:14.

34. **Saying.** From Mk 16:13, we learn that the apostles did not believe the testimony even of the two disciples from Emmaus, while it is here asserted they were saying, when they entered the room, "The Lord is risen," etc. This difficulty is removed by rendering interrogatively, "Has the Lord risen," etc.? Yet the presence of the word "indeed" indicates that this added evidence of the two disciples was the turning point which convinced the rest that the Lord was risen indeed. **the Lord.** Lk 7:13. **hath appeared.** Lk 22:54-62. Mk 16:7. 1 C 15:5.

35. **they told.** Mk 16:12, 13. **was known.** Ge =45:1. **breaking of bread.** √108H4, Is +58:7. Ac 2:42.

36. **Jesus himself.** Mk *16:14. Jn *20:19-23. 1 C *15:5. **Peace.** Lk 10:5. Is 57:18, 19. Mt 10:13. Jn *14:27. 16:33. 20:26. Ro *15:13. 2 Th 3:16. Re 1:4.

37. **terrified.** Lk 16:30. 21:9. 1 S 28:13. Jb 4:14-16. Mt 14:26, 27. Mk 6:49, 50. Ac 12:15. **affrighted.** ver. 5. Mt 17:7. **supposed.** Mt 14:26. Mk 6:49. **spirit.** Gr. *pneuma*, put for a spirit being or an angel, as in ver. 39. Yet it must be remembered that a "spirit" is distinguished from an angel in Ac 23:8, and that the context here shows the apostles thought what they saw was a disembodied spirit, not the actual person of Christ himself, a misconception Christ immediately and emphatically corrects. ver. 39. Ac 8:29, 39. 10:19. 11:12. He 1:7, 14. 1 P 3:19. 1 J 4:6a. Re 1:4. 3:1. 4:5. 5:6. For the other uses of *pneuma*, see Mt +*8:16n.

38. **and why.** Je 4:14. Da 4:5, 19. Mt 16:8. 17:7. He *4:13. **thoughts.** Lk 2:35. Ro 14:1. **arise.** Ac 7:23. 1 C 2:9.

39. **Behold my.** Mt +*27:52. 28:6. Jn +√2:19, 21, 22. √20:27. **hands.** Jn 20:20, 25, 27. Ac 1:3. 1 J 1:1. **it is I myself.** Ge=45:12. Ac +*1:11. 2:32, 36. 1 Th 4:16. **handle me.** Jn *20:27. 1 J *1:1. **for.** Lk +*23:46. Nu 16:22. Ec +*12:7. Ac *23:8. 1 Th *5:23. He *12:9. **spirit.** ver. +*37. **hath not.** A spirit is therefore an intelligent entity, and like God the Father and God the Holy Spirit, must be invisible. Mt +*28:19n. Jn 4:24. 14:17. 1 C 3:16. 6:19. **flesh and bones.** Mt ◐+*16:17. 1 C ◐*15:50. Ep *5:30. ◐6:12.

40. **And when.** Jn *20:20. **he showed.** Ac *1:3. **his.** √63A3, Mt +19:13. **hands and.** Ps 22:16.

41. **believed not.** Ge=45:26-28. Jb 9:16. Ps 126:1, 2. Mk 16:16. Jn 16:22. **for joy.** Ac 12:14. **Have.** Jn 21:5, 10-13.

43. **and did eat.** Jn *21:12, 13. Ac 1:4. *10:40, 41.

44. **These are the words.** ver. *6, *7. Lk *9:22. *18:31-33. Mt *16:21. 17:22, 23. 20:18, 19. Mk 8:31, 32. 9:31. 10:33, 34. Jn +*2:18-22. **while I.** Jn 16:4, 5, 16, 17. *17:11-13. Ac 9:39. **that all.** ver. *26, *27, *46. Lk 21:22. Mt *26:54, 56. Jn 19:24-37. Ac 3:18. 13:29-31, 33. 1 C +*15:3, 4. **in the law.** Ge +*3:15. 14:18. +*22:18. +√49:10. Le 16:2, etc. Nu *21:8, 9. *35:25. Dt *18:15-19. Jn *3:14, 15. *5:46, 47. 7:23. Ac *3:22-24. 7:37. He 3:5. 7:1-3. 9:8-12. 10:1. **in the prophets.** ver. +*27n. Is +*7:14. +*9:6, 7. *11:1-10. 28:16. *40:1-11. *42:1-4. 49:1-8. 50:2-6. *52:13-15. ch. +*53. *61:1-3. Je +*23:5, 6. 33:14, 15. Ezk 17:22-24. *34:23, 24. Da *2:44. *7:13, 14. +*9:24-27. Ho 1:7-11. *3:5. Jl +*2:28-32. Am 9:11, 12. Mi +*5:1-4. Hg *2:7-9. Zc 6:12, 13. 9:9. 11:8-13. *12:10. 13:7. *14:4. Ml *3:1-3. 4:2-6. Ac 28:23. **in the psalms.** Ps ch. 2. +*16:9-11. ch. 22. 34:20. 40:6-8. 68:18. ch. 69. 72:1-19. ch. 88. 109:4-20. ch. *110. 118:22-26. 132:11. Jn +√5:39. Ac +*17:2, 3. 1 P 1:11. Re *19:10.

45. **opened.** T#1056. Lk +*3:7. Ex *4:11. Jb 33:16. 36:10. Ps √119:18. Is 29:10-12, *18, *19. Jn *2:22. Ac *16:14. *26:18. 1 C 2:11. 2 C *3:14-18. ◐*4:4-6. Ep 5:14. 1 J 5:20. Re 3:7. **the scriptures.** ver. 27, 32. Mt 21:42.

46. **Thus it is written.** ver. 7, 26, 27, 44. Ps ch. 22. Is *50:6. *53:2, etc. Mt +26:24. Ac √4:12. *17:3. 1 P 1:3. **behoved.** Is 53:5. **to rise.** Jn 20:9. Ac 5:31. **third day.** 1 C +*15:3, 4.

47. **that repentance.** Da +*9:24. Mt 3:2. *9:13. Ac +*2:38. +*3:19. 5:31. *11:18. *13:38, 39, 46. √17:30, 31. *20:21. 26:20. 1 J *2:12. **in his name.** Lk 9:48. Ac √4:12. **among.** Lk 2:32. Ge +*12:3. Ps *22:27. 67:2-4, 7. *86:9. 98:1-3. ch. 117. Is +*2:1-3. 11:10. 19:24, 25. 42:6. *49:6, 22. 52:10, 15. 60:1-3. 66:18-21. Je *31:34. Ho *2:23. Mi *4:2. Ml 1:11. Mt +*8:10, 11. +√28:19. Ac 13:46-48. *18:5, 6. 28:28. Ro *10:12-18. 15:8-16. Ga 3:8. Ep *3:8. Col *1:27. **beginning.** ver. 49. Lk *13:34. Is 5:4. Ho 11:8. Mt *10:5, 6. Ac 1:4. 2:14-47. 3:25, 26. 10:37. 13:46. Ro 5:20. *11:26, 27. Ep 1:6.

48. **ye are witnesses.** Jn *15:27. Ac +√1:8, 22. +*2:32. 3:15. *4:33. *5:32. *10:39, 41. 13:31. 22:15. 1 C 15:15. He √2:3, 4. 1 P 5:1. 2 P √1:16. 1 J √1:2, 3.

49. **I send.** √96C7, Mt +26:24. Is *44:3, 4. 59:20, 21. Ezk *36:27. Jl +*2:28, etc. Zc 12:10. Jn *14:16, 17, 26. √15:26. *16:7-16. Ac 2:16, 17, 33. Ep 1:13.

promise. Ge 1:2. Ac √‖1:4, 5. **my Father**. Lk 10:22. 22:29. Mt 7:21. Jn 5:17. **but tarry**. Is 32:15. Ac *1:4, 8. *2:1-21. **in the city**. ver. 47. **endued**. Jb 8:22. 29:14. 39:19. Ps 35:26. 93:1. 132:9. Is 52:1. 61:10. Ro 13:12, 14. 1 C 15:53, 54. 2 C 5:2, 4. Col 3:12. 1 P 5:5. **power from**. In the parallel passage at Ac 1:5 termed *pneuma hagion*, "Holy Ghost," without articles (Mt 1:18n), showing the enduement to be his gifts, not himself. Lk 5:17. Ge 1:2. Mi 3:8. Ac √1:8. **on high**. Lk 1:78. Is 32:15.

50. **as far**. Mk 11:1. Ac 1:12. **to Bethany**. Lk 19:29. Mt 21:17. 26:6. Mk 11:1, 11, 12. 14:3. Jn 11:1, 18.

12:1. **he lifted**. Ge 14:18-20. 27:4. 48:9. 49:28. Nu √6:23-27. Mk *10:16. He 7:5-7.

51. **blessed them**. Dt=33:1. Ac 3:26. **he was parted**. 2 K *2:11. Mk *16:19. Jn *20:17. Ac *1:9, +*11. Ep *4:8-10. He 1:3. *4:14. **carried up**. Ps ✱68:16. Jn 3:13.

52. **they worshipped him**. Mt +*8:2. +*14:33. *28:9, 17. Jn +√20:28. He +*1:6. **returned**. ver. 49. **with great joy**. Ps 30:11. Jn 14:28. *16:7, 22. 1 P *1:8.

53. **continually**. ʃ171D. Mk +16:20. **in the temple**. Ac *2:46, 47. 3:1. *5:21, 41, 42. **blessing God**. Lk 1:64. 2:28. 13:13. **Amen**. Mt *28:20. Mk 16:20. Re 22:21.

JOHN

JOHN 1

The Word who was in the beginning with God and was God, is the Creator of all things, has life in himself and is the Light of men, 1-5. John a witness to that true and only Light, which was unknown to the world which he made and not received by his own, except by such as were born of God, and these were adopted as his children, 6-13. The Word became flesh and displayed his glory as the only begotten of the Father, 14. John testifies to his superior dignity and fulness whence all receive; for grace and truth came by him, 15-17. He declares the invisible God to men, 18. Various testimonies of John to the Pharisees, concerning himself and Jesus, 19-28. John points him out as "the lamb of God" and "the Son of God" who "baptizeth with the Holy Ghost," 29-34. Two of John's disciples follow Jesus, 35-39. Andrew, one of them, brings Peter to him, whom he surnames Cephas, 40-42. Philip is called, who brings Nathanael, 43-45. Jesus declares him to be "an Israelite indeed:" and he confesses Jesus as "the Son of God and the King of Israel," 46-49. Jesus promises that he shall see still greater things, 50, 51.

1. **the beginning**. Jn *8:58. *17:5. Ge *1:1. Pr *8:22-31. Is *9:6. Mi +*5:2. Ep 3:9. Col *1:17. He 1:10. 7:3. √13:8. 1 J 1:1. Re 1:2, 4, *8, 11, 17. 3:14. 21:6. *22:13. **the Word**. ʃ101, Dt +32:42. ver. 14. He 4:12. 1 J 1:1, 2. 5:7. Re *19:13. **with**. ver. 18. Jn 16:28. *17:5. Pr *8:22-30. 1 J 1:2. **and the Word**. ʃ101, Dt +32:42. By Hyperbaton, the subject, "the Word," being defined by the article which is prefixed to it, can be placed at the end of two of the clauses, and in each case we are to put the stress on "the Word." ʃ77, Ex +3:19. Bengel notes that "when the predicate precedes the subject, there is an *epitasis* (an emphatic enlargement of the subject)" as also in Jn 4:24 (*New Testament Word Studies*, vol. 1, p. 543). Jn *10:30-33. +√20:28. Ps +*45:6. Is +*7:14. +*9:6. 40:9-11. Mt 1:23. Ro *9:5. Ph *2:6. 1 T *3:16. T √2:13. He *1:8-13. 2 P √1:1g. 1 J 5:7, 20. **was God**. Not "a god," for the lack of the Greek article here does not make "God" indefinite but determines which term ("Word" or "God") is to be the subject of the linking verb "was." Greek word order is somewhat more flexible than English, for in English statement sentences the predicate nominative always follows the linking verb. But the literal order of the Greek words here is "and God was the Word" (*kai theos een o logos*), the subject "Word" follows the verb and the predicate nominative

"God" precedes the verb, the reverse of English word order. Since this clause uses a linking verb, both the subject and the predicate nominative are in the nominative case, so case endings do not serve to identify the subject in this construction; rather, the article "the" points out the subject of the clause. Greek uses the article "the" to accomplish what English does by word order. Thus, if John had placed the article "the" before "God," the meaning would be "God was the Word;" if he had placed the article "the" before both "Word" and "God," the meaning would be convertible or reversible: it would mean equally "God was the Word," and "The Word was God," but this John did not do. By placing the article "the" before "Word," "Word" must be the subject of the linking verb "was," and the statement can only be rendered "the Word was God." Just as mistaken is the rendering "the Word was divine," for "God," lacking the article, is not thereby an adjective, or rendered qualitative when it precedes a linking verb followed by a noun which does have the article. See the note on Mt 27:54 for scholarly documentation and an explanation of this construction known technically as the *anarthrous noun*. Translators and translations which choose to render this phrase "a god" or "divine" are motivated by theological, not grammatical, considerations. The phrase "a god" is particularly objectionable, because it makes Christ a lesser god, which is polytheism, and contrary to the express declaration of Scripture elsewhere (Dt 32:39). For clearly if Christ is "a god," then he must be either a "true god" or a "false god." If "true," we assert polytheism; if "false," he is unworthy of our credence. John's high view of Christ expressed throughout his gospel, climaxing in the testimony of Thomas, who addressed Christ as "my Lord and my God," is asserted from this opening statement, "the Word was God." There is no legitimate basis for understanding his declaration in any lesser sense than affirming the full deity of our Savior. Jn √5:18. 8:+*35, 58, 59. +*10:30, 33, ◑+34. 14:7. +√20:28. Dt +*32:39. Jb +*19:26. Is *43:10. √44:6. Je √23:5, 6. Mi +*5:2. Ac ◑12:22. √20:28. Ro 9:5. 2 C ◑*4:4. Ep 5:5g. Ph 2:6n. 2 Th 1:12g. T √2:13g. He +*1:8. 2 P √1:1g. Re 21:7.

2. **The same**. Supply the ellipsis, (Word). ʃ50, Ho 2:21. **in the beginning**. Ge 1:1. He 1:10. **with God**. T#969‡. Jn 8:56. Ge 17:1. Ex +*6:3. Dt ◑*32:39. Is √44:6. Da +7:13 (T#968‡). Lk ◑√3:22. Ac *7:38. He +*1:8.   *15:3.

3. A.M. 1. B.C. 4004. **All things**. ver. 10. Jn 5:17-

19. Ge 1:1, 26. Jb +*26:13. Ps 33:6. 102:25. Is 40:28. 44:24. 45:12, 18. 66:2. 1 C 8:6. Ep *3:9. Col *1:16, 17. He *1:2, 3, 10-12. 2:10. 3:3, 4. Re 1:5. 3:14. *4:11. **without.** *J*24E, Ge +30:33. **was not.** *J*144D, Ge +40:23.

4. **was.** *J*96C1, Ge +4:1. Heterosis of Tense, the past put for the present. i.e. *is.* **life.** Jn *3:16. 4:14. *5:21, 26. 6:57. *10:10, 28. *11:25. √14:6. 17:2. Ge=2:9. Ac *3:15. Ro *6:23. 1 C *15:45. Col *3:4. 2 T *1:10. 1 J 1:2. *5:1, 11, 12. Re 1:18. 4:9, 10. 22:1. **the life.** *J*50, Ho +2:21. ver. 5, 8, 9. Jn *8:12. 9:5. *12:35, 46. Ps *84:11. Is 35:4, 5. 42:6, 7, 16. 49:6. 60:1-3. Ml 4:2. Mt 4:16. Lk *1:78, 79. 2:32. Ac 26:23. Ep *5:14. 1 J 1:5-7. Re 21:23. 22:16. **was.** *J*96C1, Ge +4:1. i.e. *is.*

5. **the light.** *J*50, Ho +2:21. ver. 10. Jn √3:19, 20. *12:36-40. Jb 24:13-17. Pr 1:22, 29, 30. Ro 1:28. 8:7. 1 C √2:14. **darkness.** Jn 8:12. Is 9:2. **the darkness.** *J*50, Ho +2:21. **comprehended.** *J*139, Mt +11:17. *J*134, Mt +3:9. In Syriac the word "darkness" would be *keval* and "comprehend" would be *kabbel*, constituting this an instance of the figure Parechesis, or Foreign Paronomasia. Ep 3:18.

6. A.M. 3999. B.C. 5. **a man.** ver. 33. Jn 3:28. 17:18. Is 40:3-5. Ml *3:1. 4:5, 6. Mt 3:1, etc. *11:10. 21:25. Mk 1:1-8. Lk 1:15-17, 76. 3:2, etc. Ac 13:24, 25. **John.** Mt 3:1. Mk 1:4. Lk 1:13, 61-63. 3:2.

7. **a witness.** ver. 15, 19, 26, 27, 29, 32-34, 36. 3:26-36. 5:33-35. 10:41. 15:27. Ac *19:4. **bear witness.** ver. 32. Jn 6:69. Mk ◑+*1:24. Ac +*5:32. +*10:43. Ro +*1:4. **that.** ver. 9, 12. Jn 3:26. Ac 19:4. Ep 3:9. 1 T √2:4. T *2:11. 2 P √3:9. **believe.** Jn 5:44.

8. **that light.** ver. 20. Jn 3:28. Ac 19:4.

9. **That was the.** ver. 4. Jn 6:32. √14:6. 15:1. Is *49:6. Mt 6:23. 1 J √1:8. *2:8. *5:20. **true.** Jn 4:23. 6:32. 15:1. 17:3. 19:35. **light.** Jn *12:46. 1 J *1:5. **which lighteth.** Jn *3:19. Ps *119:105. Mt 5:14. **every.** √*J*171B, Ge +24:10. ver. 7. Jn 8:12. *12:46. Is +*8:20. 1 Th 5:4-7. T 2:11. **that cometh.** *J*142, Ge +20:16. Jn 3:19. 11:27. 12:46. **world.** Gr. *kosmos,* Mt +4:8. ver. 29. Jn 3:16, 17. 4:42. 2 C 5:19. 1 J 2:1, 2. 4:14.

10. **was in.** ver. 18. Jn 5:17. Ge 11:6-9. 16:13. 17:1. 18:33. Ex 3:4-6. Ac 14:17. 17:24-27. He *1:3. **world.** Gr. *kosmos,* Mt +4:8. **and the world.** Gr. *kosmos,* Mt +4:8. **made.** Gr. *ginomai,* S#1096g. ver. 10, 14. Jn 2:9. 5:4, 6, 9, 14a. 8:33. 9:39. Ga 3:13. 4:4, 4. Ph 2:7b. T 3:7. Ja 3:9. 1 P 2:7. **by him.** See on ver. 3. Je 10:11, 12. Col *1:16. He 1:2, 3, 10-12. Re *3:14. **world.** Gr. *kosmos,* Mt +4:8. *J*145, Jg +11:40. *J*121J9A. Metonymy of the Subject B576. The *world* is put for a portion of its inhabitants. Compare √*J*171B, Ge +24:10n. For other instances of this figure see Jn 3:17. ?6:33, 51. 7:7. 14:17. ◑*31. 15:19. 16:20, 33. 17:*9, 14, 21. Ac 17:6. 19:27. 1 C 11:32. 1 J 3:1. 4:5. 5:4, 5. **knew him not.** ver. 5. Jn 16:3. 17:25. Ge=42:8. Mt 11:27. 1 C 1:21. √2:8. 1 J 3:1.

11. **came.** Mt *15:24. Ac *3:25, 26. *13:26, 46. Ro *9:4, 5. *15:8. Ga √4:4. **his own.** Mt 21:38. **and.** Jn *3:32. 13:1. Is *53:2, 3. Lk *19:14. *20:13-15. Ac *7:51, 52. **his own.** *J*145, Jg +11:40. *J*147I. Polyptoton; or, Many Inflections B284. The repetition of the same part of speech in different inflections: adjectives. For other instances of this figure see 1 C 2:13. 2 C *9:8. **not.** Jn *3:11, 32. *5:40, 43. 12:37. Ge=37:18. Ps ✱69:8. Is ✱63:3. Je +*25:4. Lk *19:14. Ac=7:25. *13:46.

12. **as many.** T 1:4. Ju 3. **received.** Dt 30:19. Mt 10:40. 18:5. Lk *18:17 w Mt 18:3. Col √2:6, 7. Re √3:20. **to them.** Is *56:5. Je 3:19. Ho 1:10. Ro 8:14, 15. 2 C 6:17, 18. Ga 3:26. 4:6. 2 P *1:4. 1 J 3:1. 5:1. **gave he.** Mt ◑+27:43. Ph *2:13. **power.** *or,* the right, *or,* privilege. **to become.** *J*96C4, Mt +3:17. Mt 5:45. T 1:4. 1 J 3:1. **the sons.** T#584. Jn 11:52. Dt +33:9 (T#672). Ps +119:1 (T#504). Ac +13:48 (T#254). Ro *8:14-17. 2 C 6:17, 18. Ga √3:26, 29. *4:4-7. Ep 1:+4 (T#255), 5. 1 J *3:1, 2. **even.** Jn 2:23. 3:18. √20:31. Mt 12:21. Ac 3:16. 1 J *3:23. √5:12, 13. **believe.** T#183. Jn *3:16, 18, 36. 6:28, 29, 40, 53, 54. *8:24, 47. 11:25, 26. Ac +3:19 (T#601). 10:43. √16:31. Ro *10:4. Ga 2:16. 2 Th *2:10-12. He √11:6. Ja +5:20 (T#175). 1 J 2:23. √5:10-13. 2 J 9-11. 3 J 4. **on.** Gr. *eis.* Eric Sauer points out that "the word *faith* is associated with the Person of Jesus Christ in a fourfold manner. (1) We believe *on* Him, literally *into* Him (Gr. *eis*). This means that He is the object of our faith, its living goal, its magnet. Faith is always in motion towards Him" (*From Eternity to Eternity,* p. 45). Sauer notes the significance of other Greek prepositions and grammatical structure related to saving faith: (2) We believe *in* him (Col 1:4), Gr. *en,* denoting where, as a determined place, our faith is placed: we are *in* him, "*in* Christ" (Ro 8:1n). (3) We believe *upon* (Gr. *epi*) him, Ac 16:31. Ac 2:38n. (4) We believe *him* (2 T 1:12), "faith" in Greek is joined to the dative case of the person trusted, signifying "He is the person to whom our faith refers and in whom personally it centers" (*From Eternity to Eternity,* p. 46). **his name.** *J*144A4, Ge +4:26. *J*121T1, Dt +28:58. Jn 2:23. 3:18. 14:13, 14, 26. *15:16. 16:23, 24, 26. *20:31. 1 J 2:12. 3:23. √5:13. 3 J 7. Re 2:3, 13. 3:12. 14:1.

13. **were born.** Jn √3:3, 5, 7. Ja √1:18. 1 P *1:3, 23. *2:2. 1 J 2:29. 3:9. 4:7. 5:1, 4, 18. **not.** Jn 8:33-41. Mt Ro 9:7-9. 1 P 1:23. **blood.** *J*96F2, Ge +4:10. **nor.** *J*129, Ezk +34:4. **of the will of the.** Jn 3:6. Ge 25:22, 28. 27:4, 33. Ps *51:5. Ro 7:18. 9:10-16. Ga 5:17. **nor of the will of man.** Ps 110:3. Ro 9:1-5. 10:1-3. 1 C 3:6. Ph 2:13. Ja *1:18. **of God.** Jn √3:6-8. 1 C *3:7. T *3:5. 1 J 2:28, 29.

14. **the Word.** ver. 1. Is +*7:14. Mt 1:16, 20-23. Lk 1:31-35. 2:7, 11. Ro *1:3, 4. *9:5. 1 C 15:47. Ga *4:4. Ph 2:6-8. 1 T 3:16. He 2:11, 14-17. 10:5. 1 J 4:2, 3. 2 J 7. **was made.** Jn 6:51. Is +*7:14. +*9:6. Mt +*1:23. Ro 1:3. 8:3. Ga *4:4. Ph *2:7, 8. Col 1:22. He *2:14. 1 J 4:2. 2 J 7. **flesh.** *J*171Q7. Synecdoche of the Part B643. Flesh is put for the whole, true humanity of Christ. For other instances of this figure see Jn *6:53. 1 T 3:16. He 10:20. 1 P 3:18. 1 J 4:2. **and dwelt.** Jn 2:21. Zc 2:10, 11. Re 7:15. **among us.** Ps +*68:17. **we beheld.** Jn 2:11. 11:40. 12:40, 41. 14:9. Is *40:5. 53:2. 60:1, 2. Mt 17:1-5. Lk 9:32. 2 C 4:4-6. 1 T *3:16. He 1:3. 1 P 2:4-7. 2 P √1:16, 17. 1 J *1:1, 2. 4:◑12, 14. **his glory.** Jn *2:11. 7:39. 11:4. *13:31, 32. +*17:5. Mt √17:2. +*25:31. 2 P √1:16-18. **the glory.** Ex 16:10. Is 40:5. Ezk 1:28. Lk 2:32. He *1:3. **as.** *J*160B, Ge +25:31. Ps 122:3. Ho 4:4. Mt *14:5. Ro *1:21. 3:7. 9:32. 1 C 3:1. 4:1. 7:25. 8:7. 2 C 3:18. Phm 9. He *3:5, 6. 1 P 1:19. 2 P 1:3. **the only.** ver. 18. Jn √3:16, 18. Ps 2:7. Ac 13:33. He 1:5. 5:5. 11:17. 1 J 4:9. **of the Father.** Jn 6:46. 7:29. 16:27. **full.** ver. 16, 17. Ps 45:2. 2 C √12:9. Ep 3:8, 18, 19. Col 1:19. 2:3, 9. 1 T 1:14-16. **grace.** ver. 16, 17. Ro 5:21. 6:14. **and.** *J*174, Ge +18:27. **truth.** ver. 17. Jn

3:21. 5:33. 8:32, 40. √14:6. 16:13. 17:17. 18:37. Ep 4:21. 2 J 1.

15. A.M. 4030. A.D. 26. **bare witness.** See on ver. 7, 8, 29-34. Jn 3:26-36. 5:33-36. Mt *3:11, 13, etc. Mk 1:7. Lk 3:16. **and cried.** Jn 7:28, 37. 12:44. **This was.** ſ96C1, Ge +4:1. **he was before.** ver. 1, 2, 27, +*30. Jn √8:58. √17:5. Pr *8:22. Is +*9:6. Mi +*5:2. Ph *2:6, 7. Col 1:17. He √13:8. Re 1:11, 17, 18. 2:8. ſ96E5. Heterosis of Degree B528. The superlative for the comparative. Here, lit. "For he was first of me": i.e. *prior to me.* So the word *first* is used in Mk 6:21; Lk 19:47; Ac 25:2; Re 13:12; and perhaps Re 21:1, "the former heaven and earth"; and Re 20:6, the former resurrection of the two foretold in the Old Testament and in the Gospels. Not necessarily the special resurrection of the church of God revealed in 1 Th 4:16 (EWB, B528). For other instances of this figure see Jn 15:18. 1 C 14:30. 2 Th 2:3. 1 T 5:12. 1 J 4:19.

16. **of his.** Jn *3:34. 10:10. *15:1-5. Mt 3:11, 14. Lk 21:15. Ac 3:12-16. Ro *8:9. 1 C 1:4, 5. Ep 3:19. *4:7-12. Col *1:19. *2:3, 9, 10. 1 P 1:11. **fulness.** T#833. ver. 14. Ge=42:25. Is 45:24. Ac 5:31. 1 C 1:30. Ep 1:23. 3:19. 4:13. Col 1:19. 2:9. **all we.** *ſ171A, Ex +9:6. Le=7:10. **and grace.** Is 57:19. Zc 4:7. Mt 13:12. 25:29. Ro 5:2, 17, 20. Ep 1:6-8. 2:5-10. 4:7. 1 P 1:2.

17. **the law.** Jn 5:45. 7:19, 23. 9:29. Ex *20:1, etc. Dt 4:44. *5:1. 33:4. Ac 7:38. 28:23. Ro *3:19, 20. *5:20, 21. 2 C 3:7-10. Ga 3:10-13, 17. He 3:5, 6. 8:8-12. **grace.** ver. 14. Jn 8:32. √14:6. Ge +*3:15. 22:18. Ps *85:10. 89:1, 2. 98:3. Mi *7:20. Lk 1:54, 55, 68-79. Ac 13:34-39. Ro 3:21-26. 5:21. √6:14. 15:8-12. 2 C 1:20. He 9:22. 10:4-10. 11:39, 40. Re 5:8-10. 7:9-17. **and truth.** ſ174, Ge +18:27. ſ93A, Ge +1:26. By Hendiadys, true grace. **Jesus Christ.** Jn 17:3. Mt 1:1.

18. **seen God.** Jn 5:37. 6:46. 12:45. Ex *33:20. Dt 4:12. Ec *3:11. Mt 11:27. Lk 10:22. Col *1:15. 1 T *1:17. +*6:16. 1 J 4:12, 20. 3 J 11. **the only.** 1 T 1:17. *6:16. 1 J 4:9. **begotten.** ver. 14. Jn √3:16n, 18. Is +*9:6. 1 J 4:9. **Son.** Some authorities read *God* instead of "son," but "son" is the preferable reading. F. H. A. Scrivener in his *Introduction to the Criticism of the New Testament,* vol. 2, pp. 358-360, discusses the MSS. evidence and favors the Received Text, "son." Dean Burgon attributes the reading *God* to the heretical Valentius, who denied the identity of the *Word* with the *Son of God* (J. W. Burgon, *The Causes of the Corruption of the Traditional Text of the Holy Gospels,* p. 215). Edward Miller comments that this text figured in the Arian controversy. Arius reads "God," while his opponents read "son." "It is curious that with this history admirers of the Vatican and Siniaticus MSS. should extol their reading over the traditional reading on the score of orthodoxy. Heresy had and still retains associations which cannot be ignored: in this instance some of the orthodox weakly played into the hands of heretics. The reading 'son' is established by unanswerable evidence. None may read Holy Scripture just as the idea strikes them" (Miller in Burgon, *Causes,* p. 217, 218). That this matter is still of contemporary interest may be seen in discussion of the reading in Metzger's *Textual Commentary,* p. 198. Note particularly the dissenting voice of Allen Wikgren, who indicates his doubt that John would have written "only begotten God." See the note in the NIV Study

Bible, which favors, if not extols, the reading "only begotten God" as a clear statement of the deity of Christ. Clearly the Arians and their modern counterparts do not find any such significance in this textual reading. Ps 2:7. Pr 30:4. Is *9:6. 1 J *4:14. **in the bosom.** ſ22A19, Ps 74:11. Jn 13:23. 14:6, 9. Dt 13:6. Pr 8:30. Is 40:11. La 2:12. Mt *11:27. Lk 16:22, 23. **he hath.** Jn 3:11, 32. 12:41. 14:9. *17:6, 26. Ge 16:13. 18:33. 32:28-30. 48:15, 16. Ex 3:4-6. 23:21. 33:18-23. 34:5-7. Nu 12:8. Jsh 5:13-15. 6:1, 2. Jg 6:12-26. 13:20-23. Is 6:1-3. Ezk 1:26-28. Ho 12:3-5. Mt *11:27. Lk 10:22. 1 J 5:20. **him.** ſ63I1D, Nu +26:4. Here the sense is to be completed by repeating the words from the preceding clause, thus: "No man hath seen God at any time; the only begotten Son, which is in the bosom of the Father, he hath (seen God, and) declared (the Father)" B101.

19. **when.** Jn 5:33-36. Dt 17:9-11. 24:8. Mt 21:23-32. Lk 3:15, etc. **Levites.** Lk 10:32. Ac 4:36. **from Jerusalem.** Mt 15:1. **Who.** Jn 8:25. 10:24. Ac 13:25. 19:4.

20. **confessed.** ver. 8. Jn 3:28. Lk 3:15. Ac 13:25. **denied not.** ſ144D, Ge +40:23. **am not.** Jn 3:28-36. Mt 3:11, 12. Mk 1:7, 8. Lk 3:15-17. **the Christ.** ver. 25, 41. Jn 3:28. 4:25, 29. 7:26, 27, 31, 41, 42. 9:22. 10:24. 11:27. 12:34. *20:31. Mt 11:2. Mk 8:29. Lk 3:15.

21. **Art thou Elias.** Ml *4:5. Mt +*11:14n. 16:14. 17:10-12. Lk 1:17. **Art thou that.** *or,* Art thou a. ver. 25. Jn 6:14. 7:40. 9:17. Dt *18:15-18. Mt 11:9-11. 16:14. 21:11. Ac 3:22. 7:37.

22. **that we may.** 2 S 24:13. **What.** ſ144C1, Ge +21:1.

23. **I am.** ſ63H, Ge +12:15. Jn 3:28. Mt *3:3. Mk 1:3. Lk 1:16, 17, 76-79. 3:4-6. **voice.** ſ121E1, Ge +25:23. **Make straight.** Lk 1:76. **as said.** Is)40:3-5. Mk 1:2.

24. **And they.** ſ71. Epicrisis; or, Judgment B459. Addition of conclusion by way of deduction. An additional conclusion noting a cause or consequence arising from the place, occasion, end, or effect, of things, actions, or speeches. Here, this sentence is added to remind us of the fact that the Pharisees made a great point of baptism, which compelled them therefore to acknowledge the baptism of John to be a matter of great importance. For other instances of this figure see Jn 1:28. 3:24. 5:39, 40. 6:4. 7:5. 8:20, 27. 9:14, 22. 10:22, 23. 11:13, 30. 12:33, 37. Ac 19:20. 1 J 3:1. **were of.** Jn 3:1, 2. 4:1. 7:45, 47-49. 8:3, 13. 9:13. 11:46, 57. 12:19, 42. Mt 23:13-15, 26. Lk *7:30. 11:39-44, 53. 16:14. Ac 23:8. 26:5. Ph 3:5, 6.

25. **Why.** Mt 3:6. 21:23. Mk 1:4. Lk 3:3, 7. Ac 4:5-7. 5:28. **if.** ſ184A, 1 C +15:2. **that Christ.** See on ver. 20-22. Da +*9:24-26. **that prophet.** Dt 18:15.

26. **I baptize.** Mt *3:11. Mk 1:8. Lk 3:16. Ac +*1:5. 11:16. 13:25. **whom.** ver. 10, 11. Jn 8:19. 16:3. 17:3, 25. Ml *3:1, 2. 1 J 3:1.

27. **who.** See on ver. 15, 30. Ac 19:4. **after.** ſ24D, Lk +10:29. Antimereia of the Adverb, Adverb for Noun. The adverbs "after" (lit. behind, Gr. *opiso*) and "before" (Gr. *emprosthen*) never refer to time, but to position or grade. Other unmarked instances of this figure are connected with the verbs *to become* and *to be,* which with an adverb or adverbial phrase often change the signification of the adverb into that of a noun. See Jn 6:25. 2 S 11:23. Mk 4:10. Ac 5:34. 13:5.

Ro 7:3. 16:7. Ep 2:13. 2 Th 2:7. 2 T 1:17. **whose**. Mt 3:11. Mk 1:7. Lk 3:16.

28. These things. ♪71, ver. +24. This is to explain that the people had come a long way. **Bethabara**. i.e. *a ferry house; place of the desert*, ❋S#962g, only here. Jn *10:40. Jg 7:24, Bethbara. 12:5. Jsh 15:6, 61. 18:22. **beyond Jordan**. Jn 3:26. 10:40. Mt 19:1. **where**. Jn *3:23.

29. Behold. ver. 36. Ge 4:4. *22:7, 8. Ex *12:3, etc. Nu 28:3-10. Is 53:7. Je 11:19. Ac 8:32. 1 P 1:19. Re 5:6, 8, 12, 13. 6:1, 16. 7:9, 10, 14, 17. 12:11. *13:8. 14:1, 4, 10. 15:3. 17:14. 19:7, 9. 21:9, 14, 22, 23, 27. 22:1-3. **the Lamb**. ♪22E. Anthropomorphism B894. God is figured by an irrational figure: animals. Christ is called a *lamb* and a *lion*. For other instances of this figure see 1 C 5:7. 1 P 1:19. Re 5:5, 6. 13:8. **which**. Is *53:11. Ho 14:2. Mt 20:28. Ac 13:39. 1 C *15:3. 2 C √5:21. Ga 1:4. +*3:13. 1 T √2:6. T *2:14. He 1:3. 2:17. *9:28. 1 P *2:24. *3:18. 1 J √2:2. 3:5. *4:10. Re *1:5. **taketh**. *or*, beareth. Ex 28:38. 34:7. Le 10:17. 16:21, 22. Nu 18:1, 23. Ps 32:1, 5. 85:3. Is 33:24. Mi 7:18. Mt 1:21. He 10:4, 11. 1 J *3:5. **world**. Gr. *kosmos*, Mt +4:8. Jn +1:9. 3:16, 17. 4:42. 6:33, 51. 8:12. 12:47. 17:21. 1 J *2:2. *4:14.

30. This. Jn 1:15. **After me**. See on ver. 15, 27. Lk 3:16. **was before**. Jn +*1:15. *3:13. 8:42, +*58. Mi +*5:2. Is +*9:6. He 1:2. +*13:8.

31. I knew. ver. 33. Lk 1:80. 2:39-42. **but**. ver. 7. Is 40:3-5. Ml 3:1. 4:2-5. Lk 1:17, 76-79. **manifest**. Jn 7:4. **to Israel**. ver. 49. Jn 3:10. 12:13. Ac 13:23, 24. **therefore**. Mt 3:6. Mk 1:3-5. Lk 1:17, 76, 77. 3:3, 4. Ac 19:4.

32. I saw. Jn 5:32. Mt *3:16. Mk 1:10. Lk *3:22. **the Spirit**. Gr. *pneuma*, Mt +3:16. Jn 7:39. **descending**. Mk 1:10. **it abode**. Is 11:2. Ac *10:38.

33. I knew. ver. 26, 31. Mt 3:13-15. **but he**. ver. 6. Lk 3:2. **with water**. Jn 3:5. Mk *1:8. Ac +*1:5n. **the same**. Jn *3:5, 34. Mt 3:11, 14. Mk 1:7, 8. Lk 3:16. Ac +*1:5. 2:4. 10:44-47. 11:15, 16. 19:2-6. 1 C √12:13. T *3:5, 6. **Spirit**. Gr. *pneuma*, Mt +3:16. **Ghost**. Gr. *pneuma*, Mt +1:18n.

34. this. ver. 18, 49. Jn √3:16-18, 35, 36. √5:23-27. 6:69. 10:30, 36. 11:27. 19:7. +*20:28, 31. Ps *2:7. 89:26, 27. Mt 3:17. 4:3, 6. 8:29. 11:27. 14:33. 16:16. 17:5. 26:63. 27:40, 43, 54. Mk 1:1, 11. Lk +*1:35. 3:22. Ro *1:4. 2 C 1:19. He 1:1, 2, 5, 6. 7:3. 1 J 2:23. 3:8. 4:9, 14, 15. 5:9-13, 20. 2 J 9. Re 2:18.

35. next day. ver. 29. **and two**. ver. 40. Jn 3:25, 26. 8:17. Ml *3:16. **his disciples**. Jn 3:25. 4:1. Mt 9:14.

36. looking upon. ver. 42. Mk 10:21. **Behold**. An allusion to the morning and evening sacrifice, which typified the lamb of God who should bear away the sins of the world. See on ver. 29. Is 45:22. 65:1, 2. He *12:2. 1 P 1:19, 20.

37. and they followed. ver. 43. Jn 4:39-42. Pr 15:23. Zc 8:21. Ro √10:17. Ep +*4:29. Re 14:4. 22:17.

38. turned. Lk 14:25. 15:20. 19:5. 22:61. **following**. Jn 21:20. **What**. Jn 12:21. 18:4, 7. 20:15, 16. Lk 7:24-27. 18:40, 41. 19:3. Ac 10:21, 29. **Rabbi**. ver. 49. Jn 3:2, 26. 4:31. 6:25. 9:2. 11:8. Mt 23:7, 8. 26:25, 49. Mk 9:5. 11:21. 14:45. 20:16. Mk 10:51. **being interpreted**. ♪95, Ps +7:13. ❋S#2059g, *hermeneuo*. ver. 42. Jn 9:7. He 7:2. For related words, see Mk +5:41. **Master**. Jn 3:2. 8:4. 11:28. 13:13, 14. 20:16. Mt +22:24. Mk +4:38. Lk +7:40. **where**. Jn 12:21. Ru 1:16, 17. 1 K 10:8. Ps 27:4. Pr 3:18. 8:34. 13:20. SS 1:7, 8. Lk

◐*8:38, 39. √10:38, 39. **dwellest**. *or*, abidest. Is +*57:15. Lk 19:5. Ac √16:15.

39. Come. ver. 46. Jn √6:37. 14:22, 23. Pr 8:17. Mt √11:28-30. Ro +*15:7. 1 P 4:9. **abode**. Jn 4:40. Ac 28:30, 31. Re 3:20. **about**. "That was two hours before night." Lk 24:29. **tenth hour**. Our 4 p.m. Jn +*11:9n.

40. Andrew. Jn 6:8. Mt *4:18. 10:2. Mk 13:3. Ac 1:13.

41. first. ver. 36, 37, 45. Jn *4:28, 29. Ge 4:9. 2 K *7:9. Is 2:3-5. 52:7. Mk 5:19. Lk *2:17, 38. Ac *13:32, 33. 1 J *1:3. **the Messias**. i.e. *anointed*, ❋S#3323g. ver. 20. Jn *4:25g. Da +*9:25, 26. 1 C 1:23. **interpreted**. ♪95, Ps +7:13. ver. +38. **Christ**. *or*, Anointed. ♪22D5L, Ps +45:7. Jn *3:34. Ps *2:2. +*45:7. 89:20. Is *11:2. *61:1. Lk +*4:18-21. Ac *4:27. *10:38. He *1:8, 9.

42. beheld him. ver. 36. **Thou art**. ver. 47, 48. Jn +*2:24, 25. 6:70, 71. 13:18. **the son of Jona**. i.e. *dove*, ❋S#2495g. Jn 21:15-17, Jonas. Mt 16:17, Barjona. **called Cephas**. i.e. *a stone*, ❋S#2786g. 1 C 1:12. 3:22. 9:5. 15:5. Ga 1:18. 2:9g, 11, 14. **interpretation**. ♪95, Ps +7:13. ver. +38. **A stone**. *or*, Peter. Jn 21:2. Mt 10:2. *16:18. Mk 3:16. Lk 5:8. 6:14. Ep *2:20.

43. day following. ver. 29, 35. **go forth**. ver. 28. **and findeth**. Jn 5:14. Is 65:1. Mt 4:18-21. 9:9. Lk +*19:10. Ph 3:12. 1 J 4:19. **Philip**. i.e. *lover of horses*, ❋S#5376g. ver. 44, 45, 46, 48. Jn 6:5, 7. 12:21, 22. 14:8, 9. Mt 10:3. 14:3. 16:13g. Mk 3:18. 6:17. 8:27g. Lk 3:1, 19. 6:14. Ac 1:13. 6:5. 8:5, 6, 12, 13, 26, 29, 30, 31, 34, 35, 37, 38, 39, 40. 21:8. (1) The apostle. He was a native of Bethsaida and is always mentioned as the fifth of the twelve, Jn 1:43. (2) The evangelist. He was a deacon in the church at Jerusalem, Ac 6:3-5, and preached in Samaria with great success, Ac 8:6-8. (3) The tetrarch or governor of Gaulanitis, Auranitis, etc., Lk 3:1. (4) The husband of Herodias, Mk 6:17. **Follow me**. Jn 21:19, 22. Nu 10:29. Mt 8:22. 9:9. 19:21. Mk 2:14. 10:21. Lk 5:27. 9:59. 18:22.

44. Philip. Jn 12:21. 14:8, 9. Mt 10:3. Mk 3:18. Lk 6:14. Ac 1:13. **Bethsaida**. Jn 12:21. Mt *11:21. Mk 6:45. 8:22. Lk 9:10. 10:13. **Andrew**. Mk +13:3.

45. Nathanael. ver. 46-49. Jn 21:2. **found**. 2 Ch 9:6. Ps =132:6. **of whom**. Jn *5:45, 46. Ge +*3:15. *22:18. +*49:10. Dt +*18:18-22. Mk 12:19. See on Lk *24:27, 44. **Moses**. Dt ❋*18:15, 18, 19. Ac 3:22, 23. 7:37. **in the law**. Lk 16:16. +*24:27. **and the prophets**. Is 4:2. +*7:14. +*9:6. *53:2. Je +*23:5. Ezk 34:23. 37:24, 25. Mi +*5:2. Zc √6:12. *9:9. See more on Lk +*24:27. **Jesus**. Jn 18:5, 7. 19:19. Mt +*2:23. *21:11. Mk *14:67. Lk *2:4. Ac *2:22. *3:6. *10:38. *22:8. *26:9. **the son**. Jn 6:42. Mt +*13:55. Mk +*6:3. Lk 1:27. √3:23. *4:22.

46. Can. ♪138A, Ge +10:9. Jn 7:41, 42, *52. Lk 4:28, 29. **thing**. ♪96G4, Mt +1:20. **Come**. ver. 39. Jn 4:29. Lk 12:57. 1 Th +*5:21.

47. Nathanael. i.e. *given of God*, ❋S#3482g. Jn 1:45, 46, 47, 48, 49. 21:2. For ❋S#5417h, see Nu +1:8. **Behold**. Jn +*8:31, 39. Ro +*2:28, 29. 9:4, 6. Ph *3:3. **in whom**. ver. 31. Ps *32:2. *73:1. Zp 3:13. 1 P 2:1, 22. Re 14:5. **no guile**. T#659. Jn +8:50 (T#56). Ge 22:10. ◐27:35. Jb +13:15 (T#294). Ps +119:1 (T#504). Pr +21:3 (T#629). Is 49:4, 5. Ac +*6:3. 2 C 1:12. 4:1, 2. Ph +1:20 (T#460). Re 14:5.

48. Whence knowest. Jn 6:64. 8:14. **when**. Jn +*2:25. Ge 32:24-30. Ps *139:1, 2. Is +*65:24. Mt

6:6. 1 C 4:5. 14:25. Re 2:18, 19. **under the.** T#1211. 1 K 19:2-4. **I saw.** 1 K 2:24. 7:29. 16:19, 30.

49. **Rabbi.** See on ver. 38. **thou.** ver. 18, 34. Jn 6:69. 11:27. +*20:28, 29. **the Son of God.** ver. 34. Mt 14:33. **the King.** Jn 12:13-15. 18:37. 19:19-22. Ps *2:6. *110:1. Is +*9:7. *44:6. Je +*23:5, 6. Ezk 37:21-25. Da +*9:25. Ho 3:5. Mi +*5:2. Zp +*3:15. Zc √6:12, 13. *9:9. +*14:9. Mt √2:2. *21:5. √27:11, 42. Mk +*15:32. Lk *19:38. **of Israel.** ver. 31, 47.

50. **Because.** ver. 48. Jn *20:29. Lk 1:45. 7:9. **believest thou.** Jn 5:44. **thou shalt.** Jn 11:40. Mt 13:12. 25:29.

51. **Verily.** The repeated "verily" indicates the solemnity and certainty of this promise. √84, Ge +6:17. Jn *3:3, 5, 11. √5:19, 24, 25. 6:26, 32, 47, 53. √8:34, 51, 58. 10:1, 7. 12:24. 13:16, 20, 21, 38. 14:12. 16:20, 23. 21:18. Ne 8:6. Mt +√5:18. **Hereafter.** "Hereafter" indicates the promise is to be fulfilled in the future, at the appearing and kingdom, the Millennium (2 T +*4:1n. Re *20:4, 6). Ezk 1:1. Mt 3:16. √26:64. Mk 1:10. Lk 3:21. √22:69. Ac 7:56. 10:11. Re 4:1. 19:11. **shall see.** "Shall see" indicates the visibility of the promised kingdom. Da *7:13n. Mt +*16:27n. +*24:3n. 2 T *4:1n. Re +*1:7. **heaven open.** Is 64:1. Ezk 1:1. Mt 3:16. Mk 1:10. Lk 3:21. Ac 7:56. 10:11. Re 4:1. 19:11. **and the angels.** Reference to "angels" indicates the visible ministration of angels upon the Son of man. If angels ministered to Christ at the first advent, there are no grounds for denial of the doctrine that they will minister at the second advent. Jn 5:3. 12:29. 20:12. Ge *28:12. Da 7:9, 10. Mt 4:11. Lk 2:9, 13. *9:26. 22:43. 24:4. Ac +*1:10, 11. 2 Th √1:7-9. 1 T 3:16. He *1:6, 14. √12:22. Ju √14. **ascending.** Ge *28:12. **the Son of man.** √108H9. Idiom B842. With the Greek article, "Son of man" is used as a Messianic title (alluding to Ps 8:4) and so understood by the Jews in Jesus' day (Jn 8:28. *12:34), pertaining to Messiah's future universal dominion in the earth. Use of the title "Son of man" in this prophecy affirms that Christ will reign forever in his kingdom still possessed of his visible human nature. Jn 3:13, 14. 5:27. 6:27, 53, 62. 8:28. 9:35. 12:23, 34. 13:31. Da √7:13n, 14. Zc +*13:7. Mt +8:20. 9:6. 16:13-16, +*27n, 28. +*25:31. √26:64. Mk +2:10. 14:62. Lk +5:24. √22:69. Re 1:13. 14:14.

JOHN 2

At a marriage in Cana, Jesus turns water into wine, 1-11. He goes to Capernaum, 12; and thence to Jerusalem, where he drives the buyers and sellers out of the temple, 13-17. He predicts his own death and resurrection as the proof of his authority, 18-22. Many believe in him because of his miracles, but he does not commit himself to them, as "knowing what was in man," 23-25.

1. A.M. 4034. A.D. 30. **the third.** Jn 1:29, 35, 43. **a marriage.** Ge 1:27, 28. 2:18-25. Ps 128:1-4. Pr 18:22. 19:14. 31:10-12. Ep 5:30-33. 1 T 4:1-3. He +*13:4. **Cana.** i.e. *zeal; possession.* ✱S#2580g. ver. 11. Jn 4:46. 21:2. For ✱S#7071h, see Jsh +16:8. Jsh 19:28, Kanah. **the mother.** ver. 3, 5, 12. Jn 6:42. 19:25-27. Mt 12:46.

2. **both.** Mt 12:19. Lk 7:34-38. 1 C 7:39. 10:31. Col 3:17. Re *3:20. **his.** Mt 10:40-42. 25:40, 47. **disciples.** ver. 11, 12, 17, 22. Jn 1:40-49. 3:22. 4:2, 8, 27, 31, 33. 6:8, 12, 16, 22, 24, 66, 70, 71. **the marriage.** Est 5:12. Mt 22:2, 3. He +*13:4.

3. **they wanted.** Ps 104:15. Ec 10:19. Is 24:11. Mt 26:28, 29. **the mother.** Mt 12:48. **They have.** Jn 11:3. Ph *4:6.

4. **Woman.** Jn 4:21. 19:26, 27. 20:13, 15. Mt 15:28. **what have.** √85H, Jg +11:12. √108H8, 2 S +16:10. Dt 33:9. Jg +11:12. 2 S 16:10. 19:22. 1 K 17:18. 2 K 3:13. 2 Ch *35:21. Mt 8:29. 27:19. Mk 1:24. 5:7. Lk *2:49. 4:34. 8:28. 2 C 5:16. Ga 2:5, 6. **mine hour.** Jn *7:6, 8, 30. 8:20. 11:6. 12:23. 13:1. 17:1. Ec 3:1. Mt 26:18.

5. **Whatsoever.** Jn +*15:14. Ge 6:22. =41:55. Jg 13:14. Ec 8:4. Lk 5:5, 6. 6:46-49. Ac 9:6. He *5:9. 11:8. **do it.** Jn √15:14. 2 S 15:15. 2 Ch 34:16. Lk 22:23. 1 C *10:31. Col *3:17.

6. **six waterpots.** Probably several were borrowed from friends or neighbors to make up this number to accommodate the guests at the wedding. In volume they are thought to have contained from 20 to 30 American gallons apiece. Thomas O. Summers remarks that they contained "enough for sprinkling purposes, but not for immersion" and were used to contain water for baptisms, which the Jews understood to mean purifications (*Baptism,* p. 84). These baptisms "were washings or purifications by water, poured or sprinkled on the hands, or entire persons, or on the furniture, for which ceremonial purposes vessels of water, containing two or three firkins apiece, were kept in the house, as St. John expresses it—'after the manner of *purifying* of the Jews.' And yet some talk about their effecting this 'purifying' by *plunging*—the word *baptismos* meaning nothing else—as if men, women, and children, cups, pots, brazen vessels, and beds, were, or could be, *plunged into these waterpots!*" (Summers, *Baptism,* pp. 230, 231). ✱S#5201g. ver. 7. Jn 4:28, 46n. **after.** Jn √3:25. Mk +*7:2-5. Ep 5:26. He 6:2. 9:10, 19. 10:22. **the Jews.** ver. 13. **firkins.** 2 Ch 4:5.

7. **Fill.** ver. 3, 5. Nu 21:6-9. Jsh 6:3-5. 1 K 17:13. 2 K 4:2-6. 5:10-14. Mk 11:2-6. 14:12-17. Ac 8:26, etc.

8. **Draw.** ver. 9. Pr *3:5, 6. Ec *9:7. **the governor.** Ro 13:7.

9. **the water that.** Jn 4:46. Ex ◐=7:20. **but.** √81, Ge +15:13. Jn √7:17. Ps 119:100. **servants.** Jn 8:17.

10. **and when.** Ge 43:34. SS 5:1. Hg 1:6. Mt 24:49. Lk 12:45. Ac 2:15. 1 C 11:21. Ep +*5:18. 1 Th 5:7. Re 17:2, 6. **but.** Ps 104:15. Pr 9:1-6, 16-78. Lk *16:25. Re 7:16, 17. **thou hast.** Jn 14:27.

11. **beginning.** Jn 1:17. Ex 4:9. 7:19-21. Ec 9:7. Ml 2:2. 2 C 4:17. Ga 3:10-13. **miracles.** ver. 18, 23. Jn 3:2. 4:48, 54. 6:2, 14, 26, 30. 7:31. 9:16. 10:41. 11:47. 12:18, 37. 20:30. Mt 12:38. Lk 21:11. **did.** Jn 1:50, 51. 3:2. 4:46. **Cana.** ver. 1. **Galilee.** Jn 1:43. **manifested.** Jn *1:14. *5:23. 7:4. 12:41. 14:9-11, 13. Dt 5:24. Ps 72:19. 96:3. Is 40:5. 2 C 3:18. 4:6. **his glory.** Jn *1:14. **and his.** ver. 2. **believed.** Jn 4:39. 11:15. *20:30, 31. 1 J √5:13.

12. **went down.** Jn 4:47, 49, 51. **Capernaum.** Jn 4:46. 6:17, 24, 59. Mt *4:13. 11:23. **his mother.** ver. 1. **and his brethren.** Jn 7:3-5. Mt 12:46. +*13:55, 56. Mk +*6:3. Ac 1:13, 14. 1 C 9:5. Ga 1:19. **his disciples.** ver. 2.

13. **passover.** ver. 23. Jn 5:1. 6:4. 7:2. 11:55. Ex *12:6-14. Le +*23:2. Nu 28:16-25. Dt *16:1-8, 16. 1 S 15:22. Is 1:14. Lk *2:41. **went up.** Jn 5:1. 7:8, 10. 11:55. 12:20. Lk 2:4. Ac 18:22.

14. **And found.** Dt *14:23-26. Zc 14:20, 21. Ml 3:1-3. Mt 21:12. Mk 11:15. Lk 19:45, 46. Re 11:2. **oxen.**

Le 22:19. **doves**. Le 1:14. 5:7. 12:8. Lk *2:24.

15. **cords**. Ac 27:32. **he drove**. Jn 18:6. Zc *4:6.
Mk 11:15. 2 C 10:4. **poured**. Gr. *ekcheo*, ❋S#1632g.
Rendered (1) pour out: Ac 2:17, 18. Re 16:1, 2, 3, 4,
8, 10, 12, 17. (2) shed: Ac 22:20. Ro 3:15. T 3:6. Re
16:6. (3) shed forth: Ac 2:33. (4) spill: Mk 2:22. (5)
run out: Mt 9:17.

16. **make**. Is 56:5-11. Je 7:11. Ho 12:7, 8. Mt 21:13.
Mk *11:16, 17. Ac 19:24-27. 1 T 6:5. 2 P 2:3, 14, 15.
my. Jn 5:17, 18. 8:49. 10:29, 30. 20:17. Lk 2:49. **Father's house**. Jn 14:2. Lk 2:49. **house of merchandise**.
Mt 21:13. Mk 11:17. Lk 19:46.

17. **The zeal**. Ps)69:9. *119:139. **of**. ⨍181E, Ge
+3:24.

18. **the Jews**. Jn 5:10. **What**. ver. 11. Jn 4:48. *6:30.
Ex 4:1, 8. 7:9. Mt *12:38, etc. 16:1-4. Mk 8:11. Lk
*11:29. **us**. ⨍63C, Ge +25:32. Supply by ellipsis, (that
thou art the Messiah). **seeing**. Jn 1:25. Mt *21:23.
Mk 11:27, 28. Lk 20:1, 2. Ac 4:7. 5:28.

19. **Destroy**. ⨍96B, Ge +20:7. Mt *26:60, 61.
*27:40. Mk 8:31. *14:58. *15:29. Lk 9:22. Ac 6:14.
temple. ⨍103, Ge +3:13. Mt 23:16. **and in**. Mt
+*12:40n. *27:63. **three days**. ⨍108H12, 1 S +30:12.
Mt 26:61. **I will raise it**. Jn 5:19. √10:17, 18. *11:25.
Jb +*19:25, 26. Is +*26:19n. Mk *8:31. Ac *2:24-
32. 3:15, 26. Ro *4:24. *6:4. *8:11. 1 C *15:3, 4, 12.
Col 2:12. 1 P *3:18.

20. **Forty and**. Ezr 5:16. **temple**. Mt 12:6. 26:61.
three days. Ho 6:2.

21. **he spake**. Jn 1:14g. Col *1:19. *2:9. He *8:2.
temple. Mt +23:16. 1 C *3:16. *6:19. 2 C *6:16. Ep
2:20-22. Col *2:9. 1 P *2:4, 5. **his body**. Jn √20:25,
27. Ps +*16:10. ◐*49:15. Is 43:10n. Da +*12:2n. Mt
+*27:52. ❋*28:6. Lk √24:39. Ro √8:11. Ph √3:21. 1 T
*2:5. 1 J √3:2.

22. **risen from**. Jn 20:27. Mt +*27:52, 53. 28:6.
Lk *24:39. Ac 13:29, 30, 34. Ro *8:11. √10:9, 10. Ph
*3:21. **his**. ver. 2, *17. Jn *12:16. *14:26. *16:4. Lk
*24:7, 8, 44. Ac 11:16. **had said**. Ge=41:54. **and they
believed**. T#1061. ver. 11. Jn +5:47. *20:8, 9. **the
scripture**. Jn +*5:39, 46, 47. 7:38, 42. 10:35. 13:18.
17:12. 19:24, 28, 36, 37. 20:9. Ps 16:10. Mt 21:42.
Lk 4:21. +*24:27, 44, 45. Ac +*17:11. Ro 9:17.

23. **at the passover**. ver. 13. **many**. Jn 3:2. 6:14.
7:31. √8:30, 31. 12:42, 43. Mt 13:20, 21. Mk 4:16,
17. Lk +*8:13. Ga 5:6. Ep 3:16, 17. Ja 2:19, 20. 1 J
√5:13. **name**. ⨍144A4, Ge +4:26. **when they saw**. ver.
11. Jn 3:2. 4:45, 48. 7:31. 11:45, 47, 48. 12:37. 20:30.
Mt 11:4-6. Ac 8:6. **the miracles**. Jn 6:2. 20:30. Mk
1:34.

24. **did**. Jn *6:15. Mt *10:16, 17. **not commit**. ⨍145,
Jg +11:40. 1 K ◐*13:7-24. Ps ◐89:34. Lk 16:11. He
◐6:18. **because he knew**. Jn *1:42, 46, 47. 5:42. *6:61,
64. 13:11. *16:30, 31. 21:17. Ge=42:7, 8. 1 S +*16:7.
1 K 8:39. 1 Ch +*28:9. 29:17. 2 Ch *6:30. Je +*17:9.
Mt *9:4. *17:24-27. Mk *2:8. Lk 5:22. Ac *1:24. 1 C
1:24, 30. Col 2:3. He *4:13. Re 2:23.

25. **needed not**. Jn 2:4. 4:32. 6:15. Mt 17:4. Mk
6:48. Lk 20:8. 22:49. **he**. √88, Ge +5:15. **knew**. Jn
1:42, 47, 48. 4:17-19, 29. 5:42. 6:61, 64, 71. *10:14,
27. 13:1, 11, 27, 28. 16:19, +*30. 18:4. 21:17. Ge=42:7,
8. 1 S *16:7. 1 K 8:39. 1 Ch +*28:9. 2 Ch *6:30. Ps
+*40:17. *44:21. *139:2. Is *66:18. Ezk +*11:5. Mt
*9:4. 12:25. *17:25-27. 22:18. Mk 2:8. 12:15. Lk 5:22.
6:8. 9:47. 11:17. He *4:13. **what was in**. 1 K 8:39. Je
+*17:10. 20:12. Mk *7:21. Ac 1:24. Re *2:23.

*Nicodemus comes to Jesus by night, 1, 2. Jesus shows
him the indispensable necessity of being born again,
3-11. He shows the difference between earthly and
heavenly things, 12, 13, and speaks of his own death
and of faith in him, 14, 15. The great love of God,
in giving his only begotten Son to redeem the world,
16, 17. Unbelief is the great cause of men's condemnation, 18-21. Jesus baptizes in Judea and John at Aenon,
22-24. John instructs his disciples who were jealous
for his honor, concerning the glory of Christ, the salvation of those who believe in him and the wrath of
God abiding on unbelievers, 25-36.*

1. **of the Pharisees**. ver. 10. Jn 1:24. **Nicodemus**.
i.e. *innocent blood; conqueror of the populace; victorious among his people*, ❋S#3530g, (ver. 4, 9. Jn 7:50.
19:39). Jn 7:47-49. 19:39. **ruler**. Jn 7:26, 48. 12:42.
Lk 18:18. 24:20. **the Jews**. Jn 5:10.

2. **came**. Jn *7:50, 51. *12:42, 43. 19:38, 39. Jg
6:27. Is 51:7. Ph 1:14. **Rabbi**. ver. 26. Jn 1:38. 20:16.
we know. ⨍156. Protherapeia; or, Conciliation B975.
The securing of indulgence for what is about to be
said. For other instances of this figure see Mt 19:16.
Ac 17:22. 22:3-6. 26:2, 3. **thou art**. Jn 4:19. 9:24, 29.
Mt 22:16. Mk 12:14. Lk 20:21. **come from God**. Jn
16:27. **for**. Jn 5:36. 7:31. 9:16, 30-33. 11:47, 48. 12:37.
15:24. Ac 2:22. 4:16, 17. 10:38. **miracles**. Jn 2:11. **except**. ⨍184C, Mt +4:9. Jn 5:36. 9:33. 10:38. 14:10,
11. 1 S 18:14. Ac *2:22. *10:38. **him**. ⨍63D2, Ge
+30:27. Supply by ellipsis (absolute: of anantapodoton,
the latter clause, or apodosis, the "then" clause of an
"if/then" statement expressing the conclusion), "(therefore am I come to thee, that thou mayest teach me
the way of salvation)."

3. **Verily**. See on Jn +1:51. Mt +*5:18. 2 C *1:19,
20. Re *3:14. **Except**. ⨍184C, Mt +4:9. ver. 5, 6. Jn
*1:13. Mt *18:3. 1 C *2:14. Ga *6:15. Ep *2:1, 4, 5.
T √3:5. Ja +*1:18. 1 P +*1:3, 23. 1 J 2:29. 3:9. *5:1,
18. **again**. *or*, from above. ver. √7, 31. Jn +1:13. 19:11.
2 C √5:17. Ga 4:9. 6:15. Ja *1:17. *3:15, 17. 1 P 1:23.
he cannot see. ver. *5, 36. Jn 1:5. *12:40. Dt *29:4.
Je 5:21. Mt *13:11-16. 16:17. Mk +*16:16n. 1 C +*6:9,
10. +*15:50. 2 C *4:4. He +*12:14. **the kingdom of
God**. Jn +*18:36, 37. 1 Ch 28:4, 5. Mt +12:28. 25:34.
Mk +1:15. Lk +4:43. +*22:29, 30. Ac +*1:3, 6n.
8:12. *14:22. 19:8. 20:25. 28:23, 31. Ro 9:8. +*14:17.
1 C 4:20. +*6:9, 10. +*15:50n. Ga 5:21. Ep 5:5. Col
1:13n. 4:11. 1 Th 2:12. 2 Th +*1:5. 2 T +*4:1n, 18n.
He 12:28. Ja +*2:5. 2 P √1:11. Re +*5:10. 12:10.

4. **How**. ⨍85R, Jb +4:17. ver. 3. Jn 4:11, 12. 6:53,
60. 1 C 1:18. √2:14.

5. **Verily**. Jn +1:51. **Except**. ⨍184C, Mt +4:9. **born**.
ver. *3. Is *44:3, 4. Ezk *36:25-27. Mt *3:11. Mk
*16:16. Ac +*2:38. Ep √5:26. T *3:4-7. 1 P *1:2. *3:21.
1 J 5:6-8. **of water**. Jn 1:33. 7:38. 13:10. Ps *119:9,
11. Ezk √36:25. Mk 16:16. Ac +*1:5. +*2:38. 8:36.
10:47. 11:16. +*22:16. Ep *5:26. T 3:5. He +*10:22.
1 P 1:23. *3:20. 2 P 3:5, 6. 1 J 5:6, 8. Re 22:1, 17.
and. ⨍93A, Ge +1:26. Hendiadys; or, Two for One
B657. Two words are used, but one thing is meant.
By this figure *water* and *spirit* are joined by "and."
There is no *of* in the Greek, supplied here by the
translators. There is no article to either of the two
nouns. This figure gives the meaning, "born of water,
even the spirit." That only one thing is meant by the

two words is clear from verses 6 and 8, where only the Spirit (the one thing) is mentioned. The figure may also be understood to mean "born of spiritual water," where the "spiritual water" is, by the figure metonymy, put for the Holy Spirit himself, as is clear from Jn 7:38, 39. The reference is to the *real* baptism by the Holy Spirit which is the one indispensable condition of entering the kingdom of God (Ro 8:9. 1 C 12:13), not to the water of *ritual* baptism (Ac 1:5n). **of the.** Jn *1:13. *6:63. Mt 3:11. Mk 16:16. Ro 8:2. 1 C *2:12. *6:11. 1 J *2:29. *5:1, 6-8. **Spirit.** Gr. *pneuma*, ♪121A1, Lk +1:17n. Jn 6:63. Ezk √36:26, 27. Mt √3:16. 1 C 15:45. **cannot enter.** Mt *5:20. *18:3. 28:19. Lk *13:3, 5, 24. Ac 2:38. +*3:19. Ro *14:17. 1 C +*6:9, 10. 2 C *5:17, 18. Ga *6:15. Ep 2:4-10. 2 Th 2:13, 14. **the kingdom.** ver. +*3. Mt +*8:11, 12. 21:43.

6. **That.** ♪96G4, Mt +1:20. The neuter gender is used to agree with the word "thing," though person is meant, because that which is born of the flesh or spirit is rather the fleshly or spiritual nature, than the man as an individual; also, because it includes men and women (B534). **born of the flesh.** Jn 1:13. Ge 5:3. 6:5, 12. Jb 14:4. 15:14-16. 25:4. Ps 51:10. Ro 7:5, 18, 25. 8:1, 4, 5-9, *13. 1 C 15:47-49, +*50. 2 C √5:17. Ga *5:16-21, 24. Ep 2:3. Col 2:11. **is flesh.** Jn 6:63. 1 P 3:18. 4:6. **that.** Ezk 11:19, 20. 36:26, 27. Ro 8:5, 9. 1 C 6:17. Ga 5:17. 1 J 3:9. **born.** Jn +1:13. **the Spirit.** Gr. *pneuma*, Mt +3:16. Jn 7:39. **is spirit.** Gr. *pneuma*, ♪121A1, Lk +1:17n. ♪121A2, Ps +51:10. ♪145, Jg +11:40. T#592. Jn 4:24. 2 S +15:6 (T#329). Ps +119:59 (T#600). Ga 5:22. *6:8. Ep 4:22, 23. 1 J 4:7.

7. **Marvel.** ver. 12. Jn 5:28. 6:61-63. 1 J 3:13. **Ye must.** This absolute requirement for salvation is nowhere retracted in the pages of scripture and is nowhere limited to a particular favored group. To allege that this requirement applies only to a select few, the "little flock," who are the 144,000 (Re 7:4n), who alone can have a "heavenly hope" (Re +7:4n), in contrast with the rest of mankind who can only aspire to an "earthly hope" (Re +7:4n), is a human addition to the word of God which finds no support in the Bible. For any group to teach this viewpoint will certainly result in the loss of salvation for any who are led to believe this false doctrine. ver. √3. Jn 4:24. Jb *14:4. 15:14. Mt 13:33-35. Ac √4:12. Ro 3:9-19. 8:5, 7. 9:22-25. *12:1, 2. 1 C *2:14. Ep 4:22-24. Col 1:12. He *12:14. 1 P 1:14-16, 22. Re 21:27. **be born.** Ac +*13:33. Ga *6:15. 1 P *2:2. **again.** *or*, from above. ver. 3mg. Jn 1:12, 13. Ezk 36:27. 37:14. Mt +*19:28. 2 C √5:17. 1 P +*1:3, 23.

8. **wind.** or, spirit. Gr. *pneuma*, Mt +3:16. ♪66, Ge +9:3. Jb 37:10-13, 17, 21-23. Ps 107:25, 29. 135:7. Ec 11:4, 5. Ezk 37:9. Ac 2:2. 4:31. 1 C 2:11. 12:11. **the sound.** Ac 2:6. **so.** Jn 1:13. Is *55:9-13. Mk 4:26-29. Lk 6:43, 44. Ro 9:15, 16. 1 C 2:11. 1 J 2:29. 3:8, 9. **Spirit.** Gr. *pneuma*, Mt +3:16.

9. **How.** ver. 4. Jn 6:52, 60. Pr +*4:18. Is 42:16. Mk 8:24, 25. Lk 1:34.

10. **Art.** ♪60A, Ge +3:22. Is 9:16. 29:10-12. 56:10. Je +*8:8, 9. Mt 11:25. +*15:14. 22:29. **master.** Lk 2:46. 5:17. Ac 5:34. Ro 2:20. **Israel.** Jn 1:31. **and knowest not.** Since Jesus expected Nicodemus as a "master in Israel" to know these things, clearly they must be taught in the Old Testament, and in fact they are. Being "born of water" is taught in Ezk 36:25, "sprinkle

clean water" and being "born of the spirit" is taught in Ezk 36:26, 27, "a new spirit will I put within you," both expressions in Ezekiel pertaining to the spiritual awakening required for Israel to be restored to God's favor in order to receive the promised theocratic kingdom in the land of Israel (Ezk 36:28). Since the three elements "water," "spirit," and promised "kingdom of God" appear together in both passages in precisely the same connection, it is unnecessary to look elsewhere for the proper explanation of Jesus's words. Jn 9:30. Ex 33:19. Dt 10:16. 30:6. 1 Ch 29:19. Ps 51:6, 10. 73:1. Is 11:6-9. 66:7-9. Je 31:33. 32:39, 40. Ezk 11:19. 18:31, 32. √36:25-27. 37:23, 24. Mt *22:29. Ro 2:28, 29. Ph 3:3. Col 2:11.

11. **verily.** ver. 3, 5. Jn +1:51. **We.** ♪96D4, Ge +29:27. **speak.** ver. 13, 32-34. Jn 1:18. *7:16. 8:14, 28, 29, 38. *12:49. *14:24. Is 55:4. Mt *11:27. Lk 10:22. 1 J 1:1-3. *5:6-12. Re +*1:5. *3:14. **ye.** ver. 32. Jn 1:11. 5:31-40, 43. 12:37, 38. Is *49:4, 5. 50:2. *53:1. 65:2. Mt 23:37. Ac 22:18. 28:23-27. 2 C *4:4. **our.** ♪96D4, Ge +29:27.

12. **If.** ♪184A, 1 C +15:2. **earthly.** ver. 3, 5, 8. Ezk 36:25-27. 1 C 3:1, 2. 15:40. 2 C 5:1. Ph 2:10. 3:19. Col 3:2. He 5:11, 12. Ja 3:15. 1 P 2:1-3. **if I tell.** ♪184C, Mt +4:9. **heavenly.** ver. 13-17, 31-36. Jn 1:1-14. 6:51-53. +*8:58. +*10:30. 1 C 2:7-9. Ep 1:3, 20. 2:6. 3:10. 6:12. Ph 2:10. 1 T *3:16. 1 J 4:10, 14.

13. **no man.** Jn *1:18. 6:46. Dt 30:11, 12, 14. Pr *30:4. Ac ●*2:34. Ro 10:6-8. 1 C ●15:50. Ep 4:9, 10. **hath ascended.** ♪96C2, Ge +45:9. The departure of the spirit to God is never called *ascension*. This declaration of Jesus does not deny that Enoch and Elijah are in heaven (Ge 5:24. 2 K 2:11) or suggest that the thief on the cross could not be with him in paradise (Lk 23:43), or teach that believers upon their death do not now go immediately to heaven (2 C 5:8). The emphasis in context is that Christ at that time who was from heaven was the only available witness of the heavenly things about which he was speaking (ver. 12); they could appeal to no other. Jn *6:62. Ge ●5:24 w He 11:5. 2 K ●2:11. Mt √22:32. Lk 24:51. 2 C 12:1-4. 1 T *2:5. Re ●4:1. **to heaven.** ♪147F, Ezk +28:2. **but he.** ver. 31. Jn *6:33, 38, 42, 51, *62. 8:42. *13:3. 16:28-30. +*17:5. Ge +11:5. 1 C √15:47. **from heaven.** ♪147F, Ezk +28:2. **even.** Jn 1:18. Mt 28:20. Mk 16:*19, 20. Ac *20:28. Ep 1:23. *4:10. **Son of man.** The title "Son of man" does not designate the divine nature of Christ, neither does it merely denote the human nature of Christ, but relates "to His descent from David and His being the designated, pre-ordained One to whom the Kingdom, by virtue of such descent, rightfully belongs" (Peters, *Theocratic Kingdom*, vol. 1, p. 567). The ground of the title lies in the Davidic covenant (Is +*55:3. Ezk +*37:24). Jn *1:51n. 4:27. 5:27. 13:31. Ps *80:17. Da +*7:13. Mt +*16:27n. 19:28. 26:64. 25:31. Mk 8:38. 13:26. Lk 9:26. 21:27. **which is in heaven.** ?♪96C5, Mt +2:13. Some authorities omit this phrase, but its retention may be argued for on the ground that these words may have been dropped out of the text at an early date as superfluous or objectionable (Thomas Whitlaw, *Commentary on John*, p. 69). That this text is weighty and difficult, is on this very account the more certainly genuine (Scrivener, *Introduction*, vol. 2, p. 360). While missing from some MSS., it is attested to by the early

versions. The text figured early in controversy, including the Apolinarian, and in some instances even the orthodox were reluctant to cite it. The modern counterparts of the ancient Socinian and Arian heresies seem to have a particular attraction to this text. Burgon has shown that it was cited many times by the church fathers. The manuscripts which omit this clause are convicted "of the deliberate suppression of one of the most mysterious, yet one of the most glorious, glimpses afforded to us in Scripture of the nature of the Savior, on the side of His Proper Divinity" (Scrivener, p. 361). Burgon, discussing this passage, notes it teaches that "Christ 'came down from heaven' when he became incarnate: and having become incarnate, is said to have 'ascended up to Heaven,' and 'to be in Heaven,' because 'the Son of Man,' who was not in heaven before, by virtue of the hypostatical union was thenceforward evermore 'in heaven'" (*Causes of Corruption in the Traditional Text*, p. 223). "Hypostatical union" is a term representing Christ as possessing two natures in one person, human and divine. George Hutcheson explains, "The Son of God hath assumed the human nature into so strict a personal union, that what is proper to either nature is ascribed unto the person under whatsoever name; for, saith he, 'the Son of man which is in heaven,' which is not to be understood, as if either his human nature came from heaven (for he is speaking of what still is there) or that his human nature were in every place, but that the same person who is the Son of man according to our nature is in heaven according to his divine nature, and yet but one person still" (*Commentary*, p. 46). God the Son possesses the incommunicable divine attribute of immensity (Ps 139:7n. Je *23:24n. Mt +*28:19n). Jn 1:18. *7:34. Ro *8:34. He 7:25. √9:24. 1 J 2:1.

14. And as. √92B, Mt +12:40. Nu *21:7-9. 2 K 18:4. **even.** Jn *8:28. *12:32-34. Ps 22:16. Mt 26:54. Lk 18:31-33. 24:20, 26, 27, 44-46. Ac 2:23. 4:27, 28. Ac 1:16. **Son.** ƒ144A3, Ge +11:5. **lifted up.** Jn 8:28. *12:32, 34. Ac 2:33. 5:31. Ph 2:9.

15. whosoever. ver. √16, √36. Jn √1:12. *6:40, 47. 11:25, 26. 12:44-46. √20:31. Is *45:22. Mk *16:16. Ac *8:37. 10:34, 35. √16:30, 31. Ro *4:23-25. *5:1, 2. *10:9-14. Ga *2:16, 20. 3:11. He *7:25. 10:39. 1 J 5:1, √11-13. **believeth.** Jn +5:44. **in him.** Jn 15:4. 16:33. 1 J 5:12, 20. **not.** Jn √5:24. √10:28-30. Mt +*18:11. Lk +*19:10. Ac 13:41. 1 C 1:18. 2 C 4:3. **perish.** Gr. *apollumi*, Mt +2:13. **but have.** ƒ144D, Ge +40:23. **eternal.** Gr. *aionios*, Mt +18:8. Jn √17:2, 3. Ro *5:21. √6:22, 23. 1 J 2:25. √5:13, 20.

16. God. Je 31:3. Lk 2:14. Ro √5:8. 2 C *5:19-21. Ep *2:4-7. 2 Th 2:16. T *3:4-7. 1 J 3:1. √4:9, 10, 14, 19. Re 1:5. **loved.** ƒ96C1, Ge +4:1. **world.** Gr. *kosmos*, Mt +4:8. Jn +*1:9, 29. 4:42. √ƒ121J8. Metonymy of the Subject B576. The *world* is put for its inhabitants, affirmed by some to denote without distinction but not without exception. See related notes and figures listed at Ge 24:10n. For other instances of this figure see Jn 7:4. Ac 17:31. 2 C *5:19. 1 J √2:2. 5:19. Re 12:9. **gave.** ƒ96C1, Ge +4:1. Jn 1:14, 18. Ge 22:12. Is +*9:6. Mk 12:6. Ro 5:10. √8:32. **only.** ver. 18. Jn 1:14. Ge 22:2, +=12. Lk ❍+7:12. **begotten.** Gr. *monogenes*, S#3439g, Lk +7:12. lit. the only one of a family, unique of its kind. *Monogenes*, applied to Jesus, expresses the unique and eternal relationship of the Son

to the Father. As *firstborn* does not mean born first (Col 1:15n), neither does *only begotten* imply a begetting, birth, or origin in time. In His preexistence, Jesus was always uniquely the Son of God (Ps 2:7. Is +*9:6. He 1:8). When used of Christ, *only begotten* speaks of "unoriginated relationship." *Only begotten* "indicates that as the Son of God He was the sole representative of the Being and character of the One who sent Him" (Vine, *Expository Dictionary*, vol. 3, p. 140). It is a word picture which portrays the relationship of the Father to the Son in the terms of a Middle Eastern patriarchal family (Ge √21:12. 22:2, 12, 16. He 11:17). Isaac, termed Abraham's only begotten son (He 11:17), though Abraham had a prior son Ishmael by Hagar (Ge 16:15) and later sons by Keturah (Ge 25:1-4. 1 Ch 1:32, 33), sustains a unique relationship to Abraham as the son of promise (Ga 4:23). The same picture, portrayed in parable (Mt 21:37), emphasizes the unique authority of Jesus as sent by the Father (Jn 20:21. 1 J 4:9), and our responsibility to receive the truth declared by Him (Jn 1:14, 18. 3:18. Mt 17:5). 1 J ❍5:18. **Son.** ver. 35. Jn +5:25. Is +*9:6. **that whosoever.** ver. 15. Mt *9:13. 1 T *1:15, 16. Re 22:17. **believeth.** "In the New Testament, when belief is said to lead to eternal life, as is the case here, the tense expressing continuous action is always used while the tense expressing a single action is never used. The stress is thus placed on a continuous faith rather than on an isolated moment of faith. Never in these passages expressing belief in eternal life is one's eternal security said to be guaranteed by a single, isolated act of faith" (George Allen Turner and Julius R. Mantey, *The Gospel According to John*, p. 99, who for the final sentence, given as footnote 20, cite E. A. Mills, "Terms for Belief in John's Gospel"; thesis in Asbury Theological Seminary, 1952). See related notes (Mt 24:13n. Ga 2:20n. 1 T 4:1n. He 6:4n, 6n, 9n. 1 J 5:13). T#865. ver. *18, *36. Jn √1:12. +4:39. +5:44. 6:35, √47. 12:46. 20:29. Is 28:16. 45:22. Mt 11:28. Mk 9:23. Lk 7:50. Ac *10:43. √16:31. Ro √1:16. *4:5. 9:33. 10:4. Ga 3:7, 9, 22. Ep √2:8-10. 1 T 4:10. He *6:12. 10:38, 39. 1 P 2:4-6. **in him.** Jn 15:4. 16:33. 1 J 5:12, 20. **should not.** The use of "should" confuses some English readers here because the English word "should" connotes a degree of doubtfulness, as if the text said "should not perish, but maybe he will." The Greek text contains no such connotation here; "should" has no directly corresponding equivalent word in the underlying Greek text, but is used in rendering the verb "perish," to represent the subjunctive mood (aorist tense, middle voice, third person singular) of the original. The subjunctive mood in Greek does not express, as in English, doubtfulness or "conditions contrary to fact," and can be used, in fact, in the strongest possible antithesis to doubtfulness in strong denial (subjunctive aorist with *ou mee*), as in He 13:5; Mt 5:18; Mk 14:25. See related notes listed at Ga 3:14n. **perish.** Gr. *apollumi*, Mt +2:13. Jn +*10:28. Lk +*19:10. 23:35. 2 P √3:9. **everlasting.** Gr. *aionios*, Mt +18:8.

17. God. Jn 5:45. 8:15, 16. 12:47, 48. Lk *9:56. **sent.** ver. 34. Jn 4:34. 5:36, 38. 6:29, 38, 57. 7:29. 8:42. 10:36. 11:27, 42. 17:3, 8, 18, 21, 23, 25. 20:21. Ro 8:3. 1 J 4:9, 10, 14. **his Son.** ver. 35. **to condemn.** Jn 4:42. ❍5:22, 45. *8:11, 15. *12:47. Lk 9:55. **world.** Gr. *kosmos*, Mt +4:8. **but.** Jn 1:29. 6:40. Is 45:21-23. 49:6, 7. 53:10-12. Zc *9:9. Mt *1:23. +*18:11.

Lk 2:10, 11. +*19:10. 1 T +*2:5, 6. 1 J √2:2. *4:14.
world. *ſ121J9A, Jn +1:10. By Metonymy of the Subject, the *world* is put for a portion of its inhabitants: people in the world without distinction.
18. **He that.** Lk 2:34, 35. **believeth.** Jn √5:24. 1 J *5:13. **is not condemned.** ver. √36. Jn √5:24. *6:40, 47. √20:31. Ro √5:1. *8:1, 34. 1 J √5:12. **he that believeth not.** Pr +*1:29. Is +√66:4. Mk *16:16. He *2:3. 12:25. 1 J *5:10. **is condemned.** ſ121C2D2, Ge +15:14. Ge 2:17. Ga 3:10. 2 Th *2:12. **hath not.** ſ158, Mt +5:18. **the name.** ſ144A4, Ge +4:26. ſ121T1, Dt +28:58. Jn 1:12. **only begotten.** ver. 16.
19. **this.** Jn 1:4, 9-11. *8:12. 9:39-41. 15:22-25. Mt 11:20-24. Lk 10:11-16. +*12:47. Ro 1:32. 2 C 2:15, 16. 2 Th *2:12. He +*3:12, 13. **condemnation.** ſ121G, Ge +31:1. ſ121C1D, Ex +6:6. **world.** Gr. *kosmos*, Mt +4:8. Jn +1:9. 12:46. **men loved.** ſ121C2C1, Ps +11:5. 2 S 13:9. Is 30:10. Je *5:31. Ep 5:12. **darkness.** Jn 1:5, 6. 8:12. 12:35, 46. 1 J 1:5. 2:8, 9, 11. **rather than.** T#309. Jn 12:43, 48. Mt 7:26, 27. 11:20-24. 12:41. Lk 11:31, 32. *12:47, 48. Ro +5:13 (T#161). Ep +4:30 (T#348). He *10:26-29. **because.** Jn 5:44. *7:7. 8:44, 45. 10:26, 27. 12:43. Ge +*6:5. =37:2. Is 30:9-12. Je +*17:9. Mk *7:21-23. Lk 16:14, 15. Ac 24:21-26. Ro 2:8. 1 P 2:8. 2 P 3:3.
20. **every.** Jn 7:7. 1 K *22:8. Jb 24:13-17. Ps 50:17. *64:4. Pr 1:29. +*4:18. 5:12. 15:12. 22:8. Am 5:10, 11. Lk 11:45. Ro 13:12. Ja 1:23-25. **that doeth.** or, practiseth. Jn 5:29. 1 J 3:9. **reproved.** *or,* discovered. Jn 16:8. Ep +*5:11-13mg. Re 3:19.
21. **he that.** Jn 1:47. +*5:39. Ne 9:33. Jb 13:6. Ps *1:1-3. *119:80, 105. 139:23, 24. Is +*8:20. Ac √17:11, 12. 1 J 1:6. **cometh.** Ps *139:23, 24. **that his.** Jn 9:3. *15:4, 5. Is 26:12. Ho 14:8. 1 C *15:10. 2 C 1:12. Ga 5:22, 23. 6:8. Ep 5:9, 13. Ph 1:11. 2:13. Col 1:29. He 13:21. 1 P 1:22. 2 P √1:5-10. 1 J 2:27-29. 4:12, 13, 15, 16. Re 3:1, 2, 15. **they are.** 3 J 11. **in God.** Ro 16:12. Ph 2:13. 1 J 3:24.
22. **these.** Jn 2:13. 4:3. 7:3. **disciples.** Jn 2:2. **and baptized.** ver. 26. Jn *4:1, 2.
23. **was baptizing.** Mt 3:5, 6. Mk 1:4, 5. **Aenon.** i.e. *fountains, springs; to praise; cloud, darkness,* ✱S#137g, only here. Ezk 47:17. 48:1, Hazar Aenon, *the Village of Fountains.* "Aenon" is the plural form of the singular *En* or *Ain,* "fountain" or "eye" (✚S#5869h, Ge +24:13). Evidence could scarcely be more complete to establish the fact of a plurality of watercourses. As it is much less common to meet with a number of springs in close proximity than with a single spring, the plural form is much more rare than the singular form in connection with the names of places. The singular form is found in place names at Ge 14:7 (En-Mishpat, *fountain of judgment*); Jsh 15:7 (En-Shemesh, *fountain of the sun,* and En-Rogel, *fountain of the fuller*); Jsh 15:34 (En-Om, *two fountains,* and En-Gannim, *fountain of the gardens*). Jsh 15:62 (En-Geddi, *fountain of the kid*). Jsh 17:11 (En-Dor, *fountain of the dwelling*). Jsh 19:21 (En-Haddah, *fountain of swiftness*). Ezk 47:10 (En-Eglaim, *fountain of two pools*). **near to Salim.** i.e. *a fox; tossing; completed,* ✱S#4530g, only here. For ✱S#8004h, see Ge +14:18. Ge 33:18, Shalem. 1 S 9:4, Shalim. **much water.** lit. "many springs." The word "much" refers not to the quantity of water, but to the number of springs. Ex 15:27. Nu 24:7. 2 S 22:17, 18. 2 Ch √32:3, 4. Ps 18:16. 77:19. *93:4. 107:23. Is 17:13. Je +9:1. *51:13, 36.

La *2:11, 18, 19. *3:48, 49. Ezk 1:24. *19:10. *43:2. Re *1:15. *14:2. 17:1. *19:6. **and they.** Mt 3:5, 6. Mk 1:4, 5. Lk 3:7.
24. **For.** ſ71, Jn +1:24. **John.** Jn 5:35. Mt 4:12. *14:3. Mk 6:17. Lk 3:19, 20. 9:7-9.
25. **disciples.** Jn 1:35. **about purifying.** This mention of purifying in conjunction with baptism (ver. 23) shows that in the Jewish mind of this time they were equated. This reveals much about both the mode and the significance of baptism, this being the case. Jn 2:6. Nu 19:7. Mt 3:11. Mk 7:2-5, 8. Lk +*11:38. He 6:2. *9:8-10, 13, 14, 23. 1 P 3:21.
26. **Rabbi.** ver. 2. Jn 1:38. **he that.** Nu 11:26-29. Ec 4:4. 1 C 3:3-5. Ga 5:20, 21. 6:12, 13. Ja 3:14-18. 4:5, 6. **beyond Jordan.** Jn 1:28. 10:40. Mt 19:1. **to whom.** Jn *1:7, 15, 26-36. **the same.** ver. 22. **and all.** ſ102, Ge +2:24. Jn 1:7, 9. 11:48. 12:19. Ps 65:2. Is 45:23. Ac 19:26, 27.
27. **A man.** Nu 16:9-11. 17:5. 1 Ch 28:4, 5. Je 1:5. 17:16. Am 7:15. Mt 25:15. Mk 13:34. Ro 1:5. 12:6. 1 C 1:1. 2:12-14. 3:5. 4:7. 12:11. 15:10. Ga 1:1. Ep 1:1. 3:7, 8. 1 T 2:7. Ja *1:17. 1 P 4:10, 11. **receive.** *or,* take unto himself. He 5:4, 5. **except.** ſ184C, Mt +4:9. **be given.** Jn 4:10. *6:65. 17:2. 1 Ch *29:14. Is 55:11. Ro 9:16. 1 C 3:7. 4:7. Ph 2:12, 13. Ja 1:17, 18. 1 P 4:10. 1 J 5:20. **from heaven.** ſ121J20, Ps +73:9. Jn 19:11. Mt 21:25. Mk 11:30, 31.
28. **I said.** Jn *1:20, 25, 27. **but.** Jn 1:6, 15, 23. Ml *3:1. 4:4, 5. Mt 3:3, 11, 12. Mk *1:2, 3. Lk *1:16, 17, 76. 3:4-6. Ac 19:4.
29. **hath.** Ps 45:9-17. SS 3:11. 4:8-12. Is 54:5. 62:4, 5. Je 2:2. Ezk 16:8. Ho 2:19, 20. Mt 22:2. 25:1. 2 C *11:2. Ep *5:25-27. Re 19:7-9. 21:9. **the friend.** Jg 14:10, 11, 20. Ps 45:14. SS 5:1. Mt 9:15. **this.** Jn 15:11. Is 66:11. Lk 2:10-14. 15:6. 1 P *1:8.
30. **must increase.** Ps 72:17-19. Is +*9:7. *53:2, 3, 12. Da *2:34, 35, 44, 45. Mt 3:11. +*13:31-33. Lk *7:47. Re √11:15. **but.** Ac 13:36, 37. 1 C 3:5. 2 C 3:7-11. Col 1:18. He 3:2-6. **decrease.** Ro *12:3. Ph +*2:3.
31. **that cometh.** ver. √13. Jn 6:33. +*8:23, 24. 1 C 2:8. √15:47. Ep 1:20, 21. 4:8-10. Ph 2:6. Ja 2:1. **is above all.** ver. 35. Jn 1:15, 27, 30. *5:21-25. Ne +*9:6. Ps *97:9. Mt *28:18. Ac 10:36. Ro √9:5. 1 C *1:30. +*12:3. Ep 1:21. Ph *2:9-11. 1 P *3:22. Re 19:16. **he that is.** ver. 12. Mt 16:23. 1 C +*15:47, 48. He 9:1, 9, 10. **and speaketh.** 1 J 4:5. **earth.** ſ145, Jg +11:40. **he that cometh.** ver. 13. Jn 6:33, 51. 16:27, 28. **above all.** T#73. Jn 1:15. Ps 89:27. Ac +√10:36. 1 C +*2:8. +*15:47. Col 1:15, 18. He 1:4-6. Re 1:5. 3:14.
32. **what.** ver. 11. Jn 1:18. 5:20. 7:16. 8:26, 28, 38, 40. 12:49. 14:24. 15:15. 18:37. Re 1:5. **and no man.** ſ171C, Ex +20:10. ver. 11, 19, 26, 33. Jn *1:11. 5:43. 12:37. Is 50:2. 53:1. Ro 10:16-21. 11:2-6.
33. **hath set.** Jn 6:27. Ro *3:3, 4. 4:11, 18-21. 2 C 1:18. T *1:1, 2. He *6:17, 18. 1 J 5:9, 10. **seal.** Ne=9:38. Ro 4:11. 15:28. 1 C 9:2. 2 C 1:22. Ep 1:13. √4:30. 2 T *2:19. Re 7:3-8. **God is true.** Jn *8:26. Ro *3:4. 1 J *5:10.
34. **he.** ver. 32. Jn *7:16. 8:26-28, 40, 47. **hath sent.** ver. 17. Jn *20:21. 1 J *4:14. **speaketh.** Ezk 3:4. **the words.** Jn 8:47. **for God.** ver. 17. Jn 1:16. 5:26. 7:37-39. 15:26. 16:7. Nu 11:25. 2 K 2:9. Ps +*45:7. Is 11:2-5. 59:21. 62:1-3. Ro 8:2. Ep 3:8. 4:7-13. Col *1:19. √2:9, 10. Re 21:6. 22:1, 16, 17. **Spirit.** Gr. *pneuma,*

Mt +3:16. Ge +1:2. Ps ♦*45:7. Is ♦11:2. ♦61:1. ƒ121A1. Metonymy of the Cause B540. The person acting is put for the thing done: the *Spirit* is put for the gifts and operations of the Spirit. For other instances of this figure see Jn 6:63. Lk 11:13. Ac 19:2. 1 C 14:12mg, 32. Ga 3:2. Ep √5:18. 1 Th 5:19. **by measure.** Ezr 7:22. Ezk 4:11, 16. 12:19. 2 C ◑1:22. ◑5:5. Ep ◑1:13, 14. 4:7. 5:18. 1 J ◑2:20, 27.

35. **Father.** Jn *5:20-23. *15:9. *17:23, 24, 26. Pr 8:30. Is 42:1. Mt *3:17. *17:5. **the Son.** ver. 17, 36. Jn 5:19-26. 6:40. 8:36. 14:13. 17:1. Mt 24:36. 1 J 2:22. 4:14. 2 J 3, 9. **and.** Jn *13:3. *17:2. Ge 41:44, 55. Ps *2:8. 110:1, 2. Is +*9:6, 7. Mt *11:27. *28:18. Lk 10:22. 11:22. 1 C 15:27. Ep 1:22. Ph *2:9-11. He 1:2. *2:8, 9. 1 P 3:22. **all things.** Jn 5:20. Ge=39:4, 8.

36. **he that believeth on.** ver. *15, √16. Jn √1:12. √5:24. 6:40, 47-54. √10:28. 11:25, 26. *20:31. Hab +*2:4. Mt 19:16. Ro 1:17. 6:22. *8:1. 1 J 3:14, 15. √5:10-13. **everlasting.** Gr. *aionios,* Mt +18:8. **believeth.** or, obeyeth. He +*5:9. **not the Son.** Jn +*8:24. Ac √4:12. Ro *5:1. **not see.** ver. *3. Jn *8:51. Nu *32:11. Jb *33:28. Ps *36:9. 49:19. 106:4, 5. Lk 2:30. 3:6. Ro *8:24, 25. Re +*21:8. **but the wrath.** Jn 9:39. 12:40. 2 K *22:13. Ps *2:12. Mt 3:7. 22:7, 12. 24:28, 30. 25:12. Lk 19:27. Ro *1:18. 2:4-9, 17. *4:15. *5:9. +*11:22. 2 C +*5:11. Ga *3:10. Ep *5:6. Col *3:6. 1 Th *1:10. 2:16. *5:9. He √2:3. *10:29. Ju 15. Re √6:16, 17. 11:18. **abideth.** Is ◑55:7. Jon ◑4:2. Mt 12:31n, 32n. +*25:46. He +*9:27. Re +*22:11.

JOHN 4

Jesus leaves Judea, 1-3. In the absence of his disciples, he discourses with a Samaritan woman concerning the water of life, 4-15; brings her sins to remembrance, 16-19; shows her the nature of acceptable worship, 20-24; and declares himself to be the Messiah, 25, 26. The disciples return and are surprised to see him thus employed, 27. The woman goes to inform her neighbors and induces them to come and hear him, 28-30. Jesus shows his disciples his delight in his Father's work and the blessed harvest about to be reaped by them, with reference to the Samaritans coming to him, 31-38. The Samaritans believe in him, and he continues among them for two days, 39-42. He returns to Cana and heals a nobleman's son who lies sick at Capernaum, 43-54.

1. **the Lord.** Jn 6:23. 11:2. 13:13, 14. 20:2, 18, 20, 25. 21:7, 12. Lk 1:76. 2:11. 7:19. 19:31, 34. Ac +√10:36. 1 C *2:8. √15:47. 2 C 4:5. Ja *2:1. Re 19:16. **the Pharisees.** Jn 1:24. **that Jesus.** Jn 3:22, 26. 1 C *1:17.

2. **baptized not.** Ac 10:48. 1 C 1:13-17. **disciples.** Jn 2:2.

3. **left.** Jn 3:22. 7:8. 10:40. 11:54. Mt 10:23. *12:14, 15. Mk 3:7. **again.** Jn 1:43. 2:11, 12.

4. **must needs.** Mt 10:5, 6. Lk 2:49. 9:51, 52. 13:33. 17:11. **Samaria.** i.e. *watch-post, guardianship, prison,* ♦S#4540g. ver. 5, 7. Lk 17:11. Ac 1:8. 8:1, 5, 9, 14. 9:31. 15:3. For ♦S#8111h, see 1 K +16:24.

5. **a city.** Lk 9:52. **Sychar.** i.e. *city; hired; drunkenness,* ♦S#4965g. Ge=37:14. Jsh +*20:7n. **the parcel.** ver. 12. Ge 33:19. 48:22. Jsh 24:32.

6. **Now.** ƒ143, Ge +19:2. **Jacob's well.** Gr. "spring," as ver. 14. Over Jacob's well the empress Helena is said to have built a church in the form of a cross, of which "nothing but a few foundations" remained in

the time of Maundrell. He states that it is situated about one-third of an hour, or about a mile, east of Naplosa, the ancient Sychar; Mr. Buckingham says it is called *Beer Samareea,* or the well of Samaria, and "stands at the commencement of the round vale which is thought to be the parcel of ground bought by Jacob, and which, like the narrow valley east of Nablous, is rich and fertile. The mouth of the well itself had an arched or vaulted building over it; and the only passage down to it at this moment is by a small hole in the roof." "It is," says Maundrell, "dug in the firm rock, and contains about three yards in diameter, and thirty-five in depth; five of which we found full of water." **being wearied.** ver. 7. Jn 19:28. Is ◑40:28. Mt 4:2. 8:24. *21:18. Mk 4:38. 11:12. Lk 4:2. 8:23. He 2:17. +*4:15. **sat.** Ex=2:15. Lk 2:7. 9:58. 2 C √8:9. **on.** Jn 13:25. Mk 4:36. **it was.** Lk 7:36. **the sixth hour.** Our noon. Jn +*11:9n. ◑19:14. Mt +20:5. 27:45.

7. **to draw water.** Ge 24:11, 13. Ex 2:15-19. Jg 5:11. 1 S 9:11. 2 S 23:15. **saith.** Is 50:4. **Give.** ver. 10. Jn 19:28. Ge 24:43. 2 S 23:15-17. 1 K 17:10. Mt 10:42.

8. ƒ81, Ge +15:13. **the city.** ver. 5, 39. **to buy.** Three things money was spent on: the poor, food, and the feast or festival tithe (Jn 13:29. Mt 17:27). Thus money was used for daily wants, God's ordinances, and charity. Jn 6:5-7. Lk 9:13. **meat.** ƒ171I8, Ps +107:18.

9. **askest.** ver. 27. Jn *8:48. Lk 10:33. 17:16-19. **for.** Jn 8:48. 2 K 17:24, etc. Ezr ch. 4. Ne 4:1, 2. Mt 10:5. Lk *9:51-56. Ac +*1:8. *10:28. **Jews.** i.e. *confessing,* S#2453g. Jn 1:19. Mt 2:2. 27:11, 29, 37. Mk 7:3. Lk 7:3. Ac 2:5. Ro 1:16. 2:9, 10, 17, 28, 29. 9:24. 10:12. 1 C 1:22-24. 9:20. 10:32. 12:13. 2 C 11:24. Ga 2:13, 14, 15. 3:28. Col 3:11. 1 Th 2:14. Re 2:9. 3:9.

10. **If.** ƒ184B, Mt +23:30. Jn √3:16. Is +*9:6. 42:6. 49:6-8. Lk 11:13. Ro √8:32. 1 C 1:30. 2 C 9:15. Ep √2:8. **the gift.** Jn 3:34. **and who.** ver. 25, 26. Jn 9:35-38. 16:3. *17:3. 1 J 5:20. **thou wouldest.** 2 Ch 33:12, 13, 18, 19. Ps 10:17. Is √55:6-9. Mt 7:7. Lk *11:8-10. 18:13, 14. 23:42, 43. Ac 9:11. Re *3:17, 18. **would have given.** Jn 6:32, 33. 10:28. 17:2. Ac 8:20. **living.** ƒ108B, Ac +7:38. ver. 14. Jn 6:35, 51. 7:37, 38. 9:37-39. Ge 26:19. Ex 17:6. Le 14:5. Ps 36:8, 9. 46:4. Is *12:3. 35:6. 41:17, 18. 43:20. *44:3. 49:10. +*55:1-3. Je *2:13. 17:13. Ezk 47:1-9, 12. Jl *3:18. Zc *13:1. *14:8. 1 C *10:4. Re 7:17. 21:6. 22:1, 2, *17. **water.** ƒ22K4, Je +2:13.

11. **thou hast.** ver. 33. Jn 3:4. 1 C √2:14. **living.** ƒ108B, Ac +7:38.

12. **thou greater.** Jn *8:53. Is *53:2, 3. Mt 12:42. He 3:3. **father.** ƒ171G, Ge +13:8. **which gave.** ver. 5. **the well.** T#1215. Ge 24:11-14.

13. **Whosoever.** Jn 6:27, 49. Is 55:2. 65:13, 14. Lk 16:24.

14. **never.** Gr. *aion,* Mt +6:13. Jn 6:35, 58. 11:26. *17:2, 3. Is 49:10. 58:11. Ro √6:23. Re 7:16. **water.** ƒ22K4, Je +2:13. **I shall give.** Jn 7:37. **never.** ƒ158, Mt +5:18. **shall be.** Jn *7:38, 39. *10:10. 14:16-19. Ro *5:21. 8:16, 17. 2 C 1:22. Ep *1:13, 14. √4:30. 1 P 1:22, 23. 1 J 5:20. **a well.** ver. 6. Ge=49:22. Re 7:17. **springing up.** Nu=21:16-18. Pr 5:15. SS 4:15. Je 17:8. **everlasting.** Gr. *aionios,* Mt +18:8. ver. 36. Jn √3:36. +*5:39. *6:27, 68. √10:28. 12:25, 50. √17:2, 3. √20:31. Mt +19:16. Ro 2:7. 1 J 1:2. 2:25. 3:15. 5:11, 20. **life.** Jn 8:12.

15. **give me.** T#1745. ver. 10. Jn 6:26, 34. *17:2, 3. Ps 4:6. Ro √6:23. 8:5. 1 C √2:14. Ja 4:3. 1 J 5:20.

16. **Go.** ver. 18. Jn 1:42, 47, 48. +*2:24, 25. 21:17. He *4:13. Re *2:23. **call.** Jn 16:8.

18. **is not.** Ge 20:3. 34:2, 7, 8, 31. Nu 5:29. Ru 4:10, 11. Je 3:20. Ezk 16:32. Mk 10:12. Ro 7:3. 1 C 7:10, 11. He +*13:4.

19. **I perceive.** ver. 29. Jn 1:48, 49. 2 K 5:26. 6:12. Lk 7:39. 1 C 14:24, 25. **thou.** √101, Dt 32:42. **a prophet.** √101, Dt +32:42. Jn 3:2. +*6:14. 7:40. 9:17. Mt 21:11. Lk 7:16, 39. 24:19.

20. **fathers.** Ge *12:6, 7. *33:18-20. Dt *11:29. 27:12. Jsh 8:33-35. Jg *9:6, 7. 2 K 17:26-33. Ezr 4:2. **worshipped.** ver. 24. Jn 12:20. Ac 8:27. 24:11. He 11:21. Re 5:14. **this mountain.** Dt 27:4n. Jg 9:7. Ne 13:28n. **and ye.** Jn 12:20. Dt 12:5-11. 16:2. 26:2. 1 K 8:29. *9:3. *14:21. 2 K *21:4. 1 Ch 21:26. 22:1. 2 Ch 6:6. *7:12, 16. Ps 78:68, 69. 87:1, 2. 132:13, 14. Lk 9:53. **the place.** Jn 11:48. Ge 22:3. Dt 12:14. +*16:16. Jsh *22:11, 16, 21-29. **ought.** ver. 24.

21. **saith.** Ezk 14:3. 20:3. **Woman.** Jn 2:4. **hour cometh.** ver. 23. Jn 5:25, 28. 16:2, 25, 32. Lk 17:22. **when.** Zp 2:11. Ml *1:11. Mt +*18:20. Lk 21:5, 6, 24. Ac 6:14. Ep *2:13, 14. 1 T *2:8. He *9:1, 11, 12, 24. **worship.** ver. 23. Jn √14:6. Mt 28:19. Ep 2:18. 3:14. 1 P 1:17. **the Father.** Mt 24:36.

22. **ye know not.** Jn 7:28. 2 K *17:27-29, 41. Ezr 4:2, 3. Is *29:13, 14. *48:1. Mt 15:7, 8. Ac 17:23, 30. **we know.** T#1423. 1 C 14:14-20. **we worship.** 2 Ch 13:10-12. Ps 147:19, 20. Is *2:3. Ro 3:1, 2. *9:4, 5. **for salvation.** ver. 42. Ge +*49:10. Ps 68:20. Is +*2:3. *12:2, 6. 46:13. Zp *3:16, 17. Zc *9:9. Lk 24:47. Ac √4:12. Ro *9:4, 5. He 7:14. Re 7:10. 12:10. 19:1. **is of.** Mt 2:5. Ac 13:23. Ro 11:26. **the Jews.** ver. 9. Jn 13:33. 18:20, 35, 36. Ex 3:18. Ac 3:25, 26.

23. **the hour.** ver. 21. Jn 5:25. 12:23. √171T6. Synecdoche of the Part B656. *Hour* is put for a special time or season. For other instances of this figure see Jn 5:25, 28. 16:2. 17:1. 1 Th 2:17. Phm 15. 1 J 2:18. **now is.** Jn 5:25. 16:32. **true worshippers.** Ps 148:14. Is *1:10-15. √26:8, 9. *29:13. 48:1, 2. 58:2, 8-14. 66:1, 2. Je 7:7-12. Mt 15:7-9. Lk 18:11-13. Ep 1:4. He 8:2. **worship.** √171J6, Ge +4:26. **the Father.** ver. 21. **in spirit.** Gr. *pneuma*, √121A1, Lk 1:17n. 1 S *16:7. Ps *51:16, 17. Is +*57:15. Ro 1:9. 8:15, 26. Ga 4:6. Ep 2:18. *6:18. Ph *3:3. 1 P *2:5. Ju 20, 21. **and.** √93A, Ge +1:26. By Hendiadys, the sense is, worship him in a truly spiritual manner. ver. 24. **in truth.** Jn 1:17. Jsh *24:14. 1 S *12:24. 1 Ch 29:17. Ps 17:1. 32:2. *51:6. +*66:18. *145:18. Is 10:20. Je 3:10. 4:2. He *10:22. **the Father seeketh.** Jn 6:44. Ps 147:11. Pr *15:8. SS 2:14. Is 43:21. Je *5:1. Ezk *22:30. He *11:6. 1 P *2:9, 10.

24. **is.** √63B, Ge +2:10. **a Spirit.** Gr. *pneuma*, 1 C +3:16. √101, Dt +32:42. Here, *pneuma* is used of God the Father. For the other uses of *pneuma*, see Mt +*8:16n. Is 31:3. 2 C *3:17. 1 T √1:17. 1 J 1:5. 4:8. **worship.** √171J6, Ge +4:26. **must.** ver. 20g. Jn *3:7. 1 S *16:7. Ps *50:13-15, 23. *51:17. *66:18, 19. Is +*57:15. Mt *15:8, 9. 2 C 1:12. He √11:6. **worship him.** ver. 20. Dt 4:15, 16. Mt 4:10. Re 22:9. **in spirit.** Gr. *pneuma*, √121A1, Lk +1:17n. 2 C *3:17. **and.** √93A, Ge +1:26. ver. 23n. **in truth.** T#1420. ver. +*23. Ps *145:18. Je +*10:2.

25. **I know.** Jn +*6:14. **Messias.** ver. *42. Jn *1:41,

42, 49. Da +*9:24-26. **called Christ.** √22D5L, Ps +45:7. Mt 1:16. **when.** ver. *29, *39. Dt *18:15-18. **will tell.** Col *2:3.

26. **I that.** Jn *9:35-37. Mt *16:20. 20:15. *26:63, 64. Mk 8:29. *14:61, 62. Lk 13:30. Ro *10:20, 21. **am he.** Jn +*8:24, 58. 9:9.

27. **came.** ver. 8. **disciples.** Jn 2:2. **marvelled.** ver. 9. Lk 7:39. **yet.** Da 4:35.

28. **then left.** ver. 7. Mt 28:8. Mk 16:8-10. Lk 24:9, 33.

29. **Come.** ver. 17, 18, 25. Jn 1:41-49. +*16:30. 2 K 7:9. Is 52:7. 1 C 14:24, 25. Re 22:17. **is not this.** Jn 7:26, 31. Mt 12:23.

30. **went out.** Is 60:8. Mt 2:1-3. +*8:11, 12. 11:20-24. 12:40-42. 20:16. Lk 17:16-18. Ac 8:5-8. 10:33. 13:42. 28:28. Ro 5:20.

31. **Master.** Jn 1:38. Ge 24:33. Ac √16:30-34.

32. **I have.** ver. 34. Jb +*23:12. Ps 63:5. 119:103. Pr 18:20. Is 53:11. Je +*15:16. Ac 20:35. **meat.** √171I8, Ps +107:18. **to eat.** √145, Jg +11:40. **that.** Ps 25:14. Pr 14:10. Re 2:17.

33. **said.** Mt 16:6-11. Lk 9:45. **one to another.** Jn 16:17. **Hath.** ver. 11, 15. Jn 2:20. 3:4. 6:34, 42, 52.

34. **My meat.** √171I8, Ps +107:18. ver. 32. Jn 6:33, 38. Ge 24:33. Le +=23:13. Jb +*23:12. Ps *40:8. 119:103. Is *61:1-3. Mt *4:4. Lk 4:4. 15:4-6, 10. +*19:10. Ac *20:35. **to do.** Jn 5:30. *6:15, 38-40. 14:31. Mt 12:50. Mk +*1:35. Lk *2:49. **that sent.** Jn 3:17. 5:23, etc. 6:38, etc. 7:16, etc. 8:16, etc. 9:4. 12:44, etc. 13:20. 14:24. 15:21. 16:5. Lk 4:43. **and to finish.** Jn 5:36. 9:4. *17:4. *19:28, 30. Lk 2:49. He *12:2.

35. **Say not.** √85B, Ge +13:9. **There are.** √7, Allegory by continued Hypocatastasis, Ga +4:24. **four months.** Le +*23:22-24. **Lift.** Is 49:18. 60:4. Lk +6:20. +11:27. **Lift.** √144A12, Ge +22:13. **fields.** Mt 13:24, 38. 24:18. Lk 21:21. **for.** ver. 30. Mt √9:37, 38. Lk 10:2. **to harvest.** Mt *9:37, 38. Lk *10:2. Ac *8:5, 6, 12.

36. **he that reapeth receiveth.** Pr +*11:30. Da +*12:3. Am 9:13. Lk 10:7. Ro 1:13. 6:22. 1 C *3:8. 9:10, 19-23. Ph 2:15, 16. 1 Th *2:19, 20. 1 T +*4:16. 2 T 2:6. 4:7, 8. Ja *5:19, 20. **wages.** 1 C 9:17, 18. **fruit.** Ro 1:13. 15:28. Ph 4:17. **eternal.** Gr. *aionios*, Mt +18:8. ver. 14. **both he that.** ver. 38. Mt +*13:37. Mk 4:14. 1 C *3:5-9. **may rejoice.** Ps 4:7. Is 9:3. Am 9:13.

37. **One.** √138A, Ge +10:9. Le 26:16. Dt 6:11. 28:30, 38. Jg 5:3. Jb 31:8. Mi *6:15. Lk 19:21. **reapeth.** Ga ◐6:7.

38. **sent.** Jn 17:18. Mt 9:38. Lk 10:2. Ac 2:41. 4:4, 32. 5:14. 6:7. 8:4-8, 14-17. **no labor.** Jsh 24:13. **other.** Jn 1:7. 2 Ch *36:15. Je *44:4. Mt *3:1-6. *4:23. 11:8-13. Ac 10:37, 38, 42, 43. 1 P 1:11, 12. **are entered.** √96C2, Ge +45:9. Ac 8:5-17, 25.

39. **many.** Jn 10:41. 11:45. **Samaritans.** ver. 9. **that city.** ver. 5, 8. **believed.** Jn 2:11. √3:16, 18, 36. 5:44. 6:29, 35, 40. 7:5, 31, 38, 39, 48. 8:30. 9:35, 36. 10:42. 11:25, 26, 45, 48. 12:11, 36, 37, 42, 44, 46. 14:1, 12. 16:9. 17:20. Ac 10:43. 1 J √5:10, 13. **for.** ver. 29, 42. Jn 17:20. **which testified.** ver. 29.

40. **they.** Ge 32:26. Pr 4:13. SS 3:4. Je 14:8. Lk 8:38. 10:39. 24:29. Ac 16:15. **he abode.** Lk 19:5-10. 2 C 6:1, 2. Re *3:20.

41. **many.** Ge +*49:10. Ac +*1:8. 8:12, 25. 15:3. **believed.** ver. 39, 42, 48, 53. Jn 5:44. **because.** Jn

6:63. 7:46. 8:30. Mt 7:28, 29. Lk 4:32. 1 C 2:4, 5. He *4:13.

42. **we believe.** ver. +41. **thy saying.** Jn 8:43. Mt 26:73. **for.** Jn 1:45-49. 17:8. Ac √17:11, 12. **and know.** ver. 29. Jn 1:29. *3:14-18. 6:68, 69. 11:27. Is 45:22. 52:10. Lk 2:10, 11, 32. Ac √4:12. Ro 10:11-13. 2 C 5:19. 2 T *1:12. 1 J *4:14. 5:20. **the Savior.** Jn 3:17. 5:34. 12:47. Lk 2:11. 1 T 1:15. 2:4. √4:10. **world.** Gr. *kosmos*, Mt +4:8. Jn +*1:9, 29. Mt *20:28. 2 C 5:19. 1 J *4:14.

43. **two.** ver. 40. Mt 15:21-24. Mk 7:27, 28. Ro 15:8. **and.** ver. 46. Jn 1:43. Mt 4:13.

44. **testified.** Jn 18:37. **that.** Mt 13:57. Mk 6:4. Lk 4:24. **own country.** Jn 7:41, 42.

45. **the Galileans.** Mt 4:23, 24. Lk 8:40. **having.** Jn *2:13-16, 23. 3:2. **for.** ver. 20. Dt *16:16. Lk 2:42-44. 9:53.

46. **Cana.** "It is worthy of remark," says Dr. E. D. Clarke (*Travels*, part ii. c. xiv. p. 445), who visited Cana a few years ago, "that, walking among the ruins of a church, we saw large mossy pots, answering the description given of the ancient vessels of the country; not preserved, but lying about, disregarded by the present inhabitants, as antiquities with whose original use they were unacquainted. From their appearance, and the number of them, it was quite evident that a practice of keeping water in large pots, each holding from eighteen to twenty-seven gallons, was once common in the country" (compare the account of the water pots, Jn 2:6). Jn 2:1-11. 21:2. Jsh 19:28. **nobleman.** *or*, courtier, *or*, ruler. **whose.** Ps +*50:15. 78:34. Ho +*5:15. Mt 9:18. 15:22. 17:14, 15. Lk 7:2. 8:42. **Capernaum.** ver. 49, 51. Jn 2:12.

47. **he heard.** Mk 2:1-3. 6:55, 56. 10:47. **was come.** ver. 3, 54. **besought him.** T#1451. Ge 21:14-16. 2 S *12:16, 17. La 2:19. Mk 5:22, 23. **that he.** Lk 11:21, 32. Ps 46:1. Lk 7:6-8. 8:41. Ac 9:38.

48. **Except.** ver. 41, 42. Jn 2:18. 6:30. 12:37. 15:24. 20:29. Nu 14:11. Mt 16:1. 27:42. Lk 10:18. 16:31. Ac 2:22. 1 C *1:22. **signs and.** Jn 2:11. Ex 7:3. Da 4:2, 3. 6:27. Mt 24:24. Mk 13:22. Ac 2:19, 22, 43. 4:30. 5:12. 6:8. 7:36. 8:13. 14:3. 15:12. Ro 15:19. 1 C 1:22. 2 C 12:12. 2 Th 2:9. He 2:4. **will not.** √158, Mt +5:18. **believe.** ver. +41.

49. **The nobleman.** Mk 9:24. **come.** ver. 47, 51. Ps 40:17. 88:10-12. Mk 5:23, 35, 36. **ere my child die.** Jn 11:21, 32. Mk 5:35. Lk 8:49.

50. **Go.** Jn 11:40. 1 K 17:13-15. Mt 8:13. Mk 7:29, 30. 9:23, 24. Lk 17:14. Ac 14:9, 10. Ro 4:20, 21. He 11:19. **believed the word.** Jn 5:47. 2 Ch 32:8.

51. **Thy.** ver. 50, 53. 1 K 17:23.

52. **seventh hour.** Our 1 p.m. Jn +*11:9n.

53. **at the.** ver. 50. Ps 33:9. 107:20. Mt 8:8, 9, 13. **and himself believed.** ver. 41. Lk 19:9. Ac +*2:39. 16:15, 34. 18:8. **whole house.** Ac 11:14. 16:34. 18:8.

54. **This is.** Jn 2:11 w ver. 45-47. **the second.** Jn 2:1-11. **miracle.** Jn 2:11. **come out.** ver. 45, 46.

JOHN 5

Jesus goes up to Jerusalem, and at the pool of Bethesda on the Sabbath day heals one who had been diseased thirty-eight years; he orders him to carry his bed, 1-9. The Jews demand of the man, Who ordered him to carry his bed? Jesus finds him at the temple and warns him to sin no more; he informs the Jews

that Jesus has healed him, 10-15. They persecute Jesus, 16. He defends himself, asserting his personal and mediatorial dignity and authority in the most explicit and energetic language, 17-32, appealing to the testimony of John, 33-35; to his own miracles, 36; to the testimony of God by a voice from heaven, 37, 38, and to the Scriptures, 39, 40. He exposes their unbelief, ambition, and ungodliness; and shows that in disbelieving him, they disbelieved Moses also, 41-47.

1. **a feast.** Jn 2:13. 6:4. Ex 23:14-17. 34:23. Le 23:2, etc. Dt *16:16. Mt 3:15. Ga 4:4.

2. **by.** √143, Ge +19:2. **market.** *or*, gate. Ne 3:1, 32. 12:39. **pool.** Is 22:9, 11. **Hebrew.** Jn 19:13, 17, 20. Ac 21:40. Re 9:11. 16:16. **Bethesda.** The supposed remains of the pool of *Bethesda* are situated on the east of Jerusalem, contiguous on one side to St. Stephen's gate, and on the other to the area of the temple. Maundrell states, that "it is 120 paces long, and forty broad, and at least eight deep, but void of water. At its west end it discovers some old arches, now dammed up. These some will have to be the porches, in which sat that multitude of lame, halt, and blind. But it is not likely, for instead of five, there are but three."

3. **of blind.** Mt 15:30, 31. Lk 7:22. **withered.** 1 K 13:4. Zc 11:17. Mt 12:10. Mk 3:1-4. Lk 6:6, 8. **waiting.** Pr 8:34. La 3:26. Ro 8:25. Ja 5:7.

4. **an angel.** Re 16:5. **whosoever.** The sanative property of this pool has been supposed by some to have been communicated by the blood of the sacrifices, and others have referred it to the mineral properties of the waters. But, (1) The beasts for sacrifice were not washed here but in a laver in the temple. (2) No natural property could cure all manner of diseases. (3) The cure only extended to the first who entered. (4) It took place only at one particular time. (5) As the healing was effected by immersion, it must have been instantaneous; it was never failing in its effects. All of which, not being observed in medicinal waters, determine the cures to have been miraculous, as expressly stated in the text. **first.** Ps 119:60. Pr 6:4, 5. 8:17. Ec *9:10. Ho 13:13. Mt √6:33. 11:12. Lk 13:24-28. 16:16. **was made.** 2 K 5:10-14. Ezk 47:8, 9. Zc *13:1. 14:8. 1 C 6:11. 1 J 1:7.

5. **thirty.** ver. 14. Jn 9:1, 21. Mk 9:21. Lk *8:43. *13:16. Ac 3:2. 4:22. 9:33. 14:8.

6. **and knew.** Jn +*2:24, 25. 21:17. Ps *142:3. He *4:13, 15. **Wilt.** Is 65:1. Je 13:27. Lk 18:41.

7. **I have.** √63D1, Mt +16:7. By ellipsis, supply "Sir, (I am indeed willing, but) I have," etc. Dt 32:36. Ps 72:12. 142:4. Ro 5:6. 2 C 1:8-10. **when.** ver. 4. **is troubled.** Ezk 32:2. **before.** ver. 4. 1 C 9:24.

8. **Rise.** Pr 6:9. SS 2:10. Is 60:1. Mt *9:6, 7. Mk 2:9, 11, 12. 10:49. Lk 5:24, 25. 22:46. Ac 9:34. Ep 5:14. **bed.** Mk 2:4, 9, 11, 12. 6:55. Ac 5:15. 9:33.

9. **immediately.** ver. 14. Mk 1:31, 42. 5:29, 41, 42. 10:52. Ac 3:7, 8. **and on.** ver. 10-12. Jn 7:23. 9:14. Mt 12:10-13. Mk 3:2-4. Lk +*13:10-16.

10. **The Jews.** ver. 15, 16, 18. Jn 1:19. 2:18, 20. 3:1, 25. 4:22. 6:4, 41, 52. 7:1, etc. 8:22, etc. 9:18, 22. 10:19, etc. 11:8, etc. 12:9, 11. 13:33. 18:12, etc., 20, 33, 36. 19:7, etc. 20:19. **it is not lawful.** Jn 7:23. 9:16. Ex +*20:8-11. 31:12-17. Ne *13:15-21. Is +*58:13n. Je *17:21, 22, 27n. Mt 12:2, etc. Mk 2:24. 3:4. Lk 6:2. +*13:14n. 23:56.

11. **He that.** Jn 9:16, 17. Mk 2:9-11.

12. **What.** Jg 6:29, 30. 1 S 14:38, 39. Mt 21:23. Ro 10:2.

13. **he that.** Jn 14:9. **for Jesus.** Jn 6:15. **conveyed himself away.** Jn √8:59. Lk +*4:30. +*24:31. **a multitude being.** *or*, from the multitude that was.

14. **Jesus.** Jn 1:43. 9:35. **in the temple.** Le 7:12. Ps 9:13, 14. 27:6. 66:13-15. 107:20-22. 116:12-19. 118:18, 19. Is 38:20, 22. **sin.** Jn 8:11. Ezr 9:13, 14. Ne 9:28. Mt 9:2, 5. Mk 2:5. 1 P 4:3. **lest.** ver. 5. Le *26:23, 24, 27, 28. 2 Ch 28:22. Ezr 9:14. La 3:22. Mt *12:45. 1 C +*11:30. Re 2:21-23.

15. **and told.** Jn 4:29. 7:21. 9:11, 12. Mk 1:45. **which.** ver. 12. Jn 9:15, 25, 30, 34.

16. **persecute.** Jn 15:20. Ac 9:4, 5. **and sought.** ver. 13. Jn 7:19, 20, 25. 10:39. Mt 12:13, 14. Mk 3:6. Lk 6:11. **because.** Jn 7:23. 9:16. Lk +*13:14n.

17. **answered.** ver. 19. Mt 12:2-8. Mk 2:24-28. +11:14. Lk 13:14-17. **My Father.** ver. 43. Jn 2:16. 6:32, 40. 8:19, 49, 54. 10:18, 25, 29, 37. 14:2, etc. 15:1, etc. 17:1. 20:17. Mt +7:21. **worketh.** Jn *9:4. *14:10. Ge 2:1, 2. Ps 65:6. Is 40:26. Mt 10:29. Ac 14:17. 17:28. 1 C 12:6, 7. Col 1:16, 17. He 1:3. **I work.** T#63. Jn 9:4. Lk 2:49.

18. **the Jews.** ver. 10. Jn *7:19. **sought.** Jn 7:1. **broken the sabbath.** ver. 16. Jn *7:22, 23. 10:35. Mt *12:5. Lk +*13:14n. **God was.** ver. *23. Jn *8:54, 58. *10:30, 33. *14:9, 23. Zc *13:7. Ph *2:6. Re *21:22, 23. *22:1, 3. **his Father.** Ro 8:32. **making himself.** At no point does Jesus in the following discourse deny the inference drawn by the Jews but emphatically supports his claim to equality with God in his nature (ver. 18) by claiming equality in power and works (ver. 19, 20), in resurrection power (ver. 21), in judgment (ver. 22), in honor (ver. √23), in giving eternal life (ver. 24, 25), in self-existent life (ver. 26), in power over death and eternal destiny (ver. 28, 29), in absolute justice (ver. 30), supported by the witness of John (ver. 33), his own works (ver. 36), the Father (ver. 37, 38), and the Scriptures (ver. 39). Clearly their inference was correct, unlike modern day Arians who refuse to acknowledge what the words must mean. To suggest "John is describing what the unbelieving Jews *incorrectly* thought Jesus meant, that he was 'making himself equal with God,'" and that "This is evident from the fact that they also *incorrectly* accused Jesus of breaking the Sabbath" (*The Watchtower*, vol. 105, No. 3, February 1, 1984, p. 6) is to deduce from this passage the very opposite of what it says, in the effort to bolster the faulty argument "Why do we not find opposing Jews attacking the doctrine that to them would have been abhorrent?" The Jews, of course, did attack Jesus, seeking to kill him (Jn 5:18. 10:30-33) for this very doctrine. "For the Jews...it would have been blasphemous to suggest that Christ was equal to God as the second person of the Trinity" (*The Watchtower*, p. 6). In John 10:33, blasphemy is the very charge leveled at Jesus by the Jews: upon what other scriptural grounds could they justify stoning him? Clearly Jesus said what he meant, and the Jews correctly understood him. If not, why did not Jesus simply deny their accusation, and correct their alleged misunderstanding? Jn 10:33. 19:7. **equal.** T#75. ver. 17. Jn +√10:30, 33. 14:9. ◐+*28. 17:5, 10. Mt ◐+*10:32. +*27:43. Mk ◐+*13:32. 1 C ◐*11:3. 15:◐+*28, 45, √47. Ph *2:5, 6.

19. **answered.** ver. 17. **Verily.** ver. 24, 25. Jn +1:51. See on Jn 3:3. **The Son.** ver. 30. Jn 3:35. 8:28. 9:4.

12:49. 14:10, 20. **do nothing.** Jn 16:13. Ge=41:16. **of himself.** (1) Jn 1:1, 3. Ge 1:1. (2) Ne 9:6. Col 1:17. (3) Ac 2:24. Jn 2:19. (4) Jn 6:44 w 12:32. (5) Jn 5:22, 23 w Ps 50:6. (6) Ro 8:11 w Ph 3:20, 21. (7) Ps 27:14 w 2 C 12:9. (8) Pr 2:6, 7 w Lk 21:15. (9) Je 23:24 w Ep 1:23. (10) Jn 6:45 w Ga 1:12. (11) Ju 1 w He 2:11. (12) Je 17:10 w Re 2:23. (13) Is 43:11 w Jn 4:42. (14) T 1:3 w 1:4. See further on Mt +*28:19. **but what.** Ge=41:25. **for.** (1) Jn 14:16-23. Ge 1:1, 26. Is 44:24. Col 1:16. (2) Compare ver. 22 with Ps 50:6. 2 C 5:10. (3) Jn 2:19. 10:18, with Ac 2:24. Ro 6:4. 1 C 15:12. 1 P 3:18. (4) and ver. 21, 25, 26, with Ep 1:18, 19. 2:5. (5) and ver. 28, 29. Jn 11:25, 26, with Ro 8:11. 2 C 4:14. Ph 3:21. 1 Th 4:14. (6) Ps 27:14. 138:3. Is 45:24, with 2 C 12:9, 10. Ep 3:16. Ph 4:13. Col 1:11. (7) Ex 4:11. Pr 2:6, with Lk 21:15. (8) Je 17:10, with Re 2:23.

20. **the Father.** Jn *3:35. 10:17. 15:9, 10. 17:23, 24, 26. Mt *3:17. 17:5. Mk 1:11. 9:7. Lk 3:22. 9:35. Ep 1:6. Col 1:13. 2 P 1:17. **and showeth.** Jn 1:18. 10:32. 15:15. Ge=41:39. Ps=103:7. Pr 8:22-31. Mt 11:27. Lk 10:22. **all things.** Jn 3:35. +*14:28. Mt +*10:32. Mk ◐+*13:32. Lk 2:52. **greater.** ver. 21, 25, 29. Jn 12:45-47. 14:12. **works.** ver. 17, 36. Jn 4:34. 9:3, 4. 10:32, 37. 14:10. 17:4. Mt 11:2.

21. **as.** Dt +*32:39. 1 S 2:6. 1 K 17:21, 22. 2 K 4:32-35. 5:7. Ac 26:8. Ro 4:17-19. **even.** Jn *11:25, 43, 44. 17:2. Lk *7:14, 15. 8:54, 55. **the Son.** Jn 6:33. 11:25. 1 C 15:45. **quickeneth.** Ps +*71:20. 80:17, 18. Ro *4:17. *8:11, 23. Ep 2:5. Col 2:13. 1 T 6:13. **whom.** Ro 9:18. **he will.** Jn 17:24. 21:22.

22. **the Father.** ver. 27. Jn 3:35. 17:2. Ps 9:7, 8. 50:3-6. 96:13. 98:9. Ec 11:9. 12:14. Mt *11:27. +*16:27n. 25:31-46. *28:18. Ac 10:42. √17:31. Ro *2:16. 14:10-12. 2 C *5:10. 2 Th 1:7-10. 2 T 4:1. He ◐*12:23. 1 P 4:5. Re 20:11, 12. **hath committed.** ver. 27. Jn 3:17. 9:39. 17:2. Ac 10:42. **all judgment.** ver. 27. Ec *12:14. Mt +*10:15n. 2 C 5:10. 2 T 4:1.

23. **That all.** Da *7:13, 14. 1 C *8:6. Ph 2:10. **men should.** (1) Jn 14:1. Ps 146:3-5. Je 17:5-7. Mt 12:21. Ro 15:12. 2 C 1:9. Ep 1:12, 13. 2 T 1:12mg. (2) Ps *2:12. Is 42:8. 43:10. 44:6. Mt +*28:19. Ro 1:7. 1 C 1:3. 2 C 13:14. 1 Th 3:11-13. 2 Th 2:16, 17. He √1:6. 2 P √3:18. Re 5:8-14. (3) Mt 10:37. 22:37, 38. 1 C 16:22. Ep 6:24. (4) Lk 12:8, 9. Ro 6:22. 14:7-9. 1 C 6:19. 10:31. 2 C 5:14, 15. T 2:14. (5) Is 43:11. 45:15, 21. Zc 9:9. T √2:13. 3:4-6. 2 P √1:1. **honor the Son.** Mt +*14:33. Nu=12:8. Re +*5:12. **even as.** Jn 14:1. 16:15. Is 42:8. Mt *4:10. +*14:33. 1 J *2:23. **honor the Father.** Jn 8:49. Is 48:11. +*58:13. 1 T +*1:17. **He that.** Jn *15:23, 24. 16:14, 15. 17:10. Mt 11:27. Lk 10:16. Ro *8:9. 1 J 2:23. 2 J 9. **hath sent.** ver. 30, 37. Jn 4:34.

24. **Verily.** Jn +1:51. **He that.** T#1119. Jn √3:16, 18, 36. 6:40, 47. 8:51. *11:26. 12:44. √20:31. Mk 16:16. Ro *10:11-13. √14:12. 1 P 1:21. 1 J √5:1, 11-13. **heareth.** Jn 8:43. Lk +*8:18. **believeth.** Jn 20:31. Ac 16:34. 1 J 5:9-13. **hath.** Eternal life is a present possession. 1 J √5:13. **everlasting.** Gr. *aionios*, Mt +18:8. **and shall not.** Jn √10:27-30. +*17:6. Ro √8:1, 16, 17, 28-30, 33, 34. Ep √4:30. 1 Th 5:9. 2 Th *2:13, 14. 1 P 1:5. Ju *24. **but.** Mt 18:8. 1 J *3:14. **passed.** ſ144C1, Ge +21:1.

25. **The hour.** ſ171T6, Jn +4:23. Jn 4:23. 13:1. 17:1. **when.** ver. 21, 28. Lk 9:60. 15:24, 32. Ro *6:4. Ep *2:1, 5. 5:14. Col *2:13. *3:4. Re 3:1. **shall hear.** Jn

10:16. 11:43. **Son of God**. Jn 3:18. 9:35. 10:36. 11:4. 19:7. Mt +14:33. Ga 2:20. Ep 4:13. He 6:6. 7:3. 10:29. 1 J 3:8. 5:10, 12, 13, 20.

26. **hath life**. T#221. Jn *6:57. Ex 3:14. Dt 32:40. Ps *36:9. 90:2. Je 10:10. Ac 17:24, 25. 1 T *1:17. *6:15, 16. Re 1:17, 18. **so hath**. Jn *1:4. 4:10. 7:37, 38. 8:51. 11:26. √14:6, 19. 17:2, 3. 1 C *15:45. Col *3:3, 4. 1 J 1:1-3. Re 7:17. 21:6. 22:1, 17. **have life**. Mt +*28:19.

27. **hath**. See on ver. 22. Jn 17:2. Ps *2:6-9. 110:1, 2, 6. Mt +*28:18. Ac 10:42. √17:31. 1 C 15:25. Ep 1:20-23. 1 P 3:22. **judgment**. ver. 22. Ex=18:13. Mt 5:21, 22. +*10:15n. 12:41, 42. *25:31-46. Lk ●12:14. Ac √17:31. Re 20:11-15. **because**. Da +*7:13, 14. Ph 2:7-11. He 2:7-9. **the Son of man**. This appears to be a direct reference to Da 7:13, which the Jews interpret of the Messiah. So Saadias Gaon expressly affirms, "This is Messiah our righteousness." Not "a son of man," for the lack of the Greek article before "son" does not make "son" indefinite or qualitative, but is an instance of the anarthrous construction whereby nouns or pronouns which occur before the verb do not have the article (see Note on Mt 27:54 and Jn 1:1). Jn 1:51. Da 7:13. Mk *15:39. Re 1:13. 14:14.

28. **Marvel**. ver. 20. Jn *3:7. Ac 3:12. 1 J 3:13. **for the hour**. ✓171T6, Jn +4:23. ver. 25. Jn 4:23. *6:39, 40. *11:24, 25. Jb +*19:25, 26. Is +*26:19n. Ezk 37:1-10. Ho *13:14. Mt 9:22. Mk 13:11. Lk 10:21. 1 C 15:22, 42-54. Ph *3:21. 1 Th *4:14-17. 1 J 2:18. Re 20:12. **in which all**. This does not assert a simultaneous resurrection of the just and unjust. The word *hour* is frequently rendered "time" as the parallel passages (Jn 4:23. 1 J 2:18) show, equivalent to saying "a time is coming when all shall be raised," without requiring that the time be brief, and certainly not simultaneous when other Scriptures tell us "every man in his own order" (1 C 15:23). Notice the following verse describes *two* resurrections, the "resurrection of life" and the "resurrection of damnation" (Peters, *Theocratic Kingdom*, vol. 2, p. 301). **graves**. Mt +8:28 (❋S#3419g). **shall hear**. Jn 11:43-45.

29. **come forth**. T#856. Jn *6:39, 40, 54. *11:25. Jb *19:25-27. Ps *16:9, 10. 71:20. Is +*26:19n. Da +*12:2, 3. Mt *25:31-46. Lk 20:35, 36. Ac *24:15. Ro *8:11. 1 C 6:2, 3. *15:21, 42-44, 49-54. 2 C *4:14. *5:1-4, 10. Ph *3:21. 1 Th √4:14-17. 2 T 1:10. **done good**. Gr. *agatha poieesantes*, do good. Aorist active participle, nominative masculine plural. Lk *14:14. Ac 16:30, 31. Ro *2:6-10. Ga 6:8-10. Ep *2:8, 9. 1 T 6:18, 19. T *3:4-8. He 13:16. Ja *2:17. 1 P 3:11. 1 J ●3:9g. **resurrection of life**. ✓181E, Ge +3:24. Jn 6:39, 40, 44, 54. Lk +*14:14. 1 C 15:23. 1 Th +√4:16n. He *11:35. Ph +*3:11g. Re +*20:5. **done evil**. Gr. *phaula praxantes*, practice evil. Aorist active participle, nominative masculine plural. Vine comments "The distinction between 'have done' (*poieo*) and 'have practised' (*prasso*) lies in this, that *poieo* denotes an act complete in itself, while *prasso* denotes a habit. Compare Jn 3:20, 21, where the same distinction is made" (*Commentary on John*, p. 44). The words are associated in Jn 3:20, 21. 5:29. Ac 26:9, 10. Ro 1:32. 2:3. 7:15, 19, etc. 13:4, etc. **resurrection of damnation**. ✓181E, Ge +3:24. ver. 24. Is +*24:22. Da *12:2. Ac +*24:15. Re √20:5, 11-15.

30. **can**. ver. 19. Jn *7:17, 18. *8:28, 42. ●10:18. 14:10. **I judge**. Jn 8:15, 16. Ge +*18:25. Ps 96:13. Is 11:3, 4. Ro 2:2, 5. **because**. Jn *4:34. 6:38. 7:18. 8:50.

17:4. 18:11. Ps *40:7, 8. Mt *26:39. Ro 15:3. He 10:7-10. **which hath**. ver. 23, 37. Jn 4:34. Mt +*10:32.

31. **If**. ✓184C, Mt +4:9. **bear witness**. Jn *8:13, 14, 18, 54. Jn 18:37. Pr 27:2. Re *3:14.

32. **is another**. ver. 36, 37. Jn 1:33. 8:17, 18. 12:28-30. Mt *3:17. *17:5. Mk 1:11. Lk 3:22. 1 J *5:6-9. **and I**. Jn 7:28, 29. 12:50.

33. **sent**. Jn *1:7, 19-27. **he**. Jn *1:6-8, 15-18, 29-34. 3:26-36. 18:37.

34. **I receive**. ver. 32, 37, 41. Jn 8:54. 1 C *4:3. 1 Th *2:6. 1 J 5:9. **that**. Jn 3:17. 4:22, 42. 10:9. √20:31. Mt 1:21. 3:7. Lk 13:34. *19:10, 41, 42. 24:47. Ro 3:3. 10:1, 21. 12:21. 1 C 9:22. 1 T 2:3, 4. +*4:16.

35. **was**. Jn 1:7, 8. Nu *25:13. 2 S 21:17. Ps 132:17. Mt *11:11. Lk 1:15-17, 76, 77. 7:28. 2 P *1:19. **light**. Mt *5:16. Ph *2:15, 16. **and ye**. Jn 6:66. Ezk +*33:31. Mt *3:5-7. 11:7-9. 13:20, 21. 21:26. Mk 1:6. *6:20. Ga 4:15, 16.

36. **I have**. ver. 32. 1 J *5:9, 11, 12. **witness**. ver. +*39. Jn 10:25. Ac +*10:43. Ro +*1:4. **the works**. ver. 20. Jn 2:23. 3:2. 9:30-33. 10:25, 37, 38. 11:37, 38. *14:10, 11. 15:24. 17:4. Mt 11:4, 5. Lk 7:22. Ac *2:22. **to finish**. Jn 4:34. **bear witness**. Jn 3:2. **sent**. Jn 3:17.

37. **borne**. See on ver. 32. Jn 6:27. 8:18. 12:28. Mt 3:17. *17:5. Mk 1:11. 9:7. Lk 3:22. 9:35. 24:27. **his voice**. Dt *4:12. Ac 7:31. 9:4. 10:13. 2 P *1:17. **nor seen**. See on Jn 1:18. 14:9. 15:24. Ex 20:19. Dt 4:12. 1 T *1:17. *6:16. 1 J 1:1, 2. *4:12, 20.

38. **ye have**. ver. 42, 46, 47. Jn *8:37, 46, 47. 15:7. Dt 6:6-9. Jsh +*1:8. Ps *119:11. Pr 2:1, 2. 7:1, 2. Col *3:16. Ja *1:21, 22. 1 J 1:10. *2:14. 5:10. **his word**. Jn 8:31. **for**. ver. 43, 46, 47. Jn 1:11. √3:18-21. 12:44-48. Is 49:7. 53:1-3.

39. **Search**. ❋S#2045g. Jn 5:39. 7:52. Ro 8:27. 1 C 2:10. 1 P 1:11. Re 2:23. The Greek form for "search" may be indicative, a statement of fact, and so rendered "Ye search," as in many modern translations, or it may be imperative, a command, as in the A.V., "Search." Robertson thinks the following words, "ye think," which are indicative, favor taking the verb as indicative, not imperative. Alford favors taking the verb as an imperative, because of the preceding context, and its initial position in the sentence. The *Companion Bible* notes that "the indicative never commences a sentence without the pronoun or some other word, while the imperative is so used." For the same Greek construction see Jn 14:11, "*Believe* me...": Jn 15:20, "*Remember* the word..." This Greek word for "search" occurs in the Septuagint (LXX), the Greek translation of the Old Testament, in the following places: Ge 31:33, 35, 37. 44:12. Dt 13:14. Jg 6:29. 2 S 10:3. 1 K 20:6. 2 K 10:23. Pr 20:27. Je 27 (50):26. Jl 1:7. The word is defined "to seek out, trace; used of a lion who 'scours the plains and traces the footsteps of the man who had robbed him,' Homer, Iliad, xviii. 321; used of dogs tracing their game by the foot, Homer, *Odyssey*, xix. 436. Hence, to track, trace, investigate" (Bullinger, *Critical Lexicon and Concordance*, p. 672). The imperative should be adopted here; the Jews did not search, but merely read the Scriptures, as so many Christians today. Had they searched diligently, and believed, they would have accepted the claims of Jesus. Lessening the force of Christ's statement by taking it as an indicative rather than imperative seems to detract from the Bible's teaching regarding itself, that we are to

search the Scriptures, not merely read them. Some modern translations appear to weaken the force of a number of texts which contain the Bible's teaching about itself at several critical points, particularly here, John 8:31, and 2 T 3:16. T#1068. ver. *46. Jn 7:52. Dt 11:18-20. *17:18, 19. *32:46, 47. Jsh +*1:8. Ps *1:2. *119:11, 97-99. Pr 6:23. 8:33, 34. Is +√8:20n. *34:16. Je *8:9. Mt *22:29. Mk 12:10. Lk √16:29, 31. Ac 8:32-35. +√17:11. Ro 2:17, 18. 3:2. Col *3:16. 2 T √3:14-17. 1 P 1:11. 2 P √1:19-21. **the scriptures.** Mt +21:42. **for.** *71, Jn +1:24. Here we have in two verses a double Epicrisis, the first approving, and the second condemning, but both adding a solemn truth, independent of the statement that goes before. (A) Search the Scriptures, (B) For in them ye think ye have eternal life. (A) And they are they which testify of me: (B) And ye will not come to me, that ye might have life. In the first and third members (A and A), we have the Scriptures; while in the second and fourth (B and B, the Epicrisis), we have the action and conduct of those who possessed them. **in them.** 1 C 15:2. 1 Th √2:13. 2 T √3:15. Ja *1:18. 1 P *1:23. **ye think.** Gr. *dokeo*, S#1380g, Mt 3:9. Robertson cites Bernard who believes this word in John "always indicates a mistaken opinion (Jn 5:45. 11:13, 31. 13:29. 16:20. 20:15)" (*Word Pictures*, vol. 5, p. 92). The analogy of Scripture, however, flatly contradicts this position and forbids taking this as the meaning here, however correct it may be for the other passages cited, for Scripture elsewhere teaches that we are born again through the instrumentality of the written word of God (2 T √3:15. Ja 1:18. 1 P 1:23). The Pharisees rightly believed that "in them" they had eternal life, but as Jesus elsewhere states, they knew not the Scriptures nor the power of God (Mk 12:24), made them void by their traditions (Mk 7:7-9), and failed to believe them (Jn 5:46. Lk 16:31). Dt 32:47. Ps *16:11. 21:4. 36:9. 133:3. Da +*12:2. Mt 19:16-20. Lk *10:25-29. Ac 15:28g. 1 C 4:9g. 7:40g,n. He 11:16, 35. **ye have.** ver. *24. Jn 3:36. 4:14. 1 J √5:13. **eternal.** Gr. *aionios*, Mt +18:8. **which testify.** T#1020. ver. 32, 36. Jn *1:45. Dt *18:15, 18. See on Lk +√24:27n, 44. Ac 10:43. 18:28. *26:22, 23, 27. Ro *1:2. 1 C 15:3. 1 P √1:10, 11. Re *19:10.

40. **And ye.** *71, Jn +1:24. **will not.** ver. 43, 44. Jn √1:11. √3:19. 8:45, 46. 12:37-41. Ps 81:11. Is 49:7. 50:2. 53:1-3. Je 27:13. Ezk 33:11, 31, 32. Mt *22:3. *23:37. Lk 13:34. 14:18. +*19:14. Re 22:17. **come.** Jn *6:35. Is *45:22-24. *55:3. Je *3:22. Mt *11:28. Re *22:16, 17. **that.** ver. 26, 39. Jn *6:27, 37, 40, 68, 69. *7:37, 38. *11:25, 26. √20:31. Ro √6:23. He *7:25. 1 J √5:11-13.

41. **receive not honor.** T#59. ver. 34, 44. Jn 6:15. 7:18. 8:50, 54. 12:43. 16:33. 18:36. Mt 6:1, 2. 1 Th 2:6. 1 P 2:21. 2 P 1:17.

42. **I know.** Jn 1:47-49. +*2:24, 25. 21:17. Lk 16:15. He *4:12, 13. Re *2:23. **that.** ver. 44. Jn 8:42, 47, 55. 15:23, 24. Ro 8:7. 1 J √2:15. 3:17. 4:20. **the love.** Dt *6:5. Lk 11:42. 2 Th 3:5. **in you.** Jn 6:53. 1 J *2:15. 5:10.

43. **come.** Jn √3:16. 6:38. 8:28, 29. 10:25. 12:28. 17:4-6. Ex *23:21. Dt *18:18. He *5:4, 5. **Father's name.** Jn 5:43. 10:25. 12:13, 28. 14:13. 17:6, 11, 12, 26. **receive me not.** Jn *1:11. 3:11, 32. 12:37. **if.** *184C, Mt +4:9. Mt +*24:5, 24. Mk 13:5, 6, 22. Lk 21:8. Ac *5:36, 37. 21:38. 2 Th 2:2, 3, 8-12. **another.** Gr. *allos*, Mt +10:23n. Da 7:24. 8:9, 23, 24. 9:27. 11:35-

45. Mt 24:15. 2 Th 2:2, 3, 8-12. 1 J 2:18. Re 13:8, 14, 18. **him.** Da 8:25. *9:27. **ye will receive.** T#476. Is 2:6, 8. Je 5:30, 31. Ezk +*14:10n. Da 8:25. *9:27. Ho +*14:8. Ac 20:29, 30. 2 T 4:2-4. 1 J 5:21. Re 13:8, 14, 18.

44. **How can ye.** Jn 3:20. 8:43. 12:43. Je 13:23. Ro 8:7, 8. He +*3:12. **believe.** Jn 1:7, 50. 3:15. 4:39, 41, 42, 48, 53. 6:36, 47, 64. 11:15, 40. 12:39. 14:29. 19:35. 20:8, 25, 29, 31. Ac 13:12. Ro 4:11. **which receive.** lit. receiving. *15E, Mk +6:9. Note the cause/effect relationships implied in this verse (Ps +√9:10n). Mt 23:5. Ga 5:19-21. Ph +*2:3. **honor.** ver. 41. **seek not.** Jn 7:13. 12:43. 1 S *2:30. 2 Ch 6:8. Mt 25:21-23. Lk 19:17. Ro 2:7, 10, 29. 1 C 4:5. 2 C 10:18. He *11:6. Ja 2:1. 1 P 1:7. **only.** Jn 17:3. Ro 16:27. 1 T 6:15, 16. Ju 25.

45. **Do not think.** Jn 3:17. 12:47, 48. **there.** Jn 7:19. 8:5, 9. Ro *2:12, 17, etc. *3:19, 20. 7:9-14. 2 C 3:7-11. Ga 3:10. **Moses.** Mk +12:19. **in whom.** Jn 8:5, 6. *9:28, 29. Mt 19:7, 8. Ro 2:17. 10:5-10. **ye trust.** 2 C 1:10. 1 T 4:10. 5:5. 1 J 3:3.

46. **For had ye believed.** *184B, Lk +7:39. ver. 38. Lk *16:29-31. Ga 2:19. 3:10, 13, 24. 4:21-31. **for.** Jn *1:45. Ge +*3:15. +*12:3. 18:18. 22:18. 28:14. +*49:10. Nu 21:8, 9. 24:17, 18. Dt *18:15, 18, 19. Ac *26:22. Ro 10:4. He ch. 7-10. **he wrote.** Ex +√24:4.

47. **But if.** *184A, 1 C +15:2. **ye believe not.** Lk √16:29, 31. **writings.** Jn 7:15. **believe my words.** ver. 24, 38, 46. Jn 2:22. 4:50. 6:30. 8:31, 45, 46. 10:37, 38. 14:11. Ac 18:8. 1 J 3:23.

JOHN 6

Jesus feeds five thousand men with five loaves and two fishes, 1-14. He withdraws from the multitudes, who purpose to make him king, 15. His disciples put to sea without him and meet with a storm, but he comes to them walking on the sea, 16-21. Being followed to Capernaum by multitudes, he reproves their carnal motives even in their diligence about religion; and requires faith in him, 22-29. They demand a sign, like that of the manna, and he speaks copiously of himself as the Bread of Life and of living by faith in him, 30-59. Many are offended and forsake him, 60-66. Peter, in the name of the Twelve, professes steadfast faith in him as "the Son of God;" but Jesus pronounces one of them to be a devil, 67-71.

1. A.M. 4036. A.D. 32. **these.** Mt 14:13, 15, etc. ●15:32-38. Mk 6:31, 32, 34, 35, etc. ●8:1-10. Lk 9:10-12, etc. **the sea.** Nu 34:11. Jsh 12:3. See on Mt 4:18. 15:29. Lk 5:1. **Tiberias.** i.e. *good vision*, ✳S#5085g. ver. 23. Jn 21:1. (1) Sea of Tiberias, Jn 6:1; 21:1. See Galilee, Sea of, Mt +2:22. (2) A city of Palestine, on the western shore of the Sea of Galilee, Jn 6:23.

2. **a great multitude.** Mt 4:24, 25. 8:1. 12:15. 13:2. 14:14. 15:30, 31. Mk 1:34, 45. 6:33. **miracles.** ver. 14, 26, 30. Jn 2:11, 23.

3. **Jesus went.** ver. 15. Mt 5:1. 14:23. 15:29. Mk 3:13. 6:46. Lk 6:12, 13. 9:28.

4. **And.** *71, Jn +1:24. **the passover.** Jn 2:13. 5:1. 11:55. 12:1. 13:1. Ex 12:6, etc. Le 23:5, 7. Dt *16:1. 1 C 5:7, 8. **feast.** Le 23:2. 12:1. 13:1. 18:28, 39. 19:14. Ex ch. 12. 23:15. Dt 16:1-6. Mt 26:2, etc. Mk 14:1, etc. Lk 2:41. 22:1, etc. Ac 12:4. He 11:28. **the Jews.** Jn 2:6. +5:10. 19:21, 42.

5. **lifted.** *144A12, Ge +22:13. Lk 6:20. **saw.** Jn

4:35. Mt 14:14, 15. Mk 6:34, 35. Lk 9:12. **Philip.** Jn +1:43. **Whence.** Nu 11:13, 21, 22. 2 K 7:2. Mt 15:33. Mk 8:2-4. Lk 9:13.

6. **prove.** Ge 22:1. Dt 8:2, 16. 13:3. 33:8. 2 Ch 32:31. 2 C +*13:5.

7. **Two.** This sum, rating the denarius at 7 1/2*d.*, would amount to 6*l.* 5*s.*; or, reckoning the denarius, with some, at 7 3/4*d.*, it would amount to 6*l.* 9*s.* 2*d.* of our money; which appears to have been more than our Lord and all his disciples were worth of this world's goods. The denarius was the usual pay for a day's labor (Mt 20:2, 9, 13). Nu *11:21, 22. 2 K 4:43. Mk 6:37. **pennyworth.** Jn 12:5. Mt 18:28mg.

8. **disciples.** Jn +2:2. **Andrew.** Jn 1:40-44. Mt 4:18. Mk +13:3.

9. **is a.** ꟻ108E1, Mt +8:19. **which.** Mt 14:17. 16:9. Mk 6:38. 8:19. Lk 9:13. **barley.** Dt 8:8. 32:14. Jg 7:13. 1 K 4:28. 2 K 4:42, 43. 7:1. Ps 81:16. 147:14. Ezk 13:19. 27:17. 2 C √8:9. Re 6:6. **fishes.** ver. 11. Jn 21:9, 10, 13. **but.** ver. 7. Jn 11:21, 32. 2 K *4:42-44. Ps 78:19, 20, 41.

10. **Make.** Mt 14:18, 19. 15:35, 36. Mk 6:39-41. 8:6, 7. Lk 9:14-16. **Now.** No wonder, since it was the spring, being near the Passover; and from the plenty of grass, it would be a place much more suitable to the purpose. This circumstance, says Dr. Paley, is plainly the remark of an eyewitness. ver. 4. Mk 6:39.

11. **given thanks.** ver. 23. Jn 11:41. 1 S 9:13. Pr 10:21. Mt +15:36. Lk 22:17. +*24:30. Ac 27:35. Ro 14:6. 1 C *10:31. 1 Th 5:18. 1 T *4:4, 5. **as much.** Ge=44:1.

12. **they.** Ne 9:25. Mt *14:20, 21. 15:37, 38. Mk 6:42-44. 8:8, 9. Lk 1:53. 9:17. **Gather.** Le ◑=23:22. **remain.** Is=1:9. **that nothing.** T#172. Ge 41:35, 36. Ne 8:10. Pr 18:9. 21:20. Lk 15:13. 16:1. **lost.** Gr. *apollumi*, Mt +2:13.

13. **and filled.** It is scarcely possible to imagine a more wonderful proof of the creative power of Christ, than was here displayed. The loaves were of the small kind, common in the country; and the fishes were small; and yet, after the five thousand were fed, twelve times as much, at least, remained, as they at first sat down to! 1 K 17:15, 16. 2 K 4:2-7. 2 Ch 25:9. Pr 11:24, 25. 2 C *9:8, 9. Ph *4:19. **baskets.** Mt +16:9.

14. **miracle.** ver. 2. **This is.** T#1122. Jn 1:21, 41, 45, 49. 7:31, 40-42, 52. 12:34. Da +*11:33n. Mt 2:1, 2, 4-6. 10:15. 11:2-6, 22-24. 12:23. Mk 6:11. Lk 2:25-35, 36-38. 7:16, 19-23. 9:19. 10:12-16. 19:11. 23:42, 43. 24:17-21. Ac 1:6. 17:6, 7. 26:26, 27. **that prophet.** Jn 1:21, 25. 4:19, 25, 42. *7:40. 9:17. Ge +*49:10. Dt *18:15-18. Mt 11:3. +21:11. Lk 7:16. 24:19. Ac 3:22-24. 7:37. **should come.** Jn 11:27. Mt 11:3. **world.** Gr. *kosmos*, Mt +4:8.

15. **perceived.** Jn +*2:24, 25. He *4:13. **take.** Jn 7:3, 4. *12:12, 13. Mk 11:9, 10. Lk *19:38. **he departed.** Jn 2:23, 24. *5:41. *18:36, 37. Mt 8:18. 14:22, 23. Mk +*1:35. *6:46, etc. Ep 6:18. Ph 2:5. He 5:7. **a mountain.** ver. 3.

16. **disciples.** Jn +2:2.

17. **and went.** ꟻ171J14, Jon +1:3. ver. 21, 24, 25. Jn 2:12. 4:46. Mk 6:45.

18. **the sea arose.** Ps 107:25. 135:7. Jon 1:13. Mt 14:24.

19. **had rowed.** Ezk 27:26. Jon 1:13. Mt 14:24. Mk 6:47, 48. **furlongs.** Jn 11:18. Lk 24:13. Re 14:20. 21:16. **see Jesus.** Jn 5:21-23. Ro 1:4. Ep 1:20. Ep 1:20-23.

walking. Jn 14:18. Jb 9:8. Ps 29:10. 93:4. Mt 14:25, 26. Mk 6:49. Lk 24:36-39. **the sea.** Jn 21:1. **were afraid.** Mt 14:26. Mk 6:49, 50. Lk 24:37.

20. **It is.** Ps 35:3. Is 41:10, 14. √43:1, 2. 44:8. Mt 14:27-31. Mk 6:50. 16:6. Lk +*24:38, 39. Re 1:17, 18. **be not afraid.** Mt +*14:27.

21. **they willingly.** Ps 24:7-10. SS 3:4. Mt 14:32, 33. Mk *6:51. Re *3:20. **received.** ꟻ63H, Ge +12:15. **and immediately.** This appears to be another miracle, recorded only by John, that they reached their destination immediately. **whither.** ver. 17.

22. **boat.** Jn 21:8. Mk 3:9. Lk 5:2. **went not.** ver. 15-21. **but.** ver. 16, 17. Mt 14:22. Mk 6:45.

23. **there.** ver. 24. **Tiberias.** Tiberias was a celebrated city of Galilee on the western shore of the lake to which it gave name, so called because built by Herod Agrippa in honor of the Emperor Tiberius; distant 30 furlongs from Hippos, 60 from Gadara, 120 from Scythopolis, and 30 from Tarichea. It is still called *Tabaria*, or *Tabbareeah* by the natives, is situated close to the edge of the lake, has tolerably high but ill-built walls on three of its sides, flanked with circular towers and is of nearly a quadrangular form, according to Pococke, containing a population estimated at from 2000 to 4000 souls. See on ver. 1. **where.** See on ver. 11, 12. **given thanks.** ver. 11.

24. **When.** Mt 14:34-36. Mk 6:53-56. **they also.** ver. 17, 23. **Capernaum.** ver. 17, 59. Mt 14:34. Mk 6:53. **seeking.** Jn 7:11. 18:4, 5. 20:15. Mk 1:37. Lk 8:40.

25. **Rabbi.** See on Jn 1:38, 39.

26. **Verily.** ver. 47, 53. Jn +*1:51. *3:3, 5. **Ye seek.** ver. 15, 24, 64. Ps 78:37. 106:12-14. Ezk +*33:31. Ac 8:18-21. Ro 16:18. Ph 2:21. 3:19. 1 T 6:5. Ja 4:3, 4. **miracles.** ver. 2, 14, 30. Jn 2:11. **did eat.** ver. 12.

27. **Labor not.** *or*, Work not. T#742. ver. 28, 29. Pr +*23:4 (T#626). Is *55:2. Je *45:5. Mt *6:19-25, 32, 33. Mk 8:36, 37. Lk 6:24, 25. 12:19-21, 33, 34. Ro 12:2. Ga 5:6. Ph *2:13. Col 1:29. *3:2. 1 Th 1:3. Ja 1:27. 1 J *2:15. **the meat.** ꟻ17118, Ps +107:18. Jn 4:13, 14. Ec 5:11-16. 6:7. Is *55:2, 3. Hab 2:13. Mt *6:19, 20, 31-33. Lk 10:40-42. 1 C 6:13. 7:29-31. 9:24-27. 2 C 4:18. Col 2:22. 3:2. He 4:11. 12:16. Ja 1:11. 1 P 1:24. 2 P 3:11-14. **perisheth.** Gr. *apollumi*, Mt +2:13. **but for.** ꟻ96E1, Ps +118:8. i.e. *labor more for the latter than for the former*, or *rather than*. Mt +*7:13, 14. Lk *13:24. **which endureth.** ver. 35, 40, 50, 51, 54, 58, 68. Jn 4:14. Je +*15:16. **everlasting.** *aionios*, Mt +18:8. **life.** Jn *10:28. *11:25, 26. √14:6. 17:2. Pr 2:2-6. Ro *6:23. **Son of man.** Mt +*16:27n. **shall give.** ver. 33, 51. Jn 10:28. Ro *8:32. **for him.** Jn 1:33, 34. 5:36, 37. 8:18. 10:36-38. 11:42. 15:24. Ps 2:7. 40:7. Is 11:1-3. 42:1. 61:1-3. Mt 3:17. *17:5. Mk 1:11. 9:7. Lk 3:22. 4:18-21. 9:35. Ac 2:22. *10:38. 2 P *1:17. **God.** Mt +*28:19. **the Father.** ver. 37, 44-46, 57, 65. Jn 3:35. **sealed.** Jn 3:33. Ezk 9:4.

28. **What.** Dt 5:27. Je 42:3-6, 20. Mi +*6:7, 8. Mt 19:16. Lk 3:10. 10:25. Ac *2:37. 9:6. √16:30. **work.** ꟻ147D, Ge +1:29. **the works.** Nu 8:11. Ro 4:6. 1 C √15:58. 1 Th 1:3. Ja 2:22. Re 2:26.

29. **This.** Jn √3:16-18, 36. +*5:39. Dt 18:18, 19. Ps 2:12. Mt 17:5. Mk 16:16. Ac √16:31. 22:14-16. Ro *4:4, 5. 9:30, 31. *10:3, 4. He +*5:9. 1 J *3:23. 5:1. **the work.** ꟻ172, Mt +5:19. ver. 28. Ep *2:8. that. 1 J *3:23. **believe.** ver. 35, 40. Jn +4:39. **sent.** Jn *3:17.

30. **What.** Jn 2:18. 4:48. Ex 4:8. 1 K 13:3, 5. Is 7:11-14. Mt 12:38, 39. 16:1-4. Mk 8:11, 12. Lk *11:29,

30. Ac 4:30. 1 C 1:22. He 2:4. **sign**. ver. 2, 14, 26. Jn 2:11. **see**. ver. 36. Jn 5:47. 10:38. 12:37. 20:25-29. Is 5:19. Mk 15:32. 2 C ◐5:7. **and believe**. ver. 28, 29. Mt +*27:42. **what**. ver. 28, 29.

31. **fathers**. ver. 49, 58. Ex *16:4-15, 21, 35. Nu 11:6-9. 21:5. Dt 8:3. Jsh 5:12. Ne 9:20. He 9:4. **He gave**. Ne ⫫9:15. Ps *78:23-25. 105:40. 1 C *10:3. Re 2:17.

32. **Verily**. Jn +1:51. **Moses**. Ex 16:4, 8, 15. Ps 78:23. **not that**. ʃ63I2, Jsh +3:3. Supply by ellipsis (of repetition: from succeeding clause), "that (true) bread." **my Father**. ver. 40. Jn +5:17. **the true**. ver. 33, 35, 41, 50, 55, 58. Jn 1:9. 3:13, 31. 15:1. Ga *4:4. 1 J 5:20.

33. **bread**. Ps=78:24. =105:40. **cometh**. ver. 38, 48. Jn *3:13. 8:42. 13:3. 16:28. 17:8. 1 T 1:15, 16. 1 J 1:1, 2. **from heaven**. Pr 31:14. **giveth life**. ver. 27, 35, 48, 50, 51, 58. Jn 5:21. **world**. *kosmos*, Mt +4:8. *ʃ121J9A, Jn +1:10. Jn 1:29.

34. **evermore**. ver. 26. Jn 4:15. Ps 4:6.

35. **I am**. ʃ119, Ge +49:9. ver. 41, 48-58. Jn 10:7. 1 C 10:16-18. 11:23-29. **bread**. ʃ22D5M, Nu +28:2. **of life**. ver. 33. Jn 8:12. **he that cometh**. ver. 37, 44, 45, 65. Jn *5:40. *7:37. Is +*55:1-3. Mt *11:28. Re *22:17. **never**. ʃ63I2, Jsh +3:3. Supply ellipsis, "never hunger (at any time)." **hunger**. Jn *4:13, 14. *7:38. Ge=45:11. Is 49:10. Je=31:14. Lk 6:25. Re *7:16. **believeth**. ver. 29. **never**. ʃ158, Mt +5:18.

36. **That**. ver. 26, 30, 40, 64. Jn 5:43. 12:37. 15:24. ◐*20:29. Lk *16:31. 1 P ◐*1:8, 9. **believe not**. ver. 47, 64. Jn 5:44. Mt *13:13-15.

37. **All that**. ver. *39, *45. Jn *17:2, 6, 8, 9, 11, 24. **Father giveth**. Jn 10:29. *17:2, 6, 9, 11, 12, 24. **shall come**. ver. *44, *65. Jn ◐*8:31. √10:28, 29. ◐*15:1-6. Ps 110:3. Ep *2:4-10. Ph *1:29. 2 Th √2:13, 14. 2 T *2:19. T *3:3-7. **him that cometh**. Is *1:18. √55:7. Mt *11:28. Lk 23:42, 43. Ac 2:21. **I will**. Jn *9:34. Ps *86:5. *102:17. Is *1:18, 19. *41:9. *42:3. √55:7. Mt √11:28. 24:24. Lk 23:40-43. Ro *5:20. 1 T *1:16. He +*4:15. √7:25. 1 P 1:2. 1 J √2:19. Re *22:17. **no wise**. ʃ158, Mt +5:18. √175B, Ge +21:16. **cast out**. Jn *9:34. ◐15:6. Ps +√9:10. *51:11.

38. **I came**. Jn 4:34. *5:30. Ps *40:7, 8. Is 53:10. Mt +*18:11. *20:28. 26:39-42. Lk +*19:10. Ro 15:3. Ph 2:7, 8. He 5:8. 10:7-9. **down from**. ver. 33. Jn *3:13, 31. Ep 4:9. **not**. The official subordination of Jesus to the Father does not imply inequality or inferiority (Jn +*5:18, 23. +*10:33. *17:5. He 1:2, 3, 6). T#72. Jn 7:16. 8:29. 10:36. *12:49. *14:28. 17:3, 8. Ro 1:3, 4. 1 C *3:23. +*11:3. √15:27, +*28n. **to do**. Jn 5:30. **the will**. Mt √7:21. *26:39. **that sent**. ver. 44. Jn 4:34.

39. **this**. ver. 40. Jn 10:28, 29. Mt *18:14. Lk 12:32. Ro √8:28-31. 2 Th *2:13, 14. 2 T *2:19. **will**. 1 T √2:4. 2 P √3:9. **given**. See on ver. 37. **I should**. Jn √10:27-30. 17:12. 18:9. 1 S 25:29. Col *3:3, 4. 1 P *1:5. Ju 1. **lose**. Gr. *apollumi*, Mt +2:13. **raise**. ʃ8, Ps +118:1. ver. 40, 44, 54. Jn 5:21, 25, 28, +*29. 11:24-26. 12:48. Ro *8:11. 1 C 6:14. Ph *3:20, 21. 2 T *1:12. **last day**. ver. +*54n. Jn 11:24. 12:48.

40. **seeth**. ver. 36, 47. Jn 1:14. *4:14. *8:56. 12:45. 14:17, 19. 16:10, 16, 19. Is 45:21, 22. 52:10. 53:2. Lk 2:30. 2 C 4:6. He 11:1, 27. 1 P 1:8. 1 J 1:1-3. **the Son**. Jn 3:35. **and believeth**. ver. 27, 29, 35, 54. Jn √3:15-18, 36. *4:14. √5:24. √10:28. 12:50. 17:2. Mk *16:16. Ro *5:21. √6:23. 1 J 2:25. √5:11-13. Ju 21.

everlasting. *aionios*, Mt +18:8. **I will**. Jn 11:25. Ro *8:30. 1 C 15:10. 2 C 1:21, 22. Ep *1:13, 14. 2 P +√1:10, 11. **raise**. ʃ8, Ps +118:1.

41. **The Jews**. ver. 52. Jn 5:10. **murmured**. ver. 43, 52, 60, 61, 66. Jn 7:12, 32. Lk 5:30. 15:2. 19:7. 1 C 10:10. Ju 16. **I am**. ver. 33, 35, 38, 48, 51, 58. **came down**. ver. 51, 58. Jn 3:13, 31.

42. **Is not**. Jn 7:27. Mt +*13:55, 56. Mk +*6:3. Lk 4:22. Ro *1:3, 4. √9:5. 1 C √15:47. Ga *4:4. **the son**. Jn 1:45. 2:1.

43. **Murmur**. ver. 64. Jn 16:19. Mt 16:8. Mk 9:33. He *4:13.

44. **man**. ver. 65. Jn 5:44. 8:43. *12:37-40. Is 44:18-20. Je 13:23. Mt 12:34. Ro 8:7, 8. **can come**. ver. 35. Jn ◐5:40. Jb 14:4. Je *13:23. Ro 11:35, 36. 1 C √2:14. *4:7. 2 C 3:5. **except**. ver. 45, 65. Jn *3:3-7. *10:26. Mt 11:25-27. *16:17. 2 C *4:6. Ep *2:4-10. Ph *1:29. Col *2:12, 13. T 3:3-5. Ja *1:18. **sent**. ver. 38. Jn 4:34. **draw**. ver. 65. Jn 4:23. *12:32. SS *1:4. Je 31:3. Ho 11:4. **and I**. ver. 39, 40. **raise**. ʃ8, Ps +118:1.

45. **written**. Mk 1:2. Lk 1:70. 18:31. **in the prophets**. ʃ171E13, Ge +46:7. Mt 26:56. Lk 16:16. 18:31. +*24:27, 44. Ac 7:42. 10:43. 13:27, 40. 15:15. **taught of God**. T#599. Jb 36:22. Ps *25:8, 9, 12. Is +*2:3. *⫫54:13. Je *31:33, 34. Mi *4:2. Hab *2:14. 1 C 2:13. Ep 4:21, 22. Ph 3:15. 1 Th 4:9. He +*8:10, 11. 10:16. 1 J *2:20, 27. **Every**. ver. *37, *65. Jn *5:38-40. 8:26. *10:27. 16:14, 15. Mt *11:27. 16:17. 17:5. Ro +*2:12. √10:17. Ga *3:2, 5. Ep *1:17. 1 J 4:1-3.

46. **any**. Jn *1:18. 5:37. 8:19. 14:9, 10. 15:24. Col *1:15. 1 T *6:16. 1 J 4:12. **save he which**. Jn 1:14. 7:29. **he hath**. Jn 1:1. 3:32. 7:29. 8:38, 55. Mt *11:27. Lk 10:22. 1 C *2:10.

47. **Verily**. Jn +1:51. **He that**. ver. 40, 54. Jn √3:16, 18, 36. √5:24. 14:19. Ro 5:9, 10. Col 3:3, 4. 1 J √5:12, 13. **everlasting**. Gr. *aionios*, Mt +18:8.

48. **that bread**. ʃ22D5M, Nu +28:2. ver. 33-35, 41, 51. 1 C 10:16, 17. 11:24, 25. Ga *2:20. Col *3:3, 4.

49. **fathers**. See on ver. 31. **and are**. ver. 58. Nu 26:65. Zc 1:5. 1 C *10:3-5. He *3:17-19. Ju 5.

50. **the bread**. ver. 33, 42, 51, 54. Jn *3:13. Re 2:17. **cometh down**. ver. 33. **a man**. *ʃ171F, Is +53:12. **may eat**. Le=2:10. =23:6. =24:9. **not die**. ver. 51, 58. Jn 8:51. *11:25, 26. Ro 8:10.

51. **living**. Jn *3:13. 4:10, 11. *7:38. 1 P 2:4. **came down**. Jn 3:13. Ja 3:15, 17. **if**. ʃ184C, Mt +4:9. **eat**. ʃ108B, Je +15:16. ver. 53n. Le=3:11. +=23:19. **and the bread**. This was one of the things which the Jews expected from the Messiah, as we learn from *Midrash Koheleth*: "Rabbi Berechiah, in the name of Rabbi Isaac said, As was the first Redeemer, so also shall be the latter. The first Redeemer made manna descend from heaven, as it is said in Ex 16:4, 'And I will rain bread from heaven for you.' So also the latter Redeemer shall make manna descend, as it is said, Ps 72:16, 'There shall be a handful of corn in the earth,' etc." **for ever**. Gr. *aion*, Mt +6:13. ver. 50. **my flesh**. ʃ171Q6, Ge +6:12. ver. 52-57. Jn 1:14. Le +=23:13. Mt +*20:28. Lk 22:19. Ep 5:2, 25. T *2:14. He *2:14, 15. 10:5-12, 20. **the life**. ver. 33, 57. Jn 1:29. *3:16. Lk 22:19. 1 C 11:24. 2 C *5:19, 21. He 10:10. 1 J 2:2. *4:10, 14. **world**. Gr. *kosmos*, Mt +4:8. ʃ121J9A, Jn +1:10. Jn 1:29. 1 J *2:2.

52. **The Jews**. ver. 41. Jn 5:10. **strove**. ver. 41. Jn 7:40-43. 9:16. 10:19. **How**. ʃ85R, Jb +4:17. ver. 60.

Jn *3:4, 9. 4:11. Ac 17:32. 1 C √2:14.

53. Verily. ver. 26, 47. Jn +1:51. See on Jn 3:3. Mt *5:18. **Except.** Jn *3:3, 5. 13:8. 15:4. Mt 18:3. Lk *13:3, 5. **eat.** ♪108B, Je +15:16. This is not a reference to the Lord's Supper, for that had not yet been instituted, and these words in their context could not possibly have been understood to have any reference to it by the original hearers. This is an idiom which signifies except we feed on Christ in our hearts and partake of his life (for the blood is the life), we have no life in us. Careful reference to verses 47 and 40 with verses 53 and 54 will show that believing on Christ is exactly the same thing as eating and drinking of his flesh and blood (B826, 827). ver. 51, 55. Jn √3:36. Mt *26:26-28. 1 J √5:12. Re 2:7, 17. **flesh.** ♪171Q7, Jn +1:14. Here, "flesh" and "blood" are jointly as well as severally put for *humanity* as distinct from *divinity*. "Flesh" is put, not for the "body" of Christ, but for himself in his true humanity (B643). **Son of man.** ver. 27. **life.** Jn √8:24. 20:31.

54. eateth. ver. 27, 40, 63. Jn *4:14. Ex=23:33. Ps 22:26. Pr 9:4-6. Is 25:6-8. +*55:1-3. Ga *2:20. Ph 3:7-10. **hath.** See on ver, 39, 40, 47. **eternal.** Gr. *aionios*, Mt +18:8. **I will raise.** ♪8, Ps +118:1. ver. *39. Jn +*5:29. **last day.** ver. 39, 44. Jn 11:24. 12:48. 1 J 2:18. "Last day" is an idiom in John for "the age to come," that age when the Messiah will reign, including the Millennium and the eternal ages which follow. Scripture recognizes but two ages (not seven dispensations, helpful though such humanly devised distinctions may be): "this age," and "the age to come," Mt 12:32. Mk 10:30. Lk 18:30. Ro 8:38. 1 C 3:22. Ep 1:21. He 1:2. For "this age," see Jn 9:39. Mt 12:32. 13:22. Mk 4:19. 10:30. Lk 1:70. 16:8. 20:34. Ro 12:2. 1 C 1:20. 2:6, 8. 2 C 4:4. Ga 1:4. Ep 2:2. 1 T 6:17. 2 T 4:10. T 2:12. For "the age to come" see Mt 12:32. 13:39, 40, 49. +*24:3. 28:20. Mk 3:29. 10:30. Lk 18:30. 20:35. 1 C 15:23. T 2:13. He 2:5. 6:5. "This age" is sometimes represented, for rhetorical effect, as composed of a number of lesser ages or cycles (1 C 2:7. See also Ro 16:25. Ep 3:9. Col 1:26. T 1:2), using the plural form. The plural form is also used for "the age to come," Ro 1:25. 9:5. 11:36. 16:27. 2 C 11:31. Ph 4:20. Ga 1:5. 1 T 1:17. Re 1:6, 18. 4:9, 10. 5:13. 7:12, etc. Since the word *aion*, or age, in Scripture may denote either the present finite age, or the future endless age, to determine the meaning of *aionios*, "eternal," "for ever," "everlasting," it is necessary first to determine to which age, "this age," or "the age to come," the thing exists to which "everlasting" is applied. Onesimus, as a slave, existed in the world of time, and when he is called an *aionion* or "everlasting" servant (Phm 15), the term is used in a finite sense, which ends when the life in this world ends. God is a being which exists in the infinite *aion* and is therefore *aionios* (eternal) in the endless signification of the term. Since the spirits of angels and men exist in the future *aion* as well as the present one, they also are "eternal" in the infinite sense. If anything belongs solely to the present age, it is *aionion* or "everlasting" in the limited sense; if it belongs to the future age, or *aion*, it is *aionion* or "everlasting" in the infinite or unlimited sense. If, therefore, the punishment of the wicked occurs in the present *aion*, it is *aionion* in the sense of temporal; but if it occurs in the future *aion*, it is *aionion* in the sense of endless. The adjective "eternal"

or "for ever" takes its meaning from its noun. The same distinction of two ages, "this age," which is finite, and "the age to come," which is infinite or endless, holds for the Old Testament. "For ever," applied to things of this age, has the sense of perpetual (Ex 21:6. Le 16:34. 1 S 27:12n. 1 Ch *28:4. Ps +*24:9n. Ec ?1:4), in the limited sense. But otherwise, and this constitutes the majority of instances, "for ever" is used in an unlimited sense, whenever it pertains to the "age to come" (see Shedd, *The Doctrine of Endless Punishment*, pp. 79-88). Consult the note at Mt 24:3 on "end," Gr. *sunteleia*, and it will be understood that the "end" of the world or age mentioned there corresponds to the end of this present finite age, and corresponds to the beginning of the infinite age, or "age to come," *sunteleia* signifying the conjunction of the two ages, the finite and the infinite.

55. For. ver. 51. **meat.** ver. *32. Jn 1:9, 47. *8:31, 36. 15:1. Ps *4:7. He *8:2. 1 J *5:20. **indeed.** Jn 1:9. Jn 15:1. He 8:2.

56. He that. La *3:24. **dwelleth.** Jn *14:20, 23. *15:4, 5, 7. *17:21-23. Ps 90:1. *91:1-9. SS 2:16. Ro 8:1. 1 C 1:30. 10:16, 17. 12:27. 2 C *5:21. *6:16. +*13:5. Ep *2:22. *3:17. 5:30-32. Ph *3:9. Col 1:27. 1 J *2:5, 6, 24. *3:9, 24. *4:12, 13, 15, 16. 5:20. 2 J *9. Re √3:20. **and I.** Ac 9:4. Ro √8:9, 10. Ga √2:20. Ep 1:22, 23. 4:15, 16. 1 J *2:27, 28.

57. the living. Jn *5:26. Ps 18:46. Je 10:10. Mt 16:16. 1 Th *1:9. He 9:14. **Father.** Jn 10:14, 15. 15:9, 10. 17:21-23, 25, 26. **hath sent.** Jn 3:17. **I live.** Jn 5:26. 11:25. 17:21. 2 C *13:4. Re 1:18. **by the Father.** Jn +*5:19, 22, 36. 7:16, 17, *28. 8:*40, 50. 12:44. +*14:28. Mt *12:32n. *19:17. *20:23. *28:18. Mk 10:40. +*12:32. **even.** Jn *11:25, 26. *14:6, 19. Ro √6:4. 1 C 15:22. 2 C 13:4. Ga *2:20. Col *3:3, 4. 1 J 4:9.

58. that bread. See on ver. 32, 34, 41, 47-51. **which came down.** ver. +*38, 62. **for ever.** Gr. *aion*, Mt +6:13. **your fathers.** Jn 7:22. Ro 15:8.

59. in the. ver. 24. Jn 18:20. Ps 40:9, 10. Pr *1:20-23. 8:1-3. Mt 4:23. Lk 4:31. **Capernaum.** Jn 2:12.

60. of his. ver. 66. Jn √8:31. **This.** ver. 41, 42. Jn *8:43. Mt *11:6. He *5:11. 2 P √3:16. Ju 15. **hard.** ♪101, Dt +32:42.

61. knew. ver. 64. Jn +*2:24, 25. 21:17. He √4:13. Re *2:23. **murmured.** ver. 41. **offend.** Jn 16:1. Mt *11:6. 17:27. 1 C √2:14.

62. What. ♪63D2, Ge +30:27. The *Companion Bible* margin notes here, "The *Apodosis* which is wanting (by ellipsis) must be supplied thus: 'If (as in ver. 51) therefore ye should behold the Son of man ascending up where He was before (will ye be offended then)?'" **and if.** ♪184C, Mt +4:9. **ascend.** Jn *3:13. 16:28. 17:4, 5, 11. Mk *16:19. Lk *24:51. Ac +*1:9, 11. Ep *4:8-10. 1 P *3:22. **where he was.** ♪37D, Ho +9:14. By the figure Aposiopesis, or sudden silence, something more is implied than can be supplied by any specific words, such as, "Will ye believe then?" For he afterwards did ascend up, but they still refused to believe! Jn 3:13. *17:5.

63. the spirit. Gr. *pneuma*, Mt +3:16. Jn 3:6. Ge 2:7. Ro 8:2. 1 C *15:45. 2 C *3:6. Ga 5:25. 1 P *3:18. 4:6. **quickeneth.** Ps 119:50, 93, +*150. He *4:12. **the flesh.** Ro *2:25, 28, 29. 3:1, 2. 7:18. 1 C *11:27-29. Ga 5:6. 6:15. 1 T *4:8. He *13:9. 1 P 3:21. **the words.** ver. *68. Jn 3:34. +*5:39. 8:47. 12:49, 50. 17:8. Dt

*32:47. Ps 19:7-10. *119:50, 93, 130. Ro 10:8-10, √17. 1 C *2:9-14. 2 C *3:6-8. 1 Th √2:13. 2 T +*3:15. He √4:12. Ja √1:18. 1 P √1:23. **spirit**. Gr. *pneuma*, ſ121A2, Mt +26:41n. "Spirit" put for living or life-giving food by the operation of the Holy Spirit (Alford). ſ121A1, Jn +3:34. **life**. ver. 53, 68.

64. **there**. ver. 36, 60, 61. Jn 5:42. 8:23, 38-47, 55. 10:26. 13:10, 18-21. **believe not**. ver. 36, 47. Jn 5:44. Lk +*8:13. **knew**. ver. 70, 71. Jn +*2:24, 25. *13:11. Ps *139:2-4. Ac 15:18. Ro *8:29. 2 T *2:19. He *4:13. **who they**. Jn +*1:48. *13:11. **betray**. ver. 71. Jn 13:11. Mt 10:4.

65. **that no man**. ver. 37, 44, 45. Jn *3:27. 10:16, 26, 27. 12:37-41. SS 1:4. Je +*13:23. *31:3. Ep √2:8, 9. Ph 1:29. 1 T 1:14. 2 T √2:25. T *3:3-7. He *12:2. Ja *1:16-18. **except**. ſ184C, Mt +4:9. Ph 2:13.

66. **of his**. ver. 60, 64. Jn √8:31. Is 8:14. Zp 1:6. Mt 12:40-45. 13:5, 6, 20, 21. 19:22. 21:8-11. 24:11. 27:20-25. Lk +*8:13. 9:62. 1 C √11:19. 2 T *1:15. +*4:10. He +*10:38, 39. 2 P √2:20-22. 1 J √2:19.

67. **the twelve**. ver. 70, 71. Jn 2:2. 20:24. Mt 10:2, 5. 11:1. 19:28. 20:17. 26:14, 20, 47. Mk 3:14, 16. 4:10. 6:7. 9:35. 10:32. 11:11. 14:10, 17, 20, 43. Lk 6:13. 8:1. 9:1, 12. 18:31. 22:3, 30, 47. Ac 6:2. 1 C 15:5. **Will ye also**. Jsh *24:15-22. Ru *1:11-18. 2 S 15:19, 20. Lk 14:25-33.

68. **Then**. Mt 16:13-20. Mk 8:27-30. Lk 9:18-21. **to whom**. Ge=41:55. Ps *73:25. **thou hast**. ver. 40, +*63. Jn *3:34. √5:24, +*39, 40. √14:6. SS 5:10, 16. Zc 11:11. Ac √4:12. 5:20. 7:38. 1 C 3:11. 1 J √5:11-13. **words**. Jn 12:50. 17:3, 8. **eternal**. Gr. *aionios*, Mt +18:8. ver. 40. Jn *4:14. **life**. ver. 57.

69. **we believe**. Jn 1:29, 41, 45-49. 11:27. 17:8. √20:28, 31. Mt √16:16. Mk 1:1. 8:29. Lk 9:20. Ac √8:37. Ro 1:3, 4. 1 J 4:16. 5:1, 20. **are sure**. T#394. Jb 19:25. +38:33 (T#240). Pr 22:20, 21. Ro +1:19 (T#206). 2 T *1:12. 1 J 2:20, 21. √5:13. **thou art**. Mt √16:16. **the living**. See on ver. 57.

70. **Have**. ſ85B, Ge +13:9. ver. 64. Jn 13:18. 17:12. Mt 10:1-4. Lk 6:13-16. Ac 1:17. **twelve**. ver. 67. **and one**. Jn 8:44. 13:2, 21, 27. Ac 13:10. 1 J 3:8. Re 3:9, 10. **a devil**. Jn 8:44. 13:2, *27. 17:12. 1 T 3:11. T 2:3g.

71. **Judas**. Mt 26:14. **Iscariot**. Jsh 15:25. Je 48:24, 41. **Simon**. Jn 12:4. 13:2, 26. 14:22. Mt 10:4. Mk 3:19. Lk 6:16. **for**. ver. 64, 67. Ps 109:6-8. Mk 14:10. Ac 1:16-20, 25. 2:23. Ju 4. **being**. Jn 18:2-6. Ps 41:9. 55:13, 14. Mt 26:14-16. 27:3-5.

JOHN 7

Jesus, when counselled by his unbelieving brethren to show himself at Jerusalem at the Feast of Tabernacles, assigning his reason, refuses to accompany them; but afterwards goes up privately, 1-10. The Jews seek him and form different opinions of him, 11-13. He teaches in the temple, declares that his doctrine is of God, and answers objections, 14-29. Some seek to take him, others believe, and Pharisees send officers to apprehend him, 30-32. He foretells his departure to the Father, when the Jews would in vain seek him, 33-36. He invites every one who is thirsty, to come to him and drink, referring to the Holy Spirit, which would be given to believers, 37-39. Divers opinions of him, 40-44. The officers, struck with his discourse, return without him, 45, 46. The Pharisees scornfully

reproach them, the common people, and Nicodemus who took his part, 47-52. They are disconcerted, and separate, 53.

1. A.M. 4037. A.D. 33. **walked**. Jn 4:3, 54. 6:1. 10:39, 40. 11:54. Mt 10:23. Lk 13:31-33. Ac *10:38. **Jewry**. *Jewry*, or *Judea*, as distinguished from Galilee and Samaria, contained the tribes of Judah, Benjamin, Simeon, and Dan, being bounded on the north by the village Annach or Dorceus, on the borders of Samaria, on the south by a village called Jarda in Arabia, and extending in breadth from the river Jordan to Joppa and the Mediterranean, having Jerusalem in its center. ✱S#2449g. Da 5:13. Lk 23:5g. **because**. ver. 19, 25, 30, 32, 44. Jn *5:16-18. 8:37, 40, 59. 10:31, 39. 11:53, 57. Mt *10:23. 21:38, 46.

2. **feast**. Jn +2:13. 5:1. 6:4. Ex 23:16, 17. Le *23:2, 34-43. Nu 29:12-38. Dt 16:13-16. 1 K 8:2, 65. 2 Ch 7:9, 10. Ezr 3:4. Ne 8:14-18. Ezk 45:25. Ho 12:9. Zc 14:16-19. **tabernacles**. Le +23:34.

3. **brethren**. ver. 5, 10. Mt 12:46, 47. Mk +*3:31n. Lk 8:19. Ac 1:14. **Depart**. Ge 37:5-11, 20. 1 S 17:28. Je 12:6. Mt 22:16, 17. **disciples**. Jn +2:2. +6:66.

4. **For**. ſ57, Mt +26:50. **there**. Jn *18:20. Pr 18:1, 2. Mt 6:1, 2, 5, 16. 23:5. Lk 6:45. **openly**. ſ101, Dt +32:42. Jn 11:54. Col 2:15. **If thou**. ſ184A, 1 C +15:2. **show**. Jn 1:31. 2:11. 17:6. 18:20. 21:1, 14. 1 K 22:13. Mt 4:6. Mk 16:12, 14. Ac 2:4-12. 1 J 1:2. **world**. Gr. *kosmos*, Mt +4:8. ſ121J8, Jn +3:16. Jn 14:22. 18:20.

5. **neither**. ſ71, Jn +1:24. Jn *1:11-13. Mi 7:5, 6. Mk *3:21. **brethren**. ver. +*3. Nu=12:1. Ps ✱69:8. Is ✱63:3. Mt 13:55. **believe in**. ver. 31, 38, 39, 48. Jn +4:39. Ge=37:5.

6. **My time**. ver. 8, 30. Jn 2:4. 8:20. 12:23. 13:1. 17:1. Ps 102:13. Ec 3:1, etc. Lk 9:51. Ac 1:7.

7. **world**. Gr. *kosmos*, Mt +4:8. *ſ121J9A, Jn +1:10. Jn *15:19. Lk 6:26. Ja *4:4. 1 J 4:5. **but**. Jn 15:18, 19, 23-25. 17:14. Pr 8:36. Is 49:7. Zc 11:8. Ro 8:7. 1 J 3:12, 13. **because**. Jn *3:19. 1 K 21:20. 22:8. Pr 9:7, 8. 15:12. Is 29:21. Je 20:8. Am 7:7-13. Ml +*3:5. Lk 11:39-54. Ac 5:28-33. 7:51-54. Ga 4:16. Re 11:5-11. **testify**. Jn +18:37. **works**. Col 1:21. 2 T 4:18. 1 J 3:12. 2 J 11.

8. **I go not**. ver. 6, 30. Jn 8:20, 30. 11:6, 7. 1 C 2:15, 16. **my time**. ver. 6, 30. Jn +2:4.

10. **his brethren**. ver. +*3, 5. Mt 12:46. **gone up**. Jn +2:13. **then went**. Ps 26:8. 40:8. Mt 3:15. Ga *4:4. **not**. Jn 11:54. Is 42:2, 3. Am 5:13. Mt 10:16, 17.

11. **Jews**. Jn 11:56. **Where**. Jn 9:12.

12. **murmuring**. The word in this place seems to mean no more than a private conversation, in a sort of whisper or low voice with differences of opinions and disputes about those opinions, but without displeasure or irritation against Jesus (Scott). This careful attention (almost eavesdropping, Ge +*18:10) is very characteristic of John. ver. 32. Jn 6:41, 61. *9:16. Ph 2:14. **some**. ver. 25-27, 40-43. Jn +*6:14. 9:16, 17. *10:19-21. Mt 10:25. 16:13-16. *21:46. Lk *7:16. **is a good**. Mt 19:16. Mk 10:17. Lk *6:45. *18:18, 19. 23:47, 50. Ac 11:24. Ro 5:7. **deceiveth**. ver. 47, 52. Mt 27:63.

13. **spake**. Jn *3:2. *9:22, 34. *12:42, 43. 19:38. 20:19. Pr 29:25. Ga 2:12, 13. 2 T 2:9-13. Re 2:13. **openly**. Jn 11:54.

14. **the midst**. ver. 2, 37. Nu 29:12, 13, 17, 20, 23, etc. **feast**. Le +*23:34. **went up**. ver. 10. Lk 18:10. **the temple**. ver. 28. Jn 5:14. 8:2. 18:20. Hg 2:7-9. Ml *3:1. Mt 21:12. Lk 19:47.

15. **marvelled.** ver. 46. Mt 7:28, 29. 22:22, 23. Mk 6:2. 12:17. Lk 2:47. **How.** Mt *13:54. Mk 6:2, 3. Lk *4:22. +20:2. Ac 2:7, etc. 4:11, 12. **letters.** *or,* learning. Jn 5:47. Is 29:12. Am 7:14, 15. Ac 26:24. 2 T √3:15.

16. **My.** Jn 3:11, 31, 32. *8:28. 12:49, 50. 14:10, 24. 17:8, 14. 18:19. Ac 17:19. Re 1:1. **but.** Jn *5:23, 24, 30. 6:38-40, 44. **that sent.** ver. 28, 33. Jn +4:34.

17. **If any.** ∫184C, Mt +4:9. **man.** Jn 1:46-49. *8:31, 32, 43, 47. *14:21, 23. Ps √25:8, 9, 12. 119:10, 101, 102. Is 35:8. Je 31:33, 34. Ho *6:3. Mi 4:2. Ml 4:2. Mt *6:22. 13:12. Lk 8:15. Ac 8:27-29. 10:1-6. 11:13, 14. +*17:11. Ph 3:15, 16. **will.** Jn 5:40. 8:44. 2 Th √2:10. **do his will.** Jn +*13:17. Mt +*7:21. Ac +*22:14. **shall know.** Jn *3:21. 8:43. Ps 25:9, 14. Pr 3:32. Da 12:10. Ho +*6:3. Ph 1:9, 10. 3:15. He *11:6. **I speak.** ver. 18. Jn 5:30. 11:51. 12:48, 49. 14:10. 16:13.

18. **that speaketh.** ver. 17. Jn *5:41. 8:49, 50. 1 C *10:31-33. Ga *6:12-14. Ph +*2:3-5. 1 Th 2:6. 1 P 4:11. **own glory.** Jn 8:54. 12:43. **seeketh his glory.** Jn 3:26-30. 5:30, 41. 11:4. 12:28. 13:31, 32. 17:4, 5. Ex 32:10-13. Nu 11:29. Pr 25:27. Mt 6:9. **unrighteousness.** Ro 2:8. 1 C 13:6. 2 Th 2:12.

19. **not.** ver. 23. Jn 1:17. 5:45. 9:28, 29. Ex *24:2, 3. Dt 33:4. Jn 1:17. Ac 7:38. Ga 3:19. He 3:3-5. **yet.** Mt 23:2-4. Ro 2:12, 13, 17-29. *3:19-23. Ga 6:13. **Why.** ver. 25. Jn 5:16, 18. 10:31, 32, 39. 11:53. Ps *2:1-6. Mt *12:14. 21:38. Mk 3:4, 6.

20. **Thou.** Jn 8:48, 49, 52. *10:20. Mt 10:25. 11:18, 19. 12:24. Mk 3:21, 22, 30. Lk 7:33. 8:27. Ac 26:24. **who goeth.** Jn 5:15, 16.

21. **I have.** Jn 5:9-11. **one.** ∫108E1, Mt +8:19. **work.** ver. 23. Jn *5:2-9. **marvel.** Jn 5:20.

22. **circumcision.** Ge *17:10-14. 21:4. Le *12:3. Ac 7:8. Ro 4:9-11. Ga 3:17. **the fathers.** Jn 6:58. Ro 15:8.

23. **If.** ∫184A, 1 C +15:2. **that the law of Moses should not be broken.** *or,* without breaking the law of Moses. Mt 12:5. **law of Moses.** ver. 19. Jn 1:17, 45. 8:5, 17. Lk 2:22. 16:29. 20:28. 24:44. Ac 13:39. 15:5. 28:23. 1 C 9:9. He 10:28. **broken.** Jn 5:18. *10:35. **angry.** Jn 5:16. Mt 12:2. **I have made.** Rather, "I have healed a whole man," *olan anthropon,* and not the circumcised member only. This reasoning was in perfect accordance with the principles of the Jews. So *tanchuma,* "circumcision, which is performed on one of the 248 members of a man, vacates the Sabbath; how much more the *whole body* of a man!" Jn 5:8, 9, 14-16. **on the sabbath.** Lk +*13:14n.

24. **Judge.** Le +*19:15, 35. Mt +*7:1, 2, ◐16, ◐20. Ro 2:1. **according.** Jn *8:15. Ex +*23:2, 3. Dt *1:16, 17. *16:18, 19. 2 Ch 19:7. Ps 58:1, 2. 82:2. *94:20, 21. Pr *17:15. 24:23. 28:21. Is 5:23. *11:3, 4. Ml 2:9. 1 C 6:5. 2 C 10:7. Ga ◐6:1. Ja 2:1, 4, 9. **judge.** ∫147D, Ge +1:29. **righteous judgment.** ver. +*51. Hab 1:4. Zc *7:9. Lk +12:57. √16:1n. 1 C 6:5. 1 T +√5:19n. Ja 2:1, 4, 9, 13.

25. **of Jerusalem.** ver. 10, 11. Mk 1:5. **Is not.** ver. 20.

26. **he speaketh.** Jn 18:20. Ps 40:9, 10. 71:15, 16. Pr 28:1. Is 42:4. 50:7, 8. Mt 22:16. Ac 4:13. Ep 6:19, 20. Ph 1:14. 2 T 1:7, 8. **boldly.** ∫24I, Is +21:7. ver. 13. **Do.** ver. 48. Jn 9:22. *11:47-53. 12:42. Lk *7:30. **very Christ.** ver. 31, 41, 42. Jn +1:20.

27. **we know.** ver. 15. Jn 6:42. 8:14, 19. 9:29. Mt *13:54-57. Mk +*6:3. Lk 4:22. **whence he is.** Jn 19:9. **no man.** ver. 41, 42. Is 11:1. 53:8. Je +*23:5. 30:21. Mi +*5:2. Mt 2:5, 6. Ac 8:33.

28. **Then cried.** ver. 37. Jn 1:15. 12:44. **in the temple.** ver. 14. Mt 26:55. **Ye both.** Jn 1:46. 8:14. Mt 2:23. Lk 2:4, 11, 39, 51. **know me.** Jn ◐8:19, 54, 55. **and I.** Jn 3:2. 5:30, 43. 8:16, 42. 10:36. 12:49. 14:10, 31. **that sent.** ver. 16. Jn 8:26. **is true.** Jn 3:33. 5:32. 8:26. Ex +*34:6. Ro *3:4. 2 C 1:18. T *1:2. He *6:18. 1 J 5:10. **whom.** ∫60A, Ge +3:22. Jn 4:22. 8:19, 54, 55. 15:21. 16:3. 17:3, 25. 1 S 2:12. Ps +√9:10. Pr *2:3-5. Je 9:6. 31:34. Ho 4:1. 5:4. 6:3-6. Mt *11:27. Lk 10:22. Ac 17:23. Ro 1:28. 2 C 4:6. Ga 4:8. 1 Th 4:5. 2 Th 1:8. 1 J √2:3, 4.

29. **I.** Jn *1:18. 8:55. *10:15. 17:25, 26. Mt *11:27. **for.** Jn 3:16, 17. 13:3. 16:27, 28. 17:18. 1 J 1:2. 4:9, 14. **from him.** Jn 1:14. 6:46. 9:16, 33. He 5:5. **sent.** Jn 3:17.

30. **they.** ver. 19, 32, 44. Jn 8:37, 59. 10:31, 39. 11:57. Mt 21:46. Mk *11:18. Lk *19:47, 48. 20:19. **but.** ver. 6, 8, 44-46. Jn 8:20. 9:4. 11:9, 10. Ps 76:10. Is 46:10. Lk 13:32, 33. 22:53. **hour.** ver. 6, 8. Jn +2:4.

31. **many of.** ver. 40, 49. Jn 8:30. 10:42. 11:45. 12:11. Mt 21:11. Mk 11:9. **believed.** ver. +5. Jn +*2:23, 24. 4:39. +*6:14, 15. 8:30-32. 12:42. Mt *12:23. Lk +*8:13. Ac 8:13. Ja 2:26. **When.** Jn *3:2. 6:2. 9:16. 10:41, 42. Mt 11:3-6. 12:23. **Christ.** ver. 26, 27, 41, 42. Jn +1:20. **miracles.** Jn 2:11, 23.

32. **Pharisees heard.** ver. 45, 47-53. Jn +1:24. 11:47, 48. 12:19. Mt 12:23, 24. 23:13. **murmured.** ver. 12. **Pharisees and.** Jn +11:57. **sent.** ver. 30, 45, 46. Jn 18:3. Lk 22:52, 53. Ac 5:26. **officers.** ver. 45, 46. Mt +26:58. **take him.** Mt 12:14. Mk 3:6. Lk 6:11.

33. **Yet.** Jn 12:35, 36. 13:1, 3, 33. 14:19. 16:5, 16-22. 17:11, 13. Mk 16:19. **I go.** Jn 16:5. **sent.** ver. 28.

34. **shall seek.** Jn *8:21-24. 13:33-36. 14:3, 6. 17:24. Pr *1:24-31. Ho *5:6. Mt ◐7:7. 23:39. Lk ◐11:9. *13:24, 34, 35. 17:22, 23. **and where.** Jn 8:21. 12:26.

35. **will he.** Jn 8:22. **the dispersed.** Ps 147:2. Is *11:12. 27:12, 13. 56:8. Zp 3:10. Ac 21:21. Ja *1:1. 1 P *1:1. **among.** ∫181E, Ge +3:24. **Gentiles.** *or,* Greeks. ✠S#1672g. Jn 12:20. Ac 11:20. 14:1. Ro 1:16. 2:9, 10. 3:9. 1 C 1:22-24. 10:32. 12:13. **teach.** Ps 67:1, 2. 98:2, 3. Is 11:10. 49:6. Mt 12:21. Lk 2:32. Ac 11:18. 13:46-48. 22:21, 22. Ep 3:8. Col 1:27. 1 T 2:7. 2 T 1:11.

36. **manner.** Jn 3:4, 9. 6:41, 52, 60. 12:34. 16:17, 18. **Ye shall.** ver. 34. 1 C √2:14.

37. **the last.** Le 23:36, 39. Nu 29:35. 1 K 8:65, *66. Ne 8:18. **feast.** Le +*23:34. **and cried.** ver. *28. Jn 1:23. Pr *1:20. *8:1, 3. 9:3. Is 40:2, 6. *55:1. *58:1. Je 2:2. Mi 6:9. Mt 3:3. **If.** ∫184C, Mt +4:9. Jn *4:10, 13, 14. *6:35. Ex=17:3. Ps *36:8, 9. 42:2. 63:1. 143:6. Is 12:3. 41:17, 18. *44:3. *55:1. Am 8:11-13. Mt +*5:6. Re *21:6. *22:1, 17. **let.** Jn *5:40. *6:35, 37. √14:6. Is +*55:3. Je 16:19. Mt *11:28. **drink.** Jn 6:55. SS 5:1. Zc 9:15. 1 C *10:4, 21. *11:25. *12:13. Ep *5:18.

38. **He that.** ver. 5. Dt *18:15. **the scripture.** Jn 2:22. Lk 4:21. Ro 9:17. **said.** ∫63C, Ge +25:32. Supply "(concerning Jerusalem: so shall it be, Zc 13:1. 14:8)." **out.** Jn *4:14. 5:26. 6:57. Jb 32:18, 19. Pr *10:11. 18:4. Is 12:3. *44:3. 55:1. *58:11. 59:21. Ezk 3:3. 47:1-12. Zc 14:8. Mt 12:35. Ga *5:22, 23. Ep 5:9. **belly.** ∫121J22, Jb +15:35. **rivers.** Pr 5:16. Is 49:10. 58:11. **living water.** ∫22K4, Je +2:13. Jn 3:5. +4:10. Pr 5:15. SS 4:15. Je 2:13. Ep 5:26.

39. **this spake.** ∫95, Ps +7:13. Jn *14:16, 17, 26. Pr *1:23. Is 12:3. *32:15. *44:3. Jl *2:28. Lk *3:16.

*24:49. Ac *1:4-8. *2:4, 17, 38. 4:31, 32. Ro *8:9.
1 C √12:13. Ga 3:14. Ep *1:13, 14. +*4:30. **the Spirit.**
Gr. *pneuma*, ✍121A1, Lk +1:17n. ✍121A3, Nu ?11:17.
Jn 1:32, 33. 3:6, 8, 34. 16:13. Ge ●1:2. Ps 104:30.
Ac +8:29. Ro 8:16, 23, 26, 27. 15:30. 1 C 2:10, 13.
12:7-9, 11. 2 C 1:22. 3:17. 5:5. 12:18. Ga 3:2, 3, 5,
14. 5:22, 25. 6:8. Ep 4:3. 6:17. 1 Th 5:19. 1 T 4:1.
1 P 1:2. 1 J 3:24. 5:7, 8. Re 2:7, 11, 17, 29. 3:6, 13,
22. 14:13. 22:17. **which.** Jn 1:33. 20:22. Jl 2:28. Lk
24:49. Ac 2:16-18. **that believe.** ver. 5. **for.** Jn *16:7.
20:22. Ps 68:18. Is 32:15. Ac 2:4, 17, *33. 19:2. 2 C
3:8. **Ghost.** Gr. *pneuma*, Mt +1:18n. **not yet given.**
✍63G, Ge +50:23. Jn 3:34. 14:16, 17. 20:22. Lk 11:13.
Ac 2:38. 1 J 3:24. 4:13. **because.** Jn 14:16, 17. *16:7.
glorified. Jn ●1:14. ●2:11. 8:54. 11:4. *12:16, 23.
*13:31, 32. 14:13. 16:14. *17:5. Ac *3:13. Ph 2:9. He
2:9. 1 P 1:21.

40. **the people.** ver. 31. **Of.** ver. 12. Jn 1:21, 25.
+*6:14. Dt *18:15-18. Mt 16:14. 21:11. Lk 7:16. Ac
3:22, 23.

41. **This is.** ver. 26, 31. Jn 1:20, 41, 49. *4:25, 29,
42. √6:69. Mt 16:14-16. **Shall.** ver. 52. Jn *1:46.

42. **not.** ver. 27, 38. Ps √132:11. Is 11:1. Je +*23:5.
Mi +*5:2. Mt 2:5. Lk 2:4, 11. **of David.** Ps 89:3, 4.
Mt 1:1. Ac +*13:23. **Bethlehem.** Mi +*5:2. Mt 2:1,
5. Lk 2:4. **where.** 1 S *16:1, 4, 11-13, 18. 17:58.

43. **a division.** ver. 12. Jn 6:52. 9:16. 10:19. Mt
10:35. Lk 12:51, 52. Ac 14:4. 23:7-10.

44. **no man.** ver. 30. Jn 8:20. 18:5, 6. Ac 18:10.
23:11. 27:23-25.

45. **the officers.** ver. 32. Ac 5:21-27.

46. **Never.** ver. 26. Mt *7:28, 29. Lk *4:22. **spake
like.** Ps *45:2.

47. **Are.** ver. 12. Jn 9:27-34. 2 K 18:29, 32mg.
2 Ch 32:15. Mt 27:63. 2 C 6:8.

48. **Have any.** ✍85R, Jb +4:17. ver. 26, 50. Jn
*12:42. Je 5:4, 5. Mt 11:25. Ac 6:7. 1 C 1:20, 22-28.
*2:8. **the rulers.** ver. 26. Jn 3:1. **believed.** ver. 5.

49. **this people.** ver. 31. Jn 9:34, 40, 41. Is 5:21.
28:14. 29:14-19. +*65:5n. Lk *18:9, 10. 1 C 1:20, 21.
3:18-20. Ja 3:13-18. **knoweth not.** Jn ●+√6:14. Mk
●*12:24. Ro *2:17-21. **cursed.** Mt 18:17. Lk ●7:6.

50. **he that.** Jn *3:1, 2. 19:39. **to Jesus.** Gr. to him.

51. **our law.** Ex 23:1. Dt 1:17. 17:6, 8-11. 19:15-
19. Pr 18:13. Ac 23:3. **before.** ✍184C, Mt +4:9. ver.
+*24. Dt 1:16. Pr 17:15. +*18:13. Ac 26:1. 1 T
+√5:19n.

52. **Art.** ver. 41. Jn 9:34. Ge 19:9. Ex 2:14. 1 K
22:24. Pr 9:7, 8. **Search.** ver. 41. Jn 1:46. +*5:39. Is
*9:1, 2. Mt 4:15, 16. **and look.** ✍108A6. Idiom B824:
idiomatic usages of verbs. Two imperatives are sometimes united, so that the first expresses a condition
or limitation in regard to the second; by which the
latter becomes a future. Here, "search and thou wilt
see." For other instances of this idiom see 1 C 15:34.
1 T 6:12. **for out of.** 2 K ●14:25n w Jsh 19:13. Am
1:1. Mi 1:1n. **ariseth.** Mt 11:11. Lk 7:16. Ac 13:22.

53. **every man went.** Jb 5:12, 13. Ps 33:10. 76:5,
10.

JOHN 8

*Jesus teaches at the temple, 1, 2. The Pharisees lay
a snare for him in respect of a woman taken in adultery,
but he turns it to their confusion and warns the woman
to sin no more, 3-11. He declares himself to be the*

*Light of the world, 12; justifies his doctrine, shows
that his Father bore witness to him, and predicts the
doom of unbelievers, 13-29. Many believe, whom he
exhorts "to continue in his word;" promising them liberty by the knowledge of the truth, 30-32. He refutes
the cavils and detects the vain-confidence of the Jews
who opposed him, showing that they are the slaves
of sin and the children of the devil, 33-47. Being reviled, as a Samaritan and possessed, he refutes the
charge, promises life to believers, asserts his dignity,
and adds, "Before Abraham was, I AM," 48-58. He
withdraws from those who attempt to stone him, 59.*

1. **went unto.** Mt 21:1. Mk 11:1. 13:3. Lk 19:37.

2. **early.** Jn 4:34. Ec 9:10. Je 25:3, 4. 44:4. Lk 21:37,
38. **into the temple.** ver. 20. Jn 7:10, 14. Mt 26:55.
Lk 21:37, 38. Ac 5:21. **and he sat.** Mt 5:1, 2. 26:55.
Lk 4:20. 5:3. **and taught.** T#746. Jn *18:20. 2 K +*4:23.
Ne *8:8. Mk 2:1, 2. Lk 4:43, 44. Ac *18:4, 5. 1 C
+1:17 (T#430).

3. **scribes and Pharisees.** ver. 13. Jn +1:24.
brought. The genuineness of the passage contained
in the first eleven verses of this chapter is much controverted, as it is wanting in several MSS. and ancient
versions, and is found with considerable variations
in those in which it is retained. It is found, however,
in the greater part of the MSS. extant of various recen-
sions; and the learned Mr. Nolan (*On the integrity of
the Greek Vulgate*, p. 37) has shown it to be probable
that it was omitted for certain reasons by Eusebius
in that edition of the Greek Testament which he was
commanded by Constantine to prepare for public use;
likewise in subsequent editions under the influence
of his name and authority. The subject of the story,
says that eminent critic, forms as convincing a proof
of its genuineness, as it does in the subversion of the
contrary notion, that it is an interpolation. There could
be no possible inducement for fabricating such a passage, while there is an obvious motive for removing
it from the canon. It has, besides internal evidence
of authenticity, in the testimony of the Vulgate, in
which it is uniformly found; and external, in the express
acknowledgement of its genuineness by St. Chrysostome, St. Jerome, St. Augustine, and St. Ambrose.
St. Augustine has specified the reason of its having
been withdrawn from the text of the Evangelist. Add
to this, that the plain and simple style is that of the
Evangelist; and that every circumstance is completely
in character; exactly what might be expected from the
scribes and Pharisees, and from our Lord; while his
answer, though perfectly suited to the purpose, would
scarcely have ever been thought of by human ingenuity.
taken. Nu 5:13. **in the midst.** Mt 14:6. Ac 4:7.

4. **Master.** Jn +1:38. **taken.** Nu 5:13. **adultery.** Mt
19:3.

5. **Moses.** Le *20:10. Dt 22:21-24. Ezk 16:38-40.
23:47. **to stone.** Dt 22:24. Ezk 16:38, 40. 23:45. **such.**
Le ●19:20mg, "they." *20:10. Dt ●22:24, "both." **but.**
Jn *18:31. Mt 5:17. 19:6-8. 22:16-18.

6. **tempting.** Jn 6:6. Nu 14:22. Mt 16:1. *19:3. 22:18,
35. Mk 8:11. 10:2. 12:15. Lk 10:25. 11:16, 53, 54.
20:20-23. 1 C 10:9. **that they.** Lk 11:54. **But.** ver. 2.
Ge 49:9. Je 17:13. Da 5:5. **wrote.** Le *20:13. Is +*8:16,
20. **as though.** ✍63K, Ge +37:13. Ps 38:12-14. 39:1.
Pr 26:17. Ec 3:7. Am 5:10, 13. Mt 10:16. 15:23. 26:63.

7. **lifted.** ver. 10. Lk 13:11. **and said.** Jn 7:46. Pr
12:18. 26:4, 5. Je 23:29. 1 C 14:24, 25. Col 4:6. He

*4:12, 13. Re 1:16. 2:16. 19:15. **He that.** Dt 17:6. Ps 50:16-20. Mt *7:1-5. 23:25-28. Ro *2:1-3, 21-25. **him first.** Dt *17:7.

9. **being.** Ge 42:21, 22. Ex 9:27. 1 K 2:44. 17:18. Ezr 9:6. Jb 15:21. Ps 40:12. 50:21. Ec 7:22. Da 5:6. Mk 6:14-16. Lk 12:1-3. Ro 2:15, 22. 1 J 3:20. **convicted.** Ho 14:9. Lk 5:8. 2 C 7:10. **conscience.** T#125. Jn +16:2 (T#127). Pr 20:27. Is 5:3. Lk +12:57 (T#632). Ac +23:1 (T#129). Ro 2:14, 15. 2 C 4:2. **went out.** Jb *5:12, 13. 20:5, 27. Ps 9:15, 16. 40:14, 15. 71:13. Lk 13:17. **one by one.** Mk 14:19. **alone.** ver. 2, 10, 12.

10. **lifted.** ver. 7. **where.** Is 41:11, 12.

11. **Neither.** ver. 15. Jn *3:17. *18:36. Dt 16:18. 17:9. Lk *9:56. 12:13, 14. Ro 13:3, 4. 1 C 5:12. **go.** Jn 5:14. Jb 34:31, 32. Pr √28:13. Is *1:16-18. √55:6, 7. Ezk 18:30-32. Mt 21:28-31. Lk 5:32. +*13:3, 5. 15:7, 10, 32. Ro 2:4. *5:20, 21. 1 T *1:15, 16. 2 P 3:15. Re 2:21, 22.

12. **again.** Jn 7:37, 38. **I am.** ſ119, Ge +49:9. Jn 1:4-9. √3:19. *9:5. +10:7. *12:35, 36. Ne 9:12. Ps 36:9. 78:14. Is 9:2. 42:6, 7. 49:6. 60:1-3. Ho +*6:3. Ml *4:2. Mt 4:14-16. 5:14. Lk 1:78, 79. 2:32. Ac 13:47, 48. 26:+18, 23. 1 J 2:8. **light.** Jn 12:46. Ep 6:12. Re 21:23. **world.** Gr. *kosmos*, Mt +4:8. Jn +1:29. **followeth.** Jn 10:27. 12:26. 21:19. Mt +10:38. **shall not.** ſ158, Mt +5:18. Jn 12:35, 46. Ps 18:28. 97:11. Is 50:10. Ep *5:8. 2 P 2:4, 17. Ju 6, 13. **darkness.** Is +9:2. **shall have.** Jn √7:17. √14:6. Jb 33:28. Ps 49:19. Re 21:24. **the light.** Jn 1:4. 6:35. 12:35, 36. Ep 5:14. Ja 1:12. Re 21:6. 22:14. **of life.** Jn √3:15, 16, 36. *4:14. √5:24, 26, 29, 39, 40. 6:35, 40, 47, 53, 54, 63, 68. √10:10. √20:31.

13. **Pharisees.** ver. 3. **Thou.** Jn *5:31-47. **bearest record.** Jn +18:37.

14. **Though.** ſ184C, Mt +4:9. **bear record.** Jn +18:37. **yet.** Nu 12:3. Ne 5:14-19. 2 C 11:31. 12:11, 19. **for.** ver. 42. Jn 7:29. 10:15, 36. 13:3. 14:10. 16:28. 17:8. **is true.** Re *3:14. **I know.** Jn +*1:48. 13:1. 18:4. 19:28. **whence I came.** ver. *42. Jn 13:3. 16:28. **and whither.** ver. 21. Jn 7:33. **but.** Jn *7:27, 28. *9:29, 30.

15. **Ye judge.** Jn +*7:24. 1 S *16:7. Jb 10:4. Ps 58:1, 2. 94:20, 21. Am 5:7. 6:12. Hab 1:4. Mk 6:3. Ro 2:1. 1 C 2:15. 4:3-5. Ja 2:4. **after the flesh.** 1 C 1:26. 2 C 5:16. **I judge.** ver. 11. Jn *3:17. *12:47. +*18:36. Lk 12:14.

16. **yet if.** ſ184C, Mt +4:9. ſ185C, Mt +11:14. Jn *5:22-30. 1 S *16:7. Ps +*45:6, 7. 72:1, 2. 98:9. 99:4. Is +*9:7. *11:2-5. 32:1, 2. Je +*23:5, 6. Zc *9:9. Ac √17:31. Re 19:11. **for I.** ver. 29. Jn *16:32. **that sent.** ver. 18, 26, 29. Jn +4:34.

17. **also.** Jn 10:34. 15:25. Ga 3:24. 4:21. **that.** Jn +7:23. Nu 35:30. Dt *17:6. *19:15. 1 K 21:10. Mt 18:16. 2 C 13:1. 1 T 5:19. He 10:28. 1 J 5:9. Re 11:3. **of two.** Jn 2:9.

18. **one.** ver. 12, 25, 38, 51, 58. Jn 10:9, 11, 14, 30. 11:25. √14:6. Re 1:17, 18. **and the.** See on Jn 5:31-40. He 2:4. 1 J 5:6-12. **Father.** Jn +5:37. **that sent.** ver. 16, 26, 29. Jn +4:34.

19. **Ye neither.** ver. 54, 55. Jn 1:10. 7:28. 10:14, 15. 15:21. 16:3. Je 22:16. 24:7. 1 C 15:34. Ga 4:9. Col +√1:10. 1 J *5:20. **nor my Father.** ver. 49, 54. Jn +5:17. **if.** ſ184B, Mt +23:30. Jn *1:18. √14:6-9. *17:3, 25, 26. Mt 11:25, *27. Lk 10:21, 22. 2 C *4:4-6. Ep 1:17. Col +*1:15n. He 1:3. 2 J 9. **had known.**

Jn *17:3. **known my.** ver. 55. Jn +10:15.

20. **in the treasury.** 1 Ch 9:26. Mt 27:6. Mk 12:41, 43. **as he taught in.** ver. 2. **and no.** ſ71, Jn +1:24. ver. 59. Jn 7:8, 30, 44. 10:39. 11:9, 10. Lk 13:31-33. 20:19. **his hour.** Jn 2:4. 7:6. 12:23. 13:1. 17:1.

21. **I go.** Jn 7:34. 12:33, 35. 14:2, 3, 28. 15:16. 16:7. 1 K 18:10. 2 K 2:16, 17. Mt 23:39. 24:23, 24. +*25:19. **seek.** Jn 7:34. **and shall die in.** T#564. ver. 24. Ge 19:24, 25. Le 10:1, 2. Nu 16:22, *33. Jb 20:11. Ps 58:9. 73:18-20. Pr 11:7. *14:32. Is √65:20. Ezk *3:18, 19. 18:18. 33:8. Mt 27:5. Lk *16:22-26. Ac 5:5. 1 C 15:17, 18. Ep 2:1. 2 P 2:12, 13. **whither.** Jn 7:34. 13:33. Mt +*25:41, 46.

22. **the Jews.** ver. 31, 48, 52, 57. Jn +5:10. **Will.** ver. 48, 52. Jn 7:35. Mt 7:20. 10:20. Ps 22:6. 31:18. 123:4. He 12:3. 13:13.

23. **Ye are from.** ver. 44. Jn *1:14. +*3:13, 31. Ps 17:14. Ro 8:7, 8. 1 C √15:47, 48. Ph 3:19-21. Ja 3:15-17. 1 J √2:15, 16. **from above.** Jn +*3:13, 31. 1 C √15:47. **ye are of.** Jn 15:18, 19. 17:14, 16. Ja *4:4. 1 J √2:15, 16. 4:5, 6. 5:19, 20. **world.** Gr. *kosmos*, Mt +4:8. **I am not.** Jn 17:14, 16. 18:36. **world.** Gr. *kosmos*, Mt +4:8. Jn 9:39. 1 J *5:19.

24. **I said.** ver. 21. **shall die.** Ro *6:23. Col 1:14. 1 P 3:18. Re 1:5. **for if.** ſ184C, Mt +4:9. Negative condition of the third class (the more probable future condition). **ye believe not.** Jn √3:18, 36. 16:9. Pr 8:36. Mk *16:16. Ac √4:12. He *2:3. +*10:26-29. 12:25. **I am.** Gr. *ego eimi.* Used in the absolute sense (as in the LXX. of Is 43:10, where it is used of Jehovah), Jesus claiming absolute divine being, as at Jn 8:58 (A. T. Robertson, *Word Pictures*, vol. 5, p. 146). ver. +*28. Jn 13:19. 18:5. Dt 32:39, LXX. Is 46:4, LXX. **he.** ver. +*58n. Jn *17:5. Ne +*9:6. Is *43:10. Mt 3:3. 1 C *12:3. Col 1:17. He 1:3.

25. **Who.** Jn 1:19, 22. 10:24. 19:9. Lk 22:67. **Even.** Mt 17:17. Mk 9:19. Lk 9:41. **that I said.** ver. 12. Jn 5:17, etc. **from the beginning.** Jn 1:45. 16:4.

26. **have many.** Jn 16:12. Dt 18:18. He *5:11, 12. **to judge.** ver. 16. Jn 5:42, 43. 9:39-41. 12:47-50. **but he.** ver. 17. Jn 3:33. 7:28. Ro 3:4. 2 C 1:18. **that sent.** ver. 16, 18. Jn +4:34. **and I.** ver. 28, 40. Jn 3:11, 32. 7:16. 15:15. 17:8. Re 1:1. **world.** Gr. *kosmos*, Mt +4:8. Jn *18:20. **heard of him.** Jn *15:15.

27. **They.** ſ71, Jn +1:24. **understood not.** ver. 43, 47. Is 6:9. 42:18-20. 59:10. Ro 11:7-10. 2 C 4:3, 4. **of the Father.** ver. 18, 26.

28. **When.** Jn *3:14. *12:32-34. 19:18. Lk 23:48. **Son of man.** Jn +1:51. ●9:35. **then.** Jn 16:8-11. Mt √27:50-54n. Ac *2:37, 41. 4:4. Ro 1:4. 1 Th 2:15, 16. **I am.** ver. +*24n, 58n. Jn +*1:1. 4:26. 11:27. 13:19. 17:5, 24. Ex 3:14. 6:3. Dt 32:39. 1 Ch ●21:17. Ps 68:4. Is +*41:4. 43:10, 12, 13. Mk 13:6. Lk 21:8. Col 1:17. He +*13:8. Re +*1:8, 17. **and that.** Jn *5:19, 30. 6:38. 11:42. 12:49, 50. Nu 16:28-30. Ro 1:4. He *2:2, 3. **but.** Jn 3:11. 7:16, 17.

29. **he that sent.** ver. 16. Jn 11:42. *14:10, 11. 16:32. Is *42:1, 6. 49:4-8. *50:4-9. Ac *10:38. 2 T 4:17, 22. **with me.** Ex=3:12. **not left.** He=11:27. **for.** ver. 55. Jn *4:34. *5:30. *6:38. 14:31. *15:10. *17:4. Is *42:1, 21. Mt *3:17. *17:5. He *4:15. *5:8, 9. *7:26. 10:5-10. 1 J *2:1. 3:22.

30. **As he spake.** Is √55:10, 11. He *4:12. **many.** Jn 2:23. +*6:14. 7:31. 10:42. 11:45. **believed.** Jn +4:39.

31. **Then said Jesus.** Jn 7:17. 14:21, 23. **those Jews.** ver. 22, 48, 52, 57. Jn +5:10. **which believed.** Jn +5:47.

If. ✼184C, Mt +4:9. Jn 6:66-71. *15:4-9. 1 S 12:14. Mt *24:13. Ac *13:43. +*14:22. 26:22. Ro 2:7. *11:22. Col +*1:23. 1 T 2:15. +*4:16. 2 T 3:14. He +*3:14. 8:9. *10:38, 39. Ja *1:25. 1 J *2:19, 24. 2 J *9. **continue.** T#937. Jn 5:38. *15:7. Mt 10:22. ◐+*13:20, 21. 24:13. Lk ◐+*8:13. 1 C √15:58. Ga √6:9. Col +*1:23. *3:16. He +*10:35. 1 P √2:2. 2 P √3:18. 1 J 2:24, 28. 2 J 8, 9. Re *2:10. **word.** ver. +*43. Jn +*5:39n. Ps 119:93. 1 Th √2:13. 2 T +*3:15. **my disciples.** ver. 36. Jn 1:47. 6:55. *13:35. *15:8. 1 T +*4:16. 5:3-5. 2 T +*2:2.

32. **ye shall.** Jn *6:45. √7:17. √14:6. 16:13. Ps *25:5, 8, 9. Pr 1:23, 29. *2:1-7. +*4:18. SS 1:7, 8. Is +*2:3. 30:21. *35:8. 54:13. Je 6:16. *31:33, 34. Ho +*6:3. Ml 4:2. Mt *11:29. 13:11, 12. 2 T 3:7. **know the truth.** 2 J 1. **and the.** ver. *36. Jn *17:17. Ps *119:45. Is *61:1. Ro 6:7, 14-18, 22. 8:2, 15. 1 C 7:22. 2 C *3:17, 18. Ga 5:1, 13. 2 T *2:25, 26. Ja *1:25. 2:12. 1 P 2:16. **truth.** ver. 40, 44, 45. Jn 1:14, 17.

33. **We be.** ver. 37, 39. Le 25:42. Mt *3:9. Lk 3:8. 16:24-26. 19:9. Ro 9:7. **Abraham's seed.** Lk 1:55. Ro *2:29. 4:13. *9:7. +*11:1. 2 C 11:22. Ga *3:9, 16, 29. He 2:16. **and were.** Jn *19:15, 25. Ge 15:13. Ex ◐*1:13, 14. Jg 2:18. *3:8. 4:3. 2 K 25:21, 22. Ezr 9:9. Ne 5:4-8. 9:27, 28, 36, 37.

34. **Verily.** Jn +1:51. See on 3:3. Mt +*5:18. **Whosoever.** 1 K 21:25. Pr *5:22. Ac 8:23. Ro *6:6, 12, 16, 19, 20. 7:14, 25. 8:21. Ep 2:2. T 3:3. 2 P *2:19. 1 J *3:8-10. Re 1:5. **committeth.** lit. practices. ✼108B. Idiom B828. "To do (i.e. *commit*) sin" means to sin willfully and willingly. For another instance of this figure see 1 J √3:9.

35. **the servant.** Ge 21:10. Ezk 46:17. Mt 21:41-43. Ga *4:30, 31. **in the house.** Jn +*14:2. He *3:6. **for ever.** Gr. *aion*, Mt +6:13. Jn +*6:54n. **but.** Jn 14:19, 20. Ro 8:15-17, 29, 30. Ga *4:4-7. Col *3:3. He 3:5, 6. 1 P *1:2-5. **ever.** Gr. *aion*, Mt +6:13. ver. 56, 58. Jn √1:1. +*17:5. Is +*9:6. Mi +*5:2. Lk 15:31. Col *1:17. He +*1:8. *7:3. +*13:8.

36. **If the Son.** ✼184C, Mt +4:9. ver. 31, 32. Jn 3:35. Ps 19:13. 119:32, 133. Is 49:24, 25. 61:1. Zc 9:11, 12. Lk *4:18. Ro 8:2. 2 C *3:17. Ga *5:1. **free.** Nu 35:25, 27. 1 Ch=9:33. Ps 119:134. Mt 17:26. Ro 6:22. *8:1, 2.

37. **know.** ver. 33. Ac 13:26. Ro 9:7. **but.** ver. 6, 40, 59. Jn 5:16-18. 7:1, 19, 25. 10:31. 11:53. **because.** ver. 43, 45-47. Jn 5:44. 12:39-43. Mt 13:15, 19-22. 1 C √2:14. **my word.** Ro √10:17. 1 J 1:10. **no place.** Jn *5:38.

38. **speak.** ver. 26. Jn 3:11, 32. *5:19, 30. 6:46. 12:49, 50. *14:10, 24. 17:8. **have seen.** Ac 4:20. 1 J 1:3. **and ye.** ver. 41, 44. Mt 3:7. 1 J 3:8-10.

39. **Abraham.** ver. *33, 36. **father.** ✼171G, Ge +13:8. **If.** ✼184B, Mt +23:30. ver. 37. Mt √3:9. 5:45. Ro 2:28, 29. *4:12, 16. *9:6, 7. Ga *3:7, 9, 29. Ja 2:22-24. **ye would.** ✼184E, Lk +17:6.

40. **now.** ver. 37, 59. Jn +*7:1. Ps 37:12, 32. Ga 4:16, 29. 1 J 3:12-15. Re 12:4, 12, 13, 17. **a man.** ver. 26, 38, 56. Ac 2:22. *17:31. Ro 5:15. 1 T √2:5. **the truth.** Jn *1:17. **of God.** ver. 26. this. Ro 4:12.

41. **do.** ver. 38, 44. **We be.** Jn 9:29. Is 57:3-7. Ezk 23:45-47. Ho 1:2. 2:2-5. Ml 2:11. **we have.** ver. 47. Ex *4:22. Dt 14:1. 32:6. Is 63:16. 64:8. Je 3:19. 31:20. Ezk 16:20, 21. Ml *1:6.

42. **If God were.** ✼184B, Lk +7:39. Jn √5:23. 15:23, 24. Ml *1:6. 1 C 16:22. 1 J *5:1, 2. **for I proceeded.**

ver. 14. Jn 1:14. 13:3. 16:27, 28, 30. 17:8, 25. Re 22:1. **came from.** Jn +*1:1, 2. He 10:9. 1 J 5:20. **neither.** Jn 5:43. 7:28, 29. 12:49. 14:10. 17:8, 25. Ga *4:4. 1 J *4:9, 10, 14. **he sent.** Jn 3:17.

43. **do.** ver. 27. Jn 5:43. +*7:17. 12:39, 40. Pr 28:5. Is 44:18. Ho 14:9. Mi 4:12. Ro 3:11. **my speech.** Jn 4:41. Mt 26:73. **ye cannot.** Jn 6:60. Is *6:9. Je *6:10. Ac 7:51. Ro *8:7, 8. 1 C √2:14. **hear.** ✼108B, Ac +22:9. ✼121C2A1, Jb +19:25. ver. 47. Jn *5:24. 14:24. Mt *13:14, 15. **my word.** ver. 31, 37, 51, 52. Jn 12:48. 14:23. 15:3, 20. 1 J 2:5.

44. **are.** ✼62, Lk +13:32. ver. 23, 38, 41. Jn 6:70. Ge +*3:15. Mt +*13:38. Ac 13:10. 1 J *3:8-10, 12. **lusts.** ✼108K40B, Ex +15:9. **He was.** Ge *3:3-7. 4:8, 9. 1 K 22:22. 1 Ch +*21:1. Ja 4:1-7. 1 P *5:8. 1 J 3:12, 15. Re 2:10. 9:11. 13:6-8. 20:7-9. **beginning.** Ge 3:1-6. Ro 5:14-21. 1 J *3:8. **and abode.** 2 P 2:4. 1 J 2:4. Ju 6. **the truth.** Jn 1:17. 2 Th √2:9-12. **When.** Ge 3:4, 5. 2 Ch 18:20-22. Jb 1:11. 2:4-6. Ac *5:3. 13:10. 2 C √11:3, 13-15. 2 Th √2:9-11. Re 12:9. 13:14. 20:2, 3, 10. +*21:8. 22:15. **his own.** Jn 1:11. 16:32. 1 Th 4:11. **a liar.** T#416. Ge *3:4. +*27:19. Ps +5:9 (T#702). Is 59:3, 4, 13, 14. Je 9:2-8. Ezk +*13:22. Ho 4:1, 2. Mi 6:12. **it.** ✼96F1, Ge +3:8.

45. **because.** ver. 46. Jn √3:19, 20. 7:7. Ga 4:16. 2 Th √2:10. 2 T 4:3, 4. **the truth.** ver. 44. Jn 1:17. **believe me not.** Jn +5:47.

46. **Which.** ✼85C, Ge +18:14. **convinceth.** ver. 7. Jn +*14:30. 15:10. 16:8. Ge=40:15. Lk +*1:35. 2 C √5:21. He +*4:15. *7:26. 1 P *2:22. **And if.** ✼184A, 1 C +15:2. **why.** Mt 21:25. Mk 11:31.

47. **He that.** ver. 37, 43, 45. Jn *1:12, 13. 6:45, 46, 65. *10:26, 27. 17:6-8. 18:37. 1 J 3:10. *4:1-6. 5:1. 2 J 9. 3 J 11. **of God.** ✼25, Ge +4:4. Jn 3:34. **heareth.** 2 Ch=34:30. **God's words.** Jn 3:34. 15:15. 17:8. **hear them not.** ✼108B, Lk +8:15. ver. *43. Jn 10:26. 12:48. Je *6:10.

48. **Say.** ver. 52. Jn 13:13. Mt 15:7. Ja 2:19. **thou.** Jn 4:9. 7:20. 10:20. Is 49:7. 53:3. Mt 10:25. 12:24, 31. Ro 15:3. He 13:13.

49. **I have not.** Pr 26:4, 5. 1 P 2:23. **but.** ver. 29. Jn 11:4. 12:28. 13:31, 32. 14:13. 17:4. Is 42:21. 49:3. Mt 3:15-17. Ph *2:6-11. **honor my Father.** Jn √5:23. 7:18. Is +*58:13. **dishonor.** Jn √5:23. Ps 4:2.

50. **I seek not.** T#56. ver. 54. Jn *5:41. 7:18. 18:19-21. Ps +58:11 (T#630). Is 11:5. Ac 3:14. 2 C 5:21. He +*4:15. 7:26, 27. 1 P 1:21-23. Re +15:4 (T#229). **there.** Jn 5:20-23, 45. 12:47, 48.

51. **If.** ✼184C, Mt +4:9. Jn √3:15, 16. √5:24. 6:50. *11:25, 26. **keep.** ver. 55. Jn 14:23, 24. 15:20. +*17:6. 1 J +*2:3, 5. Re 1:3. **my saying.** ver. 43. **never.** Gr. *aion*, Mt +6:13. ✼158, Mt +5:18. **see.** ver. 12, 52. Ps 89:48. Mt 16:28. Mk 9:1. Lk 2:26. 9:27. Ac 2:27, 31. 13:35-37. He 2:9. 11:5.

52. **Now.** ver. 48. Jn 9:24. **Abraham.** Zc 1:5, 6. He 11:13. **If a.** ✼184C, Mt +4:9. **never.** Gr. *aion*, Mt +6:13. ✼158, Mt +5:18. **taste.** Mt 16:28. He 2:9.

53. **thou greater.** ver. √58. Jn *4:12. 10:29, 30. 12:34. Is +*9:6. Mt 12:6, 41, 42. Ro √9:5. He 3:2, *3. 7:1-7. **Abraham.** ver. 39. **whom makest.** Jn +*5:18. +*10:33. *19:7, 12. Je +*29:26.

54. **If.** ✼184C, Mt +4:9. ver. 50. Jn 2:11. 5:31, 32, 41. 7:18. Pr 25:27. 2 C 10:18. He 5:4, 5. **it is.** Jn 5:22-29, 41. 7:39. 13:31, 32. 16:14, 15. *17:1, 5. Ps 2:6-12. 110:1-4. Da *7:13, 14. Ac *3:13. Ep *1:20-23. Ph √2:9-11. He 5:5. 1 P 1:12, 21. 2 P *1:17. **my Father.**

ver. 19, 49. Jn +5:17. **ye say**. ver. 41. Is 48:1, 2. 66:5. Ho 1:9. Ro 2:17, etc.

55. ye have not. ver. 19. Jn 7:28, 29. 15:21. 16:3. 17:25. Je 4:22. 9:3. Ho 5:4. Ac 17:23. 1 C 1:21. 2 C 4:6. 1 J 3:1. 4:8. **known**. Gr. *ginosko*. Objective knowledge, such as can be improved upon or gained by study; to know by experience or effort. ver. 19. Jn 10:15. Ac 19:15n. **but**. Jn *1:18. 6:46. 7:29. 10:15. 17:25. Mt √11:27. Lk 10:22. **I know**. Gr. *oida*, full conscious or intuitive knowledge which cannot be improved upon; to know without effort. Darby suggests objective knowledge may pass into conscious knowledge, but not the reverse (*New Translation*, 1 C 8:1n). These two words for knowledge are contrasted in Jn 13:7 and He 8:11. The believer's knowledge of having eternal life is expressed by *oida*, 2 T *1:12. 1 J √5:13. Paul's knowledge of a man in Christ (2 C 12:2, 3), Timothy's knowledge of Paul (2 T 3:14), and very remarkably, Timothy's knowledge of the Holy Scriptures from a child (2 T 3:15), all use *oida*, and refer to inward conscious knowledge. Compare *epiginosko*, Mt +*11:27n. **and if**. √184C, Mt +4:9. **I shall**. ver. 44. 1 J 1:6. *2:4, 22. 5:10. Re 3:9. **and keep**. ver. 29, 51. Jn 14:31. 15:10.

56. father. √171G, Ge +13:8. **Abraham**. ver. 33, 39. Ac 7:2. **rejoiced**. Ge 17:17. *22:13, 14, 18. Mt 13:17. Lk 2:28-30. 10:24. Ga *3:7-9, 14-18. He 11:13, 39, 40. 1 P 1:10-12. **to see**. Lk 17:22. **my day**. 1 C *2:8. **he saw**. Jn 1:3. Ge √17:1. Ex +*6:3. Ac 7:38. Re +*1:8. 15:3.

57. the Jews. ver. 22, 31, 52. Jn +5:10. **not yet**. Lk 3:23. **hast thou**. ver. 52.

58. Verily. ver. 34, 51. Jn +1:51. **Before**. ver. +*35. Jn √1:1, 2. *17:5, 24. Ps 68:4. Pr *8:22-30. Is +*9:6. *43:13. Mi +*5:2. Col *1:17. He 1:10-12. +*13:8. 1 P 1:20. Re 1:+*8, 11, 17, 18. 2:8. That our Lord by this expression asserted his divinity and eternal existence as the great I AM, appears evident from the use of the present tense, instead of the preter, from its being in answer to the Jews, who inquired whether he had seen Abraham, and from its being thus understood by the multitude, who were exasperated at it to such a degree that they took up stones to stone him. The ancient Jews not only believed that the Messiah was superior to and Lord of all the patriarchs, even of angels (see Yalkut Simeoni on Is 52:13. Bereshith Rabba on Ge 28:10. Zohar, Gen. fol. 88), but that his celestial nature existed with God, from whom it emanated before the Creation (Netzach Israel, c. 35, fol. 38), and that creation was effected by his ministry (Zohar, l. fol. 128, on Ge 49:11). Ex *3:14. Is *43:13, 15. 44:6, 8. 46:9. 48:12. Re +*1:8. **I am**. ver. +*24n, +*28. Jn 4:26. 13:19. 18:5, 6.

59. took. This action on the part of these Jewish hearers demonstrates that they understood Jesus to be making claim to deity. See related notes (Jn 5:18n and 10:32n). ver. 5, 6. Jn 7:1. +*10:30-33. 11:8. 18:31. Le 24:16. Lk *4:29. 13:34. Ac 7:57, 58. **stones**. Ex= 17:4. **but**. Jn 5:13. 10:39, 40. 11:54. Ge 19:11. 2 K 6:18-20. Lk +*4:30. 24:31. Ac 8:39, 40. **hid**. Jn 10:39. 12:36. Pr +*22:3. Lk +*4:30. **passed by**. Jn 9:1.

JOHN 9

Jesus gives sight to one who was born blind, 1-7. The man shows his inquiring neighbors by what means

his eyes were opened, 8-12. He is brought to the Pharisees, who strictly examine both him and his parents, 13-23. They are offended at him for contending that Jesus is a prophet and disdainfully excommunicate him, 24-34. Jesus makes himself known to him as "the Son of God," he believes in him and worships him, 35-38. Christ declares the design of his coming to be that the blind might see and the seeing be made blind; with reference to the miracle and to the proud and willful blindness of the Pharisees, 39-41.

1. passed. Jn 8:59. **he saw**. ver. 32. **from**. Ac 3:2. 14:8.

2. disciples. Jn +2:2. **Master**. Jn +1:38. **who**. ver. 34. Mt 16:14. Lk √13:2-5. Ac *28:4. **this man**. √63I2, Jsh +3:3. Supply by ellipsis, "(that he is blind)." ver. 34. **his parents**. Ex +*20:5. 34:7. Nu 14:18. Dt 5:9. Ps 79:8. 109:14. Is 65:6, 7. Je 32:18. Ezk 18:4n.

3. Neither hath. Jb 1:8-12. 2:3-6. +*9:22n. 21:27. 22:5, etc. 32:3. 42:7. Ec 9:1, 2. Lk +*13:3n. Ac 28:4. **parents**. √63I1D, Nu +26:4. Supply by ellipsis (repetition: of preceding connected words), "(that he should be born blind)." **but**. Jn 11:4, 40. 14:11-13. Mt 11:5. Ac 4:21. **the works**. Jn +5:20. **manifest**. Jn 3:21. 5:36.

4. I. Jn 3:11. **must**. Jn 3:14. **work**. Jn *4:34. 5:19, 36. *10:32, 37, 38. *17:4. 19:30. Lk 13:32-34. Ac *4:20. **the works**. ver. 3. Jn +5:20. **that sent**. Jn +4:34. **while**. Jn 7:33. 11:9, 10. *12:35. 1 S 21:8. Ps 104:23. Ec *9:10. Is *38:18, 19. √55:6. Ro 13:12. Ga 6:10. Ep √5:16. Col √4:5. **the night**. Jb +*10:21. 36:20. **when no**. Ps +*146:4. Ec *9:10. **can work**. Ps 40:8. Ec +*1:15. +*11:3. Mt 21:28. Lk 12:37. *19:13. Re +*22:11.

5. long. Jn 1:4-9. √3:19-21. *8:12. *12:35, 36, 46. Is 42:6, 7. 49:6. *60:1-3. Ml 4:2. Mt 4:16. Lk 2:32. Ac 13:47. 26:18, 23. Ep *5:14. Re 21:23. **world**. Gr. *kosmos*, Mt +4:8. **I am**. Our Lord here claims one of the titles given by the Jews to the Divine Being. So in Bammidbar Rabba, sec. 15, fol. 229.1, "The Israelites said to God, O Lord of the universe, thou commandest us to light lamps to thee, yet thou art *the light of the world*." It was also a title of the Messiah (see Is 49:6. 60:1), and in a remarkable passage of Yalkut Rubeni, fol. 6, it is said on Ge 1:4, "From this we learn, that the holy and blessed God saw the *light of the Messiah*, and his works, before the world was created; and reserved it for the Messiah, and his generation, under the throne of his glory. Satan said to the holy and blessed God, For whom doest thou reserve that light which is under the throne of thy glory? God answered, For him who shall subdue thee, and overwhelm thee with confusion. Satan rejoined, Lord of the universe, show that person to me. God said, Come, and see him. When we saw him, he was greatly agitated, and fell upon his face, saying, Truly this is the Messiah, who shall cast me and idolaters into hell." **the light**. Mt 5:14. Ro 15:21. **world**. Gr. *kosmos*, Mt +4:8.

6. he spat. Mk 7:33. 8:23. Re 3:18. **anointed the eyes of the blind man with the clay**. or, spread the clay upon the eyes of the blind man. 2 K 20:7n. **made clay**. Is 64:8. 2 C 6:1. **the eyes**. Mt 9:29. 20:34. Mk 8:25.

7. Go. 2 K *5:10-14. **the pool**. ver. 11. Ne 3:15, Siloah. Is 8:6, Shiloah. Lk 13:4. **Siloam**. i.e. *sent forth, dart, branch, missle*, *S#4611g. ver. 11. Lk 13:4. **interpretation**. √95, Ps +7:13. Mk +5:41. **Sent**. Jn 10:36. Ro 8:3. Ga *4:4. **and came**. ver. 39. Jn 11:37. Ex

4:11. Ps 146:8. Is 29:18, 19. 32:3. 35:5. 42:7, 16-18. 43:8. Lk 2:32. +7:21. Ac 26:18.

8. **Is not**. Ru 1:19. 1 S 21:11, 12. **sat**. 1 S 2:8. Mk 10:46. Lk 16:20-22. 18:35. Ac 3:2-11.

10. **How were**. ver. 15, 21, 26. Jn 3:9. Ec 11:5. Mk 4:27. 1 C 15:35.

11. **A man**. ver. 6, 7, 27. Je 36:17, 18. **received sight**. Lk 4:18.

12. **Where**. Jn 5:11-13. 7:11. Ex 2:18-20.

13. **They brought**. Jn 8:3-8. 11:46, 47, 57. 12:19, 42.

14. **And**. ſ71, Jn +1:24. **the sabbath**. Jn 5:9, 16. 7:21-23. Mt 12:1-14. Mk 2:23-28. 3:1-6. Lk 6:1-11. +*13:10-17. 14:1-5.

15. **the Pharisees**. See on ver. 10, 11, 13, 26, 27, 40. Jn +1:24. **He put**. ver. 6, 7, 10.

16. **This man**. ver. 24, 30-33. Jn 3:2. 5:36. 14:11. 15:24. **not of God**. ver. 33. Jn 1:14. 6:46. 7:29. **because**. Jn 5:10. 7:23. Mt 12:2, 10. Mk 2:24. Lk 6:2. +*13:14n. 14:3. **How can**. ver. 33. **miracles**. Jn +2:11. **And there**. Jn 6:52. *7:12, 43. 10:19. Lk 13:51-53. Ac 14:4.

17. **blind**. ſ11, Ge +2:23. **again**. ver. 15. **He is**. Jn 3:2. *4:19. +*6:14. Mt +21:11. Lk 24:19. Ac 2:22. 3:22-26. 10:38.

18. **not believe**. Jn 5:44. 12:37-40. Ge 19:14. Is 26:11. 53:1. Lk +*16:31. He 3:15-19. 4:11.

19. **Is this**. See on ver. 8, 9. Ac 3:10. 4:14.

22. **These**. ſ71, Jn +1:24. **because**. Jn 7:13. 12:42, 43. 19:38. 20:19. Ps 27:1, 2. Pr √29:25. Is 51:7, 12. 57:11. Mt +*10:28. Mk *8:38. Lk 12:4-9. 22:56-61. Ac 5:13. Ga 2:11-13. Re +*21:8. **had agreed**. Jn 7:45-52. **if**. ſ184C, Mt +4:9. **confess**. Ro √10:9. **Christ**. Jn +1:20. **he should**. ver. 34. Jn 12:42. 16:2. Mt 18:17. Lk 6:22. Ac 4:18. 5:40. He 13:13.

23. **He is**. ver. 21.

24. **again**. ver. 17. **Give glory**. Jn √5:23. 8:49. 16:2. Jsh 7:19. 1 S 6:5-9. 1 Ch 16:28. Ezr 3:11. Ps 50:14, 15. Is 42:12. 66:5. Je 13:16. Ml 2:2. Lk 17:18. Ac 12:23. Ro 4:20. 10:2-4. Re 11:13. **we know**. ver. 16, 29, 31. Jn 3:2. 8:46. 14:30. 18:30. 19:6. Mk 15:28. Ro 8:3. 2 C √5:21. **a sinner**. Lk 7:39. 15:2. 19:7.

25. **one thing**. ver. 30. Jn 5:11. Ps 27:4. Ec 3:19. Mk 10:21. Lk +*10:42. Ph 3:13. 2 P 3:8. 1 J *5:10. **was blind**. ver. 18, 24. **now**. 2 C √5:17.

27. **I have**. ver. 10-15. Lk 22:67, 68. **hear**. ſ108B, Ac +22:9. Jn 8:43.

28. **they**. ver. 34. Jn 7:47-52. Is 51:7. Mt 5:11. 27:39. 1 C 4:12. 6:10. 1 P 2:23. **but**. Jn *5:45-47. 7:19. Ac 6:11-14. Ro 2:17.

29. **know**. ver. 24. Jn 1:17. Ex 19:20. Nu 12:2-7. 16:28. Dt 34:10. Ps 103:7. 105:26. 106:16. Ml 4:4. Ac 7:35. 26:22. He 3:2-5. **as for**. ver. 16, 24. 1 K 22:27. 2 K 9:11. Mt 12:24. 26:61. Lk 23:2. Ac 22:22. **we know not**. Jn 7:27, 28, 41, 42. 8:14, 41. 19:9. Ps 22:6. Is 53:2, 3.

30. **herein**. Jn 3:10. 12:37. Is 29:14. Mk 6:6. **and yet**. Ps √119:18. Is 29:18, 19. *35:4, 5. Mt 11:5. Lk *7:22. 2 C 4:6.

31. **heareth not sinners**. ſ101, Dt +32:42. Dt 1:45. 1 S 14:37. 28:6. 2 S +*22:42. 2 Ch=26:18. Jb *27:8, 9. *35:12, 13. *42:8. Ps *18:41. *34:15, 16. 50:16. +*66:18-20. 109:7. 140:8. Pr *1:28, 29. *15:8, 29. *21:13. *28:9. Is *1:15. *58:9. *59:2. Je *11:11. *14:12. 15:1. 18:17. La 3:8, 44. Ezk *8:18. +*14:3, 14. 20:3, 31. Ho 5:6. Mi *3:4. Zc *7:13. Ja +*4:3. 1 J 5:14, 16. **if any**. ſ184C, Mt +4:9. Ps 33:18. *34:15. Pr *15:29.

Ac 10:2-4. **and doeth**. T#534, 1325. Jn *4:34. +*7:17. √15:16. Jb 36:7. Ps 37:4. *40:8. 86:11. 119:47, 48. *143:10. Pr 28:9. Mt *7:21. 1 C +2:9 (T#289). He 10:7. 1 J *3:21, 22. **him he heareth**. Jn *11:41, 42. Ge 18:23-33. 19:29. *20:7. 1 K *17:20-22. *18:36-38. 2 Ch 32:20, 21. Ps *4:3. 10:17. +*34:15. *99:6. 106:23. 145:19. Je 15:1. Lk 18:13, 14. Jn 15:7. Ac 10:4. Ja +*5:15-18. 1 P *3:12.

32. **Since**. It is worthy of remark that from the foundation of the world, no person *born blind* had been restored to sight, even by surgical operation, till about the year 1728, when the celebrated Dr. Chesel-den, by couching the eyes of a young man fourteen years of age, restored them to perfect vision. This was the effect of well-directed surgery: that performed by Christ was wholly a miracle, effected by the power of God. The simple means employed could have had no effect in this case, and were merely employed as symbols (2 K +*13:17n. 20:7n). **the world**. Gr. *aion*, Mt +6:13. Jb 20:4. Is 64:4. Lk 1:70. Re 16:18.

33. **If this**. ſ184B, Lk +7:39. **were**. ver. 16. Jn 3:2. 10:21. Ac 5:38, 39.

34. **wast**. ver. 2. Jn 8:41. Jb 14:4. 15:14-16. 25:4. Ps *51:5. Ga 2:15. Ep *2:3. **and dost**. ver. 40. Jn 7:48, 49. Ge 19:9. Ex 2:14. 1 S +*25:17. 2 Ch 25:16. Pr 9:7, 8. 26:12. 29:1. Is +*65:5n. Mt +*7:6. Lk 11:45. 14:11. 18:10-14, 17. 1 P 5:5. **And they**. ver. 22. Jn 6:37. Pr 22:10. Is *66:5. Lk *6:22, 23. 3 J 9, 10. Re 13:17. **cast him out**. *or*, excommunicated him. ver. 22, 35. Jn √6:37. ●12:31. 2 Ch=13:9. Mt 18:17, 18. Lk *6:22, 23. 1 C 5:4, 5, 13. 3 J 10.

35. **cast him out**. ver. 34. 2 Ch=13:9. **and when**. Jn 1:43. 5:14. Ps √27:10. Ro 10:20. **Dost**. Jn 1:49, 50. √3:15-18, 36. 6:69. 8:28. 11:26, 27. +*20:28, 31. Ac 8:37. 9:20. 1 J 4:15. 5:5, 10-13, 20. **believe**. 1 J √5:13. **the Son of God**. Jn 1:18, 34. ●+51. 10:36. Ps *2:7, 12. Mt +*14:33. 16:16. Mk 1:1. Ro 1:4. He 1:2-9. 1 J √5:13.

36. **Who**. Jn 1:38. Pr 30:3, 4. SS 5:9. Mt 11:3. Ro 10:14. **might**. ſ96C1, Ge +4:1. **believe**. ver. 35. Jn +4:39.

37. **Thou**. Jn √4:26. +*7:17. 14:21-23. Ps *25:8, 9, 14. Mt 11:25. 13:11, 12. Ac 10:31-33.

38. **Lord**. Jn +√20:28. Ps 2:12. *45:11. Mt 8:2. *14:33. *28:9, 17. Lk *24:52. Re *5:9-14. **worshipped**. Mt +8:2. +*14:33. 1 P *2:9.

39. **For judgment**. Jn 2:13-16. *3:17. *5:22-27, 37-46. 8:15-55. 11:38. 12:47, 48. Je 1:9, 10. Lk 2:34. 13:30. 2 C 2:16. **I am come**. Jn +11:27. Lk +*19:10. **world**. Gr. *kosmos*, Mt +4:8. Jn 8:23. 11:9. 12:25, 31. 13:1. 16:11. 18:36. 1 J 4:17. **might see**. Ge +*3:7. **that they**. ver. 25, 36-38. Jn *8:12. 12:46. Mt 11:5, 25. Lk 1:79. 4:18. 7:21. 10:21. Ac *26:18. 2 C √4:4-6. Ep 5:14. 1 P 2:9. **and that they**. Is *5:21. Mt 9:13. *13:13-15. Mk 4:12. Lk 1:52, 53. 2 C 2:16. Re 3:17, 18. **might be**. Jn √3:19. 12:40, 41. Is 6:9, 10. 29:10. 42:18-20. 44:18. Mt *6:23. 13:13-15. +23:16. Lk 11:34, 35. Ro 11:7-10. 2 Th √2:10-12. 1 J 2:11.

40. **Pharisees which**. ver. 13, 15, 16. Jn +1:24. **Are**. ver. 34. Jn 7:47-52. Mt +*15:12-14. 23:16, 17, 19, 24, 26. Lk 11:39, 40, 45, 46. Ro *2:19-22. Re *3:17. **blind**. ver. 39. Mt +*15:14. +23:16.

41. **If**. ſ184B, Lk +7:39. Jn 15:22-24. +*19:11. Pr 26:12. Is *5:20, 21. Je 2:35. Lk 12:47. 18:14. He 10:26, 27. Ja √4:17. 1 J √1:8-10. **We see**. Pr 26:12. 29:20. Mt +*6:23. 1 C *3:18.

JOHN 10

True shepherds enter in by the door of the sheep-fold, are acknowledged by the sheep, and go before them; being thus distinguished from dishonest and corrupt teachers, 1-8. Christ is the Door, and "the good Shepherd, who lays down his life for the sheep," 9-18. Divers opinions are held concerning him, 19-21. He proves his mission by his works; shows the character of his sheep, to whom "he gives eternal life, neither shall any pluck them out of his hands;" and that "he and the Father are one," 22-30. The Jews attempt to stone him as a blasphemer, but he justifies his doctrine and escapes from them, 31-39. He goes beyond Jordan, where many believe on him, 40-42.

1. **verily.** Jn +1:51. See on 3:3. 1 P 1:11. **He.** ver. 9. Je 14:15. *23:16, 17, 21, 32. 28:15-17. 29:31, 32. Ezk *13:2-6. Mt 7:15. 23:16, etc. Ro 10:15. Ep 4:8-12. He *5:4. 1 P *1:10. 2 P 2:1. 1 J *4:1. **the same.** ver. 8, 10. Is 56:10-12. Ezk 34:2-5. Zc 11:4, 5, 16, 17. Ro 16:18. 2 C √11:13-15. T 1:11. 2 P 2:3, 14-19.

2. **he that.** ver. 7, 9. Ac √20:28. 1 T 3:2-7. 4:14. T 1:5. Re 1:20. 2:1. **the shepherd.** ver. 11, 12, 14. Ps √23:1. 80:1. Ec 12:11. Is 40:11. 63:11. Ezk 34:23. Mi 5:5. Zc 11:3, 5, 8. 13:7. He √13:20. 1 P *2:25. *5:4.

3. **the porter.** Is 53:10-12. Mk 13:34. 1 C 16:9. Col 4:3. 1 P 1:12. Re 3:7, 8, *20. **the sheep.** ver. 4, 16, 26, 27. Jn *6:37, 45. SS 8:13. **his voice.** Ps 29:3. SS 2:14. 8:13. **and he.** ver. 14, 27. Ex 33:17. Ro 8:30. Ph 4:3. 2 T *2:19. Re 20:15. **by name.** 1 Ch=16:41. Ps +*40:17. Is 43:1. 45:3, 4. 49:1. 62:2. Lk 19:5. 3 J 14. Re 3:5. **and leadeth.** ver. 9. Ps *23:2, 3. *78:52, 53. 80:1. Is *40:11. *42:16. *49:9, 10. Je 31:8, 9. *50:4-6. Ezk *34:11-16. Re *7:17.

4. **he goeth before.** Jn 12:26. 13:15. +*14:2, 3. Nu 27:16, 17. Dt 1:30. Jsh 3:11. 2 S 5:24. Is 30:12. +*40:11. 52:12. Ezk 46:10. Mi 2:12, 13. Mt 16:24. Lk 19:28. 1 C *11:1. Ep 5:1, 2. Ph *2:5-11. He 6:20. *12:2, 3. 1 P 2:21. 4:1, 2. 5:3. **for.** ver. 8, 16. Jn 3:29. 18:37. SS 2:8. 5:2.

5. **a stranger.** ver. 12, 13. 1 K 22:7. Pr +*19:27. Mk +*4:24. Lk +*8:18. Ga 1:8. Ep *4:11-15. Col *2:6-10. 1 Th 5:21. 2 T *3:5-7. 4:3, 4. 1 P 2:1-3. 1 J √2:19-21, 27. 4:5, 6. 2 J *10. Re *2:2. **not.** ſ158, Mt +5:18.

6. **parable.** Jn 16:25, 29. 2 P 2:2. **unto them.** Jn 9:40. **they understood not.** Jn 6:52, 60. 7:36. 8:27, 43. Ps 82:5. 106:7. Pr 28:5. Is *6:9, 10. 56:11. Da 12:10. Mt +*13:13, 14, 51. Mk 9:32. 1 C √2:14. 1 J *5:20. **know not.** Ex 1:8.

7. **again.** Jn 8:12, 21. **I am.** ver. 1, 9, 11, 14. Jn 6:35, 41, 48, 51. 11:25. √14:6. 15:1, 5. Ep 2:18. He *10:19-22. **the sheep.** Ps 79:13. 95:7. 100:3. Is *53:6. Ezk 34:31. Lk 15:4-6.

8. **All.** ſ171A, Ex +9:6. **came.** See on ver. 1. Is 56:10-12. Ezk 22:25-28. *34:2-4. Zp 3:3, 4. Zc 11:4-9, 16, 17. Mt 23:2-4. Ac *5:36, 37. **thieves.** ver. 1. Je 23:1, 2. Ezk 34:2. Ob 5. **but.** ver. 5, 27.

9. **am.** ſ119, Ge +49:9. **the door.** ver. 1, 7. Jn √14:6. Ro *5:1, 2. Ep *2:18. He *10:19-22. **if.** ſ184C, Mt +4:9. **be saved.** Jn 5:34. **and shall.** Ps *23:1-6. 80:1-3. 95:7. 100:3, 4. Is 40:11. 49:9, 10. Ezk *34:12-16. Zc 10:12. **go in and out.** ſ171J3, Nu +27:17. Ps 121:8. Ac 1:21.

10. **thief.** ver. *1. Jn 12:6. Is 56:11. Ezk *34:2-4. Ho 7:1. Mt *21:13. 23:14. Mk 11:17. Ro 2:21. 2 P *2:1-3. **kill.** Je 23:1. Ezk 34:3. **destroy.** Gr. *apollumi*,

Mt +2:13. **I am come.** Jn *3:17. 6:33, 51. *12:47. Mt +*18:11. +*20:28. Lk +*19:10. 1 T *1:15. **life.** T#835. Jn *5:21. 6:57. 8:12. 14:19. 20:31. Ro 6:8, 11. 2 C 13:4. Ga *2:20. Ep 2:1, 5, 6. Col *3:3, 4. 2 T 1:1, 10. 1 J √5:12. **more abundantly.** Jn 1:16. SS 5:1. Ro 5:13-21. He 6:17. *7:25. 2 P √1:11.

11. **the good shepherd.** ver. 14. Ge=37:2. Ex=3:1. Ps *23:1. 80:1. Is 40:11. 63:11. Ezk *34:12, 23. 37:24. Mi 5:4. Zc 13:7. He *13:20. 1 P *2:25. *5:4. Re 7:17. **the good.** God the Son possesses the attribute of essential goodness (Mt +*28:19n), as does God the Father (Mk +*10:18n) and God the Holy Spirit (Ps +*143:10). Jn 7:12. 8:46. Ac 10:38. **giveth.** ver. 15, 17. Jn 13:37. *15:13. Ge 31:39, 40. 1 S 17:34, 35. 2 S 24:17. Is *53:6. Mt 20:28. Mk 10:45. Ep 5:2. T *2:14. 1 P *2:24. 1 J 2:2. 3:16. **life.** Gr. *psyche*, ſ121A7, Mt +2:20. ſ121A7, Ge +9:5.

12. **he that.** ver. 13. Is 56:10-12. Ezk 34:2-6. Zc *11:16, 17. 1 T 3:3, 8. 2 T 4:10. T 1:7. 1 P 5:2. 2 P 2:3. **the wolf coming.** Mt 7:15. 10:16. Ac 20:29. **leaveth the sheep.** Zc 11:17. 13:7. **catcheth.** ver. 28, 29. Is 9:20. **scattereth.** Jn 11:52. Je 10:21. 23:1-3.

13. **hireling.** 1 P 5:2. **careth not.** Jn 12:6. Zc 11:16. Ac 18:17. Ro *16:18. Ph 2:20. 3:19. 1 P 5:7.

14. **good.** See on ver. 11. Ge=37:2. Ex=3:11. Ps 23:1. Is 63:11. Lk *18:19. **know.** ver. 27. Jn +*14:20. Ps *1:6. Na *1:7. Mt ❍*7:22, 23. 1 C *8:3. Ga 4:9. 2 T *2:19. 1 J 4:7, 8. Re 2:2, 9, 13, 19. 3:1, 8, 15. **am.** ver. 4. Jn 14:9. *17:3, 8. Is *53:11. 2 C *4:6. Ep 1:17. 3:19. Ph 3:8. 2 T √1:12. 1 J *5:20.

15. **As.** Jn 1:18. 6:46, 57. 8:55. 17:25. Mt +*11:27. Lk 10:21, 22. Re 5:2-9. **knoweth me.** Dt=34:10, 11. **so know.** Jn 7:29. 8:19. 14:7. 16:3. 1 J 2:13. 3:1. **and I lay.** ver. 11, 17. Jn 15:13. Is *53:4-6, 8, 10. Da +*9:26. Zc *13:7. Mt *20:28. Ga 1:4. *3:13. Ep 5:2, 25. 1 T 2:5, 6. T *2:14. 1 P 1:18, 19. *2:24. *3:18. 1 J *2:2. *3:16. Re 5:9. **life.** Gr. *psyche*, ſ121A7, Mt +2:20. ſ121A7, Ge +9:5.

16. **other.** Gr. *allos*, Mt 10:23n. Jn *11:52. *17:20. Ge +*49:10. Ps 22:26-31. *72:17-19. *82:8. *86:9. 98:2, 3. Is 11:10. 14:17. 24:13-16. 42:10-12. *43:6. *49:6. 52:10. *56:8. Ho *1:10. 2:23. Zc 2:11. *8:20-23. Ac 18:10. Ro *9:23-26. *15:9-13. Ep √2:14. 3:6. 4:4. He 11:40. 1 P *2:10. Re *7:9. **sheep.** ſ11, Ge +2:23. **this fold.** ver. 1. **them.** Ezk 34:11-13. Mt +*8:11, 12. Ac *15:14. Ro 8:29, 30. Ep *2:1-5, 15-18. 2 Th √2:13, 14. T 3:3-5. 1 P 2:25. **must.** Jn 3:14. **bring.** or, lead. ver. 3. **they shall.** ver. *27. Jn 5:25. *6:37. 18:37. Mt 17:5. Ac *22:14. 28:28. 1 J 4:6. Re √3:20. **there.** Ezk 37:22. Ep *2:14. **one fold.** Jn 11:52. 12:32. 17:11. Ps +*149:9. Ezk 37:22. Lk 12:32. Ac +√10:11. 1 C √12:12, 13. Ga *3:28. Ep +*4:4n. Col *3:11. He 11:40. **one shepherd.** ver. 2, *11. Jn 21:22. Ec 12:11. Ezk 34:23. 37:24. He *13:20. 1 P *2:25. 5:4.

17. **my Father love.** Jn *3:35. 5:20. 15:9, 10. 17:4, 5, 24-26. Is 42:1, 21. 53:7-12. Ph 2:9. He 2:9. 12:2. 1 P 2:23. **lay down.** ver. 11. Ep *5:2. **life.** Gr. *psyche*, ſ121A7, Mt +2:20. ſ121A7, Ge +9:5.

18. **No man.** Jn *18:5, 6. *19:11. Mt *26:53-56. **but.** ver. 11. Jn *2:19-21. Is *53:10-12. Ac *2:24, 32. *3:15. Ph 2:6-8. T *2:9, 14, 15. **of myself.** Jn 5:30. Le=1:3. He 9:14. **power to lay.** Lk 23:46. **power to take.** Jn +*2:19. Ac 2:24. Ph 2:7, 8. **This commandment.** Jn *6:38. 12:49. 14:31. 15:10. Ps *40:6-8. He *5:6-9. 10:6-10. **my Father.** ver. 25, 29, 37. Jn 5:17. 18:11.

19. **a division.** Jn 7:40-43. 9:16. Mt 10:34, 35. Lk 12:51-53. Ac 14:4. 23:7-10. 1 C 3:3. 11:18. **the Jews.** ver. 24, 31, 33. Jn +5:10.

20. **He hath.** Jn 7:20. 8:48, 52. Mt 9:34. 10:25. Mk 3:21, 22. Ac 26:24, 25. **is mad.** Mk 3:21. Ac 26:24. **why.** Jn 7:46-52. 8:47. 9:28, 29. Is 53:3. Ac 18:14, 15. 25:19, 20. 26:30-32.

21. **that hath.** Mt +4:24. **Can.** Jn 9:6, 7, 32, 33. Ex 4:11. 8:19. Ps 94:9. 146:8. Pr 20:12. Is 35:5, 6. Mt 11:5.

22. **And.** ƒ71, Jn +1:24. **it was winter.** ƒ49. Chronographia; or, Description of Time B455. The figure is used, when, by the addition of the time, something explanatory is given which helps to the understanding of what is said, supplies some important fact or implies some extra lesson. Here, this brief description of time is intended to convey to us a sense of the humiliation and rejection of the Lord Jesus. The next verse tells how he "walked in Solomon's porch," on the bleak summit of Mount Moriah, to keep himself warm; no one asking him to house or inviting him even into such of the temple chambers as had fires in them. Jn 18:18. For other instances of this figure see Mt 11:25, 26. Mk 6:48. Ac 2:15. 10:3, 9.

23. **in Solomon's.** Ac 3:11. 5:12.

24. **round about.** Ps 88:17. **How.** 1 K 18:21. Da *9:24. Mt 11:3. Lk 3:15. **make us to doubt.** or, hold us in suspense. ƒ121A9, Ge +23:8. **us.** Gr. *psyche*, ƒ171Q2, Mt +12:18. **If.** ƒ184A, 1 C +15:2. Jn 1:19. 8:25, 53. 9:22. Lk 22:67-70. 2 C 3:12. **tell us.** Mt 26:63. Lk 22:67. **plainly.** ƒ24I, Is +21:7. Jn 16:25. 18:20g.

25. **I told.** Jn 2:16. 4:26. *5:17-43. 7:38. *8:12, 24, 56, 58. 9:37. **the works.** ver. 32, 38. Jn *3:2. 5:36. 7:31. 11:47. 12:37. 14:11. 20:30, 31. Ac 2:22. *10:38. He √2:3, 4. **Father's name.** Jn +5:17, 43. Re 14:1. **bear witness.** ver. 38. Jn +*5:36, 39. Ac +*10:43. Ro +*1:4.

26. **because.** ver. 4, 27. Jn *6:37, 44, 45, 65. √8:47. *12:37-40. Ro 11:7, 8. 2 C *4:3, 4. Ep *2:8. 1 J *4:6.

27. **My sheep.** ver. 4, 8, 14, 16. Jn *5:25. *8:31, 43. Ps 119:94. Mt *17:5. Ac 3:23. He 3:7, 8. Re √3:20. **hear.** Jn *5:24. Lk +*8:18. 1 T 4:1n. **my voice.** Ge 3:8. Dt 8:20. 26:17. **and I.** ƒ148, Ge +8:22. ver. *3, 14. Mt *7:23. *25:12. Lk *13:27. 1 C *8:3. Ga 4:9. 2 T *2:19. **know.** ƒ121C2A1, Jb +19:25. **they follow.** ver. *4. Jn *8:12. *12:26. 21:22. 1 K *18:21. Ps *119:3. Mt *16:24. Mk 8:34. 10:21. Lk *9:23. Ep 5:1. He *2:1. Re *14:4.

28. **And.** ƒ148, Ge +8:22. **I give.** ver. 10. Jn √3:16, 36. +*5:39, 40. *6:27, 40, 47, 68. *11:25. *17:2, 3. 1 Ch 17:22. Ac √13:48. Ro 5:21. √6:23. 1 T *1:16. 1 J 2:25. √5:13-20. Ju *21. **eternal.** Gr. *aionios*, Mt +18:8. Jn +4:14. **they.** Jn *3:15. 4:14. √5:24. *6:37, 39, 40. 14:19. *17:12. *18:9. 1 S *2:9. Jb 17:9. Ps *37:28. 103:17, 18. *125:1, 2. Pr +*4:18. 24:16. Is 45:17. 54:17. +*55:3. Je 31:3, 34. 32:40. Mk 13:22. Ro 5:2, 9, 17. √8:1, 29, 33-39. Ph *1:6. Col *3:3, 4. 2 Th √2:13, 14. He *7:25. 1 P √1:5. 2 P +*1:10. 1 J √2:19. √5:13, 18. Ju √1, 24. **never.** Gr. *aion*, Mt +6:13. ƒ158, Mt +5:18. **perish.** Gr. *apollumi*, Mt +2:13. T#515. Jn *3:16, 36. √5:24. 6:*39, 40, 47, 51, 54. 17:12. Jb *17:9. Ps √37:23, 24. 89:30-37. +125:2 (T#95). Pr +*4:18. Is 54:10. 55:3. Je *32:40. Mt 18:14. 24:24. Ro 2:12. *8:30, 38, 39. 1 C 1:18. 8:11. Ep √4:30. Ph *1:6. 2 Th 2:14. He *6:19. 2 T *4:18. 1 P *1:3-5, 9. 2 P 3:*9, +18 (T#667). 1 J 5:18. **neither.** Jn *6:37, 39. 17:11, 12.

Dt 33:3. Jsh +*20:5. Ps 31:5. Lk *22:31, 32. 23:46. Ac 7:59. 2 T √1:12. He √7:25. **pluck.** ver. 12. **my hand.** ƒ22A14.3, Ps +31:5. ƒ22A14.6. Anthropomorphism B879. A hand is attributed to God, denoting his power of preservation. Dt 32:39. Ps +*37:24. Is 43:13. 49:2. 51:16.

29. **My Father.** ver. 18, 25, 37. Jn +5:17. **which.** Jn √6:37, 39. *17:2, 6, 9, 11. **is greater.** ƒ96E4, Mt +13:32. ƒ22I3C. Anthropomorphism B895. Comparison is used of God: He is greater than all. Jn +*14:28. Ex 18:11. Ps 145:3. Da 4:3. Ml 1:14. **hand.** ƒ22A14.3, Ps +31:5. ƒ22A14.6, ver. +28. Dt 33:3. Is 43:13.

30. **I and.** ver. 38. Jn +√1:1, 2. +√5:17, 23. √8:58. *14:9, 10, 23. *16:15. *17:10, 11, 21-23. Mt +*11:27. +√28:19. 1 T *3:16. T √2:13. 1 J *5:7, 20. **are one.** This oneness Jesus claimed with the Father must not be reduced to mere oneness in "agreement, purpose and organization," equating this degree of oneness with that of believers with the Father and the Son (Jn 17:20-22), for if this is all Christ asserted, he would not have been accused of blasphemy (ver. 33), for even the Old Testament prophets had asserted as much (Is 48:16). Jn *5:19, 23. 12:45. 14:7, 9, ⦿+*28. 17:5, 11, 21, 22.

31. **the Jews.** ver. 19, 24. Jn +5:10. **took up stones.** Jn √5:18. +*7:1. *8:59. 11:8. Ex *17:4. 1 S 30:6. Mt 21:35. 23:35. Ac 7:52, 58, 59. **to stone.** Dt 17:5.

32. **answered.** Jn 5:17, 19. Mk +11:14. **Many.** ver. 25, 37. Jn 5:19, +20, 36. Mt 11:5. Ac 2:22. *10:38. **for which.** 1 S 19:4-6. 2 Ch 24:20-22. Ps 35:12. 109:4, 5. Ec 4:4. 1 J 3:12. **stone.** Stoning was the prescribed punishment for the non-religious crimes of (1) unchastity, including adultery and rape, Le 20:10. Dt 22:21-24. (2) insubordination to constituted authorities (a) parents, Ex 21:15, 17. Le 20:9. Dt 21:18-21. (b) priest or judge, Dt 17:12. Stoning was the prescribed punishment for five capital crimes of a religious nature: (1) sacrifice to idols. Ex 22:20. Le 20:2. Dt 13:6-17. 17:2-7. 2 K 10:18-25. 11:18. 23:5, 20. (2) sorcery. Ex 22:18. Le 20:27. 1 S 28:3, 9. (3) profaning the Sabbath. Ex 31:14, 15. 35:2. Nu 15:32-36. (4) blasphemy. Le 24:10-16, 23. 1 K 21:13. (5) false prophecy. Dt 13:1-5. 18:20. 1 K 18:40. 20:27, 28. When Jesus asked upon what grounds they were about to stone him, their unequivocal answer was for blasphemy, explained in the very next verse, "because that thou, being a man, makest thyself God." As in the other two cases where the Jews were about to stone Jesus (Jn 5:18. 8:59), Jesus did not deny the correctness of their understanding of his claims. The Jews, therefore, correctly understood Christ's claim to be deity, and on this basis they charged him with blasphemy. This proves that Jesus himself asserted his own deity and equality with God the Father (see Jn 5:18n). At John 5:18 the assertion that Jesus made himself "equal with God" is John's own assertion under divine inspiration, not merely his report of the understanding of the Jews.

33. **but.** ver. *36. Jn 19:7. Le *24:14-16. 1 K 21:10, 13. Mt 9:3. 26:65, 66. Mk 2:7. 14:63, 64. **makest thyself God.** ver. *30. Jn +√5:18n. +√20:28. Ps +*82:6n. Ro *9:5. 13:1. Ph *2:6. T *2:13. He +*1:8.

34. **written.** Jn 8:17. **in.** Jn 12:34. 15:25. Ro 3:10-19. 1 C 14:21. **I said.** Ps 82:1, ⅃6, 7. **gods.** Ex *4:16. 7:1. *22:28. Ps +*86:6n. *138:1.

35. **If.** ƒ184A, 1 C +15:2. **gods.** Ex +12:12. Ps +138:1. **unto.** Ge 15:1. Dt 18:15, 18-20. 1 S 14:36,

37. 15:1. 23:9-11. 28:6. 30:8. 2 S 7:5. 1 Ch 22:8. 2 Ch 11:2, 3. *19:2. Je 1:2. 2:1. Lk 3:2. +5:1. Ro *13:1. **the scripture.** Jn +2:22. *12:38, 39. *19:28, 36, 37. Ps +*56:4. Mt +*5:18. *24:35. *26:53-56. 27:35. Lk 16:17. *24:26, 27, 44-46. Ac 1:16. **broken.** Jn +*5:39. 7:23. Mt +*5:18. *26:53-56. Lk 16:17.

36. **whom.** Jn 3:34. *6:27, 69. Ps 2:2, 6-12. Is 11:2-5. 42:1, 3. 49:1-3, 6-8. 55:4, 5. 61:1-3. Je 1:5. **sanctified.** Jn *17:19. Lk 4:18. **sent.** Jn *3:17. 5:30, 36, 37. 6:38, 39, 57. 8:42. 17:4, 5, 8, 18, 21. Ge=12:1-4. Ro 8:3. Ga *4:4. 1 J 4:9-14. **world.** Gr. *kosmos*, Mt +4:8. **blasphemest.** ver. +*33. **I said.** ver. 30. Jn 5:17, 18. **I am.** ver. *30-33. Jn +*5:17, 18. *9:35-37. 19:7. +√20:28, 31. Mt +*14:33. 26:63-66. 27:43, +*54n. Lk +*1:35. Ro *1:4. √9:5.

37. **If I do not.** ſ184A, 1 C +15:2. ver. 25, 32. Jn 5:31. 12:37-40. 14:10. 15:24. Mt 11:20-24. **the works.** ver. 32. Jn +5:20. **my Father.** ver. 18, 25, 29. Jn +5:17. **believe me not.** Jn 5:47.

38. **But if.** ſ184A, 1 C +15:2. **though.** ſ185B, Ga +6:1. ſ184C, Mt +4:9. Jn 14:11. **believe the.** ver. 25. Jn 3:2. *5:36. Ac 2:22. 4:8-12. **that ye.** ver. 30. Jn 8:29. *14:9-11, 20. 17:11, *21-23. Col *2:9. **and I.** Jn *5:17-23. 10:30. 12:45. 14:1, 7-10. *17:10, 11, 21-23.

39. **they sought.** ver. 31. Jn *7:1, 30, 44. *8:59. Lk +*4:29, 30. **escaped.** Jn *8:59. Pr +*22:3.

40. **again.** Jn 1:28. **beyond Jordan.** Mt 19:1. Mk 10:1. **the place.** Jn *1:28. *3:23, 26. **there.** Jn 7:1. 11:54.

41. **many.** Jn 3:26. Mt 4:23-25. Mk 1:37. Lk 5:1. 12:1. **resorted.** Ps 71:3. Mk 10:1. **John did.** Mt 14:2. Lk 7:26-28. **miracle.** Jn +2:11. **but.** Jn 1:7, 29, 33, 34. *3:29-36. 5:33. Mt *3:11, 12. Lk *7:29, 30.

42. **many.** Jn +7:31. **believed.** Jn 2:23. 4:39, 41. *8:30. *11:45. 12:42. **there.** ver. 40.

JOHN 11

Lazarus, the brother of Martha and Mary, is sick, 1, 2. They send to Jesus, who, declaring his "sickness not unto death, but for the glory of God," abides two days where he is, 3-6. He informs the disciples that Lazarus is dead, and intimating that he would raise him to life, proposes going to him. The disciples, fearing the Jews, express their surprise but resolve to accompany him, 7-16. Jesus arrives at Bethany, after Lazarus has been dead four days, 17, 18. He assures Martha that her brother shall rise again and requires her to believe that he is the "Resurrection and the Life," she confesses her faith in him as "the Christ, the Son of God," 19-27. She calls Mary, who comes with her, 28-31. Jesus, sympathizing with the mourners, "groans in spirit" and "weeps;" the remarks of the Jews on the occasion, 32-37. He comes to the grave, appeals to God as his Father who sent him, and calls Lazarus out of the grave, 38-44. Many Jews believe, but some inform the Pharisees, 45, 46. They hold a council; and concur with Caiaphas, who instigates them to put Jesus to death; while, as high priest, Caiaphas was led, beyond his intention, to prophesy concerning the gracious intention and extensive efficacy of his death, 47-53. Jesus retires from places of public resort, 54. Before the Passover, the Jews inquire about him, the rulers having given orders to apprehend him, 55-57.

1. **Now.** The raising of Lazarus from the dead, being a work of Christ beyond greatest measure, the most stupendous of all he had hitherto performed, and beyond all others calculated to evince his divine majesty, was therefore purposely recorded by the Evangelist John while it was omitted by the other Evangelists; probably, as Grotius supposes, because they wrote their histories during the life of Lazarus and did not mention him for fear of exciting the malice of the Jews against him. We find from Jn 12:10 that they sought to put him to death, that our Lord might not have such a monument of his power and goodness remaining in the land. **was sick.** ver. 3, 6. Ge 48:1. 2 K 20:1-12. Ac 9:37. **Lazarus.** ver. 5, +11. Jn 12:1, 2, 9, 10, 17. Lk 16:20-25. **Bethany.** ver. 18. Jn 12:1. Mt 21:17. Mk 11:1. **Mary.** Lk *10:38-42.

2. **that Mary.** Jn 12:3. Mt 26:6, 7. Mk 14:3. **anointed.** Lk 7:37, 38.

3. **Lord.** ſ171E12, Ge +14:22. **he.** ver. 1, 5, 11, 36. Jn 13:23. Ge 22:2. Ps 16:3. Ph 2:26, 27. 2 T 4:20. He 12:6, 7. Ja 5:14, 15. Re 3:19.

4. **This.** ver. 11. Jn *9:3. Mt 9:24. Mk 5:39-42. Lk 8:52. Ro 11:11. **unto death.** 2 K 20:1. **for.** ver. 40. Jn 9:24. 12:28. 13:31, 32. Ph 1:11. 1 P 4:11, 14. **that.** Jn 2:11. √5:23. 7:39. 8:54. 13:31, 32. 17:1, 5, 10. Ph 1:20. 1 P 1:21.

5. **loved.** ver. 3, 8, 36. Jn 13:23. 15:9-13. 16:27. 17:26. Mk 10:21.

6. **he abode.** Jn 2:4. 7:6, 8. Ge 22:14. 42:24. 43:29-31. 44:1-5. 45:1-5. Ps *37:7. Is +*30:18. √55:8, 9. Mt 15:22-28.

7. **Let.** Jn 10:40-42. Lk 9:51. Ac 15:36. 20:22-24.

8. **the Jews.** ver. 19, 31, 33, 36, 45, 54. Jn +5:10. 7:1. 8:59. 10:31, 39. Ps 11:1-3. Mt 16:21-23. Ac 21:12, 13. **and goest.** Ac *20:24.

9. **Are.** ſ85B, Ge +13:9. Jn *9:4. Lk 13:31-33. **twelve hours.** The Jews divided the day into twelve hours. These hours were computed from about six in the morning until six in the evening. The first hour corresponds to our 7 A.M., the second to 8 A.M., the third to our 9 P.M. (Mt 20:3. Mk 15:25. Ac 2:15. ◐23:23), the fourth hour to our 10 A.M., the fifth to our 11 A.M., the sixth to our noon (Mt 20:5. 27:45. Mk 15:33. Lk *23:44n. Jn 4:6. 19:14. Ac 10:9), the seventh hour to our 1 P.M. (Jn 4:52), the eighth to our 2 P.M., the ninth to our 3 P.M. (Mt 20:5. 27:45, 46. Mk 15:33, 34. Lk *23:44n. Ac 3:1. 10:3, 30), the tenth hour to our 4 P.M. (Jn 1:39), the eleventh hour to our 5 P.M. (Mt 20:6, 9), the twelfth hour to our 6 P.M. For the night time divisions into watches, see Mt 14:25n. **If any.** ſ184C, Mt +4:9. **he stumbleth not.** Jn 12:35. Pr 3:23. Je 31:9. **world.** Gr. *kosmos*, Mt +4:8.

10. **But if.** ſ184C, Mt +4:9. **walk in.** Jn *12:35. Ps 27:2. Pr +*4:18, 19. Ec 2:14. Je 13:16. 20:11. 1 J 2:10, 11. **night.** Is +9:2. **no light.** Mt 6:23. Ac 7:51.

11. **he saith.** Jn 3:29. 15:13-15. Ex 33:11. 2 Ch 20:7. Is 41:8. Ja 2:23. **Lazarus.** i.e. *whom God helps*, ✺S#2976g. Jn 11:1, 2, 5, 11, 14, 43. 12:1, 2, 9, 10, 17. Lk 16:20, 23, 24, 25. (1) A man of Bethany, the brother of Martha and Mary. Jesus raised him from the dead, Jn 11:1—12:11. (2) The name given by Christ to a beggar who was the subject of one of his parables, Lk 16:19-31. **sleepeth.** ſ88, Ge +15:15. ver. 13. Dt *31:16. Da +*12:2. Mt *9:24. 27:52. Mk 5:39. Ac *7:60. 1 C *15:18, 51. 1 Th 4:14, 15. 5:10. **awake.** ver. 43, 44. Jn √5:25-29. Da +*12:2. 1 C 15:34. Ep *5:14.

12. **Lord.** ſ171E12, Ge +48:16. **if he.** ſ184A, 1 C +15:2. **do well.** Mk 10:52mg.

13. **Howbeit.** ſ71, Jn +1:24.

14. **plainly.** ſ24I, Is +21:7. Jn 10:24. 16:25, 29.

15. **I am glad.** ver. 35, 36. **for.** Jn 12:30. 17:19. Ge 26:24. 39:5. Ps 105:14. Is 54:15. 65:8. 2 C 4:15. 2 T 2:10. **to.** ver. 4. Jn 2:11. 5:44. 14:10, 11. 1 J √5:13.

16. **Thomas.** i.e. *twin*, *S#2381g. Jn 14:5. *20:24-29. 21:2. Mt 10:3. Mk 3:18. Lk 6:15. Ac 1:13. **Let.** ver. 8. Jn 13:37. Mt 26:35. Lk 22:33.

17. **grave.** Mt 8:28 (*S#3419g). **four.** ver. 39. Jn 2:19. Ho 6:2. Ac 2:27-31.

18. **Bethany.** i.e. *house of affliction*, *S#963g. ver. 1. Jn 12:1. Mt 21:17. 26:6. Mk 11:1, 11, 12. 14:3. Lk 19:29. 24:50. **fifteen furlongs.** *that is*, about two miles. Jn 6:19. Lk 24:13. Re 14:20. 21:16.

19. **the Jews.** ver. 8, 31, 33, 36, 45, 54. Jn +5:10. **to comfort.** ver. 31. Ge 37:35. 1 S 31:13. 2 S 10:2. 1 Ch 7:21, 22. 10:12. Jb 2:11. 42:11. Ec 7:2. Is 51:19. Je 16:5-7. La 1:2, 9, 16, 21. 2:13. Ro *12:15. 2 C 1:4. 1 Th 2:11. *4:18. 5:11.

20. **as soon.** ver. 29, 30. Mt 25:1, 6. Ac 10:25. 28:15. 1 Th 4:17. **Mary.** Lk 10:39.

21. **if.** ſ184B, Mt +11:21. ver. *32, *37. Jn *4:47-49. 1 K *17:18. Ps *78:19, 20, 41. Mt *9:18. Lk *7:6-10, 13-15. *8:49-55.

22. **that.** ver. 41, 42. Jn *9:30, 31. Mk *9:23, 24. He *11:17-19. **God will give it thee.** ver. 42. Jn *3:35. *5:22-27. +*9:31. *17:2. Ps 2:8. Mt *28:18.

23. **Thy.** ver. 43, 44.

24. **I know.** Jn *5:28, 29. Ps *17:15. *49:14, 15. Is 25:8. +*26:19n. Ezk 37:1-10. Da +*12:2, 3. Ho 6:2. *13:14. Mt *22:23-32. Lk 14:14. Ac √17:31, 32. 23:6-9. *24:15. He 11:35. **last day.** Jn 6:39, +√54n. 12:48.

25. **I am.** Jn *5:21. *6:39, 40, 44. +10:7. Ge=47:15, 19. Ro 5:17-19. 8:11. 1 C *15:20-26, 43-57. 2 C 4:14. Ep 2:6. Ph *3:10, 20, 21. 1 Th *4:14, 15. Re *1:5. *20:5, 10-15. 21:4. **the resurrection.** ſ121E1, Ge +25:23. Jn +*5:29. 1 C 15:21. **and.** ſ93A, Ge +1:26. By this figure of Hendiadys the Lord distinguishes the resurrection for which Martha hoped as the resurrection "to everlasting life" (Da 12:2). He refers not to two things, but to one. It is as though He had said, "I am the resurrection—yea, the one that is to eternal life; he that believeth on me, though he die, he shall live again; and everyone who thus liveth again in resurrection and believeth (again Hendiadys, every believer who lives again in resurrection), shall in no wise die again for ever" (Jn 11:25, 26). No! he shall rise again in the first resurrection, and shall by no means die "the second death." That shall have no power over such (EWB, *Apocalypse*, p. 621). **the life.** ſ121E1, Ge +25:23. Jn *1:4. *5:26. *6:35, 57. *14:6, 19. Ps *36:9. Is 38:16. Ac 3:15. Ro 6:5, 8-11. 8:2. Col *3:3, 4. 1 J 1:1, 2. √5:11, 12. Re 1:18. 22:1, 17. **he that.** Jn √3:36. √5:24. Jb +*19:25-27. Is +*26:19n. Lk *23:43. Ro 4:17. *8:10, 11, 38, 39. 1 C 15:18, 29. 2 C *5:1-8. Ph *1:23. 1 Th *4:14. He 11:13-16. **though** Jn 12:25.

26. **whosoever.** Jn √3:15-18. *4:14. √5:24. 6:50, 54-58. 8:52, 53. √10:28. Ro 8:13. 1 J √5:10-12. **never.** Gr. *aion*, Mt +6:13. ſ158, Mt +5:18. **die.** Jn 6:50, 51. 8:51. 1 Th 4:17. Re 2:11. **Believest.** Jn *9:35. 14:10. Mt 9:28. 26:53. Mk 9:23.

27. **Yea.** Jn 21:15, 16. Mt 9:28. 15:27. Mk 7:28. Re 16:7. **I believe.** Jn 1:49. *4:42. *6:14, 69. 8:24. 9:36-38. 13:19. √20:28-31. Mt *16:16. Ac *8:37. 1 J

4:16. 5:1, 5. **the Christ.** Jn 1:20, 34, 49. Mt 14:33. 16:16. Mk 8:29. **which.** Jn +*6:14. Ml 3:1. Mt 11:3. Lk 7:19, 20. 1 T 1:15, 16. 1 J 5:20. **world.** *kosmos*, Mt +4:8. Jn 1:9. 9:39. 16:28. 18:37. Mt 11:3.

28. **and called.** ver. 20. Jn 1:41, 45. 21:7. Zc 3:10. Lk 10:38-42. 1 Th *4:17, 18. 5:11. He 12:12. **secretly.** Mt 1:19. 2:7. Ac 16:37. **The Master.** ſ171E12, Ge +48:16. Jn 1:38. 3:10. 13:13. 20:16. Mt 26:18. Mk 14:14. Lk 22:11. **come.** Jn 10:3. SS 2:8-14. Mk 10:49.

29. **she heard.** Ps 27:8. 119:59, 60. Pr 15:23. 27:17. SS 3:1-4. **came.** ſ171J14, Jon +1:3.

30. **Now.** ſ71, Jn +1:24. **not yet come.** ver. 20.

31. **Jews.** ver. 19. **She goeth.** Ge 37:35. 2 S 12:16-18. 1 C 2:15. **grave.** Mt +8:28 (*S#3419g). **to weep.** Jn 16:20. 20:11, 13, 15. Mt 2:18. Mk 5:38. Lk 7:13. 8:52. Ac 9:39.

32. **she fell.** Lk 5:8. 8:28, 41. 17:16. Re 5:8, 14. 22:8. **if.** ſ184B, Mt +11:21. ver. 21, 37. Jn 4:49.

33. **weeping.** Ge 23:2. **the Jews.** Ro 12:15. **he groaned.** ver. 38. Jn 12:27. Mk 3:5. 9:19. 14:33-35. He +*4:15. 5:7, 8. **spirit.** Gr. *pneuma*, ſ171Q1B, Mk +2:8n. Jn 13:21. 19:30. Mt 27:50. Mk 2:8. 8:12. Lk 23:46. **was troubled.** Gr. he troubled himself. or, was moved with indignation in the spirit. ver. 38. Jn 12:27. 13:21. Ge 43:30, 31. 45:1-5. La 2:6. Mt 9:30. Mk 1:43. 14:5.

34. **Where have.** Jn 1:39. 20:2. Mt 28:6. Mk 8:5. 11:33. ◐+*13:32. 15:47. 16:6.

35. **Jesus wept.** ver. 33. Ge 43:30. Jb 30:25. Ps 35:13-15. 119:136. Is *53:3. *63:9. Je 9:1. 13:17. 14:17. La 1:16. Lk *19:11, 41. Ro 9:2, 3. He 2:16, 17. +*4:15.

36. **Behold.** ver. 3. Jn 14:21-23. 21:15-17. 2 C *8:8, 9. Ep 5:2, 25. 1 J *3:1. *4:9, 10. Re +*1:5.

37. **Could.** Jn 9:6, 7. Ps 78:19, 20. Mt 27:40-42. Mk 15:32. Lk 23:35, 39. **have caused.** ver. 21, 32.

38. **groaning.** ver. 33. Ezk *9:4. 21:6. Mk 8:12. lit. being moved with indignation in himself. ver. 33. Jn 2:13-16. +*3:36. 5:37-46. 8:15-55. 9:39-41. Mt 23:13-33. Mk 3:5. **grave.** Mt +8:28 (*S#3419g). **It was.** Ge 23:19, 20. 49:29-31. 2 Ch 16:14. Is 22:16. Mt 27:60, 66. Mk 15:46. **a stone.** Jn 20:1. Lk 24:2.

39. **Take.** Mk 16:3. **Lord.** ver. 17. Ge 3:19. 23:4. Ps 49:7, 9, 14. Ac 2:27. 13:36, 37. Ph 3:21.

40. **Said.** ver. 23-26. Jn 5:44. 2 Ch +*20:20. Mt 17:20. Mk 5:36. 9:23, 24. Lk 17:6. Ro √4:17-25. **if.** ſ184C, Mt +4:9. **see.** ver. 4. Jn *1:14. 9:3. 12:41. Ps 63:2. 90:16. Ro 6:4. 2 C *3:18. *4:6. **glory.** ſ121N1, Ge +31:54. By Metonymy of the Adjunct, "glory" is put for the glorious work of God.

41. **And Jesus lifted.** ſ144A12, Ge +22:13. Jn 12:28-30. 17:1. Ps 123:1. Mt 14:19. Mk 6:41. Lk 6:20. 9:16. 18:13. Ac 7:55. **his.** ſ63A3, Mt +19:13. **Father.** Mt 11:25. Mk +*1:35. Lk 10:21. 22:42. Ph √4:6.

42. **I knew.** ver. 22. Jn 8:29. 12:27, 28. Ge=15:6. Mt 26:53. He 5:7. √7:25. **thou hearest.** Jn 8:29. Ps *21:2. La ◐3:8. **but.** ver. 31. Jn 12:29, 30. **that they.** T#276. ver. 45-50. Jn 9:24-34. 10:37, 38. √20:31. Ex 8:22. 9:16. Dt 4:34-39. +8:2 (T#4). Jsh 4:23, 24. 1 K *18:37-39. Ps +75:1 (T#207). +83:18 (T#570). Ezk 25:7. Da 4:25. Mt 12:22-24. **that thou.** ver. 27. Jn *3:17. 6:29, 38-40. 7:28, 29. 8:16, 42. 10:36. 17:3, 8, 21, 25. Ro 8:3. Ga *4:4. 1 J *4:9, 10, 14.

43. **Lazarus.** 1 K 17:21, 22. 2 K 4:33-36. Mt 9:25. Mk 4:41. Lk 7:14, 15. Ac 3:6, 12. 9:34, 40. 20:9-12.

44. **he that.** ver. 25, 26. Jn √5:21, 25, 28, 29. √10:30. Ge 1:3. 1 S 2:6. Ps 33:9. Ezk 37:3-10. Ho *13:14. Ac

20:9-12. Ph 3:21. Re 1:18. **bound.** "Swathed about with rollers," or bandages, *keiriais*, long strips of linen, a few inches in breadth, brought round the *sinoon*, or sheet of linen in which the corpse was involved, and by which the *aromata*, or spices, were kept in contact with the flesh. In reply to skeptical objections, it is sufficient to observe that he who could raise Lazarus from the dead could, with a much less exertion of power, have so loosened or removed the bandages of his feet and legs as to have rendered it practical for him to come forth. Tittman well observes that Lazarus was restored not only to life but also to health, as appears from the alacrity of his motion; this would constitute a new miracle. Jn 19:40. 20:5, 7. **face.** Jn 20:7. **Loose.** ver. 39. Mk 5:43. Lk 7:15.

45. **many.** Jn 7:31. 12:11. Ac 9:42. **Jews.** ver. +8, 19, 31. Jn +5:10. 10:41, 42. 12:9-11, 17-19, 42. **which came.** ver. 19. **had seen.** Jn +*2:23. **believed.** ver. 25, 48. Jn +4:39. Ac 28:24.

46. **some.** Jn 5:15, 16. 9:13. 12:37. Lk 16:30, 31. Ac 5:25. **the Pharisees.** ver. 47, 57. Jn +1:24.

47. **gathered.** Ps *2:2-4. Mt +26:3. 27:1, 2. Mk 14:1. Lk 22:2. Ac 4:5, 6, 27, 28. 5:21. **a council.** Mt +5:22. **What.** Jn *12:19. Ac *4:16, 17. 5:24. **many miracles.** Jn 2:11, 23.

48. **If.** ʃ184C, Mt +4:9. **we let.** Ac 5:28, 38-40. **all.** Jn 1:7. Lk 8:12. 11:52. 1 Th *2:15, 16. **will believe.** ver. 25, 45. Jn +4:39. **and the Romans.** Jn 6:15. 18:36, 37. Dt *28:50-68. Da +*9:26, 27. Zc *13:7, 8. *14:1, 2. Mt 21:40-42. *22:7. 23:35-38. 27:25. Lk 19:41-44. 21:20-24. 23:28-31. **take away.** Mt ◐+*21:43. **our place.** Mt 24:15. Ac 6:13, 14. 21:28.

49. **Caiaphas.** Jn 18:13, 14, 24, 28. Mt +26:3. Lk *3:2. Ac *4:6. **high priest.** ver. 51. Jn 18:13. **Ye.** Jn 7:48, 49. Pr 26:12. Is 5:20-23. 1 C 1:20. 2:6. 3:18, 19.

50. **consider.** ver. 48. Jn 18:14. 19:12. Lk *24:46. Ro 3:8. **for the people.** Lk 2:10. Ac 10:2. **nation.** Jn 18:35. Lk 7:5. 23:2. Ac +10:22. **perish.** Gr. *apollumi*, Mt +2:13.

51. **spake he not.** Nu 23:12. 1 S 19:20-24. Mt 7:22. **being.** ver. 49. Ex 28:30. Le 8:8. Nu 27:21. Jg 20:27, 28. 1 S 23:9, 10. 28:6. 30:7. Ezr 2:63. Ne 7:65. **he prophesied.** Nu 22:28. 24:2, 14-25. Mt √7:22, 23. 1 C 13:2. 2 P 2:15-17. **that Jesus.** Jn 10:15. Is *53:5-8. Da *9:26. Mt *20:28. Ro *3:25, 26. 2 C √5:21. Ga *3:13. *4:4, 5. 1 P *2:24. *3:18.

52. **not.** Jn 1:29. *12:32. Ge ✱22:18. Ps 22:15, 27. 72:19. Is *49:6. Lk 2:32. Ro 3:29. 1 J √2:2. Re 5:9. 7:9, 10. **gather.** Jn *10:16. Ge +*49:10. Dt 30:3. Ps 50:5. 102:22, 23. Is +*11:10-12. 49:18. *55:5. 56:8. 60:4. Mt *25:31-34. Ep 1:9, 10. *2:14-22. Col 1:20-23. **the children.** Jn 1:12, 13. 8:41, 47. Ho 1:10. Ac 18:10. Ro 4:17. 8:16, 29, 30. 9:25, 26. Ep 1:5. 3:11. Ph 2:15. 2 Th *2:13, 14. 1 J 2:29. 3:1, 2, 10. 5:2. 3 J 11. **were scattered.** Jn +*10:16. Ezk 11:16, 17. 34:12. Ep *2:14-17. Ja *1:1. 1 P *1:1.

53. **from.** Ne 4:16. 13:21. Ps 113:2. Mt 16:21. 22:46. **they.** ver. 47. Jn +7:1. Ge=37:18. Ps 2:2. 31:13. 71:10. Mt 26:4. 27:1. Mk 3:6. Ac 5:33. 9:23. **put.** Jn 12:10. Ps 109:4, 5. Je 38:4, 15. Mt 26:59. Mk 14:1.

54. **walked.** Jn 4:1-3. *7:1, 4, 30. 10:40. 18:20. **openly.** ʃ24I, Is +21:7. **the Jews.** ver. 8, 19, 31, 33, 36, 45. Jn +5:10. **went.** Jn 7:4, 10, 13. **Ephraim.** i.e. *doubly fruitful; double ash heap,* ✱S#2187g, only here. Ephraim appears to be the same city which is called

Ephrain, 2 Ch 13:19 (see the Note) and *Ephron*, Jsh 15:9, which was situated eight miles north of Jerusalem, near Bethel, and apparently between that city and Jericho. Accordingly we find that a desert or wilderness extended from Jericho to Bethel (Jsh 16:1), called the wilderness of Bethaven (Jsh 18:12), in which Joshua and the Israelites slew the inhabitants of Ai (Jsh 8:24). 2 S 13:23. 2 Ch 13:19.

55. **passover.** Jn *2:13. 5:1. 6:4. Ex 12:11, etc. **many went.** Lk 2:42. **before.** Jn 7:8-10. 12:1. Ezr 3:1, etc. Ne 8:1, etc. **to purify.** Jn 2:6. 18:28. Ge 35:2. Ex 19:10, 14, 15. Nu 9:6, 10. 1 S 16:5. 2 Ch *30:17-20. Jb 1:5. Ps 26:6. Ac 21:24. 24:18. 1 C 11:28. He *9:13, 14. Ja *4:8.

56. **sought.** ver. 8. Jn 7:11, 12. *11:7. **come.** ʃ96C4, Mt +3:17.

57. **Now.** ver. 46, 47. **chief priests and.** ver. 47. Jn 7:32. 18:3. Mt 21:45. 27:62. **Pharisees.** Jn +1:24. 12:10. **had.** Jn 5:16-18. 8:59. 9:22. 10:39. Ps 109:4. **if.** ʃ184C, Mt +4:9. **might take.** ver. 53. Jn +7:1. Mt 26:4.

JOHN 12

Jesus is entertained at Bethany, 1, 2. Mary anoints his feet, 3; Judas, from dishonest motives, objects, but Jesus vindicates her, 4-8. The people resort to him on account of Lazarus, and the rulers consult about putting Lazarus also to death, 9-11. Jesus enters Jerusalem as in triumph, riding on an ass, to the extreme indignation of the Pharisees, 12-19. Certain Greeks desire to see him, 20-22. He predicts his own death and its blessed effects, 23-26. Being troubled in spirit, he resigns to the Father, prays, and is answered by a voice from heaven, 27, 28. He signifies the manner of his death, 29-34; and exhorts the people to improve their present advantages, 35, 36. The unbelief of the Jews shown to be a fulfilment of Isaiah's prophecy, 37-41. Many rulers believe but dare not confess him, 42, 43. He further warns the people not to reject him, 44-50.

1. **Then Jesus.** Mt 26:6-13. Mk 14:3-9. Lk 7:37-39. **six.** Jn 11:55. **passover.** ver. 12, 20. Jn 6:4. 11:55. **came.** Jn 2:2. Mt 11:19. Lk 14:1, 12. Re 3:20. **Bethany.** Jn 11:*1, 44. Mt *21:17. Mk 11:11, 12. Lk *24:50. **where.** Jn 11:1. **Lazarus.** ver. 9, 10, 17. **he raised.** Jn 11:43, 44.

2. **they made.** SS 4:16. 5:1. Lk *5:29. *14:12. Re √3:20. **Martha.** Mt *26:6. Mk *14:3. Lk *10:38-42. 12:37. 22:27. **Lazarus.** ver. *9, *10. Jn *11:43, 44.

3. **took.** Jn *11:2, 28, 32. Mt *26:6, 7, etc. Mk *14:3, etc. Lk ◐7:37, 38. *10:38, 39. **a pound.** Jn 19:39. **ointment.** Ps 133:2. SS *1:12. 4:10, 13, 14. **spikenard.** Spikenard is a highly aromatic plant growing in India, whence was made a very valuable ointment or perfume, used at the ancient baths and feasts. It is identified by Sir W. Jones with the *sumbul* of the Persians and Arabs, and *jatamansi* of the Hindoos; he considers it a species of the *valerian* of the triandria monogynia class of plants. The root is from three to twelve inches long, fibrous, sending up above the earth between thirty and forty ears or spikes, from which it has its name; stem, lower part perennial, upper part herbaceous, sub-erect, simple, from six to twelve inches long; leaves, entire, smooth, fourfold, the inner radical pair petioled and cordate, the rest sessile and lanceo-

late; pericarp, a single seed crowned with a pappus.
very costly. 2 S √24:24. **anointed.** ver. 7. Ps 23:5.
45:7. 133:2. Mt 26:7. Mk 14:3. Lk *7:37, 38, 46. **the
feet.** Jn 11:32. Lk 10:39. **wiped.** Lk 7:38. **filled.** SS
1:3. **odor.** Ex +=30:1. SS +=1:12. Mk 14:9. 2 C 2:14,
15. **ointment.** SS 1:3, 12. Pr 27:9. Mk 14:8. 16:1.

4. **one.** 1 S 17:28, 29. Ec 4:4. **disciples.** Jn +2:2.
Judas Iscariot. Jn *6:70, 71. *13:2, 26. *18:2-5. Mt
10:4. Lk 6:16.

5. **was.** Ex 5:8, 17. Am 8:5. Ml 1:10-13. Mt *26:8,
9. Mk 14:4. Lk 6:41, 42. **three hundred.** Jn 6:7. Mt
18:28. 20:2mg. Mk 14:5. **and given.** Jn 13:29. Mt *26:9.
Lk *12:33. *18:22.

6. **not.** Jn 10:13. Ps *41:1. Pr 29:7. Ezk +*33:31.
Ga 2:10. Ja 2:2-6. **because.** Jn 10:8-10. 2 K *5:20-27.
Ps *50:16-20. Mt 21:13. 1 C *6:10. **the bag.** Jn 13:29.
2 K 12:14, 15. Ezr 8:24-34. 2 C *8:19-21. 1 Th *5:22.
and bare. Jn 19:17g. 20:15g. **what was put.** Lk 8:3.

7. **Let.** Ps *109:31. Zc 3:2. Mt *26:10. Mk 14:6,
9. **against.** Jn 19:38-42. Mt *26:12. 27:57-60. Mk *14:8.
*15:42-47. Lk 23:50-56.

8. **the poor.** Ex +*23:3. Dt +*15:11. Mt *26:11.
Mk *14:7. **but.** ver. *35. Jn 8:21. 13:33. *16:5-7. SS
5:6. Mt ◐28:20. Ac +*1:9-11. **not always.** Mt +*25:19.

9. **Much people.** ver. 12. Jn *11:43-45. Mk *12:37.
Ac 3:10, 11. 4:14. **Jews.** ver. 11. Jn +5:10. **Lazarus.**
ver. 1, 2, 17. **had raised.** ver. 1, 17, 18. Jn 11:43,
44.

10. **chief priests.** Jn 11:57. 18:35. 19:6, 15, 21. Ac
4:1. **consulted.** Jn *11:47-53, 57. Ge 4:4-10. Ex 10:3.
Jb 15:25, 26. 40:8, 9. Ec 9:3. Da *5:21-23. Mt 2:3-8,
16. Lk *16:31.

11. **by reason.** ver. 18. Jn *11:45, 48. 15:18-25. Ac
13:45. Ja 3:14-16. **many.** ver. 42. Jn 11:45. **the Jews.**
ver. 9. Jn +5:10. **believed.** ver. ◐36, ◐37, 42, 44,
46. Jn +4:39.

12. **next day.** ver. 12-15. Mt 21:4-9. Mk 11:7-10.
Lk 19:35-38. **much.** ver. 9. Jn 6:15. Mt *21:8. **come.**
Jn 11:55, 56. **the feast.** ver. 1, 20.

13. **branch.** Le *23:40. Re 7:9. **Hosanna.** Ps *72:17-
19. 118:25, *26. Mt 21:9-11. *23:39. Mk 11:8-10. Lk
19:35-38. **Blessed.** Mt 23:39. Lk 13:35. **the King.** ver.
15. Jn *1:49. 19:15, 19-22. Is *44:6. Ho 3:5. Zp *3:15.
Re *15:3. 19:16. **that cometh.** Jn 5:43.

14. **Jesus.** Mt *21:1-7. Mk 11:1-7. Lk 19:29-35. **as.**
Zc *9:9.

15. **Fear.** Is ╲35:4, 5. 40:9, 10. 41:14. 62:11. Mi
4:8. Zp 3:16, 17. Zc 2:9-11. Mt 2:2-6. **daughter of.**
Zc ╲9:9. **sitting.** Dt 17:16. Jg 5:10. 12:14. 2 S 15:1.
16:2. 1 K 1:33. Mt 25:34.

16. **understood not.** Jn 13:7. Mk 9:32. Lk 9:45.
18:34. 24:25, 26, 45. **when.** ver. 23. Jn *7:39. 13:31,
32. 17:5. Mk 16:19. Ac 2:33, 36. 3:13. He 8:1. *12:2.
then. Jn 2:22. *14:26. 16:4. Lk 24:6-8.

17. **people.** ver. 9. Jn 11:31, 45, 46. Ps 145:6, 7.
Lk 19:37. **with him.** Jn 11:42. **grave.** Mt 8:28
(*S#3419g). **bare record.** Jn 1:19, 32, 34. *5:35-39.
8:13, 14. 15:26, 27. 19:35. 21:24. Ac 1:22. 5:32. 1 J
√5:9-12. Re 1:2.

18. **this cause.** ver. 9-11. Lk 19:37. **they heard.**
ver. 11. **miracle.** Jn +2:11.

19. **Pharisees.** ver. 42. Jn +1:24. **Perceive.** Jn
*11:47-50. Mt 21:15. Lk 19:47, 48. Ac 4:16, 17. 5:27,
28. **the world.** Gr. *kosmos*, Mt +4:8. ♪102, Ge +2:24.
Jn 3:26. 4:42. 17:21. Ps 22:27. 49:1. Is 27:6. Ac 17:6.
1 J *2:2.

20. **Greeks.** Jn 7:35. Mk 7:26. Ac 14:1. 16:1. *17:4.
20:21. 21:28. Ro √1:16. 10:12. Ga 2:3. *3:28. Col *3:11.
came up. Jn +2:13. **to worship.** Jn +4:20. 1 K *8:41-
43. Is *11:10. 60:2-14. *66:19-21. Ac *8:27. 24:11. **the
feast.** ver. 1, 12.

21. **Philip.** Jn *1:43-47. 6:5-7. 14:8, 9. **Bethsaida.**
Mt +11:21. **we would.** Jn 1:36-39. 6:40. Mt 2:2. 8:9-
12. 12:19-21. 15:22-28. Lk 19:2-4. Ro 15:8-12.

22. **Andrew.** Jn 1:40, 41. 6:8. Mk +13:3. **and telleth.**
Mt 14:12. **Andrew and.** Mt 10:5. Mk 10:13, 14. Lk
9:49, 50.

23. **The hour.** ver. 27. Jn 2:4. 7:6. 8:20. 13:1, 31,
32. *17:1-5, 9, 10. Is 49:5, 6. *53:10-12. *55:5. 60:9.
Mt 25:31. Mk 14:35, 41. 1 P 2:9, 10. **that.** ver. 16.
Jn +7:39. **Son of man.** ver. 34. Jn +1:51.

24. **Verily.** Jn +1:51. **Except.** ♪184C, Mt +4:9. Ps
72:16. Ro 14:9. 1 C *15:36-38. **corn.** Le +=23:10,
11. Jsh=5:11, 12. **if.** ♪184C, Mt +4:9. ver. 32, 33.
Ps 22:15, 22-31. Is *53:10-12. He +*2:9, 10. Re 7:9-
17. **much fruit.** Jn 15:2. Ge 9:1. =41:52.

25. **that loveth.** Mt 10:39. 16:25. 19:29. Mk *8:35.
Lk 9:23, 24. 17:33. Ac 20:24. *21:13. Col *3:3. 1 T
5:6. 2 T *4:6, 8. He 11:35. Re √12:11. **life.** Gr. *psyche*,
♪121A7, Mt +2:20. ♪121A7, Ge +9:5. **lose.** Gr. *apollumi*, Mt +2:13. **he that.** Jn 11:25. **hateth.** ♪121C2C2,
Ge +29:31. Ge 29:30-33. Ec 2:17. Lk +*14:26. **life.**
Gr. *psyche*, ♪121A7, Mt +2:20. ♪121A7, Ge +9:5.
this. Notice the mention here of the two age divisions
of Scripture: this world and the world to come. Jn
+*6:54n. **world.** Gr. *kosmos*, Mt +4:8. ver. 31. Jn
+9:39. **life.** Gr. *zoe*, Mt +7:14. ♪63I2, Jsh +3:3.
Here two expressions are to be repeated (by ellipsis
of repetition: from succeeding clause) from the latter
clause, in the former: "He that loveth his life (in
this world) shall lose it (unto eternity)" (B107). **eternal.** Gr. *aionios*, Mt +18:8. ver. 50. Jn +4:14. Re
*2:10.

26. **If any.** ♪184C, Mt +4:9. **serve.** Jn 13:16. 14:15.
15:20. Lk +*6:46. Ro 1:1. 14:18. 2 C 4:5. Ga 1:10.
Col 3:24. 4:12. 2 P 1:1. 1 J 5:3. Ju 1. **let.** Jn *10:27.
21:22. Nu 14:24. 32:11. Mt 16:24. Mk 8:34. Lk 9:23.
Ep 5:1, 2. Re 14:4. **follow.** Jn +8:12. **where.** Jn 7:34,
36. +*14:3. *17:24. Ps +*17:15. Mt 25:21. Lk +*23:43.
Ro *8:17. 2 C +*5:8. Ph +*1:23. 1 Th *4:17, 18.
there shall. 2 S 15:21. **if any.** ♪184C, Mt +4:9. **serve.**
Pr +*22:29. **him.** Jn 14:21-23. 16:27. 1 S *2:30. Pr
27:18. **honor.** T#760. Dt *28:13. 1 S *2:30. Ps *91:14,
15. 112:6, 9. Pr 3:16. 22:4. 4:8. 10:7. Lk 12:37. 2 T
*2:12. Re 3:9.

27. **is.** Jn 11:33-35. 13:21. Ps 69:1-3. 88:3. Is *53:3.
Mt 26:38, 39, 42. Mk 14:33-36. Lk 22:44, 53. He *5:7.
soul. Gr. *psyche*, ♪171Q2, Mt +12:18. **troubled.**
T#1400. Jn *13:21. Ps 88:1-3, *15. 143:11. Mt *26:38,
39. **what.** Is 38:15. Lk *12:49, 50. **Father.** Jn 11:41.
Mt 26:53, 54. Lk +22:42. **save me.** Mt 26:39. Mk
14:35. Lk 22:42. He 5:7. **this hour.** ver. 23. Lk *22:53.
but for. ♪69A, Mk +9:24. Jn +*18:37. Lk 22:53. 1 T
*1:15. He *2:9, 14, 15. *5:7. *10:5-9.

28. **Father.** Jn 18:11. Mt 26:42. Mk 14:36. Lk
+22:42. **glorify.** T#1507. Jn +13:31. **thy name.** Jn
5:43. 17:6, 11, 12, 26. Mt 6:9. Lk 1:49. 11:2. Re 15:4.
Then. Mt *3:17. *17:5. Mk 1:11. 9:7. Lk 3:22. 9:35.
2 P √1:17. **I have.** Jn 9:3. 11:4, 40-44. **and will.** Jn
13:31, 32. Is 49:3-7. Ep 2:7. 3:10, 21. Ph 1:6-11. Re
5:9-14.

29. **thundered.** Ex 19:16, 19. 20:18. Jb 37:2-5. 40:9.

Ezk 10:5. Re 4:5. 6:1. 8:5. 10:3. 11:19. 14:2. **An angel.** Ac 23:8, 9. Re 18:1, 2.

30. **but.** Jn 5:34. 11:15, *42. 2 C √8:9.

31. **Now is.** ſ96C6, Mt +2:4. Jn *5:22-27. 16:8-10. **the judgment.** Jn 3:18, 19. 9:39. **this.** ver. 25. Jn 9:39. **world.** Gr. *kosmos*, Mt +4:8. ſ121J9B. Metonymy of the Subject B577. The *world* is put for the ungodly inhabitants of it, of which the devil is the prince or god. For other instances of this figure see Jn 14:30. 16:11. 2 C 4:4. Ep 2:2. 6:12. **now.** Jn +*14:30. *16:11. Ge +*3:15. Is ◑+*24:21, 22. 49:24, 25. Mt 4:9. *12:28, 29. 13:19. Mk 3:27. Lk *4:6. √10:17-19, 21, 22. Ac *26:18. 2 C √4:4. Ep *2:1, 2. *6:12. Col 2:15. He +*2:14. 1 J √3:8. 4:4. 5:19. Re √12:9-11. +*20:2, 3. **world.** Gr. *kosmos*, Mt +4:8. **cast out.** Lk 10:18. Col 2:15. 1 J 3:8.

32. **if.** ſ184C, Mt +4:9. Jn +3:14. 8:28. 19:17, 18. Dt 21:22, 23. 2 S 18:9, 10. Ps 22:16-18. Ga *3:13. 1 P *2:24. *3:18. **will draw.** Jn +*6:44. 10:16. Ps +*2:8. SS 1:4. Ezk +*17:23. Ho 11:4. **all.** √ſ171B, Ge +24:10. **men.** Jn 1:7, 29. Is 49:6. Mt ◑*20:28. Ro *5:17-19. 8:32. 1 T +*2:6. He *2:9, 10. 1 J *2:2. Re 5:9. **unto me.** Ge +*49:10. 2 C *5:15. Ep 1:10. 3:21. Col 1:20. 2 Th 2:1. He 13:13.

33. **This.** ſ71, Jn +1:24. **signifying.** Jn *18:32. 21:19. Mt +20:19.

34. **We have heard.** Jn +*6:14. **the law.** Jn +10:34. 15:25. Ro 3:19. 5:18. **Christ abideth.** 2 S *7:13. Ps *72:7, 17-19. *89:4, 36, 37. *110:4. Is +*9:7. *53:8. Ezk +*37:24, 25. Da *2:44. *7:14, 27. Mi 4:7. Lk 1:32, 33. **for ever.** Gr. *aion*, Mt +6:13. **Son of man.** ver. 23. Jn +1:20, 51. **lifted up.** ver. 32. **who is.** ſ85R, Jb +4:17. Jn √3:14-16. *5:25-27. √8:53-58. Mt 16:13. 21:10. 22:42-45.

35. **Yet.** Jn +7:33. 9:4. 16:16. He 3:7, 8. **the light.** Jn 1:4, 9. +*8:12. **with you.** Jn 1:14. Is 12:6. Ac 2:29. **Walk.** ver. 36, 46. Jn 1:5-9. *8:12. 9:5. Is *2:5. 42:6, 7. Je 13:16. Ro 13:12-14. Ga 5:16. Ep +*5:8, 14, 15. Col +*1:10. 1 Th 5:5-8. 1 J √1:6, 7. **while ye.** Ge *6:3. Ps +*146:4. 2 C *6:2. He *3:7, 8. **lest.** ver. 39, 40. Ps 69:22-28. Je *13:16, 17. Mt *21:43. Ac *13:46. Ro 11:7-10. 2 C 3:14, 15. **darkness.** Jb +38:9. Is +19:2. 1 Th 5:4. **for.** Jn 11:10. Pr +*4:18, 19. Is 9:2. 1 J 1:6. 2:8-11. **darkness.** Jb +38:9. Is +19:2. 1 J *2:11.

36. **believe.** Jn 1:7. 3:21. Is 60:1. Ac 13:47, 48. **the light.** Jn +*8:12. 2 C *4:6. **the children.** Lk +10:6. 16:8. Ep *5:8. 1 Th *5:5, 8. 1 J 2:9-11. **and departed.** Jn 8:59. 10:39, 40. 11:54. Mt 21:17. **did hide.** Pr +*22:3.

37. **though.** ſ71, Jn +1:24. Jn 1:11. 3:11, 32. 5:43. 11:42. 15:24. Mt 11:20-24. Lk 16:31. **miracles.** Jn 2:11, 23. **before them.** Ac 26:26. **believed not.** Mt ◑27:42. Lk 16:31.

38. **That.** Jn +13:18. 15:25. 17:12. 19:24, 36, 37. Mt 27:35. Ac 13:27-29. **Esaias.** 2 Ch 32:20, Isaiah. Mt 15:7. Ac 8:28-30. Ro 10:20. **who.** Ps 14:2. Is ▶53:1. Ro *10:16. **report.** lit. hearing. ſ108B, Mt +14:1. ſ121R1, Le +13:55. **the arm.** ſ22A13, Is +52:10. Dt 5:15. Ps 44:3. Is 26:11. 40:10, 11. 51:5, 9. 52:10. 63:5. Lk 1:51. Ac 13:17. Ro *1:16. 1 C *1:24. **revealed.** Mt 16:17. 2 C 3:14-18. 4:3-6. Ga 1:16. Ep 1:17-20.

39. **could not believe.** Jn *3:27. 5:44. +*6:44, 65. 10:38. Dt +*2:30. Is *44:18-20. Ac +*13:48. +*18:27. Ro +*9:18. 1 P +*2:8. 2 P *2:14. **because.** Is *6:9, 10.

40. **He hath.** ſ108A3, Is +6:10. Am +*3:6. **blinded.** Jn 9:39. 1 K 22:20-23. Is ▶6:10. 29:10-14. 44:18. Ezk

14:9. Mt +*13:13-15. +*15:14. Mk 4:12. Lk 8:10. Ac 28:26, 27. Ro 11:8-11. **hardened.** Ex 4:21. 7:3, 13. 14:4, 8, 17. Jsh 11:20. Mk +6:52. Ro +*9:18. 11:7mg. **that they.** Dt 29:4. Ps 135:10-18. Is 26:11. 42:19, 20. Je 5:21. Ezk 12:2. Mk 8:17, 18. Ro *1:21, 28. *11:8. 2 Th √2:10, 12. **and be converted.** Ac +*3:19. 15:3. Ja *5:19, 20. **heal.** Ps 6:2. 41:4. 147:3. Is *53:5. 57:18, 19. Je *3:22. Ho +*6:1. +*14:4. Lk 4:18.

41. **when.** Is *6:1-5, 9, 10. **saw his glory.** ver. 45. Jn *1:14, 18. 14:9. Ex 33:18-23. Ne +*9:6. Is +*6:3, 5. 8:13, 14. 2 C 4:6. Ph 2:6. He *1:3. 1 J 1:3. **spake of him.** Jn +*5:39. Lk +*24:27. Ac 10:43. 1 P 1:11, 12. Re *19:10.

42. **among.** Jn *3:2. 7:26, 48-51. 11:45. 19:38. **rulers.** Lk +24:20. **believed.** ver. 11. Jn +4:39. **because.** Jn *7:13. *9:22. **the Pharisees.** ver. 19. Jn +1:24. **they did not confess.** Jn +9:22. Mt √10:32, 33. Lk 12:8, 9. Ro √10:9, 10. 1 J 4:2, 15. **lest.** Jn 7:13. *9:22, 34. 16:2. Pr *29:25. Is 51:7, 8. 57:11. +*66:5. Mt 26:69-75. Lk 6:22. Ac 5:41. 1 P 4:12-16.

43. **they loved.** Jn *5:41, 44. Mt 6:2. *10:33. 23:5-7. Lk 16:15. Ro 2:29. 1 Th 2:6. **praise of men.** 1 S 15:30. Ga ◑1:10. Ro *2:29. He ◑11:27. **the praise of God.** ver. 26. Jn 8:54. 1 S *2:30. Lk 16:15. 19:17. Ro 2:7. *3:23. 1 C 4:5. 2 C 10:18. 1 P 1:7, 8. 3:4.

44. **cried.** Jn 1:15. 7:28, 37. 11:43. Pr 1:20. 8:1. Is +*55:1-3. **He.** Jn 13:20. Mt +10:40. Mk *9:37. Lk *10:16. 1 P *1:21. **on him.** Jn √5:24. *14:1. 1 P 1:21. **that sent.** ver. 49. Jn +4:34.

45. **that seeth me.** ver. 41. Jn 1:18. 6:40. *14:9, 10, 19. 15:24. 2 C 4:6. Col +*1:15. He *1:3. 1 J 5:20. **that sent.** ver. 44. Jn +4:34.

46. **am come.** ver. 35, 36. Jn *1:4, 5, 9. √3:19. +*8:12. 9:5, 39. Ps *36:9. Is *60:1. Ml *4:2. Mt 4:16. Lk 1:76-79. 2:32. Ac +*26:18. 1 J *1:1-3. 2:8, 9. **world.** Gr. *kosmos*, Mt +4:8. **believeth.** ver. 42. Jn +4:39. **abide.** Jn √3:36. Is 42:7, 16. Ep *5:14. 1 J 3:14.

47. **And if.** ſ184C, Mt +4:9. **believe not.** Jn 8:51. Mt 7:26. Lk +*11:28. **I judge him not.** ver. 48. Jn 5:45. 8:15, 16, 26. **for.** Jn +*3:17. Mt +*18:11. *20:28. Lk 9:56. +*19:10. 1 T *1:15, 16. 2 P *3:15. 1 J *4:14. **world.** Gr. *kosmos*, Mt +4:8. **to save.** Jn 3:17. 4:42. **world.** Gr. *kosmos*, Mt +4:8.

48. **rejecteth.** Dt *18:18, 19. 1 S 8:7. 10:19. Is +*53:3. Mt 21:42. Mk 8:31. 12:10. Lk +*7:30. +*8:18. 9:22, 26. +10:16. 17:25. 20:17. Ac 3:23. He √2:3. +*10:29-31. 12:25. **receiveth not.** Jn 8:47. ◑14:23. Pr 13:13. 2 C 3:14. 4:3. Ep 4:18. 2 Th *2:9-12. 1 J 4:6. **the word.** Jn √3:17-20. Mk *16:16. 2 C 2:15, 16. 4:3. 2 Th 1:8. **have spoken.** Jn *7:17. **judge.** Jn 11:24. Mt 25:31. Ro 2:16. He +*9:27, 28. **last day.** Jn +*6:54n. 11:24.

49. **not spoken.** Jn *3:11, 32. *5:30. 6:38-40. 7:16, 17. 8:26, 42. 14:10, 31. 15:15. 17:8. Ex=6:29. Dt *18:18. Is *61:1. Re 1:1. **which sent.** ver. 44, 45. Jn +4:34. **a commandment.** Jn 10:18. 14:31. 15:10. Dt 18:18.

50. **his commandment.** ſ121G, Ge +31:1. Jn *6:63, 68. √17:3. √20:31. 1 T 1:16. 1 J *2:25. √3:23, 24. √5:11-13, 20. **everlasting.** Gr. *aionios*, Mt +18:8. ver. 25. Jn √3:16. +4:14. *6:40, 68. **whatsoever.** Ex=6:29. **as the Father.** ver. 49. Jn +5:30.

JOHN 13

Jesus washes the feet of his disciples and requires them to imitate his example of humility and love, 1-

17. He declares that one of them will betray him and points out Judas as the traitor to John by a token, 18-26. Satan enters into Judas, who leaves the company, 27-30. Jesus speaks of his glorification as at hand and enjoins his disciples to love one another, 31-35. He forewarns Peter, who avows his readiness to die with him, that before the cock crows he will thrice deny him, 36-38.

1. **before.** Jn 12:1. **the feast.** Jn +6:4. Mt 26:2, etc. Mk 14:1, etc. Lk *22:1, etc. **passover.** Le +*23:5. **knew.** ver. 3, 11, 18. Jn +*1:48. 6:64. 7:6, 30. 8:+14, 20. 11:9, 10. 12:23. +16:30. 17:1, 11. 18:4. 19:28. Mt 26:45. Lk 9:51. 13:32, 33. 22:53. **his hour.** Jn 2:4. 7:6. 8:20. +12:23. 17:1. **depart.** ver. 3. Jn 14:12, 28. 16:5-7, 10, 17, 28. *17:5, 11, 13. **world.** Gr. *kosmos*, Mt +4:8. Jn +9:39. 15:19. **having.** ver. 34. Jn 15:9, 10, 13, 14. 17:9, 10, 14-16, 26. Je 31:3. Ro 8:37. Ep *5:25, 26. 1 J *4:19. Re +*1:5. **world.** Gr. *kosmos*, Mt +4:8. **loved.** ver. +34. Jn *15:13. Dt 33:3. Ep *5:2. **his own.** Jn 1:11. Ac 4:23. 24:23. 1 T 5:8. **which were.** Jn 17:6, 9-11. **unto.** Mt *28:20. 1 C 1:8. 1 Th 2:16. He 3:6, 14. 6:11. 1 P 1:13.

2. **supper.** ver. 4, 26. **the devil.** ver. 11, 27. Jn *6:70, 71. Lk 22:3, 31. Ac *5:3. Ep *2:2. 2 C *2:11. **put.** 1 Ch *21:1. Ezr 7:27. Ne 2:12. Mt *13:19. 2 C 8:16. Ja 1:13-17. Re 17:17.

3. **knowing.** ver. 1. Jn *3:35. 5:22-27. +17:2. Mt *11:27. *28:18. Lk 10:22. Ac 2:36. 1 C *15:27. Ep 1:21, 22. Ph 2:9-11. He *1:2. *2:8, 9. **and that.** ver. 1. Jn 1:18. 3:13. 7:29, 33. *8:42. *16:27, 28. 17:5-8, 11-13. **and went.** Jn 14:12.

4. **laid aside.** That is, his gown, or upper coat, *imatia*, with the girdle by which it was girded close to his tunic or inner coat; instead of this girdle, he tied a towel about him that he might have it in readiness to dry their feet, and that he might appear as a servant. Indeed the whole action was a servile one and never performed by a superior to an inferior. Lk 12:37. 17:7, 8. 22:27. 2 C √8:9. Ph *2:6-8. **girded.** Jn 21:7. Lk 12:37. 22:27.

5. **After.** Lk 22:27. **poureth.** Jn 19:34. 2 K √3:11. Ezk 36:25. Zc 13:1. Ep *5:26. 1 J 5:6. **began.** Mt 20:28. **to wash.** ver. 8. Ex 29:4. Le 14:8. 2 K 5:10-13. Ps 51:2, 7. SS +*5:3. Is *1:16. Lk +7:44. Ac +*22:16. 1 C 6:11. 1 T 5:10. T *3:3-5. He +*10:22. 1 J *1:7. Re +*1:5. *7:14. **feet.** ver. 10, 12-14. Ge 18:4. 19:2. 1 S 25:41. Lk 7:38, 44. 1 T *5:10.

6. **Peter.** Gr. he. **Lord.** Jn 1:27. Mt 3:11-14. Lk 5:8.

7. **answered.** ver. 36. **What I do.** ver. 10-12. Jn 12:16. *14:26. Ps 39:9. Is 38:15. Je 32:24, 25, 43, 44. Ezk 14:23. Da 12:8, 12. Hab 2:1-3. Mk 7:37. Ja 5:7-11. **knowest.** Gr. *oida*, Jn +8:55. ver. 12. Jn 15:15. **thou shalt.** T#398. Jn 16:25. 1 C *13:9, 10, 12. **know.** Gr. *ginosko*, Jn +8:55n.

8. **Thou shalt.** Ge 42:38. Mt *16:22. 21:29. *26:33, 35. Mk 8:32. Col *2:18, 23. **never.** Gr. *aion*, Mt +6:13. √158, Mt +5:18. **If.** √184C, Mt +4:9. ver. 6. Jn *3:5. Is 4:4. Lk 6:4-9. *36:25. Zc 13:1. Ac 22:16. 1 C *6:11. Ep *5:26. T *3:5. He *9:22, 23. *10:4-10, 22. Re *1:5. *3:17. *7:14. **hast no part.** Dt 12:12. 14:27. 2 S 20:1. 1 K 12:16. Ps 50:18. Ro √8:9. 1 C 6:11.

9. **not.** Ps 26:6. *51:2, 7. Je *4:14. Mt 27:24. He +*10:22. 1 P 3:21.

10. **He.** Le 16:26, 28. 17:15, 16. Nu 19:7, 8, *12, *13, 19-21. He 9:10g. **washed.** Ex=30:18. Gr. *louo*,

*S#3068g. Ac 9:37g. 16:33g. T 3:5. He +*10:22g. 2 P 2:22g. Re 1:5g. **needeth.** Ec √7:20. Mt *6:12. Ro *7:20-23. 2 C *7:1. Ep 4:22-24. +*5:26, 27. 1 Th √5:23. Ja 3:2. 1 J √1:7-10. **wash.** Gr. *nipto*, S#3538g, Mt +6:17. **his feet.** Ge 18:4. 19:2. 24:32. 43:24. Ex=40:30-32. Jg 19:21. **but.** Jn *15:3. SS *4:7. Je 50:20. 2 C √5:17, 20, 21. He 10:14. **ye.** Jn *15:3. **not all.** ver. 18.

11. **he knew.** ver. 1, 18, 21, 26, 27. Jn +1:48. +*2:25. *6:64-71. 16:30. 17:12. Mt 26:24, 25. **who.** ver. 2. **said.** ver. 10.

12. **Know.** ver. 7. Jn 15:15. Ezk 24:19, 24. Mt 13:51. Mk 4:13.

13. **call.** Jn 11:28. Mt 7:21, 22. 23:8-10. Lk +*6:46. Ro 14:8, 9. 1 C 8:6. +*12:3. Ph *2:11. 3:8. 2 P 1:14-16. **Master.** Jn +1:38. Ep 6:9. **Lord.** Jn +4:1. **and ye.** Je 1:12. Lk 7:43. 10:28. Ja 2:19. **for so.** 1 J 3:1.

14. **If.** √184A, 1 C +15:2. **I then.** Mt 20:26-28. Mk 10:43-45. Lk 22:26, 27. 2 C *8:9. Ph 2:5-8, 11. He 5:8, 9. *12:2. **have washed.** ver. 5. **ye also.** Ac 20:35. Ro *12:3, 10, 16. 15:1-3. 1 C 8:13. *9:19-22. 2 C 10:1. Ga 5:13. *6:1, 2. Ph +*2:2-5. 1 T 5:10. 1 P 4:1. *5:5. **to wash.** √171K2, Ex +23:4. Synecdoche of the Species: "washing the feet" is only one kind or example of humble service which one may do for another. 1 S 25:41.

15. **given.** Mt 11:29. Ro 15:5mg. Ep 5:2. 1 P *2:21. 3:17, 18. 1 J *2:6. **example.** 1 Ch=28:19. He +4:11. **should do.** Jg 7:17. Mt *11:29. Ph +*2:3, 5.

16. **Verily.** Jn +1:51. See on 3:3, 5. **The servant.** √138B, Ge +13:16. Jn 15:20. Mt 10:24, 25. Lk 6:40. **neither he.** Ac 14:4, 14. 2 C 8:23g. Ph 2:25g.

17. **If ye know.** √184A, 1 C +15:2. **happy.** Jn *15:14. Ge 6:22. Ex 40:16. Ps *19:11. *119:1-5. +*128:2. Ezk *36:27. Mt *7:24, 25. 12:50. 22:36-40. Lk *12:47, 48. 2 C *5:14, 15. Ga 5:6. He 11:7, 8. Ja *1:25. *2:20-24. √4:17. Re *22:14. **if ye.** √184C, Mt +4:9. √184E, Lk +17:6. This is an example of "mixed conditions" of Hypothetical Propositions. Here there are two *conditions* with the one *conclusion* ("happy are ye") coming in between. **do them.** T#871. Jn +*7:17. Ex 19:5. Le 25:18, 19. Dt 4:1, 6. *5:29. 6:3, 18, 19. 7:12. 11:27. 13:17, 18. +*26:16, 18. 29:9. *30:15, 16. *32:46, 47. 1 S 12:14. 1 K 2:3. 1 Ch *22:12, 13. 2 Ch *15:7. Ezr +*7:10. Ne 10:29. Jb *36:11. Ps 25:10. 50:23. 106:3. 111:10. *119:1, 2, 6. Pr *19:16. 29:18. Is *1:19. *48:18. Je *7:23. Ezk 33:14. Mt *5:19. √7:21. *12:50. Lk +*11:28. Ro *2:13. Ph *4:9. He +*5:9. Ja *1:22, 25. 1 J √2:3, *17. *3:22. Re *22:14.

18. **I know.** ver. 11. Jn *17:12. 21:17. 2 C *4:5. 2 T *2:19. He *4:13. Re 2:23. **chosen.** Jn 6:70. √15:16, 19. Mk 3:13. Lk 6:13. Ac 1:2. +*13:48. **but.** √63C, Ge +25:32. Supply by ellipsis (absolute: *brachylogia*), "but (I have done this)." ver. 21-27. Ps ❋*41:9. Mt *10:36. *26:23. Mk *14:20. **be fulfilled.** Jn +2:22. 12:38. 15:25. 17:12. 18:9, 32. 19:24, 28, 36. Mt +1:22. 26:56. Mk 14:49. Lk +21:22. **He that.** Ps ▸41:9. **eateth.** 2 S 9:10, 11. 1 K 18:19. 2 K 25:29. **bread.** √171I8, Ge +3:19. **lifted.** Ps 55:12. Je 9:4.

19. **Now.** *or,* From henceforth. **I tell.** Jn *14:29. *16:4. Is 41:23. 48:5. Mt 24:25. Lk 21:13. **before.** Jn *14:29, 16:4. Is 41:26. 48:5. Ezk 24:24. Mt 24:25. 2 P 3:17. **may believe.** Jn 8:24. **that I.** Jn 1:15. *8:23, +*24, 58. *18:5. Dt 32:39, LXX. Is 43:10. Ml 3:1. Mt 11:3. Re 1:17, 18.

20. **Verily.** Jn +1:51. **He that.** T#911. Jn 12:44-48. 2 Ch +*20:20. Mt 10:40-42. √25:40. Mk 9:37. Lk

9:48. *10:16. 2 C *5:20. Ga 4:14. Col 2:6. 1 Th 4:8. **receiveth me.** Jn *1:12. Ac *9:27. 3 J ◐*9. **that sent.** Jn +4:34.

21. **he was.** Jn 11:33, 35, 38. +12:27. Mt 26:38. Mk 3:5. Ac 17:16. Ro 9:2, 3. 2 C 2:12, 13. **spirit.** Gr. *pneuma,* ꟁ171Q1B, Mk +2:8n. Jn +11:33. **testified.** Jn +18:37. **one.** ver. 2, 18. Mt 26:21. Mk 14:18. Lk 22:21, 22. Ac *1:16, 17. 1 J *2:19.

22. **looked.** Ge 42:1. Mt 26:22. Mk 14:19. Lk 22:23. **doubting.** Ga 4:20g.

23. **leaning.** According to the mode of reclining at table adopted by the ancients, he who reclined immediately below another at table seemed to lie in his bosom; and the most favored guests, who were placed nearest the host, sometimes literally did so. ver. 25. Jn 1:18. 21:20. 2 S 12:3. **bosom.** Lk 16:22. **whom.** Jn 11:3, 5, 36. 19:26. 20:2. *21:7, 24. Re 1:16-18.

24. **beckoned.** Lk 1:22. 5:7. Ac 12:17. 13:16. 21:40.

25. **He.** Jn 21:20. **lying on.** Jn 4:6g. Mk 4:36g. **who.** Ge 44:4-12. Est 7:5, 6.

26. **He it is.** ver. 18, 30. Mt 26:23. Mk 14:19, 20. Lk 22:21. **sop.** *or,* morsel. Ru 2:14. **have dipped.** Gr. *bapto,* Lk +16:24. **had dipped.** Gr. *embapto,* ✱S#1686g. Mt 26:23. Mk 14:20. Jn 13:26. For related words see Mk +*7:4n. **he gave.** Mt 26:25. **Judas Iscariot.** Jn 6:70, 71. 12:4-6.

27. **Satan.** ver. 2. Ps 109:6. Mt 12:45. Lk 8:32, 33. 22:3. Ac 5:3. 1 C 5:5. 11:27. **That.** ꟁ83, 1 K +22:15. ver. 11. 1 K 18:27. Pr 1:16. Ec 9:3. Je 2:24, 25. Da 2:15. Mk 6:25. Lk 12:50. Ja 1:13-15.

29. **had the bag.** Jn 12:6. **Buy.** Jn 4:8. **the feast.** ver. 1. **that he.** ꟁ15F. Anacoluthon; or, Non-Sequence B724. The change from the direct form, which passes into the indirect form of speech. Note the shift from "Buy those things" to "he should give." For other instances of this figure see Ac 14:22. 23:23. **should give.** Jn 12:5. Ac 20:34, 35. Ga 2:10. Ep 4:28.

30. **went.** ver. 27. Pr 4:16. Is 59:7. Ro 3:15. **it.** 1 S 28:8. Jb 24:13-15. Lk 22:53.

31. **Now.** Jn +7:39. 11:4. 12:23. 16:14. Lk 12:50. Ac 2:36. 3:13. Col 2:14, 15. He 5:5-9. **the Son of man.** Jn +1:51. **and God.** Jn 11:4. 12:28. 14:13. 15:8. 17:1-6. 21:19. Is 49:3-6. Lk 2:10-14. Ro 15:6-9. 2 C 3:18. 4:4-6. Ep 1:5-8, 12. 2:7. 3:10. Ph 2:11. 1 P 1:21. *4:11. Re 5:9-14.

32. **If.** ꟁ184A, 1 C +15:2. **shall.** Jn *17:1, 4-6, 21-24. Is 53:10-12. He *1:2, 3. 1 P 3:22. Re 3:21. 21:22, 23. 22:1, 3, 13. **and.** Jn 12:23. Ph *2:8, 9.

33. **Little.** Jn 14:18. 21:5, 15. Mk 10:24. Ga 4:19. 1 J 2:1. 4:4. 5:21. **yet.** Jn +7:33. 12:35, 36. 14:19. *16:16-22. **Ye.** Jn 7:33, 34. 8:21-24. 14:4-6. **the Jews.** Jn +4:22. **so now.** Jn 16:4, 5.

34. **A new.** The Mosaic law commanded men to "love their neighbor as themselves;" this implied that reciprocal and social love of believers of which our Lord spake: but this was now to be explained with new clearness, enforced by new motives and obligations, illustrated by a new example, obeyed in a new manner, and carried to a new extent. They were required to love each other for his sake and in imitation of him, "even as I have loved you," and be ready on all occasions to lay down their lives for each other. By this the primitive Christians were particularly known among the Gentiles: "See, said they, how they love one another; and are ready to lay down their lives for each other" (Tertullian, in *Apol.*). Mk +2:22n.

Ga 6:2. 1 J 2:7-10. 3:11, 14-18, 23. 2 J 5. **I give.** Jn +10:28. 15:12, 17. 1 J 3:23. 4:21. **That ye love.** Jn 15:12, 13, 17. 17:21. Le √19:18, 34. Ps 16:3. +*119:63. Mt 19:19. Ro 12:10. 13:8. 1 C 12:26, 27. √13:4-7. Ga *5:6, 13, 14, 22. *6:10. Ep 5:2. Ph 2:1-5. Col 1:4. 3:12-14. 1 Th +*3:12. 4:9, 10. 2 Th 1:3. 1 T 1:5. He 13:1. Ja *2:8. 1 P +*1:22. *3:8, 9. 2 P +*1:7. 1 J *3:11, 23. *4:7-11, 21. 5:1. **one another.** Ro +12:5. **as I have.** ꟁ77, Ex +3:19. Jn 15:12. Ep 5:2. 1 J 4:10, 11. **loved you.** ver. 1. Jn 14:21. 15:9, 12. Ro *8:37. Re *1:5.

35. **By this.** Jn *17:21. Ge 13:7, 8. Ac *4:32-35. 5:12-14. 1 J 2:5, 10. 3:10-14. *4:20, 21. **if ye.** ꟁ184C, Mt +4:9. **have love.** T#912. Ps 133:1-3. Mk 9:50. Ro 15:5. 2 C 13:11. 1 P *1:22. 1 J 2:10. **one to another.** Ro +12:5.

36. **whither goest.** ver. 33. Jn 14:4, 5. 16:17. 21:21. **answered.** ver. 7. **Whither I go.** ver. 33. Jn 16:5. **thou canst not.** Jn 7:34. 14:2. 16:2. **thou shalt follow.** Jn *21:18, 19, 22. Ph *1:23. 2 P *1:14.

37. **why.** Jn 21:15. Mt 26:31-35. Mk *14:27-31. Lk *22:31-34. Ac 20:24. 21:13. **I will.** Pr *28:26. Je +*17:9. 1 C *10:12. **lay down.** Jn 10:11. 11:16. **life.** Gr. *psyche,* ꟁ121A7, Mt +2:20. ꟁ121A7, Ge +9:5.

38. **answered.** Jn 16:31. **Wilt.** Pr 16:18. *28:26. 29:23. 1 C √10:12. **life.** Gr. *psyche,* ꟁ121A7, Mt +2:20. ꟁ121A7, Ge +9:5. **The cock.** Jn 18:16, 17, 25-27. Mt *26:34, 69-75. Mk *14:30n, 66-72. Lk 22:34, 56-62. **shall not.** ꟁ158, Mt +5:18.

JOHN 14

Jesus encourages his disciples to believe in God and in him and promises them mansions in heaven, 1-3. He shows that he is the Way, the Truth, and the Life, 5, 6; and that he is one with the Father, 7-11. He promises them power to do even greater works than he had done and that he will grant all the prayers offered in his name, 12-14. He requires obedience as the proof of their love and promises to give them the Comforter, the Holy Spirit, and much security and comfort, in communion with the Father and with him, as coming and making their abode with those that love him, 15-26. He leaves his peace with them, and shows that his return to his Father was a proper ground for their rejoicing, 27-29, he informs them of his approaching conflict with the prince of this world in obedience to the Father, 30, 31.

1. **Let not.** ver. *27, *28. Jn 11:33mg. *12:27. 13:21. *16:3, 6, 22, 23. Ge=50:21. Jb 21:4-6. 23:15, 16. Ps 42:5, 6, 8-11. *43:5. 77:2, 3, 10. Is *43:1, 2. Je *8:18. La *3:17-23. 2 C 2:7. 4:8-10. *12:9, 10. 1 Th 3:3, 4. 2 Th 2:2. He 12:12, 13. 1 P 3:14. **be troubled.** Zc 8:13. **ye believe.** ver. 10, 11. Jn √5:23. *6:40. *11:25-27. *12:44. *13:19. 17:3. Is *12:2, 3. *26:3, 4. Mk 11:22. Ac 3:15, 16. Ep 1:12, 13, 15. *3:14-17. 1 P *1:21. 1 J *2:23, 24. √5:10-12. **believe also.** ver. 11, 12. Jn +4:39. +√5:23. Lk 24:38.

2. **In.** 2 C *5:1. He *11:10, 14-16. *13:14. Re *3:12, 21. *21:10-27. **my.** ver. 7, 20, 21, 23. Jn +5:17. **Father's house.** ꟁ171E4B. Synecdoche of the Genus B620. "House" is put for kingdom. The term "house" is used (1) to designate the central place or seat of dominion of a kingdom (Da *4:30). When used with *Father, God, Lord,* it denotes (2) the tabernacle, Ac 15:16. (3) the temple, Jn +2:16. *8:35. Ps 65:4. Is √2:2, 3.

Mi 3:12. 4:1. (4) Jerusalem, Ps 122:1, 2. Je 3:17. Zc 8:3, 8, 21. (5) the church, 1 C 3:9. Ep 2:19-22. 1 T 3:15. 1 P 2:4-10. 4:17. "House" can refer (6) to the government or rulership of a kingdom, He 3:2, 5, 6, and (7) to the kingdom itself, Ge +*41:30. 1 S +*7:13, 16. 1 Ch *17:11-27. Ps 36:8. 84:4, 10. 113:9. Is +*55:3. √56:5. 60:7. Mt 23:38. √26:29. Lk +*22:29, 30. Ac +*1:6. 2 P 1:11. Re 11:15 (see Peters, *Theocratic Kingdom*, vol. 3, Proposition 170, Observation 2, pp. 54-57). Jn +2:16. *8:35. Ge 24:23. Ps *23:6. *36:7, 8. 115:16. Is 2:1-4. Mi *4:1-3. Lk 14:22. 2 C 5:1. He 11:16. Re *21:2. **mansions.** or, abiding *or* dwelling places. i.e. *stations of honor and glory possessed by saints dwelling in the Father's house* (Peters, *Theocratic Kingdom*, vol. 3, p. 57). Da √7:18mg. +*12:13. Lk *16:9. Col +*1:12. He 12:22. Re 3:12. **if.** ſ184B, Mt +23:30. Jn *12:25, 26. *16:4. Lk *14:26-33. Ac *9:16. 1 Th *3:3, 4. *5:9. 2 Th 1:4-10. T √1:2. Re 1:5. **I would.** Jn 15:15. **I go.** Jn 8:21, 22. *13:33, 36. 16:7. *17:24. Nu 10:33. He *6:20. *9:8, 23-26. *11:16. Re *21:2. **a place.** T#334. Mt +√5:5. Lk ◑2:7. Ep 3:10. 1 P √1:4-7. Re *21:2.

3. **And if.** ſ184C, Mt +4:9. **I.** ſ159, Ezk +36:23. The repetition of the pronouns "I" and "you" emphasizes the fact that nothing is to come between the Lord and the hearts of his people, so that his promised return may be the object ever before them (B263). **prepare.** Mt +*25:34. Lk 22:8. Re √21:2. **a place.** ver. +*2. **I will.** ver. 18-23, 28. Jn *12:26. *17:24. Mt 25:32-34. Ac +*1:11. 7:59, 60. Ro 8:17. 2 C 5:6-8. Ph *1:23. 1 Th 4:16, 17. 2 Th 1:12. 2:1. 2 T *2:12. He *9:28. 1 J √3:2, 3. Re 3:21. 21:22, 23. 22:3-5. **come again.** Mt +*24:3, 30. 25:34. 26:64. Lk 9:52g. Ac +*1:11. 1 C 11:26. Ph +*1:26. 1 Th √2:1. T √2:13. He 9:28. 1 J √3:2. Re +*1:7. **receive you.** Zc 8:8. 1 C *15:51. Ph *3:20, 21. 1 Th √4:13-18. **unto myself.** ver. 18, 28. Jn 21:22, 23. **that where.** Jn +12:26. √17:24. Ps 132:13, 14. 1 Th *4:17. **there ye may be.** Jn *17:24. Ps +*140:13. Mt +*19:28. +*26:29. Lk *12:32. Col *3:4. 1 Th √4:17. 2 Th +*2:1, 2. Re *3:21.

4. **whither.** ver. 2, 28. Jn 13:3. 16:28. Lk 24:26. **and the.** Jn 3:16, 17, 36. 6:40, 68, 69. 10:9. 12:26.

5. **Thomas.** Jn 11:16. +*20:25-28. **we know not.** Jn 13:7, 36. 15:12. 16:18. Mk 8:17, 18. 9:19. Lk 24:25. He *5:11, 12.

6. **I am.** Jn +10:7. **the way.** ſ94, Je +4:2. By *Hendiatris*, three words are used, but one thing is meant. Two of the words are exalted to the place of emphatic adjectives, which are thus raised to equal importance with the subject itself. Here, the sense is "I am the true and living way." Of course, Christ is the "truth" as He is also the "life," but this is not what is stated in this verse. Here, only one subject is in question: "the way"; and the other two nouns are used to define its true nature and character (B673). Compare the related figure, Hendiadys (ſ93A, Ge +1:26), which differs from this figure only in having two, not three, words used when only one thing is meant. Jn √10:9. 15:3. Is 35:8, 9. Mt 11:27. Ac √4:12. Ro 5:2. Ep 2:18. He *7:25. 9:8. *10:19-22. 1 P 1:21. Ju ◑*11. **the truth.** ver. 17. Jn *1:14, 17. *8:32. 15:1, 3. *17:3, 17. 18:37, 38. Ro *15:8, 9. 2 C 1:19, 20. Ep 4:21-24. Col 2:9, 17. 1 J 1:8. 5:6, 20. Re +*1:5. 3:7, 14. 19:11. **the life.** ver. 19. Jn 1:4. 5:21, 25-29. 6:33, 51, 57, 68. 8:51. √10:28. *11:25, 26. 17:2, *3. Dt 30:20. Ac 3:15. Ro *5:21. 1 C 15:45. Col 3:4. 1 J 1:1, 2. √5:11, 12.

Re 22:1, 17. **no man cometh.** Jn *10:7, 9. Ac √4:12. Ro +√2:12. 15:16. 1 P 2:4. 3:18. 1 J 2:23. 2 J √9. Re 5:8, 9. 7:9-17. 13:7, 8. 20:15. **but by me.** Ac √4:12. He 7:25.

7. **If ye.** ſ184B, Mt +11:21. ver. 9, 10, 20. Jn *1:18. 8:19. 15:24. 16:3. 17:3, 21, 23. Mt *11:27. Lk 10:22. 2 C 4:6. Col +*1:15-17. 2:2, 3. He *1:3. **should have known.** Jn 10:15. 1 J 2:13, 14. **my Father.** ver. 2. Jn +5:17. **from.** ver. 16-20. Jn 16:13-16. 17:6, 8, 26. **have seen.** Jn 6:46.

8. **Philip.** Jn 1:43-46. 6:5-7. 12:21, 22. **show us.** T#1517. Jn 16:25. Ex 33:13-23. 34:5-7. Jb 33:26. Ps *17:15. 63:2. Mt +*5:8. Re 22:3-5.

9. **Have.** Ge=50:15-17. Mk 9:19. **known me.** Jn 10:14. **he.** ver. 7, 20. Jn 1:14. 10:30. *12:45. 15:24. Col +*1:15. Ph *2:6. He *1:3. **hath seen the.** Jn ◑1:18. 10:38. 1 T ◑1:17. ◑6:16. **how.** Ge 26:9. Ps 11:1. Je 2:23. Lk 12:56. 1 C 15:12.

10. **Believest.** ver. 11, 20. Jn 1:1-3. *10:30, 38. 11:26. *17:21-23. 1 J 5:7. **words.** Jn 3:32-34. *5:19. 6:38-40. *7:16, 28, 29. *8:28, 38, 40. *12:49. 17:8. **speak not.** ver. 24. Jn 5:19, 20. 7:17. **dwelleth.** Ps 68:16-18. 2 C *5:19. Col *1:19. √2:9. **he.** Jn 5:17. Ac *10:38.

11. **Believe.** Jn +5:47. **Father in.** ſ16, Ge +1:27. **or.** Jn *5:36. 10:25, 32, 38. 12:38-40. Mt 11:4, 5. Lk 7:21-23. Ac 2:22. He 2:4. **works'.** Jn +3:2.

12. **Verily.** Jn +1:51. **He that.** Mt 17:20. *21:21. Mk 11:23. *16:17. **believeth.** ver. 1. Jn +4:39. **the works.** Mt 21:21. Mk 11:23. 16:17. Lk *10:17-19. Ac 3:6-8. 4:9-12, 16, 33. 8:7. 9:34, 40. 16:18. 1 C 12:10, etc. **greater.** Jn 4:37, 38. 5:16, 20. Ac 2:4-11, 41, *43. 4:4. 5:15. 6:7. 10:46. 19:12. Ro *15:18, 19. **because.** ver. 28. Jn *7:39. 16:7. Ac 2:33. **I go unto.** ver. 28. Jn *5:19. 7:33. 13:1, 3. +*14:28. 16:5, 10, 17, 28. 17:11, 13. 20:17.

13. **whatsoever.** T#1746. Jn *15:7, 16. 16:23, 26. Mt √7:7, 8. √21:22. Mk √11:24. Lk √11:9. Ep 3:20, 21. Ja √1:5. √5:16. 1 J √3:21, 22. √5:14, 15. **in my name.** T#1123. ver. 6, 14. Jn 1:12. 10:7, 9. *15:16. *16:23, 24, 26, 27. 20:31. Ps 72:17. Mt +6:13 (T#1126). Lk 10:17. Ac 2:21. *16:18. Ro 8:34. 16:27. Ep 2:18. 3:11, 12, 14, 15, 21. 5:20. Ph *4:7. Col *3:17. He +*4:15, 16. *7:19, 24, 25. 9:15, 24. 10:19-22. 12:24. 13:15, 20, 21. 1 P 2:5. 1 J 2:1, 2. **will I do.** ver. 14. Jn *4:10, 14. 5:19. 7:37. +*10:30. 16:7. 1 S=20:4. 2 C 12:8-10. Ph √4:13. **that.** Jn 12:44. +13:31. 17:4, 5. Ph *2:9-11. **the Son.** Jn +3:35.

14. **If ye.** ſ184C, Mt +4:9. ver. 13. **any thing.** Mt +*18:19. *21:22. Ro +*8:32. Ep +*3:20. 1 J √5:14, 15. **in my name.** Ep +5:20.

15. **If ye love.** ſ184C, Mt +4:9. ver. 21-24. Jn 8:42. *15:10-14. 21:15-17. Mt 10:37. 25:34-40. 1 C 16:22. 2 C √5:14, 15. √8:8, 9. Ga 5:6. Ep 3:16-18. 6:24. Ph *1:20-23. 3:7-11. 1 P 1:8. 1 J √2:3-5. 4:19, 20. *5:2, 3. 2 J 6. **keep.** Jn 8:51. Lk +*11:28. 1 J +*2:3. 5:2.

16. **I will.** ver. 14. Jn 16:26, 27. 17:9-11, 15, 20. Ro 8:34. He *7:25. 1 J *2:1. **another.** ver. 18, *26. Jn 7:39. *15:26. 16:7-15. Nu=27:16, 17. Ac √9:31. 13:52. Ro *5:5. *8:15, 16, 26, 27. 14:17. *15:13. Ga *5:22. Ph 2:1. He 2:16. **Comforter.** ver. 26. Jn 15:26. ◑16:7. 1 J 2:1g. **he.** ver. 17. **abide.** Jn *4:14. 16:22. Mt *28:20. Ep *1:13, 14. Col *3:3, 4. 2 Th 2:16. **for ever.** Gr. *aion*, Mt +6:13.

17. **the Spirit.** Gr. *pneuma*, Mt +3:16. Jn +7:39. Ro *8:9. 1 C 2:12-14. 1 T 4:1. 1 J *2:27. *4:6. 5:7. **of**

truth. Jn *15:26. 16:13. whom. Pr 14:10. 1 C √2:14. Re 2:17. world. Gr. *kosmos*, Mt +4:8. *ʃ121J9A, Jn +1:10. receive. ʃ25, Ge +4:4. but. ver. 16, 23. Is +*57:15. 59:21. Ezk 36:27. Ro 8:9, 11, 13, 14. 1 C *3:16. 6:19. 2 C 6:16. Ep *2:22. 3:17. 2 T 1:14. 1 J *2:27. 3:24. 4:12, 13. he. ver. 16. dwelleth with. Ac 2:4. Ro *8:9. 1 J 2:27. shall. Mt 10:20. Ro 8:10. 1 C 14:15. 2 C √13:5. Ga 4:6. Col 1:27. 1 J *4:4, 13. 2 J 2.

18. will not. ʃ175B, Ge +21:16. ver. 16, 27. Jn 16:33. Ps *23:4. Is 43:1, 2. 51:12. 66:11-13. 2 C 1:2-6. 2 Th 2:16, 17. He 2:18. 6:18. comfortless. *or*, orphans. Jn 13:33. La 5:3. Ho 14:3. Ja 1:27. will come. ver. 3, 28. Ps 101:2. Ho +*6:3. Mt √18:20. *28:20. Re +*1:7.

19. a little. Jn +7:33. 8:21. 12:35. 13:33. *16:16, 22. world. Gr. *kosmos*, Mt +4:8. seeth me no more. Mt +√23:39. 1 J √3:2. but ye see. Jn 16:16. 2 C *5:7. 1 P *1:8, 9. because. ver. 6. Jn 6:56-58. *11:25, 26. Ro 5:10. 8:34. 1 C *15:20-22, 45. 2 C 4:10-12. Ep 2:5. Col *3:3, 4. He *7:25. 1 J *1:1-3. Re 20:4. I live. Dt 32:40. ye shall live. 1 S 22:23. Col 3:2.

20. that day. Jn 16:23, 26. ye shall know. ver. 10. Jn *10:14, 38. *17:7, 11, 21-23, 26. 2 C 5:19. Ep *3:17. Col 1:19. 2:9. 1 J √5:10, 13. I am in. ver. 10, 23. Jn +5:17. *10:30. ye in. Jn 6:56. 15:5-7. Ro *8:1. *12:5. 16:7. 1 C *1:30. 2 C √5:17. *12:2. √13:5. Ga √2:20. Ep √2:10. Col √1:27. 1 J 2:28. *3:24. 4:12, 13, 15, 16. and I. Jn 17:21, 23, 26. Ep 4:16. Re *3:20.

21. that hath. ver. 15, 23, 24. Jn 7:17. *8:31, 32. 15:14. Ge 26:3-5. Dt 10:12, 13. 11:13. 30:6-8. Ps 119:4-6. Je 31:33, 34. Ezk 36:25-27. Lk +*11:28. 2 C √5:14, 15. Ja 2:23, 24. 1 J *2:5. 3:18-24. *5:3. 2 J 6. Re 22:14. commandments. 2 Ch=8:15. and keepeth. ver. 15, 23. Lk +*11:28. 1 J 2:5. that loveth. ver. 23. Jn 15:9, 10. 16:27. 17:23. Ps 35:27. Is 62:2-5. Zp 3:17. 2 Th 2:16. 1 J √3:1. shall be loved. Jn 12:26. I will. Jn +13:34. and will manifest. ver. 18, 22, 23. Jn 16:14, 15. Ex 33:18, 19. Pr 8:17. Ac 18:9-11. 22:18. 2 C *3:18. 4:6. *12:8, 9. 2 T 4:17, 18, 22. 1 J *1:1-3. Re 2:17. √3:20.

22. Judas. Mt 10:3, Lebbeus, Thaddeus. Mk 3:18, Thaddeus. Lk 6:16. Ac 1:13. Ju 1. not. Jn 13:30. Iscariot. Jn +6:71. how. Jn 3:4, 9. 4:11. 6:52, 60. 16:17, 18. unto us. Ac *10:40, 41. world. Gr. *kosmos*, Mt +4:8.

23. If. ʃ184C, Mt +4:9. ver. 15, 21. Jn ◐12:48. keep. Jn +8:51. Dt=33:9. my words. Jn +8:43. will love. Jn 12:26. *16:27. 2 Th 2:16. 1 J *3:1. we will come. Jn 14:3. 17:21. Pr 2:10. 14:33. 1 C 1:9. 1 J *1:3. Re *3:20. 21:3. 22:3. make. ver. 17. Jn 5:17-19. 6:56. 10:30. Ge 1:26. 11:7. Ps 90:1. 91:1. Is +*57:15. Ro +*8:9-11. 2 C *6:16. Ep *3:17. 1 J *2:24. 3:24. 4:4, 15, 16. Re *3:20, 21. 7:15-17. 21:22, 23. 22:3.

24. that loveth me not. ver. 15, 21-23. Mt 19:21, 22. 25:41-46. 2 C √8:8, 9. 1 J *3:16-20. and. ver. 10. Jn 3:34. *5:19, 38. *7:16, 28. 8:26, 28, 38, 42. 12:44-50. the word. ver. 10. Jn +7:16. 8:43. which sent. Jn +4:34.

25. have. ver. 29. Jn 13:19. 15:11. 16:1-4, 6, 12, 33. 17:6-8, 13.

26. the Comforter. ver. 16. Mt 12:32. the Holy. Jn 7:39. 20:22. Ps 51:11. Is +*63:10, 11. Mt 1:18, 20. 3:11. 28:19. Mk 12:36. 13:11. Lk 1:15, +*35, 41, 67. 2:25, 26. 3:22. 11:13. Ac 1:2, 8. 2:4. 5:3. 7:51, 55. 13:2, 4. 15:8, 28. 16:6. *20:28. 28:25. Ro 5:5. 14:17. 15:13, 16. 1 C 2:13. 6:19. 12:3. 2 C 6:6. 13:14. Ep

*1:13. +*4:30. 1 Th 1:5, 6. 4:8. 2 T 1:14. T *3:5. He 2:4. 3:7. 9:8. 10:15. 1 P 1:12. 2 P 1:21. 1 J 5:7. Ju 20. Ghost. Gr. *pneuma*, Mt +3:16. whom. ver. 16. Jn 15:26. *16:7. Lk √24:49. Ac √1:4. 2:33. Ro *8:9. will send. Jn=2:10. in my name. ver. 13. he. Jn 6:45. *16:13, 14. Ge=43:19. Ps *25:8, 9, 12-14. Is 54:13. Je *31:33, 34. 1 C 2:10-13. Ep 1:17, 18. 1 J *2:20, 27. Re 2:11. shall teach. Jn 16:13, 14. Ps 119:135. Ro *8:26. 1 C 2:10, 11. 2 C 4:6. He 8:10. 1 J √2:20, 27. bring. Jn +2:22. *12:16. Ac 11:16. 20:35.

27. Peace I leave. ʃ17119B, Is +57:19. Jn *16:33. 20:19, 21, 26. Nu *6:26. Ps 29:11. 72:2, 3, 7. 85:10. Is +*9:6, 7. 32:15-17. 54:7-10, 13. 55:12. 57:19. Zc *6:13. Lk *1:79. *2:14. 10:5. 24:36. Ac +*10:36. Ro 1:7. 5:1, 10. *8:6. 15:13. 1 C 1:3. 2 C √5:18-21. Ga 1:3. 5:22. 6:16. Ep 2:14-17. Ph √4:7. Col 1:2, 20. *3:15. 2 Th 1:2. 3:16. He 7:2. 13:20. Re 1:4. I give. Jn 10:28. not. Jb 34:29. Ps 28:3. La 3:17. Da 4:1. 6:25. Lk *12:19, 20. world. Gr. *kosmos*, Mt +4:8. Let not. ver. 1. afraid. Ps 11:1. 27:1, 2. +*34:4. 56:3, 11. 91:5. 112:7. Pr 3:25. Is *12:2. 41:10, 14. Je 1:8. Ezk 2:6. Mt 8:26. *10:26-28. Mk 4:40. Lk *12:4, 5. Ac 18:9. He +*13:6. 2 T +*1:7. Re 2:10. +*21:8.

28. heard. ver. *3, *18. Jn *16:16-22. I go. Jn 8:21. *20:17. Lk 24:51. and come. ver. 3, 18. If. ʃ184B, Mt +11:21. Jn 16:7. Ps 47:5-7. *68:18, 19. Lk 24:51-53. 1 P 1:8. rejoiced. Jn 16:22. I go. ver. 12. Jn *16:16. *20:17. my Father. Jn ◐+√5:18. 6:57. Jn 10:29, ◐+*30, 38. 13:16. 16:15. +*17:5. 20:17, 21. Is 42:1. 49:5-7. *53:11. Mt 12:18. 1 C √2:8. +*11:3. +*15:24-28, √47. Ph *2:6-11. He *1:2, 3. 2:9-15. 3:1-4. Re 1:11, 17, 18. greater than. ver. *12. Jn √5:19. +*6:38n. Ge 41:40 w 44:18. Mt 24:36. Mk +√13:32. 1 C *11:3. +√15:28. T#963‡; Jn *5:19. 8:42. 13:16. Lk 22:41, 42. 1 C √15:28 (T#964‡). Ph 2:9.

29. told you before. Jn *13:19. 16:4, 30, 31. Is *41:23, 26. 48:5. Ezk 24:24. Mt 24:24, 25. that, when. Is *41:23. Ezk 33:33. believe. Jn +5:44.

30. I will not. Jn *16:12. Lk *24:44-49. Ac *1:3. the prince. Jn +*12:31. 16:11. Lk 22:53. 2 C √4:4. Ep *2:2. *6:12. Col 1:13. 1 J *4:4. 5:19g. Re *12:9. 20:2, 3, 7, 8. world. Gr. *kosmos*, Mt +4:8. ʃ121J9B, Jn +12:31. hath nothing in me. Jn 17:14. Mt 26:59, 60. Lk +*1:35. Ro ◐7:18. 2 C √5:21. He +*4:15. *7:26. 1 P *1:19. *2:22. 1 J *3:5-8.

31. that the. Jn 4:34. *10:18. 12:27, 28, 49, 50. *15:9, 10. 17:21, 23. 18:11. Ps *40:8. Is *50:5. Mt 26:39-42. Ph *2:8. He 5:7, 8. 10:5-9. 12:2, 3. world. Gr. *kosmos*, Mt +4:8. *ʃ121J9A, Jn +1:10. i.e. that the godly in the world. Arise. Jn 18:1-4. Mt 26:46. Mk 14:42. Lk 12:50.

JOHN 15

Jesus, by the parable of himself as the true vine and his disciples as the branches, shows the necessity of union and communion with him in order to fruitfulness; illustrates the conduct of God towards his church; and exhorts his disciples to abide in him, 1-8. He shows the greatness of his love to them, 9-15; and that he has chosen them, that they may bring forth fruit which may remain, 16. He commands them to love one another and warns them to expect hatred and persecution from the world, which hates both him and his father, 17-25. He promises the Comforter, to confirm the testimony which they should bear to him, 26, 27.

1. **I am**. Jn 10:7, 9, 11. **true**. Jn *1:9, 17. *3:34. 6:32, 55. 1 J 2:8. **vine**. ♪22H2B, Is +4:2. Ge +*49:10, 11,=22. Ps *80:8, etc. Is 4:2. *5:1-7. Je *2:21. 12:10. Ezk 15:2-6. 19:10-14. Ho 10:1. Zc *3:8. Mt 21:33-41. Mk 12:1-9. Lk *13:6, 7. 20:9-16. Ep *4:14-16. **my Father**. ver. 8, 10, 15, 23, 24. Jn +5:17. **husbandman**. ♪22D2A. Anthropomorphism B891. God is spoken of as a husbandman. SS 7:12. 8:11, 12. Is 27:2, 3. +*60:21. 61:3. Mt 15:13. 20:1. Mk 12:1. Ro 11:17. 1 C *3:9.

2. **branch**. ver. 6. Jn *17:12. Mt *3:10. √7:19, 21-23. *15:13. 21:19. Lk 3:9. +*8:13. *13:7-9. Ac 1:17. Ro 11:17. 1 C *3:13. 13:1. 2 T *3:5. He *6:7, 8. 2 P *1:8. 1 J *2:19. Re 3:1-3. **taketh away**. ♪135, Ps +68:28. Mt 15:13. Ro 11:22. **and every**. Jb 17:9. Ps *51:7-13. Pr +*4:18. Is +*27:6-9. 29:19. Ho +*6:3. Ml 3:3. Mt 3:12. 13:*12, 33. Ro *5:3-5. √8:28. 2 C *4:17, 18. Ph *1:9-11. 1 Th *5:23, 24. T *2:14. He 6:7. *12:10, 11, 15. Re *3:19. **may**. ver. *8, *16. Ga √5:22, 23. Ph 1:11. Col *1:5-10. **more fruit**. ver. 5. Jn 12:24. Ge 9:1.

3. **are clean**. T#1044. Jn *13:10. √17:17. Ex=30:18. Ps √119:9, 11. Pr ●20:9. Ac *15:9. Ep √5:26, 27. 1 P √1:22, 23. **the word**. Jn 8:43. 14:25. 17:17, 19. Ps +*119:9. Lk 22:61. Ep *5:26.

4. **Abide**. ver. 6, 7. Jn 6:56, 68, 69. √8:31. Jsh=18:5. SS 8:5. Lk 8:15. Ac *11:23. *14:22. Ga *2:20. Col +*1:23. *2:6, 7. 1 Th 3:5. He *10:39. 1 J *2:6, 24-28. 2 J √9. Ju *20, *21. **in me**. Jn +3:15. 14:1. 1 J *3:24. **I in you**. Jn 6:56. 14:20, 23. *17:23. Ro √8:9, 10. 2 C √6:16. +*13:5. Ep √3:17. Col 1:27. **As**. ver. 5, 6. Jn 5:19. Is 27:10, 11. Ezk 15:2-5. Ho √14:8. 2 C √12:8-10. Ga √2:16, 20. Ph 1:11. **bear fruit**. Ho 14:8. Ph 1:11. **except it**. ♪184C, Mt +4:9. **abide**. 1 Ch=9:34. Col 2:6. **except ye**. ♪184C, Mt +4:9.

5. **I am the vine**. ♪119, Ge +49:9. Ge=49:22. Ro 12:5. 1 C 10:16, 17. *12:12, 27. 1 P 2:4, 5. **ye are the**. Ro 6:5. **He that abideth**. ver. +*4. **the same**. ver. 16. Jn *12:24. Pr √11:30. Ho √14:8. Lk √13:6-9. Ro *6:22. 7:4. 2 C 9:10. Ga √5:22. Ep √5:9. Ph *1:11. *4:13, 17. Col +√1:6, 10. Ja 1:17. 2 P √1:2-18. *3:18. **without**. or, severed from. ♪24E, Ge +30:33. Ac √4:12. Ep *2:12. **can**. Jn 5:19. *9:33. 2 C √13:8. Ph √2:13. √4:13. **do nothing**. ♪171C, Ex +20:10. Ge=41:44. Ro *7:18. Ga 5:6. 2 C +*3:5.

6. **If**. ♪184C, Mt +4:9. **he is**. ver. 2. Jb 15:30. Ps 80:15, 16. Is 14:19. 27:10. Ezk 15:3-7. 17:9, 10. 19:12-14. Mt *3:10. *7:19. *13:41. 27:5. He *6:7, 8. 10:26-29, 39. 2 P √2:20-22. 1 J √2:19. Ju *12, *13. Re *20:15. +*21:8. **cast**. ♪96C4, Mt +3:17. **withered**. Is *27:11. 56:3. Mt 13:6. Mk 4:6. Lk 8:6. Ja 1:11. **gather them**. Mt +*13:40-42. Lk 12:20. **and cast**. Ezk 15:3, 4. Mt *7:19. **them**. ♪63A2, 2 S +6:6. **are burned**. Ps 1:6. √21:9, 10. *50:2, 3. 139:24. Is 5:24. +*24:6. *27:11. Je 11:16. Zp +*3:8. Ml +√4:1. Mt *3:10. +*13:40-42. He 6:8. 2 P +√3:7.

7. **If**. ♪184C, Mt +4:9. **ye abide**. T#1301. ver. 4. Zc 3:7. **my words**. Jn 8:+*31, 37. Dt 6:6. Jb +*23:12. Ps √119:11. Pr 4:4. Je +*15:16. Lk *8:15. Col √3:16. 1 J *2:14, 27. 2 J 1, 2. **abide in**. Jn 5:38. **ye shall ask**. ver. *16. Jn +*14:13. 16:23. Jb 22:26, 27. Ps *37:4. Pr 10:24. Is 45:11. 58:8, 9. Ja *4:2, 3. *5:16. 1 J *3:22. √5:14, 15. **what ye will**. Est 8:8.

8. **is**. Jn +*13:31. Ps 92:12-15. Is +*60:21. 61:3. Hg 1:8. Mt +*5:16. 1 C √6:20. √10:31. 2 C 9:10-15. Ph *1:11. T *2:5, 10. 1 P 2:12. 4:11. **bear**. ♪96B, Mt +11:6. **much fruit**. ver. 5. Mk ●11:13. **so shall**. Jn

√8:31. *13:35. Mt *5:44, 45. Lk +*6:35.

9. **As**. Jn 6:57. **the Father**. ver. 13. Jn +5:20. *17:23, 24, 26. Ep 3:18, 19. Re +*1:5. **I loved you**. Jn 13:34. **continue**. ver. 11. Mt 24:13. Ep *5:2. 1 J 2:28. Ju *20, *21. **in my love**. Jn 15:13. 1 J *3:16.

10. **If**. ♪184A, Mt +4:9. **ye keep**. Jn *14:15, 21-23. Le=8:36. 1 C 7:19. 1 Th *4:1, 2. 2 P 2:21. 1 J √2:5. √3:21-24. √5:3. Re 22:14. **my commandments**. 1 J +√2:3n. **even**. Jn 4:34. *8:29. +10:18. 12:49, 50. 14:31. *17:4. Ex=40:16. Is *42:1-4. Mt √3:15-17. Ph 2:8. He 7:26. 10:5-10. 1 J 2:1, 2.

11. **These things**. Jn 14:25. 17:13. **my joy**. Is 53:11. 62:4, 5. Je 32:41. 33:9. Zp *3:17. Lk 10:21. 15:5, 6, 9, 10, 23, 24, 32. 2 C 2:3. He 12:2. 1 J 1:4. **your joy**. Jn 3:29. 16:*24, 33. 17:13. Ro *14:17. √15:13. 2 C 1:24. Ep √5:18. Ph 1:25. 2:2. 1 Th *5:16. 1 P *1:8. 1 J *1:4. 2 J 12. **full**. Jb ●14:1. He 12:11.

12. **my commandment**. ver. 17. Jn +*13:34. Ro *12:10. 1 C 13:1, 2. Ep 5:2. 1 Th 3:12. *4:9, 10. 2 Th 1:3. 1 Th 5:15. 1 P *1:22. 3:8, 9. *4:8. 1 J 2:7-10. *3:11-18, 23. 4:21.

13. **Greater love**. Jn 10:11, 15. Is 41:8. Ro √5:6-8. Ep *5:2. Ja 2:23. 1 J 4:7-11. **lay down**. Jn *10:11. 1 J *3:16. **life**. Gr. *psyche*, ♪121A7, Mt +2:20. ♪121A7, Ge +9:5. **his friends**. Lk 12:4.

14. **my friends**. Jn *14:15, 23. 2 Ch 20:7. SS 5:1. Is 41:8. Mt 12:50. Lk 12:4. Ja *2:23. **if ye**. ♪184C, Mt +4:9. Jn 2:5. +*13:17. 14:21. 1 J 5:3. **do whatsoever**. ver. 10. Jn 2:5. +*13:17. Dt 33:2. Zc 3:7. Mt *12:50. 28:20. Mk 3:34, 35. Lk 8:21. 1 C √10:31. Col *3:17. **command**. Jn 14:21. 2 Ch=8:15. =35:10.

15. **I call**. ver. 20. Jn 12:26. 13:16. 20:17. Ro *8:15. Ga *4:6, 7. Phm 16. Ja 1:1. 2 P 1:1. Ju 1. Re 1:1. **servants**. Le=22:10. Lk 15:18, 19. **knoweth not**. Jn 13:7, 12. Ge ●18:17. Ro 7:15. **friends**. ver. 14. 2 Ch +*20:7. SS 5:16. Ja 2:23. **all things**. Jn 3:32. 4:19. 8:26, 40. *16:13. 17:6-8, 26. Ge *18:17-19. Ex *33:13. Nu *12:7, 8. 1 K 10:3. 2 K 6:8-12. Ps +*25:14. *103:7. Am +*3:7. Mt 13:11. Mk 6:30. Lk 10:23, 24. Ac 20:27. Ro 16:25, 26. 1 C 2:9-12, 16. 13:10. Ep 1:9. 3:5. Col 1:26. 1 P 1:11, 12.

16. **Ye have not**. ♪25, Ge +4:14. ver. 19. Jn 6:70. 13:18. Lk 6:13. Ac 1:24. 9:15. 10:41. 22:14. Ro 9:11-16, 21. 1 J *4:10, 19. **chosen me**. Jn +*12:39. Dt 32:10. Ac +*13:48. Ep 1:12. √2:10. 2 T +*1:9. **chosen you**. Dt 7:6-8. **ordained**. Jn 20:21-23. 21:15-17. Is 49:1-3. Je *1:5-7. Mt *28:18, 19. Mk *16:15, 16. Lk 24:47-49. Ac +*1:8. Ro 1:5. 15:15, 16. 1 C 9:16-18. Ga *1:15, 16. Ep √2:10. Col +*1:23. 1 T 2:7. 2 T 1:11. 2:2. T 1:5. **should go**. Jn 8:21. Mt +*28:19. Mk *16:15. Lk 10:3. **bring forth fruit**. ver. 8. Ge 1:12. Pr +*11:30. Is +*27:6. √55:10-13. Mi 5:7. Mk 4:28. Ac *2:41, 42. Ro +*1:13. 15:16-19. 1 C *3:6, 7. Ph +*4:17. Col *1:6, +*10. 1 Th *1:5. Ja 3:18. Ju 12. **your fruit**. Ge *18:18, 19. Ps 71:18. 78:4-6. 145:4. Zc 1:4-6. Ac *20:25-28. Ro √15:4. 1 C 10:11. 2 T √3:15-17. He 11:4. 2 P 1:14-21. 3:2, 15, 16. **should remain**. Jn √4:36. 1 C √15:58. Ga +*4:11. Ph 4:17. 1 Th +*3:5, 8. He *6:10-12. 2 P √1:8-11. 2 J 8. **that whatsoever**. ver. 7. Jn *14:13, 14. √16:23, 24. Mt *7:7. √21:22.

17. **These things**. Jn 14:25. **I command**. ver. 12. Jn 13:34. 1 P 2:17. 1 J *3:14-17. **love one another**. Mk *9:50.

18. **If the**. ♪184A, 1 C 15:2. Not implying a doubt but putting the actual case. **world**. Gr. *kosmos*, Mt +4:8. **hate you**. ver. 23-25. Jn 3:20. 7:7. 1 K 22:8. Is

49:7. *53:3. Zc 11:8. Mt +*5:11. *10:22, 25. +*24:9. Mk 13:13. Lk 6:22. He *12:2, 3. Ja √4:4. 1 J *3:1, 3, 13. **before.** lit. first of you. ✒96E5, Jn +1:15.

19. **If ye.** ✒184B, Lk +7:39. **were of the world.** Gr. *kosmos,* Mt +4:8. Jn 13:1. 18:36. Lk 6:32, 33. 1 J *4:4, 5. **because.** ver. 16. Jn *17:14-16. Lk *6:26. Ga 1:4. Ep 1:4-11. 2:2-5. T 3:3-7. Ja *4:4. 1 P 2:9-12. 4:3, 4. 1 J *3:12. *5:19, 20. Re 12:9, 17. 20:7-9. **chosen.** ver. 16. Jn 13:18. Dt=18:5. =21:5. Ac +*13:48. **world hateth.** *✒121J9A, Jn +1:10.

20. **word.** Jn 5:16. 7:32. 8:59. 10:31. 11:57. 13:16. Mt 10:24, 25. Lk 2:34, 35. 6:40. Ac 4:27-30. 7:52-60. 1 Th 2:15, 16. **The servant.** ver. 15. Jn 13:16. Mt *10:24. **If they.** ✒184A, 1 C +15:2. **persecuted me.** He *12:2-4. **persecute you.** Jn 16:33. 1 C 4:12. 2 C 4:9. Ga 4:29. 1 Th 2:15. 2 T *3:12. **if they have kept.** ✒184A, 1 C +15:2. ✒111, Ge +18:27. Jn √5:23. 8:51. 1 S 8:7. Is *53:1-3. Ezk √3:7. **my saying.** Jn +8:49. **will keep.** Lk *16:10.

21. **all.** Jn 16:3. Ps 69:7. Is 66:5. Mt +*5:11. 10:18, 22, 39. +*24:9. Lk 6:22. Ac 9:16. 1 P *4:13, 14. **for my.** Mt 10:22. 24:9. Mk 13:13. Lk 21:12, 17. Ac 4:17. 5:41. 9:14. 26:9. 1 P *4:14, 16. Re 2:3. **because.** Jn 8:19, 54, 55. 16:3. 17:25. Ac 3:17. 17:23. 28:25-27. Ro 1:28. 1 C *2:8. 15:34. 2 C 4:3-6. 2 Th 1:8. 1 J √2:3, 4. 3:1. **know not.** Jn +7:28. **that sent.** Jn +4:34.

22. **If I.** ✒184B, Lk +7:39. **they.** Jn √3:18-21. 9:41. 12:48. 19:11. Ezk 2:5. +*33:31-33. Lk 12:46, 47. Ac *17:30. 2 C *2:14-16. He *6:4-8. Ja √4:17. **not had sin.** ✒96E1, Ps +118:8. i.e. so much sin. ver. 24. Jn +9:41. 19:11. Mt *10:15. +*11:22, 24. Lk 10:13, 14. +√12:47, 48. **cloke.** *or,* excuse. Ac *17:30. 27:30g. Ro *1:20. 2:1. 1 P 1:14. 2:16.

23. **that hateth me.** ver. 18, 24. Jn √5:23. *8:40-42. *10:30. Mt 12:30. 1 J *2:23. 2 J 9. **my Father.** ver. 1. Jn +5:17. **also.** Jn √5:23. 1 J *2:23. *5:1.

24. **If.** ✒184B, Mt +23:30. Jn *3:2. 5:36. *7:31. *9:32. 10:32, 37, 38. 11:47-50. 12:10, 37-40. Mt 9:33. 11:5, 20-24. Mk 1:27. 2:12. Lk 4:36. 10:12-16. 19:37-40. 24:19. Ac 2:22. *10:38. He *2:3, 4. **the works.** Jn 3:2. +5:36. Dt=34:10, 11. **not had sin.** ver. +*22. **but.** Jn 6:36. 12:45. 14:9. Mt 21:32. **hated.** ver. 23. Ge=37:4. Ex +*20:5. Dt 5:9. Ps 69:19. 81:15. Pr 8:36. Ro 1:30. 8:7, 8. 2 T 3:4. Ja *4:4. **both me.** Lk 14:18-20.

25. **this.** ✒63C, Ge +25:32. **the word.** Jn 10:34. 19:36. Lk +*24:44. Ro 3:19. **be fulfilled.** Jn +13:18. 18:32. They hated. Ge=37:4, 5. Ps 7:4. ▶35:19. ✱▶69:4. 109:3. Is ✱49:7. **without.** Mt 10:8. Ro 3:24. 2 C 11:7. Ga 2:21. 2 Th 3:8. Re 21:6. 22:17 (All in Greek). **a cause.** Ps 35:7. 59:3, 4. 109:3. 119:161. Mt 10:8g (freely).

26. **when.** Jn *14:16, 17, 26. 16:7, √13, 14. Lk *24:49. Ac *2:33. **will send.** Mt 3:11. **Spirit.** Gr. *pneuma,* Mt +3:16. Lk 11:13. Ga 4:6. **of truth.** Jn 14:17. 1 J *2:27. **which proceedeth.** Jn *8:42. Re 22:1. he. Jn 16:14, 15. Ac *2:32, 33. 5:32. 15:8. 1 C 1:6. +*12:3. He 2:4. 1 J *5:6-10. **testify.** Jn +*5:39. Ac *5:32. Ro 1:4. 8:16. He *10:15, 16. **of me.** Jn √16:13n.

27. **ye also.** Jn 19:35. *21:24. Lk +24:48. Ac +*1:8, 21, 22. +*2:32. 3:15. *4:20, 33. *10:39-42. *13:31. 18:5. 23:11. 1 P 5:1, 12. 2 P √1:16-18. 1 J *1:2. 4:14. 3 J 12. Re 1:2, 9. **bear witness.** Is +*43:10n. Ac 5:32. **have.** Mk 1:1. Lk *1:2, 3. 1 J *1:1, 2. **from the beginning.** ✒63C, Ge +25:32. Supply by ellipsis (absolute:

brachylogia), "(and are still with me)." Lk 1:2. Ac *1:21, 22. 1 J 2:7.

JOHN 16

Jesus again warns his disciples to expect persecution, 1-3. He states that he foretells these things because he is about to leave them, kindly noticing their sorrow and assuring them that this will be expedient for them, as he will send the Comforter, 4-7. He explains the nature and effects of the Spirit's influences, 8-15. He intimates his own death, resurrection, and ascension, with assurances that their sorrow should soon be turned into joy and that their prayers in his name should be accepted, 16-28. They profess their faith in him: he foretells that they will desert him in his extremity of suffering yet promises them his peace amidst their tribulation in the world, 29-33.

1. **These things.** ver. 4, 6, 33. Jn +14:25. 15:18-27. **have I spoken.** ver. 4. Jn 6:6g. 15:11. Mt 11:6. +*13:20, 21, 57. 15:12. 24:10. 26:31-33. Ro 14:21. Ph 1:10. 1 P 2:8.

2. **shall.** Jn *9:22, 34. 12:42. Mt 18:17. Lk 6:22. 1 C 4:13. **the time.** lit. hour. ✒171T6, Jn +4:23. ver. 25, 32. Jn +4:21. **that whosoever.** Is +*65:5n. Mt +*5:11. +*10:28n. 21:35. 23:34. *24:9. Mk 13:12. Lk 6:22. 21:16. Ac 5:33. 6:13, 14. 7:56-60. *8:1-3. *9:1, 2. 22:3, 4, 19-23. *26:9-11. Ro *10:2, 3. Ga 1:13, 14. Ph 3:6. **will think.** T#127. Jb +21:14 (T#363). Is 5:20. Ac +23:1 (T#129). 26:9-11. T +1:15 (T#126). **service.** Ro 9:4. He 9:1, 6.

3. **because.** Jn 8:19, 55. 15:21, 23. *17:3, 25. Lk 10:22. 1 C *2:8. 2 C 4:3-6. 2 Th 1:8. 2:10-12. 1 T √1:13. 1 J *3:1. 4:8. 5:20. **not known.** Jn √5:23. +10:15. Ac *9:5. Ro *10:2.

4. **these things.** ver. +1. **that when.** Jn 13:19. 14:29. Is 41:22, 23. Mt 10:7. 24:25. Mk 13:23. Lk 21:12, 13. +22:53. Ac 9:16. 20:23, 24. 2 P 1:14. **remember.** Jn +2:22. **said not.** ver. *12. **at the beginning.** Jn 6:64. 8:25. 15:27. **because.** Jn 17:12, 13. Mt *9:15. Mk *2:19, 20. Lk 5:34, 35.

5. **I go.** ver. 10, 16, 28. Jn 6:62. 7:33. 13:3. 14:12, 28. 17:4, 5, 13. Ep 4:7-11. He 1:3. *12:2. **that sent.** Jn +4:34. **asketh.** ✒108A2, Is +65:1. **Whither.** Jn *13:36. *14:4-6.

6. **these things.** ver. +1. **sorrow.** ver. *20-22. Jn *14:1, 27, 28. 20:11-15. Lk *22:45. *24:17.

7. **I tell.** Jn *8:45, 46. Lk 4:25. 9:27. Ac 10:34. **It.** Jn *11:50-52. *14:3, 28. 18:14. Ro √8:28. 2 C 4:17. **the Comforter.** Jn *7:39. *14:16, 17, 26. *15:26. **for if.** ✒184C, Mt +4:9. **but if.** ✒184C, Mt +4:9. Ps 68:18. Lk *24:49. Ac 1:4, 5. *2:33. Ep *4:8-13. **I depart.** Jn 8:21, 22. 14:2. **I will send.** Jn 14:●16, +26. He 9:14. 1 P 1:11.

8. **when.** Jn 8:28. **he will.** Zc *12:10. Ac 2:37. 16:29, 30. **reprove.** *or,* convince. Jn *8:9, 46. Ge=44:16. 1 C 14:24. 1 T 5:20. T 1:9. Ja 2:9. Ju 15. **world.** Gr. *kosmos,* Mt +4:8. ver. 33. Jn 7:7. 17:21.

9. **Of sin.** Jn √3:18-21. *5:40-44. *8:23, 24, 42-47. 9:24. *12:47, 48. *15:22-25. Mk 16:16. Ac *2:22-38. *3:14-19. *7:51-54. 26:9, 10. Ro *3:19, 20, 24. 5:1. 7:9. 1 Th 2:15, 16. 1 T *1:13. He +*3:12. *10:28, 29. ✒153. Prosapodosis; or, Detailing B395. A returning for repetition and explanation. For other instances of this figure see Ro 11:22. Ph 1:15-17. **because.** Jn 8:21, *24. 9:41. Ac 2:36, 37. 1 C 12:3. **believe not.** Jn +4:39.

10. **righteousness**. Jn 5:30. 7:18. Is 42:21. *45:24, 25. Je +*23:5, 6. Da +*9:24. Ac 2:32. *3:14. 7:52. *17:31. Ro 1:17. *3:21-26. *4:25. 5:17-21. *8:33, 34. *10:3, 4. 1 C *1:30. 15:14-20. 2 C √5:21. Ga *5:5. Ph *3:7-9. 1 T 3:16. He 10:5-13. 1 P 3:18. 1 J *2:1. **because**. ver. +5, 16, 17, 19. Jn *3:14. 5:32.

11. **judgment**. Jn *5:22-27. Mt 12:18, 36. Ac 10:42. √17:30, 31. *24:25. *26:18. Ro *2:2-4, 16. *14:10-12. 1 C *4:5. *6:3, 4. 2 C *5:10, 11. He 6:2. *9:27. 2 P 2:4-9. *3:7. Re +*1:7. *20:11-15. **the prince**. Jn *12:31. *14:30. Ge +*3:15. Ps 68:18. Is *49:24-26. Ro *16:20. 2 C √4:4. Ep *2:2. 1 J *3:8. Re *12:7-10. *20:2, 3, 10. **of this**. Jn +9:39. **world**. Gr. *kosmos*, Mt +4:8. ʃ121J9B, Jn +12:31. **is judged**. Jn 12:31. Lk *10:18. Col *2:15. He *2:14.

12. **yet**. Jn 14:30. 15:15. Ac 1:3. **ye**. Jn 6:56, 60. Mk *4:33. 1 C *3:1, 2. He *5:11-14. Re 2:2, 3.

13. **when he**. ʃ96G2, Ge +2:18. ʃ163. Syllepsis; or, Change in Concord B701. Grammatical Syllepsis, by which there is a change in the ideas rather than in actual words, so that the concord is logical rather than grammatical. For other instances of this figure see Jn 21:12. 2 C 5:19. Re 17:16. The use of *ekeinos*, the masculine personal pronoun, surely marks the personality of the Holy Spirit. The fact that Greek employs grammatical gender, unlike English, which employs natural gender, all the more emphatically points to the personality of the Holy Spirit, since in Greek "spirit" or *pneuma* is neuter, and most naturally would require "it." John's departure from grammatical gender to indicate natural gender emphasizes the personality of the Holy Spirit. See Jn 14:26. 15:26. 16:8, 13, 14, where this phenomenon occurs. Some MSS. and authorities (Tischendorf's 8th edition of his Greek N.T.) read *os*, "*who* is the earnest of our inheritance" at Ep 1:14, in reference to the Holy Spirit of promise, ver. 13. Compare Ro 8:16, 26, where "the Spirit itself" reflects grammatical gender, and does not deny the personality of the Holy Spirit. See Ro 8:27, "he maketh intercession." **Spirit**. Gr. *pneuma*, Mt +3:16. Jn +7:39. *14:17. *15:26. 1 J 4:6. **of truth**. Jn +*14:17. **is come**. Jn *15:26. **will guide**. ʃ159, Ezk +36:23. In this passage (ver. 12-15) the verbs "shall" and "will" are repeated eleven times in these four verses, in order to impress us with the importance of the promise and the absolute certainty of its performance (B263). T#1057. Jn *14:26. Ps +*32:8. Ac 8:31. 1 C *2:9-14. Ep 4:7-15. 1 J *2:20, 27. **all truth**. Jn 1:17. 14:6. Ps 25:5. 86:11. Ac 20:27, 32. 1 J 2:27. Re 7:17. **for**. Jn 3:32. 7:16-18. 8:38. 12:49. **not speak of himself**. The Holy Spirit works to glorify Christ (ver. 14), he does not draw attention to himself. Just as any reading of Old Testament Scripture which fails to find Christ "in all the Scriptures" (Lk 24:27n, 44) is defective, so any work or ministry alleged to be that of the Holy Spirit, which in balance draws more attention to him or gives more emphasis to him or his manifestations and gifts than to Christ, is similarly defective. Regularly studying Scripture by means of well-chosen cross references will assist the student of the Bible to maintain the necessary and proper biblical balance in all things (Jn +*5:39. Is +*8:20n. *43:10n. Mk 7:9. Ac +*17:11. √20:27, 32. Ph 1:9, 10. Col 1:10. 2 T +*1:7. √3:16, 17. 2 P +*1:20n). The study of Scripture in this manner will soon reveal to earnest students any imbalance or wrong perception of biblical truth on their part, if they are willing to take the Bible as the sole authority for faith and practice (Ps √119:18. Is +*8:20n). This method of Bible study is "self correcting" (2 T 2:15. +*3:16), the surest corrective for the human tendency to fall into error or go off on tangents (Ga 1:6. Ep 4:14. Col 1:23. 2:7. 1 T 4:16). Note that neither Jesus nor the Holy Spirit presume to speak on their own, but speak as directed by God the Father. In this, therefore, they are both subordinate to the Father (Jn 6:38n), and the Holy Spirit is subordinate to the Son. Jn +7:17. **but**. Jn 5:19. **he will show**. Jn 15:15. Jl +*2:28. Ac 2:17, 18. 11:28. *20:23. *21:9-11. 27:24. 2 Th 2:3, 12. 1 T *4:1-3. 2 T *3:1-5. 2 P 2:1, etc. Re 1:1, √19. ch. 6-22.

14. **He**. ʃ96G2, Ge +2:18. While in some texts it could be argued that the use of the masculine personal pronoun *ekeinos* is grammatically justified because *parakleetos* (Paraclete, Comforter) may be considered as the antecedent, this is *not* the case here or in ver. 13. "Indeed *O Paraklatos* is as much personal, as *ekeinos*. In fact all the language is manifestly personal: 'He,' 'the Comforter,' 'the Spirit of truth,' 'is sent,' 'comes,' 'bears witness,' etc. as in other places he is said to *hear, speak, command, forbid*, etc." (Thomas Scott). Some who would attempt to deny the validity of this evidence to prove the personality of the Holy Spirit are forced to use the same class of evidence when they are pressed to prove the personality of Satan, or of God himself, thus exposing the fatal flaw of inconsistency in their handling of the Scriptural evidence (2 C √4:2) pertaining to the personality of the Holy Spirit. Mt √12:32n. **glorify me**. ver. 9, 10. Jn +7:39. Ac 2:32-36. 4:10-12. 1 C +*12:3. 1 P 1:10-12. 2:7. 1 J 4:1-3, 13, 14. 5:6. **for**. Jn 15:26. Zc 12:10. 1 C 2:8-10. 2 C 3:14-18. 4:6. Ga 5:5. 1 J *3:23, 24. 4:13, 14. 5:20. Re *19:10. **shall show**. Ge=42:23.

15. **All things**. Jn 3:35. *10:29, 30. 13:3. *17:2, 10. Mt +*11:27. 28:18. Lk 10:22. Col 1:19. *2:3, 9. **are mine**. Jn 1:16. +*5:18, 23. 10:30. *17:5. He +*1:8. Re 22:3. **therefore**. ver. 14.

16. **A little while**. ver. 5, 10, 17-19. +7:33. 12:35. 13:33. *14:19. **not see**. ver. 16-24. Jn 14:18-24. **a little while**. Jn 20:19-29. 21:1-23. Ac 1:3. 10:40, 41. 1 C 15:5-9. **shall see**. ver. 19, 22. He *10:37. 2 P *3:8. 1 J 2:8. **because**. ver. 28. Jn 13:3. 17:5, 13. Mk 16:19. He *12:2.

17. **said**. ver. 1, 5, 19. Jn 12:16. 14:5, 22. Mk 9:10, 32. Lk 9:45. 18:34. **a little while**. ver. 16. **Because**. ver. 5, 10, 16.

18. **we**. Mt 16:9-11. Lk 24:25. He 5:12. **know not**. Jn 14:5.

19. **Jesus**. ver. 30. Jn +*2:24, 25. 21:17. Ps 139:1-4. Mt 6:8. 9:4. Mk 9:33, 34. He *4:13. Re 2:23. **A little**. ver. 16. Jn 7:33. 18:33. 14:19.

20. **Verily**. Jn +1:51. **That**. ver. 6, 33. Jn 19:25-27. Mk 14:72. 16:10. Lk 22:45, 62. 23:47-49. 24:17, 21. **weep and lament**. Mt *9:15. Mk 2:19, 20. 16:10. Lk 5:34, 35. 23:27. **but the**. Jb 20:5. Mt 21:38. 27:39-44, 62-66. Mk 15:29-32. Re 11:10. 18:7. **world**. Gr. *kosmos*, Mt +4:8. *ʃ121J9A, Jn +1:10. **your**. ver. 22. Ps 30:5, 11. 31:25. 40:1-3. 97:11. +*126:5, 6. Is 12:1. 25:8, 9. 61:3. 66:5. Je 31:9-14, 25. Mt +*5:4. Lk 6:21. Ac 2:46, 47. 5:41. Ro 5:2, 3, 11. 2 C √4:17. 6:10. Ga *5:22. 1 Th 1:6. 2 Th 2:16, 17. Ja 1:2. 1 P 1:6-8. Ju *24. Re 7:14-17.

21. **woman**. Ge 3:16. Ps 48:6. Is 13:8. 21:3. 26:16-18. +*66:7. Je +*30:6, 7. Ho 13:13, 14. Mi 4:9, 10.

Mt +*24:8. 1 Th *5:3. Re *12:2-5. **for.** Ge 21:6, 7. 30:23, 24. 1 S 1:26, 27. Ps +*113:9. Lk 1:57, 58. Ga 4:27. **world.** Gr. *kosmos*, Mt +4:8.

22. **ye now.** ver. 6, 20. 2 C 6:10. **have sorrow.** Ps 69:20. Pr 25:15. **but.** ver. 16. Jn 14:1, 27. 20:19, 20. 21:7. Is 25:9. 65:13, 14. 66:9-14. Mt 28:8. Lk *24:41, 51-53. Ac *2:46. *13:52. 1 P *1:8. **and your heart.** Jn 14:28. 20:20. Ps 33:21. Is 66:14. Lk 24:52. Ac 2:46. 8:8, 39. 13:52. 1 P 1:8. **and your joy.** Jn *4:14. Jb 34:29. Ps 146:2. Is *12:2-4. 51:11, 12. 54:7, 8. 65:18, 19. Hab 3:17, 18. Lk 10:42. 16:25. 19:26. Ac *5:41. 16:25. √20:23, 24. Ro *8:35-39. 1 Th 3:7-9. 2 Th 2:16. He *6:18. 10:34. 1 P *1:8. *4:13, 14. Re *21:4.

23. **in that day.** ver. 26. Jn 14:20. **ask.** ver. 19. Jn 13:36, 37. 14:5, 16, 22. 15:15. 17:9, 15, 20. 21:20, 21. Ph 4:3. 1 Th 4:1. 5:12. 2 Th 2:1. 1 J 5:16. 2 J 5. **me nothing.** ver. 13, 19, 26, 30. Jn 13:36. 14:5, 22. 17:9. 1 J 2:20. **Verily.** Jn +1:51. **Whatsoever.** Jn *14:13, 14. *15:7, 16. Is +*65:24. Mt *7:7. *21:22. Ep 2:18. 3:14-20. 1 T *2:5, 6. He 4:14-16. *7:25, 26. *10:19-23. 1 J *2:1. *5:14-16. **in my name.** T#541. Jn +1:12. 1 Ch=9:30. SS=1:3. Ep 1:3. Col 3:17.

24. **in.** Ge 32:9. 1 K 18:36. 2 K 19:15. Mt 6:9. Ep 1:16, 17. 1 Th 3:11-13. 2 Th 1:2. 2:16, 17. **ask.** Mt *7:7, 8. Ps *81:10. Ja 4:2, 3. **that.** ver. 23. Jn 15:11. 1 J 1:3, 4. 2 J 12.

25. **These things.** Mk 4:33, 34. **proverbs.** *or*, parables. ver. 12, 16, 17, 29mg. Jn 10:6. Ps 49:4. 78:2. Pr 1:6. Mt 13:10, 11, 34, 35. Mk 4:13. **time cometh.** ver. 2, 32. Jn +4:21. **but.** ver. 28, 29. Lk *24:45. Ac 2:33-36. 2 C 3:12-18. 4:2. **plainly.** ſ24I, Is +21:7. ver. 29. Jn 10:24. 11:14. 18:20g. Mk 8:32g.

26. **At.** ver. 23. **that.** Jn 14:16. 17:9, 15, 19, 20, 24. Ro 8:34.

27. **the Father.** Jn +12:26. *14:21, 23. 17:23, 26. Zp 3:17. He 12:6. Ju 20, 21. Re 3:9, 19. **loveth you.** Is 63:9. La 3:33. **because.** Jn 8:42. 21:15-17. Mt 10:37. 1 C 16:22. 2 C 5:14. Ep 6:24. 1 P *1:8. 1 J 4:19. **and have believed.** ver. 30. Jn 3:13. 7:29. 17:7, 8, 25. Ro 8:3. 1 C 15:47. Ga *4:4. 1 T 1:15. **came out.** ver. 28, 30. Jn +8:42. **from.** ver. 30. Jn 1:14. 6:46. 7:29. *13:3.

28. **came.** Jn 8:14, 42. 13:1, 3. **come into.** Jn +11:27. 18:37. **world.** Gr. *kosmos*, Mt +4:8. **I leave.** ver. 5, 16. Jn 13:1, 3. 14:28. 17:5, 11, 13. Lk 9:51. 24:51. Ac 1:9-11. **world.** Gr. *kosmos*, Mt +4:8.

29. **plainly.** ſ24I, Is +21:7. ver. +25. **proverb.** *or*, parable. ver. +25.

30. **are we sure.** ver. 17-19. Jn 5:20. 21:17. He *4:13. **thou knowest.** ver. +19. Jn +1:48. +*2:24, 25. 4:29. 6:61, 64. 13:11, 18. 21:15-17. 2 S ◐14:20. 1 K 8:39. Mt 9:4. Lk ◐7:39. **ask thee.** ver. 23. **by this.** Jn 17:8. **we believe.** ver. +27. **from God.** ver. *27, 28. Jn 3:2.

31. **Do.** Jn 13:38. Lk 9:44, 45. **believe.** 1 J 5:4.

32. **the hour.** ver. 2, 25. Jn 4:21, 23. 5:25, 28. 12:23. **yea.** ſ69B, Pr +6:16. **scattered.** Jn 10:12. Zc 11:16. 13:7. Mt *26:31, 56. Mk 14:27, 50. Ac 8:1. 2 T 4:16, 17. **every.** Jn 20:10. own. *or*, own home. Jn ◐1:11. 19:27. Lk 18:28. **shall leave me.** Is 63:5. **alone.** Is *53:8n. **yet.** ſ69B, Pr +6:16. Jn *8:16, 29. *14:10, 11. Is *50:6-9. **with me.** Ge=39:2, 21, 23.

33. **These things.** ver. 1, 4, 6. Jn +14:25. **in me.** Jn 3:15. √14:27. 1 Ch=9:34. Ps 85:8-11. Is +*9:6, 7. Mi +*5:5. Lk 2:14. 19:38. Ro *5:1, 2. Ep 2:14-17. Ph *4:7. Col *1:20. 2 Th 3:16. He 7:2. *13:20, 21. **In the.** Jn *15:19-21. Ps *34:19. Ac +*14:22. Ro √8:35-

37. 2 C 7:4. 1 Th *3:3, 4. 2 T √3:12. He 11:25. 1 P 5:9. Re *7:14. **world.** Gr. *kosmos*, Mt +4:8. *ſ121J9A, Jn +1:10. **tribulation.** Ac +*14:22. Re 1:9. **but.** Jn 14:1, 27. Ge 35:17. Jl 2:21, 22. Mt 9:2, 22. 14:27. Mk 6:50. 10:49. Ac 9:31. 23:11. 27:22, 25, 36. 2 C 1:3. 13:11. 1 Th 3:7. **I have.** ver. 11. Jn 12:31. 1 S 17:51, 52. Ps 68:18. Ro 8:37. 2 C √2:14. Ga 1:4. 6:14. 1 J *4:4. *5:4, 5. Re 3:21. 5:5. 6:2. 17:14. **overcome.** Ro *8:37. 1 J √2:13, 14. Re +2:7. √12:11. **world.** Gr. *kosmos*, Mt +4:8.

JOHN 17

Jesus prays the Father to glorify him, that he may glorify the Father, and give eternal life, which is found in knowing the Father and the Son, to his disciples, 1-5; to preserve the apostles in unity of faith and love after his ascension, 6-12; and from the world and all evil, 13-16; and to sanctify them by the truth, 17-19. He intercedes for them and all who should believe in him through their word that they might be united in love, admitted to the most intimate communion with the Father and the Son, and be brought to share his glory in heaven, 20-26.

1. **and lifted.** ſ144A12, Ge +22:13. Jn 11:41. Ps 121:1, 2. 123:1. Is 38:14. Mt +14:19. Lk *18:13. **Father.** ver. 5, 11, 21, 24, 25. Jn +3:35. Lk +22:42. **the hour.** ſ171T6, Jn +4:23. Jn 2:4. 7:6, 30. 8:20. 12:+23, 27, 28. *13:1. 16:32. Ec 3:1. Mk 14:41. Lk 22:14, 53. Ga 4:4. **glorify.** T#1508. ver. 4, 5. Jn +7:39. 11:4. *12:27, 28. *13:31, 32. Is *55:5. Lk 22:43. Ac 3:13. Ph √2:9-11. 1 P 1:21. **thy Son.** Jn +5:17. Mt 27:51-54. Ro *1:4. **glorify thee.** ver. 4.

2. **As.** Jn 3:35. 5:21-29. Ps 2:6-12. 110:1. Da +*7:14. Mt +*11:27. +*28:18. Ac +*10:36. Ro *14:9. 1 C +*15:25-27. Ep 1:20-23. Ph 2:10. He *1:2. *2:8, 9. 1 P 3:22. **over.** ſ181E, Ge +3:24. **all flesh.** Je *32:27. Lk +3:6. **give.** ver. 6, 9, 24. Jn *4:14. 6:27, 54-57. √10:28. *11:25, 26. 18:9. Ro √6:23. Col *3:3, 4. 1 T 1:16. 1 J 1:2. 2:25. 5:20. Ju 21. **eternal.** Gr. *aionios*, Mt 18:8. **life.** Jn √3:14-16. Mt 19:16. **as many.** ver. 6, 9, 12, 24. Jn *6:37, 39. 10:29. He *2:13.

3. **this.** ſ121G, Ge +31:1. ver. *25. Jn *8:19, 54, 55. 1 Ch +*28:9. Ps +√9:10. Is √53:11. Je *9:23, 24. *31:33, 34. Ho +*6:3. 1 C *15:34. 2 C *4:6. 2 Th *1:8. He *8:11, 12. 1 J *4:6. *5:11, 20. **eternal.** Gr. *aionios*, Mt +18:8. **know thee.** ſ121C2A1, Jb +19:25. T#886. Jn 8:19. Jb √22:21. Ps *91:14. Ho 2:20. +*6:3. 1 C 1:21. 8:1. Ep 3:19. 2 T 3:7. 2 P 1:2, 3. **the only.** Jn 5:44. *14:9, 10. Dt +*6:4. 2 Ch 15:3. Is *44:6. Je 10:10. 1 C *8:4, 6. 1 Th *1:9. 1 T *6:15, 16. 1 J *5:20. Ju 25. T#966‡. 1 P +1:3 (T#965‡). **true God.** ſ79, Ge +21:16. Dt 32:4. Ps 31:5. Je 10:10. Mk +*12:32. 1 Th 1:9. 1 J 5:20. **and Jesus.** Jn *3:17, 34. *5:36, 37. √6:27-29, 57. *7:29. *10:36. 11:42. *12:49, 50. *14:6, 7, 26. Is *48:16. *61:1. Mk *9:37. Lk *9:48. 1 J *4:14, 15. √5:11, 12. **whom.** Jn 6:68. Ph 3:8, 10.

4. **I have.** Lk 2:49. **glorified.** Jn 12:28. 13:31, 32. 14:13. **finished.** Jn *4:34. 5:36. 9:3. 14:31. *15:10. *19:30. Ex=40:33. Jsh 11:15. Ac 20:24. 2 T 4:7. **which thou.** ver. 2.

5. **Father.** ſ101, Dt +32:42. **glorify.** ver. 24. Jn *1:18. 3:13. *10:30. *14:9. 17:23, 24. Le 5:15, 16. 6:45. Ps 69:4. Pr 8:22-31. Ph 2:6. Col +*1:15-17. He *1:3, 10. 1 J 1:2. Re 5:9-14. **the glory.** ver. ◐22. Jn *1:14. 18:6. Is √42:8. √48:11. Mt *17:2. 1 C √2:8. *12:3. Ph

*2:6-8. Col *2:9. 2 P √1:16, 17. 1 J 1:1-3. **which I had.** Jn 16:15. Le 5:15, 16. 6:4, 5. Ps 69:4. Ph *2:6-8. **with thee.** ſ101, Dt +32:42. Jn 10:30. 17:23, 24. Ge=37:14. Le 5:15, 16. 6:4, 5. Ps 69:4. Ne +*9:6. Is √42:8. 1 C √15:47. Re 3:21. **before.** Jn *1:1-3. +*8:35, 58. 17:23, 24. Pr 8:23. Mi +*5:2. Mt 25:34. 1 P 1:20. Re √13:8. **world.** kosmos, Mt +4:8.

6. **have manifested.** ver. *26. Jn *1:18. 7:4. 12:28. Ex *3:13-15. *9:16. *23:21. *34:5-7. Ps *22:22. 71:17-19. Mt *11:25-27. Lk *10:21, 22. 2 C *4:6. Mt *2:12. 1 J 5:20. **thy name.** ſ121T1, Dt +28:58. ver. 11, 12, 26. Jn +12:28. Ex *23:21. **the men.** ver. 2, 9, 11, 14, 16, 24. Jn √6:37, 39. √10:27-29. *15:19. 18:9. Ac +*13:48. **gavest.** Nu=3:9. =8:19. =18:6. **world.** Gr. kosmos, Mt +4:8. **thine.** ver. *9, *10. Ro √8:28-30. 11:2. Ep *1:4-11. 2 Th √2:13, 14. 1 P 1:1, 2. **they.** Jn √8:31, 32. *14:21-24. *15:3, 7. Ps √119:11. Pr *2:1-5, 10, 11. *3:1-4. 23:23. Col *3:16. 2 T *1:13. He 3:6. Re 2:13. *3:8, 10. **have kept.** Jn +*8:47, 51. Le=23:17. Nu 23:21. Dt +*33:9. 1 K 3:14. 11:34. 2 Ch 15:17. Jb 42:7, 8. Ezk +*18:22. Lk 1:6. Ro *4:17. 1 C +*2:6. Ja 4:11. 2 P 2:8. 1 J +*2:3.

7. **they.** Jn 7:16, 17. 14:7-10, 20. 16:27-30. **are.** ver. 10. Jn 8:28. *10:29, 30. 12:49, 50. 16:15, 16.

8. **I have.** ver. 14. Jn *6:68. *14:10. Pr 1:23. Mt 13:11. Ep 3:2-8. 4:11, 12. **the words.** ſ147G, Ps +68:16. ver. 14. Jn 6:68. 8:26. *12:49. 15:15. **received.** Jn 3:33. Dt 33:3. Pr 1:3. 2:1. 4:10. 8:10. 10:8. 1 C 11:23. 15:1, 2. 1 Th √2:13. 4:1. **and have known.** ver. 6, 7, 25. Jn *16:27, 30. 1 J 4:14. **that I came.** Jn +8:42. 16:27. **have believed.** ver. 21, 25. Jn 6:69. 11:42. 16:27, 30. Ro 10:14. **didst send.** ver. 3.

9. **pray for.** ver. 14, 16, 20. Jn 11:41. *14:16, 17. 16:26, 27. Lk *22:32. Ro *8:34. He √7:25. 9:24. 1 J √2:1, 2. *5:19. Re 12:9. 13:8. 20:15. **pray not.** ver. 20. Is ◑53:12. Mt 5:44. Lk *23:34. Ac 7:60. 1 T 2:1. **world.** Gr. kosmos, Mt +4:8. *ſ121J9A, Jn +1:10. Jn 15:18, 19. 16:8, 9. **but for.** ver. 2, 6, 24. **are thine.** ver. 6.

10. **all.** Jn *10:30. *16:14, 15. Ps 18:23. 1 C 3:21-23. Col +*1:15-19. *2:9. **thine are mine.** Jn √10:27-30. Nu=8:14, 16. Ac 15:14. Ro 14:8. He 1:2. **and I.** Jn √5:23. 11:4. 12:23. Ac 19:17. 2 C *8:23. Ga 1:24. Ph *1:20. *2:9-11. 1 Th 2:20. 2 Th *1:10, 12. 1 P *2:9. Re *5:8-14.

11. **I am.** ver. 13. Jn 13:1, 3. 16:28. Ac +*1:9-11. +*3:21. He *1:3. 9:24. **world.** Gr. kosmos, Mt +4:8. **but these.** ver. 14-18. Jn 13:1. 15:18-21. 16:33. Mt 10:16. Ja *4:4. 1 J 3:12, 13. 5:19. **world.** Gr. kosmos, Mt +4:8. **I come.** ver. 13. Jn 14:12. **Holy.** ver. 25. Le *19:2. Ps 17:8, 9. Is 27:3. Mt *5:10, 29, 30. Lk 11:2. 1 P 1:5. 1 J 2:20. Ju 1, 24. Re 6:10. **Father.** ver. 1. **keep.** ver. 12, 15. Ps 12:7. 1 P *1:5. 2 P +*1:10. Ju *1, *2. Re +*3:10. **thine own name.** Jn 5:43. 12:28. Ex *23:21. Ps 79:9. Pr 18:10. Is 64:2. Je 14:7, 21. Ezk 20:9, 22, 44. Mt +*6:9. Ro 9:17. Ph 2:9. Re 19:12. **those whom.** Jn 13:1. **be one.** T#1629. ver. 20-23. Jn *10:16, 30n. 14:20. Ps 34:14. *133:1. Ro 12:5. *15:5, 6. 1 C *1:10. 12:12, 13. Ga 3:28. Ep 1:10. √4:3, 4. 5:30. Col 3:14. **as we are.** Jn +*10:30n.

12. **world.** Gr. kosmos, Mt +4:8. **I kept.** Jn *6:37, 39, 40. √10:27, 28. 21:11. Mt ◑+*13:48. He 2:13. 1 J ◑5:18. **those that.** He 2:13. **gavest.** ver. 6, 24. Nu=18:6. **have kept.** Ph *4:7. 2 Th 3:3. 1 P 1:5. Ju *24. **and none.** Jn *6:39. √10:28. 13:18. *18:9. Lk 4:26, 27. 1 J √2:19. **lost.** Gr. apollumi, Mt +2:13. **the son.**

ſ108B, 1 S +20:31. Jn *6:70, 71. 13:2, *18, 27. Mt 23:15. *26:24. Mk 14:21. Lk +10:6. 2 Th *2:3. 1 J *2:19. **that.** Jn +13:18. Ps 41:9. *109:6-19. Ac 1:16-20, 25.

13. **come.** ver. 1. Jn 13:3. 14:12. Ge=37:14. He *12:2. **these things.** Jn +15:11. **world.** Gr. kosmos, Mt +4:8. **that.** Jn 3:29. *15:11. 16:22-24, 33. Ne 8:10. Ps 43:4. 126:5. Ac 13:52. Ro *14:17. Ga 5:22. 1 J 1:4. 2 J 12.

14. **given.** ver. 8. **thy word.** ſ147G, Ps +68:16. Ps 119:50. Mt 11:25. Mk 16:15. Ac *4:29. **the world.** Gr. kosmos, Mt +4:8. *ſ121J9A, Jn +1:10. T#740. Jn 18:36. Ps +2:2 (T#68). +42:10 (T#511). 82:2-5. Is +24:5 (T#86). Mt *10:22. +13:38 (T#690). Ep 2:1, 2. 2 T +3:12 (T#467). Ja *4:4. 1 J *2:16. **hath hated.** Jn 7:7. 15:18-21. Ge +*3:15. Pr 29:27. Zc 11:8. Mt 10:24, 25. 1 P 4:4, 5. 1 J 3:12, 13. **they.** ver. 16. Jn 8:23. 1 J 4:5, 6. 5:19, 20. **world.** Gr. kosmos, Mt +4:8.

15. **pray not.** ver. +9. **take.** Ps 30:9. Ec *9:10. Is 38:18, 19. 57:1. Lk 8:38, 39. 1 C *5:10. Ph 1:20-26. **world.** Gr. kosmos, Mt +4:8. **keep them from.** T#1479. ver. 11. Ge 28:20-22. 48:16. 1 Ch 4:10. Ps 121:7. *141:4, 9. Pr 30:7-9. Mt +*6:13. Lk 11:4. Ga *1:4. 2 Th √3:2, 3. 2 T 4:18. 1 J *5:18, 19. **the evil.** Ps 140:1. Mt +*13:19. Ga 1:4. 1 J 5:19.

16. **are not.** ver. 14. Jn *15:19. **world.** Gr. kosmos, Mt +4:8.

17. **Sanctify.** T#1040. ver. 19. Jn √8:31, 32. √15:3. Ps *19:7-9. √119:9, 11, 104. Lk *8:11, 15. Ac *15:9. 2 C √3:18. Ep √5:26. 1 Th 5:23. 2 Th *2:13. Ja 1:21. 1 P *1:22, 23. **thy truth.** Jn 1:14. √14:6. 16:13. 18:38. **word.** ſ147G, Ps +68:16. Jn *8:40. 15:3. 2 S *7:28. Ps *12:6. *19:7-9. *119:9, 142, 144, 151, 152, 172. Lk 22:61, 62. Ep *4:21. *5:26. 2 T *2:15, 25, 26. √3:16, 17. **is truth.** Ps 119:160. Pr +*22:21. Da *10:21. Ep *1:13. Ja 1:18.

18. **hast sent me.** ver. 3. Jn +3:17. √20:21. Is *61:1-3. Mt *10:40. *23:34. 2 C *5:20. Ep 3:7, 8. **world.** Gr. kosmos, Mt +4:8. **sent them.** Jn 4:38. Mt 10:5, 16. Mk 3:14. Lk 9:3. 10:3. **world.** Gr. kosmos, Mt +4:8.

19. **for.** Is 62:1. 2 C 4:15. √8:9. 1 Th *4:7. 2 T 2:10. T 2:14. **I sanctify.** Jn 10:36. Ex=29:44. Je 1:5. 1 C *1:2, 30. He 2:11. *9:13, 14, 18, 26. *10:5-10, 29. **that.** ver. 17. T *2:14. **sanctified through the truth.** or, truly sanctified. 1 C 1:2, 30. 6:11. He 2:11. 10:10.

20. **pray.** ver. 6-11. Ep 4:11. **for them.** ver. 9. Jn +*10:16. 14:19. Dt 29:15. Ac *2:41. *4:4. Ro 5:10. 15:18, 19. *16:26. 2 T 1:2. **which shall.** Jn 20:29. **believe.** Jn +4:39. **through their word.** Ro 10:14. 1 C 3:5.

21. **they all.** ver. 11, 22, 23. Jn *10:16. Je *32:39. Ezk 37:16-19, *22-25. Zp 3:9. Zc *14:9. Ac *2:46. *4:32. Ro *12:5. 1 C *1:10. *12:12, 25-27. Ga √3:28. Ep *4:3-6. Ph *1:27. *2:1-5. Col *3:11-14. 1 P *3:8, 9. **may be one.** T#1579. Jn +*10:30n. Ac 4:32. ◑15:39. 1 C ◑1:10-12. 3:6, 8. 6:17. 10:17. 12:25. Ep √4:2-6. **as.** ver. 23. Jn √5:23. *10:30n, 38. *14:9-11. Ph *2:6. 1 J *5:7. **one in us.** T#1737. Jn 14:23. 1 J 1:3. 3:24. 5:20. **that the.** Jn *13:35. **world.** Gr. kosmos, Mt +4:8. *ſ121J9A, Jn +1:10. i.e. many in the world, without distinction (B577). T#1756. ver. 23. Jn 16:8. 1 Ch 16:30, 31. **may believe.** ver. 8. Mt *5:16. 1 P *2:12. 3:1.

22. **the glory.** ver. 24. Jn 1:14, 16. 15:18, 19. 20:21-23. Ge 45:13. Mt 19:28. 25:31. Mk 6:7. 10:37. 16:17-

20. Lk 9:26. 22:30. Ac 5:41. Ro 15:15-20. 2 C *3:18.
5:20. 6:1. Ep 2:20. 5:27. Ph 1:29. *3:21. Col 1:24.
*3:4. 2 Th 1:5-10. 2 T *2:11, 12. 1 J *3:2. Re 3:21.
20:4. 21:14. **which**. ver. +2. **have given them**. Ro
*8:17, 30. 1 Th 2:12. He 2:10. **that**. ver. 21. Jn 14:20.
Ep *2:6. 1 J 1:3. 3:24.

23. **I in them**. ver. 26. Jn 6:56. 14:10, +20, 23.
Ro 8:10, 11. 1 C *1:30. 2 C √5:21. +*13:5. Ga *2:20.
*3:28. 4:19. Col √1:27. 3:3. 1 J *1:3. 4:12-16. **thou in
me**. ver. 21. Jn +10:38. 2 C 5:19. **made perfect**. Ep
4:12-16. Ph 3:15. Col 1:28. 2:2, 9, 10. *3:14. He 11:40.
12:23. 1 P 5:10. 2 P √1:4. 1 J +*2:5. 4:12, 17, 18.
that the world. Gr. *kosmos*, Mt +4:8. **may know**. ver.
21. Jn 13:35. 14:31. **hast sent**. ver. 8. Jn 6:57, 58.
loved them. ver. 24. Jn 16:27. Ep 1:6, etc. 1 J 3:1.
4:19. **loved me**. Jn +5:20.

24. **Father**. ver. +1. **I will**. Jn 5:21. *12:26. +*14:3.
21:22. Mt 25:21, 23. 26:29. Lk 12:37. 22:28-30. 23:43.
2 C +*5:8. Ph +*1:23. 1 Th √4:17. Re 3:21. 7:14-17.
given. ver. 6, 12. Nu=3:9. **with me**. T#1570.
Ge=37:14. Jn +12:26. +*14:3. Mk 5:18. 1 Th *4:17.
2 T 2:11, 12. **may behold**. T#1577. Jn 1:14. Ge 45:13.
Ac *7:55, 56. 1 C 13:12. 2 C *3:18. 4:6. 1 J 3:2. Re
21:22. **my glory**. ver. 5. Ps +*102:16. **for**. ver. 5. Pr
8:22-31. **before**. ver. 5. Mt +*13:35. Ep 1:4. 1 P 1:20.
world. Gr. *kosmos*, Mt +4:8.

25. **righteous**. ver. 11. Is 45:21. Je 12:1. Ro 3:26.
1 J 1:9. Re 16:5. **the world**. Gr. *kosmos*, Mt +4:8.
not known. 𝒥147A, Ge +50:24. T#739. Jn √3:19. *8:19,
55. 15:21. 16:3. Ps +10:4 (T#693). Mt +*11:27. Lk
10:22. Ac *17:23. 26:18. Ro *1:21, 28. *3:11, 26. 1 C
1:20, 21. 15:34. 2 C √4:4. Ga 4:8, 9. 2 Th √1:8. He
*8:11. 1 J 5:19, 20. Re *13:8. **but**. Jn *1:18. 5:19, 20.
7:29. *8:55. *10:15. **these**. ver. 8. Jn 6:69. *16:27,
30. Mt 16:16.

26. **I have**. See on ver. 6. Jn 8:50. *15:15. Ps 22:22.
He 2:12. **will declare**. 𝒥147A, Ge +50:24. **thy name**.
Dt *32:3. Ps +√9:10. Ac 3:16. **that**. Jn *14:23. 15:9.
Ro *5:5. Ep 1:6, 22, 23. 2:4, 5. √3:17-19. 5:30, 32. 2
Th 2:16. **and I**. ver. 23. Jn 6:56. 14:20. 15:4. Ro 8:10.
1 C *1:30. 12:12. Ga *2:20. Ep 3:17. Col 1:27. 2:10.
3:11. 1 J 3:24. 4:13, 14.

JOHN 18

*Jesus retires to a garden, and Judas leads a company
thither to apprehend him, 1-3. At the word of Jesus,
the officers, soldiers, and company fall to the ground,
4-6. Jesus, yielding up himself, requires that his disciples be dismissed, 7-9. Peter cuts off Malchus's ear
and Jesus reproves him, 10, 11. Jesus is bound, led
away to Annas, and then to Caiaphas, 12-14. Peter
is admitted into the palace and then denies Christ,
15-18. Jesus is examined by the high priest and struck
by an officer, 19-24. Peter again twice denies him,
25-27. Jesus is brought before Pilate and declares that
his "kingdom is not of this world," 28-37. Pilate testifies
to his innocence and offers to release him; but the
Jews prefer Barabbas the robber, 38-40.*

1. **spoken**. Jn 13:31, etc. ch. 14-17. **he went forth**.
Jn 14:31. Mt 26:30, 36. Mk 14:26, 32. Lk 22:39, 40.
the brook. 2 S=15:23, 24. 1 K 2:37. 15:13. 2 K 23:4,
6, 12. 2 Ch 15:16. 29:16. 30:14. Ne 2:15. Je 31:40,
Kidron. **Cedron**. i.e. *gloomy, dark, black, sad,*
⁑S#2748g, only here. For ⁑S#6939h, see 2 S +15:23.
a garden. ver. 26. Jn 19:41. Ge 2:15. 3:23.

2. **Judas**. Jn 13:2. **the place**. Lk 22:40. **for**. Mk 11:11,
12. Lk *21:37. *22:39.

3. **Judas**. Jn 13:2, 27-30. Mt 26:47, 55. Mk 14:43,
44, 48. Lk 22:47, etc. Ac *1:16. **a band**. ver. 12g. Ps
3:1, 2. 22:12. Ac 10:1. **officers**. ver. 12, 18, 22. Jn
19:6. Mt +26:58. **chief priests**. Jn +11:57. **Pharisees**.
Jn +1:24. **torches**. Mt 25:1.

4. **knowing**. Jn 1:17, 18, +48. +8:14. +13:1. 19:28.
Mt 16:21. 17:22, 23. 20:18, 19. 26:2, 21, 31. Mk 10:33,
34. Lk *18:31-33. 24:6, 7, 44. Ac 2:28. 4:24-28. *20:22,
23. 21:13. He *12:2. **went forth**. Lk *9:51. **Whom**.
ver. 7. Jn 1:38. 20:15. 1 K 18:10, 14-18. Ne 6:11. Ps
3:6. 27:3. Pr 28:1. 1 P 4:1.

5. **Jesus**. Jn 1:46. 19:19. Mt 2:23. 21:11. **of Nazareth**.
ver. 7. Jn 19:19. Mt +2:23. 26:71. Mk 10:47. 14:67.
16:6. Lk 4:34. 18:37. 24:19. Ac +2:22. **I am**. Jn 4:26.
6:20. 8:24, 28, 58. 13:19. **Judas**. Jn +13:2. **which betrayed**. Jn +13:2. **stood**. Is 3:9. Je 8:12.

6. **As soon**. Jn √10:18. Mt 26:53. Re 1:17. **I am**.
ver. +*5. **they went**. Doubtless by the interposition
of divine power; it was thus shown that Jesus voluntarily
resigned himself into their hands. 2 K 1:9-15. Ps 27:2.
40:14. 70:2, 3. 129:5. Lk 9:54-56. Ac 4:29, 30. **and
fell**. Jb 1:20.

7. **Whom seek**. ver. 4. **of Nazareth**. ver. 5.

8. **have told you**. Perhaps this is evidence that Jesus
was relatively indistinguishable from the generality of
men, was unrecognized, and explains why they needed
Judas to identify him. Jesus was unrecognized (1) before
the resurrection: Mt 26:48. Mk *14:44. Lk +*4:30.
(2) after the resurrection: Mk *16:12n w Lk +*24:16.
(3) and this accords with prophecy: Is +*53:2. **I am**.
ver. +*5. **if**. 𝒥184A, 1 C +15:2. Is *53:6. Ep 5:25.
let. Jn √10:28. 13:1, 36. 16:32. 1 S ●22:22. 23:10. Mt
26:56. Mk 14:50-52. 1 C √10:13. 2 C *12:9. 1 P
*5:7.

9. **be fulfilled**. Jn +13:18. Ex=8:13. **Of**. Jn *17:12.
lost. Gr. *apollumi*, Mt +2:13.

10. **and cut off**. ver. 26. Mt *26:51-54. Mk *14:30,
47. Lk *22:33, 38, 49-51. **Malchus**. i.e. *king*,
⁑S#3124g, only here. For ⁑S#4429h, see 1 Ch +8:35.

11. **Put up**. ver. 36. Dt *32:35. Mt *5:39. ‖26:52.
Lk ●+*22:36. Ro *12:19. 2 C 6:7. √10:4. Ep 6:11-
17. **the cup**. Jn *4:34. Ps 75:8. Is 51:22. Ezk 23:31.
Mt 20:22, 23. *26:39, 42. Mk 10:38, 39. 14:35, 36.
Lk 22:42. He *12:2. **my Father**. Jn 11:41, 42. 12:27,
28. 15:10. 17:24. 20:17. Lk 12:30. Ro 8:15-18. He 12:5-
10. **hath given**. Ps +*39:9.

12. **the band**. ver. 3, 18, 22. Jn 19:6. Mt *26:57,
58. Mk 14:53. Lk *22:54. **the captain**. Ac 21:31, 37.
22:24-28. 23:10, 17, etc. **the Jews**. ver. 14, 31, 38.
Jn +5:10. **bound**. Ge 22:9. 40:3. Jg 16:21. Ps 118:27.
Mt 27:2. Mk 15:1.

13. **led**. Mt 26:57. Mk 14:53. **Annas**. ver. 24. Lk
3:2. Ac 4:6. **Caiaphas**. ver. 24, 28. Jn 11:49. Mt 26:3,
57. Lk *3:2. Ac *4:6. **that same**. Jn 11:51. "And Annas
sent Christ bound unto Caiaphas the high priest, ver.
24."

14. **Caiaphas**. Jn *11:49-52. 19:11. **die**. Gr. *apollumi*, Mt +2:13.

15. **Simon**. Mt *26:58, etc. Mk 14:54. Lk 22:54.
another disciple. Jn 20:2. *21:24. **the palace**. Mt 26:3.

16. **But Peter**. Mt 26:69, 70. Mk 14:66-68. Lk 22:55-
57. **other disciple**. ver. 15. Jn 20:2. **unto her**. Ac 12:13.

17. **the damsel**. ver. 16. Mt 26:69, 70. Mk 14:66-
68. Lk *22:54, 56, 57. Ac 12:13. **Art not thou**. ver.

25. I am not. ver. 5, 8. Jn 21:15. Mt 26:33. 1 C √10:12.

18. And. ſ143, Ge +19:2. officers. ver. 3, 12, 22. Jn 19:6. Mt +26:58. who. ver. 25. Mk 14:54. Lk 22:55, 56. a fire. Jn 21:9. for. Lk 22:44. Peter. ver. 25. Mk 14:54. stood with. Ge 19:1. 49:6. 1 K 19:9. Ps +*1:1. 26:4-10. Pr 13:20. Ac 4:23. 1 C 15:33. 2 C 6:15-17. Ep *5:11, 12.

19. The high priest. Mt 26:59-68. Mk 14:55-65. Lk 22:63-71. asked. Lk 11:53, 54. 20:20. his doctrine. Jn +7:16.

20. I spake openly. ſ24I, Is +21:7. Jn *7:14, 26, 28. *8:2. 10:23-39. +16:25. Ps 22:22. 40:9, 10. Mt 4:23. 9:35. 21:23, etc. 26:65. Lk *4:15, 16. 19:45-47. 20:1, etc. 21:37. to the. Jn 8:26. world. Gr. kosmos, Mt +4:8. and in. Jn 7:4. Is 45:19. 48:16. Mt 24:26. Ac 26:26. the synagogue. Jn 6:59. Mt +4:23. the temple. ſ77, Ex +3:19. ſ171.O.11, Lk +2:46. Mt +26:55. the Jews. ver. 36. Jn +4:22. +5:10. in secret. Jn 7:4. Is 45:19. 48:16. Mt 10:27. Lk 12:3. Ac *26:26. said nothing. ſ171C, Ex +20:10.

21. ask. Mt 26:59, 60. Mk 14:55-59. Lk 22:67, 68. Ac 24:12, 13, 18-20.

22. officers. ver. 3. Mk 14:65. struck. Jb 16:10. 30:10-12. Is 50:5-7. Je 20:2. Mi 5:1. Mt 26:67, 68. Mk 14:65. Lk 22:63, 64. Ac *23:2, 3. the palm of his hand. or, a rod. Jn 19:3. Mt 5:39. Answerest. Ac 23:3-5.

23. If. ſ184A, 1 C +15:2. 2 C 10:1. 1 P *2:19-23. but if. ſ184A, 1 C +15:2. why smitest. Ac 23:3.

24. Annas. Annas was dismissed from being high priest, A.D. 23, after filling that office for fifteen years; but, being a person of distinguished character, and having had no fewer than five sons who had successively enjoyed the dignity of the high-priesthood, and the present high priest Caiaphas being his son-in-law, he must have possessed much authority in the nation. It was at the palace of Caiaphas where the chief priests, elders, and scribes, were assembled the whole of the night to see the issue of their stratagem. ver. 13. Mt 26:57. had sent. lit. sent. ſ96C3, Mt +14:3. bound. See ver. 13.

25. stood. ver. 18. Mk 14:37, 38, 67. Lk 22:56. They. Mt *26:69-72. Mk *14:68-70. Lk *22:58. Art not thou. ver. 17. He. Ge 18:15. Pr 29:25. Ga 2:11-13.

26. being. ver. 10. Did. Pr 12:19. Mt *26:73. Mk *14:70, 71. Lk *22:59, 60. see thee. Apparently Peter, in contrast to Jesus (ver. 8n), was easily recognized. in the garden. ver. 1. Jn 19:41.

27. and. Jn *13:38. Mt *26:34, 74, 75. Mk *14:30, 68, 71, 72. Lk *22:34, 60-62.

28. led. Mt *27:1, 2, etc. Mk 15:1, etc. Lk 23:1, etc. Ac 3:13. from. ver. 24. Caiaphas. ver. 13. unto. ver. 33. Jn 19:9. Mt *27:27. Mk 15:16g. Ac 23:35. Ph 1:13g. hall of judgment. or, Pilate's house. The praetorium, the Roman governor's house: see on Mk 15:16. early. Pr 1:16. 4:16. Mi 2:1. Mt 27:2. Mk 15:1. Lk 22:66. and they. Ps 35:16. Is 1:10-15. Je 7:8-11. Am 5:21-23. Mi 3:10-12. Mt *23:23-28. 27:6. Ac 10:28. 11:3. lest. Pr +*16:2. Jn 11:55. Mt √23:23, 24. Ac *10:28. 11:3. eat. ver. 39. Jn 19:14. Dt 16:2. Dt *16:2, 6. 2 Ch 30:21-24. 35:8-14. Ezk 45:21. the passover. ver. 39. Jn +6:4.

29. went out. Mt 27:11-14. Mk 15:2-5. Lk 23:2, 3. What. Mt 27:23. Ac 23:28-30. 25:16.

30. If. ſ184B, Mt +11:21. Mt 19:12. Mk 15:3. Lk 20:19-26. 23:2-5. malefactor. or, evil-doer. 1 P 2:12,

14. 3:17. 4:15. 3 J 11. delivered. Mk 10:33. Lk 24:7. Ac 3:13.

31. Take. Jn 19:6, 7. Ac 25:18-20. not lawful. Jn 19:15. Ge +*49:10. Ezk 21:26, 27. Ho 3:4, 5. to put. Lk 4:29. Ac 7:59.

32. the saying. Jn 3:14. 10:31, 33. *12:32, 33. +13:18. 15:25. Mt *20:19. 26:2. Mk 10:33, 34. Lk 18:32, 33. 24:7, 8. Ac 7:59. what. Dt 21:23. Ps 22:16. Ga *3:13.

33. again. ver. 28, 29. Jn 19:9. judgment hall. ver. +28. and said. ver. 37. Mt *27:11. Mk 15:2. Lk 23:3, 4. 1 T 6:13. Art thou. Jn 19:12. the King. ver. 39. Jn 1:49. 12:13, 15. 19:3, 19-22. Ps 2:6-12. Is +*9:6, 7. Je +*23:5, 6. Zp 3:15. Zc *9:9. Mt +27:11. Lk 19:38-40. Ac 2:34-36.

34. Sayest. ver. 36.

35. Am I. Ezr 4:12. Ne 4:2. Ac 18:14-16. 23:29. 25:19, 20. Ro 3:1, 2. Thine. ver. 28. Jn 19:11. Ac 3:13. chief priests. Jn +11:57. 12:10. 19:6, 15, 21. what hast. Jn 19:6. Ge 3:13. 4:10. 20:9. 31:26. 1 S 13:11. Ac 21:38. 22:22-24.

36. Jesus. 1 T *6:13. My kingdom. Jn 6:15. 8:15. Ps 45:3-7. Is +*9:6, 7. Da *2:34, 35, 44, 45. +*7:14, 27. Zc *9:9. Mt 12:28. +√21:43. Lk +*1:32, 33. 12:14. +*17:20, 21. *19:11. +√21:31. +√22:29, 30. 23:42. Ac 1:3, 6. Ro *14:17. Col *1:12-14. 2 T +*4:18n. Re *11:15. is not. Jn 8:23. 14:30. 15:19. 17:14, 16. Da 2:34, 35, 44, 45. +*7:14, 27. Mt 22:21. *26:64. Lk 12:13, 14. +*17:21. +*21:31. He +*11:16n. 1 P +*1:4n. 1 J 2:16. 4:5. Re +*5:10. √11:15. of this. Jn +*6:54n. +9:39. *15:19. 16:16. 17:25. world. Gr. kosmos, Mt +4:8. if my. ſ184B, Lk +7:39. then would. ſ184B, Mt +23:30. ver. 11. Le 26:7, 8. Ps 9:15-20. 10:16. *49:14. *58:10. 68:23. *110:1, 2. +*149:6-9. Je *51:20. Zc 12:3-8. *14:14. Mt +5:39. √26:53. Lk +*22:36. He 1:13. Re +*2:26, 27. 11:15-18. my servants. or, officers, as ver. 3, 12, 18, 22. fight. Is 63:3, 4. Jl *3:11. Mi *4:13. 5:8. Zc *14:14. Ml *4:3. Lk 13:24g. 22:50, 51. 1 C +9:25g. not be delivered. Jn 19:16. the Jews. ver. 20. Jn +4:22. but now. Peters observes "Will the Savior contradict the predictions of the prophets? No, for He qualifies His language, guarding it, by the "but now," i.e. at the present time, my Kingdom is not of this world and my servants do not fight, leaving the plain inference that at some future time, just as prophesied, His servants would fight" (Theocratic Kingdom, vol. 2, p. 109). Jl 2:28n. Lk 17:20n. +*21:31. +*22:29, 30. 2 T +*4:1n. Re ◖+*5:10. ◖*11:15. not from. He +*11:16n.

37. Thou sayest. Mt 26:64. +*27:11n. Mk *14:61, 62. 15:2. Lk +22:70. 23:3. 1 T 6:13. a king. Ps ✱2:6. To this end. Jn 12:27. Ro 14:9. was I. ſ16, Ge +1:27. came I. Jn +11:27. 16:28. world. Gr. kosmos, Mt +4:8. that I should. Jn +1:14. 3:11, +32. 4:44g. 5:31. 7:7g. 8:13, 14, 18. 13:21g. √14:6. Is 55:4. Ac 14:3. 1 T 6:13. Re 1:4, +5. 3:14. bear witness. T#66. Jn 5:33. Pr +28:23 (T#610). Is 11:3, 4. *55:4. Ml 3:2, 3. Lk 11:52. 12:49. Mt ch. 5, 23. Ga +2:11 (T#611). Re *1:5. *3:14. unto the truth. Jn +1:17. Every. Jn +*7:17. 8:47. 10:26, 27. 1 P 1:22, 23. 1 J 2:21. 3:14, 19. 4:6. 5:20. heareth. Jn *6:45. +*7:17. √8:47. √10:16, 26, 27.

38. What. ſ60B, Ge +20:16. Ac 17:19, 20, 32. 24:25, 26. truth. Jn √14:6. *17:17. went out again. ver. 33. Jn 19:4. I find. Jn 19:4, 6, 21, 22. Is *53:9. Mt *27:18, 19, 24. Mk 15:14. Lk 23:4, 14-16, 22. 2 C √5:21. He *7:26. 1 P 1:19. *2:22, 23.

39. **ye have**. Mt *27:15-18. Mk 15:6, 8-10. Lk *23:17, 20. **the passover**. ver. 28. Jn +6:4. **I release**. ver. 33.

40. **Then cried**. Mt 27:16, 26. Mk 15:7, 15. Lk *23:18, 19, 25. Ac *3:13, 14. **Not this**. Je *2:13. Lk √19:14, 27.

JOHN 19

Jesus is scourged, crowned with thorns, and mocked by the soldiers, 1-3. Pilate declaring his innocence, the Jews charge him with calling himself the "Son of God," 4-7. Pilate, after further examination, desires to release him, but overcome with the clamors of the Jews, delivers him to be crucified, 8-16. He is led to Golgotha and crucified between two robbers, 17, 18. The title placed over his cross, which Pilate refuses to alter, 19-22. The soldiers part his garments, 23, 24. Jesus affectionately commends his mother to the care of John, 25-27; and, receiving vinegar to drink, he expires, 28-30. The legs of the robbers are broken to hasten their death, but Jesus being previously dead, his side is pierced by a soldier, and thus the Scriptures are fulfilled, 31-37. Joseph of Arimathea, assisted by Nicodemus, buries him, 38-42.

1. **Pilate**. Mt 27:26, etc. Mk 15:15, etc. Lk 23:16, 23. **scourged**. Ps 129:3. Is ✱50:6. *53:5. Mt *20:19. 23:34. 27:26. Mk 10:33, 34. 15:15. Lk 18:33. 23:16. Ac 16:22, 23. 22:24, 25. 2 C 11:24, 25. He 11:36. 1 P *2:24.

2. **the soldiers**. ver. 5. Ps 22:6. Is 49:7. 53:3. Mt *27:27-31. Mk 15:17-20. Lk *23:11. **crown**. Ezk 16:12. **purple robe**. Is 63:1, 2. Re 19:13.

3. **Hail**. Mt 26:49. 27:29. Lk 1:28. **King**. ver. 19-22. Jn 18:33, 39. Mt 27:11. **they smote**. Jn 18:22.

4. **went forth**. Jn 18:33, 38. **that ye**. ver. 6. Jn *1:29. 18:38. Mt 27:4, 19, 24, 54. Lk 23:41, 47. 2 C √5:21. He *7:26. 1 P 1:19. 2:22. *3:18. 1 J 3:5.

5. **came Jesus forth**. Jn 18:28. **crown**. ver. 2. **purple robe**. ver. 1. **Behold**. ver. 14. Jn 1:29. Is +*7:14. 40:9. 42:1. La 1:12. He *12:2.

6. **the chief priests**. ver. 15, 21. Mt 27:22, 23. Mk 15:12-15. Lk 22:21-23. Ac 2:23. 3:13-15. 7:52. 13:27-29. **officers**. Jn 18:3. **Take**. Pilate neither did nor could say this seriously; for crucifixion was not a Jewish but a Roman mode of punishment. The cross was made of two beams, either crossing at the top, at right angles, like a T, or in the middle of their length, like an X; with a piece on the center of the transverse beam for the accusation, and another piece projecting from the middle, on which the person sat. The cross on which our Lord suffered was of the former kind, being thus represented on all old monuments, coins, and crosses. The body was usually fastened to the upright beam by nailing the feet to it, and on the transverse (or horizontal) piece by nailing the hands; and the person was frequently permitted to hang in this situation till he perished through agony and lack of food. This horrible punishment was usually inflicted only on slaves for the worst of crimes. That Christ was crucified on a cross, and not on a so-called "torture stake" or single upright pole, is proven by the fact that Jn 20:25 refers not to a single nail piercing both hands, as would be if Jesus had been crucified upon a single upright stake, but to the print of the *nails*, showing that each hand was nailed separately to the cross-arm, as usually por-

trayed. Jn 18:31. Mt 27:24, 25. **no fault**. ver. 4. Jn 18:38. Ps 59:4. 109:3. Da 6:4.

7. **The Jews**. ver. 12, 14, 20, 21, 31, 38. Jn +5:10. **We have**. Le *24:16. Dt 13:1-5. 18:20. 1 K 21:10, 13. **because**. Jn +√5:18n. *8:58, 59. √10:30-33, 36-38. Mt 26:63-66. 27:42, 43. Mk 14:61-64. 15:39. Lk 22:70. Ro 1:4. **the Son of God**. Mt +*14:33. Lk *4:41.

8. **heard**. ver. 13. Ac 14:11-19. **more afraid**. Mt 27:19.

9. **And went**. Jn 18:33. **judgment hall**. Jn +18:28. **Whence**. Jn 7:27. 8:14. 9:29, 30. Jg 13:6. Ps 38:13-15. Is *53:7. Mt 27:12-14. Mk 15:3-5. Ac 8:32, 33. Ph 1:28. **no answer**. Jn 18:37. Is *53:7. Mt +*26:63. 27:12, 14. Mk 14:61. 15:4. Lk 23:9.

10. **knowest**. Jn 18:39. Da 3:14, 15. 5:19.

11. **Thou**. Jn 3:27. *7:30. √10:17, 18. Ge 45:7, 8. Ex 9:14-16. 1 Ch *29:11, 12. Ps 39:9. 62:11. Je 27:5-8. La 3:37. Da 4:17, 25, 32, 35. 5:21. Mt +*6:13. √26:53, 54. Lk 22:53. Ac 2:23. *4:28. Ro 11:36. *13:1. Ja 1:17. **couldest have**. √184B, Mt +23:30. **except**. Is +*36:10. **given**. Ge 9:6. Ex 21:25. Ro 13:4. **from above**. Jn 3:3, 7, 31. **he that**. Jn 11:49, 50. *18:3, +14, 28-32. Mt 26:65. 27:2. Mk 14:44. **the greater**. Jn +9:41. 15:22-24. Mt +*11:22. Lk 7:41, 42. 10:11-14. +*12:47, 48. He *6:4-8. Ja √4:17.

12. **from**. Jn 6:66. Mk 6:16-26. Ac 24:24-27. **Pilate**. Mt +27:54. Ac 3:13. **If**. √184C, Mt +4:9. **thou art**. Jn 18:33-36. Mt 22:17. Lk 23:2-5. Ac 17:6, 7. **Caesar**. i.e. *one cut out; head of hair*, ✱S#2541g. ver. 15. Mt 22:17, 21, 21. Mk 12:14, 16, 17, 17. Lk 2:1. 3:1. 20:22, 24, 25, 25. 23:2. Ac 11:28. 17:7. 25:8, 10, 11, 12, 21. 26:32. 27:24. 28:19. Ph 4:22.

13. **heard**. ver. 8. Pr *29:25. Is 51:12, 13. 57:11. Lk 12:5. Ac *4:19. **and sat**. Ps 58:1, 2. 82:5-7. 94:20, 21. Ec 5:8. Am 5:7. Mt 27:19. **in the Hebrew**. ver. 17, 20. Jn 5:2. Ac 21:40. 22:2. 26:14. **Gabbatha**. i.e. *the high place, the knoll; paved with stones*, ✱S#1042g, only here.

14. **the preparation**. ver. 31, 32, 42. Jn 18:28. Mt 27:62. Mk *15:42. Lk 23:54. **passover**. Jn +6:4. Le +*23:5. **the sixth**. That is, sixth hour of the night, or midnight. See Ac 23:23. Instead of *ektee*, "sixth," several MSS. and fathers have *tritee*, "third," as in the parallel place. Mk 15:25, 33, 34. Lk 23:44. **Behold**. √60B, Ge +20:16. ver. 3, 5, 19-22.

15. **cried out**. Mt ◑21:9. **Away**. ver. 6. Lk 23:18. Ac 21:36. 22:22. **We have**. ver. 12. Jn 18:31. Ge +*49:10. Ezk 21:26, 27. Mt 22:17.

16. **delivered**. Jn 18:36. Mt *27:26-31. Mk 15:15-20. Lk 23:24, 25.

17. **he**. Mt 10:38. 16:24. 27:31-33. Mk 8:34. 10:21. 15:21, 22. Lk 9:23. 14:27. 23:26, 33. **bearing**. Ge 22:6. Lk 14:27. **went forth**. Le 16:21, 22. 24:14. Nu 15:35, 36. 1 K 21:13. Lk 23:33. Ac 7:58. He *13:11-13. **Golgotha**. *Golgotha*, of which *Kranion* and *Calvaria* are merely translations, is supposed to have been a hill or a rising on a greater hill on the northwest of Jerusalem. Mt 27:33, 34. Mk 15:21, 22. Lk 23:33.

18. **Where they crucified**. Jn 3:14, 15. *12:32, 33. 18:32. Ps ✱22:16. Is *53:12. Mt 27:35-38, 44. Mk 15:24-28. Lk 23:32-34. Ga +*3:13. He *12:2. **and two**. Lk 23:39-43.

19. **wrote**. Mt 27:37. Mk 15:26. Lk 23:38. **And the**. The apparent discrepancy between the accounts of this title given by the Evangelists, which has been urged as an objection against their inspiration and veracity,

has been satisfactorily accounted for by Dr. Townson; who supposes that, as it was written in Hebrew, Greek, and Latin, it might have slightly varied in each language; and that, as St. Luke and St. John wrote for the Gentiles, they would prefer the Greek inscription, that St. Matthew, addressing the Jews, would use the Hebrew, and that St. Mark, writing to the Romans, would naturally give the Latin. **JESUS**. ver. 3, 12. Jn 1:45, 46, 49. 18:33. Ac 3:6. 26:9. **OF NAZARETH**. Jn 18:5. **THE KING**. ver. +3.

20. **was nigh**. ver. 17. Nu 15:35, 36. He 13:12. **in**. ver. 13. Jn 5:2. Ac 21:40. 22:2. 26:14. Re 16:16. **and Greek**. Ac 21:37. Re 9:11.

21. **chief priests**. ver. 6, 15. Jn +12:10. **of the Jews**. Jn +6:4. **The King of the Jews**. ver. 3, 19. **but**. ver. 12.

22. **What**. ♪9, 2 K +5:19. ver. 12. Ge 43:14. Est 4:16. Ps 65:7. 76:10. Pr 8:29. **written**. ♪145, Jg +11:40.

23. **the soldiers**. Mt 27:35. Mk 15:24. Lk 23:34. **to every**. Ac 12:4. **now**. Such was the *Kiton*, or "coat," of the Jewish high priest, as described by Josephus (*Ant*. l. iii. c. 7. sec. 4). **woven**. *or*, wrought. Ex 28:32. 39:22, 23.

24. **that**. ver. 28, 36, 37. Jn 7:38. 10:35. 12:38, 39. 13:18. **They parted**. Ps ▶22:18. Is 10:7. Ac 13:27.

25. **his mother**. Mt +1:16. Lk 2:35. **and his**. Mt *27:55, 56. Mk 15:40, 41. Lk 23:49. **Cleophas**. *or*, Cleopas. i.e. *the whole glory*, ✱S#2832g, only here. Lk 24:18. **and Mary Magdalene**. Jn 20:1, 11-18. Mt 27:56, 61. 28:1. Mk 15:40, 47. 16:1, 9. Lk 8:2. 24:10.

26. **whom**. Jn +13:23. 20:2. 21:7, 20, 24. **Woman**. Jn 2:4.

27. **Then saith**. Lk 7:15. Col 4:1. **Behold**. Ge 45:8. 47:12. Mt 12:48-50. 25:40. Mk 3:34, 35. 1 T 5:2-4. **took**. 1 J 3:18, 19. **his**. Jn 1:11. 16:32mg. Lk 18:28. Ac 21:6g.

28. **Jesus**. ver. 30. Jn 13:1. 18:4, 32. Lk 9:31. 12:50. *18:31. *22:37. Ac 13:29. **knowing**. Jn +1:48. +8:14. +13:1. **accomplished**. ver. 30. **that the**. ver. 24. Jn 4:6, 7. Mt *26:54. **I thirst**. Ps 22:15. 69:21.

29. **was set**. Mt *27:34, 48. Mk 15:36. Lk 23:36. **hyssop**. This *hyssop* is termed a *reed* by Matthew and Mark; and it appears that a species of hyssop, with a *reedy* stalk, about two feet long, grew about Jerusalem. Ex 12:22. Le 14:6. Nu 19:18. 1 K 4:33. Ps 51:7. He 9:19.

30. **It is finished**. ver. 28g. Jn *4:34. +17:4. Ge +*3:15. Ps 22:15. Is *53:10, 12. Da +*?9:24, 26. Zc 13:7. Mt 3:15. Mk 13:57. Lk 2:49. Ac 13:29. Ro 3:25, 26. 4:25. *10:4. 1 C 5:7, 8. Ga 2:20. Ep 2:13-20. 5:2, 25. Col *2:14-17. He +*2:10. *5:9. 9:11-14, 22-28. *10:1-14. *12:2. **and he**. Jn √10:11, 18. Mt 20:28. 27:50. Mk 15:37. Lk 23:46. Ph 2:8. He 2:14, 15. **ghost**. Gr. *pneuma*, ♪121A3, Mt +27:50. Jn +11:33.

31. **The Jews**. ver. +7. **because**. ver. 14, 42. Mt 27:62. Mk *15:42. **that the**. Dt *21:22, 23. Jsh 8:29. 10:26, 27. Ga +*3:13. **that sabbath**. Le 23:7-16. **high day**. Ex 12:16. Le 23:7. Nu *28:16-18, 25. **their**. Lactantius says (l. iv. c. 26), that it was a custom to break the legs of criminals upon the cross; which was done, we are told, at the instep with an iron mallet; and appears to have been a kind of *coup de grace*, the sooner to put them out of pain. ver. 1. Pr 12:10. Mi 3:3.

32. **of the first**. ver. 18. Lk 23:39-43.

34. **pierced**. Zc ✱12:10. **came**. Jn 13:8-10. Ps 51:7.

Ezk +*36:25. Zc *13:1. Mt 27:62. Ac 22:16. 1 C *1:30. 6:11. Ep *5:26, 27. T *2:14. *3:5-7. He 9:13, 14, √22. *10:19-22. 1 P 3:21. 1 J √1:6-9. *5:6, 8. Re +*1:5. *7:14. **and water**. Ex 17:6. Le 14:5-7. Is 32:2. He=9:19. 1 J 5:6, 8.

35. **he that**. ver. 26. Jn 12:17. +15:27. 21:24. Ac 10:39. He *2:3, 4. 1 P 5:1. 1 J 1:1-3. Re 1:2. **his record**. Jn 21:24. **that ye**. Jn 11:15, 42. 14:29. 17:20, 21. √20:31. Ro √15:4. 1 J √5:13. **believe**. Jn +5:44.

36. **were done**. Mt 1:22. **that the**. ver. 24. Jn +7:38. +13:18. **fulfilled**. The passages here cited as fulfilled were not, in their original contexts, strictly prophecies, but what may be regarded as types, pictures in the Mosaic institutions which prefigured the Messiah. This shows that the distinctions we commonly make between type and prophecy are artificial distinctions imposed by us upon Scripture, not distinctions strictly maintained by Scripture. This, then, provides the Scriptural basis for the study of types, a field of study as valid as the field of prophecy, if carefully conducted. **A bone**. ♪92A, Mt +12:40. Ex *▶12:46. Nu *9:12. Ps 22:14. *34:20. 35:10. 1 C 5:7. **not be broken**. Ge +=22:12. Ex ✱▶12:46. Nu=9:12. Ps ✱34:20. 35:10.

37. **scripture saith**. Jn +7:38. 2 T 3:16. 1 P 2:6. 2 P 1:20. **They shall**. ♪92A, Mt +1:23. **look**. ♪108B, Ge +21:16. Jn *1:29. Ps ✱22:16, 17. Zc ✱▶12:10. Re +*1:7.

38. **Joseph**. Mt *27:57-60. Mk *15:42-46. Lk *23:50-54. **but secretly**. Jn 9:22. 12:42. Pr 29:25. Mk 15:43. Ph 1:14. **for fear**. Jn +7:13. **take away**. Mt 14:12. Mk 6:29. Ac 8:2.

39. **Nicodemus**. Jn *3:1, etc. *7:50-52. Mt 12:20. 19:30. **and brought**. Mk 16:1. Lk 24:1. **a mixture of**. Jn 12:7. 2 Ch 16:13, 14. SS 4:6, 14. **myrrh**. Ex 30:23. Est 2:12. SS 1:13. 3:6. 4:6, 14. 5:1, 5, 13. Mt 2:11. Mk 15:23. **aloes**. Ge 50:2. Ps 45:8. Pr 7:17. SS 4:14. **about**. Some have objected to the great quantity of spices employed on this occasion; but Josephus states (l. xvii. c. 3. sec. 4) that five hundred servants bearing spices attended the funeral of Herod; and 80 lbs. of opobalsam are said to have been used at the funeral of R. Gamaliel (Talmud, Messec. Semach, c. 8). **hundred pounds**. Jn 12:3.

40. **wound**. Jn 11:44. 20:5-7. Mt *26:12. Mk 14:8. Ac *5:6. **linen clothes**. Jn 20:5-7. Lk 24:12. **to bury**. Jn 12:7. Mt 26:12. Mk 14:8.

41. **garden**. Jn 18:1. 20:15. **and in**. Jn 20:15. 2 K 21:18, 26. 23:30. Is 22:16. Mt 27:60, 64-66. **wherein**. Mk 11:2. Lk 23:53.

42. **laid**. Ps 22:15. Is *53:9. Mt 12:40. Ac 13:29. 1 C 15:4. Col 2:12. **because**. ver. 14, 31.

JOHN 20

Mary Magdalene goes to the sepulchre and, discovering that the stone was taken away, runs to tell Peter and John, who hasten thither. They find not the body but only the graveclothes in exact order, 1-10. Mary as she weeps sees two angels, and afterwards Jesus, who sends her to inform the apostles, 11-18. Jesus meets them as assembled in the evening and speaks peace to them, 19-23. Thomas, who was absent, remains resolutely incredulous, 24, 25. Jesus again meets the assembled disciples, and satisfies Thomas, who confesses him as "his Lord, and his God," 26-29. "These things were written, that we might believe, and

... have life through his name," 30, 31.

1. first. ver. *19, 26. Ac *20:7. 1 C *16:2. Re 1:10.
cometh. Mary Magdalene, as well as Peter, was evidently at the sepulchre *twice* on the morning of the resurrection. The *first* time of her going was some short time before her companions, the other Mary and Salome (Mt 28:1); and observing that the stone had been removed, she returned to inform Peter and John. In the meantime, the other Mary and Salome came to the sepulchre, and saw the angel, as recorded by Matthew and Mark. While these women returned to the city, Peter and John went to the sepulchre, passing them at some distance, or going another way, followed by Mary Magdalene, who stayed after their return. This was her second journey; when she saw two angels, and then Jesus himself, as here related; and immediately after Jesus appeared to the other women, as they returned to the city (Mt 28:9, 10). In the meantime Joanna and her company arrived at the sepulchre, when two angels appeared to them as the one angel had done the other women (Lk 24:1-10). They immediately returned to the city, and by some means found the apostles before the others arrived, and informed them of what they had seen; upon which Peter went a *second* time to the sepulchre, but saw only the linen clothes lying (Lk *24:12). Mt *28:1, etc. Mk *16:1, 2, 9. Lk *24:1-10. **Mary Magdalene.** ver. 18. Jn +19:25. **the stone.** Jn +11:38. Mt 27:60, 64-66. *28:2. Mk 15:46. *16:3, 4. Lk 24:2.

2. **other disciple.** Jn +18:15. **whom.** Jn 13:23. *19:26. *21:7, 20, 24. **They have taken.** ver. *9, 13, 15. Mt *27:63, 64. **the Lord.** ver. 18, 20, 25. Jn +4:1.

3. **Peter therefore.** Mt +4:21. Mk +9:38. Lk 22:8. Ac 3:1, 3, 4, 11. 4:13, 19. 8:14. Ga 2:9. **went forth.** Lk *24:12, 24. **other disciple.** ver. 2.

4. **outrun.** 2 S 18:23. Lk 13:30. 1 C *9:24. 2 C 8:12.

5. **stooping.** ver. 11. Lk 24:12. Ja 1:25. 1 P 1:12g. **saw.** Jn *11:44. *19:40. **linen clothes.** Jn 19:40. Lk 24:12.

6. **Then cometh.** Jn 6:67-69. 18:17, 25-27. 21:7, 15-17. Mt 16:15, 16. Lk 22:31, 32. **went into.** Gr. *eiseelthen eis.* To signify the actual entering into a place, notice Greek repeats the preposition *eis*, *into*, by attaching it as a prefix to the verb, and repeating it after the verb. This grammatical construction serves to distinguish the mere approach to a place, as distinct from entering into it. Examples of this construction may be seen at Mt 8:5 (of entering the city Capernaum); 12:4 (of David entering the house of God); 24:38 (of Noah entering the ark). Mk 1:21 (of Jesus entering into the synagogue); 2:1; 3:1; *5:13 (of unclean spirits entering the swine); 6:56; *7:17 (into a house), 24; 11:2 (entered into a village); 11:11 (entered Jerusalem and the temple); 16:5 (entering into the sepulchre). Lk 1:40. 4:38 (entered Simon's house). 6:6; 7:1, 44; 8:30 (of demons entering the man), 33 (demons entering into swine); 9:34 (entered a cloud on the mount of transfiguration), 52 (entered a Samaritan village); 10:38; 17:12, 27 (Noah entering the ark); 22:3 (Satan entered Judas), 10. Jn 4:38 (entered into their labors); 13:27 (Satan entered Judas); 18:1 (entered the garden of Gesthemene), 33 (Pilate entered the judgment hall). Ac 3:2, 8; 5:21; 9:17 (Ananias entered into the house where Saul was); 10:24; 11:8 (of Peter, who states no unclean food ever entered his mouth), 12; 16:40; 18:19;

19:30 (entered in unto the people); 21:8 (entered house of Philip), 26 (entered the temple); 23:16 (entered the castle); 25:23. Ro 5:12 (sin entered the world); He 4:6, 10 (enter into his rest); 9:12, 24. Ja 5:4 (entered into the ears). 2 J 7. The significance of all this is that those who assert that baptism is not by immersion claim that this expression is never used of going into the water for baptism: the expressions used simply mean they went down to and came up from the water, but never entered into the water in the sense of being immersed. Thus the Reverend G. W. Hughey writes "When the Greeks wished to specifically express *motion into* a place by the force of the preposition *eis*, they used it both before and after the verb. Instances of this often occur, as *'eiselthen eis,'* or *'eiserchomai eis.'* We have numerous examples of this usage, both in the New Testament and in the Septuagint. We have a striking example of this usage in John's account of the resurrection of our Lord: John 20:4, 'and came first *to* (*eis*) the sepulchre,' (*'elthe protos eis mnemion'*); verse 6, 'Then cometh Simon Peter following him and he went into the sepulchre,' *'eiselthen eis to mnemion.' "* And again, "In not a single example of its use with *baptidzo* do we have this usage. This is a most significant fact" (*The Scriptural Mode of Christian Baptism*, pp. 128, 129).

7. **the napkin.** Jn *11:44. Lk 19:20. Ac 19:12. **in a.** ∫108E1, Mt +8:19. **by itself.** ∫24E, Ge +30:33. Jn 15:5.

8. **and he.** ver. 25, 29. Jn 1:50. **believed.** Jn +5:44.

9. **they.** Mt 16:21, 22. Mk 8:31-33. 9:9, 10, 31, 32. Lk *9:45. 18:33, 34. √24:26, 44-46. **knew not.** Mt *22:29. Mk +*12:24. **that.** Jn *2:22. Ps +*16:10. 22:15, 22, etc. Is 25:8. +*26:19n. 53:10-12. +55:3. Ho 13:14. Lk +*24:44. Ac *2:25-32. *13:29-37. 17:3. 1 C +*15:4. **must.** Jn +3:14.

10. **went.** Jn 7:53. 16:32. Lk 24:12.

11. **Mary.** ver. 1, 2. **stooped.** ver. 5.

12. **seeth.** Mt *28:3-5. Mk *16:5, 6. Lk *24:3-7, 22, 23. **in white.** 2 Ch 5:12. Da 7:9. Mt 17:2. 28:3. Mk 16:5. Ac 1:10. Re 3:4. *7:14.

13. **Woman.** ver. 15. Jn 2:4. 4:21. 19:26. **why.** ver. 15. Jn 14:27, 28. 16:6, 7, 20-22. 1 S 1:8. Ps 43:3-5, 11. Ec 3:4. Je 31:16. Lk 24:17. Ac 21:13. **Because.** ver. 2.

14. **and saw.** SS 3:3, 4. Mt 28:9. Mk 16:9. **and knew not.** Jn 8:59. 21:4. Ge +*19:11. Mt 14:26. 28:17. Mk 16:12. Lk +*4:30. +*24:16, 31.

15. **Woman.** ver. +13. **whom.** Jn 1:38. 18:4, 7. SS 3:2. 6:1. Mt 28:5. Mk 16:6. Lk 24:5. **the gardener.** Mt 19:41. **if.** 1 S 1:16. Mt 12:34. **if.** ∫184A, 1 C +15:2. **borne him.** Jn 12:6g.

16. **Mary.** Jn 10:3, 4. Ge 22:1, 11. Ex 3:4. 33:17. 1 S 3:6, 10. Is *43:1. Lk 10:41. Ac 9:4. 10:3. **She.** Ge 45:12. SS 2:8, etc. 3:4. 5:2. Mt 14:27. **Rabboni.** i.e. *great master,* *S#4462g. ver. 28. Jn 1:38, 49. 3:2. 6:25. 11:28. 13:13. Ge +*3:7. Mt 23:8-10. Mk 10:51g.

17. **Touch.** ∫108B. Idiom B827. "To touch" is used for detention, or for diverting from any purpose. Or rather, "embrace me not," or "cling not to me," *mee mou aptou,* "Spend no more time with me now in joyful gratulations: for I am not yet immediately going to ascend to my Father—you will have several opportunities of seeing me again; but go and tell my disciples that I shall depart to my Father and your Father." ver. 27. 2 K 4:29. 7:9. Mt *28:7, 9, 10. Lk 10:4. 24:39.

1 J 1:1. **am**. J96C1, Ge +4:1. **ascended**. Lk 24:51.
my brethren. Jn 21:23. Ps 22:22. Mt *12:50. *25:40.
*28:10. Ro 8:29. He *2:11-13. **I ascend**. J96C7, Mt
+26:24. Jn *13:1, 3. +*14:1-3, 6, 12, *28. *16:28.
17:5, 11, 25. Ps *68:18. 89:26. Mk 16:19. Lk *24:49-
51. Ep *1:17-23. *4:8-10. 1 P 1:3. **my Father**. Jn +5:17.
Mt 3:17. Ro *8:29. *15:6. He 2:11. Re 1:6. **your Father**.
Jn *1:12, 13. Nu=18:2. Mt 6:9. Ro *8:14-17. 2 C *6:18.
Ga *3:26. 4:6, 7. 1 J *3:2. Re *21:7. **my God**. Mt
27:46. 1 C ●3:23. Ep *1:17. He +*1:8, 9. Re 3:12.
your God. Ge 17:7, 8. Ps 43:4. *48:14. Is *41:10. Je
*31:33. 32:38. Ezk 36:28. 37:27. Zc *13:7-9. He *8:10.
+*11:16. Re *21:3.

18. **Mary Magdalene**. ver. 1. Jn 19:25. **came**. Mt
*28:9, 10. Mk 16:10-13. Lk *24:10, 22, 23. **had seen**.
ver. 25. **the Lord**. ver. 2, 20, 25. Jn +4:1.

19. **the same**. Mk 16:14. Lk 24:36-49. 1 C 15:5.
the first. Ac *20:7. 1 C *16:2. **when**. ver. 26. Ne 6:10,
11. **for fear**. Jn 7:13. **the Jews**. Jn +5:10. **came**. Jn
14:19-23. 16:22. Ac 1:3. **in the midst**. Mt +*18:20.
Peace. J171I9B, Is +57:19. ver. 21, 26. Jn *14:27.
16:33. Ps 85:8-10. Is 57:18, 19. Mt 10:13. Lk 24:36.
Ro 15:33. Ep 2:14. 6:23. Ph 1:2. 2 Th 3:16. He 7:2.
Re 1:4.

20. **he showed**. ver. 25, 27. Lk *24:39, 40. 1 J *1:1.
Then. Jn *16:22. Is 25:8, 9. Mt 28:8. Lk 24:41. Ro
*5:1, 2.

21. **Peace**. J171I9B, Is +57:19. ver. 19. Jn *14:27.
hath sent. Jn 3:+17, 34. 6:38. 17:18. He 3:1. **so send**.
Jn 13:20. 17:18, 19. 21:15-17. Is 61:1-3. Ezk 3:4. Mt
10:16, 40. 28:18-20. Mk √16:15-18. Lk 24:47-49. Ac
+*1:8. 2 T √2:2. He 3:1.

22. **he breathed**. Ge +*2:7. Jb 33:4. Ps 33:6. Ezk
37:9. **Receive**. Jn 7:39. 14:16. *15:26. 16:7. Ac √2:4,
38. *4:8. 8:15. 10:47. 19:2. Ga 3:2. 1 Th *4:8. **Ghost**.
Gr. *pneuma*, Mt +1:18n. T#967‡. The suggestion
that this and the following texts teach that the Holy
Spirit is not a person, but is a "force," is false, for it
confounds what is said of His gifts with what is asserted
of His person (Jn ●+*16:13n, 14n. Mt +*12:32n).
Mt 3:16. Ac 1:8. 2:2-4, 16, 17, 33. 1 C 12:4-13. Ep
5:18.

23. **Whose soever**. J184C, Mt +4:9. lit. "If the sins
of any ye forgive." A condition of the third class. Only
God has the power to forgive sins (Mk 2:8). Jesus asserted his authority and power to forgive sins (Mk
2:10), thus indirectly asserting his deity. There is no
evidence that Jesus by this statement intended to convey this power to Peter alone, the other apostles exclusively, or their alleged successors, for not just the
twelve disciples but other men and women were gathered in the upper room (ver. 19. Lk 24:48, 49. Ac
1:15). Rather, every Christian who shares the message
of God's terms of forgiveness recorded in the Bible
does the work of authoritatively announcing the goodness of God (Ro √11:22) by declaring the grounds of
the forgiveness of sins (Ac √10:43), so securing their
remission (Ja √5:19, 20); and by declaring the severity
of God (Ro √11:22), sharing God's terms of judgment
(Jn √3:18, 36. Ac √4:12. 17:31. 1 C 5:4, 5. 6:9, 10.
2 C 5:√11, 20), so authoritatively pronouncing the
grounds of their retention (Mt +*12:31, 32. 1 J 5:16).
sins ye. J121I1, Ge +3:7. **remit**. J121I2, Ge +2:17.
Le=13:2, 3. Mt +*16:19n. √18:18n. Mk 2:5-10. Ac
+*2:38. 10:43. 13:38, 39. 1 C *5:4, 5. 6:11. 2 C *2:6-
10. Ep 2:20. 1 T 1:20. Ja +*5:20. **are remitted**. Lk

7:48. **retain**. Je 18:23. Mt √18:18n. 1 T +*1:20. 1 J
+*5:16.

24. **Thomas**. Jn 11:16. 14:5. 21:2. Mt 10:3. **Didy-
mus**. i.e. *Twin*, *S#1324g. Jn 11:16g. 21:2g. Ge 25:24.
38:27. SS ●6:6. Ac 28:11. **was**. Jn 6:66, 67. Mt *18:20.
He *10:25. **Jesus came**. Mk 16:14.

25. **We**. ver. *14-20. Jn *1:41. 21:7. Mk *16:11.
Lk *24:34-40. Ac *5:30-32. *10:40, 41. 1 C *15:5-8.
the Lord. ver. 18. **Except**. ver. *20, 27. Jn *6:30. Jb
*9:16. Ps *78:11-22, 32. *95:8-10. *106:21-24. Mt
*16:1-4. *27:42. Lk *24:25, 39-41. He +*3:12, 18,
19. *4:1, 2. *10:38, 39. **the print**. Ps ✱22:16. **the nails**.
Notice Thomas testifies to more than one nail being
used to fasten the hands of Jesus to the cross, proving
that Christ was crucified on a cross of traditional form,
not a so-called "torture stake" (see Jn 19:6n). **not**. J158,
Mt +5:18. **believe**. ver. 8. Jn +5:44.

26. **eight**. ver. 19. Mt 17:1. Lk 9:28. **Thomas**. ver.
24. **came Jesus**. 1 C 15:50. **Peace**. J171I9B, Is +57:19.
ver. 19. Is 26:12. 27:5. 54:10.

27. **Reach hither thy finger**. ver. 20, 25. Ps 78:38.
103:13, 14. Lk +*24:39. Ro 5:20. 1 T 1:14-16. 1 J
*1:1, 2. **reach hither thy hand**. 1 J 1:1. **and be**. Mt
17:17. Mk 9:19. Lk 9:41. 1 T 1:14. **but believing**. Ep
1:1. He *10:22.

28. **and said**. Ps *35:23. 38:15. **My Lord**. x●J59,
Ge +28:16. The disbelief of the apostle is the means
of furnishing us with a full and satisfactory demonstration of the resurrection of our Lord. Throughout
the divine dispensations every doctrine and every important truth is gradually revealed; and here we have
a conspicuous instance of this progressive system. An
angel first declares the glorious event; the empty sepulchre confirms the women's report. Christ's appearance
to Mary Magdalene showed that he was alive; that to
the disciples at Emmaus proved that it was at least
the spirit of Christ; that to the eleven showed the
reality of his body; and the conviction given to St.
Thomas proved it the self-same body that had been
crucified. Incredulity itself is satisfied; and the convinced apostle exclaims in the joy of his heart, "My
Lord and my God!" ver. *16, *31. Jn 1:49. √5:23. *9:35-
38. Jsh +*5:14. Jg +*6:22. 1 S 20:12. Ps *35:23. 38:15.
*45:6, 11. *102:24-28. *118:24-28. Is +*7:14. +*9:6.
*25:9. *40:9-11. Je +*23:5, 6. Ml *3:1. Mt +*14:33.
Lk *24:52. Ac +*7:59n, 60. +√10:36. Ro √10:9, 10. 1
T *3:16. Re *5:9-14. **my God**. Jn √1:1. √5:18, 23.
+*8:24. Dt +*32:39. Jb +*19:26. Is 37:16, 20. √44:6,
8. +*45:21-23. Mt *1:23. +*14:33. Ro 1:4. *9:5. 1 C
+*8:4. Ep 5:5g. Ph 2:11. 1 Th 1:12g. T √2:13g. 2 P
√1:1g. Re ●+*22:9.

29. **Jesus saith**. Notice what Jesus did not say: he
did not disclaim or deny the truth of the confession
Thomas just made. Thomas called Jesus God. If Jesus
is not God, then here is a most dreadful and unexplained omission of needful correction on the part of
Jesus, who by not correcting the impression made by
this confession is guilty of perpetrating an untruth on
all future generations of believers who receive this
unexplained testimony. But such failure on the part
of Jesus is impossible, as being entirely out of character
with his absolute truthfulness (Jn 14:2, 6). Peter
abruptly declined the well-meaning worship of Cornelius (Ac 10:25, 26). Paul and Barnabas were acclaimed
as gods come down in the likeness of men at Lystra,
but they strenuously denied this ascription of deity

to themselves (Ac 14:11-18). When John fell down to worship before the feet of the angel which showed him things to come, the angel rebuked him, and refused to receive worship (Re 22:8, 9). But Herod, acclaimed as a god, was eaten of worms for not giving the glory to the true God (Ac 12:23). Jesus suffered no such rebuke from the Father, thus the Father confesses the truth of the claims of his Son, and those who refuse the truth of the testimony of Thomas are refusing to "honor the Son, even as they honor the Father." "He that honoreth not the Son, honoreth not the Father which hath sent him" (Jn √5:23). Jesus did not correct, but commended the testimony of Thomas, as the following words plainly show. **seen.** ♪171J15, Ge +42:1. **hast believed.** ver. 31. Jn 5:44. **blessed.** ver. 8. Jn 4:48. Mt 16:16, 17. Lk 1:45. 2 C √5:7. He *11:1, 27, 39. 1 P √1:8. **have believed.** The eye-witness testimony of Thomas satisfies for all time the need for testimony to the physical resurrection of Christ from the dead. No further continuing or repeated experience is necessary to establish the fact of the resurrection, for it is an established principle of law that eyewitness testimony, preserved in writing, is valid for all time, and the event or circumstance does not need to be repeated. This answers the frequent plea of skeptics that they have not been given the same opportunity to verify the resurrection offered to Thomas. That the doubt of Thomas was completely removed is sufficient testimony to remove all similar doubt on the part of all future skeptics, so that they are without excuse. Ro √10:9, 10.

30. **many other.** ♪166, Mt +1:17. Jn 21:25. Lk 1:3, 4. 3:18. Ro *15:4. 1 C 10:11. 2 T √3:15-17. 2 P 3:1, 2. 1 J 1:3, 4. √5:13. **signs.** Jn +2:11, 23. **in the presence.** Ac 10:41. **this book.** Ac +1:20.

31. **these.** ver. 28. Jn 1:49. 6:69, 70. 9:35-38. 19:35. Ps *2:7, 12. Mt *16:16. +*27:54n. Lk 1:4. Ac *8:37. 9:20. Ro 1:3, 4. 1 J 4:15. 5:1, 10, 20. 2 J *9. Re 2:18. **written, that.** T#1041. Ro √10:17. **might believe.** ver. 29. Jn +11:27. **that Jesus is.** Mt +1:1. Mk +8:29. **the Son of God.** Mt +14:33. **believing.** Jn √3:15, 16, 18, 36. *5:24, 39, 40. 6:40. 10:10. Mk *16:16. Ac 8:37. 1 P 1:9. 1 J 2:23-25. √5:10-13. **have life.** Jn 6:53. +8:12. 1 J √5:13. **through.** Lk *24:47. Ac 3:16. *10:43. *13:38, 39. 1 C *6:11. **his name.** ♪121T1, Dt +28:58. Jn +1:12. +14:13. 17:11, 12. Ac +3:6. 15:26. 1 C 1:10.

JOHN 21

Jesus appears to some of his disciples at the Sea of Tiberias, makes himself known by a miraculous draught of fishes, and eats with them, 1-14. He thrice demands of Peter whether he loves him, and thrice requires him to show his love, by feeding his lambs and sheep, 15-17. He foretells Peter's martyrdom, commanding him to follow him, 18, 19; and reproves his curiosity concerning John, who showed his readiness in the same way to follow him, 20-23. The truth of John's testimony affirmed, and it is stated that Jesus did many miracles besides, even too numerous to be all recorded, 24, 25.

1. **these.** Jn 20:19-29. **Jesus.** Mt 26:32. *28:7, 16. Mk 16:7. **showed himself.** ver. 14. Jn +7:4. Mk 16:12, 14. **again.** Jn 20:19, 26. **the disciples.** Ac 10:41. **the sea.** Jn 6:1, 23.

2. **Thomas.** Jn +11:16. +√20:28. **Nathanael.** Jn

*1:45-51. **Cana.** Jn 2:1, 11. 4:46. Jsh 19:28, Kanah. **the sons.** Mt *4:21, 22.

3. **I go.** 2 K 6:1-7. Mt 4:18-20. Lk 5:10, 11. Ac 18:3. 20:34. 1 C 9:6. 1 Th 2:9. 2 Th *3:7-9. **and that night.** Is +=60:2. Jl 2:2. Am 5:18, 20. Zp 1:15. Lk 5:5. 1 C 3:7.

4. **but.** Jn 20:14. Mk 16:12. Lk 24:15, 16, 31. **knew not.** Ge +*19:11. Lk +*24:16, +*31.

5. **Children.** or, Sirs. Jn 13:33. 1 J 2:13, 18g. **have.** Ps 37:3. Lk 24:41-43. Ph *4:11-13, 19. He +*13:5. **meat.** ♪171I8, Ps +107:18.

6. **Cast.** Mt 17:27. Lk 5:4-7. **the net.** Mt 4:20. +*13:47. **They cast.** Jn 2:5. Ps 8:8. He 2:6-9. **the multitude.** ver. 11. Ac 2:41. 4:4.

7. **that disciple.** ver. 20, 24. Jn 13:23. 19:26. 20:2. **unto Peter.** Jn 18:10. Mt 16:16. 26:33. **It is.** Jn √20:20, 28. Ge +*3:7. Ps 118:23. Mk 11:3. Lk 2:11. Ac 2:36. +*10:36. 1 C 15:47. Ja 2:1. **the Lord.** ver. 12. Jn +4:1. Ac +*10:36. **when.** SS 8:7. Mt 14:28, 29. Lk 7:47. 2 C 5:14. **he girt.** ver. 18. Jn 13:4. Lk 12:35. **fisher's coat.** Or, *upper coat, great coat,* or *surtout, ependuteen,* from *epi,* "upon," and *enduo,* "I clothe." **naked.** ♪171N, Ge +8:13. That is, he was only in his "vest," or under garment; for *gumnos,* "naked," like the Hebrew *arom,* is frequently applied to one who has merely laid aside his outer garment. See 1 S 19:24. 2 S 6:20, on which see the Note. To which may be added what we read in the LXX, Jb 22:6, "Thou hast taken away the covering of the *naked," amphiasin gumnon,* the "plaid," or blanket, in which they wrapped themselves, and besides which they had no other. In this sense Virgil says (Georg. l. i. v. 299), *Nudus ara, sere nudus,* "plough naked and sow naked," i.e. *strip off your upper garments.* 1 S 19:24. Is +*20:2. Am 2:16. Mi 1:8, 11. Ac +*19:16. **did cast.** Mt 14:29.

8. **And.** ♪143, Ge +19:2. **little ship.** Jn +6:22. **cubits.** Dt 3:11.

9. **they saw.** ♪143, Ge +19:2. Jn 18:18. 1 K 19:5, 6. Mt 4:11. Mk 8:3. Lk 12:29-31. **and fish.** ver. 10, 13. Jn 6:9, 11.

11. **drew the net.** Mt +*13:48. **and for.** Lk 5:6-8. Ac 2:41. **was not.** Lk ●5:6.

12. **Jesus.** Lk 24:39-43. **Come.** Ac 10:41. **dine.** The word *aristan,* like *prandere,* was used for any meat taken before the *caena,* or supper. ver. 15. Ge=43:31. Mt 22:4. Lk 11:37, 38. 14:12g. **none.** This word is singular in Greek. **durst.** Jn 4:27. 16:19. Ge 32:29, 30. Mk 9:32. Lk 9:45. **ask.** Mt 2:8. 10:11g. **knowing.** ♪163, Jn +16:13. This word is plural in Greek; note the shift here from singular to plural, an instance of the figure Syllepsis. The figure points out that *not one* asked; for *all* knew (B701). **the Lord.** ver. 7. Jn +4:1.

13. **then cometh.** Lk 24:42, 43. Ac 10:41. **taketh bread.** ver. 9. Mt 14:19. 15:36. Mk 6:41. 8:6. Lk 9:16. Ac 1:4.

14. **the third time.** Or, as some read, the third *day.* On the day the Savior rose he appeared five times; the second day was that day se'nnight; and this was the third day—or this was his third *appearance* to any considerable number of his disciples together. Though he had appeared to Mary, to the women, to the two disciples, to Cephas—yet he had but twice appeared to a company of them together. ver. 1. Jn *20:19, 26.

15. **dined.** ver. +12. **Simon.** Mt 16:17. Lk 22:31.

son. ver. 16, 17. Jn 1:42, Jona. Mt 16:17, Bar-jona.
Peter. Mt 26:33. **lovest.** Jn 8:42. 13:37. 14:15-24. 16:27.
Mt 10:37. 25:34-45. 26:33. Mk 14:29. 1 C 16:21, 22.
2 C 5:14, 15. Ga 5:6. Ep 6:24. 1 P 1:8. 1 J 4:19. 5:1.
more. ver. 7. Mt 26:33, 35. Mk 14:29. **thou knowest.**
ver. 17. Jn +*2:24, 25. 2 S 7:20. 2 K 20:3. He *4:13.
Re *2:23. **I love thee.** Jn +16:27. **Feed.** Ps 78:70-72.
Pr 10:21. +*27:23. Je 3:15. 23:4. Ezk 34:2-10, 23. Ac
+*20:28. 1 T √4:15, 16. He *13:20. 1 P 2:25. *5:1-4.
lambs. Jn 10:11-16. 13:33. Ge 33:13. Is 40:11. Mt *18:6,
10, 11. Lk 12:32. 22:32. Ro 14:1. 15:1. 1 C 3:1-3.
8:11. Ep +*4:14. He 12:12, 13. 1 P *2:2.
16. **again.** ƒ73, Zc +1:5. **the second.** Jn 18:17, 25.
Mt 26:72. **Feed.** Is 40:11. Mt 2:6. Ac +*20:28. 1 C
9:7g. 1 P *2:25. *5:2, 4. Re 7:17. **my sheep.** Jn *10:11-
16, 26, 27. Ps 95:7. 100:3. Zc 13:7. Mt 25:32. Lk 15:3-
7. +*19:10. Ac +*20:28. He *13:20. 1 P *2:25.
17. **the third.** Jn 13:38. 18:27. Mt 26:73, 74. Re
*3:19. **grieved.** 1 K 17:18. La 3:33. Mt *26:75. Mk
14:72. Lk 22:61, 62. 2 C 2:4-7. 7:8-11. Ep +*4:30.
1 P 1:6. **Lord, thou knowest all things.** God the Son is
omniscient. Jn +*2:24, 25. 6:64. 13:1, 18, 19. +16:30.
18:4. Je +*17:10. Mt +9:4 (T#76-7). √17:24-27.
+*28:19n. Lk 5:22. 22:10-12. Ac 1:24. 15:8. Re *2:23.
thou knowest that. ver. 15. Jsh 22:22. 2 S 7:20. 1 Ch
29:17. Jb 31:4-6. Ps 7:8, 9. 17:3. 2 C 1:12. **Feed.** ver.
15, 16. Jn 12:8. 14:15. 15:10. Pr +*27:23. Mt 25:40.
2 C √8:8, 9. 2 P *1:12-15. 3:1. 1 J 3:16-24. 3 J 7, 8.
18. **Verily.** Jn +1:51. **but.** Jn *13:36. Ac 12:3, 4.
another. Ac 21:11. **thou wouldest not.** Jn 12:27, 28.
2 C 5:4.
19. **signifying.** Jn 7:39. 12:33. 18:32. **by.** Ph 1:20.
1 P 4:11-14. 2 P *1:14. **glorify.** Jn 13:31. Ph 1:20.
1 P 2:12. **Follow.** ver. 22. Jn +8:12. 12:26. 13:36, 37.
Nu 14:24. 1 S 12:20. Mt *10:38. 16:21-25. 19:28. Mk
8:33-38. Lk 9:22-26.

20. **seeth.** ver. 7, 24. Jn 13:23. 20:2. **following.** Jn
1:38. **which.** Jn *13:23-26. 20:2.
21. **Lord.** Mt 24:3, 4. Lk 13:23, 24. Ac *1:6, 7.
22. **If.** ƒ184C, Mt +4:9. Jn 5:21. 17:24. Mt *16:27,
28. *24:3, 27, 29-31, 36-39, 44. 25:31. Mk 9:1. 1 C
4:5. 11:26. Re +*1:7. 2:25. 3:11. 22:7, 20. **tarry.** 1 C
15:6. Ph 1:25. **till.** Mt 10:23. *16:28. +*23:39. Mk
9:1. Lk 9:27. 1 C 4:5. 11:26. Ph 1:6. Ja 5:7. Re 2:25.
I come. Jn 14:3, 18, 28. Mt +*16:27n. He 10:37. Re
2:5, 16. 3:3, 11. 16:15. 22:7, 12, 20. **follow.** ver. 19.
23. **the brethren.** Jn 20:17. Mt 23:8. 28:10. Lk 22:32.
Ac 1:15. 6:3. 9:30. 10:23. 11:1, etc. 12:17. 14:2. 15:1,
etc. 16:2, 40. 17:6, etc. 18:18, 27. 21:7, 17. 28:14,
15. Ep +6:23. 1 J 3:14, 16. 3 J 3, 5, 10. **If.** ƒ184C,
Mt +4:9. ver. 22. **I will.** ver. 22. **what.** Dt 29:29. Jb
28:28. 33:13. Da 4:35.
24. **which testifieth.** Jn 15:27. **we know.** ƒ96D4,
Ge +29:27. Jn *19:35. 1 J 1:1, 2. 3:2, 14. 5:6, 15,
18-20. 3 J *12. **testimony.** Re 1:5. **is true.** 1 J *4:6.
25. **there.** Jn √20:30, 31. Jb 26:14. Ps 40:5. 71:15.
Ec 12:12. Mt 11:5. Ac *10:38. 20:35. He 11:32. **if they.**
ƒ184C, Mt +4:9. ƒ102C, Mt +5:29. **that even.** This
is a very strong eastern expression to represent the
number of miracles which Jesus wrought. But however
strong and strange it may appear to us of the western
world, we find sacred and other authors using hyper-
boles of the like kind and signification. See Nu 13:33.
Dt 1:28. Da 4:11. Ecclesiaticus 47:15. Basnage (Hist.
des Juifs, l. iii. c. 1. sec. 9) gives a very similar hyperbole
taken from the Jewish writers, in which Jochanan is
said to have "composed such a great number of precepts
and lessons, that if the heavens were paper, and all
the trees of the forests so many pens, and all the children of men so many scribes, they would not suffice
to write all his lessons." Am 7:10. Mt 19:24. **the world.**
Gr. *kosmos*, Mt +4:8.

ACTS

ACTS 1

*The sacred writer addresses his narrative to Theo-
philus, 1. Christ being risen, instructs his disciples;
commands them to wait at Jerusalem, for the promise
of the Holy Spirit; and ascends towards heaven in
their sight, 2-9. Two angels assure them, that he would
come again in like manner, 10, 11. The apostles and
disciples at Jerusalem continue in prayer, with one
accord, 12-14. Peter calls on them to appoint another
apostle instead of Judas, in whose awful doom the
scripture had been fulfilled, 15-22. Matthias is chosen
by lot, accompanied with prayer, 23-26.*

1. A.M. 4037. A.D. 33. **former.** Lk ch. 1-24. **O
Theophilus.** Lk *1:3. **of.** Ac 2:22. 10:38. Mt 4:23, 24.
11:5. Lk 7:21-23. 24:19. Jn 10:32-38. 18:19-21. 1 P
2:21-23.
2. **the day.** ver. 9, 11, 22. Mk *16:19. Lk 9:51.
*24:51. Jn 6:62. 13:1, 3. 16:28. 17:13. 20:17. Ep 4:8-
10. 1 T *3:16. He 6:19, 20. 9:24. 1 P 3:22. **through.**
Ac *10:38. Is 11:2, 3. 42:1. 48:16. 59:20, 21. 61:1.
Mt 3:16. 12:28. Lk 4:1, 18. Jn 1:16. *3:34. 20:21. Re
1:1. 2:7, 11, 17, 29. 3:6, 13, 22. **Ghost.** Gr. *pneuma,*
Mt +1:18n. **given.** Mt +*28:19. Mk *16:15-19. Lk
24:45-49. **the apostles.** ver. 13. Ac +5:12. 10:40-42.

Mt 10:1-4. Mk 3:14-19. 6:30. Lk 6:13-16. Jn 6:70, 71.
13:18. *20:20, 21. 1 C 12:28. Ga 1:1. Ep 2:20. 2 P
3:2. Re 21:14.
3. **he showed.** ver. 21, 22. Ac 10:40, 41. 13:31. Mt
28:9, 16, 17. Mk *16:10-14. Lk *24:30-40. Jn 20:14-
16, 19, 20, 27, 28. 21:1, etc. 1 C *15:5-7. 1 J 1:1, 2.
his passion. Ac 3:18. Lk 22:15. **forty.** Dt 9:9, 18. 1 K
19:8. Mt 4:2. **speaking.** Ac 8:12. 19:8. 20:25. 28:23,
31. Da 2:44, 45. Mt 3:2. 21:43. Lk 4:43. +*17:20,
21. 24:44-49. Ro *14:17. Col 1:13. 1 Th 2:12. **the kingdom.** ver. +*6n. Ac +14:22. Mt +12:28. Jn +3:3.
4. **being assembled together.** *or,* eating together.
Ac 10:41. Lk 24:41-43. Jn 21:13. **commanded.** Lk
*24:49. **the promise.** ƒ121R7, Ge +43:11. Ac *2:33.
Is 44:3. Ezk 36:27. Jl 2:28, 29. Mt 10:20. Lk 11:13.
12:12. √‖24:49. Jn 7:39. *14:16, 17, 26-28. *15:26. *16:7-
15. 20:22. **of the Father.** ver. 7. Ac 2:33. Mt 24:36.
Lk 9:26. Ro 6:4. 1 C 8:6. Col 1:12. **saith he.** ƒ63BA,
Ge +26:7. **have heard.** ƒ15E, Mk +6:9. Ac 14:22.
5. **John.** Ac +*11:15, 16. 19:4-6. Mt +*3:11. Lk 3:16.
Jn 1:31-34. 1 C √12:13. T *3:5. **baptized.** Ac 9:18.
+*22:16. 2 K 5:13, 14. Is 44:3. Ezk +*36:25, 27. Da
4:15, 23, 25, 36. 5:21. Ep *4:5. He 6:2. 9:10. +*10:22.
Re 19:13. **with water.** Notice the expression "with water," as opposed to "in water." New Testament bap-

tisms were performed by applying water to the person or object, not by placing the person or object in the water (Mk +*7:4n). Baptism was a rite of purification (Jn 3:23, 25), and as instituted by Christ, symbolized the believer's reception of the Holy Spirit, and the cleansing of the heart from sin by the blood of Christ (Ac 22:16 w Re 1:5. He 10:22). The mode was sprinkling or pouring, never immersion (Ac 2:41n), for to immerse a person or object into standing (as opposed to running or "living," Le 14:5, 6, 50, 51, 52. 15:13) water would render the water unclean. The New Testament speaks of one baptism (Ep 4:5), yet we find reference to ritual baptism, requiring water; real baptism; baptism of the Holy Spirit; and baptisms (He 6:2) mentioned in the plural, probably purifications. Ritual baptism is performed by one person upon another person; that is, there is a human administrator of the rite, using the natural element water. Ritual baptism must be distinguished from (1) the *real* baptism performed once by the Holy Spirit without human hands upon every believer at the time faith is placed in Christ (Ac 11:17n. Ro +*8:9n, 11. 1 C 12:13), no doubt the *one baptism* referred to by Paul (Ep 4:5), of which ritual or water baptism is the mere symbol; (2) the indwelling of the Holy Spirit (Ro +*8:9n), which is the permanent nonrepeatable experience of every believer which takes place at the moment of salvation when faith is placed in Christ; (3) the miraculous gift-producing supernatural baptism of the Holy Ghost experienced only during the lifetime of the original apostles (Ac 8:16n); and (4) the filling of the Spirit which is a repeatable experience (Ep +*5:18n). Many verses which are understood by the casual reader as references to ritual baptism will be seen, upon closer examination, to refer to *real* baptism, and can be so distinguished by the fact that (1) no human administrators are mentioned in connection, (2) the element *water* is not mentioned in the immediate context, and most important, (3) the *result* accomplished by the baptism goes far beyond what can be legitimately claimed for a humanly administered ritual (Mk 16:16. Jn 3:5. Ro 6:4. 1 C √12:13. Ga *3:27. Col 2:12). Failure to observe such distinctions has resulted in a distortion of this ordinance of Christ into something it was never intended to be, such as (1) the means of regeneration, termed "baptismal regeneration;" (2) an essential requirement for salvation, a command of Christ, obedience to which is absolutely necessary for salvation and the remission of sins, a command which if not obeyed renders salvation impossible (Mk 16:16n. Ac 2:38n. 11:17n). George N. H. Peters has wisely written "It is the part of kindness to point out the opinion that we regard erroneous, and to sustain our own by an appeal direct to Scripture, and no one who holds to the supremacy of Scripture will object to this; but to direct attention to the opinion of others merely to ridicule the same and to call into question the honesty, veracity, etc., of its upholders is unworthy of a student and of a Christian" (*Theocratic Kingdom*, vol. 3, p. 111). Mk +*1:8. **but**. Ac 2:1-4, 16-21. 10:45. 11:15. Jl +*2:28-32. 3:18. **with the Holy**. In the parallel passage in Lk 24:49 termed "power from on high," thus without articles (Mt +1:18n) a reference to His gift, rather than Himself. **Ghost**. Gr. *pneuma*, Mt +1:18n. Ge +1:2. **not many**. Ac 2:1-4, 16-21. Jl 2:28-32.

6. **Lord**. Mt +*24:3, 4. Jn 21:21, 22. **they asked**.

Mt *20:21. Lk √24:21. **wilt thou**. Jesus had just been speaking for forty days of the kingdom of God (ver. 4), and no doubt the content of his discussions prompted this question. Christ's answer must not be understood to be a denial of the hope reflected in this question, a hope firmly founded upon the provisions of the Davidic Covenant and the predictions of the prophets (Is √11:11n. +*55:3), but a confirmation of it. If the disciples were mistaken in this hope, this would have been a most opportune time to correct them, but Christ did not (Jn 14:2. 20:29n. Ro √15:8). Yet, misunderstanding this, many expositors have gone far astray in their understanding of the prophetic plan of God revealed in Scripture. Misunderstanding on this point is virtually fatal to understanding Biblical prophecy as a whole. A typical example of this misunderstanding is the comment of Thomas Walker, "They were still hankering, apparently, after a Jewish earthly monarchy. They interpreted what He had said about "the kingdom of God" (ver. 3) after an earthly and carnal manner, and they misunderstood His statement about "not many days hence" (ver. 5) as referring to a speedy establishment of a visible monarchy. It needed Pentecost to revolutionize completely their ideas and to spiritualize their conceptions. They even appear to have understood the promise of the coming of the Holy Ghost as the advent of some supernatural power for the promotion of a Jewish kingdom" (*Commentary on Acts*, pp. 9, 10). How far mistaken the otherwise excellent commentator Thomas Walker is on this point may be readily established by consulting the Scripture references pertaining to the Davidic Covenant furnished in the note above, and the references furnished for the word "restore" below. To suggest that the disciples were mistaken or carnal in their view is contrary to Mt 13:11, and to suggest they changed their viewpoint to a more spiritual one after Pentecost is an assertion which can find no support in Scripture. Rather, this very so-called carnal viewpoint is the focal point of Peter's message recorded in Ac 3:19-21 spoken *after* Pentecost (see also Ac 13:34 and 15:16), and is spoken of by Paul in Romans ch. 9-11, particularly Ro +√11:1, 2, 26. Peters calls attention to numerous passages in Paul's writings which are Jewish in conception, in which Paul speaks of Jesus as the Messiah, "locating the fulfillment of the promises held by the Jews *to the future coming* of this Jesus, by employing the *language and ideas* of the Jews applied to the Messiah" (*Theocratic Kingdom*, vol. 1, p. 439). This is positive proof that there was no change, as alleged above, in the apostolic view of the kingdom after Pentecost. Peters cites the following passages of Paul: Ro 8:19-23. 11:1-32. 13:11, 12, etc. 1 C 1:7, 8. 4:5, 8. 6:2, 3, 9, 14, etc. 2 C 1:14. 3:16. Ga 1:4. 3:16-18, etc. Ep 1:10-21. 2:12-19. 4:30, etc. Ph 1:6, 10. 2:10, 11, 16, etc. **at this time**. Ps 102:13, 16. Ho 3:4. Mt +√25:19. Lk 17:20, 22. **restore**. Ac +*3:19, 21. *15:16. Ge +*49:10. Ps 89:34. Is +*1:26. +*9:6, 7. +√11:11n. Je +*23:5, 6. *33:15-17, 26. Ezk *37:24-27. Da *7:27. Ho *3:4, 5. Jl *3:1, 2, 16-21. Am *9:11. Ob *17-21. Mi 4:8. +*5:2. Zp *3:15-17. Zc *9:9, 10. Mt 17:11. 20:21. +*26:29. Mk 9:12. Lk 1:71. √19:11. +*22:29, 30. *24:21. Ro *15:8. **the kingdom**. Ac 15:16. Da +*7:13, 14. Mt +*6:10n. 20:21. Mk 14:25. +*15:43. Lk +*1:32, 33. *19:11. +*22:18, 29. **to Israel**. Ac 2:26, 30. Ps +*132:13, 14. Mi 4:6-8. Zc 1:17. +*2:12. Mt *19:28. Lk +*22:30.

7. **not for you.** Much caution should attend the application of this text. While it has rightfully been applied as a warning against setting dates for the return of Christ, it must not be understood to mean that the time of his Second Advent will be unknown, for in Daniel (Da +*9:26, 27) the precise means of determining the very day of His coming is revealed (Mt 24:42n), and though not understood by us at the present time, will be understood by those who know the Scriptures (Da 11:33n) at the time appointed. Even the time of the rapture may be known approximately, otherwise there would have been no point for Christ to give the signs of its approach, no point to warning us to watch, lest the day come upon us unawares (Lk 21:34-36), and Paul could not have written what he did in 1 Th 5:4-6. In this matter, Peters points out, "Three extremes are to be avoided: (1) to fix definite, positive time; (2) to ignore the signs; (3) and to encourage any interpretation or application that forbids or hinders a daily posture of watching" (*Theocratic Kingdom*, vol. 3, p. 114). Add to this a fourth, that of neglecting to earnestly study the entire subject because of the extremes and mistakes of others. Ac *17:26. Dt +*29:29. Da *2:21. Mt *24:36. Mk +*13:32. Lk √21:24. Ep *1:10. 1 Th *5:1, 2. 1 T *6:15. 2 T *3:1.
to know. Mt 24:42n. √25:13. Mk +*13:32. Lk 12:40. Jn +*14:28. 1 P 1:10-12. 2 P 1:19. **the times.** ♪96F2, Ge +4:10. Da *2:21. Mt *16:3. 24:32, 33. Lk 21:+*24, 27, 28, *30. Ro +*11:25. 13:11. He 10:25, 37. 1 P 1:10. **and seasons.** ♪96F2, Ge +4:10. Da 2:21. 1 Th *5:1. T 1:2, 3. **which.** Mt *20:23. Mk *10:40.

8. **ye shall.** Ac *2:1-4. *6:8. 8:19. Mi 3:8. Zc *4:6. Lk 10:19. Re 11:3-6. **power**, etc. *or*, the power of the Holy Ghost coming upon you. Ac 10:38. Lk +*1:35. 4:14. 24:49. Ro 15:19. Ep 3:16. 1 Th 1:5. 2 T +*1:7. **Ghost.** Gr. *pneuma*, Mt +1:18. **and ye.** ♪148, Ge +8:22. ver. 22. Ac +*2:32. 3:15. *4:33. 5:32. 10:39-41. 13:31. 22:15. Mt +*28:19. Mk √16:15. Lk 24:46-49. Jn 15:27. **witnesses.** Ac +*2:24n. Is 43:10n, 12. 44:8. **unto me.** Ne +*9:6. **in Jerusalem.** Ac *5:28. 11:19. *26:20. Lk *24:46-49. Ro *15:19. **all Judea.** Ac *10:37. **in Samaria.** Ac *8:1, 5-25. Mt 10:5. **unto.** Ac 13:4, 5, 47. Ps 22:27. 98:3. Is 8:9. 42:10. 49:6. 52:10. 66:19. Je 16:19. Mt 24:14. +*28:19. Mk 13:27. √16:15. Ro 10:18. 15:19. Col *1:23.

9. **when.** ver. 2. Ps 68:18. Mk *16:19. Lk *24:50, 51. Jn 6:62. Ep 4:8-12. **a cloud.** Ex 19:9. 34:5. 2 K 2:11. 2 Ch +*5:13. Ps 104:3. Is 19:1. Ezk 1:4. Da 7:13. Mt 17:5. Mk 14:62. Lk 21:27. 1 Th +*4:17. Re +*1:7. 11:12. 14:4, 14.

10. **while.** 2 K 2:11, 12. **looked stedfastly.** Ac 3:4. 7:55. **two.** Ac *10:3, 30. Jsh 5:13. Da 7:9. 9:21. 10:5. 12:6, 7. Zc 1:8-11. Mt 17:2. 28:3. Mk 16:5. Lk 24:4. Jn *20:12. Re 3:4. 7:14. **white apparel.** Mt 28:3. Mk 16:5. Jn *20:12.

11. **Ye men.** Ac *2:7. 13:31. Mk 14:70. **why.** Ac 3:12. Lk 24:5. **from you.** ♪12111, Ge +3:7. **this same.** Ac 2:32, 36. Lk 24:39. 1 Th 4:16. **shall so come.** Ac 3:20, 21. Dt ◐33:2, 3. Ps ◐42:5mg. ◐68:1, 7, 17, 18, 23. Is ◐16:1-5. ◐63:1-3. Da +*7:13, 14. Zc +*14:4. Mt +*16:27n. +*24:7, 8, 30. +*25:31. 26:64. Mk 13:26. Lk 21:27. Jn +*14:3. 1 C *11:26. Ph +1:26. 3:20. 1 Th +*1:10. +*4:16. 2 Th √1:7-10. T +*2:13n. Re +*1:7. 11:17n.

12. **from.** Zc √14:4. Mt +21:1. +*24:3. 26:30. Lk *19:29. 21:37. *24:50, 52. **Olivet.** i.e. *olive yard,*

*S#1638g, only here. **a sabbath.** Mt *24:20. Lk 24:50. Jn *11:18.

13. **an upper room.** T#1212. Ac 9:37-39. 20:8. Mk 14:15. Lk 22:12. **Peter.** Ac 2:14, 38. 3:1, etc. 4:13, 19. 8:14-25. 9:32-43. 10:9, etc. 12:2, 3. 15:7-11. Mt 4:18-22. 10:2-4. Mk 3:16-18. 5:37. 9:2. 14:33. Lk 6:13-16. Jn 1:40-42. 13:23-25. 18:17, 25-27. 21:15-24. 1 J. 2 J. 3 J. Re 1:1, etc. **and James.** Ac +12:2. **Philip.** Jn 1:43-46. 6:5-7. 12:21, 22. 14:8, 9. **Thomas.** Jn 11:16. 20:26-29. 21:2. **Matthew.** Mt 9:9. Mk 2:14. Lk 5:27-29, Levi. **James.** Ac 12:17. 15:13. Mt 27:56. Mk 15:40. 1 C 15:7. Ga 1:19. 2:9. Ja 1:1. **Alpheus.** Mk 2:14. 3:18. **Simon.** Mt 10:4. Mk 3:18, Canaanite. Lk 6:15. **Zelotes.** Ac 21:20. **Judas.** Mt 10:3, Lebbeus whose surname was Thaddeus. Mk 3:18, Thaddeus. Jn +14:22. Ju 1.

14. **all.** Ac *2:1, 42, 46. 4:24-31. *6:4. Mt +*18:19, 20. √21:22. Lk 11:13. 18:1. *24:53. Ro 12:12. Ep *6:18. Col 4:2. **one accord.** T#1293. Ac 2:46. 4:24. 5:12. 15:25. Mt *18:19, 20. Ro 15:6. Re 5:13, 14. **with the women.** Mt *27:55, 56. Mk 15:40, 41. 16:1. Lk *8:2, 3. *23:49, 55. *24:10. Jn 19:25. **Mary.** Jn *19:25, 26. **the mother.** Mt +12:46. with his. Ps √69:8. Mt +*13:55, 56. Mk +*3:31n. +*6:3. Jn *7:5.

15. **Peter.** Ps *32:5, 6. *51:9-13. Lk *22:32. Jn *21:15-17. **the disciples.** Jn +21:23. **the number.** ♪81, Ge +15:13. **names.** ♪121T2. Metonymy of the Adjunct B608. "Name" or "names" is put for the person or persons, when the person is human. For other instances of this figure see Dt 25:10n; Re 3:4 and 11:13mg. Nu 1:2, 18, 20. 3:40, 43. Re 3:4. 11:13g. **an.** Ac 21:20g. Mt 13:31, 32. Jn *14:12. 1 C *15:6.

16. **Men.** Ac 2:29, 37. 7:2. 13:15, 26, 38. 15:7, 13. 22:1. 23:1, 6. 28:17. **this.** Ac 2:23. 13:27-29. Mt 26:54, 56. Jn *10:35. 12:38-40. 19:28-30, 36, 37. **scripture.** ver. 20. Ac 4:25. Lk +4:21. 21:22. Jn 17:12. 2 T √3:16. 2 P *1:21. **must.** ver. 22. Ac +3:21. Lk +13:33. 22:37. +*24:44. Jn +3:14. **which the.** Ac 2:30, 31. 4:25-28. 28:25. 2 S 23:2. Mk 12:36. Lk 1:70. He 3:7, 8. 9:8. 10:15. 1 P 1:11. 2 P *1:21. **Ghost.** Gr. *pneuma*, Mt +3:16. **spake.** Ps *41:9. 55:12-15. Mt 26:47. Jn *13:18. 18:2-8. 1 Th 4:6. **by the mouth.** Ac 3:18, 21. +4:25. Lk 1:70. **guide.** Mt *26:47, 48. Mk 14:43. Lk 22:47. Jn 18:3.

17. **he.** Mt 10:4. Mk *3:14, 15, 19. Lk 6:16. 22:47. Jn 6:70, 71. 13:21. 17:12. **numbered with.** Lk 22:14. **obtained part.** ver. 26. Ac *8:21. 26:18. Mt √7:22, 23. Col 1:12. 1 P 5:3. **this.** ver. 25. Ac 12:25. 20:24. 21:19. Ro 11:13. 2 C 4:1. 5:18. Ep 4:11, 12.

18. **this.** Mt *27:3-10. **purchased.** ♪121E2, Ge +42:38. ♪108A5, Ge +42:38. **with.** Nu 22:7, 17. Jsh 7:21-26. 2 K 5:20-27. Jb 20:12-15. Mt 25:15. *26:14-16. Mk 14:10, 11. Lk 22:3-6. 2 P 2:15, 16. **and falling.** Ps 55:15, 23. Mt *27:5.

19. **it was known.** Ac 2:22. Mt 28:15. **in their.** Luke's expression, "*Their* proper tongue," is supposed to exclude himself from the Jewish nation. By way of undesigned coincidence, Paley has pointed out that in Colossians it is implied that Luke is not "of the circumcision," in saying that Aristarchus, Marcus, and Justus were "of the circumcision" (Col 4:11), that Epaphras, Luke, and Demas, mentioned separately, were not (Col 4:12-14). The words "their proper tongue" are taken to be the words and observation of Luke the historian, and not a part of Peter's speech, in the midst of which they are found. Such words would not have been used

by a Jew, but are suitable to the pen of a Gentile writing concerning Jews. This coincidence is so remote from all possibility of design, that it stands as substantial evidence of the historicity of Acts, and the authenticity of Paul's epistle. Such an obscure relationship would not be the product of a forger, who would want validating relationships to be evident on the surface, or they might be missed by the intended audience, and furnish no evidence for authenticity of his document. The evidential strength of any observed undesigned coincidence is directly proportional to its obscurity. The less obvious the coincidence, the stronger evidence it furnishes for authenticity (William Paley, *Horae Paulinae*, pp. 146, 147. See related notes on Ac 11:29. +*12:12n).
tongue. Ac 21:40. **Aceldama.** i.e. *field of blood*, *S#184g, only here. 2 S 2:16mg.
20. **in.** Ac 13:33. Lk 20:42. 24:44. **the book.** Ac 7:42. Mk 12:26. Lk 3:4. 4:17. Jn 20:30. Ga 3:10. Re 22:7, 9, 18, 19. **Let his.** ♪92G, Lk +4:18. Ps ♪69:25. 109:9-15. Zc +*5:3, 4. Mt 23:38. Lk 13:35. **his.** ver. 25. Ps ♪109:8. Jn 17:12. **bishoprick.** *or*, office, *or*, charge. 1 T 3:1.
21. **these.** Lk *10:1, 2. Jn *15:27. **the Lord Jesus.** Ac 4:33. 7:59. 8:16. 11:17, 20. 15:11. 16:31. 19:5, 13, 17. 20:21, 24, 35. 21:13. Mk +16:19. **went.** ♪171J3, Nu +27:17. Ac 9:28. Nu 27:17. Dt 28:6. 31:2. 1 S 18:13. 2 S 5:2. 1 K 3:7. 2 Ch 1:10. Ps 121:8. Je 37:4. Jn *10:1-9.
22. **Beginning.** Ac 10:37. 13:24, 25. Mt ch. 3. Mk 1:1, 3-8. Lk 3:1-18. Jn 1:28-51. **baptism.** ♪171S3. Synecdoche of the Part B650. In a few passages *the baptism of John* is put for his ministry. For another instance of this figure see Ac 10:37. **unto.** See on ver. 2, 9. **taken up.** ver. 2. **us.** ♪12I1I, Ge +3:17. **must.** ver. 16. **ordained.** 2 C 12:12. Ga 1:1, 12. Ep 1:1. Re 2:2. **witness.** See on ver. 8. Ac +*2:24, 32. 3:15. *4:33. 5:32. 10:40, 41. 13:30, 31. Lk 24:48. Jn *15:27. Ro *1:4. 2 C 12:12. He *2:3. 1 P 1:3. **resurrection.** Ro 4:25. 1 C *15:13, 14, 20. 1 P 1:3.
23. **Barsabas.** Ac *15:22. **Justus.** i.e. *just*, *S#2459g. Ac 18:7. Col 4:11. **Matthias.** ver. 26.
24. **they prayed.** Ac 6:6. 13:2, 3. 14:23. Pr √3:5, 6. Lk 6:12, 13. Ph √4:6. **Thou, Lord.** Ac 15:8. Nu 27:16. 1 S +*16:7. 1 K *8:39. 1 Ch +*28:9. 29:17. Ps 7:9. 44:21. Pr 15:11. Je 11:20. +*17:10. 20:12. Jn +*2:24, 25. 21:17. Ro 8:27. He √4:13. Re *2:23. **hearts.** ♪12I1I, Ge +3:7. **show.** T#1467. 1 S 14:40-42. **chosen.** ver. 2. Ac 15:7.
25. **he may.** ver. 17, 20. **this ministry.** ver. 17. **and.** ♪93A, Ge +1:26. By *Hendiadys*, "apostolic ministry," with an emphasis upon the adjective "apostolic," which is obtained by exchange for the noun. **apostleship.** Ro 1:5. 1 C 9:2. Ga 2:8. **from.** ver. 16-21. Ps 109:7. Mt 27:3-5. **by.** 1 Ch 10:13, 14. 2 P 2:3-6. Ju 6, 7. **go.** Mt 25:41, 46. 26:24. Jn 6:70, 71. 13:27. 17:12. **own place.** Ac 4:23. Ps +*9:17.
26. **they gave.** Ac 13:19. Le 16:8. Nu 26:55. Jsh +*14:2n. 18:10. Jg 20:9. 1 S 10:20. 11:1. 14:41, 42. 1 Ch 24:5. Pr +*16:33. Jon 1:7. Lk 1:9. **the lot.** T#1775. Ac ◐13:2. Ge ◐+*24:44n. Jsh 14:2n. 1 S 14:41, 42. Ezk 21:21n. Jon 1:6, 7. **Matthias.** i.e. *gift of God*, *S#3159g. ver. 23. **the eleven.** ver. 2.

ACTS 2

The day of Pentecost being come, the Holy Spirit is poured out on the assembled disciples, with "a sound

as of a mighty wind;" while "cloven tongues as of fire" rest on each of them, 1-3. They speak divers languages, in the hearing of multitudes from many nations, who are come together on the occasion; at which most are amazed, but some deride, 4-13. Peter shows, that this is the fulfillment of a prophecy of Joel, 14-21; that Jesus, whom they had crucified, was risen from the dead, according to the prophecy of David, 22-32; and that being ascended into heaven, and exalted at the right hand of God, he had poured out the Holy Spirit, to demonstrate that he was the promised Messiah, 33-36. They are pricked to the heart, and inquire what they must do, 37. Peter exhorts and encourages them to repent, and to be baptized in the name of Jesus, 38-40. Three thousand are added to the church, 41. They continue stedfast in the faith, 42. Many miracles are wrought by the apostles, 43. The disciples have all things in common, and abound in love, joy, and praise; while numbers are daily added to them, 44-47.

1. **the day.** Ac 20:16. Ex 23:16. 34:22. Le *23:15-21. Nu 28:26-31. Dt *16:9-12. 1 C 16:8. **Pentecost.** i.e. *fiftieth*, *S#4005g. Le 23:2n. 25:9n. Ac 20:16. 1 C 16:8. **fully come.** or, being fulfilled. Ac 21:27. Lk 9:51. **one accord.** ver. 46. Ac *1:13-15. 4:24, 32. 5:12. 2 Ch 5:13, 14. 30:12. Ps *133:1, 2. Je 32:39. Zp 3:9. Ro 15:6. Ph 1:27. *2:2. **one place.** Jn 20:19. Lk 24:53.
2. **suddenly.** Ac 16:25, 26. Is +*65:24. Ml *3:1. Lk 2:13. **as.** 1 K 19:11. Jb 38:1. 40:6. Ps 18:10. SS 4:16. Ezk 1:4. 3:12, 13. *37:9, 10. Jn *3:8. **it filled.** Ac *4:31. 16:26. Lk 11:13.
3. **cloven.** He 2:4. **tongues.** ver. 4, 6, 11. Ge 11:6, 7. Ps 55:9. 1 C 12:10. Re 14:6. **like.** Is 6:5-8. Je √23:29. Ml 3:2, 3. Mt *3:11. Lk 3:16. 24:32. Ro *12:11. Ja 3:6. Re 11:3-5. **it sat.** ♪63I2, Jsh +3:3. i.e. the Holy Spirit, as is clear from the next verse. Ac 1:15. Is *11:2, 3. Mt 3:16. Jn 1:32, 33.
4. **filled.** ver. +38. Ac +*1:5, 8. 4:8, 31. 6:3, 5, 8. 7:55. 8:17. 9:17. 11:15, 24. 13:9, 52. Lk 1:15, 41, 67. 4:1. Jn *14:26. 20:22. Ro 15:13. Ep 3:19. +*5:18. **Ghost.** Gr. *pneuma*, Mt +1:18n. **began.** ver. 11. Ac *10:46, 47. *19:5, 6. Is 28:11. Mk +16:17. 1 C *12:7-11, 28-31. +*13:1, 8. 14:5, 6, 18, 21-23, 39. **tongues.** ♪121BC, Mk +16:17. **as.** Ex 4:11, 12. Nu 11:25-29. 1 S 10:10. 2 S 23:2. Is 59:21. Je 1:7-9. 6:11. Ezk 3:11. Mi 3:8. Mt 10:19, 20. Lk 12:12. 21:15. 1 C 14:26-32. Ep +*6:18, 19. 1 P 1:12. 2 P +*1:21. **the Spirit.** Gr. *pneuma*, Mt +3:16. Jn +7:39. **utterance.** 1 Ch 25:1.
5. **were.** ver. 1. Ac 8:27. Ex 23:16, 17. Is 66:18, 19. Zc 8:18-21. Lk 24:18. Jn 12:20. **devout.** Ac 8:2. 10:2, 7. 13:50. 17:4, 17. 22:12. Lk 2:25. He 5:7. 12:28. **under.** Dt *2:25. 4:19. 28:64. Mt 24:14. Lk 17:24. Col 1:23.
6. **Now.** ♪144A11, Ge +38:1. **was noised abroad.** Gr. voice was made. Jn 3:8g. **the multitude.** Ac 3:11. 1 C 16:9. 2 C 2:12. **confounded.** *or*, troubled in mind. Ac 9:22. Mt 2:3.
7. **amazed.** ver. 12. Ac 3:10. 14:11, 12. Mk 1:27. 2:12. Lk 2:47. 8:56. **are.** Ac 1:11. Mt 4:18-22. 21:11. Jn 7:52. **Galileans.** Ac 1:11. Mt 26:73. Mk 14:70. Lk 22:59.
8. **And now.** ♪136, Is +60:12. **own tongue.** Thus the gift of tongues in Acts was the gift of speaking another human language, and the evidence is nearly conclusive that this was the case when the gift is mentioned elsewhere: it was not an ecstatic speech.

9. **Parthians**. i.e. *horseman*, ✻S#3934g, only here. **Medes**. i.e. *overflowing*, ✻S#3370g, only here. For ✻S#4074h, see Ezr +6:2. 2 K 17:6. Ezr 6:2. Is 13:17. Je 51:11, 28. Da 5:28, 31. 8:20. **Elamites**. Ge 10:22. 14:1, 9. Is 11:11. 21:2. Da 8:2. **Mesopotamia**. Ac 7:2. Ge 24:10. Dt 23:4. Jg 3:8. 1 Ch 19:6. **Cappadocia**. i.e. *branded unreal*, ✻S#2587g. 1 P 1:1. **Pontus**. i.e. *the open sea*, ✻S#4195g. Ac 18:2 (S#4193g). 1 P 1:1. **Asia**. i.e. *slime, mire*, ✻S#773g. Ac 6:9. 16:6. 19:10, 22, 26, 27, 31. 20:4, 16, 18. 21:27. 24:18. 27:2. Ro 16:5, Achaia. 1 C 16:19. 2 C 1:8. 2 T 1:15. 1 P 1:1. Re 1:4, 11.

10. **Phrygia**. Ac 16:6. 18:23. **Pamphylia**. Ac 13:13. 14:24. 15:38. 27:5. **Egypt**. Ge 12:10. Is 19:23-25. Je 9:26. Ho 11:1. Mt 2:15. Re 11:8. **Libya**. i.e. *heart of the sea*, ✻S#3033g, only here. Je 46:9. Ezk 30:5. Da 11:43. **Cyrene**. i.e. *wall; coldness*, ✻S#2957g, only here. Ac 6:9. 11:20. 13:1. Mt 27:32. Mk 15:21. Lk 23:26. **strangers**. Ac 17:21. +✻28:15, 16. **Rome**. i.e. *strength*, ✻S#4516g. Ac 18:2. 19:21. 23:11. 28:14, 16. Ro 1:7, 15. 2 T 1:17. **Jews and**. Ac 6:5. 13:43. Est 8:17. Zc +✻8:20-23. Mt 23:15.

11. **Cretes**. i.e. *given to the flesh, carnal*, ✻S#2912g, here and T 1:12, Cretians. Ac 27:7, 12, 13, 21. T ✻1:5, 12. **Arabians**. 1 K 10:15. 2 Ch 17:11. 26:7. Is ✻13:20. 21:13. Je 3:2. 25:24. Ga 1:17. 4:25. **wonderful**. Ex 15:11. Jb 9:10. Ps 26:7. 40:5. 71:17, 19. 77:11. 78:4. 89:5. 96:3. 107:8, 15, 21. 111:4. 136:4. ✻138:2. Is 25:1. 28:29. Da 4:2, 3. Ho ✻8:12. Lk ✻1:49. Ro √1:16. 1 C 12:10, 28. 1 T ✻3:16. He 2:4.

12. **amazed**. ver. 7. **in doubt**. Ac 5:24. 10:17. Lk 9:7. **What**. Ac 10:17. 17:20. Lk 15:26. 18:36.

13. **mocking**. Ac 17:32. 1 C 14:23. **These**. ver. 15. 1 S 1:14. Jb 32:19. SS 7:9. Is 25:6. Zc 9:15, 17. 10:7. Ep +✻5:18.

14. **standing up**. Ac 27:21. **with**. Ac 1:26. **lifted**. ſ144A12, Ge +22:13. Ac 4:24. 14:11. 22:22. Is 40:9. 52:8. 58:1. Ho 8:1. Lk 11:27. 17:13. **and said**. ver. 4. Ac 26:25. **Ye men**. ver. 22. Ac 5:35. 13:16. 21:28. **be this**. ver. 36. Ac 4:10. 13:38. 28:28. **hearken**. Ac 7:2. Dt 27:9. Pr 8:32. Is 51:1, 4, 7. 55:2. Ja ✻2:5.

15. **these**. 1 S 1:15. **drunken**. Jn +2:10. **seeing**. Mt 20:3. 1 Th 5:5-8. **the third hour**. ſ49, Jn +10:22. Our 9 a.m. Mt 20:3. Mk 15:25. Jn +✻11:9n.

16. **the prophet**. See on Joel +✻)2:28-32. Mt +1:22. **Joel**. i.e. *the Lord is God*, ✻S#2493g, only here. For ✻S#3100h, see 1 S +8:2.

17. **And**. Jl)2:28. **in the last days**. Ge 49:1. Is +✻2:2. Da 10:14. Ho 3:5. Mi 4:1. 2 T 3:1. He +1:2. Ja 5:3. 2 P 3:3. **I will pour**. ſ22C38, Ps +79:6. ſ22K4, Je +2:13. Ac ✻10:45. Ps 72:6. Pr ✻1:23. Is 32:15, 16. 44:3. Ezk ✻11:19. +✻36:25-27. 39:29. Zc +✻12:10. Jn 7:39. Ro +5:5. T 3:4-6. **Spirit**. Gr. *pneuma*, ſ121A1, Lk +1:17n. Ge +1:2. **upon**. Is 54:13. Jn 6:45. **all flesh**. Ge 6:12. Ps 65:2. Is 40:5. 49:26. ✻66:23. Zc 2:13. Lk +3:6. Jn 17:2. **your sons**. Ac 11:28. 21:9. 1 C 12:10, 28. 14:26-31. **shall prophesy**. Ac +13:1. **see visions**. Ac +9:10.

18. **And**. Jl)2:29. **on my servants**. 1 C 7:21, 22. Ga ✻3:28. Col ✻3:11. Ja 1:1. **handmaidens**. Ac 21:4, 9, 10. **will pour**. ſ22C38, Ps +79:6. ſ22K4, Je +2:13. ver. 17. **Spirit**. Gr. *pneuma*, ſ121A1, Lk +1:17n. Ge +1:2. **and they**. See on ver. 17. Ac 11:28. 21:10. 1 C ✻12:10.

19. **And**. Jl)2:30. **wonders in heaven**. Jl +✻2:30,

31. Zp 1:14-18. Ml 4:1-6. **and signs**. ver. 22, 43. Jn +4:48.

20. **sun**. Is 13:9, 10, 15. 24:23. Je ✻4:23. Jl)2:31. ✻3:15. Am 8:9. Mt +✻24:29. 27:45. Mk ✻13:24. Lk 21:25. 2 P +✻3:7, 10. Re 6:12. 16:8. **the moon**. Re 6:12. **great**. Is 2:12-21. 34:8. Jl 2:1. 3:14. Am +✻5:18. Zp +✻2:2, 3. Ml 4:5. 1 C 5:5. 1 Th 5:2. 2 P +✻3:10. **day of the Lord**. Am +✻5:18. 1 Th 5:2. Re +✻1:10n. 16:14.

21. **whosoever**. Ac 9:11, 15. √16:31. +✻22:16. Ps 86:5. Jl +✻)2:32. Mt +✻28:19. Ro ✻10:12, 13. 1 C 1:2. He ✻4:16. **the name**. Ac 9:28. 15:26. Ps 118:26. Mt 21:9. 23:39. Mk 11:9. Lk 13:35. 19:38. Jn 12:13. Ro ✻10:13. 1 C 1:2, 10. 6:11. Ep 5:20. Ja 5:10, 14.

22. **men**. Ac 3:12. 5:35. 13:16. 21:28. Is 41:14. **Jesus**. Ac √10:38. Lk 24:19. **of Nazareth**. Ac 3:6. 4:10. 6:14. 22:8. 24:5. 26:9. Mt +2:23. Mk +1:24. Jn 1:45, 46. +18:5. 19:19. **a man**. Ac ✻10:37, 38. 26:26. Mt 11:2-6. Lk 7:20-23. 24:18, 19. Jn +✻3:2. 5:36. 6:14, 27. 7:31. 10:37, 38. 11:47. 12:17, 18. 14:10, 11. ✻15:24. He ✻2:4. **miracles**. Ac 10:38. Mt 12:28. Lk 11:20. **wonders**. Ac 8:13. Is 9:6. 28:29. Mt 21:15. Ro 15:19. 2 C 12:12. 2 Th 2:9. He ✻2:3, 4. **signs**. ver. 19, 43. Jn +4:48. **which**. Ac 10:37. 14:27. +20:18. Mt 9:8. 12:28. Lk ✻7:16. 11:20. 24:18. Jn 3:2. 5:17-20. 9:33. 11:40-42. ✻14:10, 11. Ro ✻1:4.

23. **being delivered**. Ac 3:13, 18. 4:28. 13:27. 15:18. Ps 76:10. Is 10:6, 7. 46:10, 11. Da 4:35. +✻9:24-27. Mt 20:19. ✻26:24. Lk ✻22:22, 37. ✻24:20, 44-46. Jn 19:24, 31-37. Ro 4:17. 11:33-36. 1 P 1:20. +✻2:8. Ju ✻4. Re √13:8. **determinate counsel**. ſ173, Ge +27:44. Ac ✻3:18. ✻4:27, 28. 13:27. +20:27. Lk 22:22. **foreknowledge**. T#213. Ac 3:18. 4:28. +✻13:48. 15:18. Ge=45:8. Is +✻42:9. 46:9, 10. Da 2:28. Am +✻3:6. Mt 6:8, 32. ✻24:36. Ro 8:29. 11:2. Ep +1:11 (T#260). He +4:13 (T#219). 1 P 1:2, 20. Re 13:8. **ye have taken**. ver. 36. Ac 3:13-15. 4:10, 11. 5:28, 30. 7:52. 13:28. Ge ✻50:20. Mt 27:20-25, 27, 31. Jn ✻7:30. ✻19:11. **wicked hands**. Ro 2:12, 14. 1 C 9:21. **crucified**. ſ173, Ge +27:44.

24. **Whom God**. Here Christ's resurrection is ascribed to God the Father; in John 10:18 it is ascribed to Christ himself, while in Ro 8:11 it is ascribed to the Holy Spirit. Thus we have the Trinity acting in unity in the resurrection of Christ. ver. ✻32. Jn √10:18. Ro 4:24. ✻6:4. ✻8:11. **hath raised**. Notice the single, consistent note present in all their witness: the bodily resurrection of Christ. Any religious faith which claims to be Biblical must share the same balance and emphasis the Bible itself contains (Is +✻43:10n. Jn +✻16:13n). ver. 32. Ac 3:15, 26. 4:10, 33. 5:30. 10:40, 41. ✻13:30, 33, 34, 37. √17:30, 31. Ps=105:20. Mt 27:63. Lk ch. ✻24. Jn +✻2:19-22. ✻10:17, 18. Ro 4:24. ✻6:4. ✻8:11, 34. √10:9. 14:9. 1 C ✻6:14. 15:12-15. 2 C ✻4:14. Ga 1:1. Ep 1:20. 2:5. Col 2:12. 1 Th 1:10. 2 T 2:8. He ✻13:20. 1 P ✻1:21. **loosed**. Jb 39:2. Ps ✻116:3, 4, 16. **pains of death**. Mt +✻24:8g. Ps 18:5. 116:3. Col 1:18. **because**. Lk 24:5. Jn √10:18. 20:9. 2 T 1:10. He 2:14. Re 1:17, 18. **not possible**. Ac 1:16. Is ✻25:8. +✻26:19n. 53:10. Ho ✻13:14. Lk ✻24:46. Jn ✻10:35. 12:39. He ✻2:14. Re ✻1:18. **be holden**. Ro 6:9.

25. **David**. ver. 29, 30. Ac +4:25. 13:32-36. **I foresaw**. Ps)16:8-11. **for**. Ps 73:23. 109:31. 110:5. 121:5. Is 41:13. 50:7-9. Jn 16:32. **on my right**. ſ22D3F, Ps +16:8. **I should not**. Ps 21:7. 30:6. 62:2, 6.

26. **my tongue**. Ps 16:9. 22:22-24. 30:11, 12. 63:5.

71:23, 24. **flesh**. ⌐171Q5, Ge +17:13. **shall rest.** 1 Th *4:13, 14, 18. **in hope**. Ro 4:18.

27. **leave**. Ps 49:15mg. 86:13. 116:3. Lk 16:23. 1 C *15:55mg. Re 1:18. 20:13, 14. **soul**. Gr. *psyche*, Mt +*10:28n. ⌐121A8, Ps +16:10. **hell**. Gr. *hades*, Mt +11:23. ver. 31. **neither**. Ac 13:35. **thine**. Ac 3:14. 4:27. Ps 89:19. Mk 1:24. Lk +*1:35. 4:34. He +7:26. 1 J *2:20. Re 3:7. **to see**. ver. 31. Ac 13:27-37. Jb +*19:25-27. Jon 2:6. Lk 2:26. Jn 8:51. 11:39. 1 C *15:52-54. **corruption**. Jb 17:14.

28. **made**. Ps +*16:11. 21:4. 25:4. Pr 2:19. 8:20. Jn *11:25, 26. ✓14:6. **the ways of life**. Dt 30:15. Pr 10:17. 15:24. Mt 7:14. **make**. Ps 4:6, 7. *17:15. 21:6. 42:5. He *12:2. **thy countenance**. Nu 6:25. Ps 11:7. *17:15. Mt 18:10. He 9:24. 1 P 3:12. Re 22:4.

29. **let me**. *or*, I may. ⌐63B, Ge +2:10. **freely**. Ac 26:26. **the patriarch**. Ac 7:8, 9. He 7:4. **David**. Ac 13:+*23, 36. 1 K 2:10. Mk 11:10. **his sepulchre**. Ne 3:16.

30. **being**. Ac 1:16. 2 S *23:2. Mt 22:43. 27:35. Mk 12:36. Lk +*24:44. He 3:7. 4:7. 11:32. 2 P *1:21. **knowing**. 2 S +*7:11-16. 1 Ch 17:11-15. Ps *89:3, 4, 19-37. *110:1-5. *132:11-18. Ro *1:3. 2 T 2:8. He 7:1, 2, 21. **with**. Mt *6:17. **the fruit**. Ac *13:23. Mt 1:1. 9:27. Mk 12:35-37. **according to the flesh**. Mt *16:27n. Ro *1:3. 2 J 7n. Re 22:16. **he would**. Ac 13:23. Ps 2:6-12. 72:1-19. Is +*7:14. +*9:6, 7. +✓55:3. Je +*23:5, 6. 33:14, 15. Am 9:11, 12. Mi +*5:2. Lk *1:31-33, 69, 70. 2:10, 11. Jn 18:36, 37. Ro 15:12. Re 17:14. 19:16. **raise up**. Gr. *anistemi*, ✻S#450g. ver. 24, 32. Ac 1:15. 3:22, 26. 5:6, 17, 34, 36, 37. 6:9. 7:18, 37. 8:26, 27. 9:6, 11, 18, 34, 39, 40, 41. 10:13, 20, 26, 41. 11:7, 28. 12:7. 13:16, 33, 34. 14:10, 20. 15:7. 17:3, 31. 20:30. 22:10, *16n. 23:9. 26:16, 30. Mt 9:9. 12:41. 17:9. 20:19. 22:24. 26:62. Mk 1:35. 2:14. 3:26. 5:42. 7:24. 8:31. 9:9, 10, 27, 31. 10:1, 34, 50. 12:23, 25. 14:57, 60. 16:9. Lk 1:39. 4:16, 29, 38, 39. 5:25, 28. 6:8. 8:55. 9:8, 19. 10:25. 11:7, 8, 32. 15:18, 20. 16:31. 17:19. 18:33. 22:45, 46. 23:1. 24:7, 12, 33, 46. Jn 6:39, 40, 44, 54. 11:23, 24, 31. 20:9. Ro 14:9. 15:12. 1 C 10:7. Ep 5:14. 1 Th 4:14, 16. He 7:11, 15. For the related word *anastasis*, ✻S#386g, see ver. +*31. **to sit**. Ps ◐110:1. Mt +*19:28. ✓25:31. Lk 1:33. He ◐8:1. ◐12:2. Re +*3:21. **his throne**. Lk +*1:32.

31. **seeing**. 1 P 1:11, 12. **spake**. ver. 27. Ac 13:35. Ps +*16:10. **the resurrection**. "Except for Luke 2:34, the word for 'resurrection' (*anastasis*) means bodily resurrection in its other 40 occurrences in the N.T." (Norman F. Douty, *Union with Christ*, ftn. 4, p. 225). Gr. *anastasis*, ✻S#386g. Rendered (1) resurrection: Mt 22:23, 28, 30, 31. Mk 12:18, 23. Lk 14:14. 20:27, 33, 35, 36. Jn 5:29, 29. 11:24, 25. Ac 1:22. 2:31. 4:2, 33. 17:18, 32. 23:6, 8. 24:15, 21. Ro 1:4. 6:5. 1 C 15:12, 13, 21, 42. Ph 3:10. 2 T 2:18. He 6:2. 11:35b. 1 P 1:3. 3:21. Re 20:5, 6. (2) rising again: Lk 2:34. (3) that should rise: Ac 26:23. (4) with ✻S#1537g, *ek*, raised to life again: He 11:35a. For the related word *anistemi*, ✻S#450g, see ver. +*30. **of Christ**. Lk +3:15. **that**. ver. 27. **soul**. Gr. *psyche*, Mt +*10:28n. ⌐171Q2, Nu +23:10. ⌐121A8, Ps +16:10. **hell**. Gr. *hades*, Mt +11:23. **corruption**. Ps ✦16:10.

32. **This Jesus**. ver. 36. Ac +*1:11. **hath God**. ver. 24. **raised up**. Gr. *anistemi*, ✻S#450g, ver. +*30. This is an explicit reference to bodily resurrection (Is 43:10n. Da +*12:2). Mk 5:42. Lk 8:55. **whereof**. ver. +*24. Ac +*1:8, 22. 3:15. *4:33. *5:31, 32. *10:39-41. *13:31.

Lk *24:46-48. Jn *15:27. *20:26-31.

33. **by**. Ac *5:31. Ps 89:19, 24. 118:16, 22, 23. Is 52:13. *53:12. Mt 28:18. Mk +16:19. Jn +*17:5. Ep 1:20-23. Ph *2:9-11. He 1:2-4. 2:9. *10:12. 1 P *1:21. 3:22. **right hand**. ⌐22A15C, Ps +110:1. Ex 15:6. Ps 98:1. Is 63:12. **exalted**. Jn 3:14g. **having**. Ac +1:4. Lk ✓24:49. Jn *7:38, 39. *14:16, 26. *15:26. *16:7-15. **the promise**. Ac 1:4. Lk 24:49. Ga +3:14. **Ghost**. Gr. *pneuma*, Mt +3:16. ver. 38. **he**. ver. +17, 38, 39. Ac *10:45. Ro *5:5. Ep *4:8. T *3:6. **shed forth**. ⌐22C38, Ps +79:6. ⌐22K4, Je +2:13. Jb 29:6.

34. **not ascended**. This is spoken in reference to his body, not his soul or spirit (Da +*12:2n. Mt 22:32. Jn +*2:19, 21. 1 C ◐+*15:50. 2 C +*5:8. Ep 4:8-10. Ph *1:23. +*3:21. He 12:23). "The departure of the spirit to God is never reckoned 'ascension'" (F.W. Grant, *Facts and Theories as to a Future State*, p. 127). Lk ◐23:43. Jn ◐+*3:13n. *20:17. 2 C 5:1-4, 6. **into the heavens**. ver. 33. Mt 5:12. 25:34, 46. Jn 12:26. +*14:2, 3. ✓17:24. 2 C *12:4. Ph +*1:23. 3:20. 1 Th ✓4:17. 1 P ✓1:4. Re 2:7. 3:21. +*14:12. 22:14. **but he saith**. Ac +4:25. **The Lord**. Ps ◗110:1. Mt 22:42-45. Mk 12:36. Lk 20:42, 43. 1 C 15:25. Ep 1:22. He 1:13. 10:12, 13. **Sit thou**. Mt 26:64. Ep *1:20. Col 3:1. He 1:3. 8:1. 12:2.

35. **Until**. Ps ◗110:1. Ep 1:22. He 2:8. 1 P 3:22. **thy foes**. Ge +*3:15. Jsh 10:24, 25. 1 S 17:51. Ps *2:8-12. 18:40-42. 21:8-12. 72:9. Is 49:23. 59:18. 60:14. 63:4-6. Lk *19:27. 20:16-18. Ro 16:20. 1 C *15:24-27. Re 19:19-21. 20:1-3, 8-15. **thy footstool**. Jsh 10:24. Ps 8:6. 18:38.

36. **all**. Je 2:4. 9:26. 31:31. 33:14. Ezk 34:30. 39:25-29. Zc 13:1. Ro 9:3-6. **the house of**. Ac 7:42. Ezk 36:32, 37. Mt 10:6. 15:24. Lk 1:33. He 8:8, 10. **assuredly**. Ac 16:23. Mk 14:44. **that God**. Mt 28:18. He 3:2. **hath made**. Jn +*14:28. He 3:2g. **that same Jesus**. ver. 22, 23, 32. Ac +*1:11. 4:11, 12. 5:30, 31. =7:35. 10:36-42. Ps *2:1-8, 12. Mt 22:32. 28:18-20. Jn ✓3:35, 36. *5:22-29. Ro 14:8-12. 2 C *5:10. 1 Th +*4:16n. 2 Th ✓1:7-10. **whom**. ver. +23. **both Lord**. Lk 2:11. Ro 14:9. 2 C 4:5. Ph *2:9-11. **and Christ**. Ac +18:5.

37. **when**. T#590. Ac 5:33. 7:54. Jg +10:15 (T#356). Ezk 7:16. Zc *12:10. Lk *3:10. Jn 8:9. *16:7-11. Ro 7:9-11. 1 C 14:24, 25. He *4:12, 13. **pricked**. Ps 109:16. **Men**. See on Ac 1:16. **the apostles**. ver. 42, 43. Ac 5:12. **what shall**. T#306. ver. 38. Ac *9:5, 6. ✓16:29-31. 22:10. 24:25, 26. Mk *16:15, 16. Lk 3:10, 12, 14. 2 C 5:18-20. Ga *3:10-12. Col 1:20, 21.

38. **Repent**. The English text does not adequately convey the grammar of this verse. When the grammar is understood, the verse no longer can be used to support any view of baptismal regeneration or baptismal remission of sin. The phrase "every one of you" is mistakenly understood to be the subject of the verbs "repent" and "be baptized," with the phrase "for the remission of sins" modifying this alleged compound predicate. There are three clauses in this verse: (1) *Ye*: understood subject, second person, plural number. *repent*: verb, aorist tense, active voice, imperative mood, second person, plural number. (2) *every one of you*: subject, third person, singular number. *be baptized*: verb, aorist tense, passive voice, imperative mood, third person, singular number. *for the remission of sins*. modifying phrase, expressing the ground or basis of the baptism commanded (if understood of ritual water baptism), or the result (if understood of real

baptism) of the baptism received. (3) *ye.* subject, second person, plural number. *shall receive.* verb, future tense, indicative mood, passive voice, second person, plural number. *the gift of the Holy Ghost.* direct object of the verb. Note particularly in the above analysis that the first and third clauses agree with each other in that both are in the second person and plural number for their subject and verb. The second clause does not agree in person and number of its subject and verb with the preceding or following clause. This makes it impossible to make "every one of you," which is third person singular, the subject of both "repent" (second person plural) and "be baptized" (third person singular), for subjects and verbs must agree in person and number. A. T. Robertson observes that this change in person and number "marks a break in the thought here that the English translation does not preserve" (*Word Pictures*, vol. 3, p. 34). Peter thus commanded all in his audience to repent. Upon repentance, each individual was then to be baptized on the basis that the specific individual's sin had been remitted upon their placing faith upon the name of Jesus Christ. Since the first and third clauses agree in person and number, the thought is that reception of the Holy Spirit is the consequence of faith upon the name of Christ, not ritual water baptism. Ac +*3:19. *5:31. *17:30. *20:21. 26:18, 20. Mt *3:2, 8, 9, 11. *4:17. *21:28-32. Lk 1:77. 3:3. +*13:3, 5. *15:1-32. 17:3, 4. *24:47. 2 C 7:10. 2 T +*2:25. 1 J √1:9. **and.** The force of this conjunction is neglected or misunderstood by some interpreters. The word "and" marks the gracious relation of cause and effect, as in the grammatical parallel at Ac 3:19, "Repent and be converted." The Holy Spirit who gives repentance does, therewith, confer baptism for the remission of sins (J. W. Dale, *Christic Baptism*, p. 142). This of itself proves that the reference is to real, not ritual water, baptism. **be baptized.** The traditional understanding of this command is that it refers to ritual water baptism. An alternate view is that this is a reference to real baptism by the Holy Spirit. The correctness of the alternative view is established by the fact that (1) water is not mentioned in the context. (2) The baptism is not "into water" but, literally, upon the name of Jesus Christ. (3) Believing upon Jesus Christ is the ground upon which remission of sins is received. (4) Ritual water baptism is never in Scripture said to secure for us the remission of sins, only real baptism possesses such efficacy. (5) This real baptism takes the penitent sinner out of a state of guilt and places him *into* (*eis*) a new state of remission. This placement is permanent, and can hardly be symbolized by a momentary dipping in water, for the relationship established is permanent (Col 2:12n). (6) Only real baptism by the Holy Spirit can produce the change in condition always marked by the term "baptize" (1 C 10:2n) when the subject is spiritual baptism. Ac *8:12, 36-38. 13:24. *16:15, 31-34. +*22:16. Mt +*3:11n. Mk +*16:16. Jn +*3:5. T 3:5. He +*10:22. 1 P *3:21, 22. **in.** Gr. *epi*, lit. upon. With the dative case, as here, *epi* means "*upon* (ground, reason)" (Professor Harrison, *Greek Prepositions*, p. 266, cited by J. W. Dale, *Christic Baptism*, p. 138). Eric Sauer states "Under the influence of a psalm and a prophecy which speak of the Messianic 'cornerstone' and 'foundation' (Ps 118:22. Is 28:16), Christ is described as the foundation of our life of faith 'upon' (Gr. *epi*) Whom we believe (1 P 2:6. Ro

10:11)" (*From Eternity to Eternity*, p. 46). Dale gives some additional instructive examples. From the apocryphal book of *Judith* (12:7), *epi* occurs in conjunction with the verb baptize in the expression "baptized herself upon the fountain." The preposition expresses that *upon* which Judith rested when she baptized herself. Every "fountain" as "a lip," an edge, on which one can stand and be baptized. Clement of Alexandria (I. 1352) says: "It is a custom of the Jews to be baptized *upon* (Gr. *epi*) a couch." The preposition points out that *upon* which the Jew rested when he received baptism; he *rested upon* a couch. Mt 3:13, Jesus came from Galilee toward, more literally, upon, the Jordan, meaning that when he reached it he rested upon it (every river, like every fountain, has "a lip," an edge, a bank, *upon* which one can stand) to be baptized. "These examples present a physical basis on which the baptized rested. The case under consideration (Ac 2:38) exhibits the moral basis upon which the soul must rest in receiving the baptism into the remission of sins" (*Christic Baptism*, p. 145). Dale explains "the soul to be baptized *out of* guilt *into* the remission of sins must rest, not upon repentance (as any meritorious or ultimate ground), but must *rest upon that* NAME, 'which is the only name given under heaven whereby we must be saved,' Jesus Christ," and "every penitent sinner, *resting upon* Jesus Christ, as an atoning Redeemer, shall thereby be baptized into the remission of sins" (p. 145). Lk 24:47g. Ac 16:31g. 1 C 3:11. **the name.** The question often arises, why is not the trinitarian formula of baptism given in Mt 28:19 utilized by the apostles in the book of Acts? Of several answers which have been proposed, the best sees this shortened expression as the figure of speech 𝒥171S11. Synecdoche of the Part, whereby a part is put for the whole, a shortened expression for the fuller expression. It seems to be that the apostles indeed did use the full formula, but simply referred to the act of baptism by the shorter phrase "in the name of Jesus Christ," "in the name of the Lord Jesus," or even shorter, "in the name of the Lord," in common with the wider practice of that day of being baptized "in the name" of one's spiritual teacher, as John's disciples were (Ac 19:3), just as John, as well as Jesus, taught his disciples to pray, Lk 11:1, evidently in a distinct manner. Thus the expression pertains more to this distinctiveness than to the precise formula employed. "As Waterland well puts it, 'The meaning is that the apostles baptized into the faith and religion of Christ, in that method and according to that form which our Lord Himself had prescribed'" (cited in Thomas Walker, commentary on Acts, p. 54. The citation is from Daniel Waterland, *Works*, vol. 2, Sermon viii, "Christ's Divinity Proved from the Form of Baptism," p. 173). Waterland continues, "The Apostles administered Christ's, not John's baptism; that baptism which Christ had appointed; St. Luke expresses it briefly by baptizing 'in the name of Christ;' not because it ran in his *name* only, but because it was instituted by his authority. Thus the practice of the Apostles is reconciled with the *commission* given them" (p. 173). Other answers which have been proposed are less satisfactory. Some suggest that the trinitarian formula was never used, but this would appear to place the disciples in direct disobedience to what our Lord commanded. To escape this difficulty, some (often in the name of "right division" of Scripture:

2 T 2:15. 1 Th 4:2n) would refer the practice of baptism within narrow dispensational limits—the time of the establishment of Jewish Christian churches in the early part of Acts—suspending the validity of baptism for the church age, reserving it to the millennial kingdom, a view totally out of harmony with the general practice of Bible believing Christians throughout church history. This view depends upon artificially dividing Scripture (1 Th 4:2n. 2 T 2:15n) in a manner unauthorized by its own content, by principles undiscoverable by the proverbial independent Bible reader on a desert island with no denominational "helps" to guide him, a quite sound rule for determining whether a teaching is truly Biblical (Is +*8:20n. Ac 17:11). Such a view contradicts the Bible doctrine of the perpetuity of the ordinance establishing ritual baptism (Mt 28:19n). Still further astray is the "Jesus only" viewpoint, which suggests there is one God, "Jesus," who is the Father and the Holy Spirit, into whose single name we are to be baptized. While maintaining the deity of Christ, this view is faulty by denying the existence of three distinct persons in the Godhead. Attempting to prove Jesus and the Father are one and the same person, some misapply such Scripture as Jn 10:30 and 14:7, 9, for Christ's own appeal to the Father as a witness distinct from Himself is fatal to this view (Jn 5:36-38). Ac *8:12, 16. 10:48. *19:4, 5. Mt +√28:19. Ro 6:3. 1 C 1:13-17. **for.** Gr. *eis*. Some would make this expression equivalent to the expression in Mt 26:28, where the same words "for the remission of sins" are found. This assumes that the preposition "for" (Gr. *eis*) possesses the same meaning wherever it occurs. Here *eis* expresses either the "ground or basis" for the baptism, namely, the remission of sins consequent upon repentance and believing upon the name of Christ, or far better, the result of the real (not ritual) baptism attending true repentance and faith upon Christ. In Mt 26:28, *eis* expresses the aim or purpose of the death of Christ. When *eis* expresses purpose (as Mt 26:28), grammarians term this the *telic* use of *eis*. J. W. Dale asserts "The *telic* use of *eis* with *baptidzo* (baptize) may, very confidently, be declared to have no existence, whether in the Scriptures or out of the Scriptures" (*Christic Baptism*, p. 144). In other words, Dale asserts that the proposition *eis* is never used to express purpose in conjunction with the verb "baptize" in either Classical or Biblical (Koine) Greek. Dale cites a passage from Clement of Alexandria (II. 1212), "they baptize *out of (ek)* chastity *into (eis)* fornication," commenting "Who would think of translating this phrase, 'They baptize out of temperance *unto, for, in order to*, fornication'?" (*Christic Baptism*, p. 144). Dale asserts "it is impossible for *eis* to reach over *baptized* and receive a *telic* character from *Repent* exclusively" (p. 139). Thus the grammar forbids the notion that repentance is "in order to the remission of your sins." The preposition *eis* in this verse (Ac 2:38) is one of the most debated prepositions in all the Word of God. But merely compiling long lists of scholars who translate or explain this preposition in a particular manner to defend the mistaken assertion that *eis* can only mean "unto" (or "in order to," "with a view to," "to the end that," "for," etc.) is not sound linguistic practice. A list of scholars is no more valid than the validity of logic and evidence which they marshal to support their position (2 S 5:23n): the honor of the names cited or their number have

no bearing on the strength of their case. The scholars cited do not necessarily affirm that this must be the rendering here, particularly if they are not discussing the doctrinal implications which such a translation supports. The preposition *eis* may mean "because of," as at Mt 12:41. It may also mean "as a sign or profession of," as at Mt +*3:11n. 28:19. 1 C 1:13. 10:2. Notice that in the last four passages cited, the preposition *eis* occurs in the same grammatical construction and with reference to the same subject, baptism. The preposition *eis* may be understood here to mean "the ground or basis of" (as in Mt 10:41. *12:41. See related notes at Mt 26:28n. Mk +*1:4n), or it may legitimately be understood to indicate the result of believing upon the name of Jesus Christ. Each of these alternatives is certainly to be preferred to the view that we are baptized in order to receive remission of sins, a viewpoint contrary to the rest of the Word of God, and incompatible with Greek grammar, for *eis* never possesses a *telic* sense (expressing purpose, as when rendered "for") in conjunction with the verb baptize. It is a fallacy, if not absurdity, to hold that a word in Greek or Hebrew must in every occurrence be translated by the same English word, or to suggest that at every occurrence of a word it always possesses exactly the same meaning. A reference to the classifications of the words "soul" and "spirit" (Mt +2:20n. +8:16n) will demonstrate that single words may have numerous and quite different meanings. This holds true for every part of speech. When translating from one language to another no word in one language possesses precisely the same range of meaning, connotation, and denotation as a single usually equivalent word of the other language, neither does it function with precisely the same or equivalent idioms (Ac +*8:39n. 10:11n. 1 J 2:19n). This text is a favorite of those who teach the mistaken doctrine of baptismal regeneration (along with Mk 16:16. Jn 3:5. Ac 22:16. Ga 3:27. 1 P 3:21). Lewis Sperry Chafer's remark regarding the tendency to build a whole system of belief upon one text applies equally well to those who build such a system upon several chosen texts of Scripture, "A certain type of mind seems able to construct all its confidence on an erroneous interpretation of one passage and to be uninfluenced by the overwhelming body of Scripture which contradicts that interpretation" (*Systematic Theology*, vol. 3, p. 380). Mt ●26:28n. Mk +1:4n. Lk 3:3. **remission of sins.** Ac 10:43. 13:38. Lk +7:48. Ep 1:7. Col 1:14. He 10:18. **and ye.** ver. 16-18. Ac 8:15-17. *10:44, 45. Is 32:15. 44:3, 4. 59:21. Ezk +*36:25-27. 39:29. Jl +*2:28, 29. Zc +*12:10. **the gift.** Ac 8:15, 20. 10:45. 11:17. Jn 4:10. +7:39. He 6:4. **Ghost.** Gr. *pneuma*, Mt +3:16.

39. **the promise.** Ac √3:21. Dt 30:19. Ro 9:4. Ga √3:17, 29. He 6:17. **is unto you.** Ac 3:25, 26. Ge +*17:7, 8. Dt 30:19. Ps 115:14, 15. Je 32:39, 40. Ezk 37:25. Jl +*2:28. Ro 11:16, 17. 1 C +*7:14. **your children.** "Meaning, probably, 'to your posterity for all time to come' (Ge 17:7). It may, however, also point to the fact that the promises of the new covenant include the children of believers" (Thomas Walker). T#120, 821. Ac *3:25. √16:31. Ge +*17:7, 9, 19. 26:24. Dt +*29:11n. 30:6, 19. 2 K 13:23. Ps +*102:28. 103:17, 18. Pr +22:6 (T#496). Is +*29:23. 44:3-5. *54:13. 59:21. Je *31:17. Mk *10:14, 16. 1 C √7:14n. **and to all.** Ac 10:45. 11:15-18. 14:27. 15:3, 8, 14. Is 2:2. 59:19.

Ep 2:13-22. 3:5-8. **afar off.** ƒ88, Ge +15:15. Ac 22:21. Is 49:1. 57:19. Mi 4:1-3. Zc 6:15. Ep *2:13, 17. Ja 1:1. **as many.** Jl +*2:32. Ro *8:30. 9:24. 11:29. Ep 1:18. 4:4. 2 Th 1:11. *2:13, 14. 2 T +*1:9. He 3:1. 9:15. 1 P 5:10. 2 P 1:3, 10. Re 17:14. 19:9. **shall call.** T#597. Ro 1:6, 7. *8:30. 9:23, 24. 1 C 1:9, 23, 24. 1 Th 2:12. 2 Th 2:14. 1 P 2:9.

40. **with.** Ac 15:32. 20:2, 9-11. 28:23. Jn 21:25. **did.** Ac 10:42. 20:21, 24. Ga 5:3. Ep 4:17. 1 Th 2:11. 1 P 5:12. **testify.** Lk +16:28. **Save.** ver. 21, 47. Nu 16:28-34. Pr 9:6. Lk +*21:36. 2 C 5:20. √6:17. 1 T +*4:16. He +*3:12, 13. Ja 4:8-10. Re 3:17-19. 18:4, 5. **untoward generation.** Dt 32:5. Je +*7:29. Mt *3:7-10. 12:34, 39. 16:4. 17:17. 23:33, *36. Mk 8:38. Ph 2:15. 1 P 2:18g.

41. **Then they.** For additional instances of salvation received without tongues–speaking see Ac 3:7-9. 4:4. 5:14. 6:7. 8:36. 9:42. 11:21. 13:12, 43, 48. 14:1, 21. 16:14, 34. 17:4, 11, 12, 34. 18:4, 8. 28:24. See related notes on Ac +*4:8n. Ro +*8:9n. Ep +*5:18n. **gladly.** ver. 47. Ac 8:6-8. 13:48. √16:31-34. Mt +*13:44-46. Ga 4:14, 15. 1 Th 1:6. **received.** Ac +*17:11. Lk 8:40g. *23:34. **were baptized.** See on ver. +*38. There appears no conceivable way for three thousand people to have been immersed on the streets or within the confines of Jerusalem. There was no adequate source of water available to such a crowd for this purpose. While "there were abundant pools of water in and about Jerusalem, in some of which bathing was certainly allowed (Jn 5:4. 9:7)" (Lyman Abbott, cited in J. W. Shepherd, *Handbook on Baptism*, p. 117), nothing in the text or the argument informs us how these facilities were made available for Christian use. Those who argue that there was certainly water enough to handle the many sacrifices offered at the passover (J.W. Shepherd, *Handbook on Baptism*, pp. 117, 118, citing Robert Halley, *The Sacraments*, Part I, p. 318) fail to show how three thousand persons were permitted to enter the temple to use its facilities for such a purpose. Did such a crowd come prepared for this exigency with a change of clothing? Were the men and women provided separate changing areas? And how could 12 disciples immerse so many in an afternoon, even if the facilities were available? To suggest, as Abbott, that though the 3000 were baptized immediately, Scripture doesn't specifically state they were all baptized on the same day (J.W. Shepherd, p. 117, citing Lyman Abbott, Comm. on Acts 2:41), is an unprovable assertion based upon an inference required by his theory, not deducible from the text, which directly to the contrary explicitly states "and the same day there were added...." The evidence would seem to require that some mode other than immersion be employed on this, if not every, occasion of baptism in the New Testament (see related notes on Ac 1:5n. +*22:16). **added.** ver. 47. Ac 1:15. 4:4. Ps 72:16, 17. 110:3. Lk 5:5-7. Jn 14:12. **souls.** Gr. *psyche*, ƒ121A8, Metonymy of Cause, or ƒ171Q1A, Synecdoche of the Part, where an integral part of man (individually) is put for the whole person. *Psyche* is used here of persons or individuals, as at ver. 43. Ac 3:23. 7:14. 27:37. Ro 2:9. 13:1. Ja 5:20. 1 P 3:20. 2 P 2:14. Re 18:13. For the other uses of *psyche*, see Mt +*2:20n. For other instances of ƒ121A8, see Ps +16:10. For ƒ171Q1A, see Ge +12:5. Ge 12:5. 14:21. Le 4:2. Ezk 27:13.

42. **they continued.** ver. 46. Ac +1:14. *11:23.

*14:22. Pr 4:13. Mk 4:16, 17. Jn √8:31, 32. 1 C 11:2. Ga *1:6. Ep 2:20. Col +*1:23. 2 T *3:14. He *10:39. 2 P 3:1, 2, 17, 18. 1 J √2:19. **stedfastly.** 1 C +*15:58. He *10:25. **the apostles'.** ver. 37. Ac +5:12. **doctrine.** ƒ108B, Mk +4:2. Ro 6:17. 1 C 14:6, 26. 1 T +*4:16. 2 T *2:2. 3:16. **fellowship.** Ac 4:23. 5:12-14. Ga 2:9. Ph 1:5. 1 P 2:17. 5:9. 1 J *1:3, 7. **in breaking.** ver. 46. Ac *20:7, 11. Lk 24:35. 1 C 10:16, 17, 21. 11:20-26. **bread.** ƒ171I8, Ge +3:19. **and in prayers.** Ac *1:14. *4:31. *6:4. Ro 12:12. Ep *6:18. Col *4:2. He √10:25. Ju 20.

43. **fear.** Ac 5:5, 11, 13. 19:17. Est 8:17. Ps 40:3. Je 33:9. Ho 3:5. Lk 1:65. 5:26. 7:16. 8:37. **soul.** Gr. *psyche*, ƒ171Q1A, ver. +*41n. ƒ171Q1, Ge +12:5. **many.** ver. 19, 22. Ac 3:6-9. 4:33. 5:12, 15, 16. 9:34, 40. Mk *16:17, 20. Jn 4:48. 14:12.

44. **believed.** Ac +13:12. **had.** Ac *4:32, 34, 35. 5:4. 6:1-3. Mt 19:21. 2 C *8:9, 14, 15. 9:6-15. 1 J 3:16-18.

45. **sold.** Ac 4:34-37. 5:1, 2. 11:29. Lk 12:33, 34. +*16:9. 18:22. 19:8. **parted.** Ps 112:9. Pr 11:24, 25. 19:17. Ec 11:1, 2. Is 58:7-12. Lk 11:41. 2 C 9:1, 9. 1 T +*6:18, 19. Ja *2:14-16. 5:1-5. 1 J *3:17.

46. **continuing.** Ac 3:1. 5:21, 42. Lk *24:53. **daily.** Ac *1:14. 3:1. *5:42. 1 Ch=16:37. 2 Ch=30:21. Lk 24:53. He +*3:13. **one accord.** Ac +1:14. **in the temple.** Ac 5:42. **breaking.** ƒ108H4, Is +58:7. ver. *42. Ac *20:7. Lk *22:19. **bread.** ƒ171I8, Ge +3:19. **from house to house.** or, at home. Ac 1:13. 1 C 11:20-22. 2 J +*10. **did.** Ac *16:34. Dt *12:7, 12. 16:11. Ne *8:10. Ec 9:7. 1 C √10:30, 31. **with gladness.** Ac 16:34. 2 Ch=29:30. Jn +16:22. Ro *14:17. **singleness.** Ps *86:11. Mt 6:22. Ro 12:8. 2 C *1:12. *11:3. Ep *6:5. Col *3:22.

47. **Praising.** Ps *34:1. Lk +24:53. **having favor.** Ac *4:21, 33. +5:13. Pr +*16:7. Lk *2:52. *19:48. Ro *14:18. **all.** ƒ171L2, Mt +26:59. **the Lord.** ver. *39. Ac *5:14. *11:24. *13:48. Ro *8:30. 9:27. 11:5-7. 1 C 3:6. T *3:4, 5. **added.** ver. 41. Ac 5:14. 11:24. Is √55:10, 11. 1 C *3:7. **daily.** Ac 16:5. 1 Ch=16:37. He +*3:12, 13. **should be saved.** ver. 21, 40. Ac √16:31. 1 C +1:18. Ep 2:8.

ACTS 3

Peter and John, at the temple, heal one who had been lame from his birth, 1-8. The people, being astonished, throng around them, 9-11. Peter declares, that this miracle had been wrought by the power, and through faith in the name of Jesus, whom they and the other Jews had delivered to be crucified, but whom God had raised from the dead, 12-16; he supposes that they did it ignorantly, and shows that God had thus fulfilled the scripture, 17, 18; he exhorts them to "repent and be converted, that their sins" may be pardoned, and they made partakers of the promised blessing, 19, 20; and refers them to Moses and all the prophets, whose predictions were fulfilled in Jesus the Savior, whom God had sent to bless them, in turning them from their iniquities, 21-26.

1. **Peter and John.** ver. 3, 4, 11. Ac 4:13, 19. 8:14. Mt +4:21. 17:1. 26:37. Mk +9:38. Lk 22:8. Jn 13:23-25. 20:2-9. 21:7, 18-22. Ga 2:9. **went up.** Ac 2:46. 5:25. Lk +18:10. 24:53. **together.** Gr. *epi to auto*, rather, "at the same time," or "at that time," referring to the time when the transactions took place, which

are mentioned at the close of the preceding chapter. **into the temple.** Lk +24:53. **the hour.** There were *three* stated hours for prayer among the Jews: the *third* hour, or about nine in the morning, when they offered the morning sacrifice, Ac 2:15; the *sixth* hour, or about twelve o'clock, Ac 10:9; and the *ninth* hour, answering to three in the afternoon, when they offered the evening sacrifice. Ac 10:3, 30. Ex 29:39. Nu 28:4. 1 K 18:36. Ps +*55:17. Da +*6:10. 9:21. Lk 1:10. 23:44-46. **ninth.** Our 3 p.m. T#1166. Ac 10:2, 3, 30. 1 K 18:29. Ps +*141:2. Mt +*20:5. 27:45, 46. Mk 15:34. Lk *23:44n. Jn +*11:9n.

2. **lame.** Ac 4:22. *14:8. Jn *9:1-3. **was carried.** Mt 9:2. Mk 2:3. Lk 16:22. **whom.** Lk 16:20. **the gate.** This was probably the gate without the holy house on the east, made of Corinthian brass, which far surpassed the others in size and beauty; its height being 50 cubits, and its doors 40 cubits, adorned after a more costly manner, and having more massive plates of gold and silver (See Josephus, Bel. l. v. c. 5, sec. 3). **which.** ver. 10. **to ask alms.** ver. 10. Ac 10:4, 31. Lk 18:35. Jn *9:8.

4. **fastening.** ver. 12. Ac 1:10g. 6:15. 7:55g. 10:4. 11:6. 13:9. 14:9, 10. 23:1g. Lk 4:20. 22:56g. 2 C 3:7, 13g. **Look.** ver. 12. Jn 5:6. 11:40.

6. **Silver.** ʃ121D5, Ge +23:9. Mt *10:9. 1 C 4:11, 12. 2 C 6:10. √8:9. Ja *2:5. **and.** ʃ174, Ge +18:27. **but such.** Mk 14:8. Lk +*11:41mg,n. 2 C 8:12. 1 P 4:10. **In the name.** ver. 16. Ac 4:7. 9:34. 16:18. 19:13-16. Mt √7:22. Mk +9:38. 16:17. Jn +20:31. Col *3:17. **Jesus.** Ac 2:22, 36. *4:10, 30. 9:27, 29. *10:38. +15:26. Jn 19:19. **of Nazareth.** Ac +2:22.

7. **he took.** Ac 9:41. Mk +1:31. 5:41. 9:27. *16:17, 18. Lk 13:13.

8. **he leaping.** Ac 14:10. Is *35:6. Lk 6:23. Jn 5:8, 9, 14. **praising.** Ps 103:1, 2. *107:15, 20-22. Lk 17:15-18. 18:43.

9. **the people.** Ac 4:16, 21. 14:11. Mk 2:11, 12. Lk 13:17.

10. **they knew.** Gr. *epiginosko*, Mt +11:27. ver. 2. Ac 4:13-16, 21, 22. Jn 9:3, 18-21. **they were.** Ac 2:7, 12. Lk 4:36. 9:43. Jn 5:20.

11. **held.** Ac 4:14. Lk 8:38. **all.** Ac 2:6. **in.** Ac *5:12. Jn *10:23.

12. **answered.** Ac 5:8. 10:46. Mt +11:25. Mk +11:14. Re 7:13. **Ye men.** Ac +2:22. 13:26. Ro 9:4. 11:1. **at this.** ver. 10. **or why.** ver. 4. Ac 10:25, 26. 14:11-15. Ge 40:8. 41:16. Da 2:28-30. Jn 3:27, 28. 7:18. **as though.** T#78. ver. 6. Ac 9:34. 16:18. Nu 20:10-12. Jn *15:5. ◐+√20:29n. 2 C *3:5. **holiness.** Ac +10:2. Is *64:6. 1 T 3:16. 2 P 1:3, 6, 7. 3:11.

13. **God of Abraham.** Ac 5:30. 7:32. Ex 3:6, 15. Ps 105:6-10. Mt +*22:32. Mk 12:26. Lk 20:37. He 11:9-16. **God of our fathers.** Ac 5:30. 7:32. 22:14. 24:14. Ex 3:13, 15. **hath glorified.** Ac 2:33-36. 5:31. Ps 2:6-12. 110:1, 2. Is 52:13. 55:5. Mt +*11:27. 28:18. Jn √3:35, 36. 5:22, 23. 7:39. +8:54. 12:16. 13:31, 32. 16:14, 15. 17:1-5. Ep *1:20-23. Ph *2:9-11. He *2:9. Re +*1:5, 18. **his son Jesus.** ver. 26. Ac 4:25, 27, 30. Is 42:1. 52:13. 53:11. Mt 12:18. Lk 1:54, 69. **whom ye delivered.** Mt +20:19. *27:2. **and denied.** Ac 2:23, 24. 5:30. 13:27, 28. Mt 27:2, 17-25. Mk 15:11. Lk *23:16-23. Jn 18:40. *19:7, 12, 15. **Pilate.** Mt +27:2. **when.** Lk 23:14, 16. Jn 19:12. **to let.** Ac 26:32g. Lk 6:37g.

14. **ye denied.** ver. 13. **the Holy One.** ʃ32, Ge +31:21. Ac 2:27. 4:27, 30. 22:14. Ps +*16:10. Zc *9:9.

Mk +1:24. Lk +*1:35. Ja 5:6. Re 3:7. **and.** ʃ93A, Ge +1:26. This is the figure *Hendiadys*, where two words are used, but only one thing meant. Here, it is perfectly clear that only one person is meant, although two are apparently described, since two terms connected by "and" are used: "Holy One" and "the Just." The emphasis is upon "just," in the sense of "that righteous Holy One," the figure being employed to mark the contrast between that "righteous" One and the unrighteous criminal. **the Just.** God the Son is absolutely just, as is God the Father (Ge +*18:25) and God the Holy Spirit (Jn 16:8). Ac *7:52. 22:14. Is 53:11. Mt 27:19, 24. +*28:19n. 2 C √5:21. 2 T 4:8. He 1:8, 9. 1 P *3:18. 1 J *2:1, 29. 3:7. **desired.** Mt 27:20. Mk 15:7, 11. Lk *23:19, 25. **granted.** Ac 25:11g.

15. **killed.** Ac 5:28, 30. **Prince.** *or*, Author. Ac 5:31. Jn 1:4. 4:10, 14. 5:26. √10:28. *11:25, 26. √14:6. 17:2. Ro *8:1, 2. 1 C *15:45. Col *3:3, 4. He +*2:10. √5:9. *12:2. 1 J √5:11, 12, 20. Re 21:6. 22:1, 17. **of life.** Ac 5:20. 2 T *1:10. **whom.** See on Ac +*2:24n, 32. Mt 28:2-5. Ep 1:20. **whereof.** Ac 1:22. +*2:24n, 32. 10:40, 41. 13:30-32. Lk +24:48.

16. **his name.** ʃ121T1, Dt +28:58. ver. 6. Ac 4:7, 10, 29, 30. 16:18. Dt=10:18. =18:5. *32:3. SS 1:3. Mt 9:22. Jn 17:26. Col *3:17. **through.** Ac *14:9. 19:13-17. Mt +9:2, 22. *17:19, 20. *21:21, 22. Mk *11:22, 23. 16:17, 18. Lk 17:5, 6. Jn 14:12. 1 C 13:2. **faith.** Jn *1:12. Ep *2:8. **in his name.** ver. 6. Ac +15:26. **by him.** 1 P 1:21. **perfect.** ver. 8. Ac 4:14-16. Dt 32:4. Jn 7:23.

17. **wot.** Ac 7:40. Ge 21:26. 39:8. 44:15. Ex 32:1. Nu 22:6. Ro 11:2. Ph 1:22. **through ignorance.** Ac 13:27. 26:9. Nu 15:24-31. Lk *23:34. Jn 7:26, 27, 52. +15:21. *16:3. 1 C √2:7, 8. 2 C 3:14. Ep 4:18. 1 T *1:13. **your rulers.** Lk 24:20.

18. **those.** Ac +*17:2, 3. *26:22, 23. 28:23. Lk +*24:26, 27, 44. 1 C +*15:3, 4. 1 P *1:10, 11. Re *19:10. **before.** Ac +2:23. **by the mouth.** ver. 21. Ac 1:16. **all.** Ge +*3:15. Ps *22:1, 6-8. ch. 69. Is 50:6. ch. √53. Da +*9:26. Zc +*12:10. +*13:7. **that Christ.** Lk +9:20. **should suffer.** Ac 1:3. 17:3. Mt 17:12. Mk +8:31. Lk 22:15. 24:46. 2 C +1:5. He +*2:10. 9:26. 13:12. 1 P 2:21, 23. 3:18. 4:1. **fulfilled.** Mt +1:22. 11:3.

19. **Repent.** T#867. See on Ac +*2:38. 5:30, 31. *11:18. 2 Ch +√7:14. 30:9. Jb 22:23. Ps 37:27. Pr *1:23. Is √55:7. Je 4:14. 18:8. 26:3, 13. 31:18-20. *36:3. Ezk 18:21-23, 30-32. 33:14-16, 19. Jl *2:12-14. Zc 1:3. Ml 3:7. Mt 3:2. Lk +*13:3, 5. Ep 5:14. 2 T *2:25. **be converted.** T#601. Ac *11:21. *15:3. *16:31. *26:18-20. *28:27. Dt 10:16. Jb *22:21. Ps +*51:13. Pr 23:26. Is *1:16-20. *6:10. 42:18. 45:22. √55:6, 7. Je 4:3, 4, 14. *31:18-20. La *3:40. 5:21. Ezk *18:30-32. *33:11. Da *9:13. Ho +*14:2. Jl *2:13. Mt *13:15. *18:3. 25:24-27. Lk *1:16. +13:3 (T#606). 19:20. +22:32. Jn +1:12 (T#183). Ro 12:2. *13:14. 2 C +*3:16. 5:20. Ep 4:22-24. 5:14. Ja *4:7-10. +*5:19, 20. 1 P *2:25. Ju +21 (T#288). **that.** Dt √4:29-31. 1 K 8:48-50. Ps √32:1-5. +*51:1-3, 9. *103:12. Is *1:16-18. *43:25. *44:22. Je *31:33, 34. *50:20. Mi √7:18, 19. Re *21:4. **blotted out.** "Blotting out" denotes (1) the present forgiveness of sins; (2) the forgiveness of the Jewish nation at the time of its restoration (Peters, *Theocratic Kingdom*, vol. 3, p. 459). Ne 4:5. Ps +*51:1, 9. 109:14. +*130:8. Is 4:2-4. *25:8. 43:25. 44:22. +*60:21. Je 18:23. Mi +*7:15, 19. Zc +*10:6. Col 2:14. **when.** or, so that.

Ps *37:14. 102:16. Ezk √20:33-40. Ho +*5:15. +*6:3. Mi ◐+*5:3. **times of refreshing.** "Refreshing" is closely related to the consolation and the resurrection (Lk 2:25, 34. Da 12:2). ver. +*21. Ac +*1:6n, 7n. 17:26. Ps √14:7. *72:6-19. ch. 98. Is +*2:1-3. *25:6-9. *28:12. 35:1, 6, 7, 10. 41:17, 18. 43:19, 20. *49:10-22. +*51:11. *52:1-10. *54:1-14. +*60:10. *61:3, 9-11. 62:1-5. *65:17-25. 66:10-14, 18-22. Je 30:10. 31:2, 3, 22-26. *32:37-41. *33:15-26. Ezk 11:19. *34:23-31. 36:26, 27. *37:14, 21-28. 39:25-29. Ho 2:19-23. *6:2. Jl +*2:28n, 32. *3:16-21. Am +√9:13-15. Mi *7:14, 15, 20. Zp *3:14-20. Zc +*8:20-23. Mt *11:28-30. +*19:28. Ro √8:19-23. +√11:25, 26. Ep +*1:10. 2 Th √1:7, 10. He 4:1-11. 2 P 3:8. Re 7:17. 21:4. 19:9. **presence.** ⨍144A1, Ge +11:8. Ac 1:11. Ps 16:11. +*102:16. Is +*59:20. Ezk 48:35. Zc *14:9.

20. **shall send.** ver. 26. Ac √17:31. Is √16:1. +*59:19, 20. Mt +*16:27n, 28. +*24:3, 30, 36. Mk *13:26, 30-37. Lk *11:28. *19:11. 21:27, +*28. Ro +*11:26. 2 Th 2:2, 8. He +*9:28. Re +*1:7. *19:11-16. **Jesus Christ.** Ac 2:30, 31, 36. 4:10. 5:42. 8:5, 12. 9:20, 22. *17:3. 18:5, 28. 19:4. 20:21. 28:31. 1 C 1:23. 2:2. 2 C *4:5. **which before.** Ac 22:14. 26:16.

21. **the heaven.** Ac +*1:11. Lk 24:26. **must receive.** Ac 1:16, 22. 9:6. Ho +*5:15. Lk 13:33. Jn 3:14. **until.** Mt +*23:39. He *9:28. 10:12, 13. **the times.** T#446. See on ver. *19. Is *1:26, 27. *11:6, 7. 40:4, 5. 41:18-20. *55:13. *65:25. Ml *3:3, 4. *4:5, 6. Mt *17:11, 12. Mk *9:11-13. Ep +*1:10. **of restitution.** Ac +*1:6n. +*15:16. 26:6, 7. Le=25:10. 27:24. Dt 11:21. 30:1-3. Ps *89:29-37. Is *1:25, 26. +√11:11n. *49:6. Je 24:7. 30:10. 48:47n. Ezk 16:53n, 55, 63. +*36:24. Jl *2:25. Am +*9:11-15. Zp +*3:15, 20. Zc +*10:6. Ml 3:4. 4:6. Mt +*8:11. *17:11. +*19:28. 23:37-39. Lk 1:32, 33, 74. 13:34, 35. +*21:24. Ro +*8:21-23. Re 21:1. **of all things.** Mt 13:41. Ro *8:22, 23. Ep 1:10. **God hath spoken.** Lk +1:70. **by the mouth.** ver. 18. Ac 1:16. **holy prophets.** Ac *10:43. Lk *1:70. +*24:25, 26. 2 P *1:21. *3:2. Re 18:20. 22:6. **world.** Gr. *aion*, Mt +6:13.

22. **Moses.** Ac 7:37. Ex +*24:4. Dt *▶18:15-19. Mk +12:19. **A prophet.** ⨍92A, Mt +1:23. Dt ✱18:15. Mt +21:11. Lk 13:33. 24:19. Jn +*1:45. *8:12. 12:46. Re 1:1. **of your.** Ro 8:3. *9:5. Ga *4:4. He 2:9-17. **like.** See on Dt 18:18. **him.** Is +*55:3, 4. Mt 17:4, 5. Mk 9:4-7. Lk 9:30-35. Jn 1:17. +*5:23, 24, 39-47. He *1:1, 2. 2:1. 5:9.

23. **come to pass.** ⨍144A11, Ge +38:1. **that every.** Ac 13:38-41. Dt 18:19. Mk *16:16. Jn √3:18-20. +*8:24. 12:48. 2 Th √1:7-9. He √2:3. √10:28-30, 39. 12:25. Re *13:8. 20:15. **soul.** Gr. *psyche*, ⨍171Q1A, Ac +2:41. **not hear.** Lk *10:10-12, 16. **be destroyed.** Ac 1:25. Le 23:29. **the people.** Ac +10:2.

24. **and all.** ver. 19, 21. Ro 3:21. **Samuel.** i.e. *God hath heard*, ✱S#4545g. Ac 13:20. He 11:32. For ✱S8050h, see 1 S +1:20. 1 S 2:18. *3:1, 20. Ps 99:6. Je 15:1. He 11:32. **foretold.** ver. 18.

25. **the children.** Ac +*2:39. 13:26. Ge 20:7. 27:36-40. 48:14-20. ch. 49. Ps 105:8-15. Mt 3:9, 10. Mk +2:19. Lk +10:6. **the covenant.** Ge +*17:9, 10, 19. 1 Ch 16:17. Ne 9:8. Ps +*89:34. Lk 1:72. Ro *9:4, 5. √15:8. Ga *3:16, 29. **saying unto Abraham.** Ge ▶22:18. Ga *3:8, 26. **And in.** Ge +*12:3. 18:18. +*22:18. 26:4. *28:14. Je 4:2. Ro +*4:13. Ga 3:8, 16. **all.** Ps 22:27. 96:7. Re 5:9. 7:9. 14:6. **kindreds.** Ro 9:24-26. **be blessed.** Ge=12:3. =22:18.

26. **first.** Ac +*1:8. *13:26, 32, 33, 46, 47. 18:4-6. 26:20. 28:17, 23-28. Mt *10:5, 6. *15:24. Mk 7:27. Lk *24:47. Jn 4:22. Ro +√1:16. +*2:9, 10. 11:11. 15:8, 24. Re 7:4-9. **having raised.** ver. 15, 22. Ac +*2:24n. **his Son Jesus.** ver. 13. **sent.** ver. 20, 25. Ps 67:6, 7. 72:17. Lk 2:10, 11. +*19:10. Ro 15:29. Ga 3:9-14. Ep 1:3. 1 P 1:3. 3:9. **to bless.** ver. 25. Lk 24:51. Ep *1:3, 4. **in turning.** Is 59:20, 21. Je 32:38-41. 33:8, 9. Ezk 3:19. 11:19, 20. 33:9. 36:25-29. Mt 1:21. Ro 11:26. Ep +*5:26, 27. T *2:11-14. 1 P *1:3, 4, 15, 16. 1 J 3:5-8. Ju *24. **from his.** Mt 1:21.

ACTS 4

The priests and Sadducees imprison Peter and John, 1-3. The signal success of their preaching, 4. When brought before the council, Peter boldly declares, that the late cure had been wrought in the name of Jesus, the only Savior, whom the rulers had rejected, 5-12. The council, unable to answer, dismiss them with a threatening charge to speak no more in the name of Jesus, which they avow themselves bound to disregard, 13-22. They return to their company; and all unite in prayer, for boldness in preaching, and that miracles of mercy might confirm their testimony, 23-30. The house being shaken, they are all filled with the Holy Spirit, and emboldened to speak the word of God, 31. The harmony and charity of the whole company, who had all things in common; the miraculous assistance granted to the apostles; and the pious liberality of Barnabas and others who who had possessions, in selling them, to distribute to the needy, 32-37.

1. **the priests.** ver. 6. Ac 6:7, 12. Mt 26:3, 4. 27:1, 2, 20, 41. Jn 15:20. 18:3. **the captain.** *or*, the ruler. Ac 5:24, 26. 1 Ch 9:11. 2 Ch 23:4-9. Ne 11:11. Lk 22:4, 52. **the Sadducees.** Ac 5:17. *23:6-9. Mt 16:12. 22:16, +23, 34. 1 C 15:17. **came upon.** Ac 6:12. Lk +20:1.

2. **grieved.** Ac 5:17. 13:45. 16:18. 19:23. Ne 2:10. Jn 11:47, 48. **preached.** Ac 3:15. 10:40-43. 17:18, 31, 32. 24:14, 15, 21. 26:8, 23. Ro +*8:11. 1 C 15:12-20, 23. 2 C 4:13, 14. 1 Th 4:13, 14.

3. **laid.** Ac 5:18. 6:12. 8:3. 9:2. 12:1-3. 16:19-24. Mt 10:16, 17. Lk 22:52, 54. Jn 18:12. **and put.** Lk +21:12.

4. **many.** Ac 28:24. 2 C 2:14-17. Ph 1:12-18. 2 T 2:9, 10. **believed.** ver. 32. Ac +13:12. +*17:11, 12. Ro √10:17. **the number.** Ac 2:41. Ge +*49:10. Is 45:24. 53:12. Jn 12:24.

5. **on.** Ac 5:20, 21. Mi 2:1. Mt 27:1, 2. **rulers.** ver. 8, 26. Ac 5:34. 6:12. Is 1:10. Mk 15:1. Lk 20:1. 22:66. +24:20. **elders.** ver. 8, 23. Ac 6:12. 23:14. 24:1. 25:15. **scribes.** Ac 6:12. 23:9.

6. **Annas.** Lk *3:2. Jn 11:49. *18:13, 14, 24. **Caiaphas.** Mt +26:3.

7. **when.** Ac 5:27. 1 K 21:12-14. Mt 14:6. Jn 8:3, 9. **By what power.** Ex 2:14. Mt 21:23. Mk 11:28. Lk 20:2. Jn 2:18. **by what name.** ver. 10. Ac 5:28, 40.

8. **filled with.** For instances of being filled with the Holy Spirit without speaking in tongues see ver. 31. Ac 7:55. 9:17. 11:24. 13:9, 52. See related notes on Ac 2:41n. Ro +*8:9n. Ep 5:18n. **Ghost.** Gr. *pneuma*, Mt +1:18n. **said unto.** Mt 10:19, 20. Lk *12:11, 12. 21:14, 15. **rulers.** ver. 5.

9. **If.** ⨍184A, 1 C +15:2. **examined.** Ac 12:19. **the good.** Ac 3:7, 8. Jn 7:23. 10:32. 1 P 3:15-17. 4:14-16.

to. ⨍181E, Ge +3:24. **made whole.** Mk 10:52.

10. **known.** Ac +2:14. 13:38. 28:28. Je 42:19, 20. Da 3:18. **that by.** Ac 2:22-24, 36. *3:6, 13-16. 5:29-32. **the name.** ver. 17. Ac +3:6. **of Nazareth.** Ac +2:22. **whom ye.** Ac 5:28, 30. **whom God.** Ac +*2:24. 10:40-42. 13:29-41. Mt 27:63-66. 28:11-15. Lk 16:31. Ro *1:4.

11. **the stone.** ⨍22L1, Ps +118:22. Ps *118:22, 33. Is *28:16. Mt 21:42-45. Mk 12:10-12. Lk 20:16-18. 1 C 3:11. Ep *2:20. 1 P *2:6-8. **you.** Ac 7:52. 20:26, 27. Pr 28:1. Is 58:1, 2. Ezk 2:6, 7. 3:7-11, 18, 19. 33:7-9. 2 C 3:12. 4:1. **set at nought.** Mk +9:12. **the head.** Zc 3:9. *4:6, 7. Ep *2:20-22.

12. **Neither is there.** Ac 5:31. *10:42, 43. Mt *1:21. Mk 16:15, 16. Jn √3:36. √14:6. Ro +*2:12. 1 C *3:11. 1 T √2:5, 6. He √2:3. 12:25. 1 J √5:11, 12. Re 7:9, 10. 20:15. **salvation.** ⨍77, Ex +3:19. Bengel notes that with the article in Greek, "salvation" forms an *Epitasis* with reference to verse 9. Ac 13:26. √16:31. 28:28. Jn 4:22. He *2:3. Ju 3. **in any other.** Is 43:11. 45:21, 22. 59:16. **none other.** Ge=42:6. Ga 1:7. **name.** ⨍121T1, Dt +28:58. Ac 15:26. Lk 24:47. Jn √20:31. **under.** Ac 2:5. Ge 7:19. Jb 41:11. Ps 45:17. Col +*1:23. **must.** Ac +14:22. 16:30. Jn +3:7. **be saved.** Mk *16:16.

13. **boldness.** ver. 29, 31. Ac 9:27, 29. 13:46. 14:3. 18:26. 19:8. 26:26. 28:31. 2 C 3:12. 7:4. Ep 6:19, 20. Ph 1:20. 1 Th 2:2. 1 T 3:13. Phm 8. He 3:6. *4:16. 10:19, 35. **Peter and John.** ver. 19. Ac +3:1. **were unlearned.** Ac 2:7-12. Ex 4:10. Mt 4:18-22. +*11:25. Jn 7:15, 49. 1 C *1:27. **and ignorant.** 1 C 14:16, 23, 24. 2 C 11:6. **they took knowledge.** Gr. *epiginosko*, Mt +11:27. Ac 3:10. Mt 26:57, 58, 71, 73. Lk 22:52-54, 56-60. Jn 18:16, 17. 19:26. 2 C 4:10. **with Jesus.** Mt 26:71.

14. **beholding.** ver. 10. Ac 3:8-12. **they.** ver. 16, 21. Ac 19:36. **say nothing.** Lk 21:15.

15. **to go.** Ac 5:34, etc. 26:30-32. **the council.** Ac 5:21, 34, 41. 6:12, 15. 22:30. 23:1, 6, 15, 20, 28. 24:20. Mt +5:22. **conferred.** Ac 17:18.

16. **What.** Jn *11:47, 48. 12:18, 19. **a notable.** ver. 21. Ac *3:9, 10. Da 8:5, 8. Mt 27:16. **miracle.** ver. 22. Ac +8:6. **and we.** Ac 6:10. Lk 6:10, 11. 21:15.

17. **that it.** Ac *5:39. Ps *2:1-4. Da 2:34, 35. Ro 10:16-18. *15:18-22. 1 Th 1:8. **let.** ver. 21, 29, 30. Ac *5:24, 28, 40. 2 Ch 25:15, 16. Is *30:8-11. Je 20:1-3. 29:25-32. *38:4. Am 2:12. 7:12-17. Mi *2:6, 7. Mt *27:64. Jn *11:47, 48. 1 Th *2:15, 16. **straitly.** lit. let us threaten them with a threat. i.e. threaten them very severely. ⨍108C8, Lk +22:15. **this name.** ver. 10. Ac +15:26. Lk 24:47.

18. **And they.** Ac *5:40. **commanded.** T#466-2. Am 7:12, 13. **not to speak.** Ac +*1:8. *5:20. Lk 24:46-48.

19. **Peter and John.** ver. 13. Ac +3:1. **Whether.** 2 C 4:2. Ep 6:1. 1 T 2:3. **to hearken.** Ac +*5:29. Ex *1:17. 1 S 22:17. 1 K 12:30. 14:16. 21:11. 22:14. 2 K 16:15. 2 Ch 26:16-20. Da *3:18. +*6:10, 11. Ho 5:11. Am 7:16, 17. Mi 6:16. Mt 22:21. Ga *1:10. He 11:23. Re *13:3-10. 14:9-12. **judge ye.** ⨍14, Is +5:3. Ps 58:1. Jn +*7:24. 1 C 10:15. Ja 2:4.

20. **we cannot.** Ac 2:4, 32. 17:16, 17. 18:5. Nu 22:38. 23:20. 2 S 23:2. Jb 32:18-20. Je 1:7, 17-19. 4:19. 6:11. 20:9. Ezk 3:11, 14-21, 26, 27. Am 3:8. Mi 3:8. Jn 15:27. 1 C *9:16, 17. **but speak.** Ac 2:4. 8:4. 17:16, 17. 18:5. 20:18-21, 24, 26, √27, 31, 35. Ps *116:10. Je *20:9. Ezk 40:4. 1 J 1:3. **the things.** Ac *1:8, 22. 3:15. 5:32. 10:39-41. 22:15. Lk 1:2. He *2:3, 4. 1 J *1:1-3. **have seen.** Ac 2:32. *22:14, 15. Ezk 40:4.

Jn 8:38. 2 P √1:16. 1 J *1:1, 3.

21. **when.** ver. 17, 18. Ac 5:40. **how.** Ac 5:26. Mt *21:26, 46. 26:5. Lk 19:47, 48. 20:6, 19. 22:2. **because.** Ac 5:13, 26. Mt 21:26, 46. Mk 11:32. Lk 20:6, 19. 22:2. **for all.** ver. 16. Ac 3:6-9. Mt 9:33. 15:31. Lk 5:26. 13:17. Jn 12:18, 19. **glorified God.** Ac 11:18. 21:20. Mt +9:8. Lk 13:13.

22. **forty.** Ac 3:2. 9:33. Mt 9:20. Lk 13:11. Jn 5:5. 9:1. **miracle.** ver. 16. Ac +8:6.

23. **they came.** Ac *1:13-15. *2:44-46. 12:11, 12. 16:40. Ps 16:3. 42:4. +√119:63. Pr 13:20. Ml √3:16. 2 C *6:14-17. **own company.** Ac 24:23. Jn *1:11. 13:1. 1 T 5:8. **chief priests.** Ac +5:24. **elders.** ver. 5.

24. **they.** Ac 16:25. Ps 55:16-18. 62:5-8. 69:29, 30. 109:29-31. Je 20:13. Lk 6:11, 12. 2 C 1:8-11. 1 Th 5:16-18. 2 T 4:17, 18. **lifted.** ⨍144A12, Ge +22:13. Ac 2:14. 14:11. 22:22. Lk 11:27. 17:13. **one accord.** Ac 1:14. 2:46. 5:12. 15:25. Ro 15:6. **Lord.** ver. 29. 2 K 19:15, 19. Ne +*9:6. Ps 146:5, 6. Is 51:12, 13. Je 10:10-12. 32:17. Lk 2:29. 2 P +2:1. **hast made.** Ac 17:26. Ge 1:1—2:3. Ex 20:11. 2 Ch 2:12. Ne 9:6. Ps 102:25. 124:8. 134:3. 146:6. Is *51:11-13. He 1:❷2, 10. Re 14:7.

25. **by.** Ac 1:16. 2:25, 30, 34. Mt 22:43. Mk 12:36. Lk 20:42. Ro 4:6. 11:9. He 4:7. **thy servant.** Lk 1:69. **Why.** See on Ps ❩2:1-6. **imagine vain things.** Is *8:10. *46:10. Jn *10:29.

26. **kings.** Ps 76:12. 83:2-8. 89:27. 102:15. 138:4. 148:11. Is 24:21. Jl 3:9-14. Re 17:12-14, 17. 19:16-21. **the rulers.** ver. 5. **against the Lord.** Ac *9:4. Lk *10:16. Jn √5:23. 1 Th *4:8. **against his.** Ps 84:9. 89:51. 132:17. Lk +9:20. **Christ.** Ac 10:38. Da 9:24. Lk +*4:18. He 1:9. Re √11:15. 12:10.

27. **of a truth.** Mt 26:3. Lk 22:1. 23:1, 8, etc. **against.** Pr +*21:30. **thy holy.** ver. 30. Ac 2:27. 3:13, 14. Jb 14:4. 15:14. 25:4. Lk +*1:35. He *7:26. **whom.** ver. 26. Ac *10:38. Ps 2:2, 6mg. +*45:7. Is 61:1. Lk +*4:18. Jn 10:36. **both.** Mt 2:13-16. Lk +3:1. 13:31-33. 23:7-12. **Pontius Pilate.** Ac 3:13. Mt 27:2, 11-36. Mk 15:1-28. Lk 18:31-33. 23:13-38. Jn 19:1-24, 34. **with.** Ps ✹2:1, 2. Mt +20:19. **the people.** ver. 10, 25. Ge 28:3. 35:11. 48:4. Is 49:7. *53:3. Zc 11:7, 8. Mt 20:18, 19. 21:38. 23:37. *26:3, 4, 59-68. 27:25, 40-43. Mk 10:33, 34. 14:1, 2, 43-65. 15:1-3, 31, 32. Lk 9:22. 20:13-19. 22:2-6, 47-52, 63-71. *23:1-5, 10-12. Jn *1:11. 18:1-14, 19-24, 28-40. 19:15, 16.

28. **to do.** Ac +*2:23, 33. *3:18. *13:27-29. Ge *50:20. Ps 33:11. 76:10. Pr 19:21. Is *10:7. 44:28. 46:10. Mt *26:24, 54. Lk 22:22. 24:44-46. 1 P +*2:7, 8. **thy hand.** ⨍22A14.2. Anthropomorphism B878. A *hand* is attributed to God, indicating his *purpose.* ver. 30. Ac +7:50. 13:11. 1 K 8:15. 2 Ch 30:12. Is 14:26. 1 P 5:6. **and thy counsel.** Ac +2:23. Jb 12:13. Pr +*21:30. Is 5:19. 28:29. 40:13, 14. 46:10, 11. 53:10. Ep +*1:11. He *6:17. **determined.** ⨍180C. Zeugma (Hypzeugma); or, End-yoke B134. When the verb is at the end of a clause, or sentence. Here, "determined" relates only to "counsel" and not to "hand." Lk +22:22. Ro +8:29.

29. **Lord.** ver. 24. **behold.** ver. 17, 18, 21. 2 K 19:16. Is √37:17-20. 63:15. La 3:50. 5:1. Da 9:18. **threatenings.** 2 Ch 20:11. **thy servants.** ver. 24. Ja +1:1. Re +7:3. **that.** ver. 13, 31. Ac 9:27. *13:46. *14:3. *19:8. 20:26, 27. 26:26. *28:30, 31. Is 58:1. Ezk 2:6. Mi 3:8. Ep *6:18-20. Ph *1:14. 1 Th *2:2. 2 T +√1:7, 8. 4:17. **thy word.** Ac +11:1.

30. **By stretching.** Ex 6:6. Dt 4:34. 1 S 24:6. Jb

1:12. Ps 138:7. Pr 31:20. Is 1:25. Je 15:15. 20:11, 12. Zp 1:4. Lk 9:54-56. 22:49-51. **thine hand.** ✗22A14.3, Ps +31:5. ver. +28. Ac 13:11. **to heal.** Mk +16:20. **and that signs.** Ac 2:22, 43. *5:12, 15, 16. 6:8. 9:34, 35, 40-42. **wonders.** T#1754. Jn +4:48. **the name.** ver. 10, 27. Ac 3:+6, 16. 15:26. Dt=10:8. =18:5. Mt *7:22. Mk 9:39. 16:17. Col *3:17. **thy holy.** ver. 27. Ac 3:13, 14.

31. **had prayed.** Mt *7:7. **the place.** Ac *2:2. 16:25, 26. Ps 77:18. 114:7. **they were all.** See on Ac 2:4. **Ghost.** Gr. *pneuma*, Mt +1:18n. T#1773. Ac 13:1-3. **spake.** ver. 29. Is +*65:24. Da *9:21-23. Mt +*18:19, 20. *21:22. Jn 14:12, 13. 15:7, 16. 16:23, 24. Ph 1:14. Ja +*1:5. **the word.** Ac +11:1. **boldness.** ✗24I, Is +21:7. ver. +13.

32. **the multitude.** Ac 1:14. 2:1. 5:12. 6:2. 2 Ch 30:12. Je 32:39. Ezk 11:19, 20. Jn 17:11, 21-23. Ro 12:5. 15:5, 6. 1 C 1:10. 12:12-14. 2 C 13:11. Ep 4:2-6. Ph 1:27. 2:1, 2. 1 P 3:8. **that believed.** ver. 4. Ac +13:12. **one heart.** T#111. Ac +1:14. 20:37, 38. 1 S 18:3. 2 S 1:26. 1 Ch 12:38. 2 Ch 30:12. Ps 133:1, 2. Is 52:8. Ezk 11:19. Ml +*3:16. Mt +12:25 (T#114). Jn 13:34, 35. 15:12. *17:20-22. Ro 12:10. *15:5, 6. 1 C 1:10. 2 C *13:11. Ga 6:10. Ep 4:1-3. 5:2, +25 (T#94). Ph *1:4, 5, 27. *2:1, 2. 3:16. 1 Th +3:12 (T#412). 4:9, 10. He +*13:1. 1 P 1:22. 2:17. *3:8. 2 P *1:5-7. 1 J 3:11, 12, 14, 16-19, 23. 4:7, 8, 10, 11, 21. 2 J 5. **soul.** Gr. *psyche*, ✗121A9B, Mt +22:37. Ph 1:27. **ought.** Ac 2:44-46. 1 Ch 29:14-16. Lk 16:10-12. 1 P 4:11. **neither said.** T#661. Ac +10:4 (T#407). Ec +12:13 (T#295). Lk +10:33 (T#414). +18:28 (T#674). 2 C 12:14, 15. **possessed.** Ezk=44:28. 1 C 7:30. 2 C 6:10. He 13:14. **they had.** ver. 34, 35. Ac 2:44. Mt 19:21.

33. **with great power.** ver. 30. Ac +*1:8, 22. +*2:32, 33. 3:15, 16. 5:12-16. Mk 16:20. Lk 1:48, 49. Ro 15:18, 19. 1 Th *1:5. He *2:4. **the apostles.** Ac +5:12. **witness.** Is 43:10n. **the resurrection.** Ac +*2:24n. **the Lord Jesus.** Ac +1:21. **grace.** Ac 2:47. +11:23. Lk *2:52. Jn 1:16. 1 T *1:14.

34. **was.** Dt 2:7. Ps 34:9, 10. Lk 22:35. 2 C 8:14, 15. 1 Th 4:12. **for.** ver. 37. Ac 2:45. 5:1-3. Mk 10:21. Lk *12:33. +*16:9. 1 T *6:19. Ja *1:27.

35. **And laid.** ver. 37. Ac 5:2. **at.** Ac 3:6. 5:2. 6:1-6. 2 C 8:20, 21. **distribution.** Ac 2:45. *6:1. Ga *6:6, 10. **according.** Ac 2:45.

36. **Barnabas.** i.e. *son of consolation, son of prophecy*, ⚹S#921g. Ac 9:27. *11:22, 25, 30. 12:25. 13:1, 2, 7, 43, 46, 50. 14:12, 14, 20. 15:2, 2, 12, 25, 35, 36, 37, 39. 1 C 9:6. Ga 2:1, 9, 13. Col 4:10. **interpreted.** ✗95, Ps +7:13. Mk +5:41. **The son.** Mk 3:17. Lk +10:6. **consolation.** or, exhortation. Ac 2:40. 9:31. 11:23. 13:15. 15:31. 20:12. Is 40:1, 2. Ro 12:8. 1 C 14:3. 2 C ✓1:3-7. 8:4, 17. 1 Th 2:3, 11. 3:2. 1 T 4:13. He 12:5. 13:22. **a Levite.** Ac 6:7. 2 Ch 35:3n. Lk 10:32. Jn 1:19. **of the country.** Ac 18:2, 24. **Cyprus.** Ac 11:19, 20. 13:4. 15:39. 21:3, 16. 27:4.

37. **Having land.** Je 32:7. **sold.** ver. 34, 35. Ac 5:1, 2. Mt 19:29. **laid.** ver. 35. Ac 5:2.

ACTS 5

Ananias and Sapphira, combining to tempt the Holy Spirit by a lie in respect of land sold by them, at Peter's word fall down dead, 1-11. The apostles work many and great miracles, and have much success in their ministry, 12-16. The rulers cast them all into prison, 17, 18. An angel releases them, and directs them to preach openly in the temple, 19, 20. They are at length brought before the council; and, being examined, they boldly bear testimony to Jesus, as exalted to be a Prince and Savior, 21-32. The rulers, being "cut to the heart," purpose to slay them, but are restrained by the counsel of Gamaliel, 33-39. The apostles are beaten, and dismissed with injunctions, not to speak any more in the name of Jesus, 40. They rejoice in their sufferings, and proceed diligently in preaching Jesus the Christ, 41, 42.

1. Cir. A.M. 4038. A.D. 34. **But.** Le 10:1-3. Jsh 6:1. Mt 13:47, 48. Jn 7:70. 2 T 2:20. **Ananias.** i.e. *cloud of the Lord, Jehovah is gracious*, ⚹S#367g. ver. 3, 5. Ac 9:10, 10, 12, 13, 17. 22:12. 23:2. 24:1. (1) The husband of Sapphira, Ac 5:1, etc. (2) A Christian of Damascus who restored the sight of Saul (Paul) after his vision of Christ, Ac 9:10; 22:12. (3) A high priest of the Jews, A.D. 48. Before him and the Sanhedrin Paul was summoned, Ac 23:2; 24:1. Ananias is the Greek form of Hananiah, ⚹S#2608h, 1 Ch +25:23. **Sapphira.** i.e. *beautiful; who tells or relates; sapphire*, ⚹S#4551g, only here.

2. **kept.** ver. 3. Jsh 7:11, 12. 2 K 5:21-25. 2 Ch +*29:7. Pr +*15:27. Ec +*5:13. Ezk +*33:31. Mi +*6:12. Ml 1:14. 3:8, 9. Jn 12:6. 1 T *6:10. T 2:10g. 2 P 2:14, 15. **his.** ver. 9. **laid.** Ac *4:34, 35, 37. Mt 6:2, 3. 23:5. Ph +*2:3. **apostles'.** ver. +12.

3. **why.** Ge 3:13-17. 1 K 22:21, 22. 1 Ch 21:1-3. Mt 4:3-11. 13:19. Lk *22:3. Jn 13:2, 27. Ep 6:11-16. Ja 4:7. 1 P 5:8, 9. Re 12:9-11. **Satan.** Lk 22:3. 1 C +5:5. **filled.** Est 7:5. Ec 8:11. **lie to.** or, deceive. ver. 9. Jb 22:13. Ps 94:7-9. Is 29:15. Je 23:24. Ho 11:12. **Ghost.** Gr. *pneuma*, Mt +3:16. ver. 4. Ac 28:25, 26. Jg 15:14. 16:20. 2 S ✓23:2, 3. Jb 33:4. Ps 139:7. Is 6:5. **to keep.** ver. +2. Nu *30:2. Dt *23:21. Pr 20:25. Ec *5:4. Ro 2:21, 22.

4. **was it not thine.** Ex 35:21, 22, 29. 1 Ch 29:3, 5, 9, 17. 1 C 8:8. 9:5-17. Phm 14. **conceived.** Ac *8:21, 22. Jsh 7:25, 26. Jb 15:35. Ps 7:14. Is 59:4. Je +*6:19. Ezk 38:10mg. Ja 1:15. **thou hast.** ver. 3. Ex 16:8. Nu 16:11. 1 S 8:7. 2 K 5:25-27. Ps 5:6. 139:4. Lk 10:16. 1 Th 4:8. **but unto.** ver. 3, 9. Ex *16:8. 1 S 8:7. Ps 51:4. Mt +*12:31n. **God.** This is a clear instance of the Holy Spirit being called God (Mt +*28:19). Ac 13:4 w Mt 9:38. Nu 6:24-26. Is 42:1n. Lk 2:26, 28, 29. Jn 3:6 w 1 J 5:4. Jn 6:45 w 1 C 2:13. Jn 6:63 w 5:21. Jn 15:26. 16:15. Ro 8:14 w Is 48:17. 1 C 3:16. 6:19. 12:4-11. 2 C 3:17. Ep 2:18. 2 Th 3:5. 2 T 3:16 w 2 P 1:21. He *3:7, +*12. *9:14. 1 P *1:2. Re 4:8.

5. **hearing.** ver. 10, 11. Ac 13:11. Nu 16:26-33. 2 K 1:10-14. 2:24. Je 5:14. 1 C 4:21. 2 C 10:2-6. 13:2, 10. Re 11:5. **fell down.** ver. 10. Is +*38:10. Ezk 9:8. 11:13. **gave up.** ver. 10. Ac +*7:59, 60. 12:23. 20:10. Ge +*25:8n. 1 C +*11:30. **great.** ver. 11, 13. Ac +2:43. Le 10:3. Nu 16:34. 17:12, 13. Dt 13:11. 21:21. Jsh 22:20. 1 S 6:19-21. 1 Ch 13:12. 15:13. Ps 64:9. 119:120. 2 C 7:11. 1 P 4:17. Re 11:13.

6. **wound him up.** ver. 10. Ac 8:2. Le 10:4-6. Dt 21:23. 2 S 18:17. Ezk 29:5. Jn *19:40.

8. **answered.** Ac +3:12. **for so much.** ver. +*2.

9. **How.** Ge 3:9-13. Lk 16:2. Ro 3:19. **have agreed.** Ac 23:20-22. Dt 13:6-8. Ps 50:18. Pr 11:21. 16:5. Mi 7:3. **to tempt.** ver. 3, 4. Ac 15:10. Ex 17:2, 7. Nu 14:22. Ps 78:18-20, 40, 41, 56. 95:8-11. Mt *4:7. 1 C 10:9. **Spirit.** Gr. *pneuma*, Mt +3:16. **the feet.** ver.

6. 2 K 6:32. Is 52:7. Na 1:15. Ro 10:15. **have buried**. ver. 6.

10. **fell**. ver. +*5. **yielded up**. ver. +*5. Ac 12:23. 20:10.

11. **great fear**. ver. 5. Ac +2:43. 19:17. Ps 89:7. Je 32:40. 1 C 10:11, 12. Ph 2:12. He 4:1. 11:7. +*12:15, 28, 29. 1 P 1:17. Re 15:4.

12. **by the hands**. ⨍144A5, Ge +9:5. Ac 2:43. 3:6, 7. *4:30, 33. 9:33, 40. 14:3, 8-10. 16:18. *19:11, 12. Mk 16:17, 18, 20. Ro *15:18, 19. 2 C 12:12. He *2:4. **the apostles**. ver. 2, 18, 40. Ac 1:2, 26. 2:37, 42, 43. 4:33, 35, 37. 6:6. 8:1, 14. 9:27. 11:1. 14:4, 14. +15:2. Mk +6:30. **signs**. Jn +4:48. **one accord**. Ac 1:14. 2:42, 46. 4:32. **in**. Ac 3:11. Jn 10:23. **Solomon's porch**. Josephus informs us (Ant. l. xx. c. 8. sec. 7), that Solomon, when he built the temple, finding the area of Mount Moriah too small to answer his magnificent plan, filled up a part of the adjacent valley, and built an outward portion over it toward the east. This is what was called *Solomon's porch*: it was a most noble structure, supported by a wall 400 cubits high, and consisting of stones of a vast bulk, being 20 cubits long, and 6 cubits high. It was probably left standing because of its grandeur and beauty; and Josephus speaks of it as continuing even to the time of Albinus and Agrippa.

13. **of**. ver. 5. Nu 17:12, 13. 24:8-10. 1 S 16:4, 5. 1 K 17:18. Is 33:14. Mt *10:32, 33. Lk 12:1, 2. 14:26-35. Jn *9:22. *12:42, 43. 19:38. 2 P *2:20-22. **durst**. Ps 118:6. **join**. ver. ❍*14. Ac 9:26. 10:28. 17:34. Lk 15:15. **but**. ver. 26. Ac 2:47. *4:21. 19:17. Lk 19:37, 38, 48. **magnified**. 2 C 10:15.

14. **believers**. T#651. Ac 2:41, 47. 4:4. 6:7. 9:31, 35, 42. +13:12. Is 44:3-5. 45:24. 55:11-13. 2 C 6:14. **were the more**. Ac 6:1, 2. **added**. T#619. Ac 2:41-43. 4:4. 8:5-7. 11:19-24. 14:1. Ge 4:26. 1 K 18:38, 39. 2 K 23:3, 21, 22. 2 Ch 30:11-13, 21-23, 26, 27. Ne 8:2, 3, 6, 9. Je 2:2, 3. **the Lord**. Ac +11:16. +18:8. **multitudes**. Ac 6:1, 2. 8:3, 12. 9:2. 22:4. Ex 35:22. Dt 29:11, 12. 31:11, 12. 2 S 6:19. Ezr 10:1. Ne 8:2. 1 C 11:11, 12. Ga 3:28.

15. **they brought**. Ac 19:11, 12. Mt 9:21. *14:35, 36. Mk 6:55. Jn 14:12. **into the streets**. *or*, in every street. **that at**. Ac *19:12. 2 K 4:29. 13:21. Mt 14:36. Mk 6:56. **the shadow**. Ps 91:1.

16. **bringing**. Mt 4:24. 8:16. 15:30, 31. Mk 2:3, 4. 6:54-56. Lk 4:40, 41. Jn 14:12. **vexed**. Lk 6:18. **unclean**. Mk +3:30. **spirits**. Gr. *pneuma*, Mt +8:16. **healed**. Ac 4:30. Mk *16:17, 18. Lk 5:17. 9:11. Jn 14:12. 1 C 12:9. Ja 5:16.

17. **the high**. Ac 4:26. Ps 2:1-3. Jn 11:47-49. 12:10, 11, 19. **rose up**. Ac 27:21. **all**. Ac 4:1, 2, 6. 23:6-8. **the sect**. Ac +24:5. **Sadducees**. Ac *4:1. 23:6-8. Mt +22:23. **indignation**. *or*, envy. Ac 7:9. 13:45. 17:5. 1 S 18:12-16. Jb 5:2. Pr 14:30. 27:4. Ec 4:4. Mt 27:18. Ro +13:13. Ga 5:21. Ja 3:14-16. 4:5. 1 P 2:1.

18. **laid their hands**. Ac 4:3. 8:3. 12:5-7. 16:23-27. Lk +21:12. 2 C 11:23. He 11:36. Re 2:10.

19. **the angel**. Ac 8:26. 10:3. 11:13. *12:7-11, 23. *16:26. 27:23. Jg 6:12. 13:3. Ps 34:7. 105:17-20. 146:7. Is 61:1. Mt 1:20, 24. 2:13, 19. 28:2. Lk 1:11. 2:9. He *1:14. **opened**. Ac 12:10. *16:26.

20. **stand**. Ac +27:21. Is 58:1. Je 7:2. 19:14, 15. 20:2, 3. 22:1, 2. 26:2. 36:10. Mt 21:23. Jn 18:20. **speak**. Ac 18:9. Mt *10:27, 28. **all the words**. ⨍100, Ge +10:9. Ac 11:14. 13:26. Ex 24:3. Jn *6:63, 68. 12:50. *17:3, 8. Ph *2:16. 1 J *1:1-3. √5:11, 12. **of this**. Ac 13:46.

22:4. 28:28. **life**. Ac 3:15. 11:18. 13:46, 48.

21. **entered**. ver. 25, 42. Lk 21:37, 38. 24:53. **early**. Jn 8:2. **But**. ver. 17, 24. Ac 4:5, 6. 22:2, 3, 15. Lk 22:66. Jn 18:35. **the council**. ver. 27, 34, 41. Ac +4:15. **senate**. Ps 105:22. **children of Israel**. Ac 9:15. 10:36. Lk 1:16. 2 C 3:7, 13. He 11:22. Re 2:14. 7:4. 21:12. **sent**. Ac 4:7. 12:18, 19.

22. **the officers**. ver. 26. Mt +26:58.

23. **The prison**. ver. 19. Ps 2:4. 33:10. Pr +*21:30. La 3:37, 55-58. Da 3:11-25. 6:22-24. Mt 27:63-66. 28:12-15. Jn 8:59.

24. **the captain**. ver. 26. Ac +4:1. Lk 22:4, 52. **chief priests**. Ac ❍4:1. 9:14, 21. 22:30. 23:14. 25:2, 15. 26:10, 12. Jn +12:10. **they doubted**. Ac 2:12. 4:16, 17, 21. 10:17. Lk 9:7. Jn 11:47, 48. 12:19. **this**. Is +*9:7. *53:1, 2. Da 2:34, 35, 44, 45. Zc *6:12, 13. Mk 4:30-32. **would**. ⨍184D2, Lk +1:62.

25. **Behold**. ver. 18-21.

26. **the captain**. ver. 24. Ac +4:1. **the officers**. ver. 22. Mt +26:58. **without violence**. Ac 24:6. **they feared**. ver. 13. Ac +4:21. Mt 14:5. 21:26. 26:5. Lk 20:6, 19. 22:2.

27. **set**. Ac 4:7. 6:12. 22:30. 23:1. Lk 22:66. **the council**. ver. 21, 34, 41. Ac +4:15.

28. **Did not**. ver. *40. Ac *4:18-21. **straitly**. ⨍108C8, Lk +22:15. lit. "Did we not charge you with a charge." **intend**. Ac *2:23-36. *3:14, 15. 4:10, 11. *7:52. 18:6. Jg 9:24. 1 K *18:17, 18. 21:20. *22:8. Je *38:4. Am *7:10. **blood**. Je *26:15. Mt 21:44. *23:35, 36. √27:25. 1 Th *2:15, 16.

29. **apostles**. ver. +12. **We ought**. See on Ac *4:19. Ge 3:17. 1 S 15:24. 1 K 22:14. Mk 7:7-9. Re 14:8-12. **obey God**. ver. 32. **rather than**. T#319. Ac *4:19. Ex +*1:17, 20. 1 S 14:44, 45. 22:17. Est 3:2, 4. Da *3:16-18. +*6:10, 13.

30. **God**. Ac 3:13-15. 22:14. 1 Ch 12:17. 29:18. Ezr 7:27. Lk 1:55, 72. **raised**. Ac +*2:24. 3:26. 13:33. **ye slew**. Ac 2:22-24, 32. 4:10, 11. 10:39. 13:28, 29. Lk +24:20. Ga +*3:13. 1 P *2:24. **a tree**. Ac 13:29. Jn *19:6n. 20:25n. 1 P 2:24.

31. **hath**. Ac *2:33, 36. 4:11. Ps 89:19, 24. 110:1, 2. Ezk 17:24. Mt 28:18. Ep 1:20-23. Ph *2:9-11. He +*2:10. *12:2. 1 P 3:22. **a Prince**. Ac 2:36. *3:15. Ps *2:6-12. Is +*9:6. Ezk *34:24. +*37:25. Da +*9:25. 10:21. Re +*1:5. **a Savior**. Ac √4:12. 13:23. Is 43:3, 11. 45:21. 49:26. Mt +*1:21. 20:28. Lk +*2:11. Ph 3:20. T 1:4. *2:10, 13. 3:4-6. 2 P 1:1, 11. 2:20. √3:18. 1 J 4:14. Ju *25. **to give**. T#595. Ac 3:26. √11:18. +*13:48. Je 31:31-33. Ezk *36:25-27, 31. Zc +*12:10. Lk +*24:47. Ro *2:4. 5:5. +*11:26, 27. +*12:3. Ep *2:8. Ph +*1:29. 2 T √2:25, 26. **repentance**. T#800. Ac +*2:38. *3:26. Ezk 20:43. 36:31. Ho 2:6, 7. Zc *12:10. Mt *9:13. Lk +5:32. *24:47. **forgiveness**. Ac 3:19. *13:38, 39. Je 31:19, 24. Mk 2:10. 4:12. Jn 20:21-23. Ro *5:1. 2 C 2:10. Ep *1:7. Col 1:14.

32. **are witnesses**. ver. 29. Ac +*1:8. +*2:24n, 32. *10:39-41, +*43. *13:31. Lk 2:10. 24:47, +48. Jn 15:27. 2 C 13:1. He √2:3. **and so**. The Holy Spirit is spoken of as a person (Mk 5:12n). Ac 15:28. Jn *14:26. *15:26. *16:7-14. Ro 8:16. He *2:4. 1 P *1:12. 1 J 5:7. **is also**. Ro +*1:4. **whom**. Ac *2:4, 38, 39. *10:44. Jn *7:39. *15:26. +*16:13n, 14n. **to them**. Ro 1:5. **obey him**. ver. 29.

33. **they**. Ac 2:37. 7:54. 22:22. Lk 4:28, 29. 6:11. 11:50-54. 19:45-48. 20:19. **took**. Ac 9:23. Ge 4:5-8.

Ps 37:12-15, 32, 33. 64:2-8. Mt 10:21, 25. 23:34, 35. 24:9. Jn 15:20. 16:2.

34. **stood**. Ac 23:7-9. Ps 76:10. Jn 7:50-53. **the council**. ver. 21, 27, 41. Ac +4:15. **a Pharisee**. Ac 15:5. 23:6-9. 26:5. Ph 3:5. **Gamaliel**. i.e. *benefit of God, recompense of God,* ✱S#1059g. Ac *22:3. **a doctor**. Lk 2:46. 5:17. **and commanded**. Ac 4:15.

35. **Ye men**. Ac +2:22. **take heed**. ver. 38. Ac 19:36. 20:28. 22:26. Je 26:19. Mt 27:19. Lk 12:1g. 17:3. 21:34.

36. **before**. Ac 21:38. **these days**. ♪171T2B, Ps +102:11. **Theudas**. i.e. *confession; gift of God,* ✱S#2333g, only here. This was probably the same with *Judas* (for *Jude* is called **Thaddeus**, Mt 3:18) of whom Josephus says (Ant. l. xvii. c. 12. sec. 5. Bel. l. ii. c. 4. sec. 1) that "a little after the death of Herod the great, he raised an insurrection in Galilee, and aimed at getting the sovereignty of Judea," and that he was defeated and put to death, as is implied in sec. 10. **boasting**. Ac 8:9. Mt 24:24. Ga 2:6. 6:3. 2 Th 2:3-7. 2 P 2:18. Ju 16. Re 17:3, 5. **somebody**. ♪175A, Ge +27:44. **to whom**. Ac 21:38. 2 P *2:2. **obeyed**. *or,* believed. Mt 24:26.

37. **Judas**. Judas the **Gaulonite**, as he is termed by Josephus (Ant. l. xviii. c. 1, 2. Bel. l. ii. c. 12), opposed the levying of taxes by Cyrenius; but he was soon cut off, and all his followers dispersed. Lk *2:1. 13:1. **the taxing**. Lk 2:2. **he also**. Jb 20:5-9. Ps 7:14, 15. 9:15, 16. Mt 26:52. Lk 13:1, 2. **perished**. Gr. *apollumi,* Mt +2:13. **obeyed**. *or,* believed. ver. 36mg.

38. **Refrain**. ver. 35. Jn 11:48. **for if**. ♪184C, Mt +4:9. Ne 4:15. Jb 5:12-14. Ps 33:10, 11. Pr +*21:30. Is 7:5-7. *8:9, 10. 14:25. La 3:37. Mt 15:13. 1 C 1:26-28. 3:19. **of men**. Mt 21:25. Mk 11:30. Lk 20:4.

39. **But if**. ♪184A, 1 C +15:2. Turner cites Zerwick who says in part, "Gamaliel seems strangely biased. He says doubtfully, "If it should be of men" but confidently "If (as it seems) it is of God," the one hypothetical, the other "real" (Nigel Turner and James Hope Moulton, *A Grammar of New Testament Greek*, vol. 3, p. 114). A. T. Robertson states "This condition *assumes* that the thing is so without *affirming* it to be true" (*Word Pictures*, vol. 3, p. 69). Ac 6:10. ♪184E, Lk +17:6. Ge 24:50. 2 S 5:2. 1 K 12:24. Jb 34:29. Is 43:13. *46:10, 11. Da 4:35. Mt *16:18. Lk *21:15. 1 C *1:25. Re 17:12-14. **ye cannot**. Pr +*21:30. Is 8:9, 10. Na 1:9. **to fight against**. Ac 7:51. *9:5. 11:17. 23:9. Ex 10:3-7. 2 K 19:22. 2 Ch *13:12. Jb 15:25-27. 40:9-14. Is *45:9. Je 26:19. 1 C 10:22.

40. **when**. Ac +4:18. **the apostles**. ver. 12. **beaten**. Ac 22:19. Pr 12:10. Mt *10:17. 23:34. Mk 13:9. Lk 20:10. 23:16. Jn 19:1-4. 2 C *11:24. **they commanded**. ver. 28. Ac *4:17-21. Is 30:10. Am 2:12. Mi 2:6.

41. **the council**. ver. 21, 27, 34. Ac +4:15. **presence**. ♪144A1, Ge +11:8. **rejoicing**. ♪125, Jb +22:6. Ac 16:23-25. Is 61:10. 65:14. 66:5. Mt +*5:10-12. Lk 6:22, 23. Ro *5:3. 2 C *12:10. Ph *1:29. He *10:34. Ja *1:2. 1 P √4:13-16. **counted worthy**. Lk 20:35. 2 Th 1:5. **to suffer**. Ac 9:16. 21:13. **shame**. He 12:2. **for his name**. ♪121T1, Dt +28:58. Ac +15:26. Ex 3:14, 15. Le 24:11, 16. Jn +15:21. Ph 2:9. 3 J 7.

42. **daily**. ver. 20, +21. Ac 2:46. 3:1, 2, etc. Lk 21:37. 22:53. 2 T *4:2. **in**. Ac 2:46. *20:20. **they**. Ac *4:20, 29. 2 S 6:22. Ro 1:15, 16. Ga 6:14. **teach**. Ac 15:35. Lk 20:1. **preach**. Ac 8:5, 35. 9:20. 11:20. 17:3, 18. 1 C *2:2. Ga 1:16. Ep 4:20, 21. **Jesus Christ**. Ac +18:5.

ACTS 6

On occasion of the murmurings of the Grecians, seven persons, chosen by the church, under the direction of the apostles, are appointed by them to superintend the daily ministration to the poor; that none might be neglected, and that the apostles might "give themselves to the word of God and to prayer," 1-6. The word of God greatly prevails, 7. Stephen, full of faith and the Holy Spirit, confutes those who disputed against him, 8-10. They suborn witnesses, who, before the council, falsely accuse him of blasphemy against the law and the temple, 11-14. His face shines like the face of an angel, 15.

1. **when**. ver. 7. Ac *2:41, 47. *4:4. *5:14, 28. 9:31, 35, 42. 11:21. 12:24. 13:43, 44. 14:1. 16:5. 17:4, 12. 18:8. 19:20, 26. 21:20. Ps 72:16. 110:3. Is 27:6. Je 30:19. **the disciples**. ver. 7. Ac +11:26. **there arose**. 1 C 10:10. He 13:1. Ja 4:5. 5:9. **Grecians**. i.e. *Hellenists,* ✱S#1675g. Ac 9:29. 11:20. **Hebrews**. i.e. *a region across, passed over, the other side,* ✱S#1445g. 2 C 11:22. Ph 3:5. For ✱S#5680h, see Ge +40:15. **their widows**. Ac 9:39, 41. Dt *24:19-21. 26:12. Jb 29:13. 31:16. Is 1:17. Ezk 22:7. Ml +*3:5. Mt 23:14. 1 T +*5:4, 5, 8-10, 16. Ja 1:27. **the daily**. Ac 2:45. *4:34, 35. **ministration**. Ac 11:29. 12:25. Ro 12:7. 15:31. 1 C 12:5. 2 C 8:4. 9:1, 12, 13.

2. **the twelve**. Ac 1:13, 26. 21:22. Mk +9:35. **the multitude**. ver. 5. Ac 4:32. 15:12, 30. It. Ac 4:19. 25:27. **reason**. *or,* fit. Gr. pleasing. Ac 12:3. Jn 8:29g. **we should leave**. Ex 18:17-26. Nu 11:11-13. Dt 1:9-14. Ne 6:3. 2 T 2:4. **the word of God**. ♪108B, Lk +1:2. ver. 7. Ac +11:1.

3. **brethren**. Ac 9:30. 15:23. Mt 23:8. Jn +21:23. 1 J *3:14-16. **look**. Ac 1:21. Ex +*18:21. Nu 11:16, 17. Dt *1:13. 1 C 16:3. 2 C 8:19-21. **honest report**. Ac 10:22. 16:2. 22:12. Ex +*18:21. Nu 16:15. 1 S 12:4. 2 S 18:12. 1 K 13:8. 2 K 5:16. +*12:15. Pr +*11:3. Am +*8:5. Ro *12:17. 1 C +*4:2. 2 C +*6:3. √8:19-21. 1 Th 4:12. 1 T *3:7, 8, 10. 5:10. He 13:18. 3 J 12. **full**. ver. 5. Ac +2:4. 7:55. 11:24. Ge 41:38, 39. Nu 11:17-25. 27:18, 19. Jb 32:7, 8. Is 11:2-5. 28:6, 26. Lk 1:15. 4:1. 1 C 12:8. Ep +*5:18. Ja 1:17. 3:17, 18. **Ghost**. Gr. pneuma, Mt +1:18n. **and wisdom**. T#1855. 2 K +*5:13. Pr +*22:3. Ro 12:8. Ja *4:17. **whom**. ver. 6. Ac 13:2, 3. 1 T 3:8-15.

4. **give**. Ac *2:42. *20:19-31. Ro √12:6-8. 1 C 9:16. Col 4:17. 1 T √4:13-16. 2 T *4:2. **continually**. T#1319. Ac +1:14. 10:1, 2. 12:5. Ge 32:24-26. 1 S 7:8. 1 Ch *16:11. Ps 72:15. 86:3. 88:1. 109:4. Is 62:1, 6, 7. La 2:18, 19. Ho 12:6. Mt 26:40-44. Lk √11:5-10. *18:1-6. +*21:36. Ro 1:9. 12:11, 12. 1 C 7:5. Ep *6:18. Col 1:9. *4:2. 1 Th +*5:17. 2 T 1:3. He 13:15. **prayer**. Ac *1:14. 13:2, 3. 2 Ch +*7:14. Ro *1:9. Ep *1:15-17. *3:14-21. Ph *1:4, 9-11. Col *1:9-13. 2:1. √4:12. 2 Th *3:1, 2. **the ministry**. ver. 2 (serve). **the word**. Ac +8:4. 2 T √3:16, 17. √4:2.

5. **the saying**. Ac 15:22. Ge 41:37. Pr 15:1, 23. 25:11, 12. **whole multitude**. ver. +2. **Stephen**. i.e. *a crown,* ✱S#4736g. ver. 8, 9. Ac 7:59. 8:2. 11:19. 22:20. **a man**. ver. 3, 8, 10. Ac ch. 7. 8:1, 2. 11:24. Mi 3:8. **full of faith**. Ac 11:24. **Ghost**. Gr. pneuma, Mt +1:18n. ver. 3. **Philip**. Ac *8:5-13, 26-40. 21:8. **Prochorus**. i.e. *leader of the choir or leader of praise,* ✱S#4402g, only here. **Nicanor**. i.e. *victorious,* ✱S#3527g, only here. Re ?2:6, 15. **Timon**. i.e. *honorable, valuable,*

*S#5096g, only here. **Parmenas.** i.e. *one who abides*, *S#3937g, only here. **Nicolas.** i.e. *submission*, *S#3532g, only here. Re 2:6, 15. **a proselyte.** Ac 2:10. 13:1, 43. Mt 23:15. **Antioch.** Ac +11:26.

6. **the apostles.** Ac +5:12. **when.** Ac *1:24. *8:17. 9:17. *13:3. 14:23. Ph *4:6. **they laid.** Ac 8:17. 9:17. 19:6. *13:3. Nu 8:10. 27:18. Dt 34:9. Mk +5:23. 1 T *4:14. *5:22. 2 T *1:6. He 6:2.

7. **the word.** ver. 2. Ac +11:1. *12:24. *19:20. Is √55:11. 1 C *3:6, 7. Col *1:6. 2 T 2:9. **the number.** ver. 1. Ac 21:20g. **the priests.** Ac 4:1, 36, 37. 2 Ch 29:34. 30:24. Ps 132:9, 16. Mt 19:30. Lk 2:34. Jn *12:42. **obedient.** Ro +1:5. 16:26. 2 Th √1:8. He +*5:9. 11:8. **the faith.** Ac 13:8. +*14:22. 16:5. 24:24. Lk √18:8. 1 C +16:18. √121R2. Metonymy of the Adjunct B599. *Faith* is put for the thing believed, as the doctrine. For other instances of this figure see Ga 1:23. 3:23. 5:5. Ep 4:5. 1 T 4:1. T 1:13. Ju 3. Re 2:13.

8. **full.** ver. 3, 5, 10, 15. Ac 7:55. Ep 4:11. 1 T 3:13. **of faith.** Mt *17:20. **and power.** Ac +*1:8. **did.** Ac 2:17, 18. 4:29, 30. 8:6. **wonders.** Mk +16:20. Jn +4:48.

9. **there arose.** Ac 13:45. 17:17, 18. 27:21. **the synagogue.** Ac 22:19. 26:11. Mt 10:17. 23:34. Mk 13:9. Lk 21:12. **Libertines.** i.e. *freedmen*, *S#3032g, only here. **Cyrenians.** Ac +2:10. 11:20. 13:1. Mt 27:32. **Alexandrians.** *S#221g. Ac 18:24g. 27:6. 28:11. **Cilicia.** i.e. *which rolls, or overturns*, *S#2791g. Ac 15:23, 41. 21:39. 22:3. 23:34. 27:5. Ga 1:21. **Asia.** Ac +2:9. 16:6. 19:10, 26. 21:27. **disputing.** 1 C 1:20.

10. **not able.** Ac 5:39. 7:51. Ex *4:12. Is +*54:17. Je 1:18, 19. 15:20. Ezk 3:27. Mt 10:19, 20. Lk 12:11, 12. *21:14, 15. Jn 7:46. **the wisdom.** Lk 21:15. **the spirit.** Gr. *pneuma*, √121A1, Lk +1:17n. ver. 3, 5. Jb 32:8, 18. Mi 3:8. Lk 1:17. 1 C 2:4.

11. **they suborned.** Ac 23:12-15. 24:1-13. 25:3, 7. 1 K 21:10, 13. Mt *26:59, 60. 28:12-15. Jn 16:3. Ro 3:8. **blasphemous.** ver. 13. Ac 18:6. 26:11. Le *24:16. 1 K 21:10-13. Jn +*10:33-36. 1 T 1:13. **against Moses.** Ac 7:37-39. 15:21. 21:20-22, 28. Jn 1:17. 5:45-47. 9:29. He 3:2-5.

12. **they stirred.** Ac 13:50. 14:2. 17:5, 13. 21:27. Pr 15:18. **the elders.** Ac +4:5. **came upon.** Ac 4:1. Lk +20:1. **and caught.** Ac 4:1-3. 5:18, 27. 16:19-21. 17:5, 6. 18:12. 19:29. Mt 26:57. Lk 8:29. **and brought.** Mt *10:17-19. **the council.** ver. 15. Ac +4:15.

13. **set up.** ver. +11. Ps 27:12. 35:11. 56:5. **false witnesses.** Ac 7:58. **holy place.** Mt 24:15. Jn +11:48. **the law.** Ac 21:28. 25:8.

14. **we have.** Ac 25:8. **this Jesus.** Ac +2:22. **shall destroy.** Is 66:1-6. Je 7:4-14. 26:6-9, 12, 18. Da +*9:26. Mi 3:12. Zc 11:1. 14:2. Mt *24:2. 26:61. Mk 14:58. Lk 13:34, 35. 21:6, 24. Jn *2:19. *4:21. **this place.** ver. 13. **change.** Is 65:15. 66:19-21. Ho 3:4. Mt ◑*5:17. Ga 3:19, 23. 4:3-5. He *7:11-19. 8:6-13. *9:9-11. *10:1-18. 12:26-28. **customs.** *or*, rites. Ac 15:1. 21:21. 26:3. 28:17.

15. **the council.** ver. 12. Ac +4:15. **looking.** √149, Mk +8:33. **stedfastly.** Ac +3:4. 7:55. **saw his face.** Ex *34:29-35. Jg 13:6. Ec 8:1. Mt 13:43. *17:2. 2 C *3:7, 8, 18.

ACTS 7

Stephen, being required to answer before the council, shows how God called Abraham, and promised

Canaan to him and his seed, 1-8; how Joseph was sold by his brethren, and Jacob with his family went down into Egypt, 9-16; that when they were oppressed by the Egyptians, Moses was born, and brought up by Pharaoh's daughter, 17-22; that attempting to deliver Israel he was rejected, and fled into Midian, 23-29; that at length he was sent to be their deliverer, 30-36; that he prophesied of Christ, received the law for Israel, and was grieved by their rebellion and idolatry, 37-43; that they had "the tabernacle of witness," till Solomon built the temple, 44-47; yet, according to the prophets, "the Most High dwelleth not in temples made with hands," 48-50. He boldly accuses the council and the nation of imitating the rebellion and persecution of their ancestors, who rejected and slew the prophets; and charges them with murdering Christ, in violation of their own law, 51-53. Being "cut to the heart," they hasten to stone him; while he, favored with a vision of Christ, and calling on him to receive his soul, and pardon his murderers, falls asleep, 54-60.

1. **Are.** Ac 6:13, 14. Mt 26:61, 62. Mk 14:58-60. Jn 18:19-21, 33-35.

2. **Men.** Ac 22:1. 23:7. **fathers.** √171G, Ge +13:8. **The God of glory.** ver. 55. Ex *15:11. 24:16. *40:35. Ps 24:7-10. 29:3. *84:11. Is *6:3. Mt +*6:13. Lk 2:14. Jn 1:14. 12:41. 1 C √2:8. 2 C √4:4-6. T *2:13g. He *1:3. Ja √2:1. Re *4:11. +*5:12, 13. **appeared.** Ge *12:1. 15:7. Jsh 24:3. Ne 9:7. Is 51:2. Jn √8:56-58. **Abraham.** Lk +19:9. **when.** Both Ur of the Chaldees, and Haran, were, properly speaking, in Mesopotamia, though Haran was much nearer to Canaan than Ur was. Jsh 24:2. **Mesopotamia.** i.e. *exalted, magnificent*, *S#3318g. Ac 2:9. 1 Ch 19:6. **Charran.** i.e. *heat of wrath*, *S#5488g. ver. 4. For *S#2771h, see 1 Ch +2:46; for *S#2039h, see Ge +11:26. (1) Brother of Abraham and father of Lot, Ge 11:26, 31. (2) A son of Shimei, of the tribe of Levi, 1 Ch 23:9. (3) A son of Caleb, the son of Jephunneh, 1 Ch 2:46. (4) The place to which Abram removed after leaving Ur, and before he went into Canaan, Ge 11:31; 2 K 19:12. Ge *11:31. 12:5. 29:4, Haran.

3. **Get.** Ge *⟩12:1. Mt 10:37. Lk 14:33. 2 C *6:17. He *11:8. **the land.** Ge 13:14-17. 15:7. Jsh 24:3. Ne 9:8.

4. **came.** Ge *11:31, 32. *12:4, 5. Is 41:2, 9. **Chaldeans.** i.e. *as it were demons*, *S#5466g. For *S#3778h, see Je +50:10. **was dead.** Ge 11:32. Ru 1:3. **when his father.** From Ge 11:26, it appears that Abraham was born when Terah was 70 years of age; and he departed from Haran when 75 (Ge 12:4); while Terah lived to the age of 205 years (Ge 11:32). Instead of 205, however, the Samaritan has 145, which reconciles this discrepancy; but it is not improbable, that Abram was in reality born when his father Terah was 130 years old; and that he is merely mentioned *first* in Ge 11:26 by way of *dignity*. **he removed.** ver. 43. Ge 12:4, 5. Mt 1:11, 12, 17. **land.** Je +*7:7.

5. **he gave.** Ge *23:2-4. Ps 105:11, 12. He +*11:9, 10, 13-16. **him.** The point is, that the promise was made personally to Abraham that he would himself inherit the promised land, but Abraham himself never personally possessed the land God promised to him. It is for this reason that God, who cannot lie, must resurrect Abraham and bring him personally into the promised land in order for the Abrahamic Covenant

to be fulfilled. How many Bible scholars have failed to notice the explicit statement of Scripture here, which declares that Abraham did not receive the inheritance, and have taught the opposite, and worse, have spiritualized and transformed the covenants into something they were never meant to be, taking to themselves or the church the blessings promised to Abraham and the Jews, but very carefully leaving the curses to Israel, literally interpreted at that (see related notes at Jsh √21:43n. 1 K √4:21n. Is 60:21n. Je 33:21n). Mt +*8:11, 12. Ro +*4:13. **none inheritance.** Is +*26:15. Je +7:7. Ezk ●33:24. Ob 17. Mi 7:20. Lk *1:72. He 9:8, 9. 11:9, 10, √13, √39. **not.** ∫77, Ex +3:19. Dt 2:5. **yet he promised.** Ge 12:7. *13:15. 15:3, 18. 17:8. 26:3. 28:13-15. 48:4. Ex 6:7, 8. 32:13. 33:1. Nu 32:11. Dt 6:10, 11. 9:5. 10:11. 11:9. 34:4. 2 Ch 20:7. Ne 9:8. Ps 105:8-12. Ro +*4:13. He 11:8, 9. **to him.** Ge 15:8. **when.** ∫77, Ex +3:19. Ge 15:2-5. 16:2. 17:16-19. 18:10. Ro 9:9.

6. **That.** Ge ▶15:13, 16. **sojourn.** Ex 2:22. He 11:9. **four.** Stephen here uses the round number 400, leaving out the odd tens; for it is evident, from the parallel passages, as well as Josephus (Ant. l. ii. c. 1. sec. 9. Bel. l. v. c. 9. sec. 4) that the real number of years was 430. ver. 17. Ge 15:16. Ex *12:40, 41. Ro *4:18, 21. Ga 3:17.

7. **the nation.** Ge 15:14-16. Ex ch. 7-14. Ne 9:9-11. Ps 74:12-14. 78:43-51. 105:27-36. 135:8, 9. 136:10-15. Is 51:9, 10. **will I judge.** Je 25:12. 30:20. **and serve.** Ex 3:12.

8. **the covenant.** Ge *17:9-14. 21:2-4. Jn 7:22. Ro *4:10-13. Ga 3:15-17. **and so.** Or, "and thus," *kai oitos*, in this covenant. Ge 17:12. 21:1-4. He 11:11. **circumcised.** Lk +1:59. **and Isaac.** Ge 25:21-26. 1 Ch 1:34. Mt 1:2. Ro 9:9-13. **and Jacob.** Ge 29:31-35. 30:1-24. 35:16-18, 23-26. Ex 1:1-4. 1 Ch 2:1, 2. **patriarchs.** Ac +2:29. He 7:4.

9. **moved.** Ac +5:17. Ge *37:4-11. 49:23. Mt 27:18. 1 C 13:4. Ja 4:2. **sold.** ∫63H, Ge +12:15. Ge *37:18-29. 45:4, 5. 50:15-20. Ps 105:17. **but.** Ge *39:2, 3, 5, 21-23. 49:24. Jg ●16:20. Is 41:10. 43:2.

10. **delivered.** Ge 48:16. Ps 22:24. *34:17-19. 37:40. 40:1-3. *91:14. 2 T 4:18. Ja 5:11. Re 7:14. **all.** *∫171L2, Mt +26:59. **gave.** Ge 41:37-40. Pr *3:1, 4. **Pharaoh.** i.e. *sun king,* ✳S#5328g. ver. 13, 21. Ro 9:17. He 11:24. **made him.** Ge 41:41, 43, 46. 42:6. 44:18. 45:8, 9. Ps 105:19-22. Pr 2:6. 3:4. +16:7.

11. **a dearth.** Ge *41:54-57. 42:5. 43:1. 45:5, 6, 11. *47:13-15. Ps 105:16. **Chanaan.** i.e. *merchant, servant,* ✳S#5477g. Ac 13:19. For ✳S#3667h, see Ge +10:6.

12. **Jacob heard.** Ge *42:1, etc. 43:2. **corn.** ∫121D4, Ge +27:28.

13. **at the second.** Ge 43:2-15. Zc=12:10. **Joseph.** Ge *45:1-18. 46:31-34. 47:1-10.

14. **sent.** Ge *45:9-11, 27. Ps 105:23. **all his kindred.** Ex 1:5. **threescore.** Ge 38:12. *46:10, 12, 20, 26, 27. Ex 1:5. Dt 10:22. 1 Ch 2:5, 6. **souls.** Gr. *psyche,* ∫171Q1A, Ac +2:41. ∫171Q1, Ge +12:5. Ac +27:37.

15. **Jacob.** Ge *46:3-7, 28. Nu 20:15. Dt 10:22. 26:5. Jsh 24:4. Ps 105:23. **died.** Ge 49:33. Ex *1:6. He 11:21, 22.

16. **were carried.** Of the two burying-places of the patriarchs, one was at Hebron, the cave and field which Abraham purchased of Ephron the Hittite (Ge 23:16, etc.); the other in Sychem, which Jacob (not Abraham) bought of the sons of Emmor (Ge 33:19). To remove

this glaring discrepancy, Markland interprets *para, from,* as it frequently signifies with a genitive, and renders, "And were carried over to Sychem; and afterwards *from* among the descendants of Emmor, the father, or son, of Sychem, they were laid in the sepulchre which Abraham bought for a sum of money." This agrees with the account which Josephus (Ant. l. ii. c. 8) gives of the patriarchs; that they were carried out of Egypt, first to Sychem, and then to Hebron, where they were buried. Ge 50:25. Ex *13:19. Jsh *24:32. **the father.** ∫63I1A, Ex +12:4. Ge 33:19. Jsh 24:32. **Sychem.** i.e. *place of figs,* ✳S#4966g. For ✳S#7927h, see Ge +33:18, Shechem. Ge 12:6. Jsh 17:7. **the sepulchre.** Ge 23:9-20. 35:19. 49:29-32. *50:13. Jsh *24:32. **Emmor.** i.e. *an ass,* ✳S#1697g, only here. For ✳S#2544h, see Ge +33:19. Ge 34:2, etc., Hamor, Shechem.

17. **when.** ver. 6. Ge 15:13-16. 2 P 3:8, 9. **the people.** Ac 13:17. Ge *15:5. Ex *1:7-12, 20. Ps 105:23-25.

18. **another king.** Ex ▶1:8.

19. **dealt subtly.** Ge 15:13. Ex *1:9-22. Ps 83:4, 5. 105:25. 129:1-3. Re 12:4, 5. **cast out.** Ex 1:16-18, 22. Mt=2:13-16. **not live.** Ex 1:22. Lk 17:33. 1 T 6:13g.

20. **Moses.** Ex *2:2-10. **and was.** 1 S 16:12. He 11:23. **exceeding fair.** or, fair to God. Ge 10:9. 23:6. 30:8. Ex *2:1, 2. 1 S 14:15. 1 Ch 12:22. Jon 3:3. Lk=2:40, 52. 2 C 10:4. He *11:23. **father's house.** Ex 2:1. 6:20.

21. **when.** Ex *2:2-10. Dt 32:36. **for.** He 11:24.

22. **was learned.** 1 K 4:29, 30. 2 Ch 9:22, 23. Is 19:11, 12. Da 1:4, 17-20. **wisdom.** Ex 4:10. Mt=13:54. Mk 6:2. **and was mighty.** Ac 18:24. Dt 18:15. Lk *24:19. **words and.** ∫174, Ge +18:27. Ex 4:10.

23. **when.** Ex *2:11, 12. He 11:24-26. **it came.** Ex 35:21, 29. 1 Ch 29:17-19. 2 Ch 30:12. Ezr 1:1, 5. 7:27. Pr 21:1. Is 65:17. Je 3:16. 32:35. 1 C 2:9g. 2 C 8:16. Ph √2:12, 13. Ja *1:17. Re 17:17. **to visit.** Ac 15:36. Ex 2:11, 12. 4:18. Ja 1:27. **his brethren.** ver. 26.

24. **seeing one.** ver. 28. Ex 2:13, 14. Jn 18:10, 11, 25-27. **defended.** ✳S#292g, only here. Pr 19:25. Ep 5:11. **avenged.** Nu 35:19. Dt 19:12. Jsh 20:3. 2 S 3:27. **oppressed.** Dt +*24:14. Ps +*12:5. *72:14. Ezk +*16:49.

25. **For.** *or,* Now. **God.** Ac 14:27. 15:4, 7. 21:19. 1 S 14:45. 19:5. 2 K 5:1. Ro 15:18. 1 C 3:9. 15:10. 2 C 6:1. Col 1:29. **hand.** ∫144A5, Ge +9:5. **understood not.** ver. 39, 51, 52, 53. Ps *106:7. Mk 9:32. Lk 9:45. 18:34. Jn=1:10, 11.

26. **the next.** Ex *2:13-15. **ye are.** Ge 13:8. 45:24. Ps 133:1. Pr 18:19. Jn 15:17, 18. 1 C 6:6-8. Ph 2:1, 3. 1 J 3:11-15.

27. **he that.** ver. 54. Ac 5:33. Ge 19:9. 1 S 25:14, 15. Pr 9:7, 8. **Who.** ver. 35, 39. Ac 3:13-15. 4:7, 11, 12. Mt 21:23. Lk 12:14. Jn +*18:36, 37. 19:12-15. **ruler.** Lk=12:14. √19:14.

28. **Egyptian.** i.e. *that binds or oppresses; tribulation,* ✳S#124g. ver. 22, 24. Ac 21:38. He 11:29.

29. **fled Moses.** Ex *2:14-22. **Madian.** i.e. *contention,* ✳S#3099g. For ✳S#4080h, see Ge +25:2, Midian. Ge 37:28. Ex 4:19, 20, Midian. 18:2-4. Jg 6:2. **he begat.** Ex 2:22. 18:3, 4.

30. **when forty.** ver. 17, 23. Ex 7:7. **there.** Ex 3:1. 19:1, 2. 1 K 19:8. Ga 4:25, Sinai. **an angel.** ver. 32, 35. Ge 16:7-13. 22:15-18. 32:24-30. 48:15, 16. Ex *3:2, 6. Is +*63:9. Ho 12:3-5. Ml *3:1. **in the wilderness.** Ex 3:1. **of mount Sina.** i.e. *cliffs; my thorns,* ✳S#4614g.

ver. 38. Ga 4:24, 25. For *S#5514h, see Ex +16:1. **in a flame.** Ex *3:2. Dt 4:20. Ps 66:12. Is 29:6. 30:30. 43:2. 66:15. Da 3:27. 2 Th 1:8. He 1:7. Re 1:14. 2:18. 19:12. **fire.** ✝24N, Ge +17:5. **in a bush.** ver. 35. Dt 33:16. Mk 12:26. Lk 20:37.

31. **and as.** Ex 3:3, 4. **the voice.** Ac 9:4. 1 K 19:13.

32. **I am.** Ac 3:13. Ge 50:24. Ex ▶3:6, 15. 4:5. Mt +*22:32. Mk 12:26. Lk +20:37. He +*11:16. **the God.** Ac +3:13. **Then.** Ac 9:4-6. Ge *28:13-17. Ex 33:20. 1 K 19:13. Jb 4:14. 37:1, 2. 42:5, 6. Ps 89:7. Is 6:1-5. Da 10:7, 8. Mt 17:6. Lk 5:8. Re 1:17.

33. **Put.** Ex *3:5. Jsh *5:15. Ec 5:1. Mk +1:7. 2 P 1:18.

34. **I have seen.** ✝147B, Ge +2:16. Ex 2:23-25. *3:7, 9. 4:31. 6:5, 6. Jg 2:18. 10:15, 16. Ne 9:9. Ps 106:44. Is +*63:8, 9. **have heard.** Ex +*2:24. *3:9. **and am.** Ge 11:5, 7. 18:21. Ex 3:8. Nu 11:17. Ps 144:5. Is 64:1. 66:1. Mt 5:24. Jn 3:13. 6:38. **And now.** Ex 3:10, 14. Ps 105:26. Ho 12:13. Mi 6:4.

35. **Moses.** ver. 9-15, 27, 28, 51. 1 S 8:7, 8. 10:27. Lk 19:14. Jn 18:40. 19:15. **they refused.** Ac 3:14g. **saying.** ver. +*27. **the same.** Ac 5:31. Ps 75:7. 113:7, 8. 118:22, 23. **a ruler and.** Ac=2:36. 3:22. 5:31. 1 S 12:8. Ne 9:10-14. Ps 77:20. Is 63:11, 12. Mi +*5:2. Re 15:3. **a deliverer.** Dt 7:8. 13:5. Is 59:20. Lk +1:68. Ro +*=11:26. 1 Th=1:10. **by the hand.** ✝144A5, Ge +9:5. See on ver. 30. Ac 11:21. Ex 3:2. *14:19, 24. 23:20-23. 32:34. 33:2, 12-15. Nu √20:16. Is +*63:9. Col +*1:15. He 2:2. **appeared.** ver. 30.

36. **brought.** Ex 12:41. 33:1. He 8:9. **after.** Ex ch. 7-14. Dt 4:33-37. 6:21, 22. Ne 9:10. Ps 78:12, 13, 42-51. 105:27-36. 106:8-11. 135:8-12. 136:9-15. **wonders.** Ex 7:3. 11:9. **signs.** Jn +4:48. **Egypt.** Ex ch. 7-12. Ps 78:43-51. 105:27-36. **in the Red.** Ex 14:21, 27-31. Ps 78:53. 106:9. **and in the wilderness.** Ex 15:23-25. ch. 16, 17, 19, 20. Nu 9:15, etc. ch. 11, 14, 16, 17, 20, 21. Dt 2:25-37. 8:4. Ne 9:12-15, 18-22. Ps 78:14-33. 105:39-45. 106:17, 18. 135:10-12. 136:16-21. **forty years.** ver. 42. Ac 13:18. Ex *16:35. Nu 14:33, 34. Ps 95:10. He 3:9, 17.

37. **that.** ver. 38. 2 Ch 28:22. Da 6:13. **A prophet.** Ac 3:22. Dt ✱*▶18:15-19. Mt +21:11. Jn +*1:45. **like unto me.** or, as myself. **him.** Ac 3:23. Mt *17:3-5. Mk 9:7. Lk 9:30, 31, 35. Jn 8:46, 47. 18:37.

38. **in the church.** T#116. Ac 19:32. Ex +*12:6n. *19:3-17. 20:19, 20. Nu 16:3, etc., 41, 42. Dt 4:10. 9:10. 18:16. Jsh 8:35. Ezr 2:65. Jl 2:16. Mt 16:18n. 18:17. Ro 11:11-24. 1 C 3:16, 17. 2 C 6:16. Ga 3:7-9, 29. 4:26. Ep 2:11-22. He 2:12. 12:22, 33. **with the angel.** See on ver. 30, 35, 53. Ge +*17:1. Ex *6:3. Is +*63:9. Jn 1:3. +*8:56. Ga *3:19. He *2:2. Re +*1:8. *15:3. **mount Sina.** ver. 30. **who received.** Ex 21:1, etc. Dt 5:27-31. 6:1-3. 33:4. Ne 9:13, 14. Jn +1:17. **lively.** Dt 30:19, 20. 32:46, 47. Ps 78:5-9. Mt *4:4. Jn +*5:39. *6:63, 68. Ro 3:2. 9:4. *10:6-10. He 5:12. 1 P 4:11. ✝108B. Idiom B831. "Living" was used by the Hebrews to express the *excellency* of the thing to which it is applied. For other instances of this idiom see Jn 4:10, 11. He 10:20. 1 P 2:4, 5. Re 7:17. **oracles.** Ro 3:2. He 5:12. 1 P 4:11.

39. **whom.** ver. 51, 52. Ne 9:16. Ps 106:16, 32, 33. Ezk 20:6-14. **but.** ver. 27. Jg 11:2. 1 K 2:27. **and in.** Ex *14:11, 12. 16:3. 17:3. Nu 11:4, 5. 14:3, 4. 21:5. Ne 9:17. Ezk 20:8, 24.

40. **unto.** Ex ▶32:1, 23. **go before.** Ex 13:21.

41. **they.** Ex 32:2-8, 17-20, 35. Dt 9:12-18. 1 K 12:28.

Ne 9:18. Ps 106:19-21. **offered sacrifice.** Am 6:13. **rejoiced.** Is 2:8, 9. 44:9-20. Je 1:16. 25:6, 7. 32:30. Ho 9:1, 10. Hab *2:18-20.

42. **God turned.** Jsh 24:20. Is +*63:10. **and gave.** Ac 14:16. Ps *81:11, 12. Is 66:4. Ezk 14:7-10. 20:25, 39. Ho 4:17. Ro *1:24-28. 2 Th √2:10-12. **the host.** Dt 4:19. *17:3. 2 K *17:16. +*21:3. 23:5. Jb 31:26-28. Je 8:2. *19:13. Ezk 8:16. Zp 1:5. **written.** Lk 2:13. **the book.** Ac +1:20. Jn +6:45. **prophets.** ✝171E13, Ge +46:7. **O ye.** Am ▶5:25, 26. **house of Israel.** Ac +2:36. **have ye.** Is 43:23. **of forty.** ver. 36. Ps 95:10. He 3:9, 15-17.

43. **ye took.** Le 18:21. 20:2-5. Nu 1:50. Jsh 3:6. 2 K 17:16-18. 21:6. **of Moloch.** i.e. *a king; rule,* *S#3434g. For *S#4432h, see Am +5:26. Le +*18:21. 20:2-5. Dt +*18:10. Jsh 15:8n. 1 K 11:7. 2 K 23:10. Je 7:31. 32:35. Ho 13:2mg. Zp 1:5. **the star.** Am *5:26n. **Remphan.** i.e. *the shrunken; set in array,* *S#4481g. For *S#3594h, see Am 5:26, Chiun. **figures.** ✝92F2, Mt +2:6. Ex 20:4, 5. Dt 4:16-18. 5:8, 9. **and I.** ver. 4. 2 K 17:6. 18:11. Am *5:27. **Babylon.** In the passage of Amos, to which St. Stephen refers, it is *beyond Damascus;* but as Assyria and Media, to which they were carried, were not only *beyond Damascus,* but *beyond Babylon* itself, he states that fact, and thus fixes more precisely the place of their captivity.

44. **the tabernacle.** Ex 38:21. Nu 1:50-53. 9:15. 10:11. 17:7, 8. 18:2. Jsh 18:1. 2 Ch 24:6. Re 15:5. **of witness.** Ex 25:21, 22. **speaking.** *or,* who spake. **that he.** Ex 25:9, 40. *26:30. 27:8. Nu 8:4. 1 Ch 28:11, 19. He 8:2, 5.

45. **Which.** Jsh *3:11-14. 18:1. Jg 18:31. 1 S 4:4. 1 K 8:4. 1 Ch 16:39. 21:29. **that came after.** or, having received. **Jesus.** Jsh 3:6, 7, Joshua. *11:23. He 4:8. **possession.** ver. 5. Nu 32:5. Dt 32:49. **whom.** Ac 13:19. Jsh 3:10. 18:1. 23:9. 24:18. 2 Ch 20:7. Ne 9:24. Ps 44:2. 78:55. 80:8. **unto.** 2 S ch. 6. 7:2. 1 Ch ch. 15-17.

46. **found.** Ac 13:22. 1 S 15:28. *16:1, 11-13. 2 S 6:21. 7:1, 8, 18, 19. 17:10. 1 Ch 28:4, 5. Ps 78:68-72. 89:19-37. *132:11, 12. Lk +1:30. **and desired.** 2 S *7:1-5. 1 K 8:17-19. 1 Ch 17:1-4. 22:7, 8. 28:2, 3. 29:2, 3. Ps *132:1-5. **God of Jacob.** Ge 49:24. Is 49:26. Ro +11:26.

47. **Solomon built.** 2 S 7:13. 1 K ch. 5. *6:1, 37, 38. 7:13-51. 8:20. 1 Ch 17:1. 22:10. 28:6. 2 Ch ch. 2-4. Zc *6:12, 13. **house.** ✝171E4, Lk +11:51.

48. **the most High.** Ac 16:17. Dt 32:8. Ps 7:17. 46:4. +*78:17, 35, 56. +*83:18. 91:1, 9. 92:8. Da 4:17, 24, 25, 34. 7:18. Ho 7:16. Mt 11:10. Mk 5:7. Lk 1:+32, 76. 8:28. Ro *9:5. 1 C 10:9. 1 Th 3:13. **dwelleth not.** ✝19, Dt +22:1. Ac *17:24, 25. 1 K *8:27. 2 Ch 2:5, 6. 6:18. **made with hands.** Mk +14:58. **as.** Is ▶66:1, 2.

49. **Heaven.** 1 K 22:19. Ps 11:4. 103:19. Is *66:1, 2. Je 23:24. Mt *5:34, 35. 23:22. Re 3:21. 4:2. **what house.** Je 7:4-11. Ml 1:11. Mt +*24:2. Jn *4:21.

50. **made all.** Ac 14:15. Ge 1:1. Ex 20:11. Jb 12:9. Ps 33:6-9. 50:9-12. 146:5, 6. Is 40:26, 28. 44:24. 45:7, 8, 12. Je 10:11. 32:17.

51. **stiffnecked.** ✝59, Ge +28:16. Ex *32:9. 33:3, 5. 34:9. Dt 9:6, 13. 10:16. 31:27. 2 Ch 30:8. Ne *9:16. Ps 75:5. 78:8. Is *48:4. Je 17:23. Ezk 2:4. Zc 7:11, 12. **uncircumcised.** Le *26:41. Dt *10:16. 30:6. Je *4:4. *6:10. 9:25, 26. Ezk 44:7, 9. Ro √2:25, 28, 29. Ph

3:3. Col 2:11. **always**. Gr. *aei*, Mk 15:8. **resist**. Ac 6:10. Nu 27:14. Ne 9:30. Is +*63:10. Ep +*4:30. 1 Th *5:19. He +*10:28, 29. **Ghost**. Gr. *pneuma*, Mt +3:16. *121A3, Nu +11:17. **as your fathers**. ver. 9, 27, 35, 39. Ml 3:7. Mt 23:31-33.

52. **Which of**. 1 S 8:7, 8. 1 K *19:10, 14. 2 Ch *16:10. *24:19-22. *36:15, 16. Ne *9:26. Je 2:30. 20:2. *26:8, 15, 23. Mt +*5:12. *21:35-41. *23:31-37. Lk 11:47-51. 13:33, 34. 1 Th *2:15. He *11:36-38. **which showed**. Ac 3:18, 24. 1 P 1:11. Re +*19:10. **the Just One**. Ac +*3:14. 22:14. Zc +*9:9. Ro *5:1. 1 C *1:30. 1 P *3:18. 1 J *2:1. Re 3:7. **of whom**. Ac 2:23. 3:15. 4:10. +5:28-30.

53. **have received**. ver. 38. Ex ch. 19, 20. Dt +*33:2. Ps 68:17. Ga *3:19. He *2:2. **and have**. Ezk 20:18-21. Jn 7:19. Ro 2:23-25. Ga 6:13.

54. **they were**. Ac 2:37. *5:33. 22:22, 23. **cut**. *141, Is +22:4. **they gnashed**. Jb 16:9. Ps 35:16. 37:12. 112:10. La 2:16. Mt +*8:12. +*13:42, 50. 22:13. 24:51. +*25:30. Lk 13:28.

55. **full**. Ac +*2:4. +*4:8n. 6:3, *5, 8, 10. 13:9, 10. Mi 3:8. **Ghost**. Gr. *pneuma*, Mt +1:18n. **looked up**. *149, Mk +8:33. Ac 1:10, 11. +3:4g. Lk +*21:28. Jn 11:41. 17:1. 2 C 12:2-4. Re 4:1-3. **stedfastly**. Ac 6:15. **and saw**. ver. 2. Ex 24:16. Is 6:1-3. Ezk 1:26-28. 10:4, 18. 11:23, 24. Lk 2:9. Jn 12:41. 2 C 4:6. 2 P 1:17. Re 21:11, 23. **standing**. Ps 109:31. 110:1. Mk +16:19. Jn +*14:3. He *1:3. 8:1. **right hand**. *22A15C, Ps +110:1.

56. **I see**. Ac 10:11, 16. Ezk *1:1. Mt *3:16. Mk 1:10. Lk 3:21. Jn +1:51. Re 4:1. 11:19. 19:11. **the Son of man**. Da +*7:13, 14. Mt +*16:27n, 28. +*25:31. 26:64, 65. Jn 1:51. 5:22-27. **standing**. Ps ●110:1. He *1:3. **right hand**. *22A15C, Ps +110:1.

57. **they cried out**. *141, Is +22:4. ver. 54. Ac 21:27-31. 23:27. **stopped**. Ps 58:4. Pr 21:13. Zc 7:11.

58. **cast**. Le 24:14-16. Nu 15:35, 36. 1 K 21:13. Lk *4:28, 29. He 13:12, 13. **stoned**. Ac 6:11. 14:19. Le 24:14-16. Jsh 7:25. 2 Ch 24:21. Mt 21:35. 23:37. Jn *10:23-36. **the witnesses**. Ac 6:13. Dt 13:9, 10. *17:6, 7. **laid down**. Ac 22:23. **their**. Ac 8:1. 9:1, etc. *22:4, 20.

59. **Stephen**. T#439. Mt +10:16 (T#660). +11:29 (T#62). **calling upon**. Upon whom was Stephen calling? Those who deny the deity of Christ are caught upon the horns of a fatal dilemma. If "God," then Stephen addresses Jesus as God. If "Lord," then Jesus is being directly addressed in prayer, an act of worship due only to God. In the New Testament, prayers, invocations, or doxologies are not uniformly and invariably addressed exclusively to God the Father. Thomas addressed Jesus as God (Jn +*20:28). The disciples worshipped Christ directly as he went up into heaven (Lk 24:51, 52). Paul prayed to the Father and the Lord Jesus Christ jointly: Ro 1:7. 1 C *1:3. 2 C 1:2. Ga 1:3. Ep 1:2. 6:23. Ph 1:2. Col 1:2. 1 Th 1:1. 3:11. 2 Th 1:2. 2:16, 17. 1 T 1:2. 2 T 1:2. T 1:4. Phm 3. So John prayed to the Father and Son jointly, 2 J 3, and to all three persons of the Godhead alike, Re 1:4, 5. Paul also prayed to Christ singly: Ro 16:20, 24. 1 C 16:23. Ga 6:18. Ph 2:19, 24. 1 Th 5:28. 2 Th 3:16, 18. 1 T 1:12. 2 T 4:14, 17, 18, 22. Some devotional acts Paul performed towards the Holy Ghost singly: Ro 9:1. 15:30. See Paul's noted doxology to Christ, Ro *9:5. Peter put up his doxologies to Christ: 1 P 2:3, 4. *4:11. 2 P √3:18. See the whole creation join

in the same common doxology to the Father and the Son, not to the Father through the Son, Re *5:11-13 (Daniel Waterland, *Works*, Vol. 4, pp. 8, 9). "Christ is to be worshipped with religious worship by *men* (Ac 7:59. 9:14. Jn √5:23. Re 5:8); either *singly* and by himself, or *jointly* with the Father in the *same acts* of worship. He is therefore *God by nature*, and not by *office* only, appointment, or designation. The worship of him must of consequence stand upon the same foot whereon Scripture has founded all *religious* worship; upon his real and essential *divinity*, his being *God, Jehovah, Almighty*, etc. which he must be because he is *adorable*; and which if he be, then the worship of him comes within the reason, intent, and even the *letter* of the law about worship. And it is very observable how the *Scripture rule* of worship exactly harmonizes with what the same Scripture teaches of the *divinity* of God the Son. For as, on the one hand, his claim of *worship* confirms the doctrine of his *divinity*; so, on the other hand, his *divine* titles and *attributes* confirm his claim of *worship*: and thus is Scripture uniform, consistent, and harmonious throughout" (Daniel Waterland, *Works*, vol. 3, "The Scriptures and the Arians Compared," pp. 295, 296). Ac 2:21. 9:+14, 21. 22:16. Jl 2:32. Jn √5:23. Ro 10:12-14. 1 C 1:2. 1 Th 3:11. 2 T 2:22. Re +*5:12. **God**. *63I2, Jsh +3:3. There is evidently an *Ellipsis* after the verb "calling upon," which the A.V. supplies with the word "*God*." The R.V. supplies the word "*Lord*." **Lord Jesus**. "A clear instance of prayer addressed to the second person of the Trinity" (Thomas Walker, Comm. on Acts, p. 179). H. P. Liddon observes, "Stephen would never have prayed to Jesus, if he had been taught that such prayer was hostile to the supreme prerogatives of God; and the apostles, as monotheists, must have taught him thus, unless they had believed that Jesus is God, who with the Father is worshipped and glorified" (*The Divinity of Our Lord*, Bampton Lectures, 1866, Lecture VII, p. 370). Ac +1:21. **receive**. T#1580. Ge 25:17. Ps *31:5. Ec +*3:21. +*9:5. Mt +*10:28n. Lk *23:46. Ph +*1:23. 1 P *4:19. **my spirit**. Gr. *pneuma*, *121A3, Mt +27:50. Ge +*25:8n, 9, 17. √35:18. 49:33. Dt 32:49, 50. 1 K √17:22. Jb +*14:22. +*34:14. Ec +*12:7. Lk√23:46. He +*12:23.

60. **he kneeled**. Ac *9:40. 20:36. 21:5. 1 K 8:54. Ezr 9:5. Ps *95:6. Da +*6:10. Lk 22:41. Ep *3:14. **Lord**. Mt +*5:44. Lk *6:28. √23:34. Ro 12:14-21. **lay not**. 2 Ch ●24:22. Je ●+*10:25. Lk 23:34. 1 T *1:16. 2 T 4:●14, 16. **he fell asleep**. Ac 13:36. 1 C +*11:30. 15:6, 18, 20, 51. 1 Th *4:13, 14. 5:10.

ACTS 8

Saul well approves the murder of Stephen; and the disciples, "except the apostles," are dispersed by persecution, 1. Devout men bury Stephen and lament over him, 2. Saul makes havoc of the church, 3, 4. Philip preaches in Samaria, and has great success, 5-8. Simon, who had long bewitched the people by sorceries, believes and is baptized, 9-13. Peter and John, being sent thither, by prayer and imposition of hands confer the gift of the Holy Ghost, 14-17. Simon, offering money for the like power, is by Peter rebuked, warned, and called to repent, 18-24. The apostles, having preached in the cities of Samaria, return to Jerusalem, 25. Philip is sent by an angel into the desert of Gaza, 26; where he meets with an eunuch, treasurer of Candace queen of Ethiopia, returning in his chariot from Jerusalem, and reading the prophecy of Isaiah, 27, 28. By a divine monition he joins the chariot, and preaches Jesus to the Ethiopian, 29-35; who, professing faith in him as "the Son of God," is baptized, 36-38. The Spirit conveys away Philip, who preaches in the cities on the sea coast, till he comes to Cesarea: and the eunuch returns home rejoicing, 39, 40.

1. **And Saul.** This clause evidently belongs to the conclusion of the preceding chapter; there is scarcely a worse division of chapters than this. Ac 7:58. 22:20. **consenting.** Lk 11:48. Ro +1:32. **there.** Ac 5:33, 40. 7:54. Mt 10:25-28. *22:6. 23:34. Lk 11:49, 50. Jn 15:20. 16:2. **the church.** Ac 2:47. 7:38. 11:22. 13:1. **scattered.** ver. 4. Ac *11:19-21. Mt 5:13. +10:23. Ph 1:12. Ja 1:1. 1 P 1:1. **Samaria.** ver. 14. Ac +*1:8. 9:31. Jn *4:39-42. **except.** Ac 5:18, 20, 33, 40. Ex 10:28, 29. Ne 6:3. Da 3:16-18. *6:10, 23. He 11:27. **the apostles.** ver. 14. Ac +5:12.

2. **devout.** Ac +2:5. 10:2. Lk 2:25. **carried.** Ac +5:6. **made.** Ge 23:2. 50:10, 11. Nu 20:29. Dt 34:8. 1 S 28:3. 2 S 3:31. 2 Ch 32:33. 35:25. Is 57:1, 2. Je 6:26. 22:10, 18. Jn 11:31-35.

3. **Saul.** i.e. requested; persuaded, *S#4569h. Ac 7:58. 8:1, 3. 9:1, 8, 11, 19, 22, 24, 26. 11:25, 30. 12:25. 13:1, 2, 7, 9. See *S#4549g: Ac 9:4, 17. 13:21. 22:7, 13. 26:14. Compare *S#7586h, 1 S +9:2. **made havock.** Ac 7:58. *9:1-13, 21. 22:3, 4, 19. *26:9-11. 1 C 15:9. Ga *1:13. Ph 3:6. 1 T 1:13. **haling.** Ac 14:19. 17:6g. Ja 2:6.

4. **were scattered.** ver. 1. Ac 11:19. 14:2-7. Mt 10:23. 1 Th 2:2. Ja 1:1. 1 P 1:1. **went every where.** Ge +*50:20. Ph *1:12. **preaching.** ver. 12. Ac 15:35. 2 T *4:2. **the word.** Ac 6:4. 10:36, 44. 11:19. 14:25. 16:6. 17:11. 18:5. Mk +4:14. Ga 6:6. Col 4:3. 1 Th 1:6. 1 T 5:17. 2 T 4:2. 1 P 2:8. 3:1.

5. **Philip.** ver. 1, 14, 15, 40. Ac +6:5. 21:8. **the city.** Rather, "to a city of Samaria," eis polin tas Samareios, for the city of Samaria had been utterly destroyed by Hyrcanus, and the city built by Herod on its site was called Sebastee, that is, Augusta, in honor of Augustus. Samaria comprised the tract of country formerly occupied by the tribes of Ephraim and Manasseh, west of Jordan, lying between Judea and Galilee: beginning, says Josephus (Ant. l. xiii. c. 18), at Ginea in the great plain, and ending at the toparchy of Acrabateni. Ac *1:8. Mt ◐*10:5, 6. Jn *4:39-42. **preached.** ver. 35-37. Ac 5:42. *9:20. *13:38. *17:2, 3, 18. Lk *24:47. Jn 4:25, 26. 1 C *1:23, 24. √2:2. 3:11. **Christ.** Ac +18:5. Lk +3:15.

6. **the people.** ver. 25. Jn 4:38. **with one.** Ac 13:44. 2 Ch 30:12. Mt 20:15, 16. Jn 4:41, 42. **seeing.** Jn 2:23. **the miracles.** ver. 13. Ac 4:16, 22. Mk +16:20.

7. **unclean.** Ac 5:16. Mt 10:1. Mk +3:30. 9:26. 16:17, 18. Lk 10:17. Jn 14:12. He 2:4. **spirits.** Gr. pneuma, Mt +8:16. **crying.** Mk 1:26. 5:7. **palsies.** Ac 9:33, 34. Mt +4:24. Mk 2:3-11. **lame.** Ac 3:6, 7. 14:8-10. Is 35:6. Mt 11:5. 15:30, 31.

8. **great joy.** T#621. ver. 39. Ac *2:44-47. 13:48, 52. *19:18-20. 2 K 23:24, 25. 2 Ch 31:5, 8. Ps 9:2. 14:7. 96:10-12. 98:2-6. Is 35:1, 2. 42:10-12. Lk 2:10, 11. Jn +16:22. Ro *14:17. 15:9-12. Col 2:5. 2 C +7:11 (T#605). 1 P 1:8.

9. **used sorcery.** ver. 11. Ac 13:6. 16:16-18. 19:18-20. Ex 7:11, 22. 8:18, 19. 9:11. Le 20:6. Dt +*18:10-

12. Is +47:12. Ml +*3:5. 2 T 3:8, 9. Re 13:13, 14. 22:15. **giving.** Ac +5:36. Jn 7:18. 2 Th 2:4. 2 T 3:2, 5. 2 P 2:18.

10. **all gave heed.** 2 C √11:19. Ep +*4:14. 2 P 2:2. Re 13:3. **from.** Ac 26:22. Ge 19:11. Je 6:13. 8:10. 31:34. 42:1. 44:12. Jon 3:5. He 8:11. Re 11:18. **This man.** Ac 14:11. 28:6. **the great power.** Ac 19:27, 28. 1 C 1:24.

11. **he had.** ver. 9, 13. Is *8:19. 44:25. 47:9-13. Ga 3:1.

12. **they believed.** ver. 35-38. Ac +*2:38, 41. 10:47, 48. 16:14, 15, 31-34. 18:8. 19:4, 5. 22:16. Mt +*28:19. Mk *16:15, 16. Ro √10:10. 1 P 3:21. **concerning.** Ac +1:3. 11:20. 20:21, 25. 28:31. Lk +4:43. 9:2, 60. Jn *3:3. **the name.** Ac √4:12. +15:26. **were baptized.** ver. 36-38. Mt +*28:19. Mk √16:16. **both.** Ac 5:14. 1 C 11:11. Ga *3:28. **men and women.** An objection to infant baptism has been founded on this statement, for it makes no mention of infants or children. Such an objection is not only precarious, it is invalid. It fails to take into account that an abstract statement of fact cannot be used to deny specifics which are not mentioned. The account of Joshua's destruction of Ai (Jsh 8:25, 26) makes no mention of children or infants: would any dare to assert that the city of twelve thousand contained no infants? When a thousand men and women fled to and were destroyed in the tower of Shechem (Jg 9:49), were there no children? Or the city of Thebez which fled to its tower (Jg 9:51), yet no children mentioned? Clearly the fact that children or infants are not specified does not preclude their presence and participation (see Hibbard, Christian Baptism, Part I, pp. 254-257). See related notes (Ge 6:5, √121N1. 1 P 3:21n).

13. **Simon.** This Simon was probably, as several learned men suppose, the same who is mentioned by Josephus (Ant. l. xx. c. 5. sec. 2), as persuading Drusilla to leave her husband, and live with Felix. **believed.** ver. 21, ◐37. Ps 78:35-37. 106:12, 13. Lk +*8:13. Jn +*2:23-25. √8:30, 31. 1 C +*15:2. Ja *2:19-26. **and wondered.** ver. 9, 11. Ac 3:10. 13:44. Hab 1:5. Jn 5:20. 7:21. **miracles and signs.** Gr. signs and great miracles. ver. 7. Ac +2:22. 19:11. Mt *7:22. 11:20, 21, 23. 13:54, 58. 14:2. Mk 6:2, 5, 14. 9:39. 16:17. Lk 10:13. 19:37. 1 C 12:10, 28, 29. Ga 3:5.

14. **when.** ver. 1. Ac 11:1, 19-22. 15:4. 1 Th 3:2. **the apostles.** ver. 1. Ac +5:12. **Samaria.** ver. 1. Ac 1:8. **received.** Ac 2:41. √17:11. Mt 13:23. Jn 12:48. 1 Th √2:13. 2 Th √2:10. **the word.** Ac +11:1. **Peter.** Ac +3:1-3. Ga 2:9.

15. **come down.** ver. 26. Ac 18:22. **prayed.** T#1561. Ac +*2:38. Ps *51:11, 12. Mt √18:19. Lk 11:13. Jn *14:13, 14, 16, 17. *16:23, 24. 2 C *13:14. Ph 1:19. **Ghost.** Gr. pneuma, Mt +1:18n.

16. **he was.** This probably indicates that the accompanying supernatural baptism of the Holy Spirit evidenced by the miraculous gifts was conveyed only through the ministry of the original apostles and Paul, but not through the evangelists, and was therefore limited to their lifetime, perhaps even to the time before the destruction of the Temple in A.D. 70. This baptism of the Holy Spirit must be distinguished from the filling of the Holy Spirit for service, still possible for every believer (see the related notes on Ac 1:5n. 2:41n. +*4:8n. Ro +*8:9n. Ep +*5:18n), and the indwelling of the Holy Spirit, experienced by every true

believer in Christ (Ro +*8:9, 11. 1 C √12:13). The baptism of the Holy Spirit was given as a sign to Israel (and by nature a sign must be temporary, or it would lose its effect as a sign), and as an earnest, to validate the claims of the apostles and of our Lord, that they indeed had the power and authority to bring in the restoration of Israel as promised by the prophets. The fulfillment of the promise and the establishment of the kingdom of God is postponed until the Second Advent, delayed until, and conditioned upon, the repentance of Israel (Ac +√3:19-21), when the gifts and the signs will be in evidence again (Jl √2:28n). Ac 10:44-46. 11:15-17. *19:2. 1 C 12:8-10. **only**. Ac +*2:38n. *10:47, 48. +15:26. *19:5, 6. Mt +*28:19. 1 C √1:13-15. Ga 3:27. **the Lord Jesus**. Ac +1:21.

17. **laid**. ver. 18. Ac 6:6. 9:17. 13:3. *19:6. Nu 8:10. 27:18. Mk +5:23. 1 T *4:14. 5:22. 2 T 1:6. He 6:2. **they received**. Ac +2:4. Ro 1:11. Ga 3:2-5. **Ghost**. Gr. *pneuma*, Mt +1:18n.

18. **he offered**. 2 K 5:15, 16. 8:9. Ezk 13:19. Mt 10:8. 1 T 6:5.

19. **Give me also**. ver. 9-11, 17. Mt 18:1-3. Lk 14:7-11. Jn 5:44. 1 C 15:8, 9. 3 J 9. **Ghost**. Gr. *pneuma*, Mt +1:18n.

20. **Thy money**. *f*34, Ps +50:16. Ac 1:18. Dt 7:26. Jsh 7:24, 25. 2 K 5:16, 26, 27. Da 5:17. Hab 2:9, 10. Zc 5:4. Mt *10:8. 27:3-5. 1 T +*6:9. Ja *5:3. 2 P 2:14-17. Re 18:15. **perish**. 1 C *6:10. **thou**. ver. 22. Dt 15:9. 2 K 5:15, 16. Pr 15:26. Mt 15:19. **the gift**. ver. 19. Ac *2:38. 10:45. 11:17. Mt 10:8. **with money**. Is 55:1.

21. **hast**. Jsh 22:25. Ezk 14:3. Re 20:6. 22:19. **part**. Dt 10:9. 12:12. 14:27, 29. 18:1. Is 57:6. Ep 5:5. Col 1:12. **nor lot**. Ac +1:17. **for**. 2 K 10:15. 2 Ch 25:2. Ps 36:1. 78:36, 37. Hab 2:4. Mt 6:22-24. Jn 21:17. He √4:13. Re *2:23.

22. **Repent**. T#1383. Ac +*2:38. +*3:19. √17:30. 1 K 8:46-50. 2 Ch 15:10-15. Ne 9:1-4. Jb *42:5, 6. Je 3:21, 22. 36:7. Da *4:27. Jl 2:15-19. Ro *2:4. 2 T +*2:25, 26. Ja *4:8-10. Re 2:21. **wickedness**. Ro +1:29g. **pray**. Ac 9:11. Dt 4:29, 30. 1 K 8:47, 48. 2 Ch 33:12, 13. Is √55:6, 7. Am 5:6. Mt √7:7, 8. Lk √11:9-13. Re 3:17, 18. **if**. *f*184A, 1 C +15:2. Je 18:8. Da 4:27. Jl 2:13, 14. Am 5:15. Jon 1:6. 3:9, 10. Mt *12:31n. Mk 11:13. 2 T +*2:25. **the thought**. ver. 20. Ac 5:4. Je 4:14. +*6:19. He √4:12.

23. **thou art**. 2 K 8:11, 12. **the gall**. Dt *29:18-20. 32:32, 33. Jb 20:14. Je *4:18. *9:15. La *3:5, 19. Mt 27:34. He √12:15. **bitterness**. Ro 3:14. Ep 4:31. **the bond**. Ps 116:16. Pr *5:22. Is 28:22. 58:6. Jn *8:34. Ro *6:17-22. Ep 4:3. Col 3:14. T 3:3. 2 P 2:4, *19.

24. **Pray**. Ge *20:7, 17. Ex *8:8, 28. 9:28. *10:17. 12:32. Nu *21:7. 1 S *12:19, 23. 15:25. 1 K *13:6. Ezr 6:10. 8:23. Jb +*42:8. Je 15:1. Ja √5:16.

25. **when they had**. Ac +*1:8. 18:5. 20:21. 26:22, 23. 28:23, 28, 31. Lk +16:28. Jn 15:27. 1 P 5:12. **the word**. Ac +15:35. **and preached**. ver. 6-8, 40. Ac 9:32. Jn 4:38. **in**. or, to. *f*121J19, 1 S +22:19. **villages**. Lk 9:52-56. **Samaritans**. Mt +10:5.

26. **the angel**. Ac +5:19. 10:7, 22. 12:8-11, 23. 27:23. 2 K 1:3. He 1:14. **Arise**. Ac +6:5. 1 Ch 22:16. Is 60:1, etc. **unto the way**. "There were several roads from Jerusalem to Gaza. One led via Ashkelon and then along the coast. Another passed through Hebron, across the less frequented country known as the Negeb. If the word desert refer to the road, then we must

understand that the latter route is intended" (Thomas Walker). "Besides the ordinary road from Jerusalem by Ramleh to Gaza, there was another, more favorable for carriages (Ac 8:28), further to the south, through Hebron, and thence through a district comparatively without towns, and much exposed to the incursions of people from the desert" (McClintock and Strong, vol. 3, art. "Gaza," p. 756). **Gaza**. i.e. *strong*, *S#1048g, only here. For *S#5804h, see Ge +*10:19. Jsh 11:22. 13:3. +*15:47. Jg 16:1. Zc 9:5. **desert**. It is probable, that we should refer *ereemos*, "desert," not to *Gaza*, but to *odos*, the "way;" though Gaza was situated at the entrance of the desert (Arrian, Exped. Alex. l. ii. c. 26), and the ancient city was in ruins, being destroyed by Alexander (Strabo, l. xvi). Thus, "we must understand that Philip was instructed to take the less frequented route via Hebron mentioned above" (Thomas Walker). Mt 3:1-3. Lk 3:2-4.

27. **he arose**. Mt 21:2-6. Mk 14:13-16. Jn 2:5-8. He 11:8. **a man**. 2 K 19:9. Est 1:1. 8:9. Jb 28:19. Ps 68:31. 87:4. Is 18:1. 20:3, 5. 37:9. 43:3, 6. 45:14. 60:3-6. 66:19, 20. Je 13:23. 38:7, 10. 39:16. Ezk 29:10. 30:4, 5. Na 3:9. Zp *3:10. **an eunuch**. Is +*56:3-5. Mt 19:12. **great authority**. Lk 1:52. 1 T 6:15. **Candace**. i.e. *who has contrition, pure possession*, *S#2582g. **queen**. 1 K 10:1. Mt 12:42. **the charge**. Ezr 7:21. **had come**. R. B. Rackham notes the eunuch "had come up to Jerusalem as a pilgrim to some feast, probably Pentecost" (Comm. on Acts, p. 122). W. G. Williams states "And at that season (April, after the Passover, Acts 8:27), the rains had ceased, and the country was dry, except for occasional pools" (*Baptism*, p. 22). Ac 24:11. 1 K 8:41-43. 2 Ch 6:32, 33. Ps 68:29. Is 56:3-8. Jn *12:20.

28. **and sitting**. Ac √17:11, 12. Dt 6:6, 7. 11:18-20. 17:18, 19. Jsh √1:8. Ps √1:2, 3. 119:99, 111. Pr 2:1-6. 8:33, 34. Jn +√5:39, 40. Col *3:16. 2 T √3:15-17. **Esaias**. Ac 28:25. Is 1:1, Isaiah. Mk +1:2. Lk 3:4. 4:17.

29. **the spirit**. Gr. *pneuma*, Lk +24:37. Mt +*12:32. **said**. Since the Holy Spirit is said to *speak*, the Holy Spirit must be a person. ver. 39. Ac *10:19. *11:12, 28. 13:2-4. 15:28. 16:6, 7. 20:22, 23. 21:4, 11. 28:25. Is +*65:24. Ho +*6:3. 1 C 12:11. 1 T 4:1. He 3:7.

30. **ran thither**. ver. 27. Ps 119:32. Ec +*9:10. Jn 4:34. **heard him read**. Ex 24:7. Jsh 8:34. Je 36:8. Lk 4:16. Col 4:16. 1 T *4:13. Re *1:3. **Understandest**. *f*135, Ps +68:28. Ps √119:97-105. Pr +*8:9. Mt +*13:19, 23, 51. *15:10. *24:15. Mk 13:14. Lk +*24:44, 45. Jn +√5:39. 1 C 2:9-11. *14:19. 2 C 3:2g. Ep √5:17. Re √13:18.

31. **How can I**. *f*184D2, Lk +1:62. Ps √25:8, 9. 73:16, 17, 22. Pr 30:2, 3. Is 29:18, 19. 35:8. Mt 18:3, 4. Mk 10:15. Jn +*7:17. Ro +10:14. 1 C 3:18. 8:2. 14:36, 37. Ja 1:10, 21. 1 P 2:1, 2. **except**. *f*184A, 1 C +15:2. *f*184E, Lk +17:6. In his puzzlement over the meaning of this Scripture, the Ethiopian had the humility and desire to receive instruction through a human instrument to learn its meaning. In our own efforts to understand Scripture, we must not neglect to make careful use of Bible study tools produced by godly men, and the writings and researches of devout scholars whose scholarship and industry we cannot hope to duplicate. There is no necessity to reinvent the wheel. It is the height of egotism to suppose that we can go ourselves to the Bible alone, and learn all that God has for us in His Word, never utilizing cross references,

concordances, commentaries and specialized topical studies, as though the Holy Spirit never assisted the labors of the writers and scholars that have gone before us. God will hold us responsible not only for what we know, but for what we could have known had we made the proper and diligent use of the means He has made available to us. Proper spiritual growth is dependent upon our careful and systematic study of the Word of God. A mere reading of the Bible, good and necessary as that is, is not enough. Nor is it satisfactory to derive all of our spiritual food from the labors of others, such as pastors, as valuable as they are. We are to search the Scriptures for ourselves, and test the teaching of others by the Word of God (Is +*8:20n. Ac √17:11). Ps *119:18, 21. 2 P *3:18. **some man**. 1 T +*4:16. 2 T +*2:2. 1 J ◐*2:27. **guide me**. Ps +*102:18 (T#49). Pr 4:18n. 18:1n. Is +*8:20n. Je +*23:28n. Da +*11:33n. Lk +*12:57 (T#420). Jn √16:13g,n. 2 P 1:20n. **And he**. 1 K 20:33. 2 K 5:9, 26. 10:15, 16. **come up**. *S#305g. ver. 39n. Ac 1:13. 2:34. 3:1. 7:23. 10:4, 9. 11:2. 15:2. 18:22. 20:11. 21:4, 12, 15, 31. 24:11. 25:1, 9. Mt 3:16. 5:1. 13:7. 14:23. 15:29. 17:27. 20:17, 18. Mk *1:10. 3:13. 4:7, 8, 32. √6:51. 10:32, 33. Lk 2:4, 42. 5:19. 9:28. 18:10, 31. 19:4, 28. 24:38. Jn 1:51. 2:13. 6:62. 7:8, 10, 10, 14. 10:1. 11:55. 12:20. 20:17, 17. 21:√3, 11. Ro 10:6. 1 C *2:9. Ga 2:1, 2. Ep *4:8, 9, 10. Re *4:1. 7:2. 8:4. 9:2. 11:7, 12, 12. 13:1, 11. 14:11. 17:8. 19:3. 20:9.

32. **the scripture**. Lk +4:21. **He was**. Is ❱53:7, 8. **as a**. Ps 44:11, 22. Je 11:19. 12:3. 51:40. Ro 8:36. Re 5:6. **and like**. Jn 1:29. 1 P 1:19. 2:21-24. **opened**. ℐ108H6B, Ps +38:13. Ps 39:2, 9. Mt +*26:62, 63. Lk 23:34. Jn 18:9-11.

33. **his humiliation**. Ph *2:8, 9. **judgment**. Jb 27:2. 34:5. Is 5:23. 10:2. Hab 1:4. Mt 27:12-26. Jn 19:12-16. **and who**. Ps 22:30. Is 53:8, 12. **for**. Ps 22:15. Is 53:10, 12. Da +*9:26. Zc *13:7.

34. **of whom**. Mt 2:2-4. 13:36. 15:15. **of himself**. Ac 2:29-31. 13:35-37.

35. **opened**. ℐ108H6A, Jg +11:35. Ac 10:34. Mt +5:2. 2 C 6:11. **began**. Ac 17:2. *18:28. 26:22, 23. 28:23. Lk +*24:27, 44-47. Re *19:10. **the same scripture**. Lk +4:21. **preached**. Ac 3:20. +5:42. 9:20. 11:20. √17:3, 18. 19:13. 1 C 1:23. 2:2. Ep 4:21. 1 P 1:11, 12.

36. **came unto**. The chariot stopped in the water. "The position of the chariot in relation to the water is of vital importance. This must, primarily, be determined by *epi*. The chariot stands wherever *epi ti udor* puts it. This may be either *upon, over*, the water (the wheels in the water of a streamlet running across the road), or immediately adjacent to the water. Winer says, *epi* means *upon, above, on* the shore; *beside, near*, in local sense is not established" (J. W. Dale, *Christic and Patristic Baptism*, p. 185). **a certain water**. Gr. *epi ti udor*, to some water. The pronoun *ti* has sometimes a diminutive sense, and so here. "They came to *a little* water," etc. (F. G. Hibbard, *Christian Baptism*, Part 2, p. 104). J. A. Alexander notes here "not to *a certain water*, which might seem to mean a well known lake or stream, of which the region seems to have been wholly destitute, but, as the Greek words properly denote, *to some water*, the indefinite expression, like that in Ac 5:2, suggesting naturally the idea of a small degree or quantity" (Comm. on Acts, p. 348). That this water was small in quantity may be

determined because, additionally, (2) the region was desert (ver. 28, not merely wilderness or uninhabited land. The region is the same as where Abraham and Isaac dug wells, and their herdmen strove, saying "the water is ours," Ge 26:19, 20, in the valley of Gerar). (3) The Eunuch was surprised to see water, as shown by his exclamation "See! water," "where it might have been least expected" (Alexander). (4) "The promptitude and urgency for baptism; implying that if this spot should be passed by no other such spot might be found on the road. Everything said and implied points to a limited quantity of water" (James W. Dale, *Christic and Patristic Baptism*, p. 185). Dt 21:4, 6. **See**. As observed in the note on Ac 1:6, the question fairly reveals the content of the preceding instruction. Ac 10:47. Is *52:15. Ezk 36:25. Mt 28:19, 20. Mk 16:15, 16. Jn 3:5, 23. T 3:5, 6. 1 J 5:6. **what doth hinder**. Ac *10:47.

37. **If**. ℐ184A, 1 C +15:2. ver. 12, 13, 21. Ac +*2:38, 39. Mt +*28:19. Mk *16:16. Ro √10:10. **with all**. ver. ◐21. Ezk ◐+*33:31, 32. **thine heart**. 2 K +*20:3. 1 Ch 12:38n. **he answered**. Mt 3:6. Ro √10:9, 10. 1 P 3:21. **I believe**. Ac 9:20. Mt +*16:16. Jn 6:68, 69. 9:35-38. 11:27. √20:31. 1 C +*12:3. 1 J *4:15. √5:1, 5, 10-13. **Jesus Christ**. Mt +1:1. **the Son of God**. The name "son of God" is not merely an honorary title conferred upon him, but declares (1) his eternal preincarnate relation as the second person of the Trinity to the Father: Jn 1:14, 18. Ga 4:4. (2) his unique relationship to the Father as the only-begotten Son: Jn 1:14, 18. 3:16n, 18. 1 J 4:9. (3) his full deity: Jn 5:18. √10:33, 36. (4) his unique knowledge of God: Mt +*11:27. (5) his messiahship: Mt 8:29. *26:63, 64. (6) his supernatural origin, having God for his Father in the virgin birth: Lk 1:32, 35. Jn 1:13. It is in Peter's confession of Jesus as the son of God that Peter goes beyond what others (Jn 1:45) asserted before or after (Jn 11:49-52), a perception given Peter by the Father (Mt 16:16, 17). Mt +14:33. 16:27n. 27:54n.

38. **chariot to stand still**. Luke's vivid picture is of the chariot stopping in the shallow water of the spring or wady. **went down**. The Greek term *katebeesan* pertains to dismounting from the chariot, not descent into the water. Observe the use of this term elsewhere (Jg 4:15, LXX. Mt √14:29). Keeler notes that whenever the two words *anabaino* and *katabaino* appear together in context, the motion in all such cases is directly *down* and *up* (R. F. Keeler, *Christian Baptism*, p. 235. Keeler cites numerous examples: *katabaino*: Jg 4:15. Ex 3:8. 19:11. Nu 11:17. Dt 28:24. 2 K 1:11, 12. Ps 72:6. Is 55:10. Ezk 26:16. 27:29. Mt 3:16 (descending). 7:25. √14:29. 27:40. 28:2. Mk 15:32. Lk 9:54. 19:5, 6. 22:44. Jn 3:13. 5:4, 7. *anabaino*: Ge 28:12. Jg 13:20. 1 S 28:13. Ps 24:3. 68:18. √139:8. Is 14:13, 14. Ezk 38:9. Mt 3:16 (went up). 13:7 (sprung up). 17:27 (cometh up). Mk 1:10 (coming up). 6:51 (went up). Lk 19:4 (climbed up). Jn *1:51 (ascending, descending). *3:13. Jn 6:62. 10:1. 20:17. 21:3. Ac 1:13. 2:34. 10:4, 9. Ro 10:6, 7. Ep 4:8-10. Re 7:2. 8:4. 11:7, 12. 14:11). There is no provision in the text for walking away from the chariot several steps or some distance to go into the water: they both dismounted from the chariot directly into the water. However deeply the chariot was in the water, that is how deep Philip and the Eunuch were in the water (see ver. 36n). **both**. Here the argument for immersion fails, for the evidence that the

eunuch was immersed must apply with equal force to Philip, and this no one would maintain. **into the water.** "The implication is, if they stepped down 'into the water' that it was so trifling in depth as to make it unnecessary to change the position of the chariot; certainly no one would step down out of a chariot into water *two feet nine inches* in depth; which they must have done, if at all, at one step, for there is no second step in the record beyond that which brought them out of the chariot" (Dale, p. 186). *katebasan eis to udor* does not require entrance *into* the water: Lk 8:23, a storm of wind came down to, not *into* the lake. Jn 5:4, an angel went down into the pool, and whoever first stepped into, neither phrase requiring a walking step by step into deeper water, or taking anything more than just one step within the water, and their entrance into the water certainly cannot signify that they were immersed. See further on the note to Jn 20:6. **and he baptized.** Thomas Walker notes on Ac 2:41 that "the contention that the Greek word "baptize" always means "immerse" is not borne out by Holy Scripture. For example, it is used in Mk 7:4; Lk 11:38 of pouring water over the limbs; in 1 C 10:1, 2, of the Israelites passing through the Red Sea where they were certainly not immersed; and in Ac 1:8 of the effusion of the Holy Ghost on the disciples" (Comm. on Acts, p. 57). Even if it could be proven that *baptizo* means immerse (and this cannot be proven), this would not satisfy the case, for though the word would then mean to place entirely beneath the water, there is nothing in this Greek verb which allows for being taken back out of the water, a problem which is fatal to the theory. Jn *3:22, 23n. 4:1.

39. **were.** Mt *3:16. Mk 1:10g. **come up.** The same word is used in verse 31 of Philip mounting the chariot, only here it is plural, indicating that both men remounted the chariot, the precise reverse of their both disembarking the chariot discussed in the note on ver. 38. With as much certainty that it can be affirmed that the Ethiopian re-entered the chariot, it can be affirmed that so did Philip, for the term applies equally to both. If the word means that they walked from the deeper to the shallower water, then they are both left standing there, and the chariot went on without them. **out of.** The Greek preposition *ek* does not necessitate the uniform meaning "to come out from within a place, object, group, or substance." The word *ek* also has the sense "from" with no indication of having been within: Mt 12:42, the Queen of Sheba came from (*ek*) the uttermost parts of the earth; Mt 27:38, the thieves crucified on (*ek*) Christ's right hand and left were in no sense prior to the cross "in" or "within" Christ; the preposition *ek* is used here by way of Greek idiom. Mk 11:20, the fig tree dried up from (*ek*) the roots. Lk 1:71, saved from (*ek*) our enemies, and from (*ek*) the hand of all that hate us. Jn 5:24, passed from (*ek*) death unto life. Jn 6:64, Jesus knew from (*ek*) the beginning. Jn 6:66, From (*ek*) that time many of his disciples went back. Jn 8:23, Ye are from (*ek*) beneath. Jn 8:42, For I proceeded forth and came from (*ek*) God. Jn 9:1, He saw a blind man which was blind from (*ek*) his birth. Jn 10:32, Many good works have I showed you from (*ek*) my Father. Jn 12:27, Father, save me from (*ek*) this hour. 12:32, "from the earth" does not specify Christ was in the earth. Jn 13:4, He riseth from (*ek*) supper. Jn 19:23, Now the coat was

without seam, woven from (*ek*) the top throughout. R. F. Keeler remarks, "Do not these passages prove that *from* is *a true* meaning of *ek*? Neither *eis* nor *ek* proves that they were *in the water* at all" (*Christian Baptism*, pp. 232, 233). Ac 12:7, the chains fell off (*ek*) from his hands or wrists: not *out of*, but *from* his hands; they could not have fallen out of, unless he had held them in his hands. Ac 28:3, the viper hung on (*ek*) his hand, and Paul shook it off into the fire (ver. 5). Thus *ek* need indicate no more than that the action of mounting up into the chariot began within the water, even if only the toe of the sandal of Philip or the Eunuch touched the water's edge. The preposition *ek* may therefore have different significations, just as argued for the preposition *eis* and for the same reasons, at Ac 2:38n. If the preposition *ek* can have but a single, uniform meaning, then this proves too much for the case of some who would so argue, for the preposition occurs with two significances at 1 J 2:19, or the case for unconditional "eternal security" generally advocated by many who also accept immersion is demolished, for "they went out from (*ek*) us," showing that they were not "*of* (*ek*) us." But if *ek* means only "out" from being within a place, object, substance, or group, then these individuals must have been *within* the group from which they left in the fullest sense: they thus had been genuine believers who apostatized if *ek* can have no lesser degree of significance in the first clause. See related notes (on *eis*, Ac 2:38n. on *ek*, 1 J 2:19n. Re 3:10n). **the Spirit.** Gr. *pneuma*, Lk +24:37. Ac 5:9. 1 K *18:12. 2 K 2:16. Ezk *3:12-14. 8:3. 11:1, 24. 37:1. 43:5. 2 C 12:2-4. **caught away.** Ac 23:10. Mt 13:19. Jn 10:28, 29. 2 C +12:2, 4. 1 Th 4:17. **and he.** ver. 8. Ac 13:52. 16:34. Ps *9:2. 68:31. 119:14, 111. Is 35:1, 2. √55:12, 13. 56:4-8. 61:10. 66:13, 14. Zp 3:10. Mt +*12:32. 13:44. Ro *5:1, 2. 15:10-13. Ph 3:3. 4:4. Ja 1:9, 10. 4:16.

40. **at Azotus.** i.e. *ravager,* *S#108g, only here. For *S#795h, see Jsh +11:22. 13:3. 15:46, +*47. 1 S 5:1, 5. Ne 4:7. 13:24. Je 25:20. Am 1:8. Zp 2:4. Zc 9:6, Ashdod. **he preached.** ver. 25. Ac 14:7, 21. 16:10. Lk 10:1, 2. Ro 15:19. **Caesarea.** i.e. *a bush of hair; cutting,* *S#2542g. Ac 9:30. 10:1, 24. 11:11. 12:19. 18:22. 21:8, 16. 23:23, 33. 25:1, 4, 6, 13.

ACTS 9

Saul, having sought and obtained letters from the high priest, sets out for Damascus, to persecute the disciples, 1, 2. Drawing near the city, he is surrounded by a light from heaven, and, falling to the earth, hears Jesus expostulating with him, 3-5. He submits, and is led blind to Damascus, where he continues three days, without sight or food, 6-9. Ananias is directed in a vision to go to him; by whom he is restored to sight, and baptized, 10-18. Immediately he preaches in the synagogue, with great boldness, 19-22. The Jews seek to kill him, but he escapes from them, 23-25. He goes to Jerusalem, and is by Barnabas introduced to the apostles, 26-28. Preaching boldly in the name of Jesus, his life is in danger, and he is sent to Tarsus, 29, 30. The church has rest, and is edified and multiplied, 31. Peter heals Eneas at Lydda, 32-35; and at Joppa raises Tabitha from the dead, 36-43.

1. Cir. A.M. 4039. A.D. 35. **Saul.** ver. 11-13, 19-21. Ac 7:58. *8:3. 22:3, 4. 26:9-11. 1 C 15:9. Ga *1:13.

Ph 3:6. 1 T *1:13. **breathing.** Ps 27:12. **and slaughter.** Ac +22:4. **the disciples.** ver. 10, 19, 26, 38. Ac +11:26. **the Lord.** ver. 10, 13, 15, 17, 27, 29, 35, 42. Ac +11:16. **high priest.** ver. 14, 21. Ac 22:5. 26:10.

2. **desired.** ver. 14. Ac 7:19. 22:5. 26:12. Est 3:8-13. Ps 83:2-4. **to Damascus.** i.e. *the sackcloth weaver is silent,* *S#1154g. ver. 3, 8, 10, 19, 22, 27. Ac 22:5, 6, 10, 11. 26:12, 20. For *S#1834h, see Ge +14:15. 15:2. 2 S 8:5, 6. 1 K 11:24. 2 K 8:7. SS 7:4. Is 7:8. 8:4. 10:9. 17:1, 3. Je 49:23, 24, 27. Ezk 47:17, 18. 48:1. Am 1:3, 5. 3:12. 5:27. Zc 9:1. 2 C 11:32g. Ga 1:17g. **to the synagogues.** Ac 6:9. 13:14, 15. 22:19. 28:17-21. Lk 12:11. 21:12. **if.** ʃ184C, Mt +4:9. **of this way.** Gr. of the way. Ac *16:17. *18:25, 26. 19:9, 23. 22:4, 5. *24:14, 22. 28:22. Is 30:21. *35:8. Je 50:5. Am 8:14. Mt +√7:14. Lk *1:79. Jn √14:6. He *10:20. 2 P *2:2, 15, 21.

3. **as.** ver. 17. Ac 22:6. 26:12, 13. 1 C 15:8. **a light.** Ps 104:2. 1 T *6:16. Re *21:23. 22:5.

4. **he fell.** Ac 5:10. Nu 16:45. Jn *18:6. Ro 11:22. 1 C 4:7. **Saul.** Ge 3:9. 16:8. 22:11. Ex 3:4. Lk 10:41. Jn 20:16. 21:15. **Saul.** ʃ84, Ge +22:11. **why.** Ac 22:7, 8. 26:14, 15. Is +*63:9. Zc *2:8. Mt √25:40, 45, etc. 1 C 12:12. Ep +*5:30. Col *1:18. **me.** ʃ121K5. Metonymy of the Subject B583. *Christ* is put for His people. For other instances of this figure see 1 C 12:12. Col 1:24.

5. **Who.** 1 S 3:4-10. 1 T 1:13. **I am.** Ac 26:9. Ge=45:4. **whom thou.** Mt 25:44, 45. Lk 10:16. Jn 5:16. 1 C 8:12. **it is.** ʃ138B, Ge +13:16. Ac +*5:39. Dt 32:15. Jb 9:4. 40:9, 10. Ps 2:12. Is 45:9. 1 C *10:22.

6. **trembling.** Ac 16:29. 24:25, 26. 1 S 28:5. Is 66:2. Hab +*3:16. Ph *2:12. **Lord, what.** Ac *2:37. *16:30. 22:10. Ps *25:4. Lk 3:10. Ro 7:9. 10:3. Ja 4:6. **said.** ʃ63BA, Ge +26:7. **Arise.** ver. 15. Ac 26:16. Ezk 3:22. 16:6-8. Mt 19:30. Ro 5:20. 9:15-24. 10:20. Ga 1:1, 15, 16. 1 T 1:14-16. **and it.** Ac 10:6, 22, 32. 11:13, 14. Ps √25:8, 9, 12. 94:12. Is *57:18. **what.** ver. 16. 1 C 9:16. **must do.** ver. 16. Ac 19:21. 23:11. 26:9. 27:24. Lk 13:33.

7. **the men.** Ac 22:9. 26:13, 14. Da *10:7. Mt 24:40, 41. **hearing.** Ac *22:9. Jn 12:29, 30.

8. **he saw.** ver. 18. Ac 13:11. 22:11. Ge 19:11. Ex 4:11. 2 K 6:17-20.

9. **three days.** ver. 11, 12, 17, 18. 2 Ch 33:12, 13, 18, 19. Est 4:16. Jon 3:6-8.

10. **there.** Ac 22:12. **disciple.** ver. 26, 36. Ac +11:26. 16:1. 19:1. 21:16. Jn 21:23, 24. **Damascus.** ver. +2. **Ananias.** Ac *22:12. **and to.** Ac 2:17. 10:3, 17-20. Nu 12:6. Da 2:19. **the Lord.** ver. +1. **a vision.** Ac 2:17. 10:3, 17, 19. 11:5. 12:9. 16:9, 10. 18:9. 26:19. **Ananias.** ver. 4. **Behold.** Ge 22:1. 31:11. Ex 3:4. 1 S 3:4, 8-10. 2 S 15:26. Is 6:8.

11. **Arise.** Ac 8:26. 10:5, 6. 11:13. **the street.** The street called *Straight,* says Maundrell (Journey, May 3), "is about half a mile in length, running from east to west through the city. It being narrow, and the houses jutting out in several places on both sides, you cannot have a clear prospect of its length and straightness. In this street is shown the house of Judas, with whom Paul lodged; and in the same house is an old tomb, *said* to be Ananias's." **Saul.** ver. 30. Ac 11:25. 21:39. 22:3. **Tarsus.** ver. 30. Ac 11:25. 21:39. 22:3. **for.** Ac 2:21. 8:22. Dt 4:29. 2 Ch *33:12, 13, 18, 19. Jb *33:18-28. Ps 32:3-6. 40:1, 2. +*50:15. 130:1-3. Pr 15:8. Is √55:6, 7. Je *29:12, 13. 31:18-20. Jon 2:1-

4. Zc *12:10. Mt *7:7, 8. Lk +*11:9, 10. 18:7-14. 23:42, 43. Jn 4:10.

12. **hath seen.** ver. 10, 17, 18. **hand on.** ver. 17. Mk +5:23.

13. **Lord.** Ex 4:13-19. 1 S 16:2. 1 K 18:9-14. Je 20:9, 10. Ezk 3:14. Jon 1:2, 3. Mt 10:16. **how.** ver. 1, 2. Ac 8:3. 22:4, 19, 20. 26:10, 11. Is *55:7, 8. 1 T *1:13-15. **thy saints.** ver. 32, 41. Ro 15:25, 26, 31. Col 1:26. 1 Th 3:13. 2 Th 1:10.

14. **here.** ver. 2, 3. **chief priests.** ver. 21. Ac +5:24. **call.** ver. 21. Ac +*7:59g,n. +15:26. *22:16. Ro *10:12-14. 1 C *1:2. 2 T *2:22.

15. **Go.** Ac 22:21g. Ex 4:12-14. Je 1:7. Jon 3:1, 2. **for he.** Ac *13:2. Ro 1:1. Ga 1:15. Ep 3:7. **a chosen.** Ac *13:2. 1 Ch=15:2. Je 1:5. Jn +*15:16. Ro *1:1. 9:21-24. 2 C *4:7. Ga *1:1, 15, 16. 2 T 1:11. 2:4, 20, 21. Re 17:14. **to bear.** Ac 21:19. *22:21. *26:17-20. Ro *1:5, 13-15. 11:13. 15:15-21. 1 C *15:10. Ga 2:7, 8. Ep *3:7, 8. Col 1:25-29. 1 T 2:7. **my name.** Ac √4:12. *10:43. +15:26. Is +*9:6. 42:4. Je +*23:5, 6. Mt *1:21-23. Je √3:18. 1 C *6:11. Ph √2:9, 10. **before the Gentiles.** Ac +13:46. 22:21. 26:17. Ro 1:5g. *11:13. *15:16, 19. Ga 1:16. *2:2, 7-9. Ep 3:7, 8. 1 T 2:7. 2 T 4:17. **and kings.** Ac 25:22-27. 26:1, etc., 32. 27:24. Mt 10:18. 2 T 4:16, 17. **the children.** Ac +5:21. 28:17, etc.

16. **I will.** Ac *20:22, 23. 21:4, 11. Is 33:1. Mt 10:21-25. *19:29. Jn 15:20. 16:1-4. 1 C 4:9-13. 2 C *11:23-27. 1 Th 3:3. 2 T 1:12. 2:9, 10. *3:10-12. Ph *3:8. **must suffer.** ver. 6. Ac 14:22. 2 C 6:4, 5. 11:23-28. **for.** ver. 14. Ac +5:41. Mt +*5:11. +*24:9. 1 P *4:14. Re 1:9.

17. **Ananias went.** Ac 22:12, 13. **the house.** ver. 11. **and putting.** ver. 12. Ac 6:6. +8:17. 13:3. 19:6. Mt 19:13. Mk 6:5. 1 T *4:14. 5:22. 2 T 1:6. He 6:2. **Brother Saul.** ver. 13, 14, 30. Ac +21:20. 22:13. Ge 45:4. Lk 15:30, 32. Ro 15:7. Phm 16. 1 P 1:22, 23. **the Lord.** ver. 4, 5, 10, 11, 15. Ac +*10:36. *11:21n. 22:14. 26:15. Lk 1:16, 17, 76. 2:11. 1 C 15:8, 47. **that thou.** ver. 8, 9, 12. **and be.** See on Ac 2:4. 4:31. 8:17. 13:52.

18. **immediately.** 2 C 3:14. 4:6. **received.** Ac 22:13. **arose.** Ac +*22:16. **and was baptized.** Ac +*2:38, 41. 8:12, 13, 37, 38. +*22:16.

19. **when.** Ac 27:33-36. 1 S 30:12. Ec 9:7. **Then.** Ac *26:19, 20. 1 S 10:10-12. Ga 1:17. **the disciples.** ver. +1. **Damascus.** ver. +2.

20. **straightway.** ver. 27, 28. Ga 1:23, 24. **he preached Christ.** Ac *4:2. *17:18. *26:19, 20. 2 C *4:6. **in the synagogues.** ver. 2. Ac +13:5. **that.** ver. 22. Ac 8:37. 13:33. Ps 2:7, 12. Mt 26:63-66. 27:43, 54. Jn 1:49. 19:7. 20:28, 31. Ro *1:4. Ga √2:20. 1 J *4:14, 15. Re 2:18. **the Son of God.** Ac 8:37n. Mt +14:33. 27:54n.

21. **amazed.** Ac 2:6, 12. 4:13. Nu 23:23. Ps 71:7. Is 8:18. Zc 3:8. 2 Th +*1:10. 1 J *3:1. **Is not.** Ac 3:10. Mt +*13:54, 55. Mk 5:15-20. Jn 9:8, 9. **destroyed.** ver. 1, 2, 13, 14. Ac *8:3. *22:19. Ga *1:13-24. **which called.** ver. +14.

22. **But.** ʃ106, Ge +31:7. **increased.** Ge 49:24. Jb 17:9. Ps 84:7. Is 40:29. 2 C √12:9, 10. Ph √4:13. 1 T +1:12g. **confounded.** Ac +2:6. 6:9, 10. 18:27, 28. Lk 21:15. 1 C 1:27. **proving.** Ac 16:10g. √17:3. *18:5, 28. 28:23. Lk +*24:44, 45. 1 C 2:16g. Ga *1:11, 12. **this is.** ver. 20. Ac +18:5.

23. Cir. A.M. 4040. A.D. 36. **many days.** 1 K 2:38,

39. Ga *1:17, 18. **the Jews.** ver. 16. Ac 13:50. 14:2, 19. 22:21-23. 23:12. 25:2, 3. Jsh 10:1-6. Mt 10:16-23. 2 C 11:26. 1 Th *2:15, 16.

24. **their laying wait.** ver. 29, 30. Ac 14:5, 6. √17:10-15. 20:3, 19. 23:12-21, 30. 25:3, 11. Jg 16:2, 3. 2 C *11:32. **And they watched.** Ps 21:11. *37:32, 33. 2 C 11:32, 33. **day and night.** Lk +18:7.

25. **the disciples.** Maundrel states (Journey, April 29), that after visiting *the place of vision,* "about half a mile distant from the city eastward," they returned to the city, and "were shown the gate where St. Paul was let down in a basket. This gate is at present walled up, by reason of its vicinity to the east gate, which renders it of little use." ver. 30. Mt +10:23. **let.** Jsh *2:15. 1 S *19:11, 12. 2 C 11:33.

26. **when.** √106, Ge +31:7. Ac 22:17-20. 26:20. Ga *1:17-19. **he assayed.** ver. 19. Ac 4:23. **but.** Mt 10:17-19. 24:10. 2 C +*6:9. Ga 2:4. **was.** lit. is. √96C5, Mt +2:13.

27. **Barnabas.** Ac +4:36. 11:22, 25. 12:25. *13:1, 2. 15:2, 25, 26, 35-39. 1 C 9:6. Ga 2:9, 13. **and brought.** Jn 1:40-42. Ga 1:18, 19. T +*1:8. He 13:2. 1 P +*4:9. 3 J ◐*9. **the apostles.** Ac +5:12. Ga 1:18, 19. **how he had seen.** ver. 3-6, 17. 1 C 15:8. **and how.** ver. 20-22. Ac 4:13, 29. Ep 6:19, 20. **Damascus.** ver. +2. **preached boldly.** Ac +4:13. **in the name.** Ac +3:6.

28. **coming.** Ac +1:21. Nu 27:16, 17. 2 S 5:2. 1 K 3:7. Ps 121:8. Jn *10:9. Ga 1:18.

29. **he spake boldly.** ver. 20-22, +27. Ac +4:13. **in the name.** Ac +2:21. **the Lord.** ver. 1. **disputed.** Ac 6:9, 10. 17:17. 18:19. 19:8. Ju 3, 9. **Grecians.** Ac 6:1. 11:20. **but.** ver. 23. Ac 22:18. 2 C 11:26.

30. **when.** ver. 24, 25. Ac 17:10, 15. Mt 10:23. **the brethren.** Jn +21:23. **Caesarea.** Ac +8:40. or, Mt 16:13. **Tarsus.** i.e. *hardness; flat basket,* *S#5019g. ver. +11. Ac 11:25g. *21:39. 22:3g. Ga 1:21.

31. **the churches.** Ac 5:11. *8:1. 16:5. Dt 12:10. Jsh 21:44. Jg 3:30. 1 Ch 22:9, 18. Ps 94:13. Pr +*16:7. Is 11:10. Zc 9:1. He 4:9. **were edified.** Ac 20:32. Ro 14:19. 1 C 3:9-15. 14:4, 5, 12, 26. 2 C 10:8. 12:19. 13:10. Ep 4:12, 16, 29. 1 Th 5:11. 1 T 1:4. Ju 20. **and walking.** √93B, Is +66:11. Here, in the Received Text, the verbs are not in the same inflection. But the Critical Texts (Lachman, Tischendorf, Tregelles, Alford, Wescott and Hort, and R.V.) are, making this an instance of *Hendiadys,* "being built up and progressing": i.e. being built up, yes—and increasingly so too (B671). Ne 5:9, 15. Jb 28:28. Ps 19:9. 86:11. 111:10. Pr +*1:7. 8:13. 9:10. 14:26, 27. 16:6. 23:17. Is 11:2, 3. 33:6. Lk 1:6. 2 C 5:11. *7:1. Ep 5:21. Col +√1:10. **the fear.** Ac +10:2. **and in.** Jn *14:16-18. Ro *5:5. 8:15-17. *14:17. 15:13. Ga √5:22, 23. Ep *1:13, 14. *6:18, 19. Ph 2:1. 2 Th 2:16, 17. **the comfort.** Jn 14:16. 1 C +14:3. **were multiplied.** ver. 35, 42. Ac 6:+1, 7. 12:24. Est 8:16, 17. Zc +*8:20-23.

32. Cir. A.M. 4041. A.D. 37. **as Peter.** Ac +*1:8. 8:14, 25. Ga 2:7-9. **the saints.** ver. 13, 41. Ac 26:10. Ps 16:3. Pr 2:8. Mt 27:52. Ro 1:7. 2 C 1:1. Ep 1:1. Ph 1:1. Re 8:3. **Lydda.** i.e. *strife, travail; nativity, birthplace,* *S#3069g. ver. 35, 38. For *S#3850h, see Ne +7:37, Lod. 1 Ch 8:12. Ezr 2:33. Ne 7:37. 11:35.

33. **Aeneas.** i.e. *laudable, praiseworthy, famous,* *S#132g. ver. 34. **which.** Ac 3:2. 4:22. 14:8. Mk 5:25. 9:21. Lk 13:16. Jn 5:5. 9:1, 21. **and was.** Mk 2:3-11.

34. **Jesus Christ.** Ac *3:6, 12, 16. *4:8-10. 16:18.

Mt 8:3. 9:6, 28-30. Jn 2:11. **bed.** √63A2, 2 S +6:6.

35. **all.** ver. 31, 42. Ac 4:4. 5:12-14. 6:7. 19:10, 20. Ps 110:3. Is 66:8. **Lydda.** ver. 32. **Saron.** i.e. *his song; rightness,* *S#4565g, only here. For *S#8289h, see Is +35:2, Sharon. 1 Ch 5:16. 27:29. SS 2:1. Is 33:9. 35:2. 65:10. **turned.** ver. 42. Ac +*3:19. 11:16, 21. 14:15. 15:19. *21:21. 26:18-20. Dt 4:30. Ps 22:27. Is 31:6. La 3:40. Ho 12:6. 14:2. Jl 2:13. Mt 18:3. Lk 1:16, 17. 2 C 3:16. 1 Th 1:9, 10.

36. **Joppa.** ver. 38, 42, 43. Ac 10:5, 8, 23, 32. 11:5, 13. Jsh 19:46. 2 Ch 2:16. Ezr 3:7. Jon 1:3. **disciple.** ver. +10. **Tabitha.** i.e. *gazelle; clear-sighted,* *S#5000g. ver. 40. **interpretation.** √95, Ps +7:13. Mk +5:41. **Dorcas.** or, Doe, or, Roe. *S#1393g. ver. 39. Pr 5:19. SS 2:9. 3:5. 8:14. **full.** Jn *15:5, 8. Ro 13:3. 2 C 9:8. Ep √2:10. Ph *1:11. Col +√1:10. 1 Th 4:10. 2 Th 2:17. 1 T *2:9, 10. 5:10. +6:18. 2 T 2:21. 3:17. T 1:16. 2:7, 14. √3:8. He *13:21. Ja 1:27. **almsdeeds.** Ac 10:4, 31. 24:17g. Mt 6:2, 3.

37. **she was.** Jn 11:3, 4, 36, 37. **they.** √96G1. Heterosis of Gender B533: the Masculine for the Feminine. "They" is masculine in gender (in the Greek), though the reference is to women. For another instance of this figure see He 9:16, *17. **washed.** Jn +13:10. **upper chamber.** ver. 39. Ac +1:13. 20:8. Mk 14:15.

38. **Lydda.** ver. 32, 36. **the disciples.** ver. +1. **desiring.** 2 K 4:28-30. **delay.** or, be grieved. Nu 22:16.

39. **upper chamber.** ver. +37. **and all.** ver. 41. Ac 8:2. 2 S 1:24. Pr 10:7. 1 Th 4:13. **and showing.** ver. 36. Ac +*20:35. Jb 31:19, 20. Pr *31:30, 31. Mt 25:36-39. 26:11. Mk 14:8. Jn 12:8. 2 C 8:12. Ep 4:28. 1 Th 1:3. Ja √2:15-17. 1 J *3:18. **while.** Ec +*9:10. Mt 17:17. Lk +*24:44. Jn 17:12.

40. **put them.** Mt *9:25. Mk 5:40. 9:25. Lk 8:54. **and kneeled.** Ac *7:60. 20:36. 21:5. Lk 22:41. Ep 3:14. **and prayed.** 1 K *17:19-23. 2 K *4:32-36. Mt 9:25. Ja *5:15. **said.** Mt 10:8. 11:5. Mk *5:41. Lk 7:14, 22. 8:54. Jn 11:43. **she opened.** Mk *5:41, 42. Jn *11:43, 44. **sat up.** Lk 7:15.

41. **he gave.** Ac 3:7. Mk +1:31. **the saints.** ver. +32. **widows.** Ac 6:1. Jb 29:13. Ps 146:9. Lk 7:12. **he presented.** Ac 20:12. Ge 45:26. 1 K 17:23. Lk 7:15.

42. **and many.** ver. 35. Ac 11:21. 19:17, 18. Jn 11:4, *45. 12:11, 44. **believed.** Ac +*10:43. **the Lord.** Ac +11:16.

43. **Joppa.** i.e. *lovely,* *S#2445g. ver. 36, 38, 42. Ac 10:5, 8, 23, 32. 11:5, 13. For *S#3305h, see 2 Ch +2:16. **one.** Ac 10:6, 32.

ACTS 10

Cornelius, a devout centurion in Caesarea but a Gentile, being directed by an angel, sends for Peter to instruct him, 1-8; who in the mean time is prepared by a vision, 9-16; and, being commanded by the Spirit, he, attended by certain disciples, accompanies the messengers, 17-23. Cornelius renders undue honor to Peter, who declines it, 24-26; and shows the occasion of his sending for him, avowing the readiness of himself and his friends to receive the word of God from him, 27-33. Peter preaches to them Jesus, and salvation by faith in him, 34-43. The Holy Spirit is poured out on the company, as on the apostles on the day of Pentecost; and Peter commands them to be baptized, 44-48.

1. Cir. A.M. 4045. A.D. 41. **in Caesarea.** ver. 24n. Ac +8:40. 21:8. 23:23, 33. 25:1, 13. **Cornelius.** i.e.

of horn; a sunbeam, ✳S#2883g. ver. 3, 7, 17, 21, 22, 24, 25, 30, 31. **a centurion.** ver. 22. Ac 21:32. 22:25, 26. 23:17, 23. 24:23. 27:1, 6, 11, 31, 43. 28:16. Mt +8:5, etc. 27:54. Lk 7:2. **Italian.** ✳S#2483g, only here. The *Italian band,* or rather "cohort," *speira,* (a regiment sometimes consisting of 555 to 1105 infantry), is not unknown to the Roman writers (see Tacitus, l. i. c. 59. l. ii. c. 41) and Gruter (Inscriptions, p. ccccxxxiii-iv.) gives an inscription in which it is mentioned, which was found in the Forum Sempronii, on a fine marble table. Ac 21:31. 27:1. Mt 27:27. Mk 15:16. Jn 18:3, 12.

2. **devout.** ver. 7, 22. Ac 2:5. +3:12g. 8:2. 13:50. 16:14. 22:12. Lk 2:25. 2 P 2:9g. **one that feared.** ver. 35. Ac 9:31. 13:16, 26. 1 K 8:43. 2 Ch 6:33. Jb 1:1. Ps *25:12. 102:15. Ec 7:18. Is 59:19. Da 6:26. Re +11:18. 15:4. **with all.** T#1242. ver. 7. Ac +11:14. 16:15. 18:8. Ge +*18:19. 35:1-3. Jsh √24:15. 1 S 1:19. 2 Ch 20:12, 13. Jb *1:5. Ps *101:2, 4-8. Zc 12:10-14. Lk 4:38, 39. **house.** ∫121J4, Ge +7:1. **gave much alms.** ∫121C1B, Ge +20:13. T#1245. ver. 4, 22, +31 (T#1219). Ac 9:36. Dt 26:12, 13. Ps *41:1. Pr +*11:25. Is 58:6-11. Lk 7:4, 5. 11:41n, 42n. Ro 15:26, 27. 2 C *9:8-15. **to the people.** Ac 2:47. 3:23. 12:4, 11. 21:28. 26:17, 23. 28:17. Jn 11:50. **and prayed.** Ac 9:11. Ps √25:5, 8, 9. 55:17. 86:3mg. 88:1. 119:2. Pr 2:3-5. Da *6:10, 16, 20. Mt *7:7, 8. Lk +*11:9, 10. +*18:1. Jn +√9:31. Col *4:2. 1 Th +*5:17. Ja +*1:5.

3. **saw.** ver. 17, 19. Ac +9:10. Jb 4:15, 16. Da 9:20, 21. **ninth hour.** ∫49, Jn +10:22. Our 3 p.m. ver. 30. Ac *3:1. Mt +*20:5. 27:46. Lk 23:44n-46. Jn +*11:9n. **an angel.** Ac +5:19. 11:13. 12:7-11. 27:23. Lk 1:11. 2:10, 11, 13. He *1:4, 14. **Cornelius.** Ac 9:4. Ex 33:17. Is 45:4.

4. **looked.** Ac +3:4. **he was.** Da *10:11. Lk *1:11, 12, 29, 30. *24:5. **What.** Ac 9:5, 6. 22:10. 1 S 3:10. **Thy prayers.** ver. 31. 2 Ch 6:33. 32:24. Ps 141:2. Is 43:26. Ml √3:16. Lk 1:13. Jn +*9:31. Ph *4:6. **thine alms.** ∫121C1B, Ge +20:13. T#407. ver. +31 (T#1219). Ac +4:32 (T#661). Jb +31:32 (T#355). Is 45:19. Lk +10:33 (T#414). +*11:41mg,n. Ph *4:18. He +*6:10. *13:16. Ja 2:17. **come up.** Ge 18:21. Ex 2:23. Ps 141:2. Da *10:11, 12. Lk 1:10. Re 5:8. 8:3, 4. **memorial.** ver. 31. Ph 4:18. He +*6:10.

5. **send.** ver. 32. Ac 9:38. 15:7. 16:9. **Joppa.** Ac +9:36. **whose.** Mk 3:16. Jn 1:42.

6. **one.** Ac 9:43. **he shall.** Ac *9:6. *11:13, 14. Jn +*7:17. Ro *10:14-17. Ep *4:8-12. **oughtest to do.** Ac 2:37, 38. 16:30, 31. 22:16.

7. **two.** ver. 2. Ge 24:1-10, 52. Jg 7:10. 1 S 14:6, 7. 1 T 6:2. Phm 16. **household.** Lk 16:13. Ro 14:4. 1 P 2:18. **and a.** ver. 1, 2. Mt 8:9, 10. Lk 3:14. **devout soldier.** Lk +*3:14n. 1 C √7:20.

8. **he sent.** ver. 33. Ac 26:19. Ps *119:59, 60. Ec +*9:10. Ga 1:16.

9. **Peter.** ver. 8. Ac 11:5-10. 1 S 9:25. Zp 1:5. Mt 6:6. Mk +*1:35. 6:46. 1 T *2:8. **housetop.** T#1197. Dt 22:8. 1 S 9:25. 2 S 11:2. 16:22. 2 K 23:12. Ne 8:16. Je 19:13. 32:29. Zp 1:5. Mt 10:27. 24:17. Mk 13:15. Lk 5:19. 12:3. 17:31. **the sixth hour.** ∫49, Jn +10:22. Our 12 noon. Ac 6:4. Ps +*55:17. Da +*6:10. Mt +*20:5. 27:45. Jn +*11:9n. Ep *6:18.

10. **he became.** Mt 4:2. 12:1-3. 21:18. **ready.** ∫63A2, 2 S +6:6. Supply by ellipsis (absolute: of accusative), "made ready (the food)." **he fell.** Ac 22:17. Nu 24:4, 16. Ezk 8:1-3. 11:24. 40:2. 2 C 12:2-4. Re *1:10. 4:2,

---

3. **trance.** T#1778. Ac 11:5. 13:17-21. 22:17. 2 C 12:2, 3.

11. **saw.** Ac *7:55, 56. Ezk 1:1. Lk 3:21. Jn +*1:51. Re *4:1. 11:19. *19:11. **and a.** Ge +*49:10. Is *11:6-14. 19:23-25. 43:6. *56:8. Mt +*8:11. 13:47, 48. Jn +*10:16. +*11:52. *12:32. Ro √1:16. *3:29-31. 9:4. 15:9-12. 16:25, 26. Ga 2:15. √3:28. Ep *1:10. *2:14. √3:6. √4:4. Col √3:11. **vessel.** The word *skeuos,* which corresponds to the Hebrew *kelee,* denotes every kind of *vessel* or *utensil,* any thing which may be considered as a receptacle; and is therefore applicable to a *sheet, othonee,* or any thing woven from flax, tied up at the four corners, which our word *vessel* is not (compare note at Ac 2:38).

12. **all.** √∫171B, Ge +24:10. ∫108B, Mt +4:23. **manner of.** Ge 7:8, 9. Is *11:6-9. 65:25. Jn 7:37. 1 C +*6:9-11. Ep *1:10. **fourfooted.** ∫171E8. Synecdoche of the Genus B621. *Quadrupeds* (Gr. *tetropoda*) is used for *tame* or *domestic* animals which are classed off, as distinct from "wild beasts" which are also "fourfooted." **creeping things.** Ac 11:6. Ro 1:23. Ja 3:7. **fowls.** Mt 6:26. 8:20. 13:32. Mk 4:32. Lk 8:5. 9:58. 13:19.

13. **Rise.** ver. 10. Je 35:2-5. Jn 4:31-34. **kill.** Or, "sacrifice and eat," *thuson kai phage.* The spirit of the heavenly direction seems to be this, says Dr. A. Clarke, "The middle wall of partition (Ep 2:14) is now pulled down; the Jews and Gentiles are called to become one flock (Jn +*10:16), under one shepherd and bishop of souls (1 P 2:25). Thou, Peter, shalt open the door (Mt +*16:19n. 18:18n) of faith to the *Gentiles,* and also be the minister of circumcision (Ro 15:8). Rise up; already a blessed sacrifice is prepared: go and offer it to God; and let thy soul feed on the fruits of his mercy," etc.

14. **Not.** Ge 19:18. Ex 10:11. Mt 16:22. 25:9. Lk 1:60. **for.** Le ch. 11. 20:25. Dt ch. 14. Ezk 4:14. 44:31. Da +*1:8. **common.** ver. 28. Mk +7:2. **unclean.** Le *11:2-47. *20:25. Dt 14:4-20.

15. **spake.** ∫63BA, Ge +26:7. **What.** ver. 28. Ac 11:9. 15:9, 20, 29. Mt 15:11. Mk 7:15, 19. Ro 14:2, 14-17, 20. 1 C 10:25, 26. Ga 2:12, 13. Ep *2:14. 1 T √4:3-5. T *1:15. He 9:9, 10. **God hath.** ∫108A3, Is +6:10. **cleansed.** ∫121I2, Ge +2:17.

16. **thrice.** Ge √41:32. Jn 21:17. 2 C 13:1.

17. **while.** ver. 19. Ac 2:12. 5:24. 25:20. Lk 9:7. Jn 13:12. 1 P 1:11. **vision.** ver. 3. Ac +9:10. **should mean.** ∫184D2, Lk +1:62. **the men.** ver. 7, 8. Ac 9:43. **the gate.** Ac 12:13, 14. 14:13. Mt 26:71. Lk 16:20. Re 21:12, 13, 15, 21, 25. 22:14.

18. **and asked.** ver. 5, 6. Ac 11:11.

19. **the Spirit.** Gr. *pneuma,* Lk +24:37. **said.** +8:29n. 11:12. 13:2. 16:6, 7. 21:4. Mt 12:32n. Jn +*16:13n, 14n. 1 C 12:11. 1 T 4:1. **three men seek.** ver. 7, 17.

20. **and get.** Ac 8:26. 9:15. 15:7-9. Mk *16:15. **doubting.** Ac 11:2. Mt 21:21. Mk 11:23. Ro 4:20. 14:23. Ja 1:6. 2:4. Ju 9, 22g. **for.** Ac 9:17. 13:4. Is 48:16. Zc 2:9-11.

21. **Behold.** Jn 1:38, 39. 18:4-8. **what.** ver. 29. Mk 10:51.

22. **Cornelius.** ver. 1-5. **a just.** ∫46C, Mt +8:6. Gr. *dikaios,* which is an adjective, and means strictly *righteous,* is used generally for *a good man,* like the Hebrew *tzaddeek,* which has both meanings. See Lk 1:6; 2:25. Ac 24:15. Ho 14:9. Hab 2:4. Mt 1:19. Mk 6:20. Lk 2:25. 23:50. Ro +*1:17. He *10:38. *12:23. **feareth**

God. ver. +2. **of good report.** Ac +6:3. 22:12. Lk 7:4, 5. 1 T 3:7. He 11:2. 3 J 12. **the nation.** Ac 24:2, 10, 17. 26:4. 28:19. Jn +11:50. **was warned.** Ac 11:26. Mt 2:12, 22g. Mt +*7:14. Lk 2:26g. Ro 7:3. +*11:22. 2 C +*5:11. Col *1:28. He *2:3. 8:5g. *11:7g. 12:25g. 1 P *4:18. **holy angel.** Mk 8:38. Lk 9:26. Ju 14. Re 14:10. **and to hear.** ver. 6, 33. Ac 11:14. Jb +*37:2. Lk +*8:18. +*11:28. Jn √5:24. *6:63, 68. 13:20. 17:8, 20. Ro √10:17, 18. 2 C 5:18-20. 2 P 3:2.

23. **and lodged.** Ge 19:2, 3. 24:31, 32. Jg 19:19-21. He *13:2. 1 P 4:9. **on.** ver. 29, 33. Ec +*9:10. **and certain.** ver. 45. Ac 9:38, 42. 11:12. Jn +21:23. 2 C 8:21. **Joppa.** Ac +9:36.

24. **the morrow.** ver. 9. **Caesarea.** This city, once an obscure fortress called *Strato's Tower*, was built and superbly decorated by Herod the Great, and called *Caesarea*, in honor of Augustus Caesar, to whom he dedicated it in the 28th year of his reign (Josephus, Ant. l. xv. xvi.). It was situated on the shore of the Mediterranean, between Joppa and Dora, with a haven, rendered by Herod the most convenient on the coast: according to Ibn Idris and Abulfeda, 30 miles from Jaffa, or Joppa, 32 from Ramlay, and 36 from Acco, or Ptolemais; and according to Josephus, 600 stadia, or 75 miles, from Jerusalem (Ant. l. xiii. c. 19. Bel. l. i. c. 3), though the real distance is probably not more than 62 miles. Nothing now remains of the former splendor of Caesarea: the supposed sites of the ancient edifices are mere mounds of indefinable form; the waves wash the ruins of the mole, the tower, and the port; the whole of the surrounding country is a sandy desert; and not a creature except beasts of prey, resides within many miles of this silent desolation (See Buckingham's *Travels*, pp. 126-138, and Dr. E. D. Clarke's *Travels*, P. II. c. 18, pp. 645-647). ver. 1. Ac +8:40. **called together.** Is +*2:3. Mi 4:2. Zc 3:10. +*8:20-23. Mt 9:9, 10. Mk 5:19, 20. Lk 5:29. 15:6, 9. Jn 1:41-49. 4:28, 29. 1 J *1:1-3.

25. **and fell.** Ac 14:11-13. 16:29. Da 2:30, 46, 47. Mt +*8:2. ◑+*14:33. Re +*19:10. +*22:8, 9. **and worshipped.** Ac +*7:59n. *14:11-15. Mt +8:2. 18:26. Jn +*20:29n.

26. **Stand.** Ac ◑+*7:59n. ◑√12:22, 23. √14:14, 15. Is √42:8. 48:13. Mt √4:10. Jn ◑+*20:29n. 2 Th *2:3, 4. Re *13:8. +*19:10. +*22:8, 9.

27. **he talked.** Ac +20:11. **and found.** ver. 24. Ac 14:27. Jn 4:35, 36. 1 C 16:9. 2 C 2:12. Col 4:3.

28. **that it.** Ac *11:2, 3. 22:21, 22. Jn *4:9, 27. *18:28. Ga *2:12-14. 1 P 4:3g. **come unto.** Ac 5:13. Lk 7:6. **another nation.** Dt *7:1-3. **but.** ver. 14, 15, 34, 35. Ac 11:9. *15:8, 9. Is +*65:5n. Lk *18:11. Ro *12:3. Ep √3:6, 7. +*4:4. Ph +*2:3.

29. **as soon.** ver. 19, 20. Ps *119:60. 1 P √3:15. **I ask.** ver. 21. **intent.** Gr. logos. lit. word. ſ108B, Lk +1:2.

30. **Four.** ver. 7-9, 23, 24. **I was fasting.** ver. 3. Ezr 9:4, 5. Ne 9:1-3. Da 9:20, 21. Ja *4:8. **ninth hour.** Our 3 p.m. ver. +*3. Mt +*20:5. Jn +*11:9n. **in my house.** T#1195. Ac *12:11, 12. Lk 4:38, 39. 10:38-40. **and, behold.** Ac *1:10. Da *9:21-23. Mt *28:3. Mk 16:5. Lk *24:4. **bright clothing.** Lk 23:11. Ja 2:2, 3g. Re 15:6. 19:8.

31. **thy prayer is heard.** ver. +4. Is +*38:5. Da +*9:23. *10:12. Lk 1:13. Jn +√9:31. **thine alms.** T#1219. ver. +*4. Dt 26:12, 13. Is *58:6-11. **had in remembrance.** ver. 4. Le 2:2, 9. 5:12. Mt 5:45. *10:42.

*25:34-40. Lk 6:35. Ph 4:18. He +*6:10. Re 5:8. 8:3, 4. **in the sight.** Dt 6:18. 12:25. 2 K 12:2. 2 Ch *26:4. 1 Th 1:3. 1 T 2:3. He *13:21. 1 J 3:22.

32. **Send therefore.** ver. 5-8. **Joppa.** Ac +9:36. **is lodged.** ver. 6.

33. **Immediately.** Ps *119:60. Ec +*9:10. **well done.** 2 P 1:19. 3 J 6. **are we.** Ac √17:11, 12. 28:28. Dt 5:25-29. 2 Ch 30:12. Pr 1:5. 9:9, 10. 18:15. 25:12. Mt 18:4. 19:30. Mk 10:15. 1 C *3:18. Ga 4:14. 1 Th √2:13. Ja *1:19, 21. 1 P √2:1, 2.

34. **opened.** ſ108H6A, Jg +11:35. Ac 8:35. Mt +5:2. Ep 6:19, 20. **perceive.** ſ121C2A1, Jb +19:25. **God is.** ver. 28. Ac 15:19. Dt 1:17. Ro 3:29. **no respecter.** Dt +*10:17. 16:19. 2 Ch 19:7. Jb 34:19. Ps 82:1, 2. Mt 22:16. Mk 12:14. Lk 20:21. Ro *2:10, 11. Ga *2:6. Ep 6:9. Col 3:11, 25. Ja 2:4, 9. 1 P 1:17. **of persons.** Ex +*23:2, 3. Le √19:15. Dt 1:17. 16:19. Pr 18:5. 24:23. 28:21. Ml 2:9. Ja 2:1, 9. Ju √16.

35. **in every nation.** Ac 15:9. Is 56:3-8. Ro 2:13, 25-29. *3:19-22, 29, 30. √10:12, 13. 1 C +*12:13. Ga √3:28. Ep *2:13-18. *3:6-8. Ph 3:3. Col *1:6, 23-27. √3:11. **feareth.** ver. +*2. Ac 9:31. Jb 28:28. Ps 19:9. 85:9. 111:10. Pr +*1:7. 2:5. *3:7. *8:13. 16:6. Ec √12:13. Ro ◑+*2:6-16. 2 C *7:1. Ep 5:21. 1 J 2:29. **worketh righteousness.** Ps *15:2. Is √64:5. Ro +*2:10. ◑√4:5. He *11:4-6. Ja √2:17. **is accepted.** Ge 4:5-7. Ps √50:23. *107:9. Ho 8:13. Mi +*6:8. Lk 1:28mg. 4:19, +24. 1 C +*12:13. 2 C 6:2. Ep *1:6. Ph 4:18. He √11:4-6.

36. **The word.** ſ15A, Lk +21:6. Ac +*2:38, 39. *3:25, 26. +8:4. *11:19. *13:26, 46. Ps 107:20. 147:15, 18, 19. Mt *10:6. Lk +*24:47. **children of Israel.** Ac +5:21. **preaching peace.** Ps 72:1-3, 7. 85:9, 10. Is +*9:6. 32:15-17. 52:7. 55:12. *57:19. Na 1:15. Lk *2:10-14. Ro *5:1. 10:15. 2 C √5:18-21. Ep √2:13-18. *4:3-6. 6:15. Col *1:20. He *7:2, 3. *13:20. **he is Lord of all.** Ac *2:36. 5:31. √17:24. Ps *2:6-8. *24:7-10. +*45:6, 11. *110:1, 2. Is +*7:14. *45:21-25. Je +*23:5, 6. Da +*7:13, 14. Ho 1:7. Mi +*5:2. Ml *3:1. Mt +*11:27. *22:44-46. *28:18. Jn √3:35, 36. √5:23-29. +√20:28. Ro √10:9-13. *14:9. 1 C √2:8. √15:27, 47. Ep *1:20-23. 4:5-12. Ph √2:11. Col +√1:15-18. He *1:2, 6-12. 1 P *3:22. Re +*1:5, 18. √17:14. *19:16.

37. **ye know.** Ac +2:22. 26:26. 28:22. **which.** Lk 4:14. 23:5. **began.** Lk +*24:27. **from Galilee.** Mt 4:12. Mk 1:14. Lk 4:14. Jn 4:43. **after.** Ac 1:22. 13:24, 25. Mt 3:1-3. 4:12. Mk *1:1-5, 14, 15. Jn 4:1-3. **the baptism.** ſ171S3, Ac +1:22.

38. **How God.** Jn *3:2. 8:29. 14:10. **anointed.** ſ22D5L, Ps +45:7. Ac *2:22. *4:26, 27. Ps *2:2, 6mg. +*✳45:7. Is ✳*11:2. 42:1. ✳61:1-3. Mt +*3:16. 12:28. Mk 1:10. Lk √3:22. +*4:18. Jn +*3:34. *6:27. 10:36-38. He *1:9. **Jesus of Nazareth.** Ac +2:22. Mt +2:23. **with the.** Ge=41:38. **Ghost.** Gr. *pneuma*, Mt +1:18n. Ac 1:2. Ge +1:2. Mt 12:28. Lk 4:18. Jn 1:32. Ro 1:4. **with power.** Lk 6:19. **who went.** 2 Ch 17:9. Mt 4:23-25. 9:35. 12:15. 15:21-31. Mk 1:38, 39. 3:7-11. 6:6, 54-56. Lk 7:10-17, 21-23. 9:56. 1 P ◑5:8. **healing.** Ex +*23:25. Mt 4:24. +*8:17. √12:15. Mk 5:13-15. 7:29, 30. Lk 4:33-36. 9:42. He √2:14, 15. 1 J √3:8. **oppressed.** Mt +4:24. 8:16. **for God.** Jn *3:2. +8:29. 10:32, 38. 16:32.

39. **And we.** ſ77, Ex +3:19. In reference to "ye" of ver. 37, to which this has the force of *Epitasis*, or emphatic addition (Bengel, *N.T. Word Studies*, vol. 1, p. 820). **are witnesses.** ver. 41. Ac +*1:8, 22.

+*2:24n, 32. 3:15. *5:30-32. 13:31. Lk 1:2. 24:48. Jn *15:27. **whom they slew.** Ac *2:23, 24. 3:14, 15. 4:10. +5:30. 7:52. 13:27-29. Ga +*3:13. 1 P *2:24. **a tree.** Jn 19:6n. 20:25n.

40. **God raised.** Ac +*2:24n. 13:30, 31. √17:31. Mt *28:1, 2. Ro *1:4. 4:24, 25. √6:4-11. +*8:11. 14:9. 1 C √15:3, 4, 12-20. 2 C 4:14. He *13:20. 1 P *1:21. **third day.** Mt *12:40n. Lk +9:22. 23:44n. 1 C +*15:4. **showed him openly.** Ac +*1:3.

41. **Not to all.** ver. 39. Ac *1:2, 3, 22. *13:31. Mt ✱*23:39. Jn 14:17, 19, 21, *22. 15:27. ch. *20, *21. **witnesses.** ver. +*39. **chosen before.** Jn +*15:16. **even to us.** Ac 1:4. Lk *24:30, 41-43. Jn *21:13.

42. **he commanded.** Ac +*1:8. +*4:19, 20. +*5:20, 29-32. Mt +*28:19, 20. Mk +*16:15, 16. Lk *24:47, 48. Jn 21:21, 22. **to testify.** Lk +*16:28. **it is he.** Ac √17:31. 24:25. Mt +*16:27n. 25:31-46. Jn √5:22-29. Ro *14:9, 10. 2 C *5:10. 2 T *4:1, 8. 1 P 4:5. Re +*1:7. √20:11-15. 22:12. **ordained of God.** Lk +22:22g. Ac √17:31. **the Judge.** Mt +√10:15n. Jn √5:22. Ac √17:31. **of quick.** Mt 25:31-46. 2 T 4:1. 1 P 4:5. Re 19:20. **and dead.** Jn *5:21. Ro *14:9, 10. 1 Th √4:15-17. 2 T √4:1. 1 P *4:5. Re 20:5, 12-15.

43. **To him.** Ac 26:22. Is *53:11. Je *31:34. 33:8. Da *9:24. Mi √7:18. Zc *13:1. Ml *4:2. Lk +√24:25-27, 44-46. Jn *1:45. +√5:39, 40. Ro 3:21. 1 P *1:11. Re *19:10. **all the prophets.** Ac 3:18, 24. Mt 11:13. Lk 11:50. 13:28. +*24:27. **witness.** Ac 5:32. Jn 1:7, 32. Ro 1:4. **through his name.** ♪121T1, Dt +28:58. Ac 3:16. √4:10-12. +15:26. Jn √20:31. Ro *5:1. √6:23. He *13:20. 1 J 2:12. **whosoever.** Ac 2:39. 11:17. 13:39. 15:9. Ro 9:33. 10:11. Ga 3:22. 1 T √2:4. 2 P √3:9. Re √22:17. **believeth.** Ac 9:42. 11:17. *13:38, 39. 14:23. 15:9. √16:31. 19:4. 22:19. *26:18. Mk +*16:16. Jn √3:14-17. +4:39. √5:24. *6:69. Ro 8:1, 34. 10:11, 14. **shall receive.** Ro √6:23. Ga *3:22. Ep √2:8. **remission of sins.** Ac +*2:38. Mt *26:28. Lk *7:48, 50. Ep *1:7. Col *1:14.

44. **the Holy.** Ac *2:2-4. 4:31. 8:15-17. 11:15. 15:8. 19:6. 1 Th 1:5. **Ghost.** Gr. *pneuma,* ♪121A1, Lk +1:17n. Ge +1:2. **fell.** Ac 8:16. 11:15. **the word.** ♪108B, Lk +1:2. Ac +8:4.

45. **they of.** ver. 23. Ac 11:2, 3, 15-18. Ga *3:13, 14. **which believed.** Ac +13:12. **the Gentiles.** Is ✱11:10. ✱42:1. Ga 2:15. Ep 2:11, 12. *3:5-8. +*4:4. Ga +*3:28. Col *2:13, 14. **also.** Ac 11:17. Ro 1:11. Ep 1:1. 1 T 4:12. **was poured.** Ac +2:17. Gr. *ekchuno,* ✱S#1632B,g. Rendered (1) shed: Mt 23:35. 26:28. Mk 14:24. Lk 11:50. 22:20. (2) run greedily: Ju 11. (3) shed abroad: Ro 5:5. (4) pour out: Ac 10:45. (5) gush out: Ac 1:18. (6) spill: Lk 5:37. **the gift.** Ac +2:38. **of.** If this is the genitive of apposition, then this is a reference to the gift; if it is the genitive of origin, it is the Holy Spirit as the giver of the gift. **Ghost.** Gr. *pneuma,* Mt +1:18 or +3:16.

46. **speak with tongues.** Ac 2:4, 11. 19:6. Mk 16:17. 1 C 14:20-25. **magnify.** Ac 19:17. Ps 34:2, 3. 35:27. 40:16. 69:30. 70:4. Lk 1:46. Ph 1:20. **answered.** Ac +3:12.

47. **Can any.** ♪85C, Ge +18:14. "This event settles the question of Gentile baptism. How can anyone refuse water-baptism to those on whom God has already bestowed the baptism of the Spirit?" (Ernst Haenchen, *The Acts of the Apostles,* p. 359). "The form of interrogation here used (with *meeti*) is equivalent to a strong negation. 'Surely no one will now venture to forbid,

etc.' (Compare Mt 7:16. Mk 4:21. Lk 6:37. Jn 4:49.) The same verb which, applied to persons, means *forbid,* when applied to things, is better rendered by *withhold,* as in Lk 6:29, where *to take* is supplied by the translators" (J. A. Alexander, *Commentary on the Acts of the Apostles,* vol. 1, p. 417). **forbid.** Just as Abraham was justified by faith, having believed God, and had righteousness imputed to him (Ge 15:6) before the institution of circumcision (Ge 17:10, 23. 21:4. Ro 4:10), and before any other associated outward act of obedience on his part (Ge 22:12-18. Ro *4:2, 3. He ◐11:8 w Ge 12:1, 4), and is so accounted "the father of all them that believe" (Ro 4:11), so Cornelius and his household believed and received remission of sins, as evidenced by the Holy Spirit coming upon him and all his, before they underwent the rite of water baptism. This dismisses the view of those who believe that ritual water baptism is essential to salvation (Mk 16:16n. Jn 3:5) or the remission of sins (Ac 2:38n), for Cornelius and his household received the Holy Spirit on the basis of their faith before they were water baptized. Since there is no evidence in the New Testament that after Christ's resurrection any unsaved individual was the recipient of the Holy Spirit, it can be confidently affirmed that Cornelius and his household were saved before experiencing water baptism; indeed, the indwelling of the Holy Spirit is the mark of a true believer (Ro +*8:9, 11), and the case of Cornelius proves that the Holy Spirit is received before the rite of water baptism. Ac √8:12, 36. *11:15-17. *15:8, 9. Ge 17:24-26. Ro √4:11, 12. *10:12. **water.** "Water" in Greek has the article, indicating a definite amount of water set aside, as in a pitcher or other vessel, for the use of baptism. Shedd notes "the phraseology implies that the baptismal water was brought into the room. 'Can any man forbid *the* water (*to hudor*), that these should not be baptized?' This phraseology would be unnatural, if the water in question were in a river, pond, or reservoir; but natural, if it were in a vessel" (W. G. Shedd, *Dogmatic Theology,* vol. 2, p. 584). **which.** ver. 44, 45. Ac +8:16. 11:17. 15:8. **Ghost.** Gr. *pneuma,* ♪121A1, Lk +1:17n. **as we.** Ac 2:4.

48. **commanded.** The baptism was evidently not performed by Peter, but by some minister. Walker suggests either the "six companions officiated, or some other Christian or Christians present" (Commentary on Acts, p. 247). Ac 13:5. Mt 28:19n. Jn *4:2. 1 C √1:13-17. Ga √3:27. **to be baptized.** Where were Cornelius and his household baptized? According to ver. 27, they were inside the home of Cornelius, where many were gathered. There is no notice of their having gone anywhere else to have the rite performed. Therefore, the evidence suggests that in this case Cornelius and his household were baptized in his own home. This corresponds to several other cases in Acts: Saul or Paul in a chamber at Damascus (Ac 9:17, 18), the baptism of Lydia, away from her home and from change of raiment at Philippi (Ac 16:14, 15), the Jailor at midnight in a prison (Ac 16:33, 34), the baptism of "the twelve" without warning or preparation at Ephesus (Ac 19:1-7). While the theory of immersion rests upon a sufficient quantity of water represented by a *river* (Mk 1:9n) and *much water* (Jn 3:23n) alleged in the baptism of John, the ritual baptisms under Christianity present not a single circumstance (excepting that of the Ethiopian Eunuch, Ac 8:36-39n) to which appeal

could be made to prove a dipping into water (J. W. Dale, *Christic Baptism*, p. 182). See related notes (Ac 1:5n. 2:41n. 8:36-39n). Ro ◐+*6:3, 4n. Ga 3:27. **the name.** Ac +*2:38n. *8:16. **Then prayed.** Ac 16:15. Jn 4:40.

ACTS 11

Peter is blamed by those of the circumcision, for going among the Gentiles, 1-3. He satisfies them, by relating the whole transaction; and they "glorify God, who had given to the Gentiles repentance unto life," 4-18. The gospel having spread to Phenice, Cyprus, and Antioch, 19-21; Barnabas is sent to Antioch, who rejoices over the converts, and exhorts them to persevere, 22-24. He goes to fetch Saul from Tarsus, and many are instructed at Antioch, where the disciples are first called Christians, 25, 26. Agabus foretells a famine; and the disciples at Antioch send relief to their brethren in Judea, by Barnabus and Saul, 27-30.

1. **the apostles.** Ac +5:12. 8:14, 15. Ga 1:17-22. **brethren.** ver. 29. Jn +21:23. **the Gentiles.** Ac 10:34-38. 14:27. 15:3. Ge +*49:10. Ps 22:27. 96:1-10. Is 11:10. 32:15. 35:1, 2. 42:1, 6. 49:6. 52:10. 60:3. 62:2. Je 16:19. Ho 2:23. Am 9:11, 12. Mi 5:7. Zp 2:11. 3:9. Zc 2:11. +*8:20-23. Ml 1:11. Mt +*8:11. Mk 16:5. Lk 2:32. Ro 15:7-12. **the word.** Ac 4:31. 6:2, 7. 8:14, 25. 12:24. 13:5, 7, 44, 46, 48. 17:13. 18:11. Lk +5:1. Ro 9:6.

2. **come up.** Ac +18:22. **they that.** Ac 10:9, 45. *15:1, 5. 21:20-23. Ro 4:12. Ga 2:12-14. Col 4:11. T 1:10. **contended with him.** "This fact is…an unanswerable proof, that the primitive church had no idea of Peter's supremacy and infallibility: indeed, the persons concerned by no means rendered due respect to his apostolical authority" (Scott).

3. **Thou wentest.** Ac 9:50. 10:23, *28, 48. 15:28. Mt 9:11. Mk 2:16. Lk 5:30. 15:2. 1 C 5:11. 2 C 2:7, 10. Ga *2:12, 14. 2 J 10.

4. **rehearsed.** Ac 14:27. Jsh 22:21-31. Pr 15:1. Lk 1:3. **expounded.** Ac 18:26. 28:23. **by order.** Ac 18:23. Lk 1:3.

5. **was.** T#1183. See on Ac *10:9-18. SS 3:2, 3. **Joppa.** Ac +9:36. **in a trance.** Ac 22:17. 2 C 12:1-3. **vision.** Ac +9:10. **a great sheet.** Camararius would render the word *othonee* by *mappa*, a table napkin, and Daniel Heinsius, by a shepherd's bag, or sack, in which they were accustomed to put food, platters, trenchers, and other things. It was a type of the Christian church, separated from the world; the living creatures of all kinds of which it was full, were the people of all nations included in the church; it was knit at the four corners, to show that they were gathered together from the four quarters of the globe; it descended from heaven, in the same manner as the New Jerusalem is represented in the Apocalypse, to intimate, that though the church exists in the world, it is not of the world, but of celestial origin; and the drawing back of it into heaven was designed to teach us, that, as the Church has its origin from heaven, so it shall return victorious thither. In this representation, the condition of believing Gentiles is described: they were about to constitute one Church with the believing Jews, and be made partakers of the heavenly inheritance. See a

dissertation by Bernard Duysing, Critici Sacri, vol. xiii. pp. 610-620. Jones' Works, vol. iii. pp. 44, 45. It should be noted, however, that this inheritance, though heavenly in its nature as being from heaven and under its authority, is the ultimate theocratic kingdom of our Lord and Savior Jesus Christ, which shall be established at the Second Advent here upon the earth (He +*11:16n). Ep +*4:4. **and it.** Je 1:11-14. Ezk 2:9. Am 7:4-7. 8:2.

6. **fastened.** Ac +3:4. Lk 4:20. **creeping.** Ac 10:12. Ro 1:23. Ja 3:7. **fowls.** Mt 6:26. 8:20. +*13:32. Mk 4:32. Lk 8:5. 9:58. 13:19.

8. **common.** Ac 10:28. Mk +7:2. Ro 14:14mg. **unclean.** T#1642. Le 10:10. 11:47. 20:25. Dt 14:4-20. Ezr 9:11, 12. Ho 9:3. Ro 14:14. 1 C +*7:14. **entered.** Ezk *4:14. Da +*1:8.

9. **What God.** Ac 10:28, 34, 35. 15:9. Ps *119:9. Mt 15:11. Mk 7:15, 19. Jn 15:3. Ro 14:2, 14, 20. 1 C *6:11. 10:25, 26. Ep *5:25, 26. 1 T +*4:4, 5. T 1:15. He 9:13, 14.

10. **three times.** Nu 24:10. Jn 13:38. 21:17. 2 C 12:8.

11. **immediately.** Ac 9:10-12. Ex 4:14, 27. **three men.** Ac 10:7, 17, 18. **Caesarea.** Ac +8:40.

12. **the Spirit.** Gr. *pneuma*, Lk +24:37. **bade me.** Ac +*8:29n. 10:19, 20. 13:2, 4. 15:7-9. 16:6, 7. Jn 16:13n. 2 Th 2:2. Re *22:17. **nothing doubting.** Ac 15:9. Mt 1:20. **these six.** Ac 10:23, 45.

13. **he showed.** Ac 10:3-6, 22, 30-32. 12:11. He *1:14. **to Joppa.** Ac 9:+36, 43.

14. **words.** Ac 10:6, 22, 32, 33, 43. √16:31. Ps +*19:7-11. Mk 16:16. Jn *6:63, 68. 12:50. √20:31. Ro √1:16, 17. √10:9, 10, 17. 2 T √3:15. 1 J √5:9-13. **all thy house.** √121J4, Ge +7:1. Ac +*2:39. +*16:15, 31. 18:8. Ge +*17:7. +*18:19. Ps 103:17. 112:2. 115:13, 14. Pr 20:7. Is 61:8, 9. Je 32:39. Lk +*19:9, 10. Jn 4:53. **shall be saved.** Ac √16:31.

15. **as I.** Ac 10:34-44. **the Holy.** Ac 10:45, 46. 19:6. **Ghost.** Gr. *pneuma*, √121A1, Lk +1:17n. **fell on them.** Ac 8:16. 10:44. **as on.** Ac 2:2-12. 4:31. **beginning.** Lk 1:2.

16. **remembered.** Ac *20:35. Lk 22:61. 24:8. Jn *14:26. 16:4. 2 P 3:1. **the Lord.** ver. 21n, 23, 24. Ac 2:36. 5:14. 9:1, 10, 13, 15, 17, 27, 29, 35, 42. +*10:36. Lk +7:19. **how that.** Ac +*1:5n. 19:2-4. Mt +*3:11. Mk *1:8. Lk *3:16. Jn 1:26, 33. **but.** Pr *1:23. Is 44:3-5. Ezk 36:25. Jl +*2:28n. 3:18. 1 C √12:13. T *3:5, 6. **Ghost.** Gr. *pneuma*, Mt +1:18n.

17. **as God gave.** ver. 15. Ac +*10:47. √15:8, 9. Mt 20:14, 15. Ro 9:15, 16, 23, 24. 11:34-36. **the like gift.** Ac +*2:38. **who believed.** or, when we believed. The participle rendered "when (we) believed" refers alike to "them" and to "us" (Thomas Walker). Notice it does not say that the Spirit was conferred upon their being circumcised, the point of the controversy, but upon their faith, that spiritual gifts were received. It is at the point of faith, not circumcision or ritual water baptism, that a person is saved and receives the Holy Spirit. There is no basis in Scripture to teach that the Holy Spirit gives his gifts to an unsaved individual at the point of his placing faith in Christ, but that the individual is not truly saved until after he has received water baptism. This is the point to the debate question, Do you baptize an alien sinner (an as yet unsaved person), or a saved person? The command of our Lord is to make disciples first, then baptize

them (Mt +*28:19). Nowhere in Scripture are we authorized to baptize unsaved individuals in order to save them; they are baptized as a public confession to the fact that they have been saved. In this sense the Bible teaches believer's baptism, not unbeliever's baptism, as well expressed by P. W. Grant's title, *Christian Baptism the Baptism of Christians.* The Spirit is conferred upon Jew or Gentile alike upon their faith in Christ. Ac +10:43. 1 C √12:13. Ep 1:13. +*4:4. **the Lord Jesus Christ.** Ac +1:21. +*10:36. 15:26. 20:21. 28:31. **what.** Ac +5:39. 10:47. Jb 9:12-14. 33:13. 40:2, 8, 9. Da 4:35. Ro 9:20-26.

18. **they held.** Ac 21:14g. Le 10:19, 20. Jsh 22:30. Lk 14:4. 23:56g. 1 Th 4:11g. **and glorified.** Ac 15:3. 21:20. Is +*60:21. 61:3. Mt +9:8. 2 C *3:18. Ga 1:24. **to the Gentiles.** Ac 13:47. Mt 8:11. **hath.** See on ver. 1. Ac 13:47, 48. 14:27. 22:21, 22. Ro 3:29, 30. 9:30. *10:12, 13. *15:9-16. Ga *3:26, 27. Ep 2:11-18. *3:5-8. +*4:4. Ph 2:12, 13. Ja *1:17. **granted.** Jn +*6:44, 65. 2 T +*2:25. **repentance.** Ac +*3:19, 26. +5:31. 20:21. 26:17-20. Je 31:18-20. Ezk 36:26. Zc *12:10. Mk *1:15. Ro *10:12, 13. 15:9, 16. 2 C √7:10. 2 T +*2:25, 26. Ja 1:16, 17. **unto life.** Ac +5:20. Jn 6:47. Ro *6:22, 23. Ep *2:8, 9.

19. **they.** Ac *8:1-4. Ge +*50:20. Ps *76:10. Ph *1:12. 2 T 2:9. **Phenice.** i.e. *palm country,* ✻S#5403g. Ac 15:3. 21:2. **Cyprus.** i.e. *fairness,* ✻S#2954g. Ac 13:4. 15:39. 21:3. 27:4. Compare ✻S#2953g: Ac +4:36. 11:20. 21:16. **Antioch.** i.e. *swift as a chariot, driven against,* ✻S#490g. ver. 20, 22, +26, 26, 27. Ac 13:1, 14. 14:19, 21, 26. 15:22, 23, 30, 35. 18:22. Ga 2:11. 2 T 3:11. **preaching.** ver. 20, 24. **the word.** Ac +8:4. **to none.** Ac 3:26. 13:46. Mt *10:5-7. Jn 7:35.

20. **Cyrene.** Ac 2:10. 6:9. 13:1. Mt 27:32. Mk 15:21. Lk 23:26. **spake unto.** ver. ◐19, 24. **the Grecians.** Ac 6:1. 9:29. Jn +7:35. **preaching.** Ac +5:42. 8:5, 35. 9:20. 17:18. 1 C 1:23, 24. 2:2. Ep 3:8. **the Lord Jesus.** Ac +1:21.

21. **the hand.** This Old Testament phrase is used by Luke. It was proof of God's approval of their course in preaching the Lord Jesus to Greeks (A. T. Robertson, *Word Pictures,* vol. 3, p. 157). Ac 4:28, 30. 13:11. Ex 9:3. 2 Ch 30:12. Ezr 7:9. 8:18. Ne 2:8, 18. Ps 80:17. 89:21. Is 53:1. 59:1. Lk 1:66. **with them.** Mt *28:30. 1 C 3:7. 15:10. 1 Th 1:5. **great number.** ver. 24. Ac 2:47. 4:4. 5:14. 6:7. +9:35. 15:3. 1 C 3:6, 7. 1 Th 1:5. **believed.** Ac +13:12. **turned unto.** Ac *9:35. +*10:36. 14:15. 15:3, 19. 26:18-20. Mt +*18:3. 1 Th *1:9, 10. **the Lord.** Here "Lord" refers to "the Lord Jesus," as in verse 20, though "the hand of the Lord" is the hand of Jehovah, clearly showing that the early disciples put Jesus on a par with Jehovah. His deity was not a late development read back into the early history (A. T. Robertson, *Word Pictures,* vol. 3, p. 157). ver. +16. 1 P +*2:3n.

22. A.M. 4047. A.D. 43. **tidings.** ver. 1. Ac 8:14. 15:2. 1 Th 3:6. **and they sent.** ver. 30. Ac 4:+36, 37. 9:27. 13:1-3. 15:22, 35-39. **Antioch.** ver. +26.

23. **had seen.** Mk 2:5. Col *1:6. 1 Th *1:3, 4. 2 T *1:4, 5. 2 P *1:4-9. 3 J *4. **the grace of God.** Ac 4:33. +*13:43. 14:26. 15:40. 20:24, 32. Ro 5:15. 1 C 1:4. 3:10. 15:10. 2 C 6:1. 8:1. Ga 2:21. Ep 3:2, 7. Col 1:6. 2 Th 1:12. T 2:11. He *12:15. 1 P 5:12. Ju 4. **and exhorted.** ⨍130. Paraeneticon; or, Exhortation B921. An expression of feeling by way of exhortation. This figure is employed when a direct statement is

changed, and put into the form of an exhortation. For another instance of this figure see 1 T 2:1. Ac +*13:43. +*14:22. +15:32. Jn +*8:31, 32. 15:4. 1 Th *3:2-5. He *10:19-26, 32-39. 2 P *3:17, 18. 1 J *2:28. **purpose.** Ps *17:3. Pr 23:15, 28. Da +*1:8. 2 C 1:17. 2 T *3:10. **cleave.** Ac 2:42. +13:43g. Nu=1:50. Dt *10:20. 30:20. Jsh *22:5. 23:8. 1 Ch=9:27. Pr *4:13. Mt *16:24. Jn 15:4. 1 C √15:58. Col +*1:23. **the Lord.** ver. +16.

24. **he was.** Ac 24:16. 2 S 18:27. Ps *37:23. 112:5. Pr 12:2. 13:22. 14:14. Mt 12:35. 19:17. Lk 23:50. Jn 7:12. Ro 5:7. **full.** Ac 6:3, 5, 8. Ro 15:15. **Ghost.** Gr. *pneuma,* Mt +1:18n. **and of faith.** Ac *6:5. Mt *17:20. **and much people.** ver. 19, *21, 26. Ac *5:14. 9:31. +19:26. **the Lord.** ver. +16.

25. **to Tarsus.** Ac 9:+11, 27, *30. 21:39.

26. **unto Antioch.** ver. +*19, 20, 22, 27. Ac 6:5. 13:1. 14:26. 15:22, 23, 30, 35. 18:22. Ga 2:11. **that.** Ac 13:1, 2. **with the church.** or, in the church. Ac 14:23, 27. 1 C 4:17. 11:18. 14:23. **taught.** Mt +*28:19. **much people.** ver. +24. **the disciples.** ver. 29. Ac 6:1, 2, 7. 9:1, +10, 19, 26, 38. 13:52. 14:20, 22, 28. 15:10. 18:23, 27. 19:9, 30. 20:1, 30. 21:4, 16. **were called.** Ac +10:22g. **Christians.** i.e. *followers of Christ,* ✻S#5546g. Ac 26:28g. Is √65:15. 1 C 12:12. Ep 3:15. 1 P *4:14, 16g. 1 J √2:27. Re 3:18.

27. **came.** Ac 18:22. **prophets.** Ac *2:17. +13:1. *15:32. *21:4, 9, 10. Ezr 2:46. Mt 23:34. 1 C *12:28. 14:32. Ep *4:11.

28. **Agabus.** i.e. *locust; feast of the father,* ✻S#13g. Ac 21:10. **Spirit.** Gr. *pneuma,* Mt +3:16. Ac +2:18. 8:29. 2 P *1:21. **great.** This was probably the famine which took place in the fourth year of Claudius, which continued for several years, and in which, says Josephus (Ant. lib. xx. c. 2), "many died for want of food." Ge 41:30, 31, 38. 1 K 17:1-16. 2 K 8:1, 2. Mt 24:7. **world.** Gr. *oikoumene,* Mt +24:14. **Claudius.** *Claudius Caesar* succeeded C. Caligula, A.D. 41; and after a reign of upwards of thirteen years, he was poisoned by his wife Agrippina, and succeeded by Nero. Ac 18:2. Lk 2:1. 3:1.

29. **the disciples.** ver. +*26. **every man.** Dt 16:17. Ezr 2:69. Ne 5:8. 1 C 16:2. 2 C 8:2-4, 12-14. 1 P 4:9-11. **according to his ability.** Lk +*11:41n, 42n. **to send relief.** William Paley in his *Horae Paulinae* demonstrates in an unanswerable manner that the incidental references and allusions to this relief effort found in the book of Acts compared with the same event alluded to in Paul's epistles furnish many undesigned coincidences which absolutely evince the truth of the narrative and the authenticity of the epistles, such that any doubt cast upon the authorship and authenticity of the epistles of Paul is unjustified. The details of the argument are given at the note on Ro 15:26. See the listing of related notes at Ac 12:12. Several of the specific passages Paley appeals to in his extensive argument are included in the following cross references. Ac 2:44, 45. 4:34. 6:1. 24:17. Ec 11:1, 2. Lk 12:29-33. Ro √15:25-27. 1 C 13:5. 16:1. 2 C 9:1, 2. Ga *2:10. He 13:5, 6, 16. Ja 2:15, 16. 1 J 3:17. **the brethren.** ver. 1. Jn +21:23.

30. **Which also.** Ac 12:25. **the elders.** Ac 14:23. 15:2, 4, 6, 22, 23. 16:4. 20:17. 21:18. 1 T *5:17, 19. T *1:5-7. Ja 5:14. 1 P *5:1, 2. 2 J 1. 3 J 1. **by.** Ac 12:25. 1 C 16:3, 4. 2 C 8:17-21. **Barnabas.** ver. 22. Ac +4:36. **and Saul.** Ac 12:25.

ACTS 12

King Herod persecutes the church; kills James, the brother of John; and imprisons Peter, 1-4; who, in answer to unceasing prayer, is delivered out of prison by an angel, 5-17. Herod puts the keepers to death; and leaving Jerusalem goes to Caesarea, 18, 19. Proudly receiving the honor due to God alone, he is smitten by an angel, and dies miserably, 20-23. The word of God prospers, 24. Barnabas and Saul return to Antioch, 25.

1. Cir. A.M. 4048. A.D. 44. **Herod**. Mt 14:1. **stretched forth his hands**. *or*, began. Ac 4:30. 9:31. Lk 22:53. **to vex**. Mt 10:17, 18. 24:9. Jn 15:20. 16:2.

2. **James**. Mt 4:+21, 22. *20:23. Mk 10:35, 38, 39. **with**. 1 K 19:1, 10. Je 26:23. He 11:37.

3. **he saw**. Ac 24:27. 25:9. Jn 12:43. Ga 1:10. 1 Th 2:4. **he proceeded**. Ac 2:14. 4:13. Ps 76:10. Jn 19:11. 21:18. **Then**. Ex *12:14-20. 13:3-7. *23:15. 34:18, 25. Le 23:6-14. Nu 28:17. Dt 16:3, 8. Mt 26:17. Mk 14:1, 12. Lk 22:1, 7. 1 C +*5:7, 8. **unleavened bread**. Le +*23:6.

4. **apprehended**. 1 S 20:3. **he put**. Ac 4:3. 5:18. 8:3. Mt *24:9. Lk +21:12. 22:33. Jn 13:36-38. √21:18. **delivered**. Ac 16:23, 24. Mt 27:64-66. **four quaternions**. Jn 19:23. **intending**. Ac 4:28. Est 3:6, 7, 13. Pr +*19:21. +*21:30. 27:1. La 3:37. Mt 26:5. **Easter**. Rather, *the passover, to paska.* Jn +6:4.

5. **prayer was made without ceasing**. *or*, instant and earnest prayer was made. **instant**. Ac 26:7. Lk 22:44. 1 P 1:22g. 4:8g. **earnest prayer**. T#1430. ver. 12. Ps +*50:15. Is 62:6, 7. Mt +*18:19. Lk *18:1. 1 C 12:26. 2 C *1:11. Ep *6:18-20. Ph 1:16-19. 1 Th +*5:17. He *13:3. Ja √5:16. **of the church**. Ro 15:30. 2 C 1:11. Ep 6:18. Ph 1:19. Phm 22.

6. **would have**. 1 S 20:3. **brought him**. Ac 17:5. **the same**. Ge 22:14. 32:24. Dt 32:36. 1 S 23:26, 27. Ps 3:5, 6. 4:8. Is √26:3, 4. Ph √4:6, 7. He +*13:6. **was sleeping**. Ps 127:2. **bound**. Ac 21:33. 28:20. Je 40:4. Da 3:20, 25. Ep 6:20mg. 2 T 1:16. **and the**. Ac 5:23. Mt 28:4.

7. **the angel**. ver. 23. Ac +5:19. 10:30. 27:23, 24. 1 K 19:5, 7. Ps √34:7. *37:32, 33. Is 37:36. Da 6:22. He *1:14. **came upon**. Lk 2:9. 24:4. **and a light**. Ac 9:3. 2 S 22:29. Ezk 43:2. Mi 7:9. Hab 3:4, 11. Re 18:1. **prison**. lit. building. √173E3. Synecdoche of the Genus B620. A domicile is put for prison. It is called a building, for it was no longer a prison after the angel had entered it. **he smote**. 1 K 19:7. **Arise**. Ge 19:15, 16. Is 60:1. Ep 5:14. **And his**. The two chains with which his hands were fastened to those of the two soldiers between whom he slept. This, it appears, was the Roman method of securing a prisoner, and seems to be that which is intimated in ver. 6. Ac +*2:24n. 16:26. Ps 105:18-20. 107:14. 116:16. 142:6, 7. 146:7. Da 3:24, 25. **from**. Ac 8:39n.

8. **Gird thyself**. Ps 18:32n. Lk +12:35. **bind on**. Mk 6:9.

9. **he went**. Ac 26:19. Ge 6:22. *19:16. Jn 2:5. He 11:8. **wist not**. That is, he *knew* not; *wist* being the preter tense of the obsolete verb to *wis*, from the Saxon *wissan*, in German *wissen*, and Dutch *wysen*, to *think, imagine, know*. Ac 10:3, 17. 11:5. Ge 45:26. Ps 126:1. 2 C 12:1-3. **a vision**. Ac +9:10.

10. **the first**. ver. 4. Ge 40:3. 42:17. Nu 15:34. Is 21:8. **which opened**. Ac *5:19. *16:26. Is 45:1, 2. Jn

20:19, 26. Re 3:7. **own accord**. Mk 4:28g.

11. **was come**. He was in an ecstacy; and it was only when the angel left him, that he was fully convinced that all was real. Lk 15:17. **I know**. Ge 15:13. 18:13. 26:9. **the Lord**. ver. 7. Ac *5:19. 2 Ch *16:9. Ps √34:7. *91:11. Da *3:25, 28. *6:22. He *1:14. **hath delivered**. 2 S 22:1. Jb *5:19. Ps *33:18, 19. 34:22. 41:2. *97:10. 109:31. 2 C *1:8-10. 2 P *2:9. **all**. Ac 23:12-30. 24:27. 25:3-5, 9. Jb 31:31. Lk 21:26. Jn 15:19, 20.

12. **considered**. Ac 14:6g. **he came**. Ac 4:23. 16:40. **house of Mary**. There is an indirect clue not furnished in Acts that Barnabas and Mark are related to one another, for in Col 4:10 it is mentioned that Mark is the son of the sister of Barnabas. The history (Ac 15:37, 39) mentions the fact of Barnabas's adherence to Mark, but not the reason of it; this is supplied by Paul incidentally in his epistle: Mark was his near kinsman (Col 4:10). Mark's mother, thus referred to, must have been a person of some repute. So when Peter was delivered from prison, he went to her house, "where many were gathered together praying." These are undesigned coincidences, depicting real transactions among real persons, marking the authenticity and historicity of these corresponding records. Paley notes that this "air of reality and business, as well as of seriousness and conviction, which pervades the whole" of Paul's letters and Luke's history are qualities that reveal on nearly every page "the language of a mind actuated by real occasions, and operating upon real circumstances." This "air of reality and business," of "seriousness and conviction," argues powerfully that the truthfulness of the record for anyone who is sensible to these qualities. This proof of authenticity is "not to be deemed occult or imaginary because it is incapable of being drawn out in words, or of being conveyed to the apprehension of the reader in any other way than by sending him to the books themselves" (*Horae Paulinae*, p. 197). Paley further notes that Paul's epistles "are connected with his History by their particularity, and by the numerous circumstances which are found in them." The History and Epistles are independent documents unknown to, or at least unconsulted by, each other. Yet the substance, and frequently very minute details of the History are recognized in the Epistles by allusions and references. These allusions and references cannot be imputed to design, nor, without a foundation in truth, be accounted for by accident. They are "hints and expressions and single words dropping as it were fortuitously from the pen of the writer, or drawn forth, each by the occasion proper to the place in which it occurs, but widely removed from any view to consistency or agreement. These, we know, are effects which reality naturally produces, but which, without reality at the bottom, can hardly be conceived to exist" (*Horae Paulinae*, pp. 197, 198). No forger would devise them, for undesigned coincidences, like these found in Scripture, being difficult to observe, would be largely unnoticed by the great mass of readers and students, and could not serve his purpose. I have made these available once again to Bible students in this new edition of the *Treasury of Scripture Knowledge* because of their evidential value for apologetics, and because their very nature relates to the kind of close Bible study which the cross references in the *Treaury* make possible. The alert student will find many on his own, and as

R.A. Torrey's "Introduction" to previous editions of the *Treasury* states, the *Treasury* "greatly strengthens faith" and "emphasises the truth by bringing in a multitude of witnesses" (see related notes on ver. 17n. Ac 1:19n. 11:29n. 17:2n, 16n. 18:2n, 5n, 18n. 19:20n, 21n. 20:2n, 3n, 4n, 22n, 25n, 34n. 21:21n, 26n. 22:3n, 18n. 28:20n. Mk 6:27n. Ro 15:19n, 26n. 16:3n, 4n, 23n. 2 C 8:19n). **John.** ver. 25. Ac 13:5, 13. 15:37-39. Mk ?14:51n. Col *4:10. 2 T 4:11. Phm 24. **Mark.** i.e. *shining, polite; a defense*, *S#3138g. ver. 25. Ac 15:37, 39. Col 4:10, Marcus. 2 T 4:11. Phm 24. 1 P 5:13. **where.** ver. 5. Is +*65:24. Da *9:21-23. Mt +*18:19, 20. 1 J √5:14, 15.

13. **knocked.** ver. 16. Lk 13:25. **the door.** The door was probably shut for fear of the Jews; and, as most of the houses in the East have an area before the door, it might have been at this outer gate at which Peter stood knocking. **of the gate.** Ac +10:17. **a damsel.** Jn 18:16, 17. **hearken.** *or,* ask who was there. **Rhoda.** i.e. *a rose,* *S#4498g.

14. **knew.** Gr. *epiginosko,* Mt +11:27. **she opened.** Mt 28:8. Lk 24:41. **the gate.** ver. 13. Ac +10:17. **for gladness.** Ge 45:26. Lk 24:41. **stood.** ✓96C1, Ge +4:1.

15. **Thou art mad.** Ac 26:24. Jb 9:16. Mk 16:11, 14. Lk 24:11. **constantly affirmed.** Lk 22:59. **It is.** Ge 48:16. Mt *18:10. Lk 24:37, 38. **his angel.** They spoke according to the notion, whether true or false, which has generally prevailed, that when a person is near death, or has actually expired, a spirit or angel, in his exact form, and speaking with his voice, sometimes appears to his friends. Thomas Walker notes "According to beliefs current among the Jews of that age, every man has a guardian angel assigned to him who can assume, at will, the form of the man whom he protects." Ac 23:8. Ps *91:11. Mt 18:10. Lk 16:22. 24:37. He 1:14.

16. **were astonished.** Ac 2:7. 8:9, 11, 13. 9:21. 10:45.

17. **beckoning.** Ac 13:16. 19:33. 21:40. Lk 1:22. Jn 13:24. **declared.** Ps 66:16. 102:20, 21. 107:21, 22. 116:14, 15. 146:7. **James.** Paley notes there is an exact conformity in the manner in which James is represented in the history and Paul's epistle to the Galatians. Both refer to his prominence in the Church at Jerusalem, and his stationary residence there. He is spoken of as if he were a leader in Jerusalem, in Ga 1:19 and 2:9. This idea agrees with Ac 12:17 and 21:17, 18, where he is referred to as the head of the Church there; and in the council regarding circumcision of the Gentiles, James was the person who closed the debate. This proves the truth of the circumstances, and confirms all the parts of the narrative that relate to it (see further related note on undesigned coincidences at ver. 12). Ac 15:13. *21:18. Mk +*6:3. 1 C 15:7. Ga *1:19. *2:9, 12. Ja 1:1. **the brethren.** Ac +21:23. **And he departed.** Ac ◑15:7-11. 16:40. Pr +*22:3. Mt 10:23. Jn 7:1. 8:59. 10:40. 11:54.

18. **there.** Ac 5:22-25. 16:27. *19:23g. **among the soldiers.** ver. 4, 19.

19. **sought for him.** 1 S 23:14. Ps *37:32, 33. Je 36:26. Mt 2:13. **he examined.** ver. 4, 6. Ac 4:9. 24:8. 28:18. Mt 28:11-15. Lk 23:14. **commanded.** Da 2:11-13. Mt 2:16. Jn 12:10, 11. **put to death.** Ac 16:27. 27:42. **he went.** Ac 21:8. 25:13. 1 K 20:43. Est 6:12. **Caesarea.** Ac +8:40. **abode.** Hobart notes this Greek term "was much employed in medical language in a variety of meanings:—to rub—to delay an operation—

to spend time at meals, in the bath, etc." (*Medical Language of Luke,* p. 221). Ac 14:3, 18, 28. 15:35. 16:12. 20:6. 25:6, 14. Jn 3:22. 11:54.

20. **was highly displeased.** *or,* bare an hostile mind intending war. **Tyre.** Ac 21:3, 7. Ge 10:15, 19. Jsh 19:29. Is 23:1-4. Mt 11:+21, 22. **Sidon.** Ac 27:3. Ge 10:19. Dt 3:9. Jsh 13:4. Jg 3:3. 1 K 5:6. Lk 4:26. **but.** Pr 17:14. 20:18. 25:8. Ec 10:4. Is 27:4, 5. Lk 14:31, 32. **having made.** Mt 28:14g. Ga 1:10g. **Blastus.** i.e. *germinate, sprout,* *S#986g. **the king's chamberlain.** Gr. that was over the king's bed-chamber. **because.** 1 K 5:9-11. 2 Ch 2:10, 15. Ezr 3:7. Ezk *27:17. Ho 2:8, 9. Am 4:6-9. Hg 1:8-11. 2:16, 17. Lk +*16:8.

21. **a set day.** Josephus (Ant. l. xix. c. 8. sec. 2) says that this was upon a day in which games were exhibited in honor of Claudius; and that, as Herod did not rebuke this impious flattery, he was seized with a severe pain in his bowels, which terminated his existence in five days. **arrayed.** Ge 41:42. Est 5:1. 6:8. 8:15. Da 5:29. **his throne.** Mt +27:19.

22. **gave a shout.** Ac 17:5. 19:30, 33g. **the voice.** Ac 14:10-13. Ps 12:2. Da 6:7. Jn ◑+*20:29n. Ju 16. Re 13:4. **a god.** Ro ◑8:31.

23. **the angel.** Ac +8:26. Ex 12:12, 23, 29. 1 S 25:38. 2 S *24:17. 2 K *19:35. 1 Ch 21:14-18. 2 Ch *32:21. **because.** Ac 10:25, 26. 14:14, 15. Ex 9:17. 10:3. 2 S 24:16, 17. Ps 115:1. Is 37:23. Is 42:8. √48:11. Ezk 28:2, 9. *Da 4:30-37. 5:18-24. Lk +*12:47, 48. Jn √9:24. ◑+*20:29n. 2 Th 2:3, 4. Re 13:8. **and he.** 2 Ch 21:18, 19. Jb 7:5. 19:26. Is 14:11. 51:8. +*66:24. Mk 9:44-48. **gave up.** Ac 5:5, 10.

24. **the word.** Ac 5:39. *6:7. 11:1, 21. *19:20. Pr 28:28. Is 41:10-13. 54:14-17. √55:10, 11. Da 2:24, 25, 44, 45. Mt 16:18. Col *1:6. 2 Th 3:1.

25. **Barnabas.** Ac +4:36. 11:29, 30. 13:1-3. **and Saul.** Ac 9:27. 11:25. 13:7, 43, 46, 50. 14:12, 14. 15:2, 12, 22, 25, 35, 36. 1 C 9:6. Ga 2:1, 9. **returned.** Ac 11:27-30. 13:1. **when.** Ac *11:29, 30. **ministry.** *or,* charge. Ac +6:1. **took.** Ac 9:27. 13:5, 13. 15:37. **John.** ver. +*12. Ac *13:5, 13. *15:38. Mk ?14:51n. 2 T 4:11. 1 P 5:13.

ACTS 13

Barnabas and Saul, by the command of the Holy Spirit, are set apart from among other teachers at Antioch with fasting and prayer, and sent forth to preach the gospel, 1-3. Attended by John Mark, they arrive at Cyprus, and preach at Salamis, 4, 5. At Paphos, Elymas the sorcerer, opposing them, is smitten with blindness, and the deputy, Sergius Paulus, believes, 6-12. They pass through Pamphylia (where Mark leaves them) to Antioch in Pisidia, 13, 14. Saul, now named Paul, preaches in the synagogue, showing that Jesus is the Messiah, through whom all believers are pardoned and justified; and warning his hearers not to reject him, 15-41. The Gentiles desire to hear the word again; and some Jews and proselytes join Paul and Barnabas, 42, 43. Almost the whole city throng to hear the word, 44. The envious Jews gainsay and blaspheme; and the apostles turn to the Gentiles, of whom many believe, 45-49. The Jews raise a persecution, and drive Paul and Barnabas away, who go to Iconium, 50, 51. The disciples are filled with joy and with the Holy Spirit, 52.

1. Cir. A.M. 4049. A.D. 45. **in the church.** Ac 11:22-

24. 14:26, 27. **at Antioch.** Ac +11:26. **prophets.** Ac 2:17. 11:25-27. *15:32. 19:6. 21:9, 10. Ro 12:6, 7. 1 C *12:28, 29. *14:1, 24, 25. Ep 2:20. 3:5. *4:11. 1 Th 5:20. **and teachers.** Ac *15:35. Ro 12:7. 1 C 12:28. Ep *4:11. He 5:12. Ja 3:1. **Barnabas.** Ac +4:36. *11:22-26, 30. 12:25. 1 C 9:6. Ga 2:9, 13. **Niger.** i.e. *black,* *S#3526g. **Lucius.** i.e. *luminous, light, bright, white,* *S#3066g. Ac 11:20. Ro 16:21g. **Cyrene.** *Cyrene* was a city of Libya, situated in a fertile plain about 12 miles from the Mediterranean, and the capital of *Cyrenaica,* at present called *Cairoan* in the kingdom of Balca. Ac 2:10. 6:9. 11:20. Mt 27:32. Mk 15:21. Lk 23:26. **Manaen.** i.e. *comforter; leader,* *S#3127g. Compare *S#4505h, 2 K +15:14, Menahem. **which,** etc. *or,* Herod's foster-brother. **Herod.** Mt 14:1-10. Lk 3:+1, 19, 20. 13:31, 32. 23:7-11. Ph 4:22. **and Saul.** ver. 9. Ac 8:1-3. 9:1, etc.

2. **they ministered.** Ac 6:4. Dt 10:8. 1 S 2:11. 1 Ch 16:4, 37, etc. Lk +1:23. Ro 15:16. Col 4:17. 2 T 1:11. 4:5, 11. **fasted.** ver. 3. Ac 10:30. Da 9:3. Mt 6:16. 9:14, 15. Lk +2:37. 1 C 7:5. 2 C 6:5. 11:27. **the Holy.** Ac 10:19. 16:6, 7. 1 C 12:11. **Ghost.** Gr. *pneuma,* Mt +3:16. Mt +*12:32. **said.** ver. 4. Ac +8:29n. 20:28. **Separate.** Ac 22:21. Nu 8:11-14. Ro *1:1. 10:15. 1 C *12:11. Ga *1:15. 2:8, 9. 2 T 2:2. **the work.** Ac +9:15. 14:26. Mt 9:38. Lk 10:1, 2. Ep *3:7, 8. 1 T 2:7. 2 T *1:11. He 5:4.

3. **they had.** ver. 2. Ac 1:24. 6:6. 8:15-17. 9:17. 14:23. Nu 27:23. 1 T *4:14. 5:22. 2 T 1:6. 2:2. **laid.** Ac +6:6. 9:17. ◐26:16-18. **their.** ♪63A3, Mt +19:13. **they sent.** Ac *14:26. 15:40. Ro 10:15. 3 J 6-8.

4. **being sent.** ver. 2. Ac 16:6, 7. 20:23. **Ghost.** Gr. *pneuma,* Mt +3:16. **Seleucia.** i.e. *beaten by waves, tossed; white light,* *S#4581g. **Cyprus.** Ac +4:36. *11:19. 27:4.

5. **Salamis.** i.e. *shaken, agitated,* *S#4529g. *Salamis* was a famous city on the eastern coast of Cyprus, opposite Seleucia, afterwards called *Constantia,* and now *Famagusta.* **the word of God.** ver. 7, 44, 46, 48. Ac +11:1. **in the synagogues.** ver. 14, 46. Ac 9:20. 14:1. 17:1-3, 10, 17. 18:4, 19. 19:8. **John.** ver. 13. Ac 12:+12, 25. 13:13. 15:37, 38. Mk 14:51, 52. Col *4:10. 2 T 4:11. Phm 24. 1 P 5:13. **their.** Ex 24:13. 1 K 19:3, 21. 2 K 3:11. Mt 20:26. 2 T 4:11. **minister.** Gr. assistant, used of an attendant who looked after the scriptures. Ac 19:22. Lk *4:20.

6. **Paphos.** i.e. *suffering; very hot,* *S#3974g. ver. 13. **certain.** Ac 8:9-11. 19:18, 19. Ex 22:18. Le 20:6. Dt 18:10-12. 1 Ch 10:13. Is +*8:19, 20. **sorcerer.** Gr. *Magus.* Ac 8:9, 11. Mt 2:1, 7, 16. **a false.** Dt 13:1-3. 1 K 22:22. Je 23:14, 15. Ezk 13:10-16. Zc 13:3. Mt +7:15. 24:24. 2 C 11:13. 2 T 3:8. 2 P 2:1-3. 1 J 4:1. Re 19:20. **whose.** Mt 10:3. 16:17. Mk 10:46. Jn 21:15-17. **Bar-jesus.** i.e. *son of Jesus or Joshua,* *S#919g.

7. **the deputy.** ver. 8, 12. Ac 18:12. 19:38. **Sergius.** i.e. *a net; a kind of olive; earth-born, born a wonder,* *S#4588g. **Paulus.** i.e. *to lessen,* *S#3972g. **a prudent.** Ac 17:11, 12. Pr 14:8, 15, 18. 18:15. +*22:3. Ho 14:9. Lk 10:21. 1 Th 5:21. **Barnabas.** Ac +4:36. **the word.** ver. +5.

8. **Elymas.** i.e. *magician; corruptor,* *S#1681g. **for.** ver. 6. Ac 9:36. Jn 1:41. **interpretation.** ♪95, Ps +7:13. Mk +5:41. **withstood.** Ex 7:11-13, 22. 8:7, 18. 9:11. 1 K 22:24. Je 28:1, 10, 11. 29:24-32. 2 T 3:8. 4:14, 15. **turn away.** ver. 10g. Mt +17:17. **the deputy.** ver. +7. **the faith.** Ac +6:7. 1 C 16:13.

9. **who.** ver. 7. **Paul.** i.e. *little,* *S#3972g. ver. 13, 16, 43, 45, 46, 50. Ac 14:9, 11, 12, 14, 19. 15:2, 2, 12, 22, 25, 35, 36, 38, 40. 16:3, 9, 14, 17, 18, 19, 25, 28, 29, 36, 37. 17:2, 4, 10, 13, 14, 15, 16, 22, 33. 18:1, 5, 9, 12, 14, 18. 19:1, 4, 6, 11, 13, 15, 21, 26, 29, 30. 20:1, 7, 9, 10, 13, 16, 37. 21:4, 8, 11, 13, 18, 26, 29, 30, 32, 37, 39, 40. 22:25, 28, 30. 22:25, 28, 30. 23:1, 3, 5, 6, 10, 11, 12, 14, 16, 16, 17, 18, 20, 24, 31, 33. 24:1, 31, 33. 24:1, 10, 23, 24, 26, 27. 25:2, 4, 6, 7, 9, 10, 14, 19, 21, 23. 26:1, 1, 1, 24, 28, 29. 27:1, 3, 9, 11, 21, 24, 31, 33, 43. 28:3, 8, 15, 16, 17, 25, 30. Ro 1:1. 1 C 1:1, 12, 13. 3:4, 5, 22. 16:21. 2 C 1:1. 10:1. Ga 1:1. 5:2. Ep 1:1. 3:1. Ph 1:1. Col 1:1, 23. 4:18. 1 Th 1:1. 2:18. 2 Th 1:1. 3:17. 1 T 1:1. 2 T 1:1. T 1:1. Phm 1, 9, 19. 2 P 3:15. **filled.** Ac 2:4. 4:+8, 31. 7:55. Mi 3:8. **Ghost.** Gr. *pneuma,* Mt +1:18n. **set.** Ac +3:4. Mk 3:5. Lk 20:17.

10. **said.** ♪6, Ge +3:13. **O full.** Ac 8:20-23. Ec 9:3. Mt 3:7. 15:19. 23:25-33. Lk 11:39. Ro 1:29. 2 C 11:3. **mischief.** Ac 18:14. **thou child.** ♪108B, 1 S 20:31. Ge +*3:15. Mt +*13:38. Jn √8:44. 1 J *3:8. **wilt.** Ac 20:30. Je *23:36. Mt 23:13. Lk 11:52. Ga 1:7. **pervert.** ver. 8. Pr 10:9. Is 59:8. Mi 3:9. **the right.** Ac 18:25, 26. Ge +*18:19. 2 Ch 17:6. Ho 14:9. Jn 1:23. Ro 11:33. 2 P 2:15. Re 15:3. 16:7.

11. **hand.** ♪22A14.7, Ex +9:3. Ac 11:21. Ex 7:4. 9:3. Jg 2:15. 1 S 5:6, 7, 9, 11. Jb 19:21. Ps 32:4. 38:2. 39:10, 11. Lk 1:66. He 10:31. 1 P 5:6. **thou.** Ac 9:8, 9, 17. Ge 19:11. 2 K 6:8. Is 29:10. Jn 9:39. Ro 11:7-10, 25. **for a season.** Lk 4:13. **a mist.** 2 P 2:17. **darkness.** Ex 10:21-23. **some to lead.** Ac 9:8. 22:11.

12. **the deputy.** ver. +7. Ac 28:7. **when.** Ac 19:17. Mt *27:54. Lk 7:16. **believed.** ver. 39, 48. Ac 2:44. 4:4, 32. 5:14. 10:45. 11:21. 14:1. 15:5, 7. 16:1. 17:12, 34. 18:27. 19:2, 18. 21:20, 25. Jn +5:44. Ro *4:11. **being.** Ac 6:10. Mt 7:+28, 29. Lk 4:22. Jn 7:46. 2 C 10:4, 5. **the doctrine.** ver. 49. Ac 8:25. 15:35, 36. 19:10, 20. **the Lord.** Ac +11:16.

13. **loosed.** ver. 6. Ac 27:13. **Perga.** i.e. *very earthy,* *S#4011g. Ac 2:10. 14:24, 25. 27:5. **Pamphylia.** i.e. *heterogeneous; all sorts, all tribes,* Ac 2:10. 14:24. 15:38. 27:5. **John.** ver. +*5. Ac 12:12, 15. 15:38. Col *4:10. 2 T 4:11. **departing.** Ac *15:38. Lk *9:62. 2 T √4:11. **to Jerusalem.** Ac 12:12.

14. A.M. 4050. A.D. 46. **Antioch.** Ac 14:19, 21-24. 2 T 3:11. **Pisidia.** i.e. *pitch; persuasion of right,* *S#4099g. Ac 14:24. **went.** ver. +5. Ac 16:13. *17:2. *18:4. 19:8. **on the sabbath.** ver. 42, 44. Ac 16:13. 17:2. *18:4. Mk +6:2.

15. **the reading.** ver. 27. Ac 15:21. Lk *4:16-18. 2 C 3:14, 15. **the law.** Lk +16:16. **the prophets.** ver. 27. Lk 4:17. +16:16. **the rulers.** Ac 18:8, 17. Mk +5:22. **Ye men.** Ac 1:16. 2:29, 37. 7:2. 15:7. 22:1. **if.** ♪184A, 1 C +15:2. Ac 2:4. 20:2. Ro 12:8. 1 C 14:3. He 13:22. **any word.** Ac +4:36. He 13:22.

16. **beckoning.** Ac 12:17. 19:33. 21:40. **Men.** ver. 26. Ac +2:22. 3:12. **and ye.** ver. 26, 42, 43, 46. Ac 10:+2, 35. 1 K 8:40. Ps 67:7. 85:9. 135:20. Lk 1:50. 23:40. **give.** Ac 2:14. 22:1, 22. Dt 32:46, 47. Ps 49:1-3. 78:1, 2. Mi 3:8, 9. Mt 11:15. Re 2:7, 11, 17, 29.

17. **God.** Ac 7:2, etc. Ge +*12:1-3. +*17:7, 8. Dt 4:37. 7:6-8. 9:5. 14:2. Ne 9:7, 8. Ps 105:6-12, 42, 43. 135:4. Is 29:23. 41:8, 9. 44:1. Je 33:24-26. Mt 15:31. Lk 1:68. 1 P *2:9. **chose.** Dt *7:6-8. **and exalted.** Ac 7:17. Ex 1:7-9. Nu 24:7. Dt 10:22. 2 S 5:12. 1 Ch 14:2. Ps 105:23, 24. **when.** Ac 7:17. Ex 1:1, 7, 12. Dt

26:5. Ps 105:23, 24. **and with.** Ac 7:36. Ex ch. 6-14. 15:1-21. 18:11. Dt 4:20, 34. 7:19. 1 S 4:8. Ne 9:9-12. Ps 77:13-20. 78:12, 13, 42-53. 105:26-39. 106:7-11. ch. 114. 135:8-10. 136:10-15. Is *63:9-14. Je 32:20, 21. Am 2:10. Mi 6:4. 7:15, 16.

18. **about.** Ac 7:+36, 39-43. Ex *16:2, 35. Nu *14:22, 33, 34. Dt 9:7, 21-24. Ne 9:16-21. Ps 78:17-42. *95:8-11. 106:13-29. Ezk 20:10-17. Am 5:25, 26. 1 C 10:1-10. He 3:7-10, 16-19. **suffered.** "Gr. *etropophoreesen*, perhaps for *etrophophoreesen*, bore, *or* fed them as a nurse beareth, *or* feedeth her child. Dt 1:31, according to the LXX., and so Chrysostom." Nu 11:12. Dt 1:31. Is 46:3, 4. +*63:9. 2 P √3:9.

19. **when.** Ac 7:45. Dt 7:1. Jsh 12:7, 8. *24:11, 12. Ne 9:24. Ps 78:55. **seven nations.** Dt *7:1. **Chanaan.** Ge 12:5. 17:8. Ps 135:11, Canaan. **he divided.** Nu 26:53-56. Jsh *14:1, 2. 18:10. 19:51. 23:4. Ps 78:55. 136:21, 22.

20. **And after.** Jg 11:26. 1 K 6:1. **he gave.** T#310. Ge 9:5, 6. Ex 18:25, 26. Nu 11:11, 16, 17. 27:15-20. Dt 1:9-18. 16:18, 19. Jg *2:16. *3:9, 10. Ru 1:1. 1 S 12:11. 2 S 7:11. 2 K 23:22. 1 Ch 17:6. Pr 8:12, *15, 16. Ro *13:3-6. **until.** Ac +3:24. 1 S *3:20.

21. **they desired.** 1 S 8:5-22. 12:12-19. **a king.** T#1591. 1 S *8:4, 5. 9:16. 12:19. Ho *13:11. **Saul.** 1 S *10:1, 21-26. 11:15. 15:1. **Cis.** i.e. *a snare*, ❋S#2797g. For ❋S#7027h, see 1 S 9:+1, 2. 10:21, Kish.

22. **when.** 1 S 12:25. *13:13, 14. *15:11, 23, 26, 28. *16:1, 13. 28:16, 17. *31:4, 6. 2 S 7:15. 1 Ch 10:13, 14. Da 2:21. Ho 13:10, 11. **he raised.** 1 S 16:1, 13. 2 S 2:4. *5:3-5. 7:8. 1 Ch 28:4, 5. Ps 2:6. 78:70-72. *89:19, 20, etc. Je 33:21, 26. Ezk 34:23. 37:24, 25. Ho 3:5. **David.** Mt 11:11. Lk 7:16. Jn 7:52. **to whom.** Ac 15:8. He 11:4, 5. **I have.** Ac 7:46. 1 S 13:14. 1 K 15:3, 5. Ps ⟩89:20. **a man after.** 1 S ⟩13:14. **my own heart.** √22A17, Ge +6:6. Ep 6:6. **which shall.** ver. 36.

23. **this.** Ac 2:30. 2 S ❋7:12-15, 27. Ps ❋89:3, 4, 35-37. 132:11. Is +7:13. +❋*9:6, 7. *11:1, 10. +❋*55:3, 4. Je +❋*23:5, 6. 33:15-17. Am ❋9:11, 12. Mt +❋1:1. 21:9. 22:42. Lk 1:31-33, ❋69. *2:4. Jn ❋7:42. Ro ❋1:3. 2 T ❋2:8. Re ❋22:16. **according to.** ver. 32, 33. 2 S 7:12. 1 K 8:20. Ps *132:11. Lk *1:32. **raised.** Ac 2:32-36. 3:26. 4:12. 5:30, 31. Is 43:11. 45:21. Zc +*9:9. Mt *1:21. Lk *2:10, +11. Jn 4:42. Ro +*11:26. T 1:4. 2:10-14. 3:3-6. 2 P 1:1, 11. 2:20. 3:2, 18. 1 J 4:14. Ju 25.

24. **first preached.** Ac +1:22. 10:37. 19:3, 4. Mt 3:1-11. Mk *1:2-8. Lk 1:76. *3:2, 3, etc. Jn 1:6-8, 15, etc. *3:25-36. 5:33-36. **before his coming.** Am 1:1. Zc 8:10. 1 Th 1:9. 2:1. **baptism of repentance.** Ac +*2:38. 19:4. Mt 3:11.

25. **fulfilled.** ver. 36. Ac 20:24g. Mk 6:16-28. Jn 4:34. 19:28-30. 2 T 4:7. Re 11:7. **Whom.** Ac 19:4. Mt *3:11. Mk 1:7. Lk 3:15, 16. Jn *1:20-23, 26, 27, 29, 34, 36. 3:27-29. 7:18. 2 C 4:5.

26. **children.** ver. 15, 17, 46. Ac *3:26. 2 Ch 20:7. Ps 105:6. 147:19, 20. Is 41:8. 48:1. *51:1, 2. Mt 3:9. +*10:6. Lk +*24:47. **and whosoever.** ver. 16, 43. Ac 10:35. Mt *11:28. **feareth God.** ver. 16. Ac +10:2. **to you.** Ac 16:17. 28:28. Is 46:13. Lk 1:69, 77. Ro √1:16. 2 C √5:19-21. Ep √1:13. Col 1:5. **the word.** Ac 10:36. Ep 1:13. **this salvation.** Ac 5:20. +*4:12. 28:28. **sent.** ver. 23.

27. **their rulers.** Lk +24:20. **because.** Ac +*3:17. Lk *23:34. Jn *8:28. *15:21. *16:3. Ro *11:8-10, 25.

1 C √2:8. 2 C *3:14, 15. *4:4. 1 T *1:13. **nor.** ver. +15. Ac 15:21. Mt *22:29. Lk *24:25-27, 44, 45. Jn +6:45. **which.** ver. *14, *15. Ac *15:21. **they have fulfilled.** Ac 2:23. *26:22, 23. *28:23. Ge +*50:20. Mt *26:54-56. Lk *24:20, 24, +*27, 44. Jn *19:28-30, 36, 37. 1 C √2:8.

28. **found no cause.** Ac 3:13, 14. Mt 27:19, 22-25. Mk 14:55. *15:13-15. Lk 23:4, 5, 14-16, 21-25. Jn *18:38. 19:4, 12-16. **yet desired.** Ac 2:23. 3:14, 15. Lk 23:23.

29. **when.** ver. 27. Ac 2:23. 4:28. 26:22. Mt +1:22. Lk 18:31-33. +*24:44. Jn *19:28, 30, 36, 37. **they.** √63A1, Ge +14:20. i.e. Joseph of Arimathea and Nicodemus took him down, but these are not mentioned here by name by Ellipsis (Absolute: of Nominative). Compare 1 C 15:24n. **took.** √108A4, Ge +31:7. i.e. they (the rulers, ver. 27) took, that is, they permitted Joseph of Arimathea and Nicodemus to do so. Jsh 8:29. Mt *27:57-60. Mk 15:45, 46. Lk 23:53. Jn 19:38-42. 1 C +*15:4. **him.** √63A1, Ge +14:20. **the tree.** Ac 5:30. Jn 19:6n. 20:25n. 1 P 2:24. **laid.** Jn +*2:19-22.

30. **God raised.** ver. 33, 34, 37. Ac +*2:24n, 32. 3:13, 15, 26. 4:10. 5:30, 31. 10:40. *17:31. Mt *28:6. Jn +*2:19, 21. *10:17. He *13:20. **from.** √181E, Ge +3:24.

31. **he was.** Ac +*1:3, 11. +*10:41. Mt 28:16, 17. Mk 16:12-14. Lk 24:36-42. Jn 20:19-29. 21:1, etc. 1 C √15:5-7. **came up.** Ac +18:22. Mk 15:41. **from Galilee.** Ac 1:11. 2:7. **his witnesses.** Ac +*1:8, 22. *2:32. 3:15. 5:32. 10:39. Lk +24:48. Jn *15:27. He *2:3, 4.

32. **we declare.** ver. *38. Ac 5:42. 14:15. Is *40:9. 41:27. *52:7. *61:1. Lk 1:19. *2:10. Ro 10:15. **how.** Ac 2:39. 26:6. Ge +*3:15. +*12:3. +*22:18. 26:4. +*49:10. Dt *18:15. Is +*7:14. +*9:6, 7. 11:1. Je +*23:5. Ezk *34:23. Da +*9:24-26. Mi +*5:2. Hg *2:7. Zc √6:12. +*9:9. 13:1, 7. Ml *3:1. *4:2. Lk *1:54, 55, 68-73. Ro *4:13. 9:4. Ga *3:16-18. **the fathers.** Ro +*15:8.

33. **God hath.** ver. 23. Lk 1:69-73. Ro *15:8. **fulfilled.** √77, Ex +3:19. Marked as emphatic by the addition of *ek*, with reference to ver. 29. Ac 21:26g. **raised up.** ver. 30. Ac +*2:24. 3:22, 26. **the second.** Lk 20:42. +*24:44. **Thou art.** √92A, Mt +1:23. Ps *⟩2:7. Ro 1:4. He *1:5, 6. *5:5. **begotten.** Ps +*71:20. Is +*66:7-9. Mi +*5:3, 4. Mt √19:28. Ro 4:17. +*8:29. 1 Th +*4:16.

34. **as concerning.** ver. +30. **raised.** Ac 2:23-36. 10:38-43. Ps +*16:10. Jn 2:21, 22. **from.** √181E, Ge +3:24. **now.** Ro 6:9. He 9:25-28. Re 1:18. **no more.** ver. 35-37. T#979‡. 1 C 15:50. 2 C 5:16. **I will.** Is +√55:3. **the sure.** 2 S √7:14-16. √23:5. Ps *89:2-4, 19-37. Je 33:15-17, 26. Ezk +*34:23, 24. +*37:24, 25. Ho +*3:5. Am *9:11. Zc 12:8. **mercies.** "Gr. *ta osia*, holy, *or* just, things; which word the LXX., both in the place of Is 55:3, and in many others, use for that which is in the Hebrew *mercies*." √46C, Mt +8:6. The words *holy* or *just things* are used for *promises made*, and *mercies* vouchsafed, in pure grace; the Hebrew *chasadeem* having both meanings (B679). 2 S +*7:15. Ps +*89:28, 33, 37. +√132:11. Is 38:5. +√55:3. Ro +*11:1, 2. Re *11:15.

35. **in another.** Ac *2:27-31. Ps +*⟩16:10. **Holy One.** He +*7:26. **to see.** ver. 36, 37. Ps 49:9. *89:48. Lk 2:26. Jn √3:36. 8:51. He 11:5. **corruption.** Jb 17:14.

36. **served, etc.** *or*, in his own age served the will of God. ver. 22. Ac +20:27. 1 Ch 11:2. 13:2-4. 15:12-

16, 25-29. 18:14. ch. 22-29. Ps 78:71, 72. **fell on sleep.** Ac 2:34n. 7:60. Dt 31:16. 2 S 7:12. 1 K 1:21. *2:10. Da +*12:2n. Mt +27:52. 1 C 15:6, 18. 1 Th 4:13. **and was laid.** Ac 2:29. Ge 15:15. +*25:8n. Jg 2:10. 1 Ch 17:11. 2 Ch 9:31. 12:16. 21:1. 26:28. **and saw corruption.** Clearly a reference to the body, not the soul: thus it is the *body*, not the *soul*, which "fell on sleep." Ge 3:19. Jb 17:14. 19:26, 27. 21:26. Ps +√16:10. 49:9, 14. Jn 11:39. 1 C 15:42-44, 53, 54.

37. **But he.** ver. +30. Ac +*2:24n.

38. **Be it known.** Ac 2:14. 4:10. 28:28. Ezk 36:32. Da 3:18. **that through.** Ac +*2:38. 5:31. 10:43. Ps √32:1, 2. 130:4, 7, 8. Je 31:34. Da *9:24. Mi *7:18-20. Zc *13:1. Lk +*24:47. Jn √1:29. 2 C √5:18-21. Ep *1:7. √4:32. Col *1:14. He 8:6, 12, 13. 9:9-14, 22. 10:4-18. 1 J *2:1, 2, 12. **forgiveness.** T#792. Ac +5:31. Le=23:19. Is *53:5, 6. Zc 13:1. Mt *1:21. 26:28. Jn *1:29. 1 C *15:3. Ep *1:7. 1 T 1:15. He 1:3. *9:26, 28. *10:14. 1 J *1:7, 9. 2:1, 2, +12. 3:5. 1 P 2:24. Re 1:5.

39. **by him.** ver. +12. Ac +10:43. Is *53:11. Hab *2:4. Lk 18:14. Jn √5:24. Ro *3:24-30. √4:5-8, 24, 25. *5:1, 9. *8:1, 3, 30-34. √10:10. 1 C 6:11. Ga √2:16. 3:8-11. **justified.** Le=23:12. Jb *25:4. Ro 3:26. **from which.** Jb 9:20. 25:4. Ps 143:2. Je 31:32. Lk 10:25, 28, 29. Jn 1:17. Ro 2:13. √3:19, 20, 28. 4:15. 5:20. 7:9-11. 8:3, 4. 9:31, 32. *10:4, 5. Ga 2:16, 19. *3:10-12, 21-25. 5:3, 4. Ep 2:9. Ph 3:6-9. 2 T +*1:9. T *3:5. He *7:19. 9:9, 10. *10:4, 11. **law of Moses.** Jn +7:23.

40. **Beware.** Ml 3:2. 4:1. Mt 3:9-12. He √2:3. +*3:12. *12:25. **which.** Is 29:14. Hab ▶1:5. Jn +6:45.

41. **Behold.** ℐ92C, Mt +2:15. **ye despisers.** Pr *1:24-32. 5:12. Is *5:24. 28:14-22. Hab ▶1:5. Lk 16:14. 23:35, 36. He 10:28-30. **and.** ℐ93B, Is +66:11. By *Hendiadys,* perish wonderfully. **perish.** or, vanish away. Ja 4:14. **for I work.** ver. 47. Ac 3:23. 6:14. 22:21. Is 28:21n. *29:14. 65:15. Da +*9:26, 27. Mt +*8:10, 11. 21:41-44. *22:7-10. *23:34-38. Lk *19:42-44. *21:20-27. Ro 11:7-14. Ep *3:3-8. Col *1:26, 27. 1 Th 2:16. 1 P *4:17. **no wise believe.** Hab *1:5. Lk +*16:31. **though.** ℐ184C, Mt +4:9.

42. **the Gentiles.** Ac 10:33. 28:28. Ezk 3:6, 7. Mt 11:21-23. 19:30. **the next sabbath.** Gr. in the week between, *or,* in the sabbath between. ℐ171T3, Mt +28:1. ver. 14, 44.

43. **many of the Jews.** ver. 44. Ac +6:1. **and religious.** ver. 50. Ac 16:14. 17:4, 17. 18:7. **proselytes.** Ac 2:10. 6:5. Mt 23:15. **followed.** Ac 17:34. 19:9. **Paul.** Ac 12:25. **Barnabas.** Ac +4:36. **persuaded.** Ac +*11:23. +*14:22. 18:4g. 19:8. 28:23. Jn √8:31, 32. *15:5-10. 2 C 5:11. 6:1. Ga *5:1. Ph 3:16. 4:1. Col +*1:23, 28. 1 Th 3:3-5. He *6:11, 12. 12:15. 2 P 3:14, 17, 18. 1 J 2:28. 2 J 9. **to continue.** Ac +*11:23. +*14:22. Col +*1:23. He +*10:35. Ju 21. **the grace.** Ac +11:23. 14:3. Ro 3:24. 5:2, 21. 11:6. Ga *5:4. Ep √2:8. T √2:11. He +*12:15. 13:9. 1 P *5:12. Ju 4.

44. **next sabbath.** ver. 42. **came.** Ge +*49:10. Ps *110:3. Is *11:10. 60:8. **the word.** ver. 5. Ac +11:1.

45. **But.** Ac 19:9. **when the Jews.** Ac 22:22. 1 Th 2:16. **they.** Ac +5:17mg. 17:5. Ge 37:11. Nu 11:29. Ec 4:4. Is *26:11. Mt 27:18. Lk 15:25-30. Ro 1:29. 1 C 3:3. Ga 5:21. Ja 3:14-16. 4:5. **spake.** Ac 6:9, 10. 18:6. 19:9. Mt 23:13. 1 P 4:4. Ju 10. **contradicting.** ℐ144C1, Ge +21:1. **blaspheming.** Ac 26:11. 1 T +*1:20g. Ja 2:7. 2 P 2:12.

46. **Then.** T#469. Is *49:4, 5. 53:1. Ezk 3:7. Jn *12:37-40. He +4:2 (T#435). **waxed bold.** Ac 4:13, 29-31. Pr 28:1. Ro 10:20. Ep 6:19, 20. Ph 1:14. He 11:34. **It was necessary.** ver. 26. Ac 3:21, 26. 18:5. 26:20. Mt +*10:6. Lk +*24:47. Jn 4:22. Ro √1:16. 2:10. *9:4, 5. **first.** ver. 5, 14. Ac +3:26. Ro √1:16. **seeing.** Ac 7:51. Ex 32:9, 10. Dt *32:21. Is 49:5-8. Mt 10:13-15. +21:43. 22:6-10. Lk 14:16-24. Jn 1:11. Ro *10:19-21. 11:11-13. **put it from.** T#697. Ps +58:5 (T#373). Pr 8:36. Je 23:17. Ezk 20:13. Jn *5:40. **unworthy.** Mt +22:8. **everlasting.** Gr. *aionios,* Mt +18:8. Mt 19:16. Ro 2:7. **life.** Ac +5:20. **turn.** Ac +9:15. *18:6. 22:21. 26:17, 18, 20. *28:28. Is *55:5. Mt *8:12. *21:43.

47. **so.** Ac +*1:8. 9:15. 11:18. 22:21. 26:17, 18. Mt +*28:19. Mk *16:15. Lk +*24:47. **I have.** Ac 26:23. Is *42:1, 6. ▶49:6. 60:3. Lk *2:32. Jn +8:12. **that thou.** Ac 15:14-16. Ps 22:27-29. 67:2-7. 72:7, 8. 96:1, 2. 98:2, 3. ch. 117. Is +*2:1-3. 24:13-16. 42:9-12. *45:22. 52:10. +*59:19, 20. Je *16:19. Ho 1:10. Am 9:12. Mi 4:2, 3. 5:7. Zp 3:9, 10. Zc 2:11. *8:20-23. Ml 1:11. **the ends.** Ac +*1:8. Ro *10:18.

48. **the Gentiles.** Ro 9:23, 24. **they.** ver. 42. Ac +*2:41. *8:8. 15:31. 28:28. Lk *2:10, 11. Ro *15:9-12. **glorified.** Ps √138:2. 2 Th 1:12. 3:1. **the word.** ver. 5, 44, 46. Ac +11:1. **of the Lord.** Ac +15:35. **and as many.** Ac *2:47. Jn +*10:16, 26, 27. 11:52. Ro √8:30. 11:7. Ep 1:19. √2:5-10. 2 Th √2:13, 14. **ordained.** T#254. Ac 2:47. +*11:18. 15:2. +*18:27. 20:13g. 22:10. 28:23. Ps 135:4. Mt +*11:27. 20:16. *24:22n. 28:16. Lk 7:8. Jn +1:12 (T#584). +*6:44. +*12:39. 13:18. +*15:16, 19. Ro √8:28-30. *9:10-15, +18 (T#234). 11:5, 7. 13:1g. 1 C 16:15g. Ep 1:4-6, +*11. Ph +*1:29. *2:13. 1 Th 1:4. *5:9. 2 Th +*2:13. 2 T +*2:25 (T#242). Ja 1:18. 1 P *1:2. **eternal.** Gr. *aionios,* Mt +18:8. ver. 46. **believed.** ver. +12.

49. **word of.** ver. 48. Ac +15:35. **was published.** Ac 6:7. 9:42. 12:24. 19:10, 26. Ph 1:13, 14.

50. **the Jews.** ver. 45. Ac 6:12. 14:2, 19. 17:5, 13. 18:12. 20:3, 19. 21:27. 1 K 21:25. **devout.** ver. +43. Ac 2:5. Ro 10:2. **honorable.** Ac 17:12. Mk 15:43. 1 C 1:26-29. Ja *2:5, 6. **chief men.** Mk +6:21. **and raised.** Ac 8:1. Mt 10:23. 2 T *3:11. **Barnabas.** Ac +4:36. **and expelled.** Ac 16:37-39. Is +*66:5. Am 7:12. Mk 5:17. 1 Th 2:15.

51. **they shook off.** ℐ138B, Ge +13:16. Ac 18:6. Ne 5:13. Mt 10:14. Mk *6:11. Lk 9:5. *10:11. **Iconium.** i.e. *I come; image-like,* ✱S#2430g. Ac 14:1, 19, 21. 16:2. 2 T 3:11.

52. **the disciples.** Ac +11:26. **were.** Ac *2:46. 5:41. *10:45, 46. Mt +*5:12. Lk 6:22, 23. Jn 16:22, 23. Ro 5:3. *14:17. 15:13. 2 C 8:2. 1 Th 1:6. Ja 1:2. 1 P 1:6-8. 4:13. **with the.** Ac 2:4. 4:31. Ga 5:22. Ep *1:13. 5:18-20. **Ghost.** Gr. *pneuma,* Mt +1:18n.

ACTS 14

Paul and Barnabas preach with success at Iconium; and, being driven thence by the Jews, they preach at Lystra, 1-7. They heal a man who had been a cripple from his birth, 8-10. The priests and people attempt to sacrifice to them as gods, and are hardly restrained by their most earnest expostulations, 11-18. Paul is stoned, at the instigation of the Jews from Antioch and Iconium, and left for dead; but reviving, he goes with Barnabas to Derbe, 19, 20. They return to Lystra,

Iconium, and Antioch, confirming the churches, and ordaining elders in each of them, 21-23. Passing through Pisidia, Pamphylia, and Perga, they sail to Antioch in Syria, and rehearse to the church what things God had wrought by them, 24-28.

1. **in Iconium.** Ac +13:51. **went.** Ac 9:20. 13:+5, 46. 17:1, 2, 17. 18:4. 19:8. **great multitude.** ver. 21. Ac +6:1, 2. 11:21. 13:43, 46. 17:4. 18:8. **Greeks.** ver. 2. Ac 16:1. 17:12. 18:4. 19:10, 17. 20:21. 21:28. Mk 7:26. Jn 7:35mg. 12:20. Ro √1:16. 10:12. 1 C *1:22-24. Ga 2:3. 3:28. Col 3:11. **believed.** Ac +13:12.

2. **unbelieving Jews.** ver. 19. Ac 13:45, +50. 17:5, 13. 18:12. 19:9. 21:27-30. 26:19. Mk 15:10, 11. Jn √3:36. Ro +10:21. 15:31. 1 Th 2:15, 16. **minds.** Gr. *psyche*, √121A9A, Mt +11:29. **brethren.** Jn +21:23.

3. **Long time.** ver. 28. Ac 11:26. **therefore.** Ac 18:9-11. 19:10. 1 C 16:8, 9. **speaking boldly.** Ac +4:13. 13:46. Ep *6:18-20. 1 Th *2:2. **in the Lord.** ver. 23. Mk 16:20. He 2:4. **which.** Ac 2:22. 5:32. 15:8. Mk *16:20. He *2:4. **the word.** Ac 20:24, 32. Ro √1:16. **granted.** Ac *4:29, 30. 5:12-14. 19:11, 12. **signs.** Mk *16:20. Jn +4:48.

4. **the multitude.** Ac 23:7. Mi 7:6. Mt *10:34-36. Lk 2:34. 11:21-23. 12:51-53. Jn *7:43. **part.** Ac 17:4, 5. 19:9. 28:24. **apostles.** ver. 14. Ac 13:2. Jn 13:16. 1 C 9:1, 5, 6.

5. **when.** Ac 4:25-29. 17:5. Ps *2:1-3. 83:5. 2 T 3:11. **with their rulers.** Ac 3:17. **despitefully.** Mt 5:44. 22:6. Lk 6:28. 11:45g. 18:32. 2 C 12:10. 1 Th 2:2. **to stone.** ver. 19.

6. **were.** Ac 9:24. 12:12g. 17:13, 14. 23:12, etc. 2 K 6:8-12. **and fled.** Ac 8:1. 9:25, 30. 17:10, 14. Mt *10:16, 17, 23. **Lystra.** i.e. *ransoming; dissolves or disperses,* ✻S#3082g. *Lystra* and *Derbe,* two cities of Lycaonia, were situated south of Iconium, and north of Mount Taurus, the former being to the west, and the latter to the east. ver. 8, 20, 21. Ac 16:1, 2. 2 T 3:11. **Derbe.** i.e. *tanner,* ✻S#1191g. ver. 20. Ac 16:1. 20:4. **Lycaonia.** i.e. *wolfland; wolfish,* ✻S#3071g. *Lycaonia,* now *Konieh,* was a province of Asia Minor, bounded by Phrygia on the north, Pisidia on the west, Pamphylia and Cilicia on the south, and Cappadocia on the east, made a Roman province under Augustus (Strabo, l. x. Mela, l. i. c. 2. Livy, l. xxvii. c. 54. l. xxxvii. c. 39). ver. 11.

7. **they preached.** ver. 15g, 21. Ac 8:4, +40. 11:19. 17:2, 3. 1 Th 2:2. 2 T *4:2.

8. **impotent.** Ac 4:9. Jn 5:3, 7. **being.** Ac *3:2. Jn 5:5. 9:1, 2.

9. **heard.** Ac 16:14. **who.** Ac +3:4. **he had.** Mt 8:10. *9:+2, 22, 28, 29. *13:58. 15:28. Mk 1:40, 41. 2:5, 11, 12. 9:23, 24. 10:52. **be healed.** Mk +10:52.

10. **Stand.** Ac 3:6-8. *9:33, 34. Is 35:6. Lk 7:14. 13:11-13. Jn 5:8, 9. 14:12. **he leaped.** Ac 3:8. Is *35:6.

11. **lifted up.** √144A12, Ge +22:13. Ac 2:14. 4:24. 22:22. Lk 11:27. 17:13. **the speech.** The learned P. E. Jablonski, who has written a dissertation upon the subject, is of opinion, that this was not a dialect of the Greek; but that it was the same language as the Cappadocians, which was mingled with Syriac. **The gods.** Ac 8:10. 12:22. 28:6.

12. **Jupiter.** i.e. *father who helps,* ✻S#2203g. ver. 13. *Jupiter* was the supreme god of the heathen; and *Mercury* was considered the god of eloquence. The ancients represent Jupiter as an aged man, large, noble, and majestic; and Mercury, young, light, and active;

and it is very probable that Barnabas was a large, noble, well-made man; and St. Paul, young active, and eloquent. ver. 13. Ac 19:35. 28:11. **Mercurius.** i.e. *eloquent, learned, shrewd, crafty; reciprocal activity,* ✻S#2060g. Ro 16:14, Hermes.

13. **Jupiter.** Gr. Zeus. ver. 12. **oxen.** √108C6, 2 S 20:19. **and.** √93A, Ge +1:26. By *Hendiadys,* garlanded oxen. i.e. oxen decorated with a garland, and ready to be sacrificed. **the gates.** Ac +10:17. **and would.** Ac 10:25. Da *2:46.

14. **the apostles.** ver. 4. 1 C 9:5, 6. **Barnabas.** Ac +4:36. +12:25. **they rent.** Ge 37:29. 44:13. Nu 14:6. 2 S 1:11. 3:31. 2 K 5:7. 18:37. 19:1, 2. Ezr 9:3-5. Jb 1:20. Je 36:24. Mt 26:65. Mk 14:63. **ran in.** Ac 16:29.

15. **Sirs.** Ac 7:26. 16:30. 27:10, 21, 25. **why.** Ac +*10:25, 26. Jn +*20:29n. Re +*19:10. +*22:9. **We also.** Ac 3:12, 13. +*10:26n. 12:22, 23. Ge 41:16. Da 2:28-30. Jn 7:18. **of like.** Ja *5:17. Re *19:10. **and preach.** Ac +8:40. 17:16-18, 29, 30. 26:17-20. **turn from.** Ac +9:35. 15:19. 26:18, 20. Lk 1:16. 1 Th 1:9. Ja +*5:19, 20. **these vanities.** √121N2, Ge +34:29. Dt 32:21. 1 S 12:21. 1 K 16:13, 26. Ps 31:6. Is 44:9, 10, 19, 20. 45:20. 46:7. Je *8:19. 10:3-5, 8, 14, 15. 14:22. 16:19. 51:18. Am 2:4. Jon +*2:8. Ro 1:21-23. 1 C 8:4. Ep 4:17. **the living.** Dt 5:26. Jsh 3:10. 1 S 17:26, 36. 2 K 19:4, 16. Je 10:10. Da 6:26. Mt +16:16. Jn 5:26. 1 Th 1:9. 1 T 3:15. He +*3:12. **which made.** Ac 4:24. 17:24-28. Ge +*1:1. Ex 20:11. Ps *33:6. 124:8. *146:5, 6. Pr 8:23-31. Is 45:18. Je 10:11. 32:17. Zc 12:1. Ro 1:20. Re 4:11. 10:6. 14:7.

16. **suffered.** Ac √17:30. Ps *81:12. *147:19, 20. Ho 4:17. Ro 1:21-25, 28. 3:25. Ep 2:12. 1 P 4:3. **to walk.** Dt 5:33. 10:12. 30:16. Ps 81:13. Je 7:23. Mi 4:5. 1 P *4:3.

17. **he left.** Ac 17:27, 28. Ps 19:1-4. Ro *1:19, 20. 2:14, 15. **in that.** Nu 10:32. Ps 36:5-7. 52:1. 104:24-28. 145:9, 15, 16. Lk +*6:35. **and gave.** Ac 17:25, 26. Le 26:4. Dt 11:14. 28:12. 1 K 18:1. Jb 5:10. 28:26. 37:6. 38:26-28. Ps *65:9-13. 68:9, 10. 104:10, 13. 147:7, 8, 18. Is 5:6. Je 5:24. 14:22. Ezk 34:26. Jl 2:23. Mt +*5:45. 1 T 6:17. Ja 5:17, 18. **fruitful seasons.** Ps 67:6. 85:12. Ezk 34:27. 36:30. Ho 2:22. Jl 2:24. Zc 8:12. **filling.** Dt 8:12-14. Ne 9:25. Ps 104:15. Is 22:13. 1 T 6:17. Ja 5:5. **food.** Ps 104:27. **gladness.** Ps 104:15. 18. **scarce.** Ge 11:6. 19:9. Ex 32:21-23. Je 44:16, 17. Jn 6:15.

19. **Cir. A.M. 4051. A.D. 47. there.** Ac *13:45, 50, 51. 17:13. **Antioch.** *Antioch* of Pisidia, situated 92 miles east of Ephesus, now called *Ak Shehr.* ver. 21. Ac 13:14. 2 T *3:11. **persuaded.** Mt 27:20-25. Mk 15:11-14. **having stoned.** ver. 5. Ac 7:58. 9:16. 22:20. 2 C 11:25. 2 T 3:11. **drew.** Je 22:19. He 13:12, 13. **supposing.** 1 C 15:31. 2 C *4:10-12. 11:23.

20. **as.** Ac 20:9-12. 2 C 1:9, 10. 6:9. Re 11:7-12. **came.** Ac 12:17. 16:40. 20:1. **Barnabas.** Ac +4:36. **Derbe.** ver. 6. Ac 16:1.

21. **preached.** ver. 7, 15. Ac +8:40. **taught many.** Gr. made many disciples. Mt +*28:19g. **Lystra.** ver. 1, 6, 8, 19. Ac 13:14, 51. 15:36. 16:2. 2 T 3:11.

22. **Confirming.** Ac *15:32, 41. *18:23. Is *35:3. 1 C 1:8. 1 Th 3:2-4, 13. 1 P 5:10. **souls.** Gr. *psyche*, √121A9A, Mt +11:29. **the disciples.** ver. 20, 28. Ac +11:26. **exhorting.** Ac +15:32. **to continue.** Ac +*11:23. +*13:43. Je 32:40. Jn √8:31, 32. *15:4-6, 9, 10. 1 C +*15:1, 2. Col +*1:23. 1 T +*4:16. He +*10:35. 1 J +*2:3. Ju +*3, 20, 21. **in the faith.** Ac

+6:7. **and**. √63BA, Ge +26:7. Supply by ellipsis (saying). **we must**. √15F, Jn +13:29. Ac 4:12. 9:6, 16. 16:30. **much tribulation**. Ac 9:16. 20:23. Ps +*119:75. Mt 10:21, 22, 38. *16:24. Mk 8:34. 10:30. Lk 9:23. 14:27. *22:28, 29. *24:26. Jn 12:25, 26. 15:18, 20. 16:1, 2, *33. Ro √8:17, 18. Ph √1:29. 1 Th 3:3, 4. 2 Th 1:5. 2 T 1:8. +*2:11, 12. *3:12. 1 P 2:21. *4:12-16. 5:9, 10. Re 1:9. 2:10. 7:14. **enter**. Ac 1:3. Mt *19:24. Mk *9:47. *10:24, 25. Jn *3:3, 5. 1 C +*15:50n. 2 P *1:11.

23. **they had**. Ac 1:22. Mk 3:14. 2 C 8:19. Col 4:17. 1 T 5:22. 2 T 2:2. T 1:5. **elders**. This text speaks of "elders" in every church, showing that the New Testament churches founded by the apostles had a plurality of elders, not a single pastor, in charge of each local body of believers. Ac +11:30. 15:4, 6, 23. 20:17. Ph 1:1. 1 T *5:1, 17-19. T *1:5, 6. Ja 5:14. 1 P 5:1. 2 J 1. 3 J 1. **and had**. Ac 13:1-3. 20:17. Lk +2:37. Ph 1:1. **they commended**. ver. 26. Ac 20:32. Lk 23:46. 1 Th 3:12, 13. 2 Th 2:16, 17. 2 T 1:12. 1 P 4:19. 5:10. **to the Lord**. Ac +11:16. **on whom**. Ac +*10:43.

24. Cir. A.M. 4052. A.D. 48. **Pisidia**. *Pisidia* was a province of Asia Minor, situated between Phrygia on the north and west, Lycaonia on the east, and Pamphylia on the south. Ac 13:13, 14. 15:38. **Pamphylia**. Ac 2:10. 13:13. 15:38. 27:5.

25. **the word**. Ac +8:4. **Perga**. *Perga* was a considerable city of Pamphylia, towards the sea coast, and near the Caystrus, famous for a temple of Diana. Ac 13:13. **Attalia**. i.e. *increasing; sending*, ✻S#825g. *Attalia*, now *Antalia*, or *Satalie*, was a maritime city of Pamphylia, the chief residence of the praefect.

26. **to Antioch**. Ac 11:19, +26. 13:1. 15:22, 30. Ga 2:11. **recommended**. ver. 23. Ac *13:1-3. *15:40. 20:32. 2 C 1:12. 1 P 2:23g. 3 J 6-8. **the grace**. Ac +11:23. 1 C *15:10. **the work**. Ro 15:19. Col 1:25, 28, 29. 4:17. 2 T 4:2, 5-8.

27. **and had gathered**. Ac 15:4-6, 30. 21:20-22. Mk 6:30. 1 C 5:4. 11:18. 14:23. **they rehearsed**. Ac *15:4, 12. *21:19. 1 Ch=16:4. Ro 15:18. 1 C 3:5-9. 15:10. 2 C 6:1. **that God**. Ac 10:38. Mt 28:20. Mk 16:20. **opened**. Ac 11:18. Jn 9:10. 1 C *16:9. 2 C *2:12, 14. Col *4:3. 1 Th 1:9. Re *3:7, 8. **door of faith**. Ho 2:15. Ep √2:8.

28. **abode long**. Ac 11:26. 15:35. **disciples**. ver. 22.

ACTS 15

Dissensions having been excited, in the church at Antioch, about circumcising the Gentile converts; Paul and Barnabas are sent to Jerusalem, to consult the apostles and elders on the question, 1, 2. They arrive at Jerusalem, and the apostles and elders assemble, 3-5. Peter declares his opinion, 6-11. Paul and Barnabas report what God had done by them among the Gentiles, 12. James decides against circumcising the Gentile converts, but proposes some rules for their conduct, 13-21. Letters are sent by messengers, accompanying Paul and Barnabas, to the churches, with the determination of the council, and that of the Holy Spirit also; which are received with joy, 22-31. Judas and Silas, the messengers, abide at Antioch, and labor there, 32-35. Paul and Barnabas propose to revisit the churches which they had planted; but are separated by a sharp contention about John Mark; and set out to preach the gospel in different directions, 36-41.

1. Cir. A.M. 4057. A.D. 53. **certain**. ver. 24. Ac 21:20. Ga 2:4, 12, 13. **the brethren**. ver. 3, 22, 23,

32, 36, 40. Jn +21:23. **Except**. ver. 5. Ro 4:8-12. Ga 5:1-4. Ph 3:2, 3. Col 2:8, 11, 12, 16. **circumcised**. ver. 5. 1 C 7:18. Ga 2:11, 14. 5:2. **after**. Ac ◑+6:14. Ge *17:10-14. Le *12:3. Jn *7:22. **ye**. ver. 24. Ro *2:25-29. 3:1, 2, 30. *4:8-12. 1 C *7:18, 19. Ga 2:1, 3. √5:2, 6. *6:13-16: Ep *2:11, 14, 15. Col √2:8, 11, 16, 17. *3:11. **be saved**. ver. +11.

2. **Paul**. Ac +12:25. **Barnabas**. Ac +4:36. **dissension**. ver. 7. Ga 1:6-10. *2:5. Ja *3:17. Ju +*3. **disputation**. ver. 7. **they determined**. ver. 25. Ex 18:23. Ga 2:1, 2. **certain**. ver. 22, 27. Ac 10:23. 11:12. **go up**. Ac +18:22. **to Jerusalem**. ver. 4, 22, 23. 1 S 8:7. 1 C 9:19-23. Ga 2:2. Phm 8, 9. **the apostles**. ver. 4, 6, 22, 23. Ac +5:12. 11:30. 16:4. 21:18. 1 C 1:1. 2 C 11:5.

3. **brought**. Ac 20:38. 17:15. 21:5. 28:15. Ro 15:24. 1 C 16:6, 11. 2 C 1:16. T 3:13. 3 J 6-8. **passed**. Ac 8:14. 11:19. 21:2. **declaring**. ver. 12. Ac +14:27. 21:19, 20. **the conversion**. Ac 14:15. **they caused**. Ac 11:18. 13:48, 52. Is 60:4, 5. 66:12-14. Lk *15:5-10, 23, 24, 32. **the brethren**. ver. +1.

4. **were come**. Ac 21:17. **received**. Ac 18:27. 21:17. Mt 10:40. Ro 15:7. Col *4:10. 2 J 10. 3 J 8-10. **all**. ver. 3, 12. Ac 14:27. 21:19. Ro 15:18. 1 C 15:10. 2 C 5:19. 6:1.

5. **rose up certain**. *or*, rose up, *said they*, certain. **the sect**. Ac 21:20. +24:5. 26:5, 6. Ph *3:2-8. **Pharisees**. Ac +5:34. **which believed**. ver. 7. Ac +13:12. **That it**. ver. +1, 24. Ga 5:1-3. **law of Moses**. Jn +7:23.

6. **came together**. T#108. ver. 22-29. Ac 6:2. 21:18. Pr 15:22. Mt 18:20. He 13:7, 17.

7. **much disputing**. ver. 2, 39. Ph 2:14. **ye know**. Ac 10:5, 6, 20, 32-48. *11:12-18. Mt 16:18, 19. **while ago**. ver. 21. Ac 21:16g. **God**. Ac 1:2, 24. 9:15. 13:2. 1 Ch 28:4, 5. Jn 3:27. +*15:16. Ga 2:7-9. **by my mouth**. Ac 1:16. 3:18. 4:25. *10:20. Ex 4:12. Je 1:9. Ro 10:17, 18. **should hear**. Ro 10:14. **the word**. Ep 1:13. Col 1:5. 1 Th 1:5. **the gospel**. Ac 20:24. **and believe**. ver. 5. Ac +13:12.

8. **which**. Ac 1:24. 1 S +*16:7. 1 K 8:39. 1 Ch +*28:9. 29:17. Ps 44:21. 139:1, 2. Je 11:20. +*17:10. 20:12. Jn +*2:24, 25. *21:17. He +*4:13. Re *2:23. **bare**. Ac 14:3. Jn 5:37. He 2:4. *11:4. **giving**. Ac 2:4. 4:31. √10:44, 45, 47. 11:15-17. Ga 3:2. **Ghost**. Gr. *pneuma*, √121A1, Lk +1:17n. Ac *2:37, 38. ◑8:21. Jn *7:38, 39. Ro 8:16.

9. **put**. Ac 10:28, 34. 11:12. 14:1, 27. Ro 3:9, 22-24, 29, 30. 4:11, 12. 9:24. 10:11-13. 1 C 7:18. Ga *3:28. 5:6. Ep 2:14-22. 3:6. +*4:4. Col *3:11. **purifying**. Ac *10:15, 28, 43, 44. 26:18. Ps 51:10. Mt +*5:8. 1 C *1:2. 2 C 7:1. He *9:13, 14. 1 P *1:22. **by faith**. Ac +*10:43.

10. **Now**. √38B, 2 S +1:24. **why tempt**. Ac 5:9. Ex 17:2. Dt 6:16. Ps 78:18. 95:9. 106:14. Is 7:12. Mt 4:7. Lk 4:12. 1 C 10:9. He 3:9. **put**. ver. 28. Mt *11:28-30. 23:4. Ga 3:10, 13, 14. *5:1, 3. He *10:1. Ja *2:10. **yoke**. √121S1, Ge +49:10. By Metonymy of the Adjunct, whereby the sign is put for the thing signified, "yoke" is put for "burden." **the disciples**. Ac +11:26. **which neither**. Mt 11:28. *23:4. Lk 11:46. Ga 4:1-5, 9. He 9:9, 10.

11. **believe**. Ac √16:31. **through the grace**. Jn +*6:44. Ro 1:7. 5:15. +16:20. 1 C 1:3. 2 C 1:2. Ga 1:3. *3:11. Ep 1:2. Ph 1:2. 2 Th 1:2. 1 T 1:2. 2 T 1:2. T 1:4. Phm 3. **the Lord Jesus Christ**. ver. 26. Ac +1:21. 3:20, 21. +11:17. **be saved**. Ac √4:12. Ro

*3:24. *5:20, 21. √6:23. 1 C 16:23. 2 C √8:9. 13:14. Ga 1:6. √2:16. Ep 1:6, 7. √2:7-9. 1 Th 5:9. 2 T +*1:9. T √2:11. *3:4-7. Re *5:9. **even as they.** ver. +*9.

12. **the multitude.** ver. 22. Ac +6:2. **Barnabas and.** ver. +2. **declaring.** ver. 4. Ac +14:27. 21:19. **miracles.** Mk 16:20. Jn +4:48. **God had wrought.** ver. 4.

13. **after.** 1 C 14:30-33. Ja 1:19. **James answered.** Ac +12:17n. 21:18. Mk 15:40. Ga 1:19. 2:9, 12. Ja 1:1. **Men.** Ac 2:14, 22, 29. 7:2. 22:1.

14. **Simeon.** 2 P 1:1g. **declared.** ver. 7-9. Lk 1:68, 78. 2:31, 32. **did visit.** Ac +*13:48. 16:10. **to take.** Ac 18:10. Nu=3:12. =8:16. Dt 7:6. 12:5. Is *43:21. √55:11-13. Mt *22:14. Ro 1:5. 9:24-26. 11:36. 1 P *2:9, 10. **his name.** Nu +*6:27. Ps 66:2. Je 13:11. Ezk 36:22-24. He +13:15.

15. **agree.** Ac 13:47. Ro 15:8-12. **the prophets.** Jn +6:45.

16. **After.** ♪92A, Mt +1:23. **this.** Je 12:15. Am +√♪9:11-15. **build again.** Ac +*3:19, 21. 2 S 7:11-16. 1 K 12:16. Ps 89:35-49. 147:2. Is +*9:6, 7. Je 33:24-26. Ezk 17:22-24. 21:25-27. Ho 3:4, 5. Zc 13:8. Mt 1:20-25. Lk 1:31-33, 69, 70. **the tabernacle.** 2 S *7:13. Is *16:5. *33:20. Re 21:3.

17. **the residue.** Ge 22:18. +*49:10. Ps 22:26, 27. 67:1-3. 72:17-19. Is +*2:2, 3. 11:10. 19:23-25. 24:15, 16. 49:6, 7. *55:5. 66:18-21. Je 16:19. Ho 2:23. Jl 2:32. Mi 4:1, 2. 5:7. Zc 2:11. *8:20-23. Ml 1:11. **might seek.** Ac *17:27. **the Gentiles.** Ge 48:16. Nu 6:27. Is 43:7. 65:1. **upon whom.** Dt 28:10. Is 43:7. 63:19. Je 14:9. Da 9:18, 19. Am +*♪9:12. Ja 2:7. **my name.** ver. 14. Ps 66:2. He +13:15. **who doeth.** Nu 24:23. Is 45:7, 8. Da 4:35.

18. **Known unto.** Ac *2:23. +*13:48. *17:26. Nu *23:19. Is 41:22, 23. *44:7. 45:21. *46:9, 10. Mt *13:35. *25:34. Ep +*1:4, 11. *3:9. 2 Th √2:13, 14. He +*4:13. 1 P *1:20. Re *13:8. *17:8. **beginning.** Lk +1:70. 11:50. Jn 17:24. He 4:3. **world.** Gr. *aion,* Mt +6:13.

19. **my sentence.** ver. 28. **that.** ver. 10, 24, 28. Ga 1:7-10. 2:4. 5:11, 12. **turned.** Ac +14:15. 26:20. Is √55:7. Ho +*14:2. 1 Th *1:9.

20. **abstain.** Ac 21:25. **from pollutions.** ver. 29. Ge 35:2. Ex +*20:3-5, 23. 34:15, 16. Nu 25:2. Ps 106:37-39. Ezk 4:13, 14. 20:30, 31. Da +*1:8. Ml 1:7, 12. 1 C 8:1, 4-13. *10:20-22, 28. 1 P 4:3. Re *2:14, 20. 9:20. 10:20, 28. **fornication.** T#404. ver. 29. Ac 21:25. Ge 34:7. 38:24. *39:7-9. Ex +*20:14. 22:16. Le 20:10-23. 19:29. 21:7, 9, 14. Dt 22:28. 23:17. Pr 23:27. 29:3. 31:3. Hab 2:15. Mt 5:27, 28, 32. *15:19. 19:9. Ro 13:13. 1 C 5:1, 11. +√6:9, 10, 13, 18-20. 7:1, 2. 10:7, 8. 2 C 12:21. Ga *5:19. Ep 4:19n. *5:3, 4. Col *3:5, 6. 1 Th *4:3-6n. 1 T 1:10. He 12:16. *13:4. 1 P 2:11. *4:3. Ju 7. Re 9:21. +*21:8. 22:15. **things strangled.** Ac 21:25g. Ge 9:4. Le 3:17. 7:23-27. *17:10-14. Dt *12:16, 23-25. *14:21. 15:23. 1 S 14:32. Ezk 4:14. 33:25. 1 T ◐√4:4, 5. **from blood.** Le +*3:17n.

21. **Moses.** ♪121A6, Lk +16:29. Ac 13:15, 27. Mk +12:19. 2 C 3:14, 15. **of old time.** ver. 7. **sabbath day.** Ac 13:15, 27. Ne 8:1, etc. Lk *4:16.

22. **pleased.** ver. 23, 25. Ac 6:4, 5. 2 S 3:36. 2 Ch 30:4, 12. **the whole.** ♪171L2, Mt +26:59. **to send.** ver. 27. Ac 8:14. 11:22. **the apostles.** ver. +2. **with the whole church.** ver. 12. **Antioch.** *Antioch* of Syria, now *Antakia,* was the capital of the Syro-Macedonian empire, the residence of the Macedonian kings of Syria for several hundred years, and afterwards of the Roman governors of the province. It was situated on the Or-

ontes, about 67 miles west of Aleppo, and 12 miles from the Mediterranean, and is said to have been four miles in circumference. It was totally ruined by an earthquake in 1822. Ac +11:26. **Paul and Barnabas.** Ac +4:36. 12:25. **Barsabas.** i.e. *son of the oath; son of the host; son of rest, or return,* ✱S#923g. Ac *1:23. (1) Joseph Barsabas, disciple of the Lord, who was nominated along with Matthias to succeed Judas Iscariot, Ac 1:23. Some consider him as the same person as Barnabas. (2) Judas Barsabas, a disciple sent with Silas to Antioch, Ac 15:22. **Silas.** i.e. *considerate,* ✱S#4609g. ver. 27, 32, 34, 40. Ac 16:19, 25, 29. 17:4, 10, 14, 15. 18:5. Compare ✱S#4610g: 2 C 1:19. 1 Th 1:1. 2 Th 1:1. 1 P +5:12, Silvanus. **chief men.** Lk +22:26g. **the brethren.** ver. 1, 26, 40. Jn +21:23.

23. **letters.** ♪144A5, Ge +9:5. **The apostles.** ver. +2, 4, 22. **and elders.** Ac +11:30. **brethren.** ver. 22. Jn +21:23. **greeting.** Ro 16:3, etc. Ja 1:1. 2 J 10, 11, 13. 3 J 14. **brethren.** Ac 11:18. 14:27. 21:25. **Syria.** i.e. *sublime, deceiving,* ✱S#4947g. ver. 41. Ac 18:18. 20:3. 21:3. Mt 4:24. Mk 7:26 (S#4949g, Syrophenician). Lk 2:2. Ga 1:21. **Cilicia.** ver. 41. Ac +6:9.

24. **that certain.** ver. 1. Je 23:16. Ga *2:3, 4. *5:4, 12. 6:12. 2 T 2:14. T 1:10, 11. 1 J √2:19. **troubled you.** Ga *1:7, 8. *5:10, 12. **with words.** Ep +*4:14. T 3:10, 11. 2 J 10, 11. **subverting.** Ezk 14:10n. Ep +*4:14. Col 2:4, 18. 2 P 2:14. **souls.** Gr. *psyche,* ♪121A9A, Mt +11:29. **Ye must.** ♪63B, Ge +25:28. ver. 1, 5, 10. Ga 2:3, 4. √5:2-4. *6:12, 13. Col *2:14. **keep the law.** Ro 3:20, 21. Ep 2:15. Col *2:14. He 7:18. 8:13. 10:1. 12:27. **no such commandment.** Ac +*21:25.

25. **seemed.** ver. 28. Ge +*24:50. 1 K +*13:9n. Mt 11:26. Lk 1:3. **being.** ver. 6. Ac +1:14. 2:1, 46. 1 C 1:10. **to send.** ver. 22, 27. **our.** Ro 16:12. Ep 6:21. Col 4:7, 9. Phm 16. 2 P 3:15. **Barnabas.** ver. 2, 35. Ac +4:36. Ga 2:9. **Paul.** Ac +12:25.

26. **Men that.** Ac 9:23-25. **hazarded.** Ac *13:50. *14:19. Jg 5:18. Ro 16:4. 1 C *15:30-32. 2 C *11:23-27. Ph 2:29, 30. **lives.** Gr. *psyche,* ♪121A7, Mt +2:20. ♪121A7, Ge +9:5. Ac 20:24. 21:13. 2 C 4:11. 1 J 3:16. **the name.** Ac +*2:21, 38. 3:6, 16. 4:10, 12, 17, 18, 30. 5:28, 40, 41. 8:12, 16. 9:14-16, 21, 27, 29. 10:43, 48. 16:18. 19:5, 17. *21:13. 22:16. 26:9. Lk +24:47. Jn +20:31. 1 C +1:10. Re +2:3. **our Lord Jesus Christ.** ver. 11. Ac 3:20, 21. +11:17.

27. **Judas.** ver. 22, 32. **Silas.** ver. +22. **who.** 2 J 12. 3 J 13. **mouth.** Gr. word.

28. **it seemed.** ver. 25. Ml 2:7. Lk 1:3. Jn +*16:13n. Ro 1:5. 1 C 7:25, 40. 14:37. 1 Th 4:8. 1 P 1:12. **Ghost.** Gr. *pneuma,* Mt +3:16. ver. 8. Mt 12:32. Ac 5:32. +8:29n. Jn +*16:13n, 14n. 1 C 7:40. **to us.** ver. 19. **greater.** ver. 10. Mt 11:30. 23:4. Re 2:24.

29. **ye abstain.** See on ver. 20. Ac 21:25. Le 17:14. Ro 14:14, 15, 20, 21. 1 C 10:18-20. Re 2:14, 20. **things sacrificed.** 1 C 8:1, 4, 7, 10. 10:19. Re 2:14, 20. **fornication.** ver. +√20. **if ye.** 2 C 11:9. 1 T 5:22. Ja 1:27. 1 J 5:21. Ju 20, 21, 24. **Fare.** Ac 18:21. 23:30. Lk 9:61. 2 C 13:11.

30. **Antioch.** Ac +11:26, 27. **had gathered.** ver. 4, 6. Ac 14:27. **the multitude.** Ac +6:2. 21:22. **delivered.** Ac 16:4. 23:33.

31. **they rejoiced.** ver. 1, 10. Ac 16:5. Ga 2:4, 5. 5:1. Ph 3:3. **consolation.** *or,* exhortation. Ac +4:36.

32. **Judas.** ver. 22, 27. **Silas.** ver. +22. **being.** Ac 2:17, 18. 11:23, 27. +13:1. Mt 23:34. Lk 11:49. Ro

12:6. 1 C 12:28, 29. *14:3, 29, 32. Ep 3:5. 4:11. 1 Th
5:20. **exhorted.** Ac 2:40. +4:36. +*11:23. +*14:22.
16:40. 18:23. 20:1, 2. Ro 12:8. 1 Th 2:11. 4:1. 5:14.
2 Th 3:12. 1 T 2:1. 2 T 4:2. T 2:6, etc. 1 P 5:1, 12. **the
brethren.** ver. +1. **confirmed.** ver. 41. Ac +*14:22.
Is 35:3, 4. Da 11:1. 1 C 1:8. Ep 4:12, 13. 1 Th 3:2.
1 P 5:10.

33. **tarried.** ∫171J2. Synecdoche of the Species
B630. "To make" (with time) is used for *to continue*
or *abide.* For other instances of this figure see Ac
18:23. 20:3. 2 C 11:25. Ja 4:13. **they were.** Ac 16:36.
Ge 26:29. Ex 4:18. Mk 5:34. Lk 7:50. 8:48. 1 C 16:11.
He 11:31. Ja 2:16. 2 J 10.

34. **it pleased.** Ac 11:25, 26. 18:27. 1 C 16:12.

35. **Paul.** Ac +12:25. **Barnabas.** Ac +4:36. 13:1.
continued. Ac 13:1. 14:28. **Antioch.** Ac +11:26. **teaching.** Ac +5:42. 28:31. Mt +*28:19, 20. Col 1:28. 1 T
2:7. 2 T *4:2. **the word.** ver. 36. Ac 8:25. 13:12, 49.
16:32. 19:10, 20. 1 Th 1:8. **the Lord.** Ac +11:16.

36. Cir. A.M. 4058. A.D. 54. **Let.** Ac 7:23. Ex 4:18.
Je 23:2. Mt 25:36, 43. **in every.** Ac *13:4, 5, 13, 14,
51. *14:1, 6, 21, 24, 25. **and see.** Est 2:11. Ro 1:11.
2 C 11:28. Ph 1:27. 1 Th 2:17, 18. 3:6, 10, 11. 2 T
1:4.

37. **John.** Ac 12:12, 25. 13:5, 13. Col *4:10. 2 T
*4:11. Phm *24.

38. **who departed.** Ac √13:13. Ps 78:9. Pr 25:19.
Lk 9:61. 14:27-34. Ja *1:8. **Pamphylia.** *Pamphylia* was
a province of Asia Minor, bounded on the south by
the Mediterranean, west by Lycia, north by Pisidia,
and east by Cilicia. Acts 2:10. 13:13. 14:24. 27:5.

39. **the contention.** ver. 2. Ac 6:1. *14:15. 17:16g.
Ps *106:33. 119:96. 141:3. Ec √7:20. Ro 7:18-21. Ja
3:2. **Barnabas took.** Ac +4:36. Col 4:10. **Mark.** ver.
+37. **and sailed.** Ac +4:36. 11:20. 13:4-12. 27:4. **Cyprus.** Ac +4:36.

40. **chose.** ver. +22, 32. Ac 16:1-3. **being.** Ac 13:3.
14:26. 20:32. 1 C 15:10. 2 C 13:14. 2 T 4:22. T 3:15.
1 P 2:23. 2 J 10, 11. **the brethren.** ver. +1. **the grace.**
ver. 11. Ac 11:23. Ro +16:20. **the Lord.** Ac +11:16.

41. **through Syria.** ver. +23. Ac 18:18, 23. 21:3.
Ga 1:21. **confirming.** ver. 32. Ac +*14:22. 16:4, 5.
the churches. Ac *16:5. 1 C 16:1.

ACTS 16

*Paul and Silas come to Derbe and Lystra, and Paul,
having circumcised Timothy, takes him for an assistant,
1-3. They deliver the apostolic decree to the churches,
which are established, and increased in numbers, 4,
5. Having gone through Phrygia and Galatia, the Spirit
forbids them to preach in Asia and Bithynia, and they
come to Troas, 6-8. A vision directs them to go into
Macedonia, and they arrive at Philippi, 9-12. Lydia,
being converted, entertains them, 13-15. Paul casts
out a spirit of divination, 16-18; and, in consequence,
he and Silas are seized, scourged, imprisoned, and
put in the stocks, 19-24. They pray and sing praises;
and an earthquake opens the doors of the prison, and
looses their bonds, 25, 26. The jailor, prevented by
Paul from killing himself, is converted, with his family,
27-34. Paul and Silas, being set at liberty, refuse to
leave the prison, till requested by the magistrates, 35-
39. They comfort the brethren and depart, 40.*

1. **came.** ∫171J9. Synecdoche of the Species B632.
"To meet" (Gr. *katantao*) is used of arriving at so as

to touch. For other instances of this figure see Ep
4:13. Ph 3:11. 1 Th √4:17. **to Derbe.** Ac 14:+6, 8,
21. 2 T 3:11. **disciple.** Ac +9:10. **named Timotheus.**
i.e. *honoring God,* ✱S#5095g. Ac 17:14, 15. 18:5.
*19:22. 20:4, 5. Ro *16:21. 1 C *4:17. 16:10. 2 C 1:1,
19. Ph 1:1. 2:19. Col 1:1. 1 Th 1:1. *3:2, 6. 2 Th 1:1.
1 T *1:2, 18. 6:20. 2 T *1:2. Phm 1. He 13:23. **which.**
2 T *1:5. √3:15, 16. **a Jewess.** i.e. *praise,* S#2453g.
believed. Ac +13:12. **but.** Ac 14:1. Ezr 9:2. 1 C +*7:14.

2. **well reported.** Ac +6:3. 1 T 3:7. 5:10, 25. 2 T
√3:15. He 11:2. **the brethren.** ver. 40. Jn +21:23. **Iconium.** Ac +13:51. 14:21. 2 T 3:11.

3. **would.** Ac 15:37, 40. **and took.** Ac 15:20, 21.
1 C 7:19. *9:20. Ga *2:3, 8. ◐*5:1-3, 6. **his father.**
ver. 1.

4. **they delivered.** Ac *15:6, 28, 29. **the decrees.**
Ac +17:7. **ordained.** Ac 14:23. 15:28, 29. **apostles and
elders.** Ac 15:+2, 23.

5. **so.** Ac 9:31. 15:41. 2 Ch +*20:20. Is 7:9. Ro
16:25. 1 C √15:58. 16:1. Ga *5:1. Ep 4:13-16. Col 2:6,
7. 1 Th 3:2, 13. 2 Th 2:16, 17. He 13:9, 20, 21. 1 P
5:10. **in the faith.** Ac +6:7. 1 P 5:9. **increased.** Ac
2:47. 4:4. 5:14. 6:7. 9:31. 11:21. 12:24. 13:48, 49. 19:18-
21.

6. **Phrygia.** i.e. *dry, barren,* ✱S#5435g. *Phrygia,*
a country of Asia Minor, had Bithynia and Galatia on
the north, Cappadocia on the east, Lycaonia, Pisidia,
Pamphylia, and Lycia, on the south, and Lydia and
Mysia on the west. Ac 2:10. *18:23. **region.** Ac 18:23.
1 C 16:1. Ga 1:2. 3:1. 2 T 4:10. 1 P 1:1. **Galatia.** i.e.
white as milk, ✱S#1054g. *Galatia* was situated between
Phrygia on the south, Bithynia and Paphlagonia on
the north, and Pontus on the east. Ac 18:23g. 1 C
16:1. Ga 1:2. 3:1. 4:13. 2 T 4:10. 1 P 1:1. **forbidden.**
ver. 7. Ac 5:4. *8:29n. 10:19. 11:12. 13:2-4. 20:28.
2 Ch 6:7-9. Is 30:21. Am 8:11, 12. 1 C 12:11. He 11:8.
Ghost. Gr. *pneuma,* Mt +3:16. **the word.** Ac +8:4.
Asia. That is, *Proconsular Asia,* which included Ionia,
Aeolia, and Lydia. Ac +2:9. 19:◐10, 26, 27. 20:4, 16.
2 C 1:8. 2 T 1:15. 1 P 1:1. Re 1:4, 11.

7. **Mysia.** i.e. *criminal; closure; abomination,*
✱S#3465g. *Mysia* lay between Lydia on the south,
Troas on the west, the Propontis on the north, and
Phrygia and *Bithynia* on the east; which had the Euxine
on the north, Paphlagonia on the east, and Galatia
and Phrygia on the south. ver. 8. **Bithynia.** i.e. *violent
precipitation, violent rushing,* ✱S#978g. 1 P 1:1.
Spirit. Gr. *pneuma,* Mt +3:16. Mt +12:32.

8. **Troas.** i.e. *penetrated; I perforate; a Trojan,*
✱S#5174g. ver. 11. Ac 20:5, 6. 2 C *2:12. 2 T *4:13.

9. **a vision.** ver. 10. Ac 2:17, 18. 9:+10-12. 10:3,
10-17, 30. 11:5-12. 18:9, 10. 22:17-21. 27:23, 24. 2 C
12:1-4, 7. **a man.** Ac 10:30. Ezk *9:1. Da 12:1. **of
Macedonia.** i.e. *tall, extended,* ✱S#3110g. Ac 16:9.
19:29. 27:2. 2 C 9:2, 4. **Come.** Ac 8:26-31. 9:38. 10:32,
33. 11:13, 14. Mt *9:36-38. Ro *10:14, 15. **into Macedonia.** i.e. *adoration, elevation,* ✱S#3109g. Ac 18:5.
19:21, 22. 20:1, 3. Ro 15:26. 1 C 16:5. 2 C 1:16. 2:13.
7:5. 8:1. 11:9. Ph 4:15. 1 Th 1:7, 8. 4:10. 1 T 1:3.

10. **the vision.** ver. 9. Ac +9:10. **immediately.** Ac
10:29. 26:19. Ps *119:60. Pr 3:27, 28. 2 C 2:12, 13.
we endeavored. ver. 1117. Ac 20:58, 1315. 21:118.
27:128:16. Col +4:14. **assuredly gathering.** Ac 9:22g.
the Lord. Ac 15:14. **to preach.** Ac +8:40.

11. **straight course.** Ac 21:1. **Samothracia.** i.e.
height of Thrace; a sign of rags, ✱S#4543g. *Samothra-*

cia, now Samandrachi, was an island of the Aegean sea, about 20 miles in circumference, near Thrace, where the Hebrus falls into the sea. **Neopolis**. i.e. *new city*, *S#3496g. *Neopolis*, now Napoli, was a seaport of Macedonia, a few miles from Philippi, near Thrace, to which it was formerly reckoned.

12. **Philippi**. i.e. *lover of race horses*, *S#5375g. Ac 20:6. Ph 1:1. 1 Th 2:2. **the chief**. *or*, the first. **a colony**. ver. 21. **we**. ver. +10.

13. **on**. Ac 13:+14, 42. 17:2. 18:4. 20:7. **sabbath**. Gr. sabbath-day. Ac 21:5. Lk 13:10. **river side**. T#1203. Ezr 8:15, 21. Ps 137:1. Ezk 3:15, 16. Da 10:2-5. **where**. Lk 13:10. **we sat**. ver. 6. Mt 5:+1, 2. 13:2. Lk 4:20, 21. Jn 8:2. **spake**. Mk *16:15. Ga *3:28. Col +*1:23.

14. **Lydia**. i.e. *a magnet; travailing; to firebrand*, *S#3070g. ver. 40. **purple**. Lk 16:19. **Thyatira**. Re 1:11. 2:18-24. **worshipped**. Ac 8:27. 10:2. +13:43. 18:7. Jn 12:20. **heard**. Ac 14:9. **whose heart**. Ac 11:21. 2 Ch +*18:31. Ps *110:3. √119:18. Pr *16:1. SS 5:4. Is 50:5. Lk +24:45. Jn 6:44, 45. Ro 9:16. 1 C *3:6, 7. 2 C 3:14-16. *4:4-6. Ep 1:17, 18. Ph √2:13. Ja 1:16, 17. Re *3:7, 20. **opened**. Nu 24:3, 14, 15. 1 S *10:26. **she attended**. Nothing is said here of her family having accompanied her: Lydia is spoken of alone. This far in the account we know not that she has a family. "The act of her baptism cannot be separated from that of her family. Now if her family were of mature age, capable of *attention* to the word spoken, how is it that *they* are not mentioned with her, as *attending*, since they are mentioned with her as receiving baptism? …there cannot be a clearer instance to warrant the baptism of those children who have not *attended* to the word preached" (C. Taylor, *Apostolic Baptism*, p. 61).

15. **when**. ver. 33. Ac 8:+12, 38. 11:14. 18:8. 1 C 1:13-16. **and her**. Ac +*2:39. Ge +*17:9, 10. **household**. √121J4, Ge +7:1. Gr. *oikos*, a family with small infants. Had *oikos* in reference to persons been rendered *family*, New Testament teaching on infant baptism would have been clear. *Oikos* never means a married pair not having children, or the parents distinct from the children. It sometimes refers to the children distinct from the parents (1 C 1:16 w 16:15, 17), for Paul baptized the *family* of Stephanus, but not Stephanus himself. He salutes the family of Onesiphorus (2 T 1:16. 4:19), who was apparently absent from them. *Oikos* sometimes designates the family and absolutely excludes servants or household, as Noah (He 11:7. 1 P 3:20). *Oikos* designates not only minors, but children in the youngest possible state of life (1 T 3:4, 12). It has reference to babes and sucklings, infants, in 1 T 5:14, where "guide the house" is *oikodespotein*, literally despotize the offspring or family, mentioned in connection with "younger women…bear children." Those who ask for Bible evidence for infant baptism have it right here. It is impossible that there would be no infants in all the households which were baptized in the record of Acts and elsewhere in the New Testament (Lydia, the Philippian Jailor, Stephanas, are the instances most generally noted; frequently overlooked are the instances of Cornelius, Crispus, Onesiphorus, Aristobulus, and Narcissus). Since the word itself requires the idea of infants (1 T 5:14n), and several household baptisms included *all* of the family, infants must have been included. See related notes (Ac 2:41n; 8:12n. 10:48n. 1 C 7:14n. Col 2:11n). ver. 34. Ac 8:12n. +11:14. Ge

7:1. Dt +*29:11n. Ru *4:12. 1 C +*7:14n. See 1 C 1:16 w 16:15, 17. 1 T 3:4, 12. +*5:14n. 2 T 1:16. 4:19. **If ye**. √184A, 1 C +15:2. Ep 1:1. Ph 1:7. Phm 17. 1 P 5:12. 3 J 5. **faithful**. 1 C +4:2. **the Lord**. Ac +11:16. **come**. Ge 18:4, 5. Jg 19:19, 20. Mt 10:41. Lk 9:4, 5. 10:5-7. Ro 16:23. Ga *6:10. He +*13:2. 2 J +*10. 3 J *8. **and abide**. Lk 19:5. Jn 1:38. **And she**. Ge 19:3. 33:11. Jg 19:21. 1 S 28:23. 2 K 4:8. Lk 14:23. 24:29. 2 C 5:14. 12:11. He +*13:2.

16. **as**. ver. 13. **possessed**. ver. 18. Ac 8:9-11. Ex 7:11, 12. Dt 13:1-3. 18:9-11. 1 S 28:7. 1 Ch 10:13. Is *8:19. Ga 5:20. 2 T 3:8. **spirit**. Gr. *pneuma*, Mt +8:16. Lk 13:11. **divination**. *or*, Python. Ex 22:18. Le 19:31. 20:6, 27. Dt +*18:11. 1 S 28:3, 7, 9. 2 K 21:6. 1 Ch 10:13. Is 8:19. **which**. ver. 19. Ac 19:24. 1 T *6:10. 2 P 2:3. Re 18:11-13. **soothsaying**. Dt +*18:10. 1 S 28:8. 2 K 17:17. Ezk 12:24.

17. **These**. Ac 19:13. Mt 8:29. Mk 1:24. Lk 4:34, 41. **and cried**. Ac 19:15. Mk +*1:24. Ja +2:19. **the servants**. Da 3:26, 28. 6:16, 20. Jon 1:9. Ja +1:1. 1 P 2:16. **the most high**. Ge +14:18. Ps 57:2. 78:35. Da 4:2. 5:18, 21. Mi 6:6. Mk +5:7. Lk 8:28. **the way**. ver. 30, 31. Ac √4:12. 9:2. 18:26. Mt +*7:13, 14. 22:16. Mk 12:14. Lk 1:77, 79. 20:21. Jn √14:6. He *10:19-22.

18. **being grieved**. Ac 4:2. 14:13-15. Mk 1:25, 26, 34. **spirit**. Gr. *pneuma*, Mt +8:16. ver. 16. **I command**. Ac 3:6. 9:34. 19:12-17. Mk 1:25, 34. 9:25, 26. *16:17. Lk 9:1. 10:17-19. Col 2:15. **in the name**. Ac +3:6. Mt 7:22. Mk +9:38. 2 Th 3:6. **came out**. Mt 17:18.

19. **her masters**. ver. 16. **the hope**. Ac *19:24-27. 1 T √6:10. **they caught**. Ac 9:16. 14:5, 19. 15:26. 18:12, 13. 21:30. Mt *10:16-18. +*24:9. Mk 13:9. 2 C 6:5. **Silas**. ver. 25, 29. Ac +15:22. **and drew**. Ac 8:3. 17:68. 18:12. *21:30. Lk 12:11. Ja *2:6. **marketplace**. *or*, court.

20. **magistrates**. ver. 22, 35, 36, 38. **being**. Ac 18:2. 19:34. Ezr 4:12-15. Est 3:8, 9. **do**. Ac *17:6-8. 28:22. 1 K *18:17, 18. Mt 2:3. Jn 15:18-20. Ro *12:2. Ja *4:4.

21. **customs**. Ac 26:3. Ezr 4:13. Est 3:8. Je +*10:2, 3.

22. **the multitude**. Ac 17:5. 18:12. 19:28, etc. 21:30, 31. 22:22, 23. **the magistrates**. ver. 20, 37. Ac 5:40. 22:24-26. Mt 10:17. 27:26. 2 C 6:5. 11:23-25. 1 Th 2:2. He 11:36. 1 P 2:24. Re *2:10.

23. **stripes**. 2 C 6:5. 11:23. **they cast**. Ac 5:18. 8:3. 9:2. 12:4. Lk 21:12. Ep 3:1. 4:1. 2 T 2:9. Phm 9. Re 1:9. 2:10. **jailer**. ver. 27, 36. **to keep**. Ac 5:23. 12:18. 1 S 23:22, 23. Mt 26:48. 27:63-66.

24. **the inner**. 1 K 22:27. Je 37:15, 16. 38:26. La 3:53-55. **prison**. Lk +21:12. **and made**. 2 Ch 16:10h. Jb 13:27. 33:11. Ps 105:18. Je 20:2, 3. 29:26. **stocks**. lit. wood. √121D8, Ge +40:19.

25. **at midnight**. Jb 35:10. Ps 22:2. 42:8. 77:6. 119:55, 62. Is 30:29. **prayed**. T#1202. 2 Ch 33:11-13. Ps +*50:15. 77:2. 91:15. Je *33:1-3. La 3:52-56. Mt +*5:44. 26:38, 39. Lk 22:44. He 5:7. Ja 5:13. **sang**. Ac *5:41. Jb 35:10. Ps 34:1. 77:6. Mt 5:10, 11. 26:30. Mk 14:26. Lk 6:22, 23. Ro *5:3. 12:12. 2 C 4:8, 9, 16, 17. 6:10. Ep 5:19. Ph *2:17. √4:4-7. Col *1:11, 24. *3:15-17. 1 Th √5:16-18. He 2:12. Ja *1:2. 1 P 1:6-8. *4:13, 14. **and the**. Ezr 3:12, 13. Ps 71:7. Zc 3:8.

26. **suddenly**. Ac +4:31. *5:19. *12:7, 10. Mt 28:2. Re 6:12. 11:13. **earthquake**. T#1770. Nu 16:28-32. Ps 18:6-9. **doors**. Ac 5:19. 12:10. **and every**. Ac 12:7.

Ps 34:14, 15, 17, 19, 20, 22. 79:11. 102:20. 145:18-20. 146:7. Is 42:7. 61:1. Zc 9:11, 12.

27. the keeper. ver. 23, 24, 36. **he drew.** Jg 9:54. 1 S 31:4, 5. 2 S 17:23. 1 K 16:18. Mt 27:5. **killed himself.** Ac 12:19. 27:42. 1 K 20:39. 2 K 10:24.

28. cried. Le *19:18. Ps 7:4. 35:14. Pr 24:11, 12. Mt 5:44. Lk 6:27, 28. 10:32-37. 22:51. 23:34. 1 Th 5:15. **Do.** Ex 20:13. Pr 8:36. Ec 7:17. **we are all.** "All" signifies that there were several other prisoners besides Paul and Silas (see ver. 34n).

29. sprang in. Ac 14:14. Mk 10:50. **and came.** Ac 9:5, 6. 24:25. Ps 99:1. 119:120. Is 66:2, 5. Je 5:22. 10:10. Da 6:26. **and fell.** Ac 10:25. Is 60:14. Re 3:9.

30. brought. ver. 24. Jb *34:32. Is *1:16, 17. *58:6, 9. Mt *3:8. *5:7. Ja *2:13. **Sirs.** See on Ac 14:15. **what.** ver. 17. Ac *2:37. *9:6. *22:10. Jb *25:4. Lk 3:10, 12, 14. Jn *6:27-29. **must.** Ac +*4:12.

31. Believe. Ac *2:38, 39. √4:12. *8:37. +10:43. 11:13, 14. *13:38, 39. 15:11. Is *45:22. Hab 2:4. Mk +10:52. *16:16. Lk 8:12. Jn √1:12. √3:15, 16, 36. *6:40, 47. *7:37, 38. *11:25, 26. √20:31. Ro *5:1, 2. √10:9, 10. 1 C 1:21. Ga *3:22, 26. Ep √2:7, 8. He 10:39. Ja 2:14. 1 J √5:10-13. **saved.** Ac 2:21, 47. +*4:12. 11:14. 15:1, 11. **and thy house.** √121J4, Ge +7:1. ver. *15, *32. Ac +*2:39. 10:2. +11:14. *18:8. Ge 7:1. +*17:7. +*18:19. Jsh 2:18, 19. 1 K 17:15. Je 32:39. Lk *19:9. Ro *11:16. 1 C +*7:14n. Ga 3:14.

32. they. Ac 10:33-43. Mk *16:15. Ep 3:8. Col 1:27, 28. 1 Th 2:8. 1 T 1:13-16. **the word.** Ac +15:35. Ps *19:7. Ro √1:16. 1 P *1:23. **to all.** Ro 1:14, 16.

33. same hour. ver. 25. **washed.** ver. 23. Pr +*16:7. Is 11:6-9. Mt *25:35-40. Lk 10:33, 34. Ga 5:6, 13. **and was baptized.** In the case of the Philippian jailor, he and his family (which included several members, the expression used in ver. 34 denotes a large or numerous family) were baptized immediately. There most certainly were no facilities for the immersion of the members of his family in the apartment where he lived at the jail. There is no suggestion that they left the confines of his home or the jail at midnight to find sufficient water for immersion. It is certain from the account that the mode could only have been sprinkling or pouring, that his entire family was baptized, and his family included infants. T#38. ver. 14n, 15n. Ac *2:38, +39 (T#120), 40, 41. 8:+12, 36, 37, 46-48. *18:8. Mi +7:20 (T#117). Mt 18:1-6. Lk 19:9. Ro +2:29 (T#118). +4:11 (T#119). +15:8 (T#121). 1 C 1:16. **and all his.** Ac +11:14.

34. when. Lk 5:29. 19:6. Ph 4:17. 1 Th 4:9, 10. Phm 7. Ja 2:14-17. 1 J 3:18. **set meat.** Ps 23:5. **and rejoiced.** ver. 27-29. Ac 2:46. 8:39. 1 S 2:1. Ps 9:14. 13:5. 20:5. 21:1. 35:9. Is *12:1-3. 25:9. 52:12. 57:17, 18. 58:7-11. 61:10. Lk 1:47. 15:22-25, 32. Ro *5:2, 11. 15:13. Ga 5:22. Ph 4:4. 1 P *1:6-8. **believing.** Ac +8:12. 18:8. 27:25. Jn √5:24. T 3:8. 1 J *5:10. **with all.** "All" or "whole" indicates a numerous family. In Mt 13:56, "all" indicates Jesus had at least three sisters, or the word would have been "both." ver. 28. Ac *10:2. *18:8. The youthfulness of the jailor implied by his vigor and alacrity (ver. 29) make it certain that his numerous family included infants.

35. when it was day. Ac 4:21. 5:40. Ps 76:10. Je 5:22. **the magistrates.** ver. +20, 21. **sergeants.** ver. +20.

36. the keeper. ver. 23, 27. **go in peace.** Ac +15:33.

Ex 4:18. Jg 18:6. 1 S 1:17. 20:42. 25:35. 29:7. 2 K 5:19. Mk 5:34. Jn 14:27.

37. They have. ver. 20-24. Ac 22:25-28. Ps 58:1, 2. 82:1, 2. 94:20, 21. Pr 28:1. **openly.** √24F. Antimereia of the Adjective B695: adjective for adverb. For another instance of this figure see 1 C 12:11. **uncondemned.** Ac 22:25. **being Romans.** ver. ○20. Ac *22:25, 26. **privily.** Mt +1:19g. 2:7. Jn 11:28. **let.** The apostle saw no problem with asserting that his civil rights had been violated, and insisting that appropriate redress be made. Christians have a right to claim all the civil rights and protections afforded by their governments, the duty to obey the law (Ro 13:1, 2. 1 P 2:13), and the right to violate the law when such law is contrary to the written word of God (Ac 4:19, 20. +*5:29). When forced to be violators, however, they must expect to suffer the consequences (Ro 13:4). Jesus urged following a course of action, whenever possible, which did not bring undue hardship, persecution, or reprisal, especially when living under repressive governments (Mt 5:39-42). Da 3:25, 26. 6:18, 19. Mt √10:16.

38. sergeants. ver. +20. **and they feared.** Ac 22:29. Mt 14:5. 21:46.

39. came. Ex 11:8. Is 45:14. 49:23. 60:14. Mi 7:9, 10. Re 3:9. **and brought.** Da 6:16, 23. **and desired.** Mt *8:34. Mk 5:17, 18. Lk 8:37.

40. and entered. ver. 14. Ac 4:23. 12:12-17. **the brethren.** Who were these brethren? Not Lydia's children, who were infants (ver. 14n, 15n), and may just as well have been daughters. Rather, as Timothy and Luke accompanied Paul and Silas at this point in Paul's missionary journey (ver. +10), Paul and Silas returned to Lydia's home upon being released from prison to rejoin their brethren, Luke and Timothy, who had been staying at Lydia's home. "Brethren" may also be taken to include those who were appointed "bishops and deacons" at the church of Philippi, who gathered at Lydia's home. ver. 2. Jn +21:23. Ph *1:1-5. **they comforted.** Ac 14:22. +15:32. 2 C √1:3-7. 4:8-12, 16-18. 1 Th 3:2, 3.

ACTS 17

Paul preaches at Thessalonica; and some, both Jews and Greeks, believe, 1-4. The unbelieving Jews raise disturbances, and trouble the rulers, 5-9. Paul and Silas are sent by night to Berea, 10. The Bereans ingenuously attend to the word, and "search the scriptures daily: therefore many believe," 11, 12. The Jews of Thessalonica follow Paul and Silas to Berea, to stir up persecution, 13; Paul is conducted to Athens, 14, 15. His zeal is excited by the excessive idolatry of that city; and he disputes in the synagogue, and the forum with the philosophers, 16-18. He is brought before the Areopagus, 19-21. He preaches the living God, the Creator and Lord of all, as hitherto unknown to the Athenians, 22-29. He calls on them to repent; because God will judge the world by Jesus, whom he has raised from the dead, 30, 31. Some mock, others purpose to hear him again, and a very few believe, 32-34.

1. Amphipolis. i.e. *city encompassed*, *S#295g, only here. *Amphipolis* was the capital of the first division of Macedonia, situated on the Strymon, which nearly surrounded it, from whence it took its name, about 70 miles east of Thessalonica. It is now a place of little consequence, called *Emboli.* **Appolonia.** i.e. *utter destruction,* *S#624g, only here. *Appolonia* was also a city of Macedonia, southwest of Amphipolis, between that city and Thessalonica. **Thessalonica.** i.e. *victory of God,* *S#2332g. Ac 17:1, 11, 13. Ph 4:16. 2 T 4:10. *Thessalonica,* now *Salonichi,* was a celebrated city and capital of the second part of Macedonia, situated at the head of the Thermaic gulf, now the gulf of Salonichi. It was a noble mart, and the most populous of all Macedonia; and it still retains somewhat of its ancient splendor, being five miles in circumference, and containing a population of upwards of 60,000 persons (See the travels of Dr. Clarke, etc.). ver. 11, 13. Ac 20:4. 27:2. Ph 4:16. 1 Th 1:1. 2 Th 1:1. 2 T 4:10. **where.** Ac 14:1. 15:21. 16:13.

2. **as.** Lk +*4:16. Jn *18:20. **went.** ver. 10, 17. Ac 9:20. 13:+5, 14. 14:1. *18:4, 19. *19:8. 1 Th 2:1-5. **three sabbath days.** It is implied in 1 Th 2:9, 10, that Paul dwelt at Thessalonica a long time; but from this text (Ac 17:2) it seems that he spent there only "three sabbath days." The apparent discrepancies disprove design, and are not difficult to reconcile. It is expressly stated that this was the time during which Paul went in *unto the Jews,* and that does not preclude the supposition that thereafter he preached to the Gentiles, until his success provoked the Jews, who were "filled with envy," to assault Jason's house, where Paul dwelt (Ac 17:5). It was Paul's custom in every place first to address the Jews, and afterwards to turn to the Gentiles (Ac 13:46. 18:6, 11. 19:9, 10. Ro +*1:16). In 1 Th 1:9, it is stated that Paul's preaching converted many idolatrous Gentiles (William Paley, *Horae Paulinae,* pp. 154-156). See related notes on undesigned coincidences listed at Ac 12:12n. **reasoned.** T#452. ver. +*17g. Ac 18:4, 19. 19:8, 9. 20:7g, 9, 11. *24:12, 25. *28:23. 1 S *12:7. Is √1:18. Mt +28:19 (T#458). Mk 9:34. 1 C 2:4, 5. 2 C 3:12. 4:1, 2. Ep +4:11 (T#447). 1 T +5:20 (T#461). He ch. 7-10. Ju 9. **out of.** Ac +8:35. **the scriptures.** ver. 11. Mt +21:42.

3. **Opening.** Gr. *dianoigo,* *S#1272g. Ac 2:16-36. 3:22-26. 13:26-39. 16:14g. 28:23. Is 34:16. Mk 7:34g, 35g. Lk 2:23g. 24:31g, 32g, 45g. Jn +*5:39. 2 Th 3:1. 2 T +*3:15. **alleging.** Literally "setting forth (arguments)"; i.e. bringing forward passages of Scripture to prove his points (Thomas Walker). Mt +*27:9n. Gr. *paratitheemi,* *S#3908g: Rendered (1) set before: Ac 16:34. Mk 6:41. 8:6, 6, 7. Lk 9:16. 10:8. 11:6. 1 C 10:27. (2) commit: Lk *24:48. 1 T 1:18. 2 T *2:2. (3) commend: Ac 14:23. 20:32. Lk +*23:46. (4) put forth: Mt 13:24, 31. (5) commit the keeping of: 1 P 4:19. (6) allege: Ac 17:3. **Christ.** Ac 18:5. Lk +3:15. See on *24:26, 27, 32, 44, 46. 1 C +*15:3, 4. 1 Th 1:5, 6. **must needs.** Mt 16:21, 22. Lk +13:33. 24:25-27, 45-47. 1 C 1:18, 23. 1 P 1:11. **have suffered.** Ac +3:18. Mk +8:31. Lk *24:26. **and risen.** Ac +*2:24n. Jn +20:9. 1 C 15:17. 1 Th 4:14. **this.** Ac *2:36. *9:22. *18:28. Ga 3:1. **whom I preach.** *or,* whom, *said he,* I preach. **said he.** ʃ63BA, Ge +26:7. **I preach.** ʃ15E, Mk +6:9. Ac +1:4.

4. **some.** ver. 34. Ac 2:41, 42, 44. 4:23. 5:12-14. 14:1, +4. *28:24. Pr 9:6. 13:20. SS 1:7, 8. 6:1. Zc 2:11. *8:20-23. 2 C 6:17, 18. 1 Th 2:1, 2. **believed.** Ac 18:4. 19:8, 26. 26:28. 28:23. 1 Th *1:5-9. √2:13. **consorted.** Ac +*13:48. 2 C 8:5. Ep +*1:11. **Silas.** ver. 10, 14, 15. Ac 15:+22, 27, 32, 40. **the devout.** ver. 17. Ac +13:43. 16:3, 14. 18:4. 19:10, 17. 21:28.

Greeks. Jn +7:35. **great multitude.** ver. 12. Ac +6:1, 2. **and of the chief.** ver. +12. Ac 13:50. Mk +6:21.

5. **moved.** ver. 13. Ac 7:9. 13:45, 50. *14:2, 19. 18:12. Pr 14:30. Is 26:11. Mt 27:18. 1 C 3:3. Ga 5:21, 26. 1 Th 2:14-16. Ja 4:5. **envy.** Ac +5:17. **took.** Jg 9:4. 11:3. 2 Ch 13:7. Jb 30:1-10. Ps 35:15. 69:12. Pr 12:11. **baser sort.** Ac 16:19. 2 Th 3:10-13. **and set.** Ac 19:24-34, 40. **Jason.** i.e. *healer,* *S#2394g. ver. 6, 7, 9. Ro *16:21. **to bring.** Ac 12:6. **the people.** Ac 12:22. 19:30, 33g.

6. **they drew.** Ac 6:12, 13. 8:3g. *16:19, 20. 18:12, 13. **brethren.** ver. 10, 14. Jn +21:23. **These.** Ac 21:28-31. 22:22, 23. 24:5. 28:22. 1 K 18:17, 18. Est 3:8, 9. Je 38:2-4. Am 7:10. Lk *23:+2, 5. Ga 5:12g. **world.** Gr. *oikoumene,* Mt +24:14. ver. 31. ʃ121J9A, Jn +1:10.

7. **hath received.** Lk +10:38. **and these.** Ac 16:21. 25:8-11. Ezr 4:12-15. Da 3:12. 6:13. Lk *23:2. Jn *11:48. *19:12. 1 P 2:15. **the decrees.** Ac 16:4. Lk 2:1. Ep 2:15g. Col 2:14g. **of Caesar.** Ac 11:28. 18:2. 25:8, 10-12, 21, 25. 26:32. 27:24. 28:19. Mt +22:17. Ph 4:22. **another king.** Dt=33:5. Ps +*2:2, 6mg. Mt 2:3. Mk *15:32. Lk +*23:2. Jn +*1:49.

8. **they troubled.** Mt 2:3. Jn 11:48.

9. **taken security.** Thomas Walker notes this was money or sureties for their good behavior, to prevent further disturbance in the city. Ramsay suggests that the "security" took the form of an undertaking on the part of Jason and his friends, that Paul should not return to Thessalonica, citing 1 Th 2:17, 18. **Jason.** ver. +5.

10. **the brethren.** ver. 6, 14. Ac 9:25. 23:23, 24. Jsh 2:15, 16. 1 S 19:12-17. 20:42. Jn +21:23. **sent away.** ver. 14. Mt +10:23. **Silas.** ver. 4, 14, 15. Ac +15:22. **Berea.** i.e. *region beyond,* *S#960g. *Berea* was also a city of Macedonia, not far from the Thermaic gulf, west of Thessalonica, and near Pella, the birthplace of Alexander the Great. ver. 13. Ac 20:4. **went.** ver. +2. Ac 14:6, 7. Ro +*1:16. 1 Th 2:2.

11. **more noble.** T#1099. Pr *1:5. 9:9. Je 2:21. Lk 19:12g. Jn 1:46-49. 1 C 1:26g. **Thessalonica.** ver. +1. **they received.** Ac *2:41. 10:33. 11:1. Jb +*23:12. Pr *2:1-5. √4:7, 20-22. 8:10. Mt *13:23. Lk 10:38, 39. 2 C 8:5. 1 Th 1:6. √2:13. 2 Th *2:10. Ja √1:21. 1 P √2:2. **the word.** Ac +8:4. **readiness of mind.** Ac 10:33. 16:14. 1 S ◐+*25:17. Ps √25:9. Mk 12:37. *S#4288g: Ac 17:11. 2 C 8:11, 12 (willing mind), 19 (ready mind). 9:2 (forwardness). This word is used in the New Testament (1) of a ready desire to hear God's word, and (2) of a ready desire to give to God's work (Thomas Walker). **and searched.** T#1069. Ps √1:2, 3. 119:18, 97-100, *148. Pr +*8:9. Is +√8:20n. *34:16. Lk *16:29. *24:44. Jn *3:21. +√5:39. 2 T +√3:15-16. 1 P *1:10-12. 2 P +*1:19-21. 1 J *4:5, 6. Gr. *anakrino,* *S#350g. Rendered (1) examine: Ac 4:9. 12:19. 24:8. 28:18. Lk 23:14. 1 C 9:3. (2) judge: 1 C 2:15, 15. 4:3, 3, 4. 14:24. (3) ask question: 1 C 10:25, 27. (4) search: Ac 17:11. (5) discern: 1 C √2:14. Thayer defines this word "By looking through a series (*ana*) of objects or particulars to distinguish (*krino*) or search after. Hence, to investigate, examine, inquire into, scrutinize, sift, question" (*Lexicon,* p. 39). Compare "search" at Jn 5:39, the same English but a different Greek word (*S#2045g). **the scriptures.** ver. 2. Ps *119:105. *138:2. Je +*15:16. +*23:18, 22, 28, 29. Mt +21:42. Mk +*12:24. Ro +*15:4. 2 T 2:15. **daily.** Ex 16:4.

Dt *17:18-20. Jsh +*1:8. 2 Ch 8:14. Ezr 3:4. Ne *8:18. Ps +*1:2. Pr 8:34. Lk 11:3. +*21:36. Col +√1:10. He +*3:13. *11:6. 1 P *2:2. 2 P *3:18. **whether**. ƒ184D1, Lk +22:67. A. T. Robertson notes that the Bereans "were eagerly interested in the new message of Paul and Silas but they wanted to see it for themselves. What a noble attitude. Paul's preaching made Bible students of them. The duty of private interpretation is thus made plain (Hovey)" (*Word Pictures*, vol. 3, p. 275). T#1059, 1121. Ac 8:31n. Pr +√14:15. 15:14. *18:1n, +*17. Is +√8:20n. Ezk 14:10n. Da +*11:30. Ro √14:12. 2 C *4:2. Ga 1:8, 9. 1 Th *5:21. 1 T 4:1. 2 P *3:16, 17. 1 J *4:1.

12. **Therefore**. Ps +√9:10n. **many**. ver. *2-4. Ac *13:46. 14:1. Ps +*25:8, 9. Jn 1:45-49. +*7:17. Ep *5:14. Ja *1:21. **believed**. ver. 34. Ac +13:12. **honorable**. Ac +*13:50. 1 C *1:26. Ja 1:10. **were Greeks**. ver. 4.

13. **the Jews**. ver. 5. Mt 23:13. 1 Th *2:14-16. **of Thessalonica**. ver. +1. **the word**. Ac +11:1. **at Berea**. ver. +10. **stirred**. Ac 6:12. 14:2. 21:27. 1 K 21:25. Pr 15:18. 28:25. Lk 12:51. 2 Th 2:2g.

14. **then**. ver. 10. Ac 9:25, 30. Mt 10:23. **the brethren**. ver. 6, 10. Jn +21:23. **sent away**. ver. 10. Mt +10:23. **as it**. Ac 20:3. Jsh 2:16. **but**. Ac 19:22. 1 T 1:3. T 1:5. **Silas**. ver. 4, 10. Ac +15:22. **Timothy**. Ac +16:1.

15. **they that**. Ac +15:3. **Athens**. i.e. *uncertainty*, *S#117g. Ac 17:15, 16. 18:1. 1 Th 3:1. *Athens* was the most celebrated city of Greece, not merely for political greatness and military power, but for the learning, eloquence, and politeness of its inhabitants, and for the cultivation of the arts and sciences. It was situated in a delightful plain of Attica, on the Saronic gulf, opposite the eastern coast of Peloponnesus, in a sort of penninsula formed by the two rivers, the Ilissus and Cephisus, about 35 miles east of Corinth, and four miles from the sea. The ruins of many of the splendid structures for which it was celebrated yet remain. ver. 16, 21, 22. Ac 18:1. 1 Th 3:1. **receiving**. ver. 16. Ac 18:5. 2 T 4:10, 11, 20, 21. T 3:12.

16. Cir. A.M. 4058. A.D. 54. **Paul waited**. It is not stated in Acts that Timothy joined Paul at Athens; but the supposition that he did so is not inconsistent with several things there stated: (a) that Paul sent for Timothy and Silas to come to him (Ac 17:15); (b) that "Paul waited for them at Athens" (Ac 17:16); (c) that Paul did not leave Athens abruptly. Thus an event, omitted from the History but necessary to make it complete, is supplied in 1 Th 3:2-7, which mentions Timothy at Athens, and that Timothy was sent from Athens to Thessalonica. The undesigned coincidence consists in the Epistle providing a circumstance which supplies the omission in the History, witnessing to their mutual historicity and authenticity. (William Paley, *Horae Paulinae*, pp. 151-153). See Ac 12:12n for related notes on undesigned coincidences. ver. 15. **his spirit**. Gr. *pneuma*, ƒ121A2, Mt +26:41n. ƒ121A2, Ps +51:10. Ac 18:25. 19:21. 20:22. Ro 1:9. 1 C +14:14. 2 C 2:13. **was stirred**. Ac 15:39g. Ex 32:19, 20. Nu 25:6-11. 1 K 19:10, 14. Jb 32:2, 3, 18-20. Ps 69:9. 119:136, 158. Is 63:10. Je 20:9. Mi 3:8. Mk 3:5. Lk 19:41. Jn 2:13-17. 11:33, 38. 1 C 13:5. 2 P 2:7, 8. **wholly given to idolatry**. *or*, full of idols. ver. 23mg. Is 2:8. Je 2:28.

17. **disputed**. Gr. *dialegomai*, *S#1256g. ver. 2

(reasoned). Ac 18:4, 19 (reasoned). 19:8, 9. 20:7 (preached), 9 (preaching). 24:12, 25 (reasoned). Mk 9:34. He 12:5 (speaketh). Ju 9. **in the synagogue**. ver. 1-4. Ac +13:5. 14:1-4. **devout**. ver. +4. Ac 8:2. 10:2. *13:16, 43. **daily**. Pr 1:20-22. 8:1-4, 34. Je 6:11. Mt 5:1, 2. Mk 16:15. Lk 12:3. 2 T 3:2, 5.

18. **philosophers**. Ro 1:22. 1 C 1:20, 21. Col 2:8. **Epicureans**. i.e. *assistance*, *S#1946g, only here. The *Epicureans* were the followers of *Epicurus*; who acknowledged no gods except in name, and denied that they exercised any government over the world; and held that the chief good consisted in the gratification of the appetites. **Stoicks**. i.e. *of the portico*, *S#4770g, only here. The *Stoicks* were the followers of *Zeno*, and held that all human affairs were governed by fate. Both the Epicureans and the Stoicks denied the resurrection of the body and the immortality of the soul. **encountered**. Ac 4:15g. 6:9. Mk 9:14. Lk 11:53. 14:31. **What will**. ƒ184D2, Lk +1:62. 1 C +4:10. **babbler**. *or*, base fellow. Pr 23:9. 26:12. 1 C 3:18, 19. **strange**. ver. 20. **preached**. Ac +5:42. **Jesus**. ver. 31, 32. Ac 4:2, √12. 26:23. Ro 14:9, 10. 1 C +*15:3, 4, 12. **the resurrection**. Ac +*2:24n. 1 C *15:17.

19. **unto**. ver. 6. Ac 16:19. **Areopagus**. *or*, Mars' hill. i.e. *a martial peak*, *S#697g. ver. 22. "It was the highest court in Athens." ver. 22, 34. **May**. ver. 20, 21. Ac 24:24. 25:22. 26:1. Mt 10:18-20. **new**. Mk 1:27. Jn 7:16. 13:34. He 13:9. 1 J 2:7, 8.

20. **strange**. ver. 18. Ho 8:12. Mt 19:23-25. Mk 10:24-26. Jn 6:60. 7:35, 36. 1 C *1:18, 23. √2:14. He 5:11. 13:9. 1 P 4:4, 12. **we would know**. Jn +*7:17. 1 P √3:15. **what**. Ac 2:12. 10:17. Mk 9:10. 2 T 1:10.

21. **Athenians**. i.e. *inhabitants of Athens*, *S#117g. Ac 17:21, 22. **were there**. Ac 2:10. **spent**. Ep 5:16. Col 4:5. 2 Th 3:11, 12. 1 T 5:13. 2 T 2:16, 17.

22. **stood**. Ac +27:21. **Mars' hill**. *or*, the court of the Areopagites. i.e. *a martial peak; a rocky height*, *S#697g. ver. 19, 34. **I perceive**. ƒ156, Jn +3:2. ver. 16. Ac 19:35. 25:19. Je +*10:2, 3. 50:38. **ye are**. ƒ9, 2 K +5:19. **superstitious**. *or*, religious. Ac 25:19.

23. **devotions**. *or*, gods that ye worship. Ro 1:23-25. 1 C 8:5. 2 Th 2:4. **inscription**. Mk 15:26. Re 21:12g. **TO**. ƒ92H, ver. 28. Ps 147:20. Jn 4:22. 17:3, 25. Ro 1:20-22, 28. 1 C 1:21. 15:34. 2 C 4:4-6. Ga 4:8, 9. Ep 2:12. 1 T 1:17. 1 J 5:20. **ignorantly**. ver. 30. Ps 50:21. Mt 15:9. Jn 4:22. 8:54, 55. **declare**. ƒ101, Dt +32:42.

24. **that made**. ver. 26-28. Ac 4:24. +14:15. Ps 146:5, 6. Is 40:12, 28. 42:5. 45:18. Je 10:11, 12. 32:17. Zc 12:1. Jn √1:1-3. He 1:2, 3. 3:4. **world**. Gr. *kosmos*, Mt +4:8. **seeing**. Ge 14:19, 22. Dt 10:14. 2 K 19:15. Ps 24:1. 115:16. 148:13. Je 23:24. Da 4:35, 37. Mt 5:34, 35. *11:25. Lk 10:21. Re 20:11. **Lord of heaven and**. Jn 3:13. 1 C +*2:8. +*15:47. Ja *2:1. **dwelleth**. T#958. Ac +7:48. 1 K 8:27. 2 Ch 2:6. 6:18. Is *66:1, 2. Jn 4:22, 23.

25. **is**. 1 Ch 29:14, 16. Jb 22:2. 35:6, 7. Ps 16:2. *50:8-13. Je 7:20-23. Am 5:21-23. Mt 9:13. **seeing**. ver. 28. Ac 14:17. Ge 2:7. Nu 16:22. 27:16. Jb 12:10. 27:3. 33:4. 34:14, 15. Ps 104:27-30. Is 42:5. 57:16. Zc 12:1. Mt 5:45. Ro 11:35, 36. 1 T 4:3. *6:17. Ja 1:5, 17. **life**. ver. +28. Ge +*2:7. 7:22. Jb *12:10. 27:3. 32:8. 33:4. Ec +*12:7. Ezk 37:9. Zc 12:1.

26. **hath made**. Ge *3:20. *9:18, 19. Ml *2:10. De 5:12-19. 1 C √15:22, 47. **of one blood**. ƒ171Q10, Ps +94:21. T#419. Ge 1:27, 28. Ps 8:3-6. Ml *2:10. 1 C

●15:39. He 2:11. **the face**. ✍144A1, Ge +11:8. Ge 11:8. Lk 21:35. **hath determined**. Ac 15:18. Dt +*32:7, 8. Jb 12:23. 14:5. Ps *31:15. 74:17. *115:3. Is 14:31. 45:21. Da 11:27, 35. He *2:3. **the times**. ver. 31. Ac +*1:7. 14:17. Ps 74:17. Mt +*5:45. Lk +*6:35. **before appointed**. Jb *7:1. *14:5. **the bounds**. T#484. Ge 21:13. Dt +*2:21n. 29:26n. *32:8. Ps 74:17.

27. **they should**. Ac 15:17. Ps *19:1-6. Ro *1:20. 2:4. **seek the Lord**. Is *55:1, 6. Je √29:13. He √11:6. **if haply**. ✍184D1, Lk +22:67. **might feel**. Jb 23:3, 8, 9. **he be**. Ac +14:17. 1 K 8:27. Ps *139:1-13. Je *23:23, 24. **not far**. Ac *10:4. Dt 4:7. Ps 34:18. 119:151. *145:18. Re *3:20. **of us**. *✍39. Association; or, Inclusion B900: when the writer or speaker associates himself with those whom he addresses. For other instances of this figure see Ep 2:2. T 3:3. He 3:6. 10:25, 26. 1 J √1:6, 8, 9, 10. 2:1.

28. **For**. ✍92H. Gnome; or, Quotation B800: where quotations are from secular books, or books other than the Bible. For other instances of this figure see ver. 23. 1 C 15:33. Col 2:21. T 1:12. Edgar C. S. Gibson (*The Old Testament in the New*) notes that while no formal or acknowledged quotations from the Old Testament Apocrypha are made in the New Testament, yet there are some striking parallels: (1) Ep 6:13-17 with Wisdom 5:17-20; (2) Ro 9:19-21 w Wisdom 15:7; (3) Ro 1:19-23 w Wisdom 13:1-10; (4) Ro 3:25 w Wisdom 11:23; see Ac 14:15-17 and 17:30; (5) He 11:35 w 2 Maccabees 6:18-28; (6) Lk 12:16-21 w Ecclesiasticus 11:18, 19; (7) Mt 6:12 w Ecclesiasticus 28:2; (8) Lk 6:35 w Ecclesiasticus 24:19-21; (9) Mt 7:12 w Tobit 4:14, 15. **in him**. 1 S 25:29. Jb *12:10. Ps *36:9. *66:9. Da 5:23. Lk *20:38. Jn 5:26. *11:25. Col *1:17. He *1:3. 2:11. **live**. Dt 30:20. **as**. T *1:12. **we are**. Lk *3:38. He *12:9.

29. **the offspring**. Lk 3:38. He 12:9. **we ought**. Ps 94:7-9. 106:20. 115:4-8. Is *40:12-19, 25. 44:9-20. 46:5. Hab *2:19, 20. Ro 1:20-23. **graven**. Ex 20:4. 32:4. Is 46:5, 6. Je 10:4-10.

30. **the times**. ver. 23. Ac *14:16. Ps 50:21. Ro *1:28. 3:23, *25. Ep 4:18. 1 P 1:14. **ignorance**. Lk 6:35. Jn 9:41. 15:22. Ro 1:18-21, 28. 2:12. 5:13. **winked at**. Ac +*14:16. Mt 11:21. Lk +*12:48. Ro 3:25. **but now**. Ac +*3:19. 11:18. *20:21. 26:17-20. Mt 3:2. 4:17. Mk *1:15. 6:12. Lk +*13:5. *15:10. +*24:47. Ro *2:4. 2 C √7:10. Ep 4:17, etc. 5:6-8. T √2:11, 12. 1 P 1:14, 15. *4:3. **to repent**. Ac +*2:38. 14:15. 1 Th 1:9.

31. **he hath appointed**. Ac *10:42. Mt *25:31, etc. Jn *5:22, 23. Ro *2:5, 16. *14:9, 10. 1 C *4:5. 2 C *5:10. Ga 6:7, 8. 2 T +*4:1. 2 P 3:7. Ju *14, *15. **a day**. Is 2:12. Mt +*10:15n. 11:22, 24. 12:36. Lk +10:12. Ro 2:16. 1 C 3:13. 2 P 2:9. 3:7. 1 J 4:17. Ju 6. **will judge**. Ac +10:42. Ps 9:8. 58:11. 67:4. *96:13. 98:9. Is 11:4. Mt +*10:15n. Jn 5:22, 27. Ro 3:6. 1 P 2:23. **world**. Gr. *oikoumene*, Mt +24:14. *✍121J8, Jn +3:16. ver. 6. **in righteousness**. Ge +*18:25. Ex 34:7. Ps 7:11, 12. Ro 2:12-16. Re 15:3. **that man**. Ps +*80:17. Da *7:13. Zc *6:8. Jn 5:27. 1 T +*2:5. **ordained**. ver. 26g. Ac 2:23. Lk +22:22g. **given assurance**. *or*, offered faith. *or*, furnished a guarantee. ✍121F, Ge +49:6. By the figure *Metonymy of the Effect*, faith, the effect, is put for the proofs or evidence on which it rests. "Wherefore He hath afforded evidence unto all men": and then the evidence or proof is stated, "in that he hath raised him from the dead" (B564). Jn 5:26, 27. 16:10, 11. Ro *1:4. Re 20:11-13. **in that**. ver. *18. Ac

*2:23, +*24n, 32. 3:15, 16. 4:10. *5:30-32. *10:39-41. 13:30, 31. Ps 71:20. Lk *24:46-48. 1 C +*15:3-8.

32. **the resurrection**. ver. +18. He 6:2. **some**. ver. 18. Ac 2:13. 13:41. 25:19. 26:+8, 24, 25. Ge 19:14. 2 Ch 30:9-11. *36:16. Lk 22:63. 23:11, 36. 1 C 1:23. 4:10. He 11:36. 13:13. **We will**. Ac *24:25. Lk 14:18. 2 C *6:2. He 3:7, 8.

33. **among**. ✍144A6, Ge +45:6. ✍108H3, Mt +13:49.

34. **certain**. ver. 4. Ac +*13:48. Is √55:10, 11. Mt 20:16. Ro 11:5, 6. **and believed**. ver. 12. Ac +13:12. **Dionysius**. i.e. *divinely touched*, ✱S#1354g, only here. **the Areopagite**. i.e. *member of the court of Areopagus*, ✱S#698g, only here. ver. 19, 22. Jn 7:48-52. 19:38-42. Ph 4:22. **Damaris**. i.e. *a yoke-bearing wife*, ✱S#1152g, only here.

ACTS 18

Paul goes to Corinth, meets with Aquila and Priscilla; works with them as a tentmaker; and preaches, first to the Jews, 1-5; and, when they opposed and blasphemed, to the Gentiles with more success, 6-8. Encouraged by a vision, he remains there a long time, 9-11. The Jews bring him before Gallio, the proconsul who refuses to attend to such questions, 12-17. Paul returns by Ephesus to Jerusalem, goes from thence to Antioch, and revisits the churches which he had planted, 18-23. Apollos preaches at Ephesus: and being more fully instructed by Aquila and Priscilla, he goes to Achaia, where he labors very successfully, 24-28.

1. **departed**. Ac 17:32, 33. **Athens**. Ac +17:15. **Corinth**. i.e. *ornament*, ✱S#2882g. ver. +8, Corinthians (✱S#2881g). Ac 19:1. 1 C 1:2. 2 C 1:1, 23. 2 T 4:20.

2. **Aquila**. i.e. *immovable; an eagle; I shall be nourished*, ✱S#207g. ver. 18, 26. Ro *16:3, 4. 1 C 16:19. 2 T 4:19. **born in**. ver. 24. Ac 4:36. **Pontus**. Ac 2:9. 1 P 1:1. **lately come from**. Aquila and Priscilla are greeted in Ro 16:3. Paul met them in Corinth (Ac 18:2) just after they had left Rome. They are found in Ephesus in Ac 18:19-26, where they instructed Apollos, and where they had a church which met in their home (1 C 16:19). These incidental notices fix the time of writing of some of Paul's epistles. Aquila and Priscilla are back in Rome when Paul wrote Romans (Ro 16:3). There was ample time for this: (a) Paul's stay in Ephesus after writing 1 Corinthians; (b) the time he spent in Macedonia (Ac 20:2); (c) the three months he spent in Greece, toward the close of which he wrote Romans. The points by which the time is noted are so intricate that an impostor could not have avoided going wrong. The praise of Aquila and Priscilla for their devotion agrees with what is said in Acts; but the notices in Acts are too indirect as material for a forger, and yet without the Acts the picture would have been impossible (see related notes at ver. 18 and Ac 12:12). Ac 10:1. 27:1, 6. He 13:24. **Italy**. i.e. *island of the fish or lamb*, ✱S#2482g. Ac 27:1, 6. He 13:24. Compare ✱S#2483g, Ac 10:1, Italian. **Priscilla**. i.e. *ancient, old fashioned; little old woman*, ✱S#4252g. ver. 18, 26. Ro 16:3. 1 C 16:19. Compare ✱S#4251g, 2 T 4:19, Prisca. **Claudius**. i.e. *lame, wavering*, ✱S#2804g. Ac 11:28. 23:26. **depart from**. Ac 5:37. 17:6, 7. 24:5, 6. Ro 13:1.

3. **and wrought**. Ac *20:31, 34, 35. 1 C 4:12. 9:6-

12, 15. 2 C *11:7, 9. 12:13. 1 Th 2:9. 4:11. 2 Th √3:8-12.

4. **he reasoned.** Ac +13:5. +*17:1-3, 11, 17. *19:8. Lk 4:16. **in the synagogue.** ver. 19. Ac +13:5. 14:1. 17:17. Lk 4:16. **every sabbath.** Ac +13:14. Lk +*4:16. **persuaded.** ver. 13. Ac 13:43. 19:18, 26. 26:28. 28:23. Ge *9:27mg. 2 Ch 32:11. Lk 16:31. 2 C 5:11. Ga 1:10.

5. **Silas.** Ac +15:22. 17:14, 15. 1 Th 3:2, 6. **Timotheus.** Ac +16:1. **were come.** This arrival at Corinth of brethren from Macedonia is referred to incidentally in the Epistle (2 C 11:9), but explicitly here (ver. 1, 5). Silas and Timothy were Paul's assistants at Corinth (2 C 1:19). Silas and Silvanus refer to the same person (Ac 17:10. 1 Th 1:1). The differences in the name in the two passages negatives the supposition that the name in the History was transcribed from the Epistle, or the reverse. See related notes (ver. 3, 18. Ac +*12:12n). **Macedonia.** Ac +16:9. **was pressed.** Ac 4:20. 17:16. Jb 32:18-20. Je 6:11. 20:9. Ezk 3:14. Am 3:8. Mi 3:8. Lk 12:50. 2 C 5:14. Ph 1:23g. **and testified.** ver. 28. Ac 2:36. 5:42. 9:22. 10:42. +*17:3. 20:21. Lk +16:28. Jn *15:27. 1 P 5:12. **to the Jews.** Mt *10:5, 6. **was Christ.** or, is the Christ. Ac 3:20. 8:5. Da +*9:25, 26. Mk +8:29. Lk +3:15. Jn 1:41. 3:28. 10:24.

6. **they.** Ac +*13:45. 19:9. 26:11. Lk 22:65. 1 Th 2:14-16. 2 T +*2:25. Ja 2:6, 7. 1 P 4:4, 14. **he shook.** Ac *13:51. Ne 5:13. Mt *10:14. Lk 9:5. 10:10, 11. **Your blood.** Ac *20:26, 27. Le 20:9, 11, 12. 2 S 1:16. 3:29. 1 K 2:32, 33, 37. Ezk 3:18, 19. 18:13. 33:4, 8, 9. Mt *27:25. 1 T 5:22. **heads.** √171Q12, Jg +5:30. **I am clean.** Ac 20:26g. Ge 24:8. Ezk *3:18, 19. **from henceforth.** Ac *13:+46, 47. 19:9, 10. 26:20. *28:28. Mt 8:11. 21:43. 22:10. Ro 3:29. 9:25, 26, 30-33. 10:12, 13. 11:11-15.

7. **Justus.** Ac 1:23. Col 4:11. **worshipped.** Ac 10:2, 22. 13:42. 16:14. 17:4. **synagogue.** Ac +13:43.

8. **Crispus.** i.e. curled, curly haired, crisp, *S#2921g. 1 C 1:14. **the chief.** ver. 17. Ac 13:15. Mk 5:+22, 35. **believed.** Ac 5:14. 16:34. Jn +5:47. 1 J 3:23. **the Lord.** Ac +11:16. **with all.** Ac *10:2. +11:14. +*16:14n, 15n, 34n. Ge 17:27. +*18:19. Jsh √24:15. **house.** √121J4, Ge +7:1. **many.** Ac +6:1. **Corinthians.** i.e. ornament, *S#2881g. 2 C 6:11g. **hearing.** Ac +*8:12. Ro 8:14. √10:14-17. **believed.** Ac +8:12. **were baptized.** Ac +*2:37-41. *8:12, 35-38. Mt +*28:19. Mk √16:15, 16. 1 C √1:13-17.

9. **spake.** Ac 16:9. 22:18. *23:11. 27:23-25. 2 C 12:1-3. **by.** Da +*9:2. **a vision.** Ac +9:10. 26:16. 2 C *12:1-4. **Be not afraid.** Ac 27:24. Jsh 1:5, 6. Is 43:5. Je 1:8. 1 C 2:3. **but speak.** Ac 5:20. Is 58:1. Je 1:17. Ezk 2:6-8. 3:9-11. Jon 3:2. Mi 3:8. Ep *6:19, 20. 1 Th *2:2. **hold not.** √144D, Ge +40:23. Ac √20:27. Is 62:1.

10. **I am.** Ex 4:12. Jsh 1:5, 9. Jg 2:18. 1 S 10:7. 18:14. Is 8:10. 41:10. 43:2. Je *1:18, 19. Mt 1:23. *28:20. 2 C √12:9. 2 T *4:17, 18, 22. **and no.** Is √54:17. Je 15:20, 21. Mt 10:30. Lk 21:18. Ro √8:31. 2 Th 3:2. **for.** Ac 15:14, 18. Jn 10:16. 11:52. 15:14. Ro 10:20, 21. 1 C +*6:9-11. 2 C 1:1.

11. **he.** Ac 14:3. 19:10. 20:31. **continued there.** Gr. sat there. √171J12, Is +42:7. **a year and.** Col *1:23. *2:7. **the word.** Ac +11:1.

12. Cir. A.M. 4059. A.D. 55. **Gallio.** i.e. lives on milk, *S#1058g. ver. 14, 17. **the deputy.** Ac 13:+7, 12. **Achaia.** i.e. wailing, grief, trouble, *S#882g. ver. 27. Ac 19:21. Ro 15:26. 16:5. 1 C 16:15. 2 C 1:1. 9:2. 11:10. 1 Th 1:7, 8. **the Jews.** Ac +13:50. *14:2, 19.

*17:5, 13. *21:27, etc. 1 Th *2:14-16. **brought him.** Ac +16:19. Mt *10:18. **the judgment.** ver. 16, 17. Ac 25:10. Mt 27:19. Jn 19:13. Ja 2:6.

13. **This fellow.** ver. 4. Ac 6:13. 21:28. 24:5, 6. 25:8. **the law.** ver. 15. Jn 19:7.

14. **when.** Ac 21:39, 40. 22:1, 2. 26:1, 2. Lk 21:12-15. 1 P 3:14, 15. **to open.** Mt +5:2. **If it were.** √184B, Mt +23:30. Ac 23:27-29. 25:11, 18-20, 26. **wicked lewdness.** Ac 13:10. **I should.** √184B, Mt +23:30. **bear.** Ac 13:18. Mt +17:17. Mk 9:19. Ro 13:3. 2 C 11:1, 4. He 5:2.

15. **But if.** √184A, 1 C +15:2. **a question.** Ac 23:29. *25:11, 18, 19. 26:3. 1 T 1:4. 6:4. 2 T 2:14, 23. T 3:9. **your law.** ver. 13. **look.** Mt 27:4, 24. **for.** Ac 24:6-8. Jn 18:31.

16. **he drave.** Ps 76:10. Ro 13:3, 4. Re 12:16.

17. **Sosthenes.** i.e. savior, powerful, *S#4988g. 1 C *1:1. **the chief.** ver. 8. Mk +5:22. **And Gallio.** Ac 17:32. Am 6:6. 1 C 1:23. **cared.** Jn +*7:24.

18. **then took.** ver. 21. Mk 6:46. Lk 9:61. 14:33. 2 C 2:13. **brethren.** ver. 27. Jn +21:23. **Syria.** Ac 15:23, 41. 21:3. Ga 1:21. **Priscilla.** ver. 2. **having.** Ac *21:23, 24. Nu *6:2, 5-9, 18. 1 C √9:20. **Cenchrea.** i.e. granular, millet, *S#2747g. Ro 16:1. **Cenchrea,** now Kenkri, was the port of Corinth, on the east side of the isthmus, and about nine miles from the city. Ro *16:1. Paul commends Phoebe (Ro 16:1-3), and this mention of Cenchrea here in Acts, quite incidental and clearly undesigned, suggests the probable occasion of his having become acquainted with her (see related notes at Ac 12:12). **vow.** Le +*23:38.

19. **Ephesus.** i.e. desirable, full purposed, patience, *S#2181g. ver. 21, 24. Ac 19:1, 17, 26, ●+28, ●34, ●35. 20:16, 17. ●21:29. 1 C 15:32. 16:8. Ep 1:1. 1 T 1:3. 2 T 1:18. 4:12. Re 1:11. 2:1. **synagogue.** Ac +13:5. 17:17. **and reasoned.** See on ver. 4. Ac +*17:2, 3.

20. **he consented not.** Ac 20:16. 21:13, 14. Mt 25:9. Mk 1:37, 38. 1 C 16:12.

21. **bade.** ver. 18. Ac 15:29. Lk 9:61. 2 C 13:11. **I must.** Ac *20:16. Dt 16:1. **if God will.** Ac 19:21. 21:14. Mt 26:39. Lk *22:42. Ro *1:10. *15:30, 32. 1 C *4:19. 16:7, 12. Ph *2:19-24. 1 Th *3:11. He *6:3. Ja √4:15. 1 P 3:17.

22. **Caesarea.** Ac +8:40. 10:1, 24. 11:11. 18:22. 23:23. **gone up.** √63A4, 1 K +3:22. Supply ellipsis, (to Jerusalem). Ac 11:2. 13:31. 15:2. 21:12, 15. 24:11. 25:1, 9. Lk +2:4. Jn +2:13. Ga 1:17, 18. 2:1, 2. **saluted.** √108B, 2 K +4:29. **the church.** ver. 21. Ac 11:22. 15:4. 21:17-19. **he went down.** Ac 11:19-27. 13:1. 14:26. 15:23, 30, 35. **Antioch.** Ac +11:26.

23. **spent some time.** √171J2, Ac +15:33. **the country.** Ac 16:6. 1 C 16:1. Ga 1:2. 4:14. **Phrygia.** Ac 2:10. 16:6. **in order.** Ac 11:4. Lk 1:3. **strengthening.** Ac +*14:22. *15:32, 41. 16:40. Dt 3:28. Ezr 1:6. Is 35:3, 4. Da 11:1. Lk 22:32, 43. 1 Th +3:2. 4:18. 5:14. He 12:12, 13. **the disciples.** Ac +11:26.

24. **Apollos.** i.e. destroyer, *S#625g. Ac 19:1. 1 C 1:12. √3:4-6, 22. *4:6. 16:12. T 3:13. **born at.** ver. 2. Ac +4:36. **Alexandria.** Ac +6:9. 27:6. **eloquent.** Ex 4:10. Is 3:3. 1 C 2:1, 2. 2 C 10:10. **mighty in the scriptures.** ver. 28. Ac 7:22. Ezr 7:6, 11, 12, 21. Mt +*13:52. +21:42. Mk ●+*12:24. Lk 24:19. Jn +√5:39. Ro √15:4. Col √3:16. 2 T *2:15. +√3:15, 16. T *1:9. 2 P *3:18. **Ephesus.** ver. +19.

25. **instructed.** Ac 13:10. 16:17. 19:9, 23. Ge +*18:19. Jg 2:22. 1 S *9:27. √12:23. ●+√25:17. Ps

√25:8, 9. 119:1. Is 40:3. Je *6:16. Ho *14:9. Mt 3:3. Mk 1:3. 12:14. Lk 1:4. 3:4. Jn 1:23. **the way.** ver. 26. Ac +9:2. **the Lord.** ver. 8, 9. Ac 13:10, 11. **fervent.** Ac 17:16. Ro +*12:11. Col 1:28, 29. 2 T *2:4. Ja √5:16. **spirit.** Gr. *pneuma,* here an adverbial use implying *essence;* or whatever is spoken of as possessed or done, as being so in the highest degree, as in Ac 19:21. 20:22. Ro 1:9. 2:29. 7:6. +*12:11. 1 C 5:3. Ph 3:3. Col 1:8. 2:5. √108B, Idiom, Lk +10:21. For the other uses of *pneuma* see Mt +*8:16n. **taught diligently.** lit. teaching accurately. Ac 23:15g. 2 T √2:15. *4:2. **knowing only.** Ac 19:3. Mt ch. 3. Lk ch. 3. Jn 1:19-36. **the baptism.** T#34. Ac 19:1-5. Mt +9:14. Lk 7:29.

26. **to speak boldly.** Ac +4:13. 14:3. Is 58:1. Ep *6:19, 20. **Aquila.** ver. 2, 3. **and Priscilla.** Notice the injunction for women to "keep silence" and "not to teach" did not apply here. Women may teach other women and children, as in a Sunday school, and if this case of Priscilla may be generalized, Paul's injunctions do not prohibit the private instruction of men in a private home, as in a home Bible study, particularly if done jointly with their husbands. Since other Scripture informs us that churches met in homes (2 J +*10), specifically the home of Aquila and Priscilla (Ro √16:3-5), the evidence is that women are permitted to teach men even in church. Paul's injunction may be limited to the circumstance where women are placed in a position where they teach with binding authority over men. Note that women prophesied (Ac 2:17. 21:9. 1 C +*11:5) and participated in group prayer meetings (Ac 1:14. 12:12, 13), so the command to silence is not absolute. 1 C 11:5n. ◑+*14:34n. 1 T +*2:11, 12. **they took.** 1 S *9:27. ◑+√25:17. 2 K +*5:13. Lk 10:35. 2 T 2:25. 1 P 3:15. **expounded.** Ac *8:31. +11:4. 28:23. Ps +*25:9. Pr +*1:5. √9:9. *22:17, 18. *25:12. Mt 18:3, 4. Mk 10:15. Lk 19:26. 24:27. Jn +*7:17. 1 C 3:18. 8:2. 12:21. He 6:1. 2 P √3:18. **the way.** ver. 25. Ac +9:2. 19:9, 23. 24:22. Mt 22:16. Mk 12:14. Lk 20:21. **more perfectly.** or, more accurately. ver. 25. Jn 17:3. Col +*1:10. 2 P +*3:18.

27. **Achaia.** ver. 12. Ac 19:1. **the brethren.** ver. 18. Ac 9:27. Jn +21:23. Ro 16:1, 2. 1 C 16:3. 2 C 3:1, 2. **exhorting.** Col 4:10. 3 J 8-10. **the disciples.** ver. 23. Ac +11:26. **to receive.** Lk +8:40g. **helped.** 1 C 3:6, 10-14. 2 C 1:24. Ph 1:25. **believed.** Ac +13:12. Jn *1:12, 13. Ro 1:5. 1 C 15:10. Ep √2:8-10. Ph +*1:29. Col 2:12, 13. 2 Th *2:13, 14. T 3:4-6. Ja 1:16-18. 1 P 1:2, 3. **through grace.** Ac 11:21, 23. +*13:48. 15:11. Ro 12:6. Ep √2:8. Ph +*1:29. *2:12, 13. 1 Th 1:4, 5. 2 Th *2:13, 14. 2 T +*1:9. Ja *2:5. 1 P 4:10.

28. **convinced.** ver. 5, 25. Ac 9:22. +*17:3. 26:22, 23. Mt 11:3. Lk 23:10g. +*24:27, 44. 1 C +*15:3, 4. He ch. 7-10. **showing.** Ac +8:35. Jn +√5:39. **the scriptures.** ver. 24. Mt +21:42. **was Christ.** *or,* is the Christ. See on ver. 5. Ac *9:22.

ACTS 19

Paul, arriving at Ephesus, finds disciples who knew only John's baptism; and, having instructed them, and baptized them in the name of Christ, he confers on them the miraculous gifts of the Holy Spirit, 1-7. He preaches, first in the synagogue; and then very successfully in a school for two years, God confirming his word by miracles, 8-12. Certain Jewish exorcists, attempting to cast out a devil in the name of Jesus, are

driven away naked and wounded, 13-17. Many, who had used magical arts, are converted, and burn their books, 18-20. Paul purposing to go into Macedonia, and then to Jerusalem, and afterwards to Rome, sends friends before him, 21, 22. Demetrius, and the silversmiths at Ephesus, raise a mob against him, to support their gainful traffic and the worship of Diana; and this is attended with great uproar and confusion, 23-34. The town clerk, with great difficulty and address, appeases it, 35-41.

1. **Apollos.** Ac 18:+24-28. 1 C 1:12. *3:4-7. 16:12. **Corinth.** Ac 18:+1, 27. **Paul.** Ac 18:23. **came.** Ac 18:19-21. **Ephesus.** Ac +18:19. 20:17. Ep 2:22. **disciples.** Ac +9:10.

2. **Have ye.** ver. 6. Ac 2:17, 38, 39. *8:15-17. 10:44. 11:15-17. Ro 1:11, 12. **Ghost.** Gr. *pneuma,* Mt +1:18. √121A1, Jn +3:34. **since.** or, when. lit. "having believed." Ro +*8:9, 11. **believed.** ver. 18. Ac +13:12. **We have.** Ac 8:16. 1 S 3:7. Jn 7:39. 1 C 6:19. *12:1, 8-10, etc. Ga 3:5. **Ghost.** Gr. *pneuma,* Mt +1:18n.

3. **Unto what.** Mt +*28:19. 1 C √12:13. Ga +3:27. **Unto John's.** Ac +*18:25. Mt ch. 3. Lk ch. 3.

4. **John.** Ac +*1:5. 11:16. +*13:23-25. Mt *3:11, 12. 11:3-5. 21:25-32. Mk 1:1-12. Lk 1:76-79. 3:16-18. Jn 1:15, 27, 29-34. 3:28-36. 5:33-35. He 6:2. **repentance.** Ac +10:43. 20:21. **should believe.** Jn 1:7.

5. **they were baptized.** Ac +*2:38. +*8:12, 16. Ro √6:3, 4. 1 C *1:13-15. *10:2. **in the name.** Ac 2:38n. 8:12, 16. 10:48. **the Lord Jesus.** ver. 13, 17. Ac +1:21. Ro √10:9, 10.

6. **laid.** Ac 6:6. +*8:17-19. 9:17. 1 T 5:22. 2 T 1:6. **his.** √63A3, Mt +19:13. **the Holy.** Ac *2:4. 10:45, 46. 13:2. Mk +16:17. 1 C 12:8-11, 28-30. **Ghost.** Gr. *pneuma,* Mt +1:18. **and prophesied.** Ac +13:1. 1 C *14:1, 3, 4, etc.

8. **went.** Ac 13:14, 46. 14:1. 26:22, 23. **synagogue.** Ac +13:5. **spake boldly.** Ac +4:13. **disputing.** ver. 9. Ac 1:3. 9:20-22. +*17:1-3, 17. 18:4, 19. 28:23. Ju +*3. **persuading.** Ac +18:4. 28:23. 2 C 5:11. **things concerning.** Ac +1:3. **kingdom.** Ac +*1:6n. *28:23. Mk *1:14, 15.

9. Cir. A.M. 4061. A.D. 57. **divers.** Ac 7:51. 13:45, 46. 18:6. +28:24. 2 K 17:14. 2 Ch 30:8. *36:16. Ne 9:16, 17, 29. Ps 95:8. Is 8:14. Je 7:26. 19:15. Jn 12:40. Ro 9:18. 11:7mg. 1 C 16:9. He +*3:12, 13. **were hardened.** Ps *95:7, 8. He +3:8. **believed not.** Ac +14:2. **but spake.** ver. 23. Ac *9:2. 22:4. 24:21. 28:22. 2 T 1:15. 2 P *2:2, 12. Ju *10. **that way.** ver. 23. Ac +9:2. *16:17. *18:26. *24:14, 22. **he departed.** Ac +13:46. 14:4. 17:4. 18:7, 8. Mt +*15:14. 16:4. Lk 12:51-53. 1 T 6:5. 2 T 3:5. **separated.** Mt +*15:14. 1 T *6:5. **the disciples.** ver. 30. Ac +11:26. **disputing.** ver. 8. Ac +17:17. **daily.** Ac 20:31. Pr 8:34. Mt 26:55. 2 T *4:2. **Tyrannus.** i.e. *prince, ruler, tyrant,* *S#5181g.

10. **this continued.** Ac +*18:11. 20:18, 31. Ro 10:18. **two years.** ver. 8. Ac +*18:11. *20:31. **in Asia.** ver. 22, 26, 27. Ac +2:9. ◑*16:6. 2 T 1:15. 1 P 1:1. Re 1:4, 11. **the word.** ver. 20. Ac +15:35. **both.** Ac 18:4. 20:20, 21. Ro √1:16. 10:12. 1 C 1:22-24. Ga *3:28. Col *3:11.

11. **God wrought.** Ac +5:12. *14:3. 15:12. 16:18. Mk *16:17-20. Jn 14:12. Ro 15:18, 19. Ga 3:5. He 2:4. **special.** Ac 28:2g. **miracles.** Ac +8:13.

12. **from his body.** Ac +5:15. 2 K *4:29-31. 13:20, 21. Mt 14:36. **handkerchiefs.** These were for wiping off sweat. Lk 19:20. Jn +20:7g. **aprons.** These were

half-comctires or *aprons*, which were worn by working men (Rackham). **spirits**. Gr. *pneuma*, Mt +8:16. Mk 16:17. Lk +7:21.

13. **vagabond**. Ge 4:12, 14. Ps 109:10. **exorcists**. Mt 12:27. Lk 11:19. **took**. Ac 8:18, 19. Mt *7:21-23. Mk +9:38. Lk 9:49. **to call**. ✻S#3687g. Lk 6:13, 14 (named). Ro 15:20. 1 C 5:1 (named), 11. Ep *1:21. 3:15. 5:3. 2 T 2:19. **spirits**. Gr. *pneuma*, Mt +8:16. **the Lord Jesus**. ver. 5, 17. Ac +1:21. **adjure**. Jsh 6:26. 1 S 14:24. 1 K 22:16. Mt 26:63. Mk +5:7.

14. **seven sons**. Ru 4:15. 1 S 2:5. Pr 26:16. Mk 12:20. **Sceva**. i.e. *disposed; mind reader*, ✻S#4630g, only here. **chief**. Ac 5:24. 9:14, 21.

15. **evil spirit**. Gr. *pneuma*, Mt +8:16. Ac 16:17, 18. Ge 3:1-5. 1 K 22:21-23. Mt 8:29-31. Mk +*1:24, 34. 5:9-13. Lk 4:33-35. 8:28-32. Ja *2:19. **Jesus I know**. Gr. *ginosko*, suggesting a personal knowledge and recognition; the evil spirit was well aware of the Savior's power (Walker). Jn 8:55n. **Paul I know**. Gr. *epistamai*, lit. "I am acquainted with," implying knowledge of a lower degree; "I know about Paul" (Walker). ✻S#1987g: Ac 10:28. 15:7. 18:25 (knowing). 19:25. 20:18. 22:19. 24:10. 26:26. Mk 14:68 (understand). 1 T 6:4. He 11:8. Ja 4:14. Ju 10.

16. **the man**. Mk 5:3, 4, 15. Lk 8:29, 35. **spirit**. Gr. *pneuma*, Mt +8:16. **prevailed**. Mt 20:25. Mk 10:42. 1 P 5:3. **naked**. Ex 32:25n. 2 S 6:20n. Is +*20:2, 4. Jn 21:7n. ✻S#1131g: Mt 25:36, 38, 43, 44. Mk 14:51, 52. Jn 21:7. 1 C 15:37 (bare). 2 C 5:3. He 4:13. Ja 2:15. Re 3:17. 16:15. 17:16. **wounded**. Gr. *traumatizo*, ✻S#5135g. Lk 20:12 (wounded). Compare ✻S#5134g, "trauma," Lk 10:34 (wounds).

17. **all**. ver. 10. **Ephesus**. Ac +18:19. **and fear**. Ac +2:43. 5:5, 11, 13. 13:12. Le 10:3. 1 S 6:20. 2 S 6:9. Ps 64:9. Lk 1:65. *7:16. **the name**. Ac +15:26. Ph 1:20. 2:9-11. 2 Th 1:12. 3:1. He 2:8, 9. Re 5:12-14. **the Lord Jesus**. ver. 5, 13. Ac +1:21. **was magnified**. Ac +10:46. Lk 1:46.

18. **believed**. ver. 2. Ac +13:12. **confessed**. Le 16:21. 26:40. Jb 33:27, 28. Ps √32:5. Pr √28:13. Je 3:13. Ezk 16:63. 36:31. Mt 3:6. Mk +1:5g. Ro √10:10. 14:11. Ja √5:16n. 1 J √1:9. **and showed**. Gr. *anangello*, ✻S#312g. Rendered (1) tell: Mk 5:14, 19. Jn 4:25. 5:15. Ac 16:38. 2 C 7:7. (2) show: Jn 16:13, 14, 15, 25. Ac 19:18. 20:20. (3) declare: Ac 15:4. 20:27. 1 J 1:5. (4) rehearse: Ac 14:27. (5) speak: Ro 15:21. (6) report: 1 P 1:12. **their deeds**. Mt 16:27. Lk 23:51. Ro *8:13. Col *3:9.

19. **used**. Ac 8:9-11. 13:6, 8. Ex 7:11, 22. Dt +*18:10-12. 1 S 28:7-9. 1 Ch 10:13. 2 Ch 33:6. Is *8:19. 47:12, 13. Da 2:2. **curious**. *Perierga, curious*, that is, *magical arts*, in which sense the word is used in the Greek writers. The study of magic was prosecuted with such zeal at Ephesus, that *Ephesia grammata*, the *Ephesian letters*, certain *charms*, or words used in *incantation*, became much celebrated in antiquity. **and burned**. Ge 35:4. Ex 32:20. Dt 7:25, 26. 2 Ch ●33:22n. Is 2:20, 21. 30:22. Mt 5:29, 30. Lk 14:33. He 10:34. **fifty**. Probably Attic drachms; which, at 7 1/2 *d*. each, would amount to 1562*l*. 10s. or, at 9*d*. each, to 1875*l*. A. T. Robertson suggests "probably about ten thousand dollars or two thousand English pounds" (*Word Pictures*, vol. 3, p. 320). Lk 15:8.

20. **So mightily**. ♪71, Jn +1:24. ver. 26. Ac +6:7. 9:31. 11:24-26. *12:24. 13:49. 16:5. Is √55:11. 2 Th 3:1. **grew**. This statement corresponds with 1 C 16:9,

"a great door and effectual," as pointing to the place where 1 Corinthians was written. Every note of place in the Epistle is consistent with the supposition that Paul wrote it before leaving Ephesus: "fought with the beasts" (1 C 15:32); "churches of Asia" (1 C 16:19); "Aquila and Priscilla" (1 C 16:19), who were then at Ephesus (Ac 18:11, 26); "I will tarry at Ephesus" (1 C 16:8), "a great door and effectual" (1 C 16:9), compared with "so mightily grew the word" (Ac 19:20), and the complaint of Demetrius (Ac 19:26); "many adversaries" (1 C 16:9), compared with "divers were hardened" (Ac 19:9). The agreement is complete, but there is no trace of design. See related notes listed at Ac 12:12. **the word**. ver. 10. Ac +15:35. 1 Th *2:13.

21. **Cir**. A.M. 4063. A.D. 59. **these**. Ro 15:25-28. Ga 2:1. **purposed**. Ac 16:6-10. 18:21. 20:22. La 3:37. Ro 1:13. 2 C 1:15-18. **spirit**. Gr. *pneuma*, Ac +18:25n. ♪108B, Lk +10:21. ♪121A2, Ps +51:10. Ac 17:16. **when**. Ac 20:1-6. 1 C 16:5. 1 Th 1:7, 8. **Macedonia**. ver. 22, 29. Ac +16:9. **Achaia**. Ac +18:12. **to Jerusalem**. Ac *18:21. *20:16, 22. 21:4, 11-15, 17. 24:17, 18. Ro *15:25, 26. 1 C 16:4. 2 C 1:16. **I must**. Ac +9:6. **see Rome**. Here is an undesigned coincidence which confirms the genuineness of the history in Acts and the authenticity of the Epistles of Paul such as no forger or later writer would produce. In both Romans and Acts is mentioned Paul's intended visit to Rome. But the Epistle mentions "I will come by you into Spain." Paley remarks "If the passage in the Epistle was taken from that in the Acts, why was *Spain* put in? If the passage in the Acts was taken from that in the Epistle, why was *Spain* left out? If the passages were unknown to each other, nothing can account for their conformity but truth" (*Horae Paulinae*, p. 36). See related notes at Ac 12:12. Ac 18:21. *23:11. 25:10-12. 27:1, 24. 28:16, 30, 31. Ro *1:13, 15. *15:23-29. Ph 1:12-14.

22. **Macedonia**. ver. 21, 29. Ac 16:+9, 10. 18:5. 20:1. 2 C 1:16. 2:13. 8:1. 11:9. 1 Th 1:8. **two**. ver. 29. **that ministered**. Ac 13:5. 16:3. Lk 8:3. Col 4:7. 2 T 1:18. 4:11. Phm 13. **Timothy**. Ac +16:1. 1 C 4:17. 16:10. **Erastus**. i.e. *amiable, lovely*, ✻S#2037g. Ro *16:23. 2 T *4:20. **in Asia**. ver. 10, 26, 27. Ac +2:9. **for a season**. 1 C 16:8, 9.

23. **there arose**. 2 C 1:8-10. 6:9. **no small stir**. Ac 12:18. **that way**. ver. 9. Ac +9:2. 18:26. 22:4. 24:14, 22.

24. **Demetrius**. i.e. *belonging to Ceres; of mother earth*, ✻S#1216g. ver. 38. 3 J 12. (1) A silversmith at Ephesus who opposed Paul, Ac 19:24, 38. He was a manufacturer of silver shrines, small temples, and images of Diana. (2) A convert of whom nothing is recorded except the consistency of his character, 3 J 12. **shrines**. *Naous, temples*, probably portable silver *models* of the temple of Diana, and small images of the goddess, somewhat like the *Santa Casa* purchased by pilgrims at Loretto. **Diana**. Gr. Artemis. ver. 27, 28, 34, 35. **brought**. Ac 16:16. Is 56:11, 12. 1 T *6:9, 10. **craftsmen**. ver. 38. Ac 17:29.

25. **ye know**. Ac *16:16-19. Ho 4:8. 12:7, 8. 2 P 2:3. Re 18:3, 11-19.

26. **that not**. ver. 10, 18-20. 1 C 16:8, 9. 1 Th 1:9. **Ephesus**. Ac +18:19. **all Asia**. ver. 10, 22, 27. Ac +2:9. **much people**. Ac 11:24, 26. Lk 7:12. **that they**. Ac 14:15. 17:29. Ps 115:4-8. 135:15-18. Is 44:10-20. 46:5-8. Je 10:3-5, 11, 14, 15. Ho 8:6. 1 C +*8:4. 10:19,

20. 12:2. Ga 4:8. **made**. ver. 35. Dt +*4:28. 2 K 19:18. Re 9:20.

27. **that not**. ver. 21. Zp 2:11. Mt 23:14. 1 T 6:5. **great goddess**. Ac 8:10. **Diana**. ver. +24. **whom**. 1 J 5:19. Re 13:3, 8. **all Asia**. ver. +26. **the world**. Gr. *oikoumene*, Mt +24:14. *ſ121J9A, Jn +1:10.

28. **they**. Ac 7:54. 16:19-24. 21:28-31. Ps 2:2. Re 12:12. **and cried**. ver. 34, 35. 1 S 5:3-5. 1 K 18:26-29. Is 41:5-7. Je 50:38. Re 13:4. 17:13. **Great**. Ac 8:10. **Diana**. i.e. *luminous, perfect,* *S#735g. ver. +24. The Ephesian *Diana* is represented in some statues all covered with breasts, from the shoulders down to the feet; and in others from the breast to the bottom of the abdomen; from which we find that she was widely different from Diana the huntress, and that she represented *Nature*, as is stated on two inscriptions in Mountfaucon. **Ephesians**. *S#2180g. ver. 34, 35, 35. Ac ◐+18:19. 21:29.

29. **the whole**. ver. 32. Ac 17:8. 21:30, 38. **confusion**. ver. 32. Ac 21:27g, 31. **caught**. Ac 6:12. Lk 8:29. **Gaius**. Ac *20:4. Ro *16:23. 1 C *1:14. 3 J 1. **Aristarchus**. i.e. *good prince, best ruler,* *S#708g. Ac 20:4. 27:2. Col *4:10. Phm *24. **Macedonia**. *Macedonia*, an extensive province of Greece, was bounded on the north by the mountains of Haemus, on the south by Epirus and Achaia, on the east by the Aegean sea and Thrace, and on the west by the Adriatic sea; celebrated in all histories as being the third kingdom which, under Alexander the Great, obtained the empire of the world, and had under it 150 nations. ver. 21, 22. Ac +16:9. **companions**. ver. 22. Ac 20:34. 2 C 8:19. **the theater**. 1 C 4:9g.

30. **Paul**. Ac 14:14-18. 17:22-31. 21:39. **the people**. ver. 33. Ac 12:22. 17:5g. **the disciples**. ver. 9. Ac +11:26. 2 S 18:2, 3. 21:17.

31. **the chief**. The *Asiarchai, Asiarchs*, were officers of a religious nature, who presided over the public games instituted in honor of the gods in Asia; by which is meant, in the New Testament, not the quarter of the globe so called, but either *Proconsular Asia* or *Asia Minor*, a large country in the form of a peninsula, lying between the Hellespont and Euxine sea on the north, the Mediterranean sea on the south, and the Aegean sea on the west, about 600 miles in length, and 320 in breadth. Paley states "Asia, throughout the Acts of the Apostles and the Epistles of Paul, does not mean the whole of Asia Minor or Anatolia, nor even the whole of the proconsular Asia, but a district in the anterior part of that country, called Lydian Asia, divided from the rest, much as Portugal is from Spain, and of which district *Ephesus* was the capital" (*Horae Paulinae*, pp. 47, 48). ver. 10. Ac 16:6. Pr +*16:7. 1 C 16:19. **desiring**. Ac 21:12.

32. **cried**. ver. 29. Ac 21:34. **confused**. ver. +29. **and the**. ver. 40. Mt 11:7-9. Lk 7:24-26.

33. **Alexander**. Mk ?15:21. 1 T +*1:20. 2 T +*4:14. **multitude**. Ac 21:16. Jn 7:40. 16:17. **beckoned**. Ac +12:17. 13:16. 21:40. 24:10. Lk 1:22. **his defence**. Ac 22:1. 24:10g. 25:8, 16. 26:1, 2, 24. Lk 12:11g. 21:14g. 2 C +7:11. Ph 1:7, 16. 2 T 4:16. 1 P *3:15g. **the people**. ver. +30.

34. **they knew**. Gr. *epiginosko*, Mt +11:27. ver. 26. Ac 16:20. Ro 2:22. **all**. 1 K 18:26. Mt 6:7. **cried out**. *ſ42, 1 K +18:26. **Great**. ver. 28. Je *10:14, 15. Re 13:4. **Ephesians**. Ac +18:19.

35. **appeased**. ver. 36. **Ye men**. Ep 2:12. **a worship-per**. Gr. the temple-keeper. **and of**. ver. 26. 2 Th 2:10, 11. 1 T 4:2. **Jupiter**. Ac *14:12, 13.

36. **ye ought**. Ac 5:35-39. Pr 14:29. 25:8. **be quiet**. ver. 35. **rashly**. 2 T 3:4g.

37. **these men**. ver. 29. **which**. Ac 25:8. 1 C 10:32. 2 C 6:3. **robbers**. Ro 2:22.

38. **Wherefore if**. *ſ184A, 1 C +15:2. **Demetrius**. ver. 24. **have**. Ac 18:14. Dt 17:8. 1 C 6:1. **a matter**. Gr. *logos*, lit. word. i.e., according to the Hebrew idiom, "an accusation." *ſ108B, Lk +1:2. **the law is open**. or, the court days are kept. **deputies**. Ac +13:7.

39. **But if**. *ſ184A, 1 C +15:2. **lawful**. or, ordinary.

40. **we are**. Ac 17:5-8. **uproar**. Ac 20:1. 21:31, 38. 1 K 1:41. Mt 26:5.

41. **when**. Pr 15:1, 2. Ec 9:17. **he dismissed**. Ps 65:7. 2 C *1:8-10.

ACTS 20

Paul and his friends go into Macedonia and Greece, and return to Troas, 1-6; where, as Paul preaches long, Eutychus falls from a window, and is taken up dead: but he is restored to life; and the apostles and disciples break bread, and converse till daybreak, 7-12. Paul and his friends sail to Miletus, 13-16. He sends for the elders of Ephesus, 17. He states to them his ministry, conduct, and prospects; exhorting, warning, and instructing them with great fervency, and faithful love, and "commending them to God and the word of his grace," 18-35. He prays with them; and takes a most affectionate farewell, leaving them in great sorrow, because they should see his face no more, 36-38.

1. **after**. Ac 19:23-41. **the disciples**. ver. 30. Ac +11:26. **embraced**. ver. 10, 37. Ac +15:32. 21:5, 6. Ge 48:10. 1 S 20:41, 42. Ro 16:16. 1 C 16:20. 2 C 13:12. 1 Th 5:26. **departed**. Ac +19:21. **to go**. Ac 19:21. 1 C 16:5. 2 C 7:5. 1 T 1:3. **Macedonia**. Ac +16:9.

2. **over those parts**. This would take him to the borders of Illyricum (Ro 15:19), where he gave "much exhortation," a journey mentioned in the Epistle, but omitted in this History. These labors would be fresh in his mind as he wrote at Corinth. Illyricum is quite naturally mentioned in Romans, and the coincidence is all the more striking that that place is not mentioned in Acts. For a listing of related notes pertaining to undesigned coincidences, see Ac 12:12n. ver. 6. Ac 16:12. 17:1, 10. **given**. ver. 7, 11. Ac 2:40. +*14:22. 15:+32, 41. Col 1:28. 1 Th *2:3, 11, 12. 4:1. Cir. A.M. 4064. A.D. 60. **much**. The time involved, though indefinite here, is a significant part of the undesigned coincidences discussed at Ac 18:2n. **Greece**. That is, *Greece* properly so called, bounded on the west by Epirus, on the east by the Aegean sea, on the north by Macedonia, and on the south by the Peloponnesus. In its largest acceptation it also comprehended all Macedonia, Thessaly, Epirus, Peloponnesus, and the circumjacent islands. Zc 9:13.

3. **abode**. *ſ171J2, Ac +15:33. **three months**. This time period figures in the undesigned concidences discussed at Ac 18:2n. **the Jews**. ver. 19. Ac *9:23, +24. *13:50. *14:5, 19. *17:5, 13. *23:12-15. *25:1-3. Ezr 8:31. Pr 1:11. Je 5:26. 2 C 7:5. 11:26. **sail**. Ac 18:18. 21:3. Ga 1:21. **Syria**. Ac +15:23. **he purposed**. Here is mentioned the visit to Macedonia and Greece, and the voyage to Syria, but no mention is made of the

contributions. This is part of a very significant unde-signed coincidence detailed in the note at Ro 15:26. See related notes listed at Ac 12:12. Ac 19:21. 2 C 1:15-17.

4. **Asia.** ver. 16, 18. Ac +2:9. 19:31n. **Sopater.** i.e. *saving father; who defends his father,* *S#4986g, only here. Ro 16:21, Sosipater. **of Berea.** Ac +*17:10-12. **Thessalonians.** Ac +17:1. 2 C 9:4. **Aristarchus.** Ac +19:29. 27:2. Col 4:10. Phm 24. **Secundus.** i.e. *second; favorable,* *S#4580g. **Gaius.** Ro 16:23. 3 J 1. **Derbe.** Ac 14:6, 20. 16:1. 2 C 8:23, 24. **Timotheus.** Ac +16:1. 2 C 1:1, 19. Ph 2:19. 1 T 1:1. 2 T 1:2. **Tychicus.** i.e. *casual; fortunate; fate,* *S#5190g. Ep 6:21. Col *4:7. 2 T 4:12. T 3:12. **Trophimus.** i.e. *nourishment; well educated,* *S#5161g. Ac *21:29. 2 T 4:20. Of seven names mentioned in Ro 16:21-23 as saluting the Church, three are mentioned here at Ac 20:4 as being with Paul at the time. The difference between the two lists is, in the circumstances, perfectly natural, and a mark of genuineness. A forger would have made the lists correspond. See the related notes on unde-signed coincidences listed at Ac 12:12.

5. **for us.** ver. 13, 14, 15. Ac +16:10. **Troas.** *Troas* was a maritime city and country of Phrygia, in Asia Minor, anciently called *Dardania,* lying on the Helles-pont, west of Mysia. Ac 16:+8, 11. 2 C 2:12. 2 T 4:13.

6. **we.** ver. +5. **Philippi.** Ac 16:12. Ph 1:1. 1 Th 2:2. **the days.** Ac +12:3. Ex 12:14, 15, 18-20. 13:6, 7. *23:15. 34:18. 1 C 5:7, 8. **unleavened.** Le +*23:6. **came.** 2 T 4:13. **seven.** Ac 21:4, 8. 28:14.

7. **the first day.** Mt 28:1. Mk +*16:9. Lk 24:1. Jn *20:1, 19, 26. 1 C *16:2. Re ◐+*1:10n. **the disciples.** 1 C 11:17-21, 33, 34. **came together.** Dt 16:6. 1 C 11:20. **to break.** ᶜ108H4, Is +58:7. ver. 11. Ac 2:+42, 46. Lk 22:19. 24:35. 1 C *10:16, 17. *11:20-34. **preached.** Ac +17:17. **and continued.** ver. 9, 11, 31. Ac 28:23. Ne 8:3. 9:3. 1 C 15:10. 2 T *4:2.

8. **lights.** Mt 25:1. Jn 18:3. Re 4:5. 8:10g. **in.** Ac +1:13. Lk 22:12.

9. **window.** 2 C 11:33. **being.** Jon 1:5, 6. Mt 26:40, 41. Mk 13:36. **Eutychus.** i.e. *happy, fortunate; well off,* *S#2161g. **long preaching.** Ac +17:17. **and fell.** 2 K 1:2. **the third.** 1 K 17:19. **and was.** Ac 14:19, 20. Mk 9:26.

10. **and fell.** 1 K *17:21, 22. 2 K *4:34, 35. **Trouble.** Mt *9:23, 24. Mk 5:39. Lk 7:13, 14. Jn 11:11, 40. **life.** Gr. *psyche,* ᶜ121A7, Mt +2:20. ᶜ121A7, Ge +9:5.

11. **and had.** ver. +7. **talked.** Ac 10:27. 24:26g. Lk 24:14, 15g. **even.** ver. 7, 9.

12. **they.** ver. 10. **alive.** ver. 10, 11. **were.** Ac +4:36. Is 40:1. 2 C 1:4. Ep 6:22. 1 Th 3:2. 4:18. 5:11, 14. 2 Th 2:16, 17. **not.** ᶜ175B, Ge +21:16.

13. **And we.** ver. 5-8. Ac +16:10. **Assos.** i.e. *nearer, approaching,* *S#789g. ver. 14. Ac ◐27:13g. **minding.** Mk +*1:35. 6:31-33, 46.

14. **Mitylene.** i.e. *curtailed; purity,* *S#3412g.

15. **the next.** Ac 21:26. Lk 13:33g. **Chios.** i.e. *open, opening,* *S#5508g. **Samos.** i.e. *a sandy bluff; full of gravel; height by the sea,* *S#4544g. **Trogyllium.** i.e. *cache; fruit cellar; fruitport; fruits eaten raw,* *S#5175g. **Miletus.** i.e. *cared for; scarlet, red,* *S#3399g. ver. 17. 2 T 4:20, Miletum.

16. **had determined.** ver. 13. Ac 18:21. 19:21. 21:4, 12, 13. 24:17. Ro 15:24-28. **Ephesus.** ver. 17. Ac +18:19. **not spend.** Ac +*18:20, 21. **Asia.** ver. 4, 18.

Ac +2:9. **if it.** ᶜ184D1, Lk +22:67. **at Jerusalem.** ver. 22. Ac 19:21. 24:11, *17. 1 C 16:8. **the day.** Ac +2:1. Ex 34:22. 1 C 16:8.

17. **Ephesus.** Ac +18:19. 19:1. Ep 2:22. **the elders.** ver. 28. Ac +11:30. *14:23n. 15:4, 6, 23. 16:4. 1 T 4:14. 5:17. T 1:5. Ja 5:14. 1 P 5:1. 2 J 1. 3 J 1.

18. **Ye know.** ver. 31, 34. Ac +2:22. 1 Th 1:5. **from.** Ac *18:19. *19:1, 8-10. **came into.** Ac 21:4. 25:1. **Asia.** ver. 4, 16. Ac +2:9. **after.** 2 C 1:12. 6:3-11. 1 Th 1:5, 6. 2:1-10. 2 Th 3:7-9. 2 T 3:10.

19. **Serving.** Ac 27:23. Jn 12:26. Ro *1:1, 9. +*12:11. Ga 1:10. Ep 6:7. Col +3:24. 1 Th 1:9. 2 P 1:1. Re 7:15. **the Lord.** Ac +11:16. **with all.** Mt *20:25-28. 1 C *15:9, 10. 2 C *1:12. 3:5. 7:5. 12:7-10. Ga 4:13, 14. Ep +4:2. 1 Th 2:6, 7. **humility.** Ps 119:21. Ro +*12:3. Ph +*2:3. 1 P *5:1-3, 5. **many tears.** ver. 31. Ps *119:136. Je 9:1. *13:17. Lk *19:41. 2 C *2:4. Ph *3:18. 2 T 1:4. 1 P 1:6. **temptations.** 1 C 4:9-13. 2 C 4:7-11. *11:23-30. Ja 1:2. 1 P 1:6. **by the.** ver. 3. Ac 9:23-25. 13:50, 51. 14:5, 6, 19, 20. 17:5, 13. 2 C 11:26.

20. **I kept back.** ver. 27, 31. Ac 5:2. Nu 22:18. Dt 4:5. 1 S 3:18. Ps 40:9, 10. Je *42:4. Ezk 33:7-9. 1 C +*15:3. Ga 2:12. Col 1:28. 2 T *4:2. He 10:39g. **profit-able.** 1 C 7:35. 10:33. 12:7. 14:6. Ph 3:1. 2 T √3:16, 17. **and have.** ver. 31. Ac 2:46. 5:42. Mk 4:34. 2 T *4:2. **house to.** Ac 2:46. 5:42.

21. **Testifying.** ver. 23, 24, 26. Ac 2:40. 8:25. *18:5. 28:23. Lk +16:28. 1 J √5:11-13. **to the Jews.** Ac 18:4. 19:17. Ro 1:14. 1 C 1:22. **and also.** Mk *16:15, 16. Lk *24:47. **repentance.** Ac +*2:38. +*3:19. 11:18. *17:30. 19:4. 26:20. Ezk *18:30-32. Mt 3:2. 4:17. 21:31, 32. Mk *1:14, 15. 6:12. Lk +√13:3, 5. 15:7, 10. +*24:47. Ro *2:4. 2 C √7:10. 2 T +*2:25, 26. He 6:1. **faith.** Ac +*10:43. +*13:38, 39. √16:31. 24:24. 26:18. Jn √3:15-18, 36. √20:31. Ro √1:16. √3:22-26. √4:24. *5:1. √10:9. Ga *2:16, 20. 3:22. Ep 1:15. Col 1:4. 2:5. 1 T 3:13. Phm 5. 1 J √5:1, 5, 11-13. **our Lord.** Ac +11:17. 15:26.

22. **And now.** ᶜ70, Ex +16:35. **I go.** Ac *19:21. *21:11-14. Lk *9:51. 12:50. 2 C 5:14. **spirit.** Gr. *pneuma,* Ac +18:25. ᶜ108B, Lk +10:21. ᶜ121A2, Ps +51:10. Ac 17:16. 18:5. **unto Jerusalem.** ver. +16. **not knowing.** This mention of Paul's anticipation of persecution in Judea is paralleled by his prayer request in Romans 15:30-32 regarding the same. Romans was written immediately before Paul set forward on this journey; these words in Acts were uttered by him when he had proceeded as far as Miletus. The two passages, without any resemblance between them that could in-duce us to suspect that they were borrowed from one another, represent the state of Paul's mind regarding the outcome of this journey, in terms of substantial agreement (William Paley, *Horae Paulinae,* p. 38). As Paul continued on this journey his fears increased, for the Holy Spirit testified regarding the bonds and affliction which awaited him at Jerusalem (Ac 21:4, 11). Lk *18:31-33. Jn 13:1. 18:4. Ja 4:14. 2 P 1:14.

23. **the Holy.** Ac 8:29n. 9:16. 14:22. *21:4, 11. Jn 16:33. 1 Th *3:3. 2 T 2:12. **Ghost.** Gr. *pneuma,* Mt +3:16. **witnesseth.** ver. +21. **bonds.** Ac 21:33. **afflic-tions.** Ac +*14:22. 1 Th 3:3. **abide me.** *or,* wait for me.

24. **none.** Ac +*21:13. Ro √8:35-39. 1 C √15:58. 2 C *4:1, 8, 9, 16-18. 6:4-10. 7:4. 12:10. Ep 3:13. 1 Th 2:2. 3:3. 2 T 1:12. 3:11. 3:11. 4:17. He 10:34. 12:1-3.

neither. 2 C 5:8. Ph +*1:20-24. *2:17. Col 1:24. 1 J 3:16. Re √12:11. **life.** Gr. *psyche*, ⨍121A7, Mt +2:20. **I might finish.** Ac 13:25. Jn 17:4. 1 C 9:24-27. Ph 3:13-15. 2 T √4:6-8. He √12:1, 2. **and the ministry.** Ac +1:17. 9:15. 22:21. *26:17, 18. 1 C 9:17, 18. 2 C *3:6. *4:1. *5:18, 19. Ga 1:1. 1 T √1:12. T 1:3. **received of.** Ac 26:16. Ga *1:1. 1 Th 2:4. 2 T *1:9-12. T 1:3. **the Lord Jesus.** ver. 35. Ac +1:21. Lk *2:10, 11. **to testify.** ver. +21. Jn 15:27. He 2:3, 4. **the gospel.** Ac 14:3. 15:7. Lk 2:10, 11. Ro 3:24-26. 4:4. 5:20, 21. 11:6. Ep 1:6. 2:4-10. T 2:11. 3:4-7. 1 P 5:12. **grace.** T#305, 586. ver. 32. Ac +*11:23. Ro 3:24. 5:8, 15-17, 21. 9:16. 11:5, 6. 1 C +4:7 (T#668). 15:10. Ep 1:5, 6. 2:4-10. 1 T 1:14. 2 T +*1:9. T 3:5-7. 1 P 1:10.

25. **And now.** ⨍70, Ex +16:35. **I know.** ver. 38. Ro 15:23. Ph ◑*1:25. **among whom.** Ac *19:8. **preaching.** Ac 8:12. 28:31. Mt 4:17, 23. 10:7. 13:19, 52. Lk 9:60. 16:16. **the kingdom.** Ac +*1:6n. *28:23. Mt +13:19. Mk *1:14, 15. Lk +*17:21. +*22:29, 30. Jn √3:5. +*18:36. Ro *14:17. 1 C +*6:9. **see.** Paley suggests this was Paul's inference from the prophecies he had received concerning the bonds and afflictions which awaited him at Jerusalem, about which he shows such anxiety (ver. 22n). Paul probably did revisit Ephesus, for at Rome he wrote to the Philippians that he expected to go to them shortly (Ph 2:24); and he asked Philemon at Colosse to prepare him a lodging, as he expected soon to join him (Phm 22). Paul could hardly go from Rome to Colosse, or from Colosse to Philippi, without taking Ephesus in his way. These hints that make it probable that Paul did visit Ephesus after his liberation at Rome constitute an undesigned coincidence (Paley, *Horae Paulinae*, p. 164). See related notes listed at Ac 12:12n. Ga 1:22. Ph 1:25. 2:23. Col 2:1. **face.** ⨍171Q14, Ge +3:19.

26. **I take.** ver. 21. Jb 16:19. Jn 12:17. 19:35. Ro 10:2. 2 C 1:23. 8:3. Ep +4:17. 1 Th 2:10-12. **this day.** Dt +*4:26. 8:19. Lk 23:43. **that.** Ac +*18:6. 2 S 3:28. Ezk √3:18-21. 33:2-9. 2 C 7:2. 1 T 5:22. **I am.** Ac 24:16. **pure from.** Le 19:17.

27. **I have.** ver. *20, *35. Ac *26:22, 23. 2 C *4:2. Ga *1:7-10. *4:16. 1 Th *2:4. **not shunned.** Le 19:17. **to declare.** Ac +*4:20. 22:14, 15. **all.** ver. 20. Ac 2:23. Ps *33:11. Is *46:10, 11. Je *23:22. *26:2. Ezk 33:8. Mt *28:20. Lk *7:30. Jn 15:15. 1 C 11:23. Ep +*1:11. He 6:17.

28. **Take heed.** Ac +5:35. Dt 12:30. 2 Ch *19:6, 7. Mk 13:9. Lk *21:34. 1 C √9:26, 27. Col *4:17. 1 T +*4:16. He √12:15. **all the flock.** ver. 29. SS 1:7, 8. Is *40:11. 63:11. Je 13:17, 20. 31:10. Ezk 34:31. Mi 7:14. Lk +*12:32. Jn +*10:16. Ep 4:11. 1 P *5:2-4. **over the which.** Ac *13:2. *14:23. 1 C *12:8-11, 28-31. 1 T 4:14. **Ghost.** Gr. *pneuma*, Mt +3:16. Mt +12:32. **made you.** Ac 8:29n. 1 C *12:8-11, 28. **overseers.** ver. *17. Ph 1:1. 1 T *3:2. *5:17. T *1:5, 7, 9. He *13:17. 1 P *2:25g. **to feed.** Ps 78:70-72. Pr *10:21. Is *40:11. Je +*3:15. Ezk 34:3. Mi *5:4. 7:14. Zc 11:4. Mt *2:6g. Jn *21:15-17. Ep *4:11, 12. 1 P *5:2, 3. **the church.** 1 C 1:2. *10:32. 11:22. 15:9. Ga 1:13. 1 T *3:5, 15, 16. The twelve occurrences of "church of God" and similar "churches of God" or "church of the living God" are: Ac 20:28. 1 C *1:2. 10:32. 11:◑16, 22. 15:9. 2 C 1:1. Ga 1:13. 1 Th ◑2:14. 2 Th ◑1:4. 1 T 3:5, ◑15. This can by no means be taken to be the authorized name of God's one true church, as claimed by some who would take this title to them-

selves. There are a number of other church titles in the New Testament (Ro *16:4, 5, 16. 1 C 16:1, 19. 2 C 8:1. Ga 1:2, 22. Col 4:16. 1 Th 1:1. He *12:23. 2 J +*10. Re 22:16). In thirty-eight chapters, Ambrose Serle discusses as many additional more general titles of the church in his volume *The Church of God*. **of God.** Manuscript authority for this reading is about equally divided between it and "of the Lord." Alford, who favored the reading "the Lord" in his first two editions, changed to "of God" in his last edition, and gives significant reasons to support his change of view. In favor of regarding "church of the Lord" as the original it may be argued (1) some busy scribe may have written at the side, as so often occurs, "God," and over time this gloss by degrees would become adopted into the text and supersede the original word, or become combined with it; (2) since the expression "church of the Lord" is not found elsewhere in the writings of Paul, this reading would have been corrected to make it conform to the very usual one, "church of God"; (3) possible, but very unlikely, the alteration may have been made solely in the interests of orthodoxy. In favor of regarding "church of God" as the original reading, Alford states "If 'God' was the original, but one reason can be given why it should have been altered to 'Lord,' and that one sure to have operated. It would stand as a bulwark against Arianism, an assertion which no skill could evade, which must therefore be modified. If 'God' stood in the text originally, it was sure to be altered to 'Lord.' The converse was not sure, nor indeed likely, from similar reasons, the passage offering no stumblingblock to orthodoxy." In further support of "church of God," Pauline usage favors this reading; is it probable that Paul would here use an expression which he or the other apostles are not recorded as having used anywhere else? In most of the places where Paul uses "church of God," he uses it in a precisely similar manner, in a position of peculiar solemnity or as the consummation of a climax (1 C 10:32. 15:9. Ga 1:13. 1 T 3:5, 15). The present passage loses by the substitution of "Lord" the peculiar emphasis which its structure and context seem to require. Therefore, since it is more likely that the alteration should have been to "Lord" than to "God," more likely that the speaker would have used "God" than "Lord," and more consonant to the evidently emphatic position of the word, Alford states he has decided for the reading of the received text, "church of God" (*Greek Testament*, vol. 2, p. 230, 231, on Ac 20:28). Bengel favored "church of God" as the original reading, but notes significantly that if "Lord" is to be received into the text, it means, parallel to Old Testament usage, the "Church of Jehovah" (*Word Studies*, vol. 1, p. 888). F. H. A. Scrivener notes that the Patristic evidence slightly favors "church of God;" a large number of MSS. support the conflate reading "church of the Lord and of God," a reading which vouches for the presence of "God" in the earliest codices. The preponderance in favor of "church of God," "*undoubtedly the harder form*, is very marked," and coupled with the reasoning of Alford, there remains very little room for hesitation (*Introduction to the Criticism of the New Testament*, vol. 2, pp. 374-377). Frederick Nolan relates that some of the editions of the church fathers have been "notoriously corrupted, as it is conceived, by the Arians." But he shows that the genuine works of Ignatius follows the Byzantine text, "church of God." Ireneus follows the received text, for he is discussing the subject of the mysteries of the Church (Iren. adv. Haer. Lib. iii. cap. xiv. p. 201). "Now, as there was no mystery in our *Lord's* purchasing the Church with his blood, but a great mystery in '*God's* purchasing it with his own blood,' Ireneus's allegation of this passage appears to me to be perfectly irrelevant, unless that primitive father read, with Ignatius and the Vulgar Greek, 'the church of God, which he purchased with his own blood' " (*An Inquiry into the Integrity of the Greek Vulgate, or Received Text of the New Testament*, pp. 516-518). or, the Lord. Lk +11:16. Mt *16:18. Ro +16:16. **which he.** Ps √74:2. Is *53:10-12. Ep *1:7, 14. Col *1:14. He *9:12-14. 1 P *1:18, 19. 2:9. Re *5:9. **purchased.** Le=22:11. Lk 17:33g ("to save," alternate reading, "to gain"). Ro 8:32. 1 C 4:3. 1 T 3:13g. 1 P 1:18, 19. 2 P 2:1. **with his own blood.** *f*117, Ge +19:8. Scrivener protests strongly against the interpretation found in Darby's *New Translation*, which renders this phrase "the blood of his own," and the suggestion of Dr. Hort (Notes, p. 99), who would render "through the blood that was His own," i.e. as being His Son's, for even Hort admits, "this general sense, if indicated, is not sufficiently expressed in the text as it stands" (Scrivener, *Introduction*, vol. 2, p. 377). J. H. Moulton supports such a rendering, suggesting the grammatical usage is similar to the use of *o idios* without a noun expressed, as in such passages as Jn 1:11; 13:1; Ac 4:23; 24:23 (*Grammar*, vol. 1, p. 90). Such a rendering, Nigel Turner asserts, is a "theological expedient," and is not the natural way to take the Greek (*Grammatical Insights*, p. 15). If this had been the intended force of the statement, either Paul or Luke would have placed "Son" in the text. A. T. Robertson explains "Through the agency of (*dia*) his own blood. Whose blood? If *tou theou* (God) is correct, as it is, then Jesus is here called "God" who shed his own blood for the flock. It will not do to say that Paul did not call Jesus God, for we have Ro 9:5; Col 2:9 and T 2:13 where he does that very thing, besides Col 1:15-20 and Ph 2:5-11" (*Word Pictures*, vol. 3, p. 353). B. B. Warfield notes, with regard to citing Ro 9:5 and T 2:13, "when it is objected that these are disputed passages, it is just to remind the objector that this will exclude his original statement as well as our rebuttal of it" (*Textual Criticism*, p. 188), a fallacy in logic akin to asserting "there are no absolutes," which, if true, negates the assertion. Mt *1:23. Jn +√20:28. 1 C 6:20. Ep 1:7. 1 Th 1:10. He *9:12, 14. 1 P +*1:18, 19. 1 J *1:7. Re +*5:9.

29. I know. 2 P 2:1. **after.** Dt 21:29. **wolves.** *f*103, Ge +3:13. T#475. Is *3:12. 9:15, 16. Je *23:1, 2, 14, 15, 32. Ezk *13:22. 22:25-31. *34:2-4, 10. Zp 3:3. Ml 2:8, 9. Mt *7:15. *10:16. 23:14-17, 23, 24, 27, 28, 33. Lk 6:26. 10:3. *11:52. Jn *10:12. 1 C +11:19 (T#176). Ep +*4:14. 1 T +6:5 (T#177). Ja +5:20 (T#175). 2 P *2:1-3. **not.** Je 13:20. *23:1. Ezk 34:2, 3. Zc 11:17. Jn 10:12. Col 2:8. **the flock.** ver. +28.

30. of your. Jsh 20:17. Mt *26:21-25. 1 C √11:19. 2 C *11:13. 1 T +*1:19, 20. 2 T *2:17, 18. *4:3, 4. 2 P *2:1-3. 1 J √2:19. 2 J 7. Ju *4, etc. Re 2:6. **speaking.** *f*63H, Ge +12:15. Ac 13:8. Pr *19:1. 23:33. Is 59:3. 1 T *5:13. +*6:5. 2 P 2:18. Ju *15, *16. **perverse.** Ac 13:8. Mt +17:17. **to draw.** Ac *5:36, 37. *21:38. Mt √23:15. 1 C *1:12-15. Ga 6:12, 13. 2 T *1:15. **disciples.** Ac +11:26.

31. watch. Mt +*13:25. +24:42. Mk 13:34-37. Lk +√21:36. 2 T *4:5. He *13:17. Re 16:15. **remember.** ver. +18. **by.** Ac *19:8, 10. 24:17. **warn.** ver. 20. Ezk *3:17-20. Mt 3:7. 1 C 4:14. Col *1:28. 1 Th 5:+12, *14. **night.** ver. 7, 11. Ac 26:7. Mk +4:27. 1 Th 2:9, 10. 2 Th 3:8. **with tears.** ver. +19. Ps 119:136. +*126:6. Lk 19:41. 2 C 2:4. Ph 3:18. He *13:17.

32. I commend. Ac 14:23, 26. 15:40. Ge 50:24. Je 49:11. 1 P *4:19. Ju *24, *25. **to the word of.** ver. 24. Ac 14:3. He 13:9. **to build.** T#1049. Ac +9:31. Jn 15:3. 17:17. 1 C 3:9, 10. Ep *2:20-22. 4:12, 16. Col +*2:7. 1 Th √2:13. 1 T +*4:16. 1 P √2:2. 2 P √3:18. Ju √20. **and to give.** Ac *26:18. Dt +*33:2-4. Je 3:19. Mt +*5:5. +*25:34. Ro +*8:17. Ep *1:14, 18. 5:5. Col *1:12. *3:24. He *9:15. 1 P +*1:4, 5. **which are sanctified.** Jn √17:+6, 17. 1 C 1:2. √6:11. 1 Th *4:3, 4. √5:23. He 2:11. 10:14. +*12:14. Ju 1. Re *21:27.

33. coveted. ver. 35. Ac 24:16. Ex +*18:21. Nu 16:15. 1 S *12:3-5. Ps +*10:3. Mt 10:8. Lk √12:15. 1 C *9:11, 12, 15, 18. 2 C 7:2. *11:9. 12:14, 17. 1 Th 2:5. 1 T √6:10. 1 P *5:2. **silver, or.** Ja *5:2, 3.

34. know. ver. +18. **these hands.** Consistent with this speech to the Ephesian elders are Paul's statements in his letters that he maintained himself by his own labor in Thessalonica (2 Th 3:8, 9); that of the churches in Macedonia, only the Philippians gave him aid (Ph 4:15); and correspond as to his reason, to be an example, to support the weak. The sentiment in the Epistle and that in the speech recorded in the History are so alike, though the words show so little of imitation or resemblance, that the agreement cannot be explained without supposing the speech and letter to have really proceeded from the same person (Paley, *Horae Paulinae*, pp. 158, 159). See related notes listed at Ac 12:12n. Ac +18:3. 28:3. 1 C 4:12. 1 Th *2:9. 2 Th √3:8, 9. **ministered unto.** 2 C 11:7-9. **to them.** Ac +19:22, 29.

35. showed. ver. *20, *27. 1 C *11:1. 2 Th *3:7. Ja *1:22. **how that.** Is 35:3. Jn 13:29. Ro *15:1. 1 C 9:12. 2 C 11:9, 12. 12:13. Ep *4:28. 1 Th *4:11. *5:14. He 12:12, 13. *13:3. **ought to support.** Ps +*12:5. Ezk +*16:49. Lk 1:54. Ro 14:1. *15:1. 1 C 12:28. 1 Th *5:14. Ja 2:15, 16. 1 J √3:17. **the weak.** ✻S#770g, *astheneo*. Rendered (1) be weak: Ro 4:19. 8:3. 14:1, 2. 1 C *8:9. 2 C 11:21, 29, 29. 12:10. 13:3, 4, 9. (2) be sick: Mt 25:36. Lk 7:10. Jn 4:46. 11:2, 3, 6. Ac 9:37. Ph 2:26, 27. Ja 5:14. (3) sick: Mt 10:8. Mk 6:56. Lk 4:40. 9:2. Jn 11:1. Ac 19:12. 2 T 4:20. (4) weak: Ac 20:35. 1 C 8:11, 12. (5) impotent folk: Jn 5:3. (6) impotent man: Jn 5:7. (7) be diseased: Jn 6:2. (8) be made weak: Ro 14:21. **remember.** Ac 11:16. **the Lord Jesus.** ver. 24. Ac +1:21. **It is.** *f*138C, Ge +22:14. Ps *41:1-3. *112:5-9. Pr *19:17. Is 32:8. 58:7-12. Mt *10:8. 25:34-40. Lk *14:12-14. 2 C √8:9. √9:6-12. Ph 4:+*17-20. He *13:16. **to give.** Ac +*11:29. Mt 5:42. +*10:8. Lk 3:11. +*6:38. +*11:41n, 42n. 12:33. Jn 13:29. Ro 12:8. 1 C *16:2. Ep *4:28. 1 T 5:17. 6:19. He *13:16.

36. he kneeled. Ac +*7:60. 9:40. *21:5. 2 Ch 6:13. Da +*6:10. Lk 22:41. Ep *3:14. Ph *4:6.

37. wept. 1 S *20:41. 2 S 15:30. 2 K +*20:3. Ezr 10:1. Jb 2:12. Ps √126:5. 2 T 1:4. Re 7:17. 21:4. **fell.** Ge 45:14. 46:29. Lk +15:20. **kissed.** Ro 16:16. 1 C 16:20. 2 C 13:12. 1 Th 5:26.

38. that. ver. 25. **face.** *f*171Q14, Ge +3:19. **And.** Ac 15:3. 21:5, 16. 1 C 16:11.

ACTS 21

Paul and his friends leave Miletus, and arrive at Tyre; where, finding disciples, they stay seven days, and part from them with prayer, kneeling down on the seashore, 1-6. They proceed to Caesarea, to the house of Philip the evangelist, whose four daughters prophesy, 7-9. Agabus foretells that Paul will be bound at Jerusalem: he is not however dissuaded from going thither, 10-16. Arriving at Jerusalem, he reports, to James and the elders, the success of his labors among the Gentiles, 17-19. He is persuaded to purify himself at the temple, with four men who had a vow, 20-26; where he is set upon by some Jews from Asia, and in danger of being slain in a tumult, but is rescued by the chief captain; who binds him with chains, and leads him to the castle, 27-36. He requests, and is permitted, to speak to the people, 37-40.

1. **we.** Ac +16:10. 20:6. **were gotten from.** Ac 20:37, 38. 1 S 20:41, 42. Lk 22:41g. 1 Th 2:17. **and had.** Ac 27:2, 4. Lk 5:4. 8:22. **we came.** Ac 16:11. **Coos.** i.e. *summit; a public prison; convex side uppermost,* ✱S#2972g. *Coos, Cos,* or *Co,* now *Zia,* is an island in the Aegean sea, one of those called *Cyclades,* near the southwest point of Asia Minor, and about fifteen miles from Halicarnassus. **Rhodes.** i.e. *a rose; rosy,* ✱S#4499g. *Rhodes* is a celebrated island in the same sea, southward of Caria, from which it is distant about twenty miles, next to Cyprus and Lesbos in extent, being 120 miles in circumference. It was remarkable for the clearness of the air, and its pleasant and healthy climate, and chiefly for its Colossus of brass, seventy cubits high, with each finger as large as a ordinary man, standing astride over the mouth of the harbor, so that ships in full sail passed between its legs. **Patara.** i.e. *trodden under foot; scattering cursing,* ✱S#3959g.

2. **finding.** Ac 27:6. Jon 1:3. **Phenicia.** i.e. *land of palm trees,* ✱S#5403g. Ac +11:19. 15:3. 27:2.

3. **Cyprus.** ver. 16. Ac +4:36. 11:19, 20. 13:4. 15:39. 27:4, 5. **Syria.** Ac +15:23, 41. 18:18. Jg 10:6. 2 S 8:6. Is 7:2. Mt 4:24. Lk 2:2. **Tyre.** ver. 7. Ac +12:20. Ps 45:12. 87:4. Is 23:17, 18. Mt 11:21. Lk 10:13. **for there.** ver. 2.

4. **finding.** Ac 19:1. Mt 10:11. 2 T 1:17. **disciples.** ver. 16. Ac +11:26. **we.** Ac +16:10. **tarried.** Ac 20:6, 7. 28:14. Re 1:10. **said.** ver. 10-12. Ac *20:22, +23. **Spirit.** Gr. *pneuma,* Mt +3:16. **not go up.** Ac 20:18. 25:1g.

5. **and they.** Ac 15:3. 17:10. 20:38. **with.** Dt +*29:11, 12. Jsh √24:15. 2 Ch 20:13. Ne 12:43. Mt 14:21. **we kneeled.** Ac 9:40. +20:36. 1 K 8:54. Ps 95:6. Mk 1:40. **the shore.** T#1206.

6. **taken.** 2 C 2:13. **they.** Jn 1:11g. 7:53. 16:32. 19:27.

7. **Tyre.** ver. 3. Ac +12:20. **Ptolemais.** i.e. *warlike,* ✱S#4424g. **and saluted.** √108B, 2 K +4:29. ver. 19. Ac 18:22. 25:13. 1 S 10:4. 13:10. Mt 5:47. He 13:24. **the brethren.** ver. 17. Jn +21:23. **abode.** ver. 10. Ac 28:12.

8. **we that.** Ac 16:10, 13, 16, 17. 20:6, 13. 27:1, 2. 28:11, 16. **Caesarea.** ver. 16. Ac +8:40. 9:30. 10:1. 18:22. 23:23. **Philip.** Ac +*6:5. *8:5-13, 26-40. **the evangelist.** Ep 4:11. 2 T 4:5.

9. **virgins.** 1 C 7:25-34, 38. **which.** Ac *2:17, 18. +13:1. Ex 15:20. Jg 4:4. 2 K 22:14. Ne 6:14. Jl +*2:28. Lk 2:36. 1 C +*11:4, 5. Re 2:20.

10. **as.** ver. 4, 7. Ac 20:16. **came down.** Ac 18:22. **Agabus.** Ac *11:27, 28.

11. **he took.** 1 S 15:27, 28. 1 K 11:29-31. 2 K 13:15-19. Is 20:3. Je 13:1-11. 19:1, 10, 11. 27:2. Ezk 24:19-25. Ho 12:10. Jn 21:18. **Thus.** ver. 4. Ac 13:2. 16:6. +20:23. 28:25. He 3:7. 1 P 1:12. **So shall.** ver. 33. Ac +9:16. 22:25. 24:27. 26:29. 28:20. Ep 3:1. 4:1. 6:20. 2 T 2:9. He 10:34. **and shall.** ver. 31-33. Ac 28:17. Mt 20:18, 19. 27:1, 2. Mk 10:33. Lk 18:32.

12. **we.** Ac +16:10. **besought.** ver. 4. Ac 20:22. Mt 16:21-23. Mk 8:32, 33. **to go up.** ver. 15. Ac +18:22.

13. **What.** 1 S 15:14. Ps 106:15. Is 3:15. Ezk 18:2. Jon 1:6. **to weep.** Ac 20:37. 1 S 1:8. Ph 2:26, 30. 2 T 1:4. **for.** Ac 15:26. *20:24. Lk 14:26. Ro √8:35-37. 1 C *15:31. 2 C *4:10-17. 11:23-27. 12:10. Ph 1:20, 21. 2:17. Col 1:24. 2 T 2:4-6. 4:6. 2 P 1:14. Re +*3:10. √12:11. **for the name.** Ac +5:41. **the Lord Jesus.** Ac +1:21.

14. **we ceased.** Ac 11:18g. Ru 1:18. **The will.** T#299. Ge 43:14. Le 10:1-3. Jg +10:15 (T#356). 1 S 3:14, 18. 2 S 15:25, 26. 2 K 20:19. Jb 1:19-21. Ps 39:9. Mt +*6:10. *26:39, 42. Lk +10:33 (T#414). *11:2. 15:18, 19. +18:28 (T#674). *22:42. 23:40, 41. Ja +*4:7. Re 19:1-3. **the Lord.** Ac 11:16.

15. **our carriages.** or, baggage. **and went.** ver. 12. Ac +18:22. 25:1, 6, 9.

16. **of the.** ver. 8. Ac 10:24, 48. **disciples.** ver. 4. Ac +11:26. **Caesarea.** ver. 8. Ac +8:40. **Mnason.** i.e. *remembering; diligent seeker; the number is safe,* ✱S#3416g. **Cyprus.** ver. 3. Ac +4:36. 11:19. 15:39. **an old.** A probable reference to the fact that Mnason was one of the original disciples present at Pentecost. Ac 11:15. +15:7g. Ps 71:17, 18. 92:14. Pr *16:31. Ro 16:7. Phm 9. 1 J 2:13, 14. **disciple.** Ac +9:10.

17. **the brethren.** ver. 7. Jn +21:23. **received.** Ac 15:4. Lk +8:40g. Ro 15:7. He 13:1, 2. 3 J 7, 8.

18. **unto James.** Ac +12:17. *15:13. Mt 10:2. Ga *1:19. *2:9. Ja 1:1. **all.** Ac +11:30. 15:2, 6, 23. 20:17.

19. **saluted.** √108B, 2 K +4:29. **he declared.** Ac 11:4, etc. +14:27. *15:4, 12. Ro *15:18, 19. 1 C 3:5-9. 15:10. 2 C 6:1. Ga 2:8. Col 1:29. **by.** Ac +1:17. *20:24. 2 C *12:12.

20. **they glorified.** Ac 4:21. 11:18. Ps 22:23, 27. 72:17-19. 98:1-3. Is √55:10-13. 66:9-14. Mt +9:8. Lk 15:3-10, 32. Ro 15:6, 7, 9-13. Ga 1:24. 2 Th *1:10. Re 19:6, 7. **brother.** Ac 9:17. 22:13. Ga 2:9. 2 P 3:15. **how many.** Ac 2:41. 4:4. 6:1, 7. Mt 13:31-33. Jn 12:24. **thousands.** Gr. myriads. lit. how many times ten thousand. Ac 19:19. Lk 12:1g. 1 C 4:15. He 12:22. Ju 14. Re 5:11. 9:16. **which believe.** ver. 25. Ac +13:12. **and they.** Ac 15:1, 5, 24. 22:3. Ro *10:2. Ga 1:14. **zealous.** Ac ●1:13. 22:3. Lk ●6:15. 1 C 14:12. T 2:14. 1 P 3:13.

21. **informed.** ver. 24. Lk +1:4g. **that thou.** Ac 6:13, 14. 16:3. 28:17. Ro 14:1-6. 1 C 9:19-21. Ga *5:1-6. 6:12-15. **Jews which.** Ja 1:1. **to forsake.** An undesigned coincidence here demonstrates the conformity between the argument of Paul's epistle to the Romans and this history of Paul in Acts. Here in the history he is charged with having taught the Jews to forsake Moses. This is a very natural inference from Paul's teaching in Romans, that justification is by faith alone, and not by the works of the law. His object in the Epistle was to put Gentiles on an exact parity with Jews. The effect (here in Acts) is entirely consistent with the cause (in the Epistle); but the consistency is indirect and obvi-

ously undesigned (see listing of related notes at Ac 12:12). 2 Th 2:3g. **Moses.** ♩121A6, Lk +16:20. **saying.** ver. 28. **ought not.** Ac 15:19-21. Ro 2:28, 29. 1 C 7:18, 19. **to walk.** ver. 24. Mk 7:5. Ga 2:14. **customs.** Ac +6:14.

22. **What is it.** Ro 3:9. 1 C 14:15, 26. **the multitude.** Ac 15:12, 22. 19:32.

23. **We have.** Ac +18:18. Nu 6:2-7. **vow.** Le +*23:38.

24. **and purify.** ver. 26. Ac 24:18. Ex 19:10, 14. Nu 19:17-22. 2 C 30:18, 19. Jb 1:5. 41:25. Jn *3:25. 11:55. He *9:10-14. **at charges.** That is, in furnishing sacrifices; which was a common and very popular act among the Jews. Thus Josephus (Ant. l. xix. c. 6. sec. 41) observes that Agrippa, among other acts of thankfulness for being advanced from a prison to a throne, ordered very many Nazarites to be shaven, furnishing them with money for their expenses. Mk 5:26. Lk 14:28. 15:14. 2 C 12:15. Ja 4:3. **that they.** Ac +*18:18. Nu *6:5, 9, 13, 18. Jg 13:5. 16:17-19. **are nothing.** Ac 25:11. **but.** 1 C 9:20, 21. Ga 2:12, 13. **walkest orderly.** Ro 4:12. Ga +5:25. 6:16. Ph 3:16.

25. **which believe.** ver. 20. Ac +13:12. **we have written.** See on Ac +*15:20, 29. **observe no such.** Ac *15:24. Jn 3:23, 25. Col √2:16n. 1 T *4:3, 4. T 3:9. **keep themselves.** 1 C 10:28. **from blood.** Dt *12:23-25. **from fornication.** Ep +*5:3-5.

26. **Then.** 1 C √9:19-23. Ga ❶*2:3-5. **next day.** Ac 20:15. Lk 13:33. **purifying.** ver. +24. **with them.** Paul emphatically taught the abrogation of the Jewish law in Ga 3:23-25; 4:1-5. Yet on several occasions he submitted to the law. He circumcised Timothy (Ac 16:3), and in this text purified himself in the temple; but in these cases, and always, in order to conciliate the Jews, he being unwilling to give unnecessary offense. Thus these instances in the History correspond with the doctrine in the Epistle, in a manner to constitute an undesigned coincidence (see related notes listed at Ac 12:12n). **entered.** Ac 24:18. **to signify.** Nu 6:13-20.

27. **seven days.** Nu 6:9. **almost ended.** Ac 2:1. **the Jews.** Ac 24:18. **of Asia.** Ac +2:9. **when.** Ac 24:18. 26:21. **stirred.** Ac 6:12. 13:50. 14:2, 5, 19. 17:5, 6, 13. 18:12. 19:29. 1 K 21:25. **and laid.** Ac 4:3. 5:18. 26:21. Lk 21:12.

28. **Men.** Ac +2:22. 19:26-28. *24:5, 6. **This is.** ver. 21. Ac *6:13, 14. 24:5, 6, 18. 26:20, 21. **the people.** Ac +10:2. **the law.** Ac 6:13. 25:8. **this place.** Ac 6:13. Mt 24:15. Jn 4:20. +11:48. **brought.** Je 7:4, etc. La 1:10. **hath polluted.** Ac 24:6. Ezk 44:7.

29. **Trophimus.** Ac 20:4. 2 T 4:20. **Ephesian.** Ac +18:19.

30. **all.** Ac 16:20-22. 19:29. 26:21. Ru 1:19. Mt 2:3. 21:10. **and they.** Ac 7:57, 58. 16:19. Lk 4:29. 2 C 11:26. **drew him.** Ac 26:21. 2 K 11:15. 2 Ch 23:14.

31. **as they.** Ac 22:22. 26:9, 10. Jn 16:2. 2 C 11:23, etc. **came unto.** ver. 32, +35. **chief.** ver. 32, 33, 37. Ac 22:24, 26-28. 23:10, 17. 24:7, 22. 25:23. Mk +6:21. Jn 18:12. **the band.** Ac +10:1. **that all.** ver. 38. Ac 17:5. 19:40. 1 K 1:41. Mt 26:5. Mk 14:2. **uproar.** ver. 27. Ac +19:29.

32. **took soldiers.** Ac 23:23, 24. **and centurions.** Ac +10:1. **and ran.** Ac 23:27. 24:7. **beating.** Ac 5:40. 18:17. 22:19. Is 3:15.

33. **be bound.** ver. 11. Ac 12:6. *20:23. 22:25, 29. 28:20. Jg 15:13. 16:8, 12, 21. Ep 6:20. **two chains.** Ac 12:6. 22:29. 26:29. 28:20. Ep 6:20. 2 T 1:16. 2:9.

and demanded. Ac 22:24. 25:16. Jn 18:29, 30.

34. **some cried.** Ac 19:32. **know.** Ac 22:30. 25:26. **into.** ver. 37. Ac 22:24. 23:10, 16, 32.

35. **the stairs.** ver. 40. Ac 22:30. 23:10, 15, 28. **for.** Ge 6:11, 12. Ps 55:9. 58:2. Je 23:10. Hab 1:2, 3.

36. **Away with.** Ac 7:54. 22:22. Lk *23:18. Jn *19:15. 1 C 4:13.

37. **the castle.** ver. 34. **May I.** ver. 19. Ac 19:30. Mt 10:18-20. Lk 21:15.

38. **that.** "This Egyptian rose A.D. 55." This *Egyptian* is mentioned by Josephus (Ant. l. xx. c. 7. sec. 6. Bel. l. ii. c. 13. sec. 5) who says that he pretended to be a prophet, and persuaded a multitude of people to follow him to the top of mount Olivet, telling them that they should see the walls of the city fall down before them; but Felix attacked them with horse and foot, killed 400 on the spot, took 200 prisoners, and put the Egyptian himself to flight. Ac *5:36, 37. Mt 5:11. 1 C 4:13. **madest an uproar.** Ac +17:6. **into the wilderness.** Mt 24:26. Lk 21:21.

39. **I am.** Ac 9:11, 30. 22:3. 23:34. Ro +*11:1. **Tarsus.** Ac +9:11. **Cilicia.** Ac +6:9. 15:23, 41. **a citizen.** Ac 16:37. 22:25-29. 23:27. **of no.** ♩175B, Ge +21:16. **suffer.** ver. 37. 1 P 3:15. 4:15, 16.

40. **stairs.** ver. +35. 2 K 9:13. **and beckoned.** Ac 12:17. 13:16. 19:33. **a great.** Ac 22:2. **Hebrew.** Ac 6:1. 26:14. Lk 23:38. Jn 5:2. 19:13, 17, 20. Re 9:11. 16:16.

ACTS 22

The apostle declares, before the people, the place of his birth, his education, his zeal against the gospel; his conversion, and his commission from Jesus to preach to the Gentiles, 1-21. At the mention of the Gentiles, the people furiously exclaim against him; and the chief captain orders his soldiers to examine him by scourging, 22-24; which he avoids, by pleading the privilege of a Roman citizen, 25-29. He is brought before the council, 30.

1. **brethren.** Ac 7:2. 13:26. 23:1, 6. 28:17. **my.** Ac +19:33. 24:10. 25:8, 16. 26:1, 2, 24. Lk 12:11. 21:14. Ro 2:15. 1 C 9:3. 2 C 7:11. 12:19. Ph 1:7, 17. 2 T 4:16. 1 P +*3:15.

2. **in the Hebrew.** See on Ac +21:40.

3. **I am.** ♩156, Jn +3:2. **Jew.** Ac 21:39. Ro +*11:1. 2 C *11:22. Ph *3:5. **in Tarsus.** Ac +9:11, 30. 11:25. **a city.** Ac +6:9. 15:23, 41. 23:34. Ga 1:21. **at.** Dt 33:3. 2 K 2:3, 5. 4:38. Lk 2:46. 8:35. +*10:39. **Gamaliel.** Ac *5:34. **taught.** Ac 23:6. 26:5. Ga *1:14. Ph 3:5, 6. **the fathers.** Ac 24:14. 28:17. Ro 15:8. 2 T 1:3. **zealous.** This statement in the History corresponds with that written independently in Paul's Epistle (Ga 1:14). Ac +21:20. 2 S 21:2. Jn 16:2. Ro √10:2, 3. Ga 4:17, 18. Ph 3:6.

4. **I persecuted.** ver. 19, 20. Ac 7:58. *8:1-4. 9:1, 2, 13, 14, 21. *26:9-11. 1 C *15:9. Ga *1:13. Ph 3:6. 1 T *1:13-15. **this way.** Ac +5:20. 16:17. 18:26. 19:9, 23. 24:14.

5. **also.** Ac *9:1, 2, 14. 26:10, 12. **and all.** Ac 4:5. 5:21. Lk 22:66. 1 T 4:14. **the brethren.** ver. 1. Ac 3:22. 7:23, 25. 28:21. Ro 9:3, 4. **went to.** Ac 9:1, 2. 26:11, 12. **Damascus.** Ac +9:2.

6. **And it came.** It is evident that the apostle considered his extraordinary conversion as a most complete demonstration of the truth of Christianity; and when

all the particulars of his education, his previous religious principles, his zeal, his enmity against Christians, and his prospects of secular honors and preferments by persecuting them, are compared with the subsequent part of his life, and the sudden transition from a furious persecutor to a zealous preacher of the gospel, in which he labored and suffered to the end of his life, and for which he died a martyr, it must convince every candid and impartial person that no rational account can be given of this change, except what he himself assigns; and consequently, if that be true, that Christianity is Divine. It was this very consideration which led to the conversion of Lord Lyttelton in the last century. George Lyttelton, together with Gilbert West, both skeptics, determined to assault the truth of Christianity, persuaded that the Bible was an imposture. Lyttelton chose the Conversion of Paul and Mr. West the Resurrection of Christ for the subject of hostile criticism. In the process each was converted to firm belief in the truth of the Bible and Christianity, and each produced what are still unanswerable defenses of the Bible. Lyttelton wrote *Observations on the Conversion of Saint Paul*, West wrote *Observations on the History and Evidence of the Resurrection of Jesus Christ.* Of Lyttelton's production, Dr. Samuel Johnson forcibly and justly says, it is "a treatise to which infidelity has never been able to fabricate a specious answer." Lyttelton's masterful argument, which opens with the proposition "The conversion and apostleship of St. Paul alone, duly considered, was of itself a demonstration sufficient to prove Christianity to be a divine revelation," is analyzed and condensed by J. L. Campbell in volume two of *The Fundamentals*, pp. 353-366. In his argument Lyttelton shows that Paul (1) was not an impostor deliberately proclaiming what he knew to be false with intent to deceive; (2) was not imposed upon by an overheated imagination, and (3) was not deceived by the fraud of others. "Unless, therefore, we are prepared to lay aside the use of our understanding and all the rules of evidence by which facts are determined, we must accept the whole story of Paul's conversion as literally and historically true. We have therefore the supernatural, and the Christian religion is proved to be a revelation from God" (Campbell, *The Fundamentals*, vol. 2, p. 365). **that.** See on Ac 9:3-5. 26:12-18. 1 C 15:8. **Damascus.** Ge 14:15. 15:2. 2 S 8:6. **about noon.** Ac 26:13. Is 24:23. Mt 17:2. Re 1:16.

7. **Saul.** Ge 3:9. 16:8. 22:1, 11. Ex 3:4. 1 S 3:10. **why.** Is 1:18. 43:22-26. Je 2:5, 9. Mt 27:23. 1 T 1:13. **me.** Is +*63:9. Zc *2:8. Mt *25:45. 1 C *12:26, 27.

8. **I am.** Ac 3:6. 4:10. 6:14. Mt 2:23. **of Nazareth.** Ac +2:22. 26:9. **whom.** Ac 26:14, 15. Ex 16:7, 8. 1 S 8:7. Zc 2:8. Mt 10:40-42. 25:40, 45. Lk 10:16. Jn 5:16. 1 C 8:12. 12:12, 26, 27.

9. **saw.** Ac *9:7. Da *10:7. **but.** Jn 8:43. 12:29, 30. **heard.** ƒ108B. Idiom B829. "To hear" is used idiomatically when followed by the *accusative* case to mean to *understand, to receive, to believe*, etc. what is said, having regard, not to the speaker, but to the subject matter. For other instances of this idiom see Jn 8:43. 9:27. 1 C 5:1. 14:2mg. Ga 4:21.

10. **What.** Ac +*2:37. *9:6. 10:33. +*16:30. Ps +*25:8, 9. 143:8-10. **the Lord.** Ac +11:16. **Arise.** Ezk 3:22. Ga 1:1. **Damascus.** Ac +9:2. **there.** ver. 12-16.

Ac 26:16-18. **all things.** Ac +9:16. **are appointed.** ver. 14.

11. **when.** Ac 9:8, 9. **being.** Ac 13:11. Is 42:16.

12. **one Ananias.** See on Ac 9:10-18. **a devout.** Ac 8:2. 17:4. Lk +2:25. **according to.** Ac 24:14. Ph 3:5. **having.** Ac +6:3. 10:22. 2 C 6:8. 1 T 3:7. He 11:2. 3 J 12.

13. **Came.** Ac *9:17. **and stood.** Ac 23:11. 27:23. 2 T 4:17. **Brother.** Ac 9:17, 18. +21:20. Phm 16. **same hour.** Ac 9:18.

14. **The God.** Ac +3:13. 5:30. 13:17. 24:14. Ex *3:6, 13-16. 15:2. 2 K 21:22. 1 Ch 12:17. 29:18. 2 Ch 28:25. 30:19. Ezr 7:27. Da 2:23. **hath chosen.** ver. 10. Ac 3:20. +*9:15. *26:16. Je 1:5. Jn +*15:16. Ro 1:1. Ga 1:15. 2 T 1:1. T 1:1. **know his will.** Lk 12:47. Jn +*7:17. Ro 2:18. *12:2. Ep 1:9. √5:17. Col 1:9. **and see.** ver. 15, 18. Ac 9:17. 26:16. 1 C *9:1. *15:8. **that Just One.** ƒ32, Ge +31:21. Ac *3:14. 7:52. 2 C √5:21. 1 P 2:22. 1 J √2:1. **hear.** 1 C *11:23. +*15:3. Ga √1:12.

15. **thou shalt.** Ac +*1:8, 22. 10:39-41. *23:11. 26:16, etc. 27:24. Lk +*24:47, 48. Jn 15:27. **of.** Ac +*4:20. 20:27. 26:20. Ezk 40:4. 1 J 1:1, 3.

16. **why.** Ac *8:36, 37. Ps *119:60. Je 8:14. **arise.** or, standing, he was baptized (2 aorist active participle, nominative singular masculine). Paul was water baptized in a standing position in a Jewish home. Nothing in this record or the parallel accounts suggests Paul went to a place where there was sufficient water for immersion. Jewish households had no provision for immersions, and even the six waterpots at the wedding of Cana would be insufficient for such a purpose (Jn 2:6n). Ac +*2:38. +8:12. ‖9:18. Ro √6:3, 4. 1 C *6:11. √12:13. Ga √3:27. T *3:5. He √10:22. 1 P 3:21. **wash.** Gr. *apoluo*, *S#628g. 1 C 6:11g. **away thy sins.** It was not the ritual water of literal baptism that washed away Paul's sins, but the blood of Christ. This is certain from Scripture, for Re √1:5 asserts that the blood of Christ has washed us from our sins. Now if we ask the question, "Which washing is the real, and which the symbolic, washing of our sins?" the only answer possible is that the blood cleansing is real, the water symbolic. Ritual baptism symbolizes the washing away of sins by the blood of Christ. This is the basis for asserting that ritual baptism symbolizes what is accomplished by the Holy Spirit in real baptism (Ac 1:5n). See related notes (Ac 1:5n. 2:√38n, 41n. 8:36n, 38n, 39n. 10:47n, √48n. 11:17n. 16:14n, 15n, *33n. Mk √16:16n. Ro ◐√6:4n. Col 2:11n, 12n). Ac +2:38. Ps 51:2. Ro *4:11. 1 C 6:11. He +√10:22. 1 P 3:21. 1 J √1:7. Re *1:5. **calling.** Ac *2:21. +√7:59n. +9:14. Lk 3:21. Ro *10:12-14. 1 C 1:2. 2 T 2:22.

17. **when.** Ac 9:26-28. 26:20. Ga 1:18, 19. **while.** Ac 3:1. 10:9, 10. Da *9:21-23. Lk 18:10. **trance.** Ac *10:9, 10, 30, 31. 2 C 12:1-4. Re 1:10.

18. **saw.** ver. 14. **Make.** Ac 9:29. Mt 10:14, 23. Lk 21:21. **quickly out.** The History in Acts ch. 9 might lead us to suppose that Paul's stay in Jerusalem had been longer, but this vagueness is brought by the explanation here into harmony with Ga 1:18, where we are told the time was fifteen days. Such round-about consistency is by undesigned coincidence (see related notes listed at Ac 12:12). **for.** Ex 3:19. Ezk 3:6, 7. **not receive.** ƒ175B, Ge +21:16. Mt 10:14.

19. **Lord.** Ac +11:16. **know.** ver. 4. Ac 8:3. 9:1. 26:9-12. **beat.** Ac 9:2. 26:11. Mt +10:17. **that believed.** Ac +*10:43.

20. **martyr**. Re +2:13. 17:6. **Stephen**. Ac *7:57, 58. *8:1. **consenting**. Ac 8:1. 26:10. Lk 11:48. Ro 1:32.

21. **Depart**. Ac *9:15. **for**. Ac 9:15. *13:2, 46, 47. *18:6. *26:17, 18. Ro 1:5. 11:13. *15:16. 16:26. Ga 1:15, 16. *2:7, 8. Ep *3:6-8. 1 T 2:7. 2 T 1:11. **far hence**. Ac +*2:39. **Gentiles**. Ac +9:15.

22. **they gave**. Ac +13:45. **lifted**. ſ144A12, Ge +22:13. Lk +11:27. **Away**. Ac 7:54-57. +21:36. 25:24. Lk 23:18. Jn 19:15. 1 Th *2:14-16. **for**. Ac 25:24.

23. **cast off**. Ac 7:58. 26:11. Ec 10:3. **threw dust**. 2 S 16:13.

24. **The chief**. As the chief captain did not understand Hebrew, he was ignorant of the charge against Paul, and also of the defense which the apostle had made; but as he saw that they grew more and more outrageous, he supposed that Paul must have given them the highest provocation, and therefore, according to the barbarous and irrational practice which has existed in all countries, he determined to put him to the torture, in order to make him confess his crime. Ac +21:31, 32. 23:10, 27. **the castle**. Ac 21:34, 37. 23:10, 16, 32. **that he should**. ver. 25-29. Ac 16:22, 23, 37. Jn 19:1. He 11:35. **know**. Gr. *epiginosko*, Mt +11:27.

25. **the centurion**. Ac +10:1. 23:17. 27:1, 3, 43. Mt 8:8. 27:54. **Is it lawful**. By the Roman law, no magistrate was allowed to punish a Roman citizen capitally, or by inflicting stripes, or even binding him; and the single expression, *I am a Roman citizen*, arrested their severest decrees, and obtained, if not an escape, at least a delay of his punishment (See Cicero, Orat. pro Verrem, Ac. ii. l. v. 64). ver. 27, 28. Ac *16:37n. 25:16. **Roman**. i.e. *strength*, ✻S#4514g. ver. 26, 27, 29. Ac 2:10. 16:21, 37, 38. 23:27. 25:16. 28:17. Jn 11:48. **uncondemned**. Ac +16:37.

26. **Take**. ver. 29. Ac 23:27.

28. **But**. It is extremely probable that the inhabitants of Tarsus, born in that city, had the same rights and privileges as Roman citizens, in consequence of a grant or charter from Julius Caesar, from whom it was called *Juliopolis* (Dion Cassius, l. xlvii. p. 508, ed. Reimar). But if this were not the case, St. Paul's father, or some of his ancestors, might have been rewarded with the freedom of the city of Rome, for his fidelity and bravery in some military service, as Josephus (Ant. l. xxv. c. 10) says several of the Jews were; or his father might have obtained it by purchase, as in the instance of the chief captain.

29. **examined him**. *or*, tortured him. ver. 24. He 11:35. **the chief**. ver. 25, 26. Ac 16:38, 39. +21:31. **was afraid**. Ac 16:38. **knew**. Gr. *epiginosko*, Mt +11:27. **he was a Roman**. Ac 23:27. **had bound**. Ac 21:33.

30. **because**. ver. 24. Ac 21:11, 33. 23:28. 26:29. Mt 27:2. **loosed him**. Ac 21:33. **commanded**. ver. 5. Ac 5:21. 23:15. Mt 10:17. **chief priests**. Ac +4:1. **their council**. Ac +4:15. **brought Paul down**. Ac +21:35.

ACTS 23

Paul, pleading his conscientiousness before God, is smitten at the command of the high priest, whom he reproves for his injustice, 1-3. Being censured for it, he excuses the sharpness of his language, 4, 5. Declaring himself a Pharisee, in respect of the resurrection, a division in the council is excited, 6-9. The chief cap-

tain, fearing lest he should be torn in pieces, conveys him back to the castle, 10. The Lord favors Paul by a most encouraging vision, 11. Forty Jews conspire to murder him; binding themselves by oath, not to eat or drink till they have done it, 12, 13. They avow their purpose to the chief priests, and secure their concurrence, 14, 15. The conspiracy is discovered to Paul, and from him to the chief captain, 16-22; who sends Paul, under a strong guard, and with a letter, to Felix the governor at Caesarea, 23-35.

1. **earnestly**. ver. 6. Ac +3:4g. 6:15. 22:5. Pr 28:1. **the council**. ver. 6, 15, 20, 28. Ac +4:15. **Men**. Ac 22:1. **lived**. Ph 1:27. 3:20. **good conscience**. T#129. Ac *24:16. Jb 27:5, 6. Ro 13:5. 1 C 4:4. 2 C +1:12. 4:2. 5:11. 1 T 1:5, 19. 3:9. 2 T 1:3. He 10:22. *13:18. 1 P 2:19. *3:15, 16, 21. **before God**. Ro 14:8. Ga 2:19g.

2. **Ananias**. Ac 24:1. **to smite**. 1 K 22:24. Jb 16:10. Is 50:6. Je *20:2. La 3:30. Mi +*5:1. Mt 5:39. 26:67. Mk 14:65. Jn *18:22. 19:3. 2 C 11:20.

3. **then said**. Ps *106:33. **God**. God did smite in a remarkable manner; for about five years after this, after his house had been reduced to ashes, in a tumult raised by his own son, he was besieged and taken in the royal palace; where having attempted in vain to hide himself, he was dragged out and slain. **thou whited**. Mt *23:27, 28. **wall**. Is 30:13. Ezk 13:10-14. **for**. Le *19:35. Ps 58:1, 2. 82:1, 2. 94:20. Ec 3:16. Am 5:7. Mi 3:8-11. **smitten**. Le 19:15. Dt *25:1, 2. Jn 7:51. 18:23, 24.

4. **And they**. Jn 18:22. **God's**. 1 S 2:28. Ps 106:16.

5. **I wist**. Soon after the holding of the first council at Jerusalem, Ananias, son of Nebedenus, was deprived of the high priest's office, for certain acts of violence, and sent to Rome, whence he was afterwards released, and returned to Jerusalem. Between the death of Jonathan, who succeeded him and was murdered by Felix, and the high priesthood of Ismael, who was invested with that office by Agrippa, an interval elapsed in which this dignity was vacant. This was the precise time when St. Paul was apprehended; and the Sanhedrin being destitute of a president, Ananias undertook to discharge the office. It is probable that Paul was ignorant of this circumstance. Ac 24:16, 17. **Thou**. Ex ⟩22:28. 2 S 19:21. Ec *10:20. Ro *13:1-4. T 3:1, 2. 2 P *2:10, 13-17. Ju 8, 9.

6. **Paul**. Mt 10:16. **Sadducees**. Mt +22:23. **Pharisees**. ver. 7-9. Ac +5:34. **the council**. ver. +1. **I am**. Ac *26:5. Ph 3:5. **of the hope**. Ac 2:26, 27. *24:15, 21. *26:6-8. *28:20. Col 1:5. **and**. ſ93A, Ge +1:26. By *Hendiadys*, "resurrection hope." Two words used, but one thing meant. **resurrection**. Ac 24:21. Jn +5:29. **of**. ſ181E, Ge +3:24.

7. **there**. Ac 14:4. Ps 55:9. Mt 10:34. Jn 7:40-43.

8. **Sadducees**. Ac 4:1. Mt *22:23, 24. Mk 12:18. Lk 20:27. 1 C 15:12. **spirit**. Gr. *pneuma*, ſ121A3, Mt +27:50. A "spirit" was the common term for one passed into the unseen state. The Pharisees confessed their belief in "spirits," carefully distinguished from "angels," and in opposition to Sadducean infidelity (F. W. Grant, *Facts and Theories*, p. 75). "Spirit" is taken as ordinarily applying to the spirits of men apart from the body. Ac 7:59. Ec +*12:7. Lk 23:46. He 12:23. 1 P 3:19. **confess both**. The language of the inspired writer here shows his own consent with this doctrine: "the Pharisees *confess* (or acknowledge) both." When I speak of "acknowledging" a thing, I plainly suppose

it true, what is acknowledged. And thus in these matters the Pharisaic and the Christian faith are one (F. W. Grant, p. 114, 115). Paul affirms "I am a Pharisee." Thus Scripture teaches the doctrine of conscious existence after death. Lk +*24:37.

9. **the scribes.** Ac +4:5. Mk 2:16. Lk 5:30. **arose.** Ac 27:21. **We.** ver. 29. Ac 25:25. 26:31. 1 S 24:17. Pr +*16:7. Lk 23:4, 14, 15, 22. **but if.** ſ184A, 1 C +15:2. ſ37D, Ho +9:14. ver. 8. Ac 9:4. 22:7, 17, 18. 26:14-19. 27:23. Jn 12:29. **hath spoken.** A reference to his narrative of the day before. Ac 22:6, 18. **let.** Ac 5:39. 11:17. 1 C 10:22. **not fight.** Ac *5:39. Je 26:19.

10. **chief captain.** Ac +21:31. **fearing.** ver. 27. Ac 19:28-31. 21:30-36. Ps 7:2. 50:22. Mi 3:3. Ja 1:19, 20. 3:14-18. 4:1, 2. **go down.** Ac +21:31. **to take.** Ac 22:24. **from among.** ſ108H3, Mt +13:49. **bring.** ver. 15, 28. Ac +21:35. **the castle.** ver. 16, 32. Ac 21:34, 37. 22:24.

11. **the night.** Ac 18:9. 27:23. **the Lord.** Ac 2:25. +11:16. *18:9. *27:23, 24. 1 S 3:10. Ps 46:1, 2. 109:31. Is 41:10, 14. 43:2. Je *1:19. 15:19-21. Mt *28:20. Jn 14:18. 2 C 1:8-10. **Be.** Ac 27:22, 25. Mt 9:2. 14:27. Jn +16:33. 2 T 4:17. **for.** Ac 19:21. 20:22. 22:18. 28:23-28. Ro 1:15, 16. Ph 1:13. 2 T 4:17. **testified.** Lk +16:28. **must.** Ac +9:6. 28:30, 31. Is 46:10. Jn 11:8-10. **bear witness.** Ac 22:15. 26:16. **at Rome.** Ac *28:30, 31.

12. **certain.** ver. 21, 30. Ac *25:3. Ps 2:1-3. 64:2-6. Is 8:9, 10. Je 11:19. Mt 26:4. **the Jews.** Ac 9:23. 1 Th 2:16. **bound.** T#719. ver. 14, 21. Nu +*30:2n. Jg *11:30, 31. 1 K 19:2. 2 K 6:31. Mt 14:6-9. 27:25. Mk 6:23-26. **under a curse.** *or*, with an oath of execration. ſ147D, Ge +1:29. Le 27:29. Nu +*30:2n. Jsh 6:26. 7:1, 15. Jg +*11:30. Ne 10:29. Mt 26:74g. Mk 14:71. 1 C 16:22. Ga 3:13. **that.** Such execrable vows as these were not unusual among the Jews, who, from their perverted traditions, challenged to themselves a right of punishing without any legal process, those whom they considered transgressors of the law; and in some cases, as in the case of one who had forsaken the law of Moses, they thought they were justified in killing them. They therefore made no scruple of acquainting the chief priests and elders with their conspiracy against the life of Paul, and applying for their connivance and support; who, being chiefly of the sect of the Sadducees, and the apostle's bitterest enemies, were so far from blaming them for it, that they gladly aided and abetted them in this mode of dispatching him, and on its failure they soon afterwards determined upon making a similar attempt (Ac 25:2, 3). If these were, in their bad way, *conscientious* men, they were under no necessity of perishing for hunger, when the providence of God had hindered them from accomplishing their vow; for their vows of abstinence from eating and drinking were as easy to loose as to bind, any of their wise men or Rabbies having power to absolve them, as Dr. Lightfoot has shown from the Talmud (Hieros, Avodah Zarah, fol. 40). 1 S 14:24, 27, 28, 40-44. Ps 31:13.

13. **which.** 2 S 15:12, 31. Jn 16:2.

14. **they came.** Ps 52:1, 2. Is 3:9. Je 6:15. 8:12. Ho 4:9. Mi 7:3. **chief priests.** Ac +4:1. **and elders.** Ac +4:5. **We have.** ver. +12. **bound.** Ro 9:3g. **great curse.** ſ147D, Ge +1:29.

15. **the council.** ver. +1. **signify.** ver. 22. Ac 24:1. 25:2, 15g. **chief captain.** Ac +21:31. **that he.** Ac 25:3. Ps 21:11. 37:32, 33. Pr 1:11, 12, 16. 4:16. Is 59:7. Ro 3:14-16. **more perfectly.** ver. 20. Ac 18:25, 26. +22:3. 24:22.

16. **when.** Jb 5:13. Ps *37:32, 33. Pr +*21:30. Is *8:10. La 3:37. 1 C 3:19. **Paul's sister's.** Ro ?16:7. **he went.** 2 S 17:17. **the castle.** ver. +10.

17. **Paul called.** Ac 27:24, 31. **one.** ver. 23. Ac +10:1. 22:26. Pr +*22:3. Mt 8:8, 9. 10:16.

18. **Paul.** Ac 16:25. 27:1. 28:17. Ge 40:14, 15. Ep +3:1. 4:1. Phm 9. **something.** Lk 7:40.

19. **took.** Je 31:32. Mk 8:23. 9:27. **What.** Ne 2:4. Est 5:3. 7:2. 9:12. Mk 10:51.

20. **The Jews.** ver. 12. **as.** ver. 15. Ps 12:2. Da 6:5-12. **more perfectly.** ver. +15.

21. **do not.** Ex 23:2. **for.** ver. 12-14. Ac 9:23, 24. 14:5, 6. 20:19. 25:3. Lk 11:54. 2 C 11:26, 32, 33. **an oath.** ver. 14. Ro 9:3.

22. **See thou.** ſ63BA, Ge +26:7. Jsh 2:14. Mk 1:44.

23. **two centurions.** ver. 17. Ac +10:1. **to go.** lit. that they may go. ſ15F, Jn +13:39. **Caesarea.** ver. 33. Ac +8:40. **at.** About nine o'clock in the evening, for the greater secrecy, and to elude the cunning, active malice of the Jews. Mt 14:25. Lk 12:38. See Jn 19:14. For hours of the day, see Jn +*11:9n. For watches of the night, see Mt +*14:25n.

24. **beasts.** Ne 2:12. Est 8:10. Lk 10:34. **bring.** ſ63H, Ge +12:15. **Felix.** i.e. *happy, prosperous*, *S#5344g. ver. 26g, 33-35. Ac 24:3, 22, 24, 25, 27. 25:14. **the governor.** ver. 33. Ac 24:1, 10. 26:30. Mt 27:2. Lk 3:1. +20:20.

26. **Lysias.** i.e. *releaser; dissolving, dispersing*, *S#3079g. Ac 24:7, 22. **the most.** Ac 24:3. 26:25g. Lk 1:3. **governor.** ver. +24. **greeting.** Ac +15:23. Ja 1:1. 3 J 14.

27. **was taken.** ver. 10. Ac *21:27, 31-33. 24:7. **having.** Ac 22:25-29.

28. **And when.** Ac *22:30. **I brought.** ver. +10. **council.** ver. +1.

29. **question.** ver. 6-9. Ac 18:15. 24:5, 6, 10-21. *25:19, 20. **but.** ver. 9. Ac 25:7, 8, 11, 25. *26:31. 28:18.

30. **it was.** ver. 16-24. **laid wait.** ver. 12. Ac +9:24. **and gave.** ver. 35. Ac 24:7, 8, 19. 25:5, 6, 16. **Farewell.** Ac 15:29. 2 C 13:11.

31. **as.** ver. 23, 24. Lk 7:8. 2 T 2:3, 4. **Antipatris.** i.e. *against one's country*, *S#494g.

32. **horsemen.** ver. 23. **the castle.** ver. +10.

33. **Caesarea.** ver. 23. Ac +8:40. **delivered.** ver. 25-30. **presented.** Ac 28:16.

34. **he asked.** Ac 25:1. Est 1:1. 8:9. Da 2:49. 6:1. Lk 23:6, 7. **Cilicia.** Ac +6:9. 15:41. *21:39.

35. **when.** ver. 30. Ac 24:1, 10, 22, 24-27. 25:16. **in.** Ac 12:19. Mt 2:1, 3, 16. **judgment.** Mt +27:27. Jn 18:28.

ACTS 24

The high priest and elders go to Caesarea; and, by Tertullus, accuse Paul before Felix, 1-9. Paul makes his defense, refutes the charges brought against him, and gives an account of his own conduct, 10-21. Felix defers the matter, and shows favor to Paul, 22, 23. Paul reasons before Felix, and Drusilla his wife, concerning "righteousness, temperance, and judgment to come," till "Felix trembles," and postpones the subject to a convenient opportunity, 24, 25. He hopes in vain for a bribe to release Paul; and at length, being superseded in his government, he leaves him in prison, to please the Jews, 26, 27.

1. **five**. ver. 11. Ac 21:18, 27. **Ananias**. Ac *23:2, 30, 35. 25:2. **descended**. Ac +18:22. 25:6, 7. **the elders**. Ac +4:5. **orator**. Ac 12:21. Is 3:3. 1 C 2:1, 4. **Tertullus**. i.e. *triple hardened; an impostor; a liar*, *S#5061g. ver. 2. **informed**. Ac 25:2, 15. Ps 11:2. **governor**. Ac +23:24.

2. **Seeing**. Felix, bad as he was, had certainly rendered some services to Judea. He had entirely subdued a very formidable banditti which had infested the country, and sent their captain, Eliezar, to Rome (Josephus, Ant. l. xx. c. 6. Bel. l. ii. c. 22); had suppressed the sedition raised by the Egyptian impostor (Ac 21:38); and had quelled a very afflictive disturbance which took place between the Syrians and Jews of Caesarea. But, though Tertullus might truly say, "by thee we enjoy great quietness," yet it is evident that he was guilty of the grossest flattery, as we have seen both from his own historians and Josephus, that he was both a bad man, and a bad governor. ver. 26, 27. Ps 10:3. 12:2, 13. Pr 26:28. 29:5. Ju 16. **nation**. ver. 10, 17. Ac +10:22.

3. **accept**. Lk +8:40. **most**. Ac 23:26g. 26:25. Lk 1:3g. **Felix**. Ac +23:24.

4. **that**. He 11:32. **clemency**. Ph 4:5g.

5. **we have**. Ac *6:13. *16:20, 21. *17:6, 7. 21:28. 22:22. 28:22. 1 K 18:17, 18. Je 38:4. Am 7:10. Mt 5:11, 12. 10:25. Lk *23:2. 1 C 4:13. **pestilent**. 1 S 2:12. 10:27. **and a mover**. 1 S 22:7-9. Ezr 4:12-19. Ne 6:5-8. Est 3:8. Lk 23:2, 5, 19, 25. 1 P 2:12-15, 19. **world**. Gr. *oikoumene*, Mt +24:14. **the sect**. ver. 14g. Ac 5:17. 15:5. 26:5. 28:22. 1 C 11:19g. Ga 5:20g. 2 P 2:1g. **Nazarenes**. Ac 2:22. Mt 2:23.

6. **gone**. ver. 12. Ac 19:37. *21:27-29. **whom**. Ac 21:30-32. 22:23. 23:10-15. **and**. Jn 18:31. 19:7, 8.

7. **the chief**. Ac *21:31-33. 23:23-32. Pr 4:16. **great**. Ac 5:26. 21:35. 23:10.

8. **Commanding**. Ac *23:30, 35. 25:5, 15, 16. **by**. ver. 19-21. Ac +12:19. **take knowledge**. Gr. *epiginosko*, Mt +11:27.

9. **assented**. Ac 6:11-13. Ps 4:2. 62:3, 4. 64:2-8. Is 59:4-7. Je 9:3-6. Ezk 22:27-29. Mi 6:12, 13. 7:2, 3. Mt 26:59, 60. Jn √8:44.

10. **governor**. Ac +23:24. **had**. Ac 12:17. 13:16. 19:33. 21:40. 26:1. **many**. "Felix, made procurator over Judea, A.D. 53." **a judge**. Note that the term "judge" is used in a broader sense in Scripture than in our common parlance; it is often equivalent to ruler or king (see Peters, *Theocratic Kingdom*, vol. 2, pp. 352-361). This has an important bearing upon our conception of Christ returning to judge the earth at the Second Advent. The judgeship of Christ is not limited to passing sentence, but constitutes his reign as king over the earth. Ac 18:15. Ex 18:14-16. 1 S 2:25. 8:5, 6, 20. 2 S 15:4. Is +*16:5. Da 9:21. Lk 12:14. 18:2. Re +*20:4. **this nation**. ver. 2, 17. Ac +10:22. **I do**. 1 P *3:13-17. **answer**. Ac +19:33. 1 P +*3:15.

11. **but twelve**. ver. 1. Ac 21:18, 27. 22:30. 23:11, 23, 32, 33. **went up**. Ac 8:27. +18:22. Jn +2:13. **to worship**. ver. 17. Ac 20:16. *21:26.

12. **neither found**. ver. 5. Ac *25:8. 28:17. 1 P 4:14. **disputing**. Ac +17:17g. **neither raising**. ver. 18.

13. **Neither can**. Ac 25:7. 1 P 3:16.

14. **I confess**. Ps 119:46. Mt 10:32. **after**. ver. 22. Ac +9:2. 19:9, 23. Am 8:14. 2 P 2:2. **heresy**. See on ver. 5. 1 C 11:19. Ga 5:20. T 3:10. 2 P 2:1. **so worship**. Ac 27:23. Mi 4:2. Lk 1:74. Ro 1:9. He 9:14. 12:28.

the God. Ac +3:13. 5:30. 7:32. 22:14. Ex 3:15. 1 Ch 29:18. 2 T 1:3. **my fathers**. Ac +22:3. **believing all**. Ac 3:22-24. 10:43. *26:22, 27. 28:23. Lk 1:70. See on Lk 24:27, 44. Jn +*2:22. +*5:39-47. +6:45. 1 P 1:11. Re 19:10. **which**. Ac +22:12. 26:22. 28:23. Ro 3:21. **in the law**. Ac 13:15. Mt 7:12. 22:40. Lk 16:16, 29. Jn 1:45. Ro 3:21.

15. **have**. ver. 21. Ac 23:6. *26:6, 7. 28:20, etc. **hope**. Ga 5:5. T 2:13. **resurrection**. T#617. Ac 4:1, 2. 23:6-8. Jb +*19:25, 26. Is +*26:19n. Da +*12:2. Ho 13:14. Mt 22:31, 32. Lk *20:37, 38. Jn *5:28, 29. *6:40. *11:23, 24. Ro 6:8, 9. 8:23. 1 C 6:14. 15:12-27. 2 C 4:14. Ph 3:21. 1 Th √4:14-16. Re √20:6, 12, 13. **of**. √181E, Ge +3:24. **both of**. Da +*12:2. Lk 14:14. Jn +*5:29. **the just**. Lk +*14:14. 1 Th 4:16n. **and unjust**. Is 24:22. Da +*12:2. Mt +*25:46. Jn √5:29. Ro 2:7, 8. 11:22. Ga 6:8. Re 14:9-11. √20:6, 12, 13. 21:8. 22:15.

16. **herein do**. Ac *23:1. Ro 2:15. 9:1. 1 C *4:4. 2 C *1:12. *4:2. 1 Th *2:10. 1 T *1:5, 19. *3:9. 2 T *1:3. T *1:15. *2:11-13. He *9:14. *10:22. *13:18. 1 P *2:19. *3:16, 21. **exercise**. 1 T 4:7, 15. **conscience**. Ac +23:1. **void of offense**. Ac 20:26, 27, 33, 34. 23:5. Nu 16:15. 1 S 12:3. 1 C *10:32. Ph 1:10. Ju *24. **toward God**. Lk 2:52.

17. **after**. Ac +20:31. **I came**. Ac +11:29, 30. Ro 15:25-28, 31. 1 C 16:1-3. 2 C *8:1-4. 9:1, 2, 12. Ga *2:10. **to bring**. Ac *11:29, 30. 20:16. Ro +*15:25, 26. 1 C 16:1, 2. 2 C √8:9. Ga 2:10. He 13:16. **alms**. Ac +9:36g. **my nation**. ver. 2, 10. Ac +10:22. 26:4. 28:19. **offerings**. ver. 11. Ac 20:16. 21:26.

18. **certain Jews**. Ac 21:26-30. 26:21. **from Asia**. Ac +2:9. **purified**. Ac +21:26. **neither with**. ver. 12.

19. **Who ought**. √184B, Mt +23:30. √184E, Lk +17:6. Ac +23:30. 25:16. **if they**. √184D1, Lk +22:67.

20. **the council**. Ac +4:15.

21. **Touching**. ver. +15. Ac 4:2. *23:6. 26:6-8. 28:20. **of**. √181E, Ge +3:24.

22. **Felix**. Ac +23:24. **having**. ver. 10, 24. Ac +23:15. 26:3. **that way**. ver. 14. Ac +9:2. 18:26. 19:9, 23. **When**. ver. 7. Ac 18:20. 25:26. Dt 19:18. **chief captain**. Ac +21:31.

23. **centurion**. Ac +10:1. **to keep**. Ac 28:16. **and to**. ver. 26. Ac *27:3. *28:16, 31. Pr +*16:7. **forbid none**. Ac *27:3. **his**. Ac 4:23g. 21:8-14.

24. **Drusilla**. i.e. *watered by the dew*, *S#1409g. **he sent**. Ac 26:22. Mk 6:20. Lk 19:3. 23:8. **the faith**. Ac 6:7. √16:31. +20:21. Jn √3:16. Ro 3:24. Ga √2:16, 20. 3:2. 1 J 5:1. Ju +*3. Re 14:12. **in Christ**. Ro 3:24. 6:3, 11, 23.

25. **he reasoned**. Ac +*17:2, 17. 1 S 12:7. Is √1:18. 41:21. Ro *12:1. 1 P +*3:15. **righteousness**. ver. 15, 16. Ac *10:35. 13:10. 2 S 23:3. Jb 29:14. Ps *11:7. +*45:7. 58:1, 2. 72:2. 82:1-4. Pr 16:12. Ec 3:16. Is 1:21. 16:5. 61:8. Je 22:3, 15-17. Ezk 45:9. Da 4:27. Ho 10:4, 12. Am 5:24. 6:12. Mt 7:2. Jn +*16:8. Col 3:25. 4:1. 1 T 6:11. T √2:11, 12. 1 J *3:7, 10. **temperance**. Pr 31:3-5. Ec 10:16, 17. Is 27:6, 7. Da 5:1-4, 30. Ho 7:5. Mk 6:18-24. 1 C *9:25, 27. Ga 5:23. T 1:8. *2:11, 12. 1 P 4:4. 2 P 1:6. **judgment**. Ac +*10:42. √17:31. Ps 50:3, 4. Ec 3:17. 5:8. 11:9. 12:14. Da +*12:2. Mt √25:31-46. Ro 2:16. 14:12. 1 C 4:5. 2 C *5:10. 2 Th √1:7-10. 2 T 4:1. He 6:2. +√9:27. 1 P 4:5. Re √20:11-15. **to come**. Mt *3:7. 1 C 7:29-31. **Felix trembled**. Ac *2:37. 9:6. 16:29. 1 K 21:27. 2 K 22:19. Ezr 10:3, 9. Ps 99:1. 119:120. Is 32:11. 66:2. Je √23:29. Hab

+*3:16. Ro *3:19, 20. 1 C 14:24, 25. Ga 3:22. He *4:1, 12. 12:21. Ja √2:19. **Go.** Ac *16:30-34. 26:28. 1 S 18:14. 1 K 22:26, 27. Pr *1:24-32. Je 37:17-21. 38:14-28. Mt 14:5-10. 22:5. 25:1-10. Mk 6:20. Lk 8:37. **when.** Ac *17:32. Pr 6:4, 5. Is √55:6. Hg 1:2. Lk √13:24, 25. 17:26-29. 2 C √6:2. 2 T *4:2. He √2:3. 3:7, 8, 13. 4:11. Ja √4:13, 14.

26. **hoped.** ver. 2, 3. Ex *23:8. Dt 16:19. 1 S 8:3. 12:3. 2 Ch 19:7. Jb 15:34. Ps 26:9, 10. Pr 17:8, 23. 19:6. 29:4. Is 1:23. 33:15. 56:11. Ezk 22:27. +*33:31. Ho 4:18. 12:7, 8. Am 2:6, 7. Mi 3:11. 7:3. 1 C +*6:9. Ep *5:5, 6. 1 T √6:9, 10. 2 P 2:3, 14, 15. **that money.** ver. 17, 27. **wherefore.** ver. 24. **communed.** Ac 20:11g.

27. **two.** Ac 28:30. **Porcius.** i.e. *lover of pork*, *S#4201g. **Festus.** i.e. *joyful; a festival*, *S#5347g. Porcius Festus was put into the government of Judea in the sixth or seventh year of Nero. He died about two years afterwards, and was succeeded by Albinus. Ac 25:1, 4, 9, 12-14, 22-24. 26:24, 25, 32. **Felix.** Ac +23:24. **willing.** Ac *12:3. 25:9, 14. Ex +*23:2. Pr 29:25. Mk *15:15. Lk 23:24, 25. Ga 1:10. **left Paul.** Ac 25:14. Lk +21:12.

ACTS 25

The Jews accuse Paul to Festus, first at Jerusalem, and then at Caesarea, 1-7. He answers for himself, and appeals to Caesar, 8-11. His appeal is admitted, 12. Festus being visited by king Agrippa, opens the matter to him, who desires to hear Paul, 13-22. Paul is brought forth before a most splendid assembly; and Festus states his case to them, 23-27.

1. **Festus.** Ac +24:27. **was come.** Ac 20:18. 21:4g. **into.** Ac 23:34. **the province.** By the *province*, Judea is meant; for after the death of Herod Agrippa, Claudius thought it imprudent to trust the government in the hands of his son Agrippa, who was then but seventeen years of age: and therefore, Cuspius Fadus was sent to be procurator. And when afterwards Claudius had given to Agrippa the tetrarchy of Philip, he nevertheless kept the province of Judea in his own hands, and governed it by procurators sent from Rome. **he.** ver. 5, 6. Ac 18:22. 21:15. **Caesarea.** ver. 4, 6, 13. Ac +8:40.

2. **high priest.** Ac +4:1. **chief.** Mk +6:21g. **informed him.** ver. 15. Ac 24:1. Jb 31:31. Pr 4:16. Ro 3:12-19.

3. **desired.** Ac 9:2. 1 S 23:19-21. Je 38:4. Mk 6:23-25. Lk 23:8-24. **laying.** Ac +9:24. *23:12-15. 26:9-11. Ps *37:32, 33. 64:2-6. 140:1-5. Is +*8:10. Je 18:18. Jn 16:3. Ro 3:8.

4. **Festus.** Ac +24:27. **Caesarea.** ver. 1, 6, 13. Ac +8:40.

5. **them.** ver. 16. Ac 23:30. 24:8. **are able.** 1 C 1:26g. **if.** √184A, 1 C +15:2. ver. 18, 19, 25. Ac 18:14. 1 S 24:11, 12. Ps 7:3-5. Jn 18:29, 30. **wickedness.** Lk 23:41.

6. **more than ten days.** *or*, as some copies read, no more than eight or ten days. **went down.** ver. 7. Ac 24:1. Ac +18:22. **Caesarea.** ver. 1. Ac +8:40. **sitting.** ver. 10, 17. Ac 18:12-17. Mt +27:19. Jn 19:13. 2 C 5:10. Ja 2:6.

7. **was come.** ver. 6. **and laid.** ver. 24. Ac 21:28. *24:5, 6, 13. Ezr 4:15. Est 3:8. Ps 27:12. 35:11. Mt +*5:11, 12. 26:60-62. Mk 15:3, 4. Lk 23:2, 10. 1 P 4:14-16. **which.** Ac 24:13.

8. **answered.** ver. 16. Ac +19:33. **Neither.** ver. 10.

Ac 6:+13, 14. 23:1. 24:6, 12, 17-21. 28:17, 21. Ge 40:15. Je 37:18. Da 6:22. 2 C 1:12. **the law.** Jn 19:12. **Caesar.** ver. 10, 11, 12, 21. Ac +17:7. **offended anything.** Ro 13:1-5.

9. **Festus.** Ac +24:27. **willing.** ver. 3, 20. Ac 12:3. *24:27. Mk 15:15. **go up.** ver. +6.

10. **I stand.** Every procurator represented the emperor in the province over which he presided; and as the seat of government was at Caesarea, St. Paul was before the tribunal where, as a Roman citizen, he ought to be judged. Ac 16:37n, 38. 22:25-28. **Caesar's.** ver. 8, 11, 12, 21. Ac +17:7. **judgment seat.** ver. 6, 17. Mt +27:19. **as thou.** ver. 25. Ac 23:29. 26:31. 28:18. Mt 27:18, 23, 24. 2 C 4:2. 2 T 1:18. **knowest.** Gr. *epiginosko*, Mt +11:27.

11. **if I.** √184A, 1 C +15:2. Ac 18:14. Jsh 22:22. 1 S 12:3-5. Jb 31:21, 22, 38-40. Ps 7:3-5. **but if.** √184A, 1 C +15:2. **none of.** Ac 21:24. **no man.** Ac 16:37n. 22:25. 1 Th 2:15. **deliver.** ver. 16. Ac 3:14. 27:24. Lk 7:21. Ro √8:32. 1 C 2:12. Ga 3:18. Ph 1:29. 2:9. Phm 22g. **I appeal.** An appeal to the emperor was the right of a Roman citizen, and was highly respected. The Julian law condemned those magistrates, and others, as violators of the public peace, who had put to death, tortured, scourged, imprisoned, or condemned any Roman citizen who had appealed to Caesar. This law was so sacred and imperative, that, in the persecution under Trajan, Pliny would not attempt to put to death Roman citizens, who were proved to have turned Christians, but determined to send them to Rome, probably because they had appealed (Ep. l. x. ep. 97). ver. 10, 21, 25. Ac *26:30-32. *28:17-19. 1 S 27:1.

12. **unto Ceasar shalt.** ver. 21. Ac 19:21. 23:11. 26:32. 27:1. 28:16. Ps 76:10. Is 46:10, 11. La 3:37. Da 4:35. Ro 15:28, 29. Ph 1:12-14, 20.

13. **king.** ver. 22, 23. Ac 26:1, 27, 28. **Agrippa.** i.e. *wild horse tamer; one who causes great pain at his birth*, *S#67g. ver. 22, 23, 24, 26. Ac 26:1, 2, 7, 19, 27, 28, 32. **Bernice.** i.e. *one that brings victory; victorious*, *S#959g. ver. 23. Ac 26:30. **to salute.** √108B, 2 K +4:29. 1 S 13:10. 25:14. 2 S 8:10. 2 K 10:13. Mk 15:18.

14. **declared.** Ga 2:2. **There.** Ac *24:27.

15. **when.** ver. 1-3. Est 3:9. Lk 18:3-5. 23:23. **elders.** Ac +4:5.

16. **It is not.** ver. 4, 5. **deliver.** ver. +11. **and have.** ver. 8. Ac +23:30. 26:1. Dt 17:4. 19:17, 18. Pr 18:13, 17. Jn 7:51.

17. **without.** ver. 6, 7, 24. **judgment seat.** ver. 6, 10. Mt +27:19.

18. **stood up.** Ac +27:21. **accusation.** ver. 27. Mt 27:37g.

19. **certain.** ver. 7. Ac 18:15, 19. 23:29. **superstition.** Ac 17:22, 23. **which.** Ac 1:22. 2:32. 17:31. 26:22, 23. 1 C 1:23. +*15:3, 4, 14-20. Re 1:18. **affirmed.** Ac 17:18. Ge=45:26, 28.

20. **doubted of such manner of questions.** *or*, was doubtful how to inquire hereof, etc. ver. 9. Ac 2:25. Ga +4:20. **I asked.** See on ver. 9. **whether.** √184D1, Lk +22:67.

21. **had.** ver. 10, +*11. Ac 26:32. 2 T 4:16. **hearing.** *or*, judgment. **Augustus.** ver. 25. Ac 27:1. Lk 2:1. **I commanded.** ver. 12. **Caesar.** ver. 8, 10, 11, 12. Ac +17:7.

22. **Agrippa.** Ac +9:15. Is 52:15. Mt 10:18. Lk 21:12.

23. **Agrippa.** ver. 13. Ac 26:30. **with.** Ac 12:21. Est

1:4. Ec 1:2. Is 5:14. 14:11. Ezk 7:24. 30:18. 32:12. 33:28. Da 4:30. 1 C 7:31. Ja 1:11. 1 P 1:24. 1 J *2:16, 17. **chief captains.** Mk +6:21g. **at.** Ac 9:15.

24. **King Agrippa.** *King Agrippa* was the son of Herod Agrippa; who upon the death of his uncle Herod king of Chalcis, A.D. 48, succeeded to his dominions by the favor of the emperor Claudius. Four years afterwards, Claudius removed him from that kingdom to a larger one; giving him the tetrarchy of Philip, that of Lysanias, and the province which Varus governed. Nero afterwards added Julius in Perea, Tarichea, and Tiberias. Claudius gave him the power of appointing the high priest among the Jews; and instances of his exercising this power may be seen in Josephus (Ant. l. xx. c. 7. sec. 8, 11). He was strongly attached to the Romans, and did everything in his power to prevent the Jews from rebelling; and when he could not prevail, he united his troops to those of Titus, and assisted at the siege of Jerusalem. After the ruin of his country, he retired with his sister Berenice to Rome, where he died, aged 70, about A.D. 90. **about.** ver. 2, 3, 7. **have dealt.** Ro 11:2g. **that he.** Ac *22:22. Lk 23:21-23. 1 C *4:9.

25. **committed.** Ac *23:9, 29. *26:31. Lk 23:4, 14, 15. Jn 18:38. **and that.** ver. 11, 12. **Augustus.** The honorable title of *Sebastos,* or Augustus, that is, *venerable* or *august,* which was first conferred by the senate on Octavius Caesar, was afterwards assumed by succeeding Roman emperors. ver. 21.

26. **lord.** ✗171E12, Ge +14:22. ✗32, Ge +31:21. **specially.** Ac 26:2, 3.

27. **For it.** Pr +*18:13. Jn +*7:51. **the crimes.** ver. +18.

ACTS 26

Paul, before Agrippa, Festus, and their attendants, declares his manner of life and his hope as a Pharisee, 1-8; his zeal in persecuting the church, 9-11; his wonderful conversion, and call to the apostleship, 12-18; and his subsequent preaching and testimony to Christ, according to the scriptures, 19-23. Festus claims that he is mad, but he mildly denies the charge, 24, 25; and addresses Agrippa, who owns himself "almost persuaded to be a Christian," 26-28. Paul expresses his earnest desire, that every one present were altogether Christians, 29. Agrippa and the company agree with Festus, that Paul is innocent, 30-32.

1. **Agrippa.** Ac +9:15. **Thou.** Ac 25:16. Pr *18:13, 17. Jn +*7:51. **stretched.** Pr *1:24. Ezk 16:27. Ro 10:21. **answered.** ver. 2. See on Ac 22:1.

2. **I think.** ✗156, Jn +3:2. **answer.** ver. 24. Ac +19:33. **touching.** ver. 7. Ac 25:7, 19. **accused.** 1 P 3:16, 17. **of the Jews.** Ac 25:10.

3. **because.** ver. 26. Ac 6:14. 21:21. 24:10. 25:19, 20, 26. 28:17. Dt 17:18. 1 C 13:2. **customs.** Ac +6:14. **questions.** Ac +18:15. **to hear.** Ac 24:4.

4. **My.** Ga 1:13, 14. Ph 3:5. **manner.** 2 T 3:10. **from my youth.** Ezk 4:14. **which.** Ac 22:3. **mine own.** Ac +24:17.

5. **from the beginning.** Lk 1:3. **if.** ✗184C, Mt +4:9. Ac 22:5. **that.** Ac *22:3. *23:6. Ph 3:5, 6. **sect.** See on Ac 24:+5, 14. **religion.** Ja 1:26, 27. **a Pharisee.** Ac +23:6. Lk +2:25.

6. **am.** ver. 8. Ac *23:6. 24:15, 21. 28:20. **the hope.** Ac +*1:6. +*3:19-21. **the promise.** Ac 3:24. *13:+32,

33. Ge +*3:15. +*12:3. +*22:18. 26:4. +*49:10. Dt +*18:15. 2 S +*7:12, 13. Jb +*19:25-27. Ps *2:6-12. 40:6-8. 98:2, 3. *110:1-4. 132:11, 17. Is 4:2. +*7:14. +*9:6, 7. 11:1-5. 40:9-11. 42:1-4. +*53:10-12. +√55:3. *61:1-3. Je +*23:5, 6. *33:14-17. Ezk 17:22-24. 21:27. 34:23-25. *37:24. Da *2:34, 35, 44, 45. +*7:13, 14. +*9:24-26. Ho 3:5. Jl +*2:32. Am *9:11, 12. Ob +*21. Mi +√5:2. 7:20. Zp *3:14-17. Zc 2:10, 11. √6:12. +*9:9. *13:1, 7. Ml *3:1. *4:2. Lk 1:69, 70. Ro √15:8. Ga 3:17, 18. √4:4. T √2:13. He +*6:12. 1 P 1:11, 12.

7. **Unto which.** Ac 2:33. He 10:36. 11:13, 39. **our twelve.** Ezr 6:17. 8:35. Mt +*19:28. Lk +*22:30. Ja *1:1. Re 7:4-8. 21:12. **instantly.** Ac +12:5. 20:31. Ps 134:1, 2. 135:2. Lk 2:36, +37. 1 Th 3:10. 1 T 5:5. **day and night.** Gr. night and day. Ac 20:31. Mk +4:27. **hope to come.** Ac +*1:6. +*3:19-21. Lk *2:25, 26, 37, 38. 7:19, 20. Ph 3:11. **For.** ver. 6. **accused.** ver. 2. Ac 25:19.

8. **should.** Ac 4:2. 10:40-42. 13:30, 31. *17:31, 32. 25:19. Ge 18:14. Mt 22:29-32. Lk 1:37. 18:27. Jn *5:28, 29. 1 C *15:12-20, 35-38. Ph *3:21.

9. **thought.** Ac +3:17. 2 K 5:11. **that.** Ac 9:6g. Jn *16:2, 3. Ro *10:2. Ga 1:13, 14. Ph 3:6. 1 T *1:13. **the name.** Ac +2:22. 3:6. 9:16. 21:13. 22:8. 24:5.

10. **I also.** Ac 7:58. *8:1, +3. *9:13, 14, 26. 22:4, 19, 20. 1 C 15:9. Ga *1:13. **the saints.** Ac 9:+32, 41. Ps 16:3. Ro 15:25, 26. Ep 1:1. Re 17:6. **having.** ver. 12. Ac 9:1, 2, 14, 21. 22:5. **and when.** Ac +22:14, 20.

11. **I punished.** Ac +22:19. Mt 10:17. Mk 13:9. Lk 21:12. **compelled.** Ac +13:45. 18:6. Mk 3:28. He 10:28, 29. Ja 2:7. **mad.** ver. 24, 25. Ac 9:1. Ec 9:3. Lk 6:11. 15:17. 2 P 2:16. **I persecuted.** Ac 22:5.

12. **Whereupon.** Lk 12:1g. **as.** Ac 9:1, 2. 22:5. **Damascus.** Ac +9:2. **with authority.** ver. 10. 1 K 21:8-10. Ps 94:20, 21. Is 10:1. Je 26:8. 29:26, 27. Jn 7:45-48. 11:57.

13. **midday.** Ac *9:3. 22:6. **in the way.** Ge +*24:27. Mk 10:52. **above.** Is 24:23. 30:26. Mt 17:2. Re 1:16. 21:23.

14. **all fallen.** Ac 9:7. **Hebrew.** Ac +21:40. 22:2. **Saul.** Ac *9:4, 5. *22:7-9. **me.** Is +*63:9. Zc *2:8. **hard.** ✗138B, Ge +13:16. Pr +*13:15. Zc 2:8. 12:2. 1 C 10:22.

15. **I am.** Ac *9:5. Ex 16:8. Mt *25:40, 45. Jn 15:20, 21. **whom.** Mt 25:44, 45. Lk 10:16. Jn 5:16. 1 C 8:12.

16. **rise.** Ac *9:6-9. 22:10. **stand.** Ezk 2:1. Da 10:11. **to make.** Ac +3:20. 9:15, 16. 13:1-4. 22:14, 15. **a minister.** Ac 1:17, 25. 6:4. 20:24. 21:19. Lk +1:2. Ro 1:5. 15:16. 2 C 4:1. 5:18. Ep 3:7, 8. Col 1:7, 23, 25. 1 Th 3:2. 1 T 1:12. 4:6. 2 T 4:5. **witness.** Ac 22:15. 23:11. **in the.** Ac 18:+9, 10. 22:17-21. 23:11. 27:23, 24. 2 C 12:1-7. Ga 1:12. 2:2. **I will.** Ac ◐9:17. 13:3. Ga 1:12.

17. **Delivering.** Ac 9:23-25, 29, 30. 12:11. 13:50. 14:5, 6, 19, 20. 16:39. 17:10, 14. 18:10, 12-16. 19:28, etc. 21:28-36. 22:21, 22. 23:10-24. 25:3, 9-11. 27:42-44. 1 Ch 16:35. Ps 34:19. 37:32, 33. Je 1:8, 19. 15:20. 2 C 1:8-10. 4:8-10. 11:23-26. 2 T 3:11. 4:16, 17. **the people.** Ac +10:2. **the Gentiles.** ver. 23. Ac 4:25, 27. 9:15. 22:21. 28:28. Lk 2:32. Ro 11:13. 15:10, 16. Ga 2:9. Ep 3:7, 8. 1 T 2:7. 2 T 1:11. 4:17. **unto whom.** Ac +9:15. **send.** Ro 11:13. 1 T 2:7.

18. **open.** Ac 9:17, 18. Ge +*3:7. Ps √119:18. 146:8. Is √29:18. 32:3. *35:5. *42:6, 7. 43:8. Lk +*4:18. +*24:45. Jn 9:39. 2 C √4:4, 6. Ep *1:18. **to turn.** ver. 23. Ac 13:47. Ps 36:9. Is 9:2. *42:16. 49:6. *60:1-3.

Ml=2:6. *4:2. Mt 4:16. +*6:22, 23. 13:15. Lk 1:16, 79. 2:32. Jn *1:4-9. √3:19. +*8:12. 9:5. 12:35, 36. 2 C √4:4, 6. 6:14. Ep *1:18. *4:18. *5:8, 14. Col *1:12, 13. 1 Th *5:4-8. Ja *5:19, 20. 1 P *2:9, 25. 1 J 2:8, 9. darkness. Is +*9:2. and from. Is 49:24, 25. *53:8-12. Lk 11:21, 22. *22:53. 1 C 5:5. Col 1:13. 2 T *2:26. He +*2:14, 15. 1 J √3:8. 5:19. 1 P *2:9. Re *20:2, 3. that they. Ac +*2:38. +*3:19. 5:31. +*10:43. *13:38, 39. Ps 32:1, 2. Lk 1:77. +*24:47. Ro 4:6-9. 1 C 6:10, 11. Ep *1:7. Col *1:14. 1 J √1:9. 2:12. inheritance. Ac +20:32. Mt +*5:5. Ro 8:17. Ep +*1:11, 14. Col *1:12. He 9:15. Ja *2:5. 1 P +*1:4. sanctified. Ac +*20:32. Jn *17:17, 19. 1 C *1:2, 30. 6:11. T *3:5, 6. He 10:10, 14. √12:14. Ju 1. Re *21:27. faith. Ac 15:9. +20:21. Jn *4:10, 14. *7:38, 39. Ro 5:1, 2. Ga √2:20. 3:2, 14. Ep √2:8. 2 Th 2:13. He √11:6.

19. O king. ver. 2, 26, 27. I was not. Ex 4:13, 14. Is 50:5. Je 20:9. Ezk 2:7, 8. 3:14. Jon 1:3. Ga *1:15, 16. not. √175B, Ge +21:16. disobedient. Ac 14:2. heavenly vision. ver. 13.

20. showed. Ac 17:30. first. Ac +*1:8. *9:19-22. 11:26, etc. Damascus. Ac +9:2. and at. Ac 9:28, 29. 22:17, 18. Lk *24:47. Ro √1:16. throughout. Ga 1:22. and then. ver. 17. Ac *13:46-48. 18:6. 22:21, 22. Mt ☾*10:5, 6. Ro 11:18-20. repent. Ac +*2:38. +*3:19. 11:18. √17:30. 20:21. Je 31:19, 20. Ezk *18:30-32. Mt 3:2. 4:17. 9:13. 21:30-32. Mk *1:14, 15. *6:12. Lk +*13:3, 5. 15:7, 10. 24:46, 47. Ro *2:4. 2 C √7:10. 2 T +*2:25, 26. Re *2:5, 21. 3:3. 16:11. turn. ver. 18. Ac 9:35. +14:15. 15:19. Ps 22:27. La 3:40. Ho *12:6. +*14:2. Jl +*2:13. Mt +*18:3. Lk 1:16. 2 C 3:16. 1 Th +*1:9. and do works. Is √55:7. Mt *3:8. Lk *3:8-14. *19:8, 9. Ep 4:17-32. 5:1-25. 6:1-9. T *2:2-13. 1 P 1:14-16. 2:9-12. 4:2-5. 2 P 1:5-8.

21. the Jews. Ac *21:27, 30, 31. 22:22. 23:12-15. 24:18. 25:3. went about to. Ac +21:31.

22. obtained. ver. 17. Ac 14:19, 20. 16:25, 26. 18:9, 10. 21:31-33. 23:10, 11, 16, etc. 1 S 7:12. Ezr 8:31. Ps 18:47. 66:12. 118:10-13. 124:1-3, 8. 2 C 1:8-10. 2 T 3:11. 4:17, 18. help of God. 1 Ch=15:26. Mt *28:20. He +*13:5, 6. I continue. Ep 6:13. witnessing. Ac 20:20-27. Ep +4:17. Re 11:18. 20:12. to small and great. Ac +8:10. none other. See on ver. 6. Ac 3:21-24. Je=33:18. Lk +*24:27, 44, 46. 1 C *2:2. the prophets. Ac +*10:43. 13:49. 24:14. 28:23. Mt 17:4, 5. Lk +*16:29-31. Jn 1:17, 45. 3:14, 15. +*5:39, 46. Ro *3:21. Re *15:3. and Moses. Ac +3:22. Jn *5:45-47.

23. Christ. Lk +3:15. 24:26. must suffer. Ac +*3:18. Ge +*3:15. Ps ch. *22, 69. Is ch. √53. Da +*9:24-26. Zc *12:10. +*13:7. Mt 26:42. Lk *18:31-33. +*24:26, 46. Jn 12:34. 1 C +*15:3, 4. He +*2:10. the first. ver. 8. Ac *2:23-32. 13:34. Ps +*16:8-11. Is +*53:10-12. Mt *27:53. Jn √10:18. *11:25, 26. 1 C √15:20-23. Col +*1:18. Re +*1:5. and should. See on ver. +*18. Lk *2:32. Ep 2:17. light. ver. 18. Ac 13:47. Mt *4:16. Lk +2:32. the people. ver. +17.

24. spake. ver. 1. Ac +19:33. See on Ac 22:1. Festus. Ac *17:32. 24:25, +27. 25:19, 20. thou art beside. ver. 11. Ac 12:15. 2 K 9:11. Je 29:26. Ho 9:7. Mt 10:25. Mk 3:21. Jn 8:48, 52. *10:20, 21. 1 C *1:18, 23. √2:13, 14. 4:10. 2 C *4:3, 4. 5:13. 2 T +√1:7. learning. Jn +7:15g.

25. I am not mad. Jn 8:49. 2 T +√1:7. 1 P 2:21-23. 3:9, 15. most. Ac 23:26g. 24:3. Lk 1:3g. 1 P *2:17. words. T 1:9. 2:7, 8. 2 P 1:16. soberness. Lk 8:35g. 2 C 5:13.

26. the king. ver. *2, *3. Ac 25:22. speak freely. Ac 2:29. +4:13. this thing. Ac *2:1-12. *4:16-21. *5:18-42. Is *30:20. Mt 26:5. *27:29-54. was not. 2 P +*1:16.

27. believest. ver. *22, *23. Ac 24:14. I know. √69B, Pr +6:16.

28. Almost. ver. *29. Ac *24:25. Is √55:6. Ezk +*33:31. Mt *6:24. *10:18. +*13:20-22. Mk *6:20. *10:17-23. 2 C *4:2. Ja *1:23, 24. Re *3:16, 20. persuadest. Ac +18:4g. Christian. Ac 11:26. 1 P 4:16.

29. I would. √87, Ps +118:25. √184D2, Lk +1:62. Ac +27:29g. Ex 16:3. Nu 11:29. 2 S 18:33. 2 K 5:3. 1 C 4:8. 7:7. 2 C 11:1. that not. Je 13:17. Lk 19:41, 42. Jn 5:34. Ro 9:1-3. 10:1. Col 1:28. almost. √172, Mt +5:19. altogether such. 1 C 7:7. Ph 3:8. except. Ac 12:6. +21:33. 25:14. 28:20. Ep 6:20.

30. the king. Ac 18:15. 25:23. 28:22. governor. Ac +23:24.

31. This man. Ac 23:9, +29. 25:25. 28:18. 2 S 24:17. Lk 23:4, 14, 15. 1 P 3:16. 4:14-16.

32. Festus. Ac +24:27. set at. Ac 3:13g. Lk 6:37g. if he. √184B, Mt +23:30. appealed. Ac *25:11, 12, 25. 28:18, 19. unto. Ac +9:15. Caesar. Ac +17:7.

ACTS 27

Paul, attended by some friends, sails as a prisoner towards Rome, and is kindly used by the Centurion sent with him and other prisoners, 1-8. He foretells the danger of the voyage, but is not believed, 9-11. Sailing against his advice, the company are exposed to a most violent and long continued tempest, and are in extreme danger, 10-20. Paul, encouraged by an angel, assures them that all their lives shall be preserved, but that the ship shall be wrecked, 21-26; the whole of which exactly comes to pass, 27-44.

1. when. Ac 19:21. 23:11. *25:12, 25. Ge +*50:20. Ps 33:11. 76:10. Pr +*19:21. La 3:37. Da *4:35. Ro 15:22-29. we. ver. 2-8, 15, 16, 18, 20, 27, 29, 37. Ac +16:10. Italy. ver. 6. Ac 10:1. 18:2. He 13:24. Julius. i.e. *downy*, ✻S#2457g. ver. 3. a centurion. ver. 3, 6, 11, 31, 43. Ac 10:+1, 22. 21:32. 22:26. 23:17. 24:23. 28:16. Mt 8:5-10. +*27:54. Lk 7:2. 23:47. Augustus'. Ac 25:25. band. Ac 10:1. 21:31. Mt 27:27. Mk 15:16. Jn 18:3, 12.

2. entering. ✻S#1910g. ver. 6g. Ac 20:18g. 21:2, 6g. 25:1g (come into). 28:11. Mt 21:5g (sitting upon). Adramyttium. i.e. *court of death*, ✻S#98g. *Adramyttium, now Adramyti, was a maritime city of Mysia in Asia Minor, seated at the foot of Mount Ida, on a gulf of the same name, opposite the island of Lesbos.* Asia. Ac +2:9. we. Ac 21:1. Lk 8:22. to sail. Ac 20:15, 16. 21:1-3. Aristarchus. Ac *19:29. 20:4. Col 4:10. Phm *24. Macedonian. ✻S#3110g, Ac +16:9. Thessalonica. Ac +17:1. 20:4. with us. Ac 16:10-13, 17. 20:5, 6. 21:5. 28:2, 10, 12, 16.

3. Sidon. Ac +12:20. Ge 10:15. 49:13. Is 23:2-4, 12. Zc 9:2. Julius. ver. 1, 43. Ac 1:43. 24:23. 28:16. entreated. Ac 28:2. and gave. Ac *24:23. *28:16, 30.

4. we. ver. 7. Ac 21:3. under. ver. 7, 16. Cyprus. Ac 4:36. 11:19, 20. 13:4. 15:39. 21:3, 16. the winds. Mt 14:24. Mk 6:48.

5. Cilicia. Ac +6:9. 15:23, 41. 21:39. 22:3. Ga 1:21. Pamphylia. Ac 2:10. 13:13. 14:24. 15:38. Myra. i.e. *pouring; I flow*, ✻S#3460g. *Myra was a city of Lycia, situated on a hill, twenty stadia from the sea.* Lycia. i.e. *great heat; dissolving, dispersing*, ✻S#3073g.

6. **the centurion**. ver. 1. **a ship**. Ac 28:11. **Alexandria**. i.e. *helper of men*, ✳S#222g. *Alexandria*, now *Scanderoon*, was a celebrated city and port of Egypt, built by Alexander the Great, situated on the Mediterranean and the lake Mareotis, opposite the island of Pharos, and about twelve miles from the western branch of the Nile. Ac 28:11. Compare ✳S#221g: Ac 6:9, Alexandrians. 18:24.

7. **Cnidus**. i.e. *dedicated to Venus; nettled*, ✳S#2834g. *Cnidus* was a town and promontory of Caria in Asia Minor, opposite Crete, now Cape Krio. **the wind**. ver. 4. **we sailed**. ver. 12, 13, 21. Ac 2:11. T 1:5, 12. **under**. ver. 4, 16. **Crete**. *or*, Candy. i.e. *carnal; fleshly*, ✳S#2914g. ver. 12, 13, 21. T 1:5. Compare ✳S#2912g: Ac 2:11, Cretes. T 1:12, Cretians. *Crete*, now *Candy*, is a large island in the Mediterranean, 250 miles in length, 50 in breadth, and 600 in circumference, lying at the entrance of the Aegean sea. **Salmone**. i.e. *clothed; garment; peaceable; commotion; from the surging*, ✳S#4534g. *Salmone*, now *Salamina*, was a city and cape on the east of the island of Crete.

8. **hardly passing**. ver. 13g. **The fair havens**. i.e. *goodly ports*, ✳S#2568g. The *Fair Havens*, still known by the same name, was a port on the southeastern part of Crete, near *Lasea*, of which nothing now remains. **Lasea**. i.e. *shaggy; rocky country*, ✳S#2996g.

9. **the fast**. ʃ121P11. Metonymy of the Adjunct B597. *Fast* is used for the time of year at which the Fast fell. "The fast was on the tenth day of the seventh month." Le 16:29. ✳23:27-29. Nu 29:7.

10. **I perceive**. ver. 21-26, 31, 34. Ge 41:16-25, 38, 39. 2 K 6:9, 10. Ps ✳25:14. Da ✳2:30. Am +✳3:7. **damage**. *or*, injury. ver. 20, 21, 41-44. 1 P 4:18. **lading**. Mt 11:30g. **lives**. Gr. *psyche*, ʃ121A7, Mt +2:20. ʃ121A7, Ge +9:5. ver. 22. Ac 23:11.

11. **believed**. ver. 21. Ex 9:20, 21. 2 K 6:10. Pr 27:12. Ezk ✳3:17, 18. 33:4. He 11:7. **the master**. Re 18:17g.

12. **the haven**. ver. 8. Ps 107:30. **to winter**. Ac 28:11. **if by**. ʃ184D1, Lk +22:67. Ph +3:11g. **Phenice**. *Phenice* was a seaport on the western side of Crete; probably defended from the fury of the winds by a high and winding shore, forming a semicircle, and perhaps by some small island in front; leaving two openings, one towards the southwest, and the other towards the northwest. **Crete**. ver. 7.

13. **the south**. Jb 37:17. Ps 78:26. SS 4:16. Lk 12:55. **loosing**. ver. 21. **sailed close**. ver. 8g.

14. **not**. Ex 14:21-27. Jon 1:3-5. **arose**. *or*, beat. Mk 4:37. **a tempestuous**. Ps 107:25-27. Ezk 27:26. Mt 8:24. Mk 4:37. **Euroclydon**. i.e. *an easterly tempest*, ✳S#2148g. Probably, as Dr. Shaw supposes, one of those tempestuous winds called *levanters*, which blow in all directions, from N.E. round by E. to S.E.

15. **we**. ver. 27. Ja 3:4. **drive**. ver. 17, 27.

16. **under**. ver. 4, 7. **Clauda**. i.e. *broken voice; lamentable voice*, ✳S#2802g. *Clauda*, called *Cauda* and *Gaudos* by Mela and Pliny, and *Claudos* by Ptolemy, and now *Gozo*, according to Dr. Shaw, is a small island, situated at the southwestern extremity of the island of Crete.

17. **fearing**. ver. 29, 41. **were driven**. ver. 15, 27.

18. **being**. Ps 107:27. **the next**. ver. 19, 38. Jon 1:5. Mt 16:26. Lk +✳16:8. Ph 3:7, 8. He ✳12:1.

19. **we**. Jb 2:4. Jon 1:5. Mk 8:35-37. Lk 9:24, 25.

20. **neither**. Ex 10:21-23. Ps 105:28. Mt 24:29. **and**

no. Ps 107:25-27. Jon 1:4, 11-14. Mt 8:24, 25. 2 C 11:25. **all**. Is 57:10. Je 2:25. Ezk 37:11. Ep 2:12. 1 Th 4:13.

21. **after**. ver. 33-35. Ps 107:5, 6. **stood forth**. Ac 2:14. 5:17, 20. 6:9. 17:22. 23:9. 25:18. Lk 18:11. 19:8. **ye should**. ver. 7, 9, 10. Ge 42:22. **not**. ver. 13.

22. **I exhort**. ver. 25, 36. Ac 23:11. 1 S 30:6. Ezr 10:2. Jb 22:29, 30. Ps 112:7. Is 43:1, 2. 2 C 1:4-6. 4:8, 9. **good cheer**. ver. 25, 36. Ac 24:10. Ja 5:13. **for**. ver. 31, 34, 44. Jb 2:4. **no loss**. ver. 10. Ac 23:11. **life**. Gr. *psyche*, ʃ121A7, Mt +2:20.

23. **there**. Ac 5:19. +8:26. 12:8-11, 23. 18:9. ✳23:11. Da 6:22. 2 T 4:17. He ✳1:14. Re 22:16. **whose**. Ex 19:5. Nu 16:22. Dt 32:9. 2 Ch 12:8. Jb 12:10. Ps ✳40:17. 44:4. 119:94. 135:4. SS ✳2:16. 6:3. Is ✳43:1, 15. ✳44:5. Je 31:33. 32:38. Ezk 36:28. Da 5:23. Zc +✳13:9. Ml 3:17. Jn +✳17:9, 10. 1 C 6:20. Ph +1:3. 2 T ✳2:19. T ✳2:14. He ✳8:10. Ja 1:1. 1 P ✳2:9, 10. **and**. Ac 16:17. +24:14. Ps ✳116:15, 16. 143:12. Is ✳44:21. Da ✳3:17, 26, 28. ✳6:16, 20. Jn 12:26. Ro ✳1:1, 9. 6:22. 2 T ✳1:3. 2:24. T 1:1.

24. **Fear not**. Ac 18:9, 10. Ge 15:1. 46:3. 1 K 17:13. 2 K 6:16. Is 41:10-14. ✳43:1-5. Mt +✳10:28. Re 1:17. **thou**. Ac 9:15. 19:21. 23:11. 25:11. Mt ✳10:18. Jn 11:9. 2 T 4:16, 17. Re 11:5-7. **must**. Ac +9:6. 23:11. **Caesar**. Ac +17:7. **lo**. ver. 37. Ge 12:2. 18:23-32. ✳19:21, 22, 29. 30:27. 39:5, 23. Is 58:11, 12. Ezk 14:14. Mi 5:7. Ja √5:16. **given thee**. Ac +25:11g. Jb +✳35:8. **all them**. ver. 31, 42, 44. **with thee**. Jb ✳22:30.

25. **good cheer**. ver. +22. **I believe**. ver. 11, 21. Ac +16:34. Nu +✳23:19. 2 Ch +✳20:20. Lk ✳1:45. Ro √4:20, 21. 2 T √1:12.

26. **we**. Ac ✳28:1. **must**. ver. 24, 31. **cast upon**. ver. 17, 29. **a certain**. Ac 28:1.

27. **the fourteenth**. ver. 18-20. **driven**. ver. 15, 17. **Adria**. i.e. *the Adriatic Sea*, ✳S#99g. *Adria*, strictly speaking, was the name of the *Adriatic gulf*, now the *Gulf of Venice*, an arm of the Mediterranean, about 400 miles long and 140 broad, stretching along the eastern shores of Italy on one side, and Dalmatia, Sclavonia, and Macedonia on the other. But the term *Adria* was extended far beyond the limits of this gulf, and appears to have been given to an indeterminate extent of sea, as we say, generally, the *Levant*. It is observable that the sacred historian does not say "in the Adriatic gulf," but "in Adria" (that is, the *Adriatic sea*, *pelagos* being understood); which, says Hesychius, was the same as the Ionian sea; and Strabo says that the Ionian gulf "is a part of that now called the Adriatic." But not only the Ionian, but even the Sicilian sea, and part of that which washes Crete, were called the Adriatic. Thus the scholiast on Dionysius Periegetis says, "they call this Sicilian sea Adria." And Ptolemy says that Sicily was bounded on the east by the Adriatic, *upo Adrioi*, and that Crete was bounded on the west by the Adriatic sea, *upo tou Adriatikou pelagos*. **the shipmen**. ver. 30. 1 K 9:27. Jon 1:6. Re 18:17.

29. **fallen**. ver. 17, 41. **anchors**. ver. 30, 40. He 6:19. **and wished**. Ac 26:29. Dt 28:67. Ps 130:6. Ro 9:3. 2 C 13:7, 9. Ja 5:16. 3 J 2.

30. **the boat**. ver. 16, 32. **under color**. Lk 20:47. **foreship**. ver. 41.

31. **said**. ver. 11, 21, 42, 43. **Except**. T#429. ver. 22-24, 26. Ps 91:11, 12. Je 29:11-13. Ezk ✳33:8. 36:36, 37. Lk 1:34, 35. 4:9-12. Jn ✳6:37. Ro √10:14, 15, 17. 2 Th +✳2:13 (T#257), 14.

32. **cut off.** Lk +*16:8. Ph *3:7-9. **the ropes.** Jn 2:15g.

33. **while.** ver. 29. **the day.** Ro 13:11, 12. **This.** ver. 27. **fasting.** ✓171N, Ge +8:13. **taken nothing.** ✓171C, Ex +20:10.

34. **for this.** Mt 15:32. Mk 8:2, 3. Ph 2:5. 1 T 5:23. **for there.** ✓138B, Ge +13:16. 1 S 14:45. 2 S 14:11. 1 K 1:52. Da 3:27. Mt *10:30. Lk 12:7. 21:18.

35. **gave thanks.** Ac 2:46, 47. 1 S *9:13. Mt +15:36. Mk 8:6. Lk 22:19. +*24:30. Jn 6:11, 23. Ro 14:6. 1 C ✓10:30, 31. 1 T *4:3, 4. **in the presence.** Ps 119:46. Mk ✓8:38. Ro ✓1:16. 2 T *1:8, 12. 1 P 4:16. **broken.** ✓108H4, Is +58:7.

36. **they all.** Pr 27:17. 2 C 1:4-6. **good cheer.** ver. +22.

37. **two.** ver. 24. **souls.** Gr. *psyche*, ✓171Q1A, Ac +2:41. Ac 3:23. 7:14. Ex 1:5. Ro 13:1. 1 P 3:20. Re 16:3.

38. **they lightened.** ver. 18, 19. Jb 2:4. Jon 1:5. Mt 6:25. 16:26. He *12:1. **the wheat.** The Romans imported corn from Egypt, by way of Alexandria, to which this ship belonged; for a curious account of which see Bryant's treatise on the Euroclydon.

39. **knew.** Gr. *epiginosko*, Mt +11:27. Ac 28:1. **if it.** ✓184D1, Lk +22:67.

40. **taken up,** etc. *or,* cut the anchors, they left them in the sea, etc. ver. 29, 30. **the rudder bands.** Or, "the bands of the rudders;" for large vessels in ancient times had two or more rudders, which were fastened to the ship by means of *bands* or chains, by which they were hoisted out of the water when incapable of being used. These bands being loosed, the rudders would fall into their proper places, and serve to steer the vessel into the creek, which they had in view. **and hoised.** Is 33:23.

41. **they ran.** ver. 17, 26-29. 2 C 11:25. **broken.** 1 K 22:48. 2 Ch 20:37. Ezk 27:26, 34. 2 C 11:25, 26.

42. **soldiers' counsel.** Ac 12:19. Ps 74:20. Pr 12:10. Ec 9:3. Mk 15:15-20. Lk 23:40, 41.

43. **willing.** ver. 3, 11, 31. Ac 23:10, 24. Pr +*16:7. 2 C 11:25.

44. **that.** ver. 22, 24, 31. Ps 107:28-30. Am 9:9. Jn 6:39, 40. 2 C 1:8-10. 1 P 4:18. **all safe.** Ps *107:30. 2 C 1:10. **land.** *Melita,* now *Malta,* the island on which Paul and his companions were cast, is situate in the Mediterranean sea, about fifty miles from the coast of Sicily, towards Africa; and is one immense rock of soft white freestone, twenty miles long, twelve in its greatest breadth, and sixty in circumference. Some, however, with the learned Jacob Bryant, are of opinion that this island was *Melita* in the Adriatic gulf, near Illyricum; but it may be sufficient to observe, that the course of the Alexandrian ship, first to Syracuse and then to Rhegium, proves that it was the present Malta, as the proper course from the Illyrian Melita would have been first to Rhegium, before it reaches Syracuse, to which indeed it need not have gone at all.

ACTS 28

The whole company, having escaped to the island Melita, are humanely entertained by the inhabitants, 1, 2. A viper fastens on Paul's hand, which he shakes off into the fire, without harm; and the people, who at first supposed he was a murderer, believe that he

is a god, 3-6. Publius, the chief man of the island, entertains them all three days, 7. Paul heals the father of Publius, and many other sick persons; and they meet with much respect and kindness, 8-10. Paul and his company depart; and having arrived within some miles of Rome, they are met by brethren from that city, 11-15. Paul is entrusted to a soldier, and dwells in his own lodging, 16. He sends for the chief of the Jews, and shows them the occasion of his coming, 17-22. He proves to a large company, from the scriptures, that Jesus is the Christ, 23. Some believe, and others do not, 24. He solemnly warns the unbelievers, and shows that the Gentiles would receive his word, 25-29. He continues during two years, to preach the gospel in his own hired house, without interruption, 30, 31.

1. **they.** Many MSS. read "we." ver. 2, 7, 10-16. Ac +16:10. **then.** Ac 27:39. **knew.** Gr. *epiginosko*, Mt +11:27. **the island.** Ac 27:26, 44. **Melita.** i.e. *flowing with honey,* *S#3194g.

2. **barbarous.** ver. 4. Ro 1:14. 1 C 14:11. Col *3:11. **showed.** Ac 27:3. Le 19:18, 34. Pr 24:11, 12. Mt 10:42. Lk 10:30-37. Ro 2:14, 15, 27. He *13:2. **us.** ver. +1n. **received us.** Ro 1:14. 14:1. Phm 17. He +*13:2. **no little.** Ac 19:11g. **because.** Ezr 10:9. Jn 18:18. 2 C 11:27.

3. **came.** Jb 20:16. Is 30:6. 41:24mg. 59:5. Mt 3:7. 12:34. 23:33. **fastened.** ver. 4. Am 5:19. 2 C 6:9. 11:23. **his hand.** Ac 20:34.

4. **barbarians.** ver. 2. **beast.** ver. 5. Ge 3:1. Is 13:21, 22. 43:20. Zp 2:15. **on.** Gr. *ek,* Ac 8:39n. **his hand.** Ac 20:34. **No doubt.** Jb 4:7. Lk +*13:2, 3n, 4, 5. Jn +*7:24. Jn +*9:1-3. **a murderer.** Ge 4:8-11. 9:5, 6. 42:21, 22. Nu 35:31-34. Pr 28:17. Is 26:21. Mt 23:35. 27:25. Re +*21:8. **yet.** Nu +*32:23. Pr 13:15. Is 59:12. Am 5:19. 9:3.

5. **felt.** Nu 21:6-9. Ps 91:13. Mk *16:18. Lk *10:19. Jn 3:14, 15. Ro 16:20. Re 9:3, 4. **no harm.** Ex 4:2, 5.

6. **no harm.** Lk +23:41. **changed their minds.** Ac 14:11, 19. **said.** Ac 8:10. 12:22. 14:11-13. Mt 21:9. 27:22.

7. **the chief.** ver. 17. Ac 13:7. 18:12. 23:24. **Publius.** i.e. *popular, common, public,* *S#4196g. ver. 8. **who.** ver. 2. Mt 10:40, 41. Lk 19:6-9. He 11:17g.

8. **the father.** Mk 1:30, 31. **to whom.** Ga *6:10. **prayed.** Ac 9:40. 1 K 17:20-22. Ja *5:14-16. **laid.** T#1247. Ac 6:6. 9:12, 17, 18. 13:3. 19:11, 12. Mt 9:18. Mk +5:23. *6:5. 7:32. *16:18. Lk 4:40. 13:13. **and healed.** Mt 10:1, 8. Lk 9:1-3. 10:8, 9. 1 C *12:9, 28.

9. **others.** Ac 5:12, 15. Mt 4:24. Mk 6:54-56.

10. **honored.** Mt 15:5, 6. 1 Th 2:6. 1 T 5:3, 4, 17, 18. **laded.** 2 K 8:9. Ezr 7:27. Mt 6:31-34. 10:8-10. 2 C 8:2-6. 9:5-11. Ph 4:11, 12, 19.

11. **Cir.** A.M. 4067. A.D. 63. **a ship.** Ac 6:9. 27:6. **Alexandria.** Ac 6:9. 18:24. 27:6. **whose sign.** Ac 14:12g. Is 45:20. Jon 1:5, 16. 1 C +*8:4. **Castor.** i.e. *Jupiter's twins,* *S#1359g. **Pollux.** i.e. *Jupiter's young men,* *S#1359g. lit. the Dioscuri.

12. **Syracuse.** i.e. *that draws violently; a Syrian hearing,* *S#4946g. *Syracuse* was the capital of Sicily, situated on the eastern side of the island, 72 miles S. by E. of Messina, and about 112 of Palermo. In its ancient state of splendor it was 22.5 in extent, according to Strabo; and such was its opulence, that when the Romans took it, they found more riches than they did at Carthage.

13. **Regium.** i.e. *captive; a passage; to break*

through, *S#4484g. *Rhegium*, now *Reggio*, was a maritime city and promontory in Italy, opposite Messina. **the south.** Ac 27:13. **Puteoli.** i.e. *chief justice; little springs, abounding in wells,* *S#4223g. *Puteoli*, now *Pozzuoli*, is an ancient seaport of Campania, in the kingdom of Naples, about eight miles S.W. of that city, standing upon a hill in a creek opposite to Baiae.

14. **we found.** Ac 9:42, 43. 19:1. 21:4, 7, 8. Ps +√119:63. Mt 10:11. **brethren.** ver. 15. Jn +21:23. **and were.** Ac 20:6. Ge 7:4. 8:10-12. **went.** ſ171J14, Jon +1:3. **Rome.** Ac 2:10. 18:2. 19:21. 23:11. Ro 1:7, 15. 2 T 1:17.

15. **when.** Ac 10:25. 21:5. 21:5. Ex 4:14. Jn 12:13. Ro 15:24. Ga 4:14. He 13:3. 3 J 6-8. **they came.** Ro +*12:3, 16. 1 C √12:21, 22. Ph +*2:3. **Appii forum.** i.e. *persuasive mart, the market place of Appius,* *S#675g w 5410g. *Appii Forum*, now *Borgo Longo*, was an ancient city of the Volsci, fifty miles south of Rome. **The three taverns.** The *Three Taverns* was a place in the Appian way, thirty miles from Rome. **he thanked.** Ro 1:9, 10. 2 C *2:14. 1 Th +*5:18. **took courage.** Ac 23:11. Jsh *1:6, 7, 9. 1 S *30:6. 2 Ch 15:8. Ps *27:14. Ro *1:11, 12. 2 C 7:5-7, 16. 1 Th 3:7.

16. **Rome.** *Rome*, the capital of Italy, and once of the whole world, is situated on the banks of the Tiber, about sixteen miles from the sea; 410 miles S.S.E. of Vienna, 600 S.E. of Paris, 730 E. by N. of Madrid, 760 W. of Constantinople, and 780 S.E. of London. Ro 2:10. 18:2. 19:21. 23:11. Ro 1:7-15. 15:22-29. Re 17:9, 18. **the centurion.** Ac +10:1. 27:3, 31, 43. **captain.** Ge 37:36. 2 K 25:8. Je 40:2. **but.** ver. 30, 31. Ac *24:23. *27:3. Ge *39:21-23.

17. **chief.** ver. 7. Ac +3:26. 13:46. Mk +6:21. **though.** Ac 23:1, etc. 24:10-16. 25:8, 10. Ge 40:15. **the people.** Ac +10:2. **customs.** Ac +6:14. +22:3. **was.** Ac *21:33, etc. 23:33.

18. **when.** Ac 22:24, 25, 30. 24:10, 22. 25:7, 8. 26:31. **examined.** Ac +12:19. **would have let.** Ac 26:31, 32. **no cause.** Ac +23:29. *26:30, 31.

19. **I was.** Ac 25:10-12, 21, 25. 26:32. **to appeal.** Ac √25:11. **Caesar.** Ac +17:7. **not.** Ro 12:19-21. 1 P 2:22, 23. **my nation.** Ac +24:17.

20. **this cause.** ver. 17. Ac 10:29, 33. **for the hope.** ſ121R3, Ps +71:5. Ac +*1:6. +*3:19-21. 23:6. 24:15. See on Ac +√26:6, 7. Je 17:7, 13, 17. Lk +*2:25. **I am bound.** 2 T 1:10-12. **this chain.** That is, the *chain* with which he was bound to the "soldier that kept him," (ver. 16); a mode of custody which Dr. Lardner has shown was in use among the Romans. It is in exact conformity, therefore, with the truth of St. Paul's situation at this time, that he declares himself to be "an ambassador in a *chain*," *en alusei*, (Ep. 6:20); and the exactness is the more remarkable, as *alusis*, a *chain*, is no where used in the singular number to express any other kind of custody. See Paley's *Horae Paulinae*, pp. 130, 131. In Col 4:3 a different expression is used, "I am in bonds" being expressed by the verb *dedemai*. But Colossians and Ephesians were certainly written by the same person; and if an impostor had designedly borrowed the word *alusis* in the one place, he would also have done so in the other. See listing of related notes at Ac 12:12. T#1234. Ac +21:33. 26:29. Ep 3:1.

4:1. *6:20. Ph 1:+7, 13. Col 4:18. 2 T 1:16-18. 2:9. 4:14-18. Phm 10, 13.

21. **We neither.** Ex 11:7. Is 41:11. 50:8. 54:17. **the brethren.** Ac +22:5.

22. **for.** Ac 16:20, 21. 17:6, 7. 24:5, 6, 14. Lk 2:34. 1 P 2:12. 3:16. 4:14-16. **sect.** Ac 5:17. 15:5. +24:5. 26:5. 1 C 11:19mg. **every where.** ſ171D, Mk +16:20. **spoken against.** Lk *2:34. He *12:3. 1 P *2:12. 3:16. *4:14, 16.

23. **there came.** Phm 2. **his lodging.** Phm 22. **he expounded.** Ac 11:4. +*17:2, 3. 18:4, 26, 28. *19:8. *26:22, 23. **testified.** Lk +16:28. **the kingdom of God.** ver. 31. Ac +*1:3, 6n, 7n. 19:8. Da *2:44. Mt 3:2. **persuading.** Ac +18:4. 19:8. **concerning Jesus.** Ps ch. 22. Is ch. 53. Mt 11:3. **both out of.** Ac 8:35. 24:14. See on Ac +*26:6, 22. Lk +16:16. +*24:26, 27, 44. Jn +7:23. **law of Moses.** Ge +*49:10. Dt +*18:15. **the prophets.** Is ch. +*53. Je +*23:5, 6. Ezk *34:23. Da +*9:24. Mi +*5:2. Hg *2:7. Zc +*9:9. Ml *3:1. Mt +*11:3. **from morning till.** Ac 20:9-11. Jn 4:34.

24. **some believed.** Ac 13:48-50. *14:4. 17:4, 5. 18:6-8. *19:8, 9. 23:7. Jn 11:45, 46. Ro 3:3. 11:4-6. **believed not.** Mk √16:16. Jn √3:18. 2 C 2:15, 16. He *4:2.

25. **agreed.** ver. 29. **Well spake.** Ac +*5:3, 4. 8:29n. Ex 16:7 w He 3:7-9. Mt 10:20. 15:7. Mk 7:6. Jn 12:41. 2 P √1:21. **Ghost.** Gr. *pneuma*, Mt +3:16. Ac +1:16. Mt +12:32. **by.** Mt +1:22. **Esaias.** Mk +1:2.

26. **Go.** Is ʮ6:9, 10. Ezk 12:2. Mt 13:14, 15. Mk 4:12. Lk 8:10. Jn 12:38-40. Ro 11:8-10. **Hearing.** ſ147B, Ge +2:16. Dt 29:4. Ps 81:11, 12. Is 29:10, 14. 42:19, 20. 66:4. Je *5:21. Ezk 3:6, 7. *12:2. Mt +*13:14, 15. Mk 4:12. 8:17, 18. Lk *8:10. 24:25, 45. 2 C √4:4-6. **shall not.** ſ158, Mt +5:18.

27. **For the heart.** Jn *12:40. Ro *11:8. **waxed gross.** Dt 32:15g. **they closed.** Ro +*1:28. 2 Th √2:11, 12. 2 P √3:5. **lest.** Mt +*13:14, 15. Mk 4:12. **be converted.** Ac +*3:19. Lk +22:32.

28. **it known.** Ac 2:14. 4:10. 13:38. Ezk 36:32. **the salvation.** Ac √4:12. *13:26. Ps 67:2. 98:2, 3. Is 40:5. *49:6. 52:10. La 3:26. Lk *2:30-32. 3:6. Ro 11:11. **sent.** Ac 11:18. √13:46, 47. 14:27. 15:14, 17. *18:6. *22:21. *26:17, 18. Mt √21:41-43. Ps 106:4. Ro 3:29, 30. 4:11. √11:11. 15:8-16. **they will.** T#481. Ac +*13:48. Ps 68:31. 110:3. Jl 2:28, 29. Mt +*8:11. 21:43. Mk 12:9. Lk 13:29. 20:16. Jn +*10:16. Re +11:15 (T#90). +20:4 (T#440).

29. **great reasoning.** ver. 25. Mt 10:34-36. Lk 12:51-53. Jn 7:40-53.

30. **Paul.** St. Paul, after his release, is supposed to have visited Judea, in the way to which he left Titus at Crete (T 1:5), and then returned through Syria, Cilicia, Asia Minor, and Greece, to Rome; where, according to primitive tradition, he was beheaded by order of Nero, A.D. 66, at *Aquae Salviae*, three miles from Rome, and interred in the *Via Ostensis*, two miles from the city, where Constantine erected a church. **dwelt.** ver. 16. **received all.** Lk +8:40. 1 C *9:16. Ph 1:13.

31. **Cir. A.M. 4069. A.D. 65. Preaching.** ver. 23. Ac 8:12. 20:25. **the kingdom.** ver. 23. Ac +1:3. Mt 4:23. Mk 1:14. Lk 8:1. **and teaching.** Ac 5:42. 23:11. **the Lord.** Ac +11:17. **with.** Ac 4:+13, 29, 31. Ep *6:19, 20. Ph *1:12-14. Col 4:3, 4. 2 T 4:17. **no man forbidding.** Ph 1:12, 13. 2 T *2:9.

ROMANS

ROMANS 1

The apostle shows his apostolical authority, and the great subject of his ministry, 1-5. He salutes the Christians at Rome, 6, 7; thanking God on their account, and praying for them; especially that he might come and preach among them, 8-15. The gospel is the power of God to salvation, and shows the only way of justification, 16, 17. All men of every nation are exposed to the wrath of God, for acting in opposition to the light afforded them, 18-23. A just but awful description of the Gentile world, as given up, by the just displeasure of God, to the grossest idolatries, the most degrading licentiousness, and the most atrocious iniquities, 24-32.

1. **Paul**. Ac *13:9. 21:40. 22:7, 13. 26:1, 14. **a servant**. ver. *9. Ro 15:16. 16:18. Jn *12:26. 13:14-16. 15:15, 20. Ac 27:23. 2 C 4:5. Ga *1:10. Ph 1:1. *2:11. *3:6, 7. T *1:1. Ja +1:1. 2 P 1:1. Ju 1. Re 1:1. *22:6, 9. **called**. ver. *5. 11:13. Ac *9:15. 22:14, 15, 21. *26:16-18. 1 C 1:1. 9:1, 16-18. *15:8-10. 2 C +1:1. *11:5. 12:11. Ga *1:1, 11-17. Ep 1:1. *3:5-7. 4:11. Col 1:1, 25. 1 T 1:1, 11, 12. 2:7. 2 T *1:11. T 1:1. He *5:4. **to be**. *63K, Ge +37:13. **separated**. Le 20:24-26. Nu 16:9, 10. Dt 10:8. 1 Ch 23:13. Is 49:1. Je *1:5. Ac 13:2-4. Ga *1:15. 1 T *1:15, 16. He *7:26. **the gospel**. ver. *9, √16. Ro *15:16, 29. *16:25. Mk 1:14. +*16:15, 16. Lk 2:10, 11. Ac *20:24. 2 C 11:7. Ep 1:13. 1 Th *2:2, 8, 9. 2 Th *2:13, 14. 1 T *1:11. 1 P 4:17.

2. **Which**. *133, Ge +2:8. Verses 2-6 constitute a *Parecbasis*, or digression, such that verse 7 is the continuation of verse 1, and not of verse 6. **promised**. T#1017. See on Lk +*24:26, 27. Ac +*10:43. +√26:6. Ga *3:8. T √1:2. **by**. See on Ro *3:21. Lk 1:70. 2 P *1:21. **the holy scriptures**. T#1016. Ro 3:2. *16:26. Ne 8:3. Ps 1:2. 40:7. 119:140. Is 30:9. *34:16. Da *10:21. Mt 21:42. Lk +*11:28. See on Ac *3:2. Ga 3:10. Ep *6:17. Col √3:16. 2 T +√3:15, 16. He √4:12. Ja 1:18, 21-23. 1 P √2:2. 4:11. Re 22:19.

3. **his Son**. ver. 9. Ro 8:2, 3, 29-32. Ps *2:7. Mt 3:17. 26:63. 27:43. Lk +*1:35. Jn 1:34, 49. √3:16-18, 35, 36. 5:25. *10:30, 36. +√20:28, 31. Ac 3:13. *8:37. 9:20. 1 C 1:9. Ga *4:4. Col +*1:13-15. 1 Th 1:10. 1 J 1:3. 3:8, 23. 4:9, 10, 15. 5:1, 5, √10-13, 20. Re 2:18. **our Lord**. *101, Dt +32:42. **which**. 2 S +*7:12-16. Ps +*89:36, 37. Is +*9:6, 7. Je +*3:5, 6. 33:15-17, 26. Am *9:11. Mt *1:+1, 6, 16, 20-23. 9:27. 12:23. 15:22. 22:42-45. Lk *1:31-33, 69. 2:4-6. Jn 7:42. Ac 2:30. 13:22, 23. 2 T *2:8. Re 22:16. **of David**. Ac +*13:23. **according**. Ro 4:1. 8:3. *9:3, 5. Ge +*3:15. Jn *1:14. Ac +*2:30. 1 C 10:18. Ga √4:4. 1 T √3:16. 1 J 4:2, 3. 2 J √7n.

4. **And**. lit. Who. *77, Ex +3:19. The repetition of the article *tou*, rather than the use of *kai* ("and") or *de* ("but") constitutes this an instance of the figure *Epitasis*, making these additional words emphatic (Bengel, *N.T. Word Studies*, vol. 2, p. 12). **declared**. Gr. determined. Mk 9:7. Lk 3:22. +22:22. Jn 15:26. Ac *13:33. 17:31. **the Son of God**. ver. 3. Mt *3:17. +*14:33. *16:16, 17. +*27:43, 54n. Ac *8:37n. **with power**. Mt 28:18. Jn 4:34. 6:19. Ac 10:38. 26:23. 2 C

13:4. Ep 1:19, 20. Ph 3:10. He 1:3. 1 J *4:14, 15. **according**. Lk 18:31-33. +*24:26, 27. Jn 4:34. 8:39. He 9:14. 1 P 1:11. 2 P *1:21. Re *19:10. **the spirit**. Gr. *pneuma*, used of the resurrection body here and in 1 C 15:45. 1 T 3:16. He 12:23. 1 P 3:18. 4:6. For the other uses of *pneuma*, see Mt +*8:16n. **of holiness**. Lk +*1:35. 2 C 5:21. 1 P 1:19. **by the resurrection**. Jn +*2:18-21. Ac +*2:24n, 32. 3:15. 4:10-12. 5:30-32. 13:33-35. √17:31. 2 C 13:4. Ep 1:19-23. He 5:5, 6. Re 1:18. **from**. *181E, Ge +3:24.

5. **we**. *96D4, Ge +29:27. **have received**. Ro +*12:3. 15:15, 16. Jn 1:16. 1 C *15:10. 2 C 3:5, 6. Ga 1:15, 16. Ep *3:2-9. 1 T 1:11, 12. **and**. *93A, Ge +1:26. By *Hendiadys*, whereby two words are used, but one thing meant, "apostolic grace." **apostleship**. Ac +1:25. 1 C 9:2. Ga 2:8, 9. **for obedience to the faith**. *or*, to the obedience of faith. Ro 6:16. 15:18, 19. 16:26. Ac 6:7. 2 C *10:4-6. He +*5:9. 1 P 1:2. **among**. See on Ro 3:29. Ac +9:15. **for his name**. Ml 1:11, 14. Ac 15:14. Ep 1:6, 12. 1 P *2:9, 10.

6. **are ye also**. Ep +*1:11. Col *1:6, 21. **the called**. Ro √8:28-30. 9:24. 1 C 1:2, *9, 24. Ga *1:6. Ep 4:1-7. 1 Th *2:12. 2 Th *2:14. 2 T +*1:9. He 3:1. 1 P *2:9, 21. 5:10. 2 P +*1:10. Ju +1. Re *17:14.

7. **To all**. *13, Ep +3:14. The salutation commenced in verse 1 is resumed. T#1116. Ac 15:23. 1 C *1:2. 2 C 1:1. Ph 1:1. Col *1:2. Ja 1:1, 2. 1 P *1:1, 2. 1 J 2:7, 12-14. Ju 1. Re 2:1, 8, 12, 18, 29. 3:1, 7, 14, 22. **Rome**. ver. 15. 2 T +1:17. **beloved**. Ro *9:25. Dt *33:12. Ps 60:5. SS 5:1. Col *3:12. 1 Th 1:4. 1 T *6:2. **called**. ver. 6. 1 C 1:2. Col *3:15. 1 Th *4:7. He *3:1. 1 P *1:15. 2 P *1:3. **to be**. *63K, Ge +37:13. **saints**. 2 C +1:1. **Grace**. T#1542. Ro 3:24. 16:20. Ex 33:13. 1 C 1:3, etc. 16:23. 2 C 1:2. *13:14. Ga 1:3. Ep 1:2, 7. *2:7, 8. Ph 1:2. 4:23. Col 1:2. 1 Th 1:1. 5:28. 2 Th 1:1, 2. 3:18. 1 T 1:2. 6:21. 2 T 1:2. 4:22. T 1:4. 3:15. Phm 3, 25. He *4:16. 13:25. 1 P 1:1, 2. *5:10. 2 P *1:2. 2 J +3. Ju 2. Re 1:4, 5. 22:21. **peace**. *171I9B, Is +57:19. See on Ro +*5:1. Ga *5:22. Ph *4:7. 1 Th 1:1. 1 T 1:2. 2 T 1:2. 2 J +3. **God our Father**. Ro *8:15. Mt *5:16. +*6:8, 9. Jn *20:17. 2 C *6:18. Ga 1:4. Ph 4:20. 1 Th *1:3. 2 Th 1:1. 1 J *3:1. **and the Lord**. Ac +√7:59, 60. 1 C 16:23. 2 C *12:8-10. *13:14. Ga 6:18. Ep *6:23, 24. Ph *4:13, 23. 1 Th *3:11-13. 5:28. 2 Th 2:16, 17. 3:16, 18. 2 T 4:22. Phm 25. Re 22:21.

8. **I thank**. See on Ro 6:17. 1 C 1:4. 14:18. 15:57. Ep 1:15, 16. *5:20. Ph 1:3-5. *4:6. Col 1:3, 4. 1 Th 1:2, 3. *2:13. 3:9. 2 Th 1:3. *2:13. 2 T 1:3-5. Phm 4, 5. He *13:15. 2 J 4. 3 J 3, 4. **my God**. Ph +1:3. **through**. Ep 3:21. *5:20. Ph *1:11. He *13:15. 1 P 2:5. 4:11. **that your**. Ro 16:19. Mt +24:14. 2 C *2:14. Col *1:6, 23. 1 Th *1:8, 9. **the whole**. Mt *24:14. Lk *2:1. Ac *11:28. **world**. Gr. *kosmos*, Mt +4:8.

9. **God**. Ro *9:1. Jb *16:19. 2 C 1:23. 11:10, 11, *31. Ga *1:20. Ph *1:8. 1 Th *2:5-10. 1 T 2:7. **whom**. Ac +24:14. *27:23. Ph 2:22. Col *1:28, 29. 2 T *1:3. **with**. *or*, in. Jn *4:23, 24. Ac *19:21. 1 C *14:14, 15. Ph *3:3. **spirit**. Gr. *pneuma*, Ac +18:25n. *108B, Lk +10:21. *121A2, Ps +51:10. Mk 2:8. **the gospel**. Mk *1:1. Ac *3:26. 1 C 9:18. 2 C 8:18. 10:14. Ph 2:22.

4:3. 1 J *5:9-12. **without ceasing.** 1 S √12:23. Lk *18:1. Ac *12:5. Ep *6:18. 1 Th *3:10. +*5:17. 2 T *1:3. **I make mention.** Ep *1:16-19. *3:14, etc. Ph *1:4, 9-11. Col *1:9-13. 1 Th 1:2. Phm *4.

10. **request.** Ro *15:22-24, 30-32. Ph √4:6. 1 Th 2:18. *3:10, 11. Phm 22. He 13:19. **if.** ƒƒ184A, 1 C +15:2. Ph +3:11g. **prosperous journey.** T#1658. Ge 24:12, 27. 28:20-22. Ac 19:21. ch. 27, 28. 1 C 16:2. 3 J 2. **by the will.** Ro 15:32. Ac +18:21. 21:14. 1 C 4:19. 1 Th 3:10. 4:3. Ja *4:15.

11. **I long.** Ro 15:22, 23, 32. Ge 31:30. 2 S 13:39. 23:15. Ac 19:21. 2 C 1:15. 9:14. Ph +1:8. 2:26. 4:1. **that.** Ro 15:29. Ac 8:15-19. *19:6. 1 C √12:1-11. 2 C 11:4. Ga 3:2-5. Ep √4:8-12. **spiritual.** Gr. *pneumatikos,* ✻S#4152g. Ro 7:14. 15:27. 1 C 2:13, 13, 15. 3:1. 9:11. 10:3, 4, 4. 12:1. 14:1, 37. 15:44, 44, 46, 46. Ga 6:1. Ep 1:3. 5:19. 6:12. Col 1:9. 3:16. 1 P 2:5, 5. **to the end.** Ro 16:25. 2 Ch +*20:20. Ac 16:5. 2 C 1:21. 1 Th 3:2, 13. 2 Th 2:17. *3:3. He 13:9. 1 P 5:+10, 12. 2 P 1:12. 3:17, 18.

12. **that I may.** Ro 15:24, 32. Ac +*11:23. 2 C 2:1-3. 7:4-7, 13. 1 Th 2:17-20. *3:7-10. 2 T 1:4. 2 J 4. 3 J 3, 4. **with you.** *or,* in you. **by the mutual.** Ep 4:5. T 1:4. 2 P +1:1. Ju +*3.

13. **Now.** Ro *11:25. 1 C +10:1. *12:1. 2 C 1:8. 1 Th *4:13. **not.** ƒ175B, Ge +21:16. **that oftentimes.** Ro 15:23-28. Ac *19:21. 2 C 1:15, 16. **but.** ƒ4. Aetiologia; or, Cause Shown B963. The rendering of a reason for what is said or done. For other instances of this figure see ver. 16. Ro 3:20. 4:14, 15. **was let.** Ro *15:19, 22. Ac *16:6, 7. 1 Th *2:18. 2 Th *2:7. **that I.** Ro 15:28. Is 27:6. Jn *4:36. *12:24. *15:16. Ph *4:17. Col 1:6. **among.** *or,* in. **even as.** Ro 15:18-20. Ac *14:27. 15:12. *21:18, 19. 1 C *9:2. 2 C *2:14. 10:13-16. 1 Th *1:9, 10. √2:13, 14. 2 T *4:17.

14. **debtor.** Ro 8:12. 13:8g. Ac 9:15. 13:2-4. 22:21. +*26:17, 18. 1 C *4:1, 2. *9:16-23. 2 C *5:14, 15, 20. 1 T *1:11-13. 2 T 2:10. 1 P *4:10. **Greeks.** Ac 28:4. 1 C 1:22. 14:11. Col +*3:11. **Barbarians.** Ac 28:2, 4. 1 C 14:11. Col +*3:11. **both to.** ver. 22. Ro 11:25. 12:16. 16:19. Mt +*11:25. Lk 10:21. 1 C 1:19-22. 2:13. 3:18, 19. 9:16. 2 C 10:12. 11:19. Ep 5:15-17. Ja 3:17, 18. **to the unwise.** Ro 10:19. Pr 1:22. 8:5. Is 35:8. 1 C 14:16, 23, 24. T 3:3.

15. **So.** Ro 12:18. 1 K 8:18. Mk 14:8. 2 C 8:12. **in me is.** lit. according to my ready (mind). i.e. my readiness. ƒ24G, Ge 1:9. **I am ready.** 2 S ◉18:22. Is *6:8. Mt 9:38. Jn *4:34. Ac 21:13. 1 C 9:17. 2 C 10:15, 16. **Rome.** ver. 7. 2 T +1:17.

16. **I am.** Ps 31:17. *40:9, 10. 71:15, 16. *119:46. Mk +*8:38. Lk *9:26. 1 C 2:2. 2 T *1:8, 12, 16. 1 P 4:16. **not.** ƒ175B, Ge +21:16. **the gospel.** Ro 15:19, 29. Lk 2:10, 11. 1 C 9:12, 18. 2 C 2:12. √4:4g. 9:13. Ga 1:7. 1 T 1:11. **for it is.** ƒ4, ver. +13. Ro √10:17. Ps *110:2. Is 53:1. Je √23:29. 1 C *1:18-24. *2:4. 4:20. 14:24, 25. *15:2. 2 C *2:14-16. +*10:4, 5. Col 1:5, 6. 1 Th *1:5, 6. √2:13. He √4:12. **unto salvation.** Ro 7:24, 25. Mt 1:21. Ga 1:4. He *2:14, 15. **to every.** See on Ro 4:11. Lk 2:30-32. +*24:47. Ac 3:26. 1 P 2:6. 1 J √5:10-13. **believeth.** ƒ121F, Ge +49:6. The belief is the effect of the power of God through the preaching of the gospel. **to the Jew.** See on Ro 2:9. **first.** Ro 2:9. Jl 2:28n. Da +*9:25n. Zc 13:1. Ac +*1:8. +*3:26. **and also.** Ro *3:28-30. **the Greek.** Mk 7:26. Jn +7:35.

17. **For therein.** See on Ro *3:21. +9:30. Ps

*145:17. 1 P *1:16. **from faith.** See on Ro *3:3. +9:30. **The just.** Hab *♭2:4. Jn √3:36. Ga *3:11. Ph *3:9. He *10:23, 38. √11:6, 7.

18. **the wrath.** See on Ro 4:15. *5:9. Jn +*3:36. 1 Th 1:10. 2:16. +*5:9. 2 Th 1:6-8. He 10:31. 2 P *2:9. Re +*6:16, 17. **ungodliness.** See on Ro *5:6. **unrighteousness.** See on Ro *6:13. Ga 3:10. **who hold.** ver. *19, *28, *32. Ro *2:3, 15-23. Lk 4:42. 8:15. *12:46, 47. Jn √3:19-21. Ac *24:24, 25. 1 C 11:2g. 2 Th *2:6g, 10. 1 T 4:1, 2.

19. **that which.** T#206. ver. *20. Ro +*2:14, 15. Jb 32:8. Ps *19:1-6. Is *40:26. Je 10:10-13. Jn +6:69 (T#394). Ac *14:16, 17. *17:23-30. Ro 2:14, 15. **known.** lit. the known (i.e. knowable or discoverable) of God. i.e. that which may be learnt even by the natural man. ƒ24G, Ge 1:9. **manifest.** Ps 19:1. T 2:11. **in them.** *or,* to them. **for God.** Jn *1:9.

20. **For the invisible.** Jn +*1:18. Col +*1:15, 16. 1 T 1:17. √6:16. He *11:27. **from the creation.** ver. 19. Dt *4:19. Jb 31:26-28. Ps 8:3, 4. *33:6-9. 104:5, 31. *119:90, 91. 139:13-16. 148:8-12. Mt +*5:45. Mk +10:6. **world.** Gr. *kosmos,* Mt +4:8. **clearly seen.** Nu 24:2. Jb 10:4. Ps 19:1. **being understood by.** Jb 12:9. 26:14. Ps *19:1-6. 94:9. 143:5. Je 5:21, 22. **the things.** Ep 2:10g. **even his.** Ro *16:26. Ge *21:33. Dt *33:27. Ps *90:2. Is +*9:6. *26:4. *40:26. 1 T *1:17. He *9:14. **eternal.** ✻S#126g. Ju 6g. **Godhead.** Ac 17:29. Col √2:9. **so that they are.** *or,* that they may be. Ro *2:1, 15. Jn *15:22mg. **without excuse.** See on Ac 22:1g.

21. **when.** T#162. ver. 19, 28. Mt +13:38 (T#690). Jn √3:19. **they glorified.** T#301. Ro 15:9. Ge +6:6 (T#230). 1 S *2:30. Ps 50:23. 86:9. Da 5:23-25. Ho 2:8. Hab 1:15, 16. Ml *2:2. Lk 17:15-18. Ac 12:23. 2 T 3:2. Re 14:7. *15:4. **neither were thankful.** Dt 32:6. 2 T *3:2. **but became vain.** Ge *6:5. *8:21. 2 K *17:15. Ps 81:12. Ec 7:29. Is 44:9-20. Je +*2:5. *10:3-8, 14, 15. 16:19. Ep +4:17, 18. 1 P 1:18. **their foolish.** ver. 31. Ro 10:19g. 11:10. Dt +*28:29. Is 60:2. Mt +15:16. Ac +*26:18. 1 P *2:9. **darkened.** Is +9:2. Jn √3:19. Ep *4:18.

22. **Professing.** Ro 11:25. Pr 25:14. 26:12. Is 47:10. Je √8:8, 9. 10:14. Mt +*6:23. 1 C *1:19-21. *3:18, 19. **became fools.** T#200-4. Lk +16:15 (T#703).

23. **changed.** ver. 25. Ps *106:20. Je 2:11. **uncorruptible.** 1 T *1:17. **an image.** Dt *4:15-18. 5:8. Ps 115:5-8. 135:15-18. Is 40:18, 26. 44:13. Ezk *8:10. Ac *17:29. 1 C 12:2. 1 P 4:3. Re 9:20. **made like.** ƒ144B, Dt +33:19.

24. **God also.** Ps 81:11, 12. Ho 4:17, 18. Mt +*15:14. Ac 7:42. 14:16. +*17:29, 30. Ep *4:18, 19. 2 Th 2:10-12. **gave them up.** ver. 26, 28. Ep *4:19. **through the lusts.** See on Ro +*6:12. Ps *81:12. 2 P 2:18. **to dishonor.** 1 C 6:13, 18. 1 Th ◉*4:4. 2 T 2:20-22. **between themselves.** ver. 27. Le *18:22.

25. **changed.** ver. 23. **the truth.** ver. 18. 1 Th *1:9. 1 J *5:20. **into a lie.** Is 28:15. *44:19, 20. Je *10:14, 15. 13:25. 16:19. Am 2:4. Jon +*2:8. Hab 2:18. 2 Th +*2:11. **the creature.** ver. 23. Mt 6:24. 10:37. 2 T 3:4. 1 J √2:15, 16. **more.** *or,* rather. **who is.** Ro √9:5. Ps 72:19. 145:1, 2. 2 C 11:31. Ep 3:21. 1 T 1:11, 17. **blessed.** T#215. Ro *9:5. Ps +104:31 (T#223). Mk 14:61. Ac +*7:59n. 2 C 11:31. 1 T 1:11. 6:15. **for ever.** Gr. *aion,* Mt +6:13. lit. unto the ages.

26. **gave them up.** See on ver. 24. **vile affections.** Ge 19:5. Le *18:22-28. Dt 23:17, 18. Jg 19:22. 1 C

+√6:9. Ep 4:19. *5:12. Col 3:5. 1 Th 4:5. 1 T 1:10. Ju 7, *10.

27. **natural use.** He +*13:4. **burned in their lust.** Mt √5:28. Pr 6:25. Ga 5:16. Ep 4:19. Col 3:5. 1 Th 4:5. 2 T *2:22. Ja √1:14, 15. 1 P 2:11. **toward one another.** Ge *19:4, 5. **men with men.** Le *18:22. *20:13. 1 C +*6:9. **unseemly.** Ro 6:21. Ep 5:4. **receiving in themselves.** Nu +√32:23. Dt 28:21, 22, *27, *35, *45, *60, *61. Jb *21:17. Pr 13:15. Ezk 24:16n. Ml *2:2. Ac 12:23. Ga 5:19-21. *6:7. **that recompense.** ver. 23, 24. Ge +*6:13 (T#566). Le *26:21. Dt 7:15. Is 59:18. Ezk 7:4. 9:10. 11:21. Ho 9:7. 2 Th 1:6. He 2:2. 2 P 2:13. Ju *7. **their error.** 2 P 2:19. Ju 10.

28. **as they did.** ver. 18, 21. Ro +2:18mg. Jb 21:14, 15. Pr 1:7, 22, 29. 5:12, 13. 17:16. Je 4:22. 9:6. Ho 4:6. Ac 17:23, 32. Ro 8:7, 8. 1 C 15:34. 2 C √4:4-6. *10:5. 2 Th √1:8. √2:10-12. 2 P 3:5. **not like.** Jb +*21:14. Lk *19:14. **retain.** or, acknowledge. **gave them over.** ver. 24, 26. Ex +*4:21. Is 5:4, 5. **a reprobate mind.** or, a mind void of judgment. Je 6:30. 1 C +9:27. 2 C 13:5-7. 2 T 3:8. T 1:16. **not convenient.** Ep 5:4. Phm 8.

29. **filled.** See on Ro 3:10. **unrighteousness.** ʃ168, Is +1:11. **fornication.** ʃ41, Ge +10:1. *S#4202g. Mt 5:32. 15:19. 19:9. Mk 7:21. Jn 8:41. Ac 15:20, 29. 21:25. 1 C 5:1. *6:13, 18. 7:2. 2 C 12:21. Ga 5:19. Ep 5:3. Col 3:5. 1 Th *4:3. Re 2:21. 9:21. 14:8. 17:2, 4. 18:3. 19:2. **wickedness.** *S#4189g, Mk +7:22. 1 C 5:8. Ep 6:12. **covetousness.** Ps +*10:3. 1 C 5:10. **maliciousness.** *S#2549g. Mt 6:34 (evil). Ac 8:22 (wickedness). 1 C 5:8. 14:20. Ep 4:31. Col 3:8. T 3:3. Ja 1:21 (naughtiness). 1 P 2:1, 16. Trench says this word refers to "the evil habit of mind" (Synonyms, sec. 11, p. 38). **envy.** Ph 14:30. *S#5355g: Mt 27:18. Mk 15:10. Ga 5:21. Ph 1:15. 1 T 6:4. T 3:3. Ja 4:5. 1 P 2:1. **murder.** *S#5408g. Mt 15:19. Mk 7:21. 15:7. Lk 23:19, 25. Ac 9:1 (slaughter). Ga 5:21. He 11:31 (slain). Re 9:21. **debate.** *S#2054g. Ro 13:13 (strife). 1 C 1:11 (contentions). 3:3 (strife). 2 C 12:20. Ga 5:20 (variance). Ph 1:15 (strife). 1 T 6:4 (strife). T 3:9 (contentions). **deceit.** *S#1388g, Mk 7:22. **malignity.** lit. depravity. *S#2550g, only here. Thayer defines it as "bad character, depravity of heart and life." Trench (p. 40) shows it refers to that habit of mind which attributes the worst imaginable motives to the actions of others, "the evil which we trace in ourselves makes us ready to suspect and believe evil in others" (Jb 1:9-11. *2:4, 5). **whisperers.** Ps 41:7. Pr 16:28. 26:20. 2 C 12:20.

30. **Backbiters.** Pr 25:23. 2 C 12:20. Ja 4:11. 1 P 2:1 (evil speakings). **haters of God.** ʃ41, Ge +10:1. T#650. Ro 8:7, 8. Ex ●20:6. Nu 10:35. Dt *7:10. 2 Ch 19:2. Ps ●5:5. 81:15. Pr *8:36. Ho ●9:15. Jn 7:7. 15:23, 24. T 3:3. **despiteful.** *S#5197g. 1 T 1:13 (injurious). **proud.** *S#5244g. Lk 1:51. 2 T 3:2. Ja *4:6. 1 P *5:5. **boasters.** Ro 2:17, 23. 3:27. 1 K 20:11. 2 Ch 25:19. Ps +*10:3. 49:6. 52:1. 94:4. 97:7. Ac 5:36. 2 C 10:15. 2 Th 2:4. 2 T 3:2g. Ja 3:5. 4:16. 2 P 2:18. Ju 16. **inventors.** Ps 99:8. 106:39. Pr 24:8. Ec 7:29. **disobedient.** Dt 21:18-21. 27:16. Pr 30:17. Ezk 22:7. Mt 10:21. 15:4. Lk 21:16. Ep ●+*6:1, 2. 2 T *3:2.

31. **Without understanding.** ver. 20, 21. Ro 3:11. Pr 18:2. Is 27:11. Je *4:22. Mt 15:16. **covenantbreakers.** 2 K 18:14, etc. Is 33:8. Je 3:7. 2 T 3:3. **without natural affection.** or, unsociable. 2 T *3:3. **implacable.** 2 T 3:3 (trucebreakers). **unmerciful.** Ja *2:13.

32. **knowing.** Gr. epiginosko, Mt +11:27. ver. 18,

21. Ro 2:1-5, 21-23. **judgment.** *S#1345g. Ro 2:26 (righteousness). 5:16 (justification), 18 (righteousness). 8:4. Lk 1:6 (ordinances). He 9:1, 10. Re 15:4. 19:8. **worthy.** See on Ro +*6:21. He *10:29. **have pleasure in them.** or, consent with them. Ps 50:18. Je 11:15. Ho 7:3. Mk 14:10, 11. Lk 11:48. Ac 8:1. 22:20. 1 C 7:12, 13g. 13:6. 2 Th 2:12.

ROMANS 2

Those who judge others, and yet transgress themselves, are inexcusable, and cannot escape the judgment of God, 1-6. The measure of his dealings with Jews and Gentiles as it will appear at the day of judgment, 7-16. The apostle solemnly expostulates with the Jews, who trusted in the law, and yet broke it; and shows that external forms will not profit, without a renewed heart and internal piety, which God would accept even in the uncircumcised, 17-29.

1. **Therefore.** Ro *1:18-20. **O man.** ver. *3. Ro *9:20. Mi +*6:8. Lk 12:14. 22:58, 60. 1 C 7:16. Ja 2:20. **whosoever.** ver. 26, 27. 2 S *12:5-7. Ps *50:16-20. Mt √7:1-5. *23:29-31. Lk *6:37. *19:22. Jn *8:7-9. Ja *4:11. **that judgest.** ʃ135, Ps +68:28. **another.** Ro 13:8. 1 C 6:1. 10:24, 29. Ga 6:4g. **for thou that.** ver. *3, *21-23.

2. **judgment.** ver. 5. Ro +1:32. 3:4, 5. 9:14. Ge +*18:25. Jb 34:17-19, 23. Ps 9:4, 7, 8. 11:5-7. 36:5, 6. 62:12. 96:13. 98:9. 145:17. Is 45:19, 21. Je 12:1. Ezk 18:25, 29. Da 4:37. Zp 3:5. Mt +*10:15n. Ac √17:31. 2 Th 1:5-10. Re *15:3, 4. 16:5. 19:2.

3. **thinkest.** 2 S 10:3. Jb 35:2. Ps 50:21. Mt 26:53. **O man.** ver. 1. Da 10:19. Lk 12:14. 22:58, 60. **that thou shalt.** Ro 1:32. Ps 56:7. Pr 11:21. 16:5. Ezk 17:15, 18. Mt 23:33. 1 Th 5:3. He √2:3. 12:25.

4. **despisest.** Ro 6:1, 15. Ps 10:11. Ec √8:11. Je 7:10. Ezk 12:22, 23. Mt 24:48, 49. 2 P 3:3. **riches.** ʃ22D5I, Pr +8:18. Ro *8:32. 9:23. 10:12. 11:33. Ps 86:5. 104:24. 2 C *8:2, 9. *9:8. Ep 1:7, 18. *2:4, 7. 3:8, 16. Ph √4:19. Col 1:27. 2:2. 1 T +*6:17. T √3:4-6. ʃ108B. Idiom B831. "Riches" denotes not merely money, but an *abundance* of that to which it is applied. For other instances of this idiom see Ep 1:7. 3:8. Col 1:27. 2:2. **of his.** ʃ29, Ex +19:6. lit. the go___ thing of God. i.e. the goodness of God. **goodne___ and.** ʃ173, Ge +27:44. Ro +*11:22. Is *63:7-10. Mt +*5:45. Lk +*6:35. Ep 2:7. T 3:4g. **forbearance.** T#227. Ro 3:25. 9:22. 10:21. Ge 18:32. Ex +*34:6. Nu 14:18. Ne 9:30. Ps *78:38. 86:15. Ec √8:11. Is √30:18. 63:7-10. Jon +*4:2, 11. Mk +12:12 (T#67). Ac 14:16. +*17:30. 1 T 1:16. 1 P 3:19, 20. 2 P +*3:9. **longsuffering.** Ro 9:22. Ex *34:6. Ep +4:2. 1 T 1:16. 1 P 3:20. 2 P *3:9, 15. **not knowing.** Is *30:18. 2 P *3:5, 9, 15. Re +2:21. **the goodness.** lit. the kind (thing or gift) of God. i.e. the kindness of God. ʃ24G, Ge 1:9. Ro +*11:22. Jb *33:27-30. Ps *100:5. 130:3, 4. Is √30:18. Je 3:12, 13, 22, 23. Ezk 16:63. Ho *3:5. Lk *15:17-19. 19:5-8. 1 P +2:3g. 2 P 3:9, 15. Re √3:20. **leadeth.** Ho *11:4. Ac +*5:31. 2 T +√2:25. **repentance.** Lk +*13:3.

5. **But after.** Ro 11:25mg. Ex *8:15. 14:17. Dt *2:30. Jsh 11:20. 1 S 6:6. 2 Ch *30:8. 36:13. Ps 95:8. Pr √29:1. Is 48:4. Ezk *3:7. Da *5:20. Zc *7:11, 12. He +*3:13, 15. 4:7. **treasurest.** ʃ22D5.O, Dt +28:12. Ro 9:22. Dt *32:34, 35. Jb *21:29, 30. Am 3:10. Lk +*12:48. Ja +*5:3. **wrath.** ʃ121C1C, Ps +79:6. **the**

day of wrath. Ro 1:18. Jb +*21:30. Ps *110:5. Pr +*11:4. Ezk +*7:19. Zp +*1:18. 1 Th +*5:9. 2 P *2:9. *3:7. Re +*6:17. **revelation.** ver. *2, *3. Ro *1:18. Ec *12:14. 2 Th +*1:6-8. **judgment.** T#384. Mt ◐+*10:15n. 2 Th 1:5. Ju 14, 15.

6. **will render.** Ro 14:12. Jb 34:11. Ps *62:12. Pr 24:12. Is 3:10, 11. Je +*17:10. 32:19. Ezk 18:30. Mt +*16:27n. 25:34, etc. 1 C *3:8. 4:5. 2 C *5:10. Ga √6:7, 8. Re *2:23. √20:12. *22:12. **according to.** Mt 25:15.

7. **To them.** ƒ112, Is +24:3. **patient continuance.** Ro 8:24, 25. Jb *17:9. Ps 27:14. 37:3, 34. La *3:25, 26. Mt 24:12, 13. Lk *8:15. Jn 6:66-69. √8:31. 1 C √15:58. 2 C *4:16-18. Ga √6:9. 2 T *4:7, 8. He *6:12, 15. √10:35, +36. Ja 5:7, 8. Re 2:10, 11. **glory.** ƒ173, Ge +27:44. Ro √8:18. 9:23. Jn 5:41. 2 C 4:16-18. Col √1:27. 1 P 1:7, 8. 4:13, 14. **honor.** Jn *12:25, 26. **immortality.** ƒ63B, Ge +25:28. By ellipsis, supply (he will give). 1 C *15:42, 50, 53, 54. Ep 6:24g. 1 Th 5:23n. 2 T +*1:10. **eternal.** Gr. *aionios,* Mt +18:8. Ro √6:23. Mt +19:16. Jn +4:14. Ga 6:8. 1 T 1:16. T 1:2. 3:7. 1 J *2:25. 3:15. √5:11, 13. Ju 21.

8. **contentious.** Pr 13:10. 1 C 11:16. Ph 1:17. 1 T 6:3, 4. T 3:9. Ja +*3:14. **do not obey.** Ro *1:18. 6:17. 10:16. 15:18. Jb 24:13. Is 50:10. 2 Th √1:8. √2:12. He +*5:9. *11:8. 1 P 3:1. *4:17. **but obey unrighteousness.** Jn √3:18-21. 2 Th √2:10-12. He +*3:12, 13. **indignation.** ƒ173, Ge +27:44. Ro 9:22. Ps *90:11. Is +*66:14. Na *1:6. 2 C *5:11. He +*9:27. +*10:27. Re 14:10. 16:19. **and wrath.** Ps +*7:6. Na +*1:2. Ep +4:31. 1 Th +*5:9. Re +*6:17.

9. **Tribulation.** Ro 8:35. Pr *1:27, 28. Is 8:22. 2 C 4:8. 2 Th *1:6. **upon every.** Ezk 18:20. **soul.** Gr. *psyche,* ƒ171Q1A, Ac +2:41. Ezk +*18:4. Mt 16:26. **of the Jew.** ver. 10. Ro √1:16. 3:29, 30. 4:9-12. 9:24. *10:12. +*15:8, 9. Am 3:2. Mt +*11:20-24. Lk +*2:30-32. +√12:47, 48. +*24:47. Ac 3:26. 11:18. *13:26, 46, 47. 18:5, 6. 20:21. 26:20. 28:17, 28. Ga *2:15, 16. +*3:28. Ep 2:11-17. Col +*3:11. 1 P +*4:17. **Gentile.** Gr. Greek.

10. **glory.** ƒ173, Ge +27:44. ver. 7. Ro 9:21, 23. 1 S *2:30. Ps 112:6-9. Pr 3:16, 17. 4:7-9. 8:18. Lk 9:48. 12:37. Jn 12:26. 1 P *1:7. 5:4. **honor.** 1 P *1:7. **and peace.** ƒ17119A, Ge +43:23. Ro 5:1. 8:6. 14:17. 15:13. Nu 6:26. Jb 22:21. Ps 29:11. 37:37. Is *26:12. 32:17. 48:18, 22. *55:12. 57:19. Je 33:6. Mt 10:13. Lk 1:79. 2:14. 19:42. Jn √14:27. 16:33. Ga *5:22. Ph √4:7. **to every.** Ps √15:2. Pr 11:18. Is 32:17. Ac +*10:35. Ga *5:5, 6. Ja 2:22. 3:13. **that worketh.** Ja *2:17. **to the Jew.** Ro +*1:16. Ac +*3:26. **first.** 1 P +*4:17. **Gentile.** Gr. Greek.

11. **respect of persons.** T#231. Ge +*18:25. Dt +*10:17, 18. +*16:19. 1 S +*16:7. 2 Ch *19:7. Jb 34:19. Pr *24:23, 24. Ezk 18:25. Mt +16:27 (T#556). 22:16. Lk *20:21. Ac +*10:34. Ga 2:6. √6:7, 8. Ep *6:9. Col *3:25. 1 P 1:17.

12. **For.** ver. *14, *15. Ro *1:18-21, 32. Ezk +*16:49, 50. Mt *11:22, 24. Lk *10:12-15. +*12:47, 48. Jn *19:11. Ac √17:30, 31. **sinned without.** ƒ145, Jg +11:40. Ro 10:13-15, 17. Ac 2:23. 1 C *9:21. **perish.** Gr. *apollumi,* Mt +2:13. **without law.** ƒ63I2, Jsh +3:3. Supply by ellipsis (of repetition: from succeeding clause), "shall perish without (being judged by) law." Lk *12:42-48. 16:23-31. Jn √14:6. Ac √4:12. **in the law.** ver. *16. Ro *3:19, 20. *4:15. 7:7-11. 8:3. Dt *27:26. Jn 6:45. 2 C 3:7-9. Ga 2:16-19. *3:10, 22. T 2:11. Ja

√2:10, 11. Re √20:12-15. **by the law.** Ro √3:20, 23. Ec √7:20. Ja √2:10.

13. **For not.** ver. 25. Dt 4:1. 5:1. 6:3. 30:12-14. Ezk 20:11. +*33:30-33. Mt +*7:21-27. Lk 8:21. Ja +*1:22-25. 4:11. 1 J 2:29. *3:7. **but the doers.** Ro √3:20, 23. 10:5. Mt +*7:21. Lk +*6:46. 10:25-29. Jn +*13:17. Ga *3:11, 12. Ja 4:11. **justified.** Ro 3:30. 4:2-5. Ps 143:2. Lk *18:14. Ac 13:39. Ga *2:16. 5:4. Ja 2:21-25.

14. **which have not.** ƒ68, Ge +10:1. ver. +*12. Ro 3:1, 2. Dt 4:7. Ps 147:19, 20. Ac 14:16. *17:30. Ep 2:12. **do by.** ver. 27. Ro 1:+19, 20. 1 C 11:14. Ph √4:8. **are a law.** ver. +*12. Ro 1:32.

15. **Which show.** Ro +*1:19. **the work.** Ga 2:16. **written.** Ro 1:18, 19. Je 31:33. **their conscience,** etc. *or,* the conscience witnessing with them. Ro 9:1. Jn √8:9. Ac 23:1. +*24:16. 2 C +1:12. 5:11. 1 T 4:2. T *1:15. **thoughts.** or, reasonings. 2 C *10:5. **the meanwhile.** *or,* between themselves. Mt 18:15g. **accusing.** Ge 3:8-11. 20:5. 42:21, 22. 1 K 2:44. Jb 27:6. Ec 7:22. 1 J 3:19-21. **or else.** Here is the answer to the question, Are the heathen lost? Paul (ver. 12) clearly states that those without the law will yet *perish* without the law. How can a man be justly condemned if he has never heard the gospel? Paul answers, every man has a conscience, and no one has ever lived up to what he knows to be right. Every man knows he ought to do certain things, and ought not do certain other things, evidenced every time he passes judgment on the actions of others (Ro 2:1). Yet, no man can honestly claim that he has lived up to what he believes he ought to do. On this basis, God can judge a man, and find him wanting, because no man has ever lived up to the light of his own conscience. Is God being fair? Scripture elsewhere teaches that God is absolutely just (Ge +*18:25), and will reward every man according to his works (Ro +2:6), and there will be degrees of punishment (Lk +*12:47, 48). If only those who reject the gospel are lost, it would be safer not to preach the gospel. If a person could be saved without hearing the gospel, simply because he has not heard, then it would logically be safer not to preach the gospel, so that no one would hear, and all would be saved! There would be no reason for any missionary effort. But the command of Christ is to preach the gospel to every creature, because only through faith in Christ can one have salvation (Jn √14:6. Ac √4:12). The Bible does not teach that most men will be saved; rather, Jesus himself said most will be lost, and only a few saved (Mt +*7:14). In *Mere Christianity* (Part I), C. S. Lewis has a masterful argument based largely on this passage in Romans, proving the existence of God on the basis of man's sense of moral absolutes (his sense that he ought to do some things, and ought not do other things), for only God could be the source of such universal belief and conviction based upon them. **excusing.** 2 C +7:11g.

16. **God.** ver. 5. Ro 3:6. 14:10-12. Ge +*18:25. Ps 9:7, 8. 50:6. 96:13. 98:9. Ec 3:17. 11:9. *12:14. Mt +*10:15n. +*16:27. *25:31, etc. Lk *8:17. Jn *12:48. Ac 10:42. √17:31. 1 C *4:5. 2 C *5:10. He +√9:27. 1 P 4:5. 2 P *2:9. Re √20:11-15. **the secrets.** Ec 12:14. Mk +*4:22. Lk *8:17. **by Jesus Christ.** Jn *5:22-29. Ac *10:42. √17:31. 2 T +*4:1, 8. **according.** Ro 16:25. Ga 1:11. 1 T *1:11. 2 T 2:8.

17. **thou.** ƒ38D, Ps +27:14. **art called a Jew.** ƒ169,

Je +12:1. ∫184A, 1 C +15:2. ver. 28, 29. Ro 9:4-7. Ps 135:4. Is 48:1, 2. Mt *3:9. +*8:11, 12. Jn 8:33. 2 C 11:22. Ga 2:15. Ep 2:11. Ph 3:3-7. Re 2:9. 3:1, 9. **restest**. ver. 23. Ro *9:4, 31, 32. Je 7:4-10. Ezk 29:7. Mi 3:11. Zp 3:11. Mt *19:20. Lk √10:28. Jn 5:45. 7:19. 9:28, 29. **makest**. Is *45:25. *48:2. Mi 3:11. Jn *8:41.

18. **knowest**. ∫173, Ge +27:44. **his will**. ∫63A3, Mt +19:13. Dt *4:8. Ne 9:13, 14. Ps *147:19, 20. Lk *12:47. Jn +*13:17. Ac +22:14. 1 C 8:1, 2. 16:12. Ja √4:17. **approvest the things that are more excellent**. or, triest the things that differ. Ro 1:28. *12:2. 14:22. 1 C 16:3. Ep 5:10. Ph √1:10mg. 1 Th 2:4. *5:21. He *5:14. **being instructed**. Ro +*15:4. Ps 19:8. √119:98-100, 104, 105, 130. Pr 6:23. 1 C +14:19. 2 T +√3:15-17.

19. **art confident**. Pr 26:12. Is 5:21. 56:10. Mt +*6:23. +*15:14. 23:16-26. Mk 10:15. Jn 7:46-49. *9:34, 40, 41. 1 C 3:18. 4:10. 8:1, 2. Re 3:17, 18. **a guide**. Jb 29:15. **the blind**. Mt +*6:23. +*23:16. **a light**. ∫41, Ge +10:1. Is 49:6, 9, 10. Mt 4:16. 5:14. Lk 1:79. Ac +*26:18. Ph 2:15.

20. **a teacher**. Mt *11:25. 1 C 3:1. He *5:13. 12:9g. 1 P *2:2. **of babes**. He 5:13, 14. **the form**. Ro *6:17. Ga 4:19. 2 T *1:13. *3:5. T 1:16. **knowledge**. Lk +*11:52. **and**. ∫93A, Ge +1:26.

21. **therefore**. T#1847. Ps +*50:16-21. Mt *23:3-28. Lk 4:23. 11:46. +*12:47. 19:22. 1 C 9:27. Ga 6:13. T 2:1-7. **teachest thou**. ∫147A, Ge +50:24. Pr 11:25. **dost thou steal**. ∫147A, Ge +50:24. Is 56:11. Ezk 22:12, 13, 27. Am 8:4-6. Mi 3:11. Mt 21:13. 23:14.

22. **that sayest**. Jn 8:7, 9. **adultery**. ∫147A, Ge +50:24. Je 5:7. 7:9, 10. 9:2. Ezk 22:11. Mt 12:39. 16:4. Ja *4:4. **sacrilege**. Dt 7:25, 26. Ml 1:8, 14. *3:8. Mk 11:17. Ac 19:37.

23. **that makest**. ver. 17. Ro 3:2, 27. 9:4. Je √8:8, 9. Mt 19:17-20. Lk 10:26-29. 18:11. Jn 5:45. 9:28, 29. Ja 1:22, etc. √4:16, 17. **law**. ∫147A, Ge +50:24. **through breaking**. Ga 6:13. **dishonorest**. Ml 1:6.

24. **name of God**. Is ⟩52:5. La 2:15, 16. Ezk 36:20-23. Mt 18:7. 1 T 5:14. 6:1. T 2:5, 8. **is blasphemed**. Ex +*20:7. Ga ◑1:24. Ja +2:7. **as it is written**. 2 S √12:14. Ezk *36:20-23. 2 P 2:2.

25. **circumcision**. ver. 28, 29. Ro 3:1, 2. 4:11, 12. Dt 30:6. Je 4:4. Ga *5:3-6. 6:15. Ep 2:11, 12. **if thou**. ∫184C, Mt +4:9. **but if**. ∫184C, Mt +4:9. ver. 23. Je 9:25, 26. Ac 7:51.

26. **if the**. ∫184C, Mt +4:9. **uncircumcision keep**. Ro 3:30. Is 56:6, 7. Mt +*8:11, 12. 15:28. Ac +*10:2-4, 34, 35. 11:3, etc. 1 C *7:18, 19. Ep 2:11. Ph 3:3. Col 2:11. **the righteousness**. Ro +1:32. **uncircumcision**. ∫145, Jg +11:40.

27. **if it fulfill**. Ro 8:4. 13:10. Mt 3:15. 5:17-20. Ac 13:22. Ga 5:14. **judge thee**. ∫63A4, 1 K +3:22. Ezk *16:48-52. Mt +*12:41, 42. He 11:7. **by the letter**. ver. 20, 29. Ro 7:6-8. 2 C 3:6. **and**. ∫93A, Ge +1:26. By *Hendiadys*, "literal circumcision." Render, accounting for the ellipsis (absolute: of connected words), ∫63A4, 1 K +3:22: "And shall not uncircumcision which by nature fulfilleth the law, condemn thee (though thou art a Jew), who, through the literal circumcision, art a transgressor of the law?"

28. **For he**. Ro *9:6-8. Ps 73:1. Is *1:9-15. *48:1, 2. Ho 1:6-9. Mt *3:9. Jn 1:47. *8:37-39. Ga *6:15. Re *2:9. **outwardly**. ver. 17. **neither**. Je *9:25, 26. Ro *4:10-12. 1 P *3:21.

29. **But he**. So Rabbi Lipman (Nizzachon, Num. 21, p. 19) states, that "faith does not consist in *circumcision*, but in the *heart*. He who has not genuine faith is not a partaker of the Jewish circumcision; but he who has genuine faith is a *Jew*, although *not* circumcised;" agreeably to which is the maxim of the Talmudists, "That the Jews sit in the inmost recesses of the heart" (Nidda, fol. 20. 2). **which is one inwardly**. Caution must be taken not to apply this verse in such a way as to deprive natural Israel of its covenant promises, and wrongly transfer them to "spiritual Israel" (Ro 9:6. Ga 6:16) or the Church (Is 60:21n). T#118. Ro 6:6. Ex 19:5. Le 26:41, 42. Dt +*10:16. *30:6. Ne +10:29 (T#502). 1 S +*16:7. 1 K 8:23. 1 Ch *29:17. Ps 45:13. 78:10. Je *4:14. Mt *23:25-28. Lk *11:39, 40. 17:21. Jn *4:23, 24. Ga 3:9, 29. 1 P *3:4. **circumcision**. Ro √4:11, 12. Dt 10:16. *30:6. Je *4:4. Ezk 44:7. Ac 7:51. Ph *3:3. Col *2:11, 12. **inwardly**. 1 P +3:4. **spirit**. Gr. *pneuma*, Ac +18:25n. ver. *27. Ro *7:6. *14:17. Jn *3:5-8. 2 C *3:6. Ph *3:3. **the letter**. ver. 27. Ro 7:6. 2 C *3:6. **whose praise**. Jn *5:44. *12:43. 1 C *4:5. 2 C *10:18. Ga 6:16. 1 Th 2:4. 1 P 1:7. *3:4. **not of men**. Mt +*6:1, 2. Ga 1:10. 1 Th *2:4.

ROMANS 3

The advantages which the Jews possessed, 1, 2. The unbelief of some does not render the faith of God of no effect, 3, 4; who is just in punishing sin, though he takes occasion from it to display his own glory, 5-8. Passages from the Old Testament adduced to prove that the Jews, as well as others, are "all under sin," 9-19; so that no flesh is justified by the deeds of the law, 20. The "righteousness of God without the law" is "unto all and upon all that believe," without any difference, 21, 22. As all have sinned, whether Jews or Gentiles; all must be justified by the free grace of God, through faith in Christ, and the redemption of his blood, that God may be glorified, and boasting excluded, 23-30. This establishes the law, 31.

1. **advantage**. Ro *2:25-29. Ge *25:32. Ec 6:8, 11. Is *1:11-15. Ml *3:14. 1 C *15:32. He *13:9.

2. **Much**. ver. *3. Ro 11:1, 2, 15-23, *28, 29. Ph ◑3:3. **because**. Ro *2:18. *9:4. Dt *4:7, 8. Ne *9:13, 14. Ps *78:4-7. *147:19, 20. Is +√8:20n. Ezk *20:11, 12. Lk *16:29-31. Jn +4:22. +√5:39. 2 T +√3:15-17. 2 P *1:19-21. Re *19:10. **committed**. T#1079. 1 C 9:17. 2 C 5:19. Ga 2:7. 1 T 6:20. **the oracles**. Ro 1:2. Dt 4:5, 6. Ps *119:140. Da *10:21. Ac +7:38. 2 T +*3:15, 16. He *5:12. 1 P *4:11. 2 P +*1:20n, 21. Re 22:6.

3. **what if**. ∫184A, 1 C +15:2. ∫152B, Is +49:14. **some**. ∫175A, Ge +27:44. Ro 9:6. *10:16. 11:1-7. Mk +16:16. He *4:2. **shall**. ∫85C, Ge +18:14. Ro *11:29. Nu *23:19. 1 S 15:29. Is +*54:9, 10. √55:11. *65:15, 16. Je +√33:24-26. Mt 24:35. 2 T *2:13. He 6:13-18. **faith**. or, faithfulness. Ps 36:5. 84:7. La 3:23. Jn 1:16. 2 C 3:18. Ga 5:22. 2 Th 1:3. T *1:1, 2.

4. **God forbid**. or, be it not so. ∫61, Ho +9:14. ver. 6, 31n. Ro 6:2, 15. 7:7, 13. 9:14. 11:+√1, 11. Lk +20:16. 1 C 6:15. Ga 2:17. 3:21. *6:14. **let God**. Dt *32:4. Jb 40:8. Ps *100:5. *119:160. *138:2. Mi *7:20. Jn *3:33. +8:26. 2 C 1:18. T √1:2. He *6:18. 1 J 5:*10, 20. Re 3:7. **but every**. ver. 7. Ps 62:9. 116:11. **That thou**. Jb *36:3. Ps ⟩51:4. Mt 11:19. **art judged**. Nu 35:12. Jb 9:32. Jl 3:2. 1 C 6:1g.

5. **But if.** ſ184A, 1 C +15:2. ver. 7, 25, 26. Ro 5:8, 20, 21. **commend.** Ro √5:8. Is 5:16. 2 C +3:1. 7:11. Ga 2:18g. **what shall.** Ro 4:1. 6:1. 7:7. *9:13, 14, 30. **Is God.** Ro 2:5. 3:19. *9:18-20. *12:19. Dt 32:39-43. Ps *58:10, 11. *94:1, 2. Na +*1:2, 6-8. 2 Th *1:6-9. Re *15:3, 4. *16:5-7. 18:20. **who taketh vengeance.** Ro +*2:5. **I speak.** ſ104. Hypotimesis; or, Under-estimating B480: parenthetic addition by way of apology or excuse. For another instance of this figure see 2 C 11:23. Ro *6:19. 1 C 9:8. 15:32. 2 C 11:17, 21. Ga 3:15.

6. **God forbid.** See on ver. 4. **for then.** Ro +2:16. Ge +*18:25. Jb *8:3. *34:17-19. Ps *9:8. *11:5-7. *50:6. 67:4. *96:13. 98:9. Mt +*10:15n. Ac √17:31. **world.** Gr. *kosmos*, Mt +4:8.

7. **if the truth.** ſ184A, 1 C +15:2. ver. 4. Ro 15:8. Ge 37:8, 9, 20. 44:1-14. 50:18-20. Ex 3:19. 14:5, 30. 1 K 13:17, 18, 26-32. 2 K 8:10-15. Mt 26:34, 69-75. **abounded.** 2 C *4:15. **why yet.** Ro 9:19, 20. Is 10:6, 7. Ac 2:23. 13:27-29.

8. **as.** ſ81, Ge +15:13. **we be.** Mt 5:11. 1 P 3:16, 17. **slanderously.** 1 C 10:30g. 2 C 6:8. **some affirm.** 1 C +11:16. **Let us.** Ro 5:20. *6:1, 15. 7:7. Is 5:20. Ju 4. **damnation.** Ph 3:19.

9. **What then.** ver. 5. Ro 6:15. 11:7. Ac 21:22. 1 C 10:19. 14:15. Ph 1:18. **are we.** ver. 1, 22, 23. Is +*65:5n. Lk 7:39. *18:9-14. 1 C 4:7. **proved.** Gr. charged. Ro 1:28, etc. 2:1-29. **and Gentiles.** Ro *1:18-32. **that they.** ver. 19, 23. Ro 7:14. 11:32. Ga *3:10, 22. **all under.** 1 K 8:46. 2 Ch 6:36. Jb 15:14-16. Ps 130:3. 143:2. Pr *20:9. Ec +*7:20. Is √53:6. √64:6. 1 J √1:8, 10.

10. **As it is.** ver. 4. Ro 11:8. +*15:3, 4. Is +√8:20n. 1 P 1:16. **There.** ſ92G, Lk +4:18. Ps *)14:1-3. *)53:1-3. **none.** ver. √23. Dt 4:29. Jb *14:4. *15:14, 16. *25:4. Je +*17:9. Mt *15:19. Mk +*7:21, 22. *10:18. Ac ●*8:27-31. ●√10:2, 31, 34, 35. 1 C +*6:9, 10. Ga √5:19-21. Ep *2:1-3. *5:3-6. Col 3:5-9. 1 T 1:9, 10. 2 T *3:2-5. T 3:3. 1 J √1:8-10. Re +*21:8. 22:15.

11. **none that understandeth.** Ro *1:22, 28. Ps *14:2-4. *53:2, 4. 94:8. Pr 1:7, 22, 29, 30. Is *27:11. Je *4:22. Ho *4:6. Mt +*13:13, 14, 19. T 3:3. 1 J ●*5:20. **seeketh.** Ro *8:7. 2 Ch 15:2. 19:3. Jb *21:15, 16. Is *9:13. 31:1. √55:6. 65:1. Ho 7:10.

12. **They are.** Ex 32:8. Ps *14:3. Ec *7:29. Is √53:6. *59:8. Je *2:13. Ep *2:3. 1 P *2:25. **become.** Ge *1:31. *6:6, 7. Mt *25:30. Phm 11. **there is none.** Ps *53:1. Ec √7:20. Is √64:6. Ep √2:8-10. Ph √2:12, 13. T *2:13, 14. Ja *1:16, 17.

13. **throat.** ſ121BF1, Ps +5:9. Ps)5:9. Je 5:16. Mt 23:27, 28. Lk 11:44. **with their.** ver. 4. Ps 5:9. 12:2-4. 36:3. 52:2. 57:4. Pr 2:16. 7:5. Is 59:3. Je 9:3-5. Ezk 13:7. Mt *12:34, 35. *15:18, 19. Ja 3:5-8. **the poison.** Dt 32:33. Jb 20:14-16. Ps)140:3. Ja +3:8.

14. **Whose mouth.** Ps)10:7. 59:12. 109:17, 18. Ja 3:10. **cursing.** Ro 12:14. Ex 21:17. 1 S 17:43. 2 S 16:5. Pr 20:20. *26:2. 30:11. Ec *7:22. *10:20. Mt 26:74. Lk *6:28. Ja 3:9. **bitterness.** He +*12:15.

15. **Their feet.** ſ171Q21, Pr +1:16. Pr)1:16. 6:18. Is)59:7, 8. Lk 23:40. **are swift.** T#701. Ge 40:23. 49:5, 6. Dt 32:6, 15. 2 Ch 24:22. Jb +21:15 (T#689). Ps +2:2 (T#68). +12:5 (T#523). 35:11-16. +38:11 (T#205). +42:10 (T#511). Ec 9:15. Is 1:2, +15 (T#734). Ezk +22:29 (T#488). Mt +13:38 (T#690). 2 T +3:12 (T#467).

16. **Destruction.** Ps +*9:17. *55:23. **misery.** Ps *32:10. Ja 5:1.

17. **way of peace.** Ro *5:1. Is *57:21. 59:8. Mt +*7:14. Lk 1:79.

18. **no fear.** Ge 20:11. Ps)36:1. Pr *8:13. 16:6. 23:17. Mt +*10:28. Lk 23:40. He *12:28, 29. Re 19:5.

19. **we know.** Ro 7:14. 8:22, 28. **what things.** ver. 2. Ro *2:12-18. Jn 10:34, 35. 15:25. 1 C 9:20, 21. Ga 3:23. 4:5, 21. 5:18. **that every.** ver. 4. Ro 1:20. 2:1. 1 S 2:9. Jb 5:16. 9:2, 3. Ps 63:11. 107:42. Ezk 16:63. Mt 22:12, 13. Jn 8:9. 1 C 1:29. **and all the.** ver. 9, 23. Ro *2:1, 2. Ga 3:10, 22. **world.** Gr. *kosmos*, Mt +4:8. **guilty before God.** *or*, subject to the judgment of God. T#128. Ge 42:21. Ex 9:27. Mt 22:11. Lk +16:25 (T#573-2).

20. **Therefore.** ver. *28. Ro *2:13. 4:13. 9:32. Ac +*13:39. Ga 2:*16, 19. *3:10-13. *5:4. Ep √2:8, 9. T *3:5-7. Ja *2:9, 10. **shall no.** Gr. not any. ſ108E3, Ps +103:2. **flesh.** ſ171E1, Ge +6:12. ſ171Q6, Ge +6:12. Jb *25:4. Ps *130:3. √143:2. Lk +3:6. Ja *2:20-26. **in his sight.** Jb *15:15. *25:5. **for by the.** ſ4, Ro +1:13. Ro 4:15. 5:13, 20. *7:7-9. 1 C 15:56. Ga 2:19.

21. **righteousness.** Ro √1:17. 5:19, 21. √10:3, 4. Ge +*15:6. Is *45:24, 25. 46:13. 51:8. *54:17. 61:10. Je +*23:5, 6. 33:16. Da *9:24. Ac *15:11. 1 C *1:30. 2 C √5:21. Ga 5:5. Ph *3:9. He *11:4, etc. 2 P 1:1. **manifested.** Ro 16:26. 2 T 1:10. **being.** Dt *18:15-19. Lk +*24:44. Jn *1:45. *3:14, 15. *5:46, 47. Ac *26:22. He 10:1-14. **by the law.** ſ145, Jg +11:40. Lk +*16:16. **and the.** Ro *1:2. *16:26. Ac *3:21-25. +*10:43. 26:22. *28:23. Ga 3:8. 1 P *1:10, 11.

22. **righteousness** Ro 5:19. 10:4. Je 23:6. 33:16. 1 C 1:30. Ph 3:9. 2 P 1:1. **which is.** Ro *4:3-13, 20-22. *5:1, etc. *8:1. Ph *3:9. 2 T +*3:15. **by faith of.** ſ181E, Ge +3:24 or ſ181B, Nu +24:4. **unto all.** Ro *4:6, 11, 16, 22. 10:4. Ga √2:16. *3:6. Ja *2:23. **and upon.** Is *61:10. Mt *22:11, 12. Lk *15:22. Ga 3:7-9. **for there.** Ro 2:1. *10:12. Ac *15:9. 1 C 4:7. Ga +*3:28. 5:6. Col +*3:11.

23. **all have sinned.** ver. *9-19. Ro +*1:28-32. 2:1, etc. *11:32. Ec √7:20. Ga *3:22. 1 J √1:8-10. **come short.** Da *5:27. He *4:1. **of the glory.** ſ24.O, Ge +9:5. Ro 1:23. *5:2. 15:7. Da *5:23. Jn 5:44. 11:4, 40. Ac 7:55. 1 C √10:31. 11:7. 2 C 4:6, 15. Ph 1:11. 2:11. 1 Th *2:12. 2 Th 2:14. 1 T 1:11. T 2:13. 1 P 4:13. 5:1, 10. Re 15:8. 19:1. 21:11, 23.

24. **justified.** Ro *4:16. 5:16-19. √8:30. 1 C *6:11. Ep *2:7-10. T √3:5-7. **freely.** Mt +10:8. **by his grace.** Ro 4:4, 5, 16. Ac +*11:23. +15:11. **through.** Ro *5:9. Is *53:11. Mt +*20:28. 1 C 1:30. Ga 3:13. Ep *1:6, 7. Col *1:13, 14. 1 T 2:6. T √2:14. He 9:2-15. 1 P *1:18, 19. 2:24. Re 5:9. 7:14. **redemption.** Ro 8:23. Da 4:32. Lk +1:68. 1 C *1:30. *7:23. Ep *1:7, 14. +*4:30. Col *1:14. He 9:15. 11:35. **Christ Jesus.** Ro 6:3, 11, 23. Ac 24:24.

25. **set forth.** *or*, foreordained. Ro 9:11. Ac *2:23. 3:18. *4:28. *15:18. Ga 3:1g. Ep 1:9. 3:11. 2 T +*1:9. 1 P *1:18-20. Re √13:8. **to be.** Ex 25:17-22. Le *16:15. He 9:5g. 1 J √2:2. *4:10. **through.** Ro 5:1, *9, 11. Is 53:11. Jn 6:47, 53-58. Col 1:20-23. He 10:19, 20. **faith in.** T#577. Ro 5:8, 9, 11. Le +*17:11. Is 53:5. Mt 20:28. 26:28. Jn 1:29. 3:14, 15, 36. 6:51. 10:15. Ac +√20:28n. 1 C 5:7. +*15:3. Ga 1:4. *2:20. 3:13. Ep *1:7. 2:13. Col 1:20. 1 T 1:1. He 9:12-14, 22, *26-28. 10:10-14, 19, 20. 1 P 1:18, 19. *2:24. *3:18. 1 J *1:7. Re +*1:5. 5:9. **blood.** ſ117, Ge +19:8. **to declare.**

ver. 26. Ps 22:31. 40:10. 50:6. 97:6. 119:142. 1 J 1:10. **remission.** *or,* passing over. ver. 23, 24. Ro 4:1-8. Ac +*13:38, 39. *17:30. 1 T *1:15. He 9:15-22, 25, 26. 10:4. 11:7, 14, 17, 39, 40. Re 5:9. *13:8. *20:15. **that are past.** Ac 14:16. +*17:30. He 9:15. **forbearance.** Ro 2:4.

26. **To declare.** ♪67. Epanalepsis; or, Resumption B206: the repetition of the same word after a break, or parenthesis. For other instances of this figure see 1 C 4:11, 13. 10:25, 29. Ep 3:1, 14. Ph 1:22, 24. **at this time.** Ro 11:5. **his righteousness.** Hab *1:13. **that he.** Ro 2:13. Dt 32:4. Ps *85:10, 11. Is *42:21. *45:21. Zp 3:5, 15. Zc +*9:9. Ac 13:38, 39. 1 J √1:9. Re *15:3. **the justifier.** ver. 30. Ro 4:5. *8:33. Jb *25:4. Is 43:25. *53:5. Ac *13:39. Ga 3:8-14.

27. **Where.** ♪136, Is +60:12. ver. 19-21, 28. Ro 2:17, 23. 4:2. Is *45:25. Ezk 16:62, 63. 36:31, 32. Zp 3:11. Lk 18:9-14. Ac +*13:39. 1 C +*1:29-31. 4:7. Ep √2:8-10. 2 T +*1:9. **boasting.** Ro 4:2. 5:2, 11. Ph +1:26. **of works.** Ro 9:11, 32. 10:5. 11:6. Ga *2:16. **but by.** Ro 7:21, 23, 25. 8:2. 9:31. Mk *16:16. Jn √3:36. Ga 3:22. 1 J √5:11, 12. **law.** ♪145, Jg +11:40.

28. **we conclude.** ver. 20-22, 26. Ro *4:5. *5:1. *8:3, 4. Jn √3:14-18. √5:24. 6:40. Ac +*13:38, 39. 1 C 6:11. Ga *2:16. 3:8, 11-14, 24. Ph *3:9. T 3:7. **without.** Ro *4:6. 11:6. Ga *5:4, 5. Ja +2:18.

29. **the God of.** Ro +*1:16. 9:24-26. 11:12, 13. 15:9-13, 16. Ge +*17:7, 8, 18. Ps 22:27. 67:2. 72:17. Is 19:23, 25. 54:5. Je 16:19. 31:33. Ho 1:10. Zc 2:11. *8:20-23. Ml 1:11. Mt +*22:32. +√28:19. Mk *16:15, 16. Lk *24:46, 47. Ac 9:15. +10:34. 22:21. 26:17, 18. Ga 3:14, 25-29. Ep +*3:6. Col +*3:11.

30. **one God.** ver. 28. Ro √4:11, 12. √10:12, 13. Ga *2:14-16. *3:8, 20, 28. 5:6. 6:15. Ph 3:3. Col 2:10, 11. Ja +2:19. **shall.** ♪96C9, Ge +2:10. **uncircumcision.** ♪121N1, Ge +31:54. Ro +2:26. 4:9. Ga 3:8.

31. **Do we.** Ro 4:14. Ps 119:126. Je √8:8, 9. Mt *5:17. 15:6. Ga 2:21. 3:17-19. Ja *2:26. **God forbid.** Gr. *Mee genoito,* literally, *let it not be,* and which might be rendered less objectionably, *far from it, by no means.* See on ver. 4. **yea.** Ro 7:7-14, 22, 25. 8:4. *10:4. 13:8-10. Ps *40:8. Is 42:21. Je 31:33, 34. Mt 3:15. 5:20. 1 C 9:21. Ga 2:19. 5:18-23. He *10:15, 16. Ja 2:8-12. **establish.** Mt +*5:17, 18.

ROMANS 4

Justification by faith proved, from the example of Abraham; and the words of David, 1-8. Abraham was justified before circumcision (which was "the seal of the righteousness of faith"), that he might be the father of all believers, whether circumcised or not, 9-12. The promise was not given to him through the law, else it had been void; but, being "of faith by grace," it is sure to all his spiritual seed, in every age and nation, 13-17. The nature and strength of that faith, by which he was justified, 18-22. This was recorded, not for his sake only, but to show that all who believe in Christ, as crucified and risen, are justified in like manner, 23-25.

1. **What.** Ro 6:1. 7:7. 8:31. **Abraham.** ver. 16. Is 51:2. Mt *3:9. Lk *3:8. *16:24, 25, 29-31. Jn 8:33, *37-41, 53, 56. Ac 13:26. 2 C 11:22. Ph *3:3-6. **father.** ♪171G, Ge +13:8. **as pertaining.** ver. 16. Ro +1:3. He 12:9. **found.** ♪171J4, Ge +6:8.

2. **For if.** ♪152B, Is +49:14. ♪184A, 1 C +15:2.

Abraham. See on Ro *3:20-28. Ph *3:9. **he hath.** Ro *3:27. 15:17. Ex 8:9. Je *9:23, 24. 1 C 9:16. 2 C 5:12. 11:12, 30. 12:1-9. Ga *6:13, 14. Ep *2:9. **but.** Ge 12:12, 13, 18, 20. 20:9-13. Jsh 24:2. 1 C 1:29, 31. 4:7. Ga *3:22. Ja ◐2:14.

3. **what.** Ro +9:17. 10:11. 11:2. Is +√8:20n. Mk 12:10. Ja 4:5. 2 P +*1:20n, 21. **Abraham.** ver. 9, 22. Ge √15:6. Ga *3:6-8. T +3:8. Ja *2:23. **counted.** T#182. ver. 5, 9, 11, *22-25. Le 7:8. 17:4. Ps 56:8. 106:31. Is 65:6. Ml *3:16.

4. **to him.** Ro 9:32. *11:6, 35. Dt 9:4, 5. Mt 20:1-16. Ga 5:4. **worketh.** ♪108B. Idiom B828. "To work" is used of seeking to gain salvation by human merit, as opposed to grace. **the reward.** Re 22:12. **of grace.** Ro +3:24.

5. **But to.** ver. 24, 25. Ro 3:22. 5:1, 2. √10:3, 9, 10. Ac +*13:38, 39. Ga *2:16, 17. *3:9-14. Ph *3:9. **believeth.** ver. 24. Ro 3:22, 26-30. 8:30-34. Jn √5:24. +6:29. Ga *3:8. **ungodly.** ♪11, Ge +2:23. Ro 1:17, 18. *5:6-8. Jsh 24:2. Zc *3:3, 4. 1 C +*6:9-11. 1 T *1:13-15. T *3:3-7. **his faith.** See on ver. 3. Hab +*2:4.

6. **David.** Ac +4:25. **blessedness.** ver. 9. Dt 33:29. Ps 1:1-3. 112:1. 146:5, 6. Mt +*5:3-12. Ga *3:8, 9, 14. 4:15. Ep *1:3. **imputeth.** ver. 11, 24. Ro 1:17. *3:22. 5:18, 19. Is *45:24, 25. *54:17. Je +*23:6. 33:16. Da +*9:24. 1 C *1:30. 2 C √5:21. Ph *3:9. 2 P 1:1. **without.** Ro 3:*20, 21, 27, 28. Ep √2:8-10. 2 T +*1:9.

7. **Blessed.** Ps √32:1, 2. 51:8, 9. 85:2. *130:3, 4. Is 40:1, 2. Je *33:8, 9. Mi *7:18-20. Mt 9:2. Lk 7:47-50. **they.** ♪92F3, Mt +4:7.

8. **to whom.** Is *53:10-12. 2 C √5:19-21. Phm 18, 19. 1 P *2:24. *3:18. **will not.** ♪158, Mt +5:18.

9. **Cometh.** ♪63B, Ge +25:28. **this blessedness.** ver. 6. **upon the circumcision.** Ro 3:29, +30. 9:23, 24. *10:12, 13. 15:8-19. Is *49:6. Lk 2:32. Ga 3:*14, 26-28. Ep 2:11-13. 3:8. Col *3:11. **for we.** See on ver. +3.

10. **Not in circumcision.** "Faith was reckoned to Abraham for righteousness," at least 14 years before he was circumcised; the former having taken place some time before Ishmael's birth, at which time he was 86 years old, and the other when Ishmael was 13 years of age, and Abraham 99. See Ge *15:5, 6, 16. 16:1-3. 17:1, 10, 23-27. Ac 10:47n. 1 C 7:18, 19. Ga *5:6. *6:15.

11. **the sign.** T#119. Ge *17:10-13. Ex *12:13. 31:13, 17. Ezk 20:12, 20. Ac 7:8. **a seal.** Ro *2:28, 29. Dt 30:6. Jn +6:27. 2 C *1:22. Ep *1:13. +*4:30. Re 9:4. **righteousness.** ver. 13. Ro 3:22. 9:30. 10:6. Ga 5:5. Ph *3:9. He *11:7. 2 P 1:1. **father.** ver. 12, 16-18. Ro 3:22, 26. 9:6, 33. 10:4, 11. Mt +*8:11. Mk *16:16. Lk +*19:9. Jn √3:15, 16, 36. 6:35, 40, *47. 7:38, 39. 8:33. *11:25, 26. Ga 3:7, *22, 29. 6:16. **of all them.** ver. 16. Ro 3:22. 10:4. **that believe.** Ro √1:16. 3:22. 10:4. 13:11. 15:13. Jn +5:44. Ac +13:12. 1 C 1:21. 3:5. 14:22. 15:2, 11. 2 C 4:13. Ga 3:22. Ep 1:19. 1 Th 1:7. 2:10, √13. 2 Th *1:10. He 4:3. **that righteousness.** See on ver. 6.

12. **to them.** ♪63ID, Nu +26:4. Supply ellipsis (repetition: of preceding connected words), "And the father of the circumcision (that righteousness might be imputed) to them…" Ro 9:6, 7. Mt 3:9. Lk 16:23-31. Jn 8:39, 40. Ga 4:22-31. **walk.** Ga +*5:25. **in the steps.** Jb 33:11. Pr 2:20. SS 1:8. 2 C 12:18. 1 P 2:21.

13. **For the promise.** Ro 9:8. Ge +*12:3. +*17:4, 5, 8, 16. 22:17, 18. 28:14. +*49:10. Ps *2:8. 72:11.

Ac +*13:32. +*26:6. He 6:15, 17. 7:6. 11:9, 17. **heir of the.** Ge 17:6. +*22:17. 35:11. Ex 19:6. Is 43:21. Mt +√5:5. +*24:46, 47. 25:21. Lk 19:17. Ac +*7:5. 1 C 3:21-23. 2 T 2:12. He 1:2. +*11:16. Ja +*2:5. 1 P *2:5, 9. Re 1:6. *2:26. 3:21. √5:10. **world.** Gr. *kosmos,* Mt +4:8. 1 C 6:2. He 11:7. **through the law.** Ga 3:16-18, *29. **but through.** See on ver. 11.

14. **For if.** √4, Ro +1:13. √184A, 1 C +15:2. ver. 16. Ga 2:21. *3:18-24. 5:4. Ph 3:9. He 7:19, 28. **made void.** Ro 3:31. Nu 30:12, 15. Ps 119:126. Is √55:11. Je 19:7. 1 C +1:17. Ga *5:2, 4.

15. **Because.** √4, Ro +1:13. Ro *1:17, 18. *2:5, 6. *3:19, 20. 5:13, *20, 21. *7:7-11. Nu 32:14. Dt 29:20-28. 2 K *22:13. Je 4:8. La 2:22. Ezk *7:19. Zp 1:18. Jn √3:36. 15:22. Ac √17:30, 31. 1 C *15:56. 2 C *3:7-9. Ga √3:10, 19. Ep *5:6. Col *3:6. 1 J 3:4. Re +*6:16, 17. *19:15. **wrath.** √121C1C, Ps +79:6. i.e. inflicts or executes punishments and penalties. By *Metonymy of the Cause,* the thing or action is put for that which is the effect or product of it; here, wrath is put for the punishment which results from it. **where.** Ro *2:12, 13. +3:20. *5:13. **no law.** When no *law,* or *rule* of duty, is enacted and acknowledged, there is no transgression, and consequently no punishment. "*Nomos,*" says Bp. Middleton, "is used by St. Paul of every rule of life, of every revelation, especially of the Mosaic law... Our English version by having almost constantly said *the law,* whatever be the meaning of *nomos* in the original, has made this most difficult epistle still more obscure." When without the article, it is commonly used for *law* in general, when with the article, of the Mosaic law. Checking Bruder's Concordance, "law" occurs without the Greek article in the following passages of Romans: Ro 2:12, -13, -13, 14, 14, -17, 23, 25, 25. 3:20, 20, 21a, 27, 27, 28, 31, 31. 4:13, 14, 15b. 5:13, 13, 20. 6:14, 15. 7:1a, 2a, 7b, 8, 9, 23a, 25, 25. 9:31, 31, 32. 10:4. 13:10. A minus sign (-) before the reference indicates that the Greek article is omitted by some editors of the Greek text, but is a part of the Received text. **no transgression.** Ga 3:19. 1 J 3:4.

16. **of faith.** Ro 3:24-26. 5:1. Jn *1:12, 13. Ga 3:7-12, *22. Ep 2:5, 8. T 3:7. 1 P 1:5. **by grace.** Ro +3:24. **to the end.** Ro 15:8. Ga 3:22. **the promise.** ver. +*13. He 6:13-19. 2 P 1:10. **be sure.** Ro +*15:8. 1 C 1:6. Ph 1:7. He *2:3. 6:16. 9:17g. **to all.** ver. 13. Ga 3:16. **but to.** See on ver. 11. **the father.** ver. 1. Ro *9:8. Is 51:2. Mt +3:9.

17. **I have.** ver. 18. Ge 17:4, ▷5, 16, 20. ch. 25. 28:3. He 11:12. **made.** lit. placed. √171J8. Synecdoche of the Species B631. Verbs having a special meaning are used in a more general sense; here, "to place" is put for "to make." For another instance of this figure see He 1:2. **before him.** *or,* like unto him. Ro 3:29. **whom he.** ver. 3. **who quickeneth.** ver. 2. Ro *8:11. Ps +*71:20. Mt 3:9. Jn 5:+21, 25. 6:63. 1 C 15:45. Ep *2:1-5. 1 T 6:13. He 11:19. 1 P 3:18. **calleth.** Ro √8:29, 30. 9:11, *26. Is 43:6. 44:7. 49:12. 55:12. Ac *15:18. 1 C 1:28. He 11:3, 7. 1 P *2:10. 2 P 3:8. **as though.** Jn +*17:6.

18. **against.** ver. 19. Ro 5:5. 8:24. Ru 1:11-13. Pr 13:12. Ezk 37:11. Mk 5:35, 36. Lk 1:18. Ac 27:25. **hope.** √147F, Ezk +28:2. **in hope.** Ac 2:26. **the father.** ver. 17. **So shall.** Ge √▷15:5, 6.

19. **being.** ver. 20, 21. Ro 14:21. Mt 6:30. 8:26. 14:31. Mk 9:23, 24. Jn +√20:27, 28. **not.** √175B, Ge

+21:16. **considered.** Ge 17:17. 18:11-14. He *11:11-19. **now dead.** He 11:12. **was about.** 1 C 7:26. 11:7, 18. 12:22. 2 C 8:17. 12:16. Ga 1:14. 2:14. Ph 2:6. 3:20g. **an hundred.** Ge 17:17. **deadness.** Ge +*11:30. *18:11.

20. **staggered.** Nu 11:13-23. 2 K 7:2, 19. 2 Ch +*20:15-20. Is 7:9. Je 32:16-27. Mt 21:21. Lk 1:18, 45. **but was strong.** √144D, Ge +40:23. Is 35:4. Da 10:19. 11:32. Hg 2:4. Zc 8:9, 13. 1 C 16:13. 2 C 12:10. Ep +*6:10. 2 T 2:1. **giving glory.** Jn +9:24.

21. **fully.** Ro 8:38. 14:5. Lk +1:1. 2 T 1:12. He 11:13. **had promised.** Jsh 22:4. **he was able.** Ro 14:4. Ge √18:14. Ps *115:3. Je 32:17, 27. Mt 19:26. Lk *1:37, 45. 2 C *9:8. Ep *3:20. He 2:18. *11:19. √108B. Idiom B825. Certain nouns and verbs are used in the New Testament according to Hebrew idiom. "Able," when applied to God or Christ, denotes both *willingness* and *ability.* For other instances of this idiom see Ro 11:23. 14:4. 16:25. He 2:18.

22. **it was imputed.** See on ver. 3, 6.

23. **not written.** Ro +*15:4. Ps 102:18. 1 C 9:9, 10. *10:6, 11. 2 T +√3:16, 17.

24. **for us.** Ac +*2:39. **if we.** Ro √10:9, 10. Mk *16:16. Jn √3:14-16. Ac +*2:24n. *13:30. Ep 1:18-20. He *13:20, 21. 1 P *1:21.

25. **Who was delivered.** √63BC, Ge +9:20. Ro *3:25. *5:6-8. √8:3, 32. Is *53:5, 6, 10-12. Da +*9:24, 26. Zc +*13:7. Mt +*20:28. 1 C +*15:3, 4. 2 C √5:21. Ga *1:4. *2:20. 3:13. Ep 5:2. 1 T 1:15. T *2:14. He *9:14, 15, 28. 1 P 1:18, 19. *2:24. *3:18. 1 J √2:2. 4:9, 10. Re +*1:5. 5:9. 7:14. **and was raised.** Ro √8:33, 34. Nu=18:13. Ac +*2:24n. 1 C=15:17, 20, 23. He 4:14-16. 10:12-14. 1 P *1:21. **for our justification.** Ro 5:18. 1 C 15:17.

ROMANS 5

They who are justified by faith have peace with God, rejoice in hope, and rejoice and glory in tribulations, 1-5. The abundant love of God to them when sinners and enemies, in "reconciling them to himself by the death of his Son," assures them of final salvation, and excites them to rejoice and glory in him, 6-11. As sin and death come upon all men by Adam; so the grace of God, which justifieth unto life, with all concurrent blessings, comes more abundantly on all believers by Jesus Christ, 12-19. The law proved an occasion to the abounding of sin unto death; but this made way for the still greater abounding of grace, as "reigning through righteousness unto eternal life by Jesus Christ," 20, 21.

1. **being justified.** ver. 9, 18. Ro *1:17. *3:22, 26, +28, 30. *4:5, 24, 25. 9:30. √10:10. Jb *25:4. Hab *2:4. Jn √3:16-18. √5:24. Ac +*13:38, 39. Ga *2:16. 3:11-14, 25. 5:4-6. Ph *3:9. Ja 2:23-26. **we have.** √96B, Ge +20:7. **peace.** √171I9B, Is +57:19. ver. 10. Ro +1:7. 10:15. 14:17. 15:*13, 33. Jb 22:21. Ps *85:8-10. 122:6. Is 27:5. *32:17. 54:13. 55:12. *57:19-21. Zc 6:13. Lk 2:14. 10:5, 6. *19:38, 42. Jn *14:27. 16:33. Ac *10:36. 2 C *5:18-20. Ep *2:14-17. Col *1:20, 21. *3:15. 1 Th 5:23. 2 Th 3:16. He 12:28. 13:20. Ja *2:23. **through.** Ro √6:23. Jn √20:31. Ep 2:7.

2. **whom.** Jn *10:7, 9. √14:6. Ac 14:27. Ep *2:18. *3:12. He *10:19, 20. 1 P *3:18. **wherein.** ver. *9, *10. Ro *8:1, 30-39. 14:4. Jn √5:24. 1 C +*15:1, 2. Ep *1:6. *6:13. 1 P *1:4, 5. 5:12. **stand.** √96C1, Ge

+4:1. **and rejoice.** ver. 5, 11. Ro 8:24, 25. *12:12. *15:13. Jb 19:25-27. Ps +*16:9-11. 17:15. Pr *14:32. Col 1:27. 2 Th *2:16, 17. He *3:6. *6:18, 19. 1 P *1:3-9. 1 J *3:1-3. **in hope.** Ro 4:18g. **the glory.** ⨍24N, Ge +17:5. Ro *2:7. +*3:23. √8:17, 18. Ex 33:18-20. Ps *73:24. Mt *25:21. Jn √5:24. 2 C *3:18. *4:17. Col 3:4. 1 Th 2:12. 2 Th 1:9. Re 3:21. *21:3, 11, 23. 22:4, 5.

3. **And not only.** ver. 11. Ro 8:23. 9:10. 2 C 8:19. **so.** ⨍63I1D, Nu +26:4. Supply by ellipsis (of repetition: of preceding connected words), "And not only do we (rejoice in the hope of the glory of God), but we glory also in tribulations" (B102). **but we.** Ro √8:31, 35-37. Ps 34:19. *40:1-3. Mt +*5:10-12. Lk 6:22, 23. Ac *5:41. 2 C 11:23-30. 12:9, 10. Ep 3:13. Ph *1:29. *2:17, 18. Ja *1:2, 3, 12. 1 P *3:14. *4:16, 17. **knowing.** 1 C √15:58. 2 C 4:14, 17. He *12:10, 11. **tribulation.** ⨍50, Ho +2:21. **worketh patience.** Ro 2:7. Lk +21:19. He 10:36. Ja +1:3.

4. **patience.** ⨍50, Ho +2:21. Ro +*15:4. 2 C *1:4-6. 4:8-12. 6:9, 10. Ja 1:12. 1 P *1:6, 7. 5:10. **experience.** 2 C 2:9. 8:2. 13:3. Ph 2:22g. **and experience.** ⨍50, Ho +2:21. Jsh 10:24, 25. 1 S *17:34-37. Ps 27:2, 3. 39:7. 42:4, 5. 71:14, 18-24. La √3:22-25. 2 C 4:8-10. 2 T +*4:16-18. 1 J *5:14.

5. **hope.** ⨍50, Ho +2:21. Jb 27:8. Ps 22:4, 5. *31:17. 119:16. Is 28:15-18. 45:16, 17. *49:23. Je 17:5-8. Ph 1:20. 2 Th 2:16. 2 T √1:12. He *6:18, 19. **not.** ⨍175B, Ge +21:16. **because.** Ro *8:14-17, 28. Mt 22:36, 37. 1 C 8:3. He 8:10-12. 1 J √4:19. **the love.** Ro 15:30. Ps 18:1. 146:8. Mt +*28:19n. Ga 5:22. Ep ❍+*5:2. Col 1:8. 2 Th +*3:5. 2 T 1:7. 1 J ❍+*4:16. **shed.** ⨍22C38, Ps +79:6. Is 44:3-5. Ezk 36:25-27. Ac 2:17, 18, 33. 10:45. 2 C *1:22. 3:18. 4:6. Ga *4:6. √5:22. Ep *1:13, 14. 3:16-19. +*4:30. T *3:5, 6. **holy.** Gr. *pneuma*, Mt +1:18n.

6. **For.** ver. 8, 10. Ro 8:3. Ezk 16:4-8. Ho 13:9. Ep *2:1-5. Col 2:13. T *3:3-5. **without.** ⨍175A, Ge +27:44. Jb 26:2. Is 41:1. La 1:6. Da 11:15. **in due time.** *or*, according to the time. Mk +1:15. Ga √4:4. 1 T 2:6. 6:15. T 1:3. He 9:26. 1 P *1:18-21. He 13:8. **Christ.** ver. 8. Ro +4:25. 1 Th +*5:9. **ungodly.** See on Ro 4:5. 11:26. Ps +*1:1. 1 T 1:9. T *2:12. 2 P 2:5, 6. 3:7. Ju 4, 15, 18.

7. **scarcely.** Jn 15:13. 1 J 3:16. **a good.** 2 S 18:27. Ps 112:5. Ac 11:24. **some.** Ac 16:4. 2 S 18:3. 23:14-17.

8. **God.** ⨍101, Dt +32:42. **commendeth.** ver. 20, 21. Ro +3:5. Jn *15:13. Ep 1:6-8. 2:7. 1 T 1:16. **his love.** Ro 8:39. Jn +*3:16. **in that.** ver. 6, 10. Is √53:6. 1 P *3:18. 1 J *3:16. *4:9, 10. **Christ died.** 1 C +*15:3.

9. **being.** See on ver. 1. Ro 3:24-26. *8:29, 30. Ep *2:13. He √9:14, 22. 1 J √1:7. **his blood.** ⨍117, Ge +19:8. Ro +*3:25. 1 C 1:30. **we shall.** ver. 10. Ro 1:18. 8:1, 30. Jn √5:24. 1 Th +*1:10. **be saved.** Jn 6:39, 40. 1 C 1:8, 9. Ph 1:6. Col 3:3, 4. 2 T 4:18. He 5:9. *7:25. 1 P 1:3, 5. **from wrath.** T#854. Ro +1:18. ❍2:5. 12:19. Ge 5:24. 18:23, 25. 19:14, 22. Jsh 6:16, 25. Ps *86:13. Pr 10:2. 11:4. *15:24. Is *45:17. Lk +√21:36. Jn √3:15. *8:51. 1 Th √1:10. 2:16. √5:9, 10. He 11:31. Re +*3:10. +*6:17. √20:6.

10. **For if.** ⨍184A, 1 C +15:2. **when.** ver. 6, 8. Ro 8:7. 2 C *5:18, 19, 21. Col 1:20, 21. 1 J 4:10. **reconciled.** ver. 11mg. Ro √8:32. Le 6:30. 2 Ch 29:24. Ezk 45:20. Da +*9:24. Ep *2:16. He *2:17. **the death.** He 2:9. ⨍171S8. Synecdoche of the Part B651. The death of

Christ is put for the atonement and its results. For other instances of this figure see 1 C 11:26. Col 1:22. He 2:14. **reconciled.** 2 C 5:18, 19. Ep 2:15, 16. Col *1:21, 22. **we shall.** Mt 24:13. Jn 5:26. 6:40, 57. √10:28, 29. 11:25, 26. 14:19. 2 C 4:10, 11. Col *3:3, 4. He √7:25. Re *1:18. **his life.** Jn 14:19.

11. **And not.** ver. +3. **so.** ⨍63I1D, Nu +26:4. Supply by ellipsis (repetition: of preceding connected words), "And not only (are we saved from wrath through him), but we also joy in God (as our God) through our Lord Jesus Christ" (B102). **but we.** Ro *2:17. *3:29, 30. 1 S 2:1. Ps *9:2. 32:11. 33:1. 43:4. 104:34. 149:2. Is 61:10. Hab *3:17, 18. Lk 1:46, 47. Ga 4:9. 5:22. Ph 3:1, 3. *4:4. 1 P *1:8. **by whom.** Jn *1:12. 6:50-58. 1 C 10:16. Col 2:6. **received.** Ro 11:15. **atonement.** *or*, reconciliation. ver. 10. Nu=8:21. 2 C 5:18, 19.

12. **as by.** ver. 19. Ge *3:6. Ps *51:5. **world.** Gr. *kosmos*, Mt +4:8. **and death.** Ro √6:23. Ge +*2:17. *3:19, 22-24. Ezk +*18:4. 1 C *15:21. Ja *1:15. Re 20:14, 15. **so death.** T#144. ver. 17. 1 C 15:22. **for that.** *or*, in whom. 2 C 5:4. Ph 3:12. 4:10g. **all.** Ro √3:23. Ps 14:1. Ja 3:2. 1 J √1:8-10. **have sinned.** ⨍15D, Mk +11:32.

13. **until.** Ge 4:7-11. 6:5, 6, 11, 12. *8:21. 13:13. 18:20, 21. 19:4, 32, 36. 38:7, 10. **world.** Gr. *kosmos*, Mt +4:8. **not imputed.** T#161. Ro 3:19. *4:15. Jn +3:19 (T#309). *9:41. 15:22. 1 C 15:56. Phm 18g. Ja *4:17. 1 J *3:4, 14.

14. **death.** ver. 17, 21. Ge 4:8. 5:5-31. *7:22. *19:25. Ex 1:6. He +*9:27. **even.** Ro *8:20, 22. Ex *1:22. *12:29, 30. Ho +*6:7. Jon *4:11. **who is the figure.** ⨍179. Type B768. A figure or ensample of something future and more or less prophetic, called the "Antitype." Or "type (pattern, or resemblance, *tupon*) of him who was to come," i.e. the Messiah. In this, says Beza, that each of them shares what he has with his; but they are clearly unlike in this, that Adam by nature communicates sin unto death to his posterity, but Christ by grace communicates his righteousness unto his people unto life. Mr. Baxter remarks, It is indeed interesting to compare, on Scripture authority, *Adam* as the root of sin and death to all, with Christ, who is to all true Christians the root of holiness and life. 1 C *15:21, 22, 45. **of him.** Mt 11:3. Jn +11:27. He 10:37.

15. **But not.** ver. 16, 17, 20. Is √55:8, 9. Jn √3:16. 4:10. **For if.** ⨍184A, 1 C +15:2. **many.** √⨍171F, Is +53:12. ver. 12, 18, 19n. Da +*12:2. Mt +*20:28. +*26:28n. 1 C √15:22. **much.** Ep √2:8. 2 C *5:15. **grace.** Ac +*11:23. **and the gift.** ver. 17. Ro √6:23. 2 C 9:15. He 2:9. 1 J *4:9, 10. √5:11, 12. **hath.** ver. 20. Ps *22:30. Is *53:11. √55:7. 1 J √2:2. Re *7:9, 10, 14-17.

16. **it was.** ⨍63J1, Ge +13:9. **the gift.** Ja 1:17g. **for the.** Ge 3:6-19. 1 C 11:32. Ga 3:10. Ja √2:10. **but the free.** Is *1:18. 43:25. 44:22. Lk 7:47-50. Ac +*13:38, 39. 1 C +*6:9-11. 1 T √1:13-16. **justification.** ver. 18. Ro +1:32. Re 19:8.

17. **For if.** ⨍184A, 1 C +15:2. ver. 12. Ge 3:6, 19. 1 C 15:21, 22, 49. **by one man's offence.** *or*, by one offence. **abundance.** ⨍100, Ge +10:9. ver. 20. Jn 10:10. Ro 4:24. 1 T 1:14. **of grace.** ⨍29, Ex +19:6. i.e. abounding grace. **gift.** Ro √6:23. Is 61:10. Ph *3:9. **shall reign.** Ro *8:30, 39. Mt *25:34. Jn *10:10. 1 C 4:8. 2 T 2:12. Ja *2:5. 1 P *2:9. Re 1:6. 3:21. *5:9, 10. 20:4, 6. 22:5.

18. **the offence**. *or*, one offence. **upon**. ver. 12, 15, 19. Ro 3:19, 20. 2 C *5:14, 15. **the righteousness**. *or*, one righteousness. Ro 3:21, 22. 2 P 1:1. **all men**. Mt ☾+*26:28n. Jn 1:7. 3:26. +*12:32. Ac 13:39. 1 C 15:22. 1 T *2:4-6. *4:10. He *2:9. 2 P √3:9. 1 J *2:20. **justification**. Ro 4:25. **of life**. 2 C *3:6. Ga *2:20. 1 J *5:12.

19. **as by one**. ver. 12-14. **disobedience**. √135, Ps +68:28. 2 C 10:6. He 2:2g. **many**. √√171F, Is +53:12. This is a very clear instance of "many" being used as an idiom for "all," for certainly all are sinners (Ro 3:23). ver. 15. Mt 20:28. 26:28n. **so by**. √31, Is +1:21. ver. 18. Is 53:10-12. Da 9:24. 2 C √5:21. Ep 1:6. Re 7:9-17. **obedience**. Mt 26:39, 42. Jn 5:30. 6:38. Ph *2:8. He 5:8. **righteous**. Ro 3:22. 10:4. Je +*23:5, 6. 33:16. Ac +*13:39. 1 C 1:30. Ph *3:9. 2 P 1:1.

20. **the law**. Ro *3:19, 20. *4:15. 6:14. 7:5-13. Jn 15:22. 2 C 3:7-9. Ga 3:19-25. **entered**. Ro 4:13-16. 10:4. Ga 2:4g. **But**. Ro 6:1. 2 Ch 33:9-13. Ps 25:11. Is *1:18. 43:24, 25. Je 3:8-14. Ezk 16:52, 60-63. 36:25-32. Mi +*7:18, 19. Mt 9:13. Lk *7:47. 23:39-43. Jn *10:10. 1 C +*6:9-11. Ep *1:6-8. 2:1-5. 1 T *1:13-16. T *3:3-7.

21. **That**. ver. 12, 14. Ro *6:12, 14, 16, 21. **grace**. Jn *1:16, 17. T *2:11. He *4:16. 1 P 5:10. **through**. ver. 17. Ro 4:13. 8:10. 2 P 1:1. **unto**. Ro √6:23. Jn √10:28. 1 J 2:25. √5:11-13. **eternal**. Gr. *aionios*, Mt +18:8. Ro +2:7.

ROMANS 6

Believers cannot "sin on that grace may abound," as some would object; being "dead to sin," according to the meaning of baptism, which represents their conformity to Christ in his death, burial, resurrection, and living unto God, 1-10. They should reckon themselves to be "dead to sin and alive to God," 11; and, as not being "under law, but under grace," they must not suffer "sin to reign in their bodies," but yield them to God, as "instruments of righteousness," 12-15. Being "made free from sin, and become servants to righteousness," they should serve righteousness wholly, 16-20. The service of sin is unfruitful, shameful, and destructive; but the servants of God have their "fruit unto holiness, and the end eternal life," 21, 22. This is the free gift of God in Christ; but death is the wages of sin, 23.

1. **What**. See on Ro 3:5. 9:30. **Shall we**. √152B, Is +49:14. ver. *15. Ro 2:4, 5. *3:5-8, 31. 5:20, 21. Ga 5:13. 1 P 2:16. 2 P 2:18, 19. Ju 4. **grace**. Ro 5:20. 1 T 1:14.

2. **God**. See on Ro 3:4. **How**. Ge 39:9. Ps 119:104. 1 J 3:9. **dead**. ver. 5-11. Ro 7:4, 6. Ga 2:19. *5:13, 24. *6:14. Col 2:20. 3:3. 1 P *2:24. **live**. 2 C √5:14-17. 1 P 1:14. *4:1-3. 1 J *3:8-10.

3. **Know**. ver. 16. Ro 7:1. 1 C 3:16. 5:6. 6:2, 3, 9, 15, 16, 19. 9:13, 24. 2 C *13:5. Ja *4:4. **as were**. *or*, as are. Mt +*28:19. 1 C √12:13. Ga +*3:27. 1 P 3:21. **were baptized**. ver. 4, 5, 8. 1 C *10:2. 15:29. Ga 2:20, 21. **into his death**. Ga 2:20. 21. Col √3:3. 1 P *2:24.

4. **we are**. ver. 3. Col +*2:12, 13. 3:1-3. 1 P *3:21. **buried**. Since only baptism into water by immersion constitutes a burial in water, this passage is held by many to be proof that immersion is the Scriptural mode of Christian baptism. Further evidence for immersion

includes the fact that John baptized "in Jordan" (Mt 3:6) or, more specifically, "in the river of Jordan" (Mk 1:5). It is also recorded that John baptized where there was "much water" (Jn 3:23), required for immersion, but unnecessary if the mode were sprinkling or pouring. The language used of Jesus that he came "up out of the water" would indicate he was immersed in the water. Similar language is used in regard to the baptism of the Ethiopian eunuch, for he likewise is said to have "come up out of the water" (Ac 8:39). As to the assertion that there was insufficient water in Jerusalem for the 3000 persons baptized on the day of Pentecost, there were the pools of Siloam and Bethesda available, to name but two specifically mentioned in Scripture as being in the vicinity. As for the provision that was made for appropriate privacy and a change of clothing, Ralph P. Martin (*Worship in the Early Church*, p. 101) sees this alluded to in the metaphor of "divestiture and re-clothing" in a number of passages (Ro 13:14. Ga 3:27. Ep 4:21, etc. Col 2:11, 12. 3:3, 9. 1 P 3:20—4:1). That Cornelius and Paul were baptized in private homes does not rule out immersion as the mode. As for Paul, A. T. Robertson asserts he was baptized probably by Ananias, "possibly in the pool in the house of Judas as today water is plentiful in Damascus" (*Word Pictures*, vol. 3, p. 121, on Ac 9:18), just as Naaman alluded to the plentiful water available there (2 K 5:12). Just so, the Philippian jailor's baptism "apparently took place in the pool or tank in which he bathed Paul and Silas (De Wette) or the rectangular basin (*impluvium*) in the court for receiving the rain or even in a swimming pool or bath (*kolumbethra*) found within the walls of the prison (Kuinoel)" (A. T. Robertson, *Word Pictures*, vol. 3, pp. 262, 263, on Ac 16:34). As this passage links burial to baptism, following the Lord in water baptism necessarily requires immersion into water to meet the requirements of the symbolism set forth by Paul. It may also be argued in favor of immersion that the meaning of the original word *baptizo* was to immerse. Thomas J. Conant asserts "The word *baptizein*, during the whole existence of the Greek as a spoken language, had a perfectly defined and unvarying import. In its literal use it meant, as has been shown, to put entirely into or under a liquid, or other penetrable substance, generally water, so that the object was wholly covered by the inclosing element" (*The Meaning and Use of Baptizein*, p. 187, 188). Alexander Carson asserts that *baptizo* "always signifies to dip; never expressing anything but mode" (*Baptism: Its Mode and Subjects*, ch. 2, sec. 10, p. 55). Contemporary scholarship reflected in the work of G. Kittel and Geoffrey Bromiley supports the view that *baptizo* means immerse; *baptismos* is said to denote only the act, defined as "*immersion or baptism*"; *baptisma* denotes the institution (TDNT, vol. 1, p. 530; TDNT abridged in one volume, p. 94; see Bromiley's article on baptism in *Baker's Dictionary of Theology*, "Immersion was fairly certainly the original practice and continued in general use up to the Middle Ages," p. 83). The New Testament presents a regular pattern of believer's baptism involving the sequence of "hearing," "believing," and "being baptized" (Ac 2:37, 38. 2:41. 8:12, 13. 8:35, 36. 10:44. 11:14, 15. 16:14, 15. 16:32, 33. 18:8. 19:5). Since infants are unable to "hear" and "believe," infant baptism does not appear to be a practice sanctioned by the New

Testament, either by specific example or by direct command. The command to baptize disciples (Mt 28:19) is of perpetual obligation for the church until the return of Christ, for there is no word (whether by direct command, specific example, or necessary inference) in later revelation in the epistles which repeals this ordinance. Christ's command specifically pertains to ritual water baptism, for the disciples were commanded to be the administrators of such baptism; if this were a reference to baptism of the Holy Spirit, human administrators would not be involved, for no human being can baptize another human being by or into the Holy Spirit, for this is done by the sovereign act of God when a person believes in Christ (Ro 8:9, 11. 1 C 12:13). T#39-1. Ps +51:2 (T#32). Ezk ◑34:18, 19. Mt 3:5, 6, 16. Mk ◑+*1:8. Jn 3:23. Ac ◑+*1:5n. 8:38, 39. 1 C *10:1, 2. *12:13. Ga *3:27. Col √2:12. He ◑+10:22 (T#39-2). **baptism.** Gr. *baptisma*, S#908g, Mt +3:7. After comparing the various terms used in the New Testament (dip, pour, sprinkle, and wash), J. W. Shepherd concludes: (1) In the New Testament there is no record of the sprinkling of unmixed water. (2) The only provision for sprinkling in the New Testament is the "sprinkling of the blood of Jesus Christ." (3) Water of separation, blood mingled with water, and blood are the only materials said to be sprinkled. (4) In no case whatever is *baptizo* or *bapto* translated by pouring or sprinkling. (5) While the New Testament speaks of the pouring of oil, ointment, water, oil and wine, the Holy Spirit, the wine of God's wrath, and vials of wrath, it says nothing about the pouring of water on any person for any purpose whatever. (6) After this careful and critical examination of the New Testament in Greek and English, I conclude that there is not a single case of the pouring or sprinkling of unmixed water on any person or object for any *religious* purpose whatever" (*Handbook on Baptism*, Part IV, Appendix, Chapter 7, p. 462). For a listing of all the Greek words translated by the English terms mentioned above (dip, pour, sprinkle, and wash), see the subject index entry, "Baptism, related terms." **that.** ver. 9. Ro +*8:11. 1 C *6:14. 2 C 13:4. Ep *1:19, 20. 2:5, 6. **was raised.** Ac +*2:24n. **by the glory.** "Glory" is put for power (2 C 13:4. Col 1:11). Mt 28:2, 3. Jn 2:11, 19, 20. 11:4, 40. 2 C 13:4. Col *1:11. **the Father.** Ac +1:4. **even so.** ver. 19. Ro 7:6. *12:1, 2. 13:13, 14. 2 C √5:17. Ga *6:15, 16. Ep *4:17, 22-24. 5:8. Ph 3:17, 18. Col *1:9-12. 2:11, 12. 3:10. 4:1. 1 P 4:1, 2. 2 P 1:4-9. 1 J 2:6.

5. **For if.** ∫184A, 1 C +15:2. ver. 8-12. 2 C 4:10. Ep 2:5, 6. Ph *3:10, 11. Col 2:12. 3:1. **planted.** Ro 11:17. Ps 92:13. Is 5:2. Je 2:21. Mt 15:13. Jn 12:24. √15:1-8. **in the likeness.** ∫6311A, Ex +12:4.

6. **that our.** Ga √2:20. *5:24. *6:14. Ep *4:22. Col *3:5, 9, 10. **old man.** ∫173, Ge +27:44. ∫12111, Ge +3:7. Ro 7:22. 1 P 3:4. **that the.** Ro 7:24. 8:3, 13, 23. Ph 3:21. Col *2:11, 12. **body of sin.** ∫121G, Ge +31:1. **be destroyed.** 2 T 1:10. **that henceforth.** ver. 12, *22. Ro 7:25. 8:4. 2 K 5:17. Is 26:13. Jn 8:34-36.

7. **For he.** ver. 2, 8. Ro 7:2, 4. Col 3:1-3. 1 P *4:1. **freed.** *or,* justified. ver. 18. Ro *8:1.

8. **Now if.** ∫184A, 1 C +15:2. ver. 3-5. Ga *2:20. 2 T *2:11, 12. **we believe.** Jn 1:4. *14:19. 2 C 4:10-14. 13:4. Col 3:3, 4. 1 Th 4:14-17. **shall also.** ∫31, Is +1:21.

9. **Christ.** ver. 4. Ps +*16:9-11. Ac +*2:24-28. He *7:16, 25. 10:12, 13. Re *1:18. **dieth no more.** "Christ's

particular death occurs but once" (Shedd). See He 10:10. A complete refutation of the "sacrificial" character of the "mass" (A. T. Robertson, *Word Pictures*, vol. 4, p. 363). **death.** ver. 14. Ro 5:14, 17. He 2:14, 15.

10. **he died unto.** Ro 8:3. 2 C √5:21. He *9:26-28. 1 P 3:18. **once.** Gr. once for all. He +7:27. Robertson notes (*Word Pictures*, vol. 4, p. 363), "Once (*ephapax*). Once and once only (He 9:26f.), not *pote* (once upon a time)." **he liveth unto.** ver. 11. Ro 14:7-9. Lk 20:38. 2 C √5:15. Ep 1:22. Ph 2:11. 1 P 4:6.

11. **reckon.** Ro 8:18. **be dead.** See on ver. 2. **but.** ver. 13. 1 C 6:20. Ga *2:19, 20. Col 3:3-5. **alive.** Lk +20:38. **through.** ver. 23. Ro *5:1. 16:27. Jn √20:31. Ep 2:7. Ph *1:11. *4:7. Col *3:17. 1 P *2:5. 4:11.

12. **Let not.** ver. 14, 16. Ro 5:21. *7:23, 24. Nu *33:55. Dt 7:2. Jsh 23:12, 13. Jg 2:3. Ps *19:13. √119:133. Mi 7:19. 1 C 9:27. 2 C *5:15. **mortal.** Ro +*8:11. 1 C 15:53, 54. 2 C 4:11. 5:4. **body.** Ro 8:13. **in the lusts.** ver. *16. Ro 2:8. *8:13. *13:14. Ga *5:16, 24. Ep 2:3. *4:22. 1 Th 4:5. 2 T *2:22. T *2:11, 12. 3:3. Ja *1:14, 15. 4:1-3. 1 P 1:14. *2:11. 4:2, 3. 2 P 3:2-4. 1 J √2:15-17. Ju 16, 18. 13. **Neither.** ∫136, 1 C +60:12. ver. 16, 19. Ro 7:5, 23. 1 C *6:15. Col *3:5. Ja √3:5, 6. 4:1. **instruments.** Gr. arms, *or* weapons. Ro 13:12. 2 C 6:7. 10:4g. Ep 6:11-17. **unrighteousness.** Ro 1:29. 2:8, 9. Dt 25:16. Is 3:10, 11. √55:7. Ezk +*18:4. 1 C +*6:9. 2 Th √2:12. 2 P 2:13-15. 1 J √1:9. **but yield.** Ro *12:1. 2 Ch 30:8. Da 3:28. 1 C √6:20. 2 C 8:5. √10:5. Ph 1:20. **alive.** ver. 11. Lk 15:24, 32. Jn √5:24. 2 C √5:15. Ep 2:5. 5:14. Col 2:13. 1 P *2:24. *4:2, 3. **and your.** Ps 37:30. Pr 12:18. Ja 3:5, 6.

14. **sin.** ver. 12. Ro *5:20, 21. 8:2, 12. Ps 130:7, 8. Mi *7:19. Mt *1:21. Jn *8:36. T *2:14. He *8:10. **shall not.** T#809. ver. 6. Ro 7:24, 25. 8:2-4. Ho 14:8. Jn 8:32, 34. 15:2. Ga 5:16. **have dominion.** Ps √119:133. **for ye.** Ro *3:19, 20. 7:4-11. *10:5. Jn 1:17. Ga *3:11, 12, 23. 4:4, 5, 21. *5:18. **under grace.** ver. 15. Ro 4:16. 5:21. 11:6. Jn *1:17. 2 C 3:6-9. 1 J *3:8, 9.

15. **What.** See on Ro 3:9. **shall we.** ver. 1, 2. 1 C *9:20, 21. 2 C 7:1. Ga 2:17, 18. Ep √2:8-10. T *2:11-14. Ju *4. **God forbid.** ver. +2.

16. **Know.** See on ver. 3. **to whom.** ver. 13, 20. Jsh √24:15. Mt +*6:24. Jn +*8:34. *12:26. 2 P *2:19. **to obey.** 1 P +1:2. **whether of sin.** ver. 12, 17, 19-23. **righteousness.** Is *54:17.

17. **But.** See on Ro +1:8. 7:25. 1 Ch 29:12-16. Ezr 7:27. Mt 11:25, 26. Ac 11:18. 28:15. 1 C 15:57. 2 C 2:14. 8:16. **that.** ∫63F, Ge +33:10. Ro *1:21-32. 1 C +*6:9-11. Ep 2:5-10. 1 T 1:13-16. T 3:3-7. 1 P *2:9, 10. 4:2-5. **have obeyed.** Ro 1:5. 2:8. 15:18. 16:26. Ps 18:44mg. 2 C *10:5, 6. He +*5:9. 11:8. 1 P +*1:22. 3:1. *4:17. **from the heart.** 1 S +*16:7. Pr *4:23. Is ◑29:13. Ezk ◑33:31, 32. Ep *6:5-7. **that form.** 1 T 6:3-5. 2 T 1:13. 2:2. **doctrine.** Ac 2:42. 1 C 14:6, 26. **which was delivered you.** Gr. whereto ye were delivered.

18. **made.** ver. 7, 14, 22. Ro 8:2. Ps 116:16. 119:32, 45. Lk 1:74, 75. Jn 8:32, 36. 1 C 7:21, 22. Ga 5:1. 1 P 2:16. **servants.** ver. 19, 20, 22. Ro *7:17. Nu=8:22. Is 26:13. 54:17.

19. **I speak.** Ro +3:5. 1 C *9:8. 15:32. Ga *3:15. **because.** Ro 8:26. 15:1. 1 C *3:1, 2. He +*4:15. **infirmity.** Ro 8:3. Ga 4:13. **for as ye.** ver. +13, 17. 1 C 6:11. Ep 2:2, 3. Col 3:5-7. 1 P 4:2-4. **your members.** Ro 7:23. **unto iniquity.** ∫63B, Ge +25:28. or, to (work)

iniquity. ver. 16. 1 C 5:6. +*15:33. 2 T *2:16, 17. He +*12:15. **now yield**. ver. 13. Pr 31:13. **servants**. 1 C 9:27. **unto holiness**. ver. 22. 1 Th +4:7.

20. **the servants**. See on ver. +16, +17. Jn *8:34. **from**. Gr. o.

21. **What**. Ro 7:5. Pr 1:31. 5:10-13. 9:17, 18. Is 3:10. Je 12:13. +*17:10. 44:20-24. Ga *6:7, 8. **whereof**. Ezr 9:6. Jb 40:4. 42:6. Je 3:3. 8:12. *31:19. Ezk *16:61-63. *36:26, 31, 32. 43:11. Da 9:7, 8. +*12:2. Lk 15:17-21. 2 C 4:2. *7:11. Ep +*5:12. Ph 3:19. 1 J 2:28. **for the end**. ver. 23. Ro 1:32. 8:6, 13. Dt 17:6. 21:22. 2 S 12:5-7. 1 K 2:26. Ps 73:17. Pr +*14:12. 16:25. Ga *6:8. Ph +*3:19. He *6:8, 9. 1 P *4:17. Re 16:6. 20:14. **death**. Ro 1:32. 2 S 12:13. Ezk +*18:4. Ja +*5:20.

22. **But now**. ver. 14, +18. Ro 8:2. Jn 8:32. 2 C 3:17. Ga 5:13. **free**. 1 Ch=9:33. Jn 8:36. **become**. ver. 18. Ro 7:25. Ge 50:17. Jb 1:8. Ps 86:2. 143:12. Is 54:17. Da 3:26. 6:20. Ac *27:23. 1 C 7:22. Ga 1:10. Col 4:12. T 1:1. Ja 1:1. 1 P 2:16. Re 7:3. *22:3, 5. **ye have**. Ro 7:4. Ps 92:14. Jn +3:36. 15:2, 16. Ga *5:22. Ep 5:9. Ph 1:11. +*4:17. Col +√1:10. **holiness**. ver. 19. 1 Th +4:7. He +*12:14. **and the end**. ver. 21. Nu 23:10. Ps 37:37, 38. Mt 13:40, 43. 19:29. 25:46. Jn 4:36. 1 P 1:9. **everlasting**. Gr. *aionios*, Mt +18:8.

23. **For the wages**. ver. 21. Ro *1:32. +*5:12. *7:5. *8:13. Ge +*2:17. +*3:19. Is 3:11. Ezk +*18:4, 20. Mt *25:46. Mk *9:43, 44. Lk 3:14g. 1 C +*6:9, 10. 9:7g. 15:56. 2 C 11:8g. Ga 3:10. √6:7, 8. Ja √1:15. Re +*21:8. **but**. T#1010‡. Pr +7:27 (T#1009‡). ◑√15:24. 2 C +4:12 (T#1007‡). **the gift**. Ro 2:7. *5:16, 17, 21. 11:29. Jn √3:14-17, 36. *4:14. √5:24, 39, 40. *6:27, 32, 33, *39, *40, 50-58, 68. √10:28. *17:2, 3. Ac 8:17. T *1:2. 1 P +*1:3, 4. 1 J 2:25. √5:11, 12. **eternal**. Gr. *aionios*, Mt +18:8. Ro +2:7. Jn *10:28.

ROMANS 7

The believer's state, "as dead to the law," and united to Christ that he may serve God "in newness of Spirit," as illustrated by the law concerning marriage, 1-6. Through the depravity of human nature, the moral law, though "spiritual, holy, just, and good," can only occasion sin and death, 7-13. The painful conflict of those, who "delight in the law of God," but are not able to keep it, 14-24; and their prospect of deliverance by Christ, 25.

1. **Know**. See on Ro 6:3. **brethren**. Ro 9:3. 10:1. **them that**. Ro *2:17, 18. Ezr 7:25. Pr *6:23. 1 C 9:8, 9. Ga 4:21. **the law**. ver. 6. Ro 6:14. **a man**. Or, *person*, either man or woman; *anthropos* and *homo* having this extent of signification.

2. **the woman**. Rather, *a woman*. The apostle here illustrates the position laid down in the preceding verse by a familiar instance. Ge *2:23, 24. Nu 30:7, 8. 1 C *7:4, 39. **but if**. √184C, Mt +4:9. **loosed from**. ver. 6. Ga 5:4g. **the law**. Le 14:2. Nu 6:13.

3. **So then**. Ex 20:14. Le 20:10. Nu 5:13, etc. Dt 22:22-24. Mt +*5:32. Mk 10:6-12. Jn 8:3-5. **but if**. √184C, Mt +4:9. **that law**. ver. 2. **though**. Ru 2:13. 1 S 25:39-42. 1 T 5:11-14. **another man**. √63D3. Ellipsis (Absolute: of Anantapodoton) B55: when the comparison is wanting. Here, supply (and I need not say that if she be dead, she is, of course, free from that law). For other instances of this figure see 1 T 1:3, 4. 2 T 2:20. Of two possible cases, only the death of the hus-

band is given. The death of the wife is there, but only *in thought*; and this other premiss has to be supplied in the course of the argument, by adding the other premiss in some such words as these: "And if the wife die, I need not say that she is free"; or, "but it goes without saying that if the wife die, of course she is free." This is the figure Enthymema; or, Omission of Premiss B167, Mt +27:19.

4. **ye also**. ver. 6. Ro 6:+2, 14. *8:2. Ga *2:19, 20. *3:13. *5:18. Ep *2:15. Col *2:14, 20. **the body**. Mt 26:26. Jn 6:51. 1 C 10:16. Ep 2:16. Col 1:22. He 10:10. 1 P *2:24. **that ye**. Ps 45:10-15. Is 54:5. 62:5. Ho 2:19, 20. Jn 3:29. 2 C 11:2. Ep √5:25-27. Re 19:7, 8. 21:9. **raised**. Ro +6:4. **that we**. Ro 6:22. Ps 45:16. Jn 15:8. Ga *5:22, 23. Ep 5:9. Ph *1:11. *4:17. Col +*1:6, 10.

5. **in the flesh**. Ro *8:8, 9. Jn *3:6. Ga *5:16, 17, 24. Ep *2:3, 11. T 3:3. **motions**. Gr. passions. Ro 1:26g. Ga 5:24. **which**. ver. 8. Ro *3:20. 4:15. 5:20. +6:14. 1 C 15:56. 2 C 3:6-9. Ga 3:10. Ja 2:9, 10. 1 J 3:4. **did work**. ver. 8-13. Mt 15:19. Ga *5:19-21. Ja √1:15. **members**. ver. 23. Ro 6:13, 19. Col *3:5. Ja *4:1. **bring**. Ro +6:21, 23.

6. **But**. ver. 4. Ro 6:14, 15. Ga 3:13, 23-25. *4:4, 5. **delivered**. ver. 2. Ga 5:4g. **that being dead**. *or, being dead to that*. ver. 1, 4. Ro +6:2. **serve**. Ro 1:9. +*2:27-29. 6:+4, 11, 19, 22. *12:2. Ezk 11:19. 36:26. 2 C 3:6. √5:17. Ga 2:19, 20. 6:15. Ph *3:3. Col 3:10. **spirit**. Gr. *pneuma*, Ac +18:25n. **oldness**. He *8:8, 13. **letter**. Ro 2:27, 29. 2 C *3:6.

7. **What**. √152B, Is +49:14. Ro 3:5. 4:1. 6:1, 15. 9:14, 30. **Is the law**. ver. 8, 11, 13. 1 C 15:56. **sin**. √121G, Ge +31:1. **God forbid**. ver. 13. Ro +*6:2. Lk +20:16. **I had**. √96D1, Ec +3:18. By Heterosis of Person, whereby the first person is used for the third, Paul, though speaking in the first person, is saying what is true of all who share his experience; and not merely speaking of his own case as being peculiar or different from others (B524). ver. 5. Ro *3:20. Ps *19:7-12. 119:96. **not known**. √184B, Mt +23:30. **lust**. *or, concupiscence*. Gr. *epithumia*, S#1939g. desire, craving, longing, desire for what is forbidden; the active side of a vice, a word comprehensive in meaning, not limited to sexual desire. Young renders "overdesire." √63I1D, Nu +26:4. Supply by ellipsis of preceding connected words, "I had not known lust (to be sin) except the law had said..." ver. 8. 1 Th 4:5. **the law**. Ex 20:17. Dt 5:21. **Thou shalt**. Ro 13:9. Ge 3:6. Ex 20:17. Dt 5:21. Jsh 7:21. 2 S 11:2. 1 K 21:1-4. Mi 2:2. Mt 5:28. Lk 12:15. Ac 20:33. Ep 5:3. Col *3:5. 1 J √2:15, 16. **covet**. Ex 20:14. Dt 5:18.

8. **sin**. ver. 11, 13, 17. Ro *4:15. 5:20. **taking occasion**. ver. 11. 2 C 5:12. 11:12. Ga 5:13. 1 T 5:14g. **wrought**. Ja √1:14, 15. **For without**, etc. Rather, "For without a law sin is dead." Where there is no law, there is no transgression; for sin is the transgression of the law: the very essence of sin consists in the violation of some positive law. Ro +3:20. 4:15. *8:7. Jn 15:22, 24. 1 C *15:56.

9. **For I**. Mt 19:20. Lk 10:25-29. 15:29. *18:9-12, 21. Ph *3:5, 6. **without**. Mt *5:21, etc. *15:4-6. Mk 7:8-13. **but**. Ro 3:19, 20. 10:5. Ps 40:12. *119:96. Ga 3:10. Ja 2:10, 11. **came**. √12I1I2, Ge +2:17. **sin**. ver. 21-23. Ro 8:7. **and I died**. ver. 4, 6mg, 11. Ro *3:20. Ga 2:19.

10. **the commandment**. Ro +10:5. Le *18:5. Ezk

20:11, 13, 21. Lk *10:27-29. 2 C *3:7. **unto death.** Ro *4:15. Dt *27:26. Ga *3:10-12.

11. **sin.** ver. 8, 13. **deceived.** Ge 3:13. Is 44:20. Je +*17:9. 49:16. Ob 3. 2 C *11:3. Ep 4:22. 1 T *2:14. He +*3:13. Ja 1:22, 26.

12. **the law.** T#286. ver. 14. Ro 3:31. *12:2. Dt *4:8. 6:24, 25. 10:12, 13. Ne 9:13. Ps *19:7-10, +11 (T#302), 12. +58:11 (T#630). +81:13 (T#485). 119:39, *86, 127, *128, 137, 140, 172. 1 T *1:8. 1 J 5:3. **the commandment.** ver. 7. 2 P 2:21. **just.** Ps 119:137. **good.** ver. 16. Dt *10:13.

13. **then.** Ro 8:3. Ga 3:21. **good made death.** Ja √1:13-15. **forbid.** ver. 7. **But sin.** ver. 8-11. Ro *5:20. Ja √1:13-15. **appear sin.** ƒ145, Jg +11:40. **exceeding sinful.** T#557. Ro +11:22 (T#236). Ge +6:6 (T#230). 39:9. 1 S 2:25. Ps 51:4.

14. **we know.** Ro 3:19. 8:22, 28. **the law.** Le +*19:18. Dt *6:5. Ps +*51:6. *119:5, 6. Mt *5:22, 28, 43, 44. *22:37-40. He √4:12. **spiritual.** Ro +1:11g. 1 C 3:1. 10:3, 4. **but.** ver. 18, 22, 23. Jb *42:6. Ps *119:25. Pr *30:2, 5. Is *6:5. √64:5, 6. Lk *5:8. *7:6, 7. *18:11-14. Ep *3:8. **but I.** ƒ120, 1 K +18:18. **carnal.** Mt 16:23. 1 C *3:1-3. 2 C 3:3. He 7:16g. **sold.** ver. *24. Ge 37:27, 36. 40:15. Ex 21:2-6. 22:3. 1 K *21:20, 25. 2 K *17:17. Is 50:1. *52:3. Am 2:6. Mt *18:25. **under sin.** Ro +3:9.

15. **For that.** Ro *14:22. Lk 11:48. **allow.** *or*, know. ƒ121C2A1, Jb +19:25. Ps +*1:6. Na *1:7. Jn 15:15. 2 T √2:19. **what.** ver. 16, 19, 20. 1 K 8:46. Ps *19:12. *65:3. 119:*1-6, 32, 40. Ec √7:20. Ga √5:17. Ph *3:12-14. Ja *3:2. 1 J √1:7, 8. **what I hate.** Ro *12:9. Ps *36:4. *97:10. √101:3. *119:104, 113, 128, 163. Pr 8:13. 13:5. Am *5:15. He 1:9. Ju *23.

16. **If then.** ƒ184A, 1 C +15:2. **I consent.** ver. 12, 14, 22. Ps *119:127, 128. **the law.** ver. 12. 1 T 1:8.

17. **it is no more.** ver. *20. Ro *4:7, 8. 2 C *8:12. Ph *3:8, 9. **sin.** ver. 18, 20, 23. Ja *4:5, 6.

18. **that in me.** Ro 3:23. Ge *6:5. *8:21. Jb 14:4. *15:14-16. 25:4. Ps +*51:5. Is √64:6. Je +*17:9. Mt *15:19. Mk +*7:21-23. Lk 11:13. Ep *2:1-5. T *3:3. 1 P 4:2. **in my flesh.** ver. *5, *25. Ro *8:3-13. *13:14. Jn *3:6. Ga √5:19-21, 24. **no good thing.** T#688. Ro 6:20. 8:8. Ps +5:9 (T#165). +50:16 (T#589). Is *1:5, 6. Jn *5:42. 1 C 2:14. Ep 2:12. **for to will.** ver. 15, 19, 25. Ps *119:5, 32, 40, *115-117, 173, 176. Pr 31:12. Ga *5:17. Ph √2:13. 3:12. **find.** ƒ171J5, 1 S +13:15.

19. **the good.** ver. 15. Ga 5:17. **that I do.** Jn 5:29n. 1 J √1:8.

20. **Now if.** ƒ184C, Mt +4:9. **it is no.** ver. *17.

21. **a law.** ver. 23. Ro 3:27. 6:12, 14. 8:2. 9:31. Ps 19:13. 119:133. Jn 8:34. Ep 6:11-13. 2 P 2:19. **evil.** 2 Ch 30:18, 19. Ps 19:12. 40:12. 65:3. 119:37. Is 6:5-7. Zc 3:1-4. Lk 4:1, 2. He 2:17, 18. +*4:15.

22. **I delight.** T#658. Ro *8:7. Jb +*23:12. Ps +*1:2. *19:8-10. +27:4 (T#106). *40:8. 112:1. *119:16, 20, 24, 35, 47, 48, 72, 92, +*97-104, 111, 113, 127, 128, *162, 167, 174. Is *51:7. Je +*15:16. Jn *4:34. He *8:10. **inward.** Ro *2:29. 2 C *4:16. Ep √3:16. 4:22-24. Col 3:3, 9, 10. 1 P +*3:4.

23. **another.** ver. 5, 21, 25. Ro 8:2. Ec √7:20. Ga √5:17. 1 T 6:11, 12. He 12:4. Ja 3:2. 4:1. 1 P 2:11. **law.** ƒ46A, Le +26:30. Paul means that he sees *sin:* which, through the authority with which it rules his members, he calls, by *Catachresis,* "law." **members.** Ro 6:13, 19. **warring.** Ja +4:1. **law.** ƒ145, Jg +11:40. **and.** ver. 14. Ps 142:7. 2 T +*2:25, 26.

24. **O wretched.** ƒ59, Ge +28:16. Ro *8:26. 1 K 8:38. Ps 6:6. 32:3, 4. 38:2, 8-10. 77:3-9. 119:20, 81-83, 131, 143, 176. 130:1-3. Ezk *9:4. Mt +*5:4, 6. 2 C √12:7-9. Re 21:4. **who shall.** ƒ85G, Is +6:8. Dt 22:26, 27. Ps 71:11. 72:12. 91:14, 15. 102:20. Mi *7:19. Zc 9:11, 12. Lk 4:18. 2 C *1:8-10. 2 T 4:18. T *2:14. He 2:15. **deliver.** Pr *19:19. **the body of this.** *or*, this body of. ƒ100, Ge +10:9. Ro 6:6. 8:13, 23. Ps 88:5. Ph 3:21. Col 2:11. **death.** ƒ121G, Ge +31:1. Ro 8:2.

25. **thank God.** Ro 6:14, +17. Ps 107:15, 16. 116:16, 17. Is 12:1. 49:9, 13. Mt +*1:21. 1 C *15:57. 2 C 9:15. √12:9, 10. Ep 5:20. Ph 3:3. *4:6. Col *3:17. 1 P *2:5, 9. **So then.** ver. 15-24. Ga 5:17-24. **serve.** Pr 31:12.

ROMANS 8

Those who are in Christ, and walk after the Spirit, are free from condemnation, 1-4. The carnal mind, and the spiritual mind distinguished, so that they only are the children of God, who have the Spirit of Christ, are "led by the Spirit," and mortify the flesh, 9-14. "The Spirit of adoption" testifies with their spirit, and marks them as children and heirs of God; though now exposed to suffering, 15-18. The creation, through man's sin, is subject to vanity, and waits for deliverance at "the manifestation of the children of God," 19-22; who "groan being burdened," and are saved in hope, and patiently expect deliverance, 23-25; the Holy Spirit aiding their prayers, and thus rendering them acceptable, 26, 27. All things work together for the good of those who love God, as "called according to his purpose," which springs from their predestination to life, 28-31; and is secured by the death, resurrection, and intercession of Christ, 32-34. Nothing shall separate them from the love of God through Christ, 35-39.

1. **Therefore.** Ro 7:25. **now.** Ro 7:6. **no.** ver. 33, 34. Ro 4:7, 8. 5:1. 7:17, 20. Nu 35:25, 27. Is 54:17. Jn √3:18, 19, 36. √5:24. 8:36. Ac 13:39. 2 C 5:21. Ga *3:13. **in Christ.** E. H. Gifford remarks "'To be in Christ' does not mean in St. Paul's writings 'to be dependent on Christ' (a common classical usage), nor merely…to be His follower or disciple, as Pythagoreans or Platonists were followers of their several masters. It implies that living union which Christ Himself first made known (Jn 14:19, 20). What St. Paul affirmed at Athens of all mankind in their natural relation to God (Ac 17:28), he applies in a higher sense to the spiritual union of believers with Christ. In Ga 3:26-28, we see both the inward and outward means of this union, namely, faith and baptism. In speaking of this union, St. Paul never uses the name 'Jesus' alone nor first, but gives prominence to the Divine dignity and saving power of 'Christ'" (*Comm. on Romans,* p. 146). Ro +*16:7. Jn √14:19, 20. *15:4-7. 1 C *1:30. 15:22. 2 C √5:17. 12:2. Ga +1:22. 3:26-28. *5:6. Ep 1:1. 2:10. Ph *3:9. 1 P 3:16. 5:10, 14. 1 J 2:5, 6, 24, 28. 3:24. *5:20. **who walk.** ƒ108B, Ge +5:22. ver. 4, 14. Ga *5:16-25. T *2:11-14. **Spirit.** Gr. *pneuma,* ƒ121A2. Figure of speech Metonymy of the Cause, "spirit" put for the new nature which it creates, as the greatest of His gifts: Ro 8:2, 4, 5, 5, 9, ?9, ?9, 10, 11, 11, 13, 14, 16b, 23. 1 C 2:12b. 12:3a. 14:15, 15, 16. Ga 3:2, 3, 5. 4:6, 29. 5:16, 17, 17, 18, 25, 25, 6:8a. Ep 4:23. 1 J 3:24. Ju 19. For the other uses of *pneuma,* see Mt +8:16n. For ƒ121A2, see Ps +51:10.

2. **For.** ⨍136, Is +60:12. Verses 2-15 constitute a long *Parembole*. Ro 3:27. Jn 8:36. **Spirit.** Gr. *pneuma*, ⨍121A2, ver. 1n. ⨍24N, Ge +17:5. ⨍121A2, Ps +51:10. ver. 10, 11. Jn 4:10, 14. *6:63. *7:38, 39. 1 C *15:45. 2 C *3:6. Re *11:11. 22:1. **of life.** The genitive expresses the effect wrought, as in Jn 6:35 and Ro 5:18 (Gifford). Jn 11:25, 26. 14:19, 20. 1 P *1:23. **in Christ.** Ep 1:3, 4. **hath.** ver. 12. Ro *6:14, 18, 22. 7:4. Ps 51:12. Is 61:1. Jn *8:32. 2 C 3:17. Ga *2:19. *5:1. **from.** Ro *5:21. *7:21, 24, 25.

3. **For what.** Ro *3:20. 7:5-11. Ac +*13:39. Ga *3:21. He *7:18, 19. 10:1-10, 14. **weak through.** Ro +6:19. Ga 4:9. He *7:18. **God.** ver. 32. Jn √3:14-17. Ga *4:4, 5. 2 C 5:21. 1 J *4:10-14. **own Son.** Jn +*5:18. **in the likeness.** Ro 9:3. Mk 15:27, 28. Jn +1:14. 9:24. Ga 4:4. Ph *2:7. He *7:26. **sinful.** Lk +*1:35. 2 C *5:21. He +*4:15. 10:5. 1 P 2:22. **flesh.** Ro 1:3. 9:5. Mt 24:22. Lk 3:6. Jn *1:14. 3:6. 6:51. Col 1:22. 1 T 3:16. He 2:14. *10:10, 14. **for sin.** *or,* by a sacrifice for sin. Le 4:33. 5:6, 7, 8, 9. 7:37. 16:5. Ps 40:6. 2 C √5:21. Ga *3:13. He 10:6, 8. 13:11. **condemned.** Ro *6:6-10. Mt 12:41, 42. He 11:7. 1 P *2:24. *4:1, 2. **sin.** ⨍77, Ex +3:19.

4. **That.** 1 C *6:11. Ga *5:22-24. Ep *5:26, 27. Col 1:22. He 12:23. 1 J *3:2. Ju *24. Re 14:5. **righteousness.** Ro 1:32. 2:2, 26. 5:16, 18. *10:3-6, 9. 2 C *5:21. **fulfilled.** Mt +*5:17. **who.** ver. 1. Ga 5:16, 25. Ph *3:3-7. **flesh.** ⨍171Q9. Synecdoche of the Part B644. "The flesh" is put for the *animal lusts*, and the evil desires of the Old Nature, and for the Old Nature itself. For other instances of this figure see ver. 13. Ga 5:16. Ep 2:3. **Spirit.** Gr. *pneuma*, ⨍121A2, ver. 1n.

5. **For they.** ver. 12, 13. Jn *3:6. 1 C 15:48. 2 C 10:3. Ga 6:8. 2 P 2:10. **mind.** ver. 6, 7. Mt 16:23. Mk 8:33. 1 C √2:14. Ph *3:18, 19. Col *3:2. **the things.** Ga 5:19-21. **but.** ⨍31, Is +1:21. **after the Spirit.** Gr. *pneuma*, ⨍121A2, ver. 1n. **of the Spirit.** Gr. *pneuma*, ⨍121A2, ver. 1n. ver. 9, 14. 1 C √2:14. Ga √5:22-25. Ep *5:9. Col *3:1-3.

6. **to be carnally minded.** Gr. the minding of the flesh. So ver. 5, 7, 13. Ro *6:21, 23. 7:5, 11. √13:14. Ga √6:8. Col 2:18. Ja √1:14, 15. **is death.** ⨍121G, Ge +31:1. ver. 13. Ro +6:21. Ep *2:1. **to be spiritually minded.** Gr. the minding of the Spirit. Gr. *pneuma*, ⨍121A2, ver. 1n. T#930. ver. 10. **life.** ⨍121G, +31:1. Ro 5:1, 10. *14:17. Ml=2:5. Jn √14:6, 27. +*17:3. Ga *5:22. **and peace.** ⨍93A, Ge +1:26. By *Hendiadys*, peaceful life. Two words are used, but one thing is meant. Ro 5:1. Is 57:21.

7. **the carnal mind.** Gr. the minding of the flesh. Ro +*1:28, 30. 5:10. Ge 6:5. 8:21. Ex 20:5. 2 Ch 19:2. Ps 53:1. Ec 9:3. Je +*17:9. Mk 7:21-23. Jn 3:19. 7:7. 15:23, 24. 1 C √2:14. Ep 4:17-19. 5:8. Col *1:21. 2 T 3:4. T 1:15. Ja *4:4. 1 J √2:15, 16. **enmity.** Ep 2:15. Ja *4:4. **for it.** ver. 4. Ro 3:31. 7:7-14, 22. Mt +*5:19. 1 C 9:21. Ga √5:22, 23. He +*8:10. **neither.** Ro 6:6. 8:5. Je 13:23. Mt *7:18. *12:34. Jn 14:17. 1 C √2:14. 2 P 2:14.

8. **they that.** ver. 9. Ro 7:5. 1 Ch=15:2. Jn +*3:3, 5-7. **please.** Mt 3:17. Jn 8:29. 1 C 7:32. Ph 4:18. Col +√1:10. 3:20. 1 Th 2:15. *4:1. He √11:5, 6. 13:16, 21. 1 J 3:22.

9. **But ye.** ver. 2. Ezk 11:19. 36:26, 27. Jn *3:6. **Spirit.** Gr. *pneuma*, ⨍121A2, ver. 1n. **if so be.** ⨍184A, 1 C +15:2. Condition of the first class, assumed as true. ver. 11. Lk *11:13. 1 C *3:16. *6:19. 2 C *6:16.

Ga 4:6. Ep *1:13, 17, 18. *2:22. 2 T 1:14. 1 J *3:24. 4:4. Ju 19-21. **Spirit.** Gr. *pneuma*, Mt +3:16. Mt 10:20. Jn *3:34. *14:26. 15:26. 1 C 2:11, 12. **dwell.** or, dwelleth. The present tense "denotes *constant* residence and influence: the immediate operation of the third trinitarian person upon the human soul, implying the action of spirit upon spirit" (Shedd). ver. 15, 16, 23, 26, 27. Jn *6:56. *14:16, +17, 23. 15:26. 16:7, 13, 14. 1 C 2:10, 11. *3:16. *6:17, 19. 2 C 6:16. 2 T 1:14. **in you.** 1 J √4:13. **if any man.** ⨍184A, 1 C +15:2. All believers (1) have the Holy Spirit. Ro 5:5. Ga 3:2. 4:6. (2) are indwelt by the Holy Spirit. Ro 8:11. 1 C 6:19, 20. 2 C 5:5. 1 J 3:24. (3) are sealed by the Holy Spirit. 2 C 1:22. Ep *1:13. *4:30. (4) are anointed with the Holy Spirit. 2 C 1:21. 1 J 2:20, 27. (5) are baptized by the Holy Spirit at regeneration, and thereby placed "in Christ," and in the body of Christ. 1 C *12:13. **have not.** Ps 51:11. Jn 14:17. Ju *19. **the Spirit.** Gr. *pneuma*, Mt +3:16. Jn 3:34. 2 C 3:18. Ga *4:6. Ph *1:19. 1 P *1:11. **of Christ.** The same as the "Spirit of God" just before. Incidental argument for the Deity of Christ (A. T. Robertson, *Word Pictures*, vol. 4, p. 373). Jn +*10:30. 2 C *3:3. **none of his.** Mt *7:22, 23. Jn *17:9, 10. 1 C 3:21-23. +*12:3. 15:23. 2 C 10:7. Ga *5:24. Re *13:8. 20:15.

10. **if Christ.** ⨍184A, 1 C +15:2. Jn 6:56. *14:20, 23. 15:5. +17:23. 1 C 6:17. 2 C √13:5. Ga 4:19. Ep *3:17. Col *1:27. **the body.** Paul speaks here of man's constituent parts in terms of dichotomy: body and spirit (1 C 5:5. 7:34. 2 C 7:1. Ep 2:3. Col 2:5). ver. +*11. Ro +*5:12. Ezk +*18:4, 20. 2 C 4:11. +*5:1-4. 1 Th +*4:16. He +√9:27. 2 P 1:13, 14. Re +*14:13. **is dead.** ⨍121G, Ge +31:1. Ro 5:19-21. Ga 2:20. **but.** Jn *4:14. 6:54. *11:25, 26. 14:19. 1 C 15:45. 2 C 5:6-8. Ph 1:23. Col *3:3, 4. He +*12:23. Re 7:14-17. **Spirit.** Gr. *pneuma*, ⨍121A2, ver. 1n. Ac +*7:59. **life.** ⨍121G, Ge +31:1. Ro *5:21. 2 C √5:21. Ph *3:9.

11. **But if.** ⨍184A, 1 C +15:2. **Spirit.** Gr. *pneuma*, ?⨍121A2, ver. 1n. **of him.** ver. +*9. Ro 4:24, 25. Ac +*2:24, 32, 33. Ep 1:19, 20. He *13:20. 1 P *1:21. √3:18. **dwell in.** ver. +*9. **he that raised.** ver. 2. Ro +*6:4, 5. Is +*26:19n. Ezk *37:14. Jn √5:28, 29. 1 C *6:14. 15:16, 20-22, 51-57. 2 C *4:14. Ep *2:5. Ph *3:21. 1 Th √4:14-17. 1 P *3:18. Re *1:18. *11:11. *20:11-13. **quicken.** Nu=17:3, 8. Jn 5:+*21, 29. **mortal.** Ro +*6:12. 1 C *15:53. 2 C 4:11. *5:4, 5. **bodies.** ver. *23. Jn +*2:19-22. 1 C 6:19, 20. 15:44. Ph +*3:21. **by his Spirit.** *or*, because of his Spirit. Gr. *pneuma*, ?⨍121A2, ver. 1n. Jn 6:63. 2 C 3:6. 5:5. **dwelleth.** ver. +*9. Mt 12:43, 45n. Jn *7:38, 39. +*14:17. 1 C 3:16. 2 T 1:14.

12. **we are.** Ro 6:2-15. Ps *116:16. 1 C *6:19, 20. 1 P 4:2, 3. **not to.** ver. +*2. **flesh.** ⨍171Q9, ver. +4.

13. **For if.** ⨍184A, 1 C +15:2. **ye live.** ver. 1, 4-6. Ro *6:21, 23. 7:5. Ga √5:19-21. *6:8. Ep *5:3-5. Col *3:5, 6. Ja √1:14, 15. **shall die.** ver. 6. **but if.** ⨍184A, 1 C +15:2. ⨍31, Is +1:21. ver. 2. 1 C *9:27. Ga *5:24. Ep 4:22. Col *3:5-8. T *2:12. 1 P *2:11. **through.** ver. 1. Jn *3:5. Ep +*4:30. +*5:18. 2 Th *2:13. 1 P *1:22. **Spirit.** Gr. *pneuma*, ⨍121A2, ver. 1n. **mortify.** T#929. Mt 5:29, 30. 18:8, 9. 1 C 9:26. Ga 5:24. Col 3:5. **the deeds.** Lk 23:51g.

14. **led.** ver. 5, 9. Ps 143:10. Pr 8:20. Is 48:16, 17. Ezk *36:27, 28. Lk 4:1. Jn *6:44. Ga 4:6. 5:16, *18, 22-25. Ep 5:9. **Spirit.** Gr. *pneuma*, ?⨍121A2, ver. 1n. **they are.** ver. 17. 2 C *6:18. Ga 3:26. Ep *1:5. 1 J

√3:1, 2. Re 21:7. **the sons of God**. ver. 16, 19. Ro 9:26. Dt 14:1. Ho 1:10. Mt 5:9. Lk 6:35. 20:36. Jn +11:52. Ga 3:26. 4:6, 7n. He +*2:10. 12:6. Re 21:7.

15. **not received**. ƒ64, Ps +1:1. **the spirit**. Gr. *pneuma*, ƒ121A2, Mt +5:3n. **of bondage**. Ex *20:19. Nu 17:12, 13. Lk 8:28, 37. Jn +*16:8. Ac +*2:37. 16:29. 1 C 2:12. Ga 2:4. *3:10. *4:24. 2 T +√1:7. He +*2:15. *12:18-24. Ja *2:19. 1 J *4:18. **to fear**. Ge ◐19:30. Mt *25:24, 25. 2 T +√1:7. **the Spirit**. Gr. *pneuma*, ƒ121A2, Mt +5:3n. ver. 16. **of adoption**. ver. 23. Ro 9:4. Is 56:5. Je +*3:19. 31:9. 1 C 2:12. Ga 4:5-7. Ep 1:5, 11-14. **whereby we cry**. Ro *10:12. Ps 86:9. Ep *3:12. He *4:14, 16. Ju *20. **Abba**. Mk 14:36. Lk *11:2. Jn 20:17. **Father**. Ge 48:15. Ps 48:14. *103:13. Je 3:4. Lk *15:18-20. +22:42. Ga 4:6.

16. **Spirit**. Gr. *pneuma*, Mt +3:16. ver. 9, 23, 26, 27. Jn +7:39. 2 C 1:22. 5:5. Ep +*1:13, 14. +*4:30. 1 J 3:24. *4:13. **itself**. or, himself. ver. 26. Jn ◐*15:26. ◐+*16:13n, 14n. 1 Th 3:11. He 10:15, 16. **beareth witness**. Ro *5:5. Ga *5:22, 23. 1 J *3:21. *5:10. **with our**. 2 C 1:12. 1 J 3:19-22. 5:10. **spirit**. Gr. *pneuma*, ƒ121A2, ver. 1n. **we are**. T#843. ver. 17, 21. Ro 9:8. Jn +11:52.

17. **if children**. ƒ184A, 1 C +15:2. ver. 3, 29, 30. Ro 5:9, 10, 17. Lk +*12:32. Ac +*26:18. Ga 3:29. +*4:5, 7n. Ep 3:6. T 3:7. He *1:14. 6:17. Ja +*2:5. 1 P +*1:4. **then heirs**. ƒ16, Ge +1:27. Nu=18:20. Dt=10:9. +*32:9. Mt +*25:34. Ac +*20:32. Ga 3:29. 4:7. Ep +*1:11. T 3:7. He 1:2. 1 P *1:4. **heirs of**. Mt 25:21. Lk +*22:29, 30. Jn *16:15. *17:24. 1 C 2:9. *3:22, 23. Re *3:21. *21:7. **joint-heirs**. He 11:9g. **with**. ƒ181E, Ge +3:24. **if so be**. ƒ184A, 1 C +15:2. Mt 10:38. 16:24. 20:22. Lk 24:26. Jn 12:25, 26. Ac +*14:22. 2 C 1:5, 7. 4:8-12. Ph *1:29. Col 1:24. 1 Th 3:3. 2 T *2:10-14. 1 P *1:6, 7. **with him**. Mk 8:35. Lk 24:26, 46. Ac 17:3. 26:23. Ph 3:10. He *2:9, 10. 1 P *4:13. **that we**. Ro +*1:18. +*5:9. 8:1. Jn *12:25, 26. Ph *3:20, 21. 1 Th +*5:9. **glorified together**. 1 C 15:50-52.

18. **I reckon**. Mt +*5:11, 12. Ac 20:24. 2 C √4:17, 18. He *11:25, 26, 35. 1 P 1:6, 7. **not worthy**. ƒ101, Dt +32:42. Lk +*6:23. **the glory**. Ro 2:7. Ps *16:11. 1 C 1:7. *2:9, 10. 2 C *4:17. *12:4. Col *3:4. 2 Th √1:7-12. *2:14. 2 T *2:10. 1 P *1:7, 13. *4:13. 5:1. 1 J √3:2. Re *21:23. **revealed**. ƒ101, Dt +32:42.

19. **the earnest**. ver. 23. Ph 1:20. **expectation**. ƒ155D, Ge +4:10. Is *55:12, 13. +*65:17. Ac +*3:21. 2 P +*3:11-13. Re *21:1-5. **the creature**. or, creation. The word itself is of unlimited application, and the context only can determine the extent of its meaning (Gifford). ƒ121N1, Ge +31:54. ver. 22. Ho +*2:18. Mk 13:19. **the manifestation**. Dt +*33:2. Ps +*149:9. Ho 11:12. Hab +*3:13. Zc √14:5. Ml *3:17, 18. Mt +*11:11. +*13:43. *25:31-46. 1 J √3:2. **sons of God**. ver. +14.

20. **the creature**. ver. *22. Ge +*3:17-19. *5:29. 6:13. Jb 12:6-10. Ps 39:5, 11. 102:25, 26. 144:4. Ec 1:2. Is *24:5, 6. Je *12:4, 11. 14:5, 6. Ho *4:3. Jl 1:18. 2 P +*3:7. **not willingly**. ƒ81, Ge +15:13.

21. **Because**. Is +*11:6-9. Ho +*2:18. 2 P +*3:13. **delivered**. ver. 17, 18. Ro 7:22-25. Ps +*104:29, 30. Jl *2:25. Mt +*19:28. Ac +*3:19, 21. Re 21:4. **bondage of corruption**. 1 C +15:42. 2 C 4:16. Ep 4:22. 1 T 6:5. He *2:15. Re *22:3. **into the glorious**. ver. 19. Re *22:3-5.

22. **we know**. ver. 28. Ro 3:19. 7:14. **the**, etc. *or*,

every creature. ver. 20. Ps ◐*96:12, 13. ◐*98:8, 9. Is 24:5. Mk *16:15. Col +*1:23. **groaneth**. Ps 48:6. Je *12:4, 11. Ho *4:1-3. Jl *1:18. Jn 16:21. Re 12:2.

23. **not only**. Ro 5:3, 11. 9:10. 2 C 8:19. **they**. ƒ63I1D, Nu +26:4. **which have**. See on ver. 15, 16. Ro *5:5. 2 C *1:21, 22. *5:5. Ga √5:22, 23. Ep *1:13, 14. 5:9. **firstfruits**. Ge 24:22. 2 C 5:5. Ja +1:18. **Spirit**. Gr. *pneuma*, ƒ121A2, ver. 1n. Jn +7:39. **even we**. ver. 26. Ro 7:24. 2 C *5:2-4. 7:5. Ph +*1:21-23. 1 P 1:7. **groan**. Ps *38:4, 9. 1 P *1:6. **waiting for**. ver. 19, 25. Ro 13:11. Ge *49:18. Is 25:9. Lk 18:7, 8. 20:36. Ga 5:5. Ph *1:6. *3:20, 21. 2 Th 1:5-10. *3:5. 2 T 4:8. T *2:13. He +*9:28. 10:13. 1 J √3:2. Re 6:9-11. **adoption**. ver. +15. He 2:13. **the redemption**. Ro 7:24. Ho *13:14. Lk +21:28. Ep 1:14. +*4:30. **our body**. ver. +*11. Lk *20:36. Ph +*3:21.

24. **are saved**. Jn √5:24. **by hope**. ver. 20. Ro 4:18. *5:2. 12:12. +*15:4, 13. Ps 33:18, 22. 146:5. Pr 14:32. Je 17:7. Zc 9:12. 1 C 13:13. Ga *5:5. Ep ◐*2:8. Col +*1:5, 23, 27. 1 Th √5:8. 2 Th *2:16. T √2:11-13. He *6:18, 19. 1 P *1:3, 21. 1 J *3:3. **but hope**. ƒ66, Ge +9:3. ƒ121R3, Ps +71:5. Ac 28:20. 2 C 4:18. *5:7. Col 1:5. 1 T 1:1. He √11:1. 1 P 1:10, 11.

25. **But if**. ƒ184A, 1 C +15:2. **we hope**. Ro 5:3, 4. 1 Th +1:3. **with patience**. T#1375. ver. 23. Ro +*2:7. 12:12. Ge 49:18. Ps 27:14. +*37:7-9. 40:1. 62:1, 5, 6. 130:5-7. Is *25:8, 9. 26:8. √30:18. La *3:25, 26. Lk 8:15. 21:19. Col 1:11. 1 Th 1:3. 2 Th √3:5. He √6:11, 12, 15. +*10:36. *12:1-3. Ja *1:3, 4. *5:7-11. Re 1:9. 13:10. *14:12. **wait**. ver. +*23.

26. **Spirit**. Gr. *pneuma*, Mt +3:16. Jn +7:39. Re 1:4. **helpeth**. T#1364. Lk 10:40g. **infirmities**. Ro 15:1. 2 C *12:5-10. He +*4:15. 5:2. **for we**. Mt 20:22. Lk 11:1, etc. Ja 4:3. **know not**. Mt 20:22. Mk 10:19, 20. 1 P 1:8. **what we should**. Gifford notes that the same grammatical construction is found at Ro 13:9. Lk 1:62. 9:46. 19:48. 22:2, 4, 23, 24, 37. Ac 4:24. 22:30. Ga 5:14. Ep 4:9. 1 Th 4:1. **pray for**. Better, "what we should pray," i.e. what our prayer should be (Gifford). 1 K 8:30, 48. 2 K 19:20. Lk 18:11. Ph 1:9. **as we ought**. or, according to our need. Gifford states "the Greek adverb does not refer to the *manner* of praying, but to the correspondence between the prayer and that which is really needed." Jn 12:27, 28. +14:16. Ph 1:22, 23. **but**. ver. 15. Ps 10:17. Zc 12:10. Mt 10:20. Ga 4:6. Ep 2:18. 6:18. Ju *20, *21. **Spirit**. Gr. *pneuma*, Mt +3:16. **itself**. ver. 16. 1 Th 3:11. **intercession**. Ep 2:18. 6:18. **with groanings**. J. Schneider (TDNT, vol. 7, pp. 601, 602) points out that this sighing does not take place in us; it is the sighing of the Holy Spirit who, as our Paraclete, intercedes for us according to God's will. This is not, then, a reference to the sighing of Christians in prayer, or to speaking in tongues during prayer, or to inarticulate ecstatic speech. The groaning of the Spirit takes place not in response to our prayer, but when we are not able to pray, when we do not know what we ought to pray for. In ver. 22 Paul speaks of the sighing of creation; in ver. 23 of all Christians; here, of the Holy Spirit. T#1246. Ro 7:24. Ex 2:23, 24. Jb 23:1-4. Ps 6:3-9. *38:9, 10. 42:1-5. 55:1, 2. 69:3. 77:1-3. 88:1-3. 102:5, 19, 20. 119:81, 82. 143:4-7. Lk 22:44. Jn 11:38, 41, 42. 2 C 5:2, 4. 12:8. **which cannot**. The sighs are not unspoken, or unintelligible, but cannot be grasped in human words, though understood by God the Father. 1 S 1:13. Ps 42:1-4. *77:4. 2 C 12:4.

27. **And he.** 1 S +*16:7. 1 K 8:39. 1 Ch +*28:9.
29:17. Ps 7:9. 44:21. Pr 15:11. 16:2. 17:3. Je 11:20.
+*17:10. 20:12. Mt 6:8. Lk 16:15. Jn 21:17. Ac 1:24.
15:8. 1 Th 2:4. He √4:13. Re *2:23. **knoweth.** Ps *38:9.
+*66:18, 19. Ja +*5:16g. **the mind.** ver. +6. **Spirit.**
Gr. *pneuma*, Mt +3:16. +12:32. Jn +7:39. **because.**
or, that. **he maketh intercession.** T#1411. ver. 34.
Ga 4:6. Ep 2:18. **the saints.** 2 C +1:1. **according.** Pr
*15:8. Je √29:12, 13. Jn *14:13. 2 C 7:9. Ep 4:24. Ja
*1:5, 6. 1 P 4:6. 5:2. 1 J √3:21, 22. √5:14, 15.

28. **we know.** ver. +22, 35-39. Ro *5:3, 4. Ge
+*50:20. Dt 8:2, 3, 16. Ps 46:1, 2. *119:71. Je 24:5-
7. Zc +*13:9. 2 C 4:15-17. 5:1. Ph 1:19-23. 2 Th *1:5-
7. He *12:6-12. Ja 1:3, 4. 1 P 1:7, 8. Re *3:19. **all
things.** ver. +*32. 1 C *3:21, 22. 2 C *4:15. 6:10.
2 P +*1:3. **work.** Ep +*1:11. **for good.** Ge +*45:5.
+*50:20. Dt 12:25. 23:5. Ezr 8:22. Ec *8:12. Is 3:10.
Je +√29:11. **that love.** Ro +*5:5. Ex 20:6. Dt 6:5.
Ne 1:5. Ps 69:36. Mk 12:30. 1 C √2:9. 2 C *7:10, 11.
2 T 4:8. Ja *1:12. +*2:5. 1 J *4:10, 19. 5:2, 3. **the
called.** ver. 30. Ro *1:+6, 7. *9:11, 23, 24. *11:28,
+29. Dt +*10:15. Je 51:29. Mt 20:16. 22:14. Lk 18:7.
Ac +*13:48. 1 C *1:2, 9, 24. 7:15, 17. Ga *1:6, 15.
5:8, 13. Ep 1:9, 10. 3:11. 4:1, 4. Col *3:15. 1 Th *4:7.
+*5:9. 2 Th *2:13, 14. 1 T *6:12. 2 T +*1:9. √2:19.
He *9:15. 1 P 1:15. *2:9, 21. 3:9. *5:10. 2 P 1:3. Ju
1. Re *3:20. 17:14. *19:9. **purpose.** Ro *9:11. Lk 7:30.
Ac 2:23. 4:28. 20:27. Ep 1:9, +*11. 3:11. 2 T +*1:9.

29. **foreknow.** Ro +*11:2. Ge +*18:19. Ex 2:25.
33:12, 17. Ps +*1:6. 144:3. Je *1:5. Ho 13:5. Am 3:2.
Mt 7:23. Jn 10:14, 15. Ac 2:23. *15:14-18. 1 C 8:3.
Ga 4:9. 2 T √2:19. 1 P √1:2, 20. 1 J 3:1. Re *13:8.
predestinate. Ro 9:23. Ac 4:28. 1 C 2:7. Ep *1:5, +*11.
1 P 1:20. **to be conformed.** ver. 18. Ro 12:2. *13:14.
Jn 17:16, 19, 22, 23, 26. 1 C 15:49. 2 C *3:18. Ep
1:4. *2:10. 4:24. Ph +*3:21. Col +*1:15. 3:10. 2 P
*1:3, 4. 1 J √3:2. **to the image.** 2 C *3:18. 4:4. Col
1:15. **that he might.** Ro *6:4-8. Ps +*71:20. 80:17,
18. *89:27. Mt *12:50. 25:40. Jn *20:17. Ac 13:33.
Col +*1:15-18. He 1:5, 6. *2:11-15. Re +*1:5,6. **firstborn.** 1 Ch=5:2. √22D4C. Anthropomorphism B893.
Circumstances are attributed to God as to time: Christ
is said to be the "firstborn." For other instances of
this figure see Col 1:15. He 1:6. **many.** √171F, Is
+53:12. i.e. many relatively to others; but *all* with
respect to his own brethren (B624). **brethren.** Mt 12:50.
+28:10. Re *7:9.

30. **Moreover.** ver. +29. Ro 1:6. 9:23, 24. Is 41:9.
1 C *1:2, 9. Ep 4:4. He 9:15. 1 P *2:9. 2 P +*1:10.
Re 17:14. 19:9. **predestinate.** √50, Ho +2:21. **and.**
√148, Ge +8:22. **he called.** √50, Ho +2:21. ver. +28.
Ro *3:22-26. 1 C *6:11. Ga *1:15. 2 Th *2:14. T *3:4-
7. **also justified.** √96C2, Ge +45:9. **he justified.** √50,
Ho +2:21. ver. 1, 17, 18, 33-35. Ro √5:8-10. Jn √5:24.
6:39, 40. 17:22, 24. 1 C 6:11. 2 C 4:17. Ep 2:6. Ph
*3:8, 9. Col *3:4. 1 Th *2:12. 2 Th *1:10-12. *2:13,
14. 2 T 2:11. He 9:15. 1 P 3:9. 4:13, 14. 5:10. **glorified.**
√96C6, Mt +2:4. Ps *16:11. *138:8. Jn *17:22. Ph
*3:20, 21. He 2:10.

31. **What.** See on Ro 4:1. 6:1. 7:1. **If.** √184A, 1 C
+15:2. Ge *15:1. Nu *14:9. Dt *33:29. Jsh 10:42.
1 S 14:6. 17:45-47. 2 K 6:16. 2 Ch √32:7, 8. Jb 34:29.
Ps *27:1-3. +*34:4. 46:1-3, 7, 11. 56:4, 11. *84:11,
12. *118:6. Is 50:7-9. +*54:17. Je 1:19. 20:11. Jn √10:28-
30. He +*13:5, 6. 1 J 4:4. **for us.** √76, Ge +13:6.
2 K 6:16. 2 Ch 13:12. 1 J √4:4. **who.** √85C, Ge +18:14.

2 C 4:4. **against.** √121C2D4, Lk +10:19.

32. **He that.** Ro *5:6-10. 11:21. Ge *=22:12, 16.
Is *53:10. Mt *3:17. Jn √3:16. 2 C √5:21. 2 P 2:4, 5.
1 J 4:10. **his own Son.** Jn 5:18. **delivered.** Ro +4:25.
Ac *2:23. **for us all.** Mt *20:28. 2 C √5:15. 1 T *4:10.
how. ver. 28. Ro 5:9, 10. √6:23. Ge=22:8. Ps *84:11.
freely give. Ro 6:23. Lk 7:42g. Ac 8:17. +25:11. 1 C
*2:12. Ep 3:20. 1 T 6:17. **all things.** ver. *28. Dt=33:11.
Mt *6:33. 18:19. *21:22. Jn 14:14. 1 C *2:9. *3:21-
23. 2 C *4:15. +*9:8. Ph *4:19. 2 P +*1:3. 1 J 5:14,
15. Re *21:7.

33. **Who.** √85C, Ge +18:14. ver. 1. Jb *1:9-11. *2:4-
6. 22:6, etc. 34:8, 9. 42:7-9. Ps 35:11. Is *50:8, 9.
+*54:17. Zc *3:1-4. Ep *1:3, 4. Re √12:10, 11. **of God's.**
Dt +*10:15. Is 42:1. Mt 24:24. Lk +18:7. 1 Th 1:4.
2 Th *2:13. T 1:1. 1 P *1:2. **It is.** Ro *3:24, 26. Is
*43:25. *50:8, 9. Ga 3:8. Re 12:10, 11.

34. **Who.** √85C, Ge +18:14. √18, Dt +28:4. ver.
1. Ro 14:3. Jb 34:29. Ps 37:33. 109:31. Is 50:9. Je
50:20. **It is Christ.** Ro *4:25. *5:6-10. *14:9, 10. Jb
33:24. Mt *20:28. Jn *14:19. 2 C √5:21. Ga *3:13,
14. He 1:3. 9:10-14. 10:10-14, 19-22. *12:2. 1 P *3:18.
Re *1:18. **is risen.** Ro *1:4. Le 23:11. 1 C *15:17.
who is even. Ps ✱110:1. Mk 16:19. Ac +*7:56-60. Col
*3:1. He *1:3. *8:1, 2. *10:12-14. *12:1. 1 P *3:22.
right hand. √22A15C, Ps +110:1. **who also.** ver. 27.
Is *53:12. Mt +*10:32. Jn 16:23, 26, 27. 17:20-24.
He +*4:14, 15. √7:25. *9:24. 1 J √2:1, 2. **maketh intercession.** T#516, 1315. Nu=21:7. Is *53:12. Zc ✱6:13.
Lk *22:31, 32. Jn *17:9-21. He 4:14, 15. √7:25. *9:24.
*10:19-22. 1 J *2:1, 2.

35. **Who.** √85C, Ge +18:14. **shall separate.** ver.
39. Ps 103:17. Je 31:3. Jn √10:28. 13:1. 15:10, 13.
2 Th *2:13, 14, 16. Re +*1:5, 6. **the love.** 2 C 5:14.
Ep *3:17-19. 2 T 1:13. **shall tribulation.** ver. 17. Ro
2:9. *5:3-5. Mt +*5:10-12. +*10:28-31. Lk 21:12-18.
Jn *16:33. Ac +*14:22. 20:23, 24. 2 C 4:17. 6:4-10.
11:23-27. 2 T √1:12. *4:16-18. He 12:3-11. Ja 1:2-4.
1 P 1:5-7. 4:12-14. Re *7:14-17. **or.** √129, Ezk +34:4.
distress. 2 C 12:10. **persecution.** Ac 9:4. **famine.** Dt
28:48. 2 C 11:26, 27. **nakedness.** 1 C 4:11.

36. **For thy.** Ps ▶44:22. 141:7. Mt +*5:11, 12. Jn
16:2. 1 C *15:30, 31. 2 C *4:11. Ph *3:10. **we are
killed.** Ac +21:13. 1 C 4:9. 15:30, 31. 2 C 1:9. 4:10,
11. 6:9. 11:23. **as sheep.** Is *53:7. Je 11:19. 12:3. 51:40.
Zc 11:4. Ac 8:32. **for.** √181E, Ge +3:24.

37. **Nay.** 2 Ch 20:25-27. Is √25:8. 1 C *15:54, 57.
2 C 2:14. *4:17. √12:9, 10. 1 J 4:4. *5:4, 5. Re *7:9,
10. 11:7-12. √12:11. 17:14. *21:7. **more than.** Ps 60:12.
108:13. **conquerors.** Ex =17:11. Dt=33:11. Jg=1:35.
Jn +16:33. 1 C 15:57. **him.** ver. 35. Jn +13:34. Ga
2:20. Ep *5:2, 23, 25-27. 2 Th 2:16. 1 J 4:10, 19. Ju
*24. Re +*1:5.

38. **For I.** Ro 4:21. 2 C 4:13. √5:8. 2 T √1:12. He
11:13. **that.** Ro 14:8. Jn √10:28. 1 C 3:22, 23. *15:54-
58. 2 C 5:4-8. Ph +*1:20-23. **neither death.** ver. +36.
Ro *14:8. 1 C +*15:55. He *2:14, 15. *11:35. Re √12:11.
angels. Mt *25:41. 2C *11:14. 1 P 3:22. **nor principalities.** 1 C 15:24g. 2 C 11:14. Ep 1:21. √6:11, 12. Col
1:16. *2:15. T 3:1. 1 P *3:22. 5:8-10. 2 P 2:11. **nor
powers.** Ro 13:3. 1 C 15:24. Ep 1:21. 1 P *3:22. **things
to come.** Ac *20:22-24.

39. **Nor.** Ep 3:18, 19. **height.** Ex *9:16, 17. Ps 93:3,
4. Is 10:10-14, 33. 24:21. Da 4:11. 5:18-23. Ep 3:18.
2 Th 2:4. Re *13:1-8. **depth.** Ro +*11:33. Ps 64:6.
Pr 20:5. Mt 24:24. 2 C √2:11. *11:3. 2 Th √2:9-12.

Re √2:24. 12:9. 13:14. 19:20. 20:3, 7. **creature**. ver. 19-22. Ro 1:25. Ge 1:26. Ps 8:6. He 2:8. **shall be able**. Mt *24:24. Jn √10:28-30. Col *3:3, 4. 2 T *4:18. Ja *2:5. 2 P +*1:10. *2:9. **love**. ver. 35. Ro +*5:8. Je *31:3. Lk 16:23. Jn √3:16. 16:27. 17:26. Ep 1:4. *2:4-7. Col *3:3. 2 Th +3:5. T 3:4-7. 1 J *4:9, 10, 16, 19.

ROMANS 9

The apostle deeply laments the unbelief of his countrymen, and declares his willingness to endure any thing for their salvation, 1-3. He shows the privileges of Israel as a nation, 4, 5; and the difference between Israelites according to the flesh, and the true Israel, 6-8. He illustrates his subject by the example of Isaac, Jacob and Esau, and of Pharaoh; and thus shows the freeness of the mercy of God, and his holy but absolute sovereignty in all his dispensations, 9-18. He answers objections to his doctrine, 19-23; proves it from the prophets, 24-29; and evinces, that the Jews come short of the blessing (which the Gentiles obtained by faith), because "they sought it by the works of the law," and rejected Christ, 30-33.

1. **I say**. Ro +1:9. 2 C 1:23. 11:31. *12:19. Ph 1:8. 1 Th 2:5. 1 T 2:7. 5:21. 2 T +*4:1. **lie not**. Ac 5:3, 4. 2 C *11:31. Ga 1:20. **my conscience**. Ro 2:15. 8:16. 2 C +1:12. 1 T 1:5. 2 T 1:3. 1 J 3:19-21. **Ghost**. Gr. *pneuma*, Mt +1:18.

2. **I have**. Ro *10:1. 1 S 15:35. Ps *119:136. Is 66:10. Je *9:1. 13:17. La 1:12. 3:48, 49, 51. Ezk +*9:4. Lk *19:41-44. 2 C 6:10. Ph *3:18. Re 11:3.

3. **For**. ſ81, Ge +15:13. ſ47, Ezk +16:23. **I could**. ſ17. Anamnesis: or, Recalling B918: an expression of feeling by way of recalling to mind. Here, "could wish" is in the imperfect tense, and has the sense of "I used to wish." Ex *32:32. Ga 3:15. 2 T 2:9, 10. **wish**. ſ87, Ps +118:25. ſ102C, Mt +5:29. **were**. Dt 21:23. Jsh 6:17, 18. 1 S 14:24, 44. Ga 1:8. 3:10, 13. **accursed**. *or*, separated. Mk 15:34. Lk 6:22. 21:5g. Ac 23:14g. 1 C *5:5. 12:3. Ga 1:8, 9. *3:13. my **brethren**. Ac +22:5. **my kinsmen**. Ro +*11:1. Ge 29:14. Est 8:6. Ac 7:23-26. 13:26. **according**. Ro +1:3. 11:14.

4. **Who are**. Ge 12:2, 3. 13:15. 2 S 7:16. Ps 89:36. Je 31:36. 33:21. Da 7:14. **Israelites**. ver. 6. Ro 2:28, 29. Ge 32:28. Ex 4:22. 19:3-6. Dt *7:6. Ps 73:1. Is 41:8. 46:3. Ho 12:3-5. Jn 1:47. Ga 6:16. **the adoption**. Ro +8:15. Ex 4:22. Dt *14:1. 32:6. Ps +*33:12. Je 31:9, 20. Ho 11:1. **and**. ſ148, Ge +8:22. **the glory**. Ex 40:34. Le 16:2. Nu 7:89. 1 S *4:21, 22. 1 K *8:11. Ps *63:2. *78:61. 90:16. Is 60:19. Ac 7:2. 1 C 2:8. Ja 2:1. **covenants**. *or*, testaments. ſ121L7, 1 K +8:21. Ro 11:27. Ge 15:18. +*17:2, 7, 10. 26:24. 28:13, 14. Ex 24:7, 8. 31:16, 17. 34:27, 28. Dt *29:1, 12-14. 31:16. Ne 13:29. Ps 89:3, 34. Je +*31:33. 33:20-25. Lk 1:72. Ac *3:25. 7:8. Ga 3:15. 4:24. Ep *2:12. He 7:22. *8:6-10. 9:4. 10:16. 12:24. **the giving**. Ro 2:17. 3:2. Dt 4:14. Ne 9:13, 14. Ps 147:19, 20. Ezk 20:11, 12. Jn 1:17. **the service**. Ro 12:1. Ex 12:25. Is 5:2. Mt 21:33. Col ◐√2:16, 17. He *9:1, 3, 10. **promises**. Ro +*15:8. Mt +*11:3. Lk 1:54, 55, 69-75. Jn +4:22. Ac +*2:39. 3:25, 26. *13:+32, 33. +√26:6, 7. Ep 2:12. He 6:12-17.

5. **are the fathers**. Ro *11:28. +15:8. Dt *10:15. **of whom**. Ro 1:3. 11:14. Ge +*12:3. +*49:10. Is +*7:14. 11:1. Mt 1:1, etc. Lk *3:23, etc. 2 T 2:8. Re 22:16. **who is**. Ro 10:12. Ps +*45:6. *103:19. Is +*9:6,

7. Je +*23:5, 6. Mi +*5:2. Jn +*1:1-3. +*10:30. Ac +*20:28. Ph *2:6-11. Col 1:16. 1 T 3:16. He *1:8-13. 1 J *5:20. **over**. Ps 78:17, 35, 56. 83:18. Da 7:18. Mt 11:10. Mk 5:7. Lk 1:76. 8:28. Ac 7:48. 16:12. 1 C 10:9. 1 Th 3:13. **all**. Ep 4:6. Col 1:16-19. **God**. This is a clear and unequivocal instance of Christ being called God. The rendering and punctuation given in the A.V. applying this expression to Christ is strictly correct according to the context, as well as Greek grammar and usage. Gifford asserts "It is the natural and simple construction, which every Greek scholar would adopt without hesitation, if no question of doctrine were involved. This cannot be said for any other construction" (Comm. on Romans, p. 178). Jb +*19:26. Je 23:6. Jn 1:1. +*20:28. Ac +*20:28. 1 C +*2:8. Col 2:9. T √2:13. He +*1:8. 1 J 5:20. **blessed**. Strictly speaking, as Gifford observes, this is "not a doxology at all: but a solemn declaration of Deity, exactly similar in form to 2 C 11:31; compare Ro 1:25." A. T. Robertson comments, "A clear statement of the deity of Christ following the remark about his humanity. This is the natural and the obvious way of punctuating the sentence. To make a full stop after *sarka* (or colon) and start a new sentence for the doxology is very abrupt and awkward" (*Word Pictures*, vol. 4, p. 381). Re-punctuating the verse by placing a period after "flesh" and taking the whole clause as a doxology to the Father is (1) totally inappropriate to the context, and (2) in violation of Greek grammar which requires that wherever *eulogatos* (blessed) occurs in a doxology, it stands first (Gifford). It may safely be affirmed that any translation which fails to make this an ascription of deity to Christ does so for strictly doctrinal reasons. Ro √1:25. Ps 72:19. 89:52. 104:35. Mk +*14:61. Ac +*7:59. 2 C √11:31. 1 T 6:15. **for ever**. Gr. *aion*, Mt +6:13. lit. unto the ages. **Amen**. Dt 27:15, etc. 1 K 1:36. 1 Ch 16:36. Ps 41:13. 89:52. 106:48. Je 28:6. Mt +*6:13. 28:20. 1 C 14:16. Re 1:18. 5:14. 22:20.

6. **Not**. ſ152A. Prolepsis: Tecta B980. When the objection is stated, or merely implied, but not answered, called closed Prolepsis. Sometimes the anticipated objection is answered, but not plainly stated. For other instances of this figure see Ro 10:18. 11:1, 11. **as though**. Ro *3:3. +√11:1, 2, 12. Nu *23:19. Is *55:11. Mt 24:35. Lk *1:68-70. Jn *10:35. 2 T 2:13. He *6:17, 18. **the word of God**. Ac +11:1. 1 C 14:36. 2 C 2:17. 4:2. Ep 6:17. Ph 1:14. Col 1:25. 1 Th √2:13. 1 T 4:5. 2 T 2:9. T 2:5. He √4:12. 13:7. 1 P √1:23. 2 P 3:5. 1 J 2:14. Re +1:2. **they are not**. Ro *2:28, 29n. *4:12-16. Ps 73:1. Jn *1:47. Ga *6:16. **Israel**. ver. +4. **of Israel**. ſ145, Jg +11:40.

7. **because**. ſ77, Ex +3:19. Lk 3:8. 16:24, 25, 30. Jn 8:+33, 37-39. Ga 4:23. Ph 3:3. **In Isaac**. Ge *17:20, 21. ▶21:12. Ga 3:29. He 11:18.

8. **They which**. Ro 4:11-16. Ga 4:22-31. **children of God**. Ro 8:16, 17, 21. Jn +11:52. **promise**. He +*11:13. ſ121L6. Metonymy of the Subject B585. *Promise* is put for the faith which receives it. For another instance of this figure see Ga 4:28. **are counted**. Ro 4:13, 16. Ge 31:15. Ps 22:30. 87:6. Jn 1:13. Ga *3:26-29. *4:23, 28. 1 J *3:1, 2.

9. **of**. ſ181E, Ge +3:24. **At this time**. Ge 17:21. ▶18:10, 14. 21:2, Sarah. He 11:11, 12, 17. **Sarah**. i.e. *princess of the multitude*, ✱S#4564g. For ✱S#8283h, see Ge +17:15. Ro 4:19. He 11:11. 1 P 3:6.

10. **not only**. Ro 5:3, 11. 8:23. Lk 16:26. 2 C 8:19.

this. *r*63I1D, Nu +26:4. **but when.** Ge *25:21-23, Rebekah. **Rebecca.** i.e. *to ensnare by beauty,* *S#4479g, only here. For *S#7259h, see Ge +22:23.

11. **the children.** Ro 4:17. Ps +*51:5. Ep *2:3. **not yet.** ver. 16. Ro 10:20. 1 C 1:27-29. **neither having done.** Is 7:16. **that the purpose.** Ro +*8:28-30. Is 14:24, 26, 27. 23:9. 46:10, 11. Je 51:29. Ep *1:9-11. 3:11. 2 T +*1:9. **election.** Ro *11:5, 7, 28. Ac +*13:48. 1 Th 1:4. 1 P 5:13. 2 P +√1:10. 2 J +*1. **according.** Ro *11:5, 7. Ep *1:4, 5. 1 Th 1:4. 2 P +*1:10. **not of works.** Ro 11:6. Ep √2:9. T √3:5. **but of.** Ro 4:17. +*8:28. 1 Th 2:12. 2 Th *2:13, 14. 1 T +*1:9. 1 P 5:10. Re 17:14.

12. **The elder.** *or,* The greater. Ge √25:22, ▶23. 2 S 8:14. 1 K 22:47. 1 Ch +*26:10. Col +*1:15. **younger.** *or,* lesser.

13. **Jacob.** √*r*121A5, √*r*121T3, Ge +9:27. Ml √▶1:2, 3n. **loved.** Ge 29:30, 31. Pr 13:24. Ml 1:2. Mt 6:24. Lk +*14:26. 16:13. **but.** Col +*1:15. **Esau.** √*r*121A5, √*r*121T3, Ge +9:27. **hated.** Ge 29:31, 33. Dt 21:15. Pr 13:24. Mt *10:37. Lk +*14:26. Jn *12:25.

14. **shall.** *r*152B, Is +49:14. See on Ro 3:1, 5. **Is there unrighteousness.** Ro 2:5. 3:5, 6. Ge +*18:25. Dt +*32:4. 2 Ch 19:7. Jb 8:3. 34:10-12, 18, 19. 35:2. Ps *92:15. *104:28. +*145:9, 17. Pr +*19:3. Is √29:24. Je 12:1. +*29:11. Ezk +√18:25. Ja +*1:17. Re *15:3, 4. 16:7. **God forbid.** Ro +6:2.

15. **he saith.** Ep 4:8. **to Moses.** Mk +12:19. **I will have.** ver. 16, 18, 19. Ex ▶33:19. 34:6, 7. Is 27:11. Mi +*7:18.

16. **it is.** *r*63C, Ge +25:32. Supply by ellipsis (absolute: brachylogia), "So then (election is) not of him who willeth (as Isaac wished to bless Esau according to 'the will of the flesh')," compare as Jacob was asked to bless Ephraim and Manasseh according to 'the will of man,' Joseph, Ge 48:5-14; both cases are instanced in He 9:20, 21 as acts of 'faith,' faith's exercise of gifts contrary to the will of the flesh in the case of Isaac; and contrary to the will of man in the case of Jacob, "nor of him that runneth (as Esau ran for venison that his father might eat, and bless him), but of God who showeth mercy." **not of him.** ver. 11. Ge *27:1-4, 9-14. Ps 110:3. Is 65:1. Mt 11:25, 26. Lk 10:21. Jn *1:12, 13. 3:8. 1 C 1:26-31. Ep 2:4, 5. Ph √2:13. 2 Th *2:13, 14. T *3:3-5. Ja +*1:18. 1 P *2:9, 10. **that willeth.** Jn 1:12, 13g. **that runneth.** 1 C 9:24, 26. Ga 2:2. 5:7. Ph 2:16. **of God.** 2 T +*1:9.

17. **the scripture.** Ro 11:4. Lk +4:21. Ga 3:8, 22. 4:30. **Even.** See on Ex ▶9:16. **I raised.** 1 S 2:7, 8. Est 4:14. Is 10:5, 6. 45:1-3. Je 27:6, 7. 50:41. Da 4:22. 5:18-21. Hab 1:6. Zc 11:16. **that.** Ro 10:1, 2. 14:17, 18. 15:14, 15. 18:10, 11. Jsh 2:9, 10. 9:9. 1 S 4:8. Ps 83:17, 18. Pr 16:4. Is 37:20. **that my.** Jn 17:26.

18. **hath.** ver. 15, 16. Ro *5:20, 21. Ep 1:6. **mercy.** Ex +▶33:19. **whom he will.** T#234. Ex +20:5 (T#246). Dt +32:35 (T#248). 1 S +15:3 (T#244). 1 Ch +6:15 (T#247). Jb *23:13. *33:13. +38:33 (T#240). Ps +*115:3. *135:6. Is *55:10, 11. Da *4:+17 (T#245), 35. Mt +4:10 (T#241). 11:25, 26. *20:12-16. Jn 5:21. 2 C +11:19 (T#243). Ep +*1:11. Ph *2:13. 2 T +2:25 (T#242). **he hardeneth.** √*r*108A4, Ge +31:7. Ro +*1:24-28. +*2:4, 5. 11:7, 8. See on Ex +*4:21. 7:3, 13, +*14. ◐*8:15. +*9:12. 10:20, 27. 11:10. 14:4, 8, 17. Dt +*2:30. Jsh 11:20. 2 Ch √32:31. Ne ◐*9:16. Ps ◐*95:8-11. Is 63:17. Je ◐*7:26. Ezk *18:31, 32. Am +√3:6. Mt 13:14, 15. Jn *5:40. +*12:40. Ac 28:26-

28. 2 C √4:3, 4. 1 Th ◐+*5:9. 2 Th √2:10-12. 1 T ◐√2:3, 4. He 3:+8, +*13. Ja √1:13, 14.

19. **Thou.** *r*38D, Ps +27:14. Ro *3:8. 11:19. 1 C 15:12, 35. Ja *1:13. 2:18. **wilt say.** *r*152B, Is +49:14. **Why doth.** Ro *3:5-7. **For who.** Ge +*50:20. 2 Ch 20:6. Jb 9:12-15, 19. 23:13, 14. Ps 76:10. Is *10:5-7. 46:10, 11. Da 4:35. Mk *14:21. Ac *2:23. 4:27, 28. **his will.** Ac 27:43. 1 P 4:3g.

20. **Nay but.** *r*80, Lk +9:55. **O man.** *r*38D, Ps +27:14. Ro 2:1, 3. Mi +√6:8. Lk 12:14. 1 C 7:16. Ja 2:20. **who art.** *r*21, Jg +14:18. Jb 33:13. 36:23. 38:2, 3. 40:2, 5, 8. 42:2-6. Mt 20:15. Ac 11:17. Ja 4:12. **repliest.** *or,* answerest again. Jb *9:12-15. 16:3. *33:12, 13. *34:22, 23. T 2:9. *or,* disputest with God? T#273. Jb 40:2. Is *45:9, 10. Mt 20:15. Lk *19:27. 1 C 1:20. 1 T 6:5. **Shall.** Is 29:16. ▶45:9-11. **say.** *r*155D, Ge +4:10. **Why hast.** Ex +*33:19. Mt 20:15.

21. **the potter.** ver. 11, 18. Pr 16:4. Is √64:8. Je *18:3-6. Ep *2:1-7, 10. **same lump.** Ro 11:16. 1 C 5:6, 7. Ga 5:9g. **one vessel.** ver. 22, 23. Je 22:28. Ho 8:8. Ac 9:15. 2 T 2:20, 21.

22. **if.** *r*184A, 1 C +15:2. **willing.** ver. 17. Ro 1:18. 2:4, 5. Ex *9:16. Ps 90:11. Pr 16:4. Re +*6:16, 17. **endured.** Nu 14:11, 18. Ps 50:21, 22. Ec 8:11, 12. La 3:22. 1 P *3:20. 2 P *2:3, 9. 3:8, √9, 15. Ju 4. Re 6:9-11. **longsuffering.** Ro +2:4. **the vessels.** The Apostle, by employing the appellation of the *vessels of wrath,* carries on the similitude of the potter, by which he had illustrated the sovereignty of God. ver. 21, 23. Ac 9:15. 1 Th +*5:9. 2 T 2:20. **fitted.** *or,* made up. Ge +*15:16. Jb 21:30. Pr 16:4. Mt *5:13. 23:31-33. 1 Th *2:16. 1 P 2:8. 2 P 2:9. Ju 4.

23. **might.** Ro +2:4. *5:20, 21. Ep 1:6-8, 18. 2:4, 7, 10. 3:8, 16. Col *1:27. 2 Th 1:10-12. **riches.** *r*22D5I, Pr +8:18. **vessels of mercy.** ver. 21, 22. Ac 9:15. **afore prepared.** Ro +*8:29. 11:5, 6. 1 Ch 29:18. Lk 1:17. Ac +*13:48. 1 C *6:20. Ep 2:3-5. Col +*1:10-12. 1 Th +*5:9. 2 Th *2:13, 14. 2 T *2:20, 21. T *3:3-7. 1 P *1:2-5.

24. **whom.** Ro +*8:28-30. 1 C 1:9. He 3:1. 1 P 5:10. Re 19:9. **not of the Jews.** Ro +*3:29, 30. 4:11, 12. *10:12. 11:11-13. *15:8-16. Ge +*49:10. Ps 22:27. Ac +*13:47, 48. *15:14. 21:17-20. Ga +*3:28. Ep *2:11-13. *3:6-8. Col +*3:11. **Gentiles.** *r*63D2, Ge 30:27. Here we have a remarkable *anantapodoton.* The conclusion of the argument is omitted. It begins with "if" (ver. 22), and the *apodosis* must be supplied at the end of verse 24 from verse 20, i.e., if God chooses to do this or that "who art thou that repliest against God?" What have you to say? Or, indeed, we may treat it as the *Ellipsis* of a prior member, in which case verse 22 would commence "(what reply hast thou to make), if God, willing to show his wrath," etc. (B54).

25. **in Osee.** *S#5617g, only here. For *S#1954h, see Ho 1:+1, 2, Hosea. **I will call.** Ho ▶2:23. 1 P *2:10. **not.** *r*175B, Ge +21:16. **beloved.** Ro 1:7. Ezk 16:8. Jn 16:27. **not beloved.** *r*175B, Ge +21:16.

26. **And it.** Ho ▶1:9, 10. **come to pass.** *r*144A11, Ge +38:1. **in the place.** Is 62:4. **Ye are not.** Le 26:12. **there shall.** Ro 8:16. Is 43:6. Jn 11:52. 2 C 6:18. Ga 3:26. 1 J 3:1-3. **the children.** Ro +8:14. **the living God.** Mt +16:16.

27. **Esias.** Is 1:1, Isaiah. Mk +1:2. **Though.** *r*184C, Mt +4:9. *r*92F2, Mt +2:6. *r*92C, Mt +2:15. See on Is ▶10:20-23. Ho 1:10. **as the sand.** *r*102B, *r*138B, Ge +13:16. Ge 22:17. Ezk *5:7. He +11:12. **a remnant.**

ver. +*29. Ro 11:4-6. Ezr 9:8, 14. Is 1:9. *6:13. 10:20, 21. +√11:11n. 24:13. Je 5:10. *42:2. Ezk 6:8. Mi + *5:3-8.

28. **work**. *or*, account. **and cut**. Is 28:22. *30:12-14, 17. Da +*9:26, 27. Mt +*24:21, 22. **in righteousness**. Ps 9:8. 65:5. *145:17. Is 5:16. Ac √17:31. Re 19:11.

29. **Except**. ♪92C, Mt +2:15. ♪184B, Mt +11:21. Is ▸1:9. 6:13. La *3:22. Ml 3:6. **Lord of Sabaoth**. i.e. "hosts," *S#4519g. Is +*6:5. 44:6. 54:5. Je 10:16. 50:34. 51:19. Jn 12:37-41. Ja +*5:4g. **a seed**. ♪92F2, Mt +2:6. ver. +*27. Ro 11:5. Is 1:9. *4:3. *11:16. 37:4. Je 6:9. *23:3. *31:7. Ezk *14:22. Am *9:9. Mi 2:12. Zp 2:9. **we had been**. Ge 19:24, 25. Dt 29:23. Is 13:19. Je 49:18. 50:40. La 4:6. Am 4:11. Zp 2:6, Sodom, Gomorrah. 2 P 2:6. Ju +√7. **as Sodoma**. i.e. *their secret; fettered*, *S#4670g, Lk +10:12. For *S#5467h, see Ge +10:19. **Gomorrah**. Ge +*10:19. Mt +*10:15.

30. **shall**. See on ver. 14. Ro 3:5. **the Gentiles**. ver. 24. Ro +*1:18-32. 4:11. *10:20. Is 65:1, 2. 1 C +*6:9-11. Ep 2:12. *4:17-19. 1 P 4:3. **followed not**. ver. 31. Pr 15:9. 21:21. Is 51:1. 1 T 6:11. **attained**. 1 C 9:24. Ph 3:12, 13g. **even the righteousness**. ♪16, Ge +1:27. Ro +*1:16, 17. *3:21, 22. 4:9, 11, 13, 22. 5:1. *10:6, 10. Ga *2:16. 3:8, 24. 5:5. Ph *3:8, 9. He 11:7.

31. **followed**. ver. 30-32. Ro *10:2-4. 11:7. Is 51:1. Ac *21:20. Ga 3:21. Ph 3:6. **the law**. Ro 3:27. 7:21. He *10:1. Ga 3:24. **hath not**. Ro *2:17-25. *3:20. 4:14, 15. 11:7. Dt *4:8. Mt *5:20, 27, 28. Mk *10:19-22. Ga *3:10, 11. √5:3, 4. Ja√2:10, 11. **righteousness**. ♪100, Ge +10:9.

32. **Because**. Ro *4:16. 10:3. Mt 19:16-20. Jn *6:27-29. Ac √16:30-34. 1 J √5:9-12. **as**. ♪160B, Ge +25:31. **they stumbled**. Ro 11:11. Mt 13:57. Lk *2:34. 7:23. 1 C *1:23. **stumblingstone**. ♪22L2, Is +8:14. Ro 14:13, 20. Is 8:14. 1 C 8:9. 1 P 2:8.

33. **Behold**. ♪92G, Lk +4:18. Ps *118:22. Is *8:14, 15. ▸28:16. Mt *21:42, 44. 1 P 2:6-8. **stumblingstone**. ♪173, Ge +27:44. ♪22L2, Is +8:14. **rock of offence**. Ro 11:9. 14:13. 16:17. Mt +*13:41. +15:12. 1 C 1:23. Ga 5:11. 1 P 2:8. 1 J 2:10. Re 2:14. **and whosoever**. Ro *5:5. 10:11, 13. Ps 25:2, 3, 20. Is 45:17, 26. 54:4. Jl 2:26, 27. Ph 1:20. 2 T √1:12. 1 J 2:28. **ashamed**. *or*, confounded. ♪121G2, Ps +25:2. ♪96F2, Mt +2:6. Is 49:23. 2 T 2:15. 1 P *2:6.

ROMANS 10

The apostle again shows his earnest desire of Israel's salvation; testifying that they had zeal, stating wherein it was erroneous, and distinguishing between the righteousness of the law, and that of faith, 1-11. He maintains that Jews and Gentiles are, in this respect, on equal terms, 12, 13; that the gospel must be preached to the Gentiles in order to their believing in Christ; and that the prophets had foretold the rejection of the Jews, and the calling of the Gentiles, 19-21.

1. **my heart's**. Ro 9:1-3. Ex 32:10-13. 1 S 12:23. 15:11, 35. 16:1. Je 17:16. 18:20. Lk 13:34. 19:41, 42. Jn 5:34. 1 C 9:20-22. **desire**. 2 Th 1:11. **and prayer**. 1 S +*12:23. Mt *5:44. Lk 23:34. 1 T *2:1, 3, 4.

2. **I bear them**. By this fine apology for the Jews, the Apostle prepares them for the harsher truths which he was about to deliver. 2 C 8:3. Ga 4:15. Col 4:13. **that they**. 2 K 10:16. Jn 16:2. Ac *21:+20, 28. *22:3,

22. 26:9, 10. Ga *1:14. 4:17, 18. Ph 3:6. **of**. ♪181E, Ge +3:24. **but not**. ♪175B, Ge +21:16. T#748. ver. 3. Ro 9:31, 32. 1 K 18:28. Ps 14:4. Pr 19:2. Is 27:11. Mt *23:15. Jn 5:16. Ac 22:3. 2 C *4:4, 6. Ga 1:13, 14. 4:17, ●+*18. Ph 1:9.

3. **God's righteousness**. "God's method of justification," says Abp. Newcome: God's method of saving sinners. Ro +*1:17. 3:22, 26. 5:19. 9:30. Ps 71:15, 16, 19. Is 51:6, 8. 56:1. Je +*23:5, 6. Da +*9:24. Jn 16:9, 10. 2 C √5:21. 2 P 1:1. **to establish**. Ro 9:+31, 32. Ge=43:22. Is 57:12. √64:6. Lk 10:29. 16:15. *18:9-12. Ga √5:3, 4. Ph *3:9. Re 3:17, 18. **submitted**. Le 26:41. Ne 9:33. Jb 33:27. Ps √25:8, 9. La 3:22. Da 9:6-9. Lk 15:17-21. Ja *4:7. 1 P 2:13. 5:5.

4. **Christ**. Ro 3:25-31. 8:3, 4. 13:8. Is 53:11. Mt +*3:15. +*5:17, 18. Jn 1:17. Ac +*13:38, 39. 1 C *1:30. Ga *3:10, 13, 24. Ep 2:15. Col √2:10, 14, 16, 17. He 9:7-14. *10:4-12, 14. **the end**. Gr. *telos*, the *object, scope*, or *final cause*; the *end* proposed and intended. In this sense Elsner observes that *telos* is used by Arrian. **righteousness**. Ro 3:22. 5:19. 1 C *1:30. 2 C √5:17. Ph *3:9. 2 P 1:1. **to every**. Ro 3:22. 4:11, 16.

5. **Moses**. Mk +12:19. **righteousness**. Ph 3:9. **That the man**. Ro 7:10. Le ▸18:5. Ne 9:29. Ezk 18:5-9. 20:11, 13, 21. Mt 19:17. Lk *10:27, 28. Ga *3:12.

6. **righteousness**. Ro 3:22, 25. 4:13. 9:+30, 31. Ph *3:9. He 11:7. **speaketh**. ♪155D, Ge +4:10. **Say not**. ♪92C, Mt +2:15. The Apostle here takes the general sentiment, and expresses it in his own language; beautifully accommodating what Moses says of the law to his present purpose. Dt *30:11-14. Pr 30:4. **Who**. ♪85I, Ge +18:12. **that is**. ♪81, Ge +15:13. **to bring**. Jn +*3:12, 13. *6:33, 38, 50, 51, 58. Ep 4:8-10. He 1:3.

7. **Who**. ♪85I, Ge +18:12. **the deep**. Re +9:1. **that is**. ♪81, Ge +15:13. **to bring up**. Ro +*4:25. *6:9. He *13:20. 1 P *3:18, 22. Re *1:18.

8. **The word**. Dt ▸30:14. **thy mouth**. ver. 10. Ps 119:11, 13. **the word of faith**. ver. √17. Ro +*1:16, 17. Is 57:19. Mk *16:15, 16. Ac +*10:43. +*13:38, 39. √16:31. Ga 3:2, 5. Col *1:5, 6. 1 T 4:6. 1 P *1:23, 25. **preach**. ♪63I1D, Nu +26:4. Supply by ellipsis, (is nigh thee).

9. **That if**. ♪184C, Mt +4:9. Ro *14:11. Mt +*10:32, 33. Lk *12:8. Jn 9:22. *12:42, 43. 1 C +*12:3. Ph *2:11. 1 J 4:2, 3. 2 J 7. **confess**. ♪108B, Mt +10:32. Mt +10:32g. **the Lord Jesus**. or, Jesus as Lord. Mt ●+7:21. Lk ●+*6:46. Jn +*20:28. Ac +√10:36. 1 C √2:8. +√12:3. √15:47. Ja 2:1. **and shalt believe**. Ro *8:34. Jn *6:69-71. √20:26-29. Ac √8:37. +*16:31. 1 C *15:14-18. 1 P 1:21. **raised him**. Jn +*2:22. Ac +*2:24. 1 P 1:21.

10. **For with**. Lk *8:15. Jn *1:12, 13. 3:19-21. He +*3:12. +*10:22. **heart**. ver. 8. Dt +*6:5. 1 K +*8:18. 2 K +*20:3. 1 Ch 12:38n. Jl +*2:12. **believeth**. 2 Ch +*20:20. Ga *2:16. **unto righteousness**. ♪63J1, Ge +13:9. 2 C √5:21. Ga *2:16. Ph *3:9. **and with**. ver. *9. Ja *2:18. 1 J *4:15. Re 2:13. **confession**. ♪108B, Mt +10:32. Ps *107:2. Mt +10:32g. Ac +*4:20. **salvation**. ♪63J1, Ge +13:9.

11. **the scripture**. Lk +4:21. **Whosoever**. Ro +9:33. Is *28:16. *49:23. Je 17:7. 1 P 2:6. **believeth**. ver. +*14. **ashamed**. ♪121G2, Ps +25:2.

12. **there is no**. Ro *3:22, 29, 30. 4:11, 12. 9:24. Ac 10:34, 35. 15:8, 9. 1 C 1:24. √12:13. Ga +*3:28. Ep 2:18-22. +*3:6. Col +*3:11. **Lord**. ver. 9. Ro 14:9.

15:12. Ac +√10:36. 1 C 15:47. Ph 2:11. 1 T √2:5. Re 17:14. 19:16. **rich.** ⨍22D5I, Pr +8:18. Ro +*2:4. 9:23. 2 C √8:9. Ep *1:7. *2:4, 7. 3:8, 16. Ph √4:19. Col *1:27. 2:2, 3. **call upon him.** Ps 86:5. *145:18. Is √55:6. Ac +9:14. +*10:4. 1 C 1:2. 2 T *2:22.

13. **whosoever.** Jl ▶2:32. Ac 2:21. **shall call.** Ac +*2:21. +*7:59. 1 C *1:2.

14. **How then.** Ac +*27:31. **shall they.** 1 K 8:41-43. Jon 1:5, 9-14, 16. 3:5-9. He √11:6. Ja 5:15. **call.** ⨍50, Ho +2:21. **believed.** ver. 11. Ro 4:5, 24. 9:33. Jn +4:39. Ac +*10:43. Ga *2:16. Ph 1:29. 1 T 1:16. 1 P 1:8, 21. 2:6. **and how shall.** Ro *1:5. √16:25, 26. Mk *16:15, 16. Lk *24:46, 47. Jn √20:31. Ac 19:2. +*26:17, 18. 2 T *4:17. T 1:3. **believe in.** ⨍50, Ho +2:21. T 3:8g. **not heard.** Jn 9:36. 17:20. Ep 4:21. **hear.** ⨍50, Ho +2:21. **without.** Ac 8:31. T 1:3.

15. **And how.** He 23:32. Mt *9:38. 10:1-6. 28:18-20. Lk 10:1. Jn 20:21. Ac 9:15. 13:2-4. 22:21. 1 C 12:28, 29. 2 C *5:18-20. Ep 3:8. 4:11, 12. 1 P 1:12. **preach.** ⨍50, Ho +2:21. **How beautiful.** Is ▶52:7. Na 1:15. **them.** ⨍92F3, Mt +4:7. **the gospel.** ⨍173, Ge +27:44. Is 57:19. Lk 2:14. Ac 10:36. Ep *2:17. 6:15. **and bring.** Is 40:9. 61:1. Lk *2:10. 8:1. Ac *13:26.

16. **But they.** Ro 3:3. 11:17. Jn 10:26. Ac 28:24. He √4:2. 1 P 2:8. **obeyed.** Ro 1:5. 2:8. 6:17. 16:26. Is 50:10. Ga 3:1. 5:7. 2 Th 1:8. He +*5:9. 11:8. 1 P 1:22. 3:1. **Esaias.** Mk +1:2. **Lord.** Is ▶53:1. Jn *12:38-40. **our report.** Gr. the hearing of us, or, our preaching. ⨍121R1, Le +13:55. Ac 10:36.

17. **faith.** ver. *14. Ro √1:16. Lk *16:29-31. 1 C *1:18-24. Ga 3:2, 5. Col *1:4-6. 1 Th √2:13. 2 Th *2:13, 14. He *4:2. Ja *1:18-21. 1 P 1:23-25. *2:1, 2. **by hearing.** T#888. Ro √1:16. Ps *19:7, 8, 11. *119:105, 130. Pr 6:23. 8:34. Is 2:3. 55:2, 3, 10-12. Mk *4:24, 25. Jn √5:39. √20:31. Ac 4:4. +*17:11, 12. 1 C 1:21. Ga *3:2, 5. Ja *1:21. 2 P *1:19. Re *1:3. **and hearing.** ⨍16, Ge +1:27. Je +*23:28, 29. Mk *4:24. Lk 8:11, 21. +*11:28. 2 C *2:17. He √4:12, 13. Re 1:9. **by the word.** T#1115. ver. 8. Pr *4:20-22. 1 Th √2:13. 2 T +*3:15-17. Ja *1:18. 1 P *1:23. **of God.** Lk 3:2. Jn 3:34. Ep 6:17. He 6:5. 11:3. Significant ancient authorities support the alternate reading "of Christ," but Gifford cites Meyer, De Wette, Lange, Philippi, etc., who "agree in regarding it as a gloss intended to define more precisely the meaning of "by the word of God." Furthermore, if the alternate reading is accepted, it is the only occurrence of *reema Christou* in the New Testament. Jn 5:38. 8:37. Col 3:16. 1 P 1:11. 1 J 1:10.

18. **I say.** ⨍96D1, Ec +3:18. By the Holy Spirit what David said is now repeated by Paul in the first person. **Have they.** ⨍152A, Ro +9:6. Ac *2:5-11. 26:20. 28:23. **their sound.** Similar to this elegant accommodation of these words, is the application of them in a passage of *Zohar*, Genes. f. 9. "These words are the servants of the Messiah, and measure out both the things above, and the things beneath." Ro 1:8. 15:19. Ps *▶19:4. Mt +*24:14. 26:13. +*28:19. Mk *16:15, 20. Col *1:6, 23. 1 Th 1:8. **all.** ⨍171A, Ex +9:6. **unto the ends.** Ro *15:19. 1 K 18:10. Ps *19:4, 5. 22:27. 98:3. Is 24:16. 49:6. 52:10. Je 16:19. Ml 4:2. Mt 4:8. 24:14. Mk 16:15. Ac *8:4, 25, 40. *9:19, 20. *11:19. *13:5. *20:20, 21. *26:20. *28:16, 17, 23. **world.** Gr. *oikoumene*, Mt +24:14.

19. **I say.** ver. 18. Ro 3:26. 1 C 1:12. 7:29. 10:19. 11:22. 15:50. **First.** Ro 11:11. See on Dt +*▶32:21. Ho 2:23. 1 P 2:10. **Moses.** Mk +12:19. **no people.**

⨍111, Ge +18:27. 1 P +2:10. **foolish.** Ro 1:14, 21, 22. Ps 115:5-8. Is 44:18-20. Je 10:8, 14. 1 C 12:2. T 3:3.

20. **very bold.** Pr *28:1. Is 58:1. Ac 13:46. Ep 6:19, 20. **I was found.** Ro 9:30. Is ▶65:1, 2. **I was made.** Is 49:6. 52:15. *55:4, 5. Mt 20:16. 22:9, 10. Lk 14:23. 1 J 4:19. **asked not.** Ro 9:11-13, 16. Is +*2:2, 3. 18:7. 19:19, 25. Zc 14:16. 1 C 1:27-29. 2 T +*1:9.

21. **All day long.** Pr 1:24. Is ▶65:2-5. Je 25:4. 35:15. Mt 20:1-15. 21:33-43. 22:3-7. 23:34-37. Lk=13:7. 24:47. Ac 13:46, 47. **stretched forth.** Pr 1:21. **a disobedient.** Ro 2:8. 9:30. Dt 9:13. 31:27. 1 S 8:7, 8. Ne 9:26. Je 44:4-6. Ac 7:51, 52. +14:2. 1 Th 2:16. T 1:16. 3:3. He 4:11. 1 P 2:8.

ROMANS 11

The apostle shows, that God had not so cast off Israel, but that a remnant would be saved, "according to the election of grace," by grace, not by works, 1-6; while the rest would be blinded, as foretold by the prophets, 7-10. He predicts that this exclusion would not be final; and states the consequences to the Gentiles, both of the fall of the Jews, and of their recovery, 11-15. He cautions the Gentile converts not to boast against the Jews, but humbly to profit by this example of God's severity and goodness; and foretells glorious times, which would at length arrive, 10-32. He adores the depths of God's wisdom, and the glory of his unsearchable judgments, his underived all-sufficiency, and his universal and absolute sovereignty, 33-36.

1. **I say.** ver. 11. **Hath God.** ⨍152A, Ro +9:6. Ro *9:6. 1 S *12:22. 2 K *23:27. Ps 77:7. *89:31-37. *94:14. Je *31:36, 37. *33:24-26. Ho 9:17. Am +*9:8, 9. **cast away.** 2 S 7:15. 1 K *11:39. 2 K 13:23. *14:27. Ps +*89:28, 33, 37. +√132:11. Is +√41:9. *54:9, 10. +√55:3. Je √30:11. +*33:20, 25, 26. Ho ❶1:9. Ac *13:34. He +*13:5. **God forbid.** See on Ro 3:4. 6:2. **For I also.** Ro 2:9. 3:9. 9:3, 24. Ac *22:3. *26:4. 2 C *11:22. Ph *3:5. 1 T *1:13. **Benjamin.** i.e. *fortunate; dextrous,* ✳S#958g. For ✳S#1144h, see Ge +35:18. Ac 13:21. Ph 3:5. Re 7:8.

2. **not cast way.** Le 26:44. Dt *4:31. 2 S *7:24. 1 K *11:39. 1 Ch 17:22. Ps √94:14. Is +*11:11n. +√41:9. Je +√30:11. +*31:35-37. *51:5. La +*3:31. Am +√9:14, 15. **which he foreknew.** Ro +*8:29, 30. 9:6, 23. Ac 2:23. +*13:48. 15:18. 1 P 1:2, 20. **Wot.** Ge 44:15. Ex 32:1. Ac 3:17. 7:40. 1 C 6:9g. Ph 1:22. **the scripture.** Lk +4:21. **of Elias?** Gr. in Elias? Or, *by Elias; en,* corresponding to the Hebrew letter **caph,** not unfrequently having this signification. See Ne 9:30. Mk 12:26. Lk 4:1. 20:37. 1 C 6:2. He 1:1. **how he maketh.** Or, "how he addresseth God *respecting* Israel;" *kata* having frequently this meaning (See 1 C 15:15). Nu 16:15. Je 18:19-23. Jn 4:1-3, 11. Ac 25:24g.

3. **Lord.** 1 K 18:4, 13. ▶19:10-18. Ne 9:26. Je 2:30. **they have.** ⨍92E, Mt +4:10. **digged.** 1 K 18:30, 31. **left alone.** 1 K 18:22. **life.** Gr. *psyche,* ⨍121A7, Mt +2:20. ⨍121A7, Ge +9:5.

4. **the answer.** Lk +2:26. **I have reserved.** See on 1 K ▶19:18. **Baal.** i.e. *possessor, ruler, lord; a Phoenician deity,* ✳S#896g, only here. See ✳S#1168h, Jg +6:25. Nu 25:3. Dt 4:3. Jg 2:13. 1 K 16:31. 2 K 10:19, 20. Je 19:5. Ho 2:8. 13:1. Zp 1:4.

5. **at this present.** ver. 6, 7. Ro 3:26. **a remnant.** See Ro *9:27. Je 3:14. Zc 13:8. **election of grace.** The

election which proceeds from the mercy and goodness of God. ver. 28. Ro 9:11. Nu 19:2. Dt +*10:15. Ezk 14:14. +*33:19. Ac +*13:48. +*18:27. Ep 1:5, 6. He 11:40.

6. **And if.** ℐ184A, 1 C +15:2. Ro 3:27, 28. *4:4, 5. *5:20, 21. Dt 9:4-6. 1 C 15:10. Ga 2:21. √5:4. Ep √2:4-9. 2 T +*1:9. T *3:5. **works.** ℐ121C1F, Le +19:13. **otherwise work.** That is, it loses its character, or nature, that of claiming reward as a matter of right. Mt 21:32. Lk *13:26-30. 2 T 1:12-16.

7. **What then?** Ro 3:9. 6:15. 1 C 10:19. Ph 1:18. **Israel.** Ro +*9:31, 32. *10:3. Pr 1:28. Lk 13:24. He 12:17. **but the election.** ℐ121N1, Ge +31:54. Put for elect persons. That is, *the elect;* the abstract being used for the concrete. So the Jews, or circumcised people, are called *Israel,* or the *circumcision.* ver. 5. Ro +*8:28-30. 9:23. Ac +*13:48. Ep 1:4. 1 Th 1:4. 2 Th *2:13, 14. 1 P 1:2. **and the rest.** Is 6:10. 44:18. Mt *13:14, 15. Jn 12:40. 2 C 3:14. √4:4. 2 Th √2:10-12. **blinded.** or, hardened. √ℐ108A4, Ge +31:7. ver. 25. See on Ro 9:18. Jb 17:7. Mk 3:5. 6:52. Jn 12:40. 2 C 3:14. Ep 4:18.

8. **God hath.** ℐ92G, Lk +4:18. Is *29:10. **given.** √ℐ108A4, Ge +31:7. **spirit.** ℐ121A10, Ge +26:35. **slumber.** or, remorse. Ps 60:3. **eyes.** ℐ147B, Ge +2:16. Dt *29:4. Is *6:9. 43:8. Je *5:21. Ezk *12:2. Mt +*13:14. Mk 4:11, 12. Lk 8:10. Ac 28:26, 27. Ep 4:18. **unto this day.** 2 K 17:34, 41. 2 C *3:14, 15.

9. **David saith.** Ps ꟾ69:22, 23. Ac +4:25. **their table.** Dt 6:10-12. *32:13-15. 1 S 25:36-38. Jb 20:20-23. Pr 1:32. Is 5:4-7. 8:13, 14. Lk 12:20. 16:19-25. 1 T 6:17-19. **a snare.** Lk +21:34. **stumblingblock.** Ro +9:33. **a recompence.** Dt 32:35. Ps 28:4. Is 59:18. 66:6. Lk 14:12. He 2:2.

10. **their eyes.** ver. 8. Ro 1:21. Ps 69:23. Zc 11:17. Ep 4:18. 2 P 2:4, 17. Ju 6, 13. **and bow.** Dt 28:64-68. Is 51:23. 65:12.

11. **I say.** ver. 1. **Have they stumbled.** ℐ152A, Ro +9:6. Ezk 18:23, 32. 33:11. **fall.** ℐ63A4, 1 K +3:22. Supply ellipsis, (for ever). **but rather.** ver. 12, 31. Ac *13:42, 46-48. *18:6. *22:18-21. *28:24-28. **fall.** Ro 5:15-18, 20. **salvation.** Ac 28:28. **for.** ver. 14. Ro 10:19. **to provoke them to jealousy.** Rather, "to provoke (or excite) them to emulation," *paradzeelosai,* as it is rendered ver. 14.

12. **if.** ℐ184A, 1 C +15:2. **the riches.** Ro 10:12. **the world.** Gr. *kosmos,* Mt +4:8. ver. 15, 33. Ro 9:23. Ep 3:8. Col 1:27. **diminishing.** or, decay, or, decay, or loss. 1 C 6:7. **their fulness.** ver. 25. Is 11:11-16. ch. 12, 60. *66:8-20. Mi *4:1, 2. 5:7. Zc *2:10, 11. *8:20-23. Re 11:15-19.

13. **to you.** ℐ101, Dt +32:42. **Gentiles.** ℐ38B, 2 S +1:24. **the apostle.** ℐ101, Dt +32:42. Ro *15:16-19. Ac +9:15. 13:2. *22:21. 26:17, 18. Ga *1:15, 16. 2:2, 7-9. Ep *3:8. 1 T 2:7. 2 T 1:11, 12. **I magnify mine office.** Rather, "I honor my ministry," *teen diakonian mou doxadzo.* Ac +1:17. 1 C 4:1. 12:26. 2 C 5:19, 20. 1 T *1:11, 12.

14. **If.** ℐ184A, 1 C +15:2. Ph +3:11g. **by.** 1 C 7:16. 9:20-22. 2 T 2:10. **provoke.** ver. 11. He *10:24. **my flesh.** Ro 9:3. Ge 29:14. 2 S 5:1. 19:12, 13. 1 Ch 11:1. Phm 12. **might.** Ro 10:1. 1 C 7:16. 9:22. 1 T +*4:16. Ja +*5:20.

15. **if.** ℐ184A, 1 C +15:2. **the casting.** ver. 1, 2, 11, 12. Is +*54:7. **the reconciling.** Ro 5:10, 11. Da

9:24. 2 C *5:18-20. Ep 1:10. Col *1:20, 21. Re *7:9. **world.** Gr. *kosmos,* Mt +4:8. **the receiving.** Is +*54:7. Zc +√10:6. **but life.** Ps +*71:20. Is +*26:19n. +*66:19. Ezk 37:1-14. Lk 15:24, 32. Ep *2:1. Col 2:13. Re 3:1. 11:11. 20:4-6.

16. **if.** ℐ184A, 1 C +15:2. **the firstfruit.** ℐ7, Allegory by continued Hypocatastasis, Ga +4:24. Ex 22:29. 23:16, 19. Le +*23:10. Nu *15:17-21. Dt 18:4. 26:2, 10. Ne 10:35-37. Pr 3:9. Ezk 44:30. Ja 1:18. Re 14:4. **and if.** ver. 17. Ge +*17:7. Je 2:21. 1 C +*7:14.

17. **And if.** ℐ184A, 1 C +15:2. **some.** ver. 19, 20. Ro 9:13. 1 K 11:31-33. Ps 52:8. 80:11-16. Is 6:13. 27:11. Je *11:16. Ezk 15:6-8. Mt +*8:11, 12. 21:43. Jn 15:2, 6. He 9:1. 12:16, 17. **being.** Ac +*2:39. Ga 2:15. *3:28, 29. Ep *2:11-13. +*3:6. Col 2:13. **among them.** or, for them. **and with.** Ge *17:20, 21. 25:4, 5. Dt 8:8. Jg 9:8, 9. Ps 52:8. Zc 4:3. Jn 1:16. Re 11:4. **partakest.** 1 C 9:23. Ph 1:7. **root and.** ℐ93A, Ge +1:26. By *Hendiadys,* fat or prolific root. **fatness.** Zc 4:14.

18. **Boast not.** ver. 20. Ro 3:27. 1 K 20:11. Pr 16:18. Mt 26:33. Lk 18:9-11. 1 C √10:12. **But if.** ℐ184A, 1 C +15:2. **boast.** ℐ63B, Ge +25:28. Supply by ellipsis, (I tell thee). **thou bearest.** Ro *4:16. Zc +8:20-23. Jn +*10:16. Ga 3:29. Ep 2:19, 20.

19. **Thou wilt say.** ℐ26. Antimetathesis; or, Dialogue B899. A transference of speakers, as when the reader is addressed in the second person as if actually present. For other instances of this figure see Ro 11:19. 14:15. Is 58:10. 1 C 7:16. 15:35. **then.** Ro 9:19. 1 C 15:35. Ja 2:18. **that.** ℐ83, 1 K +22:15. ver. 11, 12, 17, 23, 24.

20. **Well.** 2 S 3:13. 1 K 2:18. Jn 4:17, 18. Ja 2:19. **because.** ℐ152B, Is +49:14. Ro 3:3. Ac 13:46, 47. 18:6. He +*3:12, 19. 4:6, 11. **broken off.** ver. 17, 19. **standest.** 1 C *10:12. **by faith.** Ro *5:1, 2. 2 Ch +*20:20. Is 7:9. 1 C 16:13. 2 C 1:24. Col +*2:7. 1 P 5:9, 12. **Be.** ver. 18. Ro +*12:3, 16. Ps 138:6. Pr 28:26. Is 2:11, 17. Hab *2:4. Zp 3:11. Lk *18:14. 2 C √10:5. 2 Th *2:4. 1 T *6:17. 2 T *3:3-5. Ja *4:6. 1 P *5:5, 6. Re *3:17. *18:7, 8. **but.** Pr 28:14. Is 66:2, 5. Je 44:10. 1 C 10:12. 2 C 7:1. Ph √2:12. He 4:1. 1 P 1:17. 3:15.

21. **if God.** ℐ184A, 1 C +15:2. ver. 17, 19. Ro +*8:32. Je 25:29. 49:12. 1 C 10:1-12. 2 P 2:4-9. Ju 5. **natural branches.** ℐ132G, Ge +3:19. ver. 24.

22. **therefore.** Ro *2:4, 5. 9:22, 23. Nu *14:18-22. Dt *32:39-43. Jsh 23:15, 16. Ps *58:10, 11. 78:49-52. 136:15-22. Is 66:14. **goodness.** Ex +*34:6, 7. Ps +*145:9. Mt +*28:19n. Mk +*10:18n. Lk +*6:35. 2 Th 1:11. **on them.** ℐ153, Jn +16:9. **fell.** Lk 2:34. **severity.** The term "severity," *apotomia,* from *apo,* "from," and *temno,* to "cut off," as the gardener cuts off, with a pruning kife, dead boughs, or luxuriant stems. T#236. Ro 3:5, 6. +7:13 (T#557). 12:19. Ge +6:6 (T#230). Ex 15:3. Dt 4:24. 32:35, *39, 40-42. Ps 18:6-14. +33:5 (T#232). 78:49-51. +83:18 (T#570). 97:3. Pr +27:22 (T#569). Is +27:11 (T#559). 30:27. 35:4. 59:17-19. *66:14, 15. La 2:4. Ezk 7:8. Na +*1:2, 6. Lk +23:41 (T#571). Jn +*3:36. 2 C +*5:11. 2 Th *1:6-8. He *2:2, 3. +10:30 (T#558). 12:29. 1 P √4:18. **if.** ℐ184C, Mt +4:9. 2 P +*1:10. **thou continue.** Ro +*2:7. Lk *8:15. Jn +*8:31. √15:4-10. Ac +*11:23. +*14:22. 1 C +*15:2. Ga √6:9. Col +*1:23. 1 Th *3:5, 8. He *3:6, 14. *10:23, 35-39. 1 J √2:19. Ju *20, *21. **otherwise.** Ezk *3:20. +*18:24. *33:17-19. Mt *3:9, 10. 15:13. Jn *15:2. Re *2:5.

23. **if they.** ♪184C, Mt +4:9. **abide not.** Zc *12:10. Mt 23:39. 2 C 3:16. **able.** ♪108B, Ro +4:21.

24. **if.** ♪184C, Mt +4:9. **thou wert cut.** ver. 17, 18, 30. **contrary.** ver. 21.

25. **I would.** Ps 107:43. Ho 14:9. 1 C +10:1. 12:1. 2 P 3:8. **this.** Ro +*16:25. Ep 3:3, 4, 9. Re 10:7. **lest.** Ro 12:16. Pr √3:5-7. 26:12, 16. Is 5:21. **wise.** 1 C +4:10. **blindness.** *or,* hardness. ver. 7, 8. Is 6:9-13. 2 C 3:14-16. **in part.** Ro 15:15, 24. 1 C 12:27. 2 C 1:14. 2:5. **is happened.** 2 C 3:14. **until.** Dt 30:1-3. Ps *22:27. 72:8-14, 17. ch. 117. Is +*2:1-8. ch. 60. 66:18-23. Ho 3:4. Mi 4:1, 2. +*5:3. Zc *8:20-23. √14:9-21. Mt +√25:19. Lk +*21:24. Ac +*1:6. Re 7:9. √11:15. √20:2-4. **fulness.** Many interpreters (including Peters, *Theocratic Kingdom,* vol. 3, Proposition 173, Observation 3, p. 95. See also He 11:39, 40) understand this to refer to the specific number of individuals who are to be saved before Christ returns. But this view is not strictly supportable by any other Scripture (unless Re 6:11). Rather, as Paul is referring to specific prophecies already given in the Old Testament, the term "fulness" must be understood as the figure Metonymy of the Adjunct (♪121N2, Ge +34:29), where fulness is put for wealth, as predicted (Is √60:5mg. 61:6). When Christ returns as the Deliverer and rescues Israel from the confederated armies gathered against Jerusalem, Israel will be converted, and reap the wealth of the nations that were arrayed in battle against her. Johannes Munck suggests that the "fulness of the Gentiles" was the goal toward which Paul was striving, namely, "the full dissemination of the gospel to the Gentiles," which, when completed, allows for the end to come (Mt 24:14), the revelation of Antichrist (2 Th 2:3, 4), and the return of Christ to judge and to save (*Christ and Israel,* p. 134). But prophecy conditions the return of Christ not on the successful spread of the gospel to the Gentiles, but upon the repentance and conversion of Israel (Ac +√3:19-21. See related notes, Is √11:11n). The completion of the spread of the Gospel is predicted to take place after the return of Christ, not before (Is +√66:19), accomplished by Jewish evangelists at the start of the Millennium. ver. 12. Ro 15:15, 16, 19. Pr 13:22. Is +*18:7. +√60:5mg. √61:6. Ezk 30:3. 39:10. Mi 4:13. Zp +*3:8. Zc √14:14. Col 1:25-27. 2 T 4:17. Re 6:11. **of the Gentiles.** Ge +*22:17. Dt +*28:13. Ps +√18:43. **be come in.** or, begins.

26. **all Israel.** Dt +*28:37. Is √11:11-16. *45:17. √54:6-10. Je 3:17-23. 30:17-22. 31:31-37. √32:37-41. +√33:24-26. Ezk 34:22-31. 37:21-28. 39:25-29. ch. 40-48. Ho +*3:5. Jl *3:16-21. Am +√9:14, 15. Mi *7:15-20. Zp 3:12-20. Zc *10:6-12. **shall be saved.** T#382. ver. 15, 16, 24-27. Ro 10:13. Is 27:7, 9. +*45:17. Je 31:1, 18-20, 31-34. *33:8. Ezk 36:21-32. Ho *14:4, 8. Mi 4:2. Zc *12:10, 11. Mt 23:37-39. 2 C 3:15, 16. **There.** ♪92G, Lk +4:18. Ps 14:7. 106:47. Is ▶59:20, 21. Jn 4:22. He 8:8-12. **shall come.** Is +*26:21. Ho +*5:15. Zc 8:3. **out of Sion.** Ps 14:7. 53:6. Is +*51:11. +*59:20. Zc *8:2, 3. **the Deliverer.** Is +√59:19, 20. Lk 21:28. Ac +*3:20. =7:35. 1 Th +*1:10. **and shall.** Mt 1:21. Ac 3:26. T *2:14. **turn away.** Ps +*130:8. Is 49:5, 6. +*60:21. 63:17, 18. **from Jacob.** Lk 1:33. Ac 7:46.

27. **this.** Ro +*9:4. Is √54:9, 10. +√55:3. *▶59:21. Je *31:31-34. 32:38-40. Ezk √20:33-38. Mi *7:15-20. He *8:8-12. 10:16. **when I.** ♪92G, Lk +4:18. Dt 32:36. Is ▶27:9. 43:25. 49:5, 6. 56:8. +*60:21. Je 50:20. Ezk

34:11, 12. *36:25-29. Ho +*14:2. Am 9:11, 14. Jn *1:29. He 8:12.

28. **are enemies.** ver. 11, 30. Mt 21:43. Ac 13:45, 46. 14:2. 18:6. 1 Th *2:15, 16. **but.** ver. 7. Is 41:8, 9. **the election.** Dt +*10:15. Col 3:12. 1 Th 5:9. T 1:1. **are beloved.** Ro 9:5, 25. Ge 26:4. 28:14. Le 26:40-42. Dt 4:31. *7:7, 8. 8:18. 9:5. +*10:15. Ps 105:8-11. Je 31:3. Mi *7:20. Lk 1:54, 68-75. **the father's sake.** Ro +*15:8.

29. **the gifts.** Ro √6:23. +√8:30. Nu *23:19. Ho *13:14. Ml +*3:6. Jn 4:10. 1 J √5:10-13. **and calling.** Ro +*8:28. 1 C 1:26. 7:20, 22. Ep 1:18. 4:1, 4. Ph 3:14. 2 Th 1:11. 2:14. 2 T +*1:9. He 3:1. 2 P 1:10. **without repentance.** or, irrevocable. ver. +*1. Ro 5:9. Ge +*17:7. Nu 23:19, 21. Jg 2:1. 1 K √11:39. Ps 37:23, 24. *77:8. Hab +*3:9. Ml +*3:6. Jn 6:37, 39, 40, 47. 5:24. √10:25-33. 17:11. 20:31. 2 C *7:10. 1 Th 5:23, 24. He 2:9. +*5:9. 1 J *3:2. Ju *24.

30. **as ye.** 1 C +*6:9-11. Ep *2:1, 2, 12, 13, 19-21. 5:8. Col 1:21. 3:7. T 3:3-7. **believed.** *or,* obeyed. ver. 31mg. Ro 15:31. Jn √3:36. He +*5:9. **obtained.** ver. 31. 1 C 7:25. 2 C 4:1. 1 T 1:18. 1 P 2:10. **through.** ver. 11-19.

31. **believed.** *or,* obeyed. ver. 30mg. Ro 10:16. **that.** ver. 15, 25. Is *60:10. **your mercy.** Is +*40:1.

32. **God.** Ro *3:9, 22. Ga *3:22. **concluded them all.** *or,* shut them all up together. Ps 77:9. 78:62. **that he.** Je +*33:26. Zc √10:6. Jn 1:7. +*12:32. 1 T √2:4-6.

33. **the depth.** ♪176, Nu +24:5. T#275. 1 Ch +29:11 (T#214). Ps *36:6. 77:19. 92:5. 97:2. *107:8, etc. Pr 18:3. 25:2, 3. Ec 3:11. Ep 3:18. **riches.** ♪22D5I, Pr +8:18. Ro +*2:4. *9:23. Ep *1:7. *2:7. 3:8, 10, 16. Col +*1:27. *2:2, 3. **wisdom.** T#222. Ro 16:27. Jb 5:13. Ps 104:24. 139:6. Is 28:29. Je +10:12 (T#142). 1 C 1:25. Ep 1:8. *3:9, 10. Col *2:2, 3. Ju *25. **how unsearchable.** Jb 5:9. 9:10. *11:7-9. 26:14. 33:13. 34:24mg. 37:19, 23. Ps 36:6. 40:5. 77:19. 92:5. 97:2. 139:6. 145:3. 147:5. Pr 25:2. Ec 3:11. Is *40:28. Da *4:35. Mt +*28:19n. **his ways.** Dt *29:29. Jb 11:7. Ep 3:19. **finding out.** ♪98. Homoeopropheron; or, Alliteration B175. The repetition of the same letter or syllable at the commencement of successive words. Here, "unsearchable" and "finding out" (*anexeruneeta, anexichniastoi*). For other instances of this figure see 1 Th 1:2. 5:23. He 1:1.

34. **For who.** ♪85C, Ge +18:14. Ec *3:11. 8:17. Is *55:8, 9. **hath known.** Ex +*33:19. Jb 15:8. 36:22. Is 40:13. Mt 20:15. 1 C 2:16. **his counsellor.** Jb 36:23. 40:2. Je *23:18.

35. **who.** ♪85C, Ge +18:14. **hath first.** Jb 35:7. 41:11. 1 Ch *29:14. Mt 20:15. 1 C *4:7.

36. **of him.** ♪147F, Ezk 28:2. 1 Ch *29:11, 12. Ps 33:6. Pr 16:4. Da 2:20-23. 4:3, 34. Mt +*6:13. Jn +*6:44, 65. Ac 17:25, 26, 28. 1 C *8:6. 11:12. Ep 4:6-10. Col +*1:15-17. He 2:10. Re 21:6. **to whom.** Gr. to him. Ro 16:27. Ps 29:1, 2. 96:7, 8. 115:1. Is 42:12. Lk 2:14. 19:38. Ga 1:5. Ep 3:21. Ph 4:20. 1 T +*1:17. +*6:16. 2 T *4:18. He *13:21. 1 P 4:11. 5:11. 2 P √3:18. Ju *25. Re +*1:5, 6. 4:10, 11. 5:12-14. 7:10. 19:1, 6, 7. **for ever.** Gr. *aion,* Mt +6:13. lit. unto the ages.

ROMANS 12

The apostle exhorts Christians "by the mercies of God," to devote themselves to him; and avoiding con

formity to the world, to be conformed to his holy will,
1, 2; to think humbly and soberly of themselves, as
members of one body in Christ, 3-5; to exercise faith-
fully their different gifts, and perform the duties of
their several stations, for the common benefit, 6-8; to
mutual love, diligence, patience, hope, prayer, hospi-
tality, compassion, and condescension, 9-16; to a peace-
able, forgiving, and becoming conduct towards all men;
and to a persevering kindness to enemies, as vengeance
belongeth unto God, 17-21.

1. **beseech**. Ro 15:30. 1 C 1:10. 4:16. 2 C 5:20.
6:1. 10:1. Ep 4:1. 1 Th 4:*1, 10. 5:12. 1 T 2:1. Phm
9, 10, 19. He 13:22. 1 P 2:11. **by the**. Ro +*2:4. *5:8.
*9:23. 11:30, 31. Ps *116:12. 119:156. Lk *7:47. 2 C
1:3. 4:1. √5:14, 15. Ep *2:4-10. Ph 2:1-5. T 3:4-8.
1 P 2:10-12. **mercies**. ♪96F2, Ge +4:10. **that ye**. Ro
*6:13, 16, 19. Ps 50:13, 14, 23. 1 C *6:13-20. Ph *1:20.
He +*10:22. 1 P +2:5. **bodies**. ♪171Q4, Ex +21:3mg.
Ge=47:18. Ex=29:20. 1 C *6:19, 20. **a living**. Nu=8:11
(wave offering), 13. Dt=33:10. Ps 69:30, 31. Ho
+*14:2. Ml=3:3. 1 C 5:7, 8. 2 C 4:16. √5:14, 15. Ph
2:17. He 10:20-22. *13:15, 16. **sacrifice**. Ro +14:18.
Ph 4:18. 1 P *2:5. **holy**. Le *9:2-4. 19:2. Ml *1:14.
1 P 1:16. **acceptable**. ver. 2. Ro 15:16. Ps *19:14. Is
*56:7. Je 6:20. Ep *5:10. Ph 4:18. 1 T 2:3. *5:4. 1 P
*2:5, 20. **reasonable**. 1 P 2:2, 5. **service**. Ro +9:4.

2. **be not**. Ex +*23:2. Le 18:29, 30. Dt *18:9-14.
Jsh 23:12, 13. Mt 6:24. Jn *7:7. 14:30. *15:19. 17:14.
1 C 3:19. 2 C √4:4. √6:14-17. Ga *1:4, 10. 6:14. Ep
*2:2. *4:17-20. +*5:10, 11, 17. Ja *1:27. *4:4. 1 P
1:14, 18. 4:2. 2 P *1:4. *2:20. 1 J √2:15-17. 3:13. 4:4,
5. *5:19. Re 12:9. 13:8. **conformed**. Ro +*8:29. 1 S
8:20. **this**. ♪121P2, Mt +13:22. **world**. Gr. *aion*, Mt
+6:13. lit. age, Mt 12:32. Jn +*6:54n. 1 C +1:20. T
*2:12. **be ye transformed**. Ro *13:14. Ps +*51:10. Je
31:18. La 5:21. Ezk *18:31. 36:26. 2 C √5:17. Ep 1:18.
*4:22-24. Col 1:21, 22. 3:10. T *3:5. **renewing**. Ro
*7:12, 22. 2 C 4:16. Ep *4:23. Col *3:10. **prove**. ver.
1. Ps 34:8. Ep *5:10, 17. 1 P 2:3. **good**. ver. 1. Ro
7:12, 14, 22. Ps *19:7-11. 119:47, 48, 72, 97, 103,
128, 174. Pr 3:1-4, 13-18. Ga *5:22, 23. Ep 5:9. Col
4:12. 1 Th 4:3. 2 T +*3:16, 17. **perfect**. Ps *19:7-9.
will of God. Ro 2:18. Ac +22:14. 1 Th +4:3. 1 P
*4:2, 3.

3. **I say**. ver. 6-8. Ro +1:5. **grace**. Ro *15:15, 16.
1 C 3:10. 15:10. Ga 2:8, 9. Ep 3:2, 4, 7, 8. 4:7-12.
Col 1:29. 1 T 1:14. 1 P 4:11. **given**. ver. 6. 1 C +1:4.
not to think. ver. +*16. Ro *11:20, 25. Ps +*119:21.
Pr 16:18, 19. 25:27. 26:12. Ec 7:16. Mi +√6:8. Mt
18:1-4. Lk *18:11. Ac 20:19. 1 C *4:6-8. 2 C *12:7.
Ga 6:3. Ph √2:3-8. Col 2:13. 1 T *6:17. Ja *4:6. 1 P
*5:5. 3 J 9. **of himself**. ♪63K, Ge +37:13. EWB notes
that it is a question here whether the thinking ought
to be limited by the insertion of the words *"of himself,"*
as there is no limitation in the Greek, which means
to think more than one ought, not merely of one's
self, but of anything. It denotes especially a highmind-
edness about *any subject*, which makes one proud,
arrogant, boastful, or insolent (B126). **more highly**.
♪135, Ps +68:28. **soberly**. Gr. to sobriety. 1 T 2:9,
15. T 2:2, 4, 6, 12. 1 P 1:13. 4:7. 5:8. **according**. ver.
6. Jn 3:34. 1 C 3:5. 4:7. 7:17. *12:7-11, 18. 2 C *10:13.
12:13. Ep 4:7, 13, 16. 1 P 4:11.

4. **as we**. T#1834. Ro 16:2. 1 C 3:9. **have**. 1 C
*12:4, 12, 27. Ep 4:15, 16. **one body**. Ro 15:6. 1 C
*10:17. Ep +*4:4. **and**. ♪15G, Ge +35:3.

5. **So we**. ver. 4. 1 C 10:17, 33. 12:12-14, 20, 27,
28. Ep *1:23. 4:25. 5:23, 30. Col 1:24. 2:19. **are one
body**. Jn +17:11. 1 C 12:20. Ep 4:13. **every one**. Mk
14:19. Jn 8:9g. **in Christ**. Ga 3:28. Ep 4:25. **members**.
1 C 6:15. 12:27. Ep *4:25. **one of another**. Gr. *alleelon*,
S#240g. ver. 10. Ro 14:13, *19. *15:5, 7, 14. 16:16.
Ml 3:16. Jn *13:34, 35. 1 C *12:25. Ga 5:13. 6:2. Ep
4:2, 25, 32. *5:21. Ph *2:3. Col 3:9, 16. 1 Th +*3:12.
4:9, 18. *5:11. 2 Th 1:3. He +*3:13. *10:24, 25. Ja
4:11. 5:16. 1 P +*1:22. *4:9. 5:5. 1 J 1:7. 3:11.

6. **gifts**. These gifts may be compared with those
listed at 1 C 12:8-10 and Ep 4:11. There appears to
be an intended correspondence between the order of
the gifts listed in ver. 6-8 and the admonitions which
follow in ver. 9-15. Each admonition suits the problem
area experienced by persons who possess the associated
gift. It is probable that every believer possesses just
one spiritual gift (1 P 4:10). Studying these gifts with
the additional clues furnished by the associated admonitions may help individual believers identify their gift.
Ro *1:11. Mt *25:15. 1 C *1:5-7. 4:6, 7. *7:7. *12:4-
11, 28-31. *13:2. Ep 4:7. 1 P *4:10, 11. **differing according**. ver. 3. **whether prophecy**. See the corresponding
admonition in ver. 9. Ro 15:4. Mt *23:34. Lk *11:49.
Ac *2:17. 11:27, 28. +*13:1. *15:32. 21:9. 1 C *12:10,
28. 13:2. *14:1, 3-5, 24, 29, 31, 32. Ep 3:5. *4:11.
1 Th 5:20. 2 P 1:20. **let us prophesy**. ♪63E2, 1 S +13:8.
according to the proportion. ver. *3. Mt *9:29. Is
*8:20. Ac *18:24-28. 2 C *8:12. Ph 3:15. 2 T 2:15.

7. **ministry**. See corresponding admonition in ver.
10. Is 21:8. Ezk *3:17-21. *33:7-9. Mt *24:45-47. Lk
*12:42-44. Ac +*6:1. *20:20, 28. Col 4:17. 1 T +*4:16.
2 T *4:2. 1 P *5:1-4. **wait**. Ex =30:30. Nu=3:10.
2 Ch=35:14. **or he that teacheth**. See corresponding
admonition in ver. 11. Dt 33:10. 1 S +*12:23. Ps
*34:11. 51:13. Ec *12:9. Mt +*28:19. Jn 3:2. Ac *13:1.
Ga 6:6. Ep +*4:11. Col 1:28, 29. 1 T *2:7. *3:2. +*4:16.
*5:17. 2 T 2:√2, 24.

8. **exhorteth**. See corresponding admonition in ver.
12. Persons who possess the gift of exhortation might
find the study of the cause/effect relationships discussed
at Ps +√9:10n helpful. It is less offensive and more
effective in counseling to approach a person's problem
through a Biblically defined root cause, rather than
to directly confront the effect in their life, when attempting to lead them to a Biblical solution to their
problem. Rather than provoke resistance to our help
by confronting individuals directly about their lack of
trust in God, it might be more effective to develop
their knowledge of God's character, a knowledge of
which permits us to trust Him. A study of the cause/
effect relationships related to counseling problems
would prove very fruitful. A good start toward a collection of suitable texts for such a study will be found in
the note at Ps +√9:10n. Ac +*4:36. 13:15. 15:32. 20:2.
1 C +*14:3. 1 Th 2:3. 1 T +*4:13-16. 2 T 4:2. He
10:25. 13:22. **giveth**. *or*, imparteth. See the corresponding admonition at ver. 13. The obvious close
connection of the topic of ver. 13 with the gift of giving
supports the validity of these correspondences. ver.
13. Dt 15:8-11, 14. Jb 31:16-20. Ps 112:9. Pr 22:9.
Ec 11:1, 2, 6. Is 32:5, 8. 58:7-11. Mt +*6:2-4. 25:40.
Lk 21:1-4. Ac 2:44-46. 4:33-35. 11:28-30. +*20:35.
1 C 12:28. 16:2. 2 C 8:1-9, 12. *9:7. 1 Th 2:8. 1 P
4:9-11. **with simplicity**. *or*, liberality. 2 C 1:12. 8:2.
9:11, 13g. 11:3. Ep 6:5. Col 3:22. **ruleth**. See the corre-

sponding admonition at ver. 14. If these correspondences are valid, the admonition implies that the gift of ruling (or administration) prompts more than its share of persecution, and delineates the appropriate response. This is no doubt the same as the gift of "governments" mentioned at 1 C 12:28. Ro 13:6. Ge +*18:19. Ex √18:14-23. Ps ch. 101. Ac 13:12. +*20:28. 1 C +12:28. 2 C √1:24. 1 Th 5:12-14. 1 T 3:4, 5. 5:17. He 13:7, 17, 24. 1 P *5:2, 3. **with diligence.** T#1856. ver. 11. Ex +*15:26. +*20:15n. Pr 6:10, 11. 10:4. *12:24. 21:5. 22:29. *24:30-34. Ec 9:10. 2 C 7:11, 12. 8:7, 8, 16. Col *1:28, 29. *4:17. He +*3:12, 13. 6:11. +*12:15. **showeth mercy.** Note the corresponding admonition at ver. 15. Perhaps this gift may be associated with the gift of "helps" listed at 1 C 12:28. Dt 16:11, 14, 15. Ps 37:21. Is 64:5. 2 C 9:7. **with cheerfulness.** 2 C 9:7. Ex 25:2. 35:5, 21, 29. 36:2. Jg 5:2. 1 Ch 29:5, 6. Ezr 1:6. 2:68. 3:5. 7:16. Ne 11:2. 2 C 8:12. *9:7.

9. **love.** Ro 13:8. 2 S 20:9, 10. Ps *55:21. Pr *26:25. Ezk +*33:31. Mt *26:49. Jn 12:6. 2 C *6:6. *8:8. 1 Th 2:3. 1 T *1:5. Ja 2:15, 16. 1 P √1:22. *4:8. 1 J *3:18-20. **without.** Ja +3:17. **Abhor.** Jb 28:28. Ps *34:14. √36:4. +*45:7. *97:10. √101:2-4. *119:104, 163. Pr 4:27. *8:13. 14:16. 22:3. Am *5:15. Zc 7:10. 1 C *10:6. 1 Th √5:21, 22. He *1:9. 1 P 3:11. **cleave.** Ac +*11:23. 1 Th *5:15. He +*12:14. 1 P *3:10, 11.

10. **kindly.** Jn 13:34, 35. 15:17. 17:21. Ac 4:32. Ga 5:6, 13, 22. Ep 4:1-3. Col 1:4. 1 Th 4:9. 2 Th 1:3. He +13:1. 1 P 1:22. 2:17. *3:8, 9. 2 P *1:5, 7. 1 J 2:9-11. 3:10-18, 23. 4:11, 20, 21. 5:1, 2. **with brotherly love.** or, in the love of the brethren. Jb 1:4. Ps 133:1. **in honor.** Ro 13:7. Ge 13:9. Mt 20:26. Lk 14:10. Ph +*2:3. 1 Th 5:13. 1 P 2:17. *5:5.

11. **not slothful.** ℐ144D, Ge +40:23. T#1844. Ex 5:17. 1 Ch +*22:16 (T#1). Ne 4:6. Pr *6:6-9. 10:26. *13:4. *18:9. 22:29. *24:30-34. 26:13-16. Ec *9:10. Is 56:10. Je +*48:10mg. Ezk +*16:49. Am +*9:15. Mt *25:26. Ac *20:34, 35. Ep *4:28. 5:16. Col *3:23, 24. 4:5. 1 Th *4:11, 12. 2 Th *3:6-12. 1 T *5:13. He +*6:10-12. **in business.** or, earnest care (for others). ℐ63I1A, Ex +12:4. ver. 8. Nu=8:11n. 2 Ch=13:10. =35:14. Ne=11:22. 1 C *12:25. Ep 4:11. 1 T +*3:5. He 13:17. **fervent.** Mt *24:12. Ac 17:16. *18:25. Col *4:12, 13. Ja *5:16. 1 P *1:22. *4:8. Re *2:4. *3:15, 16. **spirit.** Gr. *pneuma*, Ac +18:25n. ℐ108B, Lk +10:21. **serving.** Nu=3:7. Pr +*22:29. Ac 20:19. 1 C 7:22. Ep 5:16. *6:5-8. Col *3:22-24. *4:1. 1 T *2:9, 10. He 12:28.

12. **Rejoicing.** Ro +*5:2, 3. *15:13. Ps +*16:9-11. 71:20-23. 73:24-26. Pr 10:28. 14:32. La 3:24-26. Hab +*3:17, 18. Mt +*5:12. Lk *10:20. 1 C 13:13. Ph 3:1. *4:4. Col +*1:27. 1 Th *5:8, 16. 2 Th 2:16, 17. T *2:13. *3:7. He *3:6. *6:17-19. 1 P *1:3-8. *4:13. 1 J √3:1-3. **patient.** Ro +*2:7. *5:3, 4. 8:25. +*15:4. Ps +*37:7. 40:1. Lk *8:15. *21:19. Col *1:11. 1 Th 1:3. 2 Th *1:4. 3:5. 1 T 6:11. 2 T 3:10. He 6:12, 15. +*10:36. *12:1. Ja *1:3, 4. *5:7, 10, 11. 1 P *2:19, 20. 2 P 1:6. Re 13:10. **continuing.** Ge 32:24-26. Jb 27:8-10. Ps 55:16, 17. +*62:8. 109:4. Je 29:12, 13. Da 9:18, 19. Lk 11:5-13. +*18:1, etc. Ac +1:14. *2:42. 6:4. *12:5. 2 C 12:8. Ep 6:18, 19. Ph *4:6, 7. Col *4:2, 12. 1 Th +*5:17. He 5:7. Ja 5:15. 1 P 4:7. 1 J √5:14, 15.

13. **Distributing.** See on ver. 8. Ro 15:25-28. Ps 41:1. Ac *4:35. 9:36-41. 10:4. +*11:29. +*20:34, 35. 1 C 16:1, 2, 15. 2 C 8:1-4. 9:1, 12. Ga *6:10. 1 T

5:8-16. 6:18. Phm 7. He +*6:10. *13:16. Ja 1:27. 1 J √3:17. 3 J 7. **of saints.** 2 C +1:1. **given.** Ge *18:2-8. 19:1-3. Mt *25:35. 1 T 3:2. 5:10. *6:18mg. T 1:8. He +*13:2. 1 P √4:9.

14. **Bless.** ver. 21. Jb 31:29, 30. Mt +*5:44. Lk 6:28. *23:34. Ac +*7:60. 1 C *4:12, 13. 1 Th 5:15. Ja 3:10. 1 P *2:21-23. +*3:9. **persecute.** ℐ145, Jg +11:40. **curse not.** ℐ144D, Ge +40:23. Lk +*9:54, 55.

15. **Rejoice.** ℐ96B, Ex +20:8. Is 66:10-14. Lk 1:58. 15:5-10. Ac +*11:23. 1 C *12:26. 2 C 2:3. Ph 2:17, 18, 28. He 13:3. **rejoice.** ℐ147B, Ge +2:16. **and weep.** ℐ97. Homoeoptoton; or, Like Inflections B177. The repetition of inflections: similar endings arising from the same inflections of verbs, nouns, etc. This figure belongs peculiarly to the original languages. For other instances of this figure see 2 C 11:3. 2 T 3:2, 3. **with them.** Ne 1:4. Jb 2:11. *30:25. Ps 35:13, 14. Je 9:1. Jn *11:19, 33-36. 2 C *11:29. Ph 2:26. He 13:3. **that weep.** ℐ147B, Ge +2:16.

16. **the same mind.** Ro *15:5, 6. 2 Ch 30:12. Je *32:39. Ac *4:32. 1 C *1:10. 2 C 13:11. Ph *1:27. +*2:2, 3. 3:16. 4:2. 1 P *3:8. **Mind.** Ps *131:1, 2. Je +*45:5. Mt *18:1-4. *20:21-28. Lk 4:6-11. 22:24-27. 1 P *5:3. 3 J 9. Re 13:7, 8. **condescend to men of low estate.** or, be contented with mean things. lit. be carried away with (Ga 2:13g. 2 P 3:17g). T#123. +*3. 2 K +*5:13. Jb *31:13-16. 36:5. Pr *17:5. *19:7, 17, 22. Mt *6:25, 26. 11:5. *20:26-28. *26:11. Lk 6:20. *14:13, 14. Jn 13:14. Ac +*28:15. Ph +*2:3. *4:11-13. 1 T *6:6-9. He *13:5. Ja *2:5, 6. **Be not wise.** Ro 11:25. 1 S +*25:17. 2 K +*5:13. Pr √3:7. 26:12. Is *5:21. 1 C *3:18. 4:10. 6:5. *8:2. Ja *3:13-17.

17. **Recompense.** ver. *19. Le 19:18. Pr *20:22. 24:29. Mt *5:39. **evil for.** 1 Th *5:15. 1 P *3:9. **Provide.** Ro *13:14. *14:16, 19. Ac +*6:3. 1 C *6:6, 7. *13:4, 5. 2 C *8:20, 21. Ph √4:8, 9. Col *4:5. 1 Th *4:12. √5:22. 1 T √5:14. T *2:4, 5. 1 P *2:12. *3:16. **honest.** Je +*48:10. Ac +*6:3. 1 C +*4:2. 2 C +*4:2. *8:21. 1 Th 4:6. **in the sight.** Pr 3:4.

18. **If it be possible.** ℐ184A, 1 C +15:2. Ro *14:17, 19. 2 S 20:19. Ps 34:14. 120:5-7. Pr 12:20. Mt +*5:5, 9. Mk +9:50. 1 C 7:15. 2 C *13:11. Ga *5:22. Ep 4:3. Col 3:14, 15. 1 Th 5:13. 2 T 2:22. He +*12:14. Ja *3:16-18. 1 P 3:11. Ju +*3. **as much.** Ro 1:15. Ge *26:22. Mt *5:39. **live peaceably.** Ge 13:8, 9. 26:31. Pr +*16:7. Mt +*5:9. Ja 4:1. He *12:14. Ju 2.

19. **avenge not.** ver. *14, *17. Le +*19:18. 1 S *25:26, 33. Pr *24:17-19, 29. Ezk 25:12. Mt 6:15. **yourselves.** ℐ101, Dt +32:42. **give place.** Ge +*6:13 (T#566). Pr 24:17, 18. Mt *5:39. Lk *6:27-29. *9:55, 56. Ep 4:27. 2 Th 1:6. **unto.** ℐ63A4, 1 K +3:22. Supply ellipsis, (God's). **wrath.** Ro +*5:9. **Vengeance.** T#558. Ro *13:4. Ge 49:5-7. Dt *32:❭35, 39, 43. Ps *94:1-3. Is 1:24. 59:18. Na *1:2, 3. 1 Th √4:6. He *10:30. **I will.** Nu 12:2. Ps *31:23.

20. **if thine enemy.** ℐ38D, Ps +27:14. ℐ184C, Mt +4:9. Ex *23:4, 5. 1 S *24:16-19. 26:21. 2 S √26:8-10. 1 K 6:27. 2 K 6:22. Jb 31:29. Pr 17:5. 24:17. ❭25:21, 22. Mt +*5:44. Lk *6:27, 35, 36. **feed him.** ℐ171K2, Ex +23:4. Surely the two things mentioned are only examples of many ways in which love may be shown to our enemies (B635). **shalt heap.** Ps 37:34. +*58:10. Pr 29:16. Lk 18:7. 2 T +*4:14. **coals.** Ps *120:4. 140:10. Pr 25:15, 22. SS *8:6, 7. Is *13:7.

21. **Be not overcome of evil.** Ro √8:18, 31. Ps +*34:4. *37:1. *73:2, 3, 13, 16, 17, 26, 28. √118:24.

Pr +*4:23. 5:14. 10:24. *16:32. 23:7. Je +*12:5. Mt 6:+*13, √34. Lk +*6:27-30. Ac 16:24, 25. 20:24. 2 C √4:17, 18. Ph √4:6, 7. Col *3:1-3. 2 T +√1:7. He 12:1, 2. 1 P √3:9. 1 J *3:8. **overcome evil.** Ro *8:37. 2 K 6:21, 22. Pr 15:1. +*16:7. 2 C *10:4, 5. Ga 5:16. 1 P *2:15. Re 12:11. **with good.** 1 S 24:17, 18. Pr ◑17:13. Mt 5:16. 1 C √15:58. Ga √6:9. Ep *4:28. Ph √4:8. Col +√1:10. *3:23, 24. T *3:8, 14. He *6:10. 1 P *2:12. *3:16.

ROMANS 13

The apostle strongly inculcates subjection to rulers, the payment of tribute, and rendering to all their dues, 1-7. He exhorts to love of each other, as the fulfilment of the second table of the law, 8-10; and in the near prospect of complete salvation, to put away all the works of darkness, and seek in all things to be conformed to the Lord Jesus, 11-14.

1. **every.** Dt 17:12. Jn 19:11. Ep 5:21. T *3:1. 1 P *2:13-17. 2 P 2:10, 11. Ju 8. **soul.** Gr. *psyche*, ✍171Q1A, Ac +2:41. +27:37. ✍171Q1, Ge +12:5. **be subject.** Ac ◑4:19. ◑+*5:29. ◑*16:36-39. ◑*22:25. T *3:1. 1 P √2:13. **higher powers.** Ro 2:9. Dt 17:15. Mt 22:17. Lk 2:51. Jn 8:33. Ac 5:37. 18:2. 1 C 16:16. Ep 5:22. 1 T 2:2. T 2:5. 1 P √2:13. **For there.** 1 S 2:8. 1 Ch 28:4, 5. Ps 62:11. Pr *8:15, 16. Je 27:5-8. Da *2:21. *4:17, 25, 32, 34, 35. 5:18-23. Mt +*6:13. Jn *19:11. Re +*1:5. 17:14. 19:16. **the powers.** ✍77, Ex +3:19. **ordained.** *or,* ordered.

2. **resisteth.** Mt 17:24-27. 22:17-21. 1 C 6:7. 7:21, 22. 1 T 6:1. **power.** Je 23:8-17. 28:14-17. T 3:1. **ordinance.** Is 58:2. 1 P 2:13. **receive.** ver. 5. Mt 23:14. Mk 12:40. Lk 20:47. Ja 3:1.

3. **rulers.** ver. 4. Dt 25:1. Pr 14:35. 20:2. Ec 10:4-6. Je 22:15-18. **terror.** ✍121E1, Ge +25:23. **to.** ✍181E, Ge +3:24. **good works.** Ac +9:36. **Wilt thou.** ✍38D, Ps +27:14. 1 P *2:13, 14. 3:13, 14.

4. **he is.** ver. 6. Dt 1:17. 1 K 10:9. 2 Ch 19:6. Ps 82:2-4. Pr 24:23, 24. 31:8, 9. Ec *8:2-5. Is 1:17. Je 5:28. Ezk 22:27. Mi 3:1-4, 9. **But if.** ✍184C, Mt +4:9. **be afraid.** Pr 16:14. 20:2, 8, 26. **sword.** ✍121S1, Ge +49:10. He does not merely wear the sign, but he has the power which it signifies. **in vain.** 1 C 15:2. Ga 3:4. 4:11. Col 2:18. **minister.** S#1249g, Mk +*9:35. **of God.** Jn 19:11. **revenger.** Ro 12:19. Ge 9:5, 6. Ex 21:25. Nu 35:19-27. Jsh 20:5, 9. Ezk 25:14. 1 Th 4:6. 1 P 2:14. **wrath.** ✍121C1C, Ps +79:6.

5. **ye.** 1 S *24:5, 6. Ec *8:2. T *3:1, 2. 1 P *2:13-15. **wrath.** ✍121C1C, Ps +79:6. **conscience.** Ec 8:2. Ac +*24:16. 1 C +10:25. 2 C +1:12. He *13:18. 1 P *2:19. *3:16.

6. **pay.** Ezr 4:13, 20. 6:8. Ne *5:4. Mt *17:24-27. 22:17-21. Mk 12:14-17. Lk *20:21-26. 23:2. **ministers.** Ro 15:16. Lk +1:23. Ph 2:25. He 1:7. 8:2. **attending.** Ro 12:8. Ex 18:13-27. Dt 1:9-17. 1 S 7:16, 17. 2 S 8:15. 1 Ch 18:14. Jb 29:7-17.

7. **therefore.** Mt 17:25. *22:21. Mk 12:17. Lk 20:25. 23:2. **is due.** ✍63E2, 1 S +13:8. **fear to.** Le 19:3. 1 S 12:18. Pr 24:21. Ep 5:33. 6:5. He *12:9, 28. 1 P 2:18. **honor to.** Ro 12:10. Ex 20:12. Le *19:32. Ac 26:25. Ep +*6:2, 3. 1 T *5:3, 13, 17. *6:1. 1 P *2:17, 18. *3:7.

8. **Owe.** ✍134, Mt +3:9. The Hebrew words which would be brought to mind underlying "owe" and "love," *achab*, and *chab*, exhibit the figure *Parechesis,*

or Foreign Paronomasia. ver. 7. Le +*19:13. Dt +*24:14, 15. 2 K √4:7n. Ps +*37:21. Pr 3:27, 28. +*22:7. Je +*22:13. Ml +*3:5. Mt 7:12. 22:39, 40. Lk 11:41n. Ja +*5:4. **but to love.** Jn 13:34. **for.** ver. 10. Mt 22:37-40. Lk 10:29. Jn 13:34. Ga *5:14. Col 3:14. 1 T *1:5. Ja *2:8.

9. **For this.** Ex ▶20:12-17. Dt 5:16-21. Mt 19:18, 19. Mk 10:19. Lk 18:20. **covet.** Ro 7:7, 8. **and if.** ✍184A, 1 C +15:2. **briefly comprehended.** Ep 1:10g. **saying.** ✍108B, Lk +1:2. **love.** Le +*19:▶18, 34. Mt 5:43. 19:19. *22:39, 40. Mk *12:31. Lk 10:27. Ga 5:13, *14. Ja 2:8-10.

10. **worketh.** 1 C √13:4-7. **no.** ✍175B, Ge +21:16. **love is.** ver. 8. Mt 22:40.

11. **that.** or, this (I exhort). ✍63B, Ge +25:28. **knowing the time.** Is 21:11, 12. Mt 16:3. 24:42-44. Ac 1:6, 7. Ga 6:10. Ep *5:16. Col 4:5. 1 Th *5:1-3. **that now.** ✍7, Allegory by continued Hypocatastasis, Ga 4:24. 1 C 7:29. 10:11. Ja +5:8. 2 P 3:9, 11. 1 J 2:18. Re 1:3. 22:10. **it is.** ✍63B, Ge +25:28. **to awake.** Jon 1:6. Mt *25:5-7. 26:40, 41. Mk 13:35-37. 1 C 15:34. Ep *5:14. 1 Th *5:5-8. **for now.** Ec +*9:10. Is 56:1. Lk 21:38. Jn *9:4. 1 C 7:29-31. 1 P *4:7, 8. 2 P 3:13-15. Re 22:12, 20. **our salvation.** Ro 8:23. 2 T +*1:9. He *9:28. 1 P *1:5. **nearer than.** Jn √5:24. Ac 27:33. Ph 2:12.

12. **night.** Jb 7:4. SS *2:17. Jn ◑*9:4. 1 C *13:12. Ga 6:10. Col *1:12, 13. 1 J 2:8. Re 22:5. **the day.** Ac +*17:31. 1 C +*3:13. 2 Th +*1:10. **is at hand.** Ph *4:5. 2 Th ◑+*2:2. He 10:25. Ja 5:8. 1 P 4:7. **cast off.** 1 S 17:38, 39. Is 2:20. 30:22. Ezk 18:31, 32. Ep 4:22. Ph 3:10, 11. Col 3:8-10, 12. Ja 1:21. 1 P 2:1. 2 P *3:11. **works.** Jb 24:14-17. Jn *3:19-21. Ga 5:19. Ep +*5:11. 1 Th 5:5-7. 1 J 1:5-7. 2:8, 9. 3:8. **of darkness.** Is +*9:2. **put on.** ver. 14. Is 59:17. 2 C *6:7. 10:4. Ep *6:11-18. Col 3:10-17. 1 Th 5:8.

13. **Let us walk.** Lk 1:6. Ga 5:16, 25. Ep 4:1, 17. 5:2, 8, 15. Ph 1:27. 3:16-20. √4:8, 9. Col +√1:10. 1 Th 2:12. 4:12. 1 P 2:12. 1 J 2:6. 2 J 4. **honestly.** *or,* decently. Ro 12:17. 2 C 7:35. 14:40. **as.** Ac 2:15. 1 Th 5:7. 2 P 2:13. **rioting.** Pr 23:20. Is 22:12, 13. 28:7, 8. Am 6:4-6. Mt 24:48-51. Lk 16:19. 17:27, 28. 21:34. 1 C 6:10. Ga 5:21. Ep +*5:18. 1 P 2:11. *4:3-5. **drunkenness.** Lk +*21:34. 1 C 5:11. +*6:10. Ga 5:21. Ep +*5:18. 1 P 4:3. **chambering.** 1 C +*6:9, 10. Ga 5:19. Ep 5:3-6. Col *3:5. 1 Th 4:3-5. He 13:4. 2 P 2:14, 18-20. Ju 23. **wantonness.** Mk +7:22. **strife.** 1 C 1:11. 3:3. 2 C 12:20, 21. Ga 5:15, 20, 21, 26. Ph +*2:3. Ja 3:14-16. 4:5. 1 P 2:1, 2. **envying.** Ac +5:17. Ga 5:21.

14. **put ye on.** ver. 12. Ro +*6:4n. +*8:29. Ex=29:8. Jb 29:14. Ps 132:9. 1 C 15:53, 54. 2 C 5:3. Ga +*3:27. Ep *4:24. Col *3:10-12, 14. 1 Th 5:8. 1 P *2:21, 22. **and.** Ro *8:12, 13. Ga *5:16, 17, 24. Col *3:5-8. 1 P *2:11. 1 J √2:15-17. **provision.** Ro ◑12:17. Lk ◑24:49. 1 T ◑+*5:8. **for the flesh.** Ro *8:13. Ga √6:8. **to fulfill.** Ga 5:16. 1 P 2:11.

ROMANS 14

Christians should receive candidly "the weak in faith," and not despise or judge one another, in respect of things doubtful or indifferent, 1-6; but consider their relation and accountableness to Christ, 7-12. Exhortations to caution, charity, humility, and self-denial, in using their Christian liberty, 13-23.

1. **weak**. ver. 21. Ro 4:19. 15:1, 7. Jb 4:3. Is 35:3, 4. 40:11. 42:3. Ezk 34:4, 16. Zc 11:16. Mt 12:20. 14:31. 18:6, 10. Lk 17:2. 1 C 3:1, 2. 8:7-13. *9:22. **receive**. ver. 3. Ro 15:7. Ps 27:10. Mt 10:40-42. 18:5. Jn 13:20. Ph 2:29. 2 J 10. 3 J 8-10. **doubtful disputations**. *or*, judge *his* doubtful thoughts. ♪101, Dt +32:42. ver. 2-5. Lk 24:38g. 1 C 12:10. Ph 2:14. He 5:14.

2. **that**. ver. 14. 1 C 8:1. 10:25. Ga 2:12. 1 T 4:4. T *1:15. He 9:10. 13:9. **another**. ver. 22, 23. **weak**. ♪63A4, 1 K +3:22. Supply ellipsis, (in the faith). **eateth**. Ge 1:29. *9:3, 4. Pr 15:17. Da *1:8, 12, 16. Ac *10:14.

3. **despise**. ver. 10, 15, 21. Zc 4:10. Mt 18:10. Lk 18:9. 1 C 8:11-13. 2 C +10:10. **judge**. ♪121C2D2, Ge +15:14. ver. 13. Mt 7:1, 2. 9:14. 11:18, 19. 1 C √10:29, 30. Col √2:16, 17. **for**. Ac +*10:34, 44. 15:8, 9. **received**. ver. 1. Ro 15:7.

4. **Who**. Ro +9:20. Pr +*30:10. Mt +*7:1. Ac 11:17. 1 C 4:4, 5. Ja 4:11, 12. **thou**. ♪38D, Ps +27:14. **servant**. Lk 16:13. Ac 10:7. 1 P 2:18. **standeth or**. 1 C √10:12. **Yea**. ♪69A, Mk +9:24. **he shall**. ver. 3. Ro 11:23. 16:25. Dt 33:27-29. Ps *17:5. +*37:17, 24, 28. 119:116, 117. Jn √10:28-30. Ro +*8:31-39. He √7:25. 1 P √1:5. Ju √24. **God is able**. Ro 4:21. 2 C √9:8. Ep *3:20. He 2:18. **make him stand**. Is +*40:29. Je 35:19. 1 C 10:12.

5. **esteemeth one**. Ga 4:9, 10. Le 23:4-7, 15, 16, 24, 27, 34, 35. Zc 7:5, 6. Col √2:16, 17. **Let**. ver. 14, 23. 1 C 8:7, 11. **another esteemeth**. The Apostle is here speaking of Jewish fasts and festivals; and of course his observations do not regard the *sabbath*, which was instituted at the creation (Ge 2:3n); and which being a type of "the rest which remaineth for the people of God," must continue in force, as all types do, till the antitype, or thing signified takes place, that is, till the consumation of all things. See related notes listed at Is +*58:13n. Col ◐√2:16. **persuaded**. *or*, assured. ver. 12. Ro 4:11. Jb *34:32. Is +√8:20n. Lk +1:1. Jn 16:2. Ac 26:9. 1 J *3:19-21.

6. **regardeth**. *or*, observeth. Ga 4:10. **regardeth it unto**. Ex 12:14, 42. 16:25. Is 58:5. Zc 7:5, 6. **regardeth not**. Col √2:16. **that eateth**. ver. 2, 3. **for he giveth God thanks**. Mt 14:19. +*15:36. Lk +*24:30. Jn 6:28. 1 C √10:30, 31. 1 T √4:3-5.

7. **For none**. ver. 9. 1 C √6:19, 20. 2 C √5:15. Ga *2:19, 20. Ph *1:20-24. 1 Th 5:10. T *2:14. 1 P 4:2.

8. **For whether**. ♪184C, Mt +4:9. **we live unto**. ♪72, Ex +32:16. 2 C √5:15. Ga 2:19. **we die unto**. Jn 21:19. Ac 13:36. 20:24. 21:13. Ph 2:17, 30. 1 Th 5:10. **whether**. Ph 1:20. **we live therefore**. 1 C 3:22, 23. 15:23. 1 Th √4:14-18. Re +*14:13. **we are**. T#239. 1 Ch 29:11. Ps *24:1. 50:10-12. *95:5-7. 100:3. Ezk *18:4.

9. **Christ**. Is +*53:10-12. Lk 24:26. 2 C 5:14. He *12:2. 1 P 1:21. Re *1:18. 2:8. **Lord both**. Mt *28:18. Jn √5:22, 23, 27-29. Ac 2:36. +√10:36, 42. Ep *1:20-23. Ph √2:9-11. 2 T +*4:1. He 12:2. 1 P *4:5. **dead**. Ac +10:42. Re +20:12. **living**. Mt *22:32. Ac +√10:36. Ro √10:9. 1 Th 5:10.

10. **thou**. ♪38D, Ps +27:14. **set at nought**. ver. 3, 4. Lk 18:9. 23:11. Ac 4:11. **for we**. Ro 2:16. Ec *12:14. Mt +*10:15n. +25:31, 32. Jn 5:22. Ac 10:42. √17:31. 1 C *4:5. 2 C √5:10. Ju *14, *15. Re √20:11-15. **stand before**. Ac 27:24g. **judgment seat**. Ro +*2:16. 2 C √5:10.

11. **As I live**. ♪92A, Mt +1:23. Nu 14:21, 28. Is ▸45:23. 49:18. Je 22:24. Ezk 5:11. 14:16, 18, 20. 17:16, 19. 18:3. 20:3, 33. Zp 2:9. **every knee**. Ps 72:11. Is √45:22-25. Ph √2:10. Re *5:14. **confess**. ♪46C, Mt +8:6.

Gr. *homologein, to confess*, is used of *to praise* or *celebrate* (see Mt 11:25; Lk 10:21; He 13:15), like the Hebrew *hodah* which has both meanings. See Ge 49:8; 2 S 22:30 (B678). Ro √10:9. 15:9. Mt +*10:32. 11:25. Lk 10:21. Ac +19:18. 1 J 4:15. 2 J *7.

12. **every one**. ver. 10. **give account**. Ec *11:9. Mt +*12:36. +*16:27n. 18:23, etc. +*25:19. Lk +*12:48. *16:2. 19:15. Ga *6:5. 1 P *4:4, 5. **of himself**. Dt 24:16. Jb *19:4. Pr 9:12. Je 31:30. Ezk 14:10n. +*18:20n. Ga 6:5. **to God**. ver. 10. Jn *10:30.

13. **judge one another**. ver. 4, 10. Mt +*7:1. Ja *2:4. *4:11. **but judge this**. Lk *12:57. Jn +*7:24. 1 C *11:13. 2 C 5:14. **that no man**. Mt *18:6-9. 1 C *8:13. **put**. ver. 20g. Ro 9:32, 33. 11:9. 16:17. Le 19:14. Is 57:14. Ezk 14:3. Mt 16:23. √18:6, 7. Lk 17:2. 1 C 8:9-13. √10:32. 2 C 6:3. Ph 1:10. He 12:13. Re 2:14. **or an occasion**. Ro +9:33. 2 S 12:14. 1 T 5:14. 1 J 2:10.

14. **am persuaded**. Ac *10:28. **by the**. Mt ▸15:11. Ga *1:12. **that there**. See on ver. 2, 20. 1 C *10:25. 1 T *4:4. T √1:15. **unclean**. Gr. common. Ac +10:14, 15. 11:8, 9. **to him it**. ver. 23. 1 C *8:7, 10.

15. **But if**. ♪184A, 1 C +15:2. ♪26, Ro +11:19. **thy brother**. Ezk 13:22. 1 C 8:12. **now**. Ro 13:10. 15:2. 1 C 8:1. *13:1, 2, 4, 5, 7. Ga *5:13. Ep *5:2. Ph +*2:2-4. **charitably**. Gr. according to charity. **Destroy**. Gr. *apollumi*, Mt +2:13. ♪121E2, Ge +42:38. ver. 20. Jn ◐*10:27, 28. 1 C *8:10, 11. Ja *1:15. 2 P 2:1. 1 J *2:2.

16. **Let not**. 1 T *4:12. **your good**. Ro +*12:17. Ac +*6:3. 1 C *10:29, 30. 2 C *8:20, 21. 1 Th √5:22.

17. **kingdom of God**. T#84. Da *2:44. Mt 3:2. √6:33. Lk 14:15. +*17:20, 21. +*22:29, 30. Mk +1:15. Jn √3:3, 5. +*18:36. 1 C 4:20. +√6:9, 10. +*15:50. Ga +*5:21. Ep 5:5. Col 1:13. 4:11. 1 Th 2:12. 2 Th +*1:5. 2 T +*4:1, 18. Re 1:9. 12:10. **is not**. i.e. does not lead or tend to, or is not involved in the questions of (see Peters, *Theocratic Kingdom*, vol. 2, p. 34). Mt 11:12. Lk 16:16. Col 1:13. **meat and drink**. ♪174, Ge +18:27. 1 C *8:8. Col √2:16, 17. He *13:9. **but righteousness**. Is √26:7-11. *45:24. Je +√23:5, 6. Da +*9:24. Mi +*6:8. Mt √6:33. +*23:23. Lk √12:31, 32. 1 C *1:30. +*6:9. 2 C √5:21. Ph √3:9. 2 P 1:1. **peace**. ♪171I9B, Is +57:19. Ro *5:1-5. 8:6, 15, 16. 15:13. Is *55:12. *61:3. Mi 4:3-5. Zc 9:10. Jn 16:33. Ac 9:31. 13:52. Ga *5:22. Ph 2:1. 3:3. √4:4, 7. Col 1:11. 1 Th 1:6. He √12:14. 1 P 1:8. **joy**. Ro *15:13. Is 2:4. 24:14-16. *65:19. Ho +*2:15. Jl 2:23. Zp 3:14. Zc +*2:10. Ac 2:46. **Ghost**. Gr. *pneuma*, Mt +1:18n. Jl +*2:28.

18. **in these**. ver. 4. Ro 6:22. 12:11. *16:17, 18. Mk 13:34. Jn *12:26. 1 C 7:22. Ga 6:15, 16. Col +3:24. T √2:11-14. **is acceptable**. Ro +*12:1, 2. Ge 4:7. Dt=33:11. Ec 9:7. Ac 10:35. 2 C 5:9. *8:12, 21. Ep *1:6. 5:10. Ph 4:18. Col 3:20. 1 T 2:3. 5:4. He 13:21. 1 P *2:4, 5, 20. **and approved**. Ro 16:10. Pr +*16:7. Lk 2:52. 2 C 4:2. 5:11. 6:4. *8:21. 1 Th 1:3, 4. Ja +1:12. 2:18-26. 1 P 3:16.

19. **follow**. Ro 12:18. Ps *34:14. 133:1. Mt 5:9. Mk +9:50. 1 C 7:15. *14:33. 2 C 13:11. Ep 4:3-7. Ph 2:1-4. Col 3:12-15. 2 T √2:22. He +*12:14. Ja 3:13-18. 1 P 3:11. **edify**. Ro 15:2. Ac +9:31. 1 C 8:1. *10:23, 33. 14:3-5. *12-17, 26. 2 C 10:8. 12:19. 13:10. Ep 4:12, 16, √29. 1 Th *5:11, 12. 1 T 1:4.

20. **For**. See on ver. 15. Mt 18:6. 1 C 6:12, 13. 8:8, 13. √10:31. **the work**. Jn *6:29. 1 C √15:58. Ep

√2:10. Ph *1:6. **All.** ver. 14. Mt 15:11. Ac 10:15. 1 T √4:3-5. T √1:15. **but.** ver. 15, 21. 1 C *8:8-13. √10:32, 33. **with offence.** ver. +13.

21. **good.** ver. 17. Ro 15:1, 2. 1 C 8:13. **eat flesh.** Da +*1:8. **nor to drink wine.** T#368. Da *1:8, 12, 15. Pr +*20:1. +*22:3. Lk 1:15. 1 C 5:11. Ph +3:19 (T#199). Ep +*5:18. **any thing.** √63G, Ge +50:23. Supply by ellipsis, (to do any thing). **whereby.** ver. 13. Ml 2:8. Mt 16:23. 18:7-10. Lk 17:1, 2. Ph 1:10. He 12:13. Re 2:14. **is offended.** Mt +15:12. 17:27.

22. **thou.** ver. 2, 5, 14, 23. Ga *6:1. Ja 3:13. **Happy.** Ro 7:15, 24. Ac +*24:16. 2 C 1:12. 1 J *3:21. **condemneth not himself.** 2 S 24:10. Jb *9:20. Mt *12:36, 37. 1 T 3:7. Ja 3:2. **alloweth.** Ro +*2:18.

23. **he that.** 1 C 8:7. **doubteth.** *or*, discerneth and putteth a difference between meats. ver. 14. Mt +21:21. T *1:15. **damned.** Rather, "is condemned," *katakekritai*; which is the proper signification of "damned," from the Latin *damno*, to condemn. Ro 13:2. 1 C 11:29-32g. **if.** √184C, Mt +4:9. **whatsoever.** T √1:15. He √11:6. **is sin.** Pr 21:4. 1 J 3:4. 5:17.

ROMANS 15

In condescension to the weak, the strong ought to give up their own inclination, for the good of others, after the example of Christ, 1-3. All scriptures were written for our instruction, 4. The apostle prays for love and harmony among believers, in the worship of God, 5-7; shows that the scriptures foretell the union of Jews and Gentiles in the service of God; and subjoins a fervent prayer, 8-13. He exhorts the Christians at Rome, as the apostle of the Gentiles, 14-16; and states his extensive labors and usefulness, 17-21. He avows his purpose of visiting Rome, in his way to Spain; desires their prayers in respect of his previous journey to Jerusalem, with the contributions of the Gentile converts, 22-32; and again prays for them, 33.

1. **strong.** Ro 4:20. 1 C 4:10. 2 C 12:10. 13:9. Ep *6:10. 2 T 2:1. 1 J *2:14. **ought.** Ro +14:1. 1 C 9:22. 12:22-24. Ga √6:1, 2. 1 Th 5:14. **please.** See on ver. 3. 1 C 9:19, 22. 10:24, 33. 13:5. Ga 1:10. Ph 2:4, 21.

2. **please his neighbor.** Ro +14:19. 1 C *9:19-22. *10:24, 33. 11:1. *13:5. Ph *2:4, 5. T 2:9, 10.

3. **Christ.** Ps *40:6-8. Mt *26:39, 42. Jn *4:34. *5:30. *6:38. *8:29. *12:27, 28. *13:14, 15. *14:30, 31. *15:10. Ph *2:5, 8. **pleased not.** He 5:5. **The reproaches.** √92A, Mt +1:23. Ps *22:6. ♦*69:7, ♦9, 20. 89:41, 50, 51. Mt *10:25. Jn *15:21.

4. **whatsoever.** Ro +*4:23, 24. 1 C *9:9, 10. *10:11. 2 T +√3:16, 17. 2 P *1:20, 21. **written.** Ps *102:18. **aforetime.** Ga 3:1. Ep 3:3g. Ju 4. **for our learning.** Rather, "for our instruction." T#1030. Ro 12:7. Ps +*119:130. Is +*8:20. Mk +*12:24. Jn +*5:39. √20:31. 1 C *10:6, 11. Col 2:17. 2 T +√3:16. He 10:1. 2 P *1:19. 1 J √5:13. **patience.** √134, Mt +3:9. In Hebrew the words "patience" and "hope" would be *sabbar* and *subar*, thus exhibiting the figure *Parechesis*, or Foreign Paronomasia. Ro +*2:7. *5:3-5. 8:24, 25. *12:12. Ps 119:81-83. Lk +*8:15. 21:19. 1 C *13:4, 5. 2 C 6:4-6. 12:12. 1 Th 1:3. 2 Th 1:4. He *6:10-19. +*10:35, 36. *13:5, 6. Ja 1:3. *5:7-11. 1 P 1:13. 2:19-23. Re 14:12. **and comfort.** √93A, Ge +1:26. T#1051. Ro 8:28. 2 Ch 31:4. 35:2. Jb 5:19. 6:10. 11:16. Ps 27:5. 30:5. 42:5. 103:13. *119:50, √52, 82, 92, 143. 138:7. Is 46:4. 61:3. 63:9. Mt +*5:4. Jn 14:1-3. Ac 15:30,

31. 1 C +14:3. 1 Th 3:7. 4:13. 1 P 4:12, 13. Re 2:10. 3:10. 7:14-17. 14:13. **the scriptures.** Mt +21:42. **hope.** T#1042. Ro 4:18. 5:2. 8:24. 12:12. Ps *71:14. *119:49, 74, 81, 114, 116. 130:5. Pr +*3:5. 14:32. Ac 23:6. 26:6. 1 C 9:10. 13:13. 2 C 3:12. Ga 5:5. Ep 1:18. 4:4. Col 1:5, 23. 1 Th 1:3. 2:19. *5:8. 2 Th +*2:16. 1 T 1:1. T *1:2. *2:13. 3:7. He *3:6. +*6:11, 18. 7:19. 1 P +*1:3, 4. +*3:15. 1 J √3:3.

5. **the God.** ver. 13, 33. Ex 34:6. Ps 86:15. Ph 4:9. 1 Th 5:23. He 13:20. 1 P 3:20. 5:10. 2 P *3:9, 15. **consolation.** 2 C *1:3, 4. 7:6. **grant.** T#1605. Ro +12:16. 2 Ch 30:12. Je 32:39. Eze 11:19. Ac 4:32. 1 C *1:10. 2 C 13:11. Ph 1:27. *2:2. 3:16. 4:2. 1 P 3:8. **likeminded.** What the Apostle prays for is not identity of opinion, but harmony of feeling (E. H. Gifford). **according to.** *or*, after the example of. ver. 3. 2 C 11:17. Ep 4:24. 5:2. Ph 2:4, 5. Col 2:8.

6. **with one mind.** Ro 12:4, 5. ver. 9-11. Zp 3:9. Zc 13:9. Jn 17:11. Ac +1:14. *4:24, 32. 1 C 10:17. Ep 4:4. 5:30. **one mouth.** 2 Ch=5:13. **glorify.** Mt +9:8. **the Father of.** Jn +*10:29, 30. 20:17. 2 C 1:3. 11:31. Ep 1:3, 17. Col 1:3. 1 P 1:3. Re 1:6.

7. **receive.** Ro 12:10. *14:1-3. Ml +*3:16. Mt *10:40. 25:40. Mk *9:37-41. Lk *9:48. 10:38, 39. Jn 13:34. Ac *9:26-28. *11:25, 26. *16:15. 17:7. 2 C +*6:9. Ga 6:1, 2. He 13:1, 2. 1 P +*4:9, 10. 1 J 3:14. 2 J ◐10. 3 J ◐9, 10. **one another.** Ro +12:5. **as Christ.** Ro 5:2. Mt +*11:28-30. Lk *15:2. Jn 1:38, 39. √6:37. *13:34. He 2:11. 11:16. **to the glory.** ver. *9. Ro +3:23. Ep *1:6-8, 12, 18. Ph 2:11. 2 Th *1:10-12.

8. **I say.** Ro 3:26. 1 C 1:12. 10:19, 29. *15:50. **Jesus.** Ro *9:4, 5. Dt *18:15. Mt *15:24. *20:28. Jn *1:11. Ac *3:25, +26. *13:46. Ga 4:4, 5. He 3:1. **of the circumcision.** √121N1, Ge +31:54. Mt √10:5, 6. √15:24. **for the.** Ro *3:3. Ps 98:2, 3. Mi *7:20. Lk 1:54-56, 70-73. 2 C 1:20. **truth.** ver. 16. Ro 3:4, 7. 9:23, 24. 11:*22, 30. Is 24:15, 16. Jn +*10:16. Ep *2:12-22. 3:1-8. 1 P *2:9, 10. **to confirm.** T#121. Ro 4:16. Ps +*89:34. Mi *7:20. Mt +*5:17, 18. +*8:11. Ac +*1:6. +*2:39. +*3:19-21. +13:33. 2 C *1:20. Ga 3:17, 29. He +*11:13, 39. **the promises.** Ro 9:4. Ge +*12:3. 22:16-18. 26:3. Ac +√26:6. Ga 3:16. He +6:12. **the fathers.** Ro 9:5. 11:28. Jn 6:58. 7:22. Ac 13:32. 22:3. He 1:1. 2 P 3:4.

9. **the Gentiles.** Ro +3:29. Ga +*3:28. **For.** 2 S *)22:50. Ps *)18:49. **confess.** Ro +14:11. **and sing.** Ps 66:4. Ja +5:13.

10. **Rejoice.** Dt)32:43. Ps 66:1-4. 67:3, 4. 68:32. 97:1. 98:3, 4. 138:4, 5. Is 24:14-16. 42:10-12. **his people.** 2 P 2:1. Ju 5.

11. **Praise.** Ps)117:1.

12. **Esaias.** Mk +1:2. **There.** √92A, Mt +1:23. Is)11:1, 10. Re *5:5. *22:16. ·**root.** √22H1D, Is +11:10. **Jesse.** Mt 1:5, 6. Lk 3:32. Ac 13:22. **and he.** Ge +*49:10. Ps 2:4-12. 22:27, 28. 72:8-10, 17. *102:15. Is 42:1-4. 49:6. Da 2:44. +*7:14. Mi 4:1-3. 5:4. **rise.** √31, Is +1:21. Is 11:10. **reign over.** Ps 2:6-9. Is 2:4. 42:1. Zc +*14:9. **in him.** Is 42:4. Je +*16:19. 17:5-7. Mt 12:21. 1 C 15:19. Ep 1:12, 13. 2 T 1:12mg. 1 P 1:21. 1 J 3:3.

13. **the God of hope.** ver. 5. Je 14:8. Jl 3:16. 1 T 1:1. **fill.** Ro +*14:17. Is 55:12. Jn *14:1, 27. Ga *5:22. Ep 1:2. +*5:18, 19. 2 Th *2:16, 17. 1 P *1:8. **all joy.** T#1587. Ro *5:1, 2. 14:17. Ge=43:23. Ps 5:11. 132:9. Jn 17:13. **in believing.** Ph 1:25. **abound in hope.** T#1563. ver. +*4. Ro +*5:4, 5. *8:23-26. *12:12.

La *3:24. 2 C *9:8. He +*6:11. **through the power.**
ver. 19. **Ghost.** Gr. *pneuma*, Mt +1:18n.

14. **I myself.** Ro 1:8. Ph 1:7. 2 T 1:5. Phm 21. He
+*6:9. 2 P 1:12. 3:1. 1 J 2:21. **full.** Ga *5:22. Ep
5:9. Ph 1:11. Col +*1:8-10. 2 Th 1:11. 2 P √1:5-8.
filled. Pr √4:7. Ml=2:7. Mk +*12:24. Jn *17:3. 1 C
1:5. 8:1, 7, 10. 12:8. 13:2. Ph *1:9. Col +√1:10. 2 P
*1:12. √3:18. 1 J *2:21. **able.** Ep 5:11, 19. Col √3:16.
1 Th 5:11, +12, 14. T 2:3, 4. He +*3:12, 13. *5:12.
√10:24, 25. Ju *20-23.

15. **I have written.** He 13:22. 1 P 5:12. 1 J 2:12-
14. *5:13. Ju 3-5. **some sort.** ver. 24. Ro +11:25. **as
putting.** 1 T 4:6. 2 T 1:6. 2:14. T 3:1. 2 P 1:12-15.
3:1, 2. Ju +5. **because.** Ro +*1:5. +*12:3, 6. 1 C
3:10. 15:10. Ga 1:15, 16. 2:9. Ep *3:7, 8. 1 T 1:11-
14. 1 P 4:10, 11. 2 P *3:15. **the grace.** 1 C +1:4.

16. **I should.** ver. 18. Ro 11:13. Ac +*9:15. 13:2.
22:21. +*26:17, 18. 1 C 3:5. 4:1. 2 C *5:18, 20. 11:23.
Ga 2:7, 8. Ep 3:1. Ph 2:17. 1 T 2:7. 2 T 1:11. **the
minister.** Ro +13:6. **ministering.** ver. 29. Ro 1:1. Ml
1:11. Ac 20:24. Ga 3:5. 1 Th 2:2, 9. 1 T 1:11. 1 P
1:12. **gospel of God.** Ro +1:1. **offering.** *or*, sacrificing.
Ro +*12:1, 2. Nu=8:11. Is *66:19, 20. 2 C 8:5. Ph
2:17. 4:18. He +*13:16. 1 P 2:5. **acceptable.** ver. 31.
2 C 6:2. 8:12. Ep *1:6. 1 P 2:5. **being.** Ro *5:5. +*8:26,
27. Ac 20:32. 1 C 1:2. *6:19. Ep 2:18, 22. √5:25-27.
1 Th +*5:23. 2 Th *2:13, 14. **Ghost.** Gr. *pneuma*,
Mt +1:18n. +3:16.

17. **whereof.** Ro 4:2. *11:13. 2 C *2:14-16. 3:4-6.
7:4. 10:17. 11:16-30. 12:1, 11, etc. Ga *6:14. Ph 3:3.
in. He 2:17. 5:1.

18. **I will.** Pr 25:14. 2 C 10:13-18. 11:31. 12:6. Ju
9. **which.** Mk 16:20. Ac 14:27. 15:4, 12. *21:19. 1 C
3:6-9. *15:10. 2 C 3:1-3. 6:1. Ga *2:8. **to make.** Ro
+1:5. 6:17. 16:26. Mt +*28:18-20. Ac +*26:20. 2 C
+*10:4, 5. He +*5:9. 11:8. **by word.** Col *3:17.
2 Th 2:17. Ja +*1:22. 1 J 3:18.

19. **mighty.** Jn +4:48. Ac +2:22. *14:8-10. 15:12.
*16:16-18. *19:6, 11, 12. *20:9, 10. 1 C +2:4. 2 C
12:12. Ga 3:5. He *2:4. **by the power.** ver. 13. Mt
*12:28. +*28:19. Lk +*1:35. Ac +*1:8. 10:38. 1 C
+1:24 (T#76-5). *12:4-11. 1 P 1:12. Re +19:6 (T#218).
Spirit. Gr. *pneuma*, Mt +3:16. **so that.** ver. 24. Ac
9:28, 29. 13:4, 5, 14, 51. 14:6, 20, 21, 25. 16:6-12.
17:10, 15. 18:1, 19. 19:1. 20:2, 3, 6. **from Jerusalem.**
Ac 22:17-21. **Illyricum.** i.e. *rejoicing*, *S#2437g, only
here. *Illyricum*, or *Illyria*, was a country of Europe,
lying N. and N.W. of Macedonia, on the eastern coast
of the Adriatic gulf, opposite Italy. It was distinguished
into two parts; Liburnia north, now Croatia; and Dalmatia south, still retaining the same name. The account
of St. Paul's second visit to the peninsula of Greece,
Ac 20:1, 2, says Dr. Paley, leads us to suppose that,
in going over Macedonia, he had passed so far to the
west, as to come into those parts of the country which
were contiguous to Illyricum, if he did not enter Illyricum itself. The history and the Epistle therefore so
far agree; and the agreement is much strengthened
by a coincidence of *time*; for much before the time
when this epistle was written, he could not have said
so, as his route, in his former journey, confined him
to the eastern side of the peninsula, a considerable
distance from Illyricum. Paley alludes to Lardner, who
incidentally on this point is citing Biscoe, who maintains
that this is "a general confirmation of the whole history
of his travels in the book of the Acts" (Lardner, *Works*,

vol. 5, *A History of the Apostles and Evangelists*, p.
522), thus constituting a most remarkable undesigned
coincidence. See related notes listed at Ac 12:12n.
Ac 20:1, 2. **fully.** √100, Ge +10:9. Ro 1:14-16. Ac
*20:20, 21. Col 1:25. 2 T 4:17. **the gospel.** 1 C 9:12.
2 C 2:12. 4:4. 9:13. 10:14. Ga 1:7. Ph 1:27. 1 Th 3:2.

20. **so.** 2 C 5:9. *10:14-16. 1 Th 4:11. **named.** Is
*26:13. Am 6:10. Ep 1:21. 2 T *2:19. **build.** 1 C 3:9-
15. 2 C 10:13-16. Ep 2:20-22. **foundation.** 1 C +3:10.

21. **To whom.** Is ▸52:15. *65:1. **shall see.** Mt 5:14.
Jn 8:29. 9:5.

22. **I have.** Ro 1:13. 1 Th *2:17, 18. **much.** *or*, many
ways, *or*, oftentimes.

23. **these parts.** 2 C 11:10. Ga 1:21. **great desire.**
ver. 32. Ro *1:10-12. 1 Th 3:10. 2 T 1:4.

24. **I take.** ver. 28. Ac 19:21. **Spain.** i.e. *land of
rabbits; rare, precious; scarceness*, *S#4681g. ver.
28. *Spain* is a large country in the west of Europe,
which anciently comprehended both Spain and Portugal, separated from Gaul or France by the Pyrenees,
and bounded on every other side by the sea. **and to.**
Ac +15:3. 21:5. 2 C 1:16. 3 J 6. **if.** √184C, Mt +4:9.
Ro 1:12. 1 C 16:5-7. **somewhat.** ver. 15. Ro +11:25
(in part). **filled.** Rather, "gratified (or enjoy) your society," as *empleestho* frequently denotes. **with your company.** Gr. with you. √121I1, Ge +3:7. ver. 32.

25. **I go.** ver. 26-31. Ac 18:21. *19:21. 20:3, 16,
22. 21:15. 24:17. 1 C 16:1-3. Ga 2:10. **to minister.**
Lk +8:3. **the saints.** 2 C +1:1.

26. **it hath.** 1 C 16:1-4. 2 C *8:1. 9:2, 13. **pleased
them.** Ac 11:27-30. 2 C ch. 8, 9. Ga 6:6-10. **Macedonia.**
√121J14, Ge +47:15. Ac +19:21. 1 Th 1:7, 8. **Achaia.**
√121J14, Ge +47:15. **a certain contribution.** The three
points mentioned here (ver. 25, 26), (1) contributions
in Macedonia, (2) contributions in Achaia, (3) Paul's
intended journey to Jerusalem, are found in incidental
hints in three other writings. Ac 20:2, 3, mentions
the visit to Macedonia and Greece, and the voyage
to Syria, but not the contributions. Ac 24:17-19 mentions the collection, but not the places. 1 C 16:1-4
mentions a collection at Corinth. 2 C 8:1-4 mentions
the liberality of the Macedonians. 2 C 9:2 mentions
the liberality of the Achaians. The *time* in all is the
same. It is incredible that a forger, writing the Epistle,
could have inserted this passage for the purpose of
securing conformity with the other writings. It is in
the highest degree improbable that this conformity
could be the effect of contrivance and design, for if
this were done to countenance his forgery, the forger
did it for the purpose of an argument which would
not strike one reader in ten thousand. Coincidences
so circuitous as this answer not the ends of forgery;
are seldom, I believe, attempted by it. Only by a close
and attentive collation of the three writings could a
forger have picked out the circumstances which he
has united in this Epistle, and by a still more accurate
examination determined them to belong to the same
period. The introduction of the passage in context is
perfectly apt and natural. It arises by a junction as
easy as any example of writing upon real business can
furnish. What could be more natural that Paul, writing
to the Romans, should speak of the time when he
hoped to visit them, should mention the business which
then detained him, and that he purposed to set forwards
upon his journey to them when that business was completed (William Paley, *Horae Paulinae*, pp. 23-28, 215.

See related notes listed at Ac 12:12n). 2 C 9:13. Phm 6. He 13:16. **the poor.** Pr 14:21, 31. 17:5. Zc 11:7, 11. Mt *25:40. 26:11. Lk 6:20. 14:13. 1 C 16:15. 2 C 9:12. Ga 2:10. Phm 5. Ja *2:5, 6.

27. **their debtors.** Ro 11:17. 1 C *9:11. Ga *6:6. Phm 19. **For if.** √184A, 1 C +15:2. **spiritual.** Ro +1:11g. **their duty.** Is +*14:2. 1 C 9:11. Ga 6:6. **to minister.** 2 C 9:12.

28. **this.** √63A2, 2 S +6:6. Supply by ellipsis, (business). **and sealed.** Jn +3:33. Ph *4:17. Col 1:6. **this fruit.** Ro +1:13. **I will.** ver. 24. Pr 19:21. La 3:37. Ja 4:13-15. **by you.** 2 C 1:16. **unto Spain.** ver. 24.

29. **when.** ver. 23. **fulness of blessing.** √108B, Ge +33:11. Ro 1:11, 12. Ps 16:11. Ezk 34:26. Ep 1:3. 3:8, 19. 4:13. 1 P 3:9.

30. **beseech.** Ro *12:1. **for the.** 2 C 4:5, 11. *12:10. 1 T 6:13, 14. 2 T 4:1. **the love.** Ps *143:10. Ga *5:22. Ph *2:1. Col *1:8. **Spirit.** Gr. *pneuma*, Mt +3:16. Jn +7:39. **that.** Ge 32:24-29. 2 C *1:11. Ep 6:19, 20. Col 2:1, 2. *4:12, 13. 1 Th 5:25. 2 Th *3:1, 2. He 13:18.

31. **I may.** Ac *15:1, 2. 20:22, 23. 21:27-31. 22:24. *23:12-24. 24:1-9. 25:2, 24. 2 C 1:10. 1 Th 2:15, 16. 2 Th 3:2. 2 T 3:11. 4:17. **do not believe.** *or,* are disobedient. Ro 11:30-32. Ac +14:2. **my service.** ver. 25, 26. 1 C 16:15. 2 C 8:4, 19, 20. 9:1, 12, 13. He 6:10. **accepted.** ver. +16. Ac 21:17-26. **the saints.** 2 C +1:1.

32. **I may.** ver. 23, 24. Ro *1:10-13. Ac 27:1, 41-43. 28:15, 16, 30, 31. Ph 1:12-14. **by the.** Ac *18:21. 1 C *4:19. 1 Th +4:3. Ja +*4:15. **and may.** Pr 25:13. 1 C 16:18. 2 C 7:13. 1 Th 3:6-10. 2 T 1:16. Phm 7, 20. **you.** √12111, Ge +3:7.

33. **the God.** ver. +5. Ro 16:20. 1 C *14:33. 2 C *5:19, 20. *13:11. Ph √4:7, 9. 1 Th +*5:23. 2 Th 3:16. He *13:20. **be with.** Ro 16:24. Ru 2:4. Mt 1:23. *28:20. 2 C *13:14. 2 T 4:22.

ROMANS 16

The apostle commends Phebe to the Christians of Rome; and sends salutations to many by name, 1-16. He warns them against those who caused divisions and offences, 17-20. He names several brethren, who joined in their salutations of them, 21-23. He concludes with prayers for them, and ascriptions of glory to God, 24-27.

1. **commend.** 2 C +3:1. **Phebe.** i.e. *radiant,* ⁂S#5402g, only here. **our sister.** ver. 6. Mt 12:50. Mk 10:30. 1 T 5:2. Ja 2:15. 1 P 1:22, 23. **a servant.** Gr. *diakonos.* The Greek term may be understood in a general sense and rendered "servant," or it may be understood in a technical sense and rendered "deacon" or "deaconess." In favor of the technical sense is its immediate connection with the phrase "of the church." Ro 13:4. 15:8. Mt 20:26. Mk 10:43. Lk 8:3. 18:14. *22:24-26. Jn 2:5, 9. 12:26. 1 C 3:5. 12:21, 22. 2 C 3:6. 6:4. Ep 3:7. 6:21. Ph 1:1g. +*2:3. Col 1:7, 23, 25. 1 Th 3:2. 1 T 3:1, 8, √11, 12. 4:6. 5:9, 10. Ja *4:10. **Cenchrea.** Ac 18:18.

2. **ye receive.** Ro 15:7. Mt 10:40-42. 25:40. Ph 2:29. Col 4:10. Phm 12, 17. 2 J 10. 3 J ◐6-10. **as becometh.** Ep 5:3. Ph 1:27. 1 T 2:10. T 2:3. **saints.** √181E, Ge +3:24. 2 C +1:1. **for.** ver. 3, 4, 6, 9, 23. Ac 9:36, 39, 41. Ph 4:14-19. 2 T 1:18.

3. **Greet.** Had the notes of time in this epistle fixed the writing of it to any date prior to St. Paul's first

residence at Corinth, the salutation of Aquila and Priscilla would have contradicted the history, because it would have been prior to his acquaintance with these persons. If they had fixed it during *that* residence at Corinth, during his journey to Jerusalem, or during his progress through Asia Minor, an equal contradiction would have been incurred, because, during all that time, they were either with St. Paul, or abiding at Ephesus. Lastly, had they fixed this epistle to be either contemporary with the first epistle to the Corinthians, or prior to it, a similar contradiction would have ensued, for they were then with St. Paul. As it is, all things are consistent. The points by which the time is noted are so intricate that an impostor could not have avoided going wrong. Thus may be observed the danger of scattering names and circumstances in writings like the present, how implicated they often are with dates and places, and that nothing but truth can preserve consistency (William Paley, *Horae Paulinae,* pp. 28-31. See listing of related notes at Ac 12:12n). **Priscilla.** 2 S +=20:16. Ac *18:+2, etc., 18, 26. 1 C +*16:19. 2 T *4:19. **my helpers.** ver. 9, 21. 2 Ch=29:34. 1 C 16:16. 2 C 4:5. 8:23. Ph 2:25. 4:3. Col 4:11. Phm 1, 24. **in.** √12111, Ge +3:7.

4. **who have.** Ro 5:7. Jn 15:13. Ph 2:30. 1 J *3:16. **for my life.** Gr. *psyche,* √121A7, Mt +2:20. √121A7, Ge +9:5. √171Q2, Nu +23:10. This praise of Aquila and Priscilla for their devotion agrees with what is said in Acts; but the notices in Acts are too indirect as material for a forger, and yet without the Acts the picture would have been impossible. In Acts 18:2 we are told they were Jews; we learn from Acts that Paul met them in Corinth, that for some time he abode in the same house with them; that the unbelieving Jews raised an insurrection against Paul; we may conclude that through all this contest Aquila and Priscilla adhered to St. Paul, for when he left the city, they went with him (Ac 18:18). Under these circumstances, it is highly probable that they should be involved in the dangers and persecutions which St. Paul underwent from the Jews, being themselves Jews; and, by adhering to St. Paul in this dispute, deserters, as they would be accounted, of the Jewish cause. They were entitled to "thanks from the churches of the Gentiles" because they had stood with Paul in the matter of admitting Gentiles to parity of religious situation with the Jews (Paley, *Horae Paulinae,* p. 32. See listing of related notes at Ac 12:12n). **laid down.** Jsh 10:24. 2 S 22:41. Mi 2:3. Ac +*15:26. **also.** Ac 15:41. 16:5. 1 C +7:17. 16:1. 1 Th 2:14. Re 1:4.

5. **the church.** ver. 14, 15. Mt +*18:20. 1 C +*16:19. Col *4:15. Phm *2. 2 J +*10. **my well-beloved.** ver. 8, 12. 3 J 1. **Epaenetus.** i.e. *praised,* ⁂S#1866g, only here. **who.** Ro 11:16. 1 C 16:15. Ja 1:18. Re 14:4. **Achaia.** Ro 15:26. Ac 18:12, 27. 2 C 1:1. 9:2.

6. **who bestowed.** ver. 12. Mt 27:55. Ga 4:11. 1 T 5:10. **much labor.** 1 Th 5:12. 1 T 5:17.

7. **Andronicus.** i.e. *who excels, or is victorious; man of victory,* ⁂S#408g, only here. **Junia.** i.e. *youthful,* ⁂S#2458g. **kinsmen.** ver. 11, 21. Ro 9:3. **fellowprisoners.** 2 C 11:23. Col 4:10. Phm 23. Re 1:9. **of note.** Mt 27:16g. Ga 2:2, 6. **the apostles.** 1 C +12:28. **were.** Ro 8:1. Is 45:17, 25. Jn 6:56. +14:20. 15:2. 1 C *1:30. 2 C √5:17, 21. 12:2. Ga 1:22. 5:6. 6:15. Ep √2:10. 1 J 4:13. 5:20. **in Christ.** √12111, Ge +3:7. Ac +*13:48.

Ep 1:4. 2 T 2:10. **before me.** Ac 21:16.

8. **Amplias.** i.e. *enlarged,* ✱S#291g. **my.** ver. 5. Ph 4:1. 1 J 3:14.

9. **Urbane.** i.e. *pleasant, courteous; of the city; refined,* ✱S#3773g. **our.** ver. 2, 3, 21. **Stachys.** i.e. *ear of corn,* ✱S#4720g.

10. **Apelles.** i.e. *exclusion, separation; seclusion,* ✱S#559g. **approved.** Ro 14:18. Dt 8:2. 1 C 11:19. 2 C 2:9. 8:22. Ph 2:22. 1 T 3:10. Ja +1:12. 1 P 1:7. **them which.** 1 C 1:11. **of.** 2 T 4:19. **Aristobulus.** i.e. *good counselor,* ✱S#711g. **household.** *or,* friends.

11. **Herodion.** i.e. *valiant,* ✱S#2267g. **kinsmen.** ver. 7, 21. **household.** *or,* friends. **Narcissus.** i.e. *a daffodil; narcotic,* ✱S#3488g.

12. **Tryphena.** i.e. *luxurious,* ✱S#5170g. **Tryphosa.** i.e. *luxuriating,* ✱S#5173g. **labor.** ver. 6. Mt 9:38. 1 C 15:10, 58. 16:16. Col 1:29. 4:12. 1 Th 1:3. 5:12, 13. 1 T 4:10. 5:17, 18. He +*6:10, 11. **Persis.** i.e. *fighting,* ✱S#4069g. **in the Lord.** C. F. Hogg notes "There is a difference between 'in Christ,' which denotes relationship with Him, and 'in the Lord,' which denotes subjection to His authority. The significance of the latter in this place should be noted. Service may be self-willed, self-chosen, self-regulated. That of Persis was of another character; it was 'in the Lord,' regulated by His Word. Compare 1 C 14:37" *(The Ministry of Women,* p. 18).

13. **Rufus.** Mk 15:21. **chosen.** Mt 20:16. Jn +*15:16. Ep *1:4-6. 2 Th *2:13. 2 J 1, 13. **his mother.** Mt 12:49, 50. Mk *3:34, 35. Jn 19:27. 1 T *5:1, 2.

14. **Asyncritus.** i.e. *incomparable,* ✱S#799g. **Phlegon.** i.e. *burning, zealous,* ✱S#5393g. **Hermas.** i.e. *mercury, sand bank, teacher for gain,* ✱S#2057g. **Patrobas.** i.e. *paternal,* ✱S#3969g. **Hermes.** i.e. *refuge,* ✱S#2060g. Ac 14:12, Mercurius. **and.** Ro +*8:29. Col 1:2. He 3:1. 1 P 1:22, 23. **brethren.** Jn +21:23. Ep +6:23.

15. **Philologus.** i.e. *lover of learning; lover of the word; argumentive,* ✱S#5378g. **Julia.** i.e. *downy, hairy,* ✱S#2456g. **Nereus.** i.e. *not flowing; a light; a water nymph,* ✱S#3517g. **Olympas.** i.e. *celestial,* ✱S#3652g. **and all.** ver. 2. Ro 1:7. Is 60:21. 2 C +1:1. Ep 1:1. 1 P 1:2.

16. **one another.** ℐ63G, Ge +50:23. The *Ellipsis* understood is: "Salute one another (men and women respectively) with a holy kiss." It was, and is, contrary to all Eastern usage for women (who were always covered, 1 C 11:5) and men to kiss each other indiscriminately (B62). **with.** Ac 20:37. 1 C 16:20. 2 C 13:12. 1 Th 5:26. 1 P *5:14. **The churches of Christ.** ver. *4, 5. Mt *16:18. Ac +*20:28n.

17. **mark them.** Ph 3:17. 2 Th 3:14, 15. **cause divisions.** Ac 15:1-5, 24. 1 C 1:10-13. 3:3. 11:18. Ga 1:7-9. 2:4. 5:20. Ph 3:2, 3. Col 2:8. 2 P 2:1, 2. 1 J √2:19. 2 J +*7-10. Ju 19. **offences.** Mt +*18:7. Lk 17:1. **contrary.** 1 T 1:3. *6:3. **avoid them.** Ps +√119:63. Mt +*15:14. *18:17. 1 C 5:9-11. 2 Th *3:6, 14. 1 T *6:3-5. 2 T *3:5. T 3:10. 2 J √10, 11.

18. **serve not.** Mt *6:24. Jn 12:26. Ga 1:10. Ph 2:21. Col +*3:24. Ja 1:1. Ju 1. Re 1:1. **but.** 1 S 2:12-17, 29. Is 56:10-12. Ezk 13:19. Ho 4:8-11. Mi 3:5. Ml 1:10. Mt 24:48-51. Ph +*3:19. 1 T *6:5. 2 T 3:4. T 1:12. 2 P 2:10-15. Ju 12. **belly.** ℐ171Q18. Synecdoche of the Part B647. The *belly* is put for *man,* in respect of his *eating.* Here, "their own belly," i.e. their own

selves. For other instances of this figure see Ph 3:19. T 1:12. **by.** 2 S +*15:6. 2 Ch 18:5, 12-17. Is 30:10, 11. Je 8:10, 11. 23:17. 28:1-9, 15-17. Ezk 13:16. Mi 3:5. Mt 7:15. 24:11, 24. 2 C 2:17. 4:2. √11:13-15. Col 2:4. 2 Th 2:10. 1 T 6:5. 2 T 2:16-18. 3:2-6. T 1:10-12. 2 P 2:3, 18-20. 1 J *4:1-3. Ju 16. **the simple.** ℐ108K54, Pr +1:4. ver. 19. Ps +*19:7. 119:130. Pr 8:5. 14:15. +*22:3. 2 C √11:3. He 7:26g.

19. **obedience.** Ro +*1:8. 1 Th 1:8, 9. **I am.** Ep 1:15-17. Col 1:3-9. 1 Th 1:2, 3. 3:6-10. **yet.** Dt +*32:29. 1 K 3:9-12. Ps 101:2. Is 11:2, 3. Mt +*10:16. 1 C 14:20. Ep 1:17, 18. 5:17. Ph 1:9. Col 1:9. √3:16. 2 T +√3:15-17. Ja 3:13-18. **wise unto.** Ps 36:3. Is 1:16, 17. Je *4:22. 1 C *14:20. **simple.** *or,* harmless. ℐ108K54, Pr +1:4. Lk 10:3. Ph 2:15.

20. **the God.** See on Ro 15:33. **shall.** Ro +*8:37. Ge +*3:15. Ps *18:39. Is +*14:12. *25:8-12. Je +*20:11. He *2:14, 15. 1 J *3:8. Re *12:9-11. *20:1-3. **bruise.** *or,* tread. Jb 40:12. Ps 44:5. Is 16:4mg. 63:3. Zc 10:5. Ml 4:3. Lk 10:19. **Satan.** 1 C +5:5. **under your feet.** Jsh *10:24. **The grace.** ver. 24. Ac +15:11. 1 C 16:2, etc., 23. 2 C √13:14. Ga 6:18. Ph 4:23. 1 Th 5:28. 2 Th 3:18. 2 T 4:22. Phm 25. Re 22:21.

21. **Timotheus.** Ac *16:1-3. 17:14. 18:5. 19:22. 20:4. 2 C 1:1, 19. Col 1:1. Ph 1:1. 2:19-23. 1 Th 1:1. *3:2, 6. 2 Th 1:1. 1 T *1:2. 6:11, 20. 2 T 1:2. He 13:23. **workfellow.** ver. +3. **Lucius.** Ac *13:1. **Jason.** Ac *17:5-7, 9. **Sosipater.** i.e. *saving of the father,* ✱S#4989g, only here. Ac *20:4, Sopater. **my kinsmen.** ver. 7, 11.

22. **Tertius.** i.e. *the third,* ✱S#5060g. **who.** Je 36:18. 1 C +16:21. Ga 6:11. **the epistle.** Col 4:16. 1 Th 5:27. 2 Th 3:14. **salute.** ver. 8. Col *3:17.

23. **Gaius.** i.e. *earthy, landholder, on earth,* ✱S#1050g. Ac 19:29. 20:4. 1 C √1:14. 3 J *1. **Erastus.** Ac 19:22. 2 T 4:20. **the chamberlain.** Or, as the Vulgate renders, *arcarius civitatis,* "the treasurer (or steward, *oikonomos),* of the city"; he to whom the receipt and expenditure of the public money were entrusted. **of the city.** What city? Here by undesigned coincidence the place where the Epistle of Romans was written is indicated. The city is undoubtedly Corinth, for Erastus is said to have "abode at Corinth" (2 T 4:20). This supposition is consistent with other statements: for example, that Paul was about to carry contributions from Greece to Jerusalem (Ro 15:25, 26); that a collection had been going on in Corinth (1 C 16:3); that he intended sailing from Greece direct to Syria (Ac 20:3). If the coincidences had been designed, the author would not have left in doubt of what city Erastus was chamberlain, or from what city the epistle was written, the setting forth of which was absolutely necessary to the display of the coincidence, if any such display had been thought of: nor could the author of the Epistle to Timothy leave Erastus at Corinth from anything he might have read in the Epistle to the Romans, because Corinth is nowhere in that Epistle mentioned either by name or description (William Paley, *Horae Paulinae,* pp. 33, 34, 216. See related notes listed at Ac 12:12n). ver. 1. Ac 18:18. **Quartus.** i.e. *fourth,* ✱S#2890g. **a brother.** 1 C +1:1.

24. **The grace.** See on ver. 20. 1 Th 5:28.

25. **to him.** Ro 14:4. Ac 20:32. Ep 3:20, 21. 1 Th *3:13. 2 Th *2:16, 17. *3:3. He √7:25. 1 P 5:10. Ju *24, *25. **of power.** ℐ108B, Ro +4:21. **stablish.** 1 P

+*5:10. **according**. Ro 2:16. **my gospel**. Ro *2:16.
2 C 4:3. Ga 1:11, 12. 2:2. 2 Th 2:14. 2 T *2:8. **and
the preaching**. Ac 9:20. 1 C *1:23. 2:2. 2 C *4:5. **according to**. Mk 4:11. 1 C 2:1, 7. +4:1. 15:51. Ep *1:9.
*3:3, 4, 9. 5:32. 6:19. 2 Th 2:7. 1 T 3:9, 16. Re 1:20.
10:7. 17:5, 7. **the revelation**. 1 C *2:7. Ep *1:9. Col
*1:26, 27. **the mystery**. The New Testament mystery
doctrines (see T. Ernest Wilson, *Mystery Doctrines
of the New Testament*, pp. 10-12) make an interesting
study, and may be listed as follows (1) the faith, 1 T
3:9. (2) the church, Ro 16:25. (3) the gospel, Ep 6:19.
(4) Jew and Gentile in one body, Ep ch. 3. (5) the
bride, Ep 5:32. Re ch. 19, 20. (6) seven stars and
seven churches, Re 1:20. (7) of godliness, 1 T 3:16.
(8) kingdom of heaven, Mt 13:11. (9) Israel's blindness,
Ro 11:25. (10) rapture of the church, 1 C 15:51. (11)
His will, Ep 1:9. (12) of God, Re 10:7. (13) the indwelling Christ, Col 1:24-29. (14) the Godhead of Christ,
Col 2:2, 9. (15) of iniquity, 2 Th 2:7. (16) Babylon,
Re 17:5. Is 2:1-4. 9:6, 7. Jn 17:20-24. 1 C 2:7. 10:32,
33. 15:53-57. Ep 1:9. 2:7, 8. 3:1-12. 6:19. Col 1:27.
2:2. 4:3. 1 Th 3:12, 13. 1 T 3:16. **which was**. 1 C 2:7.
kept secret. Ps 78:2. Da 2:22. Am 3:7. Mt +*13:17,

25. Lk 10:23, 24. Ep 3:3-5, 9, 11. 1 P 1:10-12, 20.
world. Gr. *aionios*, Mt +18:8. lit. times of the ages.
2 T 1:9. T 1:2.
26. **now**. Ro 3:21. Ep 1:9. Col 1:26. 4:4. 2 T *1:10.
T *1:2, 3. 1 P 1:20. 1 J 1:2. **and by**. Ro +*1:2. 3:21.
+*15:4. Ac *3:18. *8:32-35. +*10:43. *26:22, 23. Ga
*3:8. Ep 2:20. 2 P *1:19. Re 19:10. **according**. Mt
+*28:19, 20. Mk *16:15. Lk *24:44-47. Ac *13:46,
47. +*26:17, 18. 1 C 7:6. 2 C 8:8. **everlasting**. Gr.
aionios, Mt +18:8. God the Father is eternal. Ro *1:20.
Ge *21:33. Dt +*33:27. Ps 90:2. 93:2. Is +*9:6. √40:28.
41:4. Je 10:10. Mi +*5:2. Mt +*28:19n. Ep √4:6.
1 T *1:17. He √9:14. √13:8. 1 J *5:20. Re √1:8-11,
17. **God**. 1 C +*8:6. Ep *4:6. **to all**. T#1031. **obedience
of faith**. See on Ro 1:5. 15:18. Dt +*26:16, 18. Ac
6:7. Ga *5:6. Col 1:6.
27. **God**. Ro *11:36. Ga 1:4, 5. Ep 3:20, 21. Ph
4:20. 1 T *1:17. √6:16n. 2 T 4:18. He 13:15, 21. 1 P
2:5. 5:10, 11. 2 P √3:18. Re +*1:5, 6. 4:9-11. 5:9-14.
7:10-12. 19:1-6. **only wise**. Ro *11:33, 34. Jb +*12:13.
Ps 147:5. Ep 1:7, 8. *3:8-12. Col 2:2, 3. 1 T √6:16n.
Ju *25. **for ever**. Gr. *aion*, Mt +6:13. lit. unto the
ages.

1 CORINTHIANS

1 CORINTHIANS 1

*The apostle salutes the church at Corinth, 1-3; thanks
God for the grace and gifts conferred on the Christians
residing there, 4-7; and expresses his confidence respecting their salvation, 8, 9. He exhorts them to unity,
and reproves their dissensions, 10-16. "The preaching
of the cross is foolishness to them that perish, but
the power and wisdom of God," to the salvation of
believers, 17-25. To exclude boasting, God has not
called the wise, the mighty, or the noble; but the foolish,
the weak, and those whom man despises, 26-29. Christ
is "made of God," in those who are in him, "Wisdom,
and Righteousness, and Sanctification, and Redemption," that we may glory in the Lord alone, 30, 31.*

1. **called**. Ro +1:1. Ga 2:7, 8. **an**. 1 C 3:9. 9:1, 2.
15:9. Lk 6:13. Jn 20:21. Ac 1:2, 25, 26. 22:21. Ro
1:5. 2 C 11:5. 12:12. Ga *1:1. Ep 4:11. 1 T 1:1. 2:7.
to be. ƒ63K, Ge +37:13. i.e., by Divine calling, an
apostle (B125, 126). So also Ro 1:1. **through**. 1 C 9:16,
17. Jn +*15:16. Ro 15:32. 2 C 1:1. 8:5. Ga 1:15, 16.
Ep 1:1. Col 1:1. 2 T 1:1. **Sosthenes**. Ac *18:17. **our
brother**. 1 C 16:12. Ro 16:23. 2 C 1:1. Col 1:1. Phm
1.
2. **the church of God**. 1 C +10:32. Ac *18:1, 8-
11. +*20:28n. 2 C 1:1. Ga 1:2. 1 Th 1:1. 2 Th 1:1.
1 T √3:15. **at Corinth**. Ac +18:1. **to them**. Ju *1. **sanctified**. ver. 30. 1 C +*6:9-11. 7:14. Jn *17:17-19. Ac
15:9. +*26:18. Ro 15:16. Ep *1:4. √5:26. He 2:11.
10:10, 29. 13:12. 1 P *1:15, 16. **called**. Ro +1:7.
1 Th 4:7. 2 T +*1:9. 1 P 1:15, 16. **to be**. ƒ63K, Ge
+37:13. In other words, "by Divine calling, saints,"
as in Ro 1:7. i.e., saints by the calling of God, or by
Divine calling: those who have been Divinely selected
and appointed as saints (B126). **saints**. 1 C 14:33. Ro
+*1:7 (T#1116). Is +*8:20n. 2 C +1:1. Ep *1:1. **with
all**. Ac +*7:59, 60. 9:14, 21. +*22:16. 2 Th *2:16,
17. 2 T 2:22. **every place**. Ml 1:11. Ro +1:8. 2 C

2:14. 1 Th 1:8. 1 T 2:8. **call**. *Tois epikaloumenois to
onoma*. That these words ought not to be rendered
passively, is evident from the LXX., who translate the
corresponding Hebrew phrase, "he shall call on the
name," which is active, by *en onomati Kuriou*. Ge
4:26. 12:8. 13:4-7, etc. Ps 116:17. Jl +*2:32. Zp 3:9.
Zc 13:9. Ac +*7:59. +9:14. Ro *10:12. Re +*5:12.
the name. ver. 10. Ac +2:21. **our Lord**. 1 C +8:6.
Ps 45:11. Ac +√10:36. Ro 3:22. +*10:9, 12. 14:8, 9.
2 C 4:5. Ph 2:9-11. Re 19:16. **both theirs**. Ep 6:9.
3. **Grace**. See on Ro 1:7. 2 C 1:2. Ep 1:2. 1 P 1:2.
4. **thank**. See on Ro 1:8. 6:17. Ac +*11:23. 21:20.
the grace. ver. 3. Jn *1:16. +*10:30. 14:14, 16, 17,
26. 15:26. 1 T 1:14. **given you**. 1 C 3:10. 15:10. Ac
+*13:48. Ro 12:3, 6. 15:15. 2 C 8:1. Ga 2:9. Ep 3:2,
8. 4:7, 29. 2 T +*1:9. +*2:25. Ja 4:6.
5. **in every**. 1 C 4:7-10. Ro 11:12. 2 C 6:10. 9:11.
Ep 2:7. 3:8. **in all**. 1 C *12:8, 10. 14:5, 6, 26. Ac 2:4.
2 C *8:7. Ep 6:19. Col 4:3, 4. 1 J +2:20. **and in**. 1 C
8:11. 13:2, 8. Jn *14:26. Ro 15:+*4, 14. 2 C *4:6.
Ep 1:17. Ph 1:9. Col +*1:9, 10. *2:3. 3:10. Ja 3:13.
2 P *3:18.
6. **the testimony**. 1 C *2:1, 2. Ac 18:5. 20:21, 24.
22:18. 23:11. 28:23. 2 Th 1:10. 1 T 2:6. 2 T 1:8. 1 J
√5:11-13. Re 1:2, 9. *6:9. 12:11, 17. *19:10. **was**. Mk
*16:20. Ac 11:17, 21. Ro 15:19. 2 C 12:12. Ga 3:5.
He *2:3, 4.
7. **come behind**. 2 C 12:13. He 4:1. 12:15g. **waiting**.
1 C 4:5. Ge 49:18. Mt 25:1. Lk 12:36. +*21:36. Ro
+*8:19. Ph *3:20. 1 Th √1:10. 2 T *4:8. T √2:13. He
*9:28. +*10:36, 37. Ja *5:7, 8. 2 P +*3:12. Ju 21.
coming. Gr. revelation. Mt ◐+*24:3. Lk +*17:30.
Col *3:4. 1 T 6:14, 15. 1 P *5:4. 1 J *3:2. ✱S#602g:
1 C 14:6, 26. Lk 2:32 (lighten). Ro 2:5 (revelation).
8:19 (manifestation). 16:25. 2 C 12:1, 7. Ga 1:12. 2:2.
Ep 1:17. 3:3. 2 Th 1:7. 1 P 1:7, 13. 4:13. Re 1:1.
8. **confirm**. Ps *37:17, 28. Ro *14:4. *16:25. 2 C
*1:21. Ph √1:6. Col 2:7. 1 Th 3:13. √5:23, 24. 2 Th

*3:3. He 13:9. 1 P *5:10. 2 P +*2:10. **unto the end.** Mt +*10:22. +*24:14. 2 C 1:13. Ep +*4:30. **blameless.** Ep *5:27. Ph *2:15. Col *1:22. 1 Th *3:13. *5:23, 24. 1 T 3:10. T 1:6, 7. 2 P *3:14. Ju *24, *25. **in the day.** Lk 17:24. 1 C 5:5. 2 C 1:14. Ph *1:6, 10. *2:16. 1 Th 5:2. 2 P *3:10.

9. **God.** 1 C √10:13. Nu +*23:19. Dt 7:9. 32:4. Ps 89:33-35. 100:5. 143:1. Is 11:5. 25:1. 49:7. La 3:22, 23. Mt 24:35. 2 C 1:18. 1 Th *5:23, 24. 2 Th *3:3. 2 T 2:13. T √1:2. He 2:17. 6:18. *10:23. 11:11. 1 J √1:9. Re 19:11. **by whom.** ver. 24. Ro +*8:28, 30. 9:24. Ga 1:15. 1 Th 2:12. 2 Th 2:14. 2 T +*1:9. He 3:1. 1 P 5:10. **the fellowship.** ver. 30. Ro 10:16. Jn 14:3, 23. *15:4, 5. 17:21. Ro 11:17. Ga *2:20. Ep *2:20-22. 3:6. He 2:14. +*3:14. 1 J *1:3, 7. *4:13.

10. **I beseech.** 1 C 4:16. Ro +*12:1. 2 C 5:20. 6:1. 10:1. Ga 4:12. Ep *4:1. Phm 9, 10. 1 P 2:11. **by the.** Ac 4:30. 10:43. Ro 15:30. 1 Th 4:1, 2. 2 Th 2:1. 1 T 5:21. 2 T 4:1. **name.** ver. 2. Ac +2:21. **that ye.** Ps *133:1. Je 32:39. Jn 13:34, 35. 17:23. Ac 4:32. Ro 12:16. 15:5, 6. 16:17. 2 C *13:11. Ep *4:1-7, 31, 32. Ph *1:27. 2:1-4. 3:16. 1 Th 5:13. Ja 3:13-18. 1 P *3:8, 9. **divisions.** Gr. schisms. 1 C 11:18. 12:25. Mt 9:16. Mk 2:21. Jn 7:43. 9:16. 10:19g. Ep 4:4. 5:30. **but that.** ʃ144D, Ge +40:23. **perfectly joined.** Lk +6:40. Ga 6:1g. **same mind.** Ro +*12:16. +*15:5n. Ph *1:27. *2:2.

11. **it hath.** 1 C 11:18. Ge 27:42. 37:2. 1 S 25:14-17. **by them.** Le 19:17. Jn 8:10. Ro 16:10, 11. Ep 5:11. **Chloe.** i.e. *verdant,* ❋S#5514g. **that there.** 1 C 3:3. 6:1-7. +*11:19. Pr 13:10. 18:6. 2 C 12:20. Ga 5:15, 20, 26. Ph 2:14. 1 T 6:4. 2 T 2:23-25. Ja 4:1, 2.

12. **this.** 1 C 7:29. +*15:50. 2 C 9:6. Ga 3:17. **every one.** 1 C *3:4. Mt 23:9, 10. **I am.** 1 C 3:4-6, 21-23. 4:6. **Apollos.** 1 C 16:12. Ac *18:24-28. *19:1. **Cephas.** 1 C 3:22. 9:5. 15:5. Jn +*1:42. Ga 2:9.

13. **Christ.** 1 C 12:5. 2 C 11:4. Ga 1:7. Ep 4:5. **Paul.** 1 C *6:19, 20. Ro 14:9. 2 C √5:14, 15. T *2:14. **or.** ver. 15. Ro 10:2. Mt 28:19. Ac +*2:38. 10:48. 19:5. **in the name.** 1 C 10:2. Ac +8:16. Ga 3:27.

14. **thank.** ver. 4. 1 C 14:18. 2 C *2:14. Ep 5:20. Col 3:15, 17. 1 Th 5:18. 1 T 1:12. Phm 4. **Crispus.** Ac +*18:8. **Gaius.** Ro +16:23. 3 J *1, etc.

15. **Lest any.** Ac 10:48. **I.** Jn 3:28, 29. 7:18. 2 C 11:2. **in mine own name.** ver. 13. Ac +8:16.

16. **household.** ʃ121J4, Ge +7:1. 1 C *16:15. Ac 16:15n, 33. Ro *16:15, 17. **Stephanas.** i.e. *crowned,* ❋S#4734g. 1 C 16:15, 17.

17. **sent me.** Ac 9:15. Ga 1:15, 16. Ep 3:7-9. 1 T 2:7. **not to baptize.** This statement by Paul is fatal to any view which would make ritual water baptism necessary to salvation, for Paul by this statement shows he did not consider water baptism an essential element of the gospel (ver. 16). Jn *4:2. Ac *10:48. +*26:17, 18. **but to preach.** T#430. ver. 18, 21. Mt +28:19 (T#458). Ro *10:14. Ep *4:11-13. 2 T *4:1-5. **the gospel.** 1 C √15:1-4. Mt 4:23. 9:35. *24:14. Lk 4:18. Ac *10:38-43. 20:24, 25. 28:31. Ro 1:16. Ep 1:13, 14. **not with.** 1 C 2:1, 4, 13. 2 C +*4:2. 10:3, 4, 10. 2 P *1:16. **of.** ʃ29, Ex +19:6. i.e. eloquent language. **words.** *or,* speech. 2 C √10:10, 11. 11:6. **lest.** 1 C √2:5. 2 C *4:7. **the cross.** ʃ117, Ge +19:8. Ga 5:11. 6:12, 14. Ph 3:18. **none effect.** 1 C 9:15. Ro 4:14. 2 C 9:3. Ph 2:7g.

18. **the preaching.** ver. 23, 24. 1 C 2:2. Ga 6:12-14. **cross.** ʃ117, Ge +19:8. By *Metalepsis* "the cross" is put first for the crucifixion as an act, or for Him

who was crucified thereon: and then this is put for the resulting merits of His atonement procured thereby (B611). **to.** Ac 13:41. 2 C 2:15, 16. √4:3, 4. Ph 1:28. 2 Th 2:10. **perish.** Gr. *apollumi,* Mt +2:13. Jn +*10:29. **foolishness.** ver. 21, 23, 25. 1 C √2:14. 3:19. 4:10. Mt +25:2. Ac 17:18, 32. **unto.** ver. 24. 1 C 15:2. Ps 110:2, 3. Lk 13:23. Ac 2:47. Ro √1:16. 2 C √10:4, 5. 1 Th 1:5. He *4:12. **the power.** ver. 24. Ro +*1:16.

19. **I will.** ʃ92C, Mt +2:15. **destroy.** Gr. *apollumi,* Mt +2:13. 1 C *3:19. Jb *5:12, 13. Pr 5:22. Is 19:3, 11. ❭29:14. Je 8:9. 49:7. Mt 11:25. **bring to nothing.** Lk +*7:30 (reject).

20. **is the wise.** Is 19:12. 33:18. 53:1. **the scribe.** Is 33:18. **world.** Gr. *aion,* Mt +6:13. 1 C 2:6, 7. 3:18. Mt 12:32. 13:22, 39. Lk 16:8. 20:34. Ro 12:2. 2 C 4:4. Ga 1:4. Ep 1:21. 2:2. 1 T 6:17. **hath.** ver. 19, 26. 1 C 2:6. 3:19. 2 S 15:31. 16:23. 17:14, 23. Jb 12:17, 20, 24. Is 19:11. *44:25. Je 10:14. Mt 5:13g. Ro *1:22. **world.** Gr. *kosmos,* Mt +4:8.

21. **in.** ver. 24. Da 2:20. Ro 11:33. Ep 3:10. **the wisdom.** Dr. Lightfoot well observes, "that *sophia tou theou, the wisdom of God,* is not to be understood of that wisdom which had God for its *author,* but of that wisdom which had God for its *object.* There was, among the heathen, *sophia tas phuseos, wisdom about natural things,* that is, *philosophy;* and *sophia tou theou, wisdom about God,* that is, *divinity.* But the world, in its *divinity,* could not, by wisdom, know God." The wisest of the heathen had no just and correct views of the Divine nature; of which the works of *Cicero* and *Lucretius* are incontestable proofs. Lk +11:49. **the world.** Gr. *kosmos,* Mt +4:8. Mt 11:25. Lk *10:21. Ro 1:20-22, 28. **knew not.** 1 C 15:34. Jn 14:7. Ro 1:21. Ga 4:9. 2 Th 1:8. T 1:16. He 8:11. 1 J +4:6. **it pleased.** 1 C 10:5. Lk 12:32. Ga 1:15. Col 1:19. **the foolishness.** ʃ121Q1, Je +28:5. See on ver. 18. **of preaching.** or, the thing preached. ʃ29, Ex +19:6. 2 T 4:17g. **to save.** Ac +*16:31.

22. **the Jews.** Mt +12:38, 39. *16:1-4. Mk 8:11, 12. Lk 11:16, 20. +*17:20, 21. Jn 2:18. 4:48. **the Greeks.** Ac *17:18-21. Ro 1:14. **seek after.** Pr 2:4. 4:7. 14:6. Ec 7:25.

23. **we preach.** ver. 18. 1 C 2:2. Lk 24:46, 47. Ac 7:32-35. +*10:36-43. 2 C 4:5. Ga 3:1. 6:14. Ep 3:8. **crucified.** ʃ139, Mt +11:17. ʃ134, Mt +3:9. In Hebrew "cross" is *maskal,* "stumblingblock" is *michshol,* "foolishness" is *sechel,* "power" is *haschil,* and "wisdom" is *sechel,* thus constituting the figure *Parechesis,* or Foreign Paronomasia. 1 C 2:2. Mt 28:5. **unto the Jews.** Is *8:14, 15. Mt 11:6. +*13:57. Lk 2:34. Jn *6:53-66. Ac *13:16, 38, 39, 45. Ro 9:32, 33. Ga 5:11. **a stumblingblock.** 1 P +2:8. **foolishness.** ver. 18, 28. 1 C √2:14. Ac *17:18.

24. **called.** ver. 2, 9. Lk 7:35. Ro √8:28-30. *9:23, 24. **both Jews and.** Ro *10:4. **the power.** ʃ132G, Ge +3:19. T#76-5. ver. 18. 1 C 8:6. Is +*9:6. Mt 8:16, 28-32. 28:18, +√19. Mk 1:23-27. Lk 4:35-41. 7:12-15. 8:22-24n, 25, 33n, 41, 42, 49-55. Jn 1:3, 10. 2:19. 5:21, 25. √10:17, 18. 11:25. 16:15. 17:2. Ro 1:4, +16. ◆+*15:19. 2 C 12:9. Ep *1:19, 20. Ph 3:20, 21. Col 1:16, 17. He 1:3. 2:14. 1 P *1:5. 1 J √3:8. Re +*1:8. 18. ◆+19:6 (T#218). **the wisdom.** ver. 21, 30. Pr 1:20. 8:1, 22-30. Ro *11:33. Col *2:3.

25. **Because.** ʃ125, Jb +22:6. **the foolishness.** ʃ46A, Le +26:30. ʃ121Q1, Je +28:5. ver. +18, 27-29. Ex 13:17. 14:2-4. Jsh 6:2-5. Jg 7:2-8. 15:15, 16. 1 S 17:40-

51. 1 K 20:14, etc. Zc 4:6, 7. 12:7, 8. Ro 11:33-36. **weakness**. ſ46A, Le +26:30. It is incongruous to speak of "foolishness" or "weakness" with respect to God. So we are arrested by the use of this figure *Catachresis*.

26. **your calling**. Ro +*11:29. **how that**. ver. 20. 1 C 2:3-6, 13. 3:18-20. Zp 3:12. Mt +*11:25, 26. Mk *12:37. Lk 10:21. Jn *7:47-49. Ac *4:13. Ja 3:13-17. **not many**. Mt +*7:14. **wise**. ver. 20. 1 C 2:8. Jb 37:24. Ps *8:2. **after the flesh**. Jn 8:15. **not many mighty**. Lk 1:3g. 18:24, 25. Jn 4:46-53. 19:38, 39. Ac 13:7, 12. 17:34. 25:5g. Ph 4:22. Ja 1:9-11. *2:5. 2 J 1. **noble**. Jb 1:3. Lk 19:12. Ac +*17:11g. **are called**. or, are chosen. ſ63I2, Jsh +3:3. ſ63E2, 1 S +13:8.

27. **But God**. ſ125, Jb +22:6. **hath chosen**. Ps *8:2. Is 26:5, 6. 29:14, 19. Zp 3:12. Mt *4:18-22. *9:9, 10. 11:25. 21:16. Lk 19:39, 40. 21:15. Ac *4:11-21. 6:9, 10. 7:35, 54. 17:18. 24:24, 25. 2 C 4:7. 10:4, 5, 10. Ja +*2:5. **the foolish**. "Foolish," "weak," "base," "despised," are all instances of the adjective being put for the noun, correctly rendered as in the A.V. "foolish things," etc. ſ24G, Ge 1:9. **world**. Gr. *kosmos*, Mt +4:8. **the weak**. 1 S 17:49. Ps 8:2. **world**. Gr. *kosmos*, Mt +4:8. **to confound**. 1 P 2:6.

28. **world**. Gr. *kosmos*, Mt +4:8. **are despised**. 2 C +10:10g. **which are not**. Ro 4:17. 2 C 12:11. **to bring**. 1 C 2:6. Dt 28:63. Jb 34:19, 20, 24. Ps 32:10. 37:35, 36. Is 2:11, 17. 17:13, 14. 37:36. 41:12. Da 2:34, 35, 44, 45. Re 18:17. **that are**. ſ108B, 2 S +19:6. This is an idiom which means to be in high esteem, or of great value.

29. **flesh**. ſ171Q6, Ge +6:12. Ge +*6:3. 2 Ch *32:8. Lk +3:6. **glory**. ver. 31. 1 C *4:7. *5:6. Jg 7:2. Ps 49:6. Is 10:15. Je +*9:23. Ro 3:19, 27. 4:2. 15:17. 2 C √12:9, 10. Ep *2:9.

30. **in Christ Jesus**. 1 C 12:18, 27. Is 45:17. Jn 15:1-6. 17:21-23. Ro √8:1n. 12:5. 16:7, 11. 2 C √5:17. 12:2. Ep *1:3, 4, 10. *2:10. Col *2:3, 9, 10. **of God**. Ro 11:36. 2 C 5:18-21. **wisdom**. ver. 24. 1 C 12:8. Jb *28:12. Pr 1:20. 2:6. 8:5. 23:4. Da 2:20. Lk *11:49. 21:15. Jn *1:18. *8:12. √14:6. 17:8, 26. 2 C 4:6. Ep 1:17, 18. 3:9, 10. Col 2:2, 3. *3:16. 2 T +*3:15-17. Ja *1:5. **and**. ſ148, Ge +8:22. **righteousness**. Ps 71:15, 16. =132:9, 16. Is *45:24, 25. 54:17. Je +*23:5, 6. 33:16. Da +*9:24. Ro *1:17. *3:21-25. *4:6, 25. *5:19, 21. 10:4. 2 C √5:21. Ph *3:9. 2 P 1:1. **sanctification**. ver. +2. 1 C *6:11. Mt +*1:21. Jn *17:17-19. Ac +*26:18. Ro +*8:9. Ga √5:22-24. Ep *2:10. √5:26. Col *1:21, 22. 1 Th +4:7. 1 P 1:2. 1 J 5:6. **redemption**. 1 C *15:54-57. Ho +*13:14. Lk +21:28. Ro *3:24. +*8:23. Ga 1:4. *3:13. Ep √1:7, 14. +*4:30. Col *1:14. T *2:14. He 9:12. 1 P *1:18, 19. Re 5:9. 14:4.

31. **glorieth**. 1 C 3:21. 1 Ch 16:10, 35. Ps 34:2. 105:3. Is 41:16. 45:25. Je 4:2. +*9:23, ▶24. 2 C 10:17. Ga *6:13, 14. Ph 3:3g. **glory**. Ja 2:1.

1 CORINTHIANS 2

The apostle declares, that he had not come among the Corinthians "with excellency of speech and wisdom," but had preached Christ crucified, with plainness and humble diffidence; that their "faith might stand in the power of God" alone, 1-5. The gospel contains the hidden "wisdom of God" in bringing men to glory, which could not be discovered by any human sagacity, 6-9; but God by his Spirit had revealed it, 10-13. "The natural man" cannot receive it, because

it is spiritually discerned: but "he that is spiritual" judgeth all things, "and is judged of no man," 14-16.

1. **when**. Ac 18:1-4. **not with**. ver. 4, 13. 1 C *1:17. Ex 4:10. Je 1:6, 7. Ro 16:18. 2 C √10:10. 11:6. **wisdom**. ver. 4, 13. 1 C 1:17. 2 C 1:12. **the testimony**. 1 C 1:6. Is +*8:20. Ac √20:20, 21, 27. 22:18. 2 Th *1:10. 1 T 1:11. 2 T 1:8. 1 J 4:14. √5:11-13. Re 1:2, 9. *19:10.

2. **not to know**. ſ96A1, Mt +5:29. 1 C 1:22-25. Jn +*17:3. Ac 26:22. Ga 3:1. 6:14. Ph *3:8-10.

3. **with you**. Ac *18:1, 6, 12. **in weakness**. 1 C 4:10-13. Ac 18:1, 6-12. 20:18, 19. 2 C 4:1, 7-12, 16. 6:4. 7:5. 10:1, 10. 11:29, 30. 12:5-10. 13:4, 9. Ga *4:13, 14. **in fear**. 2 C 7:15. Ep 6:5. Ph 2:12.

4. **my speech**. Ex 4:10. Ac *20:27. **preaching**. 1 C 1:21. 2 T +4:17. **not with**. ver. 1, 13. 1 C 1:17. Jg 14:15. 16:5. 2 S 14:17-20. 15:2-6. 1 K 22:13, 14. 2 Ch 18:19-21. Pr 7:21. 20:19. Je 20:10. Ezk 13:6, 10, 11. Ro 16:18. Col 2:4. 2 P 1:16. 2:18. **enticing**. *or*, persuasible. Ac 26:28. Ga 1:10. **words of**. ver. 1, 13. 1 C 1:17. **but**. 1 C 4:20. Jn 16:8-15. Ro 15:13, 19. 2 C *3:3. 1 Th *1:5. 1 P 1:12. **Spirit**. Gr. *pneuma*, ſ121A1, Lk +1:17n. **and**. ſ93A, Ge +1:26. By *Hendiadys*, the power of the Spirit. Two words used, but one thing meant. **power**. 1 C 4:20. 2 P 1:16.

5. **stand**. Gr. be. **but**. 1 C 1:17. *3:6, 7. Zc +*4:6. Ac *16:14. 2 C *4:7. 6:7. 1 P 1:5. **the power**. 1 C 1:18, 24. Ro +*1:16.

6. **perfect**. ſ46C, Mt +8:6. Here the word *teleios* receives its true meaning, *initiated*, from the Greek mysteries, where it was used of one who had been *initiated* into them (B679). T#503. 1 C ◖3:1. 14:20g. Ge 6:9. Jb *1:1, 8. 2:3. Ps *37:37. Pr 2:21. 11:5. Mt +*5:48. 19:21. Jn +*17:6. 2 C 13:11. Ep *4:11-13. Ph 3:12-15. Col 4:12. He √5:14. *6:1. Ja 3:2. 1 P 5:10. **not the wisdom**. ver. 1, 13. 1 C 1:18-20. *3:19. Lk +*16:8. 2 C 1:12. *4:4. Ep 2:2. Ja 3:15. **world**. Gr. *aion*, Mt +6:13. ver. 7, 8. **of the princes**. ver. 8. Jb 12:19, 21. Ps *2:1-6. Is 19:11-13. 40:23. Ac 4:25-28. **world**. Gr. *aion*, Mt +6:13. **come**. See on 1 C 1:28. Ps 33:10. **nought**. Jb 34:19, 20, 24. Ps +*146:4.

7. **the wisdom**. Lk +11:49. **even**. Ps 78:2. Is 48:6, 7. Mt +*11:25. 13:35. Lk 10:21. Ro +*16:25, 26. Ep 1:4. *3:4-11. Col *1:26, 27. 1 T *3:16. 2 T +*1:9, 10. 1 P 1:11, 12. Re *13:8. **ordained**. Ro +*8:29. **before**. 2 T +*1:9. T 1:2. **world**. Gr. *aion*, Mt +6:13. **unto**. 1 P *5:1, 10. 2 P 1:3.

8. **none**. ver. 6. 1 C 1:26-28. Ex=1:8. Mt +*11:25. Jn 7:48. **the princes**. ver. 6. Lk +24:20. Ac 13:27. **this world**. 1 C +1:20. **for had**. ſ184B, Mt +11:21. Am +*3:6. Hab 1:13. Mt +*11:23n. 18:7. Lk *23:34. Jn √3:19-21. 8:19. 9:39-41. 12:40-43. 15:22-25. 16:3. Ac +3:17. *13:27. 2 C 3:14. 1 T 1:13, 16. **the Lord**. The deity of Christ is proven by the divine titles which are given him, as the following reference passages demonstrate. T#74. 1 C +*12:3. Ne +*9:6. Ps *24:7-10. 45:3. Is 9:6. 44:6. 59:16 w He 7:25. Mt 1:23. 2:6. 3:3. Jn +*3:13, 31. 13:14. 21:5. Jn 1:29, 49. Ac 3:15-17. 7:2. +√10:36. Ro +*9:5. 10:12, 13. 14:9. 1 C +*15:47. Ep 1:22. Col 2:10. 1 T 6:14-16. He 1:2. 2:10. 3:1. Ja 2:1. 1 P 2:3, 4 w Ps 34:8. 1 P 2:25. 1 J 5:20 w Ps 45:6 w He +*1:8. Ju 25. Re 1:18. 5:5. 17:14. 19:13. 22:13. **of glory**. Ps *24:7, 10. 29:3. Is *42:8. Ac 7:2. Ep 1:17. He 9:5. Ja √2:1.

9. **Eye**. ſ171Q15, Mt +13:16. This passage is not taken from the LXX., nor is an exact translation of

the Hebrew; but it gives the general sense. ♪92E, Mt +4:10. Is ♭52:15. *♪64:4. Jn √3:16. 1 P 1:12. **entered into.** ♪171J1, 2 K +12:4. Is 65:17. Je 3:16. 32:35. Lk 24:38g. Ac 7:23g. **the heart.** Pr +*4:23. Ph √4:7. **the things.** Ps +*16:11. *31:19. Mt 20:23. 25:34. He 11:16. **hath prepared.** T#340. 1 C 3:21-23. Dt +33:9 (T#672). Is *64:4. Mt +*13:43. +*19:28. +*25:34. Lk +*22:28-30. Jn +*14:2, 3. Ro 8:17, 18, 32. 2 C √4:17. He √11:6. Re +*1:5, 6. 21:2, 7. 22:5. **for them.** T#289. Ex 20:6. Dt 7:9. 11:13-15. Ps +19:11 (T#302). +58:11 (T#630). *91:14. *145:20. Pr 8:17. Jn *14:21-23. Ro +*8:28. Ja 1:12. *2:5. 1 J 4:19. **that love.** Ex 20:6.

10. revealed. 1 C 14:30. Dt +*29:29. Am +*3:7. Mt +*11:25-27. +*13:11. +*16:16, 17. Lk 2:26. 10:21. Ga 1:12, 16. Ep 3:3, 5. 1 P 1:12. Re 1:1. **by.** Is 48:16. 59:21. Jn +*14:26. *16:13n. 1 J *2:20, 27. **his Spirit.** Gr. *pneuma*, Mt +3:16. Jn +7:39. *14:26. **for the Spirit.** Gr. *pneuma*, Mt +3:16. ver. 11. 1 C *12:8-11. Mt +12:32. Ro +*8:26, 27. **searcheth all things.** ♪22C2, Ge +3:9. God the Holy Spirit is omniscient. ver. *11n, 14. Mt +9:4 (T#76-7). +*28:19n. Lk 2:26. Jn 14:26. *16:13. Ro ◐+*11:33. Ep ◐+*3:8, 19. He +4:13 (T#219). **the deep.** Jb 12:22. Ps 25:14. 92:5, 6. 139:6. Da 2:22. Lk 18:34. Ro +*11:33-36. Ep +*1:11. Re ◐2:24. **of God.** Ac √5:3, 4.

11. what. Pr 14:10. 20:5, 27. Je +*17:9. **knoweth.** This plainly intimates that the essence of personality in man is in his spirit. Since the spirit "knows," the spirit is conscious and intelligent. To man's spirit Paul refers all human knowledge. Note also that this entity is *in* man. The death of the spirit is unknown to Scripture; and while the body dies, Scripture teaches that in ordinary death the *soul* does not (Mt +*10:28n). **the things.** or, the (deep) things. ♪63I1A, Ex +12:4. **spirit.** Gr. *pneuma*, ♪121A3, Mt +27:50. Nu +*27:16n. Pr 20:27. Da 7:15. Zc +*12:1n. Mk 2:8. He +*12:9, 23. Since "spirit" is spoken of in the plural in He 12:23, it may fairly be inferred that each person has his own, and it is a separate entity in each one (F. W. Grant, *Facts and Theories as to a Future State*, p. 46. See also pp. 39, 52, 56, 66, 519, 592). **even so.** ver. 10. Ro *11:33, 34. **knoweth.** Since God's Spirit "knoweth," God's Spirit is a person who is conscious and intelligent. **Spirit.** Gr. *pneuma*, Mt +3:16. +12:32. Ro +*8:9.

12. have received. Ro 8:15. **not.** ver. 6. Ro 8:1, 5, 6. 2 C √4:4. Ep 2:2. Ja 4:5. 1 J 4:4, 5. 5:19. Re +*12:9. **spirit.** Gr. ♪121A2, Mt +26:41n. ♪121A10, Ge +26:35. Here, "spirit" is put for *reason* (see Charles Hodge, Comm. on 1 Corinthians, p. 40). **world.** Gr. *kosmos*, Mt +4:8. **but.** Ro 8:15, 16. **spirit.** Gr. *pneuma*, ♪121A2, Ro +8:1n. **is.** ♪63B, Ge +25:28. **of God.** 2 C *1:12. 1 P *1:10-12. 2 P *1:21. **that we.** Ro 8:15, 16. **freely.** Is *55:1. 1 C 3:22. Jn 16:14, 15. Ro √8:32. 1 J *2:20, 27. 5:20. Re 22:6.

13. not. ver. 1, 4. 1 C *1:17-19. 2 P 1:16. 1 J 2:20. **the words.** This is a specific claim to verbal inspiration. Divine inspiration of Scripture is asserted also at 2 T 3:16, as is the divine inspiration of the Scripture writers, 2 P 1:21. Failure to accept the Bible's own testimony to itself has closed this Book to so-called "modern scholarship" (a misnomer if ever there was one!). Much modern scholarship is dishonest, for instead of explaining the Bible, it attempts to explain away the Bible, refusing to honestly come to grips with its claims and message. In an effort to escape the Bible's obvious

message, dishonest scholarship has tried to deny its authenticity and authorship, ascribing, for example, the books of Moses to multiple late authorship; denying the unity of Isaiah; asserting that the gospels, particularly John, are of late origin, and do not reflect the so-called "historical Jesus," but views and traditions of the early Church of the third or fourth century—not explaining, of course, how books can be quoted or translated before they were written, or how such stupendous claims could be foisted upon a gullible public long after the possibility of disproof by eyewitnesses has passed. The only way to get at the message of the Bible is to be completely open to its message. To approach Scripture with humanistic and naturalistic (i.e. anti-theistic) presuppositions is to try to twist Scripture to fit a world view which it most emphatically will not support. The only valid approach to Scripture is to be honest to its claims and message and grant its right to set forth a theistic, supernaturalistic world view. To deny the possibility of miracle (as Hume and his modern counterparts) is to deny the possibility of history, for both are based upon the record of eyewitness testimony, and such denial is absurd. There are more pathways to truth and knowledge than an arbitrarily narrowly defined so-called "scientific method." Like missing the right exit on a freeway, continued advance in the wrong direction is not progress; genuine progress will require a return to where we went wrong, and a fresh start in the right direction. Much "scholarship" needs to recognize it has pursued a wrong path, and recognize that it needs to return to sound principles of former generations of reverent, truthful, believing scholarship. It is neither truthful nor fair scholarship to approach a work of literature from a consistently unsympathetic and hostile world view in the attempt to legitimately understand its message. Rather, in our attempt to understand a work of literature, we must let it speak for itself. The task of scholarship is to place the reader as close as possible in sympathetic relationship to the viewpoint of the original writer and recipients of the literary work, and not to attempt to explain it away in an effort to force it to agree with popular contemporary philosophical presuppositions. Lk √8:15. 1 Th √2:13. 2 T +*3:16. 1 P 1:10, 11. 2 P 1:20, 21. 3:1, 2. **but which.** ♪63I1A, Ex +12:4. By ellipsis supply "but (things) which." 1 C *12:1-3. 14:2. Lk *12:12. Ac 2:4. *13:32-37. 1 P 1:12. **Holy.** Gr. *pneuma*, Mt +1:18n. **comparing.** Or, as Bishop Pearce renders, "explaining (*sugkrinantes*) spiritual things to spiritual men" (*pneumatikois*). To this alternative, however, Hodge rightly objects, for it is inconsistent with the context. Paul is rather asserting that he explained spiritual things in spiritual words. The word rendered "comparing" here means interpreting or explaining. T#1033. Ge 40:8, 16. 41:12, 15. Da 5:12. Lk +*4:18n. Jn +*5:39. Ac +*17:3, 11. 2 C 10:12. **spiritual things.** ♪147I, Jn +1:11. ver. 14. 1 C 9:11. 10:3-5. Ep 5:19. Col *3:16. **with spiritual.** Ro +1:11g.

14. the natural man. *psukikos*, the *animal* man, one who lives in a natural state, and under the influence of his animal passions; for *psukee* means the inferior and sensual part of man, in opposition to *nous*, the *understanding*, or *pneuma*, the *spirit*. While the preceding explanation of the words involved has validity, it is not strictly correct for this context. Would "natural man" be in contrast with "intellectual man" or "rational man"? Rather, "natural man" refers to unrenewed or unregenerate man, without the Holy Spirit; Hodge states *spiritual*, when used in the New Testament of persons, never means *intellectual*. It always means one under the influence of the Holy Spirit. It therefore must have that meaning here" (p. 43). 1 C ●3:1. 15:44, 46. Je +*13:23. Ja 3:15. Ju 19g. **receiveth not**. ✗175B, Ge +21:16. Mt 13:11, etc. 16:23. Jn *3:3-6. 8:43. 10:26, 27. 12:37, 38. 14:17. Ro *8:5-8. 2 C *4:3, 4. 1 J 4:5. **the things**. ver. 12. Jn *14:26. 15:26. 16:8-15. **they**. 1 C 1:18, 23. Jn 8:51, 52. 10:20. Ac 17:18, 32. 18:15. 25:19. 26:24, 25. **foolishness unto**. 1 C +1:18. Ge 6:5. 8:21. Ec 9:3. Je +*17:9. Mk *7:21-23. Jn *3:19. Ac *17:18. Ro *8:7, 8. Ep 4:17-19. 5:8. T 1:15. **neither can**. Pr *14:6. Je *6:10. Jn *3:3. 5:44. +*6:44, 45. *8:43, 47. *14:17. Ac 16:14. Ro *8:7. 2 C √4:4-6. 1 J *2:20, 27. 5:20. Ju 19. **are spiritually**. T#598. Pr *25:14. Pr *1:7. 16:23. *28:5. Ec *8:5. Da *12:10. Jn +*7:17. 2 C *4:6. Ep 5:8. Col 1:12, 13. 1 Th 5:4, 5. 1 P 2:9. 2 P +3:5 (T#707). 1 J 2:8-11, *20, 21. **discerned**. 1 C 4:3, 4. 9:3. 10:25, 27. 14:24. Lk 23:14. Ac 4:9. 12:19. +*17:11. 24:8. 25:26. 28:18g.

15. **he that**. 1 C 3:1. 14:37. Pr √28:5. Ga *6:1. Col *1:9. **is spiritual**. Ro +1:11g. **judgeth**. *or*, discerneth. 1 C 10:15. 2 S 14:17. 1 K 3:9-11. Ps *25:14. Pr √28:5. Ec 8:5. Is +*8:20n. Mt +*7:1, 5. Lk 7:43. Jn +*7:17, +*24. Ep 4:13, 14. Ph 1:10g. 1 Th 5:21. He *5:14. 1 J 4:1. **yet**. 1 C *4:3, 5. 2 S 12:16-23. Ac 15:1-5. 16:3. Ga 2:3-5. **judged**. *or*, discerned.

16. **who**. Jb 15:8. 22:2. 40:2. Is ▶40:13, 14. Je 23:18. Ro *11:34. **may**. Gr. shall. **But**. Jn *15:15. 16:13-16. 17:6-8. Ga *1:11, 12. Ep 3:3, 4.

1 CORINTHIANS 3

The apostle shows that he could not impart to the Corinthians the deeper mysteries of the gospel, because they were carnal, 1-3; as it appeared from their dissensions, 4. All true ministers are servants to one Lord, 5; who employs them in cultivating his field, and in building his temple, 6-9. The apostle had laid the only true Foundation, and others should take care what they build on it: for their work would be tried as by fire, 10-15. Christians are the temple of God, and it would be extremely perilous to defile that temple, 16, 17. Worldly wisdom is foolishness with God: and none ought to glory in men; for all things belong to those who are Christ's, 18-23.

1. **as unto spiritual**. ✗63A2, 2 S +6:6. Supply by ellipsis "(men)." 1 C 2:6, 15. Ro +1:11g. 7:14. 2 C 3:3. Ga *6:1. He 7:16. **as unto carnal**. ver. 3, 4. 1 C √2:14. Mt 16:23. Ro 7:14. **babes**. 1 C 14:20. Ro 2:20. Ep 4:13, 14. He 5:13. 1 J 2:12.

2. **fed**. ✗180A, Ge +4:20. ✗171J10. Synecdoche of the Species B632. "To drink" is used of partaking of food and drink of all kinds. He √5:12-14. 1 P √2:2. **for**. Mk *4:33. Jn *16:12. He √5:11, 12. **to bear it**. ✗63BA, Ps +21:11.

3. **for whereas**. 1 C 1:11. 6:1-8. 11:18. 2 C 12:20. Ga √5:15, 19-21. Ja *3:16. 4:1, 2. **envying**. Ro 13:13. 2 C 12:20. Ga 5:20. **strife**. Ro 13:13. **divisions**. *or*, factions. Ro *16:17. **and walk**. Ho 6:7. Mk *7:21, 22. Ep *2:2, 3. 4:22-24. T 3:3. 1 P 4:2. **as men**. Gr. according to man. ver. 4. 1 C 9:8. 15:32. Ro 3:5. 7:22. Ga 1:11. 3:15.

4. **I am of**. 1 C 1:12. 4:6. **carnal**. ver. 1, 3.

5. **ministers**. ver. 7. 1 C *4:1, 2, 6, 7. Mt 20:26. Mk 9:35. Lk 1:2. Ro 10:14, 15. 2 C *3:3, 6. 4:5, 7. 6:1, 4. 11:15, 23. Ep 3:7. Col 1:7, 23, 25. 1 T 4:6. **even**. ver. 10. 1 C 9:17. 12:4-11, 28. Mt 25:15. Jn 3:27. 17:20. Ro +*12:3-6. 1 P *4:10, 11. *5:3.

6. **I have planted**. ✗7, Allegory by continued Hypocatastasis, Ga +4:24. ver. 9, 10. 1 C *4:14, 15. 9:1, 7-11. *15:1-11. Mt 15:13. Ac *18:4-11. 2 C 10:14, 15. **Apollos watered**. ✗171H, Is +63:16. Pr *11:25. Ac *18:24, 26, 27. *19:1. **God gave**. 1 C 1:30. 15:10. Ps 62:9, 11. *92:13-15. 127:1. Is √55:10, 11. 61:11. Ac 11:18. 14:27. *16:14. 21:19. Ro 15:18. 2 C *3:2-5. Col 1:18. 2:19. 1 Th 1:5. **increase**. ✗96A1, Mt +5:29.

7. **neither is**. ✗96E1, Ps +118:8. i.e. they were nothing in comparison with God. 1 C *13:2. Ps 115:1. Is 40:17. 41:29. Da 4:35. Jn *15:5, 16. 2 C *12:9, 11. Ga 2:6. 6:3.

8. **he that planteth**. ver. 9. 1 C 4:6. Jn *4:36-38. **and every**. Ga 6:4, 5. **shall receive**. ver. 14. 1 C 4:5. 9:17, 18. √15:58. Ps 62:12. Da +*12:3. Mt +*5:11, 12. 10:41, 42. +*16:27. Ro +*2:6. Ga *6:7, 8. He +*6:10. 1 P 5:4. 2 J 8. Re 2:23. *22:12. **reward**. Nu=18:31. Jn *4:36. 1 C 15:41. **labor**. Nu=4:49. =7:5, 6. He +*6:10.

9. **we**. See on ver. 6. Mt 9:37, 38. Mk *16:20. 2 C 6:1. 1 Th 3:2. 3 J 8. **ye are God's**. ✗18, Dt +28:4. ✗101, Dt +32:42. Ps 65:9-13. 72:16. 80:8-11. Is *5:1-7. *27:2, 3. 28:24-29. 32:20. 61:3, 5, 11. Je 2:21. Mt 13:3-9, 18-30, 36-42. 20:1-14. 21:23-44. Mk 4:26-29. Jn 4:35-38. *15:1-8. **husbandry**. *or*, tillage. **ye are God's building**. ver. 16. 1 C *6:19. Ps 118:22. 127:1. Am *9:11, 12. Zc *6:12, 13. Mt *16:18. Ac 4:11. 2 C *6:16. Ep *2:10, 20-22. Col +*2:7. 1 T √3:15. He 3:3, 4, 6. 1 P *2:5.

10. **to the**. ver. 5. 1 C *15:10. Ro 1:5. +*12:3. 15:15. Ep 3:2-8. Col 1:29. 1 T 1:11-14. 1 P 4:11. 2 P 3:15. **given**. 1 C +1:4. **as a wise**. 1 K 3:9-11. 2 Ch 2:12. Da +*12:3. Mt *7:24. 24:45. 2 T √2:15. **masterbuilder**. Ex 31:1-6. Is 3:3. Zc 6:15. **I have**. See on ver. 6, 11. 1 C 9:2. Zc 4:9. Ro *15:20. Ep *2:20. Re *21:14, 19. **and another**. 1 C 4:15. 15:11, 12. Ne=3:17, 22. Ac 18:27, 28. 2 C 10:15. √11:13-15. **But let every**. Ec 12:9. Lk 11:35. 21:8. Ga *1:9. Col *4:17. 1 T +*4:16. Ja 3:1g. 1 P 4:11. 2 P 2:1-3. **buildeth**. Ne=4:17, 18.

11. **other foundation**. T#93. Ps 118:22. Is *28:16. Mt *16:18. 21:42. Ac √4:11, 12. Ro 10:4. 2 C 11:2-4. Ga *1:7-9. Ep *2:20, 21. 2 T √2:19. 1 P 2:6-8.

12. **if**. ✗184A, 1 C +15:2. **build**. Lk 2:49. 2 P √1:5-7. **gold**. Ps 19:10. 119:72. Pr 8:10. 16:16. Is 60:17. 1 T 4:6. 2 T 2:20. 1 P 1:7. Re 3:18. **silver**. ✗41, Ge +10:1. **precious stones**. Is 54:11-13. Da 11:38. Re 17:14. 18:12, 16. *21:11, 18, 19. **wood**. Pr 30:6. Je +*23:28. Mt *15:6-9. Ac 20:30. Ro 16:17. 2 C 2:17. 4:2. Col *2:6-8, 18-23. 1 T *4:1-3, 7. 6:3. 2 T 2:16-18. 3:7, 13. 4:3. T 1:9-11. 3:9-11. He 13:9. Re 2:14, 15. **hay**. Ga *4:9-11. **stubble**. Ex +*5:12. *15:7. Is *5:24. 47:14. Jl 2:5. Ob 18. Na *1:10. Ml *4:1.

13. **man's**. ver. 14, 15. 1 C *4:5. 2 T 3:9. **the day**. 1 C +*1:8. 4:3. *5:5. Jb +*21:30. *24:1. Is +*2:12. 13:+*6, 9. 22:5. 37:3. Je 46:10. Ezk 7:7. *13:5. ●+*30:3. Jl 1:15. 2:1. 3:14. Ob 15. Zp ●*1:7, 14. +*2:2, 3. Zc 14:1. Ml *3:2, 17, 18. √4:1, 5. Mt *3:7. Ac +*17:31. Ro *2:5, 16. 2 C 1:14. Ph 1:6, 10. 2:16. 1 Th 5:2. 2 Th √1:7-9, +*10. 2 T 1:12, 18. +*4:8. He *10:25. 2 P √3:10. Ju ●6. Re +*1:10n. ●6:17.

√11:18. ◐20:12. **shall be revealed.** Gr. is revealed. Lk 2:35. **by fire.** ver. 15. Nu *31:23. 2 Th 1:8. **and the fire.** Is +*8:20. 28:17. Je √23:29. Ezk *13:10-16. Zc +*13:9. 1 P +*1:7. √4:12.

14. **If any.** ƒ184A, 1 C +15:2. ver. +*8. 1 C 4:5. Da +*12:3. Mt 24:45-47. 25:21-23. 1 Th *2:19. 2 T 4:7, 8. 1 P *5:1, 2, 4. Re 2:8-11. **abide.** Nu *31:23. Zc *3:2. **reward.** Ezk=44:◐13, 15. Lk +*14:14. 2 T +*4:1, 8, 18. Re √11:18.

15. **If any.** ƒ184A, 1 C +15:2. ƒ7, Allegory by continued Hypocatastasis, Ga +4:24. **work.** ver. 12, 13. Re 3:18. **burned.** 1 C 5:5. Ps 17:4. Mt +*3:12. 4:4, 6, 7. +*13:30, 40. Lk 9:26. Jn +*15:6. 1 P *4:18. 2 P 1:11. +√3:7, 10, 12. 1 J 2:28. **he shall.** Ac 27:21, 22, 44. 2 J √8. **suffer loss.** S#2210g, Mt +16:26. Ezk=44:13, ◐15. Lk +*9:25. **shall be saved.** Jn *5:24. 2 P ◐*1:11. **yet so.** Am 4:11. Zc 3:2. 1 P √4:18. Ju 23. **by fire.** ver. 13. Nu *31:23. Ps 66:12. Is 43:2. Am *4:11. Zc *3:2. Ju *23.

16. **Know.** 1 C 5:6. 6:+2, 3, 9, 16, 19. 9:13, 24. Ro *6:3. Ja *4:4. **ye are.** ver. 9. 2 C *6:16. Ep *2:21, 22. He 3:6. 1 P *2:5. **the Spirit.** Gr. *pneuma*, Mt +3:16. Ezk 36:27. Jn 4:24. *14:17. Ro +*8:11. 2 T 1:14. 1 J *4:12, 15, 16. **of God.** Ac *5:3, 4. **dwelleth in.** 1 C *6:19. Ps 51:11. Jn *14:23. Ro +*8:9.

17. **If.** ƒ184A, 1 C +15:2. **any.** 1 C *6:18-20. Le 15:31. 20:3. Nu 19:20. Ps 74:3. 79:1. Ezk 5:11. 7:22. 23:38, 39. Zp 3:4. **defile.** *or*, destroy. 2 P *2:1. Re +*22:11. for. Ge 28:17. Ex 3:5. 1 Ch 29:3. Ps 93:5. 99:9. Is 64:11. Ezk 43:12. 2 C √7:1. Ep *5:25-27.

18. **deceive himself.** 1 C +*6:9. 15:33. Pr 5:7. Is *5:21. 44:20. Je 37:9. Mt +*6:23. Lk 21:8. Ga √6:3, 7. Ep 5:6. 2 T 3:13. T 3:3. Ja *1:22, 26. 1 J √1:8. **If any.** ƒ184A, 1 C +15:2. 1 C 1:18-21. 4:10. 8:1, 2. Pr *3:5, 7. 26:12. Is 5:21. Je +*8:8, 9. Ro +*11:25. +*12:16. Ph 3:4. **in this.** 1 C +1:20. Jn +*6:54n. **world.** Gr. *aion*, Mt +6:13. **let.** Mt 18:4. Mk 10:15. Lk 18:17.

19. **the wisdom.** 1 C 1:19, 20. 2:6. Is 19:11-14. 29:14-16. 44:25. Ro 1:21, 22. **world.** Gr. *kosmos*, Mt +4:8. **is foolishness.** 1 C +1:18. **For.** Jb *5:13. **He taketh.** 1 C 1:10. Ex 1:10. 18:11. 2 S 15:31. 16:23. 17:14, 23. Est 7:10. Jb ✝5:13. Ps 7:14, 15. 9:15, 16. 60:15, 16. 141:10. Pr 5:22. +*21:30. **craftiness.** Lk 20:23. 2 C 4:2. 11:3. Ep 4:14.

20. **the Lord.** Ps ✝94:11. **that.** Jb 11:11, 12. Ps 2:1. Ro 1:21. Col 2:8.

21. **glory.** ver. 4-7. 1 C 1:12, etc. √4:6. Je +*9:23, 24. **in men.** 1 C 1:31. **For.** Nu=18:14. Is 43:4. Ezk=44:29. Ro 4:13. +*8:28, 32. 2 C 4:5, 15. Ep 1:3. Re 21:7.

22. **Paul.** ver. 5-8. 1 C +1:12. 9:19-22. 2 C *4:5. Ep +*4:11, 12. **or.** ƒ129, Ezk +34:4. **or the world.** Gr. *kosmos*, Mt +4:8. Ro 8:37-39. Ph 1:21. **all are.** Jsh 1:3. Is 43:4. Mk +*10:29, 30. Ro +*8:28. 2 C 6:10. Ph *1:21. 1 T *6:17. Re *21:7.

23. **ye are.** 1 C +*6:19, 20. 7:22. 15:23. SS *2:16. Jn 17:9, 10. Ro *14:8. 2 C 10:7. Ga *3:29. 5:24. **and Christ.** 1 C +*8:6. +*11:3. +*15:28. 1 Ch *29:11. Mt +*10:32. *17:5. Jn 17:18, 21. +20:17. Ep 1:10. Ph *2:6-11. He *1:2, 3.

1 CORINTHIANS 4

The apostles, and preachers of the gospel, should be accounted of, as ministering servants to Christ, and "stewards of the mysteries of God;" and they are required as such to be faithful, 1, 2. They must be left to the judgment of the Lord at his coming, 3-5. The apostle exhorts the Corinthians, not to be puffed up for one against another, as all have their different endowments from God, 6, 7. He contrasts their vainglory and supposed proficiency; with his own despised and afflicted state, and lowly conduct, 8-13. He warns them, as their only "father in Christ," and exhorts them to imitate him, 14-16. For this purpose he had sent Timothy unto them, 17; and intended to come himself: and to make trial of the power of those who opposed him, 18-21.

1. **account.** ver. 13. 2 C 12:6. **the ministers.** 1 C *3:5. *9:16-18. Mt +√24:45. +*28:19, 20. Lk 1:2. Jn 18:36. Ac 13:5. 26:16. 2 C *4:5. 5:18-20. *6:4, 7. 11:23. Ga *1:10. Ep *4:11, 12. Col *1:25-29. 1 T 3:6. **and stewards.** Mt +*13:52. Lk +*12:42. 16:1-3. T *1:7. 1 P +4:10. **mysteries.** 1 C 2:7. 13:2. 14:2. Mt +*13:11. Mk 4:11. Lk 8:10. Ro +*16:25n. Ep 1:9. 3:3-9. 6:19. Col 1:26, 27. 2:2. 4:3. 1 T 3:9, 16.

2. **required.** T#453. 1 T 3:2-7. 2 T 2:2, 24, 25. T 1:6-9. Mt 13:52. **stewards.** Lk 11:42. 1 P *4:10, 11. **that.** ver. 1. 1 C *2:1, 2, 4. 7:25. *10:33. Nu 12:7. Pr 13:17. Mt 25:21, 23. Lk +*12:42. *16:10-12. 2 C *2:17. *4:1, 2. Col *1:7, 9. *4:7, 17. 1 Th *2:4. He *13:17. 1 P *5:2-4. **faithful.** ver. 17. 1 C 7:25. *11:1. Nu 12:7. 1 S 22:14. 2 K +*12:15. ◐22:17. 2 Ch 31:12. Ne =13:13. Pr 13:17. Mt +*24:45. +*25:21, 23. Lk √16:10. 19:17. Ac +*6:3. 16:15. *20:18-21, 24-28. 2 C *6:3. +*7:2. *8:20. *12:19. Ep 6:21. Col 1:7. 4:7, 9. 1 Th 2:7-11. 1 T *1:3, 4, 11, 12. 3:11. 2 T *2:2, 11-16, 23-25. *4:1, 2, 5. T *2:7, 8, 15. *3:8, 9. He 3:5. 1 P 5:12. 3 J *5. Re 2:10. 17:14.

3. **it is.** 1 C 2:15. 1 S +*16:7. Je +*17:9, 10. Jn +*7:24. **judged.** 1 C +2:15g. **judgment.** Gr. day. ƒ121P4, Dt +4:32. 1 C +*3:13.

4. **For.** *ouden gar emauto sunoida*, "For I am not conscious to myself of any guilt" or neglect of duty. Wetstein has shown from the classics that this is the proper signification of *suneidein*. **I know.** Jb 27:6. Ps 7:3-5. Jn 21:17. Ac +23:1. 2 C 1:12. 1 J *3:20, 21. **by myself.** ƒ63I1A, Ex +12:4. Supply ellipsis, (of any unfaithful thing). **yet.** Jb *9:2, 3, 15, 20. 15:14. 25:4. 40:4. Ps *19:12. *130:3. *143:2. Pr *21:2. Ro 3:19, 20. 4:2. 1 J 3:21. **but.** ver. 5. Ps 26:12. 50:6. 2 C 5:10.

5. **judge.** Ec +*12:14. Mt +*7:1, 2. 13:29. Lk 6:37. Ro *2:1, 16. *14:4, 10-13. Ja 4:11. **before the time.** Mt 8:29g. **until.** T#950. 1 C 1:7, 8. *11:26. 15:23. Jb 19:25. Da +*7:13, 14. Zc 12:10. 14:4. Mt +*16:27n. 24:27, 30, 42, 46. 25:31. Mk 14:62. Jn +*14:3, 28. +21:22. Ac +*1:11. +*3:20, 21. Ro +2:16. Ph 3:20, 21. Col 3:4. 1 Th 1:10. 3:13. √4:16, 17. 5:2. 2 Th 1:7. 3:5. 2 T *4:8. T *2:13. He *9:28. Ja 5:7. 1 P 5:4. 2 P *3:3, 4, 10, 12. 1 J *3:2. Ju 14. Re +*1:7. 22:12, 20. **who.** 1 C +*3:13. Jb 20:27. Ec 11:9. *12:14. Da *7:10. Ml *3:18. Mt 10:26. Lk 12:1-3. Ro *2:16. 2 C 4:2. He *4:13. Re *20:12. **darkness.** Is +*9:2. **counsels of.** 1 K *8:39. Re 2:23. **and then.** 1 C +3:8. **praise.** Ps *37:6. Pr 31:28. Mt +*6:3, 4. √25:21, 23. Jn *5:44. Ro *2:7, 29. √8:1. 2 C √5:10. 10:18. 1 P *1:7. *5:4.

6. **these.** 1 C 1:12. *3:4-7, 22. 2 C 10:7, 12, 15. 11:4, 12-15. **for.** 1 C 9:23. 2 C 4:15. 12:19. 1 Th 1:5. 2 T 2:10. **that ye.** Jb 11:11, 12. Ps 8:4. 146:3. Is 2:22. Je 17:5, 6. Mt *23:8-10. Ro +*12:3. 2 C 12:6. **be puffed.** ver. 18, 19. 1 C *3:21. 5:2, 6. 8:1. 13:4. Nu 11:28,

29. Jn 3:26, 27. 2 C 12:20g. Col 2:18.

7. **who.** 1 C *12:4-11. *15:10. Ro 9:16-18. Ep *2:3-5. 2 Th *2:12-14. 1 T *1:12-15. T *3:3-7. **maketh thee to differ.** Gr. distinguisheth thee. T#668. Mt 5:36. 6:27. Ro 3:27. Ep 2:1-3, 8. Ph +*2:3 (T#482). **and what.** 1 C *3:5. 7:7. 1 Ch 29:11-16. 2 Ch 1:7-12. Pr 2:6. Mt 25:14, 15. Lk 19:13. Jn 1:16. *3:27. +*6:65. Ro 1:5. +*12:6. Ep *2:8, 9. Ph √2:13. He 5:4. Ja *1:17. 1 P *4:10. **now if.** √184A, 1 C +15:2. √185C, Mt +11:14. **why.** 1 C 5:6. 2 Ch 32:23-29. Ezk 28:2-5. 29:3. Da 4:30-32. 5:18-23. Ac 12:22, 23.

8. **Now.** √169, Je +12:1. **ye are full.** √12, Ps +1:1. 1 C 1:5. 3:1, 2. 5:6. Pr 13:7. 25:14. Is *5:21. Lk 1:51-53. 6:25. Ro +*12:3, 16. Ga *6:3. Re √3:17. **now.** √41, Ge +10:1. **without us.** √60B, Ge +20:16. ver. 18. Ac 20:29, 30. Ph 1:27. √2:12. **and I.** Nu 11:29. Ac 26:29. 2 C 11:1. Ga 5:12. Re 3:15. **ye did reign.** Ps 122:5-9. Je 28:6. Ro 12:15. 2 C 13:9. 1 Th *2:19, 20. 3:6-9. 2 T 2:11, 12. Re 5:10.

9. **I think.** 1 C 7:40. *15:30-32. 2 C 1:8-10. *4:8-12. 6:9. Ph 1:29, 30. 1 Th 3:3. **us the apostles last.** *or,* us the last apostles, as. Ps 44:22. Ro +*8:36. 1 Th 5:9, 10. Re *6:9-11. **we are.** Is 20:3. He *10:33. 11:36. **spectacle.** Gr. theater. √121J18. Metonymy of the Subject B579. *Theater* is put for its spectacle. Ac 19:29, 31. **world.** Gr. *kosmos,* Mt +4:8. **to angels, and to men.** He 1:14. Re 7:11-14. 17:6, 7.

10. **are fools.** 1 C 1:1, etc., 18-20, 26-28. *2:3, 14. 3:18. 2 K 9:11. Ho 9:7. Ac *17:18, 32. *26:24. **for.** Mt 5:11. 10:22-25. +*24:9. Lk 6:22. Ac 9:16. 1 P *4:14. **are wise.** ver. 8. 1 C 10:14, 15. Je +*8:8, 9. Mt +25:2. Ro 11:25. 12:16. 2 C 11:19. **we are weak.** 1 C +2:3. 2 C 10:10. 11:29. √12:9, 10. 13:3, 4, 9. **but ye.** 1 C 3:2. √10:12. 2 C 13:9. **but we.** Pr 11:12. Is *53:3. Lk 10:16. 18:9. 1 Th 4:8.

11. **unto.** 1 C 9:4. 2 C 4:8. 6:4, 5. 11:26, 27. Ph 4:12. **and are naked.** √171N, Ge +8:13. Jb 22:6. Ro 8:35. **and are buffeted.** Ac *14:19. *16:23. *23:2. 2 C *11:20, 23-25. 2 T 3:11. **and have.** Mt 8:20.

12. **labor.** 1 C 9:6. Ac +18:3. *20:34. 1 Th *2:9. 2 Th *3:8. 1 T *4:10. **being reviled.** Mt *5:44. Lk 6:28. *23:34. Ac *7:60. Ro *12:14, 20. 1 P *2:23. +*3:9. Ju 9. **being persecuted.** Mt +*5:11. Jn +15:20. 2 C 4:9g. 1 P 3:14. 4:12-14, 19.

13. **we are made.** Is 30:22. 64:6. La 3:45. Ac *22:22. *24:5. **world.** Gr. *kosmos,* Mt +4:8. **unto this day.** √67, Ro +3:26.

14. **write.** 1 C 9:15. 2 C 7:3. 12:19. **to shame.** 1 C 6:5. 15:34. 2 Th 3:14. T 2:8. **my.** ver. 15. 2 C *6:11-13. 11:11. *12:14, 15. 1 Th *2:11. 3 J 4. **I warn.** Ezk 3:21. Ac 20:31. Col 1:28. 1 Th 5:12, 14.

15. **For though.** √102C, Mt +5:29. √184C, Mt +4:9. **ye have.** 2 T 4:3. **ten thousand.** 1 C 14:19. **instructors.** Ga 3:24, 25. **I have begotten.** T#432. 1 C *3:6, 10. *9:1, 2. Da +10:12 (T#545). Ac 14:1. *18:4-11. Ro 15:20. 2 C 3:1-3. Ga *4:19. 1 Th 2:7, 8, 11. 1 T +4:16 (T#468). T 1:4. Phm 10-12, 19. Ja *1:18. 1 P 1:23.

16. **be ye followers.** 1 C √11:1. Jn 10:4, 5. Ep *5:1. Ph *3:17. +*4:9. 1 Th 1:6. 2 Th 3:9. He *13:7. 1 P *5:3.

17. **I sent.** 1 C 16:10. Ac +16:1. 19:21, 22. Ph *2:19. 1 Th *3:2, 3. **Timotheus.** 2 T 1:2. **who is.** ver. 15. 1 T *1:2. 2 T 1:2. **son.** Ph *2:22. **faithful.** ver. +*2. 1 C 7:25. Nu 12:7. Pr 13:17. Mt +*24:45. 25:21, 23. Ep 6:21. Col 1:7. 4:9. 2 T 2:2. Re 2:10, 13. **my ways.** 1 C 7:17. *11:2, 16. 16:1. 2 T 3:10. **as I teach.** 1 C

7:17. **every where.** √171D, Mk +16:20. **in.** 1 C 14:33.

18. **are puffed up.** ver. 6-8. 1 C 5:2. **as though.** ver. 21. 2 C 10:2.

19. **I will come.** 1 C 11:34. 14:5. *16:5-7. Ac *19:21. 20:2. 2 C *1:15-17, 23. 2:1, 2. **if.** √184C, Mt +4:9. Ac +*18:21. Ro *15:32. He *6:3. Ja √4:15. **know.** √121C2A3, Is +53:11. **not.** ver. 18. 2 C 13:1-4. **but.** Ga 2:6.

20. **the kingdom of God.** Mt +*6:10. Lk +*17:20, 21. +*22:29, 30. Ac +*1:6n. Ro +*14:17. Col 1:13n. 1 Th 2:12. 2 T +*4:1n. **is.** √63B, Ge +25:28. **not in word.** 1 C 2:4. **but in power.** 1 C 1:24. 2:4. Mt +*24:30. Ro √1:16. *15:19. 2 C √10:4, 5. 1 Th *1:5.

21. **will ye.** √14, Is +5:3. **shall.** ver. 18. 1 C 5:5. 2 Ch 10:2, 6, 8. 12:20, 21. 13:2, 3, 10. 2 C 1:23. 2:1, 3. 12:20. *13:2, 10. **with a rod.** Is 10:24. Ac 5:5-11. 13:8-11. Re 2:27. 12:5. 19:15. **and.** 2 C *10:1, 2. Ga *6:1. 1 Th 2:7. Ja 3:17. **spirit.** Gr. *pneuma,* √121A2, Mt +5:3n.

1 CORINTHIANS 5

The apostle sharply reproves a scandalous incest, protected from censure, in the church at Corinth, 1, 2. By the authority of Christ he orders the excommunication of the incestuous person, 3-5. He shows that the leaven of sin must be purged out, in order to keep the true "passover," by faith in Christ, 6-8. Scandalous professors of Christianity must be shunned, more decidedly than those without, 9-13.

1. **reported.** √108B, Ac +22:9. 1 C 1:11. Ge 37:2. 1 S 2:24. **fornication.** ver. 11. 1 C +*6:9, 13, +18. Ac *15:20, 29. 2 C 12:21. Ga 5:19. Ep *5:3. Col *3:5. 1 Th 4:7. Re 2:21. +*21:8. **and.** Je 2:33. Ezk 16:47, 51, 52. **that one.** Ge 35:22. 49:4. Le 18:8. 20:11. Dt 22:30. *27:20. 2 S 16:22. 20:3. 1 Ch 5:1. Ezk 22:10. Am 2:7. 2 C 7:12.

2. **ye are.** ver. 6. 1 C *4:6-8, 18. Je 5:28. **mourned.** Nu 25:6. 2 K 22:19. Ezr 9:2-6. 10:1-6. Ps 119:136. Je 13:17. Ezk +*9:4, 6. 2 C *7:7, 9-11. 12:21. **he that.** ver. 13. 2 C 2:5. *7:12. **might.** ver. 5, 7, 13. Re 2:20-22. **from among.** √108H3, Mt +13:49.

3. **as absent.** 2 C 10:1, 11. 13:2. Col 2:5. 1 Th 2:17. **in body.** Ac. Mt +*6:25. **in spirit.** Gr. *pneuma,* Ac +18:25n. ?√121A3, Mt +27:50. √121A2, Ps +51:10. **judged.** *or,* determined.

4. **In.** √63I2, Jsh +3:3. Supply by ellipsis, "(To deliver) in the name of." **the name.** Ac 3:6. 4:7-12, 30. 16:18. Ep 5:20. Col 3:17. 2 Th 3:6. 1 T *5:21. **when.** Mt 16:19. *18:16-18, 20. 28:18, 20. Jn *20:23. 2 C 2:6, 9, 10. 13:3, 10. 1 T 5:20. **spirit.** Gr. *pneuma,* √121A2, Mt *26:41. √121A2, Ps +51:10. **the power.** Lk 5:17. 2 C *12:9. 2 P 1:16.

5. **To deliver.** ver. 13. Jb √1:12. *2:6. Ps 109:6. 2 C 2:6. 10:6. 13:10. Ac +*26:18. 1 T *1:20. **unto Satan.** 1 C 7:5. 1 Ch 21:1. Jb 1:6-9, 12. 2:1-4, 6, 7. Zc 3:1, 2. Mt 4:10. 12:26. 16:23. Mk 1:13. 3:23, 26. 4:15. 8:33. Lk 10:18. 11:18. 13:16. 22:3, 31. Jn 13:27. Ac 5:3. 26:18. Ro 16:20. 2 C 2:11. 11:14. 12:7. 1 Th 2:18. 2 Th 2:9. 1 T 1:20. 5:15. Re +2:9. **for the destruction.** 1 C 3:15. 7:28. Mt +*10:28. 2 C √2:6-11. 7:8-12. 12:7. **that.** 1 C *11:32. 2 C *2:7. Ga *6:1, 2. 2 Th *3:14, 15. Ja 5:19, 20. 1 J 5:16. Ju 22, 23. **spirit.** Gr. *pneuma,* √121A3, Mt +27:50. √121A2, Ps +51:10. Is +*38:16. He 12:23. **be saved.** Pr 23:14. Ju 23. **the day.** 1 C +*1:8. +*3:13. Ph 1:6. 2 T 1:18. 2 P 3:12.

6. **glorying.** ver. 2. 1 C 3:21. 4:18, 19. Ph +1:26.
Ja 4:16. **Know ye not.** 1 C +6:2. **a little.** ✓138C, Ge
+22:14. 1 C *15:33. Mt +*13:33. 16:6-12. Lk 13:21.
Ga 5:9. 2 T 2:17. He +*12:15. **lump.** Ro 9:21. 11:16g.

7. **Purge.** ✓7, Allegory by continued Hypocatastasis,
Ga +4:24. ver. 13. Ex *12:15. 13:6, 7. Mt 16:6, 12.
Mk 8:15. Lk 12:1. Ep *4:17-19, 22. Col *3:5-9. 1 P
*4:1-3. **ye may.** 1 C *10:17. **unleavened.** Le +*±23:6.
Ac +12:3, 4. **Christ.** 1 C *15:3, 4. Ex 12:5, 6. Is *53:7-
10. Jn *1:29, 36. *19:14. Ac *8:32-35. 1 P *1:19, 20.
Re *5:6-9, 12. **passover.** ✓22E, Jn +1:29. Ex 12:13.
Le +±23:5. Nu 28:16, 17. Dt=16:1-6. 2 Ch=35:*11,
13, 14. Is 25:6. Mk 14:12. **sacrificed.** or, slain.

8. **let.** Ex 12:15. 13:6. Le +*23:6. Nu 28:16, 17.
Dt +*16:16. Is 25:6. **keep.** T#105. 1 C *11:27, 28.
La +3:40 (T#397). **feast.** or, holy day. Ps 42:4. Is
30:29. **not with.** ver. 1, 6. 1 C +*6:9-11. Ex 12:15.
13:7. 23:15. 34:18, 25. Le 23:6. Nu 28:17. Dt 16:3,
8. 2 C 12:21. Ep 4:17-22. 1 P 4:2. **neither.** 1 C 3:3.
Mt 16:6, 12. 26:4, 5. Mk 8:15. Lk *12:1. Jn 18:28-30.
2 C 12:20. 1 P 2:1, 2. **malice.** Ro +1:29. **but.** Jsh
24:14. Ps 32:2. Jn 1:47. 2 C 1:12. 8:8. Ep 6:24. 1 J
3:18-21. **unleavened.** Le +±23:6. **sincerity.**
2 Ch=29:34. 2 C 1:12. 2:17. Ph 1:10. 2 P 3:1.

9. **not.** ver. 2, 7. Ps +*1:1, 2. Pr 9:6. 2 C *6:14,
17. Ep +*5:11. 2 Th *3:6, 14. **with.** Ep *5:5.

10. **altogether.** 1 C *10:27. **fornicators.** 1 C +*6:9,
18. Ps 119:36. Ep 5:5. Col 3:5. 1 T 6:10. He 13:5. **of
this.** 1 C 1:20. Jn 8:23. 15:19. 17:6, 9, 15, 16. 2 C
✓4:4. Ep 2:2. 1 J 4:5, 7. **world.** Gr. *kosmos*, Mt +4:8.
covetous. 2 C 9:5. **extortioners.** 1 C 6:10. Lk 18:11.
idolaters. 1 C +*6:9. 10:7. Ep 5:5. Re +*21:8. 22:15.
for. Mt *5:14-16. Jn ✓17:15. Ph 2:15. 1 J 5:19. Re
12:9. **world.** Gr. *kosmos*, Mt +4:8.

11. **keep company.** ver. +*9. Ps +✓119:63. **if any.**
✓184C, Mt +4:9. **called.** 1 C 6:6. 7:12, 15. 8:11. Mt
18:17. Ac 9:17. Ro 16:17. 2 Th *3:6, 14. 2 J *10. **fornicator.** See on ver. 1-9, 10. Ps 50:16-21. 2 C 12:20, 21.
Ga *5:19-21. 1 Th 4:3-8. Re 2:14, 20. +*21:8. 22:15.
or covetous. Ps 10:3. Mk +*7:21-23. Lk +*12:15, etc.
Ep 5:5. Col +*3:5. 1 T 3:3. +*6:9, 10. 2 P 2:14, 15.
or an idolater. 1 C 10:7, 8, 14, 18-22. **or a railer.**
1 C +*6:10. Ps +*101:5. 1 P *3:9. **or a drunkard.**
1 C +*6:10. 11:21. Mt *24:49-51. Lk *12:45, 46.
+*21:34. Ro +13:13. Ga 2:12. Ep +*5:18. 1 Th 5:7,
8. **or an extortioner.** Ezk 22:12. Mt 23:25. Lk *18:11.
with such. ver. 13. Mt 18:17. Ro 16:17. 2 Th 3:6, 14.
1 T 6:5. 2 J 10.

12. **what.** Lk 12:14. Jn +*18:36. **them.** Mk +4:11.
Ep *2:12. Col 4:5. 1 Th 4:12. 1 T 3:7. **do not.** 1 C
6:1-5.

13. **God.** Ps 50:6. Ac ✓17:31. Ro +*1:18-20, 29,
32. 2:16. He +*13:4. 2 P 2:9. **Therefore put away.**
lit. ye will put away. ✓96C10, Jg +5:21. ver. 1, 2, 5,
7. Dt ▸13:5. 17:7, 12. *19:19. 21:21. 22:21, 22, 24.
24:7. Jg 20:13. Ec 9:18. Mt 18:17.

1 CORINTHIANS 6

*The Corinthians are reproved for going to law before
heathen magistrates, instead of settling their differences among themselves, 1-6, and for selfishness and
dishonesty, 7, 8. Neither fornicators, nor idolaters,
nor adulterers, nor thieves, nor covetous persons, nor
drunkards, nor revilers, nor extortioners shall "inherit
the kingdom of God," 9, 10. Some of the Corinthians*

*had been such, but they were "washed, and sanctified,
and justified," 11. All lawful things are not expedient,
12. Christians, whose bodies are members of Christ,
and the temple of the Holy Spirit, must flee fornication,
as a sin against their own bodies, 13-19; that, as bought
with a price, they may glorify God in body and soul,
20.*

1. **having.** 1 C 5:12. Mt *18:15-17. Ac *18:12-17.
19:38. **against another.** Ro +2:1. **go.** ver. 6, 7. Ro
+3:4. **and not before.** Mt *18:17. **the saints.** 1 C 1:2.
14:33. 16:1, 15. 2 C +1:1.

2. **know.** ver. 3, 9, 15, 16, 19. 1 C 3:16. 5:6. 9:13,
24. Ro 6:16. 11:2. Ja 4:4g. **the saints.** 1 C 1:2. Ps
49:14. +*149:5-9. Da *7:18, 22. Zc +*14:5. 1 Th 3:13.
Ju *14. **shall judge.** ✓147A, Ge +50:24. Ps +*149:9.
Da *7:22. Mt *19:28. Lk +*22:30. Ju *15. Re 2:26,
27. 3:21. *20:4. **world.** Gr. *kosmos*, Mt +4:8. Ro
+*4:13. **and if.** ✓184A, 1 C +15:2. **world.** Gr. *kosmos*,
Mt +4:8. **the smallest.** ver. 4. 2 C 4:18. 1 J 2:16, 17.
matters. Ja 2:6.

3. **judge.** Mt 25:41. **angels.** 2 P 2:4. Ju *6. **pertain.**
ver. 4. Ps 17:14. Lk 8:14. +*21:34. 2 T 2:4. 4:10.

4. **If then.** ✓184C, Mt +4:9. **ye have.** ✓96B, Mt
+11:6. 1:2. **judgments.** Ja 2:6g. **set.** ✓60A, Ge
+3:22. **who.** Ac *6:2-4. **least.** The apostle perhaps
meant that the meanest persons in the church were
competent to decide the causes which they brought
before the heathen magistrates. 2 K +*5:13. Jb 31:13.
Ac +*28:15. Ro +*12:3. 2 C +10:10. Ph +*2:3.

5. **to your.** 1 C 4:14. 11:14. 15:34. **Is it.** 1 C 3:18.
4:10. Pr 14:8. Ja +*1:5. 3:13-18. **brethren.** ✓96F1,
Ge +3:8.

6. **brother.** ver. 1, 7. Ge 13:7-9. 45:24. Ne 5:8, 9.
Ps ch. 133. Ac 7:26. Ph 2:14, 15. 1 J 2:9-11. 3:11-15.
before the unbelievers. 1 C *9:12. 2 S ✓12:14. Ps 50:16.
Is 52:5. Ezk 36:20. Ro 2:24.

7. **there.** Pr 25:8-10. Ho 10:2. Ja 4:1-3. **a fault.** Ro
11:12. **Why.** Pr *20:22. Mt *5:39-41. Lk *6:29. Ro
*12:17-19. 1 Th *5:13, 15. 1 P *2:19-23. *3:9.

8. **ye do wrong.** Le +*19:13. Mi 2:2. Ml +*3:5mg.
Mk *10:19. Col 3:25. 1 Th *4:6. Ja +*5:4. **your brethren.** 1 Th +*4:6.

9. **Know.** ver. 2, 3, 15, 16, 19. 1 C 3:16. 9:24. **the
unrighteous.** Ex 23:1. Le +*19:15, 35, 36. Dt *25:13-
16. Ps +*34:16. Pr 11:1. 22:8. Is 10:1, 2. *55:7. Zc
+*5:3. Ac 24:25. Ro *1:18. 1 T 1:9. **shall not inherit.**
ver. *10. 1 C *15:50. Ps +*34:16. +*37:9. Mt 19:29.
+*25:34, 41. Jn ✓3:3. Ro +*1:29-32. Ga *5:21. Ep
*5:5. He *12:14. Re +*21:8. **the kingdom of God.**
Mt +*6:10, 13. +*8:11. Ro +*14:17. 2 T +*4:1. **Be
not deceived.** 1 C 15:33. Ga *6:7. Ja 1:16, 22. **fornicators.** ver. +*18. 1 C 5:1, 10. Mt *15:19. Mk +*7:21.
Ac +✓15:20. Ga +*5:19-21. Ep +*5:4, 5. 1 T 1:9,
10. He *12:14, 16. +*13:4. Re +*21:8. *22:15. **idolaters.** 1 C 5:10. Ga 5:20. Re +*21:8. *22:15. **nor effeminate.** 2 S +*3:29n. **abusers.** Ge 19:5. Le 18:22. 20:13.
Dt 22:5. 23:17. Jg 19:22. Ro 1:26, 27. 1 T 1:10.

10. **nor thieves.** T#714. Ex 21:16. Jsh 7:11, 12. Ps
50:17, 18. Is 1:23. Je 7:11. Ezk 22:13, 27, 29. Ho
4:2, 3. Zc 5:3, 4. Mt 21:19. 23:14, 33. Jn 12:6. Ep
*4:28. 1 Th *4:6. 1 P 4:15. **covetous.** See on 1 C 5:10,
11. Ex +*20:17. Pr +*21:26. Mt *13:22. Lk +*12:15.
Ac 8:20. Col +*3:5. **drunkards.** 1 C +5:11. Ge +*9:20,
21. Dt 21:18-20. 29:19, 20. 1 S 25:36. 2 S 11:13. 1 K
16:8-10. 20:16. Pr +*20:1. *23:20, 21, 29-35. Is *5:11.
28:1-3. Da 5:1-6. Ho *4:11. Hab ✓2:15. Ep +*5:18.

revilers. Ga 5:21. extortioners. Ezk +*22:12. shall inherit. Mt +*5:5. Jn +*3:3, 5. Ep +*1:11n. kingdom of God. ver. 9. Lk +*17:20, 21. +*22:29, 30. Ro +*14:17.

11. such were. 1 C 12:2. Le=13:2, 3. Dt 10:19. Jn 20:23. Ro 6:17-19. Ep *2:1-3, 19. 4:17-22. 5:8. Col *3:5-7. T *3:3-6. 1 P 4:2, 3. but ye are washed. Ex=29:4. Ps 51:2, 7. Pr 30:12. Is 1:16. Je 4:14. Ezk *36:25-27. Zc 13:1. Jn 13:10. Ac +*22:16. Ep √5:26. T √3:5. He +*10:22. 1 P 3:21. Re +*1:5, 6. *7:14. but ye are sanctified. 1 C +*1:2, 30. Ps *4:3. Jn *17:17. Ac +*26:18. Ro *6:22. 15:16. 2 C *6:17. Ga *5:22, 23. 1 Th *4:3. *5:22-24. 2 Th *2:13. 2 T *2:21, 22. He *2:11. *10:9, 10. *13:12, 13. 1 P *1:2, 22. but ye are justified. ∱18, Dt +28:4. Is 45:25. *53:11. Lk *18:14. Ac +*13:39. Ro *3:24, 26-30. 4:5. *5:1, 9. +*8:30, 33. Ga *2:16. 3:8, 11, 24. T *3:7. Ja 2:21-26. in the name. Jn +*20:31. Ac +2:21. Spirit. Gr. pneuma, Mt +3:16.

12. All things. ∱18, Dt +28:4. ∱63I2, Jsh +3:3. Supply by ellipsis, "All (meats, ver. 13) are lawful." are lawful. 1 C +8:9. *10:23. Ro *14:14. *15:2. are not. 1 C *8:4, 7-13. *9:12. √10:24-33. Ro *14:15-23. 2 Th 3:9. but I. 1 C *9:27. Ro 7:14. He +*12:15, 16. Ju 12. brought under. 1 C 7:4 (power). Lk 22:25g (exercise authority).

13. Meats for. ∱63B, Ge +2:10. 1 C 8:8. Mt 15:17, 20. Mk 7:19. Ro +*14:17, 20, 21. belly for. ∱63B, Ge +2:10. but God. 1 C 10:3-5. Jn 6:27, 49. Col *2:22, 23. not for fornication. Ro˙ *6:12, 13. 1 Th *4:3, 7. but for. ver. 15, *19, 20. 1 C 3:16, 17. Ro *6:12, 13. 7:4. +*12:1. 14:7-9. 2 C √5:15. *11:2. Ep 5:23. Ph *3:17-21. 1 Th *4:3-7. the body. Ep *5:23.

14. God. 1 C 15:15-20. Ac +*2:24. √17:31. Ro √6:4-8. +*8:11. 2 C *4:14. Ph 3:10, 11. 1 Th 4:14. also raise. 1 C 15:22, 23. Nu=17:3, 8. Jn *6:39, 40. by. Mt +*22:29. Jn 5:28, 29. 6:39, 40. 11:25, 26. Ep 1:19, 20. Ph *3:21.

15. Know. ver. +2. your bodies. ∱171Q4, Ex +21:3mg. ver. 13, 19. 1 C 11:3. *12:27. Ro *12:5. Ep 1:22, 23. 4:12, 15, 16, 25. +*5:23, 30. Col 2:19. are members. 1 C √12:12, 13. Ep +*5:30. God forbid. Ge 44:17. Lk +20:16. Ro 3:3, 4, 6, 31. +*6:2, 15. 7:7, 13. Ga 2:17. 3:21. 6:14.

16. an harlot. Ge 34:31. 38:15, 24. Jg 16:1. Mt 21:31, 32. He 11:31. for. Ge +*❫2:24. Mt +*19:5, 6. Mk 10:8. Ep 5:31.

17. joined. Nu=18:2. Dt 10:20. 11:22. 2 K 18:6. Is +*56:3. Je 13:11. Ro 12:9. is one. 1 C √12:13. Jn *3:6. 17:21-23. Ro +*8:9, 10. ◐*12:2. Ep √4:3, 4. +*5:30. Ph 2:5. spirit. Gr. pneuma put for union with Christ. 2 C 3:17, 17, 18. For the other uses of pneuma, see Mt +8:16n. Alford states "here that inner union with Christ in spirit is meant, which is the normal state of every believer" (Jn 15:1-7. 17:21). Hodge notes "That is, has one Spirit with him. This does not mean has the same disposition or state of mind, but the same principle of life, the Holy Spirit. The Holy Spirit is given without measure unto Christ (Jn 3:34), and from him is communicated to all his people who are thereby brought into a common life with him. This being the case, it imposes the highest conceivable obligation not to act inconsistently with this intimate and exalting relationship." Ro +*8:1n.

18. Flee. Ge 39:12-18. Pr 2:16-19. *5:3-15. 6:24-32. 7:5, etc., 24-27. 9:16-18. Ro 6:12, 13. 1 Th *4:3.

2 T 2:22. He +*13:4. 1 P 2:11. fornication. ver. 9, 13. 1 C 5:1, 10, 11. +7:2. Ac +15:20. 2 C 12:21. Ga 5:19. Ep 5:3. Col 3:5. 1 T 1:10. He 12:16. +*13:4. Re 9:21. +*21:8. *22:15. sinneth. Ro *1:24. 1 Th 4:5. against. Pr 5:11.

19. What. ver. 15, 16. know. ver. +*2. your body. 1 C √3:16. Ex=29:20. Ro *12:1. 2 C √6:16. Ep *2:21, 22. 1 P 2:5. the temple. Jn *2:21. 1 P 2:5. Ghost. Gr. pneuma, Mt +1:18?; +3:16. in you. Mt *12:43, 45. Ro +*8:11. ye have of. Dt 32:6. not your own. ver. 15. 1 K 20:4. 1 Ch 29:14. Ps √12:4. 100:3mg. Ro +*14:7-9. 2 C √5:15. T *2:14.

20. ye are bought. 1 C √7:23. Ge=47:23. Ex 15:16. Le=22:11. Ac +*20:28. Ga *3:13. T *2:14. He *9:12, 14. 1 P *1:18, 19. 2 P +*2:1. Re *5:9. glorify God. 1 C *10:31. Mt *5:16. Ro 6:19. +*12:1. 2 C √5:14, 15. Ph *1:20. 1 P *2:9. your body. Is 58:7. spirit. Gr. pneuma, ∱121A3, Mt +27:50. ∱121A2, Ps +51:10. which are. Ps 33:12. Pr 23:26. Lk 20:25.

1 CORINTHIANS 7

Directions concerning marriage, as a remedy against fornication; and concerning the conduct of husbands and wives to each other, 1-5. The single state has advantages to those who are capable of it, 6-9. Instructions on how to act, when one of the married persons is an unbeliever, 10-16. Every one should abide with God, in the state in which he was called, 17-24. Further intimations of the advantages of a single life, in that troubled state of the church; and a memento concerning the shortness and uncertainty of earthly things, 25-35. Directions concerning the marriage of virgins and widows, 36-40.

1. good. ver. 8, 26, 27, 37, 38. Mt 19:10, 11. not. He +*13:4. touch. ∱108B, Ge +20:6. Ge *20:6. Ru *2:9. Pr *6:29.

2. to avoid. ver. 9. 1 C 6:18. Pr 5:18, 19. 1 T 4:3. fornication. 1 C +*6:18. Mt 15:19. Mk 7:21. 2 C 12:21. let. Pr 18:22. 19:14. Ml 2:14. Ep 5:28, 33. let every. Ge *2:18. Pr *18:22. Mt 19:5. Jn *2:1, 2. Ep *5:31, 32. He +*13:4. his own. In strictness, as Dr. Campbell observes, I have no right to call that *idion*, "own," which I enjoy in common with others; and no woman can call any man *idion aneer*, "her own husband," whom she has in common with other women. In the New Testament we have always *idios aneer*, never *idios gunee*, "his own wife;" which is the more remarkable, as no such an expression occurs in the Septuagint. For, during that dispensation, things were on a different footing. The words rendered "his own wife", are, *teen eauton gunee*; for there was not the same reason for the explicitly strong restriction, on that side, which is contained in the word *idios*. This is absolutely decisive against polygamy; and places the husband and the wife entirely on the same ground; and as much forbids him to take another woman, as it does her to cohabit with another man. wife. Ge +*2:18.

3. husband render. Ex 21:10. 1 P 3:7.

4. wife hath not. 1 C +6:12g. Ho 3:3. Mt 19:9. Mk 10:11, 12. Lk 22:25g.

5. except. Ex *19:15. 1 S *21:4, 5. Ec *3:5. Jl *2:16. Zc 7:3. 12:12-14. give yourselves. 2 Ch +√7:14. 1 P 3:7. that Satan. 1 C +5:5. Mt 19:11. 1 Th 3:5. incontinency. Mt 23:25. 2 T 3:3g.

6. **by.** ver. 7n, 10, 12, 25, 40. 2 C *8:8. *11:17. **not of.** 1 T ◐5:14.

7. **I would.** St. Paul evidently gave this advice in reference to the necessities of the church, or what he calls (ver. 26) the *present distress*; for it would be perfectly absurd to imagine that an inspired apostle would in the general, discountenance marriage, since it was of the greatest importance to the existence and happiness of future generations, and expressly agreeable to a Divine institution. 1 C 9:5, 15. Ac 26:29. **even as.** ver. 8. 1 C *9:5. **But.** 1 C 12:4, 11. Mt *19:11, 12. Ro +*12:6. 1 P 4:10. **one after.** Mt 19:11, 12.

8. **to the unmarried.** 1 C 1:26, 27, 32, 34, 35. **good.** ver. 1, 7n, *26. 1 T ◐*5:14. He ◐+*13:4. **if.** ſ184C, Mt +4:9. **abide.** Gr. *meno*, remain. Jn 15:4. **even as.** ver. 7.

9. **But if.** ſ184A, 1 C +15:2. **cannot contain.** 1 C 9:25g. Ac +24:25. **let.** ver. 2, 28, 36, 39. Ep *5:22-25. 1 T *5:11, 14. **burn.** Ro 1:27. ✱S#4448g: 2 C ◐11:29g. Ep 6:16 (fiery). 2 P 3:12 (being on fire). Re 1:15. 3:18 (tried).

10. **I command.** ſ180A, Ge +4:20. ver. 6. 1 C 11:17. **yet not.** ſ69B, Pr +6:16. ver. 12, 25, 40. **Let not.** ver. 15. Je 3:20. Ml *2:14-16. Mt *5:32. *19:6-9. Mk 10:11, 12. Lk 16:18. **depart.** Gr. *chorizo*. lit. be separated. Mt 19:6 (put asunder).

11. **and if.** ſ184C, Mt +4:9. Compare ſ185C, Mt +11:14. **remain unmarried.** ver. 39. Mk 10:12. **or be reconciled.** Jg 19:2, 3. Je 3:1. Ro 5:10. 2 C 5:18, 19, 20. **and let.** Dt 22:19. Is 50:1. Mt *5:32. *19:6. Mk 10:2. **put away.** Gr. *aphiemi*. lit. send away. ver. 13g (leave).

12. **speak I.** ver. 6, 25. 2 C 11:17. **not the Lord.** That is, Paul, speaking by divine inspiration, could not cite the teaching of Jesus for his authority on this point, for Jesus did not discuss this aspect of marriage relations. **If.** ſ184A, 1 C +15:2. Ezr 10:2, 3, 11-19. **pleased.** Ro 1:32g.

13. **if he.** ſ184A, 1 C +15:2. ſ15C, Mk +6:11. **let her not leave.** Gr. *aphiemi*, as in ver. 11. The same tense and voice, and should therefore be rendered "send away." The absolutely equal rights of husband and wife are insisted on throughout the chapter (CB). See ver. 3, 4, 5. Ge 16:6, *9.

14. **the unbelieving husband.** 1 C 6:15-17. Ezr 9:1, 2. 1 T 4:5. T *1:15. **sanctified.** ſ108B, Je +12:3. 1 C +1:2. **else were.** Dt +*29:11n. Ezr 9:2. Is 52:1. Ml 2:*15, 16. Ac 10:23. Ro √11:16. **children.** Ac +*16:15. **holy.** "When Paul writes that the children of believers are '*holy*' he certainly does not mean they are all regenerated. This is not an ethical holiness, but a covenant holiness. From the whole context it appears that the apostle regards the children as being in the Covenant of Grace in distinction from the world. To them belong the promises of the Covenant of Grace which can all be summarized in that one phrase, 'to be a God unto thee, and to thy seed after thee,' Ge *17:7. Ac +*2:39" (William Masselink, *Why Thousand Years*, p. 80). There is no evidence in Scripture to suggest that Jesus, in establishing his church, determined to confer a lesser standing to children under the New Covenant than they had under the Old Covenant. "They are included in the church, and have a right to be so regarded. The child of a Jewish parent had a right to circumcision, and to all the privileges of the theocracy. So the child of a Christian parent has a right to baptism and to all

the privileges of the church, so long as he is represented by his parent; that is, until he arrives at the period of life when he is entitled and bound to act for himself. Then his relation to the church depends upon his own act. The church is the same in all ages. And it is most instructive to observe how the writers of the New Testament quietly take for granted that the great principles which underlie the old dispensation, are still in force under the new" (Charles Hodge, Comm. on 1 Corinthians, p. 117). Ge +*17:7. Dt +*29:11n. Ne +*12:43. Is +*42:6. Ml *2:15. Mt ◐16:18n. 18:17. √19:14. 23:23n. Lk +*18:15. Ac +*2:39. 16:15n. Ro √11:16. Col 2:11, 12.

15. **But if.** ſ184A, 1 C +15:2. **depart.** Pr 21:9. **let.** ſ96B, Nu +24:21. **A brother.** Mt 12:50. Ja 2:15. **not under bondage.** Ge 24:41. **but.** 1 C *14:33. Ro *12:18. 14:19. 2 C 13:11. Ga *5:22. He +*12:14. Ja 3:17, 18. **hath called.** ver. 17. Ro +*8:28. Col 3:17. **to peace.** Gr. in peace. Ro *12:18. 14:19.

16. **knowest thou.** ſ26, Ro +11:19. 2 S 12:22. Est 4:14. Jl 2:14. Jon 3:9. **O wife.** ſ38D, Ps +27:14. 1 C 9:22. Pr +*11:30. Lk 15:10. 1 T +*4:16. Ja +*5:19, 20. 1 P √3:1, 2. **whether.** ſ184A, 1 C +15:2. Pr +*19:13. 1 P *3:1. **how.** Gr. what. **O man.** ſ38D, Ps +27:14. **whether.** ſ184A, 1 C +15:2. **shalt save.** ſ121E2, Ge +42:38. Ro +11:14.

17. **as God.** ver. 7. Mt 19:12. Ro +*12:3-8. 1 P *4:10, 11. **distributed.** ſ63A2, 2 S +6:6. Supply by ellipsis, (the gift). **as the.** ver. 18, 20, 21, 24. **called.** ver. 15. **so ordain.** 1 C 4:17. 11:34. 16:1. 2 C 11:28. T 1:5. **all the churches.** 1 C +11:16. 14:33, 34. 2 C 8:18. 11:28. Ro 16:4. Ga 1:22. Re 22:16.

18. **being circumcised.** 1 C *9:20. Ac *15:1, 5, 19, 24, 28. Ga √5:1-3. Col 3:11.

19. **Circumcision.** 1 C 8:8. Ro *2:25-29. 3:30. Ga *5:6. *6:15. Col 3:11. **but.** 1 S +*15:22. Pr 19:16. Je 7:22, 23. Mt *5:19. Jn *14:23. +*15:14. 1 J +*2:3, 4. *3:22-24. *5:2, 3. Re *22:14. **God.** ſ63F, Ge +33:10. 20. **abide.** ver. *17, 21-24. Pr 27:8. Lk *3:10-14. 1 Th *4:11. 2 Th *3:12. **same calling.** Lk 3:14n. Ro +11:29.

21. **being.** 1 C √12:13. Ga +*3:28. Col *3:11. 1 T 6:1-3. 1 P 2:18-24. **a servant.** Rather, a *slave, doulos*, the property of another, and bought with his money. In these verses the apostle shows that Christianity makes no change in our *civil* connections. Jl 2:29. **care.** Lk 10:40, 41. 12:29mg. +*21:34. Ph *4:6, 11. He +*13:5. 1 P 5:7. **if.** ſ184A, 1 C +15:2. **made free.** Ps *116:16. Jn *8:36. Ro *6:22. 2 T *2:26. **rather.** T#684. Phm 15, 16, 20, 21.

22. **in the Lord.** ver. +39. **is the.** Lk 1:74, 75. Jn *8:32-36. Ro 6:18-22. Ga 5:1, 13. Ep 6:5, 6. Col √3:22-24. Phm 16. 1 P *2:16. **freeman.** Gr. made free. **is Christ's.** 1 C 9:19, 21. Ps *116:16. Ro 1:1. Ga 1:10. Ep 6:6. Col 4:12. Ja +1:1. 1 P 2:16. 2 P 1:1. Ju 1.

23. **are.** 1 C +*6:20. Le 25:42, 55. Ac +*20:28. T *2:14. 1 P *1:18, 19. 3:18. Re 5:9. **be.** Mt 23:8-11. Ga 2:4. 5:1. Ep √6:7.

24. **let.** ver. 17, 20. **abide.** 1 C *10:31. Ge 5:22-24. 17:1. 1 S 14:45. Ep *6:5-8. Col 3:23, 24. 1 T *6:1, 2. T *2:9, 10. 1 P *2:18, 19.

25. **concerning.** ver. 28, 34, 36-38. Ps 78:63. **virgins.** The word *parthenos*, as well as the Latin *virgo*, "a virgin," though it generally signifies a *maid*, frequently denotes *unmarried persons* of *both sexes*; in which sense it is evidently used here by the apostle. **have.**

ver. 6, 10, 12, 40. 2 C 8:8-10. 11:17. **I give**. 2 C 8:10. **obtained**. 1 C 4:2. 15:10. 2 C 2:17. 4:1, 2. Ph 2:27. 1 T *1:12-16. **faithful**. 1 C +4:2.

26. **that**. ver. 1, 8, 28, 35-38. Je 16:2-4. Mt 24:19. Lk 21:23. 23:28, 29. 1 P 4:17. **good**. He ◐+*13:4. **distress**. *or*, necessity. Lk +*21:23. 2 C 6:4. 12:10.

27. **thou bound**. ver. 12-14, 20. **seek not to**. He +*13:4.

28. **But and if**. ∫184C, Mt +4:9. **thou hast**. ver. 36. He +*13:4. **and if**. ∫184A, 1 C +15:2. ∫184E, Lk +17:6. **Nevertheless**. ver. 26, 32-34. **have trouble**. 1 C 5:5. 2 C 12:7. **but**. ver. 35. Pr +*22:3. Lk *14:28. 2 C 1:23. 12:6. 13:2.

29. **the time**. 2 S 19:34mg. Jb *14:1, 2. Ps 39:4-7. 90:5-10. 103:15, 16. Ec 6:12. 9:10. Ro 13:11, 12. He 13:13, 14. 1 P *4:7. 2 P 3:8, 9. 1 J 2:17. **that both**. Ec 12:7, 8, 13, 14. Is 24:1, 2. 40:6-8. Lk 12:29-36. 14:18-20. Ja 4:13-16. 1 P 1:24.

30. **that weep**. Ps 30:5. +*126:5, 6. Ec 3:4. Is 25:8. 30:19. Lk 6:21, 25. 16:25. Jn *16:22. 1 Th *4:13, 14. Re 7:17. 18:7. 22:20. **possessed not**. ∫77, Ex +3:19. Ezk=44:20. Lk *12:19, 20. Ac 4:32. 2 C 6:10.

31. **use**. 1 C 9:18. Ec 2:24, 25. 3:12, 13. 5:18-20. 9:7-10. 11:2, 9, 10. Mt 24:48-50. 25:14-29. Lk 12:15-21. 16:1, 2. 19:17-26. +*21:34. 1 T √6:17, 18. Ja *5:1-5. **world**. Gr. *kosmos*, Mt +4:8. **not abusing it**. 1 C 9:18. **for**. Ps 39:6. 73:20. Ec +*1:4. Ja 1:10, 11. *4:14. 1 P 1:24. 4:7. 1 J *2:17. **the fashion**. *To skeema*, the *form* or *appearance*. Grotius remarks that the apostle's expression is borrowed from the theater, where *to skeema tas skeenees paragei* means that the *scene changes*, and represents an *appearance* entirely new. **world**. Gr. *kosmos*, Mt +4:8.

32. **I would**. Ps 55:22. Mt 6:25-34. 13:22. Lk +*21:34. Ph *4:6. **without carefulness**. Mt 28:14g. **He that**. ver. 34. 1 T 5:5. **careth for**. Mt +6:25g. **that belong to the Lord**. Gr. of the Lord, *as* ver. 34. **please**. Ro 8:8. 1 Th 2:15. 4:1.

33. **careth**. Ne 5:1-5. Lk 12:22. 1 Th 4:11, 12. 1 T 5:8. **world**. Gr. *kosmos*, Mt +4:8. **how**. ver. 3. 1 S 1:4-8. Ep *5:25-33. Col 3:19. 1 P 3:7.

34. **careth**. Mt *5:14-16. Lk 2:36, 37. *10:39-42. 2 C 7:11, 12. 8:16. 11:28. 1 T 3:5. 5:5. T 3:8. **both**. 1 C *6:20. Ro 6:13. +*12:1, 2. Ph 1:20. 1 Th +*5:23. **spirit**. ∫121A3, Mt +27:50. **she that**. Lk 10:40-42. **world**. Gr. *kosmos*, Mt +4:8. **how**. Pr 31:12.

35. **profit**. 1 C 10:33. Ac 20:20. **cast a snare**. This is an allusion to the *Retiarius* among the Romans, who carried a small casting net, *rete*, which he endeavored to throw over his adversary's head. ver. 2, 5-9, 28, 36. Pr 6:5. 22:25. Mt 19:12. **comely**. ver. 36. Ro *13:13. Ep 5:3. Ph √4:8, 9. 1 T 1:10. T 2:3. **attend upon**. lit. with a view to *assiduousness* unto the Lord. 1 C 9:13g. Jsh +*14:8. **without distraction**. ver. 33, 34. Lk +*8:14. *10:40-42. +*21:34.

36. **But if**. ∫184A, 1 C +15:2. **behaveth**. 1 C 13:5. **his virgin**. Some interpret this of a man's continuing in a state of celibacy, and render *parthenos* not a *virgin*, but *virginity*; but such a construction of the original appears without example. It appears most obvious to explain it of a parent, or guardian, who had the charge of a virgin (Col 2:11n); and Kypke has shown that *teen parthenon autou* is an elegant phrase for *his virgin daughter*. **if she**. ∫184C, Mt +4:9. **the flower**. 1 S 2:33. **and need**. ver. 9, 37. **he sinneth not**. ver. 28. **let them**. Ge 29:18.

37. **standeth**. Da +*1:8. Hg 2:18. **stedfast**. 1 C √15:58. Ro *14:5. Col 1:23.

38. **then**. ver. 28. **doeth well**. ver. 2. He +*13:4. **doeth better**. ver. 1, 8, 26, 32-34, 37. He ◐+*13:4.

39. **wife**. ver. 10, 11, 15. Ro 7:2, 3. **but if**. ∫184C, Mt +4:9. **be dead**. Gr. fallen asleep. Mt +27:52. **to whom**. Nu 36:6. **she will**. Ge 24:+*57, *58. **only in**. ver. 22. 1 C 9:1, 2. 11:11. *15:58. 16:19. Ge 6:2. Dt 7:3, 4. Jsh 23:12. Ml 2:11. 2 C √6:14-16.

40. **she**. ver. 1, 8, 26, 35. **if she**. ∫184C, Mt +4:9. **my judgment**. ver. +6. **I think**. Rather, "I judge (or consider) also that I have the Spirit of God;" for *dokein* is frequently used to express not what is doubtful, but what is *true* and *certain*. "Think" implies the certainty of assured belief (1 C 10:12. Lk 1:3. 10:36. 12:40. 17:9. 22:24. Jn √5:39. Ac 15:25, 28, 34. 26:9). ver. 25. 1 C 4:9. 9:1-3. *14:36, 37. 2 C 10:8-10. 12:11. 1 Th 4:8. 2 P 3:15, 16. **Spirit**. Gr. *pneuma*, ∫121A1, Lk +1:17n. "Spirit of God" (*pneuma theou*), i.e. Divine spirit, Divine power, Divine inspiration. It refers to the gift of inspiration which he had, and not the giver (E. W. Bullinger, *The Giver and His Gifts*, p. 125).

1 CORINTHIANS 8

In respect of things offered to idols; humble "love" is preferable to that "knowledge which puffeth up," 1-3. We know that idols are nothing; for we worship only one God, through one Lord and Mediator, 4-6; yet this knowledge, and the liberty connected with it, may be so used as to enfeeble or stumble weak believers, 7-11. In this case we sin against Christ, 12. The apostle would rather for ever abstain from meat, than stumble a weak brother, 13.

1. **touching**. ver. 4, 7, *10. 1 C *10:19-22, 28. Nu 25:2. Ac *15:10, 19, 20, +29. *21:25. Re *2:14, 20. **we know**. Gr. *oida*, Jn +8:55n. **we all**. ∫108B. Idiom B825. *All* often denotes *the greater part*. See *∫171A, Ex +9:6, and related note and figures listed at √∫171B, Ge +24:10. For another instance of this idiom see 1 C 11:2. ver. 2, 4, 7, 11. 1 C *1:5. 4:10. 10:15. *13:2. *14:20. *15:34. Ro *14:14, 22. Col *2:18. **have knowledge**. Gr. *gnosis*, Jn +8:55n. ver. 7, 10. Ro +15:14. **Knowledge**. 1 C 4:18. 5:2, 6. *13:4. Is *5:21. *47:10. Ro 11:25. *12:16. 14:3, 10. **puffeth up**. 1 C +4:6. **but charity**. 1 C *13:4-13. Ep *4:16. Ja *3:13-18. **edifieth**. Ro +14:19. *15:1, 2.

2. **if**. ∫184A, 1 C +15:2. 1 C 3:18. Pr 26:12. 30:2-4. Je +*8:8, 9. Ro 11:25. Ga 6:3. 1 T 1:5-7. 6:3, 4. **he knoweth**. Gr. *oida*, Jn +8:55n. **he knoweth**. Gr. *ginosko*, Jn +8:55n. 1 C *13:8, 9, 12. 1 T 6:3, 4. **to know**. Gr. *ginosko*, Jn +8:55n.

3. **But if**. ∫184A, 1 C +15:2. **love**. 1 C 2:9. Ro +*8:28. Ja 1:12. *2:5. 1 P 1:8. 1 J *4:19, 21. 5:2, 3. **is known**. Gr. *ginosko*, Jn +8:55n. 1 C 13:12. Ex *33:12, 17. Ps +*1:6. 17:3. +*40:17. 139:1, 2. Je 1:5. Na *1:7. Mt 6:32. *7:23. Jn 10:14. *17:3. 21:17. Ro +*8:29. +*11:2. Ga 4:9. 2 T √2:19. Re 2:9, 13, 19. 3:8, 9, 15, 16.

4. **those things**. ver. 1, 7, 10. Ac +15:29. **we know**. 1 C 10:19, 20. Ps 115:4-8. Is 41:24. 44:8, 9. Je 10:14. 51:17, 18. Hab 2:19, 20. Ac 14:15. 19:26. **is nothing**. Je +*8:19. 14:22. Jon +*2:8. **world**. Gr. *kosmos*, Mt +4:8. 1 C 10:26. **there is**. ver. *6. Dt 3:24. *4:35, 39. +*6:4. *32:39. Ps 86:10. Is 37:16, 20. 44:6, 8, 24. 45:5, 14. 46:5-9. Je 10:10. Mk 12:29. Ga 4:8. Ep

4:6. 1 T *1:17. 2:5. Ja +2:19. Ju *25. **but one**. Is +*37:16. Jn 20:17.

5. **that**. Dt 10:17. Je 2:11, 28. 11:13. Da 5:4. Jn 10:34, 35. Ga 4:8. 2 Th 2:4. **gods many**. Ac 17:16.

6. **one God**. T#210. See on ver. *4. Dt 4:35. +√6:4. 32:39. 2 S 7:22. 2 K 19:15. Ne 9:6. Is +*37:20. 44:6, 8. *45:5. Jon 1:9. Ml 1:10. +2:10 (T#960‡). Mk +*12:32. Jn +*10:30, ◐+*33. √14:9, 10. *17:3. 20:17. Ac +1:4. Ep 1:3. 3:14. *4:6. 1 T 1:17. 2 T *2:5. Ja 2:19. 1 P +*2:3n. **the Father**. Dt 32:6. Ml 2:10. Mt 23:9. Ro *3:29. Ep √4:6. He 12:9. 1 J 5:7. **of whom**. Ac *17:28. Ro +11:36. Ep 4:6. **and we**. Jn 14:20. *17:21-23. **in him**. *or,* for him. 1 C 6:13. **and one Lord**. 1 C 1:2. +*12:3. Ge ◐+* 19:24n. Mt +*11:27. *28:18. Jn *5:20-29. +13:13. 17:23. Ac *2:36. 5:31. +√10:26. Ro *10:9. Ep 1:20-23. 4:5. Ph *2:9-11. Col *1:16, 17. 1 T *2:5, 6. 1 P 1:21. Re 1:18. **by whom**. Ro 5:11. Re 5:9, 10. **all things**. Col 1:17. **and we by**. Jn +1:3. Col 1:6, 16. He 1:2, 3.

7. **there**. 1 C 1:10, 11. **that knowledge**. ver. 1, 10. **with**. Rather, as Dr. Doddridge renders, "with *consciousness* of (some religious regard to) the idol;" as *suneideesis*, and formerly *conscience*, also imports. ver. 9, 10. 1 C 10:25, 27, 28, 29. Ro *14:14, 22, 23. 2 C +1:12.

8. **meat**. 1 C 6:13. Ro *14:17. Col 2:20-23. He 13:9. **if**. √184C, Mt +4:9. **are we the better**. *or,* have we the more. **are we the worse**. *or,* have we the less. lit. lack, or come short. Ro 3:23.

9. **take**. ver. 10. 1 C 10:23, 24, 29. Mt 18:6, 7, 10. Lk 17:1, 2. Ro 14:20, 21. Ga 5:13. 1 P 2:16. 2 P 2:19. **liberty**. *or,* power. 1 C 9:4, 5, 6, 12, 18g. **a stumblingblock**. 1 C 10:32. Le 19:14. Is 57:14. Ezk 14:3. 44:12. Ro 9:32, 33. 14:13-15, 20. Ga 5:13. 1 P 2:8. Re 2:14. **weak**. ver. 12. 1 C 9:22. Is 35:3. Ro 14:+1, 2. 15:1. 2 C 11:21.

10. **For if**. √184C, Mt +4:9. **which hast**. ver. 1, 2. **sit**. 1 C 10:20, 21. Nu 25:2. Jg 9:27. Am 2:8. **knowledge**. Gr. *gnosis*, Jn +8:55n. ver. 1, 7. **shall not**. 1 C 10:28, 29, 32. Ro 14:14, 23. **emboldened**. Gr. edified. √27B, Le +20:9. Bengel notes (*Word Studies*, vol. 2, p. 937) that *Antiphrasis* is a form of Irony, when we say by denying what should have been affirmed. But an expression is generally so called, which signifies the contrary of what is stated: 1 C 8:10, "Shall not the conscience—be edified," Gr. *oikodomeetheesetai*, "to eat," etc. Whereas the meaning is, *shall be instigated* (to do something bad). ver. 1.

11. **shall**. ver. 13. 1 C 10:33. 11:1. Ro 14:15, 20, 21. 15:1-3. **perish**. Gr. *apollumi*, Mt +2:13.

12. **when**. Ge 20:9. 44:22. Ex 32:21. 1 S 2:25. 19:4, 5. 24:11. Mt 18:21. **the brethren**. Jn +21:23. Ep 6:23. **and wound**. Zc 2:8. Mt 18:6. Mk 9:42. Lk 17:1, 2. **conscience**. ver. 7. **ye sin against**. 1 C 12:12. Ex 16:8. Mt 12:49, 50. 18:10, 11. *25:40, 45. Lk 10:16. Ac 9:4, 5.

13. **if meat**. √184A, 1 C +15:2. 1 C 6:12. 9:12, 19-23. 10:32, 33. 11:1. 13:5. Ro 14:13, 21. 2 C 11:29. 2 Th 3:8, 9. **to offend**. Mt +*17:27. **I will**. Ro 14:21. 2 C 6:3. 11:29. **world**. Gr. *aion*, Mt +6:13.

1 CORINTHIANS 9

St. Paul asserts and proves his apostolical authority, 1-3; and shows that the ministers of the gospel have a right to marry; and, with their families, to be supported by the people, 4-14; yet, he had not availed himself of this right; and had in many things waved the exercise of his liberty, in order to promote the salvation of souls, 15-23. Alluding to the conduct of the contenders in the public games, he proposes to them the example of his own exceeding earnestness in securing the incorruptible crown, 24-27.

1. **Am I not**. ver. 2, 3. 1 C 1:1. 15:8, 9. Ac *9:15. *13:2. 14:4, 14. 22:14, 15. *26:17, 18. Ro 1:+1, 5. 11:13. 2 C 10:7. 11:5. 12:11, 12. Ga 1:1, 15-17. 2:7, 8. 1 Th 2:6. 1 T 2:7. 2 T 1:11. T 1:1-3. Re 2:2. **am I not free**. ver. *19, 21. 1 C 10:29. Ga 2:4. 4:12. *5:1. **have**. 1 C 15:8. Ac *9:3, 5, 17. 18:9. *22:6-8, 14-21. 23:11. 26:16-18. **are**. 1 C +3:6. *4:14, 15. Ac 18:8-11. 2 C 6:1. **in the Lord**. 1 C +7:39.

2. **If**. √184A, 1 C +15:2. **for the seal**. Jn +*6:27. 2 C 3:1-3. *12:12. **apostleship**. Ac 1:25. Ro 1:5. Ga 2:8. **in the Lord**. 1 C +7:39.

3. **answer**. Ac 22:1. 25:16. 2 C +7:11. Ph 1:7, 17. 2 T 4:16g. **to them**. 1 C 14:37. 2 C 10:7, 8. 12:16-19. 13:3, 5, 10. **examine**. 1 C +2:14.

4. **Have we**. ver. 7-14. Mt *10:10. Lk *10:7. Ga *6:6. 1 Th 2:6, 9. 2 Th 3:8, 9. 1 T √5:17, 18. **power**. Rather, *authority*, or *right*, as *exousia*, from *exesti*, it is *possible* or *lawful*, signifies. Power is only the ability to do a thing; whereas the apostle means a *right* to do what he is speaking of, and at their expense. 1 C 8:9g. **drink**. √63C, Ge +25:32. Supply by ellipsis, (at the expense of the church).

5. **Have we**. 1 C 7:7. **power**. ver. 4n. **to lead**. 1 T 3:2. 4:3. T 1:6. He +*13:4. **a sister**. 1 C 7:15, 39. SS 4:9, 10, 12. 5:1, 2. Ro 16:1. 1 T 5:2. **wife**. *or,* woman. *adelpheen gunaikeen;* which cannot be rendered *a sister, a woman,* without the most unmeaning tautology, as a *sister* must be a *woman,* and the latter would be wholly redundant, unless it were intended to show the relation in which she stood,—that of a wife, according to the general acceptation of the word. It is also possible to understand the expression to mean "a wife that is a believer," as in the R.V. **apostles**. 1 C +12:28. **the brethren**. Mt 12:46-50. +*13:55. Mk +*6:3. Lk 6:15. Jn 2:12. Ac 1:14. Ga 1:19. **Cephas**. 1 C 1:12. Mt *8:14. Mk 1:30. Jn +1:42.

6. **Barnabas**. Ac +4:36. 11:22. +12:25. 13:1, 2, 50. 14:12. 15:36, 37. **have**. 1 C 4:11, 12. Ac *18:3. 20:34, 35. 1 Th 2:9. 2 Th *3:7-9.

7. **Who**. √85C, Ge +18:14. **goeth**. 2 C *10:4, 5. 1 T 1:18. 6:12. 2 T 2:3, 4. 4:7. **at his own**. 1 C *9:13, 14. **charges**. A. T. Robertson notes, "To give proof of his right to receive pay for preaching Paul uses the illustrations of the soldier (ver. 7), the husbandman (ver. 7), the shepherd (ver. 7), the ox treading out the grain (ver. 8), the ploughman (ver. 10), the priests in the temple (ver. 13), proof enough in all conscience, and yet not enough for some churches who even today starve their pastors in the name of piety" (*Word Pictures*, vol. 4, pp. 143, 144). Paul has used illustrations from human life, from Old Testament Scripture, and from the teaching of Christ himself in the New Testament in his argument (ver. 14n). His plea for adequate support (1 T √5:17) was not for himself, though by right he had full title to such, and his plea included support for a minister's wife and family (ver. 5). Lk 3:14. Ro 6:23. 2 C 11:8g. **planteth**. 1 C 3:6-8. Dt 20:6. Pr 27:18. SS 8:12. **or**. Je 23:2, 3. Mt *9:36-38. Jn

*21:15-17. Ac +*20:28. 1 P *5:2. **eateth not of the milk**. Pr 27:27. Is 7:22.

8. **as**. 1 C 7:40. Ro +3:5. 6:19. 1 Th √2:13. 4:8. **or**. 1 C 14:34. Is +*8:20. Ro 3:31.

9. **law of Moses**. Jn +7:23. **Thou**. Dt ▶25:4. 1 T 5:18. **Doth**. Nu 22:28-35. Dt 5:14. Ps 104:27. *145:15, 16. 147:8, 9. Jon=4:11. Mt √6:26-30. Lk 12:24-28. **for oxen**. ∫63A4, 1 K +3:22. By ellipsis, supply "(only) for oxen?"

10. **For**. Mt 24:22. Ro +4:24. +*15:4. 2 C 4:15. 2 T +√3:16. **that ploweth**. 1 C 3:9. Lk 17:7, 8. Jn 4:35-38. 2 T 2:6.

11. **If we**. ∫184E, Lk +17:6. ∫184A, 1 C +15:2. **sown**. ver. 14. Ml 3:8, 9. Mt 10:10. Ro √15:27. Ga √6:6. **spiritual**. Ro +1:11g. **a great**. 2 K +*5:13. 2 C 11:15. **if we**. ∫184A, 1 C +15:2.

12. **If**. ∫184A, 1 C +15:2. **others**. 2 C 11:20. **this power**. ver. 4n. **over**. ∫181E, Ge +3:24. **are not**. ver. 2. 1 C 4:14, 15. **Nevertheless**. ver. 15, 18. Ac 18:3. 20:31-34. 2 C 7:2. *11:7-10. 12:13, 14. 1 Th *2:5-9. 2 Th √3:8, 9. 3 J 7. **but suffer**. 1 C 4:11, 12. 6:7. 13:7. 1 Th 3:1, 5g. **hinder**. Ge 24:56. Ne 4:8. Lk 11:52. Ro 15:22. 2 C 6:3. 11:12. **gospel of Christ**. Ro +15:19.

13. **know**. 1 C +6:2. **they**. 1 C 10:18. Le 6:16-18, 26. 7:6-8, 31-34. Nu 5:9, 10. *18:8-20. Dt 10:9. *18:1-8. 1 S 2:28. **live**. *or*, feed. Ne 10:37-40. Ml 3:8-10. **wait at**. 1 C 7:35g. He 13:10. **the altar are**. Le=10:12, 13. Dt 18:3.

14. **the Lord**. Robertson notes that "Evidently Paul was familiar with the words of Jesus in Mt 10:10; Lk 10:7f. either in oral or written form. He has made his argument for the minister's salary complete for all time" (*Word Pictures*, vol. 4, p. 146). **ordained**. See on ver. 4. Mt *10:10. Lk *10:7. Ga *6:6. 1 T √5:17. **they which preach**. ver. +11. **should live**. ver. +4. Mt 10:10. Lk 8:3. 10:1-7. Ac 16:15, 34. 28:14. Ga *6:6, 7. He *13:16.

15. **I have**. See on ver. 12. 1 C 4:12. Ac 8:3. 20:34. 1 Th 2:9. 2 Th 3:8. **neither**. 2 C 11:9-12. 12:13-18. **for**. Mt 18:6. Ac 20:24. Ph 1:20-23. **my glorying**. 2 C 1:14. 11:10. Ph 1:26. **void**. 1 C +1:17.

16. **For though**. ∫184C, Mt +4:9. **I have**. Ro 4:2. 15:17. **for necessity**. Je 1:17. 20:7, 9. Am 3:8. 7:15. Ac 4:20. *9:6, 15. 26:16-20. Ro 1:14. Ep 6:20. **laid upon**. Ezk 3:14. **woe**. Jb 10:15. Is 6:5. Je 20:9. Mi 7:1. Lk 9:62. Col 4:17. **if I**. ∫184C, Mt +4:9. Ac +*4:20.

17. **if I**. ∫184A, 1 C +15:2. 1 Ch +*28:9. 29:5, 9, 14. Ne 11:2. Is 6:8. 2 C 8:12. Phm 14. 1 P *5:2-4. **willingly**. ∫111, Ge +18:27. Paul means *gratuitously*; but lessens the wording, so as to increase his meaning, by the figure *Meiosis*. **have a reward**. ∫125, Jb +22:6. "If I do this thing willingly (*ekon*, without wages) I have a reward (*misthon*, wages)." This is the figure *Oxymoron*, a wise saying that seems foolish. 1 C 3:+8, 14. Mt 10:41. Jn 4:36g. **but if**. ∫184A, 1 C +15:2. **against**. Ex 4:13, 14. Je 20:9. Ezk 3:14. Jon 1:3. 4:1-3. Ml 1:10. **dispensation**. or, stewardship. See on ver. 16. 1 C 4:1. Mt +*24:45. Lk +*12:42. 16:2-4, *10. √17:10. Ga 2:7. Ep 1:10. 3:2-9. Ph 1:17. Col 1:25. 1 Th 2:4. 1 T 1:4g, 11-13. **committed unto**. Ga 2:7. Ph 1:16. 1 P 4:10.

18. **my reward**. ver. +17. **when**. See on ver. 6, 7. 1 C 10:33. 2 C 4:5. 11:7-9. 12:13-18. 1 Th 2:6. 2 Th 3:8, 9. **without charge**. 2 C 11:7. 12:13. **that I abuse**. 1 C 7:31. *8:9. Ro 14:15. **my power**. ver. 4n, +12. **in the gospel**. Ro 1:9. 2 C 8:18. 10:14.

19. **I be**. ver. +1. Ga *5:1. **I made**. 1 C 10:33. Mt 20:26-28. Jn 13:14, 15. Ro 1:14. 15:2. 2 C 4:5. Ga *5:13. **all**. *∫171A, Ex +9:6. **that**. ver. 20-22. 1 C 7:16. Pr +*11:30. 1 T +*4:16. 2 T 2:10. Ja +*5:19, 20. 1 P 3:1. **gain**. Mt 18:15. 1 P 3:1. **the more**. 1 C 10:5. 15:6. 2 C 2:6. 4:15. 9:2. Ph 1:14. He 7:23.

20. **unto**. Ac *16:3. +*17:2, 3. *18:18. *21:20-26. **gain**. ver. +19. **are under**. Ro 3:19. 6:14, 15. Ga 4:5, 21. 5:18.

21. **them**. Ac 2:23. 15:28. 16:4. 21:25. Ro +*2:12, 14. Ga √2:3-5, 11-14. 3:2. **not**. 1 C 7:19-22. Ps 119:32. Mt 5:17-20. Ro 7:22, 25. 8:4. 13:8-10. Ga 5:13, 14, 22, 23. Ep 6:1-3. 1 Th 4:1, 2. T 2:2-12. He 8:10. **under the law**. 1 C +7:22.

22. **To the weak**. 1 C 8:13. Ro +14:1. *15:1. 2 C 11:29. Ga *6:1. **I am**. 1 C √10:33. Ro +15:2. **all**. *∫171A, Ex +9:6. **that I might by**. See on ver. 19. 1 C 7:16. Ro +11:14. **save some**. 1 C *10:33. Pr *11:30. Mt *4:19. Ga 1:10. Col 2:6, 7.

23. **for**. ver. 12. Mk *8:35. 2 C 2:4. Ga 2:5. 2 T 1:8. *2:10. Phm 13. **that**. ver. 25-27. 1 C 10:24. 2 T 2:6. He 3:1, 14. 1 P 5:1. 1 J 1:3. **partaker**. Ro +11:17.

24. **Know ye not**. 1 C +6:2. **they which run**. The Apostle here refers to the *Isthmian* games, so called from being celebrated on the isthmus of Corinth. Ho 12:10. Ph *3:13, 14. He *12:1. **run in**. Ps 19:5. Ec 9:11. Je +*12:5. **race**. ∫121.O, Ge +28:22. **the prize**. Ph 3:14. Col 2:18. **So run**. ∫56, Is +14:16. Sermocinatio; or, Dialog. When the speaker brings forward another as speaking, and uses his words, adapting them to the object in view. Here Paul brings forward and uses that incitement which the trainers and spectators in the public contests usually employed. ver. 26. Ac 20:24. Ga 2:2. 5:7. Ph 2:13, 16. 3:14. 2 T 4:7, 8. He *12:1. Ja 1:12. Re 3:11. **obtain**. Ro 9:30. Ph 3:12, 13g.

25. **striveth**. ∫24B, Ge +23:16. Lk *13:24. Ep √6:12-18. 1 T*6:12. 2 T 2:5. √4:7. He 12:4. Ju +*3. **temperate**. T#721. 1 C 7:9g. Ro +14:21 (T#368). Ga 5:22-24. Ph +3:19 (T#199). T +1:8. 2:2. 2 P *1:5, 6. **crown**. Ja +*1:12. **but**. 1 C 15:54. 2 T √4:8. He 12:28. Ja 1:12. 1 P +*1:4. *5:4. Re 2:10. 3:11. 4:4, 10.

26. **so run**. ver. +24. **not**. 2 C 5:1, 8. Ph 1:21. 2 T √1:12. 2:5. He *4:1. 1 P 5:1. 2 P +*1:10, 11. **uncertainly**. 1 C 14:8. 1 T 6:17g. **so fight**. Gr. box. Mt 11:12. Lk *13:24. Ep 6:12. Col 1:29. He 12:4. **beateth the air**. 1 C 14:9.

27. **I keep under**. or, buffet. Gr. bruise. ver. 25. 1 C 4:11, 12. *6:12, 13. 8:13. Lk 18:5g. Ro *8:13. 2 C *6:4, 5. 11:27. Col *3:5. 1 Th *4:4. 2 T *2:22. 1 P *2:11. **and**. Ro 6:18, 19. **bring it into bondage**. *doulagogo*, "I drag off as a slave," as the victors did their conquered antagonists. **lest**. 1 C √10:12. 13:1-3. Ps *50:16. Mt *7:21-23. Lk *12:45-47. *13:26, 27. Ac *1:25. Ga *2:2. Ph √2:12, 13, 16. √3:12. 2 T ●4:7, 18. 1 P √4:18. 2 P *2:15. **I myself**. SS 1:6. **a castaway**. *adokimos*, one *disapproved* by the judge of the games, as not having fairly deserved the prize. Je 6:30. Lk *9:25. Ac 1:25. Ro +*1:28. 2 C *13:5, 6, 7. 2 T 3:8. T 1:16g. He *6:8.

1 CORINTHIANS 10

When Israel came out of Egypt, they all shared in those things, which were sacramental signs of spiritual blessings; yet most of them died in the wilderness, 1-5. Their example is recorded as a warning to professed

Christians, not to imitate their crimes, 6-12. God will not suffer his servants to be tempted, so as to have no way of escape, 13. They must flee from idolatry, 14. They cannot have fellowship with Christ and believers, in the Lord's supper; and with idolaters, in those sacrifices which are offered to devils, 15-22. In the use of things lawful, the good of others should be consulted, 23-30; that all may be done to the glory of God, and without giving any occasion of falling to men, 31-33.

1. **I would not.** ✓175B, Ge +21:16. 1 C ◐11:3. 12:1. 14:38. Ro 1:13. 11:25. 2 C 1:8. Col ◐2:1. 1 Th 4:13. **that all.** Ex 10:26. **our fathers.** Jn 4:20. Ro 4:11. Ga 3:29. **were under.** 1 C 9:20g. Ps 105:39. Jn 1:48g. Ac 4:12g. Ga 4:21g. 5:18g. **the cloud.** Ex *13:21, 22. 14:19, 20, 24. 40:34, 38. Nu 9:15-22. 10:34. 14:14. Dt 1:33. 2 Ch +*5:13. Ne 9:12, 19. Ps 78:14. 99:7. 105:39. Is 4:5. **all passed.** Ex *14:19-22, 29. 15:19. Nu 33:8. Jsh 4:11, 23. Ne 9:11. Ps 66:6. 68:22. 77:16-20. 78:13, 53. 106:7-11. 114:3-5. 136:13-15. Is 63:13. 68:11-13. He 11:29. Re 15:2, 3.

2. **baptized.** Gr. *baptizo*, Mt +3:6. ✓96A3, Lk +2:5. This, of course, is a metaphorical baptism; there is no possible reference to immersion here. In the historical account, the Israelites passed through the sea on dry ground; only the Egyptians were immersed. Neither were the Israelites immersed in the cloud; the cloud remained behind the Israelites to separate and protect them from the pursuing Egyptians. These considerations entirely sustain James W. Dale's conclusion, "Whatever is capable of thoroughly changing the character, state, or condition of any object, is capable of baptizing that object; and by such change of character, state, or condition does, in fact, baptize it" (*Classic Baptism*, p. 354). Dale amplifies this conclusion thus: "Whatever *act* is capable of thoroughly changing the character, state, or condition, of any object, *by placing it in a state of physical intusposition*, is capable of baptizing that object; and whatever *influence* is capable of thoroughly changing the character, state, or condition, of any object, *by pervading it and making it subject to its own characteristic*, is capable of baptizing that object; and by such changes of character, state, or condition, these acts and influences do, in fact, baptize their objects" (*Judaic Baptism*, p. 57). In what sense is this historical event a baptism? There was no administrator of baptism; was there then self baptism? If so, *bapto* not *baptizo* is the proper word (Carson, p. 30). There was no modal act of dipping. The only act was marching. There was no momentary covering of the dipped object; it lasted from the evening until the morning watch. There was no faith in the candidates for this baptism: the Scripture shows the multitude rampant with unbelief. In this very remarkable baptism is exhibited "the most magnificent spectacle of infant baptism that the rolling ages have ever witnessed" (Dale, *Judaic Baptism*, p. 300). 1 C 1:13-16. Ex 14:31. Jn 9:28, 29. He 3:2, 3. **unto Moses.** or, into Moses. Israel was baptized *into* Moses, and not *unto* Moses, to bring them thoroughly under his influence, subject to his leadership in his divine mission, attested to by the miracle. Dale concludes, "the baptism of Israel into Moses expresses their full subjection to his controlling influence" (*Christic Baptism*, p. 310). In this class of baptism, baptism has reference to the influence which results, "And the people believed the Lord and

his servant Moses" (see Dale, *Judaic Baptism*, pp. 306-314). Ex ✓14:31. Dt 18:15. Mt 28:19, 20. Jn 5:46. Ga +*3:27. **in the cloud.** or, by the cloud. *en*, "in," expresses agency, and is better rendered "by," as Ne ✓9:12. Ps ✓77:20. 78:14, where the Greek Septuagint uses *en*, rendered "by" and "with" in connection with this very miracle. **in the sea.** or, by the sea. The Israelites were not "in the sea," but the dry sea bed, yet here Paul again is speaking instrumentally, not locally, best rendered "by the sea," expressing the agency required for the baptism into Moses. If taken at all in a local sense, "in the cloud and in the sea" must be transferred in its reference from the Israelites to the power of Jehovah, which certainly was by miracle *in* them. By means of this double miracle the Israelites were influenced to fully acknowledge the often doubted and questioned divine mission of Moses, justifying the declaration that they were now baptized into him (see Dale, *Christic Baptism*, pp. 295, 296). Similarly, our baptism into Christ signifies our submission to Him as Lord, as being made fully subject to Him (Ac +✓10:36. Ro ✓10:9).

3. **did all.** Ex *16:4, 15, 35. Dt 8:3. Ne *9:15, 20. Ps *78:23-25. 105:40. Jn *6:22-58. He *4:2. **spiritual.** Ro +1:11g. **meat.** Ps 78:25. 105:40. Jn 6:31.

4. **all drink.** Ex *17:6. Nu *20:11. Dt 8:15. Ps 78:15, 20. 105:41. Is *43:20. 48:21. *55:1. Jn *4:10, 14. *6:55. *7:37. Re 22:17. **same spiritual.** Ro +1:11g. **that spiritual.** Ro +1:11g. **followed them.** *or*, went with them. Dt 9:21. **that Rock.** 1 C 11:24, 25. Ge 40:12. 41:26. Is *53:5. Ezk 5:4, 5. Da 2:38. 7:17. Mt 13:38, 39. 16:18. *26:26-28. Ga 4:25. Col 2:17. He 10:1.

5. **with many.** 1 C 9:19g. Nu 24:11, 12, 28-35. *26:64, 65. Dt 1:34, 35. 2:15, 16. Ps 78:32-34. ch. 90, title, 7, 8. 95:11. 106:26. He 3:17. Ju *5. **not.** ✓175B, Ge +21:16. **pleased.** 1 C +1:21. **for they.** Ju +*5.

6. **these things.** ✓92C, Mt +2:15. ver. 11. Zp 3:6, 7. He 4:11. 1 P +5:3. 2 P 2:6. Ju *7. **examples.** Gr. figures. Ro 5:14. He 9:24. 1 P 3:21. **lust.** Nu *11:4, 31-34. Ps 78:18, 27-31. *95:7-11. 106:14, 15. He *4:11.

7. **be.** ver. 14, 20-22. 1 C 5:11. +*6:9. 8:7. Dt 9:12, 16-21. Ps 106:19, 20. 1 J +5:21. **as were.** Ex *32:4. Dt 9:16. Ne 9:18. Ps 106:19. Ac 7:41. **The people.** Ex *32:◐6-8, 17-19. **to play.** Jg 16:25. 2 S 6:5. Je 38:4.

8. **Neither let us.** 1 C +*6:9, 18. Nu *25:1, 5, 9. Ps 106:29. Ac +15:20. Re 2:14. **as some.** Nu 25:1. 31:16. **and fell.** Nu *25:9. Ps 106:29. **three and twenty thousand.** Both the LXX. and Hebrew texts have twenty-four thousand, but as both Moses and Paul were using round numbers, without intending to be mathematically exact in common speech, any number between the two amounts may be stated roundly as either the one or the other, as Hodge explains.

9. **tempt.** Ex *17:2, 7. ✓23:20, 21. Nu *21:5, 6. Dt 6:16. Ps 78:18, 41, 56. 95:9. 106:14. Ac +15:10. He 3:8-11. 10:28-30. **Christ.** Ps ✓78:17, 35, 56. Ac *7:38. While some MSS. read "Lord" or "God" here, "Christ," as being the more difficult and less likely expression is undoubtedly correct. That is to say, the probability that an original reading of "Lord" or "God" would be changed to "Christ" is highly unlikely, but that the more difficult reading "Christ" would be changed to "Lord" or "God" is very probable. **and were.** Nu 21:6. Dt 8:15. Jn 3:14. **destroyed.** Gr. *apollumi*, Mt +2:13. Ju 5.

10. **murmur.** Ex 15:24. 16:2-9. 17:2, 3. Nu +*11:1. *14:2, 27-30, 36. 16:41. Dt 1:27. Jsh 9:18. Ps 106:25. Ph 2:14. Ju +*16. **were.** Nu 14:29-37. 16:46-49. **destroyed.** Gr. *apollumi*, Mt +2:13. **destroyer.** Ex *12:23. 2 S *24:16. 1 Ch 21:15. 2 Ch 32:21. Ps 78:49. Is 37:36. Mt 13:39-42. Ac 12:23. 2 Th 1:7, 8. He 11:28. Re 16:1.

11. **these things.** ⌐92C, Mt +2:15. **ensamples.** *or*, types. ver. 6mg. **written for.** T#1050. 1 C 9:10. Ps 19:11. Ro +4:23. +*15:4. **admonition.** Ep 6:4. T 3:10. **upon.** 1 C 7:29. Ro +13:11. Ph 4:5. He 10:25, 37. 1 J *2:18. **the ends.** Mt +*13:39. He 9:26. 1 P *4:7. **world.** Gr. *aion*, Mt +6:13.

12. **let.** ⌐138C, Ge +22:14. **thinketh he standeth.** 1 C 4:6-8. 8:2. 2 Ch 26:15, 16. Pr *16:18. *28:11, 14. Mt *26:33, 34, 40, 41. Ro *11:20. 2 C 1:24. Re 3:17, 18. **lest he fall.** Da +*11:35. 1 T 1:19. 2 P +*3:17. Ju ◐+*24.

13. **hath.** Je +*12:5. Mt 24:21-24. Lk 11:4. 22:31, 46. 2 C 11:23-28. Ep 6:12, 13. He 11:35-38. 12:4. Ja 5:10, 11. 1 P 1:6, 7. 5:8, 9. Re 2:10. +*3:10. **but.** 1 C +*1:9. Dt 7:9. Ps +*36:5. 89:33. Is 11:5. 25:1. 49:7. Je +*29:11. La 3:23. Ho 2:20. 1 Th 5:24. 2 Th √3:3. 2 T 2:11-13. He 6:18. 10:23. 11:11. 1 P 4:19. 1 J √1:9. Re 19:11. **common.** *or*, moderate. T#722. Ge 22:1, 2. Ga 4:14. He +*4:15. Ja 1:2, 3. **who.** Ex 3:17. Ps 125:3. Da +*3:17, 18. Lk 22:32. Jn √10:28-30. Ro +*8:28-39. 2 C *1:10. 12:8-10. 2 T *4:18. Ja *5:11. 1 P 1:5. 2 P +*2:9. **above that.** Ps *103:14. **make a way.** T#725. Ge 19:20, 21. Dt +8:2 (T#4). 1 S +2:7 (T#3). Ps +23:4 (T#6). 71:20. 124:7. 138:7. Je +*29:11. Lk 16:26. Ac 27:44. 2 C +4:17 (T#5). He 2:18. 13:7g. Ja 5:11. 2 P *9:2:9. Re *3:10. **to escape.** Lk +*21:36. Re +*3:10. **that ye.** Ps 125:3.

14. **my.** Ro 12:19. 2 C 7:1. 11:11. 12:15, 19. Ph 4:1. Phm 1. 1 P 2:11. **flee.** ver. 7, 20, 21. 2 C *6:17. 1 J +*5:21. Re 2:14. *13:8. +*21:8. *22:15.

15. **as to wise.** 1 C +4:10. *6:5. *8:1. 11:13. *14:20. Jb 34:2, 3. Pr +*1:5. 2 C 11:19. Ga 6:1. 1 Th *5:21. **judge.** ⌐14, Is +5:3. Lk 12:57. Ac 4:19.

16. **cup.** ⌐121J13, Je +49:12. ver. 21. 1 C *11:23-29. Ps 116:13. Mt 20:22, 23. *26:26-28. Mk 14:22-25. Lk 22:19, 20. Re 14:10. **bless.** Mt +14:19. Ep *1:3. **is it not.** ⌐85B, Ge +13:9. ⌐119, Ge +49:9. **the communion.** ver. 20. Ac 2:42g. **of the blood.** ver. 20. 1 C 1:9. √12:13. Ge 9:13. Jn *6:53-58. He +*3:14. 1 J *1:3, 6, 7. **The bread.** 1 C 11:23, 24. Le +=3:11. ==*21:6. =23:19. Mt 26:26. Mk 14:22. Lk 22:19. Ac 2:42, 46. 20:7, 11. **break.** ⌐108H4, Is +58:7. **is it not.** ⌐85B, Ge +13:9. ⌐119, Ge +49:9. **communion.** T#895. 1 C 12:13. SS 2:3, 4. 5:1. Is 25:6. Mt *26:26-28. Jn *6:54-57, 63.

17. **we being.** 1 C *12:12, 27. Ro *12:5. Ga *3:26-28. Ep 1:22, 23. 2:15, 16. 3:6. 4:12, 13, 25. Col 2:19. 3:11, 15. **one body.** 1 C *12:12, 13, 20. Ep 4:+*4, 16, 25. 5:30. Col 3:15. **that.** ver. 3, 4, 21. 1 C 11:26-28.

18. **Israel.** Ro 4:1, 12. 9:3-8. 2 C 11:18, 22. Ga 6:16. Ep 2:11, 12. Ph 3:3-5. **after the flesh.** Ro +1:3. *9:3-6. 2 C 11:18. **are.** 1 C 9:13. Le 3:3-5, 11. 7:11-17. Dt *12:27. 1 S 2:13-16. 9:12, 13. He 13:10.

19. **that the.** 1 C 1:28. 3:7. +*8:4. 13:2. Dt 32:21. Is 40:17. 41:29. 2 C 12:11. **that which.** 1 C +8:1.

20. **sacrifice.** Le 17:7. Dt *32:16, 17. 2 Ch 11:15. Ps *106:37-39. Is 13:21. 2 C 4:4. Re 9:20. **to devils.** Le +*17:7. **fellowship.** Is 44:11. 65:11.

21. **cannot drink.** ver. 16. 1 C 8:10. Dt *32:37, 38. 1 K 18:21. Mt 6:24. *12:30. 2 C 6:15-17. **the cup.** ⌐121J13, Je +49:12. **Lord's table.** Le=24:9. Ezk=44:16. Ml 1:7, 12. Ep=2:6.

22. **we provoke.** Ex +*20:5. *34:14. Dt 4:24. 6:15. *32:16, 17, 21. Jsh 24:19. Ps 78:58. Zp 1:18. Ro 10:19. **are.** Jb *9:4, 32. 40:9-14. Ec 6:10. Is 45:9. Ezk 22:14. He 10:31.

23. **things are lawful.** See on 1 C +*6:12. +8:9. Ro 14:15, 20. **edify.** 1 C 8:1. 14:3-5, 12, 17, 26, 40. Ro +*14:19. 15:1, 2. 2 C 12:19. Ep 4:29. 1 Th 5:11. 1 T 1:4.

24. **seek.** ver. 33. 1 C 9:19-23. 13:5. Ro +*15:1, 2. 2 C 12:14. Ph *2:4, 5, 21. **his own.** ⌐63A2, 2 S +6:6. Supply ellipsis, (advantage only). **another's.** ver. 29g. Ro +2:1.

25. **sold.** Ac +10:15. Ro 14:14. 1 T *4:4. T *1:15. **asking no.** 1 C +2:14g. **for.** ver. 27-29. 1 C 8:7. Ro 13:5. 2 C +1:12.

26. **the earth.** ver. 28. Ex 9:29. 19:5. Dt 10:14. Jb 41:11. Ps ◗24:1. 50:12. 89:11. 1 T 6:17. **the fulness.** Mk 6:43. 8:20g.

27. **If.** ⌐184A, 1 C +15:2. **bid.** 1 C 5:9-11. Lk 5:29, 30. 15:23. 19:7. **whatsoever.** Lk *10:7, 8. **asking no.** ver. 25. **for.** ver. +25. Ge 1:29. 2 C 1:12. 4:2. 5:11.

28. **But if.** ⌐184C, Mt +4:9. **eat.** See on 1 C *8:10-13. Ro 14:15. **for conscience.** ver. 25. **for the earth.** See on ver. 26. Ex 9:29. Dt 10:14. Ps 24:1. 115:16. Je 27:5, 6. Mt 6:31, 32.

29. **Conscience.** ⌐67, Ro +3:26. ver. +25. **not.** ver. 32. 1 C 8:9-13. Ro 14:15-21. **the other.** T#130. ver. +24g, 27-29. 1 C 8:10-13. Ro +2:1. *14:2-5. **why.** Ro 14:16. 2 C 8:21. 1 Th 5:22.

30. **For if.** ⌐184A, 1 C +15:2. **grace.** *or*, thanksgiving. Mt +*15:36. **evil spoken of.** Ro 3:8g. **for which.** Ro *14:6. 1 T √4:3, 4.

31. **Whether.** The apostle concludes the subject by giving them a general rule, sufficient to regulate every man's conscience and practice,—that whether they eat, or drink, or whatsoever they do, to do it all with an habitual aim to the glory of God; by considering his precepts, and the propriety, expediency, appearance, and tendency of their actions. **ye eat.** 1 C 7:34. Dt 12:7, 12, 18. Ne 8:16-18. Zc 7:5, 6. Lk 11:41. Col 3:17, 23. 1 P *4:11. **whatsoever.** 2 S 15:15. Jn 2:5. +*15:14. Col √3:17. **the glory.** Ro +*3:23.

32. **none.** ver. 33. 1 C +8:13. Ac +24:16. Ro √14:13. 2 C 6:3. Ph 1:10. **Jews.** Ge +*13:15. Mt 10:6. Ro +*9:4. 10:1. **Gentiles.** *or*, Greeks. Mt *10:5. 12:21. Ep *2:11-16. **the church of God.** 1 C 11:22. Ne 13:1. Ac +√20:28n. Ep *1:22, 23. 1 T 3:5, 15.

33. **I please.** ver. 24. See on 1 C 9:19-23. Ro +15:2, 3. 2 C 11:28, 29. 12:19. **not seeking.** ver. +24. **own profit.** 1 C 7:35. Ac 20:20.

1 CORINTHIANS 11

The apostle exhorts the Corinthians to imitate him, as he imitated Christ, 1. He praises them for observing his injunctions, 2. He gives directions concerning men and women prophesying, 3-16. He blames them for abuses in their religious assemblies; especially for their divisions, 17-19; and their profanation of the Lord's supper, 20-22; reminding them of the first institution of it; and showing the danger, and the painful effects arising from the partaking of it unworthily, 23-34.

1. **Be ye followers.** T#179. 1 C +*4:16. *10:33. Ex ❍*23:2. Mt 23:3. Ph 3:17. *4:9. 1 Th 1:6. 2 Th 3:9. He +*6:12. *13:7. Ja 5:10. 1 P 2:21. 3 J 11. **even.** Ro *15:2, 3. Ep 5:1, 2. Ph *2:4, 5.

2. **I praise.** ver. 17, 22. Pr 31:28-31. **that.** 1 C 4:17. 15:2. 1 Th 3:6. **all.** ∫108B, 1 C +8:1. **keep.** 1 C 7:17. Lk 1:6. +*11:28. 1 Th 4:1, 2. **ordinances.** *or*, traditions. Mk ❍*7:9. 2 Th *2:15. 3:6. **as I.** 1 C 7:17. 1 Th 4:1, 2. **delivered.** ver. 23. 1 C 15:3. Lk 1:2. Ac 16:4. 2 P 2:21. Ju +*3.

3. **I would.** 1 C +10:1. Col 2:1. **the head of every.** Ep 1:22, 23. 4:15. *5:23. Ph 2:10, 11. Col +*1:18. 2:10, 19. **is Christ.** Jn ❍16:23. 17:5. **head of the woman.** ∫18, Dt +28:4. 1 C 14:34. Ge *3:16. Ep *5:22-24. Col 3:18. 1 T ❍√2:11, 12. T 2:5. 1 P *3:1, 5, 6. **and the head.** ∫22A3. Anthropomorphism B873. Parts and members of man or of the human body are attributed to God: the *head* is spoken of Christ. Compare ∫22A3B, Ep +1:22. **of Christ.** 1 C *3:23. 15:24, 27, +*28. Is 49:3-6. 52:13. 55:4. 61:1-4. Mt +*10:32. *20:23. *28:18. Jn √3:34-36. *5:20-30. +*14:28. 17:2-5. Ep 1:20-22. Ph *2:7-11.

4. **or prophesying.** 1 C 12:10, +28. 14:1, etc. Ac +13:1. *15:32. **having.** ver. 14. 2 S 15:30. 19:4. **head covered.** T#1250. With his cap or turban on, "dishonoreth his head;" because the head being covered was a sign of subjection.

5. **But.** ∫77, Ex +3:19. **woman.** 1 C +*14:34, 35. Ex +*15:20n. Jg 4:4. 2 K 22:14. Ne 6:14. Ezk 13:17. **or prophesieth.** This proves women were allowed to pray and preach, but as specific directions pertaining to orderliness in the congregation do not begin until ver. 17, some interpreters, probably correctly, do not see this passage as authorizing women to preach or teach in a church meeting (See Alexander Strauch, *Biblical Eldership*, pp. 64, 72, note 10). Ex +*15:20n. Jl 2:28. Lk 2:36. Ac *2:17. *21:9. 1 C ❍+√14:34n. **uncovered.** Nu 5:18. Ru +*3:9. **shaven.** In the East, if a woman appear in public unveiled, she is immediately supposed to be deficient in modesty; and consequently she would dishonor her head, her *husband*, not only by apparently throwing off the sign of her subjection, but by appearing like those women who had their hair shorn off, or shaven, as the punishment of adultery; a custom which Tacitus informs us (Germ. 19), prevailed among the Germans. Some interpreters take this admonition literally, denying any limitation to the original cultural context was intended; others, probably more correctly, consider the admonition's specifics pertain to the then existing culture, but believe the principles underlying these admonitions are applicable for all time to culturally parallel or equivalent situations. Of necessity, there is a cultural modification of the Apostle's regulation when it is applied to wearing a hat or scarf instead of an Eastern veil (which covered the face, 2 C 3:13), a modification which can boast no Scriptural authority, and which negates the normative as opposed to the relative application of the commandment. Thus, whether a woman wears a covering in church is a matter of conscience, subjection to her husband's desire, the local spiritual authority, and her understanding of Scripture; but that she must not dress in the manner of a prostitute, if in her culture such persons have a distinctive dress, is undeniable. Contrast 1 C 14:34n. Dt 21:12, 13.

6. **For if.** ∫184A, 1 C +15:2. ∫164, 1 S +17:7. **not**

covered. Ru +*3:9. **let her also.** ∫96B, Nu +24:21. **but.** Nu 5:18. Dt 22:5. **be covered.** T#1251. ver. 13.

7. **he is the image.** 1 C 15:49. Ge *1:26, 27. 5:1. 9:6. Ps 8:6. 2 C 4:4. Ep 4:24. Col 3:10. Ja 3:9. **and glory.** ∫93A, Ge +1:26. By *Hendiadys*, glorious image. Two words used, but one thing meant. Ps 19:1. Jn 1:14. 17:22. Ro +3:23. 2 C 4:6. Ph 1:11. He 1:3. **but.** ver. 3. Ge 3:16. **the woman.** Pr 12:4.

8. **the man.** ∫25, Ge +4:4. Ge *2:21, 22. 1 T *2:13.

9. **the man.** ∫25, Ge +4:4. **for the man.** Ge *2:18, 20, 23, 24.

10. **power on.** *that is*, a covering in sign that she is under the power of her husband. *Exousia*, appears here to be used for the *sign* or *token* of being under *power* or *authority*, that is, *a veil*, as Theophylact, Oecumenius, and Photius explain; and so one MS. of the Vulgate, the Sixtine edition, and some copies of the Itala, have *velamen*. Ge 20:16. *24:64, 65. Nu=6:7n. Ru 3:+*9, 15n. **because.** Ps *138:1. Ec *5:6. Mt 18:10. Lk *15:7, 10. Ep 3:10. He *1:14. *12:1.

11. **neither is.** 1 C 7:10-14. 12:12-22. Ga +*3:28. **in the Lord.** 1 C 7:39.

12. **by the woman.** Jb *14:1. **but all.** 1 C 8:6. Pr 16:4. Ro +11:36. He 1:2, 3.

13. **Judge.** ∫14, Is +5:3. 1 C 10:15. Lk 12:57. Jn +*7:24. Ac 4:19.

14. **nature.** Ro *1:26. *2:14, 27. 11:21, 24. Ga 2:15. 4:8. Ep 2:3. **if a man.** ∫184A, Mt +4:9. 2 S *14:26. **it is.** 1 C 14:35. **a shame.** Because a proof of effeminacy and folly; and because it was considered as a mark of inferiority. It may also be remarked, that there were a set of wretched despicable beings, both at Rome and Corinth, called Pathics, who are said to have imitated the dress and manners of women. In more recent times, some men have worn long hair to identify themselves with a certain youthful subculture marked for its style of music, promiscuity, drug culture, defiance of authority, and rebellion against the surrounding culture.

15. **But if.** ∫184A, Mt +4:9. **a glory to her.** Or, an *honor* or *credit* to her; as indicating that she had done nothing to deprive her of it; and also showing that she did not object to wear it as a natural veil, and as an emblem of subjection. **covering.** *or*, veil.

16. **But if.** ∫184A, 1 C +15:2. ∫116. Metabasis; or, Transition B908. A passing from one subject to another, sometimes abruptly, but more usually when the speaker reminds his hearers or readers of what has been said, and only hints at what might be said, or remains to be said. Here, Paul only hints at the contentions of others; and then passes on, in verse 17, to the subject of the Lord's Supper. For other instances of this figure see 1 C 12:31. 15:12. He 6:1-3. But if any person puts himself forward as a defender of these points, let him know that we have no such custom either among the Jews or among the churches of Christ. 1 T 6:3, 4. **any man.** 1 C 14:37. 15:12. Ro 3:8. 2 C 3:1. 10:2, 12. 11:20, 21. Ga 1:7, 9. Col 2:√8n, 16. 2 Th 2:3. 3:10, 11. 1 T 1:3, 6. 6:3, 21. **seem.** 1 T 6:3, 4. Ja 1:26g. **such.** ver. 4, 5. Ac 21:21, 24. **the churches.** 1 C 7:17. 10:32. 14:33, 34. 16:1. 1 Th 2:14. 2 Th 1:4.

17. **I praise.** ver. 2, 22. Le 19:17. Pr 27:5. Ro 13:3. 1 P 2:14. **that ye.** ver. 20, 34. 1 C 14:23, 26. Is 1:13, 14. 58:1-4. Je 7:9, 10. He √10:25.

18. **I hear.** 1 C *1:10-12. 3:3. 5:1. 6:1. **divisions.** *or*, schisms. See on 1 C 1:10. 3:3.

19. **there must be**. T#243. Dt *13:1-3. 1 K 22:20-23. Jb 2:6, 7. Je 6:21. Ezk 3:20. +*14:10n. Mt 4:1. 18:7. Lk *17:1. Ac 20:30. 1 T 4:1, 2. 2 P *2:1, 2. **heresies**. *or*, sects. T#176. Ac 5:17. 15:5. 24:+5, 14. 26:5. 28:22. Ga 5:20. T 3:10g. 2 P 2:1. **which**. Dt 13:3. Lk 2:35. 2 C 13:5-7g. 1 J √2:19. **approved**. 2 C 10:18. 13:7. Ja +1:12. **made manifest**. 2 Ch √32:31.

20. **come together**. 1 C 14:23. Ac 20:7. **one place**. Le 23:5. Dt +*16:6. Phm +*2. **this is not to eat**. *or*, ye cannot eat. **the Lord's**. Le 23:5. Re 1:10g.

21. **in eating**. ver. 23-25. 1 C 10:16-18. **and one**. 2 P 2:13. Ju *12.

22. **have**. ver. 34. **or despise**. 1 C *10:32. 15:9. Ac +*20:28. 1 T 3:5, 15. **that have not**. *or*, that are poor. Pr 17:5. Ja *2:5, 6. **praise you not**. ver. 1, 17.

23. **I have received**. 1 C +*15:3. Dt 4:5. Mt +*28:20. Ga *1:1, 11, 12. 1 Th 4:2. **delivered**. ver. +2. **the same night**. Mt 26:2, 17, 34. **took bread**. T#104. 1 C +10:16. Mt 26:26-28. 28:19. Mk 14:22-24. Lk 22:19, 20. Ac 20:7.

24. **given thanks**. Mt +15:36. Lk +*24:30. **brake**. √108H4, Is +58:7. **eat**. 1 C 5:7, 8. Ps 22:26, 29. Pr 9:5. SS 5:1. Is 25:6. +*55:1-3. Jn 6:53-58. **this is**. √96C7, Mt +26:24. ver. 27, 28. 1 C 10:3, 4, 16, 17. **my body**. He 10:10. **broken**. √145, Jg +11:40. Le=2:4, 6. Jn ❍*19:36. **in remembrance**. *or*, for a remembrance. Ge=40:14. Ex 12:14. Jsh 4:7. Ps 111:4. SS 1:4. Is 26:8. Mt 26:13.

25. **This cup**. √121J13, Je +49:12. ver. 27, 28. **the new**. Lk 22:20. 2 C 3:6, 14. He 8:8. 9:15-20. 13:20. **in my blood**. Zc 9:11. He *9:22, 25. 1 J 5:6.

26. **as often**. 1 C 16:2. Ac 2:46. *20:7. **ye eat**. Ex 12:11, 27. **cup**. √121J13, Je +49:12. **ye do show**. *or*, show ye. **death**. √171S8, Ro +5:10. **till he come**. 1 C *4:5. 15:23. Ps +*102:16. Is 62:7. Mt 16:27n. +*23:39. +*24:30. 25:19. *26:29. Mk 2:19, 20. Lk *17:22. 19:13. Jn +*14:3. +21:22. Ac +*1:11. +*3:19, 20. Ro +2:16. Ph 3:20. 1 Th √4:16. 2 Th +*1:10. 2:2, 3. 2 T +*4:1n. T *2:13. He *9:28. 10:37. 2 P 3:10. 1 J 2:28. Ju *14. Re +*1:7. 11:17n, 18. 20:11, 12. 22:20.

27. **whosoever**. 1 C 10:21. Le 10:1-3. Nu 9:10, 13. 2 Ch 30:18-20. Mt 22:11. Jn 6:51, 63, 64. 13:18-27. **cup**. √121J13, Je +49:12. **unworthily**. Jn 13:27. **shall be guilty**. Mt 26:66. Mk 3:29. 14:64. He 2:15. *6:6. Ja 2:10g. **the body**. ver. 29. Jn 6:51, 53-56.

28. **let a man examine**. ver. 31. Ps *26:2-7. +*66:18. La 3:40. Hg 1:5, 7. Zc 7:5-7. Ac *8:36, 37. 2 C √13:5. Ga 6:4. 1 J *3:20, 21. **and so**. Nu 9:10-13. Mt *5:23, 24. **cup**. √121J13, Je +49:12.

29. **unworthily**. Ex 12:43, 44. Ep 2:13, 19. **damnation**. *or*, judgment. *Krima, judgment*, or *punishment*, not *damnation*, for it was inflicted upon the disorderly and profane for their amendment. ver. 30, 32-34. Ro 13:2g. Ja 3:1. 5:12mg. **not**. ver. 24, 27. Ec 8:5. He 5:14. **discerning**. √135, Ps +68:28.

30. **many**. ver. 32. Ex 15:26. Nu 20:12, 24. 21:6-9. 2 S 12:14-18. 1 K √13:21-24, 29. Ps 38:1-8. 78:30, 31. 89:31-34. Am 3:2. He 12:5-11. Re *3:19. **weak**. Ezr 9:14. Jn 5:14. **sickly**. Mi *6:13. **and many**. Pr +*10:27. Ec +*7:17. Is +*38:10. **sleep**. 1 C 15:51. Mt +27:52. Ac *13:36. 1 Th 4:14.

31. **if we**. √184B, Lk +7:39. ver. 28. Ps √32:3-5. Je 31:18-20. Lk 15:18-20. 1 J √1:9. Re 2:5. 3:2, 3. **judge**. √135, Ps +68:28.

32. **we are judged**. See on ver. 13, *30, 31. 1 C 4:5. 6:2, 3. Dt *8:5. Jb 33:18-30. Is 1:5. Je 7:28. Zp

*3:2. Mt 7:1, 2. Lk 19:22. Jn 3:18. 7:24. Ro *14:13, 22. 2 T 4:1. He 10:30. *12:5-11. 13:4. 1 P *1:17. 2:23. Re 11:18. **chastened of**. T#820. Dt 8:5. 2 S 7:14. Jb *5:17, 18. *34:31, 32. 36:8-10. Ps *94:12, 13. 118:18. 119:67, 71, 75. Pr *3:11, 12. Is 1:25. *27:9. *48:10. Ho 2:6, 7. Da 11:35. 12:10. Zc 13:9. Ro *5:3, 4. 2 C √4:16, 17. Ph 1:19. He 12:6, 7, 10, 11. Ja 1:3, 12. 1 P *1:7. Re 3:19. **condemned**. √135, Ps +68:28. Ro *3:19. 5:16. 1 J *5:19. **world**. Gr. *kosmos*, Mt +4:8. √121J9A, Jn +1:10. Ac 17:31. Ro 3:6. 1 J 2:17.

34. **if any**. √184A, 1 C +15:2. See on ver. 21, 22. **condemnation**. *or*, judgment. **will I set**. 1 C 7:17. T 1:5. **when I come**. 1 C +4:19. 16:2, 5.

1 CORINTHIANS 12

The apostle instructs the Corinthians in the origin, nature, variety, and use, of "spiritual gifts," 1-11. He illustrates the subject, by showing how the members in the human body perform their several functions, for the benefit of the whole, 12-26: and applies this to the church, and its different orders of ministers, and members, 27-30. He concludes with exhortation, 31.

1. **spiritual**. ver. 4-11. 1 C *1:4-7. 14:1-18, 37. Ro +1:11g. Ep *4:11. **I would not**. √175B, Ge +21:16. 1 C +10:1. 2 C 1:8. 1 Th 4:13. 2 P 3:8.

2. **that ye were**. 1 C +*6:11. Ga 4:8. Ep *2:11, 12. 4:17, 18. 1 Th 1:9. T 3:3. 1 P 4:3. **carried away**. 1 Th *1:9. **dumb**. Ps 115:5, 7. 135:16. Is 46:7. Je 10:5. Hab 2:18, 19. **even**. Mt +*15:14. 2 T *2:26. 1 P 1:18.

3. **give you to understand**. Paul here gives a test, stated both negatively and positively, for determining the source—demonic or divine—of spiritual gifts. Negatively, the counterfeit source refuses to positively confess the deity of Christ, is self-exalting, and disorderly, and stems from the soulish nature of man; positively, the true source confesses the full deity of Christ, is self-effacing, and orderly, and stems from the spiritual nature in man (Jn 4:24). As many spiritual gifts had been paralleled by demons in the false worship of pagan deities in Corinth, with which these Gentile Christians had been most familiar (ver. 2), they needed a test to distinguish false spirituality from the true. Paul's subsequent discussion affirms the unity of the Body of Christ (ver. 13), and the sovereignty of the Holy Spirit who according to His discretion distributes gifts to every believer. Paul gives further admonition and direction for the use of these gifts, that everything in the congregation may be done "decently and in order" (1 C 14:40). 1 C 15:1g. **no man**. Mk *9:39. Jn 16:14, 15. 1 J *4:2, 3. **speaking by**. Mk 12:36. Lk +4:1. 10:21. **the Spirit of**. Gr. *pneuma*, Ro +8:1n. Mt +*1:20. **calleth Jesus**. That is, to say he was a malefactor, one justly condemned to death. This the Jews said who invoked his blood upon their heads (Hodge). **accursed**. *or*, anathema. 1 C 16:22. Le 27:28, 29. Dt *21:23. Lk 21:5g. Ac 23:14g. Ro 9:3. Ga 1:8, 9. *3:13. **no man**. 1 C 8:6. Mt *16:16, 17. Jn *13:13. 15:26. 2 C *3:5. 11:4. **can say**. √108B, Pr +20:9. **the Lord**. The word *kurios*, Lord, is that by which the word Jehovah is commonly rendered in the Greek version of the Old Testament. To say Jesus is the Lord, therefore, in the sense of the apostle, is to acknowledge him to be truly God. No one can truly believe and openly confess that Jesus is God manifest in the flesh unless

he is enlightened by the Spirit of God (Hodge). Thus only those enlightened by the Holy Spirit can recognize Jesus as Jehovah. Belief in the full deity of the Lord Jesus is the positive test of orthodoxy given by the apostle. 1 C √2:8. √15:47. Ne +*9:6. Mt *7:21-23. Lk *6:46. Jn +*8:24. +√20:28. Ac +√10:37. 11:21n. Ro √10:9, 10. 1 P +√2:3n w Ps ▶34:8. **but by.** Mt 16:17. Jn 15:26. Ro √10:9. **Ghost.** Gr. *pneuma*, Mt +1:18n. Mt +*3:16.

4. **diversities.** *f*167, Is +2:7. 1 Ch=25:8. **of gifts.** Gr. *karismaton, of gracious endowments*, by the extraordinary influence of the Holy Spirit. ver. 8-11, 28. Mt 25:14-30. Ro +*12:4-6. Ep 4:4, *11. He *2:4. 1 P *4:10, 11. **the same.** Ep 4:4-6. Ph 2:13. **Spirit.** Gr. *pneuma*, Mt +3:16.

5. **differences.** Nu=1:51. =10:17, 21. **administrations.** *or,* ministries. ver. 28, 29. Ro +*12:6-8. Ep √4:11, 12. **but.** 1 C 8:6. Mt 23:10. Ac +√10:36. Ro 14:8, 9. Ph 2:11.

6. **operations.** *f*121G, Ge +31:1. ver. 10. **the same God.** Notice the mention of all three persons of the Godhead in the immediate context: God the Father (ver. 6), God the Son (ver. 5), God the Holy Spirit (ver. 4): same Spirit, same Lord, same God. Is +*42:1n. Mt +*28:19. **worketh.** ver. 11. 1 C 3:7. Jb 33:29. Mt +14:2. Jn 5:17. Ep 1:19-22. Col 1:29. Ph *2:13. He 13:21. **all.** 1 C 15:28. Ep 1:23. Col 3:11.

7. **the manifestation.** 1 C 14:5, 12, 17, 19, 22-26. Mt 25:14, etc. Ro +*12:6-8. 2 C 4:2g. Ep *4:7-12. 1 P *4:10, 11. **the Spirit.** Gr. *pneuma*, Mt +3:16. Jn +7:39. **to every man.** 1 C 14:26. Ac 13:2. +*20:28. Ro +*12:3. Ep *4:7. 1 P *4:10.

8. **Spirit.** Gr. *pneuma*, Mt +3:16. Mt +*12:32. **the word of wisdom.** 1 C 1:5, 30. *2:6-10. 13:2, 8. Ge 41:38, 39. Ex 31:3. 1 K 3:5-12. 1 Ch 25:1-3. Ne 9:20. Jb *32:8. Ps 143:10. Pr *2:6. Is *11:2, 3. 50:4. 59:21. Da 2:21. Mt *13:11. Ac 6:3. 2 C 8:7. Ep *1:17, 18. 3:3-6, 10. Col *1:9. **word of knowledge.** 1 C +1:5. 13:2, 8. 14:6. Ro 15:14. 2 C 8:7. 11:6. Col *1:9. 2 P 1:5. **by the same.** 2 C 12:18. **Spirit.** Gr. *pneuma*, Mt +3:16.

9. **To another.** *f*18, Dt +28:4. **faith.** 1 C 13:2. Mt *17:19, 20. 21:21. Mk 11:22, 23. Lk 17:5, 6. 2 C 4:13. Ep √2:8. He 11:33. 2 P 1:1. **Spirit.** Gr. *pneuma*, Mt +3:16. **the gifts of healing.** ver. 28, 30. Mt 10:8. Mk 6:13. 16:18. Lk 9:2. 10:9. Ac 3:6-8. 4:29-31. *5:15, 16. +*10:38. 19:11, 12. Ja *5:14, 15. **Spirit.** Gr. *pneuma*, Mt +3:16.

10. **the working.** ver. 6. Ga 3:5. **of miracles.** ver. 28, 29. Mk 16:17, 20. Lk 24:49. Jn 14:12. Ac +*1:8. +8:13. Ro 15:19. Ga 3:5. He *2:4. **prophecy.** ver. +*28. 1 C 13:2. 14:1, 3, 5, 24, 31, 32, 39. Nu 11:25-29. 1 S 10:10-13. 19:20-24. 2 S 23:1, 2. 1 Ch 25:1-3. Jl +*2:28. Jn 16:13. Ac 2:17, 18, 29, 30. *11:27, 28. +13:1. 21:9, 10. Ro +*12:6. 1 Th 5:20. 2 P *1:20, 21. **discerning of spirits.** Gr. *pneuma*, Mt +1:18 or +8:16. 1 C 14:29. Ac *5:3, 9, 10. *8:21. Ro 14:1g. He 5:14g. 1 J *4:1. Re *2:2. **divers kinds of tongues.** ver. 28-30. 13:1. 14:2-4, 23, *27-29, 39. Mk +16:17. Ac *2:4-12. 10:46, 47. 19:6. **to another the interpretation.** *S#2058g. Gr. *hermeneia*, from *hermeneuo* from *Hermes* (the god of speech). 1 C 14:26. From this Greek word comes our "hermeneutics," the science of interpretation. Here the word must mean *translation,* as from one language to another language. Hodge remarks "If speaking in tongues was speaking incoher-

ently in ecstasy, it is hard to see how what was said could admit of interpretation. Unless coherent it was irrational, and if irrational, it could not be translated." ver. 30. 1 C 14:26-28. For the cognate verb *hermeenuo* (*S#2059g), see Jn 1:+38, 42. 9:7. He 7:2. For the related compound verb *diermeneuo* (*S#1329g), see Lk +24:47 (expounded). Ac 9:36 (by interpretation). 1 C 12:30 (interpret). 14:5, 13, 27. For related words, see Mk +5:41.

11. **all these.** ver. 4. 1 C 7:7, 17. Jn 3:27. Ro +*12:6. 2 C 10:13. Ep 4:7. **worketh.** ver. 6. Mt +14:2. **selfsame.** ver. +8. 2 C 12:18. **Spirit.** Gr. *pneuma*, Mt +3:16. Mt +*12:32. **dividing to.** 2 C 10:13. Ac 13:2. **severally.** *f*24F, Ac +16:37. **as he will.** God the Holy Spirit is sovereign. ver. 6, 18. 1 C 15:38. 1 Ch=6:32. Da 4:35. Mt 11:26. 20:15. +*28:19n. Jn *3:8. 5:21. Ac +*8:29. Ro 9:18. Ep +*1:11. He *2:4. 6:17. Ja 1:18. 2 P 3:9.

12. **as.** ver. 20. 1 C +10:17. Ro *12:4, 5. Ep 1:23. *4:4, 12, 15, 16. 5:23, 30. Col 1:18, 24. 2:19. 3:15. **is one.** Ge 5:2. **the members.** ver. 27. **so also.** ver. 27. Ga *3:16. Ep 1:23. **Christ.** *f*121K5, Ac +9:4.

13. **by.** Gr. *en.* Mt *3:11. Mk 1:8. Lk 3:16. Jn 1:33. Ac 1:5. 11:16. The Greek preposition *en,* frequently rendered "in," is instrumental here, indicating agency, and so correctly translated "by," designating who performs the baptism. Thus five times in this chapter (ver. 3, 3, 9, 9, 13) *en* is used not of the receiving element, but is instrumental, indicative of agency, though here appearing in its accustomed relation to baptism. The preposition does not indicate the ideal element, but the source of the baptism. The agency originates in *withinness,* an aspect of agency or influence which is profoundly characteristic of the New Testament (see "in Christ," Ro +*8:1n. Also 1 C +*10:2n). Dale notes, "The ground of the use of *en to pneumati* (as also of *en Christo,* in Christ) *"in the Spirit,"* is the influence inseparable from *withinness,* where one thing is enveloped in another thing. Generally it is the inclosing substance that influences the inclosed; sometimes it is the reverse.... Both forms of influence are freely used in Scripture. Christians are said to be *in* Christ and Christ in *them* (Ro 8:1; Col 1:27). So it is said of the Spirit; "If the Spirit of God *dwell in you*" (Ro 8:9), "For David said (*en to pneumati to agio*) in *the Holy Ghost*" (Mk 12:36). This withinness is for the sake of influence" (*Christic Baptism,* p. 320), Ro √8:11. "It is in this aspect that the Holy Spirit always appears as the agent in baptism. While Christ is declared to be the Baptizer he is declared so to be on the ground that he, himself, is 'in the Holy Spirit,' and thus invested with the power of the Spirit, does baptize *by* the Spirit" (J. W. Dale, *Christic Baptism,* pp. 319, 320). Mt 3:11, 16. Mt *12:28. Jn 1:32, 33. 3:34. Ac *2:33. **one Spirit.** Gr. *pneuma*, Mt +3:16. Mt ◑+1:20. Ep 2:18. **are we.** lit. were we. In Greek the tense is first aorist passive indicative, and so a reference to a definite past event with each of them (A. T. Robertson, *Word Pictures,* vol. 4, p. 171. Robertson goes on to make this past event their water baptism, with which I firmly disagree, for the reasons given in the following note. It would hardly suit Paul's theme of the unity of the body to make this a reference to water baptism which at Corinth had been such a source of divisiveness (1 C 1:11-17). This past event must have been their regeneration,

with which event Scripture teaches the baptism in this verse coincides, thus forming a "double baptism," discussed next under the words *all baptized*). **all baptized.** Gr. *baptizo*, Mt +3:6. This baptism is not accomplished by a human administrator, but divine, the Holy Spirit himself. The result is placement into the one body (Ep +*4:4). The efficacy is complete and total, for it infallibly extends to "all" who have truly placed their faith in Jesus as Lord (ver. 3). This stated universality forbids the application or restriction of this verse to any "second work of grace" subsequent to initial salvation. This unfailing and universal efficacy goes beyond the power of any humanly administered ordinance (Ac ●8:13, 21), and is therefore a reference to real, not ritual, baptism (Ac 1:5n). Notice that water is not to be found in this verse or the immediate context. It is the baptism of all individual regenerate persons who are under the influence of the Holy Spirit, and subject to the Lordship of Christ (ver. 3). It is a baptism of unification, by the distribution of appropriate and varied gifts to every member of the body of Christ, as distinguished from the baptism of regeneration (T 3:5) which unites the individual soul to Christ and makes one a participant in his redemption. Thus the Holy Spirit continues this work of double baptism (of the individual "into Christ," and of "all *into* one body") until this wondrous work of placing Jews and Gentiles into one body is complete (Dale, *Christic Baptism*, p. 323). 1 C +*10:2. Nu 11:29. Is 32:15. 44:3-5. Ezk *36:25-27. Jl +*2:28n, 29. Mt *3:11. Lk *3:16. Jn 1:16, *33. √3:5. Ac +*1:5. Ro +*6:3-6. +√8:9-11. Ga +3:27. Ep +*4:5. 5:26. Col +*2:11, 12. T 3:4-6. 1 P 3:21. **into one body.** Ep +*4:4. Col +*1:27. **whether we be Jews.** 1 C 10:32. Jl +*2:28n. Ac +*2:17. Ro 3:29. 4:11. Ga 3:23, +*28. Ep *2:11-16, 19-22. +*3:6. Col 1:27. *3:11. **Gentiles.** Gr. Greeks. 1 C +*10:32. **bond.** 1 C *7:21, 22. Ep 6:8. Re 6:15. 13:16. 19:18. **have been all.** The assertion that the following verb *given to drink* "points to a conscious, voluntary reception of the Spirit on the part of each Spirit-baptized Christian, not something which automatically happens to him" (*The Layman's Commentary on the Holy Spirit*, John Rea, editor, on this text) must be rejected, since it denies the universality of "all." The universality of "all" forbids the limitation of the following "made to drink" to those who have become "Spirit-baptized Christians" as distinguished from those who allegedly have not; no such division into separate classes of Christians is contemplated here by Paul, who is establishing the grounds of unity, not diversity, of believers in the one body. **made to drink.** √108B, Je +15:16. ✲S#4222g. Rendered (1) give to drink: Mt 10:42. 27:48. Mk 9:41. 15:36. (2) give drink: Mt 25:35, 37, 42. Ro 12:20. (3) water: 1 C 3:6, 7, 8. (4) make to drink: 1 C 12:13. Re 14:8. (5) watering: Lk 13:15. (6) feed: 1 C 3:2. This verb has the same tense in Greek as the preceding verb "were baptized," first aorist passive indicative, and therefore refers to a one-time non-repeatable event or experience in the past, when these Christians (ver. 3) individually received the Holy Spirit in regeneration for salvation (Jn √4:10, 14. √7:37-39. T √3:5). It is, therefore, a reference to the inward reception of the indwelling Holy Spirit at conversion. 1 C 2:12. 3:2. +*6:19. SS 5:1. Is *41:17, 18. *55:1. Zc 9:15-17. Jn √4:10, 14. *6:63. √7:37-39. Ac 2:17. Ro 5:5. +*8:9, 11, 15. Ga 3:2. **Spirit.** Gr. *pneuma*,

√121A1, Lk +1:17n? or, more probably, Mt +3:16. ver. 4, 11. Ep 2:18.

14. **the body.** ver. 12, 19, 27, 28. Ep 4:25.

15. **If.** √184C, Mt +4:9. **the foot.** Jg 9:8-15. 2 K 14:9. **say.** √155A, Ge +31:35.

16. **And if.** √184C, Mt +4:9. **say.** √155A, Ge +31:35. **is it.** ver. 16, 22. Ro +*12:3, 10, 16. Ph +*2:3.

17. **If.** √184A, 1 C +15:2. **whole body.** ver. 21, 29. 1 S 9:9. Ps 94:9. 139:13-16. Pr 20:12.

18. **hath God set.** ver. 24, 28. **as it hath pleased.** See on ver. 11. 1 C 3:5. 15:38. 2 Ch=35:10. Ps 110:3. 135:6. Is 46:10. Jon 1:14. Lk 10:21. +*12:32. Ro +*12:3. Ep 1:5, 9. Re 4:11.

19. **if they.** √184B, Mt +23:30. ver. 14.

20. **many members.** ver. 4. 1 Ch=25:8. **one body.** ver. 12. 1 C +10:7. Ro 12:4. Ep +*4:4.

21. **the eye.** Nu 10:31, 32. 1 S 25:32. Ezr 10:1-5. Ne 4:16-21. Jb 29:11.

22. **much more.** Pr 14:28. Ec 4:9-12. 5:9. 9:14, 15. 2 C 1:11. T 2:9, 10.

23. **bestow.** *or,* put on. Ge 3:7, 21. Mt 27:28. Mk 15:17g.

24. **our comely.** Ge 2:25. 3:11.

25. **there.** 1 C 1:10-12. 3:3. Jn 17:21-26. 2 C 13:11. **schism.** *or,* division. 1 C 1:10. 11:18. Jn +7:43. **the same.** 2 C 7:12. 8:16. **care.** Mt +6:25g. Ac *4:32. Ro *12:11n. 1 T +*3:5. **one for another.** Ro +12:5.

26. **whether one.** Ro +*12:15. 2 C 11:28, 29. Ga 6:2. He 13:3. 1 P 3:8g. **all the members suffer.** Jsh +*22:18. **honored.** √108B, Mt +15:6.

27. **ye are the body.** See on ver. 12, 14-20. Ro *12:4, 5. Ep 1:23. 4:12. 5:23, 30. Col 1:24. **members.** Ro +12:5. Ep *5:30.

28. **God hath set.** ver. 7-11, 18. Nu=4:27. 1 Ch=4:28. Lk *6:13, 14. Ac *13:1-3. +*20:28. Ro +*12:6-8. Ep 2:20. 3:5. +*4:11-13. He 13:17, 24. 1 P *5:1-4. **in the church.** Mt 16:18. Ep 5:23, 32. Col 1:18, 24. He 12:23. **first.** √157, 1 C +15:6. **apostles.** 1 C 9:5. 15:7, 9. Ac +5:12. Ro 16:7. 2 C 8:23. 11:5, 13. 12:11. Ga 1:17, 19. Ep 2:20. 3:5. √4:11. Ph 2:25. 1 Th 2:6. 2 P 3:2. Ju 17. Re 2:2. 18:20. 21:14. **secondarily prophets.** 1 C 14:29, 32, 37. Mt 10:41. 23:34. Lk 11:49. Ac 11:27. 13:1. 15:32. 21:10. Ep 2:20. 3:5. √4:11. **thirdly teachers.** Ac 13:1. Ep √4:11. 2 T 4:3. He *5:12. Ja *3:1. **miracles.** ver. 10. Ac +8:13. **gifts of healings.** ver. 9. **helps.** √41, Ge +10:1. Nu 11:17. Ac *6:3, 4. +*20:35. Ro *16:1-3, 21. 1 Th 5:14. 2 T *4:11. **governments.** *or,* wise counsels. Pr 1:5. 11:14. 24:6. Ro +*12:8. Ph 1:1. 1 T 5:17. T *1:5. He *13:7, 17, 24. **diversities.** *or,* kinds. ver. 10. Ac *2:8-11. **of tongues.** ver. 10. 1 C 14:1, 39. Mk +16:17. Ac 2:4.

29. **Are all.** Both the logic and the grammar expect a negative answer. **apostles.** ver. 4-11, 14-20. **workers.** *or,* powers.

30. **do all.** √85C, Ge +18:14. As in ver. 29, the Greek *mee* expects and requires a negative answer. This settles, once and for all, the question as to whether speaking in tongues is the evidence of having the Holy Spirit. Since all believers do not speak in tongues, it can serve as no such universal evidence. Yet all believers have the Holy Spirit (ver. 13. Ro 8:9, 11), and all believers have been baptized into the one body by the Holy Spirit (ver. 13). **speak with tongues.** Speaking in tongues was a highly prized gift at Corinth, but was of little use without an interpreter. The miraculous gift of tongues was a gift of speaking a known language

which one had not learned naturally; tongues were not outbursts of ecstatic gibberish. Paul consistently places this troublesome gift at the bottom of the list, signifying its low priority. It is very probable that this gift, along with the rest of the miraculous or supernatural gifts discussed in this chapter and chapter 14, served a very temporary revelatory and confirmatory purpose while the early church was being founded by the original apostles, before the writing of the New Testament. In particular, tongues as a gift was intended to provoke Israel to jealousy, a sign to unbelieving Jews because it was a specific fulfillment of prophecy (1 C 14:21, citing Is 28:11, 12), warning them of their impending judgment for rejecting the truth. Since Israel was scattered and the nation and temple destroyed in A.D. 70, it is doubtful that this gift would serve this purpose beyond that date, and so would cease. This may explain why tongues are not mentioned in Paul's later epistles. Supposed modern manifestations of these gifts are likely counterfeit (being evidence of "experience centered," instead of "Bible centered" or "Christ centered" Christianity, Is 65:5n, placing an overemphasis upon the Holy Spirit, Jn 16:13n, and so failing to maintain the Biblical balance of truth, Ac 2:24n. Is 43:10n). Watchman Nee has written a volume (*The Latent Power of the Soul*) which wisely cautions that many supposed manifestations of the Holy Spirit are in reality counterfeit productions of the human spirit. Spiritual gifts are predicted to reappear in the last days after the Great Tribulation and the final restoration of Israel (Jl +*2:28n). Their supposed presence in the church today is at least problematical. Clearly the revelatory gifts are out of place now that God's written revelation is complete. Anyone who now claims to be receiving revelatory knowledge from God who is not getting it directly from the written word of God in the Bible is adding to the word of God, which is forbidden by Scripture itself (Pr 30:6. Re 22:18).

31. **covet.** 1 C *8:1. *14:1, 39. Mt 5:6. Lk 10:42. 12:31. Ga 4:17, 18. **the best gifts.** 1 C 14:5. **and yet.** ſ116, 1 C +11:16. **show.** 1 C 13:1, etc. Mt *5:48. Ph 3:8. He 11:4.

1 CORINTHIANS 13

Gifts and miraculous powers, without love, are of no worth or efficacy, 1-3. The excellent properties of love, 4-7. Love will abide, when prophecies and tongues shall cease, and knowledge shall be perfected, 8-12. It is greater than faith and hope, 13.

1. **Though.** ſ102C, Mt +5:29. ſ184C, Mt +4:9. **I speak.** ver. 2, 3. 1 C 12:8, 16, 29, 30. 14:6. 2 C ◑*10:10. 12:4. 2 P 2:18. **with the tongues.** 1 C 12:10, 28, 30. Mk +16:17. Ac 2:4. **angels.** ſ101, Dt +32:42. **have not.** 1 C 8:1. Mt *22:37-40. 25:45. Ro 14:15. Ga 5:6, 22. 1 Th +*3:12. 1 T 1:5. 1 P +*1:22. 4:8. 1 J *3:14. *4:7, 8. **as.** 1 C 14:7, 8. **tinkling cymbal.** 1 Ch 13:8. Ps 150:5.

2. **though.** ſ102C, Mt +5:29. ſ184C, Mt +4:9. **I have the gift of prophecy.** 1 C 12:8-10, 28. 14:1, 6-9, 39. Nu 24:15-24. Mt *7:22, 23. Ac +2:18. **understand all.** ſ108B. Idiom B825. "All" often means the greatest degree or quality of that to which it is applied. See related figures listed at Ge +24:10n. For other instances of this idiom see 2 T 1:15. Ja 1:2. **mysteries.**

1 C +4:1. Mt +*13:11. Ro 11:25. +*16:25n. Ep 3:4. 6:19. Col 1:26. 1 T *3:16. **all knowledge.** 1 C +12:8. **and though.** ſ102C, Mt +5:29. **I have all faith.** T#190. 1 C 12:9. Mt *7:22, 23. *17:20. 21:21. Mk *11:22, 23. Lk 17:5, 6. Ja +5:15 (T#189). **remove mountains.** ſ138B, Ge +13:16. Mt 17:20. 21:21. Mk 11:23. Lk 17:6. **and have.** ver. 1, 3. 1 C 16:22. Ga 5:6, 22. 1 J 4:8, 20, 21. **I am.** ver. 3. 1 C 7:19. 8:4. Mt 21:19. 2 C 12:11. Ga 6:3.

3. **though.** ſ102C, Mt +5:29. **I bestow.** Mt +*6:1-4. 23:5. Lk 18:22, 28. 19:8. 21:3, 4. Jn 12:43. Ga 5:26. Ph 1:15-18. **though.** ſ102C, Mt +5:29. **I give.** Da *3:16-28. Mt *7:22, 23. Jn 13:37. 15:13. Ac 21:13. Ph 1:20, 21. +*2:3. **have not.** Mk 9:41. Ga *5:6, 22. **profiteth.** Is 57:12. Je 7:8. Jn 6:63. 1 T 4:8. He 13:9. Ja 2:14-17.

4. **Charity.** ſ18, Dt +28:4. **suffereth long.** ſ155F, Ge +4:7. ver. 7. Ex 34:6, 7. Pr 10:12. 17:9. 2 C 6:6. Ga *5:22. Ep 4:2. Col *1:11. √3:12. 1 Th 5:14. 2 T 2:10, +*25. 3:10. 4:2. Ja 3:17. 1 P 4:8. **and.** ſ41, Ge +10:1. **is kind.** ſ155F, Ge +4:7. Ne 9:17. Pr 19:22. 31:20, 26. Lk +*6:35, 36. Ro *12:10. 2 C 6:6. Ga *5:22. Ep √4:32. Col 3:12. 1 P 3:8. 2 P +*1:7. 1 J *3:16-19. 4:11. **envieth.** 1 C 3:3. Ge 30:1. 37:11. Mt 27:18. Ac +7:9. Ro +*1:29. 13:13. 2 C 12:20. Ga 5:21, 26. Ph 1:15. 1 T 6:4. T 3:3. Ja 3:14-16. 4:5. 1 P 2:1. **vaunteth not itself.** *or*, is not rash. Jg +*11:30, 31. 1 S 25:21, 22, 33, 34. 1 K 20:10, 11. Ps 10:5. Pr 13:10. 17:14. 25:8-10. Ec 7:8, 9. 10:4. Da 3:19-22. **is not puffed up.** 1 C 4:+6, 18. 5:2. 8:1. Lk 7:6, 7. Col 2:18. Ph 2:1-5.

5. **behave.** 1 C 7:36g. 11:13-16, 18, 21, 22. 14:33-40. Is 3:5. Ph √4:8. 2 Th 3:7. 1 P *3:8. **seeketh.** 1 C +*10:24, 33. 12:25. Ro 14:12-15. *15:1, 2. Ga 5:13. *6:1, 2. Ph +*2:3-5, 21. 2 T 2:10. 1 J *3:16, 17. **not easily provoked.** Nu *12:3. 16:15. 20:10-12. Ps 106:32, 33. Pr +*14:17. Mt *5:22. Mk 3:5. Ac 15:39. 17:16. He 10:24g. Ja √1:19, 20. **thinketh.** ſ155F, Ge +4:7. **no evil.** Ge 31:32. 2 S 10:3. Jb 21:27. Ps 15:3. Je 11:19. 18:18-20. 40:13-16. Zc 8:17. Mt *9:4. Lk *7:39. 2 C 5:19. 2 T 2:24. T 3:2.

6. **Rejoiceth not.** ſ155F, Ge +4:7. Le +*19:17. 1 S 23:19-21. 2 S 4:10-12. Ps 10:3. *119:136, 139. Pr *14:9. +*24:17 w Mt 5:44. Je 9:1. 13:17. 20:10. Ho 4:8. 7:3. Mi 7:8. Lk *19:41, 42. 22:5. Ro +*1:32. Ph 3:18. 2 Th √2:12. **iniquity.** or, unrighteousness. Ro +*1:18. **rejoiceth.** Ex 18:9. Jsh 22:22-33. Ac *11:23. Ro 12:9. 2 C 7:9-16. Ph 1:4, 18. 2:17, 18. 1 Th 3:6-10. 2 J *4. 3 J 3, 4. **in the truth.** *or*, "with the truth."

7. **Beareth all.** ſ171A, Ex +9:6. See on ver. 4. 1 C 9:12g. Nu 11:12-14. Dt 1:9. Pr *10:12. √17:9. SS 8:6, 7. Lk 17:4. Ro 15:1. Ga *6:2. He 13:13. 1 P *2:24. √4:8. **believeth.** ſ155F, Ge +4:7. Ps *119:66. **all things.** ſ18, Dt +28:4. **hopeth.** ſ155F, Ge +4:7. Lk 7:37-39, 44-46. 19:4-10. Ro 8:24. **endureth.** ſ155F, Ge +4:7. ver. 4. 1 C 9:18-22. Ge 29:20. Jb 13:15. Mt 10:22. 2 C 11:8-12. 2 Th 1:4. 2 T *2:3-10, 24, 25. 3:11. 4:5. Ja 1:12.

8. **never faileth.** ver. 10, 13. Lk 22:32. 1 C *1:7, 8. Ga 5:6. **prophecies.** ver. 2. Ac +2:18. **whether.** ſ18, Dt +28:4. **tongues.** ver. 1. 1 C *12:10, 28-30. *14:39. Ac 2:4. *19:6. **shall cease.** Robertson notes, future middle indicative of *pauo*, to make cease. They shall make themselves cease or automatically cease of themselves (*Word Pictures*, vol. 4, p. 179). D. A. Carson notes that the argument to prove that tongues

will cease "of themselves," built upon the fact that the verb is in the middle voice, is flawed exegetically; no one would argue that when Jesus commanded the sea to be calm and the storm to cease that the winds subsided of themselves, yet the verb (ceased) used in Lk 8:24 is in the middle voice (Carson, *Exegetical Fallacies*, pp. 77-79). Some interpreters believe this passage teaches the passing away or cessation of the miraculous gifts. Those of the Pentecostal or Charismatic persuasion believe these gifts continue to the present, are valid for today, and have been in greater evidence in all sectors of the church in recent times. In view of the fact that tongues was a sign gift to unbelieving Jews (1 C 14:21, 22), its purpose may have been served by the time of the destruction of Jerusalem in A.D. 70. This gift is not mentioned in Paul's later writings. When the book of Revelation was written (no later than A.D. 95), the New Testament was complete. The gift of tongues could no longer serve as a revelational gift (Re 22:18). The gift may be among those reinstituted at the Second Advent (Jl 2:28n). See related notes (1 C 12:30n. 14:27n. Ac 3:16n). Pr √25:14. **knowledge**. Gr. *gnosis*, Jn 8:55n. ver. 2. Is 11:9. Je 31:34. 1 C +12:8. He +*8:11. **vanish**. Je 49:7. He 8:13.

9. **know in part**. ver. 12. 1 C 2:9. 8:2. Jb 11:7, 8. 26:14. Ps 40:5. 139:6. Pr 30:4. Mt +*11:27. Ro *11:34. Ep 3:8, 18, 19. Col *2:2, 3. 1 P *1:10-12. 1 J √3:2.

10. **when that**. ver. 12. Is 24:23. 60:19, 20. Ho 6:3. Hab 2:14. Mt 13:11. Jn *8:31, 32. 13:7. 14:29. 16:13, 25. 2 C 5:7, 8. He *9:28. 1 P 1:10-12. 2 P 1:19. 1 J √3:2. *4:8. Re 21:22, 23. 22:4, 5. **which is perfect**. 1 C 2:6. 14:20. Jn 15:15. Ph 3:15. Ep *4:13. He 5:14. This phrase has vexed interpreters, and no agreement upon its application has been reached. It may refer to (1) the Second Advent of Christ, ver. 12. 1 C 11:26. (2) the completion of the canon; that is, the writing of the inspired books of New Testament Scripture, so ending the need for revelatory and confirmatory gifts, Jn 15:15. Re 22:18. (3) The times of restitution of all things, the restoration of the kingdom to Israel, the times of refreshing, called "the regeneration," Mt 19:28. Ac 1:6. 3:19-21. He √11:39, 40. (4) the final maturing of the body of Christ, Ep 4:13. (5) the death and returning to be with Christ of the believer, Jn 14:2, 3. 2 C 5:8. Ph 1:21, 23. 3:12. 1 J 3:2. Re 14:13. Several of these views have staunch advocates, particularly views 1, 2, and 4. For a thorough discussion of these matters see Robert L. Thomas, *Understanding Spiritual Gifts*, Moody Press, 1978. **is come**. Ac +*3:19-21. 2 T +*4:1. T *2:13. He *9:11, 28. 1 J √3:2.

11. **I spake**. 1 C 3:1, 2. 14:20. Ec 11:10. Ga 4:1. **thought**. or, reasoned.

12. **we see**. Nu 12:8. Jb 36:26. √37:5. 2 C *3:18. 5:7. Ph *3:12. Ja 1:23. 1 J *3:2. **a glass**. or, mirror. Ja 1:23g. **darkly**. Gr. in a riddle. Nu 12:8. Jg 14:12-19. Ezk 17:2. **face**. Ge 32:30. Ex 33:11. Nu 12:8. Dt 5:4. 34:10. Jg 6:22. Ps 17:15. Pr *27:19. Is 52:8. Ezk 20:35. Mt +*5:8. 18:10. Ro 8:18. 2 C *3:18. He 12:2. 1 J √3:2. 2 J 12. 3 J 14. Re 22:4. **now**. ver. 9, 10. Jn 10:15. **know**. Gr. *ginosko*, Jn 8:55n. √96A1, Mt +5:29. **in part**. 1 C 2:9. 1 J 3:2. **then shall**. Mt +*17:3n. Lk +*16:23. **know**. Gr. *epiginosko*, Mt +11:27. or, fully know. **I am known**. Gr. *epiginosko*, Mt +11:27. or, am fully known. 1 C +8:3. Ps +*1:6. +*40:17. John 10:27. 2 T √2:19.

13. **now**. √77, Ex +3:19. **abideth**. 1 C 3:14. 1 P 1:21. 1 J 2:14, 24, 27. 3:9. **faith**. Lk +*8:13-15. 22:32. Ga 5:6. Ep √4:13-16. 1 Th √1:3. Phm √5-7. He *10:35, 39. √11:1-7. 1 J 5:1-5. **hope**. √41, Ge +10:1. Ps 42:11. 43:5. 146:5. La 3:21-26. Ro *5:4, 5. +*8:24, 25. +*15:4, 13. Col *1:5, 27. 1 Th √1:3. 5:8. He +*6:11, 19. 1 P 1:21. 1 J 3:3. **charity**. ver. 1-8. 1 C 8:1, 3. 2 C √5:14, 15. Ga 5:6. Ep √4:15, 16. 1 Th √1:3. Phm √5-7. 1 J 2:10. 4:7-18. **the greatest**. lit. greater. √96E4, Mt +13:32. ver. 8. 1 C 14:1. 16:14. Mk 12:29-31. Lk 10:27. Ga 5:13-22. Ph 1:9. Col 3:14. 1 T 1:5. 2 T +√1:7. 1 J *4:7-9. 2 J 4-6.

1 CORINTHIANS 14

The apostle exhorts the Corinthians to follow after love; and shows that prophecy, as most conducive to edification, is to be preferred to "speaking with tongues," 1-5. Speaking in a language, which the hearers do not understand, resembles indistinct musical sounds, and is of no use to the hearers, 6-11. All gifts should be used in the most edifying manner, 12-20. Tongues are intended to convince unbelievers; but prophesying is more useful in the public assembly, and to strangers who resort thither, 21-25. Rules for the orderly exercise of spiritual gifts in the church, 26-33. Women are forbidden to speak in the public assemblies of the church, 34, 35. A reproof of some teachers at Corinth, 36-38. Gifts must be exercised, and all things done "decently and in order," 39, 40.

1. **Follow**. 1 C 16:14. Pr 15:9. 21:21. Is 51:1. Ro 9:30. 14:19. 1 T 5:10. 6:11. He +*12:14. 1 P 3:11-13. 3 J 11. **charity**. 1 C 13:1-8, 13. 2 T 2:22. 2 P 1:7. **desire**. 1 C 12:1, +*31. Ep 1:3. **spiritual**. 1 C 12:1. Ro +1:11g. **prophesy**. ver. 3-5, 24, 25, 37, 39. 1 C +12:28. 13:+2, 9. Nu 11:25-29. 1 Ch 25:1-3. Ro +*12:6. 1 Th 5:20. 1 T 4:14.

2. **he that**. ver. 9-11, 16, 21, 22. Ge 11:7. 42:23. Dt 28:49. 2 K 18:26. Ac 2:4-11. 10:46. 19:6. **speaketh**. ver. 4, √18, 26, 27. 1 C +13:1. **understandeth**. Gr. heareth. √108B, Ac +22:9. Ac 22:9. **spirit**. Gr. *pneuma*, √121A1, Lk +1:17n. **speaketh mysteries**. 1 C 2:7, 10. +*4:1. 13:2. 15:51. Ps 49:3, 4. 78:2. Mt 13:11. Mk 4:11. Ro +*16:25. Ep 3:3-9. 6:19. Col 1:26, 27. 2:2. 1 T 3:9, 16. Re 10:7.

3. **he that prophesieth**. 1 C +*12:28. 13:2. **edification**. √121G, Ge +31:1. ver. 4, 5, 12, 17, 26. 1 C 8:1. 10:23. Ac 9:31. Ro +14:19. 15:2. Ep 4:12-16, 29. 1 Th 5:11. 1 T 1:4. Ju 20. **exhortation**. or, comfort. Lk 2:25. 3:18. 6:24. Ac 4:36. 9:31. 13:15. +*14:22. 15:31, 32. Ro *12:8. +*15:4, 5. 2 C *1:3-7. 7:4, 7, 13. 8:4, 17. Ph 2:1. 1 Th 2:3. 4:1. 5:11, 14. 2 Th 2:16. 3:12. 1 T 4:13. 6:2. 2 T 4:2. T 1:9. 2:6, 9, 15. Phm 7. He +*3:13. 6:18. √10:25. 12:5. 13:22. 1 P 5:12. **comfort**. or, consolation. ver. 31. 2 C 1:4. 2:7. Ep 6:22. Ph 2:1. Col 4:8. 1 Th 2:11. 3:2. 4:18. 5:11-14.

4. **He that speaketh**. ver. 2, √18, 26, 27. 1 C +13:1. **edifieth himself**. ver. +3, 14. **that prophesieth**. ver. +3. **edifieth the**. ver. 3, 18, 19.

5. **I would that**. 1 C 12:28-30. 13:4. Nu 11:28, 29. **ye all speak with tongues**. ver. +4, √18, √39. **but rather**. √15G, Ge +35:3. Nu *11:29. **for greater**. ver. 1, 3. **except**. √184C, Mt +4:9. ver. 12, 13, 26-28. 1 C 12:10, 30. **he interpret**. ver. +26. **receive edifying**. Ep *4:29.

6. **if I come**. √184C, Mt +4:9. **what shall I profit**.

1 C 10:33. 12:7. 13:3. 1 S 12:21. Je 16:19. 23:32. Mt 16:26. 2 T 2:14. T *3:8. He 13:9. **except.** ⨍184C, Mt +4:9. **revelation.** ver. 26-30. Mt +*11:25. *16:17. 2 C 12:1, 7. Ep 1:17. Ph 3:15. **knowledge.** 1 C +*12:8. 13:2, 8, 9. Ro +*15:14. 2 C 11:6. Ep 3:4. 2 P +*1:5. √3:18. **prophesying.** See on ver. 1, +3. 1 C 13:2. **doctrine.** or, teaching. ver. 26. Ac 2:42. Ro 6:17. 16:17. 2 T 3:10, +√16. √4:2. 2 J √9.

7. **things.** 1 C 13:1. **except.** ⨍184C, Mt +4:9. ver. 8. Nu 10:2-10. Mt 11:17. Lk 7:32. **sounds.** or, tunes.

8. **if the trumpet.** ⨍184C, Mt +4:9. Nu=10:8-10. Jsh 6:4-20. Jg 7:16-18. Ne 4:18-21. Jb 39:24, 25. Is 27:13. 58:1. Je 4:19. Ezk 33:3-6. Jl 2:1. Am 3:6. Ep 6:11-18. 1 Th 1:8.

9. **except.** ⨍184C, Mt +4:9. **easy.** Gr. significant. ver. 19. **for.** 1 C 9:26.

10. **it may be.** ⨍184D1, Lk +22:67. 1 C 15:37g. ❶16:6g. **world.** Gr. *kosmos*, Mt +4:8.

11. **if.** ⨍184C, Mt +4:9. **I shall.** ver. 21. Ac 28:2, 4. Ro 1:14. Col 3:11.

12. **forasmuch.** ver. 1. 1 C 12:7, 31. T *2:14. **zealous.** Lk 6:15. Ac 1:13. 21:20. 22:3. Ga 1:14. T 2:14. 1 P 3:13. **of.** ⨍29, Ex +19:6. **spiritual gifts.** Gr. spirits. Gr. *pneuma*, ⨍121A1, Lk +1:17n. ⨍24J, Dt +32:42. ⨍121A1, Jn +3:34. See on ver. 32. **seek.** ver. ⸬, 4, 26.

13. **pray.** ver. 27, 28. 1 C 12:10, 30. Mk *11:24. Jn 14:13, 14. Ac 1:14. 4:29-31. 8:15.

14. **For if.** ⨍184C, Mt +4:9. **tongue.** T#1291. **my spirit.** Gr. *pneuma*, ⨍171Q1B, Mk +2:8. ver. 2, 15, 16, 19. 1 C 2:11. 5:3, 4. Ac +17:16. **prayeth.** Ro ❶8:26n. **but.** That is, "not productive of any benefit to others."

15. **What.** ver. 26. 1 C 10:19. Ac 21:22. Ro 3:5. 8:31. Ph 1:18. **I will pray with the spirit.** Gr. *pneuma*, ⨍121A2, Ro +8:1n. ver. 19. Jn √4:23, 24. Ro 1:9. Ep 5:17-20. 6:18. Col *3:16. Ju *20. **understanding.** ⨍167, Is +2:7. **and I will sing.** Ps 47:7. Ro +*12:1, 2. Ep *5:19. Col *3:16. Ja *5:13. **spirit.** ⨍121A2, Ro +8:1n. **with the understanding.** Ps *47:7.

16. **bless.** ver. 2, 14. Mt +14:19. **spirit.** Gr. *pneuma*, ⨍121A2, Ro +8:1n. **unlearned.** ver. 23, 24. Is 29:11, 12. Jn 7:15. Ac 4:13. 2 C 11:6g. **Amen.** 1 C 11:24. 16:24. Nu 5:22. Dt +*27:15-26. 1 K *1:36. 1 Ch 16:36. Ne 5:13. 8:6. Ps 41:13. 72:19. 89:52. 106:48. Je 11:5. 28:6. Mt +*6:13. *28:20. Mk 16:20. Jn 21:25. 2 C 1:20. Re 5:14. 7:12. 19:4. 22:20. **thy giving of thanks.** 1 C 1:4-8. 11:24. Mt +*15:36. Lk +*22:30.

17. **not edified.** ver. 4, 5, 12, 26. Ro +14:19.

18. **I thank.** 1 C 1:4-6. 4:7. Ro +1:8. **I speak with tongues.** ⨍121BC, Mk +16:17. ver. +4. **more than ye all.** ver. √5, √39. 1 C 11:1.

19. **in the church.** ver. 4, 21, 22. **words.** ⨍108B, Lk +1:2. i.e. by idiom, "sentences." **teach others.** Lk 1:4. Ac 18:25. 21:21, 24. Ro 2:18. Ga 6:6g. **ten thousand.** 1 C 4:15.

20. **be not children.** 1 C 3:1, 2. 13:11. Ps 119:99. Is 11:3. Ro 16:19. Ep √4:14, 15. Ph 1:9. He *5:12, 13. 6:1-3. 2 P *3:18. **in malice.** Ro +*1:29. **be ye children.** Ps *131:1, 2. Is 28:9. Mt +*11:25. +*18:3. 19:14. Mk 10:15. Lk 10:21. Ro 16:19. 1 Th 2:7. 1 P +*2:2. **but.** Ps 119:90. **men.** Gr. perfect, or, of a ripe age. 1 C 2:6. 3:1. Mt +*5:48. Ph 3:15.

21. **the law.** The passage quoted is taken from the prophet *Isaiah*; but the term *torah*, Law, was used by the Jews to express the whole *Scriptures*, law, prophets, and hagiographia; and they used it to distin-

guish these Sacred Writings from the words of the *scribes*. It is not taken from the LXX., from which it varies as much as any words can differ from others where the general meaning is similar. It accords much more with the Hebrew; and may be considered as a translation from it; "only what is said of God in the third person, in the Hebrew, is here expressed in the first person, with the addition of *legei Kurios, saith the Lord.*"—Dr. Randolph. ver. 34. Ps 82:6. Jn +*10:34. Ro 3:19. **With.** ⨍92E, Mt +4:10. Dt √28:49. Is √5:26-29. ❱28:11, 12. *33:19. Je *5:15. **tongues.** ⨍173, Ge +27:44.

22. **tongues are for a sign.** Is 8:18. Mt 16:4. Mk 16:17. Ac 2:6-12, 32-36. **not to.** 1 T 1:9. **but prophesying.** 1 C +12:28. Ac +13:1. **serveth.** ⨍63I2, Jsh +3:3. Supply ellipsis "But prophesying (is for a sign) not for them that believe not, but for them which believe." **but for.** ver. 3.

23. **If.** ⨍184C, Mt +4:9. **the whole church.** 1 C 11:18. **come together.** 1 C +*11:20. **unlearned.** ver. +*16. **will they.** Ho 9:7. Jn 10:20. Ac *2:13. +*26:24.

24. **But if.** ⨍184C, Mt +4:9. **prophesy.** ver. 22. 1 C +12:28. Ac +13:1. **he is convinced.** 1 C 2:15. Jn 1:47-49. 4:29. +*16:8. Ac *2:37. He *4:12, 13. **is judged.** 1 C +*2:14.

25. **the secrets.** He *4:12. **falling down.** Ge 44:14. Dt 9:18. Ps 72:11. Is √45:14. 60:14. Lk 5:8. 8:28. Re 5:8. 19:4. **on his face.** Nu 16:22. 20:6. Mt 17:6. 26:39. Lk 5:12. 17:16. Re 11:16. **God is.** Is 45:14. Zc √8:23.

26. **How is it.** ver. 15. Ac 21:22. **when ye come.** 1 C +*11:20. Mt +*18:20. He *10:25. **together.** This passage gives the most complete insight into the nature of the worship services of the New Testament church. Evidently the services were characterized by individual participation and sharing of spiritual gifts by each member in the local body in ministry one to another (Ro +*12:5). Ep *5:19-21. Col *3:16. **every.** See on ver. 6. 1 C *12:8-10. 1 P +*4:10. **a psalm.** Ep 5:19. Col 3:16. **a doctrine.** or, teaching. ⨍108B, Mk +4:2. ver. +6. 2 T +*3:16. **a tongue.** ver. 1, *18. **a revelation.** ver. +6. **an interpretation.** S#2058g, *hermeenia.* ver. 5, 13. 1 C +12:10g. For related words, see Mk +5:41. **Let all.** ver. 4, 5, 12, *40. 1 C 12:7. Ro *14:19. 2 C 12:19. 13:10. Ep 4:12, 16, *29. 1 Th 5:11. **unto edifying.** ver. 4, 5, 12, 17. 1 C *10:23. Ro +*14:19.

27. **If any man.** ⨍184A, 1 C +15:2. ver. 34n. **tongue.** ver. 1, 18. **by two, or.** That is, let not more than two, or at most three, be so engaged at one time of assembling; and let this be done *by course*, one after another. **let one interpret.** ver. 5, 13, 26. 1 C +12:10.

28. **But if.** ⨍184C, Mt +4:9. **interpreter.** ver. +27. **let him keep silence.** ver. ❶34n. **speak to himself.** ver. 4. **and to God.** ver. 2.

29. **the prophets.** ver. 39. 1 C 12:10. 1 Th *5:19-21. 1 J 4:1-3. **two or three.** ver. 27n. **the other.** Rather, **the others,** *io alloi.* **judge.** 1 C 12:10. Jb *12:11. Is +*8:20n. Mk +*4:24. Ac +*17:11. 1 Th *5:20, 21. 1 J *4:1.

30. **If.** ⨍184C, Mt +4:9. **revealed.** ver. 6, 26. **let the first.** ⨍96E5, Jn +1:15. Clearly no one person, no matter how gifted, was to monopolize the service. Jb 32:11, 15-20. 33:31-33. 1 Th 5:19, 20.

31. **all may learn.** ver. 3, 19, 35. Pr 1:5. 9:9. Ep *4:11, 12. **all may be.** Ro 1:12. 2 C 1:4. 7:6, 7. Ep 6:22. 1 Th 4:18. 5:11, 14. **comforted.** or, exhorted.

32. **the spirits.** Gr. *pneuma*, ⨍121A1, Lk +1:17n.

⌐121A1, Jn +3:34. By *Metonymy of the Cause*, the person acting is put for the thing done. Here, the "spirit" is put for the spiritual gifts. ⌐24J, Dt +32:42. By *Antimereia*, a noun is used for an adjective. The noun "spirits" is used for the adjective *spiritual gifts*. ver. 29, 30. 1 S 10:10-13. 19:19-24. 2 K 2:3, 5. Jb 32:8-11. Je 20:9. Ac 4:19, 20. 1 J 4:1. **the prophets**. ver. 29. Ac +13:1. Re 22:6. **are subject**. That is, those who were actuated by the Holy Spirit in the very moments of inspiration, still retained the free use of themselves, and continued masters of their rational and persuasive faculties (Bp. Warburton). Ps *39:2, 3.

33. **God is not**. T#269. Je 7:9, 10. Ja 1:13-17. 1 J *2:16. **the author**. ⌐63B, Ge +25:28. **confusion**. Gr. tumult, *or*, unquietness. Hab +*2:20. Lk 21:9. 2 C 6:5. 12:20. Ja 1:8. 3:16. **but of peace**. 1 C 7:15. Lk 2:14. Ro +15:33. Ga 5:22. 2 Th 3:16. He 13:20. Ja 3:17, 18. **as**. ⌐63B, Ge +25:28. Supply by ellipsis, (He is). **in all the churches**. 1 C 4:17. +7:17. 11:16. **of the saints**. 2 C +1:1.

34. **women**. This injunction applies not only to married women, but to all women, since "every" modifies both "men" and "women" in the corresponding passage (1 C 11:3, 5). 1 C *7:34. +*11:5. 1 S 2:1-10. 2 K 22:14. Mk 12:42. 14:9. Lk 2:36-38. 8:3. Ro 16:1-3, 6, *12, 15. Ep 5:22. Ph √4:2, 3. Col 3:18. 1 T +*2:9, 11, 12. T 2:4, 5. 1 P 3:1-8. 2 J 1. **keep silence**. The "silence" demanded here is not absolute; it applies specifically to teaching whenever it places a woman in authority over men. This command to silence is a command of the Lord (ver. 37) for all churches of the saints (ver. 33). The grounds of authority for this command, given more explicitly in 1 T 2:11, 12 and 1 C 11:2-16, are (1) the law of God, considered in (a) the order of creation of man and woman (Ge 2:18, etc. 1 C 11:8, 9); (b) the submission of woman to the headship of man (1 C 11:8, 9. 1 T 2:11), though like the subordinate relationship of Jesus the Son of God to God the Father, this by no means denies their equality before God (1 C +*11:3. Ga 3:28); (c) the complete or thorough deception of the woman (2 C 11:3g. 1 T 2:14g), in apparent reference to the disastrous consequences of reversing God's order of submission and headship. (2) the universality of the command, uniformly given and enforced in all the churches (ver. 37) and by all the apostles (1 C 11:16, "we," "churches of God"). (3) the need for such command to maintain due order in the churches (ver. 40). To suppose that this command is for Paul's time only, for a particular condition in the culture of that day, is to neglect the specific teaching of the grounds of the command, grounds which are not local and situational but normative, and therefore valid for all time. Paul does not base his argument upon cultural factors which change over time or place, but upon the unchanging relationships determined by God at creation, the very argument Jesus adopted in answering the question about divorce in Mt 19:4, 5. Both Paul and Jesus in their arguments cite the pre-fall condition of man. 1 C ◐√11:5, 13. Pr +*19:13. Is +*58:13. Jl ◑2:29. Ac ◑1:14. ◑2:17. 12:◑12, ◑13, 17g. 15:7. ◐√18:26n. ◐21:9. 2 J ◐+*5. **in the churches**. 1 C +*16:19. Ex-+√15:20n. 2 K +*4:23. Ac 1:14. 1 T 2:9. **not permitted**. 1 C 16:7g. 1 T *2:12g. **to speak**. Some of the following references are adduced to show that in the spontaneous atmosphere of the Jewish synagogue,

the men often spoke out in a disruptive fashion during the message, raising questions or voicing objections. Some interpreters suppose this was the circumstance to which Paul's admonition to keep silence was addressed. Paul, however, as noted above, grounds his prohibition on the principle that a woman is never in the congregation to assert authority over a man. This being the issue, the prohibition does not pertain to forbidding women to disrupt the service with objections and questions, but pertains to the implicit assertion of authority over a man that being in a position of public teaching implies. The Levites were the appointed teachers under the Law (2 Ch +15:3. 35:3n. He 7:11), were always men, and under the law possessed binding authority (Ml 2:7) by virtue of their office (Mt 23:2, 3). To refuse to heed their teaching or rulings was a very serious punishable offence (Dt √17:8-13). Placing a woman in such a public position of authority over men is entirely out of place, for she is to look to the man as her head, not the man look to her. Lk 4:28, 29. Jn +*7:30. Ac *13:45-47. +*17:2. 18:6. 1 T *2:12. **they are**. ⌐180A, Ge +4:20. ver. 35. 1 C 11:3, 7-10. Ep 5:22-24, 33. Col 3:18. T 2:5. 1 P 3:4-6. **under obedience**. or, under subjection. Perhaps "submission" is an even better rendering. ver. 21. 1 C 7:36-38. +*11:3. Ge √2:18. 3:16. 16:9. Nu 30:3-13. Est 1:17-20. 1 P +5:5g. **saith the law**. Paul appeals to the law as the basis of his authoritative teaching for the church. Paul was evidently not under the misconception that since we are under grace, we have no more to do with the law, a position which, when taken to the logical extreme, is the heresy termed "antinomianism." See related notes (Ga 3:10n. Col 2:13n. 1 Th 4:2n. 1 J √2:3n). ver. 21. Ge √2:18. ?3:16. 1 T √2:13, 14.

35. **And if**. ⌐184A, 1 C +15:2. ⌐152B, Is +49:14. **they will learn**. This admonition seems designed to answer the potential objection of the women, "But what if we want to ask a question about what we don't understand?" **let them ask**. Ep 5:25-27. 1 P 3:7. **their own husbands at home**. Clearly the Biblical pattern is that the husband is to exercise the spiritual leadership in the home. This ought to be a guide in choosing a mate for marriage: a Christian woman should only marry a Christian (2 C √6:14. 1 C 7:39), and only a Christian man capable of exercising the spiritual leadership in her home. Her marriage partner, for the best marriage, must be more mature spiritually than she is. 2 S +*6:20. Jb +*1:5. Ps +*101:2 (T#492). Ep *5:22. T *2:5. 1 P *3:1. **a shame**. ver. 34. 1 C 11:6, 14. Ep 5:12. Col *3:18.

36. **came**. Is 2:3. Mi 4:1, 2. Zc 14:8. Ac 13:1-3. 15:35, 36. 16:9, 10. 17:1, 10, 11, 15. 18:1, etc. Ro +*15:19n. 2 C 10:13-16. 1 Th *1:8. **the word of God**. Ro +*9:6. **or**. 1 C 4:7.

37. **If**. ⌐184A, 1 C +15:2. 1 C 8:2. 13:1-3. Nu 24:3, 4, 16. Ro +*12:3. 2 C 10:7, 12. 11:4, 12-15. Ga 6:8. **any man**. 1 C +11:16. **think himself**. Ja +1:26. **a prophet**. ver. 29. 1 C +13:1. **or spiritual**. 1 C *2:15. *3:1. Ro +1:11g. **let**. 1 C 7:25, 40. Lk 10:16. 1 Th 4:1-8. 2 P 3:2. 1 J √4:6. Ju 17. **acknowledge**. Gr. *epiginosko*, Mt +11:27. **of the Lord**. Ro 16:12n.

38. **if any**. ⌐184A, 1 C +15:2. Ho 4:17. Mt +√7:6. +*15:14. 1 T *6:3-5. 2 T 4:3, 4. Re +*22:11, 12. **let him be**. Mt +√7:6. Re +*22:11.

39. **covet**. ver. 1, 3, 5, 24, 25. 1 C +12:31. 1 Th

5:20. **to prophesy.** 1 C +13:1, 2, 8. **forbid not.** 1 Th *5:19, 20. **to speak with tongues.** ver. +4, √5, √18. 40. **Let all.** ver. *26-33. 1 C 11:34. Ro 13:13mg. Col *2:5. T 1:5. **decently.** Ro +13:13. **in order.** T#1841. 1 Ch +15:13. 2 Ch 26:18. Ep 5:23. Col 2:5. 1 Th 5:14. 2 Th 3:6, 11.

1 CORINTHIANS 15

The apostle states that gospel, which he had preached at Corinth, and shows how fully the resurrection of Christ had been demonstrated, 1-11. He proves that the resurrection of the dead is inseparable from that of Christ; and that the denial of it is subversive of Christianity, and of all the hopes of Christians, 12-19: but "Christ, the First-fruits," being risen, all others shall arise in due order; till death the last enemy being subdued, the kingdom shall be delivered up to the Father, 20-28: otherwise it would be in vain for any to risk their lives, as the apostle did, 29-32. He warns and reproves the Corinthians, refutes objections, and illustrates his doctrine, 33-41; shows some things relating to the general resurrection; contrasts the first and the second Adam, and shows the change which will be wrought both in the dead, and those who shall at that time be found living, 42-53. As death will at length be thus swallowed up in victory, he triumphs in hope over death and the grave through Christ, 54-57; and concludes with an animated exhortation, to steady and persevering diligence, in the work of the Lord, 58.

1. **I declare.** ver. 3-11. 1 C *1:23, 24. *2:2-7. 12:3. Ac *18:4, 5. 2 C 8:1. Ga *1:6-12. Ph 1:22g. **I preached.** 1 C 3:6. 2 T 2:8. **which also.** 1 C *1:4-8. 11:23. Mk *4:16-20. Jn *12:48. Ac *2:41. *11:1. Ga 1:12. 1 Th 1:6. √2:13. 4:1. 2 Th *3:6. **ye stand.** 1 C +16:13. Jn 8:44. Ro *5:2. 2 C *1:24. Col 4:12. 1 P *5:12.

2. **by which.** Is 34:16. Jn +*5:39. 2 T +*3:15. **ye are.** 1 C 1:18, 21. Ac *2:47g. Ro √1:16. 2 C 2:15. Ep √2:8. 2 T +*1:9. **if.** Ge +*4:7. Col +*1:23. 2 P +*1:10. ƒ184A. Hypothetical Propositions; or, Conditional ("if") Sentences: First Condition; or, Simple Supposition. The First Condition is used when one wished to assume or seem to assume the reality of his premise. The First Condition *"assumes* the condition to be a reality and the conclusion follows logically and naturally from that assumption." Here, Paul assumes that they are holding it fast (A. T. Robertson, *Word Pictures*, vol. 4, p. 186). For other instances of this construction see ver. 2, 12, 13, 14, 15, 16, 17, 19, 29, 32. 1 C 3:12, 14, 15, 17, 18. 4:7. 6:2. 7:9, 12, 13, 15, 16, 21, 28, 36. 8:2, 3, 13. 9:2, 11, 12, 17. 10:27, 30. 11:6, 16, 31, 34. 12:17. 14:27, 35, 37, 38. 16:22. Mt *4:3, 6. 5:29, 30. 6:23, 30. 7:11. 10:25. 12:26, 27. 14:28. 16:24. 17:4n. 18:8, 9. 19:10. 22:45. 26:33, 39, 42. 27:40, 42, 43. Mk 3:26. 4:23. 7:16. 9:22, 23, 35. 11:13, 25, 26. 14:35. 15:44. Lk 4:3, 9. 5:36. 6:32. 9:23. 10:6, 13. 11:11, 13, 18, 19, 20, 36. 12:26. 13:9. 14:26. 16:11, 12, 30, 31. 17:2. 19:8. 22:42. 23:31, 35, 37, 39. Jn 1:25. 3:12. 5:47. 7:4, 23. 10:24, 35, 37, 38. 11:12. 13:14, 17, 32. 15:18, 20. 18:8, 23. 20:15. Ac 4:9. 5:39n. 8:22, 31, 37. 13:15. 16:15. 18:15. 19:38, 39. 23:9. 25:5, 11. Ro 1:10. 2:17. 3:3, 5. 4:2, 14. 5:10, 15, 17. 6:5, 8. 7:16. 8:9, 9, 10, 11, 13, 13, 17, 17, 25, 31. 9:22. 11:6, 12, 14, 15, 16, 17, 18, 21. 13:9. 14:15. 15:27. 2 C 2:2, 5, 10. 3:7, 9, 11. 4:3. 5:14, 17. 7:14. 8:12. 11:4, 15, 16, 20, 30. Ga 1:9. 2:14, 18, 21. 3:4, 18, 29. 4:7.

5:11, 15, 18, 25. 6:3. Ep 3:2. 4:21. Ph 1:22. 2:1. 3:15. 4:8. Col *1:23. 2:20. 3:1. 1 Th 3:8. 4:14. 2 Th 3:10, 14. 1 T 3:1, 5. 5:4, 8, 10, 16. 6:3. 2 T 2:11, 12, 13. Phm 17, 18. He 2:2. 3:11mg. 4:3, 5. 7:15. 12:7, 8. Ja 1:5, 23, 26. 2:8, 9, 11. 3:2. 4:11. 5:19. 1 P 1:6, 17. 2:3, 19, 20. 3:1. 4:11, 14, 16, 17. 2 P 2:4, 20. 1 J 3:13. 4:11. 5:9, 15. 2 J 10. Re 13:9. 14:9. For the Second Condition, see ƒ184B, Lk +7:39; ƒ184B, Mt +11:21; ƒ184B, Mt +23:20; for the Third Condition, ƒ184C, Mt +4:9; for the Fourth Condition, ƒ184D1, Lk +22:67; ƒ184D2, Lk +1:62. **keep in memory.** *or*, hold fast. ver. 11, 12. 1 C 11:2. Pr 3:1. 4:13. *6:20-23. 23:23. Col +√1:23. 2 Th 2:15. 1 T 1:19. He *2:1. 3:6, *14. 4:14. 6:6. 10:23. 2 P √3:17. **what I preached.** Gr. by what speech I preached. **unless.** ƒ184A, ver. +*2. "Condition of first class, unless in fact ye did believe to no purpose" (A. T. Robertson, *Word Pictures*, vol. 4, p. 186). ver. *14, 17. Ps *106:12, 13. Mt 13:20, 21. Lk +*8:13. Jn √8:31, 32. Ac 8:13. 2 C *6:1. Ga 3:4. Ja *2:14, 17, 19, 20, 26. **believed in vain.** "Paul holds this peril over them in their temptation to deny the resurrection" (A. T. Robertson, *Word Pictures*, vol. 4, p. 186). Lk +*8:13. Ac¡ *8:13, 21. Ro +13:4. Ga +*4:11.

3. **I delivered.** 1 C 4:1, 2. 11:2, 23. Ezk *3:17. Mt *20:18, 19. Mk *16:15, 16. Lk *24:46, 47. Ga *1:12. **sins.** Le +=5:6. Mt +*26:28. Jn 1:29. Ro 3:25. 4:25. 2 C √5:21. Ga 1:4. 3:13. Ep +*1:7. 5:2. He 5:1. 10:11, 12. 1 P *2:24. *3:18. 1 J √2:2. Re +*1:5. **according.** Ge +*3:15. Ps ch. *22, 69. Is +*53:5, 6, 8, 11, 12. Da +*9:24-26. Zc *13:7. See on Lk +*24:26, 27, 46. Ac *3:18. *26:22, 23. 1 P *1:11. *2:24. **the scriptures.** Mt +21:42.

4. **that.** Is *53:9. Mt *27:57-60. Mk *15:43-46. Lk 23:50-53. Jn 19:38-42. Ac *2:31. *13:29. Ro *6:4. Col *2:12. **he rose.** ver. *16-21. Mt *20:19. *27:63, 64. *28:1-6. Mk *9:31. *10:33, 34. *16:2-7. Lk 9:22. 18:32, 33. *24:5-7. Jn +√2:19-21. *20:1-9. Ac *1:3. *2:23, +√24n, 32. 13:30. √17:31. He 13:20. **the third day.** ƒ108H12, 1 S +30:12. ver. 23 w Le +=23:11n. Ge +*22:4. 1 S 30:12n. Mt +*12:40n. 17:23. 20:19. 26:61. 27:40, 63. Lk 13:32. 23:44n. 24:7, 21, 46. Jn +*2:19, 20, 22. **according.** Ge +*49:10. Dt 16:1n. Ps *2:7. +*16:10, 11. Is *53:10-12. Ho 6:2. Jon *1:17. Mt +*12:40n. Lk +*23:44n. *+*24:26, 46. Ac *2:25-33. *13:30-37. *26:22, 23. 1 P *1:11. **the scriptures.** Mt +21:42.

5. **that.** Lk *24:34, etc. **Cephas.** 1 C 1:12. 3:22. 9:5. Jn +1:42. **then.** Mk +9:35. 16:14. Lk 24:36, etc. Jn *20:19-26. Ac 1:2-14. *10:41. **twelve.** ƒ11, Ge +2:23.

6. **After that.** ƒ157. Protimesis; or, Description of Order B457. The figure is employed when things are enumerated according to their places of honor or importance. For other instances of this figure see 1 C 12:28. 15:22-24. Col 1:15. 1 Th 4:15-17. Re 20:5, 6. **he was.** Mt *28:10, 16, 17. Mk 16:7. **remain.** Jn 21:22, 23. Ph 1:25. **are fallen.** ver. 18, 20, 51. 1 C 7:39. Mt +27:52. Ac *7:60. 13:36. 1 Th 4:13, 15. 2 P 3:4.

7. **James.** Ac +12:17. **then.** Lk *24:50. Ac *1:2-12.

8. **he was seen.** T#*99. 1 C +9:1. Ac 1:21, 22. *9:3-5, 17. 13:30, 31. 18:9. 22:14, 18. 26:16. 2 C 12:1-6. **one born.** Is *66:8. Je 30:6, 7. Mt +*24:8. **out of due time.** *or*, an abortive. Jb 3:16. Ec 6:3. Lk +*1:44n. 1 T √1:16. +*2:6.

9. **the least.** ƒ111, Ge +18:27. 2 C ◑*11:5. ◑*12:11. Ep *3:7, 8. 1 T *1:13-15. **because.** Ac +*8:3. *9:1,

etc. 22:4, 5. 26:9-11. Ga *1:13, 23. Ph 3:6. 1 T 1:13, 14. **the church.** 1 C +10:32.

10. **by.** 1 C 4:7. Ro 11:1, 5, 6. +*12:3. Ep *2:7, 8. 3:7, 8. 1 T *1:15, 16. **the grace.** 1 C +1:4. **his grace.** ver. 2. 2 C 6:1. **but I labored.** Ro 15:17-20. 2 C 10:12-16. 11:23-30. *12:11. Col 1:29. **yet not I.** ʃ69B, Pr +6:16. 1 C 3:6. 12:6. Mt +*10:20. 2 C *3:5, 6. Ga 2:8, √20. Ep 3:7, 20. Ph √2:13. √4:13. Col *1:28, 29.

11. **whether.** ver. 3, 4. 1 C *2:2. Ac *4:2. *8:5.

12. **if.** ʃ184A, ver. +*2. ʃ116, 1 C +11:16. See on ver. 4. **Christ is preached.** Ac +17:18. **how say.** ʃ96B. Heterosis of Moods B513: indicative for subjunctive. As the Hebrew language has no subjunctive mood, the indicative is often put instead of that mood; and this is done in the New Testament, as well as in the Old Testament, inasmuch as, though the language is Greek, the thoughts and idioms are Hebrew. Here, i.e., how is it that some among you say. In verse 35, "But some men will say": i.e., may say. Verse 50, "Neither doth corruption inherit incorruption": i.e., neither *can* corruption, etc. ver. 13-19. Ac 26:8. 2 T 2:17, 18. **some among.** 1 C +11:16. **there is.** ʃ96C6, Mt +2:4.

13. **if there be no.** ʃ184A, ver. +*2. ver. 20. Jn *11:25, 26. 14:19. Ac +*23:8n. Ro *4:24, 25. +*8:11, 34. 2 C *4:10-14. Col 3:1-4. 1 Th *4:14. 2 T 4:8. He 2:14, 15. *13:20. 1 P *1:3. Re *1:18. **of.** ʃ181E, Ge +3:24.

14. **if Christ be not.** ʃ184A, ver. +*2. ver. √2, √17. Ps 73:13. Is *49:4. Je *8:8. Mt *15:9. Ac √17:31. Ga 2:2. Ja *1:26. *2:20. **your faith.** ver. 2.

15. **false witnesses.** Ex +*23:3. Jb 13:7-10. Mt 26:60. Ro 3:7, 8. **we have testified.** Ac +*2:24, 32. *4:10, 33. 10:39-42. *13:30-33. 20:21. **Christ.** Mt +11:2. **whom.** ver. 13, 20. **if so be.** ʃ184A, ver. +*2. 1 C 6:14. Mt 10:8. 11:5. Mk 12:26. Lk 7:22. Jn 5:21. Ac 26:8.

16. **For if.** ʃ184A, ver. +*2.

17. **And if.** ʃ184A, ver. +*2. **your faith.** ver. 2, 14. Ro *4:25. **ye are yet.** If Christ be not risen, ye have no evidence of God's having accepted his mediation for you, nor, consequently, of your being justified. Ezk 33:10. Jn +*8:21-24. Ac *5:31. 13:38, 39. Ro +*4:25. *5:10. 8:33, 34. He *7:23-28. *9:22-28. 10:4-12. 1 P 1:3, 21. **in your sins.** Jn 3:21, 24. 9:34.

18. **fallen.** ver. +6. 1 Th 4:13, 14, 16. Re 14:13. **perished.** Gr. *apollumi*, Mt +2:13.

19. **If in.** ʃ184A, ver. +*2. **this.** Ps 17:14. Ec 6:11. 9:9. Lk 8:14. +*21:34. 1 C 6:3, 4. 2 T 2:4. **hope.** Ep 1:12, 13. 1 Th 1:3. 2 T 1:12. 1 P 1:21. **of all.** 1 C 4:9-13. Mt 10:21-25. 24:9. Jn 16:2, 33. Ac +*14:22. 2 C *1:5. 2 T *3:12. Re +*14:13. **most.** lit. more. ʃ96E4, Mt +13:32.

20. **But now.** ʃ136, Is +60:12. See on ver. 4-8. **risen.** Nu=17:3, 8. Dt=33:2. Ro 4:25. 2 T 2:8. 1 P 1:3. 3:21. **the firstfruits.** ver. 23. Le +±23:10. Ac +*26:23. Ro +*8:11. Col +*1:18. 1 P 1:3. Re +*1:5. **them that slept.** ver. +6.

21. **by man came death.** ver. 22. Ro 5:12-17. **by man came also.** Jn +11:25, 26. Ro +*6:23. **the resurrection.** Jn +*5:29.

22. **in Adam.** T#158. ver. 45-49. Ge 2:17. 3:6, 19. Jn *5:21-29. Ro 5:12-21. **all die.** ʃ171M, Ge +6:12. Ge 3:3, 22-24. 4:8. Ro *5:12, 18, 19. **made alive.** ver. +45. Jn *5:21. Ro 4:17. +*8:11.

23. **every man.** ver. 20. Is +*26:19n. 1 Th *4:15-17. **firstfruits.** ʃ157, ver. 6. ver. +20. Ac *26:23. **afterward.** ʃ157, ver. 6. **they that are Christ's.** ver. 52. 1 C 3:23. 2 C +6:14. 10:7. Lk +14:14. Ga 3:29. 5:24. 1 Th 4:16. **at his.** This text absolutely denies the possibility of any human being since Christ, not even Mary the mother of Jesus, being assumed or resurrected bodily into heaven, for bodily resurrection does not take place until his second coming, and the destiny of the resurrected is not the third heaven, but an eternal inheritance upon this earth (Mt +*5:5. Ep +*1:11n). Jn +*14:3. Ac +*1:11. Ph +*3:20, 21. 1 Th +2:19. *4:16. **coming.** Gr. *parousia*, Mt +24:3.

24. **Then.** ʃ157, ver. 6. **cometh the end.** Care must be taken not to assume that there is only one "end" in Scripture (Jn 6:54n), for this "end," which may well be postmillennial, does not transpire at the same time as some of the other "ends," several of which are clearly premillennial (1 C 1:8. Mt 24:13, 14). Furthermore, the single English word "end" is used to render two significantly different Greek words: here, it is *telos* (✳S#5056g, Mt +10:22), but in some passages it is *suntelia* (✳S#4930g, Mt +24:3). Da 12:4, 9, 13. Mt 10:22. 13:39, 40. 24:6, 13, 14. 1 P 4:7. **when.** Mt 26:29g. Lk ◐√19:15. Re 18:9g. **shall have delivered up.** ʃ63A1. Figure of speech Ellipsis (Absolute: of the Nominative), whereby the subject must be supplied from the nature of the subject alone, or from what is elsewhere expressed, Ge +14:20. The nominative or subject of this verb is not Christ, but by a common scriptural idiom in which the verb is used without any personal nominative, the verb has reference to the purpose of God elsewhere expressed in His Word (see Peters, *Theocratic Kingdom*, vol. 2, Proposition 159, Obs. 3, p. 635). Compare for the grammatical, as opposed to rhetorical, discussion of this construction: Samuel G. Green, *Handbook to the Grammar of the Greek New Testament*, pp. 101 (sec. 101), 166, 167 (sec. 170, 171). W. H. Moulton, *Grammar*, vol. 1, p. 58, 74, 226, 236. Moulton, *Idiom Book*, pp. 27-29. Robertson, *Grammar*, pp. 802, 820. Turner, *Grammar*, vol. 3, pp. 291-293. **the kingdom.** Not his own kingdom, but those which he has subdued (Re 11:15), for the Messianic kingdom will never end (Da √7:14. Lk √1:32, 33). Note Paul's *intentional obscurity* here to avoid endangering the persons addressed who lived in the potentially hostile political environment of the Roman Empire (see other instances of obscurity at the related notes on 2 Th 2:7 and He 12:27). Peters (*Theocratic Kingdom*, vol. 1, p. 260, Proposition 40, Observation 6, note; pp. 270, 271; pp. 626, 627) notes that Jesus, and the New Testament writers taken as a whole, manifest the same reserve in their teaching regarding the kingdom of God, depending upon the hearer's or reader's knowledge of the Old Testament covenants, promises, and prophecies for information as to its details, and for the same reasons. Two additional instances of intentional obscurity are the very discreet terminology Peter used in his message recorded at Ac 3:19-21, and the use of indirect citations of Old Testament prophecies by the Apostle John in the Revelation (see especially the references to Ps 2 and Da 7 in Re 11:15-19). These citations would serve, for his original intended audience, as a kind of triggering mechanism to remind his hearers of the related context and associated well known prophecies, references which would

escape notice and not be understood should the book fall into hostile hands, ever ready to charge the Christians with political intrigue against the Roman authority (Jn 11:48. Ac 17:7). This feature may also account, in part, for John's placing the prophecy of the new heaven and earth in an apparently postmillennial chronological position, when his readers, who would be most familiar with the other Bible predictions relating to this event, were certainly aware that every other mention of this event in prophecy places it in a premillennial chronological setting (see related note, 2 P 3:12n). That citations of the Old Testament were sometimes used as a "triggering mechanism" to remind the reader of their associated context seems quite evident when one considers the context of Matthew's citation (Mt 2:18) of Jeremiah, for he cites Je 31:15, but if one considers verses 16 and 17, the relevance of the quotation is evident, for Jeremiah is predicting that the children will return to this very land in resurrection, a most appropriate consolation for those who lost children at the hand of Herod. The effectiveness of such a device becomes more probable when one considers carefully the extensive background knowledge of the Scriptures possessed by even the common people in Israel during New Testament times (T#1122, Jn +√6:14). Ps 45:6. Is +*9:7. *40:9, 10. Da +*7:14, 27. Mt *11:27. *28:18. Lk 10:22. Jn 3:35. 13:3. 1 T 6:15. He +*1:8. Re +*11:15. 19:16. **to God.** Gr. the God and Father. Ps +*22:28. *146:10. Ro +15:6. Ep 5:20. Ja 1:27. **all rule.** Ro +*8:38. Ep 1:21. 3:10. 6:12. Col 1:16. 2:10, 15. T 3:1. He 2:8. **all authority and power.** Lk 4:36. 1 P 3:22. Re 17:13.

25. **For.** √22A15D. Anthropomorphism B880. Christ's dignity is further described by the figure *theoprepos, worthy of a god.* For another instance of this figure see Ep 4:10. **he.** √63A1, Ge +14:20. Supply ellipsis (absolute: of the nominative), "(the Son) must reign, until he (the Son) shall have put all things under his (the Son's) feet." **must reign.** Ps *2:6-10. 45:3-6. *110:1. Is +*24:23. Je +*23:5. Mi +*4:7. Zc +*14:9. Mt 22:44. Mk 12:36. Lk +13:33. 20:42, 43. 24:26. Jn +3:14. Ac 2:34, 35. 3:21. Ep 1:22. 2 T *2:12. He 1:13. 2:8. *10:12, 13. 1 P 3:22. Re *11:15. **till.** This must not be understood in a manner which limits the reign of Christ to one thousand years or any other period. To limit his reign contradicts all covenant and prophecy. The Millennial reign is not terminated by the close of the thousand years. The declaration that Christ rules with his saints during the thousand years does not limit the reign to this period, but only asserts that this reign begins with this period (Peters, *Theocratic Kingdom,* vol. 2, Proposition 159, Obs. 1, p. 631). What ends is the reign over his enemies, all of which, even the last enemy, death, shall be destroyed by the end of the Millennium. The one thousand year period called the Millennium marks the length of time Satan is bound, and the length of time after the completion of the first resurrection during which the "rest of the dead" await the second resurrection (Re 20:5, 7), and it most certainly must not be understood to mark the end of the eternal reign of Christ, which would be a contradiction in terms. 2 S +*7:16. Ps √10:16. 45:6. √72:5. +*89:4. 110:4. √145:13mg. Is +*9:7. Da 2:44. √7:14. Lk √1:32, 33. Jn √12:34. 1 T √1:17g. He +*1:8. 2 P 1:11. Re √11:15. **all enemies.** Ps √10:16. Mi +*5:9. **under his feet.** Jsh *10:24.

11:23. 2 S *22:41. Is +*63:1-4.

26. **last enemy.** ver. +√55. Is +*25:8. Je *31:16, 17. Ho *13:14. Lk 20:36. 2 T *1:10. He *2:14. Re √20:13, 14. +*21:4.

27. **hath put.** √96C2, Ge +45:9. Ps √8:6, 7. 110:1. Mt +*11:27. +*28:18. Jn 3:35. 13:3. Ep *1:20, 22. Ph *2:9-11. He 1:13. ◐√2:8. 10:12, 13. 1 P *3:22. Re *1:18.

28. **all things.** Ps 2:8, 9. 18:39, 47. 21:8, 9. Da 2:34, 35, 40-45. Mt 13:41-43. Ph 3:21. Re 19:11-21. 20:2-4, 10-15. **then.** T#964‡. 1 C *3:23. +*11:3. Mt +*10:32. 20:23. Jn *5:26, 27, 30. +*14:28 (T#963‡). Ph 2:5-7. **the Son.** Mt +24:36. **himself be subject.** The subordination (the Greek term means either *subject* or *subordinate,* so Daniel Waterland, *Works,* vol. 4, pp. 23, 24) of the Son to the Father is a voluntary though evidently permanent relationship which does not detract from or deny the equal deity of the Son, any more than the divine order of the submission of the wife to the husband (1 C 11:3) in the husband/wife relationship detracts from her essential equality and humanity, or implies her inferiority. 1 C 3:23. *11:3. Mt +*10:32. *20:23. Jn 6:38n. +*14:28. T +*1:2. **that God.** Mt +√28:19. **all in all.** √145, Jg +11:40. Waterland astutely observes that God's creatures will be "subject in quite another manner and degree than Christ can be. They will be subject as *servants* to their *Lord,* as *creatures* to their *Creator*: he will be subordinate only, as a *Son* to a *Father,* and as partaking of the same common dominion with him over the whole creation. The Son therefore is represented in the heavenly Jerusalem, as making but one *temple* (Re 21:22) with the Father, and one light (Re 21:23), and seated on the same *throne* (Re 22:1, 3). It is absurd to imagine that the Son will be more subject than he is now, that his *triumphant* state shall come short of his *militant,* and that he is to *decrease,* when all his saints and servants are to increase." "There is nothing in all this that intimates any *natural* or *necessary* subjection of two of the Divine Persons to one; nor any *inequality* of nature or perfections amongst them: but there is a natural supremacy of *order* belonging to God the Father; and to him, as Fountain of the Deity, God the Son, and God the Holy Ghost, proceeding from him, are referred" (Waterland, *Works,* vol. 4, p. 24). 1 C 12:6. Ro √9:5. Ep 1:23. Col +*3:11.

29. **what.** ver. 16, 32. Mt *20:22. Ro +*6:3, 4. **shall they.** Paul's shift to the third person here seems to disassociate himself from this belief or practice. The practice of baptism for the dead may have been a short-lived error of a small group of the Corinthians who, rightfully awed by the power of the resurrection, supposed its benefits could be made available (akin to the benefit derived by infants born into a family where at least one parent was a believer, 1 C 7:14) by a kind of substitutionary baptismal rite to close friends or relatives who had lately died without receiving an opportunity to hear the saving message of Christ. **which are baptized.** That is, probably, as Ellis and Dr. Doddridge interpret, "who are baptized in the room of the dead;" referring to the case of those who presented themselves for baptism immediately after the martyrdom of their brethren or friends; as if fresh soldiers should enlist and press forward to the assault, to supply the places of those who had fallen. A. T. Robertson remarks that this passage remains a puzzle, noting that over thirty different interpretations have been suggested, perhaps no one of which is certain to be correct. Tertulian tells of some heretics who took it to mean baptized in the place of dead people (unsaved) in order to save them. (*Word Pictures*, vol. 4, pp. 192, 193). Whatever Paul may here refer to, this obscure text furnishes no basis upon which to base a doctrine of baptism for the dead. The point of Paul's argument is, that if there are those who do baptize for the dead (whatever that might have meant—the precise meaning has apparently been lost to us), it shows that *they* by so doing acknowledge the truth that there shall be a resurrection, or there is no possible point to their practice. It is not necessary to the validity of Paul's argument that this practice, whatever it was, be assumed to be correct. Ac *8:1-3, 12. **for the dead**. ∫96F2, Ge +4:10. With the article, as here, "THE dead" denotes dead bodies, corpses (Ge 23:3, 4, 5, 6, 8, 13, 15. Dt 28:26. Je 12:33. Ezk 37:19. Lk 24:5). Without the article, "for (the) dead" denotes dead persons, people who are dead (Dt 14:1. Mt 22:33. Mk 9:10. Lk 16:30, 31. 24:46. Jn 20:9. Ac 10:41. 26:23. Ro 6:13. 10:7. 11:15. He 11:19. 13:20). **if the dead**. ∫184A, ver. +*2. **baptized for**. ∫63B, Ge +2:10. EWB (B41-44) shows that this verse (29) follows immediately upon verse 19 in the literary structure, the intervening verses serving as a parenthesis. By a different punctuation of the original text, and the supply of an ellipsis, this text may be understood to say "What shall they do who are being baptized? *It is* for the dead if the dead rise not at all!" If Christ be not raised, well may those who are being baptized into Christ's burial be asked, "What shall they do?" Truly, "*It is* for the dead." For they will remain dead, as corpses. In this life they "die daily" (ver. 31); in death they perish (ver. 18); and are thus "of all men most miserable" (ver. 19).

30. **why stand**. ver. 31. Ro +*8:36-39. 2 C 4:7-12. 6:9. *11:23-27. Ga 5:1. **in jeopardy**. Lk 8:23. Ac 19:27, 40g. **every hour**. Ro +*8:36.

31. **protest**. Ge 43:3. 1 S 8:9. Je 11:7. Zc 3:6. Ph 3:3. **your**. "*Some read*, our." 2 C 1:12. 2:14. 1 Th *2:19. 3:9. **Christ Jesus our Lord**. Ro +*6:23. 8:39. 2 C 4:5. Ep 3:11. Ph 3:8. Col 2:6. **I die**. 1 C *4:9-13. Ac 15:26. 20:23. Ro *8:36. 2 C 4:10, 11. 11:23. **daily**. Lk 9:23.

32. **If**. ∫184A, ver. +*2. **after**. *or, to speak* after. Ro +3:5. 6:19. Ga 3:15. **beasts**. 2 P 2:12. Ju 10. **Ephesus**. 1 C *16:8, 9. Ac +18:19. 19:1, 23, etc. 2 C *1:8-10. **what advantageth**. Jb 35:3. Ps 73:13-15. Ml 3:14, 15. Lk 9:25. Ja 2:14, 16. **if**. ∫184A, ver. +*2. **let**. Ec 2:24. 11:9. Is *)22:13. 56:12. Lk √12:19, 20.

33. **Be not deceived**. 1 C +*6:9. Mt *24:4, 11, 24. Ga *6:7. Ep 5:6. 2 Th 2:10. Ja 1:16. Re 12:9. 13:8-14. **evil communications**. or, evil company. ∫138C, Ge +22:14. ∫92H, Ac +17:28. 1 C 5:6. Ex 23:2. 2 Ch *13:7. Jb 31:1. Ps +*1:1. 84:10. +*119:63. Pr 1:10, 11, 14, 15. 2:11, 12, 16, 19. *9:6. 12:11. √13:20. 16:29. 17:12. 20:19. 22:10, 24, 25. 23:6, 7, 20, 21. 28:7, 19. 29:24. Ec 9:18. Ezk 14:10n. Ho 4:9. Mt +*15:14. 24:12, 13. Ro 16:17, 18. 1 C 5:6, 9-11. 2 C 6:14, 15. Ep 5:11, 12. 1 T 5:22. 6:3-5, 9-11. 2 T *2:16-18. 3:2-5. He +*12:15. 2 P *2:2, 18-20.

34. **Awake**. Ge +*9:24. Jl 1:5. Jon 1:6. Mt *25:5. Ro *13:11, 12. Ep *5:14. Ph 3:10, 11. 1 Th 5:6, 8. 2 T 2:26. **sin not**. ∫108A6, Jn +7:52. Denoting, "and then ye will not sin." Ps 4:4. √119:11. Jn 5:14. 8:11.

some. 1 C 8:7. See on Ro +*1:28. 1 Th 4:5. **not the knowledge**. 1 P 2:15g. **I speak**. 1 C 4:14. 6:5. He *5:11, 12.

35. **But some**. ∫26, Ro +11:19. Ro +9:19. **will**. ∫96B, ver. +12. i.e. may say. **say**. ∫122, Ex +15:9. **How are**. ∫152B, Is +49:14. Jb 11:12. 22:13. Ps 73:11. Ec 11:5. Ezk 37:3, 11. Jn 3:4, 9. 9:10. **with**. ver. 38-53. Mt 22:29, 30. Ph 3:21. **body**. Is +*43:10n. Da +√12:2. Jn +*2:21. **they come**. Jn 5:29. 1 Th 4:14.

36. **fool**. Lk 11:40. 12:20. 24:25. Ro 1:22. Ep 5:15, 17. **that**. Jn 12:24.

37. **that which**. 1 C 14:10. 16:6. **it may chance**. ∫184D1, Lk +22:67.

38. **God giveth**. 1 C 3:7. Ge 1:11, 12. Ps 104:14. Is 61:11. Mk 4:26-29. **pleased**. 1 C +12:11.

39. **All flesh**. Ge 1:20-26. 8:17. Ac ●17:26.

40. **terrestrial**. Ja +3:15g.

41. **one glory**. Ge 1:14-16. Dt 4:19. Jb 31:26. Ps 8:3. 19:4-6. 148:3-5. Is 24:23. **and**. ∫148, Ge +8:22. **one star**. Da 12:3. Mt 13:43.

42. **So also**. ver. 50. Ro 8:21. Ga 6:8. Col 2:22. 2 P 1:4. 2:12, 19g. **is**. ∫63I1D, Nu +26:4. Supply by ellipsis (of repetition: of preceding connected words), "So the resurrection also of the dead (is with a different body)." ver. 50-54. Da +*12:3. Mt *13:43. Lk *20:35, 36. Ph *3:20, 21. **the resurrection**. Jn +*5:29. **sown**. ∫167, Is +2:7. **in corruption**. ver. 50, 53, 54. Ge +*3:19. Jb 17:14. Ps +*16:10. 49:9, 14. Is 38:17. Ac 2:27, 31. 13:34-37. Ro 1:23. +2:7. 8:21. **it**. ∫41, Ge +10:1. **is**. ∫96C6, Mt +2:4. ver. 52-54. Lk 20:35, 36. 1 P 1:4.

43. **in dishonor**. Da +*12:1. Mt 13:43. Ph 3:20, 21. **is raised**. ∫96C6, Mt +2:4. Ph 3:21. Col 3:4. **weakness**. Jb 14:10mg. Ps 49:6-15. 102:23. 2 C 13:4. **is raised**. ∫96C6, Mt +2:4. **in power**. 1 C 6:14. Mt 22:29, 30. Mk 12:24, 25. 2 C 13:4. Ph 3:10.

44. **natural**. Ja +3:15. **is raised**. ∫96C6, Mt +2:4. **spiritual body**. Jb +*19:25, 26. Ro +1:11g. +*8:11. **there is a spiritual**. Mt *17:1, 2. Lk 24:31. Jn 20:19, 26. Ro +1:11g.

45. **The first**. ver. 47-49. Ge +*)2:7. Ro *5:12-14. Re 16:3. **Adam**. ver. 22. Ge=2:7. Ps 40:7, 8. Is 53:10, 11. Ro *5:14, 15, 17, 18. Ep *1:4. *3:9. Col *1:26, 27. 2 T *1:9. T √1:2. He 2:10, 11, 14. 7:22. 10:5. 13:20. 1 P √1:20. **soul**. Gr. *psyche*, ∫171Q3. Synecdoche of the Part, *psyche* is also put for the whole creature, or animate creature, human or other, as in Re 16:3. For other instances of ∫171Q3, see Ge +1:20. For the other uses of *psyche*, see Mt +2:20n. 1 Th +5:23. T#980‡. Ge 2:7. Dt 24:7. 1 P 3:20. **the last**. Ro 5:14. **a quickening**. ver. +22. Ezk 36:27. 37:14. Jn 1:4. 4:10, 14. *5:+*21, 24-29. 6:33, 39, 40, 54, 57, 63, 68. 10:10, 28. 11:25, 26. 14:6, 19. *17:2, 3. Ac 3:15. Ro 5:17, 21. *8:2, 10, +*11. 2 C 3:17. Ph 3:21. Col 3:4. 1 J 1:1-3. √5:11, 12. Re 21:6. 22:1, 17. **spirit**. Gr. *pneuma*, Ro +1:4n.

46. **spiritual**. Ro +1:11g. **that which is natural**. Ro 6:6. Ep 4:22-24. Col *3:9, 10. **spiritual**. Ro +1:11g.

47. **first**. ver. 45. Ge +*2:7. *3:19. Jn +*3:13, 31. 2 C 5:1. **earthy**. Ge 2:7. 3:19. 2 C 4:7. 5:2. **second man**. Ge 32:24. Zc +*13:7. Mt 16:27n. 1 T +*2:5. **is**. ∫63I2, Jsh +3:3. Supply by ellipsis (of repetition: from succeeding clause, ver. 48), "the second man, the Lord from heaven, (is heavenly)." **the Lord**. 1 C √2:8. *12:3. Ex *6:3. Is +*9:6. Je +*23:6. Mt 1:23. Lk 1:16, 17. 2:11. Jn 3:12, 13, 31. 6:33. Ac +√10:36.

√17:24. Ep 4:9-11. Ph √2:11. 1 T *3:16. Ja *2:1. Re *17:14. **from heaven.** Jn √3:13, 31.

48. As is. ƒ63B, Ge +2:10. **such are they also that are earthy.** ver. 21, 22, 47. Ge 5:3. Jb 14:4. +*19:26. Jn *3:6. Ro *5:12-21. **and as.** Ph *3:20, 21.

49. as. Ge 5:3. **earthy.** ver. 47. **we shall.** Mt 13:43. Ro +*8:29. 2 C *3:18. 4:10, 11. 1 J +*3:2.

50. this I say. 1 C 1:12. 7:29. 2 C 9:6. Ga 3:17. 5:16. Ep 4:17. Col 2:4. **that.** 1 C 6:13. Mt 16:17. Lk √20:35, 36. Jn 3:3-6. 2 C *5:1. **flesh and blood.** *ƒ171Q11, Mt +16:17. There are two classes of people who will live eternally upon the earth: (1) the saints, who as co-heirs with Christ (Ro +*8:17) are given glorified bodies (1 C 15:52), who possess the kingdom (Da 7:18) and rule over the kingdom (Re 20:4, 6) as its inheritors (Mt 25:34); (2) natural people, described here as "flesh and blood" who are the eternal subjects of the kingdom, who eternally perpetuate the natural race of earthly men in the flesh (Ps 72:5. Is 59:21. Ezk *37:25. Lk 1:32, 33. 2 P *3:13n). These two distinct and separate classes are symbolized by the "barren woman" and the "married woman" (Is +*54:1), the latter depicting the body of Christ, the glorified saints, who are a fixed number, and do not increase (Lk 20:35). The "barren woman," representing Israel, depicts those who will live on the earth in the flesh and continue to multiply, eventually surpassing in number the glorified saints (see Peters, *Theocratic Kingdom*, vol. 2, pp. 130-140). Mt +*16:17. Lk ◑+*24:39. Jn ◑3:13. Ga 1:16. Ep ◑+*5:30. 6:12. **cannot.** 1 C +*6:9. Jn √3:3, 5, 7. **inherit.** Those who *inherit* the kingdom are the resurrected and glorified saints who rule and possess the kingdom as joint heirs with Christ at the second advent. "Flesh and blood" refers to the natural people in the flesh who are subjects of the kingdom (See Peters, *Theocratic Kingdom*, vol. 2, p. 573), who will live forever on the earth (2 P +*3:13n). T#976‡, 978‡. ver. 45. Mt 11:11. 21:43. Jn ◑*3:13. Ac x◑+*2:34. Ro +*8:17. Ep +*1:11n. 1 P *3:18. **kingdom of God.** Those (often of materialist and Arian persuasion) who cite this text in proof that a saved person does not go immediately upon death to be with Christ (2 C √5:8. Ph *1:23) have confused the "kingdom of God" with heaven, which it is not. Neither is the church the kingdom of God or the kingdom of heaven (Is 60:21n). The kingdom of God or Heaven is the future permanent and eternal (Da 7:14. Re 11:15) earthly reign of Jesus Christ in a theocratic kingdom whose capital is Jerusalem (Je 3:17. Mi 4:7. Zp 3:15), a reign which extends to all the earth (Zc 14:9), in fulfillment of the Abrahamic and Davidic Covenants (Ac +√7:5; Is +√55:3). The kingdom of God is identical to the kingdom of heaven. Those (particularly dispensationalists) who make a distinction between the "kingdom of heaven" and the "kingdom of God" have confused the "kingdom of God" with the "sovereignty of God." The Jehovah's Witnesses, who make much of this text, fail to note the one essential requirement to enter the earthly kingdom, the new birth (Ezk 36:25, 26. Jn √3:3, 5, 7n. Ac +√3:19-21), a requirement which they deny, which is proof enough that *they*, like the unbelieving Jews of Jesus's day, will have no part or place in it (Mt +*8:11, 12). 1 C +√6:9. Jn +√3:3, 5, 7. Ac +*14:22. Ro +*14:17. **neither doth.** ƒ96B, ver. 12. i.e. can. Paul shows that the kingdom of God is yet future (Col 1:13n. 2 T 4:1n), it is inherited (Ep

+*1:11n) only by regenerated saints as co-heirs with Christ (Ro +*8:17), who will enter the kingdom with glorified bodies, as his subsequent discussion (ver. 51-53) shows, by means of resurrection or glorification. Mt +*19:28. Ac +*3:21. **corruption.** ver. +42. **incorruption.** Mt +*6:20. 1 P *1:4.

51. I show. 1 C *2:7. 4:1. *13:2. Ep *1:9. 3:3. 5:32. **a mystery.** Ro +*16:25n. **We shall not all.** ver. 6, 18, 20. Jn +*14:3. Ph √3:20, 21. 1 Th √4:13-18. 2 Th *2:1. **sleep.** ver. 6, 18, 20. 1 C 7:39. Da +√12:2n. Mt +27:52. **changed.** ver. 49. 2 C *4:14. Ph *3:21.

52. a moment. Ex 33:5. Nu 16:21, 45. Ps 73:19. 2 P *3:10. **at the last trump.** Mt ◑√24:31. 1 Th √4:16. Re x11:15. This "last trump" must not be equated with the seventh trumpet of Re 11:15, nor is "last" to be understood absolutely, for the trumpet of Mt 24:31 is clearly *after* the tribulation (Mt 24:29) and coming of Christ. J. Finis Dake (*Annotated Reference Bible*, p. 189 of the N.T., col. 4, note *q*) suggests the "last trump" in this text is the last of two trumps at the pretribulation rapture: at the first trump, the dead in Christ will be raised to immortality (1 Th 4:16); at the second or last trump the living believers will be changed to immortality and be caught up to meet the Lord in the air (1 C 15:52. 1 Th 4:17). This rapture cannot be mid or post tribulational, for then the warnings to watch, be ready, and not be caught off guard (Lk +√21:36. T 2:13, 14. He 9:28) would be pointless, for when the tribulation begins, those who know the Bible will be aware of the fact and be able to ascertain the precise time of the Second Advent by referring to Daniel's prophecy (Da +*9:27). **the trumpet.** Le +=23:24. Nu 10:1-10. **shall sound.** Ex 19:16. 20:18. Nu 10:4. Is 18:3. 27:13. Ezk 33:3, 6. Zc 9:14. Re 8:2, 13. 9:13, 14. **for.** Mt 24:31. Jn 5:25. 1 Th *4:16. **the dead.** See on ver. 23, +*42, 50. Lk 20:36. Jn *5:25, 28, 29.

53. corruptible. ƒ63A1, Ge +14:20. Supply by ellipsis (absolute: of nominative), "For this corruptible (body)." **must.** ver. 50. Jn +*3:7. **put on.** Lk +24:49. **incorruption.** ver. 42, 50. Jn +*5:29. Ro +2:7. 13:12-14. 2 C *5:2-4. Ga 3:27. Ep 4:24. 1 J *3:2. **this mortal.** 2 C 5:2-4. **immortality.** 1 T *6:16.

54. corruptible. ƒ63A1, Ge +14:20. **this mortal.** ƒ63A1, Ge +14:20. Supply by ellipsis, (body). Ro +*2:7. 6:12. +*8:11. 2 C 4:11. 2 T 1:10. **Death.** ƒ92G, Lk +4:18. Those who believe that death is the utter extinction of being, a concept utterly incompatible with the use of the word throughout the Bible, must logically deny the possibility of future existence by means of resurrection. If man is all mortal and death returns the whole man "to dust as it was," then man is extinct—there is "dust" but no *man*. Before man was formed it was all dust, and after he returns to it, it is all dust again—all dust, no man. Hence, under this view, a *resurrection of man is impossible.* All is dust "as it was" before man existed, and there can no man exist again except by means of *creation* (Mt +*10:28. 1 Th +*4:16n). The doctrine therefore which makes man all mortal and death his extinction, is the most palpable denial of a resurrection conceivable. Is ▸25:8. Lk √20:36. He *2:14, 15. Re 20:14. 21:4. **swallowed up.** ƒ22C35, Ex +15:7. **in victory.** ƒ46C, Mt +8:6. i.e. for ever, as the Hebrew *netzach* means (Jb 4:20, S#5331h), as well as *victory*, when it has the *Lamed* prefixed. See

Is 25:8; Am 1:11; also Ps 13:1; Pr 21:28 (B679). Mt 12:20g.

55. O death. T#853. Ps *23:4. *37:37. *48:14. *49:15. *73:26. Pr *14:32. Is *25:8. Ho *13:14. Ro +√8:38, 39. 2 C 4:16. 2 T *1:12. He *2:14, 15. **sting.** Ac 9:5. 26:14. Re 9:10. **grave.** *or,* hell. Gr. *hades,* Mt +11:23. *Hades* is the New Testament Greek equivalent of the Hebrew *sheol.* Its meaning is not merely the grave, as a reference to the notes on *sheol* will prove. Ge +*37:35n. Jb 17:13. Ps 49:15. 141:7. Ec +*9:10. Is 14:9n. Lk 16:23. Ac 2:27. Re 20:13, 14g. **is thy victory.** Jb 18:13, 14. Ps 49:8-15. 89:48. Ec 2:15, 16. 3:19. 8:8. 9:5, 6. Ro 5:14.

56. sting. Ge 3:17-19. Ps 90:3-11. Pr 14:32. Jn +*8:21, 24. Ro 5:15, 17. √6:23. He +*9:27. **of death.** Note carefully that Scripture nowhere asserts that physical death is the penalty for sin; if that were the case, all—whether righteous or unrighteous, would equally suffer the penalty, a view materialists might favor, but which is not in accord with Scripture. D. B. Byers *(Physical Death Not the Penalty,* chapter 4) observes that if physical death were the threatened penalty (Ge 2:17), (1) then Adam and Eve would have had to immediately die physically. (2) Man was capable of physical immortality after the fall, a fact utterly incompatible with the notion that physical death was the penalty, Ge 3:22-24. (3) Forgiveness and the new birth do not exempt believers from physical death, therefore such death cannot be the penalty. (4) If physical death is the penalty, then all who die physically have paid the penalty and are entitled to heaven, apart from the sacrifice of Christ or any belief in it. (5) God exacts a double satisfaction, that of Christ's death, and that of the individual who has died physically. (6) Since all men are not subject to physical death, some excluded by translation, living believers by rapture, physical death cannot be the penalty, as some are subject and others are not to physical death. **is sin.** Ro *6:23. **the strength.** Ro 3:19, +20. *4:15. 5:13, 20. 6:14. *7:5-13. Ga 2:16. 3:10-13. 5:4.

57. thanks. Ac 27:35. Ro +1:8. *7:25. 2 C 1:11. 2:14. 9:15. Ep 5:20. **giveth.** ver. 51. Jsh 8:7. Jg 5:2, 3. 2 K 5:1mg. 1 Ch 22:11. Ps 24:8. 60:12. 98:1. Pr 21:31mg. Jn +16:33. Ro *8:35-37. 1 J 5:4, 5. Re 12:11. 15:2, 3. **the victory.** Dt=33:11. Ro +*8:37.

58. Therefore. 2 C *7:1. 2 P *1:4-9. √3:14. **my beloved brethren.** Mt 23:8. 25:40. Lk 8:21. Jn 21:23. Ro 8:29. He *2:11, 17. Ja 1:16, 19. *2:5. Re 12:10. 19:10. **be ye.** Ru *1:18. 2 Ch +*20:20. Ps *55:22. *78:8, 37. 112:6. Col +*1:23. 2:5. 1 Th 3:3. He +*3:14. 2 P *3:17, 18. **stedfast.** T#712. 1 C 7:37. Jsh 23:7, 8. Jb *11:14, 15. Ga 5:1. Ep +4:14 (T#364). +6:10 (T#187). Ph 1:27, 28. 4:1. Col +*1:23. *2:5-7. 2 Th 2:2, 15. 2 T 1:13. He *10:23. 1 P *5:8, 9. 2 P *3:14, 17. **unmoveable.** Nu 24:13. 1 K *13:8. 2 K 22:2. Jb *1:22. *2:10. 23:11. 27:6. Ps √1:2, 3. Pr 4:25-27. Is 50:7. Je +*12:5. Da 3:18. Hab *3:17, 18. Lk 9:51. Ac 2:42. +*4:19, 20. *20:24. Col +*1:23. +*2:7. 1 Th +*5:21. 2 T 3:14. He 3:6. 4:14. +*10:23, 39. Re 3:3. **always.** 1 Ch=9:33. **abounding.** Ec *9:10. Je +*48:10. Ro +*12:11. Ph *1:9. 4:17. Col *2:7. 1 Th 3:12. *4:1. 2 Th 1:3. **the work.** 1 C 16:10. 2 Ch=35:2. Je 48:10. Jn +*6:28, 29. Ro 14:20. Ph 2:30. 1 Th 1:3. T *2:14. He *13:21. **ye know.** 1 C +3:8. 2 Ch *15:7. Ps 19:11. Da +*12:3. Mt √16:27. 25:21. Mk 9:41. Lk 19:17. Ro 2:10. 5:3. 1 C 3:14. 2 C 4:14. Ga √6:8-10.

He +*6:10. Ja 1:25. Re √22:12. **your labor.** 1 S 30:24. He +*6:10. **is not in vain.** 2 Ch 15:7. Ps 73:13. Is *65:23. Je 31:16. Ga *4:11. Ph 2:16. 1 Th *3:5. He ◑+*10:35. **in the Lord.** 1 C +7:39. Mt *10:40-42. 25:31-40. Ph *1:11. He *13:15, 16.

1 CORINTHIANS 16

The apostle directs the Corinthians, in what way to make collections for the Christians at Jerusalem, 1-4; states his intentions about visiting them, 5-9; commends Timothy, who was coming to them, 10, 11; shows that Apollos declines visiting them at present, 12; exhorts them to vigilance, stedfastness, and love, 13, 14; recommends the household of Stephanas to their special regard, 15, 16; expresses his satisfaction at the coming of certain persons from Corinth, 17, 18; and, after salutations from the churches, concludes in the most awful, yet affectionate manner, 19-24.

1. concerning the collection. 2 Ch=24:6, 9. Ac *11:28, 30. +24:17. Ro +*15:25, 26n. 2 C ch. 8, 9. Ga *2:10. **for the saints.** Ezk +*16:49. Ac 9:41. Ro 12:13. +*15:26, 27. 2 C +1:1. 9:12-15. Ga +*6:10. Phm 5-7. He +*6:10. 1 J √3:17. **given order.** 1 C +7:17. **the churches.** Ac 15:41. +16:6. 18:23. Ga 1:2.

2. the first. Apostolic admonition and example, though stated indirectly, authorizes changing Christian worship from the Jewish sabbath to the first day of the week. Mk +*16:9. Lk 24:1. Jn *20:19, 26. Ac *20:7. Re ◑*1:10n. **week.** lit. sabbath. ♪171T3, Mt +28:1. **let every.** Ex 23:15. Dt 16:16. 1 S *9:7, 8. 2 S *24:24. 1 Ch +*21:24. **as God.** Ge 26:12. 30:27, 30. 32:10. 33:11. Dt √8:18. 15:11-14. 2 Ch 31:10. Hg 2:16-19. Ml *3:9, 10. Mk 12:41-44. 14:8. Lk +√11:41n. √16:10. *17:10. 2 C 8:1-3, 11-15. **hath prospered.** Here is stated the apostolic New Testament standard of Christian giving, with no mention of the tithe. Ge 24:12, 27. Mt ◑+*23:23n. Lk +√11:41mg,n, 42n. Ac +*20:35. Ro 1:10. 12:8. 2 C +*8:12. 9:6, 7, 12. Ga *6:6, 7. 1 T +*5:4, 8. He *13:15, 16. 3 J *2. **that.** This proves that this was a one-time collection for a special need in Jerusalem, and was not the regular apostolic practice. Any appeal to this example to justify the practice of regular tithing to support the local church is a misapplication of this passage, for Paul dealt with the right of ministerial support in chapter 9. 2 C 8:11. 9:3-5, 7n, 13.

3. when. 1 C 4:19-21. 11:34. **whomsoever.** Ac 6:1-6. 2 C 8:18-24. **approve.** Ro 2:18. **by your letters.** Ac 18:27. 2 C 3:1. **liberality.** Gr. gift. 2 C 8:4, 6, 7, 19.

4. And if. ♪184C, Mt +4:9. **it be meet.** Ro 15:25. 2 C 8:4, 19. **that I go.** Ac 19:21.

5. I will come. 1 C +4:19. **when.** Ac 19:21. 20:1-3. 2 C 1:15-17. **Macedonia.** Ac +16:9. **for I do.** Ac 19:21.

6. it may be. 1 C 14:10. 15:37g. **winter.** Ac 27:12. 28:11. T 3:12. **that ye.** Ac +15:3. 17:15. 20:38. 21:5. Ro 15:24. 2 C 1:16. 3 J 6, 7.

7. by the way. 2 C 1:15, 16. **if.** ♪184C, Mt +4:9. 1 C 4:19. Pr √3:6. *19:21. Je *10:23. Ac +*18:21. Ro 1:10. He 6:3. Ja √4:15.

8. at. 1 C *15:32. Ac +18:19. **Pentecost.** Ex 23:16. Le *23:15-21. Ac 2:1. 20:16.

9. a great. Ac *19:8, etc. **door.** Ac +14:27. 2 C

2:12. Col *4:3. Re 3:7, 8. **there**. 1 C 15:32. Ac 19:9, 10. 2 C 1:8-10. Ph 3:18.

10. **if**. ∫184C, Mt +4:9. 1 C +4:17. Ac *19:22. 2 C 1:1. **without**. ver. 11. 1 T 4:12. **for he worketh**. 1 C √15:58. Ro 16:21. 2 C 6:1. Ph *2:19-22. 1 Th 3:2.

11. **Let no**. ver. 10. Lk *10:16. 1 Th 4:8. 1 T √4:12. T 2:15. **despise**. 2 C +10:10g. **but conduct**. ver. 6. Ac +15:3, 33. 3 J 6. **in peace**. Ac +15:33. **the brethren**. Jn +21:23. Ep +6:23.

12. **our brother**. 1 C 1:1. **Apollos**. 1 C 1:12. *3:5, 22. Ac 18:24-28. *19:1. T 3:13. **the brethren**. ver. +11. **his will**. or, God's will. Ac +18:21. Ro 2:18. **when**. Ec 3:1. Mk 6:21. Ac 24:25.

13. **Watch**. Mt 24:42-44. 25:13. *26:41. Mk 13:33-37. 14:37, 38. Lk 12:35-40. +√21:36. Ep *6:18. Col *4:2. 1 Th *5:6. 2 T 4:5. 1 P 4:7. √5:8. Re *3:2, 3. *16:15. **stand fast**. 1 C 15:+1, 2, √58. 2 C 1:24. Ga *5:1. Ph *1:27. 4:1. Col +*1:23. *4:12. 1 Th 3:8. 2 Th 2:15. **in the faith**. Ac +6:7. Ga 1:23. 3:23. Ph 1:27. 1 T +1:19. **quit**. 1 C 9:25-27. 14:20. 1 S 4:9. 2 S 10:12. 1 Ch 19:13. Is 46:8. Ep 6:13-17. 1 T 6:12. 2 T 2:3-5. 4:7. He 11:32-34. **be strong**. Jsh *1:6, 7, 9, 18. 1 K 2:2. 1 Ch 28:10. Ps 27:14. Is 35:4. Da 10:19. 11:32. Hg 2:4. Zc 8:9, 13. 2 C √12:9, 10. Ep 3:16. *6:10. Ph √4:13. Col *1:11, 12. 2 T *2:1.

14. **Let all**. 1 C 8:1. 12:31. ch. 13. 14:1. Jn 13:34, 35. 15:17. Ro 13:8-10. 14:15. Ga 5:13, 14, 22. Ep 4:1-3. Ph 2:1-3. 1 Th 3:6, 12. 4:9, 10. 2 Th 1:3. 1 T 1:5. He *13:1. 1 P *4:8. 2 P 1:7. 1 J 4:7, 8.

15. **the house**. ver. 17. 1 C √1:16. **the firstfruits**. Ro *16:5. Re 14:4. **of Achaia**. Ac +18:12. **addicted**. Gr. *tasso*, ✳S#5021g. Rendered (1) appoint: Mt 28:16. Ac 22:10. 28:23. (2) ordain: Ac 13:48. Ro 13:1. (3) set: Lk 7:8. (4) determine: Ac 15:2. (5) addict: 1 C 16:15. **to the ministry**. Ac 9:36-41. Ro 12:13. 15:25, 31. 16:2. 2 C 8:4. 9:1, 12-15. 1 T 5:10. Phm 7. He +*6:10. 1 P +√4:9-11. **of the saints**. 2 C 1:1.

16. **submit yourselves**. Ep 5:21. 1 Th 5:12. He √13:17. 1 P +*5:5g. **helpeth**. 1 C 12:28. 1 Ch 12:18. Ro 16:3, 9. Ph 4:3. 3 J 8. **laboreth**. 1 C 3:9. Ro 16:6,

12. 1 Th 1:3. 2:9. 5:12. 1 T √5:17. He +*6:10. Re 2:3.

17. **coming**. Gr. *parousia*, Mt +24:3n. Ac ◐+*1:11. Ph +*1:26. ◐+*2:12. **Stephanas**. ver. 15. **Fortunatus**. i.e. *fortunate*, ✳S#5415g. **Achaicus**. ✳S#883g. **for**. 2 C √11:9. Ph 2:30. Phm 13.

18. **they**. Pr 25:13, 25. Ro 15:32. 2 C 7:6, 7, 13. Ph 2:28. Col 4:8. 1 Th 3:6, 7. Phm 7, 20. 3 J 4. **spirit**. Gr. *pneuma*, ∫171Q1B, Mk +2:8n. **therefore**. 1 Th 5:12. Ph 2:29. He 13:7. 3 J 11, 12. **acknowledge**. Gr. *epiginosko*, Mt +11:27. Ph *2:29. 1 Th 5:12.

19. **churches of Asia**. Ac +2:9. 19:10. 1 P 1:1. Re 1:11. **Aquila**. Ac *18:+2, 18, 26. Ro *16:3, 4. 2 T 4:19, Prisca. **in the Lord**. 1 C +7:39. **the church**. Ro *16:+5, 15. Col *4:15. Phm +*2.

20. **the brethren**. Jn +21:23. Ro 16:16, 21, 23. 2 C 13:13. Ep +6:23. Ph 4:22. Phm 23, 24. He 13:24. **Greet**. 2 C 13:12. Ro +16:16. 1 Th 5:26. 1 P *5:14. **one another**. ∫63G, Ge +50:23. Ro √16:16n.

21. **salutation**. Ro 16:22. Ga 6:11. Col 4:18. 2 Th *3:17. Phm 19. **hand**. ∫121BC. Metonymy of the Cause B547. The *hand* is put for the writing done by it or handwriting. For another instance of this figure see Col 4:18.

22. **If**. ∫184A, 1 C +15:2. **love**. Jsh 23:11. SS 1:3, 4, 7. 3:1-3. 5:16. Is 5:1. Mt 10:37. 25:40, 45. Jn 8:42. 14:15, 21, 23. 15:24. 16:14. 21:15-17. 2 C √5:14, 15. √8:8, 9. Ga 5:6. Ep 6:24. He +*6:10. 1 P 1:8. 2:7. 1 J 4:19. 5:1. Ju 22. **the Lord Jesus Christ**. Ac +√10:36. Ju *21. **let him**. ∫96B, Ge +20:7. 2 S +3:29. Ps *71:13. Je +*10:25. 2 T *4:14. **Anathema**. That is, *Let him be accursed; our Lord cometh*, i.e. to execute the judgment denounced. Je +*10:25. Mt 25:41, 46. Ac 23:14g. Ro +9:3g. Ga 1:8, 9g. 2 Th √1:8, 9. Ju *14, *15. **Maranatha**. i.e. "the Lord comes," ✳S#3134g, only here. Ph 4:5. Ju +*14.

23. **grace**. See on Ro 16:20, 24.

24. **love**. ver. 14. 1 C 4:14, 15. 2 C 11:11. 12:15. Ph 1:8. Re *3:19. **Amen**. See on 1 C 14:16. Mt 6:13. 28:20.

2 CORINTHIANS

2 CORINTHIANS 1

The apostle salutes the Corinthians, 1, 2; and blesses God for consolations proportioned to his tribulations, and deliverance in extreme danger, lately vouchsafed to him; being intended for the benefit and comfort of others also, as well as an earnest to him of future deliverances, 3-11. He rejoices in the testimony of his conscience; and expresses his confidence of their attachment to him, which had induced him to purpose a journey to Corinth, 12-16. His delay of this journey did not arise from fickleness, 17, 18. He states the stability of the promises of God through Christ, and the security of believers, 19-22; and declares, that he had postponed his visit from lenity towards the Christians at Corinth, 23, 24.

1. Cir. A.M. 4062. A.D. 58. **Paul**. See on Ro 1:1-5. 1 C 1:1. 1 T 1:1. 2 T 1:1. **an apostle**. Ga 1:1. Ep 1:1. Col 1:1. **by the will**. Ac 26:15-18. 1 C +1:1. **Timothy**. ver. 19. Ac +16:1. Ro 16:21. 1 C 16:10. Ph 1:1.

2:19-22. Col 1:1, 2. 1 Th 1:1. +3:2. 2 Th 1:1. He 13:23. **brother**. 1 C +1:1. **the church of God**. Ac 18:1-11. +*20:28. 1 C 1:2. +10:32. **Corinth**. Ac +18:1. **all**. 1 C 6:11. Ep 1:1. **the saints**. 2 C 8:4. 9:1, 12. 13:13. Ro +1:7 (T#1116). 8:27. 12:13. 15:25, 26, 31. 16:2, 15. 1 C 1:2. 6:1, 2. 14:33. 16:1, 15. Ep 1:1, 15, 18. 2:19. 3:8, 18. 4:12. 6:18. Ph 1:1. 4:22. Col 1:2, 4, 12. 1 T 5:10. Phm 5, 7. He 6:10. 13:24. Ju 3. Re +8:3. **Achaia**. 2 C 9:2. 11:10. Ac +18:12. Ro 15:26. 16:5. 1 C 16:15. 1 Th 1:7, 8.

2. **Grace**. See on Ro +1:7. 2 S 15:20. 1 Ch 12:18. Da 4:1. 1 C 1:3. Ga 6:16. Ep 6:23. Ph 1:2. Col 1:2. 1 Th 1:1. 2 Th 1:2. Phm 3.

3. **Blessed**. 2 C 11:31. Ge 14:20. 1 Ch 29:10. Ne 9:5. Jb 1:21. Ps 18:46. 72:19. 135:19, 20. Da 4:34. Mk 14:61. Lk 1:68. Ro 1:25. +*9:5. Ep *1:3. 1 P *1:3. **God**. ∫132G, Ge +3:19. ∫68, Ge +10:1. **the Father of our**. 2 C 11:31. Jn 5:22, 23. +*10:30. *20:17. Ro +*15:6. Ep 1:3, 17. Ph 2:11. 2 J 4, 9. **the Father of mercies**. ∫96F2, Ge +4:10. Ps *86:5, 15. Da 9:9. Mi

+*7:18. Ro 12:1. Ep 1:17. Ja +5:11. **the God**. Ro 15:5. **all comfort**. T#850. 2 C 7:6. Dt +*33:27. Jg 15:19n. Ps +23:4 (T#6). 71:21. +*90:15. Pr 14:14. Is *12:1. +41:13 (T#955). *49:13. +51:12 (T#956). *54:7, 8. 51:12. 57:18. 61:1-3. *66:11, 13. Je *6:16. +*29:11. Lk 2:25. Jn *14:18. Ac 9:31. 1 C +14:3. 2 Th *2:16, 17. He 6:18.

4. **comforteth**. 2 C 7:4, *6, 7, 13. Ps *86:17. Is 12:1. 40:1. 49:10. *51:3, 12. 52:9. 66:12, 13. Jn *14:16, 18, 26. 1 Th 3:7. 2 Th *2:16, 17. **that we**. ver. 5, 6. 2 C *7:6, 7. Ps *32:5, 6. 34:2-6. 66:16. Is 40:1. 66:14. Ac 4:36. 9:26, 27. 11:23. 14:22. 1 C +*14:3, 31. 16:18. Ph 1:14. 1 Th *4:18. *5:11. He 12:12. **comforted of God**. ver. 3. Is 66:13.

5. **as the sufferings**. 2 *C 4:10, 11. 11:23-30. Mk 8:31. Ac 3:18. 9:4. 1 C *4:10-13. Ph 1:20. 3:10. Col *1:24. He 2:9, 10. +*4:15. 5:8. 1 P 1:11. 4:13. 5:1. **so**. Lk 2:25. Ph 2:1. 2 Th 2:16, 17. **consolation**. Ge=5:28, 29.

6. **whether**. ver. 4. 2 C 4:15-18. 12:15. Ac *14:22. 1 C 3:21-23. Ep 3:13. 2 T 2:10. **it is**. Ac 21:5. **salvation**. 2 T 2:10. **effectual**. *or*, wrought. 2 C 4:17. 5:5. Ro *5:3-5. √8:28. Ph *1:14, 19. He 12:10, 11. Ja +5:16. **enduring**. 2 C 6:4. 12:12. Ro 12:12. 1 P 2:20.

7. **our**. ver. 14. 2 C 7:9. 12:20. Ph 1:6, 7. 1 Th 1:3, 4. **as ye**. Mt +*5:4, 11, 12. Lk 22:28-30. Ac +*14:22. Ro 8:17, 18. 1 C √10:13. 2 Th 1:4-7. 2 T *2:12. Ja 1:2-4, 12. 1 P *5:10.

8. **For we**. 1 C +10:1. **not**. √175B, Ge +21:16. **of our**. 2 C 4:7-12. Ac *19:23-35. 1 C 15:32. 16:9. **in Asia**. Ac +2:9. **pressed**. 2 C 5:4. 1 T 5:16g. **insomuch**. 2 C 4:8. 1 S 20:3. 27:1.

9. **we had**. Ro +8:36. **sentence**. *or*, answer. **of death**. Ro 8:36. Col 3:3. **in ourselves**. √121C2A3, Is +53:11. i.e. we experienced the feelings of those who have had the sentence of death pronounced upon them. **not trust**. 2 C *3:5. *4:7. *12:7-10. Jb *40:14. Ps *22:29. *44:5-7. Pr √3:5, 6. *28:26. Je +*9:23, 24. *17:5-7. Ezk *33:13. Lk *18:9. **in God**. 2 C *4:13, 14. Ps 2:12. 25:2. 26:1. 34:8. 84:12. Je 17:7. 39:18. Ezk *37:1-14. Zp 3:12. Ro *4:17-25. He *11:19. **which raiseth**. 2 C 4:14.

10. **delivered**. √147A, Ge +50:24. Ge=45:7. 1 S *7:12. 17:37. Jb 5:17-22. Ps *34:19, 20. Is 46:3, 4. Ac *26:21, 22. 27:44. Ro +15:31. 2 T *4:17. 2 P *2:9. **death**. √121G, Ge +31:1. **in whom**. 1 T 4:10. **trust**. √96C1, Ge +4:1.

11. **helping**. 2 C 9:14. Is 37:4. 62:6, 7. Ac 12:5. Ro *15:30-32. Ep 6:18, 19. Ph *1:19. Col 4:3, 12. 1 Th 5:25. 2 Th 3:1. Phm *22. He 13:18. Ja *5:16-18. **that**. 2 C 4:15. 9:11, 12. Ac 12:5. Ep 6:18.

12. **our rejoicing**. T#327. 2 C +7:4. Jb 13:15. 23:10-12. 27:5, 6. 31:1-40. Ps 7:3-5. 44:17-21. Is 38:3. Ac √24:16. Ro 9:1. 1 C 4:4. Ga 6:4. 1 T 1:5, 19, 20. He 13:18. 1 P 3:16, 21. 1 J 3:19-22. **the testimony**. Ac +23:1. 1 Th 2:10. **conscience**. T#131. 2 C √4:2. 5:11. Pr 14:14. 18:14. Ec 10:20. Lk +16:25 (T#573-2). Ac +23:1. Ro 2:15. 9:1. 13:5. 1 C 8:7, 10, 12. 10:25, 27, 28, 29. 1 T 1:5, 19. 3:9. 4:2. 2 T 1:3. T 1:15. He 9:9, 14. 10:2. 1 P 2:19. **simplicity**. T#927. 2 C √11:3. Ps 15:1, 3. *119:130. 131:1. Pr *19:25. 21:11. Mt 6:22. 7:1, 2. 11:25. 18:2, 3. Lk 18:17. Ro 16:18, 19. He 12:10g. **godly sincerity**. 2 C √2:17. 8:8. Jsh 24:14. Pr 20:7. 1 C *9:8. Ep 6:14. Ph 1:10. T 2:7. **not**. ver. 17. 2 C 4:2. 10:2-4. 12:15-19. 1 C *2:1, 4, 5, 13. 15:10. Ja 3:13-18. 4:6. **by the grace**. 1 C *15:10. **we have**.

That is, "we have conducted ourselves"; for *anastrepho* in Greek, and *conversatio* in Latin, are used to denote the whole of a man's conduct, the tenor and practice of his life. **world**. Gr. *kosmos*, Mt +4:8.

13. **than**. 2 C 4:2. 5:11. 13:6. Phm 6. **acknowledge**. Gr. *epiginosko*, Mt +11:27. **to the end**. Mt +10:22. 1 C 1:8.

14. **acknowledged**. Gr. *epiginosko*, Mt +11:27. **in part**. 2 C 2:5. Ac *14:4. Ro +11:25. 1 C 11:18. **that we are**. 2 C 5:12. 9:3. Ro 4:2. 1 C 3:21-23. ◐5:6. 9:15, 16. Ga 6:4. Ph +1:26g. 2:16. He 3:6. **your rejoicing**. √121E1, Ge +25:23. That is, "the cause and object of your rejoicing." **even**. 2 C 9:2. 1 C 9:15. 15:31. Ph *2:16g. 4:1. 1 Th *2:19, 20. **in the day**. 1 C +*1:8. Ph 1:6, 10. 1 Th 3:13. +*5:23.

15. **in**. 1 C +4:19. 11:34. **that**. Ro 1:11. 15:29. Ph 1:25, 26. **a second**. Ac 18:1-18. **benefit**. *or*, grace. 2 C 6:1. Ro *1:11.

16. **to pass**. Ac 19:21. 1 C 16:5-7. **by you**. Ro 15:28. **Macedonia**. Ac +16:9. **and to come**. Ac 19:21, 22. 21:5. 1 C 16:5-7. **brought on**. Ac +15:3.

17. **lightness**. Jg 9:4. Je 23:32. Zp 3:4. **according**. ver. 12. 2 C 5:16g. 10:2, 3. 11:18. Jn 8:15. 1 C 1:26. Ga 1:16. 2:2. 1 Th 2:18. **yea**. ver. 18-20. Mt 5:37. Ja 5:12.

18. **as**. ver. 23. 2 C 11:31. Jn 7:28. 8:26. 1 C +1:9. 1 J 5:20. Re 3:7, 14. **word**. *or*, preaching. 2 C 2:17.

19. **the Son of God**. Ps *2:7. Mt 3:17. +*14:33. *16:16, 17. 17:5. 26:63, 64. 27:40. +*54n. Mk 1:1. Lk +*1:35. Jn 1:34, 49. √3:16, 35, 36. 6:69. 19:7. +√20:28, 31. Ac *8:37. 9:20. Ro +*1:3, 4. 2 P 1:17. 1 J 1:3. 5:9-13, 20. 2 J *9. Re 2:18. **Jesus Christ**. Ac 9:20. *18:5, 6. **even**. Ac 18:5, Silas. **and Silvanus**. i.e. *woody*, ✱S#4610g. Ac ◐+15:22. 1 Th 1:1. 2 Th 1:1. 1 P +5:12. **Timotheus**. ver. 1. Ac +16:1. **was not**. Ex 3:14. Mt 24:35. Jn √8:58. He 1:11, 12. √13:8. Re √1:8, 11, 17.

20. **all the promises**. Ge +*3:15. 22:18. +*49:10. Ps 72:17. Is +*7:14. +*9:6, 7. Lk 1:68-74. Jn 1:17. √14:6. Ac 3:25, 26. 13:32-39. Ro √6:23. +*15:8, 9. Ga 3:16-18, 22. He 6:12-19. 7:6. *9:10-15. 10:23. 11:13, 39, 40. √13:8. 1 J 2:24, 25. √5:11, 12. **are yea**. Ro +*15:8. **Amen**. Is 65:16h. Jn 3:5g. 1 C +14:16. Re *3:14. **unto**. 2 C 4:6, 15. Ps 102:16. Mt +*6:13. Lk 2:14. Ro *11:36. 15:7. Ep 1:6, 12-14. 2:7. 3:8-10. Col 1:27. 2 Th 1:10. 1 P 1:12. Re 7:12.

21. **stablisheth**. 2 C *5:5. Dt 32:6. Ps 37:23, 24. 87:5. 89:4. Is +*9:7. 49:8. 62:7. Ro *16:25. 1 C +1:8. Col +*2:7. 1 Th 3:13. 2 Th 2:8, 17. 3:3. 1 P 5:10. 2 P +*1:10. **anointed**. √22C47, Ps +23:5. Ex=28:41. Ps +*45:7. 92:10. Is +*59:21. *61:1. Jn 3:34. Ac *10:38. Ro +*8:9. He 1:9. 1 J *2:20, 27. Re 1:6. 3:18. **is God**. Is 63:16.

22. **sealed**. Jn 3:33. *6:27. Ro 4:11. Ep *1:13, 14. +*4:30. 2 T √2:19. Re 2:17. 7:3. 9:4. **the earnest**. T#517. 2 C *5:5. Mt +7:23 (T#21). Ro *8:9, 14-16, 23. Ep *1:13, 14. *4:30. 2 T √2:19. **Spirit**. Gr. *pneuma*, √121A1, Lk +1:17n. **in our hearts**. Ro *5:5.

23. **I call**. ver. 18. 2 C 11:10, 11, *31. Ro +1:9. 9:1. Ga 1:20. Ph *1:8. 1 Th 2:5, 10. **soul**. Gr. *psyche*, √171Q2, Mt +12:18. **that**. 2 C 2:3. 10:2, 6-11. 12:20. *13:2, 10. 1 C +*4:21. 5:5. 7:28. 1 T 1:20. **Corinth**. Ac +18:1.

24. **dominion**. or, lordship. 2 C 4:5. Mt *20:25-28. *23:8-10. 24:+*45, 49. Ac ◐+*10:36. √17:11, 12. 1 C 3:5. 1 Th 2:6mg. 2 T +*2:24-26. He ◐*13:17.

1 P +*5:3. **are helpers.** 2 C 2:1-3. Ro 1:12. Ph *1:25, 26. **by faith.** 2 C 5:7. Ro 5:2. 11:20. 1 C 10:12. +15:1. Ep *6:13-18. 1 P *5:8, 9.

2 CORINTHIANS 2

The apostle shows his purpose, of not coming to Corinth in heaviness; and states the grief with which he had written his former epistle, 1-4. He directs the Corinthians to forgive and restore the incestuous person; as he had forgiven him in Christ's name, 5-11. His uneasiness, at not finding Titus at Troas, had induced him to go directly into Macedonia, 12, 13. He blesses God for the joy and triumph, which had attended his faithful preaching of the gospel in every place, which he distinguishes from that of "many who corrupt the word of God," 14-17.

1. **I determined.** 2 C 1:15-17. Ac 11:29. 15:2, 37. 1 C 2:2. 5:3. T 3:12. **that.** ver. 4. 2 C 1:23. 7:5-8. 12:20, 21. 13:10. 1 C 4:21.

2. **if.** ⨍184A, 1 C +15:2. **make you sorry.** 2 C 1:14. 7:8. 11:29. Ro 12:15. 1 C 12:26.

3. **I wrote.** 1 C 4:21. 5:1, etc. **lest.** 2 C 12:21. 13:1, 2. **I ought.** 2 C 12:11. **having.** 2 C 1:15. 7:6. 8:22. Ga 5:10. 2 Th 3:4. Phm 21. **that my joy.** 2 C 7:16. Jn 15:11.

4. **out.** Le 19:17, 18. Ps 119:136. Pr 27:5, 6. Je 13:15-17. Lk 19:41-44. Ro 9:2, 3. Ph 3:18, 19. **anguish.** ⨍141, Is +22:4. Lk 21:25. **I wrote.** 2 C 7:8, 9, 12. **many tears.** Ac 20:19, 31. Ph 3:18. **not.** 2 C 7:8, 9, 12. 12:15. **that ye might.** 2 C 11:2.

5. **But if.** ⨍184A, 1 C +15:2. **any.** Pr 17:25. 1 C *5:1-5, 12, 13. Ga 5:10. **grieved.** Ga 4:12. **in part.** 2 C 1:14. Ro +11:25. **overcharge.** 1 Th 2:9. 2 Th 3:8g.

6. **punishment.** or, censure. ⨍175A, Ge +27:44. 2 C 7:11. 1 C +5:4. **which.** 2 C 13:10. 1 C *5:4, 5. 1 T 5:20. **of many.** 1 C +9:19.

7. **So that.** Lk 9:50. Ac 11:3. **ye.** Ga *6:1, 2. Ep ⨍4:32. Col 3:13. 2 Th *3:6, 14, 15. He 12:12-15. **comfort.** Lk 15:28. **swallowed.** 2 C 5:4. 2 S 20:19, 20. Ps 21:9. 56:1, 2. 57:3. 124:3. Pr 1:12. Is 28:7. 1 C 15:54. **overmuch.** 2 C 7:10. Pr 17:22. Ph 2:27. 1 Th 4:13.

8. **that.** Ga 5:13. 6:1, 2, 10. Ju 22, 23. **confirm.** Ge 23:20. Ga 3:15g.

9. **that.** 2 C 7:12-15. 8:+2, 24. Ex 16:4. Dt 8:2, 16. 13:3. Ph 2:22. **whether.** 2 C 7:15. 10:6. Ph *2:12. 2 Th 3:14. Phm 21.

10. **whom ye.** 2 C 5:20. Mt 18:18. Lk +7:42. Jn *20:23. 1 C 5:4. **for if.** ⨍184A, 1 C +15:2. **person.** or, sight. Ac 3:19. **of Christ.** 2 C 4:6. Pr 8:30. 1 C +5:4.

11. **Lest Satan.** 2 C 11:3, 14. 1 Ch 21:1, 2. Jb 1:11, 12. 2:3, 5, 9, 10. Zc 3:1-4. Lk 22:31. Jn 13:2, 27. Ac 1:25. 1 C +5:5. 7:5. Ep 6:11, 12. 2 T +*2:25, 26. 1 P 5:8. Re 2:24. 12:9-11. 13:8. **advantage.** 2 C 7:2. 12:17, 18. 1 C 10:13. 1 Th 4:6. **not ignorant.** ⨍175B, Ge +21:16. 1 P +*5:8. **his devices.** 2 C 3:14. 4:4. 10:5. 11:3. Ep 6:10-18. Ph 4:7. 2 Th 2:9. 1 P 5:8, 9. 1 J 2:1, 2. Re 12:9, 10. 20:7, 8.

12. **when.** Ac +16:8. *20:1-6, 8. **gospel.** Ro +15:19. **a door.** Ac +14:27. 1 C 16:9. Col 4:3. Re 3:7, 8.

13. **no rest.** 2 C *7:5, 6. **spirit.** Gr. *pneuma,* ⨍171Q1B, Mk +2:8n. **Titus.** 2 C 7:6, 13, 14. 8:6, 16, 23. 12:18. Ga 2:1, 3. 2 T 4:10. T 1:4. **taking my leave.** Mk 6:46. Lk 9:61. 14:33g. Ac 18:18, 21. **I went.** Ac

20:1, 2. **Macedonia.** Ac +16:9.

14. **thanks.** 2 C 1:11. 8:16. 9:15. Ro +6:17. Ep 5:20. 1 Th 3:9. Re 7:12. **triumph.** ⨍96A1, Mt +5:29. Ps 92:4. 106:47. 148:14. Is 12:2. Ro 8:37. 1 C 15:57. Col 2:15. **the savor.** ver. 15, 16. SS *1:3. Jn 12:3. Ro 15:19. Ep 5:2. Ph 4:18. Col 1:6, 23. **knowledge.** 2 Ch=30:22. **by us.** Ro *15:18, 19. **every place.** 1 C +1:2.

15. **a sweet.** Ge 8:21. Ex 29:18, 25. 2 Ch=13:11. Ps 141:2. SS 1:3. Ezk 20:41. Jn 12:3. Ep *5:2. Ph 4:18. Re 5:8. 8:3, 4. **savor.** ⨍22C15, Ge +8:21. **in them.** 2 C 4:3, 4. Is 49:5, 6. 1 C +1:18. 2 Th 2:10. **and in.** 2 C 4:3. Ac 28:24. 1 C 1:23, 24. **perish.** Gr. *apollumi,* Mt +2:13.

16. **the savor of death.** Lk +2:34. Jn √3:19. +9:39. √15:22. Ac 13:45-47. 20:26, 27. Ro *11:22. 1 P *2:7, 8. **to the other.** Ro *11:22. 1 P *2:7, 8. **who.** 2 C *3:5, 6. 12:11. 1 C *15:10.

17. **as many.** 2 C 11:13. Ac 20:29. **which.** 2 C 4:2. 11:13-15. Is 1:18. Je 5:31. 23:27-32. Mt 24:24. 1 Th 2:3, 5. 1 T 1:19, 20. 4:1-3. 2 T 2:6-18. 4:3, 4. T 1:11. 2 P 2:1-3. 1 J 4:1. 2 J 7-11. Ju 4. Re 2:14, 15, 20. 12:9. 19:20. **corrupt.** or, deal deceitfully with. T#1102. 2 C *4:2. Mt 4:6. +*22:29. Ep √4:14. Col *2:8. 1 T 5:13. 2 T 3:6. 2 P √3:16. 2 J 9-11. Ju 3. **the word of God.** Is +*8:20n. Ro +9:6. **but as.** ⨍160B, Ge +25:31. **of sincerity.** 2 C *1:12. √4:2. Ac 20:20, 27. 1 C +5:8. He 11:27. **as of.** ⨍160B, Ge +25:31. **in the sight.** 2 C 12:19. Ro +1:9. +9:1. **speak we.** 2 C 12:19. **in.** or, of.

2 CORINTHIANS 3

To obviate the charge of self-commendation; the apostle shows, that the conversion of the Corinthians was a sufficient attestation of Christ given to his ministry, 1-3. He ascribes all his sufficiency and success to God, 4, 5; and shows the glory of the gospel to be superior to that of the law, 6-11: declaring that his plain speaking according to the nature of his ministry, which was less obscure than that of Moses, 12-14: stating the blindness of the Jews, which would be removed when they turned to the Lord, 15, 16; and describing the liberty and progressive holiness, which arose from faith in Christ, and the illumination of the Holy Spirit, 17, 18.

1. **begin.** 2 C 2:17. 5:12. 10:8, 12. *12:11, 19. 1 C 3:10. 4:15. 10:33. **commend ourselves.** 2 C 4:2. 7:11. 10:12, 18. 12:11. Ro +3:5. 16:1. **as some.** 2 C 11:4. 1 C +11:16. **epistles.** Ac *18:27. 1 C 16:3.

2. **Ye are.** ⨍7, Allegory by continued Metaphor, Ga +4:24. 2 Ch=34:13. 1 C 3:10. *9:1, 2. **in.** 2 C 7:3. 11:11. 12:15. Ph 1:7. **known.** Ac 8:30. Ro 1:8. 1 C 9:2. 1 Th 1:8.

3. **the epistle.** Ex 31:18. 2 Ch=34:13. Re *2:1, 8, 12, 18. 3:1, 7, 14, 22. **ministered.** ver. 6. 1 C *3:5-10. **the Spirit.** Gr. *pneuma,* ⨍121A1, Lk +1:17n. Ro 8:13-16. Ga 5:22. **the living.** 2 C 6:16. Jsh 3:10. 1 S 17:26. Ps 42:2. 84:2. Je 10:10. Da 6:26. Mt +*16:16. 1 Th 1:9. He 9:14. **not.** Ex *24:12. 34:1. **tables of stone.** ver. 7. Ex *24:12. 31:18. 32:16. 34:1. Dt 4:13. 5:22. 9:10, 11. 10:1, 4. **but.** Ex +*25:21. Ps 40:8. Pr 3:3. 7:3. Je 17:1. *31:33. Ezk *11:19, 20. 36:25-27. He 8:10. 10:16. **of flesh.** Ro 7:14. 1 C 3:1. He 7:16.

4. **such.** 2 C 2:14. Ep 3:12. Ph 1:6. **Godward.** Ex 18:19. 1 Th 1:8.

5. **Not that.** T#262. 2 C *2:16. 4:7. Ex 4:10. Jb

*12:10. Ps *22:29. 87:7. Je 10:23. 18:6. Jn *15:5. Ac 17:26-28. Ep 2:8. **are sufficient**. Je +*13:23. Jn +*6:44, 65. **but**. 2 C 12:9. Ex 4:11-16. Je 1:6-10. Mt 10:19, 20. Lk 21:15. 24:49. 1 C 3:6, 10. +*15:10. Ph *2:13. *4:13. Ja 1:17.

6. **also**. *77, Ex +3:19. **hath**. 2 C 5:18-20. Mt 13:52. Ro 1:5. 1 C 3:5, 10. 12:28. Ep *3:7. 4:11, 12. Col *1:25-29. 1 T *1:11, 12. 4:6. 2 T 1:11. **made us**. Col 1:12. **able ministers**. ver. 3. 2 C 4:1. 5:18. 6:4. 11:23. 1 Ch=26:8. Ep 3:7. 4:12. Col 1:23, 25. 1 T 1:12. **the new**. ver. 14. Je *31:31. Mt *26:28. Mk 14:24. Lk 22:20. 1 C 11:25. He 7:22. *8:6-10, 13. 9:15-20. 12:24. 13:20mg. **not**. Ro *2:27-29. *7:6. **spirit**. Gr. *pneuma*, *121A2, Mt +26:41n. Here, "spirit" is put for the gospel (so C. Hodge). Horne states "But by the *spirit* is intended the saving doctrine of the Gospel" (*Introduction*, vol. 2, p. 455). Mt +*26:41. Jn 6:63. Ro 8:2. **letter killeth**. *121I2, Ge +2:17. T#1054. This often cited but misapplied text is used too frequently to belittle faithful adherence to the teaching of written Scripture (misidentified as the "letter" that killeth) as opposed to following the "spirit" as identified with the nebulous experience of the objector who alleges a disdain for doctrinal teaching. More correctly, "letter" refers to the Mosaic law written on stone, which brings death because it condemns all who cannot keep it, but the gospel of Christ, here called "spirit," written in the heart, brings life to all who will receive it. ver. 7, 9. Dt 27:26. Jn 6:63. Ro 3:20. *4:15. *7:9-11. Ga *3:10-12, 21, 22. **but the**. Jn *6:63. Ro 8:2. 1 J 1:1. **spirit**. Gr. *pneuma*, *121A2, Mt +26:41n. *121A3, Nu +11:17. **giveth life**. *or*, quickeneth. Jn 5:21. *6:63. Ro 4:17. *8:2. 1 C 15:45. Ga *5:4-6. Ep 2:1, 5. 1 P 3:18.

7. **But if**. *184A, 1 C +15:2. *136, Is +60:12. **the ministration**. *100, Ge +10:9. See on ver. 6, 9. Ro +4:15. 7:10. **written**. ver. +3. Ex 24:12. 31:18. 32:15, 16, 19. 34:1, 28. Dt 4:13. 5:22. 9:9-11, 15. 10:1-4. He 9:4. **in stones**. Ex +*25:21. **was glorious**. Dt 4:8. Ne 9:13. Ps 19:7, 8. 119:97, 127, 128, 174. Ro *7:12-14, 22. Ge 3:21. **so that**. ver. 13. Ex *34:29-35. Lk 9:29-31. Ac 6:15. **children of Israel**. Ac +5:21. **stedfastly behold**. Ac +3:4g. **which**. ver. 10, 11, 14. Ro *10:4. 1 C 13:10. He *8:13. **done away**. ver. 11, 13. 1 C 13:8, 10.

8. **How shall not**. Paul in various places abounds with this device of comparison and contrast to emphasize a glorious truth. 2 C √4:16-18. √5:21. √8:9. 9:8. √12:9, 10. Ro √5:20, 21. 8:18, √32. 1 C 13:12. **the ministration**. ver. 6, 17. 2 C 11:4. Is 11:2. 44:3. 59:21. Jl +*2:28, 29. Jn 1:17. 7:39. Ac *2:17, 18, 32, 33. Ro 8:9-16. 1 C 3:16. 12:4-11. Ga 3:2-5, 14. 5:5, 22, 23. Ep *1:13, 14. 2:18. 2 Th 2:13. 1 P 1:2. Ju 19, 20.

9. **For if**. *184A, 1 C +15:2. **the ministration of condemnation**. See on ver. 6, 7. Ex 19:12-19. 20:18, 19. Ro 1:18. 8:3, 4. Ga 3:10. He 12:18-21. Ro 1:18. 8:3, 4. Ga 3:10. He 12:18-21. **the ministration of righteousness**. 2 C 5:21. ◐11:15. Is 46:13. Je +*23:6. Ro √1:16, 17. *3:21, 22. 4:11. 5:15-21. 10:3-10. 1 C 1:30. Ga 5:4, 5. Ph 3:9. 2 P 1:1. **exceed**. ver. 10, 11. 1 C 15:41. He 3:5, 6.

10. **that which**. Ex 34:29, 35. **had no**. Jb 25:5. Is 24:23. Hg 2:3, 7-9. Ac 26:13. Ph 3:7, 8. 2 P 1:17. Re 21:23, 24. 22:5. **in this respect**. 2 C 9:3.

11. **if**. *184A, 1 C +15:2. See on ver. 7, 13. Ro

5:20, 21. He 7:21-25. 8:13. 12:25-29. **much**. ver. 6. 2 C 4:1.

12. **we use**. 2 C 4:2, 3, 13. Jn 10:24. 16:25, 29. 1 C 14:19. Col 4:4. **plainness**. *or*, boldness. 2 C *7:4. 10:1. Ac 4:+13, 29-31. 9:27, 29. 14:3. Ep *6:19, 20. Ph 1:20. 1 Th 2:2. 1 T 3:13.

13. **not as Moses**. ver. 7. **which**. Ex *34:33-35. **children of Israel**. Ac +5:21. **could not**. ver. 18. **stedfastly look**. Ac +3:4g. **to the end**. Ro *10:4. Ga 3:23, 24. Ep 2:14, 15. Col √2:16, 17. He 9:1-14. 10:1-9. 1 P *1:10-12. **abolished**. ver. 7, 11.

14. **their minds**. 2 C +2:11. √4:3, 4. Ps 69:23. Is 6:10. 20:10-12. 42:18-20. 44:18. 56:10. 59:10. Je 5:21. Ezk 12:2. Mt +*6:23. 13:11, 13-15. Jn 9:39-41. 12:40. Ac 28:26, 27. Ro *11:7-10, 25. **blinded**. 2 C √4:3, 4. Mk +6:52. Jn 6:45. 7:17. 8:47. 12:48. 1 C 1:18. √2:14. 2 Th √2:9-12. Ja +*1:5. 1 J *2:27. 4:6. **in the reading**. Ac *13:15, 27-29. 15:21. **old testament**. ver. 6. **which veil**. 2 C 4:6. Is 25:7. Mt 16:17. Lk 18:31-34. 24:25-27, 44-46. Jn 8:12. 12:46. Ac 16:14. 26:18. Ep 1:17-20.

15. **when**. ver. 14. Ac 13:15. 15:21. **Moses**. *121A6, Lk +16:29. **is read**. Mk +12:19. **the veil**. Ac *13:27-29.

16. **when**. Ex 34:34. Dt 4:30. 30:10. La 3:40. Ho 3:4, 5. Ro +*11:25-27. **it**. *or*, a man. *63I1A, Ex +12:4. Supply ellipsis, (their heart). Ro 11:23. **shall turn**. Is 11:11n. +*59:20. Je +*12:14. Ho +*3:5. *5:15. *6:3. Zc *12:10. Ac +√3:19-21. +9:35. **the veil**. Is *25:7. 29:18. 54:13. 61:1, 2. Je *31:34. Jn 6:45, 46. Ga 4:6. **shall be**. Je +*29:12.

17. **the Lord**. ver. 6. Jn 6:63. 1 C *15:45. **Spirit**. Gr. *pneuma*, 1 C +6:17. Jn +7:39. **where**. Ps 51:12. Is 61:1. Ro *8:2, 15, 16. Ga *4:6. 2 T +*1:7. **Spirit**. Gr. *pneuma*, 1 C +6:17. **liberty**. Jn +*8:32, 36. Ga 5:1, 13.

18. **with open**. ver. 13. **beholding**. Ps 17:15. Ho 14:8. 1 C +*13:12. He 12:2. **as in a glass**. 1 C *13:12. Ja 1:23. **the glory**. 2 C 4:4, 6. Ps 67:1. Jn 1:14. 12:41. +*17:24. 1 T 1:11g. **are changed**. 2 C 5:17. Je ◐+*2:5. Ro +*8:29. 12:2. 13:14. 1 C 15:49. Ga 6:15. Ep 4:22-24. Col 3:10. T 3:5. 2 P √1:5-9. 1 J +*3:2. **from**. Ro 8:4, 7. **glory to glory**. Ps 84:7. Pr +*4:18n. Is 40:31. Jn 1:16. **as**. *160B, Ge +25:31. **by the Spirit of the Lord**. *or*, of the Lord the Spirit. Gr. *pneuma*, 1 C +6:17. ver. 17.

2 CORINTHIANS 4

The apostle declares his unwearied zeal and conscious integrity in preaching the gospel, 1, 2. "The god of this world blinds the minds" of unbelievers, against the light of the divine glory of Christ; which God imparts, by shining into the hearts of his people, 3-6. The weakness and sufferings of the apostle redounded to the praise of the power of God, 7-12. He states the supports, motives, and prospects of glory, by which he and his helpers were induced to persevere without fainting, 13-18.

1. **seeing**. 2 C 3:6, 12. 5:18. Ep 3:7, 8. **this**. Ac 1:17, 25. *20:23, 24. 21:19. Ro 11:13. 2 T *4:5. **ministry**. 2 C +3:6. **as**. 1 C 7:25. Ph 2:27. 1 T *1:13, 16. 1 P 2:10. **we faint not**. ver. 16. Is 40:30. Lk +18:1. Ga *6:9. Ep 3:13. Ph *4:13. 2 Th 3:13mg. He 12:3. Re 2:3.

2. **renounced**. 1 C 4:5. **dishonesty**. *or*, shame. Ro

+*1:16. +6:21. Ep 5:12. **not walking.** 2 C 1:12. +*2:17. *11:3, 6, 13-15. Ezk 14:10n. Lk 10:23. Ac 20:29, 30. 1 C 3:19. Ep +*4:14. 1 Th 2:3-5. **nor handling.** T#1074. 2 C +*2:17. 6:3. 8:20. Mk +*12:24. 1 Th 2:3. 1 T 5:13-15. 6:10. 2 T ◐√2:15. 1 P 2:2. 2 P *3:16. 2 J 9-11. **the word of God.** Dt 4:2. 12:32. Pr +*30:6. Is +*8:20n. Ro +9:6. Re *22:19. **by.** 2 C 5:11. 6:4-7. 7:14. 11:6. **manifestation.** 1 C 12:7g. **the truth.** 2 C 6:7. 7:14. Ac *20:27. **commending.** 2 C +3:1. 5:11. **conscience.** 2 C +1:12. Ac +23:1. **in the sight.** 2 C 2:17.

3. **if.** √184A, 1 C +15:2. **our gospel.** Ro 2:16. 1 Th 1:5. 1 T 1:11. **be hid.** 2 C 3:14. Jb 24:16. Mt +*13:15. 1 C √2:14. **hid to.** ver. 4. 2 C 2:15, 16. 3:14, 16. Mt +*11:25. Jn 6:45. 7:17. 8:47. 12:48. 1 C *1:18. 2 Th √2:9-12. Ja 1:5. 1 J *4:6. **lost.** √11, Ge +2:23.

4. **the god.** √121Q1, Je +28:5. Mt *4:8, 9. Jn 12:+*31, 40. 14:30. 16:11. 1 C 10:20. Ep *2:2. *6:12. 1 J *5:19g. Re *12:9. 20:2, 3. **this.** Jn +*6:54n. 1 C +1:20. **world.** Gr. *aion*, Mt +6:13. √121P2, Mt +13:22. √121J9B, Jn +12:31. **blinded.** 2 C *3:14. Ge +*19:11. 1 K 22:22. Is 6:10. Mt +*13:19. Jn 12:40. **the minds.** or, thoughts. 2 C +2:11. 3:14. **lest.** ver. 6. 2 C 3:8, 9, 11, 18. Jn *8:12. 12:35. Ac +*26:18. Col +*1:27. 1 T 1:11. T *2:13. **glorious.** √24N, Ge +17:5. 2 C 3:18. Ge=45:13. Jn +17:24. 1 T 1:11. **the image.** Jn +*1:14, 18. 12:45. *14:9, 10. 15:24. Ro 8:29. 1 C 11:7. Ph √2:6. Col +*1:15. He √1:3. **shine.** ver. 6. Ps 50:2. *119:130. Is +*8:20mg. 60:1, 2. Lk 24:45. 2 P *1:19. 1 J 2:8.

5. **we.** Mt 3:11. Jn 1:21-23. 3:27-31. 7:18. Ac 3:12, 13. 8:9, 10. 10:25, 26. 14:11-15. Ro 15:17, 18. 1 C 1:13-15, 23. 3:5, 6. *10:33. Ph 1:15. 1 Th 2:5, 6. T 1:11. 1 P 5:2-5. 2 P 2:3. **Christ.** 2 C 1:19. Mt 23:8. Lk *2:11. Ac 2:36. 5:31. +√10:36. Ro 14:8, 9. 1 C 1:23. 2:2. 8:6. +*12:3. √15:47. Ph 2:11. **and ourselves.** 2 C √1:24. √5:14, 15. Mt *20:25-28. Lk 22:25, 26. Jn 13:14, 15. Ro 15:1, 2. 1 C *9:19-23. Ga 5:13. 2 T 2:10. **your servants.** 1 Ch=23:28. Ro 16:3.

6. **who.** Ge *1:3, 14, 15. Ps 74:16. 136:7-9. Is 45:7. **light.** Ge +1:3. **to shine.** Dt 33:2. Ps 119:135. Jn 14:26. He 8:10. **darkness.** Is +*9:2. **hath.** Gr. is he who hath. **shined.** Ep 1:17, 18. 5:8. 2 P √1:19. **the light.** ver. 4. 2 C *3:18. Ex 33:18-23. 34:5-7. Ps 63:2. 90:16. Is 6:1-3. 35:2. 40:5. 60:2. Jn 11:40. Ac 7:55, 56. +*26:18. 1 P *2:9. **knowledge.** Ge +*3:7. **the glory.** √24N, Ge +17:5. ver. 15. 2 C +*3:18. **in the face.** 2 C +2:10. Lk 2:14. Jn 1:14. 12:41. 14:9, 10. Ph 2:6. Col +*1:15. He √1:3. 1 P 1:12.

7. **this treasure.** √22D5.O, Dt +28:12. ver. 1. 2 C 6:10. Mt 13:44, 52. Ep 3:8. Col 1:27. 2:3. **in earthen vessels.** 2 C 5:1. 10:10. Jg 7:13, 14, 16-20. Jb 4:19. 10:9. 13:12. 33:6. Is 64:8. La 4:2. 1 C 1:28. 4:9-13. Ga 4:13, 14. 1 Th 4:4. 2 T 2:20. 1 P 3:7. **that.** 2 C 3:5, 6. 12:7-9. 13:4. 1 C *2:3-5. Ep 1:19, 20. 2:5, 8, 9. Col 2:12. 1 Th 1:5. **not of us.** Dt 8:17. Jg 7:2. Is 10:13.

8. **troubled.** 2 C 1:8-10. 6:4. *7:5. 11:23-30. Ps 129:2. **yet.** ver. 16, 17. 2 C 6:12. 12:10. 1 S 28:15. 30:6. Ps 56:2, 3. Pr 14:26. 18:10. Ro 2:9g. 5:3-5. 8:35-37. Ja 1:2-4. 1 P 1:6, 7. 4:12-14. **not.** √114. Mesodiplosis; or, Middle Repetition B261. The repetition of the same word or words in the middle of successive sentences. **perplexed.** √135, Ps +68:28. Ga 4:20. **not in despair.** *or*, not altogether without help, *or*, means. 2 C 1:8. 1 S 31:4. Jb 2:9, 10. Ps 37:33. Jn 14:18. 1 C √10:13.

9. **persecuted.** 1 C 4:12g. **not forsaken.** Dt 4:31. 31:6, 8. Jsh 1:5. 1 Ch 28:20. Ps +√9:10. 22:1. *37:25, 28. Is 62:4. He +*13:5, 6. **cast.** 2 C 7:6. Jb 5:17-19. 22:29. Ps √37:24. 42:5, 11. Pr 24:16. Is 43:2. Mi 7:8. **destroyed.** Gr. *apollumi*, Mt +2:13.

10. **bearing.** 2 C 1:+5, 9. Dt=10:8. Ac=9:15. Ro 6:5. 8:17, 18. Ga 6:17. Ph *3:10, 11. Col 1:24. **in the body.** Le 6:28. Pr 25:4. **the dying.** Ro 4:19. +8:36. 1 C +15:31. **that.** 2 C *13:3, 4. Jn 14:19. Ac *18:9, 10. Ro 5:10. 6:8. 8:17. 2 T *2:11, 12. 1 P 4:13. Re 1:17, 18. **manifest.** Ac 4:13. 2 Th 1:12.

11. **are alway.** Gr. *aei*, Mk +15:8. **delivered.** 2 C *1:5. *11:23, 25. Ps 44:22. 141:7. Ro *8:36. 1 C 15:31, 49. **manifest.** 2 Th 1:12. **our.** 2 C 5:4. Ro +*8:11. 1 C 15:53, 54.

12. **death.** 2 C 12:15. 13:9. Ac 20:24. 1 C 4:10. Ph *2:17, 30. 1 J *3:16. **but life.** T#1007‡. 2 C *1:6. ◐√5:11. Dt 30:15, 19. Ps +*146:4. Pr ◐√15:24. 18:21. Ec +*9:5, 10. Ro +6:23 (T#1010‡). ◐√11:22. 1 J 3:14.

13. **the same.** Ac 15:11. Ro 1:12. 1 C 4:21. 12:9. Ep 1:17. T 1:4. He *11:1, etc. 2 P 1:1. **spirit.** Gr. *pneuma*, √121A1, Lk +1:17n. **I believed.** Ps ▶116:10. **therefore.** Ps 39:3. *116:8-10. Ac *4:20. **we also.** 2 C 3:12. Pr 21:28.

14. **Knowing.** Ro 5:3. 1 C √15:58. **that.** 2 C *5:1-4. Is +*26:19n. Jn *11:25, 26. Ac +*2:24n. Ro +*8:11. 1 C 6:14. 15:20-22. 1 Th 4:14. **raise up us.** 2 C 1:9. Jn +*5:29. **shall present.** 2 C 11:2. Ep 5:27. Col 1:22, 28. Ju *24.

15. **all.** 2 C *1:4-6. Ro +*8:28. 1 C *3:21-23. Col *1:24. 2 T *2:10. **the abundant grace.** 2 C 1:11. 8:19. 9:11, 12. Ps 50:14, 23. Ga 1:24. Ep 3:20, 21. Col √3:16, 17. He *13:15, 16. 1 P *2:9. 4:11. Re 4:8-11. 5:8-14. 19:4-6. **of many.** 1 C +9:19g. **redound.** Ro 3:7. **to the glory.** ver. 6. 2 C 8:19. Ro +*3:23.

16. **we faint not.** ver. 1. Ps 27:13. *84:5-7. 119:81. Is 40:29. Je +*12:5. Lk +18:1. 1 C √15:58. **but though.** √185A, Lk +11:8. 2 C 12:15. Jb +*19:26, 27. Ps 73:26. Is 57:1, 2. Mt 5:29, 30. Ac +21:13. **outward man.** √24E, Ge +30:33. Mt +*10:28. **yet.** Ps *22:26. 1 C +*15:55. **the inward.** Ro +7:22. Ep 3:16. 1 P 3:4. **is renewed.** √24E, Ge +30:33. Ps +*51:10. Is 40:30, 31. Ro +*12:2. Ep 4:23. Col *3:10. 2 Th *1:3, 4. T 3:5. **day by.** √108E4, Mk +6:7. Ne=11:23. Lk 11:3.

17. **our light affliction.** √24E, Ge +30:33. 2 C 11:23-28. Ps 30:5. Is 54:8. Ac 20:23, 24. Ro 8:√18, 34, 37. Ph 2:12g. 1 P 1:5, 6. 4:7. *5:10. **but for.** √31, Is +1:21. **moment.** T#5. Jb 11:16. +36:7 (T#585). Ps 30:5. Is 26:20. 54:7. La 3:32, 33. Ja +5:11 (T#225). 1 P *5:10. **worketh.** Ps 119:67, 71. Mt +*5:12. Ro *5:3-5. Ph 1:19. 2 Th 1:4-6. He *12:10, 11. Ja *1:3, 4, 12. **far more.** √24E, Ge +30:33. 2 C 1:8. *3:18. Ge 15:1. Ps 31:19. 73:24. Is 64:4. Lk *6:23. Ro +*2:7. 7:13. 1 C √2:9. 12:31. Ga 1:13g. 1 P 1:7, 8. 5:10. 1 J √3:2. Ju *24. **eternal.** Gr. *aionios*, Mt +18:8. Da +*12:3.

18. **look not.** 2 C √5:7. Mt 4:8. Ro 8:24, 25. He *11:1, 25-27. *12:2, 3. **not seen.** He +*11:13. **but at.** √31, Is +1:21. **for.** Mt +*25:46. Lk 16:25, 26. 2 Th 2:16. 1 J *2:16, 17, 25. **temporal.** Mt 13:21. Mk 4:17. He 11:25g. **but the.** √31, Is +1:21. **eternal.** Gr. *aionios*, Mt +18:8. 1 J *2:17.

2 CORINTHIANS 5

The apostle declares, that the assured hope and earnest desire of being present with the Lord, when absent from the body, rendered him indifferent as to this life, 1-8: that he labored to approve himself to Christ, in the prospect of a future judgment, 9, 10; "knowing the terror of the Lord," he conscientiously persuaded men, 11: that he said this, not as boasting, but to furnish the Corinthians with an answer to false pretenders, 12; that the love of Christ constrained him to live no longer to himself, but to Christ; and made him dead to all other regards, 13-16: that all who are in Christ are new creatures, 17: that God, in Christ, reconciling the world unto himself, had reconciled him and other faithful preachers, and had "committed to them the ministry of reconciliation," 18, 19: and that as ambassadors, they in the stead of Christ, besought men to be reconciled to God, through his righteousness and atonement, 20, 21.

1. **For.** *↗7,* Allegory by continued Hypocatastasis, Ga +4:24. **we know.** Jb +*19:25, 26. Ps 56:9. 2 T 1:12. 1 J √3:2, 14, 19. 5:19, 20. **that if.** *↗184C,* Mt +4:9. **our.** ver. 4. 2 C 4:7. Ge +*3:19. Jb *4:19. 1 C 15:46-48. 2 P √1:13, 14. **earthly house.** *↗142,* Ge +20:16. *↗144B,* Dt +33:19. Ja +3:15g. **tabernacle.** ver. 4. Is 38:12. 2 P 1:13, 14. **dissolved.** Jb 30:22. 2 P 3:11. **we have.** *↗96C6,* Mt +2:4. Jn +*5:29. He *6:11. **a building.** Jn +*14:2, 3. 1 C 3:9. He *11:9, 10, 16. **an house.** Mk 14:58. Ac 7:48. 17:24. Col 2:11. He 9:11, 24. 1 P 1:4. **not made with hands.** Col 2:11. **eternal.** Gr. *aionios,* Mt +18:8. This is not a reference to a temporary body possessed in the third heaven during the intermediate state, for that would not be *eternal.* It must, therefore, be a reference to the *resurrection body,* glorified. Paul here, as elsewhere (Ro 8:30. He 12:22, 23), passes over the intermediate state, referring rather to the inheritance at the Second Coming (see Peters, *Theocratic Kingdom,* vol. 2, Proposition 125, observation 8, p. 240). **in the heavens.** Ph 3:20. 1 P √1:4.

2. **we groan.** ver. 4. Ro 7:24. *8:23. 1 P 1:6, 7. **earnestly.** Ph *1:23. **clothed.** ver. 3, 4. Lk +24:49. 1 C *15:53, 54. **from heaven.** Thus the change to a resurrected, glorified body occurs on earth (Peters, *Theocratic Kingdom,* vol. 2, p. 241). The more usual interpretation of this passage, that it teaches we receive temporary bodies in heaven immediately after death, is faulty, because it makes the future resurrection of the body unnecessary and redundant.

3. **If.** *↗60A,* Ge +3:22. **being.** Ge 3:7-11. Ex 32:25. Re *3:18. 16:15. **naked.** *↗63C,* Ge +25:32. Supply by ellipsis (absolute: brachylogia), "If indeed being clothed also, we shall not be found naked (as some among you say)." There were some among the Corinthians who said "there is no resurrection of the dead" (1 C 15:12, 35), and here those assertions are thus referred to.

4. **we that.** Ro *7:24. 2 P 1:13. **tabernacle.** ver. +1. **do groan.** See on ver. 2. **being burdened.** 2 C 1:8. 1 T 5:16g. **for that.** Ro +5:12g. **unclothed.** *↗135,* Ps +68:28. **but.** ver. 3. **that mortality.** Ge *5:24. 2 K *2:11. Is 25:8. 1 C *15:53, 54.

5. **wrought.** 2 C 4:17. Is 29:23. 60:21. 61:3. Ep 2:10. **the earnest.** 2 C 1:22. Nu 13:23-27. Ac *20:23, 24. Ro 8:23. Ep *1:13, 14. +*4:30. 1 J 3:24. **the Spirit.** Gr. *pneuma,* *↗121A1,* Lk +1:17n. Jn +7:39. Ac 5:3, 4. 1 C 6:11.

6. **we are always.** ver. 8. Ps 27:3, 4. Pr 14:26. Is 30:15. 36:4. He 10:35. 1 P 5:1. Re 1:9. **whilst.** See

on ver. 1. 1 Ch 29:15. Ps 39:12. 119:19. Ph 3:20, 21. He 11:13, 14. 13:14. **in the body.** ver. 8. 2 C √12:3. Jb +*19:26. Ga 2:20. Ph 1:22. He 13:3. 2 P *1:14, 15. **absent from.** Jn *14:2, 3.

7. **we walk.** *↗108B,* Ge +5:22. 2 C *1:24. +*4:18. Dt 12:9. Ro *8:24, 25. 1 C 13:12. Ga *2:20. He 10:38. *11:1, etc., 27. 1 P 1:8. 5:9. **by faith.** T#184. Jn 20:29. Ro 4:20, 21. Ga 2:20. He 11:7-10, 13. 1 P 1:8. **not by sight.** Mk +*15:32. Lk 3:22. 9:29. Jn 5:37. 1 C +13:12. 1 Th 5:22.

8. **I say.** *↗77,* Ex +3:19. **and willing.** ver. 6. 2 C 12:2, 3. Lk 2:29. Ac 21:13. Ph *1:20-24. 2 T 4:7, 8. 2 P 1:14, 15. 3:11, 12. **rather.** Ph *1:22-24. Re +*14:13. **absent from.** He +*12:23. Ja +*2:26. Re *6:9-11. **the body.** Da +*12:2. Lk *16:22. Jn +*2:19, 21. 1 C 15:35. Ph √3:21. Ja √2:26. **to be.** *↗15C,* Mk +6:11. **present with.** ver. 9. Ps 16:11. 17:15. 73:23-26. Mt 25:21, 23. Lk 16:23. +*23:43. Jn +*14:3. 17:24. 1 Th 4:17, 18. 1 J √3:2. Re 7:14-17. 22:3.

9. **we labor.** *or,* we endeavor. Lk +*13:24. Jn 6:27. Ro 15:20. 1 C 9:26, 27. √15:58. Col 1:29. 1 Th 4:11g. 1 T 4:10. He *4:11. 2 P +*1:10, 11. √3:14. **whether.** See on ver. 6, 8. Ro 14:8. **accepted.** Ge 4:7. Dt=33:11. Is 56:7. Ac 10:35. Ro +14:18. Ep 1:6. Col +√1:10. 1 Th 4:1. He 12:28.

10. **we.** Ge +*18:25. 1 S 2:3, 10. Ps 7:6-8. 9:7, 8. 50:3-6. 96:10-13. 98:9. Ec 11:9. 12:14. Ezk 18:30. Mt *25:31-46. Ac +*10:42. √17:31. Ro 14:10-12. He +*9:27. 1 P 4:5. Ju 14, 15. Re 3:18. 20:11-15. **judgment seat.** Ec *12:14. Mt +*10:15n. Jn 5:22, 27. 9:39. Ac 12:21g. Ro √14:10. 1 C √3:13. **of Christ.** Ne +*9:6. 2 T +*4:1. **receive.** 2 C 7:3. 1 K 8:32, 39. Jb 34:11. Ps 62:12. Is 3:10, 11. Mt 7:1. +*16:27. Lk *14:14. Jn *3:18. 5:29. Ro *2:5-10. *8:1. 1 C √3:13. *4:5. Ga √6:7, 8. Ep 6:8. Col 3:24, 25. Re 2:23. *20:12, 13. *22:12. **in.** Ro 6:12, 13, 19. *12:1, 2. 1 C 6:13-20. **done.** *↗63I2,* Jsh +3:3. **good.** Mt *10:42. Mk 9:41. 10:29, 30. 1 C *3:12, 14. Ga 6:7, 9. Ep *6:8. He +*6:10. **or bad.** Mt 12:36. 1 C *3:12, 15. Ja 3:2, 8. +*4:17.

11. **the terror.** *↗121R6,* Ge +31:42. T#573-6. Ge 35:5. Jb 6:4. 18:11. 28:28. 31:23. Ps *34:11. 73:19. 76:7. 88:15, 16. 90:11. 111:10. Pr 10:24. Is 11:2. 33:14. Na 1:6. Mt +*10:28. 25:46. Mk 8:35-38. 9:43-50. Lk 12:5. Jn +*3:36. Ro *2:8, 9. +*11:22. 2 Th √1:8, 9. He *2:3. √9:27. *10:31. 1 P *4:17, 18. Ju *23. Re 6:16. 20:15. **we persuade.** ver. 20. 2 C 6:1. Mt 28:14. Lk 16:31. Ac 13:43. 18:+4, 13. 19:26. 20:18-27. 26:26. 28:23. Ga 1:10. Col 1:28, 29. 2 T +*2:24-26. **but.** 2 C 1:12-14. 2:17. +*4:1, 2. 1 C 4:4, 5. 1 Th 2:3-12. **consciences.** 2 C +1:12.

12. **we.** 2 C +3:1. 6:4. 10:8, 12, 18. 12:11. Pr 27:2. **give.** 2 C *1:14. 11:12-16. 12:1-9. **occasion.** Ro +7:8g. **to glory.** Ph +1:26. **appearance.** Gr. the face. 2 C 10:7. Ga 6:12-14. 1 Th 2:17. **in heart.** 1 S +*16:7.

13. **we be beside.** 2 C 11:1, 16, 17. 12:6, 11. Jn *10:20. See on Ac *26:24, 25. 1 C 4:10-13. 1 Th 2:3-11. 2 T +√1:7. **it is to.** 2 S 6:21, 22. **sober.** Ac 26:25. Ro +*12:3. 1 P +4:7g. **for.** 2 C 7:12. Col 1:24. 1 Th 1:5. 2 T 2:10.

14. **the love.** 2 C 8:8, 9. SS 1:4. 8:6, 7. Mt 10:37, 38. Lk 7:42-47. Jn 14:21-23. *15:12, 13. 21:15-17. Ro 8:35. 1 C 16:22. Ep *3:18, 19. 6:24. 2 T 1:13. He +*6:10. 1 P *1:8. 1 J *3:16. **of.** *↗181E,* Ge +3:24. **constraineth.** 2 S 23:16. Jb 32:18. Lk 24:29. Ac *4:19, 20. +18:5. **because.** Ro 2:2. 1 C 2:14. **if.** *↗184A,* 1 C

+15:2. **one died.** Ro 5:15. **for all.** Ex 12:6. Is 53:6. Mt ❍20:28. ❍+*26:28n. Jn 1:29. 11:50-52. Ro 5:18. 1 T √2:6. He *2:9. 2 P √3:9. 1 J √2:1, 2. **then.** 2 C 3:7, 9. Lk 15:24, 32. Jn 5:25. 11:25. Ro *5:12, 15. 14:7-9. Ep *2:1-5. Col 2:13. 1 T 5:6. T 3:3. 1 J 5:19.

15. **for all.** ver. +*14. Ro +*5:18. Ga ❍*2:20. 1 Th 5:10. 1 T +*2:6. **that they.** 2 C 3:6. Ezk 16:6. 37:9, 14. Hab 2:4. Zc 10:9. Jn 3:15, 16. 5:24. 6:57. Ro 6:2, 11, 12. 8:2, 6, 10. *14:+7, 8. 1 C √6:19, 20. Ga *2:20. 5:24, 25. 6:14. Ep 5:14. Col 2:12. *3:1-3. 1 P 4:6. 1 J 4:9. 5:18. **which live.** 1 J *5:12, 13. **henceforth.** ver. 16. 2 K 5:17. Ro 6:6. Ep 4:17. 1 P 1:14, 15. *4:2-4. **live unto.** Lk 1:74. Ro 6:13. 12:1. 14:7-9. 1 C 6:20. 10:33. Ga 2:19. Ph 1:20, 21. Col 3:17, 23. 1 Th 5:10. T *2:14. He 13:20, 21. Re 1:18. **but unto him.** 2 C 12:10. Ge +*49:10. Jn *12:32. Ro 14:8. Ga *2:20. Ep 3:21. Ph 3:7, 8. 2 Th 2:1. He 13:13. **rose again.** Jn 14:19. Ro +*4:25. 1 C 15:17. Ph 3:10.

16. **know we no.** Dt 33:9. 1 S 2:29. Mt 10:37. *12:48-50. Mk 3:31-35. Jn 2:4. 15:14. Ga 2:5, 6. Ph 3:7, 8. Col 2:11. 3:11. 1 T *5:21, 22. Ja 2:1-4. 3:17. **after the flesh.** 2 C +1:17. 11:22. Ro *9:3-5. Ga 2:11-14. **though.** √184A, 1 C +15:2. **yet.** Jn 6:63. **him.** √63A2, 2 S +6:6.

17. **if.** √184A, 1 C +15:2. **in Christ.** ver. 19, 21. 2 C 12:2. Is *45:17, 24, 25. Jn +14:20. *15:2, 5. 17:23. Ro +*8:1n, 9. 16:7, 11. 1 C *1:30. Ga 1:22. 3:28. *5:6. Ep *1:3, 4. Ph 4:21. Col 1:19, 20. 1 J *4:13. **he is.** or, let him be. or, he is created. √63E2, 1 S +13:8. **a new.** Gr. *kainos*, new in quality, not time, Mk +*2:22n. Ps 51:10. Ezk 11:19. 18:31. 36:26. Mt 12:33. Jn +*3:3, 5. Ga *6:15. Ep √2:10. Re +*2:17. **creature.** √121I1, Ge +3:7. T#591. Dt 30:6. Jb +2:3 (T#645). Ps 102:18. Ezk *36:26. Jn 1:13. +*3:3, 5. Ro 2:28, 29. +6:4. Ga 5:24. 6:15. Ep 2:15. T 3:5. Re 21:5. **old.** ver. 16. Is 43:18, 19. 65:17, 18. Mt 9:16, 17. 24:35. Ro *6:4-6. 7:6. 8:9, 10. 1 C 13:11. Ep 2:15. *4:22-24. Ph *3:7-9. Col *3:1-10. He 8:9-13. 2 P 3:10-13. Re 21:1-5. **become new.** Is 66:17, 18.

18. **all things.** √16, Ge +1:27. Jn 3:16, 27. Ro 11:26. 1 C *1:30. 8:6. 11:12. 12:6. Col 1:16, 17. Ja 1:17. **who.** Le 6:30. Ezk 45:15. Da +*9:24. Ro *5:1, 10, 11g. Ep 2:15, 16. Col 1:20-22. He 2:17. 1 J *2:2. *4:10. **hath given.** ver. 19, 20. Is 52:7. 57:19. Mk √16:15, 16. Lk 10:5. 24:47. Ac +√10:36. 13:38, 39. Ep 2:17. Col 1:20. **the ministry.** 2 C +3:6. **reconciliation.** T#793. Is 27:5. Ro *5:9-11. 11:15. Ep 2:13-17. Col *1:21-23. He 2:17.

19. **God.** Mt 1:23. Jn 14:10, 11, 20. 17:23. 1 T *3:16. **in Christ.** Jn 17:23. Col 2:9. **reconciling.** Ro *3:24-26. 11:15. 1 J 2:1, 2. 4:10. **the world.** Gr. *kosmos*, Mt +4:8. √121J8, Jn +3:16. "World" is singular, and by *Metonymy* is put for its *inhabitants*, as interpreted by the following "them." Jn +1:9. Ga 6:14. Col 2:8. 2 P 2:5. 1 J 2:1, 2. **not.** Ps *32:1, 2. Is 43:25. 44:22. Ro √4:6-8. 1 C 13:5. **trespasses.** Le +=5:6. **unto them.** √163, Jn +16:13. "Them" (plural) has reference to "world" (singular), an instance of *Syllepsis*, or change in concord. **committed.** or, put in us. **the word.** ver. 18. 2 Ch=17:9.

20. **ambassadors.** T#454. 2 C 3:6. Ge=42:23. Jb 33:23. Pr 13:17. Ml +*2:7. Jn +17:18. 20:21. Ac 26:17, 18. Ga 4:14. Ep 6:20. **as.** ver. 11. 2 C 6:1. 2 K 17:13. 2 Ch 36:15. Ne 9:29. Is √55:6, 7. Je 44:4. Ezk 18:31, 32. **you.** √63A2, 2 S +6:6. **in.** Jb 33:6. Lk 10:16. 1 C 4:4, 5. 1 Th 4:8. **be.** Jb *22:21. Pr 1:22, etc. Is 27:5.

Je 13:16, 17. 38:20. Lk 14:23.

21. **he.** Is *53:4-6, 9-12. Da +*9:26. Zc *13:7. Ro +4:25. *8:3. Ga *3:13. Ep *5:2. 1 P *3:18. 1 J *2:1, 2. **sin.** √√121L5, Ge +4:7. **for us.** Ex 12:13. Le +=23:19. Pr 17:15. Mt +*1:21. Ro 4:25. 1 P 2:24. 3:18. **who knew no sin.** √145, Jg +11:40. Is *53:9. Lk +*1:35. He *7:26. 1 P 1:19. *2:22-24. 1 J *3:5. **we.** ver. *17. Is *45:24, 25. *53:11. Je +*23:6. *33:16. Da +*9:24. Ro +*1:17. *3:21-26. √5:19. *8:1-4. √10:3, 4. 1 C +*1:30. Ph *3:9.

2 CORINTHIANS 6

The apostle earnestly exhorts the Corinthians, not to receive the grace of God in vain, but to seek salvation without delay, 1, 2. He most pathetically shows, by what labors, sufferings and patient endurance he, and his brethren, sought to render their ministry approved, 3-10. He assures them, that he spake of this the more freely, out of the great love, which he bare to them, 11, 12; requiring the like affection from them, 13. He warns them against intimate connections with unbelievers, seeing Christians are the temples of the living God, 14-16; and encourages them, by the promises of being received as the children of God, to separate from sinners and from sin, 17, 18.

1. **workers.** 2 C 5:18-20. 1 C *3:9. **together.** Is 64:8. Mk 16:20. Lk 5:7. Jn 9:6. Ac 14:27. 15:4. Ph *2:13. **with him.** √63K, Ge +37:13. EWB argues that this is a false ellipsis, the words give a totally false view of our position as workers. "We are not fellow-workers with God, but with our brethren; *with you*, not *with him*, should be the words supplied, if any" (B126, 127). The verse should read "But working together (or as fellow-workers *with you*), we exhort also that ye receive not the grace of God in vain." **beseech.** See on 2 C 5:20. 10:1. Mt 23:37. Ro +*12:1. Ga 4:11, 12. **ye.** Je 8:8. Ga 3:4. He 12:15, 26. **the grace.** 2 C 8:1, 2. Ac +*11:23. 14:3. Ga 2:21. T *2:11. 1 P 4:10, 11. **in vain.** 1 Th +*3:5.

2. **a time accepted.** T#553. Jb +27:8 (T#572). Ps +69:13 (T#1150). +90:12 (T#727). Pr √1:24-28. Ec *9:10. Is ▶49:8. √55:6. 61:2. Je *8:20. Ezk 16:8. Zc 9:12. Mt 25:10-12. Lk 4:19. +16:26 (T#390). 19:42-44. He 3:7, +*13. 4:7. **now.** T#1168. Ge +*6:3. =45:9. Jsh √24:15. 1 S +*15:23. 1 K +*18:21. Jb *9:4. 33:14. *36:11, 12. Ps 32:6. 95:7, 8. Pr √27:1. √28:13, 14. √29:1. Ec √8:11-13. *12:1. Is √1:18. √55:6, 7. 57:17. *63:10. Je 2:13, 19. *8:20. Ezk √3:18, 19. Da √9:13. Ho 4:6. 7:9, 10, 13, 14. Zp 3:2. Zc 7:11-14. Ml 2:2. 3:18. 4:1. Mt 24:44. Lk *12:19, 20. +*13:24, 25. *19:5, 42. Jn √6:37. *8:24, 47. *12:35, 48. Ac 3:23. *24:25. *26:28, 29. 2 Th 1:7, 8. √2:10-12. 2 T 4:3, 4. He √2:3. +*3:13. +*9:27. 12:25. Ja √4:13. Re √3:17-20. 10:5, 6. **accepted.** Ro +15:16. **day of salvation.** Ps +*118:24. Is 49:8.

3. **no offence.** 2 C 1:12. *8:20. 2 S ❍*12:14. Mt 17:27. 18:6. Ac +*6:3. Ro 14:13. 1 C 8:9-13. 9:12, 22. 10:23, 24, 32, 33. 1 Th +*5:22.

4. **in all.** 2 C 2:17. 7:11. Ac 2:22. Ro 14:18. 16:10. 1 C 11:19. 1 Th 2:3-11. 2 T *2:15. **approving.** Gr. commending. 2 C +3:1. 4:2. Ro *5:8. **as the ministers.** 2 C +*3:6. *4:1. 11:23. Is 61:6. Jl 1:9. 2:17. Mt *10:16-18, 22. 1 C 3:5. 4:1. 1 Th 3:2. 1 T 4:6. 2 T +*2:24, 25. **in much patience.** 2 C *12:12. Lk 21:19. Ac +9:16. Ro 5:3, 4. Col +*1:11. 1 Th 5:14. 1 T 6:11. 2 T 3:10. He 12:1. Ja *1:2-4. 5:7-10. 2 P +*1:6. Re 1:9. +*3:10.

afflictions. 2 C *4:17. Ac *20:23, 24. Col 1:24. 1 Th 3:3. 2 T 1:8. 3:11, 12. 4:5. **necessities.** 2 C 11:9, 27. 12:10. Ac *20:34. 1 C 4:11, 12. Ph 4:11, 12. **distresses.** 2 C 4:8. Ro 8:35, 36. 1 Th 3:7.

5. **stripes.** 2 C *11:23-25. Dt 25:3. Is *53:5. Ac *16:23. **imprisonments.** 1 K 22:27. 2 Ch 16:10. Je 33:1. 37:15, 16. 38:6. Mt 14:3, 10. Ac 5:18. 12:4, 5. 16:24. 22:24. *23:35. 24:27. 26:10, 29. 28:16, 17, 30. Ep 3:1. Ph 1:13. 2 T 1:8. 2:9. He 11:36. 13:23. Re 2:10. **in tumults.** *or*, in tossings to and fro. 2 C 1:8-10. Lk +21:9. Ac 14:19. *17:5. 18:12-17. *19:23-34. 21:27-35. 22:23. 23:10. **labors.** 2 C √11:23. 1 C *15:10. 1 Th 2:9. 1 T 4:10. **watchings.** 2 C 11:27. Ezk 3:17. Mk 13:34-37. Ac 20:31. 2 T 4:5. He *13:17. **fastings.** Mt 9:15. Lk +2:37. Ac 13:3. 14:23. 1 C 7:5.

6. **pureness.** 2 C +*4:2. 7:2. 11:3g. 1 Th *2:10. 1 T 4:12. 5:2. T 2:7. **knowledge.** 2 C 4:6. 11:6. 1 C 2:1, 2, 16. Ep *3:4. Col +*1:9, 10, 27. 2:3. **longsuffering.** 1 C *13:4. Ga *5:22. Ep *4:+2, 32. Col *1:11. 3:12. 2 T *3:10. *4:2. **kindness.** 1 C 13:4. Ga *5:22. Col 3:12. **by the.** 2 C 3:3. 11:4. Ro *15:19. 1 C 2:4. Ga 3:2, 5. 1 Th *1:5, 6. 1 P 1:12. **Ghost.** Gr. *pneuma*, Mt +1:18n. **love.** 2 C 2:4. 11:11. *12:15. Jg 16:15. Ezk +*33:31. Ro +*12:9. Ja +3:17. 1 P 1:22. 1 J 3:18.

7. **the word.** 2 C 1:18-20. +*4:2. 7:14. Ps 119:43. 1 C *2:4. Ep *1:13. 4:21. Col *1:5. 2 T √2:15. Ja √1:18. **the power.** 2 C √10:4, 5. 13:4. Mk 16:20. Ac 11:21. Ro +*1:16. 1 C 1:24. 2:4, +5. Ep 1:19, 20. 3:20. He 2:4. **the armor.** 2 C 10:4. Is 11:5. 59:17. Lk *1:6. Ro +*13:12, 13. Ep *6:11, 13, 14, etc. 1 Th 5:8. 2 T 4:7. **on the right.** Ex 14:22. Pr 3:16. Ep 6:16, 17.

8. **By honor.** √125, Jb 22:6. Ac 4:21. 5:13, 40, 41. 14:11-20. 16:20-22, 39. 28:4-10. 1 C 4:10-13. **by evil.** √31, Is +1:21. Mt +*5:11, 12. 10:25. Ac 6:3. 10:22. 22:12. 24:5. 28:22. Ro 3:8. 1 T 3:7. 4:10. He 13:13. 1 P 4:14. 3 J 12. Re 3:9. **as deceivers.** Mt 27:63. Jn *7:12, 17. 1 Th 2:3g. **yet.** √31, Is +1:21. **true.** Mt 22:16. Mk 12:14. Jn 7:18.

9. **unknown.** Ac *9:26, 27. 17:18. 21:37, 38. 25:14, 15, 19, 26. 1 C *4:9. 1 J *3:1. **and yet.** √31, Is +1:21. **well known.** Gr. *epiginosko*, Mt +11:27. 2 C 4:2. 5:11. *11:6. Ac 19:26. Ro 15:19. Ga 1:22-24. **as dying.** Ps 118:17. Ro +*8:36. **behold.** √31, Is +1:21. 2 C *1:8-10. *4:10, 11. Ro 8:36. 1 C 4:9. 15:31. **as chastened.** Ps *118:17, 18. Je 30:11. 1 C 11:32. **and not.** √31, Is +1:21.

10. **sorrowful.** 2 C 2:4. 7:3-10. Mt +*5:4, 12. Lk 6:21. Jn +16:22. Ac 5:41. 16:25. Ro 5:2, 3. 9:2. 12:15. 15:13. Ph *4:4. 1 Th 3:7-10. 5:16. He 10:34. Ja 1:2-4. 1 P 1:6-8. 4:13. **yet.** √31, Is +1:21. T#323. **alway.** Gr. *aei*, Mk 15:8. **poor.** See on ver. 4. 2 C *8:9. 11:8. Jg 6:15. 1 K 17:12. 2 K 4:1. Pr *13:7. Mt +*5:12. Mk *12:42. Re 2:9. **making.** √31, Is +1:21. 2 C 4:7. *8:9. 9:11. Ro 11:12. 1 C 1:5. Ep 3:8, 16. Col *3:16. 1 T 6:18. Ja +*2:5. Re 2:9. **having nothing.** Ac 3:6. Ph *3:8. **and yet.** √31, Is +1:21. 2 C 4:15. Ps *84:11. Pr 16:16. Mt 6:19, 20. Lk 16:11, 12. 1 C *3:21-23. 1 T 4:8. Ja +*2:5. Re 21:7. **possessing.** 1 C ◐7:30. Col 3:24. **all things.** Ro +*8:28.

11. **ye.** Ga 3:1. Ph 4:15. **our mouth.** 2 C *7:3, 4. 1 S 2:1. Jb 32:20. 33:2, 3. Ps 51:15. Ezk 33:22. Ep 6:19. **open.** √108H6A, Jg +11:35. **our heart.** 2 C 2:4. 7:3. 11:11. 12:15. 1 K 4:29. Ps 119:32. Is 60:5. Hab 2:5. Ep 6:8. Ph 1:8. Re 22:12.

12. **are not.** 2 C 4:8. 7:2. 12:15. Ec 6:9mg. Jb 36:16.

Pr 4:12. Mi 2:7. **in your.** 2 C 7:15. SS 5:4. Ph 1:8. Col +*3:12. 1 J 3:17. **bowels.** √46C, Mt +8:6. Gr. *splangna, bowels*, is used for *mercy*, like the Hebrew *rachameem*, which has both meanings. See Ge 43:30; Ps 51:1; Pr 12:10. When used with the word "mercies" itself, it denotes *tender mercies* (B679). 2 C 7:15. Lk 1:78. Ph 1:8. Col 3:12.

13. **recompense.** Ga 4:12. **I speak.** 1 C *4:+14, 15. Ga 4:19. 1 Th *2:11. He *12:5, 6. 1 J 2:1, 12-14. 3:7, 18. 3 J 4. **be.** 2 K 13:14-19. Ps 81:10. Mt 9:28, 29. 17:19-21. Mk 6:4-6. √11:24. Ga *4:12. Ja *1:6, 7. 1 J √5:14, 15.

14. **unequally.** Ex 34:16. Le *19:19. Dt *7:2, 3. 22:9-11. Jsh 23:12. Ru 3:10n. Ezr 9:1, 2, 11, 12. 10:3n, 19. Ne 13:1-3, 23-26. Ps 94:20. 106:35. +*119:63. Pr 22:24. Ml 2:11, 15. 1 C +*5:9. √7:39. 15:33. Ja *4:4. **what fellowship.** Jsh 9:14. 1 S 5:2, 3. 1 K 18:21. 2 Ch 19:2. Ps 16:3. 26:4, 5, 9, 10. 44:20, 21. 101:3-5. +√119:63. 139:21, 22. Pr 29:27. Jn 7:7. 15:18, 19. Ac 4:23. 1 C 10:21. Ep *5:6-10, +*11. 1 J 1:6. 3:12-14. 2 J +*11. **and what communion.** Pr 4:18, 19. Ac +*26:18. Ro 13:12-14. Ep 4:17-20. √5:8-14. Ph 2:15. 1 Th 5:4-8. 1 P *2:9, 10. 4:2-4. 1 J 1:5-7. **darkness.** Is +*9:2. Mt +*15:14.

15. **what concord.** 1 S *5:2-4. 1 K +*18:21. 1 C *10:20, 21. **Belial.** ✳S#955g, only here. For ✳S#1100h, see Dt +13:13. Dt +*15:9. Jg +*19:22. 1 S 2:12. 1 K 21:10. **or.** Ezr 4:3. Mk *16:16. Ac 8:20, 21. 1 J√5:11-13. **part.** Nu=18:20. **an infidel.** 1 T +*5:8.

16. **what.** Ex 20:3. 23:13. 34:14. Dt 4:23, 24. 5:7. 6:14, 15. Jsh 24:14-24. 1 S 7:3, 4. 1 K √18:21. 2 K 17:33, 34. 21:4, 5. 23:5-7. 2 Ch 33:4, 5. Ezk 36:25. Ho 14:8. Zp 1:5. Mt √6:24. Col +*3:5. 1 J *5:20, 21. **with idols.** √6311A, Ex +12:4. Supply ellipsis, "with (the temple of) idols." **ye are.** 1 C √3:16, 17. √6:19. Ep *2:20-22. 1 T 3:15. He 3:6. 1 P 2:5. **the temple.** 2 Ch=29:16. 1 C +3:9. **living God.** Mt +*16:16. **I will dwell.** √92G, Lk +4:18. Ex 25:8. *29:45. Le ▶26:12. 1 K 6:13. Ps 90:1. Ezk 43:7, 9. Zc 2:10, 11. Jn 6:56. 15:4. Ro +*8:9, 11. Ep 3:17. 2 T 1:14. 1 J 4:12, 15. Re 21:3. **and walk.** √22C17, Le +26:12. Col ◐2:6. Re 2:1. 7:15. 21:3. **I will be.** Ge +*17:7, 8. Ex 6:7. 2 S 7:14. Je 24:7. *31:33. 32:38. Ezk 11:20. 36:28. 37:26, 27. Ho 2:23. Zc 8:8. 13:9. Ro 9:26. Ho 8:10. Re 21:7. **my people.** Ex 33:16. Je 7:23. 11:4. 24:7. 30:22. *31:33. 32:38. Ezk 14:11.

17. **come out.** 2 C 7:1. Nu 16:21, 26, 45. Ezr 6:21. 10:11. Ps +*1:1-3. Pr 9:6. Is ▶52:11. Je 51:6. Ac 2:40. 1 C *5:10. Re *18:4. **from.** √108H3, Mt +13:49. **among.** √144A6, Ge +45:6. **separate.** T#424. Ge 6:2. Ex 33:16. Le 20:23, 24, 26. Nu=8:14. Dt √7:3, 4. Ps 4:3. 45:10. Je +*10:2. Am 3:3. 1 C 7:39. **touch not.** Is ▶52:11. 1 C *10:28. **unclean.** 2 Ch=23:19. **and I.** Nu=16:9. Is +*▶52:11. Ezk 20:34, 41. Zp 3:20. Jn 6:37, 38. Ro 15:7.

18. **a Father.** Ex 4:22. 2 S 7:8, 14. Ps 22:30. Is 43:6. Je *3:19. *31:1, 9. Ho 1:9, 10. Jn √1:12. Ro *8:14-17, 29. Ga 3:26. 4:5-7. Ep 1:5. He 1:5. Ja 1:7. 1 J √3:1, 2. Re *21:7. **my sons.** 2 S 7:14. Ga 3:28. **the Lord.** Ge *17:1. 48:3. Re +*1:8. 21:22.

2 CORINTHIANS 7

The apostle exhorts the Corinthians to follow after holiness, encouraged by the preceding promises, 1; and to receive him, who had done nothing to forfeit their esteem, but had great love for them and confidence in them, 2-4. He shows what comfort, under his troubles, Titus's good account of them gave him, 5-7; so that he does not repent of having grieved them by his former Epistle, considering the happy effects of their godly sorrow, 8-11. He wrote to approve his care of them as in the sight of God, 12; and he rejoices, especially, in the joy of Titus, and in his affection for them, as excited by their good conduct, which was answerable to the apostle's former boasting concerning them, 13-16.

1. **therefore.** 2 C 1:20. *6:17, 18. Ro 5:20, 21. 6:1, etc. He *4:1. 2 P √1:4-8. **these promises.** He +6:12. **let.** 2 C 6:17. Ps +*51:10. √119:9. Pr +*20:9. 30:12. Is *1:16. Je 13:27. Ezk *18:30-32. *36:25, 26. Mt +*5:8. *12:33. *23:25, 26. Lk 11:39, 40. 1 C 3:17. T 1:15. *2:11-14. Ja *4:8. 1 P *1:22. *2:11. 2 P √1:3-7. 1 J √1:7, 9. *3:1-3. **cleanse.** Nu=8:6, 7. He 10:22. **filthiness.** Is √55:7. Je *4:14. 1 C √6:20. Ep 2:3. 1 Th √5:23. **of the flesh.** ƒ171Q5, Ge +17:13. Ga √5:19-21. **spirit.** Gr. *pneuma*, ƒ171Q1B, Mk +2:8n. **perfecting.** T#501. 2 Ch=31:18. Pr +21:3 (T#629). Mt +*5:48 (T#285). Ro +7:12 (T#286). 12:1, 2, 9-21. Ep 4:12, 13, 25-32. 5:1-4, 11, 15, 16. *6:10-18. Ph *3:12-15. 1 Th *3:13. 4:7. He +*12:14, 23. 1 P 1:15. 2:21, 22. *5:10. 2 P *3:14. **in the fear.** 2 Ch 19:9. Ps *19:9. Pr *8:13. *16:6. Ac 9:31. He *12:28. 1 P +1:17.

2. **Receive.** 2 C *5:20. 6:12, 13. 11:16. Mt *10:14, 40, 41. Lk 10:8. Ph 2:29. Col 4:10. Phm 12, 17. 2 J 10. 3 J *8-10. **we have wronged.** 2 C 1:12. +*4:2. 6:3-7. 11:9, 20. 12:14-18. Nu 16:15. 1 S 12:3, 4. Ac 20:33. Ro 16:18. 1 C +9:12. 1 Th 2:3-6, 10. 2 Th 3:7-9. **we have.** ƒ41, Ge +10:1. **defrauded.** 2 C 2:11. √8:19-21. 12:17, 18. Ex +*18:21. Le +*19:13. 2 K +*12:15. Mk 10:19. Ac +*6:3. 1 Th 2:5. *4:6.

3. **to condemn.** ver. 12. 2 C 2:4, 5. 13:10. 1 C 4:14, 15. **for.** 2 C 6:11, 12. **ye.** 2 C *3:2. 11:11. 12:15. Ph *1:7-9. **to die.** Ru 1:16, 17. 1 Th *2:8.

4. **my boldness.** 2 C 3:12. 6:11. 10:1, 2. 11:21. Ac +*4:13. Ep 6:19, 20. Ph 1:20. 1 Th 2:2. **great.** 2 C 1:14. 9:2-4. 1 C *1:4-7. 1 Th 2:19. **my glorying.** ver. 14. 2 C 1:12. 8:24. 9:2. **I am filled.** ver. 6, 7. 2 C +*1:4. 2:14. 6:10. Ac 5:41. Ro 5:3. Ph *2:17. Col 1:24. 1 Th 3:7-9. Phm 7. Ja 1:2. **comfort.** ver. 7, 13. 1 C +14:3. **I am.** ƒ41, Ge +10:1. 2 C 12:10. **tribulation.** Mt +*5:12.

5. **when.** 2 C 1:16, 17. *2:12, 13. Ac 20:1. 1 C 16:5. **Macedonia.** Ac +16:9. our. 2 C *4:8-12. 11:23-30. Ge 8:9. Is 23:12. Je 8:18. 45:3. Mt 11:28-30. **troubled.** 2 C 4:8. Jb 18:11. Je 6:25. 20:10. **without.** Dt 32:25. La 1:20. Ezk 7:15. 1 C 15:31, 32. **within.** ƒ41, Ge +10:1. **fears.** 2 C 2:3, 9. *11:28, 29. *12:20, 21. Ga 4:11, 19, 20. 1 Th 3:5.

6. **that comforteth.** 2 C *1:3, 4. 2:14. Is 12:1. *51:12, 13. 57:15, 18. 61:1, 2. Je 31:13. Mt +*5:4. Jn *14:16. Ro *15:5. Ph 2:1. 2 Th *2:16, 17. **cast down.** Ps +*34:4. Ro +*12:21. Ja +*4:6. **comforted.** ver. 13. 2 C 2:13. 1 C 16:17, 18. 1 Th 3:2, 6, 7. 3 J 2-4. **coming.** Gr. *parousia*, Mt +24:3. Ac ❍*1:11. Ph +*1:26. **Titus.** ver. 13, 14. 2 C +2:13.

7. **coming.** Gr. *parousia*, Mt +24:3. **but.** ver. 4, 13. Ac 11:23. Ro 1:12. Col 2:5. 1 Th 3:8. 2 J 4. **when.** ver. 11. 2 C 2:9. Ps 141:5. Pr 9:8, 9. **earnest.** ver. 11. 2 C 5:2. 8:16. Lk 22:44. Ph 1:20. He *2:1. Ja 5:17. Ju +*3. **your mourning.** ƒ41, Ge +10:1. ver. 10. Jg 2:4, 5. Ps 6:1-6. 30:5. 31:9-11. 38:18. *51:1.

√126:5, 6. Je 31:18-20. Mt +*5:4. 26:75. Ja 4:9, 10. **fervent.** 2 C 1:14. 2:3, 4. 1 Th 3:6.

8. **though I made.** ƒ185A, Lk +11:8. ver. 6, 11. 2 C 2:2-11. La 3:32. Mt 26:21, 22. Lk 22:61, 62. Jn 16:6. 21:17. He 12:9-11. Re *3:19. **not repent.** ver. 10. Mt 21:29g. **though I did.** 2 C *2:4. Ex 5:22, 23. Je 20:7-9. **season.** Jn 5:35. Ga 2:5. 1 Th 2:17. Phm 15g. Re 17:12.

9. **I rejoice.** See on ver. 6, 7, 10. Ec 7:3. Je 31:18-20. Zc *12:10. Lk 15:7, 10, 17-24, 32. Ac 20:21. **ye sorrowed.** Ps 38:18. 1 C 5:2. **after a godly manner.** *or, according to God.* ver. 10, 11. 2 C 1:12g. Ro +*8:27. **that ye.** 2 C 2:16. 10:8-10. 13:8-10. Is 6:9-11. **receive damage.** Mt +16:26 (*S#2210g). Lk +9:25.

10. **godly sorrow.** Ps ch. 32, 51. Mt 26:75. **repentance.** T#603. 2 C 12:21. Jg +10:15 (T#356). 2 S *12:13. 1 K 8:47-50. Jb *33:27, 28. +40:4 (T#30). *42:5, 6. Ps *38:3-10, *18. *51:3, 4, 17. *119:59, 60. Pr +28:13 (T#124). Je 31:9. Ezk 7:16. *18:27-30. 20:43. *36:31. Jon 3:8, 10. Mt *21:28-32. *26:75. Lk 5:8. *15:10, 18, 19. *18:13. Ac +*3:19. 11:18. 2 T +*2:25, 26. Ja +4:10 (T#357). **to salvation.** Ho 14:9. **not to be.** Ro 11:29g. **the sorrow.** The sorrow of carnal men about worldly objects, loss of fortune, fame, or friends; which, being separated from the fear and love of God, and faith in his providence and mercy, frequently drinks up their spirits, breaks their proud, rebellious hearts, or drives them to lay desperate hands on themselves. T#609. Ge 4:13-15. 30:1. 1 S *30:6. 31:3-6. 2 S 13:4. *17:23. 1 K *21:4. Jb +21:15 (T#689). Ps +106:13 (T#411). Pr *15:13, 15. *17:22. *18:14. Is *17:11mg. Jon *4:9. Mt *27:3-5. Lk +18:12 (T#194). Ga +4:17 (T#623). 2 T +3:5 (T#191). He *12:17. **world.** Gr. *kosmos*, Mt +4:8. **worketh death.** Jn 8:9.

11. **ye sorrowed.** T#605. ver. 9, 10. Ps +119:6 (T#602). Is 66:2. Zc *12:10-14. Ac +8:8 (T#621). 1 C 5:2. **carefulness.** See on ver. 7, 12. Mk 6:25. Lk 1:39. Ro 12:8. 1 C 12:25. T *3:8, 18. 2 P 1:5. Ju 3g. **clearing.** 2 C 12:19. Ge 44:6, 7. Ac 22:1. 25:16. Ro 2:15g. 1 C 5:13. 9:3. Ep +*5:11. Ph 1:7, 16. 1 T 5:21, 22. 2 T 4:16. 1 P 3:15g. **yea.** ƒ18, Dt +28:4. **indignation.** 2 S 12:5-7. Ne 5:6, etc. 13:25. Jb 42:6. Je 31:18-20. Da 6:14. Mk 3:5. 1 C 5:2. Ep 4:26. **fear.** ver. 1, 15. Ps 2:11. Pr 14:16. *16:6. 28:14. Ro 11:20. 1 C +2:3. Ph *2:12. He 4:1. +*12:15, 16. 1 P 1:17. Ju *23. **vehement.** ver. 7. Ps 38:9. 42:1. 130:6. 145:19. SS 8:6. Is 26:8. 1 P *2:2. **zeal.** 2 C 9:2. Ps 69:9. 119:139. Jn 2:17. Ac 17:16. **revenge.** Ps 35:13. Mt *5:29, 30. Mk *9:43-48. Re *3:19. **approved.** 2 C +3:1. 6:4. 13:7. Ro +3:5. 14:18. 2 T √2:15. **clear.** Ja 3:17. **in this matter.** 1 Th 4:6.

12. **though.** ƒ185A, Lk +11:8. **I did.** 2 C 2:9. 1 C *5:1, 2. *6:7. **that our.** 2 C 2:4, 17. 11:11, 28. 1 T 3:5.

13. **we were.** 2 C 2:3. Ro 12:15. 1 C 12:26. 13:5-7. Ph 2:28. 1 P 3:8. **because.** ver. 15. Ro 15:32. 1 C 16:13. 2 T 1:16. Phm 20. **spirit.** Gr. *pneuma*, ƒ171Q1B, Mk +2:8n. **refreshed.** Ro +15:32.

14. **if.** ƒ184A, 1 C +15:2. ver. 4. 2 C 8:24. 9:2-4. 10:8. 2 Th 1:4. **we.** 2 C 1:18-20. **in truth.** 2 C 4:2. 6:7. **our boasting.** ver. +4. **Titus.** ver. 6, 13.

15. **inward affection is.** Gr. bowels are. 2 C +6:12. Ge 43:30. 1 K 3:26. SS 5:4. Ph 1:8. Col *3:12. 1 J 3:17. **the obedience.** 2 C 2:9. 10:5, 6. Ph *2:12. 2 Th 3:14. **with.** See on ver. 10, 11. Ezr 9:4. 10:9. Jb 21:6. Ps 2:11. 119:120. Is 66:2. Ho 13:1. Ac 16:29. 1 C +2:3.

Ep 6:5. Ph *2:12. **received him**. 2 C 11:16. Mt 10:40. Lk 10:16. Jn 13:20.

16. **that**. 2 C 2:3. 2 Th *3:4. Phm 8, 21.

2 CORINTHIANS 8

The apostle sets before the church at Corinth the liberality of the poor Christians in Macedonia, 1-5; and excites them to imitate this liberality, toward the poor saints in Judea; that they might abound as much "in this grace" as in other things; and show the sincerity of their love, as animated by the self-abasing and self-denying love of Christ to them, 6-9. They had before shown a readiness to this contribution, which would be graciously accepted by the Lord, 10-15. He commends to them Titus, and two other brethren, whom he had engaged in this service; and who were on many accounts worthy of their peculiar regard, 16-24.

1. **we**. 2 C 5:19. 1 C +15:1. **the grace**. ver. 2-7. 2 C 9:12, 14. Ac +*11:23. 1 C +1:4. 15:10. Ep 3:8. Col 1:29. **churches**. 2 C 9:2, 4. 11:9. Ac +16:9. Ro 15:26. 1 Th 1:7, 8. 4:10.

2. **in**. 1 Th 1:6. 2:14. 3:3, 4. **trial**. ver. 8. 2 C 2:9. 9:13. 13:3. Ro +5:4. **the abundance**. Ne 8:10-12. Ac 2:45, 46. 1 Th 1:6. **and**. ʃ93A, Ge +1:26. **their deep**. Mk *12:42-44. Lk 21:1-4. Ja *2:5. Re 2:9. **poverty abounded**. ʃ125, Jb +22:6. **the riches**. 2 C 6:10. 9:11, 13. Dt 15:4. Pr 11:25. Is 32:5-8. **liberality**. Gr. simplicity. 2 C 1:12. 9:11, 12. Ro +*12:8.

3. **For**. ʃ77, Ex +3:19. **to**. ver. 11. 2 C 9:6, 7. Mk 14:8. Ac *11:29. Ro *15:25, 26. 1 C *16:2. 1 P 4:11. **I bear**. Ro 10:2. Ga 4:15. Col 4:13. **beyond**. ver. 12, 16, 17. Ex 35:5, 21, 22, 29. 1 Ch 29:5, 6, 9, 13-17. Ps 110:3. 1 C 9:17. Ph √2:13. 1 Th 2:8. Phm 14. 1 P 5:2. **willing of themselves**. ver. 17.

4. **intreaty**. Ac +4:36g. **that**. ver. 18, 19. Ge 33:10, 11. 2 K 5:15, 16. Ac 16:15. 1 C 16:3, 4. **the ministering**. ver. 19, 20. 2 C 9:1, 12-14. Mt 10:42. 12:50. 25:40, 44, 45. Mk 14:7. Jn 19:26, 27. Ac 6:1, etc. 9:39-41. 11:29. +24:17. Ro *15:25, 26. +15:31. 1 C *16:1, 3, 4, 15. Ga 2:10. 6:10. 1 T 5:10. Phm 5, 6. He +*6:10. 1 J *3:16-18. **the saints**. 2 C +1:1.

5. **first gave**. 2 C √5:14, 15. 1 S 1:28. 2 Ch 30:8. Ps 76:11. 110:3. Pr 23:26. Is 44:3-5. Je 31:33. Zc 13:9. Ac +*17:11, 12. Ro 6:13. +*12:1. 14:7-9. 1 C √6:19, 20. T *2:14. **unto**. 2 C 4:5. 1 Ch 12:18. 2 Ch 30:12. **by the will**. 1 Th +4:3. 2 P ☉2:10.

6. **we**. ver. 16, 17. 2 C 12:18. **Titus**. ver. 23. 2 C +2:13. **had begun**. ver. 10. **grace**. or, gift. ver. 4, 19mg. 2 C 9:5. 1 C 15:10. 16:3. Ph 4:18. 1 P 4:10.

7. **as**. Ro 15:14. 1 C +1:5. 4:7. +*12:13. 14:12. Re 3:17. **faith**. 1 C 13:2. **utterance**. 1 P +*4:11. **knowledge**. 1 C 7:1, 2. +12:8. *13:8. **diligence**. ver. 8, *16, 17, 22. 2 C 7:11, 12g. **in your love**. ver. 24. 2 C 7:7. **see**. 2 C *9:8. Ph 1:9, 11. 1 Th 4:9, 10. 2 Th 1:3. 1 P 1:22. 2 P 1:5-8. **this**. ver. 6. 2 C 9:14. Ep 4:29. 2 T 2:1. He 12:28. 2 P √3:18.

8. **speak**. ver. 10. 2 C 9:7. 1 C 7:+6, 12, 25. **by occasion**. ver. 1-3. 9:2. Ro 11:12-14. He 10:24. **prove**. ver. 2g, 24. 2 C 6:6. Jsh *24:14. Ezk +*33:31. Ro *12:9. Ep 4:15mg. 6:24. Ja 2:14-16. 1 P 1:22. 1 J *3:17-19. **sincerity**. lit. genuine of your love. i.e. the genuineness (or genuine character of). ʃ24G, Ge 1:9. **of your**. ʃ29, Ex +19:6. i.e. your genuine love.

9. **the grace**. 2 C *13:14. Ps ☉+*84:11. Mt +*28:19n. Jn *1:14, 17. Ro 1:5, 7. *5:8, 20, 21. 1 C

1:4. Ep *1:6-8. *2:7. *3:8, 19. 1 T 1:14. He ☉10:29. **though**. 2 C 6:10. Ps *102:25-27. Jn *1:1-4, 10. *16:15. 1 C 15:47. Ph *2:6, 7. Col *1:16, 17. He *1:2, 6-14. **was rich**. ʃ22D5I, Pr +8:18. Jn *17:5. **for**. Is 62:1. 65:8. Jn *12:30. *17:19. Ga 2:20. Col *1:24. **he became**. Is 53:2. Mt *8:20. 17:27. *20:28. Mk 6:3. Lk *2:7. *8:3. *9:58. Ph *2:6-8. He=11:26. **that ye**. 2 C 6:10. Lk 16:11. Ro +*8:32. 11:12. 1 C *3:21, 22. Ep *3:8. 1 T *6:18. Ja +*2:5. Re *3:18. 21:7. **might be**. Ph 3:8. **rich**. ʃ22D5I, Pr +8:18.

10. **I give**. 1 C 7:25, 40. **expedient**. 2 C 12:1. Dt *15:7, 8. Pr √19:17. 28:27. Mt √10:42. Jn 11:50. 16:7. 18:14. 1 C 6:12. 10:23. Ph 4:17. 1 T √6:18, 19. He *13:16. Ja 2:15, 16. **to be**. ver. 8. 2 C 9:2. **forward**. Gr. willing. ʃ108B, 1 T +6:9. See on ver. 3. **a year ago**. ver. 19n. 2 C 9:2. 1 C 16:2.

11. **readiness**. ver. 19. 2 C 9:2. Ac +*17:11. **out of**. ver. 3.

12. **if**. ʃ184A, 1 C +15:2. 2 C *9:7. Ex 25:2. 35:5, 21, 22, 29. 1 Ch 29:3-18. 2 Ch 6:8. Pr +*19:22. Mk 12:42-44. 14:7, 8. Lk 7:44-46. +12:47, 48. √16:10. √21:1-4. 1 P *4:10. **accepted**. Ro +*15:16. **according**. The New Testament standard of giving is not represented as a legalistic obligation based on the tithe system under the law, but is based upon the willingness, cheerfulness, and ability of the giver (2 C 9:7. Lk +*11:41mg,n, 42n. 1 C 16:2n). Le 14:30. 27:8. Dt 16:17. Ezr *2:69. Ne *5:8. Ac √11:29. 1 C +*16:2. **a man hath**. 2 C *9:7. Ne 10:32n. Mk 12:43, 44. Lk 21:3.

13. **not**. Ac 4:34. Ro +*15:26, 27.

14. **equality**. ʃ132G, Ge +3:19. Col 4:1. **their want**. 2 C 9:12. Ac 4:34. **that**. ʃ63F, Ge +33:10. **your want**. Pr +*11:25. Ec 11:1, 2. Lk 6:38. 16:9. Ro *15:27. 1 C 9:11. Ga *6:6.

15. **He that**. Ex ▶16:18. Lk *22:35.

16. **thanks**. 2 C 2:14. 9:15. Ezr 7:27. Ne 2:12. Je 31:31. 32:40. Ro +6:17. Col *3:17. Re 17:17. **earnest care**. ver. 6, +7g. 2 C 7:7, 12. Ro +*12:5. Ph 2:20. **Titus**. ver. 6, 23. 2 C +2:13.

17. **accepted**. ver. *6. He 13:22. **but**. See on ver. 8, 10. **own accord**. ver. 3. Ph √2:12, 13.

18. **the brother**. This is generally supposed to have been St. Luke, "whose praise was in all the churches," on account of the gospel which he had written, and for many zealous services in its cause. ver. 19, 22, 23. 2 C 12:18. Col *4:14. 2 T *4:11. **in the gospel**. 2 C 10:14. Ro 1:9. 1 C 9:18. **throughout**. Ro 16:4. 1 C +7:17.

19. **And not**. Ro +5:3. **that**. ʃ63I1D, Nu +26:4. Supply by ellipsis (repetition: of preceding connected words), "And not only (is his praise throughout all the churches), but he was chosen." **but**. ver. 1-4. Ac 6:3-6. 15:22, 25. 1 C *16:3, 4. **chosen**. Ac +*14:23. 1 C 16:3, 4. **to travel**. Ac +19:29. **with this**. That is, the charitable contributions for the saints of Judea; respecting which Doctor Paley has some excellent remarks. There is, he observes, a circumstance of nicety in the agreement between the two Epistles, which I am convinced, the author of a forgery would not have hit upon, or which, if he had hit upon it, he would have set forth with more clearness. The Second Epistle speaks of the Corinthians as having begun this eleemosynary business a year before (ver. 10. 2 C 9:2). It appears, however, from other texts in the Epistle, that the contribution was not yet collected or paid; for breth-

ren were sent from St. Paul to Corinth "to make up their bounty" (2 C 9:5). They are urged to "perform the doing of it" (ver. 11), and every man was urged to "give as he purposed in his heart" (2 C 9:7). The contribution, therefore, was in readiness, yet not received from the contributors; was begun, was forward long before, yet not hitherto collected. Now this representation agrees with one, and only with one, supposition, namely, that every man had laid by in store, had already provided a fund, from which he was afterwards to contribute—the very case which the first Epistle authorizes us to suppose to have existed; for in that Epistle, St. Paul had charged the Corinthians "upon the first day of the week, every one of them, to lay by in store, as God had prospered him" (1 C *16:2). See related notes on undesigned coincidences listed at Ac 12:12n. **grace.** *or*, gift. See on ver. 4, 6, 7. 2 C *9:8. **administered.** ver. 4. Ro +15:31. **to the glory.** ver. 1, 2. 2 C 4:15. 9:12-14. Ph 4:18, 19. 1 P *4:10, 11. **ready mind.** ver. +11.

20. **Avoiding.** Ezr 8:24, 25. 1 Th +*5:22. 2 Th 3:6g. **that.** 2 C 11:12. Mt 10:16. Ro 14:16. 1 C 16:3. Ep 5:15. 1 Th +*5:22. **administered.** ver. 19. 2 C *7:2. 2 K +*12:15. Ac +*6:3.

21. **for honest.** T#1821. 2 K +*12:15. Ps 15:2, +*4. Ac 5:4. +*6:3. Ro +*12:17. Ph √4:8. 1 T 5:14. T 2:5, 8. 1 P *2:12. **not only.** 2 C 2:17. 5:9-11. Mt +*5:16. 6:1, 4. 23:5. Ro 14:18. Ph 4:8. 1 Th +*5:22.

22. **whom.** Ph 2:20-22. **proved diligent.** ver. +7. **confidence.** 2 C +2:3. **I have.** *or*, he hath.

23. **Titus.** ver. 6, 16. 2 C 7:6. 12:18. **is my.** Lk 5:7, 10. Phm 17. **our brethren.** ver. 18, 22. 2 C 9:3, 5. **and fellowhelper.** 1 C +12:28. Ph 2:25. 4:3. Col 1:7. 1 Th 2:2. Phm 1, 24. 3 J 8. **the messengers.** ver. 19. 2 Ch=24:5, 9, 11-13. Ph 2:25g. **the glory.** ver. 19. 1 C 11:7. 1 Th 2:20.

24. **show ye.** ver. 8. 2 C 9:2-4. **proof.** ver. 7, 8. **our boasting.** 2 C 7:4, 14. 9:2, 3.

2 CORINTHIANS 9

The apostle assigns his reasons for sending the brethren beforehand, to make up the collections of the Corinthians, notwithstanding his confidence in them, 1-5. He encourages their cheerful liberality; under the figure of sowing seed, from which they might expect from God a large increase, to enable them to sow still more abundantly to his glory, 6-11; for such services, not only supply the wants of the saints, but excite them to abundant thanksgivings to God, and fervent love to their benefactors, and prayers for them, 12-14. He concludes the subject by "thanking God for his unspeakable gift," 15.

1. **touching.** Ge 27:42. 1 S 20:23. 2 K 22:18. Jb 37:23. Ps 45:1. Mt 22:31. Ro 11:28. Ph 3:5, 6. **the ministering.** ver. 12-14. See on 2 C 8:4, etc. Ro +15:31. Ga 2:10. 6:10. **the saints.** 2 C +1:1. **it is.** 1 Th 4:9, 10. 5:1. 1 J *2:27.

2. **I know.** 2 C +8:4. **the forwardness.** 2 C 8:8, 10, +11, 19. 1 Th 1:7, 8. **I boast.** 2 C 8:24. **of Macedonia.** Ac +16:9. +19:21. Ro 15:26. **that Achaia.** 2 C 1:1. 8:10. Ac +18:12. 1 C 16:15. **a year ago.** 2 C 8:10. **provoked.** 2 C 8:8. He 10:24. **very many.** 1 C +9:19.

3. **have I sent.** ver. 4. 2 C 7:14. 8:6, 17-24. **the brethren.** Ep +6:23. **our boasting.** 2 C +8:24. Ph

+1:26. **in vain.** 1 C +1:17. **in this.** 2 C 3:10. **ye may.** ver. 5. 1 C *16:1, etc. T 3:1.

4. **if.** ✓184C, Mt +4:9. **they.** ver. 2. 2 C 8:1-5. Ac 20:4. **be ashamed.** 2 C 8:24. 11:17. **confident.** 2 C 11:17. He 1:3. 3:14. 11:1g.

5. **the brethren.** 2 C +8:23. **and make.** 2 C 8:6. 1 C 16:2. **bounty.** Gr. blessing. ✓108B, Ge +33:11. ver. 6. Ge 33:11. Jg 1:15. 1 S 25:27. 30:26mg. 2 K 5:15. **whereof ye had notice before.** *or*, which hath been so much spoken of before. **bounty.** Ph 4:17. **and not.** 2 C 9:7. 12:17, 18. **covetousness.** 1 C 5:10.

6. **I say.** 1 C 1:12. 7:29. 15:50. Ga 3:17. *5:16. Ep 4:17. Col 2:4. **He which.** ✓138C, Ge +22:14. **soweth.** ✓68, Ge +10:1. **sparingly.** ver. 10. Ps *41:1-3. Pr *11:18, 24, 25. *19:17. *22:9. Ec 11:1, 6. Ml *3:10. Lk +*6:38. *19:16-26. Ga √6:7-9. He +*6:10. **shall reap.** Lk +*6:38. **sparingly.** ✓16, Ge +1:27. **bountifully.** ✓16, Ge +1:27.

7. **not grudgingly.** Gr. of sorrow. Ex *25:2. Nu=18:6. Dt *15:7-11, 14. Jg 5:2. 1 Ch 29:5. Pr 23:6-8. Is 32:5, 8. Ph *4:18. Ja 5:9. 1 P *4:9. Ju 16. **for.** ✓138C, Ge +22:14. **God.** 2 C 8:12. Ex 25:2. 35:5. 1 Ch 29:17. Pr 11:25. 22:8, 9. Ac +*20:35. Ro *12:8. **cheerful giver.** The Greek term underlying "cheerful" reflects the insight that a cheerful or radiant countenance reflects a kind heart, a heart disposed to benevolence and generosity, a spirit opposite to murmuring and complaining. Motivated by our reception of God's gift, the spirit of murmuring is driven away, replaced by an inner freedom of generosity (see TDNT, vol. 3, pp. 297-299). Le +*23:38. Pr ⟩22:9. Ro +*12:8. Ph ◖2:14. 1 P 4:9. Ju 16.

8. **God is able.** T#588. Dt *33:25, 27. 2 Ch *25:9. Ps *84:11. 110:3. Pr *3:9. *10:22. *11:24. *28:27. Is *26:4. *40:31. *41:10. 48:18. *59:1. Ezk 36:26. Da *3:17. Mi 2:7. Hg 2:8. Ml √3:10. Lk 3:8. Ro √4:21. +*8:33-39. +9:18 (T#234). 14:4. Ep 1:18-20. √3:2, 20, 21. Ph *3:21. √4:18, 19. 2 T √1:12. He 2:18. √7:25. Ju +*24. Re +19:6 (T#218). **all.** ✓147I, Jn +1:11. **grace.** 2 C 8:19. Lk 10:19. Ro *14:4. Ph √4:13. 1 T 1:12. 1 P *4:10. **always.** ver. 11. 1 Ch 29:12-14. **all sufficiency.** Ps 36:8. Jn *10:10. Ep *3:20. Ph 4:+11, √19. 1 T 6:6g. 2 P √1:11. **in all things.** Le 26:5. Dt *30:9. Ps *132:15. Pr 3:10. Is 30:23. Ezk 36:30. Am 9:13. Zc 8:12. Ro +*8:32. **may abound.** 2 C 8:2, 7. Ac 9:36. 1 C 1:5. √15:58. Ep √2:10. Col +√1:10. 2 Th 2:17. 2 T √3:17. T *2:14. *3:8, 14. **good work.** Ac +9:36.

9. **He hath dispersed.** See on Ps ⟩112:9. **his righteousness.** Dt 6:25. 24:13. Ps 112:3. Pr 8:18. 21:21. Is 51:8. Da 4:27. 1 C 13:13. Ga *5:5, 6. Ja *2:17-26. **for ever.** Gr. *aion*, Mt +6:13. lit. unto the age, Mt +21:19.

10. **he that ministereth.** Ga 3:5. Ep 4:16. Ph 1:19. Col 2:19. 2 P 1:5, 11. **seed.** Ge 1:11, 12. =47:19, 23, 24. Is √55:10. **multiply.** ver. 6. Pr √11:18. Ec *11:6. Mt *6:31, 33. Ph *4:17. **increase.** Ho 10:12. Mt 6:1. Ep *5:9. Ph *1:11. 1 Th *3:12. *4:10.

11. **enriched.** 2 C 6:10. 8:2, 3. 1 Ch 29:12-14. 2 Ch 31:10. Pr *3:9, 10. Ml *3:10, 11. 1 C 1:5. 1 T √6:17, 18. **bountifulness.** *or*, liberality. Gr. simplicity. 2 C 8:2g. Ro +*12:8. **which.** ver. 12. 2 C 1:11. 4:15. 8:16, 19.

12. **the administration.** See on ver. 1. 2 C 8:4. Ro +15:31. **service.** Ro 15:27. Ph 2:30. **only.** 2 C 8:14, 15. Ph 2:25. 4:18, 19. Phm 4-7. Ja 2:14-16. 1 J 3:17,

18. **the want**. 2 C 8:14. **the saints**. 2 C +1:1. **by many**. 2 C +1:11.

13. **experiment**. 2 C 8:2g. **ministration**. Ro +15:31. **they glorify**. Ps 50:23. Mt +*5:16. Jn 15:8. Ac 4:21. 11:18. 21:19, 20. Ga 1:24. 1 P *2:9, 12. *4:11. **professed subjection**. 2 C √10:5. Lk +*6:46. Ro 10:16. 16:26. 1 T 6:12, 13. He 3:1. 4:14. +*5:9. 10:23. **the gospel**. Ro +15:19. **and for**. He *13:16. **liberal**. ver. +11. **distribution**. Ro 15:26. Phm 6. He *13:16.

14. **by**. 2 C 1:11. Ezr 6:8-10. Ps 41:1, 2. Pr 11:26. Lk *16:9. Ph 4:18, 19. 2 T 1:16-18. **long**. 2 S 13:39. Ro 1:11. Ph 1:8. 2:26. 4:1. **the exceeding**. 2 C *8:1, 6, 7. 1 C *1:4, 5. 1 T 1:14. **grace**. 2 C 8:1. **in you**. √63B, Ge +25:28. or, (bestowed) upon you.

15. **Thanks**. ver. 11. 2 C √2:14. Le=7:11, 12. +=23:19. 1 Ch 16:8, 35. Ps 30:4, 12. 92:1. Lk 2:14, 38. 1 C *15:57. Ep 5:20. Ja √1:17. Re 4:9. **his unspeakable**. Is +*9:6. 49:6. Jn 1:16. √3:16. Ro √6:23. √8:32. 11:33. Ep 3:18, 19. 1 J *4:9, 10. √5:11, 12. **gift**. Ep *2:8.

2 CORINTHIANS 10

The apostle entreats the Corinthians not to leave him any cause to exert his spiritual power, "and the weapons of his warfare," "which were mighty through God" for man's salvation, in rebuking those who despised his person and ministry, 1-6; assuring them, that when he came, he should be found as powerful in deeds, as he was in writing when absent, 7-11: and contrasting his own conduct, with the ostentatious boastings and ambitious intrusions of the false teachers, 12-18.

1. **I Paul**. 1 C 16:21, 22. Ga 5:2. 2 Th 3:17. Phm 9. Re 1:9. **beseech**. ver. 2. 2 C 5:20. 6:1. Ro +*12:1. Ep 4:1. 1 P 2:11. **by the meekness**. Ps 45:4. Is 42:3, 4. Zc +*9:9. Mt *11:29. 12:19, 20. 21:5. Ac 8:32. Ph 2:7, 8. 1 P 2:22, 23. **gentleness**. Ph 4:5. **who**. √122, Ex +15:9. **presence**. *or*, outward appearance. ver. 7, 10. **base**. Rather, *lowly*, or *humble*, *tapeinos*, which some think refers to his lowness of stature. √169, Je +12:1. ver. 10. 2 C 11:30. *12:5, 7-9. 13:4. 1 C 2:3. 4:10. Ga 4:13. 1 Th 2:7. **bold**. 2 C 3:12mg. 7:4. 11:21. 13:2, 3. Ro 10:20. 15:15.

2. **that I**. ver. 6. 2 C 12:20. *13:2, 10. 1 C *4:19-21. **some**. 1 C 4:18. +11:16. **think**. *or*, reckon. **we walked**. 2 C 11:9-13. 12:13-19. Ro 8:1, 5. Ga 5:16-25. Ep 2:2, 3. **according to**. 2 C +1:17.

3. **For though**. √7, Allegory by continued Hypocatastasis, Ga +4:24. **walk**. 2 C *1:12. Ga *2:20. 1 P 4:1, 2. **we do**. ver. 4. 2 C +1:17. Ro 8:13. 1 T 1:18. 2 T 2:3, 4. 4:7. He 12:1.

4. **the weapons**. 2 C *6:7. 1 S 17:39, 45. Is 59:17. Mt 4:4. Ro *6:13mg. *13:12. Ep *6:11, 13-18. 1 Th *5:8. He *4:12. Re *12:11. **our warfare**. 1 C +9:7. Ro 7:23. Ep 6:12. 1 T *1:18. 6:12. 2 T 2:3, 4. He 10:32. Re 12:17. **not carnal**. 2 Ch 20:1-30. Is *31:1. Ho 1:7. Zc *4:6. He *4:12. **mighty**. 2 C *2:14. *3:5. *4:7. *13:3, 4. Jg 7:13-23. 14:6. 15:14-16. 1 S *17:45-50. Ps 110:2. Is 41:14-16. Zc *4:6, 7. Ac 7:+20, 22. Ro +*1:16. +*8:35-37. *15:19. 1 C *1:18-24. *2:5. 13:3, 4. 1 Th *1:5. He *11:32, 33. 1 J 5:4. **through God**. *or*, to God. **pulling down**. ver. 8. 2 C 13:10. Jsh 6:20. 11:11. Ps 44:5. Pr *21:22. Is 30:25. Je *1:9, 10. Ml 4:3. Lk 10:19. 11:21, 22. He 11:30. Re 15:2.

5. **down**. Lk *1:51. Ac 4:25, 26. Ro *1:21. 1 C *1:19,

27-29. *3:19. **imaginations**. *or*, reasonings. Ge 6:5. 8:21. 11:6. 31:21. Le *13:44. Ps 38:12. Pr 6:18. Je *23:17. Ezk 8:12. Ro 1:21. *2:15. He √4:12. **every high**. Ex 5:2. *9:16, 17. Dt 1:28. 2 K *19:22, 28. Jb *40:11, 12. 42:6. Ps *10:4. *18:27. Is *2:11, 12, 17. 60:14. Ezk 17:24. Da *4:37. *5:23-30. Mi 2:3. Ac *9:4-6. Ph *3:4-9. 2 Th *2:4, 8. **exalteth itself**. Jb 33:9. Pr 17:19. 25:6, 7, 27. Is 14:13, 14. 47:10. Ezk 28:2. 31:10. Ob 4. Mt 23:12. Mk 10:37. Lk 18:11. Jn 9:41. 1 C 4:18. Re 3:17. **against the knowledge**. Pr 2:5. +*19:27. +*21:30. Is 11:9. Ho 6:6. Ro 11:33. 1 C 15:34. Ph 3:8. Col +√1:10. 2 P 2:20. **bringing**. Mt *11:29, 30. Ro 7:23. **every thought**. 2 C +2:11g. Ge *8:21. Dt *15:9. Ps *139:2. Pr *12:5. *15:26. 16:3. 23:7. *24:9. Is √55:7. 59:7. Je *4:14. +*6:19. Mt *15:19. Mk 5:15. Lk 15:17. Ro 8:6. 1 C 2:16. Ph 2:5. 2 T +√1:7. T 2:6. He √4:12. **the obedience**. 2 C 9:13. Ps *18:44. 110:2, 3. Lk +*6:46. +*11:28. Ro *1:5. 5:19. *16:26. He +*5:9. 1 P *1:2, 14, 15, 22. **of**. √181E, Ge +3:24.

6. **readiness**. ver. +2. 2 C 13:2, 10. Nu 16:26-30. Ac 5:3-11. 13:10, 11. 1 C 4:21. 5:3-5. 1 T 1:20. 3 J 10. **disobedience**. √135, Ps +68:28. **when**. 2 C 2:9. 7:15.

7. **ye look**. ver. 1mg. 2 C 2:3, 4. 5:12. 1 S +*16:7. Mt 23:5. Lk 16:15. Jn +*7:24. Ro *2:28, 29. **If**. √184A, 1 C +15:2. 1 C 3:23. 14:37. 15:23. Ga 3:29. **as he**. 1 C 3:23. Ga 3:29. **even**. 2 C 5:12. *11:4, 18, 23. 12:11. 13:3. 1 C 9:1. Ga 1:11-13. 2:5-9. 1 J *4:6.

8. **though**. 2 C +*1:24. +7:14. 13:2, 3, 8, 10. Ga 1:1. **authority**. T#455. 2 C ◐+*1:24. 9:7n. 13:10. Ac 20:17, 28. 1 T *5:17. 2 T 4:1, 2. T *2:15. He *13:7, 17. **for edification**. Ro +14:19. **not for**. ver. +4. **I should not**. 2 C 7:14. 12:6. 2 T *1:12.

9. **terrify**. ver. 10. 1 C 4:5, 19-21. **by letters**. 1 C 5:9.

10. **say they**. Gr. saith he. √122, Ex +15:9. ver. 11. **but**. ver. 1. 2 C 12:5-9. 1 C 2:3, 4. Ga 4:13, 14. **presence**. Gr. *parousia*, Mt +24:3. Ph +*1:26. **weak**. ver. 1. 2 C 11:21, +30. 12:7. **his speech**. 2 C 11:6. Ex *4:10. Je 1:6. 1 C 1:+17, 21. 2:1-4. **contemptible**. Lk 18:9. 23:11. Ac 4:11. Ro 14:3, 10. 1 C 1:28. 6:4. 16:11. Ga *4:14. 1 Th 5:20g.

11. **such**. 2 C 12:20. 13:2, 3, 10. 1 C 4:19, 20.

12. **we dare not**. √60B, Ge +20:16. 2 C 3:1. 5:12. Jb 12:2. Pr 25:27. 27:2. Lk 18:11. Ro 15:18. **ourselves**. √147E, Is +24:16. **compare**. 1 C 2:13. **with some**. 1 C +11:16. **commend themselves**. ver. 18. 2 C +3:1. 12:6, 11. Pr 12:15. 16:2. 20:6. 21:2. 25:27. 27:2. 30:12. Is +*65:5n. Ro +*12:3. Ga *6:3, 4. Ph +*2:3. Re 3:17. **are not wise**. *or*, understand *it* not. ver. 8. Pr *26:12. Is *5:21. Mt +*13:13. Mk 8:21. Ep 5:17.

13. **we will not**. ver. 15. Pr 25:14. **according**. ver. 14. Mt 25:15. Ro +*12:6. 15:20. 1 C *12:11. Ep *4:7. 1 P *4:10. **rule**. *or*, line. √121B, Jsh +17:14. Dt 32:9. Ps *19:4. Is *28:17. Ro *10:18. Ga 6:16. Ph 3:16. **to reach**. Ro 15:20.

14. **we stretch not**. 2 C 3:1-3. Ro 15:18, 19. 1 C 2:10. 3:5, 10. 4:15. 9:1, 2. **for we**. 1 C +3:6. **come as far**. Ac *18:1, 4. 1 Th 4:15g. **the gospel**. 2 C 4:4. 8:18. Mk 1:1. Ac 20:24. Ro +*1:16. 2:16. 16:25. 1 C 9:18. Ga *1:6-8. Col *1:5. 1 T 1:11.

15. **boasting**. ver. 13. Ro *15:20. **faith is increased**. 2 Th 1:3. **enlarged by you**. *or*, magnified in you. Ac 5:13. **our rule**. or, province, or limit. Gr. measuring rod. ver. +13.

16. **preach**. Ac 19:21. Ro 15:24-28. **in another**. Ro

*15:20. 1 C 3:10. **line.** *or*, rule. ⨍121B, Jsh +17:14. ver. 13.

17. **he that glorieth.** Ps 105:3. 106:5. Is 41:16. 45:25. 65:16. Je 4:2. +*9:23, ⧫24. Ro 5:11g. 1 C *1:29, +31. Ga *6:13, 14. Ph 3:3g. Ja 1:9, 10g.

18. **not.** ver. +12. 2 C 3:1. 5:12. Pr 21:2. *27:2. Lk 16:15. 18:10-14. **approved.** 2 C 6:4. 13:7. Ac 2:22. Ro 14:18. 16:10. 1 C 11:19. 2 T √2:15. Ja +1:12. **but.** Mt *25:20-23. Jn 5:42-44. 12:43. Ro *2:29. 1 C *3:13, 14. *4:5. 1 P 1:7.

2 CORINTHIANS 11

The apostle excuses his self-condemnation; because he used it out of "godly jealousy" over those at Corinth, whom he had espoused to Christ; lest false teachers should pervert them, as Satan did Eve, 1-3. Their new teachers had not preached another Savior, or another Spirit, or another gospel, than he had done, 4. He was not at all inferior to the "chiefest apostles;" for though "rude in speech," he was not so "in knowledge," 5, 6. He declined being chargeable to the Corinthians, not from want of love, but to counteract his opposers, 7-12; who were "false apostles, ministers of Satan," though apparently "ministers of righteousness;" even as "Satan transforms himself into an angel of light," 13-15. As many gloried, and were borne with, even while overbearing and rapacious; he would, though reluctantly, "glory also," 16-20. A most extraordinary account of his abundant labors, dangers, sufferings, and deliverances, 21-33.

1. **Would.** Nu 11:29. Jsh 7:7. 2 K 5:3. Ac 26:29. 1 C 4:8. **bear with me a.** ver. 4, 19, 20. Mt +17:17. Ac 18:14. He 5:2. **in my folly.** ver. 16, 17, 19, 21. 2 C +5:13. *12:11. Mk 7:22. 1 C 1:21. 3:18. 4:10. **bear with me.** *or*, ye do bear with me.

2. **For I.** ⨍7, Allegory by continued Hypocatastasis, Ga +4:24. **jealous.** Ga 4:11, 17-19. Ph 1:8. 1 Th 2:11. **I have.** Ge 24:2-5, 58-67. Ps 45:10, 11. Is 54:5. 62:4, 5. Je 3:14. Ezk 16:8. Ho *2:19, 20. Jn 3:29. Ro *7:4. 1 C 4:15. **I may.** Ep *5:27. Col 1:28. **to one.** Je 3:1. Ezk 16:15. **may present.** Col +1:22, 28. **a chaste.** Le 21:13-15. Ezk 44:22. Ep *5:25-27. Re 14:4.

3. **I fear.** ver. 29. 2 C 12:20, 21. Ps 119:53. Ga 1:6. 3:1. 4:11. Ph 3:18, 19. **as the serpent.** Ge *3:4, 13. Jn √8:44. 1 Th 3:5. 1 T *2:14. Re *12:9. 20:2. **beguiled.** Ge 3:13. 1 T *2:14. Re 12:9, 14, 15. **Eve.** i.e. *life giver*, ✱S#2096g. 1 T 2:13. For ✱S#2332h, see Ge +3:20. **subtlety.** 2 C 4:2. Lk 20:23. 1 C 3:19. Ep +*4:14. **so your minds.** ver. √13-15. 2 C 2:+11g, 17. *4:2. Mt 24:24. Ac *20:30, 31. Ro *16:17-19. Ga 1:6. 2:4. 3:1. Ep +*4:14. 6:24. Col *2:4, 8, 18. 2 Th 2:3-11. 1 T 1:3. *4:1-4. 2 T *3:1-9, 13. *4:3, 4. T 1:10. 2:7. He 13:9. 2 P *2:1-14. *3:3, 17. 1 J 2:18. *4:1. Ju *4. Re *12:9, 14, 15. **corrupted from.** Ga *5:4. 1 T *4:1. **the simplicity.** ⨍97, Ro +12:15. 2 C 1:12. 6:6g. Ro +*12:8. 16:18, 19. Ep 6:5.

4. **if.** ⨍184A, 1 C +15:2. **he that cometh.** 2 C 3:1. Jn *5:43. Ac 15:1, 24. Ga 2:4, 12. **preacheth.** 1 C 3:11. Ac √4:12. 1 T √2:5. **another Jesus.** ⨍121L1. Metonymy of the Subject B584: *Jesus* is put for his doctrine. Ga 1:8. **receive.** 1 C *12:4-11. Ga 3:2. Ep 4:4, 5. **another.** Gr. *heteros*, Mt +11:3n. **spirit.** Gr. *pneuma*, 1 J +4:2n. Mt 17:21. Ac 16:17. 1 C 2:12. Ep 2:2. 1 T 4:1. **another gospel.** Is +*8:20. Ga √1:6-8. **bear.** ver. +1. **with him.** *or*, with me.

5. **I was not.** 2 C 12:11, 12. 1 C *15:10. Ga *2:6-9. Ep ◑3:8. **apostles.** 1 C 12:28.

6. **though.** ⨍185A, Lk +11:18. 1 C +1:17. **rude.** 2 C *10:10. 1 C 1:17, 21. 2:1-3, *13. +14:16g. **in speech.** Ex 4:10. **not.** Ep *3:4. 2 P 3:15, 16. **in knowledge.** 1 C 1:5. 12:8. **but we.** 2 C +*4:2. 5:11. 7:2. *12:12.

7. **committed an offense.** 1 J +3:4g. **in abasing.** 2 C *8:9. 10:1. 12:13. Ac *18:1-3. 20:34. 1 C 4:10-12. 9:6, 12, 14-18. 1 Th 2:9. 2 Th 3:8. **exalted.** Ep *2:4-6. **gospel of God.** Ro +1:1. **freely.** Mt 10:8. Ac 20:34.

8. **robbed.** ver. 9. Ph *4:14-16. **wages.** Lk 3:14. Ro 6:23. 1 C 9:7g.

9. **and wanted.** 2 C 6:4. 9:12. Lk 15:14. Ph 2:25. 4:11-14. He 11:37. **I was.** 2 C *12:13, 14. Ne 5:15. Ac 18:3. *20:33. 1 Th *2:9. 2 Th *3:8, 9. **the brethren.** 2 C 8:1, 2. Ep +6:23. Ph 4:10, 15, 16. **came from.** Ac +16:9. 18:5. **supplied.** See on ver. 8. 1 C 16:17. Ph 4:15, 16. **burdensome.** 2 C 12:14-16. 1 Th 2:6.

10. **the truth.** ver. 31. 2 C 1:18, +23. 12:19. Ro +1:9. +*9:1. Ga 1:20. 1 Th 2:5, 10. 1 T 2:7. **no man shall stop me of this boasting.** Gr. this boasting shall not be stopped in me. ver. 12, 16, 17. 2 C *10:15. 1 C *9:15-18. **the regions.** 2 C 1:1. 9:2. Ac 18:12, 27. Ro 15:23. 16:5. 1 C 16:15. Ga 1:21. 1 Th 1:7, 8. **of Achaia.** Ac +18:12.

11. **because.** 2 C 6:+11, 12. *7:3. *12:15. **God.** See on ver. 10, 31. 2 C 12:2, 3. Jsh 22:22. Ps 44:21. Jn +*2:24, 25. 21:17. Ac 15:8. He √4:13. Re *2:23.

12. **what.** ver. 9. 2 C 1:17. Jb 23:13. **that will.** 2 K *10:16. **that I may.** 1 C *9:12. Col *4:5. 1 T 5:14. **occasion.** Ro +7:8. **them.** Ga 1:7. Ph 1:15, etc. **they glory.** ver. 18. 2 C *5:12, 13. 10:17. 1 C 5:6. Ga *6:13, 14. **found even.** 1 C *10:33. *11:1.

13. **For such.** 1 C +2:17. **false apostles.** ver. 15. 2 C 2:17. 4:2. Mt *7:15, 16, 19. 24:24. Ac 15:1, 24. *20:30. Ro *16:18. Ga *1:7. 2:4. 4:17. 6:12. Ep +*4:14. Ph 1:15, 16. 3:18. Col 2:4, 8. 1 T 1:4-7. 4:1-3. 6:3-5. 2 T 2:17-19. 3:5-9. 4:3, 4. T 1:10, 11. 2 P *2:1-3. 1 J *2:18. √4:1. 2 J +*7-11. Ju +*4. Re *2:2, 9, 20. 19:20. **deceitful workers.** Ph 3:2. T 1:10, 11. **transforming themselves.** Ph 3:21.

14. **for Satan himself.** ver. *3. 2 C 2:11. Ge *3:1-5. Jb *2:1. Mt *4:1-10. 1 C +5:5. Ga *1:8. Re *12:9.

15. **no great thing.** *or*, marvel. ⨍63I1A, Ex +12:4. 2 K 5:13. 1 C 9:11. **if.** ⨍184A, 1 C +15:2. **his ministers.** ver. 13. Mt 25:41. Ac 13:10. Ep *6:12. Re 9:11. 12:7. 13:2, 14. 19:19-21. 20:2, 3, 7-10. **transformed.** ver. 13. Ph 3:21. **as the ministers.** ver. 23. 2 C 3:9. 1 C +3:5. Ga 2:17. **whose end.** Is 9:14, 15. Je 5:31. *23:14, 15. *28:15-17. 29:32. Ezk 13:10-15, 22. 14:10n. Ho 4:9. Mt *7:15, 16. +*16:27. Ro +*2:6. Ga *1:8, 9. Ph 3:19. 2 Th √2:8-12. 2 P 2:3, 13-22. Ju 4, 10-13.

16. **say.** ver. 1. **Let.** ver. 21-23. 2 C 12:+6, *11. **if.** ⨍184A, 1 C +15:2. **receive me.** *or*, suffer me. ver. 1, 19. 2 C 7:15. Mt +10:40.

17. **I speak it.** 1 C 7:6, 12. **not after the Lord.** Mt *11:29. Ro +15:5. **foolishly.** ⨍134, Mt +3:9. In Hebrew "foolishly" would be *hithallel*, "boasting" would be *hitholel*, thus an instance of *Parechesis* or Foreign Paronomasia. ver. 18-27. 2 C 9:4. Ph 3:3-6.

18. **many glory.** ver. 12, 21-23. 2 C 10:12-18. Je +*9:23, 24. 1 C *1:5, 7. 4:10. *5:2. Ga *6:13. Ph *3:3, 4. 1 P 1:24. **after the flesh.** 2 C +1:17. **I will.** 2 C 12:5, 6, 9, 11.

19. **For ye suffer.** ⨍60B, Ge +20:16. ver. +1. **seeing.** 1 C +*4:10. 8:1. 10:15. Re 3:17.

20. **if**. ✸184A, 1 C +15:2. **a man bring**. 2 C 1:24. Ga *2:4. *4:3, 9, 25. 5:1, 10. 6:12. **if**. ✸184A, 1 C +15:2. **devour**. 2 C 7:2. Ps 14:4. Mt *23:14. Mk 12:40. Lk 20:47. Ga 5:15. Re 11:5g. **you**. ✸121K2, Ge +15:3. **if**. ✸184A, 1 C +15:2. **take**. 2 C 12:16. Ro *16:17, 18. Ph 3:19. 1 Th 2:5. 1 P +*5:2, 3. **of you**. ✸63A2, 2 S +6:6. **if**. ✸184A, 1 C +15:2. **a man smite**. Is 50:6. La 3:30. Lk 6:29. Ac 23:2. 1 C 4:11.

21. **as though**. 2 C *10:1, 2, 10. 13:10. **whereinsoever**. ver. 22-27. Ph 3:3-6. **I speak**. ver. 17, 23. Ro +3:5. **foolishly**. ver. 1. **I am bold**. 2 C *7:4. *13:2. 1 Th *2:2.

22. **Are they**. ✸30, Mt +15:27. **Hebrews**. Ex 3:18. 5:3. 7:16. 9:1, 13. 10:3. Jn 19:13, 17, 20. Ac 6:1. 21:40. 22:2, 3. Ro +*11:1. Ph 3:5. **am**. ✸63B, Ge +2:10. **Israelites**. Jn 1:47. Ac 2:22. 3:12. 5:35. 13:16. 21:28. Ro 9:4. +*11:1. **the seed**. Ge +*17:8, 9. 2 Ch 20:7. Mt 3:9. Jn 8:33-39. Ro 4:13-18. **so am I**. ✸75. Epiphoza; or, Epistrophe in Argument B244. The repetition of the same word or words at the end of successive sentences used in argument.

23. **ministers**. 2 C +3:6. 6:4. +10:7. 1 C 3:5. 4:1. 1 Th 3:2. 1 T 4:6. **I speak**. ✸104, Ro +3:5. **I am more**. ver. 5. 2 C 12:11, 12. 1 C +*15:10. **in labors**. 1 C *15:10. Col 1:29. **in stripes**. ver. 24, 25. 2 C *6:4, 5. Ac +*9:16. 16:23. **in prison**. Lk +*21:12. Ac +*9:16. 16:24. *20:23. 21:11. 24:26, 27. 25:14. 27:1. 28:16, 30. Ro +16:7. Ep 3:1. 4:1. 6:20. Ph 1:13. 2 T 1:8, 16. 2:9. Phm 9. He 10:34. **in deaths oft**. ✸121G, Ge +31:1. 2 C 1:9, 10. 4:11. 6:9. Ac 14:19. Ro +*8:36. 1 C *15:30-32. Ph 2:17. Col 1:24.

24. **forty stripes**. Dt *25:2, 3. Mt 10:17. Mk 13:9.

25. **beaten with rods**. Ac 16:22, 23, 33, 37. 22:24. **once was I stoned**. Mt 21:35. Ac +*7:58, 59. √14:5, 19. He 11:37. **thrice I suffered shipwreck**. Ac ch. 27. **been**. ✸171J2, Ac +15:33. **deep**. Ge +1:2·. Ps 107:24.

26. **journeyings**. Ac *9:23, 26-30. 11:25, 26. ch. 13, 14. 15:2-4, 40, 41. ch. 16, 17. 18:1, 18-23. 19:1. 20:1, etc. Ro 15:19, 24-28. Ga 1:17-21. **in perils**. ✸18, Dt +28:4. **of robbers**. Lk 10:30. **in perils by mine**. Ac 9:23-25, 29. *13:50. *14:5, 19. *17:5, 13. 18:12. *20:3, 19. *21:27-31. *23:10, 12, etc. 25:3. 28:10, 11. 1 Th *2:15, 16. **countrymen**. Gr. race. Ac 7:19. Ga 1:14. **in perils by the heathen**. 2 C 1:8-10. Ac 14:5, 19. 16:19-24. 19:23-41. 27:42. 1 C 15:32. **in perils in the city**. ✸96F1, Ge +3:8. ver. 32, 33. Ac 9:24. 17:5. 21:31. **wilderness**. ✸96F1, Ge +3:8. Ga 1:17. **among false brethren**. Ga 2:4.

27. **weariness**. ver. +23. 2 C 6:5. Ac 20:5-11, 34, 35. 1 Th 2:9. 2 Th 3:8. **in watchings**. Ac 20:31. **in hunger**. Dt 28:48. Je 38:9. 1 C *4:11, 12. Ph 4:12. **fastings**. 2 C 6:5. Lk +2:37. Ac 13:2, 3. 14:23. 1 C 7:5. **nakedness**. Ro +*8:35, 36. He 11:37. Ja *2:15, 16.

28. **those**. ver. *23-27. **the care**. Mt +6:25. 13:22g. Ac *15:36, 40, 41. *18:23. *20:2, 18-35. Ro 1:14. 11:13. 15:16. 16:4. Ga +*4:11. Col *2:1. He +*6:11. **all the churches**. 1 C +7:17.

29. **is weak**. 2 C 2:4, 5. 7:5, 6. *8:13. 13:9. Ezr 9:1-3. Ro 12:15. +14:1. 15:1. 1 C 8:13. 9:22. 12:26. Ga 6:2. 1 Th 3:5-8. **who is**. 1 C 8:13. **offended**. Mt +17:27. Ro *14:21. **and I burn**. ver. *13-15. Nu 25:6-11. Ne 5:6-13. 13:15-20, 23-25. Jn 2:17. 1 C 5:1-5. 6:5-7, 15-18. 11:22. 15:12, etc., 36. Ga *1:7-10. 2:4-6, 14. *3:1-3. 4:8-20. 5:2-4. 2 J *10, *11. Ju +*3, 4. Re 2:2, 20. 3:15-18.

30. **If**. ✸184A, 1 C +15:2. **must**. ver. 16-18. 2 C 10:10. *12:1, 5, 9, 11. Pr 25:27. 27:2. Je +*9:23, 24. **I will**. 2 C *12:5-10. Col 1:24. **mine infirmities**. 1 C +2:3.

31. **God**. 2 C 1:3, 23. Ex *3:15. Jn +*10:30. 20:17. Ro 1:9. 9:1. +15:6. Ep *1:3. 3:14. Ga 1:2, 3. Col 1:3. 1 Th 2:5. 1 P 1:3. **which is blessed**. Ne 9:5. Ps 41:13. Mk 14:61. Ro 1:25. √9:5. 1 T *1:11, 17. *6:16. **evermore**. Gr. *aion*, Mt +6:13. lit. unto the ages. **knoweth**. See on ver. 10, 11. 2 C 12:2, 3.

32. **Damascus**. ver. 26. Ac 9:+2, *24, 25. **Aretas**. i.e. *virtuous*, ✸S#702g. This *Aretas* was an Arabian king, and the father-in-law of Herod Antipas, upon whom he made war in consequence of his having divorced his daughter. Herod applied to Tiberius for help, who sent Vitellius to reduce Aretas, and to bring him alive or dead to Rome. By some means or other, Vitellius delayed his operations, and in the meantime Tiberius died; and it is probable that Aretas, who was thus snatched from ruin, availed himself of the favorable state of things, and seized on Damascus, which had belonged to his ancestors (See Josephus, Ant. l. xiii. c. 15, sec. 2. xviii. c. 5, and Pococke, *Spec. Hist. Arab.* p. 76). **Damascenes**. i.e. *inhabitants of Damascus*, ✸S#1153g.

33. **through**. Ac *9:22-25. **a window**. Ac 20:9. **I let down**. Jsh 2:18. 1 S 19:12.

2 CORINTHIANS 12

The apostle relates extraordinary revelations made to him: which had rendered such humiliating and distressing experiences necessary, as constrained him to glory, only in his own infirmities and trials, and in the all-sufficient power and grace of Christ, 1-10. As his apostleship had been fully proved, the Corinthians ought to have commended him, and not to have compelled him to self-commendation, 11-13. He was about to visit them again; but was determined to adhere to his disinterested conduct; and to spend himself in fervent love to them, though they should on that very account love him the less, 14, 15. He shows that those, whom he had sent to them, had acted in the same disinterested manner, 16-19, and expresses his fears, that he should be humbled, as well as compelled to use severity; by finding many who had grossly offended, and had not repented, 20, 21.

1. **expedient**. 2 C 8:40. Jn 16:7. 18:14. 1 C 6:12. 10:23. **to glory**. ver. 5, 9, 11. 2 C 10:10. 11:16-30. **I will come**. Gr. For I will come. **visions**. ver. 7. Nu 12:6. Ezk 1:1, etc. 11:24. Da 10:5-10. Jl 2:28, 29. Ac 9:10-17. 18:9. 22:17-21. 23:11. 26:13-19. Ga 1:12. 2:2. Ep 3:3. 1 J 5:20.

2. **knew**. lit. know. ver. 3, 5. **in Christ**. 2 C +*5:17, 21. 13:5. Is 45:24, 25. Jn 6:56. 15:4-6. 17:21-23. Ro +*8:1n. 16:7. 1 C +*1:30. Ga 1:22. 5:6. 1 T 1:12. **about**. "A.D. 46, at Lystra, Ac 14:6. 22:17." **in the body**. 2 C *5:6-8. 1 K 18:12. 2 K 2:16. Ezk 8:1-3. 11:24. Ac 8:39, 40. 22:17. Ph *1:22, 23. Re 1:10. 4:2. **out of the body**. 2 C 5:8. Jb 19:26. He 13:3. 2 P 1:14. **I cannot tell**. Wordsworth notes, "This was not therefore a *trance*, but a *local translation*. If it had been only a *trance* or *ecstacy*, he could not have *doubted* whether he was in the body or no. For in all *such* visions the soul and body *remain united*. St. Paul says he was *caught up*; his only doubt is whether this rapture

was a translation of his *body* and *soul* together, or a translation of his *disembodied spirit alone*. This sentence, therefore, shows that the *soul*, when separated from the body, has powers of perception. If not, it could not be a matter of doubt with St. Paul, whether he was out of the body or no, when he was translated to heaven and to Paradise, and heard what he did there. It therefore confirms the doctrine, that the *soul*, when separated from the body by *death*, does not sleep (*Greek Testament*, vol. 3, p. 179). Mt +*10:28n. Lk 12:4. 16:23. 23:43. **God knoweth**. ver. 3. See on 2 C 11:11, 31. **caught up**. ver. 4. Ezk 8:3. Lk 24:51. Ac *8:39. 1 Th *4:17. He *9:24. Re *4:1, 2. *12:5. **third heaven**. 2 C 5:8. Ge 1:14-20. Dt 10:14. 1 K 8:27. 2 Ch 2:6. Ne 9:6. Ps 68:33. 148:4. Is +*57:15. Lk 19:12n. 1 C 15:50n. Ep +*1:11n. 4:10. Ph 1:23. 1 Th +√4:18n. He *4:14. 7:26.

3. **God knoweth**. ver. +2.

4. **caught up**. ver. +*2. Ezk *11:24. 37:1. Re 17:3. 21:10. **paradise**. Ge 2:8. Is 51:3. Ec 2:5. SS 4:13. Ezk 31:9. Lk *23:43. Re 2:7. **unspeakable**. Ro 8:26. **lawful**. *or*, possible.

5. **such**. ver. 2-4. **yet**. ver. 9, 10. 2 C 11:30. **but in**. 1 C +2:3.

6. **I would**. 2 C 10:8. 11:16. 1 C 3:5, 9, 10. **I shall not**. ver. 11. 2 C +5:13. 11:16, 17. **I will**. 2 C 1:18. 11:31. Jb 24:25. Ro 9:1. **I forbear**. 2 C 1:23. 13:2. 1 C 7:28. **above that**. ver. 7. 2 C 10:9, 10.

7. **lest**. 2 C 10:5, 10. 11:20. Dt 8:14. 17:20. 2 Ch 26:16. 32:25, 26, 31. Da 5:20. 1 T 3:6. **the abundance**. ver. 1-4. **there was given**. ver. 5. 1 C +2:3. **a thorn**. Ge 32:25, 31. Nu 33:55. Jg 2:3. Ezk 28:24. Ga *4:13, 14. **the messenger**. Jb *2:6, 7. Lk *13:16. **of Satan**. 1 C +5:5. **to buffet**. Mt 26:67. Mk 14:65. 1 C 4:11. 1 P 2:20g.

8. **For this**. T#1722. 2 C 10:10. **I besought**. Dt *3:23-27. 1 S 15:11. 2 S 12:16-18. Ps 77:2-11. Mt *20:21, 22. *26:39-44. He *5:7. **the Lord**. 1 C 1:3. **thrice**. Mt *26:44. Mk 14:41.

9. **My grace**. ver. *10. 2 C 3:5, 6. Ex 3:11, 12. *4:10-15. Dt *3:25, 26. *33:25-27. Jsh *1:9. Ps 66:12. Is *43:2. Je 1:6-9. Mt 10:19, 20. Lk 21:15. 1 C +*10:13. 15:10. Ph *4:13. Col 1:28, 29. 1 T 1:14. He √4:16. **for my strength**. Dt 31:23. Ps 8:2. Is 35:3, 4. *40:29-31. 41:13-16. 45:24. Da 10:16-19. Jl 3:10. Ep *3:16. Ph *4:13, 19. Col 1:11. He *11:34. **Most**. ver. 10, 15. Mt +*5:11, 12. **glory**. ver. +1, 5. 2 C 11:30. **the power**. 2 C *4:7. 2 K 2:15. Is 4:5, 6. *11:2. Zp 3:17. Mt +*28:18, 20. 1 C +2:5. 1 P *4:13, 14. **may rest**. Gr. *episkeenosee ep eme*, "may *overshadow* me as a tent," or *tabernacle*, affording me shelter, protection, safety, refreshment, and rest. Re +7:15.

10. **I take**. 2 C *1:4. 4:8-10, *17. *7:4. Mt +*5:12. Ac *5:41. Ro *5:3. +*8:35-39. Ph *1:29. 2:17, 18. Col 1:24. Ja 1:2. 1 P 1:6, 7. *4:13, 14. **in infirmities**. ver. 5, 9. See on 2 C 11:23-30. **in reproaches**. Ac 14:5. **necessities**. 2 C 6:4. Lk +21:23. **persecutions**. Ro +*8:35. 2 T 3:11. **distresses**. 2 C 6:4. **for Christ's**. 2 C 4:5, 11. 5:15. Mt +*5:11. 10:18. Lk 6:22. Jn *15:21. 1 C 4:10. Re 2:3. **for when**. √125, Jb +22:6. See on ver. 9. 2 C *13:4, 9. Dt 32:36. Jl 2:13, 14. 3:10. Ep *6:10.

11. **become**. ver. 6. 2 C 1:6. 11:1, 16, 17. **commended**. 2 C +3:1. **for in nothing**. ver. 12. 2 C +11:5. 1 C 3:4-7, 22. 1 C +15:10. Ga *2:6-14. **apostles**. 1 C +12:28. **though**. √125, Jb +22:6. √185A, Lk +11:8.

Lk √17:10. 1 C *3:7. 15:8-10. Ep *3:8.

12. **the signs**. 2 C 4:2. 6:4-10. 11:4, 6. Ro *15:18, 19. 1 C 1:5-7. 9:2. 14:18. **an apostle**. Ac 1:22. 1 C +9:1. Ga 1:1, 12. Re 2:2. **in all patience**. 2 C +*6:4. **in signs**. Jn +4:48. 2 Th +2:9. **wonders**. Ro +15:19. Jn +4:48. **mighty deeds**. Ac 13:11. 14:10. 16:18. 19:11, 12.

13. **I myself**. ver. 14. 2 C *11:8, 9. Ac +20:33. 1 C 9:6, 12, 15-18. **not burdensome**. 2 C 11:9. **forgive**. √60B, Ge +20:16. 2 C 11:7.

14. **the third**. That is, the third time I have *purposed* to visit you. See the parallel passages. 2 C 1:15. 13:1, 2. 1 C 4:19. 11:34. 16:5. **for I seek**. Pr *11:30. Ac 20:33. 1 C *10:24, 33. Ph 4:1, 17. 1 Th 2:5, 6, 8, 19, 20. 1 P 5:2-4. **but you**. Mt 18:15. 1 C 9:19. **for the children**. Ge 24:35, 36. 31:14, 15. Pr 13:22. 19:14. 1 C *4:14, 15. 1 Th 2:11. **but the parents for**. T#495. Ge 37:14. Ex 2:5-10. 18:17-23. Jg 19:5. 1 S 2:18, 19. 10:2. 2 S 18:29, 33. Mt 17:16, 17. Est *2:11. Jb 1:1, 2, 4, 5. Pr *19:14. +*29:15. Ezk 34:2. Mt 15:22. Mk 9:17, 18. 1 T +*5:8. He 11:23.

15. **will very gladly**. ver. 9. 2 C 1:6, 14. 2:3. 7:3. Jn *10:10, 11. Ga 4:10. Ph *2:17. Col *1:24. 1 Th *2:8. 2 T *2:10. **you**. Gr. your souls. Gr. *psyche*, √171Q2. *Psyche* used to emphasize the personal pronoun in the second person, as at He 13:17. Ja 1:21. 1 P 1:9, 22. 2:25. For the other uses of *psyche* see Mt +2:20n. For other instances of √171Q2, see Nu +23:10 and Mt +12:18. ver. 14. Le 17:11. 26:15. 1 S 1:26. He 13:17. **though**. 2 C 6:11-13. 11:11. 2 S 13:39. 17:1-4. 18:33. 1 C 4:8-18. 16:24.

16. **I did not**. ver. 13. 2 C 11:+9, 10. **nevertheless**. √63BA, Ge +26:7. Supply by ellipsis, (you say that). **being**. That is, as my enemies represent. 2 C *1:12. +*4:2. *7:2. 10:2, 3. Mt +*5:11. 1 Th 2:3, 5. 1 P 2:3. **crafty**. √169, Je +12:1. **I caught you**. 2 C 11:20.

17. **make a gain**. ver. 18. 2 C +2:11. 2 K 5:16, 20-27. 1 C 4:17. 16:10. 2 P 2:3. **by any**. 2 C 9:5.

18. **I desired**. 2 C 8:6, 17. **Titus**. √63B, Ge +25:28. Supply by ellipsis, (to go to you). 2 C 2:12, +13. 7:2, 6. **with**. 2 C 8:6, 18. **walked we not in the same spirit**. Gr. *pneuma*, √121A2, Mt +26:41n. "Spirit" put for purpose, aim, as in Ezr 1:5. Ps 78:8. Da 5:12. Ph 1:27. Ep 4:23. Re 19:10. For other uses of *pneuma*, see Mt 8:16n. 2 C 8:6, 16-23. Jn +7:39. 1 C 12:8, 11. Ph 2:19-22. **in the same steps**. Nu 16:15. 1 S 12:3, 4. Ne 5:14. Ac 20:33-35. Ro 4:12. 1 P 2:21.

19. **think**. 2 C 3:1. 5:12. **excuse**. 2 C +7:11. **we speak**. See on 2 C 11:10, 31. Ro +1:9. +9:1. **God in Christ**. 2 C *5:19. He *1:3. **but**. 2 C 5:13. 10:8. 13:10. 1 C 9:12-23. *10:33. 14:26. **dearly**. ver. 15. 2 C 7:1. Ro 12:19. 1 C 10:14. Ph 4:1. **edifying**. Ro +14:19.

20. **when I come**. 2 C 2:1-4. 1 C +4:21. **I shall not**. ver. 21. 2 C 13:9. **and that**. 2 C 1:23, 24. 2:1-3. 10:2, 6, 8, 9. 13:2, 10. 1 C 4:18-21. 5:3-5. **debates**. 1 C 1:11. 3:3, 4. 4:6-8, 18. 6:7, 8. 11:16-19. 14:36, 37. Ga 5:15, 19-21, 26. Ep +*4:31, 32. Ja 3:14-16. 4:1-5. 1 P 2:1. **envyings**. Ro +*13:13. **strifes**. Ja +*3:14. **backbitings**. Ro +*1:30. Ja +*4:11. **whisperings**. Ps 41:7. Pr 16:28. Ro +*1:29. **swellings**. 1 C +4:6. 2 P 2:18. Ju 16. **tumults**. Lk +21:9.

21. **when I come again**. ver. +20. **my God**. ver. 7. 2 C 8:24. 9:3, 4. **that I**. 2 C 2:1-4. Ex 32:31. Dt 9:15, 25. 1 S 15:35. Ezr 9:3. 10:1. Ps 119:136. Je 9:1. 13:17. Lk 9:41, 42. Ro 9:2. Ph 3:18, 19. **sinned**. 2 C 13:2. Re 2:21. **and have not**. 2 C 2:5-11. 7:9-11. 10:6.

1 C +*6:9-11. Re 20:22. **uncleanness.** Ro 13:13. 1 C 5:1, 9-11. 6:15-18. Ga *5:19. Ep 5:5, 6. Col *3:5. 1 Th 4:3-7. He 13:4. 1 P 4:2, 3. 2 P 2:10-14, 18. Ju 7, 23. Re +*21:8. 22:15. **fornication.** 1 C *5:1. +*6:18. Re *2:21, 22. **lasciviousness.** Mk +*7:22.

2 CORINTHIANS 13

The apostle declares his expectation and purpose of inflicting miraculous punishments on those who persisted in opposing his authority, 1-4. He exhorts the people to self-examination, 5; and to disarm him of his power to use sharpness, by their previous repentance, 6-10. He concludes with exhortations, salutations, and benedictions, 11-14.

1. **the third.** See on 2 C 12:14. **In.** Nu 35:30. Dt 17:6. ⟩19:15. 1 K 21:10, 13. Mt +*18:16. 26:60, 61. Jn 8:17, 18. He *10:28, 29.

2. **told.** 2 C 1:23. 10:1, 2, 8-11. 12:20. 1 C *4:19, 21. 5:5. **before.** 1 Th 3:4. **being.** ver. 10. **heretofore.** 2 C +12:21. **if I come.** ⟋184C, Mt +4:9. ver. 10. 1 C +4:10. **not spare.** 2 C 1:23.

3. **ye seek.** 2 C 10:8-10. **a proof.** 2 C +8:2. **Christ.** 2 C 2:10. Mt +*10:20. 18:18-20. Lk 21:15. 1 C +*5:4, 5. **which.** 2 C 2:6. 3:1-3. 12:12. 1 C *1:6, 7. *9:1-3. 1 Th √2:13.

4. **he was.** Lk 22:43, 44. Jn *10:18. 1 C 15:43. Ph *2:7, 8. Col 1:22. He 5:7. 1 P *3:18. 4:1. **yet.** Ac 2:36. 4:10-12. Ro +*6:4, 9, 10. 14:9. Ep *1:19-23. Ph 2:9-11. 1 P 3:18, 22. Re 1:17, 18. **by the power.** Ro +*1:4. **we also.** ver. 9. 2 C *4:7-12. *10:3, 4, 10. 12:10. 1 C +*2:3. **in him.** *or,* with him. Ph 3:10. 2 T 2:11, 12. **but.** Ac 3:16. Ro +*6:8-11.

5. **Examine.** ⟋60A, Ge +3:22. Ps *17:3. 26:2. *77:6. *119:59. *139:23, 24. La *3:40. Ezk *18:28. Hg *1:5, 7. 1 C *11:28-31. Jn 6:6. 8:6. Ga *6:4. He *4:1. +*12:15. 1 J *3:20, 21. Re *2:2, 5. *3:2, 3. **yourselves.** ⟋101, Dt +32:42. The *Hyperbaton* by which the pronoun *heautous, yourselves,* is placed at the beginning of the sentence (the object before the subject), shows the emphasis which is to be placed upon it, and tells us that this is the serious *irony* of a grieved heart, and not a general command. These Corinthian saints, having been beguiled by the Jewish enemies of the apostle to question his apostleship, actually sought a proof of Christ speaking in him! So he meets their questionings with another question: Since ye seek a proof of Christ speaking in me...YOURSELVES examine ye, if ye are in the faith; YOURSELVES prove ye. Know ye not that Jesus Christ is in you except ye be reprobates?" The answer to this question, thus ironically put, would prove them to be the seals of his ministry, and the real proof of his apostleship. Here is no command for the saints today, no admonition to practice continual self-examination and introspection, to see whether they are in the faith; for Christ is in them. Read the words in connection with the context, and the force of this solemn *Irony* will be at once seen: and it will be used no more to vex and perplex

God's dear children, by taking words which refer to their *state* to upset their *standing,* which is perfect and complete "in Christ" (B812). **whether.** 1 C 16:13. Ga 2:20. **in the faith.** 1 C +*16:13. Col +*1:23. +*2:7. 1 T *2:15. T 1:13. 2:2. 1 P 5:9. **prove.** 1 C 11:28. Ga 6:4. **Know.** Gr. *epiginosko,* Mt +11:27. 1 C +*3:16. *6:2, 15, 19. *9:24. Ja *4:4. **Jesus Christ.** 2 C *6:16. Jn 6:56. *14:23. *15:4, 5. +*17:23, 26. Ro *8:10. Ga *2:20. *4:19. Ep 2:20-22. *3:17. Col +*1:27. 2:19. 2 T √1:12. 1 P 2:4, 5. 1 J *3:24. **reprobates.** 2 C *10:18. ver. 6, 7. Je *6:30. Ro +*1:28. 1 C +*9:27g. 2 T *3:8. T *1:16. He *6:8g.

6. **I trust.** ver. 3, 4, 10. 2 C 12:20. 1 C *9:1, 2.

7. **I pray.** T#1480. ver. 9. 2 C *10:2. 1 Ch 4:10. Ps 141:4. Mt +*6:13. Jn 17:15. Ph 1:9-11. 1 Th *5:23. 2 T 4:18. **approved.** 2 C 6:4. 10:18. Ac *2:22. Ro 16:10. 1 C 11:19. 2 T √2:15. Ja +1:12g. **honest.** 2 C 8:21. Ro 12:17. 13:13. Ph √4:8. 1 T +*2:2. 1 P 2:12. **as reprobates.** 2 C 6:8, 9. 10:10. 1 C 4:9-13.

8. **can do nothing against.** ver. 10. 2 C 10:8. Nu 16:28-35. 1 K 22:28. 2 K 1:9-13. 2:23-25. Pr +*21:30. 26:2. Mk 9:39. 16:17-19. Lk *9:49-56. Ac 4:28-30. 5:1-11. 13:3-12. 19:11-17. 1 C 5:4, 5. 1 T 1:20. He 2:3, 4.

9. **when.** ver. 8. 2 C 4:12. 11:30. 12:5-10. La *3:33. 1 C 4:10. **weak.** ver. 4. 1 C +2:3. **strong.** Ep *6:10, 11. 1 J *2:14. **even.** ver. 7, 11. 2 C 7:1. Ep √4:11-13. Ph 3:12-15. Col *1:28. 4:12. 1 Th 3:10. 2 T +*3:16, 17. He 6:1. *12:10, 23. 13:21. 1 P *5:10.

10. **I write.** 2 C 2:3. 10:2. 12:20, 21. 1 C 4:21. **lest.** See on ver. 2, 8. Ro 11:22g. T *1:13. Re *3:19. **according.** 2 C 10:8. **edification.** Ro +14:19. 1 C +14:26g.

11. **Finally.** Ph 3:1. 4:4. **farewell.** Lk 9:61. Ac 15:29. 18:21. 23:30. Ph 4:4. 1 Th 5:16g. **Be perfect.** ver. 9. Mt +*5:48. Lk +*6:40. Jn 17:23. Ja 1:4. 1 P *5:10. **be of good comfort.** 2 C +*1:4. Mk 10:49. Ro 15:13. 1 Th 4:18. 2 Th 2:16, 17. **be of one mind.** Nu +*14:24. Ac +*11:22, 23. Ro 12:+16, 18. *15:5n, 6. 1 C +*1:10. Ep *4:3. Ph 1:27. *2:1-3. 3:16. 4:2. 1 P *3:8. **live in peace.** Ge 37:4. 45:24. Mk +*9:50. Ro 12:18. +*14:19. 1 Th 5:13. 2 T 2:22. He +*12:14. Ja 3:17, 18. 1 P 3:11. **the God of love.** Ro 15:33. 16:20. Ph *4:9. 1 Th *5:23. He *13:20. 1 J *4:8-16. **and peace.** Ro +*15:33. **with.** ver. 14. Mt 1:23. 2 Th 3:16. Re 22:21.

12. **Greet one another.** ⟋63G, Ge +50:23. Ro +√16:16n. 1 C 16:20. 1 Th 5:26. 1 P *5:14.

13. **All.** Ro 16:16, 21-23. Ph 4:21, 22. Phm 23, 24. He 13:24. 1 P 5:13. 2 J 13. 3 J 14. **the saints.** 2 C +1:1.

14. **The grace.** Nu *6:23-27. Is +*42:1n. Mt +*3:16. +√28:19. Jn *1:3, 16, 17. 14:1, 23. 17:3. See on Ro 1:7. 16:+20, 24. 1 C 16:23. 1 Th 3:11. 2 Th 1:2. Re 1:4, 5. **the love.** Ro *5:5. +*8:39. Ep 6:23. 2 Th +3:5. 1 J 3:16. Ju *21. **the communion.** Jn *4:10, 14. +*7:38, 39. 14:15-18. Ro +*8:9, 14-17. 1 C *3:16. +*6:19. √12:13. Ga *5:22, 23. Ep 2:18, 22. 5:9. Ph 2:1. 1 J 1:3. 3:24. **Ghost.** Gr. *pneuma,* Mt +3:16. **Amen.** See on Mt +*6:13. 28:20. Ro 16:20, 27. 1 C 14:16.

GALATIANS

GALATIANS 1

Paul asserts his divine appointment to the apostolical office, 1. He salutes the churches of Galatia, and praises God, 2-5. He sharply reproves the Galatians for so soon turning aside to a false gospel; and denounces an awful curse on all who preach any other doctrine, than that which they had received from him, 6-10. He declares that he had his authority and instructions from Christ; and shows what his conduct had been before his conversion, and what it was afterwards, 11-24.

1. **an apostle.** T#97. Mt 4:18, 19. 10:5. See on Ro 1:1. 1 C 1:1. 2 C +1:1. **not.** ver. 11, 12, 17. **neither.** Ac 1:16-26. *13:2-4. **but.** Ac 9:6, 15, 16. 20:24. *22:10, 14-21. *26:16-18. Ro 1:4, 5. 2 C 3:1-3. Ep *3:8. 1 T 1:1, 11-14. 2 T 1:1. T 1:3. **and God the Father.** Mt +*28:18-20. Jn 5:19. +*10:30. 20:21. **who raised.** Jn +*2:19, 21. Ac +*2:24. 3:15. Ro 4:24, 25. √10:9. *14:9. Ep 1:19, 20. 6:23. Ph 2:11. Col 3:17. 1 Th 1:1. 2 T 1:2. T 1:4. He 13:20. 1 P 1:21. Re 1:5, 18. 2:8.

2. **all.** Ph 2:22. 4:21. Ep +6:23. **churches.** Ac 9:31. 15:41. *16:5, 6. 18:23. 1 C 16:1. **of Galatia.** Ac +16:6.

3. **Grace.** Ps *84:11. Jn *1:16, 17. Ro +*1:7, etc. 1 C 1:3. 2 C 1:2. 13:14. Ep 1:2. Ph 1:2. Col 1:2. 1 Th 1:1. 2 Th 1:2. 2 J 3. **and peace.** Ro *5:1. Ph *4:7. **from God.** 1 T 1:2.

4. **Who gave.** Ga *2:20. Mt +20:28. +*26:28. Mk 10:45. Lk 22:19. Jn *10:11, 15, 17, 18. 19:30. Ro +*4:25. Ep 5:2. 1 T √2:6. T √2:14. He 9:14. 10:9, 10. 1 P *2:24. *3:18. 1 J √2:2. *3:16. Re +*1:5. **for our.** Mt +*1:21. 1 C +*15:3. **sins.** Le +=5:6. **from.** T#812. Ga *6:14. Is 65:17. Jn 12:31. 14:30. 15:18, 19. 16:33. *17:14, 15. Ro +*12:2. 2 C *4:4. Ep 2:2. 6:12. He 2:5. 6:5. Ja *4:4. 1 J √2:15-17. *5:4, 5, 19, 20. Re 5:9. 7:9. **this present.** 1 C +1:20. **evil.** Jn +15:19. 1 J +5:19. **world.** Gr. *aion*, Mt +6:13. Jn 6:54n. **according.** Ps *40:8. Mt 26:42. Lk 22:42. Jn 5:30. 6:38. 14:30, 31. Ro 8:3, 27, 32. Ep +*1:3, 11. He *10:4-10. **our.** Mt *6:9. Ro *1:7. Ep 1:2. Ph 4:20. 1 Th 1:3. *3:11, 13. 2 Th *2:16.

5. **whom.** 1 Ch 29:13. Ps 41:13. 72:19. Is 24:15. 42:12. Mt +*6:13. Lk *2:14. Ro *11:36. 16:27. Ep 1:12. Ph +4:20. 1 T *1:17. 2 T *4:18. He 13:21. 1 P 5:11. 2 P √3:18. Ju *25. Re 4:9-11. *5:11-14. 7:12. 14:7. **ever.** Gr. *aion*, Mt +6:13. **and ever.** Gr. *aion*, Mt +6:13. lit. unto the ages of the ages, as at Ph 4:20. 1 T 1:17b. 2 T 4:18. He 13:21. 1 P 4:11. 5:11. Re 1:6, 18. 4:9, 10. 5:13, 14. 7:12. 10:6. 11:15. 14:11. 15:7. 19:3. 20:10. 22:5. **Amen.** See on Mt 28:20.

6. **marvel.** √176, Nu +24:5. Mk 6:6. Jn 9:30. **that ye.** 1 C 9:2. **so soon removed.** Ga 3:1-5. *4:9-15. *5:4, 7. Ps 106:13. Is 29:13. Je 2:12, 13. Ac 16:6. 18:23. **that called.** ver. 15. Ga 5:8. Ro +*8:28. 1 C 4:15. 2 Th 2:14. 2 T +*1:9. 1 P 1:15. 2 P 1:3. **the grace.** Ac 15:11. Ro *5:2. 1 T 1:14. 2 T 2:1. Re 22:21. **another gospel.** √121Q1, Je +28:5. Mt +11:3g. Ro 7:23. *10:3. 2 C 11:4. 1 T 1:3.

7. **not another.** √69B, Pr +6:16. Mt +10:23g. Ac √4:12. 1 C 3:11. **but.** Ga 2:4. 4:17. 5:10, 12. 6:12, 13, 17. Ac √15:1-5, 24. 20:30. Ro 16:17, 18. 2 C +*11:13.

some. 1 C +11:16. **that trouble.** Ga 5:10. Ac 15:24. **pervert.** Ga 5:10, 12. Je *23:26. Mt *24:24. Ac 13:10. 15:1, 24. 2 C 2:17. +*4:2. 1 T *4:1-3. 2 T 2:18. 3:8, 9. 4:3, 4. T 1:10, 11. 2 P 2:1-3. 1 J 2:18, 19, 26. √4:1. 2 J *7, *10. Ju +*4. Re 2:2, 6, 14, 15, 20. *12:9. 13:14. 19:20. 20:3. **the gospel.** Ro +15:19.

8. **though we.** √102C, Mt +5:29. √185B, Ga +6:1. ver. 9. 1 C 16:22. 2 C *11:13, 14. 1 T 1:19, 20. T 3:10. Re √22:18, 19. **an angel.** 1 K *13:18n. 2 C 11:14. **preach any other.** T#1120. Individual Christian believers are here deemed competent to judge the doctrinal correctness of the preaching of an inspired apostle or even an angel from heaven, a very clear assertion of the Bible doctrine of the perspicuity of Scripture. This doctrine holds that, in all essential matters pertaining to faith and practice, the Bible is clearly understandable upon careful study to even the humblest believer, without the interposition of an institutional or ecclesiastical authority to interpret the Scriptures for him. Closely allied to this is the doctrine of the right and necessity of private judgment, which holds that the individual is responsible directly to God for his beliefs, and that God will hold him responsible only to believe what is taught in Scripture, apart from the teachings of humanly devised creeds and institutions, or unwritten traditions however hoary with age. The doctrines of perspicuity and private judgment having been clearly established as scriptural (see the following reference passages and their notes), the conclusion to be drawn is that the ultimate authority in spiritual or doctrinal matters is the written word of God found in the Bible, not the teachings of any man or group of men. Thus there can be no "one true church," for any church is only "true" insofar as its teachings rest squarely upon and are in accordance with the teachings of the inerrant and infallible verbally inspired word of God in the Bible. Ps +102:18 (T#49). 119:105, 130. Pr +*8:9. Is +√8:20n. Je +*23:28n. Da +*11:33n. Mt 7:15. +*15:14. Mk 7:7-9. Lk +12:57 (T#420). Jn +√5:39n. 16:13n. Ac 8:31n. 15:15. +√17:11. Ro +*15:4. 1 C 10:15. 14:29. 2 C 3:14. Ep +*4:14. Col +*1:23. 2:18. 1 Th √5:21. 2 T +√3:15-17. 2 P 1:19, 20n. 1 J 2:20, 27. 4:1, 2. 2 J +*10. **than that.** or, contrary to that. Dt *4:2. *12:32. Jsh 1:7. Pr +*30:6. Re √22:18, 19. **let.** Ga 3:10, 13. Ge 9:25. Dt +*27:15-26. Jsh 9:23. 1 S 26:19. Ne *13:25. Mt +*15:14. 25:41. 2 P 2:14. **have preached.** √147A, Ge +50:24. **accursed.** Mk 14:71. Ac 23:14. Ro +9:3. 1 C +*12:3. *16:22g.

9. **so.** 2 C 1:17. 13:1, 2. Ph 3:1. *4:4. **again.** √77, Ex +3:19. **If.** √184A, 1 C +15:2. **any man.** 1 C +11:16. **preach.** √147A, Ge +50:24. √18, Dt +28:4. **than.** Dt *4:2. 12:32. 13:1-11. Pr +*30:6. Re √22:18, 19. **have received.** Ga 2:1-3. 1 C 15:1. **accursed.** Ro +9:3.

10. **do I now.** Ac *4:19, 20. +*5:29. 2 C 5:9-11. 1 Th *2:4. **persuade.** 1 S 21:7. Mt 28:14. Ac 12:20. 18:4. Ro 2:8g. 1 J 3:9. **do I seek.** 2 C 12:19. 1 Th 2:4. **for if.** √184B, Lk +7:39. Mt 22:16. Ro 2:29. 15:1, 2. 1 C *10:33. Ep 6:6. Col 3:22. Ja *4:4. **the servant.** See on Ro 1:1. 1 C 7:23. Ja +1:1.

11. **certify.** 1 C +15:1. **that.** ver. 1. 1 C *2:9, 10. 11:23. 15:1-3. Ep *3:3-8. **the gospel.** Ro +2:16.

12. **neither received.** *∫*173, Ge +27:44. Ac 22:14. 1 C 11:23. +*15:3. **by the revelation.** ver. 16. Ga 2:2. Ac ●1:21, 22. ●9:17. 26:16-18. 1 C +2:10. 15:8. 2 C 12:+1, 12. Ep *3:2-4. 2 T ●1:13, 14. ●2:2. **Jesus Christ.** Ro +*9:5.

13. **ye.** Ac 22:3-5. 26:4, 5. **conversation.** or, manner of life. Ep +4:22. Ja +3:13g. **how.** Ac 8:1, +3. *9:1, 2, 13, 14, 21, 26. 22:4, 5. *26:9-11. 1 C 15:9. Ph 3:6. 1 T 1:13. **church of God.** Ac +*20:28. 1 C +10:32. **wasted it.** ver. 23. Ac +*8:3. 9:21.

14. **profited.** Is 29:13. 57:12. **equals.** Gr. equals in years. **nation.** Gr. race. Ac 7:19. 2 C 11:26. **being.** Ac +21:20. *22:3. 26:5, 9. Ph *3:4-6. **zealous.** lit. a zealot. *∫*24J, Dt +32:42. **traditions.** Je 9:14. 15:2. Mt 15:2, 3, 6. Mk *7:3-13. Ac +22:3. Col 2:8. 2 T 1:3. 1 P 1:18.

15. **it.** Dt 7:7, 8. 1 S 12:22. 1 Ch 28:4, 5. Mt 11:26. Lk 10:21. 1 C 1:1, +21. Ep *1:5, 9. 3:11. **who separated.** Is 49:1, 5. Je *1:5. Lk 1:15, 16, +*44n. Ac 9:15. 13:2. 22:14, 15. Ro 1:1. **from my.** Ps 22:9. 71:6. Is 44:2, 24. Lk 1:15. **and called.** ver. 6. Ro 1:5. 8:30. 9:24. 1 C 1:9, 24. 15:10. 2 Th 2:13, 14. 1 T 1:12-14. 2 T +*1:9. 1 P 5:10.

16. **reveal.** ver. 12. Mt 16:17. 1 C 2:9-13. 2 C *4:6. Ep 1:17, 18. 3:5-10. **that.** Ga 2:7-9. Ac +*9:15. 22:21. 26:17, 18. Ro 1:13, 14. 11:13. 15:16-19. Ep *3:1, 8. Col 1:25-27. 1 Th 2:16. 1 T 2:7. 2 T 1:11. **immediately.** ver. 11, 12. Ga 2:1, 6. Dt 33:9. Lk 9:23-25, 59-62. Ac 26:19, 20. 2 C 5:16. **flesh and blood.** *∫*171Q11, Mt +16:17. Mt +*16:17. 26:41. Lk ●+*24:39. 1 C +*15:50. Ep +*6:12. He 2:14.

17. **Neither went.** ver. 18. Ac 9:20-25. **up to.** Ac +18:22. **apostles.** 1 C +12:28. **before me.** Ro 16:7. **into Arabia.** Ga 4:25. Ex +=3:1. Mk +=6:31, 32. Ac 2:11. **returned.** 2 C 11:32, 33. **Damascus.** Ac 9:+2, 22, 23.

18. **after.** Ac 9:22, 23. **I went up.** or, I returned. Ac *9:26-29. 22:17, 18. **to see Peter.** Ga 2:9, 11, 14. Jn +1:42. 1 C 9:5.

19. **James.** Mt *10:3. Mk 3:18. Lk 6:15. Ac 1:13, James the son of Alpheus. +12:17. Ja 1:1. Ju 1. **the Lord's.** Mt 12:46. +*13:55. Mk +*6:3. 1 C 9:5.

20. **behold.** See on Ro 9:1. 2 C 11:10, 11, 31.

21. **I came.** Ac *9:28-30. 11:25, 26. 13:1. 15:23, 41. 18:18. 21:3. **regions.** Ro 15:23. 2 C 11:10. **Syria.** Ac 9:30. 11:25, 26. 13:1. +15:23. **Cilicia.** Ac 6:9. 21:39. 22:3. 23:34.

22. **the churches.** Ac 9:31. 1 C +7:17. 1 Th 2:14. **in.** Jn *15:4, 5. See on Ro +16:7. 1 C +*1:30. Ph 1:1. 1 Th 1:1. 2 Th 1:1.

23. **he which.** Ac 9:13, 20, 26. 1 C 15:8-10. 1 T 1:13-16. **faith.** *∫*121R2, Ac +6:7. **once destroyed.** ver. 13. Ac 9:21.

24. **they glorified.** Nu 23:23. Lk 2:14. 7:16. 15:10, 32. Ac 11:18. *21:19, 20. 2 C 9:13. Col 1:3, 4. 2 Th 1:10, 12. 1 P +2:12. **in me.** Is 49:3. Ro ●2:24.

GALATIANS 2

The apostle shows for what purpose he, after many years, again went up to Jerusalem, 1, 2; and that Titus, who attended him was not circumcised; lest the freedom of the Gentile converts from the law should be doubted, 3-5. No additional knowledge or authority was communicated to him by the other apostles; but they acknowledged his divine mission to the Gentiles, 6-10. At Anti-

och, he openly withstood Peter; who dissembled, as to communion with the Gentile converts, for fear of some from among the Jews, and induced others to dissemble, 11-13; expostulating with him, because he, who himself sought justification by "faith in Christ," led others to seek it by the works of the law, 14-16. The apostle, by the law was "become dead to the law, that he might live to God," being "crucified with Christ, yet living, Christ living in him; and he living by faith in Christ, and not frustrating the grace of God," 17-21.

1. **fourteen.** Ga 1:18. **I went.** Ac 15:2-4. **up.** Ga 1:17, 18. Ac +18:22. **Barnabas.** ver. 9, 13. Ac 4:+36, 37. 11:25, 30. +12:25. 13:2, 50. 14:12. 15:25, 36-39. 1 C 9:6. Col 4:10. **Titus.** ver. 3. 2 C +2:13. 8:16, 23. T 1:4.

2. **went up.** Ac +18:22. **by.** Ga +1:12. Ac 16:9, 10. 18:9. 23:11. **communicated.** ver. 9. See on Ga 1:16. Ac 15:4, 12. 25:14g. 1 C 1:23. 2:2. **I preach.** 1 T 3:16. **privately.** or, severally. **which.** ver. 6, 9. Ec 10:1. Mk +10:42g. Ac 5:34. Ph 2:29. **I should.** Ga +*4:11. Mt 10:16. 1 C 9:26. Ph *2:16. 1 Th *3:5. **had run.** 1 C +9:24. Ph 2:16. **in vain.** 1 C *9:27.

3. **neither Titus.** Ga 5:2-6. Ac 15:24. *16:3. 1 C 9:20, 21. **compelled.** ver. 14. Ga 6:12. Ac 16:3.

4. **because.** Ga 5:10, 12. Ac 15:1, 24. 20:30. 2 C 11:13, 17, 26. 1 J √4:1. **false brethren.** Ga 5:12. 2 C 11:26. **unawares.** Ro 5:20g. 2 T 3:6. 2 P 2:1, 2. Ju +*4. **spy out.** 2 S 10:3. He 11:31. **liberty.** Ga 3:23-26. *5:1, 13. Ps 51:12. 119:45. Jn 8:31-36. 2 C 3:17. 1 P 2:16. 2 P 2:19. **bring.** Ga *4:3, 8-10, 24, 25. *5:1, 2. Is 51:23. Ro 9:15. 2 C 11:20.

5. **we.** Ga 3:1, 2. Ac 15:2. Col 2:4-8. Ja *3:17. Ju +*3. **not for.** *∫*123. Negatio; or, Negation B961. A spontaneous denial of that which has not been affirmed. Compare the figure *Repeated Negation*, *∫*158, Mt +5:18. **for an hour.** 2 C 7:8g. **that.** ver. 14. Ga 4:16. 5:7. Ep 1:13. Col *1:5. 1 Th √2:13. T 1:14. 2 J 1.

6. **those who.** ver. 2, 9. Ga 6:3. 1 C *4:6. 2 C 11:5, 21-23. 12:11. He 13:7, 17. **somewhat.** *∫*175A, Ge +27:14. Ac 5:36. 1 C +3:7. **it maketh.** ver. 11-14. Jb 32:6, 7, 17-22. Mt 22:16. Mk 6:17-20. 12:14. Lk 20:21. 2 C 5:16. **God accepteth.** See on Jb 34:19. Ac +10:34. Ro *2:11. 1 P 1:17. **in.** ver. 10. Ac 15:6-29. 2 C *12:11. **added nothing.** Ga 1:16g. For Paul's use of *nothing* as hyperbole, see Ga 4:11. 5:2. 6:3. 1 C 4:4, 5. 7:19. 8:4. 13:2, 3. 2 C 6:10. 12:11. Ph 4:6. 1 T 4:4. 6:4. Phm 4. Compare Ro 13:8. 1 C 2:2. 3:7. 10:19. 2 C 3:5. 6:3, 15. 1 Th 1:8. **to me.** 2 C 11:5. 12:11.

7. **when.** ver. 9. Ac 15:12, 25, 26. 2 P 3:15. **saw.** *∫*171J15, Ge +42:1. **the gospel of the uncircumcision.** See on Ga 1:16. Ac +9:15. 13:46-48. 18:6. 28:28. Ro 1:5. 11:13. 1 Th 2:4. 1 T 2:7. 2 T 1:11. **committed.** 1 C 9:17. 1 Th 2:4. 1 T 1:11. T 1:3. **me.** *∫*132G, Ge +3:19.

8. **he.** T#98. Ga 1:11, 12. Mt 10:19, 20. Ac +*1:8. *2:14-41. 3:12-26. *4:4. *5:12-16. 8:17. **wrought.** Ga 3:5g. Mt +14:2g. **apostleship.** Ac +1:25. **the same.** Ga 3:5. Ac 9:15. 13:2-11. 14:3-11. *15:12. 19:11, 12, 26. 21:19. 22:21. *26:17, 18. 1 C 1:5-7. 9:2. +*15:10. 2 C 11:4, 5. Col *1:25-29.

9. **James.** Ac +12:17. 15:7, 13, 22-29. **Cephas.** Ga 1:18. Jn +1:42. Ac +3:1. **pillars.** ver. 2, 6, 12-14. Mt +*16:18. Ep 2:20. Re +3:12. 21:14-20. **the grace.** Ro +*1:5. *12:3, 5, 6. 15:15. 1 C +1:4. *15:10. Ep *3:8. Col 1:29. 1 P 4:10, 11. **gave.** 2 K 10:15. Ezr

10:19. Ezk 17:18. 2 P 3:15. **Barnabas.** ver. 1. Ac +4:36. +12:25. **hands.** ✱121S3I, 1 Ch +29:24. **fellowship.** 2 C 8:4. 1 J 1:3. **we should.** ✱63C, Ge +25:32. Ac 15:23-30. **circumcision.** ✱121N1, Ge +31:54.

10. **remember the poor.** Lk 6:38. +*14:13. Jn 13:29. Ac *11:29, 30. +24:17. Ro 15:25-27. 1 C 16:1, 2. 2 C ch. 8, 9. He *13:16. Ja 2:15, 16. 1 J *3:17.

11. **to Antioch.** Ac +11:26. *15:1, 30-35. **I withstood.** ver. 5. 2 Ch 26:18. 2 C 5:16. 11:5, 21-28. 12:11. 1 T 5:20. Ju +*3. **to the face.** Dt 7:10. Jb 21:31. Ho 5:5. **because.** Ex 32:21, 22. Nu 20:12. Je 1:17. Jon 1:3. 4:3, 4, 9. Mt 16:17, 18, 23. Ac 15:37-39. 23:1-5. Ja 3:2. 1 J √1:8-10. **blamed.** ✱24C, 2 K +18:21. T#611. Le +*19:17. Ne 13:11, 17, 18. Pr 27:6. Ec +*7:20. Da 5:22-24. Ho 5:2. Mt 16:23. Lk 23:40. Jn +18:37 (T#66). Ep +*5:11. 1 T +5:20 (T#461). Ja *4:17. 1 J 3:4. 5:17.

12. **certain.** ver. 9. Ac 21:18-25. **James.** ✱121.O, Ge +28:22. **he did eat.** ver. 14. Lk +15:2. Ac 10:28. *11:2, 3. Ep 2:15, 19-22. 3:6. **he withdrew.** Is +*65:5n. Lk 15:2. Ac 20:20g. 1 Th +*5:22. **fearing.** Pr *29:25. Is 57:11. Mt *26:69-75. Ac +11:2. **circumcision.** ✱121N1, Ge +31:54.

13. **the other.** Ge 12:11-13. 26:6, 7. 27:24. Ec +*7:20. 10:1. 1 C 5:6. *8:9-11. 15:33. **carried away.** Jb 15:12. Ro 12:16g. 1 C 12:2. Ep +*4:14. He *13:9. 2 P 3:17g. **dissimulation.** Lk +12:1g.

14. **walked.** ✱96C5, Mt +2:13. Ps 15:2. 58:1. *84:11. Pr *2:7. 10:9. He 12:13. **the truth.** See on ver. 5. Ro 14:14. 1 T √4:3-5. He 9:10. **I said.** ver. 11. Le +*19:17. Ps +*141:5. Pr 27:5, 6. 1 T *5:20. **before them all.** 1 T 5:20. **If thou.** ✱184A, 1 C +15:2. ver. 12, 13. Ac 10:28. 11:3-18. **being a Jew.** Ro +*11:1. **why compellest.** ver. +3. Ga 6:12. Ac *15:1, 10, 11, 19-21, 24, 28, 29. **to live as.** Est 8:17.

15. **Jews.** Mt 3:7-9. Jn 8:39-41. Ro 4:16. Ep *2:3. **by nature.** Ga 4:8. Ep 2:3. **sinners.** ver. 17. Mt 9:11. Mk 7:26-28. Ac 22:21, 22. Ro 3:9. Ep *2:3, 11, 12. T 3:3. **of the Gentiles.** Mt 5:47. Lk 6:32, 33. 18:32.

16. **that.** ver. 19. Ga 3:10-12. 5:4. Jb 9:2, 3, 29. 25:4. Ps 130:3, 4. Lk 10:25-29. Ac +*13:38, 39. Ro 3:19, 20, 27, 28. 4:2, 13-15. Ph 3:9. **works.** Ga 3:2, 5, 10. Ro 2:15. T √3:5. **but by.** Ga 3:13, 14, 22-24. 4:5. Ro 1:17. *3:21-26, 28, 30. 4:5, 6, 24, 25. *5:1, 2, 8, 9. 8:3, 30-34. +9:30. 1 C 6:11. 2 C √5:19-21. Ph 3:9. He 7:18, 19. **we have believed.** ver. 20. Jn 6:68, 69. √20:31. Ac √4:12. Ro +*10:14. 1 P 1:2, 8, 9, 18-21. *2:24. *3:18. 2 P 1:1. 1 J *1:7. *2:1, 2. Re 7:9, 14. **for by the works.** Ga *3:11, 24. Ps *143:2. **no flesh.** Lk +3:6.

17. **But if.** ✱184B, Mt +23:30. **while.** Ro 9:30-33. 11:7. **are found.** ver. 11. Ro 6:1, 2. 1 J 3:8-10. **sinners.** ver. 15. **is.** Mt 1:21. Ro +*15:8. 2 C *3:7-9. He 7:24-28. 8:2. 1 J *3:5. **minister of sin.** 2 C 11:15. **God forbid.** Ga 3:21. 6:14g. Lk +20:16. See on Ro 3:4, 6.

18. **For if.** ✱184A, 1 C +15:2. **I build.** ver. 4, 5, 12-16, 21. Ga 4:9-12. 5:11. Ro 14:15. 1 C 8:11, 12. 2 C *3:9. **I make.** Ro +3:5. 2 C +3:1g.

19. **through.** Ga 3:10, 24. Ro *3:19, 20. 4:15. *5:20. 7:7-11, 14, 22, 23. 8:2. 10:4, 5. **dead.** Ro *6:2, 11, 14. *7:4, 6, 9. Col 2:20. 3:3. 1 P *2:24. **to the law.** ✱147F, Ezk +28:2. **that.** ver. 20. Ro 14:7, 8. 1 C *10:31. 2 C √5:15. 1 Th 5:10. T *2:14. He *9:14. 1 P 4:1, 2, 6. **live.** Lk 20:38. Ro 6:11. +14:7, 8. 1 Th 5:10. **unto God.** Ac 23:1g.

20. **crucified.** Ga *5:24. *6:14. Ro *6:4-6. 8:3, 4.

Col *2:11-14, 20. **Christ.** ✱66, Ge +9:3. **nevertheless.** Ro 6:8, 13. 8:2. Ep 2:4, 5. Col 2:13. 3:3, 4. **yet not.** ✱69B, Pr +6:16. **but.** Jn 14:19, 20. 17:21. 2 C 4:10, 11. 13:3, 5. Ep *3:16, 17. Col +*1:27. 1 Th 5:10. 1 P 4:2. Re √3:20. **in me.** Jn +17:23. 1 J *4:13. **the life.** 2 C 4:11. 10:3. 1 P 4:1, 2. **I now live.** ✱147F, Ezk +28:2. ver. *16. Ga 3:11. Jn 6:57. Ro +*1:17. 5:2. 2 C +*1:24. *5:7, 15. Ph √4:13. Col *3:17. 1 Th *5:10. 1 P 1:8. *4:2. **the Son of God.** Jn 1:49. √3:16, 35. +5:25. 6:69. 9:35-38. Ac √8:37. 9:20. 1 Th +*1:10. 1 J *1:7. *4:9, 10, 14. √5:10-13, 20. **who.** Ga 1:4. Mt 20:28. Jn *10:11. 15:13. Ro +*8:37. Ep 5:2, 25. T *2:14. Re +*1:5. **loved me.** Ep ●5:25. **gave himself.** Ga +1:4. Le=4:3. Nu=8:12. **for me.** Paul's use of the first person singular "I" and the singular personal pronoun "me" proves the promise and work of Christ applies to and is valid for each believer as an individual. Compare 1 J 5:13 (ye, plural) w 2 T 1:12 (I know, singular). Ju 24 (you, plural) w Ps 37:24 (he, singular). The promises of present assurance of salvation and the security of the believer are thus valid for each individual, and not merely to an unspecified group inapplicable or uncertain of fulfillment to particular individuals as some would claim. 2 C *8:9. T ●2:14.

21. **do not.** ver. 18. Ga 3:15. Ps 33:10. Mk 7:9mg. Lk +7:30. Ro *8:31. **frustrate.** or, esteem at a small price. **the grace.** 1 C +1:4. **for if.** ✱184A, 1 C +15:2. **righteousness.** See on ver. *16. Ga 3:21. 5:2-4. Ro *10:3. 11:6. He *7:11. **Christ.** Ga *5:4. Is 49:4. Je 8:8. 1 C 15:2, 14, 17. **in vain.** Mt +10:8g. ✱46C, Mt +8:6. Here, Gr. *dorean*, "a free gift," is put for *mateen*, "in vain;" and the A.V. so translates it. The R.V. renders it "for nought." But like the Hebrew *chinnam*, *mateen* means "in vain," while *dorean* means "without a cause." See Ps 109:3 (B679).

GALATIANS 3

The apostle sharply reproves the Galatians, for departing from that gospel which had been fully preached to them, and confirmed by the gift of the Holy Spirit, 1-5. He proves the doctrine of justification by faith alone, from the example of Abraham, and the testimony of scripture, 6-9; from the curse of the law, and the redemption of Christ, 10-14; and from the Abrahamic covenant, which the law could not disannul, 15-18. He states the use of the law, in connection with the covenant of grace; shows that all men are by the law shut up under sin, till Christ releases them; and describes the law as a schoolmaster to bring men to him, that they may be justified by faith, 19-24; and that all believers are delivered from the law, and made the spiritual seed of Abraham by faith in Christ, 25-29.

1. **Foolish.** ver. 3. Dt 32:6. 1 S 13:13. Mt 7:26. Lk 24:25. Ep 5:15. 1 T 6:4mg. **Galatians.** ✱S#1052g. Ac ●+16:6. **who.** Ga 1:6. 4:9. 5:7, 8. Mt 24:24. Ac 8:9-11. 2 C *11:3, 13-15. Ep +*4:14. 2 Th 2:9-12. 2 P 2:18. Re 2:20. 13:13, 14. 18:3. **ye should not obey.** Ga 2:14. 5:7. Ac 6:7. Ro 2:8. 6:17. 10:16. 2 C +*10:5. 2 Th 1:8. He +*5:9. 11:8. 1 P 1:22. 4:17. **before.** Nu 21:9. **Jesus Christ.** 1 C 1:23, 24. 2:2. *11:26. Ep *3:8. **evidently.** Ro 15:4. Ep 3:3g. Ju 24g. **crucified.** 1 C +*1:23.

2. **of you.** ✱14, Is +5:3. **Received.** ver. *5, *14. Ac +*2:38. *8:15. *10:44-47. *11:15-18. +*15:8. *19:2-

6. 1 C *12:7-13. 2 C 11:4. Ep *1:13, 14. He *2:3, 4. *6:4. 1 P 1:12. **Spirit**. Gr. *pneuma*, ⌐121A2, Ro +8:1n. ⌐121A1, Jn +3:34. By *Metonymy of the Cause*, the person acting is put for the thing done. Here, "Spirit" is put for the gifts of the Spirit. ver. 14. Jn +7:39. 2 C *3:8, 9. **the works**. ver. 10. Ga *2:16. **by the hearing of faith**. ⌐121R7, Ge +43:11. ⌐121R1, Le +13:55. ver. *5. Ro +*1:17. √10:16, 17.

3. **having begun**. Ga *4:7-10. 5:3-8. 6:12-14. 2 C *5:7. Ph 1:6. *2:13. *3:3-6. Col √2:6. He 7:16-19. *9:2, 9, 10. **Spirit**. Gr. *pneuma*, ⌐121A2, Ro +8:1n. **the flesh**. He 7:16. 9:10.

4. **ye suffered**. Ga +*4:11. Ezk 18:24. 1 C +*15:2. He √6:4-6. *10:32-39. 2 P √2:20-22. 2 J √8. **so many**. *or*, so great. **if**. ⌐184A, 1 C 15:2. ⌐69C. Epanorthosis; or, Correction B911: where the retraction is conditional. **if**. ⌐184A, 1 C +15:2. **in vain**. Ro +13:4. 1 C +*15:2.

5. **He therefore**. 2 C 3:8. **that ministereth**. See on ver. 2. 2 C 3:8. +9:10. **Spirit**. Gr. *pneuma*, ⌐121A2, Ro +8:1n. **worketh**. Ga 2:8g. Mt +14:2g. Ac 14:3, 9, 10. 19:11, 12. Ro 15:19. 1 C 1:4, 5. 12:10. 2 C 10:4. 12:12. 13:3. **miracles**. Ac +8:13. **by the works**. ver. 2. **hearing of faith**. ver. +*2. Ro √10:17.

6. **as**. ver. 9. Ge +*♭15:6. Ro *4:3-6, 9, 10, 21, 22. 9:32, 33. T +*3:8g. Ja *2:23. **accounted**. *or*, imputed. Ro *4:6, 11, 22, 24. 2 C √5:19-21.

7. **Know**. Ps 100:3. Lk 21:31. He 13:23. **they which**. ver. 9, *26-29. Jn *8:39. Ro 3:26. *4:11-16, 24. 9:7, 8. **children of Abraham**. Lk +19:9.

8. **the scripture**. ver. *22. Ga 4:30. Lk +4:21. Jn *7:38, 42. 19:37. Ac 28:25. Ro 9:17. 2 T +√3:15-17. 2 P *1:21. **foreseeing**. Ac *15:15-18. **God**. Ro +*3:28-30. 9:30. **preached**. Ro 1:2. He *4:2. **In thee**. ⌐92G, Lk +4:18. ver. 16. Ge +*♭12:3. 18:18. 22:18. *26:4. 28:14. +*49:10. Ps 72:7. Is 6:13. 65:9. Je *4:2. Ac 2:25, 26, 35. 3:25. Re *11:15.

9. **they which**. ver. 7, 8, 14, 29. Ga 4:28. Jn 20:27. Ro *4:11, 16, 24.

10. **as many**. ver. 11. See on Ga +*2:16. Lk *18:9-13. Ro 3:19. 4:15. 7:9-13. *8:7. **works of the law**. or, works of law. "Law" does not have the Greek article here, or in ver. 2, 5, or in Ga 2:16. When "law" lacks the Greek article, it no longer is a reference exclusively to the Mosaic law, but to law or rule as principle (See note on Ro 4:15). So while Paul as a Jew writing to Jews is doubtless alluding to the law of Moses, his assertion applies to any requirement of obedience to "law" or "rule" to merit salvation, and in principle is not limited to Mosaic law. Any system of belief which makes salvation depend upon what we do for God instead of what God in grace has already done for us violates this principle, and those who so depend upon works in any sense have fallen from grace (Ga 5:4), and cannot be saved as long as they are resting upon such a principle for salvation. Good works and obedience are the necessary and essential fruit and evidence of saving faith, not its ground (Ro 16:26. Ep 2:10. T 3:8. He +*5:9. Ja 2:17). Since Scripture does not explicitly make the distinction between ceremonial and moral law, that cannot be the intended distinction here by the use and non-use of the Greek article. Hogg and Vine assert (Comm. on Galatians, Ga 2:16, p. 88) "the Apostle asserts the freedom of the Christian from the law of Moses in its totality, making no distinction as between ceremonial and moral." ver. 2, 5. Ga 2:16.

Col √2:16. **under**. Ga 5:4. Dt *11:26-28. 29:20. Is 43:28. Mt *25:41. Ro +*4:15. **Cursed**. Dt *♭27:26. Je *11:3. Ezk +*18:4. Ro *3:19, 20. √6:23. Ja √2:9-11. **all things**. Mt 5:19. Ja √2:10. **the book**. Dt 31:26. Jsh *1:8. 2 K 22:8, 11. 2 Ch 34:14. Ac +1:20.

11. **that**. ver. 24. Ga +*2:16. 1 K 8:46. Jb 9:3. 40:4. 42:6. Ps *19:12. 130:3, 4. 143:2. Ec +*7:20. Is 6:5. +*53:6. √64:6. Ja 3:2. 1 J √1:8-10. Re 5:9. 7:14, 15. **The just**. Hab √♭2:4. Ro +*1:17. He *10:38. **by faith**. Ro +*1:17. He 10:23.

12. **the law**. Ro √4:4, 5, 14, 16. 9:30-32. 10:5, 6. 11:6. **The man**. Lk ♭18:5. Ne 9:29. Ezk 20:11, 13. Mt 19:17. Lk *10:25-28. Ezk 20:11, 13. Mt 19:17. Lk 10:25-28. Ro 10:+5, 6, 9.

13. **redeemed us**. T#834. See on ver. 10. Ga √4:4, 5. Is 42:7. 49:9. *53:5-7, 10-12. Da +*9:24, 26. Zc *13:7. Mt *10:45. +*26:28. Ro +*3:24-26. *4:25. 8:3, 4. 1 C 5:7. 2 C √5:21. Ep *1:7. 5:2, 16. Col *1:13, 14. 4:5g. 1 Th +*1:10. T *2:14. He *7:26, 27. 9:12, 14, 15, 26, 28. 10:4-10. 1 P 1:18-21. *2:24. *3:18. 2 P +2:1. 1 J √2:1, 2. 4:10. Re +*1:5. 5:9. 13:8. 22:3. **curse of the law**. ver. *10n. Ga ●*22:18. Dt √27:15-26. *28:15. Pr *3:33. √26:2. Da +*9:11. Zc +*5:3. Ml *3:9, ◐11. **being made a curse**. ⌐121N2, Ge +34:29. Le +=23:19. 2 K 22:19. Je 44:22. 49:13. Ro 9:3. 2 C *5:21. **for us**. 2 S 17:23. 18:10, 14, 15. 21:3, 9. Est 7:10. 9:14. Mt 27:5. 1 P *2:24. **Cursed**. Dt ♭21:23. Jsh 10:26, 27. **hangeth**. Dt *21:22n, 23n. Ac +5:30. **tree**. ⌐121D8, Ge +40:19.

14. **the blessing**. See on ver. 6-9, 29. Ge +*12:2, 3. 14:19. Is 41:8. 51:2, 3. Ro 4:3-17. Ja *2:23. **on the Gentiles**. ver. 28. Ro 4:9, 16. **through**. ver. 16. Ge 22:18. Is 49:6. 52:10. Lk 2:10, 11. Ac +*2:39. 3:25, 26. √4:12. Ro *10:9-15. 1 T *2:4-6. **might**. Readers of English translations and versions are often confused by the use of "might" and "should," "hope," "think," etc., for in modern English usage these words all connote a degree of doubtfulness, a connotation apparently not present in the Greek. Frequently "might" and "should" are strictly English auxiliaries used to represent tense and aspect distinctions in the original, and have no strictly corresponding word in the Greek (see notes on Jn 5:39 for "think"; on T 1:2 for "hope"; on Jn 3:16 for "should"). ver. +*2, 5. Ga 4:6. **the promise**. Is 32:15. *44:3, 4. 59:19-21. Je +*31:33. 32:40. Ezk *11:19. *36:26, 27. 37:14. 39:29. Jl +*2:28, 29. Zc *12:10. Lk 11:13. 24:49. Jn +*7:39. √14:16, 26. Ac +*1:4, 5. *2:33, 38. *5:32. *10:45-47. 11:15, 16. Ro *8:9-16, 26, 27. 1 C √12:13. 2 C 1:22. Ep +*1:13, 14. 2:18, 22. 3:16. +*4:30. 1 P 1:22. Ju 19, 20. **of the**. ⌐29, Ex +19:6. i.e. the promised Spirit. **Spirit**. Gr. *pneuma*, Mt +3:16. ver. 2, 3, 5. Jn +7:39. **through faith**. ver. 28. Ro 4:9, 16.

15. **I speak**. Ro 6:19. 1 C 15:32. **after the manner**. Ro +3:5. **it be**. He 9:17. **covenant**. *or*, testament. Ro +9:4. **confirmed**. Ge 23:20. 2 C 2:8g. **disannulleth**. Ga 2:21. Jsh +*9:19. Jg *11:25. Lk +7:30. Ro 11:29.

16. **to Abraham**. ver. 8. Ge *12:3, 7. 13:15, 16. *15:5. +*17:7, 8. 21:12. *22:17, 18. 26:3, 4. *28:13, 14. +*49:10. Lk +1:55. Ro 4:13, 16. **the promises**. Ac +13:32. He +6:12. **to thy seed**. Here, Paul's argument depends on the fact that the Hebrew word is singular, not plural, strong evidence to support the verbal inspiration and inerrancy of Scripture. Jesus similarly based his argument for the resurrection on the fact that the tense in the original was present,

not past (Mt 22:32). ver. 8. Ge 12:7. 13:15, 17. 17:7, 8, 19. ▶21:12. 22:18. 24:7. Mt +1:1. Ac 3:25. Ro *9:7, 8. **which is Christ**. ver. 27-29. Ro 12:5. 1 C *12:12, 13, 27. Ep 4:15, 16. 5:29, 30, 32. Col 2:19. +*3:11.

17. **this**. Ga 5:16. 1 C 1:12. 7:29. 10:19. 2 C 9:6. Ep 4:17. Col 2:4. **the covenant**. Ge 15:18. +*17:7, 8, 19. Lk 1:68-79. Jn 1:17. *8:56-58. Ro 3:25. 2 C 1:20. He 11:13, 17-19, 39, 40. 1 P 1:11, 12, 20. **which**. Ge 12:1-3. 15:13. Ex √12:40, 41. Ac 7:6. **cannot**. ver. 15. Jb 40:8. Is 14:27. 28:18. He 7:18. **disannul**. Mt 15:6. Mk 7:13g. **that it**. ver. 21. Nu *23:19. Ro *4:13, 14. He 6:13-18. **the promise**. ver. 29. Ge +*17:7. Ac +*2:39. He 6:17. **none**. Ga 5:4. Nu 30:8. Ps 33:10. Ro 3:3. 4:14. 1 C 1:17.

18. **if**. ∫184A, 1 C +15:2. ver. 10, 12, 26, 29. Ga 2:21. Ro 4:13-16. 8:17. **inheritance**. ver. 29. Dt 4:38. 15:4. 19:10. 20:16. 1 P √1:4. **but**. See on ver. 16. Ps 105:6-12, 42. Mi 7:18-20. Lk 1:54, 55, 72, 73. He 6:12-15. **gave**. Ac +25:11g.

19. **then**. Ro 3:1, 2. 7:7-13. **It was added**. ver. 21-24. Dt *4:8, 9. Ps 147:19, 20. Lk 16:31. Jn 5:45-47. 15:22. Ro 2:13. *3:19, 20. *4:15. 5:20, 21. 7:7-13. 1 T +*1:8, 9. **till**. ver. 16, 25. Ga 4:1-4. **by angels**. Dt 33:2. Ac +*7:53. He *2:2, 5. **in the hand**. ∫144A5, Ge +9:5. Ex *20:19-22. 24:1-12. 34:27-35. Le 1:18. 26:46. Dt *5:5, 22-34. 9:13-20, 25-29. 18:15-19. Ps 106:23. Jn 1:17. Ac 7:38. The Apostle, having just before been speaking of the promise made to Abraham, and representing that as the rule of our justification, and not the law, lest they should think he derogated too much from the law, and thereby rendered it useless— he thence takes occasion to discourse of the design and tendency of it, and to acquaint us for what purpose it was given. **a mediator**. Jb 9:33. 1 T √2:5. He 6:17. 8:6. 9:15. 12:24.

20. **a mediator is**. Jb 9:33. Ac 12:20. 1 T 2:5. **a mediator**. ∫63K, Ge +37:13. "Now a mediator is not of one (party)": there must be two parties where there is a mediator; for he is a person who stands between the two others. Now when God gave the promise to Abram (Ge 15:9-21), there was only one party; for God caused Abram to fall into a deep sleep, and He Himself "was one"—the One who, alone, was thus the one party to this glorious covenant; which is therefore unconditional, and must stand for ever (B127). **but**. ver. 17. Ge *15:18. 17:1, 2. *25:8. Ex *19:20. Dt +*6:4. Ro 3:29, 30.

21. **the law**. Mt *5:17-20. Ro *3:31. *7:7-13. **God forbid**. Ga 2:17. 6:14. Lk +20:16. Ro 3:4, 6. **for if**. ∫184B, Lk +7:39. The second condition of hypothetical proposition, stating a case which did not and could not exist. Ga *2:19, 21. Ro √3:20. 5:18-20. He 7:11. **righteousness**. Ro 3:21, 22. 9:31. 10:3-6. Ph 3:6-9. He 11:7.

22. **the scripture**. ver. 8. Ga 4:30. Lk +4:21. **concluded**. ver. 8-10, 23. Ps *143:2. Ro *3:9-20, 23. 5:12, 20. 11:32. **under sin**. Ro +3:9. **that**. ver. 14-17, 29. Ro 4:11-16. *5:20, 21. 2 T 1:1. He 6:13-17. 9:15. 2 P *1:4. 3:13. 1 J 2:25. √5:11-13. **faith. to them**. Mk *16:16. Jn √3:15-18, 36. √5:24. 6:40. 11:25, 26. 12:46. √20:31. Ac +*10:43. +*16:31. Ro √10:9. 1 J *3:23, 24. √5:13.

23. **faith**. ∫121R2, Ac +6:7. By *Metonymy of the Adjunct*, "faith" is put for the thing believed. Here, before the true doctrine of the Gospel was revealed. **came**. ∫121I2, Ge +2:17. ver. 19, 24, 25. Ga 4:1-4. He *12:2. **kept**. 2 C 11:32. Ph 4:7. 1 P 1:5g. **under**.

Ga 4:4, 5, 21. 5:18. Ro 3:19. 6:14, 15. 1 C 9:20, 21. **shut**. ver. 22. Ro 11:32. **the faith**. Lk *10:23, 24. He *11:13, 39, 40. 1 P *1:11, 12. 1 J *2:8.

24. **the law**. ver. 25. Ga 2:19. 4:2, 3. Mt √5:17, 18. Ac +*13:38, 39. Ro 3:20-22. 7:7-9, 24, 25. *10:4. Col *2:17. He 7:18, 19. *9:8-16. *10:1-14. **schoolmaster**. 1 C 4:15. **to bring us**. ∫63K, Ge +37:13. There is no need to introduce the words "bring us," the sense being complete without them: *eis, unto,* is used in its well-known sense of *up to,* or *until,* as at Ph 1:10, "without offense till the day of Christ"; Ep 1:14, "until the redemption of the purchased possession." **justified**. ver. 11. See on Ga *2:16. Ac 13:39.

25. **faith**. ver. 23. **we**. Ga 4:1-6. Mt *11:30. Ac *15:7-11. Ro *6:14. 7:4. He 7:11-19. 8:3-13. 10:15-18.

26. **ye are all**. Ga 4:5, 6. Lk 20:36. Jn *1:12, 13. 20:17. Ro *8:14-17. 2 C 6:18. Ep 1:5. 5:1. Ph 2:15. He 2:10-15. 1 J *3:1, 2. Re 21:7.

27. **as many**. Mt +*28:19, 20. Mk *16:15, 16. Ac +*2:38. 8:36-38. 9:18. 16:15, 31-33. Ro *2:28, 29. *3:21, 22. *6:3, 4. 1 C √12:13. Col 2:10-12. 1 P *3:21. **baptized into Christ**. This is a reference to real, not ritual baptism, for this baptism is declared to be into Christ, not water. Notice further that (1) the element water is not specified; (2) ritual baptism does not possess the universal efficacy ascribed here to baptism into Christ (Ac 8:13, 20-23). Baptism into Christ takes place upon placing saving faith in Him, and the baptism is that of controlling influence, as the believer is subject to the Lordship of Christ (Ac +*1:5n. +√10:36. Ro √10:9. 1 C 10:2n). Ac +8:16. 19:3. Ro 6:3, 4n. 1 C 10:2n. √12:13. **put on**. Ex=29:8. Jb 29:14. Ps=132:9, 16. Is 61:10. Lk 15:22. Ro 3:22. +*6:4n. √13:14. Ep 4:24. Col *3:9-14.

28. **neither**. ver. 14. Ga 5:6. 6:15. Ro +*1:16. 2:9, 10. +*3:29, 30. 4:11, 12. 9:24. *10:12-15. 1 C 7:19. √12:13. Ep *3:5-10. Col +*3:11. **male**. 1 C +*7:14. 11:11. **all one**. T#795. Ga 4:26, 28. Jn +*10:16. 11:52. *17:+11, 20, 21. Ro 11:17. 12:5. 1 C 12:12. Ep *2:12-22. 4:+√4, 15, 16. Ph 3:3. Col √3:11. He 12:22-24. 1 J 1:3.

29. **And if**. ∫184A, 1 C +15:2. **Christ's**. Ga 5:24. 1 C +*3:23. 15:23. 2 C 10:7. **then are**. Jn +8:33. Ro 9:7. **Abraham's**. ver. 7, 16, 28. Ga 4:22-31. Ge 21:10-12. Ro 4:12, 16-21. 9:7, 8. He 11:18. **heirs**. ver. 18. Ga 4:1, 7, 28. Ro 4:13, 14. +8:17. 1 C 3:22. Ep +*3:6. T 3:7. He 1:14. 6:17. 11:7. Ja *2:5. Re 21:7. **the promise**. ver. 17. Ge +*17:7. Ac +*2:39. 2 T 1:1. T 1:2. He 6:17. *9:15.

GALATIANS 4

The ancient church had been under the law, as a young heir under a guardian, 1-3. Christ came to "redeem those that were under the law," and to give believers both Jews and Gentiles "the adoption of sons," 4-7. The apostle shows how absurd the conduct of the Galatians was; in that, after having been delivered from idolatry by the gospel, they willingly subjected themselves to the bondage of the law: and he expresses his doubts concerning them, 8-11. He tenderly expostulates with them, for becoming alienated from him, to whom they had expressed the most fervent love; ascribes this to the influence of false teachers; and shows the ardor of his soul in longing for their salvation, 12-20. He illustrates the subject of the two covenants, by showing, that the history of Sarah and Isaac with Hagar and Ishmael was an allegorical representation of them, 21-31.

1. **That**. Ga 3:23, 29. Ge 24:2, 3. 2 K 10:1, 2. 11:12. 12:2.

2. **tutors**. Mt 20:8. Lk 8:3g. **governors**. Ge 24:2. **time appointed**. Jn *4:23.

3. **when**. Ga 3:19, 24, 25. **in bondage**. ver. 8, 9, 24, 25, 31. Ga 2:4, 23. 5:1. Mt 11:28. Jn √8:31-36. Ac 15:10. Ro 8:15. **elements**. *or*, rudiments. ver. 9. Col 2:8mg, 20mg. He 5:12. 7:16. 2 P 3:10, 12. **world**. Gr. *kosmos*, Mt +4:8.

4. **the fulness**. Ge +*49:10. Da +*9:24-26. Ml *3:1. Mk +*1:15. Ac *1:7. Ep *1:10. He 9:10. **of the**. Ϳ29, Ex +19:6. i.e. the full or completed time. **time**. Ec 3:1. Lk 22:14. Jn 17:1. **God**. Is *48:16, 17. Zc *2:8-11. Jn √3:16, 17. *6:38, 39. *8:42. +√10:36. 1 J *4:9, 10, 14. **made**. Ϳ52B. Figure of speech Introverted Correspondence, or Chiasmus, whereby in four lines or clauses the first and fourth (born of a woman, that we might receive adoption of sons) refer to mankind without distinction of nation or race, while the second and third (born under the law, that he might redeem them which were under the law) refer to the Jews alone (Hogg and Vine, Comm. on Galatians, pp. 188, 189). For other instances of this figure see Ge +43:3. Is +*9:6, 7. Mi +*5:2. Zc *6:12. Lk *2:10, 11. Jn +*1:14. 8:58g. Ro *1:3. 8:3. √9:5. Ph √2:6-8. 1 T *3:16. He *2:14. *10:5-7. 1 J *4:2. **of a woman**. Ge +*●3:15. Is +*7:14. Je *31:22. Mi 5:3. Mt +*1:23. Lk √1:31, 35. 2:7. Ro 1:3. 1 T 2:15. **made under**. Mt *3:13-15. *5:17. Lk *2:21-27. Ro +*15:8. Col 2:14.

5. **redeem**. ver. 21. Ga +*3:13. Mt +*20:28. Lk 1:68. Jn √5:24. Ac +*20:28. Ro 6:14, 15. 8:1. 2 C *5:17, 18. Ep *1:7. 2:4-10. +*4:30. *5:2. Col *1:13-20. 2:10, 13, 14. T √2:14. He *1:3. *9:12, √15. 1 P *1:18-20, 23. *3:18. Re *5:9. 14:3. **adoption of sons**. Gr. *whiothesia*, i.e. "placing among the sons," ❋S#5206g: Ro 8:15, 23. 9:4. Ep 1:5. T#794. ver. *7. Ga +*3:26. Is 63:16. 64:8. Je 31:9. Jn *1:12. Ro 5:1. 7:4. √8:14, 15, 19, 23. 9:4-6, 19, 26. Ep *1:5, 6. Col 1:13, 20. 1 J 3:1, 2.

6. **are sons**. ver. 5. Ga +3:26. Ge 48:15. Ps 48:14. Je 3:4. **God**. Lk *11:13. Jn 7:39. *14:i6. Ro 5:5. 8:15-17. 2 C 1:22. Ep *1:13. +*4:30. **the Spirit**. Gr. *pneuma*, Ro +8:1n. T#347-4. Dt +30:6 (T#594). Ps +17:5 (T#596). Is 48:16. Jn 3:34. 14:16, 17. *15:26. *16:7, 13. Ac +5:31 (T#595). +16:7. Ro *5:5. +*8:9, 14-16. 1 C +2:14 (T#598). 15:45. 2 C *3:17. Ph *1:19. He 10:15, 16. 1 P *1:11. 1 J 2:5. 3:24. 5:10. Re *19:10. **crying**. Is 44:3-5. Je 3:4, 19. Mt 6:6-9. Lk 11:2. Ro +*8:26, 27. Ep 2:18. 6:18. He 4:14-16. Ju *20. **Abba**. Mk 14:36. Ro 8:15.

7. **thou**. Ϳ96F4, Ex +10:2. Ϳ38D, Ps +27:14. ver. 1, 2, 5, 6, 31. Ga 5:1. **but a son**. Under the former dispensation, females were not recognized as heirs except by special enactment (Nu 27:7, 8). But now they are recognized as sons, and have all the rights, privileges, and inheritance of sons. Every regenerate soul (male or female, infant or adult) is in the gospel language called a "son," and "if a son then an heir of God through Christ." Under the Gospel only sons are baptized. "Ye are all sons (Greek) of God by faith in Christ Jesus" (Ga 3:26); "ye are all one (man) in Christ Jesus" (Ga 3:28; the word *one* in Greek is masculine gender); Ro 8:14; Ga 4:6; 1 Th 5:5 "all sons (Greek) of the

light and sons of the day;" He 2:10; 12:5, 6, 7. The expression "daughters of the Lord" is not found in New Testament language. The apparent exception in 2 C 6:18 is a quotation from the Old Testament (Thomas Gallaher, *Baptism*, p. 303). See on Ga 3:26. **if**. Ϳ184A, 1 C +15:2. Ga *3:29. Ro *8:16, 17. **heir**. ver. 1. Ga 3:29. Ge 15:1. +*17:7, 8. Ps +*16:5. 73:26. Je 10:16. 31:33. 32:38-41. La 3:24. 1 C 3:21-23. 2 C 6:16-18. Re 21:7.

8. **when ye**. Ϳ96F4, Ex +10:2. Ex 5:2. Je 10:25. Jn 1:10. +7:28. Ac 17:23, 30. Ro +*1:21, 28. 1 C 1:21. Ep *2:11, 12. 4:18. 1 Th 4:5. 2 Th 1:8. 1 J 3:1. **ye did**. ver. 3. Ga 2:4. Jsh 24:2, 15. Ps 115:4-8. 135:15-18. Is 44:9-20. Je 10:3-16. Ac 14:12. 17:29. Ro 1:23, 25. 1 C +*8:4. 10:19, 20. *12:2. Ep 2:11, 12. 1 Th 1:9. 1 P 4:3. **by nature**. Ga 2:15. Ep 2:3. **no gods**. 2 Ch 13:9. Is 37:19. Je 2:11. 5:7. 16:20. 1 C +*8:4.

9. **ye have**. 1 K 8:43. 1 Ch +*28:9. Ps +√9:10. Pr 2:5. Je 31:34. Hab 2:14. Mt +*11:27. Jn +*17:3. 1 C 15:34. 2 C 4:6. Ep 1:17. 2 P 2:20. 1 J 2:3, 4. 5:20. **known God**. 1 C +1:21. 1 J +4:6. **or rather**. Ϳ69B, Pr +6:16. **are known**. Ϳ96A1, Mt +5:29. Ex 33:17. Ps *1:6. Jn 10:14, 27. Ac *15:8. Ro +*8:29. 1 C +8:3. 13:12. 2 T √2:19. **how**. Ga 3:3. Ro 8:3. Col *2:20-23. He *7:18. **again**. *or*, back. He *10:38, 39. **weak and beggarly**. Ro +8:3. **elements**. *or*, rudiments. ver. +3. **desire again**. Ϳ159, Ezk +36:23. Jn 3:3.

10. **observe days**. Le ch. 23. 25:1, 13. Nu ch. 28, 29. Zc 7:5, 6. Ro 14:5. Col √2:16, 17. **months**. Nu 10:10. 28:11. 1 S 20:5. 1 Ch 23:31. 2 Ch 2:4. Ezr 3:5. Ne 10:33. Ps 81:3. Is 1:13, 14. Ezk 45:17. 46:6. Ho 2:11. Col √2:16. **seasons**. 2 Ch 8:13. **years**. Le 25:2-5, 8-17.

11. **am**. ver. 20. 2 C *11:2, 3. *12:20, 21. **lest**. Ga 2:2. *5:2-4. Is *49:4. Ac 16:6. 1 C √15:58. Ph 2:16. 1 Th *3:5. 2 J *8. **bestowed labor**. Ro 16:6. **in vain**. Ga 5:2, 4. ver. 19. Ro +13:4. 1 C 4:15. +*15:2. 2 C 11:28. 1 Th ●2:19, 20. *3:5, 8.

12. **beseech**. 2 C 6:13. 1 Th *5:12, 13. **be**. Ga 2:14. 6:14. Ge 34:15. 1 K 22:4. Ac 21:21. 1 C 9:20-23. 2 C *12:15. Ph *3:7, 8. **ye**. 2 C 2:5.

13. **through**. Ro 6:19. 1 C +*2:3. 2 C 10:10. 11:6, 30. √12:7-10. 13:4. **at**. ver. 18. Ga +1:6. Ac 16:6.

14. **ye despised not**. ver. 13. Jb 12:5. Ps 119:141. Ec 9:16. Is *53:2, 3. 1 C 1:28. 4:10. 2 C +10:10g. 1 Th 4:8. **an angel**. 1 S 29:9. 2 S 14:17, 20. 19:27. Zc 12:8. Ml +*2:7h. 2 C 5:20. He +*1:6. *13:2. **as Christ**. Mt +*10:40. 18:5. 25:40. Lk 10:16. Jn 13:20. 2 C 5:20. 1 Th √2:13.

15. **Where is**. *or*, What was. Ϳ121II, Ge +3:7. **the blessedness**. Ga 3:14. 5:22. 6:4. Lk +*8:13. Ro *4:6-9. 5:2. 15:13. **for I**. Ϳ169, Je +12:1. **bear**. Ro 10:2. 2 C 8:3. Col 4:13. **if**. Ϳ184B, Mt +23:30. Ϳ102, Ge +2:24. ver. 19. Ro 9:3. 1 Th 2:8. 5:13. 1 J 3:16-18. **plucked out**. Jg 16:21. 1 S 11:2.

16. **become**. Ga 3:1-4. 1 K 18:17, 18. 21:20. 22:8, 27. 2 Ch 24:20-22. 25:16. Ps +*141:5. Pr 9:8. Jn 7:7. 8:45. **because**. Ga 2:+5, 14. 5:7.

17. **zealously**. Ga 6:12, 13. Mt *23:15. Ro *10:2. 16:18. 1 C 11:2. +12:31g. 2 C 11:2g, 3, 13-15. Ph 2:21. 2 P 2:3, 18. **not well**. T#623. Jb +21:15 (T#689). Ps +106:13 (T#411). Mt 23:15. Lk +18:12 (T#194). 2 C +7:10 (T#609). 2 T +3:5 (T#191). **exclude you**. *or*, exclude us. Mt *23:5-7, 13. 1 C 4:8, 18.

18. **zealously**. T#749. ver. 17. Nu 25:11-13. 1 Ch 22:16 (T#1). Ps 69:9. *119:139. Is 59:17. Jn 2:17. Ac

*18:25. Ro ●+*10:2. +*12:11. 1 C √15:58. 2 C *7:11. Col *4:12, 13. T *2:14. Re *3:19. **I am.** ver. 13, 20. Ph 1:27. *2:12.

19. **little.** 1 C *4:14, 15. 1 T 1:2. T 1:4. Phm 10, 19. Ja 1:18. 1 J 2:+1, 12, 13. 5:21. **I travail.** ƒ141, Is +22:4. ver. +*11. Nu 11:11, 12. Is *53:11. Lk 22:44. Ac 20:31. 2 C 11:3, 28. Ph 1:8. 2:17. Col 2:1. 4:12. He 5:7. +*6:11. Ja *1:18. Re 12:1, 2. **in birth.** 1 C 4:15. **until Christ.** Ro +*8:29. 13:14. Ep *4:13, 24. Ph *2:5. Col +*1:27. *3:9, 10. **be formed.** Ro +2:20. +*12:2. 2 C *3:18. Ph 2:6, 7. **in you.** Jn +*17:23.

20. **desire.** ƒ141, Is +22:4. **to be.** 1 C 4:19-21. 1 Th 2:17, 18. 3:9. **stand in doubt of you.** *or*, am perplexed for you. T#29. ver. 11. Pr +5:22 (T#166). Je +10:3 (T#143). Lk +9:7. 22:31, 32. 24:4. Jn 13:22. Ac 25:20.

21. **ye that.** ƒ14, Is +5:3. ver. 9. Ga 3:10, 23, 24. Ro 6:14. 7:5, 6. 9:30-32. *10:3-10. **desire.** ƒ108B, 1 T +6:9. **do.** Mt 21:42-44. 22:29-32. Jn 5:46, 47. Ro 2:13. **hear.** ƒ108B, Ac +22:9. **the law.** Jn 10:34. 12:34. 15:25. Ro 3:19.

22. **bondmaid.** Ge *16:2-4, 15. **freewoman.** Ge *21:1, 2, 10.

23. **born.** ver. 29. Ro +*9:7, 8. **but.** ver. 28. Ge 17:15-19. *18:10-14. 21:1, 2. Ro 4:18-21. 10:8, 9. He 11:11, 12.

24. **are.** ƒ119, Ge +49:9. **an allegory.** Ezk 20:49. Ho 11:10. Mt 13:35. 1 C 10:11g. He 11:19. ƒ7. Figure of speech Allegory; or, Continued Metaphor and Hypocatastasis: continued comparison by representation or implication. In metaphor, comparison by representation, the comparison is substituted; in hypocatastasis, comparison by implication, the comparison is implied. Allegory thus differs from Parable, which is continued simile, comparison by resemblance, wherein the resemblance is stated. An allegory always refers to the past, whether fictitious or historical, and brings out further teaching from past events beyond the facts of what took place. Allegory thus differs from prophecy, which tells of events which are yet to come. For other instances of this figure see Jg 9:7-15. Is 5:1-6. 28:20. Mt 3:10, 12. 5:13. 7:3-5. 9:15. 9:16, 17. Mt 12:43-45. Lk 9:62. Jn 4:35. Ro 11:16-18. 13:11, 12. 1 C 3:6-8, 12-15. Paul uses allegory also at 1 C 5:6-8 (unleavened bread); 1 C 9:9, 10 (not muzzle plowing ox). 2 C 3:2, 3. 5:1. 10:3-5. 11:2. Ga 6:8. 6:11. **for.** ver. 25. Lk 22:19, 20. 1 C 10:4. **the two.** Ga *3:15-21. He 7:22. 8:6-13. 9:15-24. 10:15-18. 12:24. 13:20. **for these.** ƒ63E1, Le +4:2. Supply by ellipsis (absolute: of anantapodoton), "for these (two women) are the two covenants; the one, indeed, from the mount Sinai, which bringeth forth (children) unto bondage, which is Hagar." The *apodosis* or conclusion is suspended till verse 26. "But Jerusalem which is above is the free (woman), who is the mother of us all" (B57). **are.** ƒ119, Ge +49:9. **covenants.** *or*, testaments. Ro +9:4. **Sinai.** Gr. *Sina.* i.e. *rock fissures; my thorns*, ver. 25. Ac 7:30, 38g. For *S#5514h, see Ex +16:1. Dt 33:2. **which gendereth.** ver. +*3. Ga 5:1. Ro 8:15. **which is.** ver. 22. **Agar.** i.e. Greek form of Hagar, *S#28g. ver. 25g. For *S#1904h, see Ge +16:1. Ge 16:3, 4, 8, 15, 16. 21:9-13. 25:12, Hagar. 1 Ch 5:10, 19, 20. 27:31. Ps 83:6.

25. **this.** Gr. *to.* The Greek article *to* is neuter, while "Hagar" is feminine. *To*, therefore, must agree with some neuter word, which must be supplied, such

as *onoma, name*: "For this (name) Hagar is (or, denotes) Mount Sinai in Arabia." It is a fact that in Arabia the word Hagar (which means *a stone*) is the name for Mount Sinai (B57). **is.** ver. 24. Mt *26:26. **Sinai.** Dt 33:2. Jg 5:5. Ps 68:8, 17. He 12:18. **Arabia.** Ga 1:17. Ac 2:11. **answereth to.** *or*, is in the same rank with. Gr. *sustoikei.* That is, says Bp. Fell, in the same *order* or *file*, suppose in this manner: I. Covenant by Moses. (A) Bondage, (B) Hagar, (C) Ishmael, (D) Law in Sinai, (E) Jerusalem that now is, (F) Jews circumcised. II. Covenant by Christ. (A) Liberty, (B) Sarah, (C) Isaac, (D) Gospel from heaven, (E) Jerusalem above, (F) Christians baptized. Note the clear correspondence between I. F, Jews circumcised, and II. F, Christians baptized. Here, as in Col 2:11, 12, circumcision is unmistakably equated with Christian baptism, in such a manner as to affirm that baptism now takes the place of circumcision as the initiatory rite into membership in the Body of Christ. See related note (Col 2:11n). Ro 11:7-11. Re 11:8. **in bondage.** ver. +*3, 24. Mt *23:2, 4. He *10:11. **her children.** Mt 23:37. Lk 13:34. 19:44.

26. **Jerusalem.** Ps 87:3-6. Is +*2:2, 3. 52:9. 62:1, 2. 65:18. 66:10. Jl 3:17. Mi 4:1, 2. Ph √3:20. He 11:10. *12:22, 23. 13:14. Re 3:12. *21:2, 10-27. **free.** ver. 22. Ga *5:1. Jn 8:36. Ro 6:14, 18. *8:15. 1 P 2:16. **mother.** ƒ155E4, 2 S +20:19. SS 8:1, 2. Is 50:1. Ezk 16:61. Ho 2:2, 5. 4:5. Re 17:5.

27. **Rejoice.** Is ▶54:1-5. **barren.** 1 S 2:5. Ps +*113:9. **desolate.** Ru 1:11-13. 4:14-16. 2 S 13:20. Is 49:21. 62:4. 1 T 5:5. **more children.** 1 S 2:5. Ps 68:6. +*113:9. Is +*60:5.

28. **children of promise.** ƒ121L6, Ro +9:8. ver. 23. Ga +*3:29. Ac 3:25. Ro 4:13-18. *9:8, 9, 24-26.

29. **he that.** ver. 23. Ge *21:9. Ro +9:7. **persecuted.** Ge *21:9, 10. **after the Spirit.** Jn 3:5. 15:9. Ro *8:1, 13. **Spirit.** Gr. *pneuma*, ƒ121A2, Ro +8:1n. **even.** Ga 5:11. 6:12-14. Mt 23:34-37. Jn *15:20. Ac *21:27, 28. 1 Th 2:14, 15. He *10:33, 34.

30. **what.** Ga 3:8, 22. Lk +4:21. Ro 4:3. 11:2. Ja 4:5. **Cast.** Ge ▶21:10-12. Ro 11:7-11. **for.** Jn 8:35. Ro 8:15-17.

31. **we.** ver. 22. Ga 5:1, 13. Jn 1:12, 13. 8:36. He 2:14, 15. 1 J √3:1, 2. **but of.** 1 P 3:6. **the free.** Ga 2:4. 5:13. Ja +1:25.

GALATIANS 5

The apostle exhorts the Galatians to stand fast in their Christian liberty; and shows that, by being circumcised they would in fact renounce Christ; as in him "nothing availeth but faith which worketh by love," 1-6. He disclaims the preaching of circumcision himself, and condemns it in others, 7-12. He cautions them not to abuse their liberty, but "by love to serve one another;" for "love is the fulfilling of the law," 13-15. Exhorting them to "walk in the Spirit," he states the conflict between the flesh and the spirit, 16-18. He enumerates the words of the flesh, and the fruits of the Spirit, 19-23. He shows that true Christians have "crucified the flesh;" again calls on the Galatians to walk in the Spirit; and warns them against vain glory and envy, 24-26.

1. **Stand.** Pr 23:23. 1 C √15:58. +16:13. Ep 6:14. Ph *1:27. 1 Th 3:8. 2 Th 2:15. He 3:6, 14. 4:14. 10:23, 35-39. Ju +*3, *20, *21. Re 2:25. 3:3. **the liberty.**

ſ16, Ge +1:27. ver. 13. Ga 2:4. 3:25. 4:26, 31. Ps +*51:12. Is 61:1. Mt *11:28-30. Jn √8:32-36. Ro *6:14, 18. 7:3, 6. 8:2. 1 C 7:22. 2 C 3:17. Ja +1:25. 1 P 2:16. 2 P 2:19. **made us free.** Jn +*8:32. **and be not.** ſ144D, Ge +40:23. **entangled.** Ga 2:4. 4:9. Mt 23:4. Ac *15:10. 1 C 7:23. Col √2:16-22. He 9:8-11. **the yoke.** Ac 15:10. 1 T 6:1. **bondage.** Ga +*2:4.

2. **I Paul.** 1 C 16:21. 2 C 10:1. 1 Th 2:18. Phm 9. **that if.** ſ184C, Mt +4:9. ver. 4, 6, 11. Ga 2:3-5. Ac 15:1, 24. 16:3, 4. Ro 9:31, 32. *10:2, 3. 1 C +7:18. He *4:2. **profit you nothing.** Ga +*4:11.

3. **testify.** Dt 8:19. 31:21. Ne 9:29, 30, 34. Lk 16:28. Ac 2:40. 20:21. 20:26. 26:22. Ep 4:17. 1 Th 2:11. 4:6. 1 J 4:14. **again.** ſ77, Ex +3:19. **a debtor.** Ga *3:10. Dt 27:26. Mt 23:16, 18g. Ro 2:25. Ja √2:10, 11.

4. **is become.** ver. 2. Ga √2:21. Ro *9:31, 32. *10:3-5. **no effect.** ſ63H, Ge +12:15. ver. 11. Ro 7:2, 6g. **justified.** ſ108A1, Ex +8:18. Ga 2:21. 3:10. Ro √3:20. √4:4, 5. 9:31, 32. **ye are fallen.** Ga 1:6-9. Ro 11:6. 1 C +*15:2. He +*6:4-6. +*10:38, 39. +*12:15. 2 P √2:20-22. +*3:17, 18. Re *2:5.

5. **through.** Jn *3:5. 16:8-15. Ep 2:18. Ju *20, *21. **Spirit.** Gr. *pneuma,* ſ121A1, Lk +1:17n. **wait.** Ge 49:18. Ps 25:3, 5. 62:5. 130:5. La 3:25, 26. Ho 12:6. Ro 8:24, 25. 1 Th +*1:10. 2 Th 3:5. **the hope.** Ac *24:15. Ro *5:1, 2, 21. Ph 3:9. 2 T *4:8. T *2:13. **faith.** ſ121R2, Ac +6:7.

6. **in.** ver. 2, 3. Ga +*3:28. *6:15. Ro 2:25-29. 3:29-31. 1 C *7:19. Col +*3:11. **faith.** ſ174B, Ge +18:27. Mt *25:31-40. 2 C *5:14. Ep 6:23. 1 Th 1:3. He 11:8, 17-19. Ja *2:14-26. 1 P *1:8. 1 J 3:14-20. 4:18-21. 5:1. **which worketh.** Ja +*5:16.

7. **run.** Mt 13:21. 1 C +*9:24. He *12:1. **hinder you.** *or,* drive you back. Ga 3:1. **obey.** ſ147E, Is +24:16. Ac 6:7. Ro 2:8. 6:17. 10:16. 15:18. 16:26. 2 C +*10:5. 2 Th √1:8. He +*5:9. 11:8. 1 P 1:22. **the truth.** Ga +2:5.

8. **him.** See on Ga *1:6, 15. Ro +*8:28. 1 C *1:9. *4:15. Ja √1:13.

9. **little leaven.** Mt +*13:33n. 16:6-12. Mk 8:15. Lk 12:1. 13:21. 1 C 5:6, 7. 15:33. 2 T 2:17. He +*12:15. **leaveneth.** ſ147E, Is +24:16. **lump.** Ro 9:21. 11:16g.

10. **confidence.** Ga 4:11, 20. 2 C 1:15. +2:3. 7:16. 8:22. 2 Th *3:4. Phm 21. **none otherwise minded.** Ph 3:15. **but.** ver. 12. Ga +1:7. 2:4. 3:1. 4:17. 6:12, 13, 17. Ac 15:1, 2, 24. 1 J 2:18-24. **bear.** ver. 12. Jsh 7:25. 1 C 5:5. 2 C 2:6. 10:2, 6. 13:10. 1 T 1:20. **whosoever.** Ga 2:6. 2 C 5:16.

11. **if.** ſ184A, 1 C +15:2. ver. 2, 3. Ga 2:3. Ac 16:3. **why.** Ga 4:29. *6:12, 17. Jn *15:20. Ac 21:21, 28. 22:21, 22. 23:13, 14. 1 C 15:30. 2 C 11:23-26. **the offence.** Is 8:14. Ro 9:32, +33. 1 C *1:18, 23. 1 P 2:8, 9. **the cross.** 1 C +1:17. **ceased.** ver. 4.

12. **I would.** ſ124, Dt +5:29. 2 S 3:29. Ps 97:10. 101:3. 119:104, 128. 139:22. Pr 8:13. Je +*10:25. **they.** ver. 10. Ga +2:4. **cut off.** lit. cut themselves off. i.e. mutilate or castrate themselves. D. A. Hayes remarks on this passage, "There is something of 'grim ferocity' about this language. There is nothing delicate in it. It is offensive to white-fingered and white-cheeked and white-livered people who sit in their easy-chairs and read these burning words today. They blush when they read them (Ga 1:8, 9), and they blush more when they read that passage farther on in the Epistle to the Galatians in which Paul says: 'I wish that those who unsettled you on the subject of circumcision would

go off and castrate themselves! Possibly in that way they would lose all further interest in the subject.' They think that such language ought not to be used in the presence of ladies. Paul was not thinking about the ladies when he dictated those words. He was hot with anger against the Judaizers who were making trouble for him through all the Gentile field. He had to say something which would stop it; and he did. His righteous anger brought about a righteous result" (*Paul and His Epistles,* p. 51). ver. 10. Ga 1:8, 9. Ge *17:14. Ex *12:15. 30:33. Le 22:3. Dt +*23:1. Jsh 7:12, 25. Jn 9:34. Ac 5:5, 9. 27:32g. 1 C *5:13. Ph 3:2g. T 3:10. **trouble.** Ac 15:1, 2, 24. +17:6g.

13. **ye.** ver. 1. Ga 4:5-7, 22-31. Is 61:1. Lk +*4:18. Jn √8:32-36. Ro *6:18-22. **only.** 1 C *8:9. 1 P *2:16. 2 P 2:19. Ju 4, 10-12. **use.** ſ63B, Ge +25:28. **or,** misuse. **an occasion.** Ro +7:8. **but.** ver. 14, 22. Ga 6:2. Mk 10:43-45. Jn 13:14, 15. Ac +*20:35. Ro *15:1, 2. 1 C *9:19. +*13:4-7. 2 C *4:5. 12:15. 1 Th 1:3. Ja *2:15-17. 1 J *3:16-19.

14. **all the law.** T#283. Mt 5:43-48. √7:12. 19:18, 19. *22:35-40. Lk +10:33 (T#414). Ro *13:8-10. Ja *2:8-11. **Thou shalt love.** T#413. ver. 22. Ga 6:2. Le ▶19:18, 34. Jg +10:15 (T#356). Jb +21:15 (T#689). Pr +28:16 (T#137). Mt 5:43-45. *6:33. *7:12. +19:19. *22:39. Mk 12:31, 33. Lk *6:35. 10:27-37. +18:28 (T#674). Jn +*13:34. Ac +4:32 (T#111). +21:14 (T#299). Ro *8:9. 15:1-3. 1 C *10:24, 33. *13:4-7. 2 C *5:15. Ep +5:5 (T#138). Ph +*2:3, 4. 1 T 1:5. Ja 2:8, 9. 1 J 3:16.

15. **if ye bite.** ſ184A, 1 C +15:2. ver. 26. 2 S 2:26, 27. Is 9:20, 21. 11:5-9, 13. 1 C 3:3. 6:6-8. 2 C 11:20. 12:20. Ph 3:2. Ja 3:14-18. 4:1-3.

16. **I say.** Ga 3:17. 1 C 7:29. **Walk.** ver. 24, *25. Ga *6:8. Ro *6:6. *8:1, 4, 5, 12-14. Ep *4:22-24. Col +√1:10. 1 P *1:22. 4:6. Ju √19-21. **Spirit.** Gr. *pneuma,* ſ121A2, Ro +8:1n. **and.** ver. *19-21. Ro *6:12. +*13:13, 14. 2 C *7:1. Ep 2:3. Col 2:11. *3:5-10. 1 P *1:14. *2:11. 4:1-4. 1 J √2:15, 16. **ye shall not fulfill.** *or,* fulfill not. Ga 2:11, 13. Ac 21:4, 10-12. Ro √8:13. 1 J 3:8, 9. **flesh.** ſ171Q9, Ro 8:4.

17. **the flesh.** ſ25, Ge +4:4. Ps *19:12, 13. *51:1-5, 10-12. 65:3. 119:5, 20, 24, 25, 32, 35, 40, 133, 159, 176. Ec +*7:20. Is 6:5. Mt 16:17, 23. 26:41. Jn *3:6, 7. Ro √7:18, 21-25. *8:5, 6, 13. Ja 4:5, 6. **against the Spirit.** Gr. *pneuma,* ſ121A2, Ro +8:1n. **and the Spirit.** Gr. *pneuma,* ſ121A2, Ro +8:1n. **and these.** Ga 3:21. Mt 12:30. Ro *7:7, 8, 10-14. 8:5-8. **so that.** Ps *119:4-6. 130:3. Mt 5:6. Lk 21:33, 46, 54-61. Ro √7:15-23. Ph 3:12-16. Ja 3:2. 1 J √1:8-10. **cannot do.** Gr. *poieo,* Jn 5:29n. Here, present active subjunctive, "that ye may not keep on doing." **that ye would.** "whatever ye wish." Ro *7:19. 1 C √10:13.

18. **if.** ſ184A, 1 C +15:2. ver. 16, 25. Ga 4:6. Ps *25:4, 5, 8, 9. 143:8-10. Pr 8:20. Is 48:16-18. Ezk 36:27. Jn 16:13. Ro *8:12, 14. 2 T +*1:7. 1 J *2:20-27. **Spirit.** Gr. *pneuma,* ſ121A2, Ro +8:1n. **ye are not under.** Ga *3:10. *4:5. Ro *6:14, 15. +*7:4. *8:2.

19. **the works.** ver. 13, 17. Ga 6:8. Ps 17:4. Jn 3:6. Ro *7:5, 18, 25. *8:3, 5, 9, 13. 13:12. 1 C *3:3. +*6:9, 10. Ep 5:11. 1 P 4:2. 1 J 3:8. **which are.** ſ112, Is +24:3. **Adultery.** ſ173, Ge +27:44. Ex +*20:14. Ezk 22:6-13. Mt *15:18, 19. Mk +*7:21-23. Ro +*1:21-32. 1 C +√6:9, 10. 2 C *12:20, 21. Ep 4:17-19. √5:3-6. Col √3:5-8. 1 T 1:9, 10. T 3:3. Ja *3:14, 15. 1 P *4:3, 4. Re +*21:8. *22:15. **fornication.** ſ41, Ge +10:1.

Ac +√15:20. Ep *5:3. Col 3:5. **uncleanness**. 2 C 12:21. **lasciviousness**. Mk +*7:22. Ep 4:19n.

20. **Idolatry**. 1 C 10:14. Ep *5:5. Col *3:5. 1 P 4:3. **witchcraft**. ⨍41, Ge +10:1. Ex 22:18. Dt *18:10. 1 S 15:23. 1 Ch 10:13, 14. 2 Ch +*33:6. Ac *8:9-11. *16:16-19. Re 9:21. 18:23. **hatred**. ✷S#2189g. Lk 23:12 (enmity). Ro 8:7. Ep 2:15, 16. Ja 4:4. **variance**. S#2054g, Ro +1:29. **emulations**. ✷S#2205g. Jn 2:17 (zeal). Ac 5:17 (indignation). 13:45 (envy). Ro 10:2. 13:13. 1 C 3:3 (envying). 2 C 7:7 (fervent mind), 11 (zeal). 9:2. 11:2 (jealousy). 12:20 (envyings). Ph 3:6. Col 4:13. He 10:27 (indignation). Ja *3:14, 16. **wrath**. ✷S#2372g. Lk 4:28. Ac 19:28. Ro 2:8 (indignation). 2 C 12:20 (wraths). Ep *4:31. Col 3:8 (wrath). He 11:27. Re 12:12. 14:8, 10, 19. 15:1, 7. 16:1, 19. 18:3. 19:15. **strife**. ✷S#2052g. Ro 2:8 (contentious). 2 C 12:20. Ph 1:16 (contention). 2:3. Ja 3:14, 16. **heresies**. Ac +24:5. 1 C √11:19. T 3:10. 2 P 2:1.

21. **drunkenness**. Dt 21:20. Lk 21:34. Ro +*13:13. 1 C 5:11. +√6:10. Ep +*5:18. 1 Th 5:7. **revellings**. ⨍41, Ge +10:1. ✷S#2970g. Ro 13:13 (rioting). 1 P *4:3. **I tell you**. 1 Th +3:4. **that they**. Is *3:11. Ro +*2:8, 9. *8:13. 1 C +√6:9, 10. Ep *5:5, 6. Col *3:6. Re *21:27. *22:15. **which do**. Gr. *prasso*, Jn +5:29n. *Prasso* is the verb for habitual practice (our very word, in fact), not *poieo* for occasional doing. The *habit* of these sins is proof that one is not in the Kingdom of God and will not inherit it.—Gentile churches were peculiarly subject to these sins. But who is not in danger from them? (A. T. Robertson, *Word Pictures*, vol. 4, p. 313). The apostle John makes this same distinction between the commission of individual acts of sin from time to time and the habit of willfully practicing the sin, but does this by means of distinctions in the Greek tenses employed, rather than in the use of distinctive synonyms, as Paul. He +*10:26. 1 J 1:8, 10. 2:1, 2. √3:8, 9. **not inherit**. ⨍175B, Ge +21:16. Jn √3:3, 5. Ro +*1:29. 1 C +√6:9, 10. +*15:50. Ep √5:5. 1 J 3:15. Re +*21:8. **kingdom of God**. Mt +*25:34. Ro +*14:17.

22. **the fruit**. ver. 16-18. 1 Ch=9:29. Ps +*1:3. 92:14. SS 4:16. Ho 14:8. Mt 12:33. Lk 8:14, 15. 13:9. Jn *15:2, 5, 16. Ro 6:22. 7:4. 8:5. Ep *5:9. Ph 1:11. Col +√1:10. Ja 3:18. **of the Spirit**. Gr. *pneuma*, Mt +3:16. ver. +25. **is**. ⨍112, Ls +24:3. **love**. ver. 13, 14. Ga 6:2. Ro *5:2-5. 12:9-18. 15:3. 1 C √13:4-7. 2 C +6:6. Ep *4:23-32. 5:1, 2. Ph 4:4-9. Col 3:12-17. 1 Th 1:3-10. *4:9. 5:10-22. T 2:2-12. Ja *3:17, 18. 1 P 1:8, 22. 2 P √1:5-8. 1 J *4:7-16. **joy**. ⨍41, Ge +10:1. Ro 14:17. *15:13. Ph *3:3. **peace**. Ph 4:7. He *12:14. Ja *3:17. **longsuffering**. Ep +*4:2. Col 3:12. **gentleness**. ✷S#5544g. Ro 2:4 (goodness). 3:12 (good). 11:22, 22 (goodness). 2 C 6:6 (kindness). Ep 2:7 (kindness). Col 3:12 (kindness). T 3:4 (kindness). **goodness**. Ro +*15:14. **faith**. Ro 3:3. 1 C 13:7, 13. 2 Th 3:2. 1 T 3:11. 4:12. 1 P 5:12.

23. **Meekness**. Nu 12:3. Ps 22:26. *25:9. 37:11. Zp 2:3. Mt +*5:5. *11:29. Ep 4:1, 2. 2 T 2:25. Ja *1:21. 1 P *3:4. **temperance**. ⨍41, Ge +10:1. Pr 21:17. 25:16. Da +*1:8. Ac 24:25. 1 C *9:25. T 1:8. 2:2. 1 P 4:3. 2 P *1:6. **against**. 1 T 1:9.

24. **they**. Ga *3:29. Ro +*8:9. 1 C 3:23. 15:23. 2 C 10:7. **crucified**. ver. 16-18. Ga *2:20. *6:14. Ro √6:6. √8:13. √13:14. 1 P *2:11. **affections**. *or*, passions. Ro 7:5. **lusts**. Ro √13:14. 1 P *2:11.

25. **If we**. ⨍184A, 1 C +15:2. Jn 6:63. Ro *8:2,

10. 1 C 15:45. 2 C 3:6. 1 P 4:6. Re 11:11. **in the Spirit**. Gr. *pneuma*, ⨍121A2, Ro +8:1n. ver. 22. Jn +7:39. **let**. See on ver. 16. Ga 6:16. Ac 21:24. Ro 4:12. *8:4, 5. Ph 3:16. **in the Spirit**. Gr. *pneuma*, ⨍121A2, Ro +8:1n.

26. **desirous**. Lk 14:10. 1 C 3:7. Ph +*2:1-3. Ja *4:16. **provoking**. See on ver. 15. 1 Ch 21:1. He ◐10:24. Ja *3:14-16. 1 P *5:5.

GALATIANS 6

The apostle exhorts the Christians in Galatia to restore the fallen with meekness, and to bear each other's burdens, according to "the law of Christ," 1, 2; to beware of self-deception, 3-5; to provide for their teachers; and to persevere without wearying in every good work; being assured that every one will reap as he has sowed, 6-10. He shows the carnal motives and glorying of the Judaizing teachers, 11-13; and determines to "glory in the cross of Christ" alone, by which he is "crucified to the world, and the world to him," 14. Nothing in Christ avails, but a new creation, 15. He prays for peace on "the Israel of God;" desires that none of them would further trouble him, who, as an old soldier, bare the scars of his warfare; and he commends them to the grace of Christ, 16-18.

1. **if**. ⨍184C, Mt +4:9. Condition of the third class. **or**, although. ⨍185B. Concessive Clauses: Doubtful Concession. This type of concession is proposed as a possibility. Ga 1:8. Jn 10:38. **overtaken**. Ga *2:11-13. Ge *9:20-24. 12:11-13. Nu *20:10-13. 2 S *11:2, etc. Ps 141:5. Mt *26:69, 75. Ro *14:1. *15:1. 2 C 2:7. He 12:13. Ja +*5:19, 20. **ye which**. ⨍15C, Mk +6:11. T#109. Ps 141:5. Pr +28:23 (T#610). Mt *18:15-17. 1 C 5:4, 5, 9-13. 10:15. 2 Th 3:6, 14, 15. T 3:10, 11. Re 2:2, 3. **spiritual**. Ro +1:11g. *8:6. +*15:1. 1 C +*2:15. *3:1. 14:37. **restore**. 2 S *12:1, etc. Jb *4:3, 4. Is *35:3, 4. Ezk *34:16. Mt *9:13. *18:12-15. Lk +6:40. +*15:4-7. *22:32. 1 C 1:10g. He +*3:12, 13. +*12:13-15. Ja *5:19, 20. 1 J *5:16. Ju *22, *23. **in the**. Ga 5:23. Mt *11:29. 1 C 4:21. 2 C *10:1. 2 Th *3:14, 15. 2 T +*2:25. Ja *3:13. 1 P *3:15. **spirit**. Gr. *pneuma*, 121A2, Mt +5:3. **of meekness**. ⨍100, Ge +10:9. T#437. Ps +*25:9. Pr +16:7 (T#737). +19:11 (T#201). Zp *2:3. Mt *10:16. Ep *4:1-3. Ph +2:3 (T#482). Col 3:12, 13. 1 T 6:11. 2 T *2:25. He +12:13 (T#499). Ja +1:4 (T#498). 1 P *3:3, 4. **considering**. ⨍38D, Ps +27:14. 1 C *7:5. √10:12. He 13:3. Ja 3:2. **thyself**. ⨍96F4, Ex +10:2. ⨍96D2, Is +1:29. The Second Person is put for the Third, "thyself" instead of "yourselves." This is in order to emphasize the fact that those who are thus addressed stand each in the same individual danger (B524).

2. **Bear**. ver. 5. Ga 5:13, 14. Ex 23:5. Nu 11:11, 12. Dt 1:12. Ps 55:22. Is 58:6. Mt 8:17. *11:29, 30. Lk 11:46. Ro *15:1. 1 Th 5:14. 1 P *2:24. **one another's**. Ph 2:4. **burdens**. Gr. *baros*. *Baros* denotes the pressure of a weight, which may be relieved or transferred; *phortion*, also rendered "burden" (ver. 5) is specific, the "load" which each must bear for himself (Samuel Green, *Greek Grammar*, p. 385, no. 68). **so fulfill**. ⨍96B, Ge +20:7. Ga 5:14, 22. **the law**. Jn 13:14, 15, +34. *15:12. 1 C 9:21. Ja *2:8. 1 J 2:8-11. 4:21.

3. **if**. ⨍184A, 1 C +15:2. Ga 2:6. Pr 25:14. 26:12. Lk 18:11. Ro +*12:3, 16. 1 C +*3:18. *8:2. **when**. 1 C 3:7. 13:2, 3. 2 C *3:5. 12:11. **he deceiveth**. 1 C

+*3:18. 2 T 3:13. Ja *1:22, 26. 1 J *1:8.

4. **prove.** Jb 13:15mg. Ps 26:2. 1 C 11:28. 2 C +*13:5. **and then.** Ro 14:12. 1 C +3:8. **rejoicing in himself.** Ps 40:17. Pr *14:14. Mt 10:31. 16:26. Lk ●18:11. Ro 8:17, 18. *12:3. 1 C 4:3, 4. 2 C *1:12. Ph +*2:3. 1 J 3:19-22. **and not.** Ga 6:13. Lk 18:11. Ro +2:1g. 1 C 1:12, 13. 3:21-23. 4:6, 7. 2 C *10:12. 11:12, 13.

5. **every man.** Is 3:10, 11. Je +*17:10. 32:19. Ezk +*14:10n. +*18:4n. Mt +*16:27. Ro *2:6-9. 14:10-12. 1 C 3:8. 4:5. 2 C 5:10, 11. Re 2:23. 20:12-15. 22:12. **his own.** 2 K +*14:6. Pr 9:12. Je *31:30. Ezk +*18:20. **burden.** Gr. *phortion*, see ver. 2n. Nu=4:27. Mt 11:30. 23:4. Lk 11:46. Ac 27:10g.

6. **taught.** 2 Ch=30:22. Lk +1:4g. **the word.** Ac +8:4. **communicate.** T#472. Nu 18:21. Dt√12:19. 18:1, 5. 1 S +*9:7. Ml *3:10. Mt √10:9, 10. Jn 13:20. Ro *15:27. 1 C *9:7n, 9-14. 1 Th 5:12, 13. 1 T √5:17, 18. He *13:16. **that teacheth.** 2 Ch=30:22. Ezk=44:23.

7. **not deceived.** ver. 3. Jb 15:31. Je 37:9. Ob 3. Lk 21:8. 1 C 3:18. +*6:9. 15:33. Ep *5:6. 2 Th 2:3. Ja *1:16, 22, 26. 1 J √1:8. 3:7. **God.** Jb 13:8, 9. Ju 18. **for.** 1 Ch +*28:9. Jb 4:8. Pr 1:31. 6:14, 19. *11:18. Ho 8:7. *10:12. Lk 16:25. Jn ●4:37. Ro 2:6-10. 2 C *9:6. **soweth.** 2 C *9:6. **that shall.** Nu +√32:23. Dt 19:19. Jg +*1:7. Ps *7:16. Pr +*13:21. Ml 3:8-10. 1 C *9:13, 14.

8. **For he.** ſ7, Allegory by continued Hypocatastasis, Ga +4:24. **soweth to his.** Jb *4:8. Ps 7:14. Pr *22:8. Ho *8:7. *10:13. Ro *6:13. *8:13. *13:14. Ja *3:18. **shall of.** Ro +*6:21. reap. Pr *22:8. Je 12:13. Ho *10:13. 2 P 2:12, 19. Re 22:11. **corruption.** 1 C +15:42. **he that soweth.** ver. *7. Ps √126:5, 6. Ec 11:6. Is 32:20. Ho *10:12. He +*6:10. Ja +*3:18. **to the Spirit.** Gr. *pneuma*, ſ121A2, Ro +8:1n. **of the Spirit.** Gr. *pneuma*, Mt +3:16. Mt *19:29. Lk *18:30. Jn *4:14, 36. *6:27. +7:39. Ro *6:22. 1 T 1:16. T *3:7. Ju *21. **everlasting.** Gr. *aionios*, Mt +18:8. Ro +*2:7.

9. **us.** Ml *1:13. 1 C √15:58. 2 Th +*3:13. He *12:3. **be weary.** Lk +18:1g. **well.** Ro +*2:7. 1 P *2:15. *3:17. *4:19. **for.** Le *26:4. Dt 11:14. Ps *104:27. *145:15. Ja *5:7, 8. **due season.** Ec 3:1. Mt 24:45. Lk +*14:14. 1 T 2:6. +*4:8. 6:15. 2 T *4:8. T 1:3. Re *11:18. **shall reap.** 2 C +9:6. He +*10:35. **if.** Is *40:30, 31. Zp 3:16mg. Mt +10:22. *24:13. Lk *18:1. 2 C *4:1, 16. Ep 3:13. He *3:6, 14. *10:35-39. *12:3, 5. Re 2:3, 7, 10, 11, 17, 26-29. 3:5, 6, 12, 13, 21, 22.

10. **opportunity.** Pr 3:27. Ec *9:10. Jn +*9:4. *12:35. Ep *5:16. Ph 4:10. Col *4:5g. T *2:14. **do good.** Ps 37:3, 27. Ec 3:12. Mi +*6:8. Mt *5:44. Mk 3:4. Lk 6:35. Ac 6:1. 28:8. Ep 4:28. 1 Th *5:15. 1 T +*6:17, 18. T √3:8. He *13:16. 3 J 11. **unto all.** Lk 10:25-37. 1 Th +*3:12. 1 T 4:10. **especially.** Is +*58:7. Mt 10:25. 12:50. 25:40. Ro *12:13. 2 C 9:1, 2, 12-15.

Ep *2:18, 19. 3:15. 1 T 4:10. +*5:8. He 3:6. +*6:10. 10:21. 1 P 4:17. 1 J 3:13-19. 5:1. 3 J 5-8. **of faith.** Ga *3:26. Ac +6:7. 1 C +16:13.

11. **written.** Ro 16:22. 1 C 16:21-23.

12. **as desire.** ver. 13. Mt *6:2, 5, 16. 23:5, 28. Lk 16:15. 20:47. Jn 7:18. 2 C 10:12. +*11:13. Ph 1:15. 2:4. Col 2:23. **they constrain.** Ga 2:3, 14. Ac 15:1, 5. *20:30. **lest.** Ga +5:11. Ph 3:18. **the cross.** 1 C +1:17.

13. **keep the law.** Mt *23:3, 15, 23. Ro 2:17-24. 3:9-19. 2 P 2:19. **that they may.** Ro *2:28. 1 C 3:21. 5:6. 2 C 11:18. Ph 3:3, 4.

14. **God.** Ga 2:17. 3:21. Lk +20:16. Ro 3:4-6. Ph *3:3, 7, 8. **that I.** 2 K 14:9-11. Jb 31:24, 25. Ps 49:6. 52:1. Je +*9:23, 24. Ezk 28:2. Da 4:30, 31. 5:20, 21. 1 C +*1:29-31. 3:21. 2 C 11:12. 12:10, 11. **save.** Is 45:24, 25. Ro +*1:16. 1 C 1:23. *2:2. Ph 3:3g, 7, 8. **cross.** ſ117, Ge +19:8. **by whom.** *or*, whereby. **the world.** Gr. *kosmos*, Mt +4:8. Ga 1:4. *2:20. *5:24. Ac 20:23, 24. Ro *6:6. 1 C √15:58. 2 C *5:14-16, 19. Ph *1:20, 21. 3:8, 9. Col √3:1-3. 2 P 2:5. 1 J √2:15-17. 5:4, 5. **world.** Gr. *kosmos*, Mt +4:8.

15. **in.** See on Ga *5:6. Ro 8:1. 2 C √5:17. **neither.** Ro 2:28. 1 C *7:19. **but.** Jn *3:7. 2 C √5:17. Ep *2:10. *4:22-24. Col *3:10, 11. Re 21:5.

16. **walk.** Ga 5:16, +25. Ps 125:4, 5. Ph 3:16. **this rule.** Dt 32:9. Ps 19:4. 2 C 10:13g. **peace.** Ga 1:3. Nu 6:23-27. 1 Ch 12:18. Ps *125:5. 128:6. Jn 14:27. 16:33. See on Ro +*1:7. Ph √4:7. Ju 2. **the Israel of God.** T#974‡. Ga *3:7-9, 28, 29. Ps 73:1. Is 45:25. Ho 1:10. Lk +12:32 (T#959‡, 972‡). Jn *1:47. Ro +*2:28, 29n. 4:12, 16. 7:4. *9:6-9. Ph 3:3. Col 2:11. 1 P 2:5-9. Re 5:9, 10. x7:4. x14:1-4. 20:6.

17. **let no.** Ga 1:7. 5:12. Jsh 7:25. Ac 15:24. He +*12:15. **I bear.** Ga 5:11. Is 44:5. Ezk +*9:4. 2 C 1:5. √4:10. *11:23-25. Col *1:24. Re 13:16. 16:2. 19:20. 20:4. **the marks.** Gr. *stigmata*. "Stigma is a sign usually made on the body (especially on the forehead and hands) by branding or puncturing, on slaves, soldiers, etc. It was especially used as a symbol of the god whom they served (Le 19:28. 21:5. Dt 14:1), and supposed to be *protective*. This explains Paul's use of the word in Ga 6:17. Paul regarded his wounds and scars received in the service of his Lord and God as not only being marks of his servitude, but marks implying that he was under God's protection (Ex 13:9, 16. Is 49:16. Ezk 9:4). Therefore he says, beware how you trouble me! (this explains the word "for"). See also Re 14:1; 7:2; 9:4 (E. W. Bullinger, *The Apocalypse*, p. 441, footnote). *Stigma* is the Greek letter used for the number six, as in the last digit of 666 in Re 13:18.

18. **the grace.** Ro 16:+20, 24. 2 C √13:14. 2 T 4:22. Phm 25. Re 22:21. **your spirit.** Gr. *pneuma*, ſ171Q1B, Mk +2:8n.

EPHESIANS

EPHESIANS 1

The apostle salutes the Ephesians, 1, 2. He blesses God for the spiritual blessings which he had conferred on them and him, as "chosen in Christ," and "predestinated to the adoption of children," 3-5; as "accepted in the Beloved," "through the redemption of his blood,"

and "his grace abounding towards them, in all wisdom," 6-8; as gathered, and made heirs with his people, "to the praise of his glory, by first trusting in Christ," 9-12; as "sealed by the Spirit of adoption, the Earnest of their inheritance," 13, 14. He thanks God for them, and prays that God would more completely illuminate them, and give them deeper experience of the grace *and comforts of the gospel, 15-18; "according to the mighty power, by which Christ had been raised from the dead," and exalted as "Head over all things to his church," 19-23.*

1. **A.M.** 4068. A.D. 64. **an apostle.** Ep *4:11. Ac 13:4. Ro *1:1. 1 C 1:1. 2 C +1:1. Ga 1:1. **by the will.** Mk 3:13. Ac +*9:15. *26:15-18. 1 C +*1:1. 1 T *1:11-14. **to.** Col 1:2. **the saints.** Is +*8:20n. Ro +*1:7. 1 C *1:2. 2 C +1:1. Ga 1:8n. **which.** Ac +*18:19. *19:17, 20. *20:17, 28. **faithful.** Ep 6:21. Ge +*18:19. Nu *12:7. Jsh +*14:8. Pr *20:6. Mt +*24:45. Lk +*16:10. Jn +*17:6. Ac *16:15. 1 C *4:2, 17. 7:25. Ga 3:9. Col 1:2. 2 Th 2:13. 1 T *4:12. *6:2. 2 T *2:2. T 1:6. He 3:2-6. *6:11. +*10:22. 2 P *1:1. Re *2:10, 13. *17:14. **in Christ.** Ro +*8:1n.

2. **Grace.** See on Ro 1:7. 2 C 1:2. Ga 1:3. T 1:4. 2 P *1:2. **and peace.** Zc *6:13. Jn *14:26, 27. Ro *5:1. Ga *5:22. Ph *4:7. **from God our.** Lk *11:13. Re *1:4, 5.

3. **Blessed.** ʃ147E, Is +24:16. ʃ43, Dt +28:3. Ge 14:20. =39:5. Jsh=17:14. 1 Ch 29:20. Ne 9:5. Ps 72:19. =115:12. Da 4:34. Lk 2:28. 2 C +*1:3. T 3:5. 1 P *1:3. Re 4:9-11. 5:9-14. **God.** ver. 17. Jn √10:29, 30. 20:17. Ro +*15:6. 2 C 1:3. 11:31. Ph 2:11. **hath.** ʃ96C6, Mt +2:4. **blessed us.** ʃ145, Jg +11:40. Ge +*12:2, 3. 22:18. Dt 33:29. 1 S 12:22. 1 Ch 4:10. Ps 72:17. 134:3. Is *61:9. Zc 3:7. Ga 3:9. **with all.** Jn *1:16, 17. Ro +*8:32. 1 C +*1:30. 3:21. Col *2:10, 11. 2 P *1:3, 4. **spiritual.** Ro +1:11g. **blessings.** Ro 15:29. 1 P 3:9. **in heavenly.** ver. 20. Ep 2:6. 3:10. 6:12mg. He 3:1. 8:5. 9:23. 1 P *1:4n. **places.** *or,* things. Ep 6:12. **in Christ.** ver. 10. Jn 14:20. *15:2-5. +*17:21. Ro +*8:1n. 12:5. 1 C +*1:30. 12:12. 2 C √5:17, 21.

4. **According as.** Ep 2:10. 2 Th 2:13. 1 P 1:2. **chosen.** Dt 7:6, 7. 26:18, 19. 2 Ch=29:11. Ps 135:4. Is 41:8, 9. 42:1. 65:8-10. Mt +*11:25, 26. 24:22, 24, 31. Jn +*10:16. Ac +*13:48. 18:10. Ro +*8:28, 30, 33. 9:23, 24. 11:5, 6. 1 Th 1:4. 2 Th *2:13, 14. 2 T +*1:9. 2:10. T *1:1, 2. Ja +*2:5. 1 P *1:2. *2:9. Re ⬤13:8. ⬤17:8. in him. Ro 16:7. Ep 3:11. **before.** T#255. Ep 3:9. 1 Ch=23:31. 2 Ch=29:11. Mt +*13:35. +*25:34. Jn *17:24. Ac +13:48 (T#254). 15:18. 2 Th 2:13. 2 T +*1:9. +*2:10. 1 P 1:20. Re *13:8. *17:8. **world.** Gr. *kosmos,* Mt +4:8. **that we.** Ep √2:10. Lk 1:74, 75. Jn +*15:16. Ro +*8:28, 29. Col *3:12. 1 Th 4:7. √5:23. 2 Th 2:13. 2 T +*1:9. *2:19. T √2:11, 12. 2 P √1:5-10. **should be.** Nu *23:19. Je 31:3. Jn 13:1. Ro +*11:29. 2 T +*1:9. T *2:14. He *7:25. **without blame.** Ep √5:27. Jn +*17:6. 1 C 1:8. Ph *2:15. Col 1:22. He 9:14. 1 P 1:19. 2 P √3:14. Ju √24. Re 14:5. **love.** Ep 3:17. 4:2, 15, 16. *5:2. Ga 5:6, 13, 22. Col 2:2. 1 Th 3:12. 1 J 4:16.

5. **predestinated.** ver. +*11. Ro +*8:29, 30. **adoption of children.** Je 3:4, 19. Ho 1:10. Jn √1:12. 11:52. Ro *8:14-17, 23. 2 C √6:18. Ga +*4:5-7n. He *12:5-9. 1 J √3:1. Re *21:7. **by.** Jn *20:17. Ga +*3:26. He *2:10-15. **to himself.** Col 1:16. **according.** ver. 9, +*11. Da *4:35. Mt 1:26. *11:26. Lk 2:14. 10:21. +*12:32. Ro *9:11-16. 1 C 1:1, 21. Ph √2:13. 2 Th 1:11. He 2:4. **good pleasure.** Ex +*33:19. Mt 20:15.

6. **praise.** ver. 7, 8, 12, 14, 18. Ep *2:7. 3:10, 11. Pr 16:4. Is 43:21. 61:3, 11. Je 33:9. Lk *2:14. Ro *9:23, 24. 2 C *4:15. Ph 1:11. √4:19. 2 Th √1:8-10. 1 T 1:14-16. 1 P·*2:9. *4:11. **the glory.** ʃ24N, Ge +17:5. Ezk 16:14. **he.** Is 45:24, 25. Je +*23:6. Ro *3:22-26. 5:15-19. *8:1. 2 C √5:21. Ph *3:9. 1 P 2:5. **accepted.** Le

7. **In whom.** Ro +*8:1n. Ga 4:5. Col 1:14. **redemption.** ver. 14. Ep +*4:30. Jb 33:24. Ps 130:7. Da +*9:24-26. Zc 9:11. 13:1, 7. Mt +*20:28. +*26:28n. Mk 14:24. Ac +*20:28n. Ro +*3:24. 1 C +*1:30. Ga +*3:13. Col √1:14. 1 T √2:6. T √2:14. He *9:12-15, 22. 10:4-12. 1 P *1:18, 19. *2:24. *3:18. 1 J √2:2. *4:10. Re *5:9. 14:4. **through his blood.** ʃ117, Ge +19:8. Ex 12:12, 13. Le 17:11. Ac +*20:28n. He 9:14-22. 10:4-14. 1 J 1:7. **the forgiveness.** Ex 34:7. Ps √32:1, 2. 86:5. 130:4. Is *43:25. √55:6, 7. Je 31:34. Da *9:9, 19. Jon 4:2. Mi *7:18. Lk 1:77. 7:40-42, 47-50. *24:47. Jn 20:23. Ac +*2:38. +*3:19. +*10:43. +*13:38, 39. Ro √4:6-9. Col *2:13. He 10:17, 18. 1 J √1:7-9. 2:12. **sins.** Le +=5:6. **according.** to. See on ver. 6, 18. Ep *2:4, 7. 3:8, 16. Ro +*2:4. *3:24. 9:23. 2 C √8:9. Ph √4:19. Col +*1:27. *2:2. T *3:6mg. **riches.** ʃ22D5I, Pr +8:18. ʃ108B, Ro +2:4. **of his.** ʃ29, Ex +19:6. His exceeding rich grace.

8. **Wherein.** ʃ63A1, Ge +14:20. It is not "wherein," but *hees, which,* i.e., "(the knowledge) *or grace,* which he hath made to abound in us in all wisdom and prudence." **he hath abounded.** Ro *3:25, 26. √5:15, 20, 21. Ph 1:9g. **in.** ver. +*11. Ep 3:10. Ps 104:24. Pr 8:12. Is 52:13. Da 2:20, 21. Mt 11:19. Ro *11:33. 1 C 1:19-24. 2:7. Col +*1:9. *2:3. Ju *25. Re *5:12. **wisdom.** ver. 17. 1 K 4:29. Col +*2:3. **prudence.** Lk 1:17g.

9. **made known.** ver. 17, 18. Ep *3:3-9. Mt 13:11, 35. Ac +22:14. Ro +*16:25-27. 1 C 2:10-12. Ga 1:12, 16. Col *1:26, 27. 1 T *3:16. **the mystery.** ʃ100, Ge +10:9. Ro +*16:25n. **his will.** T#307. ver. 10-12. Ep 3:8-12. Jb +14:5 (T#251). **according.** See on ver. 5. **purposed.** ver. +*11. Ep 3:11. Jb 23:13, 14. Ps 33:11. Is 14:24-27. 46:10, 11. Je 2:29. La 3:37, 38. Ac 2:23. 4:28. +*13:48. Ro 3:25. +*8:28. 9:11. 2 T +*1:9. **in himself.** Jb *33:13. Ro *11:33, 34.

10. **in the dispensation.** Ep +*3:2. **fulness of times.** Is +*2:2-4. Da *2:44. +*9:24-27. Am *9:11. Mi 4:1, 2. Ml *3:1. Mt +*24:45. Mk +1:15. Lk +*21:24. Jn +√6:54n. Ac +√3:19-21. Ro +√11:25. 1 C 10:11. Ga √4:4. He *1:2. *9:10. 11:40. 1 P *1:20. **he might gather.** lit. head up. ʃ22A3B, ver. 22. ver. 22. Ep 2:15. Ge +*49:10. Da ⬤+*7:22. Mt +*13:30, 39-43. 25:32. Ro 13:9g. 1 C 3:22, 23. +*11:3. 15:24-28. Col 1:20. +*3:11. 1 Th +*4:17. 2 Th √2:1. He *12:22-24. Re *5:8-14. 7:4-12. 14:19. 19:4-6. 21:3. **in one.** Ep *2:14. +*4:4. Col +*3:11. **all things.** Ep *3:15. Mt 13:41. Ac +√3:21. Ro 8:22, 23. Ph *2:9, 10. Col 1:16, 20. **heaven.** Gr. the heavens. He *12:22-24.

11. **obtained an inheritance.** Gr. *ekleerotheemen,* ✶S#2820g, only here. See related word, *proskleroo,* Ac 17:4 (consorted). From *kleroo,* to assign by lot, to make a heritage. See Jsh +*14:2n. Ezk √45:1. Care must be taken not to spiritualize this inheritance. In Scripture there is but one inheritance, promised to Abraham, not yet accomplished (Ac +*7:5), but certain of fulfillment, being confirmed by an oath (Ge 15:8-18. Mi 7:20. He 6:13, 18), whereby Jesus Christ the Messiah (Zc 14:4, 9), and Abraham personally upon resurrection (Mt +*8:11, 12) through Him, together with we the saints as co-heirs and co-inheritors (Ro 8:17) of the same promise given in the Abrahamic cov-

enant (Ro 4:11, 12, +*13), shall inherit the land forever (Da √7:14. Lk √1:32, 33. 1 C 15:24n. Re √11:15), not some ethereal mansion (Jn +*14:2, 3) in the third heaven (2 C 12:2), as the following reference passages abundantly confirm. ver. *14, 18. Ep √5:5. Le 25:23. Nu=18:20. Dt 4:20. =10:9. *32:9. 1 S 2:8. Ps +*37:18. 68:16. √69:35, 36. +*94:14. 106:5. √132:11-14. SS=2:16. Is 8:8. *60:21. Ezk +*38:16. =44:28. Jl 2:18. Mt +√5:5. +*25:34. Jn 1:11. Ac 7:5n. +*20:32. +*26:18. Ro *8:17. Ga √3:16-18. Col *1:12. *3:24. T *3:7. He 9:15. Ja +*2:5. 1 P √1:4. *3:9. **being predestinated.** See on ver. 5. Lk 22:29. Ro +*8:30. 1 Th 2:12. **according to.** Ep *3:11. Dt +*2:30. Ps +*115:3. Pr +*21:1. Is 46:10, 11. Ro +*8:28. +*9:18. Re 4:11. **the purpose.** See on ver. 9. Lk 12:32. **all things.** T#260. Dt +2:30 (T#267). 1 S +2:7 (T#3). 2 S +7:14 (T#265). 1 Ch *29:12. 2 Ch +18:31 (T#264). Ps 135:*6, 7. 147:8, 9, 15-18. Pr *16:33. Is 26:12. +*45:7. Je 10:13. Da +1:9 (T#266). Am +*3:6. Mt *10:29, 30. Ro +*8:28. 11:36. 1 C 12:6. Ph *2:13. He *13:20, 21. **who worketh.** ver. 20g. Ep 2:2. Mt +14:2. **the counsel.** See on ver. 8. Jb 12:13. Pr 8:14. Is 5:19. 9:6. 28:29. 40:13, 14. √46:10-13. Je 23:18. 32:19. Zc 6:13. Mt 1:19g. Ac 2:23. 4:28. +*20:27. Ro *11:34. Col 2:3. He 6:17. 1 J 2:1. Re 3:18. **his own will.** God the Father is sovereign. Ps 24:1. 115:3. Is 45:9. Da 4:25, 35. Mt +*28:19n. Ro +*9:18 (T#234). Re 4:11.

12. **That we.** Ep √2:10. Jn +*15:16. Ro *2:10. **should be.** See on ver. 6, 14. Ep 2:7. 3:21. 2 Th *2:13. **to the praise.** ver. 6, 14. Ph 1:11. **who.** ver. 13. Ps 2:12. 146:3-5. Is 11:10. 12:2. 32:1, 2. 42:1-4. 45:23-25. Je *17:5-7. +*23:6. Mt 12:18-21. Jn *14:1. Ac *19:1-3. Ro 15:12, 13. 2 T *1:12. Ja *1:18. 1 P *1:21. **trusted.** *or*, hoped.

13. **ye also.** Ep √2:11, 12. Col *1:21-23. 1 P +*2:10. **after that ye heard.** Ep 4:21. Jn 1:17. Ro 6:17. √10:14-17. Col *1:4-6, 23. 1 Th √2:13. **the word of truth.** Ps *119:43. 2 C *6:7. Col 1:5. 2 T √2:15. Ja *1:18. **the gospel.** Mk *16:15, 16. Ac 13:26. 15:7. Ro +*1:16. 2 T +√3:15. T *2:11. He √2:3. **ye were sealed.** Ep +*4:30. Ezk +*9:4. Jn +3:33. +*6:27. Ro *4:11. 2 C *1:22. 2 T √2:19. Re 7:2, 3. **holy.** Jl +*2:28. Lk *11:13. *24:49. Jn *14:16, 17, 26. *15:26. 16:7-15. Ac *1:4. 2:16-22, 33. Ga 3:14. **Spirit.** ℐ121A1, Lk +1:17n. **of promise.** Ezk 36:27. *37:14. Lk +*24:49.

14. **the earnest.** Ro *8:15-17, 23. 2 C 1:22. *5:1, 4, 5. Ga *4:6. **our inheritance.** ver. +*11n, 18. Ep *5:5. Ac +*20:32. Col *3:24. **the redemption.** ver. +*7. Ep +*4:30. Le 25:24, etc. Ps 74:2. 78:54. 111:9. Is √51:11. Je 32:7, 8. Ho *13:14. Lk 21:28. Ac +*20:28. Ro √8:23. T *2:14. 1 P *2:9mg. **purchased possession.** ver. 11n. Mt +*5:5. **unto the praise.** See on ver. 6, 12. 1 P +*2:9.

15. **after.** Ro +*1:8. Col *1:3, 4. Phm 5. **faith.** Ga *5:6. 1 Th 1:3. 2 Th *1:3. 1 T 1:5, 14. Re 2:19. **love.** Ps 16:3. Col 1:4. 1 Th 4:9. He +*6:10. 1 P *1:22. *2:17. 1 J √3:17. *4:20, 21. **the saints.** 2 C +*1:1.

16. **Cease.** Ro *1:8, 9. 1 S 7:8. +*12:23. Ph √1:3, 4. Col 1:3, 9. 1 Th +*5:17. 2 Th 1:3. 2 T *1:3. **making.** Ge 40:14. Is 62:6. Ro +*1:9. 1 Th *1:2, 3.

17. **the God.** See on ver. *3. Jn *20:17. Ro +*15:6. **the Father of glory.** 1 Ch *29:11. Ps *24:7, 10. 29:3. Je 2:11. Mt +*6:13. Lk 2:14. Ac *7:2. 1 C √2:8. 2 C 1:3. He 9:5. Ja √2:1. Re 7:12. **the spirit.** Gr. *pneuma*, ℐ121A1, Lk +1:17n. Ge 41:38, 39. Is +*11:2. Da 5:11. Lk 12:12. *21:15. Jn √14:17, 26. *16:13, 14. Ac 6:10.

1 C +*12:8. 14:6. Col *1:9. *2:3. Ja *3:17, 18. **of wisdom.** ver. 8. Is 11:2. 1 C 2:6. 12:8. Col *1:9. Ja +*1:5. **and.** ℐ93A, Ge +1:26. **revelation.** Ep 3:5. Da *2:28-30. 10:1. Mt +*11:25. 16:17. 1 C *2:7-10. 14:6, 26. 2 C 12:1. **in the knowledge.** *or*, for the acknowledgment. Ep *3:18, 19. *4:13g. Pr *2:5. Je +*9:24. *24:7. *31:34. Mt +*11:27. Jn √8:54, 55. 16:3. 17:√3, 25, 26. Ro +*1:28. Col +√1:10. 2:2. 2 T +*2:25. T *1:1. 2 P *1:3. +*3:18. 1 J 2:3, 4.

18. **eyes.** Ep 5:8. Ps √119:18. Is 6:10. 29:10, 18. 22:3. *42:6, 7. Mt +*13:15. Lk √24:45. Ac *16:14. +*26:18. 2 C *3:18. √4:4, 6. He 10:32. **understanding.** Ep 4:18. **enlightened.** Ge +*3:7. Ac +*26:18. He *6:4. 10:32. Re 3:17, 18. **the hope.** Ep *2:12. √4:4. Ro +*5:4, 5. *8:24, 25. Ga *5:5. Col +*1:5, 23. 1 Th 5:8. 2 Th 2:16. T √2:13. *3:7. He *6:18. 1 P *1:3. 1 J 3:1-3. **his calling.** Ep 4:1. Ro +*8:28-30. +*11:29. Ph *3:14, 20, 21. Col 3:15. 1 Th *2:12. 2 Th 1:11. 1 T 6:12. 1 P 3:9. 5:10. **the riches.** ℐ22D5I, Pr +8:18. See on ver. 7, 11. Ep *3:8, 16. Col *1:27. **of the glory.** ℐ29, Ex +19:6. **the exceeding rich glory of his inheritance in the saints. his inheritance.** ver. +*11n, *14. Dt *32:9. **the saints.** 2 C +1:1.

19. **And what.** ℐ136, Is +60:12. **exceeding greatness.** Ep √2:10. *3:7, 20. Ps *110:2, 3. Is *53:1. Jn *3:6. Ac +*26:18. Ro +*1:16. 2 C 4:7. √5:17. Ph √2:13. Col 1:29. 2:12. 1 Th *1:5. 2 Th 1:11. Ja +*1:18. **according to.** Ep 3:7. Ro 1:4. 1 C *6:14. Ph 3:21. Col 1:29. 2:12. 2 Th 2:9. **his power.** Le=7:34. Col 1:11, 17. He 1:3. **his mighty.** Gr. the might of his. Ep 6:10. Da 2:37. 4:30. Col 1:11. 1 P *1:3-5.

20. **he wrought.** ver. 11g. Ep 2:5, 6. Mt +14:2. Ro 6:5-11. Ph 3:10. 1 P *1:3. **when.** Ps +*16:9-11. Jn √10:18, 30. Ac +*2:24-33. 4:10. 10:40. 26:8. Ro +*1:4. He *13:20. **and set.** ℐ15C, Mk +6:11. Ep 2:6. *4:8-10. Ps *110:1. Mt 22:43-45. 26:64. *28:18. Mk 14:62. +*16:19. Jn *17:1-5. Ac *2:33-36. 5:31. *7:55, 56. Ro *8:34. Col *3:1. He *1:3, 13. *2:9. 10:12. 1 P +3:22. Re *1:17. √5:11-14. **right hand.** ℐ22A15C, Ps +110:1. **heavenly.** See on ver. 3.

21. **far above all.** Ep 4:10. Jn +*3:31. Ph √2:9, 10. Col *2:10. He *1:4. **principality.** ℐ173, Ge +27:44. ℐ121N1, Ge +31:54. Ep 3:10. *6:12. Da 7:27. Ro +*8:38, 39. 1 C 15:24. Col +*1:15, 16. *2:10, 15. He 4:14. 1 P 3:22. **and power.** Ep 3:10. 6:12g. Col *2:10, 15. T 3:1. **and might.** Is +*9:6. 10:21. 49:26. 60:16. Je 32:18. Mt 11:21. Lk 9:43. Re 7:10, 12. **every name.** ℐ121T4. Metonymy of the Adjunct B608. "Name" is put for the name of the thing itself: here, dignities. For another instance of this figure see Ph 2:9. Ep 3:15. Mt +√28:19. Ac √4:12. Ph *2:9-11. He 1:4. Re 19:12, 13. **this world.** Gr. *aion*, Mt +6:13. *12:32. Mk +10:30. Jn +√6:54n. 1 C +1:20. He 6:5. **in that.** Mt 25:31-36. 28:18. Jn *5:25-29. He 2:5. Re *20:10-15.

22. **put all.** Ge +*3:15. Ps *8:6-8. 91:13. Mt +*11:27. *28:18. 1 C √15:25-27. He *2:8. **under.** ℐ22D3D2, Ps +110:1. **gave.** Ep *4:15, 16. 1 C 11:3. Col 1:8. 2:10, 19. **head.** ℐ22A3B. Anthropomorphism B873. Christ is said to be the head of the body. For other instances of this figure see ver. 10. Ep 4:15. Col 1:18. T#96. Ep 4:15. 5:23. Mt 23:8-10. 1 C ◐+*11:3. Col 1:18. +2:10 (T#76-1). **to the church.** Ep 3:10, 21. 5:23, 24, 25, 27, 29, 32. Mt +*16:18. Ac +*20:28. 1 T 3:15. He *12:22-24.

23. **his body.** ℐ22A2, Col +2:17. Ep 2:16. √4:4, 12,

16. *5:23-32. Ro *12:5. 1 C *12:12, 27. Col *1:18, 24. 2:19. 3:15. **fulness.** Ep 3:19. 4:10, 13. Ps 23:5. 94:15. Jn +*1:16. 1 C +*12:6. *15:28. Col *1:19. √2:9, 10. +*3:11. **that filleth.** Ep 4:10. **all in all.** For the omnipresence of God the Son, see Mt +18:20 (T#76-6). Je 23:24. 1 C 12:6g. Col *3:11.

EPHESIANS 2

The apostle shows the Christians at Ephesus their former ruined state, as dead in sin, slaves of Satan and "children of disobedience;" among whom he and all believers once were, being "by nature the children of wrath, even as others," 1-3. All who do not perish are saved "by grace," "in Christ," "through faith;" and are "created unto good works," 4-10. The Gentiles were once "without Christ, without hope, without God;" but by the special grace of God, through the atonement of Christ, all who believed were brought nigh, and reconciled to God; had access to him; and were formed into one church with Jewish converts, the ritual law being taken away by the death of Christ, 11-18. Thus they became one family and temple, a habitation of God through the Spirit, 19-22.

1. **you.** ver. 5, 6. Ep 1:19, 20. Jn √5:24, 25. *10:10. 11:25, 26. √14:6. Ro 8:2. 1 C 15:45. Col 1:21. *2:13. *3:1-4. **hath he quickened.** ∫63I2, Jsh +3:3. ver. 5. **dead.** ver. 5. Ep 4:18. 5:14. Ge 2:17. Ezk +*18:4, 21. Mt 8:22. Lk 15:+24, 32. Jn 5:21, 24, 25. Ro *8:6-8. 2 C *5:14. 1 T *5:6. 1 J 3:14. Re 2:11. 3:1.

2. **in time.** ver. 3, 11, 13. Ep 4:22. 5:8. Jb 31:7. Ac 19:35. Ro *11:30. 1 C +*6:11. Col 1:21. 3:7. T 3:3. 1 P 4:3. 1 J 5:19. **walked according.** Ep 4:17. Ps 17:14. Je 23:10. Lk *16:8. Jn 7:7. 8:23. 15:19. Ro +*12:2. 1 C 5:10. Ga 1:4. Col 3:7. 2 T 4:10. Ja 1:7. *4:4. 1 J √2:15-17. *5:4. **course.** Gr. *aion*, Mt +6:13. ∫121P2, Mt +13:22. Ep +1:21. Ga 1:4. **world.** Gr. *kosmos*, Mt +4:8. ∫121J9B, Jn +12:31. Col 2:8, 20. **the prince.** Ep *6:12. Jn √8:44. +*12:31. +*14:30. *16:11. 1 J *5:19. Re 9:11. *12:9. *13:8, 14. *20:2. **of the air.** Jb *1:7, 16, 19. Re 16:17. **the spirit.** Gr. *pneuma*, Mt +*8:16. Ep *6:12. Mt 12:43-45. Lk 11:21-26. *22:2, 3, 31. Jn 13:2, 27. Ac 5:3. 2 C √4:4. 1 J *3:8. 4:4. **worketh.** Ep 1:11. Mt +14:2. **the children.** ∫108B, 1 S +20:31. ver. 3. Ep 5:6. Is 30:1. 57:4. Ho 10:9. Mt 11:19. 13:38. Lk +10:6. Jn 8:34, 44. Ro 6:20. Col 3:6. 2 T +*2:25, 26. T 3:3. 1 P 1:14g. 2 P 2:14g. 1 J 3:10. *5:19.

3. **we all.** *∫39, Ac +17:27. ver. 2. Is √53:6. *64:6, 7. Da 9:5-9. Ro *3:9-19. 1 C +*6:9-11. Ga 2:15, 16. 3:22. T *3:3. 1 P *4:3. 1 J √1:8-10. **in times.** Ep 4:17-19. Ac 14:16. √17:30, 31. Ro 11:30. 1 P 2:10. 1 J 2:8. **in the lusts.** Ep 4:22. Mk 4:19. Jn *8:44. Ro 1:24. 6:12. *13:14. Ga *5:16-24. 1 T *6:9. Ja *4:1-3. 1 P 1:14. *2:11. 4:2. 2 P 2:18. 1 J *2:16. Ju 16-18. **flesh.** ∫171Q9, Ro +8:4. **fulfilling.** T#698. Le 18:24, 25. Ro 8:7, 8. 2 C *7:1. Ga *5:19-21. 2 T 3:4. T 3:3. Ja 5:5. 1 P +2:11 (T#675). 4:3, 4. **desires.** Gr. wills. Jn *1:13. **and of the.** Paul and the rest of Scripture frequently speaks in terms of dichotomy more consistently than of trichotomy. Mt ●22:37. Lk *1:46, 47. Ro +*8:10. 1 Th ●*5:23. He ●*4:12. **by nature.** T#164. Ge 5:3. 6:5. *8:21. Jb 11:12. *14:4. *15:14-16. 25:4. Ps √51:5. *58:3. Pr 22:15. Is 48:8. Mk +*7:21, 22. Jn *3:1-7. Ro *3:10, 20, 23. *5:12-19. 7:18. 2 C 5:14. Ga *2:15, 16. 4:8. **children of wrath.** ∫108B, 1 S +20:31. T#656.

See on ver. 2. Mt 13:38. Lk +10:6. Ro *9:22. 2 P 2:14. **even.** Ps 51:5. Ro *3:9, 22, 23. 5:12. 1 C 4:7. 1 Th 4:1. 5:6.

4. **rich in mercy.** ∫22D5I, Ps +8:18. ver. *7. Ep +*1:7. *3:8. Ex *33:19. *34:+√6, 7. Ne 9:17. Ps +*51:1. *86:5, 15. *103:8-11. 111:4. 118:3. 130:7. 145:8. Is √55:6-8. Je +√29:11. Da 9:9. Jon +*4:2. Mi *7:18-20. Mt +*28:19n. Lk 1:78. Ro +*2:4. *5:20, 21. 9:23. *10:12. 1 T 1:14. T 3:5. 1 P *1:3. **his.** Dt *7:7, 8. 9:5, 6. Je 31:3. Ezk 16:6-8. Jn √3:14-17. Ro √5:8. 9:15, 16. 2 Th 2:13. 2 T +*1:9. T 3:4-7. 1 J *4:10-19. **loved us.** T#826. Dt 7:13. Ps 4:3. 42:8. 103:4. 146:8. Pr 15:9. Is 43:4. 62:4, 5. Je *31:3. 32:41. Ho 14:4. Zp 3:17. Jn 16:27. 17:23, 26. Ro 9:25. 2 Th 2:16. 1 J 4:10, 16, 19.

5. **dead.** See on ver. 1. Ro *5:6, 8, 10. **quickened.** See on ver. 1. Ep 5:14. Jn *5:21. *6:63. 11:25. *14:19. Ro 8:2. Col 2:12, 13. *3:1-3. Re 20:4. **grace ye.** Gr. whose grace ye. ∫81, Ge +15:13. ver. 8. Ac +15:11. Ro +*3:24. 4:16. 8:24. 11:5, 6. 16:20. 2 C *13:14. T *2:11. *3:5. Re 22:21.

6. **hath.** ∫96C2, Ge +45:9. See on Ep 1:19, 20. Ro *6:4, 5. Col *1:18. 2:12, 13. *3:1-3. **sit.** Mt 26:29. Lk 12:37. +*22:29, 30. Jn 12:26. +*14:3. *17:21-26. Re *3:20, 21. **in heavenly.** See on ver 1:3. Le=24:9. Dt 32:13. Ps 18:33. 81:16. Pr 30:28. Ezk=44:16. 1 C=10:21. Ph *3:20. He *6:19, 20.

7. **in the.** Ep 3:5, 21. Ps 41:13. 106:48. Is *60:15. 1 T *1:17. **ages.** Gr. *aion*, Mt +6:13. **show.** See on ver. 4. 2 Th 1:12. 1 T *1:16. 1 P 1:12. Re *5:9-14. **riches.** ∫22D5I, Pr +8:18. **in his kindness.** Ro +*2:4. +*11:22. T *3:4g.

8. **by grace.** See on ver. 5. Ro +*3:24. 11:6. 2 T +*1:9. **through faith.** Mk *16:16. Lk +*7:50. Jn √3:14-18, 36. √5:24. 6:27-29, 35, 40. Ac 13:39. 15:7-9. +√16:31. Ro *3:22-27. *4:5, 16. √10:9, 10. Ga 3:14, 22. 1 P 1:5. 1 J √5:10-12. **not of yourselves.** ver. *10. Ep 1:19. Mt *16:17. Jn √1:12, 13. *6:37, 44, 65. Ac 14:27. *16:14. Ro √10:14-17. 2 C 3:5. Ph *1:29. Col 2:12. Ja *1:16-18. **the gift.** Ep 3:7. 4:7. Jn 4:10. Ac 8:20. 2 C 9:15. He 6:4.

9. **Not of works.** Ro *3:20, 27, 28. *4:2. *9:11, 16. *11:6. Ga 3:12, 13. 2 T +*1:9. T √3:3-5, ●8. **lest any.** Jg 7:2. 1 C *1:29-31. 2 C *12:9, 10.

10. **we are.** Dt 32:6, 15. Ps 95:6. 100:3. 138:8. 149:2. Is 19:25. 29:23. 43:21. *60:21. 61:3. 64:8. Je 31:33. 32:39, 40. Jn *3:3-6, 21. 1 C *3:9. 2 C *5:5, 17. Ph *1:6. √2:13. He *13:21. **workmanship.** Ro 1:20g. **created.** Ep 3:9. *4:24. Ps *51:10. 102:18. 2 C √5:17. Ga *6:15. Col 3:10. 2 T *3:15. **good works.** Ep 4:24. Mt +*5:16. Ac +9:36. 2 C *9:8. Col +√1:10. 2 Th 2:17. 1 T 2:10. 5:10, 25. 6:18. 2 T *2:21. +*3:17. T *2:7, 14. √3:1, +8, 24. He *10:24. *13:21. 1 P 2:12. **which God.** Ep +1:4. Ro +*8:29. **ordained.** *or,* prepared. Nu=4:27. 1 Ch 6:48. Jn +*15:16. **that we.** Ep 1:12. **walk.** ver. 2. Ep 4:1. Dt 5:33. Ps 81:13. 119:3. Is +*2:3-5. Ac 9:31. Ro *8:1. Col +√1:10. 1 J *1:7. +*2:6.

11. **remember.** Ep 5:8. Dt 5:15. 8:2. 9:7. 15:15. 16:12. Ps *103:2. Is *51:1, 2. Ezk 16:61-63. 20:43. 36:31. 1 C 6:11. 12:2. Ga 4:8, 9. **time past.** ver. +2. Dt 5:15. **Gentiles.** Ro +*2:28, 29. Ga 2:15. 6:12. Col 1:21. 2:13. **Uncircumcision.** Le 26:41. 1 S 17:26, 36. Je 6:10. +*9:25, 26. Ezk 44:7. Ph *3:3. Col +*3:11. **Circumcision.** Ro *2:26, 28. Col *2:11, 13. **made by hands.** Mk 14:58. Col *2:11.

12. **without Christ**. Ep 5:8. Jn +*10:16. *15:5, 6. 1 C 12:2. Col 1:21. 3:7. **aliens**. Ep 4:18. Ezr 4:3. Is 61:5. Ezk 13:9. 14:5, 7. Ga 2:15. 4:8. Col 1:21. He 11:34. **commonwealth of Israel**. ver. 19. **strangers**. Le=22:10. **the covenants**. Ge *15:18. +*17:7-9. Ex 24:3-11. Nu 18:19. Ps 89:3, etc. Is +*55:3. Je √31:31-34. *33:20-26. Ezk 37:26. Lk 1:72. Ac *3:25. Ro 9:1, +4, 5, 8. Ga +*3:16, 17. **having no hope**. Ep +1:18. Je 14:8. 17:13. Jn 4:22. Ac 28:20. Col ◑*1:5, 27. 1 Th 4:13. 2 Th *2:16. 1 T 1:1. He ◑*6:18, 19. 1 P ◑*1:3, 21. *3:15. 1 J 3:3. **without God**. 2 Ch 15:3. Is 44:6. 45:20. Ho 3:4. Lk √10:22. Ac 14:15, 16. Ro +*1:18-20, 28-32. +*2:12. *10:13-15. 1 C +*8:4-6. 10:19, 20. Ga 4:8. 1 Th 4:5. **world**. Gr. *kosmos*, Mt +4:8.

13. **in Christ Jesus**. See on Ro +*8:1n. 1 C +*1:30. 2 C √5:17. Ga *3:28. **far off**. ver. 12, 17, 19-22. Ep 3:5-8. Ps 22:27. 73:27. Is 11:10. 24:15, 16. 43:6. 49:12. 57:19. 60:4, 9. 66:19. Je 16:19. Ac +*2:39. 15:14. 22:21. +*26:18. Ro *15:8-12. **are made nigh**. ver. 16. Ep *1:7. Ge=45:4. Ex 12:44. Le +=23:19. Nu=3:5, 6. =16:10. Ezk=43:27. Ro *3:23-30. *5:9, 10. 1 C 6:11. 2 C *5:20, 21. Col *1:13, 14, 21-23. He 9:18. 1 P *1:18, 19. *3:18. Re *5:9. **by the blood**. √117, Ge +19:8. By *Metalepsis* or Double Metonymy, "blood" is put for his death and the atonement made in His obedient act in dying for His people. Ro +3:25. Col 1:20.

14. **For he**. Jb *9:33. **our peace**. ver. 17. Ep 6:15. Le +=23:19. Ps 72:7. Is +*9:6, 7. Ezk 34:24, 25. Mi 5:5. Zc 6:13. 9:10. Lk 1:79. +*2:14. Jn 16:33. Ac +√10:36. Ro *5:1. Col 1:20. 3:15. He 7:2. *13:20. **both**. ver. 15. Ep 3:15. 4:16. Is 19:24, 25. Ezk 37:19, 20. Jn +*10:16. 11:52. 1 C 12:12. Ga +*3:28. Col +*3:11. **broken down**. Ep +*4:4. Jn 2:19g. Ac +√10:11. **the middle**. Est 3:8. Mt √27:51. Ac *10:28. Col *2:10-14, 20. **partition**. Ac 10:13n.

15. **in his flesh**. Ro 7:4. Col 1:21, 22. He +*10:19-22. **the enmity**. ver. 16. Ro 8:7. Ja 4:4. **the law**. Ga 3:10. Col *2:14, 20. He 7:16. 8:13. 9:9, 10, 23. 10:1-10. **ordinances**. Lk 2:1. Ac 16:4. 17:7g. Col 2:14, 20. **one new man**. Ep 4:16, 24. 1 C √12:12, 13. 2 C √5:17. Ga √6:15. Col *3:10. **making peace**. ver. +14.

16. **reconcile**. Ro +*5:10. 1 C √12:13. 2 C *5:18-21. Col 1:20-22. **both unto God**. Ac 13:44-46. 22:21, 22. 1 Th 2:16. **one body**. Ep *3:6. +*4:4. Ro 7:4. Col 3:15. **having slain**. ver. 15. Ro *6:6. 8:3, 7. Ga √2:20. Col 2:14. 1 P 4:1, 2. **the enmity**. ver. 15. Ro *8:7. **thereby**. *or*, in himself. Col 2:15g.

17. **And came**. Jn 14:18. Ac 26:23. **and preached**. Ps *85:10. Is 27:5. 52:7. *57:19-21. Zc *9:10. Mt 10:13. Lk *2:14. 10:5, 6. Ac +*2:39. +√10:36. Ro *5:1. 2 C 5:20. **peace**. ver. +14. Le +=23:19. Ps 85:8. Zc 9:10. **that**. ver. +13, 14. Dt *4:7. Ps 75:1. 76:1, 2. 147:19, 20. *148:14. Lk 10:9-11.

18. **through him**. Ep *3:12. Jn 10:7, 9. √14:6. Ro 5:2. He 4:14-16. *7:19, 25. *10:19, 20, 22. 1 P *1:21. *3:18. 1 J √2:1, 2. **access**. T#796. Ep 1:6. *3:12. Ex 24:2. 34:4-7. Le=16:12-15 w He 10:19-22. Nu=3:5, 6. =16:10. Dt 4:7. Ps 15:1. *16:11. 23:6. 24:3, 4. 27:4. 42:1, 2. 43:3. 65:4. 73:28. 84:1, 2. 145:18. Is 2:3. 26:2. √55:3, 6. Je 31:6. Ezk 20:40, 41. Ho 14:2. Jl 2:12. Mt 6:6. Jn *10:7, 9. √14:6. Ac 14:27. Ro +5:2. Col 1:21, 22. He √4:16. 7:19, 25. 10:19, 20. √11:6. Ja 4:8. 1 P 1:17. 2:4, 5. 3:12. Re 3:8. **by one**. Ep +*4:4. 6:18. Zc *12:10. Jn *4:23. Ro *8:15, 26, 27. 1 C √12:13. Ju √20. **Spirit**. Gr. *pneuma*, Mt +3:16. **unto the Father**.

Ep 3:14. Mt +√28:19. Jn *4:21-23. 20:17. Ro *8:14, 15. 1 C *8:6. Ga 4:6. Ja 3:9. 1 P 1:17.

19. **no more**. Le +=23:19. Is 56:3. 1 C 6:11. **strangers and**. See on ver. 12. Ex 12:43. Le=22:10. Dt 10:19. He 11:13. 13:14. 1 P ◑2:11. **foreigners**. or, sojourners. Ac 7:6, 29. 1 P 1:17. 2:11. **but**. Ep 3:6. Ga 3:26-28. 4:26-31. Ph *3:20g. He *12:22-24. Re 21:12-26. **the saints**. 2 C +1:1. **household**. Ep *3:15. Mt 10:25. Ga +*6:10. 1 T 3:15. 1 J √3:1.

20. **built**. Ep *4:12. Je *12:16. 24:6. 1 C +*3:9. Col +*2:7. 1 P *2:4, 5. **the foundation**. Is *28:16. Mt *16:18. 1 C *3:9-11. Ga *2:9. Re *21:14. **apostles**. Ep *4:11-13. 1 C *12:28. He +11:9g. Re 21:14. **and prophets**. Ep 3:5. Lk +*24:44. 1 C +12:28. 2 P *1:21. **Jesus**. 1 C 3:11. **chief corner**. √22L2, Is +8:14. Ps *118:22. Is *28:16. Mt *21:42. Mk 12:10, 11. Lk *20:17, 18. Ac √4:11, 12. 1 C 3:11. 2 Th 2:16. 3:16. 1 P *2:6-8.

21. **all the building**. Ep *4:13-16. Ezk ch. 40-42. 1 C 3:9. He 3:3, 4. **fitly framed**. Ex ch. 26. 1 K 6:7. **groweth unto**. Ep 4:15, 16. **holy temple**. Ps 93:5. Ezk 42:12. 1 C *3:16, 17. *6:19. 2 C *6:16.

22. **an habitation**. Ep 3:17. Lk ◑11:21-26. Jn *14:16-23. 17:21-23. Ro +*8:9-11. 1 C *3:16. *6:19. 2 C 6:16. 1 T 3:15. 1 P 2:4, 5. 1 J 3:24. *4:13, 16. Re 18:2.

EPHESIANS 3

Paul, the prisoner of Christ for the Gentiles, 1; shows, that the mystery concerning their salvation, which was before concealed, had been made known to him by revelation, 2-7; and to him, "who was least of all saints, was this grace given, that he should preach among the Gentiles the unsearchable riches of Christ," 8, 9; that "the principalities and powers in heavenly places" might, in the church, discover "the manifold wisdom of God;" while, "according to his eternal purpose," Jews and Gentiles had "access with boldness, by Jesus Christ," 10-12. He desires that the Ephesians may not faint, because of his tribulations for them, 13; fervently prays, that they may be abundantly strengthened, enlightened, sanctified, and comforted, 14-20; and concludes with most animated praises, 21.

1. **I Paul**. 2 C 10:1. Ga 5:2. **the prisoner**. √63B, Ge +2:10. Supply by ellipsis, "(am) the prisoner." Ep 4:1. 6:20. Lk 21:12. Ac *21:13, 27, 28, 33. 23:18. 26:29. 28:17-20. 2 C 11:23. Ph 1:7, 13-16. Col 1:24. 4:3, 18. 2 T 1:8, 16. 2:9. Phm 1, 9. Re 2:10. **for**. ver. 13. Ac *22:21, 22. Ga *5:11. Col 1:24. 1 Th *2:15, 16. 2 T 2:10. **Gentiles**. ver. 8.

2. **If**. √184A, 1 C +15:2. √136, Is +60:12. **ye**. 4:21. Ga 1:13. Col 1:4, 6. 2 T 1:11. **the dispensation**. or, stewardship. ver. 8. Ep 1:10. 4:7. Ac *9:15. +11:23. *13:2, 46. 22:21. +*26:17, 18. Ro *1:5. *11:13. +*12:3. 15:15, 16. 1 C *4:1. 9:+17-22. Ga 1:15, 16. 2:8, 9. Col 1:25-27. 1 T 1:4, 11. 2:7. 2 T 1:11. **grace**. Ac *20:24. 1 C +1:4.

3. **How that**. Ep 1:17. Ac 22:17, 21. 23:9. *26:15-19. 1 C 2:9, 10. Ga *1:12, 16-19. **by revelation**. 2 C +12:1. **the mystery**. ver. 9. Ep 6:19. Da 2:29. Ro 11:25. +*16:25n. Col +*1:26, 27. **as I**. Ep *1:9-11. 2:11-22. **afore**. *or*, a little before. Ep 1:9, 10.

4. **Whereby**. 2 C 11:6. **ye may**. Mt 13:11. 1 C 2:6, 7. 13:2. 2 C 11:6. **the mystery**. Ep 1:9. 5:32. *6:19. Lk 2:10, 11. 8:10. 1 C 4:1. Col 1:27. 2:2. 4:3. 1 T *3:9, 16.

5. **in other.** ver. *9. Mt *13:17. Lk *10:24. Ac 10:28. Ro +*16:25n. 2 T *1:10, 11. T *1:1-3. He *11:39, 40. 1 P √1:10-12. **sons of men.** ∫144A3, Ge +11:5. Mt 12:31. Mk 3:28. **now revealed.** Mt ❍*23:24. **holy.** Lk +1:70. **apostles and.** See on Ep +*2:20. *4:11, 12. Lk *11:49. 1 C *12:28, 29. 2 P *3:2. Ju *17. **by.** Mt 1:22. Lk *2:26, 27. Jn *14:26. *16:13. Ac *10:19, 20, 28. 1 C *12:8-10. Re 1:10. **Spirit.** Gr. *pneuma*, Mt +3:16.

6. **the Gentiles.** Ep 2:13-22. Ro 8:15-17. Ga *3:26-29. +*4:5-7n. **fellowheirs.** Ep *1:11n. Mt +*8:11. Ro √8:17. Ga +*3:29. He 11:9. **the same body.** Ep +*2:16. 4:15, 16. 5:30. Ro 12:4, 5. 1 C √12:12, 13, 27. Col 2:19. **partakers.** Ep ❍5:7. Ga *3:14. 1 J *1:3. *2:25. **his promise.** Ep +2:18.

7. **I was.** See on ver. 2. Ro 15:16. 2 C 3:6. 4:1. Col 1:23-25. **a minister.** 1 C +3:5. **according.** ver. 8. Ro 1:5. 1 C 15:10. 1 T *1:14, 15. **the grace.** ver. +2. **by.** ver. 20. Ep +1:19. 4:16. Is 43:13. Ro 15:18, 19. 2 C *10:4, 5. Ga 2:8. Col *1:29. 1 Th √2:13. He *13:21.

8. **who am.** Pr *30:2, 3. Ro 12:10. 1 C +*15:9. Ph +*2:3. 1 T *1:13, 15. 1 P *5:5, 6. **less than.** ∫111, Ge +18:27. 2 C 10:1, 10. 1 T 1:15. **the least.** ∫125, Jb +22:6. **saints.** 2 C +1:1. **is this.** 1 Ch 17:16. 29:14, 15. Ac 5:41. Ro 15:15-17. **I should.** See on ver. 2. Ga 1:16. 2:8. 1 T 2:7. 2 T 1:11. **among the Gentiles.** ver. 1, 2. Ac +9:15. **unsearchable.** ver. 16, 19. Ep 1:7, 8. 2:7. Ge=41:49. Jb 5:9. Ps 31:19. Mt +*28:19n. Jn 1:16. Ro *11:33g. 1 C +*1:30. √2:9. Ph √4:19. Col +*1:27. *2:1-3. Re 3:18. **riches.** ∫22D5I, Pr +8:18. ∫108B, Ro +2:4. ver. 16. Ep 1:18. Ro +2:4.

9. **to make.** Mt 10:27. +√28:19. Mk *16:15, 16. Lk *24:47. Ro 16:26. Col 1:23. 2 T 4:17. Re 14:6. **fellowship.** or, dispensation, or stewardship. ver. +2, 3-5. Ep 1:9, 10. 1 T *3:16. **beginning.** Ep *1:4. Mt 13:35. 25:34. Ac 15:18. 1 C 2:7. Col 1:26. 2 Th 2:13. 2 T +*1:9. T *1:2. 1 P 1:20. Re 13:8. 17:8. **world.** Gr. *aion*, Mt +6:13. **hid.** ∫84, Ge +6:17. Col 1:26. 3:3. **created.** Ep 2:10. Ps 33:6. Is 44:24. Jn *1:1-3. 5:17, 19. +*10:30. Col *1:16, 17. He *1:2, 3. 3:3, 4. Re 4:11.

10. **intent.** Ex *25:17-22. Ps *103:20. *148:1, 2. Is *6:2-4. Ezk 3:12. 1 P 1:12. Re *5:9-14. **principalities.** See on Ep *1:21. 6:12. Ro +*8:38. 1 C +15:24g. Col 1:16. 1 P *3:22. **in heavenly.** See on Ep *1:3. **be known.** ver. 5. T 1:3. 1 P 1:12. **manifold.** Ep *1:8. Ps *104:24. Mt +*11:25-27. Ro *11:33. 1 C 1:24. 2:7. 1 T *3:16. 1 P 4:10. Re *5:12. **wisdom.** Ro *11:33.

11. **eternal.** Gr. *aion*, Mt +6:13. **purpose.** T#304. Ep *1:3, 4, 9, +*11. Dt +32:4 (T#249). Jb +14:5 (T#251). Ps +33:11 (T#250). Is 14:24-27. 46:10, 11. Je 51:29. Ro +*8:28-30. 9:11. 2 T +*1:9. T 1:2. 1 P 1:19, 20. Re 13:8. 17:8.

12. **In whom.** Ep +*2:18. Jn √14:6. Ro 5:2. He 4:14-16. +*10:19-22. **boldness.** T#1314. He *4:15, 16. *10:19, 20. 1 J *2:28. **and access.** Ep +*2:18. **with confidence.** 2 C 3:4. **faith.** Mk 11:22. Ph 3:9.

13. **ye faint not.** Dt 20:3. Is 40:30, 31. Zp 3:16. Lk +18:1. Ac +*14:22. Ga *6:9. 2 Th 3:13. He *12:3-5. **at.** ver. 1. 2 C 1:6. Ph *1:12-14. Col 1:24. 1 Th *3:2-4. **for you.** ver. 1. Ph 2:17. Col 1:24. **which is.** 2 C *1:6.

14. **For this.** ∫67, Ro +3:26. ∫13. Anachoresis; or, Regression B913. A return to the original subject after a digression. Here, resuming the subject of verse 1. For another instance of this figure see Ro 1:7. **I bow.**

Ep 1:16-19. 1 K 8:54. 19:18. 2 Ch 6:13. Ezr 9:5. Ps 95:6. Is 45:23. Da +*6:10. Lk *22:41. Ac +*7:60. 9:40. 20:36. 21:5. **the Father.** See on Ep 1:3.

15. **the whole.** Ep 1:10, 21. Ga *3:26. Ph *2:9-11. Col 1:20. Re 5:8-14. 7:4-12. **is.** Is 65:15. Je 33:16. Ac 11:26. Re 2:17. 3:12.

16. **That.** ∫63E2, 1 S +13:8. Supply ellipsis, "(Praying) that." **according.** ver. +8. Ep *1:7, 18. 2:7. Ro 9:23. Ph √4:19. Col +*1:27. **riches.** ∫22D5I, Pr +8:18. **to be.** Ep *6:10. Jb 23:6. Ps 28:8. *138:3. Is *40:29-31. *41:10. Zc 10:12. Mt +*6:13. 1 C 16:13. 2 C *12:9. Ph √4:13. Col *1:11. 2 T 4:17. He 11:34. **Spirit.** Gr. *pneuma*, Mt +3:16. **the inner man.** Je 31:33. Ro 2:29. +*7:22. 2 C *4:16. 1 P *3:4.

17. **dwell in.** T#1575. Ep *2:21, 22. Is +*57:15. Jn *6:56. *14:17, +*20, 23. *17:20-23. Ro +*8:9-11. 2 C 6:16. Ga *2:20. Col +*1:27. 2 T 4:22. 1 J 4:4, 16. Re √3:20. **being rooted.** Mt *13:6. Ro *5:5. 1 C 8:1. 2 C √5:14, 15. Ga *5:6. Col +*2:7. **grounded.** Mt *7:24, 25. Lk 6:48g. Col +*1:23. **in love.** Mt *10:37.

18. **able.** ver. 19. Ep *1:18-23. Jb 11:7-9. Ps *103:11, 12, 17. 139:6. Is *55:9. Mt *18:11. Jn 1:5. *15:13. Ga *2:20. +*3:13. Ph *2:5-8. 3:8-10. 1 T 1:14-16. *3:16. T 2:13, 14. Re 3:21. **with all.** Ep 1:10, 15. Dt 33:2, 3. 2 Ch 6:41. Ps 116:15. 132:9. 145:10. Zc 14:5. 2 C 13:13. Col 1:4. Re *5:9. **saints.** 2 C +1:1. **what.** Ro *10:3, 11, 12. **depth and.** Jb 11:8, 9. Ro +*8:39. *11:33. **height.** ∫22I1, Jb 11:8. ∫63I1A, Ex +12:4. Supply ellipsis, "height (of love is)."

19. **to know.** T#1612. ver. 18. Ep 5:2, 25. Jn *17:3. 2 C *5:14. Ga √2:20. Ph *2:5-12. Col +√1:10. 2 P +*3:18. 1 J 4:9-14. **the love.** Le=7:34. Pr *8:17. SS *2:4. Jn *11:35, 36. *13:1, 34, 35. *14:21. *15:9, 10. Ro +*8:35. 2 C 5:14. 2 T 1:13. 1 J *3:16. *4:19. Re +*1:5, 6. 3:19. **passeth knowledge.** ver. +*8. Jb 11:7. Mt +*28:19n. Ph √4:7. **that ye.** Ep *1:23. +*5:18. Ps *17:15. 43:4. Mt +*5:6. Jn *1:16. Ro *15:13, 14. Ph *1:11. Col *1:9. *2:9, 10. Re *7:15-17. *21:22-24. *22:3-5. **the fulness.** T#1504. Ep +1:23. Jn 1:16.

20. **able.** Ge 17:1. 18:4. 2 Ch 25:9. Je 32:17, 27. Da 3:17. 6:20. Mt 3:9. Jn *10:29, 30. Ac 20:32. Ro *4:21. 14:4. +*16:25. 2 C *9:8. He 2:18. *7:25. 11:19. *13:20, 21. Ja 4:12. Ju *24. **exceeding.** Ex 34:6. 2 S 7:19. 1 K 3:13. Ps 36:8, 9. SS 5:1. Is 35:2. √55:7. Jn *10:10. Ro +*8:32. 1 C √2:9. 1 T 1:14. 2 P √1:11. **above all.** 1 K 10:13. 2 K=13:18, 19. 2 Ch 1:10, 12. *25:9. Ps 37:4. Je +*33:3. Ml *3:10. **according.** ver. 7. Ep *1:19, 20. Ph *4:19. Col *1:29. **that worketh.** Mt +14:2. 1 Th √2:13. Ja +*5:16.

21. **Unto him.** Ge +*49:10. Jn 12:32. 2 C √5:15. 2 Th 2:1. He 13:13. **be glory.** Ep 1:6. 1 Ch 29:11. Ps 29:1, 2. 72:19. 115:1. Is 6:3. 42:12. Mt +*6:13. Lk *2:14. Ro *11:36. 16:27. Ga 1:5. Ph 2:11. 4:20. 2 T 4:18. He *13:15, 21. 1 P *5:11. Re *4:9-11. *5:9-14. 7:12, etc. **by.** Ph 1:11. He *13:15, 16. 1 P 2:5. **throughout.** Ep *2:7. 1 P *5:11. 2 P +*3:18. Ju *25. **ages.** or, generations. Col 1:26. **world.** Gr. *aion*, Mt +6:13. lit. the age of the ages.

EPHESIANS 4

The apostle exhorts his brethren to a consistent walk in humility and love, as united by manifold most endearing bonds, 1-6; to a peaceful improvement of gifts and endearments, and performance of duties, for the good of the church; from regard to the ascended Savior, and the nature of his communications and appoint-ments, for the edification of his saints, 7-16; to a conduct peculiarly distinguished from that of the Gentiles around them; being taught by Christ, dead to sin, and continually more and more renewed to the divine image, 17-24; to avoid deceit and anger, 25-27, to labor in what was good; and so to shun dishonesty, and to practice charity, 28; to use their tongues in holy dis-course, and not in unholy, 29; to beware of grieving the holy Spirit, 30; and to meekness, kindness, and forgiveness, after the example of the love of God in Christ, 31, 32.

1. **prisoner.** See on Ep 3:1. **of the Lord.** *or,* in the Lord. **beseech.** Je 38:20. Ro +*12:1. 1 C 4:16. 2 C 5:20. 6:1. 10:1. Ga 4:12. Phm 1, 9, 10. 1 P 2:11. 2 J 5. **walk.** ver. 17. Ep 5:2. Ge 5:24. 17:1. Ac 9:31. Ph *1:27. 3:17, 18. Col +√1:10. *2:6. 4:12. 1 Th *2:12. 4:1, 2. T *2:10. He *13:21. 1 P 1:15, 16. 1 J *2:6. **vocation.** ver. 4. Lk *3:14n. Ro +*8:28-30. Ro +*11:29. 1 C *7:20. Ph *3:14. 2 Th 1:11. 2 T +*1:9. He 3:1. 1 P 3:9. 5:10. 2 P *1:3.

2. **lowliness.** Nu 12:3. Ps 45:4. 138:6. Pr 3:34. *16:19. 29:23. Is +*57:15. 61:1-3. Zp +*2:3. Zc *9:9. Mt +*5:3-5. √11:29. Ac 20:19. 1 C √13:4, 5. Ga +*5:22, 23. Ph +*2:3. Col 2:18, 23. *3:12, 13. 1 T 6:11. 2 T +*2:25. Ja 1:21. 3:15-18. 1 P *3:8, 15. 5:5g. **meekness.** Ga +*5:22, 23. Col 3:12. **with longsuffering.** Ro +*2:4. 1 C *13:4. 2 C 6:6. Ga +*5:22. Col *1:11. *3:12. 2 T 3:10. 4:2. He 6:12. Ja 5:10g. **forbearing.** Mt +17:17. Mk 9:19. Ro 15:1. 1 C *13:7. Ga *6:2. Col *3:13.

3. **keep the unity.** ver. *4. Jn 13:34. *17:21-23. Ro *15:5n. 1 C +*1:10. √12:12, 13. 2 C 13:11. Col *3:13-15. **the Spirit.** Gr. *pneuma,* Mt +3:16. Ep 6:17. Jn +7:39. **in the bond.** Ac 8:23. Col 2:19. *3:14. **peace.** Ro *14:17-19. 1 Th 5:13. He +*12:14. Ja *3:17, 18.

4. **one body.** Since there is but one body and one hope, the teaching of Jehovah's Witnesses that there is a heavenly hope available only to 144,000 and an earthly hope available to the rest of mankind is certainly mistaken, for it obviously sets forth two hopes and makes two bodies, an earthly and a heavenly, in contra-diction to this clear Scripture. See related notes (John 3:7. 1 C 15:50). T#113. Ep 1:10. +2:16. √3:6. *5:30. Nu +*15:16. Jn +*10:16. Ac +√10:11. Ro *12:4, 5. 1 C 10:17. *12:12, √13, 20. Col 3:15. **one Spirit.** Gr. *pneuma,* Mt +3:16. Ep 2:+18, 22. Mt +√28:19. 1 C *12:4-11. 2 C 11:4. **as ye are called.** See on ver. 1. Ep +*1:18. **one hope.** Ep 1:+*11n, +18. Je 14:8. 17:7. Jn √3:3, 5, 7. Ac *15:11. Ro +*15:4. Col *1:5, 27. 2 Th *2:16. 1 T 1:1. 2 T +*4:1. T √1:2. √2:13. √3:7. He *6:18, 19. 1 P √1:3, 4, 21. 1 J √3:3. **calling.** ver. *1. Ro +*11:29. 2 T +*1:9.

5. **One Lord.** Zc √14:9. Ac *2:36. +√10:36. Ro √14:8, 9. 1 C 1:2, +13. +*8:6. *12:3, 5, 6. Ph √2:11. *3:8. **one faith.** √121R2, Ac +6:7. ver. *13. Ro *3:30. 2 C 11:4. Ga 1:6, 7. *5:5, 6. T 1:1, 4. He *13:7. Ja 2:18. 2 P 1:1. Ju +√3, 20. **one baptism.** Since the scope of the immediate context shows Paul is writing of the spiritual unity of the church, this reference to baptism has no bearing upon the mode of Christian baptism. On this text Alexander Carson asserts that as believer's baptism "cannot possibly extend to infants, if there is such a thing as infant baptism, there must be two baptisms. If then, there is but one baptism, there can be no infant baptism" (*Baptism: Its Mode and Subjects,* p. 212). As relevant to the exposition of this text as

the assertion that the moon is made of green cheese! Some wrongly assume that to accept sprinkling, pour-ing, and immersion as baptism means that would make three baptisms; therefore, since immersion is alleged to be the only biblical mode, immersion, as the only valid mode of baptism, must be the "one baptism." In the same manner as there are expressly stated to be two circumcisions, one with hands, which is the sign (Ro 4:11) of the real, made without hands (Ro 2:29. Col 2:11), Scripture teaches there are at least two baptisms: ritual baptism with water, and real bap-tism by the Holy Spirit. Since ritual baptism is the mere symbol of real baptism, the "one baptism" of this passage must refer to real baptism, by which we are all placed in the one body (1 C √12:13). Paul is not contradicting himself or the rest of Scripture when he speaks here of one baptism, since there is only one real, spiritual baptism which places all believers into the one body. J. W. Dale (*Christic Baptism,* p. 349) enumerates twelve distinctly different non-Jewish baptisms mentioned in connection with Christianity in the New Testament: (1) Baptism into repentance, Ac 2:38. He 6:2. (2) Baptism into the remission of sins, Ac 2:38. (3) The personal covenant baptism of Christ to "fulfill all righteousness," Mt 3:15. (4) The personal baptism of Christ by the Holy Ghost "without measure" in order to the fulfilment of this covenant engagement, Jn 3:34. (5) The personal baptism of Christ in the actual fulfilment of this covenant engagement, by baptism into penal death upon the Cross, Mt 20:22. Lk 12:50. (6) The baptism of the Apostles by the Holy Ghost at Pentecost, endowing them with gifts and power for the Apostleship, Ac 1:5. 2:4. (7) The ritual, symbol baptism of the Samaritans "into the name of the Lord Jesus," Ac 8:12, 16. (8) The baptism of Corne-lius and friends by the Holy Ghost endowing with miraculous gifts, but diverse from the kindred baptizing endowment of the Apostles, in that these gifts were not such as to qualify for the Apostleship, Ac 10:47, 48. (9) Baptism into Moses, 1 C 10:2n. (10) Baptism into Paul, 1 C 1:13. (11) Baptism "by one Spirit into one body," including regeneration and endowment, without either of which there can be no membership in the body of Christ, 1 C √12:13. (12) Baptism "into the name of the Father, and of the Son, and of the Holy Ghost," which is consequent upon and the con-summation of baptism "into Christ," Mt 28:19. See related notes listed at Ac 22:16. Mt +√28:19. Ac +*1:5n. +*22:16n. Ro +*6:3, 4n. 1 C √12:13n. Ga +*3:26-28. He 6:6. 1 P 3:21. Re +*1:5.

6. **One.** ver. 5. Dt +*6:4. 1 K ◐+*20:23n. 1 C +*8:6. **God and.** Note the mention of all three mem-bers of the trinitarian Godhead in the immediate con-text: Father (ver. 6), Son (ver. 5), and Holy Spirit (ver. 4), as in 1 C 12:4-6. See related notes (Is +*42:1n. Mt +√28:19). Ep 6:23. Nu 16:22. Is 63:16. Ml *2:10. Mt +*6:9. Jn *20:17. 1 C +*8:6. 12:6. Ga *3:26-28. 4:3-7. 1 J √3:1-3. **who.** Ep 1:21. Ge 14:19. 1 Ch *29:11, 12. Ps 95:3. Is 40:11-17, 21-23. +*57:15. Je 10:10-13. Da 4:34, 35. 5:18-23. Mt +*6:13. Ac *17:24-26, 28. Ro *11:36. Re *4:8-11. **above all.** or, over all. Ro +*9:5n. Col *1:16-19. **and in.** Ep *2:22. 3:17. Jn 14:23. 17:26. 2 C 6:16. 1 J 3:24. 4:12-15.

7. **unto.** ver. *8-14. Mt *25:15. Ro √12:6-8. 1 C 7:7. √12:7-11, 28-30. 1 P 4:10. **grace.** Ep 1:6. *3:2, 8. 1 C +*1:4. 2 C *6:1. 1 T 4:14. 1 P *4:10. **according**

to. ver. 16. Ex 28:21. **the measure.** Ep 3:2. Jn *3:34. Ro +*12:3. 2 C 10:13-15.

8. **he saith.** Ep 5:14. Ro 9:15. Ja 4:6. **When.** ℐ92A, Mt +1:23. See on Ps *⊅68:18. **he.** In the Hebrew of the passage Paul cites, "he" is in reference to Jehovah (Ps 68:17), another instance of many where the New Testament writers apply to Jesus what was said in the Old Testament of Jehovah (Ne +*9:6. Je +*23:6. Mk 1:3 w Is ⊅40:3. Ac 11:21n. 1 C 12:3n. 1 P +*2:3n w Ps ⊅34:8), inconceivable of strict former Jewish monotheists if they did not explicitly believe and teach that Jesus is God (Ac 7:59n). **ascended.** Ps 7:7. 24:7-10. 47:5. Is 14:17. Lk 16:22. 23:43. Jn +*3:13n, 31n. Ac *1:9. **he led.** Jg 5:12. Col *2:15. **captivity.** or, a multitude of captives. 2 C √2:14n. He *2:14, 15. **and.** 1 S 30:26. Est 2:18. **gave.** ℐ63H, Ge +12:15. ℐ92F2, Mt +2:6. An ellipsis may be supplied, "led captivity captive, and, (receiving) gifts, gave them to men." **gifts.** Jn *16:7. Ac *2:4, 29-33.

9. **that.** ℐ63B, Ge +25:28. or, "this (expression)." **he ascended.** Pr *30:4. Jn +*3:13. *6:33, 62. *20:17. Ac *2:34-36. **he also.** Ge *11:5. Ex *19:20. Jn 6:33, 38, 41, 51, 58. 8:14. *16:27, 28. **the lower.** Dt +*32:22. Ps 8:5. *63:9. 139:15. Is 44:23. Ezk 26:20. 31:14. Mt +*12:40n. He *2:7, 9.

10. **ascended.** See on Ep *1:20-23. Mk +*16:19. Ac +*1:9, 11. 1 T *3:16. **far above.** Ep 1:21. He 4:14. 7:26. 8:1. 9:23, 24. **all heavens.** 2 C 12:2. He 9:24. **that he.** ℐ22A15D, 1 C +15:25. Ep 3:19. Jn *1:16. Ac 2:33. Col 1:19. 2:9. **fill.** or, fulfil. Ep *1:23. Je 23:24. Mt 24:34. Lk +*24:44. Jn 19:24, 28, 36g. Ac 3:18. 13:32, 33. Ro 9:25-30. 15:9-13. +*16:25, 26.

11. **he gave.** ver. *8. 1 C 12:5, 6. **some.** T#447. Je +*3:15 (T#101). *15:19. Ezk *3:17. Mt 5:13, 14. Ac +*26:17, 18. Ro *10:14, 15. 1 C 1:21. 2 C 1:24. 5:20. 1 T 3:1. He *13:17. **apostles.** The term "apostles" meant what we call "missionaries" today (see Watchman Nee, *The Normal Christian Church Life*, p. 17), who minister the word in places where it has not been preached before (Ro 15:20. 1 C 3:10). Ep *2:20. 3:5. 2 S 12:7. Jn 13:16g. Ac 13:2. 14:4, 14. Ro *10:14, 15. 16:7. 1 C 4:9. +*12:28. *15:5-7. 1 Th 2:6. Ju 17. Re 2:2. 18:20. 21:14. **prophets.** Ac 11:27, 28. 15:4, 6, 22, 32, 41. 21:10, 11. 1 C 12:28, 29. 14:29, 32, 37. **evangelists.** Ac +*21:8. 2 T *4:5. **pastors.** 2 Ch *15:3. Je +*20:28. 1 C *12:29. 1 P √5:1-3. **and.** ℐ93A, Ge +1:26. By *Hendiadys*, "teaching pastors," with an emphasis upon *teaching*. Not two classes of persons, but one; implying that a shepherd who did not feed would fail in his duty; and so would a teacher who failed to be a pastor. **teachers.** Ac 11:26. *13:1. 15:35. 18:11, 25. 28:31. Ro *12:7. 1 C 12:28, 29. He *5:12. Ja 3:1.

12. **perfecting.** Lk *22:32. Jn 21:15-17. Ac *9:31. +*11:23. +*14:22, 23. +*20:28. Ro 15:*14, 29. 1 C 12:7. 2 C *7:1. 13:9, 11. Ph 1:25, 26. *3:12-18. Col *1:28. 1 Th 3:10. 5:11-14. He *6:1. *13:17. **the saints.** 2 C +1:1. **the work.** Ac 1:17, 25. *20:24. Ro *12:7. 1 C 4:1, 2. 2 C 3:+6, 8. 4:1. *5:18-20. *6:3. Col 4:17. 1 T 1:12. 2 T *4:5, 11. **the edifying.** ver. 16, *29. Ro *14:19. 15:2. 1 C 14:4, 5, 12, 14, +26. 2 C *12:19. 1 Th 5:11. **the body.** ℐ22A2, Col +2:17. ver. *4. Ep 1:23. 1 C +12:27. Col *1:24.

13. **we all.** See on ver. 3, 5. Je 32:38, 39. Ezk 37:21, 22. Zp *3:9. Zc 14:9. Jn *17:21. Ac 4:32. 1 C 1:10. Ph +*2:1-3. **come.** ℐ171J9, Ac +16:1. **in the unity.**

or, into the unity. ver. 5. Ju +*3. **the knowledge.** Ep 1:17. Is *53:11. Mt +*11:27. Jn 16:3. 17:3, 25, 26. 2 C 4:6. Ph 3:8, 10. Col 2:2g. 2 P 1:1-3. +*3:18. 1 J 5:20. **the Son of God.** Mt +*14:33. +*27:54n. Jn +*5:25. Ac 8:37n. **unto a perfect man.** ver. 12. Ep 2:15. 1 Ch=28:12, 19. Jn 13:15. 1 C 14:20. Col *1:28. He *5:14. **stature.** *or,* age. Lk +2:52. **fulness.** See on Ep 1:23.

14. **no more children.** ver. ●13. Jb 17:9. Is *28:9. Ezk +*33:31, 32. Mt 18:3, 4. Mk 4:16, 17. Lk 6:49. +*8:13. 1 C +*3:1, 2. 14:20. Ga 4:1-3. Col +*1:23. +*2:7. He *5:12-14. **tossed.** T#364. Ge 49:4. Ps ●+*119:63. Pr +*24:21. Mt 11:7. Ac 20:30, 31. Ro *16:17, 18. 1 C +15:58 (T#712). 2 C 11:3, 4. Ga +*1:6, 7. 3:1. Col *2:4-8. 2 Th 2:2-5. 1 T *3:6. *4:6, 7. 2 T 1:15. 2:17, 18. 3:6-9, 13. *4:3. He √13:9. Ja 1:6. 2 P *2:1-3. 1 J *2:19, 26. √4:1. Ju ●+*3, 12. **carried about.** 1 K +*18:21. Mt 11:7. 1 C 12:2. Ga 2:13. Col ●+*1:23. He *13:9. Ja *1:6. 3:4. **every wind.** Pr 24:21. Je 2:36. 2 T 4:3. **of doctrine.** Is √32:6. Mt 15:9. 16:12. Ac +*15:24. Ro +*16:17, 18. 1 C √11:19. 2 C 3:6n. 1 T +*4:1, 16. 2 T +*3:16, 17. 4:3. He *13:9. 2 P √2:1. √3:17. **by the sleight.** Mt *24:11, 24. 2 C *2:17. +*4:2. √11:13-15. 2 Th √2:9, 10. 2 P 2:18. Re 13:11-14. *19:20. **cunning craftiness.** Ge 3:1. 27:16. Jsh 9:4. Jb 15:5. Mt 26:4. Mk 14:1. Lk 20:23. 1 C 3:19. 2 C +*4:2. 11:3. 2 P √3:16, 17. **lie in wait.** Ps 10:9. 59:3. Mi 7:2. Ac 23:21. **to deceive.** Ep 6:11. Ezk 13:10. 14:10n. Ac 20:30. Ro 16:18. 2 C √11:13. Col 2:8. 1 T 1:7. 4:2. √6:3, 4. 2 T 3:6, 7, 13. √4:3. T 1:10, 11. 2 P √2:1, 18. 2 J 7.

15. **But.** ver. 25. Zc *8:16. 2 C +*4:2. 8:8. **speaking the truth.** *or,* being sincere. or, dealing truly. ver. 25. Jg 16:15. Ps 32:2. Ml=2:6. Jn 1:47. Ro *12:9. 2 C +*4:2. Ja 2:15, 16. 1 P *1:22. 1 J +3:18. **in love.** Jn *13:34, 35. 1 C *13:2. **may grow.** Ep 2:21. Ho 14:5-7. Ml 4:2. Ro +*8:29. 1 P √2:2. 2 P √3:18. 1 J 2:14. **which.** Ep 1:22. 5:23. Col +*1:18, 19. 2:19. **the head.** ℐ22A3B, Ep +1:22. Ep +1:22.

16. **whom.** See on ver. 12. Jn *15:5. **body.** ℐ22A2, Col +2:17. **fitly.** Jb 10:10, 11. Ps 139:15, 16. ⋅SS 7:1. 1 C *12:12-28. Col 2:19. **supplieth.** ℐ181E, Ge +3:24. **according.** ver. 7. **the effectual.** Ep 3:7. 1 Th √2:13. **edifying.** ver. 12, 15, 29. Ep 1:4. *3:17. 1 C 8:1. *13:4-9, 13. 14:1, +26. Ga *5:6, 13, 14, 22. Ph 1:9. Col 2:2. 1 Th 1:3. 3:12. 4:9, 10. 2 Th 1:3. 1 T 1:5. 1 P *1:22. 1 J 4:16.

17. **I say.** 1 C 1:12. 15:50. 2 C 9:6. Ga 3:17. Col 2:4. **testify.** Ne 9:29, 30. 13:15. Je 42:19. Ac 2:40. 18:5. 20:21, 26. 26:22. Ga 5:3. 1 Th 2:11. +4:6. **in the.** 1 Th 4:1, 2. 1 T 5:21. 6:13. 2 T 4:1. **that ye.** ver. 1, *22. Ep *2:1-3. *5:3-8. Ro 1:23-32. 1 C +*6:9-11. Ga *5:19-21. Col 3:5-8. 1 P *4:3, 4. **walk not.** 1 Th 4:5. **in the vanity.** Ps 94:8-11. Je +*2:5. 10:3. Ac 14:15. Ro *1:21. Col 2:18. 1 P 1:18. 2 P 2:18.

18. **the understanding.** Ep ●1:18. Ps 74:20. 115:4-8. Is *44:18-20. 46:5-8. Ac *17:30. +*26:17, 18. Ro *1:21-23, 28. 1 C 1:21. +*2:14. 2 C +*3:14. √4:4, 5. Ga 4:8. Col 1:21g. 1 Th 4:5. 2 Th *1:8, 9. √2:9-12. **darkened.** Pr *5:8, 11. 6:12. Mt +*6:23. Jn *3:19. Ro 11:10. Col 1:13. 1 Th 5:4, 5. 1 J 1:5, 6. 2:8, 9, 11. **alienated.** Ep 2:1, +12. Ge 2:17. +*6:5. Ro *8:7, 8. Ga 4:8. Col 1:21. 1 Th 4:5. Ja *4:4. **from the life.** Jn 1:3, 4. **through the ignorance.** Ac +*17:30. 2 P 3:5. **because.** Ro 1:21. 2:19. 1 J 2:11. **blindness.** *or,*

hardness. Da *5:20. Mt +*13:15. Mk +3:5. Jn 12:40. Ro 11:25mg.

19. **past**. Pr 23:35. 1 T *4:2. **given themselves over**. ver. 17. 1 K 21:25. Ro +*1:24-26, 28. 1 P 4:3. **lascivious-ness**. The Greek word refers to the conduct of one who is morally unprincipled, who excites disgust, by unbridled lust, excess, licentiousness, wantonness, out-rageousness, shamelessness, insolence. Used of glut-tony and venery (Ju 4), carnality, lasciviousness (2 C 12:21. Ga 5:19. Ep 4:19. 2 P 2:7). Used in the plural (Ro 13:13) of wanton acts or manners, as filthy words, indecent bodily movements, unchaste handling of males and females (Thayer, *Lexicon*, p. 79, 80). Trench argues the word encompasses more than sexual devi-ancy, that it depicts "one who acknowledges no re-straints, who dares whatsoever his caprice and wanton petulance may suggest" (*Synonyms*, Sec. 16, p. 56). ✻S#766g: Mk +*7:22. Ro 13:13 (wantonness). 2 C 12:21. Ga 5:19. Ep 4:19. 1 P 4:3. 2 P 2:7, 18. Ju 4. **uncleanness**. Ep 5:3. **with greediness**. Ep 5:3. Jb *15:16. Is 56:11. 2 P 2:12-14, 22. Ju 11. Re 17:1-6. 18:3.

20. **not so learned**. Mk +*11:29. Lk +*24:47. Jn *6:45. Ro 6:1, 2. 2 C √5:14, 15. T √2:11-14. 1 J *2:27.

21. **If**. ſ184A, 1 C +15:2. **heard**. Ep 1:13. Mt 17:5. Lk 10:16. Jn +1:14. √10:27. Ac *3:22, 23. Ro 10:14. Col 1:6. He 3:7, 8. **been taught**. Col +*2:7. **as the truth**. ver. 24. Ep 1:13. Ps 45:4. *85:10, 11. Jn *1:17. 3:21. √14:6, 17. *16:13, 14. 2 C 1:20. 11:10. 1 J 1:6. √5:10-12, 20.

22. **ye**. ver. 25. 1 S 1:14. Jb 22:23. Ezk 18:30-32. Col 2:11. *3:8, 9. He *12:1. Ja *1:21. 1 P *2:1, 2. **former**. ver. 17. Ep *2:3. Ga 1:13. Col 3:7. 1 P 1:18. 4:3. 2 P 2:7. **conversation**. Ja +3:13. **the old**. ſ12lll, Ge +3:7. Ro *6:6. Col *3:9. **corrupt**. Ro 8:21. 1 T 6:5. **deceitful lusts**. Pr 11:18. Je 49:16. Ob 3. Ro 7:11. 2 Th 2:10. 1 T +*6:9. T 3:3. He +*3:13. Ja 1:26. 2 P 2:13.

23. **be**. Ep 2:10. Ps +*51:10. Ezk 11:19. 18:31. 36:26. Ro +*12:2. Col *3:10, 12. T √3:5. **spirit**. Gr. *pneuma*, ſ121A1, Ro +8:1n. ſ144B, Dt +33:19. ſ121A2, Ps +51:10. Ro 8:6. 1 P 1:13. **mind**. Ro 7:25.

24. **put on**. Ep 6:11. Jb 29:14. Is 52:1. 59:17. Ro *13:12, +14. 1 C *15:53. Ga *3:27. Col *3:10-14. **new man**. Ep 2:15. Ro +*6:4. 2 C 4:16. √5:17. Col 3:10. 1 P √2:2. **after God**. Ge +*1:26, 27. Ro +*8:27. 2 C *3:18. Col *3:10. 1 J √3:2. **created**. See on Ep *2:10. 3:9. Ga *6:15. **righteousness**. Ep 5:9. Ps *45:6, 7. Lk 1:75. Ro +*8:29. 1 Th 2:10. T √2:14. He +*1:8, 9. √12:14. 1 J *3:3. **true holiness**. or, holiness of truth. Jn 17:17. T 1:8g. *2:11, 12.

25. **putting away lying**. ver. 22. Ge +*27:19. Ex +*20:16. Le +*19:11, 13. 1 K 13:18. Ps 52:3. 119:29. Pr *6:17. *12:19, 22. 21:6. Is 9:15. 59:3, 4. 63:8. Je 9:3-5. Ho 4:2. Mt 19:19. Mk 10:19. Jn √8:44. Ac √5:3, 4. Col *3:9. 1 T 1:10. 4:2. T √1:2, 12. Re +*21:8. *22:15. **speak**. ver. 15. Ps *15:2. Pr 8:7. 12:17. Zc 8:16, 19. 2 C 7:14. Col *3:9. **members**. Ep +*5:30. Ro +*12:5. 1 C 10:17. 12:12-27.

26. **Be ye angry**. ver. 31, 32. Ex 11:8. 32:21, 22. Nu 20:10-13, 24. 25:7-11. Ne *5:6-13. Ps 4:4. *37:8. 106:30-33. Pr +*14:29. *19:11. 25:23. Ec *7:9. Mt 5:22. Mk *3:5. *10:14. Ro 12:19-21. Ja √1:19, 20. **let**. Dt 24:15.

27. **Neither give place**. T#18. Ep +*5:11. 6:11-13, 16. 2 S +*12:14. Ps 50:16. Mt +15:14 (T#477). Mk

+*1:34. Lk +12:37 (T#738). Ac *5:3. 2 C √2:10, 11. 11:14. Ga √2:5. Ja +*4:7. 1 P *5:8, 9. 2 J +*10, 11. Ju +*3.

28. **him that stole**. Ex +*20:15, 17. 21:16. Pr +30:9 (T#1712). Je 7:9. Ho 4:2. Zc 5:3. Jn 12:6. 1 C +*6:10, 11. **steal no more**. T#713. Ex 20:15. Le 19:11. Jb 34:32. Pr √28:13. Lk 3:8, 10-14. 19:8. 1 P 4:15. **labor**. Pr 13:11. 14:23. Ac 20:34, 35. 1 Th *4:11, 12. 2 Th *3:6-8, 11, 12. T 3:8, 14. **his hands**. Pr 31:19. **good**. Ga *6:10. **that he**. Pr 21:26. Lk 3:11. 21:1-4. Jn 13:29. 2 C 8:2, 12. **give**. or, distribute. Lk +3:11. √19:7, 8. Ac +*20:35. Ro 12:12, 13. 1 C 16:2. 9:13, 14. 2 C 9:12-15. Ga *6:6, 7. 1 T √6:17, 18. He 13:16. **that needeth**. 1 J 3:17g.

29. **no corrupt communication**. Ep *5:3, 4. Ps 5:9. 52:2. *73:7-9. Mt 7:17, 18. +*12:33-37. 13:48. Lk 6:43g. Ro 3:13, 14. 1 C 15:32, 33. Col *3:8, 9. √4:6. Ja *3:2-8. 2 P 2:18. Ju 13-16. Re 13:5, 6. **out of**. Mt 12:34. Lk 6:45. Col 3:8. **but**. ſ63C, Ge +25:32. Not observing the *Ellipsis*, the word "if" was omitted to make sense. With the word "if" retained, the *Ellipsis* is properly supplied thus: "Let no corrupt communica-tion proceed out of your mouth, but, if any (speech be) good to the use of edifying, (let it be spoken) that it may minister grace unto the hearers." **that which**. Dt *6:6-9. Ps *37:30, 31. 45:2. 71:17, 18, 24. 78:4, 5. Pr 10:31, 32. 12:13. *15:2, 4, 7, *23. 16:21. *25:11, 12. Is *50:4. Ml √3:16-18. Lk 4:22. 1 C 14:19. Col √3:16, 17. √4:6. 1 Th *5:11. **to the use of edifying**. or, to edify profitably. ſ29, Ex +19:6. The meaning by the figure *Antiptosis* is "that which is good for edify-ing use." See on ver. 12, 16. Jb 4:3, 4. 1 C +14:26. 1 Th *5:11. T 3:14g. **minister grace**. Pr 22:11. Ec 10:12. Mt *5:16. 1 C +1:4. Col *3:16. √4:6. 1 P 2:12. 3:1.

30. **And**. Mk +*3:5. 1 Th 5:19. **grieve**. The linguistic and semantic category of this verb unequivocally asserts and establishes the personality of the Holy Spirit: ask "does the verb belong to the category 'animate' or 'inanimate,' 'personal' or 'nonpersonal'?" Clearly only animate persons can be grieved. For related notes es-tablishing the Holy Spirit as a person, see Mt 12:32n; Lk 3:22n; Jn 16:13n, 14n. T#348. Ge *6:3, 6. Jg 10:16. Ps 78:40. *95:10. Is *7:13. 43:24. +*63:10. Ezk 16:43. Mt 12:31, 32. Mk 3:5. Jn +3:19 (T#309). Ac *7:51. 1 Th *5:19. He *3:10, 17. 10:28, 29. **Spirit**. Gr. *pneuma*, Mt +3:16. Mt +12:32. **whereby**. See on Ep +*1:13. **ye**. Je 33:21n. Ga ●2:20n. **sealed**. T#347-5, 844. Ep +*1:13. Ge 17:11. Ezk +*9:4. Jn +*3:33. *6:27. Ro 4:11. 5:5. 2 C +*1:22 (T#517). 5:5. 2 T +*2:19. **unto the day**. Is *35:4, 10. +*51:11. Ro 8:12-14. 1 C √1:8. Ga 3:3. 5:2-4. 6:7-9. 1 Th +*4:16. He +*3:14. 6:11, 12. 10:23, 35. **of redemption**. Ep √1:+7, 14. Ps √111:9. Is +*51:11. Ho *13:14. Lk +*21:28. Ro √8:11, 23. 1 C 1:30. *15:54. Ph 3:20, 21.

31. **bitterness**. Ps 64:3. Ac 8:23g. Ro 3:14. Col *3:8, 19. He +*12:15g. Ja 3:14, 15. **and**. ſ148, Ge +8:22. **wrath**. Gr. *thumon*, S#2372g: Lk 4:28. Ac 19:28. Ro 2:8 (indignation). 2 C 12:20 (wraths). Ga 5:20. Ep 4:31. Col 3:8. He 11:27. Re 12:12. 14:8, 10, 19. 15:1, 7. 16:1, 19. 18:3. 19:15. stirring emotions, then explosions (A. T. Robertson, *Word Pictures*, vol. 4, p. 312). ver. 26. Pr 14:17. 19:12. Ec 7:9. Ro 2:8. 2 C 12:20. Ga 5:20. Col *3:8. 2 T 2:23. T 1:7. Ja √1:19. *3:14-18. *4:1, 2. **anger**. Gr. *orgee*, S#3709g. Vine notes that *orgee* "suggests a more settled or abiding condition

of mind, frequently with a view to taking revenge. *Orgee* is less sudden in its rise than *thumos*, but more lasting in its nature. *Thumos* expresses more the inward feeling, *orgee* the more active emotion" (*Expository Dictionary*, vol 1, pp. 55, 56). Mt 3:7 (wrath). Mk 3:5. Lk 3:7. 21:23. Jn 3:36. Ro 1:18. 2:5, 5, 8. 3:5 (vengeance). 4:15. 5:9. 9:22, 22. 12:19. 13:4, 5. Ep 2:3. 4:31. 5:6. Col 3:6 (wrath), 8 (anger). 1 Th 1:10. 2:16. 5:9. 1 T 2:8. He 3:11. 4:3. Ja 1:19, 20. Re 6:16, 17. 11:18. 14:10. 16:19. 19:15. clamor. 2 S 19:43. 20:1, 2. Pr 29:9, 22. Mt 25:6g. Lk 1:42g. Ac 19:28, 29. 21:30. 22:22, 23. 1 T 3:3. 6:4, 5. evil speaking. Le *19:16. 2 S 19:27. Ps *15:3. 50:20. 101:5. 140:11. Pr *6:19. 10:18. 18:8. 25:23. 26:20. Je 6:28. 9:4. Mt 15:19. Mk 7:22. Ro +*1:29, 30. Col 3:8. 1 T 3:11. 5:13. 6:4. 2 T 3:3. T 2:3. *3:2. Ja *4:11. 1 P *2:1. 2 P *2:10, 11. Ju *8-10. Re *12:10. put away. *f*180D, Ex +20:18. with. Ge 4:8. 27:41. 37:4, 21. Le +*19:17, 18. 2 S 13:22. Pr 10:12. 26:24, 25. Ec 7:9. Ro +*1:29. 1 C 5:8. 14:20. Col *3:8. T 3:3. 1 P 2:1. 1 J 3:12, 15.

32. **kind.** Ru 2:20. Ps 112:4, 5, 9. Pr 19:22. Is 57:1mg. Lk +*6:35. Ac 28:2. Ro *12:10. 1 C +*13:4. 2 C 2:10. 6:6. Col *3:12, 13. 1 P 2:3g. 2 P *1:7. **tenderhearted.** *f*41. Ge +10:1. Ps 145:9. Pr 12:10. Lk 1:78. Ja *5:11. 1 P *3:8. **forgiving.** T#203. Ep *5:1. Ge 50:17, 18. Pr +16:7 (T#737). Mt *6:+12 (T#539), +14, 15. +11:29 (T#62). *18:21-35. Mk *11:25, 26. Lk *6:37. *11:4. *17:3, 4. Ro 12:20, 21. 2 C 2:7, 10. Col *3:12, 13. 1 P *3:8, 9. 1 J √1:9. +2:12 (T#583). **as God.** Is *44:22. **for.** Ge=39:5. Nu=14:17-20. **hath forgiven.** Lk +7:42.

EPHESIANS 5

The apostle exhorts the Ephesians to imitate the love of God in Christ, 1, 2, to avoid all uncleanness, covetousness, and improper discourse, which draw down the wrath of God upon "the children of disobedience," 3-6; to have "no fellowship with the unfruitful works of darkness;" but, as the "children of light," to reprove them, 7-14; to walk with wisdom and circumspection, 15-17; not to seek exhilaration by excess of wine, but to "be filled with the Spirit," speaking and singing Psalms and praises to God, 18-20; and to submit to one another, in the several relations of life, 21. The duties of wives and husbands, enforced and illustrated by the mutual love of Christ and his church, 22-33.

1. **followers.** Ep √4:32. Le 11:45. Mt *5:7, 45, 48. Lk +*6:35, 36. Jn 10:27. 1 C +4:16. 1 P 1:15, 16. 2:21. 3:13. 1 J 4:11. **as.** Je 31:20. Ho 1:10. Mt *5:45. Jn √1:12. Col *3:12. 1 J √3:1, 2.

2. **walk.** Ep *3:17. *4:2, 15, 16. Jn *13:34. Ro *14:15. 1 C *16:14. Col *3:14. 1 Th *4:9. 1 T *4:12. 1 P *4:8. 1 J *3:11, 12, 23. *4:20, 21. **as Christ.** ver. *25, 29. Ep *3:19. Mt *20:28. Jn *15:12, 13. Ro 14:15. 2 C √5:14, 15. √8:9. Ga *1:4. √2:20. 1 T √2:6. T √2:14. He *7:25-27. *9:14, 26. 10:10, 11. 1 P *2:21-24. 1 J *3:16. Re +*1:5. *5:9. **loved us.** T#837. Ps 45:11. SS 2:4, 6. 4:9. 7:10. Mt +*28:19n. Jn 13:1, 34. 14:21. *15:9, 12. Ro *8:37. 1 J ◐+*4:16. Re +*1:5. 3:9. **given himself.** ver. 25. Ro +4:25. **an offering.** Le +=23:12 (burnt offering). He 7:27. 9:14. 10:10, 12. **a sacrifice.** Le=7:11 (peace offering). Ro *8:3mg. 1 C *5:7. He 9:23. *10:12. **for a.** Ge +*8:21. Ex 29:18, 25, 41. Le 1:*9, 13, 17. 3:16. Ezk 16:19. 20:41. Am 5:21. 2 C *2:15. Ph 4:18. **savor.** *f*22C15, Ge +8:21.

3. **fornication.** ver. 5. Ep 4:19, 20. Nu 25:1. Dt 23:17, 18. Mt 15:19. Mk +*7:21. Ac +√15:20. Ro +*1:29. 6:13. 1 C 5:10, 11. +*6:9, 10, 13, 18. 10:8. 2 C 12:21. Ga *5:19-21. Col *3:5. 1 Th *4:3, 7. He 12:16. +*13:4. 2 P 2:10. Re 2:14, 21. 9:21. +*21:8. *22:15. **all uncleanness.** Ep 4:19. Mt 23:27. 1 C +5:10. **covetousness.** ver. 5. Ex +*18:21. +*20:17. Jsh 7:21. 1 S 8:3. Ps +*10:3. *119:36. Pr *28:16. Je 6:13. 8:10. 22:17. Ezk +*33:31. Mi 2:2. Mk +*7:22. Lk +*12:15. 16:14. Ac 20:33. 1 C +*6:10. Col *3:5. 1 T 3:3. √6:6-11. 2 T 3:2. T 1:7, 11. He +*13:5. 1 P *5:2. 2 P 2:3, 14. **named.** ver. 12. Ex 23:13. Ps +*16:4. 1 C 5:1. **as.** Ro 16:2. Ph *1:27. 1 T 2:10. T 2:3. **saints.** 2 C 1:1.

4. **Neither.** Is +*58:13n. **filthiness.** Ep 4:29. Pr 12:23. 15:2. Mt +*12:34-37. Mk +*7:22. Col *3:8. Ja 3:4-8. 2 P 2:7, 18. Ju 10, 13, 15. **foolish talking.** Ec 10:13. Is 58:13n. **nor jesting.** Pr 10:23. 26:19. Is 58:13n. Ezk +*33:31mg. Ro 12:3. 1 Th 5:8. 2 T 1:7n. T 2:4, 6, 12. 1 P 5:8. **convenient.** Ro +*1:28. Col 3:18. Phm 8. **but.** ver. 19, 20. Ep 1:16. Ps 33:1. *92:1. *107:21, 22. Da +*6:10. Jn 6:23. 2 C 1:11. 9:15. Ph √4:6. Col *3:15-17. 1 Th 3:9. *5:18. He √13:15.

5. **this.** SS 5:19, 21. 1 C +*6:9, 10. **that no.** See on ver. 3. 1 C +*6:9, 10. Ga *5:21. Re +*21:8. **whoremonger.** 1 C +5:10. He +*13:4. Re *22:15. **covetous man.** T#138. ver. +*3. Ps +*10:3. Is *56:11mg. 57:17. Mi 2:2, 3. Hab 2:9. 1 C 5:11. *6:10. Ju 11. **who is.** Ezk +*14:3. Ga *5:21. Col *3:5. 1 T *6:10, 17. Re +*21:8. *22:15. **inheritance.** Ep +*1:11n. 1 C +*15:50n. **kingdom.** Mt +*13:41-43. Ro 14:17. 2 T +*4:1. 2 P 1:11. Re +*11:15. **and.** *f*93A, Ge +1:26. By Hendiadys, "the kingdom of Christ, yes—of Christ who is truly God" (B667).

6. **no.** Je 29:8, 9, 31. Ezk 13:10-16. Mi 3:5. Mt 24:4, 24. Mk 13:5, 22. Ga 6:7, 8. Col 2:4, 8, 18. 2 Th 2:3, 10-12. Ja 1:16. 1 J *4:1. **vain words.** 2 K 18:20. Je 23:14-16. Col 2:8. **cometh.** Nu 32:13, 14. Jsh 22:17, 18. Ps 78:31. Mt 3:7. Ro +*1:18. Col 3:6. **wrath.** *f*121C1C, Ps +79:6. **children.** *f*108B, 1 S +20:31. See on Ep 2:2, 3. **disobedience.** *or*, unbelief. He 3:19. 1 P 2:8g.

7. **Be not.** ver. *11. Nu *16:26. Ps 50:18. Pr *1:10-17. *9:6. *13:20. 1 T *5:22. Re *18:4. **partakers.** Ep 3:6.

8. **ye were.** Ep *2:11, 12. +*4:18. 6:12. Ps 74:20. Is 9:2. 42:16. 60:2. Je 13:16. Mt 4:16. Lk 1:79. Ac *17:30. +*26:18. Ro 1:21. 2:19. 2 C 6:14. Col 1:13. T 3:3. 1 P *2:9. 1 J 2:8. **darkness.** *f*121N2, Ge +34:29. Ge +*6:5. Is +*9:2. Jn *3:19. **but.** Is 42:6, 7. 49:6, 9. 60:1, 3, 19, 20. Jn 1:4, 5, 9. *8:12. *12:46. 1 C 1:30. 2 C 3:18. *4:6. 1 Th *5:4-8. 1 J 2:9-11. **light.** *f*121N2, Ge +34:09. **walk.** ver. 2. Is 2:5. Lk *16:8. Jn *12:35, 36. Ga 5:25. 1 P *2:9-11. 1 J *1:7.

9. **the fruit.** Ro +7:4. See on Ga +*5:22, 23. **Spirit.** Gr. *pneuma*, Mt +3:16. **is.** *f*63B, Ge +25:28. *or*, consists. **goodness.** Ps 16:2, 3. Ro 2:4. +*15:14. 2 C 1:12, 13. 1 P 2:28. 3 J 11. **righteousness.** Ep 4:24. Ph 1:11. 1 T 6:11. T 2:12. He +*1:8. 11:33. 1 P *2:24. 1 J 2:29. 3:9, 10. **truth.** Ep 4:15, 25. 6:14. Jn 1:47.

10. **Proving.** 1 S 17:39. Ro +2:18. *12:1, 2. Ph *1:10. 1 Th 2:4. *5:21. **acceptable.** Ps *19:14. Pr *21:3. Is 58:5. Je 6:20. Ro +*14:18. Ph 4:18. Col +*1:10. 3:20. 1 T 2:3. *5:4. He 12:28. 1 P 2:5, 20.

11. **no fellowship.** ver. *7. Ge 49:5-7. 2 Ch +*19:2. Ps +*1:1, 2. *26:4, 5. 94:20, 21. +*119:63. Pr *4:14,

15. 9:6. Je +*10:2. 15:17. *16:8. Mt +*15:14. Ro *16:17. 1 C *5:9-11. *10:20, 21. 2 C √6:14-18. 2 Th *3:6, 14. 1 T *6:5. 2 T *3:5. 2 J *10, *11. Re *18:4. **unfruitful.** Pr 1:31. Is 3:10, 11. Ro *6:21. Ga *6:8. 2 P +*1:8. **works.** Ep 4:22. Jb *24:13-17. Jn *3:19-21. Ro *1:22-32. +*13:12. 1 Th 5:7. **darkness.** T#167. Jb 24:14-17. Pr 7:6-9. Is +*9:2. 29:15. Ezk 8:12. Mt +*6:23. Jn *3:19. **reprove.** Ge 20:9, 16. Le ◑5:1. +√19:17. Ne +*13:11. Ps +*141:5. Pr 9:7, 8. 13:18. 15:12. *19:25. *25:12. 28:4. *29:1, ◑24. Is 29:21. Mt *18:15, +*31. Lk 3:19. 1 T +*5:20. 2 T *4:2. T 2:15.

12. **a shame.** ver. 3. 2 S 13:9. Ezk 16:25. 23:14-20. Ro 1:24-27. Ph 3:19. 1 P 4:3. **in secret.** 2 S 12:12. Pr 9:17. Ec 12:14. Je 23:24. Ezk 8:12, 14, 16. Lk 12:1, 2. Ro 2:16. Re 20:12.

13. **reproved.** *or*, discovered. La 2:14. Ho 2:10. 7:1. **for.** Mi 7:9. Jn *3:20, 21. 1 C 4:5. He 4:13.

14. **he.** *or*, it. Ep +4:8. **Awake.** Pr 6:9. SS 2:10. Is 51:17. 52:1. *60:1. Ml 4:2. Ro 13:+11, 12. 1 C 15:34. 1 Th 5:6. 2 T 2:26mg. **arise.** Ep *2:5. Is +*26:19n. 51:17. Ezk 37:4-10. Mk 10:49. Lk 22:46. Jn 5:8, 25-29. 11:43, 44. Ro *6:4, 5, 13. Col 3:1. **from the dead.** 1 T 5:6. Re 3:1, 2. **Christ.** Lk 1:78, 79. Jn *8:12. 9:5. Ac 13:47. 2 C 4:6. 2 T 1:10. **shall give.** Lk 15:32. Jn *5:40. Ph 3:10, 11.

15. **See.** ver. *33. Mt 8:4. 27:4, 24. 1 Th *5:15. He 12:25. 1 P *1:22. Re *19:10. **walk.** Ex *23:13. Pr *4:23-27. 15:21. Mt +*10:16. 1 C 14:20. Ph +*1:27. Col +*1:9, 10. *4:5. **circumspectly.** Ac 26:5g. 1 Th +*5:22. **not.** 1 S +*25:17, 25, 36, 37. 2 S *24:10. Jb *2:10. Ps 73:22. Pr *14:8, 21. Mt *25:2. Lk *24:25. Ga *3:1, 3. 1 T √6:9. Ja *3:13. **as wise.** 2 K +*5:13. Mt 10:16. Ph 2:15.

16. **Redeeming.** Ps 89:47. *90:12. Pr 22:29. Ec *9:10. Da 2:8. Jn *9:4. Ac 20:17-19, 23, 24. Ro +*13:11. Ga *6:10. Col *4:5. **the days.** ƒ121P4, Dt +4:32. Ep 6:*13, 15. Ps 37:19. Ec 11:2. *12:1. Am 5:13. Jn *12:35. Ac 11:28, 29. 1 C *7:26, 29-31. Ga 1:4.

17. **be.** See on ver. 15. Mt 25:1, 2. Col *4:5. **understanding.** Dt *4:6. 1 K 3:9-12. 1 Ch +*12:32. Jb *28:28. Ps *111:10. *119:27. Pr *2:5. 14:8. 23:23. Je 4:22. Jn +*7:17. Ro +*12:2. 2 C +10:12. Col *1:9. 1 Th *4:1-3. +*5:18. 1 P 4:2. **the will.** Ac 21:14. +22:14.

18. **be not drunk.** T#366. Ge +*9:21. 19:32-35. Dt *21:20, 21. Ps 69:12. Pr +*20:1. +*22:3. *23:20, 21, 29-35. Is *5:11-13, 22. 28:1, 7. Je 35:2, 5, 6, *8, 13, *14. Am 4:1. Mt *24:48-51. Lk 1:15. 12:45. +*21:34. Ro √13:13. +14:21 (T#368). 1 C *5:11. +√6:10. +9:25 (T#721). 11:21. Ga *5:21. Ph +3:19 (T#199). 1 Th 5:7. 1 T ◑3:8. ◑5:23. **wine.** Le=10:8, 9. Is 24:9. **excess.** Pr 7:11. Mt *23:25. Lk 15:13. T 1:6. 1 P √4:3, 4. **but.** This marks the sentence as another instance of the balanced sentence (ver. 17. Lk +*11:4n), where the command of the first clause is used to enhance the emphasis of the last clause. Ps 63:3-5. SS 1:4. *7:9. Is 25:6. 55:1. Zc 9:15-17. Lk *11:13. Ac *2:13-18. 11:24. Ga *5:22-25. **be filled.** There is a sermon in the mood, tense, voice and number of this verb: it is imperative mood, indicating a command; it is present tense, which in Greek represents aspect denoting continuous action—we are to be constantly or continuously filled; it is passive voice, indicating we are to allow this to be done to us; it is plural in number, meaning it applies to all believers. There is much needed corrective doctrinal instruction in the grammatical cases which this passive verb governs:

the Dative case designates the filler, here, the Holy Spirit, necessitating an improvement in the English rendering to show we are filled not *with* but BY the Spirit; the Genitive case denotes what the vessel is filled with. When the verb "fill" is in the active voice, a third case, the Accusative, designates the vessel or whatever is filled. Note that the Holy Spirit is never said to fill us with Himself, but with gifts specified in the immediate context; here, gifts other than wine, gifts specified by the participles in the following verses, speaking (in psalms, hymns, and spiritual songs), singing, giving thanks, and submitting. The filling of the Holy Spirit is always a reference to a filling with His gifts for service. He does not fill us with Himself, but with His gifts. Attention to these details will show how greatly mistaken are the popular conceptions of the Holy Spirit and His work. These mistaken conceptions, though taught with great sincerity, frequently supported by an appeal to misconstrued or misinterpreted experience, are in great error. Such mistaken notions lack Biblical authority because they are not based upon an accurate understanding of Scripture (Is +*8:20n. Mk √12:24. 2 T √2:15). Lk 1:15. Ac +2:4. **with the.** 1 S 10:6. Jn 3:34. **Spirit.** Gr. *pneuma*, Mt +3:16. ƒ121A1, Jn +3:34. Not with the Person of the Holy Spirit surely! but with His operations: i.e., with the gifts which come through the ministry of the Word; as is clear from Col 3:16, where this effect is produced by the same cause: occupation of the heart with God—the Word of Christ dwelling richly within us (B540).

19. **Speaking.** T#747. Le 18:30. Jg 5:12. 1 K 8:22. Ps 89:7. Ml +*3:16. Mt *26:30. Col +3:16 (T#529). He 12:28, 29. +13:15 (T#528). 1 P *4:10, 11. 2 J +*10. **to yourselves.** Ac 16:25. Ro +12:5. 1 C *14:26. Col *3:16. Ja 5:13. 1 P √4:10, 11. **psalms.** ƒ173, Ge +27:44. Psalms, *psalmoi*, from *psallo*, to *touch*, or *play* on a musical instrument, properly denotes such *sacred songs* or poems as are sung to stringed instruments, and may here refer to those of David; Alford states these are not to be confined to Old Testament hymns (1 C 14:26. Ja 5:13): the word properly signified those sacred songs which were performed with musical accompaniment; *hymns, umnoi*, from *udo*, to *sing*, *celebrate, praise*, signifies *songs* in honor of God; and *songs, odai*, from *asido*, to *sing*, denotes any regular poetic composition adapted to singing, and is here restricted to those which are *spiritual*. 1 Ch 15:22. *16:42n. Ps 95:2. 105:2. Mt *26:30. 1 C 14:26. **hymns.** Ac +16:25. **spiritual.** Ro +1:11g. **songs.** 1 Ch=6:32. =25:7. Col *3:16. Re 5:9. 14:3. 15:3. **singing.** Col 3:16. **making melody.** Ps 47:7, 8. 57:7, 8. 62:8. 86:12. 105:3. 147:7. Is 65:14. Mt 15:8. Jn 4:23, 24. Ja +5:13.

20. **thanks.** See on ver. 4. Jb *1:21. Ps *34:1. Is *63:7. Ac *5:41. 1 C 1:4. Ph *1:3. *4:6. Col 1:11, 12. 2:7. √3:17. 4:2. 1 Th 1:2. 3:9. +*5:18. 2 Th *1:3. *2:13. 1 T +*2:1. **unto God.** 1 C 15:24. Ja 1:27. **in the name.** Jn *14:13, 14. +*15:16. *16:23-26. Ac +2:21. Col *3:17. He *13:15. 1 P *2:5. 4:11.

21. **submitting.** ver. 22, 24. Ge 16:9. 1 Ch 29:24. Ro 13:1-5. 1 C *16:16. Ph +*2:3. 1 T 2:11. +3:4. He +*13:17. 1 P 2:13. +*5:5g. **one to another.** Ro +12:5. **in the fear of God.** 2 Ch 19:7. Ne 5:9, 15. Pr 24:21. 2 C 5:11. *7:1. 1 P *2:13-17.

22. **submit.** ver. 24. Ge *3:16. Est 1:16-18, 20. 1 C +11:3. +*14:34n. Col *3:18, etc. 1 T 2:11, 12. T *2:4, 5. 1 P *3:1-6. **as.** Ep 6:5. Col 3:22, 23.

23. **husband.** See on 1 C 11:3-10. **the head.** 1 C √11:3, 8, 9. *14:34n. 1 T 2:11. **even.** Ep 1:+22, 23. 4:15. Col +*1:18. **Christ is.** Col 2:10. **the church.** Note carefully that the church is not said here to be the head of anyone or anything, and no one is said to be subject to the church. All the members are directly responsible to the head of the church, who is Christ alone. Mt +*24:45. Ac +*17:11. 2 C +√1:24. Ga *1:8n. He ◐*13:7. 2 P *1:20n. **he.** ver. 25, 26. Ac +*20:28. 1 C 6:13. 1 Th 1:10. Re *5:9. **the savior.** 2 T +1:10. **the body.** Ep +1:23.

24. **in every thing.** ver. 33. Ex 23:13. 29:35. Col 3:20, 22. T 2:7, 9.

25. **love.** ver. 28, 33. Ge +*2:24. 24:67. 2 S 12:3. Pr 5:18, 19. Col *3:19. 1 P *3:7. **loved.** ver. +*2, 29. Mt 20:28. Lk 22:19, 20. Jn 6:51. Ac +*20:28. Ga 1:4. √2:20. 1 T √2:6. 1 P 1:18-21. Re +*1:5. *5:9. **gave himself.** ver. 2. Ro +4:25. 1 T *2:5, 6. T 2:14.

26. **he.** Jn *17:17-19. Ac +*26:18. 1 C *6:11. T *2:14. He *9:14. *10:10. 1 P *1:2. Ju *1. **and cleanse.** T 2:14g. 2 P +1:9. 1 J *1:7. **with the washing.** Gr. *loutron*, *S#3067g, only here and T 3:5g. Ex=29:4. =30:18. Ezk 16:9. *36:25. Zc 13:1. Jn *3:5. Ac +*22:16. 1 C +*6:11. T *3:5-7. He +*10:22. 1 P *3:21. 1 J *5:6. Re 7:14. **by the word.** Ep 6:17. Ps √119:9. Jn *15:3. 17:17. Ro +10:8, 9. He 6:5. Ja *1:18. 1 P *1:22, 23.

27. **present it.** Ep 1:4. Ge 24:67. Nu=3:6. 2 C *4:14. *11:2. Col *1:22, 28. Ju *24. **glorious.** 2 Ch=5:1. Ps 45:13. *87:3. Is *60:15-20. *62:3. Je 33:9. Jn 17:22. 2 Th 1:10. He *12:22-24. Re *7:9-17. 19:7, 8. *21:10-26. **not having spot.** SS *4:7. 5:2. 6:9. He *9:14. 1 P *1:19. 2 P ◐2:13. *3:14. **but.** ꟷ15G, Ge +35:3. Ep +*1:4. 2 C *11:2. Col *1:22, 28. 1 Th √5:23. Ju √24. Re *21:10, 11, 27.

28. **ought men.** ver. 25, 33. **as.** ver. 31, 33. Ge 2:21-24. Mt 19:5.

29. **hated.** ver. 31. Pr 11:17. Ec 4:5. Ro 1:31. **nourisheth.** Ep 6:4g. Is 40:11. Ezk 34:14, 15, 27. Mt 23:37. Jn 6:50-58. **cherisheth.** Le +*19:18. Mt +*22:39. Ph ◐+*2:3. **even as.** ver. +*2, 25. Ep *4:32. Dt 32:10. Is 62:3. Ml 3:17. Jn 14:16, 17. 16:13, 14. 17:14, 15. Ac *20:28. Ro 5:8. Col 1:24.

30. **are members.** Ep 1:23. Ge *2:23. Nu=18:2. Jn 17:11. Ro *12:4, 5. 1 C 1:10. +*6:15, 17. 10:17. *12:12-27. Col 2:19. **of his body.** Ep +1:23. +*4:4n. 1 C √12:13. **of his flesh.** Ep ◐+*6:12. Ge +*29:14. Mt ◐+*16:17. Lk +*24:39. 1 C ◐+*15:50. **of his bones.** Ge +*29:14. 2 S +*5:1.

31. **For this cause.** ꟷ92B, Mt +12:40. Ge ᐅ2:24. Ps 45:10. Mt 19:5. Mk 10:7, 8. 1 C 6:16. 7:10, 11.

32. **a great mystery.** Ep 6:19. Ro +*16:25n. Col 2:2. 1 T 3:9, 16. **speak.** Ps 45:9-17. SS ch. 1-8. Is 54:5. 62:4, 5. Jn 3:29. 2 C 11:2. Re 19:7, 8. 21:2.

33. **let.** ver. 25, 28, 29. Col 3:19. 1 P 3:7. **and.** ꟷ15G, Ge +35:3. **reverence.** i.e. fear, in the sense of reverence; spontaneous, obedient regard (*Expositor's Greek Testament*); deference. ver. 22. 1 K 1:31. Est 1:20. He 12:9. 1 P 3:2-6.

EPHESIANS 6

The apostle exhorts children and parents to their respective duties, 1-4; and also servants and masters, 5-9. He animates his brethren to resist their spiritual enemies, by putting on and using diligently "the whole armor of God," 10-17, and by persevering prayer; supplicating for all saints, and for him especially, that he might preach the gospel with all boldness, 18-20. He commends Tychicus to them, and concludes with affectionate salutations, 21-24.

1. **Children obey.** T#53, 1903. Ge 28:7. 37:13. Ex +*20:12. Le *19:3. Dt *21:18-21. 1 S 17:20. Est *2:20. Pr *1:8, 9, 20-22. *6:20-22. 13:1. *23:22. *30:11, 17. Je *35:14, 18, 19. Mt 15:4-6. Lk *2:51. Col *3:20, etc. 1 T 5:4. **in.** ver. 5, 6. Ro 16:2. 1 C √15:58. Col *3:16, 17, 23, 24. 1 P *2:13. **for.** Ne 9:13. Jb *33:27. Ps *19:8. *119:75, 128. Ho *14:9. Ro 7:12. *12:2. 1 T 5:4.

2. **Honor.** Ge 45:9-11. Ex +*)20:12. Le *19:3. Dt 5:16. *27:16. Pr *20:20. Je *35:18, 19. Ezk 22:7. Ml 1:6. Mt *15:4-6. 19:19. Mk 7:9-13. 10:19. Lk 18:20. Ro 13:7. 1 T 5:4.

3. **That.** Ps +√9:10n. *78:5-8. **may be well.** Ex 20:12. Dt 4:40. 5:16. 6:3, 18. 12:25, 28. 22:7. Ru 3:1. Ps 128:1, 2. Is 3:10. Je 42:6. **live long.** Dt +*5:16. Ps +*91:16mg. Is ◐+*38:10. **on the earth.** Mt +*5:5.

4. **fathers.** Ex +*13:8. Dt +*6:20. 1 Ch +*28:9, 10. Jb +*1:5. La 2:19. 1 C +*14:35n. 2 C 12:14. 1 T 3:4. **provoke not.** Ge 31:14, 15. +*44:30. 1 S 20:30-34. Ro 10:19g. Col √3:21. **but bring.** Ge +*18:19. Ex 12:26, 27. 13:14, 15. Dt *4:9. *6:6-9, 20-24. 11:19-21. Jsh 4:6, 7, 21-24. √24:15. 1 Ch 22:10-13. 28:9, 10, 20. 29:19. Ps 71:17, 18. √78:4-8. Pr 4:1-4. +*19:18. √22:6, 15. 23:13, 14. *29:15, 17. Is 38:19. 2 T 1:5. 3:15. He 12:7-10. **nurture.** Gr. *paideia*, Thayer states, means "1. the whole training and education of children (which relates to the cultivation of mind and morals, and employs for this purpose now commands and admonitions, now reproof and punishment: Ep 6:4; 2. whatever in adults also cultivates the soul, especially by correcting mistakes and curbing the passions; hence, a. instruction which aims at the increase of virtue: 2 T 3:16. b. according to biblical usage *chastisement*, *chastening*, (of the evils with which God visits men for their amendment): He 12:5, 7, 11; Pr 3:11; 15:5" (*Lexicon*, p. 473a). Trench states the word speaks of discipline, indicating "the laws and ordinances of the Christian household, the transgression of which will induce correction"—"training by act and by discipline" (*Synonyms*, sec. 32, p. 112). Ep 5:29g. Dt +*6:20. Is 28:9. 38:19. 2 T +√3:15. **admonition.** Gr. *nouthesia*, Trench explains, "is the training by word—by the word of encouragement, when this is sufficient, but also by that of remonstrance, of reproof, of blame, where these may be required" (*Synonyms*, p. 112); "whatever is needed to cause the monition to be taken home, to be *laid to heart*, is involved in the word" (p. 113, 114). Lightfoot discusses *nouthesia* (admonition) in its relation to teaching (*didaskein*) in his comments on Col 1:28, where the terms occur together, speaking of them as complimentary aspects of the preacher's duty, related to one another as repentance is to faith: "*warning* to repent, *instructing* in the faith" (Ac 20:21). Jg ◐8:16. 2 S ◐2:24. 3:13, LXX. 1 C +*10:11. T 3:10g. **of the Lord.** Charles Hodge on this phrase states "Children are not to be allowed to grow up without care or control. They are to be instructed, disciplined, and admonished, so that they be brought to knowledge, self control, and obedience. This whole process of education is to be religious, and not only religious, but Christian. It is 'the nurture and admonition of the

Lord,' which is the appointed and only effectual means of attaining the end of education. Where this means is neglected or any other substituted in its place, the result must be disastrous failure. The moral and religious element of our nature is just as essential and universal as the intellectual. Religion therefore is as necessary to the development of the mind as knowledge. And as Christianity is the only true religion, and God in Christ the only true God, the only possible means of profitable education is the nurture and admonition of the Lord" (Comm. on Ephesians, p. 360). 1 S ●3:13. ●8:3. 1 K ●1:6. 2 Ch +*26:4. Pr ●29:15. 2 T *1:5.

5. **Servants**. T 2:9. 1 P +*2:18. **obedient**. Ge +*16:9. Ps 123:2. Ml 1:6. Mt √6:24. 8:9. Ac 10:7, 8. Col *3:22. 1 T *6:1-3. T *2:9, 10. 1 P *2:18-21. **according**. Col 3:22. Phm 16. **with fear**. 1 C +2:3. 2 C 7:15. Ph 2:12. 1 P 3:2. **in singleness**. ver. 24. Jsh 24:14. 1 Ch 29:17. Ps 86:11. Mt 6:22. Ac 2:46. 2 C 1:12. 11:2, 3. **as unto Christ**. Ep ch. 1. 5:22. Ac +√10:36. Ro 14:9. 1 C 7:22. Col 3:17-24.

6. **eyeservice**. T#1838. Ph 2:12. Col 3:22. 1 Th 2:4. **menpleasers**. Ps 53:5. Ga +1:10. **servants of Christ**. ver. 9. 1 C 7:22. Col *3:23. Ja +1:1. **doing**. Ep 5:17. Mt 7:21. 12:50. Col 1:9. 4:12. 1 Th +4:3. Re 10:36. 13:21. 1 P 2:15. 4:2. 1 J 2:17. **from**. 2 Ch *19:6. Je 3:10. 24:7. Ro 6:17. Col 3:23. **heart**. Gr. *psyche*, √121A9B, Mt +22:37.

7. **good will**. Ge 31:6, 38-40. Jsh +*14:8. 2 K 5:2, 3, 13. **service**. 1 Ch=16:37. 1 C +*4:2. Ph *2:12. 1 P *4:10. **as to the Lord**. T#1864. ver. 5, 6. Dt=10:8. Pr +*16:7. 1 C 7:32, 34. *10:31. **not to men**. ver. +*6. Mt √6:24. Mt *23:8, 10. Ac +√10:36. 1 C √7:23. Col √3:23, 24.

8. **whatsoever**. Pr 11:18. 23:18. Is 3:11. Mt 5:12. 6:1, 4. 10:41, 42. 16:27. Lk +*6:35. 14:14. Ro *2:6-10. 2 C +*5:10. Col +*3:24, 25. He +*10:35. 11:26. **good**. √101, Dt +32:42. **the same**. Mt *10:42. 1 T +*4:8. He +*6:10. **whether**. 1 C +*12:13. Ga *3:28. Col +*3:11.

9. **ye masters**. Le +*19:13. 25:39-46. Dt 15:11-16. +*24:14, 15. Ru 2:4. Ne 5:5, 8, 9. Jb 24:10-12. 31:13-15. Is 47:6. 58:3-6. Am 8:4-7. Ml +*3:5. Mt 8:8-13. Lk 7:2-10. *10:7. Col √4:1. Ja +*5:4. **the same**. ver. 5-7. 1 S +*25:17. 2 K +*5:13. Ps 123:2. Mt √7:12. Lk 6:31. Ja 2:8, 13. **forbearing**. *or*, moderating. T#1848. Ep 4:2. Le +*25:43. 1 S *15:17. 1 K +*12:7. Pr 29:21. Ec *7:21, 22. √10:12. Je *2:14. Da *3:6, 15. *5:19, 20. Col 3:13. 1 P *2:23. **knowing**. Ps 140:12. Ec 5:8. Mt 23:8, 10. 24:48, 51. Lk 12:45, 46. Jn 13:13. 1 C *7:22. **your Master**. *Some read*, both your and their Master. Jb *31:13-15. Jn +*13:13. Ac +√10:36. 1 C 1:2. Ph 2:10, 11. **neither**. See on Ac 10:34. Ro *2:11. Col *3:25.

10. **Finally**. 2 C 13:11. Ph 3:1. *4:8. 1 P 3:8. **be strong**. T#187. ver. 10-13. Ep 1:19. *3:16. Dt *20:3, 4. 31:23. Jsh 1:6, 7, 9. 1 S *23:16. 1 Ch=26:8. 28:10, 20. 2 Ch *15:7. Jb 23:6. Ps 28:8. *138:3. Is *26:4. 35:3, 4. *40:28-31. 41:10. Na 3:11. Hg *2:4. Zc 8:9, 13. Ro 4:20g. 1 C *16:13. 2 C √12:9, 10. Ph √4:13. Col 1:11. 2 T *2:1. 4:17. 1 P 5:10. 1 J 2:14. **the power**. Col *1:11.

11. **Put on**. √7, Allegory by continued Hypocatastasis, Ga +4:24. ver. 14. Ep *4:24. Ro +6:4n. *13:12, 14. Ga 3:27. Col 3:10. **whole armor**. ver. *13. Lk 11:22. Ro *13:12. 2 C *6:7. *10:4. 1 Th *5:8. **able**.

ver. *13. Lk *14:29-31. 1 C √10:13. He *7:25. Ju *24. **the wiles**. Ep +*4:14g. Mk *13:22. 2 C *2:11. *4:4. √11:3, 13-15. 2 Th *2:9-11. 1 P *5:8. 2 P *2:1-3. Re 2:24. 12:9. 13:11-15. 19:20. 20:2, 3, 7, 8.

12. **wrestle not**. Ge 12:6. Ps *23:5. Pr *1:10. Mt 5:11. Lk +*13:24. Ro *7:22, 23. 1 C *9:25-27. 15:32. 2 T 2:5. He *12:1, 4. 1 P 1:7. 1 J *2:15. **against**. √18, Dt +28:4. **flesh and blood**. Gr. blood and flesh. *√171Q11, Mt +16:17. Ep ●+*5:30. Mt +*16:17. Lk ●+*24:39. 1 C +*15:50. Ga *1:16. **principalities**. Ep +*1:21. *3:10. Ro +*8:38. Col *2:15. 1 P *3:22. **against the**. Ep *2:2. Jb *2:2. Da √10:3, 12, 13. Lk *22:53. Jn *12:31. +*14:30. *16:11. Ac +*26:18. 2 C *4:4. Col *1:13. **darkness**. Ep +*4:18. Lk 22:53. Jn 8:12. Col 1:13. **this world**. Gr. *aion*, Mt +6:13. √121P2, Mt +13:22. √121J9B, Jn +12:31. Jn +*6:54n. **spiritual wickedness**. *or*, wicked spirits. Gr. *pneumatikos*, Ro +1:11. lit. the spiritual (powers, bands, hosts) of wickedness. i.e. wicked spirits. √24G, Ge 1:9. Da +*10:13. Mt +*8:16. 2 T *4:1. **high**. *or*, heavenly. See on Ep 1:3. 3:10. Re 12:9-11.

13. **take**. See on ver. *11-17. Ro 13:13, 14. 2 C *10:4. 1 P 4:1. **the whole**. *Panoplia*, a complete suit of armor, both offensive and defensive, from *pan*, "all," and *oplon*, "armor." ver. +*11. **in the evil day**. Ep *5:6, +16. Ec *12:1. Am 6:3. Lk +*8:13. Re *3:10. **done all**. *or*, overcome all. **to stand**. Dt=10:8. 1 Ch=6:33mg. Ml *3:2. Lk +√21:36. Ac 26:22. Col *4:12. Re *6:17.

14. **loins girt**. Ep *5:9. Ex=29:9. Ps 18:32n. Is 11:5. Je +*1:17. Lk +*12:35. 2 C *6:7. 1 P *1:13. **truth**. Jn √14:6. Ac +*6:3. 2 C *1:12. **the breastplate**. The *thorax*, or "breastplate," consisted of two parts; one of which covered the whole region of the thorax or breast, and the other the back, as far down as the front part extended. Is *59:17. 1 Th *5:8. Re 9:9, 17. **of righteousness**. Ps *119:6. =132:9. Is 61:10. Je +*23:6. Ac *24:16. 2 C 6:7.

15. **feet shod**. Ex 12:11. Dt *33:25. SS 7:1. Is *52:7. Na 1:15. Hab 3:19. Lk 15:22. Ac 10:36. Ro 10:15. **the preparation**. Is 40:3. T 3:1. **the gospel**. Is *52:7. Ro *10:15. 2 C *5:18-21. **of peace**. Ep 2:14, 17. Ro *5:1, 3.

16. **Above all**. Col 3:14. **the shield**. The *thureos* was a large oblong shield, or scuta, like a door, *thura*, made of wood and covered with hides. Ge *15:1. *39:9. Ps *56:3, 4, 10, 11. Pr *18:10. 30:5. 2 C *1:24. *4:16-18. He 6:17, 18. 11:24-34. 1 P *1:6-9. *5:8, 9. 1 J *5:4, 5. **to quench**. 1 Th 5:19. **fiery darts**. Ps 120:4. **the wicked**. √96F1, Ge +3:8. Mt +13:19.

17. **the helmet**. 1 S 17:5, 38. Ps 140:7. Is *59:17. 1 Th √5:8. **salvation**. Ps *27:1. Is 61:10. Lk 2:30. 3:6. Ac 28:28g. He *6:17-19. **the sword**. Ex=32:27. 1 S 21:9. Ps 64:3. SS 3:8. Is 49:2. Ho 6:5. 2 C 6:7. Ph *1:17. 1 T 1:18. 2 T 2:3. He √4:12. Re 1:16. 2:16. *19:15. **Spirit**. Gr. *pneuma*, Mt +3:16. Ep 4:3. Jn +7:39. **which**. Mt *4:4, 7, 10, 11. 2 C *10:4. He 12:5, 6. *13:5, 6. Re *12:11. **word of God**. T#1076. Ep 5:26. Is √55:11. Ho 6:5. Mt *4:4-10. Lk 4:4, 8, 10. Ro +9:6. 1 Th √2:13. 2 T +√3:15-17. He √4:12. 6:5. 2 P *1:21. Re 19:13.

18. **Praying always**. √147D, Ge +1:29. Ep 1:16. 1 S +*12:23. Ne 2:4. Jb 27:10. Ps 4:16, 17. 35:22. 73:28. *86:3, 6. 109:4. 116:2. Is 26:16. Da +*6:10. Lk *2:37. 3:26, 27. *18:1-7. +*21:36. Ac 1:14. *6:4. 9:11. 10:2, 9. 12:5. Ro 1:9. *12:12. Ph √4:6. Col 1:9.

*4:2. 1 Th 3:10. +*5:17. 1 T 5:5. 2 T 1:3. **all prayer.** ♪93A, Ge +1:26. By Hendiadys, "supplicating prayer." T#1307. **supplication.** 1 K 8:52, 54, 59. 9:3. Est 4:8. Da 9:30. Ho 12:4. 1 T 2:1. He 5:7. **in the.** T#1410. Ep 2:22. Zc 12:10. Jn *4:24. Ro +*8:15, 26, 27. Ga 4:6. Ju √20. **Spirit.** Gr. *pneuma*, Mt +3:16. **watching.** Mt *26:41. Mk *13:33. 14:38. Lk +√21:36. 22:46. Col *4:2. He 13:17. 1 P *4:7. **all perseverance.** Ge *32:24-29. Ex=17:11. Mt 15:25-28. Lk 11:5-8. 18:1-8. Ac +1:14. **and.** ♪93A, Ge +1:26. **supplication.** See on ver. 19. Ep 1:16. 3:8, 18. Ac 12:5. 2 C 1:11. Ph 1:4. 1 T 2:1. Col 1:4. Phm 5. **saints.** 2 C +1:1.

19. **for.** Ro *15:30. 2 C 1:11. Ph 1:19. Col *4:3. 1 Th +5:25. 2 Th *3:1. Phm 22. He 13:18. **utterance.** Is 50:4. Ac 2:4. 1 C *1:5. 2 C 8:7. 2 Th 3:1. **that I.** Ac *4:13, 29, 31. *9:27, 29. *13:46. 14:3. *18:26. 19:8. 28:31. 2 C 3:12mg. 7:4. Ph *1:20. 1 Th 2:2. **open.** Ps 51:15. Mt 5:2. **boldly.** T#1441. Ac 4:+13, *29-31. Ph 1:20. He 4:16. 13:6. **the mystery.** Ep 1:9. 3:3, 4. Ro +*16:25n. 1 C 2:7. 4:1. Col *1:26, 27. *2:2. 1 T *3:16.

20. **I am.** Pr 13:17. Is 33:7. 2 C +*5:20. Phm 9. **bonds.** *or*, a chain. See on Ep 3:1. 4:1. 2 S 10:2-6. Ac +21:33. 26:29. 28:20. Ph *1:7, 13, 14. 2 T 1:16. 2:9. Phm 10. **therein.** *or*, thereof. **boldly.** See on ver.

19. Is 58:1. Je 1:7, 8, 17. Ezk *2:4-7. Mt 10:27, 28. Ac 5:29. *22:21-24. 28:31. Ph *1:20. Col 4:4. 1 Th *2:2. 1 J 3:16. Ju +*3. **ought.** Ac +*5:29. 1 C 9:16.

21. **that.** Ph 1:12. Col *4:7. **Tychicus.** Ac *20:4. 2 T 4:12. T 3:12. **beloved.** Col 4:9. Phm 16. 2 P 3:15. **faithful.** 1 C 4:+2, 17. Col 1:2, 7. 1 T 4:6. 1 P 5:12. **minister.** Ac +19:22.

22. **I have sent.** Ph 2:19, 25. Col 2:2. 4:7, 8. 1 Th 3:2. 2 Th 2:17.

23. **Peace.** See on Ro +*1:7. 1 C 1:3. Ge 43:23. 1 S 25:6. Ps √122:6-9. Jn *14:27. Ga *6:16. 2 Th 3:16. 1 P 5:14. 3 J 14. Re 1:4. **the brethren.** Jn +21:23. 1 C 8:12. 16:11, 12, 20. 2 C 9:3, 5. 11:9. Ga 1:2. Ph 1:14. 4:21. Col 1:2. 4:15. 1 Th 4:10. 5:26, 27. 1 T 4:6. 2 T 4:21. **and love.** Ga 5:6. 1 Th 1:3. *5:8. 2 Th 1:3. 1 T 1:14. Phm 5-7. **with faith.** ♪174, Ge +18:27.

24. **Grace.** 1 C 16:23. 2 C *13:14. Col 4:18. 2 T 4:22. T 3:15. He 13:25. **all them.** T#1684. ver. 18. 2 Ch 6:41. Ps *36:10. 40:16. *70:4. 90:16. 125:4. 132:9. Mt *25:40. Jn 17:20-23. Ac 20:32. Ph 1:3-6. Col 1:3, 4, 9, 10. **love.** See on Jn *21:15-17. 1 C 16:22. **in sincerity.** *or*, with incorruption. Mt 22:37. Ro +*2:7g. 2 C 8:8, 12. T 2:7. **Amen.** See on Mt 6:13. 28:20.

PHILIPPIANS

PHILIPPIANS 1

The apostle addresses the saints at Philippi with the bishops and deacons, 1, 2: showing his thankfulness to God for their "fellowship in the gospel," to that time; his love to them; and his confidence in them as to the future, 3-8; and giving a summary of the blessings for which he prayed in their behalf, 9-11. He informs them, that his imprisonment at Rome had conduced "to the furtherance of the gospel," 12, 13: so that many had been rendered more bold in preaching it; in which he greatly rejoices, though some did it from corrupt motives, 14-18; knowing that this "will turn to his salvation, through their prayers, and by the Spirit," and trusting that "Christ will be magnified in his body, whether by life or death," 19, 20. He declares that he is prepared for either event; that "to depart, and be with Christ, would be far better" for him; but that, as his life would be useful to them, he doubts in his choice, and supposes that he shall live, and be set at liberty, that he may further their joy of faith, by coming to them, 21-26. He exhorts them to walk worthy of their profession; to be of one mind "in striving for the gospel;" and to suffer cheerfully for Christ, as they had already been called to do, 27-30.

1. **Paul.** See on Ro 1:1. 1 C 1:1. **Timotheus.** Ph 2:19. Ac 16:1-3. 1 C 16:10. 2 C 1:1. Col 1:1. 1 Th 1:1. 2 Th 1:1. 1 T 1:2. He 13:23. **the servants.** Mt *6:24. Mk 13:34. Jn *12:26. Ro *6:22. T 1:1. Ja +1:1. 2 P 1:1. Ju 1. Re 1:1. 19:10. 22:9. **the saints.** Ro 1:7. 1 C 1:2. 2 C +1:1. Ep 1:1, 15. 2 Th 1:10. **in Christ Jesus.** Ph 3:9. Ro +*8:1n. 12:5. 2 C *5:17. **Philippi.** Ac +16:12, etc. 1 Th 2:2. **the bishops.** or, overseers. Ac 1:20. +*20:28. 1 T 3:1, 2. T 1:7. 1 P 2:25. Re 1:20. 2:1, 8, 12. **and deacons.** Ac 6:1-7. 1 T 3:8, 10, 12, 13.

2. **Grace.** Ro +1:7. 2 C 1:2. 1 P 1:2.

3. **I thank.** Ro 1:+8, 9. 6:17. 1 C 1:4. **my God.** Ph 4:19. Ac 27:23. Ro 1:8. 1 Th 2:2. 2 Th 1:11. Phm 4. **upon.** Ep 1:15, 16. Col *1:3, 4. 1 Th 1:2, 3. 3:19. 2 Th 1:3. 2 T 1:3. Phm 4, 5. **remembrance.** *or*, mention.

4. **in every prayer.** ver. 9-11. See on Ro 1:9. Ep 1:14, etc. 1 Th 1:2. **with joy.** ver. 25. Ph 2:2, 17, 18, 28, 29. 3:1, 18. 4:1, 4, 10. Lk 15:7, 10. Col 2:5. 1 Th 2:19, 20. Phm 7. 2 J 4.

5. **your fellowship.** ver. 7. Ph 2:12. 4:14, 15. Ac +2:42. 16:15. Ro 11:17. 12:13. 15:26, 27. 1 C *1:9. 2 C 8:1. Ep 2:19-22. +*3:6. Col 1:21-23. Phm 17. He +*3:14. 2 P 1:1. 1 J 1:3, 7.

6. **confident.** 2 C 1:15. 2:3. 7:16. 9:4. Ga 5:10. 2 Th 3:4. Phm 21. He +*10:35. **begun.** ver. 29. Ph √2:13. Jn *6:29. Ac 11:18. 16:14. Ro +*8:28-30. Ga 3:3. Ep 2:4-10. Col 2:12. 1 Th *1:3. 2 Th √2:13, 14. T 3:4-6. He *13:20, 21. Ja *1:16-18. 1 P 1:2, 3. **will.** Ph *2:13. Ex 6:8. Ru 3:18. Ps 57:2. 138:8. Jn 6:29. Ga 3:3. Ep 4:12. Col +*2:6, 7. 1 Th √5:23, 24. 2 Th 1:11. He 6:9. 13:20, 21. 1 J 2:19. 1 P *5:10. 2 P +*1:10. **perform it.** *or*, finish *it*. Ep *1:13, 14. He +*12:2. **until.** Jn 21:22. **the day.** ver. 10. Ph 2:16. See on 1 C +*1:8. 2 P *3:10.

7. **it is.** 1 C 13:7. 1 Th 1:2-5. 5:5. He +*6:9, 10. **because.** 2 C 3:2. *7:3. **I have you in my heart.** *or*, ye have me in your heart. Ga 5:6. 1 J 3:14. **as.** ver. 13, 14, 17. Ac 16:23-25. 20:23. 26:29. 28:20. Ep +3:1. 4:1. 6:20. Col 4:3, 18. 2 T 1:8. 2:9. Phm 10, 13. He 10:33, 34. **the defense.** ver. 17. Ph 4:14. Ac +19:33. **confirmation.** He 6:16. **partakers of my.** *or*, partakers with me of. See on ver. 5. Ph 4:14. Ro +11:17. 1 C 9:23. He 3:1. 1 P 4:13. 5:1.

8. **God is.** See on Ro 1:9. 9:1. Ga 1:20. 1 Th 2:5. **how.** Ph 2:26. *4:1. Ro 1:11. 15:23. 2 C 9:14. 13:9. Ga 4:19. Col 2:1. 1 Th 2:8. 3:6. 2 T 1:4. **in.** Ph 2:1. Is 16:11. 63:15. Je 31:20. Lk 1:78mg. 2 C 6:12. 7:15mg. Col +3:12. Phm 12, 20. 1 J 3:17.

9. **this**. See on ver. 4. **love may abound**. T#1609. Ph 3:15, 16. Jb 17:9. Pr +*4:18. Mt 13:31-33. 2 C 8:7. Eph 1:8g. 3:17-19. Col 2:1, 2. 1 Th *3:12, 13. 4:1, 9, 10. 2 Th 1:3. Phm 6. 1 P 1:22. 1 J *5:2. Ju 2. **in knowledge**. T#393. Ps +19:7 (T#47). 1 C 14:20. Ep 5:17. Col +*1:9. 3:10. 2 P 1:2, 3, 5, 6. +*3:18. **judgment**. *or*, sense. Ps 119:66n. Pr 1:4, 22. Lk 9:45. He 5:14g.

10. **ye**. Is 7:15, 16. Am 5:14, 15. Mi 3:2. Jn *3:20. Ro +2:18. 7:16, 22. 8:7. +*12:2, 9. **approve things that are excellent**. *or*, try things that differ. Jb 12:11. 34:3. Ps 119:66n. Ro +*12:2. 2 C √11:13-15. Ep *5:10, 17. 1 Th +*5:21. He *5:12-14. 1 J √4:1. Re 2:2. **that ye may be**. ver. 16. Ge 20:5. Jsh *24:14. Jn 1:47. Ac *24:16. 2 C 1:12. 2:17. 8:8. Ep 4:15mg. 5:27. 6:24. 1 Th 3:13. √5:23. 2 P +*3:14. **sincere**. Gr. *eilikrineis*, from *eilee*, the *splendor of the sun*, and *krino*, *I judge*, *discern*, properly *pure* and *unsullied* to such a degree as to bear examination in the full splendor of the solar rays. 2 Ch +29:34. 1 C +5:8. 2 P 3:1. **without**. Mt 16:23. 18:6, 7. 26:33. Ro 14:20, 21. 16:17. 1 C 8:13. 10:32. 2 C 6:3. Ga 5:11. 1 Th 3:13. **till**. ver. 6. See on 1 C +*1:8. 1 Th *5:23. 2 P +*1:10, 11.

11. **filled**. Ph 4:17. Ps +*1:3. 92:12-14. Is 5:2. Lk *13:6-9. Jn *15:2, 8, 16. Ro 6:22. 15:28. 2 C 9:10. Ga +*5:22, 23. Ep 5:9. Col +*1:6, 10. He 12:11. Ja 3:17, +18. **fruits**. Ho 14:8. Jn 15:4. **are**. Ps 92:14, 15. Is +*60:21. *61:3, 11. Mt *5:16. Jn *15:4, 5. 1 C *10:31. Ep √2:10. Col 1:6. 2 Th 1:12. He *13:15, 16. 1 P 2:5, 9, 12. 4:10, 11, 14. **unto the glory**. Mt +*5:16. Jn *15:8. Ro +*3:23. **and praise**. Ep +1:12, 14.

12. **that**. Ac 21:28, etc. ch. 22, 28. **rather**. Ge +*50:20. Ex 18:11. Est 9:1. Ps +*76:10. Pr +*21:30. Ac *8:4. *11:19-21. Ro +*8:28, 37. 2 T 2:9. **furtherance**. ver. 25. 1 T 4:15.

13. **my bonds**. ſ121G, Ge +31:1. ver. +*7. Lk 21:13. Ac 20:23, 24. 21:11-13. 26:29, 31. 28:17, 20. Ep 3:1. 4:1. 6:20. Col 4:3-18. **in Christ**. *or*, for Christ. 1 P 4:12-16. **all**. ſ171L2, Mt +26:59. **the palace**. *or*, Caesar's court. Ph 4:22. Mt 27:27. Mk 15:16. Jn 18:28, 33. Ac 23:35. **in all other places**. *or*, to all others. Ac 28:30, 31. 1 Th 1:8, 9. 2 T 2:9.

14. **many**. 1 C +9:19g. **brethren**. Ph 4:1. Ep +6:23. Col 4:7. **waxing**. Ac 4:23-31. 2 C 1:3-7. Ep 3:13. 6:19, 20. Col 4:4. 1 Th 2:2. **the word**. Ro +9:6. **without**. Lk 1:74. 12:5-7.

15. **Some indeed**. 2 C +*11:13. **preach**. ver. 16, 18. Ac 5:42. 8:5, 35. 9:20. +*10:36. 11:20. 1 C 1:23. 2 C 1:19. 4:5. 1 T *3:16. **envy and strife**. Ph +*2:3. Mt 23:5. Ro +*1:29. 16:17, 18. 1 C 3:3, 4. 13:3. 2 C 12:20. Ga *1:7. 2:4. Ja 4:5, 6. **good will**. ver. 17. 1 P *5:2-4.

16. **The one**. ſ153, Jn +16:9. **contention**. Ro 2:8. Ja +3:14. **not sincerely**. See on ver. 10. 2 C 2:17. +*4:1, 2. **supposing**. Jb 6:14. 16:4. Ps 69:26. **bonds**. ſ121N1, Ge +31:54.

17. **knowing**. 1 C 9:17. **I am set**. ver. 7. Lk 2:34. Ro +*1:13-17. 1 C 9:16, 17. Ga 2:7, 8. 1 Th 3:3g. 1 T 2:7. 2 T 1:11, 12. 4:6, 7. **defense**. Nu=8:24. Lk 21:14. Ac 22:1. 26:1, 24. Ep 6:17. 1 T 1:18. 2 T 2:3. 4:16g.

18. **What**. Ro 3:9. 6:15. 1 C 10:19. 14:15. **notwithstanding**. ſ5. Affirmatio; or, Affirmation B960. Spontaneous affirmation of what no one has disputed. **whether**. ver. 14-17. Mt 23:14. Mk 12:40. **Christ**. See on ver. 15. **and I**. Mk 9:38-40. Lk 9:45, 50. 1 C 15:11. 2 J

+*9-11. **rejoice**. Mk 9:39. Lk 9:50.

19. **I know**. Ro +*8:28. 1 C 4:17. 1 P 1:7-9. **this shall turn**. Ge +*50:20. 2 C *4:17. **my salvation**. Jb 13:16. **through**. 2 C +*1:11. Ep 6:18, 19. **the supply**. 2 C +9:10. Ga 3:5. Ep 4:16. **the Spirit**. Gr. *pneuma*, Lk +1:17n. Ac +16:7. Ro +*8:9. Ga 4:6. 1 P 1:11.

20. **earnest expectation**. Ps 62:5. Pr 10:28. 23:18. Ro 8:19. **and hope**. Ps 25:3. Jl 2:27. Ro +5:5. 2 T 1:12. 2:15. **in nothing**. Ps 25:2. 119:80, 116. Is 45:17. 50:7. 54:4. Ro 5:5. 9:33. 2 C 7:14. 10:8. Ep 6:19, 20. 1 P 4:16. 1 J 2:28. **with all boldness**. T#460. See on ver. 14. Jsh +1:9 (T#134). Ps +*34:4. Je 1:7, 8, 17-19. Ezk 2:6. Jn +1:47 (T#659). Ac *4:13, 18-20, 29. 6:10. 9:29. 18:9, 10. *19:8. 2 C 2:14-16. He +*13:6. **Christ**. Ph 2:17. Jn 21:19. Ac +*10:46. Ro 6:13, 19. +*12:1. 1 C *6:20. 7:34. 2 C √5:15. 1 Th √5:23. 1 P 2:12. **whether**. ver. 23, 24. Jn 12:27, 28. 21:19. Ac 20:24. 21:13. Ro *14:7-9. 1 C 15:31. 2 C 4:10. Col *1:24. 2 T 4:5-7. 2 P 1:12-15.

21. **to live**. See on ver. 20. Ph 2:21. 1 C +*1:30. Ga *2:20. *6:14. Col *3:3, 4. **is Christ**. That is, Christ is the object of his life. **to die**. T#153. ver. 23. Jb *3:17, 18. *7:16. Ps 23:4. 31:5. *37:37. *116:15. Pr +*14:32. Is 57:1, 2. Ro +*8:35-39. 1 C 3:22. +*15:54-57. 2 C *5:1, 6, 8. 1 Th √4:13-15. Re +*14:13. **is gain**. Paul says to die is "gain," and this he says while living. If death resulted in annihilation or soul sleep, it is unaccountable how one with the mind of Paul while living would prefer *that*. Rather, contrary to the teaching of annihilationists, Paul expects upon death to go immediately to be with Christ—not to lie mouldering in the grave, "to depart into forgetfulness, and be with Christ when he woke up," insensible of the time that intervened (see related notes on Da 12:2. 1 C 15:54). Re +*14:13.

22. **if**. ſ184A, 1 C +15:2. **live**. ver. 24. 2 C 10:3. Ga √2:20. Col 2:1. 1 P 4:2. **this**. Ps 71:18. Is 38:18, 19. **I wot**. Ge 21:26. 39:8. Ex 32:1. Ac 3:17. Ro 11:2. 1 C +15:1.

23. **in a strait**. 2 S 24:14. 1 Ch 21:13. Lk 12:50. Ac +18:5. 2 C 6:12. **betwixt two**. This does not mean he was equally indifferent to the two things, and desired a third, for he specifically states he is in a strait betwixt *two*. The alternatives are clearly (1) to remain in the flesh and (2) to die. The immediately corresponding advantages are (1) to benefit the Philippians in their spiritual growth or (2) to depart this life in death and be immediately with Christ, which Paul for himself would prefer. Annihilationists and materialists find it necessary to wrest this plain scripture, and in a vain effort to maintain their system against its logic, mangle Paul's clear statement by affirming a third alternative, his desire to depart, which they claim is not a departure at all, but a reference to the returning and being with Christ. But if this were so, they are hard pressed to explain how Paul could affirm to the Philippians that it is better for him to remain in the flesh than for Christ to return. By dividing this third alternative, Jehovah's Witnesses introduce a fourth, asserting Paul's departure is a releasing, that is, "his own releasing to be with Christ at his return and the Lord's releasing of himself from heavenly restraints to return as he promised" (*New World Translation* with references, 1984 revised edition, Appendix 5D, p. 1578), which by their doctrine occurred at the second presence of Christ (Appendix 5B, pp. 1576, 1577) in 1914 (*Bible*

Topics for Discussion, p. 4; *Make Sure of All Things*, topic "Chronology," pp. 89, 90, of 1965 edition). **a desire.** Lk 2:29, 30. Jn 13:1. 2 C √5:8. 2 T √4:6. **to depart.** Gr. *to analusai*, ✱S#360g, only here and Lk 12:36 (return). ℐ88, Ge +15:15. Paul uses a beautiful *euphemism* for death, employing a Greek word which itself contains a *Metaphor*, to loose anchor. A. T. Robertson states "One may note here that Paul speaks as if he expected to be with Jesus at death without an interval. The word 'depart' (*analusai*, loosen up. The intransitive sense of depart is common in Polybius and the papyri, see p. 36 of Moulton and Milligan, *Vocabulary*, etc.) was variously used, for a ship's departure, for breaking up camp, and for death. Paul himself uses a similar word (*kataluthee*) for death under the figure of breaking up camp or striking a tent (2 C 5:1). And in 2 T 4:6 he speaks of his own death again with the same word (*analuseos*) as here" (*Paul's Joy in Christ*, p. 97, 98). See the related noun derived from this verb, ✱S#359g, *analusis*, which occurs at 2 T 4:6 (departure). Vine states for ✱S#360g, *analuo*, "lit., to unloose, undo (*ana*, up, or again), signifies to depart, in the sense of departing from life, Ph 1:23, a metaphor drawn from loosing moorings preparatory to setting sail, or, according to some, from breaking up an encampment, or from the unyoking of baggage animals" (*Expository Dictionary*, vol 1, p. 294, 295). For ✱S#359g, *analusis*, Vine states "an unloosing (as of things woven), a dissolving into separate parts (English *analysis*), is once used of departure from life, 2 T 4:6, where the metaphor is either nautical, from loosing from moorings (thus used in Greek poetry), or military, from breaking up an encampment" (*Expository Dictionary*, vol. 1, p. 295). Compare the related word *kataluo* (✱S#2647g, Mt +5:17 "destroy," rendered "dissolved" in 2 C 5:1, used of the death of the body). Since the noun derived from the verb used here is likewise used by Paul of his "departure" or death (2 T 4:6), it should be so understood here of his death, as his death is the immediate subject of the context. F. W. Grant observes "And it is true that it sometimes means 'return,' but not so often as 'depart,' so that an Annihilationist alone could tell us why it should be so translated here. The reason being only in the exigencies of a theory, which must bend Scripture to its need, or be convicted of open opposition to it" (*Facts and Theories as to a Future State*, p. 119). A modern example of just such an explanation may be found in Appendix 5D of the 1984 revised edition of the Jehovah's Witnesses *New World Translation* with references, p. 1578; p. 3591 of the six volumes in one edition of 1963; or pp. 780, 781 of the *Christian Greek Scriptures*, 1951 edition. Ja 2:26. 2 T √4:6g. *X?ℐ24A, Antimereia of the Verb: the Infinitive for a Noun, Ge +32:24. E. W. Bullinger, being a materialist, and therefore an annihilationist, supports the mistaken view discussed above with the following comments. "Having a desire unto the return": i.e., (lit.) unto the to return (i.e. the returning of Christ). 'Analuo,' *to loosen back again*, but always from there to here; hence, *to return* (not from here to there, which would be to depart). See the only occurrences of the verb: Lk 12:36. Tobit 2:1. Judith 13:1. 1 Esdras 3:3. Wisdom 2:1. 5:12. Ecclusiasticus 3:15. 2 Maccabees 8:25. 9:1. 12:7. 15:28; and Josephus Ant. vi. 4, 1. The meaning is that the Apostle knew not which to choose, whether to live or to die.

His living would be better for them than his dying, but not better than a third thing which pressed him out of the other two, *viz.*, the return of Christ, which was "far better" than either" (B492). See further on this mistaken view supported by E. W. Bullinger in the notes on *Epanalepsis*, ℐ67, ver. 24. **be with.** ver. 21. Jb +*19:26, 27. Ps *49:15. Mt +*10:28n. Mk 5:18. Lk 8:38. 12:4, 5n. 16:22. +*23:43. Jn 11:11-14. +12:26. +*14:3. 17:24. Ac +*7:59. 1 C 15:20-23. 2 C √5:8. 12:2. 1 Th √4:17. Re +*14:13. **far better.** ℐ144C1, Ge +21:1. lit. much (*pollo*) more (*mallon*) better (*kreisson*). Ps +*16:10, 11. 17:15. 73:24-26. Re 7:14-17. +*14:13.

24. **to abide.** ver. 22, 25, 26. Jn 16:7. +*21:22g. Ac 20:29-31. **in the flesh.** ℐ67, Epanalepsis; or, Resumption: the repetition of the same word after a break, or parenthesis, Ro +3:26. E. W. Bullinger explains this figure in support of his annihilationist position as follows. "In verse 20, the apostle had been speaking of glorifying God "by life, or by death." For, if he lived, it would be "Christ," and if he died, it would be "gain" to him, and would release him and give him rest from all his labors. The real conclusion is that if he continued to abide in the flesh it would be better for them. But this conclusion is interrupted by the mention, parenthetically, of a third thing, which made him unable to say which of the two (living or dying) he would really prefer, because this third thing was so much better than either of the other two; for it was—the return of Christ. Then, having mentioned this, he takes up the statement again, repeating the beginning of verse 22 ("in the flesh") and continuing it in verse 24. Verse 22:—"But if I live in the flesh, [this is the fruit of my labor (yet what I shall choose I wot not, (23) for I am being pressed out of (*ek*) these two, having a strong desire unto the return, and to be with Christ, which is a far, far better thing): but to remain in the flesh] is more needful for you" (i.e., than dying—not better than Christ's return)" (B206, 207). Bullinger then cites 1 Th 4:17 to show that "and so shall we ever be with the Lord" proves our being with the Lord will only occur at the return of Christ: "There is, therefore, no other way of being 'with the Lord.' The Spirit of God would not have written one thing to the Thessalonians and a different thing to the Philippians" (B207). Bullinger's view is mistaken, being forced by his materialist position. His identification of the figure Epanalepsis is undeniable, but he is otherwise mistaken in (1) his forced identification of "to depart" with the figure *Antimereia* (compare another theologically forced identification, Ps 16:10n); (2) his strained definition of "depart" as "unto the to return" (B492), and (3) his introduction of a "third thing" into Paul's argument.

25. **confidence.** Ph 2:24. Ac 20:25. **for.** Lk 22:32. Jn 21:15-17. Ac +*11:23. +*14:22. Ro *1:11, 12. *15:18, 29. 2 C √1:24. Ep +*4:11-13. **furtherance.** ver. 12. **joy.** ver. +4. Ps 60:6. Ro 5:2. 15:13. 1 P *1:8. **of faith.** Ac +6:7. 1 C +16:13.

26. **your rejoicing.** Ph 2:16-18. 3:1, 3. 4:4, 10. SS 5:1. Jn 16:22, 24. Ro 4:2. 1 C 5:6. 9:15, 16. 2 C 1:14. 5:12. 7:6. 9:3. Ga 6:4. He 3:6. **coming.** Gr. *parousia*, Mt +24:3. ver. 8. Ph 2:12. Mt *24:23-27. Ac +*1:11. 1 C 16:17. 2 C 7:6.

27. **let.** Ph 3:18-21. Ac 23:1. Ep +*4:1. Col +√1:10. 1 Th 2:11, 12. 4:1. T 2:10. 2 P √1:4-9. *3:11, 14. **the**

gospel. Ro *1:9, 16. 15:16, +19, 29. 2 C √4:4. 9:13. Ga 1:7. whether. Ph 2:12, 24. I may. Ep 1:15. Col 1:4. 1 Th 3:6. Phm 5. 3 J 3, 4. stand fast. Ph 2:1, 2. *4:1. Ps 122:3. 133:1. Mt 12:25. 1 C 1:10. √15:58. +16:13, 14. 2 C 13:11. in one. Je 32:39. Jn 17:20, 21. Ac 2:46 4:32. Ro 12:4, 5. 15:5n. 1 C +*1:10. 12:12, etc. Ep 4:3-6. Ja 3:18. Ju +*3. spirit. Gr. *pneuma*, ᴶ121A2, Mt +26:41. mind. Gr. *psyche*, ᴶ121A9B, Mt +22:37. striving. Ph 4:3. Ju +*3. the faith. Pr 23:23. Ac 24:24. Ro *1:5. 10:8. Ep 1:13. 1 T 1:11, 19. 2 T 4:7.

28. in. Is *51:7, 12. Mt +*10:28. Lk *12:4-7. 21:12-19. Ac *4:19-31. *5:40-42. 1 Th 2:2. 2 T *1:7, 8. He *13:6. Re 2:10. to them. 1 C 1:18. an evident token. 2 Th √1:5-10. 1 P *4:12-14. but. Mt *5:10-12. Ac +*14:22. Ro 8:17. 2 Th 1:5. 2 T 2:11, 12. and that. Ge 49:18. Ps *50:23. *68:19, 20. Is +*12:2. Lk 3:6. Ac 28:28.

29. it is given. T#801. Ph 2:9. Mt +*5:12. Jn +*6:45. Ac *5:41. +*11:18. +*13:48. +*18:27. +25:11. Ro 5:3. Ep 1:3, 4. *2:8. 2 Th *2:13. 2 T +*2:25. Ja 1:2. 1 P 4:13. the behalf. Ep ◖5:25, 26. T ◖*2:14. He ◖9:14. 13:12. not only. Mt 16:17. Jn 1:12, 13. 6:44, 45. Ac 13:39. 14:27. Ep 2:8. Col 2:12. Ja 1:17, 18. to believe. Ac 5:31. Ro +10:14. 1 C 1:30. T 3:5, 6. 1 J 1:7. to suffer. Ph *3:8. Mk *10:30. Ac +*14:22.

30. the same conflict. Jn 16:33. Ro 8:35-37. 1 C 4:9-14. 15:30-32. Ep 6:11-18. Col 1:29. 2:1. 1 Th 2:2, 14, 15. 3:2-4. 1 T 6:12. 2 T 2:10-12. 4:7. He 10:32, 33. 12:1g, 4. Re 2:10, 11. 12:11. which. Ac 16:19-40. 1 Th 2:2. now. See on ver. 7, 13.

PHILIPPIANS 2

The apostle, by the most affecting topics, exhorts his brethren to humble, condescending, and self-denying love, 1-4; after the example of Christ, in his incarnation, humiliation, and death on the cross, as introductory to his glorious exaltation, 5-11. He exhorts to diligence, "in working out their own salvation," as depending on the grace of God, 12, 13; and to profess the gospel, and adorn it among their neighbors, by a harmless and blameless example; in such a manner, that he might rejoice with them at the day of Christ, in the success of his labors, 14-16. He assures them that he should joyfully become a martyr for their sakes; and he exhorts them to rejoice with him, 17, 18. He hopes to send Timothy to them shortly, whom he highly commends, 19-23; as he does also Epaphroditus, their messenger to him; who had been sick, and was grieved that they had heard it; and who, as God had mercifully restored him, longed to return to them, 24-27. The apostle therefore sends him back; and exhorts them highly to value him and such as he, seeing he had "disregarded his life, to supply their lack of service," 28-30.

1. If. ᴶ184A, 1 C +15:2. any consolation. Ph 3:3. Lk 2:10, 11, 25. Jn 14:18, 27. 15:11. 16:22-24. 17:13. Ro 5:1, 2. 15:12, 13. 1 C +14:3. 15:31. 2 C *1:5, 6. 2:14. Ep *3:19. 2 Th *2:16, 17. He 6:18. 1 P 1:6-8. if any comfort. ᴶ184A, 1 C +15:2. Ps 133:1. Jn 15:10-12. Ac 2:46. 4:32. Ga 5:22. Ep 4:30-32. Col 2:2. 1 J 4:7, 8, 12, 16. of love. Ro 15:30. 2 Th 2:16. if any fellowship. ᴶ184A, 1 C +15:2. Ro 5:5. *8:9-16, 26. 1 C *3:16. 6:19, 20. √12:13. 2 C *13:14. Ga 4:6. Ep *1:13, 14. 2:18-22. 4:4. 1 P 1:2, 22, 23. 1 J 3:24. the

Spirit. Gr. *pneuma*, ᴶ121A2, Mt +26:41. if any bowels. ᴶ184A, 1 C +15:2. ᴶ121G1, Is +63:15. See on Ph 1:8. Col +3:12.

2. Fulfil. ver. 16. Ph 1:+4, 26, 27. Jn 3:29. +15:11. 2 C 2:3. 7:7. Col 2:5. 1 Th 2:19, 20. 3:6-10. 2 Th *2:13. 2 T 1:4. Phm 20. 1 J 1:3, 4. 2 J 4. 3 J 4. that. See on Ph 1:27. likeminded. ver. 20. Ph 3:15, 16. 4:2. Ro +12:16. 15:5n, 6. 1 C *1:10. 2 C 13:11. 1 P 3:8, 9. one accord. Ac 1:14. 2:1, 46. 5:12.

3. nothing. ver. 14. Ph 1:15, 16. Pr 13:10. Ro 13:13. 1 C 3:3. 2 C 12:20. Ga 5:15, 20, 21, *26. Col 3:8. 1 T 6:4. Ja *3:14-16. 4:5, 6. 1 P 2:1, 2. strife. Ph 1:17. Ge 13:8. Ja +3:14. vainglory. Ga 5:26. but. Lk 14:7-11. 18:14. Ro *12:10. 1 C 15:9. Ep +4:2g. *5:21. 1 P *5:5. lowliness of mind. T#482. Pr 25:6, 7. Mt +*11:29 (T#62). *20:26, 27. Jn +*3:30. Ro. +*12:3, 10. 1 C 13:4. Ga 5:26. +6:1 (T#437). Ep 4:1, 2. 1 T +*6:17. esteem. 1 S *2:30. 15:17. ◖18:23. Jb ◖+*23:12. Ps +*119:21. Pr 25:27. Is ◖53:3, 4. Mt ◖+*22:39. Jn +*5:44. Ac 20:19. +*28:15. Ro √12:3, 10, 16. 1 C ◖*4:6. ◖11:5. ◖12:11. 2 C +*10:12. Ga ◖*6:4. Ep ◖*2:10. 5:21, ◖+*29. 1 Th ◖5:13.

4. Look not. ver. 21. Mt *18:6. Ro *12:15. *14:19-22. +*15:1, 2. 1 C *8:9-13. *10:24, 32, 33. *12:22-26. *13:4, 5. 2 C 6:3. 11:29. Ja *2:8, 15, 16. 1 J 3:14-18. others. Ga *6:2. Ja 2:15, 16. 1 J 3:14-18.

5. this mind. Mt +*11:29. *20:26-28. Lk 14:11. 18:14. 22:27. Jn *13:14, 15. Ac *10:38. +*20:35. Ro 14:15. *15:3, 5. 1 C *10:33. *11:1. Ep *5:2. 1 P *2:21. *4:1. 1 J +*2:6.

6. Who. Jn +*1:1n. in the form. Is +*7:14. 8:8. +*9:6. Je +*23:6. Mi +*5:2. Mt +*1:23. Jn *1:2, 18. *17:5. Ro +*9:5. 2 C +*4:4. Col +*1:15, 16. 1 T *1:17. *3:16. T *2:13. He *1:3, 6, 8. +*13:8. of God. This is a clear assertion on Paul's part of the deity of Christ. Daniel Waterland gets to the crux of the controversy by setting forth two series of texts. The first series includes Is 43:10. 44:8. 45:5. 46:9, which declare that God is one, and to him none can be likened. The second series includes Jn 1:1. Ro 9:5. Ph 2:6. He 1:3, 8, which declare that Jesus Christ is God. The consequences of the Arian scheme are that if the texts of Isaiah exclude the Son, he is altogether excluded, and is no God at all. He cannot, upon Arian principles, be the same God, because he is not the same Person: he cannot be another God, because he is excluded by the Isaiah texts. If, therefore he be neither the same God, nor another God, it must follow, that he is no God. This is the difficulty which lies against the Arian scheme, and which Arians have not sufficiently attended to. It will not do to make Jesus Christ "a god" in a lesser sense, reserving only to the Father the title of supreme God, for neither Isaiah, nor the first commandment, allow for such a distinction. If they had allowed such a distinction, then in what sense would the worship of Baal and Ashteroth be considered idolatry, if they were merely looked upon as inferior deities, and served with a subordinate worship? The Old Testament texts cannot mean that there is merely no other *Supreme* God; but absolutely *no other*: and therefore our blessed Lord must either be included and comprehended in the one Supreme God of Israel, or be entirely excluded with the other pretended or nominal deities. In no case have the Arians proved— what must be proved if their understanding is to be received as correct—that texts which designate God

the Father as the "only true God" (Jn 17:3) or "one God" (1 C 8:6) are meant to teach that the Son is absolutely excluded also from such designations, just as the Son is emphatically designated *one Lord* (Ep 4:5) without design to exclude the Father from being Lord also (see Daniel Waterland, *Works*, vol. 1, pp. 275-280). Waterland observes that the tactics of Arians in his day were to industriously run from the point, misrepresent our sense, and artfully conceal their own—characteristics which have not changed from his day to ours. Jesus must either be entirely excluded by the Isaiah texts, or not at all: and if he be not excluded, he is comprehended in the one Supreme God, and is one with him. Arians produce texts to show that the Father *singly* is the Supreme God, and that Christ is excluded from being the Supreme God: but I insist upon it, that you misunderstand those texts; because the interpretation you give of them is not reconcilable with other texts; and because it leads to such absurdities, as are too shocking even for yourself to admit. In short, either you prove too much, or you prove nothing (Waterland, vol 1, p. 278, 281). Subsisting in the form of God proves his nature and essence to be divine. John Daille states "As then the Lord Jesus, before He took our flesh, was in the form of God, it necessarily follows that He was truly God, no one being able to have the glory of God but He who had His nature also. And what the apostle adds, that He was "equal with God," clearly also determines the same thing; it being evident that if the Son were a creature, He could not be equal to God; every creature being of necessity infinitely below the nature, power, and majesty of the Creator" (Comm. on Philippians, Sermon 9, pp. 91, 92). **thought**. Ge *32:24-30. *48:15, 16. Ex *3:2-6. Jsh *5:13-15. Ho *12:3-5. Zc +*13:7. Jn +√5:18, 22, 23. √8:58, 59. +√10:30, 33, 38. *14:9. +√20:28. He 5:5. Re *1:17, 18. *21:6. **not robbery**. or, counted it not a prize. The Greek word *harpagmos* may bear either of two meanings: (1) in the active sense, the act of seizing, robbery; (2) in the passive sense, a thing held as a prize. The orthodox position may accept of either meaning, but the Arian position requires the latter meaning only, which is the reason they contend so strongly for it. The former meaning may be understood in the sense "Who *because* He was subsisting in the essential form of God, did not regard it as any usurpation that He was on an equality of glory and majesty with God, *but yet* emptied Himself of that co-equal glory"; the latter meaning may be understood in the sense "Who *though* He was subsisting in the essential form of God, *yet* did not regard His being on an equality of glory and majesty with God as a prize and a treasure to be held fast, *but* emptied himself thereof" (Vine, *Expository Dictionary*, vol. 3, p. 216, citing Gifford, *The Incarnation*, pp. 28, 36). Waterland offers the following explanatory paraphrase for the second view: "Who being essentially God (and consequently having a rightful claim to be honored equally with God), yet did not covet or desire to be so honored, did not insist upon his right; but, for the greater glory of God, and for the good of others, chose rather (in the particular instance of his incarnation) to wave his pretensions, and, in appearance, to recede from them" (*Works*, vol. 2, p. 110). Jn +*5:18. *10:33. ◐+*14:30. **equal with**. √45, Is +40:31. √24G, Ge 1:9. i.e. on an equality with God. This is what

the first man grasped at, tempted and deceived by the Old Serpent. But Christ, the second man, the last Adam, did not think it a matter to be grasped at in this way, "but humbled Himself," and through suffering and death reached His exaltation (B496). Seven steps downward in the Savior's humiliation are followed in verses 9-11 by seven steps upward in His glorification (B433). Is 40:25. 45:5. Zc 13:7. Ml 3:6. Jn +*5:18n. Re 1:17.

7. **made**. Ps 22:6. Is 49:7. *50:5, 6. 52:14. *53:2, 3. Da 9:26. Zc *9:9. Mk *9:12. Jn *6:38. Ro *15:3. 2 C *8:9. He *2:9-18. +*12:2. *13:3. **no reputation**. or, emptied himself. Waterland explains "we are not to suppose that he lost anything which he had before; or that he ceased to be in the *form of God*, by taking on him the *form of man*. No: he had the same *essential* glory, the same *real* dignity, which he ever had, but among men concealed it; appeared not in majesty and glory like to God, but divested himself of every dazzling appearance, and every outward mark of majesty and greatness, condescending to appear, and act, and converse as a man, like unto us in all things, sin only excepted" (*Works*, vol. 2, pp. 111, 112). Various *kenosis* theories have since been devised in an attempt to define what Christ "emptied himself" of—some asserting that he emptied himself of his divine nature, exchanging it for a human nature (thus denying the doctrine of the two natures in Christ); others assert that he gave up some of his divine attributes (such as omniscience, omnipotence, essential holiness—and so could sin, though he did not, though Scripture clearly affirms Christ was not able to sin, He 4:15); or his prerogatives as deity. Waterland's observation that Christ gave up only the visible manifestation of his glory is the one explanation fully verified by Scripture. Ex=40:34. Mk +9:12g. Jn √17:5. Ac 8:33. 1 C +1:17g. 2 C *8:9. 13:4. Re *5:12, 13. **and took**. This refutes the error which maintains that Christ did not always possess a divine nature, for he had that nature, being in the form of God, before he took upon himself human nature, in the form of a servant. Is √9:6. **the form**. Is *42:1. 49:3, 6. 52:13. *53:11. Ezk *34:23, 24. Zc *3:8. Mt *12:18. *20:28. Mk *10:44, 45. Lk *22:27. Jn *13:3-14. Ro +*15:8. **a servant**. Ge=39:1. Ps=105:17. Is=49:7. Mt 20:28. **was made**. Jn +1:14. Ro 8:3. Ga 4:4. **in the**. ver. 6. Jn *1:14. Ro 1:3. *8:3. Ga *4:4. He *2:14-17. +*4:15. **likeness**. or, habit.

8. **found**. √171J5, 1 S +13:15. **in**. Mt 17:2. Mk *9:2, 3. Lk 9:29. **he humbled**. ver. 7. Pr *15:33. Lk 2:51. Ac 8:33. 2 C *8:9. He *5:5-7. *12:2. **and became**. Ps *40:6-8. Is *50:5, 6. Mt *26:39, 42, 52-54. Jn *4:34. *15:10. Ro 5:19. He *5:8, 9. *10:7-9. **the death**. √16, Ge +1:27. Dt 21:23. Ps *22:16. Jn *10:18. *12:28-32. 14:31. Ga +*3:13. T *2:14. He *12:2. 1 P *2:24. *3:18.

9. **Wherefore**. Jn 10:17. **God**. Ge +*3:15. Ps 2:6-12. 8:5-8. 45:6, 7. 69:29, 30. 72:17-19. 91:14. 110:1-5. Is +*9:7. 49:6-8. 52:13. *53:12. Da 2:44, 45. *7:14. Mt +*11:27. *28:18. Lk 10:22. Jn 3:35, 36. 5:22-27. 13:3. 17:1-3, 5. Ac 2:32-36. 5:31. Ro 14:9-11. 1 C 15:24-27. He *2:9. 12:2. 2 P 1:17. Re +*1:5. 3:21. 5:12. 11:15. 19:16. **given**. Ph 1:29g. Ps 89:27. Ep *1:20-23. Col +*1:18. He 1:4. 1 P 3:22. **a name**. √121T4, Ep +1:21. 1 S 18:30mg. SS 1:3. Ac 5:41. Ep 1:21. He 1:4. **above**. 1 Ch ◐29:11.

10. **at the name**. Is √45:23. Jn 8:24. **every knee**.

Ge=41:43. Ex=11:8. Is √45:23-25. Mt +14:33. 27:29. 28:18. Jn √5:23. Ro 11:4. 14:10, 11. 1 C *15:24, 25. Ep 3:14. Col *1:18. He 1:6. Re 1:7. 4:10. 5:+12, 13, 14. **bow.** ſ121S3H, Is +45:23. **of things.** Ep +*1:10. Re 5:3, 13. **under.** Ex 20:4. Dt 5:8. Mt +*12:40n. Jn 5:28, 29. Ep 4:9. Re 20:13.

11. **every.** Ps 18:49mg. Mt 10:32. Jn 9:22. 12:42. Ro √10:9. 15:9. 1 C 12:3. 1 J 4:2, 15. 2 J 7. Re 3:5. **Jesus Christ.** Ac +*2:36. Col 2:6. **is Lord.** Ps 110:1. Je +*23:6. Lk 2:11. Jn +13:13. +*20:28. Ac *2:36. +√10:36. Ro *10:9-12. *14:9, 11. 1 C *8:6. +*12:3n. √15:47. Col *2:9. 1 P +*2:3n. **to the.** Jn √5:23. 13:31, 32. 14:13, 23. 16:14, 15. 17:1. Ro 15:7. 1 P 1:21. **glory.** Ph 1:11. Ro +*3:23.

12. **my beloved.** Ph *4:1. 1 C *4:14. 1 P *2:11. **as ye.** Ph *1:5, 27, 29. 4:15. **always obeyed.** Ro 6:17. 2 C 10:5. He +*5:9. *13:7, 17. 1 P +*1:22. **presence.** Gr. *parousia,* Mt +24:3n. Ph 1:+26, 27. **much more.** Ge 39:6. Ex +*18:21. Le=6:13. 2 K *12:15. 22:2. Jb 27:5, 6. Ps 12:1. *15:2-5. 18:21-23. Pr 11:3. 20:6, 7. +*22:6. ❍*25:19. Je 5:1. +*12:5. 15:18mg. 35:6-10. Da 1:8. Mk 13:32-36. Lk +*16:10. Ac +*6:3. 1 C 4:2. +*15:58. Ep *6:5-8. Col √3:22-24. **in my absence.** Mt 24:46. 25:14, 15, 19. Jn 20:29. **work out.** Ph *3:13, 14. Pr *10:16. *13:4. 31:27. Mt *11:12, 29. Lk *13:23, 24. Jn *6:27-29. Ro +*2:7. 1 C *9:24-27. √15:58. 2 C 4:17g. *7:1. Ga *6:7-9. 1 Th *1:3. He +*3:14. *4:11. +*6:10, 11. *12:1. 2 P √1:5-11. +*3:18. **own.** Ph 2:19. Ro *13:11-14. 1 C 9:20-23. 2 T 2:9, 10. **with fear.** Ezr *10:3. Ps *2:11. *119:120. Is *66:2, 5. Ac +*9:6. 16:29. 1 C +*2:3. 2 C 7:15. Ep *6:5. He *4:1. *12:28, 29. 1 P √4:17, 18.

13. **For.** Jn 6:65. **it is God.** 2 Ch 30:12. Is *26:12. Je 31:33. *32:39. Jn *3:27. Ac 11:21. 1 C 12:6. +15:10. 2 C *3:5. He *13:21. Ja *1:16-18. **which worketh.** Ps 68:28. Pr 16:1. Is 26:12. 43:13. Mt +14:2. 2 C 6:1. **to will.** 1 K *8:58. 1 Ch 29:14-18. Ezr 1:1, 5. 7:27. Ne 2:4. Ps 110:3. 119:36. 141:4. Pr *21:1. Jn *6:45, 65. Ac +*13:48. Ep 2:4, 5. 2 Th *2:13, 14. T 3:4, 5. 1 P 1:3. Re 17:17. **good pleasure.** Ps +*115:3. Lk +2:14. *12:32. Ro 9:11, 16, +*18. Ep *1:5, 9, 11. *2:8. 2 Th *1:11. 1 T 2:4. 2 T +*1:9.

14. **without murmurings.** ver. 3. Ex *16:7, 8. Nu +*11:1. 14:27. Ps *106:25. 144:14. Is +√29:24. 58:13. La 3:39. Mt *20:11. Mk 14:5. Lk 10:40. Ac 6:1. 1 C *10:10. Ja *5:9. 1 P *4:9. Ju +*16. **disputings.** Pr 13:10. *15:17, 18. Mk 9:33, 34. Ac 15:2, 7, 39. Ro *12:18. 14:1. *16:17. 1 C 1:10-12. 3:3-5. 2 C 12:20. Ga 5:15, 26. Ep +*4:31, 32. 1 Th 5:13, 15. 1 T 2:8. *6:3-5. He +*12:14. Ja 1:20. *3:14-18. *4:1. 1 P 3:11.

15. **blameless.** Ph 3:6. Lk 1:6. 1 C *1:8. Ep 5:27. 1 Th *5:23. 1 T 3:2, 10. 5:7. T 1:6. 2 P √3:14. **and.** Mt *10:16. Ro *16:19. Ep 5:15. He *7:26. **harmless.** *or,* sincere. Ph 1:10. **sons of God.** Mt *5:45, 48. Lk +*6:35. Jn 1:12. 11:52. Ro 8:16, 17, 21. 9:8. 2 C √6:17, 18. Ep 5:1, 2, 7, 8. 1 P 1:14-17. 2:9. 1 J √3:1-3, 10. 5:2. **rebuke.** Ep +1:4. 1 T 5:14, 20. T *2:10, 15. **in the midst.** Jn 17:15. 1 C 5:10. 1 P +*2:12. **a crooked.** Dt=*32:5. Ps 125:5. Mt 17:17. Lk 9:41. Ac +2:40. 20:30. 1 P +2:12. Re 3:9. **ye shine.** *or,* shine ye. Is 60:1. Mt *5:14-16. Lk 5:35. 8:12. Ep *5:8. T *2:10. **as lights.** Ps 119:130. Pr +*4:18. Re 21:11. **world.** Gr. *kosmos,* Mt +4:8.

16. **Holding forth.** Ph 1:27. Dt=33:11. Ps 40:9, 10. 71:17, 18. Mt 10:27. Lk 12:8. Ro *10:8-16. 2 T 4:2. Re 22:17. **the word.** Jn *6:63, 68. Ac 5:20. 13:26. 2 T

*2:15-17. He √4:12. 1 P *1:23. 1 J 1:1. **that I may rejoice.** Ph +1:26. 2 C 1:14. 1 Th *2:19, 20. **the day of Christ.** Ph 1:6, 10. 1 C +*1:8. **not run in vain.** Is 49:4. 1 C 9:24-26. Ga 2:2. +*4:11. 5:7. **labored in vain.** Is 49:4. 65:23. Ga +*4:11. 1 Th 3:5.

17. **and if.** ſ185A, Lk +11:8. ver. 30. Ph 1:20. Ac *20:24. 21:13. 2 C 12:15. 1 Th 2:8. 2 T 4:6. 1 J 3:16. **offered.** Gr. poured forth. Le +=23:13 (drink offering). Nu 28:7. Is 53:12. 2 C +12:15. 2 T *4:6. 1 J 3:16. **the sacrifice.** Ph 4:18. Ro +*12:1. 15:16. He 13:15, 16. 1 P 2:5. **and service.** Lk +1:23. Ro 15:16. **I joy.** Ph +1:4. Mt +*5:12. 2 C 7:4. Col *1:24. 1 Th 3:7-9.

18. **do.** Ph 3:1. 4:4. Ep 3:13. Ja 1:2-4.

19. **But.** *or,* Moreover. **I trust.** ver. 24. Je 17:5. Mt 12:21. Ro 15:12. Ep 1:13. 2 T 1:12mg. Ja *4:15. 1 P 1:21. **to send.** ver. 23, 25. Ph 1:1. Ro 16:21. 1 C √4:17. Ep 6:21, 22. Col 4:8, 9. 1 Th 3:2, 6. **Timotheus.** Ph 1:1. Ac +16:1. **that I.** ver. 28. 1 Th 3:6-8. 2 Th 1:3. Phm 5-7. 3 J 3, 4.

20. **I have.** ver. 2, 22. Ps 55:13. Pr 31:29. Jn 10:13. 12:6. 1 C 1:10, 11. Col 4:11. 1 T 1:2. 2 T 1:5. **likeminded.** *or,* so dear unto me. 1 S 18:1, 3. 1 C 16:10. **naturally.** or, truly. Gr. genuinely. Ph +4:3. **care.** Mt +6:25g.

21. **all.** ſ171A, Ex +9:6. **seek.** T#136. ver. 4. Jb +*21:15 (T#689). Is 56:11. Ml 1:10. Mt *16:24. Lk 9:57-62. 14:26. Ac 13:13. ˙15:38. 1 C *10:24, 33. 13:5. 2 T 1:15. 3:2, +5 (T#191). 4:10, 16. **the things.** Ph 1:20, 21. 2 C 4:5. √5:14, 15.

22. **ye.** Ac 16:3-12. 2 C 2:9. 8:+2, 8, 22, 24. **as.** See on ver. 20. 1 C *4:17. 1 T 1:2, 18. 2 T 1:2. T 1:4. **served with me.** 2 T 3:10. **in the gospel.** Ph 4:3. Ro 1:9.

23. **to send.** ver. +19. **so soon.** 1 S 22:3.

24. **trust.** See on ver. 19. Ph 1:25, 26. Ro 15:28, 29. Phm 22. 2 J 12. 3 J 14.

25. **Epaphroditus.** Ph 4:18. Col 1:7. 4:12. Phm 23. **my brother.** 2 C 2:13. 8:22. Phm 1. **companion.** Ph 4:3. Ro +16:3. 1 C 3:9. 2 C 8:23. Col 1:7. 4:11. 1 Th 3:2. Phm 1, 24. **fellowsoldier.** 2 T *2:3, 4. Phm 2. **messenger.** Gr. apostle. Pr 25:13. Jn 17:18. 1 C +12:28. 2 C 8:23. He 3:1g. **and he.** Ph 4:18. 2 C 11:7-9. **that ministered.** Ro +13:6. **my wants.** ver. 30. Ph *4:18.

26. **he longed.** Ph 1:3, +8. 4:1. 2 S 13:39. Ro 1:11. 2 C 9:14. **full.** Jb 9:27. Ps 69:20. Pr 12:25. Is 61:3. Mt 11:28. 26:37. Mk 14:33. Ro 9:2. 1 P 1:6. **ye had.** 2 S 24:17. Jn 11:35, 36. Ac 21:13. Ro 12:15. 1 C 12:26. Ga 6:2. Ep 3:13.

27. **sick nigh.** ver. 30. 2 K 20:1. Ps 107:18. *116:15. Ec 9:1, 2. Is +*38:1. Jn 11:3, 4. Ac 9:37. **but God.** 2 K 20:5. Jb 5:19. Ps 30:1-3, 10, 11. 34:19. +*41:3. +*103:3, 4. *107:19-22. Is 38:17. 43:2. Ac 9:39-41. 1 C 7:25. 2 C 4:1. 1 T 1:13, 16. **but on.** Is *27:8. Je 8:18. 10:24. 45:3. Hab 3:2. 1 C +*10:13. 2 C 2:7.

28. **more carefully.** Lk 7:4. 2 T 1:17. T 3:13g. **ye see.** ver. 26. Ge 45:27, 28. 46:29, 30. 48:11. Jn 16:22. Ac 20:38. 2 T 1:4. **rejoice.** Ph +1:4. **and that.** See on ver. 27. 2 C 2:3. 1 J 1:3, 4.

29. **Receive.** Ph 2:19, 24, 29. Mt *10:40, 41. Lk 9:5. Jn 13:20. Ro 16:2. 1 C 16:10. 2 C 7:2. Col 4:10. 3 J 10. **gladness.** Ph +1:4. 3:1. 4:4, 10. Is 52:7. Lk 2:10, 11. Ac 2:46. 8:8. Ro 10:15. Ep 4:9-12. Col 3:17. **and.** 2 C 10:18. 1 Th *5:12, 13. He 13:17. **hold such in reputation.** *or,* honor such. Lk 7:2. Ac 28:10. 1 C 16:18. 1 T *5:17.

30. **the work.** 1 C 15:53. 16:10. **nigh.** ver. 17, 27. Ph 1:19, 20. Mt *25:36-40. Ac 20:24. Ro 16:4. 2 C

12:15. Re √12:11. **life**. Gr. *psyche*, ſ121A7, Mt +2:20. ſ121A7, Ge +9:5. **to supply**. Ph 4:10, 18. 1 C +16:17. Phm 13. **your lack**. ver. 25. **service**. Ro 15:27. 2 C 9:12.

PHILIPPIANS 3

The apostle exhorts to joy in the Lord, and gives cautions against false teachers, 1, 2; shows that the church of real Christians are the true "circumcision," 3; and that he had better grounds of carnal confidence than most of those who trusted in the law, or inward distinctions, 4-6; but he had learned to count all his gain loss for Christ; yea, that he still counted all things, as loss and dung, compared with the knowledge of Christ, and the "righteousness of God by faith" in him, 7-9; desiring also to know the power of his resurrection, and to be conformed to him, even in suffering and death; if so be he might attain to the resurrection of the just, 10, 11. He owns, that he was not yet perfect, but that he anxiously and earnestly sought "the prize of the high calling of God," 12-14. He exhorts to an imitation of his example, 15-17; as many, professing Christianity, "walked after the flesh," in the way of destruction, 18, 19; with whom he contrasts true Christians, their heavenly conversation, and their expectation of Christ to raise their "vile body," and render it "like to his glorified body," 20, 21.

1. **Finally**. Ph √4:8. 2 C 13:11. Ep *6:10. 1 Th *4:1g. 2 Th 3:1. 1 P 3:8. **rejoice**. ver. 3. Ph +1:4. *4:4. Dt *12:18. *16:11. 1 S *2:1. 1 Ch 15:28. *16:10, 31-33. 29:22. 2 Ch 30:26, 27. Ne *8:10. Jb 22:26. Ps *5:11. 32:11. 33:1. *37:4. 42:4. 97:1. *100:1, 2. 149:2. Is +*12:2, 3. 41:16. *61:10. 65:14. 66:11, 12. Jl 2:23. Hab √3:17, 18. Zp *3:14, 17. Zc 10:7. Mt +*5:12. Lk 1:47. Ro 5:2, 3, 11. 1 Th +*5:16. Ja *1:2. 1 P *1:6-8. *4:13. **To write**. Ph 2:17, 18. Ro 15:14, 15. 2 P *1:12-15. *3:1. Ju 5.

2. **Beware of dogs**. Ps 22:16, 20. Pr 26:11. Is 56:10, 11. Mt 7:+*6, 15. 24:10. Ga 5:15. 2 T 4:14, 15. 2 P √2:22. Re *22:15. **beware**. ſ18, Dt +28:4. **evil**. ver. 19. Ps 119:115. Mt *7:22, 23. 2 C √11:13. Ga 5:13. 1 T 1:19. 2 T 3:1-6. 4:3, 4. T 1:16. 2 P 2:18-20. Ju 4, 10-13. Re +*21:8. **the concision**. ver. 3. Ro +*2:28. Ga 2:3, 4. *5:1-3, 6. 6:13. Re 2:9. 3:9.

3. **we**. Ge 17:5-11. Dt *10:16. 30:6. Je 4:4. 9:26. Ro 2:25-29. *4:11, 12. Col *2:11. **circumcision**. Ex 12:48. Ro *2:29. **worship**. Ml 1:11. Lk +2:37. Jn √4:23, 24. Ro 1:9. *7:6. +*8:15, 26, 27. Ep 6:18. Ju *20. **in the spirit**. Gr. *pneuma*, Ac +18:25n. Ro 8:14. Ga 5:25. 1 P 4:14. 1 J 4:2. Ju 20. **rejoice**. See on ver. 7-9. Ps 105:3. Is 45:25. Je *9:23, 24. Ro 15:17. 1 C 1:29-31. Ga *6:13, 14. **have**. ver. 4-6. He *9:10. 1 P 1:23-25.

4. **have confidence**. 2 C *11:18-22. **If**. ſ184A, 1 C +15:2. **any other**. 1 C 3:18. 8:2. **thinketh**. ſ122, Ex +15:9.

5. **Circumcised**. Ge *17:12. Le 12:3. Lk 1:59. 2:21. Jn 7:21-24. **of the stock**. ſ41, Ge +10:1. Ac 22:3. 2 C 11:22. **of Israel**. Ro +*11:1. **of the tribe**. Ro +*11:1. **an Hebrew**. ſ147H, Ge +9:25. Ge 14:13. 40:15. 41:12. 1 S 4:6. Jon 1:9. Ac 6:1. 2 C 11:22. **as touching**. Ac 22:12. **Pharisee**. Ac +*23:6. *26:4, 5.

6. **zeal**. 2 S 21:2. 2 K 10:16. Ac 21:20. Ro +*10:2. Ga *1:13, 14. **persecuting**. Ac +*8:3. *9:1, etc. 22:3, 4. 26:9, 10. 1 C 15:9. 1 T 1:13. **touching**. ver. 9. Mt

√5:20, 27, 28. *19:17-20. 23:25. Mk 10:20, 21. Lk 1:6. Ac 26:5. Ro *7:9. 9:31, 32. 10:2-5. **blameless**. Ph 2:15.

7. **were gain**. ver. 4-6, 8-10. Ge 19:17, 26. Jb 2:4. Pr 13:8. 23:23. Mt +*13:44-46. 16:26. Lk 14:26, 33. *16:8. 17:31-33. Ac 27:18, 19, 38. Ga 2:15, 16. 5:2-5. **those**. ſ31, Is +1:21. **counted loss**. Lk 14:33. Ga √2:21. He 11:26.

8. **doubtless**. Nu 14:30. Ps +*126:6. Lk 11:20. 1 C 9:10. 1 J 2:19. **I count**. Ge 45:20. 2 Ch 25:9. Ac 20:24. Ro 8:18. 2 C *8:9. **the excellency**. ver. 10. Is *53:11. Je +*9:23, 24. Mt +*11:25-27. 16:16, 17. Lk 10:21, 22. Jn 14:7, 20. 16:3. *17:3, 8. 1 C *2:2. 2 C *4:4, 6. *5:15. +*10:5. Ga 1:16. Ep 1:17, 18. 3:8, 9, 18, 19. Col 2:2, 3. 1 P 2:7. 2 P 1:3. +*3:18. 1 J *5:20. **my Lord**. Lk 1:43. 20:42-44. Jn 20:13, +*28. **for whom**. See on ver. 7. Mt *19:27-29. Mk +*10:28-30. 1 C 4:9-13. 2 C 11:23-27. 2 T 4:6. **have suffered**. Lk +9:25g. **loss**. Ph ◐4:18. Mt +*16:26 (✱S#2210g). **but dung**. 1 K 14:10. 2 K 9:37. Jb 20:7. Ml 2:3. **win**. Mt 13:44-46. He +*3:14. 1 J 1:3.

9. **be found**. ſ171J5, 1 S +13:15. Ge *7:7, 23. Dt 19:3, 4. He *6:18. 1 P 3:19, 20. **in him**. Jn *15:4. See on Ro +*8:1n. 16:7. 1 C +*1:30. 2 C √5:17. **not having**. ſ64, Ps +1:1. ver. 6. 1 K *8:46. 2 Ch 32:25, 31. Jb 9:28-31. 10:14, 15. *15:14-16. 42:5, 6. Ps 14:3. 19:12. 130:3, 4. 143:2. Ec +*7:20. Is 6:5. +*53:6. √64:5, 6. Mt 9:13. Ro 9:31, 32. *10:1-3, 5. 2 T +*1:9. T √3:5. Ja 3:2. 1 J √1:8-10. **own righteousness**. Jb ◐27:6. Mt *5:20. **which is**. Dt 27:26. Lk 10:25-29. Ro *3:19, 20. *4:13-15. 7:5-13. 8:3. 10:4, 5. Ga 3:10-13, 21, 22. Ja *2:9-11. 1 J 3:4. **faith**. Mk +11:22. **the righteousness**. Ps 71:15, 16. Is 45:24, 25. 46:13. *53:11. Je +*23:6. 33:16. Da +*9:24. Jn 16:8-11. Ro +*1:17. *3:21, 22. 4:5, 6, 13. *5:19, 21. 9:30. *10:3, 4, 6, 10. 1 C +*1:30. 2 C √5:21. Ga *2:16. 3:11. 2 P 1:1.

10. **I may know**. ſ180D, Ex +20:18. See on ver. 8. Ro 13:11, 12. 1 C 15:34. Ep 4:13. 1 J 2:3, 5. **and the power**. Jn 5:21-29. *10:18. *11:25, 26. Ac 2:31-38. Ro +*1:4. *6:4-11. 8:10, 11. 1 C 15:21-23. 2 C 1:10. 4:10-13. 13:4. Ep 1:19-21. Col 2:13. *3:1, 2. 1 Th 4:14, 15. 1 P 1:3. 4:1, 2. Re 1:18. **and the fellowship**. Mt 20:23. Ro *6:3-5. 8:17, 29. 2 C 1:5. Ga √2:20. Col 1:24. 2 T *2:11, 12. 1 P +*4:13, 14. **made conformable**. ver. 21. 2 C *4:10, 11.

11. **If**. ſ184C, Mt +4:9. Ac 27:12g. Ro 1:10g. 11:14g. **by**. Ph *1:21. Ps 49:7. Ac 27:12. Ro 11:14. 1 C *9:22, 26, 27. 2 C *11:3. 1 Th 3:5. 2 Th 2:3. **attain**. ſ171J9, Ac +16:1. Lk *14:14. *20:35, 36. +*21:36. Jn *5:29. 11:24. Ac 23:6. 26:7. He 11:35. **resurrection**. lit. "out-resurrection." J. N. Darby affirms that "Scripture never confounds resurrection *of* and resurrection *out of* the dead" (*Collected Writings*, Vol. 11 (Prophetic No. 4, p. 364). W. J. Erdman states "It is very clear from these foregoing scriptures that believers in Christ, by virtue of their union with Him, share with Him a resurrection peculiar as to kind and as to time; it is the resurrection from among the dead, the rest of the dead waiting until their call to judgment comes. It is not a simultaneous raising of good and evil, nor a judgment of all in one brief period of time" (*The Unseen World*: A Concordance with Notes, p. 40). Ps ◐+*6:10. Is ◐+*24:21, 22. Lk +*14:14. *20:35. Jn 5:29. Ac 4:2. 26:23. 1 C 15:23. 1 Th +*4:16. 1 P 1:3. Re ◐+*20:5. **of the dead**. lit. from among *or* out of. Gr. *ek*, which expresses *out of, from, from among*, and (as noted in Peters, *Theocratic Kingdom*, vol 2, p. 298) invariably

before a genitive signifies a *whole* from which a *part* is taken (Ac 3:23. 19:33. 1 C 5:13. He 5:1). Da *12:2. Mk 9:9, 10. Lk √20:35g. Ac 4:2. 1 C 6:14g. 1 Th +*4:16n. 1 P *1:3.

12. **I had.** ver. 13, 16. Ph *1:21. Ps 119:5, 173-176. Ro 7:19-24. Ga 5:17. 1 T 6:12, 19. Ja 3:2. **either were.** Ex 23:29, 30. **already perfect.** ver. +*13. Jb √9:20. +*17:9. Ps +*37:18n. *138:8. Pr +*4:18. Ec +*7:20. Jn ●+*17:6. Ro √7:21. 1 C 13:10. 2 C +*7:1. 13:9. Ep *4:12. He 5:9. 11:40. √12:23. *13:21. Ja ●*3:2. √4:17. 1 P *5:10. 2 P √1:5-8. +*3:18. 1 J √1:8, 10. √2:1. ●√3:9. Re 3:2. **I follow.** ver. 14. Ps 42:1. 63:1-3, 8. 84:2. 94:15. Is 51:1. Ho +*6:3. 1 Th 5:15. 1 T 5:10. 6:11. He +*12:14, 15. 1 P 3:11-13. **if that.** √184C, Mt +4:9. ver. 13, 14. Ro 9:30. 1 C 9:24g. 1 T 6:12. **that for.** Ph 4:10g. **apprehended.** Ps 110:2, 3. Zc 3:2. Ac *9:3-6, 15. Ep 1:4. 2 Th 2:13.

13. **I count not.** ver. 8, +*12. Ph 1:18-21. 4:11-13. Ge *12:9. 26:13. Ps 27:4. Ec 3:19. Mk 10:21. Lk *10:42. Jn 9:25. 2 P +*3:18. **apprehended.** √63I2, Jsh +3:3. √63A2, 2 S +6:6. Supply ellipsis, (the prize). **one thing.** Ps 27:4. Lk +*10:42. 2 P 3:8. **forgetting.** Ge=45:20. Ps 45:10. Lk 9:62. 2 C 5:16. ●11:23-27. He 6:1. 12:1. **and reaching.** Ph *2:12. Jsh 13:1. Ro 15:23-29. 1 C *9:24-27. He +*12:1, 2.

14. **press.** Jsh +*14:8. Lk 16:16. 2 C *4:17, 18. 5:1. 2 T *4:7, 8. Re 3:21. **the prize.** 1 C +9:24. **the high.** Ro +*8:28-30. 9:23, 24. +11:29. Col 3:1, 2. 1 Th 2:12. 2 Th *2:13, 14. He 3:1. 1 P *1:3, 4, 13. *5:10. 2 P *1:3.

15. **as many.** Jn +*17:6. Ro *15:1, 8, 13, 14. 1 C 2:6. 14:20. 2 C 13:11. Ep +*4:13. Col *1:28. 4:12. 2 T +*3:17. He *5:14g. 6:1. Ja *1:4. 1 J *2:5. **be.** √108A1, Ex +8:18. √63B, Ge +25:28. or, supply "(desire to) be." **perfect.** ver. +*12. Mt +5:48. Jn +*17:6. 1 C +*2:6. **if.** √184A, 1 C +15:2. **otherwise.** Ga 5:10. **be thus.** ver. 12-14. **God.** Ps +*25:8, 9. Pr 2:3-6. √3:5, 6. Is 35:8. Ho *6:3. Lk 11:13. Jn +*7:17. Col +*2:7. Ja +*1:5.

16. **whereto.** Ga 5:7. He *10:38, 39. 2 P 2:10-20. Re 2:4, 5. 3:3. **let us walk.** √96B, Ex +20:8. Ro 12:16. 15:5n. Ga +5:25. 6:16. Ep 5:2-8. Col +*2:6. **let us mind.** See on Ph 1:27. 2:2. 4:2. 1 C √15:58.

17. **be followers.** Ph *4:9. 1 C +4:16. 10:32, 33. +*11:1. 1 Th 1:6. 2:10-14. 2 Th 3:7, 9. 1 T √4:12. He *13:7. 1 P +*5:3. **and mark.** Ps 37:37. Ro 16:17. 2 Th 3:14. **for an ensample.** or, example. He +*6:12.

18. **For.** √136, Is +60:12. **many walk.** Is 8:11. Da 4:37. 2 C +11:13. Ga 2:14. Ep 4:17. 2 Th *3:11. 2 P √2:10. Ju 13. **I have told.** 1 C +*6:9. Ga *5:21. Ep *5:5, 6. 1 Th +*4:6. **even weeping.** Ph 1:4. Ps *119:136. 126:6. Je 9:1. 13:17. Ezk +*9:4. Lk 19:41. Ac *20:19, 30, 31. Ro 9:2. 2 C 2:4. 11:29. He 13:17. **enemies.** Ph 1:15, 16. Ro *2:23, 24. 1 C 1:18. Ga 1:7. 2:21. √5:4. 6:12. 2 P *2:1, 2. **the cross.** 1 C +1:17.

19. **end.** √183. Hysteron-Proteron; or, Last First B703. Here, the "end" is put first, in order that the mind may dwell with greater horror on the things which lead to it. For other instances of this figure see He 3:8 and 4:2. Mt +*25:41. Lk *12:45, 46. 2 C 11:15. 2 Th √1:9. √2:8, 12. He *6:6-8. 2 P 2:1, 3, 17. Ju 4, 13. Re 19:20. 20:9, 10. +*21:8. *22:15. **destruction.** Nu 24:20. Dt +*32:29. Lk *12:45, 46. **whose God.** Ph 2:21. 1 S 2:11-16, 29. Is 56:10-12. Ezk 13:19. 34:3. Mi 3:5, 11. Ml 1:12. Lk *12:19. 16:19. Ro *16:17, 18. 1 T 6:5. 2 T 3:4. T *1:11, 12. 2 P 2:13. Ju 12.

belly. √171Q18, Ro +16:18. i.e. themselves, and what they can get. T#199. Ge 1:29. 9:3, 4. Ex 32:6, 7. Nu 11:32. Dt +*21:20, 21. Pr 21:17. 23:1-3, 20, 21. 25:16. Is 22:12, 13. √56:11. Je 35:14. Ezk +*16:49. Da 1:12, 15. Mt 6:31-33. ●11:19. Lk ●7:34. 16:19, 25. 21:34. Ro +14:21 (T#368). 1 C √3:16, 17. +*6:9, 10. 8:13. +9:25 (T#721). Ep +*5:18. 1 T 3:8. 4:3. T 1:12. 2:3. 1 P +*4:3. Ju 12. **whose glory.** Ps 52:1. Ho 4:7. Hab 2:15, 16. Lk 18:4. Ro +*1:28, 32. +6:21. 1 C 5:2, 6. 2 C 11:12. Ga 6:13. Ja *4:16. 2 P *2:18, 19. Ju 13, 16. Re 18:7. **who mind.** Ps 4:6, 7. 17:14. Mt 16:23. Ro √8:5-7. 1 C 3:3. Col ●*3:1, 2. 2 P 2:3. **earthly things.** Jn +3:12g.

20. **For our.** Ph 1:18-21. Ps +*16:11. *17:15. 73:24-26. Pr 15:24. Mt *6:19-21. 19:21. Lk 12:21, 32-34. 14:14. 2 C 4:18. 5:1, 8. Ep 2:6, 19. Col *1:5. √3:1-3. He 10:34, 35. 1 P +*1:3, 4. **conversation.** Ph 1:27. Is 26:1, 2. Ga 4:26. Ep +2:19. He *12:22, 23. Re 21:10-27. **is in.** Mt 22:32. He 11:13. **heaven.** √96F1, Ge +3:8. Ep *2:6. He +*11:16. **from whence.** Ac +*1:11. 1 Th √4:16. 2 Th *1:7, 8. Re +*1:7. **we look for.** Ph 1:10. 1 C +1:7. 15:23. 1 Th +*1:10. 2 T √4:8. T √2:13. He √9:28. 1 P 1:7. 2 P √3:12-14. **the Savior.** 2 T +1:10.

21. **shall change.** Jn +*5:29. 1 C *15:42-44, 48-54. 2 C ●11:13-15. **our vile body.** Ph 1:21, 23. Jb +*19:25, 26. Jn +*2:21, 22. Ro +6:6. 7:24. +*8:23. 1 C 15:40, 44. 2 C +*5:8. **fashioned like.** T#618. ver. 10. Ac +*2:24. Ro +*8:29. 1 C 15:35-37, 42-44, 50-54. 2 C 5:2-4. Col 3:4. 1 J √3:2. **his glorious.** Mt *17:2. Col *3:4. 1 J √3:2. Re 1:13, etc. **the working.** Is 25:8. +*26:19n. Ho *13:14. Mt 22:29. 28:18. Jn *5:25-29. *11:24-26. 1 C *15:25-27, 53-56. Ep 1:+19, 20. Re +*1:8, 18. 20:11-15. **to subdue.** 1 C 15:27, 28. Col +*3:16.

PHILIPPIANS 4

The apostle affectionately exhorts and encourages the Christians at Philippi to stedfastness in the faith, concord among themselves, and joy in the Lord, 1-4; and to moderation, confidence in God, constant prayer and thanksgiving, and positive themes for thought, 5-9. He declares his joy in the Lord, on account of their renewed care of him, in sending by Epaphroditus a supply for his wants, 10; for, though he had learned, and was able, "through Christ strengthening him," to be content in any station; they had done well in communicating with him in his affliction, 11-14. Indeed, they alone had formerly thus communicated with him: and he rejoiced that they were thus fruitful; as it would redound to their own profit; being a spiritual sacrifice particularly acceptable to God through Christ, who would abundantly supply all their needs, 15-19. To him he ascribes eternal glory, 20; and concludes with salutations and benedictions, 24-28.

1. **Therefore.** Ph *3:20, 21. 2 P √3:11-14. **and.** See on Ph 1:8. 2:26. **my joy.** Ph +1:4. 2:16. 2 C +1:14. 1 Th *2:19, 20. 3:9. **and crown.** Pr 16:31. 17:6. **so stand fast.** Ph +*1:27. Ps 27:14. 125:1. Mt 10:22. Jn √8:31. 15:3, 4. Ac *2:42. +*11:23. +*14:22. Ro +*2:7. 1 C √15:58. *16:13. Ga *5:1. Ep 6:10-18. Col *4:12. 1 Th *3:8, 9, 13. 2 Th 2:15. 2 T 2:1. He +*3:14. 4:14. 10:23, 35, 36. 2 P *3:17. Ju *20, 21, 24, 25. Re 3:10, 11.

2. **beseech.** √18, Dt +28:4. **Euodias.** i.e. *a sweet*

scent, **S#2136g. Syntyche.** i.e. *fate; well-met,* **S#4941g. same mind.** Ph +*2:2, 3. 3:16. Ge 45:24. Ps ch. 133. Mk 9:50. Ro 12:16-18. 15:5n. 1 C +*1:10. Ep 4:1-8. 1 Th 5:13. He +*12:14. Ja *3:17, 18. 1 P *2:13. 3:8-11.

3. **I.** ver. 2. Ro +*12:1. Phm 8, 9. **true.** See on Ph 2:20-25. Col 1:7. 1 T 1:2. T 1:4. **help.** Ph 1:27. Ac 9:36-41. 16:14-18. Ro 16:2-4, 9, 12. 1 T 5:9, 10. **which labored.** Ph 1:27g. **in the gospel.** Ph 2:22. Ro 1:9. **Clement.** i.e. *mild; merciful,* **S#2815g. fellow-laborers.** Ro +16:3. **whose names.** Ex 32:32. Ps 69:28. Is 4:3. Ezk 13:9. Da +*12:1. Lk +*10:20. He 12:23. Re *3:5. *13:8. 17:8. 20:12, 15. 21:27. **book.** *√*22D5K1A, Ex +32:32.

4. **Rejoice.** *√*66, Ge +9:3. See on Ph 3:1. 1 Ch=15:16. Ps *32:11. Ro *12:12. 1 Th +*5:16. 1 P *4:13. **alway.** Ps 34:1, 2. 145:1, 2. 146:2. Mt +*5:12. Ac 5:41. +*16:25. Ro 5:2, 3. 1 Th +*5:16-18. Ja *1:2-4. 1 P *4:13. **again.** *√*77, Ex +3:19. Ph +1:4. 3:1. 2 C 13:1, 2. Ga 1:8, 9.

5. **your moderation.** lit. your moderate. *√*24G, Ge 1:9. Ge 13:8. Pr 25:16. Mt 5:39-42. 6:25, 34. Lk 6:29-35. 12:22-30. *21:34. 1 C 6:7. 7:29-31. 8:13. *9:25. 2 C 10:1. Ep *4:2. T 3:2. He +*13:5, 6. Ja +*3:17. 1 P 1:11. **The.** Mt 24:48-50. 1 Th 5:2-4. 2 Th 2:2. He √10:25. Ja *5:8, 9. 1 P *4:7. 2 P *3:8-14. Re *22:7, 20. **at hand.** Dt 4:7. Ps 119:151. Ro +*13:12. 1 C *7:29-31. 16:22. 2 Th ❶+*2:2. Ja +*5:3.

6. **careful.** or, anxious. Ps +*34:4. Da 3:16. Mt *6:25-33. 10:19. *13:22. Lk 10:41. *12:22, 29. 1 C 7:21, 22, 32. 1 P √5:7. **in every thing.** T#1477. Ge *32:7-12. 1 S *1:15. *30:6. 2 Ch *32:20. *33:12, 13. Ps *34:5-7. 37:5mg. 51:15. √55:17, 22. *62:8. Pr √3:5, 6. *16:3. Je √33:3. Mt √7:7, 8. Lk +*11:9. *18:1, 7. Ep *6:18. Col *4:2. 1 Th +*5:17, 18. 1 P *4:7. Ju *20, *21. **by prayer.** Mt +17:21. **and supplication.** 1 T +2:1. **thanksgiving.** T#1415. 1 S 7:12. 2 S 22:50. Ne=11:17. Ps 30:4. 35:18. 50:14. 79:13. 100:4. 116:17, 18. 119:62. Da +*6:10. Jon 2:9. Ro +*1:8. 2 C 1:11. Ep *5:20. Col 2:7. *3:15, 17. 4:2. 1 Th *5:18. 1 T *2:1. Re 4:9-11. 7:12. 11:16, 17. **requests.** Gr. *aiteema,* **S#155g. Lk 23:34 (required). 1 J 5:15 (petitions). **known.** Pr *15:8. SS 2:14. Mt *6:8.

7. **the peace.** T#666. Ph 1:2. Nu 6:26. Jb 22:21. 34:29. Ps 29:11. 85:8. *119:165. Is √26:3, 13. 45:7. 48:18, 22. √55:11, 12. 57:19-21. Je 33:6. Lk 1:79. *2:14. Jn +*14:27. 16:33. See on Ro +*1:7. *5:1. 8:6. *14:17. 15:13. 2 C 13:11. Ga *5:22. Col 3:15. 2 Th 3:16. He +2:17 (T#582). *13:20. Re 1:4. **passeth.** Ep 3:19. Re *2:17. **shall keep.** or, guard. Dt 32:10. Ne *8:10. Pr 2:11. +*4:6, 23. √6:22. Is 26:3. 1 P +*1:5. **and minds.** 2 C +2:11g. **through.** 1 P 1:4, 5. Ju 1.

8. **Finally.** See on Ph 3:1. **whatsoever.** Ro *12:9-21. 1 C *13:4-7. Ga *5:22, 23. Ja *3:17. 2 P √1:5-7. **are true.** Mt 22:16. Jn 7:18. Ro 12:9. 2 C 6:8. Ep *4:25. 5:9. 6:14. 1 T 3:8, 11g. T 2:2g. 1 P 1:22. 1 J 3:18. **whatsoever things.** *√*18, Dt +28:4. **honest.** or, venerable. Ac +*6:3. Ro *12:17. *13:13. 2 C 8:21. 13:7. 1 Th 4:12. 1 T 2:2. 3:4, 8, 11. T 2:2, 7g. 3:14mg. He 13:18. 1 P 2:12. **are just.** Ge +*18:19. Dt 16:20. 2 S 23:3. Ps 82:2. Pr 11:1. 16:11. 20:7. Is 26:7. Mi +√6:8. Mk 6:20. Lk 2:25. 23:50. Ac 10:22. Col 4:1. T 1:8. **are pure.** Ps +*101:3. Hab 1:13. Mt +*5:8. 1 Th 5:22. 1 T √4:12. 5:2. T 2:14. Ja 1:27. 3:17. 2 P ❶2:14. 3:1. 1 J √3:3. **are lovely.** 2 S 1:23. SS 5:16. 1 C ch. 13. 1 P *4:8. **good report.** Ph *1:27. Ac +*6:3.

10:22. 22:12. Col 4:5. 1 Th +*5:22. 1 T 3:7. 5:10. T *2:10. He 11:2. **if.** *√*184A, 1 C +15:2. **virtue.** Ru 3:11. Pr 12:4. 31:10, 29. 1 P 2:9g. 2 P 1:3-5. **if.** *√*184A, 1 C +15:2. **praise.** Pr 31:31. Ro 2:29. 13:3. 1 C 4:5. 2 C 8:18. **think on.** Pr +*4:23. 16:3. 23:7. Is ❶+*66:4. Je +*6:19. Ezk ❶+*14:3. Lk 16:15. 2 C +*3:18. 10:5. 1 Th +*5:21. 1 J *4:1.

9. **which.** Ph *3:17. 1 C *10:31-33. +*11:1. 1 Th 1:6. √2:2-12, 14. 4:1-8. 2 Th *3:6-10. **learned.** *√*173, Ge +27:44. **received.** Col 2:6. **in me.** Ph 3:17. **do.** Dt 5:1. Mt *5:19, 20. 7:21, 24-27. Lk +√6:46. 8:21. Jn +*2:5. +*13:17. +*15:14. Ac 9:6. 2 Th 3:4. Ja +*1:22. 2 P √1:10. 1 J √2:3. *3:22. **the God.** ver. 7. Ro +15:33. *16:19, 20. 1 C *14:33. 2 C 5:19, 20. 13:11. 1 Th +*5:23. He *13:20, 21. **with.** Is 8:10. 41:10. Mt +*1:23. *28:20. 2 T 4:22.

10. **I rejoiced.** See on Ph 1:1, 3, +4. 2 C 7:6, 7. **your.** 2 C 11:9. Ga 6:6. **hath flourished.** or, is revived. Ph 2:30. Ps 85:6. Ho 14:7. 2 C 11:9. **wherein.** Ph 3:12g. **but ye lacked.** *√*78. Epitherapeia; or, Qualification B466. Addition of conclusion by way of modification. The figure is employed when a sentence is added at the end to heal, soften, mitigate, or modify what has been before said, so that modesty or other feeling might not be offended or injured. It may be added by way of apology. For another instance of this figure see Mt 26:41. 2 C 6:7. Ga +*6:10.

11. **in respect.** 1 C 4:11, 12. 2 C 6:10. *8:9. 11:27. **want.** Mk 12:44. **I have learned.** Ph 3:8. Ps 119:71. Is 1:16, 17. Mt 11:29. Jn 6:45. Ep 4:20-23. 1 T 5:4. He 5:8. 10:34. **therewith.** *√*63C, Ge +25:32. Supply ellipsis "to be content (with the will of God). **to be content.** T#133. Ge 28:20. Ex 2:21. Ps ❶+*77:3. Pr 15:16. ❶+*19:3. +23:4 (T#626). Is +*29:24. Mt √6:21-34. Lk *3:14. 2 C 9:8. 1 T √6:6-9. He +*13:5, 6.

12. **how to be.** Ac *20:33, 34. 1 C 4:9-13. 2 C 6:4-10. 10:1, 10. 11:7, 27. 12:7-10. **I am.** Dt 32:10. Ne 9:20. Pr *30:8, 9. Is 8:11. Je 31:19. Mt *11:29. +*13:52. Ep *4:20, 21. **suffer need.** Lk 15:14. 2 C 11:9.

13. **can do.** Nu 13:30. Jn *15:4, 5, 7. 2 C *3:4, 5. **all.** √*√*171A, Ex +9:6. **through Christ.** Is 40:29-31. *41:10. 45:24. See on 2 C √12:9, 10. Ep +*3:16. 6:10. Col *1:11. 1 T +1:12. **strengtheneth.** Dt 31:23. Jsh=17:17. Is 45:24. Zc 10:12. 2 C √12:9. Ep *3:14-17.

14. **ye have.** 1 K 8:18. 2 Ch 6:8. Mt 25:21. 3 J 5-8. **ye did communicate.** ver. 18. Ph 1:7. Ro 15:27. 1 C 9:10, 11. Ga 6:6. 1 T 6:18. He 10:33, 34. 13:16. Re 1:9.

15. **Philippians.** i.e. *war-like,* **S#5374g. beginning.** Ph +1:5. 2 K 5:16, 20. 2 C *11:8-12. 12:11-15. **I departed.** Ac 16:40. 17:1-5. **Macedonia.** Ac +16:9. **giving.** Ja 1:17g.

16. **even.** *√*63B, Ge +2:10. Supply by ellipsis (absolute: of the verb substantive), "For even (when I was) in Thessalonica." **in.** Ac +17:1. 1 Th 2:9. 2 Th 3:8. **once and again.** 1 Th 2:18.

17. **because.** ver. 11. Ml 1:10. Ac *20:33-35. 1 C 9:12-15. 2 C 9:5. 11:16. 1 Th 2:5. 1 T 3:3. 6:10. T 1:7. 1 P 5:2. 2 P 2:3, 15. Ju 11. **fruit.** Ph 1:11. Mi 7:1. Jn +*15:8, 16. Ro +1:13. 15:28. 2 C 9:9-13. T 3:14. **to your.** 1 S *30:24. Pr +*19:17. Mt √10:40-42. *25:34-40. Lk √14:12-14. Ac 10:4. 1 T √6:17-19. He +*6:10. +*10:34.

18. **I have all.** or, I have received all. Ph ❶3:8. Mt +6:2g. **abound.** ver. 12. Le=7:10. 2 Ch=31:10.

Mt 14:20. Lk 15:17. 2 Th 1:3. **having received**. Ph +2:25. **Epaphroditus**. i.e. *lovely; fascinating,* *S#1891g. Ph *2:25g, 26. **an odor**. Ex +=30:1. SS +=1:12. Jn 12:3-8. 2 C 2:15, 16. Ep +*5:2. He *13:16. 1 P *2:5. **smell**. ♪22C15, Ge +8:21. **sacrifice**. Is 56:7. **acceptable**. Ne =10:38. Ro +*12:1. 2 C 9:7, 12. **well-pleasing**. Ga *5:6. He √11:6.

19. **my God**. Ph +1:3. 2 S *22:7. 2 Ch 18:13. Ne *5:19. Ps *63:1. Da 6:22. Mi *7:7. Jn 20:17, +*28. Ro 1:8. 2 C 12:21. Phm 4. **supply**. Ge *48:15. Nu=7:5, 6. Dt *8:3, 4. Ne 9:15. Ps *23:1-5. 41:1-3. *84:11. 112:5-9. Pr *3:9, 10. *11:24, 25. Ml *3:10. Lk *12:30-33. 2 C *9:8-11. **all**. 2 Ch *25:9. Ro +*8:32. **your need**. T#1146. Ge=42:25. 2 Ch 20:12. Ps *9:18. 22:11. 25:16. 28:1. 31:9, 10. *37:3, 4. 38:1-8. 39:12, 13. 40:11, 12. 56:1. 69:1-3. 142:6. *143:7. La 1:20, 21. Mt *6:8. **according**. Ge 45:21. Ps 36:8. *84:11. *104:24. *130:7. Mt *6:33. 9:29. Ro +*2:4. +*8:32. 9:23. *11:33. Ep *1:7, 18. *2:7. 3:*8, 16, √20. Col *1:27. *3:16. 1 T *6:17. **riches**. ♪22D5I, Pr +8:18. **glory**. Ps 145:10-13. Ro √8:18. 1 C *2:9. 2 C √4:17. Col 1:12. *3:4. 1 Th *2:12. 1 P 5:1, 10.

20. **unto**. Ph 1:11. Ps 72:19. 115:1. Mt *6:9, 13. Ro +*11:36. 16:27. Ga 1:+4, 5. Ep 3:21. 1 T 1:17. 2 T 4:18. Ju *25. Re 1:6. 4:9-11. 5:12. 7:12. 11:13. 14:7. **for ever**. Gr. *aion*, Mt +6:13. **and ever**. Gr. *aion*, Mt +6:13. **Amen**. ver. 23. Mt 6:12. 28:20.

21. **Salute**. See on Ro 16:3-16. **saint**. Ph 1:1. 1 C 1:2. Ep 1:1. **The brethren**. Ro 16:21, 22. Ga 1:2. 2:3. Ep +6:23. Col 4:10-14. Phm 23, 24.

22. **the saints**. Ro 16:16. 2 C +1:1. 13:13. He 13:24. 1 P 5:13. 3 J 14. **they**. Ph *1:13. **Caesar's**. The cruel, worthless, and diabolical Nero was at this time emperor of Rome; but it is not improbable that the empress Poppaea was favorably inclined to Christianity, as Josephus relates that "she was a worshipper of the true God." Jerome states (in Philemon) that St. Paul had converted many of Caesar's family; for "being by the emperor cast into prison, he became more known to his family, and turned the house of Christ's persecutor into a church." Ac +17:7. 1 C *1:26. *7:20-22.

23. **grace**. Ro 16:20, 24. 2 C *13:14. Ga +6:18. **you all**. or, your spirit. Gr. *pneuma*, ♪171Q1B, Mk +2:8n.

COLOSSIANS

COLOSSIANS 1

The apostle salutes the saints at Colosse, 1, 2; thanks God for the good account which he had heard from Epaphras, of their faith and love, 3-8; shows how he prayed for their increasing knowledge, holiness, patience, joy, and gratitude for redeeming love, 9-14; declares in exalted terms the personal and mediatorial glory of Christ, 15-20; by whom they, who were once enemies, were now reconciled to God; and would be eternally saved, if they continued in the faith of the gospel, of which Paul was made a minister, 21-23; who rejoiced in all his labors and sufferings for their sakes, as the apostle of the Gentiles, 24-27; and labored earnestly, "according to the mighty power of God in him," 28, 29.

1. **an apostle**. See on Ro 1:1. 1 C 1:1. 2 C +1:1. Ep 1:1. **by the will**. 1 C +1:1. Ga *1:1. *2:8. **Timotheus**. Ac +16:1. Ph 1:1. 1 Th 1:1. 2 Th 1:1. Phm 1.

2. **To**. Is +*8:20n. Ro +*1:7. **the saints**. The term *agios, saint*, properly denotes a *holy person*, separated from sin, and consecrated to God, probably from *agos, a thing sacred, purity*; and such the gospel requires every man to be, and such every true believer is. To restrict it here to those who adhered to the purity of the Christian faith in opposition to the Judiazing Christians, greatly impoverishes and debases the sense, as Dr. Doddridge well remarks. Taking it in the sense of those few holy persons canonized by the church and now in heaven is of course a wholly mistaken and unscriptural view of the term. See on Ps 16:3. 1 C *1:2. Ga 3:9. Ep 1:1. 2 P *1:1. 1 J 1:3. **faithful brethren**. 1 C √4:17. Ep 1:1. 6:21. 1 J *3:14. **in Christ**. Ro 8:1n. **Colosse**. i.e. *punishment; monstrosities*, *S#2857g. **Grace**. Ro +1:7. Ga 1:3. 1 P 1:2. 2 P *1:2. Ju 2. Re 1:4.

3. **give**. Ro 1:8, 9. 1 C 1:4. Ep 1:15, 16. Ph *1:3-5. *4:6. 1 Th 1:2. **to God**. Ro +15:6. **praying**. ver. 9, 13. Ep *3:14-19. Ph *1:9-11. 1 Th 3:10-13. 2 Th *2:16, 17. 2 T 1:3.

4. **we**. ver. 9. 2 C 7:7. Ep 1:15. 1 Th 3:6. 3 J 3, *4. **faith**. Ga *5:6. 1 Th +*1:3. 4:9, 10. 2 Th *1:3. Phm *5. 1 P *1:21-23. 1 J *3:14, 23. *4:16. **the love**. He +*6:10. 2 P *1:5, 7.

5. **the hope**. ver. *23, 27. Ac +23:6. *24:15. 26:6, 7. Ro +*15:4. 1 C 13:13. *15:19. Ga *5:5. Ep *1:18, 19. +*4:4. 2 Th *2:16. T +1:2. He +3:6. 7:19. 1 P +*3:15. 1 J *3:3. **laid**. Ps *31:19. Mt √6:19-21. Lk 12:33, 34. Ph 3:20. 1 T 6:19. 2 T *4:8. 1 P √1:3, 4. **the word**. Col *3:16. Ac +*10:36. 13:26. Ro *10:8. 2 C 5:19. 6:7. Ep +*1:13. 1 Th *1:5. √2:13. 1 T 1:15. 2 T +√3:15-17. 1 P √2:2. **the truth**. Ga 2:5.

6. **is come**. ver. *23. Ps 98:3. Mt 24:14. +*28:19. Mk *16:15. Ro +1:8. *10:18. 15:19. 16:26. 2 C 10:14. **world**. Gr. *kosmos*, Mt +4:8. **bringeth**. ver. 10. Ge 39:3, 23. Dt 29:9. Jsh √1:8. Ps +*1:3. Is 44:4. Mk *4:8, 26-29. Jn +*15:16. Ac 12:24. Ro 1:13. 15:28. Ep *5:9. Ph *1:11. 4:17. 1 P *2:2. **since**. Ro √10:17. Ep 4:21. **knew**. Gr. *epiginosko*, Mt +11:27. Ps *110:3. Ac 11:18. *16:14. +*26:18. Ro 16:26. 1 C *15:10, 11. 2 C +*6:1. Ep *3:2. 4:23, 24. 1 Th *1:5. √2:13. 2 Th *2:13, 14. T √2:11, 12. 1 P 1:2, 3. *5:12. **the grace**. Ac +*11:23. *20:24. **in truth**. Jn √4:23.

7. **Epaphras**. i.e. *covered with foam*, *S#1889g. Col *4:12g. Ph 2:25. 4:18. Phm *23g. **our**. Col 4:17. See on Ph 2:19-22, 25. **faithful minister**. ver. 23, 25. Col 4:9. Nu 12:7. Mt +*24:45. *25:21. 1 C *1:17. +3:5. 4:+2, 17. *7:25. 2 C 11:23. Ep 6:21. 1 T *4:6. 2 T +*2:2. He 2:17. 3:2.

8. **love**. ver. 4. Ro *5:5. *15:30. Ga +*5:22. 2 T +*1:7. 1 P *1:7, 8, 22. *2:5. **the Spirit**. Gr. *pneuma*, Ac +18:25n.

9. **since**. ver. 3, 4, 6. Ro 1:8-10. Ep *1:15, 16. **do not cease**. 1 S √12:23. Ac *12:5. Ro +*1:9. Ep 1:16. Ph 1:4. 1 Th 1:3. +*5:17. 2 Th *1:11, 12. 2 T 1:3, 4. Phm 4. **to pray**. Mk *11:24. **that ye**. 1 C 1:5. Ep *1:15-20. 3:14-19. Ph *1:9-11. **the knowledge**. Col 2:2. 3:10. Ac +22:14. Ep 1:9. 4:13. Ph 1:9. 1 T +2:4. Phm 6. **of his will**. Col *4:12. Ps *143:10. Jn +*7:17. Ro +*12:2. Ep 5:10, *17. *6:6. 1 Th *4:3. He +*10:36.

*13:21. 1 P *2:15. 4:2. 1 J √2:17. **wisdom.** ver. 28. Col √3:16. √4:5. Ps *119:99. 1 C +12:8. Ep *1:8. Ja +*1:5. *3:17. **spiritual.** Ro +1:11g. **understanding.** Col 2:2. Ps +*119:27. Mk +12:33. Ep 5:17. 1 J *5:20.

10. **walk worthy.** T#1740. Col +*2:6. *4:5. Ps +*1:1, 3. *119:3. 128:1. Mi *4:5. Lk +√21:36. Ro 4:12. +*6:4. Ep *4:1. *5:2, 15. Ph *1:27. 1 Th *2:12. **all pleasing.** Col *3:20. Ps 147:11. 149:4. Pr +*16:7. 2 C 5:9. Ep 5:10. Ph 4:18. 1 Th *4:1. 2 T *2:4. He *11:5. *13:16, 21. 1 J *3:22. **fruitful.** T#1503. ver. 6. Ps +*1:3. Jn +*15:8, 16. 2 C 9:10. Ga +*5:22, 23. Ep √2:10. Ph *1:9-11. 4:17. T *3:1, 14. He *13:21. 1 P +*2:2. 2 P √1:8. **good work.** Ac +9:36. 2 C *9:8. T *3:1, 8, 14. **increasing.** Col 2:19. Is *53:11. Da +*12:4. Hab *2:14. Jn √17:3. 2 C 2:14. *4:6. √9:8. Ep *1:17. 4:13. 2 P 1:2, 3. +*3:18. 1 J 5:20, 21. **knowledge.** Ps +*51:6. Pr +*15:14. Ho *6:3, 6.

11. **Strengthened.** Dt *33:25. Jsh *1:9. Is 40:29, 31. See on Is 45:24. 2 C √12:9. Ep +*3:16. *6:10. Ph √4:13. He 11:34. **his glorious power.** √24.O, Ge +9:5. ver. 17, 29. Ex 15:6. Ps 63:2. Ac +*1:8. Ro 6:4. 2 C 4:7. Ep 1:19. He *1:3. Ju *25. **patience.** T#1633. Pr 24:10. Ac 5:41. Ro 2:7. *5:3-5. 2 C 6:4-6. √12:9, 10. Ep 4:2. 1 Th 3:3-5. 2 T 2:1-3. He *10:34-38. 11:34-38. +*12:1, 2. Ja *1:2-4. *5:7, 8. 2 P +*1:6. Re *14:12. **longsuffering.** T#1608. *S#3115g. Col 3:12. Ro 2:4. 9:22. 2 C 6:6. Ga *5:22. Ep +4:2. 1 T 1:16. 2 T 3:10. 4:2. He 6:12 (patience). Ja 5:10 (patience). 1 P 3:20. 2 P 3:15. **with joyfulness.** ver. 24. Mt +*5:12.

12. **Giving thanks.** Col *3:15, 17. 1 Ch 29:20. Ps 79:13. 107:21, 22. 116:7. Da 2:23. Ep 5:4, +20. **the Father.** Col 2:2. Jn √4:23. √14:6. *20:17. Ac +1:4. 1 C +*8:6. Ep 4:6. Ja 3:9. 1 J 1:3. **made us.** 1 K 6:7. Pr 16:1. Ro +*8:29, 30. *9:23. 2 C 3:6. *5:5. T √2:14. Re 22:14. **partakers.** Ro 11:17. 15:27. 1 C 9:23. Ep 3:6. He +*3:1, 14. 1 P *5:1. 1 J √3:1-3. **inheritance.** Ps 16:5. Da +*12:13. Mt +*25:34. Jn +*14:2. Ac 20:32. +*26:18. Ro √8:17. Ep +*1:11n, 18. 1 P √1:2-5. **the saints.** 2 C +1:1. **in light.** Ps 36:9. *97:11. Pr +*4:18. Is *60:19, 20. 2 C *4:6. He *12:23. Re *21:23. *22:5.

13. **delivered us.** Ps +*71:20. 86:13. Is 49:24, 25. *53:12. Mt 12:29, 30. Lk 8:27-35. Ac +*26:18. 1 Th +*1:10. He *2:14, 15. **the power.** Lk *22:53. Jn *12:31, 32. 2 C √4:4. Ep 4:18. *5:8. *6:12. 1 P *2:9. 1 J 2:8, 9. √3:8. **darkness.** Jb *10:21, 22. Ps 88:18. 143:3. Ac 6:4. Mi 7:8. Lk +*22:53. Jn 12:27. **and hath.** √96C6, Mt +2:4. Here, future blessings are spoken of as present (as *glorification*, Ro 8:30), for this kingdom is declared by Paul to be future, 2 T √4:1. The reference to the "inheritance" in the immediate context (ver. 12) verifies the reference to be future. As the inheritance is certainly future, so the kingdom with which it is associated must be future. Lk +*13:24. Jn √5:24. Ro 6:17-22. 1 C +*6:9-11. 2 C 6:17, 18. Ep *2:3-10. 1 Th 2:12. T 3:3-6. 2 P 1:11. 1 J 3:14. **the kingdom.** Ps *2:6, 7. Is +*9:6, 7. Da +√7:13, 14. Zc *9:9. Mt +*25:34. Ro *14:17. 1 C 15:23-25. 2 P √1:11. **his dear Son.** Gr. the Son of his love. √24B, Ge +9:5. Is 42:1. Mt √3:17. *17:5. Jn *3:35. *17:24. Ep 1:6.

14. **In whom.** Mt *20:28. +*26:28. Ac +*20:28. Ro *3:24, 25. Ga +*3:13. Ep √1:7. 5:2. 1 T √2:6. T √2:14. He *9:12, 22. 10:12-14. 1 P *1:19, 20. √3:18. 1 J √2:2. Re +*1:5. *5:9. 14:4. **redemption.** Ep *1:7. T *2:14. **through his blood.** √117, Ge +19:8. Ex 12:13. Ro +*3:25. 5:8. He 9:12. **the forgiveness.** Col 2:13.

3:13. Ps √32:1, 2. 130:4. Lk 5:20. 7:47-50. Ac +*2:38. +*10:43. +*13:38, 39. +*26:18. Ro √4:6-8. Ep √4:32. 1 J √1:9. *2:12. **of sins.** Le +=5:6.

15. **the image.** Ex 24:10. Nu *12:8. Ezk 1:26-28. Jn √1:18. √14:9. *15:24. Ro 8:29. 2 C *4:4, 6. Ph +*2:6. 1 T *3:16. He √1:3. **the invisible God.** Jn +*1:18. Ro 1:20. 1 T *1:17. √6:16. He 11:27. **the firstborn.** or, heir. √22D4C, Ro +8:29. √157, 1 C +15:6. Compare Ge 41:51, 52 w Je +√31:9. Ex *4:22, superiority of position, rank, priority. Dt 21:15-17. Ps +*89:20, *27. Consider Abraham's sons: Ishmael was the firstborn, but Isaac was the promised heir and seed, Ga 4:23. Consider also Jacob and Esau: Ge 25:23. Ml *1:1, 2, 3. Ro 9:12, 13. Among Jacob's sons, Reuben was the firstborn, but the birthright was Joseph's, 1 Ch 5:1, 2. Simri was made firstborn, 1 Ch 26:10, though expressly not born first. Manasseh was firstborn, but the blessing was given to Ephraim, Ge 48:14. If "firstborn" invariably means "born first," then how can Israel (Ex 4:22), David (Ps 89:27), and Ephraim (Je +√31:9), and Christ (Ro 8:29. Col 1:15, 18. He 1:6. Re 1:5) all be called by God "my firstborn"? Therefore, use of the term *firstborn* in reference to Christ says nothing concerning his origin, but declares his position, rank, and office. Note the use of "firstborn" in Jb 18:13. ver. 17, 18. Le +=23:10. Jsh √14:6n. 1 Ch 8:38n. Ps *89:27. Jn 1:14. √3:16. Ro +*8:29. He *1:2, 6. **of every creature.** ver. *16, *17. Pr *8:29-31. Re +*3:14.

16. **by him were.** ver. 15. Ps *102:25-27. Is *40:9-12. √44:24. Jn *1:3. 1 C +*8:6. Ep *3:9. He *1:2, 10-12. *3:3, 4. **all things.** Logically, if *all things* have been created by Christ, then he of necessity is uncreated, an absolute proof of His deity. This explains why the Jehovah's Witnesses in their *New World Translation* felt constrained, for doctrinal reasons, to make the unwarranted addition to the Word of God at this verse by adding "other" so as to read "all other things," making a lame attempt to justify such an addition by a reference to Lk 11:41, 42 or 13:2, 4. In the early editions (1950, 1951, and six volumes bound in one, 1963) of their translation, "other" was not even included in brackets, as it now is—a change perhaps prompted by the harsh criticism of many Bible scholars. ver. 17, 20. Is 44:24. Jn 1:3. Ep 3:9. He 1:2. 2:10. **in heaven.** ver. 20. Dt *4:39. 1 Ch 29:11. Ep +*1:10. Ph *2:10. Re *5:13, 14. **thrones.** √173, Ge +27:44. Col 2:10, 15. Ezk 10:1. Ro +*8:38. Ep *1:21. *3:10. *6:12. 1 P *3:22. **dominions.** Col 2:15. Ep +*1:21. **powers.** 1 P 3:22. **all things.** Ps 8:6. Pr 16:4. Jn +*1:3. Ph 3:21. ◖4:13. He 3:4. Re 4:11. **by him.** Pr *16:4. Is *43:21. Ro *11:36. 1 C 8:6. He *2:10. **for him.** T#76-2. Pr +16:4 (T#209). Ep 1:5. He +9:14 (T#346).

17. **he is before.** ver. *15. Pr *8:22, 23. Is *43:11-13. *44:6. Mi +*5:2. Jn +*1:1-3. √8:+*35, 58. +*17:5. 1 C +*8:6. He +*13:8. Re +*1:8, 11, 17. *2:8. **all things.** ver. 16, 20. 1 C *8:6. **and by him.** ver. 11. 1 S *2:8. Ne +*9:6. Ps 75:3. Jn +√5:17, 18. Ac *17:28. Ep 1:19. He √1:3. 2 P 3:5g. Re +*3:14.

18. **he is.** ver. 24. Col √2:10-14. 1 C +*11:3. Ep *1:10, +22, 23. *4:15, 16. *5:23. **the head.** √22A3B, Ep +1:22. **the church.** ver. 24. Ep +1:23. **the beginning.** Jn +*1:1. 1 J 1:1. Re +*1:8. +*3:14. 21:6. 22:13. **the firstborn from.** Le +±23:10. Jn *11:25, 26. Ac +*2:24. +*26:23. Ro *6:9. 8:29. 14:9. 1 C √15:20-23n. Re +*1:5, 18. **in all.** *or*, among all. ver. 16, 17, 20. Ps 45:2-5. 89:27. SS *5:10. Is 52:13. Mt 23:8. *28:18.

Jn 1:16, 27. 3:29-31, 34, 35. Ro +*8:29. 1 C *15:25. He +*1:5, 6. Re 5:9-13. √11:15. 21:23, 24. **preeminence.** Ge=37:7, 9. Ex *20:3. Jn √5:23. Ph *2:10.

19. **it pleased.** Col 2:3, 9. *3:11. Mt +*11:25-27. Lk *10:21, 22. Jn *1:16. *3:34. 1 C 1:21. 10:5. Ga 1:15. Ep *1:3, +5, 23. 4:10. Ja 1:12. 4:6. **in him.** 2 C 5:19. **fulness.** Col √2:9n. Jn 1:16. Ep 1:23.

20. **having made peace.** or, making peace. ver. 21, 22. Le 6:30. +=23:19. Ps *85:10, 11. Is +*9:6, 7. Ezk *16:63. 45:17-20. Da +*9:24-26. Mi +*5:2, 5. Zc *9:9, 10. Lk *2:14. Ac +*10:36. Ro √5:1. 2 C *5:19-21. Ep *2:13-17. He *13:20, 21. 1 J *4:9, 10. **through the blood.** ♪117, Ge +19:8. Ro +*3:25. Ep 2:13. He *10:10. **cross.** ♪117, Ge +19:8. **reconcile.** Le=16:20. Ro +5:10. 2 C *5:18. He 2:17. 1 J +2:2. **things in earth.** ver. 16-18. Ep *1:10. Ph *2:10.

21. **And you.** Col 2:13. Ep +*2:1. **alienated.** Nu=35:25. Ro +*1:30. *5:9, 10. *8:7, 8. 1 C +*6:9-11. Ep *2:1, 2, +12, 19. 4:18. T *3:3-7. He 9:15. Ja *4:4. **and enemies.** Mt *12:30. Ro 5:10. Ep 2:15. Ja *4:4. **in your mind by.** or, by your mind in. T *1:15, 16. **wicked works.** Mt *7:20. Jn +7:7. T 1:16. **reconciled.** Ro +*5:10. 2 C 5:18, 19. Ep 2:15, 16.

22. **the body.** Ro *7:4. Ep *2:15, 16. He *10:10, 20. **his flesh.** 1 P +*3:18. **death.** ♪171S8, Ro +5:10. **to present.** ver. 28. Lk 1:75. 2 C 11:2. Ep *1:4. *5:27. 1 Th *4:7. T √2:14. 2 P √3:14. Ju √24. **unreproveable.** 1 C +1:8. **in his sight.** Jb 15:15. *25:5. Ps +*51:7. Jn +*17:6. He *13:21.

23. **If.** ♪184A, 1 C +15:2. Ge +*4:7. Je +*7:5. 1 Th +*3:8. 2 P +√1:10. **ye continue.** T#514. Ps *92:13, 14. *125:5. Ezk *18:26. Ho 6:3, 4. Zp *1:6. Mt 10:22. *24:13. Lk +*8:13-15. *22:32. Jn √8:30-32. *15:+4, 6, 9, 10. Ac +*11:23. +*14:22. Ro +*2:6, 7. 1 C 9:27. *10:12. Ga +*4:11. *5:7. √6:9. 1 Th *3:5. He +*3:6, 14. *4:1, 11, 14. +*10:35, 38. 1 P √1:5. 2 P +*1:10. *2:18-22. 1 J *2:27. Re *2:7, 10, 11, 17, 26. 3:5. 12:21. 21:7. **grounded.** Col +*2:7. Mt *7:24, 25. Lk *6:48. Ep 2:21. *3:17. 4:+*14, 16. **and settled.** 1 C 7:37. +√15:58. 2 P √3:16. **not moved away.** Jn √10:27, 28. *15:6. Ac *20:24. 1 C √15:58. Ga 2:13. Ep +*4:14. 1 Th 3:3. He 10:38. 1 P √1:5. 2 P √3:17. 1 J √2:19. **the hope.** ver. +*5. Ro +*5:5. +*15:4. Ga *5:5. Ep *1:18. 1 Th *5:8. 2 Th *2:16. T *3:7. He √6:19. 1 P +*1:3, 4. 1 J √3:1-3. **to every.** ver. *6. Mt *24:14. Mk *16:15. Ro *10:18. **creature.** ♪171E2, Mk +16:15. **under.** Dt *2:25. *4:19. La 3:66. Ac *2:5. √4:12. **whereof.** ver. *25. Ac 1:17, 25. *26:16. Ro *15:16. 1 C 4:1-3. 2 C +*3:6. 4:1. *5:18-20. *6:1. *11:23. Ep *3:7, 8. 1 T *1:12. *2:7. 2 T *1:11, 12. *4:5, 6. **a minister.** 1 C +3:5.

24. **rejoice.** ver. 11. Mt +*5:11, 12. Ac *5:41. Ro *5:3. 2 C +7:4. Ep 3:+1, 13. Ph 2:17, 18. Ja *1:2. **fill up.** 2 C *1:5-8. *4:8-12. 11:23-27. Ph *3:10. 2 T 1:8. 2:9, 10. **afflictions of.** ♪181E, Ge +3:24. Lk 9:23. 2 C +1:5, 6. 1 P 4:13. **Christ.** ♪121K5, Ac +9:4. **for.** See on ver. 18. Ep 1:23. 4:12. **the church.** ver. 18. Ep +1:23.

25. **I am.** ver. +*23. 1 Th 3:2. 1 T *4:6. **according.** Ro 15:15-18. 1 C *9:17. Ga 2:7, 8. Ep *3:+2, 9. **to fulfill.** or, fully to preach. Ro *15:19. 2 T √4:2-5. **the word.** Ro +9:6.

26. **the mystery.** lit. the word concerning the mystery. ♪93A, Ge +1:26. Col 4:3, 4. Ro +*16:25n, 26. 1 C *2:7. Ep *3:3-10. 1 T *3:16. **hid.** Col 2:3. Ep 3:9. **ages.** Gr. aion, Mt +6:13. Ep 3:21. **now.** ♪15C,

Mk +6:11. Ps 25:14. Mt +*13:11. Mk 4:11. Lk 8:10. 2 T *1:10. **his saints.** Ps 30:4. *50:5. 52:9. 79:2. +*149:9. 1 Th 3:13. 2 Th 1:10.

27. **To whom.** Col 2:2. Mt +*13:11. 1 C √2:12-14. 2 C *2:14. *4:6. Ga 1:15, 16. **the riches.** ♪22D5I, Pr +8:18. ♪108B, Ro +2:4. Col √2:3. Ro 9:23. *11:33. Ep *1:7, 17, 18. *3:8-10, 16. Ph √4:19. **of the.** ♪29, Ex +19:6. **Christ.** Col 3:3, 11. Mt +*28:19n. Lk +*17:21. Jn 6:56. 14:17, 20, 23. *15:2-5. √17:22, 23, 26. Ro 8:10. 1 C √3:16. ◑+*12:13. 2 C *6:16. Ga √2:20. 4:19. Ep 1:23. 2:22. √3:17. 1 J 4:4. Re √3:20. **in you.** or, among you. A. T. Robertson states the idea is "in," not "among." "It is the personal experience and presence of Christ in the individual life of all believers that Paul has in mind, the indwelling Christ in the heart as in Ep 3:17. He constitutes also the hope of glory for he is the *Shekinah* of God" (*Word Pictures*, vol. 4, p. 485). **the hope.** ver. +*5. Ps +*16:9-11. Ro +*5:2. +*8:18, 19. 2 C √4:17. 1 T *1:1. He *6:18, 19. 1 P +*1:3, 4n. **of glory.** Col +*3:4. Ex 13:21. 40:35. Zc +*2:5. 2 P 1:17.

28. **Whom.** Ac 3:20. 5:42. 8:5, 35. 9:20. +*10:36. 11:20. +*13:38. +*17:3, 18. Ro +*16:25n. 1 C 1:23. 15:12. 2 C *4:5. 10:14. Ep *3:8. Ph 1:15-18. 1 T *3:16. **warning.** Col 3:16. Je √6:10. Ezk √3:17-21. 33:4-9. Mt 3:7. Ac +*20:27, 28, 31. Ro +*11:22. 1 C *4:14. 1 Th 4:6. 5:+12-14. **teaching.** Dt 4:5. Ezr *7:10. Ec 12:9. Mt *28:20. Mk 6:34. Ac *20:20. Ep +*4:11. 1 T 3:2. +*4:11, 16. 2 T +*2:2, 24, 25. **in all wisdom.** *♪171A, Ex +9:6. ver. +*9. Pr +*4:7. 8:5. Je +*3:15. Lk 21:15. 1 C 2:6, 15. 12:8. 2 P *3:15. **we may present.** ver. +22. 2 C 11:2. Ep *5:27. **perfect.** Col *2:10. 4:12. Mt +*5:48. Jn +*17:6. 1 C +*1:30. Ep *4:12, 13. Ph ◑+*3:12. He *10:14. *13:21.

29. **Whereunto.** 1 T 4:10g. **labor.** Col *4:12. 1 C *15:10. 2 C 5:9. 6:5. *11:23. 12:11. Ph +*2:16. 1 Th *2:9. 2 Th *3:8. 2 T 2:10. Re 2:3. **striving.** Col *2:1. 4:12mg. Lk +*13:24. Jn 18:36g. Ro 15:20, 30. 1 C *9:25-27. Ph *1:27, 30. 1 T 4:10. 6:12g. 2 T 4:7g. He 12:4. **his working.** 1 C *12:6, 11. Ep +*1:19. *3:7, 20. Ph √2:13. He *13:21. **which worketh.** Mt +14:2. Ja +5:16. **mightily.** ver. 11. 2 C √12:9, 10. 13:3.

COLOSSIANS 2

The apostle shows how earnestly he prayed for the Colossians, and the churches which had not seen him; that they might be united in love, and thus comforted; and that they might attain to a clear knowledge of the mysteries of Christ, and not be seduced by deceivers, 1-4. He rejoices, as if he saw "their order, and the stedfastness of their faith;" and exhorts them to perseverance and thankfulness, 5-7; warning them against vain philosophy and human traditions; and showing that they were complete in Christ, 8-10; having in him the true circumcision, of which baptism was the external sign, 11-13. For God "had quickened them with Christ," having forgiven their sins, and abolished the law of ordinances, by his cross, 14; on which he triumphed over principalities and powers, 15. They ought not then to submit to legal impositions, which were shadows of Christ, 16, 17; nor be induced, by vain pretences, to worship angels, or to any other observances of voluntary humility, will-worship, and self-imposed austerity, 18-23.

1. **I would.** 1 C +10:1. 11:3. **what.** Col 1:24, 29.

4:12. Ge 30:8. 32:24-30. Ho 12:3, 4. Lk 22:44. Ga 4:19. Ph 1:30. 1 Th *2:2. He 5:7. **conflict**. *or*, fear, *or*, care. Col 1:29. Ph +1:30. **at**. Col 4:13, 15, 16. Re 1:11. *3:14-22. **not**. ver. 5. Ac 20:25, 38. 1 P 1:8. **in the flesh**. ver. 5.

2. **their**. Col 4:8. Is 40:1. Ro 15:13. 2 C *1:4-6. Ep 6:2. 1 Th 3:2. *5:14. 2 Th *2:16, 17. **being**. Col 3:14. Ps *133:1. Jn *17:21. Ac 4:32. Ga +*3:28. Ph *2:1. 1 J 4:12, 16. **all**. See on Col 1:27. **riches**. ⌐108B, Ro +2:4. **of the full**. Is 32:17. Lk +1:1. 1 Th 1:5. He 6:11. 10:22. 2 P +*1:10. 1 J *3:19. **understanding**. Col +*1:9. Ps +*119:27. Jn 6:69. *17:3. Ro 16:25. 1 C *2:12. Ep *1:17-19. *3:9, 10. Ph 3:8. 2 P 1:3. 3:18. **to the**. Col 1:9. Ep 4:13. 1 J 5:7. **mystery**. Ro +*16:25n. **of the Father**. Col 1:15-17. Is *53:11. Je *9:24. Mt +*11:25, 27. Lk 10:21, 22. Jn +*1:1-3. *5:17, 23. +*10:30, 38. 14:9-11. 16:15. *17:21-23. 1 T *3:16.

3. **In whom**. *or*, Wherein. Col 1:9, 19. *3:16. Ps *68:18, Is 11:2. 45:3. Lk 11:49. Ro *11:33. 1 C +*1:24, 30. 2:6-8. Ep 1:8. 3:10. 2 T +*3:15-17. **hid**. Col 1:27. 3:3. Jb 28:21. Pr 2:4. Mt 10:26. Ep *3:8, 9. Re *2:17. **the treasures**. Dt=33:8. Ezr=2:62, 63. **wisdom**. Ge=41:39. Pr 2:6. +*4:7. 8:14. Is 9:6. Je 32:19. Ro +*11:33. 1 C *2:6, 7. Ep +*1:11. 1 J 2:1. Re 3:18. **and knowledge**. Pr 8:12, 22-30. Mt +*28:19n. Jn 1:1, 14. +*2:24, 25. 1 C 1:24, 30.

4. **lest**. ver. 8, 18. Mt *24:4, 24. Mk 13:22. Ac *20:30. Ro *16:18, 19. 2 C 11:3, √11-13. Ga 2:4. Ep +*4:14. *5:6. 2 Th 2:9-11. 1 T 4:1, 2. 2 T 2:16. 3:13. T 1:10, 11. 2 P 2:1-3. 1 J 2:18, 26. *4:1. 2 J 7. Re 12:9. 13:8. 20:3, 8. **beguile**. *or*, delude. Ja 1:22. **enticing**. 1 C *2:4.

5. **For though**. ⌐185A, Lk +11:8. **absent**. ver. 1. 1 C *5:3, 4. 1 Th *2:17. **in the flesh**. ver. 1. **with you**. 2 K 5:26. **spirit**. Gr. *pneuma*, Ac +18:25n. **and beholding**. 2 Ch 29:35. 1 C 11:34. *14:40. **stedfastness**. Ru 1:18. Ps 78:8, 37. Ac 2:42. 16:5. 1 C √15:58. 16:13. 1 Th +*3:8. He +*3:14. *6:19. 1 P 5:9. 2 P +*3:17, 18. **faith in**. Ac +20:21.

6. **received**. Mt 10:40. Jn √1:12, 13. 13:20. 1 C +*1:30. Ga 3:3. Ph 4:9. He +*3:14. 1 J √5:11, 12, 20. 2 J 8, 9. Ju +*3. Re √3:20. **Jesus**. Ph 2:11. **so walk**. T#1872. Col +*1:10. *3:17. Is 2:5. Mi 4:2. Jn √14:6. 2 C √5:7. 6:16. Ga √2:20. Ep *4:1. 5:1, 2. Ph *1:27. 1 Th *4:1. He +*10:35. Ja 3:11. 1 J √2:6. **in him**. Jn 15:4.

7. **Rooted**. Col *1:23. Ps +*1:3. 37:35mg. 92:13. Is *61:3. Je *17:8. Ezk 17:23, 24. Ro 11:17, 18. Ep *2:21, 22. *3:17. Ju 12. **built**. Col 1:23. Mt *7:24, 25. Lk +*6:48. Ac √20:32. Ro +14:19. 1 C *3:9-15. Ep *2:20-22. 1 P *2:4-6. Ju √20. **stablished**. Col *1:23. Ro 16:25. 1 C +1:8g. √15:58. 2 C *1:21. *5:7. Ep +*4:14. 2 Th 2:17. He *13:9. 1 P *5:10. 2 P *3:17, 18. Ju *24. **been taught**. Ep 4:21. **thanksgiving**. Col *1:12, 13. *3:17. Ep *5:20. 1 Th +*5:18. He *13:15.

8. **Beware**. Dt 6:12. Mt 7:15. 10:17. 16:6. 24:4. Ph 3:2. He +*3:12. 2 P 3:17. **any man**. *or*, any one. This indefinite *tis* is frequently used by St. Paul, when speaking of opponents whom he knows well enough but does not care to name (Lightfoot, Comm. on Colossians, p. 178). ver. 16. 1 C 4:18. +*11:16. Ga 1:7. 2:12. **spoil**. ver. 18. SS 2:15. Je *29:8. Ro 16:17. Ep 5:6. He *13:9. 2 J *8. **philosophy**. Ac 17:18, 32. Ro 1:21, 22. 1 C 1:19-23. *3:18, 19. 15:35, 36. 2 C 10:5g. 1 T √6:20, 21. 2 T 2:17, 18. 3:13. **and**. ⌐93A, Ge +1:26. By Hendiadys, "vain, deceitful philosophy." Two words

used, one thing meant. **vain deceit**. Ep 5:6. **after the tradition**. ver. 22. Mt 15:+2-9. Mk √7:3-13. 1 C ●11:2. Ga 1:14. 2 Th ◐*2:15. ◐*3:6. 1 P 1:18. **of men**. Ga 1:1, 11, 12. **the rudiments**. *or*, the elements. ver. 20. Ga 4:3mg, 9. Ep 2:2. **world**. Gr. *kosmos*, Mt +4:8. **after Christ**. Ro +*15:5. Ep 4:20.

9. **in him**. ver. 2, 3. Col 1:19. Is +*7:14. Mt +*1:23. Jn *1:14. 10:30, 38. *14:9, 10, 20. *17:21. 2 C *5:19. 1 T 3:16. T √2:13. 1 J 5:7, *20. **dwelleth**. Col 1:19. 1 C ●6:19. Ep ◐3:17, 19. 1 J ◐4:15. **fulness**. Ex=29:9mg. Jn +*1:16. **Godhead**. Gr. *theoteetos*. J. H. Thayer gives the definition "*deity*. i.e. the state of being God, *Godhead*" (*Lexicon*, p. 288b). Trench states "St. Paul is declaring that in the Son there dwells all the fulness of absolute Godhead.... He was, and is, absolute and perfect God...." (*Synonyms*, sec. 2, p. 8). Bengel states "not merely the Divine attributes, but the *Divine Nature* itself." Alford states "*theotees*, the abstract of *theos*, must not be confounded with *theiotees*, the abstract of *theios*, *divine*, which occurs in Ro 1:20." **bodily**. ver. 17. Jb +*19:26. Lk 3:22. 24:39. Jn 1:14. +*2:21. *3:13. 20:27. Ph *3:21. 1 T *2:5.

10. **complete**. Col 3:11. Jn *1:16. 1 C +*1:30, 31. 2 C √5:21. Ga *3:26-29. Ep *1:6, 23. 3:19. He +*5:9. **the head**. T#76-1. Col 1:16-18. Mt 10:1. Mk 2:5-11. 1 C +*11:3. Ep 1:20-23. 4:15, 16. 5:23. Ph √2:9-11. He 1:14. 1 P *3:22. Re 1:18. 5:9-13. **principality**. ver. 15. Ep +1:21.

11. **whom**. Dt 10:16. *30:6. Je *4:4. Ro +*2:29. Ph *3:3. **without**. Mk 14:58. Ac 7:48. 17:24. 2 C 5:1. Ep 2:11. He 9:11, 24. **in putting**. ver. 15. Col *3:8, 9. Ro *6:6. Ep *4:22. **the body**. Ro +6:6. *7:24. *8:13. **by**. Lk 2:21. 2 C √5:17. Ga √2:20. 4:4, 5. Ep 2:10-18. **circumcision of Christ**. The juxtaposition of baptism and circumcision in this passage (ver. 11, 12) clearly shows that there is an intended relationship between them (Ga √4:25n). As the circumcision is spiritual, so the baptism is spiritual. Here, circumcision is unmistakably equated with Christian baptism, in such a manner as to affirm that baptism now takes the place of circumcision as the initiatory rite into membership in the Body of Christ. Real baptism corresponds to circumcision of the heart; ritual baptism to circumcision with hands; circumcision under the Old Covenant and baptism under the New Covenant is the seal of the Abrahamic Covenant, associated with the Promise, not the Law, and therefore not done away in Christ, who fulfilled the Law, but not yet the Promise. Just as there is a similarity between the Jewish Passover and the Lord's Supper, so is there intended similarity between Circumcision and Baptism. As the Lord's Supper was given to Gentile converts instead of the Passover, so Baptism was given to them instead of Circumcision. The law required of worthy partakers of the Passover (Ex √12:48), "let ALL his males be circumcised, and then let him come near and keep it." A man's own personal circumcision was not sufficient passport to the Passover Table. Not only must the father of the family be circumcised, but his whole family or *oikos*. Thus in the New Testament the whole *oikos* (Ac +*16:15n), *family*, was baptized because in Christ there is neither male nor female, no distinction in behalf of either sex (Ga 3:28). Perhaps more accurately, all believers, male or female, are in the New Testament regarded as sons (Ga 4:7). Thus the objection that cir-

cumcision cannot prefigure baptism because it applies only to males is mistaken on two counts: (1) every female under the Old Covenant is represented by a male (Ge 1:27. 2:18, 24. Ex √12:48. ◑34:15, 16. Dt ◑7:3. Jg ◑14:3), regarded as circumcised, and qualified to partake of the Passover; (2) under the New Covenant, all believers partake of the "adoption of sons" (Ga +*4:5), and are spoken of, without exception, as sons (Ga +*4:7n).

12. **Buried.** Gr. *sunthaptomai*, *S#4916g, only here and Ro 6:4. This Greek word is thought by many to be decisive in regard to the mode of Christian baptism. But the word would better have been translated "entombed," then the term would not have been interjected into the baptism debate. There is no possible likeness between immersion into water and the mode of burial of the dead. When Christ was buried, he was not placed under six feet of earth, but wrapped like a mummy and laid on a shelf in a cave above ground. Roman burial involved burning the body, and placing the ashes in an urn kept in a tomb or a room prepared for the purpose. Hughey asks "Can any likeness be seen between *our mode* of *burial* and *immersion?* If there is any likeness at all between baptism and such a *mode of burial*, it would be to baptism by pouring, for the earth is *poured* upon the body, and not the body *plunged* into the earth. Plainly there can be no *physical* likeness between any of these *modes* of *burial* and *immersion in water*" (*The Scriptural Mode of Christian Baptism*, p. 194). The concept of "burial in water" may be possible in English, but in Greek this word is never used with reference to water. In this passage, and its near-parallel in Romans 6:4, water is not mentioned. The reference is to real baptism, not ritual, and those who are buried with Christ stay buried. There is no resurrection out of that into which believers were buried, for such would be apostasy from Christ. Those who favor immersion as a mode do not practice immersion, but dipping, for to leave the person immersed would be as fatal to the person as it is to their theory. To bring the issue of water baptism into Romans 6 or Colossians 2 is to extract from the message of Paul a meaning he did not intend, so as to totally miss the significance of the doctrinal truth he wished to convey. Baptism into Christ's death is not a momentary dipping, but the permanent placement in the grave where Christ was laid of every believer in his permanent union with Christ. As a result of the misapplication of these two passages by immersionists, this central message of Paul in Romans is often missed—perhaps accounting for the prevalence of such defective views of our death to sin, union with Christ, and his Lordship over our lives. 2 K 24:6n. Ps +51:2 (T#32). Mt 3:5, 6, 16. Jn 3:23. Ac 8:38, 39. Ro 6:4◑n (T#39-1), 5. He ◑+10:22 (T#39-2). **baptism.** The baptism of this verse and the circumcision of ver. 11 are one and the same thing. As the circumcision is spiritual and made without hands, so is the baptism. This is a reference to real baptism by the Holy Spirit, not ritual baptism in water (Ac +*1:5n). The burial is not into water but into the benefits of Christ's death. This baptism is accomplished by the Holy Spirit when an individual places faith in Christ (1 C √12:13n). "The being baptized into anything is the being brought under, and saturated with its influence and power" (W. R. Nicholson, *Popular Studies in Colossians: Oneness With Christ*, p. 195).

See related notes listed at Ac 22:16n. Ro √6:3. 1 C √12:13. Ga *3:27. Ep +*4:5. T 3:5, 6. He 6:2. 1 P *3:21. **wherein.** Col 3:1, 2. Ro *6:8-11. 7:4. 1 C 15:20. Ep 1:20. 2:4-6. *5:14. 1 P 4:1-3. **ye are risen.** As this resurrection is a moral or spiritual one in the individual believer through the faith of the operation of God, so the "burial" in the first half of this antithesis must likewise be a spiritual burial, not a literal burial under water. Col 3:1. Ro 6:5. **the faith.** Mk *11:22. Lk *17:5g. Jn *1:12, 13. √3:3-7. Ac 14:27. Ep *1:19. √2:8. 3:7, 17. Ph 1:29. He *12:2. Ja 1:16, 17. **the operation.** Col 1:29. 1 C 6:14. Ep +1:19. 4:16. Ph 3:21. **who.** Ac +*2:24. Ro 4:24. He *13:20, 21.

13. **dead.** Ezk *37:1-10. Lk 9:60. *15:24, 32. Ro 6:13. 2 C √5:14, 15. Ep +*2:1, 5, 6. 5:14. 1 T 5:6. He 6:1. 9:14. Ja 2:17, 20, 26. **the uncircumcision.** ver. 11. Ep 2:11. **he quickened.** Ps 71:20. +*119:50. Jn 5:21. 6:63. Ro 4:17. *6:13. +*8:11. 1 C 15:36, 45. 2 C 3:6mg. Ep +*2:5. 1 T 6:13. 1 P *1:3. **having forgiven.** It is helpful to distinguish between judicial forgiveness, where God as judge forgives the sinner of the penalty of sin, and family (or parental) forgiveness, where God as Father forgives the saint and restores the joy (Ps 51:12) of his salvation (John B. Marchbanks, *Great Doctrines Relating to Salvation*, pp. 33, 36. Charles F. Baker, *A Dispensational Theology*, pp. 276, 277). Col 3:13. Le=16:21, 22. Nu 14:18. Ps *32:1, 2. 86:5. √103:3, 12. 130:3, 4. Is *1:18. √55:7. Je 31:34. Mk 2:7. Lk +*7:43. Jn +*17:6. Ac +*10:43. +*13:38, 39. Ro 4:7, 8. 5:21. +*8:1, 32-34. 2 C 5:19. Ep 1:7. *4:32. He 8:10-12. 10:12-18. 1 J √1:7-9. 2:12. **all.** The specification of "all" includes past, present, and future trespasses. This follows logically from the fact that justification does not admit of repetition, and that the pardon granted in justification "involves the removal of all guilt and of every penalty" (L. Berkhof, *Systematic Theology*, p. 514). Confession of sin for the believer does not restore him to salvation, but to fellowship with God (1 J 1:9). If continued salvation depended upon complete confession, then by this theory the failure to confess one sin through oversight would result in loss of salvation, which is contradictory to the possibility of assurance of salvation, our placement as sons and joint-heirship with Christ (Jn 1:12. Ro 8:17. Ga +*4:5, 7n), and the close connection between (1) justification and glorification (Ro +*8:29, 30); (2) present suffering and future glory (Ro 8:17. 2 T 2:12); (3) remission of sin and future inheritance (Ac +*26:18); (4) justification and hope of glory (Ro 5:1, 2). Ps ◑25:7. √103:3, 12. Is 44:22. Zc=3:4. Ac +*26:18. Ro 5:1, 2. 2 C *5:19. He *10:14. 1 J √1:7. **trespasses.** Le +=5:6.

14. **Blotting out.** ʃ73, Zc +1:5. ʃ105, Ml +4:2. Nu 5:23. Ne 4:5. Ps 51:1, 9. 109:14. Is 43:25. 44:22. Je 18:23. Ac +*3:19. **the handwriting.** ver. 20. Est 3:12. 8:8. Da 5:7, 8. Lk 1:6. Ac *15:10. Ro +*7:4. Ga 4:1-4. Ep √2:14-16. He 7:18. 8:13. 9:9, 10. 10:8, 9. **ordinances.** Ga 3:10n. Ep +*2:15. **took.** Is 57:14. 2 Th 2:7. **out of the way.** ʃ108H3, Mt +13:49.

15. **having.** ver. 11. Ge +*3:15. Ps 68:18. Is 49:24, 25. *53:12. Mt *12:29. Lk *10:18. *11:21, 22. Jn 12:31. *16:11. 1 C *15:55-57. Ep 4:8. He √2:14. Re 12:9. 20:2, 3, 10. **principalities.** ver. 10. Col 1:16. 2 C *4:4. Ep +1:21. 6:12. **triumphing.** Lk 23:39-43. Jn 12:32. 19:30. Ac 2:23, 24, 32-36. Ro +*8:37-39. 2 C √2:14g,n. **in it.** *or,* in himself. Ep 2:16g.

16. **judge.** Ro *14:3, 10, 13. 1 C 10:28-31. Ga 2:12,

13. 3:10n. Ja 4:11. **in meat**, etc. *or*, for eating and drinking. ver. 21. Le 11:2-47. 17:10-15. Dt 14:3-20. Ezk 4:14. Mt 15:11. Ac 11:3-18. 15:20. Ro 14:2, 6, *14-17, 20, 21. 1 C *8:7-13. 1 T √4:3-5. He 9:10. *13:9. **in drink**. Le 10:9. 11:34. Nu 6:3. **in respect**. *or*, in part. 2 C 3:10. 9:3g. **of an**. 1 Ch 23:31. 2 Ch 2:4. 31:3. Is 1:13, 14. Ezk 45:17. Ho 2:11. Ga 4:10. **holy day**. or, feast day. Le 23:+√2n, 3n, +*5, +*6, +*16, +*24n, 28, +*34, 39n, 42. Nu ch. 28, 29. Dt 16:1-17. Ne 8:9. 10:31. Ps 42:4. Ro 14:5, 6. Ga 4:10. **the new moon**. Nu 10:10. 28:11, 14. 1 S 20:5, 18. 2 K 4:23. 1 Ch 23:31. 2 Ch +*2:4. Ne 10:33. Ps 81:3. Is 1:13. √66:23. Ezk 45:17. 46:1-3. Am 8:5. Ga 4:10. **or of the sabbath**. or, the sabbath days. The plural is put for the singular, Mt 12:1. Bengel notes "used here significantly, for the several days of the week are called *Sabbaths*, Mt 28:1; therefore Paul intimates here the removal of all distinctions of days; for he never wrote more openly of the Sabbath. Christ, after he himself, the Lord of the Sabbath, had come, or before his suffering, clearly taught the liberty of the Sabbath; but he asserted it more openly by Paul after his resurrection. Nor has it yet been clearly defined what is due to the Sabbath, what to the Lord's day; but this has been left to the *measure* of every one's *faith*. The Sabbath is not commended, is not enjoined; the Lord's day is mentioned, not enjoined. A stated day is useful and necessary to those who are engrossed in worldly concerns. They who keep a continual Sabbath enjoy greater liberty. The Sabbath is a type even of eternal things, He 4:3, 4; yet its obligation does not therefore continue in the New Testament, otherwise the new moons should be retained, Is 66:23" (*Word Studies*, vol. 2, p. 463). Some argue that the Sabbath, like the tithe, is a pre-Mosaic institution, and therefore our obligation to observe it did not çease with the abolition of the Mosaic law (Ep 2:15) upon the death and resurrection of Christ and the beginning of the New Covenant under grace. In answer to this argument is Paul's very clear statement here, that we are to let no one judge us in respect to the keeping of the sabbath. Furthermore, those who would place us under legalistic obligations of the law, Mosaic or not, are guilty of the Galatian heresy, a heresy which results in spiritual death and loss of salvation (Ga 2:21. 5:2-4). Nowhere in the Word of God is the Mosaic Law given as binding to the Gentiles (Ac 15:5, 10, 19, √24. √21:25. Ro 2:14. 3:2. Ep 2:12). Sabbath observance needs to be left where the inspired apostle has placed it—as a matter of individual conscience, conviction, and preference—but never as an obligation to be imposed upon others (Ro 14:5). So with tithing: in all of the apostolic appeals for Christian giving for a multitude of purposes, never once is recourse had to making the tithe obligatory for the Christian, whether by direct appeal to the law, by precept, or example (Mt ❍23:23n. Lk √11:41n, 42n). The proper basis of appeal for Christian giving is found in Ph 4:17, where Paul urges as a proper motive the eternal reward which accrues to our account as the result of our Christian giving. Le 16:31. 23:3, 24, 32, 39. Is ❍+*58:13n. Mk 2:27, 28. Ro ❍14:5n. T *3:9.

17. **a shadow**. Jn 1:17. Ro +*15:4. He *8:5. *9:9. *10:1. **things to come**. He 10:1. **the body**. ♪22A2. Anthropomorphism B872. Parts and members of man, or of the human body, are attributed to God: a *body* is used of Christ. For other instances of this figure

see Ep 1:23. 4:12, 16. **is of Christ**. ver. 9. Mt *11:28, 29. He 4:1-11.

18. **no**. ver. 4, 8. Ge 3:13. Nu 25:18. Mt 24:24. Ro 16:18. 2 C 11:3. Ep 5:6. 2 P 2:14. 1 J 2:26. *4:1, 2. 2 J *7-11. Re *3:11. 12:9. *13:8, 14. **beguile you**. *or*, judge against you. ver. 16. 1 C 9:24. Ph 3:14. **your reward**. Gr. *katabrabuo*, ✳S#2603g, only here. Compare the related root, ✳S#1018g: *brabuo*, Col 3:15 (rule), and its root ✳S#1017g: *brabion*, 1 C 9:24 (prize); Ph 3:14 (prize). 2 J 8. **in a voluntary humility**. Gr. being a voluntary in humility. ver. 23. Is 57:9. Ac 26:5. Ja 1:26, 27g. **humility**. Ep +4:2g. **and**. ♪93A, Ge +1:26. By Hendiadys, "the religious humility of angels." **worshipping**. T#80. Da 11:38h. Mt 4:10. Ac 14:13-15. Ro 1:25. 1 C 8:5, 6. 1 T 4:1g. *2:5, 8. Re 19:10. +*22:8, 9. **of angels**. ♪181E, Ge +3:24. Mt +18:10. He ❍*1:4-6. **intruding**. Dt +*29:29. 1 S=6:19. 2 S=6:6, 7. Jb 38:2. Ps 138:1, 2. Ezk 13:3, 7. Mt=11:27. 1 T 1:7. **not seen**. Ezk 13:3. **vainly**. ver. 8. Ro +13:4. 1 C 4:18. 8:1. 13:4. **puffed up**. Is 65:5n. 1 C +4:6. Ep 4:17. **fleshly**. Ro 8:6-8. 1 C 3:3. 2 C 12:20. Ga 5:19, 20. Ja 3:14-16. 4:1-6.

19. **not**. ver. 6-9. Col 1:18. Ga 1:6-9. 5:2-4. Ep +*4:15, 16. 1 T 2:4-6. 1 P +*2:2. **holding**. Re 2:13. 3:11. **all**. Ep 4:15, 16. **by**. Jb 10:9-12. Ps 139:15, 16. **bands**. Ep +4:3. **nourishment**. Jn *15:4-6. Ro 11:17. Ep *5:29. **ministered**. 2 C +9:10. **knit**. ver. 2. Jn *17:21. Ac 4:32. Ro *12:4, 5. 1 C 1:10. 10:16, 17. *12:12-27. Ep *4:3. Ph 1:27. 2:2-5. 1 P 3:8. **increaseth**. ♪147D, Ge +1:29. Col +*1:10. 1 C 3:6. Ep 4:16. 1 Th 3:12. 4:10. 2 Th 1:3. 2 P √3:18.

20. **if**. ♪184A, 1 C +15:2. Col 3:3. Ro *6:2-11. 7:4-6. Ga 2:19, 20. *6:14. 1 P 4:1-3. **from**. See on ver. 8. Ep 2:15. **rudiments**. *or*, elements. ver. 8. Ga 4:3mg. **world**. Gr. *kosmos*, Mt +4:8. **living**. Jn 15:19. 17:14-16. 2 C 10:3. Ja 4:4. 1 J 5:19. **world**. Gr. *kosmos*, Mt +4:8. **subject**. See on ver. 14, 16. Ga *4:3, 9-12. He *13:9.

21. **Touch not**. ♪81, Ge +15:13. ♪92H, Ac +17:28. Ge 3:3. Le 5:2. 11:8. Is 52:11. 2 C *6:17. **taste not**. ver. 16. 1 T √4:3, 4.

22. **to perish**. Mt 15:17. Mk *7:18, 19. Jn *6:27. 1 C 6:13. +15:42g. **after**. Is √29:13, 18. Da 11:37. Mt *15:3-9. Mk *7:7-13. T 1:14. Re 17:18.

23. **a show**. Ge +*3:5, 6. Dt *4:2. Mt *23:27, 28. 2 C 11:13-15. 1 T 4:3, 8. **will**. See on ver. 8, +18, 22. **and**. ♪93A, Ge +1:26. ver. 18. **neglecting**. *or*, punishing, *or*, not sparing. Ep 5:29. 1 T 4:8. **satisfying**. Is +*58:13. Ro *13:14. 1 C *10:31.

COLOSSIANS 3

The apostle exhorts Christians to "seek" and "set their affections on things above," as risen with Christ, and as following him to heaven, 1-4; to mortify all carnal lusts, to put away malice, and to seek conformity to Christ in holiness, 5-11; especially in love of each other, readiness to forgive injuries, and gratitude to God, 12-15; to "let the word of Christ dwell in them richly;" to abound in grateful praises; and to "do all things in the name of Christ," 16, 17. He gives exhortations to wives and husbands, 18, 19; to children and parents, 20, 21; and to servants, 22-25.

1. **If**. ♪184A, 1 C +15:2. **risen**. Col 2:+*12, 13, 20. Ro *6:4, 5, 9-11. Ga *2:19, 20. Ep 1:19, 20. *2:5, 6. **seek**. ver. 2. Ps +*16:11. *17:14, 15. *73:25, 26.

Pr 15:24. Mt √6:19, 20, 33. Lk 12:33. Ro 8:6. 2 C √4:18. Ph +*3:20, 21. He 10:34. 11:13-16. **those things.** Jn 8:23. Ph 3:14. **where.** Ps 110:1. Mt 22:44. 26:64. Mk 12:36. 14:62. *16:19. Lk 20:42. 22:69. Ac 2:34. *7:55. Ro *8:34. Ep +1:20. 4:10. He 1:3, 13. 8:1. 10:12. *12:2. 1 P 3:22. **right hand.** ſ22A15C, Ps +110:1.

2. **Set.** See on ver. 1. 1 S 22:23. 1 Ch *22:19. 29:3. Ps √62:10. 91:14. √119:36, 37. Pr *23:5. Ec 7:14. Mt *6:21. +*16:23. Jn 14:19. Ro √8:4-6. Ph 1:23. 1 J √2:15-17. **affection.** *or,* mind. **not.** ver. √5. Ge 45:20. Ps 49:11-17. Pr 23:6. Mt √6:19. Lk √12:15. *16:8, 9, 11, 19-25. Ph +*3:19. 1 J √2:15.

3. **are dead.** Col 2:20. Ro +*6:2, 6. Ga √2:20. **your.** ver. 4. Col 1:5. Jn √3:16. *4:14. *5:21, 24, 40. 6:39, 40. √10:28-30. *14:19. Ro *5:10, 21. 8:2, 34-39. 1 C 15:45. 2 C +*5:7. He 7:25. 1 P +*1:3-5. **hid.** Col +*2:3. Ge 7:16. 2 K 11:3. Ps +*83:3. Mt +*11:25. Jn 17:23. 1 C √2:14. Ph +*4:7. 1 P 3:4. 1 J √3:2. Re *2:17. **with Christ.** Jn *17:21. 1 C 12:27. 2 C √5:17. 1 J *5:20.

4. **who is.** ſ63I1D, Nu +26:4. *or,* "(with whom) our life (is hid)." **our.** Jn +*11:25. √14:6. +*20:31. Ac *3:15. 2 C 4:16. Ga √2:20. 2 T 1:1. 1 J *1:1, 2. √5:12. Re 2:7. 22:1, 14. **shall appear.** Ph 3:21. 1 T 6:14. 2 T +*4:1, 8. T √2:13. He √9:28. 1 P 1:7, 13. 4:13. *5:4. 1 J 2:28. √3:2. **ye also.** Ps *17:15. *73:24. Is *25:8, 9. Mt +*13:43. Jn 6:39, 40. +*14:3. *17:24. Ro *8:19, 29. 1 C *15:43. 2 C *4:17. Ph +*3:21. 1 Th √4:17. 2 Th +*1:10-12. Ju *24. **with him.** Ex=28:1. **in glory.** Ps √102:16. Ro *8:17, 18, 21. 1 C √15:43. 1 Th 2:12. 1 P *4:13.

5. **Mortify.** Mt 5:29. 18:9. Mk 9:47. Ro *6:6. √8:13. Ga √2:20. *5:24. Ep 5:3-6. **members.** ſ46A, Le +26:30. The members which commit the sins are put by a forcible *Catachresis* for the sins themselves. For the sins are immediately enumerated, not the members (B677). Ro 6:13. *7:5, 23. Ja 4:1. **fornication.** Mt 15:19. Mk +*7:21, 22. Ac +√15:20. Ro +*1:29. 1 C *5:1, 10, 11. +*6:9, 13, 18. 2 C 12:21. Ga *5:19-21. Ep +*5:3, 5. 1 Th *4:3. He 12:16. +*13:4. Re +*21:8. *22:15. **inordinate.** Ro 1:26. 1 Th 4:5g. **evil.** Ro 7:7, 8. 1 C 10:6-8. Ep 4:19. 1 P 2:11. **covetousness.** Ps +*10:3. 1 C +*6:10. Ga *5:19-21. See on Ep 5:3, 5. **which is.** 1 S +*15:23. **idolatry.** Jb 31:25, 26. Ezk +*14:3.

6. **which.** Ro *1:18. Ep +*5:6. Re 22:15. **children.** Is 57:4. Ezk 16:45, 46. Ep 2:2, 3. 1 P 1:14. 2 P 2:14g.

7. **also walked.** Col 2:13. Ro *6:19, 20. 7:5. 1 C +*6:11. Ep +*2:2. T 3:3. 1 P *4:3, 4. **when.** Ep +*2:11.

8. **put off.** ver. 5, 9. Ro 6:6. Ep +*4:22. He *12:1. Ja *1:21. 1 P 2:1. **anger.** Ps *37:8. Pr 17:14. 19:19. 29:22. Mt 5:22. Ro 13:13. 1 C 3:3. 2 C 12:20. Ga 5:15, 20, 26. Ep √4:26, +31, 32. 2 T 2:23, 24. Ja *1:20. *3:14-16. **blasphemy.** Le 24:11-16. Mk 7:22. 1 T 1:13, 20. Ja 2:7. Ju 8. Re 16:9. **filthy.** Ep +*4:29. *5:4. Ja *3:4-6. 2 P 2:7, 18. Ju 8, 13.

9. **Lie not.** T#417. Ge +*27:19. Ex 20:16. Le +*19:11, 12. Ps *15:1, 2. *34:13. +101:5 (T#729). Pr 4:24. Is *63:8. Je 9:3-5. Zp 3:13. Zc 8:16. Jn √8:44. Ep √4:25. 1 T 1:10. T 1:12, 13. 1 P *3:10. Ju +8 (T#730). Re +*21:8, 27. *22:15. **ye have.** Col 2:11. **put off.** ver. 8. Ro *6:6. Ep *4:22.

10. **put on.** ver. 12, 14. Jb 29:14. Is 52:1. 59:17. Ro *13:12, 14. 1 C 15:53, 54. Ga +*3:27. Ep +*4:23, 24. **the new.** Ezk 11:19. 18:31. *36:26. Ro +*6:4.

2 C √5:17. Ga *6:15. Ep √2:10, 15. 4:24. Re 21:5. **renewed.** Ps +*51:10. Ro +*12:2. Ep *4:23. T 3:5. He 6:6. **knowledge.** Col +*1:9. Jn √17:3. 2 C √3:18. *4:6. 1 J *2:3, 5. **after.** Ge +*1:26, 27. Ro +*8:29. Ep √2:10. *4:23, 24. 1 P *1:14-16.

11. **there.** Ps 117:2. Is 19:23-25. 49:6. 52:10. 66:18-22. Je *16:19. Ho 2:23. Am 9:12. Mi 4:2. Zc 2:11. *8:20-23. Ml *1:11. Mt 12:18-21. Ac *10:34, 35. *13:46-48. 15:17. 26:17, 18. Ro 3:29. 4:10, 11. 9:24-26, 30, 31. *10:12. 15:9-13. 1 C √12:13. Ga √3:28. Ep +*3:6. **circumcision.** 1 C *7:19. Ga +*5:6. *6:15. **Barbarian.** Ac 28:2, 4. Ro 1:14. 1 C 14:11. **Scythian.** i.e. *degraded,* ✳S#4658g. **bond.** 1 C 7:21, 22. Ep 6:8. **but.** Col 2:10. 1 C +*1:29, 30. 3:21-23. Ga *3:29. *6:14. Ph 3:7-9. 1 J √5:11, 12. 2 J 9. **and.** Jn 6:56, 57. 14:23. *15:5. *17:23. Ro +*8:10, 11. Ga √2:20. Ep +1:23. +*3:17. 1 J 5:20.

12. **Put on.** See on ver. 10. Ex=29:8, 9. Le=7:8. Ps=132:9. Ep 4:24. **as the elect.** Dt +*10:15. Is 42:1. 45:4. 65:9, 22. Mt 24:+*22n, 24, 31. Mk 13:20, 22, 27. Lk +18:7. Ro +*8:29-33. *9:11. *11:5-7. 1 Th *1:3, 4. 5:9. 2 T 2:10. T 1:1. 1 P *1:1, 2. 2:8, 9. 2 P +*1:10. 2 J 1, 13. Re 17:14. **holy.** Ro *8:29. Ep *1:4. 1 Th 1:3-6. 2 Th *2:13, 14. **beloved.** Je 31:3. Ezk 16:8. Ro +*1:7. Ep 2:4, 5. 2 T *1:9. T *3:4-6. 1 J 4:19. **bowels.** ſ46C, Mt +8:6. ſ121G1, Is +63:15. Is 63:15. Je 31:20. Lk 1:78mg. 2 C +*6:12n. 7:15. Ph 1:8. 2:1. Phm 7, 12, 20. 1 J *3:17. **mercies.** 1 Th 5:15. Ja *2:13. *3:17, 18. 1 P 3:8-11. 2 P √1:5-8. 1 J *3:14-20. **kindness.** Ro 12:9, 10. Ep +*4:32. **humbleness of mind.** Ph +*2:3. **meekness.** Mt +*5:5. Ga 5:23. **longsuffering.** Ga 5:22. Ep +*4:2.

13. **Forbearing.** Ro *15:1, 2. 2 C 6:6. Ga *6:2. Ep √4:2, 32. **forgiving.** Mt *5:44. *6:12, 14, 15. *18:21-35. Mk *11:25. Lk +*6:35-37. 11:4. *17:3, 4. 23:34. Ja *2:13. **if any.** ſ184C, Mt +4:9. **quarrel.** *or,* complaint. Mt *18:15-17. 1 C 6:7, 8. **even.** Mt 18:27. Lk 5:20-24. 7:48-50. 2 C 2:10. Ep √4:32. 5:2. 1 P 2:21.

14. **above all.** Ep 6:16. **charity.** Col 2:2. Jn *13:34. 15:12. Ro 13:8. 1 C ch. *13. Ep *4:15, 16. +5:2. 1 Th 4:9. 5:8. 1 T 1:5. 1 P *4:8. 2 P *1:7. 1 J *3:23. 4:21. **the bond.** Col 2:2. Ac 8:23. Ep 1:4. *4:3. He +*12:14. 1 J *4:7-12. **perfectness.** Jn 17:23. He 6:1g.

15. **the peace.** T#849. Ps 25:13. *29:11. +*34:4. 85:8. 147:3. Is √26:3. 27:5. *32:17, 18. *57:15, 19. Lk 7:50. Jn *14:27. 16:33. Ro *5:1. *14:17. 15:13. 2 C *5:19-21. Ep *2:12-18. 5:1. Ph +√4:7 (T#666). 2 Th 3:16. **to the which.** 1 C +7:15. Ep 2:16, 17. 4:4, 16. **one body.** Ep +2:16. +*4:4n. **thankful.** ver. +17. Col *1:12. *2:7. Ps 100:4. 107:22. 116:17. Jon 2:9. Lk 17:16-18. Ro 1:21. 2 C 4:15. 9:11. Ep *5:20. Ph √4:6. 1 Th *5:18. 1 T 2:1. He *13:15. Re *7:12.

16. **the word.** 2 Ch=17:9. Jn +√5:39, 40. +*8:31, 37. *15:3, 7. Ac 8:25. 2 T +√3:15, 16. He √4:12, 13. 1 P 1:11, 12. 1 J +*1:10. Re 19:10. **dwell.** T#1101. Dt *6:6-9. *11:18-20. Jb 22:22. +*23:12. Ps +*1:2. √119:11. Pr 22:18. Je +*15:16. Lk 2:51. Jn *15:7. 1 J *2:14, 24, 27. 2 J 2. **richly.** 1 T *6:17. T 3:6mg. **all wisdom.** Col +*1:9. 1 K *3:9-12, 28. Pr *2:6, 7. √4:7. 14:8. +*18:1n. Is *11:2. Ep *1:17. *5:17. Ja +*1:5. *3:17. **teaching.** Col +*1:28. Ro *15:14. 1 Th 4:18. *5:11, 12. 2 Th *3:15. He *12:12-15. **admonishing.** Col +*1:28. **in psalms.** ſ173, Ge +27:44. Mt *26:30. 1 C *14:26. Ep +*5:19n. Ja *5:13. **and spiritual.** 1 Ch *25:7. Ne *12:46. Ps *32:7. *119:54. SS 1:1. Is 5:1. 26:1. 30:29. Ro +1:11g. Ep 5:19. Re *5:9. 14:3.

*15:3. **singing**. Col *4:6. 1 Ch=6:32. =15:22. =25:7. 2 Ch=23:13. Ps *28:7. 30:11, 12. 47:6, 7. *63:4-6. 71:23. 103:1, 2. 138:1. 1 C *14:15. Ep +*4:29. **in your hearts**. T#529. 1 S +16:7 (T#333). Ps 111:1. 1 C 14:15. Ep 5:19, 20. **to the Lord**. ver. *23.

17. **whatsoever**. ver. *23. 2 Ch *31:20, 21. Pr √3:6. Ro *14:6-8. 1 C √10:31. **in word**. 2 Th 2:17. 1 J *3:18. **do all**. 2 S 15:15. Jn +*2:5. *15:14. 1 C *10:31. **in the name**. Dt=10:8. =18:5. Mi *4:5. Mt +*28:19. Ac 3:6, 16. 4:10, 18, 29, 30. 5:40. 9:27, 29. 10:48. 16:18. *19:17. 1 C 5:4. 6:11. Ep 5:20. Ph 1:11. 2:10, 29. 1 Th *4:1, 2. 2 Th 3:6. Ja 5:14. **giving thanks**. ver. 15. Col *1:12. +*2:7. *4:2. Ps 100:4. 107:1. Mt 26:27. Jn 11:41. Ro 1:8. Ep +*5:20. 1 Th +*5:18. 1 T 4:4, 5. He *13:15. 1 P *2:5, 9. *4:11. **God**. Ep 1:17. Ph 2:11. 1 Th 1:1. He 1:5. 1 J *2:23.

18. **submit**. T#197. Ge 2:18. *3:16. +*16:9. Nu 30:13. Est 1:20. 1 C +*11:3-9, 13-15. +*14:34n, 35n. Ep *5:22-24, 33. 1 T √2:11-13. T 2:+4 (T#425), 5. 1 P *3:1-7. **as**. Ac *5:29. Ep *5:3, 4. 6:1. Phm 8.

19. **love**. Ge 2:23, 24. 24:67. Pr 5:18, 19. Ec 9:9. Ml 2:14-16. Lk 14:26. 1 C *7:14-16. Ep *5:25, 28, 29, 33. 1 P *3:7. **bitter**. ver. 21. Ro 3:14. Ep *4:31. Ja 3:14.

20. **obey**. Ge 28:7. Ex +*20:12. Le +*19:3. Dt *21:18-21. *27:16. Pr *6:20-23. *20:20. *30:11, 17. Ezk 22:7. Ml *1:6. Mt 15:4-6. *19:17, 19. Lk *2:51. Ep +√6:1-3. **in all**. ver. 22. Ep 5:24. T 2:9. **well pleasing**. Col +*1:10. Ep +5:10. Ph 4:18. He *13:21.

21. **provoke not**. A. T. Robertson notes that the Greek verb translated "provoke" in its good sense means excite (2 C 9:2, to stimulate), and in its bad sense as used here means to nag. The present tense signifies nag as a habit (*Word Pictures*, vol. 4, p. 507). Ps 103:13. Pr 3:12. 4:1-4. See on Ep +√6:4. 1 Th +*2:11. He *12:5-11. **lest**. Ps *78:4, 7, 8. Pr ●3:27. ●*12:25. ●*15:1, 23, 30. ●*16:24. 22:6. Is 50:4. Je ●+*12:5. Mt 18:4-6. Lk 17:2. Ac ●+*11:23. 1 C ●*15:58. 1 Th ●+*2:11, 12. He *3:13n. *12:15.

22. **servants, obey**. T#680. ver. 20. Ps 123:2. Pr +14:35 (T#907). Ml *1:6. Mt 8:9. Lk +*6:46. 7:8. Ep +*6:5-9. 1 T √6:1-3. T 2:9, 10. Phm *16. 1 P *2:18, 19. **all things**. ver. +20. **menpleasers**. Ga *1:10. 1 Th 2:4. **in singleness**. Mt *6:22. Ac 2:46. Ep +*6:5. **of heart**. 1 S +*16:7. **fearing**. Ge 42:18. Ne *5:9, 15. Ec 5:7. *8:12. √12:13, 14. Ac *5:29. 2 C *7:1.

23. **whatsoever**. See on ver. 17. 2 Ch +*31:21. Ps 47:6, 7. 103:1. 119:10, 34, 145. Ec +*9:10. Je 3:10. 1 P 1:22. **heartily**. Gr. from the soul. *psyche*, ƒ121A9B, Mt +22:37. **as to**. 2 Ch 19:6. Zc 7:5-7. Mt 6:16. Ro *14:6, 8. Ep +*5:22. +*6:5-7. Phm 16. 1 P *2:13, 15.

24. **of the Lord**. 2 K 17:35. Jn 1:1. **shall receive**. Col 1:13n. Mt *25:34. Lk √14:14. 2 T *4:1n, 8. He 12:28n. 2 P 1:11. Re 11:18. **the reward**. Col *2:18. Ge 15:1. Ru *2:12. Pr *11:18. Mt +*5:12, 46. 6:1, 2, 5, 16. *10:41. Lk *6:35. +*14:14. Ro +*2:6, 7. *4:4, 5. 1 C *3:8. 9:17, 18. Ep *6:8. He *9:15. *10:35. √11:6. **the inheritance**. Nu=18:20. Dt +*32:9. Ps *106:5. Ac +20:32. Ro 8:17. 1 C 6:9. 2 C 6:10. Ep +*1:11n, 14. 1 Th 2:12. 2 Th 1:5. Ja 2:5. 1 P +*1:4n. 2 P 1:11. **for ye serve**. Nu=3:7. 1 Ch=16:37. Jn *12:26. Ac 20:19. Ro *1:1. +*12:11. *14:18. 16:18. 1 C 7:22. Ga *1:10. Ep +*6:6, 7. Ja +1:1. 2 P 1:1. Ju 1.

25. **he that**. 1 C 6:7, 8. 1 Th 4:6. Phm 18. **receive**. Ge +*6:13 (T#566). 2 C √5:10. He 2:2. **and**. Col 4:1.

Le +*19:15. Dt 1:17. *10:17. 2 S 14:14. 2 Ch 19:7. Jb 34:19. 37:24. Lk 20:21. Ac 10:34. Ro *2:11. Ep 6:9. 1 P *1:17. Ju 16.

COLOSSIANS 4

Masters are charged to behave properly to their servants, 1. Exhortations to perseverance in prayer, 2-4; and to prudence and edifying speech, 5, 6. The apostle commends Tychicus and Onesimus, by whom he sends the epistle, 7-9; and concludes with salutations, admonitions, and directions, 10-18.

1. **Masters**. T#679. Dt 23:15, 16. +*24:14, 15. Jb +27:13 (T#490). Pr +21:13 (T#687). +22:22 (T#636). Je *22:13. Ezk +*16:49. Ep +*6:9. 1 T 5:18. **give**. Le +*19:13. *25:39-43. Dt *15:12-15. +*24:14, 15. Ne 5:5-13. Jb 24:11, 12. *31:13-15. Is *58:3, 5-9. Je 34:9-17. Ml +*3:5. Lk 7:15. Jn 19:27. Ja *2:13. +*5:4. **just**. T#1849. Pr +*18:13. Jn +*7:51. 1 T +*5:19n. Ja +*5:4. **equal**. T#1850. Ml +*3:5. Mt √7:12. *20:9n, 13n, 25, 26. 2 C 8:14. **ye also**. Ec *5:8. Mt 23:8, 9. *24:48-51. Lk *16:1-13. 19:15. Ep 6:8, 9, etc. Re *17:14. 19:16.

2. **Continue**. ver. 12. Col 1:9. Ge *32:26. 1 S +*12:23. Jb 15:4. 27:8-10. Ps +*55:16, 17. 109:4. See on Lk 18:1. Ac +1:14. Ro *12:12. Ep *6:18. Ph √4:6. 1 Th +*5:17, 18. **watch**. Ne *4:9. Mt +24:42. *26:41. Mk 13:33. 14:38. Lk +√21:36. 1 P *4:7. **thanksgiving**. Col *1:12, 13. See on 2:7. 3:15, 17. Ep +5:20. He *13:15.

3. **praying**. Ro *15:30-32. Ep *6:19. Ph 1:19. 1 Th *5:25. Phm 22. He 13:18, 19. **that**. 1 C 16:9. 2 C 2:12. 2 Th 3:1, 2. Re *3:7, 8. **a door**. The term *door* is used metaphorically for an *entrance* to any business, or *occasion* or *opportunity* of doing any thing; and consequently "a door of utterance" is an opportunity of preaching the gospel successfully. See the parallel texts. Ac +*14:27. **of utterance**. or, for the word. Ac +8:4. **the mystery**. See on Col *1:26. 2:2, 3. Mt +*13:11. Ro +*16:25n. 1 C *4:1. Ep 6:19. **of Christ**. Ep 3:4. **for**. ver. 18. Ep 3:1. 4:1. 6:20. Ph *1:+7, 13, 14. 2 T 1:16. *2:9.

4. **I may**. Mt 10:26, 27. Ac 4:29. 2 C 3:12. 4:1-4. **as**. ver. 6. Ac 5:29. 1 C *2:4, 5. 2 C +*2:14-17. Ep 6:20.

5. **Walk**. Col +*3:16. Ps *90:12. Mt *10:16. Ro 16:19. 1 C 14:19-25. Ep +*5:15-17. Ja +*1:5. *3:13, 17. **in wisdom**. Col +*1:9. **toward them**. Col +*1:10. 2 S √12:14. Ps *39:1. Pr +*25:26. Ezk 20:9. Mk +4:11. Ac 2:47. *24:16. Ro +*2:24. 12:17. 13:7. 14:16-18. 1 C 5:12, 13. 9:12. *10:32. 14:23. 2 C 1:12. 8:21. Ga +*6:10. Ep 4:1. Ph 1:27. 2:15. 4:5, 8. 1 Th *4:12. *5:15. 1 T *3:7. 5:7, *14. 6:1. T *2:5, 8, 10. 3:2. He +*12:14. Ja 2:7. 1 P *2:12, 15, 17. *3:1, 16. **redeeming**. Da 2:8. See on Ep *5:16. **the time**. Ec +*9:10. Ro +13:11g.

6. **your speech**. Col +*3:16. Dt *6:6, 7. *11:19. 1 Ch 16:24. Jb *4:3, 4. Ps 19:14. 30:12mg,n. 34:13. *37:30, 31. √39:1. *40:9, 10. 45:2. *66:16. 71:8, 15-18, 23, 24. +*71:8. *78:3, 4. 105:2. 119:13, 46. Pr *10:21. *15:4, 7. *16:21-24. 22:17, 18. *25:11, 12. 31:26. Ec *10:12. Ml +*3:16-18. Mt +*12:34, 35. Lk *4:22. Ep +*4:29. T *2:8. Ja 3:2, 6, 8. **with grace**. Col +*3:16. **seasoned**. Le 2:13. 2 K 2:20-22. Mt *5:13. Mk +*9:50n. **how**. Pr 15:1. 26:4, 5. Mt +*7:6. Lk *20:20-40. Ro 14:19. 1 P +*3:9, 15.

7. **my**. Ep 6:21-23. **Tychicus**. Ac 20:4. 2 T 4:12. T 3:12. **a beloved**. ver. 9, 12. See on Ep 6:21. Ph 2:25. **brother**. Col 1:1. **a faithful**. ver. 9. 1 C +*4:1-4. **minister**. Ac +19:22. **fellowservant**. Col 1:7.

8. **I have**. 1 C 4:17. 2 C 12:18. Ep 6:22. Ph 2:28. 1 Th 3:5. **and comfort**. Col +2:2. Is 40:1. 61:2, 3. 2 C *1:4. 2:7. 1 Th 2:11. 3:2. 4:18. 5:11, 14. 2 Th *2:16, 17.

9. **Onesimus**. ver. 7. Phm *10-19. **faithful**. ver. 7. Col +1:7. 1 C +*4:2. 1 P 5:12. **beloved**. Phm 16. **who is**. ver. 12, 14.

10. **Aristarchus**. Ac 19:29. 20:4. 27:2. Ro 16:7. Phm 23, 24. **saluteth**. See on Ro 16:21-23. **and Marcus**. Ac +*12:12. 13:5, 13. 15:37-39. 2 T 4:11. 1 P 5:13. **sister's son**. Ac 15:37, 39. **to Barnabas**. Ac +4:36. **if he come**. ∫184C, Mt +4:9. 2 T √4:11. **receive**. Ro 16:2. 2 J 8, 9.

11. **Justus**. Ac 1:23. 18:7. **who**. Ac 10:45. +11:2. Ro 4:12. Ga 2:7, 8. Ep 2:11. T 1:10. **fellowworkers**. ver. 7. Ro +16:3. 1 C 3:5-9. 2 C 6:1. Ph 4:3. 1 Th 3:2. Phm 1, 24. **the kingdom of God**. Ro +*14:17. **a comfort**. 2 C 7:6, 7. 1 Th 3:7. Phm 7.

12. **Epaphras**. Col 1:7. Phm *23. **one of you**. ver. 9, 14. **a servant**. Jn *12:26. Ga 1:10. Ja +1:1. 2 P 1:1. **always**. See on ver. 2. Lk 22:44. Ga 4:19. He *5:7. Ja +*5:16. **laboring**. *or*, striving. Col +*1:29. ch. 2. **that**. ver. 1. See on Col +*1:9, 22, 28. Mt *5:48. Ro +*15:30. 1 C 2:6. 14:20g. 2 C 13:11. Ep +*4:11-13. Ph 3:12-15. 1 Th +*5:23. He 5:14g. 6:1. Ju *24. **perfect**. Col 1:28. Mt +*5:48. **complete**. *or*, filled. Lk +1:1g. Ro 15:14. **will of God**. Col +*1:9. 1 Th +*4:3.

13. **I bear**. Ro 10:2. 2 C 8:3. Ga 4:15. **for you**. Col 2:1. **and them**. Re 3:17. **Laodicea**. *Laodicea* and *Hierapolis* were both cities of Phrygia in Asia Minor, between which, and equidistant from each, was situated Colosse. *Laodicea* was seated near the Lycus, about 63 miles east of Ephesus; and became one of the largest and richest towns in Phrygia, vying in power with the maritime cities. It is now called *Eski-hissar*,

the old castle; and besides the whole surface within the city's wall being strewed with pedestals and fragments, the ruins of an amphitheater, a magnificent odeum (a small roofed theater for musical or dramatical performances), and other public buildings, attest its former splendor and magnificence. But when visited by Dr. Chandler, all was silence and solitude; and a fox, first discovered by his ears peeping over a brow, was the only inhabitant of Laodicea. **Hierapolis**. i.e. ⁕*temple city*, ✻S#2404g, only here. *Hierapolis*, now *Pambouk-Kaiesi*, was situated, according to the Itinerary, six miles N. of Laodicea; and its ruins are now about a mile and a half in circumference. ver. 15, 16. Col +2:1. Re 1:11. *3:14-18.

14. **Luke**. i.e. *luminous*, ✻S#3065g. Ac ◑+16:10. 2 T *4:11. Phm 24. **beloved**. ver. 9, 12. **Demas**. i.e. *popular*, ✻S#1214g. 2 T +*4:10. Phm 24.

15. **the brethren**. Ep +6:23. **Laodicea**. See on ver. 13. **Nymphas**. i.e. *bridegroom*, ✻S#3564g. This name may be feminine. **the church**. Ro +16:5. 1 C *16:9. Phm +*2. **their house**. or, some authorities read, her house. A. T. Robertson states "It is not possible to tell whether it is 'her' or 'his' house here" (*Word Pictures*, vol. 4, p. 512). Bruce Metzger in his *Textual Commentary* indicates the editorial committee for the United Bible Societies' Greek text preferred the feminine reading on the basis of the manuscript evidence cited there (p. 627).

16. **this epistle**. Ro 16:22. 2 Th 3:14. **is read**. 1 Th *5:27. **Laodiceans**. ✻S#2994g. Re 3:14.

17. **Archippus**. i.e. *horse chief*, ✻S#751g. Phm *2. **Take**. Le 10:3. Nu 18:5. 2 Ch 29:11. Ezk 44:23, 24. Ac +*20:28. 1 T +*4:16. 6:11-14, 20. 2 T 4:1-5. **the ministry**. Ac 1:17. 14:23. 1 C 4:1, 2. Ep +*4:11. 1 T 4:6, 14. 2 T 1:6. +*2:2. 4:5. **thou hast received**. Ac 14:23. T 1:5. **fulfil**. 2 T 4:5.

18. **by**. 1 C +*16:21. 2 Th 3:17. **hand**. ∫121BC, 1 C +16:21. **Remember**. 2 T 1:8. He 13:3. **my bonds**. ver. 3. Ph +1:7. **Grace**. See on Ro 16:20, 24. 2 C +*13:14. 1 T 6:21. 2 T 4:22. T 3:15. He 13:25.

1 THESSALONIANS

1 THESSALONIANS 1

The apostle salutes the church at Thessalonica, 1; and shows how he thanked God on their behalf, and prayed for them; remembering the fruits of their faith, love, and patient hope, as evidences of their "election of God," 2-4. He speaks, more particularly, concerning the happy effects of his success among them: for, "receiving the word in much affliction," copying the example of their teachers, and setting good examples to others; their conversion from idols to the service of the true God, and their patient waiting for Jesus, the Deliverer "from the wrath to come," speedily became known in every place, 6-10.

1. **Paul**. 2 Th 1:1. **Silvanus**. Silas, or Silvanus, and Timothy, did not come to the Apostle, when driven from Thessalonica and Berea, till after his arrival at Athens, nor did they continue with him in that city, being sent speedily back to Thessalonica (1 Th 3:1. Ac 17:10-15); which shows that this epistle could not have been written from Athens, but from Corinth,

where they afterwards rejoined him (Ac 18:1-6). Ac 15:+22, 27, 32, 34, 40. 16:19, 25, 29. 17:4, 15. 18:5, Silas. 2 C 1:19. 2 Th 1:1. 1 P 5:12. **Timotheus**. Ac 16:+1-3. 17:14, 15. 18:5. 19:22. 20:4. 2 C 1:1. Ph 1:1. Col 1:1. 1 T 1:2. 2 T 1:2. He 13:23. **unto the**. See on 1 C 1:2. Ga 1:2. **Thessalonians**. i.e. *victory over the tossing of the law; victory over falsity*, ✻S#2331g. Ac ◑17:+1-9, 11, 13. 20:4. 27:2. 2 Th 1:1. **in God**. Ga 1:22. 2 Th 1:1. 1 J 1:3. Ju 1. **Grace**. See on Ro +1:7. Ep 1:2.

2. **give thanks**. 1 Th 2:13. 3:9. See on Ro 1:+8, 9. 6:17. 1 C 1:4. Ep 1:15, 16. Ep +5:20. Ph 1:3, 4. Col 1:3. Phm 4. **always for**. ∫98, Ro +11:33. Alliteration is present in the Greek: "*pantote peri panton.*" **mention**. Ro +1:9. **prayers**. Ph *4:6.

3. **Remembering**. 1 Th 3:6. 2 T 1:3-5. **without ceasing**. 1 Th *2:13. +*5:17. **your work of**. ∫29, Ex +19:6. This may be understood to mean "work which proceeds from faith, labor which proceeds from love, and patience that proceeds from hope" if taken as the genitive of origin. The genitive, however, may be, by *Anti-*

mereia, faithful service, loving labor, and hopeful patience. But if the figure is *Antiptosis,* then it means a working faith (i.e. *a faith which is manifested by its works*), a laborious love, and patient hope. Probably all three interpretations are correct! (B508). 1 Th *2:13, 14. Jn 6:27-29. Ro 16:26. 1 C √15:58. Ga *5:6. 2 Th *1:3, 11. He 4:11. +*6:10. 11:7, 8, 17, 24-34. Ja *2:17-26. Re 2:19. **of faith.** √174, Ge +18:27. 1 Th *3:6. 5:8. 1 C 13:13. **and labor.** Ge 29:20. SS 8:7. Jn 14:15, 21-23. 15:10. 21:15-17. Ro 16:6. 1 C 13:4-7. 2 C √5:14, 15. 8:7-9. Ga 5:13. Phm 5-7. He +*6:10, 11. 1 J 3:18. 5:3. Re 2:2-4. **of love.** 1 Th *3:6. Col 1:4. 2 Th *1:3, 4. 1 T +1:14. Phm 5. Re 2:10. **and patience.** Ro +*2:7. +*5:3-5. 8:24, 25. 12:12. 15:+*4, 13. 1 C 13:13. 2 C √4:17, 18. Ga +*6:9. 2 Th 1:4. 3:5. He 6:15. 10:36. Ja 1:3, 4. *5:7, 8. 1 J 3:3. Re 3:10. **in the sight.** 1 Th 2:19. 3:9, 13. Is 2:5. 50:11. Ec 2:26. Ac +*3:19. 10:31. 2 C 2:17. 1 T 2:3. He *13:21. 1 P 3:4. 1 J 1:7. 3:21. **our.** Ga +1:4.

4. **Knowing.** ver. 3. Ro +*8:28-30. 11:5-7. Ep 1:4. Ph *1:6, 7. 1 P 1:2. 2 P +*1:10. **beloved, your election of God.** *or,* beloved of God, your election. **beloved.** Ro 1:7. Col 3:12. 2 Th 2:13. **election.** Mk 13:20. Lk +18:7. Ac +*13:48. +*18:27. Ro +*1:7. *9:25. Ep *1:4. 2:4, 5. Col 3:12. 2 Th *2:13. 2 T +*1:9, 10. T 3:4, 5. 2 P +*1:10. Re 13:8. 17:8.

5. **our.** Is √55:11. Ro 2:16. 2 C 4:3. Ga 1:8-12. 2:2. 2 Th 2:14. 2 T 2:8. **in word.** 1 Th √2:13. Is √55:10, 11. 1 C +*2:4. *4:20. 2 C 3:6. **but.** Ps 110:2, 3. Mk 16:20. Ac 11:21. 16:14. Ro +*1:16. 15:18, 19. 1 C 1:24. 2:4, 5. 3:6. 2 C 10:4, 5. Ep 1:17-20. 2:4, 5, 10. 3:20. Ph √2:13. Ja 1:16-18. 1 P 1:3. **in the.** Jn 16:7-15. Ac 2:33. 10:44-46. 11:15-18. 1 C 3:16. 12:7-11. 2 C 6:6. Ga 3:2-5. 5:5, 22, 23. T 3:5, 6. He 2:4. 1 P 1:12. **Ghost.** Gr. *pneuma,* Mt +1:18n. **in much assurance.** Col +*2:2. He *2:3. 6:11, 18, 19. 10:22. 2 P √1:10, 19. **what manner.** 1 Th *2:1-11. Ac 20:18, 19, 33-35. 1 C 2:2-5. 4:9-13. 10:33. 2 C 4:1, 2. 6:3-10. Ph 4:9. 2 Th 3:7-9. 1 T 4:12-16. 1 P 5:3. **for.** 1 C 9:19-23. 2 T 2:10.

6. **ye.** 1 Th 2:14. 1 C +4:16. +*11:1. 2 C *8:5. Ph 3:17. 2 Th 3:7, 9. **and of.** Mt 16:24. Jn *8:12. 13:13-15. 1 C +*11:1. Ep 5:1. 1 P 3:13. 3 J 11. **received.** 1 Th √2:13, 14. 3:2-4. Ho 2:14. Mk 10:29, 30. Ac 17:5-10. 2 C 8:1, 2. 2 Th 1:4. **the word.** Ac +8:4. **with joy.** Mt +*5:12. Jn 14:16-18. Ac 5:41. 9:31. *13:52. Ro 5:3-5. 8:16-18. 15:13. Ga *5:22. He 10:34. 1 P 1:6, 8. **Ghost.** Gr. *pneuma,* Mt +1:18.

7. **ensamples.** 1 Th 4:10. 1 T 4:12. T 2:7. 1 P +*5:3. **in Macedonia.** 1 Th 4:10. ver. 8. Ac 16:+9, 12. 17:13. 18:1. 2 C 1:1. 9:2. 11:9, 10. **Achaia.** Ac +19:21.

8. **from.** Is 2:3. 52:7. 66:19. Ro 10:14-18. 1 C 14:36. 2 Th 3:1. Re 14:6. 22:17. **sounded.** Nu=10:8-10. 1 C 14:8. **the word.** 1 Th 4:15. Ac +15:35. 2 Th 3:1. **in every.** Ro +*1:8. 2 C 2:14. 2 Th *1:4. 3 J 12. **Godward.** Ex 18:19. 2 C 3:4. Phm 5. **so that.** 2 Th 1:4.

9. **what.** ver. 5, 6. 1 Th 2:1, 13. Ac 13:24. **ye turned.** Is 2:17-21. Je 16:19. Zp 2:11. Zc *8:20-23. Ml 1:11. Ac 11:21. ✪+14:15. +*26:17, 18, 20. 1 C 12:2. Ga 4:8, 9. **from idols.** 1 C 12:2. Ga 4:8. **to serve.** Ja +1:1. **the living.** Dt 5:26. 1 S 17:26, 36. Ps 42:2. 84:2. Is 37:4, 17. Je 10:10. Da 6:26. Ho 1:10. Mt +16:16. Ro 9:26. 2 C 6:16, 17. 1 T 4:10. He 12:22. Re 7:2. **and true.** √79, Ge +21:16. Jn +*17:3.

10. **wait.** 1 Th √4:16, 17. Ge 49:18. Jb +*19:25-27. Ps 40:1. Is *25:8, 9. Mt ✪21:28 (work). Lk 2:25.

12:36, 37 (watch). +√21:36. Ac 1:4, +*11. +*3:20, 21. 10:42. 17:31. Ro +*2:7. *8:23-25. 1 C +1:7. *4:5. Ph *3:20. 2 Th 1:7. 2:7. 3:1-5. 1 T 6:14. 2 T +*4:1. T √2:13. He √9:28. *2 P √3:12, 14. Re +*1:7. **his Son.** Mt 3:17. +*16:27n. Jn 3:16. Ro 8:32. Ep 1:6. Col 1:13. **from heaven.** 1 Th +*4:16. Ps 8:1. Jn +*14:3. Ac +*1:11. Ep 4:10. 2 Th *1:7, 10. He 4:14. 9:24. 1 P 3:22. Re +*1:7. **raised.** Ac +*2:24. 3:15. 4:10. 5:30, 31. 10:40, 41. √17:31. Ro 1:4. 4:25. 8:34. 1 C 15:4-21. Col +*1:18. 1 P 1:3, 21. *3:18. Re 1:18. **Jesus.** 1 Th *5:9. Mt 1:21. Lk 3:7. Ga 3:13. He 10:27. 13:8. 1 P 2:21. **delivered.** Ex 12:13, 23. Ps +*83:3. Zp +*2:3. Ac=7:35. Ro +*11:26. Col 1:13. 1 J 1:7. **from.** Is 57:1. Re +*3:10. **wrath.** Interpreters differ as to what this reference to wrath refers. Some take it to refer to the wrath of God against the unsaved (Jn +*3:36), but others, probably more correctly, take it to mean the time of wrath called the Great Tribulation which is yet future. The reference to the Great Tribulation is confirmed by (1) the immediately preceding reference to "waiting for his Son," a statement which would lack connection if the wrath were that of God against unbelievers, (2) the mention of deliverance, which, allied closely with the similar term in Ro 11:26, certainly designates deliverance from tribulation foretold in Old Testament prophecy (Zp +*2:3), and promised by Christ (Lk +*21:36). If the identification of the "wrath to come" with the great tribulation is correct, then the pre-tribulation rapture position would be the correct prophetic position. This of itself would not answer the question whether the Rapture is promised for all believers, or only to those who are "counted worthy" (Lk +*21:36). The doctrine of the "one body" (Ep 4:4n), the declaration that "we shall all be changed" (1 C 15:51), and the extension by promise and prophecy of blessings equally to all believers (Ps +*149:9) argue for all to be raptured, as against the various partial rapture theories. However, the presence in Scripture of repeated warnings to be faithful and ready, and the exhortation of our Lord to pray that we might be counted worthy, suggest the real possibility that some believers will not be counted worthy, otherwise there would be no point to the warnings, if qualification were universal and automatic. 1 Th 2:16. √5:9. Jb *21:30. Ps +*7:6. Is 24:20, 21. +*26:20, 21. 34:2-4. 61:2. Je +*30:7. Da +*12:1. Na √1:2. Zp 1:15. +*2:3. Mt 13:49, 50. Ro 1:18. 2:5. +*5:9. Re *6:16, 17. **to come.** Ps 132:18. 149:4. Mt 3:7. Ep 5:6. Col 3:6.

1 THESSALONIANS 2

The apostle reminds the Thessalonians of his affectionate, faithful labors, and holy manner of life, among them, 1-12. He expresses his satisfaction, as to the manner in which they had received the gospel; and their constancy amidst persecution, 13, 14: and speaks of the guilt and ruin of the unbelieving Jews, especially for opposing the truth being preached to the Gentiles, 15, 16. He shows his joy on the account of the Thessalonians, his desire of seeing them again, and his hope of a joyful meeting at the coming of Christ, 17-20.

1. **our entrance.** ver. 13. 1 Th *1:3-10. Ac 13:24. 2 Th 3:1. **was not.** 2 Th 1:10. **in vain.** 1 Th 3:5. Jb 39:16. Ps 73:13. 127:1. Is *49:4. *65:23. Hab 2:13.

1 C 15:+*2, 10, √58. 2 C 6:1. Ga 2:2. +*4:11. Ph 2:16.

2. **shamefully.** Ac 5:41. 14:5g. 16:12, 22-24, 37. 2 T 1:12. He 11:36, 37. 12:2, 3. 1 P 2:14-16. **bold.** 1 Th 1:5. Ac 4:+13, 20, 31. 14:3. +*17:2, 3. Ep 6:19, 20. **at Philippi.** Ac 16:+12, 22-24, 37. **our God.** 1 Th 3:9. Ph +1:3. 2 Th 1:11, 12. **to speak.** Ac 17:2-9. **the gospel.** ver. 8, 9. Ro +1:1. Col 1:26-29. **much.** Ac 6:9, 10. 15:1, 2. 17:2-9, 17. 19:8. Ph 1:27-30. Col 2:1. Ju +*3. **contention.** The word *agon* properly denotes strife, contention, or contest for victory, such as was used in the Grecian games of running, wrestling, boxing, etc. Hence it may mean here not only a struggle, contest, or labor, but exposed to danger,—at the peril of our lives. So in a Greek phrase quoted by Rosenmuller, *agon prophasin, ouk anamenei,* "in danger, we must not delay." Ph +1:30.

3. **our exhortation.** ver. 5, 6, 11. 1 Th 4:1, 2. Nu 16:15. 1 S 12:3. Ac +4:36. 20:33, 34. 2 C *2:17. *4:2, 5. 7:2. 11:13. 12:16-18. 2 P 1:16. **deceit.** 2 C 6:8g. 2 Th 2:11. **uncleanness.** 1 Th 4:7. **in guile.** 2 C +*4:2.

4. **as we.** 1 C 7:25. Ep *3:8. 1 T 1:11-13. **allowed.** Ro +2:18. **to be.** Lk 12:42. 16:11. 1 C 4:1, 2. *9:17. Ga +2:7. 1 T *1:11, 12. 6:20. 2 T 1:14. +*2:2. T 1:3. **the gospel.** 2 Ch=17:9. 2 C 5:19. Col *3:16. **not.** 1 C 2:4, 5. 2 C +*4:2. 5:11, 16. Ga +*1:10. Ep 6:6. Col 3:22. **but God.** Nu 27:16. 1 K 8:39. 1 Ch 29:17. Ps 7:9. 17:3. 44:21. *139:1, 2. Pr 17:3. Je +*17:10. 32:19. Jn +*2:24, 25. 21:17. Ro +8:27. He √4:13. Re *2:23.

5. **flattering.** Jb 17:5. 32:21, 22. Ps *12:2, +*3. Pr 20:19. 26:28. 28:23. 29:5. Is 30:10. Mt 22:16. 2 P 2:18. 1 J *3:21. **a cloke.** Is 56:11. Je 6:13. 8:10. Mi 3:5. Ml 1:10. Mt 23:14. Ac +*20:33. Ro 16:18. 1 C +9:12. 2 C 2:17. +*4:2. 7:2. 12:17. 1 T 3:3, 8. T 1:7. 1 P 5:2. 2 P *2:3, 14, 15. Ju 11. Re 18:12, 13. **God is witness.** ver. 10. Ro +*1:9. 9:1. 2 C *1:23. 11:31. Ga 1:20. Ph 1:8.

6. **of men.** Est 1:4. 5:11. Pr 25:27. Da 4:30. Jn *5:+41, 44. 7:18. *12:43. 2 C 4:5. Ga +*1:10. 5:26. *6:13. 1 T +*5:17. **when.** ver. 9. 1 C *9:+4, 6, 12-18. 2 C 10:1, 2, 10, 11. 13:10. Phm 8, 9. **been burdensome.** *or,* used authority. 2 C +*1:24. 11:9. *12:13-15. 2 Th *3:8, 9. 1 T 5:16. **as the.** 1 C 9:+1, 2, 4-6.

7. **we.** Ge 33:13, 14. Is *40:11. Ezk 34:14-16. Mt *11:29, 30. Jn 21:15-17. 1 C 2:3. *9:22. 2 C *10:1. 13:4. Ga +*5:22, 23. 1 T *5:1, 2. 2 T +*2:24, 25. Ja *3:17. **gentle.** Mt +18:3. 1 C 14:20. **as.** ver. 11. Nu 11:12. Is 49:23. 60:16. 66:13. Ac 13:18mg. 1 C 4:15.

8. **affectionately.** Je 13:15-17. Ro 1:11, 12. 9:1-3. 10:1. 15:29. 2 C 6:1, 11-13. Ga 4:19. Ph 1:8. 2:25, 26. Col 1:28. +*4:12. He *13:17. **the gospel.** ver. 2. Ro +1:1. **but.** Ac 20:23, 24. 2 C +*12:15. Ph 2:17. 1 J +*3:16. **souls.** Gr. *psyche,* √121A7, Mt +2:20. **dear.** Lk 7:2. Ph 2:20mg. 4:1. Col 1:7. Phm 1.

9. **our labor.** 1 Th 1:3. Ac 18:3. *20:34, 35. 1 C 4:12. 9:6, 15. 2 C 6:5. 11:27. 2 Th 3:7-9. 1 T 4:10. **night.** 1 Th 3:10. Ps 32:4. 88:1. Je 9:1. Lk 2:37. 18:7. Ac +*20:31. 1 T 5:5. 2 T 1:3. **laboring.** Ac +18:3. **chargeable.** ver. 6. Ne 5:15, 18. 1 C 9:7, 18. 2 C 11:9. 12:13, 14. Ph 4:16. **the gospel.** ver. 2. Ac 20:24. Ro 1:1. 15:16, 19. 1 T 1:11.

10. **witnesses.** 1 Th 1:5. 1 S 12:3-5. Ac *20:18, 26, 33, 34. 2 C +*4:2. +*5:11. 11:11, 31. **and God.** ver. 5. Ro +1:9. **how holily.** 1 Th +1:5. Nu 16:15. Jb 29:11-17. 31:1-39. Ps 7:3-5. 18:20-24. Je 18:20. Lk +1:75. Ac +*24:16. 2 C *1:12. 6:3-10. *7:2. 2 Th 3:7. 1 T

+*4:12. 2 T 3:10. T 2:7, 8. 1 P +*5:3. **unblameably.** 1 Th 3:13. 5:23. Lk +1:6.

11. **how.** 1 Th *4:1. 5:11. Ac 20:2. 2 Th 3:12. 1 T 6:2. 2 T *4:2. T 2:6, 9, 15. He 13:22. **exhorted.** 1 Th +4:18. **and.** √148, Ge +8:22. **comforted.** 1 Th 5:14. Jn 11:19, 31. 1 C 14:3. Ph 2:1g. **charged.** Nu 27:19. Dt 3:28. 31:14. Ep +4:17. 1 T 5:7, 21. 6:13, 17. 2 T +*4:1. **as a father.** ver. 7, 17. Ge 50:16, 17. 1 Ch 22:11-13. 38:9, 20. Ps *34:11. Pr *1:10, 15. 2:1. 3:1. 4:1-12. 5:1, 2. 6:1. 7:1, 24. 31:1-9. 1 C √4:14, 15.

12. **walk worthy.** 1 Th *4:1, 12. Lk +√21:36. Ga 5:16. Ep +*4:1. 5:2, 8. Ph *1:27. Col +√1:10. 2:6. 1 P 1:15, 16. 1 J 1:6, 7. +*2:6. 3 J 6. **called you.** 1 Th 5:24. Lk ⦿*22:29. Ro +*8:28, 30. 9:23, 24. 1 C *1:9. 2 Th 1:11, 12. *2:13, 14. 2 T +*1:9. 2:14. 1 P 1:15. *2:9. 3:9. 5:10. **kingdom.** Ps *145:11, 13. Mt +*24:14. +*25:34. Col 1:13n. 2 T +*4:1n. **and.** √93A, Ge +1:26. By Hendiadys, "his glorious kingdom," with emphasis on the word "glorious." Two words are used, but one thing meant. **glory.** Ps +*102:16. Mt +*25:31. Col +*3:4.

13. **thank.** See on 1 Th +*1:2, 3. Ro *1:8, 9. **because.** Je *44:16. Mt 10:13, 14, 40. Ac *2:41. 10:33. 11:1. 13:45, 48. 16:14, 30-34. 17:+*11, 18-20, 32. Ga *4:14. 2 P *3:2. **ye received.** 1 Th *4:8. Mt *10:40. 13:23. Lk 10:39. Ac +*17:11, 12. **which ye heard.** lit. the word of hearing. √144B, Dt +33:19. Ro √10:17. Ga 3:2, 5. **received it not as.** T#1066. Mt +10:20. Lk +*8:18. Ga 4:14. **word of men.** Ga 1:11. **the word of God.** Je √23:28n, 29. Lk *5:1. *8:11, 21. +*11:28. Ac 8:14. 13:44, *46. Ro +9:6. √10:17. Ep *6:17. 2 T +√3:15, 16. He √4:12. 1 P *1:25. 2 P *1:16-21. **effectually worketh.** T#1053. 1 Th *1:5-10. Is √55:11. Je 5:14. 23:29. Jn √15:3. *17:17, 19. Ac 19:20. +*20:32. Ro +*1:16. *6:17, 18. 2 C √3:18. Ph ⦿*2:13. Col *1:6. 2 T +√3:15, 16. He √4:12. Ja +*1:18. +*5:16. 1 P +*1:23. ⁂2:2. 2 P *3:18. 1 J *3:3. *5:4, 5.

14. **became.** 1 Th +1:6. **the churches.** Ac 9:31. ⦿+*10:28. 1 C +11:16. Ga 1:22. **are in Christ.** 1 Th 1:1. Jn 15:5. 1 C 1:30. 2 Th 1:1. **ye also.** 1 Th 3:4. Ac 17:1-8, 13. 2 C 8:1, 2. 2 Th 1:4, 5. **even.** Ac 8:1, 3. 9:1, 13. 11:19. 12:1-3. He 5:33, 34. *10:33, 34.

15. **killed.** Mt +*5:12. 21:35-39. 23:31-35, 37. 27:25. Lk 11:48-51. 13:33, 34. +24:20. Ac 2:23. 3:15. 4:10. 5:30. *7:52. **own prophets.** Je 2:30. **persecuted us.** *or,* chased us out. Am 7:12. Lk 11:49g. Ac 9:22, 23. 22:18-21. 2 C +11:26. **please not.** Ac 12:3. Ro +8:8. 1 C 10:5. **contrary.** Est 3:8. Lk 11:52, 53.

16. **Forbidding.** Ac 11:2, 3, 17, 18. *13:45, 50. *14:2, 5, 19. *17:5, 6, 13. *18:12, 13. 19:9. 21:27-31. 22:21, 22. Ga 5:11. Ep *3:8, 13. **that.** Is *45:22. Mk +*16:16. Ac √4:12. Ro *10:13-15. 2 Th 2:10. 1 T +*2:4. **to fill.** Ge +*15:16. Da 8:23. Zc 5:6-8. Mt *23:32, 34. **for the wrath.** 1 Th +*1:10. Jl *2:30, 31. Ml *4:1, 5. Mt *3:7-10, 12. 12:45. 21:41-44. *22:6, 7. *24:1, 2, 6, 14, 21, 22, 34. Lk 11:50, 51. *19:42-44. +*21:20-24. He *6:8. +*10:27-30. Ja +*5:1-6. Re *22:11.

17. **being taken.** ver. 11. Ac 17:6-9. **short time.** lit. hour. √171T6, Jn +4:23. 2 C +7:8. **in presence.** 2 K 5:26. Ac 17:10. 1 C 5:3. Col *2:5. **endeavored.** 1 Th *3:6, 10, 11. Ge 31:30. 45:28. 48:11. 2 S 13:39. Ps 63:1. Lk 22:15. Ro 1:13. 15:23. Ph 1:22-26.

18. **even.** 1 C 16:21. Col 4:18. 2 Th 3:17. Phm 9. **once.** Ne 13:20. Jb 33:14. Ph 4:16. **Satan.** By raising such a storm of persecution at Berea and other places, that it was deemed prudent to delay his visit till the

storm was somewhat allayed. Some, apparently with less propriety, suppose Satan may mean some adversary, or powerful opponent, as the word denotes; others refer it to wicked men, who are the instruments of Satan; and others by a very usual figure which substitutes the concrete for the abstract (*121A11. Figure of speech Metonymy of the Cause: here, the person acting for the thing done. For other instances of the concrete put for abstract, see Ga 4:19. Ep 4:13, 22. Col 3:11. Contrast *121N1. Metonymy of the Adjunct, abstract put for concrete, Ge +31:54), understand wickedness, i.e. *the wickedness of his enemies and persecutors*. Satan, of course, is himself a created being, a person, not merely an abstract influence (see Jn 16:14n), not ominiscient, not omnipresent—only ubiquitous, everywhere present in an evil sense, but only in one place at a time. Jb +1:7 (T#15). Zc 3:1, 2. Jn *13:2, 27. Ro 1:13. 15:22. 1 C +5:5. 2 C 11:12-14. Re *2:10. 12:9-12. **hindered**. Ne 4:8. Jb 2:7. Da 10:13. Lk 11:52. 13:16. Ac 5:3. ◐16:7. 17:√9, 13, 14, 18. Ro 1:13. 15:22. 2 C 2:11. 11:3. 11:13-15. 12:7. Ep 6:11. 1 T 5:15. 1 P 5:8. Re 2:13, 24.

19. **For what**. Dr. Macknight connects this verse with the preceding by adding, "These things ye may believe; for what," etc. The fervor of affection, and the animation with which it is expressed, in this chapter, are incomparable. **our hope**. 2 C *1:14. Ph 2:16. +*4:1. **crown**. Pr 4:9. 12:4. 16:31. 17:6. Is 62:3. 2 T 4:8. Ja 1:12. 1 P 5:4. Re +*2:10. 4:10, 11. **rejoicing**. *or*, glorying. *121E1, Ge +25:23. ver. 20. Ps +*126:6. Da +*12:3. Ro 15:16-19. He +*13:17. **Are not**. Is *8:18. 1 C 15:31. 2 C +1:14. 2 Th 1:4. **even ye**. Ga ◐+*4:11. **in the presence**. 1 Th 1:3. 3:9, 13. *5:23. 1 C *4:5. 15:23. 2 C 1:14. Ph 2:16. 4:1. 2 Th 1:7-12. 2:1. 1 T 6:14, 15. 2 T *4:1, 2. T √2:13. 1 J 2:28. **our Lord**. Ju *24. **at his**. 2 T +*4:1. 1 J *3:1-3. 2 P √3:14. Re +*1:7. 11:18. *22:12. **coming**. Gr. *parousia*, Mt +24:3. 1 Th 3:13. 4:15. 5:23. 2 Th 2:1, 8. 1 C 15:23. Ja 5:7, 8. 2 P 1:16. 3:4, 12. 1 J 2:28.

20. **our glory**. *121E1, Ge +25:23. Pr 17:6. 1 C 11:7.

1 THESSALONIANS 3

The apostle shows, that his care for the Christians at Thessalonica had induced him to send Timothy, to establish and encourage them, 1-5; whose good report concerning them had been a great comfort to him in his distresses, 6-8. He thanks God, in their behalf, and shows how earnestly he desires to see them, 9, 10; and prays, that he may be enabled to visit them; and for their growth in holiness and love, and perseverance to the end, 11-13.

1. **when**. ver. 5. 1 Th 2:17. Je 20:9. 44:22. 1 C +9:12. 2 C 2:13. 11:29, 30. **forbear**. *63A2, 2 S +6:6. Supply by ellipsis (absolute: of accusative), "when we could no longer bear (our anxiety)." ver. 5. **we thought**. Ac +*17:15, 16.

2. **sent**. ver. 5. Ph +2:19. **Timotheus**. Ac +16:1. 17:14, 15. 18:5. **our brother**. Ro 16:21. 1 C 16:10, 11. 2 C 1:1, 19. 2:13. 8:23. Ep 6:21. Ph 2:19-25. Col 1:1, 7. 4:9, 12. Phm 1. He 13:23. **minister**. 2 C +6:4. **fellowlaborer**. 1 C +3:9. 16:10. **the gospel**. Ro +15:19. **to establish**. ver. 13. Lk 22:32. Ac +*14:22, 23. 16:5. Ep 6:22. Ph 1:25. 1 P +*5:10. **comfort**. 1 Th +4:18.

3. **moved**. Ps 112:6. Ac 2:25. 20:24. 21:13. Ro +*5:3.

1 C √15:58. Ep 3:13. Ph 1:28. Col +*1:23. 2 Th 1:4. 2:2. 2 T 1:8. 1 P 4:12-14. Re 2:10, 13. 3:2. **we are**. 1 Th *5:9. Mt 10:16-18. *24:9, 10. Lk 21:12. Jn 15:19-21. 16:2, 33. Ac +*9:16. +*14:22. *20:23, 24. 21:11, 13. Ro +*8:17, 35-37. 1 C 4:9. 2 T √3:11, 12. 1 P *2:21. *4:12, 13. √5:10. **appointed**. Lk 2:34. Ph 1:16g.

4. **we told**. 1 Th 4:6. Jn *16:1-3. Ac 20:24. 2 C 13:2. Ga 5:21. **suffer tribulation**. Mt 10:22. Ep *3:13. **even**. 1 Th 2:2, +14. Ac 17:1, 5-9, 13. 2 C 8:1, 2. 2 Th 1:4-6.

5. **when**. See on ver. 1. **forbear**. *63A2, 2 S +6:6. ver. 1. **I sent**. ver. 2, 6. Ac 15:36. 2 C 7:5-7. **your faith**. 2 Th *1:3, 4. He 3:6, 14. 4:14. 10:38. 2 P 2:18-22. **lest**. Mt 4:3. 1 C 7:5. 2 C 2:11. √11:2, 3, 13-15. Ga 1:6-9. Ep +*4:14. Ja 1:13, 14. 1 P *1:5-7. **the tempter**. *24B, Ge +23:16. 1 Th 2:18. Mt 4:3. **and our labor**. Paul consistently sought to conserve his gains and minimize losses through careful followup of his converts (Ac 15:36. 20:31, 32. Compare He +*3:12, 13). In our day more attention needs to be paid to spiritual growth following initial conversion. So much attention has been focused upon the "birth" that little has been done to insure growth of new believers. As a result, as many are lost silently out the "back door" as are currently being won and brought in through the front door. Warmly introduce newcomers to the fellowship to strong believers who will exercise continuing love and hospitality toward them (Ro +*12:13. 1 P *4:9, 10) to facilitate the development of deep Christian relationships (Ro +*12:5). Rather than be so efficient in dropping inactive members from the church roll, we ought to be careful to exercise our responsibility in caring for (1 T +*3:5) and feeding the sheep, seeking out the ones who have left the fold, winning them back to active life in the body of Christ, rather than abandoning them to the world, the flesh, or the devil. See related notes (Jon 4:11n. He 3:13n. 6:9n). See on 1 Th 2:1, 11-13, 19, 20. Is *49:4. Ga 2:2. +*4:11. Ph +*2:16. **in vain**. It does not appear from this remark that Paul taught or believed in unconditional eternal security. See the "if" in ver. 8. To what purpose are the warnings to believers in Scripture, if what is warned against is not possible in the first place? We need to exercise care in formulating our doctrinal systems that we do not wrest Scripture by arbitrarily denying even the possibility of what so many texts repeatedly warn against: doctrinal (1 C +*15:2) or moral (1 C +*6:9, 10) apostasy. Lk +*8:13. Jn 3:16n. 2 C 6:1. Ga 2:2. +*4:11. Ph 2:16. 1 T *4:1n.

6. **when**. 1 Th 1:1. Ac *18:1, 5. 2 C 7:6, 9. **and brought**. Pr 25:25. Is 52:7. 2 C 7:5-7. **faith**. 1 Th +1:3. 1 C 13:13. Ga +*5:6. Col 1:4. 2 Th 1:3. 1 T 1:5. Phm 5. 1 J +*3:23. **and charity**. *174, Ge +18:27. **and that**. 1 Th 1:3. 2:9. 1 C 11:2. Col 4:18. 2 T 1:3. He 13:3, 7. **desiring**. ver. 9, 10. See on 1 Th 2:17. Ph +1:8.

7. **we were**. ver. 8, 9. 2 C +*1:4. *7:6, 7, 13. 2 J 4. **in all**. Ac 17:4-10. 1 C 4:9-13. 2 C *11:23-26. 2 T *3:10-12. **distress**. Lk +*21:23.

8. **we live**. *108B, 1 S +10:24. 1 S 25:6h. Ps *30:5. 2 C 13:4, 5. Ga +*4:11, 19. Ph *1:21. He +*6:11. **if**. *184A, 1 C +15:2. Ge +*4:7. Je +*7:5. Jn *8:31. Col +*1:23. 2 P +*1:10. 3 J *4. **stand fast**. 1 Th 2:19. Jn +*8:31. *15:4, 7. Ac +*11:23. +*14:22. 1 C +√15:58. +16:13. Ga *5:1. Ep *3:17. *4:15, 16. *6:10, 11, 13, 14. Ph *1:27. *4:1. Col +*1:23. He +*3:14.

4:14. *10:23. 1 P 5:10. 2 P √3:17. Re 3:*3, 11.

9. **what**. 1 Th 1:2, 3. 2 S 7:18-20. Ne 9:5. Ps 71:14, 15. 2 C *2:14. 9:15. **for**. ver. 7, 8. See on 1 Th *2:19. **before**. ver. 13. 1 Th +1:3. Dt 12:12, 18. 16:11. 2 S 6:21. Ps 68:3. 96:12, 13. 98:8, 9. **our God**. 1 Th 2:2. Ph +1:3. 2 Th 1:11, 12.

10. **Night**. Mk +5:5. Lk 2:37. Ac 26:7. 2 T 1:3. Re 4:8. 7:15. **praying**. ver. 11. 1 Th 2:17, 18. Ro 1:10. 15:30-32. Phm 22. **exceedingly**. 2 Th 1:3. **might see**. T#1693. 1 Th 2:17. Ro 1:10. 15:23. **might perfect**. T#1486. Ro *1:11, 12. 2 C 1:15, +*24. *13:+9, 11. Ph 1:25. Col 1:28. *4:12. 2 Th 1:11.

11. **God**. ver. 13. Is 63:16. Je 31:9. Ml 1:6. Mt 6:4, 6, 8, 9, 14, 18, 26, 32. Lk *12:30, 32. Jn 20:17. 2 C *6:18. Ga +1:4. Col 1:2. 1 J √3:1. **himself**. 1 Th 4:16. 5:23. Ro 8:16, 26. 2 Th *2:16. 3:16. Re 21:3. **our Father**. 1 Th *2:16. Jn +*10:30. **and our Lord**. See on Ro 1:3. 2 Th *2:16. **direct**. *or*, guide. Lk 1:79g. 2 Th 3:5. **our way**. Ezr 8:21-23. Pr √3:5, 6. Mk 1:3.

12. **the Lord**. This invocation of Christ by all Christians, in all places, must suppose him omniscient, omnipresent, and the searcher of all hearts; and these are the properties of God alone (Whitby, cited by Scott. See Ac 7:59n). 1 Th 4:10. Ps 115:4. Lk 17:5. 2 C 9:10. Ph *2:11. Ja 1:17. 2 P +*3:18. **make you**. 2 Th 1:3. **abound**. 1 Th 4:1, 9, 10. Ph 1:9. 2 Th 1:3. **in love**. T#412, 1611. 1 Th 4:9. 5:15. Pr +21:3 (T#629). Ml +2:10 (T#685). Mt √7:12. +10:8 (T#406). 22:39. +25:35 (T#715). Jn +*13:34, 35. Ro 13:8-10. 1 C *13:13. 16:14. Ga *5:6, 13, 14, 22, 23. Col 2:1, 2. 3:14. 1 T 4:12. He +*6:10. 1 P +*1:22. 4:8. 2 P +*1:7. 1 J 3:11-19. 4:7-16. **one toward another**. Ro +12:5. **toward all**. T#1610. Mt +5:44. Ga +*6:10. 1 T 4:10. **even**. 1 Th 2:8.

13. **he may**. 1 Th √5:23. Ro 14:4. *16:25. 1 C +*1:8. Ph *1:10. 2 Th *2:16, 17. 1 P +*5:10. 1 J 3:20, 21. **unblameable**. 1 Th 2:10. +*5:23. Lk +1:6. Ep *5:27. Col *1:22. 1 J 3:20, 21. 2 P +*3:14. Ju *24. **before**. See on ver. 11. 1 Th +1:3. **at the coming**. Gr. *parousia*, Mt +24:3. 1 Th +*2:19. *4:15. *5:23. 1 C *1:7. *15:23. 2 Th √2:1. **with all**. 1 Th 4:14. Dt +*33:2. Ps +*50:5. +*149:6-9. Zc +*14:5. Mt +*25:31. 2 Th *1:7, 10. Ju *14, *15. Re 19:14. 20:6. **his saints**. Ps +*149:9. Da *7:18. Col +1:26. 2 Th 1:10.

1 THESSALONIANS 4

The apostle earnestly exhorts his brethren, to increasing in diligence in obeying Christ, 1, 2: and to chastity, and integrity in all things: as God had called them to holiness: and those who despised these admonitions, would despise God himself, 3-8. He calls on them to "abound more and more in love" of one another, 9, 10; to be industrious in their respective callings, 11, 12; and to moderate their sorrow for deceased believers, 13; from assured expectation of the coming of Christ to raise the dead in Christ, to change living believers, and receive them by the Rapture to himself, 14-18.

1. **Furthermore**. Ph +3:1. **we**. 1 Th 2:11. Ro *12:1. 2 C 6:1. 10:1. Ep 4:1. Phm 9, 10. He 13:22. **we beseech**. *or*, we request. **exhort**. *or*, beseech. **by the**. ver. 2. 1 C *5:4. Ep 4:20. 2 Th 2:1. 1 T 5:21. 6:13, 14. 2 T +*4:1. **ye have received**. ver. 11, 12. Ac *20:27. 1 C 11:23. 15:1. Ph *1:27. Ph 4:9. Col +*2:6. 2 Th 3:10-12. **ye ought**. See on 1 Th 2:12. **to walk**. Col +√1:10.

and. √93B, Is +66:11. **to please**. Ro +8:8. +*12:2. Ep +*5:17. Col +√1:10. He √11:6. *13:16. 1 J *3:22. **abound**. ver. 10. 1 Th 3:12. Jb 17:9. Ps 92:14. Pr +*4:18. Jn *15:2. 1 C √15:58. Ph 1:9. 3:14. 2 Th 1:3. 2 P √1:5-10. +*3:18.

2. **ye know**. 1 C 11:2. **what commandments**. ver. 11. Ezk 3:17. Mt *28:20. Ac 5:28g. 16:24g. 1 C 9:21. 2 Th 3:4, 6, 10. 1 T 1:5. 1 J +*2:3. **by the Lord**. The assertion that Paul never quotes the words of Christ is false (ver. 15. Ac 20:35. 1 C √9:7n, 14n. 11:23-26. 1 T 5:18); so also the assertion that his teaching was not founded upon any of the teaching of our Lord given during the earthly ministry in Palestine. On the contrary, Paul carefully distinguishes the basis of authority for his teaching, whether the known teaching of Jesus himself (see the reference passages below), the teaching of the law (1 C 14:34), or divinely inspired teaching granted Paul by the Holy Spirit (Ro 16:25. 1 C 7:40. Ga 1:12). Careful attention to this matter will serve as a proper corrective to the mistaken teaching of some that the Old Testament is not authoritative for the church, or that the teaching of our Lord's earthly ministry in the gospels does not pertain to this dispensation. Paul taught that all scripture is given by inspiration of God and is profitable (2 T +√3:16, 17); that the Old Testament was written for our learning (Ro +*15:4); to it Paul appeals as the ground of authority for his teaching for New Testament church practice and doctrine (1 C 14:34. 1 T 2:12-14); he cites the very words of Christ in Mt 10:10 at 1 T 5:18, calling them scripture. Peter calls the writings of Paul *scripture*, 2 P 3:16. Beware, therefore, of that false teaching in the name of "rightly dividing the word of truth" (apparently misread by some as "rightly subtracting") which would take whole portions of the Word of God, such as the Sermon on the Mount, the commands of Christ (1 J +*2:3n), or even the whole of Christ's earthly teaching ministry before the cross, not to mention all of Paul's early epistles written before the alleged founding of the church after Acts ch. 28, and render them inapplicable for teaching and instruction for the church today. Such an approach is certainly condemned by the consistent warning of scripture (Dt 4:2. 12:32. Pr 30:6) not to "take away from the words" of this book, lest God take away "his part out of the book of life" (Re +*22:19). 1 C √7:●6, *10, ●12, ●25, ●40.

3. **the will**. 1 Th 5:18. Ps *40:8. 143:10. Mt 7:21. 12:50. Mk 3:35. Jn 4:34. +*7:17. Ro 1:10. +*12:2. 15:32. 2 C 8:5. Ep *5:17. 6:6. Col 1:9. *4:12. 2 T 2:26. He *10:36. *13:21. 1 P 2:15. 3:17. 4:2, 19. 1 J √2:17. **your sanctification**. ver. 4. 1 Th +*5:23. Jn *17:17-19. Ac *20:32. +*26:18. Ro 6:19, 22g. 1 C +*1:30. +*6:11. Ep √5:26, 27. 2 Th *2:13. 1 T 2:15. T *2:14. He +*12:14. 1 P 1:2. **abstain**. Mt 15:19. Ac +√15:20. Ro +*1:29. 1 C 5:9-11. +*6:9, 10, 13-18. 7:2. 2 C 12:21. Ga *5:19. Ep *5:3-5. Col +*3:5. He 12:16. +*13:4. Re +*21:8. 22:15g.

4. **should know**. Ro √6:19. +*12:1. 1 C *6:15, 18-20. **possess**. Gr. *ktaomai*, to acquire, as money (Mt 10:9. Lk 18:12), lands (Ac 1:18), political liberty (Ac 22:28), or the gifts of the Holy Spirit (Ac 8:20), as noted by Hogg and Vine, *Comm. on Thessalonians*, p. 116. Boyce W. Blackwelder points out that the present tense of this infinitive requires the meaning of "acquire;" if the perfect tense of the verb had been used, then the meaning of "possess" would be correct,

but such is not the case here (*Toward Understanding Thessalonians*, p. 93). **his vessel.** ⨍46C, Mt +8:6. Gr. *skeuos*, a vase or utensil, is used for the Hebrew *klee*, which has a wider meaning, instrument or weapon. See Ho 13:15 and 1 S 21:3-6 (B679). This may be a reference to himself, his body (1 S 21:5. Ro 6:13. 1 C 9:27), or more likely, the reference is to acquiring his own wife (1 C 7:2), since one could hardly acquire himself. Ru 4:10. 1 S 21:5. Ac *9:15. Ro 9:21-23. 2 C 4:7. 2 T 2:20, 21. 1 P √3:7. **in sanctification.** ver. +*3. **honor.** Ac +*6:3. Ro 1:24. Ph +*4:8. He +*13:4.

5. **in the lust.** Ro +*1:24, 26. Col +*3:5. **concupiscence.** Gr. *epithumia*, ✱S#1939g. Mk 4:19 (lusts). Lk 22:15 (desire). Jn 8:44. Ro 1:24. 6:12. 7:7, 8. 13:14. Ga 5:16, 24. Ep 2:3. 4:22. Ph 1:23. Col 3:5 (concupiscence). 1 Th 2:17 (desire). 1 T 6:9 (lusts). 2 T 2:22. 3:6. 4:3. T 2:12. 3:3. Ja 1:14, 15. 1 P 1:14. 2:11. 4:2, 3. 2 P 1:4. 2:10, 18. 3:3. 1 J 2:16, 16, 17. Ju 16, 18. Re 18:14. Compare *epithumeo*, ✱S#1937g, Mt +5:28. **as the Gentiles.** Mt 6:32. Lk 12:30. Ep 4:17-19. 1 P +*4:3. **which.** ⨍142, Ge +20:16. **know not.** A. T. Robertson aptly observes "One of the reasons for the revival of paganism in modern life is professedly this very thing that men wish to get rid of the inhibitions against licentiousness by God" (*Word Pictures*, vol. 4, p. 29). Jg 2:10. Ps ⟩79:6. Is 45:4, 5. Je 9:3. ⟩10:25. Ho 4:1. Ac *17:23, 30, 31. Ro +*1:28. 1 C 1:21. 15:34. Ga +4:8. Ep √2:12. 2 Th √1:8.

6. **go beyond.** A command not to go beyond the fixed limits of chastity established by God's law. Ex +*20:14, 17. Le +√19:11, 13. Dt 24:7. 25:13-16. Pr *11:1. 16:11. *20:14, 23. *28:24. Is 5:7. 59:4-7. Je 9:4. Ezk 22:13. 45:9-14. Am 8:5, 6. Zp 3:5. Ml +*3:5. Mk √10:19. 1 C √6:7-9. 13:5. Ep +*4:28. Ja +*5:4. **defraud.** *or*, oppress, *or*, overreach. We are not to destroy the moral purity of fellow believers or anyone else to satisfy our own impure desires by stepping over the boundaries God has established. The practice of men having "live in" girlfriends, or women having "live in" boyfriends, is clearly and absolutely forbidden by this Scripture. Christian parents further have the responsibility to shield their children from exposure to amoral or non-Christian instruction in these matters contrary to the principles of the written word of God (Mt 18:6. 1 C 7:36-38. Ep 5:12) by whatever means are necessary (Ac +*5:29). T#732. Le 19:11, 13, 35. *25:14, 17. Dt +*24:14. 25:13-15. 27:17. 1 S 12:3, 4. Ps +*12:5. 82:2. Pr 11:1. +21:3 (T#629). +22:22 (T#636). Je 7:6. Ezk +*16:49. Mi 2:2. Zp 3:1. 2 C +*2:11g. Ep 4:19n. Ja 2:6. **his brother.** Used of mankind in general by Paul only here. Mt 7:2. 1 C 6:8. **in any matter.** *or*, in the matter. Paul delicately has reference to the sexual sin mentioned in the immediate context; in particular, adultery and pre-marital sex, sins absolutely forbidden to Christian men and women. As the preceding reference passages show, the commandment "Defraud not" elsewhere has broader application. Dt 22:25. 2 S √13:1-14. Ac 15:20. 1 C 6:9, 18, 19. 7:1,2. 13:5. 2 C 7:11. Ep 5:3, 6-11. **the avenger.** Dt √32:35. Jb 31:13, 14. Ps 94:1. 140:12. Pr +*22:22, 23. Ec 5:8. Is 1:23, 24. Ro *1:18. √12:19. 13:4. Ep 5:6. 2 Th √1:8. He +*13:4. **as we.** Lk 12:5. Ga 5:21. Ep 4:17. **forwarned.** 1 Th +3:4. Ac 1:16g. **testified.** Lk +16:28. Ep +4:17. 1 T 5:21. 2 T 2:14. 4:1. He 2:6g.

7. **God.** Le 11:44. *19:2. Ro 1:7. +*8:29, 30. 1 C

1:2. Ep 1:4. 2:10. 4:1. 2 Th 2:13, 14. 2 T +*1:9. He √12:14. 1 P *1:14-16. 2:9-12, 21, 22. 2 P √3:14. 1 J √3:3. **uncleanness.** 1 Th 2:3. Ga *5:19. Ep 4:19. 2 P 2:10. **holiness.** ver. +*3. He +*12:14.

8. **therefore.** He 12:1g. **despiseth.** *or*, rejecteth. 1 S 8:7. 10:19. Lk 7:30g. Jn 12:48. 1 C 1:19g. Ga √2:21g. **despiseth not man.** 1 Th 2:13. Pr 1:7. 23:9. Is 49:7. 53:3. Lk √10:16. Ac 13:41. Ju 8. **who.** Ne 9:30. Ezk 37:6. Ac +*5:3, 4. 1 C *2:10, 13. √6:19. 7:40. +*10:13. 2 T +*3:16. 1 P 1:12. 2 P √1:21. 1 J 3:24. **Spirit.** Gr. *pneuma*, ⨍121A1, Lk +1:17n.

9. **touching.** Le 19:8. Ps 133:1. Jn 13:34, 35. 15:12-17. Ac 4:32. Ro 12:10. Ep 5:1, 2. He +13:1. 1 P *1:22. 3:8. 2 P 1:7. 1 J 2:10. 3:11, 14-19, 23. 4:7-16. **ye need.** 1 Th 1:8. *5:1. Je 31:34. 2 C 9:1. He +*8:10, 11. 1 J *2:20-27. **for ye.** Is 54:13. Mt *22:39. Jn 6:44, 45. 13:34. *14:26. *15:12, 17. Ep *5:2. He 10:16. 1 P *4:8. 1 J *3:11, 23. 4:21. 5:1. **taught of God.** Is 54:13. Jn 6:45. 1 C 2:13. 1 J *2:20, 27. **to love.** 1 Th 3:12. Jn +*13:34.

10. **all the.** 1 Th 1:7. 2 C 8:1, 2, 8-10. Ep 1:15. Col 1:4. 2 Th 1:3. Phm 5-7. **brethren.** 1 Th 5:26, 27. Ep +6:23. **Macedonia.** 1 Th 1:7. Ac +16:9. **beseech.** ver. +18g. **that ye increase.** ver. 1. 1 Th 3:12. Ph *1:9. 3:13-15. 2 P +*3:18.

11. **that.** Pr *17:1. Ec 4:6. La 3:26. 2 Th *3:12. 1 T 2:2. 1 P *3:4. **study.** Gr. be ambitious. Ro 15:20. 2 C 5:9g. **to be quiet.** Pr 17:14. 20:3. 25:8. 2 Th 3:12. 1 T 2:2. **and to do.** Mk 13:34. Lk 12:42, 43. Ro 12:4-8. Col 3:22-24. 2 Th √3:11. 1 T √5:13. T 2:4-10. 1 P 4:10, 11, +*15. **to work.** Ac +18:3. +*20:35. Ro +*12:11. 1 C *4:12. Ep +*4:28. 2 Th √3:7-12. T 3:14mg. **commanded.** ver. 2. 2 Th 3:4.

12. **ye may walk.** 1 Th 5:22. Ro +*12:17. +*13:13. 2 C *8:20, 21. Ph +*4:8. Col *4:5. T 2:8-10. 1 P √2:12. *3:16, 17. **honestly.** Ex +*18:21. Ac +*6:3. 2 C +*6:3. *8:20, 21. **them.** ⨍142, Ge +20:16. Mk +4:11. 1 C 5:12, 13. Col 4:5. 1 T 3:7. 1 P 3:1. **nothing.** *or*, no man. 2 C 11:7-9.

13. **I would not.** ⨍175B, Ge +21:16. Ro 1:13. 1 C +10:1. 12:1. 2 C 1:8. 2 P 3:8. **which are.** ver. 15. 1 Th 5:10. 1 K 1:21. 2:10. Da +*12:2n. Mt +27:52. Lk 8:52, 53. Jn *11:11-13. Ac *7:60. 13:36. 1 C 15:6, 18. 2 P 3:4. **asleep.** Gr. *koimaomai*, to fall asleep, involuntarily: hence used (in nearly every place) of death, but only of saints. Contrast 1 Th +*5:6, "sleep," Gr. *katheudo*, to go asleep, voluntarily: hence not used of death, but either of taking rest in sleep, or of the opposite of watchfulness. EWB (B372) observes, "Thus the marked use of *koimaomai* in the *first* series, and of *katheudo* in the second series teaches us that the hope of Resurrection and Ascension before the Day of the Lord is for all who are Christ's, whether they are dead or alive, whether they are watchful or unwatchful." ✱S#2837g. ver. 14, 15. Mt 27:52. 28:13. Lk 22:45. Jn 11:11, 12. Ac 7:60. 12:6. 13:36. 1 C 7:39. 11:30. 15:6, 18, 20, 51. 2 P 3:4. **ye sorrow not.** Ge 37:35. Le 19:28. Dt *14:1, 2. 2 S √12:19-23. 18:33. Jb √1:21. Ezk 24:16-18. Mk 5:39. Jn *11:24. Ac 8:2. **as others.** ⨍142, Ge +20:16. 1 Th 5:6. Ep 2:3. **have no hope.** Jb ◑+*19:25-27. Pr +*14:32. Ezk 37:11. 1 C 15:19. See on Ep *2:12.

14. **if we believe.** ⨍184A, 1 C +15:2. Is +*26:19n. Ro +*8:11. √10:9, 10. 1 C *15:12-23. 2 C 4:13, 14. Re 1:18. **sleep in Jesus.** ver. +*13. 1 Th 3:13. 1 C +15:18. Re +*14:13. **God bring.** Jn 5:29. 1 C 15:35.

with him. ver. 17. 1 Th +*3:13. Ge +*49:10. Zc +*14:5. Mt +*24:31. 1 C √15:23. Ph +*3:20, 21. 2 Th √2:1. Ju *14, *15.

    15. by the word. ver. √2n. 1 Th +1:8. 1 K 13:1, 9, 17, 18, 22. 20:35. 22:14. Lk √20:35, 36. **that we**. Some have mistakenly drawn the inference that Paul here asserts he expected the return of Jesus in his own lifetime. This, of course, is an unwarranted inference which fails to take into account Paul's own inspired prediction regarding the great apostasy and the coming of Antichrist given in 2 Th ch. 2, events which Paul certainly did not suppose were to be compressed into his own lifespan. The fact that Christ revealed to Peter certain events which would transpire in his life (Jn 21:18-23), as well as to Paul (Ac 9:15. 20:23, 24. 27:24), must not be understood to deny the doctrine of the imminency of the return of Christ. Robertson notes Paul "was alive, not dead, when he wrote" (*Word Pictures*, vol. 4, p. 32). Paul sometimes associates himself with the living (as here, and Ph 3:20. T 2:12, 13), and sometimes with the dead, (as 1 C √6:14. 2 C √4:14. 5:8. Ph 1:21-24. 2:17. 2 T 4:6-8). By such words Paul simply associates himself with the class of the living to which he then belonged, as opposed to the dead, and was not making a statement about how soon Jesus would return, a secret which God has kept in his own counsel (Dt +*29:29. Mt 24:36. Mk +*13:32. Ac +*1:7), as Hogg and Vine well observe (*Comm. on 1 Thessalonians*, p. 138). ver. 17. 1 Th 5:10. Ps 66:6. Ho 12:4. Mt 16:28n. Mk 9:1. Lk 9:27. Ro 13:11, 13. 1 C 15:51. **which are alive**. 1 C √15:51-53. 2 C *4:14. **and remain**. Gr. ✻S#4035g, only here and ver. 17. *perileipomenoi*, present passive participle of *perileipo*, "remain, be left behind," "to leave over; to remain over, to survive," (Arndt, Gingrich; Thayer); compare citation in MM, p. 506b, "a very small portion…will be left." Is +*24:6. Mt +*7:14. Lk 18:8. **the coming**. Gr. *parousia*, Mt +24:3. 1 Th +2:19. *Parousia* has the basic meaning of presence or arrival, used in later Greek secular literature of the official visit of a king or ruler. In the New Testament it is used nontechnically of presence (1 C 16:17. 2 C 10:10. Ph 1:26. 2:12); of coming or arrival (2 C 7:6, 7. Ph 1:26); and in a technical eschatological sense of the second coming of Christ, with the connotation of ultimate presence (Mt +24:3n, 27, 37, 39. 1 C 15:23. 1 Th 2:19. 3:13. 4:15. 5:23. 2 Th 2:1, 8. Ja 5:7, 8. 2 P 1:16. 3:4, 12. 1 J 2:28). Hogg and Vine note that the usual translation, "coming," is misleading, for other Greek words are better so translated (*erchomai*, Lk 12:45. 19:23. *eleusis*, Ac 7:52. *eisodos*, Ac 13:24). "…whereas these words fix the attention on the journey to, and the arrival at, a place, *parousia* fixes it on the stay which follows on the arrival there" (*Comm. on Thessalonians*, p. 87. See also Boyce Blackwelder, *Toward Understanding Thessalonians*, p. 85). The word *parousia* does not itself denote either secrecy or invisibility (Mt 24:3n). Hogg and Vine further note (p. 88) that when used non-prophetically of Christ, *parousia* refers to a defined period (2 P 1:16, the transfiguration, see Mt 17:1-8). Where it is used prophetically, *parousia* refers to the time beginning with the descent of the Lord from heaven into the air (1 Th 4:16, 17), and ending with his revelation and manifestation to the world (2 Th 1:7). "The Parousia of the Lord Jesus is thus a period with a beginning, a course, and a conclusion. The begin-

ning is prominent in 1 Th 4:15; 5:23. 2 Th 2:1. 1 C 15:23. Ja 5:7, 8. 2 P 3:4; the course in 1 Th 2:19. 3:13. Mt 24:3, 37, 39. 1 J 2:28; the conclusion in 2 Th 2:8. Mt 24:27" (Hogg and Vine, *Thessalonians*, p. 88). **shall not**. 𝒥158, Mt +5:18. Ac +10:42. **prevent**. obsolete for **precede**. Jb 41:11. Ps 88:13. 119:147, 148. Mt 17:25. 2 C 10:14. **asleep**. See on ver. 13.

    16. the Lord. Is *25:8, 9. Mt +*16:27n. +*24:30, 31. +*25:31. 26:64. Ac +*1:11. 2 Th *1:7. 2 P *3:10. Re +*1:7. **himself**. 1 Th +3:11. **descend**. Ph *3:20. **from heaven**. 1 Th 1:10. 2 Th 1:7. **with a shout**. Nu 23:21. 2 S 6:15. Ps 47:1, 5. Jl 2:11. Zc 4:7. 9:9. Jn 5:28, 29. **the voice**. Jl *2:11. Mt +24:31. 1 C 14:7, 8. Re 1:10. 4:1. **the archangel**. Hogg and Vine note that there is no article before "voice" and "archangel" in the Greek, "so that the quality of the voice, its majesty and authority, is intended; but there is nothing to indicate that any particular angelic chief was in the writer's mind" (*Comm. on 1 Thessalonians*, p. 142). Jehovah's Witnesses argue from this text that Jesus is the archangel Michael, since Michael is the only archangel named in Scripture. This of course is shaky inference indeed, opposed to very clear declarations of Scripture as to the two natures in Christ. The motivation for such identification is to remove the basis for the doctrine of the deity of Christ and the Trinity. But such wresting of Scripture will not stand up to careful comparison of Scripture. In He 2:16 it is declared that Jesus "took not on him the nature of angels," but took on in his incarnation "the seed of Abraham." As Paul asserts Christ before the incarnation was in the form of God, Christ could not have been an archangel in time past; Scripture declares that Jesus during his earthly life "became flesh" (Jn 1:14) and was made in the likeness of men (Ph 2:7), and now as man is in heaven (1 T 2:5). These direct assertions of Scripture leave no room before, during, or after the incarnation for Jesus Christ to have been or to have since become an archangel: he is truly man, in whom the fulness of the Godhead dwells bodily (Col 2:9). The Jehovah Witness doctrine regarding the person of Christ also fails in that it requires the discontinuity of the person of Michael the archangel, and is subject to the same fatal objection noted in their doctrine of the mortality of the soul, namely, that not resurrection but new creation must take place in reconstituting the person, so that the same person does not exist before and after (see note on Mt +*10:28n. Compare 1 C 15:54n). The apostle Peter could not truthfully assert, as he did, that it was "this same Jesus" who is now exalted to the right hand of the Father, if he believed Jesus is now Michael (Ac +*2:36). Perhaps Jehovah's Witnesses would be helped to perceive the invalidity of their logic if we apply the same logic to the succeeding phrase: since Christ is to return with the "trump of God," He must be God. While on other grounds this can be proven true, Jehovah's Witnesses would rightly object to the logical form of such an argument here; and for the same reasons they find it invalid, their own argument identifying Jesus with Michael fails. Da 10:13, 21. 12:1. Ro 8:38. Ep 1:21. Col 1:16. Ju *9. Re 12:7. **with the trump**. Ex 19:16. 20:18. Le +=23:24. 2 S 6:15. Is 27:13. Jl 2:1. Zc 9:14. 1 C √15:52n. Re 1:10. 8:13. **of God**. 1 Ch 16:42. Zc 9:14. Re 15:2. **and the dead**. 1 C 15:+23, 51, 52. 2 Th 2:1. Re +*14:13. *20:5, 6. **rise first**. 𝒥157, 1 C +15:6. This proves that Scripture does not teach a single general resurrection of the righteous with the wicked at the end of the world (Jn x6:39), as so often taught. Here reference is made to the resurrection of the "dead in Christ," not all the dead. Daniel asserts that "many of," not "many," and certainly not "all" that sleep in the earth shall awake. While "many" by a figure of speech may sometimes stand for "all" (Mt 26:28n), such cannot be so for the phrase "many of" which is different (See Peters, *Theocratic Kingdom*, vol. 2, Proposition 126, Observation 2, who cites Dr. Hody to this effect, p. 245). Clearly the wicked are resurrected at another time, which Scripture elsewhere teaches is after a one thousand year interval, at the end of the Millennium (Re 20:5). Since the resurrection of the wicked is not mentioned here, this resurrection has exclusive reference to the righteous, a fact utterly opposed to a simultaneous resurrection of all the dead (Peters, *Theocratic Kingdom*, vol 2, p. 297). Is 25:6-9. +*26:19n, 21. 27:6. Da √12:2. Lk *14:14. √20:35, 36. Ac 26:6-8. 1 C *15:23. Ph *3:11g. He 11:35. Re 20:3, +*5, 6.

17. **Then.** ⌐157, 1 C +15:6. **we which.** ver. +*15. 1 C 15:52. **caught.** This clause gives the basis for belief in the rapture (from the Latin, *rapio*) of the living saints. The Rapture is clearly pretribulational, for Paul's purpose is to comfort (ver. 18) the Thessalonians by calling attention to this glorious prospect and blessed hope (T √2:13). Paul corrects the mistaken view of the Thessalonians again in the second epistle by showing that the day of Christ was not at hand. Logically, this must refer to the fact that they had been taught and correctly understood that the day of Christ was secret in its initial stage—at least unknown to the world, and not the public manifestation of Christ at his return in glory, or they could not have been confused about the day of Christ having already transpired, or being already present, without their having had a part in it, 2 Th 2:1. Paul argues they could know that the day had not yet come because the Rapture had not taken place (2 Th 2:1), nor had the great apostasy and the revelation of the Antichrist transpired (2 Th 2:3, 8). Careful students of prophecy have noted that the Second Advent of Christ takes place in two stages: at the first stage Christ's coming for his saints is unobserved by the world (Is 26:20. Zp 2:3. Mt +*24:42n. 1 Th 5:2. 2 Th 2:1. 2 P 3:10); the last stage, when Christ comes with his saints, is most public and visible (Jl 3:11. Zc +*14:5. Mt +*24:30. Re +*1:7. 19:14). The timing of the first stage is not revealed; the Rapture is imminent: it could take place at any time. The second stage takes place at the end of the Great Tribulation, therefore the precise timing will be known (Mt +*24:42n. Da 9:27. 12:7). Because many prophetic events take place between the two stages, the time interval may be greater than the usually postulated seven years. The amount of time between the Rapture and the onset of the Tribulation is apparently unrevealed. 1 K 18:12. 2 K 2:11, 16. Ps +*7:6, 7. Is 57:1. Jl 2:32. Zp +*2:3. Mt 11:12g. 13:19g. Jn 6:15g. 10:12, 28, 29g. Ac *8:39. 23:10. 2 C *12:+2-4. Ju 23. Re 11:12. 12:5. **together with.** Ep +*1:10. 2 Th √2:1. **in the clouds.** Gr. *en nephelais*, "the instrumental case, by means of clouds, portrays clouds as the vehicle by which the Rapture of the saints is executed" (Boyce W. Blackwelder, *Toward Understanding Thessalonians*, p. 101). Ellicott explains "the clouds forming

the element with which they would be surrounded, and in which they would be borne up to meet their coming Lord." "...upon which the glorified and luciform body will be caught up in the enveloping and upbearing clouds" (*Comm. on Thessalonians*, p. 65, 66). Other interpreters more generally understand this as "in clouds," as the Greek article is lacking. Ge +9:13. Ex +*13:21. +*16:10. 19:9. 24:16. Nu 11:25. 2 Ch +√5:13. Ps 18:11, 12. +*68:17. Is 19:1. Da +*7:13. Mt 17:5. +*24:30. 26:64. Mk 14:62. Ac 1:9. 1 C 10:2n. Re +*1:7. √11:12. **to meet.** ⌐171J9, Ac +16:1. Alford notes "as he descends." The word "implies meeting one who was approaching—not merely a 'meeting with' a person." "Christ is on his way to this earth: and when De W. says that there is no plain trace in St. Paul of Christ's kingdom on earth,—and Lun., that the words show that the Apostle did not think of Christ as descending down to the earth, surely they cannot suppose him to have been so ignorant of O. T. prophecy, as to have allowed this, its plain testimony, to escape him" (*Greek Testament*, vol. 3, p. 276). 1 S 13:10. 1 K 9:14. 2 Ch 15:2. 19:2. Mt 25:1g, 6g, 31. Ac *28:15g. Col 3:4. 2 Th *2:1. **in the air.** The word for "air" in Greek is *aer*, a reference to the dense atmosphere of earth, not *aither* (a word not used in the New Testament), which would refer to the upper atmosphere. Ac 22:23. 1 C 9:26. 14:9. Ep 2:2. Re 9:2. 16:17. **and so.** Ps +*16:11. *17:15. *49:15. 73:24. Is 35:10. 60:19, 20. Jn 12:26. +*14:3. 17:24. 2 C √5:8. Ph +*1:23. 2 P 3:13. Re 7:14-17. 21:3-7, 22, 23. 22:3-5. **ever be.** Wordsworth states "We shall be caught up into the air, and so be ever with Christ. There is no indication of any intervening Millennium on earth between Resurrection and heavenly glory" (*Greek Testament*, vol. 2, p. 19). His misunderstanding is grounded in his failure, among other things, to note that only the righteous are spoken of as being included in this resurrection. His careful observation earlier on the same passage, that the "circumstances of the Second Advent, and of the Last Judgment, appear to have been prefigured by those of the giving of the Law on Mount Sinai" is carefully drawn, except for the mistaken connection with the Last Judgment, and independently confirms Peters, cited below. Further confirmation of such connections is provided by the study of "Antitypical Parallels" alluded to by Peters (*Theocratic Kingdom*, vol. 2, Proposition 121, Observation 8, note 28, point 4, p. 191), but developed fully by others as in *Antitypical Parallels; or, The Kingdom of Israel and of Heaven*, by "Gershom" (Major General J. E. Goodwyn), London: S. W. Partridge, 1866, pp. xxiv, 1-501. Jn +*12:26. **with the Lord.** Paul, having accomplished his purpose of comfort by asserting that the living saints would rejoin deceased believers at the Rapture, abruptly stops the discussion. No doubt the Thessalonians had received much fuller instruction from Paul about prophecy when he was with them in person. We are left to infer from other Scripture where the saints will go once they are raptured. The usual view is that Christ takes the saints back to the third heaven, some believe forever, others suppose for the seven years of the Tribulation. Interestingly enough, Paul does not say here, nor does Scripture elsewhere state, that the saints return to heaven. Peters cogently argues (See the following references, which I have carefully noted, as they are not represented in the indexes in

Peters' volumes: *Theocratic Kingdom*, volume 3, Proposition 170, Observation 6, pp. 59, 60. Prop. 166, Ob. 6, note 1, pp. 25, 26. For other significant references to the "third heaven" in Peters not found in his indexes see: Volume 1, pp. 245, Prop. 35, Ob. 2; *596, Prop. 89, Ob. 1; 602, Prop. 90, Ob. 5; 615, Prop. 93, Ob. 6, point 2; Volume 2, pp. 11, 12, Prop. 107, Ob. 2; 13, Prop. 107, Ob. 4; 29, Prop. 108, Ob. 3, note 7; 222, Prop. 123, Ob. 4; 227, Prop. 125, p. 227; 303, Prop. 128, Ob. 12; 341, Prop. 131, Ob. 3; √346, Ob. 7; √377, Prop. 134, Ob. 2, point 15; 378, Prop. 134, Ob. 2, note 3; 411, Prop. 138, Ob. 3; *501, Prop. 148, Ob. 3; √575, 576, Prop. 154, Ob. 3, note 1 & 2; 578, Ob. 5, point 4. Volume 3, p. 25, 26, Prop. 166, Ob. 6, note 1; 46, Prop. 169, Ob. 2, note 2; 453, Prop. 196, Ob. 4, note; 459, Prop. 196, Ob. 12, point 7) that such a removal of the saints from this earth to heaven with Christ (especially if conceived of as a permanent removal) would be in violation of prophecy and covenant, which place the inheritance and kingdom of Christ here upon this earth (Mt +*5:5. Ac +*7:5n. Ep +*1:11n. He +*11:13, 16n). Peters establishes at length and in great detail that the saints will be taken by Christ to some secure appointed place upon earth (Dt +*33:2) to organize and prepare for the establishment of the kingdom, when believers will receive their training and appointments (Jn +*14:2) to posts of rulership and responsibility (Ps 149:4-9. Mt 19:28, 29. 24:47. 25:21, 23. Lk 22:29, 30. 1 C 6:2. 2 T 2:12. Re 2:26, 27. 20:4, 6) in that kingdom (*Theocratic Kingdom*, vol. 3, Proposition 166, pp. 17-28). When the preparation is complete, Christ will march (Dt +*33:2. Is *63:1-6) upon his enemies, then victorious will ascend the Mount of Olives (Zc 14:3-5) and enter Zion (Is *1:27. +*51:11. +*59:20. Jl *3:16. Zc *1:16, 17. Ro +*11:26) with all his saints, and establish his kingdom over the whole earth, ruling from Jerusalem (Zc 14:9). **with**. Jn +*14:3. 2 Th *2:1.

18. **Wherefore**. 1 Th 5:11, 14. Is 40:1, 2. Lk 21:28. He 12:12. **comfort**. 1 Th 3:2, 7. 5:11. Is 66:13. 2 C 1:4. 7:6, 7. 2 Th 2:17. *or*, exhort. ver. 1, 10. 1 Th 2:11. 5:11, 14. Is 41:6. 2 Th 3:12. He +*10:24, 25. **these words**. T 1:9.

1 THESSALONIANS 5

As the coming of Christ will be sudden, and bring inevitable destruction on the wicked; "the children of light" are especially called on to prepare for it, in vigilance and sobriety, with faith and love and hope, and to comfort and edify one another, 1-11. Various exhortations, admonitions, and encouragements, 12-25. Concluding prayers and salutations, 26-28.

1. **the times**. ⨍96F2, Ge +4:10. Da 2:21. Mt +*24:3, 36. Mk 13:30-32. Ac +*1:7n. **seasons**. ⨍96F2, Ge +4:10. **ye**. 1 Th +4:9. 2 C 9:1. Ju +*3. **you**. ⨍159, Ezk +36:13. The repetition of the pronoun "you" and "ye" in verses 1, 2, 4, 5, stands in marked contrast to the repetition of the pronouns "they" and "them" in verse 3, thus pointing out the significant lesson that those who are "waiting for God's Son from heaven" are not concerned with "times and seasons" which have to do with "the day of the Lord," and his coming as "a thief" on the ungodly.

2. **know**. 1 Th 2:1. 2 Th 3:7. Je 23:20. **the day of the Lord**. ver. 4. Is +*2:12. √13:6-13. +*34:8. Je

*46:10. Ezk +*30:3. Jl +*2:1, 11, 31. Am⸱ +*5:18, 20. Ob 15. Zp +*1:14, 15. +*2:2, 3. Mt 24:42-44. 25:13. Mk 13:34, 35. Lk *12:39, 40. Ac 2:20. 1 C +1:8. +*3:13. 2 P √3:10. Ju 14, 15. Re 3:3. *16:14, 15. **so cometh**. Mt 25:6. Lk +*21:34-36. **as a thief**. Mt +*24:43. Lk +*17:24. 2 Th 2:2. 2 P √3:10. Re 16:15. **in the night**. Mt 25:6.

3. **Peace**. Dt 29:19. Jg 18:27, 28. Ps 10:11-13. Is 21:4. 56:12. Ezk 13:10. Da 5:3-6. √8:25. Na 1:10. Mt 24:37-39. Lk 17:26-30. 21:34, 35. **then sudden**. Ex 15:9, 10. Jsh 8:20-22. Jg 20:41, 42. 2 Ch 32:19-21. Ps 35:8. 73:18-20. Pr *29:1. Is 30:13. Lk *17:26-30. +*21:34g, 35. Ac 12:22, 23. 12:41. 2 Th 1:9. 2 P 2:4. Re 18:7, 8. **destruction**. Is √13:6-11. 2 Th √1:9. 2 P 3:7. **as travail**. Ps 48:6. Is *13:8. 21:3. 26:17. 43:6-9. Je 4:31. 6:24. 13:21. 22:23. +*30:6, 7. Ho 13:13. Mi 4:9, 10. Mt +*24:8. Jn 16:21. Re 12:2. **and they**. Mt 23:33. He √2:3. 12:25. **shall not**. ⨍158, Mt +5:18. **escape**. Hab +*2:9. Lk ◑+*21:36.

4. **are not**. Ro 13:11-13. Col +*1:13. 1 P 2:9, 10. 1 J +2:8. **darkness**. Is +9:2. **overtake**. Dt 19:6. 28:15, 45. Je 42:16. Ho 10:9. Zc 1:6. Jn 12:35. **as a thief**. ver. +*2.

5. **the children**. Lk +*16:8. Jn 12:36. Ac +*26:18. Ep *5:8. **darkness**. Is +9:2. Lk +22:53. Ac +*26:18. Col *1:12, 13.

6. **let us not**. ver. ◑10. Pr 6:10, 11. 19:15. 24:33, 34. +*25:28. Is 56:10. Jon 1:6. Mt 13:25. *25:5. Mk 13:36. 14:37. Lk 22:46. Ro +*13:11-14. 1 C 15:34. Ep 5:14. Ph 3:10, 11. **sleep**. Gr. *katheudo*. ✻S#2518g. ver. 7, 7, 10. Mt 8:24. 9:24. 13:25. 25:5. 26:40, 43, 45. Mk 4:27, 38. 5:39. 13:36. 14:37, 37, 40, 41. Lk 8:52. 22:46. Ep 5:14. See related note, 1 Th 4:13. **as do others**. 1 Th *4:13. Ep *2:3. **watch**. Mt +*24:42. 25:13. 26:38, 40, 41. Mk 13:34, 35, 37. 14:38. Lk 12:37, 39. +√21:36. 22:46. Ac 20:31. 1 C 16:13. Ep *6:18. Col *4:2. 2 T 4:5. 1 P *4:7. Re 3:2. 16:15. **sober**. ver. 8. Ph *4:5. 1 T 2:9, 15. 3:2, 11. T 2:6, 12. 1 P +*1:13. √5:8.

7. **they that sleep**. Jb 4:13. 33:15. Lk *21:34, 35. Ro 13:13. 1 C 15:34. Ep 5:14. **night**. Ge 19:33. **and they**. 1 S 25:36, 37. Pr 23:29-35. Is 21:4, 5. Da 5:4, 5. Lk +*21:34. Ac 2:15. 1 C +*6:10. 2 P 2:13.

8. **Let us**. Pr +*4:18. **who**. ver. 5. Ro 13:13. Ep 5:8, 9. 1 P *2:9. 1 J *1:7. **be sober**. ver. 6. 1 P +*1:13. **putting on**. Ro +*13:12. **the breastplate**. Is 59:17. Ro 13:12. 2 C 6:7. Ep 6:11, 13-18. **of faith and**. 1 Th 1:3. 1 C 13:13. Ga *5:6. Ep 6:23. He *11:32-34. **and love**. ⨍174, Ge +18:27. Mt *22:37-40. Col 3:14. **helmet**. Ex=29:9. Ep *6:17. **the hope**. Jb +*19:23-27. Ps 42:5, 11. 43:5. *119:6. La 3:26. Ro 5:2-5. 8:24, 25. 1 C 13:13. Ga 5:5. 2 Th *2:16. 2 T √1:12. He *6:18, 19. 10:35, 36. 1 P 1:3-5, 13. 1 J √3:1-3.

9. **not appointed**. 2 Th *1:10. 3:3. Ge 19:22. Ex 9:16. Dt +*10:15. Pr *16:4. Ezk 38:10-17. Na *1:2. Mt *26:24. Ac 1:20, 25. +*13:48. Ro *9:11-23. 2 Th *2:13, 14. 2 T *2:19, 20. 1 P *2:8. 2 P *2:3. Ju *4. Re +*3:10. **wrath**. 1 Th +*1:10. Jb +*21:30. Ps +*7:6. Na 1:2. Ro *5:9. 9:22. Ph ◑1:29. Re *6:16, 17. **obtain**. Ge 19:22. Lk +17:33. Jn 3:17. Ro ◑8:17. *11:7, 30. 2 Th *2:13, 14. 1 T 1:13, 16. *2:4. 2 T 2:10, 12. He 10:39. 1 P *2:10. 2 P *1:1.

10. **died**. Mt *20:28. Jn 10:11, 15, 17. 15:13. Ro 5:6-8. 8:34. +*14:8, 9. 1 C +*15:3. 2 C √5:15, 21. Ep 5:2. 1 T √2:6. 2 T 2:11. T *2:14. 1 P *2:24. *3:18. **whether**. ⨍184C, Mt +4:9. ver. +6. See on 1 Th 4:13,

17. **should live.** Lk 20:38. Ro 14:9. 2 C 5:15.

11. **Wherefore.** See on 1 Th 4:18. **comfort.** *or*, exhort. ver. 14. 1 Th +*4:18. He +*3:13. *10:25. **together.** T#110. Ro 12:4-10. 14:19. 15:1-3. Ep 4:15, 16, 29. Col 3:16. He +*3:13. *10:24, 25. **and edify.** Ro 14:19. 15:2. 1 C 10:23. 14:5, 12, 29. 2 C 12:19. Ep 4:12, 16, +29. 1 T 1:4. Ju *20. **even.** 1 Th 4:10. Ro 15:14. 2 P 1:12.

12. **to know.** ♪121C2A2, Ge +39:6. 1 C *16:18. Ph *2:29. He 13:7, 17. **labor.** 1 Th 2:9. Mt 9:37, 38. Lk 10:1, 2, 7. Jn 4:38. Ac +*20:35. Ro 16:6. 1 C 3:9. 15:10. 16:16. 2 C 5:9. 6:1. 11:23. Ga +*4:11. Ph *2:16. Col 1:29. 1 T *5:17, 18. 2 T 2:6. Re 2:3. **are over.** 1 Ch=9:28, 29. 2 Ch=34:12, 13. Ne=11:16. Ac *14:23. +*20:28. 1 C 12:28. 16:16. 1 T 5:17. T 1:5. He *13:7, 17. 1 P *5:2, 3. Re 1:20. 2:1, 8, 12, 18. 3:1, 7, 14. **and admonish.** ver. 14. Ac 20:31. Ro 15:14. 1 C 4:14. Col 1:28. *3:16. 2 Th 3:15. 1 T 5:1, 20. T 1:13. 2:15. *3:10.

13. **esteem.** Mt *10:40. Ro 12:3. 1 C 4:1, 2. 9:7-11. Ga 4:14. 6:6. Ph +*2:3. **And be.** Ge 45:24. Ps *133:1. Mk +*9:50. Lk +*17:3-5. Jn 13:34, 35. 15:17. Ro 14:17-19. 2 C 13:11. Ga *5:22. Ep 4:3. Col 3:15. 2 Th 3:16. 2 T 2:22. He +*12:14. Ja 3:18.

14. **exhort.** *or*, beseech. ver. 11. Ro *12:1. **you.** See on ver. 12. **warn.** ver. +12. Je *6:10. Ezk *3:17-21. *33:3-9. Ac *20:27, 31. 1 C 4:14. Col 1:28. **unruly.** *or*, disorderly. 2 Th *3:6, 7, 11-13. T *1:6, 10. **comfort.** ♪41, Ge +10:1. 1 Th *2:7-12. 4:18. Is *35:3, 4. *40:1, 2, 11. Ezk *34:16. Mt *12:20. Lk *22:32. Jn *21:15-17. Ro +*15:4. 2 C +*1:3, 4. **feebleminded.** or, fainthearted. Pr √18:14g. Is *35:4. 54:6. +*57:15. He 12:15. **support the weak.** Da *11:32-34. Ac *20:35g. Ro *14:1. +*15:1-3. 1 C 6:9, 11. Ga 6:1, 2. He 12:12. **be patient.** Is +*63:9. 1 C +*13:4, 5. Ga *5:22. Ep *4:2, 32. 5:1, 2. Col *3:12, 13. 1 T 3:3. 6:11. 2 T +*2:24, 25. *4:2. He 5:2, 3. 13:3.

15. **See.** Ge 45:24. 1 C 16:10. Ep *5:15, 33. 1 P *1:22. Re 19:10. 22:9. **none.** Ex *23:4, 5. Le +*19:18. 1 S *24:13. Ps 7:4. Pr *17:13. *20:22. *24:17, 29. *25:21. Mt *5:39, 44, 45. Lk *6:35. Ro √12:17-21. 1 C *6:7. 1 P *2:22, 23. *3:9. **ever.** 1 Th *2:12. Dt *16:20. Ps *38:20. Ro 12:9. *14:19. 1 C *14:1. Ga +*6:10. 1 T *6:11. He +*12:14. 1 P *3:11-13. 3 J *11. **and to.** 1 Th 3:12. Ps *39:1. Pr +*25:26. Ro *12:17, 18. Ga +*6:10. Col +*4:5. 2 T +*2:24. T *3:2. 1 P 2:17.

16. **Rejoice.** T#296. 1 Ch 16:31, 32. Ne +8:10 (T#52). Ps 5:11. 32:11. 33:1. *37:4. *40:16. 68:3, 4. 97:1, 2. 149:2. Is 41:16. Mt +*5:12. Lk 10:20. Ro 12:12. 2 C *6:10. Ph +1:4. +3:1. √4:4.

17. **Pray.** T#1147. Ge 4:26. Dt 8:18. 1 S √12:23. 1 Ch 16:8, 10, 11, 29. 22:19. *28:9. 2 Ch +√7:14. 14:4, 7. 15:12, 13. 16:12. 17:3, 4. 26:1, 5. Jb *5:8, 9. 15:4. 22:27. 23:3, 4. 33:26. 35:10, 11. Ps 2:8. *10:4. 53:2. 55:16. 62:2. 79:6. 95:6, 7. 105:3, 4. 109:4. Is 8:17. 17:7. 43:22. √45:11. *55:6. 62:6, 7. Je 3:4. La 3:40, 41. Ezk *22:30. 36:37. Da +*6:10, 11. Ho *14:2. Jl *2:12-19. Am 5:6. 11:8. Zc 10:1. Mt *5:44. *6:6. *7:7. 9:38. 17:21. 24:20. 26:41. Mk +*1:35. 13:33. 14:37, 38. Lk 3:21. See on +*18:1. +*21:36. 22:40, 46. Jn *16:24. Ro 12:12. Ep *6:18. Ph *4:6. Col *4:2. 1 T *2:8. Ja 4:8. *5:13, 14. 1 P *4:7. **without ceasing.** T#540. 1 Th +1:3. 3:10. Ge 32:24-26. Is +*62:7. Lk 6:12. 11:5-8. 18:1, 5, 7, 8. +*21:36. Ac +6:4 (T#1319). Ro *12:12. Ep *6:18. Col +1:23 (T#514). *4:2.

18. **In.** ♪41, Ge +10:1. **every.** Jb 1:21. Ps 34:1.

See on Ep *5:20. Ph *4:6. Col *3:17. He 13:15. **give thanks.** 1 Ch=23:30. **the will.** 1 Th +*4:3. Nu=4:27. 1 Ch=6:48. Ep 2:10. 1 P *2:15. 4:2. 1 J *2:17.

19. **Quench.** SS 8:7. 1 C ◐14:30. Ep +*4:30. *6:16. **the Spirit.** Gr. *pneuma*, ♪121A1, Lk +1:17n. ♪121A1, Jn +3:34. i.e. do not hinder in yourself or in others the use of spiritual gifts (B540). Horne (*Introduction*, vol. 2, p. 455) states "The Holy Spirit is put for the Influences or Gifts of the Spirit. The similitude is borrowed from the ancient altar of burnt-offering, in which the fire was to be kept continually burning." Ge +1:2. +*6:3. 1 S 16:14. Ne 9:30. Ps 51:11. Is +*63:10. Jn +7:39. Ac 7:51. 1 C 14:30. Ep 4:39. 1 T 4:14. 2 T *1:6.

20. **Despise not.** 1 Th 4:8. Nu 11:25-29. 1 S 10:5, 6, 10-13. 19:20-24. Lk *10:16. Ac 19:6. 1 C 11:4. 12:10, 28. 13:2, 9. 14:1, 3-6, 22-25, 29-32, 37-39. 2 C +10:10g. Ep +*4:11, 12. Re 11:3-11. **prophesyings.** Ac +2:18. *15:32. Ro 12:6. 1 C 13:2. 14:6.

21. **Prove.** Jb *34:4. Pr +√14:15. +*18:17. Is +*8:20n. Mt *7:15-20. Mk *7:14-16. Lk *12:57. Jn 7:24, 51. Ac +√17:11n. Ro +*12:2. 1 C +*2:11, 14, 15. √14:29. Ga +*1:8n. Ep +*5:10. Ph *1:10mg. 1 J √4:1. Re *2:2. **hold fast.** Dt 11:6-9. *32:46, 47. Pr *3:1, 21-24. *4:13. *6:21-23. *23:23. SS *3:4. Jn +*8:31. *15:4. Ac +*11:23. +*14:22. Ro *12:9. 1 C √15:58. Ph 3:16. *4:8. 2 Th *2:15. 2 T 1:15. 3:6. 4:14. He +*10:23. Re *2:25. *3:3, 11. **which is good.** ver. +*15.

22. **Abstain.** 1 Th *4:12. Ex *23:7. Is *33:15. Je 48:10. Mt 17:26, 27. Ro *12:17. *14:21. 1 C 8:13. *10:31-33. 2 C 6:3. *8:20, 21. Ph *4:8. Ju *23. **appearance.** Ge ◐38:15. Nu 5:17n. Ac +*6:3.

23. **God.** Ro 15:5, 13, +33. 16:20. 1 C 14:33. 2 C *5:19. Ph +*4:9. 2 Th 3:16. He *13:20. 1 P 5:10. **sanctify.** T#1686. 1 Th 3:13. 4:3. Ex=28:41. 31:13. Le=8:30. 20:8, 26. Ps 17:5. *19:12-14. *51:10-12. 119:117. Ezk 37:28. Jn *17:17-19, 22, 23. Ac 20:32. +*26:18. 1 C 1:2. *6:11. Ep 3:16-21. *5:25-27. Ph *4:6, 7. He 2:11. 1 P 1:2. Ju *1. **wholly.** ♪98, Ro +11:33. In Greek the words underlying "wholly" and "whole" demonstrate the figure *Homoeopropheron*, or Alliteration: *holoteleis* and *holokleeron*. Jsh +*14:8. Ja 1:4. **your whole.** Gr. *holoteleis*, ✳S#3648g, only here and Ja 1:4 (entire). Paul in this text does not use the word "*holomereis*, 'in all your parts,' followed by the summing up of those parts, spirit, soul, and body; but that it reads *holoteleis*, which refers, not to the parts, but to the final end, *telos*" (Abraham Kuyper, *The Work of the Holy Spirit*, p. 491, note. Also cited by J. I. Marais, ISBE, vol 4, p. 2496), thus a reference to man as a unity. Paul speaks here of "body," "soul," and "spirit" by way of periphrasis to represent the whole man. This text and He 4:12 appear to teach man is *trichotomous*, that he consists of three distinct elements: body, soul, and spirit. Yet no one argues on the basis of Lk 10:27 that man's being consists of four or five elements: (body), heart, soul, strength, mind. Careful comparison of Scripture with Scripture will show that man is *dichotomous* (Ro +*8:10), and that soul and spirit are but two different aspects of the same conscious non-material eternal part of man. That they are the same element in man is proven by the fact that the terms soul and spirit are used interchangeably (Ge +*2:7). The terms soul and spirit are used with a wide degree of meaning in Scripture (see

for soul, Mt +*2:20n; for spirit, Mt +*8:16n), but it is possible to affirm absolutely that the soul is not the body (Mt +*10:28n), contrary to the frequent affirmation of materialists like the Jehovah's Witnesses. That soul and spirit as they comprise the "hidden man of the heart" are immortal is absolutely affirmed by Peter (1 P +*3:4), for the Greek word *aphthartos*, rendered "not corruptible" is rendered "immortal" at 1 T 1:17, and the closely related noun form of this word, *aphtharsia*, is rendered "immortality" at Ro 2:7 and 2 T 1:10. Yet some quibble may be raised that *aphthartos* is best translated "incorruptible," and that the rendering immortal and immortality is best reserved for *athanasia*, which occurs at 1 C 15:53, 54 and 1 T 6:16. Yet by the rule that things equal to a third thing are equal to each other, the Corinthian passage shows that the bodies of dead saints must put on incorruption, and the living saints who are mortal must put on immortality: but since both the living and the dead are one body (Ep 4:4) in Christ, at the Rapture (1 Th 4:15-17) the final form of existence for both groups is identical. Since the dead saints are raised to incorruption and the living saints ("mortals") are changed and put on immortality, incorruption and immortality are in this case one and the same thing in final result, and the objection that "incorruption" is not "immortality" has no force. For if the living are granted immortality, but the dead only incorruption, then living believers have an advantage over the dead in Christ, which is contrary to Paul's argument in 1 Th 4:13-18, for such a concept is the very error Paul wrote to correct in the Thessalonian church. Perhaps the term "immortal-

ity" with its meaning of deathlessness was reserved by Paul to living believers since they shall never experience physical death, and applied to their bodies, not their souls or spirits, both of which latter are never said in Scripture to be subject to natural (as opposed to spiritual) death in any case. Mt ❶22:37. Ro ❶+*8:10. He √4:12. **spirit**. Gr. *pneuma*, ƒ121A3, Mt +27:50. Jb 27:3. 32:8. 33:4. Lk 1:47. 1 C 5:5. 15:45. **soul**. Gr. *psyche*, Mt +*10:28n. Jb +*14:22. Lk 1:46. 1 C 15:45. **body**. Jb +*14:22. Mt 10:28. 1 C 5:5. **preserved**. T#1650. 1 Th 3:12, 13. 1 C 1:8, 9. Ep *5:26, 27. Ph *1:6, 10. *2:15, 16. Col 1:22. 2 P +*1:10. Ju +1. **blameless**. 1 Th +2:10. 1 C *1:8. 2 P +*3:14. Ju *24. **coming**. Gr. *parousia*, Mt +24:3. 1 Th +2:19. +*5:15n.

24. **Faithful**. Dt 7:9. Ps 36:5. 40:10. 86:15. 89:2. 92:2. 100:5. √138:2. 146:6. Is 25:1. La 3:23. Mi 7:20. Jn 1:17. 3:33. 1 C +*1:9. √10:13. 2 Th *3:3. 2 T 2:13. T 1:2. He *6:17, 18. **calleth**. 1 Th +*2:12. Ro +*8:30. 9:24. Ga 1:15. 2 Th 2:14. 2 T +*1:9. 1 P 5:10. 2 P 1:3. Re 17:14. **who**. Nu 23:19. 2 K 19:31. Is +*9:7. 14:24-26. 37:32. Mt 24:35. **will do**. Jsh 14:10. 23:14. Ph *1:6. *2:13. 1 P *1:5. 2 P +*1:10.

25. **pray for**. T#471, 1618. Ro 15:30-32. 2 C *1:11. Ep *6:18-20. Ph 1:19. Col *4:3, 4. 2 Th *3:1-3. Phm 22. He 13:18, 19.

26. **Greet**. See on Ro 16:16. 1 C 16:20. **the brethren**. Ep +6:23.

27. **I charge**. *or*, I adjure. 1 Th 2:11. Nu 27:23. 1 K 22:16. 2 Ch 18:15. Mt 26:63. Mk +5:7. Ac 19:13. 1 T 1:3, 18. 5:7, 21. 6:13, 17. 2 T 4:1. **that**. Col *4:16. 2 Th 3:14. **holy**. He 3:1.

28. **grace**. See on Ro +*1:7. 16:20, 24. 2 Th 3:18.

2 THESSALONIANS

2 THESSALONIANS 1

The apostle salutes the Church of the Thessalonians, 1, 2; thanks God for their growth in faith and love; encourages their perseverance under persecutions, by the prospect of the coming of Christ; and shows how glorious he will then appear in the destruction of all unbelievers, and the complete salvation of his people, 3-10. He prays for their perfect sanctification, and meetness for heavenly felicity, by the grace and for the glory of God the Father, and the Lord Jesus Christ, 11, 12.

1. Cir. A.M. 4056. A.D. 52. **Paul**. 1 Th 1:1. **and Silvanus**. Ac +15:22. See on 2 C 1:19. 1 Th 1:1, etc. 1 P 5:12. **Timotheus**. Ac +16:1. **the Thessalonians**. Ac +17:1. **in God**. 1 J 1:3.

2. **Grace**. See on Ro 1:7. 1 C 1:3, 8.

3. **are bound**. 2 Th *2:13. See on Ro 1:8. 1 C 1:4. 1 Th 1:+2, 3. 3:6, 9. **thank God**. 1 C 1:4, 5. Ep *1:15-17. Col *1:3, 4. 1 Th 3:10. **always**. Ep +5:20. **as it**. Lk 15:32. Ph 1:7. 2 P 1:13. **your**. Jb 17:9. Ps 84:7. 92:13. Pr +*4:18. Is 40:29-31. Lk 17:5. Jn 15:2. 2 C 10:15. Ph 1:9. 1 Th 4:1, 9, 10. 1 P 1:22. 2 P √1:5-10. +*3:18. **faith**. 1 Th +1:3. **groweth**. The word *uperauksano*, from *uper*, intensive, and *auksano*, to grow, increase, signifies, as Dr. Clarke remarks, to grow luxuriantly, as a good and healthy tree in a good soil; and, if a fruit tree, bearing an abundance of fruit to compensate the labor of the husbandman. Faith is one of the

seeds of the kingdom: this the Apostle had sowed and watered, and God gave an abundant increase. Their faith was multiplied, and their love abounded: and this was not the case with some distinguished characters only; it was the case with every one of them. For this the apostle felt himself bound to give continual thanks to God on their behalf, as it was "meet" and right. **the charity**. 1 Th +3:12.

4. **glory**. 2 C 7:14. 9:2, 4. 1 Th 2:+19, 20. **in the churches**. 1 C +11:16. 1 Th 1:8. **your patience**. 2 Th 3:5. Ro 2:7. *5:3-5. 8:25. 12:12. 1 Th 1:3. 3:2-8. He 6:15. 10:36. *11:32-36. *12:1-3. Ja *1:3, 4. √5:7, 8. 2 P *1:6. Re 14:12. **your persecutions**. Mk 10:30. 1 Th +*2:14. 3:3, 4. 2 T *2:12. Ja 5:11.

5. **a manifest**. ver. 6. Ph *1:28. 1 P 4:14-18. **righteous**. Jb 8:3. Ps 9:7, 8. 33:5. 50:6. 72:2. 99:4. 111:7. Je +*9:24. Da 4:37. Ro 2:5. Re *15:4. 16:7. 19:2. **counted worthy**. ver. 11. Lk √20:35. +√21:36. Ac 5:41. *13:46. Ep *4:1. Col 1:+*10, 12. He 3:3. Re *3:4. **kingdom of God**. Mt +*5:10. Lk +*22:29, 30. Ac +*14:22. Ro +*14:17. 2 T +*4:1. **for**. ver. 7. Ac +*14:22. Ro √8:17. 1 Th 2:14. 2 T √2:11, 12. He *10:32, 33. 1 P √4:12, 13.

6. **righteous**. Ge +*18:25. Ps 71:2. He +*6:10. **recompense tribulation**. Ex 23:22. Dt 32:41-43. Ps 74:22, 23. 79:10-12. 94:20-23. Is 49:26. Jl 3:4, 7. Zc √2:8. Re +*12:19. Re +*6:10. 11:18. 15:4. 16:5, 6. 18:20, 24. 19:2. **to them**. Ge +*6:13 (T#566). Je +*20:11.

7. **who**. Is 57:2. Mt +*5:10-12. Lk 16:25. Ro 8:17.

2 C 4:17. 2 T 2:12. He *4:1, 9, 11. 1 P 4:1. Re 7:14-17. 14:13. 21:4. **rest with.** Ps +*94:13. Je +*31:2. Hab +√3:16. Re 6:11. 11:18. +*14:13. **when.** Mt +*13:39-43. +*16:27n. +*25:31. √26:64. Mk 8:38. 14:62. Lk +*17:30. Jn +*1:51. Ac +*1:11. 1 Th +*4:16, 17. T √2:13. He *9:28. Ju *14, *15. Re +*1:7. 20:11. **from heaven.** 1 Th +*1:10. **his mighty angels.** Gr. the angels of his power. Ps 103:20. Jn 1:3. Ep 1:2. Col 1:16. 1 P 3:22. Ju +*14. Re 22:6, 9, 16.

8. **flaming.** Ge *3:24. Dt 4:11. 5:5. Ps 21:8, 9. 50:2-6. Da 7:10. Ml 3:2, 3. 4:1. Mt +*25:41, 46. 1 C 3:13. He *10:27. *12:29. 2 P √3:7, 10-12. Ju 7. Re 14:10. 19:20. 20:10, 14, 15. +*21:8. **fire.** Is +*33:14. *66:15, 16. Lk +*16:24. 2 C *5:11. 2 P +*3:10. **taking.** or, yielding. **vengeance.** Dt 32:35, 41, 42. Ps *2:9-12. +*9:17. 94:1. Is 35:4. 61:2. 63:4-6. Ro +*1:18. +*2:8, 9. He 10:30. Re 6:10, 16, 17. **that know not.** Ex 5:2. 1 S 2:12. Ps +*9:10. 79:6. Is 27:11. Je 9:6. Zp 1:6. Jn *3:19. 8:19. Ro +*1:28. 1 C 15:34. Ga +*4:8. 1 Th 4:5. **obey not.** Dt 4:30. Ps 18:44. Is 1:19. Ac 6:7. Ro 1:5. +*2:7, 8. 6:16. 10:16. 15:18. 16:26. 2 C *10:5. Ga 3:1. He √2:3. +*5:9. 11:8. 1 P 1:2. 3:6. *4:17.

9. **be punished.** Jb +*8:13. Is 33:14. +*66:24. Da +*12:2. Mt +*25:41, 46. 26:24. Mk +*9:43-49. Lk +*12:48. *16:25, 26. Jn 5:14. Ph +*3:19. He 10:29. 2 P 2:17. 3:7. Ju 13. Re *14:10, 11. 20:14. +*21:8. *22:15. **everlasting.** Gr. aionios, Mt +18:8. Ju +*7. **destruction.** 1 K 13:3, 4, LXX. Is *65:15-17. 1 Th 5:3. 2 P 3:7. Ju 13. Re 19:19-21. **from the presence.** √22A4, Ge +19:13. Ge 3:8. 4:16. Jb 21:14. 22:17. Ps +*16:11. +*51:11. Mt *7:23. 22:13. 25:41. Lk 13:27. Re 6:16. **the glory.** 2 Th 2:8. Dt +*33:2. Is *2:10, 19, 21. Mt +*16:27n. +*24:30. T √2:13g. Re 15:8. 20:11.

10. **he shall come.** Is +*66:5. 1 Th +*1:10. +*2:19, 20. **to be glorified.** ver. 12. Nu 23:23. 2 Ch=5:1. Ps 89:7. +*149:4. Is 28:5. 43:21. 44:23. 49:3. 60:21. Je 33:9. Mt 25:31. Jn 11:4. *17:10. Ga 1:21. Ep 1:6, 12, 14, 18. 2:7. *3:10, 16. 5:27. 1 P 2:9. Re *7:9-12. **in his saints.** Col +1:26. 1 Th 3:13. **to be admired.** Ps 68:35. **our testimony.** 1 C 1:6. 2 Th *2:13. 1 Th *1:5. √2:13. **was believed.** 1 Th 2:1, √13. 1 T *3:16. **in that day.** Ml *3:17. Mt √7:22. +*24:36. Lk *10:12. Lk +*14:14. 1 C +*3:13. 2 T √1:12, 18. √4:8.

11. **we pray.** See on Ro 1:9. Ep 1:16. 3:14-21. Ph 1:9-11. Col *1:9-13. 1 Th 1:2. 3:9-13. **our God.** Ps 48:14. 68:20. Is 25:9. √55:7. Da 3:17. Ph +1:3. 1 Th 2:2. 3:9. Re 5:10. **would.** See on ver. +*5. Col 1:12. Re 3:4. **count.** or, vouchsafe. **worthy.** ver. +*5. Lk +√21:36. **this calling.** √121R7, Ge +43:11. i.e. of that for which He has called you: viz., to deliver you out of the tribulation; so that He may be glorified in His saints before He comes forth "in flaming fire," etc. (ver. 8, 9). 2 Th 2:14. Ro +*8:30. 9:23, 24. +*11:29. Ph 3:14. 1 Th 2:12. 2 T +*1:9. He 3:1. 1 P 5:10. **fulfill.** Ps 138:8. Pr +*4:18. Is 66:9. Ho +*6:3. Zc +*4:7. Mk 4:28. 1 C 1:8. Ph *1:6. **good pleasure.** Ps 51:18. Lk +*12:32. Ro 10:1. +*15:14. Ep *1:5, 9. Ph √2:13. T *3:4-7. **of his goodness.** Je +*29:11. Mt +*28:19n. Mk +*10:18n. Ro +*11:22. **the work.** Jn 6:27-29. Ep 1:19, 20. Ph *1:6. 1 Th +1:3. √2:13. He *12:2. **with power.** 1 P +*1:5.

12. **the name.** See on ver. 10. Jn *17:10. 1 P *4:14. **glorified in you.** ver. +*10. Is *66:5. Ac *13:48. 2 C 4:11. T 2:13. **and ye.** Ge 18:18. Ps 72:17. Is 45:17,

25. Jn *17:21-26. Ph 3:9. Col 2:9, 10. 1 P 1:7, 8. **the grace.** See on Ro 1:7. 1 C 1:4. 2 C √8:9. 13:4. T √2:11. Re 1:4. **our God and.** T √2:13. 2 P √1:1.

2 THESSALONIANS 2

The apostle warns the Thessalonians against groundlessly supposing that the day of Christ was at hand, 1, 2, and shows that it must be preceded by a great apostasy; in which "the man of sin," by his blasphemies, usurpations, and impostures, would cause the destruction of numbers, and then sink himself into perdition, 3-12. He thanks God for his special and effectual grace shown in choosing and calling the Christians at Thessalonica, "unto salvation and glory," 13, 14. He exhorts them to steadfastness, 15; and prays that they may be "comforted, and established in every good word and work," 16, 17.

1. **we beseech.** See on Ro +*12:1. He *10:25. **by the coming.** Gr. parousia, Mt +24:3. ver. 8. See on 1 Th +2:19. +√4:14-16n. 2 T +*4:1n. **and by.** Ge +*49:10. Mt 24:31. 25:32. Mk 13:27. Ep +*1:10. 1 Th +*3:13. +√4:17n. 2 T +*4:1n. **our gathering.** Ps +*50:5. √102:21, 22. Ezk +*17:23. 1 Th +√4:17n. **unto him.** Ge +*49:10. Ps √102:22. Jn 12:32. 2 C 5:15. Ep 3:21. He 13:13.

2. **shaken.** Is 7:2. 8:12, 13. 26:3. Mt 24:6. Mk 13:7. Lk 21:9, 19. Jn 14:1, 27. Ac 17:13g. 20:23, 24. Ep 5:6. 1 Th 3:3. **troubled.** Mt 24:6. Mk 13:7. **neither.** √129, Ezk +34:4. **by spirit.** Gr. pneuma, Mt +8:16. √121A4, Ezk +37:1. Dt 13:1-5. Je +√23:25-28n. Mi 2:11. Mt *24:4, 5, 24. 1 C +*14:29. 1 Th 5:19, 21. 2 P *2:1-3. 1 J √4:1, 2. Re 19:20. **by word.** ver. 15. 1 C 12:8. 14:26, 29. 1 Th 5:2. **nor by letter.** Ga +*1:7, 8n. 1 Th 4:15. 2 P 3:4-8. **day of Christ.** Virtually all modern editors of the Greek text read "day of the Lord" here (Is 13:6. Am +*5:18. Zp 1:14. 1 Th +√5:2. 2 P +*3:10). Ac +*17:31. Ro 2:5. 1 C +*1:8. +*3:13. 5:5. 2 C 1:14. Ep +*4:30. Ph 1:6, 10. 1 Th +*5:2. **is at hand.** or, is now present. Ro 8:38. ◑+*13:12. Ga 1:4. 2 T 2:18. 3:1. He 9:9. 1 P ◑+*4:7. Such a belief on the part of the Thessalonians necessarily implies that they correctly understood the rapture and its associated resurrection of the righteous dead in Christ to be an event which will be secret and unobserved by the world (Peters, *Theocratic Kingdom*, vol. 2, pp. 316, 317). Mt 24:3-6, 14. 25:+√19, 31-34, 41. Lk +*19:11. Ac 17:31. 1 C 15:24. He 2:8. 2 P 3:13. Re 11:15-18.

3. **Let no man.** See on Mt +*24:4-6. Mk +*4:24. 1 C +*6:9. +11:16. Ep +*4:14. +5:6. Ph 2:5, 8. Col +*1:23. +*2:7, 18. **that day.** √63D1, Mt +16:7. **except.** 1 T *4:1-3. 2 T *3:1-3. 4:3, 4. **falling away.** Da +*11:35. Ac 21:21g. **first.** √96E5, Jn +1:15. **man of sin.** ver. √8-10. Da +*7:25. 8:24, 25. +*11:36, 40n, 41n. Mi √5:5, 6. Zc 9:13. 11:15. 1 J 2:18. Re 13:5, 6, 11, etc. 19:20. **the son.** √108B, 1 S 20:21. Jn +17:12. Re 17:8, 11.

4. **exalteth himself.** Is √14:13. Ezk √28:2, 6, 9. Da √7:8, 25. √8:9-11. +*11:36. Re *13:6. **called God.** 1 C 8:5. **worshipped.** Ac 17:23. Re 13:4. **sitteth.** Da √8:12-14. √11:45. Mt +*24:15. Re *13:6, 7. **the temple.** Da 9:27. Mt 23:16. +*24:15. 1 T x3:15. Re 11:1. **of God.** 1 C x1:2. 2 C x6:16. **showing himself.** Is 14:14. Ezk 28:2, 6, 9.

5. **Remember**. Mt 16:9. Mk 8:18. Lk 24:6, 7. Ac 20:31. **when**. 2 Th 3:10. Jn 16:4. Ga 5:21. 1 Th 2:11. 2 P 1:15.

6. **withholdeth**. *or*, holdeth. ver. 7. Lk 4:42. Ro 1:18g. **revealed**. ver. 3, 8. **in his time**. Da 11:29, 35. 1 T 6:15.

7. **the mystery**. Ro +*16:25n. 1 T 3:16. Re *17:5, 7. **doth**. Ac 20:29. Col 2:18-23. 1 T 4:1. 2 T 2:17, 18. 1 J 2:18. 4:3. **only he who**. ver. 6. Is 5:4, 5. Ro 1:24, 28. **he be taken**. ✸63A1. Figure of speech Ellipsis (Absolute: of the Nominative), whereby the subject of the verb must be supplied from the nature of the subject alone, or from what is elsewhere expressed, Ge +14:20. See 1 C 15:24n. Hogg and Vine note the nominative of *ginomai* is not expressed in the original (*Thessalonians*, p. 261). Just who or what will be taken out of the way has puzzled interpreters. The most usually suggested options are (1) human government, (2) the church, (3) the Holy Spirit, (4) God. Several considerations, faithfully applied, will narrow down the possibilities to the correct choice. First, who or whatever this was or is was already known, already existing. Second, whatever is the correct choice must correspond to identifiable prophecy in the Old Testament. Third, Paul is intentionally being obscure here, probably to protect himself and the Christians he is addressing from adverse political persecution (Jn 11:48. Ac 17:7). Similar reticence to protect the parties concerned is reflected in the fact that the synoptic gospels do not mention the resurrection of Lazarus; only John records this event, presumably long after any possible harm might occur to Lazarus himself. Paul uses similar obscurity at 1 C 15:24-28. This factor of obscurity immediately rules out the possibility that the reference is to God, the Holy Spirit, or the Church, for if any of these were what he meant, he could have unhesitatingly named any of them without risk. Grammatical considerations also remove God, the Church, or the Holy Spirit from consideration. In this passage two grammatical genders are used of the restrainer: neuter gender, and masculine gender. If the Holy Spirit were the intended reference, Paul would have consistently used the neuter gender. Since the Holy Spirit is omnipresent (Ps 139:7, 8), and does not merely indwell believers, the removal of the saints at the Rapture does not constitute his removal. His removal is not suggested here or elsewhere in Scripture. As many are to be saved during the Tribulation (Re 7:14. 15:2-4. 20:4), his presence is essential (Ro 8:9). If the Church were Paul's intended reference, Paul would have consistently used the feminine gender, for in Greek the word "church" is feminine in its grammatical gender. Note that this does not mean that the church is feminine in any sense, or that it is thereby called a woman, for Greek grammatical gender has no necessary connection with natural gender (see note on Jn 16:13n). The reference is not to the Church, for if this were the case, the Church must be present during the first half of the Tribulation, until the Antichrist is revealed, yet this cannot be, for the Church is raptured (1 Th 4:17n) before the Tribulation begins. But the masculine and neuter gender does fit the future government (neuter gender) and its king (masculine gender). This leaves human government as the only remaining choice of those given. But the reference is not to human government in general, for prophecy nowhere states that such government will cease just

prior to the revelation of the Antichrist. Rather, Paul has a specific reference to biblical prophecy in mind, Da √7:8, 24, where Daniel speaks of the Antichrist defeating three kings which until that time restrained his power. That Paul's reference is to prophecy in the book of Daniel is confirmed by his reference to Daniel in ver. 4, and his statement in ver. 5, which indicates that when he was present with the Thessalonians he had been teaching them about Bible prophecy from the book of Daniel. **out of the way**. ✸108H3, Mt +13:49.

8. **that Wicked**. ver. +3. Ps +*9:5. Mt 13:19, 38. 1 J 2:13. 3:12. 5:18. **whom**. Da *7:10, 11, 26. Re 18:8-10. 19:20. **shall consume**. Je *25:30, 31. **with the**. Is 30:28. **spirit**. Gr. *pneuma*, ✸121A2, Mt +26:41n. Jb 4:9. Ps 18:15. 29:3-6. 33:6. Is +*11:4. Ho 6:5. He 10:27. Re 1:16. 2:16. 19:15, 20, 21. **of his mouth**. He *4:12. Re 2:16. 19:15. **destroy**. This is unanswerable proof that since Antichrist exists prior to the millennial age, and is destroyed (Da √7:10, 11. 2 Th 2:8. Re √19:19-21) by the personal coming of Jesus, we then have the strongest possible proof of the personal premillennial coming of Christ (Peters, *Theocratic Kingdom*, vol. 2, Proposition 123, Observation 1, p. 208). Da √7:10, 11. Lk 13:7. 1 C 15:24. He 2:14. Re 14:6-8. 18:10, 21. √19:20. **with the brightness**. Gr. *epiphaneia*, ✸S#2015g. 2 Th 1:8, 9. Hab +*3:4. Mt √24:27. 1 T 6:14g (appearing). 2 T 1:10g. *4:1g, 8g. T √2:13. He 10:27. **of his**. Paul repeatedly asserts the personal coming of Christ. ver. 1. 2 Th 3:5. Da *7:13, 14. 1 Th 1:10. 2:19. 3:13. 4:16. 5:23. **coming**. Gr. *parousia*, Mt +24:3. ver. 1. 1 Th +2:19. 4:15n.

9. **coming**. Gr. *parousia*, Mt +24:3. **is after**. Jn 8:41, 44. Ac 8:9-11. 13:10. 2 C 4:4. 11:3, 14. Ep +1:19. 2:2. Re 9:11. 12:9, 17. 13:1-5. 18:23. 19:20. 20:10. **Satan**. 1 C +5:5. **with all**. Re 13:14. **power**. 2 Th 1:11g. **and signs**. Ex 7:22. *8:7, 18. Dt 13:1, 2. Mt +*24:24. Mk 13:22. Jn ◐+4:48. Ac ◐2:22. Ro ◐15:19. 2 C ◐12:12. 2 T 3:8. He ◐2:4. Re √13:11-15. 18:23. 19:20. **lying**. ver. 11.

10. **deceivableness**. Ro 16:18. 2 C 2:17. +*4:2. √11:13, 15. Ep +*4:14. 2 P 2:18. He +*3:13. **of unrighteousness**. ver. 12. 1 C 13:6. **in them**. 1 C +1:18. 2 C 2:15. *4:3-5. Ep 4:18. 2 P 2:12. Re ◐9:4. *13:8. **perish**. Gr. *apollumi*, Mt +2:13. **because**. Jb 21:14. Ps +√9:10n. Je +*9:6. Lk 19:14. Ac *12:23g. 2 C *4:3-5. Ep 4:18. **they received**. Pr 1:7. 2:1-6. 4:5, 6. 8:17. Mt +*13:11. Jn √3:19-21. 8:45-47. Ro 2:7, 8. 6:17. 1 C 16:22. Ja 1:16-18. **the love of**. Ps ◐119:104. **the truth**. Both "love" and "truth" have the Greek article, so that Paul is referring not to love of truth in general, but love for the specific truth of the gospel. 2 C 4:2. 13:8. **that they**. Jn 3:17. 5:34. Ro 10:1. 1 Th 2:16. 1 T √2:4.

11. **for**. Ps *81:11, 12. 109:17. Is 29:9-14. Jn 12:39-43. Ro *1:21-25, 28. 2 C *4:3, 4. **God shall send**. √✸108A4, Ge +31:7. Ex +*4:21. Dt +*2:30. 1 K 22:18-22. 2 Ch 18:18-22. See on Is 6:9, 10. *66:4. Ezk 14:5, 9. Ro *1:28. He 17:17. **strong delusion**. ver. 9. **that**. Is 30:28. 44:20. 66:4. Je 27:10. Ezk 21:29. Mt 24:5, 11. 2 Th ◐2:13. 1 T 4:1. **a lie**. lit. the lie. ver. √4. Ge 3:5. Jn 8:44. Ro +1:25. 1 Th 2:3. 1 T 4:2.

12. **they**. Dt 32:35. Mk *16:16. Jn √3:36. 1 Th +*5:9. 2 P *2:3. Ju 4, 5. **be damned**. Gr. judged. Ac 7:7g. **believed not**. 2 Th 1:8. Jn *3:18. Ro 2:8. 2 P 3:5. **the truth**. ver. 10. 1 C 13:6. **but**. Ps 11:5. 50:16-21. 52:3,

4. Ho 7:3. Mi 3:2. Mk 14:11. Jn √3:19-21. Ro +*1:32. 2:8. 8:7, 8. 12:9. 2 P 2:13-15. 3 J 11.

13. **we.** 2 Th 1:3. See on Ro 1:8. 6:17. 1 Th +1:2. **beloved.** ver. 16. Dt 33:12. 2 S 12:25mg. Je 31:3. Ezk 16:8. Da 9:23. 10:11, 19. Ro 1:7. Col 3:12. 1 Th +*1:4. 1 J 4:10, 19. **from.** Ge 1:1. Pr 8:23. Is 46:10. Mt 25:34. Jn 1:1. 8:44. Ac 15:18. T 1:1, 2. He 1:10. Re 13:8. 17:8. **chosen.** Dt 7:6, 7. 26:18. Mk 13:20. Ac +*13:48. Ro +*8:29, 30, 33. 9:11. Ep 1:+4, 5. 1 Th 1:4. 2 T +*1:9. Ja +*2:5. 1 P *1:2. 2:9. **unto salvation.** 1 Th +*5:9. **through sanctification.** ver. 10, 12. Lk 1:75. Ro *15:16. 1 C *6:11. Ep 1:1. 1 Th 4:3, +4. 2 T *2:19. He +*12:14. 1 P *1:2-5. **Spirit.** Gr. *pneuma*, Mt +3:16. Ro 8:9. 1 C 2:4. 1 P *1:2. **belief.** T#257. ver. ❍11. Mt +4:6 (T#17-3). Jn 8:45, 46. √14:6. Ac +*13:48. 15:9. 27:22-24, 30, 31. Ga 1:3. Ep √2:8. Col +*1:5. 2 T +*2:15. +√3:15. Ja +*1:18. 1 P *1:2. or, faith. 1 P *1:5. **of the truth.** lit. of truth. Jn +*7:17.

14. **he called.** See on Ro +*8:28-30. 1 Th √2:12. 1 P 5:10. **our gospel.** Ro 2:16. +*16:25. 1 Th *1:5. **to the obtaining.** Ps +*16:11. Mt √25:21. Jn +*14:2, 3. *17:22, 24. Ro √8:17. Ep +*1:18. 1 Th √2:12. +*5:9. 2 T *2:12. 1 P +*1:4, 5. *5:10. Re *3:21. *21:23. *22:3-5. **of the glory.** 2 Th +*1:10. Jn *17:22. Ro 5:2. +*8:30. Col √3:4. 1 Th √2:12. 2 T 2:10. 1 P *5:10.

15. **stand fast.** ver. ❍2. See on 1 C +√15:58. +16:13. Ph *4:1. 1 Th +*3:8. **hold.** 2 Th *3:6. 1 C 11:2. Re 2:25. **the traditions.** 2 Th 3:6. Mt 15:2. Ro 6:17. 1 C *11:2, 23. +*15:3. Ga 1:12, 14. Col 2:8. Ju +*3g. **whether.** ver. 2. 2 Th 3:14. **by word.** ver. +2. **our epistle.** 1 Th 4:15-18.

16. **our Lord.** 2 Th 1:1, 2. 3:16. Jn +*10:30. See on Ro 1:7. 2 C *13:14. Ep 2:20. 1 Th 3:11. 5:23. **himself.** 1 Th +*3:11. **and God.** 2 Th 1:1, 2. **which hath loved.** See on ver. 13. Jn √3:16. 13:1. 15:9, 13. Ro *5:8. Ep 2:4, 5. 5:2, 25. Ph 2:1. T *3:4-7. 1 J *3:16. *4:9, 10. Re +*1:5. 3:9. **everlasting.** Ps 103:17. Is +*35:10. +*51:11. +*60:19, 20. 61:7. Jn *4:14. 2 C √4:17, 18. 1 P *1:5-8. Re 22:5. **consolation.** Lk +*2:25g. *16:25. Jn 14:16-18. 16:22. 1 C +*14:3. He *6:18. Re 7:16, 17. **good hope.** Ro *5:2-5. 8:24, 25. +*15:4. Col +*1:5, 23. 1 Th 1:3. T 1:2. √2:13. 3:7. He *6:11, 12, 19. 7:19. 1 P +*1:3-5. 1 J √3:2, 3. **through grace.** Ac 15:11. 18:27. Ro 4:4, 16. 5:2. 11:5, 6.

17. **Comfort.** ver. 16. Is 51:3, 12. +*57:15. 61:1, 2. 66:13. Ro 15:13. 2 C √1:3-6. 1 Th +4:18. **your hearts.** Col +2:2. **stablish.** 2 Th 3:3. Is 62:7. Ro 1:11. 16:25. 1 C *1:8. 2 C 1:21. Col +*2:7. 1 Th 3:2, 13. He *13:9. 1 P +*5:10. Ju *24. **in every.** Ja 1:21, 22. 1 J 3:18. **good.** Mt *5:16. Ph *2:15, 16. **word.** In the Revised Version (1881) and more modern translations (NIV), the order is reversed to read "every good work and word." Hogg and Vine note "the order is significant, practice should precede precept" (Comm. on Thessalonians, p. 279). Ep *4:29. 5:4. Col ❍*3:17. *4:6. Ja 1:19. *3:2. 1 P 4:11. **and work.** Ac +9:36.

2 THESSALONIANS 3

The apostle requests the prayers of the Thessalonians, especially for the success of his ministry; expresses his confidence respecting them; and prays for them, 1-5. He charges them to censure and withdraw from disorderly walkers, who neglected their own business, and intermeddled in that of others; interspersing

suitable arguments, directions, and exhortations, 6-15. He concludes with benedictions, 16-18.

1. **Finally.** Ph +3:1. **pray.** Mt *9:38. Lk 10:2. Ro 15:30. 2 C 1:11. Ep 6:19, 20. Col *4:3. 1 Th +*5:17, 25. He 13:18, 19. **the word.** Ac 6:7. 12:24. 13:49. +*17:2, 3. 19:20. 1 C 16:9. 1 Th 1:8. 2 T 2:9. **have free course.** Gr. run. T#1755. Ps 147:15. **be glorified.** Ps √138:2. Ac +*13:48. **even.** 1 Th 1:5. 2:1, √13.

2. **delivered from.** T#1749. Ps 7:1, 2. 36:11. 43:1. 59:2-4. 71:4, 5. 74:19, 20. Ro +*15:31. 1 C 15:32. 2 C 1:8-10. 1 Th 2:18. 2 T 4:17. **unreasonable.** Gr. absurd. Lk 23:41. Ac 25:5. 28:6g. **all men have not.** Dt 32:20. Mt 17:17. 23:23. Lk *18:8. Jn 2:23-25. Ac 13:45, 50. 14:2. 17:5. 28:24. Ro 10:16. 2 C √4:3, 4. **faith.** *or*, the faith. Lk *18:8. Ac +6:7. 1 C +16:13. Ep *2:8.

3. **the Lord.** See on 1 C 1:9. √10:13. 1 Th 5:24. 1 J *1:9. **stablish.** See on 2 Th 2:17. 1 P +*5:10. 2 P +*1:10. **and keep.** Ge 20:6. 48:16. 1 Ch 4:10. Ps 19:13. 121:7. Mt +*6:13. Lk +*11:4n. Jn *17:15. 1 C *10:13. 2 T 4:18. 2 P *2:9. 1 J *5:18. Ju √24. **from evil.** 2 Th 2:17. Mt +13:19.

4. **we have.** Ro 15:14. 2 C +2:3. 7:16. 8:22. Ga 5:10. Ph *1:6. Phm 21. **that.** ver. 6, 12. Mt 28:20. Ro +*2:7. 15:18. 1 C 7:19. 14:37. 2 C 2:9. 7:15. Ph √2:12. 1 Th 4:1, 2, 10. **command.** 1 Th 4:2, 11.

5. **the Lord.** 1 K 8:58. 1 Ch 29:18. Ps 119:5, 26. Pr √3:6. Je 10:23. Ja 1:16-18. **direct.** Lk 1:79g. 1 Th 3:11. **your hearts.** 1 Ch 29:18. Ps 78:8. **into the love.** T#1532. Dt 30:6. Je 31:33. Lk 11:42. Jn 5:42. 17:26. Ro *5:5. +*8:28, 39. 1 C 8:3. 2 C 13:14. Ga *5:22. Ep 3:16-19. 6:23. Ja +*2:5. 1 J 2:5. 3:17. 4:9, 19. 5:3. Ju 2, *21. **and into.** Ps 40:1. 130:5, 6. La 3:26. Lk 12:36, 37. Ro 8:25. Ph +*3:20, 21. 1 Th *1:+3, 10. 2 T *4:8. T √2:13. He √9:28. 2 P 3:12. Re *3:10, 11. 13:10. **the patient waiting for Christ.** or, the patience of Christ. Ro 2:7. He *12:2, 3. Ja *5:7, 11. 1 P 4:1.

6. **in the name.** 1 C 5:4. 2 C 2:10. Ep 4:17. Col *3:17. 1 Th 4:1. 1 T 5:21. 6:13, 14. 2 T 4:1. **that ye.** ver. 14, 15. Mt 18:17. Ro +*16:17. 1 C 5:+9, *11-13. 1 T *6:5. 2 T 3:5. He 12:15, 16. 2 J 10. 3 J 10, 11. **withdraw.** Ps +*119:63. Mt +*15:14. 2 C 8:20g. **brother.** 1 C 5:11. **walketh.** ver. 7, 11. 1 Th 4:11. 5:14. **not after.** ver. 10, 14. 2 Th 2:15. 1 C 11:2.

7. **how.** ver. 9. Ac 20:35. 1 C 4:16. √11:1. Ph 3:17. 4:9. 1 Th 1:+6, 7. 1 T 4:12. T 2:7. 1 P 5:3. **for.** ver. 6. 1 Th +1:5. *2:10.

8. **Neither did.** 1 C +9:12. **eat.** ver. 12. Pr 31:27. Mt 6:11. **but wrought.** Ac *18:3. *20:34. 1 C *4:12. 2 C 11:9. 1 Th 4:11. **night.** Ac +5:5. See on 1 Th 2:9. **that we.** T#1860. Lk ❍10:7. 22:36. 1 C 10:24.

9. **Not.** Mt *10:10. 1 C +*9:4-14. 2 C *11:9, 12. Ga 6:6. 1 Th 2:6. 1 T *5:18. **to make.** See on ver. 7. Jn 13:15. 1 P 2:21. +*5:3. **to follow.** ver. +7. Ph *3:17. *4:9.

10. **when.** Lk 24:44. Jn 16:4. Ac 20:18. **commanded.** 1 Th 4:11. **that if.** ꟻ184A, 1 C +15:2. **any would.** ꟻ138C, Ge +22:14. T#1862. Ge *3:19. Pr 13:4. 20:4. 21:25. 24:30-34. 1 C +11:16. 1 Th 4:11. **not work.** T#1837. Ec *3:13. Ezk +*16:49. **neither.** ꟻ164, 1 S +17:7. ꟻ65, Mt +27:19. Bengel on this passage (*N.T. Word Studies*, vol. 2, p. 502) identifies this as a form of *Enthymeme*, confirmation of the argument from its contrary. "Supply, But every man eats: therefore let every man labor. Paul does not mean, that such a

man should be immediately deprived of food by others; but he proves from the necessity of eating the necessity of laboring. There is a similar *Enthymeme* at 1 C 11:6." More properly, this is the figure *Syllogismus*, or Omission of the Conclusion, the opposite of the figure *Enthymeme*, or Omission of the Premise. Pr 19:15.

11. **some**. 1 C +11:16. **walk**. See on ver. 6. **working not**. *✸*171C, Ex +20:10. Ezk +*16:49. 1 Th √4:11. 1 T +*5:8. 1 P +*4:15. **busybodies**. *✸*135, Ps +68:28. 1 T +*5:13.

12. **we**. See on ver. 6. **exhort**. 1 Th +4:18. **that with**. Ge 49:14, 15. Pr 17:1. Ec 4:6. Ep +*4:28. 1 Th +*4:11. 1 T 2:2. **eat**. See on ver. 8. Lk 11:3.

13. **ye**. Is 40:30, 31. Ml 1:13. Ro 2:7. 1 C √15:58. Ga *6:9, 10. Ph 1:9. 1 Th 4:1. He 12:3. **be not weary**. *or*, faint not. Dt 20:8. Ps 27:13. Is *40:29-31. Zp 3:16mg. Ml 1:13. Lk +*18:1. Ro +*2:7. 1 C +√15:58. 2 C 4:1, 16. Ga *6:9. He 12:5. Re 2:3.

14. **And if**. *✸*184A, 1 C +15:2. **obey**. Dt 16:12. Pr 5:13. Zp 3:2. Mt *18:17. 2 C 2:9. 7:15. 10:6. Ph √2:12. 1 Th 4:8. Phm 21. He 13:17. **by this epistle, note that man**. *or*, signify that man by an epistle. ver. 6.

Mt 18:17. Ro 16:17, 22. 1 C 5:9, 11. Col 4:16. 1 Th 5:27. T 3:10. **have no company**. ver. +*6. Ps +*119:63. **that he**. Nu 12:14. Ezr 9:6. Ps 83:16. Je 3:3. 6:15. 31:18-20. Ezk 16:61-63. 36:31, 32. Lk 15:18-21. 1 C +*4:14.

15. **count**. Le +*19:17, 18. Mt +18:15. 1 C 5:5. 2 C 2:6-10. 10:8. 13:10. Ga +*6:1. 1 Th 5:14. Ju 22, 23. **admonish**. Ps *141:5. Pr 9:9. 25:12. Mt 18:15. 1 C 4:14. 1 Th 5:12, 14. T 3:10. Ja +*5:19, 20.

16. **the Lord of peace**. Ps 72:3, 7. Is +*9:6, 7. Zc 6:13. Lk *2:14. Jn *14:27. Ro +15:33. 16:20. 1 C 14:33. 2 C *5:19-21. 13:11. Ep √2:14-17. +6:23. 1 Th *5:23. He 7:2. √13:20. **himself**. 2 Th 2:16. Ep 2:20. 1 Th +3:11. **give**. Nu 6:26. Jg 6:24mg. Ps 29:11. *85:8-10. Is *26:12. +*45:7. 54:10. 66:12. Hg 2:9. Jn 16:33. See on Ro 1:7. Ph √4:7-9. **always**. Ep 6:18. **The Lord be**. ver. 18. Ru 2:4. 1 S 17:37. 20:13. Ps 46:7, 11. Is 8:10. Mt *1:23. *28:20. 2 T 4:22. Phm 25.

17. **with mine own hand**. 1 C +*16:21. Col *4:18. **the token**. See on 2 Th 1:5. Jsh +*2:12. 1 S 17:18.

18. **grace**. See on Ro 16:20, 24.

1 TIMOTHY

1 TIMOTHY 1

The apostle salutes Timothy, 1, 2; reminds him for what purpose he was left at Ephesus, 3, 4; shows that "the end of the commandment is love, from a pure heart, a good conscience, and unfeigned faith," 5; from which some having swerved, in attempting to preach the law had perverted it, 6, 7. The law is good; but is intended to condemn transgressors, 8-10; which accords with the gospel also, 11. With deep humility and thankfulness, the apostle speaks of his own conversion, and the encouragement given by it to sinners in every age; and ascribes glory to God, 12-17. He charges Timothy to maintain faith and a good conscience; and mentions some, who had renounced the truth, and whom he had delivered unto Satan, 18-20.

1. **an apostle**. See on Ro 1:1. 1 C 1:1. 2 C +1:1. **by**. 1 T 2:7. Ac *9:15. +*26:16-18. Ro 16:26. 1 C 7:6. 9:17. 2 C 8:8. Ga 1:1, 11. 2 T 1:11. T 1:3. **God**. 1 T 2:3. *4:10. Ps 24:5. 106:21. Is +*12:2. 43:3, 11. 45:15, 21. 49:26. 60:16. 63:8. Ho 13:4. Lk 1:47. 2:11. 2 T *1:10. T 1:3. 2:10, 13. 3:4, 6. 2 P 1:1. 1 J 4:14. Ju *25. **our hope**. *✸*121R3, Ps +71:5. Ro 15:12, 13. Col +*1:27. 2 Th 2:16. 1 P 1:3, 21.

2. **Timothy**. Ac 16:1-3. 1 Th 3:2. 2 T 1:2. **my**. ver. 18. 1 C +*4:14-17. Ph *2:19-22. 2 T 1:2. 2:1. T 1:4. **Grace**. *✸*173, Ge +27:44. See on Ro 1:7. Ga 1:3. 6:16. 2 T 1:2. T 1:4. 1 P 1:2. 2 J 3. Ju 2. **and**. *✸*174, Ge +18:27.

3. **As I besought**. T 1:5. **at**. Ac +18:21. 19:1, etc. 2 T 1:18. 4:12. **when**. Ac 20:1-3. Ph 2:24. **Macedonia**. Ac +16:9. **charge**. 1 T 4:6, 11. 5:7. 6:3, 10, 17. Ga 1:6, 7. Ep +*4:14. Col 2:6-11. T 1:9-11. 2 J 7, 9, 10. Re 2:1, 2, 14, 20. **some**. 1 C +11:16. **no other**. 1 T 6:3-5. 2 C 11:4. Ga *1:6, 7, 9.

4. **Neither give heed**. Mk +*4:24. **to**. 1 T 4:7. 6:4, 20. Col *2:8. 2 T *2:14, 16-18. 4:4. T 1:14. 2 P √1:16. **fables and**. *✸*93A, Ge +1:26. **endless**. Gr. *aperantos*, ✸S#562g, only here. T *3:9. **questions**. 1 T 6:+4, 5.

2 T *2:23. **godly**. 1 T *3:16. 6:3, 11. Lk 16:2, 3, 4. 1 C +9:17. 2 C 1:12. √7:9, 10. Ep +3:2. +*4:12-16. T 1:1. He +*13:9. **in faith**. 15D, Mk +11:32. **so do**. *✸*63D3, Ro +7:3. Supply by ellipsis (absolute: of anantapodoton), "in faith (so I repeat my charge, that thou remain at Ephesus)" (B55).

5. **the end**. Ro *10:4. 13:8-10. Ga *5:13, 14, 22. 1 J 4:7-14. **commandment**. ver. 18. **charity**. Mk *12:28-34. Jn +*13:34. Ro 14:15. 1 C 8:1-3. ch. √13. 14:1. 1 P 4:8. 2 P *1:7. 1 J *3:18, 19. **a pure**. Ps 24:4. +*51:10. Je 4:14. Mt +*5:8. 12:35. Ac *15:9. 2 T *2:22. Ja +4:8. 1 P *1:22. 1 J 3:3. **a good**. ver. *19. 1 T 3:9. Ac +*23:1. *24:16. Ro 9:1. 2 C 1:12. 2 T 1:3. T *1:15. He *9:14. √10:22. 13:18. 1 P 3:*16, 21. **faith**. Ro 12:9. Ga *5:6. 2 T *1:5. He *11:5, 6. 1 J *3:23. **unfeigned**. Ja +3:17g.

6. **some**. 1 C ≠11:16. **having swerved**. *or*, not aiming at. 1 T 6:21. 2 T 2:18g. 4:10. **turned**. 1 T 5:15. 6:4, 5, 20. 2 T 2:23, 24. 4:4. T 1:10. 3:9. He 12:13g. **vain jangling**. T 1:10.

7. **Desiring**. Ja +*3:1. **to**. Lk +5:17. Ac 15:1. Ro 2:19-21. Ga 3:2, 5. 4:21. 5:3, 4. T 1:10, 11. **understanding**. 1 T 6:4. Is 29:13, 14. Je 8:8, 9. Mt +*15:14. 21:27. 23:16-24. Jn 3:9, 10. 9:40, 41. Ro 1:22. Col 2:18. 2 T 3:7. 2 P 2:12. **affirm**. T 3:8.

8. **the law**. Dt 4:6-8. Ne 9:13. Ps *19:7-10. *119:96-105, 127, 128. Ro *7:12, 13, 16, 18, 22. *10:4. +*12:2. Ga *3:11, 21. **is good**. Ro 7:16. T 1:15. **if a**. *✸*184C, Mt +4:9. **lawfully**. 2 T 2:5.

9. **the law**. Ro 4:13. 5:20. 6:14. Ga 3:10-14, 19. 5:23. **the lawless**. 2 Th 2:8g. **disobedient**. Ro 1:30. T 1:6, 10, 16. 3:3. He 11:31. 1 P 2:7. 3:20. **the ungodly**. 1 P 4:18. Ju 15. **profane**. 1 T 4:7. 6:20. Je 23:11. Ezk 21:25. 2 T 2:16. He 12:16. **murderers**. Ex *21:15. Le 20:9. Dt 27:16. 2 S 16:11. 17:1-4. 2 K 19:37. 2 Ch 32:21. Pr 20:20. 28:24. 30:11, 17. Mt 10:21. **manslayers**. Ge +*9:5, 6. Ex +*20:13. 21:14. Nu 35:30-33. Dt 21:6-9. Pr 28:17. Ga *5:21. Re +*21:8. *22:15.

10. **whoremongers**. Mk +*7:21, 22. 1 C +*6:9, 10.

Ga *5:19-21. Ep *5:3-6. He +*13:4. **defile**. Ge 19:5. Le 18:21, 22. 20:13. Ro +*1:26. Ju +*7. **menstealers**. T#682. Ge 37:27. 40:15. Ex 21:16. Dt 24:7. Jb +27:13 (T#490). +36:6 (T#631). Pr +21:7 (T#489). +22:22 (T#636). Ec +7:7 (T#491). Je 5:26. *34:17. Re 18:13. **for liars**. Je 8:44. Re +*21:8, 27. *22:15. **perjured**. Ex +*20:7. Le +*19:12. Ezk 17:16-19. Ho 4:1, 2. 10:4. Zc 5:4. 8:17. Ml +*3:5. Mt *5:33-37. **if**. J184A, 1 C +15:2. **contrary**. 1 T 6:3. Ga ◑*5:22, 23. 2 T 1:13. 4:3. T 1:9. 2:1. **sound**. Gr. healthful. 1 T 6:3. 2 T 1:13. 4:3. T 1:9, 13. 2:1, 2. **doctrine**. or, teaching. 1 T +4:6.

11. **According**. Ro 2:16. **glorious**. J24N, Ge +17:5. Ps √138:2. Lk 2:10, 11, 14. 2 C 3:8-11. √4:4, 6. Ep 1:6, 12. 2:7. *3:8, 10. 1 P 1:11, 12. **the blessed**. 1 T 6:15. **committed**. T#465. 1 T 2:7. 6:20, 21. Ezk 3:17, 19. 33:7-9. 34:8-10. Ro +2:16. *15:15. 1 C +*4:1, 2. 9:17. 2 C √5:18-20. Ga +2:7. Col 1:25. 1 Th 2:4. 2 T 1:11, 14. +*2:2. **trust**. 1 Ch=9:26mg.

12. **I thank**. Jn √5:23. Ph *2:11. Re *5:9-14. 7:10-12. **enabled**. Ac 9:22g. 1 C *15:10. 2 C 3:5, 6. 4:1. √12:9, 10. Ph √4:13. 2 T 4:17. **counted**. Ac 16:15. 1 C 7:25. **faithful**. 1 C +*4:2. **putting**. See on ver. 11. Ac *9:15. 2 C +*3:6. Col 1:25. 2 T 1:3.

13. **was**. Ac *8:3. 9:1, 5, 13. 22:4. 26:9-11. 1 C 15:9. Ga *1:13. Ph 3:6. **a blasphemer**. 2 T 3:2g. **persecutor**. Ac +8:3. **and injurious**. Ro 1:30g. **but**. ver. 16. Ho 2:23. Ro √5:20, 21. *9:18. 11:30, 31. 1 C 7:25. 2 C 4:1. He √4:16. 1 P 2:10. **because**. Nu 15:30. Lk +*12:47. 23:34. Jn *9:39-41. Ac +3:17. 26:9. He *6:4-8. √10:26-29. 2 P *2:21, 22.

14. **the grace**. Ac 15:11. Ro *5:20. 6:1. 16:20. 2 C √8:9. √13:14. Re *22:21. **our Lord**. 2 T 1:8. He 7:14. **exceeding**. Ex 34:6. Is √55:6, 7. Ro *5:15-20. 1 C *15:10. Ep 1:7, 8. *2:8. 1 P 1:3. **with faith and love**. J174, Ge +18:27. 1 T 2:15. +*4:12. 6:11. Lk *7:47-50. 1 Th +1:3. *5:8. 2 T 1:13. 2:22. 3:10. T 2:2. 1 J *4:10. **which is in**. 1 T 3:13. 2 T 1:1, 13. 2:1, 10. 3:15.

15. **a faithful**. J101, Dt +32:42. ver. 19. 1 T 3:1. 4:9. 2 T 2:11. T 1:9. √3:8. Re 21:5. 22:6. **worthy**. 1 T 4:9. Jn *1:12. √3:16, 17, 36. Ac 11:1, 18. 1 J √5:11, 12. **that**. Mt +*1:21. 9:13. +*18:11. 20:28. Mk 2:17. Lk *5:32. +*19:10. Jn *1:29. +*3:17. 12:47. Ac 3:26. Ro *3:24-26. +.4:25. *5:6, 8-10. 2 T *1:9, 10. He √7:25. 1 J 3:5, 8. *4:9, 10. Re *5:9. **world**. Gr. kosmos, Mt +4:8. **of whom**. ver. 13. Jb 42:6. Ezk 16:63. 36:31, 32. 1 C *15:9. Ep *3:8.

16. **for this**. Nu 23:23. Ps 25:11. Is √1:18. 43:25. Ep 1:6, 12. 2:7. 2 Th +*1:10. **I obtained**. See on ver. 13. 2 C 4:1. **that in me**. Ep 2:7. **first**. or, as chief (of sinners). J63I1A, Ex +12:4. **all**. Ex +*34:6. Ro 2:+4, 5. 1 P 3:20. 2 P *3:9, 15. **for a pattern**. 2 Ch 33:9-13, 19. Is √55:7. Lk 7:47. 15:10. 18:13, 14. 19:7-9. 23:43. Jn √6:37. Ac 13:39. Ro *5:20. +*15:4. 2 T 1:13g. He √7:25. **believe**. Jn √3:15, 16, 36. √5:24. 6:40, +*54n. √20:31. Ro *5:21. √6:23. 1 J √5:11, 12. **everlasting**. Gr. aionios, Mt +18:8. Ro +2:7. T 1:2. 3:7.

17. **the King**. 1 T √6:15, 16. Ps *10:16. 45:1, 6. 47:6-8. 90:2. 145:13. Je 10:10. Da *2:44. +*7:14. Mi +*5:2. Ml 1:14. Mt +*6:13. 25:34. Ro 1:23. He *1:8-13. Re 4:9, 10. √15:3. 17:14. 19:16. **eternal**. Gr. aion, Mt +6:13. Dt +*33:27. He *9:14. **immortal**. Gr. aphthartos, *S#862g. Ro 1:23 (uncorruptible). 1 C 9:25 (incorruptible). √15:52. 1 P +*1:4, 23. 3:4. This Greek word is rendered immortal only here. Nevertheless, a comparison of how this word is used in conjunction with *athanasia* (*S#110g, 1 T +6:16) in 1 C 15:52-54 shows these terms are equivalent, as discussed in the note at 1 Th 5:23. 2 T 1:10. **invisible**. J41, Ge +10:1. Jn √1:18. Ro 1:20. Col *1:15. He 11:27. 1 J 4:12. **the only**. T#962‡. 1 T ◑6:16n. Ps 90:2. Is 40:28. *44:6. Ro *16:27. Ju +*25. **be honor and**. T#300. 1 Ch 16:28, 29. +*29:11. Ne *9:5. Jb 36:24. Ps 41:13. 57:11. 72:18, 19. +79:9 (T#538). 106:48. 115:1. Pr 3:9. Je *13:16. Da *4:34, 37. Ml 1:6. Jn √5:22, 23. 8:49. 1 C 6:20. *10:31. Ep 3:20, 21. 1 P 5:11. 2 P +*3:18. Re 4:8-11. 5:9-14. 7:12. 19:1, 6. **glory**. 1 Ch 29:10, 11. Ph +4:20. **for ever**. Gr. aion, Mt +6:13. lit. unto the ages of the ages. Ga +1:5. **and ever**. Gr. aion, Mt +6:13. **Amen**. See on Mt +*6:13. 28:20.

18. **charge**. ver. 5. See on ver. 11, 12. 1 T 4:14. 6:13, 14, 20. 2 T +*2:2. *4:1-3. **son**. See on ver. 2. Ph 2:22. 2 T 1:2. 2:1. T 1:4. Phm 10. **according**. 1 T 4:14. **went before**. 1 T 5:24. Lk 1:66, 67, 76. **mightest**. 1 T *6:12. 2 C *10:3, 4. Ep *6:12-18. 2 T 2:3-5. 4:7. **war**. J147D, Ge +1:29. 1 C 9:7. 2 C *10:4. Ph +*1:17. 2 T 2:3, 4.

19. **Holding**. See on ver. 5. 1 T *3:9. 1 C +*15:2. T 1:9. He +*3:14. 1 P *3:15, 16. Re *3:3, 8, 10. **faith**. ver. +5. Mt +*7:21. Ja *2:17. Ju +*3, 4. **good conscience**. Ac *23:1. T *3:8. **which some**. Ex 32:1. Nu 14:1-4, 9, 10, 22-24. Dt 13:13. Jg 2:17. 1 S 18:12. 2 Ch 25:14, 27. Ne *9:26. Ezk 36:20. Mt 26:14-16. 27:3-5. Jn *6:66. 17:12. Ac 7:39. √8:13, 21. 20:30. Ro *6:15. Ph +*3:18, 19. 2 T 1:15. *3:1-6. 4:10. He +√10:38. 2 P *2:1-3, 12-22. Ju 10-13. **put away**. Lk +*8:13. Col +√1:23. He +√10:38. 2 P +*3:17. **concerning**. 1 T +*4:1n, 2. 1 C √11:19. Ga *1:6-8. +*5:4. 2 T 4:4. He √6:4-6. 1 J √2:19. **faith**. or, the faith. 1 T *4:1n, 6. 5:8. 6:10, 21. Lk +*18:8. Ac +6:7. 1 C +16:13. 2 T 3:8. 4:7. T 1:13. **made shipwreck**. 1 T 6:9. Mt 7:27. 1 C *10:12.

20. **Hymenaeus**. i.e. *marriage*, *S#5211g. 2 T *2:17. **Alexander**. Mk 15:21. Ac 19:33. 2 T 2:14. √4:14, 15. **I have delivered unto**. Mt *18:17. 1 C √5:4, 5. 2 C 10:6. 13:10. **Satan**. 1 C +5:5. that. 1 C 11:32. 2 Th 3:15. Re 3:19. **learn**. Gr. paideuo, *S#3811g. Lk 23:16 (chastise), 22. Ac 7:22 (learned). 22:3 (taught). 1 C 11:32 (chastened). 2 C 6:9. 2 T 2:25 (instructing). T 2:12 (teaching). He 12:6 (chasteneth), 7, 10. Re 3:19 (chasten). **blaspheme**. 2 T 3:2. Re 13:1, 5, 6. Gr. blaspheemeo, *S#987g. 1 T 6:1. Mt 9:3. 26:65. 27:39 (reviled). Mk 3:28, 29. 15:29 (railed). Lk 12:10. 22:65. 23:39 (railed). Jn 10:36. Ac +13:45. 18:6. 19:37. 26:11. Ro 2:24. 3:8 (slanderously reported). 14:16 (evil spoken of). 1 C 4:13 (being defamed). 10:30 (evil spoken of). T 2:5. 3:2 (speak evil). Ja 2:7. 1 P 4:4, 14. 2 P 2:2, 10, 12. Ju 8, 10. Re 13:6. 16:9, 11, 21.

1 TIMOTHY 2

The apostle enjoins prayers, and thanksgivings, to be made for all men; especially for kings and rulers to "God our Savior, who is willing that all should be saved," 1-4. There is "one God, and one Mediator, Jesus Christ, who gave himself a ransom for all, to be testified in due time," 5, 6. He declares his appointment, as the teacher of the Gentiles, 7: gives directions concerning prayer, and the modest apparel of women, 8-10; prohibits them to teach, and requires them to be in subjection, 11, 12; as the man was first created, and the woman was first seduced into sin, 13, 14. A promise concerning childbearing, 15.

1. **exhort.** *or*, desire. ⨍130, Ac +11:23. 2 C 8:6. Ep 3:13. He 6:11. **first.** 1 C +*15:3. **supplications.** 1 T 5:5. Ge 18:23-32. 1 K 8:41-43. Ps 67:1-4. 72:19. Mt *6:9, 10. Ep 6:18. Ph 4:4. Ja +*5:16. Gr. *de-eesis*, ❋S#1162g: Rendered (1) prayer: Lk 1:13. 2:37. 5:33. Ro 10:1. 2 C 1:11. 9:14. Ph 1:4a, 19. 2 T 1:3. He *5:7. Ja +*5:16. 1 P 3:12. (2) supplication: Ac 1:14. Ep 6:18, 18. Ph 4:6. 1 T 2:1. 5:5. (3) request: Ph 1:4b. **prayers.** Mt 6:9, 10. 1 Th +*5:17. Gr. *proseukee*, ❋S#4335g: Mt 17:21. 21:13, 22. Mk 9:29. 11:17. Lk 6:12. 19:46. 22:45. Ac 1:14. 2:42. 3:1. 6:4. 10:4, 31. 12:5. 16:13, 16. Ro 1:9. 12:12. 15:30. 1 C 7:5. Ep 1:16. 6:18. Ph 4:6. Col 4:2, 12. 1 Th 1:2. 1 T 2:1. 5:5. Phm 4, 22. Ja *5:17. 1 P 3:7. 4:7. Re 5:8. 8:3, 4. **intercessions.** Ge +*18:32. Ex 32:11. Nu +*12:13. 14:19, 20. 1 S +*12:23. 2 Ch *30:18-20. Gr. *enteuxis*, ❋S#1783g. 1 T 4:5g (prayer). **giving of thanks.** Ro 1:8. 6:17. Ep 5:20. Ph 1:3. +*4:6. 1 Th 5:18. 2 Th 1:3. **be made.** Dt +*29:29. **for all men.** T#1432. ver. 4. Is 56:7. Ac *17:30. 1 Th 3:12. 2 T 2:24. T √2:11. 3:2.

2. **For kings.** T#1592. 1 S 10:24. 15:10, 11. 1 K 1:34-37, 39. 1 Ch 29:19. Ezr *6:10. Ne 1:11. Ps 20:1-4. 72:1. Je 29:7. **for all.** T#1435. Ro *13:1, etc. 1 P 2:13, 14. **authority.** *or*, eminent place. **quiet.** T#1662. 2 Ch 20:30. **peaceable.** Ge 49:14, 15. Jsh 23:1. 2 S 20:19. 2 K 20:19. 2 Ch 15:15. Jb *34:29. Pr +*16:7. 24:21. Ec 3:12, 13. 8:2-5. Je *29:7. Ro 12:18. 1 Th 4:11. 5:13. He +*12:14. **all godliness.** 1 T +3:16. Lk 1:6. 2:25. Ac 10:22. 24:16. Ph √4:8. T √2:10-14. 1 P *2:9-13. 2 P +*1:3-7. **honesty.** *or*, gravity. 1 T 3:4. T 2:7.

3. **this.** 1 T 5:4. Ro +*12:1, 2. 14:18. Ep 5:9, 10. Ph 1:11. 4:18. Col +√1:10. 1 Th 4:1. He *13:16. 1 P 2:5, 20. **God.** See on 1 T 1:1. Is 45:21. Lk 1:47. 2 T +*1:9.

4. **Who will.** Is *45:22. *49:6. *55:1. Ezk *18:23, 32. *33:11. Mt *18:14. Lk *13:34. 14:23. Jn √3:15-17. √6:37. Ro *3:29, 30. 2 C √5:17-19. Ph *2:13. 1 Th 2:15, 16. T *2:11. 2 P √3:9. **all men.** √⨍171R, Ge +24:10. 1 T *4:10. Ezk 18:23, 32. Mt 26:28n. Jn +3:17. +4:42. Ro +*5:18. T 2:11. 2 P √3:9. **and to come.** Mt +*28:19. Mk *16:15. Lk *24:47. Ro √10:12-15. 2 T 3:7. Re *14:6. **the knowledge.** Is *53:11. Hab *2:14. Lk *1:77. Jn √14:6. *17:3, 17. Col +*1:9. 2 T +*2:25. *3:7. T 1:1. He 10:26.

5. **one God.** Dt +*6:4. Is *44:6. *45:22. Mt +√28:19. Mk +*12:29-33. Jn √17:3. Ro 3:29, 30. 10:12. 16:27. 1 C +*8:6. Ga 3:20. Ep +*4:5, 6. Ja 2:19. **and one mediator.** There is no basis in Scripture to introduce additional intermediaries such as Mary the mother of Jesus or the saints. To do so is directly contrary to the explicit teaching of God's word in Scripture in this text, and contradicts the statement of Jesus that no one can come to the Father but through him (Jn 14:6). Ex=33:8, 9. Le 16:17. Jb *9:33. Jn √14:6. Ac √4:12. Ro 8:34. Ga +3:20. He √7:25. 8:6. *9:15. *12:24. 1 J *2:1. **between.** Jn √14:6. **and men.** ⨍174, Ge +18:27. **the man.** The Jehovah's Witness doctrine that Jesus Christ is the archangel Michael (1 Th 4:16n), and is no longer a man, directly contradicts this declaration of Paul that Jesus is still a man, not an angel, though now in heaven as our one Mediator. Je +*23:5, 6. Zc +*13:7. Mt +*1:23. Lk *2:10, 11. Jn *1:14. 8:40. Ro +1:3. 1 C √15:45-47. Ph +*2:6-8. He 2:6-13. Re

1:13. **Christ Jesus.** Mt +*10:32.

6. **gave.** Jb *33:24. Is √53:6. Mt +*20:28. +*26:28n. Mk +*10:45. Jn *6:51. *10:15, 18. 2 C *5:14, 15, 21. Ep *1:7, 14. *5:2. T *2:14. He *9:12. 1 P *1:18, 19. *2:24. *3:18. 1 J √2:1, 2. *4:10. Re +*1:5. *5:9. **himself.** Is 53:10. Lk +*9:24. **a ransom.** Gr. *antilutron*, ❋S#487g, only here. Thayer gives the definition "what is given in exchange for another as the price of his redemption, ransom" (*Lexicon*, p. 50). Friedrich Buchsel in the TDNT notes that the word is a rare form, but represents a direct reference to Mk 10:45 expressed in the more elegant and forceful style of Greek found in the Pastoral epistles (TDNT, vol. 4, p. 349). A. T. Robertson states, speaking of the Greek preposition *anti* in reference to Mt 20:28 and Mk 10:45, "These important doctrinal passages teach the substitutionary conception of Christ's death, not because *anti* of itself means "instead," which is not true, but because the context renders any other resultant idea out of the question. Compare also *antilutron uper panton* by Paul (1 T 5:6) where both *anti* and *uper* combine with *lutron* in expressing this idea" (*A Grammar of the Greek New Testament*, pp. 573, 574). The Jehovah Witness *New World Translation* renders *antilutron* as "corresponding ransom." According to Jehovah Witness theology, following the pattern set by Charles T. Russell, Christ's ransom corresponded exactly to Adam, and Christ atoned for but one man, Adam, in whom we were all comprehended (He 7:10). Thus "one unforfeited life could redeem one forfeited life and no more." As F. W. Grant wryly remarks in reviewing this system, it smacks of the merchant, "with simply a clever plan for making a very large purchase with a very little money; and this trader's wit Mr. Russell credits to God as divine wisdom," but such a view of the atonement constitutes "a dreadful estimate or blasphemy of the divine nature, and in which Christ's life is valued at just the worth of any other man's!" (*Facts and Theories as to a Future State*, pp. 587, 588). The flaw in Russellism's atonement is at least twofold: (1) Scripture nowhere states Christ was Adam's substitute; this is a false deduction from Ro 5:18, 19, the commercial theory of the atonement taken to its extreme; (2) this passage does not state Christ gave his life a ransom for Adam, but Christ gave himself a ransom for all, as the very next words in the verse indicate. Le 5:15, 16. 6:4, 5. Ps 69:4. Mt *20:28. Jn 17:23, 24. **for all.** The Calvinistic doctrine of the limited atonement does not accord with the declaration of this verse, and the attempts to get around the obvious sense of this passage show the flaw to be in that system of interpretation which necessitates explaining away this text (2 P 1:20n). T#580. ver. +*4. Mt 20:28. +*26:28n. Mk *16:15. Jn *1:29. 3:17. 4:42. Ro +*5:18. 2 C √5:14, 15. He *2:9. √7:25. 1 J *2:2. Re +22:17 (T#370). **to be testified.** *or*, a testimony. ⨍63B, Ge +25:28. Supply ellipsis, (to be borne by us). 1 C +*1:6. 2 Th 1:10. 2 T *1:8. 1 J √5:11, 12. **in due time.** 1 T *1:16. *6:15. Mt 24:14. Is 26:9. 27:6. Ro *5:6. 16:26. 1 C +*15:8. Ga *4:4. Ep *1:9, 10. *3:5. T *1:3. Re 7:9, 10.

7. **I am.** See on 1 T 1:11, 12. 2 T 1:11. **a preacher.** Ec 1:1, 2, 12. 7:27. 12:8-10. Ro 10:14. Ep *3:7, 8. 2 T 1:11. 2 P 2:5. **apostle.** Ac 26:17. 1 C +9:1. **I speak.** See on Ro 1:9. 9:1. 2 C 11:31. Ga 1:20. **a teacher.** Jn 7:35. Ac +*9:15. 22:21. 26:17, 18, 20. Ro 11:13.

*15:16. 2 C *5:20. Ga 1:16. 2:9. **in faith.** Ac 14:27. Ga 2:16. 3:9. **verity.** Ps 111:7.

8. **I will.** 1 T 5:14. 1 C 7:7g. T √3:8. **pray.** 2 Ch 33:11, 12. Ps 130:1, 2. La 3:55, 56. Jon 2:1, 2. Ml 1:11. Lk 23:42, 43. Jn *4:21, 23, 24. Ac 21:5. He *10:21, 22. 1 Th +*5:17. **everywhere.** T#1189. Jn +4:21. 1 C +1:2. **lifting up.** ſ121S3, Ge +14:22. T#1248. Ge *14:22. Le +*9:22n. 1 K 8:22. Ne 8:6. Jb 11:13. 16:17. Ps 26:6. *28:2. *63:4. +*66:18. 119:48. 134:2. *141:2. 143:6. Pr 15:8. 21:27. Is *1:15. 58:7-11. Je 7:9, 10. La *2:19. *3:41. Ml 1:9, 10. Lk 24:50. Ac *10:2, 4, 31. He +*10:22. Ja *4:8. 1 J *3:20-22. **holy hands.** T#1341. Jb 16:17. 17:9. Ps 24:4. Ja 4:8. **without wrath.** T#1429. Zp +*2:3. Mt *5:23, 24. **and doubting.** T#1326. 1 K 3:11. Ps 35:13. Mt *5:22-24, 44. 6:12, 14, 15. 21:21. Mk √11:23-25. Lk 23:34. Ac *7:60. Ph +2:14. Ja *1:6-8. 1 P 3:7.

9. **like manner.** Grammatically a reference to ver. 8, "I will." **women adorn themselves.** T#173. 2 S *11:2. T 2:10. 1 P √3:3-5. **with shamefacedness.** Pr 7:10. Is 3:16. T 2:3-5. **and sobriety.** ver. 15. T 2:4, 5. **not.** Ge 24:53. Ex 35:22, 23. 2 K 9:30. Est 5:1. Ps 45:13, 14. 149:4. Pr 31:22. Is 3:18-24. 61:10. Je 2:32. 4:30. Ezk 16:9-16. Mt 6:28, 29. 11:8. **broidered.** or, plaited. 1 P *3:3. **pearls.** Mt +13:46.

10. **becometh.** Ep 5:3. **women.** 1 P *3:3-5. 2 P 3:11. **godliness.** 1 T +3:16. **with good works.** 1 T 5:6-10. +*6:18. Pr 31:31. Ac 9:+*36, 39. Ep √2:10. T √2:14. √3:8. 1 P 2:12. 2 P +*1:6-8. Re 2:19.

11. **women learn.** Ge *3:16. Est 1:20. 1 C +√11:3n. +*14:34n, 35. Ep *5:22-24. Col 3:18. 1 P 3:1, 5, 6. **in silence.** 1 Th +4:11. **subjection.** Ep *5:24. T 2:5. 1 P +3:1.

12. **I suffer not.** 1 C 14:34g. 16:7g. **a woman.** 1 T 5:14. 1 C +√14:34n. 2 T +√3:15. T 2:4, 5. **to teach.** 1 T 3:2-5. 4:11, 12. 5:17. Dt 17:8-13. 2 Ch +*15:3. 35:3n. Ml 2:6, 7. Mt 7:29. Ac 13:1. ◐18:26n. 1 C 12:29. Ep 4:11. T 2:1, *4, 7, 15. **authority.** 1 T 3:2-5. 4:11, 12. 5:17. Ge 3:16. Nu 30:8. Mt 23:2, 3. Ep 5:22. T 2:1, 7, 15. **silence.** Is +*58:13.

13. **was first.** Ge 1:27. *2:7, 8, 18, 22. 1 C *11:8, 9, 12. **then Eve.** Ge 2:18, 22. 1 C 11:8.

14. **not deceived.** Ro +7:11. **but the woman.** Ge 3:6, 12, 13. 2 C +*11:3n. **being deceived.** or, being greatly deceived. Ro 7:11. 16:18. 1 C 3:18. 2 C *11:3. 2 Th 2:3. **in the transgression.** Ge *3:6, 13, 16.

15. **she.** Ge +*3:15. Is +*7:14. +*9:6. Je 31:22. Mt *1:21-25. Lk 2:7, 10, 11. Ga *4:4, 5. **shall be saved.** Having just spoken of the curse which brought pain in childbearing to women, Paul in a rapid transition of thought marked by the "nevertheless" of this verse, here refers not to the present period but to the state of restoration or restitution (Ac +*3:19-21) of the race to the pre-Fall Edenic condition during the Millennium, at which time women who continue in faith, charity, and holiness will be spared the pain experienced now (Peters, *Theocratic Kingdom*, vol. 2, Proposition 119, Observation 3, note 2, p. 146). **in childbearing.** Ge *3:16. **if they continue.** ſ184C, Mt +4:9. ſ96D4, Ge +29:27. The presence of this condition annexed to the promise does not remove its application from the millennial period, for there are other promises attached to that time which are also conditional. Is 65:20. Zc 14:16-19. **in faith.** See on 1 T 1:5, 14. **and charity.** ſ174, Ge +18:27. **holiness.** 1 Th +4:3. **sobriety.** See on ver. 9. T 2:12. 1 P 4:7.

1 TIMOTHY 3

The office of a bishop is a "good work," and the desire of it, as such, should be encouraged, 1. The qualifications required in bishops and deacons; with directions concerning their wives and children, 2-13. The apostle wrote these things to Timothy (hoping to come to him soon), to regulate his conduct in the church of God, "the pillar and ground of the truth," 14, 15. "Great is the mystery of godliness," 16.

1. **is a.** 1 T +1:15. 4:9. 2 T 2:11. T √3:8. **true.** ſ101, Dt +32:42. **If.** ſ184A, 1 C +15:2. **desire.** 1 T 6:10. He 11:16g. **the office.** ver. 2-7. Ac 1:20. +20:28. Ph 1:1. T 1:7. 1 P 2:25. **bishop.** Ac +*20:28. He *12:15. 1 P 4:15. 5:2g. **desireth.** Pr +*11:30. Lk *15:10. Ro 11:13. Ep *4:12. 1 Th 5:14. Ja +*5:19, 20.

2. **bishop.** T +*1:6-9. **blameless.** ver. 10. 1 T 5:7. 6:14. Lk 1:6. Ph 2:15. **the husband.** ver. 12. 1 T 4:3. 5:9. He +*13:4. **of one wife.** T#426. Ge +4:19. Dt 17:15, *17. 1 K 11:1, 3. Ml *2:15. Mt 19:9. Mk 10:11, 12. **vigilant.** Is 56:10. Ac 20:29-31. 1 P 4:7. 5:8. **sober.** T 2:2, 5. **of good behavior.** or, modest. Ro +*12:3. Ph +*2:3. **given.** 1 T 5:10. Ro 12:13. T 1:8. He *13:2. 1 P 4:9. **apt to teach.** 2 T 2:24. Ep +*4:11. T 1:9.

3. **Not given to wine.** or, Not ready to quarrel, and offer wrong, as one in wine. ver. 8. Le 10:9. Is 5:11, 12. 28:1, 7. 56:12. Ezk 44:21. Mi 2:11. Mt 24:45-51. Lk 12:42-46. +*21:34-36. Ep +*5:18. T 1:7. 2:3. **no striker.** 2 T +*2:24, 25. T 1:7. **not greedy.** Ex +*18:21. Pr 1:19. 15:27. Is 56:11. Ac *20:33, 34. Ju 11. **filthy.** ver. 8. 1 S 8:3. T 1:7, 11. 1 P *5:2. **patient.** 1 T 6:11. Ec 7:8. 1 Th 5:14. 2 T +*2:24. T 3:2. Ja +*3:17. Re 1:9. **a brawler.** T 3:2. Ja 4:1mg. **not covetous.** 1 T +*6:10. Ex +*18:21. 1 S 2:15-17. 2 K 5:20-27. Je 6:13. 8:10. Mi 3:5, 11. Ml *1:10. Mt 21:13. Jn 10:12, 13. 12:5, 6. Ac 8:18-21. 20:33. Ro 16:18. He 13:5. 2 P 2:3, 14, 15. Re 18:11-13.

4. **One.** T 1:6. **ruleth.** ver. +*12. 1 T 5:17. Ge +*18:19. Jsh +*24:15. Ps *101:2-9. Ac *10:2. Ro *12:8. 1 Th 5:12. T +*1:6. **house.** ſ121J4, Ge +7:1. **having his children.** Ge +*18:19. Ex +*20:12. Le 19:3. Dt 27:16. 1 S ◐2:12, 22-25. ◐+*3:13. Pr 1:8. 6:20. 7:1. +*19:18. 23:22. ◐+*29:15. Lk *2:51. Ep +*6:1-4. Col +*3:20, 21. 1 Th +*2:11. **in subjection.** Gr. *hupotagee*, ✻S#5292g. 2 C 9:13. Ga 2:5. 1 T 2:11. For the related Greek term, *hupotasso*, ✻S#5293, see 1 P +5:5. **with.** 1 T 2:2. Ex 20:12. Pr 23:22. Ml 1:6. Ph 4:8g. T *1:6. 2:2, 7.

5. **if.** ſ184A, 1 C +15:2. 1 S *2:29, 30. *3:13. **how to.** Lk *16:10. **rule.** Gr. *proisteemi*, ✻S#4291g. Rendered (1) rule: Ro 12:8. 1 T 3:4, 5, 12. 5:17. (2) maintain: T 3:8, 14. (3) be over: 1 Th 5:12. **take care.** Lk 10:35, 36g. Jn 10:13. Ac *20:28, 31, 32. Ro *12:11n. 1 C √12:25. *16:15, 16. 2 C 7:12. *11:28. 12:20. Ga +*4:11. Ph *2:20. 1 Th 3:10. 5:12. He +*3:13n. *13:17. Ja +*5:14-16. 1 P +*4:7-11. 5:7. **the church of God.** ver. *15. Ac +*20:28. 1 C +10:32. Ep 1:22. 5:24, 32.

6. **not a novice.** or, one newly come to the faith. 1 T 5:22n. 1 C 3:1. He 5:12, 13. 1 P *2:2. **lest.** Dt 8:14. 17:20. 2 K 14:10. 2 Ch 26:16. 32:25. Pr 16:18, 19. 18:12. 29:23. Is 2:12. 1 C 4:6-8. 8:1. 2 C 12:7. 1 P *5:5. **lifted up.** 1 T 6:4. 2 T 3:4. **with pride.** 1 T +*6:17. Ps +*10:2, 4. +*119:21. Pr +*16:5, 18. Ezk +*16:49. Ro +*12:3. Ph +*2:3. **the condemnation.** ver. 7. 1 T 6:10. Is 14:12-14. Lk 10:18. 2 P 2:4. Ju 6.

7. **a good report.** 1 T 5:24, 25. 1 S 2:24. Ac +*6:3. 10:22. *22:12. 3 J 12. **them.** Mk +4:11. 1 C 5:12. Col *4:5. 1 Th *4:12. **lest.** 1 T *5:14. 1 C 10:32. 2 C 6:3. 8:21. 1 Th 5:22. T 2:5, 8. 1 P 4:14-16. **the snare.** ver. 6. 1 T 6:9. 2 T 2:26.

8. **the deacons.** T#102. ver. 12. Ac *6:3-6. Ph 1:1. **be.** See on ver. 4, 11. 1 T +*2:2. Ph 4:8g. T 2:2. **doubletongued.** 1 Ch 12:33. Ps 5:9. *12:2. 50:19. 52:2. Ro 3:13. Ja 1:8. 3:10. **not given.** See on ver. 3. 1 T *5:23. Le 10:9. Ezk 44:21. T 2:3. **not greedy.** Ex +*18:21. Pr 15:27. T 1:7, 11. 1 P 5:2.

9. **Holding.** See on 1 T 1:5, 19. **the mystery.** ver. 16. Ro +*16:25n. 2 J 9, 10. **the faith.** Ac +6:7. 1 C +16:13. **pure conscience.** Ac +*23:1. 2 T 1:3. T 1:15.

10. **let these.** ver. 6. 1 T 5:22. 1 J 4:1. **use.** ver. 13. Ac 6:1, 2. **being.** ver. 2. 1 C +1:8. Col 1:22. T 1:6, 7.

11. **their.** Le 21:7, 13-15. Ezk 44:22. Lk 1:5, 6. T 2:3. **be grave.** See on ver. 4, 8. **not slanderers.** Ps 15:3. 50:20. +*101:5. Pr 10:18. 25:23. Je 9:4. Mt 4:1. Jn 6:70. 2 T 3:3. T 2:3g. Re 12:9, 10. **sober.** ver. 2. 1 Th 5:6-8. 2 T 4:5. T 2:2. 3:2g. 1 P 5:8. **faithful.** See on 1 T 1:12. 6:2. Lk +*16:10. 1 C +*4:2. T 2:10.

12. **the husband.** See on ver. 2, 4, 5. **of one wife.** Ge +4:19. **ruling their children.** ver. +*4. Pr +*19:18. Ep +*6:4. **own houses.** 1 C +*14:35n.

13. **they.** Mt +25:21. Lk 16:10-12. 19:17. **used.** or, ministered. Mt 20:28. Ro 12:7, 8. 1 C 16:15. He +*6:10. 1 P 4:10, 11. **purchase.** Lk +*17:33. Ac 20:28. **degree.** 1 T 6:19. Ac 21:35g. **great.** Ac +4:13. *6:5, 8, 10, 15. 7:1, etc. Ph 1:14. 1 Th 2:2. 2 T 2:1. **which is.** 1 T +1:14. Col 1:4.

14. **hoping.** 1 T 4:13. 1 C 11:34. 16:5-7. 2 C 1:15-17. 1 Th 2:18. Phm 22. He 13:23. 2 J 12. 3 J 14. **shortly.** lit. more quickly. ſ96E3. Heterosis of Degree B527: the comparative for the positive. For another instance of this figure see 2 T 1:18.

15. **But if.** ſ184C, Mt +4:9. **know.** ver. 2. Dt 31:23. 1 K 2:2, 4. 1 Ch 22:13. 28:9-21. Ac 1:2. 1 C *3:16. **the house.** ſ173, Ge +27:44. Ep *2:21, 22. 2 T 2:20. He 3:2-6. 10:21. 1 P 2:5. 4:17. **the church.** T#92. See on ver. 5. Mt 5:13-16. Ep 3:10, 11. **the living.** 1 T 4:10. 6:16. Dt 5:26. Jsh 3:10. 1 S 17:26, 36. 2 K 19:4. Ps 42:2. 84:2. Je 10:10. 23:36. Da 6:26. Ho 1:10. Mt +16:16. Jn 6:69. Ac 14:15. Ro 9:26. 2 C 3:3. 6:16. 1 Th 1:9. He +*3:12. 9:14. 12:22. Re 7:2. **the pillar.** Pr 9:1. Je 1:18. Mt 16:18, 19. 18:18. Ro 3:2. Ga 2:9. **and.** ſ93A, Ge +1:26. By Hendiadys, foundation pillar. ver. 9, 16. **ground.** or, stay. **the truth.** ver. 16. Jn 1:17. √14:6. 18:37. 2 C 6:7. Ga 3:1. Ep 4:21. Col *1:5.

16. **without.** He 7:7. **great.** ſ101, Dt 32:42. **the mystery.** ſ101, Dt +32:42. T#81. ver. 9. Mt 1:23. 13:11. 22:41-46. Ro +*16:25n. 1 C 2:7. Ep 1:9. 3:3-9. 6:19. Col 2:2. 2 Th 2:7. Re 17:5, 7. 19:12. 22:16. **godliness.** 1 T 2:2, 10. 4:7, 8. 6:3, 5, 6, 11. Ac +3:12. 2 T 3:5, 12. T 1:1. 2:12. 1 J *3:1-3. **God.** All of the modern editors of the Greek text read "Who" instead of "God." The difference in the original Greek manuscripts is between the two-letter word *os* and the two-letter abbreviation for God, *Ths*, the letter *theta* in Greek differing from *omicron* only by having a horizontal line across its middle. Is +*7:14. +*9:6. Je +*23:5, 6. Mi +*5:2. Mt 1:23. Jn 1:1, 2, 14. Ac +*20:28. Ro 8:3. √9:5. 1 C √15:47. Ga 4:14. Ph *2:6-8. Col *1:16-18. He 1:3. *2:9-13. 1 J 1:2. Re 1:17, 18. **manifest.** Gr. manifested. 1 J 3:5. **in the flesh.** ſ171Q7, Jn +1:14.

Jb +*19:26. Jn +1:14. Ro 8:3. 1 P 3:18. **justified.** Is 50:5-7. Mt *3:16. Jn *1:32, 33. 15:26. *16:8, 9. Ac *2:32-36. Ro *1:3, 4. 1 P *3:18. 1 J 5:6-8. **Spirit.** Gr. *pneuma*, Ro +1:4. 1 P 3:18. **seen.** Ps 68:17, 18. Mt *4:11. 28:2. Mk 1:13. 16:5. Lk *2:10-14. *22:43. 24:4. Jn 20:12. Ac +*1:10, 11. Ep 3:10. 1 P 1:12. **preached.** Lk 2:32. Ac +9:15. 10:34. +*13:46-48. Ro 10:12, 18. Ga *2:2, 8. Ep 3:5-8. Col 1:27. **believed.** Ac 14:27. Col *1:6, 23. 2 Th 1:10. Re 7:9. **world.** Gr. *kosmos*, Mt +4:8. Ro 10:18. Col 1:27, 28. **received.** Mk +16:19. Lk *24:51. Jn 6:62. 13:3. 16:28. 17:5. Ac 1:1-9, 19. Ep 4:8-10. He 1:3. 8:1. *10:13. *12:2. 1 P *3:22. **into glory.** 1 P 1:11.

1 TIMOTHY 4

The apostle foretells a great apostasy, and corruption of Christianity, in after times, 1-3; shows that "every creature of God is good," 4, 5; and directs Timothy, in respect of his doctrine and personal conduct, that he may preach and live in such a manner as "to save himself and those that hear him," 6-16.

1. **the Spirit.** Gr. *pneuma*, Mt +3:16. Jn +7:39. 14:17. *16:13. Ac 13:2. 28:25. 1 C 12:11. 2 P *1:21. 1 J *2:18. Re 2:7, 11, 17, 29. 3:6, 13, 22. **expressly.** Ezk 1:3. **the latter.** Nu 24:14. Dt 4:30. 32:29. Is 2:2. Je 48:47. 49:39. Ezk 38:16. Da 10:14. Ho 3:5. Mi 4:1. 1 C +*11:19. 2 Th √2:3-9. 2 T 3:1, etc. 1 P 1:20. 2 P +*2:1. *3:3. Ju 4, 18. **some.** ſ175A, Ge +27:44. **depart.** Those who teach unconditional eternal security need to consider whether the direct statements of Scripture affirm apostasy is possible. One cannot logically be said to depart, fall away, or apostatize from a faith which one never held in the first place. Paul is addressing these warnings to believers, not unbelievers. One must not appeal to an isolated text such as Jn 10:28, and force it to teach unconditional security, when such a statement in its context is clearly said of those who Jesus declares "hear my voice" and "follow me" (Jn 10:27). A text like Jn 5:24 shows by the use of the present tenses in the Greek that the promise is to those who keep on hearing and believing (Jn 3:16n). In the context of Romans 8, the subject of apostasy is not in view. A text like Ro 8:30 is not addressing the unconditional security of the believer but the certainty of our glorification with Christ, despite how difficult our present circumstances might seem. In context (Ro 8:17) such confidence relates directly to our eternal inheritance with Christ as co-heirs in his earthly Messianic kingdom, an inheritance which is not rendered less certain because of present trials and tribulations, but more certain, for our reward and position is only increased by our perseverance (Mt +*5:11, 12). One does not apostatize every time a sin is committed. Moral apostasy consists of willfully persisting in known sin (1 C +*6:9-11. He 10:26. 1 J 3:9). Although one is never said in Scripture to be saved over and over again, or to be born again more than once, this fact does not remove the validity of all the warnings to believers against both moral and doctrinal (1 C +*15:2) apostasy. Certainly there would be no point in warning believers against what was impossible (1 Th 3:5n). While the Bible emphatically teaches the eternal security of the believer (Mt 24:13n), and makes the security of salvation in no sense dependent upon good works to stay saved, this security belongs to believers who

continue to place their faith in Christ for salvation, not unconditionally to persons who by a single act of faith allegedly "received Christ" but have since departed from the faith doctrinally or morally. That eternal security is not unconditional is proved by (1) repeated warnings to believers against doctrinal and moral apostasy; (2) the presence of "if" clauses (2 P +*1:10); (3) Paul's repeated concern that his labor not be in vain (1 Th 3:5n); (4) recorded instances of individuals who departed from true faith (He +*10:38); (5) that believing or saving faith is always represented in Greek as a continuing active faith, not a single or one time act of faith (Jn 3:16n). (6) Jesus said it is possible to stop believing (Lk +*8:13). To suggest, as many contemporary expositors do, that the warnings against apostasy in the book of Hebrews were addressed only to Jewish Christians who were in danger of forsaking Christianity and falling back into Judaism, and therefore cannot apply to believers today, is at best a shaky assumption, and at worst is taking away from the Word of God by wrongly rendering its warnings inapplicable to present day believers. As the warnings against apostasy are addressed with greater frequency to the Gentile Christians addressed in Paul's epistles (1 C +*15:2), such an argument has no force. To deny the force of the warning in Hebrews 6:4-6 by relegating the Apostle's argument to a "*reductio ad absurdum*," or reduction to an absurdity, is begging the question, as Spiros Zodhiates does in a footnote in his otherwise excellent work (*The Hebrew-Greek Key Study Bible*, pp. 1496, 1497). Few readers of that day or this would be in position to appreciate such a display of the niceties of rhetoric as the argument necessarily supposes was the author's intention. Such interpreters, in their mistaken effort to support the theory of unconditional eternal security, ignore, suppress, or explain away all contrary evidence. Such a procedure is invalid because, by its practice, the interpreter makes it impossible for God to assert a contrary truth. No matter how God might choose to express such a truth, the interpreter intent on defending this mistaken theory would explain the language away. An example of a clever but mistaken attempt to escape the logical consequences of this passage (1 T 4:1) is the effort to redefine the Greek terms for apostasy used here and at 2 Th 2:3 to mean "stand aloof from," making the reference to be to persons who were never believers, but simply those who associated with the Christians (Spiros Zodhiates, *The Hebrew-Greek Key Study Bible*, p. 1468, note on 2 Th 2:3). Zodhiates' redefinition also involves him in the exegetical "word study" fallacy discussed by D. A. Carson as "The Root Fallacy" (*Exegetical Fallacies*, pp. 26-32). Such a redefinition is rendered necessary by the exigencies of the theory of unconditional eternal security, as Zodhiates' ensuing arguments using Jn 10:28, Ro 8:38, 39, etc., show. This view is in error for the word "apostasy," in Greek, *apostasia*, in its religious use necessarily includes a prior turning to God (Heinrich Schlier, TDNT, vol. 1, p. 513, note 4), a concept rendered certain here by the next words "from the faith." Da 11:35. Mt 24:5-12. Lk +*8:13. 2 Th 2:3g. 2 T 3:1-5. 4:4. He +*3:12. Re *3:8. **from the faith.** ♪121R2, Ac +6:7. ver. 6. 1 T +*1:19. **seducing.** ♪168, Is +1:11. Ge 3:3-5, 13. 1 K 22:22, 23. 2 Ch 18:19-22. Mt +7:15. 2 C √11:3, 13-15. 2 Th 2:9-12. 2 T 3:13. 2 P 2:1. 1 J 4:6g. Re 9:2-11. 13:14. 16:14.

18:2, 23. 19:20. 20:2, 3, 8, 10. **spirits.** Gr. *pneuma*, Mt +8:16. **and doctrines.** ver. +6. Da 11:35-38. 1 C 8:5, 6. 10:20. Col 2:18. Ac 17:18. Ju *4. Re 9:20g.

2. **lies.** 1 K 13:18. 22:22. Is 9:15. Je 5:31. 23:14, 32. Da 8:23-25. Mt 7:15. 24:24. Ac 20:30. Ro 16:18. Ep +*4:14. 1 Th 2:3. 2 Th 2:11. 2 T 3:5. 2 P *2:1-3. Re 16:14. **hypocrisy.** Lk +12:1. **their.** Ro +*1:28. 2 C +1:12. **seared.** Ep 4:19.

3. **Forbidding.** Da 11:37. 1 C 7:28, 36-39. He +*13:4. **and commanding.** ♪180A, Ge +4:20. ♪63F, Ge +33:10. **to abstain.** Ro *14:3, 17. 1 C *8:8. Col 2:+16, *20-23. He *13:9. **which.** 1 T 6:17. Ge *1:29, 30. *9:3. Ps 104:14, 15. 145:15, 16. Ec 5:18. Mt *15:9, 11. Ac 10:13-15. 1 C 6:13. **received with thanksgiving.** ver. 4. 1 S 9:13. Mt 14:19. 15:36. Lk +*24:30. Jn 6:23. Ac 27:35. Ro +14:6. 1 C *10:30, 31. Col *3:17. **believe.** 1 T 2:4. Jn √8:31, 32. 2 Th *2:13, 14. **know.** Gr. *epiginosko*, Mt +11:27. 1 T 2:4.

4. **every.** Ge 1:31. Dt 32:4. Ec 7:29. Ac 10:15. Ro *14:14. **and.** Ac +*10:15. 11:7-9. 15:20, 21, 29. 21:25. Ro 14:14, 20. 1 C 10:23, 25. **received.** ver. 3.

5. **sanctified.** ver. 3. Lk 11:41. 1 C +*7:14. T 1:15. **the word of God.** Ge 1:25, 31. Lk 4:4. **and prayer.** 1 T 2:1. 1 S *9:13. Lk +*24:30.

6. **thou put.** Ac *20:31, 35. Ro 15:15. 1 C √4:17. 2 T 1:6. 2:14. *3:14, 15. 2 P *1:12-15. 3:1, 2. Ju 5. **the brethren.** Ep +6:23. 2 T 4:21. **a good.** Mt 13:52. 1 C +*4:1, 2. 2 C 3:6. 6:4. Ep 6:21. Col 4:7. 1 Th 3:2. 2 T +*2:15. **nourished.** Je +*15:16. Ep 4:15, 16. Col 2:19. √3:16. 2 T +*3:14-17. He *5:12. 1 P *2:2. **faith.** or, the faith. ver. 1. 1 T +1:19. **good doctrine.** ver. 1, 13g, 16g. 1 T 1:10. +*4:16. 5:17g. 6:1, 3. Ps 19:7mg. Pr 4:2. Jn +*7:16, 17. 2 T 3:10, 16g. 4:3. T 1:9. 2:1, 7-10. 2 J +*9. **thou hast.** Ph 3:16. 2 T 3:14. **attained.** Lk +1:3g. 2 T 3:10.

7. **refuse.** 1 T 1:4. 5:11. 6:20. 2 T 2:16, 23. 4:4. T 1:14. 3:9, 10. **profane.** 1 T +1:9. **fables.** 1 T +1:4. **exercise.** 1 T 1:4. 2:10. 3:16. 6:11. Ac 24:16. 2 T 3:12. T √2:12. He *5:14. 12:11. 2 P √1:5-8. 2:14. **godliness.** 1 T +3:16.

8. **bodily.** 1 S 15:22. Ps 50:7-15. Is 1:11-16. 58:3-5. Je 6:20. Am 5:21-24. 1 C *8:8. Col *2:21-23. He *13:9. **little.** or, for a little time. He 9:9, 10. **godliness.** 1 T 2:1, 2. 6:3, 6, 11. Jb 22:2. Mi +*6:8. T *2:12. √3:8. 2 P 1:3. 3:11. **is profitable.** 1 T 6:6. Dt +*4:40. 29:9. 2 Ch *26:5. Jb ●21:15. 22:2. Ec 8:12. Is 3:10. 65:22. Je 7:23. 22:15. **having promise.** Ge 49:25. Dt *28:1-14. Jb 5:19-26. Ps +*19:11. *37:3, 4, 9, 11, 16-19, 29. *84:11. *91:10-16. 112:1-3. 128:1-6. 145:19. Pr 3:16-18. 19:23. 22:4. Ec √8:12. Is 3:10. 32:17, 18. 33:16. 65:13, 14. Mt +*5:3-12. √6:33. +*19:29. Mk +√10:29, 30. Lk *12:31, 32. Ro +*8:28. 1 C 3:22. 2 P *1:3, 4. 1 J 2:25. Re 3:12, 21. **that now is.** Ps *68:19. Pr +*28:20. Mt +*12:32. Mk +√10:30. Lk +*18:30. **is to come.** Mt +*5:12. +*12:32. 20:21, 23. *25:21. Lk +*14:14. +*18:30. Ja +*2:5. Re *11:18.

9. **faithful saying.** ♪101, Dt +32:42. See on 1 T 1:15.

10. **therefore.** 1 C 4:9-13. 2 C 4:8-10. 6:3-10. 11:23-27. Col +1:29. 2 T 2:9, 10. 3:10-12. He *11:24-26. 13:13. 1 P *4:14, 15. **because.** 1 T √6:17. Ps *37:40. 52:8. 84:12. 118:8. Is +*12:2. 50:10. Je +*17:7. Da 3:28. Na *1:7. Mt 27:43. Ro 15:12, 13. 1 P *1:21. **the living God.** See on 1 T 3:15. Mt +16:16. **the savior.** 1 T 1:1. See on *2:6. Ps 36:6. 107:2, 6, etc. Is 45:21,

22. Jn *1:29. √3:15-17. +4:42. 1 J *4:14. **of all men.** See on 1 T √2:4. 2 C √5:15. 1 J √2:2. 2 P √3:9. **specially.** Jn ◑√3:18. √5:24. ◑√8:24. Ga +*6:10. 1 J √5:10-13.

11. **command.** 1 T 5:7. 6:2. 2 T √4:2. T *2:15. √3:8. **teach.** Ezk=44:23. 1 C 14:34n. Ep 4:11. 2 T *2:2. 1 P 4:11.

12. **Let no man.** Mt 18:10. 1 C *16:10, 11. 2 T 2:7, *15, *22. T 2:15. **thy youth.** 2 T 2:22. **an example.** T#178. Ps +101:2 (T#492). Ezk=44:23. Mt 5:16, 48. Lk 6:36. Jn 13:15. Ro 15:2. 1 C 8:8, 9, 13. √11:1. 2 C *6:4-6. Ph 3:17. Col *4:5. 1 Th 1:6. 2:10. 2 Th 3:7-9. 1 T 1:15, 16. 2 T 3:15. T *2:7, 8. He 13:7. Ja 5:10, 11. 1 P 2:11-15. +*5:3. **of the believers.** Jn 20:27. Ac 10:45. Ep 1:1. **in word.** Pr 15:26. Mt 12:34-37. 2 C *6:4-17. Ep 5:12. Ph √4:8. Col +*4:6. 2 T *2:22. T 2:8. Ja 3:13, 17. 2 P +*1:5-8. **in conversation.** Je +*10:2. Ro *12:2. Ph 1:27. He 13:7. Ja +3:13. 1 P 2:12. 2 P 3:11. 1 J 2:15-17. **in charity.** 1 T +1:14. Jn +*13:34, 35. 1 Th +*3:12. 1 P +*1:22. 2 P +*1:7. **in spirit.** Gr. *pneuma*, ∫121A2, Mt +5:3n. Pr +*4:23. **in faith.** Ga *5:22, 23. He 10:22. **in purity.** 1 T 1:5. 5:2, 22. Ps 24:4. +*101:3. *119:9. Pr 15:26. 20:11. 21:8. Mi 6:11. Mt +*5:8. 2 C 6:6. Ph *4:8. 1 Th 4:3-6n. T 1:15. Ja 1:27. 3:17. 4:8. 1 P +*1:22. 2 P *3:1, 14. 1 J *3:3. Ju *24.

13. **I come.** See on 1 T 3:14, 15. **give attendance.** Da +*9:2. **to reading.** Dt *17:19. Jsh +*1:8. =15:15 (*Kirjath-sepher*: city of books), 49 (*Kirjath-sannah*: city of study). Ps +*1:2, 3. √119:97-104. Pr *2:4, 5. +*4:7. Mt +*13:51, 52. Mk √12:24-27. Jn +√5:39. Ac *6:4. +√17:11. 2 T *2:15-17. 4:13. Re *1:3. **to exhortation.** 1 T 6:2. Ac +4:36. Ro 12:8. 1 C 14:3. 2 T 4:2. T 1:9. 2:15. **to doctrine.** ∫41, Ge +10:1. ver. +*6, *16. 1 C 14:6, *26. 2 T *4:2.

14. **Neglect not.** Mt √25:14-30. Lk *19:12-26. Ro √12:6-8. 1 C *14:12. 1 Th +*5:19. 2 T *1:6. 1 P 4:9-11. **gift.** Ro +*11:29. 1 C 12:4-11. Ja 1:17, 18. 1 P 4:10. 1 J 5:16. **which.** 1 T 1:18. Ep *3:7, 8. **by prophecy.** 1 T 1:18. **with.** 1 T 5:22. Ac +*6:6. *8:17. *13:3. *19:6. 2 T 1:6. **the presbytery.** 1 T 5:17, 19. Lk 22:66g. Ac 20:17. 22:5g.

15. **Meditate.** Jsh +*1:8. Ps +*1:2. *19:14. 49:3. 63:6. 77:12. 104:34. 105:5. *119:15, 23, 48, 97, 99, 148. 143:5. **give.** ∫41, Ge +10:1. Ac *6:4. *20:23, 24. 1 C 16:15. 2 C 4:14, 15. 8:5. T *2:14. **wholly.** T#464. Nu +*14:24. Jsh +*14:8. Lk 9:59, 60. Ac 6:2-4. Ro +*12:8, 11. 1 C 2:2. Ph *1:21. **that.** ver. 6. Mt *5:16. Ph 1:12, 25. 2:15, 16. 2 T 2:16. 3:9, 13. **to all.** *or*, in all things.

16. **Take heed.** 1 Ch 28:10. 2 Ch *19:6. Mk 13:9. Lk +*21:34. Ac +*20:28. 1 C *3:10, 11. Col 2:8, 18. 4:17. 2 T *4:2. T *2:7, 15. He 2:1. +*3:12. 4:1. +*12:15. 2 J *8. **unto the doctrine.** ver. +6. 1 T 1:3. Ro *16:17. Ep +*4:14. T 2:7. He *13:9. 2 J +*9. **continue.** ∫41, Ge +10:1. 1 S 12:14. 1 Ch 28:9. Ezr *7:10, 25. Je +*23:28n. Jn 8:31. Ac *6:4. 13:43. 14:22. *26:22. Ro 2:7. 11:22. 1 C +*15:2, 58. Col +*1:23. 2 T *3:14. T *1:9. He +*10:35. 1 J 2:24. **thou shalt.** T#468. Je *23:22. Ezk *3:19-21. *33:7-9. Da +*12:3. Mk 1:17. Jn *4:36. Ac 11:24. 14:1. *20:26, 27. 1 C +*4:15 (T#432). 9:27. **save thyself.** Ezk *14:10n. Ob +*21. Ml ◑2:12. Lk +*21:36. **and them.** Pr +*11:30. Is √55:11. Je √23:22. Da +*11:33n. *12:3. Ro *10:10-14. +11:14. 1 C *9:22. 1 Th 2:16, 19, 20. 2 T 2:10. Phm 19. Ja +*5:20.

1 TIMOTHY 5

Directions how to admonish elders, and younger persons, men and women, 1, 2: concerning the widows, who were provided for, or employed by the church; the conduct of Christians towards relations; and what was expedient for younger widows, 3-16. The honor to be shown to diligent rulers and teachers, 17, 18. How Timothy should behave towards accused elders, and offenders, 19, 20. A solemn charge to faithfulness and impartiality in ordaining pastors, 21, 22. Counsel to Timothy concerning his health, 23. The character of some is more easily known than that of others, yet that may by patience and careful investigation be ascertained, 24, 25.

1. **Rebuke.** ver. 19, 20. Le *19:32. Dt 33:9. Ga 2:11-14. **an elder.** ver. 17. Ac +*14:23. 15:4, 6. 20:17. T 1:5, 6. Ja 5:14. 1 P 5:1. 2 J 1. 3 J 1. Re 4:4. **intreat.** Ro 13:7. Ga 6:1. 2 T +*2:24, 25. Phm 9, 10. Ja 3:17. 1 P 5:5, 6. **younger men.** Lk 22:26. T 2:6. 1 P 5:5. **as brethren.** Mt 18:15-17. 23:8.

2. **elder.** ver. 3. Mt 12:50. Jn 19:26, 27. **with.** 1 T +*4:12. Ph √4:8. 1 Th 5:22. 2 T 2:22.

3. **Honor.** ∫108B, Mt +15:6. ver. 2, 17. Ex 20:12. Mt 15:6. 1 Th 2:6. 1 P 2:17. 3:7. **widows.** ver. 9. Dt 10:18. 14:29. 16:11, 14. 27:19. Jb 29:13. 31:16. Ps 68:5. 94:6. 146:9. Je 49:11. Mt 23:14. Lk 7:12. Ac 6:1. 9:39. Ja 1:27. **indeed.** ver. 4, 5, 9-11, 16. Lk 2:37. Jn 1:47.

4. **if.** ∫184A, 1 C +15:2. **nephews.** Jg 12:14mg. Jb 18:19. Is 14:22. **learn.** 1 S 22:3, 4. Pr 31:28. Lk 2:51. Jn 19:26, 27. **piety.** *or*, kindness. Mt 15:4-6. Mk 7:10-13. **to requite their parents.** Ge 45:9-11. 47:12, 28. Ru 2:2, 18. Mt 15:5, 6. 2 C ◑+*12:14. Ep +*6:1-3. **good.** See on 1 T 2:3.

5. **a widow.** ver. 3, 16. Ru 1:5, 12, 20, 21. 1 C 7:32. **and desolate.** Is 3:26. 49:21. 54:1. La 1:13. **trusteth.** 1 T 6:17. Ru 2:12. Ps 91:4. Is +*12:2. 50:10. Je +*49:11. 1 C 7:32. 1 P 3:5. 1 J *3:3. **in God.** Ps 4:5. 1 P 3:5. **continueth.** See on Lk *2:37. +*18:1, 7. Ac 26:7. Ep *6:18. **in supplications.** 1 T +2:1. **night and.** Mk +5:5.

6. **she that.** ∫125, Jb +22:6. 1 S 25:6. Jb 21:11-15. Ps 73:5-7. Is 22:13. Ezk +*16:49. Am 6:5, 6. Lk *12:19. 15:13. 16:19. Ja 5:5. Re 18:7. **in pleasure.** *or*, delicately. Dt 28:54, 56. 1 S 15:32. Pr 29:21. Is 47:1. Je 6:2. La 4:5. Lk 7:25. **is dead.** ∫145, Jg +11:40. Mt 8:22. Lk 15:24, 32. 2 C √5:14, 15. Ep √2:1, 5. 5:14. Col 2:13. Re 3:1, 2.

7. **these things.** 1 T 1:3. 4:11. 6:2, 17. 2 T +*4:1. T 1:13. 2:15. **blameless.** 1 T 3:2. 6:14.

8. **if.** ∫184A, 1 C +15:2. **provide not.** T#1863. Ro 12:13. 2 C ◑+*12:14. Ga *6:6, 10. 2 Th 3:10. Ja 2:15. 1 J 3:17. **his own.** Ac +4:23. **and specially.** Ge 30:30. Is √58:7. Mt 7:11. Lk 11:11-13. 2 C 12:14. Ga +*6:10. **house.** *or*, kindred. See on ver. 4. Is +*58:7. Ga +6:10. **hath denied.** 2 T 3:5. T 1:16. 2 P +2:1. Re 2:13. 3:8. **the faith.** 1 T +*1:19. **and is worse.** Mt 18:17. Lk +*12:47, 48. Jn 15:22. 2 C 2:15, 16. 6:15.

9. **a widow.** See on ver. 3, 4. **taken.** *or*, chosen. **under.** ver. 11, 14. Lk 2:36, 37. Ro 16:1. **having.** 1 T 3:2, 12. 1 C 7:10, 11, 39, 40. **wife of one.** Some interpreters suggest that this means not having been remarried, not to one husband at a time. Others hold that this refers to a "one-wife husband," denoting marital faithfulness. Still others, probably more correctly, hold this prohibition excludes from leadership in the church

those who have practiced polygamy (Mt √19:3n). Ge +*4:19. 1 C *7:39.

10. **Well reported**. 1 T 3:7. Ac +*6:3. 10:22. 22:12. 3 J 12. **good works**. ʃ171K2, Ex +23:4. ver. 25. 1 T 2:10. 6:18. Mt +*5:16. Ac +*9:36. Ep √2:10. 2 T +2:21. 3:17. T 2:7. √3:8, 14. He 10:24. 13:21. 1 P 2:12. **if she have brought**. ʃ184A, 1 C +15:2. 2 T 1:5. +*3:15. **if she have lodged**. ʃ184A, 1 C +15:2. 1 T +3:2. Ac *16:14, 15. Ro 12:13. He *13:2. 1 P *4:9. **washed**. Ge 18:4. 19:2. 24:32. 43:24. SS +*5:3. Lk *7:36, 38, +44. Jn *13:5-15. **saints'**. 2 C +1:1. **if she have relieved**. ʃ184A, 1 C +15:2. ver. 16. Le 25:35. 2 Ch 28:15. Is 1:17. Ac 9:39. **if she have diligently**. ʃ184A, 1 C +15:2. 1 T 6:18. Ps 119:4. Col +√1:10. 2 T 2:21. T √2:14. 3:1, 8g.

11. **the younger**. ver. 9, 14. **refuse**. 1 T +4:7. **to wax**. Dt 32:15. Is 3:16. Ho 13:6. Ja 5:5. 2 P 2:18. Re 18:3, 7, 9. **they will**. ver. 14. 1 T 4:3. 1 C 7:39, 40.

12. **damnation**. 1 C 11:34. Ja 3:1. 1 P 4:17g. **their**. 2 C *6:14. Ga 1:6. Re *2:4, 5. **first**. ʃ96E5, Jn +1:15.

13. **to be idle**. T#358. 1 Ch +22:16 (T#1). Pr *6:6-9. 15:19. 18:9. *19:15. 20:4, 13. 21:25, 26. *23:21. *24:30-34. ●31:27. Ec *10:18. Ezk +*16:49 (T#709). Col ●+*4:5. 2 Th √3:6-12. **wandering**. Le 19:16. Pr 7:11, 12. 20:19. +*25:17. Lk 10:7. Ac 20:20. T 1:11. *2:4, 5. **tattlers**. Pr +*11:13. Ro +*1:29. 3 J 10g. **busybodies**. 1 C 7:9. 2 Th *3:11, 12. 1 P +*4:15. **speaking**. Pr 17:9. Mt +*12:36. Ac 20:30. Col ●*4:6. T 1:11. Ja 3:10. 3 J 10.

14. **I will**. See on 1 T *2:8. **the younger**. ver. *11. 1 T 4:3. 1 C 7:8, 9. He +*13:4. **guide the house**. Gr. *oikodespotein*, ✱S#3616g, only here (see note at Ac 16:15). Ge *18:6, 9. Pr 14:1. 31:27-29. T 2:5g. **give none**. 1 T 6:1. 2 S √12:14. Da 6:4. Ro 14:13. 2 C 11:12. Col *4:5. T 2:5, 8. 1 P *4:14, 15. **occasion**. Ro +7:8. **the adversary**. 1 C 16:9. Ph 1:28. **to speak reproachfully**. Gr. for their railing. Lk 23:35-41.

15. **already turned aside**. 1 T 1:20. 4:1n. Ph +*3:18, 19. 2 T 1:15. 2:18. 4:10. He +*10:38. 2 P *2:2, 20-22. 3:16. 1 J √2:19. Ju 4, 5. Re 12:9. **Satan**. 1 C +5:5.

16. **If**. ʃ184A, 1 C +15:2. **let them relieve**. See on ver. 4, 8, 10. **church be charged**. 2 C 1:8. 5:4g. 1 Th +2:6. **widows indeed**. ver. 3, 5.

17. **the elders**. See on ver. 1, 19. 1 T +4:14. T 1:5. **rule well**. 1 T *3:4, 5. Mt +√24:45. Lk +*12:42. Ro +*12:8n. 1 C 12:28. 2 C √1:24. +*10:8. 1 Th *5:12, 13. He √13:7, 17, 24. 1 P +*5:3. **be counted worthy**. See on ver. 3, 18. Lk 10:7. +*21:36. Ac 28:10. Ro √15:27. 1 C *9:5-14. Ga +*6:6. Ph 2:29. +*4:17. Col +*1:10. 1 Th +*1:5, 11. He *13:7, 16. **double**. ʃ121L9, Ge +43:12. **honor**. ʃ108B, Mt +15:6. Ge +*14:20. Dt 15:18. 21:17. 1 S +*9:7. 2 K 2:9. Jb *42:10-12. Is +*40:2. Je 16:18. *17:18. Zc +*9:12. 1 C 9:14. +*16:2. **labor**. 1 T 4:10. 2 Ch *17:9. Mt 9:37, 38. Lk 10:1, 2, 7. Jn 4:38. Ac +*20:35. Ro 16:+6, 12. 1 C 3:9. *15:10. 16:16. 2 C 6:1. Ph 2:16. 4:3. Col *1:28, 29. 1 Th 5:12. 2 T 2:6. **word**. 1 T 4:6, 16. Ac +8:4. 2 T *4:2. **and doctrine**. 1 T +4:6g.

18. **the scripture**. Lk +4:21. Ro 4:3. 9:17. 10:11. 11:2. Ga 3:8. Ja 4:5. **Thou**. Dt ▶25:4. 1 C *9:9, 10. **The laborer**. Le +*19:13. Dt +*24:14, 15. Je +*22:13 (T#1851). Ml +*3:5. Mt *10:10. 20:13n. Lk ▶10:7. 1 C √9:7n, 14n. 1 Th *4:2n. Ja +*5:4.

19. **Against an elder**. Every servant of Christ must exercise diligence in living absolutely above reproach (Ac +*6:3. Ro 14:22. 1 Th +*5:22. T *2:8), lest the ministry be blamed (2 C +*6:3). Yet despite such care, misunderstandings and ugly situations will arise (Lk 16:1n. 2 T *3:12), frequently from lack of communication between the accuser and the accused. Words and actions are consistently misread, and wrong motives assigned, which in the imagination of the accuser run wild and rampant with no foundation in reality. And it takes but little effort to find two "witnesses" to agree in a false accusation. Any person in the church, whether elder, pastor, teacher, or custodian, will have repeated and sometimes painful experiences where his words or actions will be misinterpreted, and taken completely out of context. The corrective for such problems is to teach forthrightly the penalty Scripture assigns for the false accuser (Dt *19:18, 19). Teach the necessity of godly forbearance and suspension of judgment until all concerned parties have been fully heard, the evidence is in, and all due process appeal procedures have been exhausted. Teach the need to keep channels of communication open in both directions (1 S +*25:17. 2 K +*5:13). Teach the proper response to correction (Ps 25:9. +*141:5. Pr +*9:8, 9. Jn 15:20, 21), as well as the proper means of offering it (Le +*19:17. Pr 27:6. Ro +*12:8n. Ga √6:1. Ep +*6:9). Teach the requirement that scrupulous adherence to every principle of due process be maintained (Le +*19:13, 15. Jn +*7:51. Col 4:1). Christians in positions of management in the workplace need to follow the same principles in maintaining proper employer/employee relations. **receive not**. Accusations against an elder which cannot be substantiated by credible, disinterested witnesses are not even to be investigated, but ignored, suppressed, and silenced. Ex +*23:1mg. Le +*19:15. Ps *15:3mg. Pr +*18:13. Jn 18:29. Ac 24:2-13. *25:16. T 1:6. **an accusation**. Ge +*38:19. Ex +*23:1, 2. Ps +*101:5. Pr +*9:8. +*13:18. +*17:10. +*18:13. Mt √18:15. Lk +*16:1n. Jn +*7:24, 51. Ep +*5:11. +*6:9. Col +*4:1. **before**. *or*, under. **two**. Dt 17:6. √19:15, 18, 19. Mt +18:16. Jn 8:17. 2 C 13:1. He 10:28.

20. **Them that sin**. The present active participle refers to those that continue to sin; continue, that is, after appropriate private correction has taken place (ver. +*19n), and no change for the better has occurred. Jn 5:29n. Ga 5:21n. He +*10:26. 1 J +*3:8. **rebuke**. T#461. Le +*19:17. 1 S 13:13, 14. 2 S 12:7. 1 K 18:17, 18. 21:20. Pr +*9:8. +28:23 (T#610). *27:5. Is *58:1. Ezk 16:2. Mi 3:8. Mt 18:15. Jn 8:9. +16:8g. Ac 2:23. 7:51-53. Ga √2:+11 (T#611), 12-14. Ep +*5:11. 2 T √4:2. T *1:9-11, 13. 2:15. Ju 15g. **before all**. Public exposure and rebuke is the final stage of the disciplinary process, reserved for those elders who, after due process procedures have been exhausted, and after private rebuke has been administered, are found to be continuing obstinately in the sin. Ga 2:14. **that others**. 1 T *1:20. Dt 13:11. 17:13. +*19:20. *21:21. Ac *5:5, 11. *19:17.

21. **charge**. 1 T 6:13. 1 Th +4:6. 5:27. 2 T 2:14. +*4:1. **before**. Lk 9:26. +12:8. **the elect angels**. Zc +*3:7. Mt +*16:27. 18:10. *25:31, 32, 41. 1 C 4:9. 11:10. 2 P *2:4. Ju *6. Re 12:7-9. 14:10. **observe**. Ps 107:43. 119:34. Mt *28:20. **without preferring**. *or*, without prejudice. Le +*19:15. Dt 1:7. 33:9. Pr 18:5. Lk 20:21. Ac 15:37, 38. 2 C +*5:16. **partiality**. Ge +*44:30. Ps *15:2-5. Ml 2:9. Ja *2:1-4. 3:17.

22. **Lay hands**. This has reference to ordination. T#401. 1 T +4:14. Nu 27:22, 23. Ac 6:6. *13:2, 3.

2 T 1:6. He 6:2. **suddenly.** This applies equally to new candidates for ordination, or restoring a wayward elder to fellowship (ver. 20). 1 T √3:6, 10. Jsh 9:14. 2 T +*2:2. T 1:5-9. **neither.** Ex +*23:2. Ps +*119:63. 139:22. Pr +*1:10. 16:1. Da 1:8. Ep +*5:11. 2 J +*9-11. Re *18:4. **keep.** ſ136, Is +60:12. 1 T +*4:12. Ac 18:6. *20:26. Ja 1:27. 2 P +*3:14. 1 J *3:3.

23. **but use.** 1 T *3:3, 8. *4:4. Le 10:9-11. Ps 104:15. Pr 31:4-7. Ezk 44:21. Ep +*5:18. T 1:7. 2:3.

24. **sins.** ver. 20, 22. **are open.** Je 2:34. Ac 1:16-20. 5:1-11. *8:18. 1 C *5:3. Ga +*5:19-21. 2 T 4:10. He 7:14. 2 P *2:20, 21. **going before.** 1 T 1:18. T 3:11. **to judgment.** Mt *5:21. 18:17. Jn +*7:24. **follow after.** Nu +*32:23. Pr *13:15. Ro *2:16. 1 C 4:5. 2 C 4:2.

25. **the good works.** 1 T *3:7. +6:18. Mt √5:16. Ac +*9:36. 10:22. *16:1-3. 22:12. Ga √5:22, 23. Ph 1:11. **cannot.** Ps *37:5, 6. Pr 10:9. Mt +*6:3-6. √10:26. Lk 11:33.

1 TIMOTHY 6

The duty of servants to unbelieving and to believing masters, 1, 2. Timothy must shun those, as corrupters of the gospel, who teach things contrary to the apostle's doctrine, 3-5. The advantage of godliness with contentment, 6-8. The mischiefs arising from the love of money, 9, 10. The apostle exhorts Timothy to flee from these evils; to "follow after righteousness," and "to fight the good fight of faith," 11, 12; and most solemnly charges him to be faithful till the coming of Christ, 13, 14. He ascribes glory to the eternal God, 15, 16. Timothy must charge the rich to avoid pride, and confidence in wealth; and to abound in liberality, as seeking a treasure in heaven, against the time to come, 18, 19; and he must adhere to the faith, avoiding profane and vain controversies, 20, 21.

1. **servants.** Dt 28:48. Is 47:6. 58:6. Mt *11:29, 30. Ac 15:10. 1 C 7:21, 22. Ga *5:1. T 2:9. 1 P +*2:18. **count.** Ge +*16:9. 24:2, 12, 27, 35, etc. 2 K *5:2, 3, +*13. Ml 1:6. Ac 10:7, 22. Ep +*6:5-8. Col +*3:22-25. T 2:9. 1 P *2:17-20. **that the name.** 1 T +5:14. Ge 13:7, 8. 2 S +*12:14. Ne 9:5. Is 52:5. Ezk 36:20, 23. Lk 17:1. Ro 2:24. 1 C *10:32. T 2:5, 8, 10. Ja +2:7. 1 P *2:12. *3:16. **his.** ſ63A3, Mt +19:13. **doctrine.** ver. 3. 1 T +4:6.

2. **believing masters.** Col +*4:1. Phm 10-16. **let.** Ge 16:4, 5. Nu 16:3. Mt 6:24. 2 P 2:10. Ju 8. **because they are brethren.** 2 T 5:1. Mt 23:8. 25:40. Ro +*8:29. Ga 3:26-29. Col *3:11. Phm +16. **because they are.** Ga 5:6. Ep 1:1, 15. Col 1:2, 4. 3:12. 2 Th 1:3. Phm 5-7. **faithful.** *or,* believing. **partakers.** Jl +*2:28. Lk 1:54. Ac 20:35g. Ro 11:17. Ep 3:6. He *3:1, 14. 1 P *5:1. **These.** 1 T 4:11. 5:7. T 2:1, 15. √3:8. **exhort.** 1 T +4:13.

3. **if.** ſ184A, 1 C +15:2. **any.** 1 C +11:16. **teach otherwise.** 1 T 1:+3, 6. Ro 16:17. 2 C 13:2, 3. Ga *1:6-8. **to wholesome.** 1 T +*1:10. Pr 15:4. 2 T 1:13. 4:3. T 1:9. 2:1, 2g, 8. √3:8. **the words.** Mt *10:20. 22:21. 28:20. 1 Th 4:1, 2, 8. **the doctrine.** ver. 1. 1 T +4:6-8. T 1:1. √2:11-14. 2 P +*1:3-7. **according.** T 1:1. **godliness.** ver. 11. 1 T +*3:16.

4. **He is.** 1 T 1:7. 3:6. Pr 13:7. 25:14. 26:12. Ac 8:9, 21-23. Ro +*12:16. 1 C *3:18. 8:1, 2. Ga 6:3. Col *2:18. 2 Th 2:4. 2 T 3:4. 2 P 2:12, 18. Ju 10, 16. Re 3:17. **proud.** *or,* a fool. **knowing nothing.** ſ171C,

---

Ex +20:10. 1 T 1:7. 1 C *8:2. **doting.** *or,* sick. **about.** 1 T 1:4. 2 T *2:23. **words.** Is 58:4. Ac 15:2. Ro 2:8. 13:13. 14:1. 1 C 3:3. 11:16, 18. 2 C 11:20. Ga 5:15, 20, 21, 26. Ph 1:15. +*2:3, 14. 2 T 2:14. T 3:9. Ja 1:19, 20. 2:14-18. 4:1, 2, 5, 6. 1 P *2:1, 2. **envy.** Ro +*1:29. **railings.** Ep +4:31. **evil surmisings.** 1 C ◐13:5.

5. **Perverse,** etc. *or,* Gallings one of another. 1 T 1:6. 1 C *11:16. **men.** Mt *7:17-20. 12:33. Jn √3:19-21. Ep 4:17-19, 22. 2 Th +*2:8-11. 2 T 3:8. T *1:15, 16. He +*3:12, 13. 2 J +*8-10. **destitute of the truth.** 1 T +1:19. +*4:1n. T 1:14. **supposing that gain.** ver. 6. 1 T 3:3, 8. 2 K 5:20-27. Is *56:11. Je 6:13. *8:10. Ezk +*33:31. Zc √11:5. Mt 21:13. 23:14. Ac *8:18-20. 19:24-28. 2 C ◐11:7. Ph ◐*3:7, 8. T 1:11. 2 P 2:3, 15. Ju 11. Re √3:17. 18:3, 13. **is godliness.** ſ101, Dt +32:42. ver. 3, 11. 1 T +*3:16. **withdraw.** T#177. 2 Ch +19:2 (T#112). Ps +√119:63. Mt +*15:14 (T#477). 18:17. Ro +*16:17, 18. 1 C 5:11. Ga 1:8, 9. 2 Th *3:6. 2 T *3:5. T *3:10, 11. 2 J *10. Re +18:4 (T#115).

6. **godliness.** See on 1 T *4:8. Ps *37:16. *84:11. Pr *3:13-18. 8:18-21. *15:16. +*16:8. 30:8. Mt √6:32, 33. Lk *12:31, 32. Ro 5:3-5. +*8:28. 2 C √4:17, 18. 5:1. Ph 1:21. He +*13:5. **contentment.** T#928. ver. 8. Ex 2:21. Pr 14:30. 15:15. 17:22. 23:17, 18. Lk 3:14. 2 C *9:8g. Ph √4:11-13. He +*13:5. **great gain.** ſ145, Jg +11:40. 2 C *9:8. Ph *3:7, 8.

7. **we brought.** Jb *1:21. Pr 27:24. Ec 5:15, 16. **world.** Gr. *kosmos,* Mt +4:8. **certain.** Jb 27:19. Ps *39:6. √49:17. Lk *12:19-21. *16:22, 23.

8. **having food.** ſ171K2, Ex +23:4. Food and raiment are put by example for this world's goods. Ge +*28:20-22. 48:15. Dt 2:7. 8:3, 4. Pr 27:23-27. *30:8, 9. Ec 2:24-26. 3:12, 13. Mt √6:11, 25-33. He +*13:5, 6. 1 J 3:17. **let us.** lit. we shall. ſ96C10, Jg +5:21. **content.** T#1873. Ps +*62:10. Pr 27:26, 27. Lk +*12:15.

9. **that will.** ſ108B. Idiom B828. "To will" is an idiom used for to wish to do anything speedily and spontaneously. It is also used for eager desire. For other instances of this idiom see 2 C 8:10mg. Mk 10:35. 12:38. Ga 4:21. **be rich.** Ge √13:10-13. Nu *22:17-19. Jsh √7:21. 2 K *5:20-27. Ps +*10:3. Pr √15:27. *20:21. *21:6. √22:16. *23:4. √28:20-22. Is 5:8. Ho *12:7, 8. Am 8:4-6. Zc √11:5. Mt +*13:22. *19:22. 26:15. Mk +*4:19. Ja +*5:1-4. 2 P *2:15, 16. Ju *11. **snare.** 1 T +*3:7. Dt *7:25. Ps 11:6. Pr *1:17-19. Lk +*21:34, 35. 2 T *2:26. **many.** Mk +*4:19. Ep 4:22. 1 J √2:15-17. **which.** 1 T +1:19. Nu *31:8. Jsh √7:24-26. Mt *27:3-5. Ac *5:4, 5. *8:20. 2 P 2:3.

10. **the love of money.** 1 T 3:3. Ge 34:23, 24. 38:16. Ex *23:7, 8. Dt 16:19. *23:4, 5, 18. Jg 17:10, 11. 18:19, 20, 29-31. 2 S *4:10, 11. Pr *1:19. Is 1:23. *56:11. Je 5:27, 28. Ezk 13:19. 16:33. *22:12. Mi *3:11. 7:3, 4. Ml *1:10. Mt 23:14. Lk 16:14. Ac *1:16-19. 1 C 5:10. 2 T 3:2. T *1:11. He +*13:5. Re 18:13. **the root.** Ex 23:8. Dt 16:19. **coveted.** ver. *21. 1 T 3:1. Ps +*10:3. 2 T *4:10. He 11:16g. Ju 11. Re 2:14, 15. **erred.** *or,* been seduced. He +*3:13. +*10:38. +*12:15. **the faith.** ver. 21. 1 T +1:19. **and pierced.** Ge 19:14, 26, 31, etc. 2 K 5:27. Ps *32:10. Pr 1:31. 2 P *2:7, 8.

11. **But.** 2 T 2:22. **O man.** ver. 20. Dt 33:1. Jsh 14:6. Jg 13:6. 1 S 2:27. 9:6. 1 K 12:22. 13:1, 26. 17:18, 24. 20:28. 2 K 1:9, 13. 5:20. 23:17. 1 Ch 23:14. 2 Ch 8:14. 30:16. Ezr 3:2. Ne 12:24, 36. Je 35:4. 2 T *3:17. **flee.** 1 C +*6:18. 10:14. 2 T *2:22. **follow after.** 1 T

5:10. Dt 16:20. Ps 34:14. 38:20. Pr *15:9. 21:21. Is 51:1. Mt +*5:6. Ro 9:30. 14:19. 1 C 14:1. 2 T 2:22. He +*12:14. 1 P 3:11. **righteousness.** 1 T +*4:12. Pr *15:9. Ga +*5:22, 23. Ph √4:8, 9. T √2:11, 12. 2 P √1:5-7. **godliness.** ver. 3, 5, 6. 1 T +*3:16. **faith.** 1 T 1:14. 1 C +*4:1, 2. **love.** 2 T +*3:10. **patience.** Ro +*15:4. **meekness.** Mt *11:29. 2 T 2:25.

12. **Fight.** 1 T 1:18. Zc 10:5. 1 C +*9:25, 26. 2 C 6:7. *10:3-5. Ep *6:10-18. 1 Th 5:8, 9. 2 T *2:3. 4:7. Ju +*3. **good.** ſ101, Dt +32:42. **fight of faith.** Ph +1:30. **lay hold.** ſ108A6, Jn +7:52. Denoting, "thou shalt lay hold of." ver. 19. Ps 63:8. Pr 3:18. SS 3:4. Ph 3:12-14. He +*3:14. *6:18. 1 J 2:25. Re 3:3. **eternal.** Gr. *aionios*, Mt +18:8. Jn √17:3. Ac 13:46g. **whereunto.** Ro +*8:28-30. 9:23, 24. Col 3:15. 1 Th 2:12. 2 Th 2:14. 2 T +*1:9. 1 P 3:9. +*5:10. **hast.** ver. 13. Dt 26:3, 17-19. Is 44:5. Lk 12:8, 9. Ro √10:9, 10. 2 C +9:13. He *10:23. 2 P +*1:10, 11. **good.** ſ101, Dt +32:42.

13. **give.** See on 1 T 5:21. 2 T +*4:1, 2. **who quickeneth.** Dt 32:39. 1 S 2:6. Lk 17:33. Jn +*5:21, 26. *11:25, 26. √14:6. Ac 7:19. 17:25. Re 21:6. 22:1. **who before.** Mt 27:11. Jn +*18:36, 37. 19:11. Re +*1:5. +*3:14. **Pilate.** Mt +27:2. **confession.** *or*, profession. ver. 12. 2 C +9:13.

14. **keep.** ver. 20. 1 T 4:11-16. 1 Ch 28:9, 10, 20. Col *4:17. **without.** SS 4:7. Ep +*5:27. He *9:14. Ja 1:27. 1 P 1:19. 2 P √3:14. **unrebukable.** 1 T 3:2. 5:7. Jn +*17:6. Ph 2:15. Col 1:22. Ju √24. **until.** 1 C +*1:8. Ph *1:6, 10. 1 Th +*3:13. +*5:23. 2 Th +*2:1, 8. 2 T +*4:1n. T √2:13. He √9:28. 1 P 1:7. 1 J √3:2. Re +*1:7.

15. **times.** ſ96F2, Ge +4:10. **who.** See on 1 T 1:11, 17. Ps 47:2. 83:18. Je 10:10. 46:18. Da 2:44-47. 4:34. Mt +*6:13. **his times.** 1 T +2:6. Ac +*1:6, 7. **blessed.** 1 T 1:11. **the King.** Ezr 7:12. Pr 8:15. Da 4:34. Re √17:14. √19:16. **of kings.** ſ147H, Ge +9:25. **Lord of.** Dt 10:17. Ps 136:3. Da 2:47. Jn +*20:28. T *2:13. He 1:2.

16. **Who only.** If this limits the possession of immortality to God alone, then by a similar process of reasoning, Ro 16:27 restricts the possession of wisdom exclusively to him likewise. Of course, both statements, correctly interpreted, ascribe inherent wisdom and immortality to God, but do not limit their possession to Him alone (see Ec +*3:19n. Ezk 32:27n). See on 1 T *1:17. Ex +*3:14. Dt 32:40. Ps *90:2. Is +*57:15. Jn √8:58. He +*13:8. Re +*1:8, 17, 18. **immortality.** Gr. *athanasia*, ✱S#110g, only here and 1 C 15:53g, 54g. 1 T 1:17n. 1 Th +*5:23n. 2 T +*1:10. **dwelling.** Ps 104:2. Hab 3:4. 1 J *1:5. 1 J 1:7. Re *1:16, 17. 21:23. 22:5. **can approach.** Jb 37:23. Ec *3:11. **no man hath seen.** Ex *33:20. Jb 23:8, 9. Mt +*28:19n. Jn +*1:18. 6:46. *14:9. Col +*1:15. 1 J 4:12. **to whom.**

See on 1 T √1:17. Ro *16:25-27. Ep 3:21. Ph 4:20. Ju *25. Re *1:6. 4:11. 7:12. **honor.** 1 T +1:17. Jn √5:23. Re *4:11. **power.** 1 P +4:11. **everlasting.** Gr. *aionios*, Mt +18:8. Ro *16:26. He *9:14. Re 22:13.

17. **Charge.** See on ver. 13. 1 T 1:3. *5:21. **rich.** Ge *13:2. Jb *1:1-3. Pr +*10:22. Mt *19:23. 27:57. Lk 19:2, 9, 10. **in this world.** Gr. *aion*, Mt +6:13. Lk 16:8. Jn +*6:54n. 1 C 1:20. 2 T *4:10. T *2:12. **that they.** Dt √6:10-12. 8:17. 33:15. 2 Ch 26:16. *32:25, 26. Ps +*10:3, 4. 73:5-9. Pr *30:9. Je 2:31. *9:23. Ezk 16:+*49, 50, 56. Da 4:30. 5:19-23. Ho *13:6. Hab 1:15, 16. Ro *11:20. +*12:3, 16. Ph +*2:3. Ja *1:9, 10. Re *18:6, 7. **nor trust.** Jb 31:24, 25. Ps *52:7. +*62:10. Pr 11:28. Je +*9:23, 24. *48:7. Mk +*10:24. Lk *12:15-21. Ep +*5:5. **uncertain riches.** Gr. the uncertainty of riches. Pr *23:5. *27:24. Ec 5:13, 14. Hg *1:6. Mt +*13:22. **but.** Ps *62:8. *84:11, 12. 118:8, 9. Je +*17:7, 8. **the living.** See on 1 T *3:15. *4:10. 1 Th *1:9. **who giveth.** Ps 104:28. Pr +*10:22. Mt *6:32. Ac +14:17. *17:25. Ro +*8:32. 2 C 9:11. **richly.** Pr +*10:22. Mt √6:31, 33. Ec 5:18, 19. Ro *8:18. 1 C *2:9. Col *3:16. T *3:6mg.

18. **they do good.** T#628. 2 Ch *24:16. Ps *37:3. Ec 3:12. Mt +10:8 (T#406). Lk +*6:33-35. Ac *10:38. Ga +*6:10. He *13:16. 1 P 3:11. 3 J *11. **rich in.** 1 T 5:10. Lk √12:21. Ac +*9:36. T √2:14. √3:8. Ja +*2:5. **good works.** 1 T 2:10. 5:10, 25. Ac +*9:36. Ep *2:10. +*5:11. T 2:7, 14. √3:8, 14. He 10:24. 1 P 2:12. **ready.** Dt √15:7-11. Ps 112:9. Pr *11:24, 25. Ec *11:1, 2, 6. Is 32:8. *58:7. Mt +*6:19, 20. Lk +*6:35, 38. *14:12-14. Ac 2:44, 45. 4:34-37. *11:29. +*20:35. Ro *12:8, 13. 1 C +*16:2. 2 C 8:1, 2, *9, *12. 9:6-15. Ga *6:6. Ph *4:18, 19. He *13:16. 1 J *3:17. **willing to communicate.** *or*, sociable. *or*, ready to sympathize. Dt 10:19. Ro +*12:13, 15. He *13:16.

19. **Laying up.** ſ46B, Ex +5:21. Ps 17:14. Mt √6:19-21. √10:41, 42. *19:21. *25:34-40. Lk *12:33. *16:9. 18:2, *22. 2 C *9:6. Ga +*6:8, 9. Ph +*4:17n. **foundation.** Pr *10:25. Lk *6:48, 49. Ga 5:6. Ep *3:17. 2 T *2:19. **the time.** 1 T *4:8. Pr 31:25. Lk 16:9, 25. +*21:36. Jn +*6:54n. **lay hold.** See on ver. 12. Lk 19:9. Ph *3:14. 1 P +*1:4. **eternal.** Gr. *aionios*, Mt +18:8. 2 T 1:1.

20. **O Timothy.** ver. 11. 2 T 2:1. **keep.** ver. 14. 1 T 1:11. Ro 3:2. 2 Th 1:4. 2:15. 2 T +*1:12-14. 3:14. *4:5. T *1:9. Re 3:3. **avoiding.** ver. 4, 5. 1 T 1:4, 6. 4:7. Col 2:8. 2 T 2:14-16, 23. 3:5. 4:4. T 1:4, 14. 3:9. **profane.** 1 T +1:9. **vain babblings.** 2 T 2:16. **oppositions.** Ac 17:18, 21. Ro 1:22. 1 C 1:19-23. 2:6. *3:19. Col 2:8, 18.

21. **some.** 1 C +11:16. **have erred.** ver. *10. 1 T +*1:6, 19. 2 T 2:14, 18g. He +*3:10-12. **the faith.** ver. 10. 1 T +1:19. **Grace.** Ro +*1:7. 16:20, 24. Col +4:18. 2 T 4:22. T 3:15. He *13:25. **Amen.** Mt +*6:13.

2 TIMOTHY

2 TIMOTHY 1

The apostle affectionately salutes Timothy with thanksgiving and prayer, 1-3, and expresses a great desire of seeing him, 4; remembering his faith, and that of his grandmother and mother, 5. He exhorts him to stir up the gift of God which was in him, 6.

He charges him not to be ashamed of the divine testimony, or of him the Lord's prisoner; but to prepare for suffering; as having been saved, and called by the grace of God, according to the gospel, which fully reveals life and immortality, 7-10. Of this, Paul had been made an apostle; for which cause he suffered, without being either ashamed or afraid, as he knew the power of him in whom he trusted, 11, 12. He exhorts Timothy to steadfastness and faithfulness, 13, 14; shows that those of Asia had turned from him, 15; and commends the diligent and courageous kindness of Onesiphorus; praying fervently that he and his family might find mercy from God at the last day, 16-18.

1. **an.** Ac *26:15-18. See on Ro 1:1. 2 C +1:1. **by the will.** 1 C +1:1. **according.** Ga +3:29. **the promise.** Jn *5:24, 39, 40. 6:40, 54. √10:28. √17:3. Ro *5:21. *6:23. 2 C 1:20. Ep *3:6. T *1:2. He 9:15. 2 P 1:3, 4. 1 J 2:25. √5:11-13. **of life.** 1 T 6:19. **in Christ Jesus.** 1 T +1:14.

2. **Timothy.** i.e. *valued of God; honored of God,* ✛S#5095g. Ac +16:1. Ro 12:19. 2 C 1:1. Ph 4:1. See on 1 T 1:*2, 18. 6:20. Phm 1. He 13:23. **beloved son.** 2 T 2:1. 1 C *4:17. 3 J +4. **Grace.** ⌡173, Ge +27:44. See on Ro 1:7. 1 T +1:2. **and peace.** ⌡174, Ge +18:27.

3. **I thank.** See Ro +1:8. Ep 1:16. **whom.** ver. 5. Ac 22:3. +24:14. 26:4. *27:23. **from.** 2 T 3:15. Ac +22:3. Ga 1:14. **pure conscience.** Ac +*23:1. 24:16. Ro 1:9. 9:1. 2 C *1:12. 1 T 1:5, 19. *3:9. T 1:15. He *13:18. **that.** See on Ro *1:9. 1 Th 1:2, 3. 3:10. **night.** See on Lk 2:37. Mk +5:5.

4. **desiring.** 2 T 4:9, 21. Ro 1:11. 15:30-32. Ph +1:8. 2:26. 1 Th 2:17-20. 3:1. **being.** Ac 20:19, 31, *37, 38. Re 7:17. 21:4. **filled.** Ps 126:5. Is 61:3. Je 31:13. Jn 16:22, 24. 1 J 1:4.

5. **I call.** Ps 77:6. **unfeigned.** Ps 17:1. 18:44. 66:3. 81:15mg. Je 3:10. Jn 1:47. Ro 12:9. 2 C 6:6. 1 T 1:5. 4:6. Ja +3:17g. 1 P 1:22. **that is.** ⌡63I2, Jsh +3:3. The words "that is" should have been placed in *italics*, for there is no verb in the Greek. The ellipsis (of repetition: from succeeding clause) may be supplied: "Taking remembrance of the unfeigned faith (dwelling in thee)." **Lois.** i.e. *superior; pleasing; no flight,* ✱S#3090g. **thy mother.** 2 T +*3:15. Ps 22:10. 86:16. 116:16. Ac *16:1. **Eunice.** i.e. *good victory; well won,* ✱S#2131g. **I am.** ver. 12. Ac 26:26. Ro 4:21. 8:38. 14:5, 14. 15:14. He +*6:9. 11:13.

6. **I put.** 2 T 2:14. Is 43:26. 1 T 4:6. 2 P 1:12. 3:1. Ju 5. **that.** 2 T *4:2. Ex 35:26. 36:2. Mt 25:15, etc. Lk 19:13. Ro *12:6-8. 1 C *12:7. Col *4:17. 1 Th +*5:19. 1 T *4:14. 1 P 4:10, 11. **by the.** Ac 8:17, 18. 19:6. 1 T 4:14. He 6:2.

7. **the spirit.** Gr. *pneuma,* ⌡121A2, Mt +5:3n. Is 11:2. Ac *20:24. 21:13. Ro +*8:15. He 2:15. 1 J *4:18. **of fear.** Ge ◖+*19:30. Ps +√34:4. Is +*12:2 (T#814). Jn 14:27. 1 J *4:18. Re 21:8. **but.** ⌡63I1D, Nu +26:4. Supply ellipsis, "but (God hath given to us the spirit)." **of power.** Mi *3:8. Zc *4:6. Lk 10:19. *24:49. Ac +*1:8. 6:8. 9:22. *10:38. 1 C *2:4, 5. **of love.** Ro *5:5. Ga *5:22. Col 1:8. 1 P *1:22. **a sound mind.** ver. +*13. Ps *119:80. Pr *2:7. *8:14. Is *59:15mg. Je 29:26. Ho 9:7. Lk *8:35. *15:17. Ac *26:11, 25. 2 C 5:13, 14. Gr. *sophronismou,* ✱S#4995g, only here. The word means self-discipline, self control, and prudence in living a "measured and orderly life" (TDNT, vol. 7, p. 1103) before the world. The concept connected with the word group to which this word belongs (in terms of associated words from the same or related roots) has reference to living soberly and righteously in this present world in watchful expectation of Christ's coming, as well as reference to avoidance of ecstatic and eschatological frenzy (2 C 5:12, 13. 1 P 4:7). Trench remarks of the related word *sophrosunee* at 1 T 2:9 that it refers to "that inner self-government, with its

constant rein on all the passions and desires" (*Synonyms,* Sec. 20, p. 71, 72). Pr +*22:3. Ac 26:25. Ro +*12:3, 16. 1 T 2:9, 15. 3:2. T 1:8. 2:2, 4, 5, 12. 1 P *4:7.

8. **ashamed.** ver. 12, 16. Ps 119:46. Is 51:7. Mk +*8:38. Lk 9:26. Ac 5:41. Ro √1:16. 9:33. Ep 3:13. 1 P 4:14. **the testimony.** Ps *19:7. Is +*8:20. Jn 15:27. 19:35. 1 C +1:6. Ep 4:17. 1 T √2:6. 1 J *4:14. √5:11, 12. Re 1:2. √12:11. *19:10. **our Lord.** 1 T 1:14. He 7:14. **his prisoner.** ver. 16. 1 T 2:9. See on Ep 3:1. 4:1. Ph 1:7. **be thou partaker.** 2 T 2:3, 9, 11, 12. *4:5. Mk +8:35. Ro 8:17, 18, 36. 1 C 4:9-13. 2 C 11:23-27. Ph 3:10. Col 1:24. 1 Th 3:4. 1 P 4:13-15. Re 1:9. *12:11. **afflictions.** Ac *20:23, 24. *21:13. 2 C *12:10. **according.** 2 T 4:17. Ro 16:25. 2 C 6:7. √12:9, 10. Ph √4:13. Col *1:11. 1 P +*1:5. Ju *24.

9. **hath saved.** Mt 1:21. Ac 2:47. Ro 13:11. 1 C 1:18. Ep 2:5, 8. 1 T +1:1. T 3:4, 5. **called.** Ro +*8:28, 30. 9:24. 1 Th 1:4. 4:7. 2 Th *2:13, 14. He 3:1. 1 P 1:15, 16. 2:9, 20, 21. 2 P +1:3. **holy calling.** Ro +*11:29. 2 Th +*1:11. **not.** Ro 3:20. 9:11. 11:5, 6. Ep 2:9. Ph ◖*2:12. T *3:5. **according to his.** Dt 7:7, 8. Is 14:26, 27. Mt 11:25, 26. Lk 10:21. Ro +3:27. +*8:28. Ep 1:9, +*11. **own purpose.** Dt *7:7, 8. Jn 15:16. Ro +*8:28. 9:11-13, 16. 10:20. 1 C 1:27-29. Ep 1:3-7, *9. *3:11. **and grace.** Ac +*15:11. **which.** Jn √6:37. √10:28, 29. 17:9. 1 C +*1:4. 3:21, 22. Ep 1:3. **before.** Jn 17:24. Ac 15:18. Ro 16:25. Ep +1:4. 3:11. 2 Th +*2:13. T *1:2. 1 P 1:20. Re 13:8. 17:8. **the world.** Gr. *aionios,* Mt +18:8. lit. ages of time.

10. **now.** Is 25:7. 60:2, 3. Lk 2:31, 32. Ro +16:26. Ep 1:9. Col *1:26, 27. T 1:3. *2:11. 1 P *1:20, 21. 1 J 1:2. **the appearing.** 2 Th +*2:8. **our.** Is 43:3. 45:15, 21. Lk +2:11. Jn 4:42. Ac 5:31. 13:23. Ep 5:23. Ph 3:20. T 1:4. *2:13. 3:4, 6. 2 P 1:1, 11. 2:20. 3:2, 18. 1 J 4:14. **who.** Is 25:8. Ho 13:14. Jn *11:25, 26. Ac 2:24. 1 C √15:54, 55. He *2:14, 15. Re 20:14. **abolished.** Lk 13:7. Ro 3:31. 5:12-21. 6:6. 1 C 15:26. Ga 5:4g. **and hath brought.** ⌡63H, Ge +12:15. ver. 1. Jb 33:30. Jn *5:24-29, 40. √14:6. √20:31. Ro *2:7. 5:17, 18. 1 C 15:53. 2 C 5:4. 2 P 1:3. 1 J 1:2. Re 2:7. 22:1, 2, 14, 17. Lk 11:36. Jn 1:9. 1 C 4:5. Ep 1:18. He 10:32. Re 18:1g. **life and.** ⌡93A, Ge +1:26. By Hendiadys, immortal life, with an emphasis upon immortal. Two words used, but one thing meant. Jn +*5:29. *11:25, 26. **immortality.** Gr. *aphtharsia,* ✱S#861g. Ro 2:7. 1 C 15:42 (incorruption), 50, 53, 54. Ep 6:24 (sincerity). T 2:7 (sincerity). Compare the related word *aphthartos,* ✱S#862g, 1 T +1:17n. T#422. Ec +3:21 (T#152). Ezk 32:27n. Jn *10:27, 28. Ac +24:15 (T#617). Ro 2:6, 7. 1 Th 5:23n. 1 T 6:16. 1 P +*1:4. **to light.** Ezk 32:27n. 2 C 4:4.

11. **appointed.** Ac *9:15. Ep *3:7, 8. See on 1 T 1:7. +2:7.

12. **the which.** ver. 8. 2 T *2:9. 3:10-12. 4:16, 17. Lk 12:4. Ac 9:16. 13:46, 50. 13:46, 50. 14:5, 6. 21:27-31. 22:21-24. Ep 3:1-8. 1 Th 2:16. **I am.** ver. 8, 16. Ps 25:2. Is 50:7. 54:4. Ac 21:13. Ro √1:16. 5:4, 5. 9:33. Ph 1:20. He *12:2. 1 P 4:16. **for I know.** Jb *19:25. Ps +√9:10. 10:14. 56:9. Na 1:7. Jn 4:42. Ga 2:20n. Ph 3:8, 10. 1 P *4:19. 1 J √5:13. **believed.** *or,* trusted. Is +*12:2. Na *1:7. Mt 12:21. Ro 15:12, 13. Ep 1:12, 13. T +*3:8. 1 P 1:20, 21. **am persuaded.** See on ver. 5. **he is.** Jn √10:28-30. Ph *3:21. He 2:18. 7:25. **keep that.** 2 T +*4:18n. Ge=39:6. Is 27:3. Jn 6:39, 40, 44. 17:11, 12, 15. 1 C +*15:55. 1 T 6:20. 1 P

+*1:5. Ju *24. which I. ver. 14. Ps 31:5. Lk +*23:46n. Ac +*7:59n. 1 T 6:20. 1 P √4:19. against. ver. 18. 2 T *4:8. Mt 7:22. 24:36. Lk 10:12. 1 Th 5:4. that day. ver. 18. 2 T *4:8. 1 C +*3:13. 2 Th +*1:10.

13. Hold fast. ver. 14. 2 T *3:14. Pr 3:18, 21. 4:4-8, 13. 23:23. Mt +*15:14. Ph 1:27. 1 Th 5:21. 1 T 1:10. T *1:9. He *3:6. *4:14. 10:23. Ju +*3. Re 2:25. 3:3, 11. the form. Pr 8:14. Ro 2:20. *6:17. 1 T 1:10, 16g. 6:3. T 2:1, 8. sound words. ver. +*7. 1 T +1:10. 6:3. T 1:9. 2:1, 8. which. 2 T +*2:2. 3:10, 14. Ph *4:9. in faith. Ro *14:23. See on Col 1:4. 1 T 1:14. and love. ſ174, Ge +18:27. Jn *13:35. *14:15. 1 C *13:2. in Christ Jesus. 2 T 2:1. 1 T +1:14.

14. good. ver. +12. 2 T *2:2. Lk 16:11. Ro 3:2. 1 C 9:17. 2 C *5:19, 20. Ga 2:7. Col *4:11. 1 T 1:11. 6:20. keep. Nu=3:7. 2 T 4:7. by the. Ro 8:13, 26. Ep +*5:18. 1 Th 5:19. 1 P 1:22. Ghost. Gr. pneuma, Mt +1:18. which dwelleth in us. Jn *14:17. Ro +*8:9, 11. 1 C *3:16. *6:19. 2 C *6:16. Ep 2:22.

15. that. Ac 16:6. 19:10, 27, 31. 20:16. 1 C 16:19. all. ſ108B, 1 C +13:2. in Asia. Ac +2:9. turned away. 2 T *4:10, 11, 16. Ph 2:21. 1 T +*4:1n. He *6:4-8. 2 P *2:20-22. Phygellus. i.e. fugitive, *S#5436g. Hermogenes. i.e. begotten of Mercury, *S#2061g.

16. Lord. ver. 18. Ne 5:19. 13:14, 22, 31. Ps 18:25. 37:26. Mt +*5:7. √10:41, 42. 25:35-40. 2 C 9:12-14. He +*6:10. 10:34. the house. ſ121J4. Metonymy of the Subject, here "house" put for family, Ge +7:1. T#1564. 2 T 4:19. Ru 4:12. 2 S 7:25-29. Ac 16:15n. Onesiphorus. i.e. profit bringing, *S#3683g. 1 T 4:19. refreshed. Mt *10:42. 1 C 16:18. Phm 7, 20. not ashamed. See on ver. 8, 12. my chain. ver. 8. Ac +28:20. Ep 6:20mg.

17. Rome. Ac 18:2. 19:21. 23:11. *28:14, 16. Ro 1:7, 15. he sought. Mt 25:36-40. Ac 28:30, 31. diligently. Lk 7:4g.

18. that he. See on ver. 16. 1 K 17:20. Mt 25:31-40. find mercy. ver. 16. Ps 130:3, 4. Lk 1:72, 78. Ro √3:23, 24. 9:15-23. Ep 2:4. 1 P 1:10. in that day. See on ver. 12. 1 C +*3:13. 2 Th +*1:10. Re +*1:10n. ministered. Mt √25:40. Lk +8:3. Ac +19:22. 2 C 9:1. He +*6:10. Ephesus. 2 T 4:12. Ac +18:21. 19:1. 1 C 16:8. 1 T 1:3. Re 2:1. very well. lit. better. ſ96E3. Heterosis of Degree, 1 T 3:14. i.e. too well to need reminding of. Ac 25:10.

2 TIMOTHY 2

Timothy is exhorted to appoint faithful ministers; and to courage, fidelity, and patience, as "the good soldier of Christ," 1-7; in remembrance of Christ as risen from the dead, 8; in imitation of the apostle's example, 9, 10; and in assured faith and hope, 11-13. He must warn the flock against false teachers and vain controversies; studying, as an approved workman, "rightly to divide the word of truth," 14-16. The pernicious effects of the error of Hymeneus and Philetus, 17, 18: yet "the foundation of God stands sure," and "all who name the name of Christ" should "depart from iniquity," 19. Some are vessels of honor, others of dishonor; but Timothy must seek to be the former, 20, 21. He is taught what to flee and what to follow after, 22; to shun disputatious questions; and to instruct opposers with meekness, in hopes of their being recovered from the snare of the devil, 23-26.

1. my. 2 T +1:2. See on 1 T 1:2, 18. be. 2 T +*1:7.

Jsh *1:7, 9. Hg 2:4. See on 1 C 16:13. 2 C √12:9, 10. Ep +*6:10. Ph √4:13. 2 P √3:18. that is. 2 T 1:13. 1 T +1:14.

2. the things. 2 T *1:13. *3:10, 14. among. or, by. many. 1 T 4:14. *6:12. the same. See on 2 T 1:14. 1 T 1:18. *5:22. commit. Ex +*18:21. Ezr 7:25. Pr *11:30. Mt 28:19mg, 20. faithful. Nu *12:7. 1 S *2:35. Ne *7:2. Ps 101:6. Pr 13:17. Je +*23:28n. Mt +√24:45. Lk +*12:42. √16:10-12. Ac +*6:3. 1 C +*4:2. Col *1:7. 1 T 1:12. He 2:17. 3:2, 3. Re *2:10-13. who. ver. 24, *25. Ezr *7:10, 25. Ml 2:7. Mt +*13:52. 1 T 3:2-9. *4:6. T *1:5-9.

3. endure. ver. 10. 2 T +1:8. 3:11. *4:5. 1 C 13:7. 2 C 1:6. He 6:15. 10:32. 11:27. *12:2, 3. Ja *1:12. a good. 1 C +9:7. 2 C 10:3-5. Ep *6:11-18. Ph +*1:17. See on 1 T 1:18.

4. that warreth. Dt 20:5-7. Lk 9:59-62. entangleth. 2 T 4:10. Lk +*8:14. 1 C 9:25, 26. 1 T +*6:9-12. 2 P *2:20. that he. 1 C 7:22, 23. 2 C 5:9. 1 Th 2:4.

5. And if. ſ184C, Mt +4:9. strive. Lk 13:24. 1 C *9:24-27. Ph 1:15. Col 1:29. He 12:4. is he. 2 T *4:7, 8. He 2:7, 9. Ja 1:12. 1 P 5:4. Re 2:10. 3:11. 4:4, 10.

6. husbandman. Is 28:24-26. Mt 9:37, 38. 20:1. 21:33-41. Lk 10:2. Jn *4:35-38. 1 C *3:6-9. 9:7-11. He 6:7. laboreth must be first partaker of the fruits. or, laboring first, must be partaker of the fruits. 1 C 9:23. He 10:36.

7. Consider. Dt 4:39. 32:29. Ps 64:9. Pr 24:32. Is 1:3. 5:12. Lk 9:44. Ph √4:8. 1 T 4:15. He 3:1. 7:4. 12:3. 13:7. and. Ge 41:38, 39. Ex 36:1, 2. Nu 27:16, 17. 1 Ch 22:12. 29:19. 2 Ch 1:8-12. Ps 119:73, 125, 144. 143:8, 9. Pr 2:3-6. Is 28:26. Da 1:17. Lk 21:15. 24:45. Jn *14:26. 16:13. Ac 7:10. 1 C 12:8. Ep 1:17, 18. Col *1:9. Ja +*1:5. *3:15, 17. 1 J 5:20. understanding. Ps +*119:27.

8. Remember. ſ121C2B, Is +44:21. He 12:2, 3. Jesus. See on Mt 1:1. Ac 2:30. 13:23. Ro *1:3, 4. Re 5:5. of the seed of David. 2 S 7:12. Ac +*13:23. Mt +1:1. Ro *1:3, 4. raised. See on Lk 24:46. Ac 2:24. 1 C 15:1, 4, 11-20. 1 P 1:3. 3:21. according. Ro +2:16. +*16:25. 1 C √15:1-4. 2 Th 2:14. 1 T 1:11. 2:7.

9. I suffer. 2 T 1:8, 12, 16. Ac *9:16. as. Ep 6:20. 1 P 2:12, 14. 3:16. 4:15. even. Ac 28:31. Ep 6:19, 20. Ph *1:+7, 12-14. 2 Th 3:1. but. 2 T 4:17. Ro +9:6. Ep 3:1. Ph 1:7, 13. Col 4:3, 18. not bound. Je +*39:15.

10. I endure. See on ver. 3. 1 C 13:7. Ep 3:13. Col 1:24. for. Mt 24:22, 24, 31. Jn 11:52. +*17:9. 1 C 9:22. 2 C *1:6. 4:15. +12:15. Ep 3:13. Col *1:24. elect's. Dt 7:7, 8. Is 48:11. Da 9:19. Ho 14:4. Mt +√24:22n. Lk +*18:7. Jn 6:37, 39, 44. 10:29. 12:32. 17:2. Ac +13:48 (T#254). Ro 5:8. 9:11-13. 1 C 1:27, 28. 4:7. Ep +1:4 (T#255). 2:8. 1 J 4:10, 19. obtain. Pr 8:35. Jn 17:24. 1 Th 5:9. 1 T 1:13, 14. 1 P 2:10. salvation. Co 1:6. which is. 1 T +1:14. with. Ro *2:7. 9:23. 2 C √4:17. Col 1:27. 2 Th *2:14. 1 P *5:10. eternal. Gr. aionios, Mt +18:8. glory. T#860. Da +*12:3. Mt +*13:43. Ro √8:17, 18. 2 C √4:17, 18. Col 3:4. 1 P 4:13.

11. faithful. ſ101, Dt +32:42. 1 T +1:15. 3:1. T *3:8. For if. ſ184A, 1 C +15:2. Ro ●*6:5, 8. 1 C 15:31. 2 C *4:10. Ga *2:19, 20. Col *3:3, 4. we shall. Mt *10:32. Jn 14:19. 2 C 13:4. 1 Th *4:17. 5:10. live with. Re *20:4.

12. If we. ſ184A, 1 C +15:2. Mt +*5:10. 19:28, 29. Ac +*14:22. Ro *8:17. Ph 1:28. 2 Th 1:4-8. 1 P *4:13-16. Re 1:6, 9. *5:10. √20:4, 6. suffer. Gr. hupo-

meno, ✳S#5278g. ver. 10 (endure). Mt 10:22 (endureth). 24:13. Mk 13:13. Ac 17:14 (abode). Ro 12:12 (patient). 1 C 13:7 (endureth). He 10:32. 12:2, 3, 7. Ja 1:12. 5:11. 1 P 2:20 (patiently), 20. **we shall.** T#512. Dt +8:2 (T#4). Ps *64:10. 68:13. Mt +*5:10-12. Ro *8:17, 18. 1 P *4:12-14. Re +14:13 (T#337). 15:3. **reign with.** Ps +*149:5-9. Da 7:27. Mt +*25:34. Lk *22:28-30. Ro +*8:17. 1 C *6:2, 3. He +*10:36. Re 1:9. *3:21. +√5:10. +*20:4. 22:5. **if we deny.** ⨍184A, 1 C +15:2. Pr 30:9. Mt +*10:33. 26:35, 72, 75. Mk *8:38. 10:33. Lk 9:26. 12:9. Ac +*14:22. 1 C +*15:2. 1 T 5:8. He +*10:35. 1 J 2:22, 23. Ju 4. Re 2:13. 3:8. **deny us.** Dt +*31:17. Mt 10:33. √25:12.

13. **If we.** ⨍184A, 1 C +15:2. Lk +*8:13. Ro *3:3. 1 C +*15:2. **yet.** Is 25:1. Mt 24:35. Ro 3:3. 9:6. 1 C +1:9. +*10:13. 2 C 1:18. Ph 1:6. 1 Th 5:24. 2 Th 3:3. He 10:23. **he cannot.** Nu *23:19. 1 S 15:29. Je 10:10. Ml +*3:6. T *1:2. He *6:18. Re 3:7.

14. **put.** 2 T 1:6. T 3:1. 2 P 1:12, 13. 3:1. **charging.** 2 T +*4:1. Ep 4:17. 1 Th 4:1, +6. 2 Th 3:6. 1 T 5:21. 6:13. **that.** ver. 16, 23. Ac 18:15. Ro 14:1. 1 T 1:4, 6. *6:4, 5. T 3:9-11. **to no.** 1 S 12:21. Je 2:8, 11. 7:8. 16:19. 23:32. Hab 2:18. Mt 16:26. 1 T +*4:8. T 3:9. He 13:9. **the subverting.** Pr +*19:27. Je *23:36. Ezk 14:10n. Mt +*15:14. Mk +*4:24. Lk +*8:18. Ac 13:10. 15:24. Ga 1:7. T 3:11. 2 P 2:6g.

15. **Study.** Pr √23:12. Gr. *spoudazo,* ✳S#4704g. 2 T 4:9 (diligence), 21. Ga 2:10 (forward). Ep 4:3 (endeavoring). 1 Th 2:17 (endeavored). T 3:12 (diligent). He 4:11 (labor). 2 P 1:+*10 (give diligence), 15. √3:14. **approved.** Lk +√21:36. Ac 2:22. 27:24g. Ro *14:18. 16:10. 2 C *5:9. *10:18. Ga *1:10. Col +*1:10. 1 Th *2:4. 2 Th 1:11. Ja +1:12g. **a workman.** Mt +*13:52. 2 C *3:6. *6:3, 4. 1 T *4:6, 12-16. **ashamed.** Ph 1:20. 1 J 2:28. **rightly.** Is +*8:20n. Je +*8:8mg. Mt +*13:52. Mk *4:33. +*12:24. Lk 4:18-20. +*12:42. Jn *21:15-17. Ac *20:20, 27. 1 C 2:6. *3:1, 2. 2 C √4:2. 1 Th 4:2n. *5:14. He *5:11-14. 2 P ◯*3:16. **dividing.** "rightly dividing" is the rendering of a single Greek word, *orthotomeo,* ✳S#3718g, only here. Vine notes the word is from *orthos,* straight, and *temno,* to cut, "the meaning passed from the idea of cutting or dividing, to the more general sense of rightly dealing with a thing. What is intended here is not dividing Scripture from Scripture, but teaching Scripture accurately" (*Expository Dictionary,* vol 1, p. 327). The word occurs in the Septuagint at Pr 3:6 and 11:5, where the English has "direct." The reference is not to dividing up Scripture into dispensations, and applying to ourselves only what is allegedly valid for this dispensation. Neither is it dividing Scripture on the basis of to whom it was originally addressed or spoken of, the Jew, the Gentile, or the Church of God (citing 1 C 10:32, pressing this text far beyond the bounds of its legitimate meaning and application in context), for all Scripture is given by inspiration of God and is profitable (2 T √3:16). While all Scripture may indeed not be about us, it is all for our learning (Ro +*15:4), and we have no right by such arbitrary distinctions to eliminate from our careful consideration whole sections of the Word of God. The emphasis is not upon "right division" (which in the practice of some is "wrong subtraction," 1 Th 4:2n), but on "correct interpretation." In context Paul is directing Timothy not to strive about words to the subverting of the hearers, but to handle the Word of God accurately so as to teach them the truth.

Pr 25:12. Mt +*7:6. 2 C +*2:17. √4:2. **word of truth.** Jn +*17:17. Ep +1:13.

16. **shun.** ver. 14. Pr +*19:27. 1 T 4:7. 6:20. T 1:14. *3:9. **profane.** 1 T +1:9. **babblings.** 1 T 6:20. **for.** 2 T 3:9, 13. Ezr 10:10. Ho 12:1. 1 C 5:6. 15:33. 2 Th 2:7, 8. T 1:11. He +*12:15. 2 P 2:2, 18. Re 13:3, 14. **ungodliness.** T 2:12.

17. **their word.** Na 3:15. Ja *5:3. **canker.** *or,* gangrene. **Hymeneus.** 1 T *1:20. **Philetus.** i.e. *beloved,* ✳S#5372g.

18. **concerning.** Mt 22:29. 1 T 1:19. 6:10, 21. He 3:10. Ja 5:19. **have erred.** Mk +*12:24. 1 T 1:6. 6:21. **that.** 1 C *15:12. Col *3:1. **overthrow.** ver. 14. Mt 15:13. Lk +*8:13. 22:31, 32. Ac 5:39. 1 C √11:19. T 1:11. 1 J √2:19.

19. **the foundation.** Pr 10:25. Is 14:32. *28:16. Mt 7:25. *16:16, 18. Lk 6:48. 1 C *3:10, 11. Ep 2:20. 1 T 6:19. He 11:10. 1 P 2:5. Re 21:14. **standeth.** Mt 24:24. Mk 13:22. Ro +*8:31-35. 9:11. He *6:18, 19. 1 J *2:19. **sure.** *or,* steady. Ps 112:6. 125:1, 2. **having.** Ezk +*9:4. Hg 2:23. Zc 3:9. 4:7-9. Ro *4:11. 2 C 1:22. Ep +*4:30. Re 7:2, 3. **The Lord knoweth.** ⨍96A1, Mt +5:29. ⨍121C2A2, Ge +39:6. i.e. *loves and cares for.* Nu *16:5. Ezr=2:62, 63. Ps +*1:6. *37:18, 28. Na √1:7. Mt √7:23. Lk 13:27. Jn √10:14, 27-30. 13:18. Ro +*8:28. +*11:2. 1 C +8:3. Ga 4:9. Re 17:8. **them that are his.** ver. 10. Mt 24:24. **Let.** Nu 6:27. Is 26:13. 63:19. 65:15. Am 6:10. Mt +*28:19. Ac 9:14. 11:26. 15:17. Ro 15:9, 20. 1 C 1:2. Ep 3:15. Re 2:13. 3:8. 22:4. **depart.** Nu 16:26. Jb 28:28. Ps *34:14. *37:27. *97:10. Pr *3:7. Is 52:11. Ro *12:9. 2 C √7:1. Ga *5:24. Ep 4:17-22. 5:1-11. Col +*3:5-8. T *2:11-14. 1 P *1:13-19. 2 P √1:4-10. √3:14. 1 J *3:7-10.

20. **in a.** Mt 13:47. 1 C 3:9, 16, 17. Ep 2:22. 1 T +3:15. He 3:2-6. 1 P 2:5. **vessels.** Ex 27:3. 1 Ch=9:28, 29. Ezr 1:6. 6:5. La *4:2. Da 5:2. 2 C 4:7. **gold.** Ml=3:3. 1 P 1:7. **of wood.** 1 C ◯3:12. **earth.** 2 C 4:7. **and some to honor.** Ro 9:21-23. **dishonor.** ⨍63D3, Ro +7:3. Supply ellipsis (absolute: of anantapodoton or apodosis), "(so in the great house of the church there are not only the elect saints, which are the vessels of honor, but there are the impious and reprobate, who are the vessels of dishonor)" (B55).

21. **If.** ⨍184C, Mt +4:9. **purge.** Ps *119:9. Pr 25:4. Is *1:25. *52:11. Je *15:19. Ml *3:3. 1 C *5:7. 2 C *7:1. 1 P *1:22. 1 J *3:3. **a vessel.** ver. *20. 1 Ch=9:28, 29. Ac 9:15. 1 P *1:7. **meet.** 2 T 4:11. Ac *9:15. Phm 11. **prepared.** 2 T *3:17. Jsh 8:4. 1 T 5:10. T 3:1. **good work.** Ac +*9:36. Ep √2:10. T √3:1, 8, 14.

22. **Flee.** Pr 6:5. 1 C 6:18. 10:14. 1 T *6:11. **youthful.** Ps *119:9. Ec 11:9, 10. 1 T +*4:12. 1 P *2:11. **follow.** See on 1 T *4:12. +*6:11. He +*12:14. 3 J 11. **faith.** ⨍174, Ge +18:27. 1 C *13:13. 1 T +*1:14. **charity.** See on 1 C *14:1. **peace.** Ro *14:17, +19. 15:5, 6. 1 C 1:10. *7:15. He +*12:14. Ja *3:17. 1 P *3:11. **call.** 1 Ch 29:17, 18. Ps 17:1. 66:*18, 19. Pr *15:8, 9. See on Ac +9:14. 1 C *1:2. 1 T *2:8. **pure heart.** T#1355. Mt *15:8. 1 T *1:5. +*4:12. 1 P 1:22.

23. **foolish.** See on ver. 14, 16. 1 T 1:4. 4:7. 6:4, 5. T 3:9. **questions.** ver. 14. 1 T +6:4. **avoid.** 1 T +4:7.

24. **the servant.** Dt 34:5. Jsh 1:1. 2 Ch 24:6. Da 6:20. 1 T 6:11. T 1:1. 3:2. Ja +1:1. **must.** Is 42:1-3. Mt *12:18, 19. Ac 15:2. 2 C *10:4. Ph 2:3, 14. 1 T 3:3. T 1:7. Ja 1:19, 20. Ju +*3. **strive.** Jn 6:52. Ac 7:26. 23:9. Ja 4:2g. **but.** Is 40:11. Mt *11:29. Ac *20:31.

2 C *10:1. Ga 5:22. 1 Th 2:7. T 3:2. Ja *3:17. 1 P 3:8. **apt.** 1 T 3:2, 3. T 1:9. **patient.** *or,* forbearing. 1 C *13:5. Ep 4:2. Col 3:13.

25. **In meekness.** Mt *11:29. Ga *6:1. 1 T 6:11. T 3:2. 1 P √3:15. **instructing.** Je *13:15-17. 26:12-15. Jn 5:34. Ac ch. 22, etc. **if.** T#434. Dt +30:6 (T#594). Ps +17:5 (T#596). 51:12, 13. Je 31:18, 19, 33. Ezk *11:19. 36:26, 31. Zc *4:6. *12:10. Ac +5:31 (T#595). *11:18. Ja *1:17. 1 J *5:16. **peradventure.** Da 4:27. Ac *8:22. 1 T √2:4. **will give.** T#242. Dt +*29:4. 1 S 26:19. 2 Ch +18:31 (T#264). Ps 33:14, *15. Is 45:9. Mt +*11:27. +*13:10, 11. 20:15, 16. Jn +*6:44, 65. Ac +*11:18. +√13:48. +*18:27. Ro *9:+18 (T#234). 20-23. Ph +*1:29. He +4:2 (T#435). ◐12:17. **repentance.** 2 T *3:7. Mt 21:32. Mk *1:3, 4, 15. Ac +*2:38. *8:22. *20:21. Ro √2:4. 2 C √7:8-10. T 1:1. **acknowledging.** 1 T +*2:4.

26. **recover.** Gr. awake. ƒ63H, Ge +12:15. Supply ellipsis, (and be delivered). Lk *15:17. Ro *16:20. 1 C *15:34. Ep 5:14. **out.** Ps *124:7. Is 8:15. *28:13. Ac +*26:18. 2 C √2:11. Col *1:13. 2 Th √2:9-12. 1 T 3:7. +*6:9, 10. Re *12:9. *20:2, 3. **who are.** Is *42:6, 7. *49:25, 26. *53:12. Mt *12:28, 29. Lk 11:21. 2 P *2:18-20. **taken captive.** Gr. taken alive. Lk ◐5:10g. Jn 8:34, 44. Ro 6:20. Ep 2:1, 2. T 3:3. 1 J 3:10. 5:19. **by him.** i.e. *the devil.* Gr. *autou,* having reference grammatically to the nearest preceding noun, "devil." There is no need to attempt to connect this pronoun to a remote antecedent (see discussion in William Hendrickson, *Comm. on 2 Timothy,* p. 276, note 149). **at.** Jb *1:12. *2:6. Lk *22:31, 32. Jn *13:2, 27. Ac *5:3. 1 T 1:20. **his will.** i.e. the devil's will. Gr. *ekeinou,* having reference grammatically to the nearest preceding pronoun, "him" (*autou*). It is unnecessary to attempt to make these pronouns refer to God or to the Lord's servant, mentioned earlier in the context, for the sense is perfectly clear taking the most natural construction. Jn ◐19:11. 1 Th +4:3?.

2 TIMOTHY 3

The apostle foretells grievous times "in the last days," through the atrocious wickedness of those, who would retain "the form, without the power of godliness," 1-5; and the devices and opposition of false teachers, 6-9. He proposes his own example to Timothy, 10-13; exhorting him to continue in the faith, 14; and showing the excellency, authority, and sufficiency of the sacred scriptures which Timothy had known from his youth, 15-17.

1. **in.** 2 T 4:3. Ge 49:1. Is *2:2. Je 48:47. 49:39. Ezk 38:16. Da 10:14. Ho 3:5. Mi 4:1. Mt *24:10-12, 14. Ac 2:17. 1 T +*4:1n. 2 P *3:3. 1 J +*2:18. Ju *17, 18. **perilous.** Da 7:8, 20-25. 8:8-14. 11:36-45. 12:1, 7, 11. 2 Th 2:3-12. 1 T 4:1-3. Re ch. 8-17. **times.** ƒ121P1, 1 Ch +12:32.

2. **lovers.** ƒ168, Is +1:11. ver. 4. Ro +*12:3. 15:1-3. 2 C 5:15. Ph +*2:3, 21. Ja 2:8. **own selves.** ƒ97, Ro +12:15. Ph +*2:3. **covetous.** ƒ41, Ge +10:1. Ex +*18:21. Ps +*10:3. Lk +*12:15. 16:14. Ro +*1:29. Col +*3:5. 1 T +*6:10. 2 P 2:3, 14, 15. Ju 11, 16. Re 18:12, 13. **boasters.** Ps *10:3. 49:6. 52:1. Is 10:15. Ac 5:36. Ro 1:29-31. 11:18. 2 Th *2:4. Ja 4:16. 2 P 2:18. Ju 16. **proud.** Ps +*119:21. Pr *6:17. Lk 1:51g. 1 T 6:4. Ja *4:6. 1 P *5:5. **blasphemers.** Da 7:25. 11:36. 1 T 1:13g, 20. 2 P 2:12. Ju 10. Re 13:1, 5, 6.

16:9, 11, 21. **disobedient to parents.** Dt +*21:20. 27:16. Pr 15:20. 30:11. Mi 7:6. Ml ◐+*4:6. Mt 15:6. Mk 7:11, 12. Ro 1:30. Ep ◐+*6:1. 1 T 3:4. T 1:6. **unthankful.** Lk 17:17, 18. Ro *1:21. 1 Th ◐+*5:18. **unholy.** 1 T 1:9.

3. **natural.** Mt 10:21. Ro 1:31. **trucebreakers.** 2 S 21:1-3. Ps +*15:4. Ezk 17:15-19. Ro 1:31g. **false accusers.** *or,* make-bates. Mt 4:1. Jn 6:70. See on 1 T 3:11. T 2:3. All in Gr. **incontinent.** 1 C 7:5, 9. 2 P 2:14, 19. 3:3. Ju 16, 18. **fierce.** Ge 49:7. Da 8:23. Re 13:15, 17. 16:6. 17:6. **despisers.** ƒ41, Ge +10:1. Ps 22:6. Is *53:3. 60:14. Lk 10:16. 16:14. 1 Th 4:8. T 1:8. Ja 2:6.

4. **Traitors.** 2 P 2:10, etc. Ju 8, 9. **heady.** or, headstrong. Ac 19:36g. **highminded.** Ro 11:20. +*12:3. 1 T 3:6. 6:4, 17. **lovers.** ƒ41, Ge +10:1. **lovers of God.** Ro 16:18. Ph +*3:18, 19. 1 T 5:6. 2 P 2:13, 15. Ju 4, 19.

5. **a form.** T#191. 1 S +16:7 (T#333). Jb +21:15 (T#689). Ps +5:9 (T#702). 106:12, +13 (T#411). Pr +16:25 (T#704). Is *26:13. 29:13. *48:1, 2. *58:1-3. Je 3:10. Ezk +*33:30-32. Mt *7:15. 13:20, 21. 15:7, 8. *23:27, 28. Lk +18:12. Jn 6:26. Ac *8:13, 21. Ro 2:+20, 24. 10:2. 1 C 13:1-3. 2 C +7:10 (T#609). Ga 1:13, 14. +4:17 (T#623). 5:6. 1 T *5:8. T *1:16. Ja 2:19. **of godliness.** 1 T +*3:16. **denying the power.** 1 T +5:8. T 1:16. **from such.** 2 T *2:16, 23. Ps +√119:63. Mt +√15:14. Ro *16:17, 18. Ep +*4:14. 2 Th +*3:6, 14. 1 T *6:5, 20. T 1:14. *3:10. 2 J +*10-12.

6. **of this.** Mt 23:14. T 1:11. Ju 4. **houses.** ƒ121J4, Ge +7:1. **laden.** Ps 38:4. Is 1:4. Mt √11:28. **led.** 1 C 12:2. 2 P *3:17. **divers lusts.** 2 T 4:3. Mk +*4:19. 1 T +*6:9. T 3:3. 2 P 2:18. Ju 16, 18.

7. **learning.** 2 T *4:3, 4. Dt *29:4. Pr *14:6. Is *30:10, 11. Ezk 14:4-10. Mt +*13:11. Jn *3:20, 21. *5:44. *12:42, 43. 1 C *3:1-4. Ep +*4:14. He *5:11, 12. **never.** 1 T +*2:4. **the knowledge.** See on 2 T +*2:25.

8. **as.** ƒ106, Ge +31:7. Ex *7:11, 22. 8:7, 18. **Jannes.** i.e. *he deceived,* ✻S#2389g. **Jambres.** i.e. *the sea with poverty; foamy healer,* ✻S#2387g. **resist.** 2 T 4:15. 1 K 22:22-24. Je 28:1, etc. Ac 13:8-11. 15:24. Ga 1:7-9. 2:4, 5. Ep +*4:14. 2 Th √2:9-11. T 1:10. 2 P *2:1-3. 1 J *2:18. *4:1. Re 2:6, 14, 15, 20. **men.** Ac 8:21, 22. Ro *1:28. 16:18. 2 C √11:13-15. 1 T 1:19. 4:2. +*6:5. T 1:16. 2 P 2:14. Ju 18, 19. **reprobate.** *or,* of no judgment. Je 6:30. 1 C +9:27g. See on 2 C 13:5, 6. **the faith.** 1 T +1:19.

9. **proceed.** ver. 13g. 2 T 2:16. **their folly.** ver. 8. Ex *7:12. *8:18, 19. *9:11. 1 K 22:25. Ps 76:10. Je 28:15-17. 29:21-23, 31, 32. 37:19. Lk 6:11. Ac 13:11. 19:15-17.

10. **thou hast fully known.** *or,* thou hast been a diligent follower of. Lk 1:3. Ph 2:22. 1 T *4:6g. **my doctrine.** ver. +*16, 17. 2 T *4:3. Ac *2:42. Ro *16:17. Ep +*4:14. 1 T 1:3. +*4:6, 12, 13. T *2:7. He *13:9. 2 J +*9, 10. **manner.** ƒ41, Ge +10:1. Ac *20:18. *26:4. 1 C *2:2. √4:17. 1 Th *1:5. 2 P *3:11. **purpose.** Da +*1:8. Ac +*11:23. 2 C *1:17. Ph *1:21. **faith.** ver. 15. 2 T 2:22. 2 C *6:4-10. 1 T +1:14. +*4:12. 6:11. 2 P √1:5-7. **longsuffering.** Ep +4:2g. Col *1:11. **charity.** 2 C *12:15. T 2:2. 2 P 1:7. **patience.** Ep +1:6.

11. **Persecutions.** Ac *9:16. 20:19, 23, 24. Ro +*8:35-37. 1 C 4:9-11. 2 C *1:8-10. 4:8-11. *11:23-28. 2 C +12:10. He 10:33, 34. **afflictions.** ƒ41, Ge +10:1. **at Antioch.** Ac 13:14, 45, 50, 51. **Iconium.** Ac

14:1, 2, 5, 6, 19-21. **Lystra**. ∫41, Ge +10:1. Ac 14:6, 19. **but**. 2 T 4:7, 17, 18. Ge 48:16. 2 S 22:1, 49. Jb 5:19, 20. Ps *34:19. 37:40. 91:2-6, 14. Is 41:10, 14. 43:2. Je 1:19. Da 6:27. Ac 9:23-25. 21:32, 33. 23:10, 12-24. 25:3, 4. 26:17, 22. 2 C 1:10. 2 P 2:9. **delivered**. 2 T 4:17. Ps +*34:4. Ro +*15:31.

12. **live**. 2 C 1:12. 1 T 2:2. +*3:16. 6:3. T 1:1. √2:12. 2 P 3:11. **suffer persecution**. T#467. 2 T 2:3, 9. Jsh 17:14. Ps +2:2 (T#68). *37:12-15. +42:10 (T#511). Je 2:30. 15:10. Ezk 33:30. Da +*11:33. Mt +*5:10-12. 10:16-18, 22-25. 16:24. 23:34. Mk +10:30. Lk *14:26, 27. Jn *15:19-21. 16:2, 33. *17:14. Ac 5:40, 41. 7:52. 9:15, 16. +*14:22. 20:23. 1 C 4:9, 11-13. 15:19. 2 C 1:5-7. 4:8-11. 6:4, 5, 8-10. *11:23-27, 32, 33. Ga 1:10. 5:11. 1 Th *3:3, 4. He 11:32-38. 1 P *2:20, 21. 3:14. 4:12-16. 5:9, 10. Re 1:9, 10. 7:14. 12:4, 7-10.

13. **evil**. See on ver. 8. 2 T 2:16, 17. 2 Th 2:6-10. 1 T +*4:1. 2 P 2:20. 3:3. Re 12:9. 13:14. 18:23. 22:11. **wax worse**. ver. 9. 2 T 2:16. 1 K 12:28n. Je +*16:12. **being deceived**. ∫147A, Ge +50:24. Jb 12:16. Is 44:20. Ezk 14:9, +*10n. Mt +*15:14. Ep +*4:14. 2 Th √2:11, 12. T 3:3.

14. **continue**. 2 T +1:13. +*2:2. See on 1 T +*4:16. **learned**. ∫173, Ge +27:44. **assured**. Ac *17:31. Ro 14:5mg. Col 2:2. 1 Th *1:5. He +*6:11. +*10:22. **knowing**. Gr. *oida*, Jn 8:55n. ver. 15. Lk *10:16. 1 Th +*2:13. **thou**. ∫159, Ezk +36:23. **hast learned**. Pr +*24:21. Ep +*4:14. Ju +*3.

15. **from**. 2 T +*1:5. Ge 41:38, 46. Dt *6:6, 7. *11:19. 31:13. 32:46, 47. 1 S 2:18, 26. 3:1. 17:33, 37. 2 Ch 24:1, 2. +*26:4. *34:1-3. Ps *71:5, 17. Pr *8:17. √22:6. Ec *12:1. Is +*28:9. Lk 1:15. *2:40, 49. Jn 21:15. Ep +*6:4. **child**. T#1071, 1110. Lk +*18:15 (*S#1025g, infants). **known**. Gr. *oida*, Jn 8:55n. T#1065. 2 T +*2:15. **the holy**. Da *10:21. Mt +21:42. *22:29. Lk +*24:27, 32, 45. Jn +*5:24, 39. 15:3. Ac +*17:2. Ro 1:2. *10:17. +*15:4. *16:26. 1 C +*15:3, 4. Col 1:5, 6. *3:16. 1 Th 1:5. √2:13. Ja *1:18. 1 P *1:23. 2 P √1:20, 21. 3:16. **which**. Jn 19:7. 119:99. Jn +√5:39, 40. Ac +*10:43. *13:29, 38, 39. 1 P 1:10-12. 1 J √5:11, 12. Re 19:10. **wise**. T#1023. Da +*11:33. +*12:3. Jn +√5:39. Ja 1:21. **unto salvation**. Ro +*1:16. 1 P *1:8-11. **through faith**. Ro 3:22. 4:5. √10:17. He √11:6. **which is in**. Jn √14:6. Ac √4:12. 1 T +1:14.

16. **All**. 2 S *23:2. Mt 21:42. 22:31, 32, 43. 26:54, 56. Mk *12:24, 36. Jn *10:35. Ac 1:16. 28:25. Ro 3:2. +√15:4. Ga 3:8. He 3:7. √4:12. 2 P √1:19-21. **is**. ∫63B, Ge +2:10. This grammatical construction involves two predicate adjectives connected by *and*. The Revised Version (1881) changes one of these predicate adjectives to an attributive position, which is incorrect. The revisers do not misconstrue this construction in the other passages where it occurs. For the same grammatical construction see Ro 7:12. 1 C 11:30. 2 C 10:10. 1 T 1:15. 2:3. 4:4, 9. He 4:12, 13. In the Authorized Version text this "is" is given in italics, showing there is no word for it in the Greek, and it has therefore to be supplied. The Revised Version (1881) omits this "is," and reads "Every Scripture inspired of God *is* also profitable," thus suggesting that some Scriptures are not inspired. The American Standard Version (1901) follows the Revised Version (1881); the New American Standard Version (1960) gives this rendering as a possibility in its margin. There are nine other passages which present exactly the same construction in Greek, and

not one of these has been altered by the revisers (of 1881). Had they done so in the same manner as they have done in this case, the result would have been as follows: Ro 7:12, The holy commandment is also just. 1 C 11:30, Many weak are also sickly. 2 C 10:10, His weighty letters are also powerful. Similarly with the other passages, which are 1 T 1:15 (the faithful saying is also worthy of all acceptation). 2:3 (this good thing is also acceptable). 4:4 (every good creature of God is also nothing to be refused), 9. He 4:12 (the living word of God is also active), 13 (all naked things are also opened). "It is true that the A.V. rendering is given in the margin of the R.V., but it is difficult to see why that should be disturbed" (*Companion Bible*). This is another instance where the Scripture's own teaching about itself has been adversely affected in some modern translations (see Jn 5:39n and 8:31). **inspiration**. T#40. Ex 20:1. 2 S 23:1, 2. 2 K 17:13. 2 Ch 34:21. 36:21. Ne 9:30. Is +*8:20. Je 1:9. *36:1, 2. Ezk *1:3. Zc 7:12. Ml 4:4. Lk 1:70. 24:44. Jn 1:23. +*5:39. *10:34, 35. 14:26. 16:13. 19:36, 37. 20:9. Ac 1:16. 3:18. 7:38. 13:34. 28:25. Ro 1:2. 3:2. 4:23. 9:17. +*15:4. 1 C 2:12, 13. 6:16. 9:10. 14:37. Ga 1:11, 12. 3:8, 16, 22. 4:30. 1 Th 1:5. √2:13. He 1:1, 2. 3:7. 9:8. 10:15. 2 P *1:18-21. 3:16. 1 J 4:6. Re 14:13. 22:19. **and is profitable**. ∫52A2. Correspondence (Extended Alternation) B372. Extended alternation when there are still only two series, but each series consists of more than two members. Here, four members may be discerned: The Word of God is profitable (statement) for (A) doctrine, (B) reproof, (C) correction, (D) instruction; therefore (consequence), (A) preach the word, (B) reprove, (C) rebuke, (D) exhort. This figure occurs frequently throughout Scripture, but since the format of the *Treasury* does not lend itself to the display of this structure, only this example is given. See the margins of the *Companion Bible* for additional examples. Passages cited as illustrating this figure in B368-372 are Ps ch. 66, 72, 132. Ro 2:17-20. 1 Th 1:2-10 w 2:13-16. 4:13—5:11. T#1024, 1111. Ps *19:7-11. *119:97-104, 130. Je *23:22, 32. Mi +*2:7. Ac 20:20, *27. Ro +*15:4. 1 C 12:7. Ep 4:11-16. **for doctrine**. or, teaching. See on ver. *10. Dt 6:4-9. Ps √119:97-100. Is +*8:20n. 28:9. +√29:24. 1 T √4:+6g, 13, 16. *5:17. T *2:12. **for reproof**. The original word bears the meaning "correction," "censure," "conviction." 2 T *4:2. Ps 38:14. 39:11. +*141:5. Pr *6:23. 15:10, 31. Jn *3:20. 16:8-11. Ac 2:37, 38. 16:30, 31. Ep *5:11-13. 1 T 5:20. T 1:9, 13. 2:15. He 11:1g. **for correction**. The word literally means "restoration to an upright or a right state; hence correction and improvement" (Frank E. Gaebelein, *The Christian Use of the Bible*, p. 33). Ps √119:9. Je *23:29. Da *12:3. Jn 21:15-17. Ga *6:1, 2. **for instruction**. ∫41, Ge +10:1. Gaebelein cites Thayer (*Lexicon*, p. 473), "whatever in adults also cultivates the soul, especially by correcting mistakes and curbing passions; hence instruction which aims at increase of virtue," thus "education in righteousness" (*The Christian Use of the Bible*, p. 34). 2 T +*2:25. Dt 4:36. Ne 9:20. Ps √119:7-11. Pr *4:10-13. Mt +*13:52. Ac 18:25. Ro 2:20. +√15:4. 2 C 10:3-6. T *2:11-14. **in righteousness**. Ex +*18:21. Le +√19:2-4, 9-18, 20, 26-37. Dt +*16:20. Ps +*15:2-5. Is +*66:4. Je +*10:2. 22:13, 16. +*48:10. Ezk +*16:49. Am +*8:5. Mi +*6:8. Ml +*3:5. Mt +*23:23. Lk +*16:10. Ac +*6:3. 1 C +√6:9-11.

17. **the man**. Dt 33:1. Ne 12:24. See on Ps √119:98-100. 1 T +6:11. 2 P 1:21. **throughly furnished**. *or*, perfected. ƒ41, Ge +10:1. Holy Scripture is the only source of doctrinal and spiritual authority for the Christian. This passage teaches the sufficiency of Scripture: Scripture furnishes all that the Christian must know to be saved and to grow in grace, and tells us all we need to know to live a life which is well pleasing to God. No source of doctrine or revelation outside of Scripture is valid, for such a source would be adding to the written word of God, which is absolutely forbidden by Scripture (Re +*22:18). T#1112. 2 T +*2:21. Ne 2:18. Ps √119:104, 113, 128. Is +*8:20. Je *23:28. Lk +6:40. Ep +*4:11-14. **good works**. Mt 26:10. Ac 9:36. 2 C *9:8. Ep √2:10. 1 T 5:10. T 1:16. √2:14. 3:1, 8. He *10:24. 1 J +√2:3n.

2 TIMOTHY 4

The apostle solemnly charges Timothy to be diligent and faithful in his ministry, 1, 2; as before long, men would "not endure sound doctrine," 3, 4; and as he, Paul, had nearly finished his work, was about to suffer martyrdom, and receive the crown of righteousness, 5-8. He presses Timothy to come to him, and to bring Mark with him, as he was almost left alone; and gives him information, direction, and caution, requesting his cloak, books, and especially the parchments, 9-13. Paul warns against Alexander the coppersmith; Paul's imprecatory prayer beseeching God to reward Alexander according to his works, 14, 15. He shows Timothy, how his brethren had forsaken him, and how the Lord had supported him, when called to answer before his persecutors; expressing his confidence in God for the future, 16-18; and he concludes with salutations and benedictions, 19-22.

1. **charge**. 2 T 2:14. Dt 4:26. 30:19. 31:28. See on 1 T 5:21. 6:13. Ju 17. **and**. ƒ93A, Ge +1:26. By Hendiadys, "charge thee therefore before God, even the Lord Jesus Christ." Two words used, one person meant. Compare Ep 5:5. **the Lord**. Ne +*9:6. Ac +*10:36. **shall judge**. T#388. 1 Ch *16:14-19, 31-33. Ps 9:3, 4, 7, 8. *50:5, 6. 82:8. 94:2. 96:10, 13. 98:9. Ec *12:14. Is 9:6, 7. 16:5. 30:18, 19. Je *23:5-8. 33:15. Mi 5:1. Mt +√10:15n. +*16:27n. *25:31, etc. Lk +*14:14. Jn *5:22-27. Ac 10:40, +42. *17:31. Ro 2:16. 14:9-11. 1 C *4:4, 5. 2 C √5:9, 10. 2 Th +*1:7-10. 1 P 4:5. Re *11:17, 18. x*20:11-15. **the quick and the dead**. These are the subjects of the judgment: clearly a reference to the righteous living and the dead in Christ (1 Th 4:16n), for Scripture nowhere asserts the simultaneous resurrection of the wicked with the righteous (Lk +*14:14). Ps 9:13. Ro 14:9. Re √11:18. **at his**. This clearly specifies the time of this judgment: at Christ's appearing and kingdom. ver. +*8. Col 3:4. 1 Th +*4:15, 16. 1 T 6:14. T √2:13. He √9:27, 28. 1 P 1:7. 5:4. 1 J 2:28. Re +*1:7. **appearing and**. ƒ93A, Ge +1:26. By Hendiadys, his kingdom appearing, as distinct from his coming at the Rapture. Compare 1 Th 2:12. That Paul here links the appearing and the kingdom shows that Christ's reign will be visible, not invisible (Mt +*16:27n. +√24:3n. Da *7:13n). This further determines that this kingdom is future, and in no sense presently existing (Col 1:13n. +*3:24). 2 Th +2:8g. 3:5. **his kingdom**. Mt 13:41. +*24:14. +*25:34. Lk +*1:32, 33. 12:32. 19:12, 15. 21:31. 22:30. 23:42.

1 Th +*2:12. 2 Th +*1:5, 10. 2 P *1:11, 17.

2. **Preach**. Ps 40:9. Is *58:11. 61:1-3. Jon *3:2. Lk +*4:18, 19. *9:60. Ro *10:15. 1 C 1:21-23. 2 C 5:19, 20. See on Col *1:25, 28. **the word**. Ac 5:20. +8:4. *13:26. Ro 10:8. Ph 2:16. Ja *1:21. 1 P *4:11. **be**. Lk 7:4. 23:23. Ac 13:5. Ro *12:12. 1 T +*4:15, 16. **in season**. Ezk 2:7. Mk 14:11g. Jn *4:6-10, 32-34. Ac *16:13, 31-33. *20:7, 18-21. *28:16, 30, 31. **reprove**. Pr 15:23. Col *1:28, 29. 1 Th 2:11, 12. *5:14. 1 T +*5:20. T 1:13. 2:15. He 13:22. Re *3:19. **rebuke**. Lk 17:3. **exhort**. ƒ41, Ge +10:1. 1 T +*4:13. **all**. See on 2 T *2:21-25. 3:10. **longsuffering**. Ep +4:2.

3. **the time**. See on 2 T 3:1-6. 1 T *4:1-3. **not endure**. 1 K 22:8, 18. 2 Ch 16:9, 10. 24:20-22. 25:15, 16. Is 28:12. 33:9-11. Je 6:16, 17. 18:18. Am 7:10-13. Mt +17:17g. Lk 20:19. Jn 8:45. Ga 4:16. **sound**. 1 T +*1:10. **doctrine**. *or*, teaching. 1 T +4:6. **but**. 2 T 3:6. 1 K 18:22. 2 Ch 18:4, 5. Je 5:31. 23:16, 17. 27:9. 29:8. Mi 2:11. Lk 6:26. Jn √3:19-21. 2 P 2:1-3. **lusts**. ƒ108K40B, Ex +15:9. **heap to themselves**. 1 K +*14:23. **having**. Ex 33:32. Ac 17:21g. 1 C 2:1, 4. **itching ears**. T#466-1. Nu 24:10, 11.

4. **turn**. 2 T 1:15. Pr 1:32. Zc 7:11. Ac 7:57. 1 T +6:20. T 1:14. He 13:25. **unto**. 1 T *1:4, 6. 4:7. T *1:14-16. 2 P 1:16.

5. **watch**. Is 56:9, 10. 62:6. Je 6:17. Ezk 3:17. 33:2, 7. Mk 13:34, 37. Lk 12:37. Ac 20:30, 31. 1 Th 5:6. He √13:17. 1 P +1:13. Re 3:2. **endure**. See on 2 T 1:8. 2:3, 10. 3:10-12. **an**. Ac 21:8. Ep +*4:11. 1 T +*4:12, 15. **make full proof of**. *or*, fulfill. ver. 17. Lk 1:1g. Ac 12:25. Ro 15:19. Col 1:25. 4:17.

6. **I am**. ƒ96C7, Mt +26:24. Ph *2:17. **and the**. ƒ95, Ps +7:13. Ge 48:21. 50:24. Nu 27:12-17. Dt 31:14. Jsh 23:14. Ph *1:23. 2 P *1:14, 15. **departure**. Ph √1:23n.

7. **have fought**. ƒ147D, Ge +1:29. Nu=4:23mg, 30mg. See on 1 T +1:18. *6:12. **I have finished**. 1 Ch=23:26. Jn 4:34. Ac 13:25. +20:24. 1 C *9:24-27. Ph 3:13, 14. He 12:1, 2. **I have kept**. 2 T 1:14. Nu=3:7. Pr 23:23. Lk 8:15. 11:28. Jn 17:6. 1 T 6:20. Re 3:8, 10. **the faith**. 1 T +1:19.

8. **there**. Ps 31:19. Mt √6:19, 20. Ph +*4:17. Col +*1:5. 1 T +*6:19. **a crown**. 2 T 2:5. Pr 4:9. 1 C 9:25. 1 Th 2:19. Ja +1:12. 1 P *5:4. Re +*2:10. 4:4, 10. **the righteous judge**. See on ver. 1. Ge +*18:25. Ps 7:11. Ro 2:5. 2 Th 1:5, 6. Re 19:11. **shall give**. ver. 1n, 18n. Col +*3:24. **at that day**. 2 T 1:12, 18. Ml 3:17. Mt 7:22. 24:36. Lk 10:12. √14:14. Jn 6:54n. √11:24. 1 C +*3:13. Col *3:4. 1 Th 5:4. 2 Th +*1:10. **and not**. ƒ69B, Pr +6:16. **that love**. ƒ121C2C1, Ps +11:5. Ps *69:34-36. Is *25:8, 9. Lk +*21:28, 36. Ro 8:23. 1 C 2:9. 2 C 5:2. 1 Th +*1:10. T √2:13. He √9:28. Re +*1:7. 22:20. **his appearing**. ver. +*1.

9. **diligence**. ver. 21. 2 T 1:4. T 3:12.

10. **Demas**. Col *4:14, 15. Phm 24. **hath forsaken**. ver. 16. 2 T 1:15. Da +*11:35. Mt 26:56. Ac 13:13. 15:38. He +*10:38. 2 P 2:15. **having loved**. ƒ121C2C1, Ps +11:5. T#624. Mt 13:22. 19:21, 22. Lk 9:61, 62. √14:26, 27, 33. √16:13. 17:32. Ph 2:21. 1 T 6:10. 1 J √2:15, 16. 5:4, 5. **this present**. Jn +√6:54n. 1 C +1:20. 1 T 6:17. T 2:12. **world**. Gr. *aion*, Mt +6:13. ƒ121P2, Mt +13:22. i.e. *the course and life of this world*. **Thessalonica**. Ac +*17:1, 11, 13. **Crescens**. i.e. *increasing*, ❋S#2913g. **Galatia**. Ac +16:6. 18:23. Ga 1:2. **Titus**. 2 C +2:13. 7:6. 8:6, 16, 23. Ga 2:1-3. T 1:4. 3:12. **Dalmatia**. i.e. *vain splendor*, ❋S#1149g.

11. **Only**. See on 2 T *1:15. **Luke**. Ac 16:10. Col *4:14. Phm 24. **Take Mark**. Ho 14:4. Ac 12:+12, 25. 13:5, 13. 15:37-39. Col *4:10. 1 P 5:13. **for**. Mt 19:30. 20:16. Lk 13:30. **profitable**. 2 T 2:21. Phm 11g. **ministry**. Ac +19:22.

12. **Tychicus**. Ac 20:4. Ep *6:21, 22. Col 4:7. T 3:12. **to Ephesus**. 2 T 1:18. Ac +18:21. 20:16, 17, 25. 1 T 1:3.

13. **cloak**. This request confirms the utter poverty of Paul to the end of his life, that he should have to send so far for a garment to keep warm during the coming winter (Scott). 1 C *4:11. 2 C *11:27. **Troas**. Ac 16:+8, 11. 20:5-12. **Carpus**. i.e. *fruit*, **S#2591g**. **and the books**. "One of the great presuppositions of the Bible is that God's people will read. The existence of Scripture is in itself an argument for the necessity of reading. That God inspired a book indicates His desire that His servants should be readers" (Dinsdale T. Young, cited by Wilbur M. Smith, *Chats from a Minister's Library*, p. 176). I have somewhere read, but cannot now recall the source or the scholar alluded to, that although some have wrongfully said of such a text as this that it is unworthy of divine inspiration to have been included in Holy Writ, yet this text has been blessed to guide the life of at least one important Bible scholar to pursue a life of study which has since blessed multitudes of Christians, for, having determined to give up his library and scholarly study, he was impressed by this passage not to do so. Jsh=15:15 (*Kirjath-sepher*: city of books), 49 (*Kirjath-sannah*: city of study). 1 T +*4:13. **especially the parchments**. These may have been copies of the Hebrew Scriptures. This earnest desire of Paul to continue in earnest study to the very end of his life should impress us with the important place reading held in Paul's life. Who are we to think we need to study any less?

14. **Alexander**. Ac 19:33, 34. 1 T +1:20. **coppersmith**. Ge 4:22. **reward**. ſ110, Ezk +34:2. 1 S 24:12. 2 S *3:39. Ne 6:14. 13:29. Ps *28:3, 4. 62:12. 109:5-20. Pr 24:12. Je +√10:25. 15:15. 18:19-23. 1 C 16:22. Ga 1:8, 9. 2 Th 1:6. 1 J 5:16. Re √6:10. 18:6, 20. **according to**. Ge +√6:13 (T#566). Nu +√32:23.

15. **be**. Mt 10:16, 17. Ph 3:2. **withstood**. See on 2 T 3:8. **words**. *or*, preachings.

16. **answer**. Mt 10:18. Ac +19:33. 22:1. 25:16. 1 C 9:3. 2 C 7:11. Ph 1:7, 17. 1 P 3:15g. **no**. ver. 10. Ps 31:11-13. Mk 14:50. Jn 16:32. **forsook**. 2 T 1:15. Mt 26:56. **I pray**. 2 Ch ◑24:22. Mt +5:44. Lk 23:34. Ac +*7:60.

17. **the Lord**. Ps *37:39, 40. 109:31. Je 15:20, 21. 20:10, 11. Mt *10:19, 20. Ac 18:9, 10. *23:11. 27:23, 24. **and**. ſ148, Ge +8:22. **strengthened**. Jb 23:6. Ps 27:1. Is 41:10, 14. *43:2. 2 C √12:9, 10. Ep *6:10. 1 T +1:12. **by**. Lk 21:15. Ac 9:15. 26:17, 18. Ro 16:25, 26. Ep 3:8. Ph 1:12-14. **the preaching**. Mt 12:41. Lk 11:42. Ro 16:25. 1 C 1:21. 2:4. 15:14. T 1:3. **fully known**. ver. 5. Lk 1:1g. **all the Gentiles**. Ac +*9:15. **and I**. 2 T +3:11. 1 S 17:37. Ps 22:21. Pr 19:12. 20:2. 28:15. Je 2:30. Da 6:22, 27. He 11:33. 1 P 5:8. 2 P *2:9. **was delivered**. ſ147A, Ge +50:24. **lion**. ſ103, Ge +3:13.

18. **And**. ſ147A, Ge +50:24. **deliver**. Ge 48:16. 1 S 25:39. 1 Ch 4:10. Ps *121:7. Mt 6:13. Lk 11:4. Jn 17:15. 1 C +*10:13. 2 C 1:10. 2 Th 3:3. **evil work**. Jn +7:7. **and**. ſ148, Ge +8:22. **will preserve**. ſ63H, Ge +12:15. Supply by ellipsis, "preserve me (and bring me) unto his heavenly kingdom." Thus fixing our thought rather on the wondrous preservation than on the act of bringing (B69). "Preserve" is the usual Greek word for "save" (S#4982g: 2 T 1:9. Mt 1:21. 8:25. 9:21, 22 (whole). 10:22. 14:30. 16:25. 18:11. 19:25. 24:13, 22. 27:40, 42, 49. Jn 3:17. 5:34. 10:9. 11:12. 12:27, 47. Ac 2:21, 40, 47. 4:9, 12. 11:14. 14:9 (healed). 15:1, 11. *16:30, 31. 27:20, 31. Ro 5:9, 10. 8:24. 9:27. 10:9, 13. 11:14, 26. 1 C 15:2). 2 T *1:12. Ps *37:28. 73:24. *92:10. Mt 13:43. 25:34. Lk +*12:32. +*22:29. Jn √10:28-30. 1 Th 5:28. He 9:28n. *12:28. Ja +*2:5. 1 P +*1:5. Ju 1, *24. **me**. Ga 2:20n. Ep +*4:30. He 10:14. 1 P *1:5. 1 J √3:2. √5:10-13. **unto**. Paul's expression demonstrates that he taught that the kingdom was still future (Peters, *Theocratic Kingdom*, vol. 1, p. 600). Col 1:13n. +*3:24. *4:11. 2 Th 1:5. He 12:28. **his**. Ro *8:17. **heavenly**. "Heavenly" denotes not where the kingdom is, but its character and source from God. The kingdom is future (ver. +*1n), and our positions in it (Mt 25:21, 23. Jn +*14:2. 1 C +*6:2) are awarded "at that day" (ver. 8) when Christ appears (ver. +*1n, 8. Mt *16:27. Re 22:12). There is only one kingdom promised by prophecy and covenant (Is +*55:3), only one inheritance (Ep +*1:11n), which while heavenly in character, source, and authority, is confined by prophecy and covenant to this earth (Mt +*5:5. Ac +*7:5n. Ro √4:13. Ep +*1:11n. He +*11:16n. 1 P +*1:4n). Ps x11:4. Mt 13:44. 1 C x15:50n. He +*11:16n. 1 P +*1:4. **kingdom**. ver. +*1. Da *2:44. +*7:14. Mt +*5:5. Lk +*1:32, 33. +*17:20, 21. +*22:29, 30. Jn +*18:36. Ac +*1:6n, 7n. Ep +*1:11n. Col 1:13n. Re √11:15. **to whom**. Ro +11:36. 16:27. Ga 1:5. 1 T 1:17. 6:16. He 13:21. 1 P 5:11. Ju 25. **for ever**. Gr. *aion*, Mt +6:13. **and ever**. Gr. *aion*, Mt +6:13.

19. **Prisca**. i.e. *ancient*, **S#4251g**. Ac *18:+2, 18, 26. Ro 16:3, 4. 1 C 16:19, Priscilla. **the household**. ſ121J4, Ge +7:1. 2 T 1:16-18.

20. **Erastus**. Ac 19:22. Ro 16:23n. **Corinth**. Ac +18:1. **Trophimus**. Ac 20:4. 21:29. **Miletum**. i.e. *red; cared for*, **S#3399g**. Ac 20:15, 17, Miletus. **sick**. 2 K *13:14. 20:1. Jb 2:7. Is +*38:1. Da 8:37. Mt 8:17. Jn 9:3. 11:4, 15. Ac 10:38. Ro +*8:28. Ph 2:26, 27.

21. **thy**. ver. +9, 13. 2 T 1:4. **before winter**. Mt 24:20. **Eubulus**. i.e. *good counsellor*, **S#2103g**. **Pudens**. i.e. *modest*, **S#4227g**. **Linus**. i.e. *linen; nets*, **S#3044g**. **Claudia**. i.e. *halt, lame, wavering*, **S#2803g**. **and all**. Ro 16:21-23. 1 C 16:20. 2 C 13:13. Ph 4:22. 2 J 13. 3 J 14. **the brethren**. Ep +6:23. 1 T 4:6.

22. **The Lord**. Mt *28:20. Ro 16:20. 2 C *13:14. Ga 6:18. Phm 25. **with**. Mt 1:23. **spirit**. Gr. *pneuma*, ſ171Q1B, Mk +2:8n. **Grace**. Ro 1:7. 1 C 16:23. Ep 6:24. Col +4:18. 1 T 6:21. 1 P 5:14. Re 22:21.

Nero. Gr. Caesar Nero, *or*, the emperor Nero. i.e. *strong*, **S#3505g**.

TITUS

TITUS 1

The apostle shows the nature and importance of his office, and salutes Titus, 1-4. He states for what purpose Titus had been left in Crete, 5; and what manner of persons should be ordained to the ministry, 6-9. He exposes the dangerous principles and the self-ishness of the false teachers, "whose mouths must be stopped," 10, 11: and the bad national character of the Cretians; whom Titus must "sharply rebuke" and instruct, that "they may be sound in the faith," 12-16.

1. **a servant.** See on 1 Ch 6:49. Ro *1:1. Ph 1:1. Ja +1:1. **an apostle.** 2 C +1:1. **of Jesus.** Ac 27:23. **the faith.** Jn √10:26, 27. Ac +*13:48. Ep √2:8. 2 Th *2:13, 14. 1 T 1:5. **elect.** Dt +*10:15. Mt +*24:22n. Lk +18:7. Ep *1:4. Col 3:12. 1 Th 5:9. 2 T 2:10. 1 P 1:2. 2:8, 9. Re 17:14. **the acknowledging.** Col +1:9. 2:2. 1 T 2:4. 2 T 2:23, +*25. 3:7. He 10:26. 1 J 2:23. **truth.** 2 T 3:7. **after.** T √2:11, 12. 1 T 1:4. 3:16. 6:3. 2 P *1:3. 3:11. **godliness.** 1 T +*3:16.

2. **In.** or, For. **hope.** Readers of English translations and versions often mistakenly attribute the modern English connotation of a greater or lesser degree of doubtfulness, uncertainty, or contingency to "hope," a connotation which the biblical usage of this word most emphatically does not contain. See related note on Ga 3:14, "might." "Hope" merely distinguishes what is not yet in our full and present possession and experience; it expresses no doubtfulness of outcome. T *2:7, 13. 3:7. Jn +*5:39. *6:68. Ro 2:7. 5:2-4. Col 1:5, +*27. 1 Th 5:8. 2 T +1:1. 2:10. He 6:18. 9:15. 1 P +*1:3, 4. 1 J 2:25. √3:2, 3. √5:13. Ju *21. **eternal.** Gr. *aionios*, Mt +18:8. Mt *25:46. Mk 10:17, 30. Jn *3:15, 16. 6:54. √10:28. 17:2. Ro +2:7. *5:21. √6:23. 1 T 1:16. 6:12, 19. 1 J √5:11-13, 20. **God.** Nu *23:19. 1 S 15:29. 2 T 2:13. He *6:17, 18. **cannot lie.** The answer to the question "Can God do everything?" is No, for He cannot do that which is out of harmony with His character. The question posed by some agnostics, "Can God make a stone so great that He cannot lift it?" is nonsensical for the same and other reasons—like asking can God make a square circle, an impossibility by definition, and so an absurdity. Nu *23:19. 2 T +2:13. He *6:17. **promised.** Ro 1:2. Ep 1:9. 2 T +*1:9. 1 P √1:20. Re 17:8. **before.** Pr 8:23-31. Mt *25:34. Jn *17:24. Ac 15:18. 1 C +*15:45. Ro 16:25. 2 T +1:9. He *13:20. 1 P *1:20-23. Re 13:8. **world.** Gr. *aionios*, Mt +18:8. lit. ages of time.

3. **in.** Da 8:23. +*9:24-27. 10:1. 11:27. Hab *2:3. Ac *17:26. Ro 5:6. Ga *4:4. Ep 1:10. 1 T +*2:6. 2 T 1:10. **times.** √96F2, Ge +4:10. **manifested.** Mk 13:10. *16:15. Ac +*10:36. Ro *10:14, 15. 15:19. +*16:26. Ep 2:17. *3:5-8. Ph 1:13. Col 1:6, *23. 1 T 2:5. Re 14:6. **preaching.** Ro *16:25. 2 T +4:17g. **which.** Ro 3:2. 1 C 9:17. Ga 2:7. 1 Th 2:4. 1 T +1:11. *2:7. 2 T *1:11. **commandment.** 1 T 1:1. **God.** T *2:10, 13. *3:4-6. Is +*12:2. 45:15, 21. Lk 1:47. 1 T *1:1. 2:3. *4:10.

4. **Titus.** i.e. *honorable*, ✱S#5103g. 2 C +2:13. 7:6, 13, 14. *8:6, 16, 23. 12:18, 18. Ga 2:1, 3. 2 T 4:10. **mine.** 1 T 1:1, 2. 2 T 1:2. 3 J +4. **the common.** Jn 1:12. Ro 1:12. 2 C *4:13. 2 P *1:1. Ju +*3. **Grace.** √173, Ge +27:44. See on Ro 1:7. Ep 1:2. Col 1:2. 1 T +1:2. 2 T 1:2. **and peace.** √174, Ge +18:27. **our.** See on ver. *3. Lk *2:11. Jn *4:42. 2 T +1:10. 2 P 1:11. *2:20. *3:2, 18. 1 J 4:14.

5. **I left.** 1 T 1:3. **Crete.** ver. 12. Dt 2:23. Je 47:4. Am 9:7. Ac 2:11. 27:7, 12, 13, 21. **set.** 1 Ch 6:32. Ec *12:9. Is 44:7. 1 C 11:34. *14:40. Col *2:5. **wanting.** or, left undone. T 3:13. Lk 18:22g. **ordain elders.** Ac +*14:23. 15:22. Ph 1:1. 1 T +5:17. 2 T +*2:2. **every city.** Ac 14:23.

6. **If.** √184A, 1 C +15:2. **any.** See on 1 T *3:2-7. **blameless.** 1 C +1:8. 1 T 3:10. **the husband.** Le *21:7, 14. Ezk 44:22. Ml 2:15. Lk 1:5. 1 T *3:12. 5:9. **one wife.** Ge +*4:19. **having.** Ge +*18:19. 1 S *2:11, 22, 29, 30. *3:12, 13. 1 T *3:4, 5, 12. **faithful.** 1 C 4:17. **not accused.** Pr *28:7. **riot.** Lk 15:13. Ep +5:18. 1 P 4:3, 4. **or unruly.** lit. insubordinate, rebellious, disobedient, not submissive. ver. 10. 1 S *2:11, 22, 29, 30. *3:12, 13. *15:23. 1 Th 5:14. 1 T *1:9. He 2:8.

7. **a bishop.** ver. 5. Ac 20:28. Ph 1:1. 1 T *3:1, 2, etc. **blameless.** Ac +*6:3. 1 T 3:10. **steward.** Mt +√24:45. Lk +*12:42. 1 C +*4:1, 2. 1 P *4:10. **not selfwilled.** Ge 49:6. 1 P *5:2. 2 P *2:10. **not soon angry.** Pr *14:17. *15:18. 16:32. Ec *7:9. 2 T 2:24. Ja √1:19, 20. **not given to wine.** T 2:3. Le 10:9. Pr 31:4, 5. Is *28:7. 56:12. Ezk 44:21. Ep +*5:18. 1 T *3:3. **no striker.** 2 T *2:24, 25g. **not given to filthy.** Is 56:10, 11. 1 T *3:3, 8. 1 P *5:2.

8. **lover of hospitality.** T#354. Mt 10:40-42. +25:35 (T#715). Ro 12:10, 13. 1 T *3:2. 5:10. He *13:2. 1 P +*4:9. **a lover of good.** 1 S 18:1. 1 K 5:1, 7. 2 Ch ◑13:7. *19:2. Ps 16:3. +*119:63. Am *5:15. Ac +*6:3. 2 T 2:2. 3:3. 1 J *3:14. *5:1. **men.** or, things. Ph *4:8. **sober.** T *2:2, 5, 7. 2 C 6:4-8. 1 Th 2:10. 1 T *4:12. *6:11. 2 T *2:22. **just.** Lk 1:75. Ep 4:24. 1 Th 2:10g. **temperate.** Ac +24:25. 1 C 7:9g. 9:25. 2 P 1:6.

9. **Holding.** Jb 2:3. 27:6. Pr *23:23. 1 Th *5:21. 2 Th *2:13, 15. 2 T +*1:13. Ju +*3. Re 2:25. 3:3, *11. **fast.** 1 T 1:15. 4:9. *6:3. 2 T +*2:2. **faithful word.** 1 T +1:15. **as he hath been taught.** or, in teaching. 1 T +4:6. **sound doctrine.** T *2:1, 7, 8. 1 T +1:10. *6:3. 2 T *4:3. **exhort.** 1 T +4:13. **to convince.** ver. 11. Ac *18:28. 1 C 14:24. 1 T +5:20g. 2 T +*2:25. **the gainsayers.** Gr. *antilego*, ✱S#483g. Rendered: (1) speak against: Lk 2:34. Jn 19:12. Ac 13:45a. 28:19, 22. (2) deny: Lk 20:27. (3) contradict: Ac 13:45b. (4) gainsay: Ro 10:21. (5) gainsayer: T 1:9. (6) answer again: T 2:9.

10. **there.** ver. 6. Ac *20:29. Ro *16:17, 18. 2 C *11:12-15. Ep +*4:14. 2 Th √2:10-12. 1 T 1:4, 6. *6:3-5. 2 T 3:13. 4:4. Ja *1:26. 2 P *2:1, 2. 1 J 2:18. *4:1. Re 2:6, 14. **deceivers.** Ga 6:3. **specially.** Ac +11:2. *15:1, 24. Ga *1:6-8. 2:4. *3:1. 4:17-21. *5:1-4. Ph 3:2, 3.

11. **mouths.** ver. 9. 1 T *3:10. Ps 63:11. 107:42. Ezk 16:63. Lk 20:40. Ro 3:19. 2 C 11:10. **subvert.** Mt *23:14. 2 T 2:18. 3:6. **houses.** √121J4, Ge +7:1. **filthy.** See on ver. 7. Is 56:10, 11. Je 8:10. Ezk 13:19. Mi 3:*5, 11. Jn 10:12. 1 T *6:5. 1 P 5:2. 2 P *2:1-3.

12. **of.** Ac *17:28. **prophet.** √121Q1, Je +28:5. **Cre-**

tians. i.e. *given to the flesh*, ✱S#2912g. ♪92H, Ac +17:28. ver. ◑+5. Ac 2:11. **alway**. Gr. *aei*, Mk 15:8. **liars**. Ro *16:18. 1 T *4:2. 2 P 2:12, 15. Ju 8-13. **slow bellies**. *or*, idle gluttons. ♪171Q18, Ro +16:18. i.e. *slow persons, who by reason of large eating, have grown stout and move slowly* (B648). Ph +*3:19.

13. **rebuke**. T *2:15. Pr *27:5. Ro 11:22g. 2 C 13:10. 1 T +*5:20. ◐6:5. 2 T ◐*2:24, 25. *4:2. **that**. T *2:2. Le +*19:17. Ps *119:80. 141:5. 2 C 7:8-12. 1 T +1:10. *4:6. **sound**. 1 T 1:10. **the faith**. ♪121R2, Ac +6:7. 1 T +1:19.

14. **Jewish**. i.e. *confession*, ✱S#2451g, only here. 1 T *1:4-7. *4:7. 2 T 4:4. **commandments of men**. Is *29:13. Mt √15:6, 9. Mk √7:7. Col +2:22. **turn**. Ga *4:9. 1 T +6:20. 2 T *4:4. He 12:25. 2 P *2:22.

15. **Unto**. ♪138C, Ge +22:14. **the pure**. Mk 7:19. Lk *11:39-41. Ac +*10:15. 15:9. Ro *14:14, 20. 1 C 6:12, 13. 10:23, 25, 31. 1 T 1:8. *4:3, 4. **things**. ♪63A1, Ge +14:20. Supply (meats), for the word "clean" is being used in its ceremonial or Levitical sense, for none can be otherwise either "pure" or "clean." **but**. Pr *21:4. Hg 2:13. Zc 7:5, 6. Mt *15:11, 18. Ro *14:20, 23. 1 C 11:27-29. **their mind**. Ge +*6:5. 8:21. Ec 9:3. Je +*17:9. Mk *7:21-23. Jn *3:19. Ro 8:7, 8. 1 C *2:14. 8:7. Ep 4:17-19. 5:8. 1 T +6:5. He *9:14. *10:22. **conscience is defiled**. T#126. Je 6:15. Zp 3:5. 1 C 8:7. 2 C +1:12. 1 T 3:9. 4:2. He 9:14.

16. **profess**. Nu 24:16. Is 29:13. *48:1. 58:2. 58:2. Ezk +*33:31. Ho 8:2, 3. Ro 2:18-24. 2 T *3:5-8. 1 J 2:4. Ju 4. **but in**. Col 1:21, 22. **deny**. 1 T +5:8. **being**. Jb *15:16. Pr 17:15. Re *21:8, 27. **know**. Je 22:16. 1 J 2:3-5. 4:20. **in works**. Ps 14:1, 3. **they deny**. 2 T 3:5. **and disobedient**. T 3:3. 1 S *15:22-24. Ep *5:6. 1 T 1:9. **unto**. T 3:1. Je 6:30. Ac +9:26. Ro *1:28. 2 T 2:21. *3:8, 17. **reprobate**. *or*, void of judgment. Je ◐22:16. 1 C +9:27g.

TITUS 2

The apostle directs Titus to instruct the people in their several relative duties, for the honor of the gospel; to exemplify them in his own conduct, and to take heed to his doctrine, 1-8; to teach servants to be obedient and upright, that "in all things they may adorn the doctrine of God our Savior," 9, 10. He enforces his exhortations, by showing the holy tendency and efficacy of the gospel, and charges Titus to act with authority and firmness, 11-15.

1. **speak**. Ml=2:7. **which become**. ver. 11-14. T *1:9. 3:8. 1 T 1:10. *6:3. 2 T *1:13. **doctrine**. ver. 7, 10. 1 T +4:6.

2. **That**. ♪63I2, Jsh +3:3. **the aged**. Le 19:32. Jb 12:12. Ps *92:14. Pr *16:31. Is 65:20. Lk 1:18. Phm 9. 2 J 1, 5. **sober**. *or*, vigilant. 1 C *15:34. 1 Th *5:6, 8. 1 T 3:2, 11. 1 P 1:13. 4:7. *5:8g. **grave**. ver. 7. 1 T 3:4, +8, 11. Ph *4:8g. **temperate**. T 1:8. Mk 5:15. Lk 8:35. Ac 24:25. Ro 12:3. 1 C 9:25. 2 C 5:13. Ga *5:23. 1 T 3:2. 1 P 4:7g. 2 P *1:6. **sound**. See on T *1:13. Ro 14:1. **in faith**. 2 Th 1:4. 1 T +1:14. Ja 1:3. Re 13:10. **in charity**. See on 1 T 1:5. 6:11. 2 T 3:10. **in patience**. 2 Th 3:5. 2 T +3:10. Ja *5:8, 10.

3. **as**. Ro 16:2. Ep 5:3. 1 T *2:9, 10. 3:11. 5:5-10. 1 P *3:3-5. **holiness**. *or*, holy women. **false accusers**. *or*, makebates. See on 1 T 3:8, 11. 2 T 3:3. **not given**. See on T *1:7. **teachers**. ver. *4. He *5:12. Re 2:20.

4. **teach**. T#425. Ep 5:21-25, 28, 33. Col +3:18

(T#197). 1 T +2:9. **young women**. 1 T 5:2, 11, 14. **sober**. *or*, wise. See on ver. *2. **to love their husbands**. 1 T *5:14.

5. **discreet**. See on ver. 2. **chaste**. 1 P 3:2. **keepers at home**. T#351. Ge +*16:8, 9. 18:9. Pr *7:11. 25:17. 27:8. *31:10-31. 1 T *5:13, 14. **good**. Mt 20:15. Ac 9:36, 39. Ro 5:7. 1 T *5:10. 1 P 2:18g. **obedient**. Ge *3:16. 1 C +*11:3. *14:34. Ep *5:22-24, 33. Col *3:18. 1 T *2:11, 12. 1 P *3:1-5. **that**. 2 S *12:14. Ps 74:10. Is 52:5. Ro 2:24. 1 T *5:14. +*6:1. **the word**. Ro +9:6.

6. **Young**. Jb 29:8. Ps 148:12. Ec 11:9. *12:1. Jl +*2:28. 1 T *4:12. +5:1. 2 T 2:22. 1 P *5:5. 1 J 2:13. **soberminded**. *or*, discreet. ver. 2. 1 P +4:7g.

7. **all things**. Ac *20:33-35. 2 Th 3:9. 1 T +*4:12. 1 P 5:3. **a pattern**. 1 T +*4:12. 1 P +5:3. **good works**. ver. 14. 1 T +6:18. **doctrine**. ver. 1, 10. 1 T +4:6. **uncorruptness**. 2 C *2:17. *4:2. *11:3-5. 2 C +*2:17. +*4:2. Ga *1:8. **gravity**. See on ver. 2. 1 T 2:2. 3:4. **sincerity**. 2 C *1:12. 8:8. Ep *6:24. Ph *1:10.

8. **Sound speech**. Mk 12:17, 28, 32, 34. Col *4:5, 6. 1 T *6:3. **that he**. Ne *5:9. 1 T *5:14. 1 P *2:12, 15. *3:16. **may**. Is +*66:5. Lk *13:17. 1 C 4:14. 2 Th *3:14. **having**. Ne 5:9. Da 6:4, 5. Ph *2:14-16. 1 P 2:15.

9. **servants**. Ep *6:5-8. Col *3:22-25. 1 T *6:1, 2. 1 P *2:+18-25. **to please**. Ep 5:24. **in all**. Col 3:22. **answering again**. *or*, gainsaying. T 1:9. 1 S 15:23. Lk 21:15. Ac 19:36.

10. **purloining**. 2 K *5:20-24. Lk 16:6-8. Jn *12:6. Ac *5:2, 3. **showing**. Ge 31:37, 38. *39:8, 9. 1 S 22:14. 26:23. Ps 101:6. Mt +*24:45. Lk √16:10. 1 C +*4:2. 1 T 3:11. **adorn**. Mt +*5:16. Ep 4:1. Ph +*1:27. *2:15, 16. √4:8. 1 P *2:12. 3:16. **the doctrine**. ver. 1, 7. 1 T +4:6. *5:17. 6:1, 3. 2 J *9. **God**. T +1:3. Is +*12:2. 1 T 1:1.

11. **the grace**. T *3:4, 5, 7. Ps +*84:11. Zc *4:7. +*12:10. Jn *1:14, 16, 17. Ac +*11:23. 13:43. 15:11. 20:24. Ro *4:4, 5. 5:2, 15, 20, 21. 11:5, 6. 2 C 6:1. Ga *2:21. Ep 1:6, 7. *2:5-8. 2 Th 2:16. 1 T 1:14. He *2:9. +*12:15. 1 P 1:10-12. 5:5-12. **bringeth**, etc. *or*, bringeth salvation to all men, hath appeared. T 3:4. Ps 96:1-3, 10. 98:1-3. ch. 117. Is 2:2, 3. *45:22. *49:6. 52:10. 60:1-3. Mt +√28:19. Mk *16:15. Lk 3:6. +*24:47. Ac *13:47. Ro 10:18. 15:9-19. Ep 3:6-8. Col *1:6, 23. 1 T √2:4. 2 T 4:17. **all**. Ps 67:2. Lk +3:6. Jn 1:9. Ro 10:18. 1 T +*2:4, 6.

12. **Teaching**. Mt 28:20. Jn 6:45. Ro 6:12-16. Ga 5:16, 17. Col 3:2. 1 Th *4:9. 2 T +*3:16. He *8:11. 12:11. 1 J *2:27. **denying**. Is √55:6, 7. Ezk 18:30, 31. 33:14, 15. Mt *3:8-10. *16:24. Lk 1:75. Ro *6:1, 2, 4-6, 12, 19. 8:13. 13:12, 13. 1 C +*6:9-11. 2 C *7:1. Ga *5:24. Ep 1:4. 4:22-25. Col 1:22. 3:5-9. 1 Th *4:7. Ja 4:8-10. 1 P 2:11, 12. *4:2-5. 2 P +*1:4. *2:20-22. 1 J √2:15-17. Ju 18. **ungodliness**. 2 T 2:16. **worldly lusts**. 1 P *4:2. 1 J √2:16. **live**. Ps 105:45. Ezk 36:27. Mt √5:19, 20. Lk 1:6, 75. 3:9-13. Ac 17:30. *24:16, 25. Ro *6:19. 1 T +*4:12. 2 T 3:12. 1 P 1:14-18. 2 P √1:5-8. 3:11. 1 J *2:6. Re 14:12. **soberly**. See on ver. *4. **righteously**. Lk 1:75. **godly**. Ps *4:3. 2 C 1:12. 2 T 1:9. 2 P *2:9. **this**. Jn +√6:54n. 14:30. *17:14, 15. Ro +*12:2. Ga 1:4. Ep 2:2. 1 T 2:2. +6:17. 2 T 4:10. 1 J *5:19. **world**. Gr. *aion*, Mt +6:13.

13. **Looking**. Lk 2:25, 38g. Ac +*24:15. 1 C +1:7. Ph *3:20, 21. 2 T *4:8. He 9:28. 2 P *3:+12-14. **blessed hope**. ♪121R3, Ps +71:5. Is the "blessed hope" the Rapture of the church (1 Th 4:16, 17) before the Great

Tribulation, or is it the appearance of Christ "in the clouds of heaven with power and great glory" after the Tribulation? Misunderstanding this verse, some interpreters fail to recognize this is a reference to Christ's pretribulational "glorious appearing" for the Church (Mt 17:2. Jn √14:3. √17:5, 24. 1 Th √4:17. 1 J √3:2), to be carefully distinguished from His "coming in the clouds of heaven with power and great glory" (Mt 24:30) after the Great Tribulation at the open manifestation of the Second Advent. Paul presented the doctrine of the Rapture as a source of present comfort to the Thessalonians (1 Th 4:18). It could hardly be a source of comfort to them if Paul taught that they must endure the Great Tribulation first! A careful study of the details of prophecy confirms the doctrine of the imminent and secret pretribulation Rapture as the logical outcome of the proper combination of prophetic detail. Peters (*Theocratic Kingdom*) and other careful students of prophecy before and since have shown (1) that prophecy must be interpreted consistently in a literal manner; (2) that such a literal interpretation necessitates a distinction between the Church and Israel (Is 60:21n); (3) maintaining and observing the distinction between the Church and Israel guards against applying the Great Tribulation, called in Scripture the time of Jacob's trouble (Je 30:7) to the Church; (4) that no event of prophecy is said to occur before the first stage of the Second Advent, for to interpose any event, such as the Great Tribulation, introduces a snare to put us off our guard (see Peters, *Theocratic Kingdom*, vol. 3, p. 102); (5) Scripture most certainly does predict specific events which occur prior to the last stages of the Second Advent, such as the coming of Elijah (Ml 4:5, 6), but such events occur in the interim between the first or secret stage of the advent, and its final or open public stage, and so do not precede the Rapture; (6) that the number of events revealed in Scripture to take place on "the last day" (Jn +*6:54n) when Christ returns at the second advent are simply too numerous to compress into a single event occupying but one literal twenty-four hour day; (7) that since the events are so numerous, the second advent may be divided loosely into at least two stages (see the note on the known and unknown time of Christ's coming, Mt 24:42), which must not be misrepresented as a second and third coming, any more than prophecies of the First Advent that Christ would come as a babe to Bethlehem yet ride triumphantly to Jerusalem on a colt constitute that a first and second coming; (8) that the many passages relating to the return of Christ may be distinguished in their reference to his public manifestation in glory to the earth after the Tribulation with his saints, and the imminent return for his saints prior to the Great Tribulation; (9) careful readers have certainly noted that some passages present the world as proceeding with its affairs in very normal times ("peace and safety," 1 Th 5:3. "all things continue," 2 P 3:4) when the return of Christ comes as a surprise, while other passages represent the time immediately preceding his return as a time of great tribulation, suffering, and terror (Lk 21:26. Re 6:16), everyone very much aware of his advent (Mt 24:30); (10) many other lines of proof are developed in Peters' work, including specific prophecies (Mi 7:15) which specify a period of time involving *years* for the accomplishment of all the related events; (11) a consideration of the

prophecies of the First Advent and their manner of accomplishment will show that their fulfillment was pre-eminently literal, occupied at least 33 years, could not be compressed into a single day, yet if they were to be interpreted by the principles advocated by amillenialists for the Second Advent prophecies, we could hardly have expected a suffering Savior who was literally born of a virgin in Bethlehem, and who was crucified on a cross, for by their principles all such specific details of prophecy must not be pressed for a literal fulfillment. T 1:2. 3:7. Ac √24:15. Ro 5:5. *8:19, 24, 25, 29. 15:◑+*4, 13. Ga *5:5. Col +*1:5, 23, 27. 1 Th 2:16. He 6:18, 19. 1 P +√1:3, 4. 1 J √3:3. **and.** J93A, Ge +1:26. By Hendiadys, the "blessed hope" and "the glorious appearing" are not two things, but one: our hope is the glorious appearing (B669). The "glorious appearing" may well be one with the rapture, for Christ at the Rapture will appear gloriously for his saints. Walvoord notes, "While the appearing of the glory of Christ to the world and to Israel will not be fulfilled until the Second Coming to establish the kingdom on earth, the church will see the glory of Christ when she meets him in the air" (John F. Walvoord, *The Rapture Question*, p. 74). **the glorious appearing.** J24N, Ge +17:5. The preparations required to come with his saints require Christ to have first come for his saints; therefore, the blessed hope and glorious appearing may be applied to the Rapture of the Church prior to Christ's return in "power and great glory" (Mt 24:30), when we will be with him and share in his glory (Zc +*14:5. Ju 14, 15). The rewarding of the saints (Lk +*14:14), their appointment to positions of authority (Jn +*14:2, 3), their training and organization for posts (Mt 25:21, 23. Lk 22:29, 30) in the eternal earthly kingdom (Da 7:13. Re 11:15) of Christ, not to mention such diverse events as are comprehended in Old Testament prophecies such as Christ's pleading with Israel in the wilderness (Ezk 20:35, 36) and speaking "comfortably unto her" (Ho 2:14), and his victorious march against his enemies on the way to Jerusalem (Is 63:1-4), then his victory over the hosts gathered against Judah and Jerusalem (Zc 9:14. 12:7, 8), all require his literal physical personal presence upon the earth (Re 11:17n. 16:5) before he comes to Zion (Is +*51:11) for the victory ascent to the Mount of Olives (Zc 14:4), which are all events that take place prior to the final public victorious manifestation of Christ in clouds of glory (Mt +*24:30) with his saints (Zc +*14:5. Col 3:4. Ju 14, 15), when every eye shall see him (Re +*1:7). Now it is just such attention to prophetic details which enables the careful student to entertain a correct view of the several aspects or stages of the second advent. Of course the contention of some that this is "grasshopper theology" or "hop-skip-and-jump" prooftexting is directly refuted by the examination of the location and extent of prophecies regarding the first advent, which are likewise widely scattered through the Old Testament, and are nowhere found in a systematic arrangement (T#1874-1976). That Christ and the apostles taught Scripture by such a comparison of widely scattered texts is evident from the occurrence of composite quotations in the New Testament (Mt +*27:9n). Jb +*19:25-27. Is *25:9. Mt +*16:27n. √17:2. *25:31. *26:64. Mk 8:38. 14:62. Jn √14:3. √17:5, 24. 2 C *4:4, 6g. Col +*1:26. *3:3, 4. 2 Th 1:7, 8. +2:8g. 1 T 6:13, 14. 2 T +*4:1, 8. He

√9:28. 1 P *1:7, 13. 4:13. 1 J √3:2. Re *1:7. **great God and**. ♪93A, Ge +1:26. A. T. Robertson notes that as early as 1798 Granville Sharp laid down a rule which has not since been successfully discredited, that when two nouns (either substantive or adjective, or participle) of the same case are connected by "and" (*kai*, in Greek), nouns of personal description (respecting office, dignity, affinity, or connection, and attributes, properties, or qualities, good or ill), if the article "the" in any of its cases precedes the first of the said nouns or participles, and is not repeated before the second noun or participle, the second noun always relates to the same person that is expressed or described by the first noun or participle: i.e. it denotes a farther description of the first named person. This principle is not claimed, however, for proper names or to the plural number. Thus "the apostle and high priest of our confession" is one person, Jesus (He 3:1). John is referred to as "your brother, and companion" in Re 1:9, a reference to just one person. Such expressions as "the God and Father" (Ro 15:6. 1 C 15:24. 2 C 1:3. 11:31. Ga 1:4. Ep 5:20. Ph 4:20. 1 Th 1:3. 3:11, 13. Re 1:6) and "the Lord and Father" (Ja 1:27. 3:9) are all used of one person, not two. So likewise "the Lord and Savior Jesus Christ" (2 P 2:20. 3:2) is a reference to one person. The introduction of the word "our" in 2 P 1:11 and 3:18 does not affect the idiom. Following the same principle for the identical construction in Greek for 2 P 1:1, "our God and Savior Jesus Christ" is a reference to a single person, not two. So here at T 2:13, the same construction is correctly rendered "our God and Savior Jesus Christ," and the reference is to one person, not two. Attention to this construction thus yields two texts in support of the Deity of Christ that were not evident in some English translations (see Robertson, *The Minister and His Greek New Testament*, "The Greek Article and the Deity of Christ," pp. 61-68). When the Greek article occurs before both nouns, two persons are meant, as "let him be unto thee as an heathen man and a publican," two separate persons are implied (Mt 18:17, cited by William Hendrickson, *Comm. on 1-2 Timothy and Titus*, p. 374). Those who deny the validity of this grammatical principle are faced with the problem that if two persons are meant, then Paul is predicting the simultaneous glorious advent of both the Father and the Son at Christ's second coming. Although the advent of the Father is supportable from other prophecies (Da ●7:22. Zc √14:5. Ep *1:10), the simultaneous advent of the Father and the Son is not usually incorporated into the prophetic system of those who understand this passage to refer to two persons. Ne 1:5. 9:32. Da 2:45. 9:4. Lk *9:26. Jn *1:1. +*20:28. Ac +*20:28. Ro +*9:5. Ph *2:6. Col *2:9. 2 Th 1:12g. He +*1:8. 2 P √1:1g. **our Savior**. T *3:4, 6. Ne +*9:6. Is √43:11. Ezk 37:23. Ho 1:7. Mt *1:21. Ac 3:26. 2 T +1:10. 2 P +*3:18. 1 J 4:14.

14. **gave**. Mt +*20:28. Jn 6:51. *10:15, 18. 2 C *5:21. Ga *1:4. √2:20n. 3:13. Ep 1:7. 5:2, 23-27. Col 1:14. 1 T 1:15. √2:6. He 1:3. 7:26. *9:14. 1 P *3:18. Re +*1:5. *5:9. **for us**. Jn 10:11. 11:51, 52. Ac 20:28. Ro *5:8. √8:32. 2 C √5:15. Ep 4:23, 25-27. 1 P 1:18-21. 1 J √2:2. 4:10. **redeem**. Ge 48:16. Ex 15:16. 2 S 7:23. Ps 130:8. Ezk 36:25. 37:23. Ho 13:14. Mt *1:21. Ro 11:26, 27. 1 P +1:18. **purify**. Nu=8:21. Ml 3:3. Mt *3:12. Ac *15:9. He 9:14g. Ja *4:8. 1 P *1:22.

2 P +1:9. 1 J √3:2, 3. **unto himself**. Ac 15:14. Ro 14:7, 8. 2 C √5:14, 15. **peculiar**. T#671. Ex 15:16. *19:5, 6. Dt 7:6. *14:2. 26:18. Ps *4:3. 135:4. Ro 7:15-25. 2 C 6:8-10. 1 P +*2:9. **zealous**. Ph +*1:29. **of good works**. ♪181E, Ge +3:24. ver. 7. T √3:8. Nu 25:13. Ac +*9:36. Ep √2:10. 1 T 2:10. +6:18. He *10:24. 1 P 2:12.

15. **speak**. See on T 1:13. 2 T *4:2. **exhort**. 1 T +4:13. **rebuke**. 1 T +5:20. **with**. Mt 7:29. Mk 1:22, 27. Lk 4:36. **authority**. 2 C +*10:8. **Let**. 1 T +*4:12. **despise**. Lk *10:16.

TITUS 3

The apostle inculcates on Christians, subjection to rulers, and good behavior to all men, 1, 2; from the consideration of their own sinfulness and their salvation by God's mercy through Christ, 3-8. He cautions Titus to avoid disputes; and shows him how to deal with heretics, 9-11: and, directing him to meet him at Nicopolis, and giving instructions about other matters, 12-14, he concludes with salutations, 15.

1. **Put**. Is 43:26. 1 T *4:6. 2 T 1:6. 2:14. 2 P 1:12, 13. *3:1, 2. Ju 5. **to be subject**. T#314. Ex 22:28. Dt 17:9-12. Pr 24:21. Ec *8:2-5. 10:4. Je 27:17. Mt *17:24-27. *22:20, 21. *23:2, 3. Ac ●+*4:19. ●+*5:29. Ro √13:1-7. 1 T 2:1-3. 1 P √2:13-17. **magistrates**. Ep +1:21. **to be ready**. ver. *8, *14. T *2:14. 1 C √15:58. Ga √6:9, 10. Ep √2:10. Ph 1:11. Col +√1:10. 1 T 5:10. 2 T +2:21. He *13:21.

2. **speak**. Ps 140:11. Pr 6:19. Ac *23:5. 1 C +√6:10. 2 C 12:20. Ep +*4:31. 1 T 3:11. Ja *4:11. 1 P 2:1. 3:10. 4:4. 2 P 2:10. Ju 8, 10. **no**. Pr 19:19. 25:24. 1 T *3:3. 2 T +*2:24, 25. **gentle**. 2 S *22:36. Is 40:11. Mt *11:29. 1 C 13:5. 2 C 10:1. Ga +*5:22. *6:1. Ep 4:2. Ph 4:5. Col *3:12, 13. 1 Th 2:7. 2 T +*2:24, 25. Ja *1:19, 20. +3:17. 1 P 3:8. **showing all meekness**. 2 T +*2:25. **all men**. 1 C 9:19. Ga +*6:10. 1 Th 5:14, 15. 1 P 2:17.

3. **we ourselves**. *♪39, Ac +17:23. Ro *3:9-20. 1 C +*6:9-11. Ep *2:1-3. Col 1:21. 3:7. 1 P *4:1-3. **were**. T#574. Je +20:11 (T#513). 1 C √6:11. Ep *5:8. Re 22:15. **foolish**. Pr *1:22, 23. 8:5. 9:6. **disobedient**. T 1:16. Mt 21:29. Ac *9:1-6. *26:19, 20. Ep *2:2. 1 P *1:14. **deceived**. Is 44:20. Ob 3. Lk *21:8. Ga 6:3. 2 T 3:13. Ja *1:26. Re *12:9. 13:14. **serving**. Jn *8:+34, 44. Ro *6:17, 20, 22. Ep 2:1, 2. 2 T 2:25, 26. 1 J 3:10. 5:19. **divers lusts**. 2 T 3:6. 4:3. **living**. Ro +*1:29-31. 2 C 12:20. 2 T 3:2, 3. **hateful**. Ps 36:2. 1 J 2:9. 3:14, 15. Re 18:2.

4. **the kindness**. T *2:11. Ro 2:4. *5:20, 21. +*11:22. Ep *2:4-10. **love**. *or*, pity. 1 J *4:9, 10. **God**. See on T 1:3. *2:10. Is 45:21, 22. 1 T 1:1. 2:3. *4:10. **appeared**. T √2:11. 2 T *1:10. He *9:26.

5. **not by works**. Jb *9:20. 15:14. *25:4. Ps 143:2. Is *57:12. Lk 10:27-29. Ro *3:20, 27, 28. √4:5. 9:11, 16, 30. 11:6. Ga *2:16. 3:16-21. Ep √2:4, 8, 9. 2 T +*1:9. **according**. ver. 4. 1 S 12:22. Ps 62:12. *86:5, 15. 109:26. 130:7. Mi √7:18. Lk 1:50, 54, 72, 78. Ep 1:3, 6, 7. +*2:4. He *4:16. 1 P *1:3. 2:10. **washing**. Jn √3:3-5. 1 C *6:11. Ep *5:26. 1 P 3:21. **regeneration**. Mt +*19:28g. **renewing**. Ps +*51:10. Ro +*12:2. Ep 4:22, 23. Col *3:10. He 6:6. **Ghost**. Gr. *pneuma*, Mt +1:18.

6. **he shed**. ♪22C38, Ps +79:6. ♪22K4, Je +2:13. Pr *1:23. Is 32:15. 44:3. Ezk 36:25. Jl +*2:28. Jn *1:16.

*7:37-39. Ac *2:33. 10:45. Ro *5:5. **abundantly**. Gr. richly. See on Ep 2:4. *3:8. **through**. T 1:4. Jn *4:10. *14:16, 17. *16:7. Ro 8:2. **our Savior**. 2 T +*1:10.

7. **being justified**. T *2:11. Ro +*3:24, 28. 4:4, 16. *5:1, 2, 15-21. 11:6. 1 C 6:11. Ga *2:16. **his grace**. T 2:11. Ac +*11:23. 15:11. **made heirs**. Mt +*19:29. Ro √8:+17, 23, 24. Ga 3:29. 4:7. Ep 1:11n. He *6:17. 11:7, 9. Ja +*2:5. 1 P 3:7. **hope**. See on T +*1:2n. √2:13. Ac 23:6. +*26:6. **eternal**. Gr. *aionios*, Mt +18:8.

8. **a faithful**. √101, Dt +32:42. T 1:9. 1 T +1:15. these things. √63I1A, Ex +12:4. or, "concerning these (heirs)." **that thou**. Pr 21:28. Ac 12:15. 2 C 4:13. 1 T 1:7. **which**. Ps 78:22. Jn √5:24. 12:44. Ac +16:34g. Ro √4:3, 5. 10:14. Ga 3:6. 2 T *1:12. Ja 2:23. 1 P *1:21. 1 J √5:10-13. **be careful**. See on ver. 1, 14. T 2:14. Ep +*4:28. **maintain**. Ja *2:17. **good works**. Jb 22:2. 35:7, 8. Ps 16:2, 3. 2 C 9:12-15. 1 T +6:18. Phm 11.

9. **avoid**. See on T 1:14. 1 T 1:3-7. 4:7. 2 T 2:16, 23. **questions**. 1 T 1:4. 6:4. 2 T 2:23. **genealogies**. 1 T 1:4. **strivings about**. Col √2:16n, 17, 20-23. **the law**. Ac √21:25. **unprofitable**. Jb 15:3. 1 C 8:1. 13:2. 2 T 2:14.

10. **heretick**. 1 C √11:19. Ga 5:20. 2 P 2:1. **after**. Mt *18:+15-17. 2 C 13:2. **first and second**. Pr +*18:13. Jn +*7:24, 51. 1 T +*5:19n. **admonition**. 1 C 10:11.

Ep 6:4. 1 Th 5:12. **reject**. Ps +√119:63. Mt +*7:6. +√15:14. Ro +*16:17. 1 C 5:4-13. Ga 5:12. 2 Th +*3:6, 14. 1 T 4:7. 5:11. 2 T 2:23. *3:5. 2 J +*10.

11. **is subverted**. T 1:11. Ac 15:24. 1 T +*1:19, 20. 2 T 2:14. He 10:26. **being**. Mt 25:26-29. Lk *7:30. 19:22. Jn √3:18. Ac 13:46. Ro 3:19.

12. **Artemas**. i.e. *whole, sound; safe and sound*, *S#734g. **Tychicus**. Ac 20:4. Ep *6:21. 2 T +4:12. **be diligent**. 2 T 4:+9, 21. **Nicopolis**. i.e. *conquest of the city*, *S#3533g. 2 T ◐4:10. **for**. 1 C 16:6, 8, 9.

13. **Bring**. Ac +15:3. **Zenas**. i.e. *living; Jupiter*, *S#2211g. **the lawyer**. Mt +22:35. Lk *7:30. 10:25. 11:45, 52. 14:3. **Apollos**. See on Ac *18:24. 1 C 1:12. **on**. Ac 21:5. 28:10. Ro 15:24. 1 C 16:11. 3 J *5-8. **diligently**. Lk +7:4g. **that nothing**. T +1:5.

14. **learn**. See on ver. 8. **maintain good works**. or, profess honest trades. T 2:14. Ac 18:3. +*20:35g. Ep √4:28. 1 Th *2:9. 2 Th 3:8. 1 T 6:18. **necessary uses**. Ep 4:29g. **that**. Is 61:3. Mt 7:19. 21:19. Lk *13:6-9. Jn *15:8, 16. Ro 15:28. Ph 1:11. +*4:17n. Col +√1:10. He 6:6-12. 2 P √1:8.

15. **with me**. See on Ro 16:21-24. 2 T 4:21. **Greet**. See on Ro 16:1-20. **love**. Ga 5:6. Ep 6:23. 1 T 1:5. Phm 5. 2 J 1, 2. 3 J 1. **Grace**. See on 1 C 16:23. Ep 6:24. Col +4:18. 2 T 4:22. He 13:25.

PHILEMON

PHILEMON 1

The apostle salutes Philemon, 1-3; declares his joy at hearing of his faith and love, 4-7; earnestly and pathetically entreats him to receive into favor his fugitive servant, Onesimus, now become, by the apostle's ministry, a consistent believer, 8-21; desires him to provide for him a lodging, as he expected to be speedily released, 22; and concludes with salutations and benedictions, 23-25.

1. **a prisoner**. ver. 9. Ac *23:18. See on Ep 3:+1, 13. *4:1. *6:19, 20. Ph 1:7, 12-20. Col 4:18. 2 T 1:8. **Timothy**. Ac +16:1. See on 2 C 1:1. Ph 1:1. Col 1:1. 2 Th 1:1. **our brother**. 1 C +1:1. **Philemon**. *S#5371g. The apostle in this epistle indulges in some fine paronomasias on the proper names. Thus Philemon, *phileemon*, "affectionate," or "beloved," is "our dearly beloved;" *Apphia*, (*Apphia*, from *appha*, the affectionate address of a brother or sister, according to Suidas) is "the beloved sister," as several MSS., Vulgate, and others correctly read; *Archippus* (*Arkippos*, the ruler of the horse, for the managing of which heroes were anciently famous) is "our fellow soldier;" and *Onesimus* (*Oneesimos*, "useful" or "profitable") once unprofitable, is now profitable. **beloved**. Ac 15:25. Ro 16:5, 8. **and fellow-laborer**. ver. 24. Ro +16:3. 1 C 3:9. Ph 2:25. *4:3. Col 4:11. 1 Th *3:2.

2. **Apphia**. i.e. *dear one*, *S#682g. **Archippus**. Col *4:17. **our fellow-soldier**. Ph 2:25. 2 T *2:3, 4. **the church**. 2 C 11:28. **in thy house**. Ro +*16:5. 1 C *16:19. Col 4:15. 2 J 10.

3. **Grace**. See on Ro +*1:7. 1 C *16:23. 2 C *13:14. Ep 1:2. 1 P *5:5. **peace**. Jn *14:27. He *13:20.

4. **thank**. Ac 27:35. Ro +*1:8, 9. Ep 1:16. Ph *1:3,

4. Col 1:3. 1 Th 1:2. 2 Th *1:3. 2 T 1:3. **mention**. Ro +1:9.

5. **Hearing**. Ga *5:6. Ep *1:15. Col 1:3, 4, 9. **thy love**. Ep *6:24. 1 Th +1:3. 1 P *1:8. **and faith**. √174, Ge +18:27. Ep 1:15. **toward the Lord**. ver. 7. Ps 16:3. Ac 9:39-41. Ro 12:13. 15:25, 26. 1 C 16:1. 2 Th *1:3. He +*6:10. 1 J *3:23. 5:1, 2. **saints**. Ac 9:13. 2 C +1:1.

6. **That**. or, (praying) that. √63B, Ge +25:28. **the communication**. or, fellowship. Ac *2:42. Ro 15:26g. 1 C 1:9. 2 C 9:12-14. 13:14. Ph *1:9-11. 2:1. T *3:14. He +*6:10. 13:16g. Ja *2:14, 17. 1 J 1:3, 6, 7. **thy faith**. Ro 4:5. Ga 5:6. **effectual**. He 4:12g. Ja 5:16. **the acknowledging**. Ps 107:2. Mt +*5:16. 1 C 14:25. 2 C *9:13. Ep 1:17mg. 3:17-19. Ph 1:9. √4:8. Col +*1:9, 10. 3:10. 1 P 1:5-8. *2:12. 3:1, 16. **in you**. 2 P +*1:8.

7. **great joy**. 2 C 7:4. Ph 1:25, 26. 2:2, 17, 18. √4:4. 1 Th 1:3. √2:13, 19. 3:9. Ja 1:2. 2 J *4. 3 J 3-6. **consolation**. or, comfort. Lk 16:25. Ac 4:36. 1 C +14:3. 2 C √1:4, 6. 7:4, 13. Col 4:11. **the bowels**. *or*, hearts. ver. 12, 20. 2 C 6:12. 7:13. Col +*3:12. 2 T 1:16. **saints**. He +*6:10. **refreshed**. ver. 20. 1 Ch 22:9, 18. Mt *11:28. Ro 15:32. 1 C 16:18. 2 C 7:13. 2 T 1:16. Re 6:11. +*14:13.

8. **bold**. Ac 2:29g. 4:29. 2 C 3:12. 10:1, 2. 11:21. Ep *6:19, 20. 1 Th *2:2, 6. He 3:6g. 4:14, 16. **enjoin**. Mk 1:27g. Ac 23:2. 2 C 10:8. Col 3:18. 1 T 6:13. **convenient**. or, befitting. Ep 5:4. Col 3:18.

9. **love's sake**. Ro +*12:1. 2 C 5:20. 6:1. Ga *5:13. Ep 4:1, 2. He 13:19. 1 P *2:11. **Paul the aged**. Ps *71:9, 18. Pr *16:31. Is *46:4. Lk 1:18. 2 C +5:20. Ep 6:20. T 2:2. **a prisoner**. ver. 1. Ep 3:1. 4:1.

10. **beseech**. 2 C *10:1. **my son**. 2 S 9:1-7. 18:5. 19:37, 38. Mk 9:17. 1 T *1:2. T *1:4. 3 J +4. **Onesimus**.

i.e. *profitable*, ✱S#3682g. ver. 20. Col *4:9. **whom**. ver. 13. 1 C +*4:15. Ga *4:19. **bonds**. 2 T 2:9.

11. **time past**. Ep *2:1, 2, 12, 13. 5:8. 1 P *4:3. **unprofitable**. ✓111, Ge +18:27. Jb 30:1, 2. Ho 8:8. Mt *25:30. Lk ✓17:10. Ro *3:12. 1 P 2:10. **but now**. ✓63B, Ge +2:10. Supply (is). **profitable**. Lk *15:24, 32. 2 T 2:21. *4:11.

12. **sent**. Lk 23:7, 11, 15. Ac 25:21. **thou**. Mt *6:14, 15. *18:21-35. Mk *11:25. Ep ✓4:32. **mine**. Dt 13:6. 2 S 16:11. Je 31:20. Lk *15:20. **bowels**. ver. 7, 20.

13. **Whom**. 2 T 4:11. **in thy stead**. 1 C +16:17. Ph *2:30. **ministered**. Ac +19:22. **the bonds**. ver. 1, 10. Mk 8:35. Ep 3:1. 4:1. Ph 1:+7, 13.

14. **without**. ver. 8, 9. 2 C +*1:24. 1 P *5:3. **thy benefit**. 1 Ch 29:17. Ps 110:3. 1 C *9:7, 17. 2 C *8:12. *9:5, 7. 1 P *5:2. **necessity**. 2 C +*9:5, 7. He 7:12. **willingly**. He 10:26g. 1 P *5:2.

15. **perhaps**. Ge *45:5-8. +*50:20. Ps 76:10. Is 10:7. Ac 4:28. Ro 5:7g. +*8:28. **departed**. Mt 19:6g. 1 C 7:11, 15g. **for a season**. lit. hour. ✓171T6, Jn +4:23. Jn 5:35. 2 C +7:8. 1 Th 2:17. **receive**. Mt +6:2g. 10:40. 18:5. Lk *16:4, 9. Jn 13:20. Col 4:10. **for ever**. Gr. *aionios*, Mt +18:8. Jn +*15:16.

16. **Not now as**. 1 C 7:21-23. **a servant**. 1 C +*7:22. 1 P 2:16. **above**. Jn 15:15. Col 3:11. **a brother**. Mt *23:8. Ac 9:17. Ga 4:28, 29. Col 4:9. 1 T *6:2. He 3:1. 1 P *1:22, 23. 2:18-24. 1 J *5:1. **both in**. Ep *6:5-7. **and in**. Col *3:22, 23.

17. **If**. ✓184A, 1 C +15:2. **thou count**. Ac 16:15. 2 C 8:23. Ep 3:6. Ph 1:7. 1 T *6:2. He 3:1, 14. Ja +*2:5. 1 P 5:1. 1 J *1:3. **partner**. or, partaker. He *3:1. **receive**. ver. 10, 12. Mt *10:40. 12:48-50. *18:5. *25:40. Ac 28:2. Ro 14:1. 15:7.

18. **If**. ✓184A, 1 C +15:2. **wronged**. Mt 20:13. 1 C 6:8. **oweth**. Dt 15:2. Mt 18:28. Lk 16:5, 7. T

2:10. **put that**. Is *53:4-7h. Lk 10:35. Ro 4:23. 5:13g. **mine account**. Ph +*4:17n.

19. **I Paul**. 1 C +*16:21, 22. Ga 5:2. 6:11. **not say**. ✓35. Apophasis; or, Insinuation B486. Addition of insinuation (implied) by way of reasoning. The figure occurs when, professing to suppress certain matters, the writer adds the insinuation negatively, as if to say, "I will not mention the matter, but," etc.; or, "I will not mention another argument, which, however, if I should, you could not refute." **how thou owest**. 1 C *4:15. 6:19. *9:1, 2. 2 C *3:2. 1 T 1:2. T 1:4. Ja *5:19, 20.

20. **let me**. ver. 10. 2 C 2:2. 7:4-7, 13. Ph 2:2. *4:1. 1 Th *2:19, 20. 3:7-9. He *13:17. 3 J *4. **refresh**. ver. +7, 12. Ph 1:8. 2:1. 1 J *3:17. **the Lord**. Ro 16:7, 9.

21. **confidence**. 2 C +2:3. 7:16. 8:22. Ga 5:10. 2 Th 3:4. **obedience**. Ro 1:5. Ph ✓2:12. He 5:8. 1 P *1:2, 14, 22. **do more**. Lk ✓17:10.

22. **prepare**. Ac *28:23. **for I trust**. Ro 15:24. Ph 1:25, 26. 2:24. He 13:23. 2 J 12. 3 J 14. **through**. Ro 15:30-32. 2 C +*1:11. Ph 1:19, 25. Ja *5:16. **I shall**. He 13:19. **given unto**. Ac +25:11g. 27:24. 1 C 2:12.

23. **Epaphras**. Col 1:7. *4:12. **my fellow-prisoner**. Ro *16:7. Col 4:10.

24. **Marcus**. Ac 12:12, 25. 13:+*5, 13. 15:37-39. Col +4:10. 2 T *4:11. 1 P 5:13. **Aristarchus**. Ac *19:29. 20:4. 27:2. Col 4:10. **Demas**. Col +*4:14. 2 T +*4:10, 11. **Lucas**. i.e. *luminous*, ✱S#3065g. Col 4:14. 2 T 4:11. **my fellow-laborers**. ver. +1, 2. Ro 16:3, 9, 21. 1 C 3:9. 2 C *8:23. Ph 2:25. *4:3. 3 J *8.

25. **grace**. See on Ro 16:20, 24. Ga +*6:18. **your spirit**. Gr. *pneuma*, ✓171Q1B, Mk +2:8. 8:12. Lk 1:47. Jn 11:33. 13:21. 1 C 14:14. 16:18. 2 C 2:13. 7:1, 13. Ga 6:18. Ph 4:23mg. 2 T *4:22.

HEBREWS

HEBREWS 1

The writer declares the essential deity and mediatorial glory of the Son of God, by whom the Father speaks to men under the gospel dispensation, 1-4. He adduces several scriptures to prove that the Messiah was to be far greater than the angels, and worshipped by them as their Creator and Lord, 5-14.

1. **Cir. A.M. 4067. A.D. 63**. **at sundry times**. ✓98, Ro +11:33. Ge +*3:15. 6:3, 13, etc. 8:15, etc. 9:1, etc. +*12:1-3. 26:2-5. 28:12-15. 32:24-30. 46:2-4. Ex 3:1, etc. Lk *24:27, 44. Ac 28:23. 1 P 1:10-12. 2 P ✓1:20, 21. **in divers manners**. Nu *12:6-8. Ps *89:19. Jl +*2:28. **spake**. Mt +10:20. **the fathers**. Lk 1:55, 72. Jn 7:22. Ac 13:32. Ro +*15:8.

2. **these**. He 9:26. Ge 49:1. Nu 24:14. Dt 4:30. 18:15. 31:29. Is *2:2. Je 30:24. 48:47. Ezk 38:16. Da 2:28. 10:14. Ho 3:5. Mi 4:1. Ac 2:17. Ga ✓4:4. Ep +*1:10. 1 P 1:20. 2 P 3:3. 1 J +2:18. Ju 18. **spoken**. ver. 5, 8. He *2:3. *5:8. 7:3. Ex=20:19. Dt=5:5. Mt *3:17. *17:5. 26:63. Mk 1:1. 12:6. Jn *1:14, 17, 18. ✓3:16. *14:10. 15:15. Ro +*1:4. **by his Son**. ver. 8. He 3:6. 4:14. 5:8. 6:6. 7:3, 28. 10:29. Mt +*14:33. +*24:36. **appointed**. ✓171J8, Ro +4:17. He *2:6, 8, 9. Ps *2:6-9. Is +*9:6, 7. *53:10-12. Mt 21:38. 28:18. Jn *3:35. 13:3. 16:15. 17:2. Ac +*10:36. Ro *8:17. 1 C *8:6.

15:25-27. Ep 1:20-23. Ph ✓2:9-11. Col *1:17, 18. 1 P 3:22. **heir**. Ps *2:8. +*94:14. Mt 21:28. +*28:18. Ro ✓8:17. Ep 1:11n. **all things**. Jn 1:3. 1 C 8:6. Col 1:16. **by whom**. He 2:10. 3:3. Pr 8:22-31. Is 44:24. 45:12, 18. Jn +*1:3. 1 C *8:6. Ep *3:9. Col +*1:16, 17. **worlds**. Gr. *aions*, Mt +6:13. ✓121P2, Mt +13:22. He 11:3. 1 T +1:17.

3. **Who being**. Jn +*8:24. **the brightness**. Jn *1:14. *14:9, 10. 2 C *4:6. **his glory**. Lk *9:32. 2 C +*4:4. **express image**. Is 7:14. 43:10. Mt 1:23. Jn *14:9. 2 C *4:4. Col +*1:15, 16. ✓2:9. **his person**. or, substance. He 3:14. 11:1, 2. 2 C 9:4. 11:17g. **upholding**. He 11:3. Ne 9:6. Ps 75:3. Jn *1:4. Ep 1:19. Col ✓1:11, 17. Re 4:11. **the word**. Ec *8:4. Ro +*1:16. 2 C *4:7. **power**. Col 1:11. **by himself**. He 7:27. *9:12-14, 16, 26. Jn 1:29. 1 J *1:7. 3:5. **purged our sins**. He +*9:14. 1 P *2:24. **sat down**. ver. 13. He *4:14. *8:1. *10:12. 12:2. Ps ✱*110:1. Zc 6:13. Mt 22:44. Mk +*16:19. Lk 20:42, 43. Ac 2:33. +*7:56. Ro *8:34. Ep *1:20-22. Col *3:1. 1 P 1:21. 3:22. Re ✓3:21. **right hand**. ✓22A15C, Ps +110:1. Mt +*26:64. Lk 22:69. 1 P 3:22. **Majesty**. 1 Ch *29:11. Jb 37:22. Mi 5:4. 2 P *1:16. Ju *25. **on high**. Ps 92:8. 93:4. 113:5. Mt 21:9. Mk 11:10. Lk 2:14. 19:38.

4. **so much better**. ver. 9. He 2:9. 7:22. 8:6. 10:25. Ep 1:21. Ph 2:9. Col *1:18. 2:10, ◑18. 1 Th 4:16n.

2 Th 1:7. 1 P 3:22. Re *5:11, 12. **angels.** Col 2:18. **by inheritance.** Ps 2:7, 8. Ro *8:17. Ep +*1:11n. **more excellent name.** Is +*9:6. Lk *1:32, 35. Jn *3:18. Ep √1:21. Ph *2:9-11.

5. **which.** ſ85C, Ge +18:14. **Thou.** He 5:5. Ps *♭2:7. Ac *13:33. **begotten.** ſ22C23, Ps +2:7. **I will.** 2 S *♭7:14. 1 Ch 17:13. 22:10. 28:6. Ps +*89:26, 27. 2 C +*6:18.

6. **And again,** etc. or, When he bringeth again. He 10:5. **the firstbegotten.** ſ22D4C, Ro +8:29. ver. *5. Pr 8:24, 25. Jn *1:14, 18. √3:16. Ro +*8:29. Col +*1:15, 18. 1 J *4:9. Re +*1:5. *3:14. 19:10. **world.** Gr. *oikoumene*, Mt +24:14. ſ24B, Ge +23:16. He 2:5. **And let.** Dt *♭32:43, LXX. Ps *97:7. Mt +*14:33. Lk *2:9-14. 1 P √3:22. Re √5:9-14. **the angels.** Mt *25:31. Mk 8:38. Lk 12:8, 9. 15:10. Jn 1:51. Ac 10:3. Ga 4:14. **worship him.** T#79. Ps *2:12. Is 49:23. Mt 2:1, 2. 4:10. 8:2. +*14:33. 28:9, 16, 17, 19. Lk ◐14:10. √24:51, 52. Jn √5:23. Ac +√7:59n. ◐10:25. 2 C 13:14. Ph *2:9-11. Col ◐2:18. 2 P 1:17. 3:18. Re +*5:12.

7. **of.** Gr. unto. **Who maketh.** ver. 14. 2 K 2:11. 6:17. Ps ♭104:4. Is 6:2h. Ezk 1:13, 14. Da 7:10. Zc 6:5. **his angels.** Ps 148:8. **spirits.** Gr. *pneuma*, Lk +24:37. **ministers.** ver. 14. He 8:2, 6. 9:21. 10:11. Ps 103:20, 21. Da *9:21. Lk +1:23g. **a flame.** 2 K 1:10. 2:11. *6:17.

8. **Son.** ver. +2. Jn +*8:35. **Thy throne.** ſ92A, Mt +1:23. ſ22D3C2, Ps +45:6. Ps +*♭45:6, 7. 93:2. 110:2. Jn 16:15. Re +*3:21. **O God.** He 3:3, 4. Ex 7:1. 21:6. 22:8, 9, 20, 28. 32:31. Jsh 23:16. Jg 13:22. 16:23. 1 S 2:25. 4:7. 1 K 11:33. Jb +*19:26. Ps ♭45:6. 47:7, 8. 86:8. 97:7. Is +*7:14. +*9:6, 7. 40:9, 10. 45:21, 22, 25. Je √23:6. Ho 1:7. Zc 13:9. Ml *3:1. Mt *1:23. Lk 1:16, 17. Jn √1:1. √5:18n. 10:30, 33. +*20:28n. Ro +*9:5n. 1 C ◐+*15:24, 25. 1 T *3:16. T √2:13n, 14. 1 J *5:20. **for ever.** Gr. *aion*, Mt +6:13. **and ever.** Gr. *aion*, Mt +6:13. lit. unto the age of the age. 2 S *7:13, 16. Ps 10:16. 72:5. *89:4. 110:4. 145:13. Is +*9:7. Da *2:44. +*7:14. Mi +*5:2. Lk *1:32, 33. Jn +*8:35. 17:5. 1 C ◐+*15:24n, 25. 2 P *1:11. Re √11:15. 19:16. **a scepter.** ſ22D5R, Ps +2:9. 2 S 23:3. Ps 67:4. 72:1-4, 11-14. 96:10. 99:4. Is +*9:7. *32:1, 2. Je *23:5. *33:15. Zc *9:9. **righteousness.** Gr. rightness, or, straightness. **thy kingdom.** In this passage it is affirmed that the kingdom is eternal, that it is ruled by Messiah who is God (Je √23:6), and in accordance with covenant and prophecy, this kingdom is upon earth, the reign is upon earth, where the inheritance is located (Ep 1:11n), and not in or from heaven or the third heaven. Mt 16:28. Lk +*22:30. 23:42. Jn +*18:36. Ph 2:10. 2 T +*4:1. Re √11:15. 17:14.

9. **loved.** He 7:26. Ps 11:5, 7. 33:5. 36:5, 6. 37:28. 40:8. +*45:7. 89:14. Is 53:9. 61:8. 1 P *2:22. **hated.** Ps *119:104, 128. Pr 8:13. Am 5:15. Zc 8:17. Ro 12:9. Re 2:6, 7, 15. **God.** Is 61:1. Lk +*4:18. **thy God.** Ps 89:26. Jn *20:17. 2 C 11:31. Ep 1:3. 1 P 1:3. **anointed.** ſ22D5L, Ps +45:7. 1 K 1:39. Ps *2:2, 6mg. 89:20. Is 61:1. Lk +*4:18, 21. Jn 1:41. *3:34. Ac 4:27. *10:38. **oil.** Ge=49:25. Ps *23:5. Is 61:3. Ro 15:13. Ga *5:22. **of gladness.** Ps 21:6. Is 61:3. Lk 10:21. **above.** Re +*1:5. 17:14. 19:16. **thy fellows.** He √2:11, 16, 17. Ps 94:10. 138:4. Mi +*5:2. Zc +*14:5. Ro +*8:17. 1 C 1:9. 2 T 2:12. 1 J *1:3. Re +*5:10. *20:4, 6.

10. **Thou.** ſ92A, Mt +1:23. Ps ♭102:25-27. **Lord.** Ne +*9:6. Jn *8:24. **in.** He 11:3. Ge +*1:1. 2:1. Jb 38:4. Ps 115:15. Is 42:5. 44:24. 45:18. Jn √1:1-3. Ac

14:15. 17:24. Col 1:16, 17. Re +*3:14. 4:11. **hast.** Pr 8:29. Is 42:5. 48:13. 51:13. Je 32:17. Zc 12:1. **the heavens.** Ps 33:6. 96:5. 136:5. **the works.** Dt 4:19. Ps 8:3, 4. 19:1. Is 64:8.

11. **shall perish.** Gr. *apollumi*, Mt +2:13. He 12:27. Ec ◐+*1:4. Is 34:4. *51:6. 65:17. Mt *24:35. Mk 13:31. Lk 21:33. 2 P √3:7-10, 12. Re *20:11. *21:1. **thou remainest.** Ps 9:7. 10:16. 29:10. 90:2. 102:12. Is 41:4. 44:6. Re 1:11, 17, 18. 2:8. **shall wax.** Is 50:9. 51:6, 8.

12. **art the same.** He √13:8. Ex 3:14. Is 41:4. 48:12. Ml +*3:6. Jn √8:35, 58. Ja *1:17. Re +*1:8. **and they.** Ps 90:4.

13. **But.** ſ77, Ex +3:19. **to which.** ſ85C, Ge +18:14. ver. *5. **Sit.** ver. 3. He 10:12. Ps *♭110:1. Mt +*22:44. Mk 12:36. 14:62. +*16:19. Lk 20:42. 22:69. Ac 2:34-36. 7:55. **right hand.** Ro *8:34. Ep *1:20. Col *3:1. **until.** He 10:13. Ps 21:8, 9. 132:18. Is 63:3-6. Lk 19:27. 1 C +*15:25, 26. Re 19:11-21. 20:15. **thy footstool.** ſ22D3D2, Ps +110:1. Jsh 10:24. Ps 8:6. 18:38.

14. **Are.** ſ85B, Ge +13:9. **ministering.** T#847. ver. +7. He 8:6. 10:11. 1 K 22:19. Jb 1:6. Ps *34:7. *91:11, 12. 103:20, 21. 104:4. Is 6:2, 3. Da 3:28. 7:10. Mt 13:41, 49, 50. *18:10. Mk 1:13. Lk 1:19, 23. 2:9, 13. Ac 13:2. Ro 13:6. 15:16, 27. 2 C 9:12. Ph 2:17, 25g. 2 Th 1:7. Ju 14. **spirits.** Gr. *pneuma*, Lk +24:37. **sent.** Ge *19:15, 16. 28:12. 32:1, 2, 24. Jg 6:11. 13:3, 6, 9. Ps 34:7. +*35:6. 91:11. 103:20, 21. Da 3:28. *6:22. 10:11. Mt 18:10. Lk *1:19. +16:22. Ac 5:19. 8:26. 10:1-6. 11:22. *12:7, 15. *27:23, 24. 1 P 1:12. Re 5:6. **minister.** Ps 34:7. 91:11, 12. Da 6:22. 9:21-23. 10:11, 12. Mt 1:20. 2:13. 24:31. Lk 16:22. Ac 5:19. 10:3, 4. 12:7, 23. 16:26. 27:23. **heirs.** ſ142, Ge +20:16. He 6:12, 17. Mt +25:34. Ro √8:17. Ga 3:7, 9, 29. Ep 1:11n. 3:6. T *3:7. Ja +*2:5. 1 P +*1:4n. 3:7.

HEBREWS 2

An earnest call to attend the gospel; enforced by the consideration of the danger of "neglecting so great salvation," thus revealed and confirmed, 1-4. Further scriptural proof of Christ's superiority to angels, notwithstanding his temporary humiliation in our nature, 5-9. An explanation of the motives, reasons, condescension, and benefit, of his incarnation, temptations, sufferings, and death; as connected with his being the High Priest and Savior of his people, 10-18.

1. **Therefore.** ver. *2-4. He 1:1, 2. *12:25, 26. **the more.** Dt *4:9, 23. *32:46, 47. Jsh *23:11, 12. 1 Ch *22:13. Ps √119:9. Pr 2:1-6. 3:21. *4:1-4, 20-22. 7:1, 2. Ho *4:6, 10. Lk +*8:15. *9:44. Ac *3:22, 23. **we should.** He 12:5. Mt *16:9. Mk 8:18. 2 P 1:12, 13, 15. 3:1. **let them slip.** Gr. run out, as leaking vessels. Jb 6:15. Hag *1:6. *2:16.

2. **For if.** ſ184A, 1 C +15:2. **spoken.** Dt +*33:2. Ps *68:17. Ac +*7:53. Ga *3:19. **every.** He *10:28. Ex *32:27, 28. Le *10:1, 2. *24:14-16. Nu *11:33. *14:28, 37. *15:30-36. *16:31-35, 49. *20:11, 12. *21:6. *25:9. Dt *4:3, 4. 17:2, 5, 12. 27:26. 1 C *10:5-12. Ju *5. **recompense.** He *10:35. *11:6, 26g. Ps *31:23.

3. **How.** He *4:1, 11. √10:28, 29. *12:25. Is 20:6. Ezk 17:15, 18. Mt *23:33. Jn *12:48. Ro *2:3. 1 Th *5:3. 1 P *4:17, 18. Re 6:16, 17. **neglect.** He 8:9g. Jsh *24:15. Mt *22:5g. Ro +*2:12. 1 T 4:14g. 2 T +*3:15. 1 P ◐5:7g. 2 P 1:12g. Re +*3:20. **so great.** He *5:9. √7:25, 26. Is +*12:2. 51:5, 8. 62:11. Lk 1:69. Jn √3:16-18. Ac √4:12. 1 T *1:15. T √2:11. Re 7:10.

salvation. He +*9:28n. Mt 16:26. Lk 2:30. Ac √4:12.
2 C +*6:2. 1 J √5:11-13. Ju +*3. began. He *1:2.
Mt *4:17. Mk 1:14. Lk 24:19. Ac 2:22. and was. Mk
*16:15-20. Lk *1:2. +*24:47, 48. Jn 15:27. Ac 1:8,
22. *5:32. *10:39-42. 2 P √1:16. 1 J *1:1-3.
4. God also. Mk *16:20. Jn 15:26. Ac 2:32, 33. 3:15,
16. 4:10. *14:3. *19:11, 12. Ro *15:18, 19. signs. Jn
+4:48. Ac *2:43. divers miracles. He 6:4, 5. Ac +2:22.
1 C *2:4. gifts. or, distributions. 1 C √12:4-11. Ep
√4:8-11. Ghost. Gr. pneuma, Mt +1:18. according.
Da 4:35. Ep 1:5, 9.
5. the world. Gr. oikoumene, Mt +24:14. He 1:6.
6:5. 2 P 3:13. Re *11:15. to come. He *6:5. Is *65:17.
Jn +*6:54n.
6. in. He 4:4. 5:6. 1 P 1:11. testified. 1 Th +4:6.
What. ſ85F, Ps +8:4. Jb *7:17, 18. 15:14. 25:6. See
on Ps ▸8:4-8. *144:3. Is 40:17. mindful. Ge 8:1. 19:29.
30:22. Ex 2:24. 1 S 1:19. the son. Jb 25:6. Ps 80:17.
146:3, 4. Is 51:12. visitest. Ge *50:24. Ps 65:9. Lk
*1:+68, 78, 79. 7:16.
7. madest. ſ96C2, Ge +45:9. See on ver. 9. a little
lower than. or, a little while inferior to. Lk 22:58.
Ac 5:34. 27:28g. angels. Mt *4:11. Lk *22:43. with
glory. Ps 21:5. didst set. Ge 1:26, 28. 9:2. Ja 3:7.
8. hast. ſ151, Ge +1:28. ver. 5. He 1:13. Ps *2:6.
Da +*7:14. Mt *28:18. Jn 3:35. 13:3. 1 C +*15:27.
Ep *1:21, 22. Ph √2:9-11. 1 P 3:22. Re +*1:5, 18.
*5:11-13. under. ſ22D3D2, Ps +110:1. But. Jb 39:1-
12. ch. 41. 1 C *15:24, 25. not yet. Dt 12:9.
9. we see. 2 P 1:16. Jesus. He 8:3. 10:5. Ge +*3:15.
Is +*7:14. 11:1. *53:2-10. Ro 8:3. Ga √4:4. Ph √2:7-
9. lower. ver. 7. for the. or, by the. ſ137, Ge +13:13.
Jn +10:17. Ph 2:7-9. suffering. ver. +*10. Ro *8:17,
18. crowned. Ps *21:3-5. Zc *6:11-13. Ac +2:33. 3:13.
1 P 1:21. Re *19:12. glory. Ex 28:2. Ps *45:3, 4. 2 P
1:17. and. ſ93A, Ge +1:26. by. Jn √3:16. Ac +*11:23.
Ro *5:8, 18. √8:32. 2 C √5:21. *6:1. 1 J *4:9, 10. taste.
Mt 16:28. Mk 9:1. Lk 9:27. Jn 8:52. for every. √ſ171B,
Ge +24:10. Mt 20:28. +*26:28n. Jn +*1:29. +*12:32.
Ro *5:18. 1 C 15:22. 2 C √5:14, 15. 1 T +*2:6. 1 J
√2:2. 2 P √3:9. Re *5:9.
10. it became. He 7:26. Ge +*18:25. Lk 2:14.
+*24:26, 46. Ro *3:25, 26. Ep 1:6-8. 2:7. 3:10. 1 P
1:12. for whom. Pr *16:4. Is 43:21. Ro *11:36. 1 C
+*8:6. 2 C 5:18. Col *1:16, 17. Re 4:11. in bringing.
Nu=18:2. Ge=33:22. Ho 1:10. Jn 11:52. Ac 9:31. Ro
√8:14-18, 29, 30. 9:25, 26. 2 C *6:18. Ga 3:26. Ep
1:5. 1 J √3:1, 2. Re *7:9, 10, 14. many. √ſ171F, Is
+53:12. He 9:28. Ge=50:20. Mt +20:28. sons. Ro
+*8:14. unto glory. He 3:1. Ro 8:30. 9:23. 1 C 2:7.
2 C *3:18. √4:17. Col +*3:4. 2 T 2:10. 1 P 5:1, 10.
the captain. He 5:9. 6:20. *12:2. Jsh 5:14, 15. Is *55:4.
Mi 2:13. Ac +*3:15. 5:31. perfect. He *5:8, 9. 7:28.
11:40. 12:23. Lk 13:32. 24:26, 46. Jn 19:30. Ph 3:12.
sufferings. ver. 9. Ex 25:5. +=26:33. +*27:20.
+=30:10. Le +=2:4, 6. +=17:11. Is=53:5, 10. Ac
26:23. 2 C +1:5. 1 P *5:10.
11. he that. He *9:13, 14. *10:10, 14. *13:12. Jn
17:19. 1 J *1:7. and they. He 10:10, 14, 29. Jn 17:19.
all of one. ſ63I1A, Ex +12:4. or, all (sons) of one
(father). ver. 14. He +12:9. Jn 17:21. Ac 17:26, 28.
Ga *4:4. he is. He +*11:16. Mk 8:38. Lk *9:26. to
call. Mt +*12:48-50. 25:40. 28:10. Jn *20:17. Ro *8:29.
brethren. He 3:1. Ge=46:31. =47:1. Nu=18:2. Mt
25:40.
12. I will declare. Ps ▸22:22, 25. 102:21. Jn +*17:6.

my brethren. Mt +28:10. in. Ps 40:10. 111:1. Jn 18:20.
midst. ſ144A6, Ge +45:6. church. or, congregation.
He 12:23. Ac 7:38. sing. Ac 16:25g.
13. I will put. 2 S ▸22:3. Ps 16:1. ▸18:2. 36:7, 8.
91:2. Is *8:17. +*12:2. *50:7-9. Mt 27:43. Jn *5:30.
Behold. Is ▸8:18. *53:10. which. Ge 33:5. 48:9. Ps
127:3. Jn 10:29. *17:+*2, 6-12. 1 C 4:15.
14. the children. See on ver. 10. of flesh and.
*ſ171Q11, Mt +16:17. Ge 2:23. 2 S 5:1. Jb 33:6. Mt
+*16:17. 1 C +*15:50. he also. ver. 18. He +*4:15.
Ge +*3:15. Is +*7:14. Jn *1:14. Ro *8:3. Ga *4:4.
Ph *2:6-8. 1 T *3:16. took part. ver. 17. He 7:13. Jn
+1:14. through death. ſ171S8, Ro +5:10. He 9:15.
Is 53:12. Jn 12:24, 31-33. Ro 14:9. 1 C +*15:55. Col
2:15. Re *1:18. destroy. Is 25:8. Ho 13:14. 1 C +*15:54,
55. Col 2:15. 2 T +*1:10. of death. ſ145, Jg +11:40.
the devil. Mt 25:41. 1 J √3:8-10. Re 2:10. 12:9. 20:2.
15. deliver. Jb 33:21-28. Ps 33:19. 56:13. 89:48.
107:14. Lk 1:74, 75. 2 C 1:10. through. Jb 18:11, 14.
24:17. Ps 55:4. 73:19. 1 C +*15:50-57. death. Re
+*1:18. lifetime. ſ24A, Ge +32:24. subject. Ro 8:+15,
21. Ga 4:21. 2 T +*1:7.
16. verily. He 6:16. 12:10. Ro 2:25. 1 P 1:20. took
not, etc. Gr. taketh not hold of angels, but of the
seed of Abraham he taketh hold. ſ96C5, Mt +2:13.
He 8:9. Is 41:8, 9. 1 Th *4:16n. him the. ſ63K, Ge
+37:13. the seed. Ge 22:18. Mt *1:1, etc. Ro 4:16,
etc. Ga *3:16, 29.
17. all things. He +*4:15. it behooved. See on ver.
11, 14. Ph *2:7, 8. made like. He ◉7:26. Ps ◉*50:21.
Ph *2:7. a merciful. He 3:2, 5. +*4:15, 16. *5:1, 2,
7, 8. Is 11:5. and faithful. He 3:1, 2. Ps ◉+*36:5.
Mt +*28:19n. 2 Th 3:3. Re 1:5. 3:14. 19:11. high priest.
He 3:1. 4:14, 15. 5:5, 10. 6:20. 7:26, 28. 8:1, 3. 9:11.
10:21. in things. He 5:1. Ro 15:17. to make. T#582.
Le 6:30. 8:15. 2 Ch 29:24. Ezk 45:15, 17, 20. Da *9:24.
Lk +18:13. Ro 5:1, 2, 10. 2 C *5:18-21. Ep 2:16. Ph
+4:7 (T#666). Col *1:21. of the people. Mt 1:21. Lk
1:68, 77. 2:10.
18. suffered. He *4:15, 16. 5:2, 7-9. *12:3. Mt *4:1-
10. 26:37-39. 27:34. Lk 22:53. being tempted. He
+*4:15. Lk 22:28. he is able. ſ108B, Ro +4:21. He
*7:25, 26. Jn *10:29. Ro 4:21. 14:4. 2 C *9:8. Ep 3:20.
Ph 3:21. 2 T +*1:12. Ju *24. them. 1 C +*10:13.
2 C √12:7-10. 2 P *2:9. Re +*3:10.

HEBREWS 3

*The great superiority of Christ above Moses is
proved and illustrated, 1-6. The Hebrews are solemnly
warned not to copy the example of their unbelieving
ancestors, who perished in the wilderness, 7-19.*

1. holy. He 2:11. Col *1:22. 3:12. 1 Th *5:27. 2 T
+*1:9. 1 P 2:9. *3:5. 2 P √1:3-10. Re 18:20. partakers.
ver. *14. He *6:4. Ro 11:17. 15:27. 1 C 9:23. 10:17.
2 C 1:7. Ep *3:6. Col *1:12. 1 T 6:2. 1 P 5:1. 2 P
*1:4. 1 J *1:3. the heavenly. He 2:10. 9:15. Ro 1:6,
7. +*8:28-30. 9:24. 1 C *1:2. Ep 4:1, *4. Ph *3:14.
1 Th *2:12. *4:7. 2 Th *1:11. 2:14. 1 T 6:12. 2 T
+*1:9. 1 P 5:10. 2 P +*1:10. Ju 1. Re *17:14. consider.
Is 1:3. 5:12. 41:20. Ezk 12:3. *18:28. Hg *1:5. 2:15.
Jn 20:27. 2 T *2:7. the apostle. Jn *20:21g. Ro +*15:8.
and. He +*2:17. *4:14, 15. 5:1-10. 6:20. *7:26, 27.
8:1-3. 9:11. 10:21. Ps *110:4. profession. He 4:14.
10:23. 2 C 9:13. 1 T 6:12, 13.
2. faithful. He 2:17. Jn 6:38-40. 7:18. *8:29. 15:10.

*17:4. **appointed**. Gr. made. 1 S 12:6mg. Ac 2:36. **as**. ver. 5. Ex *40:16. Nu *12:7. Dt *4:5. 1 T 1:12. **all**. ver. *6. Ep *2:22. 1 T *3:15. **house**. Is 5:7. 1 T 3:15.

3. **this**. ver. 6. He 1:2-4. 2:9. Col *1:18. **glory**. Zc +*6:13. **who**. He 9:2, 6. 11:7. Zc 4:9. *6:12, 13. Mt *16:18. 1 C 3:9. 1 P 2:5-7. 3:20g.

4. **but**. See on ver. 3. He 1:2. Zc *6:12. Mt *16:18. Jn 1:3. Ac 7:38. Ep 2:10. 3:9. 1 P +2:5.

5. **faithful**. ver. 2. Nu 12:7. Da *6:4. Mt +*24:45. 25:21. Lk +*12:42. *16:10-12. 1 C +*4:2. 1 T +*1:12. **as a servant**. Ex 14:31. Nu 12:7. Dt 3:24. 34:5. Jsh 1:2, 7, 15. 8:31, 33. Ne 9:14. Ps 105:26. Re 15:3. **for a testimony**. He 8:5. 9:8-13, 24. *10:1. Dt 18:15-19. Lk +*24:27, 44. Jn +√5:39, 46, 47. Ac 3:22, 23. 7:37. 28:23. Ro *3:21. 1 P 1:10-12.

6. **as**. ver. ◑=5. He +*1:2. 4:14. Ps *2:6, 7, 12. Is +*9:6, 7. Jn √3:35, 36. *17:10, 12. 2 P 1:16. Re *2:18. **over**. Ge=41:40. **own house**. Ps 93:5. **whose**. ver. 2, 3. Mt *16:18. 1 C *3:16. *6:19. 2 C *6:16. Ep *2:21, 22. 1 T *3:15. 1 P *2:5. **if**. ver. +*14. He 4:11. *6:11. *10:23, 35, 38, 39. Mt *10:22. *24:13. Ga √6:9. Col +*1:23. Re *2:25. *3:11. **are we**. *√39, Ac +17:27. **if**. √184C, Mt +4:9. **hold fast**. ver. 14. He 10:23. 1 C 11:2. +*15:2. 2 P +*1:10. **confidence**. He 4:16. 10:19, 35. Ac +*4:13. **rejoicing**. Ro *5:2. *12:12. *15:13. Ph +*1:26. 1 Th +*5:16. 2 Th 2:16. 1 P *1:3-6, 8. **the hope**. He 6:11, 18. 7:19. 10:23. Ro 5:2. Col +*1:5, 23. **firm unto**. ver. 14. He +*4:14. +*6:11. *10:35, 36. Ps 119:33, 112. Mt +10:22. 1 J *2:19. Re 2:26.

7. **as**. He 9:8. 10:15. 2 S *23:2. Mt 22:43. Mk *12:36. Ac +*1:16. +8:29. 28:25. 2 P √1:21. **Ghost**. Gr. *pneuma*, Mt +3:16. **Today**. ver. 13, 15. He 4:7. Ps ▸95:7-11. Pr *27:1. Ec +*9:10. Is √55:6. Mk +16:14. Ac 19:9. Ro 9:18. 2 C +*6:1, 2. Ja *4:13-15. **if**. √184C, Mt +4:9. **hear**. Ps 81:11, 13. Is +*55:3. Mt *17:5. Jn 5:25. 10:3, 16, 27. Re √3:20.

8. **Harden**. ver. 12, 13. Ex 8:15. Dt *9:7. 1 S 6:6. 2 K 17:14. 2 Ch 30:8. 36:13. Ne 9:16. Jb 9:4. Ps ▸95:8. Pr 28:14. √29:1. Je 7:26. Ezk 3:7-9. Da 5:20. Zc 7:11, 12. Mt 13:15. Ac 19:9. Ro 2:5, 6. **as**. Ex 17:1-7. Nu *14:11, 22, 23. 20:1-13. Dt 9:22-24. Ps 78:56. **provocation**. √183, Ph +3:19. The provocation of God followed the temptation in the wilderness; but is here put first to mark out the special temptation referred to (B703). **of**. Ex 17:7. Dt 6:16. Ps 78:18. 106:14. 1 C 10:9.

9. **When**. Ps ▸95:9. **tempted**. Nu *14:22, 23. Ac +15:10. 1 C *10:9. **and saw**. Ex 19:4. 20:22. Nu *14:22, 23. Dt 4:3, 9. 11:7. 29:2. Jsh 23:3. 24:7. Lk 7:22. **forty**. Nu 14:33. Dt 8:2, 4. Jsh 5:6. Am 2:10. Ac +7:36. 13:18.

10. **I was grieved**. Ge *6:6. Jg 10:16. Ps *78:40, 41. ▸95:10. Is +*63:10. Mk 3:5. Ep +*4:30. **alway**. Gr. *aei*, Mk +15:8. **err**. ver. 12. He 5:2. Ps *78:8. Is 28:7. Ho 4:12. Jn √3:19, 20. 8:45. Ro +*1:28. 2 Th √2:10-12. **they have**. Ps 67:2. 95:10. 147:20. Je *4:22. Ro 3:17.

11. **So**. He 4:3, 5. Ps ▸95:11. **I sware**. ver. 18, 19. He 4:3. Nu *14:20-23, 24, *27-30, 35. *32:10-13. Dt 1:34, 35. 2:14. Ezk 20:15. **They shall not enter**. Gr. if they shall enter. √184A, 1 C +15:2. **my rest**. See on He 4:9.

12. **Take heed**. He *2:1-3. 4:11. *12:+*15, 25. Pr +*27:23. Mt 24:4. Mk 13:9, 23, 33. Lk *21:8. Ro 11:21. 1 C *10:12. Col +*2:8. **an evil heart**. See on ver.

10. Ge +*8:21. 1 K +*8:18. Je 2:13. 3:17. *7:24. 11:8. 16:12. +*17:9. 18:12. Mk +*7:21-23. **of unbelief**. √181E, Ge +3:24. T#708. ver. 19. He 4:6, 11. Nu 14:11. Ps 10:11, 13. +14:1 (T#22). 73:9-11. 94:5-7. Ezk 8:12. +13:22 (T#568). Zp 1:12. Mk 6:6. 16:16. Jn *3:18. 5:44. 8:43. 16:8, 9. Ro 11:20. **in departing**. He +*10:38, 39. 12:25. Jb *21:14. 22:17. Ps *18:21. *78:56, 57. Pr 1:32. Is *59:13. Je +*2:13. +*17:5. Ho 1:2. Lk +*8:13. 1 T +*1:19. +*4:1n. **the living**. He 9:14. 10:31. 12:22. Mt +16:16. See on 1 Th 1:9.

13. **exhort one another**. Our duty towards one another in watching over one another's spiritual lives (He 13:7,17) merits careful study in this context. Prompt action based upon the signs of spiritual decline given in ver. 12 is essential. Scripture furnishes much material which should form the basis of exhortation. We should encourage one another in (1) love: Ep 3:17. 4:15, 16. 1 P *1:22. (2) good works: Ep *2:10. T +*3:8. (3) regular fellowship: He √10:25. Ex 34:24. 1 S 2:30. Mt *6:33. Ac *2:42, 43. (4) avoiding willful sin: He *10:26. 1 C +*6:9-11. Ga *5:21. Ep 5:5. Re +*21:8. 21:27. (5) maintaining confidence: He +*10:35. Ac +*11:23. *13:43. +*14:22. (6) the hope of Christ's coming: 1 Th +*4:13-18. T 2:11-14. Ja 5:7, 8. 1 J 3:1-3. 2 P √3:14. (7) steadfastness and perseverance: He 10:38, 39. 1 C +*15:58. (8) in not drawing back unto perdition: He +*10:35. 1 C +*15:2. 1 T +*4:1n. 2 P *2:20-22. See the related notes pertaining to exhortation at Ps +√9:10 and Ro √12:8n, and followup evangelism, of which exhortation is a most important component, at 1 Th 3:5n. He √10:24, 25. Da +*11:33n. Ac +*11:23. Ro +√12:5. 2 C +*8:16. 1 Th 2:11. 4:18. 5:11. 2 T *4:2. **daily**. Spiritual needs should not wait until the next stated meeting of the congregation. Exhortation is to proceed on a daily basis, as the need requires, through personal contact (Ac 20:20). It is necessary to reach a person before it is too late, and spiritual hardness sets in. See on ver. 7. Pr +*19:18. Da +*11:33. Ml +*3:16. Mt 4:4. 6:11. 24:45. Lk *19:44. Jn *12:35, 36. **lest**. Col +*3:21. Ja +*5:19. **hardened**. ver. 8, 15. He 4:7. **through**. 1 T 6:10mg. **the deceitfulness**. Ge *3:4-6. Pr 28:26. Is 44:20. Ob 3. Mk *12:24. Lk *19:21. Ro *7:11. Ep 4:22. T 2:14. Ja 1:14.

14. **we are made**. √96C2, Ge +45:9. ver. 1. He √6:4. 12:10. Ro 11:17. 1 C 1:9, 30. 9:23. 10:17. Ep 3:6. 1 T 6:2. 1 P *4:13. 5:1. 1 J 1:3. Re *2:10. **if**. √184C, Mt +4:9. See on ver. +*6. He +*6:11. Ge +*4:7. Je +*7:5. Jn *8:31. Col +*1:23. 1 Th 2:19. +*3:8. 2 T +*2:12. Ja *5:19. 2 P +*1:10. **confidence**. He 11:1g. 2 C +*9:4. **stedfast**. He 6:11. *10:23, +*35. Jn *15:16. 1 C +√15:58. **unto the end**. Re *2:10. *3:21.

15. **To day**. See on ver. 7, 8. He *10:38, 39. **if**. √184C, Mt +4:9.

16. **some**. See on ver. 9, 10. Nu 14:2, 4, 11. 26:65. Dt 1:34, 35. Ps *78:17, 40. **not**. Nu 14:+*24, 30, 38. Dt *1:36, 38. Jsh *14:7-11. Ro *11:4, 5.

17. **with whom**. See on ver. 10. **forty**. Ac +7:36. **was it**. Nu 26:64, 65. 1 C *10:1-13. **whose**. Nu 14:22, 29, 32, 33. Dt 2:15, 16. Je 9:22. Ju *5.

18. **to whom**. See on ver. 11. He 4:2. Nu 14:30. Dt 1:34, 35. **but**. ver. 12, 19. He 4:6, 11. 11:31. Nu *14:11. 20:12. Dt *1:26-32. *9:23. Ps 106:24-26.

19. **could not enter**. He 4:6. Ps 78:22. *106:24-26. Mk *16:16. Jn √3:18, 36. 2 Th *2:12. 1 J *5:10. Ju *5. **unbelief**. ver. +*12.

HEBREWS 4

An admonition to humble fear, and against unbelief, 1, 2. The certainty and excellency of the heavenly rest, as typified by that of the sabbath, and of Canaan, 3-11. The energy of the word of God, the omniscience of our Judge, and the compassion of our great High Priest, used as motives to steadfastness, and earnestness in coming to the throne of grace, 12-16.

1. **Let us.** ver. 11. He √2:1-3. +*12:15, 25. 13:7. Pr 14:16. 28:14. Je 32:40. Ro 11:20. 1 C 10:12. **a promise.** ver. *9. Nu 14:34. 1 S *2:30. Ro 3:3, 4. 2 T 2:13. **entering.** ſ24A, Ge +32:24. **his rest.** ver. 3-5. See on He 3:11. **any.** Mt √7:21-23, 26, 27. *24:48-51. 25:1-3. Lk 12:45, 46. *13:25-30. Ro √3:23. 1 C *9:26, 27. **seem.** Ja +1:26. **come short.** He +*12:15. 1 C 1:7g.

2. **unto us.** Ac 3:26. *13:46. Ga *3:8, 9. 4:13. 1 P 1:12. **unto them.** ſ183, Ph +3:19. Here, the order of time is inverted, to agree with the order of thought, and for emphasis (B704). **preached.** Gr. of hearing. Ro √10:16, 17mg. 1 Th √2:13. **did not profit.** T#435. Is 6:9-12. 28:13. Je *5:14. Mi *2:7. Mk 4:3-8. Ro 2:25. 1 C *13:3. 2 C *2:15, 16. 1 T 4:8. 2 T +2:25 (T#242). **not being,** etc. *or,* because they were not united by faith to. ver. 6. He 3:*12, 18, 19. √11:6. Nu 13:27. Ro +3:3. 1 Th *1:5. √2:13. 2 Th *2:12, 13. Ja *1:21.

3. **we.** He *3:14. Is 28:12. Je 6:16. Mt √11:28, 29. Ro *5:1, 2. **As I.** See on He 3:11. Ps 95:11. **if they.** ſ184A, 1 C +15:2. ver. 5. **my rest.** 2 Th +*1:7. Re +*14:13. **the works.** Ge 1:31. Ex *20:11. **from.** He 9:26. Ge 1:31. Jb ◑26:7. Mt +13:35. Ac +*15:18. Ep *1:4. 1 P 1:20. **world.** Gr. *kosmos,* Mt +4:8.

4. **in.** See on He 2:6. **God.** ver. 10. Ge *2:1, ▶2. Ex *20:11. 31:17. Dt 5:14.

5. **If they.** ſ184A, 1 C +15:2. ver. 3. He 3:11. **shall enter.** Ps ▶95:11.

6. **it remaineth.** ver. 9. 1 C 7:29. **some.** Nu *14:12, 31. Is 65:15. Mt *21:43. *22:9, 10. Lk *14:21-24. Ac *13:46, 47. 28:28. **they.** ver. 2. He 3:19. Ga 3:8. **it was.** *or,* the gospel was. **entered not.** See on He 3:18, 19. **unbelief.** ver. 11. He 3:12, 18, 19.

7. **saying.** He 3:7, 8. 2 S 23:1, 2. Mt 22:43. Mk 12:36. Lk 20:42. Ac 2:29-31. 28:25. **in David.** Ps 95, title. Ac +4:25. **To day.** He 3:7, 8, 15. Ps 95:7. **after.** 1 K 6:1. Ac 13:20-23. **if.** ſ184C, Mt +4:9. **harden not.** He 3:15.

8. **For if.** ſ184B, Mt +23:30. The Second Class condition of Hypothetical Proposition, where the speaker denies the possibility of his assumption. **Jesus.** that is, *Joshua.* See on Ac 7:45. **had.** He *11:13-15. Dt *12:9. 25:19. Jsh 1:15. 22:4. *23:1. Ps 78:55. 105:44. **have spoken.** ſ184B, Lk +7:39. or, he would not speak (be speaking), in the passage in David. Imperfect tense, not aorist (A. T. Robertson, *Word Pictures,* vol. 5, p. 362).

9. **remaineth.** ver. 1, 3. He 3:11. Is 11:10. 57:2. 60:19, 20. Col *2:16n, 17. Re 7:14-17. *21:4. **rest.** *or,* keeping of a sabbath. Ex 16:30. 1 Ch=6:31. =23:25. 2 Ch=35:3. Is +*58:13n. Mt 11:29. **people.** He 11:25. Ps 47:9. Mt 1:21. T *2:14. 1 P 2:10.

10. **he that.** He 1:3. 10:12. Re 14:13. **hath.** He *6:20. Mt 11:28, 29. Jn *17:4. 19:30. Ph *3:9. 1 P 4:1, 2. Re 6:11. 14:13. **as.** See on ver. 3, 4.

11. **Let.** ver. 1. He *6:11. Mt *7:13. 11:12, *28-30. Lk +*13:24. 16:16. Jn *6:27. 1 C *9:24, 25. Ph √2:12. *3:14. 2 P √1:10, 11. **lest.** See on He +*3:12,

18, 19. **example.** Jn 13:15. Ja 5:10. 2 P 2:6. **unbelief.** *or,* disobedience. ver. 6. He +*5:9. Ac 26:19. Ro 11:30-32. Ep 2:2. *5:6. Col 3:6. T *1:16. 3:3g.

12. **the word of God.** He *13:7. Is *49:2. Je +*15:16. *23:29. Mt 4:4-10. Lk 8:11. Ac *4:31. Ro +9:6. 2 C *2:17. +*4:2. Ep *6:17. 2 T +*3:15. 1 P *1:23. Re *20:4. **is quick.** T#1029. Ps 110:2. *119:+*50, 130. Ec 12:11. Is √55:11. Je √23:29. Jn 6:51, 63. Ac 7:38. Ro +*1:16. 1 C 1:24. 2 C *10:4, 5. 1 Th √2:13. Ja √1:18. 1 P +*1:23. 2:4, 5g. **powerful.** Je 23:29. 2 C 10:4. 1 Th √2:13. **sharper.** Ps 45:3. 57:4. 59:7. 64:3. *149:6. Pr *5:4. Is *11:4. *49:2. Ac *2:37. *5:33. Ep *6:17. Re *1:16. *2:16. 19:*15, 21. **twoedged.** Ps 149:6. Pr 5:4. Re 1:16. 2:12. **sword.** Jsh 11:11. 1 S 21:9. Ep 6:17. Re 19:15. **dividing asunder.** This clause is often popularly understood to support "trichotomy," the doctrine that "soul" is distinct and discrete from "spirit," and that man is a trinity consisting of body, soul, and spirit. There can be no proper analogy drawn between the Divine Trinity of the Godhead who are equal in power and glory and of the same substance, and an alleged trinity in the human nature of body, soul and spirit, for to which person of the Trinity shall "body" be equated, when the body is considered inferior to the soul and spirit? Likewise, soul being considered inferior to spirit, to which person of the Trinity shall each be equated? The analogy, when pressed, breaks down immediately, and if held, is a fruitful source of heresy, as it has been throughout church history, though not all trichotomists are heretics! Elsewhere in Scripture man is consistently spoken of as *"dichotomous"* (Ro +*8:10), consisting of two elements, body and soul, sometimes expressed body and spirit, the soul and spirit being the same element. Here, the text in the original does not say soul is divided from spirit, but that soul and spirit are divided from the joints and marrow, speaking of man as *dichotomous.* Others understand the text to mean "the piercing of the soul and the spirit, even to their joints and marrow" (Strong, *Systematic Theology,* p. 485), and point out it is not stated that there is a "dividing between soul and spirit" but a dividing of, indicated in Greek by "a series of genitives, each one in itself naming something which is divided" (J. Oliver Buswell, *A Systematic Theology of the Christian Religion,* Vol. 1, p. 243). See related notes (Ge 2:7n. 1 Th 5:23n). 1 C 15:44. Ph 1:27. 1 Th 5:23. Ju 19. **soul.** Gr. *psyche,* Mt +10:28. **spirit.** Gr. *pneuma,* ſ121A3, Mt +27:50. **and is.** Ps *139:2. Je +*17:10. 1 C *14:24, 25. Ep *5:13. Re *2:23. **intents.** 1 P 4:1g.

13. **is there.** 1 S +*16:7. 1 Ch +*28:9. 2 Ch *6:30. 16:9. Ps *7:9. 33:13-15. *44:21. *90:8. √139:4, 11, 12. Pr *15:3, 11. Je +*17:10. *23:24. Jn +*2:24, 25. *21:17. 1 C *4:5. Re *2:23. **all things.** T#219. God the Father is omniscient. 1 S 2:3. √16:7. 1 K 8:39. 1 Ch 28:9. 2 Ch 16:9. Jb 11:11. 12:13, 16. 23:10. 26:6. *34:21, 22. 37:16. Ps 11:4. 44:21. *90:8. 94:9, 11. 104:24. *139:1-6, 11, 12. 147:5. Pr *5:21. 8:14. *15:3. 17:3. 21:2. 24:11, 12. Is 40:28. 42:8, 9. 48:3-5. Je 17:10. *23:23, 24. *32:19. Ezk *11:5. Mt +9:4 (T#76-7). +*28:19n. Ac 1:24. +2:23 (T#213). 15:18. Ro +*8:29. 11:33. 1 P 1:2. 1 J 3:20. Ju 25. Re *2:18, 19. **naked.** Jb *26:6. 31:4. *34:21. *38:17. **opened.** Ge=42:8. Le 1:6, 9. Ps 51:6. 139:23, 24. **with.** Ec *12:14. Mt *7:21, 22. +*10:15n. *25:31, 32. Jn *5:22-29. Ac √17:31. Ro *2:16.

*14:9-12. 2 C *5:10. Re *20:11-15. **the eyes.** ♪22A6, Ps +11:4.

14. **a great.** He +*2:17. *3:1. *5:5, 6. 7:21. 10:21. **that is.** He *1:3. *6:20. *7:25, 26. *8:1. *9:12, 24. 10:12. +*12:2. Mk *16:19. Lk *24:51. Ac +*1:11. *3:21. Ro √8:34. Ep +*4:10. 1 P *3:22. **Jesus.** He +*1:2, 8. Mk *1:1. **the Son of God.** He +*1:2. Mt +*14:33. +*27:54n. Ac 8:37n. **let.** See on He *2:1. +*3:6, 14. *10:23. **our profession.** He +3:1.

15. **we have.** He 5:2. Ex 23:9. Is *53:3-5. Ho 11:8. Mt 8:16, 17. 12:20. Ph *2:7, 8. **high priest.** ver. 14. He +2:17. 10:21. **be touched.** Is ✱40:11. ✱42:3. Mt 27:34. **tempted.** See on He 2:17, 18. Ge=39:9. Mk +*12:15. Lk *4:2. 22:28. Jn *4:6. *11:33-35, 53, 54. 22:28. **like as.** Ps +*50:21. Is 53:3. **we are.** ♪63K, Ge +37:13. or, "but was tried according to all things, according to (our) likeness, apart from sin" (B127). **yet.** He *7:26. Is *53:9. Jn 8:46. 2 C √5:21. 1 P +*2:22. 1 J *3:5. **without sin.** or, excepting sin, or, sin apart. Scripture teaches the impeccability of Christ. In answer to the question "Was Christ able not to sin, or not able to sin?" the Scripture teaches Christ was not able to sin. Since he possessed two natures (1 Th 4:16n), a human nature and a divine nature, which nature was in control? Logically, the divine nature must have been in control of the human nature. Since Jesus was both God (Jn +*20:29n) and man (Ph 2:7. 1 T 2:5), and it is impossible for God to sin or to be tempted with evil (T 1:2n. Ja √1:13), Jesus could not sin, neither could he be tempted with evil, for there was nothing of our sinful nature in him to which Satan could appeal (Jn 14:30). Though he was tempted in all points like as we, yet this temptation was never to sin. His human nature was subject to weariness and hunger, and the suffering of death, but never sin. Had Jesus been able to sin while on earth in his human nature, but merely did not, then he is still able to sin in the human nature which he still possesses, and the divine plan of redemption is ever in jeopardy—a doctrine incompatible with Scripture. Thus the significance of the qualifying phrase "without sin" can be understood to teach Jesus not only did not sin, was able not to sin, but, possessed of a divine nature, could not sin. He 7:26. 9:28g. Ge=39:9. Lk +*1:35. Jn 4:34. *8:29, *46. +*14:30. Ro 1:4. 1 P +*2:22.

16. **Let us.** Ps +*95:6. **come.** He 7:19, 25. 10:19-23. 13:6. Ro *8:15-17. Ep *2:18. *3:12. **boldly.** 1 J +2:28. **the throne.** ♪22D3C2, Ps +45:6. He 8:1. 9:5. 12:2. Ex *25:17-22. Le 16:2. 1 Ch 28:11. Zc 6:13. Mt 19:28. 25:31. Ro *3:24, 25g. **obtain.** Ps +*4:1. Is 27:11. √55:6, 7. Mt 7:7-11. 2 C √12:8-10. Ph √4:6, 7. 1 P 2:10. **mercy.** He +*2:17. **find grace.** He 12:28. Lk 1:30. Ac 7:46. **time of need.** T#1164. He +*13:6. Dt 2:7. 1 K 17:6, 16. 19:6. 2 K 3:20. 4:6. 7:8. Ps 145:15. Is *65:24. Je *33:3. Mt *6:8. 14:20. +*24:45. Ph √4:19.

HEBREWS 5

The nature of the Aaronic priesthood, and the requisite call and qualifications for it, are stated, 1-4; in order to show the pre-eminence of Christ, as a "High Priest after the order of Melchisedec," 5-10. A reproof of the Hebrews for their small proficiency in Christianity, 11-14.

1. **every.** He 10:11. Ex 28:1, etc. 29:1, etc. Le 8:2. **high priest.** He +*2:17. **is ordained.** He 8:3. **for men.**

He 2:17. Nu 16:46-48. 18:1-3. **in things pertaining.** He 2:17. Ro 15:17. **both.** He 8:3. 9:9. 10:11. 11:4. Le 9:7, 15-21. **gifts.** He 8:4. Mt +23:18g. **sacrifices.** He 10:11. Ep 5:2. **for sins.** ver. 3. He 7:27. 10:12. 1 C 15:3.

2. **Who.** He 2:18. +*4:15. **have compassion on.** or, reasonably bear with. He +2:17. **ignorant.** Nu 15:22-29. 1 T 1:13. **them.** He 3:10. 12:13. Ex 32:8. Jg 2:17. Is 30:11. **himself also.** He +*4:15. **is compassed.** He 7:28. Ex 32:2-5, 21-24. Nu 12:1-9. 20:10-12. Lk 22:32. 2 C 11:30. 12:5, √9, 10. Ga 4:13. **infirmity.** Mk 14:38.

3. **as.** He *7:27. 9:7. Ex 29:12-19. Le 4:3-12. 8:14-21. *9:7. *16:6, 15, 17, 24. **offer.** ♪63H, Ge +12:15. **for sins.** ver. +1.

4. **no man taketh.** T#449. Ex *28:1. Le 8:2. Nu *3:3, 10. 16:5, 7, 10, 35, *40, 46-48. 17:3-11. 18:1-5, 7. 1 Ch 23:13. 2 Ch √26:18, 19, 21. Jn 3:27. 1 C +*4:7. 9:16. Ga 1:15. **as was.** Ex 28:1. 1 Ch 23:13. **Aaron.** i.e. *enlightened,* ✱S#2g. He 7:11. 9:4. Lk 1:5. Ac 7:40. For ✱S#175h, see Ex +4:14.

5. **Christ.** Jn 7:18. +*8:54. **not himself.** Ro 15:3. Ph 2:6. **a high priest.** ver. 10. He +*2:17. **Thou.** ♪92A, Mt +1:23. He 1:5. Ps *)2:7. Mi +*5:2. Jn √3:16. Ac 13:33. Ro 8:3.

6. **Thou art.** ver. 10. He 6:20. 7:3, 8, 11, 15, 17, 21. Ps)110:4. Jn 1:36. Re 14:4. **a priest.** Zc 6:13. **for ever.** Gr. *aion,* Mt +6:13. He 7:24, 28. Jn 12:34. **Melchisedec.** i.e. *king of righteousness,* ✱S#3198g. ver. 10. He 6:20. 7:1, 10, 11, 15, 17, 21. For ✱S#4442h, see Ge 14:+18, 19.

7. **the days.** He 2:14. Jn *1:14. Ro 8:3. Ga *4:4. 1 T *3:16. 1 J 4:3. 2 J 7. **offered up.** Ps 22:1-21. 69:1. 88:1. Mt *26:28-44. Mk +*1:35. 14:32-39. Lk 22:41-44. Jn 17:1. **strong crying.** He 12:2. Jb 16:9, 10. 30:9-16. Ps *22:1,2, 6-8,13. 35:15,16, 25. 69:7-12. Is 49:7. 50:6-11. *52:14, 15. Mi 5:1. Mt 27:46, 50. Mk 15:34, 37. Lk *22:44, 63-65. 23:46. **tears.** Is *53:3, 11. Lk 19:41. Jn 11:35. **unto him.** Mt *26:52, 53. Mk √14:36. **was heard.** ♪63H, Ge +12:15. He *13:20. Ps *18:6, 16, 19, 20. *21:2. *22:21, 24. 40:1-3. 69:13-16. 118:5. Is 49:8. Jn *11:42. *17:4, 5. **in that he feared.** or, for his piety. He 11:7. *12:28. Ps +*5:7. Mt 26:37, 38. Mk 14:33, 34. Lk +2:25. *22:42-44. Jn *12:27, 28.

8. **he were.** He 1:+2, 5, 8. 3:6. **yet.** He 10:5-9. Is *50:5, 6. Mt 3:15. Jn 4:34. 6:38. 15:10. Ph *2:8. **learned.** Ph 2:8, 12. 4:11. **obedience.** He=11:8. **by the things.** 2 C +1:5.

9. **being.** He +*2:10. *7:26. 11:40. Da *9:24. Lk *13:32. Jn *19:30g. Ro *1:4. **he became.** He 2:10. +*12:2. Ps 68:18-20. Is *45:22. *49:6. Ac 3:15mg. √4:12. **eternal.** Gr. *aionios,* Mt +18:8. He *2:3. *9:12, 15. Is 45:17. 51:6, 8. 2 Th *2:16. 2 T *2:10. 1 J *5:20. Ju *21. **salvation.** He √9:28. **unto.** He *11:8. Is *50:10. +√55:3. Zc 6:15. Mt *7:24-27. *17:5. Ac 5:32. Ro *1:5. *2:8. *6:17. 10:16. *15:18. 2 C √10:5. 2 Th *1:8. 1 P *1:22. **that obey.** T#872. ver. 8. He 4:11mg. Ex 29:22. Is 50:10. Mt +*7:21, 24, 25. Mk 1:14, 15. 16:16. Lk +*11:28. Jn √3:36g. 5:24. 8:51. +*13:17. *14:15. *15:10. Ac +*14:22. 1 P +*1:22. 1 J +√2:3n. +*3:24.

10. **Called.** ver. 5, 6. He 6:20. **high priest.** ver. 5. He +*2:17. **after the order.** ver. +6. Ps 110:4.

11. **we.** 1 K 10:1. Jn 6:6. 16:12. **hard.** 2 P *3:16. **dull.** He 6:12g. Is *6:10. Mt +*13:15. Mk 8:17, 18, 21. Lk 24:25. Ac 28:27.

12. **for the time.** He 10:32. Mt 17:17. Mk 9:19.

teachers. Ezr *7:10. Ps *34:11. Da +*12:3mg. 1 C 14:19. Col *3:16. T 2:3, 4. **teach.** Is 28:9, 10, 13. Ph 3:1. **the first.** He *6:1. Ga +4:3. **the oracles.** 2 S 16:23. Ac +7:38. Ro *3:2. 1 P 4:11. **have need.** ver. 13. Is *55:1. 1 C +3:1-3. 1 P √2:2.

13. **useth milk.** ver. 12. 1 C +*3:2. **is unskilful.** Gr. hath no experience. **the word.** Ps *119:123. Ro *1:17, 18. 10:5, 6. 2 C 3:9. 2 T +*3:16. **of.** ſ181E, Ge +3:24. **he is.** Is *28:9. Mt +*11:25. Mk *10:15. Ro 2:20. 1 C +*3:1. *13:11. *14:20. Ep +*4:14. 1 P √2:2.

14. **of full age.** or, perfect. He 6:1. Mt +*5:48. 1 C 2:6. 14:20. Ep *4:13. Ph 3:15. Ja *3:2g. **use.** or, an habit, or, perfection. **their senses.** Jb 6:30. 12:11. 34:3. Ps *119:103. SS 1:3. 2:3. Mt +*6:22, 23. Ep 1:18. **exercised.** He 12:11. 1 T 4:7. 2 P 2:14. **to discern.** Ge +*3:5. 2 S 14:17. 1 K *3:9, 11. Jb 6:30. Pr +*14:15. Ec 8:5. Is *7:15, 16. Ml 3:18. Ro 14:1g. 1 C √2:14, 15. 12:10g. Ep 5:17. Ph √1:9, 10g. 1 Th +*5:21. **good and.** Ge 3:22. Dt 1:39. 2 S 14:17.

HEBREWS 6

The apostle purposes to lead the Hebrews forward in the knowledge of Christ, 1-3. He shows the desperate state of apostates, 4-6; and illustrates it by a simile of barren land, which no culture improves, 7, 8: but declares his favorable opinion of the Hebrew Christians, and his desire of their fruitfulness and diligence, in order to their assured hope to the end, 9-12. He expatiates on the security of the covenant of grace, as confirmed to Abraham by the promise and oath of God, for the strong consolation of all future believers, 12-20.

1. **leaving.** ſ116, 1 C +11:16. See on He *5:12-14. Ph 3:12-14. **principles of the doctrine.** or, word of the beginning. He 5:12. Mk 1:1. Jn 1:1-3. 1 T *3:16. **go on.** Ph 3:12-15. Col +√1:10. 2 P +*3:18. **unto perfection.** or, full growth. He +5:14. *7:11, 12, 18, 19. 12:13. Pr +*4:18. Mt *5:48. 1 C 13:10. 2 C *7:1. Ep 4:12. Col 1:28. 4:12. Ja 1:4. 1 P *5:10. 1 J 4:12. **laying.** Mt 7:25. Lk 6:48. 1 C *3:10-12. 1 T +*6:19. 2 T +*2:19. **repentance.** Is √55:6, 7. Ezk *18:30-32. Zc *12:10. Mt 3:2. *4:17. 21:29, 32. Mk 1:4, 15. 6:12. Ac +*2:38. +*3:19. 11:18. √17:30. *20:21. 26:20. 2 C √7:10. 2 T +*2:25, 26. **dead.** ſ121G, Ge +31:1. He 9:14. Ro *6:23. Ga +*5:19-21. Ep *2:1, 5. **and.** ſ174, Ge +18:27. **faith.** He √11:6. Jn √5:24. 12:44. 14:1. 1 P 1:21. 1 J √5:10-13.

2. **the doctrine.** He *9:9, 10. +*10:22. Mt 3:14. 20:22, 23. +√28:19. Mk +*7:3. *16:16. Lk 3:16. 12:50. Jn 1:33. *3:25, 26. 4:1, 2. Ac √1:5n. +*2:38, 41. *8:12, 13, 16, 36-38. 10:47. 16:15, 33. *19:2-5. +√22:16n. Ro +*6:3, 4n. 1 C 1:12-17. +*10:2n. +*12:13n. Col +*2:12n. 1 P 3:20, 21. Re +*19:13. **of baptisms.** He 9:10. Mk 7:4, 8. Lk 11:38g. **laying.** Nu *8:10, 11. Ac 6:6. +8:17. *13:2, 3. 19:6. **resurrection.** He 11:35. Ps +*16:9, 10. Is +*26:19n. Ezk *37:1-14. Da +*12:2. Mt 22:23-32. Lk +*14:14. √20:37, 38. Jn *5:29. 11:24, 25. Ac 4:2. 17:18, 31, 32. *23:6, 8. 24:15, 21. 26:8. Ro 6:5. 1 C *15:13-57. Ph +*3:21. 1 Th +*4:14-18. 2 T 2:18. **of.** ſ181E, Ge +3:24. **eternal.** Gr. aionios, Mt +18:8. **judgment.** Ec *12:14. Da *7:9, 10. Mt +*10:15n. *25:31-46. Ac +*10:42. √17:31. 24:25. Ro 2:5-10, 16. 2 C *5:10. 2 P 3:7. Ju *14, *15. Re √20:10-15.

3. **if.** ſ184C, Mt +4:9. Ac +18:21. Ro 15:32. 1 C 4:19. *16:7. 2 C *3:5. Ja *4:15. **permit.** ſ108B. Idiom B827. "To permit," denoting if God so orders it, and gives the needed grace and strength.

4. **impossible.** T#20. ver. √18. He 10:4, +*26-29. *11:6. +*12:15-17. Mt 5:13. +*12:31n, 32n, 45. 19:26. Lk 11:24-26. Jn *15:6. 2 T *2:25. 4:14. 2 P √2:20-22. 1 J +*5:16. ❋S#102g: Mt 19:26. Mk 10:27. Lk 18:27. Ac 14:8 (impotent). Ro 8:3 (could not do). 15:1 (weak). **for those.** The following five-fold description of the true believer is scarcely if ever equaled elsewhere in the pages of Scripture as to detail or extent, and most certainly can apply only to persons who were once genuinely saved. If such a description were to occur in any other context but this, there would be no question as to its application to true believers. This text furnishes a near-perfect measure of one's theological system: if you must work strenuously to avoid the clear implication of the text in an effort to prove these were not true believers, your system stands convicted as incorrect at this point, and the effort to explain this passage away is the hallmark of those who are guilty of mishandling the word of God in order to maintain their preconceived doctrinal system (2 C +*4:2. 2 T +*2:15). **were once.** Mt *7:21, 22. Lk +*8:13. Jn 3:27. Col +*1:23. He 12:15-17. 2 P *2:18-22. **enlightened.** He *10:32. Nu *24:3, 4, 15, 16. Ps 19:7, 8. Mt 4:16. 5:14, 15. Lk 11:34-36. 16:8. Jn 1:9. *3:20, 21. 1 C *8:1, 2. Ep 1:18. 5:8. Col 1:12. 1 Th 5:5. 1 J √1:7. 2:9, 10. **and have tasted.** Mt *7:21, 22. Lk 10:19, 20. Jn 1:12. 3:16, 27. 4:10. 6:32, 51. Ac √8:20. *10:45, 46. 11:17. Ro *1:11. 1 C *13:1, 2. Ep √2:8. 3:7. 4:7. 1 T 4:14. Ja 1:17, 18. 1 P *2:3g. **heavenly gift.** 2 C 9:15. 1 C 12:3, 8-10. Ep +2:8. **made partakers.** He *2:4. +*3:1, 14. Lk 5:7. Jn ◐14:17. Ac 15:8. Ro ◐+*8:9. Ga 3:+2, 5. Ju ◐19. **Ghost.** Gr. pneuma, Mt +1:18.

5. **tasted.** He 2:9g. Ex *24:9, 11. Ps 34:8. Je ◐+*15:16. Mt √7:22, 23. +*13:20, 21. Mk *4:16, 17. *6:20. Lk +√8:13. Jn *6:32, 51. *15:3. Ac 2:41. 4:4. 8:14. 11:1. +*17:11, 12. *24:25. Ro √10:9, 10. Ep 5:26. Ja *1:18-25. 1 P +*1:23. √2:3. 2 P √2:20. **word of God.** Ep +6:17. **the powers.** He 2:5. **world.** Gr. aion, Mt +6:13. Mt 12:32. Ep 1:21. **to come.** He 2:5. Mk +*10:30. Lk *18:30. √20:35. Jn +*6:54n.

6. **If.** lit. And. 1 C +*15:2. 2 P +*1:10. **fall away.** The Scripture frequently warns against the possibility of apostasy as a very real danger. Logically, only real believers can apostatize, unbelievers cannot. These warnings in Hebrews must not be explained away as applicable only to Hebrew Christians who were at that time in danger of falling back into Judaism, if only because the same warnings are given with equal urgency to the Gentile Christians to whom Paul wrote in his several epistles (1 C +*15:2). Nor can these individuals arbitrarily be classed as those who professed a relationship with Christ but who were never really genuinely saved (1 J 2:19n), for the Holy Spirit has closed off this possibility as completely as it is possible to do so with the language used in the preceding description identifying just who these individuals were. He *3:10, 11. Nu 3:4. Is √1:28. Jn 6:66. ◐√10:27, 28. Ac 1:25. Ga 5:4. 1 T +√4:1n. 2 P 2:15, 22. 1 J *2:19, 20. Ju *5. **to renew.** This is hardly a description of a Christian who has momentarily backslidden (Ps 37:24. Pr *24:16. Ju 24), but rather of the inveterate apostate

who, though once truly trusting in Christ for salvation, has through moral (1 C +*6:9-11) or doctrinal (1 C +*15:2) apostasy fallen away from Christ. If such a person has ceased to believe in Christ (Lk +*8:13), and no longer places faith in what Christ did on the cross for him (2 T 2:12, 13), there is no other sacrifice for sin to which he can appeal for salvation. Being removed from the only possible grounds for hope and salvation, it is impossible to renew such a person again on the basis of any other hope. This passage does not teach that it is impossible for the person who has sinned to repent and turn back to Christ, if he wills to do so (Jn 6:37). It teaches that there is no other possible alternative to which the person who has turned away from Christ for salvation can turn (Jn √14:6. Ac √4:12). Continuing to put Christ to an open shame by their flagrant disregard of His sacrifice, they cannot be renewed to repentance. See on ver. 4. Ps +*51:10, 11. Pr *21:16. *29:1. Is 1:28. Mt *12:31n, 32n. 2 T +*2:25. Ja ◐*5:19, 20. 2 P √2:20, 21. Re 3:14-22. **again unto.** He 12:17. 1 S *2:25. *3:14. Ro +*1:24, 26, 28. 2 Th +*2:9-11. 1 J +*5:16. **repentance.** Ps ◐+*51:17. Is ◐*55:6, 7. 2 C 12:21. **they crucify.** Present active participle, denoting in Greek a continuing practice, not a single unrepeated action. It has become their willful habit of life, their lifestyle. He +*10:26, 29. Zc *12:10, etc. Mt 23:31, 32. Lk 11:48. **the Son of God.** He +1:2. Mt +*14:33. **and put.** Present active participle. **an open shame.** He +*12:2. Mt 1:19g. 27:38-44. Mk 15:29-32. Lk 23:35-39.

7. **the earth.** Ge 1:11, 12. Dt 11:11. 28:11, 12. Ps *65:9-13. 104:11-13. Is √55:10-13. Jl 2:21-26. Ja *5:7. **by.** *or,* for. 1 C 9:10. 2 T 2:6. **receiveth.** Ge *27:27, 28. Le 25:21. Dt 33:13. Ps 24:5. 65:10. *126:6. Is 44:3. Ezk 34:26. Ho 10:12. Ml *3:10. Mt +*13:23. Jn *15:2.

8. **beareth.** He 12:17. Ge *3:17, 18. 4:11. 5:29. Dt 29:28. Jb 31:40. Ps 107:34. Is *5:1-7. Je *17:6. 44:22. Mk 11:14, 21. Lk √13:7-9. **rejected.** 1 C +*9:27. **nigh unto.** He 8:13g. Ge 3:17. Je 44:22. Lk 13:6-9. Ja +*5:19. **cursing.** Dt +*28:15. 29:22-28. Pr +*3:33. **whose end.** He *10:27. Is 27:10, 11. Ezk 15:2-7. 20:47. Ml 4:1. Mt *3:10. *7:19. +*25:41. Jn √15:6. 2 P 3:10, 12. Re √20:15.

9. **beloved.** ver. *4-6, 10. He 10:34, *39. Ph *1:6, 7. 1 Th *1:3, 4. **persuaded.** Ro +*15:14. **better things.** He 7:19, 22. 8:6. 9:23. 10:34, +*35. 11:+*16, 35, 40. 12:24. **things that accompany salvation.** Attention to the things which accompany salvation will provide guidance for spiritual growth beyond the initial salvation experience of the new birth, as well as provide for continuing growth or restoration, and protection against apostasy, as the individual case may require. Such things include (1) caring about spiritual things: (a) neglect not our great salvation, He 2:3. (b) care for our own steadfastness, 1 C +*15:58. 1 Th +*3:8. (c) our grounding in the faith as a guard against apostasy, Ps +*1:3. Mt 7:13-27. Lk +*8:13. Ep +*4:14. Col +√1:23. +*2:7. 1 T +*4:16. 2 T +√3:15-17. 2 P +*3:18. (d) the steadfastness of others, He +*3:13n. (e) our steadfastness in fellowship, He +*10:25. (f) guard against the danger of willful sin, He +*10:26. (g) cast not away your confidence, He *10:35-39. (2) obedience: He √5:9. Mt *7:24-27. Lk +*11:28. Jn 14:15, 23. Ro 1:5. 6:17. 15:18. 2 C 10:5. 2 Th 1:8. 1 P 1:22. 1 J +*2:3. (3) teachability, humility, and contriteness: 1 S +*25:17. Ps √25:9. Is +*57:15. (4) qualities underly-

ing spiritual maturity: Mt +*5:3-12. (5) fruit of the Holy Spirit: Ga 5:22, 23. (6) development of the composite qualities underlying true love: 1 C 13:4-7. (7) progress along the steps to steadfastness: 2 P √1:3-11. (8) regular prayer: 2 Ch +*7:14. Ps +*119:18. Da +*6:10. 1 Th +*5:17. (9) a continuing hunger for and increasing knowledge of the written Word of God: Jb +*23:12. Je +*15:16. Mt +*5:6. Jn +*5:39. Ac +*17:11. Col +√1:10. 2 T +√3:15-17. 1 P √2:2. 2 P +*3:18. (10) daily study of God's Word: Jsh *1:8. Ps +*1:2. Ac +√17:11. The book of 1 John would make a most suitable place for the new Christian to begin the study of God's Word. Read a chapter each day of 1 John on Monday through Friday every week for an entire month in order to begin to learn and master its contents. From time to time look up the cross references given in the *Treasury of Scripture Knowledge* for a favorite or striking verse encountered in that day's reading. The book of 1 John, in discussing the several characteristics of true believers (1 J 5:13n), incidentally mentions many additional things that accompany salvation. Further reading of the gospels of Mark and John, Paul's shorter letters, such as Ephesians, Philippians, and Colossians, and the concurrent reading of a chapter each day from the Old Testament book of Proverbs (read for each day the chapter number which corresponds with that day's calendar date) would provide, in about that order, an appropriate spiritual diet for a new believer. Beyond this, reading of Matthew, Luke, Acts, and the book of Romans is suggested. Once a new believer is familiar with all these books of Scripture, reading in any other books as personal interest may lead would then be profitable. In addition to the consecutive reading of whole books of the Bible, the study of particular subjects in the Bible is essential. Topics recommended for priority study are the following *Treasury* notes and references: Is +√8:20n (T#46). Ps +102:18 (T#49). Ga +√1:8n (T#1120). The reference passages given for 2 T +√3:15-17, and What the Bible teaches about itself, Topic Numbers 1014-1121. He *2:3. *5:9. Is +*57:15. Mt *5:3-12. Mk *16:16. Ac *11:18. *20:21. Ro *8:6. 2 C √5:17. *7:10. Ga *5:6, 22, 23. T *2:11-14. 2 P √1:3-11. 1 J +*2:3n. *3:14. **though.** √185A, Lk +11:8.

10. **God is not unrighteous.** Ge +*18:25. Dt 32:4. Ro 3:4, 5. 2 Th 1:6, 7. 2 T *4:8. 1 J √1:9. **to forget.** Ne 5:19. 13:*14, 22, 31. Ps 20:3. Je 2:2, 3. 18:20. Ac +*10:4, 31. **your work.** Ru 2:12. 2 Ch +*24:10. Ga 5:6. 1 Th +1:3. 1 J 3:17, 18. **and labor.** Nu=4:49. =7:5, 6. =18:31. 1 C 3:8. **of love.** 1 C *13:4-7. Ga *5:6, 13. 1 J √3:17. Re 2:19. **which ye have.** He 13:16. Pr 14:31. 19:17. 22:9. 28:27. Ec 11:1. Mt√10:42. *25:35-40. Mk 9:41. Lk 6:38. Ac *2:44, 45. *4:32, 34, 35. 9:36-39. 11:29. Ro 12:13. 15:+25-27, 31. 1 C 16:1-3. 2 C 8:1-9. 9:1, 8, 11-15. Ga *6:10. Ph 4:16-18. Col 3:17. 1 T 6:18. 2 T 1:17, 18. Phm 5-7. Ja *2:15-17. 1 J 3:14-17. **ministered to.** Nu=3:6. Mt *25:40. 27:55. Ga +*6:10. **the saints.** 2 C +1:1. **and do.** He 13:1.

11. **we desire.** He 13:17. Ps +*126:6. Ro 1:11. 2 C 11:28. Ga +*4:19. Ph *1:9-11. 3:15. 1 Th +*3:8. 4:10. **diligence.** Pr 10:4. 13:4. +*22:29. Ro 12:8g, 11. 1 C +√15:58. 2 P +*1:5-11. √3:14. **full assurance.** He +*3:6, 14. +*10:22. Is 32:17. Col +*2:2. 1 Th 1:5. 2 P +*1:10, 11. 1 J *3:14, 18, 19. √5:13. **of hope.** ver. 18-20. He +*3:6. Ac +*26:6. Ro *5:2-5. 8:24, 25. 12:12. 15:13. 1 C 13:13. Ga 5:5. Col +*1:5, 23.

2 Th 2:16, 17. 1 P 1:3-5, 21. 1 J *3:1-3. **unto the end.** He +*3:6, 14. 10:32-35. Mt 24:13. Ga +*6:9. 2 Th 3:13mg. 1 P *1:13. Re 2:26.

12. **not slothful.** He *5:11g. Jg *18:9. Pr 10:26. 12:24. *13:4. 15:19. *18:9. *24:30-34. Ec 10:18. Je +*48:10mg. Ezk +*16:49 (T#709). Mt *25:26. Ro +*12:11. 2 P +*1:10. **but followers.** He *12:1. *13:7. Jsh +*14:8. SS 1:8. Je *6:16. Ro 4:12. Ph *3:17. Ja *5:10, 11. 1 C +*11:1. 1 P *3:5, 6. **of them.** 2 Ch ❍*13:7. Ps +√119:63. **through faith.** ver. *15. He *10:36. *11:8-16. Lk *8:15. Ro +*2:7. *8:25, 26. Ga 3:7, 29. 1 Th *1:3. Re 13:10. 14:12. **and patience.** √174, Ge +18:27. T#936. He *10:35-37. Pr 10:28. La 3:26-29. Ro 5:3, 4. Ep +4:2g. Ja *1:2-4, 12. 4:10. 5:7, 8, 11. 1 P 2:20. 5:6. **inherit.** He *1:14. *10:36. 11:9, 17, 33. Mt *22:32. +*25:34. Lk 16:22. *20:37, 38. Ep +*1:11n. 1 J *2:25. Re +*14:13. **the promises.** ver. 15. He 7:6. +*10:36. 11:+*13, 17, 33. Ac +√26:6. Ro +*9:4. +*15:8. 2 C 1:20. 7:1. Ga *3:16, 18, 29.

13. **he sware.** ver. 16-18. Ge *22:15-18. Ezk 32:13. Ps 105:9, 10. Is 45:23. Je 22:5. 49:13. Mi 7:20. Lk 1:73.

14. **Surely.** Ge ▸22:17. Lk 1:73. **blessing.** √147B, Ge +2:16. **multiplying.** Ge 17:2. 48:4. Ex 32:13. Dt 1:10. Ne 9:23.

15. **after.** ver. 12. Ge +*12:2, 3. 15:2-6. 17:16, 17. 21:2-7. Ex 1:7. Hab 2:2, 3. Ro 4:17-25. **patiently endured.** ver. +*12. He 7:6. Ro +*4:13. **he obtained.** He ❍+*11:13. Dt *1:10. Lk *1:68, 69. Lk *16:22. Jn *8:56. Ac ❍+*7:5.

16. **swear.** ver. 13. Ge 14:22. *21:23, 24. *24:3. 26:20, 26, 28, 31. Mt 23:20-22. **an oath.** √101, Dt +32:42. Ge 21:30, 31. 31:53. Ex 22:11. Jsh 9:15-20. 2 S 21:2. Ezk 17:16-20. **for confirmation.** T#720. Dt 10:20. Ne 5:12. Ps 15:1, 4. Ec 8:2. Mt *26:63, 64. 2 C 1:23. Ph 1:7. **all.** √171A, Ex +9:6. **strife.** He 7:7. 12:3. Ju 11g.

17. **willing.** 1 C 12:11. Ja *1:18. 2 P √3:9. **more.** Ps 36:8. SS 5:1. Is √55:7. Jn *10:10. 1 P 1:3. **the heirs.** ver. 12. He 11:7, 9. Ro √8:17. Ga *3:29. Ep +*1:11n. Ja +*2:5. 1 P 3:7. **of promise.** Ge +*17:7. Ac +*2:39. Ga *3:17, 29. **the immutability.** lit. unchangeable. i.e. *unchangeableness.* √24G, Ge 1:9. ver. 18. Jb 23:13, 14. Ps *33:11. 110:4. Pr *19:21. Is 14:24, 26, 27. *25:1. √46:10. 54:9, 10. √55:11. Je 33:20, 21, 25, 26. Ml +*3:6. Ro *4:13, 16. +*11:29. Ja √1:17. **of his.** √29, Ex +19:6. i.e. *his unchangeable counsel.* **counsel.** Ac +*20:27. **confirmed it.** Gr. interposed himself. Gr. mediated. ver. 16. Ge 26:28. Ex 22:11. Ga +3:20. **by an oath.** He 8:6. Je=33:20, 21.

18. **two.** ver. 17. He 3:11. *7:21. Ps 110:4. Mt 24:35. 1 P *1:25. **immutable.** ver. 17. Ge +*9:16. **impossible.** Nu *23:19. 1 S 15:29. Ro 3:4. 2 T +2:13. T +*1:2n. 1 J 1:10. 5:10. **we might.** Is 51:12. 66:10-13. Lk 2:25. Ro 15:5. 2 C 1:5-7. Ph 2:1. 2 Th *2:16, 17. **strong consolation.** He 12:5. 13:22. 1 C +14:3g. **who.** He 11:7. Ge 19:22. Nu 35:11-15. Jsh 20:3. Ps 46:1. *62:8. Is 32:1, 2. Zc 9:12. Mt 3:7. 2 C *5:18-21. 1 Th +*1:10. **fled for refuge.** Nu=35:6, 11. Jsh √20:7n. Ps *46:1. Pr 14:26. Ac 14:6g. **lay hold.** 1 K 2:28. Pr 3:18. 4:13. Is 27:5. 56:4. 64:7. 1 T *6:12. **the hope.** He +3:6. Ac +√26:6. Ro *15:13. Ep +*2:12. Col +*1:5, 23, 27. 1 T 1:1. 1 P +*1:3. **set.** He *12:1, 2. Ro 3:25.

19. **we have.** Col +*1:5. 1 Th *5:8. 1 P +*1:3, 4. **as an anchor.** Ac 27:29, 40. **soul.** Gr. *psyche,* Lk +9:24. Ps +*103:1. Lk +*1:46. **both sure.** Ps 42:5, 11. 43:5.

62:5, 6. 146:5, 6. Is +*12:2. 25:3, 4. 28:16. Je *17:7, 8. Ro 4:16. 5:5-10. +*8:28-39. 1 C +√15:58. 2 T *2:19. **entereth.** He *4:16. 9:+3, 7. 10:20, 21. Le 16:2, 15. Mt *27:51. Ep 2:6. Col *3:1.

20. **the forerunner.** He 2:10. Ps *73:25. Jn +*14:2, 3. 1 C *15:20. **for.** He 1:3. *4:14. 8:1. *9:12, 24. *12:2. Ro *8:34. Ep 1:3, 20-23. 1 P 3:22. 1 J 2:12. **an high priest.** He +2:17. See on 3:1. 5:6, 10. 7:1-21. **for ever.** Gr. *aion,* Mt +6:13. He +5:6. *7:24, 15. +*13:8. lit. unto the age, Mt +21:19. **after the order.** He +5:6.

HEBREWS 7

The superiority of Melchisedec's typical priesthood, above that of Aaron, proved and illustrated, 1-10. It was intended, that the priesthood should be changed, and consequently that the ritual law of Moses should be disannulled, when the Messiah came; that a better covenant and priesthood might take place, 11-18. This was needful, for the more perfect state of the church, and for the salvation of all who come to God by Jesus Christ, to the uttermost, and forever, 19-28.

1. **this.** ver. 6. He 6:20. Ge *14:18-20. **Salem.** i.e. *at peace; perfect, complete,* ✱S#4532g. ver. 2. For ✱S#8004h, see Ge +14:18. Ge 33:18. Ps *76:2. Jn 3:23. **priest.** Zc *6:12, 13. **the most.** Ge 14:18. Nu 24:16. Dt 32:8. Ps 57:2. 78:35, 56. Da 4:2. 5:18, 21. Mi 6:6. Mk 5:7. Lk +1:32. Ac 16:17. **the slaughter.** Ge 16:14-16. Is 41:2, 3.

2. **gave.** Lk +*11:41n. **a tenth.** Ge 28:22. Le 27:32. Nu 18:21. 1 S 8:15, 17. **interpretation.** Ps +7:13. Mk +5:41. **King of righteousness.** 2 S 8:15. 23:3. 1 K 4:24, 25. 1 Ch 22:9. Ps +*45:5-7. *72:1-3, 7. *85:10, 11. Is +*9:6, 7. 32:1, 2. 45:22-25. Je +*23:5, 6. 33:15, 16. Mi 5:5. Lk 2:14. Ro 3:26. *5:1, 2. Ep 2:14-18. **peace.** Ps 76:2. Col *1:20. 2 Th *3:16.

3. **Without father.** That is, as the Syriac renders, "Whose father and mother are not inscribed among the genealogies;" and therefore it was not known who he was. **descent.** Gr. pedigree. ver. 6. Ex 6:18, 20-27. 1 Ch 6:1-3. Ezr *2:61, 62. **neither beginning.** Pr *8:23. Mi +*5:2. Jn 1:1. Re *1:8. **nor end.** Ps *102:27. **the Son of God.** ver. 28. He +1:2. Mt +14:33. **abideth.** √96C5, Mt +2:13. **a priest.** ver. 17, 23-28. **continually.** He 10:1, 12, 14.

4. **man was.** or, by ellipsis, supply (priest was). √63I1A, Ex +12:4. **the patriarch.** √101, Dt +32:42. Ac 2:29. 7:8, 9. **Abraham.** Ge *12:2. +*17:5, 6. Ro *4:11-13, 17, 18. Ga 3:28, 29. Ja 2:23. **gave.** Ge 14:20.

5. **who receive.** He *5:4. Ex 28:1. Nu 16:10, 11. 17:3-10. *18:7, 21-26. **to take.** Le *27:30-33. Nu 18:26-32. Dt 14:22. 2 Ch 31:4-6. Ne 10:37. 12:44. 13:10. **come.** ver. 10. Ge 35:11. 46:26. Ex 1:5. 1 K 8:19.

6. **descent.** Gr. pedigree. ver. 3. **received.** ver. 2, 4. Ge 14:19, 20. **had the promises.** He 6:13-15. 11:13, 17. Ge 12:2, 13. 13:14-17. 17:4-8. 22:17, 18. Ac 3:25. Ro +*4:13. 9:4. Ga 3:16.

7. **without.** He +6:16. 1 T *3:16. **the less.** √96G4, Mt +1:20. He *11:20, 21. Ge 28:1-4. 32:24-30. 47:7-10. 48:15-20. 49:28. Nu *6:23-27. Dt 32:1. 2 S 6:20. 1 K 8:55. 2 Ch 30:27. Lk 24:50, 51. 2 C *13:14. Ep *1:3.

8. **men.** ver. 23. He +*9:27. **of whom.** He 5:6. 6:20. Ps 110:4. **he liveth.** √96C5, Mt +2:13. He 3:16, 24, 25. 5:6. 6:20. Lk 24:5. Jn 6:57. *11:25, 26. *14:6, 19. Re *1:17, 18.

9. **payed tithes**. ver. 4. Ge +*14:20. Ro 5:12mg.
10. **in the loins**. ver. 5. He ◐+12:9. Ge 1:28. 2:7, 23. 35:11. 46:26. 1 K 8:19. Ps ◐104:30. Mt 1:2. Jn 1:13. 3:6. **of his father**. 1 C 11:8.
11. **If therefore**. 184B, Mt +23:30. The Second Condition of Hypothetical Propositions, to show the impossibility of the assumed condition. **perfection**. *Teleiosis*, "completion," or "fulfilment" of the plan and purpose of God. ver. 18, 19. He 8:7, 10-13. *10:1-5, 9, 11, 12, 14. Ga √2:21. 4:3, 9. Col 2:10-17. **Levitical**. ✳S#3020g. **received the law**. He 8:6g. 2 Ch +*15:3. 35:3n. 1 C +*14:34n. **what**. ver. 26-28. **another**. ver. 15, 17, 21. See on He 5:6, 10. 6:20. **after the order**. ver. 17. He +5:6.
12. **being changed**. Mt 3:15. **a change**. Is 66:21. Je 31:31-34. Ezk 16:61. Ac 6:13, 14. **the law**. Nu 8:5-7.
13. **For he**. ver. 14. **pertaineth**. He +2:14. **of which**. Nu 16:40. 17:5. 2 Ch 26:16-21.
14. **evident**. 1 T 5:24, 25g. **our Lord**. ver. 13. Lk 1:43. Jn *20:13, 28. Ep 1:3. Ph 3:8. **sprang**. Nu 24:17. **out of Judah**. Ge 46:12. +*✳49:10. Ru *4:18-22. 1 Ch +*5:2. Ps +*✳60:7. Is *11:1. Je +*23:5, 6. Mi +*✳5:2. Mt 1:3-16. 2:6. Lk 2:23-33. *3:33. Ro *1:3. 2:3. Re *5:5. *22:16. **spake nothing**. Nu 3:5-8. Dt *10:8. 2 Ch *26:1, 16, 21.
15. **after**. ver. 3, 11, 17-21. Ps 110:4. **there ariseth**. ƒ184A, 1 C +15:2.
16. **the law**. He *9:9, 10. 10:1. Ga 4:3, 9. Col *2:14, 20. **carnal commandment**. He *9:10. Ro +7:14. Ga 3:3. **the power**. ver. 3, 17, 21, 24, 25, 28. Re 1:18. **endless**. ✳S#179g, only here. **life**. Jb *19:25. Jn *5:26. Ac *3:15. 1 J *5:20. Re *1:17, 18.
17. **Thou art**. ƒ92A, Mt +1:23. ver. 15, 21. He 5:6, 10. 6:20. Ps ❭110:4. **for ever**. Gr. *aion*, Mt +6:13. lit. unto the age, Mt +21:19.
18. **a disannulling**. ver. 11, 12. He 8:7-13. 9:26. 10:1-9, 28g. Ro 3:31. Ga 3:15, 17. **the weakness**. ver. 19. He 8:7, 8. 9:9, 10. 10:1-4. 13:9. Ac 13:39. Ro +*8:3. Ga *3:23, 24. *4:9, 21. 1 T 4:8. **unprofitableness**. He +13:9.
19. **the law**. See on ver. 11. He *9:9. 10:1. Ex 29:36. Le 16:16. ◐*18:5. Ezk 45:18. Ac +*13:39. Ro *3:20, 21. 8:3. Ga +*2:16. *3:24. **made**. *Ouden eteleosen*, "completed nothing," it was the introduction, but not the completion. **the bringing in**. or, it was the bringing in. Ga 3:24. **a better hope**. He +3:6. 6:+9, 18, 19. 8:6. 11:40. Jn 1:17. Ro 8:3. Col +*1:27. 1 T 1:1. **we draw**. ver. 25. He +*4:16. *10:19-22. Le 10:3. Ps 73:28. Jn √14:6. Ro *5:2. Ep *2:13-18. *3:12. Ja 4:8.
20. **without**. ver. 21, 28g.
21. **without**. ver. 20, 28g. **an oath**. or, swearing of an oath. **The Lord**. ver. +17. Ps 110:4. **sware**. See on He *6:16-18. **repent**. Mt +21:29. **Thou art**. ƒ92A, Mt +1:23. **for ever**. Gr. *aion*, Mt +6:13.
22. **By so much**. He +1:4. **was Jesus made**. Is *53:5. **a surety**. Ge 43:9. 44:32. Jb 17:3. Pr 6:1. 20:16. **of a**. He *8:6-12. *9:15-23. *12:24. 13:20. Da 9:27. Mt 26:28. Mk 14:24. Lk 22:20. 1 C 11:25. **better**. ver. 19. He +6:9. **testament**. Rather, "covenant," *diatheekee*. Ro +9:4.
23. **were many**. ver. 8. 1 Ch 6:3-14. Ne 12:10, 11. 1 C +9:19g. **by reason**. Ex 29:29, 30. Le 16:32. Nu *20:28.
24. **But**. *O de*, "But he," that is, Christ, because "he continueth ever," hath *aparabaton ierosuneen*, "a

priesthood that passeth not away from him." **he continueth**. See on ver. 8-25, 28. He √13:8. Is +*9:6, 7. Jn 12:34. Ro 6:9. Re 1:18. **ever**. Gr. *aion*, Mt +6:13. ver. 21, 28. **hath**. 1 S 2:35. **an unchangeable priesthood**. or, a priesthood which passeth not from one to another. Ps=99:6.
25. **he is able**. He 2:18. 5:7. Is 45:22. 63:1. Je ◐=15:1. Da 3:15, 17, 29. 6:20. Mt *10:28. Jn *6:37-40. *10:29, 30. Ep 3:20. Ph 3:21. 2 T +*1:12. Ju *24. **to save**. Ge 18:32. Jn *14:19. Ro *5:10. **them**. ver. +19. He 11:6g. **to the uttermost**. or, evermore. Gr. completely. Lk 13:11g. **that come**. ver. 19. He √11:6. Jb 22:17. 23:3. Ps 68:31, 32. Is 45:24. Je 3:22. Jn √6:37, 39. **by him**. He 13:15. Jn √14:6. Ro 5:2. Ep 2:18. 3:12. 1 J *2:1, 2. **ever liveth**. See on ver. 8, 16, 24. **to make intercession**. T#836. He *4:14-16. *9:24. Ex=17:12. =30:1. Is *53:12. 59:16. Da 9:24. Mt +*10:32. Jn 14:13, 16. 16:23, 24. 17:9-26. Ro +*8:34. 1 T √2:5. 1 J √2:1, 2. Re 8:3, 4.
26. **such**. ver. 11. He 8:1. 9:23-26. 10:11-22. **a high priest**. He +2:17. **became**. He +*2:10. Lk 24:26, 46. **holy**. He +*4:15. *9:14. Ex 28:2, 36-38. Le *21:1, 6, 11. Ps *16:10. Is *53:9. Mk *1:24. Lk +*1:35. 4:34. *23:22, 41, 47. Jn *8:29. +*14:30. Ac 2:27. 3:14. 4:27. 13:35. 2 C √5:21. 1 P *1:19. *2:22. 1 J *2:2. *3:5. Re *3:7. 15:4. 16:5. **harmless**. Zc 9:9. Ro 16:18g. **undefiled**. Is *53:9. 1 P *1:19. *2:22. **separate from**. He +*4:15. Ge=49:26. Jn *8:46. 1 P 2:22. **made higher**. He *1:3. +*4:14. 8:1. *12:2. Ps 68:18. Mt 27:18. Mk +*16:19. Ep 1:20-22. *4:8-10. Ph √2:9-11. 1 P 3:22. 1 J *2:1. Re 1:17, 18.
27. **daily**. He 10:11g. Ex *29:36-42. Nu 28:2-10. **first**. He +5:3. 9:7. Le 4:3, etc. 9:7, etc. *16:6, 11, 15. **and then**. Le 4:13-16. 9:15. 16:15. **this**. He *9:12, 14, 25, 28. 10:6-12. Is *53:10-12. Ro 6:10. Ep 5:2, 25. T √2:14. **once**. He *9:12. *10:10, 12. Ro *6:10. **when**. Mt +20:28. Ro +4:25.
28. **the law maketh**. See on He 5:1, 2. Ex 32:21, 22. Le 4:3. **the word**. See on ver. 21. Ps 110:4. **maketh the Son**. See on ver. 3. He +1:2. +2:17. 3:6. 4:14. 5:5, 8. **who**. ver. 21, 24. **consecrated**. Gr. perfected. He +*2:10. +*5:9. Le 21:10. Lk 13:32. Jn 19:30g. **evermore**. Gr. *aion*, Mt +6:13. lit. unto the age, Mt +21:19.

HEBREWS 8

Further evidence of the superiority of Messiah's priesthood to that of Aaron, 1-6; and that it was predicted that the Sinai covenant would be abrogated, to make way for a new and better covenant, through a superior Mediator, 7-13.

1. **sum**. Or, chief, principal point, in both which senses *kephalaion* is used by profane writers. Ex=38:21. **We have**. See on He 7:26-28. **an high priest**. He +2:17. **who**. See on He +*1:3, 13. 10:12. *12:2. Ep 6:20. Col *3:1. Re 3:21. **right hand**. ƒ22A15C, Ps +110:1. He 1:3. Ac 7:55, 56. **the throne**. ƒ22D3C2, Ps +45:6. He +*4:16. **the Majesty**. 1 Ch *29:11. Jb 37:22. Ps 21:5. 45:3, 4. 104:1. 145:12. Is 24:14. Mi 5:4. **in the heavens**. He +*4:14. 7:26. Ep *1:20.
2. **minister**. He +1:7. 9:8-12. *10:21. Ex 28:1, 35. Lk 24:44. Ro +*15:8. **the sanctuary**. or, holy things. He 9:1, 2, 8, 12, 24, 25. 10:19. 13:11g. **the true**. He 9:11, 23, 24. 10:22. Jn 1:9. 4:23. Ep *2:19-22. 1 T *3:15. **which**. He *9:24. 11:10. Nu 24:6. 2 C 5:1. Col

2:11. **pitched**. Ex 33:7. Jsh 18:1.

3. **every**. See on He 5:1. 7:27. **to offer**. Le 1:2. 16:11, 15, 16. 23:37. **have**. He 9:14. 10:9-12. Jn 6:51. Ep *5:2. T √2:14.

4. **For if**. ⨍184B, Mt +23:30. "Now if he were on earth (which he is not), he would not even be a priest," as he is not of the tribe of Levi. Condition of the second class, determined as unfulfilled. **he should**. ⨍184B, Mt +23:30. He *7:11-15. Nu *16:40. 17:12, 13. 18:5. 2 Ch *26:18, 19. **there are priests**. *or*, they are priests. **gifts**. *dora*, gifts, or offerings, comprehended propitiatory sacrifices, as well as freewill-offerings. See He 11:4.

5. **unto**. *upodeigmati kai skia*, or, "with the representation and shadow," as Dr. Macknight renders. He 9:23. **the example**. He 9:9, 23, 24. **and shadow**. He *10:1. Col *2:17. **admonished**. He 11:7. 12:25g. Lk +2:26g. **tabernacle**. He 13:10. **See**. Ex ▸25:40. *26:30. 27:8. Nu 8:4. 1 Ch 28:11, 12, 19. Ac 7:44. **pattern**. *Tupon*, type, plan, or form.

6. **obtained**. ver. 7-13. **more excellent**. He 1:4. 2 C *3:6-11. **ministry**. He +1:7. 9:21. **the mediator**. He 7:22. 9:15. 12:24. Ga 3:+19, 20. **covenant**. *or*, testament. See on He *7:22. 9:15-20. Ex *24:6-8. Je=33:20, 21. Ml=2:4. **was established**. *Nenomotheetai*, "was ordained (or established) by law." He 7:11g. *10:8, 9. **upon**. ver. 10-12. Ro 9:4. Ga 3:16-21. T +*1:2. 2 P 1:4.

7. **For if**. ⨍184B, Mt +23:30. **had**. ver. 6. He 7:+11, 18. Ro *8:3. Ga 3:21.

8. **he saith**. See on Je *▸31:31-34. **the days**. He *10:16, 17. Je +*23:5, 7. 30:3. *31:27, 31-34, 38. Lk √17:22. **a new**. ver. 13. He *9:15. 12:24. Mt +*26:28. Mk 14:24. Lk 22:20. 1 C *11:25. 2 C 3:6. **covenant**. Is +*55:3. Je *32:40. √33:24-26. Ezk 16:60, 61. *37:26. **the house**. Ac +2:36. **Judah**. i.e. *praised*, ✚S#2455g, so rendered only here.

9. **the covenant**. He 9:18-20. Ex 24:3-11. 34:10, 27, 28. Dt 5:2, 3. 29:1, 12. Ga 3:15-19. 4:24. **I took**. He +2:16. Ge 19:16. Dt 1:31. Jb 8:20mg. SS 8:5. Is 41:13. 51:18. Mk 8:23. Ac 9:8. 13:11. **to lead**. Ex 19:4, 5. Ps 77:20. 78:52-54. 105:43. 136:11-14. Is 40:11. 63:9, 11-13. **they continued**. Ex 32:8. Dt 29:25. 31:16-18. Jsh 23:15, 16. 2 K *17:15-18. Ps 78:10, 11, 57. Is 24:5, 6. Je 11:7, 8. 22:8, 9. 31:32. Ezk 16:8, 59. 20:37, 38. **regarded**. Jg *2:20, 21. 10:13, 14. Je *15:1. La 4:16. Ho *1:9. Am 5:22. Ml 2:13.

10. **this is**. He 10:16, 17. Ro 11:27. **I will put**. Gr. I will give. Ex 24:4, 7. 34:1, 27. Dt 30:6. Ps 119:135. Je 31:33. 32:40. Ezk 11:19. *36:26, 27. 37:26. Jn *14:26. 2 C 3:3, 7, 8. *4:6. Ja +*1:18, 21. 1 P +*1:23. **into**. Ex +*25:21. **write**. ⨍22C43, Ex +31:18. **in**. *or*, upon. Ps 37:31. 40:8. Is 51:7. 2 C *3:3. **I will be**. He +*11:16. Ge +*17:7, 8. Le 26:12. SS 2:16. Je 7:23. 11:4. 24:7. 30:22. 31:1, 33. 32:38. Ezk 11:20. 14:11. 36:28. 37:27. 39:22. Ho 1:10. *2:23. Zc *8:8. +*13:9. Mt 22:32. 1 C *6:16. Re 21:7. **they shall**. Ex *19:5, 6. Ac *2:41. Ro *8:4. 9:25, 26. 2 C *6:16-18. T √2:14. 1 P *2:9, 10.

11. **they shall**. Is +*2:3. *54:13. Je *31:24. Jn +*6:45. 1 J *2:27. **Know the**. Gr. *ginosko*, Jn 8:55n. 2 K 17:27, 28. 1 Ch +*28:9. 2 Ch 30:22. Ezr *7:25. **for all**. Is *54:13. Je *24:7. Ezk 34:30. Hab *2:14. 1 J *5:20. **shall know**. Gr. *oida*, Jn 8:55n. T#443. Is *11:9. √29:18, 24. *33:6. Je *3:15. *31:34. Ezk *34:27. Hab 2:14. Jn *6:45. *17:3. 1 C 13:8. **from**.

Je 6:13. 42:1, 8. 44:12. Ac +*8:10.

12. **will be merciful**. He 10:16, 17. Ps 25:7. 65:3. Is *43:25. *44:22. +*54:7. Je 33:8. √50:20. Mi +*7:19, 20. Zc +*10:6. Ac +*10:43. +*13:38, 39. Ro +*11:27. Ep *1:7. Col *1:14. 1 J √1:7-9. √2:1, 2. Re +*1:5. **and their sins**. He 10:17. Je 31:34. Am 8:7. Col *2:13. **and their**. ⨍174, Ge +18:27. **remember no more**. ⨍158, Mt +5:18. Is +*41:9. *43:25. *44:22. Zc +*10:6. Jn √5:24.

13. **A new**. See on ver. 8. **he hath**. He 7:11, 12, 18, 19. 9:9, 10. **ready**. He +6:8g. Is 51:6. Mt *24:35. 1 C *13:8. 2 C √5:17.

HEBREWS 9

The tabernacle and its furniture, and the typical meaning of it, and of the ordinances observed at it, 1-10. An application of the subject to the priesthood, sacrifice, and covenant of Christ, 11-26. Men are appointed to die, and after death the judgment, when Christ shall come for salvation to all who "look for him," 27, 28.

1. **the first**. He 8:7,13. **covenant**. ⨍63A1, Ge +14:20. **had**. ver. 10. Le 18:3, 4, 30. 22:9. Nu 9:12. Ezk 43:11. Lk 1:6. **ordinances**. *or*, ceremonies. ver. 10mg. Ex 15:25, 26. **divine service**. ver. 6. Ro 9:4g. **and a**. ver. 10, 11. He +8:2. Ex *25:8. *29:43. Nu *10:21. Col 2:8.

2. **a tabernacle**. Ex 26:1-30. 29:1, 35. 36:8-38. 39:32-34. 40:2, 18-20. **made**. ver. 6. He +3:4g. **the first**. ver. 6. Ex 25:23-40. 26:35. 37:10-24. 39:36-38. 40:4, 22-24. **the candlestick**. Ex *25:31-39. Mt *5:15, 16. Jn *15:5. 1 J *1:3, 7. Re *1:12, 20. **the table**. Ex 25:23-29. 40:4. Le 24:5, 6. **the showbread**. Ex 25:23, 30. Le 24:5-8. 1 C *10:16-18. **the sanctuary**. *or*, holy. He +8:2. Ex 26:33.

3. **the second**. ver. 7. He +*6:19. 10:20. Ex *26:31-33, 34, 36. 36:35-38. 40:3, 21. 2 Ch 3:14. Is 25:7. Mt 27:51. Mk 15:38. Lk 23:45. **the Holiest**. ver. 8. He 10:19. Ex 26:33. 1 K 8:6.

4. **the golden censer**. Le *16:12, 13. 1 K 7:50. 2 Ch 26:19. Ezk 8:11. Re 8:3. *or*, altar of incense. Ex 30:1, 27. Le 16:20. Nu 4:13. Dt 33:10. 1 K 6:20, 22. **the ark**. Ex 25:10-16. 26:33. 37:1-5. 39:35. 40:3, 21. Re 11:19. **the covenant**. Ro +9:4. **overlaid**. Ex 25:11. **golden pot**. Ex *16:33, 34. **and Aaron's**. Nu *17:5, 8, 10. Ps 110:2, 3. **and the tables**. Ex *25:16, 21. 26:33. 34:29. *40:3, 20, 21. Dt *10:2-5. 1 K *8:9, 21. 2 Ch 5:10n.

5. **over**. Ex 25:17-22. *37:6-9. *40:20. Le 16:2. Nu 7:89. 1 S 4:4. 1 K 8:6, 7. 2 K 19:15. 1 Ch 28:18. Ps 80:1. 99:1. Ep 3:10. 1 P 1:12. **the mercyseat**. He *4:16. Le 16:2, 13, 15. 1 Ch 28:11.

6. **ordained**. ver. 2. He +3:4g. **the priests**. Ex 27:21. 30:7, 8. Nu 28:3. 2 Ch 26:16-19. Da 8:11. Lk 1:8-11. **the first**. ver. 2. **the service**. ver. 1.

7. **the second**. ver. +3. **the high priest**. ver. 24, 25. He 10:3. Ex 30:10. Le *16:2-20, 34. **alone**. Is ◉63:3. **not without**. He +5:3. 7:27. 10:19, 20. **offered**. Le +=23:27. **errors**. Le 5:18. Nu *15:27, 28, 30, 31. 2 S 6:7. 2 Ch 33:9. Ps 19:12. 95:10. Is 3:12. 9:16. 28:7. 29:14. Ho 4:12. Am 2:4.

8. **Holy Ghost**. He +3:7. 10:15. Is *63:11. Ac *7:51, 52. 28:25. Ga 3:8. 2 P √1:21. **the way**. ver. 3. He +*4:15, 16. *10:19-22. Jn *10:7, 9. √14:6. Ep 2:18.

the holiest. *J96F2*, Ge +4:10. He +8:2. Is +*57:15. Mt *27:51. Re *21:27.

9. a figure. ver. 24. He 11:19. Ro 5:14. 1 P *3:21. the time. He 7:11. 11:39, 40. 1 P 1:11, 12. gifts. See on He +5:1. that could not. ver. 13, 14. He *7:18, +19. *10:1-4, 11. Ps 40:6, 7. Ga *3:21. make. He +7:19. him that. He 10:2. 12:28g. Lk +2:37. as pertaining. ver. 14. Ps *51:16-19. conscience. ver. 14. 2 C +1:12.

10. in meats. He 13:9. Le *11:2, etc. Dt 14:3-21. Ezk 4:14. Ac 10:13-15. Col √2:16n. drinks. Le *10:8, 9. 11:34. Nu *6:2, 3. divers. This cannot mean different or diverse immersions, for under the Mosaic system different modes of purification were required, such as washing, sprinkling, and rinsing. The apostle, when writing that the Levitical institutes consisted "ONLY" of meats and drinks, and diverse baptisms, could not have meant that lustrations consist ONLY of immersion. Besides, he applied the adjective *diphorois*, different, to qualify the noun *baptisms*. This makes good sense if we suppose the noun to be generic, as purifications, but is absurd if we take the noun as specific, like immersion. Those who argue that the "one baptism" of Ep 4:5 proves their doctrine of one mode of baptism have to reckon with this passage, where "different baptisms" certainly proves different modes (See F. G. Hibbard, *Christian Baptism*, Part Two, p. 214). He 6:2g. +*10:22. Ex 29:4. 30:19-21. 40:12. Le 14:8, 9. *16:4, 24. *17:15, 16. 22:6. Nu 19:7-21. Dt 21:6. 23:11. washings. Gr. *baptismos*, *S#909g, Mk +7:4. Ex *40:31, 32. Le *8:6, 12. He 6:2. Jn 2:6. 3:25. carnal ordinances. or, ordinances of the flesh, or ordinances of the person. That is, the baptisms or Jewish purifications spoken of are restricted to those ceremonies which had an application to the body of the worshipper, not the rites for the purification of cups, skins, clothes, vessels, etc. This is clear from the context, which contemplates the effect that these ordinances were to have upon the conscience of the worshipper. It is clear from their being called ordinances of the flesh. It is clear from the antithesis drawn in the apostle's argument: the blood of bulls, and of goats, and the ashes of a heifer, sprinkling the unclean, sanctified to the purifying of the flesh, but the blood of Christ shall purge your conscience from dead works, etc. (ver. 13, 14). The fact established, then, that the ordinances spoken of as "baptisms" are with reference only to the body of the worshipper, the manner of the mode commanded for the administering of those Jewish purifications is of great significance in determining the meaning conveyed by *baptismos*. The question becomes, is immersion ever enjoined, under any circumstances, as necessary to effect a purification of a person? No immersions of persons are enjoined under the Mosaic ritual. No washings of persons are enjoined by the Hebrew word *tabal* (*S#2881h, 2 K 5:14), the Hebrew word understood by some to mean or require immersion, nor by any word that denotes immersion; but without exception washings or purifications are enjoined by the word *rahats* (*S#7364h, Ex 29:4), which denotes to wash or purify, without any reference to mode. The word *rahats* and its usual Greek equivalent in the Septuagint, *louo*, denote the application of water to the person or thing, and not of the thing or person to the water, as immersion would require. These words are synonymous with the English wash, but they are not synonymous with bathe. The Hebrew *rahats* is rendered by the Septuagint sometimes by *louo*, which denotes the washing of the body; by *nipto*, which also means to wash, and is used to denote washing of hands or feet; and sometimes by *pluno*, which is used to denote the washing of clothes, accomplished by treading them in water in a trough; and once it is translated by *cheo*, to flow, to pour forth, to shed. The word used to enjoin the washing of clothes, in the Old Testament, is *kabas*, which primarily means to tread, to trample with the feet; and hence, to wash, to cleanse, etc., as garments, by treading them in a trough; and finally, to wash in any way. It is sometimes used in a figurative sense, as Ps 51:2, 7; Je 2:22; 4:14; Ml 3:2. The Septuagint sometimes uses *pluno* which means to wash clothes, to render the Hebrew *shatap* (*S#7857h, Le +15:11), to gush, to pour out, to rush, to overflow; hence, to wash, rinse, as Ezk 16:9, "wash away thy blood"; Jb 38:25, "outpouring" of waters; Pr 27:4, anger is an "outpouring." This word is generally translated rinse in English, where it denotes washing of hands, or vessels, as in Le 15:11, 12. When in English the word bathe occurs, this does not enjoin immersion, for the original Hebrew term in every such case denotes only to wash. The most usual practice in the Old Testament was to sprinkle, as alluded to in He 9:13, and Nu 19:20 (See F. G. Hibbard, *Christian Baptism*, pp. 86-90, 210-213). For the original Hebrew and Greek terms employed with reference to baptism, see the index entry "Baptism, Related Terms." ver. 1. He +7:16. Ga 4:3, 9. Ep 2:15. Col 2:20-22. ordinances. or, rites, or, ceremonies. ver. 1. Ep *2:15. until. He 2:5. 6:5. 8:8-13. Jn *4:23. Ac *21:25. Ga *4:4. Ep 1:10. Col √2:16n.

11. Christ. Ge +*49:10. Ps 40:7. Is 59:20. Ml 3:1. Mt 2:6. 11:3. Jn 4:25. 1 J 4:2, 3. 5:20. 2 J 7. an high priest. He +*2:17. 3:1. +*4:15. 5:5, 6. 7:1, 11-26, 27. *8:1, 2. of good things. He 10:1. to come. Mt 6:10. Ro 14:17. 1 C 11:26. 13:10. by a greater. ver. 1-9, 24. He 8:2. Jn 1:14g. Ep *1:3. not made. ver. 23, 24. Mk +14:58. Jn +*2:19, 21. Ac 7:48. 17:24, 25. 2 C *5:1. Col 2:11.

12. Neither. *J111, Ge +18:27. by the. ver. 13, 19. He *10:4. Le 8:2. 9:15. *16:5-10. by his own blood. *J117, Ge +19:8. ver. 14. He 1:3. 10:9-14. *13:12, 20. Ac +*20:28. Ro +*3:25. Ep *1:7. Col *1:14. T +*2:14. 1 P *1:18, 19. Re +*1:5. *5:6, 9. he entered. ver. 7, 24-26. He +*4:14. 10:12, 19. once. ver. 26, 28. He +*7:27. 10:10. Zc 3:9. holy place. *J96F2*, Ge +4:10. ver. 8, 24. He +8:2. having. ver. 15. He 5:9. Jb 33:24. Da 9:24. Mk 3:29. 1 C 6:20. Ga 3:13, 14. 1 Th +*1:10. obtained. *J171J4, Ge +6:8. eternal. Gr. *aionios*, Mt +18:8. ver. 15. He 5:9. redemption. He 10:14. Lk +1:68. Jn 17:17. Ga 4:5. 1 P 2:24.

13. if. *J184A, 1 C +15:2. blood of. *J111, Ge +18:27. ver. +12. Le 16:14-16. and. Nu *19:2-21. sprinkling. Gr. *rantizo*, *S#4472g. ver. 19, 21. He 10:22g. the purifying. Nu 8:7. 19:12. 2 Ch 30:19. Ps 51:7. Ac 15:9. 1 P 1:22.

14. How. Dt 31:27. 2 S 4:11. Jb 15:16. Mt 7:11. Lk 12:24, 28. Ro 11:12, 24. the blood. *J117, Ge +19:8. See on ver. 12. 1 P *1:19. 1 J *1:7. Re +*1:5. *7:14. *12:11. who. Is 42:1. 61:1. Mt 12:28. Lk +*4:18. Jn *3:34. Ac 1:2. *10:38. Ro +*1:4. 1 P +*3:18. eternal. Gr. *aionios*, Mt +18:8. Dt 33:27. Is +*57:15. Je 10:10. Ro 1:20. 1 T +*1:17. Spirit. Gr. *pneuma*, Mt +3:16.

God the Holy Spirit is eternal (Mt +*28:19n). T#346. Is +6:8 (T#211). Mi 2:7. Mi +5:2 (T#76-3). Jn 14:26. Ac *5:3, 4. Ro 15:19. 1 C 2:10, 11. *12:3. Col +2:10 (T#76-1). **offered himself.** ver. 7, 28. He +7:27. 13:12. Ex 12:13. Le +=1:3. Mt +*20:28. Jn +*2:19. Jn √10:18. Ep 2:5. *5:2. Ph +*1:29. T √2:14. 1 P *2:24. *3:18. **without.** Le 22:20. Nu 19:2-21. 28:3, 9, 11. Dt 15:24. 17:1. Is +*53:9. Da +*9:24-26. 2 C √5:21. 1 P +*1:19. *2:22. 1 J *3:5. **spot.** *or,* fault. **purge.** ver. 9, 22, 23. He *1:3. *10:2, 22. T *2:14g. **conscience.** ver. 9. He *10:22. 2 C +1:12. **dead works.** √121G, Ge +31:1. See on He 6:1. Lk *15:24. Ro *6:13, 23. Ep *2:1. **to serve.** Le 12:28. Lk 1:74. Ac +24:14. Ro 6:13, 22. 16:26. Ga 2:19. 1 Th 1:9. 1 P 4:2. **the living.** He 3:12. 10:31. 12:22. Dt 5:26. 1 S 17:26. 2 K 19:16. Je 10:10. Da 6:26. Mt +16:16. Ac 14:15. 2 C *6:16. 1 T *3:15.

15. **the mediator.** He *7:22. 8:6. *12:24. Ga +3:19. 1 T *2:5. **the new.** See on He +8:8. 10:29. 12:24. 2 C 3:6. **testament.** Ro +9:4. **by means.** ver. 16, 28. He 2:14. 13:20. Nu 35:25. Is +*53:10-12. Da 9:26. Ro +4:25. Col 1:21, 22. **for.** ver. 12. He 11:40. Ro 3:+24-26. 5:6, 8, 10. Ep *1:7. 1 P *3:18. Re 5:9. 14:3, 4. **the first.** ver. 1. He 8:7, 13. **they which are called.** He 3:1. See on Ro +*8:28, 30. 9:24. 2 Th 2:14. **might receive.** He 10:36. 11:39. Ex 32:13. **promise.** √100, Ge +10:9. He 6:13. *11:+*13, +*16, 39, 40. T +*1:2. Ja 1:12. 1 J 2:25. **of.** √29, Ex +19:6. i.e. *the promised eternal inheritance.* **eternal.** Gr. *aionios,* Mt +18:8. ver. 12. He 5:9. **inheritance.** Ps +*37:18. Mt +*5:5. *19:29. 25:34, 46. Mk 10:17. Lk 18:18. Jn √10:28. Ac +*20:32. Ro √6:23. Ep +*1:11n. 2 T *2:10. T +*1:2. 3:7. 1 P +*1:2-4. *5:10.

16. **be.** *or,* be brought in. Ge *15:7-10. Je *34:18. **testator.** √63H, Ge +12:15. Supply by ellipsis, (which makes the sacrifice).

17. **a testament.** Ge 48:21. Jn 14:27g. Ga 3:15. **after.** or, over. Thus translate, "over dead victims or sacrifices" (B70). **dead.** √63H, Ge +12:15. **testator.** √24B, Ge +23:16. √96G1, Ac +9:37. Heterosis of Gender, the Masculine for the Feminine. "Testator" is masculine; but the word for sacrifice, to which it refers, is feminine: yet the masculine is used, because the sacrifice was Christ himself; otherwise it would have been feminine to agree with sacrifice (*hee thusia*). Thus, though the Greek word is feminine, the Hebrew is masculine, and "the testator" (*o diatheminos*) which is masculine agrees with the Hebrew *thought,* rather than with the Greek *word* (B533).

18. **the first.** He 8:7-9. Ex 12:22, 23. *24:3-8. **dedicated.** *or,* purified. ver. 14, 22. He 10:20. Nu 7:10, etc. 1 K 8:63. **without blood.** Ex 24:6-8.

19. **he took.** √92G, Lk +4:18. Ex ▶24:8. **the blood.** ver. +12. He 10:4. Ex 24:5, 6, 8. Le 1:2, 3, 10. 3:6. 16:14-18. **with water.** Le=14:5-7, 49, 51, 52. Nu 19:6, 17, 18. Jn=19:34. Ac 1:5n. 1 J 5:6, 8. **scarlet.** *or,* purple. Le 14:4-6, 49-52. Nu 19:6. Mt 27:28. Mk 15:17, 20. Jn 19:2, 5. **hyssop.** Ex 12:22. Nu 19:18. 1 K 4:33. Ps +*51:7. Jn 19:29. **sprinkled both.** √106, Ge +31:7. ver. 18. He 11:28. 12:24. Ex 24:8. Is *52:15. Ezk *36:25. 1 P *1:2.

20. **This.** He 10:29. *13:20. Ex ▶24:8. Zc 9:11. Mt +*26:28. Mk 14:24. Lk 22:20. 1 C 11:25. **testament.** Rather, *covenant.* Ver. 16, 17, may be better rendered, "For where a covenant is, there must necessarily be the death of that by which it is confirmed; for a covenant

is confirmed over dead victims, and does not avail while that by which it is confirmed liveth." See on Dt 29:12. Jsh 9:6.

21. **he sprinkled.** Ex 29:12, 20, 36. Le 8:15, 19. 9:8, 9, 18. *16:14-19. 2 Ch 29:19-22. Ezk 43:18-26. **tabernacle.** Ex 29:12, 36. Le 8:15, 19. 16:14, 16, 18, 19. 2 Ch 29:22. **the vessels.** Nu *4:12. 1 Ch 9:28, 29. 2 Ch 24:14. **of.** √181E, Ge +3:24. **the ministry.** He +1:7. 8:6. Lk +1:23.

22. **almost.** Le 14:6, 14, 25, 51, 52. **purged.** ver. +14. **with blood.** Ex 12:13. **and without.** Jb 8:11-15. Is 43:11. 45:22. Je 17:13. Mt 22:37, 38. Jn 3:3. √14:6. Ac √4:12. Re 20:15. **shedding of blood.** Ge=3:21. Le 4:20, 26, 35. 5:10, 12, 18. 6:7. +*17:11. Is *53:4-6, 10-12. Zc 13:1. Mt 26:28. Jn 1:29. 3:14-17. Ep √1:7. Col √1:14. 1 P 2:24. 1 J *1:7. *2:2. Re *7:14, 15.

23. **the patterns.** ver. 9, 10, 24. He 8:5. 10:1. Col 2:17. **purified.** √100, Ge +10:9. **the heavenly.** ver. 11, 12, 14, 24. He 10:4, 10-17. Lk 24:26, 46. Jn +*14:3. 1 P 1:19-21. Re 5:9. **better.** He +6:9. **sacrifices.** √√96F2, Ge +4:10.

24. **not entered.** ver. 12. He +*4:14. **the holy.** He +8:2. **made with hands.** ver. 11. Mk +14:58. Jn +*2:19-21. **the figures.** ver. 9, 23. He +8:2. 1 P 3:21g. **but.** He *1:3. 6:20. 7:26. 8:2, 5. *12:2. Ps 68:18. Mk 16:19. Lk 24:51. Jn 6:62. 16:28. Ac +*1:9-11. +*3:21. Ep 1:20-22. 4:8-11. Col *3:2. 1 P 3:22. **now to appear.** He 7:25. Ex 28:12, 29. Zc 3:1. Mt +*10:32. Ro +*8:34. 1 J *2:1, 2. Re 8:3. **the presence.** Ac +2:28. **for us.** He +*7:25. Ex=30:1. Lk 22:32. Ro +*8:34.

25. **Nor yet.** Ac 13:34. Ro 6:9, 10. **offer.** ver. 7, 14, 26. He √10:10. **as.** ver. 12. Ex *30:10. Le *16:2-34. **the holy place.** He +8:2. **blood of others.** He 10:19.

26. **For then.** √184B, Mt +23:30. **suffered.** He 13:12. Ac +3:18. **the foundation.** He +4:3. Mt 25:34. Jn 17:24. 1 P 1:20. Re 13:8. 17:8. **world.** Gr. *kosmos,* Mt +4:8. **once.** ver. 12. He 7:27. √10:10. 1 P √3:18. **in the end.** Gr. *sunteleia,* S#4930g, Mt +24:3n. He 1:2. Is *2:2. Da 10:14. Mi 4:1. Mt +*13:39. 1 C 10:11. Ga 4:4. Ep +*1:10. 1 P *1:20. **world.** Gr. *aion,* Mt +6:13. Jn +*6:54n. **he appeared.** ver. 12. He 7:27. 10:4, 10. Le 16:21, 22. 2 S 12:13. 24:10. Jb 7:21. Da +*9:24. Jn *1:29. 1 P *2:24. *3:18. 1 J +*3:5. **to put away.** He 7:18. 10:28g. Ro *5:19. *6:14. 1 C *15:56, 57. **the sacrifice.** ver. 14. He 10:12, 26. Ep *5:2. T √2:14.

27. **appointed.** Jb 7:1. +*36:18. 2 C 5:10. **once.** 2 S *14:14. Jb +*8:13. √16:22. Pr +*10:28. Lk *16:26. **to die.** T#145. Ge +*3:19. 2 S 14:14. Jb 14:5. 16:22. *30:23. 34:15. Ps 89:48. 104:29. Ec *3:1, 2, 20. *8:8. +*9:5, 10. +*12:7. Zc 1:5. Ro *5:12. **but after.** T#150. He 6:2. 2 S *12:23. Jb √7:8-10. *10:21. √14:7-12, 19-21. *16:22. 19:25. Ps +*146:4. Ec 11:9. +*12:14. Is √38:18. Mt +16:27. 21:41. 25:31, etc. Lk +*12:5. *16:27-29. Jn 5:26-29. Ac √17:31. Ro 2:5, 8, 9. *14:9-11. 1 C *4:5. 2 C *5:10, +*11. 2 T +*4:1. Ju *15. Re √20:11-15.

28. **was once.** ver. *25. Ro √6:10. 1 P √3:18. 1 J *3:5. **offered.** ver. 14. Le +=23:27. **to bear.** Le *10:17. Nu 18:1, 23. Is *53:4-6, 11, 12. Mt +*26:28n. Ro 5:15. 1 P +*2:24. **the sins.** √121C1E, Ge +19:15. **of many.** √√171F, Is +53:12. He 2:◐*9, 10. Mt 20:28. +*26:28n. Mk 10:45. Re 5:9. **unto them.** Lk +√21:36. Ph *3:20. 1 Th +*1:10. 2 T +*4:8. T √2:13. 2 P *3:12. **that look.** or, wait. Ge 49:18. Is 26:8. La 3:26. Mi *7:7. Lk +√21:28. 1 C *1:+7, 8. Ph *3:20. 2 T +*4:8.

T +*2:13n. 2 P √3:12-14. **he appear.** Zc *14:5. Jn +*14:3. Ac +*1:11. 1 Th +*4:14-16. 2 Th +*1:5-9. +*2:1. 1 J √3:2. Re +*1:7. **second time.** He 2:5. 4:9. 10:36, 37. Is ❍+*11:11. Mt 23:39. 25:19. Lk 19:12-27. Ac +*1:11. +*3:19-21. 2 T +*4:1. 1 P 1:10-13. **without sin.** He +*4:15g. Is *53:12. Ro 6:10. 8:3. 2 C √5:21. **unto salvation.** "Salvation" or "the salvation" was a Biblical term derived from the prophets (Is 25:9) descriptive of the times of Millennial blessing to be experienced when the throne and kingdom of David should be restored under Messiah (Is +*55:3). The kingdom of the Messiah and salvation were in the Jewish mind convertible terms (Mk 15:43 w Lk 2:25). From Origen's time to the present the term "salvation" has been too exclusively applied to the present life and the intermediate state. If we turn to the apostolic teaching we find, on the other hand, a full and free adoption of the Jewish phraseology (Ac 1:6n), without placing upon it another and widely differing interpretation, and its direct reference to the future, when, as prophets teach, it will be realized. The salvation which the apostles preached is related to the fulfillment of the covenant and restoration of the nation of Israel (Lk √1:69-75. Ro +*15:8). This salvation, whatever the earnest might be in the present or intermediate state, is declared by the apostles to be still future. What a contrast exists between the present prevailing spiritualistic, indefinite modern conceptions of "salvation," and the correct belief based on the oath-bound covenants. What an astonishing change, when "the Christ," "the kingdom," and even "salvation" itself are transformed from their covenanted and predicted meaning. The most selfish and mystical conceptions are adopted in preference to the simple truth (See Peters, *Theocratic Kingdom*, vol. 3, Proposition 196, Observation 1, pp. 449, 450). Ps +*37:39. 119:166, 174. +*149:4. Is +√25:9. La 3:26. Mk 15:43. Lk √1:69-75. 2:*25, 38. 21:28. Ro *8:19-23. 13:11. 1 C *15:24. Ep +*4:30. Ph *3:21. 1 Th +*4:17. *5:9. 2 Th +*1:10. 2 T *2:10.

HEBREWS 10

The inefficacy of the legal sacrifices is shown from the frequent repetition of them, 1-4. The abolition of them, and the substitution of the sacrifice of Christ, was foretold by the psalmist, 5-9; and is that by which believers obtain eternal remission, 10-18. Exhortations to faith, prayer, and constancy in the gospel; and to love and good works, 19-25. The danger of willfully renouncing Christ, after having received the knowledge of the truth; with solemn warnings, expostulations, and encouragements, 26-39.

1. **having a shadow.** See on He 8:5. *9:9, 11, 23. Ro +*15:4. Col *2:16, 17. **good things.** He 9:11. **with.** ver. 3, 4, 11-18. He 7:18, 19. 9:8, 9, 25. **continually.** ver. 12, 14. He 7:3. **perfect.** ver. 14. He +7:19.

2. **For then.** ⌐184B, Mt +23:30. **would they not have.** *or*, they would have. **worshippers.** He 9:9. 12:28g. Lk +2:37. **once.** ver. 17. He 9:13, 14. Ps 103:12. Is 43:25. 44:22. Mi *7:19. **conscience.** Our translators use the word conscience here, as elsewhere, for consciousness. 2 C +1:12.

3. **a remembrance.** He +9:7. Ex 30:10. Le 16:6-11, 21, 22, 29, 30, 34. 23:27, 28. Nu 29:7-11. 1 K 17:18. Mt 26:28.

4. **not.** ver. 8, 11. He 9:9, 13. Ps 50:8-12. 51:16.

Is 1:11-15. 66:3. Je 6:20. 7:21, 22. Ho 6:6. Am 5:21, 22. Mi +*6:6-8. Mk 12:33. **the blood.** He +9:12. **take.** There were essential defects in these sacrifices. 1st.— They were not of the same nature with those who sinned. 2nd.—They were not of sufficient value to make satisfaction for the affronts done to the justice and government of God. 3rd.—The beasts offered up under the law could not consent to put themselves in the sinner's room and place. The atoning sacrifice must be one capable of consenting, and must voluntarily substitute himself in the sinner's stead: Christ did so. The nature and requirements of Christ's office as our substitute in his work of redemption through His death on the Cross absolutely require of Him that He be divine. A substitute must meet at least these six qualifications: (1) He must honor and obey the law which those for whom he substitutes are dishonoring and disobeying, as highly as though it had never been broken, so that *justice will not be injured*. Ge 18:25. Ps 40:7, 8. Is 42:21. Jn *8:46. This demands the impeccability of Christ (He +*4:15). (2) Though giving perfect obedience to the law that is being broken, he must yet suffer its full penalty as though he had been the supreme criminal against it, so that *mercy will not be injured*. He 7:26. Is 53:3. 2 C *5:21. (3) He must do his work as a substitute voluntarily and without the slightest pressure from without, so that *he himself will not be injured*. He 12:2. Jn √10:18. (4) He must have the absolute and inherent right thus to dispose of himself, so that *no one else will be injured*. Christ has the inherent right thus to dispose of himself, provided He is Creator and not creature. No creature, not even the highest and greatest of the sinless angels, has any right over his own life. It belongs to, and is therefore wholly at the disposal of, the Creator. When Christ died, obedient to death (Ph 2:8), though he voluntarily dismissed His spirit (Lk 23:46), no man taking his life from him, yet he did not thereby commit suicide, but the very opposite. For when one suicides, he thrusts himself unbidden into the presence of God, having no right to take his life because he cannot bring it back again. No creature could qualify under this fourth requirement, for none has the right to lay his life down. Moreover, if God should grant any sinless creature that right, and he should lay his life down by the permission of God, here then would be God giving a creature instead of Himself, and this would wholly remove Him, and therefore His love, from the transaction. For love is self-giving, not the giving of someone else. God could never show His love without giving Himself (Ge 22:8). If Christ is not actually God Himself, manifest in the flesh (1 T 3:16), He was but a creature, and as such, wholly unable to qualify at this point. This fourth requirement of a substitute thus demands the *deity of Jesus Christ*. (5) A substitute must be able fully to represent and answer for both God and man in his work as a substitute, so that neither party to the transaction will be injured. In meeting this fifth requirement, Christ is fully able to answer for and represent both God and man, if He IS both God and man. That Christ is both God and Man is shown by His ability to render wholly acceptable service to God as, on the one hand, He represents Him in maintaining His Law to the last jot and tittle in qualifying before Him on behalf of the sinless; and on the other hand, as He represents man in receiving the penalty of the Law on behalf of the sinful. For no one ought to answer for man's sins but man; and no one can answer for them but God. Reason therefore demands the virgin birth of Jesus Christ. God must be his Father, else He cannot be God, just as a woman must be His mother, else He cannot be Man. Herein lies the philosophy of the incarnation. This is why the Mighty God tabernacled in the flesh. (6) His work as a substitute must be of such intrinsic moral worth as forever to satisfy the utmost demands of perfect righteousness and holiness, so that the *principles of equity will not be injured.* Christ's work as substitute was of such intrinsic moral worth as to present to God a value sufficient to cover the moral needs, not only of his own holy Law in bringing it up out of dishonor, but also of the whole sinful world. Here once more reason demands the deity of the substitute, and the Scripture declares it. And such is what gave His work its worth; such worth did His work have that no injury could ever come to the eternal principles of equity and righteousness inherent in God's holiness. Christ's suffering was the perfect satisfaction given to the justice of God by the infinite merit of the holiness of the selfsame God (Ge 22:8), who Himself became the substitute to meet on man's behalf His own just requirements. It was no third party (such as the Arians claim Michael the Archangel to be, 1 Th 4:16n) coming in between God and the sinner and changing His wrath to love. It was God Himself expressing His love, at infinite cost to Himself, in a way that gave full satisfaction both to the justice and the mercy which must be demanded by a holy and loving God. Christ did not merely offer a corresponding ransom for the sin of Adam (1 T 2:6n), for not only does his death atone for Adamic sin, but his blood has purged our sins (He 1:3), for Christ did not taste death for Adam only, but He "tasted death for every man" (He 2:9). This Christ could not do, were He merely man—even perfect man, for "None can by any means redeem his brother, nor give to God a ransom for him: (For the redemption of their soul is precious, and it ceaseth for ever:) That he should still live for ever, and not see corruption" (Ps 49:7-9). So at most, were Christ merely human, He could redeem but one man—and no more—if He himself were perfectly sinless. But as it is in truth, Christ is not merely a ransom for the sin of Adam, but He gave Himself "a ransom for all" (1 T 2:6), and this is absolute testimony for the deity of Christ: Only an infinite Savior could pay an infinite Sacrifice (adapted from J. E. Conant, *No Salvation Without Substitution*, Chapter 7, "The Nature of Substitution," pp. 112-131). ver. 11. Ho 14:2. Jn *1:29. Ro 11:27. 1 J *3:5.

5. **when.** ver. 7. He 1:6. Mt 11:3. Lk 7:19g. **world.** Gr. *kosmos*, Mt +4:8. **Sacrifice.** ♪92A, Mt +1:23. Le=7:11. +=23:19 (peace offering). 1 S *15:22. Ps ▶40:6-8. 50:8, etc. 51:16. Pr 21:3. Is 1:11. Je 6:20. 7:22, 23. Am 5:21, 22. **and offering.** Le +=23:12 (burnt offering). **but a body.** ♪92F1. Gnome; or, Quotation B793: where the words are changed by a variant reading. For another instance of this figure see He 11:21. This New Testament citation of Ps 40:6 has interpreted "ear" in the original Hebrew by the figure of speech ♪171N. Synecdoche of the Whole, where the whole (body) is put for the part (ear), taking the ear to represent the entire body of the listening and obedient servant of Jehovah. For other instances of this figure,

see Ge +8:13. For other instances of New Testament quotations which interpret rather than translate a figure of speech, see Ps +*16:9n. ver. 10. He 2:14. 8:3. Ge +*3:15. Is +*7:14. Je 31:22. Mt *1:20-23. Lk +*1:35. Jn *1:14. Ga *4:4. 1 T *3:16. 1 J 4:2, 3. 2 J 7. **hast thou prepared me.** *or,* thou hast fitted me. **me.** ♪29, Ex +19:6. It is a question whether the *Dative* is used, by *Antiptosis,* for the Accusative; to show that, while Christ's human body was prepared for Him, yet He was also constituted a servant for ever according to Ex 21:6 and Dt 15:17. This is the sense in Ps 40:6, and (*soma*), body, was used of slaves (Re 18:13), just as we use "hands" of laborers (B509).

6. **burnt.** See on ver. 4. Le ch. 1, 4, 5. 6:1-7. +=23:12. Mk 12:33. **sacrifices.** He 13:11. Ro +8:3. **for sin.** Le +=23:19 (sin offering). **thou.** 1 S *15:22. Ps 50:8-10. *51:16. 147:11. Is *1:11. Ho *6:6. Am *5:21, 22. Ml 1:10. Mt 3:17. *17:5. Ep *5:2. Ph 4:18.

7. **Then.** Ps ▶40:7. **Lo.** ver. 9, 10. Pr 8:31. Zc 2:10. Jn 4:34. 5:30. 6:38. 8:42. 1 J 5:20. in. Ge +*3:15. **the volume.** *or,* roll. lit. head. ♪171S9. Synecdoche of the Part B651. The knob of the roll is put for the manuscript or book itself. Here, "volume" is literally "head," not roll, and refers to the head or knob of the cylinder on which the manuscript was rolled, and which is put, by *Synecdoche,* for the roll and volume itself. Ezr 6:2. Is 8:1. Je 36:2, 4. Ezk 2:9. 3:1, 2, 3. Zc 5:1, 2. **written of me.** Lk +*24:26, 27.

9. **Lo.** ver. 7. He 9:11-14. Ps 40:7, 8. **He taketh.** He 7:18, 19. 8:7-13. 12:27, 28.

10. **we.** ver. 14, 29. He +2:11. *13:12. Zc 13:1. Jn *17:19. 19:34. Ro *8:29. 1 C +*1:30. *6:11. 1 J 5:6. Ju 1. **the offering.** ver. 5, 12, 14, 20. He 9:12, 26, 28. **the body.** ver. 5. Mt 26:26. Mk 14:22. Lk 22:19. 1 C 11:24. **once.** He +7:27.

11. **standeth.** ♪96C1, Ge +4:1. **daily.** He 7:27g. Ex 29:38, 39. Nu *28:3, 24. 29:6. Ezk 45:4. Da 8:11. 9:21, 27. 11:31. 12:11. Lk 1:9, 10. **ministering.** He +1:7. Lk +1:23. **offering.** He +5:1. **which.** See on ver. 1, 4. He 9:9. Ps 50:8-13. Is 1:11.

12. **this man.** See on He *1:3. 8:1. 9:12. Ac 2:33, 34. Ro +*8:34. Col *3:1. **offered.** He +7:27. **one sacrifice.** Lk 13:25. **for sins.** Le +=5:6. **for ever.** ver. 1. He 7:3g. **right hand.** He +*1:3.

13. **henceforth.** He 1:13. Ps *110:1. Da 2:44. Mt 22:44. Mk 12:36. Lk 20:43. Ac 2:35. 1 C *15:25. **till.** He 1:13. 1 C *15:25-28. **footstool.** Jsh 10:24. Ps 8:6. 18:38.

14. **one offering.** He 9:12. **he.** ver. 1. He 7:+19, 25. 9:10, 14. Ro *5:8, 9. *8:1. **them.** ver. 10, 29. He +2:11. 9:13, 14. 13:12. Ac 20:32. 26:13. Ro 15:16. 1 C 1:2. Ep *5:26. Ju 1. **are sanctified.** He ◉+*12:14. Jn *17:17. Ga 4:5.

15. **the Holy.** He 2:3, 4. +3:7. 9:8. 2 S 23:2. Ne 9:30. Jn 15:26. Ac 28:25. 1 P 1:11, 12. 2 P √1:21. Re 2:7, 11, 17, 29. 3:6, 13, 22. *19:10. **Ghost.** Gr. *pneuma*, Mt +3:16.

16. **the covenant.** He 8:8-12. Je ▶31:33, 34. Ro 11:27. **I will put.** He +8:10. Jn 15:16. Ac ◉5:3, 4. Ro ◉8:16. **into.** Ex +*25:21.

17. **And.** Some copies have: Then he said, And their, etc. He +*8:12. Ps *32:1. *103:12. Is *38:17. *44:22. Je ▶31:34. 50:20. Am ◉8:7. Mi *7:19. **and iniquities.** ♪174, Ge +18:27. **no more.** ♪158, Mt +5:18.

18. **where remission.** See on ver. 2, 14. Ac +2:38. **offering for.** Le +=23:19.

19. **Having.** ver. 35. He +*3:6. +*4:16. 12:28. Ro 8:15. Ga 4:6, 7. Ep *3:12. 2 T +*1:7. 1 J 3:19-21. 4:17. **boldness.** or, liberty. **to enter.** He *7:25. 9:3, 7, 8, 12, 23-25. Ezk=44:16. Ro 5:2. Ep *2:18. 1 J *2:1, 2. **the holiest.** He +8:2g. **blood.** ſ117, Ge +19:8.

20. **a new.** He *7:25. 9:8. Jn +*10:7, 9. √14:6. **living.** ſ108B, Ac +7:38. **consecrated.** or, new made. He +9:18. **through.** He 6:19. +9:3. Ex 26:31, etc. 36:35, etc. Le 16:2, 15. 21:23. Mt 27:50, 51. Mk 15:38. Lk 23:45. **his flesh.** ſ171Q7, Jn +1:14. Jn 6:51-56. Ep 2:15. 1 T *3:16. 1 P *3:18. 1 J *4:2. 2 J 7.

21. **an high.** ſ96E2, 1 S +17:14. See on He +*2:17. 3:1. *4:14-16. 6:20. 7:26. 8:1. Zc 6:11-13. **the house.** He *3:3-6. Mt +*16:18. 1 C *3:9-17. 2 C *6:16, 17. Ep *2:19-22. 1 T +*3:15.

22. **draw near.** He +*4:16. 7:19. Ex 12:48. Ps *73:28. Is 29:13. Je 30:21. Ja *4:8. **a true heart.** T#1361. He +8:2. 1 K *15:3. 2 K +*20:3. 1 Ch *12:33, 38n. +*28:9. 29:17. Ps 9:1. 32:11. +*51:6, 10. *84:11. 94:15. 111:1. 119:2, 7, 10, 34, 58, 69, 80, 145. Pr 23:26. Je 3:10. *24:7. Jn *1:47. Ac *8:21, 36, 37. Ep 6:5. **in full assurance.** See on ver. 19. He +*6:11. Mt 21:21, 22. Mk *11:23, 24. Ep 3:12. Col +2:2. Ja *1:6. 1 J *3:19, 21, 22. **hearts.** T#1359. He *3:5, 6. Ja *4:8. **sprinkled.** "If the real washing, the washing away of sin from the soul, is done by sprinkling, and the renewing or regeneration of the heart is done by pouring, by what rule of analogy, logic, fitness of things, or common sense would you have the emblem of this cleansing and purification done by immersion? Ought there not to be agreement between the thing done within and that which is the outward emblem of it in mode? If the inward, spiritual washing can be and is done by sprinkling or affusion, cannot and ought not the outward washing which represents it be done by affusion? Would not this be the appropriate way to represent it? It seems to me that no argument could be made clearer to prove anything than the argument here is to prove that the religious washing of baptism is Scripturally performed by affusion" (G. W. Hughey, *The Scriptural Mode of Christian Baptism*, p. 207). T#39-2. He +*9:13, 14, 19. *11:28. *12:24. Ex 29:21. Le 8:30. 14:7. Nu 8:7. +*19:13, 16-19. Ps 51:7. +72:6 (T#620). Is 44:3. 52:15. Ezk *36:25. Mk +7:4 (T#31). Ac +*22:16. Ro ◐+*6:4 (T#39-1). 2 C 7:1. 1 P *1:2. Re +*1:5. *7:13, 14. **from.** ſ63H, Ge +12:15. Supply by ellipsis (relative: of a combined word), "sprinkled (and so being delivered) from an evil conscience." **an evil.** He +9:14. Jn 8:9. Ac 23:1. 1 T 4:2. 1 P 3:21. 1 J 3:20. **our bodies.** See on He +*9:10n. Ex 29:4. Le *8:6, 22, 23. Ezk 16:9. 36:25. Jn 3:11. Mt 3:11. Jn 3:5. 13:8-10. 1 C +*6:11. 2 C +*7:1. Ep *5:26. T *3:5. 1 P 3:21. Re +*1:5. **washed.** Gr. *louo*, ✻S#3068g, Jn +13:10. He 6:2. Ex +*29:4. 30:20. *40:30. Le 8:6. *16:4. Ac 9:37. 16:33. +*22:16. 1 C +*6:11. Ep *5:26. 2 P 2:22. Re 1:5g. **with.** Ac +*1:5. **pure.** Nu 5:17. =8:6, 7. Is 1:16. Ezk 36:25. 2 C *7:1.

23. **hold fast.** See on He +*3:6, 14. +*4:14. *6:19. 1 Th +*3:8. Re *3:11. **profession.** He +3:1. **our faith.** He +3:6. **without wavering.** Ja *1:6. **for he is faithful.** See on He *6:18. *11:11. Jsh 23:14. 1 C +*1:9. +*10:13. 1 Th +*5:24. 2 Th *3:3. 2 T *2:13. T +*1:2. **that promised.** T#951. He *6:18. Nu 23:19. Dt 4:31. 7:9. Jsh *23:14. 1 S 15:29. 1 K 5:12. 8:56. Ps √9:10. 18:30. *89:34. 105:8. 119:89, 90, 160. Is 46:11. 54:10.

Ro *4:21. 2 C 1:20. 2 T 2:13. T +*1:2. 2 P *1:4. *3:9.

24. **consider.** He +*3:13. 13:3. Ps *41:1. Pr 29:7. Ac *11:29. Ro 12:15. *15:1, 2. 1 C 8:12, 13. *9:22. *10:33. Ga +*6:1. Col *3:16. 1 Th 5:11. 2 Th 3:9. **one another.** Ro +*12:5. **to provoke.** 1 S +*23:16. 1 Ch ◐21:1. Jb *4:3, 4. Pr 6:3g. Ac *15:39g. 17:16g. 1 C 13:5g. Ro *11:14. 2 C 8:8. 9:2. Ga 5:26. **love.** He +*6:10, 11. 13:1. Ga *5:6, 13, 22. Ep *3:17. *4:15, 16. Ph *1:9-11. 1 Th 1:3. *3:12, 13. 1 T 6:18. T 2:4. √3:8. 1 P *1:22. 1 J *3:18, 19. **good works.** Mt *25:40. Ga +*6:10. 1 T +6:18. 2 T +*3:16, 17.

25. **Not forsaking.** The unsteady professor has no spiritual home. No church is sound enough for him; none wholly molded to his taste. Like the wandering bird, he is always on the wing. Any one place is too strait for him. The accustomed food, even though coming down from heaven, is "loathed as light bread" (Nu 21:5). His vitiated appetite leaves him often on the sabbath morning undecided whom to hear, his own will being his only guide. He is anxious to hear from all; and, as the sure result, he learns from none (2 T 3:7). In this self-willed delusion the form and substance of the Church is destroyed. It is not a few wandering sheep, but a fold and a shepherd; not a heap of loose scattered stones, but stones cemented, fitted into their several places; and "the building thus fitly framed together groweth unto an holy temple in the Lord" (Ep 2:21, 22). The Church is "terrible" not in her single members, but "as an army with banners" (SS 6:10); close in rank, where each soldier keeps his own place. The individual profession, in the stead of collective unity, is a purely schismatical spirit, the essence of pride and selfishness (Charles Bridges, *Proverbs*, p. 509, on Pr 27:8). Ex 34:24. Ne 10:39. Pr +*27:8. Mt +*18:20. Jn 20:19-29. Ac 1:13, 14. 2:1, *42, 46. 16:16. 20:7. 1 C 5:4. 11:17, 18, 20. 14:23. Ju *19. **the assembling.** T#745. Ne 8:1-7. Ps 40:7-10. Mt *18:20. Ac 11:25, 26. 13:14-16, 42-45. **ourselves.** *ſ39, Ac +17:27. **together.** Da 11:33. Ml 3:16. Mt *18:20. Ac 19:9, 10. 1 C 14:26. 16:15, 16. Ep 5:19-21. 1 P *4:7-11. 2 J +*10. **but exhorting.** See on ver. 24. He +*3:12-14. 1 S +*23:16. Ro +*12:8. 1 C 14:3. 1 Th 4:18. *5:11mg. **so much.** Ac +1:4. **as ye.** ver. 37. Mt 24:33, 34. Mk 13:29, 30. Ro +*13:11-13. Ph 4:5. Ja *5:8. 1 P 4:7. Ja +*5:8. 2 P *3:9, 11, 14. **the day.** 1 C +*3:13. 1 Th 5:2, 4. 2 Th +*1:10. *2:2, 3. 1 T *4:1. **approaching.** Ro +*13:12. 2 Th ◐+*2:2.

26. **if we.** *ſ39, Ac +17:27. Ge +*4:7. Je +*7:5. 2 P +*1:10. 1 J 1:8, 10. **sin willfully.** See on He +*6:4-6. Le 4:2, 13. Nu ◐*15:27-31. Dt 17:12. Ps *19:12, 13. Da 5:22, 23. Mt *12:31n, 32n, 43-45. Mk 12:31. Jn 9:41. 1 T 1:13. 2 T *2:25, 26. 1 P 5:2g. 2 P 2:20-22. 1 J *3:9. +*5:16. Re +*21:8. **after.** ver. 39. He +6:4. Lk +*12:47. Jn +*13:17. 15:22-24. 2 Th 2:10. Ja √4:17. 2 P √2:20, 21. **the knowledge.** 1 T +2:4. **there remaineth.** See on ver. 3-10. He 6:6. Ac √4:12. 1 C *3:11. 1 J +*5:16. **no more.** Nu 15:30n.

27. **a certain.** He *2:3. 12:25. 1 S 28:19, 20. Is 33:14. Da 5:6. Ho 10:8. Mt 8:29. 11:24. Lk 10:14, 15. 21:26. 23:30. Ro *2:5. Re 6:15-17. **fiery.** He 12:29. Nu 16:35. Ps 21:9. 79:5. Is 26:11. Je 4:4. Ezk 36:5. 38:19. Jl 2:30. Na 1:5, 6. Zp 1:18. 3:8. Zc 8:2. Ml 4:1. Mt 3:10, 12. 13:42, 50. +*25:41. Mk *9:43-49. Lk *16:24. 2 Th √1:8. Ja +*5:3. 2 P +*3:7. Re *20:15. +*21:8. **indignation.** Is +*66:14. Ro +*2:8. **which.**

Dt 32:43. Ps 68:1, 2. Na 1:2, 8-10. Lk 19:27. 1 Th *2:14-16.

28. **despised.** See on He 2:2. +7:18. Nu 15:30, 31, 36. Dt 13:6-10. 17:2-13. 2 S 12:9, 13. Lk +7:30. **Moses' law.** Jn +7:23. **without.** Dt 19:13. Is 27:11. Je 13:14. Ro 9:15. Ja 2:13. **mercy.** ℐ96F2, Ge +4:10. **under.** Nu 35:30. Dt *17:2, 6, 7. 19:15. Mt +18:16. Jn 8:17. 2 C 13:1.

29. **how.** See on He *2:3. *12:25. **sorer punishment.** Lk +*12:48. 2 C +*5:11. 1 P *4:17. **trodden.** He 6:6. 2 K 9:33. Ps 91:13. Is 14:19. 28:3. La 1:15. Ezk 16:6mg. 23:35. Mi 7:10. Mt +*7:6. Ro 16:20. 1 C 15:25, 27. **the Son of God.** He +1:2. Jn +5:25. **the blood.** See on He +9:12, +20. *13:20. Zc 9:11. **the covenant.** ver. 16. He 9:15. Ro +9:4. **wherewith.** He 2:11. 9:13, 14. Je 1:5. Jn 10:36. 17:19. 1 C 11:27, 29. **he was sanctified.** ver. 10, 14. He +2:11. **an unholy thing.** Gr. a common thing. Mk +7:2g. **and hath done.** Ge +*6:3. Is +*63:10. Mt +*12:31n, 32n. Mk 3:28-30. Lk 12:10. Ac 7:51. Ep +*4:30. **the Spirit.** Gr. pneuma, Mt +3:16. Ps 143:10. Zc 12:10. **of grace.** Ps ◑+*84:11. Zc *12:10. Mt +*28:19n. 2 C ◑+*8:9.

30. **Vengeance.** T#558. Dt 32:◗35, 39-41, 43. Ps 94:1. Is 1:24. 35:4. 59:17, 18. 61:2. 63:4. Je 51:56. Na 1:2. Ro 12:19. 13:4. 1 Th 4:6. **I.** ℐ101, Dt +32:42. **The Lord shall.** Dt ◗32:36. Ps *50:4. 96:13. 98:9. 135:14. Ezk 18:30. 34:17. 2 C *5:10. Re *22:12.

31. **fearful thing.** T#155. ver. 27. Jb 27:19-22. Is +*33:14. Lk *12:5, 20. 21:11. Jn +8:21 (T#564). Ro ◑5:9. +*11:22. 2 C +*5:11. Re +*6:16. **to fall.** He *12:29. 2 S ◑24:14. 1 Ch ◑21:13. Ps 50:22. 76:7. 90:11. Mt +*10:28. Lk +*12:5. **the living.** He 3:12. 9:14. 12:22. Dt 32:40. Mt +16:16.

32. **call.** Ga 3:3, 4. Ph 3:16. 2 J 8. Re 2:5. 3:3. **the former days.** He 5:12. Re 2:5. **after.** See on He +*6:4. Ac +*26:18. 2 C *4:6. Ep 1:18. 1 P *2:9. **ye endured.** He 12:4. Ac 8:1-3. 9:1, 2. Ph *1:29, 30. Col 2:1. 2 T 2:3, etc. 4:7, 8.

33. **Partly.** 1 Th 2:14. **made.** He 11:36. 12:4. Ps 71:7. Na 3:6. Zc 3:8. 1 C 4:9. **by reproaches.** He 11:26. 13:13. Ps 69:9. 74:22. 79:12. 89:51. Is 51:7. 2 C 12:10. **whilst.** Ph 1:7. 4:14. 1 Th 2:14. 2 T 1:8, 16-18.

34. **had compassion.** He 13:3. Mt 25:36. 2 T 1:16. **in my bonds.** Ac 21:33. 28:20. Ep 3:1. 4:1. 6:20. Ph 1:7. 2 T 1:16. 2:9. **and took joyfully.** Ge 45:20. Mt +*5:11, 12. Ac *5:41. Ja *1:2. **goods.** ℐ135, Ps +68:28. **in yourselves that ye have.** or, that ye have in yourselves, or, for yourselves. ver. 39. Mt √6:19, 20. 19:21. Lk 10:42. 12:33. 21:19. 2 C *5:1. Col 1:5. 3:2-4. 1 T +*6:19. 2 T +*4:8. 1 P +*1:4. 1 J √3:2. **in heaven.** Mt *6:20. Ph +*4:17n. 1 P +*1:4n. **a better.** He +6:9. 1 P 1:4. **enduring.** Mt *6:19, 20. Lk 16:9. 1 P 1:4. **substance.** ℐ135, Ps +68:28.

35. **Cast.** See on He +*3:6, 14. +*4:14. +*6:9. *13:9. Jn +*8:31. Ac *13:43. +*14:22. Ro +*11:22. 1 C +*15:58. Ga +*6:9. Col +*1:23. 1 T +*4:16. 1 J *2:24. **your confidence.** ver. +19. **great recompense.** He 2:2. *11:26. Ps 19:11. Mt +*5:12. *10:32, 42. Lk 12:8. +*14:14. Ro √8:18. 1 C +√15:58. Ga √6:8-10.

36. **ye have.** He 6:+*12, 15. 12:1-7. Ps *37:7. 40:1. Mt +10:22. 24:13. Lk 8:15. *21:19. Ro +*2:7. *5:3, 4. 8:25. 12:12. +*15:4, 5. 1 C *13:7. Ga +*6:9. Col *1:11. 1 Th 1:3. 2 T 2:10, 12. Ja *1:+3, 4. *5:7-11. 2 P +1:6. Re 13:10. 14:12. **after.** He *13:21. Mt *7:21. 12:50. 21:31. Jn +*7:17. Ac *13:22, 36. Ro +*12:2.

Ep 6:6. Col 4:12. 1 J *2:17. **the will.** Lk +*11:28. 1 Th +*4:3. **ye might receive.** See on He 6:12, 15, 17. *9:15. 11:39. Col 3:24. 1 P *1:9. **the promise.** He *9:15. Ac +√26:6. Ga +*3:29. T +*1:2.

37. **For yet.** ver. 25. Lk 18:8. 2 P *3:9. Re 22:20. **a little while.** ℐ84, Ge +6:17. Ps 37:10. Is *26:20. 60:22. Hab *2:3, 4. Hg 2:6. Lk 18:8. Ja *5:7-9. 2 P *3:8, 9. Re *22:7, 20. **he that.** Hab ◗2:3, 4. Mt +11:3. *24:1-3, 34. 1 C *11:26. **will come.** ℐ147A, Ge +50:24. **tarry.** Jn +21:22.

38. **the just.** Hab +*◗2:4. Ro +*1:17. Ga *2:20. *3:11. **but if.** ℐ184C, Mt +4:9. Ge +*4:7. Je +*7:5. 2 P +*1:10. **draw back.** See on ver. *26, *27. He +*3:12. +*6:4-6. 1 Ch +*28:9. Ps *85:8. Ezk *3:20. *18:24. +*33:18. Da +*11:35. Zp *1:6. Mt *12:43-45. *13:21. Lk +*8:13, 14. *9:62. Ac +*20:20g. 1 T +√1:19. +*4:1n. +*5:15. +*6:10. 2 T *4:10. 2 P +*2:19-22. 1 J *2:19. **my.** Ps *5:4. *147:11. +*149:4. Is 42:1. Ml 1:10. Mt 12:18. 1 Th 2:15. **soul.** Gr. psyche, ℐ171Q2, Mt +12:18. ℐ22A1, Le +26:11. Le +26:11n.

39. **we are not.** He +*6:6-9. 1 S *15:11. Ps *44:18. Pr *1:32. *14:14. Lk *11:26. 1 J +*5:16. Ju *12, *13. **draw back.** ver. +*38. **unto perdition.** ver. *26. Jn *17:12. 2 Th *2:3. 1 T +*6:9. 2 P 3:7. Re 17:8, 11. **but.** He 11:1. Mk *16:16. Jn √3:15, 16. √5:24. *6:40. √20:31. Ac √16:30, +31. Ro √10:9, 10. Ep *2:8. 1 Th *5:9. 2 Th *2:12-14. 1 P +*1:5. 1 J *5:5. **believe to.** ver. +*35. Ph *1:6. 1 J *2:19, 24. **saving.** or, gaining. ver. 34. Jn *6:37, 39. Ro +*1:16. +*8:38, 39. 1 Th +5:9. **soul.** Gr. psyche, Lk +9:24.

HEBREWS 11

The nature, excellency, efficacy, and fruits of faith, illustrated by the examples of the most eminent saints, from Abel to the close of the Old Testament dispensation, 1-38. The superior advantages of Christianity, 39, 40.

1. **faith.** T#181. ver. 13. He 10:22, 39. Ac 20:21. Ro *10:9, 10. 1 C 13:13. Ga *5:6. T 1:1. 1 P 1:7. 2 P 1:1. **is the.** Ps 27:13. 42:11. **substance.** or, ground, or, confidence. He *2:3. *3:14g. 2 C 9:4. 11:17g. **hoped.** See on He 6:12, 18, 19. **things.** ver. 7, 27. Ro 8:24. 2 C √4:18. √5:7. 1 P *1:8, 9.

2. **by it.** ver. 4, 39. **the elders.** ver. 4-39. Mt 15:2.

3. **faith.** He 1:2. Ge +*1:1, etc. 2:1. Ps *33:6, 9. Is 40:26. Je 10:11, 16. Jn *1:3. Ac 14:15. 17:24. Ro 1:19-21. 4:17. 2 P 3:5. Re 4:11. **worlds.** Gr. aion, Mt +6:13. ℐ121P2, Mt +13:22. 1 T +1:17. **by.** He 1:3. 2 P +3:5. **word.** T#259. Ge 1:3. Ps 29:4-8. *33:6-9. 66:7. Re +19:6 (T#218). **things which.** Ro 4:17. 1 C 1:28.

4. **By faith Abel.** Ge *4:3-5, 15, 25. 1 J 3:11, 12. **a more.** He √9:22. Pr 15:8. 21:27. Is 1:15. T 1:16. Ju +11. **sacrifice.** He +5:1. **he obtained.** ver. 2, 39. Le *9:24. 1 K 18:38. Mt 23:35. Lk 11:51. **righteous.** Mt +*5:10. 1 J *3:12. **and by.** He 12:1, 24. Ge 4:10. Mt 23:35. Re 6:10. **yet speaketh.** or, is yet spoken of. He 12:24.

5. **Enoch.** Ge *5:22-24. Lk 3:37. Ju 14. **translated.** 2 K 2:11. Ps 89:48. Jn 8:51, 52. **not see.** Lk +2:26. **and was.** 2 K 2:16, 17. Je 36:26. Re 11:9-12. **found.** ℐ171J5, 1 S +13:15. **this testimony.** ver. 3, 4. **that he pleased.** ver. 6. He 12:28. 13:16, 21. Ge 5:22. Ps 147:11. +*149:4. Ro *8:8, 9. Col +*1:10. 1 Th 2:4. 1 J 3:22.

6. **without**. He *3:12, 18, 19. *4:2, 6. Nu *14:11. *20:12. Ps *78:22, 32. *106:21, 22, 24. Is *7:9. Mk 16:17. Jn √3:18, 19. *8:24. Ga *5:6. Re +*21:8. **faith**. T#535. He 10:22. Is +26:3 (T#293). Ja *1:5-7. **he that**. See on He *7:25. Jb *21:14. Ps *73:28. Is +*55:3. Je 2:31. Jn √14:6. **must**. 1 Ch +*28:9. Je 29:12-14. Jn *4:24. Ac *14:15. Ro *10:14. 1 Th *1:9. 1 T *4:10. **believe**. 2 Ch +*20:20. Jn √3:18. **a rewarder**. ver. 26. Ge 15:1. Ru *2:12. Ps *58:11. Pr *11:18. Mt +*5:12. *6:1, 2, 5, 16. *10:41, 42. Lk +*6:35. **diligently seek**. Ex +*15:26. 1 Ch +*28:9. Ps +*9:10. 105:3, 4. *119:10, 94. Pr *8:17. SS 3:1-4. Je √29:13, 14. Mt √6:33. Lk *12:31. 1 P +1:10g. 2 P *1:5, 10. *3:14.

7. **By faith**. Ro *3:22. Ph *3:8, 9. **Noah**. i.e. *rest*, ✸S#3575g. For ✸S#5146h, see Ge +5:29. Ge *6:13-22. 7:1, 5. Mt 24:38. Lk +17:26, Noe. 2 P *2:5. **warned**. He +8:5. Ge 6:13. 19:14. Ex 9:18-21. Pr +*22:3. 27:12. Ezk 3:17-19. Mt 3:7. 24:15-25. 2 P 3:6-8. **things**. See on ver. 1. **moved with fear**. *or*, being wary. See on He 5:7g. Ec *12:13. **prepared**. He 3:3. 9:2, 6g. Ge 6:18. 7:1, 23. 8:16. Ezk 14:14, 20. 1 P 3:20. **an ark**. Ge =7:13-17. **his house**. ſ121J4, Ge +7:1. Ac +*16:15n. **he condemned**. Mt 12:41, 42. Lk 11:31, 32. **world**. Gr. *kosmos*, Mt +4:8. **righteousness**. Ge 6:9. Ezk 14:14, 20. Ro 1:17. 3:22. 4:11, 13. +9:30. 10:6. Ga 5:5. Ph 3:9. 2 P 1:1.

8. **Abraham**. Ge 11:31. *12:1-4. Jsh 24:3. Ne 9:7, 8. Is 41:2. 51:2. Ac *7:2-4. **which**. Ge 12:7. 13:15-17. 15:7, 8. 17:8. 26:3. Dt 9:5. Ps 105:9-11. Ezk 33:24. **obeyed**. ver. 33. He 5:8, 9. Ge=12:4. 22:18. 26:5. Mt 7:24, 25. Ro 1:5. 6:17. 10:16. 2 C *10:5. Ja *2:14-16. 1 P 1:22. 3:1. *4:17.

9. **he sojourned**. Ge 17:8. *23:4. 26:3. 35:27. 1 Ch 16:19. Ac 7:5, 6. **dwelling**. Ge *12:8. *13:3, 18. 18:1, 2, 6, 9. 25:27. *26:17, 25. *33:18. *35:21. **with Isaac**. i.e. *pleasure*, ✸S#2464g. For ✸S#3327h, see Ge +17:19. ver. 17, 18, 20. Mt 1:2. 8:11. 22:32. Mk 12:26. Lk 3:34. 13:28. 20:37. Ac 3:13. 7:8, 8, 32. Ro 9:7, 10. Ga 4:28. Ja 2:21. **and Jacob**. Ge 35:27. **the heirs**. He 6:17. Ge 26:3, 4. 28:4, 13, 14. 48:3, 4. Ro 8:17. Ep 3:6. 1 P 3:7g.

10. **he looked**. He *12:22, 28. *13:14. Jn +*14:2. Ph *3:20g. Re *21:2, 10-27. **a city**. ver. 16. **foundations**. Ps 87:1. Re 21:14, 19. **whose**. ver. 16. He 3:4. 8:2. Is 14:32. 2 C *5:1. Re 21:2, 10.

11. **Sara**. i.e. *princess; noble lady*, ✸S#4564g. For ✸S#8283h, see Ge +17:15. Ge *17:17-19. *18:11-14. *21:1, 2. Lk 1:36. Ro 4:19. 9:9. 1 P 3:5, 6. **conceive**. Ge ◐11:30. 29:31. **because**. He 10:23. Ro *4:20, 21. 1 C +1:9. **promised**. ver. 17, 18. Ga +4:23.

12. **of one**. Is 51:2. Ezk 33:24. Ml 2:15. **and him**. ver. 19. Ro 4:19. **as the stars**. ſ102B, ſ138B, Ge +13:16. Ge 15:5. *22:17. 26:4. Ex 32:13. Dt *1:10. 10:22. 28:62. 1 Ch 27:23. Ne 9:23. Ro *4:17. **as the sand**. ſ102B, ſ138B, Ge +13:16. Ge 13:16. 22:17. 32:12. Nu 23:10. Jsh 11:4. Jg 7:12. 1 S 12:5. 2 S 17:11. 1 K 4:20. 2 Ch 1:9. Is 10:22. 48:19. Je 33:22. Ho 1:10. Hab 1:9. Ro 4:18. 9:27. Re 20:8. **innumerable**. Ge 32:12. 1 K 3:8.

13. **all**. ſ171M, Ge +6:12. **died**. Ge +*25:8. 27:2-4. *48:21. *49:18, 28, 33. 50:24. **in faith**. Gr. according to faith. **not**. ver. *39. Ac +√7:5. **the promises**. ſ121R7, Ge +43:11. i.e. *the things which had been promised*. The promises were what they had received, but not the things promised (B603). **but**. ver. 27. Ge +*49:10. Nu *24:17. Jb *19:25. Mt 13:17. Jn *8:56. *12:41.

2 C +*4:18. 1 P *1:10-12. **and were**. Ro 4:21. 8:24. Ge 49:18. 1 J *3:19g. **embraced**. ſ121S2, Ge +21:6. **confessed**. Ge *23:4. *47:9. 1 Ch *29:14, 15. Ps *39:12. 73:24. *119:19, 31. Ph 3:20. 1 P 1:17. *2:11. **strangers**. Ep 2:19. **pilgrims**. 1 P 1:1. 2:11g.

14. **they seek**. ver. 10, 16. He 13:14. Ro 8:23-25. 2 C 4:18. 5:1-7. Ph 1:23.

15. **if they**. ſ184B, Lk +7:39. **mindful**. ſ121C2B, Is +44:21. Ge *11:31. 12:10. 24:6-8. 31:18. 32:9-11.

16. **they desire**. See on ver. 14. He 12:22. 1 T 3:1. 6:10g. **a better**. ver. 35, 40. He +6:9. **an heavenly**. This is not a reference to either "heaven" or the "third heaven," but a reference to the heavenly kingdom or "kingdom of heaven" on earth, the restored Davidic kingdom (Is +*55:3), which involves the promised restoration of the land of Israel in theocratic millennial earthly blessing (Ac +*1:6. +*3:19, 21). He 3:11, 18. 4:9mg. Dt √11:21. Ps 37:9, 11, 22, 29, 34. 76:9. *89:29. Pr 2:21, 22. 10:30. 11:31. 12:7. Is 65:17. 66:22. Je 7:7. Mt +*5:5. 19:28. Ac +*3:21. +√7:5. Ro +*4:13. 8:19, 23. 1 P +*1:4. **God is not**. ſ175B, Ge +21:16. He 2:11. Mk +8:38. **to be**. Ge 17:7, 8. 26:24. 28:13. Ex *3:6, 15. 4:5. Is 41:8-10. Je 31:1. Mt *22:31, 32. Mk 12:26, 27. Lk 20:37, 38. Ac 7:32. **prepared**. Ps 73:24. Jn +*14:2. Ph 3:20. **a city**. ver. 10. He 13:14. Mt 25:34. Lk 12:32. Ph 3:20.

17. **faith**. Ge *17:8, 19. *22:1-12. Ja 2:21-24. **when**. Dt 8:2. 2 Ch 32:31. Jb 1:11, 12. 2:3-6. Pr 17:3. Da *11:35. Zc *13:9. Ml 3:2, 3. Ja 1:2-4. 5:11. 1 P 1:6, 7. 4:12. Re +*3:10. **received**. He 7:6. Ac 28:7g. **the promises**. ver. 11. **offered**. 2 C 8:12. Ja 2:21. **only**. Ge *22:2, 12, 16. Lk +7:12. Jn √3:16. 1 J 4:9.

18. **Of**. *or*, To. He 1:7, 8g. **That**. Ge 17:19. ✸Ↄ21:12. Ro 9:7.

19. **God**. Ge *22:5h. Mt 9:28. Ro 4:17-21. Ep 3:20. **from the**. ver. 11, 12. He 9:24. Ge *22:4, 5, 13. Mt *20:19. Ro 5:14. **a figure**. He 9:9.

20. **Isaac blessed**. Ge 27:27-40. 28:2, 3.

21. **faith**. Ge *48:5-22. **and worshipped**. ſ106, Ge +31:7. Ge *47:31. 1 K 1:47. Jn +4:20. **staff**. ſ92F1, He +10:5. Ge 32:10.

22. **faith**. Ge *50:24, 25. Ex *13:19. Jsh 24:32. Ac 7:16. **made mention of**. *or*, remembered. **children of**. Ac +5:21.

23. **faith**. Ex *2:2, etc. Ac 7:20. **was hid**. Pr +*22:3. 2 C 12:14. 1 T 5:8. **a proper child**. That is, a fine, beautiful, or fair child, as our translators render *asteios* in Ac 7:20; which was in their time the sense of proper, from the French *propre*. Ex 2:2. Lk 2:40, 52. Ac 7:20mg. **and they**. He 13:6. Ps 56:4. 118:6. Is 8:12, 13. 41:10, 14. 51:7, 12. Da 3:16-18. +*6:10. Mt +*10:28. Lk +*12:4, 5. **the king's**. Ex *1:16, 22.

24. **when**. Ex *2:10, 11. Ac *7:21-24. **refused**. Mt=4:4-8.

25. **Choosing**. He 10:32. Jb 36:21. Ps *84:10. Mt +*5:10-12. 13:21. Ac 7:24, 25. 20:23, 24. Ro 5:3. *8:17, √18, 35-39. 2 C √5:17. Col *1:24. 2 Th 1:3-6. 2 T 1:8. 2:3-10. √3:11, 12. Ja 1:20. 1 P 1:6, 7. 4:12-16. **the people**. He 4:9. Ps 47:9. 1 P 2:10. **the pleasures**. Jb *20:5. 21:11-13. Ps 73:18-20. Is 21:4. 47:8, 9. Lk *12:19, 20. *16:25. Ja 5:5. 1 J √2:17. Re 18:7. **for a season**. 2 C +4:18g.

26. **Esteeming**. Ph 3:7, 8. Re 2:9. **the reproach**. He 10:33. *13:13. Ps 69:7, 9, 20. 89:50, 51. Is 51:7. Ac 5:41. 2 C *12:10. 1 P 1:11. *4:13, 14. 2 P *3:3, 4. **of Christ**. *or*, for Christ. ſ181E, Ge +3:24. Ge *12:3.

+*49:10. **greater**. Ps 37:16. Je 9:23, 24. 2 C 6:10. =8:9. Ep 1:18. 3:8. Re 2:9. 3:18. **for he had**. See on ver. 6. He 2:2. +*10:35. =12:2. Ru 2:12. Pr 11:18. 23:18. Mt +*5:12. 6:1. 10:41. Lk +*14:14. Ro *8:17, 18. 2 T *2:12.

27. **he forsook**. Ex 10:28, 29. 11:8. 12:31, 37, etc. 13:17-21. Mt=2:15. **not fearing**. Ex *2:14, 15. 4:19. 10:28, 29. 14:10-13. **endured**. He 6:15. 10:32. 12:3. Mt 10:22. 24:13. Mk 4:17. 13:13. 1 C 13:7. Ja 5:11. **seeing**. ver. 1, 13. He *12:2. Ps 16:8. Jn=8:29. Ac 2:25. 2 C √4:18. 1 T +1:17. 6:16. 1 P 1:8. **invisible**. T#216. Jn 1:18. 4:24. Col 1:15. 1 T *6:16.

28. **he kept**. Ex *12:3-14, 21-30. Ezk +*9:4, 6. Mt 26:18. Lk ◐=22:15. Jn +6:4. **the sprinkling**. Gr. *proschusia*, *S#4378g, only here. He 9:19. 12:24. Ex 12:7, 13, 22, 23. 1 P *1:2. **of blood**. Ro *3:25. **lest he**. Ex 12:23. **firstborn**. Ex 12:29. **touch**. ∫108B, Ge +26:29.

29. **passed through**. Ex *14:13-31. 15:1-21. Nu 33:8. Jsh 2:10. Ne 9:11. Ps 66:6. 77:19. 78:13. *106:9-11. 114:1-5. 136:13-15. Is 11:15, 16. 43:16. 51:9, 10. 63:11-16. Hab 3:8-10. 1 C *10:1. **which**. Ex 14:23-29. 15:4. Dt 11:4. Ps 78:53. 106:11. 136:15.

30. **the walls**. Jsh *6:3-20. 2 C *10:4, 5. **Jericho**. Mt 20:29. Mk 10:46. Lk 10:30. 18:35, 43. 19:1. **after**. Jsh 6:15, 16.

31. **the harlot**. ∫11, Ge +2:23. ∫46C, Mt +8:6. Gr. *pornee*, a harlot, receives its true meaning from the Hebrew *zonah* which means a female hostess, or landlady, as well as harlot (B680). See related notes (Ge 38:21n. Jsh 2:1n, 13n. Jg 11:1n. 1 K 3:16n). Jsh 2:1-22. *6:22-25. Mt *1:1, 5. Ep 2:8. Ja *2:25. **Rahab**. i.e. *arrogance, insolence*, *S#4460g. For *S#7343h, see Jsh +2:1. Ja 2:25. **believed not**. *or*, were disobedient. He +3:18. 1 P 2:8. 3:20. **she had**. Jsh 1:1. 2:1, 4, 8-13. **with peace**. Ac +15:33.

32. **what shall**. Ro 3:5. 4:1. 6:1. 7:7. **more say**. ∫131. Paraleipsis; or, A Passing By B484. Addition (brief) of that which is professedly ignored. When the speaker professes a wish to pass something by in silence, but subsequently adds by a brief allusion to it. Here, the writer alludes briefly in verses 33-38 to what he professedly was about to pass by, or not mention. **the time**. Jn 21:25. **tell of**. ∫82, Ex +15:9. **Gedeon**. i.e. *a great tree trunk*, *S#1066g. For *S#1439h, see Jg +6:11. Jg ch. 6-8, Gideon. 1 S 12:11, Jerubbaal. **and**. ∫148, Ge +8:22. **Barak**. i.e. *a gleam; thunder*, *S#913g. For *S#1301h, Jg +4:6. Jg ch. 4, 5. **Samson**. i.e. *splendid sun*, *S#4546g. For *S#8123h, Jg +13:24. Jg ch. 13-16. **Jepthae**. i.e. *whom God sets free*, *S#2422g. For *S#3316h, see Jg +11:1. Jg ch. 11. 12:1-7, Jephthah. **David**. 1 S 16:1, 13. ch. 17, etc. Ac 2:29-31. 13:22-36. **Samuel**. 1 S 1:20. 2:11, 18. ch. 3-12. 28:3, etc. Ps 99:6. Je 15:1. Ac 3:24. 13:20. **the prophets**. Mt +*5:12. Lk 13:28. 16:31. Ac +3:24. +*10:43. Ja 5:10. 1 P 1:10-12. 2 P *1:21. 3:2.

33. **through**. Jsh ch. 6-13. 2 S 5:4-25. 8:1-14. Ps 18:32-34. 44:2-6. 144:1, 2, 10. **subdued**. Jg 4:24. 7:25. 16:30. 11:33. 1 S 7:13. 2 S 5:17-25. 8:1, 2. **wrought**. ∫41, Ge +10:1. See on ver. 4-8, 17. Dt *16:18. 1 S 12:3, 4. 2 S 8:15. 1 Ch 18:14. **obtained**. See on He *6:12-15. 10:36. Jsh 21:45. 2 S 7:11, 12, etc. 1 K 8:56. 1 Ch 22:9. Ga 3:16. **stopped**. Jg *14:5, 6. 1 S *17:33-36. 2 S 23:20. 1 Ch 11:22. Ps 91:13. Da *6:20-23. 2 T 4:17. 1 P 5:8.

34. **Quenched**. Ps 66:12. Is 43:2. Da *3:19-28. 1 P 4:12. **escaped**. ∫41, Ge +10:1. 1 S 18:11. 19:10, 12.

20:1. 21:10. 2 S 21:16, 17. 1 K 19:3. 2 K *6:16-18, 32. Jb 5:20. Ps 144:10. Je *26:24. 36:26. **the edge**. ∫144A2, Ge +34:26. Lk 21:24. **out of**. Jg 6:34. 7:19-25. 8:4-10. 15:14-20. *16:19-30. 2 K *20:5, 7, etc. Jb 42:10. Ps 6:8. 2 C √12:9, 10. **waxed valiant**. Jg 7:21. *15:8, 15. 1 S 17:51, 52. 2 S 10:15-19. 12:29. **turned**. 1 S 14:13, etc. *17:51, 52. 2 S 8:1, etc. 2 Ch 14:11-14. 16:1-9. 20:6-25. 32:20-22.

35. **Women received**. 1 K *17:22-24. 2 K *4:27-37. Lk 7:12-16. Jn 11:40-45. Ac 9:41. **tortured**. Ac 22:24, 25, 29. **not accepting**. Ac 4:19. **that they**. Mt 22:30. Mk 12:25. Lk +*14:14. 20:36. Jn 5:29. Ac 23:6. 24:15. 1 C 15:54. Ph √3:11. **a better**. ver. 16, 40. He +6:9. **resurrection**. Mk 9:9, 10. Ac 10:41. 13:34. 17:31, 32. 26:23. 1 C 15:12. Ph √3:11. 1 Th +*4:16n.

36. **had trial**. Re +2:10. **mockings**. Jg 16:25. 2 K 2:23. 2 Ch 30:10. 36:16. Je 20:7. Mt 20:19. Mk 10:34. Lk 18:32. 23:11, 36. **and scourgings**. 1 K 22:24. Je 20:2. 37:15. Mt 21:35. 23:34. 27:26. Ac 5:40. 16:22, 23. 2 C 11:24, 25. **bonds**. He 10:34. Ge *39:20. 1 K *22:27. 2 Ch 16:10. Ps 105:17, 18. Je *20:2. 29:26. 32:2, 3, 8. 36:5. *37:15-21. 38:6-13, 28. 39:15. La 3:52-55. Ac 4:3. 5:18. 8:3. 12:4, etc. 16:24, etc. 21:33. 24:27. 2 C 11:23. Ep 3:1. 4:1. 2 T 1:16. 2:9. Re 2:10.

37. **stoned**. 1 K 21:10, 13-15. 2 Ch *24:20, 21. Mt 21:35. 23:37. Lk 13:34. Jn 10:31-33. Ac +*7:58, 59. 14:19. 2 C 11:25. **were slain**. 1 S 22:17-19. 1 K 18:4, 13. 19:1, 10, 14. Je 2:30. 26:23. La 4:13, 14. Mt 23:35-37. Lk 11:51-54. Ac 7:52. 12:2, 3. **in sheepskins**. 2 K 1:8. Zc 13:4. Mt 3:4. Mk 2:6. Re 11:3. **being destitute**. He 12:1-3. Zc *13:9. Mt 8:20. 1 C 4:9-13. 2 C 11:23-27. 12:10. Ja 5:10, 11. **tormented**. ∫41, Ge +10:1. ver. 25. He 13:3.

38. **whom**. 1 K 14:12, 13. 2 K 23:25-29. Is 57:1. **world**. Gr. *kosmos*, Mt +4:8. **wandered**. 1 S 22:1. 23:15, 19, 23. 24:1-3. 26:1. 1 K 17:3. 18:4, 13. 19:9. Ps 142, title. **mountains**. Jg 6:2. **caves**. 1 S 22:1. 1 K *18:4. *19:9.

39. **these all**. ∫166, Mt +1:17. The apostle in the early part of the chapter having given us a general account of the grace of faith, proceeds to set before us some illustrious examples of it in Old Testament times. The leading instance and example of faith recorded is that of righteous Abel: one of the first saints and the first martyr for religion—one who lived by faith and died for it, and therefore a fit pattern for the Hebrews to imitate. It is observable that the Holy Spirit has not thought fit to say any thing here of the faith of our first parents; and yet the church of God has generally, by a pious charity, taken it for granted that God gave them repentance and faith in the promised seed; that he instructed them in the mystery of sacrificing, that they instructed their children in it, and that they found mercy with God, after they had ruined themselves and all their posterity. But God has left the matter still under some doubt, as a warning to all who have great talents given to them, and a great trust reposed in them, that they do not prove unfaithful, since God would not enroll our first parents among the number of believers in this blessed calendar (Matthew Henry). **having obtained**. See on ver. *2, *13. Lk *10:23, 24. 1 P 1:12. **received not**. ver. 13. He +10:36. Ac +√7:5. 1 P 1:12. **the promise**. Ge 12:3. Ps 111:9. Lk √1:68-73. Ac +√26:6. Ro √4:13. +*15:8. Ga *3:18.

40. **provided**. *or*, foreseen. **better**. ver. 16, 35. He

+6:9. *7:19, 22. *8:6. *9:23. *12:24. **for us.** Mt 13:16, 17. 1 P *1:10-12. **they without us.** He *9:8-15. *10:11-14. Jn +*10:16. Ro *3:25, 26. Ep *1:10. 4:8. 1 Th +*4:15-17. Ja 5:7. Re 6:9-11. **made perfect.** He +2:10. *5:9. *12:23. Ro +*8:11, 23. 1 C +*13:10n. Re *6:11.

HEBREWS 12

Exhortations to constancy, patience, and diligence, deduced from the abundant testimony of former believers, from the example of Christ, and from the loving intent and salutary effect of the Lord's corrections, 1-13; to peace and holiness, and to jealous watchfulness over ourselves, and each other, enforced by the case of Esau, 14-17; to an obedient reception of the gospel, and reverential worship of God, from the superior excellency of the promised inheritance of the eternal kingdom, and the proportionately greater guilt and danger of neglecting it, 18-29.

1. **seeing.** He 11:2-38. **compassed about.** Ps 22:4. *89:1, 8. Is 25:1. *26:3, 4. La 3:23. **a cloud.** Is 60:8. Ezk *38:9, 16. **witnesses.** Lk *16:28. Jn *3:32. *4:39, 44. Ac 22:20. 1 P 5:12. Re 2:13. 17:6. *22:16. **let us lay.** Pr *29:25. Mt *10:37, 38. Lk *8:14. *9:59-62. *12:15. *14:26-33. *18:22-25. +*21:34. Ro *13:11-14. 2 C *6:14. *7:1. Ep *4:22-24. Ph *3:7-14. Col *3:5-8. 1 T +*6:9, 10. 2 T *2:4. 1 P *2:1. *4:2. *5:7. 1 J √2:15, 16. **and the sin.** He 10:35-39. Ps *18:23. Ep +4:22. **beset.** He +*3:12. Ho 7:2. **and let us.** 1 C *9:+24-27. Ga *5:7. Ph *2:16. *3:10-14. 2 T *4:7. **with patience.** He *6:15. +*10:36. Je +*12:5. Mt *10:22. *24:13. Lk +*8:15. Ro +*2:7. *5:3-5. *8:24, 25. *12:12. Ja *1:3. *5:7-11. 2 P *1:6. Re *1:9. +*3:10. *13:10. **the race.** √121.O, Ge +28:22. 1 C *9:24. Ph +1:30g. 3:13, 14. 2 T +*4:7, 8. **set before.** He 6:18.

2. **Looking.** T#1369. ver. *3. He +*9:28. Nu 21:8, 9. Ps *17:15. 123:2. 130:6. Is *8:17. *31:1. *45:22. Mi *7:7. Zc *12:10. Jn *1:29. *3:14, 15. *6:40. *8:56. 1 C 13:12. 2 C 3:18. Ph *3:20. 2 T +*4:8. T √2:13. 1 J *1:1-3. Ju *21. **the author.** or, the beginner. or, the captain. He +2:10. Mk 9:24. Lk 17:5. Ac 5:31g. Re *1:8, 11, 17. *2:8. *3:14. **finisher.** He 7:19. *10:14g. Ps *138:8. 1 C *1:7, 8. Ph *1:6. **our.** √63K, Ge +37:13. **for the joy.** He 2:7-9. *5:9. Ge 29:20. Ps +*16:9-11. Is 49:6. +*53:10-12. Lk +*24:26. Jn *12:24, 32. 13:3, 31, 32. *17:1-4. Ac *2:25, 26, 36. Ph √2:8-11. 1 P *1:11. **endured.** He 10:5-12. Mt 16:21. *20:18, 19, 28. *27:31-50. Mk *14:36. Lk 23:33. Jn *12:27, 28. Ep 2:16. 5:2. T √2:14. 1 P *2:24. *3:18. **the cross.** Ph 2:8. **despising.** He 10:33. 11:36. Ps *22:6-8. 69:19, 20. Is 49:7. *50:6, 7. +*53:3. Mt *26:67, 68. *27:27-31, 38-44. Mk 9:12. Lk 23:11, 35-39. Ac 5:41. 1 P *2:23. *4:14-16. **the shame.** He=11:26. Ph 2:6-11. 1 P 2:23. **and is set down.** See on He *1:3, 13. *8:1. Ps *110:1. Ro 14:9. 1 P *3:22. Re +*3:21. **right hand.** He +1:3. **the throne.** He *4:16. 8:1. Mt 5:34. 23:22. Re 2:13. +*3:21. 7:15. 12:5. 16:10. 22:1, 3.

3. **consider.** ver. 2. He 3:1. 1 S 12:24. La 1:12. Mt +10:24. 2 T 2:7, 8. Re 2:3. **contradiction.** He 6:16. 7:7. Mt *10:24, 25. 11:19. 12:24. 15:2. 21:15, 16, 23, 46. 22:15. Lk 2:34g. 4:28, 29. 5:21. 11:15, 16, 53, 54. 13:13, 14. 14:1. 15:2. 16:14. 19:39, 40. Jn 5:16. 7:12. 8:13, 48, 49, 52, 59. 9:40. 10:20, 31-39. 12:9, 10. *15:18-24. 18:22. Ju 11g. **lest.** ver. 5. Dt 20:3. Pr 24:10. Is 40:30, 31. 50:4. 1 C +*15:58. 2 C 4:1, 16. Ga +*6:9. 2 Th 3:13. **minds.** Gr. *psyche*, √121A9B, Mt +22:37.

4. **resisted unto.** ver. 2. He *10:32-34. Mt +*24:9. 1 C +*10:13. 2 T 4:6, 7. 1 J *3:16. Re 2:13. *6:9-11. +*12:11. 17:6. 18:24. **striving against.** Lk 13:24. 1 C 9:25, 26. Ju +*3.

5. **ye have forgotten.** Dt 4:9, 10. Ps *119:16, 83, 109. Pr *3:1. 4:5. Mt 16:9, 10. Lk 24:6, 8. **the exhortation.** ver. 7. He 13:22. Pr *3:11, 12. Ac +4:36. **My son.** Pr ▸3:11, 12. **despise not.** Jb *5:17, 18. 34:31. Ps 94:12. 118:18. 119:75. Pr 3:11. Je 31:18. 1 C 11:32. Ja *1:12. Re *3:19. **nor faint.** ver. 3, 4. Jsh 7:7-11. 2 S 6:7-10. 1 Ch 13:9-13. 15:12, 13. Ps 6:1, 2. Pr 24:10. Je 12:5. 2 C 4:8, 9. √12:9, 10. **rebuked.** Le *26:23, 24. Ps 94:12. 119:67, 75. Je 31:18, 19. Re 3:19.

6. **whom.** Dt 8:5. Ps *32:1-5. 73:14, 15. 89:30-34. *94:12. *119:71, 75. Pr *3:12. 13:24. Is 27:9. Je 10:24. Ja *1:12. 5:11. Re *3:19. **and scourgeth.** ver. 7, 8. 2 S 7:14. **son.** He 2:10.

7. **If.** √184A, 1 C +15:2. **endure.** Jb 34:31, 32. Pr +*19:18. 22:15. 23:13, 14. 29:15, 17. Ac +*14:22. **God dealeth.** Dt *8:5. 2 S *7:14. Pr *13:24. +*19:18. 23:13. 29:17. **for what.** 1 S 2:29, 34. 3:13. 1 K 1:6. 2:24, 25. Pr 13:24. 29:15. **chasteneth not.** Am *3:2. 1 C *11:32.

8. **But if.** √184A, 1 C +15:2. **without chastisement.** ver. 6. Ps 73:1, 14, 15. Jn 16:33. 1 P *5:9, 10.

9. **fathers.** Jn 3:6. Ac 2:30. Ro 1:3. 9:3, 5. **corrected.** See on ver. 7. **we gave.** Ex +*20:12. Le *19:3. Dt *21:18-21. *27:16. Pr *30:17. Ezk 22:7. Lk +18:2g. Ep +*6:1-4. **shall we not.** Ml *1:6. Ja 4:7, 10. 1 P *5:6, 7. **the Father of.** Those who believe each soul is created separately and directly by God ("Creationism") appeal to this text and associated references. Those who believe the soul is produced by natural generation and is received through the parents ("Traducianism") appeal to He 7:10 and associated references. He 2:11. Nu *16:22. 27:16. Jb *12:10. Ps 104:30. Ec +*12:7. Is 42:5. 57:16. Da 5:23. Zc 12:1. Ac 17:28. **spirits.** Gr. *pneuma*, √121A3, Mt +27:50. **and live.** Is 38:16.

10. **after their own pleasure.** or, as seemed good, or meet, to them. **but he.** T#509. See on ver. 5, 6. Jb 36:8, 9. Is 27:7, 9. La 3:32, 33. **partakers.** Le 11:44, 45. 19:2. Ps *17:15. Ezk *36:25-27. Ep 4:24. *5:26, 27. Col 1:22. T √2:14. 1 P *1:15, 16. 2:5, 9. 2 P +*1:4. **holiness.** 2 C 1:12g.

11. **no chastening.** Ps 89:32. 118:18. Pr 15:10. 19:18. T +2:12. **for the present.** 1 P 1:6. **joyous.** lit. of joy. √24J, Dt +32:42. **but grievous.** lit. of grief. √24J, Dt +32:42. Jb 14:1. **nevertheless.** See on ver. 5, 6, 10. **afterward.** Ps *119:67. Pr +*19:18. ●20:17. +*22:6. Jn 15:11. **peaceable.** Ps *119:165. Is *32:17. Ro *5:3-5. *14:17. 2 C 4:17. Ga +*5:22, 23. Ja +*3:17, 18. **exercised.** He +5:14. 1 T 4:7, 8. 2 P 2:14g.

12. **lift up.** ver. 3, 5. 1 S +*23:16. Jb *4:3, 4. Is ▸35:3. Ezk 7:17. 21:7. Da 5:6. Na 2:10. 1 Th 5:14. **feeble knees.** Ps 109:24.

13. **make.** Pr *4:26, 27. 5:6, 21. Is 35:3, 8-10. 40:3, 4. 42:16. 58:12. Je 18:15. Lk 3:5. Ro 14:13. Ep *3:13. **straight.** or, even. **lame.** Is 35:6. Je 31:8, 9. **turned out.** Ro *14:21. 1 T 1:6. 5:15. 6:20. 2 T 4:4g. **but let.** Ga +*6:1. Ja +*5:16. Ju 22, 23.

14. **Follow peace.** T#499. Ge 13:7-9. Ps *34:14. 38:20. 120:6. *133:1. Pr *15:1. +*16:7 (T#737). 17:14. +19:11 (T#201). Is *11:6-9. Je *29:7. Mt +*5:9. +10:16 (T#660). +11:29 (T#62). Mk 9:50. Ro √12:10, 18. +*14:19. 1 C 1:10. 7:15. 2 C 13:11. Ga +*5:22, 23. +6:1 (T#437). Ep 4:1-8, √32. Ph 2:14, 15. Col

*3:8, 13-15. 1 Th 2:7. *5:13, 15. 1 T 6:11. 2 T *2:22, 24, 25. Ja √3:17, 18. 1 P 3:10, 11. **with all.** Jn 13:34. 1 C 1:10. +*12:13. Ga *6:10. **and holiness.** ver. 10. 2 Ch 31:18. Ps 94:15. Is 51:1. Lk 1:75. Ro *6:22. 2 C *6:17. *7:1. Ep 1:1. Ph 3:12. 1 Th *3:13. 4:+3, 7. 2 Th *2:13. 1 P 1:15, 16. 3:13. 2 P *3:11, 18. 3 J 11. **without which.** Ps *5:4. **no man.** Ge 32:30. Jb *19:26. 33:26. Mt +*5:8. 1 C +*6:9-11. *13:12. 2 C 7:1. Ga 5:21. Ep *5:5. 1 J √3:2, 3. Re *21:24-27. 22:3, 4, 11-15. **shall see.** Ps *15:1-5. Mt +*5:8. Jn *3:3.

15. **Looking diligently.** He *2:1, 2. +*3:12-15. *4:1, 11. +*6:11. *10:23-35. Dt √4:9. Pr +*4:23. Lk +√21:36. 1 C 9:24-27. *10:12. 2 C *6:1. *13:5. Col +√1:10. 2 P +√1:10. 3:11, *14. 2 J *8. Ju *20, *21. **any man.** Lk *22:32. 1 C 13:8. Ga *5:4. **fail of.** *or*, fall from. He +*4:1. 2 C +*6:1. Ga √5:4. 2 P +*1:10. **the grace.** Ac +*11:23. **any root.** He +*3:12. Dt *29:18. 32:32. Is 5:4, 7. Je 2:21. Mt *7:16-18. Ac 8:23. **of bitterness.** Dt 32:32. Ru +√1:13, 20, 21. Je 4:18. Ac *8:23. Ro *3:14. Ep √4:31. Ja √3:14. **trouble.** Jsh *6:18. *7:25, 26. *22:17-20. Lk 6:18g. Ep 5:3. Col 3:5. **and thereby.** Ex 32:21. 1 K 14:16. 2 Ch *13:7. Ps +√9:10n. Ac *20:30, 31. 1 C *5:6. +*15:33. Ga 2:13. 5:9. 2 T 2:16, 17. 2 P *2:1, 2, 18.

16. **any fornicator.** He +*13:4. Mk +*7:21. Ac 15:20, 29. 1 C 5:1-6, +*9-11. 6:15-20. 10:8. 2 C 12:21. Ga +*5:19-21. Ep *5:3, 5. Col +*3:5. 1 Th *4:3-7. Re 2:20-23. +*21:8. *22:15. **profane.** 1 T +1:9. **as Esau.** i.e. *rough*, ✳S#2269g. For ✳S#6215h, see Ge +25:25. He 11:20. Ge *25:31-34. 27:36. Ro 9:13. **meat.** ⨍171I8, Ps +107:18. **birthright.** T#1793.

17. **when he.** Ge *27:31-41. **he was.** He +*6:8. Pr *1:24-31. Je 6:30. Mt √7:23. 25:11, 12. Lk 13:24-27. **for he.** He +*6:4-6. *10:26-29. **found no.** 2 T +*2:25. **place for repentance.** *or*, way to change his mind. Ac *5:31. **though he sought.** He +*6:6. Ge 6:3. Ps 36:12. Pr 6:15. Is 55:6. Mk 3:29. Lk 16:26. Jn √6:37. 2 C 6:2. Re 14:11. +*22:11.

18. **For.** ⨍136, Is +60:12. **not come.** Ex *19:12-19. 20:18. 24:17. Dt *4:11. 5:22-26. Ro √6:14. *8:15. 2 C 3:9. Ga *4:24, 25. 2 T +*1:7. **touched.** ⨍24B, Ge +23:16. Ps 104:32.

19. **the sound.** Ex 19:16-19. 20:18. 1 C 15:52. 1 Th +*4:16. **and the voice.** ver. 26. Ex 19:19. 20:1-17, 22. Dt 4:12, 33. 5:3-22. **they that.** ver. 25. Ex *20:18, 19. Dt 5:24-27. 18:16.

20. **For they.** ⨍81, Ge +15:13. Dt 33:2. Ro *3:19, 20. Ga 2:19. 3:10. **And if.** ⨍184C, Mt +4:9. **so much.** Ex ⟩19:12, 13, 16.

21. **terrible.** ⨍106, Ge +31:7. **Moses.** Ex 19:16, 19. Dt 9:19. Ps 119:120. Is 6:3-5. Da 10:8, 17. Re 1:17.

22. **are come.** lit. have come. ⨍96C2, Ge +45:9. Figure of speech Heterosis of Tenses, past used for future. This figure is frequently used to assert the certainty of a future promised or prophesied benefit or event. ver. ●28n. Ge 6:13. Is 60:1. Mt 12:28. Ro *8:30. 2 C *5:1. Ep *1:3. **Mount Sion.** Ps *2:6. *48:2. 78:68, 69. *125:1. √132:13, 14. Is 12:6. 14:32. 28:16. 51:11, 16. +*59:20. 60:14. Jl +*2:32. Mi *4:7. Ro +*11:26. Ga *4:26. Re *14:1. **the city.** He 11:10. *13:14. Ps 48:2. 87:3. Mt 5:35. Ep +2:19. Ph 3:20mg. Re 3:12. 21:2, 10. 22:19. **living God.** He 3:12. 9:14. 10:31. Dt 5:26. Jsh 3:10. 2 K 19:4. Ps 42:2. 84:2. Je 10:10. Da 6:26. Ho 1:10. Mt +*16:16. Ro 9:26. 1 Th 1:9. Re 7:2. **the heavenly.** Care must be taken not to equate this "heavenly Jerusalem" with the "third heaven,"

for this Jerusalem descends from and out of (Re *21:2) heaven to the earth (Peters, *Theocratic Kingdom*, vol. 3, p. 46). Jn +*14:2. 2 P 3:13. Re *21:1, 2. **Jerusalem.** The church (ver. 23) is distinguished from, not identified as, the heavenly Jerusalem, just as Jerusalem and its people are distinguished by the prophets and other Scripture (Peters, *Theocratic Kingdom*, vol. 3, p. 44). Is *65:17, 18. Ga +4:26. Re 3:12. **an innumerable.** T#11. Dt +*33:2. Ps +*68:17. Da *7:10. Ju +*14. Re *5:11, 12. 22:14. **angels.** He *1:14. Mt 16:27. 25:31. 26:64. Lk 22:69. Jn +*1:51n.

23. **the general.** Ps 89:7. 111:1. Ac +*20:28. Ep 1:22. *5:24-27. Col 1:24. 1 T 3:5. **church.** He 2:12. Ac 7:38. **the firstborn.** Ge 49:3. Ex 4:22. 13:2. 22:29. Nu=*3:12, 13. Dt *21:17. 2 Ch 21:3. Ps *89:27. Je +*31:9. Ro √8:16, 17, 29. Ja *1:18. Re *14:4. **which.** Ex 32:32. Ps 69:28. Is 56:5, 6. Ml 3:16, 17. Lk +*10:20. Ac 13:39. Ph *4:3. Re 13:8. 20:15. **are.** Mt √22:32. **written.** *or*, enrolled. **in heaven.** 1 P +*1:4n. **God the Judge.** He +*6:10-12. +√9:27. Ge +*18:25. Ps 9:8. 50:5, 6. 58:11. 67:4. *75:7. 82:1. 94:2. 96:10, 13. 98:9. Ec *12:14. Mt 25:31-34. Jn *5:27. Ro *2:16. 3:6. 2 Th 1:5-7. 2 T +*4:8. 1 P 2:23. *4:5. **the spirits.** Gr. *pneuma*, Ro +1:4n. ⨍121A3, Mt +*27:50. He 11:4, 40. Ec +*3:21. +*12:7. Is +*38:16. Lk *23:46. Ac +*7:59. 1 C 5:3. 13:12. 15:49, 54. 2 C √5:8. Ph √1:21-23. 3:12, etc. Col 1:12. Re *6:9. *7:14-17. **made perfect.** He +2:10. Re +*14:13.

24. **Jesus.** He 7:22. 8:6, 8. 1 T √2:5. **the mediator.** He 8:6. *9:15. Ga +3:19. **new.** He +8:8. *13:20. Is +*55:3. Je *31:31-33. **covenant.** *or*, testament. He 9:15. Mt *26:28. Mk 14:24. Lk 22:20. Ro +9:4. **to the blood.** ⨍117, Ge +19:8. He 9:21. +*10:19, 22. 11:28. Ex *24:8. 1 P *1:2. 1 J √1:7. **sprinkling.** Gr. *rantismos*, ✳S#4473g, only here and 1 P 1:2g. He +*10:22n. 11:28. Le=8:30. **speaketh.** He 11:4. Ge 4:10. Mt 23:35. Lk 11:51. **better.** He +6:9. **Abel.** He 11:4. Ge=2:8-10.

25. **See that.** He 8:5. Ex 16:20. 1 K 12:16. Is 48:6. 64:9. Mt 8:4. 1 Th *5:15. 1 P *1:22. Re 19:10. 22:9. **refuse not.** He +*3:12. Pr √1:24. 8:33. 13:18. *15:32. Je *11:10. Ezk 5:6. Zc *7:11. Mt *17:5. Ac 7:35. *13:45, 46. **For if.** ⨍184A, 1 C +15:2. **escaped not.** See on He 2:1-3. 3:17. *10:28, 29. **refused him.** ver. 19. Je *13:10. **that spake.** He +8:5g. **on earth.** Re +5:10g. **turn away.** Nu 32:15. Dt 30:17. Jsh 22:16. 2 Ch 7:19. Pr *1:32. 2 T *4:4. **from him.** Ex 20:22. Dt 4:36. Ne 9:13. Lk *10:16.

26. **voice.** ver. 19. Ex *19:18. Jg 5:5. Ps 68:8. 114:6, 7. Hab 3:10. **Yet once.** ver. *27. Is *2:19. *13:13. Jl *3:16. Hg *⟩2:6, 7, 22. **I shake.** Is 2:19, 21. 13:13. *24:13, 18-23. Jl *3:16. Hg *2:21, 22. Mt 24:29. Mk 13:25. Lk 21:26. Re 11:13.

27. **signifieth.** Ps *102:26, 27. Ezk *21:27. Mt *24:35. 2 P √3:10, 11. Re *6:14. *11:15. √21:1. **the removing.** Ps 45:5. Is 34:4. *51:16. 54:10. *65:17. *66:22. Ezk 21:27. Mt +*24:35. 2 P √3:13. Re *20:11. *21:1. **those things.** Notice the writer's intentional obscurity "to avoid exciting unduly the hostility of the Roman Empire, under which the believers then lived" (Peters, *Theocratic Kingdom*, vol. 2, p. 497). Other examples of intentional obscurity can be seen at 1 C √15:24n and 2 Th 2:7n. **are shaken.** *or*, may be shaken. **be shaken.** ⨍24C, 2 K +18:21. **remain.** Ps 45:2. Da *2:44. +*7:13, 14.

28. **receiving.** ⨍96C6, Mt +2:4. Figure of speech

Heterosis of Tenses, whereby the present tense is used for the future. Peters (*Theocratic Kingdom*, vol. 1, p. 415) notes "In studying the subject of the Kingdom, we must not be misled by a striking peculiarity of Scripture, viz.: *that things still future, owing to their certainty, are spoken of as present.*" Ps 37:11. Mt +*5:5. Col √3:24. 2 T +*4:1n. **a kingdom.** Ps 2:8. Is +*9:7. Da *2:44. +*7:14, 27. Mt +*24:14. +*25:34. Lk +*1:33. +*17:20, 21. *22:28, 29. Col +*1:13n. 4:11. 1 Th 2:12. 2 Th 1:5. 2 T +*4:1n, 18. 1 P +*1:4n, 5. 2 P +*1:11. Re *1:5, 6. 3:21. *5:9, 10. **which cannot.** Da +*2:44. **have.** *or*, hold fast. See on He +*3:6. +*10:23. **grace.** or, thankfulness. He +*4:16. 13:15. Ps 50:14, 23. **we may.** He +9:14. Ps 19:14. Is 56:7. Ro +*12:1, 2. Ep 1:6. 5:10. Ph 4:18. 1 P 2:5, 20. **acceptably.** He 11:5. 13:16, 21. Lk 21:36. Col 1:10. 3:23, 24. 2 P 3:14. **with reverence.** He +*4:16. +5:7. +*10:19, 22. Le 10:3. Ps 2:11. 89:7. Pr 28:14. Ro 11:20. 1 P *1:17. Re *15:4. **godly fear.** Ml=2:5.

29. **our God is.** He *10:27. Ex *24:17. Nu 11:1. 16:35. Dt *14:24. 9:3. Ps *50:3. *97:3. Is +*9:5. 10:16-18. 29:6. 30:27, 30. *66:15. Da 7:9. Na *1:2, 3, 5, 6. Zp 1:18. 2 Th √1:8. 2 P +√3:7. **fire.** 1 K +*19:12.

HEBREWS 13

Exhortations to brotherly love, hospitality, and compassion; to chastity, contentment, and trust in God, 1-3; to recollect the faith, examples, and happy end of deceased pastors, 4-7; remembering that Christ is unchangeable and eternal, 8; to watchfulness against false doctrines, regard to the sacrifice of Christ, willingness to bear reproach for him, thanksgivings to God, liberality to men, subjection to vigilant and faithful teachers, and prayer for the apostle, 9-19. An earnest prayer to the "God of peace," through the great Shepherd, and the blood of his covenant, for the Hebrews; and concluding salutations, 20-25.

1. **brotherly love.** He +*6:10, 11. *10:24. Jn *13:34, 35. 15:17. Ac 2:1, 44-46. 4:32. Ro *12:9, 10. Ga *5:6, 13, 22. Ep 4:3. 5:2. Ph +*2:1-3. 1 Th *4:9, 10. 2 Th 1:3. 1 P √1:22. *2:17. *3:8. 4:8. 2 P *1:7. 1 J 2:9, 10. *3:10-18, 23. *4:7-11, 20, 21. 5:1. 2 J 5, 6. Re 2:4. **continue.** He +*6:10.

2. **not.** *f*175B, Ge +21:16. Le 19:34. Dt 10:18, 19. 1 K 17:10-16. 2 K 4:8. Jb 31:19, 32. Is 58:7. Mt 25:+35, 43. Ac 16:15. Ro *12:13. 16:23. 1 T 3:2. 5:10. T 1:8. 1 P +*4:9. **entertain strangers.** Ac 28:2, +*15. Ro 12:13. **some.** Ge *18:2-10. *19:1-3. Jg 13:15, etc. Mt *25:40.

3. **Remember them.** T#686. He 10:34. Ge 40:14, 15, 23. Is *58:6-11. Je 38:7-13. Mt +5:7 (T#527). *25:36, 43. Ac 16:29-34. 24:23. 27:3. Ep 4:1. Ph 4:14-19. Col *4:18. 2 T 1:16-18. **as bound with.** Ro *12:15. **which suffer.** He 11:25, 37. Ne 1:3, 4. Ro *12:15. 1 C 12:26. Ga +*6:1, 2. 1 P 3:8. **as being.** 2 C 5:6. 12:2, 3.

4. **Marriage.** T#423. Ge *1:27, 28. *2:18-22, 24. Le 21:13-15. 2 K 22:14. Ps 68:6. 107:41, 42. Pr 5:15-23. 18:22. Is 8:3. Mt *19:4-6. 1 C 7:2, etc., 38. 9:5. Ep 5:31. 1 T 3:2, 4, 12. *4:1-3. 5:14, 15. T 1:6. **honorable.** Ge 2:18. Pr *18:22. Ml *2:14, 15. Mt 19:5. Jn *2:1, 2. 1 C 7:1, *2, 8, 26, 27, 32, 33, 38, +*39. *9:5. Ep *5:23. 1 T 3:2, 12. **all.** *√171B, Ge +24:10. **and the bed.** See on He 12:16. Le *21:1, 7, 10, 13. 1 C +*6:9. Ga *5:19, 21. Ep 5:5. Col *3:5, 6. Re

22:15. **undefiled.** Ro 13:13. **but.** T#405. He 12:16. Ge 39:9. Le 20:10. Nu 25:1-9. Pr *2:18, 19. 5:3, 4, 8-12. 6:26-34. 7:22-27. 9:16-18. 29:3. Ec 7:26. Je 5:7-9. 23:14, 15. Ho 4:11. Ml +*3:5. Ro 1:27. 1 C +*5:10, 11. +√6:9, 10. 10:8. Ga *5:19-21. Ep *5:5, 6. Ju +*7. Re +*21:8. *22:15. **God will judge.** *√121C2D2, Ge +15:14. Ps 50:16-22. Ml +*3:5. Ro +*1:26-32. 1 C 5:13. 2 C *5:10. Col *3:5, 6. 1 Th +*4:6.

5. **conversation.** Ex +*18:21. +*20:17. Jsh *7:21. Ps +*10:3. 119:36. Je 6:13. Ezk +*33:31. Mk *7:22. Lk +*8:14. *12:15-21. *16:13, 14. Ro 1:29. 1 C 5:+10, 11. +*6:10. Ep 5:3, 5. Col +*3:5. 1 T 3:3. +*6:9, 10. 2 P 2:3, 14. Ju 11. **be content.** Ex 2:21. Mt +*6:25, 34. Lk *3:14. Ph √4:11, 12. 1 T +*6:6-8. **I will.** Ge *28:15. Dt 31:)6, 8, ◐+*17. Jsh *)1:5. 1 S 12:22. 1 K *8:57. 1 Ch *28:20. Ps 27:9. *37:25, 28. 38:21. Is 41:10, 17. **never.** *√158, Mt +5:18. **nor forsake.** T#831. Le 26:11. Ps +√9:10n. *37:28. 94:14. Is 42:16. 44:21. 49:14-16. *54:9, 10. La *3:31, 32. Je +*32:40. Ro +*11:1. 2 C 4:9.

6. **boldly.** He +*4:16. 10:19. Ep 3:12. **The Lord.** T#828. Ge 15:1. Ex 18:4. Dt 33:26, 27, 29. Ps *18:1, 2. *27:1-3, 9. 33:20. *40:17. 46:11. *54:4. 56:9. 63:7. 94:17. 115:9-11. *118:)6, 7, 9. 124:8. 146:3. Is *41:10, 13, 14. Ho 13:9. Ac 26:22. Ro +*8:31. **not fear.** Ge ◐+*19:30. Ps +*34:4. *56:4, 11, 12. *118:6. Is 51:12. Da *3:16-18. Zp *3:13. Mt +*10:28. Lk +*12:4, 5.

7. **which.** ver. 17, 24. Mt +*24:45. Lk +12:42. 22:26g. Ac +*14:23. 1 C 12:28. 2 C ◐+*1:24. 1 Th 5:12, 13. 1 T 3:5. **have the rule.** *or*, are the guides. 2 C +*10:8. **word of God.** Lk 8:11. Ac 4:31. 13:46. Ro +9:6. √10:17. 1 Th √2:13. Re 1:9. 6:9. 20:4. **whose faith follow.** He +*6:12. SS 1:8. 1 C *4:16. +*11:1. Ph 3:17. 1 Th 1:6. 2 Th 3:7, 9. **considering.** Ac +*7:55-60. 12:2. **the end.** 1 C +*10:13g. **conversation.** Gr. manner of life. Ja +3:13.

8. **the same.** T#76-4. God the Son is immutable. He *1:12. Ps 90:2, 4. *102:27, 28. 103:17. Is 41:4. 44:6. Ml ◐+*3:6. Mt ◐12:32. +*28:19n. Jn *8:+*35, 56-58. 2 C 1:19. Ja √1:17. Re 1:4, 8, 11, 17, 18. **yesterday.** Is *63:16. Ml +*5:2. **and.** *√148, Ge +8:22. **to day.** *√22D4B, Da +7:9. Jn +*8:58. Re +*1:8. **for ever.** Gr. *aion*, Mt +6:13. lit. unto the ages. He √7:24, 25. Is +*43:3, 11. *63:16.

9. **carried about.** Mt +*24:4, 24. Ac 17:19, 20. 20:30. Ro 16:17, 18. 2 C √11:11-15. Ga +*1:6-9. *2:13. Ep +√4:14. 5:6. Col *2:4, 8. 2 Th 2:2. 1 T *4:1-3. 6:3-5, 20. 1 J *4:1. Ju +*3, 12. **strange doctrines.** 2 T ◐1:13. ◐√3:14. T ◐1:13. 2 J ◐+*10. Ju ◐+*3. **For it is.** Ac 20:32. 2 C 1:21. Ga *6:1. 2 Th 2:17. 2 T 2:1, 2. **the heart.** Pr +*4:23. **be established.** He +*10:35. 1 C +1:8. Col +*1:23. +*2:7. **not with meats.** *√171K1, Dt +19:5. See on He 9:9, 10. Le ch. 11. Dt 14:3-21. Ac 10:14-16. Ro *14:2, 6, 17. 1 C 6:13. 8:8. Col √2:16-20. 1 T √4:3-5. T 1:14, 15. **not profited.** He 7:18. **occupied therein.** He 9:10.

10. **an altar.** *√121J6, Ps +23:5. Le=10:12, 13. 1 C 5:7, 8. 10:17-20. **no right.** Jn *6:54, 55. 1 C *9:13, 14. *11:23-26. **to eat.** Le *6:15, 16, 25, 26. **serve.** Nu 3:7, 8. 7:5. **the tabernacle.** He 8:5.

11. **the bodies.** Ex 29:14. Le 4:5-7, 11, 12, 16-21. *6:30. 9:9, 11. 16:14-19, 27. Nu 19:3, 5. **sanctuary.** He +8:2. **for sin.** Ro +8:3. **the camp.** Re 20:9.

12. **sanctify.** He 2:11. 9:13, 14, 18, 19. 10:29. Jn 17:19. 19:34. 1 C *6:11. Ep *5:26. T *2:14. 1 J 5:6-8. **own blood.** *√117, Ge +19:8. He +*9:12. Ac +*20:28.

1 J *1:7. **suffered**. He 9:26. Le 24:23. Nu 15:36. Jsh 7:24. Mt 21:39. Mk 12:8. 15:20-24. Lk 20:15. Jn *19:17, 18, 20. Ac +3:18. 7:58. Ga *3:13. Ph +*1:29. **without the gate**. Re 14:20.

13. **go forth**. He *11:26. 12:3. Ex *33:7, 8. Mt +*5:11. *10:24, 25. 16:24. 27:32, 39-44. Lk 6:22. Ac *5:41. 1 C 4:10-13. 2 C √12:10. 1 P *4:4, 14-16. **unto him**. He *12:2. Ge +*49:10. Jn 12:32. 2 C 5:15. Ep 3:21. 2 Th 2:1. **without the camp**. Ex=32:26. Le 14:3. Lk 10:33. =11:23. Jn 9:22. Re 20:9. **his reproach**. He +11:26.

14. **For here**. He 4:9. *11:9, 10, 12-16. +*12:22. Mi *2:10. 1 C 7:29. 2 C √4:17, 18. *5:1-8. Ep +2:19. Ph *3:20g. Col *3:1-3. 1 P *4:7. 2 P √3:13, 14. **no continuing city**. Nu=18:20. Dt=10:9. Ezk=44:28. **seek**. He 11:14. **one to come**. He *11:10, 16. +*12:28.

15. **By him**. He *7:25. Jn *10:9. √14:6. Ep *2:18. +5:20. Col *3:17. 1 P +*2:5. **the sacrifice**. He 12:28. Le *7:12. 2 Ch 7:6. *29:31. 33:16. Ezr 3:11. Ne 12:40, 43. Ps *50:14, 23. *69:30, 31. *107:21, 22. *116:17-19. 118:19. 119:108. 136:1, etc. 145:1, etc. Is +*12:1, 2. Je +*33:11. Ep *5:19, 20. Col 1:12. *3:16. 1 P 4:11. Re 4:8-11. 5:9-14. 7:9-12. 19:1-6. **of praise**. T#528. Ps 9:11. 22:22. 35:18. 47:6, 7. √50:23. 57:7-11. 92:1-4. 95:1-3. 96:1-4. 100:1-5. *106:12. 107:31, 32. 150:1-6. Mt 26:30. Ac 16:25. Ep +5:19 (T#747). **continually**. Je=33:18. **the fruit**. Ge 4:3, 4. Ps 119:108. Is 57:19. Ho *14:2. Ro 6:19. *12:1. Ju 12, 15, 16. **giving thanks to**. Gr. confessing to. Le=7:12. +=23:19. Ps *18:49mg. 50:14. Jon 2:9. Mt *11:25. Lk 10:21g. **his name**. Ps 113:1. Ac 15:14.

16. **to do good**. ver. 1, 2. Ps *37:3. Mt *25:35-40. Lk +*6:35, 36. Ac +√9:36. *10:38. Ga +*6:10. 1 Th 5:15. 2 Th *3:13. 1 T +*6:17-19. Ja √2:15, 16. 1 J √3:17. 3 J 11. **communicate**. Lk *18:22. Ac +*11:29. +*20:35. 24:17. Ro +*12:13. 15:26. 1 C *9:7n, 12-14n. 16:2n, 15. 2 C 8:1-4, 7. *9:12-14. Ga 2:10. +*6:6, 7. Ep *4:28. Ph 4:14. 1 T √5:17. +*6:18. Phm 6. **forget not**. Ge 29:15. Ex *23:15. Dt 16:16. 1 S 9:7, 8. 2 S +*24:24. 1 Ch +*21:24. Lk 21:4. 1 C +*16:2. **with such**. He +*6:10. Dt 10:12. Ps 51:19. Mi 6:7, +*8. Ph +*4:17, 18. **God is**. ver. 21. He 11:5. 12:28.

17. **Obey**. See on ver. 7. 1 S 8:19. 15:19, 20. Pr 5:13. Ph 2:12, 29. 1 Th *5:12, 13. 2 Th 3:14. 1 T *5:17. **have the rule over**. or, guide. ver. 7, 24. 1 Ch=9:29. 2 Ch=34:12, 13. Ne=11:16. Da +*11:33. 2 C +*1:24. +*10:8. 1 Th 5:12, 13. **submit**. Ge +*16:9. 1 C *16:16. Ep *5:21. Ja 4:7. 1 P +*5:5. **watch**. He +*3:12, 13. +*12:15. Ezk *3:17-21. 33:2, 7-9. Mk +13:33. Ac √20:24-26, 28, 31. 1 C 4:1, 2. 1 T +*4:16. 2 T *2:2. 1 P +*5:2, 3. **souls**. Gr. psyche, √171Q2, 2 C +12:15mg. **give account**. Je 13:20. Ezk 14:10n. 34:10. Ml 2:12. Lk 16:2. Ro 14:12. 1 C *4:1-5. 2 C *5:10, 11. 1 T +*4:16. **with joy**. Ps +*126:6. Da +*12:3. 2 C *2:15. Ph 1:4. 2:16. 4:1. 1 Th +*2:19,

20. 3:+*8, 9, 10. **with grief**. Ex 32:31. Je 13:17. Ac 20:31. Ga +*4:11. Ph 3:18. **unprofitable**. ⊿111, Ge +18:27.

18. **Pray**. Ro *15:30. Ep *6:19, 20. Col *4:3. 1 Th +*5:25. 2 Th *3:1. **we have**. Ac +*23:1. +*24:16. 2 C +1:12. 1 T 1:5. 1 P 3:16, 21. **in all**. Ac +*6:3. Ro *12:17. 13:13. Ph √4:8. 1 Th 4:12. 1 P 2:12.

19. **that I**. Ro 1:10-12. 15:31, 32. Phm *22.

20. **the God of peace**. Is *57:19. Ro +15:33. 16:20. 1 C *14:33. 2 C *13:11. Ph *4:9. 1 Th +*5:23. 2 Th *3:16. **brought again**. Ps 30:3. Is 63:11. Ro *10:7. **from the dead**. Ac +*2:24, 32. 3:15. 4:10. 5:30. 10:40, 41. 13:30. √17:31. Ro +*1:4. *4:24, 25. +*8:11. 1 C *6:14. *15:15. 2 C 4:14. Ga 1:1. Ep 1:20. Col *2:12. 1 Th +*1:10. 1 P *1:21. **our Lord**. Ne +*9:6. Is *40:10, 11. Jn 12:41. **that great**. ⊿96E2, 1 S +17:14. Ge=49:24. Ps +*23:1. 80:1. Is *40:11. *63:11. Ezk +*34:23. 37:24. Jn +*10:11, 14. 1 P *2:25. *5:4. **the blood**. See on He 9:20. +*10:22, 29. Ex *24:8. Zc 9:11. Mt +*26:28. Mk 14:24. Lk 22:20. **everlasting**. Gr. aionios, Mt +18:8. Ge +*9:16. +*17:7. 2 S 23:5. 1 Ch 16:17. Is *54:10. +√55:3. *61:8. Je 32:40. Ezk 37:26. 1 P *1:20. **covenant**. or, testament. T#575. See on He 9:16, 17. Ps 89:3, 4. Is +*42:6. 53:12. Zc 6:12, 13. Jn *6:39.

21. **Make you perfect**. T#1636. He 12:23. Dt 32:4. Ps 138:8. Lk +6:40. Jn 17:+*6, 22, 23. Ep 3:16-19. Col +*1:9-12. *4:12. 1 Th 3:13. +*5:23. 1 P √5:10, 11. **every good work**. Ac +*9:36. 2 C √9:8. Ep √2:10. Ph 1:11. Col +*1:10. 2 Th *2:16, 17. 1 T 5:10. 2 T +*3:15-17. T *3:1, 8, 14. **to do his will**. He *10:36. Mt +*6:10. √7:21. 12:50. 21:31. Jn +*7:17. Ro +*12:2. 1 Th *4:3. 1 P 4:2. 1 J *2:17. **working**. or, doing. He 10:36. Ph √2:13. **well pleasing**. ver. 16. He 11:5. 12:28. Ro 12:1. 14:17, +18. Ph 4:18. Col 3:20. 1 J 3:22. **through**. Jn 16:23, 24. Ep 2:18. Ph *1:11. *4:13. Col *3:17. 1 P *2:5. **to whom**. Ps 72:18, 19. Ro 16:27. Ga 1:5. Ph 2:11. +4:20. 1 T *1:17. *6:16. 2 T +*4:18. 1 P 5:11. 2 P *3:18. Ju *25. Re 4:6. *5:9, 13. **for ever**. Gr. aion, Mt +6:13. lit. unto the ages of the ages, Ga +1:5. **and ever**. Gr. aion, Mt +6:13. **Amen**. See on Mt +*6:13. 28:20.

22. **suffer**. ver. 1-3, 12-16. He *2:1. +*3:1, 12, 13. 4:1, 11. *6:11, 12. 10:19-39. 12:1, 2, 12-16, 25-28. 2 C 5:20. 6:1. *10:1. Phm 8, 9. **the word**. Ac 13:15. **of exhortation**. He 12:5. Ac +4:36. **for**. Ga 6:11. 1 P 5:12.

23. **our brother Timothy**. See on Ac +*16:1-3. 1 Th +3:2. Phm 1. **is set**. 1 T 6:12. 2 T 1:8. Re 7:14. **if**. ⊿184C, Mt +4:9. **I will**. Ro 15:25, 28. Phm 22.

24. **Salute**. See on Ro 16:1-16. **the rule**. See on ver. 7, 17. **and all**. 2 C +1:1. 13:13. Ph 1:1. 4:22. Col 1:2. Phm 5. **They**. See on Ro 16:21-23. **Italy**. Ac 18:2. +27:1.

25. **Grace**. See on Ro 1:7. 16:20, 24. Ep 6:24. Col +4:18. 2 T 4:22. T 3:15. Re 22:21.

JAMES

JAMES 1

The apostle addresses "the twelve tribes, which were scattered abroad," 1. He exhorts them to joyful patience under trials, 2-4; and to ask wisdom of God in faith, with an unwavering mind, 5-8. He counsels the poor and the rich, 9-11; and shows the happiness prepared for those who endure, 12. Men are tempted to sin, not by God, but by their own lusts, 13-15. Every good gift comes from the unchangeable God, of which good gifts regeneration is especially mentioned, 16-18. Cautions against pride, loquacity, anger, and malice, 19,

20: admonitions to receive the word of God in meekness, and to reduce it to practice, 21-25. The necessity of bridling the tongue, 26. The nature of true religion, 27.

1. James. Mt 10:3. +*13:55. Mk 3:18. Lk 6:15. Ac 1:13. +12:17. 15:13. 21:18. Ga 1:19. 2:9, 12. Ju *1. a **servant.** Gr. bondservant. Lk 2:29. 16:13. Ac 2:18. 4:29. 16:17. Jn 12:26. Ro 1:1. Ph 1:1. 1 Th 1:9. 2 T 2:24. T 1:1. 1 P 2:16. 2 P 1:1. Re +7:3. **and of.** Jn 15:15. Ro 1:1. 1 C 7:22. Ga 1:10. Ep 6:6. Ph 1:1. Col +3:24. 4:12. 2 T 2:24. 2 P 1:1. Ju 1. Re 1:1. 2:20. **to.** Ex 24:4. 28:21. 39:14. 1 K 18:31. Ezr 6:17. Mt 19:28. 22:30. Ac 26:7. Re 7:4. 21:12. **scattered.** Le 26:33. Dt 4:27. 28:25, 64. 30:3. 32:26. Est 3:8. Ezk 12:15. Am 9:8, 9. Jn +7:35. Ac *2:5, 9-11. *8:1, 4. 15:21. Ga 3:26-29. 1 P *1:1. **greeting.** Ezr 5:7. Ac +15:23. 23:26. 2 T 4:21.

2. count. ver. 12. Mt +*5:10-12. *6:13. Lk 6:22, 23. Ac *5:41. Ro *8:17, 18, 35-37. 2 C √12:9, 10. Ph 1:29. 2:17. Col 1:24. He 10:34. 12:11. 1 P *4:13-16. **all.** ♪108B, 1 C +13:2. **divers.** Mt 26:41. 1 C +*10:13. He 11:36-38. 1 P 1:6-8. 2 P 2:9. Re 2:10.

3. that. Ro *5:3, 4. +*8:28. 2 C √4:17. 1 P *1:7. **patience.** Ja 5:11. Ro +*2:7. 8:25. +*15:4. Col 1:11. 2 Th 1:4. 3:5. He +*10:36. 12:1. 2 P 1:6.

4. let patience. ♪16, Ge +1:27. ♪50, Ho +2:21. T#498. Ja *5:7-11. Jb +14:14 (T#154). 17:9. Ps 37:1, 7. 40:1. Pr +16:7 (T#737). +19:11 (T#201). Hab 2:3. Mt 10:+16 (T#660), 22. +11:29 (T#62). 24:13. Lk 8:15. *21:19. Ro *2:7. 12:12. 2 C 6:4. Ga +*6:1 (T#437), 9. 1 Th *5:14. He *6:12. *10:36. *12:1, 2. Ja 5:7-11. 1 P 2:20. 2 P *1:5, 6. **perfect and.** ♪50, Ho +2:21. Ja 3:2. Pr +*4:18. Mt +5:48. Jn 17:23. 1 C 2:6. Ph 3:12-15. Col 4:12. 2 T *3:17. He 13:21. 1 P 5:10. 1 J 4:17, 18. **entire.** Ac 3:16. 1 Th *5:23. **wanting.** ver. 5. Mt 19:20. Mk 10:21. Lk 18:22. 2 P 1:9.

5. If. ♪184A, 1 C +15:2. **any.** Ex 31:3, 6. 36:1-4. 1 K 3:7-9, 11, 12. Jb 28:12-28. Pr √3:5-7. 9:4-6. Je 1:6, 7. 2 C 2:16. **wisdom.** Ps +*51:6. +*119:27. 2 T +*2:7. **let him ask.** T#395, 1871. ver. 17. Ja 3:17. 5:16. Ex 3:13. 1 Ch 22:12. 2 Ch 1:10. Pr 2:3-7. 18:1. Is √55:6, 7. Je 29:12, 13. Da 2:18-22. Mt +*7:7-11. Lk √11:9-13. Jn 4:10. 14:13. 15:7. *16:23, 24. 1 J 3:22. √5:14, 15. **that giveth.** Ps +*32:8. Pr 28:5. Is 28:26. Ac +17:25. **and upbraideth.** Mt 11:20. Mk 16:14. Lk 15:20-22.

6. let. Ja 5:15. Mt *21:22. Mk √11:22-24. Lk 12:29. 1 T 2:8. He √11:6. **in faith.** 2 Ch +*20:20. Is 7:9mg. **nothing wavering.** Ja 2:4. 3:17. Mt 21:21, 22. He *10:23. **he.** Ge 49:4. Ep +*4:14. He *10:23. *13:9. 2 P 2:17. Ju 12, 13. **a wave.** Is 57:20. Lk 8:24g. Ep +*4:14.

7. let not. T#1812. ver. 6. Ja 4:3. Pr 15:8. 21:27. Is 1:15. 58:3, 4.

8. double minded. Ja 4:8. 1 K 18:21. 2 K 17:33, 41. 1 Ch 12:33. Ps 12:2. 119:113. Is 29:13. Ho 7:8-11. 10:2. Mt +*6:22, 24. 1 T 3:8. **unstable.** Ja 3:8g. Is *7:9mg. 2 P 2:14. 3:16.

9. the brother. Ja *2:5, 6. Dt 15:7, 9, 11. Ps 62:9. Pr 17:5. 19:1. Lk 1:52. *6:20, 21. 2 C √8:9. **rejoice.** *or, glory.* Je +*9:23, 24. Ro 5:2, 3. Ph 3:3g. **in.** Ja 2:5. 1 S 2:8. Ps 113:7, 8. Lk 9:48. 10:20. Ro *8:17. 2 C *6:10. Ph 3:14. 1 P 2:9. 1 J *3:1-3. Re 2:9. 5:9, 10. 7:9, 10.

10. the rich. Je *9:23. **in.** Is 57:15. 66:2. Mt +*5:3. Lk 16:22. Ph 3:8. 1 T +*6:17. **because.** Ja 4:14. Jb

14:2. Ps *37:2, 35, 36. 90:5, 6. 102:4, 11. 103:15. Is 40:6. 51:12. Mt 6:30. 1 C 7:31. 1 P *1:24. 1 J √2:17.

11. risen. Is 49:10. Jon 4:7, 8. Mt 13:6. Mk 4:6. **burning heat.** Mt +20:12. **it withereth.** Is ♦40:7, 8. **perisheth.** Gr. *apollumi,* Mt +2:13. **so.** Ja 5:1-7. Jb 21:24-30. Ps 37:35, 36. 49:6-14. 73:18-20. Ec 5:15. Is 28:1, 4. 40:7, 8. Lk 12:16-21. 16:19-25. 1 C 7:31. 1 P +*1:4. 5:4. **fade away.** Jb 15:30.

12. Blessed. Da 12:12. **the man.** See on ver. 2-4. Ja 5:11. Jb *5:17. Ps 94:12. 119:67, 71, 75. Pr *3:11, 12. Mt +10:22. He 6:15. 10:32. 12:5. 1 P 3:14. Re 3:19. **when.** Dt 8:2. 13:3. Pr 17:3. Zc 13:9. Ml 3:2, 3. He 11:17. 1 P 1:6, 7. 5:10. **tried.** *or,* approved. Dt 8:2. 13:1-3. Ro 5:4. 14:18. 16:10. 1 C √11:19. 2 C 10:18. 13:7. Ph 2:22g. 2 T 2:15g. 1 P 1:16. **the crown.** Zc 6:14. Mt 25:34. Lk 22:28-30. Ro 2:7-10. 1 C 9:25. 1 Th 2:19. 2 T 4:8. 1 P 1:7. 4:13. 5:4. Re *2:10. 3:11, 21. **which.** Ja *2:5. 4:6. Is 64:4. Mt 10:22. +*19:28, 29. Col 1:19. 1 T 4:5-8. **them.** Ja *2:5. Ex 20:6. Dt 7:9. Jg 5:31. Ne 1:5. Ps 5:11. 97:10. 145:20. Ro +*8:28. 1 C 2:9. 8:3. 1 P 1:8. 1 J 4:19. **love him.** T#875. Pr 8:17, 21. Jn *14:21. Ga 5:6. Ep *6:24. 2 T +*4:8.

13. no man. ver. 2, 12. Ge 3:12. Is *63:17. Hab 2:12, 13. Ro *9:19, 20. **tempted.** Mt 4:1. **cannot.** Ps *5:4, 5. Hab *1:13. T 1:2. **with.** ♪181E, Ge +3:24. **evil.** *or,* evils. ver. +*17. Ru ◖+*1:13. 2 K +*6:33. Jb +*2:10. Je +√29:11. **neither.** T#723. 1 C +14:33 (T#269).

14. when. Ja 4:1, 2. Ge 6:5. 8:21. Jsh 7:21-24. 2 S 11:2, 3. 1 K 21:2-4. Jb 31:9, 27. Pr *4:23. Is 44:20. Ho *13:9. Mt 5:28. *15:18-20. Mk *7:21, 22. Ro +*6:12. 7:11, 13. Ep 4:22. He 3:13. **own lust.** ♪50, Ho +2:21. Ge +*3:6. 1 J √2:16, 17. **and enticed.** 2 P 2:14, 18.

15. when. Ge 3:6. 4:5-8. Jb 15:35. Ps 7:14. Is 59:4. Mi 2:1-3. Mt 26:14, 48-50. Ac 5:1-3. 1 C *10:5, 6. **conceived.** ♪155F, Ge +4:7. **sin, when.** ♪50, Ho +2:21. Ge +*2:17. 3:17-19. Ps 9:17. Ro 5:12-21. *6:21-23. Re 20:14, 15. **death.** T#287. Ge +*2:17. Ps +9:17 (T#561). Pr *11:23. Ezk +*18:4. 33:11. Mt +5:20 (T#560). *25:41, +46 (T#567). Lk +12:10 (T#562). Jn +3:19 (T#309). ◖8:51. Ro *5:12. *6:23. Ga 3:10, 13. Re +2:11 (T#563).

16. Do. Mt 22:29. Mk 12:24, 27. 1 C +*6:9. 15:33. Ga 6:7. Ep +5:6. Col 2:4, 8. 2 T 2:18. **my.** ver. 19. Ja 2:5. 1 C *15:58. Ph 2:12. 4:1. He 13:1.

17. Every good. See on ver. 5. Ja 3:15, 17. Ge 41:16, 38, 39. Ex 4:11, 12. 31:3-6. 36:1, 2. Nu 11:17, 25. 1 Ch 22:12. 29:19. 2 Ch 1:11, 12. Jb ◖+*2:10. Ps +*37:24. 85:12. √104:28. +*145:9. Pr 2:6. Is 28:26. Je +√29:11. Da 2:21, 22, 27-30. Mt 7:11. 11:25, 26. 13:11, 12. Lk +*6:35. 11:13. Jn 3:27. Ac 5:31. 11:18. *17:25. Ro 6:23. 11:36. 12:6-8. 1 C 4:7. 12:4-12. Ep 2:3-5, 8. 4:8-11. Ph 1:29. 1 T *6:17. T 3:3-5. 1 J 4:10. √5:11, 12. **gift.** Ph 4:15g. **perfect gift.** Ro 5:16g. **from above.** Ja 3:15, 17. Jn 3:3g. **from the.** Ge *1:2-5, 14, 15. Dt 4:19. Ps 19:1-8. *84:11. Is 45:7. 60:19. Je 4:23. Jn *1:9. 8:12. 2 C 4:6. Ep 1:18. 1 J √1:5. Re 21:23. 22:5. **lights.** ♪96F2, Ge +4:10. ♪22J, Ps +27:1. **no variableness.** T#217. Nu *23:19. 1 S 15:29. Jb 23:13. Ps +33:11 (T#250). 102:25-27. 119:89-91. Is +*31:2. 46:10. Ml +*3:6. Ro *11:29. He 1:11, 12. +13:8 (T#76-4).

18. his own will. Jn √1:12,13. √3:3-5. Ro 4:17. +*8:29-31. 9:15-18. 1 C +12:11. Ep 2:4, 5. Col 1:20, 21. 1 Th 4:3. 2 Th *2:13, 14. 1 P *1:3, 23. **begat.**

T#1114. Ga 4:19. T *2:14. *3:5, 6. 1 P *1:3, 23. **with.** ver. 21. 1 C 4:15. Ep 1:12. 1 Th √2:13. 2 T +*3:15. 1 P √1:23. 1 J *3:9. **the word of truth.** Ps 119:43, 160. Da 10:21. 2 C 6:7. Ep 1:13. Col 1:5. 2 T 2:15. **that we.** Ep 1:12. **firstfruits.** Le +*23:10. Je 2:3. Am 6:1mg. Ro 8:19-23. He *12:23. Re *14:4.

19. **beloved brethren.** ver. +16. **let.** Ne *8:2, 3, 12-14, 18. *9:3. Pr *8:32-35. Ec *5:1. Mk 2:2. 12:37. Lk 15:1. 19:48. Ac *2:42. 10:33. 13:42-44, 48. +*17:11. 1 Th *2:13. **swift to hear.** 1 S ◐+*25:17. 2 K +*5:13. 2 Ch=34:20. Ec 5:1, 2. **slow to speak.** ver. *26. Ja *3:1, 2. Pr √10:19. *13:3. *15:2. *17:27. *18:13, 21. *21:23. Ec *5:2, 3. **slow to wrath.** √41, Ge +10:1. Ne *9:17. Ps 37:8. Pr *14:17, 29. *15:18. √16:32. 17:14. *19:11, 19. *25:15, 28. Ec *7:8, 9. Mt *5:22. Ga *5:20, 21. Ep *4:26, 31. Col *3:8, 15.

20. **wrath of man.** T#735. Ja 3:17, 18. Nu *20:11, 12. +*32:23 (T#733). Jb *5:2. Ps *37:8. 76:10. *106:33. Pr *11:17. +12:16 (T#200-21). √14:16, 17, 29. 15:18. *16:32. 19:19. 22:24. 24:17, 18. 25:28. 26:21. 27:4. 29:22. Ec 7:9. Ro 12:18-20. Ep √4:31, 32. 2 T *2:24, 25.

21. **lay.** Is 2:20. 30:22. Ezk 18:31. Ro +*1:29. 13:12, 13. Ep 4:22. Col *3:5-8. He *12:1. 1 P 2:1, 11. **filthiness.** Ja *4:8. Ezk 36:25. 2 C *7:1. Ep 5:4. Re 22:11. **and receive.** T#1067. Ja 3:13. Ps +*25:9. Is 29:19. 61:1. Zp +*2:3. Mt +*5:5. Lk +*8:15. Ac 10:33. 1 Th 1:5. √2:13. **the engrafted.** Jn 6:63, 68. Ro 6:17mg. 11:17. He 4:2. **which.** Jn √5:24. Ac 13:26. *20:32. Ro +*1:16. 1 C +*15:2. Ep 1:13. 1 Th √2:13. 2 T +√3:15-17. T *2:11. He *2:3. 1 P 1:9. **souls.** Gr. *psyche,* √171Q2, 2 C +12:15mg. Ps 103:1. Lk +*1:46.

22. **be ye doers.** Ja 2:14-20. 4:11, √17. Dt +*26:16. Mt 5:19. √7:21-25. 12:50. *28:20. Lk *6:46-48. *8:21. +*11:28. +*12:47, 48. Jn *8:31. +*13:17. Ro *2:13. Ep 2:10. Ph √4:8, 9. Col *3:17. T 3:8. 1 J 2:√3, 9, 10. 3:7. 3 J *11. Re *22:7. **the word.** ver. 21, 23. Mk 4:14. **not hearers only.** Ezk +*33:31, 32. **deceiving.** T#1078. ver. 26. Is 44:20. Ob +*3. 1 C *3:18. +*6:9. 15:33. Ga *6:3, 7. Col 2:4. 2 T 3:13. T 3:3. 2 P 2:13. 1 J √1:8. Re 12:9.

23. **if.** √184A, 1 C +15:2. **a hearer.** See on Ja 2:14-26. Je 44:16. Ezk +*33:31, 32. Mt *7:26, 27. Lk *6:47-49, etc. **natural face.** Gr. face of his birth. Ja 3:6. **mirror.** 1 C 13:12g. 2 C 3:18g.

24. **beholdeth.** √96C1, Ge +4:1. **and.** √148, Ge +8:22. **what.** Jg 8:18. Mt 8:27. Lk 1:66. 7:39. 1 Th 1:5. 2 P 3:11.

25. **looketh.** Pr 14:15. Is +*8:20n. Lk 24:12. Jn 20:5, 11g. 2 C *13:5. He *12:15. 1 P 1:12. **the perfect.** Ja 2:12. Ps √19:7-10. 119:32, *45, √96-105. Ro *7:12, 22, 23. **liberty.** Ja 2:12. Jn √8:32, 36. Ro *8:15. 2 C *3:17, 18. Ga 2:4. √5:1, 13. 1 P 2:16. 2 P 2:19. **and continueth.** 1 S *13:14. Jn +*8:31. 15:9, 10. Ac 2:42. +*13:43. 26:22. Ro *2:7, 8. +*11:22. Col +*1:23. 1 T *2:15. +*4:16. 1 J *2:24. **a forgetful.** ver. 23, 24. **but a doer.** ver. +*22. Jn +*13:17. **this.** Ps +*1:1, 2. *19:11. 106:3. 119:2, 3. Lk *6:47, etc. +*11:28. Jn +*13:17. 1 C +√15:58. Re +*14:13. 22:14. **deed.** *or,* doing.

26. **If any.** √184A, 1 C +15:2. **seem.** Pr √14:12. *16:25. Mt 3:9. Mk 10:42. Lk +*8:18. 1 C *3:18. 10:12. 11:16. 14:37. Ga 2:6, 9. 6:3. He 4:1. **bridleth not.** T#731. ver. 19. Ja 3:2-6. Ps 32:9. *34:13. *39:1, 2. 141:3. Pr *10:19, 31. *13:2, 3. 15:2. 16:10. 19:1. *21:23. Ec *10:20. Mi *7:5. Mt *12:34, 35. Ep 4:29. 5:4. Col 4:6. 1 P 3:10. **but.** See on ver. 22. Dt 11:16. Is 44:20.

Ga 6:3. **this.** Ja 2:20. Is 1:13. Ml 3:14. Mt 15:9. Mk 7:7. 1 C +*15:2, 15. Ga 3:4. **religion.** Ac 26:5. Col 2:18g.

27. **Pure.** Ja 3:17. Ps 119:1. Mt +*5:8. Lk 1:6. 1 T 1:5. 5:4. **God and.** Ja ◐3:9. 1 C 15:24. Ep 5:20. T 2:13n. **is this.** Ps *15:1-5. Is √58:6, 7. Mi +*6:8. Zc *7:9, 10. He *11:6. **To visit.** Jb 29:12, 13. 31:15-20. Ps 68:5. Is *1:16, 17. Mt *25:34-46. Ro 12:13. Ga *5:6. +*6:9, 10. 1 J √3:17-19. **the fatherless.** Ge +11:28. Dt +*10:18. Jb 29:16. *31:17, 18. Is *1:17, 23. **widows.** √171I14, Ex +22:22. **to keep.** Ja *4:4. Jn *17:14, 15. Ro +*12:2. Ga 1:4. *6:14. Col *3:1-3. 1 T 5:22. 1 J √2:15-17. 5:4, 5, 18. **unspotted.** 1 T 6:14. He +*12:14. 1 P 1:19. 2 P 2:20. √3:14. Ju *23. **world.** Gr. *kosmos,* Mt +4:8.

JAMES 2

Caution against partial regard to the rich, and contempt of the poor, especially in places of worship, as contrary to the law of love, 1-9. The transgression of one commandment violates the whole law, 10-12. No mercy will be shown to the unmerciful, 13. As love, shown by words alone, is worthless; so faith without works is dead and unprofitable, 14-20. This is illustrated by the examples of Abraham and Rahab, 21-26.

1. **the faith.** Ac *20:21. 24:24. Col 1:4. 1 T *1:19. T *1:1. 2 P *1:1. Re *14:12. **the Lord.** Ne +*9:6. **of glory.** Ps *24:7-10. 29:3. Is 42:8. Jn 1:14. +*3:13, 31. *17:5. Ac 7:2. 1 C √2:8. +*15:47. Ep 1:17. T *2:13. He *1:3. 1 P 4:14. **with respect.** ver. 3, 9. Ja *3:17. Le +*19:15. Dt *1:17. *16:19. 2 Ch 19:7. Pr *24:23. *28:21. Mt *22:16. Lk 1:52. Ac +10:34. Ro 2:11. 2 C +6:16. Ep 6:9. Col 3:25. 1 T *5:21. Ju *16.

2. **if.** √184C, Mt +4:9. **assembly.** Gr. synagogue. **gold.** Est 3:10. 8:2. Lk 15:22. **goodly.** Ge 27:15. Mt 11:8, 9. Ga 3:11. Ac 10:30. Re 15:6. 19:8. **in vile.** Is *64:6. Zc 3:3, 4. Re 22:11g.

3. **have respect.** Ro *12:16. Ju 16. **in a good place.** *or,* well, *or,* seemly. **to the poor.** See on ver. 6. Pr *14:20, 21. 18:23. Is +*65:5. Lk 7:44-46. 2 C *8:9.

4. **partial.** √135, Ps +68:28. See on ver. 1. Ja 1:6. 3:17. Jb 34:19. Ml 2:9. **judges.** √135, Ps +68:28. Ja 4:11. Jb 21:27. Ps 58:1. 82:2. 109:31. Mt 7:1-5. Lk 16:8, 9. 18:6. Jn +*7:24. **evil thoughts.** Mt 15:19.

5. **Hearken.** Jg 9:7. 1 K 22:28. Jb 34:10. 37:14. Pr 7:24. 8:32. Mk 7:14. Ac 7:2. **my beloved.** Ja +1:16. **Hath not.** Ja 1:9. Jb 34:19. Is 14:32. 29:19. Zp 3:12. Zc 11:7, 11. Mt 11:5. Lk 6:20. 9:57, 58. 16:22, 25. Jn 7:48. 1 C +1:26-28. 2 C *8:9. **chosen.** Ac +*13:48. +*18:27. 1 C +*1:27. Ep 1:4, 5. Col 3:12. 2 T +*1:9. 2 P +*1:10. **the poor.** T#524, 781. Ja 1:9. 1 S 2:8, 9. Jb 5:15, 16. 36:15. Ps *9:18. +12:5 (T#523). *68:10. 69:33. 72:2, 12, 13. 102:17. *107:41. 113:7, 8. 112:9, 10. 132:15. Is 14:30. Je *20:13. 52:16. Mt +*5:3. 11:5. Lk 1:52, 53. 4:18. 10:21. 14:21. 16:25. 1 C 1:26-29. **this.** Jn +*6:54n. **world.** Gr. *kosmos,* Mt +4:8. **rich in faith.** Pr 8:17-21. *13:7. Lk +12:21. 1 C 3:21-23. 2 C 4:15. 6:10. *8:9. Ep 1:18. 3:8. 1 T +*6:18. He 11:26. Re *2:9. 3:18. 21:7. **heirs.** Mt +*5:3. +*25:34. Lk +*12:32. +*22:29, 30. Ro +*4:13. +*8:17. 1 C ◐+*6:9. Ep *1:5, +*11n. Col *3:24. 1 Th +*2:12. 2 Th 1:5. 2 T +*4:8, 18. 1 P +*1:4. **the.** *or,* that. **kingdom.** Mt +√5:5. +*25:34. Lk 12:32. 13:29. +*22:29, 30. Ac +*1:6n. 8:12. 14:22. 20:25. 28:31.

Col +*1:13n. 4:11. 1 Th +*2:12. 2 Th 1:5. 2 T +*4:1, 18. He +*12:28. 2 P +*1:11. **which.** See on Ja 1:12. 1 S 2:30. Mt +*5:3. Lk *6:20. *12:32. 1 C √2:9. 2 T +*4:8. He +*9:28. **love him.** T#874. Ex 20:6. Dt 7:9. 11:13, 14. Jg 5:31. Ne 1:5. Ps 37:4. +*69:35, 36. 91:14. *145:20. Pr 8:17. Da 9:4. Ro *8:28. 1 C *2:9 (T#289). 8:3. 1 J 4:19, 21.

6. **ye.** ver. 3. Ps 14:6. Pr 14:21, 31. 17:5. Ec 9:15, 16. Is +*53:3. Jn 8:49. 1 C 11:22. **Do.** Ja *5:4. Jb 20:19. Ps 10:2, 8, 10, 14. 12:5. Pr 22:16. Ec 5:8. Is 3:14, 15. Am 2:6, 7. 4:1. 5:11. 8:4-6. Mi 6:11,12. Hab 3:14. Zc 7:10. **oppress.** Dt +*24:14. Jb 24:3, 4. Ps +*12:5. Ezk +*16:49. **and draw.** Ja 5:6. 1 K 21:11-13. Ac 4:1-3, 26-28. 5:17, 18, 26, 27. 8:3. 13:50. 16:+19, 20. 17:6. 18:12. **judgment seats.** 1 C 6:2, 4.

7. **blaspheme.** Ps 73:7-9. Mt 12:24. 27:63. Lk 22:64, 65. Ac +13:45. 26:11. Ro 2:24. 1 T 1:13. 6:1. T 2:5. Re 13:5, 6. 16:9. **worthy.** Ps 111:9. SS 1:3. Is +*7:14. +*9:6, 7. Je +*23:5, 6. Mt *1:23. Ac √4:12. Ph *2:9-11. Re 19:13, 16. **name.** Is 63:19. 65:1. Je 7:10. 32:34. 34:15. Am 9:12. Ml 1:11. Ac 15:17. **by.** Is 65:15. Ac 11:26. Ep 3:15.

8. **If.** √184A, 1 C +15:2. **the royal.** ver. 12. Ja 1:25. 1 P 2:9. **the scripture.** ver. 23. Ja 4:5. Lk +4:21. **Thou.** Ja 4:11. Le +*19:)18, 34. Mt +19:19. 22:39. Mk 12:31-33. Lk 10:27-37. Ro *13:8, 9. Ga *5:14. *6:2. 1 Th 4:9. **ye do.** ver. 19. 1 K 8:18. 2 K 7:9. Jon 4:4, 9. Mt 25:21, 23. Ph 4:14.

9. **if.** √184A, 1 C +15:2. See on ver. 1-4. Le +*19:15. **respect.** Ge +*44:30. Pr 24:23. **are.** Jn 8:9, 46. 16:8mg. 1 C 14:24. Ju 15. **transgressors.** Ro 2:25, 27. 3:20. 7:7-13. Ga 2:18. 1 J 3:4.

10. **For.** While the Jews taught that "he who transgresses all the precepts of the law has broken the yoke, dissolved the covenant, and exposed the law to contempt;" and so has he done who has only broken one precept;" they also taught, "that he who observed any principal command was equal to him who kept the whole law," and gave for an example the forsaking of idolatry. To correct this false doctrine was the object St. James has in view. **whosoever.** Dt *27:26. Mt 5:18, 19. Ga 3:10. **shall keep.** Le +*18:5. Dt 27:26. 2 K *22:13. **offend.** Ja 3:2. 2 P 1:10. Ju 24. **in one.** Ec +*7:20. Lk *18:22. **he is.** Mt 5:19. Ga 3:10. **guilty.** 1 C +11:27.

11. **he that said.** or, that law, which said. **Do not commit.** Ex +*)20:13, 14. Dt 5:17, 18. Mt 5:21-28. 19:18. Mk 10:19. Lk 18:20. Ro 13:9. **Now if.** √184A, 1 C +15:2. Le 4:2, 13, 22. Ps 130:3, 4.

12. **speak.** Ph √4:8. Col *3:17. 2 P 1:4-8. **the.** ver. 8. See on Ja 1:25. Ga *5:1.

13. **he.** Ja *5:4. Ge *42:21. Jg +*1:7. Jb 22:6-11. Ps 18:25, 26. Pr *21:13. Is 27:11. Ezk 25:11-14. Mt +*5:7. *6:15. *7:1, 2. *18:28-35. *25:41-46. Lk 6:38. *16:25. Ro 1:31. **and.** Ps *85:10. Je *9:24. Ezk 33:11. Mi √7:18. Ep *1:6, 7. *2:4-7. 1 J *4:8-16, 18, 19. **rejoiceth.** or, glorieth. **judgment.** √63D2, Ge +30:27. Supply by ellipsis (absolute: of anantapodoton), "mercy rejoiceth against judgment (to him that hath showed mercy)."

14. **What.** ver. 16. Je 7:8. Ro 2:25. 1 C 13:3. 15:32. 1 T 4:8. He *13:9. **profit.** √66, Ge +9:3. **though.** √184C, Mt +4:9. ver. 18, 26. Ja *1:22-25. Mt *5:20. √7:21-23, 26, 27. Lk 6:49. Ac *8:13, 21. 15:9. 1 C 13:2. 16:22. Ga *5:6, 13. 1 Th 1:3. 1 T 1:5. T 1:16. 3:8. He 11:7, 8, 17. 2 P 1:5. 1 J 5:4, 5. **faith.** √121Q1, Je

+28:5. **and.** √174, Ge +18:27. **have not.** Ja 1:22. **can.** ver. 17. Mk 16:16. Ac +*16:31. Ro 4:2. 1 C +*15:2. Ep *2:8-10.

15. **If a.** √184C, Mt +4:9. **brother or.** ver. 5. Le *25:35. Jb 31:16-21. Is 58:7, 10. Ezk 18:7. Mt *25:35-40. Mk 14:7. Lk +3:11. Ac 9:39. He 11:37. **be naked.** √171N, Ge +8:13. 2 Ch 28:15. **destitute.** Ac 11:29. +*20:35. Ro 15:26. Ga 2:10. 6:10. 1 T +*5:8. He +*13:16. 1 J √3:17.

16. **And one.** √184C, Mt +4:9. Jb 22:7-9. Pr 3:27, 28. Mt 14:15, 16. 15:32. 25:42-45. Ro 12:9. 2 C 8:8. 1 J √3:16-19. **Depart in peace.** Jg 18:6. 1 S 1:17. 20:13, 42. 2 S 15:9. Mk 5:34. Lk 7:50. 8:48. Ac 16:36. **what.** See on ver. 14.

17. **so.** ver. 14, 19, 20, 26. 1 C 13:3, 13. 1 Th 1:3. 1 T 1:5. 2 P 1:5-9. **faith.** √121Q1, Je +28:5. **if it.** √184C, Mt +4:9. **dead.** √100, Ge +10:9. **alone.** Gr. by itself.

18. **man may say.** Ro +9:19. **Thou.** ver. 14, 22. Ro 14:23. 1 C 13:2. Ga *5:6. He *11:6, 31. **show me.** Ja 3:13. **without thy works.** Some copies read, by thy works. ver. 20, 26. Ro 3:28. 4:6. He 11:33. **and I will.** ver. 22-25. Ja 3:13. Is 57:12. Mt *7:16, 17. Jn 13:35. *15:2. Ro 8:1. 2 C √5:17. *7:1. Ga *5:6. 1 Th 1:3-10. 1 T 1:5. T 2:7, 11-14. ◑3:5, 8. 1 J *1:6. *2:6, 29. 2 P *1:5-9. **my faith.** T#186. ver. 14-18. Ps +19:11 (T#302). +119:6 (T#602).

19. **Thou believest.** √169, Je +12:1. Ja 4:12. Dt +*6:4. Ne 9:6. Is 42:8. *43:10. *44:6, 8. *45:6, 21, 22. *46:9. Zc *14:9. Mk *12:29, 32. Jn +5:44. √17:3. Ro 2:17-25. *3:30. 1 C +*8:4, 6. Ga *3:20. Ep *4:5, 6. 1 T +*2:5. 2 T +*3:5. Ju 4. **thou doest.** ver. 8. Jon 4:4, 9. Mk 7:9. **the devils also.** Mt *8:28, 29. Mk +*1:24. *5:7. Lk *4:33, 34. Ac *16:16, 17. *19:15. 24:25. Ju 6. Re 20:2, 3, 10. **believe.** Ezk ◑*33:30-32. Mt 8:28, 29. Lk +*8:13. Ac *8:13, 20, 21. *26:27. 1 C +*15:2. **tremble.** Jb 4:15. Je 2:12. Mt 8:29. Mk 1:24. Lk 8:31.

20. **O vain.** Ja 1:26. Jg 9:4. Jb 11:11, 12. Ps 94:8-11. Pr 12:11. Je 2:5. Mt 5:22. Ro 1:21. 1 C 15:35, 36. Ga 3:1. 6:3. Col 2:8. 1 T 1:6. T 1:10. **that.** See on ver. 14. **faith.** √121Q1, Je +28:5. **without.** ver. +18. **dead.** or, barren. 2 P 1:8g.

21. **Abraham.** Ge 22:9, 12, 16-18. Jsh 24:3. Is 51:2. Mt 3:9. Lk 1:73. 16:24, 30. Jn 8:39, 53. Ac 7:2. Ro *4:1, 12, 16. **justified.** √121I2, Ge +2:17. ver. 18, 24. Ps 143:2. Mt 12:37. 25:31-40. Ro *3:20. Ro *11:17. **when.** Ge 22:9-12, 16-18.

22. **Seest thou.** or, Thou seest. **faith.** ver. 18. Ga *5:6. 1 Th +1:3. He 11:17-19. **faith made.** √121I2, Ge +2:17. 1 J *2:5. 4:17, 18.

23. **the scripture.** ver. 8. Ja 4:5. Mk 12:10. 15:28. Lk +*4:21. Ac 1:16. Ro 9:17. +*11:2. Ga 3:8-10, *22. 2 T +*3:16. 1 P 2:6. **fulfilled.** Mt +1:22. **Abraham.** Ge √15:6. Ro √4:3-6, 10, 11, 22-24. Ga *3:6. **believed.** T +3:8g. **the Friend.** T#649. Ex 33:11. 2 Ch *20:7. Jb 16:21mg. Is 1:24. *41:8. Mt +13:38 (T#690). Jn *15:13-15.

24. **see then.** ver. *15-18, 21, 22. **by works.** Mt *5:16. *25:34, 35, 40. Ro ◑*4:2, 20-22. *14:17, 18. Ga 3:6, 7, 12, 26, 29. Re 20:12. **justified.** √121I2, Ge +2:17. **faith.** √121Q1, Je +28:5.

25. **was.** Jsh 2:1. Mt 1:5, Rahab. **the harlot.** √11, Ge +2:23. √46C, Mt +8:6. Mt 21:31. He +*11:31n. **justified.** √121I2, Ge +2:17. ver. 18-22. **when.** Jsh 2:19-21. 6:17, 22-25. He *11:31. **received.** Lk +10:38.

26. **as the body.** Da +*12:2. Lk *16:22. Jn +*2:19, 21. 1 C *15:35. 2 C √5:8. **without.** Jb 34:14, 15. Ps 104:29. +*146:4. Ec +*12:7. Is 2:22. Lk 23:46. Ac +*7:59, 60. **spirit.** *or,* breath. Gr. *pneuma, ſ*121A3, Mt +27:50. Ps +*146:4. **so faith.** ſ121Q1, Je +28:5. See on ver. 14, 17, 20. Ep *2:8-10. **without.** ver. +18.

JAMES 3

A caution against an assuming and aspiring conduct, 1, 2. The fatal effects of an unbridled tongue, and the difficulty and duty of governing the tongue, 3-12. The nature and effects of earthly, and heavenly, wisdom contrasted, 13-18.

1. **be not.** Ml 2:12. Mt 9:11. 10:24. *23:8-10, 14. Jn 3:10. Ac 13:1. Ro 2:20, 21. 1 C 12:28, 29. Ep +*4:11. 1 T 1:7. 2 T 1:11g. 1 P +*5:3. **many masters.** Rather, "be not many of you teachers," *didaskaloi*; for many wish to be teachers who have more need to learn; and aspire to the office of teacher, without a proper call or suitable qualifications. **knowing.** Le 10:3. Ezk 3:17, 18. 33:7-9. Lk 6:37. +*12:47, 48. 16:2. Ac 20:26, 27. 1 C 4:2-5. 2 C 5:10. He *13:17. **receive.** Mk 12:40. Lk 20:47. **condemnation.** *or,* judgment. ſ37B, Ge +3:22. Mt *7:1, 2. 23:14. 1 C *11:29-32g.

2. **in.** 1 K +*8:46. 2 Ch 6:36. Pr 10:19. *20:9. Ec +*7:20. Is ◑53:9. √64:6. Ro *3:10. 7:21. Ga 3:22. 5:17. 1 J √1:8-10. **If.** ſ184A, 1 C +15:2. ver. 5, 6, √8. See on Ja 1:26. Ps *34:13. Pr 13:3. 1 P 3:10. **offend not.** Ja +2:10. Is 53:9. 1 P 2:22. **in word.** Jb *31:30. Ps *15:2-4. *39:1. Mt √12:36, 37. **a perfect.** See on Ja 1:4. Mt *12:37. Col 1:28. 4:12. He *13:21. 1 P *5:10. **to bridle.** Ja +1:26. 1 C *9:27.

3. **put bits.** Ja 1:26. 2 K 19:28. Ps *32:9. *39:1. Is 37:29.

4. **are driven.** Ps 107:25-27. Jon 1:4. Mt 8:24. Ac 27:14, etc. **governor.** ſ100, Ge +10:9.

5. **so.** Ex 5:2. 15:9. 2 K 19:22-24. Jb 21:14, 15. 22:17. Ps +*10:3. *12:2-4. 17:10. 52:1, 2. 73:8, 9. Pr 12:18. 15:2. *18:21. Je 9:3-8. 18:18. Ezk 28:2. 29:3. Da 3:15. 4:30. 2 P 2:18. Ju 16. Re 13:5, 6. **how great.** Ps 83:14. Pr 26:20, 21. Is 9:18. 10:16-18. Zc 12:6. **matter.** *or,* wood.

6. **the tongue.** T#728. Jg 12:4-6. 2 S 19:43. 20:1. 2 Ch *10:13-16. 13:17. Jb 5:21, 24. Ps +5:9 (T#702). +12:3 (T#198). 52:2, 4. *55:21. 57:4. *64:3. +*101:5. 120:2-4. *140:3. Pr *11:9, 11. *12:18. *13:13. *15:1, 4. *16:27, 28. *17:9, 28. 18:7, 8, 21. 25:18. *26:20, 21. Is ◑11:4. 30:27. ◑49:2. Je 9:3, 8. 18:18. Ho ◑6:5. Mt *15:18, 19. Jn +8:44 (T#416). **a world.** Gr. *kosmos,* Mt +4:8. ſ102, Ge +2:24. Ja 2:7. Ge +*3:4-6. Le *24:11. Nu 25:2. 31:16. Dt *13:6. Jg *16:15-20. 1 S 22:9-17. 2 S 13:26-29. 15:2-6. 16:20-23. 17:1, 2. 1 K *21:5-15. Ps 10:7. 34:13. *39:1. 52:2. Pr *1:10-14. *6:19. *7:5, 21:23. Is 3:8. 59:3. Je *20:10. *28:16. Mt *12:24, 32-36. *15:11-20. Mk +*7:15, 20-22. *14:55-57. Ac 5:3. 6:13. *20:30. Ro *3:13, 14. *16:17, 18. Ep *5:3, 4. Col *3:8, 9. 2 Th √2:10-12. T 1:11. 2 P *2:1, 2, 3.3. 3 J 10. Ju 8-10, 15-18. Re 2:14, 15. *13:1-5, 14. 18:23. *19:20. **that it.** Mt 12:34. 15:18. Mk 7:20. **defileth.** Ju 23. **body.** ſ171Q4, Ex +21:3mg. **course of nature.** Gr. *ton trochon geneseos,* literally, "the wheel of nature" or generation or birth; by which some understand the whole circle of human affairs; others, the course of man's life; and others, the successive generations of men; in all which senses the Apostle's

sentiment is true. Some think he alludes to the penal wheel of the Greeks, beneath which fire was placed; and others, that he refers to the circulation of blood. Ja 1:23g. Ezk 1:15, 16. **it is set.** Lk +*16:24. Ac *5:3. 2 C √11:13-15. 2 Th *2:9. Re *12:9. **hell.** Gr. *gehenna,* Mt +5:22.

7. **For every.** Ge 1:26. 9:2. **kind.** Gr. nature. **is tamed.** Mk 5:4g. **mankind.** Gr. the nature of man.

8. **no man.** ver. *2. 1 K +*8:46. **an unruly.** ver. 6, 16. Ja 1:8g. Ps 55:21. 57:4. 59:7. 64:3, 4. **full.** Dt 32:33. Jb 20:16. Ps 58:4. *140:3. Ec 10:11. Ro 3:13. Re 12:9.

9. **Therewith.** Ps +*16:9n. √30:12mg,n. 35:28. +*51:14. 57:8. 62:4. 71:24. 108:1. Ac 2:26. **bless.** 1 Ch 29:10, 20. Ps 34:1. 63:4. 145:1, 21. Is 29:13. Ep 1:3. 1 P 1:3. **God, even the.** ſ93A, Ge +1:26. Ja +1:27. Is *63:16. Mt 11:25. **therewith curse.** Jg 9:27. 2 S 16:5. 19:21. Ps 10:7. 59:12. 109:17, 18. Ec 7:22. Mt 5:44. 26:74. Ro 3:14. **made.** Ge *1:26, 27. 5:1. 9:6. 1 C 11:7. 15:49. 2 C 4:4. Ep 4:24. Col 3:10.

10. **Out of.** Ps 50:16-20. Pr 18:21. Je 7:4-10. Mi 3:11. Ro 12:14. 1 P 3:9. **these.** Ge 20:9. 2 S 13:12. 1 C 3:3. 1 T 5:13.

11. **Doth.** Mt 7:16-20. Lk 6:44. **place.** *or,* hole.

12. **the fig tree.** Is 5:2-4. Je 2:21. Mt 7:16-20. 12:33. Lk 6:43, 44. Ro 11:16-18. **so.** Ex 15:23-25. 2 K 2:19-22. Ezk 47:8-11.

13. **is a wise.** ver. 1. Dt 1:13. 4:6. Ps 107:43. Ec 8:1, 5. Je 9:12, 23. Ho 14:9. Mt 7:24. 1 C 6:5. Ga 6:4. **endued.** 2 Ch 2:12, 13. Jb 28:28. Is 11:3. Da 2:21. **let.** Ja 2:18. Is 60:6. 2 C 8:24. 1 P 2:9. **a good.** Ph 1:27. 1 T 4:12. He +*13:5. 1 P 2:12. 3:1, 2, 16. **conversation.** *or,* manner of life. Ga 1:13. Ep 4:22. 1 T 4:12. He 13:7. 1 P 1:15, 18. 2:12. 3:1, 2, 16. 2 P 2:7. 3:11g. **with meekness.** ver. 17. Ja 1:21. Nu 12:3. Ps +*25:9. 45:4. +*149:4. Is 11:4. 29:19. 61:1. Zp +*2:3. Mt +*5:5. √11:29. 21:5. 2 C 10:1. Ga *5:23. +*6:1. Ep 4:2. Col 3:12. 1 T *6:11. 2 T +*2:25. T 3:2. 1 P +*3:4, 15.

14. **if.** ſ184A, 1 C +15:2. ver. 16. Ja 4:1-5. Ge 30:1, 2. 37:11. Jb 5:2. Pr 14:30. 27:4. Is 11:13. Hab 1:3. Mt 27:18. Ac +5:17. 7:9. 13:45. Ro *1:29. 13:13. 1 C 3:3. 13:4. 2 C 12:20. Ga 5:15, 21, 26. Ph 1:15. +*2:3. 1 T 6:4. T 3:3. 1 P 2:1, 2. **and strife.** ver. 16. Ro 2:8. 13:13. 2 C 12:20. Ga 5:20. Ph 1:17. +*2:3. **glory.** Ro 2:17, 23, etc. 1 C 4:7, 8. 5:2, 6. Ga 6:13. **and lie.** 2 K 10:16, 31. Jn 16:2. Ac 26:9.

15. **wisdom.** ver. 17. Ja *1:5, 17. Jn 3:27. 1 C 3:3. Ph 3:19. **not from above.** Ja +*1:17. **but is.** 2 S 13:3. 15:31. 16:23. Je 4:22. Lk 16:8. Ro 1:22. 1 C 1:19, 20, 27. 2:6, 7. 3:19. 2 C 1:12. Ju 19. **earthly.** Jn 3:12. 1 C 15:40. 2 C 5:1. Ph 2:10. 3:19g. **sensual.** *or,* natural. 1 C √2:14. 15:44, 46. Ju 19g. **devilish.** Gr. demoniacal. Ge 3:1-5. 1 K 22:22. Jn √8:44. Ac 13:10. 2 C *11:3, 13-15. 2 Th 2:9, 10. 1 T 4:1. 1 J 3:8-10. Ju 19. Re 2:24. 9:11. 12:9.

16. **where.** ver. +14. 1 C *3:3. Ga 5:20. **there.** Ge 11:9mg. Ac 19:29. 1 C 14:33. **confusion.** Gr. tumult, *or,* unquietness. ver. 8. Pr 26:28. Lk 21:9g. **every.** 1 J 3:12. **evil work.** Ga √5:19, 21.

17. **the wisdom.** ver. 15. Ja 1:5, 17. Ge 41:38, 39. Ex 36:2. 1 K 3:9, 12, 28. 1 Ch 22:12. Jb 28:12, 23, 28. 32:7. Pr 2:6. 4:7. Is 11:2, 3. Da 1:17. Ho 14:9. Mt 7:24. Lk 21:15. 1 C 2:6, 7. 12:8. 2 T 3:15. **first pure.** Ja *4:8. Ml 3:3. Mt +*5:8. 2 C 7:11. Ph √4:8. T 1:15. 1 J 3:3. **peaceable.** ver. 18. Ja ◑4:4. 1 Ch

22:9mg. Pr 3:17. Is 2:4. +*9:6, 7. 11:2-9. 32:15-17. Ro 12:18. He 12:11, +*14. **gentle.** Is 40:11. 1 C 13:4-7. 2 C 10:1. Ga *5:22, 23. Ep 5:9. Ph 4:5. 1 Th 2:7. 1 T 3:3. 2 T *2:24. T 3:2. 1 P 2:18. **easy.** Ps +*19:7. +*25:9. Pr +*8:9. **to be entreated.** 1 S ◐+*25:17. 2 K +*5:13. Ro +*12:3, 10, 16. Ga ◐2:5. Ep *5:21. Ph +*2:3. 1 P *5:5. **full.** Lk +*6:36. Jn 1:14. Ac 9:36. 11:24. Ro 15:14. 2 C 9:10. Ph 1:11. Col +*1:10. **good fruits.** Ga +*5:22, 23. **without.** Ja 1:6. 2:4. Ml 2:9. 1 T 5:21. **partiality.** or, wrangling. Ge +*44:30. **hypocrisy.** Is 32:6. Mt 23:28. Lk 12:1, 2. Jn 1:47. Ro +*12:9. 2 C 6:6. 1 T 1:5. 2 T 1:5. 1 P 1:22g. 2:1. 1 J 3:18.

18. **the fruit.** ver. 17. Ja *1:20. Pr *11:18, 28, 30. Is 32:16, *17. Ho *10:12. Am 6:12. Mt *5:9. Jn *4:36. Ph *1:11. Re *12:11. **is sown.** Pr +*11:30. Mt +*5:9. Ga +*6:7, 8. **make.** Is +*45:7. Mt +*5:9. Ep 2:15.

JAMES 4

Wars and contentions spring from the lusts of the human heart, which produce the most fatal effects, and always end in disappointment, 1, 2; because men do not ask good gifts from God; or because "they ask amiss," 3. "The friendship of the world is enmity against God," 4. "The spirit that is in us lusteth to envy" and pride; but "God resisteth the proud, and showeth favor to the humble," 5, 6. Exhortations to repentance and submission to God, 7-10. Cautions against destruction and censoriousness, and against carnal security; with instructions to consider the uncertainty of life, and to trust God in every undertaking, 11-17.

1. **whence.** Ja 3:14-18. **wars.** Je 1:19. 15:20. **wars.** ✓102, Ge +2:24. **fightings.** or, brawlings. **come they.** Ja 1:14. Ge 4:5-8. Je 17:9. Mt 15:19. Mk +*7:21-23. Jn ✓8:44. Ro 8:7. 1 T 6:4-10. T 3:3. 1 P 1:14. 2:11. 4:2, 3. 2 P 2:18. 3:3. 1 J ✓2:15-17. Ju 16-18. **lusts.** or, pleasures. So ver. 3. **that war.** Ro 7:23. 1 P 2:11. **in your.** Ro *6:12, 13. 7:5, 23. Ga *5:17. Col *3:5.

2. **lust.** Ja 5:1-5. Pr 1:19. Ec 4:8. Hab 2:5. 1 T +*6:9, 10. **kill.** or, envy. Ja 5:6. **desire.** or, covet. Gr. desire to have. ✓93B, Is +66:11. Ps +*10:3. Ac +7:6. **ye have not.** ver. +*3. Jn +*9:31. **because.** Ja 1:5. Is 7:12. Mt *7:7, 8. Lk ✓11:9-13. Jn 4:10. 16:24. **ye ask not.** Jsh +*9:14. Jg 20:23, 26. 2 K=13:18, 19. Is 29:15. Je +✓10:25.

3. **ask, and.** Ja 1:6, 7. Jb 27:8-10. 35:12. Ps 18:41. *66:18, 19. Pr *1:28. 15:8. 21:13, 27. Is 1:15, 16. Je 11:11, 14. 14:12. Mi 3:4. Zc 7:13. Mt +7:7. *20:22. Mk 10:38. Jn +*9:31. 1 J 3:22. *5:14. **receive not.** For a summary of Scriptural reasons for unanswered prayer, see T#1792-1813. Ja 1:6, 7. Dt 1:45. 1 S 14:37. 28:6. Ps *66:18. Pr *1:28. 21:13. 28:9. Is 1:15. ✓59:2. Mi 3:4. Zc 7:13. 2 C 12:8. Jn 9:4. **ask amiss.** T#1792. Nu 11:15. 1 K ◐3:11, 12. 19:4. Ps ◐84:11. *106:15. Pr ◐30:8, 9. Jon 4:3. Mt 5:23, 24. 20:21. Lk 12:13. Jn 18:23g. 1 J ✓5:14. **ye may.** Lk 15:13, 30. 16:1, 2. **consume.** Lk 15:14g. **lusts.** or, pleasures. ver. 1. Lk +*8:14.

4. **adulterers.** Ps 50:18. 73:27. Is 57:3. Je 9:2. Ho 3:1. Mt +12:39. 16:4. **and adulteresses.** Is 54:5. Je 2:2. Ezk 16:32. 2 P 2:14. **the friendship.** Jn 7:7. *15:19, 23. 17:14. 2 C *6:14, 17, 18. 1 J ✓2:15, 16. **world.** Gr. kosmos, Mt +4:8. **enmity.** Ja ◐3:17. Ge +*3:15. Mt 10:34-38. Jn 15:18, 19. Ro *8:7. Ep 2:15. 1 P 4:12-19. 1 J ✓2:15-17. 3:7-10. 4:1-6. **whosoever.** Mt 6:24. Lk 16:13. Jn *15:19. Ga *1:10. 1 J ✓2:15. **world.** Gr.

kosmos, Mt +4:8. **is the.** Ps 21:8. Lk 19:27. Jn 15:23, 24. Ro 5:10.

5. **think that.** Nu 23:19. **the scripture.** Lk +4:21. Jn 7:42. *10:35. 19:37. Ro 9:17. Ga 3:8. **The spirit.** Gr. *pneuma,* ✓121A3, Mt +27:50. Ge 4:5, 6. 6:5. 8:21. 26:14. 30:1. 37:11. Nu 11:29. Ps 37:1. 106:16. Pr 21:10. Ec 4:4. Is 11:13. Ac 7:9. Ro 1:29. T 3:3. **that dwelleth.** 1 C 6:19. 2 C 6:16. **lusteth.** Ga 5:19-24. **to envy.** or, enviously. Je 3:14. Ho 2:19. 2 C *11:2.

6. **he giveth.** Ja +1:12. Is 54:7, 8. Mt +13:12. **more grace.** 1 C +1:4. 2 C ✓12:9, 10. **God resisteth.** Ex 10:3, 4. 15:9,10. 18:11. 1 S 2:3. Jb 22:29. 40:10-12. Ps *138:6. Pr ⟩3:34. 6:16, 17. +*13:15. 29:23. Is 2:11, 12, 17. 10:8-14. 16:6, 7. Da 4:37. 5:20-23. Mt 23:12. Lk *1:52. 14:11. 18:14. 2 C 7:6. 1 P *5:5. **the proud.** Ps +*119:21. **giveth grace.** 2 Ch 32:26. 33:12, 19, 23. *34:27. Jb 22:29. Ps 9:12. Pr 15:33. 18:12. 22:4. Is +*57:15. **the humble.** T#932. Jb 22:29. Ps 9:12. 10:17. 138:6. Pr ⟩3:34. 11:2. 15:33. 16:19. 18:12. 22:4. 29:23. Mt *18:4. *23:12. Lk 18:14. 1 P 5:5, 6.

7. **Submit.** T#298. Le 26:41-43. Dt 27:26. 1 S 3:18. 2 S 15:26. 2 K 1:13-15. 2 Ch 30:8. 33:12, 13. Jb 1:21. 40:3-5. 42:1-6. Ps 32:3-5. +37:7 (T#536). +39:9 (T#278). 66:3. 68:30. Is 45:9. Je 13:18. Da 4:25, 32, 34-37. Mt 6:9,10. 11:29. Ac 9:6. 16:29-31. 26:19. Ro 10:3. 14:11. Ep 5:21. He 12:9. 1 P 2:13. **Resist.** Mt 4:3-11. Lk 4:2-13. Ep *4:27. *6:11, 12. 1 P *5:8, 9. Re 12:9-11. **will flee.** T#813. Ge 3:15. Lk 22:31, 32. Ro *16:20. 1 J 2:14. *5:18.

8. **Draw nigh to God.** Ge 18:23. 45:4. 1 Ch +*28:9. 2 Ch 15:2. Ps 73:28. 145:18. Is 29:13. 48:16. ✓55:6, 7. La 3:57. Da *9:3. Ho +*6:1, 2. *14:1, 2. Zc 1:3. Ml 3:7. Lk 15:20. He 7:19. +*10:22. **Cleanse.** T#1316. Ex=30:18. Jb 9:30. 16:17. 17:9. Ps 18:20. 24:4. 26:6. 73:13. Is *1:15, 16. 33:15. Je 2:22. Mt 15:2. 27:24. 1 T 2:8. 1 P 3:21. **hands.** 2 S 22:21, 25. Jb 17:9. Ps 24:3, 4. 26:6. **purify.** Ps 51:6, 7, 10. Je 4:14. Ezk *18:31. 36:25-27. Mt 12:33. 23:25, 26. Lk 11:39, 40. Ac 15:9. 2 C *7:1. 1 P ✓1:22. 1 J *3:3. **ye double.** See on Ja 1:8. Ho 10:2. Mt *6:24.

9. **afflicted.** Ja 5:1, 2. Ps 119:67, 71, 136. +*126:5, 6. Ec 7:2-5. Is 22:12, 13. Je 9:18. 31:9, 13, 18-20. Ezk 7:16. 16:63. Jl 1:13. Mi 3:4. Zc 12:10, etc. Mt +*5:4. Lk 6:21, 25. 23:28. 2 C *7:10, 11. **let.** Jb 30:31. Pr 14:13. Ec 2:2. 7:6. La 5:15. Lk 6:25. 16:25. Re 18:7, 8.

10. **Humble.** T#357. See on ver. 6, 7. Le 26:41, 42. 1 K 21:27. 2 Ch +✓7:14 (T#607). 12:7. Jb 5:11. 22:29. Ps 9:12. 10:17. 138:6. Pr 3:34. 15:33. 22:4. 29:23. Is +*57:15. Ezk 21:26. Da 9:3. Mi +*6:8. Mt +*5:3. Lk 1:52. +13:3 (T#606). 18:14. 2 C 11:7. 1 P *5:5, 6. **he.** 1 S 2:9. Jb 22:29. Ps 27:6. 28:9. 30:1. 113:7. 147:6. Mt +23:12. Lk 14:11. 18:14. 1 P 5:6.

11. **Speak.** Ja 5:9. Ex 20:16. Ps 50:20. 101:5. 140:11. Ro 1:30. 2 C 12:20. Ep *4:31. 1 T 3:11. 2 T 3:3. T 3:2. 1 P 2:1, 12. 3:16. **and judgeth.** Mt +*7:1, 2. Lk *6:37. Ro 2:1. *14:3, 4, 10-12. 1 C +*4:5. **speaketh evil of the law.** Ja 2:8. Ro *7:7, 12, 13. **if.** ✓184A, 1 C +15:2. **a doer.** Ja *1:22, 23, 25. 1 K 11:34. Jn +*17:6. Ro 2:13. 1 J +*2:3.

12. **is one.** Ja 2:19. **lawgiver.** Is 33:22. **able.** 2 K 5:7. Mt +*10:28. Lk +*12:5. He *7:25. **destroy.** Gr. *apollumi,* Mt +2:13. **who.** 1 S 25:10. Jb 38:2. Ro 2:1. +9:20. 14:4, 13.

13. **Go to.** Ja 5:1. Ge 11:3, 4, 7. Ec 2:1. Is 5:5. **To day.** Pr *27:1. Is 56:12. Lk 12:17-20. **will go.** ✓96B,

Mt +11:6. **and.** ✔148, Ge +8:22. **continue.** ✔171J2, Ac +15:33. Mt 20:12. Re 13:5g. **and buy.** Is 24:2. 56:11. Ezk 7:12. 1 C 7:30.

14. **morrow.** Pr 27:1. Mt 6:34. **It is.** *or*, For it is. **a vapor.** Ja 1:10. Jb *7:6, 7, 9. 8:9. 9:25, 26. 14:1, 2. Ps 39:5. 89:47. 90:5-7. *102:3. 144:4. Is 38:12. 1 P 1:24. 4:7. 1 J 2:17. **a little time.** T#148. Ge *47:9. Dt ◐+*5:16. 2 S 19:34mg. 1 Ch *29:15. Jb 7:+1 (T#146), 6. *8:9. 9:25, 26. 14:1, 2. Ps *39:5. +89:47 (T#726). *90:10, +12 (T#727). *102:11. *103:15, 16. 109:23. 144:4. Ec 6:12. Is +*38:10. 40:6, 7. *64:6. 1 C *7:29-31. +*11:30. 1 P 1:24. 1 J *2:17. **vanisheth.** Ac 13:41.

15. **If.** ✔184C, Mt +4:9. 2 S 15:25, 26. Ps 31:15. Pr *19:21. La *3:37. Ac +*18:21. Ro *1:10. *15:32. 1 C 4:19. *16:7. He *6:3. **we shall.** ✔96B, Mt +11:6.

16. **ye rejoice.** Ja 3:14. Ps 52:1, 7. Pr 25:14. 27:1. Is 47:7, 8, 10. 1 C 4:7, 8. 5:6. Re 18:7. **boastings.** 1 J 2:16. **all such.** Ja 1:9. 1 C 5:6.

17. **knoweth.** Lk +*12:47, 48. Jn 5:39. +9:41. +*13:17. 15:22. Ro 1:20, 21, 32. 2:17-23. 7:13. 2 T 2:15. 2 P 2:21. 3:18. **to do good.** Ja 1:27. 3:17. Ps 1:1-3. 15:1-5. 34:14. 37:3, 27. 122:6. Is +*66:4. Mi 2:7. +*6:8. Lk +*6:35. √16:10. Ro 13:3. 1 C *15:58. Ga +*6:10. Ph √3:12. 1 T *4:13. +*6:18. He +*13:16. 1 P 2:15. 3:11, 17. 2 P *3:18. **doeth it not.** Ja 3:2, 8. Jg 5:23. 21:8. Ne 3:5. 9:35. Ps *109:16. Pr 21:13. Je 8:20. +*48:10. Ezk +*16:49. 34:4. Mt 7:26. 23:23. 25:27, 45. Lk 11:42. +*12:47. √17:10. 1 T *4:14. **sin.** Ja 2:10, 11. Pr 10:19. 14:21. *24:9. Ho 6:8. Mt 5:28. Ro 3:10. 4:15. 5:12. *14:23. 1 C 8:12. 1 J √1:8, 10. *3:4. *5:17.

JAMES 5

Judgments are denounced on the rich and wicked Jews, 1-6. Christians are exhorted to patience and meekness under their trials, in hope of a speedy deliverance, 7-11. A caution against swearing; and an admonition to prayer and praise, 12, 13. Instructions concerning the elders visiting the sick, 14, 15; and concerning Christians confessing their sins to each other, with prayer for one another; and a declaration of the efficacy of fervent prayer, 17, 18. An encouragement to attempt the conversion of sinners, and the recovery of offending brethren, 19, 20.

1. **Go.** See on Ja 4:13. **ye rich.** ✔38B, 2 S +1:24. Ja 1:11. 2:6. Dt 8:12-14. 32:15. Ne 9:25, 26. Jb 20:15-29. Ps 17:14. 49:6-20. 73:3-9, 18-20. Pr *11:4, 28. Ec 5:13, 14. Je +*9:23. Am 6:1. Mi 6:12. Zp 1:18. Mt 19:23, 24. Lk *6:24. 12:16-21. 16:19-25. 1 T +*6:9, 10. Re 6:15-24. **weep.** ✔96B, Ge +20:7. Ja 4:9. Is 13:6. 15:2, 3, 8. 16:7. 22:12, 13. Je 4:8. 51:8. Ezk 19:2. 30:2. Jl 1:5, 11, 13. Am 6:6, 7. Zc 11:2, 3. Lk 6:25. 23:28, 29. **miseries.** Ro 3:16. **that shall come.** Pr +*11:4. Ezk √7:19. Zp +*1:11. Mt *24:1, 2, 21.

2. **Your riches.** Je 17:11. Ezk 17:9, 10. Mt *6:19, 20. Lk 12:33. 1 P 1:4. **your garments.** Ja 2:2. Jb 13:28. Ps 39:11. Is 50:9. 51:8. Ho 5:12.

3. **is.** ✔96C6. Heterosis of Tenses, Present put for Future. "The present tense is often put for the future, to show that the thing spoken of shall as certainly happen as if it were already present" (Peters, *Theocratic Kingdom*, vol. 1, p. 415, citing Macnight). For other instances of this figure, see Mt +2:4. Ro 8:30. He 12:22n. **cankered.** 2 T 2:17. **the rust.** Mt *6:20. **a wit-**

---

ness. Ge 31:48, 52. Jsh 24:27. Jb 16:8. Mt +8:4. Lk 9:5. **and shall.** Je 19:9. Mi 3:3. Re 17:16. 20:15. +*21:8. **Ye have.** Dt 32:33, 34. Jb 14:16, 17. Mt 6:19. Lk 12:21. Ro *2:5. 1 T ◐+*6:19. 2 P 3:7. **heaped treasure.** ✔63A2, 2 S +6:6. By ellipsis, supply "ye have treasured up (wrath) for the last days." **the last days.** ver. 8, 9. See on Ge 49:1. Is +*2:2. Mi 4:1. Jn +*6:54n. Ac 2:17. 2 T 3:1. 2 P 3:3. 1 J +2:18.

4. **the hire.** Le +*19:13. Dt +*24:14, 15. Jb 24:10, 11. 31:38, 39. Is 5:7. Je *22:13. Hab 2:11. Zc *8:10. Ml +*3:5. Mt 10:10. Lk *10:7. Col +*4:1. 1 T +*5:18. **fields.** Lk 21:21. Jn 4:35g. **kept back.** Le +*19:13. Dt +*24:15. Pr *3:27, 28. **by fraud.** Le +*19:13. Je 22:13. Ml +*3:5. Mk 10:19. Lk 3:13. 1 Th 4:6. **the cries.** Ge +*4:10. Ex *2:23, 24. *3:9. +*22:22-24, 27. Dt *15:9. +*24:15. Jb *34:28. 35:9. Ps *9:12. +*12:5. *34:15-17. Pr +*22:22, 23. 30:10. Lk *18:7. **the ears.** ✔22A8, Ps +10:17. **Lord.** Ro *9:29. Is *1:9h. **of sabaoth.** Is +*6:5. 44:6. 54:5. Je 10:16. 50:34. 51:19. Jn 12:37-41. Ro 9:29.

5. **have lived.** 1 S 25:6, 36. Jb *21:11-15. Ps 17:14. 73:7. Ec 11:9. Is 5:11, 12. 47:8. 56:12. Am 6:1, 4-6. Lk *16:19, 25. 1 T 5:6. 2 T 3:4. 2 P 2:13. Ju 12. Re 18:7. **been wanton.** Is 3:16. Ro 13:13. 1 T +5:6. **your hearts.** Jg 19:5. Ps 104:15. Lk 21:34. Ac 14:17. **as in.** Pr 7:14. 17:1. Is 22:13. 34:2, 6. Je 12:3. 25:34. Ezk 21:15. 39:17. Re 19:17, 18.

6. **have condemned.** Ja 2:6. Mt 21:38. 23:34, 35. 27:20, 24, 25. Jn 16:2, 3. Ac 2:22, 23. 3:14, 15. 4:10-12. *7:52. *9:5. 13:27, 28. 22:14. 1 Th 2:15, 16. **killed.** Ja 4:2. 1 Th *2:14-16. **the just.** Ac 3:14. *7:52. 22:14. 1 P 3:18. 1 J 2:1. **and he.** ✔41, Ge +10:1. Is *53:7. Mt 5:39. √26:53, 54. Lk 22:51-53. Jn 19:9-11. Ac 8:32. 1 P 2:22, 23.

7. **Be patient.** *or*, Be long patient, *or*, Suffer with long patience. ✔18, Dt +28:4. Lk *8:15. Ro 2:7. 8:24, 25. +*15:4. 2 C 6:4, 5. Ga 5:5. +*6:9. Col *1:11. 1 Th 1:3. 2 Th 1:4-10. 3:5. He 6:15. 10:36, 37. *12:1-3. 1 P 4:12, 13. **unto.** ver. 8, 9. Mt 24:27, 44. Lk 18:8. 21:27. Jn +21:22. 1 C 1:7. 1 Th 2:19. 3:13. 2 P 3:4. **coming.** Gr. *parousia*, Mt +24:3. 1 Th +2:19. 2 P 3:9. **waiteth for.** Ro 5:1, 2. *8:24. 2 Th 1:5-11. 1 P 1:5, 7, 13. 4:13. 5:1, 4, 10. 1 J 2:28. *3:2. **patience for.** Lk 18:7g. **the early.** Dt 11:14. Je 5:24. Ho *6:3. Jl *2:23. Zc *10:1. **latter rain.** Jb 29:23. Pr 16:15.

8. **ye also.** Ge 49:18. Ps *37:7. 40:1-3. 130:5. La 3:25, 26. Mi 7:7. Hab 2:3. Ro 8:25. Ga 5:22. 1 Th +*1:10. 2 Th 3:5. He 10:35-37. **stablish.** Ps 27:14. 1 Th 3:13. 1 P +5:10. **for.** ver. 9. Ph 4:5. He +*10:25, 37. 1 P 4:7. Re 22:20. **coming.** Gr. *parousia*, Mt +24:3. Mt *24:2, 30. **draweth nigh.** Is 54:7. Jl 2:1. Ro +*13:11, 12. 1 C 7:29-31. 10:11. Ph *4:5. 2 Th ◐+*2:2. He 10:25, 27. 1 P 4:7. Re 1:1. *22:7, 12, 20.

9. **Grudge not.** *or* grieve not. *or*, murmur not. Ja 4:11. Le +*19:18. Nu +*11:1. Ps 59:15. *73:3, 19, 24. Mk 6:19mg. 2 C 9:7. Ga 5:14, 26. Ph *2:14. 1 P 4:9. **lest.** Mt 6:14, 15. *7:1, 2. Lk 6:37. **the Judge.** Ja +4:12. Ge 4:7. Mt 24:33. Jn 5:22. 1 C +*4:5. 10:11. 1 P 4:5. Re 22:12. **before the door.** Mt *24:33. Mk 13:29. Re *3:20.

10. **the prophets.** Da 12:12. Mt 5:10. +12. 1 P 3:14. **who have spoken.** Is 39:8. Je 23:22. 26:16. Mt 1:22. Ac +*3:21. He *13:7. **in the name.** ver. 14. Ac +2:21. **for.** 2 Ch *36:16. Je *2:30. Mt +*5:11, 12. 21:34-39. 23:34-37. Lk 6:23. 13:34. Ac 7:52. 1 Th 2:14, 15. He

*11:32-38. **example**. He +4:11g. **patience**. Ep +4:2g.
11. **we count**. Ja *1:3, 4, 12. Ps *94:12. Mt +*5:10,
11. *10:22. Ro +*2:7. He +*3:6, 14. 10:39. **Ye**. Jb
*1:21, 22, etc. √2:10. *13:15, 16. *23:10. **Job**. i.e. *the
persecuted; he that weeps or cries*, ✻S#2492g. For
✻S#347h, see Jb +1:1. **seen the end**. √121P6, Pr
+23:18. Jb *42:10-17. Ps 37:37. Ec 7:8. Je +*29:11.
1 P 1:6, 7, 13. 2 P *2:9. **the Lord is**. Ex +*34:6. Nu
*14:18. 1 Ch 21:13. 2 Ch 30:9. Ne 9:17, 31. Ps *25:6,
7. +*51:1. 78:38. 86:5, 15. *103:8, 13. 111:4. 116:5.
119:132. 136:1, etc. 145:8. Is √55:6, 7. 63:7, 9. Je
+*29:11. La 3:22. Da 9:9, 18, 19. Jl 2:13. Jon 4:2.
Mi +*7:18. Lk 1:50. 6:36. Ro 2:4. 2 C 1:3. Ep 1:6.
2:4. **pitiful**. *or*, compassionate. T#225. Ex 32:14. Jg
10:16. Jb +36:7 (T#585). Ps 25:6. 36:7. 69:16. 78:38.
86:15. 103:13. +140:12 (T#522). 145:8, 9. La +*3:22,
32, 33. Ho 11:8. Jon +4:2 (T#233). Lk +*6:35. 1 P
3:8.
12. **above**. 1 P 4:8. 3 J 2. **swear not**. Ex 20:7. Le
19:12. See on Mt *5:33-37. *23:16-22. **but**. See on
2 C 1:17-20. **lest**. Ja 3:1, 2. 1 C 11:34.
13. **afflicted**. T#1217. Dt 4:27, 29, 30. 2 Ch 33:10-
13. Jb 33:26. Ps *18:4-6. +*50:15. 91:15. 106:44.
*116:3-6. 118:5. 119:107, 153. 142:1-3. La 1:9-11. 2:18,
19. 3:55, 56. Ho *5:15. 6:1. Jon 2:1, 2, 7. Mt 26:38,
39. Lk 22:44. 23:42. Ac 16:24, 25. 2 C √12:7-10. He
5:7. **pray**. Ps 50:14, 15. **Is any**. √18, Dt +28:4. **merry**.
Jg 16:23-25. Da 5:4. Ac +27:22. **let him sing**. 1 Ch
16:9. Ps 95:2. 105:2. Mi 4:5. Mt 26:30. Ac *16:25.
Ro 15:9. 1 C 14:15, 26. Ep 5:19g. Col *3:16, 17. Re
5:9-14. 7:10. 14:3. 19:1-6.
14. **any sick**. T#1280. 2 K *20:1-6. Ps 107:17-20.
2 T +*4:20. **for the elders**. T#103. Ac +11:30. *14:23.
15:4, 6. 16:4. *20:17. Ph 1:1. T 1:5. **pray**. 1 K 17:21.
2 K 4:33. 5:11. Ac 9:40. 28:8. **anointing**. T#1221. Mk
*6:13. +16:18. **in the name**. ver. 10. Mt +*28:19.
Ac 2:+21, 38. 10:48. 19:5. 1 C 1:13, 15.
15. **the prayer of faith**. T#189. See on ver. 13,
16. Ja 1:6. Mt *9:+2, 6, 7. +10:1 (T#100). 14:29-31.
17:20, 21. *21:20-22. Mk *11:22-24. *16:17, 18. Jn
*14:12, 13. Ac 9:40. 28:8. 1 C 12:8-10, 28-30. **shall
save**. Mk +10:52. **and if**. √184C, Mt +4:9. Mt 21:21g.
have committed. Is 33:24. Mt 9:2-6. Mk 2:5-11. Lk
+7:48. 13:2-5. Jn 5:14. *9:2, 3. 1 C 11:30-32. 1 J +3:4g.
*5:14-16. **forgiven**. Ps +*103:3. 130:4. Ezk 18:22. Mt
6:14. Mk 3:28. Ac 5:31. 13:38. 26:18. Ep 1:7. 1 J
√1:9.
16. **Confess**. Gr. *exomologeo*, S#1843g, Mk +1:5.
To confess from the heart, freely, publicly, openly
(Thayer). It denotes full and unreserved confession
or acknowledgment (Cremer, p. 772). The confession
specified is voluntary (though not optional, the verb
here is second person, plural number, middle voice,
imperative mode, and so a command), not one-way
auricular confession to a pastor or priest, not merely
to the elders, nor to the church in a public meeting,
not just to those we have offended, but to one another,
to one in right standing with God, with the purpose
of securing mutual informed interest, counsel, and
prayer support. T#1235. Ge 41:9, 10. Ex 10:16, 17.
Nu 21:7. Jsh 7:19. 2 S 12:13. 19:19. Ps 106:33n. *119:26.
Pr +*28:13. Mt 3:6. 5:24. √18:15-17. Lk 7:3, 4. 17:4.
Ac +*19:18. **faults**. Ps 19:12. Gr. *paraptoma*,
✻S#3900g. A falling aside, when one should have stood
upright. Hence (morally) a fall, a falling aside from
truth and equity; a fault, or trespass (CB). Mt 6:14

(trespasses), 15, 15. 18:35. Mk 11:25, 26. Ro 4:25 (offenses). 5:15, 15, 16, 17, 18, 20. 11:11 (fall), 12. 2 C
5:19 (trespasses). Ga *6:1 (fault). Ep 1:7 (sins). 2:1 (trespasses), 5 (sins). Col 2:13 (sins), 13 (trespasses). **one
to another**. Ps 106:33n. Mt 5:23, 24. √18:15-17. Ro
+12:5. 15:1. Ga +*6:1. He +*3:12, 13. 10:24, 25.
pray one for another. 1 S *12:23. Ro 15:30. Ep 6:18.
Col 1:9. 1 Th 5:*17, 23, 25. He *13:18. **that ye**. ver.
14. Ge *20:17. 2 Ch *30:20. Ps +*103:3. Mt 8:14-
17. 13:15. Lk 9:6. Ac *10:38. He 12:13. 1 P 2:24.
The effectual. "On the word *energoumenee*, inwardly
energizing in devotion and love to God, so as to produce
external effects in obedience" see the following reference passages. "Observe, therefore, how happily the
two emphatic words *dikaiou* (righteous) and *energoumenee* are (in the Greek text) reserved for the end
of the sentence, to give weight and force to the whole;
and to make it sink into the ears and hearts of hearers
and readers of the Epistle; and to teach the faithful
of every age, that it is holiness of life and devotion of
heart which give efficacy to Prayer" (Wordsworth,
Greek Testament, vol. 4, p. 34). Zc 12:10. Ro 8:26.
2 C 1:6. Ga *5:6. Ep 3:20. Col 1:29. 1 Th √2:13. **fervent
prayer**. Ge 18:23-32. 19:29. *20:7, 17. *32:28. Ex 9:28,
29, 33. *17:11. 32:10-14. Nu *11:2. *14:13-20. *21:7-
9. Dt *9:18-20. Jsh 10:12. 1 S *12:18. 1 K *13:6. *17:18-
24. 2 K *4:33-35. *19:15-20. √20:2-5. 2 Ch 14:11, 12.
*32:20-22. Jb +*42:8. Ps 10:17, 18. +*34:15. +√62:8.
*145:18, 19. Je 15:1. *29:12, 13. √33:3. Da 2:18-23.
*9:20-22. Ho 12:3, 4. Mt √7:7-11. *21:22. Lk 11:11-
13. *18:1-8. Ac *4:24-31. *12:5-12. 1 P 3:12. 1 J *3:22.
a righteous. Pr +*15:8, 29. *28:9. Jn +*9:31. Ro 3:10.
*5:19. He 11:4, 7. 1 J *3:7. **availeth much**. On this
passage, Wordsworth notes "It is the inner working
of the heart, moved by a spirit of love, that prevails
with God. The wrestlings of Jacob in prayer, the yearn-
ings of Hanna's heart, these gain a blessing from Him."
Ge 18:23. Ex 8:13. 32:10-14. *33:17. 1 S 12:18. 1 K
13:6. Jb 42:8-10. Is 45:11, 19. Lk +*11:9, 10. 18:7,
8. Ac *10:4. 2 C 1:11. Ph *1:19. Col 4:12. Phm *22.
He 5:7. 1 J *5:14.
17. **Elias**. 1 K 17:1, Elijah. **subject**. Ac 10:26. 14:15.
and he prayed. √106, Ge +31:7. Ro +*11:2. Re 11:6.
earnestly. *or*, in prayer. √147D, Ge +1:29. T#1327.
Lk *22:44. Ps +*119:145. Ro 8:26. Col 2:1, 2. 1 Th
3:10. Mt *5:7. **not rain**. T#1666. 1 K 17:1. **and it
rained not**. Lk 4:25.
18. **he prayed**. 1 K *18:18, 42-45. Je 14:22. Ac 14:17.
gave rain. T#1665. 1 S 12:16-18. 1 K 18:42-45. 2 Ch
6:26, 27. +*7:13, 14. Zc *10:1.
19. **if**. √184A, 1 C +15:2. Col +*1:23. 2 T *2:12.
He *3:14. 2 P +*1:10. **err from**. Ps 119:21, 118. Pr
+*19:27. Is 3:12. Mk +*12:24. 1 C +*15:2. Ep +*4:14.
1 Th +*3:5n. 1 T +*4:1n. *6:10, 21. 2 T *2:18, 25,
26. 2 P *3:17. Ju 11. **and one convert him**. ver. *20.
Le +*19:17. 1 S *9:27. Ps +*51:13. Ezk 34:4, 16.
Da +*12:3. Ml 2:6. Mt *18:15. Lk 1:16. *15:3-7.
*22:32. Ga +*6:1. 1 Th *2:13. He +*3:12, 13. 6:◑+*6,
*9n. *10:24. 12:12, 13. 1 J +*5:16. Ju *22, *23. Re
3:14-22.
20. **that he**. ver. *19. **the sinner**. Ja +*4:17. **the
error of**. T#175. Ps 19:12. Pr +*19:27. Ec 7:29. Mt
+15:14 (T#477). 16:12. Jn +1:12 (T#183). 1 C +*6:9-
11. 15:33. Ga 1:6, 7. 5:9, 19-21. 2 Th 2:11, 12. 2 T
*2:16-18, 26. He +*3:12, 13. *10:26. *12:15. 2 P *2:1.
*3:17. **shall save**. Pr *11:30. Ezk 13:19. Da +*12:3.

Ro 11:14. 1 C 7:16. *9:22. 1 T +*4:16. Phm 19. Ju *23. **soul.** Gr. *psyche*, ⨍171Q1A, Ac 2:41. **from death.** Ja *1:15. Pr *10:2. *11:4. Jn √5:24. 2 T +*2:25. 1 J

+*5:16. Re *20:6. **hide.** Ne 4:5. Ps *32:1. 85:2. Pr *10:12. Is *43:25. 1 P *4:8. 1 J *1:7. **a multitude.** Ezk 28:18.

1 PETER

1 PETER 1

The apostle addressed the strangers of the dispersion in Pontus, etc., with salutations, and thanksgivings to God for his abundant mercy, and the inestimable blessings bestowed on them, 1-5. He shows the nature and benefit of their trials, and the joy by which they were counterbalanced, 6, 7. Through faith, they loved and rejoiced in an unseen Savior, and received his salvation, 8, 9. The ancient prophets had most diligently inquired into this salvation; angels desired to look into it; and the Holy Spirit confirmed and prospered the preaching of it by the apostles, 10-12. This should animate Christians to a holy and circumspect conduct, as the worshippers of a holy God, 13-17; and as redeemed by the precious blood of Christ, through whom they believed and hoped in God, 18-21. Exhortations to the pure and fervent love of Christians to one another; being brethren by regeneration, through the Word of God, which, as "an incorruptible seed," "endureth forever," in the endeared relation thus formed, and in all things, 22-25.

1. Cir. A.M. 4068. A.D. 64. **Peter.** See on Mt 4:18. *10:2. Jn 1:41, 42. *21:15-17. **an apostle.** 2 P 1:1. **strangers.** 1 P 2:11. Ac 2:5-11. Ep *2:12, 19. He 11:13. **scattered.** Le 26:33. Dt 4:27. 28:64. 32:26. Est 3:8. Ps 44:11. Ezk 6:8. Jn 7:35. 11:52. Ac *8:1, 4. Ja +*1:1. **Pontus.** Ac 2:5, +9, 10. 18:2. **Galatia.** Ac +16:6. 18:23. Ga 1:2. **Cappadocia.** Ac 2:9. **Asia.** Ac 6:9. 16:6. 19:10. 20:16-18. 1 C 16:19. 2 C 1:8. 2 T 1:15. Re 1:11. **Bithynia.** Ac 16:7.

2. **Elect.** 1 P *2:8, 9. Dt 7:6. +*10:15. Is 65:9, 22. Mt 24:22, 24, 31. Mk 13:20, 22, 27. Lk +18:7. Jn 15:16-19. Ac +*13:48. Ro +*8:29, 33. +*11:2, 5-7, 28. Ep *1:4, 5. Col 3:12. 1 Th 5:9. 2 T 2:10. T 1:1. 2 J 1, 13. **the foreknowledge.** ver. 20. Ac 2:23. 15:18. Ro +*8:29, 30. 9:23, 24. 11:2. Re 13:8. **through.** 2 Th +*2:13. **sanctification.** Ex=28:41. Le=8:30. Ac 20:32. Ro 15:16. 1 C +*1:30. +*6:11. 1 Th +4:3. 5:23. 2 Th √2:13. **Spirit.** Gr. *pneuma*, Mt +3:16. Jn +7:39. Ro +*8:9. **unto obedience.** ver. 14, 22. Ro 1:5. 6:16. 8:13. 16:19, 26. 2 C *10:5, 6. He +*5:9. **sprinkling.** Ex *24:8. Le=8:30. 16:14-16. See on He *9:19-22. +*10:22. 11:28. 12:24. **blood of.** ⨍117, Ga +19:8. He *9:13, 14. 12:24. 13:12. 1 J *1:7. **Grace.** 2 P 1:2. See on Ro 1:7. 2 C *13:14. 2 J +3. **peace.** Da 4:1. 6:25. Ju 2. **be.** Is 55:7mg. Da 4:1. 6:25. 2 P 1:2. Ju 2.

3. **Blessed.** 1 K 8:15. 1 Ch 29:10-13, 20. Ps 41:13. 72:18, 19. 2 C +1:3. Ep 1:3, 17. 3:20. **the God and.** T#965‡. Mk 15:34. Jn +17:3 (T#966‡). 20:17. Ro +15:6. 1 C 11:3. T ◐+*2:13. Re 1:6. **which.** Ex 34:6. Ps 86:5, 15. Jsh 4:2. Ro 5:15-21. Ep 1:7. 2:4, 7-10. 1 T 1:14. T*3:4-6. **abundant.** Gr. much. **mercy.** Ps 118:3. Ep *2:4-6. **hath begotten.** ver. +23. 1 P *2:2. Jn *1:13. *3:3-8. Ac +*13:33. Ja *1:18. 1 J 2:29. 3:9. 4:7. 5:1, 4, 18. **unto.** Ro 5:4, 5. 8:24. 12:12. 15:13. 1 C 13:13. Col +*1:23, 27. 1 Th 1:3. T √2:13. He *3:6. *6:18,

19. 1 J 3:3. **hope.** Ro +*15:4. Ep ◐2:12. 2 Th *2:16. T 3:7. He *6:19, 20. **by.** 1 P *3:21. Is +*26:19n. Ac 1:22. +*2:24. Ro *4:25. 5:10. +*8:11. 1 C *15:20. Ep *2:6. 1 Th *4:13, 14. **from.** ⨍181E, Ge +3:24.

4. **an inheritance.** T#862. 1 P 3:9. Mt +*25:34. Ac +*20:32. 26:18. Ro *8:17. Ga 3:18. Ep 1:+*11n, 14, 18. Col *1:12. He 9:15. Ja +*2:5. **incorruptible.** ⨍99, Mk +12:30. Mt +*6:20. Lk 12:33. 1 C 9:25. 15:52-54. 2 T 1:10. **undefiled.** Re 21:27. **fadeth.** 1 P 5:4. Is 40:7, 8. Ezk 47:12. Ja 1:11. **reserved in heaven.** The inheritance is not in heaven, for by prophecy and covenant confirmed by oath the inheritance is upon earth (Mt +*5:5. Ep +*1:11n. He +*11:16n). The inheritance is not in heaven, but from heaven (2 T 4:18n), and is not present but future (Col 1:13n. 2 T +*4:1n). The inheritance is not in heaven, but is reserved in heaven, just as Scripture elsewhere teaches that our names are written in heaven (Da *7:10. *12:1. Lk +*10:20. Re 3:5. 20:12, 15). Ps 31:19. Mk +*10:40. Jn +*14:3. Ph 3:20, 21. Col *1:5. 3:3, 4. 2 T *4:8. He +*10:34. +*12:23. 2 P +*3:13. Ju 1. Re 3:12. 21:2. **for you.** or, for us.

5. **kept.** 1 S 2:9. Ps *37:23, 24, 28. *97:10. 103:17, 18. *121:7, 8. 125:1, 2. Pr 2:8. Is 54:17. Je 32:40. Jn 4:14. √5:24. √10:28-30. 17:11, 12, 15. Ro √8:31-39. 1 C *1:8. 2 C 11:32. Ga 3:23. Ep *1:13, 14. +*4:30. Ph 1:6. 4:7g. 1 Th *5:24. 2 P +*1:10. Ju *1, 24. **power of.** Ps *18:2. 1 C 1:24. 2:5. 2 C 6:7. **through faith.** Ro 11:20. 2 C *1:24. Ga *2:20. Ep √2:8. 3:17. 2 Th 2:13. 2 T +*3:15. He 6:12. **unto.** Is 45:17. 51:6. 1 Th 1:3, 4. 2 Th *2:13, 14. He +*9:28. **ready.** ver. 13. 1 P 5:10. Ro 8:18. 2 C 4:17. 1 T 6:14, 15. T √2:13. He 12:11. 1 J √3:2. **revealed.** Mt +*25:34. Ro √8:17. Col *3:4. T +*2:13. **in.** Jb 19:25. Jn 12:48. 2 Th +*1:10. 1 J +2:18.

6. **ye greatly.** ver. 8. 1 P 4:13. 1 S 2:1. Ps 9:14. 35:19. 95:1. Is *12:2, 3. 61:3, 10. Mt +*5:12. Lk 1:47. 2:10. 10:20. Jn 16:22. Ro *5:2, 3, 11. *12:12. 2 C 6:10. √12:9, 10. Ga *5:22. Ph 3:3. √4:4. 1 Th 1:6. Ja 1:2, 9. **for a season.** 1 P 4:7. *5:10. 2 C √4:17. **if.** ⨍184A, 1 C +15:2. ver. 7. Ps +*119:75. La *3:32, 33. He 12:7-11. **ye are.** Jb 9:27, 28. Ps 69:20. 119:28. Is 61:3. Mt 11:28. 26:37. Ro 9:2. Ph 2:26. He 12:11. Ja 4:9. **manifold.** Ps 34:19. Jn 16:33. Ac 14:22. 1 C 4:9-13. 2 C 4:7-11. 11:23-27. He 11:35-38. Ja 1:2.

7. **the trial.** 1 P *4:12, 13. Ge=12:6. Dt 8:2. Jb 23:10. Ps 23:5. 66:10-12. Pr 17:3. Is 48:10. Je 9:7. Zc *13:9. Ml 3:3. Ro *5:3, 4. Ep 6:12. Ja *1:3, 4, 12. Re 2:10. +*3:10. **precious.** 1 P 2:4, 7. Pr 3:13-15. 8:19. 16:16. 2 P 1:1, 4. **gold.** Ml=3:3. 2 T 2:20, 21. **that.** Ec 5:14. Je 48:36. Lk 12:20, 21, 33. Ac 8:20. Ja 5:2, 3. 2 P 3:10-12. Re 18:16, 17. **perisheth.** Gr. *apollumi*, Mt +2:13. **tried.** 1 P 4:12. Jb 23:10. Ps 66:10. Pr 17:3. Is 48:10. Da 11:35. Zc *13:9. Ml=3:3. 1 C 3:13. Re 3:18. **with fire.** 1 P 4:12. 1 C 3:13. **might.** 1 S 2:30. Mt 19:28. 25:21, 23. Jn 5:44. 12:26. Ro 2:7, 10, 29. 1 C +*4:5. 2 Th √1:7-12. Ju *24. **glory.** 1 P 2:7. Ro *2:7, 10. 1 T 1:17. He 2:7, 9. 2 P 1:17. Re +4:9. **at.**

See on ver. 5. Re 1:7. **the appearing.** ver. 13. 1 P 4:13. Lk 17:30. 1 C 1:7. Ph 3:20. Col 3:4. 2 Th 1:7. T +*2:13n.

8. **having.** Jn *20:29. 2 C *4:18. √5:7. He *11:1, 27. 1 J 4:20. **ye love.** T#325. 1 P 2:7. Ps 45:11. SS 1:7. 5:9, 16. Mt 10:37. 25:35-40. Jn 8:42. 14:15, 21, 24. 21:15-17. 1 C *16:22. 2 C *5:14, 15. Ga *5:6. Ep 6:24. 1 J √4:19. **yet believing.** T#664. See on ver. 6, 21. Hab √3:17, 18. Ac 16:34. Ro +10:14. 14:17. 15:13. 2 C +5:7 (T#184). Ga 2:20. Ph 1:25. 3:3. √4:4. **ye rejoice.** T#852. ver. 6. 1 P 4:13. Jb 22:26. Ne *8:10. Ps 4:7. *33:21. 63:5. 64:10. *68:3. *89:15, 16. 97:11. 118:15. +*126:5, 6. SS *1:4. Is 9:3. 41:16. +*51:11. 55:12. 61:7, 10. 62:5. 65:14. Hab 3:18. Jn *15:11. 16:22. Ac +16:34. Ro 5:2. Ph *3:8, 9. **with joy.** T#297. 1 S 2:1. Ne 8:10. Hab 3:17-19. **unspeakable.** Jn 16:22. Ro 8:26. 2 C 9:15. 12:4. **full.** 1 P 5:4. 2 C 1:22. Ga *5:22. Ep 1:13, 14.

9. **Receiving.** Ro *6:22. He *11:13. Ja *1:21. **the end.** √121P6, Pr +23:18. Ro 6:22. **salvation.** Jn √5:24. Ro 8:1. **souls.** Gr. *psyche*, √171Q2, 2 C +12:15mg. √171Q2, Nu +23:10.

10. **which.** Ge +*49:10. Da *2:44. Hg *2:7. Zc *6:12. Mt *13:17. Lk *10:24. *24:25-27, 44. Ac *3:22-24. *7:52. +*10:43. *13:27-29. *28:23. 2 P *1:19-21. **the prophets.** Da 8:15. Mt 13:17. Lk 10:24. 2 P 1:19. **inquired.** ✳S#1567g. Lk 11:50, 51 (required). Ac 15:17 (seek after). Ro 3:11. He *11:6 (diligently seek). 12:17. **and searched.** ver. *11. Pr 2:4. +*15:14. Da 9:2, 3. Jn +*5:39. *7:52. Ac +*17:11. **the grace.** He *11:13, 40.

11. **Searching what.** Pr 15:14. Da 9:2, 24-26. Mt 13:17. **the Spirit.** Gr. *pneuma*, Mt +3:16. 1 P 3:18, 19. Jn 14:17. 16:7. Ac +16:7. Ro +*8:9. Ga *4:6. He 9:14. 2 P *1:21. Re *19:10. **when it testified.** Mt +26:24. **the sufferings.** Ps *22:1-21. *69:1-21. ch. 88. Is *52:13, 14. *53:1-10. Da *9:24-26. Zc *13:7. Lk +*24:25-27, 44. Ac +3:18. 1 C +*15:3, 4. 2 C 1:5. **the glory.** Ge +*3:15. +*49:10. Ps *22:22-31. 45:3-7. *69:30-36. *72:17-19. +*102:16. *110:1-6. *145:11. Is +*9:6, 7. Is *11:10mg. *49:6. *53:11, 12. Da *2:34, 35, 44. +*7:13, 14. Zc √2:8-12. +√6:13. +*14:9. Mt 6:13. Lk √24:26. Jn *12:41. Ac *26:22, 23. 1 Th +*2:12.

12. **it was revealed.** Is 53:1. Da 2:19, 22, 28, 29, 47. 10:1. 12:4, 9, 13. Am +*3:7. Mt +*11:25, 27. 16:17. Lk 2:26. Ro 1:17, 18. 1 C 2:10. Ga 1:12, 16. **that not.** Da *24. 12:9, 13. Mt 13:17. Lk 10:24. He *11:13, 39, 40. **that have.** Mk *16:15. Lk 9:6. Ac 8:25. 16:10. Ro 1:15. 10:15. 15:19. 1 Th 2:9. He 4:2. **with.** Mk *16:20. Jn 15:26. 16:7-15. Ac *2:2-4, 33. 4:8, 31. 10:44. 2 C *1:22. 6:6. 1 Th 1:5, 6. He 2:4. **Ghost.** Gr. *pneuma*, Mt +1:18. **sent.** Pr *1:23. Is 11:2-6. 32:15. 44:3-5. Jl +*2:28. Zc *12:10. Jn 15:26. Ac 2:17, 18. **which things.** Ex 25:20. Da 8:13. 12:5, 6. Lk 15:10. Ep *3:10. Re 5:11. **to look into.** Ja +1:25.

13. **gird.** Ex 12:11. 1 K 18:46. 2 K 4:29. Jb 38:3. 40:7. Is 11:5. Je 1:17. Lk +*12:35. 17:8. Ep *6:14. **be sober.** 1 P *4:7. 5:8. Lk +*21:34, 35. Ro 13:13. 1 Th *5:6-8. 2 T 4:5. T +*2:13. **hope.** ver. 3-5. 1 P *3:15. Ro +*15:4-13. 1 C 13:13. 1 Th 5:8. He 3:6. 6:19. 1 J *3:3. **to the end.** Gr. perfectly. **the grace.** ver. 4-9. Lk 17:30. 1 C 1:7. 2 Th 1:7. 2 T *4:8. T +*2:11-13. He +*9:28. *10:35. **at the revelation.** ver. +7. 1 J √3:2.

14. **obedient children.** T#654. ver. +2. Lk +10:6. Ep ❶2:2. 5:6g. **not fashioning.** 1 P 4:2, 3. Ro *6:4.

+*12:2. Ep 4:18-22. Col 3:5-7. 1 J *3:3. **according to.** 1 P *4:2, 3. T 3:3. **in.** Ac 17:23, 30. Ep 4:18. 1 Th 4:5. T *3:3-5.

15. **as.** 1 P 2:9. 5:10. Ro +*8:28-30. 9:24. Ph 3:14. 1 Th 2:12. 4:7. 2 T 1:9. 2 P 1:3, 10. **is.** Is 6:3. Re 3:7. 4:8. 6:10. **so.** Ps 93:5. Mt 5:48. Lk 1:74, 75. 2 C *7:1. Ep *5:1, 2. Ph 1:27. 2:15, 16. 1 Th *4:3-7. T √2:11-14. *3:8, 14. He +*12:14. 2 P 1:4-10. 1 J 3:3. **in.** ver. 18. 1 P 2:12. 3:16. Ph 3:20. 1 T 4:12. He +*13:5. Ja +3:13. 2 P *3:11-14.

16. **Because.** T#1062. 1 C 1:31. **Be ye holy.** Le *❶11:44. 19:2. 20:7, 26. Am 3:3.

17. **if.** √184A, 1 C +15:2. **call.** Je 3:19. Zp 3:9. Mt *6:9. *7:7-11. Lk 11:2. 2 C 1:2. Ep 1:17. 3:14. **the Father.** Je 3:19. Ml 1:6. 2 C 6:18. **who.** Dt *10:17, 20. 2 Ch 19:7. Jb 34:19. Mt 22:16. Ac *10:+34, 35. Ro *2:10, 11. Ga 2:6. Ep 6:9. Col 3:25. **judgeth.** Ec *12:14. Mt +*10:15n. 2 C *5:10. **according.** Mt +*16:27. **pass.** Ge 47:9. 1 Ch 29:15. Ps 39:12. He +*11:13-16. **sojourning.** 1 P 2:11. Ep 2:19. He *13:14. **in fear.** 1 P 3:15. Ps *2:11. *119:120. Pr 14:16. *28:14. Ro 11:20. 2 C 5:6. 7:1, 11. Ph 2:12. He 4:1. +*12:28.

18. **redeemed.** Ex 15:16. =30:11-16. Le=22:11. Nu 3:51. Ps *49:7, 8. 130:8. Is 52:3. Mt 20:28. Lk 24:21. Ac *20:28. 1 C 6:20. 7:23. T 2:14. 2 P 2:1. Re 5:9. **corruptible.** See on ver. 7. **vain.** Ps 39:6. 62:10. Je 4:11. Ro 1:21. 1 C 3:20. Ep +4:17. **conversation.** ver. 15. Ja +3:13g. **received.** 1 P 4:3. Je 9:14. 16:19. 44:17. Ezk 20:18. Am 2:4. Zc 1:4-6. Mt 15:2, 3. Ac 7:51, 52. 19:34, 35. Ga 1:14. *5:1.

19. **with.** 1 P 2:22-24. 3:18. Da 9:24. Zc 13:7. Mt 20:28. +*26:28n. 1 C *6:20. Ep 1:7. Col 1:14. He 9:12-14. 1 J *1:7. *2:2. Re +*1:5. *5:9. **precious.** Ps *49:7, 8. 116:15. 139:17. Is 28:16. **blood.** √117, Ep +19:8. Ac +*20:28. He *9:12. Re 1:5. **as.** Ex 12:5. Is *53:7, 9. Jn *1:+29, 36. Ac 8:32-35. 1 C 5:7, 8. 1 J *4:10. Re 5:6. 7:14. 14:1. **lamb.** √22E, Jn +1:29. **without blemish.** T#579. Ex *12:5. Le 22:19, 20. Ml 1:8. Ep 5:27. He 7:26, 27. 9:14. **without spot.** Ja +1:27. 1 J *3:5.

20. **foreordained.** Ge +*3:15. Pr 8:23. Mi +*5:2. Ro +3:25. 8:29. 16:25, 26. Ep 1:4. *3:9, 11. Col 1:26. **before the.** Ge 17:7. Mt 13:35. Jn +17:24. 1 C +*15:45. 2 T *1:9, 10. He 13:20. T √1:2, 3. Re 13:8. **world.** Gr. *kosmos*, Mt +4:8. **but.** Ac 3:25, 26. Col 1:26. 1 J 1:2. 3:5, 8. *4:9, 10. **manifest.** He 1:3. Ro +16:26. **in.** Ga *4:4, 5. Ep 1:10. He +1:2. 9:26.

21. **by.** Jn √5:24. +*12:44. √14:6. Ac 3:16. He 6:1. 7:25. **do believe.** ver. 8. Ro +10:14. **that raised.** Ac +*2:24, 32. 3:15. 4:10. Ro *8:32, 34. √10:9. **gave.** ver. 11. 1 P 3:22. Mt 28:18. Jn 3:34. 5:22, 23. 13:31, 32. 17:1. Jn +7:39. Ac 2:33. 3:13. Ep *1:20-23. Ph √2:9-11. He *2:9. **your faith.** Ps 42:5. 146:3-5. Je 17:7. Jn 14:1. Ep 1:12, 13mg, 15. Col 1:27. 1 T 1:1. **and hope.** T#352. Ps 42:5. Ro 5:2.

22. **have purified.** Jn 15:3. 17:17, 19. Ac *15:9. Ro 6:16, 17. 1 C *6:11. 2 Th *2:13. Ja *4:8. **souls.** Gr. *psyche*, √171Q2, 2 C +12:15mg. **in obeying.** ver. +2. 1 P 3:1. *4:17. Ezk ◑*33:31, 32. Ac 6:7. Ro 1:5. 2:8. Ga 3:1. 5:7. Ph +*2:12, 13. 1 Th *2:13. T *3:5. He +*5:9. 11:8. Ja 1:18, 21, 22. **through.** Ro 8:13. Ga 5:5. 2 T 1:14. He 9:14. **Spirit.** Gr. *pneuma*, Mt +3:16. **unto unfeigned love.** 1 P 2:17. *3:8. *4:8. Jn +*13:34, 35. 15:17. Ro *12:9, 10. 2 C 6:6. Ga +*6:10. Ep 4:3. 1 Th 4:8, 9. 1 T 1:5. He +*6:10. +13:1. Ja 2:15, 16. +3:17. 2 P +*1:7. 1 J *3:+11, 14-19, 23. *4:7, 12,

20, 21. *5:1, 2. **see**. Jn *13:35. Ep *1:4. Ph 1:9. 1 Th +*3:12. 2 Th 1:3. 1 J *3:18. Re 2:4. **one another**. Ro +12:5. **a pure**. Mt +*5:8. Ac 15:9. 1 T 1:5. +*4:12. 5:2. 2 T 2:22. Ja 4:8. **fervently**. 1 P *4:8. Ac +12:5g.

23. **born**. See on ver. 3. 1 P *2:2. Ps *119:50. Jn 1:13. *3:5. Ja *1:18. 1 J *3:9. 4:7. 5:1, 4, 18. **not**. Ml 2:3. Ro 1:23. 1 C *15:53, 54. **but of incorruptible**. Le +=11:37. 1 J *3:9. *5:18. **by the word**. T#1035. ver. *25. Je *23:28, 29. Mt *24:35. Jn *6:63. Ro +9:6. 1 Th √2:13. 2 T +*3:15. He *4:12. Ja *1:18. **which liveth**. Da ◑4:34. ◐6:26. ◐12:7. Jn ◑6:51. Ac 7:38. He +*4:12. Re ◑4:10. **forever**. Gr. *aion*, Mt +6:13. lit. unto the age, Mt +21:19.

24. **For**. *or*, For that. √92E, Mt +4:10. **all flesh**. √171Q6, Ge +6:12. Ge +*6:3. 2 K 19:26. Ps *37:2. *90:5. *92:7. 102:4. *103:15. 129:6. Is *♦40:6-8. *51:12. Lk +3:6. Ja *1:10, 11. *4:14. 1 J *2:17.

25. **the word**. See on ver. *23. Ps 102:12, 26. *119:89. Is *40:8. Mt *5:18. *24:35. Lk *16:17. **for ever**. Gr. *aion*, Mt +6:13. lit. unto the age, Mt +21:19. **this**. ver. 12. 1 P *2:2. Jn *1:1, 14. Ro 10:8. 1 C 1:21-24. 2:2. *15:1-4. Ep 2:17. *3:8. T 1:3. 2 P *1:19. 1 J *1:1, 3. **the gospel**. Is 40:9.

1 PETER 2

Christians are exhorted to lay aside selfish and angry passions; that they may long for "the sincere milk of the word," and grow by it, having "tasted that the Lord is gracious," 1-3. The preciousness of Christ, the chief corner stone, to believers as builded on him, by faith, and thus made a holy temple and a spiritual priesthood, according to the scriptures; while unbelievers stumble and perish, 4-8. The sacred character and invaluable privileges of believers, as called out of darkness into light, to show forth the praises of God, 9, 10. The apostle beseeches them to abstain from fleshly lusts, and by their good conversation to glorify God among the Gentiles, 11, 12. He enforces obedience to magistrates, 13-17, and that of servants to their masters; exhorting them to suffer patiently even for well-doing after the example of Christ, and from love to him, 18-25.

1. **Wherefore**. 1 P 1:18-25. **laying**. 1 P 4:2. Is 2:20. 30:22. Ezk 18:31, 32. Ro 13:12. Ep 4:22-25. Col *3:5-8. He 12:1. Ja +*1:21. 5:9. **malice**. ver. 16. 1 C 5:8. 14:20. Ep +*4:31. T *3:3-5. **guile**. ver. 22. 1 P 3:10. Ps 32:2. 34:13. Jn 1:47. 1 Th 2:3. Re 14:5. **hypocrisies**. Jb 36:13. Mt 7:5. 15:7. 23:28. 24:51. Mk 12:15. Lk 6:42. 11:42. +12:1. Ja 3:17. **envies**. 1 S 18:8, 9. Ps 37:1. 73:3. Pr 3:31. 14:30. 24:1, 19. Mt 27:18. Mk 15:10. Ro 1:29. 13:13. 1 C 3:2, 3. 2 C 12:20. Ga √5:21-26. Ph 1:15. 1 T 6:4. T 3:3. Ja 3:14, 16. 4:5. **all evil**. 1 P 4:4. Ml=2:6. 2 C 12:20g. Ep 4:31. Col 3:8. 1 T 3:11. T 2:3. Ja +4:11.

2. **newborn babes**. T#1113. 1 P *1:23. Le=22:11. Mt +*18:3. Mk *10:15. Ro *6:4. 1 C *3:1. 14:20. 2 T +*3:15. **desire**. Jb *23:12. Ps 112:1. 119:165. Je ◑6:10. √15:16. Mt 5:6. **the sincere**. *or*, spiritual. Gr. reasonable. Ps *19:7-10. Ro 12:1g. 1 C *3:2. He *5:12, 13. **milk**. He 5:12. **of the word**. Ex=16:15. 1 T 4:6. **grow**. T#1048. 2 S 23:5. Jb *17:9. Pr +*4:18. Ho *6:3. *14:5, 7. Ml *4:2. Ac *20:32. Ep 2:21. *4:15. Col 1:6, +*10. 2:19. 1 Th *2:13. 2 Th 1:3. 2 T +√3:16, 17. 2 P √3:18.

3. **If**. √184A, 1 C +15:2. **tasted**. Ps +√9:10. ♦34:8.

63:5. SS *2:3. Zc 9:17. He *6:5, 6. 1 J *5:10. **the Lord**. The Hebrew text underlying this quotation from the Old Testament reads "Jehovah" (Ps 34:8h); this is therefore a very clear instance of the divine name of Jehovah being applied directly to Jesus Christ by the apostles in the New Testament, for the following verse (ver. 4) shows unmistakably that this reference is to Jesus (Ac 11:21n). The following pairs of references will show that this identification is very frequently made in the New Testament: (1) Mt 3:3 w Is 40:3. (2) Jn 12:41 w Is 6:1. (3) Ep 4:7, 8n w Ps 68:18. (4) 1 P 3:15 w Is 8:13. (5) 1 C 2:8 w Ps 24:7, 10. (6) Ja 2:1 w Ps 24:7, 10. (7) 1 C 1:30 w Je √23:5, 6. (7) Jn 3:31 w Ps 97:9. (8) Re 1:17 w Is 44:6. (9) Ph 2:6 w Zc 13:7. (10) He 13:20 w Is 40:10, 11. (11) Col 1:16 w Pr 16:4. (12) Lk 7:27 w Ml 3:1. (13) He 1:8, 10-12 w Ps 102:24-27. (14) T 2:13 w Ho 1:7. (15) 2 T 4:1 w Ec 12:14. (16) Re 1:5 and 17:14 w Da 2:47. (17) Jn 1:3 w Is 40:28. (18) Col 1:17 w Ne +*9:6. For Scripture evidence establishing the divinity or deity of Christ, see Topic Numbers 74-82, the sets of references gathered at Mt 28:19n, and the following related notes and references: (1) Deity of Christ, Col 1:16n. (2) Christ received worship, Mt +*14:33. Jn +*20:28, 29n. Ac +*7:59n. (3) Christ is not a lesser god, or entitled to a lesser degree of worship, Jn +*1:1n. Ph 2:6n. (4) Jesus called God, Jn +√20:28, 29n. (5) Charged with blasphemy for his claim to deity, Jn 10:32n. (6) Only a divine Savior possessing full deity could qualify as our substitute in the atonement for sins, He 10:4n. Je √23:5, 6. **gracious**. Mt 11:30. Lk 6:35. Ro 2:4. Ep +*4:32g.

4. **To whom coming**. Dt 12:5, 6. Is +*55:3. Je 3:22. Mt 11:28. Jn *5:40. √6:37. He √7:25. **a living**. √108B, Ac +7:38. Jn 5:26. 6:57. 11:25, 26. *14:6, 19. Ro 5:10. Col 3:4. **stone**. √22L2, Is +8:14. Is 28:16. Da 2:34, 45. Zc 3:9. 4:7. **disallowed**. Ps *118:22, 23. Is 8:14, 15. Mt 16:16-18. 21:42. Mk *12:10, 11. Lk 20:17, 18. Ac 4:11, 12. 1 C *3:11. **chosen**. Is 42:1. Mt 12:18. **precious**. ver. 7. 1 P 1:7, 19. 2 P 1:1, 4.

5. **also**. 1 C *3:16. *6:19. 2 C *6:16. Ep √2:19-22. He *3:6. Re 3:12. **lively**. √108B, Ac +7:38. **are built**. *or*, be ye built. 1 C 3:9. **spiritual**. Ro +1:11g. **house**. Ro +1:11g. 1 C *6:19. Ep 2:22. He *3:4, 6. **an holy priesthood**. ver. 9. Ex=29:9. Is 61:6. 66:21. Re 1:6. 5:10. 20:6. **spiritual**. Ro +1:11g. **sacrifices**. Ps 50:14, 23. 141:2. Is 8:13, 14. 56:7. Ho *14:2. Ml 1:11. =3:3. Jn 4:22-24. Ro +*12:1, 2. Ph 2:17. 4:18. He *13:15, 16. **acceptable**. 1 P 4:11. Le +=23:12. Mi +*6:6-8. Ro +*12:1. +15:16. Ph 1:11. 4:18. Col 3:17.

6. **it**. Da 10:21. Mk 12:10. Jn 7:38. 19:37. Ac 1:16. Ro 9:17. 2 T 3:16. 2 P 1:20. 3:16. **is contained**. lit. contains. i.e., *there is a passage in the Scripture*. √96A2. Heterosis of Voice B512: the active for the passive voice. **Behold**. √92A, Mt +1:23. ver. 4. Is ♦28:16. Zc 10:4. Ro 9:32, 33. Ep 2:20. **elect**. Ps 89:19. Is 42:1. Mt 12:18. Lk 23:35. Ep 1:4. **corner stone**. √22L2, Is +8:14. Is ✱28:16. Ep 2:20. **believeth**. Ro 9:3310:11. 1 J 3:23. **shall not**. √158, Mt +5:18. Ps 40:14. Is 41:11. 45:16, 17. 50:7. 54:4. 1 C 1:27. **confounded**. √121G2, Ps +25:2.

7. **you**. 1 P 1:8. SS 5:9-16. Hg 2:7. Mt 13:44-46. Jn 4:42. 6:68, 69. Ph √3:7-10. **which believe**. √101, Dt +32:42. **precious**. *or*, an honor. 1 P +*1:7, 19. Is 28:5. 43:4. Lk 2:32. **but unto them**. Ex 14:20. 1 S 5:11. Ho 6:5. 14:9. 2 C 2:16. **which be**. ver. 8. Mk +16:16. Ac 26:19. Ro 10:21. *15:31mg. T 3:3. He 4:11.

11:31mg. **the stone.** ✻22L1, Ps +118:22. ✻92G, Lk +4:18. Ps ▸118:22, 23. Is 28:16. Mt +21:42. Mk +8:31. 12:10, 11. Lk 20:17. Ac ⟍4:11, 12. **the head.** Zc 4:7. Col 2:10.

8. a stone. ✻22L2, Is +8:14. Is ▸8:14. 57:14. Mt 21:44. Lk *2:34. Ro 9:32, 33. 1 C 1:23. 2 C 2:16. **of stumbling.** Da 2:45. Ho 14:9. Da 2:45. Ga 5:11. **of offense.** Ex=10:7. **stumble at.** T#1105. Ps 119:*155, 171. Pr 28:5. Is 26:9. +*66:4, 5. Je *6:19. Ezk 12:2. *33:31. Da *9:13. *12:10. Ho 13:6. Mi ◑+*2:7. Hab 1:4. Jn 7:17. 2 C ⟍4:3, 4. 2 P 3:16. **the word.** Ac +8:4. **being disobedient.** See on ver. 7. 1 P 3:1. Ezk *33:11. **whereunto.** T#252. Ge +*50:20. Ex 9:16. Ac +*2:23. 4:27, 28. 13:29. Ro 9:22. 1 Th 5:9. 2 P *2:3. Ju 4. Re 17:17. **appointed.** 1 P 1:2. Dt +*10:15. Re 17:14.

9. a chosen. 1 P +1:2. Dt 10:15. =21:5. Jg 2:1. Ps 22:30. 33:12. 73:15. Is 41:8. 43:20. 44:1. Ep *1:4, 5. **generation.** Ps 22:30. 24:6. Mt 24:34. **a royal priesthood.** ver. 5. Ex 19:6. 20:5, 6. =29:9. Is 61:6. 66:21. Re 1:6. 5:10. 20:4, 6. **an holy.** Ex *19:6. Dt 7:6. Ps 106:5. Is 26:2. Je 2:3. Jn 17:19. 1 C 3:17. 2 T 1:9. **peculiar.** *or,* purchased. Ex 6:7, 8. *19:5. Dt 4:20. 7:6. 14:2. 26:18, 19. Ps 135:4. Ezk 37:23. Ml 3:17. Ac +*20:28. Ep 1:14. T *2:14. **show.** 1 P 4:11. Ps 9:13, 14. 96:2. Is 42:12. *43:21. 60:1-3. 63:7. Mt *5:16. Jn *15:8. Ep 1:6. 3:21. Ph 2:15, 16. **praises.** *or,* virtues. 2 P 1:3g. **who.** Is 9:2. 60:1, 2. Mt 4:16. Lk 1:79. Ac 26:18. Ro +*8:28. 9:24. 13:12. Ep 5:8-11. Ph 3:14. Col *1:13. 1 Th 5:4-8. **out of darkness.** Ps 107:14. Is +*9:2. 42:16. Ac +*26:18. **his marvellous.** Ps 36:9. 1 J *1:7.

10. were not. ✻111, Ge +18:27. Ho *1:9, 10. 2:23. Ro *9:25, 26. 10:19. **obtained.** Ho 1:6. *2:23. Ro 11:6, 7, 30. 1 C 7:25. 1 T 1:13. He +*4:16.

11. I beseech. Ro +*12:1. 2 C 5:20. 6:1. Ep 4:1. Phm 9, 10. **as strangers.** 1 P 1:1, +17. Ge 23:4. 47:9. Le 25:23. 1 Ch 29:15. Ps 39:12. 119:19, 54. Ac 7:6, 29. Ep ◑2:19. He 11:13. **and pilgrims.** Ge 12:8. He 11:13. **abstain.** 1 P 4:2. Lk *21:34. Ac *15:20, 29. Ro ⟍8:12, 13. ⟍13:13, 14. 2 C *7:1. Ga ⟍5:16-21. 2 T 2:22. 1 J ⟍2:15-17. **fleshly lusts.** T#675. Am *6:3-7. Ro 6:12. *13:13, 14. 2 C *7:1. Ga 5:24. Ep +2:3 (T#698). +5:18 (T#366). T *2:11, 12. 1 J +*2:16. **war.** Ro 7:23. 8:13. Ga 5:17, 24. 1 T +*6:9, 10. Ja 4:1. **soul.** Gr. *psyche,* ✻121A9C, Lk +21:19.

12. Having. ver. 15. 1 P 3:16. 2 C 8:21. Ph 2:15. T 2:8. Ja +4:11. **your conversation.** 1 P 3:2. Ps 37:14. 50:23. 2 C 1:12. Ep 2:3. 4:22. Ph 1:27. 1 T *4:12. He 13:5. Ja +3:13g. 2 P 3:11. **honest.** Ps *5:8. Ac *24:16. Ro 12:17. 13:13. 2 C 8:21. 13:7. Ph ⟍4:8. 1 Th *4:12. 1 T 2:2. He 13:18. **among.** Ge 13:7, 8. Ph 2:15, 16. **that.** 1 P *3:1, 16. 4:14-16. Mt 5:11. 10:25. Lk 6:22. Ac 24:5, 6, 13. 25:7. **whereas.** *or,* wherein. **they may.** Mt *5:16. T 2:7, 8. **good works.** 1 T +*6:18. **glorify.** 1 P 4:11. Ps 50:23. Jn 21:19. Ro 15:9. 1 C 14:25. 2 C 9:13. Ga 1:24. **the day.** Is ⟍10:3. 34:8. *61:2. Je 8:12. Ho +*9:7. **of visitation.** Jb 10:12. Je *6:15. 51:18. Lk 1:68, 78. ⟍19:44. Ac 15:14.

13. Submit. T#909. Pr 17:11. 24:21. Ec 8:4, 5. Je 29:7. Mt 22:21. Mk 12:17. Lk 20:25. Ac ◑+*4:19. ◑+*5:29. Ro ⟍13:1-7. Ep ⟍5:21. 1 T 2:1, 2. T *3:1. 2 P 2:10. Ju 8-10. **ordinance.** ✻171E2, Mk +16:15.

14. for the punishment. Ro *13:3, 4.

15. so. 1 P +3:17. **the will.** 1 P 4:2. Ep 6:6, 7. 1 Th +4:3. 5:18. **with.** See on ver. 12. Jb 5:16. Ps 107:42. T *2:8. **well doing.** Ne 5:9. **put to silence.** Da *6:4,

---

5. T *2:8. **the ignorance.** 1 C 15:34g. 1 T 1:13. 2 P 2:12. Ju 10. **foolish.** Dt 32:6. Jb 2:10. Ps 5:5. Pr 9:6. Je 4:22. Mt 7:26. 25:2. Ro 1:21. Ga 3:1. T 3:3.

16. free. Jn 8:32-36. Ro *6:14, 18, 22. *8:1. 1 C 7:22. *8:9. Ga *5:1, 13. Ja +*1:25. 2:12. 2 P 2:19. **and.** Ju 4. **using.** Gr. having. **a cloak.** Mt 23:14. Jn 15:22. 1 Th 2:5. **but as.** Ro 6:22. 1 C 7:22. Ep *6:6. Col +*3:23, 24. **servants.** Ja +1:1.

17. Honor. *or,* Esteem. 1 P *5:5. Ex 20:12. Le *19:32. 1 S 15:30. Ro *12:10. *13:7. Ph +*2:3. 1 T *6:1. **Love.** See on 1 P 1:22. Zc 11:14. Jn *13:35. He +13:1. **the brotherhood.** ✻121N1, Ge +31:54. 1 P 5:9g. Ga +*6:10. **Fear.** See on Ge 20:11. *22:12. 42:18. Ps *111:10. Pr *1:7. *23:17. *24:21. Ec 8:2. Mt *22:21. Ro 13:7. 2 C *7:1. Ep *5:21. Re 14:7. **Honor.** 1 S 15:30. 1 Ch *29:20. Pr *24:21.

18. Servants. Lk 16:13. Ac 10:7. Ro 14:4. **be subject.** Ge 16:9. Ep *6:5-7. Col *3:22-25. 1 T *6:1-3. T 2:9, 10. **the good.** 2 C 10:1. Ga 5:22. T 3:2. **and gentle.** Ja +*3:17. **but.** Ps 101:4. Pr 3:32. 8:13. 10:32. 11:20. Ac +2:40.

19. this. ver. 20. Lk 6:32. **thankworthy.** *or,* thank. Lk 6:32-34. Ac 11:23. 1 C 15:10. 2 C 1:12. 8:1g. **if.** ✻184A, 1 C +15:2. **for conscience.** 1 P 3:14-17, 21. 4:14-16. Mt +*5:10-12. Jn 15:21. Ro 13:5. 1 C 4:4. 2 C +1:12. 2 T 1:12. He 10:2. **toward.** ✻181E, Ge +3:24. **suffering.** Jb 21:27. Ps 35:19. 38:19. 69:4. 119:86.

20. For. 1 P 3:14. 4:14-16. Mt 5:47. **if.** ✻184A, 1 C +15:2. **buffeted.** Mt 26:67. Mk 14:65. 1 C 4:11. 2 C +12:7. **if.** ✻184A, 1 C +15:2. **when.** See on ver. 19. 1 P 3:17, 18. 4:13, 16. **and suffer.** Mt 11:29. **take it patiently.** 1 P 1:6. 4:12, 13, 19. Jb 5:17. 13:15. Mt 26:39. Ro 5:3. 12:12. 2 C 12:9. 1 Th 3:3, 4. 2 Th 1:4. 2 T 4:5. He 10:34. 12:3-12. **this.** Mt +*5:10-12. Ro +*12:1, 2. Ep 5:10. Ph 4:18. **acceptable.** *or,* thank. See on ver. 19. Lk 6:32.

21. even. 1 P *3:9. Mt 10:38. 16:24. Mk 8:34, 35. Lk 9:23-25. 14:26, 27. Jn 16:33. Ac 9:16. 14:22. Ro +*8:28. 1 Th 3:3, 4. 2 T 3:12. **because.** ver. 23, 24. 1 P 3:18. 4:1. Lk 24:26. Ac +3:18. *17:3. He 2:10. **for us.** Some read, for you. 1 P 1:20. **leaving.** Ps 85:13. Mt +11:29. Jn 13:15. Ro 8:29. 1 C +*11:1. Ep *5:2. Ph 2:5. He +*12:1, 2. 1 J 2:6. 3:16. Re ⟍12:11. **follow.** Jn 12:26. 2 T 3:12.

22. did no sin. Is 53:9. Da=6:4. Mt *27:4, 19, 23, 24. Lk 23:41, 47. Jn *8:46. 2 C ⟍5:21. He +*4:15. *7:26, 27. +*9:28. 1 J *2:1. *3:+4g, 5. **guile.** Ps 32:2. Is ✽53:7, 9. Jn *1:47. Ja 3:2. Re 14:5.

23. when he was. 1 P 3:9. Ps 38:12-14. Is *53:7. Mt *27:12, 39-44. Mk 14:60, 61. 15:29-32. Lk 22:64, 65. *23:9, 34-39. Jn *8:48, 49. 19:9-11. Ac 8:32-35. He *12:3. **reviled not.** Mt +*26:63. **suffered.** ver. +21. **threatened.** Ac 4:17, 29. 9:1. Ep 6:9. **but committed.** 1 P 4:19. Ps 10:14. 31:5. 37:5. Lk 23:46. Ac +*7:59. 14:26g. 2 T 1:12. **himself.** *or,* his cause. ✻63A2, 2 S +6:6. **judgeth.** Ge +*18:25. Ps 7:11. 96:13. Ac +*17:31. Ro 2:5. 2 Th 1:5. 2 T 4:8. Re 19:11.

24. his own self. Ex *28:38. ◑=32:30, 32. Le *16:22. 22:9. Nu *18:22. Ps *38:4. Is ⟍53:4-6, 11. Mt *8:17. Jn *1:29. T *2:14. He +*9:28. **bare.** ✻121C1E, Ge +19:15. **sins.** 1 P 3:18. Le +=5:6. Ro +*3:25. +4:25. 2 C ⟍5:21. **his own.** He 9:12. **on.** *or,* to. **the tree.** ✻121D8, Ge +40:19. Dt *21:22, 23. Ac *5:30. 10:39. 13:29. Ga *3:13. **being.** 1 P 4:1, 2. Ro *6:2, 7, 11. *7:4, 6mg. 2 C *6:17. Col *2:20. 3:3g. He *7:26. **live.** Mt *5:20. Lk *1:74, 75. Ac 10:35. Ro *6:11, *13, 16,

22. Ep *5:9. Ph 1:11. 1 J *2:29. *3:7. **by.** Is *53:5, 6. Mt *27:26. Mk *15:15. Jn *19:1. **healed.** Ps *147:3. Ml *4:2. Mt √8:17. Lk +*4:18. Re 22:2.

25. **as sheep.** ſ160A, Ps +1:3. Ps *119:176. Is *53:6. Je 23:2. Ezk *34:6. Mt *9:36. *18:12. Lk *15:4-6. **returned.** Ac +9:35. **The Shepherd.** 1 P *5:4. Ps √23:1-3. 80:1. SS 1:7, 8. Is *40:11. Ezk *34:11-16, 23, 24. 37:24. Zc 13:7. Jn *10:11-16. He *13:20. **Bishop.** He 3:1. Ac +*20:28g. **souls.** Gr. *psyche*, ſ171Q2, 2 C +12:15mg.

1 PETER 3

Exhortations to wives and husbands, concerning their respective duties, 1-7; and to all Christians to live in amity, to forgive injuries, to be constant under persecutions, to profess and defend the truth with meekness; and to maintain a good conscience: enforced, by the nature of their calling, their privileges, and the example of Christ, 8-18. The case of those to whom Christ, by his Spirit in Noah, had preached, who yet perished in the deluge; and that of Noah and his family saved in the ark: an emblem of the destruction of the wicked, and the salvation of those, who had not only the sign of baptism, but the thing signified by it, through a risen and glorified Redeemer, 18-22.

1. **Likewise.** ver. 7. 1 P 2:13. **ye wives.** Ge 3:16. Est 1:16-20. Pr +*19:13. Ro 7:2g. 1 C +*11:3. +*14:34n. Ep √5:22-24, 33. Col 3:18. 1 T +*2:11, 12. T 2:3-6. **if.** ſ184A, 1 C +15:2. **obey.** 1 P 1:22. 2:8. 4:17. Ro 6:17. 10:16. 2 Th 1:8. He +*5:9. 11:8. **the word.** ſ145, Jg +11:40. Ac +8:4. **they.** 1 C √7:16. Col 4:5. **won.** Pr +*11:30. *18:19. Mt 18:15. 1 C 9:19-22. Ja +*5:19, 20. **the conversation.** or, manner of life. ver. 16. Ja +3:13.

2. **they behold.** ver. 16. 1 P 1:15. 2:12. Ph 1:27. 3:20. 1 T *4:12. 2 P 3:11. **chaste.** T 2:5. **conversation.** ver. 1. **with fear.** ver. 5, 6, 15. Ep 5:33. 6:5. Col 3:22.

3. **adorning.** Gr. *kosmos*, Mt +4:8. **let it not.** Je 31:34. Ro 2:29. 7:22. 2 C 4:16. Ep 3:16. 1 T *2:9, 10. T 2:3, etc. Re 21:2. **that outward.** Ge 24:22, 47, 53. Ex 3:22. 32:2. 33:4. 35:22. 38:8. 2 K 9:30. Est 5:1. Ps 45:9. Is *3:18-24. 52:1. 61:10. Je 2:32. 4:30. Ezk 16:7-13. 23:40. **plaiting.** ſ86, Is +3:16. **putting on.** Ge ◑38:14, 15. Le 19:19.

4. **the hidden.** Ps 45:13. +*51:6. Mt 23:26. Lk 11:40. Ro 2:29. 6:6. 7:22. 2 C 4:16. Ep 3:16. 4:22-24. Col *3:3, 9, 10. 1 T 2:10. **heart.** ſ121J21, Ps +24:4. **which is.** 1 P 1:23. **not corruptible.** 1 Th +*5:23n. **a meek.** ver. 15. Ps +*25:9. 147:6. +*149:4. Is 11:4. 29:19. +*57:15. 61:1. Mt +*5:5. *11:29. 21:5. 2 C 10:1. Ga *5:23. Ep 4:2. Col 3:12. 1 T 2:11, 12. 2 T +*2:25. T 3:2. Ja *1:21. *3:13-17. **quiet.** Ps 131:2. Je 51:59. 1 Th 4:11. 2 Th 3:12. 1 T 2:2. **spirit.** Gr. *pneuma*, ſ121A2, Mt +5:3. ſ121A2, Ps +51:10. **which is in.** 1 S +*16:7. Ps 147:10, 11. +*149:4. Lk 16:15.

5. **the holy.** Pr 31:10, 30. Lk 8:2, 3. Ac 1:14. 9:36. 1 T 2:10. 5:10. T 2:3, 4. **who.** 1 S 2:1. Je 49:11. Lk 2:37. 1 T 2:15. 5:5. He 11:11. **adorned.** ver. 2-4.

6. **as Sara.** Ge 18:12. **calling him.** Ge *18:12. **daughters.** Gr. children. Ro 9:7-9. Ga 3:6. 4:22-26, 31. **and.** ver. 14, 15. Ge 18:15. Pr 3:25. *29:25. Is 57:11. Da 3:16-18. Mt 26:69-75. Ac 4:8-13, 19. Ep 5:33.

7. **Likewise.** ver. 1. **ye husbands.** Ge 2:23, 24. Pr *5:15-19. Ml *2:14-16. Mt *19:3-9. 1 C *7:3. Ep √5:25-

28, 33. Col √3:19. **knowledge.** 1 Th *4:5. *2 P 1:5, 6. **giving.** 1 C 12:22-24. 1 Th *4:4. **honor.** ſ108B, Mt +15:6. **vessel.** 1 Th +4:4. **heirs.** Ep *3:6. T *3:7. He *1:14. +11:9g. **grace of life.** 1 P 1:4, 13. Ro *6:23. Ga 3:28. **that your prayers.** T#1252. Jb *42:8. Ps 66:18. Is 59:1, 2. Da *10:12, 13. Mt *5:23, 24. +*18:19. Ro *8:26, 27. 1 C 7:5. Ep +*4:30. *6:18. Ja +4:3.

8. **be ye.** See on Ac 2:1. 4:32. Ro +12:16. 15:5n. 1 C +*1:10. Ph *2:2. 3:16. **having.** Zc 7:9. Mt 18:33. Lk 10:33. Ro 12:15. 1 C 12:26. Ja 2:13. 3:17. **love as brethren.** or, loving to the brethren. See on 1 P *1:22. 2:17. Ro *12:10. He +13:1. 2 P 1:7. 1 J *3:14, 18, 19. **pitiful.** Ps 103:13. Pr 28:8. Mt 18:33. Ep *4:32. Ja *5:11. **courteous.** T#135. Pr 29:23. Mt +17:27 (T#459). 26:50. Ac 27:3. 28:7. Ep √4:+2, 31, 32. 5:1, 2. Ph √4:8, 9. Col 3:12. 4:6.

9. **not rendering.** 1 P 2:20-23. Pr 17:13. 20:22. Mt *5:39, 44. Lk 6:27-29. Ro *12:14, +17, 19-21. 1 C *4:12, 13. Ep √4:32. 1 Th *5:15. **or railing.** 1 P 2:23. 1 C 5:11. 6:10. **blessing.** Mt 5:44. Lk 6:28. Ro 12:14. 1 C 4:12. **called.** 1 P 2:21. 5:10. See on Ro *8:28, 30. **inherit.** Mt 19:29. +*25:34. Mk 10:17. Lk 10:25. 18:18. **a blessing.** Mt +6:33. Ro 15:29. Ep 1:3.

10. **he.** See on Ps ▶34:12-16. **love.** Dt 32:47. Jb 2:4. Pr 3:2, 18. 4:22. 8:35. Mt 19:17. Mk 8:35. Ja 12:25. **life.** ſ108B, 1 S +10:24. **see.** Jb 7:7, 8. 9:25. 33:28. Ps 27:13. 49:19. 106:5. Ec 2:3. Mt 13:16, 17. **refrain.** 1 P 2:1, 23. Ps 15:3. 39:1. 141:3. Pr 13:3. *18:21. 21:23. Ep *4:26. See on Ja *1:26. 3:1-10. **speak.** 1 P 2:1, 22. Zp 3:13. Jn 1:47. Re *14:5.

11. **eschew.** Jb 1:1. 2:3. 28:28. Ps 34:14. *37:27. Pr *3:7. 16:6, 17. Is *1:16, 17. Mt *6:13. Jn 17:15. Ro *12:9. **do good.** Ps 125:4. Mt 5:45. Mk 14:7. Lk +*6:9, 35. Ro 7:19, 21. Ga +*6:10. 1 T +*6:18. He +*13:16. Ja +*4:17. 3 J 11. **seek peace.** Ps 120:6, 7. Mt +*5:9. Lk 1:79. Ro *5:1. 8:6. √12:18. *14:17, +19. Ga *5:22. Col 3:15. He +*12:14. Ja *3:17, 18.

12. **the eyes.** ſ22A7, Dt +11:12. Dt 11:12. 2 Ch *16:9. Jb 36:7. Ps 11:4. 33:18. +*▶34:15, 16. Pr +*15:3. Zc 4:10. **his ears.** Ex +*22:23. 2 Ch 7:15. Ps 65:2. Pr *15:8, 29. Jn +*9:31. Ja +*5:4, 16. **but.** Le 17:10. 20:3, 5, 6. 26:17. Ps *66:18. 80:16. Je 21:10. 44:11. Ezk 14:8. 15:7. Am 9:4. **the face.** ſ22A4, Ge +19:13. Ac +2:28. **against.** Gr. upon. Ge +6:13 (T#566). Ps +34:16 (T#303). **do evil.** Ps +*34:16.

13. **who.** Pr +*16:7. Is 50:9. Ro +*8:28. 13:3. **if ye.** ſ184C, Mt +4:9. **followers.** Ps 38:20. Pr 15:9. 1 C 14:1. Ep 5:1. 1 Th 5:15. 2 T 5:10. 3 J 11.

14. **if.** ſ184D1, Lk +22:67. lit. if even ye were to suffer. The Apostle does not assume that they so suffered, as the A.V. suggests. 1 P 2:19, 20. 4:13-16. Je 15:15. Mt +*5:10-12. 10:18-22, 39. 16:25. 19:29. Mk 8:35. 10:29. Lk 6:22, 23. Ac 9:16. 2 C 12:10. Ph 1:29. Ja *1:12. **righteousness' sake.** ſ46C, Mt +8:6. "Righteousness" (Gr. *dikaiosunee*) is used of ordinary piety, kindness, etc. So 2 C 9:9. Mt 6:1 according to one reading (B680). **happy.** Ja 5:11. **and be not afraid.** ver. 6. Is *8:12, 13. 29:23. 41:10-14. 51:12. Je 1:8. Ezk 3:9. Mt +*10:28, 31. Lk +*12:4, 5. Jn 14:1, 27. Ac 18:9, 10. **their terror.** Je +*10:5. **neither.** Jn 14:1, 27.

15. **sanctify.** ſ108B, Je +12:3. Nu 20:12. 27:14. Is *5:16. *8:13. 29:23. Mt 6:9g. **and be ready.** Ps *119:46. Pr 15:28. Je *26:12-16. Da *3:16-18. Am 7:14-17. Mt *10:18-20. Lk *21:14, 15. Ac *4:8-12. *5:29-31. 21:39, 40. 22:1, 2, etc. 24:14. 26:22. Col *4:6. 2 T +*2:25.

always. Gr. *aei*, Mk 15:8. **to give**. 2 C +7:11. 2 T 2:25. **an answer**. One of the most effective approaches possible in witnessing and personal evangelism is to become involved in the lives and activities of others who are not part of the Christian community, and let our lives prompt others to ask us questions about our faith. When this happens, we have earned a right to be heard, and can be more effective for Christ when we answer their questions about our faith, than if we try to force our faith upon persons who do not have an immediate interest in our message. Le +*19:17. Dt +6:7 (T#1073). Pr +*22:21. Ac +19:33. 24:10. T 1:13. **a reason**. 1 S *12:7. Is *1:18. *41:21. Ac *24:25. Ph 1:7, 16, 27. 2 T +*2:24, 25. T 1:9-11. 2 P 1:16. 1 J 1:1-3. Ju +*3, 22. **the hope**. 1 P *1:3, 4. Ac +*26:7. Ro +*15:4. Col *1:5, 23, 27. T *1:2. He 3:6. *6:11, 18, 19. **with meekness**. See on ver. *2, *4. 2 T +*2:25, 26. **fear**. *or*, reverence. 1 P +1:17. He *12:28, 29.

16. **Having**. He 13:18. **a good conscience**. ver. +21. 1 P 2:19. Ac 24:16. Ro 9:1. 2 C +*1:12. 4:2. 1 T 1:5, 19. 2 T 1:3. He 9:14. 13:18. **whereas**. See on 1 P 2:12. T 2:8. **be ashamed**. Da 6:4. Lk 13:17. Ac *24:13. **falsely**. Mt +*5:11. **accuse**. 1 P 4:4. Lk 6:28g. **good**. See on ver. 1, 2. **conversation**. ver. 1. Ja +3:13.

17. **if**. ʃ184D1, Lk +22:67. 1 P 2:15. 4:2, 19. Mt 26:39, 42. Ac +18:21. 21:14. **the will**. 1 Th +4:3. **suffer**. See on ver. 14. Ac 26:2, 3.

18. **once**. He 9:26, 28. **suffered**. 1 P *2:21-24. *4:1. Is *53:4-6. Ro +4:25. *5:6-8. 8:3. 2 C √5:21. Ga *1:4. *3:13. T *2:14. He *9:26, 28. **for sins**. 1 P 2:24. Le +=5:6. **the just**. Zc *9:9. Mt *27:19, 24. Ac *3:14. *22:14. 2 C *5:21. Ja *5:6. 1 J *1:9. **that**. Ep √2:16-18. **bring**. Nu=18:2. He 2:10. **being**. 1 P *4:1, 6. Da *9:26. Ro *4:25. 2 C *13:4. Col *1:21, 22. **the flesh**. ʃ171Q7, Jn +1:14. 1 P 4:6. Jn 3:6. 6:63. **but quickened**. Ps +*71:20. Jn +*2:22. Ro *1:4. 4:17. *8:11. 1 C 15:45. **by**. The Greek article *to* in the dative case is omitted by many modern textual authorities, but most certainly is the correct text. No apostle would assert that Jesus Christ died physically but was raised as a spirit being (rendered, following the modern Greek textual authorities, by the *New World Translation*, "made alive in the spirit"), for such an assertion is a denial of the most basic or fundamental doctrine of the gospel, the physical, bodily resurrection of Jesus Christ on the third day (Jn +*2:19, 21. Ro 10:9, 10. 1 C 15:4). Scripture asserts the physical death of the body of Christ, but not the death of his or anyone else's spirit, so that not spirits but bodies are made alive by resurrection. The resurrection of Christ is attributed to each member of the Trinity by Scripture (Jn 2:19 and 10:18. Ac 2:24, 32. 1 P 3:18 and Ro 8:11). **Spirit**. Gr. *pneuma*, Mt +3:16; see Ro ◐+1:4. Ps +*146:4. Lk ◐23:46. Jn 10:18. Ro *8:11. He 1:10.

19. **By which**. ʃ136, Is +60:12. 1 P 1:11, 12. √4:6. Ne 9:30. 2 P *1:21. Re 19:10. **he went**. Christ, as God, had gone, by his Spirit, inspiring his servant Noah, to denounce the approaching deluge, and preach repentance to incorrigible antediluvians, who perished in their sins, and whose "spirits" were in "the prison" of hell, when the apostle wrote; being confined there till the judgment of the great day. This appears to be the genuine sense of the passage, as it is perfectly agreeable to the whole of the context. This passage does not teach Christ's alleged "descent into hell," to preach the gospel to those who had never heard (Ezk

16:55), as some mistakenly interpret. In this text only the antediluvians are mentioned as having been preached to: does anyone assert that when Christ allegedly went to hades to preach to the unsaved dead that he selectively preached only to those who had been living in Noah's day in the time before the flood? Scripture positively forbids the notion that there is any second chance for salvation after death (He +*9:27). Christ upon his death went to paradise, according to his promise to the dying thief (Lk 23:43). Ps +*16:9-11. Jn 20:17. He 9:12. **and preached**. Ps 68:18. Ep 4:9. **spirits**. Gr. *pneuma*, Lk +24:37. He +*12:23. Re ◐6:9. 20:4. **in prison**. Ge=39:20. Is 42:7. 49:9. 61:1. 2 P 2:4, 5. Ju 6. Re 20:7.

20. **sometime**. Ge *6:3, 5, 13, 14. 2 P +3:9. **the longsuffering**. Is *30:18. Ro 2:4, 5. 9:22. 2 P 3:15. **of God**. ʃ29, Ex +19:6. i.e. *the longsuffering God*. **the days**. Mt *24:37-39. Lk 17:26-30. **of Noah**. 2 P 2:5. **while**. Ge 6:14-22. He 11:7. **preparing**. He +3:3g. **wherein few**. Ge 6:14-22. 8:1, 18. Mt +√7:14. Lk *12:32. +*13:24, 25. 2 P 2:5. **eight**. Ge 7:1, 7, 23. 8:18. He √11:7. 2 P 2:5. **souls**. Gr. *psyche*, ʃ171Q1A, Ac +2:41. ʃ171Q1, Ge +12:5. Ac +27:37. **were saved**. ʃ63H, Ge +12:15. Supply ellipsis, (and delivered). Saved from what? Clearly, saved from the water. Does the apostle assert "the flood of water saved from the flood water"? Rather, Noah and his family were saved by the ark from the water, thus water was not the saving but the destructive element. **by**. or, through. 1 P 1:7. 1 C 3:15. **water**. Ge 7:17-23. 2 C 2:15, 16. Ep *5:26.

21. **like**. Ro 5:14. 1 C 4:6. He *9:24g. *11:19. **figure**. or, antitype. R. L. Keeler asks, "What saves us? Peter says 'the antitype baptism now saves us.' What is this antitype baptism, and how does it save us? By examining the type or figure we will better understand the antitype. Water and the ark together saved Noah's family in the type. In the antitype it is the blood of Christ (of which water is the type), and Christ himself (of which the ark is the type), by which we are saved—saved from sin and everlasting death" (*Christian Baptism*, p. 285). **baptism**. ʃ101, Dt +32:42. This is a reference to real, not ritual baptism, for ritual baptism does not save us, it being only a humanly administered ordinance, and Peter's parenthetical words seem expressly given to guard against such a misapplication of his words to the ritual ordinance. Real baptism accomplished by the Holy Spirit saves us, placing us in the body of Christ, and applying the cleansing blood of Christ to our hearts (Ac +*1:5n. +*22:16. 1 C 12:13. T 3:5. He 10:22. Re 1:5) upon our calling upon Christ (Ro 10:13) and placing faith in his resurrection (Ro 10:9). Mt +*28:19. Mk √16:16. Lk *12:50. Ac √2:38. 16:33. +*22:16. Ro √6:3-6. 1 C √12:13. Ga √3:27. Ep *5:26. Col √2:12. T √3:5-7. **save us**. T *3:5. **not the putting**. Ezk *36:25, 26. Zc 13:1. 2 C *7:1. 2 P 1:14. **filth**. 2 C 7:1. Re 22:11. **the answer**. or, interrogation, or inquiry, or appeal. Gr. *eperoteema*. As used by Peter, *eperoteema* appears to answer to the passive participle (paul) of *shael*, viz. something asked for; (hence applied to anything borrowed. See 2 K 6:5). That which is sought for by an interrogation being an answer, *eperoteema* by an obvious metonymy would mean "answer" (B. W. Newton, *Baptism*, p. 86). This is therefore an instance of ʃ121C2E. Figure of speech Metonymy of the Cause, where the thing or action is

put for that which is the effect or product of it, in certain verbs, here of asking, where the verb *eperoteema* which means an interrogation is put for the answer to such interrogation. Compare 2 K 6:5 (borrow) and 1 S 1:28 (lent). For other instances of this figure see Jb +19:25. Some (as Benjamin Wills Newton, *The Doctrine of Scripture Respecting Baptism*, pp. 36, 45, 51, 58, 114, 136) have urged this text as proof against infant baptism: "even if it were specially revealed to us that any particular infant or infants were in a state of salvation, yet we should not be authorized to baptize them until they could themselves return 'the answer of a good conscience unto God'" (p. 58). Such an objection is founded upon the error of confounding what is asserted in the abstract with an application made in the concrete, or specific instance. The error would be quickly perceived were any one to assert that when "God saw the wickedness of man" (Ge 6:5, *f*121N1. See for this figure Ge +31:54), women were not included, for only the masculine gender is employed. Every one sees that it is the fact, in the abstract—the fact of a general depravity of morals—that is asserted, without any attempt to distinguish between the comparative corruption of the sexes. A distinction is therefore to be made between a general question and a given case: language applicable to an abstract question cannot be applied to a specific case. In this case Peter is speaking of adults, but such language cannot exclude the applicability of baptism to infants or children. Language is often addressed to adults which seems only appropriate to them, and yet that same language does not imply an exclusion of infants (see Ac 8:12n). Circumcision is sometimes spoken of in language applicable only to adults (Dt 10:16. Ro 2:28, 29), but such language cannot be used to exclude the ordinance from its applicability to infants (See Hibbard, *Christian Baptism*, Part I, pp. 257-260). 2 K 6:5 (borrowed). Da 4:17 (demand), LXX. Ac √8:37. Ro √10:9, 10. 2 C *1:12. 1 T *6:12. **good conscience.** *f*101, Dt +32:42. ver. 16. 1 P 2:19. Ac 15:9. +23:1. 24:16. Ro 2:28, 29. *8:1. 2 C +1:12. He 9:13, 14. +*10:22. 13:18. **by the resurrection.** 1 P *1:3. Ac +*2:24. Ro *1:4. 1 C *15:17. Ep 2:1, 4-6. Col 2:12.

22. **is gone.** Mk 16:19. Ac +*1:11. 2:33-36. +*3:21. He 6:20. 8:1. 9:24. **is on the right hand.** 1 P +1:21. Ps 110:1. Mt 22:44. Mk 12:36. Lk 20:42. Ro *8:34. Ep *1:20, 21. Ph *2:9, 10. Col *3:1. He 1:3, 13. 8:1. 10:12. 12:2. **angels.** Ro 8:38. 1 C 15:24. Ep 1:21. **authorities.** Ge=45:8. 1 C 15:24g. **and powers.** Ep 1:21. Col 1:16. 2:10. **made subject.** Mt +28:18.

1 PETER 4

Exhortations to cease from sin, in conformity to Christ who had suffered for it; and to live holy lives, though reproached for it; in expectations of a future judgment, 1-6; to sobriety, watchfulness, and prayer; because "the end of all things is at hand," 7; and to love, hospitality, and a due improvement of talents, as the stewards of God, and in order to glorify him, 8-11. Encouragements to patience, and confidence in God, amidst persecutions; with cautions and instructions, 12-19.

1. **Christ.** See on 1 P *2:21. 3:18. **arm.** Ro 13:12-14. Ep 6:13. Ph 2:5. He *12:3. **mind.** or, thought. He 4:12g. **for.** 1 P 2:24. Ro *6:2, 7, 11. Ga √2:20.

*5:24. Col *3:3-5. **ceased.** Is *1:16. Ezk 16:41. He 4:10. 2 P 2:14. 1 J *3:6.

2. **no.** 1 P 2:1, 14. Ro 6:14. 7:4. 14:7. 2 C √5:15. Ep 4:17, 22-24. 5:7, 8. Col 3:7, 8. T 3:3-8. **the rest.** 1 P +1:14. **the lusts.** Ho 6:7mg. Mk *7:21. Ep 2:3. T *2:12. 1 J *2:16. **the will.** 1 P 2:15. Ps 143:10. Mt 7:21. 12:50. 21:31. Mk 3:35. Jn 1:13. +*7:17. Ro 6:11. +*12:2. 2 C √5:15. Ga *2:19, 20. Ep 5:17. 6:6. Col *1:9. 4:12. 1 Th +*4:3. 5:18. He 13:21. Ja *1:18. 1 J *2:17.

3. **the time past.** 2 S 3:17, 18. 5:1, 2. Ezk 21:27. 44:6. 45:9. Ac +14:16. *17:30. Ro 8:12, 13. 1 C 6:11. **to have.** 1 P 1:14. Dt 12:30, 31. Ro 1:20-32. 1 C 12:2. Ep *2:2, 3. 4:17-19. 1 Th 4:5. T *3:3. **will of.** Ac 27:43. Ro 9:19g. **lasciviousness.** *f*168, Is +1:11. Mk +*7:22. Ro 13:13. 2 C 12:21. Ga 5:19. Ep 4:19. 2 P 2:2, 18. Ju 4. **excess.** 2 S 13:28. Pr 23:29-35. Is *5:11. 28:7. Ep +*5:18. **revellings.** Ro 13:13. Ga 5:21. **and.** 1 K 21:26. 2 Ch 15:8. Is 65:4. Je 16:18. Re 17:4, 5. **idolatries.** *f*79, Ge +21:16. Ga 5:20.

4. **they think.** ver. 12. **strange.** Ac 17:18-20. **excess.** Mt 23:25. Lk 15:13. Ro 13:13. Ep +*5:18. 2 P 2:13. **speaking evil.** See on 1 P 2:12. 3:16. 18:6. Ac +13:45g. 2 P 2:12-19. Ju 10.

5. **give account.** *f*108B, Mt +12:36. Ml 3:13-15. Mt 12:36. Lk 16:2. Ro 14:12. Ju *14, *15. **that.** Ps *1:6. Ec *12:14. Ezk 18:30. Mt +*10:15n. 25:31, etc. Jn 5:22, 23, 28, 29. Ac +10:42. *17:31. Ro *14:10-12. 1 C 15:51, 52. 1 Th +*4:16n. 2 T +*4:1. Ja *5:9.

6. **to them.** 1 P 3:19. Jn 5:25, 26. **that they.** ver. 1, 2. Mt 24:9. Ro +*8:9-11. 1 C 11:31, 32. **in the flesh.** 1 P +3:18. Jn 3:6. 6:63. **but live.** Ro 8:2. Ga 2:19. 5:25. Ep 2:3-5. T 3:3-7. Re 14:13. **according to God.** 1 P +5:2. **spirit.** Gr. *pneuma*, Ro +1:4.

7. **the end.** Ec 7:2. Je 5:31. Ezk 7:2, 3, 6. Mt 24:13, 14. Ro *13:12. 1 C 7:29. 10:11. 15:24. Ph 4:5. He *10:25. Ja +*5:8, 9. 2 P *3:9-11. 1 J *2:18, 19. **at hand.** Ro +*13:12. Ph *4:5. 2 Th ❶+*2:2. He *10:25. Ja 5:8. **sober.** T#711, 1389. See on 1 P 1:13-15. 5:8. Pr +14:13 (T#479). Mk 5:15. Lk 8:35. Ro 12:3. 2 C 5:13. 1 Th 5:6-8. 2 T +*1:7. T 2:6, 11-13. **and watch.** 1 P 3:7. Mt 24:42. 25:13. 26:38-41. Mk 13:33-37. 14:37, 38. Lk +*21:34, 36. 22:46. Ro 12:12. Ep 6:18. Col 4:2. 2 T 4:5. Re 16:15. **unto prayer.** Lk +18:1. Ph *4:6. 1 Th +*5:17.

8. **above.** Col *3:14. Ja 5:12. 3 J 2. **fervent.** *Agapeen ektenee*, "intense love; for love shall cover (or covers, *kaluptei*, in the present tense, as several copies read) a multitude of sins;" which seems a reference to the proverb, "love covereth all sins," Pr *10:12. 1 P *1:22. Ac +12:5. 1 C 13:1-13. 14:1. 1 Th 3:12. 4:9, 10. 2 Th 1:3. 1 T 1:5. He 13:1. 2 P 1:6, 7. **for.** Pr 10:12. 12:16. 17:9. 28:13. 1 C *13:5-7. Ja +*5:20. **shall.** or, will. **cover.** Lk 7:47. **multitude of.** Mt 18:21, 22. Ga *6:1. Ep *4:32.

9. **hospitality.** Pr 3:27, 28. Ml +*3:16. 9:27, 28, 43. 11:25, 26. *16:15. 17:7. Ro *12:13. +√15:7. 16:23. 1 T +3:2. T +*1:8. He *13:2, 16. 1 J 3:14. 3 J *8. **one to another.** ver. 10. Ro +*12:5. **without.** Le 19:18. Nu +*11:1. Ac 6:1g. 2 C *9:7. Ph √2:14. Phm 14. Ja *5:9. Ju +*16.

10. **every.** Mt 25:14, +15. Lk 19:13. Ro √12:3, 6-8. 1 C *4:7. 7:7. *12:4-11. Ep 4:7. **minister.** ver. 11. Jb 29:15, 16. Ezk 16:49. Da *11:33n. Mt 20:28. 25:44. Mk 10:45. Lk 8:3. Ro 15:25, 27. 16:3-5. 1 C *14:26. 16:15. 2 C 9:1. Ga 5:13. *6:10. Ep *5:19-21. 1 T +*6:17,

18. 2 T 1:18. He +*6:10. **one to another.** ver. 9. Ro +12:5. **good stewards.** Mt +√24:45. *25:14, 21. Lk +*12:42. 16:1-8. 1 C *4:1, 2. +9:17. T 1:7. **the manifold.** 1 C 3:10. 12:4. 15:10. 2 C 6:1. Ep 3:8. 4:11.

11. **If.** √184A, 1 C +15:2. **any.** Is +√8:20n. Je *23:22, 28. 1 C *4:1, 2. 2 C *9:1, 7, 8. Ep *4:29. Col *4:6. Ja *1:19, 26. 3:1-6. **as the oracles.** T#1060. Is +*8:20. Je *23:28. Ac 7:38. Ro 3:2. He *5:12. **of God.** √63B, Ge +25:28. Supply ellipsis, "the oracles of God (require)." **if.** √184A, 1 C +15:2. See on ver. *10. **the ability.** 1 Ch *29:11-16. Ro √12:+3, 6-8. 1 C 3:10. 4:7. 12:4. **God giveth.** Is 43:7. **that.** 1 P 2:5. 1 C *6:20. √10:31. 2 C 9:13. Ep 3:20, 21. *5:20. **through.** 1 P 2:5. Ph *1:11. *2:11. **to whom.** 1 P 5:11. Ro +11:36. 16:27. Ep 3:21. 1 T 1:17. 6:16. Ju *25. Re *1:5, 6. **dominion.** 1 P 5:11. Ps *145:13. Da 4:3, 34. +*7:14. Mt +*6:13. 1 T *6:16. Ju 25. Re 1:6. *5:12-14. **for ever.** Gr. *aion,* Mt +6:13. **and ever.** Gr. *aion,* Mt +6:13. lit. unto the ages of the ages, Ga +1:5.

12. **think.** ver. 4. Is 28:21. **the fiery.** See on 1 P *1:7. Pr 27:21. Da *11:35. 1 C √3:13. **trial.** Ps *66:10. Jn *15:20. 2 Th 1:4-10. 3:5. Ja 5:7, 8. **as though.** 1 P 5:9. 1 C +*10:13. 1 Th 3:2-4. 2 T 3:12.

13. **rejoice.** 1 P 1:6. Mt +*5:12. Lk 6:22, 23. Ac 5:41. 16:25. Ro *5:3. 2 C √4:17. √12:9, 10. Ja *1:2, 3. **ye are partakers.** 1 P *5:1, 10. Lk 9:23. Ac +5:41. Ro √8:17. 2 C *1:7. 4:10. Ph 3:10, 11. Col *1:24. 2 T *2:12. Ja *1:12. Re 1:9. **sufferings.** 1 P 5:1. 2 C +1:5. **when.** 1 P 1:5, 6, 13. 5:1. Mt +*16:27. +*25:31. Mk *8:38. Lk 17:30. Ro *8:17, 18. 2 Th √1:7-10. Ju 24. Re +*1:7. **be glad.** T#328. 1 P 1:7, 8, 13. Dt +33:9 (T#672). Is 25:9. 35:10. +*51:11. Mt 25:21, 23, 34. Col 3:4. T +*2:13. Ju +24 (T#339). **exceeding joy.** Ps 16:11. Is 35:10. Ju +*24.

14. **If.** √184A, 1 C +15:2. **ye be.** 1 P 2:19, 20. 3:14, 16. **reproached.** T#778. ver. 4, 5. Ps 69:9. 89:51. Is *51:7, 8. Mt *5:11, 12. Lk 6:22. Jn 7:47-52. 8:48. 9:28, 34. Ac 24:12. 2 C 12:10. **for the name.** ver. 16. Mk 9:41. Jn 15:21. He 11:26. **happy.** 1 K 10:8. Ps *32:1, 2. 146:5. Ja *1:12. 5:11. **for.** Nu 11:25, 26. 2 K 2:15. Is 11:2. **spirit.** Gr. *pneuma,* Mt +3:16. **of glory.** 2 C *3:18. Ja *2:1. **and of God.** Is 11:2. Ph +3:3. **on their part.** Ac 13:45. 18:6. 2 P 2:2. **but.** 1 P 2:12. 3:16. Mt *5:16. Ga 1:24. 2 Th *1:10-12.

15. **suffer.** 1 P *2:19, 20. 3:14, 17. Mt +*5:11. 2 T 2:9. **a busybody.** *Allotrioepiskopos,* an inspector of another; meddling with other people's concerns. Pr 20:3. 1 Th *4:11. 2 Th 3:11, 12. 1 T 5:13g.

16. **if.** √184A, 1 C +15:2. **as.** ver. 19. 1 P 3:17, 18. Ac 11:26. 26:28. Ep 3:13-15. **a Christian.** Ac +26:28. **let him not.** Is 50:7. 54:4. Ph 1:20. 2 T 1:12. Re 12:2, 3. **but.** ver. +14. Is 24:15. Ac *5:41. Ro 5:2-5. Ph 1:29. Ja 1:2-4.

17. **the time.** Jn *16:2. **judgment.** Is *10:12. Je 25:29. 49:12. Ezk √9:6. Am 3:2. Ml +*3:5. Mt 3:9, 10. Lk +*12:47, 48. Ro 2:9. 1 C *11:32. **the house.** 1 T +3:15. **and if.** √184A, 1 C +15:2. Lk 23:31. **what.** Mt 11:20-24. Lk 10:12-14. 1 Th *2:14-16. He *2:2, 4. *12:24, 25. **obey.** 1 P 2:8. Ro 2:8. Ga 3:1. 5:7. 2 Th √1:8. He +*5:9. 11:8. **gospel of God.** Ro +1:1.

18. **if.** √184A, 1 C +15:2. 1 P 5:8. Pr 11:31. Je 25:29. Ezk 18:24. Zc *13:9. Mt 24:22-24. Mk 13:20-22. Lk 23:31. Ac +*14:22. 27:24, 31, 42-44. 1 C 10:12. He 4:1. 10:38, 39. **scarcely.** Ps 17:4. Mt 4:4, 6, 7. +*7:14. Lk +*21:36. Ro *11:22. 1 C 3:15. +*9:27. 1 T *6:12. He +*2:2, 3. **where.** Ps *1:4, 5. Ro 1:18.

5:6. 2 P 2:5, 6. 3:7. Ju *15. **ungodly and.** 1 T 1:9. Ju 15. **the sinner.** Ge 13:13. 1 S 15:18. Lk 15:1. Ro *5:8.

19. **let.** ver. *12-16. +*3:17. Ps +*119:75. Ac 21:11-14. **the will.** 1 Th +*4:3. **commit.** Ps 10:14. *31:5. *37:5. Lk 23:46. Ac *7:59. +*14:23. 20:32. Ep +*4:30. 2 T √1:12. 1 J *5:13. Ju *24. **souls.** Gr. psyche, √171Q2. Psyche used to emphasize the personal pronoun in the third person, as in 2 P 2:8. For the other uses of psyche, see Mt +2:20n. For other instances of √171Q2, see Nu +23:10 and Mt +12:18. Ex 30:12. Jb 32:2. **in.** 1 P *2:15. Est 4:16. Je *26:11-15. Da √3:16-18. +*6:10, 11, 22. Ro +*2:7. **a faithful.** T#226. Ex +34:6 (T#235). Dt 7:9. +8:2 (T#4). Jsh *21:45. *23:14. Ps 36:5. 89:2, 33, 34. *119:75, 90. *138:8. *146:5, 6. Is *40:27, 28. 43:7, 21. *51:12, 13. *54:16, 17. Jn +10:28 (T#515). Ro +8:34 (T#516). 1 C +10:13 (T#725). 2 C +1:22 (T#517). Col 1:16-20. 1 Th 5:24. He 1:2, 3. Re *4:10, 11. 5:9-14.

1 PETER 5

The apostle exhorts "the elders to feed the flock of God," willingly, cheerfully, disinterestedly, and humbly; and to be examples to it; expecting from the chief Shepherd, at his appearance, an unfading crown of glory, 1-4. He requires the younger to submit to the elder; and all of them to be "clothed with humility," "casting all their care on" God, 5-7; and to be "sober and vigilant;" and steadfastly, by faith, to "resist the devil," and bear tribulation, 8, 9. He concludes with prayers, salutations, and benedictions, 10-14.

1. **elders.** Ac +11:30. *14:23. 15:4, 6, 22, 23. 20:17, 28g. 21:18. 1 T 5:1, 19. T 1:5. **who.** Phm 9. 2 J 1. 3 J 1. **am also.** T#519. Mt 16:23. 20:25-28. Ac 8:14, 15. 15:6, 7, 12, √13, 14-20. **an elder.** *Sumpresbuteros,* a fellow-elder, one on a level with yourselves. 2 J 1. 3 J 1. **and a witness.** 1 P 1:12. Mt *26:37. Lk +*24:48. Jn 15:26, 27. Ac *1:8, 22. 2:32. 3:15. 5:30-32. 10:39-41. **the sufferings.** 1 P 4:13. 2 C +1:5. **a partaker.** Gr. *koinonos,* ✱S#2844g. Mt 23:30. Lk 5:10 (partners). 1 C 10:18, 20 (fellowship). 2 C 1:7. 8:23 (partner). Phm 17. He 10:33 (companions). 2 P 1:4. **of the glory.** ver. 4. 1 P 1:3-5. Ps 73:24, 25. Jn *13:36. Ro *8:17, +18. 2 C 5:1, 8. Ph 1:19, 21-23. Col 3:3, 4. 2 T *4:8. 1 J *3:2. Re 1:9.

2. **Feed.** Pr +*27:23. SS 1:8. Is 40:11. Ezk 34:2, 3, 23. Mi 5:4. 7:14. Jn √21:15-17. Ac +*20:28. Ju 12. **the flock.** Is 63:11. Je 13:17, 20. Ezk 34:31. Zc 11:17. Lk +*12:32. 1 C 9:7. **which is among you.** or, as much as in you is. Ps 78:71, 72. Ac 20:26, 27. **taking.** He 12:15g. **the oversight.** Ac +*20:28. **not by constraint.** Is 6:8. 1 C *9:16, 17. Phm 14. **not for.** Is 56:11. Je 6:13. 8:10. Mi 3:11. Ml 1:10. Ac 20:33, 34. 2 C 12:14, 15. 1 T 3:3, 8. T *1:7, 11. 2 P 2:3. Re 18:12, 13. **of.** Ac 21:13. Ro 1:15. 2 C 8:11, 12. T 2:14. 3:1.

3. **as.** T#456. Ezk *34:4. Mt *20:25-28. *23:8-10. Mk 10:42-45. Lk 22:24-27. 1 C 3:5, 9. 2 C +*1:24. 4:5. 3 J *9, 10. **being lords over.** or, over-ruling. 2 C +*1:24. **heritage.** √96F2, Ge +4:10. 1 P 2:9. Dt 4:20. 9:29. *32:9. Ps 33:12. 74:2. Mi 7:14. Ac 1:17g. +*20:28. **but.** 1 C 10:6, 11. Ph 3:17. 4:9. 1 Th 1:5, 6. 2 Th 3:9. 1 T +*4:12. T *2:7.

4. **the chief.** ver. 2. 1 P 2:25. Ps 23:1. Is 40:11. Ezk +*34:23. 37:24. Zc 13:7. Jn +10:11. He *13:20. **appear.** Mt +*25:31, etc. Col *3:3, 4. 2 Th 1:7-10. 1 J 2:28. √3:2. Re +*1:7. 20:11, 12. **a crown.** 1 P 1:4.

Da +*12:3. 1 C 9:25. 2 T 4:8. Ja +1:12. Re +*2:10. 3:11.

5. **ye younger.** Le *19:32. Lk *22:26. 1 T 5:1. T 2:6. He 13:17. **submit.** Gr. *hupotasso*, ✳S#5293g. Rendered (1) put under: 1 C 15:27, 27, 27, 28c. Ep 1:22. He 2:8c. (2) be subject unto: Lk 2:51. 10:17, 20. Ro 13:1. 1 C 15:28b. Ep 5:24. (3) be subject to: Ro 8:7. 1 C 14:32. T 3:1. 1 P 2:18. 5:5b. (4) submit (one's) self unto: Ro 10:3. 1 C 16:16. Ep 5:22. Col 3:18. 1 P 5:5a. (5) submit (one's) self to: Ep 5:21. Ja 4:7. 1 P 2:13. (6) be in subjection unto: He 12:9. 1 P 3:5. (7) put in subjection under: He 2:8b. (8) Miscellaneous renderings: Ro 8:20a, be made subject to; Ro 8:20b, subject; Ro 13:5, be subject; 1 C 14:34, be under obedience; 1 C 15:28a, subdue unto; Ph 3:21, subdue unto; T 2:5, obedient to; T 2:9, be obedient unto; He 2:5, 8a, put in subjection; 1 P 3:1, be in subjection to; 1 P 3:22, be made subject unto. For a related word, ✳S#5292g, rendered "subjection," see 1 T +3:4. **the elder.** T#10. Le 19:32. Ps +71:9 (T#772). Is +*58:7. 1 T 5:1, 2. Ju +8 (T#730). **all.** 1 P 4:1, 5. Ro *12:10. Ep *5:21. Ph +*2:3. **be subject.** Ge 16:9. Ro 13:1. 1 C *16:16. Ep *5:21. *6:1, 5. Ph +*2:3. He +*13:17. **be clothed.** 1 P 3:3, 4. 2 Ch 6:41. Jb 29:14. Ps 132:9, 16. Is 61:10. Ro *13:14. Col 3:12. **one to another.** Ro +12:5. 1 C 12:25. 1 P +*4:10. **with humility.** Mt 20:26, 27. Jn 13:4, 5, 14. Ep 4:2g. **God resisteth.** Jb 22:29. Ps +*119:21. Pr *16:5. Da 11:12. Lk 18:4. See on Ja 4:6. **giveth.** Ps +*25:9. Is +*57:15. *66:2.

6. **Humble yourselves.** Ex 10:3. Le 26:41. 1 K 21:27, 29. 2 K 22:19. 2 Ch +*7:14. 12:6, 7, 12. 30:11. 32:26. 33:12, 19, 23. 36:12. Pr 29:23. Is 2:11. +*57:15. Je 13:18. 44:10. Da 5:22. Mi +*6:8. Lk 14:11. 18:14. Ja +*4:10. 5:10. **the mighty.** Ex 3:19. 32:11. Ps *89:13. 1 C 10:22. **hand of God.** Ac +13:11. **that.** Jb 36:22. Ps 75:10. 89:16, 17. Is 40:4. Ezk 17:21. 21:26. Mt 23:12. Lk 1:52. Ja 1:9, 10. **in.** Dt 32:35. Ro 5:6. 1 T 2:6. T 1:3.

7. **Casting.** 1 S 1:10-18. 30:6. Ps 27:13, 14. 34:+*4, 5. √37:5mg. √55:22. 56:3, 4. Mt *6:25, 31, 34. 13:22g. Lk 12:11, 12, 22, 26. Ph √4:6. He +*13:5, 6. **for he careth.** T#829. Dt 32:11, 12. Ps 33:18. 34:15. *103:13, 14. 142:4, 5. Is 46:3, 4. *63:9. Zc *2:8. Mt *6:26-33. 10:30. Mk 4:38. Lk 12:30-32. 21:18. Jn 10:13. **for you.** Ps *40:17.

8. **sober.** 1 P +1:13. *4:7. Mt 24:48-50. Lk 12:45, 46. +*21:34, 36. Ro 13:11-13. 1 Th 5:6-8. 1 T 2:9, 15. 3:2, 11. T 1:8. 2:2, 4, 6, 12. **be vigilant.** Mt +24:42.

Lk +*21:36. **your.** Est 7:6. Jb 1:6. 2:2. Ps 109:6mg. Is 50:8. Zc 3:1. Lk 22:31. **adversary.** 1 K ❍+11:14. Mt 5:25. Lk 12:58. 18:3. **the devil.** Jb 1:9-12. Mt 4:1, 11. 13:39. 25:41. Jn *8:44. 2 C *2:11. Ep 4:27. 6:11. Ja 4:7. 1 J 3:8-10. Re 12:9, 12. 20:2, 10. **as.** Jg 14:5. Ps 22:21. 104:21. Pr 19:12. 20:2. 28:15. Is 5:29, 30. 42:13. Je 2:15. 51:38. Ezk 19:7. Ho 11:10. Jl 3:16. Am 1:2. 3:4, 8. Zc 11:3. 2 T 4:17. Re 12:12. **walketh.** Dt ❍23:14. 2 Ch ❍16:9. Jb *1:7. *2:2. Lk 22:31, 32. Ac ❍10:38. **seeking.** Mt 12:43-45. Lk *22:31-34. 2 C 2:11. **devour.** Ezk 22:25. Da 6:24. Ho 13:8.

9. **resist.** Lk 4:3-12. Ep 4:27. *6:11-13. Ja √4:7. **steadfast.** Lk 22:32. Ac 16:5g. Ep 6:16. Col 2:5. 1 T 6:12. 2 T 4:7. He 11:33. **the same.** 1 P 1:6. 2:21. 3:14. 4:13. Jn 16:33. Ac +*14:22. 1 C +*10:13. 1 Th 2:15, 16. 3:3. 2 T *3:12. He 12:3. Re 1:9. 6:11. 7:14. **brethren.** Gr. brotherhood. 1 P 2:17. **world.** Gr. *kosmos*, Mt +4:8.

10. **the God.** Ex 34:6, 7. Ps 86:5, 15. Mi +*7:18, 19. Ro *5:20, 21. 15:5, 13. 2 C 13:11. He *13:20, 21. **grace.** Jn 1:17. Ro 5:21. Ep 2:8. T 2:11, 12. **who.** 1 P 1:15. Ro +*8:28-30. 9:11, 24. +*11:29. 1 C 1:9. Ph 3:14. 1 Th 2:12. 2 Th 2:14. 1 T 6:12. 2 T 1:9. 2 P 1:3. **eternal.** Gr. *aionios*, Mt +18:8. 2 C √4:17. 2 T +*1:9. *2:10. He 9:15. 2 P 1:3. 1 J 2:25. **after.** 1 P 1:+6, 7. Ex +*23:29. Ps +*119:75. 2 C √4:17. **make.** Ps *138:8. Lk +6:40. 2 C 13:11. Ga 6:1. 2 Th 2:17. He 13:21. Ju 24. **stablish.** Ac *14:22. Ro 1:11. 16:25. Col +*2:7. 1 Th 3:2, 13. 2 Th 2:17. 3:3. Ja 5:8. 2 P 1:12. Re 3:2. **strengthen.** Ps 138:7. Zc *10:6, 12. Lk 22:32. Ph √4:13. Col 1:22, 23. **settle.** 1 P 4:11.

11. **To him.** 1 P +4:11. Re 1:6. 5:13. **for ever.** Gr. *aion*, Mt +6:13. **and ever.** Gr. *aion*, Mt +6:13.

12. **Silvanus.** Ac +15:22. 2 C 1:19. 1 Th 1:1. 2 Th 1:1. **a faithful.** 1 C +4:2. Ep 6:21. Col 1:7. 4:7, +9. **I suppose.** Ro 8:18. 2 C 11:5. Ph 3:13g. **I have.** Ep 3:3. He 13:22. **exhorting.** He 13:22. Ju 3. **testifying.** Jn 21:21. Ac 20:24. 1 J 5:9, 10. 3 J 12. **true grace.** Ac +*11:23. 20:24. 1 C 15:1. Ga 1:8, 9. Col 1:6. 2 P 2:15. **wherein.** Ro 5:2. 1 C +*15:1, 2. 2 C 1:24. 2 P 1:12.

13. **at.** Ps 87:4. Re 17:5. 18:2. **elected.** 2 J 1, 13. **Marcus.** i.e. *a defense*, ✳S#3138g. See on Ac 12:12, 25. Col 4:10. Phm 24.

14. **one another.** √63G, Ge +50:23. **with a.** See on Ro *16:16n. 1 C 16:20. 2 C 13:12. 1 Th 5:26. **Peace.** 1 P 1:2. Jn 14:27. 16:33. 20:19, 26. See on Ro 1:7. Ep +6:23. **in.** See on Ro 8:1. 1 C 1:30. 2 C *5:17.

2 PETER

2 PETER 1

The apostle salutes his brethren, 1, 2. He shows the blessings to which God had called them; and earnestly exhorts them to diligence in every good work, in order to make "their calling and election sure;" intermixing suitable warnings and encouragement, 3-11. He states, that, aware of his approaching martyrdom, he is the more diligent, in thus admonishing them, that they might remember these things after his decease, 12-15. He urges the evidence of what he had seen and heard "in the holy mount," in confirmation of his testimony concerning the power and coming of

Christ, 16-18; referring them to the "more sure word of prophecy," 19; and instructing them, concerning the interpretation and source of it, 20, 21.

1. Cir. A.M. 4069. A.D. 65. **Simon.** or, Symeon. Ac 15:14. **Peter.** Mt 4:18. 10:2. Lk 22:31-34. Jn 1:42. 21:15-17. Ac *15:7. 1 P 1:1. **a servant.** Jn 12:26. Ro 1:1. Ja +1:1. **an apostle.** Lk 11:49. Jn 20:21. 1 C 9:1, 2. 15:9. Ga 2:8. Ep 3:5. 4:11. 1 P 1:1. 5:1. **have obtained.** ver. 4. Ac *15:8, 9. Ro 1:12. 2 C 4:13. Ep *2:8. 4:5. Ph 1:29. 2 T 1:5. T 1:1, 4. 1 P 1:7. 2:7. 1 J √5:13. **precious.** ver. 4. Ps 49:7, 8. 116:15. 139:17. Is 28:16. 1 P 1:19. **through.** Je 23:6. 33:16. Ro 1:17. *3:21-26. 5:19. 1 C 1:30. 2 C 5:21. Ph 3:9. **of God and our**

Savior. Gr. of our God and Savior. ver. 11. 2 P 3:18. Is *12:2. Lk 1:47. Jn +*20:28. 2 Th 1:12. 2 T +1:10. T +*2:13n. Ju +*4.

2. **Grace**. Nu *6:24-26. Da 4:1. 6:25. See on Ro 1:7. 1 P +1:2. Ju 2. Re *1:4. **the knowledge**. ver. 3, 8. 2 P 2:20. *3:18. Jb *22:21. Is *53:11. Lk 10:22. Jn *17:3. 2 C 4:6. Ph 3:8. 1 J *5:20, 21.

3. **his divine power**. Ps *110:3. Mt *28:18. Jn 1:16. 17:2. 2 C *12:9. Ep 1:19-21. Col *1:16, 19. He 1:3. **all things**. Ps *84:11. Ro +*8:32. 1 C 3:21-23. 2 C √12:9. 1 T 4:8. **godliness**. ver. 6, 7. 2 P 3:11. 1 T +*3:16. T 1:1. **through**. See on ver. *2. Jn *17:3. **called**. Ro +*8:28-30. 9:24. 1 C 1:9. Ep 4:1, 4. 1 Th 2:12. 4:7. 2 Th 2:14. 2 T *1:9. 1 P *1:15. 2:9, 21. 3:9. 5:10. **to**. *or*, by. **and**. ♪93A, Ge +1:26. **virtue**. ver. *5. Ru *3:11. Pr *12:4. 31:10, 29. Ph √4:8.

4. **are given**. ver. 1. Ezk 36:25-27. Ro 9:4. 2 C 1:20. 6:17, 18. 7:1. Ga 3:16. He 8:6-12. 9:15. 1 J 2:25. **precious promises**. T#786. Ps *25:10, 14. Is +*55:3. Ac +*26:6. Ro *8:30. +*15:8. 2 C *7:1. Ga 6:16. Ep 1:3, 4, 7, 8. **partakers**. Jn *1:12, 13. 2 C *3:18. Ep *4:23, 24. Col 3:10. He 12:10. 1 J √3:2. **having escaped**. 2 P 2:18-20. Ga *6:8. Ja *4:1-3. 1 P 4:2, 3. 1 J √2:15, 16. **the corruption**. 2 P 2:12, 19. 1 C +15:42. **world**. Gr. *kosmos*, Mt +4:8.

5. **And**. ♪148, Ge +8:22. **beside**. Lk 16:26. 24:21. **giving**. ver. 10. 2 P 3:14, 18. Ps 119:4. Pr +*4:23. Is 55:2. Zc 6:15. Jn 6:27. Ph 2:12. He +*6:11. √11:6. +*12:15. Ju 3. **add**. ver. 11. 2 C +9:10. **to your faith**. 1 T *6:11, 12. **virtue**. See on ver. 3. Ph √4:8. **to virtue**. ♪50, Ho +2:21. **knowledge**. ver. 2. 2 P √3:18. 1 C 14:20. Ep 1:17, 18. 5:17. Ph *1:9-11. Col +*1:9, 10. 1 P 3:7.

6. **And**. ♪148, Ge +8:22. **knowledge**. ♪50, Ho +2:21. **temperance**. Ac 24:25. 1 C *9:25-27. Ga 5:23. T 1:8. 2:2. **to temperance**. ♪50, Ho +2:21. **patience**. Ps *37:7. 2 C 6:6. He 6:12, 15. Ja 5:7-10. *S#5281g: Lk +*8:15. 21:19. Ro +*2:7. *5:3, 4. 8:25. +*15:4, 5. 2 C 1:6 (enduring). 6:4. 12:12. Col *1:11. 1 Th 1:3. 2 Th 1:4. 3:5. 1 T 6:11. 2 T 3:10. T 2:2. He +*10:36. +*12:1. Ja *1:3, 4. *5:11. Re +1:9. 2:2, 3, 19. 3:10. 13:10. *14:12. **to patience**. ♪50, Ho +2:21. **godliness**. ver. +3. 2 P 3:11. Ge 5:24. Is 57:1. 1 T 2:2, 10. +*3:16. 4:7, 8. 6:3, 6, 11. 2 T 3:5. T 1:1. He *12:28.

7. **And**. ♪148, Ge +8:22. **to godliness**. ♪50, Ho +2:21. **brotherly kindness**. Jn *13:34, 35. Ac +4:32 (T#111). Ro *12:10. 1 Th 3:12. 4:9, 10. He +*13:1. 1 P 1:22. 2:17. 1 J *3:14, 16. **to brotherly kindness**. ♪50, Ho +2:21. **charity**. 1 C √13:1-8. Ga +*6:10. Col 3:14. 1 Th 5:15. 1 T +*4:12. 1 P +*1:22. 3:8. 1 J *4:16, 21.

8. **be in you**. Jn 5:42. 2 C 9:14. *13:5. Ph 2:5. Col *3:16. Phm 6. **and abound**. 1 C +√15:58. 2 C 8:2, 7. Ph 1:9. Col +*2:7. *3:16. 1 Th 3:12. 4:1. 2 Th 1:3. **they**. Jn 15:7, 8. 2 C 5:13-17. **barren**. *or*, idle. Pr 19:15. Mt 20:3, 6. 25:26. Ro 12:11. 1 T 5:13. He *6:12. Ja 2:20g. **nor unfruitful**. T#815. Ps +*1:3. Je 31:12. Ho 14:5, 8. Mt 13:22. Mk 4:19. Jn *15:+2, 5, 6, 8, 14. Ep 5:11. T +3:14. Ju 12. **in the knowledge**. See on ver. 2.

9. **lacketh**. ver. 5-7. Mk 10:21. Lk 18:22. Ga *5:6, 13. Ja *2:14-26. **blind**. Jb 5:14. 12:25. Is 59:10. Zp 1:17. Mt +*6:23. +*15:14. +23:16. Jn *9:40, 41. 2 C √4:3, 4. 1 J *2:9-11. Re *3:17. **he was purged**. ver. 4. 2 P 2:18-20. Ro √6:1-4, 11. 1 C 6:11. Ep *5:26. T 2:14. He +*9:14. 1 P *3:21. 1 J √1:7. Re 1:5. 7:14.

10. **give diligence**. See on ver. 5. 2 P *3:17. Ph 2:12, 13. **to make**. 2 C 6:1. Ga 2:21. Ph √2:12. 2 T *2:19. He 3:14. *6:11, 19. 1 J 3:19-21. **your calling**. Ro +*11:29. **election**. Lk +18:7. Ro +*8:28-31. 1 Th *1:3, 4. 2 Th *2:13, 14. 1 P *1:2, 5. **sure**. Ro *8:16. 2 C 1:12. He +*6:11. 1 J 2:5, 6. **for if**. Ge +*4:7. Je +*7:5. Col +*1:23. 1 Th +*3:8. He +*3:14. Ja +*5:19. **ye do**. Ps +*15:5. Is 56:2. Mt *7:+*21, 24, 25. Lk +*6:47-49. +*11:28. 1 J *3:18, 19. Re *22:14. **never fall**. ♪158, Mt +5:18. T#819. 2 P *3:17. 2 Ch *20:20. Ps √37:24. 62:2, 6. 94:18. 112:6. *121:3. 138:8. Pr 10:25. Mi *7:8. Jn √10:28, 29 (T#515). 17:11. Ac *20:24, 25. Ro *8:38, 39. 1 C *1:8. ◐√10:12. 2 C 1:21. Ga 5:4. Ep *4:30. Ph *1:6. 1 Th *5:23, 24. 2 Th 3:3. He 12:15mg. Ja 2:10. 3:2. 1 P *1:5. 1 J 2:10. 5:18. Ju *24. Re *3:10, 11.

11. **an entrance**. Mt 25:34. Lk ◐9:26. Ac 14:22. 1 C◐3:15. 2 C5:1. 2 T4:8. 1 J*2:28. Re 3:21. **ministered**. ver. 5. 2 C +9:10. **abundantly**. Ps 36:8. SS 5:1. Is 35:2. Mt +*5:12. 20:23. √25:21. Lk +*18:30. Jn 10:10. Ep 3:20. Ph 3:14. He 6:17. **everlasting**. Gr. *aionios*, Mt +18:8. Da +*7:14. Re √11:15. **kingdom**. T#861. 2 S *23:1, 5. Is +*9:7. Da +*7:14, 27. Mt +*24:14. +*25:34. 26:29. Lk 12:32. 22:29, 30. Col +*1:13n. 1 Th 2:12. 2 Th 1:5. 2 T +*4:18. He +*12:28. Ja +*2:5. Re *5:10. √11:15. **our Lord and**. See on ver. 1. 2 P 3:18. T 2:13n. **Savior**. ver. 1. 2 T +1:10.

12. **I will not**. ver. 13, 15. 2 P 3:1. Ro *15:14, 15. Ph *3:1. 1 T 4:6. 2 T 1:6. He 10:32. Ju +*3, 17. **always**. Gr. *aei*, Mk +15:8. **in remembrance**. 2 T 2:14. T 3:1. **though**. 1 J *2:21. Ju 5. **and be established**. 2 P *3:17. Ac 16:5. Col +*2:7. He *13:9. 1 P *5:10, 12. **present truth**. 2 J 2.

13. **as long**. ♪142, Ge +20:16. ver. 14. 2 C 5:1-4, 8. He 13:3. **to stir**. 2 P 3:1. Hg 1:14. 2 T 1:6. **by**. See on ver. 12.

14. **shortly**. Dt 4:21, 22. 31:14. Jsh 23:14. 1 K 2:2, 3. Ac 20:25. 2 T *4:6-8. **put off**. ♪142, Ge +20:16. 1 P 3:21. **even**. Jn 13:36. *21:18, 19.

15. **I will**. Dt 31:19-29. Jsh 24:24-29. 1 Ch 29:1-20. Ps 71:18. 2 T +*2:2. He 11:4. **decease**. or, departure. Lk 9:31. **these**. See on ver. 4-7, 12.

16. **we have**. 2 P *3:3, 4. Jb *36:4. 1 C 1:17, 23. *2:1, 4. 2 C *2:17. +√4:2. 12:16, 17. Ep +*4:14. 2 Th 2:9. 1 T *1:4. *4:7. T 1:14. **cunningly devised**. This verse contains one of the most significant texts for apologetics to be found in the Word of God. Christian faith is not a blind leap into the dark, but is established upon firm evidence, for unlike other world religions, Christianity "rests on definite, historical facts and events—facts and historical events of such nature that if they really took place, the religion is true, and established by so direct, so strong and so great a variety of independent and converging proofs that it has been said again and again by great lawyers that they cannot but be regarded as proved under the strictest rules of evidence used in the highest American and English courts" (Irwin H. Linton, *A Lawyer Examines the Bible*, p. 16). Linton states that he had never found a single unbelieving lawyer or layman who had made a careful, lawyer-like, two-sided investigation of the claims of the Bible and its Christ. He was never able to find a single unbeliever who had read carefully even one of the old classics on the Christian Evidences.

Professor G. W. Wright has said, "All history is fragmentary. Each particular fact is the center of an infinite complex of circumstances. No man has intelligence enough to insert a suppositious fact into circumstances not belonging to it, and make it fit exactly. This only Infinite Intelligence could do. A successful forgery, therefore, is impossible if only we have a sufficient number of the original circumstances with which to compare it" (cited in Fred John Meldau, 57 *Reasons*, p. 37). Linton cites Simon Greenleaf to the same effect: "Every event which actually transpires has its appropriate relation and place in the vast complication of circumstances of which the affairs of men consist: it owes its origin to the events which have preceded it, is intimately connected with all others which occur at the same time and place, and often with those of remote regions, and in its turn gives birth to numberless others which succeed. In this almost inconceivable contexture and seeming discord there is perfect harmony; and while the fact which really happened tallies exactly with every other contemporaneous incident related to it in the remotest degree, it is not possible for the wit of man to invent a story which, if closely compared with the actual occurrences of the same time and place, may not be shown to be false" (Linton, pp. 53, 54). "In a number of concurrent testimonies, where there has been no previous concert (utterly negatived in the case of the Gospels by the apparent but completely reconciled discrepancies between them. Linton) there is a probability distinct from that which may be termed the sum of the probabilities resulting from the testimony of the witnesses; a probability which would remain even though the witnesses were of such character as to merit no faith at all. This probability arises from the concurrence itself. That such a concurrence should spring from chance is as one to infinity; that is, in other words, morally impossible. If, therefore, concert be excluded, there remains no cause but the reality of the fact" (Linton, citing George Campbell, against Hume, p. 55). "Now, in historical researches, a reconciled inconsistency becomes a positive argument. First, because an impostor generally guards against the appearance of inconsistency; and secondly, because when apparent inconsistencies are found, it is seldom anything but truth renders them capable of reconciliation. The existence of the difficulty proves the want or absence of that caution which usually accompanies the consciousness of fraud; and the solution proves that it is not the collusion of fortuitous propositions which we have to deal with, but that a thread of truth winds through the whole, which preserves every circumstance in its place" (Linton, p. 88, citing Paley. See further related notes on undesigned coincidences listed at Ac 12:12n).

We now come to an argument for the credibility of the facts contained in Scripture which has never been answered and never can be. Infidels have repeatedly been challenged to answer it but they have never even made the attempt. It is the argument of Leslie in his *Short and Easy Method with the Deists.* This argument rests solely upon the peculiarity of Christian evidence, already mentioned, by which the truth of the religion is indissolubly connected with certain matters of fact which could originally be judged of by the senses, and also upon the fact that there exist in the Church certain ordinances commemorative of those facts. Thus the truth of our religion seems to be embodied in institutions that now exist, and in observances

that pass before our eyes. The object of Leslie is to show, from the nature of the case—for here we make very little reference to written testimony—that the matters of fact stated could not have been received at the time unless they were true, and that the observances could never have been originated except in connection with the facts. In showing this, he lays down four rules, and asserts that any matter of fact in which these four rules meet must be true, and challenges the world to show any instance of any supposed matter of fact, thus authenticated, that has ever been shown to be false. His four rules are these: (1) That the matter of fact be such that men's outward senses, their eyes and ears, may be judges of it. (2) That it be done publicly, in the face of the world. (3) That not only public monuments be kept up in memory of it, but some outward actions be performed. (4) That such monuments, and such actions, or observances, be instituted, and do commence from the time that the matter of fact was done.

The first two rules. The first two rules make it impossible for any such matter of fact to be imposed upon men at the time, because every man's eyes, and ears, and senses, would contradict it. For example, if any man should affirm that all the inhabitants of this city yesterday, or last year, walked to Governor's Island and returned on dry ground, while the water was divided and stood in heaps on each side of them, it would be impossible that he should be believed, because every man, woman, and child would know better. It would be one of those things respecting which the unlearned and the young could judge as well as the learned and more experienced. Equally impossible is it that the children of Israel, of that generation, should have believed that they passed through the Red Sea, or went out and gathered manna every morning, or drank water from the rock, or that the law was given with the terror and solemnity described in the Bible, if these things did not happen. Not less impossible is it that the five thousand should have believed they were fed by Christ; or that the relatives of Lazarus, and the Jews who knew him, should have believed that he was raised from the dead, or the parents and friends of the man born blind, that he was made to see; or that the multitudes before whom he healed the lame, and the sick of every description, should have believed that these events took place, if they did not. These miracles are of such a nature that, unless they were really wrought, it is impossible they should have been believed at the time. Leslie further says: "Therefore it only remains that such matter of fact might have been invented some time after, when the men of that generation wherein the thing was said to be done are all past and gone; and the credulity of after ages might be imposed upon to believe that things were done in former ages which were not."

The last two rules. And for this the last two rules secure us as much as the first two rules in the former case; for, whenever such a matter of fact came to be invented, if not only monuments were said to remain of it, but likewise that public actions and observances were constantly used ever since the matter of fact was said to be done, the deceit must be detected by no such monuments appearing, and by the experience of every man, woman, and child, who must know that no such actions or observances were ever used by them.

For example, suppose I should now invent a story of such a thing done a thousand years ago; I might perhaps get some to believe it; but if I say that not only such a thing was done, but that, from that day to this, every man, at the age of twelve years, had a joint of his little finger cut off; and that every man in the nation did lack a joint of such a finger; and that this institution was said to be part of the matter of fact done so many years ago, and vouched as a proof and confirmation of it, and as having descended without interruption, and been constantly practiced, in memory of such a fact, all along from the time that such matter of fact was done;—I say it is impossible I should be believed in such case, because everyone could contradict me as to the mark of cutting off the joint of the finger; and that, being a part of my original matter of fact, must demonstrate the whole to be false.

Application to the books of Moses. The case here put is not stronger than that either of the books of Moses, or of the New Testament. For, at whatever time it might have been attempted to impose the books of Moses upon a subsequent age, it would have been impossible, because they contain the laws and civil and ecclesiastical regulations of the Jews, which the books affirm were adopted at the time of Moses, and were constantly in force from that time; and because they contain an account of the passover, which they assert to have been observed in consequence of a particular fact. If, then, a book had been put forth at a particular time, stating that the Jews had obeyed certain very peculiar laws, and had a certain priesthood, and had observed the Passover from the time of Moses, while they had never heard of these laws, or of this priesthood, or of a Passover, it is impossible the book should have been received. Nothing could have saved such a book from scorn or utter neglect.

Application to the New Testament. But what the Levitical law, and the priesthood, and the passover were to the Jews, baptism, and the Christian ministry, and the Lord's Supper are to Christians. It is a part of the records of the Gospels that these were instituted by Christ; that they were commanded by Him to be continued till the end of time, and were actually continued and observed at the time when the Gospels purport to have been written—that is, before the destruction of Jerusalem. But if these books were fictions invented after the time of Christ, there would have been at that time no Christian baptism, nor order of Christian ministers, nor sacrament of the supper, thus derived from His appointment; and that, alone, would have demonstrated the whole to be false. Our books suppose these institutions to exist; they give an account of them; and it is impossible they should have been received where they did not exist. It is, therefore, impossible that these books should have been received at the time the facts are said to have taken place, or at any subsequent time, unless those facts really did take place. We now regard the sacrament of the supper as an essential part of the religion; it was so regarded by our fathers; nor can we conceive that it should have been otherwise up to the very time when the religion was founded. Thus we have a visible sign and pledge of the truth of our religion, handed down, independently of written testimony, from age to age; and the force of which age has no tendency to diminish.

Strength of the evidences. Perhaps we do not suffi-

ciently dwell on the great strength of which the Christian evidences derive from this proof, or notice the contrast it makes between the evidence for the facts of Christianity and those of ordinary history. Not only is it impossible to point out any statement of fact, substantiated by these four marks, that can be shown to be false, but none of the best authenticated facts of ancient history have them all. The Fourth of July, as observed by us, may illustrate the effects of such commemorative ordinances as guarding against false historical accounts. For any man to have invented the New Testament after the time of Christ, and to have attempted to cause it to be received, would have been as if a man had written an account of the revolution, and of the celebration of this day from the first, when no revolution was ever heard of, and no one had ever celebrated the Fourth of July. Nor, when such a festival was once established, would it be possible to introduce any account of its origin essentially different from the true one. But the case of the Christian religion is much stronger; because we have several different institutions which must have sprung up at its origin; because baptism and the Lord's Supper have occurred so much more frequently; and because the latter has always been considered the chief rite of a religion to which men have been more attached than to liberty or to life.

Credible because no others. But again: our books are credible because there are no others. That such a movement as Christianity must have been, involving the origin of so many new institutions, and such ecclesiastical and social changes should have originated at such a time and in such a place, and that no written documents should have been drawn forth by it, is incredible. And that the true account should have perished, leaving not a single vestige behind it, and that false ones, and such as these, should have been substituted, is impossible. Of the origin of such institutions we should expect some account. That of our books is adequate and satisfactory. There is nothing contradictory to it, for even spurious writings confirm the truth of our books, and there is no vestige of any other (Linton, pp. 161-164, citing Mark Hopkins, who is citing Leslie). **fables.** 1 T +1:4. **the power.** Mt *28:18. Mk *9:1. Jn *17:2. Ac *3:12, 13, 16. Ro *1:4. 1 C +2:4. *5:4. Ph 3:21. **and.** ✗93A, Ge +1:26. **coming.** Gr. *parousia,* Mt +24:3n. 2 P 3:4, 12. Ml *3:2. *4:5. Mt *16:28. +*24:3n, 27. Ac +*3:19-21. 1 C *1:7. 1 Th +2:19. 2 Th *1:7-10. Ju *14. Re +*1:7. **were eyewitnesses.** Simon Greenleaf wrote of the apostles, "It was impossible that they could have persisted in affirming the truths they have narrated had not Jesus actually risen from the dead, and had they not known this fact as certainly as they knew any other fact" (Wilbur Smith, *Have You Considered Him,* p. 19, citing Simon Greenleaf, *The Testimony of the Evangelists Examined by the Rules of Evidence Administered in Courts of Justice,* pp. 28-31). Jsh 24:17. Pr 1:20. Mt √17:1-5. 26:55. Mk 9:2. Lk 9:28-32. Jn *1:14. Ac 26:26. He 2:9. 1 J √1:1-3. *4:14. **majesty.** Lk 9:43. Jn 1:14. +*17:5. Ep *1:20-22.

17. **God.** Mt +*11:25-27. +*28:19. Lk 10:22. Jn 3:35. 5:21-23, 26, 36, 37. 6:27, *37, 39. 10:15, 36. 13:1-3. 14:6, 8, 9, 11. 17:21. 20:17. Ro 15:6. 2 C 1:3. 11:31. 2 J 3. Ju 1. **honor and glory.** ✗93A, Ge +1:26. By Hendiadys, glorious honor. Two things mentioned,

one thing meant. Ex 28:2. 1 T 1:17. He 2:9. Re +4:9.
there came. Mt 17:3. Mk 9:7. Lk 9:34, 35. Jn 12:28,
29. **This**. Mt 3:17. √17:5. Mk 1:11. 9:7. Lk 3:22. 9:35.
Son. Col 1:13. 1 J 5:9. **in whom**. Is 42:1. 53:10. Mt
12:18. Ep 1:6.

18. **this**. Mt √17:6. **the holy**. Ge 28:16, 17. Ex *3:1,
5. Jsh 5:15. Is 11:9. 56:7. Zc 8:3. Mt 17:6.

19. **We have**. 1 P +1:10. **a more sure word**.
T#1022. Ge 15:13. Ps *19:7-9. 119:105. Pr 6:23. Is
+*8:20n. *41:21-23, 26. Lk *16:29-31. Jn +*5:39n.
Ac +*17:11. **of prophecy**. T#1019. ver. 11. Lk
+*24:27. Ro 16:26. **ye do well**. Ac 10:33. 15:29. Ja
*2:8. 3 J 6. **take heed**. Ho +*4:10. **as**. ʃ137, Ge +13:13.
a light. ʃ22K2, 2 S +22:29. Ps √119:105. Pr +*4:18n.
*6:23. Is *9:2. *60:1, 2. Mt *4:16. Lk *1:78, 79. Jn
*1:7-9. 5:35. *8:12. Ep *5:7, 8. **dark place**. Jb 24:16.
1 C *13:12. Ep 6:12. **the day dawn**. Ps +*49:14. 2 C
*4:4-6. 1 J *5:10. Re 2:28. *22:16. **the day star**. Ml
4:2. Re 2:28. 22:16. **arise**. 2 C *4:6.

20. **Knowing**. 2 P 3:3. Ro 6:6. 13:11. 1 T 1:9. Ja
1:3. **that**. Ro 12:6. **of the scripture**. Ro 9:17. 1 P 2:6.
private. Rather, its own, or less likely, their own, understanding the text to mean that the writers of Scripture did not merely pen their own opinion, but were
divinely inspired by the Holy Spirit. Understanding
"its own" fits the immediate context of taking heed
to the more sure word of prophecy, and the manner
of taking heed is to interpret the individual prophecies
of Scripture in the light of every other prophecy which
bears upon the same theme. "Private" is an unfortunate
rendering of the Greek word *idios* (S#2398g), a word
which occurs 113 times in the Greek New Testament,
most often rendered "his own" (48 times) and "their
own" (13 times), but nowhere else rendered "private,"
though rendered by the word "privately" 8 times. This
rendering has been used to attack the Biblical doctrine
of the perspicuity of Scripture (Is +*8:20n) and to
deny the duty of each individual believer to exercise
the right of private judgment to determine for himself
the correctness of a proposed interpretation of Scripture (Je +*23:28n). While Scripture elsewhere teaches
the individual to maintain fellowship with other believers (He 10:25), to "hear the church" (Mt 18:17), to
"hold the traditions which ye have been taught" (2
Th 2:15), and to "obey them that have the rule over
you" (He 13:17), yet he must do so only insofar as
such teachers are faithful to the written Word of God.
The final authority in spiritual matters is never an organization or church, but the written Word of God as
found in the Bible, correctly interpreted. The Bible
warns that followers of false teachers will share in their
reward (Ezk +*14:10n). The final obligation remains
for each individual to judge truth for himself (Ro 14:12).
This, then, is the major justification for the right of
private judgment, for God holds each of us individually
and directly accountable to him and his Word. We
cannot pass off our responsibility to others by saying
"I simply believed what my church taught me" (Is
+*8:20n. Ezk 14:10n). "Private" is better rendered
"its own," so that we then read "no Scripture is of its
own interpretation." The meaning is that every statement in Scripture must be understood in the light of
what the rest of Scripture teaches which bears upon
the same theme. Of absolute importance to the correct
interpretation of Scripture is to make a full and proper
induction of all related passages, and develop from

them an interpretation which accounts for and agrees
with the whole. This is the very opposite of the deductive approach, which comes to the Bible with a predetermined belief (whether a creedal statement, a system of doctrine or philosophy, any "ism"—whether
Calvinism, Arminianism, dispensationalism, amillen-
nialism, Russellism, liberalism, humanism, scientism,
etc.) which already has decided what the Bible can
or must teach, then searches its pages for supporting
"proof texts." Such an approach is grievously in error
(Mk √12:24), and can be detected by its tendency to
ignore, suppress, explain away, or circumvent those
texts which do not "fit" the system. Adherents of deductive systems are in danger of wresting Scripture to
their own destruction (2 P 3:16), and handling Scripture
deceitfully (2 C 4:2). Those who adhere to a deductive
approach to Scripture are marked by an inability to
come to the Bible with an open mind, ready to adjust
their belief to what is newly learned. In fact, such
persons are unable to freely study Scripture and grow
in their knowledge, for they have adopted a closed
system of belief, which can never admit to anything
new to be learned, or admit a former mistake in understanding, the correction of which is based upon additional light received by a fresh study of the Word of
God. Certainly such an attitude toward Scripture makes
it a closed book, and is the very opposite of that humility
required for the reception of spiritual truth (Ps 25:9.
119:18). Jn *16:13. **interpretation**. Gr. *epilusis*,
❋S#1955g, only here, from ❋S#1956g, *epiluo*, Mk
4:34 (expounded); Ac 19:39 (determined). Vine defines
epilusis to mean "to loose, solve, explain, denotes a
solution, explanation, lit., a release. '(of private) interpretation;' i.e., the writers of Scripture did not put
their own construction upon the 'God-breathed' words
they wrote" (*Expository Dictionary*, vol. 2, p. 268).
An understanding of the principles of the correct interpretation of Scripture is of supreme importance. Formally known as the science of biblical hermeneutics,
the correct application of such principles is essential
to arrive at the correct interpretation of Scripture. Most
wrong interpretations of Scripture will be found to
violate one or more of the following ten general rules
of interpretation: (1) Interpret the words and sentences
of an author literally unless such an interpretation results in a contradiction, absurdity, or nonsense. Be
very careful not to label as nonsense what might merely
be strange or contrary to your own personal point of
view or frame of reference. Sometimes the immediate
context will indicate a non-literal interpretation must
be understood ("trees clapped their hands," Is 55:12).
In such cases watch for the literal truth or meaning
which is being figuratively expressed. (2) Do not attribute a meaning to a text that would be foreign to the
knowledge or understanding of the author or the original audience, or give a meaning which would be outside
the purpose of the original author (Thus there are no
trains or flying saucers in the Bible). (3) Do not interpret
one statement in the Bible in a way which makes it
contradict another part. All the parts must agree without contradictions. Authors write to be understood,
not to confuse their audience. Sometimes an author
may write an intended ambiguity. Sometimes our own
perception of the truth, or our knowledge of the cultural
context which produced a document, is incomplete,
and our own deficiency of knowledge may lead us to

find ambiguity, paradox, and contradiction where there is none. An author, particularly when treating of philosophical and religious subjects, may intentionally introduce paradox (determinism versus free will). (4) A correct interpretation takes account of all the material in the text, and all related material in other texts of the Bible. You cannot legitimately pick and choose separate statements and combine them arbitrarily (The Bible says, Judas went and hanged himself; go and do thou likewise; what thou doest, do quickly). You cannot leave out material which, if included, would require or necessitate a change in the interpretation. Whenever an interpretation involves the comparison of two or more subjects, the interpretation must take into account not only the similarities but also the differences which may exist. (5) Read what comes before and after the verse you are interpreting. A correct interpretation always fits into the scope, meaning, and purpose of the surrounding passage or context. A text out of context is a pretext. (6) An interpretation must be in harmony with the grammar of the sentences involved, and in harmony with the meanings of the words which make up the sentences. (7) Always interpret obscure, difficult texts in the light of other passages on the same topic which are clear in meaning. (8) A correct and authoritative interpretation must be based upon what the text itself says, not upon what someone else claims it says. (9) All that is required to establish an interpretation as correct is evidence (which is in harmony with these rules) from the text sufficient to convince an adequately informed, neutral, unbiased person. (10) When there are two differing interpretations of a passage, if the interpretations are contradictory, they cannot both be correct. One or the other interpretation must be wrong, or they may both be wrong, but they cannot both be right. A correct interpretation must comply with the rules of interpretation; an incorrect interpretation will always be found not to comply with the rules.

21. **the prophecy.** Lk *1:70. 2 T +*3:16. 1 P *1:11. **in old time.** *or*, at any time. **holy.** Dt *33:1. Jsh 14:6. 1 K 13:1. *17:18, 24. 2 K 4:7, 9, 22. *6:10, 15. 1 Ch *23:14. 2 Ch 8:14. **spake.** Nu 16:28. 2 S *23:2. Mi +*3:7. Lk 1:70. 2 T +√3:15-17. 1 P *1:11. Re *19:10. **they were.** or, being. ✦63K, Ge +37:13. **by the Holy.** Mk 12:36. Ac 1:16. 3:18. 28:25. He 3:7. 9:8. 10:15. **Ghost.** Gr. *pneuma*, Mt +1:18.

2 PETER 2

The apostle foretells the coming of false teachers; showing in general their corrupt principles and selfishness, and the fatal effects of their influence, 1-3. He adduces the severity of God in punishing apostate angels, the inhabitants of the old world, and those of Sodom, with his kindness to Noah and Lot, in proof that he would certainly preserve his people, and execute vengeance on the wicked, 4-9. A more particular account of the seducers above mentioned, of their vile character and practices, and of the hopeless conditions of many, who were deceived by them, 10-22.

1. **there were.** Dt 13:1-3. 1 K 18:19-22. *22:6, 11, 12. Ne 6:12-14. Is 9:15. 56:10, 11. Je √5:30, 31. 14:13-15. 23:16, 17, 25-32. 27:14, 15. 28:15-17. 29:8, 9, 31, 32. 37:19. La 2:14. Ezk 13:3-18. Ho 9:8. Mi 2:11. 3:5, 11. Zc 13:3, 4. Mt +*7:15. Lk 6:26. Ro 16:18. 1 J *4:1. **the people.** Ro 15:10. Ju 5. **false teachers.** 2 P

3:3. Ezk 14:9, 10. Mt *24:5, 11, 24. Mk 13:22. Lk 21:8. Ac *20:29, 30. 1 C √11:19. 2 C √11:13-15. Ga 4:17. Ep +*4:14. Col 2:8, 18. 2 Th 2:3-12. 1 T *4:1-3. 2 T 3:1-9. 4:3, 4. T 1:11. 1 J 2:18, 19, 26. √4:1. Ju 18. Re 2:9. 13:14. **privily.** ver. 3. Ga 2:4. **bring in.** Ga 2:4. Ju 4. **damnable.** ver. 3. Ga 5:20. T 3:10. **heresies.** Ac +24:5. 1 C √11:19. Ga 5:20. **denying.** Mt 10:33. Lk 12:9. Ac 3:13, 14. 1 T +5:8. 2 T 2:12, 13. T √1:16. Ju *4. Re 2:13. 3:8. **the Lord.** Mt 10:25. Lk +2:29. 2 T 2:21g. Ju 4. **bought.** Ex 15:16. Dt 32:6. Ac +*20:28. 1 C +*6:19, 20. 7:23. Ga *3:13. 4:5. Ep 1:7. 1 T *2:5, 6. He 10:29. 1 P *1:18, 19. Re 5:9. 14:3, 4. **and bring.** ver. 3. Ml +*3:5. Ph +*3:19.

2. **many.** Mt 24:10-13, 24. Mk 13:22. 1 J 2:18, 19. Re 12:9. 13:8, 14. **pernicious ways.** *or*, lascivious ways, as some copies read. 1 P +4:3. **by reason.** Ro 2:24. 1 T 5:14. T 2:5, 8. **way.** ver. 15, 21. Ps 18:21. Is 35:8. Je 6:16. Mt +*7:14. 22:16. Mk 12:14. Jn √14:6. Ac 13:10. 16:17. 18:26. 19:9. 24:14. **the way.** Ps 119:29, 30. **of truth.** Re 15:3. **evil.** ver. 12. Is 52:5. Ac 14:2. Ro 2:24. 3:8. T 2:5. Ja 2:7. 1 P 2:12. Ju 10, 15.

3. **through covetousness.** ver. 14, 15. Is 56:11. Je 6:13. 8:10. Ezk 13:19. Mi 3:11. Ml 1:10. Ro *16:18. 1 C +5:10. 2 C 12:17, 18. 1 T 3:3, 8. +*6:5. T *1:7, 11. 1 P 5:2. Ju 11, 16. **with feigned.** 2 P 1:16. Ps 18:44. 66:3. 81:15mg. Lk 20:20. 22:47. Ro 16:18. Col 2:4. 1 Th 2:5. **make.** Dt 24:17. Jn 2:16. 2 C +*2:17. Re 18:11-13. **whose.** ver. 1, 9. Dt 32:35. Is 5:19. 30:13, 14. 60:22. Hab 2:3. Lk 18:8. Ph +*3:19. 1 Th 5:3. 1 P 2:8. Ju 4, 7, 15. **now of.** ✦63B, Ge +25:28. or, (threatened). **a long time.** 2 P 3:5.

4. **For if.** ✦184A, 1 C +15:2. **spared.** ver. 5. Dt 29:20. Ps 78:50. Ezk 5:11. 7:4, 9. Ro +*8:32. 11:21. **the angels.** T#13. Ge 6:1, 2. Jb 4:18. Lk 10:18. Jn *8:44. 1 J *3:8. Ju *6. Re 12:7, 8. 20:2, 3, 10. **that sinned.** ✦63D2, Ge +30:27. Supply ellipsis, (neither will he spare the false prophets and teachers). **but cast.** Is 14:12. Mt 8:29. 25:41. Mk 5:7. Lk 8:31. Re 12:7-9. *20:2, 3, 10. **hell.** Gr. Tartarus. Jb 40:20. 41:24. Pr 30:16. **into chains.** ver. 11. Ju 6. **of darkness.** Pr +*20:20. **to be.** ver. 9. Jb 21:30. Mt +*25:41. Ju 13.

5. **spared.** Ge ch. 6-8. Jb 22:15, 16. Mt 24:37-39. Lk 17:26, 27. He 11:7. **the old.** Ezk 26:20. **world.** Gr. *kosmos*, Mt +4:8. **the eighth.** Ge 7:1, etc. 1 P +3:20. **a preacher.** 1 T 2:7. 2 T 1:11. 1 P 3:19. Ju 14, 15. **bringing.** 2 P 3:6. Jb 22:16. **world.** Gr. *kosmos*, Mt +4:8. 2 C 5:19. Ga 6:14.

6. **turning.** Ge *19:24, 25, 28. Dt 29:23. Is 13:19. Je 20:16. 50:40. La 4:6. Ezk *16:49-56. Ho 11:8. Am 4:11. Zp 2:9. Lk 17:28-30. Ju *7. **of Sodom.** Lk +10:12. **and Gomorrah.** Ro +9:29. **overthrow.** 2 T 2:14g. **making.** Nu +*26:10. Dt 29:23. 1 C *10:6, 11. **an ensample.** He +4:11. **live ungodly.** Le +*18:22n. Ro +*1:27. Ju *15.

7. **delivered.** Ge *19:16, 22, 29. 1 C 10:13. **just.** Ge ●19:33-35. Jn +*17:6. **Lot.** Lk 17:28, 29, 32. **vexed.** Ge 13:13. 19:7, 8. Ps 120:5. Je 9:1-6. 23:9. **filthy.** Mk +*7:22. Ju 4. **conversation.** 2 P 3:11g. Ja +3:13. **the wicked.** 2 P *3:17.

8. **that righteous.** ver. 7. Ge ●19:33-35. Pr 25:26. 28:12. Jn +*17:6. 1 T 1:9. Ja +*5:16. **in seeing.** Ps *119:53, 136, 139, 158. Ezk +*9:4, 6. Ml *3:15-17. **vexed.** Ne 13:25. Ezk +*9:4. **soul.** Gr. *psyche*, ✦171Q2, 1 P +4:19.

9. **knoweth.** Jb 5:19. Ps 1:6. *34:15-19. 1 C +*10:13. **deliver.** T#810. Ps *34:19. *73:3. Pr 12:13. Ec 7:18.

Ac 12:11. Ro 8:37. 1 C +*10:13. 2 C *12:9. He 2:18.
1 J 4:4. **the godly**. Ps 4:3. 12:1. 32:6. Ac 10:2, 7g.
2 T 3:12. T *2:14. **out of temptations**. Ps 37:33. Zp +*2:3.
Lk +*21:36. Ro 15:31. Re +*3:10. **reserve the unjust**.
ver. 4. Jb 21:30. Pr 16:4. Na *1:2. Ju *14, *15. **unto
the day**. 2 P 3:7. Mt +*10:15n. 11:22, 24. 12:36. Ac
+*17:31. Ro 2:5. 2 C 5:10, 11. 1 J 4:17. Ju 6.

10. **that walk**. 2 P 3:3. Ro 8:1, 4, 5, 12, 13. 2 C
10:3. He +*13:4. Ju 16, 18. **after the flesh**. Ju 7. **in
the lust**. Ro 1:24-27. 1 C +*6:9. Ep 4:19. 5:5. Col
3:5. 1 Th 4:7. Ju 4, 6-8, 10, 16. **uncleanness**. ver.
20. Ju 8. **despise**. Nu 16:12-15. Dt *17:12, 13. 21:20,
21. 1 S 10:27. *15:23. 2 S 20:1. 1 K 12:16. Ps 2:1-5.
12:4. Je 2:31. Lk 19:14. Ro 13:1-5. 1 P *2:13, 14, 17.
government. *or*, dominion. T#317. Ex 22:28mg. Nu
16:3-7, 32. Dt 17:12, 13. 2 S *19:21. Ec √10:20. Lk
+*19:14. Ac 23:5. Ro +*13:1. 2 C ◑8:5. 1 P *2:13.
Ju *8. **Presumptuous**. Nu 15:30. Dt 17:13. Ju 8. **self-
willed**. Ge 49:6. T 1:7. **to speak**. Ex 22:28. Ec 10:6,
7, √20. Ac 23:5. 3 J *9, *10. Ju *8, *10.

11. **angels**. Ps 103:20. 104:4. Da 6:22. 2 Th 1:7.
Ju +*9. **against them**. "Some read, against themselves."

12. **as natural**. Ps 49:10. 92:6. 94:8. Je 4:22. 5:4.
10:8, 21. 12:3. Ezk 21:31. Ju 10. **made**. or, born. Pr
+*16:4. Je 12:3. Ph 3:19. **taken**. 2 T 2:26. **speak evil**.
Ac +13:45g. **perish**. ver. 19. 2 P 1:4. Pr 14:32. Jn
8:21. Ga 6:8. **own corruption**. ver. 19. 2 P 1:4. 1 C
+15:42.

13. **the reward**. ver. 15. Is 3:11. Ac 1:18g. Ro 2:8,
9. Ph +*3:19. 2 T 4:14. He *2:2, 3. Ju 12, etc. Re
18:6. **as they**. *√*58. Diexodos; or, Expansion B58. A
lengthening out by copious exposition of facts by digression in order to expand. For other instances of this
figure see 2 P 2:15, 17. Ju 12, 13, 16. **to riot**. Ro
13:13. 1 Th 5:7, 8. Ja +*5:5. 1 P 4:4. **Spots**. SS 4:7.
Ep 5:27. Ju *12. **while**. 1 C *11:20-22.

14. **eyes full**. 2 S √11:2-4. Jb ◑√31:1, 7, 9. Pr *6:25.
Ezk 23:16. Mt √5:28. 1 J *2:16. **adultery**. Gr. an adulteress. *√*155A, Ge 31:35. Ja +4:4. **that cannot cease**. Is
1:16. Je *13:23. Mt 12:34. *15:19. Jn 5:44. *12:39.
Ro *1:28. He *10:26. 1 P *4:1. **beguiling**. ver. 18. 2
P 3:16. Ezk 13:18. Mk 13:22. Ro 16:18. 1 C √11:19.
Ep +*4:14. Col 2:18. Ja *1:14. Re 12:9. **unstable**.
1 P *3:16. Ja +*1:8. **souls**. Gr. psyche, *√*171Q1A, Ac
+2:41. **an heart**. See on ver. 3. Ju 11. **exercised**.
1 T 4:7. He 5:14. 12:11. **with covetous practices**. ver.
+*3. Ps +*10:3. Ezk +*16:49. Ml +*3:5. Ja +*5:1-
5. **cursed**. Is 34:5. 65:20. Mt 25:41. Lk +10:6. Ep
2:3.

15. **forsaken**. 1 S 12:23. 1 K 18:18. 19:10. Is +*66:4.
Ezk 9:10. Pr 28:4. Ho 14:9. Ac +*13:10. **gone astray**.
Ezk 14:11. **following**. *√*58, ver. +13. **Balaam**. i.e. *de-
struction of the people*, ✻S#903g. Nu 22:5-7, son of
Beor. Ju 11. Re 2:14. For ✻S#1109h, see Nu +22:5.
Bosor. i.e. *consuming*, ✻S#1007g. For ✻S#1160h, see
Nu +22:5. **who**. Nu 22:18-21, 23, 28. 31:16. Dt 23:4,
5. Ne 13:2. Ps +*62:10. Mi 6:5. 1 T +*6:9. Ju *11.
Re 2:14. **wages**. ver. +13. Ac 1:18. **of unrighteousness**.
Pr *16:8. Zc *11:5. Ja +*5:4.

16. **the dumb**. Nu 22:21-33. **the madness**. Ec 7:25.
9:3. Ho 9:7. Lk 6:11. Ac 26:11, 24, 25.

17. **are wells without**. T#1832. Jb 6:14-17. Je 14:3.
Ho 6:4. Ro *12:3. Ju *12, *13. **clouds**. Jb 7:9. 30:15.
Ho 6:4. 13:3. Ep +*4:14. **to whom**. or, for whom.
Mi 3:6. Ju 13. **the mist**. "The blackness, *dzophos*, of

darkness," darkness itself, says Leigh. **darkness**. ver.
4. Mt +*8:12. 22:13. 25:30. Ju 6, 13. **reserved**. Mt
+*25:41. Jn 3:18, 36. Ju 10-13. **for ever**. Gr. *aion*,
Mt +6:13. lit. unto an age.

18. **they speak**. Ps 52:1-3. 73:8, 9. Da 4:30. 11:36.
Ac 8:9. 2 Th 2:4. Ja 3:5. Ju 13, 15, *16. Re 13:5, 6,
11. **great swelling**. *uperogka*, "things puffed up with
wind"—Leigh. **of vanity**. Ep +4:17. **they allure**. ver.
+14. **through the lust**. 1 J +*2:16. **wontonness**. Ro
13:13. Ja 5:5. 1 P +*4:3. **that were**. ver. 20. 2 P 1:4.
Ac 2:40. **clean**. *or*, for a little, *or*, a while, as some
read.

19. **they promise**. Ga 5:1, 13. 1 P 2:16. **liberty**. Ja
+*1:25. **they themselves**. *√*31, Is +1:21. Jn +*8:34.
Ro *6:12-14, 16-22. T 3:3. **corruption**. ver. 18. **overcome**. ver. 20. Is 28:1. Je 23:9. 2 T 2:26.

20. **For if**. *√*184A, 1 C +15:2. **after**. Mt *12:43-
45. Lk *11:24-26. He +*6:4-8. *10:26, 27. **escaped**.
ver. *18. 2 P √1:4. Ac 2:40. 1 C *6:11. **the pollutions**.
ver. 10. Ju 8. **world**. Gr. *kosmos*, Mt +4:8. **through**.
ver. 21. 2 P +1:2. **the knowledge**. 2 C +*10:5. He
6:4. **the Lord and**. 2 P +3:2. T +*2:13n. **Savior**. 2 T
+*1:10. **again entangled**. Pr +*21:16. Ph +*3:19.
2 T 2:4. **and overcome**. ver. 19. 2 C 12:13g (inferior).
He *6:6. +*10:26, 38. **the latter**. Nu *24:20. Dt *32:29.
Mt 12:45. Lk 11:26. Ph +*3:19. Re 2:19. **is worse**.
Mt *12:45. He 10:26.

21. **better**. Ezk 18:24. Mt *11:23, 24. Lk +*12:47,
48. Jn *9:41. *15:22. He +*6:4-6. +*10:26, 27. Ja
+*4:17. Re 3:15. **known**. Gr. *epiginosko*, Mt +11:27.
ver. 20. **the way**. Pr *12:28. *16:31. Mt +*21:32.
known. Gr. *epiginosko*, Mt +11:27. **to turn from**.
2 P *3:17. Jsh=23:12. Ps *36:3, 4. *125:5. Ezk *3:20.
*18:24. 23:13. Zp *1:6. Lk +*8:13. √9:62. 11:52. 1 C
+*15:2. Ga 4:11. Col +*1:23. He +*3:14. 1 J *2:19.
holy commandment. *√*171I6. Synecdoche of the Species B626. "Commandment" is put for all commandments and doctrines. For another instance of this figure
see 2 P 3:2. Ro *7:12. 1 Th *4:2. 1 J *3:23. **delivered**.
1 C 11:2. +*15:3. Ju +*3.

22. **proverb**. *√*138A, Ge +10:9. Ps ◑*68:13. Pr
❱26:11. Jn +10:6. **The dog**. Pr *❱26:11. Mt +*7:6.
the sow. Mt *7:6.

2 PETER 3

*The apostle reminds his brethren of the promised
coming of Christ; and predicts that scoffers will ridicule
their expectation of that event, 1-4; being willingly
ignorant of the truth in that respect, 5-7. He shows
the reason of its being delayed, and the awful manner,
circumstances, and consequences of it; with exhortations and encouragements to diligence and holiness,
8-14. He shows that "his beloved brother Paul" had
taught them the same doctrine; commends his epistles;
and shows how "ignorant and unstable men wrested"
some parts of them, as they did "the other scriptures,
to their own destruction," 15, 16: and concludes with
warning the readers against seducers; and exhorting
them to "grow in grace, and in the knowledge of
Christ," 17, 18.*

1. **second epistle**. 2 C 13:2. 1 P 1:1, 2. **both**. *√*63A1,
Ge +14:20. Supply ellipsis, "in (both) which (epistles)
I stir up." **I stir**. 2 P *1:13-15. 2 T 1:6. **pure**. Ps 24:4.
73:1. Mt +*5:8. 1 C +5:8. Ph 1:10. 1 T 5:22. 1 P
1:22. **way**. 2 P +1:12. 1 J *2:21.

2. **ye may.** 2 P *1:19-21. Lk 1:70. +*24:27, 44. Ac 3:18, 21, 24-26. +*10:43. *28:23. 1 P *1:10-13. Re *19:10. **and of.** ver. 15. 2 P 2:21. Ep 2:20. Ja *5:8. 1 J *4:6. Ju *17. **commandment.** ſ171I6, 2 P +2:21. **the Lord and.** 2 P 2:20. T 2:13n. **Savior.** ver. 18. 2 T +1:10.

3. **Knowing.** 2 P 1:20. **that there.** 1 T *4:1, 2. 2 T *3:1. 1 J +2:18. Ju *18. **scoffers.** Pr 1:22. *3:34. *14:6. Is 5:19. 28:14. 29:20. Ho 7:5. **walking.** 2 P *2:10. 2 C *4:2. Ju *16, *18.

4. **Where.** Ge *19:14. Ex=32:1. Ec *1:9. *8:11. Is *5:18, 19. Je 5:12, 13. *17:15. Ezk 11:3. *12:22-27. Ml 2:17. Mt *24:48. Lk +*12:45, 46. **coming.** Gr. *parousia*, Mt +24:3. ver. 12. 1 Th +2:19. **the fathers.** Ro +15:8. **fell asleep.** Da +*12:2. Mt +27:52. Ac +*13:36n. **from the beginning.** Mk +10:6. 13:19. Re 3:14.

5. **they willingly.** T#707. Jb 5:14. 12:25. Ps +10:4 (T#693). 50:*17, 21. 58:4, 5. *82:5. Pr 1:22, 29, 30. 4:19. *14:6. 17:16. Is +59:2 (T#26). Je 17:23. 32:33. Da 12:10. Zc 7:11, 12. Lk +*19:14 (T#695). Jn √3:19, 20. +17:25 (T#739). Ac 26:17, 18. Ro +*1:21, 28. 1 C *2:14. Ep 4:18. 2 TH √2:10-12. 1 J 4:8. **by the word.** Ge *1:6, 9. Ps 24:2. *33:6. 136:6. Ro +9:6. He *11:3. **were of old.** 2 P 2:3. **standing.** Gr. consisting. Ps 24:2. 136:6. Col *1:17g.

6. **the world.** Gr. *kosmos*, Mt +4:8. **being over-flowed.** 2 P +2:5. Ge *7:10-23. 9:15. Jb 12:15. Mt 24:38, 39. Lk 17:27. **perished.** Gr. *apollumi*, Mt +2:13.

7. **the heavens.** ver. 10, 12. Ps *50:3. *102:25, 26. Is *51:6. Zp 3:8. Mt 24:35. 25:41. 2 Th 1:8. Ju 7. Re 20:11. 21:1. **the same word.** Ge 9:15. **reserved.** Jb 21:30. Ju 6. **unto fire.** Dt 32:22. Ps 11:6. *21:9. 50:3. *97:3. Is 24:1-6. ◐43:2. √66:15, 16, 24. Ezk 38:22. Da 7:10, 11. Jl 2:30. Mi 1:4. Na 1:5. Hab 3:5. Zp 2:3. Ml 4:1. Mt 3:12. *13:30, 39, 40. 2 Th *1:8. He 10:27. Ja +5:3. Re +*8:5. *16:9. **against.** 2 P +2:9. Mt +*10:15n. 11:22, 24. 12:36. Mk 6:11. 1 J 4:17. Re *20:11, 12, 14, 15. **day.** ſ171T2, Ge +2:4. **judgment.** Ro *2:5. Ju 6. **and perdition.** Is 13:9. Ro 2:5. Ph 1:28. 1 Th 5:3. 2 Th 1:9. 2:3. 1 T +*6:9. Re 11:18. 17:8, 11.

8. **be not ignorant.** Ro *11:25. 1 C *10:1. *12:1. 1 Th 4:13. 5:1-4. **one thing.** Ps 27:4. Ec 3:19. Mk 10:21. Lk +*10:42. Jn 9:25. Ph 3:13. **that one.** Ps *90:4.

9. **not slack.** T#238. Dt *7:10. Ps +7:11 (T#208). Is 9:7. 40:28. *46:13. 59:17. Ezk 5:13. Hab √2:3. Lk *18:7, 8. Ro +13:11. He *10:37. **as some.** Ec *8:11. Re 2:21. **but is long suffering.** ver. 15. Ex 34:6. Ps *86:15. Is √30:18. Lk 18:7. Ro +*2:4. 9:22. 1 T *1:16. 1 P *3:20. **not willing.** Ezk *18:23, 32. *33:11. Ro 11:32. 1 T √2:4. T 2:11. **perish.** Gr. *apollumi*, Mt +2:13. Jn +10:29. **but that all.** √ſ171B, Ge +24:10. Ro 2:4. +*5:18. 1 T +*2:4. Re 2:21. **should come.** Mt *11:28-30. 20:16. Jn 1:12. 3:16-20. √6:37, 65. Ac ◐+*18:27. Ep 1:4. Ph 1:29. 2 Th *2:13. 1 T +*2:4. Ja +*2:5. Re 17:14. 22:17.

10. **the day of the Lord.** Is +*2:12. Jl 1:15. *2:1, 31. 3:14. Ml *4:1, 5. Lk 17:22, 24, 30. 1 C 1:8. *3:13. 4:3mg. 5:5. 2 C 1:14. Ph 2:16. 1 Th 5:2. 2 Th 2:2. Ju 6. **as a thief.** Mt *24:42, +43. Lk 12:39. +17:24. 1 Th *5:2, 3. Re *3:3. *16:15. **in the which.** ver. 7, 12. Ps 102:26. Is 51:6. Mt +*24:35. Mk 13:31. Ro 8:20. He 1:11, 12. Re 6:14. 20:11. *21:1. **the elements.** ver. 12. Is 24:19. 34:4. Mi 1:4. Na 1:5. Ga 4:3. **melt.**

Ps 46:6. 97:5. Am 9:5, 13. Na 1:5. **the earth.** See on ver. 7. 1 Ch ◐√16:30. Ec ◐+*1:4. Mt ◐+*5:5. **burned up.** ver. +√7. Is √24:6. √66:15, 16. Da 7:10, 11. 1 C +3:15g.

11. **all these.** ver. 12. Ps 75:3. Is 14:31. *24:19. 34:4. 1 J *2:17. **shall be.** ſ96C6, Mt +2:4. **what manner.** Mt 8:27. 1 Th 1:5. Ja 1:24. Ps 37:14. 50:23. 2 C 1:12. Ph 1:27. 3:20. 1 T +*4:12. He +*13:5. Ja 3:13. 1 P 1:15. 2:12. 1 J 3:1. **conversation.** ſ96F2, Ge +4:10. 2 P 2:7g. Ja +3:13. **godliness.** ſ96F2, Ge +4:10. 2 P 1:3, 6, 7. 1 T +*3:16. *6:3, 6, 11.

12. **Looking.** Lk √12:36. 1 C *1:7. 1 Th +*1:10. T +*2:13n. Ju 21. **hasting unto.** *or,* hasting the. or, earnestly desiring. ſ93B, Is +66:11. Everywhere else (Lk 2:16. 19:5, 6. Ac 20:16. 22:18) the verb "hasting" (Gr. *speudo*) is intransitive; but here it is transitive to correspond with "looking for," and means to be eager or earnest for a thing. It qualifies the "looking for" and not the "coming" itself: looking for, yes—and earnestly looking for that coming too. We cannot hasten that day, which is fixed in the counsels of God. This is the figure *Hendiadys*, "earnestly looking for," with the emphasis on earnestly. See on ver. 10. 1 C 1:8. Ph 1:6. He +*9:28. **coming.** Gr. *parousia*, Mt +24:3. ver. 4. 1 Th +2:19. **the heavens.** See on ver. 7, *10. Ps *50:3. Is 34:4. Lk *21:25-28. Re 6:13, 14. **on fire.** Is 51:6. **shall melt.** ſ96C6, Mt +2:6. See on ver. 10. Is ch. 2, 64. Mi 1:4.

13. **according to his promise.** Peter specifically states that these predictions are "according to his promise." To properly understand the predictions, we must carefully consider the promise to which he refers. The only passages of the Old Testament which refer to the creation of a new heavens and earth preceded by a destruction by fire are found in Isaiah 65:17-19 and 66:16, 17, *22. Interpreters differ widely in their understanding of these predictions. Some advocate a post-millennial conflagration which totally destroys the earth, supposing that after the Millennium God will create a new heaven and a new earth, which will exist forever in the eternal ages which follow the Millennium. This view is radically defective in a number of points. First, the conflagration is placed by Peter and by Isaiah prior to the millennial reign of Christ, for the wicked and the scoffers continue right down to this time of destruction, the purpose of which (2 P 3:7) is stated to be the destruction and perdition of ungodly men. Such a purpose is incongruous to the conditions established by Christ during the Millennium. Second, Scripture declares that this earth will last forever, so it will never be totally destroyed (Ec +*1:4). Third, Christ's kingdom is established upon the earth, the saints are to inherit the earth, and this kingdom and this inheritance are to last forever, and will never be destroyed (Da +*7:14. Mt +*5:5. Ep +*1:11n. He *9:15. 1 P *1:4n. Re *11:15). Therefore, to suggest that this earth will be destroyed at the end of the Millennium is to contradict the oath-bound covenants and promises of God (Is +*55:3). The end of the Millennium does not mark the end of Christ's kingdom (1 C +*15:24n), but marks the duration of the binding of Satan and of the time before the resurrection of the rest of the dead (Re 20:3, 5). The time of the conflagration is therefore established as premillennial. The time of this fire corresponds to the the harvest, when the tares shall be burned up (Mt 13:30, 39, 40),

but this harvest (Re 14:14-20) occurs under the seventh trumpet preceding the Millennial age (Peters, *Theocratic Kingdom*, vol. 2, p. 516). The extent of the conflagration must not be understood to be such as to make this present earth uninhabitable, or to totally destroy all animate life on earth. Although Peter's language, if taken apart from other predictions in Scripture, may appear to be universal in its scope, yet it must be remembered that universal language in Scripture is often used where a limitation is to be understood (Ge +*7:19n. 1 K √18:10), and in this instance this single passage in 2 Peter must not be taken in a sense to contradict the rest of the prophecies in the Word of God, especially when Peter expressly refers these predictions to well-known Scripture promises, promises which do not necessitate a universal and unlimited destruction. Other predictions describe a change and a shaking, but not absolute destruction for this period (Ps 102:25-27. He 1:10-12. +*12:26). The fact that eternal generations of human beings in the flesh (Ps 72:5. 89:4, 29, 36, 37. 102:28. 145:13. 146:10. Is 34:17. 51:8. *59:21. 60:15. 65:23. 66:22. Je 33:22. Ezk *37:25. Lk 1:32, 33) will live on this earth after the Second Coming of Christ proves that not all people will be destroyed. Those who argue that "flesh and blood cannot inherit the kingdom" (1 C 15:50n) forget that these natural generations are subjects of the kingdom, not inheritors, for only the resurrected saints in glorified bodies are co-heirs with Christ in His eternal kingdom (Ro +*8:17). Is 51:6. √65:17-19. √66:22. Ac +*3:21. Ro 8:21. 1 P 1:11, 13. Re √21:1, 27. **look for.** Lk +*21:36. He +*9:28. Re 11:15-18. **new.** Gr. *kainos*, S#2537g, Mk +2:22n. The Greek word denotes a renewal or restoration of something previously existing (Peters, *Theocratic Kingdom*, vol. 2, p. 499). **heavens and.** Perhaps because the creation of a new heavens and earth is mentioned in Re 21:1, a text which occurs after the prediction of the Millennium (Re 20:3-7) and the Great White Throne Judgment (Re 20:11-15), many interpreters make the new heaven and earth postmillennial. Since all concede the new heavens and earth are preceded by the conflagration mentioned by Peter, interpreters argue that the conflagration must be postmillennial. However, the three references (Is 65:17 and 66:22. 2 P 3:13. Re 21:1) are to the same new heavens and earth, to one event, not two events separated by a millennium, for the "first" not "second" heaven and earth were passed away (Re 21:1). The references to the conflagration by Peter were proven to be premillennial. The new heavens and new earth must also be premillennial, since they immediately follow upon the conflagration. The fact that the new heavens and earth are mentioned in Revelation after a passage describing the Millennium and Great White Throne Judgment is no sure proof that the new heavens and earth are postmillennial, because it is very common in Scripture for prophecies and even histories to be

out of chronological sequence (See ✱107. Hysterologia, Ge +10:5). The predictions of a new heaven and earth in Isaiah are seen in context to be premillennial, for the millennial blessedness immediately follows upon their creation (Is 65:17-25). **wherein dwelleth.** 2 P 1:11. Ps *69:34-36. Is 32:16. +*60:21. Ac +*3:19-21. Re *21:27. *22:14, 15. **righteousness.** Ps 96:11-13. √98:4-9. Is 26:9.

14. **seeing.** Ph *3:20. He +*9:28. **be diligent.** 2 P √1:5-10. Lk 21:34. 1 C +√15:58. 1 J √3:3. **found of him.** 1 P 1:7, 13. **in peace.** Mt +*24:46. Lk 2:29. *12:43. Ro *5:1. 1 Th *5:13. **without spot.** 1 T 6:14. Ja +*1:27. 1 J *3:3. **blameless.** 1 C *1:8. Ph 1:10. +*2:15. Col *1:22. 1 Th *3:13. +*5:23. 1 T 3:10. T 1:6, 7. 1 J *2:28, 29.

15. **account.** ver. +9. Ro *2:4. 1 T 1:16. 1 P 3:20. **salvation.** He +*9:28. **our beloved.** Ac 15:25. **brother.** Ps *141:5. Ac 9:17. 21:20. Ga 2:9, 11. **according.** Ex 31:3, 6. 35:31, 35. 1 K 3:12, 28. 4:29. Ezr +*7:25. Pr *2:6, 7. Ec 2:26. Da *2:20, 21. Lk *21:15. Ac 7:10. 1 C √2:13. 3:10. *12:8. Ja +*1:5. +*3:17. 1 P 4:11.

16. **in all.** See on 1 P 1:1. **speaking.** Ro +*8:19. 1 C *15:21, 23, 24. Col *3:4. 1 Th +*4:14-18. *5:1-10. 1 T *6:14. 2 T *1:7, 8. +*4:1, 8, 18. He *9:28. **of these things.** 2 K ch. 1. **hard.** 1 K 10:1. Ro 8:29, 30. 9:18-20. 11:33. He *5:10, 11. **unstable.** 2 P 2:14. Ge 49:4. 2 T 3:5-7. Ja +*1:8. **wrest.** T#1107. Ex 23:2, 6. Dt 16:19. Ps 56:5. Je +*8:8mg. 23:36. Hab 1:4. Mt 4:5, 6. 22:29. 2 C +*2:17. +*4:2. **as they do.** Is 28:16. **the other.** Mt 15:3, 6. 22:29. 1 T +*5:18. 2 T +*3:16. **scriptures.** Mt +21:42. **unto their own.** 2 P 2:1. Ph +*3:19. 1 P 2:8. Ju 4.

17. **seeing ye know.** 2 P 1:12. Pr 1:17. Mt *24:24, 25. Mk 13:23. Jn 16:4. Ju 5. **beware.** Pr +*14:15. Mt *7:15. 16:6, 11. Ph 3:2. Col 2:8. 2 T 4:15. **led away.** 2 P √2:18-20. 2 Ch 10:8. 13:7. Ezk +*14:10n. Mt 24:24. Mk 13:22. Ro 16:18. 2 C √11:3, 13-15. 1 T +*1:19. +*4:1n. 2 T 3:6. 4:4. He +*3:12. **the error.** 2 P √2:18-22. Ps +*119:63. Pr +*19:27. *21:30. Je +*10:2. Ezk 14:10n. Mt +*15:14. 16:6, 11. Mk +*12:24. Ep +*4:14. 2 J +*10. **of the wicked.** 2 P 2:7. Ps 119:53. 2 C *6:14, 17. **fall.** 2 P +*1:10, 11. Da +*11:35. 1 C *10:12. Ga 5:4. 1 T +√1:19. +*4:1n. He +√10:38. **stedfastness.** Ac *2:42. 1 C +*15:58. Col 2:5. He +*3:14. 1 P 5:9.

18. **grow.** T#667. Ps *92:12-14. Ho 14:5. Ml 4:2. Mt 13:33. Mk 4:26-28. Jn +10:28 (T#515). 2 C 4:16. Ep *4:15. Col +√1:10. 2 Th *1:3. 1 P √2:2. **the knowledge.** 2 P *1:3, 5, 8. *2:20. Pr +*18:15. Ho +*6:3. Jn √17:3. 2 C 4:6. Ep +*1:17. Ph *3:8. Col +√1:10. 3:10. **our Lord and.** 2 P *1:1, 11. T +*2:13n. **Savior.** ver. 2. 2 T +*1:10. **To him.** Jn √5:23. Ro +11:36. 2 T +*4:18. 1 P *5:10, 11. Ju *25. Re 1:6. √5:9-14. **for ever.** Gr. *aion*, Mt +6:13. lit. unto the day of eternity, or, unto a day of an age. ver. 8. ✱22D4B, Da +7:9. **Amen.** Mt +*6:13. 28:20.

1 JOHN

1 JOHN 1

The apostle declares, what he had seen and heard of Christ, the Word of Life; that others might have fellowship with him, and with God and Christ, and might share his joy, 1-4. He shows that those who have communion with God, and are cleansed from sin by the blood of Christ, walk in the light of holiness, 5-7; and that the faithfulness and righteousness of God are engaged for the pardon and cleansing of those

who "confess their sins;" but that all who "say they
have no sin," or "have not sinned," are deceived or
deceivers, 8-10.

1. **That.** ✓96G4, Mt +1:20. **which.** ✓18, Dt +28:4.
1 J 2:13, 14. Pr *8:22-31. Is 41:4. Mi +*5:2. Jn +*1:1,
2, etc. +*8:58. Re *1:8, 11, 17, 18. 2:8. **from the.**
✓12, Ps +1:1. **which we have heard.** 1 J 4:14. Lk
1:2, 35. Jn *1:14. Ac 1:3. *4:20. 2 P √1:16-18. **have
seen.** Jn 19:35. 2 P 1:16. **looked upon.** 1 J 4:14. Jn
+1:14. **and our.** Lk *24:39. Jn *20:27. **handled.** Le=1:4
(burnt offering). **the Word.** 1 J 5:7. Jn *1:14. 5:26.
Re 19:13. **of life.** Jn +*1:4.

2. **For.** ✓136, Is +60:12. **the life.** 1 J 5:11, 20. Jn
+1:4. *11:25, 26. √14:6. **was manifested.** 1 J *3:5, 8.
Jn +7:4. Ro 16:25, +26. 1 T *3:16. 2 T 1:10. T 1:2.
1 P 1:20. **and bear.** 1 J 4:14. Jn +15:27. 21:24. Ac
1:22. +*2:32. 3:15. 5:32. 10:41. 1 P 5:1. **show.** 1 J
5:20. **that eternal.** Gr. *aionios*, Mt +18:8. 1 J 2:25.
3:15. 5:11, √13, 20. Jn +4:14. See on Jn *17:3. **which
was.** Pr 8:22-30. Jn *1:1, 2, 18. *3:13. 7:29. 8:38. 16:28.
*17:5. Ro 8:3. Ga *4:4.

3. **which.** See on ver. 1. Ezk 40:4. Jn 1:14. 8:38.
12:41. +*17:5. Ac *4:20. 20:27. 22:14, 15. 2 P *1:16.
declare. ver. *5. Ne 2:18. Ps 2:7. 22:22. Is 66:19. Jn
17:25. Ac 13:32, 41. *20:27. 1 C *15:1. He 2:12. **ye
also.** Ac +*2:42. Ro 15:27. Ep *3:6. Ph 1:7. 2:1. 1 T
6:2. He *3:1. 1 P 5:1g. **our fellowship.** ver. *7. 1 J
2:23, 24. Le=2:3 (meal offering). Ml=2:6. Jn *14:3,
20-23. *17:3, 11, 21. 1 C 1:9, 30. 2 C *13:14. Ep
2:18. Ph *2:1. *3:10. He 2:14. *3:14. 12:10. 2 P 1:4.
Re *3:20. 21:3. 22:3. **the Father.** Jn *16:27. **with his
Son.** 1 J *5:10, 11. Col *1:13. 1 Th +*1:10.

4. **that.** Is *61:10. Hab *3:17, 18. Jn +*15:11.
*16:24. 2 C 1:24. Ep 3:19. Ph 1:25, 26. 2 J *12. **joy.**
Le=3:1, 11. =21:6 (peace offering).

5. **the message.** 1 J 3:11. 1 C 11:23. **that God.** 1 J
4:8. Ps *27:1. *36:9. *84:11. Is *60:19. Jn *1:4, 9.
4:24. *8:12. 9:5. *12:35, 36. Ro 11:33. 1 T *6:16. Ja
*1:17. Re *21:23. *22:5. **light.** Ps 119:105. Mt 5:14.
Jn 1:9. **no darkness.** ✓144D, Ge +40:23. Is +*9:2.

6. **If.** ✓184C, Mt +4:9. ver. *8, *10. 1 J *2:4. 4:20.
Mt 7:22. Ja 2:14, 16, 18. Re 3:17, 18. **we.** *✓39, Ac
+17:27. **fellowship.** See on ver. 3. Ps 5:4-6. 94:20.
2 C *6:14-16. **walk.** 1 J *2:9-11. Ps 82:5. Pr 2:13.
+*4:18, 19. Jn √3:19, 20. 11:10. 12:+35, 46. **darkness.**
Is +*9:2. Ep +*5:8-11. **we lie.** ver. 10. 1 J 2:4. 4:20.
Jn 8:44, 55. 1 T 4:2. **do not.** Ne 9:33. Jn *3:21. Ep
4:21. Re 21:27.

7. **if we.** ✓184C, Mt +4:9. 1 J 2:9, 10. Ps 56:13.
89:15. 97:11. Is 2:5. 50:11. Jn *12:35, 36. Ro 13:12.
Ep 5:8. 1 Th 1:3. 2 J 4. 3 J 4. **as.** See on ver. 5. Ps
104:2. 1 T *6:16. Ja √1:17. 1 P 2:9. **we have.** See on
ver. 3. Am 3:3. **and the blood.** ✓117, Ge +19:8. 1 J
√2:1, 2. 5:6, 8. Ex 12:13. Zc 13:1. Jn *1:29. Ac +*20:28.
1 C *6:11. Ep *1:7. He *9:14. 1 P 1:19. Re +*1:5.
*7:14. **cleanseth.** Le=4:3 (sin offering). +=23:19. Ps
+*51:2. He +*9:14. 2 P +1:9. **from all.** Ezk 33:16n.
Col 2:13n. He 1:3.

8. **If.** ✓184C, Mt +4:9. **we say.** *✓39, Ac +17:27.
T#507. ver. *6, √10. 1 J 3:5, 6. 1 K *8:46. 2 Ch *6:36.
Jb √9:20. *14:4. *15:14. *25:4. 40:4. *42:5, 6. Ps 14:3.
*19:12, 13. 38:4, 5. 119:◐+3 (T#505), 96. 143:2. Pr
+5:22 (T#166). √20:9. Ec √7:20. Is *6:5. +*53:6. √64:6.
Je 2:22, 23, √35. Mt 6:12. +8:8 (T#663). 26:72-74.
Ro √3:23. *7:14, 15. Ga *5:17. Ph √3:12. Ja +*3:2.
have no sin. This refers to those who deny they have

a sin nature. The verb is present tense. However,
Thomas Scott remarks that this verse addresses the
error of those who imagine that through the gospel,
they are so perfectly sanctified as to have no spot or
blemish of sin in them. Those who claim they are
perfectly pure, and as holy in heart and life as the
law of God required are certainly deceived in a most
awful manner; the truth is not in them, or they could
never have fallen into a mistake, which implied gross
ignorance of God, of his spiritual law, and of their
own hearts. Some commentators take this, however,
to be the particular sense of the tenth verse. Ro 5:12.
7:20. **we deceive.** 1 C 3:18. Ga 6:3. 2 T 3:13. Ja 1:22,
26. 2 P 2:13. **the truth.** ✓144D, Ge +40:23. 1 J *2:4.
1 T *6:5. 2 J 2. 3 J 3.

9. **If.** ✓184C, Mt +4:9. **we.** *✓39, Ac +17:27. Ga
2:11. **confess.** The verb is present tense, with the idea
of keep on confessing. T#870. Le *16:21. *26:40-42.
2 S 12:13. 1 K 8:47. 2 Ch 6:37, 38. 30:22. Ezr ch. 9.
10:1. Ne 1:6. 9:2, etc. Jb *33:27, 28. Ps √32:5, 7. 38:18.
+*51:2-5. 130:1-3. Pr √28:13. Is 6:5. 57:15. Je *3:12,
13. Da 9:4-20. Ho *14:2. Mt 3:6. +10:32g. Mk◐+1:5g.
Lk *15:21, 22. 18:13, 14. +*19:8. Ac 2:38. +*19:18.
1 C 11:31. 2 C 7:11. 1 T 2:5. **our sins.** 1 J 3:4. 5:17.
Le 5:2, 17. Ps 19:12. 66:18. 90:8. Is 66:4. Ac 3:17.
Ro 14:23. 1 C 2:8. Ja 1:15. 2:9. 3:2, 8. +*4:17. **he is
faithful.** Dt 7:9. Ps +*36:5. 143:1. La 3:23. 1 C +1:9.
+*10:13. 1 T *1:15. He *10:23. 11:11. **and just.** 1 J
2:1, 29. 3:7. Is 45:21. Zc *9:9. Jn 17:25. Ro 3:26. He
+*6:10. Re *15:3. 16:5. **to forgive.** Le =5:6n (trespass
offering). 2 Ch +*7:14. Ps 130:4. Ho 14:4. Mt 6:14,
15. Col 2:13n. **our sins.** Is *59:2. Lk 15:18. Ro *3:23-
26. **and to cleanse.** ver. 7. Ps 19:12. 51:2. Je 33:8.
Ezk 36:25. 37:23. 1 C +*6:11. Ep *5:26. T *2:14.
unrighteousness. 1 J *5:17.

10. **If.** ✓184C, Mt +4:9. **we say.** *✓39, Ac +17:27.
ver. 8. Ps 130:3. **have not sinned.** This refers to those
who deny they have committed individual acts of sin.
The verb is in the past tense. The fact that the verb
is past tense has led to the explanation by some who
believe in sinless perfection that this refers to the time
in a person's life before he was saved, not to the presumption that a Christian sins, This, however, seems
contrary to the drift of the apostle's argument in the
light of verse nine and the first two verses of chapter
two. Ps 37:18n. +*51:3, 4. Ec +*7:20. Je 2:29. 3:13.
Ph +*3:12. Ja 2:10. *3:2, 8. +*4:17. **we make.** ✓108A1,
Ex +8:18. 1 J 5:10. Jb 24:25. Ro ◐3:4. **his word.** ver.
8. 1 J 2:4. 4:4. Jn 5:38. 8:37. Col *3:16. 2 J 2.

1 JOHN 2

*The apostle warns his "dear children" not to sin:
yet points out to them Christ, the Advocate with the
Father, and the propitiation for their sins, and the
sins of the world, 1, 2. He shows that the knowledge
of Christ, and union with him, must be evidenced by
obeying and imitating him, and by love of the brethren;
that thus "the love of God is perfected in us;" and
that those are deceived, blind, and hypocritical, who
live in hatred and malice, 3-11. He warns believers
of every age and attainment, against "the love of the
world," showing the vanity of all that is in the world,
compared with the eternal happiness of those who do
the will of God, 12-17. He cautions them against many
antichrists, who fatally seduce some professed Chris-*

tians, 18, 19; declares that the unction of the Holy Spirit is the effectual preservative against them, 21, 22; points out to them the true doctrine of Christ, and exhorts them to adhere to his truth, and abide in him, in expectation of his coming; and to prove their regeneration by an habitual righteous conduct, 23-29.

1. **little.** ver. *12, *13, 28. 1 J *3:7, 18. *4:4. *5:21. Jn 13:33. 21:5. 1 C *4:14, 15. Ga *4:19. 1 Th *2:11. **these.** 1 J *1:3, 4. 1 T 3:14. **that.** Ps *4:4. Ezk *3:21. Jn *5:14. *8:11. Ro *6:1, 2, 15. 1 C *15:34. Ep *4:26. T √2:11-13. 1 P *1:15-19. *4:1-3. **And if.** ſ184C, Mt +4:9. See on 1 J √1:8-10. 1 S 2:25. **sin.** Je 2:29. Ja +*4:17. **we have.** *ſ39, Ac +17:27. Ro *8:34. 1 T *2:5. He *7:24, 25. *9:24. **an advocate.** Gr. Paraclete. Nu=27:5. Pr 8:14. Is 9:6. Je 32:19. Jn 14:16, 26. 15:26. 16:7g. Ep 1:11. Col 2:3. Re 3:18. **with.** Mt ◑+*10:32. He 6:20. **Father.** Lk *10:22. Jn *5:19-26, 36. *6:27. *10:15. √14:6. Ep *2:18. Ja *1:27. 3:9. **Jesus.** Mt 1:21. **the righteous.** ver. 29. 1 J +1:9. *3:5. Zc *9:9. Ac +3:14. Ro 3:25. 2 C √5:21. He *7:26. 1 P *2:22. *3:18.

2. **he is.** 1 J 1:7. *4:10. Ro *3:25, 26. 2 C *5:18, 19. Col 1:20. 1 P 2:24. 3:18. **and not.** ſ69B, Pr +6:16. **for our's.** Gr. *heemeteros*. A special possessive pronoun used of that which is peculiarly ours as distinct from that which belongs to others. 1 J 1:3. Ac 2:11. 24:6. 26:5. Ro 15:4. 2 T 4:15. T 3:14. **also.** Le=16:10. **the sins.** ſ63I1A, Ex +12:4. **of the whole.** 1 J 4:14. 5:19. Jn 1:+*9, 29. 4:42. 11:51, 52. 12:32. 2 C 5:18-21. Re 12:9. **world.** Gr. *kosmos*, Mt +4:8. *ſ121J8, Jn +3:16.

3. **hereby.** ver. *4-6. 1 J *3:14, 19, 24. *4:2, 13. 5:2, 19. **we know.** 1 J 3:6. 4:7, 8. Is *53:11h. Jn *17:3. 2 C 4:6. **know him.** Mt +*11:27. Jn 6:44. 8:19. 14:6, 9. *17:3. **if.** ſ184C, Mt +4:9. 2 P +*1:10. **we keep.** 1 J *3:22, 23, +*24. *5:3. 1 K 11:34. Zc +*6:15. Ps *119:6, 32. Lk √6:46. +*11:28. Jn 8:51. +*13:17. *14:15, 21-24. *15:10, 14. +*17:6. 1 C 7:19. 1 Th *4:1, 2. He +*5:9. Re 1:3. 12:17. 14:12. *22:14. **his commandments.** Note that this word is plural; it cannot be confined exclusively, therefore, to the single command of Christ to "love one another" (Jn 13:34), as so many would have it. John is countering the problem of antinomianism, a heresy very much still with us, that lessens our obligation to obey God since we are saved by grace alone. This tendency is so much a part of evangelical thinking, that I fail to find a single work devoted to a serious, exhaustive study of the commands of Christ. I thought I would find at least a comprehensive list of such commands in *A Complete Index to the Thought and Teachings of Christ* by W. S. Harris, but the topic is dismissed under the relevant heading "Commandments and Precepts of Christ" with the statement "These are incorporated in other subjects" (p. 36). Of these commandments, R. F. Horton states "notwithstanding the unsystematic form in which the precepts are given, the commandments of Jesus constitute a complete and sufficient code of morality." Horton further notes "All His commandments center in His person. They are defined by His character and practice. They are explained by the fundamental truths which He reveals. And they can only be obeyed by virtue of that supernatural indwelling of His Spirit which it is His peculiar promise to give." Horton concludes, "But the most remarkable fact about these commandments of Jesus is that the world, in its moral progress, never gets beyond them. It is not possible to bring

any moral truth discovered since which was not already contained in His code." Most devastating is Horton's observation that "there is a Jesuitry of the conscience always at work; indolence and unbelief are constantly finding modes of slipping through the meshes of Christ's commandments. Few, perhaps, would venture to say that His demands are impossible, but many cover their failures by a vague notion that the standard is ideal rather than practical (and here Horton cites Bruce in a footnote, "To many, the creed which resolves all religion into impracticable ideals is very convenient. It saves a world of trouble and pain; it permits them to think fine thoughts, without requiring them to do noble actions; and it substitutes romancing about heroism in the place of being heroes." *Training of the Twelve*, p. 379), and are content if they obey the Ten Commandments without any special thought concerning the commandments of their Lord. Then the substitution of a doctrinal system and theoretical tests of orthodoxy for the plain truth of Jesus that He would judge men by the degree in which they had kept His commandments, has transferred the momentum of the religious life from the moral to the metaphysical sphere. Thus, in accepting the truth that faith in Jesus Christ, without works, justifies, Protestants have often failed to notice that without obedience to His commandments there can be no genuine faith in Jesus Christ" (*The Commandments of Jesus*, p. 362, 365, 368, 371, 372). The following reference passages contain a fairly complete unclassified list of the commands of Christ. 1 J 3:23. Mt 4:17, 19. 5:3-12, 16, 22, 24, 28, 37, 39, 42, 44, 48. 6:1, 3, 5, 6, 7, 8, 16, 19, 20, 25, 31-33, 34. 7:1-5, +*6, 7-12, *13, +*14, 15. 8:22. 9:9, 12, 13, 38. 10:8, 11-13, 16, 17, 26, 27, +*28, 31, 42. 11:28, 29. 15:10, 11, +*14. 16:24. 18:3, 8, 10, 15-17, 21. 19:6, 14, 17, 21. 20:25, 26. 22:21, 36-40. 23:3, 9, 26. 24:4, 42, 44. 25:34-36. 26:52. 28:19, 20. Mk 1:15, 17. 4:23, +*24. 5:19. 8:34. 9:35, 43. 10:21. 11:22, 25. 13:11, 33-37. 14:38. 16:15. Lk 6:27, 30, 32-35, 37, 38. +*8:18. 10:2, 37. 11:9, 35. 12:7, 15, 24, 27-29, 32, 33, 35, 36. 16:9-12. 17:3, +*10. 18:20. +√21:36. 22:32, *36. 24:49. Jn 2:16. 4:24. +√5:39. 7:24. 8:11. 12:35, 36. 13:34. 14:1, 15. 15:4, 9, 12. 16:23, 24. 21:15, 21. Ac 1:4, 5, √8. 18:9, 10. +*20:35. 1 C 7:10. 9:14. 11:23-25. Ga 6:2. 1 Th *4:2n. 1 T 4:6. 5:18. 6:3. 2 J 9. Re 2:7, 11, 16, 17. 3:3, 11, 19. A classified list of the commandments of Christ follows (developed from *Nave's Study Bible*, pp. 297-299, and other sources). Commandments admonishing against: Apostles preaching to Gentiles or Samaritans, Mt 10:5, 6. Hypocrisy, Mt 6:1-5, 16. Lk 20:46, 47. Commandments concerning: indissolubility of marriage, Mt 19:6. Mk 10:9. Commandments enjoining: Abiding in Christ, Jn 15:4, 9. Agreement in prayer, Mt 18:19. Agreement with adversaries, Mt 5:25, 26. Almsgiving, Lk 11:41. 12:33. Altruistic service, Mt 20:26. Mk 9:35. 10:42-45. Lk 22:26. Jn 13:14. Ambition, selfish. Mt 20:22. 23:8. Mk 10:38. Lk 22:24-27. Anointing when fasting, Mt 6:17. Baptism, Mt 28:19. Belief in Christ, Jn 6:29. 14:1. 1 J 3:23. Beware of false prophets, Mt 7:15. Beware of leaven, Mt 16:6. Mk 8:15. Lk 12:1. Beware of scribes, Mk 12:38. Lk 20:46. Beware when all speak well of you, Lk 6:26. Buy a sword, Lk 22:36. Charitableness, Mt 18:10. Lk 6:37, 38. Chastity, Mt 5:27, 28. Cheerfulness, Mt 14:27. Jn 16:33. Children to come to Christ, Mt 19:14. Mk 10:14. Children not to be despised or offended, Mt 18:6, 10. Children to be fed spiritually, Jn 21:15. Closet prayer, Mt 6:6. Clothing to be shared with needy, Mt 5:40. Lk 6:29. Clothing, undue display condemned, Mt 23:5. Compassion, Mt 18:33. Lk 10:33. Compel to come in, Lk 14:23. Confession of Christ, Mt 10:32. Mk 5:19. Confession of Christ forbidden at times, Mt 9:30. Mk 1:44. 8:26. Conscience, guard the light of, Mt 6:22. Lk 11:34, 35. Consistency, Mt 6:24. 12:33. Contentment, Mt 6:25, 34. Cost must be considered, Lk 14:28. Cross-bearing, Mt 16:24. Mk 8:34. Dead to bury the dead, Mt 8:22. Lk 9:60. Diligence, Lk 12:58. *17:10. Jn 9:4. Discipleship, Mt 19:21. Mk 10:21. Lk 18:22. Disciplining of children, Mt 19:14. Mk 10:14. Lk 18:16, 17. Do more than is asked, even under coercion, Mt 5:41, 42. Lk 6:29, 30. 17:10. Dust, shake off feet, Mt 10:14. Mk 6:11. Lk 9:5. Eat what is set before you, Lk 10:8. Endurance, Mt 10:22. 24:13. Mk 13:13. Enter strait gate, Lk 13:24. Evangelism, Mt 28:19. Faith, Mt 1:15. 5:36. 11:22. Jn 6:29. 12:36. 14:1, 11. 20:27. 1 J 3:23. Faithfulness, Mt 24:45. Lk 12:42. *16:10. Fear God, Mt 10:28. Lk 12:4, 5. Fidelity in marriage, Mt 19:6. Mk 10:8. Fidelity to God, Mt 22:21. Fidelity to government, Mt 22:21. Flee persecution, Mt 24:16. Mk 13:14. Lk 21:21. Following Christ, Mt 4:19. 8:22. 9:9. 16:24. Forgiveness, Mt 5:24. 18:22. Mk 11:25. Lk 6:36. 17:3, 4. Forsake all for Christ, Lk 14:33. Fortitude under persecution, Mt 5:10-12. 10:26-28. Mk 13:9, 11-13. Re 2:10. Footwashing, Jn 13:14. Fraternal reproof, Mt 18:15-17. Lk 17:3, 4. Fruitfulness, Jn 15:16. Giving, Mt 5:42. 10:42. 19:21. Lk 6:30, 38. Ac +*20:35. Give according to ability, Lk 11:41n. Go and do likewise, Lk 10:37. Golden Rule, in conduct, Mt 7:12. Lk 6:31. Greeting, Lk 10:4, 5. Hallow God's name, Mt 6:9. Harmless as doves, to be, Mt 10:16. Hear evidence before judging, Jn 7:51. Hearing, Mt 11:15. 13:9, 43. 17:5. Heed, Mt 6:1. 24:4. Mk +*4:24. Lk +*8:18. +*11:35. 17:3. 21:8. Heed to instruction, Mk +*4:24. Lk +*8:18. Heed to the truth, Mt 11:15. Mk 4:9. Re 2:7. Holiness, Mt 5:48. Honesty, Mk 10:19. Lk 6:31. 8:15. Honor the Son, Jn 5:23. Hospitality, Lk 14:12. Humility, Lk 17:10. 18:14. Ideal character, Mt +*5:3-12. Influence for righteousness, Mt 5:16. Invite poor for meals, Lk 14:13. Invest wisely, Mt 25:27. Justice, Mt +*23:23. Keep the commandments, Mt 19:17. Kindness to enemies, Lk 6:35. Kindness to needy, Mt 25:35, 36. Lk 14:12. Labor, Jn 6:27. Laying up treasure in heaven, Mt 6:20. Lending, Mt 5:42. 6:34, 35. Liberality, Mt 5:42. 6:30. 12:33, 34. Mk 12:41-44. Lk 12:33. Ac +*20:35. Listen to God's Word, Lk 10:39, 42. Look up, Lk 21:28. Love Christ supremely, Mt 10:37. Love for enemies, Mt 5:44. Lk 6:27-29. Love for God, Mt 22:37. Mk 12:30. Lk 10:27. Love for man, Mt 19:19. 22:39. Mk 12:31. Lk 10:27. Jn 13:34. 15:12, 17. Love yourself, Mt 22:39. Make friends of the mammon of unrighteousness, Lk 16:9. Marriage, Mk 10:7, 9. Meekness, Mt 5:39, 40. Lk 6:29. Mercy, Mt 9:12, 13. Lk 6:36. Nations to humble themselves under judgments, Mt 23:34-39. New birth, Jn 3:7. Obedience, Mt 7:21. Lk 6:46. Jn 13:15, 17. Obedience to civil government, Mt 17:24-27. Mk 12:17. Lk 20:25. Occupy, Lk 19:13. Overcoming, Re 2:7, 11, 17. Patience, Lk 21:19. Pay adequate wages, Mt 10:10. Lk 10:7. Peace, Mk 9:50. Peace, seek things belonging to, Lk 19:42. Perfection, Mt 5:48. Perseverance, Mt 24:14. Jn 15:9. Prayer, Mt 7:7-11. Lk 11:9-13. Prayer for daily bread, Mt 6:11. Lk 11:3. Prayer for deliverance from evil, Mt 6:13. Lk 11:4. Prayer for more laborers in the vineyard, Mt 9:38. Prayerfulness, Mt 6:5. Lk 18:1. 22:40. Preach, Ac 10:42. Preach upon house tops, Mt 10:27. Preparedness, Mt 24:44. 25:13. Lk 12:35. Provide for parents, Mt 15:5. Mk 7:11. Prudence, Mt 10:16. Lk 14:28. Rebuke, Lk 17:3. Reconciliation between brethren, Mt 5:23-25. Remember, Lk 17:32. 22:19. Jn 15:20. Renounce all for Christ, Lk 14:33. 18:29, 30. Renunciation of sources of temptation, Mt 5:29, 30. 18:8, 9. Mk 9:43-48. Repentance, Mt 4:17. 7:13, 14. 18:3. Mk 1:15. Lk +*13:3, 5. Re 2:16. 3:19. Rest, Mk 6:31. 14:41. Returning good for evil, Mt 5:4. Reverence for parents, Mt 15:4. 19:19. Lk 18:20. Righteousness, Mt 5:6, 20. Lk 13:24. Salt, have in yourselves, Mk 9:50. Salute, Mt 10:12. Lk 10:5. Scripture to be searched and known, Mk 12:24. Jn +*5:39. Secrecy in giving alms, Mt 6:3. Seeking the kingdom of God, Mt 6:33. Lk 12:31. Self-denial, Mt 16:24. Mk 8:34. 10:21. Lk 9:23. 18:22. Self-discipline, Mt 5:29, 30. Mk 9:45-48. Sell what you have, Mk 10:21. Lk 12:33, 34. Serve God, Mt 4:10. Settle out of court, Lk 12:58. Silence, Mt 8:4. Simplicity in worship, Mt 6:7. Steadfastness, Jn 15:9. Strengthen thy brethren, Lk 22:32. Support of family, Mt 15:5. Mk 7:10, 11. Support of the ministry, Lk 10:7. Support of the oppressed, Mt 25:35-40. Support of the poor, Lk 14:13, 14. Surrender, Mt 8:22. 16:24. Mk 10:21. Sword, buy one, Lk 22:36. Sword, put in its place, Mt 26:52. Take the last or the lowest place, Mk 9:35. Lk 14:10. Take up the cross, Mk 8:34. Temperance, Lk 21:34. Tithing, Mt 23:23. Trust God for needs, Mt 6:30-32. Turn the other cheek, Lk 6:29. Understand prophecy, Mt 24:15. Understand Scripture, Lk 24:45. Watchfulness, Lk +*21:36. Watchfulness against covetousness, Lk 12:15. Watchfulness against false christs, Mt 24:23-26. Mk 13:21-23. Lk 17:23. Weep for yourselves and your children, Lk 23:27, 28. Wise as serpents, be, Mt 10:16. Witnessing for Christ, Mk 1:17. 5:19. Ac 1:8. Work for Christ, Lk 19:13. Jn 4:36, 38. 9:4. Worship God, Mt 4:10. Jn 4:24. Zeal for righteousness, Lk 8:39. Jn 6:27. Commandments forbidding: Adultery, Mt 5:27. 19:18. Mk 10:5, 19. Lk 18:20. Anxiety, Mt 6:25-34. 10:19-23. Lk 12:11, 22-32. Jn 14:27. Casting pearls before swine, Mt +*7:6. Covetousness, Lk 12:15. Desecration of church edifices by worldly business, Mt 21:12, 13. Lk 19:46. Despising little ones, Mt 18:10. Divorce, Mt 5:32. 19:9. Mk 10:11, 12. Lk 16:18. Doubt, Lk 12:29. Drunkenness, Lk 12:45. 21:34. Exercise of lordship over brethren, Mt 20:25-28. 2 C +*1:24. False witness, Mt 19:18. Lk 18:20. Falsehood, Mk 10:19. Lk 18:20. Fear, Mk 5:36. Lk 8:50. Fellowship with the wicked, Mt +*15:14. Fraud, Mk +*10:19. Going house to house, Lk 10:7. Going into the way of the Gentiles or entering any city of the Samaritans, Mt 10:5. Heed to false teachers, Mt +*15:14. Mk +*4:24. Inconsistency, Mt 7:3-5. 23:3. Lk 6:46. Jn 7:23. Indecision, Lk 9:62. Idle words, Mt 12:36. Ingratitude, Mt 18:28-32. Lk 17:17. Injustice, Mt +*23:23. Instability, Mt 6:24. Jesting, Mt 12:36. Murder, Mt 5:21. 19:18. Murmuring, Jn 6:43. Ostentation in giving, fasting, or prayer, Mt 6:1, 5, 6, 17, 18. Profane swearing, Mt 5:34-36. Resistance, Mt 5:39. Retaliation, Mt 5:38-42. Saluting men on the way, Lk 10:4. Theft, Mt 19:18. Lk 18:20. Troubling others doing good work for Christ, Mt 26:10. Mk 14:6. Uncharitable judgments, Mt 7:1-5. Lk 6:37, 42. Uncharitableness, Mt 18:10.

Unrighteous anger, Mt 5:22. Vain repetitions in prayer, Mt 6:7, 8. Worldliness, Mt 6:19. Commandments which are implied: Enjoining an exact conscience, Mt 6:22-24. Against self-righteousness, Mt 7:3. Commandments warning against: Anger, Mt 5:22. Covetousness, Lk 12:15. False teachers, Mt 7:15. Lawsuits, Mt 5:25, 26. Looking back, Lk 9:62. Lust, Mt 5:28. Oaths, Mt 5:34. Offending, Lk 17:1, 2. Offending little ones, Mt 18:6. Mk 9:42. Revenge and vengeance, Mt 5:39. Sadness, Mt 6:16. Lk 24:17. Self-deception, Lk 11:35. Sinful indulgence, Lk 21:34. Stealing, Mt 19:18. Mk 10:19. Lk 18:20. Strife, Mt 12:25. Unfaithfulness, Lk 12:46. 16:11, 12. Vindictiveness, Lk 9:55, 56. Worry, Mt 6:34.

4. **that saith.** ver. *9. 1 J *1:6, 8, 10. *4:20. Ja *2:14-16. **I know.** Ho 8:2, 3. T *1:16. **keepeth not.** ver. 3. **his commandments.** ver. +*3. **is a.** See on 1 J *1:6, 8. Jn 8:44. **the truth.** ∫144D, Ge +40:23. ver. 3. Jn 1:14, 17. 8:32, 40, 45, 46. 16:13. *17:17. 18:37. Ro 1:18.

5. **whoso.** ver. 3, 4. Ps 105:45. 106:3. 119:2, 4, 146. Pr 8:32. 28:7. Ec 8:5. Ezk 36:27. Lk +*11:28. Jn +8:51. *14:21, 23. Re 12:17. 14:12. **his word.** Lk 5:1. Jn 17:6. Ac 4:29, 31. 8:14. 1 C 14:36. 2 C +*4:2. Col 1:25. 1 Th √2:13. T 1:3. He 13:7. Ja +*1:21. 1 P *2:8. Re 12:11. **in him.** 1 J 4:12, 18. Ja 2:22. **love of God.** i.e. *love of men to God*, as in ver 15. ∫181E, Ge +3:24. 1 J 3:17. ◐4:9, 10. 5:3. Jn 5:42. 15:10, 13. **hereby.** ver. +*3, 27, 28. 1 J 3:24. *4:11-13, 15, 16. 5:20. Jn 6:56. 15:5. Ro 8:1. 1 C 1:30. 2 C √5:17, 21. Col *2:9, 10. 2 Th +3:5. 2 T 1:12. He +*6:11. **in him.** Col +*2:6, 7.

6. **that saith.** See on ver. 4. 1 J *1:6. **he abideth.** ver. 28. 1 J 3:6. Jn *15:4-7. 2 J 9. **in him.** ver. 10, 24. 1 J 3:17, 24. 4:15, 16. Jn 6:56. 14:10. Ga 3:26. **to walk.** 1 J 1:7. Ps 85:13. Mt +11:29. Jn 8:12. 13:15. 14:12. 1 C 11:1. 2 C *4:2. Ep 5:2. Col +*1:10. √2:6. 1 P 2:21. 2 J 4. 3 J 3, 4.

7. **I write.** 1 J 3:11. Ac 17:19. 2 J 5. **no new commandment.** Dt 5:22. 2 J 5. **but.** Le *19:2, 18, 34. Dt 6:5. Mt 5:43. 19:19. 22:37-40. Mk 12:29-34. Ro 13:8-10. Ga 5:13, 14. Ja 2:8-12. **which ye had.** ver. 24. 1 J 3:11. 2 J 5, 6. **the word.** Mk 4:14.

8. **a new.** 1 J 3:23. 4:21. Jn +13:34. 15:12. **which.** 1 J *3:14-16. 4:11. Jn 15:12-15. 2 C √8:9. Ep 5:1, 2. 1 P 1:21. 4:1-3. **the darkness.** SS 2:11, 12. Is +*9:2. 60:1-3. Mt 4:16. Lk 1:79. Jn +8:12. 12:46. Ac *17:30. +*26:18. Ro 13:12. 2 C *4:4-6. Ep *5:8. 1 Th 5:4-8. **true light.** Ps 27:1. 36:9. *84:11. Ml *4:2. Jn +1:4, 5, 9. *8:12. 12:35. 2 T *1:10.

9. **that saith.** See on ver. 4. **he is.** 1 J 1:6. Jn 9:41. Ro 2:18-21. **and hateth.** 1 J 3:13-17. 4:20. T 3:3. 2 P 1:9. **is in.** ver. 11. Ps 82:5. 1 C *13:1-3. 2 P *1:9.

10. **that loveth.** 1 J *3:14. Ho 6:3. Jn +*8:31. Ro *14:13. 2 P +*1:10. **occasion of stumbling.** Gr. scandal. Ps 119:165. Pr 4:19. Mt 13:21. 18:7. Lk 17:1, 2. Jn 11:10. Ro 9:32, +33g. Ph 1:10. 2 P *1:10.

11. **he that.** See on ver. 9. Jn *12:35. T 3:3. **and walketh.** 1 J +1:6. Pr +*4:19. Jn 12:35. **because.** Is 6:10. Jn 12:40. 2 C 3:14. 4:4. Re 3:17.

12. **write.** ver. 7, 13, 14, 21. 1 J *1:4. 5:13. **little.** See on ver. 1. **sins are forgiven.** T#583. 1 J 1:7, 9. Ps √32:1, 2. 85:2, 3. 130:4. Is 43:25. 44:22. +45:25 (T#787). *55:7. Mi *7:18, 19. Lk 5:20. 7:47-50. 24:47. Ac 4:12. *10:43. 13:38. Ro 3:24. 4:6, 7. 6:14. 8:1, 2, 28, 29, 30, 33, 34, 37. 1 C *6:11. 15:57. Ga 5:18. Ep

*1:6, 7. 2:18, 19. 3:12. *4:32. Col *1:14, 21. 2:13n, 14. **for.** Ps 25:11. 106:8. Je 14:7. Jn +1:12. Ep √4:32. **name's.** ∫121T1, Dt +28:58.

13. **I write.** 2 P *1:12, 13. **fathers.** ver. 14. 1 T 5:1. **because.** ver. 3, 4. 1 J 5:20. Ps 91:14. Lk 10:22. Jn 8:19. 14:7. *17:3. **him that.** See on 1 J 1:1. Ps 90:2. **young.** ver. 14. Ps 148:12. Pr 20:29. Jl +*2:28. Zc 9:17. T 2:6. **because.** 1 J 4:4. 5:4, 5. Jn +16:33. Ep 6:10-12. 1 P 5:8, 9. **the wicked.** 1 J 3:12. 5:18, 19. Mt 13:+19, 38. **little.** See on ver. 1, 12, 18. Jn 21:5g. **ye have known.** Mt +*11:27. Lk 10:22. Jn 8:54, 55. *14:7, 9. 16:3. 17:21. 2 C 4:6.

14. **fathers.** See on ver. 13. **because ye are.** Ep *6:10. Ph *4:13. Col 1:11. 2 T *2:1. **the word.** Ps *119:11. Jn 5:38. +*8:31. *15:7, 8. Ro +9:6. Col *3:16. He *8:10. 2 J 2. 3 J 3. **abideth in.** Ps *119:11. **ye have overcome.** ver. +13. Re 2:7, etc. *3:7, 8, 12.

15. **Love not.** 1 J *4:5. *5:4, 5, 10. Jn *15:19. Ro +*12:2, 10. Ga *1:4, 10. *6:14. Ep *2:2. Col *3:1, 2. 1 T *6:10. 2 T 4:10. **world.** Gr. *kosmos*, Mt +4:8. **the things.** Le=10:8, 9. Col 3:1-3. **world.** Gr. *kosmos*, Mt +4:8. **If.** ∫184C, Mt +4:9. Mt *6:24. Lk *14:26. 16:13. Ja *4:4. **world.** Gr. *kosmos*, Mt +4:8. ∫132E, Is +65:21. **the love.** ver. +5. 1 J *3:17.

16. **world.** Gr. *kosmos*, Mt +4:8. **the lust of the flesh.** Nu *11:4, 34. Ps *78:18, 30. Pr *6:25. Mt *5:28. Mk +*4:19. Ro *8:5. *13:14. 1 C *10:6. Ga *5:16, 17, 24. Ep *2:3. T *2:12. *3:3. 1 P *1:14. *2:11. *4:2, 3. 2 P *2:10, 18. Ju *16-18. **and the lust of the eyes.** ∫121R5, Ge +27:15. ∫155A, Ge +31:35. ∫108K40B, Ex +15:9. Ge +*3:6. *6:2. Jsh *7:21. Jb *31:1. Ps *119:36, 37. Ec 4:8. *5:10, 11. Ezk +*23:16. 24:16. Mt *4:8. *5:28. Lk *4:5. 2 P *2:14. **and the pride.** Est 1:3-7. Ps 73:6. +*119:21. Da *4:30. Ja 4:16g. Re *18:11-17. **is not.** 1 C +*14:33. Ja *3:15. **is of.** Jn 18:36. **world.** Gr. *kosmos*, Mt +4:8.

17. **the world.** Gr. *kosmos*, Mt +4:8. **passeth away.** Ps *39:6. 73:18-20. *90:9. 102:26. Is *40:6-8. Mt *24:35. 1 C +*7:31. Ja *1:10, 11. *4:14. 1 P *1:24. **but.** Ps *143:10. Mt +*7:21. 21:31. Mk *3:35. Lk √6:46. *16:22. Jn +*7:17. +*13:17. Ro +*12:2. Col *1:9. *4:12. 1 Th +*4:3. *5:18. He *10:36. Ja *4:14. 1 P *4:2. **abideth.** Ps *125:1, 2. Pr *10:25. Mt *7:24, 25. Jn *4:14. 6:58. √10:28-30. He 11:25, 26. 1 P *1:5, 25. **for ever.** Gr. *aion*, Mt +6:13. lit. unto the age, Mt +21:19.

18. **Little.** See on ver. 1. Jn 21:5. **it is.** 2 T 3:1. He *1:2. Ja 5:3. 1 P 1:5, 20. 2 P 3:3. Ju 18. Re 1:3. **last.** ∫25, Ge +4:4. **time.** lit. hour. ∫171T6, Jn +4:23. **ye have.** 1 J 4:3. Mt *24:5, 11, 24. Mk 13:6, 21, 22. Ac *20:29, 30. 2 Th *2:3-12. 1 T *4:1-3. 2 T 3:1-6. 4:3, 4. 2 P *2:1. **antichrist.** ver. 22. Mt *24:5, 24. Lk +21:8. 1 J *4:3. 2 J *7. **many antichrists.** 1 J 4:1. Mt 24:5. 2 J 7. **whereby.** 2 Th 2:6, 7. 1 T 4:1. 2 T 3:1. **time.** lit. hour. ∫171T6, Jn +4:23.

19. **They.** i.e., *the antichrists, the exponents of Gnostic teaching* (A. T. Robertson, *Word Pictures*, vol. 6, p. 215, on ver. 18). **went out.** Dt 13:13. Ps 41:9. Mt 13:20, 21. Mk 4:5, 6, 16, 17. Lk +*8:13. Jn 15:2. Ac 15:24. +20:30. 2 P 2:20, 21. Ju 19. **from us.** "From us" and "of us" are the same idiom in Greek, the preposition *ek* with *hemon*, the preposition used in different senses, expressed by A. T. Robertson "they went out from our membership" and "they were not of us in spirit and life." Robertson points out that a similar difference in the meaning of the preposition

ek is seen in Jn 17:14, "of the world" in the sense of likeness, and Jn 17:15, "out of the world" in the sense of origin (*Word Pictures*, vol. 6, p. 215). See the related notes (Ac 2:38n. *8:39n). **not of us.** Mt +*12:44. 22:11, etc. Ro 9:6. **for if.** √√184B, Mt +11:21. Jb 17:9. Ps 37:28. 125:1, 2. Je *32:38-40. Mt 24:24. Mk 13:22. Jn 4:14. √6:37-39. √10:28-30. +17:12. 2 T 2:10, 19. 1 P *1:2-5. Ju 1. **have continued.** Le=22:10. 1 C +*15:2. Col +*1:23. He 6:11. +*10:39. **they went out.** √63I1D, Nu +26:4. Here the ellipsis is correctly supplied in the A.V. **they might.** 1 J *3:9, 10. Ro *9:6. 11:5, 6. 1 C √11:19. 2 T 3:9. He +*10:39. **they were not all.** A common error in the application of this verse is to assert that *all* those who turn back (1 T +*4:1n) from true faith in Christ were never saved, and were never true believers in the first place. This view is not in accord with the rest of Scripture, however, for it fails to (1) recognize the instances where true believers "stopped believing" (Lk +*8:13. 1 T +*1:19, 20); (2) recognize the seriousness of the warnings against apostasy throughout God's Word (1 C +*15:2), and (3) define apostasy biblically or logically, for one cannot fall from a faith which was never possessed (1 T +*4:1n. He 6:4-6. 2 P 2:20). While John applies his statement to "all," the "all" refers in context specifically to false teachers, who taught the Gnostic heresy, whom he called antichrists. No doubt many false teachers of today deserve this identification, as Robertson suggests, but in no way can this passage be stretched to include all individuals who have ever turned away or apostatized from Christ, to assert that none of them were ever really saved. On other themes careful interpreters rightly assert that we must take into account all Scripture which bears on a subject, and arrive at a position which agrees with the whole body of applicable evidence. They properly caution not to overgeneralize or explain all possibilities on the basis of a single prooftext. This very interpretive fallacy has fostered a whole host of error ranging from minor matters of doctrine to absolute heresy, and is used by some to support: (1) sinless perfection: one who is born of God cannot commit sin (1 J 3:9); (2) baptismal regeneration (Jn 3:5); (3) ritual water baptism required for salvation (Ac 2:38n); (4) baptism unto repentance (Ac 2:38); (5) ritual water baptism symbolizes the death, burial, and resurrection of Christ (Ro 6:4); (6) the alleged spiritual nature of the kingdom of God (Lk 17:21); (7) the "church" as "spiritual Israel" has replaced natural Israel in the plan of God (Ro 2:28, 29. Ga 6:16); (8) there is no conscious existence after death (Ps +*146:4. Ec +*9:5); (9) no one goes to heaven at death to be with Christ (Jn 3:13. Ac 2:34. 1 C 15:50. Da 1:23n), (10) but sleeps until the resurrection (Da +*12:2n), (11) unaware of any passing of time, explaining the sense of going immediately to be with Christ (2 C 5:8. Ph 1:23n); (12) since there is only one God (Dt 6:4), the Father (1 C 8:4, 6), Jesus cannot be God because he called God the Father his God (Jn 20:17), and the only true God (Jn 17:3), thus excluding himself; (13) God dispenses his truth by means of his "faithful and true servant," the one true church, and outside of this divinely provided earthly visible organization there can be no salvation (Mt 24:45); (14) No individual has the right to interpret the Bible for himself, for Scripture is not "of any private interpretation" (2 P 1:20). The most apt description of this interpretive

error I have found is that of Lewis Sperry Chafer, who wrote "A certain type of mind, however, seems able to construct all its confidence on an erroneous interpretation of one passage and to be uninfluenced by the overwhelming body of Scripture which contradicts that interpretation" (*Systematic Theology*, vol. 3, p. 380). Mt +*7:21-23.

20. ye have. ver. *27. 1 J *4:13. Ps *22:5. *45:7. 92:10. Is *61:1. Lk +*4:18. Ac *10:38. 2 C *1:21, 22. He 1:9. **an unction.** *or,* anointing. ver. 27. Ex=40:15. 1 C 2:13. 2 C *1:21. **the Holy.** Ps +*16:10. 71:22. Is 43:3. Mk +*1:24. Lk *4:34. Ac *3:14. Re 3:7. 4:8. **and ye.** ver. 27. Pr *28:5. Mt 13:11. Lk 8:10. Jn 10:4, 5. +*14:26. *16:13. Ro 15:14. 1 C 1:5. *2:15. He *8:11. 2 P 1:12. Ju 5.

21. because ye know not. Pr 1:5. 9:8, 9. Ro 15:14, 15. 2 P *1:12. **the truth.** 1 J 3:19. Jn 18:37.

22. Who. ver. 4. 1 J 1:6. 4:20. Jn *8:44. Re 3:9. **he that.** ver. 23. 1 J *4:3. 1 C *12:2, 3. 2 J 7. Ju 4. **Jesus is.** 1 J 5:1. Da *9:25, 26. Mk +8:29. Ac +18:5. **He is.** See on ver. 18. **Father and.** 1 J 4:14. Jn +3:35. √5:23. 2 J 3, 9.

23. denieth. ver. 22. 1 J *4:15. 5:1. Mt *11:27. Lk 10:22. Jn √5:23. 8:19. *10:30. 14:9, 10. *15:23, 24. 2 J √9-11. **but.** Ps *73:25, 26.

24. abide. √101, Dt +32:42. Ps *119:11. Pr 23:23. Lk 9:44. Jn 15:7. Col *3:16. He *2:1. +*3:14. 2 J 2. 3 J 3. Re *3:3, 11. **which.** ver. *7. 1 J 3:11. Lk *1:2. Jn 8:25. Ph 4:15. 2 J 5, 6. **If.** √184C, 1 C +15:2. 2 P +*1:10. **shall remain.** ver. +*3. 1 J 5:2. Jn 8:51. *14:21-24. 1 C +*15:2. **shall continue.** √101, Dt +32:42. 1 J *1:3, 7. 4:13, 16. Jn +*8:31. *14:23. 15:9, 10. 17:21-24. **in the Son.** ver. 22.

25. the promise. 1 J +1:2. √5:11-13, 20. Da +*12:2. Lk 18:30. Jn +*5:39. 6:*27, *47, 54, *68. √10:28. 12:50. √17:2, 3. Ro 2:7. 5:21. +*6:23. Ga *6:8. 1 T 1:16. *6:12, 19. T 1:2. *3:7. Ju *21. **eternal.** Gr. *aionios,* Mt +18:8.

26. concerning. 1 J 3:7. Pr 12:26. Ezk 13:10. Mt *24:24. Mk *13:22. Ac *20:29, 30. 2 C √11:13-15. Col 2:*8, 18. 1 T +*4:1. 2 T *3:13. 2 P *2:1-3. 2 J *7. **that seduce.** √108A1, Ex +8:18.

27. the anointing. √22D5L, Ps +45:7. See on ver. *20. 1 J *3:24. Le 8:12, 30. 1 S √16:22. Ps 92:10. 133:2. Jn *1:16. 3:34. *4:14. Ac *10:38. 1 Th 4:9. 1 P *1:23. 2 J *2. **received of.** Lk 11:13. Ac 2:38, 39. 5:32. **abideth in you.** √101, Dt +32:42. 1 J +3:24. √5:10-13. Ro +*8:9, 14, 16. **any man teach.** T#1117. ver. *20, 21. Is +*8:20n. *54:13. Je *31:33, 34. Ezk 14:10n. Jn *14:26. *16:13. Ac ●8:31n. Ro √14:12. Ga 1:8n. He *8:10, 11. 2 P 1:20n. **but.** 1 C *2:13. Ep *4:21. 1 Th √2:13. 1 T 2:7. 2 P *1:16, 17. **same anointing.** Ex=28:41. 2 C 1:21. **teacheth you.** T#841. Ps +*32:8. Pr *1:23. Lk 12:12. Jn 6:45. *16:13. 1 C 2:10. **is truth.** Jn +14:17. **ye shall.** ver. *28. Jn *8:31, 32. *15:4-7. Col *2:6. **abide.** √101, Dt +32:42. **him.** *or,* it.

28. little. See on ver. 1. **abide.** ver. 27. **when.** 1 J *3:2. Mk 8:38. Col *3:4. 1 T *6:14. 2 T +*4:8. T +*2:13. He +*9:28. 1 P *1:7, 13. *5:4. Re +*1:7. **have confidence.** 1 J 3:21. *4:17. 5:14. Is *25:9. *45:17. Ac +4:13. Ro *5:5. *9:33. Ep 3:12. Ph 1:20. 1 T 3:13. He 3:6. 4:16. 10:19, 35. **not be ashamed.** Lk 9:26. 1 C 3:15. Ph *2:15, 16. 2 P 1:11. **at his.** Ml *3:2. 4:5. 1 C 1:7. *15:23. 1 Th *3:13. *5:23. 2 P *3:4-12. **coming.** Gr. *parousia,* Mt +24:3.

29. If ye. √184C, Mt +4:9. **he is.** ver. 1. 1 J +1:9.

3:5. Zc *9:9. Ac 3:14. 22:14. 2 C √5:21. He +*1:8, 9. 7:2, 26. 1 P *3:18. **ye know.** *or,* know ye. **that every.** 1 J 3:7, 10. Je 13:23. Mt 7:16-18. Jn *15:5. Ac 10:35. T *2:12-14. 3 J 11. **is born.** √22C23, Ps +2:7. 1 J *3:9. 4:7. *5:1, 4, 18. Jn 1:13. √3:3-6, 8. +11:52. Ja +*1:18. 1 P *1:3, 23. 2 P *1:4.

1 JOHN 3

The apostle breaks out in admiration of the love of God, in making us his children, and giving us present privileges with the hope of an inconceivable felicity; and shows that all who have this hope "purify themselves as he is pure," 1-3. He shows how the children of God, and the children of the devil, may be distinguished, 4-10. He exhorts his readers to "love one another," contrasting this love with the example of Cain, and warning them to expect the hatred of the world, 11-13. He points out "the love of the brethren," as distinguishing evidence of conversion; explains the nature and effects of it, contrasting it with enmity and selfishness; and enforces the practice of it, by the example of Christ, 14-17. He exhorts his readers to love "in deed and in truth," and shows that confidence in God is connected with the consciousness of upright obedience, 18-24.

1. **what.** 1 J *4:9, 10. 2 S 7:19. Ps 31:19. 36:7-9. 89:1, 2. Jn √3:16. Ro √5:8. +*8:32. Ep 2:4, 5. 3:18, 19. 2 P 3:11. **love.** √121C1A. Metonymy of the Cause B549: in certain nouns, where the feeling or affection is put for the effects resulting or proceeding from the feeling. Here, love is put for the benefits and blessings flowing from it. The reference is not merely to the feeling of love, but the manifestation of it in all it has done for us. **that.** ver. 10. 1 J 5:2. Je 3:19. Ho 1:10. Jn √1:12. 11:52. 13:13. Ro √8:14-17, 21. 9:8, 25, 26. 2 C *6:18. Ga 3:26, 29. +*4:5-7n. Ep *1:5. Ph 2:15. Re *21:7. **called.** √108B. Idiom B830. "Called" is used of being acknowledged, accounted, or simply of being. **the sons of God.** Some authorities add, "and such we are." √71, Jn +1:24. **the world.** Gr. *kosmos,* Mt +4:8. *√121J9A, Jn +1:10. 1 J 4:17. Jn +8:55. *15:18, 19. *16:3. 17:25. 1 C 1:21. Col *3:3. **knoweth us not.** 2 C 6:9.

2. **now are we the.** See on ver. 1. 1 J 5:1. Is 56:5. Ro *8:14, 15, 18. Ga *3:26. 4:5, 6. Ep 1:5. 2 P 1:4. **it.** Ps 31:19. 83:3. Ro *8:18, 23. 1 C √2:9. *13:12. 15:37, 38. 2 C √4:17, 18. Ph +*3:21. Col 3:5, 6. **what.** Ps *17:15. Ro *8:29. 1 C 15:49. 2 C *4:6. Ph *3:21. 2 P 1:4. **we know.** ver. 14. 1 J 5:15, 18, 19, 20. Jn 19:35. 21:24. **when.** 1 J 2:28. Ml 3:2. Col *3:4. He +*9:28. **shall appear.** Ac +*1:11. Re 1:7. **like.** Ex=28:2, 41. Zp 3:13. Ro +*8:29. 2 C 3:18. 4:11. Ph +*3:21. 1 P 2:22. 2 P 1:4. **for.** Jb *19:26. Ps +*16:11. Mt +*5:8. Jn 17:24. 1 C 13:12. 2 C 3:18. √5:6-8. Re 21:23, 27. *22:3, 4.

3. **every.** Ro 5:4, 5. Col *1:5. 2 Th 2:16. T *3:7. He *6:18. **in him.** Ro 15:12. **purifieth.** Jn 15:5. Ac *15:9. 2 C +*7:1. 1 T 6:14-16. He +*12:14. 2 P 1:4. √3:14. **even.** ver. 5. 1 J *2:6. 4:17. Mt +*5:48. Lk *6:36. He *7:26. 1 P 1:15.

4. **committeth.** ver. 8, 9. 1 K 8:47. 1 Ch 10:13. Jn 8:34. 2 C 11:7. 12:21. Ja 5:15. 1 P 2:22g. **transgresseth.** Nu 15:31. 1 S *15:24. 2 Ch 24:20. Is 53:8. Da 9:11. Mt 13:41g. Ro *3:20. 4:15. Ja *2:9-11. **for sin is.** 1 J *5:17. Ro 4:15. 7:7-13. Ja +*4:17.

5. **he.** 1 J +1:2. 4:9-14. Jn 1:31. 1 T *3:16. 1 P 1:20. **was manifested.** √18, Dt +28:4. ver. 8. **to.** 1 J *1:7. Is *53:4-12. Ho 14:2. Mt *1:21. Jn +*1:29. Ro *3:24-26. Ep *5:25-27. 1 T 1:15. T √2:14. He *1:3. +*9:26, 28. 1 P *2:24. Re +*1:5. **in.** ver. 3. 1 J 2:1. Lk 23:41, 47. Jn *8:46. +*14:30. 2 C √5:21. He +*4:15. *7:26. +*9:28. 1 P *1:19, 20. +*2:22. *3:18.

6. **abideth.** 1 J *2:28. Jn *15:4-7. **sinneth not.** ver. +*9n. 1 J ◐+*1:8, 10. 5:18. Ec ◐+*7:20. Ro *6:14, 17, 18. Ja ◐+*3:2. **whosoever.** ver. 2, 9. 1 J 2:4. 4:8. 5:18. 2 C 3:18. 4:6. 3 J 11. **not seen.** √96C1, Ge +4:1. He ◐11:1, 27. **neither known.** √96C1, Ge +4:1. 1 J +√2:3. 3 J *11.

7. **Little children.** 1 J +2:1. **let.** 1 J 2:26, 29. Mt +24:4. Ro 2:13. 1 C +*6:9. Ga 6:7, 8. Ep 5:6. Ja 1:22. 2 J 7. **he that.** 1 J *2:29. *5:1-3. Ps 106:3. Ezk 18:5-9. Mt 5:20. Lk 1:75. Ac 10:35. Ro 2:6-8, *13. 6:16-18. Ep 5:9. Ph 1:11. Ja *2:18. 1 P 2:24. **doeth.** √108B. Idiom B828. "To do justice" or "righteousness" is used for willingly, earnestly, and joyfully walking and living as one whom God has justified. **even.** ver. 3. 1 J *2:1, +29. Ps *45:7. 72:1-7. He +*1:8. 7:2. 1 P 1:15, 16. **is righteous.** √147A, Ge +50:24.

8. **He that.** ver. 10. 1 J *2:1, 2. 5:19g. Mt +*13:38. Jn √8:44. Ro 7:14-25. 1 C 4:4, 5. 5:5. Ga +*2:11. Ep *2:2. 2 P 2:4. **committeth.** ver. +4. Mt 12:30. Jn 8:44. **for.** Is 14:12-15. Ezk 28:12-19. 2 P 2:4. Ju 6. **beginning.** √63C, Ge +25:32. Supply ellipsis, (and still sinneth). **this purpose.** ver. 5. Ge +*3:15. Is 27:1. Mk *1:24. Lk *10:18. +*19:10. Jn 12:31. 16:11. Ro *16:20. Ep 1:11. Col 2:15. 2 T *2:26. He √2:14. Re *20:2, 3, 10, 15. **the Son of God.** Jn +5:25. **destroy.** Ge ✱3:15. **the works.** Jn 8:41. 10:10. Ac 10:38.

9. **born.** √22C23, Ps +2:7. 1 J *2:29. 4:7. 5:1, 4, 18. Jn *1:13. 3:3. Ja *1:18. 1 P *1:23. **doth not.** 1 J *5:18. Ac ◐20:22, 23. ◐21:12-14. Ph ◐3:12. Ga ◐2:11-13. **commit.** √108B, Jn +8:34. ver. +4. **for.** Jb 19:28. 1 P *1:23. **seed.** Le +=11:37. **and he.** Mt 7:18. Ac *4:20. Ro 6:2. Ga 5:17. T *1:2. **cannot sin.** Gr. *ou dunatai hamartanein. Hamartainein* is the present active infinitive, and can only mean "and he cannot go on sinning" (A. T. Robertson, *Word Pictures,* vol. 6, p. 223). This is not a declaration that the Christian possesses sinless perfection, or is unable to commit a sin, but a declaration that a Christian does not freely and habitually practice sin, or live a life of sin. Had the apostle John intended to teach sinless perfection, he would have selected the second aorist or first aorist active infinitive here. Robertson observes, "A great deal of false theology has grown out of a misunderstanding of the tense of *hamartanein* here. Paul has precisely John's idea in Ro 6:1 *epimenomen tei hamartiai* (shall we continue in sin, present active linear subjunctive) in contrast with *hamartesomen* in Ro 6:15 (shall we commit a sin, first aorist active subjunctive)" (*Word Pictures,* vol. 6, p. 223). See the related notes for other examples of the present tense used to represent habitual practice of sin (1 T 5:20n. He 6:6n). See the related notes on a similar distinction obtained in a different way (Jn 5:29n. Ga 5:21n). ver. 6. 1 J ◐+√1:8, 10. Ps +*119:3. Ro *7:19. 2 P ◐+*2:14. **born.** 1 J +2:29.

10. **In this.** √62, Lk +12:32. **the children of God.** ver. +1. 1 J 5:2. Lk 6:35. Ro *8:16, 17. Ep 5:1. **and.** ver. 8. 1 J 5:19. Mt 13:38. Jn *8:34, 44. Ac 13:10. Ro 6:20. Ep 2:1, 2. 2 T 2:25, 26. T 3:3. **whosoever.** See

on ver. 7, 8. 1 J *2:29. **is.** 1 J 4:3, 4, 6. 5:19. Jn 8:47. 3 J 11. **neither.** ver. 14, 15. 1 J 2:9, 10. *4:7, 8, 21. **loveth not.** 1 J 4:20, 21. He +*13:1.

11. **this.** 1 J 1:5. 2:7, 8. **message.** *or,* commandment. 1 T 1:5g. **heard from.** 1 J *2:7, 10, +24. **that we.** ver. 23. 1 J 4:7, 11, 12, 21. Mt +19:19. Jn 13:34, 35. *15:12, 17. Ro 13:8. Ga 6:2. Ep 5:2. Col 3:14. 1 Th 4:9. 1 T 1:5. 1 P 1:22. 3:8. 4:8. 2 J *5.

12. **Not as Cain.** i.e. *spear or lance,* ✶S#2535g. For ✶S#7014h, see Ge +4:1. Ge 4:4-15, 25. He *11:4g. Ju +11g. **of.** See on ver. 8. 1 J 2:13, 14. 5:18, 19. Mt +*13:19, 38. **And.** 1 S 18:14, 15. 19:4, 5. 22:14-16. Ps 37:12. Pr 29:27. Mt 27:23. Jn 10:32. 15:19-25. 18:38-40. Ac 7:52. 1 Th 2:14. 1 P 4:4. Re 17:6. **Because.** Ps 38:20. 109:4. Pr 29:10. **works were.** Jn +7:7. **and his.** Mt 23:35. Lk 11:51. He 11:4. 12:24.

13. **Marvel not.** Ec +*5:8. Jn *3:7. 5:28. Ac 3:12. Re 17:7. **if.** ✸184A, 1 C +15:2. Mt 10:22. 24:9. Mk 13:13. Lk 6:22. 21:17. Jn 7:7. *15:+18, 19. 16:2, 33. 17:14. Ro 8:7. 2 T *3:12. Ja *4:4. **world.** Gr. *kosmos,* Mt +4:8.

14. **We know.** ver. +2. 1 J +√2:3. 5:2, 13, 19, 20. 2 C 5:1. **we have.** 1 J 2:9-11. Lk 15:24, 32. Jn √5:24. Ep *2:1, 5. **because.** ver. *23. 1 J 2:10. 4:7, 8, 12, 21. 5:2. Ps 16:3. Mt 25:40. Jn 13:35. 15:12, 17. Ga *5:6, 22. Ep 1:15. Col 1:4. 1 Th 4:9. He +*6:10, 11. 13:1. 1 P 1:22. 3:8. 2 P *1:7. **the brethren.** Ep +6:23. 3 J 10. **that loveth not.** 1 J *2:9, 11. 4:20. Pr 21:16.

15. **hateth.** Ge 27:41. Le *19:16-18. 2 S 13:22-28. Pr 26:24-26. Mt *5:21, 22, 28. Mk 6:19. Ac 23:12, 14. Ja 1:15. 4:1, 2. **is a murderer.** Jn 8:44. **hath.** Jn 4:14. Ga +*5:21. 1 P *1:23. Re +*21:8. **eternal.** Gr. *aionios,* Mt +18:8. **life.** 1 J 5:11, 13, 20. Mt +19:16. Jn +4:14. Ro +2:7.

16. **perceive.** 1 J *4:9, 10. Mt *20:28. Jn √3:16. 10:15. +*15:13. Ac +*20:28. Ro √5:8. Ep *5:2, 25. T +*2:13, 14. 1 P 1:18. *2:24. 3:18. Re +*1:5. *5:9. **of God.** ✸63J, Ge +37:13. **laid down.** Jn 10:15. **life.** Gr. psyche, ✸121A7, Mt +2:20. ✸121A7, Ge +9:5. **and we ought.** 1 J 2:6. 4:11. Pr 24:11. Jn *13:34. 15:12, 13. Ro 16:4. 1 C 15:31. Ph 2:17, 30. 1 Th 2:8. **lives.** Gr. psyche, ✸121A7, Mt +2:20. ✸121A7, Ge +9:5.

17. **whoso.** Dt *15:7-11. Pr *19:17. Is 58:7-10. Lk *3:11. Ac 11:29. +*20:35. 2 C *8:9, 14, 15. *9:5-9. 1 T +*6:17, 18. He +*13:16. **world's.** Gr. *kosmos,* Mt +4:8. **good.** ✸111, Ge +18:27. **his brother.** Is +*58:7. Ga +*6:10. 1 T +*5:8. **have need.** 2 Ch 28:15. Ja 2:15, 16. **shutteth.** Le +*25:35. Dt *15:7. Pr +*11:24, 26. 12:10mg. +*15:27. 28:9. Lk +*12:15. **compassion.** Col +2:12. **how.** 1 J *4:20. 5:1. **the love.** 1 J +2:5. Lk 11:42.

18. **My.** See on 1 J 2:1. **let.** Ps *78:36, 37. Is 29:13. Je 12:2. Ezk +*33:31. Mt *25:41-45. Ro *12:9. 1 C 13:4-7. Ga 5:13. 6:1, 2. Ep 4:1-3, 15. 1 Th 1:3. Ja 2:15, 16. 1 P *1:22. **in truth.** 2 J 1. 3 J 1.

19. **hereby.** See on ver. 14. 1 J *1:8. Jn √13:35. 18:37. **of the truth.** 1 J 2:21. Jn 18:37. **shall.** ver. 21. Is 32:17. He +*6:10, 11. +*10:22. 1 P √1:5, 7, 10, 11. **assure.** Gr. persuade. Ro *4:21. *8:38. 2 T +*1:12. He +*11:13.

20. **if.** ✸184C, Mt +4:9. Jb 27:6. Jn 8:9. Ac 5:33. Ro 2:14, 15. 1 C 4:4. 14:24, 25. T 3:11. **condemn.** ✸135, Ps +68:28. **us.** ✸63B, Ge +25:28. Supply ellipsis, (we know that). **God is greater.** God knows us better than we know ourselves. Our feelings of assurance are not a certain guide to the security or status of

our salvation. God is greater than our feelings, and knows our hearts absolutely. When in doubt, our hearts would dwell on the negative evidence, glossing over the positive fruit that our spiritual life has shown. "This would seem to make God's knowing all things not the cause of his condemning us more than our hearts do, but the reason why he spares us. He knows all our weaknesses, and his greater knowledge of our motives and infirmities will prevent Him from condemning or accusing us" (W. Graham, *The Spirit of Love,* p. 232). Graham prefers, however, the interpretation that if our own heart condemn us, much more will God condemn us, for God is greater than our heart, and knoweth all things, a view supported, says Graham, by the following verse. Haupt (Comm. on 1 John, p. 223), however, argues convincingly that the former view is correct; that "God is greater than our heart" in respect to his greater tenderness, not severity, for this is the ground of the consolation ("assure," mg. persuade, ver. 19, which Haupt shows means *soothe*). So Wescott, who summarizes the meaning of the passage: "The sense within us of a sincere love of the brethren, which is the sign of God's presence with us, will enable us to stay the accusations of our conscience, whatever they may be, because God, who gives us the love, and so blesses us with His fellowship, is greater than our heart; and He, having perfect knowledge, forgives all on which the heart sadly dwells" (*Comm. on 1 John,* p. 118). Haupt suggests that what the heart sadly dwells upon is its failure to measure up absolutely to the standard of "doing righteousness," ver. 7. 1 J 4:4. Jb 33:12. Jn 10:29, 30. 1 C *4:4. He 6:13. **and knoweth.** ✸135, Ps +68:28. 1 Ch +*28:9. Ps 44:20, 21. 90:8. *139:1-4. Je +*17:10. 23:24. Jn +*2:24, 25. *21:17. He √4:13. Re *2:23.

21. **if our heart.** ✸184C, Mt +4:9. T#1344. 1 J 2:28. 4:17. Jb 22:26. *27:6. Ps 7:3-5. 101:2. 1 C *4:4. 2 C 1:12. 1 T 2:8. **condemn us not.** Not a reference to sinless perfection, but to consciousness of fellowship with God (see A. T. Robertson, *Word Pictures,* vol. 6, p. 227). ver. 20. Ga 2:11. **confidence.** or, boldness. The Greek word signifies freedom to speak, and thus ties right in with the subject of prayer in the succeeding verse. T#1318. 1 J +2:28. √5:14, 15. Jb 11:15. 22:26. Ps 6:8, 9. 20:5, 6. 25:1-3. 27:3, 10. 31:1, 3, 14. +*34:4. 40:3, 4. 60:11, 12. 71:1. 86:7. Ro 14:22. 1 T 2:8. He +*4:16. +*10:22.

22. **whatsoever.** 1 J √5:14. Ps 10:17. 34:+*4, 15-17. *37:4. +*50:15. √66:18, 19. *145:18, 19. Pr 15:29. 28:9. Is *1:15. √55:6, 7. Je √29:12, 13. √33:3. Mt +*7:7, 8. *21:22. Mk √11:24. Lk √11:9-13. Jn +*9:31. *14:13. *15:7. *16:23, 24. Ja +*1:5. +*5:16. **because.** ver. 23, 24. Mt 7:24, 25. 17:5. Jn 15:10. Ac *17:30. 20:21. **we keep.** T#1374. Dt 4:29-31. 30:1, 2. Ps 119:8, 47, 48, 57-61. Is 50:10. Je *42:2, 3, 6. Mt √7:21. Jn *9:31. +*13:17. **his commandments.** 1 J +√2:3n. **do.** Jn 6:29. 8:29. +*9:31. Ph 4:18. Col +√1:10. He *13:21. **in his sight.** Nu=3:4.

23. **should believe on.** 1 J *5:13. Dt 18:15-19. Ps 2:12. Mk *9:7. Jn +5:47. *6:29. *14:1. √17:3. Ac √16:31. 18:8. 1 T *1:15. **the name.** Jn +1:12. **love.** See on ver. 11. 1 J 2:8-10. 4:21. Mt 22:39. Jn *13:34. 15:12. Ep 5:2. 1 Th 4:9. 1 P 1:22. 4:8.

24. **he that keepeth.** ver. 22. Jn +*13:17. *14:15, 21-23. 15:7-10. **his commandments.** 1 J +√2:3n. **dwelleth.** 1 J 2:27, 28. 4:7, 12, 13, 15, 16. Jn 6:54-56.

14:23. 15:4, 5. 17:21. 1 C 3:16. 6:19. 2 C *6:16. 2 T 1:14. Re √3:20. **and he in.** 1 J 1:3. Jn 14:20. 17:21. **hereby.** 1 J 4:13. **we know.** 1 J +*2:3n. 4:13. Ps *62:7. Ro +*8:9-17. Ga *4:5, 6. **the Spirit.** Gr. *pneuma,* ſ121A1, Ro +8:1n. Jn +7:39. **hath given.** Jn 14:16, 17.

1 JOHN 4

The apostle warns Christians against those who falsely professed to be inspired; and gives directions for distinguishing the Spirit of truth from that of error, 1-6. He exhorts them to "love one another," from the example of God in giving his Son for sinners; and from various considerations, tending to show the necessity, benefit, and efficacy of this sacred affection, 7-21.

1. **believe not.** Dt *13:1-5. Pr +√14:15. +*18:17. Je *5:31. *29:8, 9. Mt *7:15, 16. *24:4, 5. Mk +*4:24. Ro 16:18. 2 P 2:1. **spirit.** ſ121A4, Ezk +37:1. Mt +8:16. **try.** Dt *18:22. Jb 34:4. Pr +*18:17. Is √8:20. Lk 12:57. Ac +*17:11. Ro 16:19. 1 C 12:10. √14:29. 1 Th +√5:21. Re *2:2. **spirits.** Gr. *pneuma,* Mt +8:16. **many false prophets.** T#473. 1 J +2:18. 1 K 18:22. Je 10:21. Ezk *14:10n. Mt 7:+15, 22, 23. 24:5, 11, 23-26. Mk 13:21, 22. Lk *21:8. Ac *20:29, 30. 1 T +*4:1. 2 T *3:13. 2 P *2:1. 2 J *7. **world.** Gr. *kosmos,* Mt +4:8.

2. **Hereby know.** Mt 11:27. **Spirit.** Gr. *pneuma,* Mt +3:16. Jn +7:39. Ph +3:3. **Every.** 1 J 5:1. Jn 16:13-15. 1 C +*12:3. **spirit.** Gr. *pneuma.* B. F. Wescott states, "There is an endless variety in the operations of the Spirit (1 C 12:4). These severally appear to find characteristic organs in 'spirits' which are capable of acting on man's spirit. Compare 1 C 12:10. 14:12, 32. He 1:14. (12:9, 23), (1 P 3:19), (Re 22:6); Re 1:4. 3:1. 4:5. 5:6" (*The Epistles of St. John,* p. 141). Ac 23:9. 1 C 12:10. 2 C 11:4. For the other uses of *pneuma,* see Mt +8:16n. **come.** ſ108B, Mt +11:3. Note the three forms of the verb "come" (*erchomai*). Here, it is the perfect participle (*eleeuthota*), "being come." In 1 J 5:6, it is the aorist participle (*ho elthon*), "this is he that came." While in 2 J 7 it is the present participle (*erchomenon*), "who confess not that Jesus Christ is coming in the flesh": i.e., in his human nature, the same Jesus, in like manner as he went into heaven (Ac 1:11). ver. 3. Jn +*1:14. 1 T *3:16. 2 J 7. **flesh.** ſ171Q7, Jn +1:14. i.e. in His real human nature.

3. **spirit.** Gr. *pneuma,* Mt +8:16. **that confesseth not.** 1 J 2:22. 2 J 7. **flesh.** T#69. Mt 1:1. 8:20. Lk 2:52. Jn *1:14. 1 T 2:5. He 2:14-18. **of antichrist.** See on 1 J 2:18, 22. 2 Th 2:7, 8. 2 J 7. **world.** Gr. *kosmos,* Mt +4:8.

4. **are.** ver. 6, 16. 1 J 3:9, 10. 5:19. **little children.** 1 J +2:1. **have overcome.** 1 J +2:13. *5:4. Ro *8:37. Ep 6:10, 13. Re 12:11. **greater.** ver. 13, 16. 1 J 3:24. 2 K 6:16. 2 Ch 13:12. Jn √10:28-30. 14:17-23. 17:23. Ro +*8:10, 11, 31. 1 C 6:13. 2 C *6:16. Ep 3:17. **in you.** Col 1:27. **than.** 1 J 5:19g. Jn +*12:31. 14:30. 16:11. 1 C *2:12. 2 C *4:4. Ep *2:2. 6:12. **world.** Gr. *kosmos,* Mt +4:8.

5. **are.** Ps 17:4. Lk *16:8. Jn 3:31. 7:6, 7. 8:23. *15:19, 20. 17:14, 16. +18:36. Re 12:9. **world.** Gr. *kosmos,* Mt +4:8. *ſ121J9A,* Jn +1:10. **therefore speak.** Jn 3:31. 1 C +*2:14. **world.** Gr. *kosmos,* Mt +4:8. **and.** Is 30:10, 11. Je 5:31. 29:8. Mi 2:11. Jn

+15:19. 17:14. 2 T 4:3. 2 P *2:2, 3. **world.** Gr. *kosmos,* Mt +4:8.

6. **We are.** See on ver. 4. Mi 3:8. Ro 1:1. 1 C 2:12-14. Ga *1:1. 2 P 3:2. Ju 17. **he that.** Jn *8:47. 10:16. 18:37. 1 C *14:37. **knoweth God.** ver. 8. 1 J 5:20. Lk 10:22. Jn 8:19, 45-50. *10:27. 13:20. *17:3. 18:37. *20:21. Ro 1:21. 1 C 1:21. 14:37. 2 C 10:7. Ga +4:9. 2 Th 1:8. **heareth us.** Jn *8:47. **heareth not.** Jn *8:47. **Hereby.** See on ver. 1. Is +*8:20n. **the spirit.** Gr. *pneuma,* Lk +24:27. **of truth.** 1 J 2:27. 5:7. Jn 14:17. 15:26. 16:13. Ro +*8:9. 1 C 2:12-14. 1 T 4:1. **and.** Is 29:10. Ho 4:12. Mi 2:11. Ro 11:8. 2 Th 2:9-11. **the spirit.** Gr. *pneuma,* Mt +8:16.

7. **let.** ver. 11, 12, 20, 21. See on 1 J 2:10. 3:10-23. 5:1. **love is.** ver. 8. Dt 30:6. Ga *5:22. 1 Th 4:9, 10. 2 T +*1:7. 1 P *1:22, 23. **every.** ver. 12. See on 1 J 2:29. *3:14. 5:1. **is born.** 1 J +2:29. 5:1. 1 P +*1:23. **and knoweth.** Jn √17:3. 2 C 4:6. Ga 4:9.

8. **He that.** 1 J 3:10. **knoweth.** ſ96C4, Mt +3:17. 1 J 2:4, 9. 3:6. Jn 8:54, 55. **God is.** ver. 7, 16. 1 J 1:5. Ex *34:6, 7. Ps 86:5, 15. Jn 4:24. 2 C 13:11. Ep 2:4. He 12:29.

9. **was.** 1 J +2:5. *3:16. Jn √3:16. Ro *5:8-10. +*8:32. **toward us.** ver. 16. **God sent.** ver. 10. 1 J 3:1. 5:11. Ge=45:5, 7. Lk +*4:18. Jn +*3:16, 17. √5:23. 6:29. 8:29, 42. Ga ◖4:6. **only.** Ps *2:7. Mk 12:6. Jn *1:14-18. 3:16n, 18. He 1:5. **world.** Gr. *kosmos,* Mt +4:8. **we.** 1 J *5:11. Jn 6:51, 57. *10:10, 28-30. 11:25, 26. √14:6. Col *3:3, 4.

10. **Herein.** See on ver. 8, 9. 1 J 3:1. **not.** ver. 19. Dt 7:7, 8. Jn √15:16. Ro *5:8-10. +*8:29, 30. 2 C *5:19-21. Ep 2:4, 5. T *3:3-5. **he loved.** Jn 3:16. **and sent.** 1 J *2:2. Da 9:24. Ro *3:25, 26. 1 P *2:24. *3:18. **propitiation.** 1 J +*2:2. Ro 3:25.

11. **if God.** ſ184A, 1 C +15:2. 1 J *3:16, 23. Mt *18:32, 33. Lk 10:37. Jn *13:34. *15:12, 13. 2 C √8:8, 9. Ep √4:31, 32. *5:1, 2. Col 3:13. **love one another.** ver. +7.

12. **seen.** ver. 20. Ge 32:30. Ex *33:20. Nu 12:8. Jn +*1:18. *14:9. 1 T *1:17. *6:16. He 11:27. **If we.** ſ184C, Mt +4:9. **love one.** ver. 16. See on 1 J 3:24. **dwelleth in.** 1 J +3:24. **and his.** ver. 17, 18. See on 1 J *2:5. 1 C 13:13.

13. **know we.** ver. 15, 16. See on 1 J *3:24. Jn *14:20-26. Ro +*8:9-17. 1 C 2:12. *3:16, 17. *6:19. Ga *5:22-25. Ep 2:20-22. **Spirit.** Gr. *pneuma,* ſ121A1, Lk +1:17n. Jn +7:39.

14. **we have.** 1 J 1:1-3. 5:9. Jn *1:14. 3:11, 32. +*5:39. 15:26, 27. Ac 18:5. 1 P 5:12. **the Father.** See on ver. 10. Jn 3:34. 5:36, 37. 10:36. **sent.** Jn +*3:17. **the Son.** 1 J 2:22-24. Jn +3:35. 2 J 3, 9. **the Savior.** 1 J 2:1, 2. Jn +*1:29. √3:16, 17. +4:42. 12:47. 2 T +1:10. **of the.** 1 J +*2:2. Jn +*1:9. Ro +*5:18. **world.** Gr. *kosmos,* Mt +4:8.

15. **confess.** ſ108B, Mt +10:32. ver. 2. 1 J +2:23. 5:1, 5. Mt *10:32. Lk 12:8. Ro √10:9. Ph *2:11. 2 J 7. **that Jesus.** 1 J 5:5. Mt +14:33. **God dwelleth.** See on ver. 12. 1 J 3:24. Is +*57:15. 2 C *6:16. Ep *2:22.

16. **we.** See on ver. 9, 10. 1 J 3:1, 16. Ps 18:1-3. 31:19. 36:7-9. Is 64:4. Jn 6:69. 1 C √2:9. **to us.** ver. 9. **God is love.** See on ver. +8, 12, 13. Je 31:3. Mt +*28:19n. Jn √3:16. Ro √5:◖+*5, 8. Ep ◖+*5:2. T 3:4. **and he.** ver. 12. 1 J 3:24.

17. **our love.** Gr. love with us. **made.** See on ver. 12. 1 J 2:5. Ja 2:22. **we may.** 1 J +2:28. *3:19-21. Ja 2:13. **the day.** Mt +*10:15n. 11:22, 24. 12:36. 2 P

+2:9. +*3:7. **as he.** 1 J 3:1, 3. Mt 10:25. Jn 15:20. Ro *8:29. He *12:2, 3. 1 P 3:16-18. 4:1-3, 13, 14. **in this.** Jn +9:39. **world.** Gr. *kosmos*, Mt +4:8.

18. **no fear.** Ge=43:18. Ps +*34:4. 56:3. Is 12:2. Lk 1:74, 75. Ro *8:15. 2 T +*1:7. He +*12:28. 1 P *1:17. **perfect love.** Jn 3:18. Ro 8:15. **fear hath.** Jb 15:21. Ps 73:19. 88:15, 16. 119:120. Ja *2:19. **torment.** T#1012‡. ver. 8. Ps 145:20. Ec +9:5 (T#998‡). Mt 25:46g. **He that.** See on ver. 12, 17. 1 J 2:5.

19. **We love.** See on ver. 10. Lk 7:47. Jn √3:16. +*15:16. 2 C √5:14, 15. Ga 5:22. Ep *2:3-5. T *3:3-5. **he first.** ƒ96E5, Jn +1:15. Ro 5:8.

20. **If.** ƒ184C, Mt +4:9. **a man say.** See on 1 J 2:4. √3:17. T 1:16. **and hateth.** 1 J +2:9, 11. **not.** See on ver. 12. Jn +*1:18. 1 P 1:8.

21. **this commandment.** ver. 11. 1 J 3:11, 14, 18, 23. Le +*19:18. Mt *22:37-40. Mk 12:29-33. Lk 10:37. Jn *13:34, 35. 15:12. Ro 12:9, 10. 13:9, 10. Ga *5:6, 14. 6:2. 1 Th 4:9. 1 P 3:8. 4:8. **That he.** ver. +7.

1 JOHN 5

The apostle shows the connection between faith in Christ, regeneration, love to God and his children, obedience to his commandments, and victory over the world, 1-5. He states the manifold testimonies, by which the doctrine of Christ is proved; and declares the inseparable union between faith and eternal life, 6-13. He reminds Christians of the Lord's readiness to hear their prayers, for themselves and each other, 14, 15; gives an intimation of "a sin unto death," and the regenerate man's security against committing it, 16-18; he strongly marks the difference between the "world that lieth in wickedness," and true believers, 19, 20; and cautions Christians against idolatry, 21.

1. **believeth.** 1 J 2:22, 23. 4:2, 14, *15. Mt 16:16. Jn √1:12, 13. 6:69. Ac *8:37. Ro √10:9, 10. Ga *3:26. **that Jesus is the.** 1 J 2:22. Mk +8:29. Ac +18:5. is **born.** ver. 4, 18. 1 J +2:29. 3:9. 4:7. Jn 1:12, 13. √3:3, 5, 7. 1 P +*1:23. **and every.** 1 J 2:10. 3:14, 17. 4:20. Jn 15:23. Ja +*1:18. 1 P *1:3, 22, 23. **loveth him.** Jn *8:42.

2. **Hereby.** 1 J +√2:3n. **we know.** 1 J 3:22-24. 4:21. Jn *13:34, 35. 15:17. **we love.** 1 J *4:7. **the children.** 1 J +3:1. **keep.** Jn 14:15.

3. **this is.** Ex 20:6. Dt 5:10. 7:9. 10:12, 13. Da 9:4. Mt 12:47-50. Jn *14:+15, 21-24. *15:10, 14. 2 J 6. **the love.** 1 J +2:5. **keep.** 1 J +*2:3. Ps *119:4, 5. Jn 14:21. **and his.** Ps *19:7-11. 119:45, 47, 48, 103, 104, 127, 129, 140, 143, 174. Pr 3:17. Mi +*6:8. Mt *11:28-30. Ro 7:+*12, 22. He *8:10.

4. **whatsoever.** ƒ96G4, Mt +1:20. See on ver. 1. 1 J *3:9. 4:4. Jn +16:33. **is born.** ver. +1. **overcometh.** ver. 5. 1 J *2:13-17. 4:4. Jn 16:33. Ro *8:35-37. 1 C 15:57. Re *2:7, 11, 17, 26. *3:5, 12, 21. √12:11. 15:2. **world.** Gr. *kosmos*, Mt +4:8. ƒ121J9A, Jn +1:10. **the victory.** 1 C 15:57. **that overcometh.** 1 J 4:4-6. Re 12:9-11. **world.** Gr. *kosmos*, Mt +4:8. ƒ121J9A, Jn +1:10. T#743. 1 J √2:15-17. Jn *5:41 (T#59). Ro +*12:2. Ga 6:14. Ja 4:4. He *11:24-26. **victory.** ƒ121F, Ge +49:6. By Metonymy of the Effect, "victory," the effect, is put for "our faith," which accomplishes it. From Ep 6:16 we learn that it is through Christ; who is the shield which faith uses (B564). **our faith.** T#185, 1870. Jn 16:31. Ro √10:17. Ep 6:16. He 11:32-34. 1 P 1:8, 9.

5. **world.** Gr. *kosmos*, Mt +4:8. *ƒ121J9A, Jn +1:10. **but.** See on ver. 1. 1 J 4:15. Mt +14:33. 1 C *15:57.

6. **is he.** Jn 19:34, 35. **came.** ƒ108B, Mt +11:3. **by water and.** ver. 7, 8. Is 45:3, 4. Ezk 36:25. Mt 3:13-15. Jn 1:31-33. 3:5. 4:10, 14. *7:38, 39. √19:34. Ac 8:36. 1 C *6:11. Ep *5:25-27. T √3:5. 1 P 3:21. **blood.** 1 J *1:7. 4:10. Le +*17:11. Zc 9:11. Mt +*26:28n. Mk 14:24. Lk 22:20. Jn 6:55. Ro 3:25. Ep *1:7. Col 1:14. He 9:7, 14, +*22. 10:29. 12:24. 13:20. 1 P 1:2. Re +*1:5. *5:9. 7:14. **the Spirit** Gr. *pneuma*, Mt +3:16. **that beareth.** ver. 7, 8. Jn *14:17. *15:26. *16:13. Ac *5:30-32. 1 T 3:16. He *2:3, 4. **the Spirit.** Gr. *pneuma*, Mt +3:16. **is truth.** ƒ24J, Dt +32:42. Mt +*28:19n. Jn 14:√6, 17. 15:26. *16:13.

7. **three.** Ge +*1:26. **bear.** ver. 10, 11. Jn 8:13, 14. **the Father.** The genuineness of the latter part of this verse, and the first clause of the next, it is well known has divided the opinions of learned men for nearly four centuries, nor is it yet decided. It is certainly wanting in many of the ancient MSS. and versions; and is not quoted by many of the Fathers: but the number of MSS. collated is but small, only about 400; it exists in some ancient confessions of faith and liturgies; is quoted by numerous Latin Fathers; and appears necessary from the connection in which it stands. It also seems more probable that the Arians should silently omit it in their copies, or that it should be left out by mistake, than that the trinitarians should forge and insert it; for the latter would only gain one argument for a doctrine which is abundantly taught in other Scriptures; but if it was admitted as the Word of God, all the ingenuity and diligence of opponents could scarcely avoid the inference naturally deducible from it. Contemporary scholarship, however, fails to support this reading in any form, suggesting it was added to a late Greek manuscript made for the purpose to influence Erasmus to include it in his Greek text, for Erasmus had promised he would include the text if even one Greek manuscript could be found which contained it. Ps 33:6h. Is 48:16, 17. 61:1. Mt *3:16, 17. *17:5. +*28:19n. Jn 5:26. 8:18, 54. 10:37, 38. *12:28. 1 C 12:4-6. 2 C *13:14. Re 1:4, 5. **the Word.** See on 1 J 1:1. Jn *1:1, 32-34. He *4:12, 13. Re *19:13. **the Holy.** See on ver. 6. Mt 3:16. Jn *1:32, 33. Ac 2:4, 33. 5:32. He 2:3, 4. *10:15. Re 19:10. **Ghost.** Gr. *pneuma*, Mt +3:16. **and these.** Dt +*6:4. Mt +√28:19n. Jn *10:30. 14:9, 11. Ac *5:3, 4. 1 T 3:16.

8. **there.** See on ver. 7. **the Spirit.** ƒ96G4, Mt +1:20. See on ver. 6. Mt 26:26-28. +*28:19. Jn *15:26. Ro 8:16. Ga 5:22, 23. He *6:4. **the water.** Ac 2:2-4. 2 C *1:21, 22. **the blood.** 1 C *10:16. *11:26. He 13:12. 1 P 3:21. **and these.** ƒ96G2, Ge +2:18. Although "Spirit," "water," and "blood" are all neuter gender, the pronoun "these" is masculine, because persons are meant. Mk 14:56. Jn *16:13n, 14n. Ac 15:15.

9. **If.** ƒ184A, 1 C +15:2. **we receive.** ver. 10. Jn 3:32, 33. *5:31-36, 39. 8:17-19. *10:38. Ac *5:32. √17:31. He *2:4. *6:18. for. Mt *3:16, 17. *17:5. **witness of God.** Jn 5:37. 8:18. **testified of.** Mt +*3:17.

10. **that believeth on.** See on ver. 1. Jn √3:16, 33. +4:39. **the Son of God.** ver. 12, 13, 20. Jn +5:25. **hath the witness.** Ps 25:14. Pr 3:32. Ro *5:5. √8:16. 2 C *1:22. Ga *4:6. Col *3:3. 2 P 1:19. Re *2:17, 28. 12:17. 19:10. **in himself.** Jn 10:14. +*14:20. **believeth not.** Jn +5:24. T +3:8. **hath made.** ƒ108A1, Ex +8:18.

1 J 1:10. Nu 23:19. Jb 24:25. Is *53:1. Je 15:18. Jn 3:33. 5:38. He +*3:12. **because**. Jn 5:38. **gave of**. Ro 1:3.

11. **this**. ver. 7, 10. Jn 1:19, 32-34. 8:13, 14. 19:35. 3 J 12. Re 1:2. **God**. ver. 13. 1 J 2:25. Mt 25:46. Jn *3:15, 16, 36. 4:4, 36. 6:40, 47, 68. √10:28. 12:50. √17:2, 3. Ro *5:21. √6:23. 1 T 1:16. T +*1:2. Ju *21. **eternal**. Gr. *aionios*, Mt +18:8. **this life**. ver. 12, 20. 1 J 1:1-3. *4:9. Jn +*1:4. 5:21, 26. *10:28. 11:25, 26. √14:6. *17:2. Col *3:3, 4. Re 22:1.

12. **that hath the**. 1 J 2:23, 24. Jn √1:12. √3:15, 16, 36. √5:24. Ac 2:47. 1 C +*1:30. Ga +*2:20n. 2 T +*1:12. He +*3:14. 2 J +*9. **hath life**. Jn +*20:31. **and he**. Mk √16:16. Jn √3:36. **the Son of God**. ver. 10, 20. Jn +5:25.

13. **have I**. 1 J 1:4. 2:1, 13, 14, 21, 26. Jn √20:31. 21:24. 1 P 5:12. **believe**. 1 J *3:23. Jb 19:25. Jn *1:12. 2:23. √3:18. Ac 3:16. √4:12. 1 T 1:15, 16. **ye**. This pronoun is plural, and it is argued by some that assurance is not valid for any specific individual, but only for the group, namely, the "body of Christ," the Church. Such a view does not accord with those Scriptures which affirm such assurance of the individual, such as Ga 2:20n, and 2 T 1:12. **may know**. Gr. *oida*, Jn 8:55n. This is certainly one of the clearest statements in Scripture affirming that we may know in this life that we now have everlasting life—we are not left to wait until we die to discover whether we have eternal life or not. ver. 10. 1 J 1:1, 2. Jn 14:20. Ro 8:15-17. 2 C 5:1. Ga 4:6. 2 T *1:12. 2 P +*1:10, 11. Re *3:20. **ye have**. Present tense, active voice, indicative mode, second person plural verb. Not will have, or merely hope we might have, but now have in the present: such is our assurance of eternal life. Yet, this assurance is grounded upon the individual believer possessing the marks of a true believer discussed throughout this epistle. A true believer lives (1) in constant fellowship with God, 1 J 1:8. 2:2. (2) true to the Gospel, 1 J 2:24. (3) with love for others, 1 J 3:18, 19. 4:7. (4) in obedience to God, 1 J +√2:3n. 3:23. 5:2-5. (5) untainted by the world, 1 J 2:15-17. 5:4, 5. (6) consistently victorious over Satan, 1 J 3:8, 9. 4:4. 5:18. (7) concerned about souls, 1 J 5:16; see Ja +*5:20. (8) assured of personal salvation, 1 J 4:17. √5:13. **eternal**. Gr. *aionios*, Mt +18:8. **believe on**. 1 J 3:23. Jn 1:12. 2:23. 3:18. +4:39. 9:35. **the name**. Jn +1:12. **the Son of God**. ver. 12. Jn +5:25.

14. **this**. 1 J +2:28. *3:21. Ep 3:12. He 3:6, 14. 10:35. **in him**. *or*, concerning him. **if we ask**. ∫184C, Mt +4:9. See on 1 J 3:22. Jb 27:9. Ps 18:41. Pr 10:24. Je √29:12, 13. √33:3. Mt √7:7-11. *21:22. Lk √11:9. Jn +*9:31. 14:13. 15:7. *16:24. Ja +*1:5, 6. +*4:3. +*5:16. **according to**. T#1302. Jg 10:15. 1 S 3:18. 2 S 10:12. 15:25, 26. Jb 1:20, 21. Ps 39:8, 9. Mt 6:10. 26:42. Mk 14:35, 36. Lk 11:2. 22:42. Ac 21:14. Ro 1:10. *8:26, 27. 15:30-32. Ga 1:4. Ja 4:3, 13, 14. **he heareth**. ∫22C14, Ge +16:11. T#797. 1 J 3:22. Jb *22:27. 34:28. 2 Ch=30:27. Ps *4:3. 31:22. 34:6, 15, 17. +*50:15. 65:2. 69:33. 91:15. *145:19. Pr *15:29.

Is *30:19. 58:9. *65:24. Je √29:12. Zc 13:9. Mt 7:7, 8, 11. *21:22. Jn +*9:31. 11:42. *14:13, 14. 15:7. *16:23, 24. Ja *5:15, 16.

15. **if**. ∫184C, Mt +4:9. Pr 15:29. Je 15:12, 13. **ask**. ∫63I1D, Nu +26:4. Supply ellipsis, (according to his will). **we know**. ver. 18, 19, 20. 1 J +3:2. Mk √11:24. Lk √11:9, 10.

16. **If**. ∫184C, Mt +4:9. **he shall ask**. T#1442. Ge +*18:32. 20:7, 17. Ex 32:10-14, 31, 32. 34:9. Nu 12:13. 14:11-21. Dt 9:18-20. 2 Ch 30:18-20. Jb *42:7-9. Ps 106:23. +*126:5, 6. Ezk 22:30. Am 7:1-3. Ja *5:14, 15. **and he**. i.e. *God*. ∫63A1, Ge +14:20. **give him life for**. Ja +*5:20. **There is**. Nu 15:30. 16:26-32. 1 S 2:25. Je 15:1, 2. Mt +*12:31n, 32n. Mk 3:28-30. Lk 12:10. 2 T 4:14. He *6:4-6. +*10:26-31. 2 P *2:20-22. **unto death**. Ge +*2:17. 2 S +*12:13. **I do not**. Ex 32:10. Dt 9:14. +*28:32mg,n. Je *7:16. 11:14. 14:11. 18:18-21. Jn +*17:9. 2 T +*4:14.

17. **all**. 1 J +3:4. Dt 5:32. 12:32. **unrighteousness**. 1 J √1:9. **is sin**. 1 J 3:4. Ja +*4:17. **and**. ver. 16. Is *1:18. Ezk 18:26-32. Ro *5:20, 21. Ja 1:15. 4:7-10. **unto death**. Ge +*2:17. Pr +*16:25. Je +*15:2. Ezk +*18:26.

18. **We know**. ver. 15. 1 J +3:2. **whosoever**. ver. 1, 4. 1 J +2:29. 3:9. 4:6. Jn 1:13. 3:2-5. Ja 1:18. 1 P +*1:23. **sinneth not**. 1 J *3:9n. Ro *7:17. **keepeth**. ver. 21. 1 J 3:3. Ps 17:4. 18:23. 39:1. 119:101. Pr +*4:23. Jn *15:4, 7, 9. 17:11, 12, 15. Ac +*11:23. Ja 1:27. 1 P √1:5. 2 P +*1:10. Ju *21, *24. Re 2:13. 3:8-10. **himself**. 1 T 5:22. Ja 1:27. **wicked one**. 1 J 2:13, 14. 3:12. Mt +*13:19. Ro *16:20. **toucheth him not**. ∫108B, Ge +26:29. Jb 1:12. Lk *22:31, 32. Ep 6:11. Ja 4:7.

19. **we know**. ver. 10, 13, 20. 1 J 3:14, 24. 4:4-6. Ro 8:16. 2 C 1:12. 5:1. 2 T 1:12. **of God**. 1 J +*3:10. **and the**. 1 J 4:4, 5. Lk 4:6. Jn +12:31. 15:18, 19. Ro +*1:28-32. 3:9-18. Ga 1:4. T 3:3. Ja *4:4. **world**. Gr. *kosmos*, Mt +4:8. ∫121J8, Jn +3:16. **in wickedness**. ver. 18. Jn *8:44. 12:31. +*14:30. 16:11. 2 C *4:4. Ep *2:2. 2 T *2:25, 26. Re *12:9. *13:7, 8. 20:3, 7, 8.

20. **we know**. ver. 1. Re 4:2, 14. **the Son of God**. ver. 10, 12, 13. Jn +5:25. **is come**. Jn 8:42. He 10:7, 9. **and hath given**. Mt 13:11. Lk 21:15. +*24:45. Jn *17:3, 14, 25. 1 C +*1:30. 2 C *4:6. Ep 1:17-19. 3:18, 19. Col *2:2, 3. **an understanding**. 1 J +*2:27. Ps +*32:8. Pr +*8:9. Jn 16:13. Ja +*1:5. **know him**. 1 J +4:6. **that is true**. Jn √14:6. +*17:3. Re 3:+7, 14. 6:10. *15:3. 19:11. **and we**. 1 J 2:6, 24. 4:16. Jn 10:30. 14:20, 23. 15:4. 17:20-23. 2 C √5:17. Ph 3:9. **This is**. ver. 11-13. 1 J 1:1-3. 2:22. Jn 6:50. Ac 1:22. 2 J 7. **the true God**. ∫79, Ge +21:16. Is +*9:6. *44:6. 45:14, 15, 21-25. 54:5. Je 10:10. +*23:5, 6. Jn √1:1-3. *14:9. *17:3. +√20:28n. Ac +√20:28n. Ro +*9:5n. 1 T *3:16. T +*2:13n. He +*1:8. **eternal**. Gr. *aionios*, Mt +18:8.

21. **Little**. See on 1 J 2:1. **keep**. Ex +*20:3, 4. 22:20. Mt √6:24. Ac 19:27, 35. 1 C *10:7, 14. 2 C *6:16, 17. Ga 5:20. Col +*3:5. Re 9:20. 13:14, 15. 14:11. **Amen**. See on Mt 6:13.

2 JOHN

The apostle addresses, with expressions of affection-ate regard, and with salutations, "the elect lady and her children," declaring his joy in their good behavior, 1-4. He exhorts them to brotherly love and obedience, 5, 6. He warns them against deceivers, that neither they, nor he, may lose their full reward, 7, 8; and against giving the least countenance to those, who did not bring the true doctrine of Christ, 9-11. He hopes to see them shortly, and concludes with salutations, 12, 13.

1. A.M. 4094. A.D. 90. or, A.M. 4073. A.D. 69. **elder.** Ac +*11:30. +*14:23. Phm *9. 1 P *5:1. 3 J *1. **the elect lady.** *eklektee kuria,* which some, with the Peshitta Syriac and Arabic versions, render "to Kyria the elect," considering *kuria* a proper name; while others, with the Vulgate, render "to the Lady Electa," considering *eklektee* a proper name, which seems more correct. ver. 5, 13. Is ◐42:1. ◐+*45:4. Lk 1:3. Jn +*15:16. Ro *8:33. ◐+*9:11. *16:13g. Ep *1:4, 5. 2:10. 1 Th *1:3, 4. 2 Th *2:13, 14. 1 T ◐5:21. 1 P *1:2. ◐2:6. 5:13. 2 P ◐+*3:9. **whom.** ver. 2, 3. Jn 11:5. 1 C 16:14. Ep 4:15. Phm 13. 1 P *1:22, 23. 1 J *3:18. 5:1. 3 J 1. **I love.** Jn 11:5. 1 J *5:1. **in the truth.** Phm 13. **known.** Jn *8:31, 32. Ga 2:5, 14. *3:1. *5:7. Col 1:5. 2 Th 2:13. 1 T *2:4. He *10:26. 1 J 2:21. **the truth.** Jn 1:17. 8:32. √14:6. Ga +2:5. Ep 4:15. 2 T 3:7.

2. **the truth's.** Jn 8:31, 44. 1 C *9:23. 13:6. 2 C 4:5. 13:8. 2 P 1:12. 1 J +*2:4. 3:15. **which dwelleth.** Jn 8:31, 44. *15:7. Col *3:16. 2 T 1:5. 1 P *1:23-25. 1 J *2:4, 14, 17. 3:15. **in us.** 1 J 1:8. **with us.** Ps *119:89. Mt *24:35. Jn 14:16. 17:17. **for ever.** Gr. *aion,* Mt +6:13. lit. unto the age, Mt +21:19.

3. **Grace.** Ro +*1:7. 2 C 1:2. Ga 1:3. Ph 1:2. Col 1:2. 1 Th 1:1. 2 Th 1:2. 1 T 1:2. 2 T 1:2. Ju 2. Re 1:4. **be.** Gr. shall be. **mercy.** Ju 2. **and.** ♪174, Ge +18:27. **peace.** T 1:4. Phm 3. 1 P 1:2. 2 P 1:2. **the Son.** ver. 9. Jn 1:14, 18. 3:16, 35. 16:28. 1 J *2:22-24. 4:1, 4, 10. **in truth.** ver. 1. Zc *8:19. Jn 1:17. Ga *5:6. Ep 4:15. 1 T 1:14. 2 T *1:13.

4. **rejoiced.** Ro +*1:7. 1 Th *2:19, 20. 3:6-10. Phm 7. 3 J *3, *4. **thy children.** Ge +*18:19. 1 K *2:1, 3, 4. 1 C 4:15. 7:14. Ga 4:19. Ep 6:1. Phm 10. 1 J *2:13. **walking.** Ho *14:9. Ml 2:6. Ga *2:14. Ep *5:2, 8. Col +√1:10. 1 J *1:6, 7. √2:6. **in truth.** Is 38:3. 3 J 3, 4. **commandment.** Ro 6:17. 2 C 5:7. Ga 5:16. 1 Th 4:1. 1 J *2:6.

5. **And now.** The mode of address here shows, that it was a person, not a church, as some suppose, to whom the Apostle wrote. **beseech.** Ge 42:21. Ex 32:11. Ezr 8:23. Ps 80:14. 116:4. 118:25. 119:108. Mt 8:5. Mk 5:17. 7:32. Ac 19:31. Ro *12:1, 2. 15:30. 1 C 16:12. 2 C 12:8. Ga 4:12. Ep 4:1. Phm *9, 10. He 13:19. 1 P *2:11. **lady.** ver. 1, 13. Jg 4:4. 1 S 2:1-10. Jl 2:28, 29. Lk 2:36-38. Ac 1:14, 15. *2:17, 18. Ro *16:1-7, 13, 15. 1 C *11:4, 5. ◐*14:34, 35. Ga *3:28. 1 T ◐+*2:12. **not.** 1 J *2:7, 8. *3:11. 5:3. **new.** Gr. *kainos,* new in quality, use, application, or character, as op-posed to being new in time; see Mt 9:17 where contrast-ing terms occur together, *kainos* being second, applied to wineskins which were not brand new (as was the wine), but simply not having been used before, unused. See the use of *kainos* at Jn 13:34. Mk 2:22n. Jn 19:41. 1 C 11:25. 2 C *5:17. Ga 6:15. Ep 2:15. 4:24. He 8:8, 13. 9:15. 2 P *3:13. 1 J 2:7, 8. Re 2:17. *3:12. 5:9. 14:3. *21:1, 2, 5. **commandment.** Jn *13:34. **had from.** Le +*19:18. **that we love.** Le +*19:18. Jn *13:34, 35. *15:12. Ga 5:22. Ep *5:2. 1 Th *4:9. He 13:1. 1 P *1:22, 23. *4:8. 2 P 1:7. 1 J *2:7-10. *3:11, 14-18, 23. *4:7-12, 20.

6. **this is love.** Jn *14:+15, 21. *15:10, 14. Ro 13:8, 9. 1 C 13:4. Ga *5:13, 14. 1 J 2:5. *5:3. **walk.** ♪25, Ge +4:4. **This is the.** See on ver. 5. 1 J +*2:24. **begin-ning.** 1 J 2:7. **walk.** See on ver. 4.

7. **many.** Je 14:14. 23:21, 25. Mt *24:4, 5, 23, 24. Jn 5:43. Ac 5:36. 8:9. Ep 5:6. Col 2:8, 18. 2 Th 2:3. See on 2 P *2:1-3. 1 J *2:18-22, 26. *4:1. **deceivers.** Mt 27:63. 2 C 6:8. 1 T 4:1g. **entered.** or, gone forth. Mt 24:24. Ac 20:29. 1 J *2:19. *4:1. **who.** Jn *1:14, 20. 1 T *3:16. 1 J 4:2, 3. Re 12:9. 13:14. **is come.** lit. is coming. John affirms Jesus Christ at his Second Ad-vent "is coming in the flesh": i.e., *in his human nature, the same Jesus, in like manner as he went into heaven.* See related notes (Mt 16:27n. 1 J 4:2n). Peters affirms the validity of applying this text to the Second Advent, not the first, citing Alford and other scholars (*Theocratic Kingdom,* vol. 1, p. 570; vol. 2, p. 347, 698. vol. 3, p. 49). So B. F. Westcott states "The thought centers upon the present perfection of the Lord's manhood which is still, and is to be manifested, and not upon the past fact of His coming, 1 J 4:2" (*The Epistles of St. John,* p. 229). Scripture affirms He is coming to the earth (Zc 14:4. Re +*5:10n), to reign upon the earth (not merely over it from heaven) from Jerusalem (Is √24:23. Mi +*4:7). Christ will be personally present (Ps 102:16. Is +*24:23. Mi +*4:7. Ac +*3:20, 21) in his humanity (Mt 16:27n) to rule forever (Lk +*1:32, 33) over his kingdom, his inheritance, which is upon earth (Mt +*5:5. 6:10. Ro 4:13. Ep +*1:11n. 2 T +*4:18n). He 11:16n. 1 P 1:4n). The throne of David, which Christ inherits (Lk 1:32), is upon earth (Am +√9:11. Zc 1:16, 17. 2:12. Ac 15:16), not in heaven (See Peters, *Theocratic Kingdom,* vol. 1, Proposition 52, Observation 12, pp. 350-351). Zc 13:6. Jn 3:31g. 11:27g. 21:14. Ac +*1:11. 1 C 15:1-23, 35g. Ph *3:21. Col 3:6g. 1 J *3:1-3. ◐4:2n, 3. x◐3 J 3g. Re 1:4g. 22:16, 20g. **world.** Gr. *kosmos,* Mt +4:8. **who confess not.** Jn *1:14. 1 T *3:16. 1 J 2:23. 4:2, 3. **that Jesus.** Jn +1:14. 1 J 4:2. **This is.** 1 J *2:22, 26. *4:3. ◐+*5:20. **antichrist.** 2 Th *2:7-11. 1 J 2:18.

8. **Look.** Mt *24:4, 24, 25. Mk 13:5, 6, 9, 23. Lk 21:8. He +*12:15. Re *3:11. **that we lose.** Gr. *apollumi,* Mt +2:13. 1 C *3:8-15. Ga *3:4. +*4:11. *6:9. Ph *2:15, 16. 3:16. He *10:32, 35. Re *3:11. **wrought.** or, gained. "Some copies read, which ye have gained, but that ye receive, etc." Ga 4:19. 1 Th 2:19, 20. He 10:39. **that we receive.** Da +*12:3. Lk ◐*12:48. +*14:14. Jn *4:36. 1 C *3:+8, 14, 15. +√15:58. Ga 6:9. He 3:14. 6:11, 12. 10:36. 11:26. Re 11:18. *22:12. **full reward.** Ru 2:12.

9. **transgresseth.** He 3:13. Ja *5:19, 20. 1 J 5:16.
3 J 9. Ju 23. or, goeth onward. Pr 3:7. Ph 2:3. 1 T
1:18. 5:24. 6:3. 2 T 1:13. 3:14. He 7:18. Ja 3:1. 4:10.
3 J 9. **abideth not.** Ps *119:57. Jn 7:16. See on +*8:31.
+*15:6. 1 J *2:22-24. **the doctrine.** Jn *7:16, 17. *8:42.
18:19. Ac *2:42. Col *3:16. 1 T 1:10. 4:13, 16. 6:3.
2 T 1:13. +*2:2. 4:3, 4. T *2:10. He *6:1. Re 2:14,
15, 24. **hath not.** Mt +*11:27. Lk 10:22. Jn √5:23.
√14:6. 1 J 2:23. 4:15. 5:1. 3 J 9. **He that.** Ps 119:57.
Jn 15:10. He *3:6, 14. **he hath.** 1 J *1:3. *2:23. **the
Father.** ver. +3.
10. **If.** ♪184A, 1 C +15:2. **come.** ver. *11. Mt 10:13,
etc. Lk 10:5, etc. Ac *20:29, 30. Ro *16:17, 18. 1 C
*5:11. 11:19. *16:22. 2 C *11:3, 4, 13-15. Ga *1:8, 9.
2 T +*3:5, 6. T *3:10. **doctrine.** Ga *1:8, 9. 1 T *4:16.
T *3:10. Ju +*3. **receive.** 1 K 13:16, etc. Ps 119:+*63,
115. *139:21, 22. Mt 10:13, 14. +*15:14. Lk +*10:38.
Ac 19:9. Ro ◖15:7. *16:17, 18. 1 C *5:11. 16:22. Ga
1:8, 9. 2 Th 3:6, 14. 1 T ◖1:10. ◖*6:3. 2 T ◖*2:22.

3:5-7. T ◖1:1. He +*10:35. 3 J 8. **house.** Ro *16:5.
1 C 16:19. Col *4:15. Phm *2. **neither.** Ge 24:12.
2 Ch +√19:2. Ps *129:8. Ac +15:23. **bid.** Mt
26:49g.
11. **he that.** ver. 10. Ac 15:23. **partaker.** Jsh 7:24,
25. Ps +*50:18. ◖*119:+63, 115. 139:21, 22. Ro 15:27.
1 C 5:6. Ep +*5:11. 1 T *5:22. Ju 23. Re *18:4. **evil
deeds.** Jn +7:7.
12. **many.** Jn *16:12. Ga 4:20. Ju 3. **I would.** He
*21:25. 3 J *13, 14. **ink.** 2 C 3:3. **I trust.** Jn 16:22.
Ro 1:11, 12, 13. 15:24, 29, 30, 32. 1 C 13:12. 16:5-7.
Phm *22. He *13:19, 23. 3 J 14. **to come.** Jn 16:22.
Ro 15:29, 30, 32. Ga 4:20. **face to face.** Gr. mouth
to mouth. Nu *12:8. Je 32:4g. 1 C *13:12. **that.** Jn
+*15:11. *16:24. 17:13. 2 T 1:4. 1 J *1:4. **our.** or,
your. **joy.** Jn 3:29. Jn +*15:11. 17:13. Ro 15:13. 1 J
1:4.
13. **children.** See on ver. 1. 1 P 5:13. **elect.** See
on ver. 1. **sister.** See on ver. *5. Mt 12:50. 13:56.

3 JOHN

3 JOHN

*The apostle addresses Gaius, with good wishes, com-
mendations, and exhortations to persevere, in his liberal and zealous support of those who went forth to
preach the gospel, 1-8. He cautions him against the
presumptuous and malicious designs of Diotrephes;
and highly commends Demetrius, 9-12. Giving intimations of an intended visit, he concludes with salutations,
13, 14.*

1. **elder.** 1 P 5:1. See on 2 J 1. **Gaius.** Ac ?19:29.
?20:4. Ro ?16:23. 1 C ?1:14. **the well-beloved.** 2 T
1:2. Phm 1, 2. **whom.** 1 J 3:18. See on 2 J 1. **in the
truth.** or, truly.
2. **wish.** or, pray. Ro 9:3. **above.** Ja 5:12. 1 P 4:8.
that. Ps 20:1-5. Ph 2:4, 27. **prosper.** Jsh +*1:8. 2 Ch
+*20:20. Ps +*1:3. Mt +*6:33. Ro +1:10. 1 C 16:2.
be in health. Ex *15:26. +*23:25. Dt 7:15. Ps +*103:3.
Pr *4:20-22. 17:22. Is 33:24. Je 30:17. Mt *8:17. Mk
1:41. Lk 5:31. 7:10. 15:27. Ac *10:38. 1 T ◖1:10g.
4:8. ◖6:3g. **even as.** ver. 3-6. Col 1:4-6. 1 Th 1:3-10.
√2:13, 14, 19, 20. 3:6-9. 2 Th 1:3. *2:13. Phm 5-7.
2 P √1:3-9. +*3:18. Re 2:9. **soul.** Gr. psyche, ♪121A9C,
Lk +21:19. Jn 12:27.
3. **I.** ver. 4. Ph 1:4. 4:10. 1 Th *2:19, 20. See on
2 J 4. **when.** Ro 1:8, 9. 2 C 7:6, 7. Ep 1:15, 16. Col
1:7, 8. 1 Th 3:6-9. **in the truth.** Ps √119:11. Is 38:3.
See on 2 J 2, 4.
4. **have.** Pr 23:24. **to hear.** Ph 1:27. **that.** Is 8:18.
1 C *4:14, 15. Ga 4:19. 1 T 1:2. T 1:4. Phm 10. **walk.**
1 K 2:4. 3:6. 2 K +*20:3. Ps 26:1-3. Is 38:3. Jn 12:35,
36. Ga 2:14. **in truth.** ver. 12. Ps 119:3. Is 38:3. 2 J
+1, 4.
5. **thou doest faithfully.** Nu 12:7. 2 K 12:15. 2 Ch
19:9. 31:12. 34:12. Mt +√24:45. Lk +*12:42. √16:10-
12. 2 C *4:1-3. Col *3:17. 1 P *4:10, 11. **to the brethren.**
ver. 10. Ga +*6:10. He *13:1. **strangers.** Mt +25:35.
He *13:2.
6. **have borne witness of thy charity.** ver. 12. Phm
5-7. **before the church.** 1 C 14:19, 35. **whom.** Ac 15:3.
21:5. Ro 15:24. 2 C 1:16. T 3:13. **bring forward.** Ac
+*15:3. 20:38. 21:5. Ro 15:24. 1 C 16:6, 11. 2 C 1:16.

T 3:13. **after a godly sort.** or, worthy of God. This is
a literal and proper rendering of the original *axios
tou theou*; by which the antecedent to the possessive
pronoun his, in the next verse, becomes immediately
apparent. "In a manner worthy of God, and of your
relations and obligations to Him, and such as He can
approve." Jn 13:20. Ro 16:2. Ep 4:1. Ph 1:27. Col
+*1:10. 1 Th *2:12g. **do well.** Ge 4:7. Jon 4:4. Mt
25:21-23. Ac 10:33. 15:29. 1 C 7:37, etc. Ph 4:14. Ja
2:19. 1 P 2:20. 2 P 1:19.
7. **that.** Ac *8:4. *9:16. 2 C 4:5. Col 1:24. Re *2:3.
name's. Ac +5:41. **taking nothing.** Ex +*18:21. 2 K
*5:15, 16, 20-27. Ps +*50:16. Ac +*6:3. +20:33. Ro
12:13. 1 C 9:12-15, 18. 2 C 11:7-9. 12:13, 16-18. Ga
6:6, 7. 1 Th 2:6. +*5:22. T 1:7.
8. **to receive.** ver. 10. Mt 10:14, *40. Lk 9:48. 10:7-
12. Ro *15:7. 2 C 7:2, 3. **fellowhelpers.** 1 S 30:24.
1 C 3:5-9. 16:10, 11. 2 C 6:1. 8:23. Ph 4:3. Col 4:11.
1 Th 3:2. Phm 2, 24.
9. **Diotrephes.** i.e. *nourished by Jupiter,*
*S#1361g. **who loveth.** *o philprotuon,* "who loveth
the presidency," or chief place, doubtless in the church,
of which Diotrephes was most probably an officer; and
being one, magnified himself in his office: he loved
such pre-eminence, and behaved haughtily in it. Mt
√20:20-28. *23:4-8. Mk 9:34. *10:35-45. Lk 22:24-27.
Ro +*12:3, 10, 16. 2 C +*1:24. Ph +*2:3-5. T 6:3,
4. 2 J 9. **receiveth.** See on ver. 8. Mt 10:40-42. Mk
9:37. Lk 9:48. Jn 5:43. ◖+*13:20. 15:20. Ac *9:26,
27.
10. **if I come.** ♪184C, Mt +4:9. ver. 14. 2 J 12. **I
will.** 1 C 4:21. 5:1-5. 2 C 10:1-11. *13:2, 10. **prating.**
Pr 10:8, 10. 1 T 5:13g. **not content.** 1 T 6:8. He 13:5.
neither doth. ver. +5. **the brethren.** Ep +6:23. 1 J
3:14, 16. **forbiddeth.** Mt 3:14g. **and casteth.** Is +*66:5.
Lk 6:22. Jn 9:22, 34, 35. 1 J ◖2:19.
11. **Beloved.** Beloved, *agapeete,* is in the vocative
singular, and therefore refers to Gaius. **follow.** Rather,
imitate, Gr. *mimou,* *S#3401g. 2 Th 3:7, 9. He 13:7.
not that. Ex +*23:2. 2 Ch 13:7. Ps 34:14. *37:27.
+*101:4. Pr *12:11. *13:20. Is *1:16. Je +*10:2. 1 C
15:33. **evil.** ♪25, Ge +4:4. ♪68, Ge +10:1. **but that.**

Est +*1:12. Ps 34:14. 37:27. +*119:63. Pr √13:20. Is 1:17. Jn *10:27. 12:26. 1 C 4:16. +*11:1. Ep 5:1. Ph 2:12. *3:17. 1 Th 1:6. 2:14. 2 Th 3:7, 9g. 2 T 3:10mg, +*14. He +*6:12. 13:7g. 1 P 3:13. **He that doeth good.** Mk 3:4. Lk 6:9. Ro 2:10. ◐7:20. 1 T +*4:8. Ja ◐+*3:2. 1 P 3:11. See on 1 J +2:29. 3:6-9. **of God.** Jn +11:52. **he that doeth evil.** Jn *3:20. Ro +*12:21. 1 P 3:17. **hath not seen.** 1 J +3:6.

12. **Demetrius.** Ac ?19:21, etc. Col ?4:4. 2 T ?4:10. Phm ?24. **good report.** Ac +*6:3g. 10:22. 22:12. 1 Th 4:12. 1 T 3:7. **the truth.** ver. 4, 8. 1 J ?5:6. **and**

we. Jn 19:35. 21:24. **ye know.** Jn 5:32. 21:24.

13. **many things.** See on 2 J 12. **with ink.** 2 J 12. **and pen.** Mt 11:7.

14. **face to face.** Gr. mouth to mouth. 2 J +12. **Peace.** Ge 43:23. Da 4:1. Lk 10:5. 24:36. Jn 20:19, 21, 26. Ga 6:16. Ep +6:23. 1 P 5:14. **Our.** Ro 16:10, 11mg. **friends.** Instead of *philoi* and *philous*, "friends," an appellation used no where else as a mutual address among Christians, several MSS. read *adelphoi* and *adelphous*, "brethren." **Greet.** See on Ro 16:1-16. **by name.** Ps *40:17. Lk 10:20. Jn +*10:3g.

JUDE

JUDE

The address and salutation; and the writer's purpose in the epistle, namely, to establish Christians against certain false teachers, who were men of a very bad character, and to excite them to "contend earnestly for the faith once delivered to the saints," 1-4. The example of the Israelites who perished in the wilderness, that of fallen angels, and that of Sodom, are adduced, as showing the danger to which those who apostatized, or perverted the gospel, were exposed, 5-7. The vile character of these seducers further shown, and their doom denounced; with reference to some traditions, concerning Michael contending with the devil about the body of Moses; and an ancient prediction delivered by Enoch, concerning the "day of judgment and perdition of ungodly men," 8-16. Warnings, counsels, and exhortations suited to the occasion, whereby the godly, by the assistance of the Holy Spirit and prayers to God, may persevere and grow in grace and keep themselves and recover others out of the snares of the deceivers; and a concluding ascription of glory "to the only wise God our Savior," 17-25.

1. A.M. 4069. A.D. 65. **Jude.** i.e. *praised; confession*, ✳S#2455g, so rendered only here. Mt 10:3, Lebbeus, Thaddeus. Mk 3:18, Thaddeus. +*6:3. Lk 6:16. Jn 14:22. Ac *1:13. **the servant.** Jn 12:26. Ac 27:23. Ro 1:1. 6:22. 16:18. Ja +1:1. 2 P 1:1. **to them.** Jn +*15:16. *17:17, 19. Ac *20:32. Ro 1:7. 1 C 1:2. *6:11. Ep *5:26. Col 3:12. 1 Th +*5:23. 1 P 1:2. **preserved.** Jn 6:39. √10:28-30. *17:11, 12, 15. 1 Th +*5:23. 2 T +*4:18. 1 P +*1:4, 5. **and called.** Ro +*8:30. 9:24. 1 Th 1:4. 2:12. 2 Th *2:13, 14. 2 T +*1:9. He 3:1. 1 P *2:9. *5:10.

2. **Mercy.** See on Ro 1:7. Ga 6:16. 1 T 1:2. 2 T 1:2. T 1:4. 1 P 1:2. 2 P 1:2. 2 J 3. Re 1:4-6. **and.** ƒ174, Ge +18:27. **peace.** Da 4:1. 6:25. 1 P 1:2. 2 P 1:2.

3. **Beloved.** 3 J 2. **when.** Ro 15:15, 16. Ga 6:11. He 13:22. 1 P 5:12. 2 P √1:12-15. 3:1. **all diligence.** 2 P 1:5. **the common.** Is 45:17, 22. Jn *1:12. Ac √4:12. 13:46, 47. 28:28. Ga *3:28. Ep +*4:4. T *1:4. 2 P *1:1. **salvation.** Ac √4:12. He *2:3. +*9:28. **needful.** Lk 14:18. He 7:27. **earnestly contend.** T#188. Ne +*13:11, 25. Je *9:3. Mt +*15:14. +28:19 (T#458). Lk 13:24. Jn 18:37. Ac 6:8-10. 9:22, 29. +*17:3, 16, 17. 18:4-6, *28. 19:8-10. 1 C 9:25. Ga 2:11. Ph *1:17, 27. 1 Th 2:2. 1 T 1:18. *6:12. 2 T *1:13. *4:7, 8. T 1:13. He 12:4. Re 2:10. +*12:11. **the faith.** ƒ121R2, Ac +6:7. ver. 20. Lk +*18:8. Ga 1:23. 3:23. Ep 4:5,

13. Ph 1:27. **once delivered.** Dt 9:10. 31:9. Ac *20:27. 1 C 11:2. +*15:3. Ga 2:5. 2 Th 2:15. 1 T 6:20. 2 P 2:21. *3:2. **the saints.** 2 C +1:1. See on Ep 1:1. Ph 1:1. Col *1:2.

4. **are certain.** 2 P +2:1. **crept.** Mt *13:25. Ac 15:24. Ga 2:4. Ep +*4:14. 2 T 3:6. 2 P *2:1, 2. **who.** Ro 9:21, 22. 1 P *2:8. 2 P 2:3. **of old.** Ro 15:4. **ordained.** Ac +*2:23. Ga 3:1. Ep 3:3g. 1 P +*2:8. **this condemnation.** Ro *9:22. 2 P 2:3. **ungodly.** ver. *15. 2 S 22:5. Ps +*1:1. 1 P *4:18. 2 P *2:5, 6. 3:7. **turning.** Ro *6:1, 2. Ga 5:13. T *2:11, 12. He +*12:15, 16. 1 P 2:16. 2 P √2:10, 18-22. **the grace.** Ac +*11:23. +*13:43. 1 T *2:3, 4. **into lasciviousness.** Mk +7:22. Ro 3:8. 6:1. 2 P 2:7. **denying.** T *1:15, 16. 2 P +*2:1. 1 J 2:22. **only Lord.** Lk 2:29. Ac 4:24. Re 6:10. **God.** Jb 19:26. Ps 45:6. 62:2. Is 25:9. 52:7. Jn +*1:1. √17:3. +*20:28. Ro +*9:5. 2 C 5:19. Col *2:8, 9. 1 T 3:16. *6:15, 16. T +*2:13n. He +*1:8. 2 P +*1:1. Re *15:4. 21:7.

5. **put.** Ro 15:14, 15. Ph 3:1. 2 P *1:12, 13. 3:1. **though.** 2 P 3:17. 1 J 2:20, 21. **having.** See on 1 C *10:1-12. **the people.** Ro 15:10. 2 P 2:1. **afterward.** Gr. the second time. Nu *14:22-37. *26:64, 65. Dt 2:15, 16. Ps 106:26. He *3:16-19. *4:1, 2. **destroyed.** Gr. *apollumi*, Mt +2:13.

6. **angels.** Jn *8:44. **first estate.** or, principality. Ep 1:21. 3:10. *6:12. Col 1:16. 2:15g. **he hath reserved.** Jb 21:30. Mt *25:41. See on 2 P *2:4. +*3:7. Re 20:2. **everlasting.** Gr. *aidios*, ✳S#126g, only here and Ro 1:20. **darkness.** Pr +*20:20. **unto.** Mt *8:29. He 10:27. Re *20:10. **judgment.** Ac +*17:31. 1 C *6:3. 2 P 2:9. **of the great day.** Ac 2:20. Re 6:17.

7. **as Sodom.** Ge 13:13. 18:20. *19:24-26. Dt 29:23. Is 1:9. 13:19. Je 20:16. 50:40. La 4:6. Ezk +*16:49, 50, 55, 60. Ho 11:8. Am 4:11. Lk +10:12. 17:29. 2 P *2:6. **Gomorrah.** Ro +9:29. **the cities.** Ge 14:2. 19:25. Dt 29:23. Ho 11:8. **going after.** ver. 8. 2 P 2:10. **strange.** Gr. other. Ge 19:5. Mt +11:3g. Ro +*1:26, 27. 1 C +*6:9. **are set.** Mt 11:24. 2 P 2:6. +3:7. **eternal.** Gr. *aionios*, Mt +18:8. Dt 29:23. Is +*33:14. Mt +*25:41. Mk *9:43-49.

8. **these.** Je 33:25-28. **defile.** 1 C *3:16, 17. 1 T 1:10. See on 2 P *2:10-12. **despise.** Ge 3:5. Nu 16:3, 12, 13. 1 S 10:27. Ps 2:1-6. 12:3, 4. Lk √19:14. Ac 7:27, 39. Ro *13:1, 2. 1 Th 4:8. He +*13:17. **speak evil.** T#730. ver. 9, 10. Ex *22:28. Pr 30:11, 17. Ec √10:20. Ac 23:4, 5. 1 P 2:17. +5:5 (T#10). 2 P 2:9-11.

9. **Michael.** It is most probable that the Apostle took this account concerning Michael, and that of the

prophesying of Enoch, from an ancient tradition preserved and well known among the Jews. T#1013‡. Ex ‡23:20, 21, 23. ‡32:34. Da 10:13, 20, 21. 11:40. 12:+*1, 7, 10, 12. Mt ‡28:18. 1 Th ‡4:16n. Re 12:7. ‡17:14. **archangel.** 1 Th √4:16. 2 P *2:11. **when.** ſ106, Ge +31:7. **the body.** Dt *34:6. 2 K *18:4. Mt=27:65. **durst.** Ex 22:28. Is 36:13-21. Mk 15:29. Lk 23:39, 40. 1 P 3:9. 2 P 2:11. Re *12:7. **The Lord.** 1 Ch 12:17. Is 37:3, 4, 10-20. Zc *3:2.

10. **speak.** See on 2 P *2:12. **know not.** Mk 14:68. **in those.** See on Ro 1:21, 22. Re 19:2.

11. **Woe.** Is 3:9, 11. Je 13:27. Ezk 13:3. Zc 11:17. Mt 11:21. 23:13-16. Lk 11:42-47. **for.** Ge 4:5-14. 1 J *3:12. **gone.** ſ132A, Ge +4:23. **in the way.** Jn ◑*14:6. **of Cain.** Mt ◐23:35. He 11:4. 12:24. **ran greedily.** Nu ch. 22-24. 31:16. Dt 23:4. Jsh 24:9-11. Ps +*10:3. Mi 6:5. 1 T +*6:9. T *1:11. 2 P +*2:15. Re 2:14. **perished.** Gr. *apollumi,* Mt +2:13. Nu 16:1-3, 31-35. Ps 106:16-18. **the gainsaying.** Ac *13:45. Ro 10:21. He 6:16. 7:7. 12:3g. **Core.** i.e. *thin; frozen; ice; bald,* **⁕**S#2879g. For **⁕**S#7141h, see Ge +36:5. Nu 16:1, etc. 26:9, 10, Korah.

12. **are spots.** ver. 15, 16. See on 2 P *2:13, 14. **feasts.** 1 C *11:21, 22. **when.** ſ58, 2 P +2:13. **feeding themselves.** Ps 78:29-31. Is 56:10-12. Ezk *34:2, 8, 10, 18. Lk 12:19, 20, 45. 16:19. +*21:34. Ph +*3:19. 1 Th 5:6, 7. Ja 5:5. 1 P 5:2. **clouds.** Pr 25:14. Ho 6:4. 2 P *2:17. **carried.** Ep +*4:14. He 13:9. **trees.** Ps +*1:3. *37:2. Mt *13:6. 21:19, 20. Mk 4:6. 11:21. Lk 8:6. Jn *15:4-6. **without fruit.** Mt 12:36. Lk 13:6. He ◐13:15. 2 P +*1:8. **twice.** 1 T 5:6. He *6:4-8. See on 2 P *2:18-20. **plucked.** 2 Ch 7:20. Ezk 17:9. Mt *15:13. Mk 11:20.

13. **Raging.** Jb 3:17. Ps 65:7. 93:3, 4. Is *57:20. Je 5:22, 23. **foaming.** 2 C 4:2. Ph 3:19. 2 T 3:13. **wandering.** Is 14:12. Re 8:10, 11. **to whom.** See on 2 P *2:17. Re 14:10, 11. 20:10. +*21:8. **reserved.** Na *1:2. **darkness.** Pr +*20:20. Mt +*8:12. **for ever.** Gr. *aion,* Mt +6:13. lit. unto the age, Mt +21:19.

14. **Enoch.** Ge *5:18, 24. 1 Ch *1:1-3. He *11:5, 6. **the seventh.** Ge 5:18. Lk 3:37. **prophesied.** ſ106, Ge +31:7. **Behold.** Dt +*33:2. Jb *19:25-27. Ps *50:3-5. Is 26:21. Da *7:9, 10. Mi 1:3. Zc +*14:5. Mt +*16:27. +*24:30, 31. +*25:31. Mk 8:38. Lk 9:26. 1 C 16:22. 1 Th *3:13. 2 Th *1:7, 8. Re +*1:7. **with.** Ps +*68:17. Da 7:10. He 12:22. Re 5:11. 9:16. **his saints.** Ps +*149:9. Zc +*14:5. Col 1:26. 1 Th 3:13. 2 Th 1:10.

15. **execute.** Ps 9:7, 8. *37:6. 50:1-6. 98:9. +√149:7, 9. Ec 11:9. +*12:14. Mt *25:32, 33. Jn 5:22, 23, 27. Ac *17:31. Ro 2:16. 14:10. 1 C *4:5. 5:13. 2 P 2:5. Re *20:12-15. 22:12. **convince.** Ro 2:5. 3:19, 20. 1 T +5:20g. **ungodly.** 1 T 1:9. 1 P 4:18. **ungodly committed.** Zp 3:11. 2 P 2:6. **and of all.** ver. 16. Ex 16:8. 1 S 2:3. Ps 31:18. 73:9. 94:4. Is 37:22-36. Da 7:20. 11:36. Ml 3:13-15. Mt *12:31-37. Jn 6:60. Re 13:5, 6, 11.

16. **murmurers.** T#700. Ex 16:2, 3, 8. Nu +*11:1. 14:36. 16:11. 17:10. Dt 1:27. Ps 106:25. 144:14. Pr +12:25 (T#171). 19:3. Is +9:13 (T#171). *29:24. 58:13. La 3:39. Ezk +33:20 (T#272). Mt 20:11, 12. Lk 5:30. 10:40. 15:2. 19:7. Jn 6:41, 61. 1 C 10:10. Ph √2:14. **complainers.** Ps 144:14. **walking.** ver. 18. Ga 5:16, 24. 1 Th 4:5. 2 T 4:3. Ja 1:14, 15. 1 P 1:14. 2:11. 4:2. 2 P 2:10. 3:3. **their mouth.** ſ58, 2 P +2:13. ver. 15. Jb 17:4, 5. Ps 12:4. 17:10. 73:8-11. Ja 3:5. 2 P *2:18.

having. Ge 19:21. Ex +*23:3. Le +*19:15. Dt 10:17. Jb 13:10. 32:21. 34:19. Ps *15:4. Pr *28:21. Ac +*10:34. Ph +*2:3. 1 T +*6:5. Ja 2:1-9. 2 P 2:1-3. 3 J 9.

17. **remember.** Ml 4:4. Ac 20:35. Ep 2:20. 4:11. 2 P 3:2. 1 J 4:6.

18. **there.** Ac 20:29. 1 T 4:1, 2. 2 T 3:1-5, 13. *4:1-3. 2 P 2:1. *3:3. 1 J +2:18. **who.** ver. 16. Ps 14:1, 2. 2 P 2:10. 3:3.

19. **who.** Pr 18:1. Is +*65:5n. Ezk 14:7. Ho 4:14. 9:10. He +*10:25. 1 J *2:18, 19. **sensual.** 1 C √2:14. 15:44. Ja 3:15g. **having not.** Jn *3:5, 6. Ro +*8:9. 1 C *6:19. 7:40. Ph 3:3. **the Spirit.** Gr. *pneuma,* ſ121A2, Ro +8:1n.

20. **building.** Ac +9:31. Ro 15:2. 1 C 1:8. 10:23. 14:4, 5, 26. Ep 4:12, 16, 29. Col +*2:7. 1 Th *5:11. 1 T 1:4g. **most.** Ac *15:9. +*26:18. 2 T 1:5. T 1:1. Ja 2:22. 2 P 1:1. 1 J *5:4. Re 13:10. **praying.** T#1363. Zc *12:10. Ro *8:15, +26, 27. 1 C 14:15. Ga 4:6. Ep *6:18. **Ghost.** Gr. *pneuma,* Mt +1:18.

21. **Keep.** ver. √24. Jn +*14:21. *15:9, 10. Ac +*11:23. 13:43. 2 C 13:14. 1 J *4:16. 5:18, 21. Re *12:11. **in the love.** T#288. Dt 6:5. 11:1. 30:15, 16. Jsh 22:5. 23:11. Pr 23:26. Mt 22:37, 38. Mk 12:30. Lk 10:27. Ac +3:19 (T#601). Ro *5:5. +*8:39. 1 C 16:22. Ga +5:14 (T#283). 2 Th +*3:5. 1 J √3:16, 17. **looking for.** Jb *14:14. La *3:25, 26. Mt *24:42-51. Lk *12:36-40. Ga *5:5. 2 T +*4:8. T +*2:13, 14. He +*9:28. 2 P +*3:12, 14. **the mercy.** Mt +*28:19n. Mk 5:19. Jn 1:17. Ga ◑5:22, 23. Ep ◑+*5:4. 1 T 1:2. 2 T 1:2, 16, 18. He *4:16. **unto.** Ro +*2:7. 5:21. √6:23. 1 J √5:10, 11. **eternal.** Gr. *aionios,* Mt +18:8.

22. **of some.** ver. 4-13. Ezk 34:17. Ga 4:20. +*6:1. He *6:4-8. Ja +*5:19, 20. 1 J +*5:16-18.

23. **save.** Ro 11:14. 1 C 5:3-5. 2 C 7:10-12. 1 T +*4:16. Ja +*5:20. **with fear.** 2 C 5:11. 7:1. Ph 2:12. 1 P 1:17. +*3:15. **pulling.** Am ▶4:11. Zc ▶3:2, 3. **the fire.** Ps *106:18. 1 C *3:15. 2 P +*3:7. **hating.** ſ102C, Mt +5:29. Le 13:47-59. 14:47. 15:17. Nu +*19:10. Pr 8:13. Is 30:22. √64:6. La 4:14. Zc *3:3-5. Ro *12:9. 1 C 5:9-11. 15:33. Ep +*5:11. 1 Th *5:22. 2 Th 3:14. 1 T 5:22. Re 3:4, 18. **spotted.** Ja +*1:27. 3:6g.

24. **is able.** ver. ◑*21. Jn √10:28-30. Ac *20:32. Ro +*8:31. *14:4. *16:25-27. 2 C *9:8. Ep *3:20. Ph 2:13. 2 T +*4:18. **to keep.** Jn +17:12. **from falling.** Ps *37:24. Pr 24:16. 28:18. Jn 6:37. Ac 24:16. Ro 11:29. 14:4. 16:25, 26. He ◑+*10:35. Ja 2:10. 3:2. 2 P +*1:10. **present.** Ge 24:67. Nu=8:21. Ps 43:4. 45:14, 15. SS 3:11. 2 C *4:14. *11:2. Ep *5:27. Col *1:22, 28. *3:4. He *13:20, 21. **faultless.** Jn +*17:6. Ro 5:9, 10. Ep 1:4. 5:27. Ph 2:15. 2 T 4:18. He 13:20, 21. Re *14:5. **the presence.** Ps 22:22. Mt +*16:27n. +*19:28. +*25:31. Lk *9:26. 1 Th +*4:16, 17. 1 P *4:13. **his glory.** Mt +*16:27. 19:28. 25:31. Lk 9:26. **exceeding joy.** T#339, 859. Ps +*16:11. *21:6. 36:8. *43:4. 84:11. 97:11. Is +*51:11. Mt +*5:12. 25:21. Lk 1:14. 15:6. 2 C √4:17. 1 P *4:13. Re *7:15-17. *21:3, 4.

25. **the only.** Jn 5:44. 1 T 1:17. **wise.** Ps 104:24. 147:5. Ro +*11:33. 16:27. Ep 1:8. 3:10. 1 T 1:17. *6:16n. **God.** Ps 68:20. Is +*12:2. √45:21. Lk +1:47. Jn 4:22. 1 T 2:3. T 1:3, 4. *2:10, 13. 3:4. 2 P +*1:1. **be glory.** 1 Ch *29:11. Ps 72:18, 19. Da 4:37. See on Mt 6:13. Ro +11:36. Ep 3:21. 1 P +4:11. 5:10, 11. 2 P +*3:18. Re *1:6. *4:9-11. *5:13, 14. **and majesty.** He 1:3. 8:1. **both now.** Pr 8:23. 1 C 2:7. **ever.** Gr. *aion,* Mt +6:13. lit. unto all the ages.

REVELATION

REVELATION

The source and design of the book; with a blessing pronounced on those who duly attend to it, 1-3. The apostle salutes the seven churches in Asia; ascribes glory to God; and predicts the coming of Christ to judgment, with the terror and distress of his enemies, 4-7. The Lord declares his own eternity and omnipotence, 8. The place, time, and circumstances of John's vision; with what he heard of the words, and saw of the glory, of Christ; and the commandment given him to write these things to the churches, 9-20.

1. A.M. 4100. A.D. 95. **Revelation** Da 2:28, 29. Am 3:7. Ro 16:25. Ga 1:12. Ep 3:3. **which God.** Jn 3:32. 8:26. 12:49. **gave.** Jn 17:7, 8. Jn *3:35. *5:20. 7:16. 8:26. 12:49. 14:10. +17:2. **to show.** Re 4:1. *22:6. Ps 25:14. Is *46:9, 10. Da *2:20-22. 9:22, 23. Am +*3:7. Jn *1:18. *15:15. *16:13. **his servants.** Re +7:3. Jsh 1:2. Ja +1:1. **things.** Da 2:⟩28, 47. **which must.** ver. 3, 19. Re 4:1. 22:10. Mt 24:6. Lk +13:33. Jn +3:14. 2 P 3:8. **shortly.** ver. 3. Lk *18:8g. **and he.** Re 22:6, 16. Da 8:16. 9:21, 23. **and signified.** *S#4591g. Jn 12:33. 18:32. 21:19. Ac 11:28. 25:27. **by his angel.** Re 22:6, 16. Da 9:23. He *1:14. **John.** ver. 4, 9. Re 21:2. 22:8.

2. **bare.** ver. 9. Re 6:9. 12:11, 17. 1 K *22:14. 1 Ch=16:4. Jn 1:32. 12:17. *15:27. +*19:35. 21:24. Ac *10:41. 1 C 1:6. 2:1. 2 P *1:16-21. 1 J 1:1-3. 5:7-11. 3 J 12. **the word.** ver. 9. Re *12:11. 20:4. Ro +9:6. **the testimony.** Re 6:9. 12:17. 17:6, 7. 19:9, 10, 13. 20:4. 1 C +1:6. **and of all.** ver. 11, 19. Jn 3:11. Ac *4:20. 22:15. 26:16. 1 J 1:1. 4:14.

3. **Blessed.** ſ43, Dt +28:3. Re +*14:13. 16:15. 19:9. 20:6. 22:7, 14. Ps +*1:1. Pr 8:34. Da 12:12, 13. Lk +*11:28. **that readeth.** Jsh +*1:8. Ps +*1:1. Da *9:2. Jn +*5:39. Ac +*17:11. Ro +*15:4. 2 T +√3:15-17. **the words.** Jn *6:63. 2 T +*3:16. **and keep.** Re *22:7. Ps *119:4, 103, 105, 111, 129, 130, 162, 167. Lk +*11:28. Jn 8:51. 1 J +√2:3. **for.** ver. 1. Re 3:11. 22:6, 7, *10, 12, 20. Ro +13:11. Ja *5:8, 9. 1 P *4:7. 2 P *3:8, 9. 1 J 2:18.

4. **John.** See on ver. 1. **to the.** ver. 11, 20. Re 2:1, 8, 12, 18. 3:1, 7, 14. Ac 19:10. 1 P 1:1. **in Asia.** Ac +2:9. **Grace.** Nu *6:23-26. See on Ro 1:7. *5:20. 1 C 1:3. 2 C 1:2. *9:8. √12:9. 1 P 1:2. 2 J +3. **and peace.** Ps *29:11. Lk *24:36. Jn *14:27. Ac *10:36. Ro *5:1. 14:17. **from him.** ver. *8, 17. Re 4:8. 11:17. 16:5. Ex *3:14. *6:3. Ps *90:2. *102:25-27. Is 41:4. +*57:15. Mi +*5:2. Jn *1:1. He *1:10-13. +*13:8. Ja *1:17. **which is.** Ex ⟩3:14. Is ⟩41:4. Jn +8:24, 58. 18:5, 6. **which was.** Jn +1:1. **from the.** Re *3:1. *4:5. *5:6. Zc 3:9. 4:10. 6:5. 8:2. 1 C *12:4-13. **Spirits.** Gr. *pneuma*, Lk +24:37. **his throne.** Ac *2:32, 33.

5. **And from.** ſ29, Ex +19:6. **who is.** Re *3:14. Ps 89:36, 37. Is *55:4. Jn *1:18. 3:11, 32. 8:14-16. *18:37. 1 T 6:13. 1 J 5:7-10. **faithful.** Re 2:13. 19:11. Ezk 33:5, 9. Mt 24:4, 25. 1 T 4:16. **witness.** Ps ⟩89:37. Jn *8:55. 1 J *5:9. **and the first.** ver. 18. Re 3:14. Ps ⟩89:27. Ac 26:23. Ro *8:29. 1 C *15:20-23. Col +*1:18n. He *1:5, 6. **of the dead.** Ac +26:23. Ro *1:4. *8:34. **and the prince.** Re √11:15. 15:3. +17:14. *19:16. Ex 15:1. Ps 2:1-6. *72:11. 89:27. Pr *8:15, 16. Da 2:44. √7:14. Mt 28:18. Ep 1:20-22. 1 T 6:15. **him that loved.** Re 3:9, 19. Dt 7:8. 23:5. SS 8:6, 7. Jn 13:1, 34. 14:29. 15:9. Ro *5:8. *8:35, +37. Ga *2:20. Ep 2:4. *3:19. *5:2, 25-27. 1 J *4:10. **washed.** Re *7:14. Ps +*51:1, 2. Zc *13:1. Jn *13:8-10. Ac +*22:16n. 1 C *6:11. He +*9:14. +*10:22. 2 P +1:9. Some authorities read "redeemed" instead of "washed." Jb 42:9. Ps ⟩130:8. Is ⟩40:2. Jn 8:34. **from our sins.** Mt 1:21. **in.** ſ108D, Mt +3:11. The preposition "in" (Gr. *en*) may be better translated "by" or "through" to conform to the underlying Hebrew idiom, as was properly done at Re 5:9. Compare for this meaning of *en*: Mt 5:34, 35. 9:34. 1 C 10:2n. Ga 3:11. 2 T 2:10. **blood.** ſ117, Ge +19:8. We lose nothing of the facts, but gain immensely as to their meaning, when we understand that, by *Metalepsis*, "blood" is put for death, and "death" for the atonement made by it and all its infinite merits (B611). Re *5:9. 7:14. *12:11. 19:13. Ex 12:13. Ac +*20:28. Col *1:20. He +*9:14. 1 P *1:18, 19. 1 J *1:7.

6. **made us.** Re *5:9. Ep 1:3. **kings.** T#848. ver. ◑9. Re *3:21. *5:10. *20:4, 6. Ex ⟩19:6. Is 9:6, 7. 61:6. 62:3. Lk +*12:32. +*22:29, 30. Ro *12:1. 1 P 2:5-9. **and priests.** Re 20:6. Ex=29:9. Is *61:6. 66:21. 1 P *2:5, 9. **unto God.** Jn *20:17. Ro *12:1. +15:6. **to him.** Re 4:11. 5:12-14. Ps 72:18, 19. Da 4:34. Mt +*6:13. Jn √5:23. Ph 2:11. 1 T 6:16. He *13:21. 1 P *4:11. 5:11. 2 P *3:18. Ju *25. **glory.** T#1576. Re *5:11-14. Ro +11:36. 1 P *4:11. **dominion.** T#1573. He 4:14-16. 1 P +4:11. **for ever.** Gr. *aion*, Mt +6:13. ſ147H, Ge +9:25. **and ever.** Gr. *aion*, Mt +6:13. lit. unto the ages of the ages, Ga +1:5. ver. 18. Re 4:9, 10. 5:13, 14. 7:12. 10:6. 11:15. 14:11. 15:7. 19:3. 20:10. 22:5.

7. **he cometh.** Re 14:14-16. Ps 97:2. *98:9. Is 19:1. Da +*7:13. Na 1:3. Mt +*24:30. 26:64. Mk 13:26. 14:62. Lk *9:26. 21:27. Jn *14:3. Ac +*1:9-11. Ph +*1:26. 1 Th +*4:17. *5:23. **with.** Da ⟩7:13. Mt 24:29-31. +*25:31, 32. **clouds.** Ge +9:13. **and every.** Ph 2:10. **eye.** Re 22:4. Nu *24:17. Jb √19:25-27. 33:26. Mt 20:34. 1 Th *1:10. 1 J √3:2. Ju *14. **shall see.** ſ108B, Ge +21:16. Zc *12:10. Mt +*16:27n. +*24:3n, 30. *26:64. Mk +*1:2n. Ac +*1:11. 2 T *4:1n. 1 J *3:2. **and they.** ſ92C, Mt +2:15. Ps *22:16. Zc *12:10. Jn 19:34, 37. He 6:6. 10:29. **and all.** Re *6:15-17. 18:15-19. Is +*2:19. Mt +*24:30. Lk 23:28-30. **shall wail.** Le=23:22. Zc ⟩12:10, 12, 14. **Even so.** Re 18:20. 19:1-3. *22:20. Jg 5:31. Ps 68:1.

8. **I am.** This text, according to Daniel Waterland, "is to be interpreted (with all antiquity) of God the Son," which he proves (1) from the context; (2) from antiquity; (3) from the weaknesses of the reasons for applying this text to the Father. As to the context, all acknowledge that verse 7 applies to the Son; there is insufficient contextual warrant for making a sudden shift in this verse to avoid the application of divine titles to the Son, as the Arians argue for. As to antiquity, both ante-Nicene and post-Nicene writers concur in applying this text to Christ, such that "never were men more unanimous than the ancients were in this matter; there being no one exception, on record,

against it." As to reasons for applying this text to the Father, some argue that since in verse 4 the title "which is, which was, and which is to come" applies to the Father, the same title used here must likewise. But this fails to recognize that the same titles are often given to both, as the title "Alpha and Omega" most certainly is (Re 1:11, 17. 2:8. 22:13. See related note on Re 3:14). The objection that the title "the Almighty" is always in Scripture applied to the Father, never the Son, is mistaken, for (1) "it is mere groundless presumption to suppose that as often as that title is applied to the one *God* in the Old Testament, it is applied to the Father only: since it may often be understood indifferently either of Father, or Son, or of the whole Trinity"; (2) "there are several texts of the Old Testament, which we have good reason to believe are to be understood particularly of God the Son. Psalm 24 has by the primitive Fathers been interpreted of Christ. The title Lord of hosts (*Kurios dunameon*), applied to Christ in that Psalm, is equivalent to Almighty (*Kurios pantokrator*), as the LXX Interpreters render the same words indifferently by one or other, as may easily be seen in a multitude of instances, by looking into Trommius's Concordance." John himself in his Apocalypse, Re 4:8, alluding to Is 6:3, where it reads "Holy, holy, holy, is the Lord of hosts," gives not *Kurios dunameon*, (or *sabaoth*), but *Kurios o Theos o pantokrator*, Lord God Almighty. John likewise applies the title "Lord of hosts" to Christ, as can be seen by comparing Jn 12:41 with Is 6:5. Compare Zc 2:8 and 12:5, 10 with Jn 19:34, 37. "These instances are sufficient to check the confidence of such as roundly affirm, without a syllable of proof, that the title of *pantokrator*, Almighty, is in holy Scripture applied always to the Father only" (Waterland, *Works*, vol. 2, Sermon VI, "Christ's Divinity proved from his Titles," pp. 141-143; "A Second Defence of Some Queries," pp. 562-565). Waterland continues his argument at length with the astute observation, that the arguments used by the Arians to deny the eternity of the Son left no remaining valid arguments to assert the eternity of the Father. Re 21:6. *22:13. Ex)3:14. Ps 68:4. Is 43:3, 11. *44:6. 45:5, 6. 63:16. Jn +*8:28, 58. **Alpha**. ver. *11, *17. Re *2:8. *21:6. √22:13. Is 41:4. *43:10. *44:6. *48:12. **Omega**. i.e. *the last; finality*, ✱S#5598g. ver. 11. Re 21:6. 22:13. **the beginning**. Pr *8:22, 23. Is)41:4. Hab *1:12. Jn *1:1-3. Col *1:17. **and ending**. Ps *102:27. He *12:2. **the Lord**. Re +4:8. **which is**. See on ver. *4. Re 16:5. Ex +*)3:14. **the Almighty**. Re 4:8. 11:17. 15:3. 16:7, 14. *19:6, 15. *21:22. 22:12-16. Ge *17:1. 28:3. 35:11. 43:14. 48:3. 49:25. Ex +*6:3. Nu 24:4. Is +*9:6. Ho 12:5. Am)4:13, LXX. Jn 1:3. 8:56. Ac 7:38. 2 C *6:18.

9. **John**. See on ver. 4. **companion**. Re *2:9, 10. *7:14. Jn 16:33. Ac +*14:22. Ro *8:17. 1 C 4:9-13. Ph 1:7. 4:14. 2 T 1:8. 2:3-12. **in tribulation**. Jn 16:33. Ac +*14:22. Ro 8:17. 2 T √2:12. **in the kingdom**. ver. 6. Re 3:+*10, 21. 5:10. 13:10. 14:12. *20:4, 6. 22:5. Mt *13:43. +*25:34. Lk *23:42. Ac +*1:6. +*3:21. Col +*1:13n. 2 Th 1:5. 2 T√2:12. +*4:1n. **and patience**. Re 2:2, 3, 19. 3:10. 13:10. 14:12. Ps *37:7. Lk *21:19. Ro +*2:7, 8. *5:3, 4. *8:25. 1 C 1:7. 2 Th 1:4, 5. *3:5. He +*10:36. Ja 1:3, 4. *5:7, 8. 2 P +1:6. **of Jesus**. He *10:12, 13. **in the isle**. Ex +*3:1. Mt 20:23. Mk 10:39. **Patmos**. i.e. *mortal*, ✱S#3963g. **for the word**. ver. +2. Re 6:9. 11:7. 12:11, 17. 19:10.

10. **I was**. Da 9:3, 20, 21, etc. **in**. Re 4:2. 17:3. 21:10. Nu 24:2. 1 K 18:12. Ezk 2:2. 3:12. 11:5. Mt 22:43. Lk 4:1. Ac 10:10, etc. 2 C *12:2-4. 2 P *1:21. **the Spirit**. Gr. *pneuma*, Mt +3:16. √121A4, Ezk +37:1. **on the Lord's day**. Mk +*16:9. Lk 24:1. Jn 20:19, 26. Ac +20:7. 1 C 11:20g. *16:2. Most of the preceding and original references of the *Treasury* assume that "Lord's day" refers to the Christian Sabbath, the first day of the week, or Sunday. However, such an interpretation is open to the objection that (1) such a meaning has no relevance to the context; (2) the term is never so applied in Scripture, where the day of Christian worship is uniformly called the "first day of the week"; (3) such an interpretation does not agree with the Patristic understanding of the verse; (4) the interpretation is a reading back into the text of a term subsequently applied to Sunday. The term "Lord's day" is better understood as John's way of expressing the common Hebrew term "day of the Lord," in a manner in Greek which places the emphasis upon "Lord's" (by placing it in an initial position) in the same manner as the Hebrew expression places emphasis upon "Lord" (by placing it in the final position) in "day of the Lord." Supposing the expression refers to Sunday cannot account for the presence of the Greek article "the" used in the expression. When the article is lacking, there are several possible explanations to account for the fact, but when an interpretation cannot account for the presence of the Greek article, the interpretation stands self-condemned (J. B. Smith, Comm. on Revelation, Appendix 5, p. 320). The expression "on the Lord's day" would better be translated "in the Lord's day," as a reference to this specific prophetic time period. The Greek preposition *en* is more usually rendered "in," only once in Revelation is it translated "on," in the expression "on the earth," Re 5:13. Everywhere else where *en* is followed by the word "day" it is rendered "in" (Re 2:13. 9:6. 10:7. 11:6. 18:8). Understanding this term to refer to the "day of the Lord" emphasizes that the events which transpire in the third division of the book ("things which shall be hereafter") are events which take place during the "day of the Lord," a future time which begins at the Great Tribulation and concludes with the judgment of the Great White Throne at the end of the Millennium, and specifically ties in the prophecies of this book with the rest of Scripture relating to this coming day. This being the case, a more appropriate set of relevant references reflecting this understanding follows (For "day of the Lord": Is 13:6. Ac 2:20. 1 Th 5:2. 2 Th 2:2. 2 P 3:10. For "the last days": Is 2:2. For "in that day": Is 2:11. For "day of the Lord of hosts": Is 2:12). A careful comparison of the Scripture passages adduced may well show that the "day of the Lord" does not start with the beginning of the tribulation, or the beginning of Daniel's Seventieth Week, as commonly held, but some time in the latter half of this week, a time marked by cosmic disturbances which immediately precede the onset of the "day of the Lord" (Joel *2:30, 31. Re 6:17. 16:14). Jb +*21:30. Pr 6:34. +*11:4. Is +*2:12. +*13:6. 61:2. 63:4. Je 51:6. Ezk +*7:19. Am +*5:18. Na *1:2. Zp 1:11, 15, 18. 2:2, 3. Mt 24:42. Lk 17:24. Ro +*2:5. 1 C +√3:13. ◑4:3mg. 1 Th +*5:9. 2 Th +*1:10. Ja 5:3. **great voice**. Ps *18:13. *46:6. *68:33. as. Re 4:1. 10:3-8. Ex 19:16. 20:18. 1 Th +*4:16.

11. **I am**. See on ver. 8, 17. Re 21:6. 22:13. **the**

first. ver. 17. Re 2:8. √22:13. Is 41:4. √44:6. 48:12. **and**. ♪148, Ge +8:22. **What**. ver. 2, 19. Re 2:1. 10:4. 14:13. 19:9. 21:5. Dt 31:19. Is 30:8. Je 30:2. Hab 2:2. **write in**. Ex 17:14. Dt 17:18. **seven**. See on ver. 4, 20. Re 2:1, 8, 12, 18. 3:1, 7, 14. **Ephesus**. Ac 18:+19-21, 24. ch. 19. 20:17. 1 C 15:32. 16:8. Ep 1:1. 1 T 1:3. **Smyrna**. i.e. *myrrh; tribulation,* ✳S#4667g. Re 2:8. **Pergamos**. i.e. *fortified,* ✳S#4010g. Re 2:12. **Thyatira**. Re 2:18, 24. Ac 16:14. **Sardis**. Re 3:1, 4. **Philadelphia**. i.e. *brotherly love,* ✳S#5359g. Re 3:7. **Laodicea**. i.e. *justice; the people's rights; just or religious people,* ✳S#2993g. Re ●3:14. Col 2:1. 4:13, 15, 16.

12. **see**. ♪46B, Ex +5:21. ♪171J15, Ge +42:1. Ezk 43:5, 6. Mi 6:9. **the voice**. ♪121E1, Ge +25:23. **I saw**. ver. 13, 20. Re 2:1. 11:4. Ex 25:36, 37. 37:23. 2 Ch 4:20. Zc *4:2. **candlesticks**. Gr. lampstands. Ex *25:31-40. Zc 4:1-6. Mt 5:14. Jn 8:12. He 9:2.

13. **midst**. Re 2:1. Nu=1:50. 1 Ch=9:27. Mt +*18:20. **like**. Re 14:14. Ezk 1:♪26-28. ♪8:2. Da 7:9, 13. 10:5, 6, 16. Ph 2:7, 9. He *2:14-17. +*4:15. **Son of man**. Re 14:14. Ezk 1:26. Da ●3:25. +*7:♪13, 14. 8:15. 10:16. Mt *16:13. Jn +*1:51. 5:27. Ac *7:56. 1 T *2:5. He *2:14. **clothed**. Ezk ♪9:2, 3, 11. Da 10:5. **a garment**. Ge=41:42. Da 7:9. **and girt**. Re 15:6. Ex 28:6-8. *39:5. Le 8:7. Is 11:5. Da ♪10:5. Zc *6:13. Ep 6:14. He 6:20. *7:24.

14. **and his hairs**. Da ♪7:9. Mt 28:3. **white**. Mt 17:2. Mk 9:3. Lk 9:29. **and his eyes**. Re 2:18, 23. 19:12. 1 S +*16:7. 2 Ch *16:9. Jb *10:4. Ps *139:1-3. Pr 20:8. Ezk 1:28. Da ♪10:6. Zc *4:10. He *4:13.

15. **his feet**. Re 2:18. 10:1. Ezk 1:7. *40:3. Da 10:6. **his voice**. Re *14:2. *19:6. Ps *93:4. Is *17:13. Ezk *43:2. **many waters**. Re 17:1. 19:6. Ezk ♪1:24. ♪43:2. Da 10:6. Jn +*3:23.

16. **he had**. ver. 20. Re 2:1. 3:1. 12:1. Jb 38:7. Da 8:10. +*12:3. **seven stars**. Re 3:1. **out**. Re 2:12, 16. 19:15, 21. Is *11:1, 4, 5. 49:2. Ep *6:17. He +*4:12. **his mouth**. Is 49:2. **two-edged**. Re 2:12. He +*4:12. **sword**. Re 2:16. *19:15. **and his countenance**. Re 10:1. 2 S *23:4. Is 24:23. 60:19, 20. Ml *4:2. Mt *17:2. Ac 26:13-15. **as the sun**. Jg ♪5:31. **that shineth**. Da +*12:3. 1 C *15:41.

17. **when I saw**. Ex *3:6. Jg *6:22, 23. *13:22. Is *6:5. Lk 24:37. Jn 21:12. **I fell**. Ge=43:26. Ezk 1:28. 3:23. 43:3. 44:4. Da 8:17, 18. 10:8, 9, 15, 17-19. Hab +*3:16. Mt 17:2-6. Lk 5:8. Jn 13:23. 21:20. **And he**. Da 8:18. 10:10. **hand upon**. T#399. Ge 48:14-16. Mt 17:7. 19:13-15. **Fear not**. Ge 15:1. 26:24. Ex 14:13. 20:20. Is 41:10. Da ♪10:12, 19. Mt 28:4, 5. Mk 16:5, 6. Lk 24:37-39. **I am**. ♪92C, Mt +2:15. See on ver. 4, 8, 11. Re 2:8. 22:13. Ne +*9:6. Is 41:4. √44:6. 48:12. Jn 3:31. **the first**. Gr. *protos.* Thayer states "first, with the article, i.e. *the eternal One,* Re 1:17. 2:8. 22:13" (*Lexicon,* p. 554). Is ♪44:6. ♪48:12.

18. **that liveth**. Re 4:9, 10. Ge=45:26. Jb *19:25. Ps 18:46. Lk 24:5. Jn 1:4. +6:57. 14:19. Ro 6:9. 2 C 13:4. Ga *2:20. Col *3:3. He *7:25. **was dead**. Re 2:8. Ro *6:9. 14:8, 9. 2 C √5:14, 15. He *1:3. +*12:2. **I am alive**. Re 4:9, 10. 5:14. 10:6. 15:7. Da 4:34. 12:7. Ac +*2:24. *17:31. Ro *1:4. *6:4. 1 C 15:12-17, 20, 23-27, 45, 47, 55-57. He 7:16, 25. **for evermore**. Gr. *aion,* Mt +6:13. lit. unto the ages of the ages, Ga +1:5. ver. 6. **the keys**. Re 3:7. 9:1. 20:1, 2, 14. Ps 68:20. Is 22:22. Mt 16:18, 19. **hell**. Gr. *hades,* Mt +11:23. Re 6:8. Pr 15:11. **death**. Re 6:8. 20:13, 14. Ps 68:20. He 2:15.

19. **Write**. This verse provides the outline of the entire prophecy of Revelation. ver. 2, 11. Re 10:4. 14:13. 19:9. 21:5. **the things**. See on ver. 11-16. **and the things which are**. Re ch. 2, 3. **and the things which shall be**. Re ch. 4-22. **hereafter**. Is ♪48:6. Da ♪2:29.

20. **mystery**. Re 10:7. 17:5, 7. Da ♪2:29. See on Mt 13:11, 35. Lk 8:10. Ro +*16:25n. **the seven stars**. See on ver. 13, 16. **the seven golden**. ver. +12. **The seven stars**. Re 2:1, 8, 18. 3:1, 7, 14. ●9:1. ●12:4. **the angels of**. Re 2:1, 8, 12, 18. 3:1, 7, 14. Ml +*2:7. **the seven churches**. ver. 4, 11. **and the**. ver. +12. Zc 4:2. Mt *5:14-16. Ep *5:13. Ph *2:15, 16. 1 T 2:14-16.

REVELATION 2

The epistle of Christ to the angel of the church of Ephesus; consisting of a commendation and reproof, a call to repentance, a solemn warning, and a gracious promise to those who overcame, 1-7. That to Smyrna, replete with commendation, and encouraging exhortations to faithfulness under tribulation, 8-11. That to Pergamos; in which are warnings against the Nicolaitans, threatenings of judgments on the impenitent, and promises to the victorious, 12-17. That to Thyatira, nearly of similar import, 18-29.

1. **the angel**. ver. 8, 12, 18. Re +1:20. 3:1, 7, 14. 2 C 5:20. 1 T 3:1. **church**. See on Re 1:11. **Ephesus**. Re 1:11. Ac +18:19. 20:16-38. **holdeth**. Re 1:16, 20. 8:10-12. 12:1. Jn 5:35. **walketh**. See on Re 1:12, 13. Ezk 28:13, 14. Mt +*18:20. *28:20. **candlesticks**. Re 1:+12, 13, 20.

2. **know**. ver. 9, 13, 19. Re 3:1, 8, 15. Ps *1:6. Mt 7:23. 1 Th 1:3. 2 T 2:19. He +*6:10. **labor**. Re 14:13g. **patience**. ver. 19. Re +1:9. **how**. ver. 6, 14, 15, 20, 21. 2 Ch 19:2. ●20:35. Mt 7:15. Jn 16:12. Ga *1:7-9. Ep +*4:14. 1 Th +*5:21. 2 P *2:1-3. 1 J √4:1. **thou hast**. 2 C √11:13-15. 1 J 2:21, 22. *4:1. **apostles**. Ac 1:22. 1 C 9:1. 12:28. 2 C 12:12. Ga 1:1, 12. Ep 1:1. **found them**. Ep *5:13.

3. **hast borne**. Ps 69:7. Mi 7:9. Mk 15:21. Lk 14:27. 1 C 13:7. Ga 6:2. He 13:13. **hast patience**. Re 1:9. 3:10. Ps *37:7. Lk +*8:15. 21:19. Ro +*2:7. *5:3, 4. 8:25. 12:12. +*15:4, 5. Col *1:11. 2 Th 3:5. He 6:12, 15. 10:36. 12:1. Ja 1:3, 4. *5:7-11. 2 P 1:6. **and for my**. Mt +*5:11. +10:22. 19:29. Jn +1:12. √15:21. **hast labored**. Ro 16:12. 1 C 16:16. 2 C 5:9. 6:5. 10:15. 11:23. Ph 2:16. 4:3. 1 Th 1:3. 2:9. 5:12. 2 Th 3:8. 1 T 4:10. 5:17. He +*6:10. **hast not**. Pr *24:10. Je +*12:5. Lk 18:1. 2 C *4:1, 16, 17. *12:10. Ga +*6:9. 2 Th 3:13. He *12:3-5.

4. **I have**. ver. 14, 20. **because**. Re 3:14-17. 1 K *11:4. Ps *85:8. Je 2:2-5. Mt *24:12, 13. Ph 1:9. 3:13-16. 1 Th 4:9, 10. 2 Th 1:3. He +*6:10, 11. **first**. Ge 13:3. 2 Ch 17:3. **love**. 1 C 13:1-3.

5. **Remember**. Re 3:3, 19. Ezk 16:61-63. 20:43. 36:31. 2 P 1:12, 13. **thou art fallen**. 2 Ch 16:7, 9. Pr *6:23. Is 14:12. Ho 14:1. Ga +*5:4. Ep *5:14. Ju *24. **and repent**. ver. 16, 21, 22. Re 3:3, 19. 9:20, 21. 16:9. Ezk *18:30-32. Ac *17:30, 31. **and do**. ver. 19. Re 3:2, 3. Is 1:26. Je 2:2, 3. Ho 9:10. Ml 3:4. 4:6. Lk 1:17. **the first works**. ver. 2, 19. Ge 13:3. Jn √6:29. He 10:32. **else**. ver. 16. Re 3:3. Mt 21:41-43. 24:48-51. Mk 12:9. Lk 12:45, 46. 20:16. Jn +21:22. **repent**. Le 26:40-42. Dt √30:1-3. 1 K 8:33, 35, 37. Da 9:3, 4.

Ho 5:15. 14:2. Zc 1:3. Mt 3:2. 4:17. Ac 2:38. +*3:19-21.

6. **But this.** ∫127. Palinodia; or, Retracting B978. Approval of one thing after reproving for another thing. For other instances of this figure see Re 3:4, 5. 2 Ch *15:17. *19:3. Ps 89:33. 106:8, 44. **that thou hatest.** ver. 14, 15. 2 Ch 19:2. Ps *26:5. *97:10. 101:3. *139:21, 22. Ep +*5:11, 12. 2 J +*9, *10. **Nicolaitans.** i.e. *conqueror of the people,* ❋S#3531g. ver. 15g. Ac 6:5? 2 C +*1:24? **I also.** Is 61:8. Je 44:4. Am 5:21. Zc 8:17.

7. **He that.** ∫8, Ps +118:1. **hath an.** ver. *11, *17, *29. Re *3:6, 13, 22. *13:9. Mt *11:15. +*13:9, 13. Mk *7:16. **let him.** Re *14:13. *22:17. 1 C *2:10. *12:4-12. Ep *5:17. **hear what.** ∫147A, Ge +50:24. Re 13:9. Mt +11:15. **the Spirit.** Gr. *pneuma,* Mt +3:16. Jn +7:39. **that overcometh.** T#938. ver. *11, *17, *26-28. Re *3:5, 12, 21. *12:10, 11. 15:2. *21:7. Jn +*16:33. Ro ◐+*8:37. +*12:21. Ja *1:12. 1 J 2:13. 4:4. *5:4, 5. **the tree.** ∫46C, Mt +8:6. In the Greek *xylon* means wood; but receives its meaning of "tree" from the Hebrew *eytz,* tree, which is frequently rendered *xylon* in the Septuagint (B680). Re *22:2, 14, 19. Ge *❩2:9. *3:❩22-24. Pr *3:18. +*11:30. *13:12. *15:4. **the paradise.** Ge 2:8. 13:10. Ps +*16:11. Is 51:3. Ezk 28:13. ❩31:8. Jl 2:3. Lk +*23:43. 2 C +*12:4.

8. **the angel.** See on ver. 1. Re +1:20. **Smyrna.** Re 1:11. **the first.** Re 1:8, +*11, +17, 18. Is *41:4. √44:6. ❩48:12. **which was.** Re +1:18.

9. **know.** See on ver. 2. Ro 14:10-12. **tribulation.** Re *7:14. Jn 16:33. Ac +*14:22. Ro *5:3. *8:35. 12:12. 1 Th 3:4. 2 Th *1:6, 7. **poverty.** Pr *13:7. Mt +*5:3. Lk +*4:18. 6:20. 1 C 1:26. 2 C *8:2, 9. Ja +*2:5, 6. **thou art.** Re 3:17, 18. Pr *13:7. Mk ◐10:25. Lk *12:21. Ro √8:18. 1 C *3:21, 23. 2 C *6:10. Ph +*4:17. 1 T +*6:18. He 10:34. 11:26. Ja +*2:5, 6. **the blasphemy.** Lk 22:65. Ac 26:11. 1 T 1:13. **which say.** Ro 2:17, 28, 29. *9:6. Mt *7:21-23. **are not.** Jn *8:39, 44. Ro *2:28, 29. 10:2. **but are.** Ac 13:50. 14:2, 5, 19. 17:5. **the synagogue.** Re 3:9. **of Satan.** ver. 13, 24. Re 3:9. 12:9. 20:2, 7. 1 C +5:5.

10. **Fear none.** Ps *27:3. Da +*6:10. Mt +*10:28. 28:20. Jn *14:27. Ac 9:16. **shalt.** Da *3:16-18. Mt +*10:28. Lk +*12:4-7. **the devil.** Re *12:9-11. *13:2, 7, 15-17. Lk 21:12. Jn 13:2, 27. Ep 2:2. 6:12. 1 P *5:8, 9. **into prison.** Ps 69:33. **tried.** Re 3:10. Da ❩1:12. +*11:35. He 11:36. 1 P *5:10. **ye shall.** See on ver. 9. Mt 24:9, 21, 29. Jn *15:20, 21. *16:33. 1 C +*10:13. Ph *1:28, 29. 1 Th *3:3, 4. **ten days.** Ge 24:55. Nu 11:19. 1 S 25:38. Da ❩1:12, 14. Hab *2:3. 1 P √1:6, 7. **be thou faithful.** ver. 13. Re *12:11. 17:14. Mt +10:22. *24:13. Mk 8:35. 13:13. Lk 21:16-19. Jn 12:25. Ac 20:24. 21:13. 1 C +*4:2. *15:50-58. 2 T *4:7, 8. He +*3:6. **a crown.** Re 3:11. 4:4, 10. 6:2. 9:7. 12:1, ◐3. 14:14g. 1 Th 2:19. 2 T *4:8. Ja +*1:12. 1 P *5:4.

11. **He that.** ∫8, Ps +118:1. **hath.** See on ver. 7. Re 13:9. Mt 11:15. 13:9, 43. **hear.** ∫147A, Ge +50:24. **the Spirit.** Gr. *pneuma.* Mt +3:16. **the second death.** T#563. Re √20:6, 11-15. +*21:8. Ezk 18:31, 32. Ja +1:15 (T#287).

12. **the angel.** See on ver. 1. Re 1:11, +20. **Pergamos.** Pergamos, now Bergamo, the ancient metropolis of Mysia, and the residence of the Attalian kings, is situated on the river Ciacus, about sixty miles north of Smyrna, in long. 27 degrees East lat. 39 degrees 11 minutes North. It still retains some measure of its

ancient importance; containing a population of about 15,000 souls, and having nine or ten mosques, two churches, and one synagogue. Re 1:11. **which hath.** ver. 16. Re *1:16. 19:15, 21. Is 11:4. He +*4:12.

13. **know.** See on ver. 2, 9. Jb *23:10. 1 C *3:13-15. He +*6:10. **where thou dwellest.** Ps *120:5. **Satan's.** ver. 9, 10, 24. Re 3:9. **thou holdest.** ver. 25. Re 3:3, 11. Mt *10:32. Ro √10:9, 10. 1 Th +*5:21. 2 T 1:13. *2:11, 12. He +*3:6. +*10:23. **my name.** Re 3:8. Mt 24:9. Lk 21:17. Jn +1:12. Ac 9:14. Ja 2:7. **not denied.** Re 3:8. Mt *10:23. 1 T +*5:8. 2 T 2:12. Ju +*3, 4. **faith.** ∫121R2, Ac +6:7. **Antipas.** i.e. *against all,* ❋S#493g. **was.** ver. +10. Re 1:5. 11:3. 17:6. Ac 22:20.

14. **I have.** See on ver. 4, 20. **Balaam.** Nu 24:14. *25:1-3. *31:8, ❩16. Jsh 24:9. 2 P +2:15. Ju *11. **who taught.** ver. 20. Pr *28:10. **Balac.** i.e. *waster,* ❋S#904g. For ❋S#1111h, see Nu +22:2. **a stumblingblock.** Is 57:14. Je 6:21. Ezk 3:20. 44:12. Mt 18:7. Ro 9:32, +33. 11:9. 14:13, 21. 1 C 1:23. *8:9. 1 P 2:8. **children of Israel.** Re 7:4. 21:12. Ac +5:21. **eat.** ver. 20. Ps *106:28. Ac *15:20, 21, +29. 21:25. 1 C 8:4-13. *10:18-31. **to commit.** Re +*21:8. *22:15. Nu ❩25:1. 31:16. Ac +15:20. 1 C *6:13-18. *7:2. He +*13:4.

15. **So hast.** ver. 4, 21. 1 C *5:11. **the doctrine.** See on ver. 6. Ro *6:1, 2. Ju *4. **which thing.** Ps *97:10.

16. **Repent.** ver. 5, 21, 22. Re *3:3, 19. 16:9. Mt *3:2, 10. Ac *17:30, 31. **else.** See on ver. 5. **will come.** Re 22:7. Jn +21:22. **will fight.** ver. 12. Re 1:16. 19:15, 21. Is *11:4. 49:2. Ho *6:5. Ep *6:17. 2 Th +*2:8. **the sword.** ver. 12. Re 1:16. *19:15, 21. He *4:12.

17. **He that hath.** ∫8, Ps +118:1. ver. +7, 11. Re 3:6, 13, 22. Mk 4:9, 23. **hear.** ∫147A, Ge +50:24. **the Spirit.** Gr. *pneuma,* Mt +3:16. Jn +7:39. **I give.** 1 K ◐*18:19. Ps 78:19, 24, 25. **to eat.** Ps *25:14. 36:8. Pr *3:32. 14:10. Is 65:13. Mt 13:11. Jn 4:32. 6:48-58. Col *3:3. **hidden.** Re 19:9. Ex *16:23. Ezr 1:7n. Ps 87:4. Is 18:3, 7. Je 3:16n. He 9:4. **manna.** Re *16:15, 32-35. =40:23. Ps ❩78:24. Jn 3:12. 4:32. *6:31, 48-50, 56, 58. 13:17. **white stone.** Re 13:18. Ex ?28:30, 36. Le 8:8. Nu 11:7. Ac 26:10. **a new.** Gr. *kainos,* new in quality, not in time; unfailing freshness, the like of which has never existed before (Mk +2:22. ❋S#2537g. 2 J 5n). Re *3:12. 5:9. 14:3. *19:12, 13. 21:1, 2, 5. Is 56:4. ❩62:2. *❩65:15. 2 C *5:17. Ep 4:24. 1 J *3:1. **no man knoweth.** Re 19:12. Dt 29:29. **saving.** Ps *25:14. Mt +*11:27. 1 C √2:9, 10, 14. **that receiveth.** Ro 5:1. *8:15, 16. 2 C *1:22. Ph 2:1. 1 J +*5:10.

18. **unto.** See on ver. 1. Re 1:11, +20. **Thyatira.** i.e. *sacrifice of labor; odor of affliction,* ❋S#2363g. ver. 24. Re 1:11. Ac *16:14. ◐19:10. **the Son of God.** Ps 2:7. Mt 3:17. 4:3-6. +14:33. 17:5. 27:54. Lk +*1:35. Jn *1:14, 34, 49. √3:16, 18, 35, 36. 5:25. *10:30, 36. Ac *8:37. Ro *1:4. +*8:32. He *1:1-3. **his eyes.** See on Re 1:14, 15. *19:12. Ps *139:23, 24. He *4:12. **his feet.** Re +1:15. Da ❩10:6.

19. **know.** See on ver. 2, 9, 13. Jn *1:48, 49. **thy works.** ver. 4, 5. **charity.** 1 C 13:1-8. Ga *5:22, 23. Ep 1:15. Col 3:14. 1 Th +1:3. 3:6. 2 Th *1:3, 4. 1 T 1:5. 1 P 4:8. 2 P 1:7. **service.** He +*6:10. **faith.** He *11:1. **patience.** See on ver. 2, 3. Re +1:9. **the last.** ver. 4. Jb 17:9. Ps 92:14. Pr +*4:18. Mt 12:45. Lk 11:26. Jn *15:2. 2 P 2:20. +*3:18. **the first.** ver. 5.

20. **I have.** See on ver. 4, 14. **that woman.** 1 K *16:31. 17:4, 13. ch. 18. 19:1, 2. 21:7-15, 23-25. 2 K

9:7, 30-37. **Jezebel**. i.e. *a dunghill; without cohabitation*, ✻S#2403g. For ✻S#348h, see 1 K +16:31. **calleth herself**. Pr 27:2. Mt=13:33. 2 C ◑√10:18. **a prophetess**. Ex +✻15:20. Jg 4:4. 2 K 22:14. Ne 6:14. Is 8:3. Ezk 13:17. Lk 2:36. Ac +21:9. **and to seduce**. ver. 14. Ex 34:15. Nu 25:1, 2. 2 K ✻21:9. Ac 15:20, 29. 1 C 8:10-12. 10:18-21, 28. **my servants**. Re +7:3. 1 S ✻2:24. **to commit**. ver. +14, 22. Re 17:1, 2. Nu ▸25:1. 1 C 5:1. **to eat**. 1 C ✻10:28.

21. **space**. Re 9:20, 21. Je 8:4-6. Da 4:28, 29. Lk ✻13:6-9. Ro +✻2:4, 5. 9:22. 1 P 3:20. 2 P ✻3:9, 15. **to repent**. Lk +✻13:3, 5. **repented not**. ver. 4, 15. Re ✻9:20, 21. 16:9, 11. Ro +2:4.

22. **will cast**. Mt 8:6, 14. 9:2. Mk 7:30g. **a bed**. Ex 21:18. Ps ◑41:3. **and them**. Re 17:2. 18:3, 9. 19:18-21. Pr ✻6:26. Ezk 16:37-41. 23:29, 45-48. Ro ✻2:5. 1 C ✻5:9. He +✻13:4. Ja ✻4:4, 5. ✻5:5. **great tribulation**. Mt +✻24:21. **except**. Re ✻9:20, 21. Je 36:3. Ezk ✻18:30-32. ✻33:11-15. Zp 3:7. Lk +✻13:3, 5. Ac ✻8:22. 1 C 3:13-15. ✻11:32. 2 C 12:21. 2 T +✻2:25, 26.

23. **will kill**. Ge ✻2:17. 2 K 10:7. Ezk 18:20. 33:27. Mt +✻10:28. Ro ✻6:23. Re ✻20:14. **her children**. Ps 137:9. **with death**. Re 6:8. 18:8. Ex 5:3. Le 26:25. 2 S 24:13. **and all**. ver. 7, 11. Dt 13:11. 17:13. 19:20. 21:21. Zp 1:11. **I am he**. Ne +✻9:6. Mt +✻3:3. **which searcheth**. ♫22C2, Ge +3:9. 1 S +✻16:7. 1 K 14:5, 6. ◑✻8:39. 2 K 5:25, 26. √6:12. 8:11, 12. 1 Ch +✻28:9. 29:17. 2 Ch 6:30. Ps ▸7:9. 26:2. 44:21. 139:1. Je 11:20. +✻▸17:10. 20:12. Da ✻2:28, 29. Ml 3:2. Jn +✻2:24, 25. 4:19. +✻21:17. Ac 1:24. 5:4. Ro +✻8:27. He +✻4:13. **the reins**. ♫121I1, Ge +3:7. **and hearts**. 1 S +✻16:7. Ps ✻66:18. Pr 15:11. 16:2. Ezk 11:5. Mt 9:4. **and I will**. Re 20:12. Ps 62:12. Is 3:10, 11. Mt +✻16:27. Lk +✻14:14. Ro ✻2:5-11. √14:12. 2 C ✻5:10. Ga 6:5. 1 P 1:17. **according**. Re 18:6. 20:12. 22:12. Ps 7:9. ▸62:12. Je 11:20. ✻17:10.

24. **Thyatira**. ver. +18. **known**. ♫121C2A1, Jb +19:25. **the depths of Satan**. ver. +9. Re ✻12:9. 13:14. Is 28:14-18. Da 7:25. 8:23-25. Ro 8:38, 39. 1 C ◑2:10. 2 C √2:11. √11:3, 13-15. Ep ✻6:11, 12. 2 Th ✻2:9-12. **I will**. 2 K 9:25, 26. Is 13:1. Mt 11:28-30. Ac 15:28.

25. **that**. Re ✻3:3, 11. Ac +✻11:23. Ro ✻12:9. 1 C +✻15:2. 1 Th +✻5:21. He +✻3:6. +✻4:14. +✻10:23. **hold fast**. ver. 13. Re 3:11. Ps 119:33. Ga 5:1. ✻6:9. 2 T ✻1:13, 14. **till I come**. Re +✻1:7. ✻22:7, 20. Jn +✻14:3. +21:22, 23. 1 C ✻4:5. ✻11:26. 2 P ✻3:10.

26. **he**. See on ver. ✻7, ✻11, ✻17. Re ✻3:5, 12, 21. ✻21:7. Ro ✻8:37. 1 J ✻5:5. **overcometh**. Re ✻12:11. **keepeth**. Mt ✻24:13. Lk +✻8:13-15. Jn ✻6:29. √8:31, 32. Ro +✻2:7. 16:26. 1 Th ✻3:5. He +✻10:38, 39. Ja ✻2:20. 1 J ✻2:19. ✻3:23. **my works**. Jn +6:28, 29. **unto the end**. Mt +10:22. He +3:6. **to him will I give**. Re ✻3:21. +✻5:10. ✻20:4. ✻22:5. Ps ▸2:8. ✻49:14. Da ✻7:18, 22, 27. Mt +✻19:28. Lk +✻22:29, 30. 1 C ✻6:2-4. **power over**. Ps +✻149:7-9. Mt ✻25:21, 23. Lk ✻19:17, 19.

27. **he shall rule**. Re ✻12:5. ✻19:15. 20:6. Ps ✻2:8, 9. ✻49:14. +✻149:5-9. Is 9:6. Da ✻7:22. Mt +2:6. 28:18. **rod of iron**. Re 12:5. 19:15. Ps ▸2:9. +✻149:9. Is 10:24. 1 C 4:21. He ✻1:8. **be broken**. Is ✻30:14. 60:12. Je 19:11. Da ✻2:44, 45. Mi 4:13. **even**. Mt +✻11:27. Lk +✻22:29. Jn ✻17:24.

28. **give him**. Re ✻22:16. Da 12:3. Lk ✻1:78, 79. 2 P ✻1:19. **morning star**. This is an admittedly obscure text. Peters writes, "The 'morning star' comes before 'the day' dawns; the 'sun' shines during 'the day'; Jesus is both. As the morning star, He is seen by few: as

the sun, He is seen by all. Those who watch not merely for the sun, but for the morning star, properly heed the cautions and injunctions relating to the posture of watching" (*Theocratic Kingdom*, vol. 2, p. 317). In another place Peters states "We have in the 'Morning Star' an implied reference to the first stage of the Advent, the thief-like coming for the saints, and to obtain it indicates that we are worthy of the better resurrection, or (if living) of the translation. The mention of this in such a connection is also exceedingly significant of the exaltation of the saints to coheirship with the Christ when the morning breaks" (Peters, *Theocratic Kingdom*, vol. 2, p. 418). Re ✻22:16. Nu 24:17. 2 S √23:4, 5. Jb 7:21. 38:7. Ps 30:5. 46:5mg. 49:14, 15. 59:16. 88:13. 90:14. 101:8. 110:2, 3. 130:6. 143:8. Is 8:19, 20mg. 17:14. 21:11, 12. 26:19. 60:3. Ho 5:15. ✻6:3. Zp ✻2:2, 3. 3:5. Ml 4:1-3. Lk +✻21:36. Ro 13:12. 1 Th 4:13-18. 2 P √1:19.

29. **hath an ear**. ♫8, Ps +118:1. See on ver. ✻7. Re 13:9. Ne ✻8:3. Je 13:15. Lk 8:8. 14:35. **hear**. ♫147A, Ge +50:24. **the Spirit**. Gr. *pneuma*, Mt +3:16. Jn +7:39. **unto the churches**. Re 22:16. 1 Th 4:13-18. 2 P 1:19.

REVELATION 3

The epistle of Christ to the angel of the church of Sardis; consisting of reproofs, exhortations, warnings, and promises to the pious remnant, 1-6. That to the angel of the church in Philadelphia, replete with encouragement, 7-13. That to Laodicea; comprising severe rebukes of lukewarmness and spiritual pride; connected with instruction, counsels, calls to repentance, invitations, and promises, 14-22.

1. **unto**. See on Re 1:11, +20. **the church**. ver. 7n. Re 1:4, 20. **Sardis**. i.e. *the sun; red ones; prince of joy*, ✻S#4554g. ver. 4. Re 1:11. Sardis, the once proud capital of Lydia, and the residence of its opulent monarchs, is now reduced to a wretched Turkish village called Sart, the habitation of herdsmen, buffaloes, and oxen, situated at the foot of mount Tmolus, on the banks of the Pactolus, between 30 and 40 miles east from Smyrna. The ruins of Sardis are peculiarly grand, and lift up their heads, as if to assert their ancient glory; but it now contains not a single Christian family. Re +1:16. **he that**. See on Re 1:4. 4:5. ✻5:6. Jn ✻1:16, 32, 33. 3:34. ✻7:37-39. ✻15:26, 27. 20:22. Ac ✻2:33. ✻10:38. 1 P 1:11. **Spirits**. Gr. *pneuma*, Lk +24:37. **seven stars**. Re ✻1:+16, 20. ✻2:1. **I know**. ver. 8, 15. See on Re ✻2:2, 9, 13, 19. Ps ✻44:21. **hast a name**. Ge +✻11:4. **art dead**. Lk 8:14. ✻15:+24, 32. 1 C +✻11:30. Ep ✻2:1, 5. ✻5:14. Col ✻2:13. 1 T ✻5:6. 2 T 3:4. He 6:1. 9:14. Ja ✻2:26. Ju ✻12.

2. **watchful**. Re 16:15. Is 56:10. 62:6, 7. Ezk 34:8-10, 16. Zc 11:16. Mt 24:+42-51. 25:13. ✻26:41. Mk ✻13:33-37. 14:37, 38. Lk +✻21:36. Ac +✻20:28-31. 1 C ✻16:13. 1 Th ✻5:6. 2 T ✻4:1-5. 1 P ✻4:7. 5:8. **strengthen**. Re 2:4. Dt 3:28. Jb 4:4, 5. 16:5. Is 35:3. Ezk 34:4, 16, 21. Lk 22:31, 32. Ac 18:23. 1 Th 3:3. T ✻1:16. He ✻2:1. ✻10:38. **ready to die**. Zc 11:9. **thy works**. 1 K ✻11:4. ✻15:3. 2 Ch ✻25:2. Is ✻57:12. Da ✻5:27. Mt 6:2-4. ✻23:5, 28-38. **perfect**. Ge 6:9. +✻17:1. Dt ✻18:13. Mt +✻5:48. Ac 14:26. 2 C ✻13:9. Ph ◑√3:12. He ✻6:1. **before God**. ver. 12. Jn +20:17.

3. **Remember**. See on Re ✻2:5. Ezk 16:61-63. ✻20:43. ✻36:31. Ga 5:7. He ✻2:1. +✻3:14. ✻10:32. 2 P

1:13. 3:1. **received**. Mt *10:8. Col +*2:6. **and heard**. Dt *4:9. Mk +*4:24. Lk +*8:18. Ac 19:10. Col 1:5, 6. **and hold fast**. ver. *11. See on Re *2:25. Jn +*8:31. 1 T *6:20. 2 T *1:13. *3:14. T 1:9. Ja +*1:25. **repent**. ver. *19. See on Re *2:5, 16, 21, 22. Je 18:8. **If**. ꟿ184C, Mt +4:9. **watch**. Lk +*21:36. 1 C 16:13. 1 P 5:8. **I will come**. Note ver. 5, Re 13:10 and 21:6 for other marked allusions of Revelation to known sayings of Christ. ver. 11. Re +1:3. +2:5. *16:15. Mt *24:42, ▸43. Lk *12:39, 40. 1 Th *5:2, 4, 5, 6. 2 P *3:10. **as a thief**. Christ's coming as a thief has no reference to His coming for the church at the rapture. His thief-like coming occurs at the day of the Lord. Since Paul tells the Thessalonians they were well acquainted with the prophetic truth concerning the day of the Lord, this day is not to be identified with the Rapture, about which Paul did need to write to clarify their understanding. The day of the Lord begins with the Great Tribulation, and ends with the close of the Millennium. Those who shall "not escape" (1 Th 5:3) are those who are not brethren, who fail to watch and pray (Lk +*21:36), are not counted worthy to escape, and therefore go on into the tribulation period (see J. B. Smith, *A Revelation of Jesus Christ*, Appendix 8, pp. 328, 329). Re 16:15. Mt *24:42-44. Lk 12:39, 40. 1 Th *5:2. 2 P *3:10. **not know**. Mt 24:42n. *25:13. Mk *13:32n, 33, 36. Ac 1:6n, 7n. 1 Th ◐5:4. **I will come**. Ro 13:11.

4. **Thou hast**. ꟿ127, Re +2:6. **a few**. Mt +√7:14. **names**. ꟿ121T2, Ac +1:15. Re 11:13g. Ac 1:15. **even**. 1 K √19:18. Is 1:9. Ezk +*9:4. Ro 11:4-6. **which**. Re 7:14. 14:4. 19:8. Is 52:1. 59:6. 61:3, 10. √64:6. Zc 3:3-6. Mt *22:11. 2 T 3:5. Ju *23. **with me**. Jn 17:24. **in white**. ver. 5, 18. Re 4:4. 6:11. *7:9, 13, 14. *19:8, 14. Est 8:15. Ps *45:14. 68:14. Ec *9:8. SS *4:7. Is 61:10. Zc 3:4. Mk 16:5. Ep *5:25-27. **are worthy**. Re 16:6. Is 56:3-7. Mt 10:11. +22:8. Lk *20:35. +√21:36. 2 Th 1:5.

5. **overcometh**. See on Re +2:7. *12:11. 1 S 17:25. Mt *7:21. **the same**. See on ver. 4. Re 19:8. **clothed**. Mt ◐22:11-13. Ro 4:5. **in white**. ver. +*4. **blot**. Logically, a name cannot be blotted out of the Book of Life unless it has been written in the Book of Life. The Book of Life is not merely the book of the living, but the book of the redeemed. God has kept such a book from the beginning, witness the expression "my book" (Ex 32:33), a book therefore not to be identified as the census list of the nation of Israel! A person's name is blotted out because of sin (Ex 32:33), but here it is promised that those who are overcomers will not be blotted out of the Book of Life. Ex *32:32, ▸33. Dt 9:14. 25:19. 29:20. Ne *13:14. Ps *▸69:28. 109:13. Ac ◐3:19. Ro 9:3. **the book of life**. ꟿ22D5K1A, Ex +32:32. Re *13:8. 17:8. *20:12, 15. *21:27. 22:19. Ps 33:16-22. 56:8. 139:16. Is 4:3. 65:6. Ezk 13:9. Da 12:1. Lk *10:20. Ph *4:3. He 12:23. **confess**. Ml *3:17. Mt +*▸10:32. Lk 12:8. Ju *24. **my Father**. Mt +*25:21, 34. **before his angels**. Lk +12:8.

6. **hath an ear**. ꟿ8, Ps +118:1. See on Re 2:7. Mt 11:15. 13:9, 43. **let him hear**. ꟿ147A, Ge +50:24. Pr *1:23. **the Spirit**. Gr. Mt +3:16.

7. **to the angel**. See on Re 1:11, +20. 2:1. **the church**. Though each of the seven letters is addressed to a specific church, Gerald B. Stanton notes that "very probably each letter went to all seven (*cf*. Re 2:29, "what the Spirit saith unto the churches")" so that "it is evident that the letter to the church in Philadelphia

has more than local application" (*Kept From The Hour*, pp. 47, 48). **Philadelphia**. Philadelphia, so called from its founder, Attalus Philadelphus, still exists in the town called Allah-shear, "the city of God," "a column in a scene of ruins." It is situated on the slopes of three or four hills, the roots of mount Tmolus, by the river Cogamus, twenty-seven miles E.S.E. from Sardis, about long. 28 degrees 40 minutes, lat. 38 degrees 23 minutes. The number of houses is said to be about 3000, of which 250 are Greek, the rest Turkish; and the Christians have twenty-five places of worship, five of them large and regular churches, a resident bishop, and twenty inferior clergy. Re 1:11. **he that is holy**. Re *4:8. 6:10. Le *20:26. Ps +*16:10. *22:3. 30:4. 89:18. *145:17. Is 6:3. 30:11. 41:14, 16, 20. 47:4. 48:17. 49:7. 54:5. 55:5. +*57:15. Mk +*1:24. Lk 4:34. Jn *10:30. Ac *3:14. *4:27. **he that is true**. ꟿ41, Ge +10:1. ver. 14. Re +*1:5. 6:10. *15:3. 16:7. *19:2, 11. 21:5. Pr *8:7. Mt 24:35. Jn √14:6. +*17:3. 1 J *5:20. **the key**. ꟿ121S1, Ge +49:10. By Metonymy of the Adjunct, whereby the sign is put for the thing signified, "key" is put for governmental authority, of which it is the sign. Re +1:18. Is ▸22:22. Lk +*1:32. **of David**. Re *5:5. Is +*9:7. **he that openeth**. ꟿ121S3B, Jb +12:14. Re 5:3-5, 9. Jb 11:10. 12:14. Mt *16:19. Lk +*24:45. Ac *16:14. **no man shutteth**. Mt 23:13. **and shutteth**. Mt *25:10. Lk *13:25.

8. **I know**. ver. 1, 15. See on Re 2:2, 19. Ps 33:16-22. **an open door**. ver. 7. Re *4:1. Jn *10:9. Ac +14:27. 1 C *16:9. 2 C *2:12. Ep *2:18, 19. Col *4:3. He *10:19, 20. **a little strength**. Da 11:34. 2 C √12:8-10. Ph *4:13. **and hast kept**. ꟿ148, Ge +8:22. ver. 10. Re 22:7. Jn *14:21-24. 15:20. +*17:6. 2 T *1:14. 4:7. **hast not denied**. See on Re 2:13. Pr 30:9. Mt *10:32, 33. 26:70-72. Lk 12:9. Ac 3:13, 14. 1 T +*5:8. 1 J *2:22, 23. Ju *4.

9. **the synagogue**. See on Re 2:9. **are not**. Ro *2:28, 29. **I will make them to**. Ex 11:8. *12:30-32, 36. 1 S 2:36. 2 K *1:13. Est 6:13. *8:17. Jb *42:8-10. Is ▸45:14. ▸49:23. ▸60:14. ▸66:23. Da *2:46, 47. Zc *8:20-23. Ac 16:37-39. **and worship**. Re 4:10, 11. Mt 8:2. 12:36. +*14:33. Ph *2:10, 11. **I have loved**. ver. 19. Re +*1:5. Ps *146:8. Is ▸43:4. Je 31:3.

10. **hast kept**. Jn +*17:6. 1 T ◐*4:1, 2. **the word**. Re 1:9. 13:10. 14:12. **of**. ꟿ181E, Ge +3:24. **my patience**. Re +1:9. 2:2, 19. 13:10. 14:12. Lk *21:19. He *12:1, 2. Ja 1:3, 12. 1 P *1:6, 7. **I also**. Pr *1:10. *3:25, 26. +*4:23. Mt +*6:13. *26:41. 1 C +*10:13. Ep *6:13. 2 P +*2:9. **will keep**. Ge 19:28, 29. Ex +*12:13. Ps 12:7. +17:5. 91:8. *94:18. Pr *2:8. Is +*26:20. 33:16. +*57:2. Hab 3:16. Zp 2:3. Lk +√21:36. 22:31, 32. Jn 17:11. Ro +*5:9. 1 C +*10:13. 1 Th 5:9. **from**. Gr. *ek*, lit. out of. Some who favor a post-tribulational rapture of the church understand the primary force of this preposition to mean "out from within" (Robert Gundry, *The Church and the Tribulation*, p. 55). Gundry asserts "the preposition *ek* appears in John's writings approximately 336 times, far more often than in the writings of any other NT author. There is not a single instance where the primary thought of emergence, or origin, cannot fit, indeed, does not best fit the thought of the context. Surely the invariability of meaning in such a high number of occurrences establishes the Johannine usage" (p. 57). Gundry's unexamined universal assertion is not supported by a careful examination of the particular instances. We have met

this claim for a universal meaning for *ek* in other connections, and fully proved by the citation of specific instances, that *ek* may sometimes mean not "out of," as from within, but *from*, as here (Ac 8:39n). J. B. Smith points out that if *ek* means "out of," in the sense of being preserved in the hour of temptation, applying this construction to the acclaimed parallel in Jn 17:15, "shouldst keep them out of (the evil one)," the words "would really mean safe in the evil one, that is, safe in the devil. Thus the absurdity of such an interpretation becomes apparent" (Comm. on Revelation, Appendix 10, p. 333). A much more satisfactory parallel is Jn √12:27, which, taken with its parallels (Mt 26:38. Mk 14:36. Lk 22:42. Jn 18:11. Ps 42:5, 6) proves that, when Jesus in his human nature prayed "remove this cup from me," and the parallel or equivalent request, "save me from this hour," he was not praying to be spared during the hour, but to be kept from it, which settles the meaning of the expression here. Ps 27:5. 32:6. Jn √12:27. 17:15g. Ro +*5:9. 2 C 1:10. 1 Th +*1:10. 2 P 2:9. **the hour**. Re 2:10. **of temptation**. Da +*12:1. Zp 1:14-18. Mt √24:21, 22. **come upon**. Da *7:21, 25. 2 Th √2:8-12. **all the world**. Gr. *oikoumene*, Mt +24:14. The use of this phrase shows this testing is not to be confined to "an hour of trial or tribulation upon the churches of John's day" (Dake), for no such world-encompassing tribulation occurred in John's day. Rather, this time of testing "may be equated with the tribulation yet to come," which proves that the Philadelphian church, "as well as the other churches, is representative of the church universal" (J. B. Smith, *Comm. on Revelation*, p. 88). Re 13:3, 8. Mk 14:9. Lk 2:1. Ro *1:8. **to try**. Is *24:17. Da +*11:35. *12:10. Zc *13:9. Mk *13:13, 19. Ja *1:3, 12. 1 P *4:12. **that dwell**. Re 6:10. 8:13. 11:10. *12:12. *13:◐6, 8, 12, 14. 14:6. 17:2, 8. Is 24:17. He ◐11:13. **upon the earth**. Re +*6:10.

11. **I come**. ver. 3. Re 1:1, 3. 2:5. *22:7, 12, 20. Zp *1:14. Mt 24:27. 25:6. 1 C 15:52. Ph *4:5. Ja *5:9. 2 P *3:8-10. **hold**. See on ver. *3. Re *2:13, 25. He *10:35-39. **that no man**. 1 C 3:8, 14. 9:17. Col *2:18. 3:24. 2 J +*8. **thy crown**. Re *2:10. 4:4, *10. 1 C *9:25. 2 T 2:5. *4:8. Ja +*1:12. 1 P *5:3, 4.

12. **overcometh**. See on Re 2:+7, 10. *12:11. 17:14. Ps 125:1. 1 J 2:13, 14. 4:4. **pillar**. 1 K *7:21. 2 Ch 3:17. Is 22:23. Je 1:18. Ga 2:9. 1 T 3:15. **the temple**. or, sanctuary. Re 7:15. 11:1, 2, 19. 14:15, 17. 15:5, 6, 8. 16:1, 17. 21:22. Ps *23:6. *65:4. *92:13. Mt +23:16. 1 C *3:9. Ep *▶2:19-22. 1 P *2:5. **no more out**. 𝄋158, Mt +5:18. 1 Ch=23:25, 26. Ps *23:6. 27:4. **I will write**. Re *2:17. 14:1. *22:4. **him the name**. Nu +*6:27. Jn +1:12. 14:13. **my God**. ver. 2. Jn +20:17. **and the name**. Ezk ▶48:35. **the city**. Re *21:2, 10-27. Ps 48:8. 87:3. Ga *4:26, 27. He *12:22. 13:14. **new Jerusalem**. Re √21:2. **cometh down**. Re 21:2, 10. **out of heaven**. Is 11:9. Ph 3:20, 21. 1 P +*1:4n. **my God**. Jn +20:17. **my new name**. Re +2:17. 22:4. Is ▶62:2. ▶65:15. Mt 1:21, 23. Ac 11:26. Ep 3:15.

13. **hath an ear**. 𝄋8, Ps +118:1. Re 2:7. Pr 1:17, 33. Mk 4:9, 23. 7:16. **hear**. 𝄋147A, Ge +50:24. **the Spirit**. Gr. *pneuma*, Mt 3:16.

14. **the angel**. Re 1:11, +20. 2:1. **of the Laodiceans**. or, in Laodicea. Re 1:11. Col *2:1. *4:13-16. **the Amen**. Is ▶65:16. Jn 8:14. 2 C *1:20. **the faithful**. ver. 7. Re +*1:5. 19:11. 21:5. 22:6. Ps ▶89:37. Is *11:5. Je 42:5. **and true**. Is *65:16. **witness**. Is 55:4. Mt 24:35. Jn

1:18. *18:37. **the beginning**. This is a favorite Arian prooftext, cited to prove that Jesus is not eternal, but had a beginning, Jesus being understood by them to be the first-created creature of God, through whom God created all else in the universe. The underlying Greek word, *arche*, may be understood in a passive sense, and rendered "the beginning," as the A.V., or more correctly understood in the active sense, and rendered "the beginner," source, origin, or principle of creation. Since God is eternal, and Jesus is God, the passive sense is not suited to the context, as being out of harmony with the many representations of Christ John has already given, whereby he in citing or alluding to Old Testament passages has applied to Jesus Christ in the book of Revelation what is in the Old Testament spoken of Jehovah (see related notes at Ac 11:21n. Col 1:16n. 1 P +*2:3n). Herman Gebhardt states "that qualities, actions, and conditions which belong specifically to God, are also ascribed to Christ, and to Him only," and "in Old Testament expressions things which otherwise belong to God are frequently affirmed of Christ. It is said of Christ that 'His head and His hairs were white like wool,' Re 1:14; and in Da 7:9, God is so represented. The eyes of Christ are as a flame of fire, Re 1:14; 2:18; 19:12; and in the same words God's omniscience is symbolized as directed with holy indignation against all unrighteousness, Da 10:6. The feet of Christ are 'like unto fine brass, as if they burned in an oven,' Re 1:15; 2:18; the same image represents God's power in treading down the wicked, Da 10:6; Ezk 1:7. The voice of Christ is as the voice of many waters, Re 1:15; and we find a similar representation of God's power against His enemies, Da 10:6; Ezk 1:24; 43:2; Ps 93:3. Christ's countenance is as the sun shining in his strength, Re 1:16; and so it is said of God, Da 10:6 (compare Jg 5:21). The seer fell down before Christ as if dead, Re 1:17; a similar effect was wrought by the appearance of God, Ex 33:20; Is 6:5; Ezk 1:28; Da 8:17, 18; 10:7-9. Christ says, 'I am He that searcheth the reins and hearts, and will give unto every one of you according to your works,' Re 2:23; and we read that 'the righteous God trieth the hearts and reins,' Ps 7:9, and that He 'renders to every man according to his work,' Ps 62:12. Christ says, 'As many as I love I rebuke and chasten,' Re 3:19; and in Pr 3:12 we read 'whom the Lord loveth He correcteth.' Christ calls Himself 'the Amen,' Re 3:14; and the same expression is used of God, Is 65:16. The Lamb has 'seven horns and seven eyes, which are the seven Spirits of God sent forth into all the earth,' Re 5:6; and in Zc 4:10 we read of 'the eyes of the Lord, which run to and fro through the whole earth.' According to Re 7:17, the Lamb will feed His people, and lead them to fountains of living waters; and the same thing is said of Jehovah in Is 49:10. What is said of the anger of Christ, Re 19:15 (compare Re 14:10, 14-16), is drawn from a similar passage respecting God in Is 63:1-6. The 'vesture dipped in blood,' worn by Christ, Re 19:12, is said to have been worn by God, Is 63:1, 2" (*The Doctrine of the Apocalypse*, pp. 85, 86). Gebhardt asks, "What exposition is demanded by the laws of language? Without further delay I reply, that had the seer written 'the beginning of the creatures (*ktismata*) of God,' or had he written 'the first, or the first-born, or the first-fruit (*protos, prototokos, aparxee*) of the creation of God,' then the expression might be understood to denote the first created, or that which precedes all things, the first creature in time and rank. But the seer has written *ee arkee tees ktiseos tou theou*, which can mean nothing else than *principium creationis*, the principle, the *en o, di ou, eis o*, of the creation of God. After this affirmation of the literal sense, I may remark that it finds confirmation in Re 1:17, 18; 2:8" (p. 92, 93). "Are not all the expressions concerning Christ, quoted above, so many proofs that John, by 'the beginning of the creation of God,' cannot have meant the earliest and greatest of creatures, but a being above creation?" (Gebhardt, *The Doctrine of the Apocalypse*, p. 93). Waterland defines *Arkee* (beginning), "that is, author or efficient cause" (*Works*, vol. 2, p. 53). T#961‡. Re 21:6. 22:13. Ge 1:1. 49:3, LXX. Dt 21:17. Pr ▶8:22. Jn 1:◑+*1, ◑2, ◑3, 18. 5:17, 19. ◑+*8:35. 1 C √8:6. Ep 3:9. Col *1:13, ▶15, 16, 18. He 1:2, 10.

15. **I know.** ver. 1, 8. Re 2:2, 19. **art neither.** Re *2:4. 2 K *17:41. Mt *24:12. Ph *1:9. 2 Th *1:3. 1 P 1:22. **I would.** Dt *5:29. Ps *81:11-13. 1 C 4:8g. 2 C 12:20. **thou.** Jsh *24:15-24. 1 K *18:21. Pr 23:26. Ezk *20:39. Ho 7:8. *10:2. Zp *1:5, 6. Mt *6:24. *10:37. *12:30. Lk 14:27, 28. 1 C 16:22. Ja *1:8. **wert cold.** Mt 24:12. 2 P 2:21. **or hot.** Nu 14:14. Jsh 14:8. Mt *5:16. Ro +*12:11.

16. **lukewarm.** Nu 32:6. Jsh 18:3. Jg 5:16, 17, 23. 2 Ch 24:5. Ne *3:5. 13:11. Ps 123:4. Is 32:9. 47:8. *64:7. +*66:4. Je *9:3. +*48:10. Ezk +*16:49. +*33:31, 32. Ho 10:2. Am 6:1. Zp *1:12. Hg *1:2-11. Mt 22:5. 24:12. Ro ◑+*12:11. **and neither.** Jsh +*24:15. 1 K *18:21. **I will spue thee out.** Re *2:5. Le *18:25, 28. 20:22. Dt *32:19. Je 14:19. *15:1-4. Zc 11:8, 9. He 10:28, 29.

17. **I am rich.** Re *2:9. Pr *13:7. Je *9:23. Ho ▶12:8. Am 6:1-7. Zc √11:5. Mt *6:8. Lk 1:53. *6:24. *12:21. 18:11, 12. Ro 11:20, 25. +*12:3. 1 C 4:8-10. 2 C *8:9. 1 T +*6:9. **and.** ʃ148, Ge +8:22. **increased.** Ps 62:10. **have need.** Dt 8:12-14. Pr *26:12. *30:9. Je 2:31. Mt *9:12. **knowest not.** T#25. Pr +16:25 (T#704). Ho 7:8, *9. Lk *6:42. Ro 2:17-23. 1 C *8:1, 2. **wretched.** Is *1:5, 6. Zc 3:3. Mt +*5:3. Ro *7:24. **blind.** Is *42:18-20. Mt +23:16. Jn √9:39-41. Ep 1:18. 2 P *1:5-9. **naked.** Re 16:15. Ge *3:7, 10, 11. Ex 32:25.

18. **counsel.** Ps 16:7. +*32:8. 73:24. 107:11. Pr 1:25, 30. 8:14. 19:20. Ec 8:2. Is 9:6. Je *32:19. Ho *13:9. Ep *1:11. Col 2:3. 1 J *2:1. **buy.** Pr 3:13-17. *8:18, 19. 23:23. Is *55:1. Mt *13:44. 25:9. **gold.** Ml 3:3. 1 C 3:12, 13. 1 P +*1:7. **that thou.** Re 2:9. Lk 12:21. 2 C *8:9. 1 T +*6:18. Ja +*2:5. **white raiment.** ver. +*4, 5. Re *7:13, 14. 16:15. *19:8, 14. Ps 51:7. 2 C 5:3. **be clothed.** Re 16:15. Ge *3:7, 21. Is *61:10. 2 C 5:3. Ph 3:9. **the shame.** Re 16:15. Is 47:3. Je 13:26. Da +*12:2. Mi 1:11. Na 3:5. **not appear.** 2 C 5:10. **anoint.** Jn 9:6-11. 1 C *1:21. 1 J +*2:20, 27. **mayest see.** Is *42:7.

19. **as many.** ver. 9. Dt *8:5. 2 S *7:14. Jb *5:17. Ps 6:1. *39:11. 94:10. *119:67, 71, 75. Pr *▶3:11, 12. 15:10, 32. *22:15. Is *26:16. Je *7:28. 10:24. *30:11. *31:18. Zp *3:2. 1 C *11:32. 2 C 6:9. He *12:5-11. Ja *1:12. **I rebuke.** T#508. Dt +8:2 (T#4). Jb +5:7 (T#2). 1 S +2:7 (T#3). Pr 27:6. He 12:5-8. **and chasten.** 2 S *7:14. Ps *94:12. He 12:5-13. **be zealous.** Nu 25:11-13. Ps 69:9. Jn 2:17. Ro *12:11. 2 C *7:11. Ga *4:18. T √2:14. **repent.** ver. 3. Re *2:5, 16, 21, 22.

20. **I stand.** SS *5:2-4. Lk *12:36. **at the door.** Jb 23:3. Mt 24:33mg. Ac 17:27. Ja +*5:9. **and knock.** Mt 7:7. Lk 11:9. *12:36. **if any man.** ʃ184C, Mt +4:9. Re 22:17. Da 11:33n. Jn *6:37. Ro √14:12. 2 P *3:9. **hear.** Mk +*4:24. Lk +*8:18. Jn √5:24. Ro √10:17. **my voice.** Pr 1:20. 9:3. SS 5:2. Jn +*10:3, 5, 27. **and open.** Dt *30:19. Jsh +*24:15. 1 K *18:21. SS 5:6. Jn √1:12. **I will come in.** T#839. Mt +*18:20. Lk *19:5, 6. 24:29, 30. Jn *14:18, +*20, 21-23. Ep *3:17. 1 J 1:3. **will sup.** Re *19:9. 2 S *9:7. SS *2:4. Lk *12:37. 17:8.

21. **overcometh.** See on Re 2:7. *12:11. Ga 3:3. 2 T *4:7. 1 J 5:4, 5. **will I grant.** Re 1:6. 2:26, 27. Mt 19:28. 24:46, 47. 25:21. Lk 19:17. 2 T 2:12. He 2:8, 10, 12, 13. 10:12, 13. **to sit.** Re 1:6. 2:26, 27. 20:4. 1 S *2:8. Zc *3:7. Mt +*19:28. Lk *12:43, 44. +*22:28-30. Jn 12:26. Ro +*8:17, 37. 1 C *6:2, 3. Ep 4:8. 2 T *2:12. **with me.** Re 20:6. Is +*55:1-3. Jn *12:26. Ep 1:3. **my throne.** ʃ22D3C2, Ps +45:6. Re 22:1. Ps 89:3, 4, 14, *29, 35, *36. Is 9:7. *16:5. Je 33:15, 17. Ezk *37:24, 25. Zc *6:13. Mt +*25:31. Lk +*1:32. Ac +*2:30. 2 T +*4:1. He 1:8. 2:8. **even.** Jn 16:33. **overcame.** Re 5:5. 6:2. *12:11. 17:14. Jn +*16:33. He *12:1-3. **and am set.** Re 5:6-8. 7:17. Ps *110:1. Da +*7:13, 14. Mt *26:64. 28:18. Mk +16:19. Jn 5:22, 23. 17:5, 22. Ep 1:20-23. Ph 2:9-11. **in his throne.** Re 1:4. 4:4. 22:1. Ps +*103:19. He 8:1. *10:12, 13. 12:2.

22. **hath an ear.** ʃ8, Ps +118:1. ver. 6, 13. See on Re 2:7, 11, 17. Lk 8:8. 14:35. **let him hear.** ʃ147A, Ge +50:24. Pr *1:20-23. **Spirit.** Gr. *pneuma*, Mt +3:16.

REVELATION 4

John, in vision, beholds heaven open, and the glory of God, as seated on an exalted throne, 1-3; surrounded by twenty-four elders, and four living creatures, who unite in adoring Him, as the Creator and Lord of all, 4-11.

1. **After.** Re ch. 1-3. **a door.** Ezk *1:1. 8:3. 11:24. Mt 3:16. Mk 1:10. Lk 3:21. Ac *7:56. 10:11. 22:17. 2 C *12:1, 2. **the first voice.** Re 1:10. 16:17. **I heard.** Is *6:8. Jn 5:25, 28. **trumpet.** Re 1:10. 8:2. Ex *19:19, 20. 1 C 15:52. 1 Th *4:16. **Come up hither.** This phrase is taken by many to prove the pretribulation Rapture of the church. This text, however, cannot prove anything about the Rapture, for to apply this to the Rapture one must take John to be a type of the church, the call to "come up hither" a type of the shout-command at the Rapture, and the third heaven as the destination of believers at the Rapture, all of which are tenuous connections at best. One cannot base a doctrine on a type, and proof of the timing of the Rapture must rest upon the direct statements of Scripture elsewhere. There is no need to search the Apocalypse for a direct mention of the pretribulation Rapture of the church, when the doctrine is clearly stated elsewhere. After all, the church or repentance is not mentioned in the entire gospel of John, but that need not be cause for concern that the doctrine of repentance or the church suffers thereby. Re 11:12. Ex ▶19:16, 20, 24. 24:12. 34:2, 3. 1 Th ?=4:13-18. **and I.** Re 1:19. 22:6. Jn 16:13. **things which.** This phrase is crucial to understanding the structure of the book of Revelation. In the light of Revelation 1:19, this phrase marks the third grand division of the book as the "things which must be here-

after." Interpreters differ widely in their understanding of the book of Revelation. Four major schools or systems of interpretation have been (1) the preterist, which takes all the events in the book to have been fulfilled in John's own day, the position held by many respected scholars and critics; (2) the historicist, which understands the prophecy to be in continuous fulfillment from John's day to the end of history; (3) the idealist, or spiritual scheme of interpretation, which takes the prophecies not as prophetic of future events but places a "spiritual" interpretation upon them, believing they reveal timeless truth about the conflict between good and evil, the spiritual history of the church, the ultimate victory of Christ over the powers of darkness, and are meant to provide spiritual comfort in times of trial; (4) the futurist, which holds that the majority of the book deals with end-time events which are still future. Most Bible-believing Christians today would probably opt either for the historicist or the futurist position of interpretation. The historicist position, reflected in the original notes of the *Treasury*, suffers from the inability of interpreters of this school to establish a specific verifiable criterion of judgment whereby positive identification for the fulfillment of specific prophecies can be proved to be historically fulfilled by specific events in world history, in historical instances of fulfillment to which most of the interpreters of this school could agree. The method requires the student of Revelation to go outside the Bible and seek for the fulfillment of predictions in the past events of world history, and to one not well taught in history the method is impossible to carry out, leaving the book of Revelation largely closed to the ordinary reader. The futurist position suffers, in the opinion of some, because it makes the book largely inapplicable to the original readers of the book, or to anyone since then, since the events are all placed in the future. A sufficient answer to such an objection is that the practical object of prophecy is to motivate us to holy living in watchful expectation of our Lord's return (Lk +√21:36. 2 P √3:14), and Scripture itself teaches us that we have "a more sure word of prophecy" to serve as a light in dark times (2 P 1:19). All Bible prophecy was written with both a near and a distant vantage point. A prophet predicted some things which transpired during his own lifetime, as verification that he was a true prophet of God (Dt 18:22), but also spoke of things in the distant future, which only the passing of time could verify (see the excellent discussion of these matters in R. B. Girdlestone, *The Grammar of Prophecy*, Chapter 3, "Tests of the Truth of Prophecy," pp. 16-24). The futurist position is the only position which can be entirely consistent in interpreting the prophecies of the book of Revelation in harmony with the rest of the prophecies of the Bible. Any system of prophetic interpretation, to be correct, must follow a consistent principle of literal interpretation for all of Scripture (using the same principle for prophetic as is used for non-prophetic portions), and must appeal to Scripture (not tenuous and unsubstantiated historic parallels) for its justification (Is +*8:20). What John writes in Revelation corresponds to the predictions in the Old Testament (Is 11:11n), the prophetic Discourses of Christ himself, such as the most significant Olivet discourse in Matthew 24 and parallels, and the prophetic teaching of the apostle Paul (T 2:13n). Futurists, consistent with the

divinely provided divisions of the book of Revelation (Re 1:19), place the events of chapters 4-22 in the future, understanding them to be events particularly connected with the Seventieth Week of Daniel's prophecy (Da +*9:27n), and the time of the Great Tribulation. Futurists are correct in understanding Bible prophecy to be a self-consistent whole, and interpret the book of Revelation in the light of the rest of the covenants and prophecies of Scripture, and find the explanation of the book of Revelation to be contained in the rest of Scripture, and the method of interpretation which is most satisfactory to be a comparison of Scripture with Scripture (2 P 1:20n). Re √1:19. Ge *41:25. Da ▶2:29.

2. **I was.** See on Re 1:10. *17:3. *21:10. Ezk 2:2. 3:12-14. 10:1. **the spirit.** Gr. *pneuma*, Mt +3:16. √121A4, Ezk +37:1. **a throne.** ver. 5, 9, 10. Re 5:1, 6, 7, 13. 6:16. 7:10, 15. 16:17. 19:4. 20:11-15. 21:5. 1 K *22:19. Ps *11:4. 103:19. Is *6:1. Je 17:12. Ezk *1:26, 28. 10:1. Da 7:9. Mt +5:34. 23:22. **and one sat.** ver. 9. Re 3:21. 5:1, 6, 7, 13. 6:16. 7:9-17. 12:5. 19:4. 21:5. 22:1-3. Ps ▶47:8. Is ▶6:1. Da 7:9. He 8:1.

3. **And he.** Da 7:13, 14. **like a jasper.** Re 21:11, 18, 19, 20. Ex *24:10. 28:20. 39:13. Ezk 1:26. 28:13. **sardine stone.** Re 21:20. Ex 28:17. 39:10. Ezk 28:13. **a rainbow.** Re 10:1. Ge *9:8-17. Ps *85:10. Is +*54:9, 10. Ezk 1:28. 1 Th 5:9. **round about.** Ezk ▶1:26. **like unto an emerald.** Re 21:19g. Ex 28:18. 39:11. Ezk 27:16. 28:13.

4. **round about.** ver. 6. Re 5:11. 7:11. **were four.** Re 11:16. 20:4. Mt +*19:28. Lk +*22:30. **four and twenty.** ver. 10. Re *5:5, 6, 8, 11, 14. 7:11, 13. 14:3. 19:4. 21:12-14. 1 Ch 24:1, 4, 5. **elders.** Ac 20:17. **clothed.** Re 3:+4, 5. 6:11. 7:9, 13, 14. 19:14. **white raiment.** Re 19:8. **crowns.** ver. 10. Re *1:5, 6. 2:10. *3:11. 9:7. Est 8:15. Ps 21:3. 2 T *4:8. He *12:23. 1 P 2:5, 9. **of gold.** Ex 39:27-30.

5. **proceeded.** Re *8:5. 11:19. *16:17, 18. Ex ▶19:16. 20:18. Ps 18:13, 14. 68:35. 77:18. Ezk ▶1:13. Jl 3:16. He 12:18-29. **thunderings.** Re 8:5. 10:3, 4. 11:19. 19:6. Ex 19:16. **voices.** Re 8:5. 10:3, 4. 11:19. 16:18-21. **seven lamps.** Ex *25:37. 37:23. 2 Ch 4:20. Ezk 1:13. Zc *4:2, 3, 11-14. Mt +25:1g. **burning.** Ge *15:17. **which are.** Re +1:4. **the seven.** Re *1:4. 3:1. 5:6. Mt *3:11. Ac 2:3. Ro +*8:9. 1 C 12:4-11. **Spirits.** Gr. *pneuma*, Lk +24:37.

6. **a sea.** Re *15:2. 21:18, 21. Ex *38:8. 1 K *7:23. Ps 77:19. **crystal.** Re 21:11. 22:1. Jb 28:17. Ezk ▶1:22, 26. ▶10:1. 1 C 13:12. **the midst.** Re 5:6. 7:17. Is ▶6:1. Ezk 1:4, 5. **round about.** ver. 4. Re 5:11. 7:11. **four.** Re 7:1. Zc 6:1, 5. **beasts.** Gr. living creatures. ver. 8, 9. Re 5:6, 8, 11, 14. 6:1, 6. 7:11. ◯13:1. 14:3. 15:7. 19:4. Ex 25:17-22. *26:1, 31. Nu 7:89. 1 S 4:4. 2 S 6:2. 1 K 6:29. Ps 80:1. 99:1. Is 37:16. Ezk ▶1:5, etc. 10:14. He 8:5. 9:5. **full.** ver. 8. Ezk ▶1:18. 10:12. **behind.** Re 5:1.

7. **the first beast.** ver. 6. Ge 49:9. Nu 2:2, etc. 23:24. 24:9. 1 K √7:29. Pr 28:2. Ezk ▶1:10. ▶10:14, 21. **like a calf.** Ezk 1:10. 1 C 9:9, 10. **as.** 1 C 14:20. **a flying.** Dt 28:49. 2 S 1:23. Is 40:31. Ezk 1:8, 10. Da 10:14. Da 7:4. Ob 4.

8. **the four beasts.** ver. +6. **six wings.** Ge *3:24. Ex 26:1. 25:18-22. 37:7-9. Is ▶6:2, etc. Ezk *1:6. 10:21, 22. 2 T 4:2. **full of eyes.** ver. 6. Ezk ▶1:18. ▶10:12. 1 T +*4:16. **and they.** Re 7:15. Is 62:1, 6, 7. Ac 20:31. 1 Th 2:9. 2 Th 3:8, 9. **rest not.** Gr. have no rest. Re

14:11. **day and night**. Lk +18:7. **Holy**. Re 3:7. Ex 15:11. Le *20:26. Ps *20:6. *22:3. *28:2. *99:5. Is)6:3. **Lord God**. Re 11:17. 15:3. 16:7, 14. 18:8. 19:6, 15. 21:22. 22:5, 6. Ge *17:1. Ps 91:1. Is 13:6. Jl 1:15. Am)4:13, LXX. Mt 4:7, 10. 22:37. Mk 12:30. Lk 1:16, 32, 68. 4:8, 12. 10:27. 20:37. Ac 2:39g. 2 C *6:18. **Almighty**. Re +*1:8. **which was**. ver. 4. Re +1:4, 8, 11. 11:17. 16:5. Is 43:3, 11. *48:12. 63:16. He +*13:8. **and is**. Re 1:18. Ex)3:14. Is)41:4. Jn +*8:58. *18:6.

9. **when**. Re *5:13, 14. 7:11, 12. **beasts**. ver. +6. **give**. Re +11:13. **glory**. ver. 11. Re √5:12, 13. 7:12. 19:1. 21:24, 26. Ro +11:36. 1 T 1:17. 2 P 1:17. **honor**. ver. 11. Re √5:12, 13. 7:12. 21:26. Jn √5:23. 1 T 1:17. 6:16. 2 P 1:17. **thanks**. Re 7:12g. **sat on**. ver. 2. Ps)47:8. Is)6:1. **who liveth**. Re +1:18. 5:14. 10:6. 15:7. Ex 15:18. Ps 48:14. Da)4:34.)6:26.)12:7. 1 T 1:17. He 7:8, 25. **for ever**. Gr. *aion*, Re +1:6.

10. **The four**. ver. +4. 1 Ch 25:1-31. **fall**. Re 5:8, 14. 7:11. 11:16. 19:4. Jb 1:20. Ps 72:11. Mt 2:11. **worship**. ver. 9. Re 7:11. 15:4. 22:8, 9. 1 Ch 29:20. 2 Ch 7:3. Ps 95:6. Mt 4:9, 10. Lk 24:52. **for ever**. Gr. *aion*, Re +1:6. **cast**. ver. 4. 1 Ch 29:11-16. Ps 115:1. 1 C 15:10. **crowns**. ver. 4. Re 2:10. 1 Th 2:19. 2 T 4:8. Ja 1:12. 1 P 5:4.

11. **worthy**. Re 5:2, 9, *12. 2 S 22:4. Ps 18:3. **O Lord**. ver. +8. **to receive**. Re 14:7. Dt 32:4. 1 Ch 16:28, 29. Ne 9:5. Jb 36:3. Ps *29:1, 2. 68:34. 96:7, 8. Da *7:13, 14. Mt 4:10. **glory**. ver. +9. Re 1:6. 3:14. Ps *115:1. **honor**. 1 T *6:14-16. **power**. Re 5:12. 7:12. 12:10. 19:1. 1 Ch +*29:11. Ju *25. **for thou**. Re 10:6. 14:7. Ge +*1:1. Ex *20:11. Ne +*9:6. Ps 102:25. 124:8. Pr 8:23-31. Is *40:26, 28. Je 10:11. 32:17. Jn *1:1-3. Ac +14:15. 17:24. Ro 1:25. Ep *3:9. Col *1:16, 17. He *1:2, 10. **and for**. Ge 1:31. Ps *33:9-11. Pr *16:4. Is 43:7. Da *4:34, 35. Mt 6:10. Jn 1:3. Ro *11:36. Ep +*1:11. He 1:2.

REVELATION 5

The apostle beholds a sealed book, which none could open, and he weeps on that account, 1-4. He is assured by one of the elders, that the Lamb had prevailed to open it; who accordingly comes and takes it, 5-7. He hears the living creatures and the elders adoring the Redeemer; while angels, and all creatures, join in the praises of "him who sits on the throne, and of the Lamb that was slain," 8-14.

1. **right hand**. Ps 20:6. *89:13. 98:1. **of him**. ver. 7, 13. Re +4:2. **that sat**. See on Re 4:3. Ps)47:8.)6:1. Da 7:9, 10. **a book**. ver. 7-9. Re 10:2, 8-11. Ex 32:15. Is *29:11. 34:16. Ezk)2:9, 10. **on the back**. Re 4:6g. **sealed**. Re 6:1. Dt 32:34. Is 8:16.)29:11. Je 32:14, 15. Da 8:26. *12:4-9. Mt 24:36. Ac 1:7.

2. **a strong**. Re 10:1. 18:21. Ps 103:20. **Who**. ver. 5. Le 25:25. Dt 25:5. Ru 4:1-6. Ps 24:3-5. Is 29:11, 12. 41:22, 23. **to open**. Re 3:7. Jb 11:10. **loose the seals**. Re 22:10. Da)12:4.

3. **no man**. ver. 13. Is 40:13, 14. 41:28. 63:5. Ro 11:34. **in heaven**. Ph 2:10.

4. **because**. Re 4:1. Da 12:8, 9. **no man**. Is 53:6. 64:6. Ro 3:23.

5. **one**. ver. 6, 8, 11, 14. Re 4:+4, 10. 7:13. **Weep**. Je 31:16. Lk 7:13. 8:52. 23:28. Jn 20:13. **the Lion**. √22E, Jn +1:29. Ge +*49:9, 10. Nu 24:9. He *7:14. **of Judah**. Ge 49:)9, +*10. Jg 20:18. 1 Ch +✱5:2. Ps +✱60:7. Mi +✱*5:2. Mt 1:2. 2:6. He +7:14. **the Root**.

√22H1D, Is +11:10. Re *22:16. Is)11:1, 10. Je +*23:5, 6. Ro 1:3. 15:12. **of David**. Ru 4:14, 21, 22. Ps 89:20-29. Is +*9:7. **hath prevailed**. Re 1:1. +3:21. 6:1. Jb 19:25. Ps 74:2. Pr 23:11. Is 43:14. Je 50:34. Lk 24:21. **to open**. Da *7:15, 16. **seven seals**. ver. 1. Re 6:1.

6. **in the midst of the throne**. Re *3:21. See on Re 4:4-6. **four beasts**. ver. 11, 14. Re +4:6. **the elders**. ver. 5, 11, 14. Re +4:4. **a Lamb**. An emblematical representation of our Savior's high-priesthood. √22E, Jn +1:29. ver. 9, 12, 13. Re 6:1, 16. 7:9-17. *12:11. +*13:8, 11. 14:1, 4, 10. 15:3. *17:14. 19:7, 9. 21:9, 14, 22, *23, 27. 22:1, 3. Ex *12:3-13. Is *53:7, 8. Jn *1:+29, 36. Ac 8:32. He 7:26. 1 P *1:19, 20. **slain**. Re *13:8. Ge 4:4. 22:8. 1 S 7:9. Is)53:7. Zc 12:10. Jn 20:25. **seven horns**. As a horn is the emblem of power, and seven the number of perfection, the seven horns may denote the almighty power of Jesus Christ. 1 S 2:1, 10. 2 S 22:3. Ps 75:4. 132:17. 148:14. La 2:3. Ezk 29:21. Da *7:14. 8:5, 20, 21. Mi 4:13. Hab 3:4. Lk 1:69. Ph *2:9-11. **seven eyes**. His infinite knowledge and wisdom; and especially "the treasures of wisdom" laid up in him, to be communicated to the Church by "the seven Spirits of God," i.e. *the Holy Spirit*. 2 Ch 16:9. Zc *3:9. 4:10. Jn +*2:24, 25. Col *2:3. **the seven Spirits**. Gr. *pneuma*, Lk +24:37. Re +1:4. See on Re 4:5. 1 C 12:4. **sent forth**. Zc 4:10. **all the earth**. Zc)4:10.

7. **took**. Zc 13:7. Jn 5:22. *16:15. Ac *4:12. Ph 2:6. **out**. ver. 1. See on Re 4:2, 3. **of him**. ver. 1, 13. Re +4:2. **that sat**. Ps)47:8. Is)6:1. Da 7:13, 14.

8. **the four**. ver. 14. See on Re 4:4, 8, 10. 7:10-12. 19:4. Jn √5:23. Ro *14:10-12. Ph *2:9-11. He *1:6. **fell down**. ver. 14. Re +4:10. ◐+*19:10. Mt *2:11. **harps**. Re 14:2, 3. 15:2. 1 S 10:5. 1 Ch 25:3. 2 Ch=5:12. 29:25. Ps 33:2. 43:4. 49:4. 71:22. 81:2. 92:3. 149:3. 150:3. Is ◐24:8. **golden vials**. Re +15:7. Ex 25:23-29. 27:3. 37:10-16. 1 K 7:45, 50. 2 Ch 4:22. Zc 14:20. **odors**. *or*, incense. Re 8:3, 4. 18:13. Ex 30:7, 8. 2 Ch=13:11. Ps)141:2. Ml 1:11. Lk *1:10. 2 C 2:15. **the prayers**. Re 8:3, 4. Ps 141:2. Ml 1:11. Lk 18:7, 8. Ac 10:4. **the saints**. Re +8:3. Da 7:18, 22, 27.

9. **sung**. Re 7:10-12. 14:3. Ex 15:1. Ps 33:3. *40:3. 96:1. 98:1. 107:1, 2. 144:9. 149:1. Is *42:10. 44:23. +*51:11. **new song**. Re *14:3. 15:3. 2 Ch=5:13. Ps)144:9. Ep 5:19. Col 3:16. **Thou art**. See on ver. 2, 3, 12. Re 4:11. **slain**. ver. 6, 12. Re *13:8. Ex 12:13. Ga 3:13. He *2:9. **redeemed us**. Most modern authorities omit "us," though it has considerable, if not overwhelming, authority in the MSS. Alford notes that it is more likely to have been inserted, considering the prevalent early interpretation of the elders as apostles and prophets, than omitted because they were imagined to be angels. For similar constructions with *ek* and the object not expressed, see Mt 25:8; 1 J 4:13. Tregelles retains "us," remarking "in verse 9, *eemas*, "us," should certainly be read. There was an opinion, many years ago, that it rested on but slight authority. This arose through an error in a reprint of Griesbach's text; so that he was supposed to have excluded it. On this misprint interpretations were based. Now of all collated MSS. the *Codex Alexandrinus* alone omits *eemas* (and this is thought to have some support from the Ethiopic version); and one MS. has *eemon* instead. The consent of the ancient versions has much weight in a case of this kind. It is surprising that some later editors have omitted it only on the authority men-

tioned" (S. P. Tregelles, *The Hope of Christ's Second Coming*, p. 69, 70 note). Hoskier, the greatest authority on the Greek text of the book of Revelation, calls this omission "and that huge blunder at v. 9" when listing a few of the solecisms of the Alexandrian MSS., further remarking, "Surely we ought not to be asked ever to follow A alone (as we *have* at v. 9, more is the pity)" (H. C. Hoskier, *Concerning the Genesis of the Versions of the N.T.*, p. 392, 393). A further issue in interpretation for some seems to be that this is one of the clearest texts to show that the twenty-four elders are saints, redeemed believers in heaven, significant evidence that they represent the raptured church in heaven during the tribulation period. Alexander Reese, opposing the pretribulation rapture, evidently placed much weight on this mistaken omission of "us," to support the view that the elders cannot represent the redeemed, acknowledging, however, that the ancient readings of this passage do indicate the elders to be of the redeemed, stating "Certainly these words seem conclusive that here we have the redeemed" (*The Approaching Advent of Christ*, p. 92). But even with a change of the pronouns involved (some modern critics supplying "them" here and in verse 10, in reference to the last word in verse 8, "saints") it is clear elsewhere that the twenty-four elders are redeemed men (Re 1:1. 5:5-7. 7:13-15. *19:10. *22:8, 9). For a fine and very complete discussion of this matter see J. B. Smith (*Comm. on Revelation*, Appendix 11, pp. 334-339). Re 14:4, 6. Ex 14:10, 30. Le 25:30, 54. Is 47:4. 53:11. *62:12. Mt *20:28. +*26:28n. Ac +*20:28. Ro 3:24-26. 1 C 6:20. 7:23. Ep 1:7. Col *1:14. T √2:14. He 11:14. 1 P 1:18, 19. 2 P +2:1. 1 J *1:7. 2:2. **to God.** Re 21:3. **by thy blood.** ∫108D, Mt +3:11. Re +1:5. 7:9, 10, 14. Jn 11:51, 52. Ac +*20:28. Ep 1:7. He 9:12, 14. 1 P *1:18, 19. **out of.** Re 7:9. 10:11. 11:9. 13:7. 14:6. 17:15. Is 56:7. Da 3:4, 7, 29. 4:1. 5:19. 6:25. 7:14. Mk *16:15, 16. Col +*1:23.

10. **made us.** T#973‡. Re 7:4n. 20:4, 6. Mt +7:14 (T#669). Lk +12:32 (T#959‡, 972x). **kings.** Re *1:6. 20:4. 22:5. Ex 19:6. Ro +*4:13. 1 P *2:5-9. **and.** ∫93A, Ge +1:26. By Hendiadys, "a great priestly kingdom." Two words used, one thing meant. **priests.** ∫96F2, Ge +4:10. The plural form "priests" is put by *Heterosis* for the singular, denoting greatness. Re *20:6. Ex ◖19:6. 2 Ch=5:11. Is *61:6. 66:21. **we shall reign.** Re +1:9. 2:26. *3:21. 20:4, 6. Ge 17:6. 35:11. Ex 19:6. Jg 5:13, 31. 1 S 2:8, 9. Ps 23:5. 45:16. 47:7-9. 75:10. 112:9, 10. 113:8. +*149:7-9. Pr 14:11, 19. Is 32:1. Je 3:17. Da *7:14, 18, 22, 27. Zc 14:5, 9. Mt +*19:28. 24:47. 25:21, 23, 34. Lk 19:17. +*22:29, 30. 1 C 6:2. 2 T 2:12. +*4:1. Ja +*2:5. 1 P 2:5, 9. 5:4. Ju 14, 15. **on the earth.** Gr. *epi tees gees*, prepositional phrase correctly rendered "on the earth" (F. Blass and A. Debrunner, *A Greek Grammar of the New Testament*, p. 96, sec. 177, genitive with verbs of ruling and surpassing). *Epi* with the genitive, of place, lit. on, upon, answering the question "where?" as on (the) earth, Mt 6:10, 19. 9:6. 23:9. Mk 6:47 (Arndt and Gingrich, *Lexicon*, p. 285, I. 1. a. Compare p. 286, I. 1. B. a). Re +*6:10g. ◖x9:11g. ◖x11:6g. Ps *37:9. 45:16. *96:13. Is +*24:23. Je 23:5. Mt 3:13g,n. +*5:5. Lk √18:8g. Ac 2:38n. +*7:5. Ro *4:13. *8:17. He 12:25g.

11. **many.** Re 7:11. 1 K 22:19. 2 K 6:16-18. Ps +*68:17. *103:20. 148:2. Mt *26:53. Lk *2:13, 14. **the throne.** See on Re 4:4, 6, 9, 10. **the beasts.** ver.

6, 8. Re +4:6. **the elders.** ver. 5. Re +4:4. **was.** Re 19:6. Dt +*33:2. Jb *25:3. Ps +*68:17. Da *7:10. He *12:22. **ten thousand.** Re ◖9:16. Da ◗7:10. Ju +14.

12. **Worthy.** See on ver. 9. Re 4:11. Zc 13:7. **the Lamb.** ver. +6. **slain.** Is ◗53:7. **to receive.** Re +4:11. 7:12. 19:1. Ne +*9:6. Mt 28:18. Jn √3:35, 36. 17:2. Ro *14:11. 2 C *8:9. Ph *2:9-11. Col *2:9. 1 T 1:17. **power.** Power, glory, and honor are mentioned in Re 4:11 as being given to the God the Father (O Lord, i.e. *Jehovah*) as an act of worship (Re 4:10). In this text, the Lamb, or Christ, is given power, glory, and honor in what must equally be understood as worship. Therefore, it is proper to worship the Son, even as it is proper to worship the Father, for here it has been shown that Father and Son receive the same worship. 1 Ch *29:11-13. Ps 62:11. Mt 6:13. Jn √5:23. 1 C 1:24. **riches.** Re 3:18. Pr *8:18. Ep *3:8. **wisdom.** 1 C *1:24. Ep *3:10. **strength.** ver. 6. Jb 9:19. Ps *68:34. Is *26:4. **honor.** Re 4:10, 11. Ps 8:5. *66:2. *104:1. Pr 8:18. Jn √5:23. 8:24. Ac +*7:59. 1 C 1:2. Ph *2:9-11. He *2:7, 9. **glory.** Re +4:9. Ps *29:2, 9. *138:5. Is *42:8. Da 7:10, 14. 2 C *4:6. 1 T *1:17. **blessing.** Ps 72:18, 19. 103:21, 22. 135:19, 20. Ro +*9:5. 1 T *1:11. *6:15, 16.

13. **every.** ver. 3. Re 7:9, 10. Ps 96:11-13. 145:21. 148:2-13. 150:6. Lk *2:14. Ph *2:10. Col +*1:23. **creature.** Re 8:9g. **in heaven.** T#1193. ver. 3. Re 6:9-11. Zc 1:12, 13. Ro 8:26, 27. *8:34. Ph 2:10. **such.** Is 24:14. 42:10. **Blessing.** ver. 12. Re 1:6. 1 Ch *29:11. Ps 72:18, 19. Mt +*6:13. Ro +*9:5. *11:36. 16:27. Ep 3:21. 1 T +*6:16. 1 P 4:11. 5:11. Ju *25. **honor.** Is +*58:13. Jn √5:23. 1 T 1:17. **glory.** Re +1:6. Lk 2:13, 14. Jn *17:24. **him.** ver. 1, 7. See on Re 4:+2, 3. **that sitteth.** Ps ◗47:8. Is ◖6:1. **and unto.** See on ver. 6, 9. Re 6:16. 7:10. Mt +*14:33. Ro 14:11. He 1:6. **for ever.** Gr. *aion*, Re +1:6.

14. **the four.** Re 19:4. **said.** Re 7:12. 1 C +14:16. **And the four and.** See on Re 4:9-11. **fell down.** ver. 8. Re +4:10. **worshipped him.** ver. 12n, 13. Re ◖4:10, 11. Dt *32:43, LXX. Ps *150:1-6. Mt 8:2. 9:18. 14:33. 15:25. 28:9. Jn +4:20. Ac +*7:59n. 1 C 1:2. He +*1:6. **for ever.** Gr. *aion*, Re +1:6.

REVELATION 6

The opening of six of the seven seals, and the emblematic discovery of future events made after each of them, 1-17.

1. **when.** ver. 16. See on Re 5:5-7. **the seals.** Re 5:1, 5-7. **noise of thunder.** Re 4:5. 10:3, 4. 11:19. 14:2. 19:6. Ex 19:16. Jb *37:5. Ezk 1:24, 25. 10:5. **one of.** ver. 3, 5, 7. Re 4:6, 7. Ac 4:20. **the four.** ver. 6. Re +4:6. **Come.** ∫171J14, Jon +1:3. In verses 1, 3, 5, and 7, the verb "and see" is not in many modern critical Greek texts. In this case the verb "come" is used in the sense of "go," as a command from the throne to the horsemen, rendered "saying, Go! and I saw and behold a white horse...and he went forth."

2. **a white.** This seems to be a representation of the person and dignity of Christ, and the mild and beneficent triumphs of his gospel over all the powers of paganism. In contrast to the preceding original *Treasury* note (which reflects the historicist school of interpretation, Re 4:1n), H. B. Swete states (in reference to the rider and white horse of Re 19:11) that "the two riders have nothing in common beyond the white

horse.... A vision of the victorious Christ would be inappropriate at the opening of a series which symbolizes bloodshed, famine, and pestilence" (*The Apocalypse of St. John*, p. 86). The rider on the white horse is more probably to be identified as the Antichrist. If this is not Antichrist, then Revelation does not place Antichrist on the scene of events before the middle of Daniel's Seventieth Week (in Re ch. 13), and the rider is virtually unidentifiable. The first seal corresponds to Mt 24:4, 5 (the false Messiah or Antichrist). Re ◐19:11, 14, 19, 21. Zc ❯1:8. ❯6:2, 3, etc., ❯6. Mt 24:4, 5, 23, 24. Jn 5:43. 2 C 11:13-15. **horse**. Jb 39:19, 25. Ps 76:6. Pr *21:31. Is 43:17. Je 6:23. Zc 9:10. 10:3. **and he that**. Ps 45:3-5, LXX. Is 41:2. 49:2, 3. Hab 3:8, 9, 13. Zc 9:13, 14. **had a bow**. Re ◐1:16. ◐19:15, 21. Ps 7:12. 11:2. 37:14. 46:9. 58:7. Je 49:35. **and a crown**. Re ◐2:10. 9:7. *13:2, 4. ◐14:14. ◐19:12. Da *8:24. *11:38, 39. Zc 6:11-13. Mt 28:18. **was given unto him**. Re 13:7. **and he went forth**. Re ◐1:18. 11:15, 18. 13:4. 15:2. 17:14. Ps 98:1. 110:2. Is 25:8. Da 9:27. 11:37. Mt 7:15. 24:4, 5. Jn 5:43. Ro 15:18, 19. 1 C 15:25, 55-57. 2 C 10:3-5. **conquering**. Re +3:21. 13:1-18. 14:9-11. 16:13-16. 17:1-17. 19:19, 20. Is 14:16, 17. Da 7:7, 8, 20, 21, 23, 24. 8:23-25. 9:27. 11:36-45. **and to conquer**. The following references (largely from the *Commentary Wholly Biblical*) assume the rider of this white horse is Christ, and that the scene portrays the conquest of the world by the spread of the gospel during this age, in harmony with the idealist or spiritual view (Re 4:1n). Re 11:15. Ps 21:13. *24:8. 45:3-5. Is 63:1. Ezk 21:27. 47:1-5. Zc 9:14. Mt 28:18. Ac 19:20. 1 C 15:25. Ep 4:8.

3. when he. See on ver. 1. Re 4:7.

4. horse. Re 12:3. 17:3, 6. Zc ❯1:8. ❯6:2, 6. **red**. Re 17:3, 6. **power**. Re 13:10. Ex 9:16, 17. Is 37:26, 27. Ezk 29:18-20. Da 2:37, 38. 5:19. Jn 19:11. **to take peace**. The second seal corresponds to Mt 24:6, 7, wars. Le 26:25. 2 Ch *15:5, 6. Je *25:29, 31. Ezk 38:21. Mi ch. *7. Mt √24:6, 7. Mk 13:7, 8. **should kill**. Mt 24:6, 7. **and there**. Ps 17:13. Is 10:5, 6. 34:5, 6. Je 12:12. 47:6, 7. Ezk 14:17. 21:9-11. 30:24, 25. Da 11:33. **sword**. Gr. *maxaira*, any sword or long knife. ver. ◐8. Mk 14:43. Jn 18:10, 11. He 4:12.

5. he had. See on ver. 1. Re 4:6, 7. 5:5, 9. **a black**. Black symbolizes famine. The third seal corresponds to Mt 24:7, famines. 2 K 8:1. Je 4:1, 2. 16:4. La 4:4-8. 5:10. Hg 1:11. 2:16, 17. Zc ❯6:2, 6. **had**. Le 19:36. 26:26. Pr 16:11. La 5:10. Is 40:12, 15. Ezk *4:10, 16, 17. 45:10. Ho 12:7. Am 8:5. Mi 6:11.

6. I heard. √18, Dt +28:4. **four beasts**. ver. 1. Re +4:6. **A measure**. "The word *chenix* signifieth a measure containing one wine-quart and the twelfth part of a quart." ver. 8. Le *26:26. Dt *32:23-25. 2 K *6:25. 7:1, 16, 18. *25:3. Ps *105:16. Pr 11:1. 16:11. Ezk 4:10, 11, *16. 5:10, 16. 14:15, 17, 19, 21. Mt 24:7, 8. Mk 13:8. **for a penny**. This was a day's wage (Mt 20:13n), which in this time of famine is sufficient to purchase a day's provision of food for only one person. Mt 18:28. 20:2. **and see**. Re 7:3. 9:4. Ps 76:10. **hurt not**. The law of God forbids the destruction of these agricultural resources during war (Dt 20:19n). **the oil and**. Some interpreters have suggested that the brunt of the suffering falls upon the poorer classes, but the rich are left largely untouched, but this is a less likely interpretation, for while fine wine and oil could be understood of the luxuries belonging to the rich, the

poorer quality product may be in view here as descriptive of the ordinary provisions used by the common people. Dt 7:13. 11:14. 28:51. 2 Ch 32:28. Ne 5:11. Ho 2:8, 22. Jl 2:19. Hg 1:11.

7. when. See on ver. 1, 35. Re 4:7.

8. pale. Zc 6:3. **was Death**. Re +1:18. 9:15. 20:13, 14. Is 25:8. 28:15, 18. Ho ❯13:14. Hab 2:5. 1 C 15:26, 55mg. **Hell**. Gr. *hades*, Mt +11:23. Re 1:18. 20:13. Ho ❯13:14. **power was given**. Re 13:5. **unto them**. *or*, to him. **over**. Re 8:7-12. 9:15, 18. 12:4. **kill**. Le 26:22-33. Je 15:2, 3. 16:4, 16. 43:11. Ezk 5:15-17. 14:13-21. ❯33:27. **with sword**. Gr. *romphaia*, a large blade of Thracian origin. Re 1:16. 2:12, 16. 19:15, 16. Ge 3:24. Ezk 12:16. Lk 2:35. **with hunger**. ver. 6. Re 18:8. Je 14:12. Ezk ❯5:12. 7:15. ❯14:21. Lk 21:10, 11. **death**. *or*, pestilence. √121G1. Metonymy of the Effect, the effect (death) put for the cause producing it (pestilence). For other instances of this figure, see Ge +31:1. Re +2:23. The fourth seal corresponds to Mt 24:7, pestilences. 1 K 8:37. 1 Ch 21:12. Je 14:12. 21:7. 24:10. *38:2. 44:13. Ezk 5:12. 6:11, 12. Hab *3:5. Mt √24:7. **beasts of**. Le 26:22. Nu 21:6. Dt 32:24. Jsh 24:12. 2 K 2:24. 17:25. Je 5:6. Ezk 5:17. *14:15, 21. ❯29:5. 33:27. ❯34:28.

9. I saw. Re 8:3. 9:13. 14:18. Le 4:7. Jn 15:20. 16:2g. Ph *2:17. 2 T *4:6. **under**. Ex 29:12. Le 4:7. 8:15. Mt +*12:40. **the altar**. Re 8:◐3, 5. ◐9:13. 11:1. 14:18. 16:7. Ro 12:1. **the souls**. Gr. psyche. Here used of disembodied man, as in Re 20:4. For the other uses of psyche, see Mt +2:20n. √√171Q1, Ge +12:5. √121A8, Ps +16:10. Re 20:4. 2 C *5:3, 4, 8. *12:2. Ph 1:23. He ◐+*12:23. **slain**. Re 1:9. 2:13. 5:6. 11:3-7. 12:11-17. 19:10. Ph 2:17. 2 T 1:8. 4:6. **word of God**. Re 1:+2, 9.

10. they cried. √155D, Ge +4:10. Ge +*4:10. Ps 9:12. Is *64:1-4. Lk 18:7, 8. He 12:24. **loud voice**. Re 7:10. **How long**. Ps 13:1. 35:17. 74:9, 10. 89:46. *94:1, 3, 4. SS *8:14. Is 6:11. Da 8:13. 12:6. Zc ❯1:12. Jn 11:24-26. Ro *8:23. **Lord**. Gr. *despotees*, rendered (1) Lord: Re 6:10. Lk 2:29. Ac 4:24. 2 P +2:1. Ju 4. (2) Master: 1 T 6:1, 2. 2 T 2:21. T 2:9. 1 P 2:18. **holy and**. See on Re 3:7. 15:3, 4. Ps 89:28, 34, 35. Is +*55:3. **dost**. Re 11:18. 16:5-7. 18:20, 24. 19:2. Dt 32:36-43. Jg 16:28. 1 S 24:12. Ps 58:10, 11. Is 61:2. *63:1-6. Lk 21:22. Ro 12:19. 2 Th 1:6-8. **avenge**. This seal seems a prediction of the terrible persecution of the church under Dioclesian and Maximian, from A.D. 270 to 304, which lasted longer, and was far more bloody, than any or all by which it was preceded, whence it was called the "aera of the martyrs." The futurist interpretation takes these as the first martyrs of the tribulation of Daniel's 70th Week. The fifth seal corresponds to Mt 24:8-28, martyrdoms. Re *14:12-20. 18:20. 19:2. Dt 32:35, ❯43. 2 K ❯9:7. Ps 79:10. *94:1-4. 119:84. Is=54:4, 5. *63:4. Je +√10:25. La=1:1. Lk *18:7, 8. Ro *12:19. **that dwell**. Re +*3:10. Ho ❯4:1. **on the earth**. Re *3:10. +*5:10n. 8:13. 11:10. 12:12. 13:8, 12, 14. 14:6. 17:2.

11. white. Re *3:+4, 5. *7:9, 14. Da *12:10. **robes**. Ge 41:42. 45:22. Est 6:8, 9. Is 3:7. Zc 3:5. **should rest**. Re 14:13. Is +*26:20, 21. Da 12:13. 2 Th ◐+*1:7. **a little season**. Re 10:6. 20:3. **until**. Re 7:14. 13:15. 17:6. *22:20. Hab *2:3. Mt 10:21. 23:34, 35. Lk *18:7, 8. Jn 16:2. Ep +*1:11. He *10:36, 37. 11:40. Ja 5:8. 1 P *4:19. **and their brethren**. √93A. Figure of speech Hendiadys of Nouns. "Fellow servants and brethren" denote by this figure not two separate classes of persons, but one class, their fellow servants who were their brethren. For other instances of this figure see Ge +1:26. fulfilled. Ge +*15:16.

12. earthquake. Re 8:5. 11:13, 19. 16:18. Ex 19:18. 20:18. Jg 5:4. 2 S 22:8. 1 K 19:11-13. Is 29:6. Am 1:1. Hg +*2:6, 7, 21, 22. Zc 14:5. Mt 24:7. *27:54. 28:2. Mk 13:8. Lk 21:11. Ac 16:26. He 12:26. the sun. The sixth seal corresponds to Mt 24:29, 30, signs in heaven of the Advent. Re 8:12. 16:8. Is 13:9, 10. 24:23. *50:3. ◐60:19, 20. Ezk *32:7, 8. Jl *2:10, 30, ▶31. *3:15. Am 8:9. Hab 3:11. Hg 2:6, 7, 21, 22. Zc 14:6. Mt +*24:29. 27:45. Mk 13:24, 25. 15:33. Lk 23:44, 45. Ac 2:19, 20. sackcloth. Is 50:3. Zc 13:4. the moon. Re 8:12.

13. the stars. Re *8:10-12. 9:1. Is ▶13:10. Ezk 32:7. Da 8:10. Lk 21:25. as a fig tree. Is ▶34:4. untimely figs. or, green figs. SS 2:13. shaken. Is *13:13. Hg 2:6. He +*12:26, 27. of a. Is 7:2. 33:9. Da 4:14. Na 3:12.

14. the heaven. Re 20:11. 21:1. Ps *102:25, 26. Is 34:4. *51:6. He 1:11-13. 2 P +*3:7, 10. as a scroll. Is *34:4. and every. Re √16:20. Is 2:14-17. 54:10. Je 3:23. *4:23-26. 51:25. Ezk *38:20. Na 1:5. Hab *3:6, 10.

15. And. ♪148, Ge +8:22. the kings. Re 18:9-11. 19:13-21. Jb 34:19, 20. Ps 2:2, 10-12. *49:1, 2. 76:12. *110:5, 6. Is *24:21, 22. the great men. or, princes. Re 18:23. +*19:18g. Is 34:12. Mk 6:21g. the rich. Re 13:16. bondman. Re 13:16. +*19:18g. hid. Jsh 10:16, 17. Jg 6:2. 1 S 13:6. Is 2:10, 19, 21. 42:22. Mi 7:17. He 11:38.

16. and rocks. Ps 97:5. Is √2:19. Fall on. Re 10:6. Is √24:19-23. Je 8:3. Ho ▶10:8. Lk √23:30. hide us from. Re 9:6. *20:11. Ex 20:19. Jb *34:22. Pr *1:27. Is *2:10, 12, 19, 21. *63:4-6. Je *3:23. Lk 13:24, 25. the face. Re 4:2, 5, 9. *20:11. Ps 17:15. that sitteth. Re +4:2. Ps ▶47:8. Is ▶6:1. the wrath. ver. 10, 17. Re 11:18. 14:9, 10, 19. 15:1, 7. 16:1, 19. 17:1. 18:10. 19:2, 15. Dt 7:9, 10. Ps 2:9-12. 14:5. 21:8-12. 110:5, 6. Is +*1:9. Zc 1:14, 15. Mt 26:64. Mk 3:5g. 2 Th *1:7-9. He 10:31. the Lamb. Re +5:6.

17. the great day. Re 11:18. 16:14. Jb +*21:30. Is +*13:6, etc. √34:8. Je +*30:7. Jl *1:15. *2:1, 2, ▶11, 31. 3:14. Zp ▶1:14, etc., 18. Ml *3:2. *4:1. Ro 2:5. Ju 6. of his wrath. Ro 1:18. 2:3, 5, 8, 9. *5:9. 1 Th +*5:9. 2 Th √1:6-8. is come. Re 19:17. Mk 14:41. and who. Re 7:4-8. 14:1. Ezr *9:15. Ps *2:12. *76:5-9. *130:3, 4. Is +*33:14. Jl *2:11. Na *1:6. Hab +*3:16. Ml *▶3:2. to stand. Ps *1:5. Lk +*21:36.

REVELATION 7

The four winds are restrained, by four angels, from hurting the earth, till "another Angel" seals the servants of God in the forehead, 1-3. The number of the sealed from the several tribes of Israel, 4-8. An innumerable multitude of all nations are seen before the throne, 9-12; with an account of the way in which they came thither, and the blessedness which they enjoy, 13-17.

1. after. Re ch. 4-6. these. ver. 9. Re 15:5. Jn 2:12g. 6:1. 7:1. 19:28g. four angels. Re 4:6. 9:14. Ezk 7:2. 37:9. Zc 1:18-20. 6:1. Mt 24:31. Mk 13:27. four corners. Re 20:8. Is 11:12. Je 49:36. Ezk ▶7:2. holding. Ps *76:10. Is 27:8. Je 49:36. Da 7:2. 8:8. Jon 1:4. Mt 8:26, 27. 24:31. four winds. Je 49:36. Ezk ▶37:9. Da *7:2. 8:8.

11:4. Zc 2:6. ▶6:5. Mt 24:31. Mk 13:27. the wind. ver. 3. Re 6:6. 9:4. SS 4:16. Is 27:3. should not. Mt 8:27. the sea. Re 4:6. 8:7, 8.

2. And I. Re 8:3. 10:1. Ml 3:1. 4:2. Ac 7:30-32. from the east. Re 16:12. Ezk 40:6. having. ver. 3-8. Re 5:2. 9:4. 10:4. SS 8:6. Jn 6:27. 2 C 1:22. Ep +*1:13. +*4:30. 2 T *2:29. the living God. See on Dt 5:26. Jsh 3:10. 1 S 17:26, 36. 2 K 19:4. Je 10:10. Da 6:26. Mt +16:16. 26:63. 1 Th 1:9, 10. He 12:22. to whom. Re 1:3. 8:7-12. earth and. Re 8:7, 8.

3. Hurt not. ver. 1. Re 6:6. 9:4. 2 K +*10:23. Ps 105:15. Is 6:13. 27:8. 65:8. Mt 24:22, 31. till. ver. 2. Re 9:4. 14:1. Ge √19:22. Ex *12:13, 23. 2 K 10:23. Is +*26:20, 21. Ezk +*9:4-6. Am 9:9. Zp +*2:3. sealed. Re ◐13:16-18. SS *8:6. Ezk +*9:6. 2 C *1:21, 22. Ep *1:13. +*4:30. 2 T *2:19. the servants. Re 1:1. 11:18. 15:3. *19:2, 5, 10. 22:3, 6, 9. Ge 50:17. Dt 32:36. Is 54:17. 61:6. +*66:19. Da 3:17, 26. 6:16, 20. +*11:33. Mi *5:5. Ml 3:18. Mt 24:31. Jn +*12:26. Ro 6:22. Ja +1:1. in their foreheads. Re 13:16. 14:1. 20:4. *22:4. Ex 28:38. Ezk 3:8, 9. ▶9:4.

4. I heard. Re 9:16. the number. Ps +*68:11. Is +*27:6. +*66:19. of them. Dt +*4:30. an hundred and forty and four thousand. What is the significance of the number? Reginald T. Naish, in his volume *Spiritual Arithmetic*, suggests that since this number contains the square of twelve, it "is naturally associated with that number, which is perfect government. It emphasizes it, and expresses spiritually the fact that perfect government of the life is only possible through the agency of the Holy Spirit. Hence it may well be called, the number of the Spirit-guided life." In Ge 1:2, the Hebrew word translated "move" (*rachaph*) has a numerical value or gematria of 288, or 144 x 2. Its next occurrence is Dt 32:11, where it is translated "fluttered." Naish states "In both these passages the gracious work of the heavenly dove, the Holy Spirit of God, is described." Other occurrences of this number are to be found in the word "eastward" (Ge 2:8) in the phrase "eastward in Eden," showing that God intended man "should live a life of perfect government, a wonderful garden life, bringing forth the fruit of the Spirit, and finding their chief joy in communion with their loving God." The cubic capacity of the ark, found by multiplying its three dimensions of 300 cubits, 50 cubits, and 30 cubits, was 450,000 cubic cubits, a number whose prime factors are 5x5x5x5x5x144. The number appears here in Re 7:4 of the number "sealed by the Holy Spirit before God's judgments fall on earth. It does not of course mean that this identical number are saved in that time of tribulation. It is only using the numbers 144 and 10 in the spiritual sense in which these numbers are used through Scripture to tell of those who by the power of the Holy Spirit are kept from that time of trouble." The same number occurs in Re ch. 14. "Again, we are given a symbolical picture of those who have yielded their lives wholly to the guidance of the Holy Spirit. They are taken up to be with Christ, their Savior, before the actual 'harvest of the earth' is reaped" (*Spiritual Arithmetic*, pp. 107-109).

Who are the 144,000? The Jehovah's Witnesses teach that the 144,000 is the body of spirit-begotten believers who have a "heavenly hope" (Ro 8:24. Ep 4:4. Col 1:5. He 7:19. 1 P 1:3. 1 J 3:3). All other believers can have only an "earthly hope" (Jb 14:7. Je 31:17.

Ac 26:6). Once the Watchtower organization had more than 144,000 adherents, the teaching was developed that the "great multitude" mentioned later in the chapter (ver. 9) referred to those Christians who had only an earthly hope. Jehovah's Witnesses teach that members of the "great multitude" who have only an earthly hope do not need to be born again (see related note, Jn 3:7). Peters remarks "It is a matter of amazement how coolly and deliberately men can appropriate Scripture to themselves which relates to the future. Sects, at various times, have professed to be those sealed ones" (*Theocratic Kingdom*, vol. 2, p. 323, note 1). Not considering that the number sealed refers to a time yet future, Jehovah's Witnesses claim the number represents the total number of those who can be born again and have a heavenly hope. How long would it take for the apostolic church of the New Testament to reach the size of 144,000 converts? Suppose we assume that the first converts were zealous witnessing Christians during the lifetime of the apostles. Suppose each convert was able to win just one person to Christ each year of his new life in Christ, and that each of these converts continued to win an additional convert each year. Take into account only the growth theoretically possible for the new converts won by the original group of 5,000 converts mentioned in the book of Acts. Exclude from consideration any additional converts won through the ministry of the apostles (Paul, Barnabas, Apollos, and the original twelve disciples) to compensate for any of the original 5000 who may not have been active soul winners. In the year A.D. 33, the size of the church would be 5,000. In 34 A.D., 10,000; 35 A.D., 20,000; 36 A.D., 40,000; 37 A.D., 80,000; 38 A.D., 160,000—assuming each new convert continued to win one additional convert per year. Thus before Paul began his first missionary journey in A.D. 45, the New Testament church could easily have surpassed the figure of 144,000 genuine converts. If any converts beyond that figure were limited to an earthly hope without opportunity for new birth and "heavenly hope," this most certainly would be reflected in the teaching of the New Testament epistles of Peter or Paul. The earliest of Paul's epistles was written in A.D. 52 or 54, fourteen or more years after the time the New Testament church exceeded the 144,000 maximum number the Jehovah's Witnesses teach can have a heavenly hope. Is this situation reflected in the writings of Paul? At the time Paul wrote 2 Thessalonians (A.D. 52 or 54), he specifically confirms that the "falling away" or apostasy had not yet occurred (2 Th 2:3). This Scripture evidence would lead us to believe that the vast body of believers had remained faithful. What few that fell away during this time would be more than made up by any converts won beyond the first five years after Pentecost. If the claim of Jehovah's Witnesses that the heavenly hope is limited to 144,000 has any validity, the significance of that hope for anyone today is purely historical, for since this number was reached within five years of Pentecost, no person alive today could possibly lay claim to be one of that fixed number, not even the leaders of the Watchtower in Brooklyn, New York. Following Jehovah Witness doctrine to its logical conclusion, the apostle Paul must have been mistaken in his theology, for he continued to emphasize the "heavenly hope" and the necessity of the "new birth" (1 C 6:2. 2 C 5:17. Ga 6:14)

long after the "heavenly class" was complete in number. The 144,000 of Revelation 7:4 and 14:1 do not pertain to persons who have lived before now, but to a specific group in the future. The book of Revelation supplies its own outline in Re 1:19. The 144,000 are mentioned well after Re 4:1, where the third grand division of the book pertaining to "things which must be hereafter" commences. Therefore, these events must take place during the "day of the Lord" (Re 1:10n), *after* the Rapture of the church (1 Th 4:16-18), and during the Great Tribulation. The 144,000 are all males (Re 14:4), and are all Jews (Re 7:4, "of all the tribes of the children of Israel"). Scripture speaks of three categories of persons its contents concern: the Jews, the Gentiles, and the church of God (1 C 10:32). What is stated in Re 7:4 pertains to Israel—it *cannot* pertain to any other group. The names of the tribes of Israel are nowhere in Scripture ever applied to the Gentiles or the church of God. Furthermore, the 144,000 are not the only saints in heaven. They were preceded by all those who died in Christ before the Rapture (2 C +*5:8. 1 Th 4:14). They are preceded by those who have been martyred for Christ (Re *6:9-11). There are *five* raptures in the first resurrection; the 144,000 constitute only one of these five. The five raptures are: (1) Christ and the saints in Jerusalem at his first resurrection, 1 C 15:20, 23. Mt 27:52, 53. Ep 4:8-10. (2) Afterward, they that are Christ's at his coming, 1 C 15:23, 51-54. Lk +*21:34-36. Jn +*14:1-3. 2 C 5:1-8. Ep 5:27. Ph 3:11, 20, 21. Col 3:4. 1 Th 2:19. 3:13. 4:13-17. 5:9, 23. 2 Th 2:1, 7. Ja 5:7, 8. 1 P 5:4. 1 J 2:28. 3:2. (3) The 144,000 Jews saved in the first 3 1/2 years of the tribulation (of Daniel's 70th week), caught up to heaven as the manchild, Re 12:5. 14:1-5. Is 66:7, 8. Da 12:1. (4) The great multitude of tribulation saints saved after rapture number two above, during Re 6:1—19:21. (5) The rapture of the two witnesses, ending the first resurrection which began with the resurrection of Christ, Re 11:7-11. 1 C 15:20, 23. The 144,000 do not comprise the totality of all saints possessing a "heavenly hope" throughout this age. All of the 144,000 are on the earth at the same time. This is evidenced by the fact that they are as a group "sealed" and protected from the tribulation by the angel. The 144,000 do not constitute the "little flock." The "little flock" is comprised of all born-again believers. The flock is little because there are "few that be saved" (Mt +*7:14). The term "flock" is used in the New Testament for the true church made up of born-again believers (Ac 20:28). The "other sheep" are the Gentile Christians who, in addition to the Jewish believers, are now being constituted one body in Christ, the church (Ac 10:45. 15:7, 17. Ep +*4:4). The Great Tribulation is still future, and pertains to Israel. The church is raptured prior to the manifestation of the Antichrist, 2 Th 2:8n, and prior to the Great Tribulation (Jn 14:1-3. 1 C 15:51, 52. Ph 3:21. 1 Th 4:16-18. 2 Th +*1:7. 2:1. T +*2:13n). Christ's Second Advent occurs at the end of tribulation, when Christ personally destroys the Antichrist. Since it is certain that Antichrist is destroyed before the Millennium, this proves absolutely that Christ's coming is premillennial (2 Th 2:8n). At the Second Advent, Christ returns visibly in power and great glory (Mt +*16:27n) with his saints to rule over His eternal kingdom on this earth (Da +*7:13, 14. Zc 14:5, 9. 2 T +*4:1n). Since the rapture of the Church and the Great Tribulation are future, and the 144,000 are protected during the first half of the Tribulation, the 144,000 must constitute a group that is yet future, and cannot pertain to any denomination or other religious group of today. Re √14:1, 3. Ge 15:5. Ro *9:27. *11:5, 6. **all the tribes.** The tribes of Dan and Ephraim are omitted from the list which follows, being replaced by Levi and Joseph. The reason for Ephraim's omission is suggested see by Ho 4:17. For possible reasons for Dan's omission see the related texts and note (Le 24:10-16. Dt 29:18-21. Jg 18:2-31. 1 K 12:26-33. 1 Ch 7:12n). Dan and Ephraim are included in Ezekiel's prophecy of their inheritance in the eternal earthly kingdom of Christ (Ezk 48:1, 2, 5, 6, 32), demonstrating God's faithfulness to his covenant and promise (Le 26:44. Ml 3:6. Ro 11:29. 15:8). Re 21:12. 1 Ch 7:12n. Ezk 47:13. 48:19, 31. Zc 9:1. Mt +*19:28. Lk +*22:30. Ac 26:7. Ja 1:1. **children of Israel.** Re 2:14. 21:12. Ac +5:21.

5. **tribe of Juda.** Ex 1:2-4. Nu 1:4-15. 10:14-27. 13:4-16. 1 Ch 2:1, 2. **Reuben.** i.e. *son of a vision*, ❋S#4502g. For ❋S#7205h, see Ge +29:32. **sealed.** ♪76, Ge +13:6. **Gad.** i.e. *troop*, ❋S#1045g. For ❋S#1410h, see Ge +30:11.

6. **Aser.** Lk 2:36. **sealed.** ♪76, Ge +13:6.

7. **sealed.** ♪76, Ge +13:6. **Issachar.** i.e. *he will be hired; he brings wages*, ❋S#2466g. For ❋S#3485h, see Ge +30:18.

8. **sealed.** ♪76, Ge +13:6. **Joseph.** Ge 48:14.

9. **After this.** 1 T +*2:6. **a great multitude.** T#975‡. ver. ◑+*15 (temple). Re x21:1-4. Ge +*49:10. Le +=23:22. Ps 2:8. 22:27. x37:9, 11. 66:4. 67:2. 72:7-11. 76:4. 77:2. 98:3. 110:2, 3. ch. 117. Pr x2:21, 22. Is +*2:2, 3. +√27:6. 49:6-8, 12. *60:1-14. Je 3:17. 16:19. Zc 2:11. 8:20-23. Mt 8:11. Ro 15:9-12. Ga 4:27. **no man.** Re 5:11. 11:15. Ge 13:16. Ho 1:10. Lk 12:1. Ro +*11:25. He 11:12. 12:22. **of all.** Re 5:9. Da 4:1. 6:25. Ro +*11:25. **nations.** Re +5:9. Ge +*12:3. Ps 67:1, 7. *68:31, 32. 98:3. Is *11:10. 49:6. 52:9, 10. Lk *2:32. Jn *11:51, 52. Ro *3:29, 30. *9:23-26. Ga 3:7. **stood before the throne.** This shows that the "great multitude" are in heaven, not upon earth, at the time spoken of in this vision of John. Lk +*21:36. Ep 6:13. **the Lamb.** Re +5:6. **clothed.** ver. 13, 14. See on Re 3:+4, 5, 18. 4:4. 6:11. Mt 22:11. Lk 15:22. **palms.** Le *23:10, 39-43. 1 K 6:29. Jn *12:13.

10. **cried.** Zc 4:7. **Salvation.** Re 12:10. 19:1. Ex 15:2. Ps *3:8. 37:39. 62:7. *68:19, 20. 115:1. 118:25. Is 12:2. *43:11. 45:15, 21, 22. Je 3:23. Ho 13:4. Jon 2:9. Zc 9:9. Mt 21:9. Lk 3:6. Jn 4:22. Ac *4:12. Ep √2:8. T *3:5, 6. He +*9:28. **our God.** ver. 3, 12. **sitteth upon.** Re 4:+2, 3, 9-11. 5:7, 13, 14. 21:5. Ps ▶47:8. Is ▶6:1. **unto.** Re 5:6, 9. 22:3. Jn *1:29, 36.

11. **all the angels.** Re 4:6. *5:11-13. 19:4-6. Ps 103:20, 21. 148:1, 2. He *1:6. 1 P *1:9, 10, 12. **round about.** Re 4:4, 6. 7:11. **the elders.** Re +4:4. **four beasts.** Re +4:6. **and fell.** Re +4:10. 11:16. **and worshipped.** Re +4:10. 15:4. 19:4. 19:4. 22:9. Ps 29:2. 45:11. 95:6. 97:7. Mt *4:10. Jn 4:23. √5:23. He *1:6.

12. **Amen.** Re 1:18. 5:13, +14. 19:4. Ps 41:13. 72:19. 89:52. 106:48. Mt +*6:13. Ju *25. **Blessing.** See on Re 5:+12, 13. **glory.** Re +4:9. **wisdom.** Re +5:12. **thanksgiving.** Re 4:9g. Ne 12:8, 46. Ps 50:14. 95:2. 100:4. 107:22. 116:17. 147:7. Is 51:3. Je 33:9, 11. Jon 2:9. 2 C 4:15. 9:11, 12. Col 2:7. 3:17. **honor.** Re +4:9. **power.** Re +5:12. **might.** Re 5:12. Is 9:6. +*10:21.

49:26. 60:16. Je *32:19. Mt 11:21. Lk 9:43. Ep 1:21. **for ever.** Gr. *aion*, Re +1:6. **Amen.** Je 11:5. Lk 10:21.

13. **one.** Re 4:4, 10. 5:5, 11. **answered.** Ac +3:12. **arrayed.** See on ver. 9. Re +*3:4. *6:9, 11. Da *11:35. *12:10. **whence.** Ge 16:8. Jg 13:6. Jn 7:28.

14. **thou.** Ex 37:3. **came.** Re 2:9. *6:9-11. 15:2. 17:6. Ps 34:19. *66:12. Jn 16:33. Ac +*14:22. Ro *5:3. 8:35-37. 2 Th 1:4. **great tribulation.** Da ▶12:1. Je √30:7. Mt 24:+21, 29. Ro ◑5:3. ◑8:35. **and have.** Re 1:5. 22:14. Is √1:18. Zc *3:3-5. 13:1. Jn *13:8-14. 1 C *6:11. Ep *5:25-27. He +*9:14. 1 J √1:7. Ju *24. **washed.** Gr. *pluno*, ❋S#4150g, only here. Re *1:5. Ge ▶49:11. Ps 51:7. Da 12:10. Ep 5:26, 27. 2 P 1:9. 1 J 1:7. **made them white.** Da 11:35. **the blood.** ♪117, Ge +19:8. Re *5:9. *12:11. Le *17:11. He 13:12. 1 P *1:18, 19. 1 J 1:7.

15. **are.** Re 4:4. 14:3-5. He 8:1. *12:2. **serve.** Re 20:10. *22:3-5. 2 Ch=35:3. Ps 134:1, 2. Pr +*22:29. **day and night.** 1 Ch=9:33. Lk 2:37. +18:7. **his temple.** Re +3:12. √11:19. √14:17. Ps *65:4. **that sitteth.** Re +4:2. Ps ▶47:8. Is ▶6:1. **dwell.** Re 12:12. 13:6. *21:3, 4. 22:3. Ex 29:45. Le 26:11. 1 K 6:13. 1 Ch 23:25. Ps +*16:11. 68:16-18. Is 4:5, 6. *12:6. Ezk *37:26, 27. 43:7. 48:35. Mt 1:23. Jn *1:14. 1 C *3:16. 2 C *6:16. 12:9.

16. **hunger.** Ps 42:2. 63:1. *107:9. 143:6. Is 41:17. ▶49:10. 65:13. Mt +*5:6. Lk 1:53. 6:21. Jn +*4:14. *6:35. **the sun.** Re 21:4. 2 K 4:18, 19. Ps 121:6. SS 1:6. Is 4:5, 6. 25:4. 32:2. *60:19, 20. Jon 4:8. Mt 13:6, 21. Mk 4:6, 17. Ja 1:11. **nor any heat.** Jb *11:16. Is *4:6.

17. **in the.** See on Re 5:6. **feed.** Ps 22:26. *23:1, 2, 5. 28:9. 36:8. SS *1:7, 8. Is 25:6. *40:11. 49:9. Ezk ▶34:23. Mi +*5:4. 7:14. Mt 2:6mg. Jn *10:+11, 14. 21:15-17. Ac +*20:28. 1 P *5:2. **shall lead.** Re 21:6. Ps 23:2. 36:9. Is *12:3. 30:25. 35:6, 7. 49:10. Je 2:13. 31:9. Jn *4:11, 14. *7:37, 38. +*10:3, 4. **living.** ♪108B, Ac +7:38. **fountains.** Re 22:1. Je ▶2:13. Zc 13:1. Jn *4:14g. **of waters.** Re 21:6. *22:1. Ezk *47:12. Zc *14:8. **God.** Re 4:21. 21:4. Is 25:8. 30:19. 35:10. 60:20. Ep *3:20, 21. Ju +*24. **wipe away.** Is ▶25:8. *35:10. +*51:11. *65:19. 66:13. **from their eyes.** Re *21:4. Je ▶31:16.

REVELATION 8

The seventh seal is opened; and, after a short silence, seven angels appear with seven trumpets prepared to announce approaching judgments; with reference to Christ's intercession, and the prayers of his saints, 1-6. The sounding of four of the trumpets, with the emblematical predictions following each of them; and an intimation of more awful calamities, under the other three, 7-13.

1. **And.** Re *5:1, 9. 6:1, 3, 5, 7, 9, 12. **silence.** Jb 4:16. Ps 22:2, 3. 37:7. 39:2. 62:1mg. 75:1. La 3:26. Hab +*2:20. Zc *2:13.

2. **the seven.** ver. 6, 7, 8, 10, 12, 13. Re 1:4. 3:1. 4:5. 5:6. **angels.** Re 9:1, 13. 11:15. 15:1. 16:1. Ps 103:20. Da 4:13, 17, 23. Mt *18:10. Lk *1:19. He 1:7. **which stood.** Re 7:11. Lk *1:19. **trumpets.** ver. 6-12. Re 9:1, 13, 14. *11:15. 14:14. Le 25:9, 10. See on Nu 10:1-10. Jsh *6:4. Jg 3:27. 6:34. 7:8, 16, 18. 1 S 13:3. 1 Ch 15:24, 28. 16:6. 2 Ch 5:12, 13. 7:6. 13:14. 29:25-28. Ezr 3:10. Ne 12:35, 41. Jb 39:25. Je 4:5. Am 3:6-8. Zp 1:14-16. 1 C 15:52.

3. **another.** Re 7:2. 10:1. See on Ge 48:15, 16. Ex 3:2-18. Ac 7:30-32. **stood.** Re 9:13. Ex 30:1-8. 2 Ch 26:16-20. Am ▶9:1. Ro *8:34. He *7:25. **having.** Le 16:12. 1 K 7:50. He +9:4. **censer.** ℐ121.O, Ge +28:22. **much.** Le 16:13. Nu 16:46, 47. Ml 1:11. **incense.** Re 5:8mg. 18:13. Ex 30:7, 8. Ps ▶141:2. **offer it with the prayers.** or, add it to the prayers. ver. 4. Re +5:8. Ps 141:2. Lk 1:10. Jn *16:24. He +*4:15, 16. *10:19-22. 1 J *2:1, 2. **saints.** 11:18. 13:7, 10. 14:12. 16:6. 17:6. 18:20, 24. 19:8. 20:9. 22:21. 2 C +1:1. **the golden.** Re *6:9. 9:13. 11:1. Ex 30:1, 3. 37:25, 26. 40:26. **before.** Ex 30:6. 40:5, 26.

4. **smoke.** ver. 3. Re 15:8. Ex 30:1. Ps *141:2. Lk *1:10. **incense.** Re *5:8. 2 Ch=13:11. Ps 141:2. 2 C 2:15. He *13:15. **with.** 2 Ch *30:27. Ps *141:2. Ac +10:4.

5. **the angel.** Ex 9:8. Nu 16:46. Ezk 10:2. **censer.** Le ▶16:12. Nu 16:46. **and filled.** Re 16:1, etc. Le 16:12. Is 66:6, 14-16. Je 51:11. Ezk *10:2-7. Lk *12:49. **with fire.** Le *6:13. Dt 32:22. Ps 18:4, 6-8. Ezk 10:2. 38:22. 39:6. Ho 8:14. Am 1:4, 7, 10, 12. 2:5. 2 P +*3:7. **of the altar.** Is *6:6, 7. **into.** or, upon. **the earth.** 2 S *22:8. Ps *104:32. **and there.** See on Re 4:5. 11:19. 16:18. 2 S 22:7-9. Ps 18:7, 8, 13. Is 30:30. He 12:18, 19. **thunderings.** Re +4:5. 11:19. 16:18. Ex ▶19:16. 20:18. Ps 18:13. **earthquake.** Re +6:12. 11:13, 19. 1 K 19:11. Is 29:6. Zc 14:5. Mt *24:7. 27:52-54. Ac 4:31. 16:26.

6. **seven angels.** See on ver. 2. Ps *103:20, 21. **prepared.** Ex 34:10. Dt 28:10. Ps 79:11, 12. Is 11:15, 16. Je 23:7, 8. Mi 7:15.

7. **hail.** Re 11:19. *16:21. Ex *9:▶23-25, 33. Jsh 10:11. Ps 11:5, 6. 18:12, 13. 78:47, 48. *105:32. Is 28:2. 29:6. 30:30. 32:19. Ezk 13:10-15. ▶38:22. Mt 7:25-27. **fire.** Re 13:13. **blood.** Jl ▶2:30. **cast.** Re 16:2. **the third part.** ℐ159, Ezk +36:23. ver. 9, 10, 12. Re ◑6:8. 9:15, 18. 12:4. Zc 13:8, 9. **the trees.** Re 9:4. Is 2:12, 13. 10:17, 18. **green grass.** Ja 1:11. 1 P 1:24.

8. **and as.** Ps *46:2. Je *51:24, 25. Zc 4:7. Mk *11:23. **burning.** Je ▶51:25. Am *7:4-6. **into the sea.** Re 16:3. **the third.** ver. +7. Re 16:3, etc. Ex 7:17-21. Ezk 14:9. **became blood.** Re 11:6. *16:4. Ex ▶7:19. Ps 78:44. *105:29. Ezk *38:22.

9. **the third part of the creatures.** ver. 7, 10, 12. Re 5:13. 16:3. Ex 7:21. Ho 4:1-3. Zp 1:3. Zc 13:8. **life.** Gr. psyche, ℐ121A7, Mt +2:20. **died.** Ex 7:21. **the ships.** Ps 48:7. Is 2:16. 23:1.

10. **third angel.** Re 16:4-6. **a great.** Re 1:20. 6:13. *9:1. 12:4. Is ▶14:12. Lk 10:18. Ju 13. **lamp.** Mt 25:1g. **the fountains.** Re 14:7. 16:4. Ex 7:20, 21. Jg 5:11. 2 K 2:19-22. 2 Ch 32:3. Is *12:3. Ho 13:15, 16.

11. **Wormwood.** Re 15:25. Dt 29:18. Ru 1:20. 2 K *2:19-21. Pr 5:4. Je 8:14. *9:15. *23:15. La 3:5, 15, 19. Am 5:7. 6:12. He +*12:15. **many.** Ex 7:18-24. *15:23.

12. **fourth angel.** Re 16:8. **and the third part of the sun.** ver. +7. Re *6:12, 13. 16:8, 9. Is 5:30. *13:10. 24:23. ◑30:26. ◑60:19, 20. Je 4:23, 28. Ezk 32:7, 8. Jl 2:10, 31. 3:15. Am √5:20. *8:9. Zp 1:14-16. Mt 24:29. 27:45. Mk 13:24. 15:33. Lk 21:25. 23:44, 45. Ac 2:20. **darkened.** Re 9:2. *16:10. Pr +*20:20. **and the day.** Ex *10:21-23. 2 C *4:4. 2 Th *2:9-12.

13. **an.** Gr. one. Re 9:13. 18:21. 19:17g. **an.** ℐ108E1, Mt +8:19. **angel.** Re 14:6. Many authorities read eagle. Dt 28:49. 2 S 1:23. Is 40:31. Je 4:13. Ho 8:1. Hab 1:8. **flying.** Re 14:3, 6. 19:17. Ge 1:20. Ps 103:20. He

1:14. **saying.** Nu ◑22:28. **Woe.** Re 9:1, 12. 11:14. Ezk 2:10. Da *12:1. Ho *7:13. Mt *24:21, 22. **woe.** Re 12:12. **inhabiters.** Re +3:10. **the three.** ver. +2.

REVELATION 9

At the sounding of the fifth angel, a star falls from heaven, to whom is given the key of the bottomless pit, 1. He opens the pit, and there come forth locusts like scorpions, 2-11. The first woe is past, 12. The sixth trumpet sounds, 13. Four angels are let loose, that were bound, 14-21.

1. **the fifth.** ver. 12, 13. Re 8:+2, 6-8, 10, 12. 11:14, 15. **a star fall.** Re 1:20. +8:10. *12:4, 12. Jsh 5:14. 1 K 22:19. 2 Ch 18:18. Jb 38:7. Ps 148:2. Is 14:12. Lk *10:18. 2 Th 2:3-8. 2 T 3:1-5. **the key.** Re +1:18. 20:1. Mt 16:19. **the bottomless.** ver. 2, 11. Re 11:7. 17:8. *20:1, 3, 10. Lk 8:28, 31. Ro 10:7g. Ju *6. **pit.** Nu +*16:30n, 33. Ps 55:23.

2. **there.** ver. 17. Re +14:11. Ge 15:17. 19:28. Is 14:31. Jl 2:30. Ac 2:19. **smoke of a.** Re 18:9, 18. 19:3. Ge ▶19:28. Ex ▶19:18. Is 34:10. Mt 13:42, 50. Lk 16:24. **and the sun.** See on Re 8:12. Ex 10:21-23. Jl 2:2, ▶10. **darkened.** Re 8:12. 16:10. Pr +*20:20.

3. **there came.** Re 12:7. 16:13, 14. Lk 8:30-33. 1 T 4:1. **the smoke.** Jb 41:19-21. **locusts.** ver. 7. Ex ▶10:12, 15. Jg 6:5. *7:12. Ps *105:34, 35. Pr 30:27. Is 33:4. Jl 1:4. 2:25. Na 3:15, 17. **scorpions.** ver. 5, 10, 11. Dt 8:15. 1 K 12:11, 14. Ezk 2:6. Jl *2:3. Lk 10:19. 11:12.

4. **that they.** Re 6:6. *7:3. Jb 1:10, 12. Ps 76:10. Mt 24:24. 2 T 3:8, 9. **not hurt.** Re 3:10. 8:7. Ex 12:23. 15:26. Dt 33:29. Jb *5:19-22. Ps *91:1. **green thing.** Ex 10:15. **but only.** Ex *8:22, 23. **which.** See on Re *7:3, 4. *13:8. 14:1. Ex 12:23. Jb 2:6. Ezk *9:▶4, 6. 2 C 1:22. Ep 1:13. +*4:30.

5. **it was.** Re 13:5, 7. Da 5:18-22. 7:6. Jn 19:11. **they should not.** Re 11:7. Jb 2:6. **tormented.** Re 11:10. 14:10. 20:10. Mt √8:29. 12:43-45. 17:15, 18. Mk 5:2-5. Lk *8:29. Ac 5:16. **five months.** ver. 10. **and their.** See on ver. 3.

6. **shall men.** Re 6:16. 2 S 1:9. 1 K 19:4. Jb ▶3:20-22. *7:15, 16. Is 2:19. Je *8:3. Ho 10:8. Jon 4:8, 9. Lk 23:30.

7. **the shapes.** Jb 39:20. Jl ▶2:4, 5. Na 3:17. **heads.** Na *3:17. **horses.** Je *8:16, 17. **crowns.** Re +6:2. **their faces.** Da *7:4, 8.

8. **hair.** 2 K 9:30. Is 3:24. Je 51:27. 1 C 11:14, 15. 1 T 2:9. 1 P 3:3. **women.** Zc 5:7-11. **and their teeth.** Ps 57:4. Da 7:19. Jl ▶1:6.

9. **they had.** ver. 17. Jb 40:18. *41:1, 7, 15-17, 23-30. Jl 2:8. **and the.** Jb 39:25. Is 9:5. Jl 2:5-7. Na 2:4, 5. **sound of chariots.** Jl ▶2:5. **horses.** Jb 39:21-25. Je 8:6. **to battle.** 1 C 14:8.

10. **tails.** See on ver. 3, 5. Re 12:4. **five months.** ver. 5.

11. **a king.** Re 12:9. Jb 18:14. *41:33, 34. Pr 30:27. Jn 12:31. *14:30. 16:11. 2 C 4:4. Ep *2:2. 1 J 4:4. 5:19. **the angel.** Re 20:2. Ezk *38:17. ver. +1. Jb 26:6. **the angel.** ver. 1. **whose name.** ℐ121N1. Metonymy of the Adjunct. The name of the pit is given to the angel of the pit, by this figure, by which the abstract is put for the concrete. For other instances of this figure, see Ge +31:54. **Hebrew.** Re 16:16. Jn +5:2. **Abaddon.** that is, *a destroyer.* ℐ121N1, Ge +31:54. ✳S#3g. For ✳S#11h, see Jb +26:6. 28:22. 31:12. Ps *17:4. 88:11. Pr 15:11. 27:20. Is 16:4. Je

4:7. 6:26. Da 8:24, 25. 9:26. 11:44. Jn *8:44. 2 C *11:14, 15. Ja 3:14, 15. 1 J *3:12. **Apollyon**. i.e. *destroyer,* *S#623g. ʃ24B, Ge +23:16. Jb 28:22.

12. **woe**. See on ver. 1, 2. Re 8:13. **two**. ver. 13-21. Re *8:13. 11:14.

13. **the sixth**. See on ver. 1. Re +8:2. **a**. Gr. one. Re +8:13. **voice**. See on Re *8:3-5. Ps 118:27. He 9:24. 10:21. **horns**. Ex *30:3. 1 K 1:50-53. 2:13-25. **golden altar**. Re +8:3. Ex 30:6. 40:3.

14. **to the**. Re 8:2, 6. **Loose**. ver. 15. Re 7:1. *16:12. **which are bound**. Re 20:2-7. 1 P 3:19. 2 P 2:4. Ju 6. **the great**. Re 14:8. Ge 2:14. ▶15:18. Dt ▶1:7. Jsh ▶1:4. 2 S 8:3. Je 51:63. **Euphrates**. i.e. *unlimited,* *S#2166g. Re 16:12. For *S#6578h, see Ge +2:14. Je 46:4-10.

15. **prepared**. Is 46:8-11. Ep 1:11. **for**. *or,* at. **an hour**. ver. 5, 10. Re 14:7. Mk 13:32. Ac 1:7. **a day**. Is 34:8. 61:2. 1 C 3:13. **month**. Ho 5:7. **year**. Is 34:8. 61:2. **for to slay**. ver. 18. Re 6:8. 8:7, 9, 11, 12. **the third**. Re 9:18.

16. **the number**. Re 5:11. Ps 68:17. Da 7:10. Ju +14. **army**. Ezk *38:4. 39:11. Jl *2:11. **horsemen**. Ezk 23:6. 38:4. Da 11:40. **I heard**. Re 7:4.

17. **horses**. Re 9:7-10. Is ◑31:3. Je 8:17. **having**. ver. 9. **of fire**. Ezk 28:14, 16. **jacinth**. Re 21:20. **the heads**. 1 Ch 12:8. Is 5:28, 29. **out of**. Re 11:5. **fire**. Re 16:8. **brimstone**. ver. 18. Re 14:10. 19:20. 20:10. +*21:8. Ge 19:24. Ps 11:6. Is +*30:33. Ezk 38:22. Lk 17:29. **as the**. 1 Ch 12:8. Is 5:28, 29.

18. **the third**. See on ver. 15, 17. Re +8:7. 9:15. **by the fire**. ver. 17. **and smoke**. ver. +2.

19. **their mouth**. 1 K *22:21, 22. Is 5:26-30. Da 7:20, 25. Ja 3:6-8. **in their tails**. ver. 10. Re 9:10. Is 9:15. Ep +*4:14. **do hurt**. Ex 34:10. Dt 28:59.

20. **yet repented not**. ver. 21. Re 2:21, 22. 16:8. Ex 8:32. 10:7. *11:9. Dt 31:29. 2 Ch 28:22. Pr *27:22. Je *2:30. *5:3. *8:4-6. Am *4:6-13. Mt 21:32. 2 C 12:21. **works of their hands**. Dt *4:28. *31:29. 2 K 19:18. Ps 115:4. *135:15. Is 2:8. ▶17:8. 37:19. 44:10-20. Je 1:16. 10:3. 25:6, 7, 14. Ac 7:41. 19:26. **worship devils**. Re 13:4. Le 17:7. Dt ▶32:17. 2 K 22:17, 22, 23. 2 Ch 18:21, 22. 34:25. Ps 106:37. Is 2:8. Je 25:6. 44:8. Mt 10:1-8. 12:43-45. Ac 7:41. 19:26. 1 C 10:20, 21. 1 T *4:1. **and idols**. Ps 115:4-8. 135:15-18. Is 40:19, 20. 41:7. 42:17, 18. 44:9-20. 46:5-7. Je 10:3-5, 8, 9, 14, 15. 16:19, 20. 51:17. Da ▶5:4, 23. Hab *2:18-20. Ac 17:29. Ro 1:21-23. **which neither**. Ps ▶115:7. Is 46:5-7.

21. **Neither repented**. Re *16:10, 11. Je 18:8. Lk *16:29-31. Ro 1:18-32. 3:10-18. **their murders**. Re 11:7-9. 13:7, 15. 16:6. 18:24. 21:8. 22:15. Da 7:21-25. 11:33. **their sorceries**. Re 13:13. 18:23. +*21:8. *22:15. Ex 7:22. 22:18. Le 19:31. 20:6, 27. Dt +*18:10. 1 S 28:7. 2 K ▶9:22. 1 Ch 10:13. Is 8:19. 47:9, 12. 57:3. Mi 5:12. Na 3:4. Ml +*3:5. Ac 16:16. Ga 5:20. **nor of their fornication**. Re 14:8. 17:2, 5. 18:3. 19:2. Mt 15:19. 1 C +6:18. 2 C 12:21.

REVELATION 10

The apostle in vision beholds a mighty Angel, with a little book open in his hand; and hears the voice of seven thunders, which he was ordered to seal up, 1-4. The angel swears by the eternal Creator, that at an appointed time, when the seventh trumpet shall begin to sound, the mystery of God shall be finished,

5-7. The apostle receives and eats the little book, 8-11.

1. **another**. ver. 5, 6. Re *5:2. 7:1, 2. 8:2-5, 13. 9:13, 14. 14:14, 15. **mighty angel**. Re 18:21. Is 63:9. Da 8:16. 9:21. √10:21. 12:1. Lk 1:19, 26. **come down**. Re 18:1. 20:1. 21:2, 10. **clothed**. Re +*1:7. Ex 16:10. Le 16:2. 2 Ch ◑+*5:13. Ps 18:11. *97:2. 104:3. Is 19:1. La 3:44. Ezk 1:4. Da +*7:13. Mt +*17:5. +*24:30. Lk 21:27. Ac 1:9. 1 C 10:1. **a rainbow**. Re +4:3. Ge 9:11-17. Is +*54:9. Ezk 1:28. **his face**. Re *1:16. Da 10:6. Ml 3:1, 2. *4:2. Mt √17:2. Ac *26:13, 15. **his feet**. Re +1:15. 2:18. Da 10:5, 6. **pillars**. Re 1:15. SS 5:15.

2. **a little**. ver. 8-10. Re 5:1-5. 6:1, 3. Ezk 2:9, 10. **book**. Re 5:5-7. 6:1—8:1. **he set**. ver. 5, 8. Dt √11:24. Ps *2:8. 65:5. 72:8. *89:25. Pr 8:15, 16. Is 59:19. Zc *9:10. Mt *28:18. Ep 1:20-22. Ph 2:10, 11. **foot upon**. Da 10:4. 12:7.

3. **loud**. Jb *40:9. Pr 19:12. Is 5:29. *42:13. Je √25:29-31. Ho 11:10. Jl +*3:16. Am 1:2. **a lion**. Is *31:4. Am *3:8. **seven**. Re *4:5. +6:1. 8:5. 11:19. 14:2. 15:1, 7. 19:6. Ps *81:7. **thunders**. These may have been angel voices, the effect (thunder) being put, by Metonymy, for the cause. Jn 12:29.

4. **I was**. Re 1:11. ch. 2, 3. Is 8:1. Hab 2:2, 3. **I heard**. ver. 8. **Seal up**. Re ◑22:10. Dt +*29:29. Pr *25:2. Is +*8:16. 29:11. Da ▶8:26. 12:▶4, 9. Am *3:7. Mt 8:4. 2 C 12:4. **write**. Re +1:19.

5. **the angel**. Da 10:4-6. **stand**. See on ver. 2, 8. **upon the sea**. Da ▶12:7. **lifted up**. Ge ▶14:19, 22. 22:15, 16. Ex 6:8. 17:16mg. Nu 14:30. Dt *32:40. Ezk 20:5, 6, 15, 23, 28, 42. *36:7. 47:14. Da 12:7. He *6:13, 17.

6. **by him**. Re +1:18. 4:9. Je 10:10. **for ever**. Gr. *aion,* Re +1:6. **who created**. Re +4:11. 14:7. Ge ch. 1, 2. Ex *▶20:11. Ne +*▶9:6. Ps 95:3-6. ▶146:6. 148:1-7. Je 10:11-13. Ac 14:15. 17:23. Ro 1:20. **that there**. Rather, "the time should not be yet," *kronos ouk esti eti,* that is, the time of those glorious things with which the mystery of God should be finished. Re 12:12. 16:17. 21:6. Da 12:7. **time no longer**. Signifying not the abolition of time, which is impossible, but that there would be no further delay or waiting (Re 6:10) for the accomplishment of God's covenanted and promised purposes. Hab *2:3. Mt 24:22. Mk 13:20. 1 T ◑*6:14, 15.

7. **in the days**. Re +*11:15-18. **seventh angel**. Re *11:15. *16:17. **the mystery**. Re +1:20. Mt 13:10, 11, 34, 35. Ro √11:25. +*16:25n. 1 C 15:51, 52. Ep 3:3-9. **should be finished**. This "mystery" which is to be finished involves (1) the resolution of the problem of evil, which was first manifest in the Garden of Eden, as the first sin seemingly interrupted the purpose for Adam and Eve in the Garden of Eden. The fall brought the attendant curse upon man and all creation, the curse now announced to be removed. The prophets speak unitedly of the coming messianic kingdom as a time of regeneration, restitution, and restoration, when earth will be restored to its paradaisical state, a time when the curse is removed (Re +*22:3. Ge +*3:15. Is 11:6-9. +*60:21. Zc 14:11. Ac +√3:19-21). (2) the resolution of the apparent paradox of election and free will, and a clarification to us of the orderings of providence (1 C 13:12. Ep +*1:11). (3) the consummation of the mystery of godliness, involving the human and divine cooperating in establishing the Davidic theocratic kingdom (Is +*54:1. Mt 22:41-46. Jn +*1:51.

1 C +*15:50n. Ep 1:10. 1 T +*3:16). (4) the completion of our redemption and the establishment of our inheritance (Mt 19:27-30. Ro +*8:23. Ep +*1:11n. +*4:30. He +*9:28n. 1 J √3:2). (5) the pre-tribulational, premillennial personal appearance of Christ for believers to prepare the organization of, and to set up, his kingdom before its open, public manifestation (Dt +*33:2. Is 11:11n. 1 C 15:51, 52. 1 Th +*4:16-18. T +*2:13n. Re +*11:17n, 18). (6) the accomplishment of divine vengeance and retribution in the Day of the Lord (Is +*61:2. +*63:4. Re +*1:10). (7) the open revelation of Christ, the overthrow of Antichrist, the investiture of the kingdom, the exaltation of the saints, the overthrow of Satan (Da +*7:13, 14. Lk 10:18. Col +*3:4. 2 Th 1:10. +*2:8. Re 20:10). Because this finishing occurs at the beginning of the seventh trumpet (which itself is clearly premillennial), the finishing is necessarily premillennial, not postmillennial. The theme of all the prophets is the fulfillment of the covenants and promises in the "sure mercies of David" in establishing the messianic kingdom, which is the kingdom of God upon earth, as our eternal inheritance (Is +*55:3. Mt +*5:5. Ac 1:3, 6. +*13:34. 15:14-18. 28:31. Ro +*4:13. +*8:17). Re +*16:17. 17:17. Dt √32:43. Ps 102:13-22. Ezk √39:8. Da 9:24, 27. 12:7. **as he.** Is +*65:17. Da 7:25, 26. Am +*3:7. See on Lk +*24:44-47. Ac +√3:21. 2 P +*3:7-10, 13. **hath declared.** Re 14:6g. **his servants the.** 2 K 21:10. 24:2. Ezr 9:11. Is +*65:17. Je 7:25. 25:4. 29:19. 35:15. 44:4. Da ▶9:6, 10. Am √▶3:7. Zc ▶1:6.

8. **the voice.** See on ver. 4, 5. Is 30:21. **book.** ver. 2. **which standeth.** ver. 2, 5.

9. **book.** Ezk *2:9, 10. **Take.** Jb +*23:12. Je +*15:16. Ezk 2:8. *3:1-3, 14. Col *3:16. **eat.** Je *15:16-18. Ezk ▶3:1. **honey.** Ps 19:10. *119:103. Ezk 3:1-4, 14.

10. **and ate.** "Eating" is a Hebrew idiom for receiving knowledge; just as we idiomatically use the word digesting of considering what we have learned (E. W. B., *Apocalypse*, p. 342). Dt 31:26. Je 31:33. Ezk 3:4, 10. Jn 6:47, 48, 53, 54. **sweet.** Ps *19:10. 104:34. 119:103. Pr 16:24. Ezk 3:3. **my belly.** Ezk 2:10. 3:14mg.

11. **Thou.** Re 11:9. 14:6. 17:15. Je *1:9, 10, 17. 25:15-30. Lk *12:11, 12. **prophesy.** Re *12:11. Je ▶25:30. Ezk 37:4. **before.** *or,* concerning. Je 1:10. 46:1. This word is several times rendered "against" in Lk 12:52, 53. **peoples.** Re +5:9. Da ▶7:14. **nations.** Je ▶1:10. Mt *24:14. **tongues.** Da ▶3:4. **kings.** Ps *119:46. 2 T 4:16, 17.

REVELATION 11

The apostle is directed to measure the temple, the altar, and the worshippers; but to leave "the outer court to the Gentiles"; with a prediction of their prevalence for forty-two months, 1, 2. Power is given to two witnesses, who prophesy in sackcloth, during twelve hundred and sixty days, 3-6. The beast makes war upon them, and slays them: but after three days and a half, overtake their enemies, 13, 14. The seventh trumpet sounds; and the announcement is made of the glorious events which shall follow, including the great power of God and the eternal reign of Christ, the anger of the nations, the wrath of God, the resurrection of the righteous, the time of their rewards, and the destruction of the earth-destroyers, 15-18. An

introduction to the prophecies of the subsequent chapter, 19.

1. **was given.** Re 6:11. 8:2. **a reed.** Re *21:15, 16. Ps 74:2. Is *28:17. Je 10:16. 31:39. 51:19. Ezk 40:▶3-5. 42:15-20. Zc *2:1, 2. Ga 6:14-16. **the angel.** Re 10:1-5. **Rise.** Nu 33:18. Ezk ch. 40-48. 1 C *3:16, 17. 2 C 6:16. Ep *2:20-22. 1 P 2:5, 9. **and measure.** ∫180A. *Zeugma.* The verb measure is by this figure "yoked" to a second object which does not fit it as equally as the first, for worshippers would not be measured but taken account of. For other instances of this figure, see Ge +4:20. 2 K 21:13. Is 34:11. La *2:8. Ezk 40:5. Am 7:7-9. Zc 2:2, 4. **the temple.** ver. 19. Re +3:12. Mt 24:15. 2 Th *2:4. **the altar.** Re 8:3. 9:13. Ezk 41:22. Da 9:27. Mt 24:15. 2 Th 2:3, 4.

2. **the court.** Ezk 40:17-20. 42:20. Mt +26:3. **the temple.** Ps ▶79:1. **leave out.** Gr. cast out. **it is given.** Re ch. 13-18. Ps *74:1-7. *79:1. La 1:10. Lk +*21:24. 2 Th 2:3-12. 1 T 4:1-3. 2 T 3:1-6. **unto the Gentiles.** Ho *8:8. Ep ◐2:14. Col ◐*3:11. **the holy city.** Re 21:2, 10. 22:19. Is 48:2. 52:1. Mt +4:5. 27:53. **tread.** Is 60:15. *▶63:18. Da 7:19, 22, 26, 27. *8:10, ▶13, 24, +*25. Zc ▶12:3, LXX. Mt +*5:13. 24:15, 29-31. Lk +*21:24. He 10:29. **forty.** ver. 3, 11. Re 12:6, +*14. 13:5. Nu 14:34. Da *7:25. +*9:27. *12:7, 11, 12. Ro +*11:25.

3. **I will give,** etc. *or,* I will give unto my two witnesses, that they may prophesy. Jn 3:27. 1 C 12:28. Ep 4:11. **two.** Nu 30:30. Dt 17:6. 19:15. Mt 18:16. 2 C 13:1. **witnesses.** ver. 10. Re 2:13. 19:10. 20:4. Is 8:2. 43:10. 55:4. Lk 24:48. Jn 15:27. Ac +*1:8. +*2:32. 3:15. 13:31. **they shall.** Re 19:10. **a thousand.** See on ver. 2. Re 12:6, +*14. 13:5. Da +*9:27. **days.** The duration of man is often reckoned in days (Ge 47:9, 28. Ps 90:10, 12. 119:84), whereas judgments are sometimes reckoned in months (Ge 8:5. Re 9:5, 10. 13:5). Lk 4:25. Ja 5:17. **clothed.** Ge 37:34. 2 S 3:31. 1 K 20:31. 21:27. 2 K 6:30. 19:1, 2. 1 Ch 21:16. Ne 9:1. Est 4:1, 2. Jb 16:15. Ps 35:13. 69:11. Is 20:2. 22:12. 32:11. 37:1, 2. Je 4:8. 6:26. La 2:10. Ezk 7:18. Jl 1:13. Am 8:10. Jon 3:5-8. Mt 11:21. Lk 10:13.

4. **These are.** ∫92C, Mt +2:15. **two olive.** Ps 52:8. Je *11:16. Zc ▶4:2, 3, *11-14. Ro 11:17. **two candlesticks.** Re 1:12, 20. Zc ▶4:2. Mt *5:14-16. Lk 11:33. Jn 5:35. Ph 2:15, 16. 1 J 2:20. **standing.** Dt 10:8. 1 K 17:1. Mt 20:23. **the God.** Ex 8:22. Jsh 3:11, 13. Is *54:5. Mi 4:13. Zc *4:14. 6:5.

5. **And if.** ∫184C, Mt +4:9. **fire.** Re 9:17, 18. Nu *16:28-35. Jg 9:19, 20, 56, 57. 2 K *1:▶10-12, 14. 6:15-17. Ps *18:8. Is 11:4. Je 1:10. *5:14. =23:29. Ezk 43:3. Ho 6:5. Jl 2:3. Zc 1:6. 2:8. Ac 2:3. 9:4, 5. **devoureth.** 2 S ▶22:9. Ps ▶97:3. Je ▶5:14. **and if.** ∫184C, Mt +4:9. **he must.** Nu 16:35.

6. **These have.** 2 K 2:11. Mt 11:14. *17:3. Lk 1:17. Ju 9. **power.** 1 K *17:1. Lk 4:25. Ja *5:16-18. **have power over.** Ex ch. 7-12, 14. Ps 78:43-51. 105:26-36. **to turn.** Re +8:8. **plagues.** 1 S ▶4:8.

7. **when.** ver. 3. Lk 13:32. Jn 17:4. 19:30. Ac 20:24. 2 T 4:7. **the beast.** Re *9:11. 13:1, 7, 11. *17:6-8. 19:19, 20. Da ▶7:3, 7, 8 LXX. 21, 22, 25. 8:23, 24. Zc 14:2, etc. 2 Th 2:8, 9. **out.** Re 9:+1, 2. 20:1-3. **make war.** Re 12:17. *13:1-8. 19:19. Da *7:21. 2 T *3:12. **overcome them.** Re ◐12:11. Da 11:35.

8. **their dead.** ver. 9. Ps 9:9. 10:1. √79:2, 3. Je 26:23. Ezk 37:11. **the great city.** ver. 13. Re 14:8. 16:19. 17:1, 5, 18. 18:2, 10, 16, 18, 19, 21. 2 Ch 32:6. Ne

*7:3, 4. Je 5:1. 22:5, *7-9. **Sodom**. Ge 13:13. 19:24. Dt +*32:30-33. Is ▶1:10. 3:9. Je *23:14. Ezk 16:2, 46, +*53-55. Am 4:11. Zp 2:9. Mt 10:15. Lk +10:12. 2 P 2:6. Ju +*7. **Egypt**. Ex 1:13, 14. 3:7. 20:2. Ps 78:43-51. Ezk 23:3, 4, 8, 19, 27. **where also**. Re 14:20. Jn *19:20. **our Lord**. Re 18:24. Lk 13:33, 34. Ac 9:4. He 6:6. 13:12.

9. **the people**. Re +5:9. 10:11. 13:7. 17:15. **shall see**. 1 S 31:9, 10. **three**. See on ver. 2, 3, 11. **and shall not**. Re 5:8. 19:17, 18. 2 K 9:10. Ps *79:2, 3. Ec 6:3. Is 14:20. 33:1. Je 7:33. 8:2. 14:16. Mt 7:2. 23:29-34. Lk *13:34. **graves**. Gr. *mneuma*, Mk +5:5. This Greek word is found in the LXX at Ex 14:11. Nu 11:34, 35. 19:16, 18. 33:16, 17. Dt 9:22. Jsh 24:31. 2 Ch 16:14. 34:4, 28. Jb 10:19. Is 65:4. Je 26:23. Ezk 32:22, 24, 26. 37:12, 12.

10. **dwell**. Re +*3:10. 12:13. 13:8, 14. Mt 10:22. **rejoice**. Jg 16:23, 24. Jb ◑*20:5. Ps 13:4. 35:19, 24-26. 89:42. Pr 24:17. Je 50:11. Ob 12. Mi 7:8. Mt *24:48-51. Lk 23:12. Jn 16:20. **make merry**. Ne 8:10-12. Est 9:19-22. Ps ▶105:38. Lk +15:23. 1 C 13:6. **send gifts**. Ne 8:10, 12. Est 9:19, 22. **two prophets**. ver. +3, 5, 6. Re 16:10. 1 K 18:17. 21:20. 22:8, 18. Is 14:16, 20. Je 38:4. Jn 7:7. Ac 5:33. 7:54-57. 17:5, 6.

11. **three**. ver. 9. **the spirit**. Gr. *pneuma*, ⌐121A3, Mt +27:50. Ge +*2:7. Jb 33:4. Ezk *37:5-14. Lk 8:55g. Jn 6:63. Ro +*8:2, 11. **entered**. Ezk ▶37:5, 10. **they stood**. Ezk 37:10. **great fear**. ver. 13. Jsh 2:9. Je 33:9. Ho 3:5. Mt 27:54. Ac 5:5, 11.

12. **Come**. Re 4:1. Ps 15:1. 24:3. Is 40:34. Jn *12:26. **And they ascended**. Re *3:21. *12:5. 2 K 2:11. Is 14:13. Ac +*1:9. Ro *8:34-37. Ep 2:5, 6. **up to heaven**. 2 K ▶2:11. **in a cloud**. Is 60:8. Ac +*1:9. 1 Th +*4:17. **and their**. Ex 14:25. 2 K 2:1, 5, 7. Ps 86:17. 112:10. Ml *3:18. Lk *16:23.

13. **great earthquake**. ver. 19. Re +6:12. 8:5. 16:18-21. Ezk ▶38:19. Zc *14:3-5. He +*12:26, 27. **and the tenth**. Re 8:9-12. 13:1-3. 16:10, 19. **men**. Gr. names of men. ⌐121T2, Ac +1:15. Re 3:4. Ge 6:4. Ac 1:15. **and the remnant**. See on ver. 11. **were affrighted**. Pr +*19:25. Is +*26:9. **gave glory**. Re 4:9. 14:7. *15:4. 16:9. 19:7. Ex 8:19. Dt *32:3. Jsh 7:19. 1 S 6:5. Ps 9:16. 106:12-15. Is 26:15, 16. Je 13:16. Ml 2:2. Lk 4:15, ◑29. 5:26. 17:12-18. 18:43. 23:47. Jn +9:24. Ac 12:23. 24:25. Ro 4:20. **God of heaven**. Re 16:11. 2 Ch 36:23. Ezr 1:2. 5:11, 12. 6:9. 7:12, 23. Ne 1:4, 5. 2:4. Ps 136:26. Da 2:18, ▶19, ◑28, 37, 44. Jon 1:9.

14. **second woe**. Re *8:13. 9:12. 15:1. 16:1, etc.

15. **the seventh**. "Each seventh seal, trumpet and vial is marked off from the preceding six by unmistakable signs, sufficient to show us that they are resumptive rather than continuous. Each going over the same ground to give particulars not contained in the others, bringing us up to a crisis; and giving the other events in the corresponding period, but from a different point of view" (E.W.B. *Apocalypse*, pp. 370, 371). This seventh trumpet is the last of this series of seven, but not the last absolutely, and is not to be confused with the "last trump" of 1 C 15:52n. Chronologically, the trumpet of Mt 24:31 must follow this seventh trumpet of Revelation, for it occurs after the Tribulation, at the open manifestation of Christ's Second Advent (Mt 24:30), which in the book of Revelation is recorded in Re 19:11-16, which is after the time expressed here. In the book of Revelation the seventh trumpet is never called "last" (Re 1:11, 17. 2:8, 19. 15:1. 21:9. 22:13).

Re 8:+2-6, 12. 9:1, 13. +*10:7. **sounded**. The sounding of the seventh trumpet does not mark the Rapture of the church, but proclaims the coming coronation of earth's rightful king, the answer to the prayer of the ages, "thy kingdom come." 2 S 15:10. 1 K *1:39. 1 C 15:52n. 1 Th +*4:16n. **and there**. Re 4:5. 12:10. 16:17. 19:1, 6. Is 27:13. 44:23. Lk 15:6, 10. **The kingdoms**. Re 12:10. 15:4. 17:14. +*20:4. 1 Ch +*29:11. Ps *22:27, ▶28. 72:11. +*82:8. 86:9. 89:15-17. Is +*2:2, 3. 49:6, 7, 22, 23. 55:5. 60:3-14. Je 16:19. Da *2:34, 35, 44, 45. +*7:13, 14, 18, 22, 27. Ho 2:23. Am *9:11, 12. Ob +*21. Mi 4:1, 2. Zp 3:9, 10. Zc 2:11. *8:20-23. +*14:9. Ml 1:11. **world**. Gr. *kosmos*, Mt +4:8. Jn 18:36. **are become**. T#90. Re 12:10. 19:16. +20:4 (T#440). Ps 72:8-11. Is *9:7. Da 2:35, 44, 45. +*7:13, 14. Zc +*14:9. Mt 13:31-33. 1 C 15:27, 28. **our Lord**. Re 19:16. Ps 45:6. 47:7, 8. Is 40:9, 10. Mt 26:29. 1 C 15:24, 25. **He** +*1:8. **and of**. Re 22:3. Ep 5:5. **his Christ**. Ps ▶2:2. Mk *14:61, 62. Lk +9:20. Ac 4:26. 17:30, 31. 1 C +*1:7, 8. 15:21-23. Ph 3:20. 1 Th 2:19. +*3:13. +*5:9, 23. 2 Th 1:1, 2. T +*2:12, 13. 1 P 1:7, 13. 2 P 1:11. 1 J 2:22. **shall reign**. ver. 17. Re 20:4. Ex ▶15:18. Ps ▶10:16. 110:4. 146:10. Is +*9:7. Ezk +*37:25. Da *▶2:44. +*7:▶14, 18, 27. Mi +*4:7. Zc +*14:9. Mt +*6:13. Lk +*1:33. He +*1:8. **for ever**. Gr. *aion*, Re +1:6. Ge +9:12. 2 S 7:16. Is √9:7. Da 2:44. +*7:14. Lk √1:32. 2 P *1:11.

16. **elders**. Re *4:4, 10. 5:5-8, 14. 7:11. 19:4. **which sat**. Re 4:4. **fell upon**. Re +4:10.

17. **We give**. Re 4:9. Ps *95:1-3. *97:1, 12. Da 2:23. +*6:10. Mt +*11:25. Lk 10:21. Jn 11:41. 2 C 2:14. 9:15. 1 T 1:12. **Lord God Almighty**. See on Re +*1:8. +4:8. 15:3. 16:7, 14. Ge 17:1. Am ▶4:13, LXX. **which art**. See on Re 1:4, 8. 16:5. Ex ▶3:14. Is ▶41:4. He +*13:8. **and art to come**. Many significant authorities omit this phrase and "and shalt be" at Re 16:5. Peters says of this omission, "This omission, as the weightiest MSS. (admitted by Anti-Millenarians, as Prof. Stuart, *Com.*) prove, is not accidental but intentional, showing that the coming one is no longer expected to come, but has already come." Peters notes "the omission is most significant of presence" (*Theocratic Kingdom*, vol. 2, p. 185, 191). See related notes (Re 10:7n, point 5. Is 11:11n, points 4, 24. T 2:13n). Re 1:4, 8. Mt 11:3. 21:9. 23:39. Lk 7:19. 13:35. He 10:37. **thou hast reigned**. See on ver. 15. Re *19:6, 11-21. *20:1-3. Ps 21:13. 57:11. 64:9, 10. 97:1. 98:1-3. 102:13-18. Is *51:9-11. 52:10. **reigned**. Ps ▶99:1.

18. **the nations**. ver. 2, 9, 10. Re 17:12-15. 19:19, 20. Ps 2:▶1-3. ▶46:6. Is 34:1-10. 63:1-6. Ezk 38:9, 23. Jl 3:9-14. Mi 7:15-17. Zc 14:2, 3. **were angry**. Ac 4:26. **and thy wrath**. See on Re +*6:15-17. 14:10. 15:1, 7. ch. 16. 19:15. Ps ▶2:5. 99:1. 110:5. Is *24:17-21. +*26:19, 20. 30:27, 28, 30-33. Ezk 38:16-23. Zp 1:2, 3, 14-16. 3:8. **time of the dead**. See on Re 6:10, 11. *20:4, 5, +*6, 12, 15. Is +*26:19-21. Da *7:9, 10. +*12:1, 2. He +*9:27. **be judged**. Re +*6:10. 14:7. 18:8. Da 7:10. Mt +*10:15n. Jn √3:18. √5:24. Ro *2:2, 6-11. *8:1. *14:10, 12. 2 C √5:10. **give reward**. T#857. Re *2:10, 23. 3:4. *7:15-17. *21:22, 23. *22:5, 12. Ps 49:14. Is *40:10. 60:19, 20. Mt +*5:12. *10:41, 42. +*16:27. *25:34. Lk *14:14. Jn +*14:2, 3. 17:22, 24. Ro +*2:7. 5:10, 17. 1 C √2:9. 2 Th *1:5-7, 10, 12. 2 T +*4:8. He *4:9. *9:15. 11:9, 10, 16, 25, 26. 1 P 1:9, 13. 2 P +*3:13n. 2 J +*8. **thy servants the**. Re +7:3. +*10:7. 2 K *9:7. 17:13, 23. 21:10. 24:2. Da

)9:6, 10. Am)3:7. Zc)1:6. Jn *12:26. **prophets.** Re 16:6. 18:20, 24. 2 K *9:7. Hab +*3:16, 19. Lk +*13:28. **the saints.** Re +8:3. Ex 22:31. Dt +*33:2. Ps 16:3. 30:4. 31:23. 34:9. 50:5. Da *7:18. 2 Th *1:7, 8. **and them.** Re 19:5. Jsh 24:14. 1 S 12:24. Ps 34:9. 85:9. 102:15. 103:11. 115:13, 14. 147:11. Ec 8:12. 12:13. Mi 6:9. Lk 1:50. **small and.** Re 13:16. 19:5, 18. 20:12. Ge 19:11. Ps)115:13. Je 16:6. Ac +8:10. **shouldest destroy them.** Re 13:10. 18:6, 16-24. 19:19, 21. Ge +*6:13 (T#566). Da 7:26. 8:25. 11:44, 45. He 12:27. 2 P +*3:7. **which destroy.** *or,* which corrupt. Re +*10:7. Is *24:21. 2 Th 2:7.

19. **the temple.** ver. 1, 2. Re +3:12. 14:15-17. 15:5-8. 19:11. Is *6:1-4. **was opened.** Re 4:1. 6:1-9. 9:2. *15:5-8. *19:11. 20:12. **in heaven.** Re +*7:15. *14:17. **the ark.** Ex *25:21, 22, 40. Nu 4:5, 15. 10:33. Dt 31:24-26. 1 K)8:1, 6. 2 Ch)5:7. 2 C 3:14-16. He 9:+4-8, 23. **his testament.** Ge *15:7. 2 S 7:12-16. Is +*55:3. Lk 1:68-79. Ac +*7:5. Ro +*4:13. 11:29. *15:8. **and there were.** ver. 13, 15. See on Re +4:5. 8:5. 10:3. 16:18. 19:6. Ex)19:16. 20:18. **an earthquake.** ver. 13. Re +6:12. **and great.** Re 8:7. 16:17-21. Ex 9:18-29. Jsh 10:11. Jb 38:22, 23. Ps 18:12. 105:32. Is 28:2. 30:30. 32:19. Ezk 13:11. 38:22. **hail.** Ex)9:24.

REVELATION 12

The apostle sees in vision a travailing woman, watched by a red dragon, that he might devour her offspring: she is delivered of a son; he is caught up to the throne of God, and she flees into the wilderness, 1-6. Michael overcomes, and casts out Satan; joy in heaven on that occasion; and woe denounced on the earth, through Satan's rage and malice, 7-12. The dragon persecutes the woman; she having wings given her flies into the wilderness, and is preserved from his unwearied and varied efforts, 13-17.

1. **And.** ſ107. Hysterologia, Ge +10:5. **there.** ver. 3. Re 11:19. 15:1. 2 Ch 32:31. Mk 13:25. Ac 2:19. **wonder.** *or,* sign. Mt 12:38. 24:30. Lk 21:+11, 25. **a woman.** Is 49:14-23. 54:5-7. 60:1-4. Ho 2:19, 20. Jn 3:29. 2 C 11:2. Ep 5:25-27, 32. **clothed.** Re 21:23. Ps *84:11. 104:2. Is 60:19, 20. 61:10. Ml 4:2. Ro 3:22. 13:14. Ga 3:27. **and the moon.** SS 6:10. Ga 6:14. T 2:11, 12. **crown.** Re 1:20. 21:14. Is 62:3. Zc 9:16. **twelve.** Ge 37:9, 10.

2. **And.** ſ148, Ge +8:22. **with child.** Ro 9:4, 5. **travailing.** ver. 4. Ge 3:16, 20. Ps *87:5. Is 53:11. +*54:1. +*66:)7, 8. Je +*30:7. Da +*12:1. Mi 4:10. +*5:3. Mt +√24:8, 15-21. Jn +*16:21. Ga 4:19, 27.

3. **wonder.** *or,* sign. See on ver. 1. **in heaven.** Jb 1:6. 2:1, 2. **a great.** ver. 4, 9, 17. Re *13:2, 4. 16:13. *17:3, 4. 20:2. Is *27:1. 51:9. Ep *2:2. **red.** Re 6:4. 17:3. **dragon.** Re *12:9. *13:2, 4, 11. 16:13. 20:2. Ps 74:13. 91:13. Is 27:1. 51:9. Ezk 29:3. **seven heads.** Re 13:1, 3. *17:3, 9, 10, 11. **ten horns.** Re 17:3, 7, 12, 16. Is 9:15. Da 2:42, 44.)7:7, 8, 20, 24. **seven crowns.** Re ●2:10. 13:1. 19:12. Is 62:3.

4. **his tail.** Re 9:10, 19. Da *8:9-12. **the third part.** Re +8:7. **of the.** Re 17:18. **stars of heaven.** Da)8:10. **cast.** Da)8:10. **the dragon.** ver. 2. Ex *1:16. Mt *2:3-16. Jn 8:44. 1 P 5:8. **the woman.** ver. 1, 2. Ge +*3:15. **devour.** Mt *2:16.

5. **she.** ver. 2, 13. Ge +*3:15. Is +*7:14. +*9:6. Je 31:22. Mi *5:3. Mt 1:25. Ac *4:30. Ga *4:4. **brought forth.** Is)66:7. **manchild.** Interpreters vary widely in

their understanding of who the manchild is. Many believe that this verse is retrospective, and that the manchild refers to the birth of Christ. More probably, the manchild refers to a group of resurrected saints (Peters, *Theocratic Kingdom*, vol. 2, p. 285). J. Finis Dake has argued ably that the group of saints involved are the 144,000 of chapter 7. This group is found in heaven in chapter 14, and this passage appears to provide the Rapture that brought them there. That this is not a reference to Christ seems evident, for this occurs in the section past Re 4:1, which has to do with future events. Christ's ascension did not occur in the middle of Daniel's Seventieth Week. The basis for identifying the manchild with Christ is that he was born of a woman, but in this passage the woman is Israel, not Mary, for it is Israel that is predicted to flee for protection into the wilderness (ver. +*6. Ob +*3). That the manchild is to rule with a rod of iron is taken by many to indicate that this is a reference to Christ, for He will do so. But Scripture clearly shows that Christ (Ps 2:8), the manchild (Re 12:5), the church saints (Re 2:26, 27), the tribulation saints (Re 20:4-6), and indeed all the saints (Ps +*149:6-9) are to so rule, so this does not necessarily indicate that the manchild is Christ. Ex 13:12. Is 66:7. **rule.** See on Re +*2:26, 27. *19:15, 16. Ps *2:9, 10. **rod of iron.** Ps)2:8. **her child.** Re 11:12. **caught up.** Re 5:6. See on 11:12. Mk 16:19. Ac +*3:21. 2 C +12:2. **unto God.** Ac 7:55.

6. **the woman.** ver. 1, 4, 14. **fled.** ver. 14, 16. Re 17:3. Is +*16:3, 4. +*26:20. Zc 13:8, 9. Mt 2:13. *24:16-21. **into the wilderness.** ver. +*14. 2 K 14:7n. Ps 9:9. 60:6-12. 108:8-13. Is +*16:1-5. +*26:20, 21. 42:11-13. 63:1-5. Je +*31:2. 49:16n. Ezk √20:33-44. 35:9n. Da 11:36-45. Ho 2:14-23. Ob +*3. Mt 24:15-22, 27. Ac 7:38. **a place.** 2 K 14:7n. Is +*16:1-4. Da 11:41. Jn +*14:2, 3g. **prepared.** Re 8:6. 9:7, 15. 12:6. 16:12. 19:7. 21:2. **that.** Re *2:17. 1 K *17:3-6, 9-16. *19:4-8. Mt 4:11. **a thousand.** See on Re *11:2, 3. 13:5.

7. **war.** Re 13:7. 19:11-20. Is 34:5. Ep 6:12g. **Michael.** i.e. *who is as God,* ✱S#3413g. Is 55:4. Da)10:13, 21. 12:1. He 2:10. Ju +9g. **and his.** Ps +*68:17. *103:20, 21. Da *7:10. Mt 13:41. 16:27. 24:31. 26:53. 2 Th 1:7. He *12:22. **fought against.** Da)10:20. **the dragon.** ver. 3, 4. Re 20:2. **his angels.** ver. 9. Re *9:11. Ps 78:49. Mt +*25:41. 2 C 12:7g. 2 P 2:4. Ju *6.

8. **prevailed not.** ver. 11. Ps 13:4. 118:10-13. 129:2. Je 1:19. 5:22. Mt *16:18. Ro *8:31-39. **neither.** ver. 9, 12, 13. Lk +10:18. **their place.** Re 20:11. Jb 7:10. 8:18. 20:9. 27:21-23. Ps 37:10. Da 2:35. Jn *12:31. Ac 1:25. Ju 6. **in heaven.** Ep 6:12.

9. **the great.** ver. 3, 7. Ps 74:12-14. Is *51:9. **cast out.** Lk *10:18. Jn *12:31. **serpent.** ver. 14, 15. Re *20:2. Ge *)3:1, 4, 13. Is 27:1. 65:25. 2 C 11:3. **the Devil.** Re 9:20. 16:14. 18:2. Mt 4:1, 5, 8. 13:39. Lk 8:12. Jn √8:44. 1 T 3:6, 7. He *2:14. 1 J *3:8-10. Ju 9. **and Satan.** Re 2:+9, 13, 24. 3:9. 1 Ch 21:1. Jb 1:6-12. 2:1. Ps 109:6. Zc)3:1, 2. Mt 4:10. Lk 13:16. 22:3, 31. Ac 5:3. 26:18. Ro 16:20. 2 C 2:11. *11:14. 12:7. 2 Th 2:9. **deceiveth.** Re 13:14. 18:23. 19:20. 20:3, 8, 10. Mt *24:24. Jn *8:44. Ro 16:18. 2 C *11:3. Ep +*4:14. 2 Th *2:3, 9-11. 1 T *2:14. 2 T 3:13. 1 J 5:19. **world.** Gr. *oikoumene,* Mt +24:14. *ſ121J8, Jn +3:16. **he was.** Re +9:1. Ezk √28:16. Lk √10:18. Jn *12:31. **into.** Jb 1:7. 2:2. Is √14:12, 13. 65:25. Jn *14:30. 16:11. 2 C *4:4. 1 P *5:8. **his angels.** 2 P *2:4.

10. **I heard.** See on Re +*11:15. 19:1-7. **salvation.** Re +7:10. He +*9:28. **the kingdom.** Re +*11:15. 1 Ch *29:11. Ps *22:28. 45:6. 145:11-13. Da *2:44. Mt +*6:10. Lk 11:2. **the power.** Re 2:26. +4:11. Ps *2:8-12. 110:5, 6. Mt 26:64. 28:18. 1 C 5:4. 2 C *12:9. his Christ. Re +*11:15. **the accuser.** Jb *1:9. *2:5. Zc 3:1, 2. Lk 22:31. Ro 8:33, 34. T 2:3. 1 P +*5:8. **day and night.** Lk +18:7.

11. **they overcame.** Re *2:7, 11, 17, 26. *3:5, 12, 21. 15:2. Jn +16:33. Ro *8:33-39. *16:20. 1 C *15:57. 2 C *10:3-5. Ep *6:13-18. 2 T *4:7, 8. He *2:14, 15. 1 J *2:13, 14. 4:4. *5:4, 5. Ju +*24, 25. **the blood.** ℐ117, Ge +19:8. Re +1:5. 7:10-14. 14:1-4. Ex 12:13. He +*9:22. **the Lamb.** Re +5:6. 15:3. Ex 12:3. and. ℐ148, Ge +8:22. **the word.** ver. 17. See on Re *1:2, 9. *6:9. 11:7. *19:10. **they loved not.** ℐ175B, Ge +21:16. Re 2:10, 13. *20:4. SS *8:6. Mt *16:25. Lk +*14:26. Ac *20:24. *21:13. He *11:35-38. **lives.** Gr. psyche, ℐ121A7, Mt +2:20. ℐ121A7, Ge +9:5. **unto the death.** Re 2:10.

12. **rejoice.** Re 18:20. 19:1-7. Ps 96:11-13. 148:1-4. Is ▶44:23. ▶49:13. *55:12, 13. Lk 2:14. 15:10. **ye that.** Re +3:10. 13:6. **dwell.** Re +7:15. Woe. Re 8:13. 9:12. 11:10, 14. **the devil.** ver. 8, 9. Mt *13:19, 25, 39. 1 P *5:8. **because.** Re *10:6. He 10:37. 2 P 3:8. **short time.** Mt *8:28, 29.

13. **the dragon.** ver. +3. **he was.** ver. 8, *9, 12. Re +9:1. Lk +10:18. **he persecuted.** ver. 4, 5. Ge +*3:15. Ne *4:7, 8. Ps 37:12-14. Jn 15:19, 20. *16:33. Ac 8:1. 12:1-3. 1 J 3:10. **the woman.** ver. 5.

14. **wings of.** Ex *19:4. Dt 32:11, 12. Ps 55:6. Is *40:31. Ezk 17:3, 7. **that.** Re ◐3:10. 2 P 2:4-9. **she might.** See on ver. 6. Re 17:3. **fly.** i.e. flee. Ex *14:5. Jsh 24:6. Ps 35:1-5. La *4:19. Mt 10:23. *24:15-28. Mk 13:13-23. Lk ◐21:12, 20-24. **into the wilderness.** ver. +*6. Jsh 7:26. Ps +*83:3. Is *11:16. +*26:20. *27:8. 32:16. Je +*31:2. Ezk √20:35-38. Ho √2:14, 15. Mi 4:10. √7:15. Zp +*2:3. Mt 24:16. **her place.** ver. +*6. **nourished.** Ps 23:5. Ps +*74:14. *78:19. **for a time.** ver. 6. Re *11:2, 3. *13:5. Je +*30:4-7. Da▶7:25. +*9:27. ▶12:7. Mt 24:15-22. **from the face.** ℐ144A1, Ge +11:8. Jg 9:21.

15. **the serpent.** Re 12:10. **cast.** Re 17:15. Ps 18:4. 65:7. 93:3, 4. Is 8:7. 28:2. *59:19. **the flood.** Ps 32:6. 69:2, 15. Is *8:7. *59:19. Je 46:7, 8. Da √11:21, 22. Mt 7:25, 27.

16. **the earth.** Ex 12:35, 36. 1 K 17:6. 2 K 8:9. Is 11:15, 16. Mi *7:15. **swallowed up.** Ge 8:13, 14. Nu 16:28-33. 26:10. Ps *76:10. *93:3, 4. *124:1-5.

17. **the dragon.** ver. 12. Jn *8:44. 1 P *5:8. **make war.** Re +11:7. 13:7. 17:6, 14. 18:20. 19:19. *20:7-9. Ge +*3:15. Da 7:23-26. 11:36. **the remnant.** 1 K 19:14, 18. Je 23:3. Zc *13:8, 9. **her seed.** Ge +*3:15. Ga *3:26. He *2:11. **which keep.** Re 14:12. 22:14. Mt 28:20. 1 J +√2:3. *5:2, 3. **and have.** See on ver. 11. Re 1:2, 9. *6:9. 19:10. 20:4. 1 C 2:1. 1 J +5:10. Many authorities take the succeeding clause that begins chapter 13 and place it as part of this verse, to read "and he stood upon the sand of the sea." Da 7:2, 7, 8, 19-27.

REVELATION 13

A vision of "a beast rising out of the sea"; with an account of its power, rage, and success, 1-10: of a "second beast, rising out of the earth," exercising the power of the former beast, making an image of it, and compelling all to worship it, 11-17. The number of the beast, 18.

1. **And.** ℐ148, Ge +8:22. **upon.** Je 5:22. **and saw.** Re 11:7. 17:8. Da *7:2, 3. **a beast.** Gr. vicious, wild beast. ver. 14, 15. Re ◐4:6. +11:7. 15:2. 16:13. Da 7:3, 7, 24. **the sea.** Da ▶7:3. **having.** See on Re 12:3. 17:3, 7-12, 16. Da 7:▶7, 8, 19, 20, 23, 24. **ten.** Re 17:12. **crowns.** Re +12:3. **name.** or, names. **blasphemy.** ver. 5, 6. Re 17:3, 5. Da 7:25. 11:36. 2 Th *2:3, 4.

2. **beast.** Da ▶7:5. **was like.** SS 4:8. Is 11:6. Je 5:6. 13:23. Da *7:▶6, 7. Ho 13:7. Hab 1:8. **and his feet.** 1 S 17:34-37. 2 K 2:24. Pr 17:12. 28:15. Da *7:4, 5. Ho 13:8. Am 5:19. **a bear.** Da ▶7:5. **and his mouth.** Ps 22:21. Is 5:29. Ho 11:10. Am 3:12. 2 T 4:17. 1 P *5:8. **a lion.** Da ▶7:4. **dragon.** ver. 4, 11. See on Re 12:3, 4, 13, 15. **gave.** Re 16:10. 17:12. 19:20. 20:2. Jn ◐5:30. **great authority.** ver. 4, 5, 7, 12. Mt 9:34. Lk +4:6. 2 C *4:4. Ep *2:2. 6:12.

3. **one.** ver. 1, 12, 14. Re 17:10. 2 Th 2:6-12. **wounded.** Gr. slain. Re *13:14. 17:16-18. Ezk=21:25. **and his.** Ezk 30:24. **deadly wound.** ver. 14. Zc 11:17. **all.** Re 17:6, 8, 13, 17. Lk 2:1. Jn 12:19. Ac 8:10, 11, 13. 2 Th 2:9-12. **wondered.** ℐ63H, Ge +12:15. Supply by ellipsis, (and followed).

4. **And they.** ver. 2. Re 9:20. Ps 106:37, 38. 1 C 10:20-22. 2 C 4:4. 2 Th 2:4. **worshipped.** Da 3:15. Mt *4:8, 9. **and they.** ver. 12, 13, 15. Da 11:36, 37. 2 Th 2:4. **Who is like.** Re 18:18. Ex 15:11. Ps 89:8. **who is able.** Re 17:14. Dt 9:2. 1 S 17:24.

5. **a mouth.** Da ▶7:8, 11, 20, 25. ▶11:36. **speaking great.** ver. 1. Da *7:25. 2 Th 2:4. **things and.** ℐ93A. Hendiadys, Ge +1:26. i.e. *great blasphemous things.* **and power.** See on Re 11:2, 3. 12:6, 14. **to continue.** or, to make war. ver. 7. Re 11:7. Da ▶7:12. Mt 20:12g. Ja 4:13g. **forty and.** Re *11:2. *12:6, 14. Da +*9:25, 27.

6. **he opened.** ℐ108H6A, Jg +11:35. Jb 3:1. Ps *52:1-7. Da *7:8, 11, 20. 11:36. Mt 12:34. 15:19. Ro 3:13. 2 Th *2:4. **blasphemy.** Re 17:3. **to blaspheme.** Re 16:9. Is 52:5. Ro 2:24. 1 T 6:1. Ja 2:7. **and his tabernacle.** Re 21:3. Jn 1:14g. Col 1:19. *2:9. He 9:2, 11, 12, 24. **and them.** Re 4:1, 4. 5:13. 7:9. 11:12. 12:12. 18:20. 19:1-6. He 12:22, 23. **that dwell.** Re ◐+3:10. +7:15. Da *8:10, 11.

7. **was given.** Jn *19:11. **to make.** Re +11:7. 12:17. Da *7:▶21, 25. 8:12, 24, 25. 11:36-39. 12:1. **the saints.** ver. 10. Re +8:3. **overcome.** Re ◐+*6:16, 17. 14:9, 10. 20:12, 15. Is +*1:9. Da 7:21. *8:12. **and power.** ver. +2. Re 10:11. 11:18. 17:15. Ex 9:16. Is 10:15. 37:26. Je 25:9. 27:6, 7. 51:20-24. Da 5:18-23. Lk 4:6. Jn 19:11. **all.** ℐ171A, Ex +9:6. **kindreds.** Re +5:9.

8. **all.** ℐ171A, Ex +9:6. See on ver. 3, 4, 14, 15. **that dwell.** ver. 12, 14. Re +3:10. **upon the earth.** Re +*6:10. He +*11:13. **shall worship.** Re 14:9-11. Da *3:7. **whose names.** Re +*3:5. 20:12, 15. 21:27. Ex *32:32. Is 4:3. Da +*12:1. Lk *10:20. Ph 4:3. **are not.** Re 17:8. Mk 13:20. Ep 1:4. 1 Th 1:4. 2 Th 2:13. 2 T 1:9. **written.** Re +*3:5. *20:12, 15. *21:27. 22:19. Ex 32:32. Ps *56:8. ▶69:28. 139:16. Da▶12:1. Lk *10:20. Ph 4:3. He 12:23. **book.** ℐ22D5K1A, Ex +32:32. **Lamb.** ℐ22E, Jn +1:29. See on Re 5:6-9, 12. Is ▶53:7. Jn *1:29. **slain.** Ac 2:23. 1 P 1:19, 20. **from.** ℐ101, Dt +32:42. Re 17:8. Mt +13:35. Ep 1:4. T 1:2. 1 P *1:19, 20. **world.** Gr. kosmos, Mt +4:8.

9. **If**. ʃ184A, 1 C +15:2. **any man**. Notice that this expression differs from the similar formula found earlier in the book of Revelation, in that no reference is made to the church, significant evidence supporting the view that the church is not in view in this context. Re +2:◐7, 11, 17, 29. Je *13:15. Mt *11:15. **hear**. ʃ147A, Ge +50:24.

10. **that leadeth**. Ex 21:23-25. Is 14:2. 33:1. Je +*30:16. *43:11. Zc 11:9. Mt 7:2. Ep ◐4:8. **into captivity**. Je ⟩15:2. **shall go**. Re 17:8, 11. **he that killeth**. Re 11:18. 16:6. Ge +*9:5, 6. Is 26:21. Ezk 5:2, 12. Mt +⟩26:52. 1 C 15:26, 27. **Here is**. Re +1:9. 2:2, 19. 3:3, 10. *12:11, ◐+*14. 14:12. 17:14. La 3:26. Hab +*2:3. Lk 18:1-8. *21:19. Col *1:11. He *6:12. *10:36, 37. 12:3, 4. Ja 1:2-4. +*5:7, 8. **and**. ʃ174, Ge +18:22. **the saints**. ver. 7. Re +8:3.

11. **I saw**. ver. 1, 14. Re 16:13. **another beast**. Re 16:13. *19:20. 20:10. **coming**. ver. 1. Re 11:7. 17:8. **and he had**. Mt *7:15. 24:5, 11, 24. Mk 13:22. Ac 20:29. Ro 16:18. 2 C √11:13-15. **and he spake**. ver. 17. Re 12:3, 4, 17. 17:6. Ge 3:1. 49:17. Ps *12:3, 4. Da 7:8, 24, 25. Zc 11:16, 17. Ac 16:16-18. 19:15, 16. 2 C 11:3. 2 Th 2:4. **a dragon**. ver. +2.

12. **all the power**. ver. 2-5, 7. Jn ⟩16:13, 14. **before him**. ver. 14. **causeth**. ver. 3, 14-17. Re 17:10, 11. 2 Th 2:4. **dwell**. ver. 8, 14. Re +3:10. **to worship**. ver. 4, 8, +15. Re 20:4. Ac 12:21-23. **healed**. ver. +3.

13. **he doeth**. Re 16:14. 19:20. Ex 7:11, 12, 22. 8:7, 18, 19. 9:11. Dt 13:1-3. Mt *24:24. Mk 13:22. Lk 21:11. Ac 8:9-11. 2 Th 2:9, 10. 2 T 3:8. **great wonders**. 2 Th 2:9. **he maketh fire**. Re 8:7. 11:5. 20:9. Nu 16:35. 1 K 18:38. 2 K 1:9-16. Mt 16:1. Lk 9:54-56. 2 T 3:8.

14. **deceiveth**. Re 12:9. 18:23. 19:20. 20:3, 10. 2 K 22:20mg. Jb 12:16. Is 44:20. Ezk 14:9. 2 Th 2:9-12. 1 T 4:1-3. **dwell**. See on ver. 3, 8. Re +3:10. **miracles**. Miracles are no sure proof of divine mission. Christ's miracles were generally called signs, and served as such because they were the fulfillment of prophecy, as these shall be. B. B. Warfield has written an excellent volume on *Counterfeit Miracles*, but these miracles are not counterfeit, but are used to establish false claims. Students of Scripture will be able to tell the difference and not be deceived. 2 Th +2:9. **power**. ver. 12. Re 19:20. **make an image**. ver. 3, 4, 11, 12, 15. Re 14:9, 11. 15:2. 16:2. 19:20. 20:4. 2 K 20:7. Ezk 8:10. 16:17. Da 11:36. 2 Th 2:4. **wound by**. ver. 3, 12. Zc 11:17.

15. **life**. Gr. breath. *pneuma*, ʃ121A3, Mt +27:50n. Ge +*2:7. Ps 135:17. Je 10:14. 51:17. Hab 2:19. Ja 2:26g. **the image**. ver. +14. Re 14:9, 11. 15:2. 16:2. 19:20. 20:4. Ps 73:20. Da 9:27. 12:10, 11. Mt 24:15. **speak**. Ps 115:5. 135:16. Je 10:5. **cause**. See on ver. 14. Re 16:2, 5. 17:6, 14, 17. 18:20, 24. 19:20. 20:4. Da 7:20, 25. **as many**. Da ⟩3:5. **not worship**. ver. 12. Re 14:9, 11. 16:2. 19:20. 20:4. **should be**. Re 16:6. Mt 5:10-12.

16. **all**. ʃ171A, Ex +9:6. **both small**. Re +*11:18. 19:5, 18. 20:12. 2 Ch 15:13. Ps 115:13. Ac 26:22. **rich**. Jb 34:19. Ps 49:2. Pr 22:2. **and poor**. ʃ174, Ge +18:27. **free**. Re 6:15. 19:18. 1 C +*12:13. Ga *3:28. Ep 6:8. Col 3:11. **receive**. Gr. give them. **a mark**. Gr. *charagma*, brand. It was an official seal, found on all sorts of documents and bills of sale, making them valid, having the name and likeness of the Emperor, with the year of his reign. It was necessary for buying and

selling (see E. W. Bullinger, *Apocalypse*, p. 439). Re *14:9-11. 15:2. 16:2. 19:20. 20:4. Zc 13:6. 2 C ◐1:22. Ga ◐+6:17. **or**. Re 7:3. Ex 13:9. Dt 6:8. 11:18. Ezk +*9:4. 2 T 3:8. **foreheads**. Re ◐+7:3.

17. **mark**. See on ver. 16. Ga ◐+*6:17n. **name**. Re 3:12. 14:11. 17:5. 22:4. **the number**. ver. 18. Re 15:2. **of his name**. The letters of the name of the Antichrist, in Greek, will total 666, using the normal mathematical valuation of the Greek letters, by a process known as *gematria*, of which this is the only mention in Scripture. Numerical values were assigned to all the letters of the Greek alphabet by the Greeks themselves, ranging from 1 for *alpha* to 800 for *omega*. See the tables for the Hebrew and Greek alphabets giving the numerical values assigned in E. W. Bullinger, *Number in Scripture*, pp. 48, 49. The number six has identifiable spiritual significance (Da 3:1n). It has long been known that several of the names of Satan, for example, have mathematical values evenly divisible by the number thirteen. "Dragon" has a numerical value of 975, or 13x3x5x5. "Tempter" has a value of 1053 (13x3x3x3); a place value of 91 (13x7); and a total value of 1144 (13x11x2x2x2). "Belial" has a numerical value of 78 (13x3x2); a place value of 39 (13x3); a total value of 117 (13x3x3). "Murderer" has a numerical value of 1820 (13x7x5x2x2). "Serpent" has a numeric value of 780 (13x3x2x2x5). The phrase in Re 12:9, "called the devil and satan" has a numerical value of 2197 (13x13x13). That this many names of Satan should all demonstrate the factor thirteen seems beyond what is reasonable to attribute to mere chance.

Beyond the spiritual significance of the numbers in the Bible, is another interesting and valuable study which involves the mathematical structure of the original Greek and Hebrew text of the Scripture. It often appears that the mathematical structure of the original text, taken by sentences, not verses, possesses a structure where the number seven is the consistent or predominant factor. Seven is a consistent prime factor in the numerical value of the sentence, in the place value of the sentence, and in the total value of the sentence. By "factor" is meant what in mathematics is called the "prime factor," a set of numbers which are divisible by themselves and one only, which multiply to give a specific number. Every number has only one set of prime factors, and these may be found listed in standard mathematical tables (such as the *British Association for the Advancement of Science, Mathematical Tables, Volume 5, Factor Table*, giving the complete decomposition of all numbers less than 100,000, prepared by J. Peters, A. Lodge, and others, London, 1935, 1963). The numerical structure is displayed in the prime factors of the numbers involved, and I have shown these in parentheses in the examples above and below. The numerical value is simply the sum of all the arithmetical values of the Greek or Hebrew letters in the sentence. The place value is the sum of the individual letter place values (which in Greek range from 1 to 24, the Greek alphabet having 24 letters). The total value is simply the sum of the numerical and place values. The sentence "But remember Lot's wife" (Lk 17:32) contains five words in Greek. Their numerical value is 3374 (7x2x241); place value is 322 (7x2x23); total value is 3696 (7x2x2x2x2x3x11). Romans 10:13, "For whosoever shall call upon the name of the Lord shall be saved" contains eight words in Greek. Their numerical value is 4459 (7x7x7x13); place value is 490 (7x7x2x5); total value is 4949 (7x7x101). Romans 10:17, "So then faith cometh by hearing, and hearing by the word of God" contains eleven words in Greek. Their numeric value is 3276 (7x2x2x3x3x13); place value is 420 (7x2x2x3x5); total value is 3696 (7x2x2x2x2x3x11). Romans 11:26, 27, "There shall come out of Zion the Deliverer, and shall turn away ungodliness from Jacob: for this is my covenant unto them, when I shall take away their sins" contains 23 words in Greek. Their numeric value is 12180 (7x3x2x2x5x29); place value is 1176 (7x7x2x2x2); total value is 13356 (7x3x2x2x3x53).

Just as the names and titles of Satan frequently possess a significant mathematical structure, so Christ's titles often possess significant structure. In the passage just cited (Ro 11:26), the title "the Deliverer" possesses an extensive structure involving the number five. The name "Jesus" has a numerical value of 888, which is quite a contrast to 666. The number 8 has spiritual significance (Mi 5:5n). It is unlikely that this many instances of structure by seven could occur by chance in such a limited section of text as Romans chapter 11. The frequency with which this mathematical phenomena is found is greater than what can be attributed statistically to chance, and is believed by many who have devoted considerable time and study to the subject to be an evidence of design, supporting the Bible claim to divine inspiration. I am indebted to Mr. G. E. Hoyer, formerly of Chicago, Illinois, with whom I have studied for over twenty-five years, for my knowledge of this subject. Much more could be said about the usefulness of this research. The results of this study have a bearing upon deciding consistently matters of orthography (spelling). Findings of this research lend support to some texts in the Greek New Testament which have been marked as doubtful, but space allotment in this reference work will not allow more than this brief sampling of the evidence. Acts 8:37, marked doubtful in some modern translations, has a numerical value of 16170 (7x7x3x11x2x5); a place value of 1617 (7x7x3x11); a total value of 17787 (7x7x3x11x11). I found, upon my own investigation, that the text of 1 P 3:18 with the article in the dative case ("raised by the Spirit") possesses a consistent structure by seven: the numerical value of this text is 13230 (7x7x3x3x3x2x5); the place value is 1281 (7x3x61); the total value is 14511 (7x3x691). There is no structure when the article is omitted. In my file I have perhaps 100 examples of this pervasive structure by seven for texts from the New Testament. Mr. Hoyer has, I would suppose, several times this number which I have seen in his files.

On the supposition that perhaps this structure could be found in any Greek literature of the period, I tested sample passages from *the LXX., the Apostolic Fathers*, sample passages from *Scripture Parallels in Ancient Classics*, and entire books and chapters from the Old Testament Apocrypha. The results were comparatively meager. The closest and best example I have found of "structure" is in the Epistle of Jeremy, verse 13, which has a numeric value of 9163 (7x7x17x11); a place value of 952 (7x17x2x2x2); a total value of 10115 (7x17x17x5). I do not argue from this example that this verse is "inspired," however. Neither do I conclude that texts in the Bible which do not contain this structure are uninspired. Examining the text in Jeremy for what Mr. Hoyer has called "detail structure," even

this text does not possess the richness to be found in every New Testament example he has shown me. That I should be able to find an occasional random text which has in all three values a multiple of seven is not beyond the realm of statistical possibility, for theoretically something less than one sentence in every forty-nine samples should have such a structure. Mr. Hoyer has found for the New Testament far more examples than can be attributed to this normal chance distribution, and his examples seem to demonstrate a grammatical and orthographical consistency which supports the thesis of intentional design. For example, the name "David" has several possible spellings in Greek, according to accepted MSS. evidence, but only one of these alternatives (*Daueid*) is consistently selected in such texts as Mt 9:27, which has a numerical value of 1456 (7x2x2x2x2x13); place value of 189 (7x3x3x3); total value of 1645 (7x5x47). So for Mt 12:23, which has a numerical value of 6664 (7x7x2x2x2x17); a place value of 756 (7x2x2x3x3x3); a total value of 7420 (7x2x2x5x53). When a different spelling of "David" is selected for these texts, they no longer possess a discernible mathematical structure. I call attention to these facts because it ought to be more generally recognized that there is much more to know and understand about even apparently insignificant matters related to the Bible than most people—even scholars—are aware, and to offer the caution that one must not arbitrarily dismiss the validity of a branch of study without having thoroughly personally investigated the subject (Ps 25:9. Jn 7:24, √51). To my knowledge none of this research has been published, as the research is incomplete and still in progress. There are other books which have appeared in the past which are related to this subject, but apparently none pursue the study with the mathematical consistency and rigor of Mr. Hoyer's work. The common flaw underlying many studies of this subject appears to be the arbitrary selection of evidence. Given a large enough mass of raw data, one could find many amazing "patterns" and combinations if one looked long enough, and devised enough ways of finding them. The common regard for thirteen as an "unlucky" number is based upon this flaw, for instances are gathered which favor the hypothesis, but those that do not are ignored. For the spiritual significance of this number in the Bible see Ge 14:4, where at its first mention it is associated with rebellion.

Another flaw which may be present in the work of Del Washburn and Jerry Lucas (in their work titled *Theomatics*), is their rather cavalier attitude toward Greek grammar, particularly in their conceptual understanding of the use and non-use of the Greek article. They state "There is not a Greek scholar or theologian alive that can prove that the definite Greek article has any meaning (interpretive significance) whatsoever" (*Theomatics*, p. 340). While it must be candidly admitted that the use and non-use of the Greek article is not fully understood, my years of study of American English linguistics lead me to confidently affirm that our knowledge and understanding of English grammar is no better. Contemporary scholars are not in complete agreement as to the significance of the Greek article in some of its uses (D. A. Carson in *Exegetical Fallacies*, p. 84, criticizes R. H. Lenski as "notoriously unreliable" when Lenski attempts to distinguish articular *nomos* to represent Mosaic law, anarthrous *nomos* to represent the principle of law; see my related notes on Ro 4:15 and Ga 3:10; see Boyce W. Blackwelder, *Light from the Greek New Testament*, p. 148, where he has a fine study of the issue, "The Article and 'Law.'" For a related scholarly study, see Arthur Wakefield Slaten, *Qualitative Nouns in the Pauline Epistles and Their Translation in the Revised Version*, particularly pages 35-40. The authors of *Theomatics* have misquoted Dana and Mantey. They cite in quotation marks as from Dana and Mantey "in rare cases it is possible that the writer employed the article at random" (*Theomatics*, p. 341), whereas Dana and Mantey actually wrote "It is precarious to suppose in any instance that a writer is employing an idiom at random, though in rare cases this is possibly true" (*Manual Grammar*, p. 143). Lucas and Washburn point to William Webster as "A perfect example of a scholar trying to attach a mystical significance to the article," citing Dana and Mantey's quotation of Webster. Though Dana and Mantey state "This analysis is doubtless more exact and detailed than the facts will support, but it certainly shows admirable discrimination," Lucas and Washburn comment "Webster was hard-pressed to establish a rule and fails to do so" (*Theomatics*, p. 341). Both Dana and Mantey as well as Lucas and Washburn err in regard to "the facts will support," if they mean to imply that William Webster was unable to adduce satisfactory evidence to support his distinctions, for this fine Cambridge scholar devotes nearly forty lines of index to the uses of the Greek article in his *Greek Testament with notes Grammatical and Exegetical*, vol. 2, p. 869). My acquaintance with Mr. Hoyer has taught me to respect the advances in Greek scholarship represented by the work of Nigel Turner and others, and not dismiss so quickly the intricacies of Greek grammar as being superfluous or insignificant (See related notes on the Greek article at Mt 27:54. Jn 1:1. See entries under "Nigel Turner" in the index).

In the examples I have cited above of mathematical structure found in the text of the Greek New Testament using the procedures refined by Mr. Hoyer in his lifetime of research on the subject, the mathematical pattern is exact (not based upon "neighbor values" as found in the works of Ivan Panin and Jerry Lucas, though the Lucas volume provides valuable mathematical and statistical justification for ascribing design even if their use be allowed), and is found consistently in the same manner for every passage, so I believe Mr. Hoyer's basic research possesses greater validity than the other approaches alluded to. What has all this to do with ascertaining the meaning of 666? I believe that this number will be found in the manner described, commonly referred to as gematria, and not by the many other approaches esoteric followers of mysticism have devised to find this number, or in contemporary occurrences of this number allegedly found on Social Security checks, computer bar codes, etc., so prevalent in the literature of prophetic sensationalism (2 K 20:11n).

I am well aware that most serious Bible scholars would place these matters of the symbolism of numbers and the alleged mathematical structure of the Greek text in the same class as prophetic sensationalism. Oswald T. Allis has written a booklet titled *Bible Numerics*, which criticizes the whole subject, particularly the work of Ivan Panin. Allis also authored the article on "Numerics, Bible" in Baker's *Dictionary of Theology*,

edited by Everett F. Harrison, 1960, p. 381. The writings of John J. Davis (*Biblical Numerology*, 1968; *Contemporary Counterfeits*, pp. 23-29) are quite critical of this approach. Davis limits his acknowledgment of any symbolic use of number in Scripture to the number seven (*Biblical Numerology*, p. 116). E. C. Colwell, famous as a Greek scholar, wrote a little book on Bible study which contains some pointed paragraphs against the work of Ivan Panin. Colwell claims such structures as Panin found can be found anywhere, and adduces an example from the opening paragraph of *Gone with the Wind* (*The Study of the Bible*, p. 109). I have analyzed the same passage using the procedures Mr. Hoyer adopts for the Greek text of the N.T., only giving mathematical values for the English alphabet in a similar fashion to those given by the Greeks. No mathematical structure is evident. I have also tried numerous verses from the King James Version and other English translations, and have yet to find a single example in English which possesses structure. No doubt one could be found, if enough examples were tested—but I have run out of time. I do not believe the strictures of Allis, Colwell, and Davis, among others, entirely apply to the study as Mr. Hoyer has pursued it, though no doubt there are broader philosophic grounds for objecting to any such study (no matter what evidence might be produced in its support) which would lead them to reject any validity that might be claimed for it. But that noted scholars can be decidedly wrong is evident when one compares the interpretations of Bible prophecy expressed by Allis in his *Prophecy and the Church* with those of George N. H. Peters in his three volume study, *The Theocratic Kingdom of Our Lord Jesus, the Christ*. Rather than commit the logical fallacy of appeal to authority, I submit the evidence given in this extensive note (which could easily be extended to book length) to the judgment of the reader. For further study of the number 666 see the fascinating information in David Chilton's commentary on the book of Revelation, *The Days of Vengeance*, pp. 344-352.

18. **Here.** Re 1:3. 17:9. Dt +*29:29. Ps 107:43. Pr *25:2. Da *12:9, 10. Ho 14:9. Mk 13:14. **count.** Re 15:2. **the number.** Re 21:17. Dt 3:11. Ro 3:5. **of a man.** Re ☉21:17. This would seem to restrict the application of this number to an individual.

REVELATION 14

A prophetical view of the remnant of believers, during the reign of the beast, 1-5. An angel preacheth the Gospel, 6, 7. The fall of Babylon, 8-12. The immediate felicity of those who die in the Lord, 13. The harvest of the world, and putting in of the sickle, 14-19. The vintage and winepress of the wrath of God, 20.

1. **I looked.** ver. 14. Re 4:1. 6:8. 15:5. Je 1:11. Ezk 1:4. 2:9. 8:7. 10:1, 9. 44:4. Da 12:5. Am 8:2. Zc 4:2. **a Lamb.** See on Re 5:5-9, 12, 13. 7:9-17. **mount.** 2 S 5:7. Ps 2:6. 132:13, 14. Is 49:14. Jl 2:32. Mi 4:7. Ro 9:33. He *12:22-24. **Sion.** i.e. *peak*, ✻S#4622g. For ✻S#6726h. 2 S +5:7. Mt 21:5. Jn 12:15. Ro 9:33. 11:26. He 12:22. 1 P 2:6. **with him.** Is 35:10. +*51:11. Jn *17:24. **an hundred forty and.** ver. 3. See on Re *7:4-8. **having.** Re *3:12. *7:3. 13:16, 17. Lk 12:8. Jn +1:12. **his Father's.** Je 31:9, 10. Mt 6:1, 32. Jn *20:17. 2 C

6:17, 18. **name.** Re *3:12. *22:4. Dt ◐32:5. **foreheads.** Re 7:3. Ezk ▶9:4.

2. **a voice.** Re 10:4. 11:12, 15. 19:1-7. **the voice.** Da ▶10:6. **of many waters.** Re +*1:15. ◐17:1. *19:6. Ps *93:4. Is *17:13. Ezk ▶1:24. *▶43:2. Jn +*3:23. **the voice.** Re 1:10. 8:7-13. 9:1. 10:3, 4. +*11:15. Ex 19:16. 20:18. Zc 9:14. **of thunder.** Re 6:1. 10:3, 4. 19:6. **harpers.** See on Re 5:8. 15:2. 18:22. 2 S 6:5. 1 Ch 25:1-7. Ps 33:2. 43:4. 57:8. 92:3. 98:5. 147:7. 149:3. 150: 3-6.

3. **they sung.** Re 5:12. 15:3. Ps 87:5, 7. Je 31:11, 12. **a new song.** See on Re 5:9. 15:3. Ps 33:3. *40:3. 96:1. *98:1. 137:3. ▶144:9. 149:1. Is 42:10. +*65:14. Mt ◐24:51. **throne.** See on Re 4:2-11. **four beasts.** Re +4:6. **the elders.** Re +4:4. **no man.** ver. 1. Re 2:17. 19:12. Ps 25:14. Mt +*11:25-27. 1 C 1:18. √2:14. Ep 3:9. **the hundred and.** ver. 1. Re 7:4. **redeemed.** See on Re 5:9. Ex 14:10, 30. 15:1. Ps 107:2. 1 C 7:23. 2 P +2:1.

4. **not defiled.** Re 3:4. **are virgins.** Ps 45:14. SS 1:3. 6:8. Mt *25:1. 1 C 7:25, 26, 28. 2 C +11:2. 1 T 4:3. **which follow.** Re 3:4. 7:15-17. *17:14. Nu 14:24. Jsh 1:16. 2 S 15:15. Ps *18:23, 24. Mt 8:19. Lk 9:57-62. Jn 1:36. *8:12. √10:27. 12:26. 13:37. **These were.** Re 5:9. **redeemed.** Gr. bought. Ps 74:2. Ac +*20:28. 1 C *6:20. Ep *1:14. T *2:13, 14. 1 P 2:9mg. **the firstfruits.** Le +*23:10. Is +*66:19. Je *2:3. Am 6:1mg. Zc 12:10. Ro 11:26, 27. 1 C 16:15. Ja +1:18. **the Lamb.** Re +5:6.

5. **in their mouth.** Re 21:8, 27. 22:15. Ps *32:2. *34:13. 55:11. Pr *8:8. Is 6:5-7. *53:9. 63:8. Zp *▶3:13. Mt 12:34. Jn 1:47. 1 P *3:10. **no guile.** Ps 32:2. Is ▶53:9. Jn 1:47. 1 P 2:22. **without fault.** Nu 23:21. Ps ▶15:1, 2. SS *4:7. Is *38:17. Da 6:4. Ho 10:2. Mt *5:48. Lk *23:4. Jn +*17:6. Ep *5:27. Col *1:22. Ju +*24.

6. **another.** Re 8:13. 19:17. Is 6:2, 6, 7. Ezk 1:14. Da 9:21. **in the midst.** Ge 1:6. **having.** Re 10:7g. **everlasting.** Gr. aionios, Mt +18:8. 2 S √23:5. Ps 119:142. 139:24. 145:13. Is √40:8. 45:17. 51:6, 8. Ep 3:9-11. 2 Th 2:16. T 1:1-3. He *13:20. **preach.** Is *52:7. Mt 10:27. Mk *16:15. Ro 16:25. Col +*1:23. **unto them.** Re +3:10. **to every.** Re +5:9. 10:11. 13:7. Da 4:1. 6:25, 26. Mt *24:14. Mk 13:10. Ep 3:9. Col *1:5, 6.

7. **with.** Is 40:3, 6, 9. 44:23. 52:7, 8. *58:1. Ho 8:1. **Fear.** See on Re +*11:18. *15:4. 19:5. Ge *22:12. 42:18. Ex 1:17-21. Jb 1:1. Ps 36:1. *76:7, 9. 89:7. Ec 12:13, 14. Ac 13:16, 26. 1 P *2:17. **give glory.** Re 4:9. +11:13. 16:9. Jsh 7:19. 1 S 6:5. Is 42:12. Ml 2:2. Lk 17:18. Ro 1:21. **the hour.** ver. 15. Re +*11:18. *15:4. 18:10, 17, 19. Ezk 7:2, 6. Da 8:19. Mt 25:13. Jn *5:25-29. 1 P 4:7. **worship.** Re +4:10, 11. **that made.** Re 4:11. Ex ▶20:11. Ne +*9:6. Ps 33:6. 95:5. 124:8. 146:5, ▶6. Pr 8:22-31. Je 10:10. Ac *14:15. 17:23-25. **fountains.** Re 8:10. 16:4. Pr 8:24.

8. **Babylon.** i.e. confusion, ✳S#897g. For S#894h, see 2 K +17:24. **is fallen.** Re *16:19. *17:5, 18. 18:2, 3, 10, 11, 18-21. Is ▶21:9. Je *50:2. 51:7, 8, 64. **great.** Da ▶4:30. **because.** ver. 10. Re 11:8. *17:2-5. 18:3, 10, 18, 21. 19:2. Jb 21:20. 60:3. 75:8. Is 51:17, 22. 63:6. Je 25:15. ▶51:7. La 4:21. Ezk 16:15, etc. Ob 16. Na 3:19. **the wine.** Re 18:3. **wrath.** ſ46C, Mt 8:6. Gr. thumos, wrath, means heat, as well as anger; like the Hebrew cheymah, heat, venom, or poison. See Jb 6:4, where the LXX renders it thumos, evil or affliction, as Mt 6:34. So that the meaning is "the heating

or poisonous wine of her fornication" (B680). Re 13:15-17. 17:6.

9. **the third.** ver. 6-8. Je 44:4. **If.** ſ184A, 1 C +15:2. ver. 11. See on Re 13:3-6, 11-17. **worship.** ver. 11. Re +13:15. **his image.** ver. 11. Re +13:14. Ex *20:4, 5. **his mark.** ver. 11. Re +13:16. **forehead.** Re +7:3.

10. **The same.** ver. +8. **drink.** Re 16:19. 18:3. 19:15. Jb 21:20. Ps 11:6. 60:3. 75:8. Is 29:9. 51:▶17, 21, 22. Je 25:15-17, 27. 51:57. **wrath.** ver. 19. Re +*6:16. +*11:18. 15:1, 7. 16:1. **which is.** Re 18:6. Is 1:22. **poured.** Gr. kerannumi, ✳S#2767g. Re 18:6 (filled), 6 (fill). **into the cup.** Re 18:6. Ps 73:10. ▶75:8. Is *51:17, 22, 23. Je 49:12. La 4:21. Hab 2:16. Zc 12:2. Mt 20:22. 26:39. **indignation.** Is 10:5, 6. Je 10:10. Da 8:19. Mi 7:9. **be tormented.** Re 9:17, 18. 19:20. 20:10. +*21:8. Ge 19:24, 28. Dt 29:23. Jb 18:15. Ps 11:6. Is +*30:33. 34:9, 10. Mt +*25:41. Ju +*7. **with fire and brimstone.** Re +9:17. 20:15. Ge ▶19:24. Ezk ▶38:22. 2 Th +1:8. **in the presence.** Ps *37:34. 52:6. 91:8. Is +*66:24. Ezk 20:48. Mt 13:41, 42, 49, 50. Lk +*13:28. 16:23. 2 Th *1:8, 9. **the holy angels.** Mk 8:38. **the Lamb.** Re +5:6.

11. **smoke.** Re 9:2. 18:9, 18. 19:3. Ge 19:28. Is +*33:14. ▶34:10. Jl 2:30. Mt 13:50. Lk *16:23. **torment.** Re *20:10. Mt 18:34. Lk 16:23-28. **for ever.** Gr. aion, Re +1:6. Re 4:9, 10. 5:13, 14. 7:12. +*11:15. 20:10. 22:5. Ex 15:18. Ps 10:16. 145:1. Mt +*25:41, 46. He +*1:8. Ju *7. **no rest.** T#573-3. Re 4:8. Dt 28:65. Ps 95:11. Is *57:20, 21. Mt 11:28. Mk *9:43-49. Lk 16:24, 25. He 3:18. **day nor night.** Lk +18:7. **who worship.** ver. 9. Re +*13:14-16. **the mark.** Re 13:17. *19:20.

12. **is the patience.** Re +1:9. See on 13:10. He *6:12. **the saints.** Re +8:3. **that keep.** See on Re 12:17. Jn +*17:6. 1 J +√2:3. **the faith.** Re 3:8, 10. 2 T 4:7.

13. **a voice.** Re *11:15, 19. 16:17. Mt 3:17. **Write.** Re 1:11, +19. 2:1. 10:4. 19:9. 21:5. **Blessed.** ſ43, Dt +28:3. Re +*1:3. 16:15. 19:9. 20:6. 22:7, 14. Mt 5:11, 12. 10:28. 2 C 5:6-8. **are the dead.** T#855. Re 20:6. Jb *3:17, 18. Ps 49:15. 73:24. Ec 4:1, 2. Is 57:1, 2. Lk *16:25. +*23:43. 2 C √5:8. Ph √1:21-23. He *12:22, 23. **which die.** Jb 36:18. Ro 14:8. 1 C 15:18. 1 Th 4:14, 16. 5:10. He +*9:27. **in the Lord.** Ps *116:15. 1 C 15:18. 1 Th +*4:16n. **from henceforth: Yea, saith the Spirit.** or, from henceforth saith the Spirit, Yea. **Spirit.** Gr. pneuma, Mt +3:16. Jn +7:39. **rest.** The righteous who die "in the Lord" do not suffer torment or punishment after death, as in purgatory. There is no such place as purgatory known to Scripture, and even the Apocrypha contains firm testimony against such a view in a remarkable statement at Wisdom 3:1, "But the souls of the righteous are in the hand of God, and there shall no torment touch them." See related note, Ezk 33:16n. T#337. Re +6:11. 7:14-17. ◐20:11-15. 21:27. 1 Ch=6:31. =23:25, 26. 2 Ch=35:3. Jb *3:17-19. Is 35:10. *57:2. Da +*12:2, 13. Mt +*25:46. Lk 16:19-31. +*23:43. Ro 8:1. 2 C 5:+*8, 21. 2 Th +*1:6, 7. 2 T +2:12 (T#512). He *4:3, 9-11. 10:10-14. 1 P +*1:4. 1 J 1:7. **their labors.** Re 2:2g. Mt ◐11:17g. 26:10. 1 C +*15:58. He +*6:10. **and their works.** ſ121C1F, Le +19:13. Ps 19:11. 85:13. Mt 25:35-40. Lk 16:9. 1 C +√15:58. Ga +*6:7, 8. Ph 2:17. 2 T *4:7, 8. He +*6:10, 11.

14. **behold.** ver. 15, 16. Re +*1:7. 10:1. 20:11. Ps 97:2. Is 19:1. Mt *17:5. +*24:30. *26:64. Lk 21:27. **like.** Re +1:13. Ps 8:5. Ezk *1:26. Da +*▶7:13. ▶10:16. Mt 8:20. *13:37. Jn +*1:51. 5:27. **a golden.** Re +6:2.

11:17. *17:14. *19:12. Ps *21:3. He 2:9. **a sharp**. ver. 15-17. Jl 3:12, 13. Mt 13:30. Mk 4:29.

15. **came**. Re 15:6. 16:17. **the temple**. Re +3:12. **crying**. Re 6:10. Is 62:1, 6, 7. **to him**. ver. 14. **Thrust**. See on ver. 14, 18. Re 19:21. Is 11:4. Je *51:33. Ho 6:11. Jl √3:▶12-16. Mt +*13:30, 39. Mk 4:29. 2 Th 2:8. **the time**. ver. 7. Am 8:2. 2 P *3:9. **harvest**. Re 13:12. 19:11-21. Is 11:4. *34:1-8. Je 51:33. Ezk ch. 38, 39. Jl 3:13. Zc 14:1-3. Mt +*13:30, 39-43, 47-50. 24:29-31. 2 Th 1:7-10. 2:8-12. Ju 14, 15. **ripe**. *or*, dried. ver. 18. Ge +*15:16. Zc 5:6-11. Mt *23:32. 1 Th *2:16.

16. **he**. ver. 14. Mt +*16:27. Jn *5:22, 23. **thrust**. ver. 19. Re 16:1, etc. Mt 13:41. 24:37-42. Mk *4:29. 2 Th *1:6-8. **was reaped**. Je *51:33. Mt *3:12. *13:30, 38-42.

17. **came**. ver. 14, 15, 18. Re 15:5, 6. 16:1.

18. **came**. Re *6:9, 10. **the altar**. Re +6:9. 8:3-5. 9:13. 16:7. He 8:6. 9:23. **which had power**. Re 16:8. **over fire**. Mt *13:30, 39, 40. 2 P +*3:7. **and cried**. See on ver. 15, 16. **to him**. ver. 17. **Thrust**. ver. +*15. Re 19:15. Is 63:1-6. Jl *▶3:13. Lk *18:8. **the vine**. Dt *32:32, 33. **for her grapes**. Jl 3:13. **fully ripe**. Ge *15:16.

19. **and cast**. Re *19:15-21. Dt 32:32, 33. **the wrath**. ver. +10. Re +*6:16.

20. **the winepress**. Is *34:1-8. √63:1-3. La 1:15. Jl 3:12-15. Zp 3:8. **without**. Re 11:8. He 13:11, 12. **and blood**. ver. 18. Re *16:5, 6. *19:13-21. Is *34:5-7. *49:26. 66:24. Ezk 38:21-23. *39:17-21. **horse bridles**. Re 19:14.

REVELATION 15

The seven angels with the seven last plagues, 1, 2. The song of them that overcame the beast, 3-6. The seven vials full of the wrath of God, and the temple is filled with smoke, 7, 8.

1. **I saw**. Re 12:1-3. Da 4:2, 3. 6:27. **seven angels**. ver. 6-8. Re 8:2, 6. 10:3. 16:1-17. 17:1. 21:9. Mk 13:41, 42, 49, 50. **the seven**. Le *26:28. **last**. Re 8:13. 11:14. 16:17-21. 17:1. **plagues**. Le ▶26:21. Ex *34:10. **is filled**. ver. 7. Re 14:10, 19. 16:19. 19:15. Da 12:6, 7, 11, 12. **the wrath**. ver. 7. Re +*6:16. +14:10.

2. **a sea**. Re +4:6. 21:18. Ex=15:19, 20. 2 K 16:17. 2 Ch *4:2, 4, 15. Je *27:19. 49:23. **of glass**. Re +4:6. 21:21. Ex 24:10. **mingled**. Is 4:4, 5. Mt 3:11. 1 P 1:7. 4:12. **and them**. Re 7:9-17. 12:17. 14:1-5. **victory over**. Re 11:11, 12. +*12:11. 13:14-18. 14:1-5. **the beast**. Re +13:1. **his image**. Re +13:14. **the number**. Re 13:17. **stand**. Ezk 14:30, 31. **sea of glass**. Re +4:6. **having**. See on Re 5:8. *14:2. 19:1-7.

3. **they sing**. Re +5:9. Ps *106:12. **song of Moses**. Ex=15:▶1-18. Dt 31:19-22, 28-30. √32:1-43. **the servant**. Re +7:3. Dt 34:5. 1 Ch 6:49. 2 Ch 24:6. Ne 9:14. Da 6:20. 9:11. Jn 1:17. He 3:5. **and the song**. Re *5:9-13. 7:10, 11. 14:3, 8. **Great**. Ex 15:11. Dt 32:4. Jb *5:9. 37:5. Ps 66:3. 78:12. 92:5. 105:5. ▶111:2. 118:22, 23. *139:14. 145:6, 17. Da 4:2, 3. **marvelous**. Ex ▶34:10. Ps ▶139:14. **thy works**. Ps 111:7. Da 4:37. **Lord God**. See on Re +*4:8. 11:17. **Almighty**. Re +*1:8. Ge 17:1. Ex 6:3. Am ▶4:13, LXX. Jn 1:3. 8:56. Ac 7:38. **just**. Re 16:5-7. 19:2. Dt *32:4. Ps *85:10, 11. 99:4. 100:5. 145:17. Is 45:21. Ho 14:9. Mi *7:20. Zp 3:5. **true**. Ex +*34:6. Dt ▶32:4. **thou King**. Ps 22:28. Is +*9:6, 7. 32:1, 2. 33:22. Je ▶10:7, 10. Zc *9:9. 1 T +1:17. **saints**. *or*, nations, *or*, ages. Re 17:14. 19:16.

4. **Who shall**. Re +*14:7. Ex 15:14-16. Ps 19:9. 72:5. *89:7. *111:10. 130:4. Is 60:5. Je 5:22. ▶10:7. Ho 3:5. Mi *7:16, 17. Lk 12:4, 5. **and glorify**. Re +11:13. Ps 22:23. ▶86:9. √102:13-22. Is 24:15. 25:3. Ml *2:2. Ro 15:9. 2 Th 1:10-12. **thou only**. Re 3:7. 4:8. 6:10. 1 S 2:2. Ps 22:3. 99:5, 9. 111:9. Is *6:3. +*57:15. Hab 1:12. Mk√10:18. Lk *18:19. 1 T ●*6:16n. 1 P 1:16. **art holy**. T#229. Re 16:5. Ex 15:11. Le 11:44. 1 S 2:2. 6:20. Jb 4:17, 18. 34:10. Ps *5:4, 5. 22:3. 27:4. *45:7. 71:22. 90:17. 99:9. *111:9. *145:17. Is *6:3. 28:5. 33:17. Hab *1:13. Zc 9:17. He +7:26. **for all nations**. Re +*11:15. Ps 22:27, 31. *46:10. *48:10. 65:2. 66:4. 72:1-4. 86:9. ch. 117. Is 45:23. 66:18-20, 22, 23. Je 16:19. Zp 2:11. Zc 2:11. *8:20-23. 14:16, 18. Ml ▶1:11. **shall come**. Zc 8:22. **for thy judgments**. Re 16:7. 19:2, +8. 21:4g. Dt ▶32:4. Ps 76:8, 9. 97:6, 8. 98:2. 105:7. ▶145:17. Is √26:9. *59:18, 19. Ezk *39:17-21. Lk 1:6g. Ro 1:32g. 5:16g. He 9:1, 10g.

5. **the temple**. Re +3:12. *11:19. Ex 25:21. Nu 1:50, 53. Mt 27:51. **the tabernacle**. Ex 31:7-11. 38:21. ▶40:34. Nu 1:50, 53. 9:15. 10:11. 17:7, 8. 18:2. 2 Ch 24:6. Ac 7:44. **the testimony**. Ex 25:21, 22. 27:21. **was opened**. Re 11:19. 19:11.

6. **the seven angels**. See on ver. 1. **came out**. Re 14:15. 16:17. Nu 11:24. **plagues**. Le ▶26:21. **clothed**. Re *1:13. Ex 28:5-8. 39:1, 2, 5. Ezk *44:15, 17, 18. Lk 24:4. **linen**. Westcott and Hort read, after some MSS., "stone" here, but such a reading without a modifying word such as "precious" (*timion*) is impossible, and manifestly an error, as Hoskier, roundly criticizing Hort's defective note on this passage, points out, charging that Hort "caused the Revisers to invent Scripture, as at Re 15:6: 'arrayed with precious stone'" (H. C. Hoskier, *Concerning the Genesis of the Versions of the N.T.*, vol. 1, p. 388). Bruce M. Metzger calls the reading an early transcriptional error, and labels Ezk 28:13 a "superficial parallel" (*A Textual Commentary on the Greek New Testament*, p. 756). Ezk ?▶28:13. Da 10:6. **pure**. Re 19:8. Ac 10:30. **girded**. Re +1:13.

7. **one**. See on Re 4:6-9. **seven angels**. ver. +1, 6. **golden**. Re 5:8. 16:2, etc. 17:1. 21:9. Ps *75:8. Je 25:15. **vials**. Re 16:1-4, 8, 10, 12, 17. 17:1. 21:9. Ne 7:70. **wrath**. ver. 1. Re +*6:16. +14:10. **who liveth**. Re +1:18. See on 4:9. 10:6. 1 Th 1:9. **for ever**. Gr. *aion*, Re +1:6.

8. **the temple**. ver. 5. Re +3:12. **was filled**. Ex 19:18. 29:43. *40:34, 35. Le 16:2. Nu 9:15. 1 K *8:10, 11. 2 Ch=5:1, 11-14. 7:2. Ps 18:8-14. Is ▶6:4. Ezk 43:5. Hg *2:7. **from the glory**. Re 21:11, 23. Ex ▶40:34. Le *9:23, 24. Nu 14:10. Ps 29:9. Ro +3:23. 2 Th +*1:9. **no man**. Ex 40:35. 1 K 8:11. Je 15:1. La *3:44. Ro 11:33. **till**. See on ver. 1. **plagues**. Le ▶26:21. **fulfilled**. Ge 15:16.

REVELATION 16

The first angel pours out his vial on the earth, and the worshippers of the beast are plagued with a noisome sore, 1, 2; the second, on the sea, which becomes blood, 3; the third, on the rivers and fountains, which also become blood; and the angel of the waters celebrates the justice of God, in thus visiting bloody persecutors, which is confirmed by one from the altar, 4-7. The fourth angel pours his vial on the sun; and men, scorched with fire, blaspheme God, 8, 9; the fifth, on the seat of the beast, with the miseries caused, and the blasphemies excited, 10, 11. The sixth angel pours his vial on the Euphrates, to prepare the way of eastern kings, 12. Three unclean frogs, from the mouth of the beast, stir up kings to war against God, 13, 14. A warning that Christ comes as a thief. Blessed are they that watch, 15. The seventh angel pours his vial into the air, and the last plagues are tremendously finished on Babylon, etc. 16-21.

1. **I heard.** Re 14:15, 18. 15:5-8. **voice.** Re 1:15. 14:15. Is ▶66:6. **the temple.** Re +3:12. **the seven.** ver. 2, 3, 4, 8, 10, 12, 17. Re 8:6. See on 15:+1, 6. **and pour.** ver. 2-12, 17. 14:9-11. 15:7. 1 S 15:3, 18. Ps ▶69:24. *79:6. Je *6:11. ▶10:25. 42:18. 44:6. Ezk 9:5-8. 10:2. *22:22. Da 9:11, 27. Zp ▶3:8. Mt *13:41, 42. **the vials.** Re +15:7. **the wrath.** Re +*6:16. +14:10.

2. **poured out.** Ps *79:1-6. La 4:11. **upon the earth.** Re *8:5, 7g. 14:16. Is 13:9. **a noisome.** Ex *9:8-11. Le 26:16. Nu 12:10. Dt 7:15. 28:15, 27, 35. 1 S 5:6, 9. 2 Ch 21:15, 18. Jb 2:7, 8. Ps 78:66. Is 1:5, 6. 3:17, 24. Lk 16:20-22. Ac 12:23. **sore.** ver. 11. Ex ▶9:9. Dt *28:27, ▶35. **had the mark.** See on Re *13:15-18. **worshipped.** Re +13:15. Ex *20:4, 5. **his image.** Re +13:14.

3. **second angel.** Re 8:8, 9. **upon.** Re 8:8. 10:2. 13:1. **it became.** Re 11:6. Ex 7:17-21. Ps *78:41, 44. *105:29. Is 50:2. Ezk 16:38. Na 1:2-4. **as the blood.** Re +8:8. Ex ▶7:20, 21. **and every.** Re *8:9. Ge 1:30. 7:22. **soul.** Gr. psyche, ℓ171Q3, 1 C +15:45.

4. **third angel.** Re *8:10, 11. **upon.** Re 8:10, 11. **the rivers.** Ps ▶78:44. **fountains.** Re 14:7. **became blood.** ver. 5. Re 14:7. Ex ▶7:20. 8:5. Is 50:2. Ezk 35:8. Ho 13:15.

5. **the angel.** ver. 4. Jn 5:4. **Thou art.** ver. 7. Re 15:3. 19:2. Ge +*18:25. Ezr 9:15. Ne 9:33. Ps ▶119:137. 129:4. 145:17. Je 12:1. La 1:18. Da 9:7, 14. Jn 17:25. Ro *2:2, 5. *3:5, 26. 2 Th 1:5, 6. 1 J +*1:9. **which art.** Re 1:4, 8. 4:8. 11:17. Ex ▶3:14. Is ▶41:4. 43:3, 11. 63:16. He 13:8. **and shalt be.** Re 11:17n. **hast judged.** Dt ▶32:4. Ps ▶145:17.

6. **they have shed.** Re 6:10, 11. 13:10, 15. *17:6, 7. 18:24. 19:2. Dt *32:42, 43. 1 K *18:4. *19:14. 2 K 24:4. 2 Ch 24:20, 21. Ps ▶79:3. Is 49:26. 51:22, 23. Je 2:30. 26:22, 23. La 4:13. Mt 7:2. 21:35-41. *23:30-37. **of saints.** Re +11:18. **and prophets.** Re +*11:18. 18:20. **blood to drink.** Is ▶49:26. Lk 11:49, 50. **for they are worthy.** Re ●3:4. +*11:18. *18:20. Jg 1:7. Ps 74:18-23. 79:10-13. Je 26:11, 16. Ezk 16:38. 35:6. Lk +*12:48. He 10:29.

7. **out.** Re *6:9. 8:3-5. 14:18. Is 6:6. Ezk 10:2, 7. **Even.** Re *15:3, 4. **Lord God.** Re +4:8. **Almighty.** ver. 14. Re +*1:8. Am ▶4:13, LXX. **true.** Re 13:10. 14:10. 15:3. 19:2. Ps ▶19:9. ▶119:137. **righteous are.** Ge *18:23-33. Ps *50:6. Ro *9:14. 2 Th 1:6.

8. **fourth angel.** Re *8:12. **upon the sun.** Re 6:12. 8:12. 9:2. Is 24:23. Ezk 8:16. Lk *21:25. Ac 2:20. Ro 1:18-23. **and power.** Re 7:16. *9:17, 18, 20, 21. 14:18. Jon 4:8. Mt 13:6. **with fire.** Re *9:17. 14:18.

9. **scorched.** *or,* burned. Is *24:6. 42:25. Ml 4:1. 2 P +*3:7. ℓ147D, Ge +1:29. **blasphemed.** ver. 10, 11, 21. Re +13:6. 2 K 6:33. 2 Ch 28:22. Is 1:5. 8:21. 52:5. Je 5:3. 6:29, 30. Ezk 24:13. **they repented not.** ver. 11. Re +2:21. 9:20. Ex 9:34, 35. Je 8:6. Da 5:22, 23. Lk +*13:3, 5. 2 C 12:21. **to give.** Re +11:13. 14:7. Ex 8:15. Jsh 7:19. 2 K 6:33. Jb 1:11, 20-22. Je 13:16. Da *5:22, 23. Am 4:6-12.

10. **upon.** Re 11:2, 8. *13:2-4. 17:9, 17. *18:2, 21-23. **the seat.** *or,* throne. Re 2:13. 13:2. **his kingdom.**

Re 8:12. 9:2. Ps 105:28. **full of darkness.** Re 9:2. 18:11-19. Ex ▶10:21-23. Ps 78:49. Is 8:21, 22. Jl +*2:1, 2, 31. Zc *14:12. Mt 8:12. 22:13. Mk *13:24, 25. 2 P 2:17. **they.** Re 11:10. Mt 13:42, 50. *24:51. Lk 13:28.

11. **blasphemed.** See on ver. 9, 21. **the God.** Re +11:13. 2 Ch 36:23. Ezr 1:2. 5:11, 12. 6:10. 7:12, 21, 23. Ne 1:4. 2:4. Ps 136:26. Da 2:18, 19, 44. Jon 1:9. **because.** ver. 2, 9. **and repented not.** ver. 9. 2 Ch *28:22. Pr *27:22. Da *12:10. Lk 23:39, 40. 2 T 3:13. **their deeds.** Re 2:13.

12. **upon.** Re *9:14. 11:14. Is 8:7. **great river.** Ge ▶15:18. Dt ▶1:7. Jsh ▶1:4. Is *11:15. 27:12. 44:27. Je 50:38. 51:32, 36. Zc *10:10, 11. **Euphrates.** Ge 2:10, 14. **and the water.** Re *17:15. Is 11:15. 42:15. ▶44:27. Je 50:▶38-40. 51:36. **dried up.** Ex 14:21, 22. Jsh 3:15-17. 4:22. Ps 74:15. Is *44:27. Hab 3:8. **that the way.** Is 41:2, 3, 25. 45:1-3. 46:11. Ezk ch. *38, 39. Da 11:43-45. **kings of.** Is ▶41:2, 25. **the east.** Re 7:2. Mt 2:1.

13. **I saw.** Ex 7:10-13, 22. three. ver. 14. 2 Th *2:9-11. 1 T 4:1-3. 2 T 3:1-6. 2 P 2:1-3. 1 J 4:1-3. **unclean.** Re 18:2. Mk +3:30. **spirits.** Gr. *pneuma*, Mt +8:16. **like frogs.** Ex ▶8:2-7. Ps 78:45. 105:30. **come out of.** Re *12:+3, 4, 9-13. *13:1-7, 11-18. **the beast.** Re +13:1. **the false prophet.** Re 13:11, 14. *19:20. 20:10. Mt +7:15.

14. **the spirits.** Gr. *pneuma*, Mt +8:16. Re 12:9. 1 K *22:19-23. 2 Ch 18:18-22. Ezk 14:9. Jn *8:44. 2 C √11:13-15. 1 T +*4:1. Ja 3:15. **working miracles.** Re 13:+13, 14. 19:20. Dt 13:1, 2. Mt 24:24. Mk 13:22. 2 Th *2:9. **which.** 1 K 22:6, 10, 11, 19-22. Ac 13:8-10. **the whole.** Re +*3:10. 12:9. 13:3. Lk 2:1. Ro 1:8. 1 J 5:19. **world.** Gr. *oikoumene*, Mt +24:14. **to gather.** ver. 16. Re *17:14. *19:19. 20:8. 1 K *22:20. Ps 2:1-3. Is 34:1-8. 63:1-6. Ezk *38:8-12. Jl *3:2, 9-14. Zc *14:1-3. **great day.** Re +6:17. Ac 2:20. Ro +*2:4, 5. 1 Th 5:2. **God Almighty.** See on ver. 7. Re +*1:8. Am ▶4:13, LXX.

15. **Behold.** ℓ136, Is +60:12. ℓ161, Mk +15:13. **I come.** Re +3:3. Mt *24:43. *25:6. Jn +21:22. 1 Th √5:2-4. 2 P *3:10. **Blessed.** ℓ43, Dt +28:3. Re 1:3. +14:13. 19:9. 20:6. 22:7, 14. **that watcheth.** Re 3:2, 3. Mt +*24:42, 46. 25:13. 26:41. Mk 13:33-37. 14:38. Lk 12:37-43. +√21:36. Ac 20:31. 1 Th 5:6. 1 P 4:7. **keepeth.** SS 5:3. **garments.** Re 3:18. **lest.** Re *3:4, 18. Ge *3:10. Ex 32:25. Is 47:3. Ezk 16:37. Ho 2:3, 10. Na 3:5. Hab 2:15. 2 C 5:3.

16. **he gathered.** Re 14:20. 16:14. 17:14. 19:17-21. Jg 4:7. Is 14:24-27. Ezk 38:8-19. Da *11:35—12:1. Jl 3:2, 9-14. Mi *4:11-13. Zp +*3:8. Zc *12:3. *14:2, 3. **the Hebrew.** Re 9:11. Jn +5:2. 19:13, 17. Ac 26:14. **Armageddon.** i.e. *hill of slaughter,* *S#717g. Jsh 12:21. 17:11. Jg 1:27. *5:19-22. 2 K 9:27. 23:29, 30. 2 Ch 35:22. Is 10:28, LXX. Zc *12:11.

17. **seventh angel.** Re +*11:15-19. **into the air.** Re *20:1-3. Ep *2:2. 6:12. **there.** ver. 1. Re 11:+15, 19. 14:17. 15:5, 6. **voice out.** Is ▶66:6. **the temple.** Re +3:12. 15:8. ●21:22. **the throne.** Re +4:2. **It is.** Re +*10:6, 7. *21:6. Ezk √39:8. Da 12:7-13. Jn 19:30. 1 P *4:7.

18. **were voices.** Re +4:5. *8:5. *11:19. **and thunders.** Ex ▶19:16. **great earthquake.** Re +6:12. 11:13. Ezk *38:20. Is *2:19, 21. Da 12:1. Hg +*2:6, 21, 22. Zc √14:4, 5. He +*12:26-28. **such as.** Da ▶12:1. Jl 2:2. Mt 24:21.

19. **great city.** Re +11:8. *14:8. 17:18. 18:2, 10, 16-19, 21. **was divided.** Re 11:13. Zc *13:8, 9. **cities**

of. ver. 14. Re 17:13-17. **great Babylon.** Re +14:8. 17:5. Is 14:4. Da)4:30. **in remembrance.** See on Re 14:8-10. *18:5. Ps 74:18. 89:50. 98:3. *105:8, 42. *137:7-9. Is 49:26. 51:17-23. Je 25:15, 16, 26. 44:21. Ho *9:7. **the cup.** Re 14:10. Je)25:15. Zc 12:2-8. **fierceness.** √144B, Dt +33:19. Re 18:4. Is)51:17. **wrath.** Re +*6:16. 19:15.

20. **every island.** Re *6:14. 20:11. Ps *102:25, 26. Is 2:14-17. *34:3. **the mountains.** Ps 18:7. *46:1-3. ☽*72:3, 16. ☾148:9. Is ☾2:2. ☾44:23. Je *4:23-25. Ezk ☾36:8. Hab *3:6, 10.

21. **there fell.** Re 8:7. *11:19. Ex *9:23-26. Jsh *10:11. Jb *38:22, 23. Ps *18:12-14. 78:47. 105:32. Is 28:17. *30:30. Ezk *13:11, 13. *38:21, 22. **hail.** Ex)9:24. **blasphemed.** ver. 9, 11. Is 8:21. **the plague.** Ex 9:23-25.

REVELATION 17

A woman arrayed in purple and scarlet, with a golden cup in her hand, sitteth upon the beast, 1-4; which is great Babylon, the mother of all abominations, 5-8. The interpretation of the seven heads, 9-11; and the ten horns, 12, 13. The victory of the Lamb, 14, 15. The punishment of the whore, 16-18.

1. **one.** Re 15:1, 6. 16:1-17. 21:9. **seven angels.** Re +15:1. **seven vials.** Re +15:7. **talked.** Re 4:1. 21:15. Lk 9:30. 24:32. **Come hither.** Re 21:9. **I will.** Re 16:19. 18:16-19. **the judgment of.** Je *51:11, 13, 33. **the great.** ver. 4, 5, 15, 16. Re 19:2. Dt 31:16, 17. Ps *73:27. Is 1:21. 23:15-17. 57:3. Je 2:20. 3:1. Na *3:4, 5. **that sitteth.** ver. *15. Je *51:13. **many waters.** ver. 15. Re ☾1:15. Je)51:13. Jn +*3:23.

2. **the kings.** ver. 13, 17. Re 14:8. 18:3, 9, 23. **committed fornication.** Is)23:17. **inhabitants.** ver. 8. Re +3:10. **were made.** ver. 4. Re +14:8. **drunk.** ver. 6. Je *)51:7. Da 3:1, 4-6. Zc 5:5-11. Jn +2:10.

3. **he carried.** Re +*1:10. 4:2. 21:10. 1 K 18:12. 2 K 2:16. Ezk 3:12. 8:3. 11:24. Ac 8:26, 29, 39. **spirit.** Gr. *pneuma*, Mt +3:16. √121A4, Ezk +37:1. Lk +24:37. **into the wilderness.** Re +*12:6, 14. SS 8:5. **a woman.** ver. 4, 6, 18. Re *12:3. **scarlet.** Re *12:3. Mt +27:28. **full.** See on Re 13:1-6. Da 7:8, 20, 25. 11:36. 2 Th 2:4. **having.** ver. 7, 9-12. Re +12:3. *13:1. **ten horns.** Da 7:)7, 20.

4. **arrayed.** Re 18:7, 12, 16. **purple.** Re 18:12, 16. Jg 8:26. Est 1:6. **scarlet.** ver. 3. Re 12:3. Mt 27:28. **decked.** Gr. gilded. Da 11:38. **pearls.** Re 21:21. Mt +13:46. **golden.** Re 14:8. 18:6. 19:2. Ps 75:8. Je *)51:7. 2 Th 2:3-10. **full of.** Mt 23:25, 26. **abominations.** ver. 5. Re 21:27. Dt 18:9. *29:17. 32:16. 1 K *14:24. 2 K 16:3. 21:2. 23:13, 24. Is 44:19. 66:3. Ezk 8:6, 9, 13, 15, 17. 11:18. 14:6. 16:2. *20:7, 8, 30. Ho 9:10. Lk 16:15. **filthiness.** Ezr 9:11. La 1:9. Ezk 24:11, 13. 36:25.

5. **upon.** Re 7:3. 13:16. Is 3:9. Ph 3:19. **written.** Re ☾3:12. **Mystery.** T#518. ver. 7. Re +1:20. 13:11-18. Da 7:8, 24-26. Ep 5:32. 2 Th *2:3-10. 1 T *4:1-3. 2 T 3:1-5. **Babylon.** Re 11:8. +14:8. 16:19. 18:2, 10, 21. Ge 10:10. Je 51:47, 48. Da)4:30. **The Mother.** Re 18:9. 19:2. Pr 9:13-18. Ezk *16:44, 45. Harlots. *or,* fornications. ver. +1. Le 20:5. Nu 25:1. 2 Ch 21:11. Is 1:21. 23:17. Je 2:20. 3:1, 6, 8. Ezk *16:15-17, 28, 29, 31, 34, 35, 41. 20:30. *23:5, 9, 43, 44. Ho 2:5. 3:3. 4:5, 10, 13-15. Mi 1:7. **Abominations.** ver. +4. 1 K 11:5. 2 K 23:11. Is 66:17n. Am 5:25, 26. Ac 7:43.

6. **drunken.** ver. 2. Re 13:7, 15. 16:6. 18:20-24. Is

34:7. Da *7:21, 25. Mt 23:32-36. Jn +2:10. **the blood.** Re +16:6. **the saints.** Re +8:3. Ps *79:2, 3. 83:1-5. Da +*11:33, 35. **the martyrs.** Re +2:13. *6:9, 10. 11:7, 8. 12:+*11, 13, 17. 13:7. 18:24. 20:4. Ps 9:5, 9, 10, 12, 13, 19. 10:2, 3, 8, 14-18. 44:22. 79:2, 3. 94:5, 6. Da 7:21, 25. 8:27. 11:33, 35. Ac 22:20. He 11:33-40. **of Jesus.** Re +1:2. **I saw.** Ec *5:8. **I wondered.** √147D, Ge +1:29. Da *7:28. *8:27. Hab 1:13.

7. **I will.** See on ver. 1-6, 8. **mystery.** ver. +5. 2 Th *2:7. **of the woman.** ver. +3. **the beast.** ver. +3. **ten horns.** Da *7:7.

8. **beast that thou.** Re 9:2, 3. 11:7. 13:1-11. Da)7:3. *10:20. **was.** That is, *had existence before John's day.* ver. 10, 11. Re 1:4. √13:3, 12. **is not.** Ge 5:24. **shall ascend.** This beast is the eighth and last kingdom in the times of the Gentiles, the revived Grecian kingdom. Re *11:7. *13:1, 2. 17:8-11. Da 10:12-21. Jl 3:6. Zc 9:13. **bottomless pit.** Re +9:1. **go into.** ver. 11. Re 13:10. 14:8-20. ch. 16, 18. 19:15-21. 20:10. Da *7:11, 26. 11:45. 2 Th 2:3-8. **that dwell.** ver. 2. Re +3:10. **shall wonder.** Re *13:3, 4. **whose names.** Re +*13:8. 20:12, 15. **written.** Re *21:27. Da)12:1. **the book.** √22D5K1A, Ex +32:32. Re +3:5. Ps)69:28. Ph 4:3. **from.** Re 13:8. Mt +13:35. 25:34. Jn 17:24. Ac 15:18. Ep +*1:4. T *1:2. 1 P 1:20. **world.** Gr. *kosmos*, Mt *4:8. **the beast that was.** Re 13:1-4, 11, 12. **yet is.** Re 7:11. *8:23, 24. *9:27. *11:36, 45.

9. **here.** Re *13:18. Pr 9:10. Da *12:4, 8-10. Ho 14:9. Mt *13:11. 24:15. Ja *1:5. 1 J 2:20, 27. **The seven heads.** ver. +3, 7, 18. 13:1. **mountains.** Je 51:25. Da 2:35. Zc 4:7.

10. **are fallen.** The word is always used of violent death, when speaking of individuals, or violence when referring to kingdoms. Jg 3:25. 5:27. 2 S 1:19, 25. Is 21:9. Je 50:15. 51:8. Ezk 29:5. 30:6. **short space.** Re 12:12.

11. **that was.** See on ver. 8. **goeth into.** ver. 8. Re 13:10. 2 Th *2:6-9.

12. **the ten.** ver. 3, 16. Re 12:3. 13:1. Da 2:40-43. *7:7, 8, 20,)24. Zc 1:18-21. **received no kingdom.** Lk 19:12, 15. He 12:28. **receive power.** Da *4:34, 35. **one hour.** Re 3:10. 14:7, 15. 18:10, 17, 19. Is 61:2. Mt 14:15. 18:1. Mk 6:35. 2 C +7:8. Phm 15.

13. **one.** Re 16:14. Ph 1:27. 2:2. **shall.** ver. 17. Is 10:5-7. Ezk 38:10. Ac *4:28.

14. **shall make war.** Re 11:7. 12:6, 7. +16:14. √19:15-21. Is *8:9, 10. Da 7:21, 25. *8:25. *11:31. 13:9-12, 24, 25. Zc 2:8. Mt 25:40. Ac 4:26. 9:4, 5. **the Lamb.** Re +5:6. **the Lamb shall.** Re +3:21. 6:12-17. Ps 2:8, 9. *21:8-12. 110:5. Is *8:9, 10. Je *50:44. Da *2:44. 7:26, 27. 1 C 15:24n, 25n. **overcome.** T#82. Re 12:11. Ps 24:7. *110:5, 6. Is 13:3-9. +*24:21-23. Zc 6:13. Mt 24:30. 25:31, 32. Ep 1:19-21, +22 (T#96). Ph *2:9-11. He 1:1-4. **Lord of lords.** √147H, Ge +9:25. Re *1:5. *19:16. Dt)10:17. Ps 136:2, 3. Pr 8:15, 16. Da)2:47. Mt 28:18. Jn 8:24. Ac +*10:36. 1 T +6:15. 2 T +*4:1. **King of kings.** √147H, Ge +9:25. Re 1:5. Mt 25:34. 1 T *6:14, 15. **and they.** Re 14:1-4. 19:14. Ps +*149:5-9. Je 1:44, 45. Mi 5:7-9. Jn +*15:16. Ro 8:30, 37. 2 T 2:4. He 3:1, 2. 1 P 2:9. **with him.** Re 3:4. 14:4. 19:14. Ps +*149:5-9. Da *7:13, 14, 21, 22. **called.** Mt 22:14. Ro +1:6. *8:28. 2 T *1:9. **and chosen.** Dt +*10:15. Mt 22:14. Lk +*18:7g. Jn +*15:16. Col 3:12. 1 Th 5:9. 1 P *1:1, 2. 2:8, 9. **and faithful.** Re 2:10, 13. 1 C +4:2. 2 T *1:12.

15. **The waters.** See on ver. 1. Ps *18:4, 16. 65:7.

*93:3, 4. 124:4. Is *8:7, 8. Je *51:»13, 42, 55. Ezk 27:26. **the whore.** Re 17:2. **are.** Re 10:11. 11:9. 13:7, 8. Ps 18:4, 16. 124:4. Is 8:7. **peoples.** Re +5:9.

16. **the ten.** See on ver. 2, 10, +12. **these.** ƒ163. Syllepsis, Jn +16:13. By the figure Syllepsis, the concord of the pronoun is logical rather than grammatical. "These" (masculine) links "the horns" and "the beast" (which are neuter) together. **shall hate.** ver. 1, 2, 13. Re 16:12. Is 13:17, 18. 14:4-6. Je 25:14. 50:41, 42. **the whore.** T#520. Re *18:4, 8. 19:1-3, 20. Da 7:11, 26. 2 Th 2:8. **desolate.** Re 18:17, 19. **and naked.** Re 18:16, 17. Ezk 16:37-44. 23:45-49. 23:29, 45-49. Ho 2:2, 3. **eat.** Re 19:18. Jb 31:31. Ps 14:4. 27:2. Da 7:5. Mi 3:3. Ja 5:3. **and burn.** Re 18:8, 16. Le 20:14. 21:9.

17. **God hath.** See on ver. 13. Dt +*2:30. Pr 21:1, +*30. Is 10:5-7. *14:27. *46:9-11. *66:4. Am +*3:6. Ac +*2:23. 4:27, *28. Ro 9:19-22. 2 C 8:16. Ep +*1:11. Ph 2:13. 2 Th +*2:11. 1 P +*2:8. **put.** Ezr 7:27. Ps 105:25. Pr 21:1. Je 32:40. 2 Th 2:10-12. Ja 1:13-17. **to fulfil.** Is *55:11. Lk 22:3, 22, 37. Jn 13:2, 18. **to agree.** ver. 13. **give their kingdom.** 2 Th 2:11. **until.** Re 6:11. +*10:7. 15:1. Pr 19:21. Is 45:27. 46:10, 11. Je 27:6, 7. Ezk *38:16, 17. Da 12:7. Jn *10:35. 12:39, 40. 19:24, 28. **the words.** Ps *119:89. Je 1:12. Jn 17:17. **be fulfilled.** Lk +21:22.

18. **the woman.** ver. 5, 9. Re 16:19. 18:2. Da 2:37, 38, 40, 41. 7:23. Lk 2:1. **great city.** Re 11:8. 16:19. Ge 11:9. Je 25:26. Da 1:1, 2. Zc 5:1-11. **which reigneth.** Re 12:4. Je 27:2-7. Lk 2:1. Jn 19:15. **the kings of.** Re *16:14. Ps »2:2. »89:27.

REVELATION 18

A mighty angel announces the fall of Babylon, and its utter desolation, because of its abominations, 1-3. A voice from heaven calls on the people of God to come out of her, lest they should be involved in her destruction, 4-8. The kings and merchants connected with her lament her fall, 9-19. The apostles and prophets are called to rejoice over it, 20. Her final and total overthrow first signified by a millstone cast into the sea; and then is emphatically described, 21-24.

1. **I saw.** See on Re 17:+1, 7. **come down.** Re +10:1. **and the earth.** Re 21:23. Is 60:1-3. Ezk 10:4. 43:2. Hab *3:3, 4. Lk 2:9. 17:24. Ac 9:3. 12:7. 2 Th 2:8.

2. **cried.** Re 1:15. 5:2. 10:3. 14:15. Je 25:30. Jl *3:16. **Babylon.** ver. 10, 21. Re +14:8. 16:19. 17:5, 18. Is *13:19. *21:9. Je *51:8, 60-64. Da »4:30. **is fallen.** Re *14:8. Is ◐13:17. »21:9. Je *51:8. Da ◐5:28-31. **become.** Le 11:13-19. Is 13:20-22. 14:23. 21:8. *34:11-15. Je *50:39, 40. *51:37. Mk 5:3-5. Lk 8:27, 28. **habitation of devils.** Le »17:7. 2 Ch »11:15. Is »13:21. »34:14. Je 50:39. 51:37. Zp 2:14, 15. **every foul.** Re 16:13. Mt 8:28. Mk +3:30. 5:2, 3. Lk 8:27. **spirit.** Gr. *pneuma*, Mt +8:16. **every unclean.** Is 14:23. 34:11.

3. **all nations.** ver. 9. Re +14:8. *17:2. Je 51:7. **have drunk.** Is »51:17, 22. Je »25:16, 27. »51:7. **wrath.** ƒ24N, Ge +17:5. **committed fornication.** Is »23:17. **the kings.** ver. 9. Re 17:2. **the merchants.** ver. 11-17, 19, 23. Is 47:15. Ezk 27:33. 2 P 2:1-3. **abundance.** *or,* power. Pr 23:1-3. **her delicacies.** ver. 7, 9. Je 51:34. La 4:5. Lk 7:25. 1 T 5:11.

4. **Come out.** T#115. Ge *19:12, 13, 16, 17, 29. Nu *16:21, 26, 27. 2 Ch +19:2 (T#112). Ps +26:4 (T#122). Is *48:20. *52:11. Je *50:8. »51:6, 9, 45, 50. Zc *2:6, 7. Mt 24:15, 16. Lk 12:51. 2 C +*6:17. *7:1.

---

1 T +6:5 (T#177). Ju *23. **partakers.** Ps 50:18. Mt 23:30. 1 T 5:22. 2 J *11. **her plagues.** Re 15:1.

5. **reached.** ƒ155F, Ge +4:7. Ge 4:10. 18:20, 21. 19:13. 2 Ch 28:9. Ezr 9:6. Je *51:9. Jon 1:2. **remembered.** ƒ22C3, Ge +8:1. See on Re *16:19. Is 47:10.

6. **Reward her.** Re 13:10. 16:5, 6. Ex 21:23-25. Ps 28:4. »137:8. Je *50:15, 29. 51:24, 49. 2 T 4:14. **double unto.** Ex *22:4. Is +*40:2. 61:7. Je 16:18. 17:18. Zc 9:12. **according to.** Re 2:23. 20:12. 22:12. Je »50:29. **the cup.** See on Re 14:10. 16:19. *17:2, 4. Ps *11:6. *75:8. Je 25:15, 16, 26. 51:7. **hath filled.** Re 14:10.

7. **much she.** Is 22:12-14. 47:1, 2, *7-9. Je *50:31, 32. Ezk 28:2-10. Zp 2:15. 2 Th 2:4-8. **lived deliciously.** ver. +3. Ps *73:3, 16, 20. Lk *9:25. **so much.** Lk +*12:47, 48. **for she.** Re 17:18. Ps 10:6, 11, 13. 49:11. Is »47:7. Ob 3. Zp 2:15. **I sit.** Ps 45:9. Is *47:5. Je 13:18. La 1:1. **a queen.** Je 7:18. *44:17. Ac 8:27. **no widow.** ƒ175B, Ge +21:16. Is 47:7, 8. La 1:1.

8. **shall her plagues.** ver. 10, 17, 19. Ex 9:14. Is *47:9-11. Je 51:6. **death.** Re 6:8. **and she.** ver. 9. Re 17:+16, 19. *19:3. Je 51:58. **for strong.** Re 11:17. 15:1. Jb 9:19. Ps 2:1-5, 9. 62:11. *89:8, 13. Is 27:1. Je *50:31, »34, 54-56. Ezk 16:59. Am 3:6. 1 C 10:22.

9. **the kings.** ver. 3, 7. Re 17:2, 12, 13. Ps 2:2. »48:4, LXX. Is 23:14. Ezk 26:16, 17. »27:33. **committed fornication.** Is »23:17. **lived deliciously.** ver. +3. **shall bewail.** ver. 20. Ps 58:10. Je *50:46. Ezk »26:16, 17. 27:»30, 35. 32:9, 10. Da 4:14. Zc 11:2, 3. **the smoke.** ver. 18. Re +14:11. 19:3. Ge *19:28. Dt 29:23. Is 13:19. 30:33. 34:9, 10. Je 50:40. 51:31, 32. Ju *7.

10. **Standing afar.** ver. 15, 17. Nu 16:34. **Alas.** ver. 16, 19. Je +*30:7. Jl 1:15. Am 5:16. **that great.** Re +14:8. Ge +=11:4. Is 21:9. Ezk »26:17. Da »4:30. **for.** See on ver. 8, 17, 19. Re +17:12. Je 51:8, 9.

11. **the merchants.** ver. +3, 9, 15, 20, 23. Re 13:16, 17. Is 23:1-15. 47:15. Ezk 26:17-21. 27:27-»36. Zp 1:11, 18. **shall weep.** Ezk »27:30, 31. **buyeth.** Pr 3:14. Mt 22:5. Jn 2:16. Ac 19:24-34. 2 P 2:3.

12. **merchandise.** Re 17:4. 1 K 10:11, 12. Pr 8:10, 11. Ezk 27:5-25. **of gold.** Re +17:4. **and.** ƒ148, Ge +8:22. **fine linen.** ver. 16. Re 19:8, 14. Est 1:6. 8:15. Lk 16:19. **purple.** Re 17:4. Mk 15:17, 20. Jn 19:2, 5. Ac 16:14. **thyine.** *or,* sweet. 1 K 10:11. 2 Ch 2:8.

13. **And.** ƒ148, Ge +8:22. **cinnamon.** 1 K 10:10, 15, 25. 2 Ch 9:9. Pr 7:17. SS 1:3. 4:13, 14. 5:5. Am 6:6. Jn 12:3-8. **frankincense.** Le 2:1, 2. 6:15. Mt 2:11. **fine flour.** Ge 18:6. Nu 6:15. 1 S 1:24. **slaves.** *or,* bodies. Ge 36:6. Ex 21:16. Dt 24:7. 28:68. Ne 5:4, 5, 8. Is 50:1. Ezk 27:13. Am 2:6. 8:6. 1 T 1:10. **and souls.** Gr. psyche, ƒ171Q1A, Ac +2:41. Nu 31:35. 1 Ch 5:21. Ezk »27:13. 2 P 2:3, 9.

14. **thy soul.** Gr. psyche. Here psyche is the seat of appetite. ƒ121A9C. Metonymy of Cause. For the other uses of psyche see Mt +2:20n. For other instances of ƒ121A9, see Ge +23:8. Nu 11:4, 34. Ps 78:18. 106:14. 107:9. Pr 6:30. Is 5:14. 29:8. 1 C 10:6. Ja *4:2. 1 J *2:16, 17. **lusted after.** 1 J *2:15-17. **departed.** Ec 2:1-11. 5:10-17. Mt 6:19-24. Lk 12:20. 16:25.

15. **merchants.** ver. +3. Ezk »27:36. **which.** ver. 3, 11. Ho 12:7, 8. Zc 11:5. Mk 11:17. Ac 16:19. 19:24-27. **shall stand.** See on ver. 11, 17. Jg 18:23, 24. Ezk 27:31. Am 5:16, 17. **weeping.** Ezk »27:30, 31.

16. **Alas.** See on ver. 10, 11, 19. Re 17:4. Lk 16:19, etc. **that great.** Re +14:8. **city.** Ge +=11:4. **clothed.** Re 17:4. **fine linen.** ver. +12. **scarlet.** ver. 12. Re +17:4.

17. **in one hour.** ver. +10. Is 47:9. Je 51:8. La 4:6. **come to nought.** ver. 19. Re 17:16. Is 13:19. Je 49:18. 50:40. Mt 7:26, 27. **And every.** ver. 11. Is *23:14. Ezk *27:27-36. Jon 1:6. Ac 27:11. **sailors.** Ezk ▶27:29. Ac 27:27, 30g. **stood afar.** ver. 10, 15.

18. **cried.** Ezk 27:30. **when.** See on ver. 9. Re +14:11. **What.** ver. 10. Re 13:4. Is 23:8, 9. Je 51:37. Ezk ▶27:30-32. **this great.** Re +14:8.

19. **they cast dust.** Jsh 7:6. 1 S 4:12. 2 S 1:2. 13:19. 15:32. Ne 9:1. Jb 2:12. La 2:10. Ezk ▶27:30. **weeping.** See on ver. 10, 15, 16. Ezk ▶27:31. **Alas.** ver. 10, 16. **wherein.** ver. +3. Ezk ▶27:36. **ships.** Is 23:14. Ezk ▶27:9. **the sea.** Ezk ▶27:33. **for.** ver. 8. **one hour.** ver. +10. **desolate.** ver. 17. Re 17:16. Je 51:37, 43. Ezk ▶26:19.

20. **Rejoice.** Re +12:12. 19:1-3. Dt 32:43. Jg 5:31. Ps 48:11. *58:10. 96:11-13. 107:42. 109:28. Pr 11:10. Is *26:1, 5-8. 44:23. 49:13. Je 51:47, 48. **and ye holy.** Re +8:3. +*11:18. Ep 2:20. 3:5. 4:11. 2 P 3:2. Ju 17. **apostles.** Lk 11:49. 1 C +12:28. **God.** Re +*6:10. *19:2. Dt 32:42, ▶43. Ps 18:47. *58:11. *79:10. 94:1. Is 26:21. Je 50:15. Lk 11:49, 50. *18:7, 8. Ro 12:19.

21. **a mighty angel.** Re 5:2. +8:13g. 10:1. **took up.** Je *51:63, 64. **a great millstone.** Mt 18:6. Mk 9:42. Lk 17:2. **and cast.** Re *8:8. Jg 9:53. Je ▶51:63. Lk 17:2. **Thus.** Ex *15:5, 6. Ne *9:11. Je 51:63, ▶64. **great city.** Re +14:8. Da ▶4:30. **and shall.** ver. 22. Re 12:8. 16:20. 20:11. Jb 20:8. Ps 37:36. Ezk ▶26:21. Da 11:19. Mt 24:37-39. **no more.** ƒ8, Ps +118:1.

22. **the voice.** Is 14:11. *24:1, 8, 9. Je 7:34. 16:9. 25:10. 33:11. Ezk 26:13. **of harpers.** Re 14:2. 15:2. **pipers.** Mt 9:23. **be heard.** Ezk ▶26:13. **no more.** ƒ167, Is +2:7. **the sound.** Je ▶25:10n. **millstone.** Ec 12:4. Mt 24:41. **no more.** ƒ8, Ps +118:1. ƒ76, Ge +13:6.

23. **the light.** Re 22:5. Jb 21:17. Pr +*4:18, 19. 24:20. Je 25:10. **the voice.** See on ver. 22. Ps 78:63. **bridegroom.** Mt 24:38. **no more.** ƒ8, Ps +118:1. ƒ76, Ge +13:6. **thy merchants.** ver. +3, 11-19. Is *23:8, 9. Ezk 27:24, 25, 33, 34. **great men.** Re 6:15g. Is 34:12. **sorceries.** ver. 3, 9. Re +9:21. 12:9. 13:13-16. 17:2, 5. +*21:8. *22:15. 2 K 9:22. Is ▶47:9. Na 3:4. Ac 8:11.

24. **in her.** Re 11:7. 16:6. 17:6. 19:2. Je 2:34. Ezk 22:9, 12, 27. Da 7:21. Mt 23:27, 35, 36. Lk 11:47-51. Ac 7:52. 1 Th 2:15. **the blood.** Ge *4:10. *9:6. Ps *79:2, 3. Je *51:35. **prophets.** Re +*11:18. **were slain.** Re *6:9-11. Je *▶51:49. Mt 23:29-38.

REVELATION 19

The apostle hears in vision all the servants of God praise him with loud acclamations, 1-6. The marriage of the Lamb, 7-9. John, about to worship the angel, is reproved, and forbidden, 10. Christ and his followers, on white horses, are seen obtaining great and decisive victories, and utterly destroying all opposers, especially the beast and the false prophet and their adherents, who are cast alive into a lake of fire and brimstone, 11-21.

1. **after.** See on Re ch. 18. **I heard.** ver. 6. Re +*11:15. 18:20. **saying.** Ps 66:1, 3-5, 8. **Alleluia.** ver. 3, 4, 6. Ps +*68:4. ▶104:35. 105:45. 106:1, 48. 111:1. 112:1. 113:1, 9. 115:18. 116:19. 117:2. 135:1, 3, 21. 146:1, 10. 147:1, 20. 148:1, 14. 149:1, 9. 150:1mg, 6. **Salvation.** Re 4:10, 11. 5:9-13. 7:+10-12. 11:15. 12:10. 1 Ch 29:11. Ps 3:8. Is 12:2. Jon 2:9. Mt +*6:13. 1 T

1:16, 17. **glory.** Re +4:9. **honor.** Re +4:9. Jn +*5:23. **power.** Re +4:11. Ps 62:11.

2. **true.** See on Re 15:3. +16:7. Dt 32:4. Ps ▶19:9. ▶119:137. Is 25:1. **and righteous.** Re 16:5-7. Ge +*18:25. Ps 58:11. 145:17. Is 45:21. **judged.** Re +6:10. 17:1, 2, 15, 16. 18:3, 9, 10, *20, 23. **the great.** Re 14:8. 17:+1, 6, 15. **and hath avenged.** See on Re +*6:10. 16:6. 18:20, 24. Dt 32:35, ▶43. 2 K ▶9:7. Ps 149:1, 7-9. **his servants.** Re +7:3. **hand.** ƒ144A5, Ge +9:5.

3. **Alleluia.** See on ver. 1. Re +14:11. Ps ▶104:35. **And her smoke.** See on Re 14:11. 18:9, 18. Ge 19:28. Is ▶34:10. He 12:29. Ju 7. **for ever.** Gr. *aion*, Re +1:6.

4. **the four and.** Re 4:+4-10. 5:8-11, 14. 11:15, 16. 15:7. **four beasts.** Re 4:+6, 8. **fell down.** Re +4:10. **that sat.** Re +4:2. Ps ▶47:8. Is ▶6:1. **Amen.** Re 5:14. 7:12. 1 Ch 16:36. Ne 5:13. 8:6. Ps 41:13. 72:19. 89:52. 106:48. Je 28:6. Mt +*6:13. 28:20. 1 C +14:16. **Alleluia.** See on ver. 1.

5. **a voice.** Re 7:15. 11:19. 16:17. **Praise.** Ps *50:1, 14, 23. 103:20-22. 113:1. 134:1. 135:1, 19, 20. 148:11-13. 150:6. Zc 4:7. **our God.** Ps *22:22, 23, 25. Jn 20:17. He *2:11-13. 5:6. 8:1. **all ye.** Ps 148:11, 12. **his servants.** Ps ▶134:1. ▶135:1. **that fear.** Re +*11:18. Ac +10:2. **both small.** See on Re +*11:28. 20:12.

6. **voice of a great.** ver. 1. Da ▶10:6. **and as the voice of many waters.** Re +1:15. *14:2. Ezk ▶1:24. *▶43:2. Jn +*3:23. **and as the voice of mighty.** Re 4:5. +6:1. 8:5. 40:19. Jb 40:9. Ps 29:3-9. 77:18. **Alleluia.** ver. 1. Ps ▶104:35. **for.** Re *11:15-18. 12:10. 21:22. Ps 47:2, 7. 93:1. 97:1, 12. 99:1. Is 52:7. Mt +*6:13. **the Lord God.** Re +4:8. **omnipotent.** T#218. Re +*1:8. 11:17. Ge 17:1. 18:14. 1 Ch *29:11. 2 Ch 20:6. Jb 9:12. +*42:2. Is +*40:12. 43:13. Je *32:17-19, 27. Am ▶4:13, LXX. Mt *19:26. +*28:19. Mk 10:27. Lk 1:37. Ro +9:18 (T#234). +*15:19. 1 C +1:24 (T#76-5). 2 C +9:8 (T#588). He +11:3 (T#259). 1 P 1:5. **reigneth.** Re *11:15, 17. Ps ▶93:1. 96:10. 97:1. ▶99:1. 146:10. Is 52:7.

7. **be glad.** Dt 32:43. 1 S 2:1. Ps 9:14. 48:11. 95:1-3. 100:1, 2. 107:42. Pr 29:2. Is *25:9. 66:10, 14. Zc *9:9. Jn 3:29. Ph 3:3. **and rejoice.** Mt +*5:12. 1 P 4:13g. **give honor.** Re +11:13. **the marriage.** ver. 9. Re 21:2, 9. Ps 45:10-16. SS 3:11. 5:9-16. Is 4:5. ◑54:5-8. ◑62:4, 5. Je ◑3:14. Ho ◑2:16, 19, 20. Mt 22:2. 25:1-13. Lk 12:36. 14:8. Jn 2:1. 2 C 11:2. Ep 5:22-32. **and his wife.** Re *21:2, 9. SS 7:1-5. Is 52:1. 54:+*1, 5. Ezk 16:8. Ho *2:16, 19, 20. Zp 3:17. 2 C 11:2. Ep 5:25-27. **ready.** Ro 8:19-23. Ep 1:6. Col ◑1:10, 12, 28.

8. **to her.** Re 3:4, 5, 18. Ps *45:13, 14. Is *61:10. Ezk 16:10. Mt 22:12. Ro 3:22. 13:14. Ep *5:26, 27. **fine linen.** ver. 14. Re +18:12. Pr 31:24. Is *52:1. Ezk=44:17. Zc *3:4. **clean and.** ver. 14. Re 4:4. **white. or, bright.** Re 15:6. Mt 17:2. Mk 9:3. Lk 24:4. Ac 1:10. **the fine.** Re 7:13, 14. Ps 132:9. **the righteousness.** Re 7:14. +*15:4. Ps 132:9. Is 61:10. Lk 1:6g. Ro 1:32. 2:26. 3:21-28. 5:16, 18g. 8:4g. He 9:1, 10g. **saints.** Re +8:3.

9. **Write.** Re +1:19. 2:1, 8, 12, 18. 3:1, 7, 14. 10:4. 14:13. Is 8:1. Hab 2:2. **Blessed.** ƒ43, Dt +28:3. See on ver. 7, 8. Re +*1:3. +14:13. 16:15. 20:6. 22:7, 14. SS *1:4. **are called.** Ps 45:14. Jn 3:29. **marriage supper.** Re *3:20. SS 2:4. Is *25:6-9. Mt 9:15. *22:2-4. Lk *14:15-17. 22:15-18, 29, 30. Ac +*3:19. **the Lamb.** Re +5:6. **he saith.** Re 17:1. **These.** ver. 11.

Re 21:5. 22:6. 1 T 1:15. 4:9. 2 T 2:11. T 3:8.

10. I fell. Re 1:17, 18. 22:8, 9. Jsh ●5:14. Mk 5:22. 7:25. Lk 5:8, 10. Ac 10:25, 26. 14:11-15. 1 J 5:21. **to worship.** When used with the Dative case this Greek word means to worship with divine honor (Re 4:10. 5:14. 7:11. 11:16. 14:7. 19:4, 10, 10. 22:9). When followed by the accusative case it means merely to do homage or obeisance to another, as from man to man. This shows that divine worship will be actually offered to the Beast (13:4, 4, 15. 16:2. 19:20); though the Accusative case is also used of the worship of the Beast (Re 9:20. 13:8, 12. 14:9, 11. 20:4). In the other passages where *proskuneo* occurs the case is not shown on account of some other part of speech being used with the verb (E. W. Bullinger, *Apocalypse*, pp. 594, 595). Mt ●+*14:33. He ●1:6. **See.** 2 C 8:7. Ep 5:15, 33. 1 Th 5:15. He 12:25. **do it not.** Ex +*34:14. Ac *10:25, +26. **I am.** Re 5:9n. Ps 103:20, 21. Da 7:10. Lk 1:19. He *1:14. **that have.** Re 12:17. 1 J +5:10. **the testimony.** See on Re 1:+2, 9. 12:11, 17. 22:9. 1 J 5:10. **worship God.** Re 4:10. √5:8, 12n, 13. 14:7. *15:4. Ex 34:14. 2 K 17:36. Ps 45:11. Da 3:14. Mt +*4:10. Jn *4:22-24. Ph 3:3. **for the.** Lk *24:25-27, 44. Jn +*5:39. Ac 3:12-18. +*10:43. 13:27. Ro 3:21, 22. 1 P *1:10-12. 2 P *1:19-21. **of.** √181E, Ge +3:24. **spirit.** Gr. *pneuma*, √121A2, Mt +5:3n. Jsh 5:13-15. Zc 12:10. **of prophecy.** Re +11:3. Is +*9:6. Mi +*5:2.

11. heaven. See on Re 4:1. 11:19. 15:5. Jn +1:51. **opened.** Ezk ●1:1. **a white.** ver. 19, 21. See on Re ●6:2. Zc 1:8. 6:3. **he that.** √105, Ml +4:2. **Faithful.** ver. 9. Re +1:5. 3:7, 14. Jn √14:6. **and in righteousness.** Re 15:3-7. Ps *45:3-7. 50:6. 72:2-4. *96:13. 98:9. 99:4. Pr 16:12. Is *11:3-5. 32:1. 45:21. 63:1-5. Je +*23:5, 6. 33:15. Zc *9:9, 10. He 7:1, 2. **doth he judge.** Ps 50:2, 3. +*94:15. ●96:13. 110:1, 2. Is *16:5. 28:5, 6. *61:2. Je *5:26, 27. Mt *24:30, 31. Ac 24:10n. **make war.** Zc 14:1-4.

12. eyes. See on Re *1:14. *2:18. Da ●10:6. Ml *3:2. **on his.** Re 6:2. +12:3. 13:1. Ps 8:5. *21:3. 132:18. SS 3:11. Is 62:3. Zc 9:16. Mt 21:5. 28:18. He 2:9. **a name.** ver. 16. Re *2:17. *3:12. Ge 32:29. Ex 23:21. Jg 13:18. Is +*9:6. Mt +*11:27. Lk 10:22. Ph *2:8-11. **no man knew.** Re 2:17. 14:3. Pr 30:4.

13. clothed. ver. 16. Re 14:20. Ps 58:10. Is 9:5. 34:3-8. *59:16-18. √63:1-6. **dipped.** Gr. *bapto*, Lk +16:24. Le 14:51. Is 44:3. *63:3. Ezk 36:25. Lk *19:27. Jn 13:26g. Ac +*1:5. He +*6:2. **his name.** Jn 14:7-11. Ro 13:14. Ep 6:17. Mt *1:3. **The Word.** Ps 33:6. *138:2. See on Jn +*1:1, 14. 12:48. He 11:3. 1 P 1:23. 2 P 3:5-7. 1 J 1:1. *5:7.

14. the armies. Re 14:1, 20. 17:14. Dt +*33:2. 2 K 6:17. Ps 68:17. +*149:6-9. Hab +*3:16. Zc *14:5. Mt 16:27. 24:30, 31. *25:○1. 26:53. 2 Th +*1:7. Ju *14, 15. **in heaven.** Re 7:9. **white horses.** See on ver. 11. Zc 1:8. 6:2-7. **clothed.** See on ver. 8. Re 4:4. 7:9. Is ●64:6. Mt ●22:11-14. 28:3. **white and.** ver. 8. Re +3:4. 15:6.

15. out. ver. 21. Re +1:16. 2:12, 16. Nu 24:17, 19. Is *11:4. +*30:33. 2 Th +2:8. **sword.** Ep *6:17. He *4:12. **smite.** Is ●11:4. **and he shall rule.** Re +2:27. 12:5. Ps 2:9. **rod of iron.** Re 2:27. +*12:5n. Ps ●2:9. Da 2:44. **and he treadeth.** Re 14:17-20. Is *63:2-6. **winepress.** Re 14:14-20. Jl ●3:13. **and wrath.** Re +*6:16. 14:+10, 14-16. Is *63:1-6. **Almighty.** Re +1:8. Am ●4:13, LXX.

16. on his vesture. ver. 12, 13. **King.** √147H, Ge

+9:25. Re *11:15. +17:14. Ps +*22:28. 45:6. *47:7, 8. 72:11. 138:4, 5. Pr 8:15, 16. Is +*9:6, 7. 40:9, 10. Da 2:47. 1 C 15:24, 25. Ph *2:9-11. 1 T 6:15. He 1:8. **Lord of.** √147H, Ge +9:25. Dt ●10:17. Ps *136:3. Da ●2:47. Ac +*10:36.

17. an angel. Re +8:13g. 14:6. Is 34:1-8. **saying.** ver. 21. Is *56:9. Je 12:9. Ezk 39:●17-20. **fly in the midst.** Re 8:13. 14:6. **Come and.** 1 S 17:44, 46. Is 18:6. Je 12:9. Ezk 39:17. Mt +*24:28. **the supper.** Is 34:6. Je 46:10. Ezk *39:19.

18. ye. Re 17:16. Dt 28:26. 1 S *17:44, 46. Ps 110:5, 6. Is 34:5-8. Je 7:33. 16:4. 19:7. 34:20. Ezk 29:5. *39:●18-20. Mt +*24:28. Lk *17:37. **captains.** Or, military tribunes. Gr. *chiliarchs*. **S#5506g. Re +6:15. Mk 6:21. Jn 18:12. Ac 21:31, 32, 33, 37. 22:24, 26, 27, 28, 29. 23:10, 15, 17, 18, 19, 22. 24:7, 22. 25:23. **of mighty.** Ezk ●39:20. **of all.** Re 6:15. 13:16. **free.** Re 6:15. 13:16. **small and.** Re +11:18.

19. I saw. Re 13:1-10. 14:9. 16:+14, 16. **the beast.** Re 11:7. 13:1. **kings of.** Ps ●2:2. **gathered.** Re *16:12-16. 17:12-14. 18:9. Ps *2:1-3. 110:5, 6. Is *8:9, 10. *13:4. Ezk *38:8-18. Da 7:21-24. 8:25. 11:40-45. Jl 3:9-14. Zp *3:8. Zc *14:1-3. Ac 4:26. 2 Th 2:9-12. **against him.** See on ver. 11-14.

20. the beast. ver. 19. Re 13:1-8, 18. +16:13. *17:3-8, 12. Is 27:1. Da 2:40-45. 7:7, 12-14, 19-21, 23. **the false.** Re *13:11-17. 16:13, 14. √20:10. *22:15. 1 K 18:40. 2 K 10:18-28. Da *7:8-11, 24-26. 8:24, 26. 2 Th *2:8-11. **that wrought miracles.** Re +13:13. +16:14. **before him.** Re 13:14. **the mark.** Re 20:4. Ga +6:17n. **worshipped.** Re +13:15. **his image.** Re +13:14. **were cast.** Re 20:10, 14. Ps 21:8, 9, 11, 12. Da 7:11. 11:45. **alive.** Re 20:10. Mt +*10:28. **lake of fire.** Is +*66:24. Mt +*25:41. 2 Th +1:8. **burning.** Re 14:10. +*21:8. Ge 19:24. Dt 29:23. Jb 18:15. *31:3. Ps 11:6. Is +*30:33. 34:9. Ezk 38:22. **brimstone.** Re +9:17. Ge ●19:24. Ps +*11:6. Is ●30:33. Ezk ●38:22.

21. the remnant. ver. 11-15. Re 1:16. 1 K ●19:18. Is ●10:20-22. Zc ●13:8, 9. Ro ●9:27. **were slain.** Re *14:14-20. Dt +*32:39. Jg *5:31. Ps 119:119. *139:19. Is *34:1-3. He 10:31, 35-39. **out of his.** ver. 15. Re +1:16. Lk 4:22. **and all.** ver. 17, 18. Re 17:16. **the fowls.** Ezk ●39:17, 20.

REVELATION 20

An angel binds Satan, and imprisons him in the abyss, for a thousand years, 1-3. The reign of Christ with his saints commences during the time Satan is bound, until the resurrection of the rest of the dead at the end of the thousand years, 4-6. Satan, being loosed, again deceives the nations, Gog and Magog, and excites terrible war against the saints, 7, 8. The assailants are destroyed by fire from heaven, and Satan cast into hell, 9, 10. Christ raises the rest of the dead to final judgment, with the condemnation and punishment in the lake of fire of all who are not written in the book of life, 11-15.

1. I saw. ver. 4. Re +10:1. 18:1. **from heaven.** 1 C 15:47. **having.** Re ●+1:18. *3:7. 9:1, 2. Lk 8:31. **bottomless pit.** Re +9:1. **a great.** 2 P 2:4. Ju *6. **chain.** 2 K 25:7.

2. he laid. Ge +*3:15. Is 27:1. 49:24, 25. Mt *8:29. 12:29. Mk 5:7. Lk *8:30, 31. *11:20-22. Jn *12:31. 16:11. Ro *16:20. He *2:14. **the dragon.** See on Re 9:11. *12:+3, 9, 13, 15, 17. 13:2, 4. Jb 1:7. 2:1, 2.

Ps 91:13. 1 P 5:8. 2 P 2:4. Ju 6. **serpent**. Re +12:9. Ge)3:1. **the Devil**. Re 12:9. **and Satan**. Re +2:9. Zc)3:1. **bound him**. ♪63H, Ge +12:15. Supply by ellipsis, (and kept him bound). This binding is yet future; the Apostle Peter authoritatively declares some years after the crucifixion and resurrection of our Lord that Satan goeth about, seeking whom he may devour (1 P 5:8), so there is no sense in which Satan can be said to have been literally bound then as he will be in the future as described in this prophecy. Is √24:22. 2 P 2:4. Ju 6. **a thousand years**. Nathaniel West, a great prophetic scholar in America from the nineteenth century, notes that it is "due to the superficial knowledge of so many in our day...that they have not recognized ...in their study of the Scriptures" that "'the 1000 years' of John are found in the Old Testament prophets," "but still keep harping on the old and tuneless string that 'the Millennium is found in *only one passage* of the Bible, and that in a very obscure book called the Apocalypse!'" (*The Thousand Years in Both Testaments*, p. 78). Ps ◐+*90:4. Is 11:6-9. 12:3. +*24:22n. Ezk 37:25, 26, 28. Ho 3:3-5.

3. **cast**. See on ver. 1. Re 17:8. **and shut him**. Jb 38:1, 8, 11. Is 24:21, √22, 23. 27:1. **and set**. Da 6:17. 12:4. Mt 27:66. **that he**. 1 P 5:8. **should deceive**. ver. 8, 10. Re 12:9. 13:14. 16:14-16. 17:2. Mt 24:24. 2 C *11:3, 13-15. 2 Th *2:9-11. **the thousand**. Ps 90:4. Is 14:7. 2 P 3:8. **and after**. ver. 7-10.

4. **thrones**. Ps √49:14. √122:5. Is 31:8, 9. 32:1-4. Da *7:)9, 10, 18, *22, 27. Je *3:17. Ezk 43:7. Jl *3:12. Zc 6:13. Mt +*19:28. +*25:31. Lk +*1:32, 33. +*22:30. 1 C +*6:2, 3. **they sat**. Re 1:4. +3:21. Mt +*25:31. 1 T 5:21. **judgment was given**. Ps 94:15. +*149:9. Da)7:22. Ac +*24:10n. 1 C +*6:2, 3. 2 T +*4:1. **the souls**. Gr. *psyche*, Re +6:9. √♪171Q1, Ge +12:5. ♪121A8, Ps +16:10. These souls, once disembodied (Re 6:9), but here clearly resurrected, for they live and reign with Christ a thousand years. Thus, this is the figure of speech Metonymy of the Cause, whereby "soul" is put for the person, ♪121A8, Ps +16:10. Compare ♪171Q1A, Ge +12:5. The use of "soul" here provides no basis for asserting a spiritual, as opposed to a literal, reign or resurrection. Ps 49:15. Je 2:34. Ml 4:5. Mt 17:10-13. Mk 9:11. Lk 1:17. 9:7-9. **of them**. Re +*6:9. 7:13, 14. **beheaded**. Mt 14:10. Mk 6:16, 27. Lk 9:9. **the witness**. Re 1:9. 6:9. *11:+3, 7. +*12:11. **for the word**. Re +1:2. **and which**. Gr. *hoitines*. Mt 5:39, 41. 7:24. 10:32, 33. 13:12. 18:4. Mk 8:34. Lk 14:27. Ga 5:4. Ja 2:10g. **not worshipped**. Re 13:12-17. 14:11. 15:2. 17:8. **his image**. Re +13:14, 15. **his mark**. Re 13:15-17. 19:20. Ga +6:17. **they lived**. Re 1:18. 2:8. Mt 10:39. Lk 15:32g. Jn 5:21. 11:25. 14:19. Ro 14:9. 2 T 2:11. **and reigned**. ♪93B, Is +66:11. ver. 6. Re 5:9, 10. 11:11, 15. 22:5. Ps 45:16. +√149:5-9. Is *24:23. Da *2:44. *7:18, 27. Mt 13:43. 20:21, 27. Mk 10:37, 43, 44. Lk 19:17, 19. 22:29. Ro 5:17. +*8:17. 11:15. 2 Th 1:10. 2 T *2:12. *4:8. **with Christ**. Is +*9:7. +*24:23. Je 3:17. *23:5. Ezk 43:7. Mi *4:7. Zc +*14:9. Lk +*1:32, 33. **a thousand years**. T#440. Re +*11:15 (T#90). 15:4. Nu *14:21. Ps 22:27. *37:11. *67:4-7. 72:6, 7, 11. 82:8. 86:9. Is *2:2, 4, 17, 20. √24:22. 25:6-8. 29:18, 19. 32:1, 15, 16. 33:6, 24. 45:22, 23. 49:6, 8, 9. 60:18. 65:17-23. 66:23. Da *7:27. Mi *4:1, 2. Hab *2:14. Ml 1:11. Ac +√3:19-25. Ro +*11:25-27. 2 P +*3:13n.

5. **the rest**. Since all of the righteous are raised

during the first resurrection, these designated as "the rest of the dead" must refer to the unrighteous, who are not raised until after the first thousand years of the reign of Christ have transpired. That the resurrection of the righteous is an event distinct from the resurrection of the wicked has been shown from other Scripture (1 Th 4:16n). ver. 8, 9. Re 19:20, 21. 1 S *2:9. Jb √21:30. 27:13, 19. 40:12, 13. Ps 49:14. 59:13. Pr 20:20. √21:16. Is √24:21, 22. √26:14. 43:17. Da +*12:2. Hab 1:12. Ml 3:18. **the dead**. Is 65:20. **lived**. ver. +4. Re 2:8. Ro 14:9. **not**. Ps *31:17. 37:9, 20, 22, 28, 34. 52:5. 88:10-13. 115:17, 18. Pr 12:7. **until**. Ps +*6:10. 59:14. *109:28. **This is**. or, supplying the ellipsis differently, This completes. Re 11:11, 15. Ezk 37:2-14. Ro 11:15. **the first resurrection**. ♪157, 1 C +15:6. The first resurrection must not be spiritualized into the new birth experienced in this life by every believer, for such is not called a resurrection in Scripture. Many interpreters have been confused by failing to understand the meaning of "first." "First" is here a term of priority, and the first resurrection includes all the several resurrections of the righteous dead which have occurred, many students having enumerated at least five such resurrections which are included in the "first resurrection" (see related note listing these at Re 7:4). Re 7:9-17. *11:18. Ps √49:14. Is +*26:19n. Ezk *37:9-14. Da +*12:2. Ho *6:2. Mt *27:52, 53. Lk √14:14. +*20:35. Jn 5:21, 28, 29. 11:24. Ac *24:15. 26:6-8. 1 C 15:23, 24. Ph 3:10, 11. 1 Th +*4:16n, 17. 2 T 2:11, 12. He *11:35.

6. **Blessed**. ♪43, Dt +28:3. ver. 5. Re +*1:3. +14:13. 16:15. 19:9. 22:7, 14. Da 12:12. Lk 14:15. **and holy**. Is 4:3. **is he**. Re +*3:10. 7:14. 12:11, 17. Ps +*149:9. 1 C 15:51, 52. 1 Th 3:13. He ◐9:28. **the first**. ♪157, 1 C +15:6. ♪96E5, Jn +1:15. Lk 14:14. *20:35, 36. Jn 5:29. Alford remarks, "As regards the text itself, no legitimate treatment of it will extort what is known as the spiritual interpretation now in fashion. If, in a passage where two resurrections are mentioned, where certain persons lived at the first, and the rest of the dead only at the end of a specified period after that first—if, in such a passage, the first resurrection may be understood to mean spiritual rising with Christ, while the second means literal rising from the grave; then there is an end of significance in language, and Scripture is wiped out as a definite testimony to anything. If the first resurrection is spiritual, then so is the second, which I suppose none will be hardy enough to maintain; but if the second is literal, so is the first, which, in common with the whole primitive church and many of the best modern expositors, I do maintain, and receive as an article of faith and hope" (Cited in Peters, *Theocratic Kingdom*, vol. 2, p. 291, from Alford, vol. 4, p. 732). See related notes on spiritual interpretation (ver. 5. Is 60:21n). **the second**. ver. 14. Re 2:11. +*21:8. **priests**. Re +1:6. +*5:10. Is *61:6. 66:21. Ro +*12:1. 1 P *2:5, 9. **and shall reign**. ver. +4. Re 1:6. +*5:10. Da ◐*7:19. Ro +*8:17. 2 T *2:12.

7. **when**. See on ver. 2. **Satan**. ver. 2.

8. **to deceive**. See on ver. 3, 10. Is 65:20. **the nations**. Is 65:20. Zc 14:16-21. **four quarters**. Re +7:1. Ezk)7:2. **Gog**. i.e. *roof; extension; to cover; surmount*, ✳S#1136g. For ✳S#1463h, see 1 Ch +5:4. Ge *10:2. 1 S *2:10. Ezk)38:2. 39:1. **Magog**. i.e. *expansion, extension, covering*, ✳S#3098g. For ✳S#4031h, see Ge +10:2. *Gog* and *Magog* seem to have been anciently

the name of the northern nations of Europe and Asia, as the Scythians have been since, and Tartars are at present; but this seems to refer to a different nation from that mentioned in Ezekiel, which was to come exclusively from "the north quarters," while this comes from the "four quarters of the earth"; and the events in Ezekiel's prophecy relate to the times previous to the Millennium, while this refers to the transactions subsequent to that period. Ezk ch. 38, 39. **to gather**. Re +*16:14. Is √54:15, 17. Hab 2:5. Jn 11:47. **the number**. Jg 7:12. 1 S 13:5. 1 K 4:20. Is 10:22. Je 33:22. He +11:12. **as the sand**. ♪102B, ♪138B, Ge +13:16.

9. **went up**. Is 8:7, 8. Ezk *38:9, 16. **the breadth of**. Is 8:8. Hab ►1:6. **and compassed**. 2 K 6:15. Ps 59:14. Mi 2:13. Hab 1:4. 2:5. Mt 16:16-18. Lk 19:43. 21:20. **the camp**. Ps 48:1-3. 74:2-4. 125:1, 2. He 13:11, 13. **the saints**. Re +8:3. Da ◐2:44. **beloved**. Ps ►78:68. ►87:2. 132:13. Je ►11:15. ►12:7. **city**. Zc 8:22. **and fire**. Re 11:5. +13:13. Ge 19:24. Ex 9:23, 24. Le 10:2, 3. Nu 11:1. 16:35. 2 K ►1:10-15. Jb *34:20. Ps *9:16. *11:6. *18:8. *21:9, 11. 97:3. 106:18. Is +*30:33. 37:36. 51:13. 66:16. Ezk 38:22. 39:6. Lk *9:54. 17:29. 2 Th *1:8.

10. **the devil**. See on ver. 2, 3, 8. Re *12:3, 9. **that deceived**. ver. 3, 8. Re 12:9. 13:14. 19:20. 1 T 2:14. **cast into**. ver. 14, 15. Re +19:20. Nu 16:31-35. **the lake**. ver. 14, 15. Re 19:20. **brimstone**. Re +14:10. Ge ►19:24. Ezk ►38:22. **where**. Re 19:20. Lk ◐+*16:23. **the beast**. Re 13:1, 11, 12. 14:9-11. +16:13. 19:20. **tormented**. Re 14:10. Mt +*25:41, 46. **day and night**. Lk +18:7. **for ever**. Gr. *aion*, Re +1:6. lit. unto the ages of the ages, Ga +1:5. Re +1:6. √22:5.

11. **I saw**. ver. 2. Re 19:11. Ge +*18:25. Ps 9:7, 8. 14:6, 7. 47:8. 89:14. 97:2. Mt 25:31. Ac 17:30, 31. Ro 2:5. **throne**. Re +4:2. Ps *9:7. *96:13. Da 7:9, 13, 14. He +*1:8. **and him**. Jn *5:22, 27-30. **that sat**. Is ►6:1. Da ►7:9. **from**. Re 6:14. 16:20. 21:1. Je 4:23-26. Da 2:35. Mt 24:35. 2 P +*3:7, 10-12. **whose face**. Re *6:16. **the earth**. Re 6:14. 21:1, 4. He +12:27. 2 P *3:10. **fled**. Re *6:16. Ps ►114:3, 7. Is 6:5. Lk 5:8. **and there**. Re 12:8. Jb 9:6. **no place**. Da *►2:35.

12. **I saw**. ver. 11. Da +*12:2. Jn *5:28, 29. 11:25, 26. Ac *24:15. 1 C 15:21-23. 1 Th +*4:15-17. He 6:2. **small**. See on Re 19:5. **the great**. Re +11:18. **stand**. Ro 14:10-12. 1 C *4:5. 2 C *5:10. **the books**. ♪22D5K1B, Da +7:10. Re 17:8. Da ►7:10. **and another**. Re 3:5. 13:8. 17:8. 21:27. Ps ►69:28. Da *12:1. Ml *3:16. Lk 10:20. Ph 4:3. **book**. ♪22D5K1A, Ex +32:32. **book of life**. ver. 15. Re +3:5. 13:8. 21:27. Ph *4:3. **the dead**. Re +11:18. Ro 14:10. 2 C 5:10. **were judged**. Dt 30:15. Je 21:8. Mt 25:14, 15, 19-29. Jn √3:18. √5:24. Ro *8:1. He +*9:27. Ju *6. **according**. ver. 13. Re 2:23. 18:6. 22:12. Ps ►28:4. ►62:12. Pr 24:12, 29. Ec 12:14. Je +*►17:10. 32:19. Mt +*16:27. Ro 2:6. 2 C *5:10.

13. **the sea**. Jn *5:28, 29. **and death**. ver. 14. Re +1:18. 6:8. Ho 13:14. 1 C 15:50-58. **hell**. *or*, the grave. Gr. hades, Mt +11:23. 1 C 15:55mg. **delivered up**. 1 K 17:17-24. Mt 22:23-33. Lk 7:11-17. 8:49-56. Jn 11:25, 26, 43, 44. **and they**. See on ver. 12. **according**. ver. 12. Ps ►28:4.

14. **death**. See on Re 19:20. Jb *28:22. Ho *13:14. 1 C *15:26, 53, 54. **hell**. Gr. hades, Mt +11:23. Mt 5:22, 29, 30. 7:21-23. **were cast**. T#1004‡. ver. +10. Re 21:4. Lk 20:36. 1 C 15:26. **This**. See on ver. 6. Re 2:11. +*21:8.

15. **whosoever**. Ex *32:33. Mt +*7:13. Mk *16:16.

Jn 3:18, 19, 36. √14:6. Ac √4:12. He √2:3. 12:25. 1 J √5:11, 12. **written**. ver. 12. Re +*3:5. 13:8. 17:8. Ps ►69:28. Da ►12:1. Ph 4:3. **book**. ♪22D5K1A, Ex +32:32. **was cast**. ver. 14. See on Re *19:20. Ps *9:17. Pr 5:3-5. 7:27. Mt +*7:13. *13:40-42, 50. √25:41, 46. Mk *9:43-48. **lake**. T#997‡. Re +*21:8. Lk +12:5 (T#995‡). 2 Th *1:8, 9.

REVELATION 21

The new heaven and the new earth, and the inheritance of overcomers, 1-7. Dreadful warning of the second death for unbelievers, 8. The new Jerusalem, descending out of heaven to earth, with a full description thereof, 9-22. The city needs no sun, the glory of God being her light, 23. The redeemed dwell in the presence, light, and glory of God and the Lamb, and the kings of the earth bring their riches unto it, 24-27.

1. **a new heaven**. ver. 5. Dt √11:21. Is √65:►17-19. √►66:22. Ep 1:10. 2 P √3:13n. **for the first**. Most interpreters understand the new heaven and new earth to be postmillennial, as this description succeeds the account of the last judgment. It is necessary, however, in interpreting prophecy to take into account all that the rest of the prophets have written. If this is done, it will be seen that the new heaven and new earth are distinctly revealed to be premillennial in the only other passages which contain the prediction (Is 65:17-19. 66:22. 2 P √3:13n). Every student of prophecy knows that there are numerous instances of prophecies given out of their chronological sequence. The order of events must be determined by a careful comparison of all the related Scripture. Many times in Scripture it will be noticed that a succeeding prophecy is really a further explanation, elaboration, and expansion of what has been mentioned on the same topic previously (this, in fact, is the fundamental feature which must be understood to discover the meaning of prophecy, and makes the study of its details by the comparison of Scripture, and a thorough induction of all related evidence, absolutely essential). Just because a prediction is mentioned in a context subsequent to another prediction, does not necessitate a corresponding chronological relationship between them. This feature, common to prophecy and history (♪107. Hysterologia, Ge +10:5), is to be seen in the opening chapters of Genesis, where the account in chapter two is an expansion of what was more briefly given in chapter one. As to this feature being a negation of the evidential value of predictive prophecy, as Scott maintains at this place in his commentary, one need only consider the fact that the many predictions regarding the first advent of Christ are nowhere stated in chronological order, but their evidential value is not diminished by this circumstance. If the contrary view is insisted upon, holding that the first heaven and earth are passed away in a great conflagration which destroys all natural life, and all spiritual life continues in the new heaven and earth after the Millennium, then such a view contradicts the oath bound covenants and the promises of God that Christ will reign personally on this earth for ever upon the throne of David, for the earthly kingdom of God ruled by Christ is to last for ever, not merely one thousand years, and this earth, not some other, is to be our eternal inheritance. See related notes and references

(Mt +*5:5. Ac +*7:5. Ro +*4:13. 1 C 15:24n, 25n, 50n. Ep +*1:11n. 2 P √3:13n). See on Re 20:11. Ge 1:1. Ps *102:25, 26. **passed away**. Mt 5:18. 24:34, 35. Mk 13:30, 31. Lk 16:17. 21:33. **and there**. Re 13:1. Ps +*65:7. Is 27:1. 57:20. Da 7:3.

2. **I.** Re 1:1, 4, 9. **the holy.** ver. 10. Re 3:12. 22:19. Ps 48:1-3. 87:3. Is 1:21. *)52:1. Je 31:23. Mt +4:5. He *11:10. 12:22. *13:14. **new Jerusalem.** Re +3:12. **coming.** ver. 10. Re 3:12. +10:1. Ga 4:25, 26. He *11:10. **prepared.** Jn +*14:2, 3. **as a bride.** See on Re *19:+7, 8. 22:17. Ps *45:9-14. SS 4:7, 11. 6:4. Is *54:5.)61:10. 62:4. Ho 2:16, 19, 20. Jn *3:29. 2 C 11:2. Ep 5:25-27, 30-32.

3. **a great.** Re 10:4, 8. 12:10. **the tabernacle.** ver. 7. Re 7:15. 13:6. Le 26:11, 12. 1 K 8:27. 2 Ch 6:18. Is 12:6. Je 24:7. 30:22. 31:33. 32:38. Ezk *)37:27. 43:7. Zc 8:8. Jn 1:14. 14:23. Ac +*15:16. 2 C 6:16. **will dwell.** Re +7:15. Ex *25:8, 9. 29:45, 46. 1 K 6:11-13. 9:3-9. 1 Ch 17:5, 6. Ps *68:18. 135:21. Ezk 37:23-28. *48:35. Zc)2:10, 11. *8:3. Jn 1:14. **with them.** Re 22:3. Is)8:8, LXX. w Mt 1:23. Jn 14:3, 23. 1 C 1:9. 1 J 1:3. **they shall.** ver. 7. See on Ge 17:7, 8. Je 31:33. 32:38. Zc 13:9. 2 C 6:18. He 8:10. 11:16. **God himself.** Zc 8:8. **their God.** ver. 7. Re 7:15. Ge +*17:7. 28:13. Ex 6:7. 19:5, 6. *29:45. Le *26:12. Is 25:9. Ezk 11:20. 14:11. +*34:24, 30. *36:28. *37:23, 27. Zc *8:8. 2 C *6:16, 18. He *8:10.

4. **God shall wipe.** Re +7:17. Ps 23:2. Is +*)25:8. Je +*31:)16, 17. **all tears.** Mt 8:12. **no more death.** Re +20:14. 22:3. 2 K=2:21. Is +*25:8. Ho *13:14. Lk +*20:36. 1 C √15:26, 54-58. 2 T *1:10. He +*2:14, 15. **neither sorrow.** T#858. Is 30:19. +*35:10. 51:11. *60:20. 61:3. *65:18, 19. Je *31:13. Mt 6:20. Ju +*24. **nor crying.** Ps 30:11. Is)65:19. **pain.** Is 33:24. **the former.** ver. 1. Re +20:11. Ps 144:4. Is)65:17. Mt 24:35. 1 C 7:31. 2 C √4:17, 18. 6:17. 2 P +*3:10. 1 J √2:17.

5. **that sat.** Re 4:+2, 9. 5:1. 20:11. Ps)47:8. Is)6:1. **Behold.** Is 42:9.)43:19. *64:4. 1 C √2:9. 2 C +5:17. **Write.** See on Re 1:11, +19. **these words.** See on Re 19:9. 22:6. Ps *119:89, 90. Mt *24:35. 1 P 1:23, 25. **true and.** Re 3:14. 19:11. **faithful.** 1 T +1:15.

6. **It is.** Re +10:6. See on 16:17. Ezk +*39:8. Jn 19:30. Ac +*3:21. **I am Alpha.** Re 1:+8, 11, 17. 22:13, 16. **the beginning.** Re +*3:14. **I will.** Re 7:17. 22:1, 17. Ps 87:7. Is 12:3. +*55:)1-3. Jn 4:+)10, 14. 7:37, 38. **the fountain.** Re *7:17. Ps +*16:11. *36:8, 9. Je 2:13. Jl 3:18. **water of life.** Zc)14:8. **freely.** Ho 14:4. Mt 10:8g. Ro 3:24. *8:32. 1 C 2:12. 3:5, 12, 21. 1 J 5:4, 5.

7. **overcometh.** Re 2:+7, 11, 17, 25. **shall inherit.** 1 S 2:8. Pr 3:35. Is 65:9. Mt 19:29. +*25:34. Mk 10:17. Lk +*22:29, 30. Ro +*8:17. 1 C *3:21-23. Ep +*1:11n. 1 P 1:3, 4. 3:9. **all things.** or, these things. Is 64:4. Mt *6:33. Mk +*10:29, 30. Ro √8:32. 1 C √2:9. Ep 1:22. **and I.** See on ver. +3. Zc 8:8. Ro 8:15-17. He 8:10. 1 J 3:1-3. **will be.** 2 S)7:14. Ps)89:26. **his God.** ver. 3. Ge +*17:7. Jb 19:26. Ps 45:6. Is 25:9. 52:7. Jn +*1:1. +*20:28. Ro +*9:5. 2 C 5:19. Col *2:8, 9. 1 T 3:16. T *2:13. He +*1:8. 2 P 1:1. Ju 4. **my son.** Je *3:19. Jn √1:12. Ro +8:14. 2 C +6:18. Ga +*4:7n. 1 J √3:1, 2.

8. **the fearful.** Dt 20:8. Jg *7:3. 1 S *15:24. Is 51:12. 57:11. Mt 8:26. +*10:28. √25:25. Mk 4:40g. Lk *12:4-9. *19:21. Jn 12:42, 43. 2 T ()+*1:7. 1 P 3:14, 15. 1 J 5:4, 5, 10. **unbelieving.** Mt 11:20-24. Lk +*8:13.

12:46g. Jn √3:36. 2 Th *2:12. T *1:15. 1 J *5:10. **abominable.** ver. 27. Re +17:4. 22:15. Le *18:22, 26, 27, 29, 30. Ho 9:10g. Ml +*3:5. 1 C +√6:9, 10. Ga +*5:19-21. Ep *5:5, 6, 12. 1 T 1:9, 10. T *1:16. He 10:26. 12:24. 13:4. 1 J 3:+*8, 15. **murderers.** Re +9:21. 22:15. 1 J +*3:15. **whoremongers.** 1 C +*6:9. **sorcerers.** Re +9:21. Le *19:31. Ac 8:9-21. 16:16, etc. **and idolaters.** Re +22:15. Ezk +*14:3. 1 C 10:20, 21. **and all liars.** ver. 27. Re 2:2. Ge +*27:19. Ps 4:2. 5:6. Pr 19:5, 9. Is 9:15. Jn *8:44. 2 Th 2:9. 1 T 1:10. 4:2. 1 J 2:22. **the lake.** Re +19:20. 20:6, 14, 15. **burneth with.** Ge)19:24. Is)30:33. Ezk)38:22. **fire.** Lk +*16:23, 24. **which is.** See on Re 20:14.

9. **one of.** Re 17:1. **the seven angels.** Re +15:1. **which had.** Re 15:1-7. 16:1-17. **seven vials.** Re +15:7. **seven last.** Le)26:21. **Come.** Re 22:17. **the Lamb's.** See on ver. 2. Re +5:6. +*19:7.

10. **he carried.** Re +1:10. 4:2. 17:3. 1 K 18:12. 2 K 2:16. Ezk 3:14. 8:3. 11:1, 24.)40:1-3. 43:5. Mt ()4:8. Ac 8:39. 2 C 12:2-4. **spirit.** Gr. *pneuma*, Mt +3:16. ʃ121A4, Ezk 37:1. **great and.** Ps 87:1. Ezk 40:2. Mt 4:8. **that.** See on ver. 2. Ezk ch. 40. 48:15-22. **the holy.** ver. +2. Is)52:1. Jl *3:17. **Jerusalem.** Ps 48:1, 2. SS *6:4. Is *2:2. Zc *8:3. Ga *4:26.

11. **the glory.** ver. 22, 23. Re 15:8. 22:5. Ps 84:11. SS *6:10. Is 4:5.)58:8.)60:1, 2, 19, 20. *62:3. Ezk 43:2, 4. *48:35. Ml *3:17. Ro +3:23. **her light.** ver. 19. Ezk 1:26. 28:13, 14, 16. Mt 5:14. Ph 2:15. **like unto.** SS 1:10, 11. *7:1. Ezk 16:10-13. Zc 9:16. **jasper.** ver. 18, 19. Re +4:3. **clear.** ver. 18. Re +4:6. 22:1. Jb 28:17. Ezk 1:22. Ep *5:27.

12. **a wall.** ver. 17-20. Ezk 9:9. Ne 12:27. Ps 51:18. 122:7. Is 56:5. 60:18. Ezk ()38:11. **had twelve.** ver. 21, 25. Is 54:12. 60:18. Ezk)48:31-34. **at the.** 1 Ch 15:23, 24. 26:1-19. Ps *84:10. **gates.** ver. 13, 15, 21, 25. Re 22:14. Mt +26:71. **twelve angels.** Ps 103:20, 21. Mt 18:10. Lk *15:10. 16:22. He *1:14. **and names.** Re 7:4-8. Nu 2:2-32. Ac 26:7. **written thereon.** Ac +17:23g. **which are.** Re 7:4. Ezk *48:31. **twelve tribes.** Ac +26:7. Ex 28:15, 21. Nu 7:84. **children of Israel.** Re 2:14. 7:4. Ac +5:21.

13. **On the east.** Ps *48:12-14. Ezk 48:31-34.

14. **foundations.** ver. 19-21. Ps 87:1. Is 54:11. Ro 15:20. 1 C 3:10. He *11:10. **and in.** Re 18:20. Mt *10:2-4. *16:18. 1 C 3:10, 11. Ga 2:9. Ep +2:20. 3:5. 4:11. Ju 17. **the Lamb.** Re +5:6.

15. **a golden.** See on Re 11:1, 2. Ezk)40:3-5. 41:1, etc. Zc 2:1.

16. **four square.** Ezk 11:47.)43:16. 48:20. **twelve.** Ezk 48:8-19. **the length.** Zc 2:1, 2. **are equal.** 1 K 6:19, 20.

17. **an hundred and.** Re *7:4. 14:1, 3. **of a man.** Re 13:18. Dt 3:11. **the angel.** ver. 9.

18. **the city.** Ge ()+11:4. **was of jasper.** See on ver. 11, 19. Re +4:3. **pure gold.** ver. 21. Re 3:18. Ge 2:11, 12. 1 K 6:21, 22. Jb *23:10. Ps 45:9. 72:15. Is √60:17, 18. La 4:2. Zc 13:9. Ml 3:2, 3. 2 C *4:17, 18. 1 P 1:7. **like.** ver. 11, 21. Re +4:6.

19. **the foundations.** Jb 28:16-19. Pr 3:15. Is)54:11, 12. **precious stones.** Is *54:11, 12. **sapphire.** Ex 24:10. See on Ex 28:17-21. 39:10-14. Jb 28:6, 16. SS 5:14. Is 54:11. La 4:7. Ezk 1:26. 10:1. 28:13.

20. **sardonyx.** *Sardonyx*, as well as onyx, is a kind of chalcedony, generally marked with alternate stripes of white and black. Ge 2:12. Ex 39:13. Ezk 28:13. **sardius.** The *sardius*, or *Sardine* stone, is a precious

stone of a blood-red color. **chrysolite**. The *chrysolite*, or gold stone, now called the Oriental topaz, is of a dusky green, with a cast of yellow, and is very beautiful. Ex 28:20. 39:13. Ezk 28:13. **beryl**. Ex 28:20. 39:13. SS 5:14. Ezk 1:16. 10:9. 28:13. Da 10:6. **topaz**. Ex 28:17. 39:10. Jb 28:19. Ezk 28:13. **chrysoprasus**. The *chrysoprasus*, which Pliny reckons among the beryls, is generally considered a kind of chalcedony, and is an extremely hard stone, of a clear and delicate apple-green color. **jacinth**. The *jacinth, hyacinth,* or *ligure,* is a dark orange-red variety of jargoon. Re +9:17. **amethyst**. Ex 28:19. 39:12.

21. **the twelve gates**. ver. +12. Re 17:4. Mt 13:45, 46. **pearls**. Re 17:4. Mt +13:46. **the street**. ♪96F1, Ge +3:8. Re 22:2. Am +*5:16n. Zc 8:4, 5. **the city**. Re 22:14. Ge ◑+11:4. Ps 84:10. **pure gold**. ver. 18. Re 17:4. 18:16. 22:2. 1 K 6:20. Is 60:17, 18. **as it**. ver. 11, 18. **glass**. Re +4:6.

22. **I saw**. ver. 4, 5. 1 K 8:27. 2 Ch 2:6. *6:18. Is *66:1, 2. Ml *1:11. Jn √4:21, 23, 24. **no temple**. 2 Ch ch. 7. Ml ◑3:1. Ac *7:48-50. *17:24. **the Lord**. See on Re +*1:8. +4:8. 11:17. 15:3. 16:7, 14. 19:15. **Almighty**. Re +1:8. Am ⫤4:13, LXX. **the Lamb**. Re +5:6. **are the temple**. ♪22L7. Anthropomorphism B897. God is figured by things which pertain to the earth: a temple. Mt *27:39, 40, 43. 26:61. Jn *2:19-21. 10:30. Col 1:19. 2:9. He 9:1-12.

23. **the city**. ver. 11. Re 22:5. Ps *87:3. *102:16. Is 4:5. 24:23. ◑30:26. *60:19, 20. **no need of**. ver. 25. Is 60:19. 1 C *13:10. **for the glory**. See on ver. 11. Re *15:8. 18:1. Nu 16:41, 42. 2 Ch 7:1-3. Ps 72:19. 90:16. √102:16. Is 2:10, 19, 21. ⫤60:1, 2. Ezk 1:26-28. *43:5-7. Hab 3:3. Mt +*16:27. Mk 8:38. Jn 12:41. 17:24. Ac 22:11. **did lighten**. Ps *36:9. Col *1:12. **the Lamb**. Re +5:6. Lk 2:32. Jn 1:4, 9, 14, 18. √5:23. **is the light**. Is ⫤60:19. Jn 1:4, 5. 8:12. 10:30. Col 2:9. 1 J *1:5.

24. **the nations**. Re 22:2. Dt 32:43. Ps 22:27. Is 2:2. 52:15. 55:5, 10. ⫤60:11. *66:12, 18. Je 4:2. Zc 2:11. *8:22, 23. 14:16-19. Mt 25:31-46. Ro 15:10-12. 16:26. **saved**. ♪100, Ge +10:9. **walk**. Is 2:5. 60:3. **in the light**. Is *2:2-5. Ac *13:47. **the kings**. Ps *72:8-11. ⫤89:27. Is *60:3-10, 13. 66:11, 12. **do bring**. Is 60:+*5, ⫤13, 16. **their glory**. Re +4:9. Ro +*11:25.

25. **the gates**. Is *33:20. +*⫤60:11. Mi *4:4. Zc *14:11. **for**. ver. +23. Re 22:5. Is 60:20. Zc *14:6, 7. 26. **shall bring**. Mi *4:13. Zc 14:16-21. **the glory**. See on ver. 24. Ro +*11:25.

27. **there**. Le 13:46. Nu 5:3. 12:15. 2 Ch 23:19. Ps 101:8. Is *35:8. *52:1. +*60:21. Jl 3:17. Zc 14:21. Mt *13:41. 1 C +*6:9, 10. Ga *5:19-21. Ep 5:5. He +*12:14. 2 P +*3:13. **no wise enter**. ver. +*8. Re 22:14, 15. 2 Ch 23:19. Is ⫤52:1. Ezk 44:9. Jn *3:3. **that defileth**. Mk +7:2. **worketh abomination**. See on Re 17:4, 5. Le 18:20-30. Dt 12:31. 27:15. Is 44:9-18. 46:6. Je 8:12. 11:15. Ezk 7:20. 22:3. 33:26. **or maketh**. See on ver. +*8. Re 22:14, 15. **they**. See on Re +*3:5. +13:8. ◑17:8. 20:12, 15. Da ⫤12:1. Ph *4:3. **book of life**. Ps *⫤69:28.

REVELATION 22

The river of the water of life, 1. The tree of life, 2-4. The light of the city of God is himself, 5-8. The angel attests these things to be faithful and true, and again forbids John to worship him, 6-9. Christ himself

shows the apostle, that the state of men would soon be unchangeably fixed, by his coming to judgment, 10-12. He declares who would enter heaven, and who would be excluded, 13-15. He urgently invites all who are athirst, yea all who are willing, to accept of his salvation, 16, 17. Nothing may be added to the Word of God, nor taken therefrom, 16-19. The apostle desires the speedy advent of Christ; and concludes with a benediction on his readers, 20, 21.

1. **a pure**. Ps 36:8. *46:4. *65:9. Is 41:18. 48:18. 66:12. Ezk 47:1-9. Jl *3:18. Zc *14:8. Jn *7:38, 39. **river of**. Zc ⫤14:8. **water**. ver. 17. Re 7:17. 21:6. Ps 36:8, 9. Je 2:13. 17:13. Jn *4:+10, 11, 14. **clear**. See on Re 21:11. **as crystal**. Re +4:6. **proceeding**. Re 3:21. 4:5. 5:6, 13. 7:10, 11, 17. Jn 14:16-18. 15:26. 16:7-15. Ac 1:4, 5. 2:33. **and of**. ver. 3. **the Lamb**. Re +5:6.

2. **the midst**. ver. 1. Re 21:21. Ezk 47:1, 12. **the street**. Re *21:21. **the river**. Ex 17:6. Ezk ⫤47:1, 7, 12. Zc 14:8, 9. Jn 4:13, 14. 1 C 10:4. **the tree of life**. Rather, the definite article not being in the original, "a tree of life"; for there were three trees; one in the street, and one on each side of the river. ver. 14, 19. Re +2:7. Ge ⫤2:9, ◑17. 3:⫤22-24. Pr *3:18. SS *2:3. Ac ◑5:30. Ga ◑3:13. 1 P ◑2:24. **fruits**. SS *7:13. **the leaves**. Ge ◑3:7. Mt ◑21:19. **healing**. Re 21:24. Ps 147:3. Is 6:10. 57:18, 19. Je 17:14. Ezk 47:8-11. Ho 14:4. Ml 4:2. Lk 4:18. 1 P 2:24.

3. **no more curse**. Re 6:15-17. 21:4. Ge √3:10-19. ◑4:12. Dt 27:15-26. 2 K=2:21. Jl 2:22. Zc ⫤14:11. Mt 25:41. Ro √8:21, 22. Ga +*3:13. **but the throne**. Re *7:15-17. 21:+3, 22, 23. Ps +*16:11. *17:15. Is 12:6. Ezk 48:35. Mt 25:21. Jn +*14:3. 17:24. **and of**. ver. 1. Re 3:21. +*11:15. Re *1:3. **the Lamb**. Re +5:6. **his**. ver. 6. Re 7:+3, 15. Jn *12:26. **shall be in it**. Ezk *48:35. **shall serve**. Re 7:15. Ex 21:6. Jsh ◑9:22-27. Pr +*22:29. Ro +1:1. 1 C 7:22.

4. **they**. Ezk 33:18-20, 23. Jb 33:26. Ps 4:6. Is 33:17. 35:2. 40:5. Mt +*5:8. Jn 12:26. 17:24. 1 C 13:12. He +*12:14. 1 J *3:2, 3. **shall see**. T#338, 863. Ex ◑33:20, 23. Jb +*19:27. Ps ⫤17:15. 36:9. Mt +*5:8. Jn ◑1:18. *14:23. *17:22-24. 1 C *13:12. 2 C 4:6. 1 Th 4:17. He 1:2, 3. 1 J √3:2. **his name**. See on Re *3:12. ◑13:16. *14:1. Ex ◑28:30. **their foreheads**. Re +7:3. ◑13:16. Ex ◑28:36-38.

5. **no night**. Re 18:23. See on *21:22-+25. Ps *36:9. 84:11. Pr +*4:18, 19. Is 60:19, 20. **candle**. Re ◑18:23. **neither light**. Re +21:23. Is ⫤60:19. **giveth them light**. Re +21:11. Ps 36:9. Hab *3:4. Ml *4:2. Mt *17:1, 2. 1 J *1:5. **shall reign**. Re 3:21. +*11:15. +*20:4. Da 7:⫤18, 27. Mt 25:34, 36. Ro 5:17. 2 T *2:12. 1 P 1:3, 4. **for ever**. Gr. *aion,* Mt +6:13. lit. unto the ages of the ages, Ga +1:5. Re +1:6. √20:10. Ge +*9:12. Da *7:18, 22, 27.

6. **These**. See on Re 19:9. 21:5. **faithful and**. Re 3:14. 19:11. Is 11:5. 1 T +1:15. **Lord God of**. Nu 16:22. **the holy**. or, spirits of the. Gr. *pneuma,* ♪121A1, Lk +1:17n. 1 C 14:32. **prophets**. Re 18:20. Lk 1:70. 16:16. Ac 3:18. Ro 1:2. 1 C *12:7, 8, 28. 1 P 1:11, 12. 2 P +*1:21. 3:2. **sent**. See on Re 1:1. Da 3:28. 6:22. Mt 13:41. Ac 12:11. 2 Th *1:7. **to show**. Re 1:1. **his servants**. ver. +3. **the things**. Da ⫤2:28. **which**. ver. 7. Ge 41:32. 1 C 7:29. 2 P 3:8, 9.

7. **I come**. ver. 10, 12, 20. Re +*1:7. 2:16. See on 3:11. Is ⫤40:10. Mt +*24:3. Jn +21:22. Ac +*1:11. He 10:37. **quickly**. Re *3:11. Mt *24:27. 2 P 3:8.

blessed. ✒43, Dt +28:3. ver. 9. See on Re +*1:3. 14:13. **keepeth.** Mt 23:3. Jn 2:5, 10. +*5:39. Ac +*17:11. 1 Th 5:20. 2 T +√3:16, 17. **this book.** ver. 20. Ac +1:20.

8. **John.** Re 1:1, 4, 9. **saw.** Lk 1:1-4. 2 P 1:16. 1 J 1:1-3. **these things.** Jn 21:24. **I fell.** See on Re 19:10, 19. **worship.** Mt 4:8-10.

9. **do it not.** Re +*19:10. Ex +*34:14. Dt 4:19. Mt ◑+*14:33. 28:5, 17. Lk ◑*24:52. Jn 4:23, 24. +*20:28. Ac *10:25, +26. *14:11-18. Col 2:18, 19. 1 J 5:21. **worship God.** Re 4:10. 9:20. 14:7. 15:4. Ex 34:14. 2 K 17:36. Ps 45:11. Mt *4:9, +10. Lk 4:7. Jn *4:22, 23.

10. **he saith.** ver. 12, 13, 16, 20. **Seal not.** Re 5:1, 5. *10:2, ◑4. Dt +*29:29. Is +*8:16. Da 8:26. ◑12:◗4, 8, 9. Mt 10:27. **for the time.** See on Re +1:3. Is 13:6. Ezk 12:23. Da ◗12:4. Ro 13:12. 2 Th 2:3. 1 P 4:7.

11. **that is unjust.** Re 16:8-11, 21. Ps 81:12. Pr *1:24-33. 14:32. Ec √11:3. Ezk *3:27. Da 12:10. Mt +*15:14. *21:19. *25:10-13, 46. Jn 8:21. 2 T 3:13. Ja 1:21. **unjust still.** ✒76, Ge +13:6. Ec 1:15. 11:3. Is *32:6. Da +*12:10. Mt 23:31. Jn 9:4. Ac *24:25. 2 C ◑+*6:2. He +*12:17. **is filthy.** Ps *69:24-28. Ezk *24:13. 47:11. **and he that is righteous.** ver. 3. Re 7:13-15. Jb 17:9. Pr +*4:18. *11:30, 31. Is 32:17. Mt +*5:6. Ep *5:27. Col 1:22. Ju +*24. **is holy.** Ro *12:1. 1 C *3:17.

12. **I come.** See on ver. +7. Is ◗40:10. ◗48:12. Zp 1:14. Ja +*5:8. **my reward.** Re +*11:18. ◑19:20. Is 3:10, 11. 40:10. 62:11. Mt 7:21-23. 25:31-46. Lk *14:14. Ro √14:10, 12. 1 C 3:8, 12-15. 9:17, 18. 2 C 5:10. Col *3:24. **to give.** See on Re 20:12. Mt +*16:27. Ro *2:6-11. *14:12. **according.** Re 2:23. Jb *34:11. Ps ◗28:4. ◗62:12. Je ◗17:10. Mt 12:36. *16:27. Ro 2:2, 6, 16. Ep 6:8. Ga 6:7.

13. **I am.** Ne +*9:6. **Alpha.** See on Re +*1:8, 11. 21:6. Is 41:4. 44:6. 48:12. **beginning and.** God the Son is eternal. Re +*1:8, 17. +*3:14. 21:6. Is +*9:6. Mi +*5:2 (T#76-3). Mt +*28:19n. Jn √1:1-3. *8:58. 17:5. Col 1:17. He *12:2. +*13:8. **the first.** Re +1:17. Is 41:4. 43:10. *◗44:6. *48:12.

14. **Blessed.** ✒43, Dt +28:3. ver. 7. Re +14:13. Ex 12:50, 51. Ps *1:1-3. 106:3-5. 112:1. 119:1-6. Is 56:1, 2. Da 12:12. Mt √7:21-27. Lk 12:37, 38. Jn 14:15, 21-23. 15:10-14. 1 C 7:19. Ga 5:6. 1 J 3:3, 23, 24. 5:3. **that do.** Some authorities read, that wash their robes. Re +7:14. Ge ◗49:11. **his commandments.** Ezr +*7:10. Lk √6:46. Jn *3:36. +*13:17. *14:21. Ro *16:26. 1 J √2:3. *3:23. **may have right.** or, authority over. Re 6:8. Jn *1:12. 1 C *8:9. 9:5g. **to the.** See on ver. 2, 19. Re +2:7. **tree of life.** Ge ◗2:9. ◗3:22, 24. **may enter.** See on Re +21:27. Ps √15:1-5. +*16:11. 24:3-5. *118:19, 20. Jn 10:7, 9. √14:6. **through the gates.** Re 21:+12, 24-26. **the city.** Re 3:12. 21:21. He 11:16. +*12:22.

15. **without.** Re 9:20, 21. +*21:8, 27. Is +*66:24. Mt +*8:12. Jn *3:36. 1 C +*6:9, 10. Ga *5:19-21. Ep 5:3-6. Ph *3:19. Col 3:6. T 3:3. **dogs.** See on Ph +3:2. **sorcerers.** Re 9:21. 18:23. +21:8. Is 47:9, 12. 57:3. Ml +*3:5. Ac 8:11. 13:6-11. **whoremongers.** See

on Re 17:1-6. **whosoever.** Re +*21:8, 27. 1 K 22:8, 21-23. Is 9:15, 16. Je 5:31. Jn *3:18-21. 8:46. 2 Th 2:10-12.

16. **I Jesus.** See on ver. 6. Re 1:1, 4. **to testify.** ver. 20. See on ver. 1, 11. Re 2:7, 11, 17, 29. 3:6, 13, 22. **the churches.** 1 C +7:17. **I am.** See on Re 5:5. Is 11:1. Zc 6:12. Mt 22:42, 45. Ro 1:3, 4. 9:5. **the root.** ✒22H1D, Is +11:10. Re +5:5. Is ◗11:10. **offspring.** Mt +1:1. **of David.** Is +*9:7. +√55:3. Mt *22:41-44. Ac +*13:23. Ro *1:3, 4. **morning star.** Re 2:28. Nu +*24:17. 2 S +*23:4. Is 60:3. Ml *4:2. Mt 2:2, 7-10. Lk *1:78, 79. 2 P +*1:19.

17. **the Spirit.** Gr. *pneuma*, Mt +3:16. See on ver. 16. Is +*55:1-3. Jn +7:39. *16:7-15. Ac 8:29, 39. 11:12. 16:7. Ro 8:4, 5, 9, 14, 16, 19, 26, 27. **the bride.** See on Re 21:+2, 9. **Come.** ✒76, Ge +13:6. T#370. Re 1:3. *3:20. 2 K *7:9. Is 2:5. 45:22. 52:7. *55:1-3. Mt *11:28-30. 22:2-4. Lk 14:17. Jn 1:41, 45. 4:29. *6:37. 7:37. **let him that heareth.** Ps 34:8. Is 2:3, 5. 48:16-18. Je 50:5. Mi 4:2. Zc 8:21-23. Jn 1:39-46. 4:29. 1 Th 1:5-8. **let him that is athirst.** See on Re 21:6. Ps 42:1, 2. Is ◗55:1. Mt +*5:6. Jn +4:10. ◗7:37. **And whosoever will.** ✒93B, Is +66:11. By Hendiadys of the Verb, "willing thirsty ones." Not two classes of persons, but one. Not thirsty ones who do not will; or willing ones who do not thirst; but willing thirsty ones, let them come (B672). **let him take.** Is 12:3. Jn 4:10, 14. **water of life.** ver. +1. Zc ◗14:8. **freely.** Mt +10:8g. Ro 3:24. 1 C 2:12.

18. **testify.** See on ver. 16. Re *3:14. Ep 4:17. 1 Th 4:6. **heareth.** See on Re 1:3. **this book.** ver. 7, 9. Ac +1:20. **If.** ✒184C, Mt +4:9. **add unto these.** Dt ◗4:2. ◗12:32. Jsh 1:7. 1 S 12:19. 1 K 12:11. Pr 19:27. +*30:6. Is +*8:20. Je √23:28, 29. Mt 7:15-20. √15:6-9, 13. 24:11, 24. 28:20. 1 C 3:12, 13. **God shall add.** T#1108. Re 14:10, 11. 15:1. ch. 16. 19:20. 20:10, 15. Le 26:18, 24, 25, 28, 37. Pr ◑10:22. **the plagues.** Dt ◗29:20.

19. **And if.** ✒184C, Mt +4:9. **take away from.** See on Re 2:18. Je *26:2. Mt 19:9n. Lk 11:52. Jn 3:7n. Ga +*1:8, 9. 1 Th 4:2n. **God.** See on Re +*3:5. +13:8. Ex 32:33. Ps √69:28. **shall take.** Lk *8:18. **his part.** Dt ◑18:1. Jsh 22:25, 27. Ep +*1:11. **out of the book of life.** Re 13:8. Ps ◗69:28. *or*, from the tree of life. See on ver. 2, 14. Re +2:7. Ge ◗2:9. ◗3:22. **and out.** See on Re 21:2, 22-27. **holy city.** Re 21:2, 10. Is ◗52:1. Mt +4:5. He *12:22. **and from.** ver. 12. Re 1:3. 2:7, 11, 17, 26. 3:4, 5, 12, 21. 7:9-17. 14:13. 20:15.

20. **which testifieth.** See on ver. 18. Re 3:14. Jn *21:24. **Surely.** See on ver. +7, 10, 12. **I come.** Is *25:9. ◗40:10. Ph *3:20. 1 T 1:1. 2 T *4:8. T +*2:13. 1 P 1:3. **Amen.** Mt +6:13. **Even so.** ✒74, Jg +5:31. **come.** T#1572. Re 1:18. Ps 40:17. 70:5. *144:5. SS *8:14. Is *25:9. 64:1. Jn 21:25. 2 T *4:8. He +*9:28. 2 P *3:12-14.

21. **The grace.** Re 1:4. Ps *45:2. Zc 4:7. Jn *1:16, 17. See on Ro 1:7. *5:20. 16:+20, 24. 2 C √12:9. *13:14. Ep *2:7. *6:23, 24. 2 Th 3:18. **Lord Jesus Christ.** Mk +16:19. **Amen.** 1 C 14:16.

BIBLIOGRAPHY

Adams, Jay E. *The Meaning and Mode of Baptism.* Phillipsburg, New Jersey: Presbyterian and Reformed Publishing Company, 1975.

Alexander, Joseph Addison. *The Psalms Translated and Explained.* Edinburgh: Andrew Elliot and James Thin, 1864.

———. *Commentary on the Prophecies of Isaiah.* Zondervan reprint, 1962.

———. *Commentary on the Gospel of Mark.* New York: Scribner, 1864.

———. *Commentary on the Acts of the Apostles.* Scribner, Armstrong & Company, 1875.

Alford, Henry. *The Book of Genesis, and Part of the Book of Exodus: A Revised Version, with Marginal References, and an Explanatory Commentary.* Originally published by Strahan & Company, 1872.

———. *The Greek Testament.* Chicago: Moody Press, 1968.

Allis, Oswald T. *Bible Numerics.* Philadelphia: Presbyterian and Reformed Publishing Company, 1961.

———. *The Old Testament: Its Claims and Its Critics.* Nutley, New Jersey: The Presbyterian and Reformed Publishing Company, 1972.

———. *Prophecy and the Church.* Philadelphia: Presbyterian and Reformed Publishing Company, 1969.

Anderson, Robert. *The Coming Prince.* London: Hodder and Stoughton, 1909.

———. *The Lord from Heaven: A Study of the Deity of the Lord Jesus Christ.* Wheaton, Illinois: Van Kampen Press, Inc., n.d.

Andrews, Samuel J. *The Life of Our Lord Upon the Earth.* Zondervan reprint of the 1891 edition.

Arndt, W. F. and F. W. Gingrich. *A Greek English Lexicon of the New Testament.* Chicago: University of Chicago Press, 1957.

Baird, Samuel J. *The Great Baptizer: A Bible History of Baptism.* Richmond, Virginia: Presbyterian Committee of Publication, 1892.

Baker, Charles F. *A Dispensational Theology.* Grand Rapids: Grace Bible College Publications, 1971.

Barndollar, W. W. *Jesus' Title to the Throne of David: A Study in Biblical Eschatology.* Findlay, Ohio: The Dunham Publishing Company, 1963.

Bengel, John Albert. *New Testament Word Studies.* Grand Rapids: Kregel Publications, 1971. Reprint of the 1864 edition.

Berkhof, Louis. *Systematic Theology.* Grand Rapids: Wm. B. Eerdmans Publishing Company, 1941.

Blackwelder, Boyce W. *Light from the Greek New Testament.* Anderson, Indiana: The Warner Press, 1958.

Blackwelder, Boyce W. *Toward Understanding Thessalonians.* Anderson, Indiana: The Warner Press, 1965.

Blass, F. and A. Debrunner. *A Greek Grammar of the New Testament and Other Early Christian Literature.* Chicago: The University of Chicago Press, 1961.

Bridges, Charles. *Psalm 119: An Exposition.* Banner of Truth Trust, 1974 reprint of the 1827 edition.

———. *A Commentary on Proverbs.* Banner of Truth Trust, 1968 reprint of the 1846 edition.

———. *A Modern Study in the Book of Proverbs: Charles Bridges' Classic Revised for Today's Reader* by George F. Santa. Milford, Michigan: Mott Media, 1978.

———. *The Christian Ministry.* Banner of Truth Trust, 1967 reprint of the 1830 edition.

Brown, John. *An Exposition of Our Lord's Intercessory Prayer.* Minneapolis: Klock and Klock Christian Publishers, 1978 reprint of the 1866 edition.

Bullinger, E. W. *Apocalypse or The Day of the Lord.* London: Eyre and Spottiswoode, 1935.

———. *The Chief Musician: Studies in the Psalms and Their Titles.* London: Eyre and Spottiswoode, 1908.

———. *The Church Epistles.* London: Eyre and Spottiswoode, 1905.

———. *Figures of Speech used in the Bible Explained and Illustrated.* London: Eyre and Spottiswoode, 1898.

———. *The Giver and His Gifts: The Holy Spirit and His Work.* London: The Lamp Press, 1953.

———. *How to Enjoy the Bible.* London: The Lamp Press, 1955.

———. *Number in Scripture.* London, 1894.

Burgon, John William. *The Causes of the Corruption of the Traditional Text of the Holy Gospels.* London: George Bell and Sons, 1896.

———. *"Inspiration and Interpretation." Seven Sermons by the Rev. John W. Burgon.* London: Marshall Brothers, 1905.

———. *The Last Twelve Verses of the Gospel According to Saint Mark.* 1871.

———. *The Traditional Text of the Holy Gospels Vindicated and Established.* London: George Bell and Sons, 1896.

———. *The Woman Taken in Adultery and God Was Manifested in the Flesh.* n.p., n.d.

Burnap, George W. *Expository Lectures on the Principal Passages of the Scriptures which Relate to the Doctrine of the Trinity.* Boston: James Munroe and Company, 1845.

Burton, Ernest De Witt. *Syntax of the Moods and*

Tenses in New Testament Greek. Edinburgh: T. & T. Clark, 1894.

Buswell, J. Oliver. *A Systematic Theology of the Christian Religion*. Grand Rapids: Zondervan Publishing House, 1962, 1963. Two volumes.

Byers, D. B. *Physical Death Not the Penalty: A Complete Refutation of the Doctrine of Annihilation*. Freeport, Illinois: Journal Steam Printing House, 1869.

Carr, Arthur. *Horae Biblicae: Short Studies in the Old and New Testaments*. London: Hodder and Stoughton, 1903.

Carson, Alexander. *Baptism: Its Mode and Subjects*. Philadelphia: American Baptist Publication Society, 1853.

Carson, D. A. *Exegetical Fallacies*. Grand Rapids: Baker Book House, 1984.

_____. *The King James Version Debate: A Plea for Realism*. Grand Rapids: Baker Book House, 1979.

Chafer, Lewis Sperry. *Systematic Theology*. Dallas: Dallas Seminary Press, 1947.

Chaney, Johnston M. *The Life of Christ in Stereo*. Portland, Oregon: Western Baptist Seminary Press, 1969.

Chilton, David. *The Days of Vengeance: An Exposition of the Book of Revelation*. Fort Worth, Texas: Dominion Press, 1987.

_____. *Paradise Restored: A Biblical Theology of Dominion*. Fort Worth, Texas: Dominion Press, 1985.

Clark, Samuel. *Precious Bible Promises*. New York: Grosset & Dunlap, n.d. reprint of original edition of 1750.

Colwell, Ernest Cadman. *The Study of the Bible*. Chicago: University of Chicago Press, 1964.

The Commentary Wholly Biblical: An Exposition in the Very Words of Scripture. London: Samuel Bagster and Sons, n.d.

Conant, J. E. *No Salvation Without Substitution*. Grand Rapids: Wm. B. Eerdmans Publishing Company, 1941.

Conant, Thomas Jefferson. *The Meaning and Use of Baptizein*. New York: American Bible Union, 1864.

Countess, Robert H. *The Jehovah's Witnesses' New Testament: A Critical Analysis of the New World Translation of the Christian Greek Scriptures*. Phillipsburg, New Jersey: Presbyterian and Reformed Publishing Company, 1982.

Cremer, Hermann. *Biblico-theological Lexicon of New Testament Greek*. Edinburgh: T. & T. Clark, 1895.

Custer, Stuart. *Does Inspiration Demand Inerrancy?* Nutley, New Jersey: The Craig Press, 1968.

Dabney, Robert L. *Lectures in Systematic Theology*. Grand Rapids: Zondervan Publishing House. 1972 reprint of the 1878 edition.

Daille, John. *An Exposition of Philippians*. MacDill Air Force Base, Florida: Tyndale Bible Society, n.d.

Dake, J. Finis. *Dake's Annotated Reference Bible*. Atlanta, Georgia: Dake Bible Sales, 1963.

Dale, James Wilkinson. *Classic Baptism: Baptizo, An Inquiry into the Meaning of the Word as Determined by the Usage of Classical Greek Writers*. Philadelphia: Presbyterian Board of Publication, 1867.

_____. *Classic Baptism*. Phillipsburg, New Jersey: Presbyterian and Reformed Publishing Company, 1989.

_____. *Judaic Baptism*. Philadelphia: Presbyterian Board of Publication, 1869.

_____. *Johannic Baptism*. Philadelphia: Presbyterian Board of Publication and Sabbath-School Work, 1898.

_____. *Christic and Patristic Baptism*. Philadelphia: Presbyterian Board of Publication, 1874.

Darby, J. N. *The Collected Writings of J. N. Darby*. Edited by William Kelly. Oak Park, Illinois: Bible Truth Publishers, 1972 reprint.

Davis, John D. *A Dictionary of the Bible*. Grand Rapids: Baker Book House, 1968 reprint.

Davis, John J. *Biblical Numerology: A Basic Study of the Use of Numbers in the Bible*. Grand Rapids: Baker Book House, 1968.

_____. *Contemporary Counterfeits*. Grand Rapids: Baker Book House, 1973.

DeHoff, George W. *Alleged Bible Contradictions Explained*. Murfreesboro, Tennessee: DeHoff Publications, 1950.

Dexter, Henry V. *The Shining Way; or, Unerring Guide, Being Scripture Precepts, Topically Arranged*. Augusta, Maine: E. C. Allen, n.d.

Ditzler, J. *Baptism*. 1880.

Douglas, Claude C. *Overstatement in the New Testament*. New York: Henry Holt and Company, 1931.

Douty, Norman F. *The Death of Christ*. Swengel, Pennsylvania: Reiner Publications, 1972.

_____. *Has Christ's Return Two Stages?* New York: Pageant Press, 1956.

_____. *Union with Christ*. Swengel, Pennsylvania: Reiner Publications, 1973.

Drummond, William Hamilton. *The Doctrine of the Trinity, Founded Neither on Scripture, Nor on Reason and Common Sense, but on Tradition and the Infallible Church*. London: R. Hunter, 1831.

Ellicott, Charles John. *Commentary on the Epistle to the Thessalonians*. Grand Rapids: Zondervan reprint of the 1861 edition.

Eerdman, W. J. *The Unseen World: A Concordance with Notes*. Chicago: F. H. Revell, n.d.

Fairfield, Edmund B. *Letters on Baptism*. Boston and Chicago: Congregational Sunday-School and Publishing Society, 1893.

Fereday, W. W. *Josiah and Revival*. Kilmarnock: John Ritchie Limited, n.d.

Finegan, Jack. *Handbook of Biblical Chronology*. Princeton, New Jersey: Princeton University Press, 1964.

Ford, David B. *Studies on the Baptismal Question: Including a Review of Dr. Dale's "Inquiry into the Usage of Baptizo."* New York: Ward & Drummond, 1879.

Freeman, James M. *Manners and Customs of the Bible*. New York: Nelson and Philips.

Gaebelein, Frank E. *The Christian Use of the Bible*. Chicago: Moody Press, 1946.

Gallaher, Thomas. *Baptism: A Short Method with the Dipping Anti-pedobaptists, in Three parts: Part I, What is Baptism? Part II, Who Are the Proper Subjects of Baptism? Part III, Perversions of Fact and History*. St. Louis: Presbyterian Publishing Company Print, 1878.

Garner, Albert. *Defense of the Faith: Or, Christian Doctrine*. Texarkana, Arkansas-Texas: Baptist Sunday School Committee of the American Baptist Association, 1962.

Gebhardt, Herman. *The Doctrine of the Apocalypse, and Its Relation to the Doctrine of the Gospel and Epistles of John*. Edinburgh: T. & T. Clark, 1878.

Gibson, Edgar C. S. *The Old Testament in the New*. London: Wells Gardner, Darton & Co., Ltd., 1907.

Gifford, E. H. *The Epistle of St. Paul to the Romans, with Notes and Introduction*. London: John Murray, 1886.

Girdlestone, R. B. *The Grammar of Prophecy: A Systematic Guide to Biblical Prophecy*. Kregel Publications, 1955 reprint.

_____. *Synonyms of the Old Testament: Their Bearing on Christian Doctrine*. London: J. Nisbet & Co., 1897.

_____. *Synonyms of the Old Testament*. Numerically Coded to *Strong's Exhaustive Concordance*. Grand Rapids: Baker Book House, 1983.

Grant, F. W. *Facts and Theories as to a Future State: The Scripture Doctrine Considered with Reference to Current Denials of Eternal Punishment*. Charlotte, North Carolina: Books for Christians, 1972.

Grant, F. W. *The Numerical Bible*. New York: Loizeaux Brothers, Bible Truth Depot, 1890.

_____. *Papers on Eternal Punishment*. New York: Loizeaux Brothers, n.d.

Grant, P. W. *Christian Baptism the Baptism of Christians: Or, Primitive, Apostolic Baptism, the Immersion of Believers in Jesus Christ, into the Name of the Father, and of the Son, and of the Holy Ghost*. Edinburgh: Lorimer & Gillies, Printers, 1900.

Green, Samuel G. *Handbook to the Grammar of the Greek Testament*. London: The Religious Tract Society, 1886.

Greenfield, W. (Ed.) *The Comprehensive Bible*. London, 1826.

Greenleaf, Simon. *The Testimony of the Evangelists Examined by the Rules of Evidence Administered in Courts of Justice*. New York: James Cockroft & Company, 1874.

Gundry, Robert H. *The Church and the Tribulation*. Grand Rapids: Zondervan Publishing House, 1973.

Guy, A. M. *Concordance to Prophecy*. London: The Sovereign Grace Advent Testimony, 1942.

Habershon, Ada R. *Outline Studies of the Tabernacle*. Grand Rapids: Kregel Publications, 1974 reprint.

_____. *The Study of the Miracles*. Grand Rapids: Kregel Publications, 1968 reprint.

_____. *The Study of the Parables*. Grand Rapids: Kregel Publications, 1967 reprint.

_____. *The Study of the Types: A New Enlarged Edition. Containing Priests and Levites: A Type of the Church*. Grand Rapids: Kregel Publications, 1974 reprint.

Haley, John W. *An Examination of the Alleged Discrepancies of the Bible*. Chicago: W. G. Holmes, 1875.

Hamilton, Frank. *Evidences that Jesus Is the Messiah*. Ventnor, New Jersey, n.d.

Hamilton, William. *A Compend of Baptism*. New York: Funk & Wagnalls, 1883.

Harris, W. S. *A Complete Index to the Thought and Teachings of Christ Alphabetically and Topically Arranged*. Nashville: Cokesbury Press, 1939.

Harrisville, Roy A. *The Concept of Newness in the New Testament*. Minneapolis: Augsburg Publishing House, 1960.

Hayes, D.A. *Paul and His Epistles*. Grand Rapids: Baker Book House, 1969 reprint of the 1915 edition.

Henry, Matthew. *Matthew Henry's Commentary on the Whole Bible*. Old Tappan, New Jersey: Fleming H. Revell Company, n.d.

_____. *The Complete Works of the Rev. Matthew Henry*. Grand Rapids: Baker Book House, 1979 reprint of the 1855 edition.

_____. *Bible Themes from Matthew Henry*. Passages Selected and Edited by Selwyn Gummer, with Sermon Outlines on Each Subject by Frank Colquhoun. Wheaton, Illinois: Van Kampen Press, 1953.

_____. *A Topical Index to Matthew Henry's A Commentary on the Whole Bible*. William T. Summers, Compiler. Old Tappan, New Jersey: Fleming H. Revell Company, 1982.

Hibbard, F. G. *Christian Baptism: in Two Parts. Part First: Infant Baptism; Part Second: Mode, Obligation, Import, and Relative Order*. New York: Nelson and Phillips, 1841, 1843.

Hislop, Alexander. *The Two Babylons*. Neptune, New Jersey: Loizeaux Brothers, 1959 reprint of 1858 edition.

Hobart, William Kirk. *The Medical Language of St. Luke*. Grand Rapids: Baker Book House, 1954 reprint of the 1882 edition.

Hodge, Charles. *Commentary on the Epistle to the Romans*. Grand Rapids: Wm. B. Eerdmans Publishing Company, 1964 reprint of the 1886 edition.

_____. *An Exposition of the First Epistle to the Corinthians*. Grand Rapids: Wm. B. Eerdmans Publishing Company, 1965 reprint.

_____. *An Exposition of the Second Epistle to the Corinthians*. Grand Rapids: Wm. B. Eerdmans, n.d.

_____. *A Commentary on the Epistle to the Ephesians*. Grand Rapids: Wm. B. Eerdmans Publishing Company, 1969 reprint.

_____. *Systematic Theology*. Grand Rapids: Wm. B. Eerdmans Publishing Company, n.d.

Hogg, C. F., W. E. Vine, W. R. Lewis. *The Ministry of Women: A Study in the Scriptures*. A

Careful Consideration of the Many Passages of Scripture Bearing on the Subject. Kansas City, Kansas: Walterick Publishers, n.d.

Hogg, C. F. and W. E. Vine. *The Epistles to the Thessalonians with Notes Exegetical and Expository*. Fincastle, Virginia: Scripture Truth Book Company, 1959 reprint of 1929 edition.

Hoekema, Anthony A. *The Four Major Cults*. Grand Rapids: William B. Eerdmans Publishing Co., 1963.

Holliday, F. C. *A Bible Handbook, Theologically Arranged: Designed to Facilitate the Finding of Proof-texts on the Leading Doctrines of the Bible*. New York: Hunt and Eaton, 1869.

Horne, Thomas Hartwell. *An Introduction to the Critical Study and Knowledge of the Holy Scriptures*. London, 1834.

Horton, Robert F. *The Commandments of Jesus*. London: Isbister and Company Limited, 1898.

Hoskier, H. C. *Concerning the Genesis of the Versions of the New Testament*. London: Bernard Quaritch, 1910, 1911.

_____. *Concerning the Text of the Apocalypse: Collations of all Existing Available Greek Documents with the Standard Text of Stephen's Third Edition, together with Versions, Commentaries and Fathers. A Complete Conspectus of All Authorities*. London: Bernard Quaritch, Ltd., 1929.

Hughey, G. W. *Baptismal Remission; or, The Design of Christian Baptism*. New York: Hunt & Eaton, 1891.

Hughey, G. W. *The Scriptural Mode of Christian Baptism*. Kansas City: Hudson Press, 1907.

Jackson, J. B. *A Dictionary of the Proper Names of the Old and New Testament Scriptures*. New York: Loizeaux Brothers, 1946.

Jenkins, Ferrell. *The Old Testament in the Book of Revelation*. Grand Rapids: Baker Book House, 1976.

Kay, William. *The Psalms Translated from the Hebrew with Notes Chiefly Exegetical*. London: Rivingtons, 1871.

Keach, Benjamin. *Tropologia; A Key to Open Scripture Metaphors*. London: William Hill Collingbridge, 1856.

Keeler, R. F. *Christian Baptism; The Mode, Design, and Subjects*. Cleveland: The Imperial Press, 1901.

Kittel, Gerhard. *Theological Dictionary of the New Testament*. Grand Rapids: Wm. B. Eerdmans Publishing Co., 1964.

Kuyper, Abraham. *The Work of the Holy Spirit*. New York: Funk and Wagnalls, 1900.

Laidlaw, John. *The Biblical Doctrine of Man*. Edinburgh: T. & T. Clark, 1895.

Lansdell, Henry. *The Sacred Tenth; Or, Studies in Tithe-giving Ancient and Modern*. Grand Rapids: Baker Book House, 1955 reprint of the 1905 edition.

_____. *The Tithe in Scripture*. London: Society for the Promotion of Christian Knowledge, 1908.

Lardner, Nathaniel. *The Works of Nathaniel Lardner*. London: Holdsworth and Ball, 1831.

Leeser, Isaac. *Twenty-four Books of the Holy Scriptures Carefully Translated after the Best Jewish Authorities by Isaac Leeser*. New York: Hebrew Publishing Company, n.d.

LeMahieu, D. L. *The Mind of William Paley: A Philosopher and His Age*. Lincoln, Nebraska: University of Nebraska Press, 1976.

Liddon, H. P. *The Divinity of Our Lord and Saviour Jesus Christ*. London: Rivingtons, 1871.

Lightfoot, J. B. *Saint Paul's Epistles to the Colossians and to Philemon*. Grand Rapids: Zondervan, 1965 reprint of the 1879 edition.

Linton, Irwin H. *A Lawyer and the Bible. With an introduction by Charles Gallaudet Trumbull*. New York: Harper and Brothers, 1929.

_____. *A Legal Man and the Bible*. London: Marshall, Morgan & Scott Ltd., n.d.

_____. *A Lawyer Examines the Bible: An Introduction to Christian Evidences*. Boston: W.A. Wilde Company, 1943.

Locke, John. *A Commonplace Book to the Holy Bible: Or, the Scripture's Sufficiency Practically Demonstrated, Wherein the Substance of Scripture, Respecting Doctrine, Worship, and Manners, Is Reduced to Its Proper Heads: Weighty Cases Are Resolved, Truths Confirmed, and Difficult Texts Illustrated and Explained*. New York: American Tract Society, n.d.

Lucas, Jerry and Del Washburn. *Theomatics: God's Best Kept Secret Revealed*. New York: Stein and Day, 1977.

Marchbanks, John B. *Great Doctrines Relating to Salvation*. Neptune, New Jersey: Loizeaux Brothers, 1970.

Martin, Ralph P. *Worship in the Early Church*. Westwood, New Jersey: Fleming H. Revell, 1964.

Martin, Walter. *Cults Reference Bible*. Santa Ana, California: Vision House, 1981.

_____. *The Kingdom of the Cults: An Analysis of the Major Cult Systems in the Present Christian Era*. Grand Rapids: Zondervan Publishing House, 1965.

_____. *The Kingdom of the Cults*. Minneapolis, Minnesota: Bethany Fellowship, 1969.

Masselink, William. *Why Thousand Years? Or Will the Second Coming be Pre-Millennial?* Grand Rapids: Wm. B. Eerdmans Publishing Company, 1930.

McClintock, John and James Strong. *Cyclopedia of Biblical, Theological, and Ecclesiastical Literature*. Grand Rapids: Baker Book House, 1968 reprint.

Memes, J. S. *Christian Literature: Evidences. Consisting of: Watson's Apology for Christianity; Watson's Apology for the Bible; Paley's Evidences of Christianity; Paley's Horae Paulinae; Jenyns' View of the Internal Evidence of the Christian Religion; Leslie's Truth of Christianity Demonstrated; Leslie's Short and Easy Method with the Deists; Leslie's Short and Easy*

Method with the Jews; Chandler's Plain Reasons for Being a Christian; Lyttelton's Observations on the Conversion of Saint Paul; Campbell's Dissertation on Miracles; Sherlock's Trial of the Witnesses, with the Sequel to the Trial; West on the Resurrection. Edinburgh: A & C Bloch, 1840.

Menzies, Mrs. Stephen. *How to Mark Your Bible.* London: Pickering and Inglis Ltd, 1917.

Metzger, Bruce M. *The Jehovah's Witnesses and Jesus Christ.* Princeton, New Jersey: The Theological Book Agency, 1953.

_____. *The Text of the New Testament: Its Transmission, Corruption and Restoration.* New York: Oxford University Press, 1964.

_____. *A Textual Commentary on the Greek New Testament.* London: United Bible Societies, 1971.

Monser, Harold E. *The Cross-Reference Bible.* Grand Rapids: Baker Book House, 1959. Reprint of the 1910 edition.

_____. *Monser's Topical Index and Digest of the Bible.* New York: Cross Reference Bible Company, 1914.

Moody, Clement. *The New Testament Expounded and Illustrated According to the usual Marginal References in the very words of Holy Scripture. Together with the Notes and Translations, and a Complete Marginal Harmony of the Gospels.*

Mooney, S. C. *Usury: Destroyer of Nations.* Warsaw, Ohio: Theopolis, 1988.

Morgan, James. *The Scripture Testimony to the Holy Spirit.* Edinburgh: T. & T. Clark, 1865.

Morris, T. D. *A Grouped and Annotated Subject-Index to St. Paul's Episles. With an Accessory Forepart.* 1910.

Moule, C. F. D. *An Idiom Book of New Testament Greek.* Cambridge: Cambridge University Press, 1959.

Moulton, James Hope. *A Grammar of New Testament Greek. Four Volumes:* Edinburgh: T. & T. Clark, 1908.

Moulton, James Hope and Albert William Greenup. *The New Testament in the Revised Version of 1881 with Fuller References.* Oxford: Oxford University Press, 1910.

Moulton, James Hope, and George Milligan. *A Vocabulary of the Greek Testament.* London: Hodder and Stoughton Limited, 1930.

Munk, Johannes. *Christ and Israel: An Interpretation of Romans 9-11.* Philadelphia: Fortress Press, 1967.

Nave, Orville J. and Anna Semans Nave. *Nave's Study Bible.* Chicago: Moody Press reprint, n.d.

Nee, Watchman. *The Normal Christian Church Life.* Washington, D.C.: International Students Press, 1962.

Newmark, Herman. *Prophecies of Centuries Fulfilled in a Day.* London: Eduth Le-Israel, n.d.

Nicholson, W. R. *Popular Studies in Colossians: Oneness With Christ.* Fincastle, Virginia: Scripture Truth Book Company, n.d.

Nicoll, W. Robertson. *The Expositor's Greek Testa-*

ment. Five volumes. Grand Rapids: Wm. B. Eerdmans Publishing Co., 1961 reprint.

Nolan, Frederick. *An Inquiry into the Integrity of the Greek Vulgate, or Received Text of the New Testament.* London: Printed for F. C. and J. Rivington, 1815.

Orr, James. (Ed.) *The International Standard Bible Encyclopedia.* Five volumes. Grand Rapids: Wm. B. Eerdmans Publishing Company, 1960.

Paley, William. *Horae Paulinae; or, the Truth of the Scripture History of St. Paul Evinced by a Comparison of the Epistles Which Bear His Name with the Acts of the Apostles and with one another.* London: T. Nelson and Sons, 1879.

_____. *The Works of William Paley.* Philadelphia: Crissy & Markley, n.d.

Panin, Ivan. *Bible Chronology.* Aldershot, Ontario: Bible Numerics, 1950.

Parsons, J. U. *The Biblical Analysis; or a Topical Arrangement of the Instructions of the Holy Scriptures.* Boston: Whipple & Damrell, 1837.

Peters, George N.H. *The Theocratic Kingdom of our Lord Jesus, the Christ, as Covenanted in the Old Testament and Presented in the New Testament.* Grand Rapids: Kregel Publications, 1957.

Pick, Aaron. *The Bible Student's Concordance.* London: Hamilton, Adams & Company, 1845.

Pink, Arthur W. *The Prophetic Parables of Matthew Thirteen.* Covington, Kentucky: Kentucky Bible Depot, 1946.

_____. *Exposition of the Gospel of John.* Grand Rapids: Zondervan Publishing House, 1968.

Poole, Matthew. *A Commentary on the Holy Bible.* London: Banner of Truth Trust, 1962 reprint of 1805 edition.

Potts, Cyrus A. *Dictionary of Bible Proper Names.* Addison, Illinois: Bible Truth Publishers, 1981.

Price, A. C. *Biblical Studies: A Guide to What the Bible Actually Says as to the Nature and Meaning of Christianity.* London: Hodder and Stoughton Limited, 1939.

Pusey, E. B. *The Minor Prophets: A Commentary, Explanatory and Practical.* Grand Rapids: Baker Book House, reprinted 1956.

Rackham, Richard Belward. *The Acts of the Apostles: An Exposition.* London: Methuen, 1901.

Rea, John. (Ed.) *Layman's Commentary on the Holy Spirit.* Plainfield, New Jersey: Logos International, 1972.

Reese, Alexander. *The Approaching Advent of Christ.* Grand Rapids: Grand Rapids International Publications, 1975.

Ritchie, John. *Scripture Proper Names.* Kilmarnock: John Ritchie, Limited, n.d.

Robertson, A. T. *The Divinity of Christ in the Gospel of John.* New York: Fleming H. Revell Company, 1916.

Robertson, A. T. *A Grammar of the Greek New Testament in the Light of Historical Research.* Nashville: Broadman Press, 1934.

_____. *The Minister and His Greek New*

Testament. London: Hodder & Stoughton, 1923.

Robertson, A. T. *Paul's Joy in Christ: Studies in Philippians*. Grand Rapids: Baker Book House, 1970 reprint of 1917 edition.

_____. *Studies in the Text of the New Testament*. New York: George H. Doran Company.

_____. *Word Pictures in the New Testament*. Nashville, Tennessee: Broadman Press, 1930. Six volumes.

Russel, Bertrand. *Why I Am Not a Christian*. New York: Simon and Schuster, 1967.

Ryle, John Charles. *Old Paths: Being Plain Statements on Some of the Weightier Matters of Christianity*. London: James Clarke & Company Ltd., 1972 reprint.

Sauer, Eric. *From Eternity to Eternity*. Grand Rapids: Wm. B. Eerdmans Publishing Co., 1954.

Scott, Thomas. *The Holy Bible, containing the Old and New Testaments, According to the Authorized Version, with Explanatory Notes, Practical Observations, and Copious Marginal References*. Boston: Crocker and Brewster, 1864. Six volumes.

_____. *Scott's Commentary*. London, 1851. Six volumes.

Scrivener, F. H. A. *Introduction to Textual Criticism. A Plain Introduction to the Criticism of the New Testament for the use of Biblical students*. London: George Bell & Sons, 1894.

Serle, Ambrose. *The Church of God; Or, Essays Upon Some Descriptive Names and Titles*. Glasgow: J. Kirk, & Co., 1814.

Serle, Ambrose. *Horae Solitariae: or, Essays Upon Some Remarkable Names and Titles of Jesus Christ and the Holy Spirit Occurring in the Old and New Testaments, and Declarative of their Essential Divinity and Gracious Offices in the Redemption and Salvation of Men: to Which is Annexed, an Essay, Chiefly Historical, Upon the Doctrine of the Trinity; and a Brief Account of the Heresies Relative to the Doctrine of the Holy Spirit, Which Have Been Published Since the Christian Era*. New York: Robert Carter, 1842.

Shedd, William G. T. *The Doctrine of Endless Punishment*. New York: Charles Scribner's Sons, 1886.

_____. *Dogmatic Theology*. Grand Rapids: Zondervan Publishing House, 1969 reprint of the 1888 edition.

Shepherd, J. W. *Handbook on Baptism*. Nashville, Tennessee: Gospel Advocate Company, 1972 reprint of the 1912 edition.

Simmons, Charles. *A Scripture Manual; Alphabetically and Systematically Arranged, Designed to Facilitate the Finding of Proof Texts*. New York: M. W. Dodd, Brick Church Chapel, 1850.

Slaten, Arthur Wakefield. *Qualitative Nouns in the Pauline Epistles and Their Translation in the Revised Version*. Chicago: The University of Chicago Press, 1918.

Smith, J. B. *Greek-English Concordance to the New Testament. A Tabular and Statistical Greek-English Concordance Based on the King James Version with an English-to-Greek Index*. Scottdale, Pennsylvania: Herald Press, 1955.

Smith, J. B. *A Revelation of Jesus Christ: A Commentary on the Book of Revelation*. Scottdale, Pennsylvania: Herald Press, 1961.

Smith, Wilbur M. *The Biblical Doctrine of Heaven*. Chicago: Moody Press, 1968.

_____. *Chats from a Minister's Library*. Boston: W. A. Wilde, 1951.

_____. *Egypt in Biblical Prophecy*. Grand Rapids: Baker Book House, 1957.

_____. *Israeli/Arab Conflict and the Bible*. Glendale, California: Regal Books, 1967.

_____. *The Minister in His Study*. Chicago: Moody Press, 1973.

_____. *A Preliminary Bibliography for the Study of Biblical Prophecy*. Boston: W. A. Wilde Co., 1952.

_____. *Profitable Bible Study. Seven Simple Methods with an Annotated List of the First One Hundred Best Books for the Bible Student's Library*. Boston: W.A. Wilde Co., 1939.

_____. *Therefore Stand. A Plea for a Vigorous Apologetic in This Critical Hour of the Christian Faith*. Boston: W. A. Wilde Co., 1945.

_____. *A Treasury of Books for Bible Study*. Natick, Massachusetts: W. A. Wilde Company, 1960.

_____. *World Crises and the Prophetic Scriptures*. Chicago: Moody Press, 1950.

_____. *You Can Know the Future*. Glendale, California: Regal Books, 1971.

Smith, William. *Dictionary of the Bible*. Grand Rapids: Baker Book House, 1971 reprint of the 1896 edition.

Stanton, Gerald B. *Kept from the Hour: Biblical Evidence for the Pretribulational Return of Christ*. London: Marshall, Morgan and Scott, 1964.

Stoner, Peter W. *Science Speaks. Scientific Proof of the Accuracy of Prophecy and the Bible*. Chicago: Moody Press, 1958.

Strauch, Alexander. *Biblical Eldership: An Urgent Call to Restore Biblical Church Leadership*. Littleton, Colorado: Lewis and Roth Publishers, 1986.

Strong, Augustus Hopkins. *Systematic Theology*. Westwood, New Jersey: Fleming H. Revell Company, 1907.

Summers, Thomas O. *Baptism: A Treatise on the Nature, Perpetuity, Subjects, Administrator, Mode, and Use of the Initiating Ordinance of the Christian Church. With an Appendix, Containing Strictures on Dr. Howell's "Evils of Infant Baptism," etc*. Richmond, Virginia: John Early, for the Methodist Episcopal Church, South, 1853.

Swete, Henry Barclay. *The Apocalypse of St. John*. London: MacMillan and Company, 1906.

Taylor, C. *Apostolic Baptism: Facts and Evidences on the Subjects and Mode of Christian Baptism*. New York: Saxton and Miles, 1844.

Taylor, Fred E. *A Christian's Bill of Responsibilities In Business. Rules of Business Conduct to help*

Christian Workers, Pastors, and Christians in Secular Employment. Portland, Oregon: Christian Supply Center, 1959.

Terry, Milton S. *Biblical Hermeneutics*. Grand Rapids: Zondervan Publishing House, reprint of the 1883 edition.

Thayer, Joseph Henry. *A Greek-English Lexicon of the New Testament*. Grand Rapids: Zondervan Publishing House, 1963 reprint of 1889 edition.

Thirtle, James William. *The Lord's Prayer: An Interpretation Critical and Expository*. London: Morgan and Scott, 1915.

_____. *The Titles of the Psalms: Their Nature and Meaning Explained*. London: Henry Frowde, 1904.

Thomas, F. W. *Masters of Deception. A Christian Analysis of the Anti-Biblical Teachings of the Jehovah's Witnesses*. Grand Rapids: Baker Book House, n.d.

Thomas, Robert L. *Understanding Spiritual Gifts: An Exegetical Study of 1 Corinthians 12-14*. Chicago: Moody Press, 1978.

Torrey, R. A., A. C. Dixon, and others (Eds.) *The Fundamentals: A Testimony to the Truth*. Grand Rapids: Baker Book House, 1972 reprint of the 1917 edition.

Tregelles, S. P. *The Hope of Christ's Second Coming*. London: The Sovereign Grace Advent Testimony, 1964 reprint of the 1864 edition.

Trench, R. C. *Synonyms of the New Testament*. Grand Rapids: Wm. B. Eerdmans Publishing Co., 1953 reprint of the 1880 edition.

Trueblood, Elton. *The Humor of Christ*. New York: Harper and Row, 1964.

Turner, Nigel. *Grammatical Insights into the New Testament*. Edinburgh: T. & T. Clark, 1965.

Turpie, David McCalman. *The Old Testament in the New*. London: Williams and Norgate, 1868.

Unger, Merrill F. *Unger's Bible Dictionary*. Chicago: Moody Press, 1973.

Vincent, Marvin R. *Word Studies in the New Testament*. Grand Rapids: Wm. B. Eerdmans Publishing Co., 1965 reprint of the 1887 edition.

Vine, W. E. *Expository Dictionary of New Testament Words*. Westwood, New Jersey: Fleming H. Revell, 1966.

Walker, Thomas. *The Acts of the Apostles*. Chicago: Moody Press, 1965 reprint of the 1910 edition.

Walvoord, John F. *The Blessed Hope and the Tribulation: A Historical and Biblical Study of Posttribulationism*. Grand Rapids: Zondervan Publishing House, 1976.

_____. *The Rapture Question*. Revised and Enlarged Edition. Grand Rapids: Zondervan Publishing House, 1979.

Wardlaw, Ralph. *Lectures on the Book of Proverbs*. London: A. Fullerton & Co., 1861.

Warfield, Benjamin B. *Counterfeit Miracles*. London: Banner of Truth Trust, 1972 reprint of the 1918 edition.

_____. *An Introduction to the Textual Criticism of the New Testament*. London: Hodder and Stoughton, 1907.

_____. *The Lord of Glory: A Study of the Designations of Our Lord in the New Testament with Especial Reference to His Deity*. New York: American Tract Society, 1907.

Waterland, Daniel. *The Works of the Rev. Daniel Waterland, D. D*. Oxford: Oxford University Press, 1856.

Watters, Philip. *The Prayers of the Bible*. New York: Phillips and Hunt, 1883.

Webster, William, and William Francis Wilkinson. *The Greek Testament with Notes Grammatical and Exegetical*. London: John W. Parker and Son West Strand, 1855.

West, Nathaniel. *The Thousand Years in Both Testaments*. Fincastle, Virginia: Scripture Truth Book Company, n.d.

Whitelaw, Thomas. *The Gospel of John: An Exposition Exegetical and Homiletical*. Fincastle, Virginia: Scripture Truth Book Company, n.d.

Whitla, William. *Sir Isaac Newton's Daniel and the Apocalypse*. London: John Murray, 1922.

Wigram, George V. *The Englishman's Hebrew and Chaldee Concordance of the Old Testament*. London: Samuel Bagster and Sons, Limited, n.d.

_____. *The Englishman's Hebrew and Chaldee Concordance of the Old Testament: Numerically Coded to Strong's Exhaustive Concordance*. Grand Rapids: Baker Book House, 1980.

Wilmore, J. A. *Wilmore's New Analytical Reference Bible*. New York: Funk & Wagnalls Company, 1891.

Wilson, Daniel. *The Divine Authority and Perpetual Obligation of the Lord's Day*. London: Lord's Day Observance Society, 1956.

Wilson, Robert Dick. *Studies in the Book of Daniel*. Grand Rapids: Baker Book House, 1972 reprint of the 1917 edition.

_____. *Is Higher Criticism Scholarly?* Grand Rapids: Grand Rapids International Publications, 1970.

Wilson, T. Ernest. *Mystery Doctrines of the New Testament*. Neptune, New Jersey: Loizeaux Brothers, 1975.

Wilson, William. *Old Testament Word Studies: An English and Chaldee Lexicon and Concordance*. London: Macmillan, 1870.

Wordsworth, Chr. *The New Testament of Our Lord and Saviour Jesus Christ, in the Original Greek: with Introductions and Notes*. London: Rivingtons, 1867.

Wright, William Heber. *New Testament Quotations from the Old*. Swengel, Pennsylvania: Reiner Publications, n.d.

Young, Edward J. *The Prophecy of Daniel: A Commentary*. Grand Rapids: Wm. B. Eerdmans Publishing Company, 1949.

Young, Robert. *Analytical Concordance to the Bible*. New York: Funk and Wagnalls Company, n.d.

_____. *Concise Critical Comments: Young's Bible. Concise Commentary on the Holy Bible, Being a Companion to the New Translation of the Old and New Covenants*. Edinburgh: Geo.

Adam Young & Co., n.d.

Young, Robert. *Dictionary and Concordance of Bible Words and Synonyms: A Key to the Hidden Meanings of the Sacred Scripture.* Edinburgh: George Adam Young and Company, 1883.

Young, Robert. *Twofold Concordance to the New Testament.* Edinburgh: George Adam Young and Company, 1884.

_____. *Young's Literal Translation of the Holy Bible.* Grand Rapids: Baker Book House, 1956 reprint of the 1898 edition.

Zodhiates, Spiros. *The Hebrew-Greek Key Study Bible.* Grand Rapids: Baker Book House, 1984.

SUBJECT INDEX

Abide. lit. "lodge for a night," Ps 49:12n.
Ability of God to sanctify. T#588, 2 C 9:8.
Ability of man to do right. T#421, Ezk 12:2.
Abomination of desolation. Da 9:27.
Abortion. Jb 3:16mg. Lk +*1:44n.
Abrahamic church. T#116, Ac 7:38.
Abrahamic covenant. T#117, Mi 7:20. T#118, Ro 2:29. T#119, Ro 4:11. T#120, Ac 2:39. T#121, Ro 15:8.
Abrahamic covenant presently unfulfilled. (1) Abraham never personally possessed the land promised. Jsh 21:43n. Ac +*7:5n. (2) Israel never possessed the full geographical extent of the land promised. 1 K *4:21n. Is +26:15. Ob 17.
Abstinence, total, the better course. 1 K 20:16n.
Abstinence, total, from alcoholic beverage, commended. Je 35:14. Ep +*5:18.
Abstinence from strong drink. Pr 23:31.
Abstract put for concrete. Ge 6:5n. +*31:54 (ʃ121N1). Jg 20:42n.
Acceptable sacrifices involve personal cost. 2 S 24:24.
Acceptance with God. T#583, 1 J 2:12. T#584, Jn 1:12.
Access to God. Ep +*2:18.
Accusation, false. Mt 5:11.
Accusation, false, subjects accuser to punishment intended for the accused. Dt √19:18, 19.
Acknowledge. Ps +51:3.
Acqueducts. 2 S 5:23n. 1 K 1:45n. 2 K 18:17n. 20:20. 2 Ch 32:30n. Ne 2:14n. Jb +38:25 (*S#8585h).
Activity in conversion. T#600, Ps 119:59.
Activity required. T#1, 1 Ch 22:16.
Adam and Eve, probable salvation of, Matthew Henry on. He 11:39n.
Adam's fall. T#157, Ec 7:29.
Adam's fall, effects of. T#158, 1 C 15:52.
Adoption of believers. T#584, Jn 1:12.
Adultery forbidden. Ex +*20:14. T#402, Je 9:2. T#403, Pr 5:3. T#404, Ac 15:20. T#405, He 13:4.
Advent of Christ, Second, predicted. Ac 1:11.
Advent of God the Father. First, Da +7:22. Second, Ep +1:10.
Advent, long period of time between First and Second. Mt +*25:19.
Adverse circumstances, trust God despite. Hab +*3:18.
Adversity, not a sign of God's punishment. Lk *13:3n.
Advice, refusal to hear. 1 S +25:17. 2 S ◑19:8n. 2 K ◑5:13, 14.
Afflictions, benefits of. T#4, Dt 8:2.
Afflictions, common. T#2, Jb 5:7.
Afflictions, demand sympathy. T#7, Jb 6:14.
Afflictions, divine support under. T#6, Ps 23:4.
Afflictions, from God. Ps +*119:75. T#3, 1 S 2:7.
Afflictions, often misimproved. T#9, Is 9:13.
Afflictions, try mankind. T#8, Dt 8:2.
Afflictions of the righteous numerous. Ps +*34:19.
Afflictions of the righteous short. T#5, 2 C 4:17.
Age discrimination, evil effects of. 2 Ch +*10:8n.
Age segregation, evil effects of. 2 Ch +*10:8n.
Aged persons. T#10, 1 P 5:5.
Agency, moral. T#271, Dt 30:19. T#329, 2 S 15:6. T#373, Ps 58:5. T#600, Ps 119:59.

Agency of God. T#264, 2 Ch 18:31. T#265, 2 S 7:14. T#266, Da 1:9. T#267, Dt 2:30.
Agency of God's judgment, heathen nations as. Is +10:5.
Agency of the Spirit. T#347-1, Jb 36:9. T#347-2, 1 S 10:10. T#347-3, Dt 31:19. T#347-4, Ga 4:6. T#594, Dt 30:6. T#595, Ac 5:31. T#596, Ps 17:5.
AIDS (Acquired Immune Deficiency Syndrome). Ezk 24:16n.
Alexander, J. A. Cited: Is 5:26. 22:24. 30:32n. 45:11n. 47:18n. Mk 16:12n. Ac 8:36n. 10:47n.
Alford, Henry. Cited: Ge 25:8n. 43:34n. Jn 6:63n. Ac 20:28n, Col 2:9n. 1 Th 4:17n.
Alien sinner, baptism of. Ac 11:17n.
All, limited to purview of author. Ge 41:56, 57. 1 Ch √14:17. Ps 118:10.
All. Term not always a universal affirmation. For the several distinctions in its use see Ge +*7:19 (ʃ102, hyperbole/overstatement). Ge +24:10 (ʃ171B, synecdoche of genus). 2 K +24:13.
Alliances with the ungodly in unscriptural causes forbidden. 2 Ch *19:2.
Allis, Oswald T. *Bible Numerics.* Re 13:17n.
Allis, Oswald T. *Prophecy and the Church.* Re 13:17n.
Almsgiving, required. T#406, Mt 10:8. T#407, Ac 10:4. T#526, Da 4:27.
Altar of burnt offering. Am +9:1.
Altar of incense. Lk +1:11.
Ambidextrousness. 1 Ch 12:2. Jb 36:32.
Ambiguity of pagan prophecy, instance of. 1 K 22:6n, 15n. Na 3:18n.
Ambition, selfish or worldly. Mt 16:26.
Amen. Je +11:5 (*S#543h).
Amusement, see Mirth. T#479, Pr 14:13.
Andrews, Samuel J. *The Life of Our Lord.* Mk 14:30n.
Angel of Jehovah. Da +*3:25n, +28.
Angels, apostate. T#13, 2 P 2:4.
Angels, some assigned to specific geographical territory. Da 12:1. Ac 16:9.
Angels, character and employment of evil. T#15, Jb 1:7.
Angels, devices of. T#16, 1 Ch 21:1.
Angels, employment of. He 1:14.
Angels, expressive names of. T#14, Mt 4:3.
Angels, how employed. T#12, 2 S 24:16.
Angels, not to be worshipped. Re 19:10.
Angels, numerous. T#11, He 12:22.
Angels, suggestions of. T#17, Mt 4:6.
Angels, to be judged by saints. 1 C 6:3.
Angels, to be resisted. T#18, Ep 4:27.
Anger, sin and folly of. T#735, Jb 5:2.
Anger, wrath, to be avoided. Ps +37:8.
Annihilation, doctrine of referred or alluded to. Ge 37:35n. Jb 14:20n. Is 14:9n. Ezk 18:4n. Am 9:2n. Na 3:11n. Mt *10:28n. 1 C 15:54n. Ph 1:21n, 23n.
Annihilation, possible Old Testament reference to. Is 26:14? Ob 16. Na *3:11n.
Another (of a different kind), Gr. *heteros,* S#2087g. Mt 11:3n.
Another (of the same kind), Gr. *allos,* S#243g. Mt 10:23n.

Boldness exemplified. T#460, Ph 1:20.
Borrowing. Pr 22:7.
Bottle. (1) S#178h, Jb 32:19n. (2) S#1228h, Je 19:1.
(3) S#2534h, Ho 7:5. (4) S#2573h, Hab 2:15. (5)
S#4997h, Jsh 9:4n. (6) S#5035h, Je 13:12n.
Breach of trust. Lk 16:12.
Brethren put for kinsmen. 1 Ch 7:22n. +15:5. 23:22.
Bribery. Pr 17:23.
Bridges, Charles. *Commentary on Proverbs.* cited: Pr
6:30n, 31n. 25:26n. He 10:25n.
Bridges, Charles. Cited upon misapplication of proof-
texts, Pr 24:16n.
Brotherly love required. T#111, Ac 4:32.
Bullinger, E. W. *Apocalypse.* Cited: Re 10:10n. 11:15n.
13:16n. 19:10n.
Bullinger, E. W. *Figures of Speech Used in the Bible.*
1 K 21:10n.
Bullinger, E. W. *The Giver and His Gifts.* 1 C 7:40n.
Bullinger, E. W. Materialist bias of, noted and corrected.
Ps 16:10n.
Bullinger, E. W. *Number in Scripture.* Re 13:17n.
Burgon, Dean John William. Cited: Jn 1:18n. 3:13n.
Burnt offering. Le +*23:12.
Burton, Ernest De Witt. *Syntax of the Moods and
Tenses in New Testament Greek.* Cited: Mt 11:14n.
18:18n.
Business responsibilities to the consumer: defraud not.
Am +*8:5.
Busy people, God calls. Am +*7:15.
Busybody. 1 P 4:15.
By the hand of, mg. 1 K +16:12mg. 2 Ch √34:14mg,n.
Byers, D. B. *Physical Death Not the Penalty.* 1 C 15:56n.
Call to preach. T#449, He 5:4.
Calling, abide in same. 1 C +*7:20.
Calling, effectual. T#597, Ac 2:39.
Calves often born during a storm, Ps 29:9n.
Campbell, J. L. Ac 22:6n.
Capital punishment under Mosaic law. Ex +*21:15
(T#316).
Care, spiritual. 1 T +*3:5.
Carr, Arthur. *Horae Biblicae.* Cited: Ge 24:44n. Is
65:11n.
Carson, Alexander. *Baptism: Its Mode and Subjects.*
Cited: Ep 4:5n.
Carson, D.A. *Exegetical Fallacies.* Cited: 1 C 13:8n.
1 T 4:1n. Re 13:17n.
Castle. 1 Ch +*27:25 (*S#4026h).
Cause/Effect relationships. Ps +√9:10n.
Causes of the ungodly (when contrary to Scripture) not
to be supported. 2 Ch *19:2.
Cautions and warnings against:
Apostasy. T#19, 1 S 15:11.
Backsliding. T#23, 1 K 11:4.
Bad company. T#179, 1 C 11:1.
Covetousness. T#137, Pr 28:16.
The devices of Satan. T#18, Ep 4:27.
Error and errorists. T#177, 1 T 6:5.
False teachers. T#477, Mt 15:14.
Intemperance. T#366, Ep 5:18.
Lewdness. T#405, He 13:4.
Perverting Scripture. T#50, Pr 30:6.
Self-deception. T#704, Pr 16:25.
Soul-murder. T#555, 1 Ch 28:9.
Suretiship. T#717, Pr 17:18.
Tempters and temptation. T#724, Mt 26:41.
Trusting in man. T#170, Pr 25:19.
Unrighteousness. T#733, Nu 32:23.
Worldly idols. T#741, Mt 13:22. T#742, Jn 6:27.
See also *Threats of evil* in this Index.

Caves. Ge +19:30.
Censoriousness forbidden. T#729, Ps 101:5.
Chafer, Lewis Sperry, cited against narrowly conceived
doctrinal prooftexting. Ac 2:38n. 1 J 2:19n.
Chamber, upper, etc. Jg +3:20n. 2 K 4:10n.
Chance, exclusion of. Ge +√24:44n. Jsh ⚫14:2n. Jg
20:22n. 1 S +6:9. 2 S +1:6. Ec +9:11. Is *65:11n.
Lk ⚫10:31.
Chance, games of, reproved. Is 65:11n.
Chance excluded by Divine Providence. Ps 91:3, etc.
Pr 16:33. Mt *6:26. *10:29, 30. Lk *12:6.
Character flaws in children.
Cursing. Le 20:9.
Disrespectful to aged. Is 3:5.
Disrespectful to parents. Pr 15:20.
Foolishness. Pr 22:15.
Mockery. 2 K 2:23. Pr 30:17.
Murder. Ex 21:15.
Scornfulness. Pr 30:17.
Stubbornness. Dt 21:18-21.
Theft. Pr 28:24.
Ungratefulness. Pr 30:11.
Unreliablility. Pr 25:19.
Unthankful. 2 T 3:2.
Character flaws in parents.
Favoritism. Ge +44:30. 2 S 13:21.
Hostility. Ep 6:4.
Neglectfulness. Ex 4:24-26. 1 K *1:6. Pr +*29:15.
Overindulgent. 2 S 13:5.
Overstrictness. Col 3:21.
Permissiveness. 1 S +*3:13.
Poor example. 1 K 15:26.
Pride. Est 5:11. Mt 20:21.
Sinfulness. Ex 20:5.
Character traits. See Christian graces.
Characteristics of true believers named in 1 John. 1 J
5:13n.
Chariots of God. Ps +*68:17.
Charitableness. Pr 17:9.
Charity, see Love. T#412, 1 Th 3:12. T#413, Ga 5:14.
T#414, Lk 10:33.
Charity, see also Liberality. T#406, Mt 10:8. T#407,
Ac 10:4. T#408, Lk 6:38.
"Charity begins at home," Is +58:7.
Chastisement of children. T#494, Pr 13:24.
Chastisement of saints. T#2, Jb 5:7. T#3, 1 S 2:7. T#4,
Dt 8:2.
Chastity required. T#404, Ac 15:20. T#405, He 13:4.
Cheerfulness. T#52, Ne 8:10.
Cheney, Johnston M. *The Life of Christ in Stereo.* Mk
14:30n.
Childlessness. 1 Ch 2:+*30, 32, 34.
Children, character flaws in. See under *Character flaws
in children*
Children, correction of. T#54, Dt 27:16.
Children, correction and discipline of. Pr +*19:18.
Children, duties of. T#53, Ep 6:1.
Care for parents. 1 T 5:4.
Comfort parents. Ge 5:29.
Hear parental counsel. Ge 49:2.
Honor parents. Ex 20:12.
Obedience. Ep 6:1.
Obey God. Dt 30:2.
Pride in parents. Pr 17:6.
Remember Creator. Ec 12:1.
Respect for age. 1 P 5:5.
Show affectionate kindness. Ge 45:3.
Children, good, of good parents. Ge 22:7 (Isaac), Jg
11:36 (Jepthah's daughter), 1 S 2:26 (Samuel), Lk

Contentiousness. Ps 35:20.

Contentment, a duty. T#133, Ph 4:11.

Contingency, as opposed to absolute predestination. Ps 81:13, 14. Is +30:15. Mt +*11:23n.

Contradictions, alleged presence of in the Bible. Mk 14:30n.

Contrast (law and gospel). T#306, Ac 2:37.

Contrast, saints and sinners. T#645, Jb 2:3. T#646, Ps 4:3. T#647, Pr 29:27. T#648, Ml 3:18. T#649, Ja 2:23. T#650, Ro 1:30. T#651, Ac 5:14. T#652, Mt 23:33. T#653, Mt 13:38. T#654, 1 P 1:14. T#655, Lk 16:8. T#656, Ep 2:3.

Controversy, God's. T#230, Ge 6:6.

Controversy with God. T#272, Ezk 33:20. T#695, Lk 19:14.

Conversion necessary. T#589, Ps 50:16.

Conversion of the Jews. T#382, Ro 11:26.

Conversion of St. Paul, evidential value of. Ac 22:6n.

Conviction of sin. T#590, Ac 2:37.

Convictions, courage of. Est +*1:12.

Corban. Le +19:5n. Le 1:2n. Mk 7:11n.

Corporal punishment of children by parents commanded. Pr +*13:24.

Correction of children. Pr +*19:18.

Correction of others. Pr +28:23.

Counsel, instance of heeding unwise. 2 Ch 10:8.

Counsel, sources of unwise. 1 K +√12:10n.

Counsel, sources of wise. 1 K +√12:7n.

Counsel, unwillingness to receive. 1 S +√25:17. 2 K ◖5:13, 14.

Counsel, unwise. 1 K +*12:10.

Counsel, wise. 1 K +*12:7.

Counsel to be wisely sought. 1 K +*12:6.

Counseling, Biblical, using Biblically defined root causes in cause/effect relationships. Ro 12:8n.

Countess, Dr. Robert H. Mt 27:54n. Mk 7:4n.

Counterfeit prophesying. 1 S 18:10n.

Courage of convictions. Est +*1:12n.

Courage required. T#134, Jsh 1:9.

Courtesy required. T#135, 1 P 3:8.

Covenant of grace. Is +*42:6.

Covenant of redemption. T#575, He 13:20. 1 C 15:45.

Covenant of works. Ho +6:7.

Covenant with Abraham. T#117, Mi 7:20. T#118, Ro 2:29. T#119, Ro 4:11. T#120, Ac 2:39. T#121, Ro 15:8.

Covenanting with God. T#502, Ne 10:29.

Covenants, vows, promises: inviolability of. Jsh 9:19. Jg *11:35. Ps 15:4. Ga 3:15. Ro *11:29.

Covenants of Scripture enumerated. Dt 30:1n.

Covetousness. T#136, Ph 2:21.

Covetousness, evils of. T#408, Lk 6:38.

Covetousness, warnings against. Ps +*10:3.

Covetousness prohibited. T#137, Pr 28:16.

Covetousness punished. T#138, Ep 5:5.

Creation, time employed in. T#140, Ex 20:11.

Creation indicates wisdom. T#142, Je 10:12.

Creation produced. T#139, Is 42:5.

Creation of the orbs, for lights. T#141, Je 31:35.

Cremation. Jsh +7:25. 2 Ch ◖16:14.

Cremer, Hermann. *Biblico-Theological Lexicon of New Testament Greek*. Mk 2:22n.

Crimes, capital. T#315, Ge 9:5. T#316, Ex 21:15.

Cross, not a single pole or "torture stake." Jn *19:6n. 20:25n.

Crucifixion of Christ. T#68, Ps 2:2.

Cruelty of sinners. T#701, Ro 3:15.

Cruelty to servants forbidden. T#679, Col 4:1.

Cruelty of warriors. T#734, Is 1:15.

Cryptogram, instance of a Hebrew. Je 25:26n.

Curse. Ne +10:29 (*S#423h).

Curses of God, result from disobedience and failure to hear God's word. Dt +*28:15.

Cursing. Ro +*3:14.

Custer, Stuart. *Does Inspiration Demand Inerrancy?* Mk 14:30n.

Custom, its power. T#143, Je 10:3.

Customs of Christ. Lk +*4:16.

Cymbals. 1 Ch +13:8.

Cypher, instance of a Hebrew. Je 25:26n.

Daille, John. Cited: Ph 2:6n.

Dake, J. Finis. *Annotated Reference Bible*. 1 K 10:10, 16. 1 C 15:52n. Re 3:10n. 12:5n.

Dale, J. W. *Classic Baptism*. Cited: 1 C 10:2.

Dale, J. W. *Judaic Baptism*. Cited: 1 C 10:2.

Dale, J. W. *Christic Baptism*. Cited: Ac 8:36n, 38, 39. 10:48n. 1 C 10:2n. 12:13n. Ep 4:5n.

Dan not sealed. 1 Ch 7:12n.

Dana and Mantey. *A Manual Grammar of the Greek New Testament*. Cited: Mt 11:14n. Re 13:17n.

Dances, mixed, not used by the people of God. Jg 21:21n.

Dancing in worship, separation of the sexes during. Ex 15:20n. Jg 21:21n. 1 Ch +15:29 (skipping).

Danger, prudent to hide or flee from. Pr +*22:3.

Darby, J. N. Cited: Mt 24:34n. Ph 3:11n.

Darkness, figurative of the abode of the lost. Mt 8:12.

Darkness, figurative of the divine inscrutability. 2 S 22:10.

Darkness, figurative of judgments. Pr +20:20.

Darkness, figurative of powers of evil. Lk 22:53.

Darkness, figurative of spiritual blindness. Is +9:2.

Darkness, God dwells in. Ex 20:21.

Darkness, natural. Jb 38:9.

Darkness, natural, created by God. Ps 104:20.

Darkness, works of. T#167, Ep 5:11.

Darwin, Charles, alleged conversion. 2 K 20:11n.

Daughter put for granddaughter, 2 K 8:26. 1 Ch 7:24n. 2 Ch 11:18n, 20. 13:2.

Daughters (Hebrew and mg), put for towns or villages. Nu +21:25mg.

David, sure mercies of. Is +√55:3.

David in future prophecy, contrasting viewpoints. (1) king over future Israel, name of the coming Messiah. Ezk 34:23n. (2) David will be a literal king over Israel reigning in Jerusalem during the Millennium, Ho 3:5n, at the same time that Christ reigns over the world from Jerusalem (Zc +*14:9).

David "not ascended." Ac 2:34n.

David to rule literally in Jerusalem, Israel, during the Millennium. Mi +2:13.

Davis, J. D. *Dictionary of the Bible*. Ge 36:35. 46:21. 2 S 5:23. 1 Ch 6:36. 15:11. Ne 12:14.

Davis, John J. *Biblical Numerology*. Re 13:17n.

Davis, John J. *Contemporary Counterfeits*. Re 13:17n.

Day, in plural put for a long time. Jg 21:19 (S#3117h). Nu +9:22n.

Day, the last. Jn +*6:54n.

Day of judgment. T#383, Mt 11:24. T#384, Ro 2:5. T#385, Mt 25:13. T#386, Ps 102:26. T#387, Mt 25:32. T#388, 2 T 4:1. T#389, Ec 12:14. T#390, Lk 16:26.

Day of the Lord. Is +13:6. 1 C +*3:13.

Day of the Lord, connection with the Great Tribulation. Am +*5:18. Re +*1:10n.

Day of the Lord, extends from the Great Tribulation to the close of the Millennium. Re +*1:10n.

Day of the Lord, figurative of times of adversity. Is +2:12.

Day of worship changed from the seventh to the first day of the week. 1 C 16:2n.

Day of wrath. (1) general references to, Jb +*21:30. Ro +*2:5. (2) directed especially at wealthy oppressors, Ezk +*7:19. Zp +*1:11, 18. Ja +*5:1. (3) wealth will not save or deliver from, Pr +*11:4. (4) true believers exempt from, Na *1:2. 1 Th +*5:9. (5) extends in time from the Great Tribulation until the close of the Millennium, Re +*1:10n.

Day, unto this. Ge +19:38. Dt +29:4, 28. Jsh +*4:9.

Deacons appointed. T#102, 1 T 3:8.

Dead, destiny and state of the. Re 14:13.

Death, by sin. T#144, Ro 5:12.

Death, demands preparation. T#156, Ps 90:12.

Death, destroys not the soul. T#152, Ec 3:21.

Death, dreadful to the wicked. T#155, He 10:31.

Death, early. Is +*38:10.

Death, the end of earth. T#150, He 9:27.

Death, fear of overcome. T#153, Ph 1:21.

Death, late in life, desirable. T#151, Ps 91:16.

Death, the lot of all. T#145, He 9:27.

Death, often sudden. T#149, Ec 9:12.

Death, ordered by God. T#147, 1 S 2:6.

Death, to be patiently waited for. T#154, Jb 14:14.

Death, the second. T#563, Re 2:11.

Death, shameful if by the hands of (1) a child, Jg 8:21n. (2) a woman, Jg 9:54n. (3) a heathen, 1 S 31:4. (4) the uncircumcised, Ezk 28:10.

Death, sin unto. 1 J *5:16.

Death, sin unto physical. 1 C +*11:30.

Death, sin unto spiritual. 1 C +*6:9. He 10:26.

Death, soon approaches. T#148, Ja 4:14.

Death, spiritual. T#165, Ps 5:9. Ezk +*18:4n.

Death, time of appointed. T#146, Jb 7:1.

Death in impenitence. T#564, Jn 8:21.

Death of false hopes. T#590, Ac 2:37.

Death penalty. (1) authorized as a provision of the Noahic covenant establishing human government, Ge +*9:5, 6. (2) capital crimes under the Mosaic code, Ex +*21:15 (T#316). Dt +27:16 (T#54). Jn +*10:32n. (3) methods of capital punishment. (a) stoning, Le 20:2. Jn +*10:32n. (b) burning after stoning, Le 20:14. Dt 21:22, 23. (c) sword, spear, or arrow. Ex 19:13. 32:27. Nu 25:7. 1 K 2:25.

Debt, divine curse of national and individual. Dt +*28:44.

Debt, obligation to keep current in our payment of. Lk 11:41n.

Debt, to get out of, is first financial priority. 2 K 4:7n.

Decalog. T#281, Ex 20:1. T#282, Ex 19:10. T#283, Ga 5:14.

Deceit. Mk 7:22.

Deceit of sinners. T#702, Ps 5:9.

Deceivers. T#16, 1 Ch 21:1. T#474, Mt 7:15.

Deceiving ourselves. T#704, Pr 16:25.

Deceptive business practices forbidden, condemned. Am +*8:5.

Decision, necessity of specific for salvation. Re 3:20.

Decrees of God. T#249, Dt 32:4. T#250, Ps 33:11. T#251, Jb 14:5. T#252, 1 P 2:8. T#253, Ps 33:12. T#254, Ac 13:48. T#255, Ep 1:4. T#256, Pr 16:4. T#257, 2 Th 2:13. T#258, Da 9:2.

Deductive contrasted with inductive approach to Biblical interpretation. 2 P 1:20n.

Degrees. Am +9:6mg, ascensions, or spheres (*S#4609h).

Degrees, songs of. Is 38:20n.

Degrees of punishment in eternity. Ezk +*18:4n. Mt 11:24n. Lk +*12:47, 48.

Degrees of reward. Mt +*5:12.

DeHoff, George W. *Alleged Bible Contradictions Explained*. Mk 14:30n.

Deity of Christ. 1 P +*2:3n.

Demons, personality of. Mk 5:12n.

Departed saints unaware of what transpires upon earth. Is 63:16.

Dependability. Ph +*2:12.

Dependence of Christ. T#70, Mk 13:32.

Dependence on God. T#261, Mt 5:45. T#262, 2 C 3:5. T#263, Ps 36:6.

Dependence on God for sanctification. T#594, Dt 30:6. T#595, Ac 5:31. T#596, Ps 17:5.

Dependence on God in using means. T#434, 2 T 2:25.

Dependence on God consistent with freedom. T#271, Dt 30:19.

Depravity—the fall. T#157, Ec 7:29.

Depravity, consequences of. T#158, 1 C 15:22.

Depravity, guilt of, personal. T#159, 2 K 14:6.

Depravity, its connection with law. T#161, Ro 5:13.

Depravity, its hateful nature. T#160, Ho 10:1.

Depravity, its native origin. T#164, Ep 2:3.

Depravity, its perpetuity. T#169, Mt 23:31.

Depravity, its restraints. T#168, Ec 8:11.

Depravity, its strength and obstinacy. T#166, Pr 5:22.

Depravity, its total dominion. T#165, Ps 5:9.

Depravity, its universality. T#163, Ec 7:20.

Depravity, its works of darkness. T#167, Ep 5:11.

Depravity, makes men untrusty. T#170, Pr 25:19.

Depravity, man's total. Ps +14:1.

Depravity, not founded in mere ignorance. T#162, Ro 1:21.

Despondency reproved. T#171, Pr 12:25.

Destiny and state of the dead. Re 14:13.

Destiny of all unacquainted with the gospel. Ro 2:16.

Destiny of deceased infants. 2 S 12:23.

Destroyed, utterly. Jsh +8:26.

Destruction, devoted to. Le *27:29n. Jg 21:11.

Deterrence, capital punishment a, to others committing a crime. Dt *13:11. 17:13. +19:20. 21:21.

Devices of Satan. T#16, 1 Ch 21:1.

Devil, character of. T#14, Mt 4:3. T#15, Jb 1:7. T#16, 1 Ch 21:1. T#17, Mt 4:6.

Devil to be resisted. T#18, Ep 4:27.

Devil will be defeated. T#277, Ps 46:10.

Devoted to destruction. Le *27:29n. Jg 21:11. Is +34:2.

Devotion to God required. T#295, Ec 12:13.

Dew, type of the resurrection. Is +*26:19n.

Dialect. Jg 12:6n. 2 K 8:21n. 1 Ch 6:36n. Ne 13:24. Mt *26:73. Mk *14:70. Ac 2:6, 7.

Dichotomy. Ge 41:8n. Nu 27:16n. Ro 8:10n.

Diet, see Food. T#199, Ph 3:19.

Differences to be accounted for, not glossed over, when comparing things that are similar. Mt 10:15n.

Dignity of man. T#419, Ac 17:26. T#420, Lk 12:57. T#421, Ezk 12:2. T#422, 2 T 1:10.

Dignity of the saints. T#672, Dt 33:9.

Diligence. T#1, 1 Ch 22:16. Ex +*15:26. +*20:15n. Pr 10:4. +*22:29. He 11:6.

Directions to sinners. T#601, Ac 3:19.

Discretion required. T#172, Pr 19:11.

Discipleship. Jon 4:11n. 1 Th 3:5n. He 3:13n. 6:9n.

Discipline of children. Pr +*19:18.

Discipline of the church. T#109, Ga 6:1.

Discontent manifest toward God. Ps +*77:3.

Discontinuity of the person, fatal flaw in materialist view of resurrection. Mt 10:28n. 1 C 15:54n. 1 Th 4:16n.

Discrepancies, alleged presence of in the Bible. Mk 14:30n.

Gate, gates. Ge +14:7. 2 S 19:8n. 2 K 7:1n. 2 Ch 18:9n.

Gebhardt, Herman. *The Doctrine of the Apocalypse.* Re 3:10n.

Gehenna. Jsh +*15:8n.

General resurrection of all the dead, righteous and wicked simultaneously, not sustained by Scripture. 1 Th +*4:16n.

Generation gap, harmful outcome of age segregation. 2 Ch +*10:8n.

Generation shall not pass. Mt 24:34.

Generations, eternal, of natural people on earth. 2 P 3:13n.

Generosity
  According to ability. Dt 16:17.
  Encouraged. Ac 20:35.
  Enjoined. 2 C 9:7.
  Rewards for. Pr 11:24, 25. 19:17. Mt 25:40. Lk 14:12-14.
  Toward Jesus. Lk 8:3.
  Toward the poor. Dt 15:7-11. Mk 10:21.
  With humility. 1 Ch 29:14.
  Without ostentation. Mt 6:1-4.

Gentleness exemplified. T#62, Mt 11:29. T#660, Mt 10:18.

Gentleness required. T#499, He 12:14.

Geographical and geological changes in Palestine, Israel, Jerusalem prophesied. Ps 46:2, 3. Ezk +*42:16n. 45:1n. 47:1n. Hab 3:6. Zc 14:4, 10.

Giants. Dt +*2:20. Jsh +17:15.

Gibeon. Jsh +10:2.

Gibson, Edgar C.S. *The Old Testament in the New.* Ac 17:28n.

Gifford, E.H. *Commentary on Romans.* Cited: Ro 8:1n, 19n, 26n. 9:5n. 10:17n. 15:5n.

Girdle, use in eastern dress. Ps 18:32n.

Girdlestone, R. B. *The Grammar of Prophecy.* Re 4:1n.

Girdlestone, *Synonyms of the Old Testament.* Cited: Ge 37:35n. Ho 10:12n. 13:14n. Ml 2:12n.

Giving, proper motive and basis exemplified. Ph +*4:17.

Glorified bodies, saints shall possess. Ph 3:21.

Glorifying God. T#300, 1 T 1:17. T#301, Ro 1:21.

Glory, Messianic, divine, Shekinah. Zc +*2:5.

Glory of Christ. T#82, Re 17:14.

Glory of God. T#214, 1 Ch 29:11. T#277, Ps 46:10.

Glory put for man's tongue which gives it. Ps 30:12mg,n.

Glory of saints in heaven. T#672, Dt 33:9.

Gluttony reproved. T#199, Ph +*3:19.

God, faithfulness of. Ps +36:5.

God, goodness of. Ex +*34:6. Ps +136:1.

God, his chief end. T#209, Pr 16:4.

God, his mode of existence. T#210, 1 C 8:6. T#211, Is 6:8.

God, plurality of Divine Beings or Persons in one. Ge 1:26.

God, transcendence of. Ps 139:7n. Is +*57:15.

God, Unity of. Dt 6:4. Mk 12:32. 1 C 8:6.

God calls busy people. Am +*7:15.

God is said to "do" what he only *permits,* an idiom in both Testaments. See √108A4, Ge +31:7. Ezk 14:9n. 20:25n. Am +√3:6.

God the Father of all men. 1 C +*8:6.

God the Father eternal. Ro 16:26 w Ep 4:6.

God the Father omnipotent. Re +*19:6.

God made known by His works. T#207, Ps 75:1.

God a moral agent. T#208, Ps 7:11.

God seen by intuition. T#206, Ro 1:19.

God's attributes:
  Eternity. T#212, Dt 33:27.
  Foreknowledge. T#213, Ac 2:23.

Greatness and supremacy. T#214, 1 Ch 29:11.
  Essential happiness. T#215, Ro 1:25.
  Immutability. T#217, Ja 1:17.
  Invisibility. T#216, He 11:27.
  Omnipotence. T#218, Re 19:6.
  Omnipresence. T#220, Pr 15:3.
  Omniscience. T#219, He 4:13.
  Self-existence. T#221, Jn 5:26.
  Natural wisdom. T#222, Ro 11:33.
  Transcendence. Ps 8:5n.

God's law:
  Supreme. T#280, Ps 22:28.
  The Decalog. T#281, Ex 20:1.
  Its promulgation. T#282, Ex 19:10.
  Summaries of. T#283, Ga 5:14.
  Very sacred. T#284, Is 42:21.
  Requires perfection. T#285, Mt 5:48.
  Is reasonable. T#286, Ro 7:12.
  Its penalty. T#287, Ja 1:15.
  Requires true love to God. T#288, Ju 21. T#289, 1 C 2:9.
  Requires the fear of God. T#290, Ec 12:13. T#291, Jb 28:28.
  Requires trust in God. T#292, Pr 3:5. T#293, Is 26:3. T#294, Jb 13:15.
  Requires supreme devotion. T#295, Ec 12:13.
  Requires joy in God. T#296, 1 Th 5:16. T#297, 1 P 1:8.
  Requires submission. T#298, Ja 4:7. T#299, Ac 21:14.
  Requires honoring God. T#300, 1 T 1:17. T#301, Ro 1:21.

God's moral government:
  Requires obedience. T#302, Ps 19:11.
  Punishes disobedience. T#303, Ps 34:16.

God's moral perfection:
  Blessedness. T#223, Ps 104:31.
  Benevolence. T#224, Ps 119:68.
  Compassion. T#225, Ja 5:11.
  Faithfulness. T#226, 1 P 4:19.
  Forbearance. T#227, Ro 2:4.
  Goodness. T#228, Ps 145:9.
  Holiness and beauty. T#229, Re 15:4.
  Holy hatred of iniquity. T#230, Ge 6:6.
  Impartiality. T#231, Ro 2:11.
  Justice and righteousness. T#232, Ps 33:5.
  Mercy and kindness. T#233, Jon 4:2.
  Sovereignty and independence. T#234, Ro 9:18.
  Truth. T#235, Ex 34:6.
  Vindicative justice. T#236, Ro 11:22. T#237, Dt 32:43.
  Zeal. T#238, 2 P 3:9.

God's prerogatives:
  To own us as his property. T#239, Ro 14:8.
  To fix natural law. T#240, Jb 38:33.
  To give supreme moral law. T#241, Mt 4:10.
  To regenerate or not. T#242, 2 T 2:25.
  To employ tempters. T#243, 1 C 11:19.
  To require human life. T#244m 1 S 15:3.
  To set up rulers to scourge us. T#245, Da 4:17.
  To visit iniquity. T#246, Ex 20:5.
  To use men instrumentally. T#247, 1 Ch 6:15.
  To vindicate himself. T#248, Dt 32:35.

God's providence:
  Nature and efficacy of. T#259, He 11:3.
  Extent of. T#260, Ep 1:11.
  Supplies our wants. T#261, Mt 5:45.
  Upholds all creatures. T#262, 2 C 3:5.
  Preserves all. T#263, Ps 36:6.
  Governs the heart. T#264, 2 Ch 18:31.

Uses moral instruments. T#265, 2 S 7:14.
Controls popular favor. T#266, Da 1:9.
Controls moral evils. T#267, Dt 2:30.
Brings good out of evil. T#268, Ge 45:5.
Approves not sin. T#269, 1 C 14:33.
Has motives above ours. T#270, Ge 50:20.
Disturbs not our freedom. T#271, Dt 30:19.
Objections against. T#272, Ezk 33:20. T#273, Ro 9:20.
Wonders of. T#274, Da 4:3.
Incomprehensible. T#275, Ro 11:33.
Makes men know the Lord. T#276, Jn 11:42.
Will secure his glory. T#277, Ps 46:10.
A solid ground of joy. T#278, Ps 39:9.
Demands attention. T#279, Ps 36:9.
God's purposes:
  Best. T#249, Dt 32:4.
  Eternal and immutable. T#250, Ps 33:11.
  Universal and particular. T#251, Jb 14:5.
  Include moral evils. T#252, 1 P 2:8.
  Include national election. T#253, Ps 33:12.
  Include individual election. T#254, Jn 13:48.
  Place election prior to faith. T#255, Ep 1:4.
  Include vessels of wrath. T#256, Pr 16:4.
  Include means and ends. T#257, 2 Th 2:13.
  Encourage the use of means. T#258, Da 9:2.
Godliness. 1 T +*4:8.
gods/god. Heb. elohim, special uses of, in reference to: (1) angels, Ps +8:5n. (2) judges, magistrates, Ps +82:6n. (3) false gods, pagan deities, 2 Ch +35:22n.
gods. Considered local, provincial, tribal, national, etc. by pagan or heathen nations surrounding Israel. Dt 29:26n. Jg 11:24n. 1 K 20:23n. 2 K 17:26. 18:33. 2 Ch 32:13, 19. Is 36:18n.
gods, false, mentioned in the Bible. Molech, Le +18:21.
Golden Rule. Mt 7:12. Lk 6:31.
Good works the fruit and evidence, not ground of faith. Ga 3:10n.
Goodness of God. Ps +136:1.
Gospel:
  Its origin. T#304, Ep 3:11.
  Its gracious design. T#305, Ac 20:24.
  Its distinctive terms. T#306, Ac 2:37.
  Its plan comprehensive. T#307, Ep 1:9.
  Its high standard of duty. T#308, Mt 5:20.
  Its fearful penalty. T#309, Jn 3:19.
  Its provisions. T#576, Ps 143:2. T#577, Ro 3:25. T#578, Is 53:6. T#579, 1 P 1:19. T#580, 1 T 2:6. T#581, Is 53:6. T#582, He 2:17. T#583, 1 J 2:12. T#584, Jn 1:12. T#585, Jb 36:7. T#672, Dt 33:9.
Gospel of "health, wealth, prosperity" mistaken in focus. 1 T +*6:5, 17-19.
Gospel of wealth and prosperity is heresy, command to withdraw from such. 1 T 6:5.
Gospel to be proclaimed to "the Jew first." Da 9:25n. Jl 2:28n. Ro √1:16.
Gossip. Le 19:16.
Government, civil. T#310, Ac 13:20.
  Expedient and necessary. T#311, Pr 26:3.
  Demands qualified rulers. T#312, Ex 18:21.
  Includes duties for rulers. T#313, Dt 16:18.
  Includes duties for subjects. T#314, T 3:1.
  Its penalty for crimes. T#315, Ge 9:5. T#316, Ex 21:15.
  Its penalty for treason. T#317, 2 P 2:10.
  Its wicked rulers injurious. T#318, Pr 28:15.
  Sometimes to be resisted. T#319, Ac 5:29.
Government, moral. T#302, Ps 19:11.

Grace of God. T#233, Jon 4:2. T#305, Ac 20:24. T#586, Ac 20:24.
Grace of God opposed by sinners. T#696, Ps 10:4.
Graces, Christian. See under Christian Graces.
Grant, F.W. Le 23:17n. 25:9n. Zc 12:1n. Mt 10:28n. 13:33n. Lk 23:43n, 46n. Ac 2:34n. 23:8n. 1 C 2:11n. Ph 1:23n. 1 T 2:6n.
Grant, P.W. Christian Baptism the Baptism of Christians. Cited: Ac 11:17n.
Gratitude exemplified. T#320, 2 S 9:7.
Grave, original language words rendered. (1) S#7585h, sheol, Ge 37:35n. (2) S#6913h, qeber, Ge 23:4. (3) S#6900h, qeburah, Ge +35:20. (4) S#86g, hades, Mt 11:23. (5) S#3419g, mnemeion, Mt 8:28 (tombs).
Gravity required. T#711, 1 P 4:7.
Great Pyramid, the. Is 19:19n.
Greek prepositions discussed. (1) eis, Mt 26:28n. Mk 1:4n. Ac 2:38n. (2) ek, Ac 8:39n. 1 J 2:19n. Re 3:10n.
Greek prepositions, multiple senses of. Ac 2:38n. 1 J 2:19n.
Green, Samuel. Greek Grammar. 1 C 15:24n. Ga 6:2n.
Grief, divine. T#230, Ge 6:6.
Grief of saints. T#662, Ps 119:158.
Grounds of ministerial support. 1 C 9:7n.
Guidance, example of, in marriage. Ge +24:44.
Guidance, false, example of. 1 S +24:4n. 2 S 4:8.
Guidance, hand of providence in. 1 S 14:15n.
Guidance, request for confirmation of. 1 S +23:4.
Guidance, sources of unwise, false. 1 K 13:18n.
Guidance, sources of wise, true. 1 K 13:9n.
Guidance confirmed. Ge 24:50.
Gundry, Robert. The Church and the Tribulation. Re 3:10n.
Habershon, Ada. Outline Studies of the Tabernacle. Ex 25:19n. Lk 23:44n.
Habershon, Ada. The Study of the Types. Le 23:11n.
Habits. See Custom. T#143, Je 10:3.
Haley, John W. An Examination of the Alleged Discrepancies of the Bible. Cited: Mk 14:30.
Hand of God in blessing. Ps +*37:24.
Hand of God in disfavor. Ru +*1:13.
Hands, laying on of. T#399, Re 1:17. T#400, Mk 16:18.
Happiness:
  Sensual. T#321, Ec 2:1.
  Intellectual. T#322, Pr 3:13.
  Of self-denial. T#323, 2 C 6:10.
  Of holy obedience. T#324, Pr 29:18.
  Of loving God. T#325, 1 P 1:8.
  Of trusting in God. T#326, Ps 40:4.
  Of a good conscience. T#327, 2 C 1:2.
  Of heaven. T#328, 1 P 4:13. T#339, Ju 24. T#672, Dt 33:9.
  Of God. T#215, Ro 1:25. T#223, Ps 104:31.
Hardness of heart defined. Ex 9:12n.
Harlot, better rendered "tavern keeper." Ge 38:21n. Jsh 2:1n, 13n. Jg 11:1n. 1 K 3:16n. He 11:31n.
Harps. 1 Ch +13:8n.
Harrisville, Roy A. The Concept of Newness in the New Testament. Mk 2:22n.
Hatred. Le 19:17.
Hayes, D. A. Paul and His Epistles. Cited: Ga 5:12n.
Healing, divine, physical. Ex +23:25.
Healing, intercessory prayer for. Nu +12:13.
Hear, failure to. Je +*29:19.
Hear, refusal to. Je +*29:19. 44:16. Zc 7:11.
Hear, take heed how you. Lk +*8:18.
Hear, take heed what you. Mk +*4:24.

Hearing, spiritual importance of attentive, selective. Jb +*37:2.

Hearing, true, involves and requires obedience. Lk +*11:28.

Heart:
Voluntary. T#329, 2 S 15:6.
Sometimes divided. T#330, Ps 12:2.
Has moral qualities. T#331, 1 K 8:18.
Its controlling influence. T#332, Pr 4:23.
Sincerity of demanded. T#333, 1 S 16:7.
Divine control of. T#264, 2 Ch 18:31.

Heart, perfect. 2 K +*20:3. 1 Ch 12:38n. Ps 37:18n.

Heart, turn to God with all your. Jl +*2:12.

Heart, whole. Dt +*6:5.

Heathen, are they lost? Ro 2:15n.

Heathen nations as instruments of God's judgment. Is +10:5.

Heathenism described. T#359, 2 K 16:3.

Heave offering, distinguished from wave offering. Ex +29:27n.

Heaven:
A place. T#334, Jn 14:2.
Its pure light. T#335, Ps 36:9.
Its perfect holiness. T#336, Ps 17:5.
Its everlasting rest. T#337, Re 14:13.
Its nearness to God. T#338, Re 22:4.
Its pure happiness. T#339, Ju 24.
Its high rewards. T#340, 1 C 2:9. T#672, Dt 33:9.
Its perpetuity. T#341, Mt 6:20.
Its rewards, unmerited. T#342, Ezk 36:32.

Heaven, the third. Lk 19:12n. 1 C 15:50n. Ep +*1:11n. 1 Th +√4:18n.

Hell:
A place of fire. T#343, Lk 16:24.
Its dreadful misery:
Complete despair, no hope. T#573-1, Jb 8:13.
Bitter reflections. T#573-2, Lk 16:25.
Deprivation of rest. T#573-3, Re 14:11.
Banishment from all lovely beings, and suffering, while saints are rejoicing. T#573-4, Lk 13:28.
Darkness and gloom. T#573-5, Mt 8:12.
Painful fears and terrors. T#573-6, 2 C 5:11.
Enduring the just scorn of the universe forever. T#573-7, Da 12:2.
Pains of body from fire. T#573-8, Lk 16:24.
Its degradation. T#574, T 3:3.

Henry, Matthew. Note on the importance of reading Scripture, 2 Ch 29:7n. Cited, 2 K 21:10n. 2 Ch 29:7n. La 1:12n. He 11:39n.

Heresies. See *Error.* T#176, 1 C 11:19.

Heresy, God's purpose in permitting. 1 C *11:19.

Heretofore, mg. "yesterday, the third day." Jsh +4:18.

Hezekiah's predicament. Is 38:19n.

Hibbard, F. G. *Christian Baptism.* Cited: Ge 6:5n. Ex 12:22n. Mt 28:19n. Ac 8:12n, 36n. He 9:10n.

Hiding from danger, evil. Pr +*22:3.

Hinderer of lawlessness identified. 2 Th 2:7n.

Hinnom, valley of. Jsh +15:8n.

Hinnom, valley of the sons of. Jsh +*15:8n. Ne 2:13n.

His land. Dt +*32:43.

His people. Dt +*32:43.

Hislop, A. *The Two Babylons.* Cited: Ezk 8:14n.

Hittites, Biblical reference to military might of, vindicated. 2 K 7:6n.

Hobart, William Kirk. *The Medical Language of Luke.* Cited: Lk 17:20n. 22:44n, 45n. Ac 12:19n.

Hodge, Charles. Cited: 1 C 6:17n. 7:14n. 10:8n. 12:3n. Ep 6:4n.

Hogg, C. F. Cited: Ro 16:12n. Ga 3:10n.

Hogg, C. F. and Vine. Cited: 1 Th 4:4 (possess), 15n (parousia), 16n (the archangel).

Holiness, value of. T#344, Pr 8:11.

Holiness of God. T#229, Re 15:4. T#230, Ge 6:6.

Holy Spirit. T#345, Lk 3:22.
His divinity. T#346, He 9:14.
His official work. T#347-1, Jb 36:9 (to awaken and convince sinners). T#347-2, 1 S 10:10 (to confer miraculous gifts). T#347-3, Dt 31:19 (to reveal divine truth, as a witness against sinners, and for God and his people). T#347-4, Ga 4:6 (to cause holy affections, which become the "witness of the Spirit" that saints "are the children of God").
Sinning against. T#348, Ep 4:30.
Judicial departure of. T#349, Ge 6:3.
Promised believers. T#350, Lk 11:13.
Outpouring of. T#620, Ps 72:6.
Agency of. T#594, Dt 30:6. T#595, Ac 5:31. T#596, Ps 17:5.

Holy Spirit does not draw attention to Himself. Jn 16:13n.

Holy Spirit omnipotent. Ro +*15:19.

Holy Spirit, an influence. Ge x1:2.

Holy Spirit, an intelligence. Mt 12:32.

Holy Spirit, personality of, proved by (1) the use of the personal pronoun, Jn +*16:13n, 14n. (2) blasphemy against, Mt √12:32n. (3) can be grieved, a verb only predicated of persons, Ep 4:30n. (4) has knowledge, only possible of a person, 1 C 2:11n.

Holy Spirit, proofs he is a person outlined. Lk 3:22n.

Holy Spirit, sin of blasphemy against. Mt √12:31n, 32n.

Holy Spirit, subordinate to the Father and the Son. Jn 16:13n.

Home, keeping at. T#351, T 2:4.

Home fellowships. 1 C 16:19.

Home schooling, father's involvement in and responsibility for, Dt +6:7.

Homer. Le +27:16n. S#2563h, Nu +11:32. Contrast with "omer."

Homonyms, Hebrew, instances/examples of. Is +59:10 (night). Is +60:5 (fear). Je 16:5 (taken away). 31:32 (husband). 49:25 (not left). Jl 2:2 (morning). Am 2:7 (pant). 6:8 (abhor). Jon 2:8 (mercy).

Homosexuality. Le 18:22n.

Honest business practices required. Am +*8:5.

Honesty. Ro +*12:17.

Honesty required. T#629, Pr 21:3.

Honesty, rewards of. T#630, Ps 58:11.

Honesty of saints. T#659, Jn 1:47.

Honey. Dt +8:8.

Honoring God required. T#300, 1 T 1:17.

Hope, earthly. Re +*7:4n.

Hope, eternal, spiritual. Ro +*15:4.

Hope, heavenly. Re +*7:4n.

Hope in God. T#292, Pr 3:5 (required). T#293, Is 26:3 (encouraged, promises). T#294, Jb 13:15 (examples). T#352, 1 P 1:21. T#353, Jb 19:25 (full assurance of).

Horne, Thomas H. *Introduction.* Cited: Is 51:16n.

Hoskier, H. C. *Concerning the Genesis of the Versions of the New Testament.* Cited: Re 5:9. 15:6.

Hospitality, a duty. T#354, T 1:8.

Hospitality, examples of. T#355, Jb 31:32.

Hours, Jewish division into twelve daytime. Jn +*11:9n.

House. Gr. *oikos.* Ac 16:15n.

House churches. 2 J +*10.

House fellowship. Ac 2:46.

House put for *family* (by Metonymy of the Subject, √121J4, Ge +7:1), Ac 16:15n.

Household, baptism of. Ac 16:15n.

Rejected by sinners. T#373, Ps 58:5.
Irony, examples of. T#374, Jg 10:14.
Iscariot, Judas, possible birthplace of. Jsh 15:25n.
Israel, spiritual. Ro 2:29n.
Israel forsaken. Is +*54:7.
Israel of God, the. Ga 6:16.
Israel his inheritance. Is 19:25.
Israel his land. Dt +*32:43.
Israel his people. Dt +*32:43.
Israel not cast away. Is +√41:9. Zc √10:6. Ro +√11:1, 2.
Israel not permanently forsaken. 1 S +*12:22. Is +*60:20. Je +*4:27. Zc *10:6. Ml +*3:6.
Israel regathered. Is +√52:12mg. +*54:7. Zc √10:6.
Israel regathered in unbelief. Zp 2:1.
Israel's final restoration to involve at least a period of forty years. Mi 7:15.
Israel's full restoration not accomplished with the return from the Babylonian captivity, but still future. Is √11:11n.
Israel's severe punishment a sign of its exclusive relationship to God. Am *3:2.
Jealousy. Pr 6:34.
Jehoiachim, fourth year of. Je 45:1n.
Jehovah. Ex 3:15n.
Jehovah, early Christian disciples placed Jesus on a par with. Ac 11:21n.
Jehovah, why this name was not pronounced by Jews. Le 24:16n.
Jehovah titles. Ex +*15:26. Is 60:16.
Jehovah's Witnesses, Alluded to in notes, but unnamed: Le 3:17. Pr 4:18. 18:1. Is 8:20. 43:10. 65:5. Ezk 14:10. 18:4, 20. 32:27. Mt 10:28. Lk 24:16. Jn 1:1, 18. 3:7, 13. 5:18. 10:30. 19:6. 20:25. Ac 2:34. 1 C 15:54. Ga 2:20. Col 1:15.
Jehovah's Witnesses: Answers to Doctrinal Errors. (1) *Bodily resurrection of Christ*, Is 43:10. Da 12:2. Jn 2:19, 21. Ac 2:24, 31, 34. (2) *Trinity*, Is 42:1. Mt +√28:19n. (3) *Deity of Christ*, Col 1:16n. (a) Christ received worship, Mt +*14:33. Jn +*20:29n. Ac +*7:59n. (b) Lesser degrees of worship untenable, Ph 2:6n. (c) Not a lesser "god," Jn +*1:1n. Ph 2:6n. (d) Called God, Jn +√20:28n. (e) Charge of blasphemy for claim to deity, Jn 10:32n. (f) Deity required to qualify as our substitute in the atonement, He 10:4n. (4) *Holy Spirit*, (a) is a person, Mt √12:32n. Lk 3:22n. Jn 16:13n, 14n. Ep +*4:30n. (b) is God, Ac 5:3, 4. (5) *Salvation*. (a) denial of necessity of new birth, Jn 3:7n. (b) division of Body of Christ into more than the one body of Scripture, Ep 4:4n. (c) denial of assurance, Ga 2:20n. 1 J ●√5:13. (6) *The Cross*, Jn 20:25n. (7) *Blood transfusions*, Le 3:17n. (8) *Military Service*, Lk 3:14n. (9) *Political involvement, participation*, Lk 3:14n. 1 Ch +*12:32n. 1 C 7:20. (10) *Absolute pacifism unscriptural*, Lk +*22:36. (11) *Denial of conscious eternal punishment in hell*, Ezk 18:4n. Mt +*25:46. (12) *Immortality of the person*, Ec +*3:19n. Mt +*10:28n. (13) *Conscious existence after death*, Da +*12:2n. Lk +*23:43n. (14) *Doctrine of annihilation foreign to Biblical world view and totally unscriptural*, Mt +*10:28n. Lk 12:5n. 1 C 15:54n. (15) *Wrongfully deny the perspicuity of Scripture*, Is +*8:20n. (16) *Deny right of private judgment*, Ro 14:12. Ga +*1:8n. 2 P 1:20n. (17) *Sustain wrong relationship to followers, as lording it over their faith, contrary to apostolic example*, Mt ●+√24:45. 2 C +√1:24. (18) *Practice wrong mode of Christian baptism*, Col 2:12n. (19) *Deny visible personal re-*

turn of Christ at a future second advent, Jn +*1:51n. Ac +*1:11. (20) *Deny natural Israel's place in unfulfilled Bible prophecy*, Is +√11:11n. +√41:9. +*55:3. 60:21n. Zc √10:6. Ro +*11:1, 2. (21) *The Person of Christ*, (a) wrongly identified as archangel Michael, 1 Th 4:16n. (b) denial of two natures in Christ, 1 Th 4:16n. (c) deny Christ is now a man, 1 Th 4:16n. 1 T *2:5. (d) wrongly limit the extent of the atonement to a "corresponding ransom," whereby Christ as one man substituted for one man only, Adam, 1 T 2:6n. He 10:4n.
Jehovah's Witnesses, doctrine contradicts one body, one hope of Scripture. Ep +*4:4n.
Jehovah's Witnesses, mentioned by name in notes at 1 C 15:50n. Ep 4:4n. Ph 1:23n. Col 1:16n. 1 Th 4:16n. 1 T 2:5n, 6n.
Jehovah's Witnesses, misconceive the qualifications essential to enter the kingdom of God. 1 C 15:50n.
Jehovahs, two, one on earth speaking to the other in heaven. Ge 19:24n.
Jesus, see *Christ*. T#56, Jn 8:50.
Jesus, teachings of, specifically cited by Paul. 1 Th 4:2n.
Jesus Christ. Ro +1:1.
Jesus identifiable as Jehovah. Ne +9:6. Ac 11:21n. 1 P +*2:3n. Re 3:14n.
Jesus indistinguishable from the members of the surrounding crowds. Mk 14:44. Lk +4:30.
"Jesus only" position, mistaken. Ac 2:38n.
Jesus unrecognized. (1) before the resurrection, Mt 26:48. Mk 14:44. Lk +4:30. (2) after the resurrection, Mk *16:12 w Lk +24:16. (3) prophesied, Is +53:2.
Jesus worshipped. Ne +9:6. Re +*5:12.
Jewish evangelists to the world during the Tribulation. Is +*27:6.
Jewish evangelists to the world at the start of the Millennium. Is +*66:19.
Jews:
Numerous. T#375, Ho 1:10.
Their territory. T#376, Jsh 1:4.
Their dispersion. T#377, Ho 9:17.
Their return to Palestine. T#378, Ezk +*34:13.
Obstacles removed. T#379, Is 11:15.
Enlarged possessions. T#380, Is 54:3.
Their future trials. T#381, Zc 10:11.
Their conversion. T#382, Ro 11:26.
Johnson, Samuel. Ac 22:6n.
Jordan, baptism in the region, not water of. Mk 1:9n.
Jordan, edge of. Mt 3:13. Ac 2:38n.
Joy in God required. T#296, 1 Th 5:16.
Jubilee. (1) definition, Le 25:11n. (2) institutional purpose, typical meaning, prophetic significance, Le 25:52n.
Judgment:
General. T#383, Mt 11:24.
Its design. T#384, Ro 2:5.
Its suddenness. T#385, Mt 25:13.
Its final conflagration. T#386, Ps 102:26.
Its final separations. T#387, Mt 25:32.
Its final Judge. T#388, 2 T 4:1.
Its particular disclosures. T#389, Ec 12:14.
Its final decisions. T#390, Lk 16:26.
Judgment, instruments of God's, heathen nations as. Is +10:5.
Judgments of Scripture. Mt +*10:15n.
Judicial visitations. T#349, Ge 6:3. T#497, 1 S 3:13.
Judith baptized resting on the edge of a fountain. Ac 2:38n.
Justice, absolute, of God. Ge +18:25.

Justice, vindicative. T#236, Ro 11:22. T#237, Dt 32:43.

Justice of God. T#232, Ps 33:5.

Justice required. Le +*19:15.

Justice and equity required. T#629, Pr 21:3.

Justice towards servants required. T#679, Col 4:1.

Justification by faith. T#583, 1 J 2:12.

Kay, William. *The Psalms with Notes*. Cited: Ps 37:18n. Ps 83, title, 10n, 12n. 146:4n.

Keeler, R.F. *Christian Baptism*. Cited: Ac 8:38n.

Kind, after his. Ge +1:11. Dt +14:13.

Kindness required. T#354, T 1:8 (hospitality). T#610, Pr 28:23 (in faithful reproof). T#715, Mt 25:35 (to strangers). Ep 4:32.

Kingdom, theocratic, Sinai possible site of reorganization at Second Advent, Dt +*33:2.

Kingdom of Christ. T#83, Ps 2:6.

Kingdom on earth, not in heaven. Re +*5:10.

Kingdom not present, but future. 2 T +*4:1n.

Kingdom of God, sometimes confused with the sovereignty of God. 1 C 15:50n.

Kingdom of heaven identical to kingdom of God. 1 C 15:50n.

Kingdom of heaven is not heaven, or in heaven, but from heaven. 2 T +*4:18n.

Kingdom of heaven will be upon earth. 2 T +*4:18n. Re +*5:10.

Knew, used of conjugal intimacy. Ge +4:1.

Knowledge:
   Required. T#391, Pr 8:10.
   Benefits of. T#392, Pr 16:22.
   Essential to true love. T#393, Ph 1:9.
   Admits of certainty. T#394, Jn 6:69.
   How attained. T#395, Ja 1:5.
   To be imparted. T#396, Mt 5:19.
   Of ourselves required. T#397, La 3:40.
   More perfect hereafter. T#398, Jn 13:7.
   Intuitive. T#206, Ro 1:19. T#420, Lk 12:57.

Kuyper, Abraham. *The Work of the Holy Spirit*. Cited: 1 Th 5:23n.

Labor/management relations, Biblical guidelines for. Lk 16:1n. 1 T +*5:18n.

Laidlaw, John. *Biblical Doctrine of Man*. Cited: Ps 30:12n. Mt 27:50n.

Land covenanted to Israel never yet possessed. 1 K 4:21n.

Land of the living. Ps 27:13.

Language of appearance used by Scripture, rather than scientific language. 2 S 22:8n (♪121Q3).

Lardner. Cited: Ro 15:19n.

Last day, the. Jn +*6:54n.

Last trumpet, the. 1 C 15:52n.

Laughter and mirth. T#479, Pr 14:13.

Laver, not used for immersion. 1 K 7:23n.

Law, division into ceremonial and moral not technically a Biblical distinction. Ga 3:10n.

Law, use of term without the Greek article. Ro +*4:15n. Ga 3:10n.

Law of double reference. Ho +11:1. Mt +16:23.

Law of God. T#280, Ps 22:28. T#281, Ex 20:1. T#282, Ex 19:10. T#283, Ga 5:14. T#284, Is 42:21. T#285, Mt 5:48. T#286, Ro 7:12. T#287, Ja 1:15.

Law of Moses, appealed to by Paul as the ground of his instruction in matters of New Testament church order. 1 C 14:34n.

Law of Moses extant and well known. 2 K *14:6n. 22:8n. Je 2:8n.

Law of prophetic double reference. Ho 11:1.

Law of prophetic perspective. Is 61:2n.

Laying on of hands. T#399, Re 1:17.

In working miracles. T#400, Mk 16:18.
In giving charges. T#401, 1 T 5:22.

Laziness. Je +*48:10. Ezk +*16:49. Mt 25:26.

Leaven, symbolism of. Le 23:17n. Mt 13:33n.

Leeser, Isaac. Cited: Ge 49:10n. Pr 18:1n. Is 45:11n. Je 37:12.

Left hand, position of less favor, etc. Ge +48:13.

Letter changes (Hebrew) affecting meanings of words, etc. 2 K 11:6n. 1 Ch 2:7 (where "Achan" is purposely respelled to draw attention to the resultant meaning, "trouble"). 6:70n.

Letters, elision of (Hebrew), source of variation of spelling and sound of the same or similar names. 1 Ch 26:24. 2 Ch 24:1n. Ezr 2:10n, 44n. Ne 11:10n. 12:5n.

Letters, mutation of (Hebrew). Ezr 2:45n. Ne 7:31n, 52n, 58n.

Letters, transposition of (Hebrew). 1 Ch 25:23n. 2 Ch 2:8n. 22:6n.

Letters, similar Hebrew, mistaken for each other. Ps 22:16n.

Levites, officially constituted teachers of the law. 1 Ch 25:7n, 8n. 26:32n. 2 Ch +15:3. 35:3n. 1 C 14:34n.

Levity, sinful. T#479, Pr 14:13.

Lewdness. Ezk +*22:9. Ho +6:9.
   Frequent. T#402, Je 9:2.
   Deceitful and alluring. T#403, Pr 5:3.
   Sinful and forbidden. T#404, Ac 15:20.
   Guilt and condemnation of. T#405, He 13:4.

Liberality. T#406, Mt 10:8 (duty of). T#407, Ac 10:4 (examples of). T#408, Lk 6:38 (rewards of).

Liberty, civil. Je +*34:8.

Licentiousness. T#402, Je 9:2.

Liddon, H.P. *The Divinity of Our Lord*. Cited: Ac 7:59n.

Life. Lk +10:25 (S#222g, Gr. *zoe*).

Lifespan shortened. Is +*38:10.

Light, sinning against. T#309, Jn 3:19.

Light, speed of. Ps 139:9n.

Light of nature. T#207, Ps 75:1.

Lightfoot. Cited: Col 2:8n.

Lightning. (1) S#216h, Jb 37:3. (2) *S#1300h, Jb +38:35. (3) *S#2385h, Jb +38:25. (4) *S#3940h, Jb +41:19. (5) *S#7565h, *S#7565h, Dt +32:24. Ps *78:48mg.

Limited atonement, Calvinistic doctrine of is not in accord with the clear assertions of Scripture. 1 T 2:6n.

Lip. Heb. put for "shore," "bank," "brim," etc. S#8193h. Jg +7:22mg. 1 K 9:26.

Litotes. Ge 18:27n. Lk 11:4n.

Local deities, pagan belief in. 1 K 20:23n.

Loneliness. He +*13:5.

Long life (longevity) promised. Dt +*5:16. Ps +*91:16mg.

Long time to intervene between first and second coming of Christ. Mt +*25:19.

Longsuffering of God. T#227, Ro 2:4.

Lord of hosts. Ex 15:26n. 1 S +1:3. Ps +24:10. Is +44:6.

Lord's day, worship on, changed from seventh to the first day of the week. 1 C 16:2n.

Lord's Supper. T#104, 1 C 11:33.

Lordship of Christ. Ac +*10:36.

Lot, casting. Jsh +*14:2n. 1 Ch 24:5. 25:8. Ne 11:1. Ps 22:18. 125:3. Ezk 21:21n. 45:1. Jl 3:3. Mi 2:5.

Love. T#413, Ga 5:14 (disinterested). T#414, Lk 10:33 (examples of). T#415, Mk 10:30 (rewards of).

Love of Christ. T#60, Mt 14:14 (to mankind). T#370, Re 22:17. T#371, Is 1:18. T#372, Lk 19:42.

Love of God. T#94, Ep 5:25 (to Zion, to church). T#224, Ps 119:68 (benevolent). T#585, Jb 36:7 (merciful). T#672, Dt 33:9 (to saints).

Love to brethren required. T#111, Ac 4:32.
Love to God. T#288, Ju 21. T#409, Mt 22:37 (our primary duty). T#410, Ps 99:9 (reasons for). T#411, Ps 106:13 (often spurious).
Love to man. T#412, 1 Th 3:12.
Lowliness of Christ. T#62, Mt 11:29.
Lowliness required. T#482, Ph 2:3.
Loyalty, political, resisting influences detrimental to. 2 S +*15:6.
Lucas, Jerry and Del Washburn, *Theomatics*. Re 13:17n.
Luck. See entry for *Chance* in this Index. Ge +*24:44n.
Lying:
   Prevalent. T#416, Jn 8:44.
   Forbidden. T#417, Col 3:9.
   Offensive to God. T#418, Pr 19:9.
Lyttelton, George. Ac 22:6n.
Maiden (also rendered "damsel"). *S#5291h. Ge +24:14 (damsel).
Majesty of God. 1 Ch +*29:11.
Mammon. Mt 6:24.
Man, constituent elements of. Nu 27:16n. Ro 8:10n. 1 Th 5:23n.
Man, frailty of. Ps 103:14.
Man, principal Hebrew and Greek words used for. Da 3:1n.
Management style, Biblical. 1 K +*12:7.
Man's:
   Common origin. T#419, Ac 17:26.
   Power of intuition. T#420, Lk 12:57.
   Power of reason. T#421, Ezk 12:2.
   Immortality. T#422, 2 T 1:10.
"Many" an idiom which signifies "all." Mt +*26:28n.
Marchbanks, John B. *Great Doctrines Relating to Salvation*. Cited: Col 2:13n.
Marriage. T#423, He 13:4. T#424, 2 C 6:14 (directions respecting). T#425, T 2:4 (its mutual duties). T#426, 1 T 3:2 (forbids polygamy). T#427, Lk 16:18 (forbids divorce).
Marriage approved. Ge 2:18.
Marriage customs. Ge +21:21. +24:57. Ex +2:21. Nu +12:1. +36:6.
Marriage disparaged. 1 C 7:1.
Marriage standards/qualifications: Christians are to marry only Christians. 1 C *7:39. 14:35n. 2 C √6:14.
Marriage standards/qualifications: Christian girls to marry husband capable of exercising the spiritual leadership of the home. 1 C *14:35n.
Martin, Ralph P. *Worship in the Early Church*. Cited: Ro 6:4n.
Massada. 1 S 23:19n.
Materialism. Pr ◐15:16 (alternative to). Ezk 16:49 (root sin of Sodom). Ezk 33:31 (hinders response and obedience to God's Word). Am 3:10 (blinds ability to do right). Mt 13:22 and Lk 8:14 (chokes the Word, and it becomes unfruitful). Lk 12:15 (beware of covetousness). 1 T 6:5-11 (mistaken notion that gain is godliness). He 13:5 (follow alternative lifestyle devoid of covetousness).
Materialist theory of man's constitution, alluded to. Ge 25:8n. 37:35n. Ps 16:10n. Ec 3:19n. Ezk 18:20n. 32:21n, 27n. Zc 12:1n. Mt √10:28n. 1 C 15:56n.
McClintock and Strong. *Encyclopedia*. Cited: Am 5:16n. Hab 2:15n. Ac 8:26n.
Means of grace:
   Means and instruments of appointed. T#428, Mk 4:14.
   Use of indispensable. T#429, Ac 27:31.
   Preaching, the principal. T#430, 1 C 1:17.
   Use of encouraged. T#431, Ps 126:5.
   Success in using. T#432, 1 C 4:15.

Superiority of the true. T#433, Lk 16:31.
   Made effectual by God's omnipotence. T#434, 2 T 2:25.
   Their effects, different. T#435, He 4:2.
   Use of sometimes hopeless. T#436, Mt 7:6.
Means and ends connected. T#257, 2 Th 2:13.
Meat offering. Le +*23:13.
Mediation, instance of wise. 2 S 20:16-22.
Meditation exemplified. T#665, Ps 1:2.
Meekness:
   Required. T#437, Ga 6:1.
   Encouraged. T#438, Mt 5:5.
   Examples of. T#439, Ac 7:59.
   Of Christ. T#62, Mt 11:29.
   Of saints. T#660, Mt 10:16.
Meeting, appointed place of. Dt 12:14.
Megiddo. Jsh +17:11.
Mercy. Mi 6:8.
Mercy of God. T#233, Jon 4:2.
Meshech. Is 66:19n.
Messianic prophecy, first. Ge +*3:15.
Messianic prophecy, First Advent. Ge +*3:15. See Topic Number Index, T#1874-1976.
Messianic prophecy, Second Advent. Is 11:11n.
Messianic prophecies, fulfilled. See T#1874-1976.
Metzger, Bruce. *A Textual Commentary on the Greek New Testament*. Cited: Jn 1:18n. Col 4:15n. Re 15:6n.
Middleton on *The Doctrine of the Greek Article*, cited. Mt 27:54n. Ro 4:15n.
Mighty man of valor. Jg +6:12. 2 S +2:7mg. 1 Ch 26:6n.
Military service, not forbidden by Scripture. Lk 3:14n.
Military service not forbidden to Christians. Lk 3:14n.
Millennial sacrifices, Is +56:7. Je 33:18n. Ezk 40:38.
Millennial temple, Is 2:2. 60:13n. 66:1. Ezk +*37:26. 40:2n. Jl 2:1. Mi 4:1, 2. Hg 2:7. Zc *1:16. √6:12, 13.
Millennium:
   On earth. T#440, Re 20:4.
   Its holiness. T#441, Is 60:21.
   Its peace and unity. T#442, Ps 37:11.
   Its light and knowledge. T#443, He 8:11.
   Its general prosperity. T#444, Is 35:2.
   Its great enjoyment. T#445, Is 35:10.
   Contrasted with former times. T#446, Ac 3:21.
Mind, one. Ro 15:5n. 1 C +*1:10.
Minister's duties:
   To take heed to themselves. T#369, Pr 31:4. T#457, Mt 10:16.
   To preach faithfully. T#458, Mt 28:19.
   To be inoffensive. T#459, Mt 17:27.
   To be fearless. T#460, Ph 1:20.
   To point out sins. T#461, 1 Th 5:20.
   To discriminate. T#462, Ml 3:18.
   To pray for others. T#463, Je 23:2.
   To be devoted to the calling. T#464, 1 T 4:15.
Ministerial calling:
   Responsibleness. T#465, 1 T 1:11.
   Temptations: T#466-1, 2 T 4:3 (to please their hearers). T#466-2, Ac 4:18 (to avoid the frowns of the influential). T#466-3, Is 30:10 (to conceal the true God). T#466-4, Am 2:12 (to countenance popular errors, delusions and vices).
   Trials. T#467, 2 T 3:12.
   Success in preaching. T#468, 1 T 4:16. T#469, Ac 13:46.
   Rewards. T#470, Ezk 3:8.
   Demands prayer and sympathy. T#471, 1 Th 5:25.
   Pecuniary support. T#472, Ga 6:6.

Ministerial parity. T#101, Je 3:15.
Ministerial support, grounds of. 1 C 9:7n.
Ministers of Satan:
    Very numerous. T#473, 1 J 4:1.
    Very deceitful. T#474, Mt 7:15.
    Cruel and dangerous. T#475, Ac 20:29.
    Much sought after. T#476, Jn 5:43.
    To be avoided. T#477, Mt 15:14.
    Ruin themselves and others. T#478, Mt 15:14.
Ministry:
    Design of. T#447, Ep 4:11.
    Divinely appointed. T#448, Lk 10:1.
    Call to preach. T#449, He 5:4.
    Ordination of ministers. T#450, Mk 3:14.
    Pre-mosaic priesthood. T#451, Ex 3:1.
    Primitive preaching. T#452, Ac 17:2.
    Qualifications for. T#453, 1 C 4:2.
    Expressive names of. T#454, 2 C 5:20.
    Authority of. T#455, 2 C 10:8. T#456, 1 P 5:3.
Ministry, one-another. 1 P 4:10.
Miracles, prove the Bible. T#43, Mk 16:20.
Mirth and laughter. T#479, Pr 14:13.
Misconceiving God's character vitiates fruitfulness. Mt
    +*25:24n.
Missions appointed. T#480, Mk 16:15.
Missions encouraged. T#481, Ac 28:28.
Mitchell, Margaret. *Gone with the Wind*. Re 13:17n.
Mizpeh. Ge 31:49. Jsh +11:3n.
Mocking. Ge +21:9.
Modest apparel. 1 T 2:9.
Modesty required. T#482, Ph 2:3.
Modesty in good works. T#483, Mt 6:1.
Modesty of Christ. T#62, Mt 11:29.
Molech, human sacrifices made to. Le +*18:21. Jsh
    15:8n. Ho 13:2mg.
Money
    Brass introduced as, by the Romans. Mt 10:9.
    Changing of, a trade. Mt 21:12. Jn 2:15.
    Custom of presenting a piece of. Jb 42:11.
    Gold and silver used as. Ge 13:2. Nu 22:18.
    Jews forbidden to take usury for. Le 25:37.
    Love of, the root of all evil. 1 T 6:10.
    Of the Jews, regulated by the standard of the sanctu-
        ary. Le 5:15. Nu 3:47.
    Of the Romans, stamped with the image of Caesar.
        Mt 22:20, 21.
    Pieces of, Mentioned
        Farthing. Mt 5:26. Lk 12:6.
        Fourth of a shekel. 1 S 9:8.
        Gerah, the twentieth of a shekel. Nu 3:47.
        Half shekel or bekah. Ex 30:15.
        Mite. Mk 12:42. Lk 21:2.
        Penny. Mt 20:2. Mk 6:37.
        Pound. Lk 19:13.
        Shekel of silver. Jg 17:10. 2 K 15:20.
        Talent of gold. 1 K 9:14. 2 K 23:33.
        Talent of silver. 1 K 16:24. 2 K 5:22, 23.
        Third of a shekel. Ne 10:32.
    Power and usefulness of. Ec 7:12. 10:19.
    Usually taken by weight. Ge 23:16. Je 32:10.
    Was current with the merchants. Ge 23:16.
    Was given
        As alms. 1 S 2:36. Ac 3:3, 6.
        As offerings. 2 K 12:7-9. Ne 10:32.
        As wages. Ezr 3:7. Mt 20:2. Ja 5:4.
        For lands. Ge 23:9. Ac 4:37.
        For merchandize. Ge 43:12. Dt 2:6.
        For slaves. Ge 37:28. Ex 21:21.
        For tribute. 2 K 23:33. Mt 22:19.

Money. See related topics: acceptable sacrifices involve
    personal cost, almsgiving, avarice, beneficence, be-
    nevolence, borrowing, bribery, business responsi-
    bilities (T#1821-1873), causes of the ungodly not
    to be supported, charity, covetousness, debt, dili-
    gence, economy required, employer-employee rela-
    tionships, extortion, extravagance, financial plan-
    ning—wisdom of, financial responsibilities—
    priorities in, financial secrecy in giving, firstfruits,
    fiscal accountability of church officers, forethought,
    frugality, gain—unjust, gambling, generosity, giv-
    ing, greed, honest business practices required, in-
    terest, laziness, liberality, mammon, management
    style—Biblical, materialism, ministerial support—
    grounds of, money—how used by Christ, national
    debt, offerings, oppression of poor and needy forbid-
    den, parsimony, poor, poverty curse, poverty of
    the righteous, prosperity, prudence, restitution,
    riches, slothfulness, stewardship, support—pecuni-
    ary of ministry, suretiship, stealing, taxes, theft,
    tithe, usury, wage, wages, wealth.
Money, how used by Christ. Jn 4:8n.
Monogamy. Jg 21:23n.
Moon, new, feast of. 2 Ch +2:4.
Mooney, S. C. *Usury: Destroyer of Nations*. Ge 31:15n.
    Dt 23:20n.
Moral agency of God. T#208, Ps 7:11.
Moral agency of mankind. T#271, Dt 30:19.
Moral evils controlled. T#267, Dt 2:30.
Moral government. T#302, Ps 19:11. T#303, Ps 34:16.
Moral inability. T#166, Pr 5:22.
Moral necessity. T#271, Dt 30:19.
Morning, resurrection and the. Ps +*49:14.
Morning star. 2 P +*1:19. Re +*2:28.
Mosaic authorship affirmed, Ex +√24:4.
Mosaic law not differentiated in Scripture into moral
    and ceremonial law. Ga 3:10n.
Mosaic writings, well known and extant when 2 Kings
    was written. 2 K *14:6n. 22:8n. Ho 9:9n. Am 4:5n.
Mosaic writings, frequently cited in the Prophets. Is
    1:2n. Je +*1:5.
Most high, (name of God). Ps +*7:17. +77:10.
Mother put for grandmother. 1 K +15:10mg,n. 2 Ch
    15:16mg.
Moulton, James Hope, and George Milligan. *A Vocabu-
    lary of the Greek Testament*. Cited: Mk 2:22n.
    1 Th 4:15n.
Much water. Jn +*3:23.
Mulberry trees. 2 S √5:23n. 2 K 18:17n. 1 Ch √14:15n.
Munck, Johannes. *Christ and Israel*: An Interpretation
    of Romans 9-11. Cited: Ro 11:25n.
Murder. Mt 19:18.
Murmuring (complainers). Nu +11:1. Ps 144:14. Is
    +*29:24. 58:13. Ph √2:14. Ju +*16.
Murmurs of sinners. T#700, Ju 16.
Musical instruments. (1) cymbals, 1 Ch +13:8. (2) harps,
    1 Ch 13:8n. Da 3:15n. (3) psalteries (viols or lutes),
    Am +5:22 (S#5053h). (4) tabret, Ezk +28:13. (5)
    timbrel, Ex +15:20n. (6) trumpets, 2 Ch +5:12.
Musical instruments, used in worship. 1 Ch 16:42n. Ne
    12:36.
Musical instruments, used in New Testament worship,
    Ep 5:19n.
Muster (military). 1 S +11:8.
Mystery doctrines of the New Testament listed. Ro
    16:25n.
Mystery of Providence. T#275, Ro 11:33.
Nails (plural), proof Christ was executed on a traditional
    cross, not a single upright "torture stake." Jn 20:25n.

Numbers, special use of. (1) once, Ps 89:35. (2) once, twice. Jb +40:5n. (3) three...four, Am +1:3n. (4) *five* favored in Egypt, Ge +43:34n. (5) *seven,* used as a "round, sacred number," Jb 2:13; 5:19n. Used as "any indefinite number," Jb 5:19n. Used to denote "many times" or "frequently" in the phrase "seven times," Ps 119:164n. (6) *ten,* used for "any number of," 1 S 1:8n. Ne 4:12. Jb 19:3. Jb +40:5n.

Numbers, symbolism of. **two.** (1) the number of testimony, Dt 17:6. (2) confirmation, Ge +22:15. *41:32. (3) distinguishing truth from error, Dt +14:6n. (4) fellowship, Le +*23:17. **three.** in reference to resurrection on the *third* day, Ge +22:4. 1 C +*15:4. **three and one half.** Lk 4:25n. **six.** Da 3:1n. **seven.** Ge 21:+28, 31. Mt 18:22n. **eight.** Mi 5:5n. Lk 24:1n. **twelve.** Ge +14:4. **thirteen.** Ge +14:4. 17:25. 1 Ch 10:10 (Dagon occurs 13 times in Scripture). Re 13:17n. **forty.** Jon +3:4n. **one hundred forty-four thousand.** Re 7:4n.

Oath (*S#7621h), Ne +10:29.

Oath, inviolability of. Nu +*30:2n. Jg +*11:◐31n, 35. Ezk 17:18n.

Oaths of confirmation. T#720, He 6:16.

Obedience accompanies salvation. He +*5:9.

Obedience associated with hearing God's voice. Ex 15:26. Zc 6:15.

Obedience brings blessing. Ge 22:18. Dt *28:1, 2.

Obedience of children to parents. T#53, Ep 6:1.

Obedience of Christ. T#57, Mt 3:17.

Obedience to Christ. He +*5:9.

Obedience to God, evidence of piety. T#602, Ps 119:6.

Obedience to magistrates enjoined. T#313, Dt 16:18.

Obedience marks true believers. Lk +*6:46. 1 J +*2:3.

Obedience our title to pardon and life. T#302, Ps 19:11.

Obedience required. Zc +*6:15.

Obedience to law, Christian obligation of. Ac 16:37n.

Obeisance. 2 Ch +29:28.

Objections against God. T#272, Ezk 33:20.

Objectors reproved. T#273, Ro 9:20.

Obligation denied. T#705, Ps 12:4.

Obscurity, intentional, used by Paul. 1 C 15:24n. 2 Th 2:7n. He 12:27n.

Occult and pagan practices: (1) Asherah, Dt 16:21. 2 K 21:3n. Is +*66:17n. (2) Astrologers, Is 47:13. (3) Astrologers, astrology, Is 47:13n. (4) Baal, 2 K +23:4. (5) Charmer, *S#2267h, Is +47:12. Dt *18:11. (6) Divination, *S#7081h, Pr +16:10mg. (7) Diviners, *S#7080h, Is +44:25. (7) Enchantments, *S#5172h, Ge +30:27. 2 K +21:6. Is +47:12 (*S#2267h, charmer). (8) Familiar spirits, Dt +*18:11. 2 K +21:6. (9) Fire, passing through, 2 K +21:6. (10) Green tree, 2 K 16:4n. +17:10. (11) Groves, 2 K +17:10. 21:3n. 23:6. (12) High hill, 2 K 16:4n. +17:10. (13) High places, 2 K +21:3. (14) Hills, 2 K 16:4n. +17:10. (14) Horoscopes, Is 47:13n. (15) Host of heaven, 2 K +21:3. (16) Idols, 2 K +23:24. (17) Images (carved or graven), 2 Ch +34:3. (18) Images (molten), 2 Ch +34:3. (19) Images, Heb. statues, or, standing pillars, 2 K +17:10. (20) Images, lit. sun images, Le +26:30. (21) Images. or, teraphim. Ge +*31:19mg,n. 2 K +23:24. (22) Oak trees, used in idolatry, groves. Is +*57:5mg. (23) Observed times, lit. observed clouds, 2 K +21:6. (24) Phallic worship, Is +66:17n. Ezk +16:17n. (25) Planets, 2 K 23:5n. (26) Saturn, Am 5:26. (27) Sodomites, 2 K +23:7. (28) Soothsayers, Is +2:6. (28) Sorceries, sorcerers, Is +47:12 (*S#3785h). Ml +3:5 (*S#3784h). (29) Totem pole, Is 66:17n. (30) Twelve signs, 2 K 23:5mg,n. (31) Witchcraft, 2 Ch +33:6. (32) Wizards, Dt +*18:11. 2 K +21:6. (33) Zodiac, 2 K +23:5n. Ec 1:6n. Is 47:13n.

Occult and pagan practices, deities, etc., to be avoided. Je +*10:2.

Offence to be avoided. T#459, Mt 17:27.

Offerings. (1) burnt, Le +*23:12. (2) drink, Le +*23:13. (3) meat, Le +*23:13. (4) peace, Le +*23:19. (5) sin, Le +*23:19. (6) trespass, Le +*5:6. (7) wave, Le +*23:15. (8) freewill, Le +*23:38. (9) heave, Ex 29:27n. Ezr +8:25. (10) whole burnt, Ps 51:19.

Offspring, numerous. Ge +29:31. Ps +127:3. See also "families, large," 1 Ch +25:5; "fruitfulness (in bearing children)," Ge +29:31.

Olam, Heb. "for ever," etc. S#5769h, Ex +12:24.

Old age, reverence or honor for. Le +*19:32.

Old man. Ge 43:27.

Old Testament Scripture authoritative in matters of doctrine and practice for the New Testament church. 1 Th 4:2n.

Omnipotence of God the Father. Re +*19:6.

Omnipotence of God the Holy Spirit. Ro +*15:19.

Omnipotence of God the Son. 1 C +*1:24.

"One," Heb. *echad,* S#259h, Dt +6:4n.

One-another ministry. 1 P 4:10.

One-another relationships. Ro +12:5.

Only. Ge 22:2. Ps 22:20mg.

Only begotten. Mk 3:31n. Lk +7:12. Jn 3:16n.

"Open places," lit. rendering of Hebrew for A.V. "streets," S#7339h, Am +5:16n.

Ophir. 1 K +9:28n. 2 Ch +8:18n.

Opportunity. Pr 1:24. He 2:3.

Opposition to Christ. T#85, Is 53:3. T#86, Is 24:5.

Opposition to God. T#740, Jn 17:14.

Opposition to ministers. T#467, 2 T 3:12.

Opposition to saints. T#511, Ps 42:10. T#740, Jn 17:14.

Oppression:
  Examples of ancient. T#488, Ezk 22:29.

Effects of. T#489, Pr 21:7.
Displeasing to God. T#490, Jb 27:13.
Infatuates oppressors. T#491, Ec 7:7.
Threats against. T#523, Ps 12:5.
Oppression of poor and needy forbidden. Dt +*24:14.
Ps +*12:5. Ezk +*16:49.
Oracle, name of the sanctuary or holy of holies. 1 K
6:16n.
Ordeal, trial by. Nu 5:17n.
Ordinances of the gospel. T#104, 1 C 11:23. T#105,
1 C 5:8. T#106, Ps 27:4. T#107, Is 44:5.
Ordination of ministers. T#450, Mk 3:14.
Ornaments in dress. T#173, 1 T 2:9.
Ostentation exemplified. T#703, Lk 16:15.
Orphans, instances of. Ge +11:28.
Overcoming evil with good. T#737, Pr 16:7.
Over-eating, reproved. Ph +*3:19.
Overstatement. Ge +√7:19 (√102, hyperbole/overstate-
ment). 1 K √18:10. 2 K *20:13. Mt *5:29.
Pacifism, absolute, unscriptural. Lk +*22:36.
Palanquins. SS 3:9. Is 66:20n.
Paley, William. Cited: Is 58:13n. Ac +*12:12n. 19:31.
Panic. 1 K 20:20n.
Panin, Ivan. *Bible Chronology*, cited. Je 45:1n.
Panin, Ivan. Re 13:17n.
Parental consent. 1 S 18:20, 21. 1 C *7:36-38.
Parental duties:
To set good examples. T#492, Ps 101:2.
To instruct and govern children. T#493, Pr 22:6.
To chastise for disobedience. T#494, Pr 13:24.
To correct children. Pr 23:13.
To encourage and comfort children. 1 Th 2:11.
To invest quality time with children. Pr 29:15.
To protect children. He 11:23.
To provide for children. T#495, 2 C 12:14.
To reprove children. Pr 29:15.
To teach children. Ex +*13:8. Dt +*6:7.
Happy result of faithfulness. T#496, Pr 22:6.
Sad result of unfaithfulness. T#497, 1 S 3:13.
Parental favoritism. Ge +44:30. 2 S 13:21n.
Parental permissiveness. 1 S 3:13.
Parental support by children. 1 T 5:8.
Parity, ministerial. T#101, Je 3:15.
Parousia (S#3952g), Mt 24:3n. 1 Th 4:15n.
Parsimony. Pr 11:24.
Partial rapture alluded to. 1 Th 1:10n. 4:13n.
Partiality forbidden. Le +*19:15. T#526, Le 25:35.
Passing through fire in human sacrifice to Molech. Le
+*18:21. Dt +*18:10. Jsh 15:8n.
Past tense used of the future. √96C2, Ge 45:9.
Patience, a grace of the righteous. Ro +*15:4.
Patience of Christ. T#62, Mt 11:29.
Patience required. T#498, Ja 1:4.
Patriotism of Jeremiah. Je 40:6n.
Paul, citation of teachings of Jesus by. 1 Th 4:2n.
Paul not antinomian. 1 C 14:34n.
Paul not mistaken about the timing of the Second Coming
of Christ. 1 Th 4:15n.
Paul's use of Mosaic law as his ground of authority in
his directions regarding New Testament church or-
der. 1 C 14:34n.
Paul's use of words of Jesus's pre-cross earthly ministry
as authoritative for doctrine and practice. 1 Th 4:2n.
Peace, false. Ezk 13:10.
Peace in believing. T#666, Ph 4:7.
Peace offering. Le +*23:19.
Peace required. T#499, He 12:14.
Peace with God. T#582, He 2:17.
Peacemakers, false. T#500, Je 6:14.

Peer pressure, youth subject to. 2 Ch 13:7.
Penalty:
Of the law. T#287, Ja 1:15.
Of the gospel. T#309, Jn 3:19.
Of civil laws. T#315, Ge 9:5. T#316, Ex 21:15.
Of disobeying parents. T#494, Pr 13:24.
Perfect heart. 2 K +*20:3. 1 Ch 12:38n. Ps 37:18n.
Perfection. Ps +119:1 (T#504).
Duty of. T#501, 2 C 7:1.
Pledged in covenants. T#502, Ne 10:29.
Of saints. T#503, 1 C 2:6. T#504, Ps 119:1.
Of true love. T#505, Ps 119:3.
Millennial. T#506, Dt 30:6.
Inconstancy of, in saints. T#507, 1 J 1:8.
United with trials. T#508, Re 3:19. T#509, He 12:10.
In pretence. T#510, Pr 30:12.
Permissiveness, parental. 1 S 3:13.
Perpetuation of the race, eternal. 2 P 3:13n.
Persecution:
Of the righteous. T#511, Ps 42:10.
Of Christ. T#68, Ps 2:2.
Of faithful ministers. T#467, 2 T 3:12.
Followed by triumph. T#512, 2 T 2:12.
Persecutors humbled. T#513, Je 20:11.
Perseverance. T#514, Col 1:23.
Perseverance divinely promised. T#515, Jn 10:28.
Perseverance prayed for by Christ. T#516, Ro 8:34.
Perseverance sealed by the Spirit. T#517, 2 C 1:22.
Person, discontinuity of, fatal flaw in Jehovah Witness
identification of Jesus as the archangel Michael.
1 Th 4:16n.
Person, discontinuity of, fatal flaw in materialist view
of resurrection. Mt 10:28n.
Personal Christian Work. Ps 107:2. Pr 11:30. Da 12:3.
Ja 5:20.
Personality of the Holy Spirit proved by (1) use of per-
sonal pronoun, Jn +*16:13n, 14n. (2) possibility
and nature of blasphemy against, Mt √12:32n. (3)
certain actions are ascribed to Him which can only
be attributed to persons, Ep 4:30. (4) for an outline
of proofs He is a person, see Lk 3:22n.
Personnel relations, Biblical guidelines for proper. 1 T
5:19n.
Perspicuity of Scripture. Ps +102:18 (T#49). Pr +*8:9.
Is +*8:20n. Je +*23:28n. Da +*11:33n. Lk +12:57
(T#420). Jn 16:13n. Ac 8:31n. Ga 1:8n. 2 P 1:20n.
Pestilence. Ezk 24:16n. +38:22.
Peters, George N. H. *The Theocratic Kingdom.* Cited:
Ge 49:10n. Ps 27:13n.· 149:5n. Is 26:15n. 60:5n.
60:21n. Je 33:18n. Ezk 20:36n. Mi 7:15n. Mt 16:27n,
28n. Mk 1:2n. Lk 17:21n, 37n. Jn 18:36n. Ro 14:17n.
1 C 15:24n, 50n 1 Th 4:16n, 17n. 2 Th 2:8n. 1 T
2:15n. He 9:28n. 12:28n. 2 P 3:12n. 2 J 7n. Re
11:17n. 12:5n.
Peters, George N.H., *The Theocratic Kingdom*, Materially influenced the selection of references and the
addition of explanatory notes for the following passages. Dt +*33:2. Is 40:31. Mt +*5:5. Lk +*12:32n.
+*16:16n. 17:20. 21:36. 22:29, 30. Jn 1:51. +*14:2n,
3. +*18:36. Ac 1:6n, 7n. +√3:19-21. +*7:5n. 8:16n.
1 C 15:24n. Ep +*1:11n. Col 1:13n. 2 T +*4:1n,
18n. He +*11:16n. 1 P +*1:4n. 2 P +*3:7, 13n.
Re +*5:10. 10:7n.
Petra. 2 K 14:7n. Je 49:16n. Ezk 35:9n. Ob +*3.
Piety, evidence of. T#602, Ps 119:6.
Piety in early life. T#55, 1 S 3:8.
Pillar and altar in Egypt, Millennial. Is 19:19n.
Pillar of cloud. Ex +*13:21.
Pink, A.W. Cited: Le 23:17n. Is 53:7n.

Pit. (1) S#875h, *be-er*, Ge 16:14. (2) *S#953h, *bor*, Ge +37:20. Is +14:19. (3) S#6354h, *pachath*, 2 S 17:9. (4) S#7585h, *sheol*, Ge +37:35n. (5) S#5421g, *phrear*, Lk 14:5.

Pity, divine, to the poor. T#522, Ps 140:12.

Place, God's appointed, as for worship. Ge 22:3. Dt 12:14. +*16:16. Jsh *22:11, 16, 21-29.

Plain. Zc +7:7 (S#8219h).

Pleasure. Pr 21:17.

Pleasures, mirthful. T#479, Pr 14:13.

Pleasures, sensual. T#675, 1 P 2:11.

Plural of majesty, instances of. ♪96F2, Ge +4:10. Is 16:8. 44:27. 50:2. 58:11mg.

Politeness and courtesy. T#135, 1 P 3:8.

Political service and participation not forbidden to Christians. Lk 3:14n.

Politics, need for involvement and skill in. 1 Ch +*12:32n.

Polygamy. Ge +*4:19.

Polygamy, not favored in Israel. Jg 21:23n.

Polygamy forbidden. T#426, 1 T 3:2.

Poole, Matthew. Cited: Ge 7:13. 49:25. Nu 12:1. Dt 24:4, 16. 25:10. 31:16. 33:24, Jsh 3:8. 5:11. 11:21. 12:23. 15:8, 63. 21:43. Jg 11:39, 40. 20:46. 20:22. 21:23. 1 S 28:13. 30:6. 2 S 24:24. 1 K 16:34. 2 K 5:18. 1 Ch 3:16, 19. 8:8. Ezr 7:10. Est 3:7. Jb 14:20. 35:10. Ps 30:12. 84:6. Is 5:26. 14:9, 12. 45:1. Je 20:1. 38:27. Ezk 16:25. Da 3:25.

Poor. See *Poverty*. T#521, Pr 10:15.

Poor, kindness to and support of, enjoined. Lk +*14:13.

Poor, oppression of, forbidden. Ezk +*16:49.

Popery. T#518, Re 17:5 (predicted). T#519, 1 P 5:1 (false claim of). T#520, Re 17:16 (fearful end of).

Popular favor bestowed upon Christ. T#67, Mk 12:12.

Popular favor from God. T#266, Da 1:9.

Pornography. Ps +*101:3.

Porters. 1 Ch +23:5.

Positive and negative assertion, instances of. ♪144D, Pleonasm. Ge +*40:23. Is 38:1. 45:21, 22.

Postponement of the Kingdom to the Second Advent. Jl 2:28n. Lk 17:20n. +*21:31.

Posture (standing) during praise, singing, in the worship of God. Ex 15:20n. Jg ◐20:26n.

Poverty:
  Its evils. T#521, Pr 10:15.
  Excites God's pity. T#522, Ps 140:12.
  Oppression of, forbidden. T#523, Ps 12:5.
  United with grace. T#524, Ja 2:5.
  Will triumph over tyrants. T#525, Lk 16:25.
  Calls for present aid. T#526, Le 25:35.
  Relieving it encouraged. T#527, Mt 5:7.

Poverty, divine curse of. Dt 28:48n.

Poverty curse. Dt +28:48n.

Poverty of the righteous. 2 C +*6:10.

Praise, sacrifice of. Je +*33:11.

Praise to God. T#528, He 13:15.

Praise to be offered with devout feelings. T#529, Col 3:16.

Prayer:
  Important. T#530, Lk 18:1.
  In secret, required. T#531, Mt 14:23.
  Mental, exemplified. T#532, 1 S 1:13.
  Verbal and audible required. T#533, Ps 55:17.
  With love to God. T#534, Jn 9:31.
  With faith in God. T#535, He 11:6.
  With submission to God. T#536, Ps 37:7.
  With humble confession. T#537, Lk 18:14.
  With a supreme regard for God. T#538, Ps 79:9.
  With forgiveness. T#539, Mt 6:12.

  With perseverance. T#540, 1 Th 5:17.
  In Christ's name. T#541, Jn 16:24.
  With godly sincerity. T#542, Ps 145:18.
  With devout sympathy. T#543, Pr 21:13.
  Postures in. T#544, Mk 11:25.
  Efficacy of. T#545, Da 10:12.
  Of sinners, not heard. T#546, Ps 66:18.
  Neglected by sinners. T#547, Jb 27:10.
  Neglect of, threatened. T#548, Je 10:25.

Prayer, appeal to promise in. Ge 32:12. Ex 32:13. 2 S 7:25. 1 K 8:25. Ps +119:58.

Prayer, ask largely. Ep +*3:20.

Prayer, commanding God in. Is 45:11n.

Prayer, elements of. (1) adoration, Ps +*71:8. (2) confession, Ps +32:5 (T#1317). Lk +18:14 (T#537). Ja +5:16 (T#1235). 1 J √1:9. (3) petition, 1 T +*2:1. (4) intercession, 1 T +*2:1. (5) thanksgiving, 1 T +*2:1.

Prayer, imprecatory. Je +*10:25.

Prayer, intercessory. Ge +18:32. Nu +12:13.

Prayer, instances of returning to the Lord again for more guidance. 1 S +23:4.

Prayer, persevering. Is 62:7.

Prayer, posture during. (1) kneeling, Da +6:10 (T#1259). Ps 95:6. (2) sitting, Jg 20:26n, congregation seated. 1 Ch 17:16, individual seated.

Prayer, prevailing. Is 62:7.

Prayer, prompt answer requested. Ps +*40:17.

Prayer, urgency in. Ps +*40:17.

Prayer answered. Ps +*27:7.

Prayer answered, examples of. Ps +*99:6.

Prayer by divine aid. Lk +*11:1.

Prayer before meals. Lk +*24:30.

Prayer before meals in public exemplified. Ac +*27:35.

Prayer forbidden. T#1788, Je +*7:16.

Prayer for Jerusalem. Ps +√122:6. Is *62:7.

Prayerfulness of Christ. T#64, Mt 14:23.

Prayerfulness of saints. T#665, Ps 1:2.

Prayerlessness. Jsh +*9:14. Je +√10:25.

Preaching:
  By Christ. T#65, Mt 4:23.
  Faithfully. T#458, Mt 28:19.
  Primitive mode of. T#452, Ac 17:2.
  The primary means of grace. T#430, 1 C 1:17.
  Success of. T#468, 1 T 4:16. T#469, Ac 13:46.

Prejudice forbidden. T#526, Le 25:35.

Premarital sex forbidden. Ac 15:20. 1 Th *4:6n.

Premature death. Is +*38:10.

Premillennial Second Advent of Christ proven. 2 Th 2:8n.

Prepositions (Greek) discussed. (1) *eis*, Ac 2:38n. (2) *ek*, Ac 8:39n. 1 J 2:19n. Re 3:10n. (3) *epi*, Mt 3:13n. Ac 2:38n. 8:36n.

Presence. Gr. *parousia*. Mt +*24:3n. 1 Th 4:15n.

Present tense used of the future. ♪96C6, Mt +2:4.

Presumption of sinners. T#710, Ps 49:11.

Price, A. C. *Biblical Studies*. Cited: Ex 20:15n.

Pride:
  Common. T#549, Ps 10:2.
  Offensive to God. T#550, Pr 16:5.
  Tends to a fall. T#551, Pr 16:18.
  Of sinners. T#696, Ps 10:4.

Pride, curse of. 1 T +*3:6.

Priorities:
  Appearance. 1 S 16:7.
  Application of Scripture. Lk 11:28.
  Character. Pr 4:23.
  Children. Ps 127:3.

Commitment to God and His Word. Jsh 14:8. Is 8:20. Jn 5:39. Ro 14:12. 1 Th 2:13.

Discipleship (spiritual investment in the lives of others). 2 T 2:2.

Education. Pr 4:7.

Excitement. Jn 10:10. Ac 17:21.

Family life. Ge 18:19.

Feeling good. Ps 4:7.

Fellowship. Ro +12:5.

Freedom from stress. Ps 4:8.

Health. 3 J 2.

Heritage. Pr 20:7.

Integrity. Ac 6:3.

Intellectual activity. Pr 15:14.

Knowledge of Scripture. Mk 12:24.

Money. 1 T 6:17.

Ownership. Pr 10:22.

Physical activity. 1 T 4:8.

Physical comfort, convenience. Ec 2:24.

Pleasure. Ps 16:11.

Power. Lk 19:17.

Prestige. Pr 18:16.

Quality of time. Ps 90:12.

Recognition. Pr 22:29.

Relaxation. Mk 6:31.

Romance. Pr 18:22.

Security. Ps 4:8.

Sociability. Pr 18:24.

Solitude. Pr 18:1.

Spiritual hunger. 1 P 2:2.

Tradition. Je 6:16.

Work. Pr 14:23.

See related subject listings, "Christian Graces" and "Values" in this index.

Priorities, financial. 2 K 4:7n.

Priority studies. Topics and notes recommended for. Ps +102:18 (T#49). Is +√8:20n (T#46). Ga +√1:8n (T#1120). He √6:9n.

Private judgment, scriptural right and obligation of individual. Ga +*1:8n.

Probation:

Retribution imperfect during this life. T#552, Ps 103:10.

Limited to this life. T#553, 2 C 6:2.

Includes dangers eternal. T#554, Lk 9:24.

Determines our final state. T#555, 1 Ch 28:9.

Its awards accord with deeds. T#556, Mt 16:27.

Probation, death ends. He +*9:27.

Procrastination. T#710, Ps 49:11 (sinners put death far away). T#727, Ps 90:12 (forbidden).

Prodigality forbidden. T#180, Ec 2:10.

Profanity forbidden. T#718, Ex 20:7.

Profession of religion. T#107, Is 44:5.

Progress of doctrine. Ezk 32:27n.

Promises. See Topic Number Index, T#751-957.

Promises absolute:

To bind Satan. T#440, Re 20:4.

To convert the Jews. T#382, Ro 11:26.

To keep saints from final ruin. T#515, Jn 10:28.

To aid them under temptation. T#725, 1 C 10:13.

To raise saints above angels. T#672, Dt 33:9.

To the persecuted. T#512, 2 T 2:12.

Promises conditional:

To faith in Christ. T#183, Jn 1:12.

To the fear of God. T#291, Jb 28:28.

To humility. T#357, Ja 4:6.

To liberality. T#408, Lk 6:38.

To loving God. T#289, 1 C 2:9.

To meekness. T#438, Mt 5:5.

To obedience. T#302, Ps 19:11. T#485, Ps 81:13.

To parental fidelity. T#496, Pr 22:6.

To perseverance. T#514, Col 1:23.

To prayer. T#545, Da 10:12.

To repentance. T#607, 2 Ch 7:14.

To reprovers. T#610, Pr 28:23.

To righteousness. T#630, Ps 58:11.

To sabbath keeping. T#642, Je 17:24.

To searching the Bible. T#48, Jsh 1:8.

To self-denial. T#674, Lk 18:28.

To sympathy with the oppressed. T#686, He 13:3.

To trust in God. T#293, Is 26:3.

To using means. T#431, Ps 126:5.

Promises of assurance and security valid for individual believers, not merely unspecified group. Ga 2:20n.

Promises of temporal blessings: (1) direction, Ge +24:44. (2) prosperity, Ge +39:3. Dt +29:9.

Pronouns, use of singular personal and first person validate promises of assurance and security of salvation to individual believers. Ga +*2:20n.

Prooftexting, danger of narrowly conceived. 2 K 22:8n. Ac 2:38n. 1 J 2:19n.

Prooftexts, caution against misapplication of in supporting the truth, Bridges and Scott cited upon. Pr 24:16n.

Prophecy, apologetic value of. Jn +14:19.

Prophecy, double reference in. Ho 11:1.

Prophecy, counterfeit gift of. 1 S 18:10n.

Prophecy, Messianic, First Advent. Ge +*3:15. See Topic Number Index, T#1874-1976.

Prophecy, Messianic, Second Advent. Is 11:11n.

Prophecy confirms the Bible. T#44-1, Ps 16:10. T#44-2, Is 14:22.

Prophecy in the book of Proverbs. Pr +*2:21, 22. +*13:22. +28:8.

Prophet, Hebrew definition. Ex 15:20n.

Prophetesses, instances of enumerated. Ex 15:20n.

Prophetic perspective, law of. Is 61:2n.

Prophetic sensationalism, harmfulness of. 2 K 20:11n.

Prophetic time gaps (involving passages where an unannounced interval of time interrupts the fulfillment of apparently successive or adjacent prophecies). Is 61:2n.

Prosperity, gospel of, mistaken in focus, heretical, 1 T +*6:5, 17-19.

Prosperity corrupting and dangerous. T#625, Mk 4:19.

Prosperity of the wicked. T#565, Mt 6:5.

Providence of God. T#259, He 11:3 (nature of). T#260, Ep 1:11 (particularity and extent). T#261, Mt 5:45 (supplies temporal wants). T#262, 2 C 3:5 (all creatures dependent upon). T#263, Ps 36:6 (preserves creatures). T#264, 2 Ch 18:31 (forms, turns and governs the heart). T#265, 2 S 7:14 (employs men instrumentally). T#266, Da 1:9 (controls popular favor). T#267, Dt 2:30 (moral evils and delusions, hardening hearts). T#268, Ge 45:5 (brings good out of evil). T#269, 1 C 14:33 (God not the actor or instigator of sin). T#270, Ge 50:20 (God and mankind often have different motives in effecting the same events). T#271, Dt 30:19 (freedom and activity under).

Provisions of the Gospel. T#576, Ps 143:2 (necessity of atonement; salvation through obedience to the law of God hopeless). T#577, Ro 3:25 (redemption through the death or blood of Christ). T#578, Is 53:6 (efficacy of the atonement). T#579, 1 P 1:19 (redemption requires a perfect Redeemer). T#580, 1 T 2:6 (the Redeemer a ransom for all). T#581, Is 53:6 (the Father's agency in making atonement).

T#582, He 2:17 (redemption includes peace with God). T#583, 1 J 2:12 (forgiveness, justification, access). T#584, Jn 1:12 (Redemption includes adoption as "sons of God"). T#585, Jb 36:7 (Redemption includes mercy, faithfulness, lovingkindness).

Proximity of place of worship to residence instanced. Jsh 21:4n.

Psalteries. 1 S 10:5.

Prudence. Pr +*22:3.

Prudence required. T#172, Pr 19:11.

Public worship. T#745, He 10:25.

Punish, or visit, or inspect, or charge. Ex +*20:5n. Je +9:25mg. +*11:22mg,n.

Punishment, capital. T#315, Ge 9:5.

Punishment, capital, authorized and commanded by Scripture. A provision of the Noahic covenant. Ge +*9:5, 6.

Punishment, corporal, of children by parents. Pr +*13:24.

Punishment, degrees of, in eternity. Ezk +18:4n. Mt 11:24n. Lk +*12:47, 48.

Punishment, purpose of: (1) deterrence, on the part of others, Dt +19:20. (2) amendment, of the sinner, Dt 25:3n. (3) Avoidance or non-repetition of behavior, Ec *8:11.

Punishment, timely, of children required. Pr +*19:18.

Punishment of evildoers in this life, executed by God as a warning and foretaste of future punishment in the next life. Ge +*6:13 (T#566).

Punishment future:
Deserved by sinners. T#557, Ro 7:13.
The prerogative of God. T#558, He 10:30.
Consistent with love. T#559, Is 27:11.
Heaven lost. T#560, Mt 5:20.
Banishment to hell. T#561, Ps 9:17.
Unpardonable sin. T#562, Lk 12:10.
The second death. T#563, Re 2:11.
Death in impenitence. T#564, Jn 8:21.
Evinced by prosperity. T#565, Mt 6:5.
Evinced by temporal judgments. T#566, Ge +√6:13.
To continue forever. T#567, Mt 25:46.
Denied by some. T#568, Ezk 13:22.
Will fail to purify. T#569, Pr 27:22.
Why inflicted. T#570, Ps 83:18.
Approved by the righteous. T#571, Lk 23:41.
Cries for relief unavailing. T#572, Jb 27:8.
Sources of future misery. T#573-1, Jb 8:13 (complete despair). T#573-2, Lk 16:25 (bitter reflections). T#573-3, Re 14:11 (deprivation of rest). T#573-4, Lk 13:28 (banishment from all lovely beings, and suffering, while saints are rejoicing). T#573-5, Mt 8:12 (darkness and gloom). T#573-6, 2 C 5:11 (painful fears and terrors). T#573-7, Da 12:2 (enduring the just scorn of the universe forever). T#573-8, Lk 16:24 (pains of body in eternal fire).
Degradation of. T#574, T 3:3.

Punishment of Israel a sign of God's exclusive relationship to her. Am *3:2.

Purgatory, no basis for in Scripture. Ezk 33:16n.

Purity. Mt 5:8.

Purposes of God. See God's Purposes. T#249, Dt 32:4. T#250, Ps 33:11. T#251, Jb 14:5. T#252, 1 P 2:8. T#253, Ps 33:12. T#254, Ac 13:48. T#255, Ep 1:4. T#256, Pr 16:4. T#257, 2 Th 2:13. T#258, Da 9:2.

Pusey, E.B. Cited: Ho 10:10n. Jl 2:20n, 23n. Mi 5:5n. Zc 9:7n. Ml 2:16n.

Pyramid, the Great. Is 19:19n.

Queen of heaven. 1 K +11:5. Je 7:18.

Questions of infidelity, Bishop Horne on. Mk 14:30n.

Quotations, composite, in the New Testament. Mt +*27:9n.

Quotations in the New Testament from the Old which interpret rather than literally translate a figure of speech present in the Old Testament text, examples of. Ps +*16:9n.

Quotations in the New Testament from the Septuagint. Lk +*4:18n.

Rackham, R.B. Commentary on Acts. Cited: Ac 8:27n. 19:12n.

Rahats, S#7364h, Ex 29:4 (wash).

Railing forbidden. T#729, Ps 101:5. T#730, Ju 8.

Rain, former. Dt +11:14.

Rain, latter. Dt +11:14.

Rapture, partial, theory alluded to. 1 Th 1:10n. 4:13n.

Rapture, possible O.T. mention. Zp +*2:3.

Rapture, premillennial and pretribulational. 1 Th 1:10n. 4:17n.

Rapture's imminency not denied by intervening prophesied events. 1 Th 4:15n.

Rash vows or promises. Nu +*30:2n. Jg 11:30-40. 11:31n. Ezk ◐17:18n. Ac +*23:12.

Reason, power of. T#421, Ezk 12:2.

Reasoning, instance of faulty. Est 1:16n.

Rebellion. 1 S 15:23. Ps 78:8.

Rebuke of sin. T#66, Jn 18:37 (by Christ). T#461, 1 T 5:20 (duty to expose, required). T#610, Pr 28:23 (faithful reproof required).

Recognition of each other in heaven. Lk 16:23.

Reconciliation by Christ. T#582, He 2:17.

Reconciliation to God. T#306, Ac 2:37.

Redemption:
Covenant of. T#575, He 13:20.
Requires atonement. T#576, Ps 143:2.
Through Christ's death. T#577, Ro 3:25.
Made effectual. T#578, Is 53:6.
Through a perfect sacrifice. T#579, 1 P 1:19.
Through a "ransom for all." T#580, 1 T 2:6.
The Father's agency in. T#581, Is 53:6.
Includes peace with God. T#582, He 2:17.
Includes forgiveness. T#583, 1 J 2:12.
Embraces adoption. T#584, Jn 1:12.
Its signal mercies. T#585, Jb 36:7.
Its astonishing grace. T#586, Ac 20:24.
Honorable to God. T#587, Ps 85:10.

Reese, Alexander. The Approaching Advent of Christ. Re 5:9n.

Refuge from danger, evil. Pr +*22:3.

Regathering of Israel. Ezk +*34:13 (T#378). +*37:25 (T#949).

Regeneration:
God able to sanctify us, and to keep us from sin. T#588, 2 C 9:8.
Indispensable. T#589, Ps 50:16.
Preceded by conviction. T#590, Ac 2:37.
A radical change. T#591, 2 C 5:17.
A moral change. T#592, Jn 3:6.
Alarming to sinners. T#593, Ps 40:3.
Creative power in. T#594, Dt 30:6. T#595, Ac 5:31.
Dependence in. T#596, Ps 17:5.
An effectual call. T#597, Ac 2:39.
Its illumination. T#598, 1 C 2:14.
Its divine teaching. T#599, Jn 6:45.
Human activity in. T#600, Ps 119:59.
Required as a duty. T#601, Ac 3:19.
Evidences of. T#602, Ps 119:6.

Reign of Christ, future earthly with saints. Re +*5:10.

Reincarnation. Jb ◐7:8, +*9, 10. ◐10:21. ◐+*16:22. Ps ◐39:13. Mt +*11:14n. He ◐+*9:27.

Relationships, harmful. 2 Ch 13:7. 1 C 15:33. 2 C 6:14.

Relationships, positive constructive. Ps +*119:63.

Relics of saints, wrongfully venerated. 2 Ch 34:5n.

Remarriage after divorce, when permitted. Mt 19:3n.

Remarriage does not exclude from holding church office. Mt 19:3n. 2 T 3:2.

Remnant of Israel will remain. Ro +*9:29.

Repentance:
   Nature of. T#603, 2 C 7:10.
   Its moral dignity. T#604, Is 57:15.
   Its signal effects. T#605, 2 C 7:11.
   Its necessity. T#606, Lk 13:3.
   Encouraged by promises. T#607, 2 Ch *7:14.
   Ascribed to God. T#608, Jon 3:10.
   Is often spurious. T#609, 2 C 7:10.

Repentance required. Lk +13:3.

Repression, governmental, appropriate Christian response to. Ac 16:37n.

Reprobation. T#256, Pr 16:4.

Reproof:
   Required. T#610, Pr 28:23.
   Examples of. T#66, Jn 18:37. T#461, 1 T 5:20. T#611, Ga 2:11.
   Received by the humble. T#612, Pr 28:23.
   Rejected by the proud. T#613, Pr 13:1.
   Wisdom of receiving. T#614, Pr 12:1.
   Demands self-correction. T#615, Mt 7:5.

Reputation, value of. T#616, Pr 22:1.

Requirements, divine. See under *God's Law*, T#288-300.

Resolution required. T#134, Jsh 1:9.

Respect of persons avoided. T#231, Ro 2:11.

Responsibility, individual. Ezk 18:20. Ro *14:12.

Responsibility of man. T#555, 1 Ch 28:9.

Rest of heaven. T#337, Re 14:13.

Restitution. Lk +*19:8.

Restoration, Millennial. (1) of the site of Sodom, Ezk 16:53n, 55. (2) of Moab, etc., Je 48:47n. (3) of remnant of the Philistines, Zc 9:7n.

Restoration of natural Israel to God's favor prophesied. Is +*60:10. Zc +*10:6. Ac +√3:19, 21.

Restoration to fellowship and service of wayward leaders only after appropriate time of probation has passed. 1 T 5:22n.

Resurrection. T#617, Ac 24:15.

Resurrection, bodily, of Christ, belief in required for salvation. Is +43:10n.

Resurrection, bodily, Old Testament revelation of and faith in. 1 S +*2:6.

Resurrection, doctrine of a general or simultaneous, of the righteous and the wicked, refuted. 1 Th +*4:16n.

Resurrection, general or simultaneous, of the righteous and wicked not taught in Scripture. 1 Th +*4:16n.

Resurrection, morning and the. Ps +*49:14.

Resurrection always *bodily*, never of soul or spirit. Is +*43:10n. Da +*12:2. Ac *2:34n.

Resurrection bodies changed. T#618, Ph 3:21.

Retaliation forbidden. T#737, Pr 16:7.

Return of Christ (Second Advent) literal in his human nature. Mt 16:27n. 1 J 4:2n. 2 J 7n.

Return of Christ (Second Advent) visible, personal. Ac +*1:11.

Return of Christ (Second Advent) will be to the earth. Re +*5:9n.

Revenge forbidden. T#735, Ja 1:20. T#736, Mt 26:52.

Reverence. Ex 20:12. Ps 34:7. Hab 2:20. He 12:28.

Revival of systematic personal Bible study is the revival most to be desired. 2 K 22:13n.

Revivals:
   Ancient. T#619, Ac 5:14.
   By the Holy Spirit. T#620, Ps 72:6.
   Happy effects of. T#621, Ac 8:8.
   To be prayed for. T#622, Ps 85:6.
   Sometimes spurious. T#623, Ga 4:17.

Revivals of the Old Testament:
   Household of Jacob. Ge 35:1-15.
   Sinai, under Moses. Ex 32:1-35. 33:1-23.
   Under Samuel. 1 S 7:1-17.
   Mount Carmel, under Elijah. 1 K 18:1-46.
   Nineveh, under Jonah. Jon 3:5-10.
   Asa, king of Judah. 2 Ch 15:1-15.
   Jehoash, king of Judah. 2 K ch. 11, 12. 2 Ch ch. 23, 24.
   Hezekiah, king of Judah. 2 K 18:4-7. 2 Ch ch. 29-31.
   Josiah. 2 K ch. 22, 23. 2 Ch ch. 34, 35.
   Zerubbabel, after the Exile. Ezr ch. 5, 6.
   In the days of Nehemiah, in which Ezra was the outstanding figure. Ne 8:9. 12:44-47.
   Jehoshaphat. 2 Ch 17:6-9.

Revivals of the New Testament:
   Sychar. Jn ch. 4.
   Jerusalem, Pentecost. Ac ch. 2.
   Samaria, under Philip. Ac ch. 8.
   Caesarea, under Peter. Ac ch. 10.
   Antioch of Pisidia, under Paul. Ac 13.
   Philippi, under Paul. Ac ch. 16.
   Ephesus, under Paul. Ac ch. 19.
   Future revival. Is 2:1-5. Zc 13:14, etc.

Revolution, political, "from the Lord." 1 K 12:15n.

Rewards, degrees of, in eternity. Mt +*5:12.

Rewards future. T#556, Mt 16:27.

Rewards in this present life. 1 T +*4:8.

Riches:
   Idolized. T#624, 2 T 4:10.
   Are corrupting. T#625, Mk 4:19.
   Not to be eagerly sought. T#626, Pr 23:4.
   Vain and transitory. T#627, Pr 23:5.
   Proper use of. T#628, 1 T 6:18.

Riches, uncertainty and danger of. 1 T +*6:17.

Riches result from diligence and God's blessing. Pr +*10:4, 22.

"Right division" of Scripture not to be confused with "wrong subtraction" of ultradispensationalism. 1 Th 4:2n.

Right hand, position of honor, etc. Ge +48:13. Ec 10:2. Is 9:20. Ezk 21:21n.

Righteous, fall of, newsworthy. Pr 25:26n.

Righteousness:
   In spiritual and temporal things required and exemplified. T#629, Pr 21:3.
   Present and future rewards of. T#630, Ps 58:11.
   Of Christ. T#56, Jn 8:50. T#578, Is 53:6.
   Of saints. T#503, 1 C 2:6. T#504, Ps 119:1. T#659, Jn 1:47.

Rights, women's. (1) To inherit property, Nu 36:1-13. (2) Against false accusation of unchastity by husband, Dt 22:13-21. (3) Against broken marriage promise, Ge 38:11, 26. (4) Instance of an attempt to legislate against, based on faulty or prejudiced reasoning, Est 1:16n.

Rights of God. See under *God's Prerogatives*, T#239-248.

Rights of man. T#631, Jb 36:6. T#632, Lk 12:57 (to inquire freely). T#633, Lk 11:52 (to mental culture).

T#634, Ec 3:22 (to fruits of labor). T#635, Ec 9:9 (family).

River. (1) S#2975h, *yeorim*, a canal, branch of the Nile, the Nile, or other alluvial stream, Na +3:8n. (2) S#5104h, *nahar*, a perennial river, 2 K 5:12n; Ezk +32:2. (3) S#5158h, *nachal*, an intermittent stream, brook or summer watercourse; a winter torrent, Am 5:24n. (4) S#7883h, *shichor*, "Sihor," a reference to the Nile river, Jsh +13:3; 1 Ch +13:5 (Sihor); Je +2:18.

River (or, brook *or* stream) of Egypt. Is +*27:12.

River put for Euphrates. 1 Ch 19:16. 2 Ch +9:26. Ezr 4:20. 7:25. Is +*27:12.

Robbery forbidden. T#636, Pr 22:22.

Robertson, A. T. *A Grammar of the Greek New Testament in the Light of Historical Research.* Cited: Mt 11:14n. 1 T 2:6n.

Robertson, A. T. *The Minister and His Greek New Testament.* Cited: T 2:13n.

Robertson, A. T. *Paul's Joy in Christ: Studies in Philippians.* Ph 1:23.

Robertson, A. T. *Word Pictures in the New Testament.* Cited: Mt 16:19n. 18:24n, 28n. 27:9n, 11n. Lk 16:8n. 17:20n, 21n. 23:43n. Jn 5:39n. Ac 5:39n. 11:21n. 20:28n. Ro 6:4n, 9n, 10n. 9:5n. 1 C 9:7n, 14n. 12:13n. 13:8n. Ga 5:21n. 1 Th 4:5n, 15n. 1 J 3:9n.

Romanism. T#518, Re 17:5.

Romanism, doctrinal positions of which are not in accord with Scripture. (1) That Mary the mother of Jesus had no other children, Mk 3:31n. (2) Veneration of relics, 2 Ch 34:5n. (3) Purgatory, Ezk 33:16n. (4) Denial of the perspicuity of Scripture, Is 8:20n. (5) Denial of the right of private judgment, Ga 1:8n. (6) Denial of the sufficiency of Scripture, 1 T +*3:15-17. (7) Mary and the saints intermediaries, 1 T 2:5n. (8) Intercession of saints, 2 K 2:9n.

Ruach, Heb. for "spirit." Ge +41:8.

Rule of faith. T#46, Is 8:20.

Rulers, civil. T#310, Ac 13:20. T#311, Pr 26:3. T#312, Ex 18:21. T#313, Dt 16:18.

Rulers, civil, to be chief objects of our corporate prayer. 1 T 2:1, 2.

Ruling elders. T#101, Je 3:15. T#103, Ja 5:14. T#455, 2 C 10:8.

Rumors, false. 2 S 13:30.

Running water. Le +*14:5. Ac +*1:5n.

Russel, Bertrand. Lk 6:30n.

Sabbath, proper observance of. Is +*58:13n.

Sabbath, used for instruction. 2 K 4:23.

Sabbath, worship on, changed to first day. 1 C 16:2n.

Sabbaths:
  Instituted. T#637, Ex 20:11.
  Enrolled in the Decalog. T#638, Ex 20:8.
  Recognized by Christ. T#639, Mk 3:4.
  Appropriate duties of. T#640, Mk 6:2.
  To be kept holy. T#641, Mt 24:20.
  Rewards for keeping. T#642, Je 17:24.
  Its profanation punished. T#643, Ex 35:2.
  The first day of the week. T#644, Mk 16:9.

Sackcloth. Ge +37:34 (*S#8242h). Da +*9:3.

Sacrifice, human, made to Molech. Le +*18:21. Jsh 15:8n. Ho 13:2mg.

Sacrifices, offerings, feasts, reinstituted in the Millennium. Is +56:7.

Sacrifice of praise, Je +33:11.

Saint, Biblical use of term explained. Col 1:2n.

Saints:
  Renewed. T#645, Jb 2:3.
  Contrasted with sinners by opposite appellations.

T#646, Ps 4:3. T#647, Pr 29:47. T#648, Ml 3:18. T#649, Ja 2:23. T#650, Ro 1:30. T#651, Ac 5:14. T#652, Mt 23:33. T#653, Mt 13:38. T#654, 1 P 1:14. T#655, Lk 16:8. T#656, Ep 2:3.
  Rejoice in God. T#657, 1 S 2:1.
  Delight in truth. T#658, Ro 7:22.
  Practice honesty. T#659, Jn 1:47.
  Are meek and forgiving. T#660, Mt 10:16.
  Are disinterested, self-denying, benevolent. T#661, Ac 4:32.
  Grieve when God is dishonored. T#662, Ps 119:158.
  Feel their own guilt. T#663, Mt 8:8.
  Live by faith. T#664, 1 P 1:8.
  Delight in prayer. T#665, Ps 1:2.
  Have internal peace. T#666, Ph 4:7.
  Make progress. T#667, 2 P 3:18.
  Cannot boast. T#668, 1 C 4:7.
  Not numerous, but will be. T#669, Mt 7:14.
  The light of the world. T#670, Mt 5:14.
  Their singularity. T#671, T 2:14.
  Their final dignity. T#672, Dt 33:9.

Salvation, assurance and security, promises of valid for individual believers. Ga 2:20n.

Salvation, danger of neglecting, delaying, rejecting. 2 C +*6:2.

Salvation, family or household. Ac 16:31.

Salvation, necessity of the instrumentality of God's written word in. 1 Th 2:13. 2 T 3:15.

Salvation, necessity of specific decision for. Re 3:20.

Salvation, plan of. Ezk 33:16n.

Salvation, way of. See under *Redemption*, T#575-586.

Salvation in no sense dependent upon works. Ga 3:10n.

Sanctification. See under *Regeneration*. T#588-597.

Sanctification by the Spirit. See under *Regeneration*, T#594-596.

Satan:
  Character of. T#15, Jb 1:7.
  Will be defeated. T#277, Ps 46:10.
  His devices. T#16, 1 Ch 21:1 (falsehood). T#17, Mt 4:6 (evil suggestions, insinuations).
  His ministers. See under *Ministers of Satan*, T#473-478.

Sauer, Eric. Jn 1:12n. Ac 2:38n.

Saved, to be proportionately few in number. Mt +*7:14.

Scholarship, task of. 1 C 2:13n.

Scientific language replaced in Scripture by the timeless language of appearance. 2 S 22:8n (*121Q3).

Scorn and contempt. T#673, Mt 18:10.

Scott, Thomas. Cited: 2 K 22:20n. Jb 9:22n. Is 14:9n, 12n. Je 17:27n. 23:25n. 33:21n. 38:24n. Ezk 28:15n. 32:21n. 47:17n. Ac 11:2n.

Scott, Thomas, cited against narrow prooftexting. 2 K 22:8n.

Scott, Thomas, cited upon misapplication of prooftexts. Pr 24:16n.

Scrip. Dt +23:24. 1 S +17:40.

Scripture, perspicuity of. Pr +8:9. Is +*8:20n.

Scrivener, F.H.A. *Introduction to Textual Criticism.* Cited: Jn 1:18n. 3:13n. Ac 20:28n.

Sealing of the Spirit. T#517, 2 C 1:22.

Season, appointed. Je +8:7.

Season, due. Mt +*24:45.

Second Advent, Christ on earth during first stage of. Ezk 20:36n. Re 11:17n.

Second Advent, two stages of. 1 Th 4:17n.

Second chance after death, no. Is +*38:18.

Second Coming of Christ literal, physical, bodily in his human nature. Mt 16:27n. Ac 1:11. 1 J 4:2n. 2 J 7n.

Second Coming not asserted by Paul to take place in his own lifetime. 1 Th 4:15n.

Secrecy in financial giving enjoined. Mt 6:3.

Security of believer, promises valid for specific single individuals. Ga +2:20n.

Seed faith gospel of prosperity and wealth is heresy; command to withdraw from such who teach this doctrine. 1 T +*6:5.

Seer. 2 S +24:11.

Segregation by age groups, harmful effect of. 2 Ch +*10:8n.

Selah. Ps +*9:16 (*S#5542h).

Self-conceit. T#510, Pr 30:12. T#549, Ps 10:2.

Self-deception. T#704, Pr 16:25.

Self-denial. T#674, Lk 18:28.

Self-denial of Christ. T#58, Mt 8:20.

Self esteem. Ps 40:17. Mt 10:31. 16:26. Ro 8:17, 18. Ph +√2:3.

Self-examination. T#105, 1 C 5:8 (preparatory to Lord's Supper). T#397, La 3:40 (self-knowledge required).

Selfishness. 1 S +30:22. T#136, Ph 2:21. T#137, Pr 28:16. T#138, Ep 5:5.

Selfishness of sinners, stupid. T#689, Jb 21:15.

Selfish religion. T#191, 2 T 3:5. T#194, Lk 18:12. T#411, Ps 106:13.

Self-justification. T#706, Pr 14:9.

Self-knowledge. T#397, La 3:40.

Self-righteousness. T#550, Pr 16:5. T#696, Ps 10:4.

Sensationalism, prophetic, does harm to the cause of truth, 2 K 20:11n.

Senses, verbs pertaining to one of the, frequently applied to another. Ge 42:1n.

Sensuality:
  Reproved. T#675, 1 P 2:11.
  Of sinners. T#698, Ep 2:3.

Separation, Scriptural, for doctrinal reasons. 2 J +*10.

Separation, Scriptural, in fellowship. Ps +√119:63.

Separations final. T#387, Mt 25:32.

Seriousness. See Sobriety. T#711, 1 P 4:7.

Serle, Ambrose. The Church of God. Ac 20:28n.

Servanthood. Mt 20:27.

Service. Mk 9:35.

Servitude:
  Oriental. T#676, Jb 31:13.
  Laws to regulate. T#677-1, Ex 21:5. T#677-2, Ex 21:2. T#677-3, Le 25:44. T#678, Ex 21:20. T#679, Col 4:1.
  Apostolic precepts. T#680, Col 3:22.
  Ancient sale of men. T#681, Ezk 27:13.
  Manstealing forbidden. T#682, 1 T 1:10.
  Freedom of the Jubilee. T#683, Le 25:10.
  Freedom desirable. T#684, 1 C 7:21.
  General precepts. T#685, Ml 2:10.
  Promises to kindness. T#686, He 13:3.
  Duty to the oppressed. T#687, Pr 21:13.

Sevenfold, figurative use of term. Pr 6:31n.

Seventh day worship changed to first day. 1 C 16:2n.

Sharp, Granville. Grammatical rule of. T 2:13n.

Shedd, William G. T. Cited: Je 23:24n. Jn √6:54n. Ac 10:47n.

Shekinah glory. Ex 13:21. +*40:35. Zc +*2:5. Col 1:27n. 2 P 1:17.

Sheol. *S#7585h, Ge +37:35n. Nu 16:30n. Is 14:9n. Ezk 32:27n. Am 9:2n.

Sheol, weapons placed in. Ezk 32:27n.

Shibboleth. Jg 12:6n.

Ships of Tarshish. 2 Ch +9:21n.

Signposts. Nu 35:32n. Dt 27:8. Jsh 20:7n. Is 35:8. Je 31:21. Hab *2:2.

Silence of Scripture, alleged. (1) Allegedly, the Sabbath is not mentioned during the Patriarchal age, but see Ge 29:27, where a reference is made to a week, which necessarily implies a division of time into seven days, the first of which would be a sabbath. See also Ex 16:26n. In Ge 15:10 the manner of making a covenant is described, but is not clearly mentioned again until Je 34:18, though possibly alluded to at Dt 29:12mg and Jsh 9:7. Does such silence indicate the practice did not continue those long ages? Then why and how would Jeremiah mention it—out of the blue? (2) A chief Arian argument against the Trinity is that the word "Trinity" does not occur in the Bible, but this is true of many matters connected with Bible truth. The term "rapture" is not in the Bible either, nor "age of accountability," nor "eternal security." Some other things not named in the Bible in terms with which we speak of them today include shekinah glory, theophany, incarnation, supernatural, battle of armageddon, personality, spiritual Israel, last judgment or general judgment, second coming, legalism, intermediate state, infant baptism, believer's baptism, to follow the Lord in baptism, baptism in or into water, real or ritual water baptism. Watson remarks "So the word Trinity is not to be found in Scripture, but there is there that which is equivalent to it." "Though the word infant baptism is not in Scripture, yet the thing is," Body of Divinity, p. 381. (3) Tithing is often said not to be mentioned in the New Testament, but see Mt 23:23. (4) Infant baptism, but see Ac 16:15n. (5) Mode of water baptism, but see Ro 6:4n and Col 2:12n. (6) Use of musical instruments in New Testament worship, 1 Ch 16:42n; Ep 5:19n. (7) No mention in Scripture is to be found of women receiving the sacrament of the Lord's Supper. (8) There is no command or example in the New Testament to baptize adults that come from Christian homes. (9) There is no express command to worship God on Sunday, or to observe Sunday as the Sabbath, but see 1 C +*16:2. (10) The virgin birth is not mentioned in the Gospel of Mark, but neither is Christ's birth mentioned there at all. And so instances could be multiplied, such as the fact that repentance is not mentioned in the Gospel of John, etc. (11) The Gospel of John says nothing about Christ having cast out devils. (12) Only Luke records the raising of the son of the widow of Nain. Only John records the raising of Lazarus. (13) Only John mentions the healing of the man at the pool of Bethesda. (14) Where is it ever in Scripture explicitly stated that Jesus ever laughed or made use of humor? Does that mean that we are not to do so? See on Mt +*6:2n. (15) Where does Paul in his epistles ever refer to the resurrection of the unjust? But see Acts 24:15.

Silence of Scripture, argument fallacious. 1 Ch 16:42n. 1 C 14:34n.

Silent prayer. 1 S +1:13.

Similarities do not prove identity when differences are not accounted for, or are glossed over. Mt 10:15n.

Similes. Nu +*21:27.

Sin:
  See Depravity. T#157, Ec 7:29.
  Cannot be blended with good. T#505, Ps 119:3.
  Its ill desert. T#557, Ro 7:13.
  Its destructive tendencies. T#733, Nu +*32:23. Overruled for good. T#267, Dt 2:30. T#268, Ge 45:5.
  What kind is unpardonable. T#562, Lk 12:10.

Sin, willful practice of. Jn 8:34 (∫108B25).

Sin against the Holy Spirit. Mt 12:31n, 32n.

Sin offering. Le +*23:19.

Sincerity. Ps 32:2.

Singers. 2 Ch +35:15.

Singing a prominent feature of the Second Advent. Is +*51:11. Zc +*2:10.

Singing to accompany the Second Advent. Is 35:10. Zc +*2:10.

Single mention or alleged obscure source no ground to reject clear Scripture statement. Mt 19:9n. (1) Note the *single mention* of taking rest outside of the observance of the Sabbath (Mk 6:31). Would this indicate that we must all be "workaholics"? (2) Where is it explicitly stated in Scripture that Jesus ever laughed or made use of humor? But see on Mt 6:2n. (3) The conception of Christ as the antitype of the mercy seat is found only in Ro 3:25. (4) The Old Testament figure of the "Rock" is applied to Christ only at 1 C 10:4. (5) The only instance of the Old Testament figure of "the serpent" applied to Christ is found at Jn 3:14. (6) Only at 1 C 10:2 is the New Testament idea applied to Old Testament history, "baptized into Moses." (7) It has been alleged by some interpreters (though incorrectly) that St. Paul never applies *theos* as a predicate to Christ. See Ro 9:5n. (8) The institution of the Lord's Supper and the appearances of the risen Christ appear in the whole of Paul's epistles only once each. (9) The Holy Spirit is mentioned as being *eternal* only once (He 9:14). (10) Only in one passage, in an allegedly very obscure book, does Scripture state that there will be a Millennium (Re 20:6), though certainly there the assertion is very clear and unequivocal, and is repeated several times.

Singular first person pronouns, use of, validates promises of assurance and security to specific individual believers. Ga 2:20n.

Sinlessness. Predicted of natural generations of Israel on future restored earth, Jb +5:24. Ps +*130:8. Is +60:21. Zp *3:13.

Sinners:

Unholy. T#688, Ro 7:18.

Full of selfishness. T#689, Jb 21:15.

Enemies to God. T#690, Mt 13:38.

Disobedient to God. T#691, Pr 1:25.

Prone to forget God. T#692, Ps 9:17.

Stupid and inattentive to God. T#693, Ps 10:4.

Depart from God. T#694, Ho 7:13.

Hate the divine government. T#695, Lk 19:14.

Opposed to grace. T#696, Ps 10:4.

Rather die than submit. T#697, Ac 13:46.

Inclined to sensuality. T#698, Ep 2:3.

Prone to idolatry. T#699, Je 44:17.

Apt to murmur. T#700, Ju 16.

Ungrateful and cruel. T#701, Ro 3:15.

Deceitful. T#702, Ps 5:9.

Boastful. T#703, Lk 16:15.

Fond of deception. T#704, Pr 16:25.

Deny obligation. T#705, Ps 12:4.

Excuse their sins. T#706, Pr 14:9.

Cherish blindness. T#707, 2 P 3:5.

Cherish unbelief. T#568, Ezk 13:22. T#708, He 3:12.

Inclined to idleness. T#709, Ezk 16:49.

Are presumptuous. T#710, Ps 49:11.

Sins and vices. See *Threats.*

Skepticism. Ps 14:1. Jn 20:24-29.

Slander. See *Lying.* T#416, Jn 8:44.

Slander forbidden. T#729, Ps 101:5.

Slaten, Arthur Wakefield. *Qualitative Nouns in the Pauline Epistles and Their Translation in the Revised Version.* Re 13:17n.

Slave trade, allusion to. Ezk 27:13.

Slavery. See *Servitude,* T#676-687.

Slaying of witnesses. T#86, Is 24:5.

Sleep, restful promised. Ps 4:8.

Sleep and sloth. T#1, 1 Ch 22:16. T#358, 1 T 5:13.

"Sleep" of death refers only to the body, not the soul or spirit, Da +*12:2n.

Sleeplessness. Ec 2:23.

Slept with his fathers. Ge +*25:8n. Dt 31:16n. 1 K +*11:43. +14:20. 2 K ◐+√24:6n. 2 Ch ◐26:23. +*28:27n.

Slothfulness. Ec +10:18. Ezk 16:49. Mt 25:26. Ro 12:11. He +*6:12.

Small-group fellowships encouraged. Mt +*18:20.

Smith, J. B. *A Revelation of Jesus Christ: A Commentary on the Book of Revelation.* Re 1:10n. 3:10n. 5:9n.

Snares laid by sinners. T#702, Ps 5:9.

Sobriety required. T#711, 1 P 4:7.

Son, put for: (1) descendant, 1 Ch 7:15n, 17n. (2) grandson, Ge 29:5 (∫171G2). 1 K 15:10n. 1 Ch 3:19n. 6:20n. 7:6n. Ezr 5:1n. 7:1n. (3) uncle, 1 K +15:10n. 1 Ch 3:16.

Sons, died having no. 1 Ch +2:34. 23:22. 24:28. Ne 3:12n.

Son of God. Mt +*14:33. +*27:54n. Ac 8:37n.

Son of man. Mt 16:27n.

Songs of degrees. Is 38:20n.

"Soul" (Gr. *psyche*, ✱S#5590g), New Testament uses. Mt +2:20n.

"Soul" (Heb. *nephesh*, S#5315h), Old Testament uses. Ge +2:7n.

Soul, eternal nature of. Ezk +*18:20n.

Soul, immortal. T#422, 2 T 1:10.

Soul, immortality of. See on "Immortality of the person." Ge +5:24. Jn +8:51.

Soul, origin of. (1) Creationism. He 12:9. (2) Traducianism (by natural generation), He 7:10.

Soul, used of the physical body. Le +*19:28n.

Soul. Heb. *nephesh.* (1) used of lower creatures, Ge +2:19.

Soul and spirit, natural death never asserted of. 1 Th 5:23.

"Soul" and "spirit" sometimes used interchangeably. Ge +2:7n.

Soul ascribed to God. Le +*26:11n.

"Soul sleep" not taught in Scripture. Da +*12:2n.

Soul sleeps not, after death. T#152, Ec 3:21.

Sound, speed of. Jb 38:26n.

South, put for Negeb. Is +30:6.

Sovereignty of God. T#234, Ro 9:18. T#240, Jb 38:33. T#241, Mt 4:10. T#242, 2 T 2:25. T#243, 2 C 11:19. T#244, 1 S 15:3. T#245, Da 4:17. T#246, Ex 20:5.

Sowing and reaping. Jb 4:8.

"Spirit" (Heb. *ruach*, S#7307h), Old Testament Uses. Ge 6:3n.

"Spirit" (Gr. *pneuma*, ✱S#4151g), New Testament uses. Mt +*8:16n.

Spirit, agency of. See Agency of the Spirit, T#594-596.

Spirit, Holy. See Holy Spirit, T#345-350.

Spirit, invisible power from on high, Ge +41:38.

Spirit, outpouring of. T#620, Ps 72:6.

"Spirit" and "soul" sometimes used interchangeably. Ge +*2:7n.

Spirit of man possesses life, is not merely "breath." Is +*38:16.

"Spirit" is referred by Scripture to the immaterial part of man's being, as distinguished from "breath" or "flesh." Nu 27:16n.

Spiritual death. Ezk +*18:4n. Ep +2:1.

Spirituality required. T#156, Ps 90:12.

Spirituality manifested by saints. T#664, 1 P 1:8.

Sprinkling bowls. 1 K +7:40 (*S#4219h).

Spurious:
 Faith and religion. T#191, 2 T 3:5.
 Fasting. T#194, Lk 18:12.
 Love to God. T#411, Ps 106:13.
 Repentance. T#609, 2 C 7:10.
 Revivals. T#623, Ga 6:17.

Stability required. T#712, 1 C 15:58.

Stage, first of Second Advent, Christ upon earth during. Ezk 20:36n. Re 11:17n.

Standard of faith. T#46, Is 8:20.

Standards, false, condemned. T#46, Is 8:20.

Standing alone. Est +*1:12. Ps +*101:4. +*119:63.

Stanton, Gerald B. *Kept From The Hour*. Re 3:7n.

Steadfastness required. T#712, 1 C 15:58.

Stealing, punishment of. T#714, 1 C 6:10.

Stealing forbidden. T#713, Ep 4:28.

Stewardship. 1 C 4:2.

Stoning, prescribed means of capital punishment under Mosaic law for seven capital crimes. Jn +*10:32n.

Stranger. (1) S#1616h, Ge +23:4. (2) S#5236h, Ex +12:43. (3) S#8453h, Ge +23:4.

Strangers, duty to. T#715, Mt 25:35.

Strauch, Alexander. *Biblical Eldership*. Cited: 1 C 11:5n.

Street. (1) S#2351h, *chuts*, Am +5:16n. (2) S#7339h, *rechob*, Am +5:16n. (3) S#7784h, *shuk*, Pr +7:8.

Strength put for wealth, riches, abundance, substance. Ge +34:29, ⌐121N2, Metonymy of the Adjunct.

Stress, remedy for. Ps 34:4. Mk 6:31. Lk 10:41, 42. 1 P 5:7.

Stubbornness. Pr 29:1.

Stupidity of sinners. T#693, Ps 10:4.

Submission, unconditional. T#298, Ja 4:7. T#299, Ac 21:14.

Submission to God. T#278, Ps 39:9. T#298, Ja 4:7.

Submission to one another. 1 P 5:5.

Submission to one-another ministry. 1 C 16:16.

Submission to parents. 1 T 3:4.

Subordination does not imply inferiority or inequality. Jn +*6:38n.

Subordination of the Holy Spirit to the Father and the Son. Jn 16:13n.

Subordination of the Son to the Father. Mt +10:32. *20:23. Jn +*6:38n. 14:28. 16:13n. 1 C 3:23. 11:3. +√15:28n. Ph 2:5-8.

Subordination of the Son to the Father does not imply inferiority. Jn √5:18, 23. 10:33. √17:5. He 1:2, 3, 6.

Substitutionary Atonement of Christ. He 10:4n.

Substitutionary, Christ's death was. 1 T 2:6n.

Suing at the law. T#716, Mt 5:40.

Sufficiency of Scripture. 2 T +*3:17.

Suicide, instances of. 2 S +*17:23.

Summers, Thomas O. *Baptism*. Cited: Jn 2:6n.

Sunstroke. 2 K 4:19n.

Supper of our Lord. T#104, 1 C 11:23.

Support of the ministry. T#472, Ga +6:6. 1 C 9:7n.

Support of ungodly causes forbidden. 2 Ch *19:2.

Sure mercies of David. Is +*55:3.

Suretiship. Pr 11:15.

Swearing forbidden. T#718, Ex 20:7.

Swearing rashly. T#719, Ac 23:12.

Swearing, oaths of confirmation. T#720, He 6:16.

Swete, H. B. *The Apocalypse of St. John*. Re 6:2n.

Sword, command to buy one (anti-pacifism). Jg 3:2. 1 Ch +5:22. Ne *4:13. Ps 18:34. Lk +√22:36.

Symbolic action. 2 K 13:17n.

Synonyms, Greek, distinguished. (1) "do" versus "practice," *poieo* vs. *prasso*, Jn 5:29n. (2) "nurture" versus "admonition," Ep 6:4n. (3) "burden," Ga 6:2n, 5. (4) "new," *kainos* versus *neos*, Mk 2:22n. (5) "end," *sunteleia*, Mt +24:3, versus *telos*, Mt +10:22. (6) "know," *ginosko*, *epiginosko*, and *oida*, Jn 8:55n. (7) "asleep," *koimaomai*, 1 Th +4:13n, versus "sleep," *katheudo*, 1 Th +5:6.

Sympathy:
 In afflictions. T#7, Jb 6:14.
 For the oppressed. T#687, Pr 21:13.
 For the poor. T#526, Le 25:35.
 Of females. T#196, Mt 27:55.

Tabal, S#2881h, 2 K +*5:14 (dipped).

Tabernacle, boards of, description. Ex 36:21n.

Tabernacle, description of. Ex 26:1n.

Tabernacle, hanging for the door of. Ex 36:37n.

Tabernacle, imitations of. Ex 40:2n.

Tabernacle, plan of. Ex 40:33n.

Tabernacle, removal of. Nu 4:5n.

Tabernacle, vail of, description. Ex 36:35n.

Tabernacle, weight and value of the gold, etc., employed in. Ex 38:24n.

Tabernacle of the Congregation, description. Ex 33:7.

Table, eastern posture at, reclining. Lk 7:38n.

Tact. Pr 15:1.

Talebearing. Le 19:17.

Tarshish, ships of. 2 Ch +9:21n.

Tattling forbidden. T#729, Ps 101:5.

Taxes, Christ paid. Mt 17:24.

Taxes, duty to pay. Ro 13:6.

Taylor, C. *Apostolic Baptism*. Cited: Ac 16:14n.

Taylor, C. Affected information in notes or references to the following passages, though not specifically cited: Ac 16:15n, 33n, 34n. Col 2:11n.

Teachers, false. See *Ministers of Satan*, T#473-477.

Teachers, official, Levites constituted the. 2 Ch +15:3. 35:3n.

Teachers from among the people. Da +*11:33n. (1) Prove the perspicuity of Scripture, (2) the right of private judgment, (3) the validity of informal Bible study and teaching, (4) the value of house fellowships. (5) Will be used of God in future times of tribulation.

Teaching, divine. T#599, Jn 6:45.

Teaching of Jesus, cited by Paul. 1 Th 4:2n.

Tears, for others. Je +9:1.

Tears, fountain of. Je +9:1.

Tears, none in heaven. Re 21:4.

Temperance, a duty. T#721, 1 C 9:25.

Temperance in food. T#199, Ph 3:19.

Temptation:
 Common. T#722, 1 C 10:13.
 Not of God. T#723, Ja 1:13.
 Watching against. T#724, Mt 26:41.
 Overcome through grace. T#725, 1 C 10:13.

Tents, women's distinct from that of the men in the East. Ge 24:67n. 2 K 17:30.

Terms of salvation:
 Faith in Christ. T#183, Jn 1:12.
 Forgiveness. T#203, Ep 4:32.
 Love to God. T#288, Ju 21.
 Love to man. T#412, 1 Th 3:12.
 Love disinterested. T#413, Ga 5:14.
 Obedience to God. T#302, Ps 19:11.
 Perseverance. T#514, Col 1:23.

Reconciliation to God. T#306, Ac 2:37.
Regeneration. T#589, Ps 50:16. T#601, Ac 3:19.
Repentance. T#606, Lk 13:3.
Righteousness. T#629, Pr 21:3.
Submission to God. T#278, Ps 39:9. T#298, Ja 4:7.
Terms of the law and gospel. T#306, Ac 2:37.
Terms not in Scripture. See the list in this index under the entry for "Silence of Scripture."
Testimony. Mk 5:19.
Thank offering. Je +*33:11.
Thankfulness. Col 3:17.
Thayer, *Lexicon*, cited. Mt 24:3. Lk 12:42. Jn 5:29. Ac 17:11. Ro 1:29. Ep 4:19. 6:4. Col 2:9. 1 Th 4:15. 1 T 2:6. 2 T 3:16n. Ja 5:16n.
Theft. Ex 20:15.
"Then" as a signal of prophetic time element. Ezk 36:25n. 39:28n. Jl +2:18.
Theological Dictionary of the New Testament. Cited: Lk 12:36n. Ro 6:4n. 8:26n. 2 C 9:7n. 1 T 2:6n. 4:1n. 2 T 1:7n.
Theophany. Ge +12:7. 16:13. +17:1.
Third heaven. Lk 19:12n. 1 C 15:50n. 2 C +*12:2. Ep 1:11n. 1 Th +*4:18n.
Third heaven. Extended index to references in Peters, *Theocratic Kingdom*. 1 Th 4:17n.
Thirtle, James W. *Titles of the Psalms.* Cited: Ps 46, title, note.
Thomas, Robert L. *Understanding Spiritual Gifts.* 1 C 13:10n.
Thousands, as "of Judah," etc. Ex +18:21. Jg 12:6mg,n. ●15:15n. 1 S +23:23. 1 K 20:30n. 1 Ch 12:20. 15:25. 2 Ch +*17:14. Mi +*5:2.
Threats of evil:
    To backsliders. T#27, Ezr 8:22.
    To disobedience. T#303, Ps 34:16.
    To capital offenders. T#315, Ge 9:5. T#316, Ex 21:15.
    To covetousness. T#138, Ep 5:5.
    To despisers of the gospel. T#309, Jn 3:19.
    To idolaters. T#362, Ex 22:20.
    To the implacable. T#203, Ep 4:32.
    To the intemperate. T#366, Ep 5:18. T#367, Hab 2:15.
    To the lewd. T#405, He 13:4.
    To liars. T#418, Pr 19:9.
    To mansteakers. T#682, 1 T 1:10.
    To murderers. T#315, Ge 9:5. T#316, Ex 21:15.
    To nations, for vices. T#486, Ezk 39:23.
    To oppressors. T#490, Jb 27:13. T#523, Ps 12:5.
    To Papists. T#520, Re 17:16.
    To parents, unfaithful. T#497, 1 S 3:13.
    To persecutors. T#513, Je 20:11.
    To the proud. T#550, Pr 16:5.
    To sabbath breakers. T#643, Ex 35:2.
    To sacrilege. T#50, Pr 30:6. T#301, Ro 1:21.
    To slanderers. T#729, Ps 101:5.
    To swearers. T#718, Ex 20:7.
    To teachers, false. T#475, Ac 20:29.
    To thieves. T#714, 1 C 6:10.
    To unbelievers. T#708, He 3:12.
    To the unrighteous. T#733, Nu +*32:23.
    To warriors. T#736, Mt 26:52.
    To works of darkness. T#167, Ep 5:11.
Three days and three nights. Jsh 5:11n. 1 S 30:12n. 1 K 16:8n. Mt *12:40n.
Threshingfloor. Ge +50:10. Dt +*16:13mg.
Throne of Christ. Re +*3:21.
Throne of David. Lk +*1:32.
Throne of God. Ps +*103:19.
Tidings, evil. 2 S +13:30.

Time, appointed. Je +8:7.
Time, long, implied between first and second advent. Mt +*25:19.
Time, short. T#726, Ps 89:47.
Time element signaled by (1) "when," Ezk 32:7. 34:27. +*39:28n. Lk 21:31. (2) "then," Ezk 36:25n. (3) "before," Ml 4:5. (4) "after," Jl 2:28n. Zc 2:8. Mt 24:29. (5) "until," Is 32:15.
Time gaps, prophetic (passages where an unannounced time period occurs between successive statements). Is +*61:2n.
Time to be improved. T#727, Ps 90:12.
Time interval between stages of the Second Advent. Mi 7:15. T 2:13n. Re 10:7n. 11:17n.
Time intervals, unannounced prophetic, between adjacent clauses of prophecy. Is +*61:2n.
Time, Jewish reckoning of days, etc. Jsh 5:11n. 1 S *30:12n. Est 4:16.
Time, Jewish reckoning of in the New Testament. (1) day time, hours, Jn +*11:9n. (2) night time, watches, Mt +*14:25n.
Time, measured by moon. Ps 89:37n.
Time of second advent, precise, known and unknown aspects of. Mt 24:42n.
Time prophecies. (1) pertaining to the jubilee, Le 25:52n. (2) pertaining to Christ's death, Le +23:11n. Dt +16:1n. Lk +23:44n. 1 C +15:4.
Time, set. Je +8:7.
Tithe. Ge +*14:20.
Title to life. T#302, Ps 19:11.
Tolerance. Lk 9:49, 50. Ro 14:10, 13.
Tongue:
    Mischievous. T#728, Ja 3:6.
    Its sins forbidden. T#729, Ps 101:5. T#730, Ju 8.
    Power of. Pr 18:21.
    Should be bridled. T#731, Ja 1:26.
Tongue, keep from evil. Ps +*34:13.
Tongue, world of iniquity. Ja +*3:6.
Tongue spoken of as man's glory. Ps 30:12mg,n.
Tongues, confusion of. Ge 11:1-9.
Tongues, gift of. Ac 2:3-11. 10:46. 19:6. 1 C 12:10-14.
Tophet. Is +*30:33. Je +7:31.
Torrent, rapid. Dt 21:4n.
Total abstinence from alcoholic beverages commended. Je 35:14. Ep +*5:18.
Total commitment exemplified. Jsh +*14:8.
Tower, castle. 1 Ch +27:25 (*S#4026h).
Trade. Le 25:14.
Tradition, false. T#46, Is 8:20.
Traditions of men. Mk 7:8.
Transcendence of God. Ps +8:5n. 139:7n. Is +*57:15.
Tregelles, S. P. *The Hope of Christ's Second Coming.* Re 5:9n.
Trench, R. C. *Synonyms of the New Testament.* Cited: (1) Mk 2:22 (new). (2) Ro 1:29 (malignity, maliciousness). (3) Ep 4:19 (lasciviousness). (4) Ep 6:4 (nurture, admonition). (5) Col 2:9 (Godhead). (6) 2 T 1:7 (sound mind).
Trespass offering. Le +*5:6.
Trial by ordeal. Nu 5:17n.
Trials. See *Afflictions.* T#2, Jb 5:7.
Trials of the Jews, to come. T#381, Zc 10:11.
Trials of ministers. T#467, 2 T 3:12.
Tribulation, deliverance or exemption from the Great. Hab +*3:16.
Tribulation, the Great. Mt +*24:21.
Tribulation, the Great, titles of. (1) the great tribulation, Mt 24:21. (2) time of Jacob's trouble, Je 30:7. (3)

tribulation, Dt 4:30. (4) their affliction, Ho 5:15. (5) the time of trouble, Jb 38:23. (6) furnace of affliction, Is 48:10. (7) sea with affliction, or sea of affliction, Zc 10:11. (8) time of trouble such as never was, Da 12:1. (9) a day of trouble, Zp 1:15. (10) the day of trouble, Na 1:7.

Trichotomy. 1 Th 5:23n. He 4:12n.

Trinity. T#210, 1 C 8:6. T#211, Is 6:8.

Trinity, all three persons named together. Is 42:1n.

Trinity, attributes shared by the. Mt +√28:19n.

Trinity, a term not in the Bible. See index entry, "Silence of Scripture."

True believers, characteristics of. 1 J 5:13n.

Trumpet, the last. 1 C 15:52n.

Trumpet, the seventh. Re 11:15n.

Trumpets. 2 Ch +5:12.

Trust in God. T#292, Pr 3:5. T#293, Is 26:3. T#294, Jb 13:15.

Trust in God, encouraged. Ps +*11:1.

Trust not in man. T#170, Pr 25:19.

Truth, belief in, indispensable. T#183, Jn 1:12.

Truth, importance of maintaining the Biblical balance of. Jn +*16:13n.

Truth, Samuel directed by God to conceal or not tell the whole. 1 S 16:2n. ◑21:2n.

Truth of God. T#235, Ex 34:6.

Truth the means of grace. T#47, Is 8:20.

Truth required of all. T#629, Pr 21:3.

Turner, Nigel. *A Grammar of New Testament Greek,* Vol. 3. Cited: Mt 27:54n. Ac 5:39n.

Turner, Nigel. *A Grammar of New Testament Greek,* Vol. 4, *Style.* Cited: Mt 16:18n.

Turner, Nigel. *Grammatical Insights into the New Testament.* Cited: Mt 16:18n. 27:11n. Ac 20:28n.

Turpie, David McCalman. *The Old Testament in the New.* Lk 4:18n.

Twins. Jn 20:24.

Two Jehovah's in one context. Ge 19:24n.

Two natures in Christ. 1 Th 4:16n.

Types of Christ:
   Persons, before the law: Adam, Ge 1:26. Ro 5:14. 1 C 15:45. Abel. Ge 4:8, 10 w Ac 2:23. He 12:24. Melchizedek. Ge 14:18-20 w He 7:1-17. Abraham. Ge 17:5 w Ep 3:14, 15. Isaac. Ge 22:1-14 w He 11:17-19. Joseph. Ge 50:19, 20 w He 7:25. Ps 106:17-22 w Ph 2:6-11, etc.
   Persons, under the law. Moses. Ex 32:11-13, 30-32 w Ro 8:34 and 1 P 2:24. Nu 12:7 w He 3:2. Dt 18:15 w Ac 3:20-22. Joshua 1:5, 6 w Ac 20:32. Samson. Jg 16:30 w Col 2:14, 15. David. 2 S 8:15 w Ezk 37:24. Ps 89:19, 20 w Ph 2:9, etc. Solomon. 2 S 7:12, 13 w Lk 1:32, 33. Jonah. Jon 1:17 w Mt 12:40. Zerubbabel. Zc 4:7-9 w He 12:2, 3.
   Orders of Persons. Firstborn. Ex 13:2 w Ro 8:29. Nazarites. Nu ch. 6 w He 7:26. Prophets. Lk 24:19. Jn 7:40. Priests. He 4:14, etc. Kings. Mt 2:2. 21:5. 1 T 6:15. Re 17:14.
   Things. Jacob's ladder. Ge 28:12 w Jn 1:51. Manna. Jn 6:32, 33, 48-51. The rock. 1 C 10:4. The brazen serpent. Jn 3:14, 15. The vail. Ex 40:21. 2 Ch 3:14 w He 10:20.
   Actions. Deliverance out of Egypt. Ga 1:4. Passage over the Jordan. Jsh ch. 3, 4 w Ps 16:9-11. He 2:14, 15. Entrance into Canaan. He ch. 4.
   Rites. Circumcision. Col 2:11, 12. Sacrifices. He 9:12-14, 19-26. Firstfruits. Le 23:10-12. Jn 20:1, 17. 1 C 15:20. Purifications. Le 16:30 w Jn 15:3. Baptism. Ro 6:3-5. 1 P 3:21. The sabbath. He 4:3.
   Places. Cities of refuge. Nu 35:6 w He 6:18. Jsh 20:7n.

Tabernacle. Ex 40:2, 34 w Col 2:9. He ch. 8, 9.

Temple. Jn 2:19-21. Ep 2:20-22.

Types not distinguished from prophecy in Scripture, establishing the validity of their proper study. Jn 19:36n.

Ultra-dispensationalism's misapplication of "right division" of Scripture. 1 Th 4:2n.

Ultra-dispensationalism's mistaken denial of the perpetuity of the ordinance of ritual water baptism during the church age. Ac 2:38n.

Unbelief in future punishment. T#568, Ezk 13:22.

Unbelief of sinners. T#708, He 3:12.

Undesigned coincidence, instance of. Mk 6:27n.

Undesigned coincidences between Acts and Paul's epistles, instances of. Ac +*12:12n.

Unforgivable sin, the. Mt 12:31n.

Unger, Merrill F. *Bible Dictionary.* 2 Ch 8:18n.

Union with Christ:
   As the head of the Church. 1 C 12:12, 27. Ep 1:22, 23. 4:15. 5:30. Col 1:18, 24.
   As the cornerstone. Ep 2:20-22. 1 P 2:4-7.
   As a vine. Jn 15:4-8.
   As the bridegroom. Jn 3:29. Ep 5:23-32.
   Wondrous nature of. Jn 17:11, 21-23. Ro 8:38, 39. 1 C 6:17. Ep 2:4-6. Col 3:1-3.

Unity, Union. See under *Church Order, Church Unity,* T#111-115.

Unity of feeling and purpose, not opinion, the subject of Paul's prayer. Ro 15:5n. 1 C +*1:10.

Unity of God. T#210, 1 C 8:6.

Unity during the millennium. T#442, Ps 37:11.

Unjust gain. Pr 28:8.

Unpardonable sin, the. Mt 12:31n. T#562, Lk 12:10.

Unregenerate works. T#546, Ps 66:18. T#589, Ps 50:16.

Unrighteousness. T#732, 1 Th 4:6.

Unrighteousness tends to ruin. T#733, Nu +*32:23.

Unseen World, Related Terms. (1) Abaddon, Jb 26:6 (*S#11h). (2) Abraham's bosom, Lk 16:22. (3) deep, Lk 8:31 (*S#12g, *abussos*, abyss). (4) destruction, Mt 7:13 (*S#684g, *apoleia*). (5) destruction, Jb 9:31 (*S#7845h, *shachath*). (6) gates of death, Jb 38:17. (7) *gehenna*, Mt 5:22 (*S#1067g, hell). (8) grave, Ge 23:4 (*S#6913h, *qeber*). (9) grave, Ge 35:20 (*S#6900h, *qeburah*). (10) hades, Mt 11:23 (*S#86g). (11) heavenly Jerusalem, He 12:22. (12) lake of fire, Re 19:20. (13) lowest, Dt 32:22 (*S#8482). (14) many mansions, Jn 14:2. (15) "outresurrection," Ph 3:11. (16) outer darkness, Mt 8:12. (17) paradise, Lk 23:43. (18) perish, Mt 2:13 (*S#622g, *apollumi, destroy*). (19) pit, Ge 37:20 (*S#953h, *bor*). (20) pit, Lk 14:5 (*S#5421g, *phrear*). (21) prison, Is 24:22 (*S#4525h). (22) *rephaim*, Pr 21:16 (*S#7496h). (23) resurrection, Is +*26:19n. (24) resurrection of the just, Lk 14:14. (25) resurrection of the unjust, Jb 21:30. Da 12:2. Re *20:5. (26) shadow of death, Ps 23:4 (*S#6757h). (27) *sheol*, Ge 37:35n (*S#7585h). (28) third heaven, 2 C 12:2. (29) tomb, Mt 8:23 (*S#3419g, *mnemeion*). (30) weeping and gnashing of teeth, Mt 8:12. (31) well, Ge 16:14 (*S#875h, *be-er*).

Unto this day. Ge +19:38. Dt +29:4. Jsh +*4:9. 2 K 8:22n. 1 Ch +4:43. 2 Ch 5:9n.

Urgency in prayer. Ps +*40:17.

Usury. Is +24:2.

Utility of the right. T#630, Ps 58:11.

Utility of the truth. T#47, Ps *19:7. T#51, Dt 29:29. T#279, Ps 36:9. T#433, Lk 16:31. T#458, Mt 28:19.

Valley, mg. brook. or, brook, mg. valley. Jg +*16:4mg. Nu +*13:23mg, 24mg.

Valley of the sons of Hinnom. Jsh +*15:8n.
Values (Terminal, Biblical life goals):
  Abundant life. Jn 10:10.
  Accomplishment. Jsh 1:8.
  Beauty, perfection. 1 P 3:3, 4.
  Contentment. Ph 4:11.
  Equality. Ga 3:28.
  Family security. Ge 18:19. 30:30. Ps 37:25. 1 T 5:8.
  Freedom. Pr 22:7. Je 34:8. Lk 4:18. Jn 8:32. Ro 6:18.
    14:12. 1 C 7:21. 10:29. 2 C 1:24. Ga 5:1.
  Friendship. Ps 119:63. Pr 27:10. Ml 3:16.
  Fruitfulness. Ps 1:3. Pr 11:30.
  Happiness. Pr 16:20. Jn 13:17.
  Impartiality. Le 19:15. Pr 21:3. Ga 6:10. Ja 2:1.
  Love, mature. Jn 13:34, 35.
  National security. Le 25:18.
  Oneness. Ps 133:1. Jn 17:21, 23.
  Peacefulness. Ro 12:18.
  Perfection. Ge 17:1.
  Pleasure. Ps 16:11.
  Prosperity. Ps 1:3.
  Righteousness. Mt 6:33.
  Salvation. He 2:3.
  Self esteem. Ga 6:4.
  Self respect. Mt 19:19.
  Social recognition. Ac 6:3. 9:39. 1 P 3:10, 16.
  Tranquility. Mt 11:29.
  Wisdom. Ja 3:17.
  See entries on *Priorities*.
Values (Instrumental, Biblical guides for conduct):
  Benevolence. Mt 10:8.
  Cheerfulness. Pr 17:22.
  Compassion. Ro 12:15.
  Competence. Pr 22:29.
  Compliance. Ph 2:12.
  Consistency. Lk 16:10. Ph 2:12.
  Courage. Jsh 1:6.
  Courtesy. Ep 4:32.
  Diligence. Ex 20:15n.
  Forgiveness. Ep 4:32.
  Frugality. Pr 13:22.
  Helpfulness. 1 P 4:10.
  Honesty. Ro 12:17.
  Humility. Ja 4:10.
  Independence. Ga 6:4.
  Industriousness. Ro 12:11.
  Kindness. Ep 4:32.
  Learning. Pr 15:14.
  Logicalness. Pr 14:15. Ep 4:14. 1 Th 5:21. 1 P 3:15.
  Love. Ga 5:13.
  Obedience. 1 J 2:3n. 3:22.
  Orderliness. 1 C 14:40.
  Patriotism. 1 Ch 12:32. Je 30:6n. Lk 3:14.
  Perseverance. Je 12:5. 1 C 15:58.
  Piety. Ja 1:27. 3:17, 18.
  Prayerfulness. 1 Th 5:17.
  Proper speech. Col 4:6.
  Punctuality. Ep 5:16. Col 4:5.
  Rationality. Is 1:18. Pr 22:3. Ro 12:1. 2 T 1:7.
  Reasonableness. Is 1:18. Ro 12:1.
  Receptivity. 1 S ●25:17. 2 K 5:13. Ps 25:9. Ac 17:11.
  Responsibility. Lk 16:10. Ac 6:3. Ph 2:12.
  Reverence. Pr 1:7.
  Self control. Pr 16:32. 25:28. 1 T 3:4.
  Self discipline. 1 C 9:27.
  Self restraint. Pr 29:11.
  Spirituality. Ga 6:1. Col 3:1, 2.
  Standing alone. Ex 23:2. Est *1:12. Pr 1:10. Da *6:10.
    Ac 5:29.

  Temperance. 1 C 9:25.
  Wisdom. Pr 2:6. 4:7. 15:14. Ja 1:5.
  See further under *Christian Graces*.
Vanities, lying. Term used of idols, Ps +31:6.
Vanities, lit. "nothings," a term for heathen deities, idols,
  gods. Je +14:22 (S#1892h).
Vanity of life. T#148, Ja 4:14.
Vanity of riches. T#627, Pr 23:5.
Various readings, minimal effect upon N.T. text, Dr.
  Bently on. Mk 14:30n.
Vengeance. Ro 12:19.
Vengeance of God upon the wicked in this life. T#566,
  Ge +*6:13.
Venereal disease. Ezk 24:16n.
Verbal inspiration. 1 C 2:13n. Ga 3:16n.
Vessels of wrath. T#256, Pr 16:4.
Vices. See *Threats*.
Vincent, Marvin R. *Word Studies in the New Testament*.
  Mt 10:32n. Lk 12:36n.
Vindicative justice. T#236, Ro 11:22. T#237, Dt 32:43.
Vine, W. E. *Expository Dictionary of New Testament
  Words*. Cited: Mt 18:19n. 20:13n. 24:3n. Mk 2:8n.
  Ph 1:23n. 2:6n. 2 T 2:15n.
Virgin. (1) *S#1330h, Ge +24:16. (2) *S#5959h, Ge
  +24:43.
Virginity. *S#1331h, Le +21:13.
Virtue. Ph 4:8. 2 P 1:5.
Virtues, Christian. See *Christian Graces*.
Visit, or punish, or charge. Ex +*20:5n. Je +9:25mg.
  +*11:22mg,n.
Visitation. He 3:13n.
Visiting the flock. T#463, Je 23:2.
Vocation, occupation, or calling. Becoming a Christian
  does not usually necessitate change in. 1 C 7:20.
Volunteerism, or self-appointment to spiritual office dis-
  countenanced. 1 K 14:33. 2 C 3:1. 5:12. 10:12.
  2 T *4:3. 3 J 9.
Vows. Le +*23:38.
Vows, rash. Nu +30:2n. Jg +*11:31n.
Vultures, prophetic mention of. Mt 24:28. Lk 17:37.
Wage fraud forbidden. Le +*19:13.
Wages, prompt payment commanded. Le +*19:13.
Waiting, saints are, for the time of rewards, crowns,
  etc., at the second advent. 2 T 4:8.
Waiting God's time, no time lost while. Nu 9:18n.
Waiting on God. Is 30:18.
Waiting as a spiritual condition of prayer. Ps 37:34.
Walker, Thomas. *The Acts of the Apostles*. Cited: Ac
  1:6n. 2:38n, 39n. 7:59n. 17:3n, 11n.
Walvoord, John F. *The Rapture Question*. T 2:13n.
Wanderers. Je +14:10.
War, common. T#734, Is 1:15.
War, conducted at a set time of the year. 2 S +*11:1n.
War, divination practiced for direction in. Ezk 21:21n.
War, how to prevent it. T#737, Pr 16:7.
War, sin and folly of. T#735, Ja 1:20. T#736, Mt 26:52.
War was of God. 1 Ch +5:22.
Warfare, Christian. T#738, Lk 12:37.
Wardlaw, Ralph. *Lectures on the Book of Proverbs*.
  Cited: Pr 18:1n.
Warfield, B. B. *Counterfeit Miracles*. Re 13:14n.
Warfield, B. B. *Textual Criticism*. Ac 20:28n.
Warning, general. T#89, Mt 24:14.
Warning against the second death. T#554, Lk 9:24.
Warning against self-deception. T#704, Pr 16:25.
Washing, Biblical mode of. Ex 30:19n. 2 K √3:11n. Lk
  7:44n.
Washing of feet. SS +5:3.
Watch, Jewish division of night time. Mt 14:25n.

Watchfulness. T#738, Lk 12:37.
Watchfulness against temptation. T#724, Mt 26:41.
Water, living or running. Le +*14:5. Ac 1:5n.
Water, much. Jn +3:23.
Waterland, Daniel. Cited: Ac 2:38n. 7:59n. 1 C 15:28n.
  Ph 2:6n, 7n. Re 1:8n.
Wave offering. Le +*23:15.
Wealth, see strength put for. Ge +34:29 (ɡ121N2, Me-
  tonymy of the Adjunct). Ezk 28:4, 5. Ro 11:25n.
Wealth laid up for the just. Pr +*13:22.
Wealth no measure of godliness, 1 T +*6:5.
Weaning of children. 1 S +1:22.
Weapons, placed in sheol. Ezk 32:27n.
Weather. Ge +9:14.
Webster, William, and Wilkinson, William Francis. *The
  Greek Testament with Notes Grammatical and Exe-
  getical.* Mk 14:30n.
Weeping, for tribulation. Je +22:10.
Weights and measures. Standards of, kept in sanctuary.
  Honesty and piety thus closely connected. 1 Ch
  23:29n.
Well. (1) S#875h, *be-er*, Ge +16:14. (2) S#953h, *bor*,
  Ge +37:20. (3) S#5869h, *ayin*, Ge +24:13.
West, Gilbert. Ac 22:6n.
West, Nathaniel. *The Thousand Years in Both Testa-
  ments.* Is 24:21n. Da 3:1n. Re 20:2n.
"When" as a signal of prophetic time element. Is 29:23.
  Ezk +*39:28n.
Whitla, William. Cited: Ezk 14:14n, on the historicity
  of Daniel the prophet.
Wholly followed the Lord, example of those who. Jsh
  +*14:8.
Wickedness of sinners. T#690, Mt 13:33.
Widow and fatherless. See under *Poverty,* T#522-527.
Widows. Is +1:17.
Wilderness, flight into. Re +*12:6, 14.
Williams, W.G. *Baptism.* Cited: Ac 8:27n.
Wilson, Daniel. *The Divine Authority and Perpetual
  Obligation of the Lord's Day.* Cited: Is 58:13n. Lk
  13:14n.
Wilson, Robert Dick. Cited at 2 S 5:23n.
Wilson, T. Ernest. *Mystery Doctrines of the New Testa-
  ment.* Ro 16:25n.
Wilson, William. *Old Testament Word Studies.* Ps
  37:34n. 69:3n. Is 30:18n.
Wine. (1) S#2531h, *chemed,* Is 27:2. (2) S#2561h,
  chemer, Is 27:2. (3) S#3196h, *yayin,* Hab 2:5n. (4)
  S#3342h, *yekeb,* Dt 16:13. (5) S#4469h, *mimsak,*
  Pr 23:30, mixed wine. (6) S#5435h, *sobe,* Is 1:22.
  (7) S#6025h, *ashishah,* Ho 3:1. (8) S#6071h, *asis,*
  Is 49:26mg, new wine. (9) S#7941h, *shekar,* Pr
  +*20:1, strong drink. (10) S#8105h, *shemarim,* Is
  25:6, wine on the lees. (11) S#8492h, *tirosh,* Ge
  +*27:28.
Wisdom, its basis. Pr 9:10.
Wisdom, its importance. Pr 4:6.
Wisdom in creation. T#142, Je 10:12.
Wisdom of God. T#222, Ro 11:33.
Witness, false, subjects accuser to punishment intended
  for the accused. Dt *19:18, 19.
Witness of the word. T#347-3, Dt 31:19.
Witness of the Spirit. T#347-4, Ga 4:6.
Women. See *Females.* T#195, Ac 9:39.
Women, in attendance at religious feasts or festivals.
  Ex 15:20n. Jg +21:21n. 2 K *4:23. 1 Ch 15:20n.
  Ne +12:43.

Women, ministry in public and in the assembly. 2 J
  +5.
Women, ministry of. Ac 18:26n.
Women, wise. 2 S +*20:16.
Word, personal, distinguished from word, spoken. 2 Ch
  34:27n.
Wordsworth, Ch. *Greek Testament* (notes). Cited: Mt
  5:23n. 17:3n. 18:22n. Mk 9:49n, 50n. Lk 4:25n.
  24:1n. 2 C 12:2n. 1 Th 4:17n. Ja 5:16n.
Works of darkness. T#167, Ep 5:11.
Works the fruit and evidence, not ground of faith. Ga
  3:10n.
World:
  Ignorant. T#739, Jn 17:25.
  Opposed to God. T#740, Jn 17:14.
  Corrupting and dangerous. T#741, Mt 13:22.
  Its idols forbidden. T#742, Jn 6:27.
  Overcome by grace. T#743, 1 J 5:4.
"World," Greek words translated. (1) S#165g, *aion,* Mt
  +13:39. (2) S#2889g, *kosmos,* Mt +4:8. (3)
  S#3625g, *oikoumene,* Mt +24:14.
Worldliness. 1 J 2:15-17.
Worship:
  Of God. T#744, Mt 4:10.
  Should be public. T#745, He 10:25.
  With proper instruction. T#746, Jn 8:2.
  With prayer and praise. T#747, Ep 5:19.
Worship, constituent aspects of. (1) prayer, Ac 7:59.
  1 C 1:2. (2) glory, honor, power, Re 4:10, 11.
Worship, day of, changed from seventh to first day of
  week. 1 C 16:2n.
Worship, Father and Son receive identical. Re 5:12n.
Worship, received by Jesus Christ. Ne +9:6. Mt
  +*14:33. Jn +*20:29n. Ac +*7:59n. Re +5:12n.
Worship declined. Jn +*20:29n. Ac +*10:25, 26.
Worship due to God alone, exclusively. Is 42:8. Mt 4:10.
Worship of creatures forbidden. T#80, Col 2:18.
Worship received wrongly by (1) Herod, Ac 12:22, 23.
  (2) Antichrist, 2 Th 2:3, 4. Re 13:8. (3) idols, Is
  42:8.
Worshipers become like what they worship. Je +*2:5.
  2 C 3:18.
Wrath, day of. Jb +*21:30.
Wrath, fierceness of. 2 Ch +24:18. 30:8.
Wresting scripture. T#50, Pr 30:6.
Year, part of, reckoned as a whole year. 1 K 16:8n.
  22:51. Compare similar usage with Day, Jsh 5:11n.
  1 S 30:12n.
Years of life shortened. Is +*38:10.
Yesterday, third day (mg. rendering). Ge +*31:2mg.
  Jsh +4:18mg.
Young, Edward J. Cited: Da 11:30n.
Young, Robert. *Concise Critical Comments.* Cited: Ex
  15:20. 18:21. 30:19. Le 19:20, 28. 23:2. Nu 8:16.
  16:41. 33:10. Dt 31:12. Jsh 15:25. 1 K 9:28. 20:30.
  2 K 2:9. 16:4. Ps 45:13. Is 34:16. Je 11:22.
Youth. See *Children.* T#53, Ep 6:1.
Zeal:
  False. T#748, Ro 10:2.
  The true exemplified. T#749, Ga 4:18.
  Is indispensable. T#750, Lk 13:24.
Zion, Christ comes victorious to during his Second Ad-
  vent. Is +*51:11.
Zion, Christ reigns from at second advent. Is +*24:23.
Zodhiates, Spiros. *The Hebrew-Greek Key Study Bible.*
  Cited: 1 T 4:1n.

TOPIC NUMBER INDEX

1. Activity and diligence required and encouraged; inactivity reproved. 1 Ch +22:16. +63, Jn 5:17. +358, 1 T 5:13. +738, Lk 12:37. +749, Ga 4:18.
2. Afflictions common to man. Jb 5:7.
3. Afflictions from God. 1 S 2:7. +147, 1 S 2:6. +260, Ep *1:11.
4. Benefit of afflictions and fatherly chastisements. Dt +8:2. +508, Re 3:19. +512, 2 T 2:12. +515, Jn 10:28.
5. The afflictions of the righteous short. 2 C +4:17. +225, Ja 5:11. +585, Jb 36:7.
6. God, the believer's support and helper under afflictions. Ps +23:4. +657, 1 S 2:1. +725, 1 C *10:13.
7. Afflictions demand sympathy—examples. Jb +6:14. +526, Le 25:35.
8. Afflictions try mankind. Dt +8:2. +4, Dt 8:2.
9. Afflictions often misimproved and magnified. Is +9:13. +569, Pr 27:22. +700, Ju 16.
10. Duties to the aged. 1 P +5:5. +730, Ju 8.
11. Angels numerous. He +12:22.
12. Employment of good angels. 2 S +24:16.
13. Apostasy of angels. 2 P +2:4.
14. Names of apostate angels. Mt +4:3.
15. Character, employment and agency of evil spirits. Jb +1:7.
16. By what means and devices do apostate angels lead mankind into sin and death? 1 Ch +21:1. +474, Mt 7:15. +702, Ps 5:9.
17. Suggestions of the adversary:
    17-1. That sinners will escape threatened punishment. Ge +3:4.
    17-2. That there is nothing but selfishness in religion. Jb 1:9.
    17-3. That means are useless, where the end is divinely appointed. Mt +4:6. +257, 2 Th 2:13.
    17-4. Forbidding matrimony and the use of meats. 1 T +4:3.
18. Apostate angels to be resisted. Ep +4:27. +477, Mt 15:14. +738, Lk 12:37.
19. Cases of real and supposed apostasy—warnings—fearful end of apostates. 1 S +15:11. +23, 1 K 11:4. +27, Ezr 8:22.
20. Apostates hard to reclaim. He +6:4.
21. Were Apostates ever truly regenerated? Mt +7:23. +515, Jn 10:28. +516, Ro 8:34. +517, 2 C 1:22.
22. Theoretical and practical Atheism. Ps +14:1. +200-1, Ps 14:1. +200-2, Pr 29:11. +200-3, Ps 74:18. +200-4, Ro 1:22. +200-5, Pr 15:5. +200-6, Pr 12:15. +200-7, Pr 13:19. +200-8, Pr 20:1. +200-9, Pr 15:2. +200-10, Pr 18:2. +200-11, Je 17:11. +200-12, Pr 7:22. +200-13, Pr 20:3. +200-14, Pr 1:32. +200-15, Pr 14:9. +200-16, Pr 17:24. +200-17, Pr 10:18. +200-18, Pr 17:16. +200-19, Pr 21:20. +200-20, Pr 10:23. +200-21, Pr 12:16. +568, Ezk 13:22. +692, Ps 9:17.

+693, Ps 10:4. +695, Lk 19:14. +705, Ps 12:4. +708, He 3:12.
23. Examples of backsliding—cautions. 1 K +11:4. +19, 1 S 15:11. +695, Lk 19:14.
24. Backsliders prone to murmur, despond, and distrust providence. 1 K +19:4. +9, Is 9:13. +171, Pr 12:25. +272, Ezk 33:20. +700, Ju 16.
25. Backsliders insensible of their state. Re +3:17. +704, Pr 16:25.
26. Backsliders walk in darkness. Is +59:2. +707, 2 P 3:5.
27. Backsliders threatened and visited with evils. Ezr +8:22. +19, 1 S 15:11.
28. Backsliders called to repentance. Je +3:14.
29. Backsliders hard to reclaim—need re-conversion. Ga +4:20. +143, Je 10:3. +166, Pr 5:22.
30. Backsliders, when reclaimed, heartily repent and confess their sins. Jb +40:4. +124, Pr 28:13. +356, Jg 10:15. +603, 2 C 7:10.
31. Mosaic baptisms. Mk +7:4.
32. Figurative baptism and circumcision. Ps +51:2.
33. John's baptism, a token of repentance, inward purity, and preparation for Christ's advent. Mk +1:4.
34. Was John's baptism in the name of the Holy Ghost? Ac +18:25.
35. Did Christ solicit baptism, to be introduced into the Aaronic priesthood, or to sanction the divine ordinance of John's baptism, and "be made manifest to Israel"? Mt +3:13.
36. Christian baptism instituted, and enjoined upon believers. Mk +16:16.
37. The proper administrators of Christian baptism. Mt +28:19.
38. The proper subjects of baptism. Ac +16:33.
39. Mode of baptism.
    39-1. Passages referred to by those who immerse. Ro +6:4. +32, Ps 51:2.
    39-2. Passages referred to by those who sprinkle or pour. He +10:22. +31, Mk 7:4. +620, Ps 72:6.
40. Bible, the inspired word of God. 2 T +3:16.
41. Bible, the everlasting truth of God. Is +40:8.
42. Bible will be fulfilled. Mt +5:18. +284, Is 42:21.
43. Miracles wrought to confirm the word of God. Mk +16:20. +77, Mk 4:41.
44. Bible confirmed by prophecy.
    44-1. Messianic prophecy. Ps +16:10.
    44-2. Non-messianic prophecy. Is +14:22.
45. Bible confirmed by its internal evidences.
    45-1. By revelations above reason and human capacity. Ps +19:12.
    45-2. By the purity of its requirements. Ps +19:7. +47, Ps 19:7. +285, Mt 5:48.

46. Bible, the true standard of faith and practice—danger of false standards. Is +√8:20n.
47. Bible, the true means of grace. Ps +19:7. +428, Mk 4:14. +429, Ac 27:31. +430, 1 C 1:17. +431, Ps 126:5. +432, 1 C 4:15.
48. Studying and teaching the Bible required and encouraged. Jsh +1:8. +279, Ps 36:9. +458, Mt 28:19. +493, Pr 22:6.
49. Bible a written revelation, and intelligible. Ps +102:18.
50. Sin and danger of altering or wresting the Bible. Ps +30:6. +284, Is 42:21.
51. The whole Bible profitable and important. Dt +29:29. +47, Ps 19:7. +279, Ps 36:9. +433, Lk 16:31.
52. Duty and advantage of cheerfulness. Ne +8:10. +296, 1 Th 5:16. +634, Ec 3:22.
53. Duties of children to parents. Ep +6:1. +10, 1 P 5:5.
54. Penalties for disobeying and abusing parents. Dt +27:16. +494, Pr 13:24.
55. Early piety exemplified and encouraged. 1 S +3:8.
56. Christ Jesus, his holiness, frankness, and disinterested ness. Jn +8:50. +229, Re 15:4. +630, Ps 58:11.
57. Christ obeyed, pleased, and honored God. Mt +3:17.
58. Christ's poverty and self-denial. Mt +8:20.
59. How did Christ regard the world and its honors? Jn +5:41. +626, Pr 23:4. +743, 1 J 5:4.
60. Christ's love and compassion towards mankind. Mt +14:14. +224, Ps 119:68. +225, Ja 5:11. +228, Ps 145:9. +370, Re 22:17. +372, Lk 19:42. +583, 1 J 2:12. +584, Jn 1:12. +585, Jb 36:7. +586, Ac 20:24.
61. Christ a pattern of condescension. Lk +22:27. +228, Ps 145:9.
62. Christ's meekness, forbearance, forgiveness, lowliness, modesty, and patience. Mt +11:29. +482, Ph 2:3. +498, Ja 1:4. +660, Mt 10:16.
63. Christ diligent in His work. Jn +5:17. +1, 1 Ch 22:16.
64. Christ's prayerfulness, and prevalence in prayer. Mt +14:23. +516, Ro 8:34.
65. Christ a preacher. Mt 4:23.
66. Christ a searching reprover. Jn +18:37. +610, Pr 28:23. +611, Ga 2:11.
67. Christ secured some popular favor. Mk +12:12.
68. Christ reviled and persecuted unto death. Ps +2:2. +467, 2 T 3:12. +511, Ps 42:10. +690, Mt 13:38.
69. Christ's humanity. Christ's human soul and body. 1 J +4:3.
70. Christ's dependence for preservation, knowledge, etc. Mk +13:32. +64, Mt 14:23.
71. Christ called the Son of God in reference to His incarnation. Lk +1:35.
72. Christ's official subjection to his Father. Jn +6:38.
73. Preeminence of "the Man Christ Jesus." Jn +3:31.
74. Christ's Divinity. Christ's divine names, titles, and offices. 1 C +2:8.
75. Christ's claim to equality and unity with God. Jn +5:18.

76. Divine attributes and prerogatives claimed and exercised by Christ and ascribed to him.
76-1. Authority supreme. Col +2:10.
76-2. Authority to seek his own glory supremely. Col +1:16. +209, Pr 16:4. +346, He 9:14.
76-3. Eternity. Mi +*5:2.
76-4. Immutability. He +13:8.
76-5. Omnipotence. 1 C +1:24. +218, Re 19:6.
76-6. Omnipresence. Mt +18:20. +220, Pr 15:3.
76-7. Omniscience. Mt +9:4. +219, He *4:13.
77. Christ wrought miracles, in his own name, to confirm his divinity and mission. Mk +4:41. +43, Mk 16:20.
78. The prophets and apostles acceptably wrought miracles, not in their own names. Ac +3:12.
79. Divine honors paid Christ, and received and claimed by him. He +1:6.
80. Mere creatures not to be divinely honored or worshipped. Col +2:18.
81. Mystery respecting Christ. 1 T +3:16.
82. Christ's final triumph and glory. Re +17:14. +96, Ep 1:22.
83. Christ's kingdom. Christ a king. Ps +2:6.
84. Nature of Christ's kingdom. Ro +14:17.
85. General opposition to Christ's kingdom, before the flood, and before the First Coming of Christ. Is +53:3.
86. Will there be another "falling away," or general opposition to Christ's kingdom before the Millenium? Is +24:5.
87. Will the foes of Christ's kingdom be cut off before the millennium? Ps +37:9. +381, Zc 10:11. +486, Ezk 39:23. +513, Je 20:11. +566, Ge 6:13. +630, Ps 58:11. +733, Nu *32:23.
88. Joy in view of the overthrow of Christ's enemies. Zp +3:14. +237, Dt 32:43. +571, Lk 23:41.
89. Christ and His friends warn the wicked before their overthrow. Mt +24:14.
90. Progress and final triumph of Christ's kingdom upon earth. Re +11:15. +440, Re 20:4.
91. Duration of Christ's kingdom. Lk +1:33.
92. Design of the church of God. 1 T +3:15.
93. Foundation of the church. 1 C +3:11.
94. The church an object of love and prayer. Ep +5:25. +111, Ac 4:32. +504, Ps 119:1. +585, Jb 36:7. +672, Dt 33:9.
95. The church safe. Ps +125:2. +515, Jn *10:28. +516, Ro 8:34. +517, 2 C 1:22. +585, Jb 36:7.
96. Christ the head of the church. Ep +1:22. +76-1, Col 2:10.
97. Church officers. Apostles, or extraordinary officers, called directly by Christ. Ga +1:1.
98. The apostles, instructed by direct revelations. Ga +2:8.
99. Apostles, eyewitnesses of Christ's resurrection. 1 C +15:8.
100. Miraculous gifts and authority of the apostles. Mt +10:1. +189, Ja 5:15.
101. Elders, Overseers, Ministers, Bishops, Preachers, Teachers, Pastors, Evangelists (one office), to instruct, admonish, edify, lead and guide. Je +3:15. +447, Ep 4:11.

170. Human nature untrusty—Cautions. Pr +25:19.

171. Despondency exemplified and reproved. Pr +12:25. +24, 1 K 19:4. +700, Ju 16.

172. Duty and advantage of discretion, etc. Pr +19:11.

173. Plain dress recommended. 1 T +2:9.

174. Envy a common and foolish sin—prohibitions. Ps +37:1. +137, Pr 28:16.

175. Error prevalent, corrupting and ruinous. Ja +5:20. +183, Jn 1:12. +477, Mt 15:14.

176. Heresies and errors designed and adapted to try mankind. 1 C +11:19. +243, 1 C 11:19.

177. Fellowship with errorists to be avoided. 1 T +6:5. +112, 2 Ch 19:2. +115, Re 18:4. +477, Mt 15:14.

178. Good examples required. 1 T +4:12.

179. Good examples to be followed—bad, to be avoided. 1 C +11:1.

180. Extravagance and prodigality sinful—Examples. Ec +2:10. +173, 1 T 2:9. +199, Ph 3:19. +625, Mk 4:19.

181. Nature of true faith. He +11:1.

182. Faith counted for righteousness. Ro +4:3.

183. Faith in Christ, and belief of the truth, required as necessary to salvation. Jn +1:12. +175, Ja 5:20. +601, Ac 3:19.

184. Examples of faith. 2 C +5:7. +664, 1 P 1:8.

185. Effects of faith. 1 J 5:4.

186. Evidence of faith. Ja +2:18. +302, Ps 19:11. +602, Ps 119:6.

187. Strength of faith required. Ep +6:10. +712, 1 C *15:58.

188. Contending for the faith exemplified and required. Ju +*3. +458, Mt 28:19.

189. Faith of miracles, and the peculiar promises to it. Ja +5:15. +100, Mt 10:1.

190. Was the faith of miracles saving faith? 1 C +13:2.

191. Spurious faith, formalism, and selfish religion common and ruinous to the soul. 2 T +3:5. +194, Lk 18:12. +333, 1 S 16:7. +411, Ps 106:13. +609, 2 C 7:10. +623, Ga 4:17. +689, Jb 21:15. +702, Ps +5:9. +704, Pr 16:25.

192. Directions for fasting. Mt +6:16.

193. Fasting exemplified. Mt +4:2.

194. Spurious fasting. Lk +18:12. +191, 2 T 3:5. +411, Ps 106:13. +609, 2 C 7:10. +623, Ga 4:17. +689, Jb 21:15.

195. Female industry and enterprise. Ac +9:39.

196. Female piety, sympathy, and kindness. Mt +27:55.

197. Female subordination and speaking. Col +3:18. +425, T 2:4.

198. Flattery a common and dangerous sin. Ps +12:3. +474, Mt 7:15. +475, Ac 20:29. +702, Ps 5:9. +728, Ja 3:6.

199. Instructions respecting food—gluttony reproved. Ph +3:19. +368, Ro 14:21. +721, 1 C 9:25.

200. Who are fools? (A looking glass)

200-1. Atheists. Ps +14:1. +22, Ps 14:1.

200-2. Blabbers. Pr +29:11. +729, Ps 101:5.

200-3. Blasphemers. Ps +74:18. +718, Ex 20:7.

200-4. Boasters. Ro +1:22. +703, Lk 16:15.

200-5. Children, disobedient. Pr 15:5. +54, Dt 27:16.

200-6. Deceivers—self-deceivers—hypocrites. Pr +12:15. +702, Ps 5:9.

200-7. Obstinate offenders. Pr +13:19. +488, Ezk 22:29.

200-8. Drunkards. Pr +20:1.

200-9. Gossips. Pr +15:2. +729, Ps 101:5.

200-10. Ignoramuses. Pr +18:2. +363, Jb 21:14.

200-11. Knaves. Je +17:11.

200-12. Libertines. Pr +7:22. +405, He 13:4.

200-13. Meddlers. Pr +20:3.

200-14. Misers. Pr +1:32. +625, Mk 4:19. +626, Pr 23:4.

200-15. Mockers. Pr +14:9.

200-16. Rovers. Pr +17:24.

200-17. Slanderers. Pr +10:18.

200-18. Sots. Pr +17:16. +693, Ps 10:4.

200-19. Spendthrifts. Pr +21:20.

200-20. Sportsmen. Pr +10:23. +479, Pr 14:13.

200-21. Warriors. Pr +12:16. +735, Ja 1:20.

201. Forbearance required and commended. Pr +19:11. +203, Ep *4:32. +437, Ga 6:1. +438, Mt +5:5. +439, Ac 7:59. +498, Ja 1:4. +499, He 12:14. +737, Pr 16:7.

202. Sinners abuse forbearance. Ec +8:11.

203. Duty to forgive, as we hope to be forgiven—Threats to the implacable. Ep +4:32. +62, Mt 11:29. +539, Mt 6:12. +583, 1 J 2:12. +737, Pr 16:7.

204. True friendship desirable—how to make friends. Pr +17:17. +737, Pr 16:7.

205. Spurious friendship—Ingratitude. Ps +38:11. +701, Ro 3:15.

206. Has mankind any intuitive knowledge of God? Ro +1:19. +394, Jn 6:69.

207. God made known by His works. Ps +75:1.

208. God a moral agent, with affections and passions. Ps +7:11. +223, Ps 104:31. +230, Ge 6:6. +238, 2 P 3:9.

209. God's chief end—His regard for Himself. Pr +16:4. +276, Jn 11:42. +277, Ps 46:10. +570, Ps 83:18.

210. Divine unity, or only one true God. 1 C +8:6.

211. Are there more persons than one in the Godhead? Is +6:8. +75, Jn 5:18. +76-1, Col 2:10. +346, He 9:14.

212. Eternity of God. Dt +33:27. +76-3, Mi 5:2.

213. Foreknowledge of God. Ac 2:23. +219, He 4:13.

214. Greatness, majesty, and supremacy of God. 1 Ch +29:11. +45-1, Ps 19:12. +45-2, Ps 19:7. +234, Ro 9:18. +275, Ro 11:33.

215. Essential happiness of God. Ro 1:25. +223, Ps 104:31.

216. Invisibility of God. He +11:27.

217. Immutability of God. Ja +1:17. +76-4, He 13:8. +250, Ps 33:11.

218. Omnipotence of God. Re +19:6. +76-5, 1 C 1:24. +234, Ro 9:18. +259, He 11:3. +588, 2 C 9:8.

219. Omniscience of God. He +4:13. +76-7, Mt 9:4. +213, Ac 2:23.

220. Omnipresence of God. Pr +15:3. +76-6, Mt 18:20.

221. Self-existence of God. Jn +5:26.
222. Wisdom of God. Ro +11:33. +142, Je 10:12. +275, Ro 11:33.
223. Blessedness or joy of God, arising from his benevolent designs and works. Ps +104:31. +208, Ps 7:11. +215, Ro 1:25.
224. Benevolence of God—He desires good, and deprecates evil. Ps +119:68. +60, Mt 14:14. +228, Ps 145:9. +233, Jon 4:2. +254, Ac 13:48. +370, Re 22:17. +371, Is 1:18. +372, Lk 19:42. +585, Jb 36:7. +672, Dt 33:9.
225. Compassion of God. Ja +5:11. +233, Jon 4:2. +522, Ps 140:12. +585, Jb 36:7.
226. Faithfulness of God. 1 P +4:19. +4, Dt 8:2. +235, Ex 34:6. +515, Jn 10:28. +516, Ro 8:34. +517, 2 C 1:22. +725, 1 C 10:13.
227. Forbearance and long-suffering of God. Ro +2:4. +67, Mk 12:12.
228. Goodness and condescension of God. Ps +145:9. +60, Mt 14:14. +61, Lk 22:27. +224, Ps 119:68. +233, Jon 4:2.* +254, Ac 13:48. +372, Lk 19:42. +672, Dt 33:9.
229. Holiness and beauty of God. Re +15:4.
230. God's holy grief, displeasure and controversy with sinners. Ge +6:6. +208, Ps 7:11. +236, Ro 11:22. +362, Ex 22:20. +418, Pr 19:9. +548, Je 10:25. +557, Ro 7:13. +558, He 10:30. +559, Is 27:11.
231. Impartiality of God. Ro +2:11. +556, Mt 16:27.
232. Justice and righteousness of God. Ps +33:5. +236, Ro 11:22.
233. Mercy, grace, and kindness of God. Jon 4:2. +225, Ja 5:11. +228, Ps 145:9. +585, Jb 36:7. +672, Dt 33:9.
234. Sovereignty, freedom, and independence of God. Ro +9:18. +240, Jb 38:33. +241, Mt 4:10. +242, 2 T 2:25. +243, 2 C 11:19. +244, 1 S 15:3. +245, Da 4:17. +246, Ex 20:5. +247, 1 Ch 6:15. +248, Dt 32:35.
235. Truth of God. Ex 34:6. +226, 1 P 4:19.
236. Vindicative justice of God. Ro +11:22. +230, Ge 6:6. +232, Ps 33:5. +557, Ro 7:13. +558, He 10:30. +559, Is 27:11. +569, Pr 27:22. +570, Ps 83:18. +571, Lk 23:41.
237. God's vindicative justice amiable, desirable, and comforting. Dt +32:43. +88, Zp 3:14. +571, Lk 23:41.
238. Zeal of God. 2 P +3:9. +208, Ps 7:11.
239. God's right of property in his creatures. Ro +14:8.
240. God's right to establish and control natural law. Jb +38:33.
241. God's right to give supreme moral law. Mt +4:10. +280, Ps 22:28.
242. God's right to regenerate, or not—to give or withhold success to means—and to form, turn and control the hearts of men. 2 T +2:25. +234, Ro 9:18. +264, 2 Ch 18:31. +435, He 4:2.
243. God's right to try us by tempters, temptations, and stumblingblocks. 1 C +11:19.
244. God's right to require human life at His pleasure. 1 S +15:3.
245. God's right to appoint rulers and statutes in judgment. Da +4:17.
246. God's right to visit the iniquity of fathers upon children, etc. Ex +20:5. +497, 1 S 3:13.

247. God's right to use men instrumentally. 1 Ch +6:15. +265, 2 S 7:14.
248. God's right to vindicate Himself and servants. Dt +32:35. +558, He +10:30.
249. God has a perfect plan of operations. Dt +32:4. +304, Ep 3:11.
250. The purposes of God eternal and immutable. Ps +33:11. +217, Ja 1:17.
251. The purposes of God universal and particular. Jb +14:5. +307, Ep 1:9.
252. Purposes of God include natural and moral evil. 1 P +2:8. +3, 1 S 2:7. +264, 2 Ch 18:31. +265, 2 S 7:14. +266, Da 1:9. +267, Dt +*2:30.
253. National election. Ps +33:12.
254. Individual election. Ac +13:48. +234, Ro 9:18. +242, 2 T 2:25. +584, Jn 1:12.
255. Election previous to faith. Ep +1:4.
256. Purposes respecting the "vessels of wrath"—reprobation. Pr +16:4. +252, 1 P 2:8. +260, Ep √1:11. +267, Dt √2:30. +435, He 4:2. +436, Mt *7:6. +560, Mt 5:20.
257. God's purposes include means and ends. 2 Th +2:13. +17-3, Mt 4:6.
258. God's purposes encourage the use of means. Da +9:2. +431, Ps 126:5.
259. Nature and efficacy of God's providence. He +11:3. +218, Re 19:6.
260. Particularity and extent of God's providence. Ep +*1:11. +3, 1 S 2:7. +264, 2 Ch 18:31. +265, 2 S 7:14. +266, Da 1:9. +267, Dt +*2:30.
261. Providence supplies temporal wants. Mt +5:45.
262. All creatures dependent upon God's providence. 2 C +3:5.
263. All creatures preserved by God's providence. Ps +36:6.
264. God forms, turns and governs the heart. 2 Ch +18:31. +242, 2 T 2:25. +243, 2 C 11:19. +244, 1 S 15:3. +245, Da 4:17. +246, Ex 20:5.
265. God employs men as His instruments. 2 S +7:14. +278, Ps 39:9.
266. God's control of popular favor and frowns. Da +1:9.
267. God's providence in moral evils and delusions. Dt +*2:30. +252, 1 P 2:8. +256, Pr 16:4. +435, He 4:2.
268. God brings good out of evil—or sin the occasion of good. Ge +45:5. +277, Ps 46:10.
269. God not the actor, or instigator of sin. 1 C +14:33.
270. God and mankind often have different motives in effecting the same events. Ge +50:20.
271. Freedom and activity under the providence of God. Dt +30:19. +128, Ro 3:19. +329, 2 S 15:6. +373, Ps +58:5. +556, Mt 16:27. +600, Ps 119:59. +601, Ac 3:19.
272. Objections against God's providential government. Ezk +33:20. +273, Ro 9:20. +695, Lk 19:14. +706, Pr 14:9.
273. Objectors against Providence reproved. Ro +9:20.
274. The works and ways of Providence wonderful. Da 4:3.
275. The Providence of God incomprehensible. Ro +11:33. +214, 1 Ch 29:11. +222, Ro 11:33.
276. Revelations and wonders of Providence make

396. Knowledge should be imparted. Mt +5:19. +110, 1 Th 5:11.
397. Self-knowledge required. La +3:40. +105, 1 C 5:8. +704, Pr 16:25.
398. Knowledge more perfect hereafter. Jn +13:7.
399. Laying on of hands in communicating ordinary blessings. Re +1:17.
400. Laying on of hands in working miracles. Mk +16:18.
401. Laying on of hands in giving charges and designating to office. 1 T +5:22.
402. Lewdness a common vice. Je +9:2.
403. Lewdness deceitful and alluring. Pr +5:3.
404. Lewdness forbidden. Ac +15:20.
405. Guilt and condemnation of lewdness—cautions. He +13:4.
406. Liberality enjoined. Mt +10:8. +412, 1 Th 3:12. +526, Le 25:35.
407. Liberality exemplified. Ac +10:4. +355, Jb 31:32. +414, Lk 10:33. +661, Ac 4:32.
408. Rewards of liberality, and evils of covetousness. Lk +6:38. +415, Mk 10:30. +527, Mt 5:7. +630, Ps 58:11. +674, Lk 18:28.
409. Love to God our primary duty. Mt 22:37. +288, Ju 21.
410. Why should we love God? Ps +99:9.
411. Spurious love to God. Ps +106:13. +191, 2 T 3:5. +194, Lk 18:12. +609, 2 C 7:10. +623, Ga 4:17. +689, Jb 21:15. +702, Ps 5:9.
412. Love to man an essential duty. 1 Th +3:12. +406, Mt 10:8. +629, Pr 21:3. +685, Ml 2:10. +715, Mt 25:35.
413. Disinterested love required as indispensable. Ga +5:14. +111, Ac 4:32. +137, Pr 28:16. +138, Ep 5:5. +283, Ga 5:14. +299, Ac 21:14. +356, Jg 10:15. +674, Lk 18:28. +689, Jb 21:15.
414. Examples of disinterested love. Lk +10:33. +56, Jn 8:50. +299, Ac 21:14. +356, Jg 10:15. +407, Ac 10:4. +674, Lk 18:28.
415. Disinterested love rewarded. Mk +10:30. +408, Lk 6:38. +527, Mt 5:7. +630, Ps 58:11.
416. Lying a prevalent sin. Jn +8:44. +702, Ps 5:9.
417. Lying forbidden. Col +3:9. +729, Ps 101:5. +730, Ju 8.
418. Lying displeasing to God. Pr +19:9. +230, Ge 6:6.
419. Man's common origin and dignity. Ac +17:26.
420. Man's power of intuition, or perception of self-evident truths. Lk +12:57. +206, Ro 1:19.
421. Man's power of reason, and capacity for knowledge, holiness, and progress. Ezk +12:2. +667, 2 P 3:18.
422. Man's immortality. 2 T +1:10. +152, Ec 3:21. +617, Ac 24:15.
423. Marriage instituted and recommended. He +13:4.
424. Matrimonial instructions and warnings. 2 C +6:14.
425. Mutual duties of husbands and wives. T +2:4. +197, Col 3:18.
426. Polygamy forbidden—its tendency. 1 T +3:2.
427. Divorce discountenanced. Lk +16:18.
428. Means and instruments of grace appointed. Mk +4:14. +47, Ps 19:7.

429. Use of means required as indispensable. Ac +27:31. +257, 2 Th 2:13.
430. Preaching, the principal means of grace. 1 C +1:17. +458, Mt 28:19.
431. Use of means encouraged by promises and predictions. Ps +126:5. +1, 1 Ch 22:16. +258, Da 9:2. +545, Da 10:12.
432. Means, successfully used. 1 C +4:15. +468, 1 T 4:16. +545, Da 10:12.
433. Superiority of the true means of grace. Lk +16:31. +47, Ps 19:7.
434. Use of means made effectual by divine power. 2 T +2:25. +594, Dt 30:6. +595, Ac 5:31. +596, Ps 17:5.
435. The means of grace have different and sometimes destructive effects. He +4:2. +242, 2 T 2:25.
436. Cases of discouragement in using means. Mt +7:6. +256, Pr 16:4. +562, Lk 12:10.
437. Meekness required. Ga +6:1. +201, Pr 19:11. +482, Ph 2:3. +498, Ja 1:4. +499, He 12:14. +737, Pr 16:7.
438. Meekness encouraged. Mt +*5:5.
439. Meekness exemplified. Ac +7:59. +62, Mt 11:29. +660, Mt 10:16.
440. A millennium of holiness and happiness upon this earth predicted. Re +20:4. +90, Re 11:15.
441. Millennium a time of general holiness. Is +60:21. +506, Dt 30:6.
442. Millennium a time of peace and unity. Ps +37:11.
443. Millennium a time of true knowledge. He +8:11.
444. Millennium a time of prosperity. Is +35:2. +446, Ac 3:21.
445. Millennium a time of enjoyment. Is +35:10.
446. Millennium a contrast to previous times. Ac +3:21.
447. Design and use of the Christian ministry. Ep +4:11. +101, Je 3:15.
448. Ministers divinely appointed and qualified. Lk +10:1. +480, Mk 16:15.
449. Call to preach the gospel. He +5:4.
450. Ordination of ministers. Mk +3:14. +401, 1 T 5:22.
451. Oriental or pre-Mosaic priesthood. Ex +3:1.
452. Primitive mode of preaching. Ac +17:2. +447, Ep 4:11. +458, Mt 28:19. +461, 1 T 5:20.
453. Ministerial qualifications. 1 C +4:2.
454. Significant names of ministers. 2 C +5:20.
455. Ministerial authority and rights. 2 C +10:8.
456. Limits of ministerial authority. 1 P +5:3.
457. Ministerial duties. The cultivation of knowledge, piety, and wisdom required and exemplified. Mt +10:16. +369, Pr 31:4. +463, Je 23:2.
458. Preaching faithfully as "ambassadors for Christ" required and exemplified. Mt +28:19. +48, Jsh 1:8. +65, Mt 4:23. +188, Ju 3. +279, Ps 36:9. +430, 1 C 1:17. +462, Ml 3:18.
459. Duty to be properly inoffensive. Mt +17:27. +67, Mk 12:12. +135, 1 P 3:8.
460. Duty to fear not man—boldness exemplified. Ph +1:20. +134, Jsh 1:9. +659, Jn 1:47.
461. Exposing sins, and reproving transgressors required and exemplified. 1 T +5:20. +610, Pr 28:23. +611, Ga 2:11.

462. Duty to distinguish saints from sinners. Ml +3:18. +458, Mt 28:19. +645, Jb 2:3.

463. The duties of praying, watching and visiting required and exemplified—negligence reproved. Je +23:2.

464. Entire devotion to the calling required and exemplified. 1 T +4:15.

465. Ministerial responsibility. 1 T +1:11.

466. Ministerial temptations
    466-1. To please their hearers. Nu +24:10.
    466-2. To avoid the frowns of the influential. Ac +4:18.
    466-3. To conceal the true God. Is +30:9.
    466-4. To countenance popular errors, delusions and vices. Am +2:12.

467. Trials and persecutions of faithful ministers. 2 T +3:12. +68, Ps 2:2. +511, Ps 42:10.

468. Success in preaching promised, encouraged, and exemplified. 1 T *4:16. +432, 1 C 4:15.

469. Is present success always in proportion to faithfulness? Ac +13:46. +435, He 4:2.

470. Faithful ministers encouraged and rewarded by God. Ezk +3:8. +630, Ps 58:11.

471. Faithful ministers to be prayed for. 1 Th +5:25.

472. Faithful ministers should be supported. Ga +6:6.

473. Ministers of Satan. False and unfaithful ministers numerous. 1 J 4:1.

474. False and unfaithful ministers deceitful. Mt +7:15. +15, Jb 1:7. +198, Ps 12:3. +702, Ps 5:9.

475. False and unfaithful teachers cruel, dangerous and despicable—Threats. Ac +20:29. +175, Ja 5:20. +176, 1 C 11:19. +177, 1 T 6:5.

476. False and unfaithful teachers, sought after. Jn +5:43. +175, Ja 5:20. +704, Pr 16:25.

477. False teachers to be avoided—cautions. Mt +15:14. +18, Ep 4:27. +112, 2 Ch 19:2. +175, Ja 5:20. +176, 1 C 11:19. +177, 1 T 6:5.

478. False teachers destroy themselves and others. Mt +15:14.

479. Mankind prone to mirth—nature and tendency of. Pr +14:13. +698, Ep 2:3. +711, 1 P 4:7.

480. Missions needed and divinely appointed. Mk +16:15. +359, 2 K 16:3. +448, Lk 10:1.

481. Encouragement of missions. Ac +28:28. +90, Re 11:15. +440, Re 20:4.

482. Modesty and lowliness required. Ph +2:3. +62, Mt 11:29. +437, Ga 6:1.

483. Modesty in good works. Mt +6:1. +703, Lk 16:15.

484. National organizations appointed. Ac +17:26.

485. National promises and favors to the obedient. Ps +81:13. +302, Ps 19:11. +630, Ps 58:11. +642, Je 17:24. +686, He 13:3.

486. National threats and calamities for disobedience. Ezk +39:23. +87, Ps 37:9. +303, Ps 34:16. +362, Ex 22:20. +381, Zc 10:11. +490, Jb 27:13. +523, Ps 12:5. +566, Ge 6:13. +630, Ps 58:11. +643, Ex 35:2. +733, Nu *32:23.

487. Neutrality towards Christ and his cause apparent, not real. Mt +12:30.

488. Specimens of ancient oppression. Ezk +22:29. +200-7, Pr 13:19. +681, Ezk 27:13. +682, 1 T 1:10.

489. Effects of oppression upon oppressors. Pr +21:7. +733, Nu *32:23.

490. God notices and hates oppressors—threats. Jb +27:13. +523, Ps 12:5. +636, Pr 22:22. +679, Col 4:1.

491. Infatuation of oppressors. Ec +7:7. +707, 2 P 3:5.

492. Parents should set a good example. Ps +101:2. +178, 1 T 4:12.

493. Parents should instruct and govern their children. Pr +22:6. +48, Jsh 1:8.

494. Parents should correct children for disobedience. Pr +13:24. +54, Dt 27:16.

495. Parents should provide for their children. 2 C +12:14.

496. Happy result of parental faithfulness. Pr +22:6. +120, Ac 2:39.

497. Sad result of parental unfaithfulness—judicial visitation. 1 S +3:13. +733, Nu *32:23.

498. Patience required. Ja +1:4. +62, Mt 11:29. +154, Jb 14:14. +201, Pr 19:11. +437, Ga 6:1. +660, Mt 10:16. +737, Pr 16:7.

499. A peaceable and gentle spirit required, encouraged, and exemplified. He +12:14. +62, Mt 11:29. +201, Pr 19:11. +437, Ga 6:1. +660, Mt 10:16. +737, Pr 16:7.

500. False peace-makers. Je +6:14. +191, 2 T 3:5.

501. Commands and exhortations to be perfect in all good works. 2 C +7:1. +285, Mt 5:48. +286, Ro 7:12. +629, Pr 21:3.

502. Should perpetual moral perfection be pledged in a covenant with God? Ne +10:29. +118, Ro 2:29.

503. The appellation, "perfect," applied to saints. 1 C +2:6.

504. Do saints attain any moral perfection in which God delights? Ps +119:1. +94, Ep 5:25. +505, Ps 119:3. +584, Jn 1:12. +585, Jb 36:7. +659, Jn 1:47. +672, Dt 33:9.

505. Can the "perfect love" of saints be blended with sin? Ps +119:3. +503, 1 C 2:6.

506. Millennial perfection. Dt +30:6. +441, Is *60:21.

507. Inconstant perfection of saints in this life. 1 J +*1:8. +166, Pr 5:22. +663, Mt 8:8.

508. Real saints subjected to occasional afflictions and chastisements. Re +3:19. +2, Jb 5:7. +3, 1 S 2:7. +4, Dt 8:2.

509. Would God afflict His people, had they attained permanent moral perfection? He +12:10.

510. Self-deceived perfectionists. Pr +30:12. +696, Ps 10:4. +703, Lk 16:15. +704, Pr 16:25.

511. The righteous reproached and persecuted. Ps +42:10. +68, Ps 2:2. +86, Is 24:5. +467, 2 T 3:12. +740, Jn 17:14.

512. Ultimate triumph of those persecuted for righteousness' sake. 2 T 2:12. +4, Dt 8:2. +337, Re 14:13.

513. God will abase persecutors. Je +20:11. +87, Ps 37:9. +525, Lk 16:25. +550, Pr 16:5. +573-7, Da 12:2.

514. Perseverance in holiness indispensable. Col +1:23. +19, 1 S 15:11. +20, He 6:4. +540, 1 Th 5:17.

515. Predictions and promises of saints' perseverance. Jn +*10:28. +95, Ps 125:2. +667, 2 P 3:18.

516. Christ's intercession for the saints. Ro +8:34.

517. Sealing and "earnest of the Spirit." 2 C 1:22.
518. Popery or the Romish hierarchy predicted. Re +17:5.
519. Was Peter made head of the apostles, or universal bishop? 1 P +5:1.
520. Dreadful end of Popery and mystery Babylon. Re +17:16.
521. Evils of poverty. Pr +10:15.
522. God pities and helps the poor. Ps +140:12. +224, Ps 119:68. +225, Ja 5:11.
523. Oppression of the poor forbidden—Threats. Ps +12:5. +490, Jb 27:13. +679, Col 4:1.
524. The poor often distinguished by God's special grace. Ja +2:5.
525. Future contrast between the humble poor, and their oppressors. Lk +16:25. +513, Je 20:11. +550, Pr 16:5.
526. Duty to help the poor and the afflicted, and to avoid prejudice and partiality. Le +25:35. +7, Jb 6:14. +687, Pr 21:13.
527. Encouragements to help the poor. Mt +5:7. +354, T 1:8. +408, Lk 6:38. +630, Ps 58:11. +686, He 13:3.
528. Praising God in private and social worship required and exemplified. He +13:15. +747, Ep 5:19.
529. Praise should be offered with a devout heart. Col +3:16. +333, 1 S 16:7.
530. Prayer an important and necessary duty. Lk +18:1. +64, Mt 14:23.
531. Secret prayer required and exemplified. Mt +14:23. +665, Ps 1:2.
532. Mental prayer exemplified. 1 S +1:13.
533. Prayer, verbal and audible, required and exemplified. Ps +55:17.
534. Devout prayer includes love and obedience to God. Jn +9:31. +289, 1 C 2:9.
535. Acceptable prayer includes faith in God. He +11:6. +293, Is 26:3.
536. True prayer includes submission to God. Ps +37:7. +278, Ps 39:9. +298, Ja +4:7.
537. Prayer includes humility, confession, and repentance. Lk +18:14. +124, Pr 28:13. +356, Jg 10:15. +357, Ja 4:10. +663, Mt 8:8.
538. Prayer includes a supreme regard for God's glory. Ps +79:9. +300, 1 T 1:17. +662, Ps 119:158.
539. Acceptable prayer includes a forgiving temper. Mt +6:12. +203, Ep *4:32.
540. Prayer includes importunity and perseverance. 1 Th +5:17. +514, Col 1:23.
541. Prayer should be offered in Christ's name. Jn +16:24.
542. Prayer implies godly sincerity. Ps +145:18. +333, 1 S 16:7.
543. Prayer implies holy sympathy and compassion. Pr +21:13.
544. Various postures in prayer—(no sitting). Mk +11:25. ◐+1283, 1 Ch 17:16.
545. Prayer heard and answered—its efficacy. Da +10:12. +431, Ps 126:5. +670, Mt 5:14.
546. Prayer and worship of the ungodly not acceptable. Ps +66:18. +165, Ps 5:9. +589, Ps 50:16.
547. Prayer not agreeable to the wicked. Jb +27:10. +22, Ps 14:1.
548. God displeased with prayerless persons. Je +10:25. +230, Ge 6:6. +1820, Jsh 9:14.

549. Pride and self-conceit prevalent evils. Ps +10:2. +696, Ps 10:4. +703, Lk 16:15.
550. Pride and self-conceit offensive to God— threats. Pr +16:5. +513, Je 20:11.
551. Pride tends to a fall. Pr +16:18. +733, Nu *32:23.
552. Retribution imperfect during this life. Ps +103:10. +565, Mt 6:5.
553. Probation limited to this life—its immeasurable importance. 2 C +6:2. +390, Lk 16:26. +572, Jb 27:8. +727, Ps 90:12.
554. Probation includes danger of losing the soul. Lk +9:24. +563, Re 2:11.
555. Probationary conduct determines our final state; or salvation conditional. 1 Ch +*28:9. +183, Jn 1:12. +203, Ep 4:32. +278, Ps 39:9. +298, Ja 4:7. +302, Ps 19:11. +514, Col +*1:23. +567, Mt 25:46. +589, Ps 50:16. +601, Ac 3:19. +606, Lk +*13:3. +629, Pr 21:3.
556. Rewards and punishments according to probationary conduct. Mt +16:27. +231, Ro 2:11. +232, Ps 33:5.

PUNISHMENT IN A FUTURE STATE

557. Sins against God, "exceeding sinful." Ro +7:13. +230, Ge 6:6. +236, Ro 11:22.
558. God's prerogative to punish according to desert. He +10:30.
559. Will God's love and compassion save unbelievers? Is +27:11. +230, Ge 6:6. +572, Jb 27:8. +573-7, Da 12:2.
560. The finally impenitent to be separated from the saints, and shut out of heaven. Mt +5:20. +256, Pr 16:4. +287, Ja 1:15. +387, Mt 25:32. +390, Lk 16:26. +554, Lk 9:24.
561. The wicked to be cast into hell. Ps +9:17. +236, Ro 11:22. +237, Dt 32:43. +287, Ja 1:15. +343, Lk 16:24. +387, Mt 25:32.
562. Future punishment evinced by the unpardonable sin. Lk +12:10.
563. Future punishment evinced by the second death. Re +2:11. +287, Ja 1:15.
564. Future punishment evinced by death in impenitence. Jn +8:21.
565. Future punishment evinced by the present prosperity of the wicked, and sufferings of the righteous. Mt +6:5. +511, Ps 42:10. +552, Ps 103:10.
566. Future punishment presaged by temporal judgments. Ge +6:13. +87, Ps 37:9. +486, Ezk 39:23. +630, Ps 58:11. +733, Nu *32:23.
567. Punishment everlasting. Mt +*25:46. +287, Ja 1:15. +390, Lk 16:26. +553, 2 C 6:2. +554, Lk 9:24. +555, 1 Ch *28:9. +572, Jb 27:8. +573-1, Jb 8:13.
568. Future punishment denied or disbelieved by some. Ezk +13:22. +22, Ps 14:1. +708, He 3:12.
569. The wicked not always purified by punishment. Pr +27:22. +9, Is 9:13.
570. The wicked punished according to their desert, to make known and glorify God. Ps +83:13. +209, Pr 16:4. +276, Jn 11:42.
571. Punishment approved by the righteous. Lk +23:41. +88, Zp 3:14. +237, Dt 32:43.
572. The cries of lost souls unavailing. Jb +27:8. +390, Lk 16:26. +553, 2 C 6:2. +554, Lk

9:24. +555, 1 Ch *28:9. +559, Is 27:11.
+567, Mt *25:46.

573.   Sources of future misery
573-1.   The loss of all hope, or complete
            despair. Jb +8:13. +390, Lk
            16:26. +567, Mt *25:46.
573-2.   Bitter reflections. Lk +16:25. +128,
            Ro 3:19. +131, 2 C 1:12.
573-3.   Deprivation of rest. Re +14:11.
573-4.   Banishment from all lovely beings,
            and suffering, while saints are
            rejoicing. Lk +13:28. +387, Mt
            25:32.
573-5.   Darkness and gloom. Mt +8:12.
573-6.   Painful fears and terrors. 2 C +5:11.
573-7.   Enduring the just scorn of the
            universe forever. Da +12:2.
            +513, Je 20:11.
573-8.   Pains of body by fire. Lk +16:24.
            +343, Lk 16:24.
574.   Degradation of the wicked, here and hereafter.
        T +3:3. +513, Je 20:11.

REDEMPTION OF SAINTS

575.   Redemption—covenant of. He +13:20.
576.   Necessity of atonement, or the salvation of sin-
        ners through obedience to the law of God,
        hopeless. Ps +143:2. +183, Jn 1:12.
577.   Redemption through the death or blood of
        Christ. Ro +3:25.
578.   Efficacy of the atonement, or "the Lord our
        righteousness." Is +*53:6.
579.   Redemption requires a perfect Redeemer.
        1 P +1:19.
580.   The Redeemer "a ransom for all." 1 T +2:6.
        +370, Re 22:17.
581.   Agency of the Father in making atonement.
        Is +53:6.
582.   Redemption includes peace with God. He
        +2:17. +666, Ph 4:7.
583.   Redemption includes forgiveness or justifica-
        tion, and access. 1 J +2:12.
584.   Redemption includes adoption as "sons of
        God." Jn +*1:12. +254, Ac 13:48. +255,
        Ep 1:4. +504, Ps 119:1. +672, Dt 33:9.
585.   Redemption includes peculiar mercy, faithful-
        ness, and loving kindness to Zion. Jb +36:7.
        +60, Mt 14:14. +94, Ep 5:25. +95, Ps 125:2.
        +233, Jon 4:2. +672, Dt 33:9.
586.   Redemption or salvation by grace. Ac +20:24.
        +305, Ac 20:24. +668, 1 C 4:7.
587.   Redemption honorable to God and his law.
        Ps +85:10. +277, Ps 46:10.

REGENERATION AND SANCTIFICATION

588.   God able to sanctify us, and to keep us from
        sin. 2 C +9:8. +218, Re 19:6. +234, Ro
        9:18.
589.   Regeneration necessary, or the total sinfulness
        of unregenerate doings. Ps +50:16. +165,
        Ps 5:9. +546, Ps 66:18. +688, Ro 7:18.
        +689, Jb 21:15.
590.   Regeneration preceded by conviction, and the
        death of false hopes. Ac +2:37. +356, Jg
        10:15.
591.   Regeneration, a radical change. 2 C +*5:17.
        +645, Jb 2:3.
592.   Regeneration a moral or spiritual change. Jn
        +*3:6. +329, 2 S 15:6. +600, Ps 119:59.

593.   Regeneration alarming to sinners. Ps +40:3.
594.   Creative or omnipotent power exerted in re-
        generation and sanctification. Dt +30:6.
        +347-4, Ga 4:6. +434, 2 T 2:25.
595.   Particular holy exercises the gift of God. Ac
        +5:31.
596.   Saints as dependent as sinners, for holy affec-
        tions. Ps +17:5. +262, 2 C 3:5.
597.   Effectual calling. Ac +2:39.
598.   Regeneration and sanctification illuminate.
        1 C +*2:14. +707, 2 P 3:5.
599.   Regeneration connected with divine teaching.
        Jn +6:45.
600.   Are men active, under the influence of means
        and instruments, and the agency of the Holy
        Spirit? Ps +119:59. +271, Dt 30:19. +329,
        2 S 15:6. +332, Pr 4:23. +432, 1 C 4:15.
        +592, Jn *3:6.
601.   Sinners required to "be converted," and holy.
        Ac +3:19. +183, Jn 1:12. +288, Ju 21. +606,
        Lk 13:3.
602.   Obedience to God, the evidence of regenera-
        tion. Ps +119:6. +186, Ja 2:18.
603.   Nature and manifestations of repentance.
        2 C +7:10. +30, Jb 40:4. +124, Pr 28:13.
        +356, Jg 10:15. +357, Ja 4:10.
604.   Moral dignity of true penitence for sin. Is
        +57:15. +672, Dt 33:9.
605.   Effects of repentance and godly sorrow. 2 C
        +7:11. +602, Ps 119:6. +621, Ac 8:8.
606.   Repentance required—its necessity. Lk
        +13:3. +357, Ja 4:10. +601, Ac 3:19.
607.   Repentance encouraged—promises. 2 Ch
        +*7:14. +357, Ja 4:10.
608.   Repentance, as ascribed to God. Jon +3:10.
609.   Spurious repentance. 2 C +7:10. +191, 2 T
        3:5. +194, Lk 18:12. +411, Ps 106:13. +623,
        Ga 4:17. +689, Jb 21:15.
610.   Faithful reproof required and encouraged. Pr
        +28:23. +109, Ga 6:1.
611.   Reproving others exemplified. Ga +2:11. +66,
        Jn 18:37. +461, 1 T 5:20.
612.   Reproof gratefully received by the humble.
        Pr +28:23.
613.   Reproof rejected by the proud. Pr +13:1.
614.   Wisdom of receiving reproof—folly of rejecting
        it. Pr +12:1.
615.   Reprovers should correct their own faults. Mt
        +7:5.
616.   Value of reputation—sin of abusing it. Pr
        +22:1. +729, Ps 101:5. +730, Ju 8.
617.   General resurrection of the dead. Ac +24:15.
618.   The dead raised with incorruptible bodies. Ph
        +3:21.
619.   Ancient revivals of religion. Ac +5:14.
620.   The influences of the Spirit compared to rain,
        or the pouring of water. Ps +72:6.
621.   Happy effects of genuine revivals. Ac +8:8.
        +605, 2 C 7:11.
622.   Praying for revivals required and exemplified.
        Ps +85:6.
623.   Spurious revivals. Ga +4:17. +191, 2 T 3:5.
        +194, Lk 18:12. +411, Ps 106:13. +609,
        2 C 7:10. +689, Jb 21:15.
624.   Riches, the idol of many. 2 T +4:10.
625.   Riches and prosperity have a corrupting and
        dangerous tendency. Mk +4:19. +741, Mt
        13:22.
626.   The eager pursuit of riches forbidden and dis-

couraged. Pr +23:4. +133, Ph 4:11. +742, Jn 6:27. +743, 1 J 5:4.

627. Riches vain and transitory. Pr +23:5. +148, Ja 4:14.

628. Proper use of riches. 1 T +6:18. +406, Mt 10:8.

629. Righteousness, impartiality, truth, and honesty in spiritual and temporal things required and exemplified. Pr +21:3. +56, Jn 8:50. +501, 2 C 7:1. +659, Jn 1:47. +732, 1 Th 4:6.

630. Righteousness and honesty rewarded, or the "gain of godliness" and loss by ungodliness. Ps +58:11. +87, Ps 37:9. +286, Ro 7:12. +344, Pr 8:11. +362, Ex 22:20. +470, Ezk 3:8. +550, Pr 16:5. +551, Pr 16:18. +566, Ge 6:13. +733, Nu *32:23.

631. A right to liberty and justice—threats for infringing these rights. Jb +36:6. +682, 1 T 1:10.

632. A right to inquire freely, and to express opinions. Lk +12:57.

633. A right to pursue mental culture. Lk +11:52. +363, Jb 21:14. +391, Pr 8:10.

634. A right to enjoy the fruits of our own industry. Ec +3:22.

635. A right to our own wives and children. Ec +9:9.

636. Robbery forbidden and denounced. Pr +22:22. +490, Jb 27:13. +682, 1 T 1:10. +732, 1 Th 4:6. +733, Nu *32:23. +736, Mt 26:52.

637. The Sabbath instituted in Paradise. Ex +20:11.

638. Sabbath enjoined and recognized in the Decalogue, and other parts of the Old Testament. Ex +20:8.

639. Sabbath recognized, and its proper works of mercy asserted by Christ, the "Lord of the Sabbath." Mk +3:4.

640. Appropriate Duties of the Sabbath. Mk +6:2.

641. Sabbath to be kept holy; secular labor forbidden. Mt +24:20.

642. Rewards to sabbath-keepers. Je +17:24.

643. Punishment of sabbath-breakers. Ex +35:2.

644. The first day of the week distinguished and observed after the resurrection of Christ. Mk +16:9.

645. Saints radically differ from sinners. Jb +2:3. +591, 2 C *5:17.

SAINTS DISTINGUISHED FROM SINNERS BY OPPOSITE APPELLATIONS

646. The godly and ungodly. Ps +4:3.

647. The just and the unjust. Pr 29:27.

648. The righteous and wicked. Ml 3:18.

649. Friends of God and enemies of God. Ja +2:23. +690, Mt 13:38.

650. Lovers of God—haters of God. Ro +1:30.

651. Believers and unbelievers. Ac +5:14.

652. Sheep, and wolves or serpents. Mt +23:33.

653. Children of God, and children of the devil. Mt +13:38. +690, Mt 13:38.

654. Children of obedience and children of disobedience. 1 P +1:14.

655. Children of light, and children of darkness. Lk +16:8.

656. Children of the kingdom and children of wrath. Ep +2:3.

PECULIAR CHARACTERISTICS OF SAINTS

657. Saints hope and delight in God, have fellowship and communion with him, and desire his presence. 1 S +2:1. +6, Ps 23:4. +294, Jb 13:15.

658. Saints love and obey God's law, and delight in all his truth and institutions. Ro +7:22. +106, Ps 27:4.

659. Honesty, integrity, and firmness of saints, leaving consequences to God. Jn +1:47. +56, Jn 8:50. +294, Jb 13:15. +460, Ph 1:20. +504, Ps 119:1. +629, Pr 21:3.

660. Saints have a meek, gentle, forbearing, and forgiving spirit. Mt +10:16. +62, Mt 11:29. +437, Ga 6:1. +499, He 12:14. +737, Pr 16:7.

661. Saints are self-edifying, disinterested, and devoted to God and His cause. Ac +4:32. +295, Ec 12:13. +407, Ac 10:4. +414, Lk 10:33. +674, Lk 18:28.

662. Saints grieve when sinners dishonor and offend God. Ps +119:158. +538, Ps 79:9.

663. Saints feel their unworthiness, and desire to learn their guilt. Mt +8:8. +507, 1 J *1:8. +537, Lk 18:14.

664. Saints believe in Christ, and live by faith in Him. 1 P +1:8. +184, 2 C 5:7.

665. Saints delight in devout meditation and prayer. Ps +1:2. +64, Mt 14:23. +531, Mk 14:23.

666. Saints have peculiar internal peace. Ph +4:7. +582, He 2:17.

667. Saints make progress in knowledge and holiness. 2 P +3:18. +515, Jn *10:28.

668. Saints made to differ—boasting excluded. 1 C +4:7. +482, Ph 2:3.

669. Real saints have been comparatively few, but will be very numerous. Mt +7:14. +440, Re 20:4.

670. Saints, the light and salvation of the world. Mt +5:14. +545, Da 10:12.

671. Singularity of Saints. T +2:14.

672. God's delight in saints, and prospective view of their perfection, preeminence and glory. Dt +33:9. +94, Ep 5:25. +340, 1 C 2:9. +504, Ps 119:1. +584, Jn 1:12. +585, Jb 36:7.

673. Unhallowed scorn and contempt reprobated. Mt +18:10.

674. Self-denial required, exemplified, and encouraged. Lk +18:28. +356, Jg 10:15.

675. Improper sensual indulgences forbidden and reproved. 1 P +2:11. +366, Ep 5:18. +698, Ep 2:3.

676. Were the civil rights and religious privileges of the patriarchal servants so secured, as to gain their confidence? Jb +31:13.

677. Hebrew laws and usages on procuring, holding, and releasing servants.

677-1. Voluntary servants, and service for life, or for a term, and laws of release. Ex +21:5.

677-2. Hebrews and their children, sometimes sold for debt—laws of release, of reward, etc. Ex +21:2.

677-3. Permanent servants were of the heathen, or of strangers, and not Hebrews. Le +25:44.

678. Mosaic penalty for maiming servants. Ex +21:20.

679. Justice and kindness to servants enjoined—oppression forbidden. Col +4:1. +490, Jb 27:13. +636, Pr 22:22. +687, Pr 21:13.

680. Apostolic precepts respecting the duties of masters and servants. Col +3:22.

681. Ancient merchandise in "slaves and the souls of men." Ezk +27:13. +488, Ezk 22:29. +636, Pr 22:22.

682. Penalties for man-stealing, and infringing human liberty, in procuring and holding servants. 1 T 1:10. +489, Pr 21:7. +490, Jb 27:13. +491, Ec 7:7. +631, Jb 36:6. +636, Pr 22:22.

683. Freedom at the year of jubilee for servants. Le +25:10.

684. Freedom recommended as preferable to servitude. 1 C +7:21.

685. General precepts respecting the duty of man to man in all the relations of life. Ml +2:10. +412, 1 Th 3:12. +413, Ga 5:14. +414, Lk 10:33. +631, Jb 36:6. +632, Lk 12:57. +633, Lk 11:52. +634, Ec 3:22. +635, Ec 9:9.

686. Encouragement to treat those "in bonds," and in poverty and oppression, with sympathy and liberality. He +13:3. +527, Mt 5:7.

687. Duty to espouse the cause of the injured and oppressed. Pr +21:13. +490, Jb 27:13. +526, Le 25:35. +527, Mt 5:7.

688. Sinners destitute of holiness. Ro +7:18. +165, Ps 5:9. +589, Ps 50:16.

689. Sinners full of selfishness and unrighteousness. Jb +21:15. +137, Pr 28:16. +191, 2 T 3:5. +194, Lk 18:12. +411, Ps 106:13. +609, 2 C 7:10. +623, Ga 4:17. +728, Ja 3:6. +732, 1 Th 4:6. +733, Nu *32:23.

690. Sinners enemies to God, children of the adversary, and prone to wicked works. Mt +13:38. +68, Ps 2:2. +86, Is 24:5. +165, Ps 5:9. +166, Pr 5:22. +511, Ps 42:10. +702, Ps 5:9. +740, Jn 17:14.

691. Sinners disobedient to God. Pr +1:25.

692. Sinners prone to forget God. Ps +9:17. +22, Ps 14:1.

693. Sinners stupid, and inattentive to God. Ps +10:4. +132, Pr 6:6. +707, 2 P 3:5. +739, Jn 17:25.

694. Sinners depart from God. Ho +7:13.

695. Sinners hate the divine presence, government, and restraints. Lk +19:14. +22, Ps 14:1. +23, 1 K 11:4. +272, Ezk 33:20. +705, Ps 12:4.

696. Sinners self-righteous, proud, and opposed to grace. Ps +10:4. +373, Ps 58:5. +510, Pr 30:12. +549, Ps 10:2. +550, Pr 16:5.

697. Sinners rather perish, than come to Christ. Ac +13:46. +373, Ps 58:5.

698. Sinners inclined to sensual pleasures and lusts. Ep +2:3. +675, 1 P 2:11.

699. Sinners naturally inclined to idolatry. Je +44:17. +362, Ex 22:20.

700. Sinners inclined to murmur. Ju +16. +9, Is 9:13. +171, Pr 12:25. +272, Ezk 33:20.

701. Sinners ungrateful and cruel. Ro +3:15. +68, Ps 2:2. +205, Ps 38:11. +467, 2 T 3:12. +488, Ezk 22:29. +511, Ps 42:10. +523, Ps 12:5. +689, Jb 21:15. +690, Mt +13:38. +734, Is 1:15.

702. Sinners deceitful, and inclined to flatter, and lay snares. Ps +5:9. +191, 2 T 3:5. +194, Lk 18:12. +198, Ps 12:3. +411, Ps 106:13. +416, Jn 8:44. +474, Mt 7:15. +728, Ja 3:6.

703. Sinners inclined to ostentation, boasting, and glorying in their shame. Lk +16:15. +482, Ph 2:3. +549, Ps 10:2. +550, Pr 16:5.

704. Sinners inclined to self-deception—warnings. Pr +16:25. +25, Re 3:17. +397, La 3:40. +476, Jn 5:43. +510, Pr 30:12.

705. Sinners inclined to deny or resist obligation to God. Ps +12:4. +22, Ps 14:1. +695, Lk *19:14.

706. Sinners prone to deny or palliate their sins. Pr +14:9. +272, Ezk 33:20. +373, Ps +58:5.

707. Voluntary ignorance, blindness, and infatuation of sinners. 2 P +3:5. +26, Is 59:2. +693, Ps 10:4.

708. Sinners are inclined to theoretical and practical unbelief— Threat. He +3:12. +22, Ps 14:1. +568, Ezk 13:22.

709. Idleness of sinners. Ezk +16:49. +358, 1 T *5:13.

710. Presumption and procrastination of sinners—death put far away. Ps +49:11. +22, Ps 14:1. +479, Pr 14:13. +726, Ps 89:47. +727, Ps 90:12.

711. Sobriety and gravity required. 1 P +4:7. +479, Pr 14:13.

712. Steadfastness and firmness required. 1 C +*15:58. +187, Ep 6:10. +364, Ep 4:14.

713. Stealing forbidden. Ep +4:28.

714. Punishment of stealing—Threats. 1 C +6:10.

715. Justice, kindness and hospitality to strangers required. Mt +25:35. +354, T 1:8.

716. Suing, especially before the unbelieving and unjust, discountenanced. Mt +5:40.

717. Suretyship discountenanced—cautions. Pr +17:18.

718. Profane swearing forbidden and punished—Threats. Ex +20:7.

719. Examples of rash swearing. Ac +23:12.

720. Oaths of confirmation—examples. He +6:16.

721. Temperance required—its importance. 1 C +9:25. +199, Ph 3:19. +368, Ro 14:21.

722. Temptation, in the sense of trial, common to man. 1 C +*10:13.

723. Temptation, or solicitation to sin, not of God. Ja +1:13. +269, 1 C 14:33.

724. Duty to pray and watch against tempters and temptations. Mt +26:41. +18, Ep 4:27. +738, Lk 12:37.

725. Believers shall be helped out of all their temptations—promises. 1 C +*10:13. +3, 1 S 2:7. +4, Dt 8:2. +5, 2 C 4:17. +6, Ps 23:4.

726. Time short. Ps +89:47. +148, Ja 4:14.

727. Time should be improved; or procrastination forbidden. Ps +90:12. +156, Ps 90:12. +553, 2 C 6:2. +554, Lk 9:24. +555, 1 Ch *28:9. +556, Mt 16:27. +710, Ps 49:11.

728. The tongue often very injurious and mischievous. Ja +3:6. +198, Ps 12:3. +416, Jn 8:44. +702, Ps 5:9.

729. Censoriousness, railing, tale-bearing, whispering, backbiting, slander, and other sins of the tongue forbidden—Threats. Ps +101:5. +200-2, Pr 29:11. +200-3, Ps 74:18. +200-4, Ro 1:22. +200-9, Pr 15:2. +200-15, Pr 14:9. +200-17, Pr 10:18. +417, Col 3:9.

730. Railing at dignities, and reviling superiors, forbidden. Ju +8. +10, 1 P 5:5.
731. Bridling the tongue enjoined and exemplified. Ja +1:26.
732. Unrighteousness and dishonesty forbidden. 1 Th +4:6. +629, Pr 21:3. +636, Pr 22:22.
733. Unrighteousness, extortion, etc., inexpedient, or the tendency of sin to ruin sinners here and hereafter— Threats. Nu +*32:23. +87, Ps 37:9. +138, Ep 5:5. +303, Ps 34:16. +362, Ex 22:20. +381, Zc 10:11. +478, Mt 15:14. +486, Ezk 39:23. +489, Pr 21:7. +497, 1 S 3:13. +513, Je 20:11. +551, Pr 16:18. +555, 1 Ch *28:9. +556, Mt 16:27. +630, Ps 58:11. +735, Ja 1:20.
734. War and fighting have been prevalent. Is +1:15. +488, Ezk 22:29. +701, Ro 3:15.
735. Sin and folly of anger, and other warlike passions—wisdom of suppressing them. Ja +1:20. +200-21, Pr 12:16. +733, Nu *32:23.
736. Carnal fighting, and returning evil for evil, foolish and forbidden—Threats. Mt +26:52. +488, Ezk 22:29. +489, Pr 21:7. +490, Jb 27:13. +630, Ps 58:11. +733, Nu *32:23.
737. How to treat enemies, and to prevent war and fighting. Pr +16:7. +62, Mt 11:29. +201, Pr 19:11. +203, Ep 4:32. +204, Pr 17:17. +437, Ga 6:1. +498, Ja 1:4. +499, He 12:14. +660, Mt 10:16.
738. Watchfulness. Lk +12:37. +18, Ep 4:27. +477, Mt 15:14. +724, Mt 26:41.
739. The world ignorant of God. Jn +17:25. +693, Ps 10:4.
740. The world opposed to God and to his people. Jn +17:14. +68, Ps 2:2. +86, Is 24:5. +467, 2 T 3:12. +511, Ps 42:10. +690, Mt 13:38.
741. The world corrupting and dangerous—cautions. Mt +13:22. +122, Ps 26:4. +625, Mk 4:19.
742. Worldly idolatry forbidden—the contrary required. Jn +6:27. +626, Pr 23:4.
743. World, overcome by grace. 1 J +5:4. +59, Jn 5:41.
744. God the only proper object of religious worship. Mt +4:10. +80, Col 2:18. +280, Ps 22:28. +295, Ec 12:13.
745. Public worship of God required, encouraged, and exemplified. He +*10:25.
746. Public worship with religious instruction exemplified. Jn +8:2. +430, 1 C 1:17.
747. Public worship with social prayer, praise, and reverence. Ep +5:19. +528, He 13:15. +529, Col 3:16.
748. False Zeal exemplified. Ro +10:2.
749. True Zeal exemplified and required. Ga +4:18. +1, 1 Ch 22:16.
750. Zeal neccessary, to overcome "the world, the flesh, and the devil," and obtain the heavenly inheritance. Lk +13:24.

PRECIOUS BIBLE PROMISES

Promises of Temporal Blessings
751. Promises of temporal blessings to believers. Ps +84:11.
752. Temporal blessings in general. Ps +34:9.
753. Food. Ps +37:3.
754. Raiment. Mt +6:25.
755. Long life. Dt +5:16.
756. Health. Ps +103:3.

757. Safety under divine protection. Pr +1:33.
758. Peace. Ps +119:165.
759. Direction. Pr +3:6.
760. Honor. Jn +12:26.
761. Success and prosperity. Ps +1:3.
762. Plenty and riches. Pr +3:16.
763. Children. Ps +127:3.
764. A blessing upon all the believer has. Pr +10:22.
765. A blessing upon children of believers. Pr +20:7.
766. A blessing upon the families of the good. Pr +12:7.

Promises Relating to the Troubles of Life
767. Preservation from trouble. Ps +91:10.
768. Deliverance from trouble. Ps +34:19.
769. Support in trouble. Ps +9:9.
770. Deliverance from sickness. Ex +23:25.
771. Support in sickness. Ps +41:3.
772. Support in old age. Ps +71:9.
773. Deliverance from famine and want. Ps +33:19.
774. Deliverance from war. Jb +5:20.
775. Deliverance from enemies. Pr +16:7.
776. Deliverance from oppression and injustice. Is +54:14.
777. Deliverance from slander. Jb +5:21.
778. Deliverance from reproach. 1 P +4:14.
779. Deliverance from witchcraft. Nu +23:23.
780. Promises to the stranger and exile. Ps +146:9.
781. To the poor and helpless. Ja +2:5.
782. Promises to the fatherless and widow. Dt +10:18.
783. To the childless. Ps +113:9.
784. To the prisoner and captive. Ps +146:7.
785. Deliverance from death. Jb +33:28.

Promises of Spiritual Blessings in This Life
786. In general. 2 P +1:4.
787. Justification. Is +45:25.
788. Pardon of sin. Ps +130:4.
789. Forgiveness of the most heinous sins. Is +1:18.
790. Forgiveness of all sins. Ps +103:3.
791. Forgiveness of backsliding. Ho +14:4.
792. Forgiveness through Christ. Ac +13:38.
793. Reconciliation through Christ. 2 C +5:18.
794. Adoption. Ga +4:5.
795. Union and communion with the church. Ga +3:28.
796. Free access to God, with acceptance. Ep +2:18.
797. Of hearing prayer. 1 J +5:14.
798. Sanctifying grace in general. Ps +84:11.
799. Of converting grace. Ezk +36:26.
800. The grace of repentance. Ac +5:31.
801. The grace of faith. Ph +1:29.
802. Grace to fear God. Je +32:39.
803. Knowledge. Pr +2:5.
804. Wisdom. Pr +2:6.
805. Divine teaching. Ps +32:8.
806. Divine guidance. Ps +23:3.
807. The means of grace. Je +3:15.
808. A blessing upon ordinances. Ps +65:4.
809. Grace to mortify sin. Ro +6:14.
810. Grace against temptation. 2 P +2:9.
811. From the enticement of sinners. Ec +7:26.
812. Victory over the world. Ga +1:4.
813. Victory over the devil. Ja +4:7.
814. Strength, courage, resolution. Is +12:2.
815. Fruitfulness. 2 P +1:8.

816. Fruitfulness in old age. Ps +92:14.
817. Increase of grace. Pr +*4:18n.
818. The grace of meekness. Ps +22:26.
819. Grace to persevere. 2 P +1:10.
820. Sanctified afflictions. 1 C +11:32.
821. Grace to the children of believers or Israel. Ac +2:39.
822. An interest in God—as our God. Is +41:10.
823. God as our portion. Ps +16:5.
824. God as our glory. Is +28:5.
825. His presence with us. Ps +140:13.
826. An interest in his love. Ep +2:4.
827. His mercy. Is +30:18.
828. His help. He +13:6.
829. His care. 1 P +5:7.
830. His covenant with his people. 2 S +23:5.
831. God will not forsake them. He +13:5.
832. An interest in Christ. SS +2:16.
833. All grace from Christ. Jn +1:16.
834. Redemption by Christ. Ga +3:13.
835. Life from him. Jn +10:10.
836. His intercession. He +7:25.
837. His love. Ep +5:2.
838. His care of his church. Is +40:11.
839. His presence with his people. Re +3:20.
840. Promises of the Spirit. Pr +1:23.
841. His teaching. 1 J +2:27.
842. Help in prayer. Zc +12:10.
843. To witness our adoption. Ro +8:16.
844. To seal our redemption. Ep +4:30.
845. To be our comforter. Ac +9:31.
846. The joys of the Holy Spirit. Ro +14:17.
847. The ministry of angels. He +1:14.
848. That we shall be kings and priests unto God. Re +1:6.
849. Peace of conscience. Col +3:15.
850. Comfort. 2 C +1:3.
851. Hope. Ps +31:24.
852. Delight and joy in God. 1 P +1:8.
853. Support in death. 1 C +√15:55.

Promises of Blessings in the Future World

854. Deliverance from hell. Ro +5:9.
855. Happiness immediately after death. Re +14:13.
856. A glorious resurrection. Jn +5:29.
857. Everlasting happiness in heaven. Re +11:18.
858. Freedom from all sorrow in heaven. Re +21:4.
859. Joy in heaven. Ju +24 (T#339).
860. Glory in heaven. 2 T +2:10.
861. The kingdom of heaven. 2 P +1:11.
862. The heavenly inheritance. 1 P +1:4.
863. Enjoyment of God. Re +22:4.
864. Eternal life. Mt +25:46.

Promises for the exercise of duties and graces in the fulfillment of duty toward God

865. To faith in Christ. Jn +3:16.
866. Confessing Christ. Mt +10:32.
867. To repentance. Ac +3:19.
868. To them that mourn for the wickedness of the land. Ezk +9:4.
869. Repenting in affliction. Ho +6:1.
870. Confession of sin. 1 J +√1:9.
871. Obedience. Jn +*13:17.
872. Obeying Christ. He +*5:9.
873. To sincerity and uprightness. 1 Ch +29:17.
874. To the love of God. Ja +2:5.
875. To the love of Christ. Ja +1:12.

876. To trusting and patiently waiting on God. Ps +56:4.
877. To the fear of God. Pr +3:7.
878. Honoring God. Pr +3:9.
879. To prayer. Je +*33:3.
880. Seeking God. Je +*29:13.
881. Secret prayer. Mt +6:6.
882. Praising God. Ps +135:3.
883. Desires of grace. Mt +5:6.
884. To the wise. Pr +19:8.
885. Love and study of wisdom. Pr +19:20.
886. Knowledge of God and Christ. Jn +17:3.
887. Learning of Christ. Mt +11:29.
888. To a due regard to the word of God: to hearing and reading the word. Ro +10:17.
889. Loving the word. 1 P 2:2.
890. Trembling at the word. Is +66:2.
891. Meditation. Jsh +1:8.
892. To fasting. Jl +2:15.
893. Fasting in secret. Mt +6:18.
894. To baptism. Mk +16:16.
895. To the Lord's Supper. 1 C +10:16.
896. To good discourse. Pr +16:24.
897. The government of the tongue. Pr +21:23.
898. To watchfulness. Pr +28:14.
899. To keeping good company. Pr +13:20.
900. Avoiding evil company. Ps +1:1.
901. To performing oaths. Ps +15:4.
902. To the keeping of the Sabbath. Ezk +20:20.

Promises for the exercise of duties and graces in the performance of duty toward men

903. To obedience of parents. Ep +6:1.
904. To good education. Pr +22:6.
905. Correction of children. Pr +23:13.
906. To a good wife. Pr +12:4.
907. To faithful servants. Pr +14:35.
908. To good kings and magistrates. Pr +29:14.
909. To obedient subjects. 1 P +2:13.
910. To faithful ministers. Is +32:20.
911. To them that receive and hearken to ministers. Jn +13:20.
912. To love and unity. Jn +13:35.
913. To the peacemakers. Mt +5:9.
914. Love to God's people. Ps +15:4.
915. To the charitable. Mt +10:42.
916. To alms in secret. Mt +6:3.
917. To the supporting of God's ministers and worship. Pr +3:9.
918. To the merciful. Mt +5:7.
919. To the giving and the receiving of reproofs. Pr +28:23.
920. To forgiving injuries. Mk +11:25.
921. To chastity and purity. Mt +5:8.
922. To diligence. Pr +10:4.
923. To improving our talents. Mt +25:23.
924. Moderation in sleep. Pr +20:13.
925. To the just and honest. Ps +16:8.
926. To truth. Pr +12:19.
927. To candor. 2 C +1:12.
928. Contentment. 1 T +6:6.
929. Mortification of sin. Ro +8:13.
930. To the spiritually minded. Ro +8:6.

Promises for the exercise of duties and graces: in the cultivation of Christian character.

931. To the meek. Mt +5:5.
932. To the humble. Ja +4:6.
933. The contrite and mourners. Mt +5:3.

934. To them that suffer for righteousness' sake. Mt +5:10.
935. To them that are excommunicated unjustly. Lk +6:22.
936. To patience and submission. He +6:12.
937. To perseverance. Jn +8:31.
938. To him that overcomes. Re +2:7.

Promises of the growth and glory of the church

939. The enlargement of the church, and spread of the gospel and kingdom of Christ. Ps +2:8.
940. Glory of the church. Ps +87:3.
941. Increase of light and knowledge, and of the means of grace. Da +12:4.
942. Increase of purity, holiness and righteousness. Is +61:11.
943. Peace, love, and unity. Ps +72:3.
944. Submission and destruction of the enemies of the church. Is +59:19.
945. Destruction of Antichrist, Babylon, etc. Ezk +26:21.
946. Favor and submission of kings to the kingdom of Christ. Is +52:15.
947. The security, tranquility, and prosperity of the church or Israel. Je +33:16.
948. The perpetual continuance of the church (or, rather, natural Israel). Is +66:22.
949. The conversion and restoration of the Jews. Ezk +37:25.
950. That Christ will come again. 1 C +4:5.
951. Conclusion: that God will perform all His promises. He +10:23.
952. For a birthday. Ps +31:19.
953. The new home. Ps +101:2.
954. For sickness. Ps +6:2.
955. Times of anxiety. Is +41:13.
956. In affliction. Is +51:12.
957. Thanksgiving Day. Ps +66:16.
958‡. Church spiritual, built upon Christ. Ac +17:24.
959‡. Church limited to 144,000. Lk +12:32.
960‡. God the Father is one person. Ml +2:10.
961‡. Son of God, Jesus, created, had a beginning. Re +3:14.
962‡. Only Jehovah is from everlasting to everlasting. 1 T +1:17.
963‡. Jesus not equal to the Father in power and glory, but subject to Him. Jn +14:28.
964‡. Even in heaven, Jesus is subject to the Father. 1 C +15:28.
965‡. Jehovah the Father is Jesus' God. 1 P +1:3.
966‡. Jesus called His Father the "only true God," excluding himself. Jn 17:3.
967‡. Holy Spirit not a person, but a force. Jn +20:22.
968‡. Heavenly visions of God and his Son reveal no personal holy spirit. Da +7:13.
969‡. Only two persons, not three, mentioned in Jn 1:1, +2.
970‡. Scriptures mentioning Father, Son, and Holy Spirit together do not say they are equal, co-eternal, or one God. Mt +28:19.
971‡. Heaven, Jehovah's dwelling place. Is +66:1.
972‡. Hope of share in heavenly kingdom held out to "little flock" of Christians. Lk +12:32.
973‡. A limited number destined for heaven, to be kings and priests with Christ. Re +5:10.
974‡. 144,000 in special position no others have, are spiritual Israelites. Ga +6:16.

975‡. Other faithful servants of God to be rewarded with life on earth, not in heaven. Re +7:9.
976‡. Men of faith who lived and died before Jesus' death and resurrection not in heaven. 1 C +15:50.
977‡. Elijah's ascension in a windstorm did not mark the end of his earthly life. 2 Ch +21:12.
978‡. Jesus raised a spirit, left flesh behind. 1 C +15:50.
979‡. Jesus will never return in flesh. Ac +13:34.
980‡. Man himself is a soul. 1 C +15:45.
981‡. Soul subject to death, not immortal. Ezk +18:4.
982‡. Soul can be killed with the sword. Jsh +11:11.
983‡. "Soul" may refer to one's own self as a soul. Is +61:10.
984‡. "Soul" sometimes refers to life one enjoys as a soul. Mt +16:26.
985‡. "Soul" may refer to future life. Lk +21:19.
986‡. Lower animals also called souls. Nu +31:28.
987‡. Lower animal souls also die. Le +24:18.
988‡. Soul distinguished from spirit. Jb +12:10.
989‡. Soul requires breath to keep alive. Jsh +11:11.
990‡. Souls have blood. Je +2:34.
991‡. "Spirit" is active life force in earthly creatures; sustained by breathing. Ec +3:19.
992‡. Spirit that returns to God is active life force, which is sustained by breathing. Ec +12:7.
993‡. Spirit does not produce intelligence apart from the physical body. Ps +146:4.
994‡. "Spirit" is one's mental disposition. Pr +25:28.
995‡. Jesus Christ used "Gehenna" to represent the worst punishment that could befall a human, complete destruction with no hope of resurrection. Lk +12:5.
996‡. Being cast into Gehenna was contrasted with gaining life in the kingdom of God. Mt +18:9.
997‡. "Lake of fire" symbolizes everlasting destruction without hope of resurrection, as does Gehenna. Re +20:15.
998‡. Impossible for the dead to be tormented; they are unconscious. Ec +9:5.
999‡. Hell provides relief from suffering. Jb +14:13.
1000‡. Hell not a place of fiery torment. Jb +14:13.
1001‡. Fire is a symbol of annihilation. Ps +21:9.
1002‡. Hope held out for those in hell; deliverance possible. Ho +13:14.
1003‡. Upright as well as wicked people go to hell. Ge +37:35.
1004‡. Hell (hades) not a lake of fire, but eventually cast into lake of fire, meaning eternal destruction. Re +20:14.
1005‡. Hell, or sheol-hades, is the grave. Ezk +√32:27.
1006‡. Hell is the grave, for "gone down to sheol with their weapons of war;" "dig down to sheol," indicate a physical place. Ezk +√32:27.
1007‡. Scriptures contrast life with death, not torment. 2 C +4:12.
1008‡. Any suffering one experiences is before death, in this life; afterward he is aware of no "pain of loss" or "separation from God." Ec +9:5.
1009‡. Hell is associated with death and the dead, not life and the living. Pr +7:27.
1010‡. God set life and death, not heaven and hell, before man. Ro +6:23.
1011‡. Torture not in the mind of God. Je +7:31.

1012‡. Love, not fear of hell, pleases God. 1 J +4:18.
1013‡. "Michael" is the name applied to God's son before he left heaven to become Jesus Christ, and also after his return to heaven. Ju +9.

THE SCRIPTURES

1014. Scriptures given by inspiration of the Holy Spirit. 2 P +1:21.
1015. Christ taught out of. Lk +24:27.
1016. Names of. Ro +1:2.
1017. Contain the promises of the gospel. Ro +1:2.
1018. Reveal the laws, statutes, and judgments of God. Dt +4:5.
1019. Record divine prophecies. 2 P +1:19.
1020. Testify of Christ. Jn +*5:39.
1021. Are full and sufficient. Lk +16:31.
1022. Are an unerring guide. 2 P +1:19.
1023. Make wise unto salvation. 2 T +3:15.
1024. Are profitable for doctrine and practice. 2 T +3:16.
1025. Scriptures described as pure. Pr +30:5.
1026. True. Ps +119:160.
1027. Perfect. Ps +19:7.
1028. Precious. Ps +19:10 (desired).
1029. Quick and powerful. He +4:12.
1030. Written for our instruction. Ro +15:4.
1031. Intended for the use of all men. Ro +16:26.
1032. Nothing to be taken from or added to the Scriptures. Pr +30:6.
1033. One portion to be compared with another. 1 C 2:13.
1034. Christ sanctioned, by appealing to them. Mt +4:4.
1035. Scriptures designed for regenerating. 1 P +1:23.
1036. Scriptures designed for quickening. Ps +119:93.
1037. Illuminating. Ps +119:130.
1038. Converting the soul. Ps +19:7.
1039. Making wise the simple. Ps +19:7.
1040. Sanctifying. Jn +17:17.
1041. Producing faith. Jn +20:31.
1042. Hope. Ro +15:4.
1043. Obedience. Dt +17:19.
1044. Cleansing the heart. Jn +15:3.
1045. Cleansing the way. Ps +119:9.
1046. Keeping from destructive paths. Ps +17:4.
1047. Supporting life. Mt +4:4.
1048. Promoting growth in grace. 1 P +2:2.
1049. Building up in the faith. Ac +20:32.
1050. Admonishing. 1 C +10:11.
1051. Comforting. Ro +15:4.
1052. Rejoicing the heart. Ps +19:8.
1053. The Scriptures work effectually in them that believe. 1 Th +2:13.
1054. Letter without spirit, killeth. 2 C +3:6.
1055. Ignorance of the Scriptures a source of error. Mt +22:29.
1056. Christ enables us to understand the Scriptures. Lk +24:45.
1057. The Holy Spirit enables us to understand the Scriptures. Jn +16:13.
1058. No prophecy of the Scripture is of any private interpretation. 2 P +1:20.
1059. Everything should be tried or tested by the Scripture. Ac +17:11.
1060. The Scriptures should be the standard of teaching. 1 P +4:11.

1061. The Scriptures should be believed. Jn +2:22.
1062. Appealed to. 1 P +1:16.
1063. Read. Is +34:16.
1064. Read publicly to all. Ne +8:3.
1065. Known. 2 T +3:15.
1066. Received, not as the word of men, but as the word of God. 1 Th +2:13.
1067. Received with meekness. Ja 1:21.
1068. Searched. Jn +*5:39.
1069. Searched daily. Ac +*17:11.
1070. Laid up in the heart. Ps +119:11.
1071. Taught to children. 2 T +3:15.
1072. Taught to all. 2 Ch +17:9.
1073. Talked of continually. Dt +6:7.
1074. Not handled deceitfully. 2 C +4:2.
1075. Not only heard, but obeyed. Mt +7:24.
1076. Used against our spiritual enemies. Ep 6:17.
1077. All should desire to hear the Scriptures. Ne +8:1.
1078. Mere hearers of the Scriptures deceive themselves. Ja +1:22.
1079. Advantage of possessing the Scriptures. Ro +3:2.
1080. Saints love the Scriptures exceedingly. Ps +119:97.
1081. Delight in. Ps +1:2.
1082. Regard as sweet. Ps +119:103.
1083. Esteem, above all things. Jb +*23:12.
1084. Long after. Ps +119:82.
1085. Stand in awe of. Ps +119:61.
1086. Keep in remembrance. Ps +119:16.
1087. Saints grieve when men disobey the Scriptures. Ps +119:158.
1088. Saints hide Scripture in their hearts. Ps +119:11.
1089. Saints hope in. Ps 119:81.
1090. Meditate in. Ps +1:2.
1091. Rejoice in. Je +*15:16.
1092. Trust in. Ps +119:42.
1093. Obey. Lk +8:21.
1094. Speak of. Ps +119:172.
1095. Esteem, as a light. Ps +119:105.
1096. Pray to be taught. Ps +119:12.
1097. Pray to be conformed to. Ps +119:133.
1098. Plead the promises of in prayer. Ps +119:25.
1099. They who search, are truly noble. Ac +17:11.
1100. Blessedness of hearing and obeying. Lk +*11:28.
1101. Let them dwell richly in you. Col 3:16.
1102. The wicked corrupt the Scriptures. 2 C +2:17.
1103. The wicked make the Scriptures of none effect through their traditions. Mk +7:13.
1104. Reject the Scriptures. Je +8:9.
1105. Stumble at. 1 P +2:8.
1106. Obey not. Ps +119:158.
1107. Frequently wrest, to their own destruction. 2 P +3:16.
1108. Denunciations against those who add to, or take from, the Scriptures. Re +22:18.
1109. Destruction of the Scriptures punished. Je +36:31.

PERSPICUITY OF THE SCRIPTURES: THE BIBLE UNDERSTANDABLE

1110. Taught to children. 2 T +3:15.
1111. Bible understandable, for it is profitable. 2 T *3:16.
1112. For it equips for every good work. 2 T +3:17.
1113. For it is milk for babes. 1 P +2:2.

1114. For it is instrumental in producing the new birth. Ja +1:18.
1115. For it is the source of faith. Ro √10:17.
1116. For it is addressed to ordinary believers, often called "saints," not to kings, priests, or religious leaders. Ro +1:7.
1117. For we have no need of a human authority to teach us. 1 J 2:27.
1118. For it declares itself to be plain. Pr +*8:9.
1119. The Bible is understandable for each individual is held responsible to hear and believe for himself. Jn +5:24.
1120. The Bible is understandable for individuals are deemed competent to recognize false doctrine. Ga +1:8.
1121. The Bible is understandable for individuals are deemed competent to judge the truthfulness and correctness of the teaching of the apostles. Ac +*17:11.
1122. The knowledge of the Scriptures incidentally noticed of the leaders and the populace in the time of Christ. Jn +6:14.

THE BIBLE'S TEACHING ABOUT PRAYER

The Grounds of Prayer
1123. Through Jesus Christ. Jn +14:13.
1124. God's name. Ps +25:11.
1125. God's promises. 2 Ch +6:16.
1126. God's glory. Mt +6:13.
1127. God's great mercy. Ne +13:22.
1128. God's righteousness. Da +9:16.
1129. God's justice. Nu +16:22.
1130. God's great power. Mt +6:13.
1131. For the sake of covenant. Da +9:4.
1132. Keeping the commandments. Ps +119:56.
1133. For ancient servants' sake. Ps +132:10.
1134. God's faithfulness. Ps +143:1.
1135. God's goodness. Ps +25:7.
1136. God's lovingkindness. Ps +25:6.
1137. God's truthfulness. 2 Ch +6:17.
1138. For the sake of God's people. Ps +7:7.
1139. For the sake of past blessings. Ps +119:132.
1140. Faith. 2 Ch +14:11.
1141. Past good life. Ne +5:19.
1142. Future good works. 1 Ch +16:35.
1143. Rejoicing of enemies. Ps +13:4.
1144. Forgiving others. Mk +11:25.
1145. Fatherhood of God. Mt +6:8.
1146. Our need. Ph +*4:19.
1147. Duty of prayer. 1 Th +5:17.
1148. Preparation from God. Ps +10:17.
1149. God's willingness to hear prayer. Ps +4:3.

Times of Prayer
1150. Accepted time. Ps +69:13.
1151. Always. Lk +18:1.
1152. Betimes. Jb +8:5.
1153. Continually. 1 Ch +16:11.
1154. Daily. Ps +86:3.
1155. Day and night. Ps +88:1.
1156. Daybreak. Ps +119:147.
1157. Daytime. Ps +22:2.
1158. Day of battle. 2 Ch +13:14.
1159. Day of trouble. Ps +50:15.
1160. Early. Mk +*1:35.
1161. Evening. Mt +14:23.
1162. Midnight. Ps +119:62.
1163. Morning. Ps +5:3.
1164. Time of need. He +*4:16.

1165. Night. Ps +119:55.
1166. Ninth hour. Ac +3:1.
1167. Noon. Ps +55:17.
1168. Now. 2 C +6:2.
1169. Often. Lk 5:33.
1170. When overwhelmed. Ps 61:2.
1171. Three times a day. Da +6:10.
1172. Today. Ps 95:7.
1173. While he is near. Is +55:6.
1174. While he may be found. Is +55:6.
1175. In youth. Je +3:4.

Places of Prayer
1176. At the altar. Is +19:19.
1177. By the ark. Ex +25:22.
1178. In battle. 1 Ch +5:20.
1179. In bed. Ps +4:4.
1180. Captivity. Je +29:14.
1181. In a cave. 1 K +19:9.
1182. In a chamber. Da +6:10.
1183. In a city. Ac +11:5.
1184. In the closet. Mt +6:6.
1185. On the cross. Mt +27:46.
1186. Out of the depths. Ps 130:1.
1187. The low dungeon. La 3:55.
1188. End of the earth. Ps 61:2.
1189. Everywhere. 1 T *2:8.
1190. In the belly of a fish. Jon 2:1.
1191. In a garden. Mt 26:36.
1192. A grove. Ge 21:33.
1193. Heaven. Re +5:13.
1194. Hell. Lk 16:23.
1195. A house. Ac +10:30.
1196. House of God. 2 Ch +20:5.
1197. Housetop. Ac 10:9.
1198. A loft. 1 K 17:19.
1199. Mercy seat. Ex 25:22.
1200. Mountain. Mt 14:23.
1201. Palace. Ne 2:4.
1202. Prison. Ac +16:25.
1203. By the riverside. Ac +16:13.
1204. At sea. Ps +107:28.
1205. Bottom of sea. Jon 2:5.
1206. Seashore. Ac 21:5.
1207. Solitary place. Mk 1:35.
1208. Streets. Mk 6:56.
1209. Tabernacle. Ex 33:7.
1210. Threshingfloor. 1 Ch +21:18.
1211. Under a tree. Jn 1:48.
1212. Upper room. Ac 1:13.
1213. Rough valley. Dt 21:4.
1214. By the wayside. Mt 20:30.
1215. By a well. Jn 4:12.
1216. Wilderness. Lk 5:16.

Outward Conditions of Prayer
1217. Affliction in. Ja +5:13.
1218. Alone. Mt +14:23.
1219. Almsgiving. Ac +10:31.
1220. Rearing an altar. 1 Ch 21:18.
1221. Anointing with oil. Ja 5:14.
1222. In ashes. Da 9:3.
1223. Asking. Mt +7:7.
1224. With atonement. Ex 32:30.
1225. Baptism. Lk 3:21.
1226. Going to battle. 1 Ch +14:10.
1227. In battle. 1 Ch +5:20.
1228. In bondage. Ex +2:23.
1229. Bowing. 1 Ch 29:20.

1230. Smiting breast. Lk 18:13.
1231. Brevity. Ec 5:2.
1232. In captivity. 2 Ch +6:37.
1233. Casting away garments. Mk 10:50.
1234. In chains. Ac +28:20.
1235. Confessing. Ja +5:16.
1236. Crying. Ps +3:4.
1237. In distress. Ne +9:37.
1238. Dying. Ps +107:19.
1239. With earth. Ne +9:1.
1240. After eating. Dt +8:10.
1241. Falling on face. Mt +26:39.
1242. With family. Ac +10:2.
1243. Fasting. Mt +17:21.
1244. Gathering of people. 2 Ch +20:4.
1245. Giving to the poor. Ac 10:2.
1246. Groaning. Ro +8:26.
1247. Laying on of hands. Ac +28:8.
1248. Hands lifted up. 1 T +2:8.
1249. Hands stretched out. Ps +88:9.
1250. Head of man uncovered. 1 C 11:4.
1251. Woman's head to be covered. 1 C 11:6.
1252. Hindrances avoided. 1 P 3:7.
1253. Hindrances overcome. Da 6:10.
1254. Hungry and thirsty. Ps 107:5.
1255. Not as the hypocrite. Mt 6:5.
1256. Incense. Lk +1:10.
1257. Inviting others. Ps +95:6.
1258. Toward Jerusalem. Da +6:10.
1259. Kneeling. Da +6:10.
1260. With letter spread out. 2 K 19:14.
1261. Not with lips only. Mt +15:8.
1262. Man and beast. Jon 3:8.
1263. Mightily, cry. Jon 3:8.
1264. Mourning. Jl +2:12.
1265. Needy. Ps +72:12.
1266. With oath. Ps +132:2.
1267. With offerings. 1 Ch +16:29.
1268. Under oppression. Ps +119:134.
1269. With due order. 1 Ch +23:31.
1270. Before meals. Lk +24:30.
1271. Poor. Is +41:17.
1272. With proclamation. Jon 3:7.
1273. Rending garments. Ezr +9:5.
1274. Without repetition. Mt 6:7.
1275. Running. Mk 10:17.
1276. In sackcloth. Da +9:3.
1277. Sacrificing. Is +43:23.
1278. In secret. Mt +6:6.
1279. Shaving head. Jb 1:20.
1280. In sickness. Ja +5:14.
1281. Sighing. Ps +12:5.
1282. Silently. 1 S +1:13.
1283. Sitting. 1 Ch +*17:16.
1284. Standing. Lk +18:13.
1285. Sweating blood. Lk 22:44.
1286. With tears. Ps +119:136.
1287. In tempest. Mt +8:24.
1288. Giving testimony. Ps 34:11.
1289. Thirsty. Ps +63:1.
1290. Giving tithes. Lk +18:12.
1291. In unknown tongues forbidden. 1 C 14:14.
1292. In torment. Lk 16:23.
1293. United. Ac +1:14.
1294. Washing. Ps +26:6.
1295. Pouring out water. 1 S 7:6.
1296. Setting a watch. Ne 4:9.
1297. Weak. Ps +6:2.
1298. Weeping. Ps +56:8.

1299. Good works. Is 58:6.
1300. Wrestling. Ge 32:24.

Spiritual Conditions of Prayer

1301. Abiding in Jesus. Jn 15:7.
1302. Accordance with the will of God. 1 J +5:14.
1303. Afraid. Hab 3:2.
1304. Agony. Lk 22:44.
1305. Agreement. Mt 18:19.
1306. All the heart. 2 Ch +15:12.
1307. All prayer. Ep 6:18.
1308. Angry. Jon 4:1.
1309. Anguish of spirit. Jb 7:11.
1310. Ashamed. Ezr 9:6.
1311. Backslidden. Je 14:7. +1437, Ps 119:176.
1312. Believing. Mk +*11:24.
1313. Beseeching. Ne +1:5.
1314. Boldness. Ep +3:12.
1315. Christ interceding. Ro +8:34.
1316. Clean hands. Ja +4:8.
1317. Confessing. Ps +32:5.
1318. Confidence. 1 J 3:21.
1319. Continuance. Ac +6:4.
1320. Courage. Ps +27:14.
1321. Covenant. 2 Ch +15:12.
1322. In darkness. Is 1:10.
1323. With delight in the Lord. Ps +37:4.
1324. Doing justly. Mi 6:8.
1325. Doing the will of God. Jn +9:31.
1326. Not doubting. 1 T 2:8.
1327. Earnestness. Ja +5:17.
1328. Eyes failing. Ps 119:123.
1329. Fainting. Jon +2:7.
1330. Faith. Mk +11:22.
1331. Fallen. Mi 7:8.
1332. In fear of death. Mk +5:23.
1333. In fear of enemies. Ps +18:3.
1334. In fear of God. Ps +5:7.
1335. In fear of punishment. Lk +16:28.
1336. In fear of trouble. 2 Ch +20:3.
1337. In the fire. Zc 13:9.
1338. Forgiving. Mk +*11:25.
1339. Without fretfulness. Ps 37:7.
1340. In gladness. Ps +30:11.
1341. With holy hands. 1 T 2:8.
1342. Broken heart. Ps +34:18.
1343. Contrite heart. Ps +*51:17.
1344. Heart not condemning. 1 J 3:21.
1345. Heart crying out. Ps +84:2.
1346. Heart desolate. Ps 143:4.
1347. Heart fixed. Ps 57:7.
1348. Heart on fire. Ps 39:3.
1349. Heart lifted up. La 3:41.
1350. Heart melted. Jsh 7:5.
1351. Heart overwhelmed. Ps 61:2.
1352. Heart panting. Ps 38:10.
1353. Heart poured out. Ps 62:8.
1354. Heart prepared. Jb 11:13.
1355. A pure heart. 2 T 2:22.
1356. Heart rejoicing. 1 S 2:1.
1357. Rending heart. Jl 2:13.
1358. Heart sore pained. Ps 55:4.
1359. Heart sprinkled. He 10:22.
1360. A tender heart. 2 K 22:19.
1361. A true heart. He 10:22.
1362. A wounded heart. Ps 109:22.
1363. In the Holy Ghost. Ju 20.
1364. Holy Spirit helping. Ro 8:26.
1365. Hoping. Ps +42:11.

1366. Humility. 2 Ch +*7:14.
1367. With importunity. 1 S +7:8.
1368. Knocking. Mt 7:7.
1369. Looking to Jesus. He 12:2.
1370. With love to God. Ps 116:1.
1371. Loving God's house. Ps 26:8.
1372. With meekness. Zp 2:3.
1373. Loving mercy. Mi 6:3.
1374. With obedience. 1 J +3:22.
1375. With patience. Ro +8:25.
1376. Pleading. Jb +16:21.
1377. With power. Ho 12:4.
1378. Praising. Ps +63:3.
1379. With purity. Jb +16:17.
1380. Putting away sin. Ps +66:18.
1381. Rejoicing. Ps +40:16.
1382. Remembrance of past mercies. Ps +119:52.
1383. Repenting. Ac +8:22.
1384. With resignation. Mt +6:10.
1385. Righteous. Pr +15:29.
1386. Seeking. 2 Ch +*7:14.
1387. In sin. Lk +18:13.
1388. With sincerity. 2 Ch +*7:14.
1389. Soberly. 1 P 4:7.
1390. In sorrow. Da 10:16.
1391. Sorrow for sin. Ps +38:18.
1392. With the soul. Is 26:9.
1393. Soul among lions. Ps 57:4.
1394. Soul athirst. Ps +42:2.
1395. Soul bowed down. Ps 44:25.
1396. Soul broken. Ps 119:20.
1397. Soul in bitterness. Jb +7:11.
1398. Soul chastened. Ps 69:10.
1399. Soul fainting. Ps +119:81.
1400. Soul full of trouble. Jn 12:27.
1401. Soul following hard after. Ps 63:8.
1402. Soul longing. Ps 84:2.
1403. Soul lifted up. Ps 143:8.
1404. Soul melted. Ps +119:28.
1405. Soul in prison. Ps 142:7.
1406. Soul poured out. Ps 42:4.
1407. Soul sorrowful unto death. Mt 26:38.
1408. Soul trusting. Ps 57:1.
1409. Soul waiting. Ps 130:6.
1410. With the spirit. Ep +6:18.
1411. Holy Spirit interceding. Ro +8:27.
1412. Broken spirit. Ps 51:17.
1413. Taking hold. Is 64:7.
1414. In temptation. Mt 26:41.
1415. With thanksgiving. Ph +4:6.
1416. In trial. Zc 13:9.
1417. In tribulation. Dt +4:30.
1418. In trouble. Ps +107:6.
1419. Trusting in God. Is +50:10.
1420. In truth. Jn 4:24.
1421. Turning from sin. Is 55:7.
1422. Turning to God. Ps +78:34.
1423. With the understanding. Jn 4:22.
1424. Hating vanity. Ps +31:6.
1425. With vow. Ps +50:14.
1426. Waiting. Ps +37:34.
1427. Watching. Mk +14:38.
1428. Way committed to God. Ps +37:5.
1429. Without wrath. 1 T 2:8.

Objects of Prayer

1430. The afflicted. Ac +12:5.
1431. Deliverance from affliction. Ps +119:153.
1432. All men. 1 T 2:1.

1433. All things whatsoever. Mt +21:22.
1434. Answers to prayer. Ps +27:7.
1435. All authorities. 1 T 2:2.
1436. To be avenged. Lk +18:7.
1437. Recovery from backsliding. Ps +119:176.
         +131l, Je 14:7.
1438. Bless. Ps +67:1.
1439. Blessing on food. Mk +6:41.
1440. Deliverance from bloodguiltiness. Ps +51:14.
1441. Boldness to speak. Ep +6:19.
1442. A brother sinning. 1 J 5:16.
1443. Against being cast away. Ps +51:11.
1444. Against chastening. Ps +6:1.
1445. Children, to have. Lk +1:13.
1446. Blessing on children. Ps +144:12.
1447. To heal children. Mk +5:23.
1448. Help for children. 2 K 4:1.
1449. How to bring up children. Jg 13:8.
1450. To restore children to life. Mt +9:18.
1451. To spare lives of children. Jn +4:47.
1452. Little children. Mt 19:13.
1453. To be cleansed. Ps +19:12.
1454. To be comforted. Ps +119:82.
1455. Aid in keeping commandments. Ps +119:10.
1456. Communion with God. La +5:20.
1457. For correction. Je 10:24.
1458. Counsel. Jg +18:5.
1459. Cup to pass, be removed. Mt 26:39.
1460. Remembrance of covenant. Je 14:21.
1461. To be saved from covetousness. Ps 119:36.
1462. Deliverance from danger. Ps +116:4.
1463. Death. 1 K +19:4.
1464. A happy death. Nu 23:10.
1465. Deliverance from death. Jon +1:14.
1466. Preparation for death. Ps +39:4.
1467. Decision of choice by lot. Ac +1:24.
1468. Casting out devils. Mk +9:29.
1469. Direction. Ps +25:4.
1470. Deliverance in distress. Ps +25:17.
1471. To divide an inheritance. Lk 12:13.
1472. The dying. Ps +79:11.
1473. Enemies. Mt +5:44.
1474. Destruction of enemies. Ps +5:10.
1475. To be saved from enemies. Ps +59:1.
1476. How to inherit eternal life. Mk 10:17.
1477. Every thing. Ph *4:6.
1478. Deliverance from evil. Mt +6:13.
1479. To be kept from evil. Jn +17:15.
1480. To be kept from doing evil. 2 C +13:7.
1481. Explanation. Ge +25:22.
1482. Eyes to be opened. Ps +√119:18.
1483. Faith. Lk +17:5.
1484. Faith to increase. Lk 17:5.
1485. Faith fail not. Lk 22:32.
1486. Faith perfected. 1 Th 3:10.
1487. To be kept from falling. Ps +56:13.
1488. Family. 2 S +7:25.
1489. Deliverance from famine. 1 K 8:37.
1490. The fatherless. Ps 10:18.
1491. Favor of the good. Ps 119:79.
1492. Fear of God. Ps +86:11.
1493. To be saved from fear. Lk +1:74.
1494. Fire to consume a company. 2 K 1:12.
1495. Fire to consume a sacrifice. 1 K 18:24.
1496. Flesh to eat. Nu +11:18.
1497. Food. Mt +6:11.
1498. Forgiveness. Mt +6:12.
1499. Not to be forgotten. Ps +13:1.
1500. Not to be forsaken. Ps +27:9.

1501. To realize frailty. Ps +90:12.
1502. Friends. Ps 35:27.
1503. To be fruitful of good works. Col +*1:10.
1504. All the fulness of God. Ep 3:19.
1505. God to come down. Ps 144:5.
1506. God to fight for us. Ps 144:11.
1507. God to glorify his name. Jn 12:28.
1508. God to glorify his son. Jn 17:1.
1509. God to be gracious. Nu +6:25.
1510. God to judge between. 1 S 24:12.
1511. God to keep. Ps +17:8.
1512. God to leave us not. Ps +27:9.
1513. God to look upon. Ps +25:18.
1514. God to plead. Ps +35:1.
1515. God to return. Ps +6:4.
1516. God to send. Is 6:8.
1517. To see God. Jn 14:8.
1518. God to seek. Ps 119:176.
1519. God to be surety. Ps 119:122.
1520. God to think upon us. Ne 5:19.
1521. God to visit. Je +15:15.
1522. God's anger to be turned away. Da +9:16.
1523. God's eyes to be upon his house. 2 Ch 6:20.
1524. God's face to shine upon. Ps 31:16.
1525. God's favor. Ps +119:58.
1526. To see God's glory. Ps 63:2.
1527. God's hand to be with. Ps 119:173.
1528. To fall into God's hand. 2 S 24:14.
1529. God's house. Is +64:11.
1530. To dwell in God's house. Ps 27:4.
1531. God's kingdom. Mt +6:10.
1532. God's love. 2 Th +3:5.
1533. God's lovingkindness. Ps +17:7.
1534. God's Name. Ge 32:29.
1535. God to make his name known. Ps 83:18.
1536. God's presence. Ps +51:11.
1537. God's strength. 1 Ch 16:11.
1538. God's will to be done. Lk +11:2.
1539. To be taught to do God's will. Ps 143:10.
1540. To be taught God's way. Ps +27:11.
1541. Good things. Mt +7:11.
1542. Grace. Ro +1:7.
1543. Guidance. Ps +*32:8.
1544. Hand to be restored. 1 K 13:6.
1545. Haste in helping. Ps +22:19.
1546. Healing. Je +17:14.
1547. Healing of spring. 2 K 2:22.
1548. A clean heart. Ps 51:10.
1549. Heart enlarged. Ps 119:32.
1550. A perfect heart. 1 Ch 29:19.
1551. An understanding heart. 1 K 3:9.
1552. The heathen. Ps +2:8.
1553. To be held up. Ps +17:5.
1554. Help. Mt +15:25.
1555. Help in old age. Ps +71:9.
1556. Help to pay debt. 2 K 4:1.
1557. Help from sister. Lk 10:40.
1558. Help in trouble. Ps +60:11.
1559. God to hide from evil. Ps +64:2.
1560. Against the hiding of God's face. Ps +27:9.
1561. The Holy Spirit. Ac +8:15.
1562. That the Holy Spirit not be taken away. Ps
       +51:11.
1563. To abound in hope. Ro 15:13.
1564. One's house. 2 T +1:16.
1565. The humble. Ps 10:12.
1566. Deliverance from hunger and thirst. Ps 107:5.
1567. Instruction. Ge +25:22.
1568. Jerusalem. Ps +*122:6.

1569. Jesus to abide. Lk 24:29.
1570. To be with Jesus. Jn 17:24.
1571. To come to Jesus. Mt 14:28.
1572. Jesus to come quickly. Re 22:20.
1573. Jesus to have dominion. Re 1:6.
1574. Jesus to depart. Mk 5:17.
1575. Jesus to dwell in us. Ep +3:17.
1576. Jesus to be glorified. Re 1:6.
1577. To behold the glory of Jesus. Jn 17:24.
1578. Jesus to lay his hand on. Mt 9:18.
1579. To be one in Jesus. Jn 17:21.
1580. Jesus to receive spirit. Ac 7:59.
1581. Jesus to send away woman. Mt 15:23.
1582. Jesus not to send away into deep. Lk 8:31.
1583. To sit beside Jesus. Mk 10:37.
1584. Jesus to speak a word. Mt 8:8.
1585. Jesus to touch blind man. Mk 8:22.
1586. Joy. Ps +51:8.
1587. To be filled with joy. Ro +15:13.
1588. Judgment. Ps +7:8.
1589. Removal of judgments. Nu +21:7.
1590. To justify the righteous. Ps 7:9.
1591. A king. Ac +13:21.
1592. The king. 1 T +*2:2.
1593. Knowledge. Jb +34:32.
1594. Knowledge of future life. Jb 14:14.
1595. Knowledge of God. Ps +25:4.
1596. Knowledge of things to come. Is 45:11.
1597. Laborers in harvest. Mt 9:38.
1598. To send Lazarus. Lk 16:24.
1599. A leader. Nu 27:16.
1600. Cure of leprosy. Mk +1:40.
1601. Life. Ps +21:4.
1602. Long life. Ps 21:4.
1603. Restoration to life. Ac +9:40.
1604. Light of God's countenance. Ps +4:6.
1605. To be likeminded. Ro 15:5.
1606. Door of the lips to be kept. Ps 141:3.
1607. Lips to be opened. Ps 51:15.
1608. Longsuffering among Christians. Col 1:11.
1609. Love to abound. Ph +1:9.
1610. Love toward all men. 1 Th 3:12.
1611. Love between Christians. 1 Th 3:12.
1612. To know the love of Christ. Ep 3:19.
1613. A lunatic. Mt 17:15.
1614. To be saved from lying. Ps 119:29.
1615. Not to fall into the hands of man. 2 S 24:14.
1616. Master. Ge 24:12.
1617. Mercy. Ps +4:1.
1618. Ministers. 1 Th +5:25.
1619. Moses to speak instead of God. Ex +20:19.
1620. Murderers. Lk 23:34.
1621. To understand mysteries. Is +45:11.
1622. Nation. Ge +20:4.
1623. National pardon. 1 K +8:34.
1624. The nations. Ps +9:20.
1625. Nearness to God. Ps +22:11. +1536, Ps
       +51:11.
1626. For the needy. Ps +40:17. +1265, Ps +72:12.
1627. Obedience. Ps +143:10.
1628. To be without offence. Ph 1:10.
1629. All believers to be one. Jn 17:11.
1630. The oppressed. Ps 10:18.
1631. Deliverance from oppression. Ps +119:134.
1632. Cure of palsy. Mt 8:6.
1633. Patience. Col 1:11.
1634. Peace. Je +29:7.
1635. The people. Ps +28:9.
1636. To be made perfect. He +13:21.

1637. To be saved from perishing. Mt +8:25.
1638. Deliverance from persecution. Ps +7:1.
1639. Persecutors. Mt 5:44.
1640. Deliverance from pestilence. 2 Ch +*7:14.
1641. Removal of plague. Nu 16:46.
1642. To avoid pollution. Ac +11:8.
1643. The poor. Ps +72:12.
1644. To be saved from poverty. Pr 30:8.
1645. Mouth to be filled with praise. Ps 71:8.
1646. Hearing of prayer. Ps +4:1.
1647. How to pray. Lk 11:1.
1648. Ps +109:7.
1649. Prayer to be accepted as incense. Ps 141:2.
1650. To be preserved blameless. 1 Th 5:23.
1651. To be kept back from presumptious sins. Ps 19:13.
1652. Priests. 2 Ch 6:41.
1653. Deliverance from prison. Ps +142:7.
1654. Prisoners. Ps +79:11.
1655. Promises to be fulfilled. 2 Ch +1:9.
1656. Remembrance of promises. Ps 119:49.
1657. Prosperity. Ps +*35:27.
1658. Prosperous journey. Ro 1:10.
1659. Protection. Ge +28:20.
1660. To be proved. Ps 26:2.
1661. To be punished instead of the innocent. 1 Ch 21:17.
1662. A quiet life. 1 T 2:2.
1663. Quickening. Ps 80:18.
1664. Raiment. Ge 28:20.
1665. Rain. Ja +5:18.
1666. To prevent rain. Ja 5:17.
1667. Redemption. Ps +26:11.
1668. Refuge. Ps +57:1.
1669. Regeneration. Ps 51:10. +1453, Ps 19:12. +1742, Ps 51:7.
1670. Remembrance. Lk +23:42.
1671. Removal of contempt. Ps 119:22.
1672. Removal of reproach. Ps +119:39.
1673. Removal of rod. Jb 9:34.
1674. Removal of stroke. Ps 39:10.
1675. To be reproved by the righteous. Ps 141:5.
1676. Rest. Ps 55:6.
1677. Revelation of secret. Da 2:18.
1678. Revival. Ps +85:6.
1679. Against riches. Pr 30:8.
1680. Righteous not to be punished with wicked. Ge 18:23.
1681. Righteousness. Ps +5:8.
1682. Permission to bow before Rimmon. 2 K 5:18.
1683. Safety. Ps 4:8.
1684. All saints. Ep +6:24.
1685. Salvation. Ps +31:16.
1686. Sanctification. 1 Th +5:23.
1687. To be satisfied. Ps +90:14.
1688. To be saved. Ps +119:94.
1689. How to be saved. Lk +3:10.
1690. Deliverance at sea. Jon +1:6.
1691. Searching. Ps +139:23.
1692. To be cleansed from secret sin. Ps +19:12.
1693. To see the brethren. 1 Th 3:10.
1694. Servants. Lk 7:7.
1695. Recovery from sickness. Ps +30:2. +1546, Je 17:14.
1696. Sight. 2 K +6:20.
1697. A sign. Is +7:11.
1698. Conviction of sin. Jb 13:23.
1699. To be delivered from sin. Ps +39:8.
1700. To be kept from sin. Ps +19:13.

1701. To know our sins. Jb 13:23.
1702. That footsteps slip not. Ps 17:5.
1703. The righteous to smite. Ps 141:5.
1704. Deliverance from sorrow. Ps +69:29. +1390, Da 10:16.
1705. To deliver soul. Ps 116:4.
1706. Heal soul. Ps 41:4.
1707. To preserve the soul. Ps 86:2.
1708. Power to speak. Je 1:6. +1441, Ep 6:19.
1709. Commending spirit to God. Lk 23:46.
1710. A double portion of the Spirit. 2 K 2:9.
1711. A right spirit. Ps 51:10.
1712. To be kept from stealing. Pr 30:9.
1713. Steps to be ordered. Ps 119:133.
1714. Strangers. Ps +119:19.
1715. Strength. Ps +86:16.
1716A. Against being a stumbling block. Ps 69:6.
1716B. Success in business. Ps +144:13.
1717. Sun and moon to stand still. Jsh 10:12.
1718. To enter into swine. Mt 8:31.
1719. To be taught. Ps +86:11.
1720. Deliverance in temptation. Lk 22:32.
1721. To be saved from temptation. Mt +6:13.
1722. For thorn in flesh to depart. 2 C 12:8.
1723. Thummim and Urim. Dt 33:8.
1724. Thunder and hail to cease. Ex 9:28.
1725. Thunder and rain. 1 S 12:17.
1726. To touch the garment of Jesus. Mk 6:56.
1727. For a tribe. Jg 21:3.
1728. For deliverance in tribulation. 1 S 26:24.
1729. Deliverance from trouble. Ps +34:17.
1730. To be preserved from trouble. Ps +32:7.
1731. Truth to be sent out. Ps 43:3.
1732. To understand the truth. Da 9:13. +1736, Ps 119:27.
1733. To try. Ps 139:23.
1734. To be turned. Ps +80:3.
1735. Help in unbelief. Mk 9:24.
1736. Understanding. Ps +119:27.
1737. Union with God in Christ. Jn 17:21.
1738. Removal of vanity. Pr 30:8.
1739. Victory in war. 2 Ch 6:34.
1740. To walk worthy of the Lord. Col 1:10.
1741. To be saved from wandering. Ps 119:10.
1742. Washing. Ps 51:7.
1743. A watch before the door of the mouth. Ps 141:3.
1744. Water. Is 41:17.
1745. Living water. Jn 4:15.
1746. Whatsoever ye will. Jn +14:13.
1747. What to do. Ac 9:6.
1748. The wicked. Is 53:12.
1749. Deliverance from the wicked. 2 Th +3:2.
1750. Not drawn away with the wicked. Ps 28:3.
1751. Punishment of the wicked. 1 K +8:32.
1752. Wings. Ps 55:6.
1753. Wisdom. Ps +51:6.
1754. Wonders. Ac 4:30.
1755. Word to have free course. 2 Th 3:1.
1756. The world. Jn 17:21.
1757. Zion. Ps +51:18.

Time Spent in Prayer

1758. All day. Ps 25:5.
1759. All night. Lk +6:12.
1760. Certain days. Ne 1:4.
1761. Forty days and nights. Dt 9:18.
1762. Seven days. 2 S 12:18.
1763. Three weeks. Da 10:2.
1764. Until evening. Jg +20:26.

1765. Encouragements to prayer. 2 Ch +14:7.

How Prayer Answered
1766. By angels. Lk +22:43.
1767. By cloudy pillar. Ps 99:7.
1768. By dreams. 1 S +28:6.
1769. By ephod. 1 S 30:7.
1770. By earthquake. Ac +16:26.
1771. By fire. 1 Ch +21:26.
1772. By God Himself in human form. Ge 32:30.
1773. By the Holy Ghost. Ac 4:31.
1774. The Lord in human form. Ge 18:1.
1775. By lot. Ac +1:26.
1776. By prophets. 1 S +28:6.
1777. By thunder. 1 S 12:18.
1778. By trance. Ac 10:10.
1779. By Urim and Thummim. 1 S 28:6.
1780. By visions. Ac +9:10.
1781. By a voice. Lk +3:22.
1782. By a strong east wind. Ex 14:21.
1783. Sometimes immediately. 2 K +20:4.
1784. Sometimes delayed. Ps +13:1.
1785. Heard and answered in part. 2 Ch +12:7.
1786. Beyond all expectation. Je +*33:3.
1787. Prayer too late. Pr +1:28.
1788. Prayer forbidden. Je +7:16.
1789. Prayer denied but subsequently granted. Jg 10:10.
1790. Prayer heard but not granted. Je +15:1.
1791. Heard, but punishment inflicted. Ps +106:15.

Prayer not heard because of:
1792. Asking amiss. Ja 4:3.
1793. Contempt of birthright. He 12:16.
1794. Bloodguiltiness. Is +1:15.
1795. Disobedience. Dt +1:43.
1796. Door shut. Lk 13:25.
1797. Enemies of his people. 2 S 22:42.
1798. Forsaking God. Je 14:10.
1799. Hypocrites. Jb 27:8.
1800. Idolatry. Ezk +14:3.
1801. Regarding iniquity in heart. Ps *66:18.
1802. Too late. Lk 16:25.
1803. Disregard of the law. Pr 28:9.
1804. Love to his people. Dt 23:5.
1805. Oppression. Mi +3:4.
1806. Pollution. Ml 1:7.
1807. Disregard of the poor. Pr 21:13.
1808. Pride. Jb 35:12.
1809. Self-righteousness. Lk 18:14.
1810. Sinfulness. Is *59:2.
1811. Vanity. Jb 35:13.
1812. Wavering. Ja 1:7.
1813. Wickedness. Pr +15:29.

1814. Prayer become sin. Ps +109:7.
1815. Duty to pray for others. 1 S +*12:23.
1816. Prayer besought (requested). Je +37:3.
1817. Prayer necessary to secure certain gifts. Mt 17:21.
1818. All shall pray. Ps +65:2.
1819. Worldly advantages of prayer. Ps +37:9.
1820. Evil of neglect of prayer. Jsh +9:14. +548, Je 10:25.

Business Responsibilities
1821. Honor your commitments. 2 C +8:21.
1822. Be prompt. Pr +10:26.

1823. Respect the customer. Pr +12:22.
1824. Show no partiality. Pr 28:21.
1825. Avoid encumbering personal obligations (debts). Pr 22:7.
1826. Avoid patronage, kick-backs, tips. Pr 17:23.
1827. Pay your bills (on time, promptly). Ps +37:21.
1828. Be careful and accurate. Pr 18:9.
1829. Get the facts, face realities. Pr 18:13.
1830. Use statistics wisely. Pr 27:23.
1831. Be alert. Pr 20:12.
1832. Know your limitations. 2 P 2:17.
1833. Pay the price for wisdom. Pr 17:16.
1834. Show teamwork. Ro 12:4.
1835. Don't tolerate "yes men." Pr 12:15.
1836. Be constant. Pr +28:20.
1837. Find contentment in work. 2 Th 3:10.
1838. Be loyal to your company/employer. Ep 6:6.
1839. Know your business. Pr 22:29.
1840. Be qualified. Pr 25:14.
1841. Keep the lines straight: follow organizational protocol, the "line of command." 1 C 14:40.
1842. Be realistic and conservative in your proposals for action. Do your "homework" well. Pr 2:2.
1843. Alert employer of potential problems. Pr 22:3.
1844. Demonstrate commitment. Ro 12:11.
1845. Give credit to worthy executive leadership. Is 10:15.

Responsibilities to the employee
1846. Give credit when it is due. Pr 3:27.
1847. Set an example. Ro 2:21.
1848. Be considerate. Ep 6:9.
1849. Be just. Col 4:1.
1850. Honor contracts, agreements. Col 4:1.
1851. Pay adequate wages. Je *22:13.
1852. Pay wages on time. Le +*19:13.
1853. Be open to advice, suggestions, criticism. 1 S +*25:17.
1854. Provide safe working conditions. Pr 12:10.
1855. Be willing to change and improve procedures when past or present practices fail to solve the problem. Ac 6:3.
1856. Exercise diligence. Ro 12:8.

For young people starting a career
1857. Have a clear purpose in life. Ec 9:10.
1858. Don't be a person with much zeal and little knowledge. Pr +17:28.
1859. Do not steal time. Pr 12:24.
1860. Pay your own freight (be self-supporting, not a burden to others). 2 Th 3:8.
1861. Do not pamper young Christians. Lk 22:36.

Responsibilities of Christian Students
1862. Be industrious. 2 Th 3:10.
1863. Be responsible. 1 T 5:8.
1864. Have a sense of duty toward your work. Ep 6:7.
1865. Do more than is required. Lk 17:10.
1866. Be faithful even in small matters. Lk 16:11.
1867. Exploit your business experience. Pr 10:4.
1868. Train to be a servant. Mt 20:28.

Responsibilities toward God
1869. Justify from God's viewpoint your place in business. Ps 127:1.
1870. Commit facts to God in faith ("Going out on faith" not a substitute for common sense and good judgment). 1 J 5:4.

1871. Pray about your business. Ja +1:5.
1872. Act like a Christian. Col 2:6.
1873. Set not your heart upon riches. 1 T 6:8.

MESSIANIC PROPHECY

1874. Messiah to be the seed of the woman. Ge +3:15.
1875. The family of Shem. Ge 9:26.
1876. The seed of Abraham. Ge +22:18.
1877. The seed of Isaac. Ge +17:19.
1878. The son of Jacob. Nu +24:17.
1879. Judah in the line of descent. Ge +49:10.
1880. Through the family line of Jesse. Is +11:1.
1881. Through David. 2 S +7:12.
1882. Messiah to come at a set time. Ml +3:1.
1883. Messiah to come to the second temple. Ml +3:1.
1884. Time Messiah would come and the time of His kingdom was told to Daniel by the angel Gabriel. Da +9:25.
1885. Christ was the Prophet that was to come. Dt +18:15.
1886. Christ born of a virgin. Is +7:14.
1887. Christ to be born in Bethlehem of Judea. Mi +5:2.
1888. Death of the innocents (babies). Je +31:15.
1889. Great persons to come to adore Messiah. Is +60:6.
1890. Messiah favored by God and men. 1 S +=2:26.
1891. Messiah to be brought forth out of Egypt. Ho +11:1.
1892. Messiah to be preceded by a Harbinger. Is +40:3.
1893. While John the Baptist was not the person of Elijah risen from the dead, he was the Elijah that was to come. Ml +3:1.
1894. Messiah to live at Capernaum and give light to the land of Zebulun and Naphtali. Is +9:2.
1895. Messiah to be a healer of many. Is +53:5.
1896. Under the Messiah's ministry the deaf should hear and the blind should see. Is +35:5.
1897. Messiah to be known and to save by His knowledge. Is +53:11.
1898. Messiah to teach by the use of parables. Ps +78:2.
1899. The Messiah to confound His questioners. Is +52:13.
1900. Messiah to teach of the resurrection from the dead. Is +26:19.
1901. Messiah's teaching of the resurrection from the dead extended to the prediction of His own death and resurrection. Is +26:19.
1902. Messiah to lead the people as the faithful shepherd. Is +40:11.
1903. Messiah to be the liberator of the race. Is +61:1.
1904. Messiah to be the Prince of Peace. Is +9:6.
1905. His zeal for the house of God to greatly endanger Him. Ps +69:9.
1906. Messiah to be sinless. Is +53:9.
1907. Messiah not to lift up His voice in the streets: His meekness and lack of ostentation. Is +42:2.
1908. The innocence and meekness of the Messiah. Is +53:7.
1909. Tenderness and compassion of the Messiah. Is +40:11.
1910. Messiah to be without guile. Is +53:9.

1911. Messiah to be rejected by His brethren. Ps +69:8.
1912. Triumphal entry into Jerusalem of the Messiah. Zc +9:9.
1913. Messiah to be the son of God. Ps +2:7.
1914. Messiah the Son of man. Da +7:13.
1915. Messiah the holy one, or saint. Ps +16:10.
1916. Messiah the saint of saints. Da +9:24.
1917. Messiah the just or righteous one. Zc +9:9.
1918. Messiah the wisdom of God. Pr +8:1.
1919. Messiah the word (or oracle) of God, or the Lord. Mi +4:2.
1920. Messiah is the redeemer or savior. Is +47:4.
1921. Messiah as shepherd of the flock, would be smitten, and the sheep would be scattered. Zc +13:7.

One day in prophecy (Ac *13:29)

1922. Messiah to pray in sorrow, foreknowing his death. Ps +55:17.
1923. Messiah to die, knowing beforehand the manner of his death. Ps +102:10.
1924. Messiah's death to be voluntary. Ps +40:8.
1925. Messiah to be betrayed by a friend. Ps +55:12.
1926. Messiah's betrayer to eat bread with him. Ps +41:9.
1927. Messiah's betrayer to greet him with soft words. Ps +55:21.
1928. Messiah to be sold for thirty pieces of silver. Zc +11:12.
1929. The money obtained was to be cast down to the potter. Zc +11:13.
1930. Messiah's disciples to forsake Him. Zc 13:7.
1931. A familiar friend would fear to acknowledge Him. Ps 31:11.
1932. Counsel would be taken to kill the Messiah. Ps +2:2.
1933. Rulers to be gathered against the Messiah. Ps +2:2.
1934. Messiah's accusers to be liars, hating Him without a cause. Ps +35:19.
1935. Messiah to be accused by false witnesses. Ps +35:11.
1936. Messiah to be falsely condemned. Ps +35:11.
1937. Messiah to be hated without a cause. Ps +69:4.
1938. Messiah to be led as a lamb to the slaughter. Is +53:7.
1939. Messiah to be dumb (silent) before His accusers. Is +53:7.
1940. Messiah to be guiltless. Is +53:9.
1941. Justice was to be denied the Messiah. Is +53:8.
1942. Messiah to be rejected by His own people. Is +53:3.
1943. Messiah to be rejected by His nation. Is 49:7.
1944. Messiah to evidence physical weakness. Ps +109:24.
1945. Messiah to be smitten. Is +53:4.
1946. Messiah to be spat upon. Is +50:6.
1947. Messiah's visage (or face) to be marred. Is +52:14.
1948. Messiah to be wounded and bruised. Is +53:5.
1949. Messiah to be smitten with a rod upon the cheek. Mi +5:1.
1950. Messiah, as God, was to be pierced. Zc +12:10.
1951. Messiah's hands and feet were to be pierced. Ps +22:16.
1952. Messiah to be crucified with thieves. Is +53:12.
1953. Messiah to pray for His persecutors. Is 53:12.

1954. Messiah to be despised by the people. Ps +22:6.
1955. Messiah to be mocked by the people. Ps +35:16.
1956. The people were to shake their heads. Ps +22:7.
1957. Messiah to be stared upon. Ps +22:17.
1958. The people were to ridicule Him. Ps +22:8.
1959. Messiah to be derided. Ps +22:7.
1960. The people to be astonished. Is +52:14.
1961. Messiah's garments to be parted and lots cast for them. Ps +22:18.
1962. Messiah to bear shame. Ps +69:19.
1963. Messiah's friends to stand afar off. Ps +38:11.
1964. Messiah to thirst. Ps +69:21.

1965. They were to give Him gall. Ps +69:21.
1966. They were to give Him vinegar. Ps +69:21.
1967. Messiah to cry aloud. Ps +55:17.
1968. Messiah to cry: "My God, my God, why hast thou forsaken me?" Ps +22:1.
1969. Messiah to cry, "It is finished." Ps +22:31.
1970. Messiah to commit Himself to God. Ps +31:5.
1971. Messiah's bones were not to be broken. Ps +34:20.
1972. Messiah's heart was to be broken. Ps +22:14.
1973. Messiah to be cut off in the prime of life at the time specified. Is +53:8.
1974. He was to be buried in a rich man's tomb. Is +53:9.
1975. Darkness to be over the land. Am +8:9.
1976. His death to be subtitutionary. Da +9:26.

PRAYER INDEX

Abiding in Jesus. T#1301. Jn 15:7.
Accepted time. T#1150. Ps 69:13.
Accordance with the will of God. T#1302. 1 J 5:14.
Afflicted, The. T#1430. Ac 12:5.
Affliction, In. T#1217. Ja 5:13.
Affliction, deliverance from. T#1431. Ps 119:153.
Afraid. T#1303. Hab 3:2.
Age, Help in old. T#1555. Ps 71:9.
Agony. T#1304. Lk 22:44.
Agreement, With. T#1305. Mt 18:19.
Aid in keeping commandments. T#1455. Ps 119:10.
All day. T#1758. Ps 25:5.
All men. T#1432. 1 T 2:1.
All night. T#1759. Lk 6:12.
All prayer. T#1307. Ep 6:18.
All saints. T#1684. Ep 6:24.
All shall pray. T#1818. Ps 65:2.
All the heart. T#1306. 2 Ch 15:12.
All the fulness of God. T#1504. Ep 3:19.
All things whatsoever. T#1433. Mt 21:22.
Almsgiving. T#1219. Ac 10:31.
Alone. T#1218. Mt 14:23.
Altar, At. T#1176. Is 19:19.
Altar, Rearing. T#1220. 1 Ch 21:18.
Always. T#1151. Lk 18:1.
Amiss, Asking. T#1792. Ja 4:3.
Angels. T#1766. Lk 22:43.
Anger of God to be turned away. T#1522. Da 9:16.
Angry. T#1308. Jon 4:1.
Anguish of spirit. T#1309. Jb 7:11.
Anointing with oil. T#1221. Ja 5:14.
Answered beyond expectation. T#1786. Je 33:3.
Answers sometimes delayed. T#1784. Ps 13:1.
Answers to prayer. T#1434. Ps 27:7.
Ark, By the. T#1177. Ex 25:22.
Ashamed. T#1310. Ezr 9:6.
Ashes, In. T#1222. Da 9:3.
Asking. T#1223. Mt 7:7.
Asking amiss. T#1792. Ja 4:3.
Athirst, Soul. T#1394. Ps 42:2.
Atonement, With. T#1224. Ex 32:30.
Authorities. T#1435. 1 T 2:2.
Avenged, To be. T#1436. Lk 18:7.
Backslidden. T#1311. Je 14:7.
Backsliding, Recovery from. T#1437. Ps 119:176.
Baptism. T#1225. Lk 3:21.
Battle, In. T#1178, 1 Ch 5:20. T#1227, 1 Ch 5:20.
Battle, Day of. T#1158. 2 Ch 13:14.
Battle, Going to. T#1226. 1 Ch 14:10.
Bed, In. T#1179. Ps 4:4.
Believers, All to be one. T#1629. Jn 17:11.
Believing. T#1312. Mk 11:24.
Beseeching. T#1313. Ne 1:5.
Betimes. T#1152. Jb 8:5.
Birthright, Contempt of. T#1793. He 12:16.
Blameless, To be preserved. T#1650. 1 Th 5:23.
Bless. T#1438. Ps 67:1.
Blessing on food. T#1439. Mk 6:41.
Blessing on children. T#1446. Ps 144:12.
Bloodguiltiness. T#1794. Is 1:15.

Bloodguiltiness, Removal of. T#1440. Ps 51:14.
Blood, Sweating. T#1285. Lk 22:44.
Boldness. T#1314. Ep 3:12.
Boldness to speak. T#1441. Ep 6:19.
Bondage, In. T#1228. Ex 2:23.
Bowing. T#1229. 1 Ch 29:20.
Breast, Smiting. T#1230. Lk 18:13.
Brethren, To see. T#1693. 1 Th 3:10.
Brevity. T#1231. Ec 5:2.
Broken heart. T#1342. Ps 34:18.
Broken soul. T#1396. Ps 119:20.
Broken spirit. T#1412. Ps 51:17.
Brother, Sinning. T#1442. 1 J 5:16.
Business, Success in. T#1716. Ps 144:13.
Captivity, In. T#1232. 2 Ch 6:37.
Captivity, Place of. T#1180. Je 29:14.
Cast away, Not to be. T#1443. Ps 51:11.
Cast out devils. T#1468. Mk 9:29.
Casting away garments. T#1233. Mk 10:50.
Cave, In. T#1181. 1 K 19:9.
Certain days. T#1760. Ne 1:4.
Chains, In. T#1234. Ac 28:20.
Chamber, In a. T#1182. Da 6:10.
Chastening, Against. T#1444. Ps 6:1.
Chastened soul. T#1398. Ps 69:10.
Children, Blessing on. T#1446. Ps 144:12.
Children, For. T#1445. Lk 1:13.
Children, Help for. T#1448. 2 K 4:1.
Children, To heal. T#1447. Mk 5:23.
Children, How to bring up. T#1449. Jg 13:8.
Children, Little. T#1452. Mt 19:13.
Children, To restore lives of. T#1450. Mt 9:18.
Children, To spare. T#1451. Jn 4:47.
Choice, decision of. T#1467. Ac 1:24.
Christ Jesus, Through. T#1123. Jn 14:13.
Christ, Interceding. T#1315. Ro 8:34.
City, In a. T#1183. Ac 11:5.
Clean hands. T#1316. Ja 4:8.
Clean heart. T#1548. Ps 51:10.
Cleansed, To be. T#1453. Ps 19:12.
Cleansed from secret sin. T#1692. Ps 19:12.
Closet, In the. T#1184. Mt 6:6.
Comforted, To be. T#1454. Ps 119:82.
Commandments, Aid in keeping. T#1455. Ps 119:10.
Commandments, Keeping. T#1132. Ps 119:56.
Communion with God. T#1456. La 5:20.
Confessing. T#1235, Ja 5:16. T#1317, Ps 32:5.
Confidence. T#1318. 1 J 3:21.
Contempt, Removal of. T#1671. Ps 119:22.
Continually. T#1153. 1 Ch 16:11.
Continuance. T#1319. Ac 6:4.
Contrite heart. T#1343. Ps 51:17.
Conviction of sin. T#1698. Jb 13:23.
Correction, For. T#1457. Je 10:24.
Counsel, For. T#1458. Jg 18:5.
Courage. T#1320. Ps 27:14.
Covenant, For sake of. T#1131. Da 9:4.
Covenant, Remembrance of. T#1460. Je 14:21.
Covenant, With. T#1321. 2 Ch 15:12.
Covetousness, To be saved from. T#1461. Ps 119:36.

Cross, On. T#1185. Mt 27:46.
Crying. T#1236. Ps 3:4.
Crying out, Heart. T#1345. Ps 84:2.
Cup to pass from. T#1459. Mt 26:39.
Daily. T#1154. Ps 86:3.
Danger, Deliverance from. T#1462. Ps 116:4.
Darkness, In. T#1322. Is 1:10.
Day, All. T#1758. Ps 25:5.
Day of battle. T#1158. 2 Ch 13:14.
Day and night. T#1155. Ps 88:1.
Day of trouble. T#1159. Ps 50:15.
Daybreak. T#1156. Ps 119:147.
Daytime. T#1157. Ps 22:2.
Days, Certain. T#1760. Ne 1:4.
Death. T#1463. 1 K 19:4.
Death, Deliverance from. T#1465. Jon 1:14.
Death, In fear of. T#1332. Mk 5:23.
Death, For happy. T#1464. Nu 23:10.
Death, Preparation for. T#1466. Ps 39:4.
Debt, Help to pay. T#1556. 2 K 4:1.
Decision of choice by lot. T#1467. Ac 1:24.
Delayed, Answers sometimes. T#1784. Ps 13:1.
Delight in Lord. T#1323. Ps 37:4.
Depths, Out of. T#1186. Ps 130:1.
Desolate heart. T#1346. Ps 143:4.
Devils, To cast out. T#1468. Mk 9:29.
Direction. T#1469. Ps 25:4.
Disobedience. T#1795. Dt 1:43.
Disregard of the law. T#1803. Pr 28:9.
Distress, In. T#1237. Ne 9:37.
Distress, Deliverance in. T#1470. Ps 25:17.
Divide an inheritance, To. T#1471. Lk 12:13.
Doing justly. T#1324. Mi 6:8.
Doing the will of God. T#1325. Jn 9:31.
Door of lips to be kept. T#1606. Ps 141:3.
Door shut. T#1796. Lk 13:25.
Doubting, Not. T#1326. 1 T 2:8.
Dreams. T#1768. 1 S 28:6.
Dungeon, In. T#1187. La 3:55.
Duty of prayer. T#1147. 1 Th 5:17.
Duty of prayer for others. T#1815. 1 S 12:23.
Dying. T#1237. Ne 9:37.
Dying, The. T#1472. Ps 79:11.
Early. T#1160. Mk 1:35.
Earnestness. T#1327. Ja 5:17.
Earthquake, By. T#1770. Ac 16:26.
Earth, End of. T#1188. Ps 61:2.
Earth, With. T#1239. Ne 9:1.
Eating, After. T#1240. Dt 8:10.
Encouragements to pray. T#1765. 2 Ch 14:7.
End of earth. T#1188. Ps 61:2.
Enemies. T#1473. Mt 5:44.
Enemies, In fear of. T#1333. Ps 18:3.
Enemies, Destruction of. T#1474. Ps 5:10.
Enemies of his people. T#1797. 2 S 22:42.
Enemies, To be saved from. T#1475. Ps 59:1.
Ephod. T#1769. 1 S 30:7.
Eternal life, How to inherit. T#1476. Mk 10:17.
Evening. T#1161. Mt 14:23.
Evening, Until. T#1764. Je 20:26.
Every thing. T#1477. Ph 4:6.
Every where. T#1189. 1 T 2:8.
Evil, Deliverance from. T#1478. Mt 6:13.
Evil, To hide from. T#1559. Ps 64:2.
Evil, To be kept from. T#1479. Jn 17:15.
Evil, To be kept from doing. T#1480. 2 C 13:7.
Evil of neglect of prayer. T#1820. Jsh 9:14.
Expectation, Answered beyond all. T#1786. Je 33:3.
Explanation. T#1481. Ge 25:22.

Eyes failing. T#1328. Ps 119:123.
Eyes of God to be upon his house. T#1523. 2 Ch 6:20.
Eyes to be opened. T#1482. Ps 119:18.
Face to shine upon, God's. T#1524. Ps 31:16.
Fainting. T#1329. Jon 2:7.
Fainting soul. T#1399. Ps 119:81.
Faith. T#1140, 2 Ch 14:11. T#1330, Mk 11:22. T#1483, Lk 17:5.
Faith to increase. T#1484. Lk 17:5.
Faith to not fail. T#1485. Lk 22:32.
Faith perfected. T#1486. 1 Th 3:10.
Faithfulness, God's. T#1134. Ps 143:1.
Fallen. T#1331. Mi 7:8.
Falling on face. T#1241. Mt 26:39.
Falling, To be kept from. T#1487. Ps 56:13.
Family. T#1488. 2 S 7:25.
Family, With. T#1242. Ac 10:2.
Famine, Deliverance from. T#1489. 1 K 8:37.
Fasting. T#1243. Mt 17:21.
Fatherhood of God. T#1145. Mt 6:8.
Fatherless, The. T#1490. Ps 10:18.
Favor of God. T#1525. Ps 119:58.
Favor of the good. T#1491. Ps 119:79.
Fear of death. T#1332. Mk 5:23.
Fear of enemies. T#1333. Ps 18:3.
Fear of God. T#1334, Ps 5:7. T#1492, Ps 86:11.
Fear of punishment. T#1335. Lk 16:28.
Fear of trouble. T#1336. 2 Ch 20:3.
Fear, to be saved from. T#1493. Lk 1:74.
Fight for, God to. T#1506. Ps 144:11.
Fire, By. T#1771. 1 Ch 21:26.
Fire, Heart on. T#1348. Ps 39:3.
Fire, In the. T#1337. Zc 13:9.
Fire to consume a company. T#1494. 2 K 1:12.
Fire to consume a sacrifice. T#1495. 1 K 18:24.
Fish, In belly of. T#1190. Jon 2:1.
Flesh to eat. T#1496. Nu 11:18.
Food. T#1497. Mk 6:11.
Food, Blessing on. T#1439. Mk 6:41.
Footsteps slip not. T#1702. Ps 17:5.
Forbidden, Prayer. T#1788. Je 7:16.
Forgiveness. T#1498. Mt 6:12.
Forgiving. T#1338. Mk 11:25.
Forgiving others. T#1144. Mk 11:25.
Forgotten, Not to be. T#1499. Ps 13:1.
Forsaken, Not to be. T#1500. Ps 27:9.
Forsaking God. T#1798. Je 14:10.
Forty days and nights. T#1761. Dt 9:18.
Frailty, To realize. T#1501. Ps 90:12.
Fretfulness, Without. T#1339. Ps 37:7.
Friends. T#1502. Ps 35:27.
Fruitful of good works. T#1503. Col 1:10.
Future good works. T#1142. 1 Ch 16:35.
Future life, Knowledge of. T#1594. Jb 14:14.
Garden, In a. T#1191. Mt 26:36.
Gathering of people. T#1244. 2 Ch 20:4.
Giving to poor. T#1245. Ac 10:2.
Giving alms. T#1219. Ac 10:31.
Gladness, With. T#1340. Ps 30:11.
Glory, God's. T#1126. Mt 6:13.
Glory of God, To see. T#1526. Ps 63:2.
God, All the fulness of. T#1504. Ep 3:19.
God Himself in human form. T#1772. Ge 32:30.
God, Communion with. T#1456. La 5:20.
God, to come down. T#1505. Ps 144:5.
God, Fatherhood of. T#1145. Mt 6:8.
God, Favor of. T#1525. Ps 119:58.
God, to fight for. T#1506. Ps 144:11.
God, In fear of. T#1334. Ps 5:7.

God, Forsaking. T#1798. Je 14:10.
God, to glorify his name. T#1507. Jn 12:28.
God, to glorify his Son. T#1508. Jn 17:1.
God, to be gracious. T#1509. Nu 6:25.
God, to judge between. T#1510. 1 S 24:12.
God, to keep. T#1511. Ps 17:8.
God, Knowledge of. T#1595. Ps 25:4.
God, to leave us not. T#1512. Ps 27:9.
God, to look upon. T#1513. Ps 25:18.
God, Nearness to. T#1625. Ps 22:11.
God, to plead. T#1514. Ps 35:1.
God, to return. T#1515. Ps 6:4.
God, To see. T#1517. Jn 14:8.
God, To seek. T#1518. Ps 119:176.
God, to send. T#1516. Is 6:8.
God, to be surety. T#1519. Ps 119:122.
God, to think upon. T#1520. Ne 5:19.
God, Turning to. T#1422. Ps 78:34.
God, Union with. T#1737. Jn 17:21.
God, to visit. T#1521. Je 15:15.
God's ancient servant's sake. T#1133. Ps 132:10.
God's anger to be turned away. T#1522. Da 9:16.
God's eyes to be upon his house. T#1523. 2 Ch 6:20.
God's face to shine upon. T#1524. Ps 31:16.
God's faithfulness. T#1134. Ps 143:1.
God's favor. T#1525. Ps 119:58.
God's goodness. T#1135. Ps 25:7.
God's glory. T#1126. Mt 6:13.
God's glory, to see. T#1526. Ps 63:2.
God's hand to be with. T#1527. Ps 119:173.
God's hand, To fall into. T#1528. 2 S 24:12.
God's house. T#1529. Is 64:11.
God's house, To dwell in. T#1530. Ps 27:4.
God's justice. T#1129. Nu 16:22.
God's kingdom. T#1531. Mt 6:10.
God's love. T#1532. 2 Th 3:5.
God's lovingkindness. T#1136, Ps 25:6. T#1533, Ps 17:7.
God's mercy. T#1127. Ne 13:22.
God's name. T#1124, Ps 25:11. T#1534, Ge 32:29.
God's name to be made known. T#1535. Ps 83:18.
God's people's sake. T#1138. Ps 7:7.
God's power. T#1130. Mt 6:13.
God's presence. T#1536. Ps 51:11.
God's promises. T#1125. 2 Ch 6:16.
God's righteousness. T#1128. Da 9:16.
God's strength. T#1537. 1 Ch 16:11.
God's truthfulness. T#1137. 2 Ch 6:17.
God's way, To be taught. T#1540. Ps 27:11.
God's will to be done. T#1538. Lk 11:2.
God's will, To be taught to do. T#1539. Ps 143:10.
God's willingness to hear prayer. T#1149. Ps 4:3.
Good, Favor of. T#1491. Ps 119:79.
Good life, Past. T#1141. Ne 5:19.
Good things. T#1541. Mt 7:11.
Good works. T#1299. Is 58:6.
Good works, Future. T#1142. 1 Ch 16:35.
Grace. T#1542. Ro 1:7.
Gracious, God to be. T#1509. Nu 6:25.
Groaning. T#1246. Ro 8:26.
Grove, A. T#1192. Ge 21:23.
Guidance. T#1543. Ps 32:8.
Hand to be restored. T#1544. 1 K 13:6.
Hand to be with, God's. T#1527. Ps 119:173.
Hand, to fall into God's. T#1528. 2 S 24:12.
Hands, Clean. T#1316. Ja 4:8.
Hands, Holy. T#1341. 1 T 2:8.
Hands, Laying on. T#1247. Ac 28:8.
Hands lifted up. T#1248. 1 T 2:8.
Hands stretched out. T#1249. Ps 88:9.

Happy death. T#1464. Nu 23:10.
Harvest, Laborers in. T#1597. Mt 9:38.
Haste in helping. T#1545. Ps 22:19.
Hating vanity. T#1424. Ps 31:6.
Heads of men uncovered. T#1250. 1 C 11:4.
Heads of women covered. T#1251. 1 C 11:6.
Heal children. T#1447. Mk 5:23.
Heal soul, To. T#1706. Ps 41:4.
Healing. T#1546. Je 17:14.
Healing of spring. T#1547. 2 K 2:22.
Heard and answered in part. T#1785. 2 Ch 12:7.
Hearing of prayer. T#1646. Ps 4:1.
Heart, All the. T#1306. 2 Ch 15:12.
Heart, Broken. T#1342. Ps 34:18.
Heart, A clean. T#1548. Ps 51:10.
Heart, A contrite. T#1343. Ps 51:17.
Heart not condemning. T#1344. 1 J 3:21.
Heart crying out. T#1345. Ps 84:2.
Heart desolate. T#1346. Ps 143:4.
Heart enlarged. T#1549. Ps 119:32.
Heart fixed. T#1347. Ps 57:7.
Heart on fire. T#1348. Ps 39:3.
Heart lifted up. T#1349. La 3:41.
Heart melted. T#1350. Jsh 7:5.
Heart overwhelmed. T#1351. Ps 61:2.
Heart panting. T#1352. Ps 38:10.
Heart perfect. T#1550. 1 Ch 29:19.
Heart poured out. T#1353. Ps 62:8.
Heart prepared. T#1354. Jb 11:13.
Heart, Pure. T#1355. 2 T 2:22.
Heart, Regarding iniquity in. T#1801. Ps 66:18.
Heart rejoicing. T#1356. 1 S 2:1.
Heart rending. T#1357. Jl 2:13.
Heart sore pained. T#1358. Ps 55:4.
Heart sprinkled. T#1359. He 10:22.
Heart, Tender. T#1360. 2 K 22:19.
Heart, True. T#1361. He 10:22.
Heart, Understanding. T#1551. 1 K 3:9.
Heart, Wounded. T#1362. Ps 109:22.
Heathen, For the. T#1552. Ps 2:8.
Heaven. T#1193. Re 5:13.
Held up, To be. T#1553. Ps 17:5.
Hell. T#1194. Lk 16:23.
Help. T#1554. Mt 15:25.
Help for children. T#1448. 2 K 4:1.
Help in old age. T#1555. Ps 71:9.
Help to pay debt. T#1556. 2 K 4:1.
Help from sister. T#1557. Lk 10:40.
Help in trouble. T#1558. Ps 60:11.
Help in unbelief. T#1735. Mk 9:24.
Helping, Haste in. T#1545. Ps 22:19.
Helping, Holy Spirit. T#1364. Ro 8:26.
Hide from evil. T#1559. Ps 64:2.
Hiding of God's face, Against. T#1560. Ps 27:9.
Hindrances avoided. T#1252. 1 P 3:7.
Hindrances overcome. T#1253. Da 6:10.
Holy Ghost. T#1773. Ac 4:31.
Holy Ghost, In the. T#1363. Ju 20.
Holy Spirit, The. T#1561. Ac 8:15.
Holy Spirit, helping. T#1364. Ro 8:26.
Holy Spirit, interceding. T#1411. Ro 8:27.
Holy Spirit, Not to take away. T#1562. Ps 51:11.
Hope to abound. T#1563. Ro 15:13.
Hoping. T#1356. Ps 42:11.
House, A. T#1195. Ac 10:30.
House of God. T#1196, 2 Ch 20:5. T#1529, Is 64:11.
House, To dwell in God's. T#1530. Ps 27:4.
House, For one's. T#1564. 2 T 1:16.
Housetop. T#1197. 1 K 17:19.

PROVERBS INDEX

Acceptable words. Pr 10:31, 32. +*25:11.
Access to neighbors. Pr 25:17.
Accusation rebuked. Pr 30:10.
Affliction, value of. Pr 15:10. 17:3.
Affliction, powerless to correct a fool. Pr 27:22.
Affliction, support in. Pr 15:15.
All-seeing eye of God. Pr 15:3, 11. 16:2.
Anger, quick, is foolish. Pr 14:17.
Anger, soft answer turns away. Pr 15:11.
Anger, discretion defers. Pr 19:11.
Anger, great, brings repeated punishment. Pr 19:19.
Anger, a bar to friendship and fellowship. Pr 22:24.
Anger, a bad influence, snare to others. Pr 22:25.
Anger brings strife. Pr 29:22. 30:33.
Angry countenance drives away backbiting tongue. Pr 25:23.
Anger, control over, a great asset. Pr 16:32.
Anger, control over, possessed by man of understanding. Pr 17:27.
Anger, controlled by prudence. Pr 19:11.
Anger, controlled, by those who are honorable. Pr 20:3.
Angry man, warning against friendship with. Pr 22:24, 25.
Ants, pattern of industry. Pr 30:25.
Appetite for the Word. Pr 4:7. 8:9, 34. 27:7.
Appetite, rules for. Pr 23:1-3.
Appetite, insatiable. Pr 30:15.
Appetite for sin. Pr 17:4.
Apostasy. Pr 1:32.
Apostasy, moral. Pr 2:16-19. 26:11.
Attention to the Bible. Pr 22:17. 23:12.
Babbling. Pr 10:8, 19.
Backbiter, described. Pr 25:18.
Backsliding. Pr 14:14.
Balance, false and true. Pr 11:1. 20:10, 14.
Beauty, vanity of. Pr 11:22. 31:30.
Behavior acceptable to God. Pr 11:20.
Bible, completeness of, Pr +*30:5, 6.
Bible, holiness of, Pr +*30:5, 6.
Bible, perspicuity (clarity) of, Pr +*8:9.
Bible, continued study brings increasing light. Pr +*4:18.
Bible, God's "medicine bottle." Pr 4:20-22.
Bible, importance of studying. Pr 2:1-6. 4:7, 21-23. 7:1-5.
Blessing of God. Pr 10:6, 22. 11:26.
Boastful spirit. Pr 25:14. 27:1.
Bountiful spirit. Pr 11:24. 22:9. 31:20.
Brawling woman. Pr 21:9, 19. 25:24. 27:15. 30:23.
Buying the truth. Pr 22:23.
Care for souls. Pr 24:11.
Character. Pr 27:19.
Character and its consequences. Pr 10:24.
Charity, Christian. Pr 3:27. 19:17.
Chastening of God. Pr 3:11. 12:31. 13:24. 15:10. 18:6, 7. 19:18.
Chastening, parental. Pr 3:11, 12. 12:31. 13:24. 15:10. 18:6, 7. 19:18.
Children, anxiety of. Pr 10:1. 15:20. 17:25. 19:26. 23:15, 16. 29:3. 31:1.

Children, blessing of. Pr 18:6.
Children, joy in. Pr 10:1. 15:20. 23:15, 16. 29:3. 31:3-7.
Children, promise to. Pr 8:17. 20:11.
Children, sorrow in. Pr 10:1. 17:21, 25. 19:13. 28:24. 29:15.
Christian, dignity of. Pr 12:26. 21:8.
Communion of saints. Pr 16:24. 27:9. 27:17.
Company, good and bad. Pr 13:20.
Competency. Pr 12:8. 22:29.
Concealment, the glory of God. Pr 25:2, 3.
Conceit, evil of. Pr 12:15. 19:20. 26:42. 28:11.
Confession of sin. Pr 28:13.
Confidence, Christian. Pr 2:32. 3:23, 24. 10:30. 14:26. 22:17. 24:13. 28:5.
Conies (badgers), description of. Pr 30:26.
Consideration, importance of. Pr 3:27. 15:28. 22:7. 25:17.
Contention, evil of. Pr 13:10. 18:19. 25:8-10. 26:20-22. 30:32, 33.
Contention, uselessness of. Pr 29:9.
Contentment, value of. Pr 15:15. 16:8. 17:1.
Conversation, vain. Pr 14:23.
Corruption of human nature. Pr 20:9. 21:4. 22:15.
Corruption, total. Pr 30:11-14.
Counsel, value of. Pr 11:14. 15:22. 20:5, 18.
Counselor, the Great. Pr 8:14. 12:15. 15:23. 20:18.
Counsels, divine certainty. Pr 19:12. 20:24. 21:25, 26.
Covering of sins. Pr 28:13.
Covetousness, evil of. Pr 15:27. 16:8. 28:8, 22, 27.
Creation, work of. Pr 3:19, 20. 8:22-31.
Credulity, evil of. Pr 14:15. 26:23-27.
Cruelty. Pr 15:20. 30:11-14.
Cruelty, punishment of. Pr 11:17.
Cruelty and compassion. Pr 12:10.
Curses. Pr 26:2.
Death of wicked and righteous contrasted. Pr 14:32.
Deceit, evil of. Pr 8:7. 14:8. 20:17.
Dependence on God. Pr 16:1. 19:16.
Depression of spirits. Pr 12:25. 15:13. 17:22.
Desires, insatiable. Pr 13:25. 27:20.
Desires of the righteous. Pr 11:23. 13:19. 18:1. 19:22.
Desires of the slothful. Pr 13:4. 19:21.
Despair, temptation to. Pr 18:14.
Despising chastening, sin of. Pr 3:11, 12.
Despising neighbor. Pr 11:12. 14:21.
Despising of parents. Pr 15:5, 20. 28:24. 30:11-14, 17.
Despising reproof. Pr 1:24-31. 29:1.
Despising our ways. Pr 19:16.
Despising wisdom. Pr 1:7. 23:9.
Despising the Word of God. Pr 13:13.
Destruction of sinners, willful. Pr 1:32. 8:34-36. 17:15.
Devices, wicked. Pr 14:17, 22.
Diligence, value of. Pr 11:27. 12:11. 21:5. 23:29. 27:23-27. 30:24.
Diligent and slothful compared. Pr 10:4. 12:24. 13:4.
Discretion, lack of. Pr 11:22.
Discretion, value of. Pr 2:10. 19:11.
Dishonesty, sin of. Pr 11:1. 20:14. 20:23. 21:6. 29:24.
Diversion of mind, evil of. Pr 17:23.
Divine omniscience. Pr 15:3.

Will, liberty of. Pr 19:21. 20:24.
Wine, evil of. Pr 20:1.
Wisdom, attribute of. Pr 3:19, 20.
Wisdom, call of. Pr 1:20-23. 8:1-4.
Wisdom, heavenly. Pr 2:7. 3:35. 8:1-4. 10:13, 31, 32.
  12:8. 14:33. 15:2, 7, 24. 17:16, 24. 19:8.
Wisdom, Personal, type of Christ. Pr 8:14, 22-31.
Wisdom, rules for study of. Pr 2:1-6. 7:1-5.
Wisdom and folly. Pr 14:1. 26:12.
Wise men, value of. Pr 15:7. 29:9.
Wise servant. Pr 14:35. 17:2.
Wise son. Pr 10:1.
Wise men and fools. Pr 10:8.

Witness, faithful. Pr 12:17. 14:5. 21:28.
Witness, false. Pr 12:17. 14:5, 25. 19:5, 28, 29. 21:28.
  24:28, 29. 25:18.
Women and marriage. Pr 11:16. 25:24.
Work and idleness. Pr 10:26.
Wounded spirit. Pr 18:14.
Young, addressed. Pr 2:16-18, 20-22. 8:17. 13:15, 18.
  18:12. 19:16, 27. 23:26-28. 27:11. 28:7, 24. 29:3.
Young, Christian word to. Pr 4:10-13. 10:8. 14:7.
Young, Proverbs book for. Pr 22:14, 15.
Young, snares for. Pr 2:12-15.
Young, teachers of, addressed. Pr 2:20-22.

NAME INDEX

1. Aaron. 175h, Ex 4:14.
2. Aaron. 2g, He 5:4.
3. Aaronites. 175h, 1 Ch 12:27.
4. Abaddon. 3g, Re 9:11.
5. Abagtha. 5h, Est 1:10.
6. Abana. 71h, 2 K 5:12.
7. Abarim. 5682h, Nu 27:12.
8. Abba. 5g, Mk 14:36.
9. Abda. 5653h, Ne 11:17.
10. Abdeel. 5655h, Je 36:26.
11. Abdi. 5660h, 1 Ch 6:44.
12. Abdiel. 5661h, 1 Ch 5:15.
13. Abdon. 5658h, Jg 12:13.
14. Abednego. 5664h, Da 1:7.
15. Abel. 1893h, Ge 4:2.
16. Abel. 59h, 1 S 6:18.
17. Abel. 6g, Mt 23:35.
18. Abelbethmaachah. 62h, 1 K 15:20.
19. Abelmaim. 66h, 2 Ch 16:4.
20. Abelmeholah. 65h, Jg 7:22.
21. Abelmizraim. 67h, Ge 50:11.
22. Abelshittim. 63h, Nu 33:49.
23. Abez. 77h, Jsh 19:20.
24. Abi. 21h, 2 K 18:2.
25. Abia. 7g, Mt 1:7.
26. Abia. 29h, 1 Ch 3:10.
27. Abiah. 29h, 1 S 8:2.
28. Abialbon. 45h, 2 S 23:31.
29. Abiasaph. 23h, Ex 6:24.
30. Abiathar. 54h, 1 S 22:20.
31. Abib. 24h, Ex 13:4.
32. Abida. 28h, 1 Ch 1:33.
33. Abidah. 28h, Ge 25:4.
34. Abidan. 27h, Nu 7:60.
35. Abiel. 22h, 1 S 9:1.
36. Abiezer. 44h, Jsh 17:2.
37. Abiezrite. 33h, Jg 6:11.
38. Abigail. 26h, 1 S 25:3.
39. Abihail. 32h, Nu 3:35.
40. Abihu. 30h, Ex 6:23.
41. Abihud. 31h, 1 Ch 8:3.
42. Abijah. 29h, 1 K 14:1.
43. Abijam. 38h, 1 K 15:1.
44. Abilene. 9g, Lk 3:1.
45. Abimael. 39h, Ge 10:28.
46. Abimelech. 40h, Ge 20:2.
47. Abinadab. 41h, 1 S 16:8.
48. Abinoam. 42h, Jg 4:6.
49. Abiram. 48h, Nu 16:1.
50. Abishag. 49h, 1 K 1:3.
51. Abishalom. 53h, 1 K 15:2.
52. Abishua. 50h, 1 Ch 6:4.
53. Abishur. 51h, 1 Ch 2:28.
54. Abital. 37h, 2 S 3:4.
55. Abitub. 36h, 1 Ch 8:11.
56. Abiud. 10g, Mt 1:13.
57. Abner. 74h, 1 S 14:50.
58. Abraham. 11g, Lk 3:34.
59. Abraham. 85h, Ge 17:5.
60. Abram. 87h, Ge 11:26.
61. Absalom. 53h, 2 S 13:1.
62. Accad. 390h, Ge 10:10.
63. Accho. 5910h, Jg 1:31.
64. Aceldama. 184g, Ac 1:19.
65. Achaia. 882g, Ac 18:12.
66. Achaicus. 883g, 1 C 16:17.
67. Achan. 5912h, Jsh 7:1.
68. Achar. 5917h, 1 Ch 2:7.
69. Achaz. 881g, Mt 1:9.
70. Achbor. 5907h, Ge 36:38.
71. Achim. 885g, Mt 1:14.
72. Achish. 397h, 1 S 21:10.
73. Achmetha. 307h, Ezr 6:2.
74. Achor. 5911h, Jsh 7:24.
75. Achsa. 5915h, 1 Ch 2:49.
76. Achsah. 5915h, Jsh 15:16.
77. Achshaph. 407h, Jsh 11:1.
78. Achzib. 392h, Jsh 15:44.
79. Adadah. 5735h, Jsh 15:22.
80. Adah. 5711h, Ge 4:19.
81. Adaiah. 5718h, Ne 11:5.
82. Adalia. 118h, Est 9:8.
83. Adam. 120h, Ge 2:19.
84. Adam. 76g, Lk 3:38.
85. Adam. 121h, Jsh 3:16.
86. Adamah. 128h, Jsh 19:36.
87. Adami. 129h, Jsh 19:33.
88. Adar. 143h, Est 3:7.
89. Adar. 146h, Jsh 15:3.
90. Adbeel. 110h, Ge 25:13.
91. Addan. 135h, Ezr 2:59.
92. Addar. 146h, 1 Ch 8:3.
93. Addi. 78g, Lk 3:28.
94. Addon. 114h, Ne 7:61.
95. Ader. 5738h, 1 Ch 8:15.
96. Adiel. 5717h, 1 Ch 4:36.
97. Adin. 5720h, Ezr 2:15.
98. Adina. 5721h, 1 Ch 11:42.
99. Adino. 5722h, 2 S 23:8.
100. Adithaim. 5723h, Jsh 15:36.
101. Adlai. 5724h, 1 Ch 27:29.
102. Admah. 126h, Ge 10:19.
103. Admatha. 133h, Est 1:14.
104. Adna. 5733h, Ezr 10:30.
105. Adnah. 5734h, 1 Ch 12:20.
106. Adonai. 136h, Ge 18:3.
107. Adonibezek. 137h, Jg 1:5.
108. Adonijah. 138h, 1 K 1:5.
109. Adonikam. 140h, Ne 7:18.
110. Adoniram. 141h, 1 K 4:6.
111. Adonizedec. 139h, Jsh 10:1.
112. Adoraim. 115h, 2 Ch 11:9.
113. Adoram. 115h, 2 S 20:24.
114. Adrammelech. 152h, 2 K 19:37.
115. Adramyttium. 98g, Ac 27:2.
116. Adria. 99g, Ac 27:27.
117. Adriel. 5741h, 1 S 18:19.
118. Adullam. 5725h, Jsh 12:15.
119. Adullamite. 5726h, Ge 38:1.
120. Adummim. 131h, Jsh 15:7.

121. Aeneas. 132g, Ac 9:33.
122. Aenon. 137g, Jn 3:23.
123. Agabus. 13g, Ac 11:28.
124. Agag. 90h, Nu 24:7.
125. Agagite. 91h, Est 3:1.
126. Agar. 28g, Ga 4:24.
127. Agee. 89h, 2 S 23:11.
128. Agrippa. 67g, Ac 25:13.
129. Agur. 94h, Pr 30:1.
130. Ahab. 256h, 1 K 16:28.
131. Aharah. 315h, 1 Ch 8:1.
132. Aharhel. 316h, 1 Ch 4:8.
133. Ahasai. 273h, Ne 11:13.
134. Ahasbai. 308h, 2 S 23:34.
135. Ahasuerus. 325h, Est 1:1.
136. Ahava. 163h, Ezr 8:15.
137. Ahaz. 271h, 1 Ch 8:35.
138. Ahaziah. 274h, 1 K 22:40.
139. Ahban. 257h, 1 Ch 2:29.
140. Aher. 313h, 1 Ch 7:12.
141. Ahi. 277h, 1 Ch 5:15.
142. Ahiah. 281h, 1 Ch 8:7.
143. Ahiam. 279h, 2 S 23:33.
144. Ahian. 291h, 1 Ch 7:19.
145. Ahiezer. 295h, 1 Ch 12:3.
146. Ahihud. 282h, Nu 34:27.
147. Ahihud. 284h, 1 Ch 8:7.
148. Ahijah. 281h, 1 K 14:6.
149. Ahikam. 296h, 2 K 22:12.
150. Ahilud. 286h, 2 S 8:16.
151. Ahimaaz. 290h, 1 S 14:50.
152. Ahiman. 289h, 1 Ch 9:17.
153. Ahimelech. 288h, 2 S 8:17.
154. Ahimoth. 287h, 1 Ch 6:25.
155. Ahinadab. 292h, 1 K 4:14.
156. Ahinoam. 293h, 1 S 14:50.
157. Ahio. 283h, 2 S 6:3.
158. Ahira. 299h, Nu 1:15.
159. Ahiram. 297h, Nu 26:38.
160. Ahiramites. 298h, Nu 26:38.
161. Ahisamach. 294h, Ex 31:6.
162. Ahishahar. 300h, 1 Ch 7:10.
163. Ahishar. 301h, 1 K 4:6.
164. Ahithophel. 302h, 2 S 15:12.
165. Ahitub. 285h, 1 S 14:3.
166. Ahlab. 303h, Jg 1:31.
167. Ahlai. 304h, 1 Ch 11:41.
168. Ahoah. 265h, 1 Ch 8:4.
169. Ahohite. 266h, 2 S 23:9.
170. Aholah. 170h, Ezk 23:4.
171. Aholiab. 171h, Ex 31:6.
172. Aholibah. 172h, Ezk 23:4.
173. Aholibamah. 173h, Ge 36:41.
174. Ahumai. 267h, 1 Ch 4:2.
175. Ahuzam. 275h, 1 Ch 4:6.
176. Ahuzzath. 276h, Ge 26:26.
177. Ai. 5857h, Jsh 7:2.
178. Aiah. 345h, 2 S 3:7.
179. Aiath. 5857h, Is 10:28.
180. Aija. 5857h, Ne 11:31.
181. Aijalon. 357h, Jsh 21:24.
182. Aijeleth Shahar. 365h, Ps 22:Title.
183. Ain. 5871h, Nu 34:11.
184. Ajah. 345h, Ge 36:24.
185. Ajalon. 357h, Jsh 10:12.
186. Akan. 6130h, Ge 36:27.
187. Akkub. 6126h, 1 Ch 3:24.
188. Akrabbim. 6137h, Nu 34:4.
189. Alameth. 5964h, 1 Ch 7:8.

190. Alammelech. 487h, Jsh 19:26.
191. Alamoth. 5961h, 1 Ch 15:20.
192. Alemeth. 5964h, 1 Ch 6:60.
193. Alexander. 223g, Mk 15:21.
194. Alexandria. 221g, Ac 27:6.
195. Alexandrians. 221g, Ac 6:9.
196. Aliah. 5933h, 1 Ch 1:51.
197. Alian. 5935h, 1 Ch 1:40.
198. Allon. 438h, 1 Ch 4:37.
199. Allon-bachuth. 439h, Ge 35:8.
200. Almodad. 486h, Ge 10:26.
201. Almon. 5960h, Jsh 21:18.
202. Almon-diblathaim. 5963h, Nu 33:46.
203. Aloth. 1175h, 1 K 4:16.
204. Alphaeus. 256g, Mt 10:3.
205. Alush. 442h, Nu 33:13.
206. Alvah. 5933h, Ge 36:40.
207. Alvan. 5935h, Ge 36:23.
208. Amad. 6008h, Jsh 19:26.
209. Amal. 6000h, 1 Ch 7:35.
210. Amalek. 6002h, Ex 17:8.
211. Amalekites. 6003h, Nu 14:45.
212. Amam. 538h, Jsh 15:26.
213. Amana. 549h, SS 4:8.
214. Amariah. 568h, Ezr 7:3.
215. Amasa. 6021h, 2 S 17:25.
216. Amasai. 6022h, 2 Ch 29:12.
217. Amashai. 6023h, Ne 11:13.
218. Amasiah. 6007h, 2 Ch 17:16.
219. Amaziah. 558h, 1 Ch 4:34.
220. Ami. 532h, Ezr 2:57.
221. Aminadab. 284g, Lk 3:33.
222. Amittai. 573h, 2 K 14:25.
223. Ammah. 522h, 2 S 2:24.
224. Ammi. 5971h, Ho 2:1.
225. Ammiel. 5988h, 1 Ch 3:5.
226. Ammihud. 5989h, 2 S 13:37.
227. Amminadab. 5992h, 1 Ch 15:11.
228. Ammishaddai. 5996h, Nu 1:12.
229. Ammizabad. 5990h, 1 Ch 27:6.
230. Ammon. 5983h, Ge 19:38.
231. Ammonites. 5984h, 1 S 11:11.
232. Amnon. 550h, 2 S 3:2.
233. Amok. 5987h, Ne 12:7.
234. Amon. 526h, Ne 7:59.
235. Amon. 300g, Mt 1:10.
236. Amorites. 567h, Dt 20:17.
237. Amos. 5986h, Am 1:1.
238. Amos. 301g, Lk 3:25.
239. Amoz. 531h, 2 K 19:2.
240. Amphipolis. 295g, Ac 17:1.
241. Amplias. 291g, Ro 16:8.
242. Amram. 2566h, 1 Ch 1:41.
243. Amram. 6091h, Ex 6:18.
244. Amramites. 6020h, Nu 3:27.
245. Amraphel. 569h, Ge 14:1.
246. Amzi. 557h, Ne 11:12.
247. Anab. 6024h, Jsh 11:21.
248. Anah. 6034h, Ge 36:20.
249. Anaharath. 588h, Jsh 19:19.
250. Anaiah. 6043h, Ne 8:4.
251. Anak. 6061h, Nu 13:33.
252. Anakims. 6062h, Dt 1:28.
253. Anamim. 6047h, Ge 10:13.
254. Anammelech. 6048h, 2 K 17:31.
255. Anan. 6052h, Ne 10:26.
256. Anani. 6054h, 1 Ch 3:24.
257. Ananiah. 6055h, Ne 3:23.
258. Ananias. 367g, Ac 5:1.

397. Aspatha. 630h, Est 9:7.
398. Asriel. 844h, Nu 26:31.
399. Asrielites. 845h, Nu 26:31.
400. Asshur. 804h, Ge 10:22.
401. Asshurim. 805h, Ge 25:3.
402. Assir. 617h, Ex 6:24.
403. Assos. 789g, Ac 20:13.
404. Assur. 804h, Ezr 4:2.
405. Assyria. 804h, Ge 2:14.
406. Astaroth. 6252h, Dt 1:4.
407. Asuppim. 624h, 1 Ch 26:15.
408. Asyncritus. 799g, Ro 16:14.
409. Atad. 329h, Ge 50:10.
410. Atarah. 5851h, 1 Ch 2:26.
411. Ataroth. 5852h, Nu 32:3.
412. Atarothadar. 5853h, Jsh 18:13.
413. Ater. 333h, Ezr 2:16.
414. Athach. 6269h, 1 S 30:30.
415. Athaiah. 6265h, Ne 11:4.
416. Athaliah. 6271h, 1 Ch 8:26.
417. Athenians. 117g, Ac 17:21.
418. Athens. 116g, Ac 17:15.
419. Athlai. 6270h, Ezr 10:28.
420. Atroth. 5855h, Nu 32:35.
421. Attai. 6262h, 1 Ch 2:35.
422. Attalia. 825g, Ac 14:25.
423. Augustus. 828g, Lk 2:1.
424. Ava. 5755h, 2 K 17:24.
425. Aven. 206h, Ezk 30:17.
426. Avim. 5761h, Jsh 18:23.
427. Avims. 5757h, Dt 2:23.
428. Avith. 5762h, Ge 36:35.
429. Azal. 682h, Zc 14:5.
430. Azaliah. 683h, 2 Ch 34:8.
431. Azaniah. 245h, Ne 10:9.
432. Azarael. 5832h, Ne 12:36.
433. Azareel. 5832h, 1 Ch 12:6.
434. Azariah. 5838h, 1 Ch 6:36.
435. Azaz. 5811h, 1 Ch 5:8.
436. Azaziah. 5812h, 1 Ch 27:20.
437. Azbuk. 5802h, Ne 3:16.
438. Azekah. 5825h, Jsh 10:10.
439. Azel. 682h, 1 Ch 8:37.
440. Azem. 6107h, Jsh 15:29.
441. Azgad. 5803h, Ezr 2:12.
442. Aziel. 5815h, 1 Ch 15:20.
443. Aziza. 5819h, Ezr 10:27.
444. Azmaveth. 5820h, 2 S 23:31.
445. Azmon. 6111h, Nu 34:4.
446. Aznothtabor. 243h, Jsh 19:34.
447. Azor. 107g, Mt 1:13.
448. Azotus. 108g, Ac 8:40.
449. Azriel. 5837h, 1 Ch 5:24.
450. Azrikam. 5840h, 1 Ch 3:23.
451. Azubah. 5806h, 1 K 22:42.
452. Azur. 5809h, Je 28:1.
453. Azzah. 5804h, Dt 2:23.
454. Azzan. 5821h, Nu 34:26.
455. Azzur. 5809h, Ne 10:17.
456. Baal. 1168h, 1 Ch 5:5.
457. Baal. 1168h, Jg 6:25.
458. Baal. 896g, Ro 11:4.
459. Baalah. 1173h, Jsh 15:9.
460. Baalath. 1191h, Jsh 19:44.
461. Baalathbeer. 1192h, Jsh 19:8.
462. Baalberith. 1170h, Jg 8:33.
463. Baale. 1184h, 2 S 6:2.
464. Baalgad. 1171h, Jsh 11:17.
465. Baalhamon. 1174h, SS 8:11.

466. Baalhanan. 1177h, Ge 36:38.
467. Baalhazor. 1178h, 2 S 13:23.
468. Baalhermon. 1179h, Jg 3:3.
469. Baali. 1180h, Ho 2:16.
470. Baalim. 1168h, Jg 2:11.
471. Baalis. 1185h, Je 40:14.
472. Baalmeon. 1186h, Nu 32:38.
473. Baalpeor. 1187h, Nu 25:3.
474. Baalperazim. 1188h, 2 S 5:20.
475. Baalshalisha. 1190h, 2 K 4:42.
476. Baaltamar. 1193h, Jg 20:33.
477. Baalzebub. 1176h, 2 K 1:2.
478. Baalzephon. 1189h, Ex 14:2.
479. Baana. 1195h, 1 K 4:12.
480. Baanah. 1195h, 2 S 4:5.
481. Baara. 1199h, 1 Ch 8:8.
482. Baaseiah. 1202h, 1 Ch 6:40.
483. Baasha. 1201h, 1 K 15:16.
484. Babel. 894h, Ge 10:10.
485. Babylon. 894h, 2 K 17:24.
486. Babylon. 895h, Ezr 5:12.
487. Babylon. 897g, Re 14:8.
488. Babylonians. 896h, Jsh 7:21.
489. Baca. 1056h, Ps 84:6.
490. Baharumite. 978h, 1 Ch 11:33.
491. Bahurim. 980h, 2 S 3:16.
492. Bajith. 1006h, Is 15:2.
493. Bakbakkar. 1230h, 1 Ch 9:15.
494. Bakbuk. 1227h, Ezr 2:51.
495. Bakbukiah. 1229h, Ne 11:17.
496. Balaam. 1109h, Nu 22:5.
497. Balaam. 903g, 2 P 2:15.
498. Balac. 904g, Re 2:14.
499. Baladan. 1081h, 2 K 20:12.
500. Balah. 1088h, Jsh 19:3.
501. Balak. 1111h, Nu 22:2.
502. Bamah. 1117h, Ezk 20:29.
503. Bamoth. 1120h, Nu 21:19.
504. Bamothbaal. 1120h, Jsh 13:17.
505. Bani. 1137h, Ezr 2:10.
506. Barabbas. 912g, Mt 27:16.
507. Barachel. 1292h, Jb 32:2.
508. Barachias. 914g, Mt 23:35.
509. Barak. 1301h, Jg 4:6.
510. Barak. 913g, He 11:32.
511. Barhumite. 1273h, 2 S 23:31.
512. Bariah. 1282h, 1 Ch 3:22.
513. Barjesus. 919g, Ac 13:6.
514. Barjona. 920g, Mt 16:17.
515. Barkos. 1302h, Ezr 2:53.
516. Barnabas. 921g, Ac 4:36.
517. Barsabus. 923g, Ac 15:22.
518. Bartholomew. 918g, Mt 10:3.
519. Bartimaeus. 924g, Mk 10:46.
520. Baruch. 1263h, Je 32:12.
521. Barzillai. 1271h, 2 S 21:8.
522. Bashan. 1316h, Nu 21:33.
523. Bashanhavothjair. 2334h, Dt 3:14.
524. Bashemath. 1315h, Ge 36:3.
525. Basmath. 1315h, 1 K 4:15.
526. Bathrabbim. 1337h, SS 7:4.
527. Bathsheba. 1339h, 2 S 11:3.
528. Bathshua. 1340h, 1 Ch 3:5.
529. Bavai. 942h, Ne 3:18.
530. Bazlith. 1213h, Ne 7:54.
531. Bazluth. 1213h, Ezr 2:52.
532. Bealiah. 1183h, 1 Ch 12:5.
533. Bealoth. 1175h, Jsh 15:24.
534. Bebai. 893h, Ezr 2:11.

535. Becher. 1071h, Ge 46:21.
536. Bechorath. 1064h, 1 S 9:1.
537. Bedad. 911h, Ge 36:35.
538. Bedan. 917h, 1 Ch 7:17.
539. Bedeiah. 912h, Ezr 10:35.
540. Beeliada. 1182h, 1 Ch 14:7.
541. Beelzebub. 954g, Mt 10:25.
542. Beer. 876h, Nu 21:16.
543. Beera. 878h, 1 Ch 7:37.
544. Beerah. 880h, 1 Ch 5:6.
545. Beerelim. 879h, Is 15:8.
546. Beeri. 882h, Ge 26:34.
547. Beerlahairoi. 883h, Ge 16:14.
548. Beeroth. 881h, Jsh 9:17.
549. Beeroth of the children of Jaakan. 885h, Dt 10:6.
550. Beerothite. 886h, 2 S 4:2.
551. Beersheba. 884h, Ge 21:31.
552. Beeshterah. 1203h, Jsh 21:27.
553. Bel. 1078h, Is 46:1.
554. Bela. 1106h, Ge 14:2.
555. Belah. 1106h, Ge 46:21.
556. Belaites. 1108h, Nu 26:38.
557. Belial. 1100h, Dt 13:13.
558. Belial. 955g, 2 C 6:15.
559. Belshazzar. 1113h, Da 5:1.
560. Belteshazzar. 1095h, Da 1:7.
561. Ben. 1122h, 1 Ch 15:18.
562. Benaiah. 1141h, 1 Ch 15:24.
563. Benammi. 1151h, Ge 19:38.
564. Beneberak. 1139h, Jsh 19:45.
565. Benejaakan. 1142h, Nu 33:31.
566. Benhadad. 1130h, 1 K 15:18.
567. Benhail. 1134h, 2 Ch 17:7.
568. Benhanan. 1135h, 1 Ch 4:20.
569. Beninu. 1148h, Ne 10:13.
570. Benjamin. 1144h, Ge 35:18.
571. Benjamin. 958g, Ro 11:1.
572. Beno. 1121h, 1 Ch 24:26.
573. Benoni. 1126h, Ge 35:18.
574. Benzoheth. 1132h, 1 Ch 4:20.
575. Beon. 1194h, Nu 32:3.
576. Beor. 1160h, Nu 22:5.
577. Bera. 1298h, Ge 14:2.
578. Berachah. 1294h, 1 Ch 12:3.
579. Berachiah. 1296h, 1 Ch 6:39.
580. Beraiah. 1256h, 1 Ch 8:21.
581. Berea. 960g, Ac 17:10.
582. Berechiah. 1296h, Zc 1:7.
583. Bered. 1260h, Ge 16:14.
584. Beri. 1275h, 1 Ch 7:36.
585. Beriah. 1283h, 1 Ch 7:23.
586. Beriites. 1284h, Nu 26:44.
587. Berites. 1276h, 2 S 20:14.
588. Berith. 1286h, Jg 9:46.
589. Bernice. 959g, Ac 25:13.
590. Berodach-baladan. 1255h, 2 K 20:12.
591. Berothah. 1268h, Ezk 47:16.
592. Berothai. 1268h, 2 S 8:8.
593. Berothite. 1307h, 1 Ch 11:39.
594. Besai. 1153h, Ezr 2:49.
595. Besodeiah. 1152h, Ne 3:6.
596. Besor. 1308h, 1 S 30:9.
597. Betah. 894h, 2 S 8:8.
598. Beten. 991h, Jsh 19:25.
599. Bethabara. 962g, Jn 1:28.
600. Bethanath. 1043h, Jsh 19:38.
601. Bethanoth. 1042h, Jsh 15:59.
602. Bethany. 963g, Jn 11:18.
603. Betharabah. 1026h, Jsh 15:61.

604. Betharam. 1027h, Jsh 13:27.
605. Betharbel. 1009h, Ho 10:14.
606. Bethaven. 1007h, Jsh 7:2.
607. Bethazmaveth. 1041h, Ne 7:28.
608. Bethbaalmeon. 1010h, Jsh 13:17.
609. Bethbarah. 1012h, Jg 7:24.
610. Bethbirei. 1011h, 1 Ch 4:31.
611. Bethcar. 1033h, 1 S 7:11.
612. Bethdagon. 1016h, Jsh 15:41.
613. Bethdiblathaim. 1015h, Je 48:22.
614. Beth-eden. 1004h, Am 1:5mg.
615. Bethel. 1008h, Ge 12:8.
616. Bethelite. 1017h, 1 K 16:34.
617. Bethemek. 1025h, Jsh 19:27.
618. Bether. 1336h, SS 2:17.
619. Bethesda. 964g, Jn 5:2.
620. Bethezel. 1018h, Mi 1:11.
621. Bethgader. 1013h, 1 Ch 2:51.
622. Bethgamul. 1014h, Je 48:23.
623. Bethhaccerem. 1021h, Je 6:1.
624. Bethharan. 1028h, Nu 32:36.
625. Bethhogla. 1031h, Jsh 15:6.
626. Bethhoglah. 1031h, Jsh 18:19.
627. Bethhoron. 1032h, Jsh 10:10.
628. Bethjeshimoth. 1020h, Jsh 12:3.
629. Bethjesimoth. 1020h, Nu 33:49.
630. Bethlebaoth. 1034h, Jsh 19:6.
631. Bethlehem. 1035h, Jsh 19:15.
632. Bethlehem. 965g, Mt 2:1.
633. Bethlehemite. 1022h, 1 S 16:1.
634. Bethmaachah. 1038h, 2 S 20:14.
635. Bethmarcaboth. 1024h, 1 Ch 4:31.
636. Bethmeon. 1010h, Je 48:23.
637. Bethnimrah. 1039h, Jsh 13:27.
638. Bethpalet. 1046h, Jsh 15:27.
639. Bethpazzez. 1048h, Jsh 19:21.
640. Bethpeor. 1047h, Dt 3:29.
641. Bethphage. 967g, Mt 21:1.
642. Bethphelet. 1046h, Ne 11:26.
643. Bethrapha. 1051h, 1 Ch 4:12.
644. Bethrehob. 1050h, 2 S 10:6.
645. Bethsaida. 966g, Mk 6:45.
646. Bethshan. 1052h, 1 S 31:10.
647. Bethshean. 1052h, Jsh 17:11.
648. Bethshemesh. 1053h, Je 43:13.
649. Bethshemite. 1030h, 1 S 6:14.
650. Bethshittah. 1029h, Jg 7:22.
651. Bethtappuah. 1054h, Jsh 15:53.
652. Bethuel. 1328h, Ge 22:22.
653. Bethul. 1329h, Jsh 19:4.
654. Bethzur. 1049h, Jsh 15:58.
655. Betonim. 993h, Jsh 13:26.
656. Beulah. 1166h, Is 62:4.
657. Bezai. 1209h, Ne 7:23.
658. Bezaleel. 1212h, Ex 31:2.
659. Bezek. 966h, Jg 1:4.
660. Bezer. 1221h, Dt 4:43.
661. Bichri. 1075h, 2 S 20:1.
662. Bidkar. 920h, 2 K 9:25.
663. Bigtha. 903h, Est 1:10.
664. Bigthan. 904h, Est 2:21.
665. Bigthana. 904h, Est 6:2.
666. Bigvai. 902h, Ezr 2:2.
667. Bikath-aven. 1237h, Am 1:5mg.
668. Bildad. 1085h, Jb 2:11.
669. Bileam. 1109h, 1 Ch 6:70.
670. Bilgah. 1083h, Ne 12:5.
671. Bilgai. 1084h, Ne 10:8.
672. Bilhah. 1090h, Ge 29:29.

673. Bilhan. 1092h, Ge 36:27.
674. Bilshan. 1114h, Ezr 2:2.
675. Bimhal. 1118h, 1 Ch 7:33.
676. Binea. 1150h, 1 Ch 8:37.
677. Binnui. 1131h, Ezr 10:30.
678. Birsha. 1306h, Ge 14:2.
679. Birzavith. 1269h, 1 Ch 7:31.
680. Bishlam. 1312h, Ezr 4:7.
681. Bithiah. 1332h, 1 Ch 4:18.
682. Bithron. 1338h, 2 S 2:29.
683. Bithynia. 978g, Ac 16:7.
684. Bizjothjah. 964h, Jsh 15:28.
685. Biztha. 968h, Est 1:10.
686. Blastus. 986g, Ac 12:20.
687. Boanerges. 993g, Mk 3:17.
688. Boaz. 1162h, Ru 2:1.
689. Bocheru. 1074h, 1 Ch 8:38.
690. Bochim. 1066h, Jg 2:1.
691. Bohan. 932h, Jsh 15:6.
692. Booz. 1003g, Mt 1:5.
693. Boscath. 1218h, 2 K 22:1.
694. Bosor. 1007g, 2 P 2:15.
695. Bozez. 949h, 1 S 14:4.
696. Bozkath. 1218h, Jsh 15:39.
697. Bozrah. 1224h, Ge 36:33.
698. Bukki. 1231h, Nu 34:22.
699. Bukkiah. 1232h, 1 Ch 25:13.
700. Bul. 945h, 1 K 6:38.
701. Bunah. 946h, 1 Ch 2:25.
702. Bunni. 1138h, Ne 9:4.
703. Buz. 938h, Ge 22:21.
704. Buzi. 941h, Ezk 1:3.
705. Buzite. 940h, Jb 32:2.
706. Cabbon. 3522h, Jsh 15:40.
707. Cabul. 3521h, Jsh 19:27.
708. Caesar. 2541g, Jn 19:12.
709. Caesarea. 2542g, Ac 8:40.
710. Caesarea Philippi. 2542g, 5375g, Mt 16:13.
711. Caiaphas. 2533g, Mt 26:3.
712. Cain. 7014h, Ge 4:1.
713. Cain. 2535g, 1 J 3:12.
714. Cainan. 7018h, Ge 5:9.
715. Cainan. 2536g, Lk 3:36.
716. Calah. 3625h, Ge 10:12.
717. Calcol. 3633h, 1 Ch 2:6.
718. Caleb. 3612h, Nu 13:6.
719. Calebephratah. 3613h, 1 Ch 2:24.
720. Calneh. 3641h, Ge 10:10.
721. Calno. 3641h, Is 10:9.
722. Calvary. 2898g, Lk 23:33.
723. Camon. 7056h, Jg 10:5.
724. Cana. 2580g, Jn 2:1.
725. Canaan. 3667h, Ge 10:6.
726. Canaan. 5478g, Mt 15:22.
727. Canaanite. 2581g, Mt 10:4.
728. Canaanites. 3669h, Ge 24:3.
729. Candace. 2582g, Ac 8:27.
730. Canneh. 3656h, Ezk 27:23.
731. Capernaum. 2584g, Mt 4:13.
732. Caphthorim. 3732h, 1 Ch 1:12.
733. Caphtor. 3731h, Je 47:4.
734. Caphtorim. 3732h, Ge 10:14.
735. Caphtorims. 3732h, Dt 2:23.
736. Cappadocia. 2587g, Ac 2:9.
737. Carcus. 3752h, Est 1:10.
738. Carchemish. 3751h, Is 10:9.
739. Careah. 7143h, 2 K 25:23.
740. Carmel. 3760h, Jsh 15:55.
741. Carmelite. 3761h, 1 S 30:5.

742. Carmelitess. 3762h, 1 S 27:3.
743. Carmi. 3756h, 1 Ch 4:1.
744. Carmites. 3757h, Nu 26:6.
745. Carpus. 2591g, 2 T 4:13.
746. Carshena. 3771h, Est 1:14.
747. Casiphia. 3703h, Ezr 8:17.
748. Casluhim. 3695h, Ge 10:14.
749. Castor. 1359g, Ac 28:11.
750. Cedron. 2748g, Jn 18:1.
751. Cenchrea. 2747g, Ac 18:18.
752. Cephas. 2786g, Jn 1:42.
753. Chalcol. 3633h, 1 K 4:31.
754. Chaldaeans. 5466g, Ac 7:4.
755. Chaldea. 3778h, Je 50:10.
756. Chaldean. 3779h, Da 2:10.
757. Chaldees. 3778h, 2 K 25:26.
758. Chanaan. 5477g, Ac 7:11.
759. Charashim. 2798h, 1 Ch 4:14.
760. Charchemish. 3751h, 2 Ch 35:20.
761. Charran. 5488g, Ac 7:2.
762. Chebar. 3529h, Ezk 1:1.
763. Chedorlaomer. 3540h, Ge 14:1.
764. Chelal. 3636h, Ezr 10:30.
765. Chelluh. 3622h, Ezr 10:35.
766. Chelub. 3620h, 1 Ch 4:11.
767. Chelubai. 3621h, 1 Ch 2:9.
768. Chemarims. 3649h, Zp 1:4.
769. Chemosh. 3645h, Nu 21:29.
770. Chenaanah. 3668h, 1 Ch 7:10.
771. Chenani. 3662h, Ne 9:4.
772. Chenaniah. 3663h, 1 Ch 15:22.
773. Chephar-haammonai. 3726h, Jsh 18:24.
774. Chephirah. 3716h, Jsh 9:17.
775. Cheran. 3763h, Ge 36:26.
776. Cheethims. 3774h, Ezk 25:16.
777. Cheerthites. 3774h, 2 S 8:18.
778. Cherith. 3747h, 1 K 17:3.
779. Cherub. 3743h, Ezr 2:59.
780. Chesalon. 3693h, Jsh 15:10.
781. Chesed. 3777h, Ge 22:22.
782. Chesil. 3686h, Jsh 15:30.
783. Chesulloth. 3694h, Jsh 19:18.
784. Chezib. 3580h, Ge 38:5.
785. Chidon. 3592h, 1 Ch 13:9.
786. Chileab. 3609h, 2 S 3:3.
787. Chilion. 3630h, Ru 1:2.
788. Chilmad. 3638h, Ezk 27:23.
789. Chilham. 3643h, 2 S 19:40.
790. Chinnereth. 3672h, Dt 3:17.
791. Chinneroth. 3672h, Jsh 11:2.
792. Chios. 5508g, Ac 20:15.
793. Chisleu. 3691h, Zc 7:1.
794. Chislon. 3692h, Nu 34:21.
795. Chisloth-tabor. 3696h, Jsh 19:12.
796. Chittim. 3794h, Nu 24:24.
797. Chiun. 3594h, Am 5:26.
798. Chloe. 5514g, 1 C 1:11.
799. Chorashan. 3565h, 1 S 30:30.
800. Chorazin. 5523g, Mt 11:21.
801. Chozeba. 3578h, 1 Ch 4:22.
802. Christ. 5547g, Mt 16:16.
803. Christians. 5546g, Ac 11:26.
804. Chub. 3552h, Ezk 30:5.
805. Chun. 3560h, 1 Ch 18:8.
806. Chushanrishathaim. 3573h, Jg 3:8.
807. Chuza. 5529g, Lk 8:3.
808. Cilicia. 2791g, Ac 6:9.
809. Cinneroth. 3672h, 1 K 15:20.
810. Cis. 2797g, Ac 13:21.

949. Elasah. 501h, Ezr 10:22.
950. Elath. 359h, Dt 2:8.
951. Elbethel. 416h, Ge 35:7.
952. Eldaah. 420h, Ge 25:4.
953. Eldad. 419h, Nu 11:26.
954. Elead. 496h, 1 Ch 7:21.
955. Elealeh. 500h, Nu 32:3.
956. Eleasah. 501h, 1 Ch 2:39.
957. Eleazar. 499h, Ex 6:23.
958. Eleazar. 1648g, Mt 1:15.
959. Elelohe:Israel. 415h, Ge 33:20.
960. Eleph. 507h, Jsh 18:28.
961. Elhanan. 445h, 2 S 21:19.
962. Eli. 5941h, 1 S 1:3.
963. Eli. 2241g, Mt 27:46.
964. Eliab. 446h, Nu 1:9.
965. Eliada. 450h, 2 S 5:16.
966. Eliadah. 450h, 1 K 11:23.
967. Eliah. 452h, 1 Ch 8:27.
968. Eliahba. 455h, 2 S 23:32.
969. Eliakim. 471h, 2 K 18:18.
970. Eliakim. 1662g, Lk 3:30.
971. Eliam. 463h, 2 S 11:3.
972. Elias. 2243g, Mt 11:14.
973. Eliasaph. 460h, Nu 1:14.
974. Eliashib. 475h, 1 Ch 3:24.
975. Eliathah. 448h, 1 Ch 25:4.
976. Elidad. 449h, Nu 34:21.
977. Eliel. 447h, 1 Ch 8:20.
978. Elienai. 462h, 1 Ch 8:20.
979. Eliezer. 461h, Ge 15:2.
980. Eliezer. 1663g, Lk 3:29.
981. Elihoenai. 454h, Ezr 8:4.
982. Elihoreph. 456h, 1 K 4:3.
983. Elihu. 453h, 1 S 1:1.
984. Elijah. 452h, 1 K 17:1.
985. Elika. 470h, 2 S 23:25.
986. Elim. 362h, Ex 15:27.
987. Elimelech. 458h, Ru 1:2.
988. Elioenai. 454h, 1 Ch 26:3.
989. Eliphal. 465h, 1 Ch 11:35.
990. Eliphalet. 467h, 2 S 5:16.
991. Eliphaz. 464h, Ge 36:4.
992. Elipheleh. 466h, 1 Ch 15:18.
993. Eliphelet. 467h, 1 Ch 3:6.
994. Elisabeth. 1665g, Lk 1:5.
995. Eliseus. 1666g, Lk 4:27.
996. Elisha. 477h, 1 K 19:16.
997. Elishah. 473h, Ge 10:4.
998. Elishama. 476h, Nu 1:10.
999. Elishaphat. 478h, 2 Ch 23:1.
1000. Elisheba. 472h, Ex 6:23.
1001. Elishua. 474h, 2 S 5:15.
1002. Eliud. 1664g, Mt 1:14.
1003. Elizaphan. 469h, Nu 3:30.
1004. Elizur. 468h, Nu 1:5.
1005. Elkanah. 511h, Ex 6:24.
1006. Elkoshite. 512h, Na 1:1.
1007. Ellasar. 495h, Ge 14:1.
1008. Elmodam. 1678g, Lk 3:28.
1009. Elnaam. 493h, 1 Ch 11:46.
1010. Elnathan. 494h, 2 K 24:8.
1011. Eloi. 1682g, Mk 15:34.
1012. Elohim. 430h, Ge 1:1.
1013. Elon. 356h, Ge 26:34.
1014. Elon-beth-hanan. 358h, 1 K 4:9.
1015. Elonites. 440h, Nu 26:26.
1016. Eloth. 359h, 1 K 9:26.
1017. Elpaal. 508h, 1 Ch 8:11.
1018. Elpalet. 467h, 1 Ch 14:5.
1019. Elparan. 364h, Ge 14:6.
1020. Eltekeh. 514h, Jsh 21:23.
1021. Eltekon. 515h, Jsh 15:59.
1022. Eltolad. 513h, Jsh 15:30.
1023. Elul. 435h, Ne 6:15.
1024. Eluzai. 498h, 1 Ch 12:5.
1025. Elymas. 1681g, Ac 13:8.
1026. Elzabad. 443h, 1 Ch 26:7.
1027. Elzaphan. 469h, Ex 6:22.
1028. Emims. 368h, Ge 14:5.
1029. Emmanuel. 1694g, Mt 1:23.
1030. Emmaus. 1695g, Lk 24:13.
1031. Emmor. 1697g, Ac 7:16.
1032. Enam. 5879h, Jsh 15:34.
1033. Enan. 5881h, Nu 1:15.
1034. Endor. 5874h, Jsh 17:11.
1035. Eneglaim. 5882h, Ezk 47:10.
1036. Engannim. 5873h, Jsh 19:21.
1037. Engedi. 5872h, Jsh 15:62.
1038. Enhaddah. 5876h, Jsh 19:21.
1039. Enhakkore. 5875h, Jg 15:19.
1040. Enhazor. 5877h, Jsh 19:37.
1041. Enmishpat. 5880h, Ge 14:7.
1042. Enoch. 2585h, Ge 5:21.
1043. Enoch. 1802g, Lk 3:37.
1044. Enos. 583h, Ge 4:26.
1045. Enos. 1800g, Lk 3:38.
1046. Enosh. 583h, 1 Ch 1:1.
1047. Enrimmon. 5884h, Ne 11:29.
1048. Enrogel. 5883h, Jsh 15:7.
1049. Enshemesh. 5885h, Jsh 15:7.
1050. Entappuah. 5887h, Jsh 17:7.
1051. Epaenetus. 1866g, Ro 16:5.
1052. Epaphras. 1889g, Col 1:7.
1053. Epaphroditus. 1891g, Ph 4:18.
1054. Ephah. 5891h, Ge 25:4.
1055. Ephai. 5778h, Je 40:8.
1056. Epher. 6081h, Ge 25:4.
1057. Ephes-dammin. 658h, 1 S 17:1.
1058. Ephesians. 2180g, Ac 19:28.
1059. Ephesus. 2181g, Ac 18:19.
1060. Ephlal. 654h, 1 Ch 2:37.
1061. Ephod. 641h, Nu 34:23.
1062. Ephphatha. 2188g, Mk 7:34.
1063. Ephraim. 669h, Ge 41:52.
1064. Ephraim. 2187g, Jn 11:54.
1065. Ephraimites. 669h, Jsh 16:10.
1066. Ephrain. 6085h, 2 Ch 13:19.
1067. Ephratah. 672h, 1 Ch 2:50.
1068. Ephrath. 672h, Ge 48:7.
1069. Ephrathites. 673h, Ru 1:2.
1070. Ephron. 6085h, Ge 23:8.
1071. Epicureans. 1946g, Ac 17:18.
1072. Er. 6147h, Ge 38:3.
1073. Er. 2262g, Lk 3:28.
1074. Eran. 6197h, Nu 26:36.
1075. Eranites. 6198h, Nu 26:36.
1076. Erastus. 2037g, Ac 19:22.
1077. Erech. 751h, Ge 10:10.
1078. Eri. 6179h, Ge 46:16.
1079. Erites. 6180h, Nu 26:16.
1080. Esaias. 2268g, Mt 3:3.
1081. Esarhaddon. 634h, 2 K 19:37.
1082. Esau. 6215h, Ge 25:25.
1083. Esau. 2269g, He 12:16.
1084. Esek. 6230h, Ge 26:20.
1085. Eshbaal. 792h, 1 Ch 8:33.
1086. Eshban. 790h, Ge 36:26.

1087. Eshcol. 812h, Nu 13:23.
1088. Eshean. 824h, Jsh 15:52.
1089. Eshek. 6232h, 1 Ch 8:39.
1090. Eshkalonites. 832h, Jsh 13:3.
1091. Eshtaol. 847h, Jsh 15:33.
1092. Eshtaulites. 848h, 1 Ch 2:53.
1093. Eshtemoa. 851h, 1 S 30:28.
1094. Eshtemoh. 851h, Jsh 15:50.
1095. Eshton. 850h, 1 Ch 4:11.
1096. Esli. 2069g, Lk 3:25.
1097. Esrom. 2074g, Lk 3:33.
1098. Esther. 635h, Est 2:8.
1099. Etam. 5862h, 1 Ch 4:32.
1100. Etham. 864h, Ex 13:20.
1101. Ethan. 387h, 1 Ch 2:6.
1102. Ethanim. 388h, 1 K 8:2.
1103. Ethbaal. 856h, 1 K 16:31.
1104. Ether. 6281h, Jsh 19:7.
1105. Ethiopia. 3568h, 2 K 19:9.
1106. Ethiopian. 3569h, Je 13:23.
1107. Ethnan. 869h, 1 Ch 4:7.
1108. Ethni. 867h, 1 Ch 6:41.
1109. Eubulus. 2103g, 2 T 4:21.
1110. Eunice. 2131g, 2 T 1:5.
1111. Euodias. 2136g, Ph 4:2.
1112. Euphrates. 6578h, Ge 2:14.
1113. Euphrates. 2166g, Re 9:14.
1114. Euroclydon. 2148g, Ac 27:14.
1115. Eutychus. 2161g, Ac 20:9.
1116. Eve. 2332h, Ge 3:20.
1117. Eve. 2096g, 2 C 11:3.
1118. Evi. 189h, Nu 31:8.
1119. Evil-merodach. 192h, 2 K 25:27.
1120. Ezar. 687h, 1 Ch 1:38.
1121. Ezbai. 229h, 1 Ch 11:37.
1122. Ezbon. 675h, Ge 46:16.
1123. Ezekias. 1478g, Mt 1:9.
1124. Ezekiel. 3168h, Ezk 1:3.
1125. Ezel. 237h, 1 S 20:19.
1126. Ezem. 6107h, 1 Ch 4:29.
1127. Ezer. 687h, Ge 36:21.
1128. Ezer. 5829h, 1 Ch 4:4.
1129. Ezer. 5827h, 1 Ch 7:21.
1130. Ezion-gaber. 6100h, Nu 33:35.
1131. Ezion-geber. 6100h, 1 K 9:26.
1132. Eznite. 6112h, 2 S 23:8.
1133. Ezra. 5830h, Ezr 7:12.
1134. Ezrahite. 250h, 1 K 4:31.
1135. Ezri. 5836h, 1 Ch 27:26.
1136. Fair Havens. 2568g, Ac 27:8.
1137. Felix. 5344g, Ac 23:24.
1138. Festus. 5347g, Ac 24:27.
1139. Fortunatus. 5415g, 1 C 16:17.
1140. Gaal. 1603h, Jg 9:26.
1141. Gaash. 1608h, Jsh 24:30.
1142. Gaba. 1387h, Jsh 18:24.
1143. Gabbai. 1373h, Ne 11:8.
1144. Gabbatha. 1042g, Jn 19:13.
1145. Gabriel. 1403h, Da 8:16.
1146. Gabriel. 1043g, Lk 1:19.
1147. Gad. 1410h, Ge 30:11.
1148. Gad. 1045g, Re 7:5.
1149. Gadarenes. 1046g, Mk 5:1.
1150. Gaddi. 1426h, Nu 13:11.
1151. Gaddiel. 1427h, Nu 13:10.
1152. Gadi. 1424h, 2 K 15:14.
1153. Gadites. 1425h, Dt 3:12.
1154. Gaham. 1514h, Ge 22:24.
1155. Gahar. 1515h, Ezr 2:47.

1156. Gaius. 1050g, Ro 16:23.
1157. Galal. 1559h, 1 Ch 9:15.
1158. Galatia. 1054g, Ac 16:6.
1159. Galatians. 1052g, Ga 3:1.
1160. Galeed. 1567h, Ge 31:47.
1161. Galilaeans. 1057g, Lk 13:1.
1162. Galilee. 1551h, Jsh 20:7.
1163. Galilee. 1056g, Mt 2:22.
1164. Gallim. 1554h, 1 S 25:44.
1165. Gallio. 1058g, Ac 18:12.
1166. Gamaliel. 1583h, Nu 1:10.
1167. Gamaliel. 1059g, Ac 5:34.
1168. Gammadims. 1575h, Ezk 27:11.
1169. Gamul. 1577h, 1 Ch 24:17.
1170. Gareb. 1619h, 2 S 23:38.
1171. Garmite. 1636h, 1 Ch 4:19.
1172. Gashmu. 1654h, Ne 6:6.
1173. Gatam. 1609h, Ge 36:11.
1174. Gath. 1661h, Jsh 11:22.
1175. Gath-hepher. 1662h, 2 K 14:25.
1176. Gath-rimmon. 1667h, Jsh 21:25.
1177. Gaza. 5804h, Jg 10:19.
1178. Gaza. 1048g, Ac 8:26.
1179. Gazathites. 5841h, Jsh 13:3.
1180. Gazer. 1507h, 2 S 5:25.
1181. Gazez. 1495h, 1 Ch 2:46.
1182. Gazites. 5841h, Jg 16:2.
1183. Gazzam. 1502h, Ezr 2:48.
1184. Geba. 1387h, 1 S 13:3.
1185. Gebal. 1380h, Ps 83:7.
1186. Geber. 1398h, 1 K 4:19.
1187. Gebim. 1374h, Is 10:31.
1188. Gedaliah. 1436h, 1 Ch 25:3.
1189. Gedeon. 1066g, He 11:32.
1190. Geder. 1445h, Jsh 12:13.
1191. Gederah. 1449h, Jsh 15:36.
1192. Gederathite. 1452h, 1 Ch 12:4.
1193. Gederite. 1451h, 1 Ch 27:28.
1194. Gederoth. 1450h, Jsh 15:41.
1195. Gederothaim. 1453h, Jsh 15:36.
1196. Gedor. 1446h, Jsh 15:58.
1197. Gehazi. 1522h, 2 K 4:12.
1198. Geliloth. 1553h, Jsh 18:17.
1199. Gemalli. 1582h, Nu 13:12.
1200. Gemariah. 1587h, Je 36:10.
1201. Gennesaret. 1082g, Mt 14:34.
1202. Gentiles. 1471h, Ge 10:5.
1203. Gentiles. 1672g, Jn 7:35.
1204. Genubath. 1592h, 1 K 11:20.
1205. Gera. 1617h, Ge 46:21.
1206. Gerar. 1642h, Ge 20:1.
1207. Gergesenes. 1086g, Mt 8:28.
1208. Gerizim. 1630h, Dt 11:29.
1209. Gershom. 1647h, Ex 2:22.
1210. Gershon. 1648h, Ge 46:11.
1211. Gershonites. 1649h, Nu 3:21.
1212. Gesham. 1529h, 1 Ch 2:47.
1213. Geshem. 1654h, Ne 6:1.
1214. Geshur. 1650h, 2 S 3:3.
1215. Geshuri. 1651h, Dt 3:14.
1216. Geshurites. 1651h, Jsh 12:5.
1217. Gether. 1666h, Ge 10:23.
1218. Gethsemane. 1068g, Mt 26:36.
1219. Geuel. 1345h, Nu 13:15.
1220. Gezer. 1507h, 1 K 9:16.
1221. Gezrites. 1511h, 1 S 27:8.
1222. Giah. 1520h, 2 S 2:24.
1223. Gibbar. 1402h, Ezr 2:20.
1224. Gibbethon. 1405h, Jsh 19:44.

1225. Gibea. 1388h, 1 Ch 2:49.
1226. Gibeah. 1390h, Jg 19:12.
1227. Gibeath. 1394h, Jsh 18:28.
1228. Gibeathite. 1395h, 1 Ch 12:3.
1229. Gibeon. 1391h, 1 Ch 14:16.
1230. Gibeonites. 1393h, 2 S 21:1.
1231. Giblites. 1382h, Jsh 13:5.
1232. Giddalti. 1437h, 1 Ch 25:4.
1233. Giddel. 1435h, Ezr 2:47.
1234. Gideon. 1439h, Jg 6:11.
1235. Gideoni. 1441h, Nu 1:11.
1236. Gidom. 1440h, Jg 20:45.
1237. Gihon. 1521h, Ge 2:13.
1238. Gilalai. 1562h, Ne 12:36.
1239. Gilboa. 1533h, 1 S 28:4.
1240. Gilead. 1568h, Ge 31:23.
1241. Gileadites. 1569h, Nu 26:29.
1242. Gilgal. 1537h, Jsh 4:19.
1243. Giloh. 1542h, Jsh 15:51.
1244. Gilonite. 1526h, 2 S 15:12.
1245. Gimzo. 1579h, 2 Ch 28:18.
1246. Ginath. 1527h, 1 K 16:21.
1247. Ginnetho. 1599h, Ne 12:4.
1248. Ginnethon. 1599h, Ne 10:6.
1249. Girgashites. 1622h, Ge 15:21.
1250. Girgasite. 1622h, Ge 10:16.
1251. Gispa. 1658h, Ne 11:21.
1252. Gittah-hepher. 1662h, Jsh 19:13.
1253. Gittaim. 1664h, 2 S 4:3.
1254. Gittite. 1663h, 2 S 6:10.
1255. Gittites. 1663h, Jsh 13:3.
1256. Gittith. 1665h, Ps 8:Title.
1257. Gizonite. 1493h, 1 Ch 11:34.
1258. Goath. 1601h, Je 31:39.
1259. Gob. 1359h, 2 S 21:18.
1260. God. 430h, Ge 1:1.
1261. Gog. 1463h, 1 Ch 5:4.
1262. Gog. 1136g, Re 20:8.
1263. Golan. 1474h, Dt 4:43.
1264. Golgotha. 1115g, Mt 27:33.
1265. Goliath. 1555h, 1 S 17:4.
1266. Gomer. 1586h, Ge 10:2.
1267. Gomorrah. 6017h, Ge 10:19.
1268. Gomorrha. 1116g, Mt 10:15.
1269. Goshen. 1657h, Jsh 10:41.
1270. Gozan. 1470h, 2 K 17:6.
1271. Grecia. 3120h, Da 8:21.
1272. Grecians. 1675g, Ac 6:1.
1273. Greece. 3120h, Zc 9:13.
1274. Greek. 1674g, Mk 7:26.
1275. Gudgodah. 1412h, Dt 10:7.
1276. Guni. 1476h, Ge 46:24.
1277. Gunites. 1477h, Nu 26:48.
1278. Gur. 1483h, 2 K 9:27.
1279. Gurbaal. 1485h, 2 Ch 26:7.
1280. Haahashtari. 326h, 1 Ch 4:6.
1281. Habaiah. 2252h, Ezr 2:61.
1282. Habakkuk. 2265h, Hab 1:1.
1283. Habaziniah. 2262h, Je 35:3.
1284. Habor. 2249h, 2 K 17:6.
1285. Hachaliah. 2446h, Ne 1:1.
1286. Hachilah. 2444h, 1 S 23:19.
1287. Hachmoni. 2453h, 1 Ch 27:32.
1288. Hachmonite. 2453h, 1 Ch 11:11.
1289. Hadad. 1908h, Ge 36:35.
1290. Hadad. 2301h, 1 Ch 1:30.
1291. Hadad. 111h, 1 K 11:17.
1292. Hadadezer. 1909h, 2 S 8:3.
1293. Hadadrimmon. 1910h, Zc 12:11.

1294. Hadar. 1924h, Ge 36:39.
1295. Hadarezer. 1928h, 2 S 10:16.
1296. Hadashah. 2322h, Jsh 15:37.
1297. Hadassah. 1919h, Est 2:7.
1298. Hadid. 2307h, Ezr 2:33.
1299. Hadlai. 2311h, 2 Ch 28:12.
1300. Hadoram. 1913h, Ge 10:27.
1301. Hadrach. 2317h, Zc 9:1.
1302. Hagab. 2285h, Ezr 2:46.
1303. Hagaba. 2286h, Ne 7:48.
1304. Hagabah. 2286h, Ezr 2:45.
1305. Hagar. 1904h, Ge 16:1.
1306. Hagarenes. 1905h, Ps 83:6.
1307. Hagarites. 1905h, 1 Ch 5:10.
1308. Hagerite. 1905h, 1 Ch 27:31.
1309. Haggai. 2292h, Hg 1:1.
1310. Haggedolim. 1419h, Ne 11:14mg.
1311. Haggeri. 1905h, 1 Ch 11:38.
1312. Haggi. 2291h, Ge 46:16.
1313. Haggiah. 2293h, 1 Ch 6:30.
1314. Haggites. 2291h, Nu 26:15.
1315. Haggith. 2294h, 2 S 3:4.
1316. Hai. 5857h, Ge 12:8.
1317. Hakkatan. 6997h, Ezr 8:12.
1318. Hakkoz. 6976h, 1 Ch 24:10.
1319. Hakupha. 2709h, Ezr 2:51.
1320. Halah. 2477h, 2 K 17:6.
1321. Halak. 2510h, Jsh 11:17.
1322. Halhul. 2478h, Jsh 15:58.
1323. Hali. 2482h, Jsh 19:25.
1324. Hallohesh. 3873h, Ne 10:24.
1325. Halohesh. 3873h, Ne 3:12.
1326. Ham. 2526h, Ge 5:32.
1327. Haman. 2001h, Est 3:1.
1328. Hamath. 2574h, Nu 13:21.
1329. Hamathite. 2577h, 1 Ch 1:16.
1330. Hamathzobah. 2578h, 2 Ch 8:3.
1331. Hammath. 2575h, Jsh 19:35.
1332. Hammedatha. 4099h, Est 3:1.
1333. Hammelech. 4429h, Je 36:26.
1334. Hammoleketh. 4447h, 1 Ch 7:18.
1335. Hammon. 2540h, Jsh 19:28.
1336. Hammothdor. 2576h, Jsh 21:32.
1337. Hamonah. 1997h, Ezk 39:16.
1338. Hamon-gog. 1996h, Ezk 39:15.
1339. Hamor. 2544h, Ge 33:19.
1340. Hamran. 2566h, 1 Ch 1:41mg, n.
1341. Hamuel. 2536h, 1 Ch 4:26.
1342. Hamul. 2538h, Ge 46:12.
1343. Hamulites. 2539h, Nu 26:21.
1344. Hamutal. 2537h, 2 K 23:31.
1345. Hanameel. 2601h, Je 32:7.
1346. Hanan. 2605h, 1 Ch 9:44.
1347. Hananeel. 2606h, Zc 14:10.
1348. Hanani. 2607h, 1 Ch 25:4.
1349. Hananiah. 2608h, 1 Ch 25:23.
1350. Hanes. 2609h, Is 30:4.
1351. Haniel. 2592h, 1 Ch 7:39.
1352. Hannah. 2584h, 1 S 1:2.
1353. Hannathon. 2615h, Jsh 19:14.
1354. Hanniel. 2592h, Nu 34:23.
1355. Hanoch. 2585h, Ge 25:4.
1356. Hanochites. 2599h, Nu 26:5.
1357. Hanun. 2586h, 2 S 10:1.
1358. Haphraim. 2663h, Jsh 19:19.
1359. Hara. 2024h, 1 Ch 5:26.
1360. Haradah. 2732h, Nu 33:24.
1361. Haran. 2039h, Ge 11:26.
1362. Haran. 2771h, 1 Ch 2:46.

1777. Jeezerites. 373h, Nu 26:30.
1778. Jegarshadutha. 3026h, Ge 31:47.
1779. Jehaleleel. 3094h, 1 Ch 4:16.
1780. Jehalelel. 3094h, 2 Ch 29:12.
1781. Jehdeiah. 3165h, 1 Ch 24:20.
1782. Jehezekel. 3168h, 1 Ch 24:16.
1783. Jehiah. 3174h, 1 Ch 15:24.
1784. Jehiel. 3273h, 1 Ch 9:35.
1785. Jehiel. 3171h, Ezr 8:9.
1786. Jehieli. 3172h, 1 Ch 26:21.
1787. Jehizkiah. 3169h, 2 Ch 28:12.
1788. Jehoadah. 3085h, 1 Ch 8:36.
1789. Jehoaddan. 3086h, 2 K 14:2.
1790. Jehoahaz. 3059h, 2 K 10:35.
1791. Jehoash. 3060h, 2 K 12:1.
1792. Jehohanan. 3076h, 2 Ch 17:15.
1793. Jehoiachin. 3078h, 2 K 24:8.
1794. Jehoiada. 3077h, 2 K 11:4.
1795. Jehoiada. 3111h, Ne 3:6.
1796. Jehoiakim. 3079h, 1 Ch 3:15.
1797. Jehoiarib. 3080h, 1 Ch 24:7.
1798. Jehonadab. 3082h, 2 K 10:15.
1799. Jehonathan. 3083h, 1 Ch 27:25.
1800. Jehoram. 3088h, 2 K 1:17.
1801. Jehoshabeath. 3090h, 2 Ch 22:11.
1802. Jehoshaphat. 3092h, 2 S 8:16.
1803. Jehosheba. 3089h, 2 K 11:2.
1804. Jehoshua. 3091h, Nu 13:16.
1805. Jehoshuah. 3091h, 1 Ch 7:27.
1806. Jehovah. 3068h, Ex 6:3.
1807. Jehovah-jireh. 3070h, Ge 22:14.
1808. Jehovah-nissi. 3071h, Ex 17:15.
1809. Jehovah-shalom. 3073h, Jg 6:24.
1810. Jehozabad. 3075h, 1 Ch 26:4.
1811. Jehozadak. 3087h, 1 Ch 6:15.
1812. Jehu. 3058h, 2 K 9:2.
1813. Jehubbah. 3160h, 1 Ch 7:34.
1814. Jehucal. 3081h, Je 37:3.
1815. Jehud. 3055h, Jsh 19:45.
1816. Jehudi. 3065h, Je 36:14.
1817. Jehudijah. 3057h, 1 Ch 4:18.
1818. Jehush. 3266h, 1 Ch 8:39.
1819. Jeiel. 3273h, 1 Ch 5:7.
1820. Jekabzeel. 3343h, Ne 11:25.
1821. Jekameam. 3360h, 1 Ch 24:23.
1822. Jekamiah. 3359h, 1 Ch 2:41.
1823. Jekuthiel. 3354h, 1 Ch 4:18.
1824. Jemima. 3224h, Jb 42:14.
1825. Jemuel. 3223h, Ge 46:10.
1826. Jepthae. 2422g, He 11:32.
1827. Jephthah. 3316h, Jg 11:1.
1828. Jephunneh. 3312h, Nu 13:6.
1829. Jerah. 3392h, Ge 10:26.
1830. Jerahmeel. 3396h, 1 Ch 2:9.
1831. Jerahmeelites. 3397h, 1 S 27:10.
1832. Jered. 3382h, 1 Ch 1:2.
1833. Jeremai. 3413h, Ezr 10:33.
1834. Jeremiah. 3414h, Je 1:1.
1835. Jeremias. 2408g, Mt 16:14.
1836. Jeremoth. 3406h, Ezr 10:26.
1837. Jeremy. 2408g, Mt 2:17.
1838. Jeriah. 3404h, 1 Ch 23:19.
1839. Jeribai. 3403h, 1 Ch 11:46.
1840. Jericho. 3405h, Nu 22:1.
1841. Jericho. 2410g, Mt 20:29.
1842. Jeriel. 3400h, 1 Ch 7:2.
1843. Jerijah. 3404h, 1 Ch 26:31.
1844. Jerimoth. 3406h, 1 Ch 7:7.
1845. Jerioth. 3408h, 1 Ch 2:18.

1846. Jeroboam. 3379h, 1 K 11:26.
1847. Jeroham. 3395h, 1 S 1:1.
1848. Jerubbaal. 3378h, Jg 6:32.
1849. Jerubbesheth. 3380h, 2 S 11:21.
1850. Jeruel. 3385h, 2 Ch 20:16.
1851. Jerusalem. 3389h, Jsh 10:1.
1852. Jerusalem. 2419g, Mt 2:1.
1853. Jerusha. 3387h, 2 K 15:33.
1854. Jerushah. 3388h, 2 Ch 27:1.
1855. Jesaiah. 3470h, 1 Ch 3:21.
1856. Jeshaiah. 3470h, 1 Ch 25:3.
1857. Jeshanah. 3466h, 2 Ch 13:19.
1858. Jesharelah. 3480h, 1 Ch 25:14.
1859. Jeshebeab. 3428h, 1 Ch 24:13.
1860. Jesher. 3475h, 1 Ch 2:18.
1861. Jeshimon. 3452h, Nu 21:20.
1862. Jeshishai. 3454h, 1 Ch 5:14.
1863. Jeshohaiah. 3439h, 1 Ch 4:36.
1864. Jeshua. 3442h, Ne 8:17.
1865. Jeshuah. 3442h, 1 Ch 24:11.
1866. Jeshurun. 3484h, Dt 32:15.
1867. Jesiah. 3449h, 1 Ch 12:6.
1868. Jesimiel. 3450h, 1 Ch 4:36.
1869. Jesse. 3448h, 1 Ch 2:12.
1870. Jesse. 2421g, Mt 1:5.
1871. Jesui. 3440h, Nu 26:44.
1872. Jesuites. 3441h, Nu 26:44.
1873. Jesurun. 3484h, Is 44:2.
1874. Jesus. 2424g, Mt 1:16.
1875. Jether. 3500h, 1 Ch 2:32.
1876. Jetheth. 3509h, Ge 36:40.
1877. Jethlah. 3494h, Jsh 19:42.
1878. Jethro. 3503h, Ex 3:1.
1879. Jetur. 3195h, Ge 25:15.
1880. Jeuel. 3262h, 1 Ch 9:6.
1881. Jeush. 3266h, Ge 36:5.
1882. Jeuz. 3263h, 1 Ch 8:10.
1883. Jew. 3064h, Est 2:5.
1884. Jews. 2453g, Jn 4:9.
1885. Jewess. 2453g, Ac 16:1.
1886. Jewish. 2451g, T 1:14.
1887. Jewry. 3061h, Da 5:13.
1888. Jewry. 2449g, Jn 7:1.
1889. Jezaniah. 3153h, Je 40:8.
1890. Jezebel. 348h, 1 K 16:31.
1891. Jezebel. 2403g, Re 2:20.
1892. Jezer. 3337h, Ge 46:24.
1893. Jezerites. 3340h, Nu 26:49.
1894. Jeziah. 3150h, Ezr 10:25.
1895. Jeziel. 3149h, 1 Ch 12:3.
1896. Jezliah. 3152h, 1 Ch 8:18.
1897. Jezoar. 3328h, 1 Ch 4:7.
1898. Jezrahiah. 3156h, Ne 12:42.
1899. Jezreel. 3157h, 1 Ch 4:3.
1900. Jezreelite. 3158h, 1 K 21:1.
1901. Jezreelitess. 3159h, 1 S 27:3.
1902. Jibsam. 3005h, 1 Ch 7:2.
1903. Jidlaph. 3044h, Ge 22:22.
1904. Jimna. 3232h, Nu 26:44.
1905. Jimnah. 3232h, Ge 46:17.
1906. Jimnites. 3232h, Nu 26:44.
1907. Jiphtah. 3316h, Jsh 15:43.
1908. Jiphthahel. 3317h, Jsh 19:14.
1909. Joab. 3097h, 1 S 26:6.
1910. Joah. 3098h, Is 36:3.
1911. Joahaz. 3099h, 2 Ch 34:8.
1912. Joanna. 2490g, Lk 3:27.
1913. Joanna. 2489g, Lk 8:3.
1914. Joash. 3135h, 1 Ch 7:8.

1915. Joash. 3101h, Jg 6:11.
1916. Joatham. 2488g, Mt 1:9.
1917. Job. 347h, Jb 1:1.
1918. Job. 3102h, Ge 46:13.
1919. Job. 2492g, Ja 5:11.
1920. Jobab. 3103h, Ge 10:29.
1921. Jochebed. 3115h, Ex 6:20.
1922. Joed. 3133h, Ne 11:7.
1923. Joel. 3100h, 1 S 8:2.
1924. Joel. 2493g, Ac 2:16.
1925. Joelah. 3132h, 1 Ch 12:7.
1926. Joezer. 3134h, 1 Ch 12:6.
1927. Jogbehah. 3011h, Nu 32:35.
1928. Jogli. 3020h, Nu 34:22.
1929. Joha. 3109h, 1 Ch 8:16.
1930. Johanan. 3110h, 2 K 25:23.
1931. John. 2491g, Lk 1:13.
1932. Joiada. 3111h, Ne 12:10.
1933. Joiakim. 3113h, Ne 12:10.
1934. Joiarib. 3114h, Ezr 8:16.
1935. Jokdeam. 3347h, Jsh 15:56.
1936. Jokim. 3137h, 1 Ch 4:22.
1937. Jokmeam. 3361h, 1 Ch 6:68.
1938. Jokneam. 3362h, Jsh 12:22.
1939. Jokshan. 3370h, Ge 25:2.
1940. Joktan. 3355h, Ge 10:25.
1941. Joktheel. 3371h, Jsh 15:38.
1942. Jona. 2495g, Jn 1:42.
1943. Jonadab. 3122h, Je 35:6.
1944. Jonadab. 3082h, Je 35:8.
1945. Jonah. 3124h, Jon 1:1.
1946. Jonan. 2494g, Lk 3:30.
1947. Jonas. 2495g, Mt 12:39.
1948. Jonathan. 3129h, 1 S 13:2.
1949. Jonathan. 3083h, 1 S 14:6.
1950. Jonathelemrechokim. 3128h, Ps 56:Title.
1951. Joppa. 3305h, 2 Ch 2:16.
1952. Joppa. 2445g, Ac 9:43.
1953. Jorah. 3139h, Ezr 2:18.
1954. Jorai. 3140h, 1 Ch 5:13.
1955. Joram. 3141h, 1 Ch 26:25.
1956. Joram. 2496g, Mt 1:8.
1957. Jordan. 3383h, Jsh 2:7.
1958. Jordan. 2446g, Mt 3:5.
1959. Jorim. 2497g, Lk 3:29.
1960. Jorkoam. 2421h, 1 Ch 2:44.
1961. Josabad. 3107h, 1 Ch 12:4.
1962. Josaphat. 2498g, Mt 1:8.
1963. Jose. 2499g, Lk 3:29.
1964. Josedech. 3087h, Hg 1:1.
1965. Joseph. 3130h, Ge 30:24.
1966. Joseph. 2501g, Mt 1:16.
1967. Joses. 2500g, Mt 13:55.
1968. Joshah. 3144h, 1 Ch 4:34.
1969. Joshaphat. 3146h, 1 Ch 11:43.
1970. Joshaviah. 3145h, 1 Ch 11:46.
1971. Joshbekashah. 3436h, 1 Ch 25:4.
1972. Joshua. 3091h, Ex 17:9.
1973. Josiah. 2977h, 1 K 13:2.
1974. Josias. 2502g, Mt 1:10.
1975. Josibiah. 3143h, 1 Ch 4:35.
1976. Josiphiah. 3131h, Ezr 8:10.
1977. Jotbah. 3192h, 2 K 21:19.
1978. Jotbath. 3193h, Dt 10:7.
1979. Jotbathah. 3193h, Nu 33:33.
1980. Jotham. 3147h, Jg 9:5.
1981. Jozabad. 3107h, 2 Ch 31:13.
1982. Jozachar. 3108h, 2 K 12:21.
1983. Jozadak. 3136h, Ezr 3:2.

1984. Jubal. 3106h, Ge 4:21.
1985. Jucal. 3116h, Je 38:1.
1986. Juda. 2455g, Lk 3:30.
1987. Judaea. 2449g, Mt 19:1.
1988. Judah. 3063h, Ge 35:23.
1989. Judah. 2455g, He 8:8.
1990. Judas. 2455g, Lk 6:16.
1991. Jude. 2455g, Ju 1.
1992. Judea. 3061h, Ezr 5:8.
1993. Judith. 3067h, Ge 26:34.
1994. Julia. 2456g, Ro 16:15.
1995. Julius. 2457g, Ac 27:1.
1996. Junia. 2458g, Ro 16:7.
1997. Jupiter. 2203g, Ac 14:12.
1998. Jushabhesed. 3142h, 1 Ch 3:20.
1999. Justus. 2459g, Ac 1:23.
2000. Juttah. 3194h, Jsh 15:55.
2001. Kabzeel. 6934h, Jsh 15:21.
2002. Kadesh. 6946h, Ge 14:7.
2003. Kadesh barnea. 6947h, Nu 34:4.
2004. Kadmiel. 6934h, Ezr 2:40.
2005. Kadmonites. 6935h, Ge 15:19.
2006. Kallai. 7040h, Ne 12:20.
2007. Kanah. 7071h, Jsh 16:8.
2008. Kareah. 7143h, Je 40:8.
2009. Karkaa. 7173h, Jsh 15:3.
2010. Karkor. 7174h, Jg 8:10.
2011. Kartah. 7177h, Jsh 21:34.
2012. Kartan. 7178h, Jsh 21:32.
2013. Kattath. 7005h, Jsh 19:15.
2014. Kedar. 6938h, Ge 25:13.
2015. Kedemah. 6929h, Ge 25:15.
2016. Kedemoth. 6932h, Jsh 13:18.
2017. Kedesh. 6943h, Jsh 15:23.
2018. Kedesh naphtali. 5321h, Jg 4:6.
2019. Kehelathah. 6954h, Nu 33:22.
2020. Keilah. 7084h, Jsh 15:44.
2021. Kelaiah. 7041h, Ezr 10:23.
2022. Kelita. 7042h, Ezr 10:23.
2023. Kemuel. 7055h, Nu 34:24.
2024. Kenan. 7018h, 1 Ch 1:2.
2025. Kenath. 7079h, Nu 32:42.
2026. Kenaz. 7073h, Ge 36:11.
2027. Kenezite. 7074h, Nu 32:12.
2028. Kenite. 7014h, Nu 24:22.
2029. Kenizzites. 7074h, Ge 15:19.
2030. Kerenhappuch. 7163h, Jb 42:14.
2031. Kerioth. 7152h, Jsh 15:25.
2032. Keros. 7026h, Ezr 2:44.
2033. Keturah. 6989h, Ge 25:1.
2034. Kezia. 7103h, Jb 42:14.
2035. Keziz. 7104h, Jsh 18:21.
2036. Kibrothhattaavah. 6914h, Nu 11:34.
2037. Kibzaim. 6911h, Jsh 21:22.
2038. Kidron. 6939h, 2 S 15:23.
2039. Kinah. 7016h, Jsh 15:22.
2040. Kir. 7024h, Am 9:7.
2041. Kirharaseth. 7025h, 2 K 3:25.
2042. Kirharesh. 7025h, Is 16:11.
2043. Kirheres. 7025h, Je 48:31.
2044. Kiriathaim. 7156h, Je 48:1.
2045. Kirioth. 7152h, Am 2:2.
2046. Kirjath. 7157h, Jsh 18:28.
2047. Kirjathaim. 7156h, Nu 32:37.
2048. Kirjatharba. 7153h, Jsh 15:54.
2049. Kirjatharim. 7157h, Ezr 2:25.
2050. Kirjathbaal. 7154h, Jsh 15:60.
2051. Kirjathhuzoth. 7155h, Nu 22:39.
2052. Kirjathjearim. 7157h, Jsh 9:17.

2191. Mahalath. 4257h, Ps 53:Title.
2192. Maahali. 4249h, Ex 6:19.
2193. Mahanaim. 4266h, Ge 32:2.
2194. Mahanehdan. 4265h, Jg 18:12.
2195. Maharai. 4121h, 2 S 23:28.
2196. Mahath. 4287h, 2 Ch 29:12.
2197. Mahavite. 4233h, 1 Ch 11:46.
2198. Mahazioth. 4238h, 1 Ch 25:4.
2199. Mahershalalhashbaz. 4122h, Is 8:1.
2200. Mahlah. 4244h, Nu 26:33.
2201. Mahli. 4249h, Nu 3:20.
2202. Mahlites. 4250h, Nu 3:33.
2203. Mahlon. 4248h, Ru 1:2.
2204. Mahol. 4235h, 1 K 4:31.
2205. Makaz. 4739h, 1 K 4:9.
2206. Makheloth. 4722h, Nu 33:25.
2207. Makkedah. 4719h, Jsh 10:10.
2208. Maktesh. 4389h, Zp 1:11.
2209. Malachi. 4401h, Ml 1:1.
2210. Malcham. 4445h, 1 Ch 8:9.
2211. Malchiah. 4441h, Je 38:1.
2212. Malchiel. 4439h, Ge 46:17.
2213. Malchielites. 4440h, Nu 26:45.
2214. Malchijah. 4441h, 1 Ch 9:12.
2215. Malchiram. 4443h, 1 Ch 3:18.
2216. Malchishua. 4444h, 1 Ch 8:33.
2217. Malchus. 3124g, Jn 18:10.
2218. Maleleel. 3121g, Lk 3:37.
2219. Mallothi. 4413h, 1 Ch 25:4.
2220. Malluch. 4409h, Ne 10:4.
2221. Mamre. 4471h, Ge 14:13.
2222. Manaen. 3127g, Ac 13:1.
2223. Manahath. 4506h, Ge 36:23.
2224. Manahethites. 2679h, 1 Ch 2:52.
2225. Manasseh. 4519h, Ge 41:51.
2226. Manasses. 3128g, Mt 1:10.
2227. Manassites. 4520h, Dt 4:43.
2228. Manoah. 4495h, Jg 13:2.
2229. Maoch. 4582h, 1 S 27:2.
2230. Maon. 4584h, Jsh 15:55.
2231. Maonites. 4584h, Jg 10:12.
2232. Mara. 4755h, Ru 1:20.
2233. Marah. 4785h, Ex 15:23.
2234. Maralah. 4831h, Jsh 19:11.
2235. Maranatha. 3134g, 1 C 16:22.
2236. Marcus. 3138g, 1 P 5:13.
2237. Mareshah. 4762h, Jsh 15:44.
2238. Mark. 3138g, Ac 12:12.
2239. Maroth. 4796h, Mi 1:12.
2240. Marsena. 4826h, Est 1:14.
2241. Mars Hill. 697g, Ac 17:22.
2242. Martha. 3136g, Lk 10:38.
2243. Mary. 3137g, Mt 1:16.
2244. Maschil. 7919h, Ps 32:Title.
2245. Mash. 4851h, Ge 10:23.
2246. Mashal. 4913h, 1 Ch 6:74.
2247. Masrekah. 4957h, Ge 36:36.
2248. Massa. 4854h, Ge 25:14.
2249. Massah. 4532h, Ex 17:7.
2250. Mathusala. 3103g, Lk 3:37.
2251. Matred. 4308h, Ge 36:39.
2252. Matri. 4309h, 1 S 10:21.
2253. Mattan. 4977h, 2 K 11:18.
2254. Mattanah. 4980h, Nu 21:18.
2255. Mattaniah. 4983h, 2 K 24:17.
2256. Mattatha. 3160g, Lk 3:31.
2257. Mattathah. 4992h, Ezr 10:33.
2258. Mattathias. 3161g, Lk 3:26.
2259. Mattenai. 4982h, Ne 12:19.

2260. Matthan. 3157g, Mt 1:15.
2261. Matthat. 3158g, Lk 3:24.
2262. Matthew. 3156g, Mt 9:9.
2263. Matthias. 3159g, Ac 1:26.
2264. Mattithiah. 4993h, Ezr 10:43.
2265. Mazzaroth. 4216h, Jb 38:32.
2266. Meah. 3968h, Ne 3:1.
2267. Mearah. 4632h, Jsh 13:4.
2268. Mebunnai. 4012h, 2 S 23:27.
2269. Mecherathite. 4832h, 1 Ch 11:36.
2270. Medad. 4312h, Nu 11:26.
2271. Medan. 4091h, Ge 25:2.
2272. Medeba. 4311h, Nu 21:30.
2273. Mede. 4075h, Da 11:1.
2274. Medes. 4074h, Ezr 6:2.
2275. Medes. 3370g, Ac 2:9.
2276. Media. 4074h, Est 1:3.
2277. Median. 4077h, Da 5:31.
2278. Megiddo. 4023h, Jsh 12:21.
2279. Megiddon. 4023h, Zc 12:11.
2280. Mehetabeel. 4105h, Ne 6:10.
2281. Mehetabel. 4105h, Ge 36:39.
2282. Mehida. 4240h, Ezr 2:52.
2283. Mehir. 4243h, 1 Ch 4:11.
2284. Meholathite. 4259h, 1 S 18:19.
2285. Mehujael. 4232h, Ge 4:18.
2286. Mehuman. 4104h, Est 1:10.
2287. Mehunim. 4586h, Ezr 2:50.
2288. Mehunims. 4586h, 2 Ch 26:7.
2289. Mejarkon. 4313h, Jsh 19:46.
2290. Mekonah. 4368h, Ne 11:28.
2291. Melatiah. 4424h, Ne 3:7.
2292. Melchi. 3197g, Lk 3:24.
2293. Melchiah. 4441h, Je 21:1.
2294. Melchisedec. 3198g, He 5:6.
2295. Melchishua. 4444h, 1 S 14:49.
2296. Melchizedek. 4442h, Ge 14:18.
2297. Melea. 3190g, Lk 3:31.
2298. Melech. 4429h, 1 Ch 8:35.
2299. Melicu. 4409h, Ne 12:14.
2300. Melita. 3194g, Ac 28:1.
2301. Melzar. 4453h, Da 1:11.
2302. Memphis. 4644h, Ho 9:6.
2303. Memucan. 4462h, Est 1:14.
2304. Menahem. 4505h, 2 K 15:14.
2305. Menan. 3104g, Lk 3:31.
2306. Mene. 4484h, Da 5:25.
2307. Menucha. 4496h, Je 51:59mg.
2308. Meonenim. 6049h, Jg 9:37.
2309. Meonothai. 4587h, 1 Ch 4:14.
2310. Mephaath. 4158h, Jsh 13:18.
2311. Mephibosheth. 4648h, 2 S 21:8.
2312. Merab. 4764h, 1 S 14:49.
2313. Meraiah. 4811h, Ne 12:12.
2314. Meraioth. 4812h, Ne 12:15.
2315. Merari. 4847h, Ge 46:11.
2316. Merarites. 4848h, Nu 26:57.
2317. Merathaim. 4850h, Je 50:21.
2318. Mercurius. 2060g, Ac 14:12.
2319. Mered. 4778h, 1 Ch 4:17.
2320. Meremoth. 4822h, Ezr 8:33.
2321. Meres. 4825h, Est 1:14.
2322. Meribah. 4809h, Ex 17:7.
2323. Meribah-Kadesh. 6946h, Dt 32:51.
2324. Meribbaal. 4807h, 1 Ch 9:40.
2325. Merodach. 4781h, Je 50:2.
2326. Merodach-baladan. 4757h, Is 39:1.
2327. Merom. 4792h, Jsh 11:5.
2328. Meronothite. 4824h, 1 Ch 27:30.

2467. Nagge. 3477g, Lk 3:25.
2468. Nahalal. 5096h, Jsh 21:35.
2469. Nahaliel. 5160h, Nu 21:19.
2470. Nahallal. 5096h, Jsh 19:15.
2471. Nahalol. 5096h, Jg 1:30.
2472. Naham. 5163h, 1 Ch 4:19.
2473. Nahamani. 5167h, Ne 7:7.
2474. Naharai. 5171h, 1 Ch 11:39.
2475. Nahash. 5176h, 1 S 11:1.
2476. Nahath. 5184h, Ge 36:13.
2477. Nahbi. 5147h, Nu 13:14.
2478. Nahor. 5152h, Ge 11:22.
2479. Nahshon. 5177h, 1 Ch 2:10.
2480. Nahum. 5151h, Na 1:1.
2481. Nain. 3484g, Lk 7:11.
2482. Naioth. 5121h, 1 S 19:18.
2483. Naomi. 5281h, Ru 1:2.
2484. Naphish. 5305h, Ge 25:15.
2485. Naphtali. 5321h, Ge 30:8.
2486. Naphtuhim. 5320h, Ge 10:13.
2487. Narcissus. 3488g, Ro 16:11.
2488. Nathan. 5416h, 2 Ch 9:29.
2489. Nathan. 3481g, Lk 3:31.
2490. Nathanael. 3482g, Jn 1:47.
2491. Nathan-melech. 5419h, 2 K 23:11.
2492. Naum. 3486g, Lk 3:25.
2493. Nazarene. 3480g, Mt 2:23.
2494. Nazareth. 3478g, Mt 4:13.
2495. Nazarite. 5139h, Nu 6:2.
2496. Neah. 5269h, Jsh 19:13.
2497. Neapolis. 3496g, Ac 16:11.
2498. Neariah. 5294h, 1 Ch 3:22.
2499. Nebai. 5109h, Ne 10:19.
2500. Nebaioth. 5032h, Is 60:7.
2501. Nebajoth. 5032h, Ge 25:13.
2502. Neballat. 5041h, Ne 11:34.
2503. Nebat. 5028h, 1 K 11:26.
2504. Nebo. 5015h, Nu 32:3.
2505. Nebuchadnezzar. 5019h, 2 K 24:1.
2506. Nebuchadrezzar. 5019h, Je 21:2.
2507. Nebuschasban. 5021h, Je 39:13.
2508. Nebuzaradan. 5018h, 2 K 25:8.
2509. Necho. 5224h, 2 Ch 35:20.
2510. Nedabiah. 5072h, 1 Ch 3:18.
2511. Neginah. 5058h, Ps 61:Title.
2512. Neginoth. 5058h, Ps 4:Title.
2513. Nehelamite. 5161h, Je 29:24.
2514. Nehemiah. 5166h, Ne 1:1.
2515. Nehiloth. 5155h, Ps 5:Title.
2516. Nehum. 5149h, Ne 7:7.
2517. Nehushta. 5179h, 2 K 24:8.
2518. Nehushtan. 5180h, 2 K 18:4.
2519. Neiel. 5272h, Jsh 19:27.
2520. Nekeb. 5346h, Jsh 19:33.
2521. Nekoda. 5353h, Ezr 2:48.
2522. Nemuel. 5241h, Nu 26:12.
2523. Nemuelites. 5242h, Nu 26:12.
2524. Nepheg. 5298h, 2 S 5:15.
2525. Nephish. 5305h, 1 Ch 5:19.
2526. Nephishesim. 5300h, Ne 7:52.
2527. Nephthalim. 3508g, Mt 4:13.
2528. Nephtoah. 5318h, Jsh 15:9.
2529. Nephusim. 5304h, Ezr 2:50.
2530. Ner. 5369h, 1 Ch 9:36.
2531. Nereus. 3517g, Ro 16:15.
2532. Nergal. 5370h, 2 K 17:30.
2533. Nergalsharezer. 5371h, Je 39:3.
2534. Neri. 3518g, Lk 3:27.
2535. Neriah. 5374h, Je 32:12.

2536. Nero. 3505g, 2 T Subscription.
2537. Nethaneel. 5417h, Nu 1:8.
2538. Nethaniah. 5418h, 1 Ch 25:12.
2539. Nethinims. 5411h, 1 Ch 9:2.
2540. Netophah. 5199h, Ezr 2:22.
2541. Netophathi. 5200h, Ne 12:28.
2542. Netophathite. 5200h, 2 S 23:28.
2543. Neziah. 5335h, Ezr 2:54.
2544. Nezib. 5334h, Jsh 15:43.
2545. Nibhaz. 5026h, 2 K 17:31.
2546. Nibshan. 5044h, Jsh 15:62.
2547. Nicanor. 3527g, Ac 6:5.
2548. Nicodemus. 3530g, Jn 3:1.
2549. Nicolaitanes. 3531g, Re 2:6.
2550. Nicolas. 3532g, Ac 6:5.
2551. Nicopolis. 3533g, T 3:12.
2552. Niger. 3526g, Ac 13:1.
2553. Nimrah. 5247h, Nu 32:3.
2554. Nimrim. 5249h, Is 15:6.
2555. Nimrod. 5248h, Ge 10:8.
2556. Nimshi. 5250h, 1 K 19:16.
2557. Nineve. 3535h, Lk 11:32.
2558. Nineveh. 5210h, Ge 10:11.
2559. Ninevites. 3536g, Lk 11:30.
2560. Nisan. 5212h, Ne 2:1.
2561. Nisroch. 5268h, 2 K 19:37.
2562. No. 4996h, Na 3:8.
2563. Noadiah. 5129h, Ne 6:14.
2564. Noah. 5146h, Ge 5:29.
2565. Noah. 5270h, Nu 26:33.
2566. Noah. 3575g, He 11:7.
2567. Nob. 5011h, 1 S 22:11.
2568. Nobah. 5025h, Nu 32:42.
2569. Nod. 5113h, Ge 4:16.
2570. Nodab. 5114h, 1 Ch 5:19.
2571. Noe. 3575g, Lk 3:36.
2572. Nogah. 5052h, 1 Ch 3:7.
2573. Nohah. 5119h, 1 Ch 8:2.
2574. Non. 5126h, 1 Ch 7:27.
2575. Noph. 5297h, Is 19:13.
2576. Nophah. 5302h, Nu 21:30.
2577. Nun. 5126h, Ex 33:11.
2578. Nymphas. 3564g, Col 4:15.
2579. Obadiah. 5662h, Ob 1.
2580. Obal. 5745h, Ge 10:28.
2581. Obed. 5744h, Ru 4:17.
2582. Obed. 5601g, Lk 3:32.
2583. Obededom. 5654h, 2 S 6:10.
2584. Obil. 179h, 1 Ch 27:30.
2585. Oboth. 88h, Nu 21:10.
2586. Ocran. 5918h, Nu 1:13.
2587. Oded. 5752h, 2 Ch 15:1.
2588. Og. 5747h, Nu 21:33.
2589. Ohad. 161h, Ge 46:10.
2590. Ohel. 169h, 1 Ch 3:20.
2591. Olivet. 2132h, 2 S 15:30.
2591. Olivet. 1638g, Ac 1:12.
2592. Olympas. 3652g, Ro 16:15.
2593. Omar. 201h, 1 Ch 1:36.
2594. Omega. 5598g, Re 1:8.
2595. Omri. 6018h, 1 K 16:16.
2596. On. 203h, Nu 16:1.
2597. Onam. 208h, Ge 36:23.
2598. Onan. 209h, Ge 38:4.
2599. Onesimus. 3682g, Phm 10.
2600. Onesiphorus. 3683g, 2 T 1:16.
2601. Ono. 207h, Ezr 2:33.
2602. Ophel. 6077h, 2 Ch 27:3.
2603. Ophir. 211h, Ge 10:29.

2604. Ophni. 6078h, Jsh 18:24.
2605. Ophrah. 6084h, 1 Ch 4:14.
2606. Oreb. 6159h, Jg 7:25.
2607. Oren. 767h, 1 Ch 2:25.
2608. Orion. 3685h, Jb 9:9.
2609. Ornan. 771h, 1 Ch 21:15.
2610. Orpah. 6204h, Ru 1:4.
2611. Osee. 5617g, Ro 9:25.
2612. Oshea. 1954h, Nu 13:8.
2613. Othni. 6273h, 1 Ch 26:7.
2614. Othniel. 6274h, Jsh 15:17.
2615. Ozem. 684h, 1 Ch 2:15.
2616. Ozias. 3604g, Mt 1:8.
2617. Ozni. 244h, Nu 26:16.
2618. Oznites. 244h, Nu 26:16.
2619. Paarai. 6474h, 2 S 23:35.
2620. Padan. 6307h, Ge 48:7.
2621. Padan-aram. 6307h, Ge 25:20.
2622. Padon. 6303h, Ezr 2:44.
2623. Pagiel. 6295h, Nu 1:13.
2624. Pahath-moab. 6355h, Ezr 2:6.
2625. Pai. 6464h, 1 Ch 1:50.
2626. Palal. 6420h, Ne 3:25.
2627. Palestina. 6429h, Ex 15:14.
2628. Palestine. 6429h, Jl 3:4.
2629. Pallu. 6396h, Nu 26:5.
2630. Palluites. 6384h, Nu 26:5.
2631. Palmoni. 6422h, Da 8:13mg.
2632. Palti. 6406h, Nu 13:9.
2633. Paltiel. 6409h, Nu 34:26.
2634. Paltite. 6407h, 2 S 23:26.
2635. Pamphylia. 3828g, Ac 13:13.
2636. Pannag. 6436h, Ezk 27:17.
2637. Paphos. 3974g, Ac 13:6.
2638. Parah. 6511h, Jsh 18:23.
2639. Paran. 6290h, Ge 21:21.
2640. Parbar. 6503h, 1 Ch 26:18.
2641. Parmashta. 6534h, Est 9:9.
2642. Parmenas. 3937g, Ac 6:5.
2643. Parnach. 6535h, Nu 34:25.
2644. Parosh. 6551h, Ezr 2:3.
2645. Parshandatha. 6577h, Est 9:7.
2646. Parthians. 3934g, Ac 2:9.
2647. Paruah. 6515h, 1 K 4:17.
2648. Parvaim. 6516h, 2 Ch 3:6.
2649. Pasach. 6457h, 1 Ch 7:33.
2650. Pasdammim. 6450h, 1 Ch 11:13.
2651. Paseah. 6454h, 1 Ch 4:12.
2652. Pashur. 6583h, Je 20:1.
2653. Patara. 3959g, Ac 21:1.
2654. Pathros. 6624h, Is 11:11.
2655. Pathrusim. 6625h, Ge 10:14.
2656. Patmos. 3963g, Re 1:9.
2657. Patrobas. 3969g, Ro 16:14.
2658. Pau. 6464h, Ge 36:39.
2659. Paul. 3972g, Ac 13:9.
2660. Paulus. 3972g, Ac 13:7.
2661. Pedahel. 6300h, Nu 34:28.
2662. Pedahzur. 6301h, Nu 1:10.
2663. Pedaiah. 6305h, 2 K 23:36.
2664. Pekah. 6492h, 2 K 15:25.
2665. Pekahiah. 6494h, 2 K 15:22.
2666. Pekod. 6489h, Ezk 23:23.
2667. Pelaiah. 6411h, Ne 8:7.
2668. Pelaliah. 6421h, Ne 11:12.
2669. Pelatiah. 6410h, 1 Ch 3:21.
2670. Peleg. 6389h, Ge 10:25.
2671. Pelet. 6404h, 1 Ch 12:3.
2672. Peleth. 6431h, Nu 16:1.

2673. Pelethites. 6432h, 2 S 8:18.
2674. Pelonite. 6397h, 1 Ch 11:27.
2675. Peniel. 6439h, Ge 32:30.
2676. Peninnah. 6444h, 1 S 1:2.
2677. Pentecost. 4005g, Ac 2:1.
2678. Penuel. 6439h, 1 Ch 4:4.
2679. Peor. 6465h, Nu 23:28.
2680. Perazim. 6556h, Is 28:21.
2681. Peres. 6537h, Da 5:28.
2682. Peresh. 6570h, 1 Ch 7:16.
2683. Perez. 6557h, 1 Ch 27:3.
2684. Perezuzza. 6560h, 1 Ch 13:11.
2685. Perezuzzah. 6560h, 2 S 6:8.
2686. Perga. 4011g, Ac 13:13.
2687. Pergamos. 4010g, Re 1:11.
2688. Perida. 6514h, Ne 7:57.
2689. Perizzite. 6522h, Ge 13:7.
2690. Persia. 6539h, 2 Ch 36:22.
2691. Persian. 6543h, Da 6:28.
2692. Persians. 6539h, Est 1:19.
2693. Persians. 6540h, Da 5:28.
2694. Persis. 4069g, Ro 16:12.
2695. Peruda. 6514h, Ezr 2:55.
2696. Peter. 4074g, Mt 16:18.
2697. Pethahiah. 6611h, Ne 11:24.
2698. Pethor. 6604h, Nu 22:5.
2699. Pethuel. 6602h, Jl 1:1.
2700. Peulthai. 6469h, 1 Ch 26:5.
2701. Phalec. 5317g, Lk 3:35.
2702. Phallu. 6396h, Ge 46:9.
2703. Phalti. 6406h, 1 S 25:44.
2704. Phaltiel. 6409h, 2 S 3:15.
2705. Phanuel. 5323g, Lk 2:36.
2706. Pharaoh. 6547h, Ge 12:15.
2707. Pharaoh. 5328g, Ac 7:10.
2708. Pharaoh-hophra. 6548h, Je 44:30.
2709. Pharaoh-necho. 6549h, Je 46:2.
2710. Pharaoh-nechoh. 6549h, 2 K 23:29.
2711. Phares. 5329g, Mt 1:3.
2712. Pharez. 6557h, Ge 46:12.
2713. Pharisees. 5330g, Mt 3:7.
2714. Pharosh. 6551h, Ezr 8:3.
2715. Pharpar. 6554h, 2 K 5:12.
2716. Pharzites. 6558h, Nu 26:20.
2717. Phaseah. 6454h, Ne 7:51.
2718. Phebe. 5402g, Ro 16:1.
2719. Phenice. 5403g, Ac 11:19.
2720. Phenicia. 5403g, Ac 21:2.
2721. Phichol. 6369h, Ge 21:22.
2722. Philadelphia. 5359g, Re 1:11.
2723. Philemon. 5371g, Phm 1.
2724. Philetus. 5372g, 2 T 2:17.
2725. Philip. 5376g, Jn 1:43.
2726. Philippi. 5375g, Ac 16:12.
2727. Philippians. 5374g, Ph 4:15.
2728. Philistia. 6429h, Ps 87:4.
2729. Philistim. 6430h, Ge 10:14.
2730. Philistines. 6430h, Je 47:4.
2731. Philologus. 5378g, Ro 16:15.
2732. Phinehas. 6372h, Ex 6:25.
2733. Phlegon. 5393g, Ro 16:14.
2734. Phrygia. 5435g, Ac 16:6.
2735. Phurah. 6513h, Jg 7:10.
2736. Phut. 6316h, Ge 10:6.
2737. Phuvah. 6312h, Ge 46:13.
2738. Phygellus. 5436g, 2 T 1:15.
2739. Pibeseth. 6364h, Ezk 30:17.
2740. Pihahiroth. 6367h, Ex 14:2.
2741. Pilate. 4091g, Mt 27:2.

2742. Pildash. 6394h, Ge 22:22.
2743. Pileha. 6401h, Ne 10:24.
2744. Piltai. 6408h, Ne 12:17.
2745. Pinon. 6373h, Ge 36:41.
2746. Piram. 6502h, Jsh 10:3.
2747. Pirathon. 6552h, Jg 12:15.
2748. Pirathonite. 6553h, Jg 12:15.
2749. Pisgah. 6449h, Nu 21:20.
2750. Pisidia. 4099g, Ac 13:14.
2751. Pison. 6376h, Ge 2:11.
2752. Pispah. 6462h, 1 Ch 7:38.
2753. Pithom. 6619h, Ex 1:11.
2754. Pithon. 6377h, 1 Ch 8:35.
2755. Pleiades. 3598h, Jb 9:9.
2756. Pochereth. 6380h, Ezr 2:57.
2757. Pollux. 1359g, Ac 28:11.
2758. Pontius. 4194g, Lk 3:1.
2759. Pontus. 4195g, Ac 2:9.
2760. Poratha. 6334h, Est 9:8.
2761. Porcius. 4201g, Ac 24:27.
2762. Potiphar. 6318h, Ge 39:1.
2763. Potipherah. 6319h, Ge 41:45.
2764. Prisca. 4251g, 2 T 4:19.
2765. Priscilla. 4252g, Ac 18:2.
2766. Prochorus. 4402g, Ac 6:5.
2767. Ptolemais. 4424g, Ac 21:7.
2768. Pua. 6312h, Nu 26:23.
2769. Puah. 6326h, Ex 1:15.
2770. Publius. 4196g, Ac 28:7.
2771. Pudens. 4227g, 2 T 4:21.
2772. Puhites. 6336h, 1 Ch 2:53.
2773. Pul. 6322h, 2 K 15:19.
2774. Punites. 6324h, Nu 26:23.
2775. Punon. 6325h, Nu 33:42.
2776. Pur. 6332h, Est 3:7.
2777. Purim. 6332h, Est 9:26.
2778. Put. 6316h, Na 3:9.
2779. Puteoli. 4223g, Ac 28:13.
2780. Putiel. 6317h, Ex 6:25.
2781. Quartus. 2890g, Ro 16:23.
2782. Raamah. 7484h, Ge 10:7.
2783. Raamiah. 7485h, Ne 7:7.
2784. Raamses. 7486h, Ex 1:11.
2785. Rabbah. 7237h, Jsh 13:25.
2786. Rabbath. 7237h, Dt 3:11.
2787. Rabbi. 4461g, Mt 23:7.
2788. Rabbith. 7245h, Jsh 19:20.
2789. Rabboni. 4462g, Jn 20:16.
2790. Rabmag. 7248h, Je 39:3.
2791. Rabsaris. 7249h, Je 39:3.
2792. Rabshakeh. 7262h, 2 K 18:17.
2793. Raca. 4469g, Mt 5:22.
2794. Rachab. 4477g, Mt 1:5.
2795. Rachal. 7403h, 1 S 30:29.
2796. Rachel. 7354h, Ge 29:28.
2797. Rachel. 4478g, Mt 2:18.
2798. Raddai. 7288h, 1 Ch 2:14.
2799. Ragau. 4466g, Lk 3:35.
2800. Raguel. 7467h, Nu 10:29.
2801. Rahab. 7343h, Jsh 2:1.
2802. Rahab. 4460g, He 11:31.
2803. Raham. 7357h, 1 Ch 2:44.
2804. Rahel. 7354h, Je 31:15.
2805. Rakem. 7552h, 1 Ch 7:16.
2806. Rakkath. 7557h, Jsh 19:35.
2807. Rakkon. 7542h, Jsh 19:46.
2808. Ram. 7410h, Jb 32:2.
2809. Rama. 4471g, Mt 2:18.
2810. Ramah. 7414h, Je 31:15.

2811. Ramath. 7418h, Jsh 19:8.
2812. Ramathaimzophim. 7436h, 1 S 1:1.
2813. Ramathite. 7435h, 1 Ch 27:27.
2814. Ramathlehi. 7437h, Jg 15:17.
2815. Ramathmizpeh. 7434h, Jsh 13:26.
2816. Rameses. 7486h, Ge 47:11.
2817. Ramiah. 7422h, Ezr 10:25.
2818. Ramoth. 7216h, 1 Ch 6:73.
2819. Ramoth-gilead. 7433h, 1 K 4:13.
2820. Rapha. 7498h, 1 Ch 8:2.
2821. Raphu. 7505h, Nu 13:9.
2822. Reaia. 7211h, 1 Ch 5:5.
2823. Reaiah. 7211h, 1 Ch 4:2.
2824. Reba. 7254h, Nu 31:8.
2825. Rebecca. 4479g, Ro 9:10.
2826. Rebekah. 7259h, Ge 22:23.
2827. Rechab. 7394h, 2 S 4:2.
2828. Rechabites. 7397h, Je 35:2.
2829. Rechah. 7397h, 1 Ch 4:12.
2830. Reelaiah. 7480h, Ezr 2:2.
2831. Regem. 7276h, 1 Ch 2:47.
2832. Regem-melech. 7278h, Zc 7:2.
2833. Rehabiah. 7345h, 1 Ch 23:17.
2834. Rehob. 7340h, Nu 13:21.
2835. Rehoboam. 7346h, 1 K 14:21.
2836. Rehoboth. 7344h, Ge 10:11.
2837. Rehum. 7348h, Ne 12:3.
2838. Rei. 7472h, 1 K 1:8.
2839. Rekem. 7552h, 1 Ch 2:43.
2840. Remaliah. 7425h, 2 K 15:25.
2841. Remeth. 7432h, Jsh 19:21.
2842. Remmon. 7417h, Jsh 19:7.
2843. Remmon-methoar. 7417h, Jsh 19:13.
2844. Remphan. 4481g, Ac 7:43.
2845. Rephael. 7501h, 1 Ch 26:7.
2846. Rephah. 7506h, 1 Ch 7:25.
2847. Rephaiah. 7509h, 1 Ch 9:43.
2848. Rephaim. 7497h, 2 S 5:18.
2849. Rephaims. 7497h, Ge 14:5.
2850. Rephidim. 7508h, Ex 17:1.
2851. Resen. 7449h, Ge 10:12.
2852. Resheph. 7566h, 1 Ch 7:25.
2853. Reu. 7466h, Ge 11:18.
2854. Reuben. 7205h, Ge 29:32.
2855. Reuben. 4502g, Re 7:5.
2856. Reubenites. 7206h, Nu 26:7.
2857. Reuel. 7467h, Ge 36:4.
2858. Reumah. 7208h, Ge 22:24.
2859. Rezeph. 7530h, 2 K 19:12.
2860. Rezia. 7525h, 1 Ch 7:39.
2861. Rezin. 7526h, 2 K 15:37.
2862. Rezon. 7331h, 1 K 11:23.
2863. Rhegium. 4484g, Ac 28:13.
2864. Rhesa. 4488g, Lk 3:27.
2865. Rhoda. 4498g, Ac 12:13.
2866. Rhodes. 4499g, Ac 21:1.
2867. Ribai. 7380h, 2 S 23:29.
2868. Riblah. 7247h, Nu 34:11.
2869. Rimmon. 7417h, 2 K 5:18.
2870. Rimmon-parez. 7428h, Nu 33:19.
2871. Rinnah. 7441h, 1 Ch 4:20.
2872. Riphath. 7384h, Ge 10:3.
2873. Rissah. 7446h, Nu 33:21.
2874. Rithmah. 7575h, Nu 33:18.
2875. Rizpah. 7532h, 2 S 3:7.
2876. Roboam. 4497g, Mt 1:7.
2877. Rogelim. 7274h, 2 S 17:27.
2878. Rohgah. 7303h, 1 Ch 7:34.
2879. Romamtiezer. 7320h, 1 Ch 25:4.

2880. Roman. 4514g, Ac 22:25.
2881. Rome. 4516g, Ac 2:10.
2882. Rosh. 7220h, Ge 46:21.
2883. Rufus. 4504g, Mk 15:21.
2884. Ruhamah. 7355h, Ho 2:1.
2885. Rumah. 7316h, 2 K 23:36.
2886. Ruth. 7327h, Ru 1:4.
2887. Ruth. 4503g, Mt 1:5.
2887. Sabachtani. 4518g, Mt 27:46.
2888. Sabaoth. 4519g, Ro 9:29.
2889. Sabeans. 7614h, Jb 1:15.
2890. Sabeans. 5436h, Is 45:14.
2891. Sabeans. 5433h, Ezk 23:42.
2892. Sabeans. 7615h, Jl 3:8.
2893. Sabta. 5454h, 1 Ch 1:9.
2894. Sabtah. 5454h, Ge 10:7.
2895. Sabtecha. 5455h, Ge 10:7.
2896. Sabtechah. 5455h, 1 Ch 1:9.
2897. Sacar. 7940h, 1 Ch 11:35.
2898. Sadducees. 4523g, Mt 3:7.
2899. Sadoc. 4524g, Mt 1:14.
2900. Sala. 4527g, Lk 3:35.
2901. Salah. 7974h, Ge 10:24.
2902. Salamis. 4529g, Ac 13:5.
2903. Salathiel. 7597h, 1 Ch 3:17.
2904. Salathiel. 4528g, Mt 1:12.
2905. Salcah. 5548h, Jsh 13:11.
2906. Salchah. 5548h, Dt 3:10.
2907. Salem. 8004h, Ge 14:18.
2908. Salem. 4532g, He 7:1.
2909. Salim. 4530g, Jn 3:23.
2910. Sallai. 5543h, Ne 12:20.
2911. Sallu. 5543h, 1 Ch 9:7.
2912. Salma. 8007h, 1 Ch 2:11.
2913. Salmon. 8009h, Ru 4:20.
2914. Salmon. 8012h, Ru 4:21.
2915. Salmon. 6756h, Ps 68:14.
2916. Salmon. 4533g, Lk 3:32.
2917. Salmone. 4534g, Ac 27:7.
2918. Salome. 4539g, Mk 15:40.
2919. Salu. 5543h, Nu 25:14.
2920. Samaria. 8111h, 1 K 16:24.
2921. Samaria. 4540g, Jn 4:4.
2922. Samaritans. 4541g, Mt 10:5.
2923. Samgarnebo. 5562h, Je 39:3.
2924. Samlah. 8072h, Ge 36:36.
2925. Samos. 4544g, Ac 20:15.
2926. Samothracia. 4543g, Ac 16:11.
2927. Samson. 8123h, Jg 13:24.
2928. Samson. 4546g, He 11:32.
2929. Samuel. 8050h, 1 S 1:20.
2930. Samuel. 4545g, Ac 3:24.
2931. Sanballat. 5571h, Ne 2:10.
2932. Sansannah. 5578h, Jsh 15:31.
2933. Saph. 5593h, 2 S 21:18.
2934. Saphir. 8208h, Mi 1:11.
2935. Sapphira. 4551g, Ac 5:1.
2936. Sara. 4564g, He 11:11.
2937. Sarah. 8283h, Ge 17:15.
2938. Sarah. 4564g, Ro 9:9.
2939. Sarai. 8297h, Ge 16:6.
2940. Saraph. 8315h, 1 Ch 4:22.
2941. Sardis. 4554g, Re 3:1.
2942. Sardites. 5625h, Nu 26:26.
2943. Sarepta. 4558g, Lk 4:26.
2944. Sargon. 5623h, Is 20:1.
2945. Sarid. 8301h, Jsh 19:10.
2946. Saron. 4565g, Ac 9:35.
2947. Sarsechim. 8310h, Je 39:3.

2948. Saruch. 4562g, Lk 3:35.
2949. Satan. 7854h, Jb 1:6.
2950. Satan. 4567g, Mt 4:10.
2951. Saul. 7586h, 1 S 9:2.
2952. Saul. 4569g, Ac 8:3.
2953. Sceva. 4630g, Ac 19:14.
2954. Scythian. 4658g, Col 3:11.
2955. Seba. 5434h, Ge 10:7.
2956. Sebat. 7627h, Zc 1:7.
2957. Secacah. 5527h, Jsh 15:61.
2958. Sechu. 7906h, 1 S 19:22.
2959. Secundus. 4580g, Ac 20:4.
2960. Segub. 7687h, 1 Ch 2:21.
2961. Seir. 8165h, Ge 36:20.
2962. Seirath. 8167h, Jg 3:26.
2963. Sela. 5554h, Is 16:1.
2964. Selah. 5554h, 2 K 14:7.
2965. Selah. 5542h, Ps 9:16.
2966. Selahammahlekoth. 5555h, 1 S 23:28.
2967. Seled. 5540h, 1 Ch 2:30.
2968. Seleucia. 4581g, Ac 13:4.
2969. Sem. 4590g, Lk 3:36.
2970. Semachiah. 5565h, 1 Ch 26:7.
2971. Semei. 4584g, Lk 3:26.
2972. Senaah. 5570h, Ezr 2:35.
2973. Seneh. 5573h, 1 S 14:4.
2974. Senir. 8149h, 1 Ch 5:23.
2975. Sennacherib. 5576h, 2 K 18:13.
2976. Senuah. 5574h, Ne 11:9.
2977. Seorim. 8188h, 1 Ch 24:8.
2978. Sephar. 5611h, Ge 10:30.
2979. Sepharad. 5614h, Ob 20.
2980. Sepharvaim. 5617h, 2 K 17:24.
2981. Sepharvites. 5616h, 2 K 17:31.
2982. Serah. 8294h, Ge 46:17.
2983. Seraiah. 8304h, 2 S 8:17.
2984. Sered. 5624h, Ge 46:14.
2985. Sergius. 4588g, Ac 13:7.
2986. Serug. 8286h, Ge 11:20.
2987. Seth. 8352h, Ge 4:25.
2988. Seth. 4589g, Lk 3:38.
2989. Sethur. 5639h, Nu 13:13.
2990. Shaalabbin. 8169h, Jsh 19:42.
2991. Shaalbim. 8169h, Jg 1:35.
2992. Shaalbonite. 8170h, 2 S 23:32.
2993. Shaaph. 8174h, 1 Ch 2:47.
2994. Shaaraim. 8189h, 1 S 17:52.
2995. Shaashgaz. 8190h, Est 2:14.
2996. Shabbethai. 7678h, Ezr 10:15.
2997. Shachia. 7634h, 1 Ch 8:10.
2998. Shadrach. 7714h, Da 1:7.
2999. Shage. 7681h, 1 Ch 11:34.
3000. Shaharaim. 7842h, 1 Ch 8:8.
3001. Shahazimah. 7831h, Jsh 19:22.
3002. Shalem. 8003h, Ge 33:18.
3003. Shalim. 8171h, 1 S 9:4.
3004. Shalisha. 8031h, 1 S 9:4.
3005. Shallecheth. 7996h, 1 Ch 26:16.
3006. Shallum. 7967h, 2 K 15:10.
3007. Shallun. 7968h, Ne 3:15.
3008. Shalmai. 8073h, Ezr 2:46.
3009. Shalmai. 8014h, Ne 7:48.
3010. Shalman. 8020h, Ho 10:14.
3011. Shalmaneser. 8022h, 2 K 17:3.
3012. Shama. 8091h, 1 Ch 11:44.
3013. Shamariah. 8114h, 2 Ch 11:19.
3014. Shamed. 8106h, 1 Ch 8:12.
3015. Shamer. 8106h, 1 Ch 6:46.
3016. Shamgar. 8044h, Jg 3:31.

3017. Shamhuth. 8049h, 1 Ch 27:8.
3018. Shamir. 8053h, 1 Ch 24:24.
3019. Shamir. 8069h, Jsh 15:48.
3020. Shamma. 8037h, 1 Ch 7:37.
3021. Shammah. 8048h, 1 S 16:9.
3022. Shammai. 8060h, 1 Ch 2:28.
3023. Shammoth. 8054h, 1 Ch 11:27.
3024. Shammua. 8051h, Nu 13:4.
3025. Shammuah. 8051h, 2 S 5:14.
3026. Shamsherai. 8125h, 1 Ch 8:26.
3027. Shapham. 8223h, 1 Ch 5:12.
3028. Shaphan. 8227h, 2 K 22:3.
3029. Shaphat. 8202h, 1 Ch 3:22.
3030. Shapher. 8234h, Nu 33:23.
3031. Sharai. 8298h, Ezr 10:40.
3032. Sharaim. 8189h, Jsh 15:36.
3033. Sharar. 8325h, 2 S 23:33.
3034. Sharezer. 8272h, 2 K 19:37.
3035. Sharon. 8289h, Is 35:2.
3036. Sharonite. 8290h, 1 Ch 27:29.
3037. Sharuhen. 8287h, Jsh 19:6.
3038. Shashai. 8343h, Ezr 10:40.
3039. Shashak. 8349h, 1 Ch 8:14.
3040. Shaul. 7586h, Ge 46:10.
3041. Shaulites. 7587h, Nu 26:13.
3042. Shaveh. 7740h, Ge 14:17.
3043. Shavehkiriathaim. 7741h, Ge 14:5.
3044. Shavsha. 7798h, 1 Ch 18:16.
3045. Sheal. 7594h, Ezr 10:29.
3046. Shealtiel. 7597h, Hg 1:1.
3047. Sheariah. 8187h, 1 Ch 8:38.
3048. Shearjashub. 7610h, Is 7:3.
3049. Sheba. 7614h, 1 K 10:1.
3050. Sheba. 7652h, 2 S 20:1.
3051. Shebah. 7656h, Ge 26:33.
3052. Shebam. 7643h, Nu 32:3.
3053. Shebaniah. 7645h, 1 Ch 15:24.
3054. Shebarim. 7671h, Jsh 7:5.
3055. Sheber. 7669h, 1 Ch 2:48.
3056. Shebnah. 7644h, 2 K 18:18.
3057. Shebuel. 7619h, 1 Ch 23:16.
3058. Shecaniah. 7935h, 1 Ch 24:11.
3059. Shechaniah. 7935h, 1 Ch 3:22.
3060. Shechem. 7927h, Ge 33:18.
3061. Shechemites. 7930h, Nu 26:31.
3062. Shedeur. 7707h, Nu 1:5.
3063. Shehariah. 7841h, 1 Ch 8:26.
3064. Shelah. 7956h, Ge 38:5.
3065. Shelah. 7974h, 1 Ch 1:18.
3066. Shelanites. 8024h, Nu 26:20.
3067. Shelemiah. 8018h, 1 Ch 26:14.
3068. Sheleph. 8026h, Ge 10:26.
3069. Shelesh. 8028h, 1 Ch 7:35.
3070. Shelomi. 8015h, Nu 34:27.
3071. Shelomith. 8019h, Le 24:11.
3072. Shelomoth. 8013h, 1 Ch 24:22.
3073. Shelumiel. 8017h, Nu 1:6.
3074. Shem. 8035h, Ge 5:32.
3075. Shema. 8090h, Jsh 15:26.
3076. Shema. 8087h, 1 Ch 2:43.
3077. Shemaah. 8094h, 1 Ch 12:3.
3078. Shemaiah. 8098h, 1 Ch 9:16.
3079. Shemariah. 8114h, 1 Ch 12:5.
3080. Shemeber. 8038h, Ge 14:2.
3081. Shemer. 8106h, 1 K 16:24.
3082. Shemida. 8061h, Nu 26:32.
3083. Shemidah. 8061h, 1 Ch 7:19.
3084. Shemidaites. 8062h, Nu 26:32.
3085. Sheminith. 8067h, 1 Ch 15:21.

3086. Shemiramoth. 8070h, 1 Ch 15:18.
3087. Shemuel. 8050h, Nu 34:20.
3088. Shen. 8129h, 1 S 7:12.
3089. Shenazar. 8137h, 1 Ch 3:18.
3090. Shenir. 8149h, Dt 3:9.
3091. Shepham. 8221h, Nu 34:10.
3092. Shephathiah. 8203h, 1 Ch 9:8.
3093. Shephatiah. 8203h, 2 S 3:4.
3094. Shephi. 8195h, 1 Ch 1:40.
3095. Shepho. 8195h, Ge 36:23.
3096. Shephuphan. 8197h, 1 Ch 8:5.
3097. Sherah. 7609h, 1 Ch 7:24.
3098. Sherebiah. 8274h, Ezr 8:18.
3099. Sheresh. 8329h, 1 Ch 7:16.
3100. Sherezer. 8272h, Zc 7:2.
3101. Sheshach. 8347h, Je 25:26.
3102. Sheshai. 8344h, Nu 13:22.
3103. Sheshan. 8348h, 1 Ch 2:31.
3104. Sheshbazzar. 8339h, Ezr 1:8.
3105. Sheth. 8352h, Nu 24:17.
3106. Shethar. 8369h, Est 1:14.
3107. Shetharboznai. 8370h, Ezr 5:3.
3108. Sheva. 7724h, 2 S 20:25.
3109. Shibboleth. 7641h, Jg 12:6.
3110. Shibmah. 7643h, Nu 32:38.
3111. Shicron. 7942h, Jsh 15:11.
3112. Shiggaion. 7692h, Ps 7:Title.
3113. Shigionoth. 7692h, Hab 3:1.
3114. Shihon. 7866h, Jsh 19:19.
3115. Shihor. 7883h, 1 Ch 13:5.
3116. Shihorlibnath. 7884h, Jsh 19:26.
3117. Shilhi. 7977h, 1 K 22:42.
3118. Shilhim. 7978h, Jsh 15:32.
3119. Shillem. 8006h, Ge 46:24.
3120. Shillemites. 8016h, Nu 26:49.
3121. Shiloah. 7975h, Is 8:6.
3122. Shiloh. 7886h, Ge 49:10.
3123. Shiloh. 7887h, Jg 21:19.
3124. Shiloni. 8023h, Ne 11:5.
3125. Shilonite. 7888h, 1 K 11:29.
3126. Shilshah. 8030h, 1 Ch 7:37.
3127. Shimea. 8092h, 1 Ch 3:5.
3128. Shimea. 8092h, 2 S 21:21.
3129. Shimeah. 8093h, 2 S 13:3.
3130. Shimeah. 8039h, 1 Ch 8:32.
3131. Shimeam. 8043h, 1 Ch 9:38.
3132. Shimeath. 8100h, 2 K 12:21.
3133. Shimeathites. 8101h, 1 Ch 2:55.
3134. Shimei. 8096h, 2 S 16:5.
3135. Shimeon. 8095h, Ezr 10:31.
3136. Shimhi. 8096h, 1 Ch 8:21.
3137. Shimi. 8096h, Ex 6:17.
3138. Shimites. 8097h, Nu 3:21.
3139. Shimma. 8092h, 1 Ch 2:13.
3140. Shimon. 7889h, 1 Ch 4:20.
3141. Shimrath. 8119h, 1 Ch 8:21.
3142. Shimri. 8113h, 1 Ch 4:37.
3143. Shimrith. 8116h, 2 Ch 24:26.
3144. Shimrom. 8110h, 1 Ch 7:1.
3145. Shimron. 8110h, Ge 46:13.
3146. Shimronites. 8117h, Nu 26:24.
3147. Shimronmeron. 8112h, Jsh 12:20.
3148. Shimshai. 8124h, Ezr 4:8.
3149. Shinab. 8134h, Ge 14:2.
3150. Shinar. 8152h, Ge 10:10.
3151. Shiphi. 8230h, 1 Ch 4:37.
3152. Shipmite. 8225h, 1 Ch 27:27.
3153. Shiphrah. 8236h, Ex 1:15.
3154. Shiphtan. 8204h, Nu 34:24.

FIGURE OF SPEECH INDEX

63B1A. The verb "to say." Ge 26:7.
63B2A. When the Infinitive of the verb is wanting: after "able." Ps 21:11.
63B2B. After the verb "to finish." 1 S 16:11.
63B2C. When the infinitive is wanting after another verb, personal or impersonal. Ge 9:20.
63B3. When the Verb Substantive is omitted. Ge 2:10.
63B4. When the Participle is wanting. Nu 24:19.
63C. When certain connected words are omitted in the same member of a passage (Brachylogia). Ge 25:32.
63D1. When a whole clause is omitted in a connected passage: when the first member of a clause is omitted. Mt 16:7.
63D2. The ellipsis of a latter clause, called *Anantapodoton*, i.e., without *apodosis*. Ge 30:27.
63D3. When the comparison is wanting. This is a kind of *anantapodoton*. Ro 7:3.
63E1. Relative Ellipsis, where the omitted word is supplied from a cognate word occurring in the immediate context, where the noun is suggested by the verb. Le 4:2.
63E2. Where the verb is to be supplied from the noun. 1 S 13:8.
63F. Where the omitted word is to be supplied from a contrary word. Ge 33:10.
63G. Where the omitted word is to be supplied from analogous or related words. Ge 50:23.
63H. Where the omitted word is contained in another word, the one combining the two significations. Ge 12:15.
63I1A. Ellipsis of Repetition (simple), where the omission is to be supplied by repeating a word or words out of the preceding clause, involving nouns and pronouns. Ex 12:4.
63I1B. Where the omitted verb is to be repeated from a preceding clause. Ge 4:24.
63I1C1. Where an omitted particle is to be repeated from the preceding clause, involving negatives. Ge 2:6.
63I1C2A. Interrogatives: Why. Ps 2:1.
63I1C2B. How oft? Jb 21:17.
63I1D. Where the omission of connected words is to be supplied by repeating them out of a preceding clause. Nu 26:3.
63I2. Where the omitted word is to be supplied out of a succeeding clause. Jsh 3:3.
63J1. Ellipsis of Repetition (Complex), where both clauses are involved, of single words. Ge 13:9.
63J2. Where Sentences are involved. Ps 1:6.

63K. False Ellipsis. Ge 37:13.
64. Enantiosis; or, Contraries. Ps 1:1.
65. Enthymema; or, Omission of Premise. Ro 7:6.
66. Epanadiplosis; or, Encircling. Ge 9:3.
67. Epanalepsis; or, Resumption. Ro 3:26.
68. Epanodos; or, Inversion. Ex 9:31.
69A. Epanorthosis; or, Correction. Where the retraction is absolute. Mk 9:24.
69B. Where it is partial or relative. Pr 6:16.
69C. Where it is conditional. Ga 3:4.
70. Epibole; or, Overlaid Repetition. Ex 16:35.
71. Epicrisis; or, Judgment. Jn 1:24.
72. Epidiplosis; or, Double Encircling. Ex 32:16.
73. Epimone; or, Lingering. Zc 1:5.
74. Epiphonema; or, Exclamation. Jg 5:31.
75. Epiphoza; or, Epistrophe in Argument. 2 C 11:22.
76. Epistrophe; or, Like Sentence Endings. Ge 13:6.
77. Epitasis; or, Amplification. Ex 3:19.
78. Epitherapeia; or, Qualification. Ph 4:10.
79. Epitheton; or, Epithet. Ge 21:16.
80. Epitimesis; or, Reprimand. Lk 9:55.
81. Epitrechon; or, Running Along. Ge 15:13.
82. Epitrochasmos; or, Summarizing. He 11:32.
83. Epitrope; or, Admission. 1 K 22:15.
84. Epizeuxis; or, Duplication. Ge 6:17.
85A. Erotesis; or, Interrogating. In positive affirmation. Ps 56:13.
85B. In negative affirmation. Ge 13:9.
85C. In affirmative negation. Ge 18:14.
85D. In demonstration. Ps 25:12.
85E. In wonder and admiration. Ge 17:17.
85F. In rapture or exultation. Ps 8:4.
85G. In wishes. Is 6:8.
85H. In refusals and denials. Jg 11:12.
85I. In doubts. Ge 18:12.
85J. In admonition. Ru 2:8.
85K. In expostulation. Ge 3:9.
85L. In prohibitions. Ge 27:45.
85M. In pity and commiseration. La 1:1.
85N. In disparagements. 1 K 9:13.
85O. In reproaches. Je 23:33.
85P. In lamentation. Ge 27:46.
85Q. In indignation. Ps 2:1.
85R. In absurdities and imposibilities. Jb 4:17.
85S. Double questions. Jb 4:17.
86. Ethopoeia; or, Description of Manners. Is 3:16.
87. Euche; or, Prayer. Ps 118:25.
88. Euphemismos; or, Euphemy. Ge 15:15.
89. Exemplum; or, Example. Lk 17:32.
90. Exergasia; or, Working Out. Ps 17:1.
91. Exouthenismos; or, Contempt. 2 S 6:20.
92A. Gnome; or, Quotation. Where the sense of the Hebrew intended by the Holy Spirit is preserved, though the words may vary. Mt 1:23.
92B. Where the original sense is modified in the quotation or reference. Mt 12:40.
92C. Where the sense is accommodated, being quite different from that which was first intended, and the sense is accommodated by analogy to quite a different event or circumstance. Mt 2:15.

121A8. Soul is put for the person, as when we say a city contains so many thousand souls. Ps 16:10.

121A9. Soul is put for the will, affection, or desire, which are its operations and effects. Ge 23:8.

121A10. Spirit is put for the soul or life in its manifestations. Ge 26:35.

121A11. Satan is put for wickedness, etc. 1 Th 2:18.

121B. The organic cause or instrument is put for the thing effected by it: the organs of speech are put for the testimony borne. Dt 17:6.

121B1A. The mouth is put for the command or precept given. Ge 45:21.

121B1B. The tongue is put for what is spoken by it. Ps 5:9.

121B1C. The tongue is also put for the language peculiar to any people or nation. Mk 16:17.

121B1D. The lip is put for the language. Ge 11:1.

121B1E. The palate is put for the words spoken. Pr 5:3.

121B1F1. The throat is put for the words spoken. Ps 5:9.

121B1F2. The throat is put for loud speaking. Is 58:1.

121B2A. The hand is put for the actions performed by it. Dt 32:36.

121B2B. The hand is put for instrumentality or agency, especially in connection with Inspiration. Ezr 9:11.

121B2C. The hand is put for the writing done by it or handwriting. 1 C 16:21.

121B2D. The hand is put for a gift given to anyone. Ps 68:31.

121B3. The sword is put for war or for slaughter. Ex 5:3.

121B4. A line is used for the territory divided up or marked out by it. Jsh 17:14.

121B5. Silver is put for the thing procured by it. Ex 21:21.

121B6. Hyssop is put for the sprinkling which was effected by it. Ps 51:7.

121C1A. The thing or action is put for that which is the effect or product of it, in certain nouns, where the feeling or affection is put for the effects resulting or proceeding from the feeling: love is put for the benefits and blessings flowing from it. 1 J 3:1.

121C1B. Mercy is put for the offices and benefits which are the outcome of it. Ge 20:13.

121C1C. Anger and wrath are put for punishment, and various acts which flow from them. Ps 79:6.

121C1D. Justice is put for the judgment or punishment which manifests it. Ex 6:6.

121C1E. Sin and its synonyms are put for the effects or punishment of sin. Ge 19:15.

121C1F. Work is put for the wages paid for it. Le 19:13.

121C1G. Divination is put for the money received from it. Nu 22:7.

121C1H. Labor is put for that which is produced by it. Dt 28:33.

121C1I. Strength is put for that which it effects or produces. Ge 4:12.

121C1J. Hunting is put for the flesh of the animal that is caught. Ge 25:28.

121C1K. Guilt is put for penalty. Le 20:9.

121C1L. The holding back of rain is put for the famine caused by it. Je 14:1.

121C2A1. In certain verbs. Verbs of knowing are used of the effect of knowing: i.e., understanding, caring for, approving. Jb 19:25.

121C2A2. Verbs of knowing are put for caring for or manifesting affection to. Ge 39:6.

121C2A3. Verbs of knowing are used also of experiencing, either by saving faith or by personal dealing. Is 53:11.

121C2A4. Verbs of knowing. Ge 19:5.

121C2B. Verbs of remembering. Is 44:21.

121C2C1. Verbs of loving and hating are put for the actions consequent upon them: to love is put for to expect, or desire, or take. Ps 11:5.

121C2C2. To love is used of the exercise of the greatest possible care for whatever is the object of the love. To hate is used in the opposite sense, of exercising less care, or of neglect. Ge 29:31.

121C2C3. To love is used not merely for the act itself, but for the effect of it. Ps 109:17.

121C2D1. Verbs of operation. The verb To Do often denotes the effect rather than the act. Ge 12:5.

121C2D2. Certain verbs are used of the actions or effects consequent upon them: to judge is put for punish or condemn. Ge 15:14.

121C2D3. To judge is used in the sense of acquit, an effect of judging. Ps 35:24.

121C2D4. To hurt or to injure is put for the hurt or injury done. Lk 10:19.

121C2D5. To hear or hearing is used of fame, the effect of hearing or being heard. Mt 14:1.

121C2E. Verbs of asking. An answer is put for that which is sought for by an interrogation. 1 P 3:21.

121D1. The material is put for the thing made of or from it. Trees are put for the arms or instruments made from them. 2 S 6:5.

121D2. Brass is put for fetters. Jg 16:21.

121D3. Curtains are put for tents. 2 S 7:2.

121D4. Corn is put for bread or food generally. La 2:12.

121D5. Gold and silver and other substances are put for what is made with them. Ge 23:9.

121D6.   Iron is put for things made of it. 2 K 6:5.

121D7.   Stones are put for things made of them. Ex 7:19.

121D8.   Wood is put for things made of wood. Ge 40:19.

121D9.   Flax is put for the wick made of it. Is 42:3.

121D10.   Dust and ashes for man, who is made of dust. Ge 3:19.

121D11.   Seed is put for son or posterity. Ge 4:25.

121D12.   Forest or wood is put for the houses, etc., made of its trees. Je 21:14.

121D13.   Wine is put for all liquids (beverages). Ge 27:28.

121D14.   Bread is put for all food. Ps 104:14.

121E1.   Metonymy of the effect, the action or the effect is put for the person producing the effect, or for the author of it, in nouns. Ge 25:23.

121E2.   In verbs. Ge 42:38.

121F.   The thing effected by an instrument is put for the instrument or organic cause of it. Ge 49:6.

121G1.   The effect is put for the thing or action causing or producing it, in nouns. Ge 31:1, glory put for wealth.

121G2.   In verbs. Ps 25:2.

121H.   The thing made is put for the material from which it is made or produced. Ps 74:15.

121I1.   Metonymy of the subject. The subject (i.e. the Thing or Action) is put for that which is connected with it (i.e. the adjunct). Nouns. Ge 3:7.

121I2.   In verbs. Ge 2:17.

121J1.   The container is put for the contents, and the place for the thing placed in it. Circuit is put for what is contained in it. Nu 22:4.

121J2.   Basket is put for its contents. Dt 28:5.

121J3.   Wilderness is put for the wild beasts in it. Ps 29:8.

121J4.   House is put for household. Ge 7:1.

121J5.   Islands are put for their inhabitants. Is 41:1.

121J6.   Table is put for the things on it. Ps 23:5.

121J7A.   Mountain is put for the mountainous region. Jsh 13:6.

121J7B.   Mountains are put for idols worshipped there; or for their inhabitants. Je 3:23.

121J8.   The world is put for its inhabitants. Jn 3:16.

121J9A.   The world is put for a portion of its inhabitants. Jn 1:10.

121J9B.   The world is put for the ungodly inhabitants of it. Jn 12:31.

121J10.   Ships are put for the souls in them. Is 23:1.

121J11.   Nests are put for the birds in them. Dt 32:11.

121J12.   Ophir is put for the gold of Ophir. Jb 22:24.

121J13.   Cup is put for the wine in it. Je 49:12.

121J14.   A region is put for its inhabitants. Ge 47:15.

121J15.   The grave is put for the dead buried in it. Is 38:18.

121J16.   Tents, etc., are put for the dwellers therein. Ge 13:5.

121J17.   The land or earth are put for its inhabitants. Ge 6:11.

121J18.   Theater is put for its spectacle. 1 C 4:9.

121J19.   A city is put for its inhabitants. 1 S 22:19.

121J20.   Heaven is put for God, who dwells there. Ps 73:9.

121J21.   Heart is put for nature and character. Ps 24:4.

121J22.   Belly is put for heart or thoughts. Jb 15:35.

121J23.   Heart is put for understanding. Jb 12:3.

121K1.   The possessor is put for the thing possessed. Nations are put for countries. Dt 9:1.

121K2.   Person is put for possessions. Ge 15:3.

121K3.   Princes are put for the thousands whom they led. Mi 5:2.

121K4.   God is put for the sacrifices offered to Him. Jsh 13:33.

121K5.   Christ is put for His people. Ac 9:4.

121K6.   God is put for the power manifested by Him. Lk 1:35.

121L1.   The object is put for that which pertains or relates to it. Jesus is put for His doctrine. 2 C 11:4.

121L2.   A god is put for his worship. Ex 32:1.

121L3.   Attributes are put for the praise and celebration of them. Ps 8:2.

121L4.   Burden is put for the prophecy. Is 21:1.

121L5.   Sin is put for the offering for sin. Ge 4:7.

121L6.   Promise is put for the faith which receives it. Ro 9:8.

121L7.   Covenant is put for the two tables of stone. 1 K 8:21.

121L8.   Blood is put for blood-shedding. Is 33:15.

121L9.   Double is used for that which is complete, thorough, or ample; and of full compensation, whether of judgment or of blessing. Ge 43:12.

121L10.   Border is put for cities which comprise the border. Jsh 13:23.

121L11.   Throne is put for any royal abode. Ne 3:7.

121M.   The thing signified is put for the sign. Ex 8:23.

121N1.   Metonymy of the Adjunct. The adjunct or accident is put for the subject. The abstract is put for the concrete, or the attribute is

121N2. Other adjuncts are put for the subjects to which they pertain: light for the sun, oil for anointing, etc. Ge 34:29, strength put for wealth.

121O. The contents for that which contains them: and what is placed, for the place where it is located. Ge 28:22.

121P1. Time is put for the things done in it, or existing in it. The word Time or Times. 1 Ch 12:32.

121P2. Age, a period of time, is put for what takes place in it. Mt 13:22.

121P3. Years is put for what happens in them. Pr 5:9.

121P4. Day, or days, is put for what transpires in them, the context showing what it is. Dt 4:32.

121P5. Hour is put for what is done at the time. Mk 14:35.

121P6. End is put for that which takes place at the end. Pr 23:18.

121P7. Feast-day is put for the sacrifices offered at the Festival. Ex 23:18.

121P8. Passover is put for the Lamb slain at the Passover. Ex 12:21.

121P9. Summer is put for the fruits gathered in it. Is 16:9.

121P10. Harvest is put for the fruits of the harvest. Dt 24:19.

121P11. Fast is used for the time of year at which the Fast fell. Ac 27:9.

121P12. Blood is put for guilt. Le 20:9.

121Q1. The appearance of a thing, or an opinion about it, is put for the thing itself. In nouns. Je 28:5.

121Q2. In verbs. Mt 14:9.

121Q3. Connected words or sentences. 2 S 22:8.

121R1. The action or affection relating to an object is put for the object itself. The senses are put for the object of them, or for the things which are perceived by the senses. Le 13:55.

121R2. Faith is put for the thing believed. Ac 6:7.

121R3. Hope is put for God, or for the object on which it is set. Ps 71:5.

121R4. Love is put for the person or object loved. Je 2:33.

121R5. Desire is put for the person or thing desired. Ge 27:15.

121R6. Fear is put for God who is feared, or for any object of fear. Ge 31:42.

121R7. Other actions are put for the object connected with, or related to them; which object is shown by the context. Ge 43:11.

121S1. The sign is put for the thing signified. Nouns. Ge 49:10.

121S2. Verbs. Ge 21:6.

121S3A. Connected words and phrases. To bind and loose. Mt 16:19.

121S3B. To open and shut. Jb 12:14.

121S3C. To be stiff-necked. Ps 75:5.

put for that to which anything is attributed. Ge 31:54.

121S3D. Cleanness of teeth. Am 4:6.

121S3E1. To lift up the eyes. Ps 121:1.

121S3E2. To lift up the head. Jg 8:28.

121S3E3. To lift up the face. Nu 6:26.

121S3F1. To strengthen the face. Pr 7:13.

121S3F2. To cover the face or head. 2 S 15:30.

121S3F3. The face to wax pale. Is 29:22.

121S3G. To have a whore's forehead. Je 3:3.

121S3H. To bow the knee. Is 45:23.

121S3I. To give the hand. 1 Ch 29:24.

121S3J. To place the hand on. Le 6:2.

121S3K. To lift up the hand, or hands. Ge 14:22.

121S3L. To strike hands. Jb 17:3.

121S3M. To put hands on the head. 2 S 13:19.

121S3N. To put the hand or hands on the mouth. Jg 18:19.

121S3O. To pour water on the hands. 2 K 3:11.

121S3P. To fill the hand or hands. Ex 28:41.

121S3Q. To cover the feet. Jg 3:24.

121S3R. Eating and drinking. Ex 24:11.

121S3S. Looking. Ge 16:13.

121S3T. The breaking of bonds. Ps 2:3.

121S3U. The clothing in sackcloth. Jb 16:15.

121S3V. Making bald. Mi 1:16.

121S3W. Licking the dust. Ps 72:9.

121S3X. Smiting the thigh. Je 31:19.

121S3Y. Sitting on the ground. La 2:10.

121S3Z. Not discerning the right hand from the left. Jon 4:11.

121S3AA. To loose the loins. Is 45:1.

121S4. The whole utterance, which may consist of admonition, instruction, etc., sometimes consists of sign or symbol, and the signs are thus put for the things signified. 2 K 4:29.

121T1. The name of a person is put for the person himself; or the name of a thing for the thing itself. The person, when that person is Divine. Dt 28:58.

121T2. When the person is human. Ac 1:15.

121T3. The name of a man for his posterity. Ge 9:27.

121T4. The name of a thing for the thing itself. Ep 1:21.

122. Mimesis; or, Description of Sayings. Ex 15:9.

123. Negatio; or, Negation. Ga 2:5.

124. Oeonismos; or, Wishing. Dt 5:29.

125. Oxymoron; or, Wise Folly. Jb 22:6.

126. Paeanismos; or, Exultation. Dt 32:43.

127. Palinodia; or, Retracting. Re 2:6.

128. Parabola; or, Parable, i.e., Continued Simile. Lk 14:16.

129. Paradiastole; or, Neithers and Nors. Ezk 34:4.

130. Paraeneticon; or, Exhortation. Ac 11:23.

131. Paraleipsis; or, a Passing By. He 11:32.

132A. Parallelism; or, Parallel Lines. Simple. Synonymous or Gradational. Ge 4:23.

132B. Antithetic, or Opposite. Pr 10:1.

132C. Synthetic, or Constructive. Ps 19:7.

132D. Complex. Alternate. Ge 19:25.

132E. Repeated Alternation. Is 65:21.

132F. Extended Alternation. Jg 10:17.

132G. Introverted Parallelisms. Ge 3:19.

133. Parecbasis; or, Digression. Ge 2:8.

171E9.   Statute is put for allowance, or necessary food. Ge 47:22.

171E10. The bowels are put for the heart. Ps 40:8.

171E11. The living are put for men. Ge 3:20.

171E12. A common name is sometimes put for a proper one. Ge 14:22. 31:21. 48:16.

171E13. The plural number is put for the singular. Ge 46:7.

171F.   Synecdoche of the Species. Many is sometimes put for all. Is 53:12.

171G1.   Words of a limited and special sense are used with a wider and more universal meaning. Man is used for both sexes, men and women. Ps 32:2.

171G2.   One relationship is put for, and includes others. Ge 13:8.

171G3.   Cessation of tongue's motion put for cessation of any other motion or action. Jsh 10:13.

171H.   A proper name is put for a common; an individual is put for many; and the particular is put for the universal. Is 63:16.

171I1.   A species of a thing is put for the whole genus. Bow, spear, etc., are put for all kinds of arms. Ps 44:6.

171I2.   The ass is put for all kinds of animals not sacrificed. Ex 13:13.

171I3.   Gold is put for gifts. Ps 72:15.

171I4.   Stones are put for whatever is hurtful to the soil. Jb 5:23.

171I5.   Lion is put for all kinds of wild beasts. Is 15:9.

171I6.   Commandment is put for all commandments and doctrines. 2 P 2:21.

171I7.   Honey is put for whatever is sweet and delicious. Ex 3:8.

171I8.   Bread is put for all kinds of food, including fish. Ge 3:19.

171I9A. Peace is used for plenty, and happiness; and of all kinds of earthly good and blessing. Ge 43:23.

171I9B. Peace is used of all heavenly and spiritual blessing. Is 57:19.

171I10. Prey (that which is taken in hunting: i.e., one kind of food) is put for any and all kinds of food. Ps 111:5.

171I11. Blood (Heb. often *bloods*) is put for murder or cruelty; or death generally. Dt 19:12.

171I12. Blood is also put for guilt. Le 20:9.

171I13. Clothing is put for all necessary things. Is 3:6.

171I14. Widows and fatherless are put for all kinds of afflicted. Ex 22:22.

171I15. Nether and upper millstone is put for all necessary means of livelihood. Dt 24:6.

171J1.   Verbs having a special meaning are used in a more general sense. "To ascend" is used for to come, or to enter into the thoughts, or the mind. 2 K 12:4.

171J2.   To Make (with time) is used for *to continue* or *abide*. Ac 15:33.

171J3.   To go out and come in is used of official actions or of life in general. Nu 27:17.

171J4.   To find is used for to receive, to obtain. Ge 6:8.

171J5.   To find is also used of to have, or to be present with. 1 S 13:15.

171J6.   To call upon the Lord is used of Divine worship. Ge 4:26.

171J7.   To pass the night is used for abiding. Ps 49:12.

171J8.   To place is put for to make. Ro 4:17.

171J9.   To meet is used of arriving at so as to touch. Ac 16:1.

171J10. To drink is used of partaking of food and drink of all kinds. 1 C 3:2.

171J11. To answer, or open the mouth is put for speaking. Jb 3:1.

171J12. To sit is used of a permanent condition in which one is placed. Is 42:7.

171J13. To sit down and rise up is used for all the ordinary acts of life which come between them. Ps 139:2.

171J14. To come is used of going as well as coming. Jon 1:3.

171J15. Verbs expressing the operation of one sense are in Hebrew often put for those of another. Ge 42:1.

171K1.   One example or specimen is put for all kinds of similar things: in human actions. Dt 19:5.

171K2.   In Divine precepts. Ex 23:4.

171L1.   Synecdoche of the Whole. The whole is put for every part of it. Nu 16:3.

171L2.   "Every" is used for the whole. Mt 26:59.

171M.   The collective is put for the particular. What is said of the whole, collectively, is sometimes said (by Synecdoche) only of a part; and not all of the parts, precisely and singularly. Ge 6:12.

171N.   The whole is put for one of its parts. Ge 8:13.

171O1.   A place is put for a part of it. The World is put for persons in all parts of it. Jn 12:19.

171O2.   The world is put for a primary part of it. Is 13:11.

171O3.   All the earth is put for the greater part of its inhabitants. Ge 41:57.

171O4.   The earth is put for the land of Judea. Ho 1:2.

171O5.   The land is put for city. Mt 2:6.

171O6.   The East is put for Persia, Media, and other countries east of Jerusalem. 1 K 4:30.

171O7.   The South is put for Egypt, with respect to Palestine. Da 11:5.

171O8.   The South is put for the Negeb, or the hill country of Judea, with respect to Jerusalem. Ge 12:9.

171O9.   The North is put for Chaldea and its chief city Babylon, because all armies from beyond the

171O10. Euphrates crossed high up and entered Palestine from the North. Je 13:20.

171O10. The North is put for Media and Persia, with respect to Babylon. Je 6:1.

171O11. The temple is put for certain of the parts comprehended in it. Lk 2:46.

171O12. Cities (plural) is put for one of them. Ge 13:12.

171O13. Manasseh is put for half Manasseh. Jsh 16:4.

171P. Time is put for a portion of time. Ex 21:6.

171Q1A. Synecdoche of the Part. An integral part of man (individually) is put for the whole man. The soul ('nephesh' and 'psyche') is put for the whole person. Ge 12:5.

171Q1B. The spirit (Heb. 'ruach' and Gr. 'pneuma') is put for the whole person. Mk 2:8.

171Q2. The expression My Soul, His Soul, etc., becomes by *Synecdoche* the idiom for *me, myself, himself*, etc. Nu 23:10.

171Q3. Soul is also used of animals. Ge 1:20.

171Q4. The body is put for the person himself. Ex 21:3.

171Q5. The flesh, an integral part of man, is put for the whole. Ge 17:13.

171Q6. The flesh is put for the whole person. Ge 6:12.

171Q7. Flesh is put for the whole, and true, humanity of Christ. Jn 1:14.

171Q8. Flesh is put for all living things. Ge 6:13.

171Q9. The Flesh is put for the animal lusts, and the evil desires of the Old nature, and for the Old nature itself. Ro 8:4.

171Q10. Blood is put for man. Ps 94:21.

171Q11. Flesh and blood is put for the human nature as distinct from the Divine Nature: or for the body of man as animal, mortal, and corruptible. Mt 16:17.

171Q12. The head is put for the man himself. Jg 5:30.

171Q13. The skull, as a part of the man, is put for the man himself. Ex 16:16.

171Q14. The face is put for the whole man, especially marking and emphasizing his presence. Ge 3:19.

171Q15. The eye is put for the man himself, in respect to his vision, mental or physical. Mt 13:16.

171Q16. The eye lifted up is put for a proud man, and his high looks. Ps 18:27.

171Q17. The mouth is put for the whole man, in respect of his speaking. Pr 8:13.

171Q18. The belly is put for man, in respect of his eating. Ro 16:18.

171Q19. The womb is put for a female, in respect to her being marriageable. Jg 5:30.

171Q20. The heart is put for the whole man, in respect to his knowledge or affection. Ge 31:20.

171Q21. The feet are put for the whole man, in respect to carefulness, quickness, etc. Pr 1:16.

171Q22. A person (servant) is described by a part of his service. 2 K 3:11.

171Q23. Hand is put for the whole person. Ps 7:3.

171Q24. Spirit put for the whole person. Ps 106:33.

171R. An integral part of men (collectively) is put for the whole, or others associated with them. Ex 12:40.

171S1. A part of a thing is put for the whole of the thing. A field is put for a country or region. Ge 14:7.

171S2. Corner is put for tower, which was usually placed at the corner. Zp 1:16.

171S3. The baptism of John is put for his ministry. Ac 1:22.

171S4. Stones is put for the restored buildings. Ps 102:14.

171S5. Wall is put for the whole city encompassed by it. Am 1:7.

171S6. In like manner Gate is put for the whole city. Ge 14:7.

171S7. Gate is also put for the inhabitants of the city, or for the people who assemble at its gates. Ru 3:11. Ge 14:7.

171S8. The death of Christ is put for the atonement and its results. Ro 5:8.

171S9. The knob of the roll is put for the MS. or book itself. He 10:7.

171S10. Sacrifices made by fire put for all the tithes, etc., assigned to the Levites. Jsh 13:14.

171S11. A shortened expression put for the fuller expression. Ac 2:38.

171T1. A part of time is put for the whole time. A year is put for time, definite and indefinite. Is 61:2.

171T2A. In the day is put for an indefinite time. Ge 2:17.

171T2B. Days are used for time. Ps 102:11.

171T2C. The plural days is put for a full year. Ge 24:55.

171T3. The sabbath is sometimes put for the full week. Mt 28:1.

171T4. The morning is put for a more lengthened period or continuous time. Jb 7:18.

171T5. Evening and morning are put for the full day; or, the whole of a day and night. Ge 1:31.

171T6. Hour is put for a special time or season. Jn 4:23.

171T7. In chronology a part of a time or period is sometimes put for the whole of such period. 2 K 24:8.

171T8. A part of a day is accounted a whole day. 1 S 30:12.

171T9. A part of a year is accounted a whole year. 1 K 16:8.

172. Synoeceiosis; or, Cohabitation. Mt 5:19.

Strong's Numbers Index: Hebrew

5237. Ge 31:15	6264. Dt 32:35	7496. Pr 21:16
5251. Ex 17:15	6313. Hab 1:4	7497. Ge 14:5
5258. 2 S 23:16	6354. 2 S 17:9	7499. Pr 3:8
5275. Is 11:15	6388. Pr 21:1	7500. Pr 3:8
5278. Ps 27:4	6437. Le 19:31	7565. Dt 32:24
5291. Ge 24:14	6475. Ps 66:14	7585. Ge 37:35
5315. Ge 2:7	6485. Je 11:22	7602. Is 42:14
5331. Jb 4:20	6496. Ge 41:34	7621. Ne 10:29
5341. Is 65:4	6599. 2 Ch 34:27	7650. Ge 21:31
5347. Je 31:22	6600. 2 Ch 34:27	7651. Ge 21:31
5352. Is 3:26	6617. Ps 18:26	7667. Jg 7:15
5362. Jb 19:26	6694. Is 26:16	7726. Is 57:17
5392. Dt 23:19	6703. Is 32:4	7745. Pr 22:14
5397. Ge 2:7	6711. Ge 21:9	7784. Pr 7:8
5413. Ex 9:33	6725. Ezk 39:15	7836. Jb 8:5
5437. Dt 32:10	6745. 2 Ch 32:13	7845. Jb 9:31
5461. Ne 12:40	6757. Ps 23:4	7857. Le 15:11
5462. 2 Ch 9:20	6807. Is 3:20	7872. Dt 32:25
5542. Ps 9:16	6900. Ge 35:20	7879. 1 S 1:16
5564. Ge 27:37	6913. Ge 23:4	7891. 2 Ch 35:15
5592. 1 K 14:17	6921. Ge 41:6.	7902. Le 15:16
5631. Ge 37:36	6924. Mi 5:2	7919. Dt 29:9
5637. Ho 9:15	6927. Is 23:7	7922. 1 S 25:3
5641. Zp 2:3	6931. 1 S 24:13	7966. Ho 9:7
5670. Hab 2:6	6944. Ex 3:5	8003. 2 K 20:3
5671. Hab 2:6	6951. Ex 12:6	8058. 2 K 9:33
5703. Ps 9:18	6960. Ps 37:34n	8074. Ho 2:12
5712. Ex 12:3	6973. Is 7:6	8081. Dt 33:24
5756. Je 4:6	7043. Ge 16:4. Ne 13:25	8082. Ge 49:20
5763. Ps 78:71	7069. Pr 8:22	8163. Is 34:14
5769. Ex 12:24	7080. Is 44:25	8210. Ex 4:9
5848. Ps 77:3	7081. Pr 16:10	8211. Le 4:12
5869. Ge 24:13	7095. Jon 2:6	8219. Zc 7:7
5959. Ge 24:43	7218. Je 13:18	8302. Ne 4:16
5971. Hab 2:13	7281. Is 26:20	8414. Is 45:18
6049. 2 K 21:6	7301. Is 34:5	8415. Jon 2:5
6090. Ps 139:24	7307. Ge 6:3	8438. Is 66:24
6106. Ge 7:13	7324. Ml 3:10	8453. Ge 23:4
6160. Da 11:30	7339. Am 5:16	8482. Dt 32:22
6168. Le 20:18	7358. Ex 34:19	8537. Ge 20:5
6172. Is 20:4	7364. Ex 29:4	8543. Jsh 4:18
6174. Is 20:2	7367. SS 4:2	8548. Is 58:11
6184. Ps 86:14	7386. Ne 5:13	8550. Ex 28:30
6190. Jsh 5:3	7411. 1 S 28:12	8585. Jb 38:25
6209. Je 51:58	7440. 1 K 8:28	8643. Le 23:24
6213. Je 3:16	7451. Is 45:7	8655. Ge 31:19
6233. Is 30:12	7494. 1 K 19:11	

Strong's Numbers Index: Greek